49.95
90E

CRIME FICTION
1749–1980

GARLAND REFERENCE LIBRARY
OF THE HUMANITIES
(VOL. 371)

CRIME FICTION
1749–1980
A Comprehensive Bibliography

Allen J. Hubin

GARLAND PUBLISHING, INC.
NEW YORK & LONDON
1984

© 1984 Allen J. Hubin
All rights reserved

Library of Congress Cataloging in Publication Data

Hubin, Allen J.
  Crime fiction, 1749–1980.

  (Garland reference library of the humanities ; vol. 371)
  Enl. ed. of: The bibliography of crime fiction, 1749-1975. c1979.
  Bibliography: p.
  Includes indexes.
  1. English fiction—Bibliography.   2. Detective and mystery stories—Bibliography.   3. American fiction—Bibliography.   4. Crime and criminals—Fiction—Bibliography.   5. Detective and mystery plays—Bibliography.   6. Gothic revival (Literature)—Bibliography.
  I. Title.   II. Series: Garland reference library of the humanities ; v. 371.
  Z2014.F4H82   1984   [PR830.D4]   016.823′0872   82-48772
  ISBN 0-8240-9219-8 (alk. paper)

Cover design by Laurence Walczak

Printed on acid-free, 250-year-life paper
Manufactured in the United States of America

DEDICATION
To all those who find crime fiction fun

CONTENTS

Preface / ix

Introduction / xi

Abbreviations / xvii

Author Index / 1

Title Index / 411

Settings Index / 635

Series Index / 689

Series Character Chronology / 703

PREFACE

The present volume is based on my book, *The Bibliography of Crime Fiction, 1749-1975*. Extending the coverage five years added some 6,000 titles, a perhaps surprising 10% of the total of about 60,000 titles presented here. Many corrections have been made, including the addition of about 2,600 titles for the years 1749-1975, titles which I did not know about when the first volume went to press. A number of these corrections and additions were suggested by the faithful correspondents acknowledged at the end of the introduction.

I am especially pleased to be able to include here a completely new Settings Index identifying 343 locations. Two other features are also new: one involves the identification of reference works in which authors listed here are cited, as well as the provision of biographical information for some authors not so cited; the other is a chronology of "durable" series characters, identifying them by type, country of origin, nature of publication, and number of appearances.

INTRODUCTION

Crime fiction, for the purpose of this bibliography, is defined very broadly as fiction intended for adult readers, in which crime or the threat of crime is a major plot element. Thus included are mystery, detective, suspense, thriller, gothic (romantic suspense), police, and spy fiction. The intent is to cover all such fiction in the English language published in book form (both soft and hard covers) through the end of 1980. Magazine and dime novel fiction, juvenile and children's material, omnibus collections, and anthologies are not included.

Since fiction—all literature, in fact—can be thought of as a continuum, any attempt to carve out a portion of it, like crime fiction, is almost impossible and necessarily raises troublesome questions of the categorization of borderline material. Mysteries and tales of Royal Canadian Mounted Police (covered in this book) merge into adventure fiction (not covered); romantic suspense (covered) merges into straight romance, historical fiction, and supernatural or horror fiction (not covered); crime fiction merges into mainstream fiction, science fiction and fantasy, westerns, pornography, and nonfiction (not covered). Since the line between any of the covered and not covered types is a fine one involving subjective individual judgment, users of this bibliography will probably find that coverage is extended at least a small way into some of these other types of literature, especially where crime or detection is significantly present.

The alphabetization practice in this work is unusual only in that Mc, Mac, and M' entries are considered to be the same and are collected together before the other M's.

AUTHOR INDEX

The main body of this bibliography comprises the author index, to which all other sections refer. Here all authors identified with crime fiction published through the end of 1980 are arranged in alphabetical order. Books are listed alphabetically under the byline under which they were first published. Cross-referencing is provided to the author's real name, where different from the crime fiction byline, and to any other pseudonyms used for crime fiction.

The headnotes to byline entries provide author birth and death dates, where known. They also identify series characters (protagonists recurring in two or more books) and provide a means to show in which of the listed books the characters appear. When all appearances of a character are believed identified, the notation so indicates (with an equal sign); when unidentified appearances may exist, the headnote indicates this uncertainty ("in at least those titles marked . . .").

Headnotes also indicate settings used by the books listed under that byline when some general statement can be made. They identify any special way in which the titles are organized, as in the Rex Stout and James Reach entries.

In addition, headnotes identify in which of eight selected general reference works the author is significantly cited, or, if the author is not so cited, provide brief biographical information if such was obtained from other sources. The other sources include primarily the dust jackets of the author's books, and so the biographical information should be understood to relate principally to the author's active writing period; in a few other cases biographical information has come directly from the authors themselves. The identification of general reference works or provision of biographical information is done only once for an author: either in the headnote for the author's real name, when this was used for crime fiction, or in the headnote for the author's principal crime fiction pseudonym.

The general reference works (and the abbreviations) used are:

A Catalogue of Crime (CC), by Jacques Barzun and Wendell Hertig Taylor (1971)
Contemporary Authors (CA), Volumes 1-105
The Development of the Detective Novel (DD), by A.E. Murch (revised edition, 1968)
Encyclopedia of Mystery and Detection (EM), edited by Chris Steinbrunner and Otto Penzler (1976)
Masters of Mystery (MM), by H. Douglas Thomson (1931)
Mortal Consequences (MC), by Julian Symons (1972; published as *Bloody Murder* in England)
Murder for Pleasure (MP), by Howard Haycraft (1941)
Twentieth Century Crime and Mystery Writers (TC), edited by John M. Reilly (1980)

Numerous other studies of crime fiction have been published, both general and specific to single authors or types of fiction within the broad field. Those wishing to explore beyond the eight works cited here will find *What About Murder?* by Jon L. Breen (1981) a very valuable guide, and the compilations by Ronald Burt De Waal *(The World Bibliography of Sherlock Holmes and Dr. Watson*, 1974, and *The International Sherlock Holmes*, 1980) are indispensable to dealing with the abundant Sherlockian materials.

The books listed under each byline are normally identified with their first American publisher and date of first United States publication, and/or with their first British publisher and date of first British publication, depending on whether the books were published in both countries. When both British and American editions exist, the United States is given first when the book was intended primarily for the United States market, and the British first when Great Britain was the primary market. In most cases, this means that the authors were American and British, respectively.

The nature of the book content is also defined. Collections of short stories (ss), collections of novelets, plays (with the number of acts given when known), criminous book-length poetry, translations (with the original title and place and date of publication given when known), and novelizations of stage, radio, TV, or screen plays (with the original source given) are identified. Those not so identified can be understood to be un-derived novels.

Settings information is also given for each title where this was obtained. More than 25,000 volumes were examined for this purpose, either directly or indirectly. Many books have settings not clearly identified, or have changing settings, but those found to be set at least about 50% (by page count) in an identifiable city (understood as the entire metropolitan area), state, country, or region are noted by giving that setting in brackets with the title entry.

American authors most commonly use United States settings, so titles by such authors listed without setting may be assumed with some confidence to be set in the United States. British authors have the comparable tendency and the same assumption can be made. In addition, rather than attempting the individual identification of all books by British authors set in England, shorthand notation is used both in author index headnotes and in the settings index.

Many books have different titles in their various editions—for example, different titles in the United States and in England, and different titles relating to movie editions. All such variant titles are listed and cross-referenced to the original title, where publisher and date for all the editions are to be found.

A dash in front of a title indicates it to be either a marginal inclusion or one whose criminous content and eligibility for inclusion remain unconfirmed.

All titles are given in full in this index, as the title appears on the title page of the first

Introduction / xiii

edition. For compactness in presentation and to aid in scanning, titles having initial articles (A, An, The) omit those articles in all other sections of this bibliography.

All bylines are given in full in this index, as they appear on the title pages of the first editions, with parentheses used to identify portions of names not used in bylines. In all other sections of this bibliography, authors are identified only by last names and initials, except in those instances where giving the byline in full would remove an ambiguity produced by a coincidence of initials.

As indicated above, the appearance of an English-language book edition before the end of 1980 satisfies the time requirement for inclusion in this bibliography. Once this requirement is met, a later edition, such as a 1981 first appearance in England of a book published in 1980 in the United States, or a later retitled edition, is also identified.

Despite endless checking and cross-checking, errors doubtless persist in this bibliography. In addition, some titles were included based on incomplete or second-hand information, and all books could not be inspected for settings information. Corrections, additions, and recommended deletions which are based on first-hand information and come with supporting detail from users of this bibliography will be most welcome. Further settings information, or more specific settings identification, is also invited. Such confirmed contributions will be incorporated in future editions or supplements of this bibliography, and their contributors acknowledged.

TITLE INDEX

This lists alphabetically all titles given in the author index, and relates each title to the byline under which it first appeared, thus providing total title access to the principal index of this bibliography.

SETTINGS INDEX

This lists settings alphabetically, with appropriate cross-references to related or overlapping settings. It identifies—alphabetically by author, and alphabetically by title under the author—the books known to use each setting, and thus provides extensive guidance for those interested in fictional treatments of specific settings.

No book is cited for both a specific and a more general geographical setting, e.g., a book listed as set in Philadelphia is not also listed as set in Pennsylvania, although of course the latter is also true. To make this index reasonably compact, summary notations are used: when the number of books using a given setting under a single byline exceeds four this is stated rather than the specific titles themselves, and when all titles under a given byline share a common setting this also is stated instead of the specific titles. Reference to the author index will identify the individual titles in such cases.

Certain non-geographical settings are also identified, and in these instances the book may also be listed under a geographical setting. Non-geographical settings comprise those related to time (past and future, where date and place of setting are also given when known), as well as certain specialized settings (academia, aircraft, church, hospital, train, ship, theatre).

In the very few cases in which books use approximately equally two different geographical settings, the books are listed under both.

SERIES INDEX

Here listed alphabetically are all series and series characters identified in the author index, together with the byline(s) under which books forming part of these series are found, thus providing complete series access to the principal index of this bibliography. In addition, those characters such as Sherlock Holmes and Sexton Blake who are found in the works of large numbers of authors can best be traced to all those works through this index.

SERIES CHARACTER CHRONOLOGY

A chronological listing of the more durable series characters may serve usefully to place a given series in time, to identify trends in types of characters, countries of origin, and types of publication, as well as to allow for comparisons in lengths of series.

These features are provided by this listing, in which "durable" series characters are defined as those having five or more book appearances through the end of 1980. The order of listing is by year, from oldest to most recent, with characters cited alphabetically within a given year.

The year of first book appearance is given for each character. When this year is in doubt, and may in fact be earlier, the year is given in parentheses.

Characters are categorized according to one of the following types, where information is available:

1. Adventurer (a character who acts out of love for intrigue or danger or revenge, rather than primarily for a fee; a knight-errant);
2. Amateur (a character whose activity—detection, primarily—arises out of abundant "accidental" encounters with crime and corpses, and who takes no fee);
3. Criminal;
4. Police (a member of a local, state, or national law enforcement agency);
5. Private (an investigator who seeks clients and takes a fee; a private eye or lawyer);
6. Spy.

It is important to note that each character is categorized here only according to his first appearance, and that changes in type can sometimes be observed in the books comprising a series. As examples: Peter Clancy is categorized as an amateur even though he functioned as such for only one book, and after a brief stint as a policeman he operated as a private detective for more than 50 books; other policemen have retired to private or amateur detection; spies have become private eyes in their later years; criminals have reformed and subsequently operated on the side of the godly.

The market for which each series was primarily written is identified (A = America; B = Britain, including Australian series; F = France; S = Sweden), as is the form of publication (hb = hardback; pb = paperback). Note that here too categorization is only according to initial appearance: some series have changed "nationalities" in midstream (such as J.M. Fox's stories about John Marshall), and others have moved from soft to hard covers (such as Ed McBain's 87th Precinct series, and John D. MacDonald's Travis McGee series) or switched from hard covers to paperback (such as the Johnny Liddell series by Frank Kane and the Mike Shayne series by B. Halliday).

When the number of appearances is in doubt, and may in fact be larger (but not smaller), it is given in parentheses. The byline(s) under which each series was issued is cited.

SOURCES AND ACKNOWLEDGMENTS

The primary sources of data for this bibliography were my own library of some 25,000 volumes of crime fiction, extensive researches in the reference literature, and the generous assistance of many knowledgeable students, readers, and authors of crime fiction.

Reference works consulted include *The National Union Catalogue*, *Cumulative Book Index*, *Paperback Books in Print*, *Cumulative Paperback Index 1939-1959* by R. Reginald and M.R. Burgess, *Forthcoming Books*, *British Museum Catalogue*, *English Catalogue*, *British National Bibliography*, *British Books in Print*, *Whitaker's Cumulative Book Lists*, *Contemporary Authors*, *A Catalogue of Crime* by Jacques Barzun and Wendell Hertig Taylor, *The Encyclopedia of Science Fiction and Fantasy* by Donald H. Tuck, *Encyclopedia of Mystery and Detection* edited by Chris Steinbrunner and Otto Penzler, *The Men Behind Boys' Fiction* by W.O.G. Lofts and D.J. Adley, *The Detective Short Story* by Ellery Queen, Victorian Detective Fiction by Eric Osborne, *A Gothic Bibliography* by Montague Summers, *The Detective Short Story: A Bibliography and Index* by E.H. Mundell and G. Jay Rausch, *The Science Fiction Encyclopedia* edited by Peter Nicholls, *The Paperback Price Guide* by Kevin Hancer, *The Complete Paperback Shopper*, *Drury's Guide to Best Plays* (Third Edition) by James M. Salem, *Twentieth Century Crime and Mystery Writers* edited by John M. Reilly, *Author Bibliographies Master Index*, *Sequels* by Frank Gardner, *Index to Full Length Plays*, *Twentieth Century Science Fiction Writers* edited by Curtis C. Smith, *A Spectrum of Fantasy* by George Locke, *Twentieth Century Romance and Gothic Writers* edited by James Vinson, *Gothic Novels of the Twentieth Century* by Elsa J. Radcliffe, *An Annotated Bibliography of California Fiction 1664-1970* by Newton D. Baird and Robert Greenwood, *The Checklist of Science-Fiction and Supernatural Fiction* by E.F. Bleiler, *Who's Who in Spy Fiction* by Donald McCormick, *Horror Literature* edited by Marshall B. Tymn, *The Bookseller*, *Publishers' Weekly*, and *Library Journal*.

Among individual contributors, I acknowledge particularly the pioneering bibliographic work of Ordean A. Hagen (*Who Done It?*, 1969), and the extensive assistance of Francis M. Nevins in preparing the first book version of this bibliography and my son Loren Hubin for invaluable help with the title index of that version. My sincere thanks also to the following and to all others who helped—this bibliography is much the more complete and accurate because of them: R.C.S. Adey, Helen Arvonen, Robert Aucott, Ivon Baker, John Ball, R. Jeff Banks, Jacques Barzun, Brian Bearshaw, Robert Beasecker, Tasman Beattie, Mrs. Otto Beeby, Norman Berrow, Peter E. Blau, E.F. Bleiler, Sydney Box, Jon L. Breen, Robert E. Briney, Douglas Browne, Joe Coffey, Kathryn Collins, J. Randolph Cox, Bill Crider, Michael Cropper, Ed Demchko, Richard Deming, Theodore Dukeshire, Bill Dunn, Herbert Eaton, Julie Ellis, Jim Finzel, L. Foulkes, James M. Fox, Niels H. Frandsen, Brian Garfield, Marilyn Granbeck, Douglas Greene, Elliott Greenfield, Mary Groff, John Hamister, Robert Hatch, Iwan Hedman, Daniel L. Higgins, Edward D. Hoch, Robert Hoffman, Don Ireland, Kenneth R. Johnson, Amnon Kabatchnik, Nancy Kingman, Herbert Kleist, Marvin Lachman, Richard M. Lackritz, Robert Lauritzen, Vernon Lay, Lionel Leventhal, Steve Lewis, Dennis Lien, Ethel Lindsay, George Locke, William R. Loeser, W.O.G. Lofts, William Lyles, Frank D. McSherry, Jr., James Malone, Mavis Marsh, Michael L. Masliah, Stephen Mertz, Jeff Meyerson, Harald Mogensen, Nigel Morland, Howard S. Mott, Will Murray, Ellen Nehr, Stanley Pachon, Lauran Paine, Madelyn Palmer, Angelo Panagos, Ruth Pattison, Hayford Peirce, Otto Penzler, B.A. Pike, Bill Pronzini, N.C. Ravenscroft, Becky Reineke, William Reynolds, W.E. Dan Ross, James Sandoe, W.A.S. Sarjeant, Tom and Enid Schantz, Stephen Schultheis, Arthur C. Scott, Charles Shibuk, Walter and Jean Shine, Patterson Smith, Aaron Marc Stein, Steven A. Stilwell, Ola Strom, Wendell H. Taylor, Michael J. Tolley, Valdis Treimanis, Edith Turner, John D. Vining, Howard Waterhouse, Charles G. Waugh, Hillary Waugh, J.F. Whitt, Camille Wolff, Neville W. Wood, and George Wuyek.

Allen J. Hubin
3656 Midland Ave.
White Bear Lake, MN 55110
June 5, 1983

ABBREVIATIONS

A = America
acad. = academia
Afghan. = Afghanistan
Afr. = Africa
Afr., E. = Africa, East
Afr., N. = Africa, North
Afr., W. = Africa, West
air. = aircraft
Ala. = Alabama
Alb. = Albania
Albuq. = Albuquerque, New Mexico
Amst. = Amsterdam, Holland
Arg. = Argentina
Ariz. = Arizona
Ark. = Arkansas
B = Britain
Balt. = Baltimore, Maryland
Bel. Congo = Belgian Congo
Belg. = Belgium
Brus. = Brussels, Belgium
Buch. = Bucharest, Rumania
Buda. = Budapest, Hungary
Buen. A. = Buenos Aires, Argentina
Bulg. = Bulgaria
CA = *Contemporary Authors*
ca. = circa
Calif. = California
Camb. = Cambodia
Can. = Canada
Can. Is. = Canary Islands
Capt. = Captain
Carib. = Caribbean
Casa. = Casablanca, Morocco
CC = *A Catalogue of Crime*
Cent. Am. = Central America
Cey. = Ceylon
Chan. Is. = Channel Islands
Chi. = Chicago, Illinois
Cin. = Cincinnati, Ohio
Cleve. = Cleveland, Ohio
Colo. = Colorado
Colom. = Colombia
Conn. = Connecticut
Copen. = Copenhagen, Denmark
Cors. = Corsica
Czech. = Czechoslovakia
D.A. = District Attorney
DD = *The Development of the Detective Novel*
Del. = Delaware

Den. = Denmark
Dep. = Deputy
Det. = Detroit, Michigan
Dom. Rep. = Dominican Republic
Dub. = Dublin, Ireland
Ecua. = Ecuador
Edin. = Edinburgh, Scotland
EM = *Encyclopedia of Mystery and Detection*
Eng. = England
Ethio. = Ethiopia
F = France
Fin. = Finland
Fla. = Florida
Fr. = France
Fr. Ant. = French Antilles
Frank. = Frankfurt, West Germany
Ga. = Georgia
Ger. = Germany
Gib. = Gibraltar
GM = Gold Medal (publisher)
Green. = Greenland
Guat. = Guatemala
H. Kong = Hong Kong
Hamb. = Hamburg, West Germany
Haw. = Hawaii
hb = hardback
Holl. = Holland
hosp. = hospital
Hung. = Hungary
Ia. = Iowa
Ice. = Iceland
Ida. = Idaho
Ill. = Illinois
Ind. = Indiana
Ind. O. = Indian Ocean
Indon. = Indonesia
Ire. = Ireland
Isr. = Israel
Istan. = Istanbul, Turkey
It. = Italy
Jack. = Jacksonville, Florida
Jam. = Jamaica
Jap. = Japan
Jerus. = Jerusalem, Palestine
Johan. = Johannesburg, South Africa
Kan. = Kansas
Kan. City = Kansas City, Missouri
Kor. = Korea
Kuw. = Kuwait

Ky. = Kentucky
La. = Louisiana
L.A. = Los Angeles, California
Las Veg. = Las Vegas, Nevada
Leb. = Lebanon
Leip. = Leipzig, East Germany
L.I. = Long Island, New York
Lith. = Lithuania
Maced. = Macedonia
Maj. = Majorca
Mal. = Malaysia
Mars. = Marseilles, France
Mass. = Massachusetts
MC = *Mortal Consequences*
Md. = Maryland
Med. Is. = Mediterranean Island
Melb. = Melbourne, Australia
Mesop. = Mesopotamia
Mex. = Mexico
Mex. City = Mexico City, Mexico
Mich. = Michigan
Mid. East = Middle East
Midway Is. = Midway Island
Milw. = Milwaukee, Wisconsin
Minn. = Minnesota
Miss. = Mississippi
MM = *Masters of Mystery*
Mo. = Missouri
Mong. = Mongolia
Mont. = Montana
Montr. = Montreal, Canada
Mor. = Morocco
Mozam. = Mozambique
MP = *Murder for Pleasure*
Mpls. = Minneapolis, Minnesota
N.C. = North Carolina
n.d. = no date
N. Dak. = North Dakota
N.H. = New Hampshire
N.J. = New Jersey
N. Mex. = New Mexico
N.W. = northwest (United States)
N.Y. = New York (state)
N.Z. = New Zealand
NAL = New American Library (publisher)
Nashv. = Nashville, Tennessee
Neb. = Nebraska
Nev. = Nevada
New Eng. = New England
New Or. = New Orleans, Louisiana
Nic. = Nicaragua
Nig. = Nigeria
Nor. = Norway
NYC = New York City, New York
Okla. = Oklahoma
Okla. City = Oklahoma City, Oklahoma

Oreg. = Oregon
P. Rico = Puerto Rico
Pa. = Pennsylvania
Pak. = Pakistan
Pan. = Panama
Parag. = Paraguay
pb = paperback
PB = Pocket Books (publisher)
Phil. = Philadelphia, Pennsylvania
Philip. = Philippines
Pitt. = Pittsburgh, Pennsylvania
Pol. = Poland
Port. = Portugal
pp = pages
Prof. = Professor
R.I. = Rhode Island
Ref = reference(s)
Rhod. = Rhodesia
Rio de J. = Rio De Janeiro, Brazil
Roch. = Rochester, New York
Rum. = Rumania
Russ. = Russia
S = series
S = Sweden (in series chronology)
S. Afr. = South Africa
S. Am. = South America
S.C. = South Carolina
S. Dak. = South Dakota
S.F. = San Francisco, California
S. Pac. = South Pacific
S.W. = southwest (United States)
S.W. Africa = South West Africa
Sard. = Sardinia
Saud. Arab. = Saudi Arabia
SC = series character(s)
Scand. = Scandinavia
Scot. = Scotland
Sen. = Senegal
Set = setting(s)
Sgt. = Sergeant
Sic. = Sicily
Sing. = Singapore
Sol. Is. = Solomon Islands
Sp. = Spain
ss = short stories
Stock. = Stockholm, Sweden
Sum. = Sumatra
Supt. = Superintendent
Suri. = Surinam
Swed. = Sweden
Switz. = Switzerland
Syd. = Sydney, Australia
Syr. = Syria
Tang. = Tanganyika
Tanz. = Tanzania
Tas. = Tasmania
TC = *Twentieth Century Crime and Mystery Writers*

Tenn. = Tennessee
Tex. = Texas
Thai. = Thailand
Tib. = Tibet
Trans. = Transvaal, South Africa
Trin. = Trinidad
Tun. = Tunisia
Turk. = Turkey
U = University
U.S. = United States
Urug. = Uruguay
Va. = Virginia
Van. = Vancouver, Canada
Venez. = Venezuela
Vir. Is. = Virgin Islands

Vt. = Vermont
W.I. = West Indies
W. Va. = West Virginia
Wash. = Washington (state)
Wash. D.C. = Washington, D.C.
WDL = World Distributors, Ltd. (publisher)
Wis. = Wisconsin
WWI = World War I
WWII = World War II
Wyo. = Wyoming
Yugos. = Yugoslavia
Zanz. = Zanzibar

Author Index

Author Index

AALBEN, PATRICK. Pseudonym of Noel Jones, 1939-   . Ref: CA.
The Grab. Hale, 1977

AARONS, EDWARD S(IDNEY). 1916-1975. Pseudonyms: Paul Ayres, Edward Ronns, qq. v. Ref: CA, CC, EM, TC. Many titles published originally as by Ronns were later reprinted as by Aarons. SC: Sam Durell = SD (see also: Will B. Aarons).
Assignment—Afghan Dragon. GM, 1976; Coronet, 1979 SD [Mid. East]
Assignment—Amazon Queen. GM, 1974; Coronet, 1975 SD [Brazil]
Assignment—Angelina. GM, 1958; Fawcett (London), 1959 SD
Assignment—Ankara. GM, 1961; Muller pb, 1962 SD [Turk.]
Assignment—Bangkok. GM, 1972; Coronet, 1972 SD [Bangkok]
Assignment—Black Gold. GM, 1975; Coronet, 1977 SD [Afr.]
Assignment—Black Viking. GM, 1967; Coronet, 1968 SD [Swed.]
Assignment—Budapest. GM, 1957; Fawcett (London), 1959 SD [Buda.]
Assignment—Burma Girl. GM, 1961; Muller pb, 1962 SD [Burma]
Assignment—Carlotta Cortez. GM, 1959; Muller pb, 1960 SD [NYC]
Assignment—Ceylon. GM, 1973; Coronet, 1974 SD [Cey.]
Assignment—Cong Hai Kill. GM, 1966 SD [Thai.]
Assignment—Golden Girl. GM, 1972; Coronet, 1972 SD [Afr.]
Assignment—Helene. GM, 1959; Muller pb, 1960 SD [Far East]
Assignment—Karachi. GM, 1962; Muller pb, 1963 SD [Mid. East]
Assignment—Lili Lamaris. GM, 1959; Muller pb, 1960 SD [It.]
Assignment—Lowlands. GM, 1961 SD [Holl.]
Assignment—Madeleine. GM, 1958; Muller pb, 1960 SD [Algiers]
Assignment—Maltese Maiden. GM, 1972; Coronet, 1973 SD
Assignment—Manchurian Doll. GM, 1963; Muller pb, 1964 SD [China]
Assignment—Mara Tirana. GM, 1960; Jenkins, 1966 SD [Rum.]
Assignment—Moon Girl. GM, 1968 SD [Iran]
Assignment—Nuclear Nude. GM, 1968; Coronet, 1969 SD [Sing.]
Assignment—Palermo. GM, 1966; Coronet, 1967 SD [It.]
Assignment—Peking. GM, 1969; Coronet, 1970 SD [Peking]
Assignment—Quayle Question. GM, 1975; Coronet, 1976 SD
Assignment—School for Spies. GM, 1966; Coronet, 1967 SD
Assignment—Silver Scorpion. GM, 1973; Coronet, 1974 SD [Afr.]
Assignment—Sorrento Siren. GM, 1963; Muller pb, 1963 SD [It.]
Assignment—Star Stealers. GM, 1970; Coronet, 1970 SD [Afr.]
Assignment—Stella Marni. GM, 1957; Fawcett (London), 1958 SD [NYC]
Assignment—Suicide. GM, 1956; Fawcett (London), 1958 SD [Russ.]
Assignment—Sulu Sea. GM, 1964 SD [Far East]
Assignment—Sumatra. GM, 1974; Coronet, 1975 SD [Sum.]
Assignment—The Cairo Dancers. GM, 1965 SD [Egypt]
Assignment—The Girl in the Gondola. GM, 1964; Coronet, 1969 SD [Venice]
Assignment to Disaster. GM, 1955; Fawcett (London), 1956 SD
Assignment—Tokyo. GM, 1971; Coronet, 1971 SD [Tokyo]
Assignment—Treason. GM, 1956; Fawcett (London), 1957 SD [Va.]
Assignment—White Rajah. GM, 1970; Coronet, 1970 SD [Mal.]
Assignment—Zoraya. GM, 1960; Muller, pb, 1961 SD [Mid. East]
Come Back, My Love. GM, 1953; Fawcett (London), 1954 [Mex.]
The Defenders. GM, 1961; Jenkins, 1962 (Novelization of the TV series.) [NYC]
Escape to Love. GM, 1952; Fawcett (London), 1957 [NYC]
Girl on the Run. GM, 1954 [Fr.]
Nightmare. McKay, 1948 [NYC]
The Sinners. GM, 1953; Fawcett (London), 1954 [ship]

AARONS, WILL B. SC: Sam Durell, in all titles (see also: Edward S. Aarons, 1916-1975).
Assignment Mermaid. GM, 1979
Assignment Sheba. GM, 1976 [Ethio.]
Assignment 13th Princess. GM, 1977 [Mid. East]
Assignment Tiger Devil. GM, 1977 [Guy.]
Assignment Tyrant's Bride. GM, 1980 [Zanz.]

ABBEY, EDWARD. 1927-   . Ref: CA.
The Monkey Wrench Gang. Lippincott, 1975; Canongate, 1978 [S.W.]

ABBEY, KIERAN. Pseudonym of Helen Reilly, 1891-1962, q.v.
And Let the Coffin Pass. Scribner, 1942 [Vt.]
Beyond the Dark. Scribner, 1944 [NYC]
Run with the Hare. Scribner, 1941 [NYC]

ABBEY, RUTH. Pseudonym of Ruth Pattison. British author of ss, articles, and novels. Set: Eng.
Bridge of Tears. Hale, 1974; Ace, 1975
Dream of Terror. Hale, 1976
Evil at Nunnery Manor; see The Story of Rachel
Girl from the Sea. Hale, 1973. U.S. title: Portrait of Doubt. Ace, 1973 [past]
House by the Tarn. Hale, 1975
Portrait of Doubt; see Girl from the Sea
Prisoner of the Manor. Hale, 1971; Ace, 1973 [past]
The Sound of the Sea. Hale, 1978
The Story of Rachel. Hale, 1972. U.S. title: Evil at Nunnery Manor. Ace, 1973

ABBOT, ANTHONY. Pseudonym of (Charles) Fulton Oursler, 1893-1952, q.v. See also: Anonymous ("Dark Masquerade"). Ref: CC, DD, EM, MP, TC. SC: Thatcher Colt, in all titles.
About the Murder of a Man Afraid of Women. Farrar, 1937. British title: The Murder of a Man Afraid of Women. Collins, 1937 [NYC]
About the Murder of a Startled Lady. Farrar, 1935. British title: The Murder of a Startled Lady. Collins, 1936 [NYC]
About the Murder of Geraldine Foster. Covici, 1930. British title: The Murder of Geraldine Foster. Collins, 1931 [NYC]
About the Murder of the Circus Queen. Covici, 1932. British title: The Murder of the Circus Queen. Collins, 1933 [NYC]
About the Murder of the Clergyman's Mistress. Covici, 1931. British title: The Crime of the Century. Collins, 1931. Also published as: Murder of the Clergyman's Mistress. Popular Library, 1950 [NYC]
About the Murder of the Night Club Lady. Covici, 1931. British title: The Murder of the Night Club Lady. Collins, 1932. Also published as: The Night Club Lady. Grosset, 1932; Collins, 1932 [NYC]
The Creeps. Farrar, 1939. British title: Murder at Buzzards Bay. Collins, 1940 [Cape Cod]
The Crime of the Century; see About the Murder of the Clergyman's Mistress
Deadly Secret; see The Shudders
Murder at Buzzards Bay; see The Creeps
The Murder of a Man Afraid of Women; see About the Murder of a Man Afraid of Women
The Murder of a Startled Lady; see About the Murder of a Startled Lady
The Murder of Geraldine Foster; see About the Murder of Geraldine Foster
Murder of the Clergyman's Mistress; see About the Murder of the Clergyman's Mistress
The Murder of the Circus Queen; see About the Murder of the Circus Queen
The Murder of the Night Club Lady; see About the Murder of the Night Club Lady
The Night Club Lady; see About the Murder of the Night Club Lady
The Shudders. Farrar, 1943. British title: Deadly Secret. Collins, 1943 [NYC]

ABBOT, WILLIS J(OHN). 1863-1934.
Philip Derby, Reporter. Dodd, 1922; Hurst, 1923 [NYC]

ABBOTT, ALICE. Joint pseudonym of Kathryn Kilby Borland, 1916-   , and Helen Ross Speicher, 1915-   . Ref on Borland: CA.
Goodbye, Julie Scott. Ace, 1975
The Third Tower. Ace, 1974 [Maine]

ABBOTT, ALICE IRVING
Circumstantial Evidence. Smith, 1882

ABBOTT, BRUCE
The Sign of the Scorpion. Grove, 1970

ABBOTT, KEITH (GEORGE). 1944-
Rhino Ritz. Blue Wind, 1979

ABBOTT, ROSA [ROSA ABBOTT PARKER]
The Young Detective; or, Which Won? Lee & Shepard, 1870

ABBOTT, SANDRA. Pseudonym of Robert Devaney.
Castle of Evil. Avon, 1974 [Rum., 1953]
Castle of Fear. Avon, 1974
The River and the Rose. Signet, 1967 [South, 1860s]
Whispering Gables. Paperback Library, 1968 [Maine]

ABDULLAH, ACHMED. Pseudonym of Alexander Nicholayevitch Romanoff, 1881-1945. Ref: EM.
-Alien Souls. McCann, 1922; Hutchinson, 1923 ss
The Benefactor's Club. Lloyd, 1921 (U.S. title?)
The Blue-Eyed Manchu. Shores, 1917; Hutchinson, 1923
-A Buccaneer in Spats. Hutchinson, 1924 (U.S. title?)
The Bungalow on the Roof. Mystery League, 1931 [NYC]
-Fighting Through. Warne, 1933 (U.S. title?)
The Honorable Gentleman and Others. Putnam, 1919 ss
The Lady in the Veil; see The Veiled Woman
The Man on Horseback. McCann, 1919 [Ger.]
-The Mating of the Blades. McCann, 1920; Hutchinson, 1921
The Red Stain. Hearst, 1915; Simpkin, 1916 [India]
The Remittance-Woman. Garden City, 1924, in "Four in One Mysteries" [China]
The Trail of the Beast. McCann, 1919; Hutchinson, 1921 [Paris]
-The Veiled Woman. Liveright, 1931. British title: The Lady in the Veil. Hurst, 1931

ABE, KOBO. 1924-   . Ref: CA.
The Ruined Map. Knopf, 1969; Cape, 1972

A'BECKETT, ARTHUR W(ILLIAM). 1844-1909.
Fallen Among Thieves. Chapman, 1870
The Ghost of Greystone Grange. Bradbury Agnew, 1878
Hard Luck; or, A Murder at Monte Carlo. Arrowsmith, 1890 [Fr.]
The Mystery of Mostyn Manor. Moxon's Christmas Annual, 1878
Tracked Out: A Secret of the Guillotine. Arrowsmith, 1888
The Tunnel Mystery and Its Solution. Routledge, 1905

ABEL, JOEL S.
The Jonah Game. Curtis, 1973

ABERCROMBIE, BARBARA (MATTES)
Good Riddance. Harper, 1979; Macdonald, 1979 [L.A.]

ABIO, RUFUS O. 1946-   .
Angels of Double Faces. Exposition, 1977

A

ABLEMAN, PAUL. 1927-   . Ref: CA. Both titles are novelizations of the British TV series. SC: Eddie Shoestring, in both titles.
- Shoestring. BBC, 1979
- Shoestring's Finest Hour. BBC, 1980

ABRAHALL, CLARE (CONSTANCE DRURY) H(OSKYNS). Ref: CA.
- Butler in a Box. Steele's, n.d. (3-act play.)

ABRAHAMS, DORIS CAROLINE. 1901-1982. Pseudonym: Caryl Brahms, q.v.

ABRAHAMS, GERALD. 1907-   .
- Conscience Makes Heroes. Eyre, 1945

ABRAHAMS, PETER
- The Fury of Rachel Monnet. Macmillan, 1980; Muller, 1981

ABRAHAMS, ROBERT D(AVID). 1905-   . Ref: CA. SC: Pete Taylor, in both titles.
- Death After Lunch. Phoenix, 1941
- Death in 1-2-3. Phoenix, 1942 [NYC]

ABRAHAMSON, CHRISTINE ELIZABETH. 1916-   Pseudonym: Kathleen Westcott, q.v.

ABRO, BEN. Pseudonym.
- July 14 Assassination. Cape, 1963. U.S. title: Assassination. Morrow, 1963 [Fr.]

ACHARD, MARCEL. Pseudonym of Marcel Auguste Ferreol, 1899-1974. See: Harry Kurnitz, 1907-1968. Ref: CA.

ACHESON, EDWARD (CAMPION). 1902-   .
- The Grammarian's Funeral. Macrae, 1935; Hutchinson, 1935
- Murder by Suggestion; see Red Herring
- Murder to Hounds. Harcourt, 1939; Harrap, 1939 [Va.]
- Red Herring. Morrow, 1932. British title: Murder by Suggestion. Hutchinson, 1933 [Conn.]

ACKLAND, RODNEY. 1908-   . Ref: CA.
- Before the Party. French (London), 1950. (2-act play based on the story by W. Somerset Maugham, 1874-1965, q.v.)
- Crime and Punishment. Marston, 1948; Holt, 1948. (Play based on the novel by Fedor Mikhailovich Dostoevskii, 1821-1881, q.v.)
- A Dead Secret. French (London), 1958 (Play.)

ACOTT, J. H.
- The Rawdon Murder Case. Thacker, ca. 1944

ACRE, STEPHEN. Pseudonym of Frank Gruber, 1904-1969, q.v. Other pseudonyms: Charles K. Boston, John K. Vedder, qq.v.
- Fall Guy for a Killer; see The Yellow Overcoat
- The Yellow Overcoat. Dodd, 1942; Boardman, 1945. Also published as: Fall Guy for a Killer, as by Frank Gruber. Jonathan Press, 1955. Reprinted under original title as by Frank Gruber. Popular Library, 1949 [Chi.]

ACTON, HAROLD (MARIO MITCHELL). 1904-   Ref: CA.
- The Betrayal and other stories. (Author), n.d. ss, some criminous

ADAIR, DENNIS. Pseudonym of Bernard Charles Cronin, 1884-   . Other pseudonym: Eric North, q.v.
- Death Rides the Desert. Hutchinson, 1940

ADAM, MICHAEL
- The Admiralty Murders. Sentinel, 1947

ADAM, NICHOLAS
- The Tripleship Cracksman. Cape, 1977

ADAM, ROBIN. Pseudonym of Robert James Adams, 1924-   . Other pseudonym: Paul MacTyre, q.v.
- Stalk to Kill. Hodder, 1970

ADAM, RUTH (AUGUSTA). 1907-   . Ref: CA.
- Look Who's Talking. Muller, 1960
- Murder in the Home Guard. Chapman, 1942

ADAMS, CHRISTOPHER. Pseudonym of (Hector) Kenneth Hopkins, 1914-   , q.v.
- Amateur Agent. Boardman, 1964

ADAMS, CLEVE F(RANKLIN). 1895-1949. Pseudonym: John Spain, q.v. Joint pseudonym with Robert Leslie Bellem, 1902-1968, q.v.: Franklin Charles, q.v. Ref: CC, EM, MP, TC. SC: Rex McBride = RM; John J. Shannon = JS.
- And Sudden Death. Dutton, 1940 RM [ship]
- The Black Door. Dutton, 1941 [San Diego]
- Borderline Cases; see Contraband
- Contraband. Knopf, 1950. British title: Borderline Cases. Cassell, 1952 [San Diego]
- The Crooking Finger. Reynel, 1944 RM [Nev.]
- Death at the Dam; see Sabotage
- Death Before Breakfast; see Sabotage
- Decoy. Dutton, 1941 RM [L.A.]
- Murder All Over; see Up Jumped the Devil
- No Wings on a Cop. Handi-Books, 1950. (Expanded by Robert Leslie Bellem, 1902-1968, q.v., from a pulp novelet by Adams.) JS
- The Private Eye. Reynel, 1942 JS [Ariz.]
- Sabotage. Dutton, 1940. British title: Death at the Dam. Cassell, 1946. Also published as: Death Before Breakfast. Mystery Novel of the Month, 1942 RM [Nev.]
- Shady Lady. Ace, 1955 RM [Mont.]
- Up Jumped the Devil. Reynel, 1943. Also published as: Murder All Over. Signet, 1950 RM [S.F.]
- What Price Murder. Dutton, 1942 [L.A.]

ADAMS, CLIFTON. 1919-   . Pseudonym: Jonathan Gant, q.v. Ref: CA.
- Death's Sweet Song. GM, 1955
- The Very Wicked. Berkley, 1960
- Whom Gods Destroy. GM, 1953; Red Seal, 1958

ADAMS, ELIHU
- Operation Homicide. Mill, 1947

ADAMS, EUSTACE L(ANE). 1891-   . Born in Maine; pulp writer; author of hundreds of ss, numerous adventure books for boys.
- Death Charter. Coward, 1943; Crowther, 1945 [ship]
- Gambler's Throw. Dial, 1930; Hamilton, 1931 [Fla.]
- Murder in the Hurricane. Methuen, 1938 [ship]

ADAMS, FRANCIS (WILLIAM LAUDERDALE). 1862-1893.
- Australian Life. Chapman, 1892 ss, some criminous [Australia]
- John Webb's End; see Strong As Death
- Madeline Brown's Murderer. Kemp, 1887
- Strong as Death. Also published as: John Webb's End. Remington, 1891

ADAMS, FRANK R(AMSEY). 1883-1963.
- For Valour. Paul, 1933
- Help Yourself to Happiness. Macaulay, 1929; Newnes, 1929
- King's Crew. Long & Smith, 1932; Constable, 1932 [Calif.]
- The Long Night. Paul, 1932 [Arctic]
- -Men on Foot. Newnes, 1937
- -Pleasure Island. Paul, 1935
- -The Secret Attic. Paul, 1930

ADAMS, FREDERICK UPHAM. 1859-1921.
- The Bottom of the Well. Dillingham, 1906; Unwin, 1906 [NYC]
- The Kidnapped Millionaires. Lothrop, 1901; Kelly, 1901 [NYC]

ADAMS, GERALD. See: Cortland Fitzsimmons, 1893-1949.

ADAMS, HERBERT. 1874-1958. Pseudonym: Jonathan Gray, q.v. Ref: CC, EM. SC: Roger Bennion = RB; Jimmie Haswell = JH. Set: Eng.
- The Araway Oath. Collins, 1942 RB
- Black Death. Collins, 1938 RB
- The Body in the Bunker. Collins, 1935; Lippincott, 1935
- By Order of the Five. Methuen, 1925
- Caroline Ormsby's Crime. Methuen, 1929; Lippincott, 1929
- The Case of the Stolen Bridegroom. Collins, 1940 RB
- The Chief Witness. Collins, 1940 RB
- Comrade Jill. Methuen, 1926; Lippincott, 1927
- The Crime in the Dutch Garden. Methuen, 1931; Lippincott, 1930 JH
- Crime Wave at Little Cornford. Macdonald, 1948 RB
- The Crooked Lip. Methuen, 1926; Lippincott, 1926 JH
- The Damned Spot. Collins, 1938 RB
- The Dean's Daughters. Macdonald, 1950 RB
- Death of a Viewer. Macdonald, 1958 RB
- Death Off the Fairway. Collins, 1936 RB
- Death on the First Tee. Macdonald, 1957 RB
- Diamonds Are Trumps. Macdonald, 1947 RB
- The Empty Bed. Methuen, 1928; Lippincott, 1928 JH
- Exit the Skeleton. Macdonald, 1952 RB
- Fate Laughs. Collins, 1935; Lippincott, 1935
- Four Winds. Collins, 1944 RB
- The Golden Ape. Methuen, 1930; Lippincott, 1930 JH
- The Golf House Murder; see John Brand's Will
- John Brand's Will. Methuen, 1935. U.S. title: The Golf House Murder. Lippincott, 1933
- The Judas Kiss. Macdonald, 1955 RB
- The Knife. Collins, 1934. U.S. title: The Strange Murder of Hatton, K.C. Lippincott, 1933
- Murder Without Risk; see A Word of Six Letters
- Mystery and Minette. Collins, 1934; Lippincott, 1934
- The Nineteenth Hole Mystery. Collins, 1939 RB
- Oddways. Methuen, 1930; Lippincott, 1929
- The Old Jew Mystery. Collins, 1936 RB
- One to Play. Macdonald, 1949 RB
- The Paulton Plot. Methuen, 1932; Lippincott, 1931 JH
- The Perfect Round. Methuen, 1927 ss, some criminous
- The Queen's Gate Mystery. Methuen, 1927; Lippincott, 1927 JH
- Roger Bennion's Double. Collins, 1941 RB
- Rogues Fall Out. Methuen, 1928; Lippincott, 1928 JH
- The Scarlet Feather. Cherry Tree, 1943
- The Secret of Bogey House. Methuen, 1924; Lippincott, 1925 JH
- Signal for Invasion. Collins, 1942 RB
- A Single Hair. Collins, 1937 RB
- The Sleeping Draught. Macdonald, 1951 RB
- Slippery Dick. Macdonald, 1954 RB
- The Sloane Square Mystery. Methuen, 1925; Dial, 1926
- The Spectre in Brown. Macdonald, 1953 RB
- Stab in the Back. Collins, 1941 RB
- The Strange Murder of Hatton, K.C.; see The Knife
- Victory Song. Collins, 1943 RB
- Welcome Home! Macdonald, 1946 RB
- The Woman in Black. Methuen, 1933; Lippincott, 1932 JH
- A Word of Six Letters. Collins, 1936. U.S. title: Murder Without Risk. Lippincott, 1936
- The Writing on the Wall. Collins, 1945 RB

ADAMS, IAN. 1937-   .
- End Game in Paris. Doubleday, 1979 [Paris]
- S—Portrait of a Spy. Gage, 1977

ADAMS, J. T.
- Mountain Murder. Pan, 1945

ADAMS, JOEY. 1911-   . Ref: CA.
- You Could Die Laughing, and The Swingers. Bobbs, 1968

ADAMS, JOHN F(ESTUS). 1930-   . Ref: CA.
- Two Plus Two Equals Minus Seven. Macmillan, 1969; Joseph, 1969 [Colo.]

Author Index

ADAMS, LETA ZOE. 1902- .
   The Mirror Murder. Phoenix, 1937
   [Wash.]

ADAMS, MARYE. Pseudonym of Marie B.
   Goodner.
   He Wouldn't Talk. Vantage, 1959

ADAMS, NATHAN M(ILLER). 1934- . Ref:
   CA.
   The Fifth Horseman. Random, 1967; Macmillan (London), 1968

ADAMS, O. L. Pseudonym: Old Hutch, q.v.

ADAMS, REX
   The Star of Persia. Harrap, 1942 [Iran]

ADAMS, ROBERT JAMES. 1924- . Pseudonyms: Robin Adam, Paul MacTyre, qq.v.

ADAMS, SAMUEL HOPKINS. 1871-1958. See also: Stewart Edward White, 1873-1946. Ref: CC, EM, MP.
   Average Jones. Bobbs, 1911; Palmer, 1913 ss
   The Flying Death. McClure, 1908 [L.I.]
   The Secret of Lonesome Cove. Bobbs, 1912; Hodder, 1913 [New Eng.]

ADAMS, SHIPLEY. SC: Inspector Harrow, in all titles. Set: Eng.
   Money by Menaces. Fiction House, 1948
   Murder in the First Person. Boardman, 1948
   Murder Unsolved. Boardman, 1947
   Murder Well Done. Boardman, 1950

ADAMS, WILLIAM T(AYLOR). 1822-1897. Pseudonym: Warren J. Ashton, q.v.
   Living Too Fast; or, The Confessions of a Bank Officer. Lee, 1876
   Three Millions! or, The Way of the World; see The Way of the World
   -The Way of the World. Lee, 1867. Also published as: Three Millions! or, The Way of the World. Lee, 1891

ADCOCK, ALMEY ST. JOHN. 1894- . Ref: CA.
   The Woman at Iron Crag. Hodder, 1934

ADDEO, EDMOND G. Served as newspaper feature writer, worked in advertising and engineering. See: Richard M(cClellan) Garvin, 1934- .

ADDIS, ERIC ELRINGTON. Pseudonym: Peter Drax, q.v.

ADDIS, HUGH. 1909- .
   Dark Voyage. Dodd, 1944; Jarrolds, 1947 [ship]
   Night over the Wood. Dodd, 1943; Jarrolds, 1944

ADDISCOMBE, JOHN. Pseudonym of (Alfred) John Hunter, 1891-1961, q.v. Other pseudonyms: L. H. Brenning, Anthony Dax, Anthony Drummond, Peter Meriton, qq.v.
   Drums of Death. Hurst, 1929
   Fighting Blood. Mowl, 1935
   Marked Cards. Gramol, 1935
   The Secret of the Graveyard. Gramol, 1937
   The Silk Scarf Murders. Gramol, 1937
   The Speed King. Gramol, 1935
   The Triangle of the Grey Wolf. Gramol, 1937

ADDISON, GWEN. Joint pseudonym of Alfred Harris, 1928- , q.v., and Arthur Moore, q.v. For Arthur Moore, see also: Don Hoyt. Joint pseudonyms of Arthur Moore and Marilyn Granbeck, 1927- , q.v.: Adam Hamilton, Van Saxon, qq.v.
   Storm over Fox Hill. PB, 1974

ADDISON, H(ENRY) R(OBERT). 1805?-1876.
   Behind the Curtain. Maxwell, 1865
   Diary of a Judge, Being Trials of Life Compiled from the Note-Book of a Recently Deceased Judge. Ward, 1860 ss
   Recollections of an Irish Police Magistrate and Other Reminiscences of the South of Ireland. Ward, 1862 ss [Ireland]

ADDLEMAN, D. R.
   A Contract on Stone. Major, 1977

ADDUCI, FRANK, JR. Pseudonym: Nick Carter, q.v.

ADDYMAN, ELIZABETH. 1900- .
   Green Shutters, with J(une) Wyndham Davies. English Theatre, 1964 (3-act play.)
   The Secret Tent. English Theatre, 1964 (3-act play.)

ADE, GEORGE. 1866-1944.
   Bang! Bang! Sears, 1928 ss

ADEE, DAVID GRAHAM
   The Blue Scarab. Laird, 1892. Also published as: The Lost Diamond. Laird, 1899
   The Lost Diamond; see The Blue Scarab
   No. 19 State Street. Cassell, 1888

ADKINS, BILL. SC: Dave Hill, in all titles. Set: Mex., in all titles.
   The Entry from San Sebastian. Popular Library, 1976
   Prison at Obregon. Popular Library, 1976
   The Rivera Collection. Popular Library, 1976

ADKINS, CLEO
   The Case of the Ebony Queen. Arcadia, 1955

ADLEMAN, ROBERT H. 1919- . Ref: CA.
   -Annie Deane. World, 1971 [Calif.]
   The Bloody Benders. Stein, 1970; Joseph, 1971 [Kan.]

ADLER, TERRY
   On Murder's Skirts. Phoenix, 1947 [Ind.]

ADLER, WARREN. 1927- . Ref: CA.
   The Casanova Embrace. Putnam, 1978 [Wash. D.C.]
   -Natural Enemies. PB, 1979 [Colo.]
   -The Sunset Gang. Viking, 1977; Macmillan (London), 1977
   Trans-Siberian Express. Putnam, 1977; Macmillan (London), 1977 [Russ., train]

ADSIT, BYRON D.
   A Mystery of the Fast Mail. Lovell, 1890
   The P.O. Detective; see Uncle Sam's Bad Boys
   Uncle Sam's Bad Boys; or, Leaves from a Diary of a Post-Office Inspector. Eagle, 1888. Also published as: The P.O. Detective. Eagle, 1891

ADYE, MAJOR GENERAL SIR JOHN. 1857-1930. Pseudonym: John Daye, q.v. SC: Oliver Smaile, in all titles.
   At the House of the Priest. Jenkins, 1925
   A Flash of Lightning. Methuen, 1927
   -The Golden Scarab. Jenkins, 1926

AEBY, JACQUELYN. Ref: CA.
   Cottage on Catherina Cay. Dell, 1976
   Falconer's Hall. Dell, 1976
   Linnet's Folly. Dell, 1973
   Never Look Back. Dell, 1976
   The Pipes of Margaree. Manor, 1978
   The Sea Gate. Leisure, 1977
   Serena. Dell, 1975 [New Mex.]
   Sign of the Blue Dragon. Dell, 1976

AESCULAPIUS. Pseudonym.
   The Magnetism of Sin. Greening, 1901

AFFORD, MAX. 1906- . SC: Jeffery Blackburn, in all novels.
   Blood on His Hands! Long, 1936 [Melb.]
   The Dead Are Blind. Long, 1937
   Death's Mannikins. Long, 1937; Appleton, 1937
   Fly by Night. Long, 1942. Also published as: The Owl of Darkness. Angus, 1942
   Lady in Danger. Mulga (Sydney), 1944; with Alexander Kirkland and some variations in text: French, 1946 (3-act play.)
   Mischief in the Air. U. of Queensland, 1974 (Plays, some criminous.)
   The Owl of Darkness; see Fly by Night

AFGHAN. Pseudonym. SC: Asaf Khan, in both titles.
   -Exploits of Asaf Khan. Jenkins, 1922 ss
   -The Wanderings of Asaf. Jenkins, 1923

AFTEREM, GEORGE. Pseudonym of Harold Williams, 1853-1926.
   Silken Threads. Cupples, 1885

AGEL, JEROME and EUGENE BOE
   22 Fires. Bantam, 1977; Corgi, 1977

AGG, HOWARD. See also: Mabel Constanduros.
   A Shot in the Dark. French, 1954 (1-act play.)

AGNEW, SPIRO T(HEODORE). 1918- .
   The Canfield Decision. Playboy, 1976; Allen, 1977 [Wash. D.C., 1983]

AGNIEL, LUCIEN D. 1919- . Ref: CA.
   Code Name "Icy". Paperback Library, 1970
   Pressure Point. Paperback Library, 1970 [Far East]

AHERN, JERRY. Pseudonym: Nick Carter, q.v.

AICKMAN, ROBERT (FORDYCE). 1914- .
   Ref: CA. Grandson of Richard Marsh, 1867-1915, q.v.
   -Cold Hand in Mine. Gollancz, 1975; Scribner, 1977 ss
   -Tales of Love and Death. Gollancz, 1977 ss

AIDE, (CHARLES) HAMILTON. 1829(?)-1906.
   The Cliff Mystery. Arrowsmith, 1888
   Morals and Mysteries. Smith Elder, 1872 ss

AIKEN, ALBERT W. 1846-1894. SC: Joe Phoenix = JP. Set: NYC, all titles.
   Chin Chin, the Chinese Detective; or, The Dark Work of the Black Hands. Westbrook, 1927
   Joe Phoenix, the Police Spy. Westbrook, 1927 JP
   Joe Phoenix, Private Detective; or, The League of the Skeleton Keys. Westbrook, 1927 JP
   he Wolves of New York; or, The King of Detectives. Westbrook, 1927

AIKEN, EDNAH. 1872- .
   -Love and I. Dodd, 1928 [S.F.]

AIKEN, GEORGE L. 1830-1876.
   -The Household Skeleton. American News, 1865

AIKEN, JOAN (DELANO). 1924- . Ref: CA, CC, TC. Set: mostly Eng.
   Beware of the Bouquet; see The Trouble with Product X
   The Butterfly Picnic. Gollancz, 1972. U.S. title: A Cluster of Separate Sparks. Doubleday, 1972 [Greece]
   Castle Barebane. Gollancz, 1976; Viking, 1976 [Scot., 1800s]
   A Cluster of Separate Sparks; see The Butterfly Picnic
   -Come Flee with Me. Gollancz, 1978
   The Crystal Crow; see The Ribs of Death
   Dark Interval; see Hate Begins at Home
   Died on a Rainy Sunday. Gollancz, 1972; Holt, 1972
   The Embroidered Sunset. Gollancz, 1970; Doubleday, 1970
   The Far Forests. Viking, 1977 ss, some criminous (British title?)
   -The Five-Minute Marriage. Gollancz, 1977; Doubleday, 1978
   The Fortune Hunters. Doubleday, 1965
   The Green Flash and other tales of horror, suspense and fantasy; see The Windscreen Weepers and other stories of horror and suspense
   Hate Begins at Home. Gollancz, 1967. U.S. title: Dark Interval. Doubleday, 1967
   Last Movement. Gollancz, 1977; Doubleday, 1977 [Greece]
   The Lightning Tree. Gollancz, 1980. U.S. title: The Weeping Ash. Doubleday, 1980 [1700s, Eng.]
   -Midnight Is a Place. Cape, 1974; Viking, 1974
   The Ribs of Death. Gollancz, 1967. U.S. title: The Crystal Crow. Doubleday, 1968
   -The Shadow Guests. Cape, 1980; Delacorte, 1980
   The Silence of Herondale. Gollancz, 1965; Doubleday, 1964

A

-The Smile of the Stranger. Gollancz, 1978; Doubleday, 1978 [Fr., 1790s]
A Touch of Chill. Gollancz, 1979; Delacorte, 1980 ss
The Trouble with Product X. Gollancz, 1966. U.S. title: Beware of the Bouquet. Doubleday, 1966
-Voices in an Empty House. Gollancz, 1975; Doubleday, 1975
The Weeping Ash; see The Lightning Tree
The Windscreen Weepers and other stories of horror and suspense. Gollancz, 1969. U.S. title: The Green Flash and other tales of horror, suspense and fantasy. Holt, 1971 ss

AIKEN, JOHN (KEMPTON). 1913-   .
The Lid Off. Hale, 1969
Nightly Deadshade. Macmillan (London), 1971

AIKEN, RALPH
The Ghost Hunters. McBride, 1934 [Conn.]

AINSWORTH, CYRUS
The Disappearance of Nicholson. Ousley, 1908

AINSWORTH, ED(WARD MADDIN). 1902-1968. Ref: CA.
Death Cues the Pageant. Arcadia, 1954 [Calif.]

AINSWORTH, HARRIET. Pseudonym of (Violet) Elizabeth Cadell, 1903-   , q.v.
Consider the Lilies. Hodder, 1955
Death Among Friends. Hodder, 1964
Shadow on the Water. Hodder, 1958. U.S. title: Shadows on the Water, as by Elizabeth Cadell. Morrow, 1958
Shadows on the Water; see Shadow on the Water

AINSWORTH, MILO. Pseudonym of Peter Fison.
Murder Is Catching. Hammond, 1959

AINSWORTH, PATRICIA. Pseudonym of Patricia Nina Bigg, 1932-   . Ref: CA.
The Devil's Hole. Hale, 1971 [1877, Australia]

AINSWORTH, W(ILLIAM) HARRISON. 1805-1882.
Jack Sheppard. Bentley, 1839; Colyer, 1839. Also published as: King of Crooks. Collins, 1930
King of Crooks; see Jack Sheppard
Rookwood. Bentley, 1834; Carey, 1834

AIRD, CATHERINE. Pseudonym of Kinn Hamilton McIntosh, 1930-   . Ref: CA, CC, EM, TC. SC: Insp. C. S. Sloan = CS. Set: Eng.
The Complete Steel. Macdonald, 1969. U.S. title: The Stately Home Murder. Doubleday, 1970 CS
Henrietta Who? Macdonald, 1968; Doubleday, 1968 CS
His Burial Too. Collins, 1973; Doubleday, 1973 CS
A Late Phoenix. Collins, 1970; Doubleday, 1971 CS
A Most Contagious Game. Macdonald, 1967; Doubleday, 1967
Parting Breath. Collins, 1977; Doubleday, 1978 CS [acad.]
Passing Strange. Collins, 1980; Doubleday, 1981 CS
The Religious Body. Macdonald, 1966; Doubleday, 1966 CS
Slight Mourning. Collins, 1975; Doubleday, 1976 CS
Some Die Eloquent. Collins, 1979; Doubleday, 1980 CS

AIRTH, RENNIE. 1935-   . Born in Johannesburg; reporter and foreign correspondent.
Snatch. Cape, 1969; Simon, 1969   [Rome]

AITKEN, ROBERT. 1872-   . Pseudonym: Hudson Douglas, q.v.
-Beyond the Skyline. Murray, 1909 ss
The Golden Horseshoe. Greening, 1908; McBride, 1907
-A Maid of Honour. Greening, 1908
-The Redding Straik. Morton, 1905

AIX. Pseudonym of Frederick Bausman, 1861-1931.
Adventures of a Nice Young Man. Duffield, 1908; Richards, 1909
Thieves. Duffield, 1911; Palmer, 1912

ALAIS, E(RNEST) W. 1864-1922. All titles were published by Amalgamated Press and feature Sexton Blake.
Camouflage! 1919
A Case of Blackmail. 1917
The Doctor's Double. 1921
In the Shadow of Night. 1922
The Lease of Convict 308. 1916

ALAN, A. J. Pseudonym of Leslie Harrison Lambert, 1883-1940.
A. J. Alan's Second Book. Hutchinson, 1933 ss, some criminous

ALAN, MARJORIE. Pseudonym of Doris Marjorie Bumpus, 1905-   , q.v. Set: Eng.
Dark Legacy. Hale, 1953
Dark Prophecy; see Masked Murder
The Ivory Locket. Hale, 1951
Masked Murder. Hale, 1945. U.S. title: Dark Prophecy. Mill, 1945
Murder at Puck's Cottage. Hale, 1951
Murder in a Maze. Hale, 1956
Murder in November. Hale, 1946. U.S. title: Rue the Day. Mill, 1946
Murder Looks Back. Hale, 1955
Murder Next Door. Hale, 1950
Rue the Day; see Murder in November

ALAN, RAY. Pseudonym of Joseph Lawrence Valls-Russell.
The Beirut Pipeline. Collins, 1980; Farrar, 1980 [Beirut]
My Bonny Lies Under the Sea. Joseph, 1963

ALBERT, ANDREW I. SC: Paul Decker, in both titles.
The Maori Murder Case. Vulcan, 1944
Murder for a Hollow Shell. Vulcan, 1945

ALBERT, EDWARD. 1890-   .
As Good As a Mile. Nicholson, 1934

ALBERT, MARVIN H(UBERT). 1924-   . Pseudonyms: Mike Barone, Al Conroy, Albert Conroy, Ian MacAlister, Nick Quarry, Anthony Rome, qq.v. Ref: CA.
The Dark Goddess. Doubleday, 1978; Deutsch, 1978
The Gargoyle Conspiracy. Doubleday, 1975; Deutsch, 1975 [Fr.]
Goodbye Charlie. Dell, 1964. (Novelization of the movie.)
Party Girl. Fawcett (London), 1959. (Novelization of the movie.)
The Pink Panther. Bantam, 1964. (Novelization of the movie.) [Fr.]

ALBRAND, MARTHA. Pseudonym of Heidi Huberta Freybe Loewengard, 1914-1981. Ref: CA, CC, EM, TC.
After Midnight. Random, 1949; Chatto, 1949 [It.]
A Call from Austria. Random, 1963; Hodder, 1963 [Austria]
A Day in Monte Carlo. Random, 1959; Hodder, 1959 [Fr.]
Desperate Moment. Random, 1951; Chatto, 1951
A Door Fell Shut. NAL, 1966; Hodder, 1966 [Ger.]
Endure No Longer. Little, 1944; Chatto, 1945
Final Encore. St. Martin's, 1978. British title: Intermission. Hodder, 1978 [NYC]
The Hunted Woman. Random, 1952; Hodder, 1953 [Switz.]
Intermission; see Final Encore
The Linden Affair. Random, 1956. British title: The Story That Could Not Be Told. Hodder, 1956 [Ger.]
Manhattan North. Coward, 1971; Hodder, 1972 [NYC]
The Mask of Alexander. Random, 1953; Hodder, 1956 [Paris, Venice]
Meet Me Tonight. Random, 1960; Hodder, 1961. Also published as: Return to Terror. Ace, 1964 [Brus.]
Nightmare in Copenhagen. Random, 1954; Hodder, 1954 [Copen.]
No Surrender. Little, 1942; Chatto, 1943 [Holl.]
None Shall Know. Little, 1945; Chatto, 1946 [Fr.]
Remembered Anger. Little, 1946 [Paris]
Return to Terror; see Meet Me Tonight
Rhine Replica. Random, 1969; Hodder, 1970 [Ger.]
The Story That Could Not Be Told; see The Linden Affair
A Taste of Terror. Putnam, 1977; Hodder, 1976 [L.I.]
Wait for the Dawn. Random, 1950; Chatto, 1950
Whispering Hill. Random, 1947; Chatto, 1948
Without Orders. Little, 1943; Chatto, 1944 [It.]
Zurich/AZ 900. Holt, 1974; Hodder, 1975 [Zurich]

ALCANTER DE BRAHM, JEANNE ICHORD. 1890-   . Pseudonym: Jean Rosmer, q.v.

ALCOTT, CYNTHIA
The Dungeons of Crowley Hall. Ace, 1973 [N.Y.]
Storm over Windmere. Ace, 1973

ALCOTT, LOUISA MAY. 1832-1888.
Behind a Mask: The Unknown Thrillers of Louisa May Alcott. Morrow, 1975; Allen, 1976 (4 novelets.)
Plots and Counterplots. Morrow, 1976; Allen, 1977 ss

ALDANOV, MARK. Pseudonym of Mark Aleksandrovich Landau, 1886-1957. Born in Kiev, educated in chemistry; most noted for historical novels.
-The Escape. Scribner, 1950; Cape, 1952
The Fifth Seal. Scribner, 1943; Cape, 1945. (Translation of "Nachalo Kontsa." Paris, 1939.)
The Key. Harrap, 1931 [Russ., 1917]
Nightmare and Dawn. Duell, 1957
-The Scoundrel. Barker, 1960

ALDEN, WINTHROP. Pseudonym.
The Lost Million. Dodd, 1913 [NYC]

ALDERSON, A. J.
The Harding Mystery. Falcon, 1949

ALDERSON, ALEXANDER
The Subtle Minotaur. Gifford, 1954

ALDERSON, ALFRED JAMES
The Crime of Wilfred Hanson. Stockwell, 1942

ALDHOUSE, ERIC
The Crime at the Quay Inn. Allan, 1934

ALDING, PETER. Pseudonym of Roderic (Graeme) Jeffries, 1926-   , q.v. Other pseudonyms: Jeffrey Ashford, Roderic Graeme, Graham Hastings, qq.v. SC: Constable Kerr and Insp. Robert Fusil, in all titles. Set: Eng., in all titles.
All Leads Negative; see The C.I.D. Room
Call Back to Crime. Long, 1972
The C.I.D. Room. Long, 1967. U.S. title: All Leads Negative. Harper, 1967
Circle of Danger. Long, 1968
Despite the Evidence. Long, 1971; Saturday Review Press, 1972
Field of Fire. Long, 1973
Guilt Without Proof. Long, 1970; McCall, 1971
Murder Among Thieves. Long, 1969; McCall, 1970
Murder Is Suspected. Long, 1977; Walker, 1978
The Murder Line. Long, 1974
Ransom Town. Long, 1979; Walker, 1979
Six Days to Death. Long, 1975

ALDIS, DOROTHY (KEELEY). 1896-1966. Ref: CA.
Murder in a Haystack. Farrar, 1931; Cassell, 1931

ALDOUS, ALLAN (CHARLES). 1911-   .
Danger on the Map. Cheshire (Melbourne), 1947
It's Murder If You Say So! Skeffington, 1952
The Lady's Eyes Were Green. Skeffington, 1951

ALDRICH, EARL AUGUSTUS. 1886-   . Pseudonym: A. B. Leonard, q.v.

ALDRICH, THOMAS BAILEY. 1836-1907. Ref: CC, DD, EM.
Marjorie Daw and Other People. Osgood, 1873; Routledge, 1873. Also published as (with altered contents): Marjorie Daw and other stories. Houghton, 1885; Douglas, 1894. And as (with differently altered contents): Marjorie Daw and other tales. Tauchnitz, 1879 ss

Marjorie Daw and other stories; see
  Marjorie Daw and Other People
Marjorie Daw and other tales; see
  Marjorie Daw and Other People
Out of His Head. Carleton, 1862 [N.H.]
The Stillwater Tragedy. Houghton, 1880;
  Douglas, 1886 [New Eng.]

ALDRIDGE, (HAROLD EDWARD) JAMES.
  1918- . SC: Kit Quayle = KQ;
  Rupert Royce = RR. Ref: CA.
-A Captive in the Land. H. Hamilton,
  1962; Doubleday, 1963 RR
-The Diplomat. Bodley Head, 1949;
  Little, 1950
 Mockery in Arms. Joseph, 1974; Little,
  1974 [Mid. East]
-A Sporting Proposition. Joseph, 1973;
  Little, 1973 KQ
-The Statesman's Game. H. Hamilton,
  1966; Doubleday, 1966 RR
-The Untouchable Juli. Joseph, 1975;
  Little, 1976 KQ

ALDYNE, NATHAN. Joint pseudonym of
  Michael McDowell, 1950- , q.v.,
  and Dennis Schuetz.
  Vermilion. Avon, 1980 [Boston]

ALEXANDER, MRS. Pseudonym of Annie French
  Hector, 1825-1902.
-At Bay. Warne, 1885; Holt, 1885
-A Choice of Evils. White, 1894
 The Crumpled Leaf. Drane, 1911
-A False Scent. White, 1889; Lovell,
  1889
 The Yellow Fiend. Unwin, 1901; Dodd,
  1901

ALEXANDER, COLIN JAMES. 1920-   . Pseudonym: Simon Jay, q.v.

ALEXANDER, DAIR
  Penelope's Daughter. Hale, 1975

ALEXANDER, DAVID. 1907-1973. Ref: CA, CC,
  EM. SC: Bart Hardin = BH; Marty Land
  = ML; Lt. Romano = R; Tommy Twotoes =
  TT.
 Bloodstain. Lippincott, 1961; Boardman,
  1962 ML [South]
 The Corpse in My Bed; see Most Men
  Don't Kill
 Dead, Man, Dead. Lippincott, 1959;
  Boardman, 1960 BH,R [NYC]
 The Death of Daddy-O. Lippincott, 1960;
  Boardman, 1960 ML [NYC]
 The Death of Humpty-Dumpty. Random,
  1957; Boardman, 1959 BH,R [NYC]
 Die, Little Goose. Random, 1956; Board-
  man, 1957 BH,R [NYC]
 Hangman's Dozen. Roy, 1961; Boardman,
  1961 ss
 Hush-a-Bye Murder. Random, 1957; Board-
  man, 1958 BH,R [NYC]
 The Madhouse in Washington Square. Lip-
  pincott, 1958; Boardman, 1959 [NYC]
 Most Men Don't Kill. Random, 1951; Ham-
  mond, 1953. Also published as: The
  Corpse in My Bed. Ace, 1954 TT,R
  [NYC]
 Murder in Black and White. Random,
  1951; Hammond, 1954 TT, R [NYC]
 The Murder of Whistler's Brother. Ran-
  dom, 1956; Boardman, 1958 BH,R [NYC]
 Murder Points a Finger. Random, 1953;
  Boardman, 1955 R [NYC]
 Paint the Town Black. Random, 1954;
  Boardman, 1957 BH [NYC]
 Pennies from Hell. Lippincott, 1960;
  Boardman, 1961 [NYC]
 Shoot a Sitting Duck. Random, 1955;
  Boardman, 1957 BH,R [NYC]
 Terror on Broadway. Random, 1954;
  Boardman, 1956 BH [NYC]

ALEXANDER, DAVID M(ICHAEL). 1945- .
  Ref: CA.
 The Chocolate Spy. Coward, 1978

ALEXANDER, GRACE
  Prince Cinderella. Bobbs, 1921

ALEXANDER, HOLMES (MOSS). 1906- .
  Ref: CA.
 Shall Do No Murder. Regnery, 1959;
  Hammond, 1960

ALEXANDER, IAN
 The Disappearance of Archibald Forsyth.
  Hutchinson, 1933

ALEXANDER, IRENE
 Crooked Alley. Penn, 1933
 Ninth Week. Penn, 1935 [L.I.]
 Revenge Can Wait. Putnam, 1941 [Calif.]
 Villa Caprice. Penn, 1932

ALEXANDER, JAN. Pseudonym of Victor Jer-
  ome Banis, 1937- . Other pseudo-
  nym: Lynn Benedict, q.v. Ref: CA.
 The Bishop's Palace. Popular Library,
  1973 [Brazil]
 Blood Moon. Lancer, 1970
 Blood Ruby. Ballantine, 1975
 Darkwater. PB, 1975 [South, 1860s]
 The Devil's Dance. Avon, 1972 [Tenn.]
 The Girl Who Never Was. Lancer, 1972
 The Glass House. Popular Library, 1971
 The Glass Painting. Popular Library,
  1972
 Green Willows. PB, 1977
 The Haunting of Helen Wren. PB, 1975
 House at Rose Point. Avon, 1972
  [Calif.]
 House of Fools. Lancer, 1971 [Calif.]
 The Jade Figurine. Curtis, 1973 [S.F.]
 The Lion's Gate. Berkley, 1976
 Moon Garden. Popular Library, 1972
  [Ga.]
 The Second House. Beagle, 1972 [N.Y.]
 Shadows. Lancer, 1970
 White Jade. Popular Library, 1971
 The Wolves of Craywood. Lancer, 1970

ALEXANDER, JOAN. Pseudonym of Joan Alexander Wetherell Pepper, 1920- .
  Ref: CA.
 One Sunny Day. Heinemann, 1974; Coward,
  1974

ALEXANDER, JOHN. Pseudonym of John Alexander Vlasto, 1877-1958. Other pseudonym: John Remenham, q.v. Set: Eng.
 The House of Shayle. Low, 1933
 Murder at the Eclipse. Low, 1934

ALEXANDER, KARL. Born in California, professor of English and drama, playwright and screenwriter.
 A Private Investigation. Delacorte,
  1980; Severn, 1981 [Calif.]
 Time After Time. Delacorte, 1979; Panther, 1980 [S.F.]

ALEXANDER, MARSHA
 Birthmark of Fear. Major, 1976
 The Curtis Wives. Major, 1979
 House of Shadows. Major, 1977
 Whispers in the Wind. Major, 1977

ALEXANDER, MARTIN
 Death Is Too Good for You. Hale, 1969
 A Dream Before Dying. Hale, 1970

ALEXANDER, PATRICK. 1926- . Reporter
  and TV writer.
 Death of a Thin-Skinned Animal. Macmillan (London), 1976; Dutton, 1977
 Show Me a Hero. Macmillan (London),
  1979; Viking, 1980 [ca.1990, Eng.]

ALEXANDER, ROBERT. 1928- .
 The Soul Eater. Souvenir, 1979

ALEXANDER, ROBERT WILLIAM. 1905-1980.
  Pseudonym: Joan Butler, q.v.

ALEXANDER, ROSS
 The Mask of Fear. Blackfriars, 1948

ALEXANDER, RUTH. Pseudonym of Ruth
  Rogers, 1890- .
 Blackmail. Readers Library, 1929; World
  Wide, ca.1929. (Novelization of the
  play by Charles Bennett.)
 The Ghost Train. Arrowsmith, 1927;
  Small, 1926. (Novelization of the
  play by Arnold Ridley, 1896- ,
  q.v.)
 The Man Who Knew Too Much. Arrowsmith,
  1936. (Novelization of the movie.)
 Rome Express. Readers Library, 1932.
  (Novelization of the movie.) [train]
 The Wrecker. Selwyn, 1928. (Noveliza-
  tion of the play by Arnold Ridley,
  1896- , q.v., and Bernard Meri-
  vale, 1882-1939.)

ALEXANDER, MRS. THOMAS
 Irene. Ponsonby, 1895

ALEXANDRE, PHILIPPE. 1932- . Ref: CA.
 The President Is Dead. Hutchinson, 1967.
  (Translation of "Le President Est
  Mort." Paris, 1965.)

ALGER, HORATIO, JR. 1832-1899.
 Dan, the Detective. Carleton, 1884
 Dean Dunham; or, The Waterford Mystery.
  U.S. Book Co., 1891
 $500; or, Jacob Marlowe's Secret. U.S.
  Book Co., 1890

ALGIE, JAMES. Pseudonym: Wallace Lloyd,
  q.v.

ALIBRANDI, TOM. 1941- . Ref: CA.
-Killshot. Pinnacle, 1979; Corgi, 1979

ALINGTON, ADRIAN (RICHARD). 1895-1958.
  SC: Insp. "Steady as a Rock" Posse,
  in both titles. Set: Eng., both
  titles.
 The Amazing Test Match Crime. Chatto,
  1939
 The Vanishing Celebrities. Chatto, 1938

ALINGTON, CYRIL A(RGENTINE). 1872-1955.
  Pseudonym: S. C. Westerham, q.v. Ref:
  CC. SC: John Craggs and James
  Castleton = C&C; Mr. Birtley = B.
  Set: Eng.
 The Abbot's Cup. Jenkins, 1930
 Archdeacons Afloat. Faber, 1946 C&C,B
 Archdeacons Ashore. Faber, 1947 C&C
 Blackmail in Blankshire. Faber, 1949
  C&C
 The Count in Kensington. Jenkins, 1926
 Crime on the Kennet. Collins, 1939
 Gold and Gaiters. Faber, 1950 C&C,B
 Midnight Wireless. Macdonald, 1947 B
 Mr. Evans: A Cricketo-Detective Story.
  Macmillan (London), 1922
 The Nabob's Jewel. Faber, 1953
 Ten Crowded Hours. Macdonald, 1944

ALLAIN, MARCEL. 1885-1970. SC: Fantomas
  = F (a continuation of the series
  begun by Pierre Souvestre, 1874-1914,
  q.v., in collaboration with Allain).
 Bulldog and Rats. Paul, 1928 F [Eng.]
 Fantomas Captured. Paul, 1926; McKay,
  1926 F [Fr.]
 Juve in the Dock. Paul, 1925; McKay,
  1926 F [Fr.]
 The Lord of Terror. Paul, 1925; McKay,
  1925 F [Fr.]
 The Revenge of Fantomas. Paul, 1927;
  McKay, 1927 F
 The Yellow Document; or, "Fantomas of
  Berlin." Paul, 1920; Brentano's,
  1919 [Fr., Ger.]

ALLAN, A. W.
-Devil's Drive: A Tale of Four Bad'uns.
  Dodd, Eyton, 1910

ALLAN, DENNIS. Pseudonym of Elinore Den-
  niston, 1900-1978. Other pseudonym:
  Rae Foley, q.v.
 Born to Be Murdered. Mill, 1945; Ham-
  mond, 1952 [NYC]
 Brandon Is Missing. Mill, 1940; Hamil-
  ton, 1938 [NYC]
 The Case of the Headless Corpse. Mill,
  1945
 Dead to Rights. Mill, 1946; Hammond,
  1953 [NYC]
 House of Treason. Greystone, 1936 [NYC]

ALLAN, DINA
 Melody of Murder. Zebra, 1979 [New
  Eng.]

ALLAN, FRANCIS K. ca.1917- .
 Death in Gentle Grove. Mason/Charter,
  1976 [Texas]
 First Come, First Kill. Reynal, 1945;
  Boardman, 1947 [NYC]
 The Invisible Bridge. Reynal, 1947
  [NYC]

ALLAN, HENRY
 The Tragic Case of John Renold. Dorrance, 1935 [NYC]

ALLAN, JOAN. SC: Valerie Lambert, in all
  titles.
 Who Killed Me? Zebra, 1979
 Who's Next? Zebra, 1979 [Paris]
 Who's on First? Zebra, 1979

ALLAN, LUKE. Pseudonym of William Lacey
  Amy, q.v. SC: Gordon Muldrew, in at
  least those marked GM; Blue Pete, in
  titles containing his name, which are
  set in Can.
-The Beast. Cape, 1924; Small, 1924

A

Behind the Wire Fence. Arrowsmith, 1935 GM [Can.]
Beyond the Locked Door. Jenkins, 1938 GM
The Black Opal. Arrowsmith, 1935 [Can.]
Blue Pete. Jenkins, 1938
Blue Pete and the Kid. Jenkins, 1953
Blue Pete and the Pinto. Jenkins, 1948
Blue Pete at Bay. Jenkins, 1952
Blue Pete Breaks the Rules. Jenkins, 1943
Blue Pete: Detective. Jenkins, 1928
Blue Pete: Half-Breed. Jenkins, 1921
Blue Pete in the Badlands. Jenkins, 1954
Blue Pete: Indian Scout. Jenkins, 1950
Blue Pete: Outlaw. Jenkins, 1944
Blue Pete Pays a Debt. Jenkins, 1942
Blue Pete: Rebel. Jenkins, 1940
Blue Pete Rides the Foothills. Jenkins, 1953
Blue Pete to the Rescue. Jenkins, 1947
Blue Pete, Unofficially. Jenkins, 1949
Blue Pete Works Alone. Jenkins, 1948
Blue Pete's Dilemma. Jenkins, 1945
Blue Pete's Vendetta. Jenkins, 1947
The Case of the Open Drawer. Arrowsmith, 1936 [Eng.]
The Dark Spot. Arrowsmith, 1932
The End of the Trail. Arrowsmith, 1931 [Can.]
Five for One. Arrowsmith, 1934 [NYC]
The Fourth Dagger. Arrowsmith, 1932 GM
The Ghost Murder. Jenkins, 1937
The Jungle Crime. Arrowsmith, 1931 GM [NYC]
The Lone Trail. Jenkins, 1922 [Can.]
The Man on the Twenty-Fourth Floor. Jenkins, 1937 [NYC]
The Many-Coloured Thread. Jenkins, 1932
The Masked Stranger. Arrowsmith, 1930 GM [NYC]
Murder at Midnight. Arrowsmith, 1930 GM
Murder at the Club. Arrowsmith, 1933 GM
-The Pace. Hutchinson, 1926
The Return of Blue Pete. Jenkins, 1923; Doran, 1922
Scotland Yard Takes a Holiday. Arrowsmith, 1934 [Eng.]
-The Sire. Hutchinson, 1927
-The Tenderfoot. Jenkins, 1939
The Traitor. Arrowsmith, 1933
The Vengeance of Blue Pete. Jenkins, 1939
-The Westerner. Jenkins, 1924
-The White Camel. Jarrolds, 1926

ALLAN, MABEL ESTHER. 1915- . Ref: CA.
Murder at the Flood. Paul, 1957

ALLAN, STELLA
A Dead Giveaway. Collins, 1980; St. Martin's, 1981
An Inside Job. Collins, 1978; Scribner, 1978
A Mortal Affair. Collins, 1979; Scribner, 1979
No Marks for Trying. Macdonald, 1975; Avon, 1982

ALLARDYCE, PAULA. Pseudonym of Ursula Torday, 1888- . Other pseudonyms: Charity Blackstock, Charlotte Keppel, qq.v., Lee Blackstock. Set: Eng.
-Adam and Evelina. Ward, 1956
-Adam's Rib. Hodder, 1963
-After the Lady. Ward, 1954
-Beloved Enemy. Ward, 1958
-Death, My Lover. Ward, 1959
-The Doctor's Daughter. Ward, 1955
-A Game of Hazard. Ward, 1955
-The Gentle Highwayman. Ward, 1961
The Ghost of Archie Gilroy. Hodder, 1970
Haunting Me. Hodder, 1978; St. Martins
-Johnny Danger. Ward, 1960
-The Lady and the Pirate. Ward, 1957
-The Man of Wrath. Ward, 1956
-A Marriage Has Been Arranged. Ward, 1959
-My Dear Miss Emma. Ward, 1958
-The Respectable Miss Parkington-Smith. Hodder, 1964
-Southarn Folly. Ward, 1957
-Witches' Sabbath. Hodder, 1961; Macmillan, 1962

ALLBEURY, TED [THEODORE EDWARD LE BOUTHILLIER ALLBEURY]. 1917- . Pseudonyms: Richard Butler, Patrick Kelly, qq.v. Ref: CA, TC.
The Alpha List. Hart-Davis, 1979; Methuen (NYC), 1980
A Choice of Enemies. Davies, 1973; St. Martin's, 1973
Consequence of Fear. Granada, 1979
The Lantern Network. Davies, 1978 [WWII, Fr.]
The Man with the President's Mind. Davies, 1977; Simon, 1978 [Russ., U.S.]
Moscow Quadrille. Davies, 1976
Omega-Minus; see Palomino Blonde
The Only Good German. Davies, 1976
Palomino Blonde. Davies, 1975. U.S. title: Omego-Minus. Viking, 1975
Snowball. Davies, 1974; Lippincott, 1974
The Special Collection. Davies, 1975
The Twentieth Day of January. Granada, 1980

ALLEN, A. WHATOFF
Exit an Admiral. Low, 1938

ALLEN, ADDISON J.
New England Gothic. Chilton, 1960. Also published as: Thunder over South Parish. Dell, 1964 [New Eng.]

ALLEN, ANITA [ANITA ALLEN SCHENCK]. 1909- . Ref: CA.
The False Face of Death. Doubleday, 1979 [Calif.]
The Spell of Choti. Berkley, 1977
Thunder Rock. Berkley, 1974

ALLEN, AUSTEN. 1887- . SC: Insp. Ord, in all titles, set in Eng.
The Dead Mouse. Bles, 1930
Live Wires. Bles, 1931
The Loose Rib. Bles, 1932; Kinsey, 1933
Menace to Mrs. Kershaw. Bles, 1929; Harper, 1930

ALLEN, ARTHUR BRUCE. 1903-1975. Pseudonym: Borough Trice, q.v.

ALLEN, CLIFFORD (EDWARD). 1902- . Ref: CA.
The Dark Places. Redman, 1958

ALLEN, E. C. Pseudonym of Elizabeth Campbell Ward, 1936- . Ref: CA.
The Laguna Contracts. Pyramid, 1973 [L.A.]

ALLEN, ELISABETH OFFUTT. 1895- . Ref: CA.
The Hounds of the Moon. Popular Library, 1974 [N.Y., 1940s]
This Tangled Web. Bouregy, 1966

ALLEN, ERIC. Pseudonym of Eric Allen-Ballard.
Canaries Also Sing. Hammond, 1960
Death on Delivery. Hammond, 1958 [Afr.]
Eric Allen's Broadcast Stories. Cowan, 1947 ss, some criminous
The Man Who Chose Death. Hammond, 1959
Passport to Murder; see Perilous Passport
Perilous Passport. Hammond, 1958. Also published as: Passport to Murder. Corgi, 1959

ALLEN, ERIC VAUGHN. Pseudonym: Erika Vaughan Allen, q.v.

ALLEN, ERIKA VAUGHAN. Pseudonym of Eric Vaughn Allen.
Voices in the Wind. Signet, 1967 [Mo.]

ALLEN, F.
The Whitechapel Murder. Ogilvie, n.d.

ALLEN, GERTRUDE M.
House of Dark Secrets. Rich, 1934
Nightshade. Rich, 1934; Macaulay, 1935

ALLEN, (CHARLES) GRANT (BLAIRFINDIE). 1848-1899. Ref: CC, EM, MP. Set: Eng.
An African Millionaire. Richards, 1897; Arnold, 1897 ss
-An Army Doctor's Romance. Tuck (London), 1894; Tuck (New York), 1893
-At Market Value. Chatto, 1894; Neely, 1894
-Babylon. Chatto, 1885; Appleton, 1885
-The Backslider. Lewis Scribner (London & NYC), 1901 ss
The Beckoning Hand and other stories. Chatto, 1887 ss
-Blood Royal. Chatto, 1893; Cassell (New York), 1892
A Bride from the Desert. Fenno, 1896. (3 stores, one or two criminous.)
The Cruise of the Albatross; see Wednesday the Tenth
-Desire of the Eyes and other stories. Digby, 1895; Fenno, 1895 ss
The Devil's Die. Chatto, 1888; Lovell, 1888
-The Duchess of Powysland. Chatto, 1892; U.S. Book Co., 1891
-Dr. Palliser's Patient. Mullen, 1889
-Dumaresq's Daughter. Chatto, 1891; Harper, 1891
For Maimie's Sake: A Tale of Love and Dynamite. Chatto, 1886; Appleton, 1886
-The General's Will. Butterworth, 1892 ss
Hilda Wade. Richards, 1900; Harper, 1900 ss (Completed by A. Conan Doyle, 1859-1930, q.v.)
-In All Shades. Chatto, 1886; Rand, 18??
-The Incidental Bishop. Pearson, 1898; Appleton, 1898
The Indian Mystery; or, Kalee's Shrine; see Kalee's Shrine
Ivan Greet's Masterpiece. Chatto, 1893 ss
The Jaws of Death. Simpkin Marshall, 1889; New Amsterdam, 1896 [West]
Kalee's Shrine, with May Cotes. Arrowsmith, 1886; New Amsterdam, 1897. Also published as: The Indian Mystery; or, Kalee's Shrine. New Amsterdam, 1902
-Linnet. Richards, 1898; New Amsterdam, 1900
Michael's Crag. Leadenhall, 1893; Rand, 1893
Miss Cayley's Adventures. Richards, 1899; Putnam, 1899 ss
Recalled to Life. Arrowsmith, 1891; Holt, 1891
The Reluctant Hangman and other stories of crime. Aspen, 1975 ss
The Scallywag. Chatto, 1893; Cassell (NYC), 1893
Sir Theodore's Guest and other stories. Arrowsmith, 1902 ss
A Splendid Sin. White, 1896; Buckles, 1899
Strange Stories. Chatto, 1894 ss
-The Tents of Shem. Chatto, 1889; Rand, 1889
A Terrible Inheritance. SPCK, 1887; Crowell, 18??
This Mortal Coil. Chatto, 1888; Appleton, 1889
Twelve Tales. Richards, 1899 ss
Under Sealed Orders. Chatto, 1895; Collier, 1894
-Wednesday the Tenth. Lothrop, 1890. Also published as: The Cruise of the Albatross. Lothrop, 1898. (British title?)
What's Bred in the Bone. Tit-Bits, 1891; Tucker, 1891

ALLEN, JAN
Double Deception. Hale, 1975

ALLEN, JOHN. Pseudonym of Ritchie (John Allen) Perry, 1942- , q.v.
Copacabana Stud. Hale, 1977
Up Tight. Hale, 1979

ALLEN, LESLIE. Pseudonym of Horace Brown, 1908- , q.v.
Murder in the Rough. Five Star, 1946; Boardman, 1948, as by Horace Brown

ALLEN, LUCY DOREEN
Innocent Murder. Stockwell, 1953

ALLEN, MARCUS. See: Anne Fuller.

ALLEN, MICHAEL (DEREK). 1939- . SC: Supt. Ben Spence, in both titles. Ref: CA. Set: Eng.
Spence and the Holiday Murders; see Spence in Petal Park
Spence at the Blue Bazaar. Constable, 1979; Walker, 1979
Spence in Petal Park. Constable, 1977. U.S. title: Spence and the Holiday Murders. Walker, 1978

ALLEN, ROBERT. Pseudonym of Allen Robert Dodd, 1887-
Captain Gardiner of the International Police. Dodd, 1916; Hodder, 1917 [future]

ALLEN, THOMAS B(ENTON). 1929- . Ref: CA.
A Short Life. Putnam, 1978 [Okla.]

ALLEN, TREVOR
Jade Elephants. Bles, 1934 [Maced.]

ALLEN, (HERBERT) WARNER. 1881-1969. See also: E(dmund) C(lerihew) Bentley, 1875-1956. SC: Mr. Clerihew = C (see also Bentley entry). Ref: CC, MP.
Death Fungus. Constable, 1937 [Fr.]
The Devil That Slumbers. Hamilton, 1925
Mr. Clerihew: Wine Merchant. Methuen, 1933 C
The Uncounted Hour. Constable, 1936

ALLEN, WILL
Contraband Cruises. Heritage, 1935 [ship]

ALLEN, WILLIS BOYD. 1855-1938.
  The Head of Pasht. Dutton, 1900

ALLEN, WOODY. 1935-   .
  -Death. French, 1975. (1-act play.)

ALLEN-BALLARD, ERIC. Pseudonym: Eric Allen, q.v.

ALLERTON, BERRIDGE
  Who Killed Roger Whitely? Georgian House, 1946

ALLERTON, MARK. Pseudonym of William Ernest Cameron, 1881-   . Set: Eng.
  The Case of Richard Eden. Hodder, 1918
  -False Witness. Thomson, 1921
  -The Girl in the Web. Thomson, 1927
  Let Justice Be Done. Hurst, 1912
  The Maitland Street Murder. Skeffington, 1919
  The Mill. Skeffington, 1919
  The Mystery of Beaton Craig. Skeffington, 1919
  -The Woman in the Case. Thomson, 1924

ALLERTON, MARY. Pseudonym of (Mary) Christine Noble Govan, 1898-   , q.v. Other pseudonym: J. N. Darby, q.v.
  The Shadow and the Web. Bobbs, 1940; Hale, 1942 [South]

ALLINGHAM, FRANCIS
  Crooked Paths. Longmans, 1897

ALLINGHAM, MARGERY (LOUISE). 1904-1966. Ref: all except MM. SC: Albert Campion = AC (continued by her husband, Youngman Carter, 1904-1969, q.v.) Set: Eng.
  The Allingham Case-Book. Chatto, 1969; Morrow, 1969 ss, some about AC
  The Allingham Minibus. Chatto, 1973; Morrow, 1973 ss, some about AC
  The Beckoning Lady. Chatto, 1955. U.S. title: The Estate of the Beckoning Lady. Doubleday, 1955 AC
  The Black Dudley Murder; see The Crime at Black Dudley
  Black Plumes. Heinemann, 1940; Doubleday, 1940
  Cargo of Eagles. Chatto, 1968; Morrow, 1968 AC
  The Case Book of Mr. Campion. Mercury, 1947. (ss, many of which also appear in the 1950 edition of Mr. Campion and others, q.v.) AC
  The Case of the Late Pig. Hodder, 1937. (A long novelet published in Britain as a separate volume and in the U.S. as part of Mr. Campion: Criminologist, q.v.) AC
  The China Governess. Chatto, 1963; Doubleday, 1962 AC
  Coroner's Pidgin. Heinemann, 1945. U.S. title: Pearls Before Swine. Doubleday, 1945 AC
  The Crime at Black Dudley. Jarrolds, 1929. U.S. title: The Black Dudley Murder. Doubleday, 1930 AC
  Dancers in Mourning. Heinemann, 1937; Doubleday, 1937. Also published as: Who Killed Chloe? Avon, 1943 AC
  Deadly Duo; see Take Two at Bedtime
  Death of a Ghost. Heinemann, 1934; Doubleday, 1934 AC
  The Estate of the Beckoning Lady; see The Beckoning Lady
  The Fashion in Shrouds. Heinemann, 1938; Doubleday, 1938. Revised edition: Heinemann, 1965 AC
  The Fear Sign; see Sweet Danger
  Flowers for the Judge. Heinemann, 1936; Doubleday, 1936. Also published as: Legacy in Blood. Mercury, 1949 AC
  The Gyrth Chalice Mystery; see Look to the Lady
  Hide My Eyes. Chatto, 1958. U.S. title: Tether's End. Doubleday, 1958. Also published as: Ten Were Missing. Dell, 1959 AC
  Kingdom of Death; see Sweet Danger
  Legacy in Blood; see Flowers for the Judge
  Look to the Lady. Jarrolds, 1931. U.S. title: The Gyrth Chalice Mystery. Doubleday, 1931 AC
  The Mind Readers. Chatto, 1965; Morrow, 1965 AC
  Mr. Campion and Others. Heinemann, 1939; Penguin, 1950. (The Penguin edition differs in contents from the Heinemann; while the Heinemann overlaps but does not completely correspond to Mr. Campion: Criminologist, below, the Penguin overlaps but does not completely correspond to The Case Book of Mr. Campion, above.) AC ss

Mr. Campion: Criminologist. Doubleday, 1937. (Includes the novelet The Case of the Late Pig, above, and several ss.) AC
More Work for the Undertaker. Heinemann, 1948; Doubleday, 1949. Revised edition: Heinemann, 1964 AC
Mystery Mile. Jarrolds, 1930; Doubleday, 1930. Revised edition: Penguin, 1968 AC
No Love Lost. World's Work, 1954; Doubleday, 1954. (Two novelets.)
Pearls Before Swine; see Coroner's Pidgin
Police at the Funeral. Heinemann, 1931; Doubleday, 1932 AC
The Sabotage Murder Mystery; see Traitor's Purse
Sweet Danger. Heinemann, 1933. U.S. title: Kingdom of Death. Doubleday, 1933. Also published as: The Fear Sign. Macfadden, 1961 AC
Take Two at Bedtime. World's Work, 1950. U.S. title: Deadly Duo. Doubleday, 1949 (Two novelets.)
Ten Were Missing; see Hide My Eyes
Tether's End; see Hide My Eyes
The Tiger in the Smoke. Chatto, 1952; Doubleday, 1952 AC
Traitor's Purse. Heinemann, 1941; Doubleday, 1941. Also published as: The Sabotage Murder Mystery. Avon, 1942 AC
Wanted: Someone Innocent. Pony Books, 1946. (A rare paperback, containing the title novelet, also found in Take Two at Bedtime, and three ss uncollected until the appearance of The Allingham Minibus, q.v.)
The White Cottage Mystery. Jarrolds, 1928. Revised edition: Chatto, 1975
Who Killed Chloe?; see Dancers in Mourning

ALLIS, SARAH. Born in Wisconsin; educated in zoology and literature.
  Nightwind. Bobbs, 1975 [Wis.]

ALLISON, CLYDE. Pseudonym of William Knowles. Other pseudonym: Clyde Ames, q.v.
  Have Nude, Will Travel. Berkley, 1962

ALLISON, WILLIAM. Pseudonym: Blinkhoolie, q.v.

ALLISON, WILLIAM
  Alias Richard Power. Doubleday, 1921 [Eng.]
  A Secret of the Sea. Doubleday, 1920 [ship]
  The Turnstile of Night. Doubleday, 1920 [Eng.]

ALLSOP, KENNETH. 1920-1973. Ref: CA.
  -The Leopard-Paw Orchid. Quality, 1954

ALLVINE, GLENDON. 1893?-1977. Pseudonym: Dana Sage, q.v.

ALLWOOD, MARGARET
  Reap What You Sow. Stockwell, 1979

ALLWRIGHT, MICHAEL. ca.1945-   . South African freelance journalist.
  The Roundabout. Macmillan (London), 1968. U.S. title: Neighbors. Walker, 1968

ALLYSON, ALAN. Son of a police inspector; writes crime fiction under several pen names; writer for newspapers and periodicals. SC: Martin Ross, in at least those marked MR.
  Bright as a Diamond. Hale, 1973
  Do You Deal in Murder? Hale, 1972 MR
  Don't Mess with Murder. Hale, 1972 MR
  The Lady Said No. Hale, 1972; Drake, 1972 MR

ALLYSON, KYM. Pseudonym of John M. Kimbro, 1929-   . Other pseudonyms: Ann Ashton, Charlotte Bramwell, Jean Kimbro, Katheryn Kimbrough, qq.v.
  The Moon Shadow. Berkley, 1976

ALMHAIN. Pseudonym.
  The Jewels of Prince de Janville. Swan, 1888

ALNER, JAMES Z.
  The Capital Murder. Knopf, 1932; Hurst, 1933 [Wash. D.C.]

ALONSO, RICARDO
  The Candidate. PB, 1972 (Translation of "El Candidato." Barcelona, 1970, as by Luis Ricardo Alonso.) [U.S.]

ALPERT, HOLLIS. 1916-   . Pseudonym: Robert Carroll, q.v.

ALROY, LIONEL
  -Shut Out the Sun. Longmans, 1955

ALTER, ROBERT EDMOND. 1925-1965. Ref: CA.
  Carny Kill. GM, 1966 [Fla.]
  The Red Fathom. Avon, 1967
  Swamp Sister. GM, 1961; Muller, 1963 [Fla.]
  Thieves Like Us. Avon, 1968 [Egypt]

ALTMAN, THOMAS. Pseudonym of Campbell Black, 1944-   , q.v. Joint pseudonym with Jeffrey (Andrew) Caine, 1944-   , q.v.: Jeffrey Campbell, q.v.
  Kiss Daddy Goodbye. Bantam, 1980

ALVAREZ, A(LFRED). 1929-   . Ref: CA.
  Hunt. Macmillan (London), 1978; Simon, 1979

ALVERSON, CHARLES. 1935-   . Ref: CA. SC: Joe Goodey = JG.
  Fighting Back. Bobbs, 1973; H. Hamilton, 1978 [NY]
  Goodey's Last Stand. Houghton, 1975; H. Hamilton, 1976 JG [S.F.]
  Not Sleeping, Just Dead. Houghton, 1977; H. Hamilton, 1978 JG [Calif.]

AMADI, ELECHI (EMMANUEL). 1934-   . Ref: CA.
  The Slave. Heinemann, 1978

AMARE, ROTHAYNE. Pseudonym of Stuart James Byrne, 1913-   . Ref: CA.
  The Visitation. Major, 1977

AMBERLEY, RICHARD. Pseudonym of Paul Henry James Bourquin, 1916-   . SC: Insp. Martin, in at least those marked M. Ref: CC.
  Dead on the Stone. Hale, 1969 M
  Incitement to Murder. Hale, 1968 M
  An Ordinary Accident. Hale, 1971

AMBERLEY, SIMON
  Murder at Quay Cottage. English Theatre, 1962. (3-act play.)

AMBLER, DAIL. Pseudonym: Danny Spade, q.v. SC: Danny Spade, in many (all?) titles.
  A Curtain of Glass. Milestone, 1954
  Danny Spade Sees Red. Milestone, 1954
  Danny Spade Spells Danger. Milestone, 1953
  Duet for Two Guns. Scion, 1952
  Hold That Tiger. Scion, 1952
  Johnny Gets His! Scion, 1952
  The Lady Says When. Scion, 1952
  Not Killed, Just Dead. Scion, 1952
  Someone Falling. Milestone, 1954
  Three Men for the Job. Hale, 1975
  The Virgin Collector. NEL pb, 1971
  What's with You? Scion, 1952
  Wildcat. Comyns, 1952

AMBLER, ERIC. 1909-   . Joint pseudonym with (Percival) Charles Rodda, 1891-   , q.v.: Eliot Reed, q.v. Ref: CA, CC, EM, MC, MP, TC. SC: Arthur Abdel Simpson = AS; Charles Latimer = CL; Valeshoff and Tamara = V&T.
  Background to Danger; see Uncommon Danger
  Cause for Alarm. Hodder, 1938; Knopf, 1939 V&T [Milan]
  A Coffin for Dimitrios; see The Mask of Dimitrios
  The Dark Frontier. Hodder, 1936
  Dirty Story. Bodley Head, 1967; Atheneum, 1967 AS [Afr.]
  Doctor Frigo. Weidenfield, 1974; Athenium, 1974 [Fr. Ant.]
  Epitaph for a Spy. Hodder, 1938; Knopf, 1952 [Fr.]
  The Intercom Conspiracy. Weidenfeld, 1970; Atheneum, 1969 CL
  Journey into Fear. Hodder, 1940; Knopf, 1940
  Judgment on Deltchev. Hodder, 1951; Knopf, 1951 [Balkans]
  A Kind of Anger. Bodley Head, 1964; Athenum, 1964 [Fr.]
  The Levanter. Weidenfeld, 1972; Atheneum, 1972 [Mid. East]
  The Light of Day. Heinemann, 1962; Knopf, 1963. Also published as: Topkapi. Bantam, 1964 AS [Istan.]
  The Mask of Dimitrios. Hodder, 1939. U.S. title: A Coffin for Dimitrios. Knopf, 1939 CL
  The Night-Comers. Heinemann, 1956. U.S. title: State of Siege. Knopf, 1956 [Far East]
  Passage of Arms. Heinemann, 1959; Knopf, 1960 [Far East]
  The Schirmer Inheritance. Heinemann, 1953; Knopf, 1953

Send No More Roses. Weidenfeld, 1977. U.S. title: The Siege of the Villa Lipp. Random, 1977 [It.]
The Siege of the Villa Lipp; see Send No More Roses
State of Siege; see The Night-Comers
Topkapi; see The Light of Day
Uncommon Danger. Hodder, 1937. U.S. title: Background to Danger. Knopf, 1937 V&T [Austria]

AMBLER, JOHN. 1911- . Born in England.
The Hunters. Exposition, 1969 [Eng.]

AMBOFILIUS. Pseudonym.
Claude Beauclerc, A Story of Modern Morality. Tinsley, 1881

AMBROSE, MISS ADELAIDE
Kinks. Adelaide Ambrose, 1927

AMES, CLYDE. Pseudonym of William Knowles. Other pseudonym: Clyde Allison, q.v.
Gorgonzola, Won't You Please Come Home? Lancer, 1967 [L.A.]

AMES, DELANO (L.). 1906- . Ref: CC.
An American who has lived for many years in England and Spain; a playwright, translator and musician. SC: Jane and Dagobert Brown = B; Juan Llorca = JL. Set: many Eng.
The Body on Page One. Hodder, 1951; Rinehart, 1951 B
Coffin for Christopher; see Crime, Gentlemen, Please
The Cornish Coast Conspiracy. Amalgamated Press, 1942 (Sexton Blake)
Corpse Diplomatique. Hodder, 1950; Rinehart, 1951 B
Crime, Gentlemen, Please. Hodder, 1954. U.S. title: Coffin for Christopher. Washburn, 1954 B
Crime Out of Mind. Hodder, 1956; Washburn, 1956 B [Switz.]
Death of a Fellow Traveller. Hodder, 1950; Rinehart, 1950. Also published as: Nobody Wore Black. Dell, 1951 B
For Old Crime's Sake; see Lucky Jane
He Found Himself Murdered. Swan, 1947
Landscape with Corpse. Hodder, 1955; Washburn, 1955 B
Lucky Jane. Hodder, 1959. U.S. title: For Old Crime's Sake. Lippincott, 1959 B [Med. Is.]
The Man in the Tricorn Hat. Methuen, 1960; Regnery, 1966 JL [Sp.]
The Man with Three Chins. Methuen, 1965; Regnery, 1968 JL [Sp.]
The Man with Three Jaguars. Methuen, 1961; Regnery, 1967 JL
The Man with Three Passports. Methuen, 1967 JL
Murder Begins at Home. Hodder, 1949; Rinehart, 1950 B [New Mex.]
Murder, Maestro, Please. Hodder, 1952; Rinehart, 1952 B [Andorra]
No Mourning for the Matador. Hodder, 1953; Washburn, 1953 B [Sp.]
No Traveller Returns. Nicholson, 1934
Nobody Wore Black; see Death of a Fellow Traveller
Not in Utter Nakedness; see They Journey by Night
She Shall Have Murder. Hodder, 1948; Rinehart, 1949 B
She Wouldn't Say Who. Hodder, 1957; Washburn, 1958 B
They Journey by Night. Hodder, 1932. U.S. title: Not in Utter Nakedness. Dial, 1932 [Tangier]

AMES, EDNA
The House of Secrets. Major, 1976

AMES, JENNIFER. Pseudonym of Maysie Greig, 1902- , q.v.
Danger in Eden; see Danger Wakes My Heart
Danger Wakes My Heart. Collins, 1949. U.S. title: Danger in Eden. Bouregy, 1950
Dark Carnival. Collins, 1951; Random, 1950, as by Maysie Greig [Fr.]
Date with Danger; see Frightened Heart
Fear Kissed My Lips. Collins, 1947
The Fearful Paradise. Collins, 1953. U.S. title: This Fearful Paradise. Random, 1953, as by Maysie Greig [Bermuda]
Flight into Fear. Collins, 1954; Bouregy, 1954
The Frightened Heart. Collins, 1952. U.S. title: Date with Danger. Random, 1952, as by Maysie Greig
I Married Mr. Richardson. Collins, 1945
Journey in the Dark. Collins, 1945
Lovers in the Dark. Collins, 1946
Perilous Quest. Avalon, 1960. (British title?) [H. Kong]
Rough Seas to Sunrise. Collins, 1955.
U.S. title: Winds of Fear. Avalon, 1956, as by Maysie Greig
This Fearful Paradise; see The Fearful Paradise
Winds of Fear; see Rough Seas to Sunrise

AMES, JOSEPH B(USHNELL). 1878-1928.
The Emerald Buddha. Small, 1921 [China]

AMES, LESLIE. Pseudonym of Orlando Joseph Rigoni, 1907- . Ref: CA.
The Angry Wind. Lenox, 1970
Bride of Donnybrook. Arcadia, 1966
Castle on the Island. Arcadia, 1969; Hale, 1970
The Hidden Chapel. Arcadia, 1967
The Hill of Ashes. Arcadia, 1968
The House of Haddon. Arcadia, 1969 [Calif.]
The Hungry Sea. Arcadia, 1967 [Calif.]
Journey to Romance. Hale, 1966 (U.S. title)
King's Castle. Lenox, 1970
The Phantom Bride. Lenox, 1972
Sinister Love. Hale, 1968 (U.S. title?)
To Shadow Our Love. Hale, 1968 (U.S. title?)
Wind over the Citadel. Lenox, 1971

AMES, NORMA. Pseudonym of Ames Norman, 1920- . Ref: CA.
My Path Belated. Avon, 1970 [West]
Whisper in the Forest. Avon, 1971 [New Mex.]

AMES, ROBERT. Pseudonym of Charles Clifford.
Awake and Die. GM, 1955 [N.J.]
The Dangerous One. GM, 1954; Fawcett (London), 1959 [Mex.]
The Devil Drives. GM, 1952; Red Seal, 1959 [N.J.]

AMES, SARAH RACHEL STAINER. 1922- . Pseudonym: Sarah Gainham, q.v.

AMHERST, FRANCES. See: Helen (Rosen) Woodward, 1882- .

AMIDON, BILL. See: Paul Ross.

AMIEL, J(OSEPH) J. 1937- . Ref: CA.
Hawks. Putnam, 1979; Macmillan (London), 1980

AMINO, L.
Death Is So Lonely. Scion, 1954
Masks of Malevolence. Scion, 1953

AMIS, KINGSLEY (WILLIAM). 1922- . Ref: CA, TC.
The Anti-Death League. Gollancz, 1966; Harcourt, 1966
The Darkwater Hall Mystery. Tragara (Edinburgh), 1978 (37 pp., 165 copies printed.)
The Riverside Villas Murder. Cape, 1973; Harcourt, 1973 [1930s, Eng.]
Russian Hide-and-Seek. Hutchinson, 1980

AMOS, ALAN. Pseudonym of Kathleen Moore Knight, q.v.
Borderline Murder. Doubleday, 1947 [Texas]
Fatal Harvest. Doubleday, 1957; Hammond, 1958, as by Kathleen Moore Knight [Panama]
Jungle Murder; see Pray for a Miracle
Panic in Paradise. Doubleday, 1951 [Panama]
Pray for a Miracle. Duell, 1941. Also published as: Jungle Murder. Adventure Novel Classic, 194? [Guat.]

AMOS, RUSSELL BOOTH. 1928- .
Perhaps I Look Simple. Longmans, 1960
Wasp in the Web. Longmans, 1961

AMY, W(ILLIAM) LACEY. Pseudonym: Luke Allan, q.v.
The Blue Wolf. Hodder, 1913. Also published as by Luke Allan: Jenkins, 1921

ANDERS, E. J. Pseudonym of E. J. Anders Lype.
-Behind the Door. Philosophical Library, 1966

ANDERSCH, ALFRED. 1914-1980. Ref: CA.
-Flight to Afar. Coward, 1958; Gollancz, 1958. (Translation of "Sansibar; oder, Der Letzte Grund." Germany, 1957.)
The Redhead. Pantheon, 1961; Heinemann, 1961. (Translation of "Die Rote." Germany, 1960.) [Vienna]

ANDERSEN, IAN. Pseudonym.
The Big Night. Simon, 1979; Hale, 1981 [Las Veg.]

ANDERSON, U(ELL) S(TANLEY). 1917- . Ref: CA.
Hard and Fast. Popular Library, 1956 [L.A.]
-The Smoldering Sea. Wyn, 1953

ANDERSON, A(RTHUR) J(AMES). 1863- .
Professor Aylmer's Experiment. Hurst, 1922

ANDERSON, ANN
The Affair at Timber Lake. Hurst, 1972; Dell, 1975 [Can.]
House of Gold. Hurst, 1969; Dell, 1974

ANDERSON, BETTY. Pseudonym: Claudia Canyon, q.v.

ANDERSON, EDWARD. 1905- .
Thieves Like Us. Stokes, 1937; Heinemann, 1937. Also published as: Your Red Wagon. Bantam, 1948 [Okla.]

ANDERSON, FRANCES
The Will to Die. Hale, 1976

ANDERSON, FREDERICK IRVING. 1877-1947. Ref: EM, MP, TC. SC: Deputy Parr = DP.
Adventures of the Infallible Godahl. Crowell, 1914 ss
The Book of Murder. Dutton, 1930 ss DP
The Notorious Sophie Lang. Heinemann, 1925 ss DP

ANDERSON, GEORGE
The Sit-In. Ace, 1970 [Chi.]

ANDERSON, IAIN F(LEMING). 1902- .
The Commerce Patrol. Jenkins, 1937 ss
Cypher 8. Heath Cranston, 1939 [future]

ANDERSON, J(OHN) R(ICHARD) L(ANE). 1911-1981. Ref: CA. Journalist and editor. SC: Major Peter Blair, in at least those marked PB; Insp. Piet Deventer = PD. Set: mostly Eng.
Death in the Caribbean. Gollancz, 1977; Stein, 1978 PB [W.I.]
Death in the Channel; see Redundancy Pay
Death in the City. Gollancz, 1977 PB
Death in the Desert. Gollancz, 1976; Stein, 1977 PB
Death in the Greenhouse. Gollancz, 1978 PB
Death in the North Sea. Gollancz, 1975; Stein, 1976 PB [ship]
Death in the Thames. Gollancz, 1974; Stein, 1975 PB
Death on the Rocks. Gollancz, 1973; Stein, 1975 PB
Festival. Gollancz, 1979; St. Martin's, 1980 PD
The Nine-Spoked Wheel. Gollancz, 1975
Reckoning in Ice. Gollancz, 1971
Redundancy Pay. Gollancz, 1976. U.S. title: Death in the Channel. Stein, 1976
A Sprig of Sea Lavender. Gollancz, 1978; St. Martin's, 1979 PD

ANDERSON, JAMES. 1936- . Ref: TC.
The Abolition of Death. Constable, 1974; Walker, 1975
The Affair of the Blood-Stained Egg-Cosy. Constable, 1975; McKay, 1977 [1930s, Eng.]
The Alpha List. Constable, 1972; Walker, 1973
Angel of Death. Constable, 1978
Appearance of Evil. Constable, 1977
Assassin. Constable, 1969; Simon, 1971
Assault and Matrimony. Muller, 1980; Doubleday, 1981

ANDERSON, JAN
Storm Castle. Pyramid, 1967 [Fr.]

ANDERSON, JESSICA (MARGARET QUEALE). Ref: CA.
The Last Man's Head. Macmillan (London), 1970
An Ordinary Lunacy. Macmillan (London), 1963; Scribner, 1964

ANDERSON, M(ARY) D(ESIREE). 1902- .
Grey Sisters. Chatto, 1972

ANDERSON, MARY
Tales of the Rock. Downey, 1897 ss

ANDERSON, MAXWELL. 1888-1959. Ref: CA.
The Bad Seed. Dodd, 1955. (2-act play based on the novel by William March, q.v.)

Gods of the Lightning, with Harold Hickerson. Longmans, 1928 (3-act play.)

ANDERSON, PATRICK. 1936-   . Ref: CA.
The President's Mistress. Simon, 1976; Secker, 1976 [Wash. D.C.]

ANDERSON, POUL (WILLIAM). 1926-   .
Ref: CA. SC: Trygve Yamamura = TY; all set in S.F.
-After Doomsday. Ballantine, 1962; Gollancz, 1963
Murder Bound. Macmillan, 1962 TY
Murder in Black Letter. Macmillan, 1960 TY
Perish by the Sword. Macmillan, 1959 TY

ANDERSON, R. A. and R. L. SWEENEY
He Isn't Dead Yet. Eldridge, 1962 (1-act play.)
Run, Robber, Run. Eldridge, 1964 (1-act play.)

ANDERSON, REX
Cover Her with Roses. Simon, 1969; Hale, 1973 [S.W., acad.]

ANDERSON, SUE LYNN
Shadows Across the Bayou. Manor, 1977

ANDERSON, W(ALTER) W(ADSLEY). 1904-
Kill 1 Kill 2. Morrow, 1940

ANDERSON, WILLIAM C(HARLES). 1920-
Ref: CA.
Penelope, the Damp Detective. Crown, 1974 [Calif.]

ANDOM, R. Pseudonym of Alfred Walter Barrett, 1869-   .
The Burglings of Tutt. Jarrolds, 1905
The Genial Rascal, with William Reginald Hodder, q.v. Jarrolds, 1909

ANDOVER, HENRY. Pseudonym of Henry Hope. SC: Henry Holland, in both titles. Set: Eng.
Death on the Pack Road. Eyre, 1931
The Dennisdale Tragedy. Eyre, 1936

ANDRAU, MARIANNE. Pseudonym of Suzanne Guillaud.
Love's Testimony. Mystique, 1980 (Translation of "Gunther L'Absent." Paris, 1965.)
Out of the Night. Mystique, 1980 (Translation of "Un Garcon Troublant." Paris, 1967.)
A Tangled Web. Mystique, 1980 (Translation of "Le Cavalier de Sienne." Paris, 1963.)

ANDRE, ALIX
Deadly Inheritance. Mystique, 1980 (Translation of "L'Infidele." Paris, 1975.)
Ghosts of Ardnamore. Mystique, 1979 (Translation of "Ce Mal S'Appelle L'Amour." Paris, 1969.)
Island of Deceit. Mystique, 1977 (Translation of "Un Tres Brillant Pirate." Paris, 1974.)
Legacy of Danger. Mystique, 1980 (Translation of "On Demande un Amour." Paris, 1957.)
Legend of Hatred. Mystique, 1980 (Translation of "Les Cent Chevaux du Roi." Paris, 1971.)
Lured by Greed. Mystique, 1980 (Translation of "L'Homme des Solitudes." Paris, 1951.)
Secret at the Abbey. Mystique, 1980 (Translation of "Tout L'Amour du Monde." Paris, 1962.)
Snows of Offenburg. Mystique, 1979 (Translation of "Les Neiges d'Offenburg." Paris, 1977.)

ANDRE, R(ICHARD) and G. LEITCH WALKER
The Ace of Spades. Ward, 1900

ANDREAE, PERCY. 1858-   .
-A Life at Stake. Ward, 1902
-The Mask and the Man. Smith, 1894
-The Signora. Smith, 1895
Stanhope of Chester. Smith, 1894; Rand, 1896
The Vanished Emperor. Ward, 1896; Rand, 1896

ANDREAS, FRED. 1898-   . Set: Ger., in all titles.
Alias. Bles, 1933. U.S. title: Death at Heel. Holt, 1933 (Translation of "Der Mann der Zweimal Leben Wollte." Germany, 1932.)
Captain Overboard. Bles, 1936 (Translation of "Einer Zuviel an Bord." Germany, 1935.)
Death at Heel; see Alias
In Court. Bles, 1931. U.S. title: The Trial of Gregor Kaska. Holt, 1932 (Translation of "Prozess Gregor Kaska." Germany, 1930.)
The Theatre Crime. Bles, 1932 (Translation of "Die Flucht ins Dunkle." Germany, 1927.)
The Trial of Gregor Kaska; see In Court

ANDREOPOULOS, SPYROS. 1929-   . See: Eugene Dong, M.D.

ANDRESS, LESLEY. Pseudonym of Lawrence Sanders, 1920-   , q.v.
Caper. Putnam, 1980; Granada, 1980 [NYC]

ANDREWS. Pseudonym: Nicholas Carter, q.v.

ANDREWS, CHARLTON. 1874-1939. SC: Drexel Ware = DW.
The Affair of the Malacca Stick. Washburn, 1936 DW [Eng.]
The Affair of the Syrian Dagger. Washburn, 1937 DW [Paris]
The Butterfly Murder. Sears, 1932; Allan, 1934 [L.A.]
Murder at the Class Reunion. Denison, 1938. (1-act play.)
The Resources of Mycroft Holmes. Aspen, 1973 ss

ANDREWS, DOROTHY C(RAIGHEAD)
Death at Springtime. Empire, 1935

ANDREWS, HORACE J.
The Indian Idol Mystery. Modern, 1938
-The Luck of the Golden Star. Mellifont, 1934. (64 pp.)

ANDREWS, ISOBEL
Exit with Emeralds. Hale, 1971

ANDREWS, LUCILLA. Pseudonyms: Diana Gordon, Joanna Marcus, qq.v.

ANDREWS, MARK
Blackout. Leisure, 1978
Body Rub. Leisure, 1976
Bomb Squad. Leisure, 1977 [NYC]
The Return of Jack the Ripper. Leisure, 1977 [NYC, 1888]
Satan's Manor. Leisure, 1977

ANDREWS, MICHAEL
Caracol Reef. Hale, 1972

ANDREWS, MILES PETER.   -1814.
The Mysteries of the Castle. Longmans, 1795. (3-act play.)

ANDREWS, PETER J.
Hoods Incorporated. Badger, 1958

ANDREWS, PHILLIP and BARNETT ST. JOHN
Cop Story. Zebra, 1977 [NYC]

ANDREWS, (CHARLES) R(OBERT) D(OUGLAS). 1903-   .
The Stolen Husband. Grosset, 1931

ANDREWS, V. and H. PENN. SC: Sherlock Holmes, in both titles.
The Mystery of the Sealed Room. Magico, 1980
Sherlock Holmes and the Arthritic Clergyman. Magico, 1980

ANDREWS, V(IRGINIA) C(LEO). Ref: CA. SC: Chris & Cathy Dollanganger, in both titles.
Flowers in the Attic. PB, 1979; Fontana, 1980 [Va.]
Petals on the Wind. PB, 1980; Piatkus, 1980

ANDREZEL, PIERRE. Pseudonym of Baroness Karen Christence Blixen-Finecke, 1885-1962. Ref: CA.
-The Angelic Avengers. Putnam (London), 1946; Random, 1947. (Translation of "Gengaeldelsens Veje." Copenhagen, 1944.)

ANDRZEYEVSKI, JERZY (GEORGE). 1909-1983. Ref: CA.
-Ashes and Diamonds. Weidenfeld, 1962. (Translation of "Popiol i Diament." Warsaw, 1960.)

ANGEL, ROSS
Bullet Proof. Scion, 1951
Call Me Sometime. Scion, 1953
The Dame Came Late. Scion, 1952
Dame Trouble There. Scion, 1953
Dames Don't Dictate. Scion, 1953
Dead Easy. Scion, 1950
Drop That Gun. Scion, 1951
Excuse My Gun. Scion, 1951
Get Out and Stay Out. Scion, 1952
Give Me a Gun. Scion, 1952
Hot Ice. Scion, 1951
I'll Fry Yet. Scion, 1951
It's All Yours. Scion, 1952
It's Murder She Says. Scion, 1951
Jail Bait! Milestone, 1953
K.O. for Keeps. Scion, 1950
Let's Shoot This Out. Scion, 1951
Live Till You Die. Scion, 1952
Luger Lullaby. Scion, 1951
Misguided Angel. Scion, 1954
Mr. Forty-Five. Scion, 1951
No Percentage in Death. Scion, 1953
One-Way Trip. Scion, 1953
Over My Dead Body. Scion, 1950
Reckless. Scion, 1954
To Sleep No More. Scion, 1951
Tomorrow—the Chair. Scion, 1950
Voice of Vice. Scion, 1951
You Don't Die Twice. Scion, 1952

ANGELL, BRYAN MARY. 1877-   . Pseudonym: H. Ripley Cromarsh, q.v.

ANGELLOTTI, MARION POLK
Three Black Bags. Century, 1922 [Ger.]

ANGELO, TONY
Honey, Hold That Scream. Harborough, 1952; Leisure Library, 1952
Satan's Sister. Archer, 1951
Sinner's Shroud. Archer, 1950

ANGREMY, JEAN-PIERRE. 1937-   . Pseudonym: Pierre-Jean Remy, q.v.

ANGUS, DOUGLAS (ROSS). 1909-   . Ref: CA, CC.
Death on Jerusalem Road. Random, 1963 [Mass.]

ANGUS, JOHN and FIELDING HOPE, 1897-   q.v.
The Scorpion's Nest. Selwyn, 1929 [India]

ANGUS, SYLVIA. 1921-   . Ref: CA.
Arson and Old Lace. World, 1972 [Maine]
Dead to Rites. Crown, 1978 [Mex.]
Death of a Hittite. Macmillan, 1969 [Turk.]

ANGUS, WILLIAM
Murder in Mallorca. Vantage, 1977 [Maj.]

ANKER, JENS. Pseudonym of Robert Hansen, 1883-1957.
Two Dead Men. Knopf, 1922. (Translation of "To Dode Maend." Copenhagen, 19??.) [Copen.]

ANKRUM, M(ORRIS) and V(INCENT) DUFFY
The Mystery Man. French, 1928. (3-act play.)

ANNE, DAVID
The Folly. Allen, 1978

ANNE-MARIEL. Pseudonym of Anne Goud, 1917-   . Ref: CA.
Murder in Venice. Pinnacle, 1974 [Venice]
One Evening I Shall Return. Pinnacle, 1973. (Translation of "Un Soir, Je Reviendrai." Paris, 1963.)
Rendezvous in Peking. Pinnacle, 1974 [China]
Tigress of the Evening. Pinnacle, 1976 [Viet Nam]

ANNESLEY, MICHAEL. SC: Lawrie Fenton, in at least those marked LF.
An Agent Intervenes. Paul, 1944 LF [Fr.]
Fenton of the Foreign Office; see Room 14
The Lights That Did Not Fail. Paul, 1949
The Missing Agent. Harrap, 1938 LF
Room 14. Harrap, 1935. U.S. title: Fenton of the Foreign Office. Speller, 1937 LF [Warsaw]
Spies Abounding. Paul, 1945 LF
Spies in Action. Harrap, 1937 LF
Spies in the Web. Harrap, 1936 LF [Lith.]
Spy Against the Reich. Harrap, 1940 LF [Ger.]
Spy Corner. Paul, 1948 LF
Spy-Counter Spy. Paul, 1946 LF [Paris]
Spy Island. Paul, 1950 LF
Suicide Spies. Paul, 1944 LF
They Won't Lie Down. Paul, 1947 LF
Unknown Agent. Harrap, 1940 LF
The Vanished Vice-Counsel. Harrap, 1939 LF [Pol.]

A

ANONYMOUS. See also: Charles Brockden Brown, 1771-1810; Anthony Berkley. SC: Lady Kate = LK; Thad Burr = TB; Dixon Hawke = DH; Joe Phoenix = JP (see also Albert W. Aiken, 1846-1894.)

The Actress Detective; or, The Invisible Hand. Aldine
Adventures of an Attorney in Search of Practice. Saunders, 1839; Lea, 1839 ss (Variously ascribed to Sir George Stephen, 1794-1879, Sir James Stephen, 1789-1859, and Samuel Warren, 1807-1877, q.v.)
Alexena; or, The Castle of Santa Marco. Minerva, 1817
-All for Him. Carleton, 1877; Low, 1877. Also published as: Sweetheart and Wife. Carleton, 1882; Low, 1882
Almagro and Claude; or, Monastic Murder. Dean, 1803
The Animated Skeleton. Minerva, 1798
Annals of the Age; or, The Crimes of London. Pattie, ca.1840 ss
The Artist Detective. Aldine
The Attorney; or, The Correspondence of John Quod. Hueston, 1853
Austenbury Castle. Minerva, 1896 (by "An Unpatronized Female")
Autobiography of an Italian Police-Officer. Maxwell, 18?? ss
The Avenger; or, The Sicilian Vespers. Stockdale, 1810 [Sic.]
The Bat of the Battery; or, Joe Phoenix, King of Detectives. Aldine   JP
Beautiful Jack, the Double-Edged Detective. Aldine
Begumbagh: A Tale of the Indian Mutiny and other stories. Chambers, 1888 ss, at least one criminous
Belle Starr, the Bandit Queen; or, The Female Jesse James. Fox, 1889
Benjamin Butts Junr. Aldine
Binnacle Jack; or, The Cavern of Death. DeWitt, 1876
The Black Band; or, Mysteries of Midnight. Blackett
The Black Box Murder. Remington, 1889; Lovell, 1890. (by Maarten Maartens, pseudonym of Joost Marius Willem van der Poorten Schwartz, 1858-1915, q.v.) Reprinted as by William Ward, q.v.: Westbrook, 192?
The Black Castle; or, The Spectre of the Forest. Dean, ca.1808
The Black Monk; or, The Secret of the Grey Turret. Peirce, 1842
The Black Troopers and other stories. Religious Tract Society, 1862 ss
The Blind Beggar of Bethnal Green and Bessy. (London), 1848
Blindights. Edmonston, 1868
The Bloody Hand; or, The Fatal Cup. Stevens
Bob Bridger, Detective. Aldine
Bob Younger's Fate. Aldine
Born Bad; or, The Countess and the Convict. DeWitt, 1876
The Bottle; or, The First Step to Crime. DeWitt, 1876
The Boy Detective; or, The Crimes of London. Howe, 1860-70
Brant Adams, the Emperor of Detectives. Aldine
Broadway Bob, the Bounder Detective. Aldine
Bruce Angelo, the Old Time Detective. Aldine
The California Detective. Aldine
Captain Clew, the Flying Detective. Aldine
The Castle of St. Vallery. Robinson, 1792
Caught in Mid-Ocean. Ogilvie, 1903
The Cavern of Horrors; or, The Miseries of Miranda. Hurst, 1802 [Naples]
The Celebrated Detective. Aldine
The Champion Clue-Finder. Aldine
Charley Hunter; or, The Fate of a Forger. Dick, 1876
A Chase Around the World. Aldine
Chillers and Thrillers. Street, 1945 (11 dramatized puzzle problems.)
The Chosen Man. Aldine
The Circus Detective. Aldine
The City of Purple Dreams. Browne, 1913
Columbia; or, Among the Corsican Bandits. Donohue, ca.1897 [Cors.]
The Combination-Lock Mystery; or, Little Lightning. Aldine
Confessions of a Detective Policeman. Elliot, 1852 ss
Confessions of a Ticket of Leave Man. Blackwood, 1879
The Convict's Sweetheart. Ogilvie
Count Roderic's Castle; or, Gothic Times. Minerva, 1794; Bradford, 1795
The Crackshot Detective. Aldine
The Crime Club. Stevens, ca.1907
The Crime of Henry Vane. Scribner, 1884 (by Frederick Jesup Stimson)
The Crime of Monte Carlo. Stevens, ca. 1906
A Cruel Secret. Carleton, ca.1883
Danton, the "Shadow-Sharp"; or, The Queen of the Hidden Hands. Aldine
Dark Masquerade. Green Circle, 1936 (by Fulton Oursler, 1893-1952, q.v.) [NYC]
The Dark Woman; or, Plot and Passion. 1860 (by Malcolm J. Rymer.)
The Dashing Female Detective; or, Lady Kate. Aldine LK
The Dastard "Dr." Aldine
Dead or Alive. Stevens, ca.1904
The Death Deal. Aldine
The Death Trust. (Author), 1889 (by Laura Eugenia Newhall.)
The Decoy Detective. Aldine
The Demon Detective; or, The Gipsy Gentleman. Aldine
Detective Burr's Seven Clues. Aldine TB
Detective Fleet of London. Aldine
The Detective for Vengeance. Aldine
Detective Gordon's Grip. Aldine
Detective Sketches. Tousey, 1881 ss
Detective Stories. Henderson ss (5 different volumes bear this title.)
The Detective's Notebook. Ward, 1860
The Detective's Victory. Aldine
Diary of a Great French Detective. Tousey, 188? ss
Dixon Hawke's Case Book. Nos. 1-20. Thomson DH
Doc Grip, the Sporting Detective; or, The Vendetta of Death. Aldine
The Dog Detective. Aldine
Don Algonah; or, The Sorceress of Montillo. Hurst, 1802
A Double Tragedy. Aldine
The Dream of Raven. Theosophical Publishing Co., 1895
Driven from Home. Amalgamated, ca.1910
The Drop Detective. Aldine
The Dumb Detective. Boys of England, 1887
The East Side Detective. Aldine
Edith Heron; or, The Earl and the Countess. 1860
Eileen the Spy. Aldine
Eliza Grimwood. (London), 1844
The Emperor of Detectives. Aldine
Eugenia; or, A Friend's Victim. Minerva, 1889
Euthanasia; or, Turf, Text and Tomb. Routledge, 1893
The Experiences of a Lady Detective. Clarke, 1884 (by William Stephens Hayward, q.v.) ss
Experiences of an American Detective. Infield, 1883 (by William Stephens Hayward, q.v.) ss
The Fair Mystery. Brett, 1870
The Famous Burdick Case. Ogilvie, ca. 1895
-Fanny White and Her Friend Jack Rawlings. Vickers
The Far West Detective. Aldine
The Fatal Secret; or, Crime and Retribution. Jay, 1852; Barclay, 1852
Female Depravity; or, The House of Death. DeWitt, 1876
The Ferret Detective. Aldine
Fireside Omnibus. Hutchinson, 1937 (Puzzle ss.)
Five Hundred Pounds Reward. Bentley, 1867 (by A Barrister.)
Foiled. Clark, 1885
The Four Pools Mystery. Century, 1908
The Frisco Detective. Aldine
Gabrielle de Vergy. Hookham, 1790
The Gambler's Last Throw. Ward
Gasparoni Detective. Aldine
The Georgia Detective. Aldine
The Ghost in the Bank of England. Hogg, ca.1888
The Giant City Swindle. Amalgamated, 1927
The Giant Detective. Aldine
The Giant Detective in Ireland. Aldine
The Gold Star Detective from Kentucky. Aldine
The Gothic Story of Courville Castle; or, The Illegitimate Son. Fisher, 1804
The Government Special Detective. Aldine
-The Grasp of the Sultan. Houghton, 1916
The Great Buxton Mystery. 1889 (by William Thomas Standen.)
The Great Cronin Mystery; or, The Irish Patriot's Fate. Laird, ca.1888 (by A Chicago Detective.)
-Greyslaer. Harper, 1840; Bentley, 1840 (by Charles Fenno Hoffman, 1806-1884.)
Guy Fawkes. ca.1880
The Gypsy Detective. Aldine
Hardenbrass and Harverill; or, The Secret of the Castle. Sherwood, 1817
Hidden, Not Lost. Newnes, 1903
A Hidden Terror. Stevens, ca.1904
The Hollwood Mystery. Stevens, ca.1905
Horatio and Camilla; or, The Nuns of St. Mary. (London)
The Hypnotist Detective. Aldine
The Idol of Lost Chance. Aldine
The "Impenetrable Mystery" of Zora Burns. (Chicago), 1888 (by Will Bone, Jr.)
In the Force; or, Confessions of a Policeman. Bryce ss
The Independent Detective. Aldine
The Irish Detective. Aldine
Iron Burgess, the Government Detective. Aldine
Ironsides Abroad. Aldine
Jack o' the Cudgel; or, The Hero of a Hundred Fights. (London), 18??
Jack Shepard, the Bandit King. Ogilvie, 1903
Jack Vinton, the Boy Detective. Aldine
Jaqueline of Olzeburg; or, Final Retribution. Chapple, 1800
The Jew Detective; or, The Beautiful Convict. Aldine
Joe Phoenix Puzzled; or, The League of the Skeleton Keys. Aldine JP
Kate Scott, the Decoy Detective; or, Joe Phoenix's Still Hunt. Aldine JP
John Jasper's Secret. Peterson, 1871; Wyman, 1872 (by Henry Morford, 1823-1881.)
The Kentucky Detective. Aldine
The King of Detectives. Aldine
The Lady Detective; see Revelations of a Lady Detective
Lady Kate, the Dashing Female Detective. Aldine LK
Leaves from the Notebook of a New York Detective. Dick, 1876 ss
The Library of Fiction. Routledge, 1841 ss, some criminous
The Life, Adventure and Opinions of a Liverpool Policeman and His Contemporaries. Booker, 1841
The Life and Anecdotes of the Black Dwarf. (Edinburgh), 1820
The Life of Anson Bunker, "The Bloody Hand." Barclay, 1886
Llewellin. Cawthorn, 1799
London by Night. Oliver
A London Detective's Thrilling Adventures. Tousey, 1883 ss
The Long Branch Detective. Aldine, 1897
The Loom and the Law. Stevenson, 1923
Love and Death in a Barn. Old Franklin, 1876
-A Love Spell. Carleton, 1883
Lovel Castle; or, The Rightful Heir Restored. Dean, 1818
The Magic Change Detective. Aldine
The Magnate Detective. Aldine
The Man from the West; or, From the Chaparral to Wall Street. Texas Siftings, 1886 (by "A Wall Street Man," pseudonym of David Law Proudfit.) [NYC]
The Man Trap. Riverton, 1909
Manfred the Magic Trick Detective. Aldine
The Mantrapper. Aldine
Marianne the Outcast: The Sorrowful Tale of a Betrayed Woman Taken from the Diary of Detective Thorn. Eichler, ca.1880 (Issued in 100 parts, totalling 3200 pages.)
The Masked Detective; or, The Dead Alive. Aldine
The Masked Motorist. Thomson
The Master of Mysteries. Bobbs, 1912 ss (by Gelett Burgess, 1866-1951, q.v.)
The Matchless Detective; or, Thad Burr's Marvellous Case. Aldine TB
A Maze of Crime. Aldine
Midnight Horrors; or, The Bandit's Daughter. Dean, 1807
A Midnight Mystery; or, The Double Detective. Aldine
The Midnight Queen. Dick, 1876
The Miner Detective. Aldine
Mrs. Druse's Case, and Maggie Houghtaling. Old Franklin, 1877
The Mrs. Guiness Mystery. (NYC), 1908
Mort Castle. Wallis, 1798
The Mountaineer Detective. Aldine
The Muddles of Solon Mudhen, the Blacksmith Detective. Tydfil, 1902 ss
Mura, the Western Lady Detective. Aldine
My Fourteen Cases. Tousey, 1887 ss
The Mysteries of Chicago. Rand, 1889 (by A Reporter.) [Chi.]
Mysteries of Crime, As Shown in Remarkable Capital Crimes. Walker, 1870
The Mysteries of Nashua; or, Revenge Punished and Constancy Rewarded. Gill, 1844

The Mysteries of New Orleans. Peterson, 1876 [New Or.]
The Mysteries of Oakendale Abbey. Perry, 1856
The Mysterious Crime at Burleigh Mansion. Barclay, 1887
The Mysterious Dagger; or, The Avengers. Peirce, 1842
The Mysterious Marksman; or, The Outlaws of New York. James, 1876 [NYC]
The Mysterious Murder of Pearl Bryan; or, The Headless Horror. Barclay
Mystery Crime Cases. Spencer, 1949
The Mystery of a Madstone. Aldine
The Mystery of Black Pit. Stevens, 1907
The Mystery of Lady Chetwynd's Spectre. Henderson
The Mystery of Woodcroft. Stevens, ca. 1906
The Mystery of Woodleigh Grange. Donohue, ca.1906
The Mystery; or, Forty Years Ago. (London), 1820 (by Thomas Gaspey)
Mystery upon Mystery. Minerva, 1808
The Naval Detective's Chase. Aldine
The Nevada Detective. Aldine
Nicky Nimble; or, The Night Prowlers. DeWitt, 1876
Nighthawk the Mountain Detective. Aldine
Norma Danton; or, The Lighthouse Murder. Hurst, 1876
Not Guilty. Ogilvie, 1888
Obi; or, Three Fingered Jack. Peterson, 1876
The Old Detective's Pupil. Aldine
Old Electricity, the Lightning Detective. Aldine
Old Harry Hawks. Aldine
Old Phenomenal. Aldine, 1894
Old Puritan, the Old Time Detective. Aldine
Old Sleuth, the Protean Detective; or, The Bay Ridge Mystery. Aldine
Old Stonewall, the "Shadower." Aldine
Old Terrible, the Iron Arm Detective. Aldine
Old Transform, the Secret Special Detective. Aldine
Olive Varcoe. Multiple, ca.1910
On Her Majesty's Secret Service. Maxwell, 1878
On the Scent; or, Hawkeye the London Detective. Aldine
On Trial for His Life. Ogilvie, 1903
O'Neil McDarragh. Aldine
Our Island. Bull, 1832 (by Humphrey William Woolryth.)
Paul Deverell; or, Two Judgments for One Crime. Dick, 1876
Paul Ferroll. Saunders, 1855; Redfield, 1856 (by Mrs. Archer Clive.)
Phantasmagoria; or, The Development of Magical Deception. Tegg, ca.1825
Piping a Detective. Aldine
Pitiless as Death; or, Crowningshield the Detective. Aldine
Plot and Counterplot. Aldine
The Poisoned Letter; or, The Lost and the Redeemed. DeWitt, 1876
The Post Office Detective. Aldine
The Prairie Detective. Aldine
The President Vanishes. Farrar, 1934 (by Rex Stout, 1886-1975, q.v.) Also published as by Rex Stout: Pyramid, 1967 [Wash. D.C.]
The Princely Detective. Butler
The Prophetic Warning; or, The Castle of Lindendorff. Ker, 1800
-The Queen of the Outlaw's Camp. Ogilvie, 1903
The Queen of the Secret Seven. Ogilvie, 1903
A Race for Life and other tales. Leisure Hour, ca.1872 ss, at least one criminous
The Railway Detective. Butler
Ralph Wildhawk; or, Alone Among the Brigands. (London), 18??
Reaping the Whirlwind. Aldine
Red-Light Will, the River Detective. Aldine
Reminiscences of a Great French Detective. Tousey, 188? ss
The Return of Dick Barton. Atlas, 1952
The Revelations of a Lady Detective. Vickers, 1864. Also published as: The Lady Detective
The Revenue Detective; or, Old Rattlesnake. Aldine
Richmond; or, Scenes in the Life of a Bow Street Runner. Colburn, 1827; Dover, 1976
Rival Lovers; or, The Midnight Murder. DeWitt, 1876
-Road to Ruin; or, The Dangers of the Tongue. James, 1876
-Robert Macaire. Routledge, 1888
Romances of Mayfair. Paul, 1925 ss, some criminous
The Rookery Detective. Aldine

Round the Block. Appleton, 1864 (by John Bell Bouton, 1830-1902.)
Running Down a Double; or, Lynx-Eye the Pacific 'Tec. Aldine [Calif.]
Sarah Brown, Detective; or, The Mystery of the Pavilion. Aldine
The Secret Oath; or, Blood-Stained Dagger. Hurst, 1802
The Secret of the Black Mere. Aldine
The Secretary; or, Circumstantial Evidence. DeWitt, 1852
Sergeant Von; or, A Long Chase. Cassell, 1889
The Shadow on the Purple. Lynwood, 1911 ss (by A Peeress = Kate Everest.)
The Sham Detective. Aldine
Shrewtzer Castle; or, The Perfidious Brother. Neil, 1802 [Ger.]
Silas Sharp, the Silent Detective. Aldine
Silver Tom, the Detective; or, Link by Link. Aldine
Slick Detective Yarns. Swan, 1951 ss
The Smiling Corpse. Farrar, 1935 (by Philip Wylie, 1902-1971, q.v., and Bernard A. Bergman.) [NYC]
The Society Detective. Aldine
Some Queer Stories. Tousey, 1888 ss
Something Better. Lee, 1878
The Spectre Mother; or, The Haunted Tower. Borradaile, 1823
The Spies Abroad; or, The Perils of the Gold Coast. Boys of England
The Spirit of Turrettville; or, The Mysterious Resemblance. Dutton, 1800
Stories and Reminiscences. Howell, 1900 ss, some criminous (by A Lieutenant-Colonel)
Stories of a World Renown Detective. Tousey, 188? ss
A Strange Case. Tinsley, 1870
Strange Stories of a Detective; or, Curiosities of Crime by a Retired Member of the Detective Force. Dick, 1863 ss
Struck Dead. Boys of England, 1888
Suppressed Sensations; or, Leaves from the Note Book of a Chicago Reporter. Rand, 1879 ss (by James Maitland, q.v.)
The Suspected Governess. Aldine
Sweetheart and Wife; see All for Him
A Tale of Mystery; or, The Castle of Solitude. Tegg, 1803
Tales and Sketches. Harper, 1829 ss (by "A Country Schoolmaster," pseudonym of William Leggett, 1801-1839.)
Tales of an Antiquary. Colburn, 1828 ss, some criminous
Tales of Heroism, and Records of Strange and Wonderful Adventures. 1847
Tales of the Coastguard and other stories. Chambers ss, at least one criminous
Tales of the R.I.C. Blackwood ss
Tales of the Wild and Wonderful. Hurst, 1825 ss, one criminous (by George Borrow.)
The Thrilling Adventures of a New York Detective. Lupton, 1893 ss
Thrilling Stories. Tousey, 1886 ss
Through a Glass Darkly. Aldine
A Titled Counterfeiter. Aldine [Fr.]
-The Toltec Cup. Vanderpoole, 1890 (by Andrew Carpenter Wheeler.)
Tom and Jerry; or, The Double Detective. Aldine
Tom Fox; or, The Revelations of a Detective. Vickers, 1860 ss
The Traditions. Minerva, 1795 (by "A Young Lady.")
The Trail of the Barrow; or, The Brother's Revenge. International
Trench's Wives; or, The Carrington Mystery. Pollard, 1887 (by "The Family Lawyer.")
-Trial and Triumph; or, A Fortune at Stake. MacCrellish, 1868
Trials of a City Detective. Munro, 1883 ss
Tried for His Life; or, The Charles River Mystery Solved. Aldine
-The Truly Remarkable Life of the Beautiful Helen Jewett. Barclay, 1878
The Twin Detectives "Which Wins". Aldine
The Ugly Man. Downey
The Unclaimed Daughter. Binns, ca.1852
Under His Thumb. Aldine
The Van Peltz Diamonds; or, 'Tec Against 'Tec. Aldine
A Wall Street Haul. Aldine
Walter Duerell. Saunders, 1838
The Wandering Spirit; or, Memoirs of the House of Moira. (London), 1802
Was It a Ghost? The Murders in Bussey's Wood: An Extraordinary Narrative. Loring, 1868
The White Witch's Warning; or, The League of Three. Aldine

Who Did It?; or, Austin, the Detective. Aldine
Who Killed Peter Trueman? Brett, 1900
Who Shot the Spy? Boys of England, 1887
The Widow's Walk; or, The Mysteries of Crime. Garrett, 1852
The Wolves of Washington. Aldine, 1895
The Woman with the Yellow Hair and Other Modern Mysteries. Saunders, 1862 ss
XX—A Fatal Clue; or, Detective Burr's Master Case. Aldine TB

ANOUILH, JEAN (MARIE LUCIEN PIERRE). 1910-   . Ref: CA.
Thieves' Carnival. Methuen, 1952; French, 1952 (4-act play.) (Translation of "Le Bal des Voleurs." Paris, 1938.)

ANSLE, DOROTHY PHOEBE. Pseudonyms: Laura Conway, Hebe Elsna, Lyndon Snow, qq.v.

ANSON, BARBARA
Golem. Leisure, 1978

ANSON, LINDSAY. SC: Peter Allen = PA. Set: Eng.
Even Doctors Die; see Such Natural Deaths
Hung by an Eyelash. Collins, 1939
I Don't Like Cats. Collins, 1940; Doubleday, 1940 PA
Such Natural Deaths. Collins, 1938. U.S. title: Even Doctors Die. Doubleday, 1939 PA

ANSTEY, EDGAR (CARNEGIE). 1882-   .
The Mystery of the Blue Inns. Longmans, 1937
The Vanishing Yacht. Longmans, 1936

ANSTRUTHER, GERALD. Pseudonym of Brandon Fleming, 1889-   , q.v.
Third Visitor. English Theatre, 1950 (3-act play.)

ANTHEIL, GEORGE JOHANN CARL. 1900-1959. Pseudonym: Stacey Bishop, q.v.

ANTHONY, DAVID. Pseudonym of William Dale Smith, 1929-   . Ref: CA. SC: Stanley Bass = SB; Morgan Butler = MB.
Blood on a Harvest Moon. Coward, 1972; Collins, 1972 [Va., W. Va.] MB
The Long Hard Cure. Collins, 1979 MB
The Midnight Lady and the Mourning Man. Bobbs, 1969; Collins, 1970 MB [acad., Ohio]
The Organization. Coward, 1970; Collins, 1971 SB [Calif.]
Stud Game. PB, 1978; Collins, 1977 SB [Calif.]

ANTHONY, ELIZABETH
Dramatic Murder. Hodder, 1948 [Scot.]
Made for Murder. Hodder, 1950

ANTHONY, ELIZABETH. SC: Pauline Lyons, in both titles.
Ballet of Death. Zebra, 1979 [theatre, Atlanta]
Ballet of Fear. Zebra, 1979 [theatre]

ANTHONY, EVELYN. Pseudonym of Evelyn Bridget Patricia Stephens Ward-Thomas, 1928-   . Ref: CA, TC.
The Assassin. Hutchinson, 1970; Coward, 1970 [NYC]
The Defector. Hutchinson, 1980; Coward, 1981
The Grave of Truth. Hutchinson, 1979. U.S. title: The Janus Imperative. Coward, 1980
The Janus Imperative; see The Grave of Truth
The Legend. Hutchinson, 1969; Coward, 1969
The Malaspiga Exit. Hutchinson, 1974. U.S. title: Mission to Malaspiga. Coward, 1974 [It.]
Mission to Malaspiga; see The Malaspiga Exit
The Occupying Power. Hutchinson, 1973. U.S. title: Stranger at the Gates. Coward, 1973 [Fr.]
The Persian Price; see The Persian Ransom
The Persian Ransom. Hutchinson, 1975. U.S. title: The Persian Price. Coward, 1975
The Poellenberg Inheritance. Hutchinson, 1972; Coward, 1972
The Rendezvous. Hutchinson, 1967; Coward, 1968 [NYC]
The Return. Hutchinson, 1978; Coward, 1978 [Paris]
The Silver Forest. Hutchinson, 1977; Coward, 1977
Stranger at the Gates; see The Occupying Power

The Tamarind Seed. Hutchinson, 1971; Coward, 1971

ANTHONY, MICHAEL
-Her Own Affair. Methuen, 1944
Men Need Sympathy. Methuen, 1943

ANTHONY, NORMAN
The Diamond Racket. Low, 1937 [S. Afr.]
Who Is the Ace? Low, 1938

ANTHONY, PIERS and ROBERTO FUENTES. Piers Anthony is the pseudonym of Piers Anthony Dillingham Jacob, 1934-   . Ref: CA. SC: Jason Striker, in all titles.
Amazon Slaughter. Berkley, 1976 [Brazil]
Kiai! Berkley, 1974
Mistress of Death. Berkley, 1974
Ninja's Revenge. Berkley, 1975

ANTHONY, ROBERT
The Widow of Zanzibar. Hale, 1979

ANTHONY, WILDER
Deep Valley. Dorrance, 1940
Hidden Gold. Macaulay, 1922; Collins, 1924
Men of Mystery. Macaulay, 1926; Collins, 1925 [West]

ANTILL, ELIZABETH. Pseudonym of Elizabeth Middleton. Born in Australia; wife of an English diplomat. SC: Insp. Simon Ashton, in both titles.
Death on the Barrier Reef. Hammond, 1952
Murder in Mid-Atlantic. Hammond, 1950 [ship]

ANTONIO, SAN. See: San Antonio.

ANTONISEN, OLE ARTHUR JUEL. 1887-1967. Pseudonym: Arthur Omre, q.v.

ANTONY, PETER. Joint pseudonym of Anthony (Joshua) Shaffer, 1926-   , q.v., and Peter (Levin) Shaffer, 1926-   . SC: Mr. Verity, in both titles. Set: Eng.
How Doth the Little Crocodile? Evans, 1952; Macmillan, 1957, as by Anthony and Peter Shaffer
The Woman in the Wardrobe. Evans, 1951

APPEL, BENJAMIN. 1907-1977. Ref: CA.
Alley Kids; see Hell's Kitchen
-A Big Man, A Fast Man. Morrow, 1961
Brain Guy. Knopf, 1934; Constable, 1937. Also published as: The Enforcer. Belmont, 1972 [NYC]
But Not Yet Slain. Wyn, 1947
The Dark Stain. Dial, 1943 [NYC]
The Death Master; see The Funhouse
Dock Walloper. Lion, 1953 ss, some criminous
The Enforcer; see Brain Guy
Four Roads to Death. Knopf, 1935. Also published as: Gold and Flesh. Macfadden, 1972 [China]
The Funhouse. Ballantine, 1959. Also published as: The Death Master. Popular Library, 1974
Gold and Flesh; see Four Roads to Death
Hell's Kitchen. Lion, 1952. Also published as: Alley Kids. Lion, 1956 ss, some criminous
Life and Death of a Tough Guy. Avon, 1955. Also published as: Teen-Age Mobster. Avon, 1957 [NYC]
Plunder. GM, 1952
The Power-House. Dutton, 1939
-The Raw Edge. Random, 1958
-Sweet Money Girl. GM, 1954
Teen-Age Mobster; see Life and Death of a Tough Guy
-A Time of Fortune. Morrow, 1963

APPELL, DON
Hot Shot. French (London), 1977 (2-act play).

APPLE, A. E.   -1933. SC: Mr. Chang, in both titles.
Mr. Chang of Scotland Yard. Chelsea, 1926 [Can.]
Mr. Chang's Crime Ray. Chelsea, 1928 [Montr.]

APPLEBY, JOHN. English reporter and BBC writer and editor.
Aphrodite Means Death. Laurie, 1951. U.S. title: The Arms of Venus. Coward, 1951 [Greece]
The Arms of Venus; see Aphrodite Means Death
The Bad Summer. Hodder, 1958; Washburn, 1958 [Cyprus]
Barbary Hoard; see The Singing Cave
The Captive City. Hodder, 1955; Sloane, 1955 [Athens]

The Dark Corsican. Laurie, 1953
Grounds for Murder; see Stars in the Water
The Secret Mountains. Hodder, 1955; Washburn, 1957 [Andorra]
The Singing Cave. Laurie, 1952. U.S. title: Barbary Hoard. Coward, 1952 [Algeria]
Stars in the Water. Laurie, 1952; Coward, 1953. Also published as: Grounds for Murder. Dell, 1958
The Stuffed Swan. Hodder, 1956
Tin Trumpets at Dawn. Laurie, 1950
Venice Preserve Me. Hodder, 1954

APPLETON, G(EORGE) W(EBB). 1845-1909. Set: mostly Eng.
-Catching a Tartar. Tinsley, 1879
-A Comedy of the Unexpected. Long, 1910
-The Co-Respondent. Downey, 1894
-Doctor Dale's Dilemma. Long, 1909
The Down Express. Long, 1908
The Duchess of Pontifex Square. Long, 1907
Francois the Valet. Pearson, 1899
Frozen Hearts. Tinsley, 1878; Appleton, 1890 [Paris]
The House on the Thames. Long, 1907
The Ingenious Captain Cobbs. Long, 1906
-Jack Allyn's Friends. Tinsley, 1880
The Lady in Sables. Chatto, 1904
The Luck of Bella Barton. Digby, 1905
-Miss White of Mayfair. Digby, 1906
The Mysterious Miss Cass. Long, 1904
Rash Conclusions. Chatto, 1902
-The Rook's Nest. Long, 1905
The Silent Passenger. Long, 1905
-A Terrible Legacy. Ward, 1887; Appleton, 1887
The Willoughby Affair. Long, 1908

APPLIN, ARTHUR. 1883-1948? Set: mostly Eng.
The Actress. Hurst, 1927; Duffield, 1930
-Adventure for Two. Wright, 1930
-Belle of the Ballet. Leng, 1938
The Black Nail. Hurst, 1932
Blackmailed. Everett, 1915
-The Butcher of Bruton Street. Richards, 1908. Rewritten and published as: The Nursing Home. Mills, 1915
-The Children of the Gutter. Richards, 1908
The Chinese Cabinet. Ward, 1921
Cold Cream. Hurst, 1923
Crash! Wright, 1935
The Dangerous Game. Mellifont, 1935
-Dangerous Lovers. Mellifont, 1933
Daring Anna Alcott. Wright, 1935
Death in the Limelight. Mellifont, 1939
The Death Mask. Hurst, 1928; Duffield, 1930
-Diana Defiant. Mellifont, 1934 (64 pp.)
-Diana's Luck. Leng, 1939
The Eternal Instinct. Wright, 1931
Fallen Among Thieves. Ward, 1914
The Fatal Ace. Hale, 1936
-The Fearless Lovers. Ward, 1922
-Fedora of the Halls. White, 1911
-The Final Payment. Hurst, 1927
-Footlights. Mellifont, 1934
-The Gamble of Life. Pearson, 1922
-The Gay Adventure. Wright, 1939
-The Gold Trap. Hurst, 1930
-The Greater Claim. Mills, 1919
-Her Sacrifice. Ward, 1912
-His Final Choice. Wright, 1933
-His Mexican Wife. Ward, 1917
-The Immediate Jewel. Bohemian, 1910
-Into Thy Hands. White, 1912
-The Irresistable Stranger. Leng, 1931
-Ladies Prefer Bruisers. Wright, 1936
-Lady Dorothy's Indiscretion. Ward, 1912
-The Man Pays. Everett, 1912
-The Marriage of Margot. Ward, 1921
-No Limit. White, 1917
The Nursing Home; see The Butcher of Bruton Street
-The Pantomime Girl. Everett, 1911
-The Path of a Star. Long, 1928
-The Pearl Necklace. Ward, 1911
Picked Up. Hurst, 1935
-The Price of Love. Readers Library, 1930
-The Priest of Piccadilly. White, 1910
-Rags. White, 1910
-The Revue Girl. Hurst, 1927
-The Scared Nymph. Wright, 1934
-The Secret Sister. Ward, 1924
-Shadowed Lives. Long, 1928
-She Asked for Adventure. Hurst, 1939
-Sin. Everett, 1912
-The Sins of the Fathers. Long, 1928
-Sister Susie—Spinster. Mills, 1915. Also published as (abridged): Wilful Susie. Mellifont, 1933
-The Stage Door. White, 1909
-Stage-Struck. Leng, 1935
Storm Driven. Mellifont, 1933
Sweeter Than Honey. Hurst, 1936; Green Circle, 1936

-Tempting Anne Brayton. Long, 1929
-Too Married. Wright, 1931
-The Unforgiving Sin. Long, 1930
The Van Dylk Diamonds. Ward, 1909
-Where Are You Going? Wright, 1931
Wicked. Mills, 1920
Wilful Susie; see Sister Susie—Spinster
-Winning Through. Wright, 1933
-The Woman Who Was Not. Ward, 1917

AQUIN, HUBERT. 1929-1977. Ref: CA.
The Antiphonary. Anasi (Toronto), 1973. (Translation of "L'Antiphonaire." Montreal, 1969.)
Blackout. Anasi (Toronto), 1974. (Translation of "Trou de Memoire." Montreal, 1968.)
Prochain Episode. McClelland, 1967. (Translation of "Prochain Episode." Montreal, 1965.)

ARANA, RIC
Big Dano. Powell, 1969
The Silent Seducers. Challenge, 1967

ARBUTHNOT, K(ATHLEEN) P(HYLLIS)
"...And Hang Him." Skeffington, 1936

ARCH, E. L. Pseudonym of Rachel (Ruth) C(osgrove) Payes, 1922-   , q.v.
The Deathstone. Avalon, 1964 [future]
The First Immortals. Avalon, 1965 [2000s]

ARCHER, A. A. Pseudonym of Archie (Lynn) Joscelyn, 1899-   , q.v. Other pseudonym: Evelyn McKenna, q.v.
Three Men Murdered. Phoenix, 1936
The Week-End Murders. Phoenix, 1938

ARCHER, C(HARLES) S(TANLEY). 1902-   .
China Servant. Collins, 1946
Hankow Return. Collins, 1941; Houghton, 1941

ARCHER, FRANK. Pseudonym of Richard O'Connor, 1915-1975. Other pseudonym: Patrick Wayland, q.v. SC: Joe Delaney = JD.
The Malabang Pearl. Doubleday, 1964; Hale, 1966 JD [S.F.]
-The Naked Crusader. Brandon, 1972
Out of the Blue. Doubleday, 1964; Hale, 1966
The Turquoise Spike. GM, 1967; Jenkins, 1968 JD [S.F.]
The Widow Watchers. Doubleday, 1965; Hale, 1967 JD [S.F.]

ARCHER, JEFFREY (HOWARD). 1940-   . Ref: CA.
-Kane and Abel. Hodder, 1979; Simon, 1980
Not a Penny More, Not a Penny Less. Cape, 1976; Doubleday, 1976
Shall We Tell the President? Cape, 1977; Viking, 1977 [Wash. D.C.]

ARCHER, LANE. Pseudonym of Louise Platt Hauck, 1883-1943. Other pseudonym: Louise Landon, q.v.
Mystery Mansion. Penn, 1931

ARCHER, MARGARET
Canter's Chase. Jarrolds, 1945
Flowers for Teacher. Jarrolds, 1948
The Gentle Rain. Jarrolds, 1952
Gull Yard. Jarrolds, 1947 [1840, Eng.]
Jonathan Guest. Jarrolds, 1952
The Silent Sisters. Jarrolds, 1950

ARCHER, MARY
The Body on the Line. Blackfriars, 1947
Concerning Miss Duncan. Cosmo, 1945
What—No Body? Blackfriars, 1947
What—No Witnesses? Locker, 1947

ARCHER, ROBERT. Set: NYC, in both titles.
The Case of the Vanishing Women. Howell, 1942; Swan, 1950
Death on the Waterfront. Doubleday, 1941; Swan, 1948

ARCHIBALD, WILLIAM. 1924-1970. Ref: CA.
The Innocents. Coward, 1950. (Play based on "The Turn of the Screw" by Henry James, 1843-1916, q.v.)

ARCTANDER, JOHN W(ILLIAM). 1849-1920.
Guilty? Cochrane, 1910 [Minn.]

ARD, WILLIAM (THOMAS). 1922-1960. Pseudonyms: Ben Kerr, Mike Moran, Thomas Wills, qq.v. Ref: CC. Born Brooklyn; copywriter and publicist; free-lance writer. SC: Timothy Dane = TD; Danny Fontaine = DF; Lou Largo = LL.
All I Can Get. Monarch, 1959 LL [Fla.]

And So to Bed. Monarch, 1962 LL
  (Ghost-written by John Jakes,
  1932-   , q.v.)
As Bad As I Am. Rinehart, 1959; Board-
  man, 1960. Also published as: Wanted:
  Danny Fontaine. Dell, 1960 DF (but
  called Mike Fontaine in the hard-
  cover edition)
Babe in the Woods. Monarch, 1960 LL
  (Ghost-written by Lawrence Block,
  1938-   , q.v.) [ship]
Cry Scandal. Rinehart, 1956; Digit,
  1960 TD [NYC]
Deadly Beloved; see The Root of His
  Evil
The Diary. Rinehart, 1952; Hammond,
  1954 TD [NYC]
Don't Come Crying to Me. Rinehart,
  1954 TD [NYC]
A Girl for Danny. Popular Library, 1953
  [ship]
Give Me This Woman. Monarch, 1962 LL
  (Ghost-written by John Jakes,
  1932-   , q.v.)
Hell Is a City. Rinehart, 1955 TD [NYC]
Like Ice She Was. Monarch, 1960 LL
  [N.Y.]
Make Mine Mavis. Monarch, 1961 LL
  (Ghost-written by John Jakes,
  1932-   , q.v.)
Mr. Trouble. Rinehart, 1954 TD
  [Las Veg.]
The Naked and the Innocent. Digit,
  1960 (U.S. title?)
No Angels for Me. Popular Library, 1954
  [N.J.]
The Perfect Frame. Mill, 1951; Hammond,
  1953 TD [NYC]
A Private Party. Rinehart, 1953. Bri-
  tish title: Rogue's Murder. Hammond,
  1955 TD [NYC]
Rogue's Murder; see A Private Party
The Root of His Evil. Rinehart, 1957;
  Boardman, 1958. Also published as:
  Deadly Beloved. Dell, 1958 TD [NYC]
The Sins of Billy Serene. Monarch, 1960
.38. Rinehart, 1952. British title:
  This Is Murder. Hammond, 1954. Also
  published as: You Can't Stop Me.
  Popular Library, 1953 TD [NYC]
This Is Murder; see .38
Wanted: Danny Fontaine; see As Bad As I
  Am
When She Was Bad. Dell, 1960 DF [NYC]
You Can't Stop Me; see .38

ARDEN, ANDREW
  The Motive Not the Deed. Talmy Franklin, 1975

ARDEN, WILLIAM. Pseudonym of Dennis
  Lynds, 1924-   , q.v. Other pseudo-
  nyms: Michael Collins, John Crowe,
  Carl Dekker, Maxwell Grant, Mark
  Sadler, qq.v. SC: Kane Jackson, in
  all titles.
  A Dark Power. Dodd, 1968; Hale, 1970
  [N.J.]
  Deadly Legacy. Dodd, 1973; Hale, 1974
  [NYC]
  Deal in Violence. Dodd, 1969; Hale,
  1971 [Calif.]
  Die to a Distant Drum. Dodd, 1972.
  British title: Murder Underground.
  Hale, 1974
  The Goliath Scheme. Dodd, 1970; Hale,
  1973 [Ohio]
  Murder Underground; see Die to a Dis-
  tant Drum

ARDIES, TOM. 1931-   . Ref: CA, TC.
  SC: Charlie Sparrow = CS.
  Kosygin Is Coming. Doubleday, 1974;
  Angus, 1975. Also published as:
  Russian Roulette. Panther, 1975
  [Van.]
  Palm Springs. Doubleday, 1978 [Calif.]
  Pandemic. Doubleday, 1973; Angus, 1974
  CS
  Russian Roulette; see Kosygin Is Coming
  Their Man in the White House. Double-
  day, 1971; Macmillan (London), 1971
  CS [Mex.]
  This Suitcase Is Going to Explode.
  Doubleday, 1972; Macmillan (London),
  1972 CS

ARDMAN, HARVEY
  Endgame. Avon, 1975 [Copen.]

ARENT, ARTHUR. 1904-1972. Ref: CA.
  Gravedigger's Funeral. Grossman, 1967;
  Macdonald, 1968
  The Laying On of Hands. Little, 1969;
  Joseph, 1971

ARESBYS, THE. Pseudonym of Helen R. Bam-
  berger, 1888-   , and Raymond S.
  Bamberger. SC: Parrish Darby = PD.
  The Mark of the Dead. Washburn, 1929;
  Skeffington, 1929 PD [Haw.]
  Murder at Red Pass. Washburn, 1930
  [Haw.]

Who Killed Coralie? Washburn, 1927;
  Skeffington, 1929 PD [S.F.]

ARICHA, AMOS
  A Man Called Jordan. Spearman, 1976
  Phoenix, with Eli Landau, 1939-   .
  Futura, 1979; NAL, 1979 [Mid. East]

ARKELL, W(ILLIAM) J. and A(LONZO) T.
  WORDEN
  Napoleon Smith. Judge, 1888

ARKHAM, CANDICE. Pseudonym of Alice
  Ramirez.
  Ancient Evil. Popular Library, 1977
  Deadly Friendship. Avon, 1973 [La.]

ARKINS, FRANK J. [FRANCIS JOSEPH ARKINS].
  1866-   .
  The Mystery of the Bonanza Trail. General Publishing Syndicate, 1910

ARKWRIGHT, RICHARD
  The Queen Anne's Gate Mystery. White,
  1889; Arno, 1976

ARLEN, MICHAEL. 1895-1956. Birth name:
  Dikran Kuyumjian. Ref: CC, EM.
  The Crooked Coronet. Heinemann, 1937;
  Doubleday, 1937 ss
  The Flying Dutchman. Heinemann, 1939;
  Book League, 1939
  Hell! Said the Duchess. Heinemann,
  1934; Doubleday, 1934 [future]

ARLEO, JOSEPH. 1933-   . Ref: CA.
  The Grand Street Collector. Walker,
  1970; Sphere, 1972 [NYC]

ARLEY, CATHERINE. 1935-   . Ref: CA.
  Dead Man's Bay. Collins, 1959; Award,
  1971 [Fr.]
  A Matter of Opportunity. Putnam, 1968
  [Holl.]
  Ready Revenge. Collins, 1960; Random,
  1961. (Translation of "Le Talion.")
  [Fr.]
  Woman of Straw. Collins, 1957; Random,
  1958. (Translation of "La Femme de
  Paille." Paris, 1956.)

ARLISS, JOEN. SC: Kate Graham = KG.
  Beloved Victim. Popular Library, 1980
  [1925, Eng.]
  The Lady Killer Affair. Zebra, 1980 KG
  [Sp.]
  Nightmare's Nest. Popular Library, 1979
  Shadow over Seventh Heaven. Popular
  Library, 1980
  The Shark Bait Affair. Zebra, 1979 KG
  [ship]

ARMAGNAC, A. L. Pseudonym: Nicholas
  Carter, q.v.

ARMAT, MRS. MARY
  River House. Dorrance, 1958

ARMFELT, ROGER
  County Affairs. Pilot, 1945
  -Village Affairs. Pilot, 1946

ARMISTEAD, LORNA MARGARET
  Death of Henrietta. Cape, 1934

ARMITAGE, FLORA
  The Five Deceivers. Dodd, 1963

ARMONT, PAUL. See: Louise Jordan Miln,
  1864-1933.

ARMOUR, JOHN. Pseudonym of Lauran Bos-
  worth Paine, 1916-   . Other pseudo-
  nyms: Reg Batchelor, Kenneth Bedford,
  Frank Bosworth, Mark Carrel, Robert
  Clarke, Richard Dana, J. F. Drexler,
  Troy Howard, Jared Ingersol, John
  Kilgore, Hunter Liggett, J. K. Lucas,
  John Morgan, qq.v.
  Death of a Doctor. Hale, 1969
  A Killer's Category. Hale, 1973 [L.A.]
  Murder in Hawthorn. Hale, 1975
  Run with the Killer. Hale, 1969
  The Saturday Night Massacre. Hale, 1976

ARMOUR, R. C(OUTTS). Australian by birth.
  Pseudonym: Coutts Brisbane, q.v. All
  titles below were published by Amal-
  gamated Press and feature Sexton
  Blake.
  The Adventure of the Egyptian Student.
  1925
  The Adventure of the Oil Pirates. 1924
  The Adventure of the Silk Smugglers.
  1926
  The Affair of the Atlantic Mail Rob-
  bery. 1929
  The Affair of the Crook Explorer. 1928
  The Affair of the Trade Rivals. 1926
  The Baboon's Paw. 1922
  The Bootlegger's Victim. 1929

By the Skin of His Teeth. 1922
The Case of the Eccentric Will. 1924
The Case of the Island Princess. 1923
The Case of the Kidnapped Legatee.
  1924. Also published as: The Secret
  of the Gold Locket. 1935, as by
  Pierre Quiroule
The Case of the Millionaire Newspaper
  Owner, 1924
The Case of the Mysterious Germs. 1923
Certified Insane. 1924
The Clue of the Cloakroom Ticket. 1925
Dead Man's Shoes. 1927
The Desert Trail. 1923
The Diamond Flood. 1922
The Episode of the Stolen Voice. 1921
In Savage Hayti. 1923
The Leopard Man. 1921
The Lighthouse Mystery. 1922
The Man Who Forgot. 1921
The Masked Raiders. 1930
The Movie Mystery. 1927
The Mystery of Bullen Point. 1926
The Mystery of the Isle of Fortune.
  1928
The Mystery of the Sunken Road. 1922
The Pirates of the Air Way. 1927
The Platinum Smugglers. 1924
The Prisoner of the Buddha. 1923
The Riddle of the Dead Man's Pit. 1929
The Riddle of the Great Art Exhibition.
  1929
The Riddle of the Lost Emigrant. 1926
The Secret of the Cask. 1929
The Secret of the Gold Locket; see The
  Case of the Kidnapped Legatee
The Secret of the Lagoon. 1923
The Secret of Torre Island. 1926
The Studio Mystery. 1922
The Sun God. 1923
Terror Island. 1921
Through Fire and Water. 1921
The Trail of Doom. 1928
The Trail of the Tiger. 1924
The Treasure of the Manchus. 1926
The Werewolf of Elphinstone. 1922
The White Refugees. 1922

ARMOUR, TONY
  Blood Tells. Curtis, 1973 [Afr.]

ARMSTRONG, ANNE (WETZELL). See: Guy
  C(ameron) Pollock

ARMSTRONG, ANTHONY. Pseudonym of George
  Anthony Armstrong Willis, 1897-1976.
  Ref: CA, CC, EM. Series character:
  Jimmie Rezaire = JR. Set: mostly Eng.
  -The Eleventh Hour. London Play Co.,
  1933. (Play.)
  -The End of the Road. Todd, 1943
  (16 pp.)
  He Was Found in the Road. Methuen, 1952
  --In the Dentist's Chair. French, 1933
  (Play.)
  Jimmie Rezaire. Paul, 1927. U.S.
  title: The Trail of Fear. Macrae-
  Smith, 1927 JR
  Mile-Away Murder. London Play Co.,
  1937. (Play.)
  No Higher Mountain. Methuen, 1951
  One Jump Ahead. Eyre, 1972
  The Poison Trail. Benn, 1932 JR
  A Room at the Hotel Ambre; see Spies in
  Amber
  The Secret Trail. Methuen, 1928;
  Macrae-Smith, 1929 JR
  Spies in Amber. Methuen, 1956. U.S.
  title: A Room at the Hotel Ambre.
  Doubleday, 1956 [Paris]
  The Strange Case of Mr. Pelham.
  Methuen, 1957; Doubleday, 1957
  Ten Minute Alibi. Gollancz, 1933.
  (Play.) Novelization with Herbert
  Shaw: Methuen, 1934
  The Trail of Fear; see Jimmie Rezaire
  The Trail of the Black King. Methuen,
  1931; Macrae-Smith, 1931 JR
  The Trail of the Lotto. Methuen, 1929;
  Macrae-Smith, 1930 JR
  Well Caught. Butler & Tanner, 1932.
  (Play.)
  Without Witness, with Harold Simpson.
  Gollancz, 1934. (Play.)

ARMSTRONG, CHARLOTTE. 1905-1969. Pseudo-
  nym: Jo Valentine, q.v. See also:
  Robert Brome, 1917-   . Ref: CA,
  CC, EM, TC. SC: MacDougal Duff = MD.
  The Albatross. Coward, 1957; Collins,
  1958 ss (The title novelet in this
  collection was reprinted separately
  as: Mask of Evil. Crest, 1958.)
  Alibi for Murder; see The Dream Walker
  The Balloon Man. Coward, 1968; Collins,
  1968 [L.A.]
  The Better to Eat You. Coward, 1954;
  Davies, 1954. Also published as: Mur-
  der's Nest. PB, 1955 [Calif.]

A

The Black-Eyed Stranger. Coward, 1951; Davies, 1952 [N.Y.]
The Case of the Weird Sisters. Coward, 1943; Gifford, 1944   MD [Mich.]
Catch-as-Catch-Can. Coward, 1952; Davies, 1953. Also published as: Walk Out on Death. PB, 1954 [L.A.]
The Chocolate Cobweb. Coward, 1948; Davies, 1952 [Calif.]
Death Filled the Glass; see The Innocent Flower
A Dram of Poison. Coward, 1956; Davies, 1956 [Calif.]
Dream of Fair Woman. Coward, 1966; Collins, 1966 [L.A.]
The Dream Walker. Coward, 1955; Davies, 1955. Also published as: Alibi for Murder. PB, 1956
Duo. Coward, 1959; Davies, 1960. (Two novelets, each reprinted separately: The Girl with a Secret. Crest, 1960; Incident at a Corner. Ace, 1963.) [L.A.]
The Gift Shop. Coward, 1967; Collins, 1967 [Calif.]
The Girl with a Secret; see Duo
I See You. Coward, 1966 ss
Incident at a Corner; see Duo
The Innocent Flower. Coward, 1945. British title: Death Filled the Glass. Cherry Tree, 1945   MD [N.Y.]
Lay On, MacDuff! Coward, 1942; Gifford, 1943   MD [NYC]
Lemon in the Basket. Coward, 1967; Collins, 1968 [Calif.]
A Little Less Than Kind. Coward, 1963; Collins, 1964 [L.A.]
The Mark of the Hand. Ace, 1963
Mask of Evil; see The Albatross
Mischief. Coward, 1950; Davies, 1951
The One-Faced Girl. Ace, 1963
The Protege. Coward, 1970; Collins, 1970 [Calif.]
Seven Seats to the Moon. Coward, 1969; Collins, 1969 [L.A.]
The Seventeen Widows of San Souci. Coward, 1959; Davies, 1959
Something Blue. Ace, 1962
Then Came Two Women. Ace, 1962 [L.A.]
The Turret Room. Coward, 1965; Collins, 1965 [Calif.]
The Unsuspected. Coward, 1946; Harrap, 1946 [Conn.]
Walk Out on Death; see Catch-as-Catch-Can
Who's Been Sitting in My Chair? Ace, 1963
The Witch's House. Coward, 1963; Collins, 1964 [Calif.]

ARMSTRONG, LEROY. 1854-1927.
 -Dan Gunn, the Man from Mauston, A Countryman Who Did Up the Town. Rand, 1898

ARMSTRONG, MARGARET (NEILSON). 1867-1944. Ref: MP.
 The Blue Santo Murder Mystery. Random, 1941; Hale, 1943 [New Mex.]
 The Man with No Face. Random, 1940; Hale, 1941
 Murder in Stained Glass. Random, 1939; Hale, 1939 [Conn.]

ARMSTRONG, RAYMOND. Pseudonym of Norman Lee, 1905-1962. Other pseudonyms: Mark Corrigan, Robertson Hobart, qq.v. SC: Insp. Dick Mason = DM; Laura Scudamore = LS; J. Rockingham Stone = JS.
 Cavalier of the Night. Long, 1956   JS
 Dangerous Limelight. Long, 1947   DM
 Midnight Cavalier. Long, 1954   JS
 Murder of a Marriage. Long, 1960
 Sinister Playhouse. Long, 1949   DM
 The Sinister Widow. Long, 1951   LS,DM
 The Sinister Widow Again. Long, 1952   LS,DM
 The Sinister Widow at Sea. Long, 1959   LS,DM
 The Sinister Widow Comes Back. Long, 1957   LS,DM
 The Sinister Widow Down Under. Long, 1958   LS,DM
 The Sinister Widow Returns. Long, 1953   LS,DM
 They Couldn't Go Wrong. Long, 1951
 The Widow and the Cavalier. Long, 1956   JS,DM

ARMSTRONG, VICTOR
 The Free-Lance Spy. Major, 1976

ARNALDI, JEAN. Pseudonym: Jean Arnold, q.v.

ARNAUD, GEORGES. Pseudonym of Henri Georges Girard, 1917-   .
 -Flesh and Fire. Avon, 1958
 -Journey Past Repentence. Bodley Head, 1953. (Translation of "Le Voyage du Mauvais Larron." Paris, 1951.)
 The Wages of Fear. Bodley Head, 1952; Farrar, 1952. (Translation of "Le Salaire de la Peur." Paris, 1950.)

ARNOLD, A(DELAIDE) V(ICTORIA). Byline also: Mrs. J. O. Arnold, q.v
 The Clue. Arnold, 1927

ARNOLD, ALEX S.
 His Fortunate Foe. Earle, 1915

ARNOLD, SIR EDWIN. 1832-1904.
 The Queen's Justice. Burleigh, 1899 [India]

ARNOLD, ELLIOTT. 1912-1980. Ref: CA.
 Code of Conduct. Scribner, 1970; Longmans, 1970 [Switz.]
 Forests of the Night. Scribner, 1971; Longmans, 1972
 Quicksand. Simon, 1977 [NYC]

ARNOLD, JEAN. Pseudonym of Jean Arnaldi.
 Prettybelle. Dial, 1970 [South]

ARNOLD, MRS. J. O. Byline also: A(delaide) V(ictoria) Arnold, q.v.
 The Merlewood Mystery. Nelson, 1928

ARNOLD, JOHN. 1903-   . Set: mostly Eng.
 The London Bridge Mystery. Jenkins, 1932
 Murder! Jenkins, 1926; Small, 1927
 The Murders in Surrey Wood; see The Surrey Wood Mystery
 The Surrey Wood Mystery. Jenkins, 1928. U.S. title: The Murders in Surrey Wood. Dutton, 1928
 Tumult in San Benito. Jenkins, 1934
 What Happened at Andals? Jenkins, 1929; Dutton, 1930

ARNOLD, MARGOT. Pseudonym of Petronelle Marguerite Mary Cook, 1925-   . SC: Penelope Spring and Tobias Glendower, in all titles.
 The Cape Cod Caper. Playboy pb, 1980 [Cape Cod]
 Exit Actors, Dying. Playboy pb, 1979 [Turk.]
 Zadok's Treasure. Playboy pb, 1980; Chivers, 1982 [Israel]

ARNOLD, RALPH (CRISPIAN MARSHALL). 1906-1970. Director of publishing company. Set: mostly Eng.
 Death of a Sinner. Heinemann, 1933
 -Despair and Delight. Constable, 1939
 -Fire on the Seven Peaks. Blackie, 1938
 Fish and Company. Heinemann, 1951; Macmillan, 1951
 -Fortune Favors Fools. Heinemann, 1932
 -The Hundred of Hoo. Constable, 1947
 Jenkin's Green. Heinemann, 1953
 The Kidnapped King. Blackie, 1937
 On Secret Service. Blackie, 1935
 The Pelican Strikes Back. Nicholson, 1936
 Skeletons and Cupboards. Heinemann, 1952; Macmillan, 1951

ARNOLD, SAMUEL JAMES. 1774-1852.
 The Creole; or, The Haunted Island. Law, 1796 [Carib.]

ARNOT, ALLEN
 The Dempsey Diamonds. Lane (London & NYC), 1912

ARNOTHY, CHRISTINE. 1930-   .
 The Black Garden. Holt, 1969; H. Hamilton, 1969 (Translation of "Le Jardin Noir." Paris, 1966.)

ARNOULD, ARTHUR. Pseudonym: A. Matthey, q.v.

ARONSON, HARVEY, 1929-   , and MIKE McGRADY, 1933-   . Ref: CA, both authors.
 Establishment of Innocence. Putnam, 1975 [L.I.]

ARPINO, GIOVANNI. 1927-   .
 A Crime of Honor. Braziller, 1963; Weidenfeld, 1963 (Translation of "Un Delitto d'Onore." Milan, 1961.) [It.]

ARRE, HELEN. Pseudonym of Z(ola) H(elen Girdey) Ross, 1912-   , q.v. Other pseudonym: Bert Iles, q.v.
 The Corpse by the River. Arcadia, 1953
 The Golden Shroud. Arcadia, 1958 [Seattle]
 Murder by the Book. Arcadia, 1960
 No Tears at the Funeral. Arcadia, 1954
 Write It Murder. Arcadia, 1956

ARRIGHI, MEL. 1933-   . Ref: CA.
 Conscience of a Killer; see Navona 1000
 The Death Collection. Curtis, 1973; Hale, 1976 [NYC]
 Freak-Out. Putnam, 1968. British title: A Wild Trip. Hale, 1969 [NYC]
 The Hatchet Man. Harcourt, 1975; Hale, 1976 [NYC]
 Navona 1000. Bobbs, 1976. British title: Conscience of a Killer. Hale, 1977 [Rome]
 An Ordinary Man. Weyden, 1970; Wingate, 1970
 Turkish White. Harcourt, 1977; Hale, 1978
 A Wild Trip; see Freak-Out

ARRIGIO, FRANK
 Mobster. Belmont, 1975

ARROYO, SANTANA
 Hustle into Death. Manor, 1977

ARTHUR, BUDD
 The Big Squeeze. Bouregy, 1956
 Swiftly to Evil. World Distributors, 1960 [NYC]

ARTHUR, FRANK. Pseudonym of Arthur Frank Ebert, 1902-   . Ref: CA, CC, TC. SC: Insp. Spearpoint = S.
 Another Mystery in Suva. Heinemann, 1956   S [Fiji]
 Confession to Murder. United Writers, 1973
 Murder in the Tropic Night. Jenkins, 1961   S [Fiji]
 The Suva Harbour Mystery; see Who Killed Netta Maul?
 The Throbbing Dark. Jenkins, 1963   S [Fiji]
 Who Killed Netta Maul? Gollancz, 1940. Also published as: The Suva Harbour Mystery. Penguin, 1948   S [Fiji]

ARTHUR, HARRY. Pseudonym of Harry Arthur Bates.
 Summer Showers. Pageant, 1952

ARTHUR, ROBERT. Pseudonym of Robert Arthur Feder, 1909-1969.
 Somebody's Walking over My Grave. Ace, 1961 [Calif.]

ARTHUR, WILLIAM. Pseudonym of W(illiam) Arthur) Howard Baker, 1925-   , q.v. Other pseudonyms: W. A. Ballinger, Julie Wellsley, Peter Saxon, Richard Williams, qq.v.
 Murder with Variety. Amalgamated Press, 1957 (Sexton Blake.)

ARUNDALE, PAMELA
 Break and Olives. Chatto, 1957 ss [Greece]

ARVAY, HARRY. 1925-   . Ref: CA. SC: Max Roth, in at least those marked MR.
 Blow the Four Winds. Corgi, 1977
 Damascus Countdown. Corgi, 1976   MR [Damascus]
 Eleven Bullets for Mohammed. Corgi, 1975; Bantam, 1975   MR
 The Meirovitz Plan. Corgi, 1975   MR
 The Moscow Intercept. Corgi, 1975; Bantam, 1975   MR [Moscow]
 Operation Kuwait. Corgi, 1975; Bantam, 1975   MR [Kuw.]
 The Piraeus Plot. Corgi, 1975; Bantam, 1975   MR [Mid. East]
 Society of Fear. NEL, 1979
 Stranglehold. Corgi, 1976   MR [Mid. East]
 The Swiss Deal. Corgi, 1976   MR
 Togo Commando. Corgi, 1976   MR
 Triad 21. NEL, 1977

ARVONEN, HELEN. Pseudonym: Margaret Worth, q.v.
 A Choice of Angels. Ace, 1974
 Circle of Death. Ace, 1967
 Doorway to Death. Ace, 1973 [Can.]
 Garden of Grief. Ace, 1974 [Can.]
 The Least of All Evils. Ace, 1970 [Can.]
 Outpost of Eternity. Tower, 1966
 Remember with Tears. Ace, 1968
 Rickshaw Bend. Ace, 1973 [Can.]
 Shadow of the Truth. Paperback Library, 1973
 A Sorrow for Angels. Ace, 1973 [Can., 1890]
 Stranger in Her House. Paperback Library, 1970
 The Summer of Evil. Ace, 1965 [Can.]
 The Two Mrs. Carrolls. Tower, 1967. (Novelization of the movie.)
 Whistle at My Window. Ace, 196?
 The Witches of Brimstone Hill. GM, 1971

ASBURY, HERBERT. 1891-1963. SC: Insp. Thomas Conroy, in both titles.
  The Crimson Rope; see The Devil of Pei-Ling
  The Devil of Pei-Ling. Macy-Masius, 1927. British title: The Crimson Rope. Jarrolds, 1928 [NYC]
  The Tick of the Clock. Macy-Masius, 1928; Brentano's (London), 1928 [NYC]

ASCHER, EUGENE. Pseudonym of Harold Ernest Kelly, 1899- . Other pseudonyms: Darcy Glinto, Gordon Holt, Buck Toler, qq.v. SC: Lucian Carolus, in all titles.
  The Grim Caretaker. Everybody's, 1944
  There Were No Asper Ladies. Mitre, 1944. Also published as: To Kill a Corpse. World Distributors, 1959
  To Kill a Corpse; see There Were No Asper Ladies
  Uncanny Adventures. Everybody's, 1944 ss (48 pp.)

ASCOTT, JOHN. Pseudonym of John William Bobin, -1935, q.v. Other pseudonym: Mark Osborne, q.v.
  The Great Shipyard Mystery. Amalgamated Press, 1931 (Sexton Blake.)

ASH, WILLIAM (FRANKLIN). 1917- .
  Ref: CA. SC: Kyle Brandeis = KB.
  -Incorporated. Harvester, 1980
  Ride a Paper Tiger. Hutchinson, 1968; Walker, 1969 [Cent. Am.] KB
  Take-Off. Hutchinson, 1969; Walker, 1970 [Paris] KB

ASHBAUGH, NANCY. 1929- . Ref: CA.
  Turn Left or Be Killed. Vanguard, 1973

ASHBROOK, H(ARRIETTE CORA). 1896-1946. Pseudonym: Susannah Shane, q.v. Ref: MP. SC: Philip "Spike" Tracy, in all titles.
  A Most Immoral Murder. Coward, 1935; Eyre, 1935 [L.I.]
  Murder Comes Back. Coward, 1940; Eyre, 1942 [NYC]
  Murder Makes Murder. Coward, 1937 [L.I.]
  The Murder of Cecily Thane. Coward, 1930; Eyre, 1930 [NYC]
  The Murder of Sigurd Sharon. Coward, 1933; Eldon, 1934 [Vt.]
  The Murder of Steven Kester. Coward, 1931; Eyre, 1933 [L.I.]
  Murder on Friday; see The Purple Onion Mystery
  The Purple Onion Mystery. Coward, 1941; Eyre, 1950. Also published as: Murder on Friday. Arrow, 1944 [NYC]

ASHBY, KAY
  Briarwood. Major, 1976
  Climb a Dark Cliff. Dell, 1972 [Calif.]
  The Cold Chill of Coptos. Ballantine, 1974
  Crown Valley. Dell, 1973 [Calif.]
  Marcadia. Dell, 1974

ASHBY, R(UBIE) C(ONSTANCE). 1899- .
  Ref: CC, EM, MP.
  Death on Tiptoe. Hodder, 1930 [Wales]
  He Arrived at Dusk. Hodder, 1933; Macmillan, 1933
  Out Went the Taper. Hodder, 1934; Macmillan, 1934 [Wales]
  Plot Against a Widow. Hodder, 1932

ASHCROFT, GENE
  The Black Vulture. Burnett, 1941

ASHDOWN, CLIFFORD. Joint pseudonym of R(ichard) Austin Freeman, 1862-1943, q.v., and John James Pitcairn, 1860-1936. SC: Romney Pringle = RP.
  The Adventures of Romney Pringle. Ward, 1902; Train, 1968 ss RP
  From a Surgeon's Diary. Ferret Fantasy, 1975; Train, 1977 ss
  The Further Adventures of Romney Pringle. Train, 1970 ss RP
  -The Queen's Treasure. Train, 1975

ASHE, B. D.
  Test Case. Dell, 1970 (Novelization of "The Young Lawyers" TV series.)

ASHE, DOUGLAS. Pseudonym of John Franklin Bardin, 1916-1981, q.v. Other pseudonym: Gregory Tree, q.v.
  A Shroud for Grandmama. Scribner, 1951; Gollancz, 1951, as by Gregory Tree. Also published as: The Longstreet Legacy. Paperback Library, 1970 [NYC]

ASHE, GORDON. Pseudonym of John Creasey, 1908-1973, q.v. Other pseudonyms: M. E. Cooke, Norman Deane, Robert Caine Frazer, Patrick Gill, Michael Halliday, Charles Hogarth, Brian Hope, Colin Hughes, Kyle Hunt, Abel Mann, Peter Manton, J. J. Marric, Richard Martin, Rodney Mattheson, Anthony Morton, Jeremy York, qq.v. SC: Patrick Dawlish = PD; Patrick Dawlish and the Crime Haters = PD*. Set: mostly Eng.
  The Big Call. Long, 1964; Holt, 1975 PD*
  A Blast of Trumpets. Long, 1975; Holt, 1976 PD*
  A Clutch of Coppers. Long, 1967; Holt, 1969 PD*
  Come Home to Death. Long, 1958. U.S. title: The Pack of Lies. Doubleday, 1959 PD
  The Crime Haters. Long, 1961; Doubleday, 1960 PD*
  The Croaker; see The Speaker
  The Dark Circle. Evans, 1950 PD
  Dark Mystery. Long, 1948 PD
  Day of Fear. Long, 1956; Holt, 1978 PD
  Death from Below. Long, 1963; Holt, 1968 PD* [Fr.]
  Death in a Hurry. Evans, 1952 PD
  Death in Diamonds. Evans, 1951 PD
  Death in Flames. Long, 1943 PD
  Death in High Places. Long, 1942 PD
  Death in the Trees. Long, 1954 PD [Wash.]
  Death on Demand. Long, 1939 PD
  Death on the Move. Long, 1945 PD
  Don't Let Him Kill. Long, 1960. U.S. title: The Man Who Laughed at Murder. Doubleday, 1960 PD
  Double for Death. Long, 1954; Holt, 1969 PD
  Drop Dead; see The Long Search
  Elope to Death. Long, 1959; Holt, 1977 PD [Fr.]
  Engagement with Death. Long, 1948 PD
  Give Me Murder. Long, 1947 PD
  A Herald of Doom. Long, 1974; Holt, 1975 PD*
  Here Is Danger. Long, 1946 PD
  Invitation to Adventure. Long, 1945 PD
  The Kidnapped Child. Long, 1955; Holt, 1971. Also published as: The Snatch. Corgi, 1965 PD
  Kill or Be Killed. Evans, 1949 PD
  A Life for a Death. Long, 1973; Holt, 1973 PD* [It.]
  The Long Search. Long, 1953. U.S. title: Drop Dead. Ace, 1954 PD [S.W.]
  The Man Who Laughed at Murder; see Don't Let Him Kill
  The Man Who Stayed Alive. Long, 1955 [NYC]
  The Masked Gunman; see Who Was the Jester?
  Missing or Dead. Evans, 1952 PD
  Murder Most Foul. Long, 1942 PD
  Murder Too Late. Long, 1947 PD
  Murder with Mushrooms. Evans, 1950; Holt, 1974 PD
  A Nest of Traitors. Long, 1970; Holt, 1971 PD*
  No Need to Die. Long, 1956. U.S. title: You've Bet Your Life. Ace, 1957 [NYC]
  The Pack of Lies; see Come Home to Death
  A Plague of Demons. Long, 1976; Holt, 1977 PD*
  A Promise of Diamonds. Long, 1965; Dodd, 1964 PD* [S. Afr.]
  A Puzzle in Pearls. Long, 1949 PD
  A Rabble of Rebels. Long, 1971; Holt, 1972 PD* [Calif.]
  Rogues Rampant. Long, 1944 PD
  Rogue's Ransom. Long, 1962; Doubleday, 1961 PD* [Fr.]
  A Scream of Murder. Long, 1969; Holt, 1970 PD*
  Secret Murder. Long, 1940 PD
  A Shadow of Death. Long, 1968; Holt, 1976 PD*
  Sleepy Death. Long, 1953 PD
  The Snatch; see The Kidnapped Child
  The Speaker. Long, 1939. U.S. title: The Croaker. Holt, 1973 PD
  A Taste of Treasure. Long, 1966; Holt, 1966 PD* [Australia]
  Terror by Day. Long, 1940 PD
  There Goes Death. Long, 1942 PD
  Two Men Missing. Long, 1943 PD
  Wait for Death. Long, 1957; Holt, 1972 PD [Fr.]
  'Ware Danger. Long, 1941 PD
  Who Was the Jester? Newnes, 1940. Also published as: The Masked Gunman.
  You've Bet Your Life; see No Need to Die

ASHE, MARY ANN. Pseudonym of Mary Christianna Milne Lewis, 1907- . Other pseudonyms: Christianna Brand, China Thompson, qq.v. SC: Inspr. Chucky (see also Christianna Brand) = C.
  Alas for Her That Met Me! Star, 1976
  A Ring of Roses. Star, 1977 C

ASHE, NICHOLAS
  Danger Aft. Low, 1935
  Preface to a Killing; see Prelude to a Killing
  Prelude to a Killing. Low, 1936. U.S. title: Preface to a Killing. Macaulay, 1937

ASHE, ROSALIND
  The Hurricane Wake. Hutchinson, 1977; Holt, 1977 [Jam.]
  Moths. Hutchinson, 1976; Holt, 1976

ASHE, SAXON. Pseudonym. SC: Saxon Ashe, in both titles.
  I Am Saxon Ashe. Hodder, 1940; Alliance, 1941 [Ger.]
  Saxon Ashe...Secret Agent. Hodder, 1941; Alliance, 1942 [Holl.]

ASHENHURST, JOHN
  The World's Fair Murders. Houghton, 1933 [Chi.]

ASHER, MIRIAM
  Black Wind. PB, 1976 [Eng.]
  Nightmare in Eden. PB, 1974 [Maj.]

ASHFORD, F(RANCIS) U(RQUHART)
  A Packet of Trouble. Hale, 1971

ASHFORD, JEFFREY. Pseudonym of Roderic (Graeme) Jeffries, 1926- , q.v. Other pseudonyms: Peter Alding, Roderic Graeme, Graham Hastings, qq.v. SC: Insp. Don Kerry = DK. Set: mostly Eng.
  The Anger of Fear. Long, 1978; Walker, 1979
  Bent Copper. Long, 1971; Walker, 1971
  The Burden of Proof. Long, 1962; Harper, 1963
  The Colour of Violence. Long, 1974; Walker, 1974
  Consider the Evidence. Long, 1966; Walker, 1966
  Counsel for the Defense. Long, 1960; Harper, 1961
  The D.I.; see Investigations Are Proceeding
  The Double Run. Long, 1973; Walker, 1973 [Maj.]
  Enquiries Are Continuing. Long, 1964. U.S. title: The Superintendent's Room. Harper, 1965 DK
  Forget What You Saw. Long, 1967; Walker, 1967
  The Hands of Innocence. Long, 1965; Walker, 1966
  Hit and Run; see Will Anyone Who Saw the Accident...
  Hostage to Death. Long, 1977; Walker, 1977
  Investigations Are Proceeding. Long, 1961. U.S. title: The D.I. Harper, 1962 DK
  A Man Will Be Kidnapped Tomorrow. Long, 1972; Walker, 1972
  Prisoner at the Bar. Long, 1969; Walker, 1969
  A Recipe for Murder. Long, 1980; Walker, 1980
  Slow Down the World. Long, 1976; Walker, 1976
  The Superintendent's Room; see Enquiries Are Continuing
  Three Layers of Guilt. Long, 1975; Walker, 1976
  To Protect the Guilty. Long, 1970; Walker, 1970
  Will Anyone Who Saw the Accident... Long, 1963; Harper, 1964. Also published as: Hit and Run. Arrow, 1966

ASHLEY, ARTHUR ERNEST. 1906- . Pseudonym: Francis Vivian, q.v.

ASHLEY, KATE
  The Cinnabar Shroud. Long, 1956

ASHLEY, KENNETH H.
  Death of a Curate. Lane, 1932

ASHLEY, LANE
  Skeleton's Holiday. Long, 1940

ASHLEY, MARTIN
  Checkmate and Deathmate. Vantage, 1973

ASHLEY, MICHAEL
　Weird Legacies. Star, 1977

ASHLEY, STEVEN. Pseudonym of Donald McCaig. Ref: CA.
　Caleb, Who Is Hotter Than a $2 Pistol. McKay, 1975
　Stalking Blind. Dial, 1976　[W. Va.]

ASHMAN, HOWARD
　Mandrake the Magician. Ace, 1979. (Novelization of the TV movie.)

ASHTON, ANN. Pseudonym of John M. Kimbro, 1929-　. Other pseudonyms: Kym Allyson, Jean Kimbro, Kathryn Kimbrough, qq.v.
　The Haunted Portrait. Doubleday, 1976
　The Phantom Reflection. Doubleday, 1978　[L.A., 1935]
　Three Cries of Terror. Doubleday, 1980

ASHTON, CHARLES. 1884-　. SC: Jack Atherley, in at least 8 titles, including those marked JA. Set: mostly Eng.
　Calamity Comes to Flenton. Nicholson, 1936　JA
　Dance for a Dead Uncle. Museum, 1948
　Death for Two. Hale, 1940
　Death Greets a Guest. Nicholson, 1936
　Fate Strikes Twice. Cherry Tree, 1944 (96 pp.)
　Here's Murder Done. Hale, 1943
　Murder at Melton Peveril. Hale, 1946
　Murder in Make-Up. Nicholson, 1934　JA
　Stone Dead. Hale, 1939
　Tragedy After Tea. Nicholson, 1935

ASHTON, HELEN (ROSALINE). 1891-1958.
　People in Cages. Macmillan, 1937; Collins, 1937

ASHTON, HERBERT, JR.
　The Locked Room. French (NYC), 1934 (3-act play.)

ASHTON, MARK
　Draw the Teeth of a Dragon. Hale, 1979
　A Plague on Both Your Houses. Hale, 1980
　A Silence of Birds. Hale, 1979
　Try to Find a Dead Man. Hale, 1980

ASHTON, SHARON. Pseudonym of Helen Van Slyke,　-1979.
　The Santa Ana Wind. Doubleday, 1974; New English Library, 1975. Also published as by Helen Van Slyke: New English Library pb, 1982 [Calif.]

ASHTON, WARREN J. Pseudonym of William T(aylor) Adams, 1822-1897, q.v.
　-Hatchie the Guardian Slave; or, The Heiress of Bellevue. Mussey, 1852

ASHTON, WINIFRED. 1888-1965. Pseudonym: Clemence Dane, q.v.

ASHTON-WOLFE, H(ARRY). 1881-　.
　Warped in the Making. Hurst, 1928; Houghton, 1928　ss

ASIMOV, ISAAC. 1920-　. Ref: CA, DD, TC. SC: Black Widowers = BW; Elijah Baley = EB.
　Asimov's Mysteries. Doubleday, 1968; Rapp, 1968　ss
　Authorized Murder; see Murder at the ABA
　Casebook of the Black Widowers. Doubleday, 1980; Gollancz, 1980　ss　BW
　The Caves of Steel. Doubleday, 1954; Boardman, 1954　EB　[future]
　The Death Dealers. Avon, 1958. Also published as: A Whiff of Death. Walker, 1968; Gollancz, 1968　[acad.]
　More Tales of the Black Widowers. Doubleday, 1976; Gollancz, 1977　ss　BW
　Murder at the ABA. Doubleday, 1976. British title: Authorized Murder. Gollancz, 1976　[NYC]
　The Naked Sun. Doubleday, 1957; Joseph, 1958　EB　[future]
　Tales of the Black Widowers. Doubleday, 1974; Gollancz, 1975　ss　BW
　A Whiff of Death; see The Death Dealers

ASINOF, ELIOT. 1919-　. Ref: CA.
　The Name of the Game Is Murder. Simon, 1968　[NYC]

ASKEW, ALICE and CLAUDE ASKEW,　-1917.
　-The Actor Manager. Newnes, 1913
　The Adventures of Police Constable Vane, M.A. Hutchinson, 1908
　-Anna of the Plains. White, 1906
　-The Apache. Everett, 1912
　-Araby's Husband. Hurst, 1914
　-The Baxter Family. White, 1907
　-Behind Shuttered Windows. C. H. White, 1910
　-Bess of Bentley's. White, 1912
　　The Blue Diamond. C. H. White, 1909
　-The Bride in Black. Ward, 1918
　　By Order of the King. Aldine, 1914
　　A Deadly Revenge. Mellifont, 1934
　-Destiny. Hurst, 1911
　-The Devil and the Crusader. White, 1909
　-The Dream Daughter. Ward, 1912
　-The Englishwoman. Cassell, 1912
　-The Etonian. White, 1906; Bell, 1906
　-Eve—and the Law. Chapman, 1905
　-Evelyn. Long, 1923
　-Fate—and Drusilla. Everett, 1910
　-Felix Stone. Everett, 1909
　-The Footlight Glare. Ward, 1916
　-Freedom. Hurst, 1914
　-The Garment of Immortality. Long, 1917
　-Gilded London. Ward, 1915
　-God's Clay. Unwin, 1913
　-The Golden Girl. Ward, 1913
　-The Golden Quest. Ward, 1915
　-The Grip of Sin. Lloyds, 1920
　　Helen of the Moor. Ward, 1911
　-Her Empty Triumph. Leng, 1926
　-Her Father's Daughter. Ward, 1916
　-Her Mother's Child. Ward, 1915
　-The House Next Door. Ward, 1911
　-In Lover's Lane. Ward, 1912
　-In Strange Shoes. Ward, 1914
　-The Inscrutable Miss Stone. Long, 1917
　-Jennifer Pontefracte. Hurst, 1906
　　John Heriot's Wife. White, 1909
　　The King's Signature. Chapman, 1912
　　Kitty Shafton—Swindler. Ward, 1911
　-Lady Borradale's Ordeal. Ward, 1918
　　Lavender's Inheritance. United Press, 1922
　-The Legacy. Ward, 1914
　-The Lily and the Devil. Everett, 1912
　　The Lost Idol. Ward, 1917
　-The Love Stone. Sisley's, 1907
　-Love the Jester. Ward, 1914
　　The Lurking Shadow. Ward, 1915
　-Master and Man. Aldine, 1915
　-Milly the Actress. Aldine, 1913
　　The Missing Million. Ward, 1915
　　The Mystery of Helmsley Grange. Pearson, 1913
　　Not Proven. Ward, 1908
　-Nurse. Hodder, 1916
　-The Orchard Close. Hurst, 1908
　-The Ordeal of Ann Curtis. Jarrolds, 1918
　　Out of the Running. Everett, 1907
　-Outlaw Jess. Ward, 1912
　-The Paignton Honour. Ward, 1917
　-The Path of Lies. White, 1908
　-The Pearl of Great Price. White, 1911
　-The Plains of Silence. Cassell, 1907
　-Poison. Nash, 1913
　-A Preacher of the Lord. Cassell, 1913
　-The Premier's Daughter. White, 1905
　-The Quest of El Dorado. Cassell, 1910
　-The Rod of Justice. Unwin, 1910; Brentano's, 1910
　-Salvation. Chapman, 1917
　-The Scarlet Sin. Ward, 1913
　-Scarlet Town. C. H. White, 1910
　-The Secret Pathway. Collins, 1919
　-The Shulamite. Chapman, 1904. Revised edition: Unwin, 1907; Brentano's, 1907
　-A Society Marriage. Ward, 1911
　-Souls Adrift. Ward, 1913
　-The Sporting Chance. Ward, 1910
　-The Stolen Lady. Ward, 1911
　　The Sword of Peace: The Story of a Secret Society. Everett, 1907
　-The Telephone Girl. Ward, 1918
　-The Tempting of Paul Chester. Unwin, 1908; Fenno, 1910
　-Through Folly's Mill. Ward, 1914
　-The Tocsin. Long, 1915
　-Trespass. Ward, 1915
　-Two Apaches of Paris. Rickey, 1911 (British title?)
　-The Weavers. Ward, 1915
　-Wild Sheba. Ward, 1910
　-A Woman's World. Leng, 1926
　-The Work of Her Hands. Chapman, 1918
　-The Yellow Yoke. Aldine, 1919

ASKIN, JULIAN. See: Robin Moore.

ASPINALL, (HONOR) RUTH (ALASTAIR). 1922-　. Ref: CA.
　The Dark Side of Magic. Harrap, 1971

ASPINWALL, MARGUERITE. See: Elsie Janis, 1889-1956.

ASPLER, TONY. 1939-　. See: Gordon Pape, 1937-　.

ASPREY, ROBERT B(ROWN). 1923-　. Ref: CA.
　Operation Prophet. Doubleday, 1977; Hale, 1979

ASQUITH, HERBERT. 1881-1947.
　Wind's End. Hutchinson, 1924; Scribner, 1924

ASSINDER, PETER
　The Paying Guest. Kenyon House, 1954 (1-act play.)

ASTERLEY, H(UGH) C(ECIL)
　Tale of Two Murders. Jarrolds, 1932. U.S. title: Mortmain. Sears, 1932

ASTLEY, JULIET. Pseudonym of Norah (Robinson) Lofts, 1904-　, q.v. Other pseudonym: Peter Curtis, q.v.
　The Fall of Midas. Coward, 1975 [ca.1900, Eng.]

ASWAD, BETSY. 1939-　　Ref: CA.
　Winds of the Old Days. Dial, 1980 [Pa.]

ASWELL, MARY LOUISE (WHITE). 1902-
　See also: Q. Patrick.
　Far to Go. Farrar, 1957

ATCHESON, GEORGE. 1923-
　The Peking Incident. Prentice-Hall, 1973; Bantam (London), 1974

ATHEN, ASTOR
　The Ladies Leave the Castle. Gifford, 1948

ATHERTON, GERTRUDE (FRANKLIN HORN). 1857-1948. Ref: CA.
　The Avalanche. Stokes, 1919; Murray, 1919　[S.F.]
　The Foghorn: Stories. Houghton, 1934. British title: The Foghorn and other stories. Jarrolds, 1935　ss
　Mrs. Balfame. Stokes, 1916; Murray, 1916
　-The Sophisticates. Liveright, 1931; Chapman, 1931

ATHOLL, JUSTIN. All titles are booklets of less than 70 pp.
　The Perfect Murder. Everybody's, 1943
　There Goes His Ghost. Everybody's, 1944
　The Trackless Thing. Everybody's, 1944

ATIYAH, EDWARD (SELIM). 1903-1964. Born in Syria; history lecturer; government-official; later lived in England.
　-Black Vanguard. Davies, 1952
　　The Crime of Julian Masters. Hale, 1959
　　The Cruel Fire; see Donkey from the Mountains
　　Donkey from the Mountains. Hale, 1961. U.S. title: The Cruel Fire. Doubleday, 1962　[Leb.]
　-The Eagle Flies from England. Hale, 1960
　-Lebanon Paradise. Davies, 1953　[Leb.]
　　Murder, My Love; see The Thin Line
　　The Thin Line. Davies, 1951; Harper, 1951. Also published as: Murder, My Love. Avon, 1957

ATKEY, BERTRAM. 1880-1952. Ref: EM, MP. SC: Smiler Bunn = SB; Prosper Fair = PF. Set: Eng.
　The Amazing Mr. Bunn. Newnes, 1912　SB　ss (A later edition, Macdonald, 1949, contains the first 5 of 6 ss in the first edition and the first 7 ss from Smiler Bunn, Gentleman-Crook, q.v.)
　Arsenic and Gold. Jenkins, 1939; Penn, 1939　SB
　Crooks' Castle. Newnes, 1908; Estes, 1908
　Easy Money. Richards, 1908; Estes, 1908
　-The Golden Lady. Ward, 1914
　-Harvest of Javelins. Cassell, 1922; Brentano's, 1923
　　Hercules—Sportsman. Robinson & Birch, 1922
　　The House of Clystevill. Jenkins, 1940　SB
　　The House of Strange Victims. Appleton, 1930　(British title?)
　　The Man with Yellow Eyes. Newnes, 1923; Dial, 1927
　　The Midnight Mystery. Appleton, 1928　PF　(British title?)
　　Mr. Dass. Hodder, 1929
　　The Mystery of the Glass Bullet. Appleton, 1931　SB　(British title?)
　　The Pyramid of Lead. Hutchinson, 1924; Appleton, 1925　PF
　　The Smiler Bunn Brigade. Hodder, 1916　SB　ss
　　Smiler Bunn, Byewayman. Newnes, 1925　SB　ss
　　Smiler Bunn, Crook. Newnes, 1929　SB (40 ss, 1016 pp., includes Smiler Bunn, Gentleman Crook, q.v., and presumably ss from other collections.)
　　Smiler Bunn, Gentleman-Adventurer. Dial, 1927　(= Smiler Bunn, Gentleman-Crook?)　SB　ss

Smiler Bunn, Gentleman-Crook. Newnes, 1923 SB ss
Smiler Bunn, Manhunter. Newnes, 1920 SB ss

ATKEY, PHILIP. 1908-   Pseudonym: Barry Perowne, q.v. Ref: EM, TC.
Blue Water Murder. Cassell, 1935 [Sp.]
Heirs of Merlin. Cassell, 1945
Juniper Rock. Cassell, 1952 [Cors.]

ATKINS, FRANCIS HENRY. 1840-1927. Pseudonym: Frank Aubrey, q.v.

ATKINS, (ARTHUR) HAROLD. 1910-   Ref: CA.
Sinister Smith. Duckworth, 1938

ATKINS, MEG [MARGARET] ELIZABETH. Ref: CA. SC: Insp. Henry Beaumont = HB.
By the North Door. Harper, 1975 HB
Samain. Cassell, 1977; Harper, 1976 HB
Secret Loving Shadows; see The Shadows of the House
The Shadows of the House. Hodder, 1969; Viking, 1969. Also published as: Secret Loving Shadows. Ballantine, 1977

ATKINS, THOMAS (RADCLIFFE). 1939-   Ref: CA.
The Blue Man. Doubleday, 1978   [Va., 1952]

ATKINSON, ALEX. 1916-1962. Ref: CC.
Exit Charlie. Davies, 1955; Knopf, 1956
Four Winds. French (London), 1954 (3-act play.)

ATKINSON, GEORGE SCOTT. 1899-   Pseudonym: Ralph Scott, q.v.

ATKINSON, HUGH. 1923-   Educated in Australia; living in Malta in the 1970s.
Big Money. PB, 1978
Crack-Up. Hart-Davis, 1974
-Low Company. Cheshire, 1961
The Man in the Middle. Hart-Davis, 1973; Putnam, 1973
-The Manipulators. Angus, 1978; Simon, 1978
The Most Savage Animal. Hart-Davis, 1972; Simon, 1972
-The Pink and the Brown. Gollancz, 1957
The Reckoning. Bodley Head, 1965. Also published as: Weekend to Kill. Angus 1977. And as: Weekend of Shadows. Angus, 1978
Unscheduled Flight. Hart-Davis, 1976
Weekend of Shadows; see The Reckoning
Weekend to Kill; see The Reckoning

ATLEE, BENGE. 1890-   .
Black Feather. Scribner, 1939 [Balkans]

ATLEE, PHILIP. Pseudonym of James Atlee Phillips, 1915-   , q.v. SC: Joe Gall, in all titles (see also Phillips entry).
The Black Venus Contract. GM, 1975 [S. Am.]
The Canadian Bomber Contract. GM, 1971 [Montr.]
The Death Bird Contract. GM, 1966; Coronet, 1968 [Mex.]
The Fer-de-Lance Contract. GM, 1970 [Carib.]
The Green Wound. GM, 1963; Muller, 1964. Also published as: The Green Wound Contract. GM, 1967 [New Or.]
The Green Wound Contract; see The Green Wound
The Ill Wind Contract. GM, 1969 [Indon.]
The Irish Beauty Contract. GM, 1966; Coronet, 1968 [Bolivia]
The Judah Lion Contract. GM, 1972 [Ethio.]
The Kiwi Contract. GM, 1972 [Australia]
The Kowloon Contract. GM, 1974 [H. Kong]
The Last Domino Contract. GM, 1976 [Indon.]
The Makassar Strait Contract. GM, 1976 [Indon.]
The Paper Pistol Contract. GM, 1966; Coronet, 1968 [Tahiti]
The Rockabye Contract. GM, 1968 [Carib.]
The Shankill Road Contract. GM, 1973 [Ire.]
The Silken Baroness. GM, 1964. Also published as: The Silken Baroness Contract. GM, 1966; Coronet, 1967 [Can. Is.]
The Silken Baroness Contract; see The Silken Baroness
The Skeleton Coast Contract. GM, 1968 [Afr.]
The Spice Route Contract. GM, 1973 [Mid. East]
The Star Ruby Contract. GM, 1967; Coronet, 1969 [Burma]

The Trembling Earth Contract. GM, 1969; Coronet, 1970
The Underground Cities Contract. GM, 1974 [Turk.]
The White Wolverine Contract. GM, 1971 [Van.]

ATTIWILL, KEN(NETH). See also: Evadne Price.
Sky Steward. Long, 1936

ATWATER, JAMES D(AVID). 1928-   . Ref: CA.
Time Bomb. Viking, 1977; Prior, 1978 [Eng.]

ATWATER, MARY M(EIGS). 1878-1956.
Crime in Corn-Weather. Houghton, 1935. British title: Murder in Midsummer. Gollancz, 1935 [Ia.]

AUBREY, EDMUND. Pseudonym of Edmund S. Ions. British political scientist; author of works on American history and politics. SC: Sherlock Holmes.
Sherlock Holmes in Dallas. Dodd, 1980 [Dallas]

AUBREY, FRANK. Pseudonym of Francis Henry Atkins, 1840-1927.
A Studio Mystery. Jarrolds, 1897

AUBREY-FLETCHER, HENRY LANCELOT. 1887-1969. Pseudonym: Henry Wade, q.v.

AUDEMARS, PIERRE. 1909-   . Ref: CA, CC, TC. SC: Monsieur Pinaud = P; Hercule Renard = HR. Set: mostly Fr.
And One for the Dead. Long, 1975 P
Walker, 1981 P
The Confession of Hercule. Low, 1947 HR
The Crown of Night. Long, 1962; Harper, 1962 P
Dead with Sorrow. Long, 1965. U.S. title: A Woven Web. Doubleday, 1965 P
The Delicate Dust of Death. Long, 1973 P
The Dream and the Dead. Long, 1963 P
Fair Maids Missing. Long, 1964; Doubleday, 1965 P
-Fate and Fernand. Polybooks, 1945 (16 pp.)
The Fire and the Clay. Long, 1959 P
The Flame in the Mist. Long, 1969; Curtis, 1971 P
The Healing Hands of Death. Long, 1977; Hutchinson (U.S.), 1977 P
Hercule and the Gods. Pilot, 1944; Rinehart, 1946 HR
A Host for Dying. Long, 1970; Curtis, 1972 P
Nightmare in Rust. Long, 1975 P
No Tears for the Dead. Long, 1974 P
Now Dead Is Any Man. Long, 1978; Walker, 1980 P
The Obligations of Hercule. Low, 1947 HR
A Sad and Savage Dying. Long, 1978 P
Slay Me a Sinner. Long, 1979; Walker, 1980 P
Stolen Like Magic Away. Long, 1971 P
The Street of Grass; see The Wings of Darkness
The Temptation of Hercule. Pilot, 1945 HR
Thieves of Enchantment. Chambers, 1956
A Thorn in the Dust. Long, 1967 P
Time of Temptation. Long, 1966; Doubleday, 1966 P
The Turns of Time. Long, 1961; Harper, 1962 P
The Two Imposters. Long, 1958 P
The Veins of Compassion. Long, 1967 P
-When the Gods Laughed. Foster, 1946
The White Leaves of Death. Long, 1968 P
The Wings of Darkness. Long, 1963. U.S. title: The Street of Grass. Harper, 1963 P
A Woven Web; see Dead with Sorrow

AUDOUARD, YVAN
-Little Pig-Alee. Ace, 1961

AUDRENN, JOEL
House of Lies. Mystique, 1980 (Translation of "La Sordane de Minuit." Paris, 1975.)

AUFRICHT-RUDA, HANS. 1899-   .
The Case for the Defendant. Allen, 1929; Little, 1929 [Fr.]

AUGUST, JOHN. Pseudonym of Bernard Augustine DeVoto, 1897-1955.
Advance Agent. Little, 1941; Selwyn, 1943 [Mass.]
Rain Before Seven. Little, 1940
Troubled Star. Little, 1939 [acad., Midwest]
The Woman in the Picture. Little, 1944; Selwyn, 1944

AUGUST, LEO. Pseudonym of Don Segall.
Superdoll. Award, 1969

AUGUSTA, CLARA. Pseudonym of Clara Augusta Jones, 1856-   . Other pseudonym: Hero Strong, q.v.
-The Adventures of a Bashful Bachelor. Ogilvie, 1890
The Fatal Glove. Lupton, 1892
The Lost Bride; or, The Price of Silence. Street, 1889
Nobody's Daughter; or, The Hidden Crime at Fernwood. Street, 1891
-Patience Pettigrew's Perplexities. Burt, 1887

AUMONIER, STACY. 1887-1928. Ref: CC, EM, MC.
The Baby Grand and other stories. Heinemann, 1926; Holt, 1927 ss
Miss Bracegirdle and others. Hutchinson, 1923; Doubleday, 1923 ss

AUSLANDER, JOSEPH. 1897-1965.
Hell in Harness. Doubleday, 1929 (Short crime story in verse.)

AUSTEN-LEIGH, LOIS (E.). Set: Eng.
The Gobblecock Mystery. Jenkins, 1938
The Haunted Farm. Jenkins, 1932
The Incredible Crime. Jenkins, 1931
Rude Justice. Jenkins, 1936

AUSTIN, ALEX
Salt and Pepper. Popular Library, 1968 (Novelization of the movie.) [Eng.]

AUSTIN, ANNE. 1895-   . Ref: CC. SC: James F. ("Bonnie") Dundee = JD.
The Avenging Parrot. Greenberg, 1930; Skeffington, 1931 JD [Midwest]
The Black Pigeon. Greenberg, 1929; Skeffington, 1932 [NYC]
Murder at Bridge. Macmillan, 1931; Skeffington, 1931 JD
Murder Backstairs. Macmillan, 1930; Skeffington, 1930 JD [Midwest]
Murdered But Not Dead. Macmillan, 1939 JD [Midwest]
One Drop of Blood. Macmillan, 1932; Skeffington, 1932 JD [Midwest]
A Wicked Woman. Macmillan, 1933; Hurst, 1934 [Tex.]

AUSTIN, BENJAMIN FISH. 1852-1930. Pseudonym: Benjamin Nitsua, q.v.

AUSTIN, F(REDERICK) BRITTEN. 1885-1941.
According to Orders. Melrose, 1918; Doran, 1918 ss
On the Borderland. Hurst, 1922; Doubleday, 1923 ss
Thirteen. Doubleday, 1925 (ss culled from According to Orders, On the Borderland, and Under the Lens, qq.v.)
Told in the Marketplace. Butterworth, 1935 ss
Under the Lens. Hurst, 1924 ss

AUSTIN, HUGH. Pseudonym of Hugh Austin Evans. SC: MP. Peter Quint = PQ; Wm. Sultan (Sultan's Harem) = WS.
The Cock's Tail Murder. Doubleday, 1938 PQ
Death Has Seven Faces. Scribner, 1949 [Ariz.]
Drink the Green Water. Scribner, 1948 WS [NYC, L.I.]
It Couldn't Be Murder. Doubleday, 1935; Heinemann, 1936 PQ
Lilies for Madame. Doubleday, 1938; Heinemann, 1938 [ship]
The Milkmaid's Millions. Scribner, 1948 WS
Murder in Triplicate. Doubleday, 1935; Heinemann, 1936 PQ
Murder of a Matriarch. Doubleday, 1936; Heinemann, 1937 PQ
The Upside Down Murders. Doubleday, 1937; Heinemann, 1938 PQ

AUSTIN, LILIAN EDNA
Shudders. Meador, 1931 ss

AUSTIN, MARILYN
Blackwater Bayou. Manor, 1979

AUSTIN, MAX
Out. Corgi, 1978 (Novelization of the TV series.)

AUSTIN, PHYLLIS. 1888-   .
Concerto. Nicholson, 1934

AUSTIN, THOMAS R.
The Week of the Succubus. Vantage, 1979

AUSTIN, WILLIAM. 1778-1841.
  Peter Rugg, the Missing Man. Rice, 1882; Polybooks, 1943

AUSTWICK, JOHN. Pseudonym of Austin Lee, 1904-1965, q.v. Other pseudonym: Julian Callender, q.v. SC: Insp. Parker, in at least those marked P. Set: Eng.
  The Borough Council Murders. Hale, 1965
  The County Library Murders. Hale, 1962
  Highland Homicide. Hale, 1957 P
  The Hubberthwaite Horror. Hale, 1958
  The Mobile Library Murders. Hale, 1964
  Murder in the Borough Library. Hale, 1959 P

AUSWAKS, ALEX
  A Trick of Diamonds. Collins, 1980

AUTUMN, AGNESE
  The Gold and Copper Delamonds. Methuen, 1930

AVALLONE, MICHAEL (ANGELO, JR.). 1924-   . Pseudonyms: Nick Carter, Priscilla Dalton, Mark Dane, Jean-Anne de Pre, Dora Highland, Stuart Jason, Steve Michaels, Dorothea Nile, Edwina Noone, Sidney Stuart, Max Walker, qq.v. Ref: CA, EM, TC. SC: April Dancer (The Girl from U.N.C.L.E., novels based on the TV series) = AD; Ed Noon = EN; Satan Sleuth (Philip St. George) = SS; Napoleon Solo (The Man from U.N.C.L.E., novels based on the TV series, with many other authors) = NS.
  The Alarming Clock. Curtis, 1973; Allen, 1961 EN [NYC]
  Assassins Don't Die in Bed. Signet, 1968 EN [ship]
  The Bedroom Bolero. Belmont, 1963; Digit, 1964. Also published as: The Bolero Murders. Hale, 1972 EN [NYC]
  The Big Stiffs. Hale, 1977 EN
  The Birds of a Feather Affair. Signet, 1966; Four Square, 1967 AD [NYC]
  The Blazing Affair. Signet, 1966 AD [S. Afr.]
  The Bolero Murders; see The Bedroom Bolero
  The Brutal Kook; see Lust Is No Lady
  A Bullet for Pretty Boy. Curtis, 1970 (Novelization of the movie.)
  -Carquake. Star, 1977
  The Case of the Bouncing Betty. Ace, 1957; Allen, 1959 EN
  The Case of the Violent Virgin. Ace, 1957; Allen, 1960 EN
  The Coffin Things. Lancer, 1968
  The Crazy Mixed-Up Corpse. GM, 1957; Fawcett (London), 1959 EN [NYC]
  Dark on Monday. Hale, 1978 EN
  Dead Game. Holt, 1954; Allen, 1959 EN [NYC]
  Death Dives Deep. Signet, 1971; Hale, 1971 EN [NYC]
  Devil, Devil. Warner, 1975; New English Library pb, 1976 SS [NYC]
  The Doomsday Bag. Signet, 1969. British title: Killer's Highway. Hale, 1970 EN [Wash. D.C.]
  Ed Noon in London; see London, Bloody London
  Fallen Angel. Warner, 1974; New English Library pb, 1976 SS [N.Y.]
  The Fat Death. Curtis, 1972; Allen, 1966 EN [NYC]
  The February Doll Murders. Signet, 1967; Allen, 1966 EN [NYC]
  The Felony Squad. Popular Library, 1967 (Novelization of the movie.)
  The Flower-Covered Corpse. Curtis, 1972; Hale, 1969 EN
  The Girl in the Cockpit. Curtis, 1972; Hale, 1974 EN [NYC]
  Hawaii Five-O. Signet, 1968. (Novelization of the TV series.) [Haw.]
  The Horrible Man. Curtis, 1972; Hale, 1968 EN [NYC]
  The Hot Body. Curtis, 1973 EN
  The Incident. Popular Library, 1968 (Novelization of the movie.) [NYC]
  Kaleidoscope. Popular Library, 1966 (Novelization of the movie.)
  Killer on the Keys. Curtis, 1973 EN [NYC]
  Kill Her—You'll Like It! Curtis, 1973; Hale, 1974 EN [NYC]
  Killer's Highway; see The Doomsday Bag
  The Killing Star. Hale, 1969
  Little Miss Murder. Signet, 1971. British title: The Ultimate Client. Hale, 1971 EN
  The Living Bomb. Curtis, 1972; Allen, 1963 EN
  London, Bloody London. Curtis, 1972. British title: Ed Noon in London. Hale, 1974 EN [Eng.]
  Lust Is No Lady. Belmont, 1964. British title: The Brutal Kook. Allen, 1965 EN [Wyo.]
  Madame X. Popular Library, 1966 (Novelization of the movie.)
  The Man from AVON. Avon, 1967 [N.H.]
  The Man from U.N.C.L.E. (The Thousand Coffins Affair). Ace, 1965; Four Square, 1965 NS
  Mannix. Popular Library, 1968 (Novelization of the TV series.) [NYC]
  Meanwhile Back at the Morgue. GM, 1960; Muller, 1961 [NYC]
  Missing! Signet, 1969 [Wash. D.C.]
  The Moving Graveyard; see Shoot It Again, Sam
  One More Time. Popular Library, 1970 (Novelization of the movie.) [Eng.]
  Shock Corridor. Belmont, 1963. (Novelization of the movie.)
  Shoot It Again, Sam. Curtis, 1972. British title: The Moving Graveyard. Hale, 1973 EN
  The Spitting Image. Holt, 1953; Barker, 1957 EN [NYC]
  The Tall Dolores. Holt, 1953; Barker, 1956 EN [NYC]
  Terror in the Sun. Signet, 1969. (Novelization of the "Hawaii Five-O" TV series.) [Haw.]
  There Is Something About a Dame. Belmont, 1963 EN [NYC]
  The Thousand Coffins Affair; see The Man from U.N.C.L.E.
  The Ultimate Client; see Little Miss Murder
  Violence in Velvet. Signet, 1956; Allen, 1958 EN [NYC]
  The Voodoo Murders. GM, 1957; Fawcett (London), 1959 EN [NYC]
  The Werewolf Walks Tonight. Warner, 1974 SS
  The X-Rated Corpse. Curtis, 1973 EN

AVELINE, CLAUDE. 1901-   . Ref: CA, MP. SC: Insp. Frederic Belot = FB.
  Carriage 7 Seat 15. Dobson, 1968; Doubleday, 1969 (Translation of "Voiture 7, Place 15." Paris, 1937.) [Fr.]
  The Cat's Eye. Dobson, 1972; Doubleday, 1973 (Translation of "L'Oeil-de-Chat." Paris, 1970.) FB [Fr.]
  The Double Death of Frederic Belot. Dobson, 1949; Holt, 1940 (Translation of "La Double Mort de Frederic Belot." Paris, 1932.) FB [Fr.]
  The Fountain at Marlieux. Dobson, 1954; Roy, 1954 (Translation of "Le Jet d'Eau.") FB [Fr.]
  The Passenger on the U. Dobson, 1968; Doubleday, 1969 (Translation of "L'Abonne de la Ligne U." Paris, 1963.) FB [Paris]
  Prisoner Born. Hutchinson, 1960; Doubleday, 1971 (Translation of "Le Prisonnier." Paris, 1936.) [Fr.]

AVERILL, CHARLES E.
  -The Secret Service Ship; or, The Fall of San Juan d'Ulloa. Gleason, 1848

AVERY, A. A. 1895-   .
  Anything for a Quiet Life. Farrar, 1942 [NYC]

AVERY, IRA. 1914-   . Pseudonym: Mavis Hathaway, q.v.

AVERY, ROBERT. Magazine writer. SC: Joe Kelly, in at least those marked JK.
  The Corpse in Company K. Swift, 1942 JK
  A Fast Man with a Dollar. Arcadia, 1947
  A Murder a Day! Mystery House, 1940 JK [Conn.]
  Murder on the Downbeat. Mystery House, 1943 [NYC]

AVRACH, JOSEPH
  Murder in Oil. Westhouse, 1948

AWIN, MARGERY
  Silence over Sinai. Pyramid, 1976 [Mid. East]

AXELROD, GEORGE. 1922-   . Ref: CA.
  Blackmailer. GM, 1952; Fawcett (London), 1959 [NYC]

AXTON, DAVID. Pseudonym of Dean R(ay) Koontz, 1945-   , q.v. Other pseudonyms: Brian Coffey, Deanna Dwyer, K. R. Dwyer, Leigh Nichols, Anthony North, qq.v.
  Prison of Ice. Lippincott, 1976; Allen, 1976 [Green.]

AYER, FREDERICK, JR. 1916-1974. Ref: CA.
  The Man in the Mirror. Regnery, 1965; Gollancz, 1965
  Where No Flags Fly. Regnery, 1960

AYERS, RONALD. 1948-   . Ref: CA.
  The Case of the Deadly Triangle. Holloway, 1975

AYLING, KAYE
  Who Was Ellen Smith? Lancer, 1967

AYLING, (HAROLD) KEITH (OLIVER). 1898-1976. Ref: CA.
  The Last Enemy. Pyramid, 1971

AYRAUD, PIERRE. 1908-   . Pseudonym: Thomas Narcejac. See: Pierre (Prosper) Boileau, 1906-

AYRES, PAUL. Pseudonym of Edward S(idney) Aarons, 1916-1975, q.v. Other pseudonym: Edward Ronns, q.v.
  Dead Heat. Bell, 1950 (Based on the radio series "Casey, Crime Photographer" and on the character of Flash Casey, created by George Harmon Coxe, 1901-   , q.v.)

AYRTON, ELIZABETH (WALSHE). 1918-   .
  The Cretan. Hodder, 1963. U.S. title: Silence in Crete. Morrow, 1964 [Crete]

AYSCOUGH, JOHN. Pseudonym of Francis Browning Bickerstaffe-Drew, 1858-1928.
  Prodigals and Sons. Chatto, 1913; Kenedy, 1914 ss

AYVAZIAN, L. FRED. 1919-   . Pseudonym: Fred Levon, q.v.

B. and R.
  Helen Elwood, the Female Detective; or, A Celebrated Forger's Fate. Ogilvie, 1885 [Australia, Eng.]

B., B. Pseudonym of Cuthbert Morley Headlam, 1876-   .
  A Strange Delilah. Murray, 1921

B., C. R. Pseudonym of Charles Hull.
  -Redeemed. Dillingham, 1894

B., M. A. A.
  Clouded in Mystery. McKinney, 1874

BABBIN, JACQUELINE
  Prime Time Corpse. Curtis, 1972 [NYC]

BABCOCK. Pseudonym: Nicholas Carter, q.v.

BABCOCK, DWIGHT V(INCENT). 1909-   . Born in Iowa; magazine writer. SC: Hannah Van Doren, in all titles.
  The Gorgeous Ghoul. Knopf, 1941; United Authors, 1947. Also published as: The Gorgeous Ghoul Murder Case. Avon, 1943 [L.A.]
  The Gorgeous Ghoul Murder Case; see The Gorgeous Ghoul
  Hannah Says Foul Play. Avon, 1946 [Calif.]
  A Homicide for Hannah. Knopf, 1941. British title: Murder for Hannah. Hale, 1941 [L.A.]
  Murder for Hannah; see A Homicide for Hannah

BABER, DOUGLAS GORDON. 1918-   . Pseudonym: John Ritson, q.v.

BABSON, MARIAN. Ref: CA, TC. SC: Douglas Perkins, in at least those marked DP. Set: mostly Eng.
  Cover-Up Story. Collins, 1971 DP
  Dangerous to Know. Collins, 1980; Walker, 1981
  Line Up for Murder; see Queue Here for Murder
  The Lord Mayor of Death. Collins, 1977; Walker, 1979
  Murder, Murder, Little Star. Collins, 1977; Walker, 1980
  Murder on Show. Collins, 1972 DP
  Murder Sails at Midnight. Collins, 1975 [ship]
  Pretty Lady. Collins, 1973
  Queue Here for Murder. Collins, 1980. U.S. title: Line Up for Murder. Walker, 1981
  So Soon Done For. Collins, 1979
  The Stalking Lamb. Collins, 1974
  There Must Be Some Mistake. Collins, 1975
  Tightrope for Three. Collins, 1978
  The Twelve Deaths of Christmas. Collins, 1979; Walker, 1980
  Unfair Exchange. Collins, 1974
  Untimely Guest. Collins, 1976

BACHELIN, ANITA
    Mask of Death. Ermine, 1978
BACHELLER, IRVING A(DDISON). 1859-1950.
    The House of the Three Ganders. Bobbs,
    1928; Hutchinson, 1929 [N.Y.]
BACHMAN, RICHARD
    Rage. Signet, 1977
BACHMANN, LAWRENCE P(AUL). 1912-   .
    Born in New York; active in film
    writing and production; later living
    in France. See also: Hannah Lees.
    The Kiss of Death. Knopf, 1946
    The Legend of Joseph Nokato. Little,
    1971
    The Lorelei. Doubleday, 1958; Collins,
    1957 [Ger.]
    The Phoenix. Collins, 1955. Revised
    edition: Ten Seconds to Hell. Crest,
    1958 [Ger.]
    Ten Seconds to Hell; see The Phoenix
    The Ultimate Act. Atheneum, 1972; Col-
    lins, 1972 [Paris]
BACHMANN, ROBERT
    The Hand of a Thousand Rings. Cosmopol-
    itan, 1924; Hutchinson, 1925 ss,
    some criminous
BACKHOUSE, (ENID) ELIZABETH. SC: Insp.
    Christopher Marsden, in at least
    those marked CM; Insp. Prentis, in at
    least those marked P.
    Death Came Uninvited. Hale, 1957 CM
    Death Climbs a Hill. Hale, 1963 P
    Death of a Clown. Hale, 1962
    The Mists Came Down. Hale, 1959
    [Australia]
    The Night Has Eyes. Hale, 1961 CM
    The Web of Shadows. Hale, 1960 P
    [Australia]
BACKUS, JEAN LOUISE. 1914-   . Pseudo-
    nym: David Montross, q.v.
BACON, JOSEPHINE DASKAM. 1876-1961.
    Ref: CA.
    Medusa's Head. Appleton, 1926 [NYC]
    The Strange Cases of Dr. Stanchon.
    Appleton, 1913 ss
BACON, PEGGY [MARGARET FRANCES BACON
    BROOK]. 1895-   . Ref: CA.
    The Inward Eye. Scribner, 1952. Also
    published as: Lady Marked for Murder.
    Mercury, 1953 [NYC]
BACON, ADMIRAL SIR REGINALD. 1863-1947.
    A Social Sinner. Nash, 1928
    The Stolen Submarine. Nash, 1926
BADGER, ALEXANDER (JOHNSON). 1893-   .
    The Bomb. Bakers, 1958 (1-act play.)
    Quickie Mysteries. Citadel, 1960 (50
    mini-ss mystery puzzles.)
BADGETT, LLOYD W.
    The Mystery of the Colored Circles.
    Vantage, 1976
BADGLEY, ANNE V. Born in New England,
    living in Virginia.
    The Rembrandt Decisions. Dodd, 1979;
    Hale, 1980 [N.H.]
BAER, HOWARD. 1921-   .
    -O Huge Angel. Roy, 1949
BAER, JILL
    House of Whispers. Paperback Library,
    1971
BAER, MRS. LUCY A. 1884?-1925. Pseudo-
    nym: K(ate) F. Hill, q.v.
BAERLEIN, ANTHONY
    Daze, the Magician. Barker, 1936
BAGBY, GEORGE. Pseudonym of Aaron Marc
    Stein, 1906-   , q.v. Other pseudo-
    nym: Hampton Stone, q.v. SC: Insp.
    Schmidt, in all titles.
    Another Day—Another Death. Doubleday,
    1968; Hale, 1968 [NYC]
    Bait for a Killer; see Dirty Pool
    Better Dead. Doubleday, 1978; Hale,
    1979 [NYC]
    A Big Hand for the Corpse; see Give the
    Little Corpse a Big Hand
    Bird Walking Weather. Doubleday, 1939;
    Cassell, 1940 [NYC]
    Blood Will Tell. Doubleday, 1950 [NYC]
    The Bloody Wig Murders; see The Corpse
    Wore a Wig
    A Body for the Bride; see The Original
    Carcase
    The Body in the Basket. Doubleday,
    1954; Macdonald, 1956 [Madrid]
    Coffin Corner. Doubleday, 1949 [NYC]
    Cop Killer. Doubleday, 1956; Boardman,
    1957 [NYC]
    Corpse Candle. Doubleday, 1967; Hale,
    1968 [New Eng.]
    The Corpse with the Purple Thighs.
    Doubleday, 1939 [acad.]
    The Corpse with the Sticky Fingers.
    Doubleday, 1952 [NYC]
    The Corpse Wore a Wig. Doubleday, 1940.
    Also published as: The Bloody Wig
    Murders. Best Detective Selection,
    1942 [NYC]
    Country and Fatal. Doubleday, 1980;
    Hale, 1981 [NYC]
    Dead Drunk. Doubleday, 1953; Macdonald,
    1954 [NYC]
    Dead on Arrival. Doubleday, 1946 [NYC]
    Dead Storage. Doubleday, 1956; Board-
    man, 1959 [NYC]
    Dead Wrong. Doubleday, 1957; Boardman,
    1958 [NYC]
    Death Ain't Commercial. Doubleday, 1591
    [NYC]
    Dirty Pool. Doubleday, 1966. British
    title: Bait for a Killer. Hammond,
    1967 [NYC]
    A Dirty Way to Die. Doubleday, 1955;
    Macdonald, 1956. Also published as:
    Shadow on the Window. Detective Book
    Club, 1955 [NYC]
    Drop Dead. Doubleday, 1949 [NYC]
    Evil Genius. Doubleday, 1961; Hammond,
    1964 [NYC]
    Give the Little Corpse a Great Big
    Hand. Doubleday, 1953; Macdonald,
    1954. Also published as: A Big Hand
    for the Corpse. Detective Book Club,
    1953 [NYC]
    Guaranteed to Fade. Doubleday, 1978;
    Hale, 1979 [NYC]
    Here Comes the Corpse. Doubleday, 1941;
    Long, 1943 [NYC]
    Honest Reliable Corpse. Doubleday,
    1969; Hale, 1969 [NYC]
    I Could Have Died. Doubleday, 1979;
    Hale, 1980 [NYC]
    In Cold Blood. Doubleday, 1948 [NYC]
    Innocent Bystander. Doubleday, 1977;
    Hale, 1978 [NYC]
    Killer Boy Was Here. Doubleday, 1970;
    Hale, 1971 [NYC]
    Mugger's Day. Doubleday, 1979; Hale,
    1980 [NYC]
    Murder at the Piano. Covici, 1935; Low,
    1936 [NYC]
    Murder Calling "50". Doubleday, 1942
    [NYC]
    Murder Half Baked. Covici, 1937; Cas-
    sell, 1938 [NYC] Set: Eng.
    Murder in Wonderland; see Mysteriouser
    and Mysteriouser
    Murder on the Nose. Doubleday, 1938;
    Cassell, 1939 [NYC]
    Murder's Little Helper. Doubleday,
    1963; Hammond, 1964 [NYC]
    My Dead Body. Doubleday, 1976; Hale,
    1978 [NYC]
    Mysteriouser and Mysteriouser. Double-
    day, 1965. British title: Murder in
    Wonderland. Hammond, 1965 [NYC]
    The Original Carcase. Doubleday, 1946;
    Aldor, 1947. Also published as: A
    Body for the Bride. Jonathan Press,
    1954 (abridged) [NYC]
    The Real Gone Goose. Doubleday, 1959.
    British title: A Real Gone Goose.
    Boardman, 1960 [NYC]
    Red Is for Killing. Doubleday, 1941;
    Long, 1944 [NYC]
    Ring Around a Murder. Covici, 1936
    [N.Y.]
    Scared to Death. Doubleday, 1952 [NYC]
    Shadow on the Window; see A Dirty Way
    to Die
    The Starting Gun. Doubleday, 1948 [NYC]
    The Three-Time Losers. Doubleday, 1958;
    Boardman, 1958 [NYC]
    The Tough Get Going. Doubleday, 1977;
    Hale, 1978 [NYC]
    The Twin Killing. Doubleday, 1947 [NYC]
    Two in the Bush. Doubleday, 1976; Hale,
    1976 [NYC]
BAGLEY, DESMOND. 1923-1983. Ref: CA, TC.
    SC: Slade, in at least those marked
    S.
    Bahama Crisis. Collins, 1980 [Bahamas]
    The Enemy. Collins, 1977; Doubleday,
    1978
    Flyaway. Collins, 1978; Doubleday, 1979
    [Afr.]
    The Freedom Trap. Collins, 1971;
    Doubleday, 1972. Also published as:
    The Mackintosh Man. Crest, 1973. Re-
    vised edition: Fontana, 1973 S
    [Malta]
    The Golden Keel. Collins, 1963; Double-
    day, 1964
    High Citadel. Collins, 1965; Doubleday,
    1965 [S. Am.]
    Landslide. Collins, 1967; Doubleday,
    1967 [Can.]
    The Mackintosh Man; see The Freedom
    Trap
    Running Blind. Collins, 1970; Double-
    day, 1971 S [Ice.]
    The Snow Tiger. Collins, 1975; Double-
    day, 1975 [N.Z.]
    The Spoilers. Collins, 1969; Doubleday,
    1970 [Mid. East]
    The Tightrope Men. Collins, 1973;
    Doubleday, 1973 [Scand.]
    The Vivero Letter. Collins, 1968;
    Doubleday, 1968 [Mex.]
    Wyatt's Hurricane. Collins, 1966;
    Doubleday, 1966 [Carib.]
BAGNOLD, ENID. 1889-1981. Ref: CA.
    The Chalk Garden. Heinemann, 1956;
    French, 1956 (Play.)
BAGOT, RICHARD. 1860-1921.
    The House at Serraville. Methuen, 1910;
    Lane (NYC), 1911
    The Passport. Methuen, 1905; Harper,
    1905
    A Roman Mystery. Digby, 1899 [Rome]
BAHADUR, K. P.
    The Case of the Poisoned Cat. Sterling
    (New Delhi), 1974
    Murder in the Delhi Mail. Sterling (New
    Delhi), 1976 [New Delhi]
BAHARAV, I. D.
    The Winds of April. Primary Sources,
    1965
BAHR, EDITH-JANE. 1926-   . Ref: CA.
    Help, Please. Doubleday, 1975; Collins,
    1975 [N.J.]
    A Nice Neighborhood. Dell, 1975; Col-
    lins, 1973
BAHR, JEROME. 1909-   . Ref: CA.
    Holes in the Wall. Luce, 1970 [Berlin]
BAILEY, ALICE WARD. 1857-
    -Mark Heffron. Harper, 1896
BAILEY, ANTHONY. 1933-   . Ref: CA.
    Making Progress. Dial, 1959; Joseph,
    1959
BAILEY, CHARLES W(ALDO), II. 1929-
    Ref: CA. See: Fletcher Knebel,
    1911-
BAILEY, ELLIOT. 1887-   . SC: Insp.
    Geoffrey Fraser, in at least those
    marked GF. Set: Eng.
    The Campden Hill Mystery. Bles, 1926
    The Cheng Ling Mystery. Gramol, 1937
    Death in Piccadilly. Gramol, 1936
    Death in Quiet Places. Eldon, 1933 GF
    The Maplethorpe Tangle. Bles, 1926
    The Metcalfe Mystery. Bles, 1928
    Mr. Benson's Business. Bles, 1925
    No Crime So Great. Eldon, 1936 GF
    Revenge at Nightfall. Eldon, 1937 GF
    The Secret Valley. Bles, 1927
    The Spider. Gramol, 1936
BAILEY, ERIC. 1933-   . Ref: CA.
    Cradle's Revenge. Long, 1969 [Can.]
    Leave of Absence. Long, 1968
BAILEY, F(RANCIS) LEE. 1933-   .
    Secrets. Stein, 1978; Melbourne, 1979
    [Boston]
BAILEY, H(ENRY) C(HRISTOPHER). 1878-1961.
    Ref: all except CA. SC: Reggie For-
    tune = RF; Joshua Clunk = JC. Set:
    Eng.
    The Apprehensive Dog; see No Murder
    The Best of Mr. Fortune. PB, 1943 (A
    pb original consisting of 12 ss from
    earlier hardcover collections.) RF
    The Bishop's Crime. Gollancz, 1940;
    Doubleday, 1941 RF
    Black Land, White Land. Gollancz, 1937;
    Doubleday, 1937 RF
    Call Mr. Fortune. Methuen, 1920; Dut-
    ton, 1920 RF ss
    Case for Mr. Fortune. Ward, 1932;
    Doubleday, 1932 RF ss
    The Cat's Whisker; see Dead Man's
    Effects
    A Clue for Mr. Fortune. Gollancz, 1936;
    Doubleday, 1936 RF ss
    Clunk's Claimant. Gollancz, 1937. U.S.
    title: The Twittering Bird Mystery.
    Doubleday, 1937 JC; RF in minor role
    Dead Man's Effects. Macdonald, 1945.
    U.S. title: The Cat's Whisker.
    Doubleday, 1944 RF
    Dead Man's Shoes. Gollancz, 1942. U.S.
    title: Nobody's Vineyard. Doubleday,
    1942 JC
    The Garston Murder Case; see Garstons
    Garstons. Methuen, 1930. U.S. title:
    The Garston Murder Case. Doubleday,
    1930 JC
    The Great Game. Gollancz, 1939; Double-
    day, 1939 RF; JC in very minor role

B

Honour Among Thieves. Macdonald, 1947; Doubleday, 1947 JC
The Life Sentence. Macdonald, 1946; Doubleday, 1946 RF
The Little Captain. Gollancz, 1941. U.S. title: Orphan Ann. Doubleday, 1941 JC
The Man in the Cape. Benn, 1933
Meet Mr. Fortune. Doubleday, 1942 (An omnibus comprising The Bishop's Crime, q.v., and 12 RF ss from earlier collections.)
Mr. Clunk's Text; see The Veron Mystery
Mr. Fortune Explains. Ward, 1930; Dutton, 1931 RF ss
Mr. Fortune Finds a Pig. Gollancz, 1943; Doubleday, 1943 RF [Wales]
Mr. Fortune Here. Gollancz, 1940; Doubleday, 1940 RF ss
Mr. Fortune Objects. Gollancz, 1935; Doubleday, 1935 RF ss
Mr. Fortune, Please. Methuen, 1928; Dutton, 1928 RF ss
Mr. Fortune Speaking. Ward, 1930; Dutton, 1931 RF ss
Mr. Fortune Wonders. Ward, 1933; Doubleday, 1933 RF ss
Mr. Fortune's Practice. Methuen, 1923; Dutton, 1924 RF ss
Mr. Fortune's Trials. Methuen, 1925; Dutton, 1926 RF ss
No Murder. Gollancz, 1942. U.S. title: The Apprehensive Dog. Doubleday, 1942 RF
Nobody's Vineyard; see Dead Man's Shoes
Orphan Ann; see The Little Captain
The Queen of Spades; see Slippery Ann
The Red Castle. Ward, 1932. U.S. title: The Red Castle Mystery. Doubleday, 1932 JC
The Red Castle Mystery; see The Red Castle
Save a Rope; see Saving a Rope
Saving a Rope. Macdonald, 1948. U.S. title: Save a Rope. Doubleday, 1948 RF
Shadow on the Wall. Gollancz, 1934; Doubleday, 1934 RF
Shrouded Death. Macdonald, 1950 JC
Slippery Ann. Gollancz, 1944. U.S. title: The Queen of Spades. Doubleday, 1944 JC
The Sullen Sky Mystery. Gollancz, 1935; Doubleday, 1935 JC
This Is Mr. Fortune. Gollancz, 1938; Doubleday, 1938 RF ss
The Twittering Bird Mystery; see Clunk's Claimant
The Veron Mystery. Gollancz, 1939. U.S. title: Mr. Clunk's Text. Doubleday, 1939 JC
The Wrong Man. Macdonald, 1946; Doubleday, 1945 JC

BAILEY, HILEA. Pseudonym of Ruth Lenore Marting, 1907-   . SC: Hilea Bailey and Hilary Dunsany Bailey III, in all titles.
Breathe No More, My Lady. Doubleday, 1946
Give Thanks to Death. Doubleday, 1940
The Smiling Corpse. Doubleday, 1941
What Night Will Bring. Doubleday, 1939; Davies, 1940

BAILEY, SETH
The Hand in the Cobbler's Safe. Bart, 1944

BAILIE, ALEXANDER DUKE. Pseudonym: Inspector Murray, q.v.

BAILLIE-SAUNDERS, MARGARET (ELSIE CROWTHER). 1873-1949.
Answer That Bell! Hutchinson, 1935
-The Sign of the Swan. Hutchinson, 1938

BAIN, GRAHAM WARD
Round Robin. Harrap, 1937; Lippincott, 1937

BAINBRIDGE, BERYL. 1933-   . Ref: CA.
Harriet Said... Duckworth, 1972

BAINES, CUTHBERT (EDWARD). SC: Dennis Doyne, in at least those marked DD.
-The Black Circle. Hodder, 1921
The Blue Poppy. Arnold, 1926
A Drug in the Market. Arnold, 1928 DD
The Slip Coach. Arnold, 1927 DD

BAIR, PATRICK
Gargantua Falls. Eyre, 1951
The Gypsum Flower. Eyre, 1959 [1944, Fr.]
Open Your Hand and Close Your Eyes. Eyre, 1964
The Tribunal. Macdonald, 1970

BAIRD, EDWIN. 1886-   .
The Mystery of the Locked Door. Sales Tales, 1928
Paul Pry's Poison Pen. Grafton, 1945 (with "The Castle of Death" by J. B. O'Sullivan, 1919-   , q.v.)

BAIRD, THOMAS. 1923-   . Ref: CA.
Poor Millie. Harper, 1978 [Wyo.]
The Way to the Old Sailor's Home. Harper, 1977 [1939, Can.]

BAKER, AGNES MONICA. 1899-   . Pseudonym: Monica Hill, q.v.

BAKER, AMY J(OSEPHINE). 1895-   .
-The Dangerous Age. Long, 1933

BAKER, ASA. Pseudonym of Davis Dresser, 1904-1977. Other pseudonym: Brett Halliday, q.v. Joint pseudonym with Kathleen Rollins Dresser: Hal Debrett, q.v. Joint pseudonym with (Walter) Ryerson Johnson, 1901-   , q.v.: Matthew Blood, q.v. SC: Jerry Burke, in both titles.
The Kissed Corpse. Carlyle, 1939 [Tex.]
Mum's the Word for Murder. Stokes, 1938; Gollancz, 1939 (Dell pb reprints as by Brett Halliday.) [Tex.]

BAKER, BETH
Mystery Evans. DeWolfe, 1890

BAKER, CARLOS (HEARD). 1909-   . Ref: CA.
The Gay Head Conspiracy. Scribner, 1973 [Mass.]

BAKER, ELLIOTT. 1922-   . Ref: CA.
-Pocock & Pitt. Putnam, 1971; Joseph, 1974

BAKER, FRANK. 1908-   .
Talk of the Devil. Angus, 1956

BAKER, H(ENRY) BARTON. 1845-1906.
Two Men from Kimberley. Ward, 1904

BAKER, HUGH. Pseudonym.
Cartwright Is Dead, Sir! Houghton, 1936 [ship]

BAKER, IVON. 1928-   . Ref: CA. SC: David Meynell = DM. Set: Eng.
The Blood on My Sleeve. Hale, 1979; St. Martin's, 1979 DM
Days Among the Dead. Hale, 1971
Death and Variations. Hale, 1977; St. Martins, 1977 DM
Death in Sanctuary. Hale, 1970
Grave Doubt. Hale, 1972; Washburn, 1972 DM
Justice for Judas. Hale, 1974 [Isr.]
The Pandora Feature. Hale, 1973
Peak Performance. Hale, 1976; St. Martin's, 1976 DM

BAKER, JAY
Night of the Fair. Macdonald, 1961

BAKER, LEDRU, JR.
And Be My Love. GM, 1951
The Cheaters. GM, 1952 [L.A.]
The Preying Streets. Ace, 1955 [Naples]

BAKER, LUCINDA. 1916-   . Ref: CA.
The Place of Devils. Putnam, 1976 [Ariz., 1879]
Walk the Night Unseen. Putnam, 1977 [S.F., ca.1900]

BAKER, MARC(EIL GENEE KOLSTAD). 1911-   . Pseudonym: Marc Miller, q.v.
The Hilltop Murders. Avalon, 1965 [Calif.]

BAKER, (HOWELL) NORTH, 1912-   , and WILLIAM BOLTON
Dead to the World. Doubleday, 1944 [Chi.]

BAKER, PETER. 1921-   . TV editor and producer.
A Killing Affair. Houghton, 1971

BAKER, RICHARD M(ERRIAM). 1896-   . Ref: CC. SC: Franklin Russell, in all titles.
Death Stops the Bells. Scribner, 1938
Death Stops the Manuscript. Scribner, 1936
Death Stops the Rehearsal. Scribner, 1937; Cassell, 1937 [theatre]

BAKER, ROBERT (MELVILLE), 1868-1929, and JOHN EMERSON, 1874-1956.
The Conspiracy. Rosenfield, 1912; Dramatic Typing, 1912 (Play.) The novel: Duffield, 1913 [NYC]

BAKER, SAMM SINCLAIR. 1909-   . Ref: CA. SC: Clark Clark Clark, in both titles, both set in NYC.
Murder—Very Dry! Graphic, 1956
One Touch of Blood. Graphic, 1955

BAKER, SIDNEY J.
Time Is an Enemy. Mystery House, 1958

BAKER, W(ILLIAM ARTHUR) HOWARD. 1925-   . Pseudonyms (not necessarily exclusively held): William Arthur, W. A. Ballinger, Peter Saxon, Julie Wellsley, Richard Williams, qq.v. See also: Desmond Reid. SC: Richard Quintain, in at least those marked RQ; Sexton Blake (with many other authors) = SB. Note: Many of the books under this byline were actually written by Wilfred (Glassford) McNeilly, 1921-   , q.v. Other McNeilly pseudonyms: W. A. Ballinger, Errol Lecale, Desmond Reid, qq.v.
The Angry Night. Amalgamated, 1960. Revised edition: Fire over India. Mayflower, 1966 SB [Calcutta]
Appointment with Danger. Amalgamated, 1958 SB
Battle Song. Amalgamated, 1956 SB
The Big Smear. Amalgamated, 1962 SB
The Big Steal. Mayflower, 1964
Blood Trail. Mayflower, 1966
Brussels Dossier. Lancer, 1968. (British title?) [Brus.]
The Cellar Boys. Consul, 1965
The Charge Is Treason. Baker, 1973; Lancer, 1968 RQ
Crime Is My Business. Amalgamated, 1958 SB
Cry from the Dark. Consul, 1956
Dark Mambo. Amalgamated, 1956 SB
The Dead and the Damned. Mayflower, 1967 RQ
Departure Deferred. Consul, 1965; Macfadden, 1965 (Novelization of the "Secret Agent" TV series.)
Destination Dieppe. Mayflower, 1965 RQ
Devil's Can-Can. Amalgamated, 1956 SB
The Dirty Game; see The Guardians
The Dogs of War. Mayflower, 1966 RQ
Every Man an Enemy; see Walk in Fear
Expresso Jungle. Amalgamated, 1959 SB
Fire over India; see The Angry Night
The Frightened Lady. Amalgamated, 1956. Revised edition: The Fugitive. Mayflower, 1965 SB
The Fugitive; see The Frightened Lady
The Girl, the City, and the Soldier; see The Rape of Berlin
The Girl in Asses' Milk. Mayflower, 1967 RQ
The Guardians. Mayflower, 1966. U.S. title: The Dirty Game. Lancer, 1967 RQ [Tangier]
The Hero Game. Lancer, 1965 (British title?)
The Imposter, with Peter Chambers, q.v. Amalgamated, 1963 SB
The Inexpendable. Consul, 1965 RQ
It Happened in Hamburg. Amalgamated, 1956 SB [Hamb.]
The Judas Diary. Baker, 1969; Lancer, 1969 RQ [Viet Nam]
The Man Who Knew Too Much. Amalgamated, 1955 SB
Murder Most Intimate. Amalgamated, 1958 SB
The Night of the Wolf. Baker, 1969; Lancer, 1967 RQ [Italy, 1945]
No Place for Strangers. Consul, 1965 RQ
No Time to Live. Amalgamated, 1958 SB
Passport into Fear. Amalgamated, 1959 SB
The Rape of Berlin. Consul, 1965; Lancer, 1967. Also published as: The Girl, the City, and the Soldier. Baker, 1968 RQ [Berlin, 1945]
The Reluctant Gunman. Amalgamated, 1962 SB
Requiem for Redheads. Amalgamated, 1956 SB
Scandal Street. Consul, 1963
Shoot When Ready. Amalgamated, 1957 SB
Storm over Rockall. Consul, 1965; Macfadden, 1966 (Novelization of the "Secret Agent" TV series.)
Strike North. Mayflower, 1965; Lancer, 1968 RQ [1941, ship]
Take Death for a Lover. Consul, 1965 RQ
Traitor! Lancer, 1967 RQ [Fr., 1942]
Treason by Truth. (London), 1964
Treason Remembered. Mayflower, 1967 SB
The Treasure Hunters. Mayflower, 1970
Walk in Fear. Amalgamated, 1957. Revised edition: Every Man an Enemy. Mayflower, 1966; Macfadden, 1967 SB
Without Warning. Amalgamated, 1955 SB

BALCHIN, NIGEL (MARLIN). 1908-1970. Ref:
    CA.
    -The Borgia Testament. Collins, 1948;
        Houghton, 1949
    -Darkness Falls from the Air. Collins,
        1942
    -The Fall of the Sparrow. Collins, 1955;
        Rinehart, 1956, as The Fall of a
        Sparrow
    In the Absence of Mrs. Petersen. Col-
        lins, 1966; Simon, 1966
    -Lightbody on Liberty. Collins, 1936
    -Lord, I Was Afraid. Collins, 1947
    Mine Own Executioner. Collins, 1945;
        Houghton, 1946
    -No Sky. H. Hamilton, 1934
    -Seen Dimly Before Dawn. Collins, 1962;
        Simon, 1962
    -Simple Life. H. Hamilton, 1935
    -The Small Back Room. Collins, 1943;
        Houghton, 1945
    A Sort of Traitors. Collins, 1949. U.S.
        title: Who Is My Neighbor? Houghton,
        1950
    A Way Through the Wood. Collins, 1951;
        Houghton, 1951
    Who Is My Neighbor?; see A Sort of
        Traitors

BALDERSTON, JOHN L(LOYD). 1889-   . See:
    Hamilton Deane.

BALDRY, W(ALTER) B(URTON), 1888-   , and
    H(ERBERT) SLADE
    The Brooklands Mystery. Car Publishing,
        1911

BALDWIN, AUDREY. See: J(ames) M(organ)
    Walsh, 1897-   .

BALDWIN, MICHAEL
    The Gamecock. Faber, 1980

BALFOUR, EVA. Joint pseudonym with Beryl
    Hearnden: Hearnden Balfour, q.v.

BALFOUR, F.
    The League of Crime; or, The Twelve
        Temptations. Brady, 1870

BALFOUR, HEARNDEN. Joint pseudonym of Eva
    Balfour and Beryl Hearnden. SC: Insp.
    Jack Strickland, in all titles. Set:
    Eng.
    Anything Might Happen. Hodder, 1931.
        U.S. title: Murder and the Red-Haired
        Girl. Houghton, 1933
    The Enterprising Burglar. Hodder, 1928;
        Houghton, 1928
    A Gentleman from Texas; see The Paper
        Chase
    Murder and the Red-Haired Girl; see
        Anything Might Happen
    The Paper Chase. Hodder, 1927. U.S.
        title: A Gentleman from Texas.
        Houghton, 1927

BALFOUR, JAMES. Pseudonym.
    Court Short. Hutchinson, 1969 ss

BALHAM, JOE. SC: Jack Regan, in all
    titles, which are novelizations of
    "The Sweeney" TV series.
    The Blag. Futura, 1978
    Regan and the Bent Stripper. Futura,
        1977
    Regan and the High Rollers. Futura,
        1978
    Regan and the Human Pipeline. Futura,
        1977
    Regan and the Lebanese Shipment. Fu-
        tura, 1977
    Regan and the Snout Who Cried Wolf.
        Futura, 1977
    Regan and the Venetian Virgin. Futura,
        1978

BALL. Pseudonym: Nicholas Carter, q.v.

BALL, A(LEXANDER) G(EORGE)
    Kill 'Em All. Stockwell, 1976

BALL, BRIAN (NEVILLE). 1932-   . Ref:
    CA. SC: Keegan = K. Set: Eng.
    Death of a Low-Handicap Man. Barker,
        1974; Walker, 1978
    Keegan: The No-Option Contract. Barker,
        1975 K
    Keegan: The One-Way Deal. Barker, 1976
        K
    Montenegrin Gold. Barker, 1974; Walker,
        1978
    Witch Finder, The Evil at Monteine.
        Mayflower, 1977

BALL, DORIS BELL COLLIER. 1897-   .
    Pseudonym: Josephine Bell, q.v.

BALL, EDWARD. 1792-1873.
    The Black Robber. Newman, 1819

BALL, EUSTACE HALE. 1881-1931.
    The Scarlet Fox. Grosset, 1927 [NYC]
    Traffic in Souls. Dillingham, 1914
        (Novelization of the movie.) [NYC]
    The Voice on the Wire. Hearst's, 1915
        [NYC]

BALL, JOHN (DUDLEY, JR.). 1911-   .
    Ref: CA, CC, EM, MC, TC. SC: Virgil
    Tibbs = VT.
    The Cool Cottontail. Harper, 1966;
        Joseph, 1967 VT [Calif.]
    Death for a Playmate; see Johnny Get
        Your Gun
    The Eyes of Buddha. Little, 1976;
        Joseph, 1976 VT [L.A.]
    The First Team. Little, 1971; Joseph,
        1972 [future, U.S.]
    Five Pieces of Jade. Little, 1972;
        Joseph, 1972 VT [L.A.]
    In the Heat of the Night. Harper, 1965;
        Joseph, 1966 VT [S.C.]
    Johnny Get Your Gun. Little, 1969;
        Joseph, 1970. Revised edition: Death
        for a Playmate. Bantam, 1972 VT
        [L.A.]
    The Killing in the Market, with Bevan
        Smith. Doubleday, 1978; Hamlyn, 1980
        [NYC]
    Mark One: The Dummy. Little, 1974
    The Murder Children. Dodd, 1978 [L.A.]
    Police Chief. Doubleday, 1977; Hale,
        1982 [Wash.]
    Then Came Violence. Doubleday, 1980;
        Joseph, 1981 VT [L.A.]

BALLANTYNE, R(OBERT) M(ICHAEL). 1825-
    1894.
    -The Iron Horse; or, Life on the Line.
        Nisbet, 1871

BALLARD, ERIC ALAN. Pseudonym: Edwin Har-
    rison, q.v.

BALLARD, HELEN MABRY
    To the Tune of Murder. Mill, 1952

BALLARD, K. G. Pseudonym of Holly Roth,
    1916-1964, q.v. Other pseudonym:
    P. J. Merrill, q.v.
    Bar Sinister. Doubleday, 1960; Board-
        man, 1961 [N.Y., Sp.]
    The Coast of Fear. Doubleday, 1957.
        British title: Five Roads to S'Agaro.
        Boardman, 1958 [Sp.]
    Five Roads to S'Agaro; see The Coast of
        Fear
    Gauge of Deception. Doubleday, 1963;
        Boardman, 1964 [Ger., Fr.]
    Trial by Desire. Boardman, 1960

BALLARD, P. D. Pseudonym of W(illis)
    T(odhunter) Ballard, 1903-1980, q.v.
    Other pseudonyms: Nick Carter, Neil
    MacNeil, John Shepherd, Robert Wal-
    lace, qq.v. Joint pseudonym with
    Norbert Davis, q.v.: Harrison Hunt,
    q.v.
    Age of the Junkman. GM, 1963; Muller
        pb, 1964
    Angel of Death. GM, 1974
    Brothers in Blood. GM, 1972 [NYC]
    The Death Brokers. GM, 1973 [NYC]
    End of a Millionaire. GM, 1964

BALLARD, W(ILLIS) T(ODHUNTER). 1903-
    1980. Pseudonyms: P. D. Ballard,
    Nick Carter, Neil MacNeil, John
    Shepherd, Robert Wallace, qq.v. Joint
    pseudonym with Norbert Davis, q.v.:
    Harrison Hunt, q.v. Ref: CA, TC.
    SC: Bill Lennox = BL (see also the
    John Shepherd entry); Max Hunter =
    MH.
    Chance Elson. Cardinal, 1958
    Dealing Out Death. McKay, 1948 BL
        [Las Veg.]
    The Demise of a Louse; see Say Yes to
        Murder
    Murder Can't Stop. McKay, 1946 BL
        [Calif.]
    Murder Las Vegas Style. Tower, 1967
        [Las Veg.]
    Pretty Miss Murder. Permabooks, 1961
        MH [L.A.]
    Say Yes to Murder. Putnam, 1942. Also
        published as: The Demise of a Louse,
        as by John Shepherd. Belmont, 1962
        BL [L.A.]
    The Seven Sisters. Permabooks, 1962
        MH [Las Veg.]
    Three for the Money. Permabooks, 1963
        MH [Las Veg.]
    Walk in Fear. GM, 1952; Red Seal, 1957
        [L.A.]

BALLEM, JOHN (BISHOP). 1925-   . Ref:
    CA.
    The Devil's Lighter. General (Ontario),
        1974
    The Dirty Scenario. General (Ontario),
        1974
    The Judas Conspiracy. Musson (Canada),
        1976

BALLENGER, DEAN. SC: Mike Gannon, in all
    titles.
    Blood Beast. Manor, 1974
    The Blood Fix. Manor, 1974
    Blood for Breakfast. Manor, 1973
        [Cleve.]

BALLEW, CHARLES. Pseudonym of Charles
    H(orace) Snow, 1877-   , q.v. The
    character Rim-Fire appears in at
    least 23 of Ballew's 55 western no-
    vels; the title below appears to have
    the strongest detective interest.
    Rim-Fire, Detective. Wright, 1936

BALLINGER, BILL S(ANBORN). 1912-1980.
    Pseudonyms: Frederic Freyer, B. X.
    Sanborn, qq.v. Ref: CA, EM, TC. SC:
    Barr Breed = BB; Joaquin Hawks = JH.
    Beacon in the Night. Harper, 1958;
        Boardman, 1960 [Greece]
    The Beautiful Trap; see Rafferty
    The Body Beautiful. Harper, 1949; World
        Distributors, 1950 BB [Chi.]
    The Body in the Bed. Harper, 1948;
        World Distributors, 1960 BB [Chi.]
    The Chinese Mask. Signet, 1965 JH
        [China]
    The Corsican. Dodd, 1974; Hale, 1976
    The Darkening Door. Harper, 1952 [NYC]
    The Deadlier Sex; see Portrait in Smoke
    Formula for Murder. Signet, 1958 [NYC]
    The 49 Days of Death. Sherbourne, 1969
    The Fourth of Forever. Harper, 1963;
        Boardman, 1963
    The Heir Hunters. Harper, 1966; Board-
        man, 1967 [L.A.]
    Heist Me Higher. Signet, 1969; Hale,
        1971 [NYC]
    The Law. Warner, 1975. (Novelization of
        the TV movie.) [L.A.]
    The Longest Second. Harper, 1957; Rein-
        hardt, 1958 [NYC]
    The Lopsided Man. Pyramid, 1969 [Ber-
        lin]
    Not I, Said the Vixen. GM, 1965 [L.A.]
    Portrait in Smoke. Harper, 1950; Rein-
        hardt, 1951. Also published as: The
        Deadlier Sex. Corgi, 1958 [Chi.]
    Rafferty. Harper, 1953; Reinhardt,
        1953. Also published as: The Beauti-
        ful Trap. Signet, 1955 [NYC]
    The Source of Fear. Signet, 1968; Hale,
        1971 [Mid. East]
    The Spy in Angkor Wat. Signet, 1966 JH
        [Camb.]
    The Spy in Bangkok. Signet, 1965 JH
        [Thai.]
    The Spy in the Java Sea. Signet, 1966
        JH [Far East]
    The Spy in the Jungle. Signet, 1965 JH
        [Viet Nam]
    The Tooth and the Nail. Harper, 1955;
        Reinhardt, 1955 [NYC]
    The Wife of the Red-Haired Man. Harper,
        1957; Reinhardt, 1957

BALLINGER, W. A. House name. Used by
    W(illiam Arthur) Howard Baker,
    1925-   , q.v., and Wilfrid (Glass-
    ford) McNeilly, 1921-   , q.v.
    Other Baker pseudonyms: William
    Arthur, Peter Saxon, Julie Wellsley,
    Richard Williams, qq.v. Other
    McNeilly pseudonyms: W. Howard Baker,
    Errol Lecale, Desmond Reid, qq.v. SC:
    Sexton Blake (with many other
    authors) = SB; Richard Quintain (also
    under the Baker byline) = RQ.
    -Call It Rhodesia. Mayflower, 1966
    -The Carrion Eaters. Joseph, 1971
    -Congo. Mayflower, 1970
    A Corpse for Christmas. Amalgamated,
        1962 SB
    Down Among the Ad Men. Amalgamated, 1968
        SB
    Drums of the Dark Gods. Mayflower, 1966;
        Paperback Library, 1967 RQ [Haiti]
    Epitaph to Treason. Amalgamated, 1960
        SB
    The Exterminator. Consul, 1966; Mac-
        fadden, 1966 (Novelization of the
        "Secret Agent" TV series.)
    -The Galaxy Lot. Mayflower, 1966
    -The Green Grassy Slopes. Corgi, 1969
    I, the Hangman. Mayflower, 1965; Mac-
        fadden, 1967 SB
    The Last Tiger. Amalgamated, 1963 SB
    Murder in Camera. Amalgamated, 1962 SB
    Murderer at Large. Mayflower, 1965 SB
    -Naked from a Well. Mayflower, 1967
    -Rebellion. Mayflower, 1966
    Savage Venture. Amalgamated, 1962 SB
    -The Shark Hunters. Baker, 1970
    A Starlet for a Penny. Mayflower, 1966
        SB [Rome]

B

BALLOU, MATURIN M. (continued)
The Strange Face of Murder. Mayflower, 1965 SB
Studio One Murder. Amalgamated, 1962 SB
The Television Murders. Amalgamated, 1961 SB
This Man Must Die! Amalgamated, 1960 SB
Unfriendly Persuasion. Consul, 1964 RQ
-The Waters of Madness. New English Library, 1974
The Witches of Notting Hill. Mayflower, 1965; Macfadden, 1967 SB
-Women's Battalion. Mayflower, 1967

BALLOU, MATURIN M. 1820-1895. Pseudonym: Lieutenant M. M. Murray, q.v.

BALMER, EDWIN. 1883-1959. Ref: EM, MP, TC. See also: William (Briggs) MacHarg, 1872-1951.
The Achievements of Luther Trant, with William (Briggs) MacHarg, 1872-1951, q.v. Small, 1910 ss [Chi.]
The Breath of Scandal. Little, 1922; Arnold, 1923 [Chi.]
-The Candle of the Wicked. Longmans, 1956
Dangerous Business. Dodd, 1927; Long, 1928
Dragons Drive You. Dodd, 1934 [Chi.]
Five Fatal Words, with Philip (Gordon) Wylie, 1902-1971, q.v. Smith, 1932; Paul, 1933 [Conn.]
Flying Death. Dodd, 1927
The Golden Hoard, with Philip (Gordon) Wylie, 1902-1971, q.v. Stokes, 1934 [Ga.]
-Her Great Moment. Paul, 1921 (U.S. title?)
Keeban. Little, 1923; Arnold, 1923 [Chi.]
-Ruth of the U.S.A. McClurg, 1919
The Shield of Silence, with Philip (Gordon) Wylie, 1902-1971, q.v. Stokes, 1936; Collins, 1937 [Ill.]
That Royle Girl. Dodd, 1925
The Torn Letter. Dodd, 1941; Nicholson, 1943 [N.J.]
Waylaid by Wireless. Small, 1909 [Eng.]

BALNAVE, JAMES
Lynch's Law. Hale, 1980

BALNEAVES, ELIZABETH
Murder in the Zoo. Chivers, 1975

BALZAC, HONORE DE. 1799-1850. Ref: CC, DD, EM, MC. Although crime and mystery elements are scattered throughout Balzac's work, it seems appropriate to mention only the following. (Note that since English translations and editions of Balzac's fiction form an impenetrable maze, the list below keys to the original French title and omits U.S. and British first edition data.)
Histoire des Treize. Published in English in various forms, including in total as: "The Thirteen"; part one as "Ferragus", and as "The Mystery of the Rue Soly"; part two as "The Duchesse de Langeais"; and part three as "The Girl with the Golden Eyes."
Le Pere Goriot. Published in English under titles including: "Daddy Goriot", "Father Goriot", "Old Goriot", "Old Man Goriot", "Pere Goriot", and "Unrequited Affection."
Une Tenebreuse Affaire. Published in English as "The (A) Gondreville Mystery."

BAMBERGER, HELEN R. 1888-   . Joint pseudonym with Raymond S. Bamberger: The Aresby's, q.v.

BAMBERGER, RAYMOND S. Joint pseudonym with Helen R. Bamberger, 1888-   : The Aresby's, q.v.

BAMBURG, LILIAN. SC: Septimus March = SM. Set: Eng.
Beads of Silence. Selwyn, 1926; Dutton, 1927 SM
Rays of Darkness. Selwyn, 1927 SM
The Riddle of the Dead, with Charles Platt. Gardner, 1930

BAMFORD, FRANCIS
A Question of Taste. Longmans, 1949
Return to Cottington. Longmans, 1946 [Eng., 1768]
This Chequered Floor. Longmans, 1941
What Stranger Cause? Longmans, 1944

BANBURY, G(EORGE) A(LEXANDER) LETHBRIDGE
The Lumley Wood Mystery. Hutchinson, 1890

BANCAL, J(EAN). See: J. Guil.

BANCROFT, GEORGE PLEYDELL. 1868-1956. Pseudonym: George Pleydell, q.v.

BANDOLIER, STEPHEN
Murder Manana. Duell, 1941 [S. Am.]

BANDY, (EUGENE) FRANKLIN (JR.). 1914-   Pseudonym: Eugene Franklin, q.v. Ref: CA. SC: Kevin MacInnes = KM.
The Blackstock Affair. Charter, 1980 KM [Ohio]
Deceit and Deadly Lies. Charter, 1978; Magnum, 1979 KM
The Farewell Party. Charter, 1980
The Shannonese Hustle. Avon, 1978

BANGS, JOHN KENDRICK. 1862-1922. Ref: EM, MP.
The Dreamers. Harper, 1899 ss
The Enchanted Type-Writer. Harper, 1899 ss
Ghosts I Have Met and Some Others. Harper, 1898 ss
Mrs. Raffles. Harper, 1905 ss
The Pursuit of the House Boat. Harper, 1897
R. Holmes & Co. Harper, 1906 ss
Shylock Holmes: His Posthumous Memoirs. Dispatch-Box Press, 1973 ss

BANIM, JOHN. 1798-1842. Joint pseudonym with Michael Banim, 1796-1874: The O'Hara Family, q.v.

BANIM, MICHAEL. 1796-1874. Joint pseudonym with John Banim, 1798-1842: The O'Hara Family, q.v.

BANIS, VICTOR JEROME. 1937-   . Pseudonyms: Jan Alexander, Lynn Benedict, qq.v.

BANKO, DANIEL. Born in Portland, Oregon.
Not Dead Yet. GM, 1972
Very Dry with a Twist. Saturday Review, 1975 [Miami]

BANKS, BARBARA
Dragonseeds. Hale, 1977; St. Martin's, 1977

BANKS, CAROLYN. 1941-   . Ref: CA.
The Darkroom. Viking, 1980; Corgi, 1981
Mr. Right. Viking, 1979; Corgi, 1981

BANKS, ELIZABETH (L.)
The Mystery of Frances Farrington. Hutchinson, 1909 [NYC]

BANKS, LYNNE REID
The Killer Dies Twice. Deane, 1956 (3-act play.)

BANKS, OLIVER (T.). Has Ph.D. in Art History; professor; art consultant and writer.
The Rembrandt Panel. Little, 1980 [Boston]

BANKS, RAYMOND E. 1918?-   . SC: Sam King, in both titles.
The Computer Kill. Popular Library, 1961 [L.A.]
Meet Me in Darkness. Popular Library, 1961 [L.A.]

BANNER, HUBERT STEWART. 1891-1964. Ref: CA.
Hell's Harvest. Hurst, 1934
The Mountain of Terror. Butterworth, 1928
Red Cobra. Butterworth, 1929
Terror Wave. Hurst, 1935

BANNER, MICHAEL
Q37. Knopf, 1937 [Eng.]

BANNERJEE, MANIK
The Primeval and other stories. People's (New Delhi), 1958 ss

BANNERMAN, W. B. SC: Domingo Santos = DS.
Bad End Valley. Low, 1937 DS
Legionnaire Spy. Low, 1939
Santos, Border Detective. Quality, 1940 [Tex.]
The Whispering Riders. Low, 1937 DS

BANNING, JOHN
Goodbye to Istanbul. New English Library pb, 1977

BANNISTER, PAT. Pseudonym of Lou Ellen Davis, 1936-   . Other pseudonym: Elizabeth Davis, q.v.
Seven Votes for Death. GM, 1964

BANNISTER, WILLIAM
Counterfeit Murder. Lancer, 1967
Portrait of Death. Lancer, 1966 [L.A.]

BANNON, DON
Killer at Large. Pinnacle, 1975

BANNON, PETER. Pseudonym of Paul Durst, 1921-   , q.v. Other pseudonym: John Chelton, q.v.
If I Should Die. Jenkins, 1958
They Want Me Dead. Jenkins, 1958
Whisper Murder Softly. Jenkins, 1963 [Mo.]

BANVILLE, JOHN
Birchwood. Secker, 1973; Norton, 1973 [Ire., ca.1850]
-Long Lankin. Secker, 1970 ss
-Nightspawn. Secker, 1971; Norton, 1971

BAOL, SAM
The Man from the Diner's Club. Lancer, 1963 (Novelization of the movie.)

BAR-ZOHAR, MICHAEL. 1938-   . Pseudonym: Michael Barak, q.v. Ref: CA. SC: Jeff Saunders = JS.
The Deadly Document. Delacorte, 1980; Weidenfeld, 1980
The Spy Who Died Twice. Houghton, 1975; Weidenfeld, 1976 (Translation of "Ha-Ish She-met Pa's Mayim." Israel, 1973.)
The Third Truth. Houghton, 1973; Hodder, 1973 (Translation of "La Troisieme Verite." Paris, 1972.)

BARAK, MICHAEL. Pseudonym of Michael Bar-Zohar, 1938-   , q.v.
The Enigma. Morrow, 1978. British title: The Enigma Sacrifice. Weidenfeld, 1978 [Paris, 1944]
The Enigma Sacrifice; see The Enigma
The Phantom Conspiracy. Morrow, 1980; Weidenfeld, 1981, as by Michael Bar-Zohar
The Secret List of Heinrich Roehm. Morrow, 1976; Weidenfeld, 1976

BARBEE, LINDSEY. 1876-   .
All in a Day. Baker, 1937 (3-act play.)
Contents Unknown. Denison, 1922 (3-act play.)
The Four of Us Meet Again. Penn, 1944 (1-act play.)
The Last of the Ruthvens. Dramatic, 1936 (3-act play.)
A Light-Fingered Lady. Penn, 1931 (1-act play.)
The Mallory Case. Dramatic, 1937 (3-act play.)
The Mystery of the Third Gable. Denison, 1926 (3-act play.)
The Rajah's Ruby. Northwestern, ca.1950 (1-act play.)
The Strangers. Northwestern, 1940 (1-act play.)
Ten Days Before the Wedding. Baker, 1929; French (London), 1931 (3-act play.)
Three Taps on a Wall. Northwestern, 1935 (1-act play.)
Thunder in the Air. Denison, 194? (3-act play.)

BARBER, ALEX. 1906-   .
Room with No Escape. Hutchinson, 1932

BARBER, D(ONALD) H(ERBERT). 1907-   .
Fortune for Four. Barker, 1937 ss, some criminous

BARBER, DULAN F. 1940-   . Pseudonym: David Fletcher, q.v.

BARBER, MARCIN
Britz of Headquarters. Moffat, 1910 [NYC]

BARBER, WILLETTA ANN, 1911-   , and R(UDOLPH) F(REDERICK) SCHABELITZ, 1884-1959. SC: Christopher Storm, in all titles.
The Deed Is Drawn. Scribner, 1949 [NYC]
Drawback to Murder. Scribner, 1947 [NYC]
Drawn Conclusion. Doubleday, 1942 [Maine]
Murder Draws a Line. Doubleday, 1940 [NYC]
Murder Enters the Picture. Doubleday, 1942 [Vt.]
The Noose Is Drawn. Scribner, 1945 [NYC]
Pencil Points to Murder. Doubleday, 1941 [Conn.]

BARBETTE, JAY. Joint pseudonym of Bart Spicer, 1918-   , q.v., and Betty Coe Spicer. SC: Harry Butten, in all titles.
The Deadly Doll. Dodd, 1958; Long, 1959

Dear, Dead Days. Dodd, 1953; Barker, 1954. Also published as: Death's Long Shadow. Bantam, 1955
Death's Long Shadow; see Dear, Dead Days
Final Copy. Dodd, 1950; Barker, 1952
Look Behind You. Dodd, 1960; Long, 1961

BARBOUR, A(NNA) MAYNARD. Pseudonym of Anna Mary Barbour, 186?-1941.
At the Time Appointed. Lippincott, 1903 [West]
The Award of Justice; see Told in the Rockies
Breakers Ahead. Lippincott, 1906
That Mainwaring Affair. American News, 1900; Ward, 1901 [NYC]
Told in the Rockies. Rand, 1897. Also published as: The Award of Justice. Rand, 1901

BARBOUR, ANNA MARY. 186?-1941. Pseudonym: A(nna) Maynard Barbour, q.v.

BARBOUR, MILDRED
Sybil, Trapper of Men. Grosset, 1927

BARBOUR, R(ALPH) H(ENRY). 1870-1944.
Death in the Virgins. Appleton, 1940 [Vir. Is.]

BARCELO, E. C.
Love Is Murder. Zebra, 1980

BARCLAY, BEN
The Empty Palace. Barker, 1976

BARCLAY, BILL. Pseudonym of Michael (John) Moorcock, 1939- , q.v. Other pseudonym: Desmond Reid, q.v. SC: Nick Allard, in both titles (but changed to Jerry Cornelius when both titles were revised and reissued as by Moorcock, q.v.). Set: Eng.
Printer's Devil. Compact, 1966
Somewhere in the Night. Compact, 1966

BARCLAY, JOHN (FRANCIS ST. BARBE). 1902- .
The Gilchrist Case. Methuen, 1930
The Unknown. London Book Co., 1928 [Sp.]

BARCLAY, WILFRID
The Club of Skulls. Modern, 1938
The Secret Menace. Modern, 1938
Tracked Across the Seas. Modern, 193?

BARCLAY, WILSON
The Seventh Man. Ward, 1933; Dial, 1935

BARD, DANIEL
The Aquanauts. Popular Library, 1961 (Novelization of the TV series.)

BARDIN, JOHN FRANKLIN. 1916-1981. Pseudonyms: Douglas Ashe, Gregory Tree, qq.v. Ref: CA, MC, TC.
The Deadly Percheron. Dodd, 1946; Gollancz, 1946
Devil Take the Blue-Tail Fly. Macfadden, 1967; Gollancz, 1948 [NYC]
The Last of Philip Banter. Dodd, 1947; Gollancz, 1947 [NYC]
Purloining Tiny. Harper, 1978 [NYC]

BARDON, MINNA (FEIBLEMAN). 1900- .
Blood Red Death. Phoenix, 1947
The Case of the Advertised Murder. Hillman-Curl, 1939
The Case of the Blood-Stained Dime; see Murder Does Light Housekeeping
The Case of the Dead Grandmother. Phoenix, 1937
Murder Does Light Housekeeping. Phoenix, 1941. Also published as: The Case of the Blood-Stained Dime. Bleak House, 194?
Murder for Real. Black Knight, 194? (Retitled reprint of ?)

BARDOS, MARIE (DUPUIS). 1935- . Ref: CA.
Nightlight. Doubleday, 1964; Gollancz, 1965

BARDSLEY, MICHAEL. SC: Supt. Donald Martin, in at least those marked DM.
Caught in Terror. Hale, 1969
Hit It Rich. Hale, 1972 DM
Murder for Sale. Hale, 1970; Roy, 1971 DM
Murder on Fire. Hale, 1969
Murder on Ice. Hale, 1972 DM

BARGONE, FREDERIC CHARLES EDOUARD. 1876-1957. Pseudonym: Claude Farrere, q.v.

BARING, MAURICE. 1874-1945.
Lost Diaries. Duckworth, 1913 ss, one criminous (Sherlockian parody)

BARK, CONRAD VOSS. Newspaper and BBC correspondent. SC: William Holmes, in all titles. Set: mostly Eng.
Mr. Holmes and the Fair Armenian. Macdonald, 1965
Mr. Holmes and the Love Bank. Macdonald, 1964
Mr. Holmes at Sea. Macdonald, 1962; Macmillan, 1962
Mr. Holmes Goes to Ground. Macdonald, 1963; Macmillan, 1964
The Second Red Dragon. Gollancz, 1968; Walker, 1968
See the Living Crocodiles. Gollancz, 1967; Walker, 1968 [Fr.]
The Shepherd File. Gollancz, 1966; Dutton, 1966

BARKER, ALBERT (W.). 1900- . Ref: CA. SC: Reefe King = RK; Hawk Macrae = HM.
The Apollo Legacy. Award, 1970 RK [NYC]
The Big Fix. Curtis, 1973 HM [Fr.]
The Blood of Angels. Curtis, 1973 HM
The Diamond Fix. Curtis, 1974 HM
The Dragon in Spring. Curtis, 1973 HM [China]
Gift from Berlin. Award, 1969 RK
If Anything Should Happen to Me. Curtis, 1973 HM [Sp.]
The Straw Virgin. Popular Library, 1975

BARKER, C(LARENCE) HEDLEY. Pseudonyms: Frank Hedley, Seafarer, qq.v.
Blue Water. Cassell, 1933
The Case of the Secret Plans. Lloyds, 1921
Dark Road to Danger. Cherry Tree, 1943
Devil's Brood. Cassell, 1941 [Fr.]
Eight Went Cruising. Hale, 1946
The Hallam Moor Mystery. Cherry Tree, 1944
Hangman's Honeymoon. Hale, 1943
The Man They Could Not Kill. Cherry Tree, 1942 (by Hedley Barker.)
They Stole a Ship. Hale, 1945
The Wayward Nymph. Cassell, 1933

BARKER, DUDLEY. 1910-1980. Pseudonyms: Lionel Black, q.v., Anthony Matthews.

BARKER, ELSA. 1869-1954. SC: Dexter Drake, in all titles.
The C.I.D. of Dexter Drake. Sears, 1929; Hamilton, 1931 ss
The Cobra Candlestick. Sears, 1928; Hamilton, 1930 [Conn.]
The Redman Cave Murder. Sears, 1930

BARKER, HEDLEY. See: C(larence) Hedley Barker.

BARKER, JOSEPH. 1929- . Ref: CA.
Fourth at Junction. Hale, 1979; St. Martin's, 1980

BARKER, LEONARD NOEL. 1882- . Pseudonym: L. Noel, q.v.

BARKER, PATRICK
Carver. Popular Library, 1973 [Calif.]

BARKER, RONALD (ERNEST). 1920-1976. Pseudonym: E. B. Ronald, q.v. Ref: CA. Born in England, raised in Scotland; active in publishing field.
Clue for Murder. Abelard (London & NYC), 1962
The Days Are Long. Cassell, 1959; British Book Service, 1959
Tendency to Corrupt. Cassell, 1957; British Book Service, 1957

BARKLEY, DEANNE. Vice-president of NBC's programming department.
Freeway. Macmillan, 1978; Sphere, 1980 [L.A.]

BARLAY, BENNETT. Pseudonym of Kendell Foster Crossen, 1910-1981, q.v. Other pseudonyms: M. E. Chaber, Richard Foster, Christopher Monig, Clay Richards, qq.v.
Satan Comes Across. Eerie, 1945 [NYC]

BARLAY, STEPHEN. Pseudonym. 1930- . Born in Budapest; escaped to England in 1956; journalist.
Blockbuster. H. Hamilton, 1976; Morrow, 1977
Crash Course. H. Hamilton, 1979

BARLING, CHARLES. Pseudonym of Muriel Vere Mant Barling, 1904- . Other pseudonym: Pamela Barrington, q.v. SC: Insp. George Marshall, in at least those marked GM (see also the Barrington entry); Insp. Henderson = H (see also the Barrington entry). Set: Eng.

Afternoon of Violence. Hale, 1963 GM
Appointment with Death. Hale, 1964 GM
Confession of Murder. Hale, 1967 GM
The Crime Against Judy Bishop. Hale, 1966
Death of a Shrew. Hale, 1968 H
A Marked Man. Hale, 1968
Motive for Murder. Hale, 1963 GM
Time to Kill. Hale, 1965 GM

BARLING, MURIEL VERE MANT. 1904- . Pseudonyms: Charles Barling, Pamela Barrington, qq.v.

BARLING, TOM
Bergman's Blitz. Allen, 1973
Goodbye Piccadilly. Eyre, 1980
The Olympic Sleeper. Eyre, 1979; GM, 1980 [Moscow]
The Shooter Man. Allen, 1974
The Snowdon Labyrinth. Allen, 1976

BARLOW, HILARE EDITH
The Mystery of Jeanne Marie. Lynwood, 1913
The Sentence of the Judge. Lynwood, 1912

BARLOW, JAMES (HENRY STANLEY). 1921-1973. Ref: CA, CC. Set: mostly Eng.
The Burden of Proof. H. Hamilton, 1968; Simon, 1968
The Hour of Maximum Danger. H. Hamilton, 1962; Simon, 1963
The Man with Good Intentions. Cassell, 1958
One Half of the World. Cassell, 1957; Harper, 1957
-One Man in the World. H. Hamilton, 1966; Simon, 1966
The Patriots. H. Hamilton, 1960; Harper, 1960
The Protagonists. Cassell, 1956; Harper, 1956
Term of Trial. H. Hamilton, 1961; Simon, 1962
-This Side of the Sky. H. Hamilton, 1964; Simon, 1964

BARLOW, JOHN S.
Dene of the Secret Service. Mellifont, 1939

BARLOW, VERNON. 1899- .
-Cloudy Ladder. Heath, 1932
The Green Murder. Heath, 1931

BARMBY, CUTHBERT
James Cope; The Confessions of a United States District Attorney. New Amsterdam, 1899; Ward, 1899 [Calif.]

BARNABY, PETER
Long Deadly Summer. Millington, 1977

BARNARD, MELVILLE CLEMENS
The Mystery of the Sandal-Wood Box. Mayhew, 1907

BARNARD, ROBERT. 1936- . Ref: CA. Set: Eng.
Blood Brotherhood. Collins, 1977; Walker, 1978
Death in a Cold Climate. Collins, 1980; Scribner, 1981 [Nor.]
Death of a Literary Widow; see Posthumous Papers
Death of a Mystery Writer; see Unruly Son
Death of an Old Goat. Collins, 1974; Walker, 1977 [Australia, acad.]
Death on the High C's. Collins, 1977; Walker, 1978 [theatre]
A Little Local Murder. Collins, 1976; Scribner, 1983
Posthumous Papers. Collins, 1979. U.S. title: Death of a Literary Widow. Scribner, 1980
Unruly Son. Collins, 1978. U.S. title: Death of a Mystery Writer. Scribner, 1979

BARNES, DALLAS. Member of Los Angeles Police Department. SC: Det. Sgt. John Stryker = JS.
Badge of Honor. Signet, 1974; Hodder, 1976 JS [L.A.]
"See the Woman." Signet, 1973; Hodder, 1974 JS [L.A.]
Yesterday Is Dead. Signet, 1976; Coronet, 1977 [L.A.]

BARNES, JAMES. 1866-1936.
The Clutch of Circumstance. Appleton, 1908
Outside the Law. Appleton, 1906 [NYC]

BARNES, JULIAN. 1946- . Pseudonym: Dan Kavanagh, q.v.

BARNES, MARGARET AYER. 1886-1967. Ref: CA. See: Henry Kitchell Webster, 1875-1932.

BARNES, MICHAEL. Pseudonym: Ricky Drayton, q.v.
  Landscape with Corpses. Merit, 1954
  You Can Run So Far. Scion, 1952

BARNES, ROBERT C.
  Silent Thunder. Tower, 1980 [Neb.]

BARNES, RONALD GORELL. 1884-   . Also Lord Gorell, q.v. Ref: CC, MP. SC: Evelyn Temple = ET (see also the Lord Gorell entry).
  In the Night. Longmans, 1917 ET

BARNETT, GLYN. SC: Insp. Gramport, in at least those marked G. Set: Eng.
  The Call-Box Murder. Low, 1935 G
  Death Calls Three Times. Low, 1936
  Find the Lady. Low, 1946 G
  I Know Mrs. Lang. Low, 1937 G
  Murder on Monday. Low, 1936 G
  The Silent Street. Barker, 1958
  There's Money in Murder. Chapman, 1939

BARNETT, JAMES. 1920-   . Born and raised in Scotland; spent 30 years with the Metropolitan Police of London. SC: Supt. Owen Smith = OS. Set: Eng.
  Backfire Is Hostile! Secker, 1979; St. Martin's, 1979 OS
  Head of the Force. Secker, 1978; St. Martin's, 1979
  Palmprint. Secker, 1980 OS

BARNETT, REGINALD
  The Devil's Whisper. Walter Scott, 1889
  Police Sergeant C21. Walter Scott, 1888
  Rubbed Out. Everett, 1904

BARNS, GLENN M(ILLER). Born in Wash.; practicing attorney. SC: Jonathan Marks, in at least those marked JM.
  Deadly Summer. Lippincott, 1957; Hale, 1959 [Calif.]
  Lawyers Don't Hang. Arcadia, 1953
  Masquerade in Blue. Ace, 1956
  Murder Is a Gamble. Phoenix, 1952; Foulsham, 1954 JM
  Murder Is Insane. Lippincott, 1956; Foulsham, 1958 JM
  Murder Walks the Stairs. Arcadia, 1954; Foulsham, 1955 JM [Wash.]
  Murderous Suspense. Foulsham, 1960 (U.S. title?)
  Only the Losers Win. GM, 1968 [Wash.]

BARON. Pseudonym of Benjamin Anthony Ronzone, 1848-   .
  The Marquis of Murray Hill. Roxburgh, 1909

BARON, BETTY. See: J. J. Parnell.

BARON, PETER. Pseudonym of Leonard Worswick Clyde, 1906-   . Set: Eng.
  Jerry the Lag. Selwyn, 1928. U.S. title: Murder in Wax. Macaulay, 1931
  Murder in Wax; see Jerry the Lag
  The Opium Murders; see Who?
  The Poacher. Selwyn, 1929. U.S. title: The Round Table Murders. Macaulay, 1931
  The Round Table Murders; see The Poacher
  Who? Selwyn, 1927. U.S. title: The Opium Murders. Macaulay, 1930

BARON, STANLEY (WADE). 1922-   . Born in Philadelphia; in U.S. Government service for many years.
  All My Enemies. Ballantine, 1952; Hart-Davis, 1952
  End of the Line. Knopf, 1951; Hart-Davis, 1952 [Paris]

BARONE, MIKE. Pseudonym of Marvin H(ubert) Albert, 1924-   , q.v. Other pseudonyms: Al Conroy, Albert Conroy, Ian MacAlister, Nick Quarry, Anthony Rome, qq.v.
  Crazy Joe. Bantam, 1974 (Novelization of the movie.)

BARONI, M.
  Wreath for a Lady. Spencer, 1957

BARR, A. J.
  Let Tomorrow Come. Norton, 1929

BARR, DENNIS. Pseudonym of Felix Denny.
  The Crimson Quest; see A Dock Brief
  A Dock Brief. Cape, 1928. U.S. title: The Crimson Quest. Sears, 1928
  A Rope Broke. Jarrolds, 1932

BARR, ELIZABETH. Pseudonym of Irene Edwards.
  Castle Heritage. Hale, 1977; Doubleday, 1978 [1896, Eng.]
  The Flowers of Darkness. Hale, 1979
  Master of Roxton. Hale, 1973
  The Opal Pendant. Hale, 1972
  The Sea Treasure. Hale, 1978; Doubleday, 1979
  The Storm Witch. Hale, 1976; Doubleday, 1976

BARR, JUSTIN
  Hellinger's Law. Jove, 1980 (Novelization of the TV movie.)

BARR, ROBERT. 1850-1912. Pseudonym: Luke Sharp. Ref: CC, DD, EM, MP.
  The Adventures of Sherlaw Kombs. Aspen, 1979 ss
  -A Chicago Princess. Stokes, 1904
  -The Face and the Mask. Stokes, 1895; Hutchinson, 1894
  From Whose Bourne? Stokes, 1896; Chatto, 1893, as by Luke Sharp
  The Girl in the Case. Nash, 1910 (U.S. title?)
  Jennie Baxter, Journalist. Stokes, 1899; Methuen, 1899 [Eng.]
  Lady Eleanor, Lawbreaker. Rand, 1911
  -The Mutable Many. Stokes, 1896; Methuen, 1897
  -Over the Border. Stokes, 1903; Isbister, 1903
  -A Prince of Good Fellows. Stokes, 1902; Chatto, 1902
  Revenge! Stokes, 1896; Chatto, 1896 ss
  -A Rock in the Baltic. Authors & Newspapers, 1906
  -The Strong Arm. Stokes, 1899; Methuen, 1900
  Tales of Two Continents. Mills, 1920 ss
  The Triumphs of Eugene Valmont. Appleton, 1906; Hurst, 1906 ss [Fr.]
  The Watermead Affair. Altemus, 1906
  A Woman Intervenes. Stokes, 1896; Chatto, 1896
  -The Woman Wins. Stokes, 1904 ss

BARR, ROBERT. Reporter, BBC foreign correspondent, writer and producer of TV scripts. SC: Nick Nicholson, in both titles.
  The Dark Island. Allen, 1972; Bobbs, 1973 [Hebrides]
  The Edge of the Forest. Allen, 1973

BARRATT, ROBERT
  The Fatal Entrance. Hale, 1975

BARREN, CHARLES MacKINNON. 1913-   Pseudonym: Thomas Rainham, q.v.

BARRETT, ALFRED WALTER. 1869-   Pseudonym: R. Andom, q.v.

BARRETT, ALFRED WILSON. 1871-   SC: Justus Wise = JW.
  -The Blue Taxi. Ward, 1915
  Father Pink. Ward, 1907; Small, 1906
  The French Master. Ward, 1903
  The Golden Lotus. Macqueen, 1901
  -The House over the Way. Ward, 1906
  -The Jew of Prague. White, 1912
  Justus Wise. Ward, 1911 JW
  The Man with the Opals, with Austin Fryers (pseudonym of William Edward Clery). Ward, 1906
  The Secret Marriage. Ward, 1912
  The Shadow on the House. Everett, 1909
  The Silver King. Everett, 1914; Dillingham, 1914
  The Silver Pin. Ward, 1905; Saalfield, 1905
  -A Soldier's Love. Everett, 1912
  -The Third Mistake. Aldine, 1917
  The Tower Hill Mystery. Ward, 1912 JW

BARRETT, C. F.
  Douglas Castle; or, The Cell of Mystery. Neil, 1803 [Scot.]

BARRETT, EATON STANNARD. 1786-1820.
  The Heroine. Colburn, 1813; Carey, 1815

BARRETT, FRANK. 1848-1926.
  -The Admirable Lady Biddy Fane. Cassell (London), 1888; Cassell (New York), 1889
  Between Life and Death. Chatto, 1890; U.S. Book Co., 1890
  Breaking the Shackles. Macqueen, 1900; Page, 1900
  By Misadventure. Rand, 1888 (British title?)
  -The Error of Her Ways. Chatto, 1905
  -Fantoccini. Tinsley, 1874
  Fettered for Life. Chatto, 1889; Munro, 1889. Also published as: Kit Wyndham; or, Fettered for Life. Lovell, 1889
  -Folly Morrison. Bentley, 1881
  For Love and Honour. Chatto, 1892; U.S. Book Co., 1892
  Found Guilty. Ward, 1887; Lovell, 1892
  The Great Hesper. Ward, 1887; Appleton, 1887
  -The Harding Scandal. Chatto, 1896
  -Hidden Gold. Digby Long, 1904
  -His Helpmate. Ward, 1887; Appleton, 1887
  His Own Law. Ward, 1914
  -Honest Davie. Bentley, 1883; Harper, 1883
  Jockey Club Stories. Fun, 1888 ss
  -John Ford: His Faults and His Follies. Ward, 1885
  The Justification of Andrew Lebrun. Heinemann, 1894; Appleton, 1894
  Kit Wyndham; or, Fettered for Life; see Fettered for Life
  Kitty's Father. Heinemann, 1893; U.S. Book Co., 1892
  Lady Judas. Chatto, 1903
  -Lieutenant Barnabas. Bentley, 1881; Lovell, 1888
  -Little Lady Linton. Bentley, 1884
  -Maggie? Tinsley, 1876
  A Missing Witness. Chatto, 1897
  The Night of Reckoning. Long, 1905
  -The Obliging Husband. Chatto, 1907
  Olga's Crime; see The Sin of Olga Zassoulich
  Out of the Jaws of Death. Cassell (London & NYC), 1892
  -Perfidious Lydia. Chatto, 1910
  -A Prodigal's Progress. Bentley, 1882
  A Recoiling Vengeance. Ward, 1888; Appleton, 1888
  A Set of Rogues. Innes, 1895; Macmillan, 1895
  The Sin of Olga Zassoulich. Chatto, 1891. U.S. title: Olga's Crime. Lovell, 1891
  The Smuggler's Secret. Griffith, 1893; Lovell, 1890
  Two Knaves and a Queen. Tinsley, 1877
  Under a Strange Mask. Cassell, 1889; Lovell, 1889
  -Was She Justified? Chatto, 1898
  The Woman of the Iron Bracelets. Chatto, 1893; Tait, 1893

BARRETT, G(EOFFREY) J(OHN). 1928-   . SC: Insp. Blessingay, in at least those marked B. Set: Eng.
  Concerto of Death. Hale, 1969
  A Cup That Kills. Hale, 1969 B
  Danger in Diamonds. Hale, 1968
  The Evil Ones. Hale, 1968
  Guilty Be Damned. Hale, 1969 B
  He Died Twice. Hale, 1968 B
  A Hearse for McNally. Hale, 1969
  His Own Funeral. Hale, 1972 B
  Lonely Is the Grave. Hale, 1968
  Murder Road. Hale, 1968

BARRETT, GRADY
  The Barker Case. Vantage, 1966

BARRETT, JOAN
  Monte Carlo Stories. Chatto, 1896 ss, some criminous [Fr.]

BARRETT, MARIANNE. See: The Edingtons.

BARRETT, MARY ELLIN. 1927-   . Ref: CA.
  -Castle Ugly. Dutton, 1966

BARRETT, MAX. Ref: CA. Pseudonym: Maye Barrett.
  The House Across the Park. Hale, 1977. U.S. title: The Crystal Palace. Berkley, 1978, as by Maye Barrett

BARRETT, MAYE. Pseudonym of Max Barrett, q.v.

BARRETT, MICHAEL (JOHN). 1924-   . Born in England; trained as electrical engineer; served in British Army and the War Office.
  Appointment in Zahrein. Joseph, 1960. U.S. title: Escape from Zahrein. GM, 1960
  Escape from Zahrein; see Appointment in Zahrein
  -The Gold of Lubra Rock. Hale, 1967
  -The Heroes of Yuca. Hale, 1968
  -The Hunt at Desolacion. Hale, 1969
  The Last Flowers. Longmans, 1956; Farrar, 1957 [S. Am.]
  The Man in the Spike. Joseph, 1961
  The Return of the Cornish Soldier. Joseph, 1962
  The Reward. Longmans, 1955; Farrar, 1956 [Arg.]
  Stranger in Galah. Longmans, 1958; Norton, 1959
  Task of Destruction. Joseph, 1963
  Ten Against Nura. Hale, 1965 [Mid. East]
  -Tonight in Sacarra. Hale, 1972
  -Zakari's Skull. Hale, 1966

BARRETT, MONTE. 1897?-1949. Ref: CC.
    SC: Peter Cardigan = PC.
    Knotted Silk; see Murder Off Stage
    Murder at Belle Camille. Bobbs, 1943;
       Boardman, 1956 [Miss.]
    Murder Off Stage. Bobbs, 1931. British
       title: Knotted Silk. Paul, 1932 PC
       [NYC]
    The Pelham Murder Case. White House,
       1930 PC [L.I.]
    A Scream in the Night. Merit, 1954
       (Retitled reprint?)
    The Wedding March Murder. Bobbs, 1933;
       Paul, 1933 PC [NYC]

BARRETT, SUSAN
    Rubbish. Joseph, 1974

BARRETT, WILLIAM E(DMUND). 1900-   .
    Ref: CA.
    The Shape of Illusion. Heinemann, 1972;
       Doubleday, 1972

BARRIE, JAMES M(ATTHEW). 1860-1937. Ref:
    CA, DD.
    Better Dead. Sonnenschein, 1888;
       Lovell, 1892
    Shall We Join the Ladies? Hart-Davis,
       1967 (3-act play.)

BARRINGER, MICHAEL
    Inquest! Deane, 1935; Baker, 1935
       (3-act play.)

BARRINGTON, CHARLES F.
    Emily; or, The Orphan Sisters. French,
       1853

BARRINGTON, HOWARD. 1906-   . Pseudonym:
    Simon Stone, q.v.

BARRINGTON, JOHN H. Pseudonym of John
    Henry Harvey. Other pseudonym: Opera-
    tor 1384, q.v. SC: Ken Williams, in
    both titles. Set: Eng.
    The Moving Finger. Langdon, 1947
    Murder in White Pit. Langdon, 1947

BARRINGTON, MAURICE. Pseudonym of Denis
    William Brogan, 1900-1974. Ref: CA.
    Stop on the Green Light! H. Hamilton,
       1941; Harper, 1942 [N.Y.]

BARRINGTON, P. V. See: Pamela Barrington

BARRINGTON, PAMELA. Byline sometimes:
    P. V. Barrington. Pseudonym of Muriel
    Vere Mant Barling, 1904-   . Other
    pseudonym: Charles Barling, q.v. Ref:
    CA. SC: Insp. Henderson, in at least
    that title marked H (see also Barling
    entry); Insp. George Marshall, in at
    least those marked GM (see also Bar-
    ling entry); Insp. George Travers, in
    at least those marked GT.
    Accessory to Murder. Hale, 1968 H
    Account Rendered. Barker, 1953 GT
    Among Those Present. Barker, 1953 GT
    By Some Person Unknown. Hammond, 1960
       GM
    Cage Without Bars. Hale, 1966 GM
    The Changing Heart. Long, 1948
    Final Judgement. Hale, 1964
    Forty-Three Candles for Mr. Beamish.
       Evans, 1950
    The Fourth Victim. Barker, 1958
    A Game of Murder. Hale, 1967 GM
    The Gentle Killer. Hammond, 1961 GT
    Mr. Hedley's Private Hell. Long, 1950
    The Mortimer Story. Barker, 1952 GT
    My Friend Judas. Hale, 1968
    Night of Violence (by P. V. Barring-
       ton). Hammond, 1959 GM
    The Rest Is Silence. Evans, 1951 GM
    Saga of a Scoundrel. Long, 1947
    Slow Poison. Hale, 1967 GM
    The Triangle Has Four Sides. Evans,
       1949
    -White Pierrot. Long, 1932

BARROLL, CLAIRE
    A Strange Place for Murder. Scribner,
       1979 [Cape Cod]

BARRON, ANN (FORMAN). Ref: CA.
    Bride of Menace. GM, 1973 [Tex.]
    Dark Vengeance. GM, 1973 [Tex.]
    Gentle Kiss of Murder; see Murder Is a
       Gentle Kiss
    Maybe It's Murder; see Murder Is a
       Gentle Kiss
    Murder Is a Gentle Kiss. Bouregy, 1960.
       British title: Maybe It's Murder.
       Hammond, 1963. Also published as:
       Gentle Kiss of Murder. Tower, 1966
       [Tex.]
    Serpent in the Shadows. Berkley, 1973
       [La.]
    Spin a Dark Web. Bouregy, 1961
    Strange Legacy. GM, 1969 [Tex.]

BARRON, DONALD G(ABRIEL). 1922-   . Born
    in England of Russian parents; a
    practicing architect.
    The Man Who Was There. Chatto, 1969;
       Atheneum, 1969
    The Zilov Bombs. Deutsch, 1962; Norton,
       1963 [Eng., future]

BARRON, ELWYN (ALFRED). 1855-1929
    Marcel Levignet. Duffield, 1906
    The Triple Scar. Sisley's, 1907

BARRON, HUGH
    Bonnie. New English Library pb, 1970
    The Corrupter. New English Library pb,
       1969
    Doll Baby. New English Library pb, 1969
    Fun City. New English Library pb, 1969
    The Goddess Game. New English Library
       pb, 1971
    High Cost of Murder. New English Li-
       brary pb, 1971 [NYC]
    The Love Thing. New English Library pb,
       1971
    The Mercenary. New English Library,
       1970

BARRY, BOB
    Murder Among Friends. French (London),
       1976 (2-act play.)

BARRY, CHARLES. Pseudonym of Charles
    Bryson, 1877-   . Ref: CC. SC:
    (Supt.) Lawrence Gilmartin, in at
    least those marked LG. Set: Eng.
    The Avenging Ikon. Methuen, 1930; Dut-
       ton, 1930 LG
    The Boat Train Mystery. Hurst, 1938 LG
    A Case Dead and Buried. Hurst, 1938 LG
    The Case for Tressider. Hodder, 1937
    The Clue of the Clot. Hutchinson, 1928;
       Dutton, 1929 LG
    The Corpse on the Bridge. Methuen,
       1927; Dutton, 1928 LG
    The Dead Have No Mouths. Hurst, 1940
    Death in Darkness. Hurst, 1933; Dutton,
       1933
    Death of a First Mate. Hurst, 1935;
       Dutton, 1935 [ship]
    Death Overseas. Hurst, 1937 LG
    The Detective's Holiday. Methuen, 1926;
       Dutton, 1926 LG [Fr.]
    The Ghost of a Clue. Methuen, 1931 LG,
       in very minor role
    The Mouls House Mystery. Methuen, 1926;
       Dutton, 1927 LG
    Murder on Monday..? Eyre, 1932; Dutton,
       1932 LG
    Nicholas Lattermole's Case. Hurst, 1939
       LG
    Poison in Public. Hurst, 1936
    The Red Star Mystery. Mellifont, 1933
    Secrecy at Sandhurst. Hurst, 1951
       [acad.]
    The Shot from the Door. Hurst, 1934;
       Dutton, 1934 LG
    The Smaller Penny. Holden, 1925; Dut-
       ton, 1928 LG
    The Thirteenth House. Mellifont, 1935
    The Witness at the Window. Methuen,
       1927; Dutton, 1927 LG
    The Wrong Murder Mystery. Hurst, 1933;
       Dutton, 1933 LG

BARRY, IRIS. 1895-1969. Ref: CA.
    The Darkness at Mantia. Berkley, 1974
       [Wash.]
    The House of Deadly Night. Belmont,
       1970 [Oreg.]
    The Mandura Mystery. Hale, 1966
    Seven Guests of Fear. Hale, 1970
    The Unprotected. Berkley, 1973; Rem-
       ploy, 1974

BARRY, JEROME (BENEDICT). 1894-1975. Ref:
    CA. SC: Chick Varney = CV.
    The Cat's Cradle Murder; see Leopard
       Cat's Cradle
    Extreme License. Doubleday, 1958;
       Boardman, 1959. Also published as:
       Murder Is No Accident. Dell, 1960
       [NYC]
    Fall Guy. Doubleday, 1960 [NYC]
    Lady of Night. Doubleday, 1944; Board-
       man, 1945 CV [NYC]
    Leopard Cat's Cradle. Doubleday, 1942;
       Boardman, 1943. Also published as:
       The Cat's Cradle Murder. Mystery
       Novel Classic, 1944 CV [NYC]
    Malignant Stars. Doubleday, 1960 [NYC]
    Murder Is No Accident; see Extreme
       License
    Murder with Your Malted. Doubleday,
       1941; Boardman, 1942 CV [NYC]
    Strange Relations. Doubleday, 1962;
       Boardman, 1963 [L.I.]
    This Will Kill You. Merit, 1954
       (Retitled reprint?)

BARRY, JO HANNOLD
    Murder Mansion. Exposition, 1959

BARRY, JOE. Pseudonym of Joe Barry Lake.
    Radio announcer, sportscaster, pro-
    ducer and script writer. SC: Rush
    Henry, in at least those marked RH.
    The Clean Up. Arcadia, 1947 RH
    The Fall Guy. Mystery House, 1945 RH
       [Chi.]
    Homicide Hotel. Phantom, 1951 [NYC]
    Kiss and Kill. Ace, 1954
    The Pay-Off. Mystery House, 1953 RH
       [Ill.]
    The Third Degree. Mystery House, 1943
       RH [Chi.]
    Three for the Money. Handi-Books, 1950
    The Triple Cross. Mystery House, 1946
       RH [Chi.]

BARRY, JOHN BROOKS
    The Michaelmas Girls. Deutch, 1975

BARRY, JOHN E(VARTS). 1906-   .
    Skeleton in Concrete. Gifford, 1952
       [Tex.]
    The Uranium Murders. Long, 1951
       [Calif.]

BARRY, LORETTA
    Sudden Silence. Zebra, 1975 [Jap.]

BARRY, MIKE. Pseudonym of Barry (Norman)
    Malzberg, 1939-   . Other pseudonyms:
    Lee W. Mason, q.v. See also: Bill
    Pronzini, 1943-   . Ref: CA. SC:
    Burt Wulff (The Lone Wolf), in all
    titles.
    Bay Prowler. Berkley, 1973 [S.F.]
    Boston Avenger. Berkley, 1973 [Boston]
    Chicago Slaughter. Berkley, 1974 [Chi.]
    Desert Stalker. Berkley, 1974
       [Las Veg.]
    Detroit Massacre. Berkley, 1975 [Det.]
    Harlem Showdown. Berkley, 1975 [NYC]
    Havana Hit. Berkley, 1974 [Havana]
    The Killing Run. Berkley, 1975
       [Mex. City]
    Los Angeles Holocaust. Berkley, 1974
       [L.A.]
    Miami Marauder. Berkley, 1974 [Miami]
    Night Raider. Berkley, 1973 [NYC]
    Peruvian Nightmare. Berkley, 1974
       [Peru]
    Philadelphia Blow-Up. Berkley, 1975
       [Phil.]
    Phoenix Inferno. Berkley, 1975
       [Phoenix]

BARRY, NORA. Pseudonym.
    Sherbourne's Folly. Doubleday, 1978
       [Eng.]

BARRY, WILLIAM EDWIN
    The Jade God. French (NYC & London),
       1930 (3-act play, based on the novel
       by Alan Sullivan, 1868-1947, q.v.)

BARTER, JOHN P(RIMROSE)
    The Secret Place. Hodder, 1952

BARTH, LOIS. Pseudonym of Lois Diane
    Freihofer, 1933-   . Ref: CA.
    Dark Labyrinth. Lenox, 1971
    Epitaph for a Teddy Bear. Lenox, 1973
    Run from the River. Bouregy, 1965

BARTH, RICHARD. 1943-   . Ref: CA.
    The Rag Bag Clan. Dial, 1978 [NYC]

BARTHOLOMEW, CECILIA. 1907-   . Ref: CA.
    Outrun the Dark. Putnam, 1977; Hale,
       1979
    Second Sight. Putnam, 1980 [S.F.]

BARTLETT, E. DE VERE
    Why? Stock, 1917

BARTLETT, E(RIC) G(EORGE). 1920-   .
    Ref: CA.
    The Case of the 13th Coach. Staples,
       1958

BARTLETT, JEAN ANNE [JEAN ANNE BARTLETT
    LUSTBERG]. 1927-   .
    Angelica. Popular Library, 1977
    Eliza. Popular Library, 1977
    Theodosia. Popular Library, 1977
    Valago Crest. Popular Library, 1979
    Willow Grove. Popular Library, 1979

BARTLETT, VERNON. 1894-   . Joint pseu-
    donym with Per Jacobsson, 1894-1963:
    Peter Oldfeld, q.v.

BARTON, D.
    Black Panther. Paladin, 1953
    Jail Break. Paladin, 1953

BARTON, GEORGE. 1866-1940. SC: Bromley
    Barnes = BB.
    The Ambassador's Trunk. Page, 1919 BB
       [Va.]
    The Mystery of the Red Flame. Page,
       1918 BB

The Pembroke Mason Affair. Page, 1920 BB [Wash. D.C.]
The Strange Adventures of Bromley Barnes. Page, 1918 ss BB [Wash. D.C.]
The True Stories of Celebrated Crimes. Winston, 1909 ss, of true crime in fictionalized form

BARTON, J. C.
The Corrupt Ones. Badger, 1961
The Pay-Off. Badger, 1960

BARTON, ROBERT EUSTACE. 1854-1943. Pseudonym: Robert Eustace, q.v. See also: L. T. Meade, Dorothy L(eigh) Sayers, 1893-1957, and Gertrude Warden.

BARTON, S. W. Pseudonym of Barton Whaley. See: Michael (J.) Kurland, 1938- .

BARTRAM, A. V.
Purple Shadows. Modern, 1935

BARTRAM, GEORGE. Pseudonym of Kenneth M. Cameron, 1931- .
The Aelian Fragment. Putnam, 1976 [Turk.]
Fair Game. Macmillan, 1973; Millington, 1976 [Turk.]
A Job Abroad. Macmillan, 1975
White Peril. Popular Library, 1977 [Wash. D.C.]

BARWICK, JAMES. Joint pseudonym of Tony Barwick, 1934- , and Donald James, 1931- , q.v.
The Hangman's Crusade. Macmillan (London), 1980; Coward, 1981 [1941, Europe]

BASHFORD, H(ENRY) H(OWARTH). 1880-1961. Ref: CC.
Behind the Fog. Heinemann, 1926; Harper, 1927

BASIL, DON
Cat and Feather. Earle, 1931; Holt, 1931

BASILE, GLORIA VITANZA. 1929- . Ref: CA.
The Manipulators. Pinnacle, 1979

BASINGER, DONALD
The Devil Within Us. Dobson, 1963; London House, 1964

BASINSKY, EARLE. 1921- .
The Big Steal. Dutton, 1955; Boardman, 1956 [NYC]
Death Is a Cold, Keen Edge. Signet, 1956

BASKERVILLE, BEATRICE and ELLIOT MONK
SC: Briconi, in at least those marked B.
The Amethyst Button. Hutchinson, 1926
By Whose Hand? Hutchinson, 1922 B [It.]
The St. Cloud Affair. Hutchinson, 1931 B [Fr.]

BASS, CHARLES BECK
Head Held High. Vantage, 1958

BASS, MILTON R(ALPH). 1923- . Ref: CA.
Force Red. Putnam, 1970 [Wash. D.C.]

BASS, RONALD JAY
The Perfect Thief. Jove, 1978

BATCHELOR, DENZIL (STANLEY). 1906-1969. Newspaper columnist, book reviewer, magazine editor, author of many books on sports. SC: Insp. Johnson, in at least those marked J. Set: Eng.
Everything Happens to Hector. Heinemann, 1958
The Man Who Loved Chocolates. Heinemann, 1961 J
On the Brink. Macdonald, 1964 J
The Sedulous Ape. Macdonald, 1965 J
The Taste of Blood. Heinemann, 1958
The Test Match Murder. Angus, 1936

BATCHELOR, REG. Pseudonym of Lauran Bosworth Paine, 1916- . Other pseudonyms: John Armour, Kenneth Bedford, Frank Bosworth, Mark Carrel, Robert Clarke, Richard Dana, J. F. Drexler, Troy Howard, Jared Ingersol, John Kilgore, Hunter Liggett, J. K. Lucas, John Morgan, qq.v. SC: Sgt. Fenwick, in at least those marked F.
-Achilles' Isle. Hale, 1974
-Blue Sea & Yellow Sun. Hale, 1967
Inspector Cole. Hale, 1970
-A Legacy of Shadows. Hale, 1972
The Murder Game. Hale, 1970 F
Murderer's Row. Hale, 1970 F
-The Time of Assassins. Hale, 1969

The Triangle Murder. Hale, 1973
The Twilight People. Hale, 1970

BATE, SAM. 1907- . Ref: CA.
Black Tulip. Deane, 1961 (3-act play.)
Escape to Fear. Kenyon, 1955 (1-act play.)
Motive for Murder. Deane, 1962 (Play.)
Murder at Deem House. French (London), 1980 (Play.)
Murder at Eight. French (London), 1977 (Play.)
Stage Door Murder. New Playwrights, 1979 (Play.)

BATES, H(ERBERT) E(RNEST). 1905-1974. Ref: CA.
-Dear Life. Little, 1949; Joseph, 1950

BATES, HARRY ARTHUR. Pseudonym: Harry Arthur, q.v.

BATESON, DAVID. 1921- . SC: Larry Vernon, in at least those marked LV.
The Big Tomorrow. Hale, 1956 LV
I'll Do Anything. Hale, 1960 LV
I'll Go Anywhere. Hale, 1959 LV
It's Murder, Senorita. Hale, 1954 LV
The Man from the Rock. Hale, 1955 LV
Night Is for Violence. Hale, 1958
The Soho Jungle. Hale, 1958 LV
This Side of Terror. Hale, 1959

BATISTA-OLIVIERI, ISRAEL
Hurt Me No More. Vantage, 1970

BATSON, GEORGE (DONALD). 1918-1977. See also: Peter Hoar. Ref: CA.
Dangerous Nan McGrew. French (NYC & London), 1949 (3-act play.)
Design for Murder. French, 1960 (3-act play.)
Gift of Murder! Dramatists, 1974 (3-act play.)
Hangman's Noose. French, 1947 (3-act play.)
House on the Cliff. French, 1957 (3-act play.)
Miss Private Eye. French, 1951 (3-act play.)
Murder on Arrival. French (NYC), 1960; French (London), 1958 (3-act play.)
Ramshackle Inn. Dramatists, 1944 (3-act play.)
Rehearsal for Death. French, 1949 (3-act play.)
Strange Boarders, with Jack Kirkland, 1901- . Dramatists, 1947 (3-act play.)
Two Faces of Murder. French (London), 1961 (3-act play.)

BATTYE, GLADYS STARKEY. 1915- . Pseudonym: Margaret Lynn, q.v.

BAUBIE, WILLIAM EDW(ARD)
-The Man Condemned. Stratford, 1936

BAULSIR, EDITH
Within Four Walls. Century, 1921

BAUM, VICKI. 1888-1960.
-Secret Sentence. Doubleday, 1932; Bles, 1932 (Translation of "Feme." Berlin, 1926.)

BAUMAN, CAROLYN (BUSEY)
The Secret of Haverly House. Bantam, 1966 [Calif.]
The Woman Who Would Not Die. Signet, 1969

BAUSMAN, FREDERICK. 1861-1931. Pseudonym: Aix, q.v.

BAVIN, BILL [WILLIAM STANLEY BAVIN]. 1919- .
Dead Regimental. Jarrolds, 1968
Destructive Vice. Tandem, 1977
The Extortionists. Tandem, 1970
One Man's War. Jarrolds, 1968

BAWDEN, NINA. Pseudonym of Nina Mary Mabey Kark, 1925- . Ref: CA, CC, TC. Set: Eng.
Change Here for Babylon. Collins, 1955
Devil by the Sea. Collins, 1957; Lippincott, 1959
Eyes of Green; see Who Calls the Tune
The Odd Flamingo. Collins, 1954
The Solitary Child. Collins, 1956; Lancer, 1966
Who Calls the Tune. Collins, 1953. U.S. title: Eyes of Green. Morrow, 1953

BAX, ROGER. Pseudonym of Paul Winterton, 1908- . Other pseudonyms: Andrew Garve, Paul Somers, qq.v. SC: Insp. James = J.
Blueprint for Murder. Hutchinson, 1948. U.S. title: The Trouble with Murder. Harper, 1948 J

Came the Dawn. Hutchinson, 1949. U.S. title: Two If by Sea. Harper, 1949 [Russ.]
Death Beneath Jerusalem. Nelson, 1938 [Isr.]
Disposing of Henry. Hutchinson, 1947; Harper, 1947
A Grave Case of Murder. Hutchinson, 1951; Harper, 1951 J
Red Escapade. Skeffington, 1940 [ship, Russ.]
The Trouble with Murder; see Blueprint for Murder
Two If by Sea; see Came the Dawn

BAXT, GEORGE. 1923- . Ref: CA, TC. SC: Sylvia Plotkin and Max Van Larsen = P&L; Pharoah Love = PL.
The Affair at Royalties. Scribner, 1972; Macmillan (London), 1971 [Eng.]
Burning Sappho. Macmillan, 1972; Macmillan (London), 1972
"I!" Said the Demon. Random, 1969; Cape, 1969 P&L [NYC]
The Neon Graveyard. St. Martin's, 1979 [L.A.]
A Parade of Cockeyed Creatures. Random, 1967; Cape, 1968 P&L [NYC]
A Queer Kind of Death. Simon, 1966; Cape, 1967 PL [NYC]
Swing Low, Sweet Harriet. Simon, 1967 PL [NYC]
Topsy and Evil. Simon, 1968 PL [NYC]

BAXTER, GREGORY. Joint pseudonym of John Sellar Mathison Ressich, 1877- , and Eric de Banzie, 1894- . SC: Supt. Daniels, in at least those marked D. Set: Eng.
The Aincesworth Mystery. Benn, 1929; Appleton, 1930 D
Blue Lightning. Cassell, 1926
Calamity Comes of Age. Hutchinson, 1936; Macaulay, 1935 D
Climax at the Falls. Benn, 1932
Death Strikes at Six Bells. Benn, 1930; Macaulay, 1934 D
Murder Could Not Kill. Benn, 1932; Macaulay, 1934
-The Narrowing Lust. Selwyn, 1928 D

BAXTER, J. K.
The Big Frame. Badger, 1960
Gun Fury. Badger, 1962
The Set-Up. Badger, 1962

BAXTER, JOHN. 1939- .
The Bidders. Lippincott, 1979. British title: Bidding. Granada, 1980

BAXTER, OLIVE. Pseudonym of Helen (Baker) Eastwood, 1892- , q.v.
The Jewel in the Crypt. Hale, 1969

BAY, ROGER
Deadly Jigsaw. Hale, 1971
Paid in Full. Hale, 1970

BAYARD, FRED. Joint pseudonym of Margaret Elizabeth Baird Campbell and Johanna Frederika Jansen.
Death and Lilacs. Phoenix, 1948; Modern Publishing, 1950 [NYC]

BAYER, ELEANOR ROSENFELD. 1914-1981. Joint pseudonym with Leo Grossberg Bayer, 1908- : Oliver Weld Bayer, q.v.

BAYER, LEO GROSSBERG. 1908- . Joint pseudonym with Eleanor Rosenfeld Bayer, 1914-1981: Oliver Weld Bayer, q.v.

BAYER, OLIVER WELD. Joint pseudonym of Eleanor Rosenfeld Bayer, 1914-1981, and Leo Grossberg Bayer, 1908- . Ref on ERB: CA.
Brutal Question. Doubleday, 1947 [Wash. D.C.]
An Eye for an Eye. Doubleday, 1945 [NYC]
No Little Enemy. Doubleday, 1944; Hutchinson, 1945
Paper Chase. Doubleday, 1943; Hutchinson, 1944

BAYER, WILLIAM. 1939- . Ref: CA.
Punish Me with Kisses. Congdon, 1980; Severn, 1981
Tangier. Dutton, 1978 [Tangier]

BAYFIELD, WILLIAM J(OHN). 1871-1958. Pseudonyms: Allan Blair, Allan Maxwell, qq.v. All titles below were published by Amalgamated Press and feature Sexton Blake (with many other authors).
The Adventure of the Man "On Bail." 1928
The Adventure of the Red-Headed Man. 1926

The Affair of the Demobilized Soldier. 1919
The Affair of the Family Diamonds. 1921
The Affair of the Seven Mummy Cases. 1923
All Suspected. 1927
The Architect's Secret. 1921
The "Black Maria" Mystery. 1929
The Bungalow Tragedy. 1919
The Case of the Bogus Ingots. 1920
The Case of the Deported Aliens. 1925
The Case of the Deserted Wife. 1921
The Case of the Double Tangle. 1921
The Case of the Income-Tax Frauds. 1924
The Case of the Millionaire's Blackmail. 1924
The Case of the Press Photographer. 1925
The Case of the Vanished Husband. 1922
The City of Horrors. 1927
The Clue of the Charred Diary. 1919
The Council of Crooks. 1926
The Covent Garden Mystery. 1929
The Crook's Double. 1926
The Crumblerock Crime! 1925
The Death Duty Swindle. 1926
The Death of Duboyne. 1929
The Doctor's Secret. 1923
Down and Out. 1929
False Scents. 1921
The Farrowshot Park Affair. 1924
Flat No. 4. 1924
The "Flying Squad" Tragedy. 1928
The Fourth Theory. 1919
The Home of His Children. 1920
The Last Clue. 1923
The Lincoln's Inn Tragedy. 1920
The Marble Arch Mystery. 1920
The Masked Dancer. 1930
The Masked Forgers. 1929
A Matter of Millions. 1918
The Mint Mystery. 1929
The Mystery of Hanging Sword Alley. 1926
The Mystery of the Missing Journalist. 1922
The Mystery of the Pot-Bank. 1925
The Mystery of the Seaside Hotel. 1926
The Oath of Fear. 1927
The Old Tollgate Mystery. 1924
The Riddle of the Million Pound Bet. 1928
The Secret of the Mansions. 1925
The Secret of the Tomb. 1927
The Strange Case of Habberton's Mile. 1924
The Trail of the Old Lag. 1927
The Twist in the Trail. 1920
When Conscience Sleeps. 1917
Whose Was the Hand? 1918

BAYLISS, HELEN
An Act of Impulse. Greening, 1904

BAYLUS, ROBERT F.
A Midsummer Night's Murder. Carlyle, 1979 [Balt.]
The People Exchange. Carlyle, 1980 [NYC]

BAYLY, A. ERIC. Set: Eng.
The House with Strange Secrets. Sands, 1899; Dutton, 1899
The Man with the Parrots. Sands, 1901
The Secret of Scotland Yard. Sands, 1900

BAYNE, ISABELLA. Nurse and social worker. SC: Benedict Breeze, in both titles. Set: Eng.
Cruel As the Grave. Jarrolds, 1956
Death and Benedict. Laurie, 1952

BAYNE, NEIL
Innoculate! Leisure, 1979

BAYNE, SPENCER. Pseudonym. SC: Hendrik Van Kill, in all titles.
Agent Extraordinary. Dutton, 1942; Eyre, 1944 [Syr.]
Murder Recalls Van Kill. Harper, 1939
The Turning Sword. Harper, 1941 [NYC]

BAYNE-POWELL, ISABELLA
Death Enters the Ward. Francis James, 1947 [hosp.]

BAYNE-POWELL, ROSAMOND. 1879-   . Set: Eng.
Crime at Cloysters. Murray, 1947
Crime at Porches Hill. Macdonald, 1950

BAYNES, JACK. SC: Morocco Jones, in all titles.
Hand of the Mafia. Crest, 1958
Meet Morocco Jones. Crest, 1957
Meet Morocco Jones in the Case of the Syndicate Hoods. Crest, 1957 [Chi.]
Morocco Jones in the Case of the Golden Angel. Crest, 1959

The Peeping Tom Murders. Crest, 1958 [L.A.]

BAZAL, JEAN and PAUL-CLAUDE INNOCENTI
The Corsican. Ballantine, 1978 (Translation of "Le Corse." Paris, 1976.)

BAZAN, EMILIA PARDO. 1852-1921.
-The Mystery of the Lost Dauphin. Funk, 1906

BEACH, EDGAR R(ICE). 1841-   .
Hands of Clay; see Stranded: A Story of the Garden City
-Joshua Humble; A Tale of Old St. Louis. Eddins, 1889 [St. Louis]
-Stranded: A Story of the Garden City. Donohue, 1890. Also published as: Hands of Clay. Eddins, 1904

BEACH, EDWARD L(ATIMER). 1919-   . Ref: CA.
Cold Is the Sea. Holt, 1978; Hodder, 1979 [ship]

BEAL, M(ARY) F. 1937-   .
Angel Dance. Daughters, 1977

BEAM, MAURICE and SUMNER BRITTON, 1902-   .
Murder in a Shell. Messner, 1939 [N.Y.]

BEAMAN, EMERIC HULME. See: HULME-BEAMAN, EMERIC

BEAMAN, J. FRANK
Dotmakers. Book Co. of America, 1965

BEAR, DAVID
Keeping Time. St. Martin's, 1979 [NYC, 1999]

BEARD, MAY
The Murder at Chartres Towers. Mitre, 1943

BEARDMORE, GEORGE (CEDRIC). 1908-   .
Pseudonyms: Cedric Stokes, George Wolfenden, qq.v. Ref: CA.
-A Tale of Two Thieves. Macdonald, 1947
-A Thousand Witnesses. Macdonald, 1953

BEARDMORE, G. RUSSELL
A White Lie. Long, 1909

BEARDSLEY, CHARLES N. Pseudonym: Jocelyn Radcliffe, q.v.

BEARDWOOD, ROGER. 1932-   .
The Winner's Share. Muller, 1980; Doubleday, 1980

BEARE, GEORGE. Born in Australia; journalist; living in England. SC: Vincent Stallard and Cynthia Godwin, in at least those marked S&G.
The Bee Sting Deal. Long, 1972; Houghton, 1972 S&G [Mid. East]
Chain of Infamy. Long, 1972
Night of the Savage. Long, 1976
Prey! Long, 1978
The Snake on the Grave. Long, 1973; Houghton, 1974 [Fr.]
The Very Breath of Hell. Long, 1971; Houghton, 1971 S&G [Mid. East]

BEARE, PETER
Devil or Man? Jenkins, 1932

BEARSHAW, BRIAN. English sports journalist. SC: Supt. Robert Townley and Sgt. Roger Newman = T&N.
The Day of Murder. Hale, 1978 T&N
The Order of Death. Hale, 1979
Practice Makes Murder. Hale, 1979 T&N

BEATTIE, TASMAN. 1930-   . Pseudonym: Alistair Hamilton, q.v. Fourth generation Australian with roots in Scotland. Retired after 30 years as commercial airline pilot.
Judas Flight. Eyre, 1979
Panic Button. Eyre, 1978
The Tillinger Codicil. Eyre, 1980
The Zambesi Break. Eyre, 1977

BEATTY, ELIZABETH. Pseudonym of Teresa Bragunier Holloway, 1906-   . Ref: CA.
The Jupiter Missile Mystery. Bouregy, 1960 [Fla.]
Murder at Auction. Bouregy, 1961

BEATY, BETTY. 1922-   . Pseudonym: Karen Campbell, q.v.

BEATY, (ARTHUR) DAVID. 1919-   . Pseudonym: Paul Stanton, q.v. Ref: CA.
Cone of Silence. Secker, 1959; Morrow, 1959
-Electric Train. Secker, 1975

Excellency. Secker, 1977; Morrow, 1977 [Afr.]
-The Proving Flight. Secker, 1956; Morrow, 1957
The Siren Song. Secker, 1964; Morrow, 1964
-Sword of Honour. Secker, 1965; Morrow, 1966
The Temple Tree. Secker, 1971; Morrow, 1971 [Cey.]
The Wind off the Sea. Secker, 1962; Morrow, 1962

BEAUCHAMP, HENRY
The Lost Emeralds of Zarinthia. Sands, 1899; Knight, 1900

BEAUMONT, CHARLES. Pseudonym of Charles Nutt, 1929-1967. Joint pseudonym with John (E.) Tomerlin, 1930-   , q.v.: Keith Grantland, q.v. Ref: CA.
The Hunger and other stories. Putnam, 1957 ss, some criminous
Night Ride and Other Journeys. Bantam, 1960 ss, some criminous

BEAUMONT, GERMAINE. 1891-   .
-Within This Circle. Laurie, 1950

BECHDOLT, FREDERICK R(ITCHIE). 1874-1950. See also: James (Marie) Hopper, 1876-   .
-Mutiny. Chelsea, 1927 [Calif.]

BECHDOLT, JACK [JOHN ERNEST BECHDOLT]. 1884-1953.
The Wages of Peril. Altemus, 1927 [NYC]

BECHER, ULRICH. 1910-   .
The Woodchuck Hunt. Crown, 1977 (Translation of "Murmeljagd." Switzerland, 19??) [Switz., 1938]

BECK, HENRY CHARLTON. 1902-   .
Cakes to Kill. Dutton, 1932
Death by Clue. Dutton, 1933 [N.J.]
Murder in the News Room. Dutton, 1931
Murder in the Newspaper Guild. Dutton, 1937
Society Editor. Dutton, 1932

BECK, ROBERT. 1918-   .
Death Wish. Holloway, 1976
The Long White Con. Holloway, 1977

BECKE, (GEORGE) LOUIS. 1855-1913.
Tom Gerrard. Unwin, 1905

BECKER, STEPHEN (DAVID). 1927-   . Ref: CA.
A Covenant with Death. Atheneum, 1964; H. Hamilton, 1965 [1923, S.W.]
-Juice. Simon, 1958; Muller, 1959
The Last Mandarin. Random, 1979; Chatto, 1979 [Peking]
Season of the Stranger. Dell, 1966; Panther, 1967

BECKETT, CHARLES HENRY. 1859-   .
Who is John Noman? Cassell, 1887

BECKETT, J.
-One for the Road. Stockwell, 1977

BECKETT, JENIFER
The Trap. St. Martin's, 1975

BECKETT, MARK. Pseudonym of Marcus George Truman, 1890-   . SC: Major Dick Burton, in all titles. Set: Eng.
The Bullet in the Cornice. Eldon, 1937
The Dower House Mystery. Eldon, 1935
Escape from Dartmoor. Eldon, 1936
The Murder at the Flower Show. Eldon, 1933
The Murder of a Magnate. Eldon, 1934
Tea Time Tragedy. Eldon, 1935

BEDFORD, JOHN. 1935-   .
The Generals Died Together. Hale, 1980
Operation Trigeminal. Hale, 1978

BEDFORD, KENNETH. Pseudonym of Lauran Bosworth Paine, 1916-   . Other pseudonyms: John Armour, Reg Batchelor, Frank Bosworth, Mark Carrel, Robert Clarke, Richard Dana, J. F. Drexler, Troy Howard, Jared Ingersol, John Kilgore, Hunter Liggett, J. K. Lucas, John Morgan, qq.v.
The Mathematics of Murder. Hale, 1969; Roy, 1969
The Merchant of Menace. Hale, 1969

BEDFORD, SIDNEY. Pseudonym of Laurence (Walter) Meynell, 1899-   , q.v.
The Man Who Escaped. Paul, 1940

BEDFORD-JONES, H(ENRY JAMES O'BRIEN). 1887-1949. Pseudonym: Allan Hawkwood, q.v.
   The Mardi-Gras Mystery. Doubleday, 1921 [New Or.]
   The Shadow. Fiction League, 1930 [S.F., Mex.]
   The Trail of the Shadow. Hurst, 1924 (U.S. title?)

BEDWELL, BETTINA
   Yellow Dusk. Hurst, 1937

BEEBY, OTTO. 1906-1981. SC: Tony Spencer, in all titles, set in Syd.
   A Blank Cheque for Murder. Long, 1968
   The Faceless Men. Long, 1969
   No Profit in Dying. Long, 1970
   Too Many Innocents. Long, 1972

BEECH, WEBB. Pseudonym of W(illiam) E(dmund) Butterworth (III), 1929-   . Ref: CA.
   Article 92: Murder-Rape. GM, 1964 [Ger.]

BEECHAM, JOHN CHARLES. SC: Koyala, in both titles, set in Borneo.
   -The Argus Pheasant. Watt, 1918; Methuen, 1920
   The Yellow Spider. Watt, 1920; Methuen, 1921

BEECHING, JACK. 1922-   . Ref: CA.
   The Dakota Project. Delacorte, 1968; Cape, 1968 [N. Dak.]

BEECHWOOD. Pseudonym.
   The Burglar's Accomplice. SPCK, 1894

BEECKMAN, ROSS
   The Last Woman. Watt, 1909; Greening, 1912 [NYC]
   -Princess Zara. Watt, 1909; Greening, 1912

BEEDING, FRANCIS. Ref: CC, EM, MP, TC. Joint pseudonym of John (Leslie) Palmer, 1885-1944, q.v., and Hilary (Aiden) St. George Saunders, 1898-1951, q.v. Pseudonym of Palmer: Christopher Haddon, q.v. Joint pseudonym of Saunders and Geoffrey Dennis: Barum Browne, q.v. SC: Ronald Briercliffe = RB; Colonel Granby = G; Professor Kreutzmark = K; Insp. George Martin = GM; Insp. Wilkins = W. Set: Eng., where not indicated otherwise.
   The Big Fish. Hodder, 1938. U.S. title: Heads Off at Midnight. Harper, 1938
   The Black Arrows. Hodder, 1938; Harper, 1938 G [It.]
   Coffin for One; see The Eight Crooked Trenches
   Death in Four Letters. Hodder, 1935; Harper, 1935
   Death Walks in Eastrepps. Hodder, 1931; Mystery League, 1931 W
   The Eight Crooked Trenches. Hodder, 1936; Harper, 1936. Also published as: Coffin for One. Avon, 1943 G
   Eleven Were Brave. Hodder, 1940; Harper, 1941 G [Fr.]
   The Emerald Clasp. Hodder, 1933; Little, 1933
   The Erring Under-Secretary. Hodder pb, 1937. (A separately published pb novelet, in the same series with Allingham's "The Case of the Late Pig" and Carr's "The Third Bullet", qq.v.)
   The Five Flamboys. Hodder, 1929; Little, 1929 G
   The Four Armourers. Hodder, 1930; Little, 1930 G [Sp.]
   He Could Not Have Slipped. Hodder, 1939; Harper, 1939 GM
   Heads Off at Midnight; see The Big Fish
   Hell Let Loose. Hodder, 1937; Harper, 1937 G [Sp.]
   The Hidden Kingdom. Hodder, 1927; Little, 1927 K [Sp.]
   The House of Dr. Edwardes. Hodder, 1927; Little, 1928. Also published as: Spellbound. World, 1945 [Fr.]
   The League of Discontent. Hodder, 1930; Little, 1930 G [Fr.]
   The Little White Hag. Hutchinson, 1926; Little, 1926 [Geneva]
   Mr. Bobadil. Hodder, 1934. U.S. title: The Street of the Serpents. Harper, 1934 [Sp.]
   Murder Intended. Hodder, 1932; Little, 1932 W
   Murdered: One by One; see No Fury
   The Nine Waxed Faces. Hodder, 1936; Harper, 1936 G [Austria]
   No Fury. Hodder, 1937. U.S. title: Murdered: One by One. Harper, 1937 GM
   The Norwich Victims. Hodder, 1935; Harper, 1935 GM
   Not a Bad Show. Hodder, 1940. U.S. title: The Secret Weapon. Harper, 1940 G [Ger.]
   The One Sane Man. Hodder, 1934; Little, 1934 G
   Pretty Sinister. Hodder, 1929; Little, 1929 G
   The Secret Weapon; see Not a Bad Show
   The Seven Sleepers. Hutchinson, 1925; Little, 1925 K [Geneva]
   The Six Proud Walkers. Hodder, 1928; Little, 1928 G [It.]
   Spellbound; see The House of Dr. Edwardes
   The Street of the Serpents; see Mr. Bobadil
   Take It Crooked. Hodder, 1932; Little, 1932 G [Fr.]
   The Ten Holy Horrors. Hodder, 1939; Harper, 1939 G
   There Are Thirteen. Hodder, 1946; Harper, 1946 G
   The Three Fishers. Hodder, 1931; Little, 1931 RB [Fr.]
   The Twelve Disguises. Hodder, 1942; Harper, 1942 G [Fr.]
   The Two Undertakers. Hodder, 1933; Little, 1933 G,RB

BEEDLE, JOHN. 1909-   .
   You Can Only Die Once. Sun (Australia), 1978

BEEKMAN, E(RIC) M(ONTAGUE). 1939-   . Ref: CA.
   The Killing Jar. Houghton, 1976

BEELEY, JAMES
   Murder's for the Birds. Vega, ca.1962

BEER, OLIVIER
   Pas de Deux. Gollancz, 1980 (Translation of "Le Chant des Enfants Morts." Paris, 1978.)

BEESTON, L. J.
   Every Night About Half Past Eight, and other stories. Hutchinson, 1923 ss

BEEVOR, ANTONY. 1946-
   The Violent Brink. Murray, 1975

BEGBIE, ERNEST
   The Mystery of the Three B Syndicate. Houghton (London), 1933

BEGBIE, GARSTIN. SC: Supt. Samuel Quan, in at least those marked SQ. Set: Eng.
   Murder Mask. Jenkins, 1934 SQ
   Sudden Death at Scotland Yard. Jenkins, 1933 SQ
   Trailing Death. Jenkins, 1932

BEHENNA, KATHLEEN
   Sidartha. Digby Long, 1896

BEHM, MARC. 1925-   . Ref: CA.
   The Eye of the Beholder. Dial, 1980

BEHN, NOEL. 1928-   . Ref: CA, MC, TC.
   Big Stick-Up at Brink's! Putnam, 1977. British title: Brink's. Allen, 1977 (Dramatized true crime.) [Boston]
   Brink's; see Big Stick-Up at Brink's!
   The Kremlin Letter. Simon, 1966; Allen, 1966 [Russ.]
   The Shadowboxer. Simon, 1969; Hart-Davis, 1970 [Ger., 1944]
   The Kremlin Letter. Simon, 1966; Allen, 1966 [Russ.]
   The Shadowboxer. Simon, 1969; Hart-Davis, 1970 [Ger., 1944]

BEHR, EDWARD. 1926-   . Ref: CA.
   Getting Even. Harper, 1980; H. Hamilton, 1980 [Paris]

BEHREND, ARTHUR
   The House of the Spaniard. Heinemann, 1935; Doubleday, 1936
   The Samarai Affair. Eyre, 1973
   Unlucky for Some. Eyre, 1955

BEIZER, BORIS. 1934-   . Pseudonym: Ethan I. Shedley, q.v.

BEKESSY, JEAN. 1911-1977. Pseudonym: Hans Habe, q.v.

BELANGER, CHUCK
   The Five Man War. Playboy pb, 1976 [Chi.]

BELASYSE, E.
   The Ventriloquist. Davies, 1935

BELGRAVE, DALRYMPLE J.
   A Great Turf Fraud. Hogg, 1888
   Jack Warleigh: A Tale of the Turf and the Law. Chapman, 1891
   Turf and Veldt. Marsden, 1893 ss

BELIARD, JEAN. Pseudonym: Jean Francois Vignant, q.v.

BELL, ABBAN
   Out of Circulation. Popular Library, 1965 [NYC]

BELL, GERARD
   Villains Galore. Cassell, 1972; PB, 1976

BELL, J(OHN) J(OY). 1871-1934.
   Some Plain—Some Coloured. Hodder, 1923 ss, some criminous
   Till the Clock Stops. Hodder, 1917; Duffield, 1917

BELL, JAY
   One More Time. GM, 1969 [Tex.]

BELL, JOHN
   In the Shadow of the Bush. Sands, 1899

BELL, JOHN KEBLE. 1875-1928. Pseudonym: Keble Howard, q.v.

BELL, JOSEPHINE. Pseudonym of Doris Bell Collier Ball, 1897-   . Ref: CA, CC, DD, EM, TC. SC: Dr. Henry Frost = HF; Insp. Steven Mitchell = SM; Amy Tupper = AT; Claude Warrington-Reeve = CW; Dr. David Wintringham = DW. Set: mostly Eng.
   Adventure with Crime. Hodder, 1962
   The Alien. Bles, 1964
   All Is Vanity. Longmans, 1940 DW
   The Backing Winds. Methuen, 1951
   Bones in the Barrow. Methuen, 1953; Macmillan, 1955 DW,SM
   The Catalyst. Hodder, 1966; Macmillan, 1967 [Greece]
   The China Roundabout. Hodder, 1956. U.S. title: Murder on the Merry-Go-Round. Ballantine, 1965 DW,SM
   Curtain Call for a Corpse; see Death at Half-Term
   Death at Half-Term. Longmans, 1939. U.S. title: Curtain Call for a Corpse. Macmillan, 1965 DW,SM [acad.]
   Death at the Medical Board. Longmans, 1944; Ballantine, 1964 DW
   Death in Clairvoyance. Longmans, 1949 DW,SM
   Death in Retirement. Methuen, 1956; Macmillan, 1956
   Death of a Con Man. Hodder, 1968; Lippincott, 1968
   Death of a Poison-Tongue. Hodder, 1972; Stein, 1977
   Death on the Borough Council. Longmans, 1937 DW
   Death on the Reserve. Hodder, 1966; Macmillan, 1967 HF
   Double Doom. Hodder, 1957; Macmillan, 1958
   Easy Prey. Hodder, 1959; Macmillan, 1959 CW,SM
   Fall over Cliff. Longmans, 1938; Macmillan, 1956 DW,SM
   The Fennister Affair. Hodder, 1969; Stein, 1978
   Fiasco in Fulham; see A Flat Tyre in Fulham
   Fires at Fairlawn. Methuen, 1954

A Flat Tyre in Fulham. Hodder, 1963.
  U.S. title: Fiasco in Fulham. Macmillan, 1963. Also published as: Room for a Body. Ballantine, 1964 CW,SM
From Natural Causes. Longmans, 1939 DW
A Hole in the Ground. Hodder, 1971; Ace, 1973
The House Above the River. Hodder, 1959
The Hunter and the Trapped. Hodder, 1963
A Hydra with Six Heads. Hodder, 1970; Stein, 1978
Murder in Hospital. Longmans, 1937 DW,SM [hosp.]
Murder on the Merry-Go-Round; see The China Roundabout
New People at the Hollies. Hodder, 1961; Macmillan, 1961
No Escape. Hodder, 1965; Macmillan, 1966 [hosp.]
A Pigeon Among the Cats. Hodder, 1974; Stein, 1978
The Port of London Murders. Longmans, 1938; Macmillan, 1958 SM
A Question of Inheritance. Hodder, 1980; Walker, 1981 AT
Room for a Body; see A Flat Tyre in Fulham
The Seeing Eye. Hodder, 1958 DW,SM
Stranger on a Cliff; see To Let, Furnished
A Stroke of Death; see Such a Nice Client
Such a Nice Client. Hodder, 1977. U.S. title: A Stroke of Death. Walker, 1977
The Summer School Mystery. Methuen, 1950 DW,SM [acad.]
A Swan-Song Betrayed. Hodder, 1978. U.S. title: Treachery in Type. Walker, 1980
To Let, Furnished. Methuen, 1952. U.S. title: Stranger on a Cliff. Ace, 1964
Treachery in Type; see A Swan-Song Betrayed
Trouble at Wrekin Farm. Longmans, 1942 DW
The Trouble in Hunter Ward. Hodder, 1976; Walker, 1977 [hosp.]
The Upfold Witch. Hodder, 1964; Macmillan, 1964 HF
Victim. Hodder, 1975; Walker, 1976
A Well-Known Face. Hodder, 1960; Washburn, 1960 CW,SM
The Wilberforce Legacy. Hodder, 1969; Walker, 1969 [Carib.]
Wolf! Wolf! Hodder, 1979; Walker, 1980 AT [hosp.]

BELL, LESLIE. 1916-   .
  The Laughing Fish. Meridian, 1952
  Ring the Bell, Sister! Laurie, 1956

BELL, MALCOLM
  His Fatal Success; Being the Strange Adventures of John Stuart. Belford, 1889

BELL, MARY HAYLEY
  Duet for Two Hands. French (London), 1947 (2-act play.)

BELL, NEIL. Pseudonym of Stephen Southwold, 1887-1964. Other pseudonym: Paul Martens, q.v.
  -Alpha and Omega. Hale, 1946 ss
  Corridor of Venus. Redman, 1960 ss, some criminous
  -The Dark Page. Eyre, 1951
  The Disturbing Affair of Noel Blake. Gollancz, 1932; Putnam, 1932
  The Endless Chain. Redman, 1956
  The House at the Crossroads. Redman, 1946 ss, some criminous
  The Ninth Earl of Whitby. Redman, 1966 ss, some criminous
  Precious Porcelain. Gollancz, 1931; Putnam, 1931
  -Thy First Begotten. Redman, 1957
  -Who Walk in Fear. Redman, 1953 (3 stories.)

BELL, RAMSEY. Joint pseudonym of Agnes Rosemary Cooper and Mary Elizabeth Phyllis Weller.
  Dangerous Promise. Hodder, 1939
  Dragon Under Ground. Hodder, 1937
  -The Lake of Ghosts. Hodder, 1940

BELL, SALLIE LEE (RILEY). Ref: CA.
  -The Barrier. Zondervan, 1957
  The Long Search. Zondervan, 1958

BELL, VICARS (WALKER). 1904-   . Ref: CA, CC. SC: Dr. Baynes, in all titles. Set: Eng.
  Death and the Night Watches. Faber, 1955; British Book Centre, 1962
  Death Darkens Council. Faber, 1952
  Death Has Two Doors. Faber, 1950
  Death Under the Stars. Faber, 1949
  Death Walks by the River. Faber, 1959
  Two by Day and One by Night. Faber, 1950

BELL, WYATT
  The Magnolia Murder. GM, 1961

BELLAH, JAMES. See: Robert G. Stimson.

BELLAH, JAMES WARNER. 1899-1976. Ref: CA.
  The Bones of Napoleon. Appleton, 1940 [Md.]
  The Brass Gong Tree. Appleton, 1936 [Jap.]
  7 Must Die. Appleton, 1938

BELLAIRS, GEORGE. Pseudonym of Harold Blundell, 1902-   . Ref: CA, CC, EM, TC. SC: Supt. (Chief Insp., Det. Insp.) Thomas Littlejohn, in all the following except "Turmoil in Zion." Set: mostly Eng.
  All Roads to Sospel; see Close All Roads to Sospel
  The Body in the Dumb River. Gifford, 1961. U.S. title: Murder Masquerade. Tower, 1981
  Bones in the Wilderness. Gifford, 1959 [Fr.]
  Calamity at Harwood. Gifford, 1943; Macmillan, 1945
  The Case of the Demented Spiv. Gifford, 1950
  The Case of the Famished Parson. Gifford, 1949; Macmillan, 1949
  The Case of the Headless Jesuit. Gifford, 1950. U.S. title: Death Brings in the New Year. Macmillan, 1951
  The Case of the Scared Rabbits. Gifford, 1947
  The Case of the Seven Whistlers. Gifford, 1948; Macmillan, 1948
  Close All Roads to Sospel. Gifford, 1947. U.S. title: All Roads to Sospel. Walker, 1981 [Fr.]
  Corpse at the Carnival. Gifford, 1958 [Isle of Man]
  Corpses at Enderby. Gifford, 1954
  The Crime at Halfpenny Bridge. Gifford, 1946
  Crime in Lepers' Hollow. Gifford, 1952
  The Cursing Stones Murder. Gifford, 1954
  Dead March for Penelope; see Dead March for Penelope Blow
  Dead March for Penelope Blow. Gifford, 1951; Macmillan, 1951. Also published as: Dead March for Penelope. Viking (London), 1956
  The Dead Shall Be Raised. Gifford, 1942. U.S. title: Murder Will Speak. Macmillan, 1943
  Death Before Breakfast. Gifford, 1962; British Book Centre, 1962
  Death Brings in the New Year; see The Case of the Headless Jesuit
  Death Drops the Pilot. Gifford, 1956
  Death in Dark Glasses. Gifford, 1952; Macmillan, 1952
  Death in Desolation. Gifford, 1967
  Death in Despair. Gifford, 1960
  Death in High Provence. Gifford, 1957 [Fr.]
  Death in Room Five. Gifford, 1955 [Fr.]
  Death in the Fearful Night. Gifford, 1960
  Death in the Night Watches. Gifford, 1945; Macmillan, 1946
  Death in the Wasteland. Gifford, 1963; British Book Centre, 1964 [Fr.]
  Death of a Busybody. Gifford, 1942; Macmillan, 1943
  Death of a Shadow. Gifford, 1964
  Death of a Tin God. Gifford, 1961 [Fr.]
  Death on the Last Train. Gifford, 1948; Macmillan, 1949
  Death Sends for the Doctor. Gifford, 1957
  Death Spins the Wheel. Gifford, 1965 [Fr.]
  Death Stops the Frolic; see Turmoil in Zion
  Death Treads Softly. Gifford, 1956 [Isle of Man]
  Devious Murder. Gifford, 1973; Walker, 1980
  Downhill Ride of Leeman Popple. Gifford, 1978
  Fatal Alibi. Gifford, 1968
  Fear Round About. Gifford, 1975; Walker, 1981
  The Four Unfaithful Servants. Gifford, 1942
  Half-Mast for the Deemster. Gifford, 1953 [Isle of Man]
  He'd Rather Be Dead. Gifford, 1945
  Intruder in the Dark. Gifford, 1966
  A Knife for Harry Dodd. Gifford, 1953
  Littlejohn on Leave. Gifford, 1941
  Murder Adrift. Gifford, 1972
  Murder Gone Mad. Gifford, 1968 [Fr.]
  Murder Makes Mistakes. Gifford, 1958
  Murder Masquerade; see The Body in the Dumb River
  Murder of a Quack. Gifford, 1943; Macmillan, 1944
  Murder Will Speak; see The Dead Shall Be Raised
  The Night They Killed Joss Varran. Gifford, 1970
  Old Man Dies. Gifford, 1980
  Outrage on Gallows Hill. Book Club Edition, 1948
  Pomeroy, Deceased. Gifford, 1971 [Fr.]
  Single Ticket to Death. Gifford, 1967 [Fr.]
  Strangers Among the Dead. Gifford, 1966
  Surfeit of Suspects. Gifford, 1964
  Toll the Bell for Murder. Gifford, 1959 [Isle of Man]
  The Tormenters. Gifford, 1962 [Isle of Man]
  Turmoil in Zion. Gifford, 1943. U.S. title: Death Stops the Frolic. Macmillan, 1944
  Tycoon's Death-Bed. Gifford, 1970

BELLAMANN, HENRY. 1882-1945.
  The Gray Man Walks. Doubleday, 1936
  Victoria Grandolet. Simon, 1943; Cassell, 1945 [La.]

BELLAMY, CHARLES JOSEPH. 1852-1910.
  -A Moment of Madness. Burt, 1888

BELLAMY, JEAN
  Ghost of Coquina Key. Lancer, 1970
  Mistress of Ghosthaven. Lancer, 1969 [Utah]
  The Prisoner of Ingecliff. Dell, 1971 [Eng., 1500s]

BELLAMY, R(OBERT) L(OWE). SC: Scout Grey, in both titles.
  The Adventures of Scout Grey. Low, 1924
  Scout Grey—Detective. Low, 1927

BELLEM, ROBERT LESLIE. 1902-1968. Joint pseudonym with Cleve F(ranklin) Adams, 1895-1949, q.v.: Franklin Charles, q.v. See also: John A. Saxon, 1886-1947. Ref: TC.
  Blue Murder. Phoenix, 1938
  The Window with the Sleeping Nude. Handi-Books, 1950

BELLINGER, MARTHA (IDELL FLETCHER). 1870-   .
  The Stolen Singer. Bobbs, 1911

BELLOC, (JOSEPH) HILAIRE (PIERRE RENE). 1870-1953. Ref: CC. Versatile British man of letters: wrote children's stories, political tracts, parodies, travel and historical works. Set: Eng.
  But Soft—We Are Observed. Arrowsmith, 1928. U.S. title: Shadowed! Harper, 1929 [future, Eng.]
  The Emerald of Catherine the Great. Arrowsmith, 1926; Harper, 1926
  The Green Overcoat. Arrowsmith, 1912; McBride, 1912
  The Haunted House. Arrowsmith, 1927; Harper, 1928
  The Missing Masterpiece. Arrowsmith, 1929; Harper, 1929
  Shadowed!; see But Soft—We Are Observed

BELMAR, CHARLES. 1890-   .
  Finnegan's Dilemma. Vantage, 1950

BELOT, ADOLPHE. 1829-1890.
  Alphonsine; or, The Criminal Charm. General Publishing, 1882
  The Drama of the Rue de la Paix; see Men Are What Women Make Them
  Fedora; or, The Tragedy in the Rue de la Paix; see Men Are What Women Make Them
  Flower of Crime. Newberry, 1892 [Fr.]
  Men Are What Women Make Them; or, The Drama of the Rue de la Paix. Peterson, 1872. British title: A Tragedy Indeed. Remington, 1878. Also published as: Fedora; or, The Tragedy in the Rue de la Paix. Rand, 1883. And as: The Drama of the Rue de la Paix. Vizetelly, 1880. And as: The Tragedy in the Rue de la Paix. Street, 1891 [Fr.]
  The Tragedy in the Rue de la Paix; see Men Are What Women Make Them
  A Tragedy Indeed; see Men Are What Women Make Them

BELVEDERE, LEE. Pseudonym of V(alerie) Merle (Spanner) Grayland, q.v. Other pseudonym: Valerie Subond, q.v.
  Meet a Dark Stranger. Dell, 1973

BENASSI, MARK
  The Thor Option. Dell, 1980

BENCHLEY, ALEXANDRA JANE
The Dream of Romy Jackson. Leisure, 1971

BENCHLEY, NATHANIEL (GODDARD). 1915-1981. Ref: CA.
Catch a Falling Spy. McGraw, 1963 [N.Y.]
The Hunter's Moon. Little, 1972
-The Off-Islanders. McGraw, 1961; Hutchinson, 1962
Sail a Crooked Ship. McGraw, 1960; Hutchinson, 1961 [ship]
Sweet Hostage; see Welcome to Xanadu
The Wake of the Icarus. Atheneum, 1969
Welcome to Xanadu. Atheneum, 1968; Hutchinson, 1968. Also published as: Sweet Hostage. PB, 1977

BENDER, WILLIAM, JR.
Tokyo Intrigue. Ace, 1957; Digit, 1958 [Tokyo]

BENEDICT, GERALD
The Case of the Deadly Drops. Phoenix, 1941 [NYC]

BENEDICT, LYNN. Pseudonym of Victor Jerome Banis, 1937- . Other pseudonym: Jan Alexander, q.v.
Bloodstone. Beagle, 1973
A Family Affair. Avon, 1973
The Fatal Flower. Avon, 1973 [Fla.]
The Lucifer Cult. PB, 1974 [New Eng.]
Moon Fire. Avon, 1973
The Twisted Tree. Avon, 1973
Whisper of Heather. PB, 1974

BENEDICT, MIRIAM
To Seek Where Shadows Are. Avon, 1973

BENEDICTUS, DAVID. 1938- .
The Rabbi's Wife. Blond, 1976; Evans, 1976

BENET, JAMES (WALKER). 1914- . Ref: CA.
The Knife Behind You. Harper, 1950
A Private Killing. Harper, 1949; Corgi, 1951 [Calif.]

BENET, WILLIAM ROSE. 1886-1950.
The First Person Singular. Doran, 1922

BENFIELD, ERIC
Poison in the Shade. Heinemann, 1953

BENJAMIN, EDLA. Daughter of Aline Bernstein; writer and scenic designer.
Murder Without Makeup. Random, 1940 [NYC]
A Well-Born Corpse. Random, 1939

BENJOYA, MITCHELL
Final Judgment. Contemporary, 1978 [Boston]

BENNET, ROBERT AMES. 1870-1954.
Which One? McClurg, 1912 [Calif.]

BENNET-THOMPSON, LILIAN, 1883-1942, and GEORGE HUBBARD, 1884- .
The Beak of Death. Chelsea, 1929
The Death Fire. Chelsea, 1929
Fruit of Folly. Macaulay, 1934
The Golden Ball. Chelsea, 1929

BENNETT, ALFRED GORDON. 1901- .
-Whom the Gods Destroy. Pharos, 1946

BENNETT, (ENOCH) ARNOLD. 1867-1931. Byline also: E. A. Bennett. Ref: CC, DD, EM, MP. Set: Eng.
The Ghost. Chatto, 1907; Turner, 1907
The Grand Babylon Hotel. Chatto, 1902; Doran, 1902. Also published as: T. Racksole and Daughter. New Amsterdam, 1902
-The Grim Smile of the Five Towns. Chapman, 1907 ss
The Loot of Cities. Rivers, 1904; Train, 1972 ss (British reprint editions contain an additional 7 ss.)
The Night Visitor and other stories. Cassell, 1931; Doubleday, 1931 ss
Sidney Yorke's Friend (by E. A. Bennett). Wells Gardner, 1901
T. Racksole and Daughter; see The Grand Babylon Hotel
Teresa of Watling Street! Chatto, 1904
The Woman Who Stole Everything and other stories. Cassell, 1927; Doran, 1927 ss

BENNETT, BARBARA CURRY
Berryhill. Manor, 1979

BENNETT, CHARLES. 1899- . See also: Ruth Alexander.
Blackmail. Rich, 1934 (3-act play.)
The Last Hour. Rich, 1934 (3-act play.)

BENNETT, DOROTHEA [DOROTHEA BENNETT YOUNG]. 1924- . Ref: CA.
The Dry Taste of Fear. Barker, 1960
The Jigsaw Man. Bodley, 1977; Coward, 1976
The Maynard Hayes Affair. Macmillan (London), 1981; Coward, 1979
Under the Skin. Barker, 1961; Mill, 1962 [Switz.]

BENNETT, DOROTHY. 1906- . SC: Dennis Devore, in at least those marked DD.
Come and Be Killed. Select, 1942 DD
How Strange a Thing. Caxton, 1935 (A detective novel in verse.)
Murder Unleashed. Doubleday, 1935 DD [S.F.]

BENNETT, DOROTHY
The Carrion Crows. Hutchinson, 1950
The Curious Were Killed. Hutchinson, 1947 [It.]
Game Without Winners. Hale, 1972
State Puppet. Hale, 1971
Stranger in His Grave. Hale, 1966

BENNETT, E. A. See: (Enoch) Arnold Bennett, 1867-1931.

BENNETT, EDWIN. See: Sylvia (G. L.) Dannett.

BENNETT, ELIZABETH DEARE. Pseudonym of Sam(uel Kimball) Merwin, Jr., 1910- , q.v.
Gower Court Manor. Dell, 1976 [Eng.]

BENNETT, EMERSON. 1822-1905.
The Female Spy; or, Treason in the Camp. Stratton, 1851
The Forged Will; or, Crime and Retrobution; see Oliver Goldfinch; or, The Hypocrite
The Heiress of Bellefront; see Walde-Warren; a Tale of Circumstantial Evidence
Oliver Goldfinch; or, The Hypocrite. Stratton, 1850. Also published as: The Forged Will; or, Crime and Retribution. Peterson, 1853
Rosalie Du Pont. Stratton, 1851 (Sequel to "The Female Spy," q.v.)
The Unknown Countess; or, Crime and Its Results. Peterson, 1852
Walde-Warren; a Tale of Circumstantial Evidence. Peterson, 1852. Also published as: The Heiress of Bellefront. Peterson, 1855

BENNETT, ERIC
Murder at the Admiralty. Hutchinson, 1941

BENNETT, F. E.
Fred Bennett, the Mormon Detective. Laird, 1888

BENNETT, GEOFFREY MARTIN. 1909- .
Pseudonym: Sea-Lion, q.v.

BENNETT, GEORGE HAROLD. 1930- . Pseudonym: Hal Bennett, q.v.

BENNETT, HAL. Pseudonym of George Harold Bennett, 1930- . Ref: CA.
Wait Until the Evening. Doubleday, 1974 [Va., WWII]

BENNETT, JACK. 1934- .
Dragon. Joseph, 1969
Ocean Road. Joseph, 1966; Little, 1966

BENNETT, JAMES (WILLIAM). 1891- .
-Chinese Blake. Skeffington, 1930
-Dragon Shadows. Duffield, 1928 ss
The Manchu Cloud. Hamilton, 1927; Duffield, 1927
Son of the Typhoon. Skeffington, 1929; Duffield, 1928
Spinach Jade. Skeffington, 1939 [Peking]
The Yellow Corsair. Hamilton, 1928; Duffield, 1927

BENNETT, JANICE N.
The Haunted. Ace, 1974 [Eng.]
House of Athena. Ace, 1970 [Greece]
To the Castle. Ace, 1975

BENNETT, JAY. 1912- . Pseudonym: Steve Rand, q.v. Ref: CA.
Catacombs. Abelard, 1959 [NYC]
Death Is a Silent Room. Abelard, 1965 [N.Y.]
Murder for Money; see Murder Money
Murder Money. Crest, 1962. British title: Murder for Money. Muller pb, 1963

BENNETT, JOHN
Revelations of a Sly Parrot. Ward, 1862 ss, some criminous

BENNETT, KEM(YS DEVERELL). 1919-
Dangerous Knowledge. Collins, 1955. U.S. title: Passport for a Renegade. Doubleday, 1955
The Devil's Current. Collins, 1953; Doubleday, 1953 [Mid. East]
The Fabulous Wink; see The Wink
Passport for a Renegade; see Dangerous Knowledge
-The Wink. Hart-Davis, 1951. U.S. title: The Fabulous Wink. Pellegrini, 1951

BENNETT, MARGOT. 1912-1980. Ref: CC, MC, TC. SC: John Davies, in at least those marked JD. Set: Eng.
Away Went the Little Fish. Nicholson, 1946; Doubleday, 1947 JD
Farewell Crown and Goodbye King. Eyre, 1953; Walker, 1961
The Golden Pebble. Nicholson, 1948
The Man Who Didn't Fly. Eyre, 1955; Harper, 1956
Someone from the Past. Eyre, 1958; Dutton, 1958
That Summer's Earthquake. Eyre, 1964
Time to Change Hats. Nicholson, 1945; Doubleday, 1946 JD
The Widow of Bath. Eyre, 1952; Doubleday, 1952

BENNETT, MARY
The Broken Heart; or, The Village Bridal. Lofts, ca.1880

BENNETT, RICHARD (LAURENCE)
The Whispering Money. Heinemann, 1953

BENNETT, ROLF
The Web. Hodder, 1917

BENNETT, W(ILLIAM) R(OBERT). 1921- .
Ref: CA. SC: Adam Kane, in both.
Dossier on a Mantis. Hale, 1972
The Man from Checkmate. Hale, 1971

BENNETTS, PAMELA. 1922- . Byline on U.S. editions: Margaret James.
Amberstone. Hale, 1980; St. Martin's, 1980
Death of the Red King. Hale, 1976; St. Martin's, 1977
Footsteps in the Fog. Hale, 1979; St. Martin's, 1980 [Eng., 1800s]
The Haunting of Sara Lessingham; see The House in Candle Square
The House in Candle Square. Hale, 1977. U.S. title: The Haunting of Sara Lessingham. St. Martin's, 1978
Marionette. Hale, 1979; St. Martin's, 1980
One Dark Night. Hale, 1978
The Quick and the Dead. Hale, 1979
Ring the Bell Softly. Hale, 1978; St. Martin's, 1978 [1865, Eng.]
A Voice in the Darkness. Hale, 1977; St. Martin's, 1979 [1870, Eng.]

BENNEY, MARK. Pseudonym of Henry Ernest Degras, 1910- .
The Scapegoat Dances. Davies, 1938

BENOIT, PIERRE. 1886-1962. Ref: CA.
Count Philip. Hutchinson, 1920. U.S. title: The Secret Spring. Dodd, 1920. Also published as: Konigsmark. Hutchinson, 1924
Konigsmark; see Count Philip
The Secret Spring; see Count Philip

BENSEN, D(ONALD) R. 1927- . Pseudonym: Julia Thatcher, q.v. Ref: CA.
Sherlock Holmes in New York. Ballantine, 1976 (Novelization of the TV movie.) [1901, NYC]

BENSON, B(LACKWOOD) K(ETCHUM). 1845-
Who Goes There? Macmillan, 1900 [ca.1860, U.S.]

BENSON, BEN(JAMIN). 1915-1959. Ref: CC, EM, TC. SC: Capt. Wade Paris = WP; Ralph Lindsay = RL. Set: Mass., in all books.
The Affair of the Exotic Dancer. Mill, 1958 WP
Alibi at Dusk. Mill, 1951; Corgi, 1952 WP
Beware the Pale Horse. Mill, 1951; Muller, 1952 WP
The Black Mirror. Mill, 1957; Collins, 1958
The Blonde in Black. Mill, 1958; Collins, 1959 WP
Broken Shield. Mill, 1955; Collins, 1957 RL
The Burning Fuse. Mill, 1954; Collins, 1956 WP [Cape Cod]
The End of Violence. Mill, 1959; Collins, 1959 RL
The Frightened Ladies. Mill, 1960 (2 novelets.)

The Girl in the Cage. Mill, 1954; Collins, 1955   RL
The Huntress Is Dead. Mill, 1960   WP
Lily in Her Coffin. Mill, 1952; Boardman, 1954   WP
The Ninth Hour. Mill, 1956; Collins, 1957   WP
The Running Man. Mill, 1957; Collins, 1958   RL
Seven Steps East. Mill, 1959   RL
The Silver Cobweb. Mill, 1955; Collins, 1956   RL
Stamped for Murder. Mill, 1952; Gannet, 1955   WP
Target in Taffeta. Mill, 1953; Collins, 1955   WP
The Venus Death. Mill, 1953; Muller, 1954   RL

BENSON, DANIEL. Pseudonym of Colin Symons Cooper, 1926-   . Ref: CA.
The Argyll Killings. Hale, 1980

BENSON, E(DWARD) F(REDERIC). 1867-1940. Ref: CC, TC.
The Blotting Book. Heinemann, 1908; Doubleday, 1908
The Countess of Lowndes Square. Cassell, 1920   ss, some criminous
The Luck of the Vails. Heinemann, 1901; Appleton, 1901
The Room in the Tower and other stories. Mills, 1912; Knopf, 1929   ss, some criminous
Visible and Invisible. Hutchinson, 1923; Doran, 1924   ss, some criminous

BENSON, EUGENE P(ATRICK)
The Bulls of Ronda. Eyre, 1976

BENSON, GODFREY R(ATHBONE) [LORD CHARNWOOD]. 1864-1945. Ref: CC, DD, EM, MP.
Tracks in the Snow. Longmans, 1906; Dial, 1928, as by Lord Charnwood

BENSON, JOHN R.
Death Opens the Ball. Cassell, 1935

BENSON, MATTHEW
Crimson Poppies. Detective Tales

BENSON, O. G.
Cain's Woman. Dell, 1960   [Chi.]

BENSON, (ELEANOR) THEODORA (ROBY). 1906-1968.
Rehearsal for Death. Gollancz, 1954

BENSON, THERESE. Pseudonym of Emilie Benson Knipe, 1870-1958.
Death Wears a Mask. Harper, 1935   [NYC]
Gallant Adventuress. Dodd, 1933
Strictly Private. Dodd, 1931   [NYC]

BENSTEAD, C(HARLES) R(ICHARD). 1896-   .
The Strange Adventures of Richard Conway Bowen. Hurst, 1927

BENT, SILAS. 1882-1945. Born in Kentucky; newspaperman and professor of journalism; author of biography of Oliver Wendell Holmes.
Buchanan of "The Press". Vanguard, 1932   [St. Louis]

BENTINCK, HENRY
Isoworg. Joseph, 1971

BENTINCK, RAY
Top Spot for Danger. Oracle, 1964

BENTLEY, E(DMUND) C(LERIHEW). 1875-1956. Ref: CC, DD, EM, MC, MP, TC. SC: Philip Trent = PT; Mr. Clerihew = C (see also: Warner Allen, 1881-1969). Set: Eng.
The Chill; see Elephant's Work
Elephant's Work. Hodder, 1950; Knopf, 1950. Also published as: The Chill. Dell, 1953
Trent Intervenes. Nelson, 1938; Knopf, 1938   ss   PT
Trent's Last Case. Nelson, 1913. U.S. title: The Woman in Black. Century, 1913   (Later U.S. editions have the British title.)   PT
Trent's Own Case, with (Herbert) Warner Allen, 1881-1969, q.v. Constable, 1936; Knopf, 1936   PT,C
The Woman in Black; see Trent's Last Case

BENTLEY, H. CUMBERLAND
-A Dream's Fulfillment. Macqueen, 1895

BENTLEY, JOHN. Ref: CC, MP. SC: Glen Gibson = GG; Sir Richard Herrivell = RH; Dick Marlow = DM. Set: Eng.
The Berg Case. Eldon, 1934. U.S. title: The Eyes of Death. Doubleday, 1934   RH
Bullets Make Holes. Hutchinson, 1945   GG
Call Off the Corpse. Hutchinson, 1947. U.S. title: Kill Me Again. Dodd, 1947   GG   [L.I.]
Dangerous Waters. Hutchinson, 1939   DM
Dark Disguise. Hutchinson, 1946
The Dead Do Talk. Hutchinson, 1944   DM
The Eyes of Death; see The Berg Case
The Fairbairn Case. Chapman, 1936   RH
Front Page Murder. Hutchinson, 1940. U.S. title: Mr. Marlow Stops for Brandy. Houghton, 1940   DM
The Griffith Case. Eldon, 1935   RH
The Hartland Case. Chapman, 1939   RH
The Iron Orchid. Hutchinson, 1950
It Was Murder, They Said. Hutchinson, 1948   GG
Kill Me Again; see Call Off the Corpse
The Landor Case. Chapman, 1937   RH
The L'Estrange Case. Eldon, 1935   RH
Macedonian Mixup. Hutchinson, 1943   DM   [Rome]
Mr. Marlow Chooses Wine. Houghton, 1941   DM (British title?)   [Fr.]
Mr. Marlow Stops for Brandy; see Front Page Murder
Mr. Marlow Takes to Rye. Houghton, 1942   DM (British title?)   [ship]
Obsession for Two. Hutchinson, 1949
The Opperman Case. Chapman, 1936   RH
Pattern for Perfidy. Hutchinson, 1946   GG
Prelude to Trouble. Hutchinson, 1939   DM
The Radcliffe Case. Chapman, 1938   RH
Rendezvous with Death. Hutchinson, 1941   DM
The Whitney Case. Chapman, 1937   RH

BENTLEY, JOYCE
Dangerous Refuge. Hurst, 1974
Secret of Strangeways. PB, 1976   [1793, Eng.]

BENTLEY, NICOLAS (CLERIHEW). 1907-1978. Ref: CA, CC, TC. Set: Eng.
The Events of That Week. Collins, 1972; St. Martin's, 1972
The Floating Dutchman. Joseph, 1950; Duell, 1951
Gammon and Espionage. Cresset, 1938
Inside Information. Duetsch, 1974; Penguin (U.S.), 1978
Third Party Risk. Joseph, 1953   [Fr.]
The Tongue-Tied Canary. Joseph, 1948; Duell, 1949

BENTLEY, PHYLLIS (ELEANOR). 1894-1977. Ref: CA, EM, TC.
The House of Moreys. Gollancz, 1953; Macmillan, 1953   [1809, Eng.]

BENTLEY, ROBERT
Here There Be Dragons. Ontario, 1972

BENTON, JOHN. 1933-   .
Marji and the Kidnap Plot. Spire, 1980   [NYC]
Sherri. Spire, 1980

BENTON, JOHN L. Pseudonym of Thomas Albert Curry, 1900-1976. Other pseudonym: Albert Jeffers, q.v. SC: Stephen Duane = SD.
The Art Treasure Murders. Gateway, 1940. British title: Duane and the Art Murders. Cassell, 1939   SD   [Boston]
Duane and the Art Murders; see The Art Treasure Murders
Duane of the FBI. Dodge, 1937. British title: Duane of the G-Men. Cassell, 1938   SD   [L.I.]
Duane of the G-Men; see Duane of the FBI
Talent for Murder. Gateway, 1942   [NYC]

BENTON, KENNETH (CARTER). 1909-   . Ref: CA, TC. SC: Peter Craig, in at least those marked PC.
Craig and the Jaguar. Macmillan (London), 1973; Walker, 1974   PC   [Peru]
Craig and the Midas Touch. Macmillan (London), 1975; Walker, 1976   PC   [Mid. East]
Craig and the Tunisian Tangle. Macmillan (London), 1974; Walker, 1975   PC   [Tun.]
The Red Hen Conspiracy. Macmillan (London), 1977   [Arg.]
A Single Monstrous Act. Macmillan (London), 1976
Sole Agent. Collins, 1970; Walker, 1974   PC   [Lisbon]
Spy in Chancery. Collins, 1972; Walker, 1973   PC   [Rome]
24th Level. Collins, 1969; Dodd, 1970   PC   [Brazil]

BERARD, L.
A Servant of Satan. Street, 1889

BERCKMAN, EVELYN (DOMENICA). 1900-1978. Ref: CA, CC, EM, TC.
Be All and End All; see Journey's End
The Beckoning Dream. Dodd, 1955; Eyre, 1956. Also published as: Worse Than Murder. Dell, 1957
The Blessed Plot; see The Crown Estate
Blind Girl's Buff. Dodd, 1962; Eyre, 1962
The Blind Villain. Dodd, 1957; Eyre, 1957. Also published as: House of Terror. Dell, 1960
A Case in Nullity. Doubleday, 1968; Eyre, 1967
The Crown Estate. Doubleday, 1976. British title: The Blessed Plot. H. Hamilton, 1976
Do You Know This Voice? Dodd, 1960; Eyre, 1961
The Evil of Time. Dodd, 1954; Eyre, 1955   [Ger.]
A Finger to Her Lips. Doubleday, 1971; Hale, 1971
The Fourth Man on the Rope. Doubleday, 1972; H. Hamilton, 1972
The Heir of Starvelings. Doubleday, 1967; Eyre, 1968   [Eng.]
House of Terror; see The Blind Villain
The Hovering Darkness. Dodd, 1957; Eyre, 1958   [ship]
Indecent Exposure; see The Nightmare Chase
Jewel of Death; see The Strange Bedfellow
Journey's End. Doubleday, 1977. British title: Be All and End All. H. Hamilton, 1976
Keys from a Window; see A Thing That Happens to You
Lament for Four Brides. Dodd, 1959; Eyre, 1960   [Fr.]
The Long Arm of the Prince. Hale, 1968   [Eng., ca.1600]
The Nightmare Chase. Doubleday, 1975. British title: Indecent Exposure. H. Hamilton, 1975   [Eng.]
No Known Grave. Dodd, 1958; Eyre, 1959
She Asked for It. Doubleday, 1969; H. Hamilton, 1970   [L.A.]
A Simple Case of Ill-Will. Dodd, 1965; Eyre, 1964
The Stake in the Game. Doubleday, 1973; H. Hamilton, 1971
Stalemate. Doubleday, 1966; Eyre, 1966
The Strange Bedfellow. Dodd, 1956; Eyre, 1957. Also published as: Jewel of Death. Pyramid, 1968   [Ger.]
A Thing That Happens to You. Dodd, 1964. British title: Keys from a Window. Eyre, 1965
The Victorian Album. Doubleday, 1973; H. Hamilton, 1973   [Eng.]
The Voice of Air. Doubleday, 1970; Hale, 1971   [Fr.]
Wait; see Wait, Just You Wait
Wait, Just You Wait. Doubleday, 1974. British title: Wait. H. Hamilton, 1973
Worse Than Murder; see The Beckoning Dream

BERCOVICI, ALFRED. Pseudonyms: Alberta Simpson Carter, Alberta Simpson, qq.v.
The Falmont Claiments. Curtis, 1973

BERCOVICI, ERIC. Born in NYC; film and TV writer and producer.
Wolftrap. Atheneum, 1979; Gollancz, 1979

BERENT, MARK. Joint pseudonym with Peter Lars Sandberg, 1934-   , q.v.: Berent Sandberg, q.v.

BERESFORD, ELIZABETH
Love Remembered. Hale, 1970; Dale, 1978

BERESFORD, HUGH and C. S. ST. BRELADE SEALE
The Second Guest. Baker, 1949   (1-act play.)

BERESFORD, J(OHN) D(AVYS). 1873-1947. Ref: CC.
The Decoy. Collins, 1927   [Fr.]
An Innocent Criminal. Collins, 1931; Dutton, 1931
The Instrument of Destiny. Collins, 1928; Bobbs, 1928
The Meeting Place and other stories. Faber, 1929   ss
Nineteen Impressions. Sidgwick, 1918   ss

BERESFORD, LESLIE (GEORGE). 1899-   .
Murder Can Be Such Fun! Long, 1947
The Other Mr. North. Long, 1926
The Way of Deception. Odhams, 1922

The Web of Wan Li. Gramol, 1935
What's at the End? Jenkins, 1937 [Fr.]

BERESFORD, MARCUS. 1919-   . Pseudonym:
Marc Brandel, q.v.

BERG, ADAM W.
Cassandra, Goodbye. Carlyle, 1980

BERGER, THOMAS (LOUIS). 1924-   . Ref:
CA.
Killing Time. Dial, 1967; Eyre, 1968
Sneaky People. Simon, 1975
Who Is Teddy Villanova? Delacorte,
1977; Eyre, 1977 [NYC]

BERGES, MAX L.
Woman of Shanghai. Digit, 1959
[Shanghai]

BERGIUS, C. C. Pseudonym of Egon Maria
Zimmer, 1910-   .
The Noble Forger. Barker, 1962 (Translation of "Der Falscher." Germany, 1960.)

BERGMAN, ANDREW. ca.1946-   . Ref: TC.
SC: Jack LeVine, in both titles.
The Big Kiss-Off of 1944. Holt, 1974;
Hutchinson, 1975 [NYC, 1944]
Hollywood and LeVine. Holt, 1975;
Hutchinson, 1976 [L.A., 1947]

BERGMAN, LEE
Walk Softly, Walk Deadly. Belmont, 1963
[NYC]

BERGNER, JAY
A Terrible Performance. Tandem, 1967

BERGQUIST, LILLIAN and IRVING MOORE
Your Shot, Darling! Morrow, 1948; Low,
1949 [L.A.]

BERGSON, LEO and ROBERT McMAHON. Leo
Bergson is the pseudonym of S(idney)
L(eo) Stebel, 1924-   , q.v. Robert
McMahon is the pseudonym of Robert
Weverka, 1926-   , q.v.
The Widowmaster. GM, 1967

BERGSTROM, LOUISE. 1914-   . Ref: CA.
The Pink Camellia. Bouregy, 1968
Strange Legacy. Bouregy, 1968

BERK, THEODORE GEORGE. Pseudonym: Theodore George, q.v.

BERKELEY, ANTHONY. Pseudonym of A(nthony)
B(erkeley) Cox, 1893-1970. q.v. Other
pseudonym: Francis Iles, q.v. Ref:
CC, EM, MC, MM, MP, TC. SC: Roger
Sheringham = RS; Ambrose Chitterwick
= AC. Set: Eng.
Dead Mrs. Stratton; see Jumping Jenny
Death in the House. Hodder, 1939;
Doubleday, 1939
Jumping Jenny. Hodder, 1933. U.S.
title: Dead Mrs. Stratton. Doubleday,
1933 RS
The Layton Court Mystery. Jenkins,
1925, as by "?"; Doubleday, 1929 RS
Mr. Pidgeon's Island; see Panic Party
Murder in the Basement. Hodder, 1932;
Doubleday, 1932 RS
The Mystery at Lover's Cave; see Roger
Sheringham and the Vane Mystery
Not to Be Taken. Hodder, 1938. U.S.
title: A Puzzle in Poison. Doubleday,
1938
Panic Party. Hodder, 1934. U.S. title:
Mr. Pidgeon's Island. Doubleday,
1934 RS
The Piccadilly Murder. Collins, 1929;
Doubleday, 1930 AC
The Poisoned Chocolates Case. Collins,
1929; Doubleday, 1929 RS,AC
A Puzzle in Poison; see Not to Be Taken
Roger Sheringham and the Vane Mystery.
Collins, 1927. U.S. title: The Mystery at Lover's Cave. Simon, 1927 RS
The Second Shot. Hodder, 1930; Doubleday, 1931 RS
The Silk Stocking Murders. Collins,
1928; Doubleday, 1928 RS
Top Storey Murder. Hodder, 1931. U.S.
title: Top Story Murder. Doubleday,
1931 RS
Trial and Error. Hodder, 1937; Doubleday, 1937 AC
The Wychford Poisoning Case. Collins,
1926; Doubleday, 1930 RS

BERKELEY, AUGUST
A Modern Quixote. American Publishing,
1884

BERLINER, ROSS. Pseudonym of a physician
and teacher at an eastern U.S. university.
The Manhood Ceremony. Simon, 1978 [Va.]

BERMAN, ARNOLD. Pseudonym: Anne-Marie
Bretonne, q.v.

BERNANOS, GEORGES. 1888-1948. Ref: CA,
MP.
A Crime. Dutton, 1936. British title:
The Crime. Hale, 1936 (Translation
of "Un Crime." Paris, 1935.) [Fr.]

BERNARD, GEORGE
Moment of the Predator. Leisure, 1980

BERNARD, JAY. Pseudonym of Raymond
H(arold) Sawkins, 1923-   , q.v.
Other pseudonyms: Colin Forbes,
Richard Raine, qq.v.
The Burning Fuse. Harcourt, 1970 [Ger.]

BERNARD, JOEL
The Thinking Machine Affair. Four
Square, 1967; Ace, 1970 (Novelization of the "Man from U.N.C.L.E."
TV series.)

BERNARD, RAFE
The Halo Highway. Corgi, 1967. U.S.
title: Army of the Undead. Pyramid,
1967 (Novelization of "The Invaders"
TV series.)

BERNARD, ROBERT. Pseudonym of Robert Bernard Martin, 1918-   . Ref: CC.
Born in Illinois; member English department of Princeton University
1951-1975; author of works on Victorian literature. SC: Millicent
Hetherege = MH.
Deadly Meeting. Norton, 1970 MH [New
Eng., acad.]
Death Takes a Sabbatical. Norton, 1967.
British title: Death Takes the Last
Train. Constable, 1967 [Eng.]
Death Takes the Last Train; see Death
Takes a Sabbatical
Illegal Entry. Norton, 1972; Faber,
1973 MH

BERNARD, THELMA RENE. 1940-   . Ref: CA.
Blue Marsh. Pinnacle, 1972
Moonshadow Mansion. Pinnacle, 1973
[Eng.]
Winds of Wakefield. Pinnacle, 1972

BERNARD, TREVOR
Brightlight. Manor, 1977

BERNEDE, A(RTHUR). 1871-1937. SC: Chantecoq, in both titles, set in Fr.
The Haunted House. Reader's Library,
1930
The Mystery of the Louvre. Reader's
Library, 1929; World Wide, 1929

BERNERS, LORD [GERALD HUGH TYRWHITT-
WILSON]. 1883-1950.
The Camel. Constable, 1936

BERNHARD, RITA SAMSON. 1945-   .
The Girls in 5J. Dial, 1977; H. Hamilton, 1978 [NYC]

BERNHARD, ROBERT. ca.1930-   . Born in
Brooklyn; educated in sciences;
designer of electronic brains, then
freelance medical and science writer.
The Ullman Code. Putnam, 1975

BERNIER, JOHN M.
Mission to Burundi. Manor, 1979 [Afr.]

BERNSTEIN, KEN. Overseas NBC-TV correspondent.
Intercept. Coward, 1971 [Russ.]
The Senator's Ransom. Coward, 1971
[Rio de J.]

BERRIDGE, ELIZABETH. 1921-   . Ref: CA.
Across the Common. Heinemann, 1964;
Coward, 1965

BERROW, (CYRIL) NORMAN. 1902-   . Born
in England; has lived most of his
life in Australia and New Zealand.
SC: Det.-Insp. Courtenay, in at
least those marked C; Michael Revel,
in at least those marked MR; Det.-
Insp. Lancelot Carolus Smith, in at
least those marked LS. Set: Eng.
The Bishop's Sword. Ward, 1948 LS
The Claws of the Cougar. Ward, 1957
[S. Am.]
Don't Go Out After Dark. Ward, 1950 LS
Don't Jump, Mr. Boland! Ward, 1954
The Eleventh Plague. Ward, 1953 [Syd.]
Fingers for Ransom. Ward, 1939 MR
The Footprints of Satan. Ward, 1950 LS
Ghost House. Ward, 1940. Revised edition: Hale, 1979; St. Martin's, 1980
It Howls at Night. Ward, 1937 [Sp.]
The Lady's in Danger. Ward, 1955
Murder in the Melody. Ward, 1940 MR
Oil Under the Window. Ward, 1936

One Thrilling Night. Ward, 1937 C
The Secret Dancer. Ward, 1936 C
The Singing Room. Ward, 1948 MR
The Smokers of Hashish. Eldon, 1934
The Spaniard's Thumb. Ward, 1949 LS
The Terror in the Fog. Ward, 1938
[Gib.]
The Three Tiers of Fantasy. Ward, 1947
LS
Words Have Wings. Ward, 1946 MR

BERRY, ARTHUR
Take Death for a Lover. Five Star,
ca.1946

BERRY, J(OHN) L(OUIS)
A Close Call. Ogilvie, 1888
-Linked with Fate. H. J. Smith, 1892

BERRY, JOHN (EDGAR)
Don't Betray Me. Signet, 1963; Jenkins,
1964 [Fr.]

BERTHOLD, MARY PADDOCK. 1909-   . Ref:
CA.
A Local Call. Vantage, 1969 [Mont.]

BERTON, GUY. Joint pseudonym of Guy Robert La Coste and Eadfrid A. Bingham.
Art Thou the Man? Dodd, 1905

BERWICK, JOHN
The Secret of Saint Florel. Macmillan
(London), 1897

BESANT, WALTER, 1836-1901, and JAMES
RICE, 1843-1882.
This Son of Vulcan. Low, 1876; Dodd,
1888

BESSELL, J. PERCIVAL. Set: Eng.
John Rutland's Romance. Low, 1921;
Macaulay, 1921
Paid Out. Low, 1919; Macaulay, 1919
The Price of an Impulse. Palmer, 1927

BESSIE, ALVAH (CECIL). 1904-   .
Bread and a Stone. Modern Age, 1941;
Swan, 1948

BEST, (OSWALD) HERBERT. 1894-   . Ref:
CA. Set: Afr., W., in both titles.
The Mystery of the Flaming Hut. Cassell, 1932; Harper, 1932
The Skull Beneath the Eaves. Grayson,
1933

BESTE, R(AYMOND) VERNON. 1908-   . Ref:
CA.
Faith Has No Country. Hodder, 1961.
U.S. title: The Moonbeams. Harper,
1961 [Fr., WWII]
The Moonbeams; see Faith Has No Country
Next Time I'll Pay My Own Fare. Allen,
1969; Simon, 1969 [Sp.]
Repeat the Instructions. Allen, 1968;
Harper, 1967
Seeds of Destruction. Hodder, 1964

BESTER, ALFRED. 1913-   . Ref: CA.
The Computer Connection. Berkley, 1975.
British title: Extro. Eyre, 1975
The Demolished Man. Shasta, 1953;
Sidgwick, 1953
Extro; see The Computer Connection
Golem 100. Simon, 1980; Sidgwick, 1980
The Rat Race; see Who He?
Who He? Dial, 1953. British title: The
Rat Race. Panther, 1959. Reprinted in
the U.S. under the British title:
Berkley, 1956

BESTOR, CLINTON. See: George Clinton
Bestor.

BESTOR, GEORGE CLINTON
The Corpse Came Calling (by Clinton
Bestor). Phoenix, 1941
Postage Stamp Murder. Dial, 1935; Low,
1936 [Tahiti]
Prelude to Murder. Dial, 1936; Low,
1936 [Minn.]

BETCHERMAN, BARBARA. Born in Toronto;
has degrees in philosophy and law;
was federal prosecutor in Canada.
Suspicions. Putnam, 1980; Macdonald,
1980 [NYC]

BETHUNE, J. G. Pseudonym of Edward
S(ylvester) Ellis, 1840-1916, q.v.
The "F" Cipher. Price McGill, 1892
The Great Berwyck Bank Burglary; see
Hands Up!
Hands Up! or, the Great Bank Burglary.
U.S. Book Co., 1890. Also published
as: The Great Berwyck Bank Burglary.
Collier, 1893
The Third Man. Cassell (NYC), 1893

BETTANY, GEORGE (KERNAHAN GWYNNE). 1891- .
  Dangerous Haven. Skeffington, 1949
  Man Hunt. Skeffington, 1951
  Murder at Benfleet. Skeffington, 1946
  Scarbrow. Skeffington, 1934
  The Secret of the Swamp. Skeffington, 1931
  Silent Mountain. Skeffington, 1935 [Can.]
  Valley of the Lost Gold. Skeffington, 1934
  Villainy. Skeffington, 1936

BETTAUER, HUGO. 1872-1925. Shot by a fanatical student who thought this novel gave too morbid a view of life in Vienna.
  Viennese Love. Macaulay, 1929; Cassell, 1929 (Translation of "Die Freudlose Gasse." Vienna, 1924.) [Vienna]

BETTERIDGE, ANNE. Pseudonym of Margaret (Edith) Newman, 1926-   , q.v.
  Sirocco. Hurst, 1970; Beagle, 1973

BETTERIDGE, DON. Pseudonym of Bernard (Charles) Newman, 1897-1968, q.v. SC: "Tiger" Lester = TL.
  Balkan Spy. Jenkins, 1942 TL [Balkans]
  The Case of the Berlin Spy. Hale, 1954 TL
  Cast Iron Alibi. Jenkins, 1939
  Contact Man. Hale, 1960 TL
  Dictator's Destiny. Jenkins, 1945 TL [Ger.]
  The Escape of General Gerard. Jenkins, 1943 TL [Ger.]
  The Gibralter Conspiracy. Hale, 1955 TL [Gib.]
  Not Single Spies. Hale, 1951 TL
  The Package Holiday Spy Case. Hale, 1962 TL
  The Potsdam Murder Plot. Jenkins, 1947 TL [Ger.]
  Scotland Yard Alibi. Jenkins, 1938
  Spies Left! Hale, 1950 TL
  The Spies of Peenemunde. Hale, 1958 TL
  Spy—Counter Spy. Hale, 1953 TL

BETZ, INGRID
  The Mourning of the Dove. Nelson (Toronto), 1976; Hale, 1976

BEUTTLER, EDWARD IVAN OAKLEY. Pseudonym: Ivan Butler, q.v.

BEVERLEY, BARRINGTON
  The Air Devil. Allan, 1934

BEVIS, JAMES. See: Marten Cumberland, 1892-   .

BEYER, WILLIAM GRAY
  Death of a Puppeteer. Mystery House, 1946
  Eenie, Meenie, Minie—Murder! Mystery House, 1945. British title: Murder by Arrangement. Partridge, 1948. Also published as: Murder Secretary. Bart, 1946
  Murder by Arrangement; see Eenie, Meenie, Minie—Murder!
  Murder Secretary; see Eenie, Meenie, Minie—Murder!

BEYMER, WILLIAM GILMORE. 1881-   .
  12:20 P.M. McGraw, 1944. Also published as: The Middle of Midnight. Whittlesey, 1947 [Ger.]

BEYNON, JANE. 1915-   . Pseudonym: Lange Lewis, q.v. Ref: CA, CC.
  Cypress Man. Bobbs, 1944

BEYNON, JOHN. Pseudonym of John Wyndham Parkes Lucas Beynon Harris, 1903-1969. Ref: CA.
  Foul Play Suspected. Newnes, 1935

BEYNON-HARRIS, VIVIAN
  Trouble at Hanard. Partridge, 1948

BEZZERIDES, A(LBERT) I(SAAC). 1908-   .
  Thieves Market. Scribner, 1949 [S.F.]

BICKEL, MARY (DUPUY)
  Brassbound. Coward, 1934. British title: The Trial of Linda Stuart. H. Hamilton, 1935

BICKERS, RICHARD (LESLIE) TOWNSHEND. 1917-   . Pseudonym: David Richards, q.v. Ref: CA. SC: Mark Stratton, in at least those marked MS.
  The Hellions. Hale, 1965 MS
  Hunt and Kill. Hale, 1969
  Maraskar Bound. Hale, 1969
  My Enemy Came Nigh. Hale, 1970
  Scent of Mayhem. Hale, 1965 MS [Brus.]

BICKERSTAFFE-DREW, FRANCIS BROWNING. 1858-1948. Pseudonym: John Ayscough, q.v.

BICKERTON, DEREK. 1926-   . Ref: CA.
  The Gold Run. Eyre, 1960
  King of the Sea. Granada, 1980; Random, 1979 [Haw.]
  Payroll. Eyre, 1959

BICKHAM, JACK [JOHN MILES BICKHAM]. 1930-   . Pseudonym: John Miles, q.v. Ref: CA. SC: Charity Ross = CR.
  -The Excalibur Disaster. Doubleday, 1978; Macmillan (London), 1979
  The Regensburg Legacy. Doubleday, 1980; Hale, 1981 [Afr.]
  Target: Charity Ross. Doubleday, 1968 CR
  -The War Against Charity Ross. Doubleday, 1967 CR

BICKNELL, FRANK MARTIN. 1854-1916.
  The Bicycle Highwayman. Estes, 1900

BIDDLE, A(NTHONY) J(OSEPH) DREXEL. 1874-1948.
  Word for Word and Letter for Letter. Gay & Bird, 1898 [Phil.]

BIDMEAD, CHARLES
  The Man in the Shadows. Rich, 1954
  The Silent Men. Rich, 1955

BIDSTON, LESTER. 1884-   . Liverpool schoolmaster. All titles below feature Sexton Blake and were published by Amalgamated Press.
  Crooks Ltd. 1929
  The Cup Final Crime. 1932
  The Fatal Alibi. 1931
  Gang's Prisoners. 1931
  The Mill of Fear. 1932
  The Motor Coach Murder. 1933
  The Mystery of Oldham. 1930
  The Phantom of the Mill. 1927
  The Silent Syndicate. 1931

BIDWELL, MARGARET. SC: Mr. Hodson, in both titles, set in Eng.
  Death and His Brother. Hurst, 1940 [acad.]
  Death on the Agenda. Hurst, 1939

BIDWELL, MARJORY ELIZABETH SARA. Pseudonym: Mary Anne Gibbs, q.v.

BIER, JESSE. 1925-   . Ref: CA.
  -Trial at Bannock. Harcourt, 1963

BIERSTADT, EDWARD HALE. 1891-   . Born in NYC; amateur criminologist and author of books on crime and prison reform.
  Satan Was a Man. Doubleday, 1935. British title: Murder by Inspiration. Chapman, 1935 [NYC]

BIGDEN, HENRY
  Late into the Night. Cassell, 1962

BIGELOW, JOHN MASON
  Death Is an Early Riser. Scribner, 1940

BIGG, PATRICIA NINA. 1932-   . Pseudonym: Patricia Ainsworth, q.v.

BIGGERS, EARL DERR. 1884-1933. See also: George M(ichael) Cohan, 1879-1942. Ref: CC, DD, EM, MC, MP, TC. SC: Charlie Chan = CC (continued by Dennis Lynds, 1924-   , q.v.).
  The Agony Column. Bobbs, 1916. Also published as: Second Floor Mystery. Grosset, 1930 [Eng.]
  Behind That Curtain. Bobbs, 1928; Harrap, 1928 CC [S.F.]
  The Black Camel. Bobbs, 1929; Cassell, 1930 CC [Haw.]
  Charlie Chan Carries On. Bobbs, 1930; Cassell, 1931 CC
  The Chinese Parrot. Bobbs, 1926; Harrap, 1927 CC [Calif.]
  Earl Derr Biggers Tells Ten Stories. Bobbs, 1933 ss
  Fifty Candles. Bobbs, 1926 [S.F.]
  The House Without a Key. Bobbs, 1925; Harrap, 1926 CC [Haw.]
  Inside the Lines, with Robert Welles Ritchie. Bobbs, 1915 [Gib.]
  Keeper of the Keys. Bobbs, 1932; Cassell, 1932 CC [Calif.]
  Love Insurance. Bobbs, 1914 [Fla.]
  Second Floor Mystery; see The Agony Column
  Seven Keys to Baldpate. Bobbs, 1913; Mills, 1914 [N.Y.]

BIGGLE, LLOYD (JR.). 1923-   . Ref: CA. SC: Jan Darzek, in all titles, set in the future.
  All the Colors of Darkness. Doubleday, 1963; Dobson, 1964
  Silence Is Deadly. Doubleday, 1977; Millington, 1980
  This Darkening Universe. Doubleday, 1975; Millington, 1979
  Watchers of the Dark. Doubleday, 1966; Chapp, 1968
  The Whirligig of Time. Doubleday, 1979

BIGGS, JOHN (JR.). 1895-1979.
  Seven Days Whipping. Scribner, 1928; Heinemann, 1929

BILLANY, DAN. 1913-1945. Born in England; a teacher.
  It Takes a Thief; see The Opera House Murders
  The Opera House Murders. Faber, 1940. U.S. title: It Takes a Thief. Harper, 1940
  -The Trap. Faber, 1950

BILLETDOUX, FRANCOIS (PAUL). 1927-   . Ref: CA.
  Chez Torpe. Secker, 1963; Hill, 1964, in "Two Plays" (3-act play.) (Translation of "Va Donc Chez Torpe." Paris, 1962.)

BILLETT, MABEL (BROUGHTON). 1892-   .
  Calamity House. Hutchinson, 1927
  The Robot Detective. Hutchinson, 1932
  The Shadow on the Stepps. Hutchinson, 1930
  Smooth Silence. Ryerson, 1936

BILLING, GRAHAM
  The Alpha Trip. Allen, 1969

BINDER, FREDERICK MOORE. 1920-   . Pseudonym: Andrew Moore, q.v.

BINDER, OTTO O(SCAR). 1911-1974. Pseudonym: Ione Frances Turek, q.v.
  The Hospital Horror. Popular Library, 1973 [hosp.]

BINDLOSS, HAROLD (EDWARD). 1866-1945. Set: mostly Can.
  The Border Trail; see Carter's Triumph
  -The Broken Net. Ward, 1925. U.S. title: Prairie Gold. Stokes, 1925
  The Broken Trail; see Sour Grapes
  Carmen's Messenger. Ward, 1917; Stokes, 1917
  Carter's Triumph. Ward, 1931. U.S. title: The Border Trail. Stokes, 1931
  The Coast of Adventure; see A Risky Game
  -The Firm Hand. Ward, 1928. U.S. title: The Lone Hand. Stokes, 1928
  The Frontiersman; see Frontiersmen
  Frontiersmen. Ward, 1929. U.S. title: The Frontiersman. Stokes, 1929
  -Halford's Adventure. Ward, 1928. U.S. title: Mystery Reef. Stokes, 1928
  Harden's Escape. Ward, 1930. U.S. title: The Man at Willow Ranch. Stokes, 1930 [Can.]
  The Lean Years. Ward, 1931. U.S. title: The Prairie Patrol. Stokes, 1931
  The Lone Hand; see The Firm Hand
  The Long Portage; see The Pioneer
  The Man at Willow Ranch; see Harden's Escape
  -The Mistress of Bonaventure. Chatto, 1903; Stokes, 1907
  -The Mountaineers. Ward, 1922. U.S. title: Northwest! Stokes, 1922
  Mystery Reef; see Halford's Adventure
  Northwest! see The Mountaineers
  -The Pioneer. Ward, 1912. U.S. title: The Long Portage. Stokes, 1912
  Prairie Gold; see The Broken Net
  The Prairie Patrol; see The Lean Years
  -A Risky Game. Ward, 1915. U.S. title: The Coast of Adventure. Stokes, 1915
  Sour Grapes. Ward, 1926. U.S. title: The Broken Trail. Stokes, 1926
  The Wilderness Patrol. Ward, 1923; Stokes, 1923
  -Winston of the Prairie. Stokes, 1907 (British title?)
  Wyndham's Pal; see Wyndham's Partner
  -Wyndham's Partner. Ward, 1919. U.S. title: Wyndham's Pal. Stokes, 1919

BINGHAM, CARSON. Pseudonym of Bruce (Bingham) Cassiday, 1920-   , q.v. Other pseudonyms: Nick Carter, Mary Anne Drew, Annie Laurie McAllister, Annie Laurie McMurdie, Michael Stratford, qq.v.
  The Gang Girls. Monarch, 1963
  It Happened in Hawaii. Monarch, 1962 [Haw.]
  Run Tough, Run Hard. Monarch, 1961

BINGHAM, EADFRID A. Joint pseudonym with Guy Robert La Coste: Guy Berton, q.v.

BINGHAM, JOHN (MICHAEL WARD). 1908- . Ref: CA, CC, MC, TC. SC: Ducane (also called Vandoren) = D.
A Case of Libel. Gollancz, 1963
Deadly Picnic. Macmillan (London), 1980
The Double Agent. Gollancz, 1966; Dutton, 1967 D
Five Roundabouts to Heaven. Gollancz, 1953. U.S. title: The Tender Poisoner. Dodd, 1953
A Fragment of Fear. Gollancz, 1965; Dutton, 1966
God's Defector. Macmillan (London), 1976. U.S. title: Minister of Death. Walker, 1977 D
Good Old Charlie; see I Love, I Kill
I Love, I Kill. Gollancz, 1968. U.S. title: Good Old Charlie. Simon, 1969
Inspector Morgan's Dilemma; see The Paton Street Case
Marion. Gollancz, 1958. U.S. title: Murder off the Record. Dodd, 1957
The Marriage Bureau Murders. Macmillan (London), 1977
Minister of Death; see God's Defector
Murder of a Witch; see The Third Skin
Murder off the Record; see Marion
Murder Plan Six. Gollancz, 1958; Dodd, 1959
My Name Is Michael Sibley. Gollancz, 1952; Dodd, 1952
Night's Black Agent. Gollancz, 1961; Dodd, 1961 [Nor.]
The Paton Street Case. Gollancz, 1955. U.S. title: Inspector Morgan's Dilemma. Dodd, 1956
The Tender Poisoner; see Five Roundabouts to Heaven
The Third Skin. Gollancz, 1954; Dodd, 1954. Also published as: Murder Is a Witch. Dell, 1957
Vulture in the Sun. Gollancz, 1971 D

BINGLEY, D(AVID) E(RNEST). 1920- . Pseudonyms: Henry Chesham, George Fallon, qq.v. Ref: CA.
-Caribbean Crisis. Hale, 1966 [Carib.]
The Elusive Witness. Hale, 1966

BINKLEY, ANNE
-What Shall I Cry. Harcourt, 1968; Gollancz, 1968

BINNIE, STEWART
Across the Water. Secker, 1979

BINNS, OTWELL. 1872- . Pseudonym: Ben Bolt, q.v.
An Adventurer of the Bay. Ward, 1926
Behind the Ranges. Ward, 1928
The Blue Sash. Ward, 1935
By Papuan Waters. Ward, 1938 [New Guinea]
Clancy of the Mounted Police. Ward, 1923 [Can.]
The Diamond Trail. Ward, 1928 [Fr.]
Doc Churston. Ward, 1933
The Drums of Doom. Ward, 1927
The Far Pursuit. Ward, 1936
The Flaming Crescent. Ward, 1931
Flotsam of the Line. Ward, 1926
Forest Exile. Ward, 1933
A Gipsy of the North. Ward, 1924
Gold Is King. Ward, 1934
The Grey Rat. Ward, 1931
A Hazard of the Snows. Ward, 1921
In the Flashlight. Ward, 1937
Java Jack. Ward, 1925
Jim Trelawney. Ward, 1930
The Lady of the Miniature. Ward, 1918
The Lady of the North Star. Ward, 1919; Knopf, 1922 [Can.]
The Last Door. Ward, 1935
The Law of the Hills. Ward, 1925
The Lifting of the Shadow. Ward, 1921
The Love That Believeth. Ward, 1920
The Man from Maloba. Ward, 1917
A Man of Dartmoor. Ward, 1939
-A Mating in the Wilds. Ward, 1920; Knopf, 1920
The Mystery of the Heart. Ward, 1919
The Nets of Fate. Mellifont, 1932
The Poisoned Pen. Ward, 1937
The Red Token. Ward, 1934 [Far East]
Ringing Sands. Ward, 1927
The Secret Adventure. Ward, 1933
The Secret Pearls. Ward, 1930 [S. Pac.]
The Shining Trail. Ward, 1935
A Shot in the Woods. Ward, 1938
A Sin of Silence. Ward, 1918
Snowbird. Ward, 1931
A Soldier of the Legion. Ward, 1937
A Tamer of Men. Ward, 1929
The Three Black Dots. Ward, 1929 [Mor.]
The Three Blue Anchors. Ward, 1934
Trader Random. Ward, 1932
The Trail of Adventure. Ward, 1923
The Treasure of Christophe. Ward, 1922 [Haiti]
The Vanished Guest. Ward, 1930
Weeds of Hate. Ward, 1936
White Gold. Ward, 1932
The White Hands of Justice. Ward, 1922

BIOY-CASARES, ADOLFO. 1914- . Ref: CA.
A Plan for Escape. Dutton, 1975

BIRCH, BRUCE
Subway in the Sky. Four Square, 1959 (Novelization of the movie.)

BIRCHALL, ROBERT. See: Jonathan Troy

BIRD, AL. Pseudonym.
Murder So Real. Coward, 1978

BIRD, BRANDON. Joint pseudonym of George Bird Evans, 1906- , and Kay Harris Evans, 1906- . Other joint pseudonym: Harris Evans, q.v. SC: Hampton Hume = HH.
Dead and Gone; see Downbeat for a Dirge
Death in Four Colors. Dodd, 1950; Constable, 1951 HH [NYC]
Downbeat for a Dirge. Dodd, 1952. Also published as: Dead and Gone. Dell, 1955 HH [NYC]
Hawk Watch. Dodd, 1954; Boardman, 1955 [W. Va.]
Never Wake a Dead Man. Dodd, 1950; Constable, 1952 HH [W. Va.]

BIRD, KENNETH. 1916- . Pseudonym: Peter Bloxham, q.v.
Bishop Must Move. Cassell, 1967
The Mozart Fiddle. Hale, 1969 [Sp.]
Murder in Vision. Hale, 1969
The Rainbow Coloured Hearse. Hale, 1970
Smash a Glass Image. Cassell, 1968

BIRD, MICHAEL J. 1928- .
Aphrodite Inheritance. Wingate, 1979

BIRKIN, CHARLES (LLOYD). 1907- . Ref: CA.
Dark Menace. Tandem, 1968 ss
-Devil's Spawn. Allan, 1934 ss
The Kiss of Death. Tandem, 1964; Award, 1969 ss
My Name Is Death. Panther, 1966; Award, 1970 ss
The Smell of Evil. Tandem, 1965; Award, 1969 ss
So Pale, So Cold, So Fair. Tandem, 1970 ss
Spawn of Satan. Award, 1970 ss
Where Terror Stalked. Tandem, 1966 ss

BIRKLEY, DOLAN. Pseudonym of (Julia Clara Catherine) Dolores (Birk Olsen) Hitchens, 1907-1973, q.v. Other pseudonyms: Noel Burke, D. B. Olsen, qq.v.
The Blue Geranium. Simon, 1941 [Calif.]
The Unloved. Doubleday, 1965; Hale, 1967 [Calif.]

BIRMINGHAM, GEORGE A. Pseudonym of James Owen Hannay, 1865-1950. Ref: CC.
-Adventurers of the Night. Doran, 1921 (British title?)
-Fed Up. Methuen, 1931; Bobbs, 1931
-Fidgets. Hodder, 1927. U.S. title: Gold, Gore and Gehenna. Bobbs, 1927 [Ire.]
Gold, Gore and Gehenna; see Fidgets
The Hymn Tune Mystery. Methuen, 1930; Bobbs, 1931 [church]
-The Island Mystery. Methuen, 1918; Doran, 1918 [Med. Is.]
The Lost Lawyer. Methuen, 1921 [Ire.]
-Miss Maitland's Spy. Methuen, 1940
The Search Party. Methuen, 1909; Doran, 1911 [Ire.]
Wild Justice. Methuen, 1930; Bobbs, 1930

BIRMINGHAM, MAISIE. 1914- . Ref: CA.
The Heat of the Sun. Collins, 1976
Sleep in a Ditch. Collins, 1978; Scribner, 1979
You Can Help Me. Collins, 1974

BIRMINGHAM, STEPHEN. 1932- . Ref: CA.
-The Towers of Love. Little, 1961; Collins, 1962

BIRNEY, HERMAN HOFFMAN. 1891-1958. Pseudonym: David Kent, q.v.

BISHOP, CASEY. See: Betty Black, 1927-

BISHOP, CECIL
Adventures of Ah Foo, the Chinese Sherlock Holmes. Mitre, 1943
The Blackmail Gang. Mellifont, 1937
Black Terror. Miller, 1945
Chinese Brown of Scotland Yard. Mellifont, 1937
Claws of the Red Dragon. Mellifont, 1937
Crime and the Underworld. Mitre, 1944 ss
Crime in a Big Way. Mitre, 1944 ss
The Kidnapper. Mellifont, 1937
Murder on the Second Floor. Everybody's, 1944
The Prince of Blackmail. Miller, 1945
The Shadow of Li Tong Su. Miller, 1945
Terror Comes to London. Everybody's, 1944

BISHOP, GEORGE
Destination: Death. Vega, ca.1962

BISHOP, GEORGE. Born in Montreal; radio emcee; writer for TV, motion pictures and magazines.
The Apparition. Bantam, 1979 [Calif.]

BISHOP, MALDEN GRANGE
Scylla. Ace, 1954 [L.A.]

BISHOP, MARY. Pseudonym of Beverly Mason.
Killraven. Dell, 1975 [Scot., past]
Widow's Walk. Dell, 1975 [Maine, 1870s]

BISHOP, MORRIS GILBERT. 1893-1973. Pseudonym: W. Bolingbroke Johnson, q.v.

BISHOP, R. F.
Camerton Slope; A Story of Mining Life. Cranston, 1893

BISHOP, SHEILA (GLENCAIRN)
The Durable Fire. Ace, 1972 (British title?)
-Goldsmith's Row. Hurst, 1969
House with Two Faces. Hurst, 1960; Ace, 1971
The Onlooker. Hurst, 1970; Ace, 1972 [Sic.]

BISHOP, STACEY. Pseudonym of George Johann Carl Antheil, 1900-1959. Ref: MC.
Death in the Dark. Faber, 1930

BISS, GERALD
Branded. Greening, 1908
The Door of the Unreal. Nash, 1919; Putnam, 1920
The Dupe. Greening, 1907; Brentano's, 1909
The Fated Five. Greening, 1910
The House of Terror. Greening, 1909
The White Rose Mystery. Greening, 1907

BISSAGAR, FREDERICK GEORGE
Entrapped; or, Charlie's First Crime. Aldine, 1894

BISSELL, ELAINE. Ref: CA.
-Women Who Wait. Evans, 1978

BITTLE, CAMILLA R.
The Boy in the Pool. Lippincott, 1962

BJERKE, ANDRE. 1918- . Pseudonym: Bernhard Borge, q.v.

BJORGUM, KENNETH L.
Bloodstone. Jove, 1980

BLACK, BETTY. 1927- , and CASEY BISHOP
The Sisterhood. Allen, 1977

BLACK, CAMPBELL. 1944- . Pseudonym: Thomas Altman, q.v. Joint pseudonym with Jeffrey (Andrew) Caine, 1944- q.v.: Jeffrey Campbell, q.v. Born in Glasgow; educated in philosophy; an editor, teacher of creative writing; came to U.S. in 1971.
Assassins and Victims. Macmillan (London), 1969; Harper's Magazine Press, 1970
Asterisk Destiny. Joseph, 1979; Morrow, 1978 [Wash. D.C.]
Brainfire. Joseph, 1980; Morrow, 1979
Death's Head. Collins, 1972; Lippincott, 1972 [Berlin, 1945]
Dressed to Kill. Bantam, 1980 (Novelization of the movie.)
The Punctual Rape. Macmillan (London), 1970; Lippincott, 1971

BLACK, DAVID
The Strangler. Manor, 1974

BLACK, E(LIZABETH) BEST. 1894- . SC: Peter Strangely, in both titles.
The Crime of the Chromium Bowl. Loring, 1934; Newnes, 1937 [Paris]
The Ravenelle Riddle. Loring, 1933 [Eng.]

BLACK, GAVIN. Pseudonym of Oswald (Morris) Wynd, 1913- , q.v. SC: Paul Harris, in all titles.

A Big Wind for Summer. Collins, 1975; Harper, 1976. Also published as: Gale Force. Fontana, 1978 [Hebrides]
The Bitter Tea. Collins, 1973; Harper, 1972 [Far East]
The Cold Jungle. Collins, 1969; Harper, 1969 [Scot.]
Dead Man Calling. Collins, 1962; Harper, 1962
A Dragon for Christmas. Collins, 1963; Harper, 1963 [China]
The Eyes Around Me. Collins, 1964; Harper, 1964 [H. Kong]
Gale Force; see A Big Wind for Summer
The Golden Cockatrice. Collins, 1974; Harper, 1975 [Macao]
Killer Moon; see A Moon for Killers
A Moon for Killers. Collins, 1976. Also published as: Killer Moon. Fontana, 1977
Night Run from Java. Collins, 1979 [Far East]
Suddenly, at Singapore... Collins, 1961 [Sing.]
A Time for Pirates. Collins, 1971; Harper, 1971 [Mal.]
A Wind of Death. Collins, 1967; Harper, 1967 [Thai.]
You Want to Die, Johnny? Collins, 1966; Harper, 1966 [Borneo]

BLACK, HAZELTON. Pseudonym: Scott Graham, q.v.

BLACK, HERMINA
Enmeshed. Eldon
Romance Comes to Scotland Yard. Hodder, 1969

BLACK, IAN STUART. 1915- . Ref: CA. SC: Peter Munro, in at least those marked PM.
Caribbean Strip. Constable, 1978 [Carib.]
Evan Less Legal! Evans, 1964 (Play.)
-The High Bright Sun. Hutchinson, 1962
In the Wake of a Stranger. Dakers, 1953
Journey to a Safe Place. Constable, 1979; St. Martin's, 1979 PM [Beirut]
The Man on the Bridge. Constable, 1975; St. Martin's, 1977 PM [Greece]
-The Passionate City. Heinemann, 1958; Viking, 1958
We Must Kill Toni. Evans, 1953; French (NYC), 1966 (3-act play.)
-The Yellow Flag. Hutchinson, 1959

BLACK, JOHN D. F.
Trouble Man. Dell, 1972 (Novelization of the movie.) [L.A.]

BLACK, JONATHAN. Pseudonym of Bela William von Block, 1922- . Other pseudonyms: Mercedes Endfield, E. L. McGinnis, qq.v.
Ride the Golden Tiger. Morrow, 1976; Hart-Davis, 1976

BLACK, LADBROKE (LIONEL DAY). 1877-1940. Pseudonym: Paul Urquhart, q.v. See also: T. C. St. J. Morton. SC: Sexton Blake (with many other authors): SB; Mr. Preed, in at least those marked P. Set: Eng.
The Case of the Crook Banker. Amalgamated, 1930 SB
-The Gorgon's Head. Low, 1932
-Her Convict Husband. Tinling, 1941
The Informer. Amalgamated, 1930 SB
The Killer at Large. Paul, 1937 P
Mr. Preed Investigates. Nelson, 1939 P
Mr. Preed's Gangster. Nelson, 1939 P
The Mystery Militiaman. Amalgamated, 1940 SB
-The Poison War. Paul, 1933
The Prince of Poisoners. Nicholson, 1932; Dial, 1932
The Wager. Methuen, 1927

BLACK, LAURA
Castle Raven. H. Hamilton, 1978. U.S. title: Ravenburn. St. Martin's, 1978 [Scot., 1800s]
Glendraco. H. Hamilton, 1977; St. Martin's, 1977 [1860, Scot.]
Ravenburn; see Castle Raven
Wild Cat. H. Hamilton, 1979; St. Martin's, 1979 [1862, Scot.]

BLACK, LIONEL. Pseudonym of Dudley Barker, 1910-1980. Other pseudonym: Anthony Matthews. Ref: CA, CC, TC. SC: Supt. Francis Foy, in at least those marked FF; Emma Greaves, in at least those marked EG; Kate Theobald, in at least those marked KT. Set: Eng.
Arafat Is Next! Collins, 1975; Stein, 1975 [Mid. East]
The Bait. Cassell, 1966 EG
Breakaway. Collins, 1970. U.S. title: Flood. Stein, 1971 FF

Chance to Die. Cassell, 1965 EG [Afr.]
Death by Hoax. Collins, 1974; Avon, 1978 KT
Death Has Green Fingers. Collins, 1971; Walker, 1971, as by Anthony Matthews KT
The Eve of the Wedding. Collins, 1980; Avon, 1981 KT
Flood; see Breakaway
The Foursome. Collins, 1978
A Healthy Way to Die. Collins, 1976; Avon, 1979 KT
The Lady Is a Spy; see Two Ladies in Verona
The Life and Death of Peter Wade. Collins, 1973; Stein, 1974 FF
Outbreak. Cassell, 1968; Stein, 1968
The Penny Murders. Collins, 1979; Avon, 1980 KT
A Provincial Crime. Cassell, 1960
Ransom for a Nude. Collins, 1972; Stein, 1972 FF
Swinging Murder. Cassell, 1969; Walker, 1969, as by Anthony Matthews KT
Two Ladies in Verona. Cassell, 1967. U.S. title: The Lady Is a Spy. Paperback Library, 1969 EG [It.]

BLACK, MANSELL. Pseudonym of Elleston Trevor, 1920- , q.v. Name originally: Trevor Dudley Smith, q.v. Other pseudonyms: Adam Hall, Howard North, Simon Rattray, Warwick Scott, Caesar Smith, qq.v. SC: Richard Vaness, in all titles.
Dead on Course. Hodder, 1951. Reprinted as by Elleston Trevor: White Lion, 1974
Shadow of Evil. Hodder, 1953
Sinister Cargo. Hodder, 1951
Steps in the Dark. Hodder, 1954

BLACK, PETER. Pseudonym.
Which of Them? Benn, 1932

BLACK, R(OBERT) JERE. 1892- .
The Killing of the Golden Goose. Loring, 1934 [Pa.]

BLACK, THOMAS B. 1910- . Born in Kansas. SC: Al Delaney, in all titles.
Four Dead Mice. Rinehart, 1954. Also published as: Million Dollar Murder. Bantam, 1955
Million Dollar Murder; see Four Dead Mice
The Pinball Murders. Reynal, 1947
The 3-13 Murders. Reynal, 1946
The Whitebird Murders. Reynal, 1946

BLACK, VERONICA. Pseudonym of Maureen Peters, 1935- . Ref: CA.
Dangerous Inheritance. Hale, 1969; Paperback Library, 1970
Echo of Margaret. Hale, 1978
The Enchanted Grotto. Hale, 1972
Fair Kilmeny. Hale, 1972; Berkley, 1973
Flame in the Snow. Hale, 1980
A Footfall in the Mist. Hale, 1971; Lenox, 1971
Greengirl. Hale, 1972
The House That Hated People. Hale, 1974
Master of Malcarew. Hale, 1971; Lenox, 1972
Minstrel's Leap. Hale, 1973
Moonflete. Hale, 1972; Berkley, 1973
Pilgrim of Desire. Hale, 1979
Portrait of Sarah. Hale, 1969; Berkley, 1973
Spin Me a Shadow. Hale, 1974
The Wayward Madonna. Hale, 1970; Lenox, 1970

BLACKBURN, BARBARA [EVELYN BARBARA BLACKBURN LEADER]. 1898- . Ref: CA.
City of Forever. Hale, 1963; Ace, 1966

BLACKBURN, JOHN (FENWICK). 1923- . Ref: CA, CC, TC. SC: Gen. Charles Kirk, in at least those marked CK. Set: mostly Eng.
Blow the House Down. Cape, 1970
Blue Octavo. Cape, 1963. U.S. title: Bound to Kill. Mill, 1963
Bound to Kill; see Blue Octavo
Broken Boy. Secker, 1959; Mill, 1962 CK
Bury Him Darkly. Cape, 1969; Putnam, 1970
Children of the Night. Cape, 1966; Putnam, 1969
Colonel Bogus. Cape, 1964. U.S. title: Packed for Murder. Mill, 1964 CK
The Cyclops Goblet. Cape, 1977
Dead Man Running. Secker, 1960; Mill, 1961
Dead Man's Handle. Cape, 1978
Deep Among the Dead Men. Cape, 1973 [Afr.]
Devil Daddy. Cape, 1972
The Face of the Lion. Cape, 1976

The Flame and the Wind. Cape, 1967 [ca. 30 A.D., Jerus.]
For Fear of Little Men. Cape, 1972
The Gaunt Woman. Cape, 1962; Mill, 1962 CK
The Household Traitors. Cape, 1971
Mister Brown's Bodies. Cape, 1975
Murder at Midnight; see Winds of Midnight
Nothing But the Night. Cape, 1968 CK
Our Lady of Pain. Cape, 1974
Packed for Murder; see Colonel Bogus
The Reluctant Spy; see A Scent of New-Mown Hay
A Ring of Roses. Cape, 1965. U.S. title: A Wreath of Roses. Mill, 1965 CK [Ger.]
A Scent of New-Mown Hay. Secker, 1958; Mill, 1958. Also published as: The Reluctant Spy. Lancer, 1966 CK
The Sins of the Father. Cape, 1979
A Sour Apple Tree. Secker, 1958; Mill, 1959 CK
The Winds of Midnight. Cape, 1964. U.S. title: Murder at Midnight. Mill, 1964 CK
A Wreath of Roses; see A Ring of Roses
The Young Man from Lima. Cape, 1968 CK [Mex.]

BLACKBURN, THOMAS
A Good Day to Die. Popular Library, 1967

BLACKER, IRWIN R(OBERT). 1919- . Ref: CA. SC: Richard Le Grande = RL.
Chain of Command. Cassell, 1965
The Kilroy Gambit. World, 1960 RL [Wash. D.C.]
Search and Destroy. Random, 1966. British title: The Valley of Hanoi. Cassell, 1966 RL [Hanoi]
To Hell in a Basket. Cassell, 1967
The Valley of Hanoi; see Search and Destroy

BLACKLEDGE, ETHEL H. 1920- . Ref: CA.
An Hour Is Forever. Avon, 1977

BLACKLEDGE, LEONARD
Behind the Evidence. Hutchinson, 1935

BLACKLEDGE, W(ILLIAM) J(AMES). 1886- .
A Girl in the Spy Racket. Laurie, 1939
Give the Lady a Camel. Nimmo, 1948

BLACKMON, ANITA. 1893- . Ref: MP. SC: Adelaide Adams, in both titles.
The Hotel Richelieu Murders; see Murder a la Richelieu
Murder a la Richelieu. Doubleday, 1937. British title: The Hotel Richelieu Murders. Heinemann, 1938 [South]
The Riddle of the Dead Cats; see There Is No Return
There Is No Return. Doubleday, 1938. British title: The Riddle of the Dead Cats. Butterworth, 1939 [South]

BLACKMORE, JANE. The books below, published at least for the most part as romances in England, have at least mostly been identified as gothics in U.S. editions. Set: Eng.
And Then There Was Georgia. Collins, 1975; Ace, 1975
Angel's Tear. Ace, 1974 (British title?) [Paris]
Beloved Stranger. Collins, 1953; Dell, 1973
Beware the Night. Collins, 1958; Ace, 1968
Bitter Honey. Collins, 1960
Bitter Love. Collins, 1956; Ace, 1973
The Bridge of Strange Music. Collins, 1952; Ace, 1974
Broomstick in the Hall. Collins, 1971; Ace, 1970
The Closing Door. Collins, 1955
The Cressely Inheritance. Collins, 1973; Ace, 1974
Dance on a Hornet's Nest. Collins, 1970
Dangerous Love. Collins, 1958
The Dark Between the Stars. Collins, 1961; Ace, 1967
Deed of Innocence; see Gold for My Girl
The Deep Pool. Collins, 1972; Ace, 1972
Flight into Love. Collins, 1964
Girl Alone. Collins, 1965
Gold for My Girl. Collins, 1967. U.S. title: Deed of Innocence. Ace, 1969
Hawkridge; see Lord of the Manor
Hunter's Mate. Collins, 1971
It Couldn't Happen to Me. Collins, 1962; Dell, 1973
It Happened to Susan. Collins, 1944; Dell, 1973
Joanna. Collins, 1963; Dell, 1972
The Lilac Is for Sharing. Collins, 1969
The Lonely House. Collins, 1957
Lord of the Manor. Collins, 1975. U.S. title: Hawkridge. Ace, 1976
A Love Forbidden; see The Other Room

Man of Power. Collins, 1966
Miranda. Collins, 1966; Dell, 1973
The Missing Hour. Collins, 1959; Ace, 1975
My Sister Erica. Collins, 1973; Ace, 1975
Night of the Bonfire. Collins, 1974; Ace, 1974
The Night of the Stranger. Collins, 1961; Ace, 1967
The Nine Commandments. Collins, 1950
Of Wind and Fire. Piatkus, 1980; Dell, 1979
The Other Mother. Ace, 1972 (British title?)
The Other Room. Collins, 1968; Ace, 1969. Also published as: A Love Forbidden. Coronet, 1974
Perilous Waters. Collins, 1954; Dell, 1973
Ravenden. Collins, 1976; Ace, 1977
Raw Summer. Collins, 1967; Dell, 1972
Return to Love. Collins, 1964. U.S. title: Stephanie. Ace, 1972
The Room in the Tower. Collins, 1972; Ace, 1973
Silver Unicorn. Collins, 1977
Snow in June. Collins, 1947
So Dark the Mirror. Collins, 1949
The Square of Many Colours. Collins, 1948; Ace, 1975
Stephanie; see Return to Love
Storm in the Family. Collins, 1956
Tears in Paradise. Collins, 1959; Dell, 1973
That Night. Collins, 1963; Lancer, 1969
They Carry a Torch. Collins, 1943
Three Letters to Pan. Collins, 1955; Ace, 1972
Towards Tomorrow. Collins, 1941
A Trap for Lovers. Collins, 1960. U.S. title (?): The Velvet Trap. Ace, 1969
Two in Shadow. Collins, 1963
The Velvet Trap; see A Trap for Lovers
Wildfire Love. Piatkus, 1980
A Woman on Her Own. Collins, 1957; Ace, 1971

BLACKSTOCK, CHARITY. Pseudonym of Ursula Torday, 1888- . Other pseudonyms: Paula Allardyce, Charlotte Keppel, qq.v., Lee Blackstock. Ref: CC, TC.
All Men Are Murderers; see The Shadow of Murder
The Bitter Conquest. Hodder, 1959
The Briar Patch. Hodder, 1960. U.S. title: Young Lucifer. Lippincott, 1960
Dewey Death. Heinemann, 1956; London House, 1958
The English Wife; see The Factor's Wife
The Exorcism. Hodder, 1961. U.S. title: A House Possessed. Lippincott, 1962
The Factor's Wife. Hodder, 1964. U.S. title: The English Wife. Coward, 1964 [1816, Scot.]
The Foggy, Foggy Dew. Hodder, 1958; London House, 1959
The Gallant. Hodder, 1962; Ballantine, 1966 [Fr.]
Ghost Town. Hodder, 1976; Coward, 1976
A House Possessed; see The Exorcism
I Met Murder on the Way. Hodder, 1977. U.S. title: The Shirt Front. Coward, 1977 [1936, Eng.]
The Knock at Midnight. Hodder, 1966; Coward, 1967 [1938, Hung.]
The Lemmings; see The Melon in the Cornfield
The Melon in the Cornfield. Hodder, 1969. U.S. title: The Lemmings. Coward, 1969 [acad.]
-Miss Charley. Hodder, 1979
Miss Fenny. Hodder, 1957. U.S. title: The Woman in the Woods, as by Lee Blackstock. Doubleday, 1958
Mr. Christopoulos. Hodder, 1963; London House, 1964 [Cyprus]
Monkey on a Chain; see When the Sun Goes Down
-Party in Dolly Creek. Hodder, 1967. U.S. title: The Widow. Coward, 1967
The Shadow of Murder. Hodder, 1958. U.S. title: All Men Are Murderers, as by Lee Blackstock. Doubleday, 1958 [Scot.]
The Shirt Front; see I Met Murder on the Way
When the Sun Goes Down. Hodder, 1965. U.S. title: Monkey on a Chain. Coward, 1965 [Bangkok]
The Widow; see Party in Dolly Creek
-With Fondest Thoughts. Hodder, 1980
The Woman in the Woods; see Miss Fenny
Young Lucifer; see The Briar Patch

BLACKSTOCK, LEE. See: Charity Blackstock.

BLACKWELL, DONALD. See: William A. Miles.

BLACKWOOD, ALGERNON (HENRY). 1869-1951. Ref: CA, EM, MP, TC. SC: John Silence (JS), in both titles.
Day and Night Stories. Cassell, 1917; Dutton, 1917. Also published as: Tales of the Mysterious and Macabre. Spring, 1968 ss, including one about JS
John Silence. Nash, 1908; Luce, 1909 ss
Tales of the Mysterious and Macabre; see Day and Night Stories

BLACKWOOD, JOY ANN. Pseudonym of Evan Lee Heyman. Other pseudonym: Evelyne Hayworth, q.v.
The Ghost of Lost Lover's Lake. Popular Library, 1973

BLACKWOOD, STEPHANIE. Pseudonym of Sigmund (Stephen) Miller, 1917- , q.v.
Lamontane. Popular Library, 1972 [S.C.]

BLADES, J. K.
The Norwood Mystery. Stockwell, 1933

BLAGOWIDOW, GEORGE. 1923- . Ref: CA.
The Last Train from Berlin. Doubleday, 1977; H. Hamilton, 1977 [Ger., WWII]

BLAIR, ALLAN. Pseudonym of William J(ohn) Bayfield, 1871-1958, q.v. Other pseudonym: Allan Maxwell, q.v. All titles feature Sexton Blake, q.v. All were issued by Amalgamated Press (one exception noted).
The Arterial Road Murder. 1933
The Bathing Pool Mystery. 1935
The Blazing Garage Crime. 1934
The Case of the Blackmailed Banker. 1937
The Case of the Crook Councilor. 1935
The Case of the Dictator's Double. 1940
The Case of the Kidnapped Prisoner. 1939
The Case of the Murdered Taxi Driver. 1935
The Case of the Stolen Police Dossier. 1939
The Crime at the Quay. 1936
The Crime at the Seaside Hotel. 1934
Crooks Convoy. 1939
The Death Ship. Red Mask, 194? (British title?)
Exhumed! 1931
The Fatal Wager. 1931
The Great Tunnel Mystery. 1931
The Great Turf Fraud. 1933
The Kidnapped Witness. 1931
The Law Courts Mystery. 1930
The Lincoln's Inn Tragedy. 1932
The Lombard Street Mystery. 1930
The Lord Mayor's Show Mystery. 1933
The Man from Dublin. 1933
The Man with the Glaring Eyes. 1936
The Murder of Constable Cartwright. 1930
The Mystery of Beckers' Brook. 1935
The Mystery of the Missing Constable. 1938
The Mystery of the Monument. 1930
The Old Bailey Mystery. 1936
The Policeman Mystery. 1932
The Riddle of Five Needle Creek. 1937
The Secret Inquest. 1935
The Town Hall Crime. 1932
The Waiting Room Mystery. 1932

BLAIR, CHARLES (RAWDON)
The Malefactors. Everett, 1903

BLAIR, CHARLES F., JR. See: A(rthur) J(ames) Wallis.

BLAIR, DOROTHY. 1903- . Joint pseudonym with Evelyn Page, 1902- : Roger Scarlett, q.v.

BLAIR, E. P. See: H. L. Blair.

BLAIR, H. L. and E. P. BLAIR
Three Saw the Murder. Spiller, 1938 [New Eng.]

BLAIR, IAIN
Bone. Sphere, 1977
Duff. Sphere, 1977
Hooligan's Rant. New English Library pb, 1979
True. Sphere, 1977

BLAIR, JENNIFER. Pseudonym of (Elizabeth) Adeline McElfresh, 1918- , q.v. Other pseudonym: John Cleveland, q.v.
Assignment in the Islands. Dell, 1970
Danger at Olduvai. Dell, 1972 [Tanz.]
Dangerous Assignment. Dell, 1975
Evil Island. Dell, 1974
Kanesbrake. Dell, 1974
Skye Manor. Dell, 1972

BLAIR, MARCIA. SC: Tory Baxter, in all titles.
The Final Appointment. Zebra, 1979
The Final Fear. Zebra, 1979
The Final Guest. Zebra, 1979
The Final Lie. Zebra, 1978
The Final Pose. Zebra, 1978
The Final Ring. Zebra, 1978 [S.F.]
The Final Target. Zebra, 1979
Finale. Zebra, 1980

BLAIR, WALTER. 1900- . Pseudonym: Mortimer Post, q.v.

BLAIS, MARIE-CLAIRE. 1939- . Ref: CA.
The Execution. Talonbooks, 1976 (Translation of "L'Execution." Montreal, 1970.) (2-act play.)

BLAISDELL, ANNE. Pseudonym of (Barbara) Elizabeth Linington, 1921- , q.v. Other pseudonyms: Lesley Egan, Dell Shannon, qq.v. All titles published in the U.S. as by Elizabeth Linington are issued in England as by Anne Blaisdell.
Nightmare. Harper, 1961; Gollancz, 1962 [Wales]

BLAISDELL, E(LIJAH) W(HITTIER). 1825-1900.
The Hidden Record; or, The Old Sea Mystery. Peterson, 1882

BLAKE, BERNARD CECIL
At the Change of the Moon. Greening, 1902 ss, some criminous

BLAKE, CHRISTINA. Pseudonym of Mary D. Halpin. Worked for many years in the theatre; lives in Toronto.
A Fragrant Death. Raven, 1980

BLAKE, ELEANOR. Pseudonym of Eleanor Blake Atkinson Cox Pratt, 1899- .
Death Down East. Putnam, 1940 [New Eng.]
The Jade Green Cats. McBride, 1931 [Chi.]

BLAKE, KATHERINE. Pseudonym of Dorothy Blake Walter, 1908- . Ref: CA.
-My Sister, My Friend. Reynal, 1965
Night Stands at the Door. Stein, 1974; Hutchinson, 1975 [Austria]

BLAKE, KEN. Pseudonym of Kenneth Bulmer, 1921- , q.v. Ref: CA. All titles are novelizations of "The Professionals" TV series.
Blind Run. Sphere, 1979. Reprinted as by Kenneth Bulmer: Severn, 1980
Dead Reckoning. Sphere, 1980
Fall Girl. Sphere, 1979. Reprinted as by Kenneth Bulmer: Severn, 1981
Hiding to Nothing. Sphere, 1980
Hunter Hunted. Sphere, 1978
Long Shot. Sphere, 1978. Reprinted as by Kenneth Bulmer: Severn, 1979
Stake Out. Sphere, 1978
Where the Jungle Ends. Sphere, 1978. Reprinted as by Kenneth Bulmer: Severn, 1978

BLAKE, LESLIE
The Wapping Butt. Allen, 1964

BLAKE, LILLIE D(EVEREUX). 1835-1913.
A Daring Experiment and other stories. Lovell, 1892 ss

BLAKE, NICHOLAS. Pseudonym of Cecil Day-Lewis, 1904-1972. Ref: all except MM. SC: Nigel Strangeways = NS. Set: mostly Eng.
The Beast Must Die. Collins, 1938; Harper, 1938 NS
The Case of the Abominable Snowman. Collins, 1941. U.S. title: The Corpse in the Snowman. Harper, 1941 NS
Catch and Kill; see The Whisper in the Gloom
The Corpse in the Snowman; see The Case of the Abominable Snowman
The Deadly Joker. Collins, 1963
Death and Daisy Bland; see A Tangled Web
The Dreadful Hollow. Collins, 1953; Harper, 1953 NS
End of Chapter. Collins, 1957; Harper, 1957 NS
Head of a Traveler. Collins, 1949; Harper, 1949 NS
Malice in Wonderland. Collins, 1940. U.S. title: The Summer Camp Mystery. Harper, 1940. Also published as: Malice with Murder. Pyramid, 1964. Also published in the U.S. under the British title: Penguin, 1946 NS
Malice with Murder; see Malice in Wonderland

Minute for Murder. Collins, 1947; Harper, 1948 NS
The Morning After Death. Collins, 1966; Harper, 1966 NS [acad., Mass.]
A Penknife in My Heart. Collins, 1958; Harper, 1959
The Private Wound. Collins, 1968; Harper, 1968 [Ire.]
A Question of Proof. Collins, 1935; Harper, 1935 NS [acad.]
The Sad Variety. Collins, 1964; Harper, 1964 NS
Shell of Death; see Thou Shell of Death
The Smiler with the Knife. Collins, 1939; Harper, 1939 NS
The Summer Camp Mystery; see Malice in Wonderland
A Tangled Web. Collins, 1956; Harper, 1956. Also published as: Death and Daisy Bland. Dell, 1960
There's Trouble Brewing. Collins, 1937; Harper, 1937 NS
Thou Shell of Death. Collins, 1936. U.S. title: Shell of Death. Harper, 1936 NS
The Whisper in the Gloom. Collins, 1954; Harper, 1954. Also published as: Catch and Kill. Bestseller, 1955, abridged NS
The Widow's Cruise. Collins, 1959; Harper, 1959 NS [ship]
The Worm of Death. Collins, 1961; Harper, 1961 NS

BLAKE, PATRICK. Pseudonym of Clive (Frederick) Egleton, 1927- , q.v.
Escape to Athena. Fontana, 1979; Berkley, 1979 (Novelization of the movie.) [Greece, 1945]

BLAKE, ROGER
Stripped for Murder. Comet, 1963 (Mark Sade is given as author on the cover.) [Wash. D.C.]

BLAKE, STACEY. 1878-1964. All titles feature Sexton Blake and were published by Amalgamated Press.
The City of Crooks. 1930
On Ticket of Leave. 1933
Prisoners of the Desert. 1929

BLAKE, VANESSA. Pseudonym of Mary Brown, 1913- .
Blood Emerald. Hale, 1970; PB, 1975
Bride of Chance. Hale, 1972. U.S. title: Bride of Misfortune. PB, 1974
Bride of Misfortune; see Bride of Chance
The Dark Guardian. Hale, 1973; PB, 1974 [past, Eng.]
The Gay Gallant. Hale, 1971. U.S. title: Master of Evrington. PB, 1974
The Lady from Lisbon. Hale, 1971. U.S. title: Pentallion. PB, 1974
Master of Evrington; see The Gay Gallant
Pentallion; see The Lady from Lisbon

BLAKE, WALTER. Pseudonym of Wilbur Braun, 1896- , q.v. Other pseudonyms: Bruce Brandon, Fred Caldwell, Raymond Dumkey, Marsha Grable, Edwin F. Hornung, Jed Parish, Basil Ring, Orville Snap, Mortimer Sprague, Bert Stoner, qq.v.
The Foolproof Murder. French (NYC), 1947 (3-act play.)
Who Would A-Murdering Go? French (NYC), 1948 (3-act play.)

BLAKE, WILLIAM DORSEY
My Time or Yours. Manor, 1979 [NYC, 1846]

BLAKEMAN, WILBERT C.
The Black Hand. Broadway, 1908

BLAKEMORE, TREVOR (RAMSEY VILLIERS)
-Through a Glass Darkly. Gay, 1913

BLAKER, RICHARD, 1893-1940.
The Jefferson Secret. Doubleday, 1929 [Eng.]
Night Shift. Appleton, 1934; Heinemann, 1934

BLAKESLEY, STEPHEN. Pseudonym of F. Bond. All titles feature Sexton Blake and were published by Amalgamated Press.
The Man with a Number. 1952
The Riddle of the Blazing Bungalow. 1951
The Trail of Raider No. 1. 1952

BLAKESTON, OSWELL. 1907- . Joint pseudonym with Roger d'Este Burford, 1904- : Simon, q.v.
And Then the Screaming Started. Hutchinson, 1968
Ever Singing Die Oh! Die. Hutchinson, 1970
For Crying Out Shroud. Hutchinson, 1969
Hop Thief. Blond, 1959
The Night's Moves. Gaberbocchus, 1961
Pink Ribbon, as Told to the Police. Quality, 1950

BLANC, SUZANNE. Ref: TC. SC: Insp. Menendez = M.
The Green Stone. Harper, 1961; Cassell, 1962 M [Mex.]
The Rose Window. Doubleday, 1967; Cassell, 1968 M [Mex.]
The Sea Troll. Doubleday, 1969 [ship]
The Yellow Villa. Doubleday, 1964; Cassell, 1965 M [Mex.]

BLANCHET, LISE
Shadow of Evil. Mystique, 1980 (Translation of "Le Fantome des Whitness." Paris, 1977.)

BLANCO, L. W.
Spy Kill. Lancer, 1966

BLAND, E. A. Pseudonym: E. A. B. D., q.v.

BLAND, EDITH NESBIT. 1858-1924. Joint pseudonym with Hubert Bland, 1856-1914: Fabian Bland, q.v.

BLAND, FABIAN. Joint pseudonym of Edith Nesbit Bland, 1858-1924, and Hubert Bland, 1856-1914.
The Prophet's Mantle. Drane, 1889; Belford, 1889

BLAND, HUBERT. 1856-1914. Joint pseudonym with Edith Nesbit Bland, 1858-1924: Fabian Bland, q.v.

BLAND, JENNIFER. Pseudonym of Jean Bowden, 1925- . Other pseudonym: Avon Curry, q.v.
Accomplice. Barker, 1974
Death in Waiting. Barker, 1975; St. Martin's, 1975 [Scot.]

BLAND, OLIVER
Outwitted. Odhams, 1921

BLANE, FERGUS. Pseudonym.
Money-Lender in Gloves. Newnes, 1939

BLANEY, CHARLES E. 1865?-1944. Pseudonym: Harry Clay Blaney, q.v.
-Across the Pacific. Ogilvie, 1904
The Boy Behind the Gun. Ogilvie, 1905
The Boy Detective. Ogilvie, 1907
-A Child of the Regiment. Ogilvie
The Child Slaves of New York, with Howard Hall. Ogilvie, 1904 [NYC]
-The Curse of Drink. Ogilvie, 1907
-The Dancer and the King, with J. S. Dawley. Ogilvie, 1907
-Dion O'Dare. Ogilvie, 1907
-The Factory Girl. Ogilvie, 1904
For His Brother's Crime. Ogilvie, 1904
The Girl and the Detective, with J. Searle Dawley. Ogilvie, 1909
-The Girl from Texas. Ogilvie, 1909
The Girl Raffles. Ogilvie, 1906
-The Hired Girl's Millions. Ogilvie, 1907
His Terrible Secret; or, The Man Monkey. Ogilvie, 1907
Kidnapped for Revenge, with Will H. Vedder. Ogilvie, 1907
The King of the Opium Ring. Ogilvie, 1905
-The Little Terror. Ogilvie, 1909
-Lottie, the Poor Saleslady. Ogilvie, 1907
The Millionaire Detective, with Howard Hall. Ogilvie, 1905
-Mrs. Blarney from Ireland. Ogilvie, 1905
-More to be Pitied Than Scorned. Ogilvie, 1904
-My Tom-Boy Girl. Ogilvie, 1906
-Old Isaacs from the Bowery. Ogilvie, 1905
-The Sheriff of Angel Gulch. Ogilvie, 1908
-The Sporting Deacon. Ogilvie, 1909
-Tennessee Tess. Ogilvie, 1909
-Young Buffalo. Ogilvie, 1905
-Young Buffalo in New York. Ogilvie, 1909 [NYC]

BLANEY, HARRY CLAY. Pseudonym of Charles E. Blaney, 1865?-1944, q.v.
From Sing Sing to Liberty. Ogilvie, 1907

BLANKENSHIP, WILLIAM D(OUGLAS). 1934- . Ref: CA.
The Helix File. Walker, 1972 [Ariz.]
The Leavenworth Irregulars. Bobbs, 1974; Barker, 1975 [Kan.]
The Programmed Man. Walker, 1973; Barker, 1973 [Calif.]
Tiger Ten. Putnam, 1977; Mayflower, 1977 [Burma]
-Yukon Gold. Dutton, 1977; Souvenir, 1978 [Can.]

BLANKFORT, DOROTHY and MICHAEL (SEYMOUR) BLANKFORT, 1907-1982, q.v.
Monique. French (NYC and London), 1957. (2-act play based on the novel "Celle Qui n'Etait Plus" by Pierre Boileau, 1906- , q.v., and Thomas Narcejac.)

BLANKFORT, MICHAEL (SEYMOUR). 1907-1982. See also: Dorothy Blankfort. Ref: CA.
-Behold the Fire. NAL, 1965; Heinemann, 1966
-I Met a Man. Bobbs, 1937; Hale, 1938
The Widow-Makers. Simon, 1946; Dobson, 1949 [NYC]

BLASSINGAME, WYATT (RAINEY). 1909- . Ref: CA.
John Smith Hears Death Walking. Bart, 1944 ss

BLATCHFORD, ROBERT. 1851-1943.
Tales for the Marines. Clarion, 1901 ss, some criminous

BLAU, ERNEST E.
The Queen's Falcon. McKay, 1947

BLAYN, HUGO. Pseudonym of John Russell Fearn, 1908-1960, q.v. Other pseudonyms: Spike Gordon, Volsted Gribdan, Griff, Nat Karta, John Slate, qq.v. SC: Insp. Garth, in all titles (see also the Nat Karta entry). Set: Eng.
Except for One Thing. Paul, 1947
The Five Matchboxes. Paul, 1948
Flashpoint. Paul, 1950
The Silvered Cage. Dragon, 1955
What Happened to Hammond? Paul, 1951

BLAYNE, SEBASTIAN. SC: Sebastian Blayne, in both titles.
Gay Ghastly Holiday. GM, 1951 [NYC]
Terror in the Night. GM, 1953; Muller pb, 1954 [Conn.]

BLAZER, J. S. Pseudonym of Justin (Blazer) Scott, q.v. SC: Donald Bracken and James Rowland Woodward VII, in both titles.
Deal Me Out. Bobbs, 1973 [NYC]
Lend a Hand. Bobbs, 1975

BLEACKLEY, HORACE (WILLIAM). 1868-1931.
-A Gentleman of the Road. Lane (NYC and London), 1911
-The Lost Diary. Nash, 1919
Night of Peril. Lane, 1926

BLEECK, OLIVER. Pseudonym of Ross Thomas, 1926- , q.v. SC: Philip St. Ives, in all titles.
The Brass Go-Between. Morrow, 1969; Hodder, 1970
The Highbinders. Morrow, 1974; H. Hamilton, 1974 [Eng.]
No Questions Asked. Morrow, 1976; H. Hamilton, 1976
The Procane Chronicle. Morrow, 1972. British title: The Thief Who Painted Sunlight. Hodder, 1972. Also published as: St. Ives. PB, 1976 [NYC]
Protocol for a Kidnapping. Morrow, 1971; Hodder, 1971 [Belgrade]
St. Ives; see The Procane Chronicle
The Thief Who Painted Sunlight; see The Procane Chronicle

BLICKLE, KATRINKA
-Dark Beginnings. Doubleday, 1978; New English Library, 1979
Heart of the Harbor. Doubleday, 1979
North Sea Mistress. Doubleday, 1977 [Scot.]

BLIGH, G.
Death Came by Night. Pemberton, 1951

BLIGH, GORDON
The Curse of Scotland. French, 1939 (1-act play.)

BLINKHOOLIE. Pseudonym of William Allison
"Blairmount?" International Horse Agency, 1909

BLISS, ADAM. Joint pseudonym of Robert Ferdinand Burkhardt, 1892-1947, and Eve Burkhardt, 1899- . Other pseudonym: Rex Jardin, q.v. SC: Alice Penny = AP.
The Camden Ruby Murder. Barse, 1931; Rich, 1934 [NYC]

Four Times a Widower. Macrae, 1936; Hamilton, 1938 AP
Murder Upstairs. Macrae, 1934; Hamilton, 1935 AP

BLISS, EDGAR JANES
The Peril of Oliver Sargent. Webster, 1891

BLISS, TIP
The Broadway Butterfly Murders. Greenberg, 1930 [NYC]

BLIXEN-FINECKE, BARONESS KAREN CHRISTENCE. 1885-1962. Pseudonym: Pierre Andrezel, q.v.

BLIZARD, MARIE. SC: Eve MacWilliams = EM.
Conspiracy of Silence. Mill, 1954; Hammond, 1957 [Conn.]
The Dark Corner. Mill, 1950; Hammond, 1956 [Md.]
The Late, Lamented Lady. Mystery House, 1946 EM [Conn.]
The Men in Her Death. Mystery House, 1947 EM [Maine]
The Watch Sinister. Mill, 1951; Hammond, 1956 [NYC]

BLOCH, BLANCHE. 1890-1980. Ref: CA.
The Bach Festival Murders. Harper, 1942

BLOCH, DON(ALD). 1943-   .
Double Take. Gollancz, 1979

BLOCH, ROBERT (ALBERT). 1917-   . See also: Collier Young, 1908-1980. Ref: CA, EM, TC.
American Gothic. Simon, 1974; Allen, 1975 [Chi., 1893]
Atoms and Evil. GM, 1962; Muller pb, 1963 ss
Blood Runs Cold. Simon, 1961; Hale, 1962 ss
Bogey Men. Pyramid, 1963 ss
Chamber of Horrors. Award, 1966; Corgi, 1977 ss
Cold Chills. Doubleday, 1977; Hale, 1978
The Couch. GM, 1962 (Novelization of the movie.)
The Cunning; see There Is a Serpent in Eden
The Dead Beat. Simon, 1960; Hale, 1961
Fear Today—Gone Tomorrow. Award, 1971
Firebug. Regency, 1961; Corgi, 1977
Horror-7. Belmont, 1963; Four Square, 1964 (7 ss from "Pleasant Dreams—Nightmares" and "The Opener of the Way," qq.v.)
The House of the Hatchet and other tales of horror; see House of Horror, Jack the Ripper: Tales of Horror
The Kidnapper. Lion, 1954
The King of Terrors. Mysterious Press, 1977; Hale, 1978 ss
The Living Demons. Belmont, 1967; Sphere, 1970 ss
More Nightmares. Belmont, 1962 (10 ss from "Pleasant Dreams—Nightmares" and "The Opener of the Way," qq.v.)
Nightmares. Belmont, 1961 (10 ss from "Pleasant Dreams—Nightmares," q.v.)
Night-World. Simon, 1972; Hale, 1974 [L.A.]
The Opener of the Way. Arkham, 1945 ss
Out of the Mouths of Graves. Mysterious Press, 1979; Hale, 1980 ss
Pleasant Dreams—Nightmares. Arkham, 1959; Whiting, 1967 ss
Psycho. Simon, 1959; Hale, 1960
The Scarf. Dial, 1947. Also published as: Scarf of Passion. Avon, 1948; New English Library, 1972
Scarf of Passion; see The Scarf
Shooting Star. Ace, 1958
The Skull of the Marquis de Sade and other stories. Pyramid, 1965 ss
Spiderweb. Ace, 1954
The Star Stalker. Pyramid, 1968
Such Stuff As Screams Are Made Of. Ballantine, 1979; Hale, 1980 ss
Tales in a Jugular Vein. Pyramid, 1965; Sphere, 1970 ss
Terror. Belmont, 1962; Corgi, 1964 [Midwest]
Terror in the Night and other stories. Ace, 1958 ss
There Is a Serpent in Eden. Zebra, 1979. Also published as: The Cunning. Zebra, 1981
This Crowded Earth & Ladies' Day. Belmont, 1968 (2 novelets.)
The Will to Kill. Ace, 1954
Yours Truly, Jack the Ripper: Tales of Horror. Belmont, 1962. British title: The House of the Hatchet and other tales of horror. Tandem, 1965 (9 ss from "Pleasant Dreams—Nightmares" and "The Opener of the Way," qq.v.)

BLOCHMAN, LAWRENCE G(OLDTREE). 1900-1975. Ref: CA, CC, EM, TC. SC: Insp. Leonidas Prike = LP; Dr. Coffee = C.
Bengal Fire. Dell, 1948; Collins, 1937 LP [India]
Blow-Down. Harcourt, 1939; Collins, 1940 [Carib.]
Bombay Mail. Little, 1934; Collins, 1934 LP [India]
Clues for Dr. Coffee. Lippincott, 1964 C ss [Midwest]
Death Walks in Marble Halls. Dell, 1951 (A novelet, published separately in Dell's 10¢ pb series.)
Diagnosis: Homicide. Lippincott, 1950 C ss [Midwest]
Menace; see Pursuit
Midnight Sailing. Harcourt, 1938; Collins, 1939 [ship]
Pursuit. Handi-Books, 1951. British title: Menace. Comyns, 1951
Rather Cool for Mayhem. Lippincott, 1951; Cassell, 1952 [N.Y.]
Recipe for Homicide. Lippincott, 1952; Hammond, 1954 C [Midwest]
Red Snow at Darjeeling. Saint Mystery Library, 1960; Collins, 1938 LP [India]
See You at the Morgue. Duell, 1941; Cassell, 1946 [NYC]
Wives to Burn. Harcourt, 1940; Collins, 1940 [India]

BLOCK, C(ANDACE) BURKE. NYC film critic.
Art for Keeps. Raven, 1980 [NYC]

BLOCK, LAWRENCE. 1938-   . Pseudonyms: Chip Harrison, Paul Kavanagh, qq.v. See also: William (Thomas) Ard, 1922-1960. Ref: CA, TC. SC: Bernie Rhodenbarr = BR; Matt Scudder = MS; Evan Tanner = ET.
After the First Death. Macmillan, 1969; Hale, 1981 [NYC]
-Ariel. Arbor, 1980; Hale, 1981
The Burglar in the Closet. Random, 1978; Hale, 1980 BR [NYC]
The Burglar Who Liked to Quote Kipling. Random, 1979; Hale, 1981 BR [NYC]
Burglars Can't Be Choosers. Random, 1977; Hale, 1978 BR [NYC]
The Canceled Czech. GM, 1966 ET [Czech.]
The Case of the Pornographic Photos. Belmont, 1961; Consul, 1965 (Novelization of the "Markham" TV series.) [N.H.]
Deadly Honeymoon. Macmillan, 1967; Hale, 1981 [NYC]
Death Pulls a Doublecross. GM, 1961
The Girl with the Long Green Heart. GM, 1965; Muller, 1967
Here Comes a Hero. GM, 1968 ET [Afghan.]
In the Midst of Death. Dell, 1976; Hale, 1979 MS [NYC]
Me Tanner, You Jane. Macmillan, 1970 ET [Afr.]
Mona. GM, 1961; Muller, 1963
-Ronald Rabbit Is a Dirty Old Man. Manor, 1974
The Sins of the Father. Dell, 1976; Hale, 1979 MS [NYC]
The Specialists. GM, 1969; Hale, 1980 [N.J.]
Tanner's Tiger. GM, 1968 ET [Montr.]
Tanner's Twelve Swingers. GM, 1967; Coronet, 1968 ET [Russ.]
The Thief Who Couldn't Sleep. GM, 1966 ET
Time to Murder and Create. Dell, 1977; Hale, 1979 MS [NYC]
Two for Tanner. GM, 1968 ET

BLOCK, LIBBIE. 1910?-1972. Ref: CA.
Bedeviled. Doubleday, 1947 [NYC]

BLODGETT, MICHAEL
-Captain Blood. Stonehill, 1980; New English Library pb, 1981 [L.A.]

BLOM, ERIC WALTER. 1888-1959. Pseudonym: Sebastian Farr, q.v.

BLOM, K(ARL) ARNE. 1946-   . Ref: CA.
The Limits of Pain. Ram, 1979; Raven, 1980
The Moment of Truth. Harper, 1977

BLOOD, ADELE and TAM MARRIOTT
The Jade Rabbit. Diamond, 1926; Dial, 1927 [Jap.]

BLOOD, MATTHEW. Joint pseudonym of Davis Dresser, 1904-1977, and (Walter) Ryerson Johnson, 1901-   , q.v. Pseudonyms of Davis Dresser: Asa Baker, Brett Halliday, qq.v. Joint pseudonym with Kathleen Rollins Dresser: Hal Debrett, q.v. SC: Morgan Wayne, in both titles, both set in NYC.
The Avenger. GM, 1952
Death Is a Lovely Dame. GM, 1954

BLOODWORTH, DENNIS. Raised in London; with British Intelligence during WWII; reporter and foreign correspondent.
Any Number Can Play. Secker, 1972; Farrar, 1973 [Far East]
The Clients of Omega. Secker, 1975
Crosstalk. Secker, 1978; Coward, 1978
Trapdoor. Weidenfeld, 1980

BLOOM, MURRAY TEIGH. 1916-   . Ref: CA.
The 13th Man. Macmillan, 1977. British title: The Last Embrace. Star, 1979 [NYC]

BLOOM, ROLFE. See: Allan Ullman

BLOOMFIELD, ANTHONY (JOHN WESTGATE). 1922-   . Ref: CA.
Delinquents. Hogarth, 1958
Life for a Life. Hogarth, 1971; Scribner, 1971
Russian Roulette. Hogarth, 1955; Harcourt, 1956
The Tempter. Hogarth, 1961; Scribner, 1962
Throw. Hogarth, 1965; Scribner, 1965

BLOOMFIELD, ROBERT. Pseudonym of Leslie Edgley, 1912-   , q.v. Joint pseudonym with Mary Edgley: Brook Hastings, q.v.
From This Death Forward. Doubleday, 1952 [Calif.]
Kill with Kindness. Doubleday, 1962 [Calif.]
Lust for Vengeance; see Vengeance Street
Portrait of Murder. French (London), 1964 (Play.)
The Shadow of Guilt. Doubleday, 1947 [Calif.]
Stranger in Town. Doubleday, 1953; Boardman, 1954 [Midwest]
Vengeance Street. Doubleday, 1952. Also published as: Lust for Vengeance. Bestseller, 1953 [Calif.]
When Strangers Meet. Doubleday, 1956; Boardman, 1957 [Calif.]

BLORE, TREVOR
The House of Living Death. Aldor, 1946

BLOUNDELLE-BURTON, JOHN EDWARD. 1850-1917.
A Dead Reckoning. White, 1904
Mystery of St. James' Park; see The Silent Shore
The Silent Shore. Maxwell, 1886; Munro, 1887. Also published as: Mystery of St. James' Park. Ivers, 1888

BLOUNT, MARGARET. Pseudonym of Mary O'Francis.
A Dangerous Woman. Brady, 1864
Downe Reserve; or, The Mystery of Wishing Well. Brady, 1864
Hollow Ash Hall. Brady, 1864
Kitty Atherton; or, A Broken Life. Brady, 1863

BLOW, LYNTON. Set: Eng.
The Bournewick Murders. Butterworth, 1935
The "Moth" Murder. Alexander-Ouseley, 1931; Holt, 1932

BLOXHAM, PETER. Pseudonym of Kenneth Bird, 1916-   , q.v.
Death for a Dropout. Hale, 1970
Funeral for a Physicist. Hale, 1966

BLOXSAM, PETER. See: Leslie Charteris, 1907-   .

BLUM, RALPH. 1932-   .
The Simultaneous Man. Little, 1970; Deutsch, 1970 [Phil.]

BLUM, RICHARD (HOSMER ADAMS). 1927-   . Ref: CA.
Death and Festivals. Hale, 1968

BLUM, RICHARD H. Pseudonym: Hartshorne, q.v.

BLUMBERG, GARY. 1938-   . Pseudonym: Michael Bradley, q.v. Ref: CA.
Blood Red Gold. Dell, 1977
Glover Undercover. Dell, 1973
Hit Woman. Dell, 1975 [N.Y.]
A Killer in My Mind. Warner, 1975
Two in the Bush. Medallion, 1973

BLUMGARTEN, JAMES
The Astronaut. Warner, 1974

BLUNDELL, HAROLD. 1902-   . Pseudonym: George Bellairs, q.v.

BLUNDELL, PETER. Pseudonym of Frank
   Nestle Butterworth.
   Mr. Pond of Borneo. Laurie, 1920

BLUNT, DON. Pseudonym of Edwin Booth,
   1906-   , q.v.
   Dead Giveaway. Avalon, 1963 [Calif.]
   Short Cut. Avalon, 1962

BLY, NELLIE. Pseudonym of Elizabeth J.
   Cochrane, 1867-1922.
   The Mystery of Central Park. Dillingham, 1889 [NYC]

BLYTH, JAMES. 1864-1915. See also: Barry
   (Eric Odell) Pain, 1864-1928. Set:
   Eng.
   The Aerial Burglars. Ward, 1906
   Brumblingham Hall, White, 1911
   The Diamond and the Lady. Digby, 1908
   The Expropriators. Digby, 1919
   The Golden Hole. White, 1913
   The Hidden Fear. White, 1912
   Jack Ranworth. Ward, 1919
   The Mystery of the Common. Ward, 1920
   The Riddle of the Marsh. Ward, 1922
   With a View to Matrimony, and other
      stories. Richards, 1904 ss, at
      least one criminous

BLYTHE, E. J. See: J(ames) M(organ)
   Walsh, 1897- .

BOARDMAN, NEIL S(ERVIS). 1907-   .
   Ref: CA.
   The Wine of Violence. Simon, 1964;
      Cape, 1965

BOAST, PHILIP
   The Assassinators. Millington, 1976

BOBIN, JOHN WILLIAM.   -1935. Pseudonyms: John Ascott, Mark Osborne,
   qq.v. All titles below feature Sexton Blake and were published by
   Amalgamated Press.
   The Banker's Trust. 1916
   The Boy Without a Memory. 1919
   The Case of the Bogus Laird. 1922
   The Case of the Bookmaker Baronet. 1926
   The Case of the Cultured Pearls. 1922
   The Case of the Girl Reporter. 1918
   The Case of the Head Dispenser. 1924
   The Case of the International Adventurer. 1917
   The Case of the Island Trader. 1921
   The Case of the Long-Firm Frauds. 1926
      Reprinted in 1936 as by Mark Osborne
   The Case of the Trade Secret. 1922
   The Case of the Two Bankers. 1918
   Daylight Robbery. 1919
   The Fatal Pit. 1927. Reprinted in 1938
      as by Mark Osborne
   The Great Diamond Bluff. 1920
   The Great "Tote" Fraud. 1929
   The Grip of the Law. 1916
   The Hidden Menace! 1919
   His Son's Honour. 1920
   The Hooded Riders. 1922
   In the Grip of the Tong. 1922
   In the Shadow of the Guillotine. 1918
   The Island Mystery. 1919
   A Legacy of Shame. 1917
   A Legacy of Vengeance. 1923
   Link by Link. 1920
   The Matador's Fortune. 1919
   The Merchant's Secret. 1916
   The Mystery Mandarin. 1923
   The Mystery of the "Agony." 1919
   The Mystery of the Grey Car. 1919
   The Only Son. 1920
   Out of the Reach of the Law. 1920
   Payment in Full. 1916
   Payment Suspended. 1921
   The Problem of the Derby Favorite. 1919
   The Riddle of Riverdale. 1919
   The Secret of the Surgery. 1929
   Sexton Blake—Special Constable. 1917.
      Reprinted in 1940 as by Mark Osborne
   The Shadow of His Crime. 1915
   The Stolen Crown. 1918
   The Stolen Partnership Papers. 1919
   Ten Years After. 1917
   The Tour of Terror. 1927. Reprinted in
      1939 as by Mark Osborne
   Twice Wronged! 1920

BOBKER, LEE R. 1925-   . Ref: CA.
   The Unicorn Group. Morrow, 1979; Constable, 1980

BOCCA, AL. Pseudonym of Bevis Winter,
   1918-   , q.v. Other pseudonyms:
   Peter Cagney, Gordon Shayne, qq.v.
   All or Nothing. Milestone, 1953
   Any Minute Now. Scion, 1952
   Black Morning. Scion, 1952
   Blonde Dynamite. Scion, 1950
   City Limit Blonde. Scion, 1950
   The Coffin Fits. Scion, 1951
   A Corner in Corpses. Milestone, 1954
   Curves for Danger. Scion, 1950
   A Dame Ain't Safe. Scion, 1950
   Dead on Delivery. Scion, 1950
   Dead on Time. Scion, 1950
   Deadly Ernest. Scion, 1951
   Double Trouble. Milestone, 1953
   Dressed to Kill. Milestone, 1952
   Easy Come, Easy Go. Scion, 1951
   A Gun for Company. Scion, 1952
   The Harder They Fall. Scion, 1951
   It's Your Funeral. Scion, 1950
   Let's Face It. Scion, 1951
   Let's Not Get Smart. Scion, 1952
   The Long Sleep. Scion, 1950
   No Dice! Scion, 1951
   No Room at the Morgue. Milestone, 1954
   Requiem for a Redhead. Milestone, 1953
   She Was No Lady. Scion, 1950
   Sinner Takes All. Scion, 1950
   Slaughter in Satin. Scion, 1950
   The Slick and the Dead. Milestone, 1953
   Sorry You've Been Shot. Scion, 1952
   Sudden Death! Scion, 1951
   Ticket to San Diego. Scion, 1953
   Trouble Calling. Milestone, 1953
   Wait for It, Pal. Scion, 1951

BOCCA, GEOFFREY. ca.1924-1983.
   The Fourth Horseman. Random, 1980
      [Calif.]
   Nadine. Putnam, 1974; Hart-Davis, 1976
      [Fr.]

BODEEN, DeWITT. 1908-   . Ref: CA.
   13 Castle Walk. Pyramid, 1975

BODELSEN, ANDERS. 1937-   . Ref: CC.
   Consider the Verdict. Harper, 1976
      (Translation of "Bevisets Stilling."
      Copenhagen, 1973.) [Den.]
   Hit and Run, Run, Run; see One Down
   One Down. Harper, 1970. British title:
      Hit and Run, Run, Run. Joseph, 1970
      (Translation of "Haedeligt Uheld."
      Copenhagen, 1968.) [Copen.]
   -Operation Cobra. Pelham, 1976 (Translation of "Operation Cobra." Copenhagen, 1975.)
   The Silent Partner; see Think of a Number
   Straus. Harper, 1974 (Translation of
      "Straus." Copenhagen, 1971.) [Den.]
   Think of a Number. Harper, 1969;
      Joseph, 1969. Also published as: The
      Silent Partner. Penguin, 1978
      (Translation of "Taenk pa et Tal."
      Copenhagen, 1968.) [Copen.]

BODEN, L.
   And the Body Came Too. Hamilton & Co.,
      1946

BODINGTON, NANCY HERMIONE. 1912-   .
   Pseudonym: Shelley Smith, q.v.

BODKIN, M(ATTHIAS) McDONNELL. 1850-1933.
   Ref: DD, EM, MC, MP, TC. SC: Paul
   Beck = PB; Dora Myrl = DM. Set: Eng.
   A Bear Squeeze; or, Her Second Self.
      Ward, 1901
   Behind the Picture. Ward, 1914
   The Capture of Paul Beck. Unwin, 1909;
      Little, 1911 PB,DM
   Dora Myrl, the Lady Detective. Chatto,
      1900 ss DM
   Guilty or Not Guilty? Talbot, 1929
   -His Brother's Keeper. Hurst, 1913
   -Kitty the Madcap. Talbot, 1927
   A Modern Robyn Hood. Ward, 1903 ss
   -Old Rowley. Holden, 1917
   Pat o' Nine Tales. Gill, 1894 ss, some
      criminous
   Paul Beck, Detective. Talbot, 1929 PB
      ss
   Paul Beck, the Rule of Thumb Detective.
      Pearson, 1898 PB ss
   Pigeon Blood Rubies. Nash, 1915 PB
   The Quests of Paul Beck. Unwin, 1908;
      Little, 1910 PB ss
   A Stolen Life. Ward, 1898
   The Test. Everett, 1914
   Young Beck. Unwin, 1911; Little, 1912
      PB,DM in very minor roles ss

BODWELL, RICHARD. Pseudonym of Gerald Max
   Spring, 1897-   . Ref: CA.
   The Mystery of Fernridge Manor. Vantage, 1974

BOE, EUGENE. See: Jerome Agel.

BOGAR, JEFF. Pseudonym of Ronald Wills
   Thomas, 1910-   . Other pseudonym:
   Ronald Wills, q.v.
   Concrete Curtain. Hamilton & Co., 1954
   Confessions of Chinatown Doll. Universal, 195?
   Dinah for Danger. Hamilton & Co., 1952.
      U.S. title: My Gun, Her Body. Lion,
      1952
   Fire Zone. Hamilton & Co., 1953
   Hoodmen's Bait. Hamilton & Co., 1953
   The Land Pirate. Hamilton & Co., 1955
   My Gun, Her Body; see Dinah for Danger
   Painted on a Donkey Cart. Hamilton &
      Co., 1955
   Payoff for Paula. Hamilton & Co., 195?.
      U.S. title: The Tigress. Lion, 1952
   Pink Film. Hamilton & Co., 1954
   The Speed Queens. Hamilton & Co., 1955
   The Tigress; see Payoff for Paula
   Undercurrent. Hamilton & Co., 1953

BOGARD, DALE
   Double Kill. World Distributors, 1952
   It's Lonely on the Sidewalk. World Distributors, 1952
   Lead Her Gently to the Grave. World
      Distributors, 1951
   Make Sure I'm Dead. World Distributors,
      1951
   9 Times Dead. World Distributors, 1951
   Nobody Died for Honnie. World Distributors, 1952
   Pardon My Body. Harlequin, 1951 [NYC]
   Speak Softly to the Dead. World Distributors, 1951

BOGART, WILLIAM (G.). 1903-1977. See
   also: Kenneth Robeson. SC: Johnny
   Saxon, in at least those marked JS.
   Hell on Friday. Swift, 1941 JS [NYC]
   Murder Is Forgetful. Mystery House,
      1944 JS [L.I.]
   Murder Man. Swift, 1941 JS [NYC]
   The Queen City Murder Case. Mystery
      House, 1946 JS
   Sands Street. Swift, 1942
   Singapore. Century, 1947 (Novelization
      of the movie.) [Sing.]

BOGGIS, DAVID
   Killer Instinct. Macmillan (London),
      1980

BOGGON, MARTYN
   -The Inevitable Hour. Tandem, 1968;
      Award, 1968
   Undercurrent. Tandem, 1967

BOGGS, WINIFRED
   Murder on the Underground. Jenkins,
      1929

BOGNER, NORMAN. 1935-   . Ref: CA.
   Snowman. Dell, 1977; New English Library, 1978

BOGUE, HOGAN
   The Dog and Duck Mystery. Jarrolds,
      1921
   -The Golden Helmet. Hodder, 1928

BOHLE, EDGAR (HENRY). 1909-   . Ref:
   CA, CC.
   The Man Who Disappeared. Random, 1958;
      Boardman, 1960
   The Wife Who Died Twice. Random, 1962;
      Boardman, 1962 [NYC]

BOHNSTEDT, HANS
   No Corpus Delecti. Exposition, 1962

BOILEAU, PIERRE (PROSPER), 1906-   , and
   THOMAS NARCEJAC, pseudonym of Pierre
   Ayraud, 1908-   . See also: Dorothy
   Blankfort. Ref: CC, MC
   Choice Cuts. Barker, 1966; Dutton,
      1966 (Translation of "Et Mon Tout
      est un Homme." Paris, 1965.) [Fr.]
   The Evil Eye. Hutchinson, 1959 (Translation of "Le Mauvais Oeil." Paris,
      1956.)
   Faces in the Dark. Hutchinson, 1955
      (Translation of "Les Visages de L'
      Ombre." Paris, 1953.) [Fr.]
   The Fiends; see The Woman Who Was
   Heart to Heart. H. Hamilton, 1959
      (Translation of "A Coeur Perdu."
      Paris, 1959.)
   The Living and the Dead. Hutchinson,
      1956; Washburn, 1957. Also published
      as: Vertigo. Dell, 1958 (Translation
      of "D'Entre les Morts." Paris, 1954.)
      [Paris]
   The Prisoner. Hutchinson, 1957 (Translation of "Les Louves." Paris, 1955.)
      [Fr.]
   Sleeping Beauty. Hutchinson, 1959
      (Translation of "Au Bois Dormant."
      Paris, 1956.)
   Spells of Evil. H. Hamilton, 1961
      (Translation of "Malefices." Paris,
      1961.)
   The Tube. H. Hamilton, 1960 (Translation of "L'Ingenieur Aimait Trop les
      Chiffres." Paris, 1958.)
   Vertigo; see The Living and the Dead
   The Victims; see Who Was Clare Jallu?
   Who Was Clare Jallu? Barker, 1965.
      Also published as: The Victims. Panther, 1967 (Translation of "Les Victims." Paris, 1964.)

B

The Woman Who Was. Hutchinson, 1954.
U.S. title: The Woman Who Was No
More. Rinehart, 1954 (Translation of
"Celle Qui N'Etait Plus." Paris,
1952.)
The Woman Who Was No More; see The
Woman Who Was

BOISSIERE, ALBERT. 1866-   .
The Man Without a Face, with Florence
Crew-Jones. Dillingham, 1911; Unwin,
1911 (Translation of "L'Homme Sans
Figure." Paris, 1909.) [Fr.]
The Missing Finger. Dodd, 1911 (Translation of "Un Crime a ete Commis."
Paris, 1908.) [Fr.]

BOK. Pseudonym.
Dragons to Slay. Jenkins, 1937
[Far East]
Piracies, Ltd. Jenkins, 1938
Tong. Jenkins, 1933
-Vampires of the China Coast. Jenkins,
1932 [Far East]

BOLAND, (BERTRAM) JOHN. 1913-1976. See
also: Philip King, 1904-   . Ref:
CA, TC. SC: John George Norman Hyde
= JH; Kim Smith = KS. Set: Eng.
The Big Job. Cassell, 1970
Bitter Fortune. Boardman, 1959
Breakdown. Cassell, 1968
The Catch. Harrap, 1964; Holt, 1966
Counterpol. Harrap, 1963; Walker, 1965
KS
Counterpol in Paris. Harrap, 1964;
Walker, 1965 KS [Paris]
The Disposal Unit. Harrap, 1966
Fatal Error. Boardman, 1962
The Fourth Grave. Cassell, 1969
The Gentlemen at Large. Boardman, 1962;
Award, 1968 JH
The Gentlemen Reform. Boardman, 1961;
Macmillan, 1964 JH
The Golden Fleece. Boardman, 1961
The Good Citizens. Harrap, 1965
The Gusher. Harrap, 1967
Inside Job. Boardman, 1961
Kidnap. Cassell, 1970
The League of Gentlemen. Boardman,
1958; Beacon, 1961 JH
The Midas Touch. Boardman, 1960
The Mysterious Way. Boardman, 1959
Negative Value. Boardman, 1960
No Refuge. Joseph, 1956
Operation Red Carpet. Boardman, 1959
Painted Lady. Cassell, 1967
Queer Fish. Boardman, 1958
The Shakespeare Curse. Cassell, 1969;
Walker, 1970
Vendetta. Boardman, 1961
White August. Joseph, 1955; Arcadia,
1955

BOLDREWOOD, ROLF. Pseudonym of Thomas
Alexander Browne, 1826-1915.
Robbery Under Arms. Remington, 1888
[Australia]

BOLES, PAUL DARCY. 1916-   . Ref: CA.
The Limner. Crowell, 1975 [1870, Va.]
-The Mississippi Run. Crowell, 1977
[1800s, Miss.]

BOLT, BEN. Pseudonym of Ottwell Binns,
1872-   , q.v. SC: Capt. Grandison,
in at least those marked G; Insp.
Godbold, in at least those marked IG;
Bob Ponting, in at least those marked
BP; John Scarlett, in at least those
marked JS. Set: Eng.
The Badge. Ward, 1928
The Buccaneer's Pride. Ward, 1929
The Burnt Caravan. Ward, 1934
The Bushmaster. Ward, 1932
By Breathless Ways. Ward, 1937
Captain Lucifer. Ward, 1928
The Coil of Mystery. Ward, 1930
The Crooked Sign. Ward, 1935
A Desperate Rememdy. Ward, 1938
The Diamond-Buckled Shoe. Robinson,
1921
Diane of the Islands. Robinson, 1921
The Empty House Mystery. Ward, 1936
The Five Red Stars. Ward, 1936 BP
The Forest Ranger. Ward, 1931
The Gay Pilgrimage. Jenkins, 1924
The Girl in the Train. Ward, 1939 JS
The Green Arrow. Ward, 1933 G
The Green Lantern. Ward, 1935 IG
The Impossible Lover. Robinson, 1921
The Jewels of Sin. Ward, 1928
The Lavenham Mystery. Ward, 1933
Linked by Peril. Ward, 1939
Masked Danger. Ward, 1937
A Modern Delilah. Mellifont, 1943
The Mystery Hand. Ward, 1932 G
The Mystery of Airedale Hall. Mellifont, 1944
The Mystery of Belvoir Mansions. Ward,
1927
The Other Three. Ward, 1929
The Pride of the King. Robinson, 1921
The Sealed Envelope. Ward, 1931
The Shadow of the Yemen. Robinson, 1921
A Shot in the Night. Ward, 1934 IG,BP
The Snapshot Mystery. Ward, 1933
The Subway Mystery. Ward, 1930
The Sundial Clue. Ward, 1937
The Sword of Fortune. Ward, 1927
The Unseen Witness. Ward, 1935
Wayland of the Guides. Ward, 1934
[Afghan.]

BOLT, CAROL
One Night Stand. Playwrights, 1977
(2-act play.)

BOLTON, CAROLE. 1926-   . Ref: CA.
Little Girl Lost. Nelson, 1980

BOLTON, GEORGE G.
A Specialist in Crime. Richards, 1904

BOLTON, GUY (REGINALD). 1884-1979. See
also: Max Marcin, 1879-1948. Ref:
CA.
The Enchantress. Doubleday, 1964; Hale,
1966
Nine Coaches Waiting. Dramatic, 1966
(Play based on the novel by Mary
Stewart, 1916-   , q.v.)

BOLTON, JOHN. Set: Eng.
The Air Sleuth. Wright, 1936
The Air Smugglers. Wright, 1938
The Desert Flyer. Wright, 1936
The Island Mystery. Wright, 1938
The Mystery Plane. Wright, 1935
Perils in Persia. Wright, 1939 [Iran]
The Spy Hunters. Wright, 1943
The Swimming Pool Murder. Wright, 1940

BOLTON, MAISIE SHARMAN. 1915-   . Pseudonyms: Stratford Davis, Miriam
Sharman, qq.v.

BOLTON, WILLIAM. See: (Howell) North
Baker, 1912-   .

BOMBAL, MARIA LUISA. 1910-1980. Born in
Chile; educated in France; living in
NYC in the 1940s.
The Shrouded Woman. Farrar, 1948; Cassell, 1950

BOMMART, JEAN (EMILE GEORGES). 1894-   .
The Chinese Fish. Longmans, 1935

BOND, A. CURTIS.   -1923.
Mrs. Sparks of Paris. Pollard, 1888

BOND, EVELYN. Pseudonym of Morris Hershman, 1920-   , q.v. Other pseudonym:
Jess Wilcox, q.v. SC: Ira Yedder, in
at least those marked IY.
Beloved Traitor. Lancer, 1967
Bride of Terror. Lancer, 1968
The Clouded Mirror. Lancer, 1967 [N.Y.]
The Crimson Candle. Avon, 1973
Dark Sonata. Beagle, 1972 IY
The Devil's Footprints. Beagle, 1972 IY
Doomway. Beagle, 1971 IY
Evil in the House. Lancer, 1965 [NYC,
1860s]
The Girl from Nowhere. Beagle, 1972 IY
Heritage of Fear. Belmont, 1966
Hornet's Nest. Avon, 1972
House of Distant Voices. Belmont, 1965
House of Shadows. Lancer, 1965
Imperial Blue. Beagle, 1973
Lady in Darkness. Lancer, 1965
Raven's Eye. Avon, 1972
Thirteen O'Clock. Berkley, 1970
The Venetian Secret. Lancer, 1967
The Waiting Eyes. Ballantine, 1976
[R.I.]
Widow in White. Lancer, 1967

BOND, F. Pseudonym: Stephen Blakesley,
q.v.

BOND, FLORENCE DEMAREST FOOS. Pseudonym:
Anne Demarest, q.v.

BOND, J. HARVEY. Pseudonym of Russell
Robert Winterbotham, 1904-1971. Ref:
CA. SC: Mike Lanson, in all titles.
Bye, Bye, Baby! Ace, 1958
If Wishes Were Hearses. Ace, 1961
Kill Me with Kindness. Ace, 1959;
Digit, 1960
Murder Isn't Funny. Ace, 1958; Digit,
1958

BOND, NOREEN
Hide Away. Hodder, 1936
Take Care. Hodder, 1938

BOND, RUSKIN. 1934-   . Ref: CA.
An Axe for the Rani. Hind Pocket Books
(Delhi), 1972

BOND, WALTER
The Kill Squad. Lancer, 1968

BONETT, EMERY. Pseudonym of Felicity
Winifred Carter Coulson, 1907-   .
See also: John and Emery Bonett.
High Pavement. Heinemann, 1944. U.S.
title: Old Mrs. Camelot. Blakiston,
1944
-Make Do with Spring. Heinemann, 1942
-Never Go Dark. Heinemann, 1940
Old Mrs. Camelot; see High Pavement

BONETT, JOHN and EMERY. Joint pseudonym
of John Hubert Arthur Coulson,
1906-   , and Felicity Winifred
Carter Coulson, 1907-   . See also:
Emery Bonett. Ref: CA, CC, EM, TC.
SC: Insp. Borges = B; Professor
Mandrake = M. Set: Eng.
A Banner for Pegasus. Joseph, 1951.
U.S. title: Not in the Script.
Doubleday, 1951 M
Better Dead. Joseph, 1964. U.S. title:
Better Off Dead. Doubleday, 1964 B
[Sp.]
Dead Lion. Joseph, 1949; Doubleday,
1949 M
Murder on the Costa Brava; see This
Side Murder
No Grave for a Lady. Joseph, 1960;
Doubleday, 1959 M
No Time to Kill. Harrap, 1972; Walker,
1972 B [Sp.]
Not in the Script; see A Banner for
Pegasus
The Private Face of Murder. Joseph,
1966; Doubleday, 1966 B [Sp.]
The Sound of Murder. Harrap, 1970;
Walker, 1971 B
This Side Murder. Joseph, 1967. U.S.
title: Murder on the Costa Brava.
Walker, 1968 B [Sp.]

BONFIGLIOLI, KYRIL. 1929(?)-   . Lives
in Ireland; an art dealer by trade.
SC: Charlie Mortdecai, in all titles.
After You with the Pistol. Secker,
1979; Doubleday, 1980
Don't Point That Thing at Me. Weidenfeld, 1972. U.S. title: Mortdecai's
Endgame. Simon, 1973
Mortdecai's Endgame; see Don't Point
That Thing at Me
Something Nasty in the Woodshed. Macmillan (London), 1976 [Chan. Is.]

BONHAM, BARBARA THOMAS. 1926-   . Pseudonym: Sara North, q.v. Ref: CA.

BONHAM, FRANK. 1914-   . Ref: CA.
By Her Own Hand. Monarch, 1963
One for Sleep. GM, 1960; Muller pb,
1961
The Skin Game. GM, 1962; Muller pb,
1963

BONHAM, MARGARET. 1913-   .
The House Across the River. Joseph,
1950; Macmillan, 1951

BONHOTE, ELIZABETH. 1744-1818.
Bungay Castle. Minerva, 1796

BONIFACE, MARJORIE. SC: Sheriff Hiram
Odom, in all titles.
Murder As an Ornament. Doubleday, 1940
[Tex.]
Venom in Eden. Doubleday, 1942 [Tex.]
Wings of Death. McBride, 1946 [N. Mex.]

BONNAMY, FRANCIS. Pseudonym of Audrey
Boyers Walz, 1906-1983. SC: Peter
Shane, in all titles.
Blood and Thirsty. Duell, 1949; Murray,
1952 [Maine]
Dead Reckoning. Duell, 1943 [Wash.
D.C.]
Death by Appointment. Doubleday, 1931
[Chi.]
Death on a Dude Ranch. Doubleday, 1937
[West]
The King Is Dead on Queen Street.
Duell, 1945 [Wash. D.C.]
The Man in the Mist. Duell, 1951;
Murray, 1952 [Can.]
Murder As a Fine Art; see Portrait of
the Artist As a Dead Man
Portrait of the Artist As a Dead Man.
Duell, 1947. British title: Self-
Portrait of Murder. Murray, 1944.
Also published as: Murder As a Fine
Art. Signet, 1949 [Wash. D.C.]
A Rope of Sand. Duell, 1944 [Ind.]
Self-Portrait of Murder; see Portrait
of the Artist As a Dead Man

BONNECARRERE, PAUL. 1925?-1977. See also:
Joan Hemingway, 1951-   . Free-
lance journalist.
The Golden Triangle. Ellis, 1977
(Translation of "Le Triangle D'Or."
Paris, 1976.)

The Lost Victory. Ellis, 1979 (Translation of "Une Victoire Perdue." Paris, 1978.)
Ultimatum. Ellis, 1976; Ballantine pb, 1976 (Translation of "Ultimatum." Paris, 1975.)

BONNELL, JAMES FRANCIS
   Death Flies West. Scribner, 1941 [air.]
   Death over Sunday. Scribner, 1940 [L.I.]

BONNER, GERALDINE. 1870-1930. SC: Molly Morganthau, in at least those marked MM.
   The Black Eagle Mystery. Appleton, 1916 MM [NYC]
   The Castlecourt Diamond Case. Funk, 1906 [Eng.]
   The Girl at Central. Appleton, 1915 MM [N.J.]
   The Leading Lady. Bobbs, 1926
   Miss Maitland, Private Secretary. Appleton, 1919
   -Taken at the Flood. Bobbs, 1927; Mathews, 1928 [Calif.]

BONNER, MARGERIE [MRS. MALCOLM LOWRY]
   The Last Twist of the Knife. Scribner, 1946 [Calif.]
   The Shapes That Creep. Scribner, 1946 [Van.]

BONNER, PAUL HYDE. 1893- . Ref: CA.
   -S.P.Q.R. Scribner, 1952; Verschoyle, 1953. Also published as: Summer in Rome. Permabooks, 1953 [Rome]

BONNEY, JOSEPH L. SC: Simon Rolfe = SR.
   Death by Dynamite. Carrick, 1940 SR [L.I.]
   Look to the Lady! Lippincott, 1947
   Murder Without Clues. Carrick, 1940. British title: No Man's Hand. Heinemann, 1940 SR [NYC]
   No Man's Hand; see Murder Without Clues

BOOCOCK, D. E.
   Murder for Love. Long, 1939

BOORE, W(ALTER) H(UGH). 1904- . Ref: CA, CC.
   Cry on the Wind. Collins, 1967 [Wales]
   The Valley and the Shadow. Heinemann, 1963 [Wales]

BOORSTIN, PAUL (TERRY). 1944- . Ref: CA.
   Savage. Marek. 1980 [S. Am.]

BOOTH, ANTHONY
   Element of Doubt. Evans, 1952 (1-act play.)
   It Could Happen to You. Evans, 1965 (1-act play.)
   Ride a Tiger. Evans, 1960 (1-act play.)
   The Sky Is Overcast. Evans, 1951 (1-act play.)

BOOTH, CHARLES G(ORDON). 1896-1949. Ref: CC. SC: Anatole Flique = AF.
   At Ten Paces; see Those Seven Alibis
   The Cat and the Clock. Doubleday, 1935; Cassell, 1938 AF [L.A.]
   The General Died at Dawn. PB, 1941; Bell, 1937 [Shanghai]
   Gold Bullets. Morrow, 1929; Hodder, 1929 [Calif.]
   Kings Die Hard. Hammond, 1949 (U.S. title?) [Cuba]
   Mr. Angel Comes Aboard. Doubleday, 1944; Hammond, 1946
   Murder at High Tide. Morrow, 1930; Hodder, 1930 AF [Calif.]
   Murder Strikes Thrice. Bond, 1946
   Sinister House. Morrow, 1926; Hodder, 1927 [Calif.]
   Those Seven Alibis. Morrow, 1932. British title: At Ten Paces. Hodder, 1933 [S.F.]

BOOTH, CHRISTOPHER B. See also: Isabel (Egenton) Ostrander, 1883-1924. SC: Jim Bliss = JB; Amos Clackworthy = AC.
   The Amateur Detectives. Chelsea, 1926 [Kan.]
   Deceiver's Door. Chelsea, 1929 [NYC]
   The Fatal Record. Hutchinson, 1929 (U.S. title?)
   The House of Rogues. Chelsea, 1923; Hutchinson, 1927 [L.I.]
   The Kidnaping Syndicate. Chelsea, 1925; Skeffington, 1926 [Midwest]
   Killing Jazz. Chelsea, 1928 JB
   Mr. Clackworthy. Chelsea, 1926 AC ss [Chi.]
   Mr. Clackworthy, Con Man. Chelsea, 1927 AC ss

A Seaside Mystery. Chelsea, 1925 JB [L.I.]
The Telltale Print. Chelsea, 1927 [L.I.]
$10,000 Reward. Chelsea, 1926

BOOTH, CLARE [CLARE BOOTH LUCE]. 1903- . Ref: CA.
   Margin for Error. Dramatists, 1940 (Play.)

BOOTH, EDWIN. 1906- . Pseudonym: Don Blunt, q.v. Ref: CA.
   The Broken Window. Arcadia, 1960 [S.F.]
   Death on a Summer Day. Arcadia, 1960

BOOTH, ERNEST. 1899- .
   With Sirens Screaming. Doubleday, 1945 [L.A.]

BOOTH, HILLIARD
   Nine Points of the Law. French, 1928 (3-act play.)

BOOTH, J. W.
   Murder by Stealth. Cole, 1943
   Queen of the Underworld. Cole, 1943
   Riddle of Crooked Creek. Cole, 1944
   Science Traps the Criminal. Cole, 1943

BOOTH, LOUIS F. SC: Maxwell Fenner, in both titles.
   The Bank Vault Mystery. Dodd, 1933; Hutchinson, 1933 [NYC]
   Broker's End. Dodd, 1935; Hutchinson, 1935 [NYC]

BOOTH, MARTIN. 1944- . Ref: CA.
   The Bad Track. Collins, 1980

BOOTH, MAUD BALLINGTON CHARLESWORTH. 1865-1948. Pseudonym: M. E. Charlesworth, q.v.

BOOTHBY, BEN
   The Centipede. Ward, 1907

BOOTHBY, GUY (NEWELL). 1867-1905. Ref: EM. SC: Dr. Nikola = N; Jacob Burrell = JB.
   -Across the World for a Wife. Ward, 1898
   The Beautiful White Devil. Ward, 1896; Appleton, 1897 [Far East]
   A Bid for Fortune; or, Dr. Nikola's Vendetta. Ward, 1895; Appleton, 1895. Also published as: Enter Dr. Nikola. Newcastle, 1975 N
   A Bid for Freedom. Ward, 1904 [Mid. East]
   -Billy Binks, Hero, and other stories. Chambers, 1898 ss
   -A Bride from the Sea. Long, 1904
   A Brighton Tragedy. White, 1905
   -Bushigrams. Ward, 1897 ss [Australia]
   A Cabinet Secret. White, 1901; Lippincott, 1901
   The Childerbridge Mystery. White, 1902
   -Connie Burt. Ward, 1903
   A Consummate Scoundrel. White, 1904
   The Countess India. White, 1903 ss
   A Crime of the Under-Seas. Ward, 1905 ss
   The Curse of the Snake. White, 1902
   A Desperate Conspiracy. White, 1904
   Doctor Nikola. Ward, 1896; Appleton, 1896. Also published as: Dr. Nikola Returns. Newcastle, 1976 N [China]
   Dr. Nikola Returns; see Doctor Nikola
   Dr. Nikola's Experiment. Hodder, 1899; Appleton, 1899 N
   Enter Dr. Nikola; see A Bid for Fortune
   Farewell Nikola. Ward, 1901; Lippincott, 1901 N [It.]
   For Love of Her. Ward, 1905 ss, some criminous
   -In Spite of the Czar. Long, 1905
   In Strange Company. Ward, 1894; Neely, 1894 [Chile]
   The Kidnapped President. Ward, 1902; Munro, 1902 [Carib.]
   The Lady of the Island. Long, 1904 ss [S. Pac.]
   The League of Twelve. White, 1903
   Long Live the King. Ward, 1900; Stone, 1900
   -A Lost Endeavor. Dent, 1895; Macmillan, 1895
   -Love Made Manifest. Ward, 1899; Stone, 1899 [Australia]
   The Lust of Hate. Ward, 1898; Warwick House, 1898 N
   A Maker of Nations. Ward, 1900; Appleton, 1899
   -The Man of the Crag. White, 1907
   The Marriage of Esther. Ward, 1895; Appleton, 1895
   A Millionaire's Love Story. White, 1901; Buckles, 1901 JB
   -My Indian Queen. Ward, 1901; Appleton, 1901

My Strangest Case. Ward, 1902; Page, 1901
The Mystery of the Clasped Hands. White, 1901; Appleton, 1901 JB
An Ocean Secret. White, 1904 [ship]
-The Phantom Stockman. Phono, 1897 (A ss printed in shorthand!)
Pharos, the Egyptian. Ward, 1899; Appleton, 1899 [Egypt]
A Prince of Swindlers. Ward, 1900. U.S. title: The Viceroy's Protege. New Amsterdam, 1903 ss
A Queer Affair. White, 1903
The Race of Life. Ward, 1906; Buckles, 1906 [Australia]
The Red Rat's Daughter. Ward, 1899; New Amsterdam, 1900
-A Royal Affair and other stories. White, 1906 ss
-A Sailor's Bride. White, 1899 [Afr.]
Sheilah McLeod. Skeffington, 1897; Stokes, 1897 [Australia]
A Stolen Peer. White, 1906
A Two-Fold Inheritance. Ward, 1903
Uncle Joe's Legacy and other stories. White, 1902 ss, some criminous
The Viceroy's Protege; see A Prince of Swindlers
The Woman of Death. Pearson, 1900 [Fr.]

BOOTON, (CATHERINE) KAGE. 1919- . Ref: CA.
   Andrew's Wife. Doubleday, 1964 [Conn.]
   Lady in Darkness. Berkley, 1974
   Place of Shadows. Dodd, 1959; Gollancz, 1960
   Quite by Accident. Doubleday, 1972; Davies, 1974 [Pa.]
   Runaway Home! Doubleday, 1967; Hale, 1968 [N.J.]
   Time Running Out. Doubleday, 1968; Hale, 1969 [Pa.]
   The Toy. Doubleday, 1975 [Pa.]
   The Troubled House. Dodd, 1958; Gollancz, 1959 [N.Y.]
   Who Knows Julie Gordon? Doubleday, 1980; Hale, 1981 [Phil.]

BORBOLLA, BARBARA MARTYN. Pseudonym: Don Martyn, q.v.

BORDAGES, ASA
   The Glass Lady. Godwin, 1932

BORDEAUX, DELMAR E(MIL). 1912- .
   So Thin Is the Veil. Bellevue, 1948

BORDEAUX, HENRY (CAMILLE). 1870-1963.
   The House That Died. Duffield, 1922; Unwin, 1923 (Translation of "La Maison Morte." Paris, 1922.) [Fr.]
   Murder Party. Dial, 1931; Gollancz, 1931 (Translation of "Murder-Party; ou, Celle Qui N'Etait Pas Invitee." Paris, 1931.) [Switz.]

BORDEN, LEE. Pseudonym of Borden Deal, 1922- , q.v.
   The Devil's Whisper. Avon, 1961
   The Secret of Sylvia. GM, 1958

BORDEN, LOWELL MASON
   The Counterfeit Bridegroom. Vantage, 1956

BORER, MARY (IRENE) CATHCART. See: Arnold Ridley, 1896- .

BORGE, BERNHARD. Pseudonym of Andre Bjerke, 1918- .
   Death in the Blue Lake. Macdonald, 1961 (Translation of "De Dødes Tjern." Oslo, 1942.)

BORGEN, JOHAN. 1902- .
   The Red Mist. Calder, 1973 (Translation of "Den Rode Taken." Oslo, 1967.)

BORGENICHT, MIRIAM [MIRIAM BORGENICHT KLEIN]. 1915- . Ref: TC.
   A Corpse in Diplomacy. Mill, 1949; Panther, 1956 [Wash. D.C.]
   Don't Look Back. Doubleday, 1956; Hale, 1958 [Midwest]
   Extreme Remedies. Doubleday, 1967; Hale, 1968 [N.H.]
   Margin for Doubt. Doubleday, 1968; Hale, 1969 [N.Y.]
   No Bail for Dalton. Bobbs, 1974
   Ring and Walk In. Harper, 1952; H. Hamilton, 1952 [NYC]
   Roadblock. Bobbs, 1973
   To Borrow Trouble. Doubleday, 1965; Hale, 1966
   The Tomorrow Trap. Doubleday, 1969; Hale, 1970 [N.Y.]
   A Very Thin Line. Doubleday, 1970; Hale, 1972

BORGES, JORGE LUIS. 1899- . Ref: CA, MC, TC.
Ficciones. Grove, 1962; Weidenfeld, 1962 ss
Labyrinths. New Directions, 1962 ss

BORLAND, KATHRYN KILBY. 1916- . Joint pseudonym with Helen Speicher: Alice Abbott, q.v.

BORNEMAN, ERNEST (WILLIAM JULIUS). 1915- . Pseudonym: Cameron McCabe, q.v. Ref: CA, MC.
Tremolo. Harper, 1948; Jarrolds, 1948 [New Eng.]

BORNICHE, ROGER
Flic Story. Doubleday, 1975; Hart-Davis, 1976 (Translation of "Flic Story." Paris, 1973.)

BORROW, GEORGE. See: Anonymous

BORTH, WILLAN G. Pseudonym of Willan George Bosworth, 1904- . Joint pseudonym with Maurice H. B. Mash: Maurice Worth, q.v.
The Monk's Bridge Mystery. Selwyn, 1929

BORTNER, NORMAN STANLEY. SC: Prof. Clifford Wells, in both titles.
Bond Grayson Murdered! Macrae, 1936 [Balt.]
Death of a Merchant of Death. Macrae, 1937 [Balt.]

BOSSE, M(ALCOLM) J(OSEPH). 1926- . Professor of English at City College of New York.
The Incident at Naha. Simon, 1972; Macmillan (London), 1972 [NYC]
The Man Who Loved Zoos. Putnam, 1974; Gollancz, 1975. Also published as: Stricken. Dell, 1977 [S.F.]
Stricken; see The Man Who Loved Zoos

BOSTON, CHARLES K. Pseudonym of Frank Gruber, 1904-1969, q.v. Other pseudonyms: Stephen Acre, John K. Vedder, qq.v. SC (continued under the Frank Gruber byline): Otis Beagle = OB.
The Silver Jackass. Reynal, 1941; Cherry Tree, 1952, as by Frank Gruber. Reprinted in the U.S. as by Gruber OB

BOSWELL, JOHN. SC: Christopher Kent, in both titles.
The Blue Pheasant. Collins, 1958
Lost Girl. Collins, 1959

BOSWORTH, ALLAN R(UCKER). 1901- . Ref: CA.
Full Crash Dive. Duell, 1942. British title: Murder Goes to Sea. Bodley, 1948. Also published as: The Submarine Signalled...Murder! Select, 1942 (abridged) [ship]
Murder Goes to Sea; see Full Crash Dive
The Submarine Signalled...Murder!; see Full Crash Dive

BOSWORTH, FRANK. Pseudonym of Lauran Bosworth Paine, 1916- . Other pseudonyms: John Armour, Reg Batchelor, Kenneth Bedford, Mark Carrel, Robert Clarke, Richard Dana, J. F. Drexler, Troy Howard, Jared Ingersol, John Kilgore, Hunter Liggett, J. K. Lucas, John Morgan, qq.v.
Murder Now, Pay Later. Hale, 1969

BOSWORTH, WILLAN GEORGE. 1904- . Pseudonym: Willan G. Borth, q.v. Joint pseudonym with Maurice H. B. Mash: Maurice Worth, q.v.

BOTEIN, BERNARD. 1900-1974. Ref: CA.
The Prosecutor. Simon, 1956 [NYC]

BOTTOME, PHYLLIS. Pseudonym of Phyllis Forbes-Dennis, 1884-1963. Ref: CA.
Danger Signal; see Murder in the Bud
-The Lifeline. Faber, 1946; Little, 1946
-The Mortal Storm. Faber, 1937; Little, 1938
Murder in the Bud. Faber, 1939. U.S. title: Danger Signal. Little, 1939
The Rat. Allan, 1927; Doran, 1927 (Novelization of the play by Ivor Novello and Constance Collier.)

BOUCHER, ANTHONY. Pseudonym of William Anthony Parker White, 1911-1968. Other pseudonyms: H. H. Holmes, q.v. See also: Theo Durrant. Ref: CA, CC, EM, MC, MP, TC. SC: Fergus O'Breen = FO.
Blood on Baker Street; see The Case of the Baker Street Irregulars
The Case of the Baker Street Irregulars. Simon, 1940. Also published as: Blood on Baker Street. Mercury, 1953 FO [L.A.]
The Case of the Crumpled Knave. Simon, 1939; Harrap, 1939 FO [L.A.]
The Case of the Seven of Calvary. Simon, 1937; H. Hamilton, 1937 [S.F.]
The Case of the Seven Sneezes. Simon, 1942; United Authors, 1946 FO [Calif.]
The Case of the Solid Key. Simon, 1941 FO [L.A.]
The Compleat Werewolf and other tales of fantasy and science fiction. Simon, 1969; Allen, 1970 ss, including two FO tales and two others combining fantasy and murder
Far and Away. Ballantine, 1955 ss, including one FO tale and others combining science fiction and detection

BOUCHER, BERNARD. 1934- . Born in England; moved to Australia in 1965; journalist.
The Megawind Cancellation. Macmillan (London), 1979; Atheneum, 1979 [Australia]

BOUCHIER, WILLIAM. Set: Eng.
The Exploits of Black Thumb. Bles, 1936
The Little Grey Man. Bles, 1935
The Strange Fellowship of Maxwell Gale. Pawling, 1934

BOUCICAULT, DION(YSIUS LARDNER). 1820-1890. See: Charles Reade, 1814-1884.

BOULGER, THEODORA HAVERS. -1887. Pseudonym: Theo Gift, q.v.

BOULLE, PIERRE. 1912- . Ref: CA, TC.
The Chinese Executioner; see The Executioner
Desperate Games. Vanguard, 1973 (Translation of "Les Jeux d'Esprit." Paris, 1973.)
Ears of the Jungle. Vanguard, 1972; Cassell, 1974 (Translation of "Les Oreilles de Jungle." Paris, 1972.)
The Executioner. Vanguard, 1961. British title: The Chinese Executioner. Secker, 1962 (Translation of "Le Bourreau." Paris, 1954.)
Face of a Hero. Vanguard, 1956. British title: Saving Face. Secker, 1956 (Translation of "La Face." Paris, 1953.)
For a Noble Cause; see A Noble Profession
An Impartial Eye; see The Photographer
A Noble Profession. Vanguard, 1960. British title: For a Noble Cause. Secker, 1961 (Translation of "Un Metier de Seigneur." Paris, 1960.) [Fr., WWII]
Not the Glory. Vanguard, 1955. British title: William Conrad. Secker, 1955. Also published as: Spy Converted. Fontana, 1960 (Translation of "William Conrad." Paris, 1950.)
The Photographer. Vanguard, 1968. British title: An Impartial Eye. Secker, 1968 (Translation of "Le Photographe." Paris, 1967.) [Paris]
Saving Face; see Face of a Hero
Spy Converted; see Not the Glory
The Virtues of Hell. Vanguard, 1974; Cassell, 1975 (Translation of "Les Vertus de l'Enfer." Paris, 1974.)
William Conrad; see Not the Glory

BOUNDEN, JOSEPH
The Murderer; or, The Fall of Lecas. Minerva, 1808

BOURGEAU, ART
A Lonely Way to Die. Charter, 1980 [Tenn.]

BOURGEOIS, CAMILLE. Pseudonym: Robin Carol, q.v.

BOURGET, PAUL (CHARLES JOSEPH). 1852-1935.
Andre Cornelis. Spencer Blackett, 1889; Brentano's, 1909

BOURJAILY, VANCE (NYE). 1922- . Ref: CA.
A Game Men Play. Dial, 1980 [NYC]

BOURNE, HESTER. Pseudonym of Molly Troke
After the Island. Hurst, 1969. U.S. title: Haunted Island. Pyramid, 1971
Haunted Island; see After the Island
-The House Across the Water. Hurst, 1972
In the Event of My Death. Hurst, 1964; Doubleday, 1964

-The Red Raincoat. Hurst, 1970
-A Scent of Roses. Hurst, 1971; Pyramid, 1976
The Spanish House. Hurst, 1962; Pyramid, 1965
-Where Is Evie Alton? Hurst, 1968

BOURNE, LAWRENCE R.
Stark Naked. Muller, 1934

BOURQUIN, PAUL HENRY JAMES. 1916- . Pseudonym: Richard Amberley, q.v.

BOUSFIELD, H(ENRY) T(HOMAS) W(ISHART)
The God with Four Arms and other stories. Barker, 1939 ss, some criminous
Vinegar—and Cream. Murray, 1941 ss, some criminous

BOUTELL, ANITA (DAY KEARNEY). 1895- . Ref: MP.
Cradled in Fear. Putnam, 1942; Joseph, 1943
Death Brings a Storke. Putnam, 1938 [Eng.]
Death Has a Past. Putnam, 1939; Joseph, 1939
Tell Death to Wait. Putnam, 1939; Joseph, 1938 [Eng.]

BOUTELLE, CLARENCE (MILES). -1903.
An Artificial Fate. Ivers, 1891 [NYC]
Beyond the End. Lupton, 1892 [NYC]
The Grave Between Them. Ivers, 1891

BOUTON, JOHN BELL. 1830-1902. See: Anonymous.

BOUVIER, ALEXIS. 1836-1892.
The Convict's Marriage. Vizetelly, 1888
A Wily Widow. Vizetelly, 1888

BOVA, BEN(JAMIN WILLIAM). 1932- . Ref: CA.
The Multiple Man. Bobbs, 1976; Gollancz, 1977

BOVE, EMMANUEL. 1898-1945.
The Murder of Suzy Pommier. Little, 1934 (Translation of "Le Meurtre de Suzy Pommier." Paris, 1933.) [Paris]

BOWDEN, JEAN. 1925- . Pseudonyms: Jennifer Bland, Avon Curry, qq.v.

BOWEN, E. M.
Murder Will Out. Fiction House, 1945
On the Run. Fiction House, 1946
Ticket for Death. Fiction House, 1946

BOWEN, ELIZABETH (DOROTHEA COLE). 1899-1973.
-The Heat of the Day. Cape, 1949; Knopf, 1949

BOWEN, IVOR IAN. 1908- . Joint pseudonym with John Creasey, 1908-1973, q.v.: Charles Hogarth, q.v. Ref: CA.

BOWEN, JOSEPH. ca.1871- . Pseudonym of "a well-known Western cattleman, born in Colorado; known throughout the state of Texas; has a collection of nearly 10,000 first editions of detective fiction."
The Man Without a Head. Covici, 1936; Butterworth, 1937 [N. Mex.]

BOWEN, MARJORIE. Pseudonym of Gabrielle Margaret Vere Campbell Long, 1886-1952. Other pseudonyms: George R. Preedy, Joseph Shearing, qq.v., Margaret Campbell.
The Bishop of Hell. Bodley, 1949 ss
-Old Patch's Medley. Selwyn, 1930 ss
The Shadow on Mockways. Collins, 1932
Withering Fires. Collins, 1931

BOWEN, NAN. Reporter and magazine writer.
Hear No Evil. Macmillan, 1968 [Fla.]

BOWEN, ROBERT SIDNEY. 1900-1977. Pseudonym: Robert Wallace, q.v. Ref: CA. SC: Gerry Barnes, in both titles.
Make Mine Murder. Crown, 1946 [NYC]
Murder Gets Around. Crown, 1947 [NYC]

BOWEN-JUDD, SARA HUTTON. 1922- . Pseudonyms: Anne Burton, Mary Challis, Margaret Leek, Sara Woods, qq.v.

BOWEN-ROWLANDS, ERNEST (BROWN). 1866- .
You Can't Kill the Dead. Allan, 1937

BOWER, B. M. Pseudonym of Bertha Muzzy Bowen Sinclair Cowan, 1874-1940.
The Haunted Hills. Little, 1934; Hodder, 1935
The Voice of Johnnywater. Little, 1923; Hodder, 1923

BOWER, MARIAN and LEON M. LION
  The Chinese Puzzle. Hutchinson, 1919; Holt, 1919

BOWERS, DOROTHY (VIOLET). 1904-   . SC: Insp. Pardoe = P. Set: Eng.
  The Bells at Old Bailey. Hodder, 1947. U.S. title: The Bells of Old Bailey. Doubleday, 1947
  The Bells of Old Bailey; see The Bells at Old Bailey
  A Deed Without a Name. Hodder, 1940; Doubleday, 1940 P
  Fear and Miss Betony; see Fear for Miss Betony
  Fear for Miss Betony. Hodder, 1941. U.S. title: Fear and Miss Betony. Doubleday, 1942 P
  Postscript to Poison. Hodder, 1938 P
  Shadows Before. Hodder, 1939; Doubleday, 1940 P

BOWERS, PAUL E(UGENE). 1886-   .
  The Pawns of Fate. Cornhill, 1918

BOWICK, DOROTHY MULLER. 1901-   . Ref: CA.
  Tapestry of Death. Hale, 1973; Walker, 1975 [Paris]

BOWMAN, CLELL EDGAR. 1904-   . Ref: CA.
  Human Equation. Exposition, 1976
  Male Order. Exposition, 1976

BOWMAN, GERALD.   -1967. SC: Michael Shannon = MS.
  The Devil's Own. Amalgamated, 1937 (Sexton Blake.)
  The Hunchback of Hatton Garden. Amalgamated, 1937 (Sexton Blake.)
  The Iron Apple. Amalgamated, 1935
  Pattern in Poison-Ivy. Laurie, 1948 MS
  The Quick and the Wed. Laurie, 1950 MS
  Sawdust Angel. Laurie, 1949 MS

BOWMAN, JEANNE
  The House of Hate. Arcadia, 1969. Also published as: Doomed to Hate. Magnum, 197? [West]

BOWSER, JIM. Pseudonym: Nick Carter, q.v.

BOWYER, JOHN
  Death Works to Rule. Hale, 1978

BOX, EDGAR. Pseudonym of Eugene Gore Vidal, 1925-   . Ref: CA, CC, EM, MC, TC. SC: Peter Sergeant, in all titles.
  Death Before Bedtime. Dutton, 1953; Heinemann, 1954 [Wash. D.C.]
  Death in the Fifth Position. Dutton, 1952; Heinemann, 1954 [NYC]
  Death Likes It Hot. Dutton, 1954; Heinemann, 1955 [L.I.]

BOX, MURIEL (VIOLETTE). 1905-   . See: Sydney Box, 1907-   .

BOX, SYDNEY. 1907-   . Founded Verity Films in 1939—this made 100 documentaries for the War Office and other British government departments; after war became prolific British film producer; won Academy Award (with Muriel Box) for best original screenplay ("The Seventh Veil"); living in Australia.
  Alibi in the Rough. Hale, 1977
  -Diary of a Drop-Out. Triton, 1969
  Forbidden Cargo, with Muriel Box, 1905-   . Heinemann, 1957
  -The Golden Girls. Triton, 1970
  Murder Trial. French (London), 1955 (Play.)
  Second Only to Murder. Hale, 1976

BOYCE, DAVID
  I'll Die Too Soon. World Distributors, 1951

BOYD, AUBREY
  No Man's Woman. Dutton, 1931; Hutchinson, 1934 [Can.]

BOYD, CATHERINE BRADSHAW. A teacher with degrees in piano and Latin; frequent contributor of articles and poetry to periodicals.
  Revenge in "The Convent". Exposition, 1955 [Ia.]

BOYD, DEREK
  The Man Who Was Bormann. Hale, 1970

BOYD, DON
  Fear Stalks the Footlights. Stanley Baker, 1952

BOYD, EDWARD. See also: Bill Knox, 1928-   . Scriptwriter for radio, TV and films; lives in Glasgow.
  The Dark Number, with Roger Parkes, 1933-   , q.v. Constable, 1973; Walker, 1974 [Glasgow]

BOYD, ERIC FORBES
  -The House of Whipplestaff. Hodder, 1924
  Merlin Hold. Jarrolds, 1927
  -A Stranger in These Parts. Skeffington, 1952

BOYD, EUNICE MAYS. SC: F. Millard Smyth, in all titles, all set in Alaska.
  Doom in the Midnight Sun. Farrar, 1944
  Murder Breaks Trail. Farrar, 1943
  Murder Wears Mukluks. Farrar, 1945

BOYD, FRANK. Pseudonym of Frank Kane, 1912-1968, q.v.
  The Flesh Peddlers. Monarch, 1959 [NYC]
  Johnny Staccato. GM, 1960; Consul, 1964 (Novelization of the TV series.) [NYC]

BOYD, HAMISH
  One Night of Murder. Mystery House, 1958; Ward, 1959 [Can.]

BOYD, JANE. Pseudonym. Ref: CC.
  Murder in the King's Road. Harvill, 1953; British Book Centre, 1954

BOYD, MARION [MARION MARGARET BOYD HAVIGHURST].   -1974. Educated at Smith College and Yale; member of English department, Miami University of Ohio; poet and mainstream novelist.
  Murder in the Stacks. Lothrop, 1934 [Midwest, acad.]

BOYD, MARY STUART. 1860-   .
  Backwaters. Chapman, 1906
  -The First Stone. Hodder, 1909
  -The Man in the Wood. Chapman, 1904
  The Mystery of the Castle. Nisbet, 1911
  -With Clipped Wings. Hutchinson, 1902

BOYD, OSCAR
  The Case of the Poisoned Cocktails. Modern Fiction, 1946

BOYD, PETER
  Slips Sees Red. Melrose, 1950

BOYD, R(OBERT) S. 1928-   . Ref: CA. See: David Kraslow, 1926-   .

BOYD, RAYMOND. SC: Paul Scarf = PS.
  Death Joins the Party. Mellifont, 1944
  Fetch Me a Rope. Hammond, 1947 PS
  Murder Is a Furtive Thing. Hammond, 1950 PS

BOYDSTUN, JACKSON BENJAMIN. 1908-   .
  On the Wings of Truth. Vantage, 1978

BOYER, BRIAN (D.). 1939-   . Ref: CA. See: John Weisman, 1942-   .

BOYER, BRUCE HALTON. 1946-   . Ref: CA.
  The Solstice Cipher. Lippincott, 1979; New English Library, 1980 [1944, Eng.]

BOYER, COLUMBIA. Pseudonym of Nell Columbia Boyer Martin, 1890-   .
  The Mosaic Earring. Henkle, 1927. Reprinted as by Nell Martin: International Fiction, 1927 [L.A.]

BOYER, RICHARD L(EWIS). 1943-   . Ref: CA.
  The Giant Rat of Sumatra. Warner, 1976; Allen, 1977 (Sherlock Holmes.) [1893, Eng.]

BOYERS, AUDREY. See: Bettina Boyers.

BOYERS, BETTINA
  Murder by Proxy, with Audrey Boyers. Doubleday, 1945 [L.A.]
  The White Mazurka. Doubleday, 1946 [Conn.]

BOYLAN, MALCOLM STUART. 1897-   . Newspaperman; Hollywood writer, editor and producer.
  The Passion of Gabrielle. Crown, 1961; Gollancz, 1962 [Carib.]

BOYLE, ANN
  Moon Shadows. Manor, 1978

BOYLE, C(ONSTANCE ANTO)NINA. 1865-   . Set: Eng.
  Anna's. Allen, 1925; Seltzer, 1925
  A Desperate Expedient. Paul, 1932
  -Good Old Potts! Paul, 1934
  How Could They? Paul, 1932
  The Late Unlamented. Paul, 1931
  -Moteley's Concession. Allen, 1926
  -My Lady's Bath. Paul, 1930
  Out of the Frying Pan. Allen, 1920; Seltzer, 1923
  -The Rights of Mallaroche. Allen, 1927
  The Stranger Within the Gates. Allen, 1926; Seltzer, 1926
  What Became of Mr. Desmond. Allen, 1922; Seltzer, 1922

BOYLE, DENIS. SC: Commander Moreton, in both titles.
  Death at Devil-Fish Point. Hale, 1961
  Strange Corpse on Murder Mile. Hale, 1960

BOYLE, JACK. Ref: TC.
  Boston Blackie. Fly, 1919 [S.F.]

BOYLE, KAY. 1903-   . Ref: CA.
  Avalanche. Simon, 1944; Faber, 1944
  A Frenchman Must Die. Simon, 1946; Faber, 1946 [Fr.]
  Monday Night. Harcourt, 1938; Faber, 1938

BOYLE, ROBERT. Pseudonym of Jennifer Jenkins.
  The Baby Sitter. Macdonald, 1975; Walker, 1974
  Cry Rape. Macdonald, 1976

BRACE, TIMOTHY. Pseudonym of Theodore Pratt, 1901-1969. Ref: CC. SC: Anthony Adams, in all titles, which were published in Britain as by Theodore Pratt.
  Murder Goes Fishing. Dutton, 1936; Selwyn, 1936. Reprinted in the U.S. under the Pratt byline: Diamond, 1945 [Miami]
  Murder Goes in a Trailer. Dutton, 1937; Eldon, 1951 [Fla.]
  Murder Goes to the Dogs. Dutton, 1938; Readers Library, 1939 [Fla.]
  Murder Goes to the World's Fair. Dutton, 1939; Eldon, 1951 [NYC]

BRACEWELL, W. HARTLEY
  Tales of the Cliffs. Henderson, 1904 ss, some criminous

BRACEY, AXEL. Set: Eng.
  Public Enemies. Rich, 1934
  School for Scoundrels. Rich, 1934

BRACKEEN, STEVE. Educated in the Midwest; living in Tennessee in the 1960s.
  Baby Moll. Crest, 1958; Fawcett (London), 1959
  The Body on the Beach. Mystery House, 1957
  Danger in My Blood. Crest, 1959
  Delfina. GM, 1962; Muller pb, 1963
  The Guardians. Holt, 1964; Hale, 1966

BRACKEN, C(ATHERINE) P(HILIPPA). 1918-   .
  Roman Ring. Cassell, 1968 [Rome]

BRACKETT, LEIGH (DOUGLAS) [MRS. EDMOND HAMILTON]. 1915-1978. Ref: CA. See also: George Sanders, 1906-1972.
  An Eye for an Eye. Doubleday, 1957; Boardman, 1958 [Ohio]
  Fear No Evil; see The Tiger Among Us
  No Good from a Corpse. Coward, 1944 [L.A.]
  Silent Partner. Putnam, 1969 [Iran]
  13 West Street; see The Tiger Among Us
  The Tiger Among Us. Doubleday, 1957; Boardman, 1958. Also published as: 13 West Street. Bantam, 1962. And as: Fear No Evil. Corgi, 1960 [Ohio]

BRADBURY, OSGOOD
  -The Banker's Victim; or, The Betrayed Seamstress. DeWitt, 1857
  -The Fair Quakeress; or, The Perjured Lawyer. DeWitt, 1857
  Female Depravity; or, The House of Death. DeWitt, 1857
  -The Flower of the Forest; or, The Discarded Daughter. DeWitt, 1857
  The Haunted Castle; or, The Abducted Niece. DeWitt, 1857
  Julia Bicknell; or, Love and Murder. Williams, 1845
  -Louise Martin, the Village Maiden; or, The Dangers of City Life. Williams, 1853
  The Rival Lovers; or, The Midnight Murder. DeWitt, 1857

BRADBURY, PARNELL. 1904-   . See: Philip King, 1904-   . Ref: CA.

BRADBURY, RAY (DOUGLAS). 1920-   . Ref: TC.
 The Stories of Ray Bradbury. Knopf, 1980; Granada, 1981 ss, some criminous

BRADBURY, WILL [WILBUR]. Pseudonym: Will Squerent, q.v.
 The God Cell. Putnam, 1976

BRADBY, G(ODFREY) F(OX). 1863-1947.
 The Face in the Mirror. Hodder, 1923

BRADDON, GEORGE. Pseudonym of George Alexis Milkomanovich Milkomane, 1903-   . Other pseudonyms: Peter Conway, Alec Redwood, George Sava, qq.v. Ref: CA, CC. SC: Michael Gaunt = MG.
 Death Doubles Death. Jenkins, 1952 MG
 Death in the Picture. Jenkins, 1951 MG
 Death Rings No Bell. Jenkins, 1951 MG [Bulg.]
 The Dog It Was That Died. Garnett, 1948
 Judgment Deferred. Trelawney, 1948
 Lady Death. Regular Publications, 1955
 Microbe's Kiss. Faber, 1940
 Murdered Sleep. Garnett, 1949
 That He May Die. Cassell, 1945
 They Stand Accused. Cassell, 1945
 Time Off for Death. Jenkins, 1952; Roy, 1958 MG

BRADDON, M(ARY) E(LIZABETH) [MRS. JOHN MAXWELL]. 1837-1915. See also: Constance Cox, 1915-   . Ref: CC, DD, EM, TC. Here listed is the book fiction attributed to this British author. No attempt has been made to distinguish among her works on the basis of criminous content. Note that a number of U.S. titles remain uncorrelated with their British originals. SC: Valentine Hawkehurst = VH.
 All Along the River. Simpkin, 1893; Cassell (NYC), 1893
 Asphodel. Maxwell, 1881; Harper, 1881
 Aurora Floyd. Tinsley, 1863; Harper, 1863
 Barbara; or, Splendid Misery; see The Story of Barbara
 Beyond These Voices. Hutchinson, 1910
 Birds of Prey. Ward, 1867; Harper, 1867 VH
 The Black Band; or, The Mysteries of Midnight. DeWitt, 1869 (British title?)
 The Blue Hand; or, A Story of a Woman's Vengeance. DeWitt, 187? (British title?)
 Bound to John Company; or, The Adventures and Misadventures of Robert Ainsleigh; see Robert Ainsleigh
 The Captain of the Vulture. Ward, 1862. U.S. title: Darrell Markham; or, The Captain of the Vulture. Dick, 1863
 Charlotte's Inheritance. Ward, 1868; Harper, 1868 VH
 The Christmas Hirelings. Simpkin, 1894; Harper, 1894
 The Cloven Foot. Maxwell, 1879; Harper, 1879
 The Conflict. Simpkin, 1903
 Cut by the County; see One Thing Needful
 Darrell Markham; or, The Captain of the Vulture; see The Captain of the Vulture
 The Day Will Come. Simpkin, 1889; Harper, 1889
 Dead Love Has Chains. Hurst, 1907
 Dead Men's Shoes. Maxwell, 1876; Harper, 1876
 Dead Sea Fruit. Ward, 1868; Harper, 1868
 Diavolo; or, Nobody's Daughter. Dick, 1867 (British title?)
 The Doctor's Wife. Maxwell, 1864; Dick, 1864
 Dudley Carleon; see Ralph the Bailiff
 During Her Majesty's Pleasure. Hurst, 1908
 Eleanor's Victory. Tinsley, 1863; Harper, 1863
 The Factory Girl; or, All is Not Gold That Glitters. DeWitt, 1869 (British title?)
 The Fatal Marriage; or, The Shadow in the Corner. Munro, 1885 (British title?)
 The Fatal Three. Simpkin, 1888; Harper, 1888
 Fenton's Quest. Ward, 1871; Harper, 1871
 Figure in the Corner and other stories; see Shadow in the Corner
 Flower and Weed. Maxwell, 1884; Harper, 1882
 George Caulfield's Journey. Munro, 1879 (British title?)
 Gerard; or, The World, the Flesh and the Devil. Simpkin, 1891
 The Golden Calf. Maxwell, 1883; Lovell, 1883
 Great Journey and other stories. Ogilvie, 1882 ss (British title?)
 The Green Curtain. Hutchinson, 1911
 Henry Dunbar; the Story of an Outcast. Maxwell, 1864; Dick, 186?
 Her Convict. Hurst, 1907
 His Darling Sin. Simpkin, 1899
 His Secret. Ogilvie, 1881 (British title?)
 Hostages to Fortune. Maxwell, 1875; Harper, 1875
 In Great Waters. Tauchnitz, 1877 ss
 In High Places. Hutchinson, 1898
 The Infidel. Simpkin, 1900; Harper, 1900
 Ishmael. Maxwell, 1884; Munro, 1884. Also published as: An Ishmaelite. Lovell, 1884
 An Ishmaelite; see Ishmael
 Jasper Dane's Secret. Peterson, 1885 (British title?)
 John Marchmont's Legacy. Tinsley, 1863; Harper, 1863
 Joshua Haggard's Daughter. Maxwell, 1876; Harper, 1877
 Just As I Am. Maxwell, 1880; Harper, 1880
 Lady Audley's Secret. Tinsley, 1862; Dick, 1863
 The Lady Lisle. Ward, 1862; Dick, 1863
 The Lady's Mile. Ward, 1866; Dick, 1878
 The Lawyer's Secret. Peterson, 1864 (British title?)
 Leighton Grange; or, Who Killed Edith Woodville? DeWitt, 187? Also published as: The Mystery of Leighton Grange. Munro, 1878 (British title?)
 Like and Unlike. Blackett, 1887; Munro, 1887
 The Little Woman in Black. Dunn, 1886 (British title?)
 London Pride; or, When the World Was Younger. Simpkin, 1896. U.S. title: When the World Was Younger. Fenno, 1897. Reprinted under British title: Fenno, 1898
 A Lost Eden. Hutchinson, 1904
 Lost for Love. Chatto, 1874; Harper, 1875
 The Lovels of Arden. Maxwell, 1871; Harper, 1872
 Lucius Davoreen; or, Publicans and Sinners. Maxwell, 1873. U.S. title: Publicans and Sinners; or, Lucius Davoreen. Harper, 1874
 Married in Haste. Munro, 1883 (British title?)
 Mary. Hutchinson, 1916
 Meeting Her Fate; see Milly Darrell and other tales
 Milly Darrell and other tales. Maxwell, 1873; Carleton, 1877. Also published as: Meeting Her Fate. Carleton, 1881 ss
 Miranda. Hutchinson, 1913
 The Missing Witness. Maxwell, 1880 (Play.)
 Mohawks. Maxwell, 1886; Harper, 1886
 Mount Royal. Maxwell, 1882; Harper, 1882
 My Sister's Confession and other stories. Gill, 1876 ss (British title?)
 The Mystery of Leighton Grange; see Leighton Grange; or, Who Killed Edith Woodville?
 The Octoroon; or, The Lily of Louisiana. DeWitt, 1869 (British title?)
 One Life, One Love. Simpkin, 1890
 One Thing Needful, and Cut by the County. Maxwell, 1886; Harper, 1885. Also published as: Penalty of Fate; or, The One Thing Needful. Illustrated Publishing, 1886
 Only a Clod. Maxwell, 1865; Dick, 1865
 Only a Woman. Munro, 1885 (British title?)
 An Open Verdict. Maxwell, 1878; Harper, 1878
 Oscar Bertrand. DeWitt, 1869 (British title?)
 Our Adversary. Hutchinson, 1909
 The Outcast; or, The Brand of Society. Dick, 1864 (British title?)
 Penalty of Fate; or, The One Thing Needful; see One Thing Needful, and Cut of the County
 Phantom Fortune. Maxwell, 1883; Harper, 1883
 Ralph the Bailiff and other tales. Ward, 1862. U.S. title: Dudley Carleon. Dick, 1864 ss
 Robert Ainsleigh. Maxwell, 1872. U.S. title: Bound to John Company; or, The Adventures and Misadventures of Robert Ainsleigh. Harper, 187?
 The Rose of Life. Hutchinson, 1905; Brentano's, 1905
 Rough Justice. Simpkin, 1898
 Run to Earth. Ward, 1868
 Rupert Godwin. Ward, 1867; Dick, 1867
 Shadow in the Corner. Munro, 1879. Also published as: Figure in the Corner and other stories. Ogilvie, 1881 ss (British title?)
 Sir Jasper's Tenant. Maxwell, 1865; Dick, 1865
 Sons of Fire. Simpkin, 1895
 The Story of Barbara. Maxwell, 1880. U.S. title: Barbara; or, Splendid Misery. Harper, 1880
 A Strange World. Maxwell, 1875; Harper, 1875
 Strangers and Pilgrims. Maxwell, 1873; Harper, 1873
 Taken at the Flood. Maxwell, 1874; Harper, 1874
 Thou Art the Man. Simpkin, 1894
 Three Times Dead; or, The Secret of the Heath; see The Trail of the Serpent; or, The Secret of the Heath
 To the Bitter End. Maxwell, 1872; Harper, 1875
 The Trail of the Serpent; or, The Secret of the Heath. Ward, 1861. U.S. title: Three Times Dead; or, The Secret of the Heath. Dick, 1864. Reprinted in England under the U.S. title: Clark, 1861
 Under Love's Rule. Simpkin, 1897
 Under the Red Flag. Maxwell, 1883; Harper, 1883
 The Venetians. Simpkin, 1892; Harper, 1892
 Vixen. Maxwell, 1879; Harper, 1879
 Wages of Sin. Ogilvie, 1881 (British title?)
 Weavers and Weft, and other tales. Maxwell, 1877; Harper, 1877 ss
 What Is the Mystery? Hilton, 1866 (British title?)
 When the World Was Younger; see London Pride; or, When the World Was Younger
 The White House. Hurst, 1906
 The White Phantom. Williams, 1868 (British title?)
 Whose Was the Hand? Munro, 1889 (British title?)
 The World, the Flesh, and the Devil. Lovell, 1891 (British title?)
 Wyllard's Weird. Maxwell, 1885; Harper, 1885

BRADDON, RUSSELL (READING). 1921-   . Ref: CA.
 Committal Chamber. Hutchinson, 1966; Norton, 1967
 End Play. Joseph, 1972. U.S. title: The Thirteenth Trick. Norton, 1973
 The Finalists. Joseph, 1977; Atheneum, 1977
 -Gabriel Comes to 24. Hutchinson, 1958
 -Out of the Storm. Hutchinson, 1956
 The Predator. Joseph, 1980
 The Thirteenth Trick; see End Play
 -Will You Walk a Little Faster? Joseph, 1969

BRADFORD, ERNLE (DUSGATE SELBY). 1922-   .
 The Touchstone. Cassell, 1962

BRADLEY, CHARLES
 The Belgrade Case. Mills (Melbourne), 1891
 The Red Cripple. Robertson (Melbourne), 1891

BRADLEY, J(OHN JAMES) FOVARGUE
 The Black Abolitionist. Greening, 1910
 -The Passing of Night. Long, 1907

BRADLEY, JACK
 If Hate Could Kill. Ace, 1960 [N.J.]

BRADLEY, MARION ZIMMER. 1930- . Ref: CA.
Bluebeard's Daughter. Lancer, 1968
Can Ellen Be Saved? Tempo, 1975
Castle Terror. Lancer, 1965
Dark Satanic. Berkley, 1972
Drums of Darkness. Ballantine, 1976
Souvenir of Monique. Ace, 1967

BRADLEY, MARY (WILHELMINA) HASTINGS. 188?- .
A Hanging Matter. Appleton, 1937 [Eng.]
Murder in Room 700. Appleton, 1931 [NYC]
Murder in the Family. Longmans, 1951 [Tenn.]
Nice People Murder. Longmans, 1952 [Maine]
Nice People Poison. Longmans, 1952
The Road to Desperation. Appleton, 1932
Unconfessed. Appleton, 1934

BRADLEY, MICHAEL. Pseudonym of Gary Blumberg, 1938- , q.v. SC: Johnny Adrano, in all titles.
The Blood Bargain. Paperback Library, 1974 [Beirut]
The Corsican Cross. Paperback Library, 1974 [Fr.]
Kill the Hack! Paperback Library, 1974
The Swiss Shot. Paperback Library, 1974

BRADLEY, MICHAEL (ANDERSON). 1944- .
Imprint. Dorset (Toronto), 1978; Warner, 1980
The Mantouche Factor. Dorset (Toronto), 1979; Warner, 1980

BRADLEY, MURIEL (DEMENS)
Affair at Ritos Bay. Doubleday, 1947; Harborough, 1953 [Calif.]
Death for My Neighbor. Doubleday, 1951; Hammond, 1954 [Calif.]
Devil in the Sky. Doubleday, 1948; Hammond, 1955 [Calif.]
Murder in Montana. Doubleday, 1950; Foulsham, 1951 [Mont.]
Murder Twice Removed. Doubleday, 1951; Hammond, 1954 [Calif.]
Waltz in Scarlet. Hammond, 1958

BRADSHAW, MRS. ALBERT S. Byline also: Annie (Cropper) Bradshaw, q.v.
Murder at the Boarding House. Allan, 1936

BRADSHAW, ANNIE (CROPPER). Byline also: Mrs. Albert S. Bradshaw, q.v.
A Crimson Stain. Cassell, 1885; Munro, 1885

BRADSHAW, GEORGE (FLOING). 1907- .
Practice to Deceive. Harcourt, 1962; Hart-Davis, 1962

BRADSHAW, HOWARD
The Pasha's Web. Watt, 1921

BRADSHAW, OLIVE
Dead Man's Booty. Diamond, 1927

BRADSHAW-JONES, MALCOLM HENRY. Pseudonym: Bradshaw Jones, q.v.

BRADY, CHARLES
Seven Games in October. Little, 1979

BRADY, CYRUS TOWNSEND. 1861-1920.
-The Corner in Coffee. Dillingham, 1904 Unwin, 1904 [NYC]
Secret Service. Dodd, 1912; Hodder, 1916 (Novelization of the play by William Gillette, 1885-1937, q.v.)

BRADY, JAMES. 1928- .
-Paris One. Delacorte, 1977 [Paris]

BRADY, JASPER EWING
The Case of Mary Sherman. Britton, 1917

BRADY, LEO. 1917- . Ref: CA.
Brother Orchid. French (NYC and London), 1940 (3-act play based on a ss by Richard Connell, 1893-1949, q.v.)
The Edge of Doom. Dutton, 1949; Cresset, 1950
-The Love Tap. Popular Library, 1979 [1972, Wash. D.C.]

BRADY, MATT
Take Your Last Look. GM, 1954; Red Seal, 1959

BRADY, MICHAEL. 1928- . Ref: CA.
American Surrender. Delacorte, 1979; Joseph, 1979

BRADY, NICHOLAS. Pseudonym of J(ohn) V(ictor) Turner, 1900-1945, q.v. Other pseudonym: David Hume, q.v. SC: Ebenezer Buckle, in at least those marked EB. Set: Eng.
The Carnival Murder; see Fair Murder
Coupons for Death. Hale, 1944
Ebenezer Investigates. Bles, 1934 EB
Fair Murder. Bles, 1933. U.S. title: The Carnival Murder. Holt, 1933 EB
The House of Strange Guests. Bles, 1932; Holt, 1932 EB
Week-End Murder. Bles, 1933

BRADY, NICHOLAS. Apparently a house name.
Bad Guy. Belmont, 1977
The Homecoming. Belmont, 1977
Inside Job (by Leonard Levinson, 1935- , q.v.). Leisure, 1978
The Master Planner. Belmont, 1977
The Microwave Factor. Belmont, 1977
Shark Fighter (by Leonard Levinson, 1935- , q.v.). Leisure, 1976

BRADY, (SALLY) RYDER. 1939- . Ref: CA.
Instar. Doubleday, 1976; New English Library, 1977

BRAEME, CHARLOTTE M(ONICA). 1836-1884. Pseudonym: Bertha Clay, q.v.
The Mystery of Colde Fell; or, Not Proven. Munro, 1887. Also published as by Bertha M. Clay: Lovell, 1887

BRAHAM, HAL. Pseudonyms: Mel Colton, Merrill Trask, qq.v.
Call Me Deadly. Graphic, 1957 [L.A.]

BRAHMS, CARYL and S. J. SIMON. Caryl Brahms is the pseudonym of Doris Caroline Abrahams, 1901-1982; S. J. Simon is the pseudonym of Simon Jasha Skidelsky. Ref: MP, TC. SC: Insp. Quill, in at least those marked Q.
A Bullet in the Ballet. Joseph, 1937; Doubleday, 1938 Q
Casino for Sale. Joseph, 1938. U.S. title: Murder a la Stroganoff. Doubleday, 1938 Q [Fr.]
Envoy on Excursion. Joseph, 1940 Q
Murder a la Stroganoff; see Casino for Sale
Six Curtains for Stroganova. Joseph, 1945

BRAIN, LEONARD. Pseudonym of Leonard Peck, 1906- , q.v.
A Case of Identity. Hale, 1971
It's a Free Country. Longmans, 1965; Coward, 1968

BRAINE, JOHN (GERARD). 1922- . Ref: CA. SC: Xavier Flynn, in both titles.
Finger of Fire. Eyre, 1977
The Pious Agent. Eyre, 1975; Atheneum, 1976

BRAINERD, MRS. EDITH RATHBONE JACOBS. -1922. Joint pseudonym with J. Chauncey Corey Brainerd, 1874-1922: E. J. Rath, q.v.

BRAINERD, J. CHAUNCEY COREY. 1874-1922. Joint pseudonym with Edith Rathbone Jacobs Brainerd, -1922: E. J. Rath, q.v.

BRALY, MALCOLM. 1925-1980. Ref: CA.
Felony Tank. GM, 1961 [S.W.]
It's Cold Out There. GM, 1966
The Master. Paperback Library, 1973 (Novelization of the movie "Lady Ice.") [Fla.]
On the Yard. Little, 1967 [Calif.]
The Protector. Jove, 1979
Shake Him Till He Rattles. GM, 1963 [S.F.]

BRAMAH, ERNEST. Pseudonym of Ernest Bramah Smith, 1868-1942. Ref: all except CA. SC: Max Carrados = MC. Set: Eng.
The Bravo of London. Cassell, 1934 MC
The Eyes of Max Carrados. Richards, 1923; Doran, 1924 MC ss
Max Carrados. Methuen, 1914; Hyperion, 1975 MC ss
Max Carrados Mysteries. Hodder, 1927; Penguin (U.S.), 1964 MC ss
The Specimen Case. Hodder, 1924; Doran, 1925 ss, including some crime and one about MC

BRAMBLE, FORBES. 1939- . Ref: CA.
The Strange Case of Deacon Brodie. H. Hamilton, 1975; Coward, 1976 [1788, Edin.]

BRAMHALL, MARION. SC: Kit (Marsden) Acton, in all titles.
Button, Button. Doubleday, 1944 [Cape Cod]
Murder Is an Evil Business. Doubleday, 1948 [Cape Cod]
Murder Is Contagious. Doubleday, 1949 [Mich., acad.]
Murder Solves a Problem. Doubleday, 1944 [New Eng.]
Tragedy in Blue. Doubleday, 1945 [Mass.]

BRAMLETT, JOHN. Pseudonym of John Leonard Pierce, Jr., 1921- .
The Devil in Broad Daylight. GM, 1967

BRAMLETTE, PAULA. 1917- . See: Margaret (Polk) Yates, 1915- .

BRAMLEY, CHARLES
The Adventures of a Social Detective. Diprose, 18?? ss

BRAMPTON, JOAN
Dilemma. Dramatists, 1958 (3-act play.)

BRAMSON, KAREN (ADLER). 1875-1936.
The Case of Dr. Morel. Philpot, 1926. U.S. title: Dr. Morel. Greenberg, 1927 [Fr.]

BRAMWELL, CHARLOTTE. Pseudonym of John M. Kimbro, 1929- . Other pseudonyms: Kym Allyson, Ann Ashton, Jean Kimbro, Kathryn Kimbrough, qq.v.
Brother Sinister. Beagle, 1973
Cousin to Terror. Beagle, 1972 [Ariz.]
Stepmother's House. Beagle, 1972

BRANCH, FLORENZ. Pseudonym of Florence Stonebraker, 1896- .
Bedroom Bargain. Phoenix, 1940

BRANCH, PAMELA (JEAN). 1920-1967. Ref: EM, MC.
Lion in the Cellar. Hale, 1951
Murder Every Monday. Hale, 1954
Murder's Little Sister. Hale, 1958; Penguin (U.S.), 1963
The Wooden Overcoat. Hale, 1951

BRAND, CHRISTIANNA. Pseudonym of Mary Christianna Milne Lewis, 1907- . Other pseudonyms: Mary Anne Ashe, China Thompson, qq.v. Ref: CA, CC, DD, EM, MC, TC. SC: Insp. Chucky = ICh (see also Mary Anne Ashe entry); Insp. Charlesworth = Ch; Insp. Cockrill = C. Set: Eng.
Brand X. Joseph, 1974 ss
Cat and Mouse. Joseph, 1950; Knopf, 1950 ICh [Wales]
The Crooked Residence; see Suddenly at His Residence
Death in High Heels. Lane, 1941; Scribner, 1942 Ch
Death of Jezebel. Bodley, 1949; Dodd, 1948 C,Ch [theatre]
Fog of Doubt; see London Particular
Green for Danger. Lane, 1945; Dodd, 1944 C [hosp.]
Heads You Lose. Lane, 1941; Dodd, 1942 C
The Honey Harlot. Allen, 1978
London Particular. Joseph, 1952. U.S. title: Fog of Doubt. Scribner, 1953 C,Ch
The Rose in Darkness. Joseph, 1979 Ch
Suddenly at His Residence. Bodley, 1947. U.S. title: The Crooked Wreath. Dodd, 1946 C
Tour de Force. Joseph, 1955; Scribner, 1955 C [Med. Is.]
What Dread Hand? Joseph, 1968 ss C

BRAND, MAX. Pseudonym of Frederick Schiller Faust, 1892-1944. Other pseudonyms: Walter C. Butler, Frederick Frost, qq.v. Ref: EM, TC.
Big Game. Paperback Library, 1973
Dead Man's Treasure. White Lion, 1975
The Granduca. Paperback Library, 1973 [N.Y.]
The Phantom Spy. Dodd, 1973; White Lion, 1975 [Berlin]
Six Golden Angels. Dodd, 1937; Hodder, 1938 [NYC]

BRAND, (CHARLES) NEVILLE. 1895- .
Death in the Forest. Lane, 1933; Kendall, 1933 [Cent. Am.]
Death of a Designer. Lane, 1938
The Winning Trick. Lane, 1931; Putnam, 1932
Winter Landscape. Hale, 1949

BRAND, SUSAN. Pseudonym of Susan Bonthron Roper, 1948-   . Ref: CA.
  Shadows on the Tor. Simon, 1977; Prior, 1978

BRANDE, DOROTHEA [DOROTHEA THOMPSON BRANDE COLLINS]. 1893-1948.
  Most Beautiful Lady. Farrar, 1935. British title: Beauty Vanishes. Bell, 1935 [It.]

BRANDEL, MARC. Pseudonym of Marcus Beresford, 1919-   . Born in St. Louis, educated abroad.
  The Choice. Dial, 1950; Eyre, 1952. Also published as: The Moron. Avon, 1951
  -The Lizard's Tail. Simon, 1979; Secker, 1980
  Maniac Responsible; see Rain Before Seven
  The Moron; see The Choice
  -Rain Before Seven. Harper, 1945. Also published as: Maniac Responsible. Avon, 1951 [NYC]
  Survivor. Simon, 1976; H. Hamilton, 1976
  The Time of the Fire. Random, 1954; Eyre, 1954

BRANDES, RHODA. Pseudonym: Diana Ramsay, q.v.

BRANDNER, GARY. 1933-   . Ref: CA. SC: Colin Garrett ("Big Brain") = CG.
  The Aardvark Affair. Zebra, 1975; New English Library pb, 1976 CG
  The Beelzebub Business. Zebra, 1975; New English Library pb, 1976 CG
  -Death Walkers. Hamlyn, 1980
  Energy Zero. Zebra, 1976 CG
  The Howling. GM, 1977; Hamlyn, 1978
  The Howling II. GM, 1979. British title: Return of the Howling. Hamlyn, 1979
  London. PB, 1976 [Eng.]
  Return of the Howling; see The Howling II
  The Sterling Standard. Popular Library, 1980

BRANDON, BEATRICE. Pseudonym of Robert Wilson Krepps, 1919-1980.
  The Cliffs of Night. Doubleday, 1974; Hodder, 1975 [Ire.]
  The Court of Silver Shadows. Doubleday, 1980

BRANDON, BRUCE. Pseudonym of Wilbur Braun, 1896-   , q.v. Other pseudonyms: Walter Blake, Fred Caldwell, Raymond Dumkey, Nan Fleming, Marsha Grable, Edwin F. Hornung, Jed Parish, Basil Ring, Orville Snap, Mortimer Sprague, Bert Stoner, qq.vs.
  On the Bridge at Midnight. French (NYC), 1937 (3-act play.)

BRANDON, CHARLES. SC: John Fortescue, in all titles. Set: Eng.
  The Missing Banker. Jenkins, 1927
  The Mystery of King's Everard. Jenkins, 1924
  The Phantom Musketeer. Jenkins, 1929

BRANDON, GORDON. SC: Arthur Stukeley Pennington and Insp. Patrick Aloysius McCarthy (following John G. Brandon, 1879-1941, q.v.), in at least those titles marked ASP,PAM; Michael and "Terry" Terrence, in at least those marked T. Set: Eng.
  Death of a Mermaid. Wright, 1960 ASP,PAM
  Here Comes the Corpse. Wright, 1949
  Homicidal Holiday. Wright, 1954 T
  A Mild Case of Murder. Wright, 1951 T
  Murder and Marigold. Wright, 1956
  Murder Comes Smiling. Wright, 1959 ASP,PAM
  Murder in Maytime. Wright, 1950 T
  A Swell Night for Murder! Wright, 1947

BRANDON, JOHN G. 1879-1941. Ref: TC. All titles below without indication of publisher feature Sexton Blake and were published by Amalgamated Press; many were retitled and given a new chief character and reissued by Wright, but correlations are not available. SC (see also Gordon Brandon): Arthur Stukeley Pennington, in at least those marked ASP; Sgt./Det. Insp. Patrick Aloysius McCarthy, in at least those marked PAM. Set: Eng.
  The Big City. Methuen, 1931; Brentano's, 1930
  The Big Heart. Methuen, 1924; Brentano's, 1923
  The Black Joss. Methuen, 1931 PAM
  The Black Swastika. 1940
  The Blue Print Murders. Wright, 1942 PAM
  The Bond Street Murder. Wright, 1937 ASP,PAM
  The Bond Street Raiders. 1937
  Bonus for Murder. Wright, 1938 PAM
  By Order of the Tong. 1935
  The Call Girl Murders. Wright, 1954 ASP,PAM
  Candidate for a Coffin. Wright, 1946 PAM
  The Case of the Gangster's Moll. 1934
  The Case of the Murdered Commissionaire. 1935
  The Case of the Night Club Queen. 1936
  The Case of the Withered Hand. Wright, 1936 PAM
  The Case of the Would-Be Widow. Wright, 1950 ASP
  The Championship Crime. 1934
  The Chink's Victim. 1934
  The Clue of the Tattooed Man. 1938
  The Cork Street Crime. Wright, 1938 ASP,PAM
  The Corpse from "The City". Wright, 1958 ASP,PAM
  The Corpse Rode On. Wright, 1951 ASP,PAM
  The Crime in the Kiosk. 1937
  The Crooked Five! Wright, 1939 PAM
  Crook's Cargo. 1940
  Dead Man's Evidence. 1936
  Death Comes Swiftly. Wright, 19?? PAM
  Death in "D" Division. Wright, 1943 ASP,PAM
  Death in Downing Street. Wright, 1937 PAM
  Death in Duplicate. Wright, 1945 PAM
  Death in Jermyn Street. Wright, 1942 ASP,PAM
  Death in the Ditch. Wright, 1940 ASP
  The Death in the Quarry. Wright, 1941 PAM
  Death of a Greek. Wright, 1955 ASP,PAM
  Death of a Socialite. Wright, 1957 ASP,PAM
  Death on Delivery. Wright, 1939 PAM
  Death Stalks in Soho. Wright, 1959 ASP,PAM
  Death Tolls the Gong. Wright, 1936 ASP,PAM
  The Diamond of Ti Lingo. 1937
  The Downing Street Discovery. 1935
  The Dragnet. Wright, 1936 PAM
  The Espionage Killings. Wright, 19?? PAM
  The False Alibi. 1938
  Fatal Forgery. 1939
  The £50 Marriage Case. Wright, 1938. Also published as: The £250 Marriage Case. Mellifont, 1954 PAM
  Finger-Prints Never Lie! Wright, 1938 PAM
  The Frame-Up. Wright, 1938 PAM
  Gang War. Wright, 1940
  The Girl Who Knew Too Much. 1936
  The Glass Dagger. 1934
  The Great Taxi-Cab Ramp. 1939
  The Gunboat Mystery. 1939
  The Hand of Seeta. Wright, 1937 PAM
  In the Hands of Spies. 1939
  The Joy Ride. Methuen, 1927
  McCarthy, C.I.D. Wright, 1936 PAM
  M for Murder. Wright, 1949 PAM
  The Mail Van Mystery. Wright, 1937 PAM
  The Man from Italy. 1937
  The Man from Singapore. 1939
  The Man with Jitters. 1939
  The Mark of the Tong. Wright, 1938 PAM
  The Melbourne Mystery. 1937
  Mr. Pennington Barges In. Wright, 1941 ASP,PAM
  Mr. Pennington Comes Through. Wright, 1939 ASP,PAM
  Mr. Pennington Goes Nap. Wright, 1940 ASP,PAM
  Mr. Pennington Sees Red. Wright, 1942 ASP,PAM
  Murder at the Yard! Wright, 1936 PAM
  Murder for a Million. Wright, 1942
  Murder in Mayfair. Methuen, 1934 ASP
  Murder in Pimlico. Wright, 1958 ASP,PAM
  Murder in Soho. Wright, 1937 PAM
  Murder in Y Division. 1935
  Murder on the Beam. Wright, 1956 ASP,PAM
  Murder on the Fourth Floor. 1936
  Murder on the High Seas. 1938 [ship]
  Murder on the Ice Rink. 1939
  Murder on the Stage. 1934 [theatre]
  Murderer's Stand-In. Wright, 1953 ASP,PAM
  The Mystery of the Dead Man's Wallet. 1938
  The Mystery of the Green Bottle. 1939
  The Mystery of the Murdered Blonde. 1936
  The Mystery of the Murdered Ice Cream Man. 1938
  The Mystery of the Murdered Sentry. 1937
  The Mystery of the Street Musician. 1938
  The Mystery of the Three Acrobats. 1936
  The Mystery of the Three City's. 1934
  The Mystery of X20. 1937
  The Night Club Murder. Wright, 1938 PAM
  Nighthawks! Methuen, 1929; Brentano's, 1930
  On the Midnight Beat. 1934
  On Ticket of Leave. 1940
  The One-Minute Murder. Methuen, 1934; Dial, 1935 ASP,PAM
  The Pawnshop Murder. Methuen, 1936 ASP,PAM
  The Pigeon Loft Crime. 1938
  Red Altars. Cassell, 1928. U.S. title: The Secret Brotherhood. Dial, 1928 PAM
  The Red Boomerang. 1935
  The Regent Street Raid. Wright, 1938 ASP,PAM
  The Riddle of the Dead Man's Bay. 1940
  The Riddle of the Greek Financier. 1940
  The Riverside Mystery. Methuen, 1935 ASP,PAM
  The Roadhouse Mystery. 1938
  A Scream in Soho. Wright, 1940 PAM
  The Secret Brotherhood; see Red Altars
  The Silent House. Cassell, 1928; Dial, 1928 (Novelization of the play by John G. Brandon and George Pickett.)
  The Snatch Game. Wright, 1936 ASP,PAM
  The Spy from Spain. 1937
  The Survivor's Secret. 1933
  The Tattooed Triangle. 1937
  The Taxi-Cab Murder. 1933
  The Terror of the Pacific. 1940
  The Tragedy of the West End Actress. 1933
  The Transport Murders. Wright, 1942 PAM
  The £250 Marriage Case; see The £50 Marriage Case
  Under Police Protection. 1934
  Under Secret Orders. 1941
  The Victim of the Secret Service. 1937
  The Victim of the Thieves' Den. 1936
  West End. Methuen, 1933 ASP,PAM
  Yellow Gods. Wright, 1940 PAM
  The Yellow Mask. 1935
  -Young Love. Methuen, 1925

BRANDON, MARGARET
  Hypnotized; or, The Doctor's Confession. Hutchinson, 1891

BRANDON, WILLIAM (E.). 1914-   . Ref: CA.
  The Dangerous Dead. Dodd, 1943 [Vt.]

BRANDRETH, CHARLES A.
  A Fenland Mystery. Jarrolds, 1925
  -The Honourable Roger. Hutchinson, 1925
  -The Lady of the Swamp. Hutchinson, 1927
  -Under the Goad. Hutchinson, 1926

BRANDT, ROGER. Pseudonym of William (Elbert) Crawford, 1929-   , q.v. Other pseudonyms: Don Logan, Jim Peterson, Paul Ross, Steve Scott, qq.v.
  The Death Connection. Playboy pb, 1976

BRANDT, TOM. Pseudonym of Thomas B(lanchard) Dewey, 1915-   , q.v.
  Kiss Me Hard. Popular Library, 1953
  Run, Brother, Run! Popular Library, 1954; Consul, 1961 [Colo.]

BRANSCOMB, ALEXANDER C.
  -Mystic Romances of the Blue and Grey. Mutual Publishing, 1883 ss

BRANSON, H(ENRY) C. Ref: CC, EM, TC. SC: John Bent, in all titles.
  Beggar's Choice. Simon, 1953
  Case of the Giant Killer. Simon, 1944; Bodley Head, 1949 [N.Y.]
  The Fearful Passage. Simon, 1943; Bodley, 1950 [N.Y.]
  I'll Eat You Last. Simon, 1941; Lane, 1943. Also published as: I'll Kill You Last. Mystery Novel of the Month, 1942
  I'll Kill You Last; see I'll Eat You Last
  Last Year's Blood. Simon, 1947; Bodley, 1950
  The Leaden Bubble. Simon, 1949; Bodley, 1951
  The Pricking Thumb. Simon, 1942; Bodley, 1949

BRANSTON, FRANK. 1939-   . Born in England; freelance journalist and writer. SC: Tommy Tompkins, in both titles. Set: Eng.
  Sergeant Ritchie's Conscience. Deutsch, 1978; St. Martin's, 1978

An Up and Coming Man. Deutsch, 1977; St. Martin's, 1977

BRAUN, LILIAN JACKSON. Ref: TC. SC: Jim Qwilleran, in all titles.
The Cat Who Ate Danish Modern. Dutton, 1967; Collins, 1968 [Midwest]
The Cat Who Could Read Backwards. Dutton, 1966; Collins, 1967 [Midwest]
The Cat Who Turned On and Off. Dutton, 1968; Collins, 1969 [Midwest]

BRAUN, M. G. SC: Al Glenne, in all titles.
Apostles of Violence. Berkley, 1966 (Translation of "Apotres de la Violence." Paris, 1962.) [Venez.]
Operation Atlantis. Berkley, 1966
Operation Jealousy. Berkley, 1966 (Translation of "Plan 'Jalousie'." Paris, 1965.) [Fr.]
That Girl from Istanbul. Berkley, 1966

BRAUN, MATTHEW
Bloody Hand. Popular Library, 1975

BRAUN, R(EINHARD) A.
Murder, Four Miles Up. Arcadia, 1954 [Calif.]

BRAUN, WILBUR. 1896-   . Pseudonyms: Walter Blake, Bruce Brandon, Fred Caldwell, Raymond Dumkey, Nan Fleming, Marsha Grable, Edwin F. Hornung, Jed Parish, Basil Ring, Orville Snap, Mortimer Sprague, Bert Stoner, qq.v.
Curse You, Jack Dalton! French (NYC), 1936 (1-act play.)
Drop Dead! Bakers, 1956 (1-act play.)
Find the Woman! French (NYC), 1935 (3-act play.)
Murder in Hollywood. French (NYC), 1935 (1-act play.) [L.A.]
Murdered Alive! French (NYC), 1934 (3-act play.)
"The Orchid Limousine." Northwestern, 1933 (3-act play.)
The Tiger's Claw. French (NYC), 1936 (1-act play.)
The White Phantom. French (NYC), 1935 (1-act play.)

BRAUTIGAN, RICHARD. 1935-   . Ref: CA.
Dreaming of Babylon. Delacorte, 1977; Cape, 1978 [1942, S.F.]
The Hawkline Monster. Simon, 1974; Cape, 1975 [1902, Oreg.]
Willard and His Bowling Trophies. Simon, 1975; Cape, 1976 [S.F.]

BRAWNER, HELEN. 1902-   . Joint pseudonym with (Francis) Van Wyck Mason, 1897-1978, q.v.: Geoffrey Coffin, q.v.

BRAXTON, HENRY [HANK]
The Committee. Zebra, 1979

BRAY, ARTHUR
The Clue of the Postage Stamp. Thom, 1913

BRAYSHAW, EILEEN RUTH
The Eye of Kali. Waterloo (Calcutta), 1934

BRAZA, DAVID
The Man of Many Colours. Modern Fiction, 1953

BREAN, HERBERT (J.). 1907-1973. Ref: CA, CC, EM, TC. SC: William Deacon = WD; Reynold Frame = RF.
The Clock Strikes Thirteen. Morrow, 1952; Heinemann, 1954 RF [Maine]
Collar for the Killer; see A Matter of Fact
The Darker the Night. Morrow, 1949; Heinemann, 1950 RF [NYC]
Dead Sure; see A Matter of Fact
Hardly a Man Is Now Alive. Morrow, 1950; Heinemann, 1952. Also published as: Murder Now and Then. Macmillan (London), 1965 RF [Mass.]
A Matter of Fact. Morrow, 1956. British title: Collar for the Killer. Heinemann, 1957. Also published as: Dead Sure. Dell, 1958 [NYC]
Murder Now and Then; see Hardly a Man Is Now Alive
The Traces of Brillhart. Harper, 1960; Heinemann, 1961 WD [NYC]
The Traces of Merrilee. Harper, 1966 WD [ship]
Wilders Walk Away. Morrow, 1948; Heinemann, 1949 RF [Vt.]

BREBNER, PERCY (JAMES). 1864-1922. Pseudonym: Christian Lys, q.v. Ref: CC. SC: Christopher Quarles = CQ. Set: Eng.
The Black Card. Lawrence, 1899
The Brown Mask. Cassell, 1911
Christopher Quarles, College Professor and Master Detective. Holden, 1921; Dutton, 1914 ss CQ
The Crucible of Circumstance. Warne, 1906
The Fountain of Green Fire. Hutchinson, 1923; Moffat Yard, 1923
-The Gate of Temptation. Long, 1920
-A Gentleman of Virginia. Macmillan (London), 1910
The Ivory Disc. Duffield, 1920 (British title?)
-The Light That Lures. Fly, 1911 (British title?)
The Little Grey Shoe. Hodder, 1913; Little, 1913
A London Cobweb. Trischler, 1892
The Master Detective. Holden, 1922; Dutton, 1916 ss CQ
Mr. Quixley of the Gate House. Warne, 1904
Peril Island. Hutchinson, 1924
Princess Maritza. Cassell, 1907; McBride, 1906
The Silver Medallion. Mills, 1912
Suspicion. Ward, 1889
The Testing of Olive Vaughn. Doscher, 1909 (British title?)
-The Top Landing. Unwin, 1921
-The Turbulent Duchess. Hodder, 1915; Little, 1915
-The White Gauntlet. Cassell, 1912

BRECHIN, DAVID
Nic Barker I.D.B. Nasionale Boekhandel (Cape Town), 1963
Uncut Diamonds. Nasionale Boekhandel (Cape Town), 1969

BREDE, ARNOLD. SC: Bull Rogers, in at least those marked BR.
The Climbing Corpse. Cooper, 1952 BR
An Outside Job. Cooper, 1952 BR
Vintage Stuff. Cooper, 1952

BREEM, WALLACE
-The Leopard and the Cliff. Gollancz, 1978; St. Martin's, 1979 [India, 1919]

BREEN, PHILLIP. Joint pseudonym with Chester Krone: Wynn L. Morgan, q.v.

BREEN, RICHARD
Adam's Child. Dell, 1978 [Fla.]

BREEN-BOND, PATRICIA
The President's Grass Is Missing. Belmont, 1980

BREIT, WILLIAM. Joint pseudonym with Kenneth Gerald Elzinga, 1946-   : Marshall Jevons, q.v.

BREMNER, MARJORIE (K.). 1916-   . Ref: CC.
Murder Amid Proofs. Hodder, 1955
Murder Most Familiar. Hodder, 1953; Detective Book Club, 1954

BRENN, GEORGE J. 1888-   .
Disappearing Bullets. Detective Tales, n.d. (61-pp. mini-paperback.)
Voices. Century, 1923; Jenkins, 1925 [NYC]

BRENNAN, ALICE
The Brooding House. Lancer, 1965 [Mich.]
Candace. Paperback Library, 1970
Castle Mirage. Belmont, 1971 [Oreg.]
Devil Take All. Popular Library, 1974 [Mich.]
The Devil's Dreamer. Lancer, 1971
Fear No Evil. Lancer, 1967 [Mich.]
Ghost at Stagmere. Paperback Library, 1973
The Haunted. Lancer, 1971
House of the Fiery Cauldron. Berkley, 1975
Litany of Evil. Lancer, 1970
A Matter of Witchcraft. Berkley, 1975
Never to Die. Lancer, 1971
Sleep Well, Christine. Avon, 1973
Thirty Days Hath July. Avon, 1975
To Kill a Witch. Lancer, 1972

BRENNAN, ANTHONY
The Carbon Copy. McClelland (Toronto), 1973

BRENNAN, BILL
The Faster We Live. Monarch, ca.1962

BRENNAN, DAN
The Badge of Honor. Belmont, 1974 [Mpls.]
Doomed Sinner. Newsstand, 1961
The Godfather Killer. Belmont, 1973

Insurrection! Belmont, 1970 [Minn.]
Lay-Over Town. Caravelle, 1968 [Minn.]
Operation Sky Drop. Tower, 1975
They Can Only Kill You Once. Leisure, 1977; New English Library pb, 1979

BRENNAN, FREDERICK HAZLITT. 1901-1962.
Memo to a Firing Squad. Knopf, 1943 [Lisbon]
One of Our H-Bombs Is Missing. GM, 1955

BRENNAN, JAMES HERBERT. Pseudonym: Jan Brennan, q.v.

BRENNAN, JAN. Pseudonym of James Herbert Brennan.
The Greythorn Woman. Collins, 1979; Doubleday, 1979

BRENNAN, JOHN NEEDHAM HUGGARD. 1914-   . Pseudonym: John Welcome, q.v.

BRENNAN, JOSEPH PAYNE. 1918-   . Ref: CA, EM. SC: Lucius Leffing = LL.
The Casebook of Lucius Leffing. Macabre House, 1973 LL ss
The Chronicles of Lucius Leffing. Grant, 1977 LL ss [Conn.]
The Dark Returners. Macabre House, 1959 ss, some criminous
Nine Horrors and a Dream. Arkham, 1958 ss, some criminous
Scream at Midnight. Macabre House, 1963 ss, some criminous
Stories of Darkness and Dread. Arkham, 1973 ss, some criminous

BRENNAN, LOUIS A(RTHUR). 1911-1983. Ref: CA.
Death at Flood Tide. Dell, 1958 [Ohio]
More Than Flesh. Dell, 1957

BRENNAN, ROBERT. 1881-   .
The Man Who Walked Like a Dancer. Rich, 1951 [U.S.]
The Toledo Dagger. Hamilton, 1927 [Fr.]

BRENNER, MARLENE
Cynthia. Baker's, 1963 (1-act play.)
Four Hours. Baker's, 1970 (1-act play.)
Middle of Nowhere. Baker's, 1959 (1-act play.)
My Aunt Agatha. Baker's, 1954 (1-act play.)
The Trap. Baker's, 1966 (1-act play.)

BRENNING, L. H. Pseudonym of (Alfred) John Hunter, 1891-1961, q.v. Other pseudonyms; John Addiscombe, Anthony Dax, Anthony Drummond, Peter Meriton, qq.v.
Boulevard. Cassell, 1931 [Paris]
The Butterfly of Paris. Cassell, 1925 [Paris]
Cabaret; see Parisian Adventure
The Channel Mystery. Gramol, 1935
The Death Plot. Cassell, 1931 [Paris]
Devil's Laughter. Cassell, 1929
Parisian Adventure. Cassell, 1934. U.S. title: Cabaret. Greenberg, 1934 [Paris]
Parisian Love. Cassell, 1926 [Paris]

BRENT, A. D.
The Organization. Belmont, 1973

BRENT, LORING. Pseudonym of George F(rank) Worts, 1892-   , q.v.
-No More a Corpse. King, 1932. British title: The Return of George Washington. Hodder, 1928
The Return of George Washington; see No More a Corpse
Who Dares? Chelsea, 1927 [Nev.]

BRENT, LYNTON WRIGHT
Daughter of Bonnie & Clyde. Producer Books, 1971 (Novelization of the movie.)
Death of a Detective. Powell, 1969
Detective on the Prowl. Powell, 1969
One Man's Crime. Powell, 1969 [L.A.]

BRENT, MADELEINE. Pseudonym.
The Capricorn Stone. Souvenir, 1979; Doubleday, 1930 [Eng., 1900]
Kirkby's Changeling. Souvenir, 1975. U.S. title: Stranger at Wildings. Doubleday, 1976 [1900, Eng.]
Merlin's Keep. Souvenir, 1977; Doubleday, 1978
Moonraker's Bride. Souvenir, 1973; Doubleday, 1973 [China]
Stranger at Wildings; see Kirkby's Changeling
Tregaron's Daughter. Souvenir, 1971; Doubleday, 1971 [Venice, ca.1900]

BRENT, NIGEL. Pseudonym of Cecil Gordon Eugene Wimhurst, 1905-   . SC: Barney Hyde, in all titles. Set: Eng.

Badger in the Dusk. Muller, 1959
Blood in the Bank. Muller, 1954
Dig the Grave Deep. Muller, 1955
The Golden Angel. Muller, 1958
The Leopard Died Too. Muller, 1957
Motive for Murder. Muller, 1954
No Space for Murder. Muller, 1960 [Holl.]
The Scarlet Lily. Muller, 1953
Spider in the Web. Muller, 1960

BRENT, PETER (LUDWIG). 1931- . Pseudonym: Ludovic Peters, q.v. Ref: CA, TC.
No Way Back from Prague. Hodder, 1970

BRENT, R. L. Pseudonym of Larry Powell. SC: Jake Brand (The Liquidator), in all titles.
The Cocaine Connection. Award, 1974; Tandem, 1975 [Ga.]
Contract for a Killing. Award, 1974; Tandem, 1974
The Exchange. Charter, 1978
Invitation to a Strangling. Award, 1975 [N.C.]
The Liquidator. Award, 1974; Tandem, 1974 [Fla.]

BRENTANO, LOWELL. 1895-1950. See: Grace (Perkins) Oursler, 1900-1955.

BRENTER, JAY G.
Blood on the Shrine. Brandon, 1967

BRENTFORD, BURKE. Pseudonym of Nathan D(ane) Urner, 1839-1893, q.v.
Gold Dust Darrell; or, The Wizard of the Mines. Street, 1890

BRENTON, HOWARD. 1942- . Ref: CA.
Christie in Love, and other plays. Methuen, 1970 (3 plays, the title play criminous.)
Revenge. Methuen, 1970 (2-act play.)

BRESLIN, CATHERINE. 1936- . Ref: CA.
-Unholy Child. Dial, 1979

BRESLIN, HOWARD. 1912- . Pseudonym: Michael Niall, q.v.

BRESLIN, JIMMY [JAMES]. 1930- . Ref: CA.
.44, with Dick Schaap, 1934- . Viking, 1978. British title: Son of Sam. Futura, 1978 [NYC]
The Gang That Couldn't Shoot Straight. Viking, 1969; Hutchinson, 1970
Son of Sam; see .44

BRETNOR, REGINALD. 1911- . Ref: CA.
A Killing in Swords. PB, 1978 [S.F.]

BRETON, FREDERIC
-The Black Mass. Hutchinson, 1897
The Crime of Maunsell Grange. Osgood, 1893

BRETONNE, ANNE-MARIE. Pseudonym of Arnold German.
The Cry of Neptune. Berkley, 1977
Dark Talisman. Popular Library, 1975 [Carib.]
A Gallows Stands in Salem. Popular Library, 1975 [Mass.]

BRETT, DAVID
Black Folder. Hodder, 1976

BRETT, JOHN MICHAEL. Pseudonym of Miles (Barton) Tripp, 1923- , q.v. Other pseudonym: Michael Brett, q.v. SC: Hugo Baron = HB (see also Michael Brett entry).
A Cargo of Spent Evil. Barker, 1966
A Plague of Dragons. Barker, 1965 HB [Afr.]

BRETT, MARTIN. Pseudonym of (Ronald) Douglas Sanderson, 1922- , q.v. Other pseudonym: Malcolm Douglas, q.v. SC: Mike Garfin, in at least those marked MG.
Blondes Are My Trouble; see The Darker Traffic
The Darker Traffic. Dodd, 1954; Reinhardt, 1954. Also published as: Blondes Are My Trouble. Popular Library, 1955 MG [Montr.]
A Dum-Dum for the President. Hammond, 1961 MG [Montr.]
Exit in Green. Dodd, 1953. British title: Murder Came Tumbling. Hammond, 1959
Flee from Terror. Popular Library, 1957 [Yugos.]
Hot Freeze. Dodd, 1954; Reinhardt, 1954 MG [Montr.]
Murder Came Tumbling; see Exit in Green

BRETT, MICHAEL. Pseudonym of Miles (Barton) Tripp, 1923- , q.v. Other pseudonym: John Michael Brett, q.v. SC: Hugo Baron = HB (see also John Michael Brett entry).
Diecast. Barker, 1964; GM, 1963 HB

BRETT, MICHAEL
Key Witness. Evans, 1964 (3-act play.)

BRETT, MICHAEL. 1921- . SC: Pete McGrath = PM. All titles set in NYC.
Another Day, Another Stiff. PB, 1967 PM
Cry Uncle!; see Lie a Little, Die a Little
Dead, Upstairs in the Tub. PB, 1967 PM
Death of a Hippie. PB, 1968 PM
Diamond Kill. Putnam, 1977
An Ear for Murder. PB, 1967 PM
The Flight of the Stiff. PB, 1967 PM
Kill Him Quickly, It's Raining. PB, 1966 PM
Lie a Little, Die a Little. PB, 1968. Also published as: Cry Uncle! PB, 1971 PM
Slit My Throat, Gently. PB, 1968 PM
Turn Blue, You Murderers. PB, 1967 PM
We, the Killers. PB, 1967 PM

BRETT, MIKE. SC: Sam Dakkers, in both titles, both set in NYC.
The Guilty Bystander. Ace, 1959; Digit, 1960
Scream Street. Ace, 1959; Digit, 1960

BRETT, SIMON (ANTHONY LEE). 1945- . Ref: CA, TC. SC: Charles Paris, in all titles.
An Amateur Corpse. Gollancz, 1978; Scribner, 1978
Cast, in Order of Disappearance. Gollancz, 1975; Scribner, 1976
A Comedian Dies. Gollancz, 1979; Scribner, 1979 [theatre]
The Dead Side of the Mike. Gollancz, 1980; Scribner, 1980
So Much Blood. Gollancz, 1976; Scribner, 1977 [theatre, Edin.]
Star Trap. Gollancz, 1977; Scribner, 1978 [theatre]

BRETT, STEPHEN. Pseudonym of Stephen Mertz.
Some Die Hard. Manor, 1979 [Colo.]
The Vampire Chase. Manor, 1979

BREUER, GUSTAV J. Joint pseudonym with Gwen Leys Davenport, 1910- : Michael Hardt, q.v.

BREWER, GIL. Ref: TC. SC: Al Mundy (in novelizations of "It Takes a Thief" TV series) = AM.
—And the Girl Screamed. Crest, 1956; Fawcett (London), 1959 [Fla.]
Angel. Avon, 1960 [Fla.]
The Angry Dream. Bouregy, 1957. Also published as: The Girl from Hateville. Zenith, 1958
Appointment in Cairo. Ace, 1970 AM [Cairo]
Appointment in Hell. Monarch, 1961 [Brazil]
Backwoods Teaser. GM, 1960 [Ga.]
The Bitch. Avon, 1958
The Brat. GM, 1957; Fawcett (London), 1958 [Fla.]
The Devil in Davos. Ace, 1969 AM [Switz.]
Flight to Darkness. GM, 1952 [Fla.]
The Girl from Hateville; see The Angry Dream
Hell's Our Destination. GM, 1953; Fawcett (London), 1955
The Hungry One. GM, 1966
A Killer Is Loose. GM, 1954; Moring, 1956 [Fla.]
Little Tramp. Crest, 1957; Red Seal, 1959
Mediterranean Caper. Ace, 1969 AM [Fr.]
Memory of Passion. Lancer, 1963
Nude on Thin Ice. Avon, 1960
Play It Hard. Monarch, 1960 [Fla.]
The Red Scarf. Mystery House, 1958; Digit, 1959
Satan Is a Woman. GM, 1951; New Fiction, 1952
77 Rue Paradis. GM, 1955; Red Seal, 1959
Sin for Me. Banner, 1967
So Rich, So Dead. GM, 1951; New Fiction, 1952 [Fla.]
Some Must Die. GM, 1954; Moring, 1956
The Squeeze. Ace, 1955
Sugar. Avon, 1959
A Taste of Sin. Berkley, 1961
The Tease. Banner, 1967 [Fla.]
13 French Street. GM, 1951; New Fiction, 1952
The Three-Way Split. GM, 1960 [Fla.]
The Vengeful Virgin. Crest, 1958; Muller pb, 1960 [Fla.]
Wild. Crest, 1958; Fawcett (London), 1959 [Fla.]
Wild to Possess. Monarch, 1959 [Fla.]

BREWER, JORDAN
Get Dumm! Banner, 1967 [NYC]

BREWER, MARK
Windward Passage. Crown, 1978 [ship]

BREWER, MIKE
Man Against Fear. Hale, 1966

BREWSTER, DAVID. Pseudonym.
-The Heart's Grown Brutal. Coward, 1972 [Ire.]

BREWSTER, EUGENE V(ALENTINE). 1869-1939.
Surprise Party Murder. Greenberg, 1936 [L.I.]

BRICE, MONICA
Green Wood Burns Slow. Lothrop, 1938

BRICKHILL, PAUL (CHESTER JEROME). 1916- . Ref: CA.
The Deadline. Collins, 1962. U.S. title: War of Nerves. Morrow, 1963 [Paris]

BRIDGE, ANN. Pseudonym of Lady Mary Dolling Saunders O'Malley, 1889-1974. Ref: CA, TC. SC: Julia Probyn (Jamieson) = JP.
The Dangerous Islands. Chatto, 1964; McGraw, 1963 JP [Hebrides]
Emergency in the Pyrenees. Chatto, 1965; McGraw, 1965 JP [Fr.]
The Episode at Toledo. Chatto, 1967; McGraw, 1966 JP [Sp.]
The Lighthearted Quest. Chatto, 1956; Macmillan, 1956 JP [Afr., N.]
The Malady in Madeira. Chatto, 1970; McGraw, 1969 JP [Port.]
The Numbered Account. Chatto, 1960; McGraw, 1960 JP [Switz.]
A Place to Stand. Chatto, 1953; Macmillan, 1953 [Hung.]
The Portuguese Escape. Chatto, 1958; Macmillan, 1958 JP [Port.]
The Tightening Screw. Chatto, 1962; McGraw, 1962 [Hung.]

BRIDGES, HILDA
House of Storms. Wright, 1931 [Tas.]
The House with Black Blinds. Popular Publications (Melbourne), 193?

BRIDGES, ROY(AL). 1885-1952.
The Alden Case. Hutchinson, 1937
-And All That Beauty—. Hutchinson, 1929
-The Black House. Hodder, 1920
-The Bubble Moon. Hodder, 1915
The Case for Mrs. Heydon. Hutchinson, 1945
-Cloud. Hutchinson, 1932
-Dead Man's Gold. Hodder, 1916
-The Fires of Hate. Hodder, 1915
-The Fugitive. Hodder, 1914
-Gates of Birth. Hutchinson, 1926
-The House of Fendon. Hutchinson, 1936
-The Immortal Dawn. Hodder, 1917
-Legion: For We Are Many. Hutchinson, 1928
-Merchandise. Hodder, 1918
-A Mirror of Silver. Hutchinson, 1927
-Negrohead. Hutchinson, 1930
Old Admiral Death. Hutchinson, 1940
The Owl Is Abroad. Hutchinson, 1941
-Rats' Castle. Hutchinson, 1924; Appleton, 1924
Rogues' Haven. Hodder, 1922; Appleton, 1922
-Soul of the Sword. Hutchinson, 1933
This House Is Haunted. Hutchinson, 1939
Through Another Gate. Huthcinson, 1927
-Trinity. Hutchinson, 1931

BRIDGES, T(HOMAS) C(HARLES). 1868-1944.
The Crime on the Moor. Amalgamated, 1935 (Sexton Blake) ss
Criminal Yarns. Hutchinson, 1925 ss
Killer's Contract. Amalgamated, 1934
-The Mystery Message. Harrap, 1927
-The Secret of the Baltic. Collins, 1919

BRIDGES, VICTOR (GEORGE DeFREYNE). 1878-1972. Set: Eng.
Accidents Will Happen. Macdonald, 1948
All Very Irregular. Macdonald, 1953
Another Man's Shoes. Hodder, 1913; Doran, 1913
Blue Silver. Hodder, 1936
The Creaking Gate. Macdonald, 1958
Dusky Night. Hodder, 1940
Exit Mr. Marlowe. Macdonald, 1957
The Girl from Belfast. Macdonald, 1961
The Girl in Black. Mills, 1926; Lippincott, 1927

Greensea Island. Mills, 1922; Putnam, 1922
The Gulls Fly Low. Hodder, 1943
The Happy Murderers. Hodder, 1933
The House on the Saltings. Hodder, 1941
I Did Not Kill Osborne; see Three Blind Mice
It Happened in Essex. Hodder, 1938
It Never Rains—. Macdonald, 1944
Jetsam. Mills, 1914 ss
The King Comes Back. Hodder, 1930
The Lady from Long Acre. Mills, 1918; Putnam, 1919
The Man from Nowhere. Mills, 1913
The Man Who Butted In. Hodder, 1942
The Man Who Limped. Macdonald, 1947
The Man Who Vanished. Macdonald, 1954
Mr. Lyndon at Liberty. Mills, 1915. U.S. title: A Rogue by Compulsion. Putnam, 1915
Peter in Peril. Hodder, 1935; Penn, 1935
Quite Like Old Days. Macdonald, 1949
The Red Lodge. Mills, 1924; Doubleday, 1924
A Rogue by Compulsion; see Mr. Lyndon at Liberty
Secrecy Essential. Macdonald, 1959
The Secret of the Creek. Hodder, 1930; Houghton, 1930
The Secret of the Saltings. Macdonald, 1955
The Seven Stars. Hodder, 1939
The Tenth Commandment. Macdonald, 1951
Three Blind Mice. Hodder, 1933. U.S. title: I Did Not Kill Osborne. Penn, 1934
Trouble on the Thames. Macdonald, 1945
We Don't Want to Lose You. Macdonald, 1952
What the Doctor Ordered. Macdonald, 1956

BRIDGMONT, (JAMES) LESLIE. 1901- .
Unbriefed Mission. Falcon, 1953

BRIERLEY, DAVID. SC: Cody, in both titles.
Blood Group O. Faber, 1980
Cold War. Faber, 1979

BRIGHT, ALFRED
The Golden Earnest. Hocage, 1938 [Fr.]

BRIGHT, JOHN. See: Kubec Glasmon.

BRIGHTON, LAURA. Pseudonym of Jane Corby, 1899- , q.v. Other pseudonyms: Jean Carew, Jeanne Holden, qq.v.

BRILEY, JOHN
Last Dance. Secker, 1978

BRILLANT, J. MAURICE. Native of Quebec; with the Canadian National Railway in the 1950s.
Vision of Murder. Comet, 1954 [Can.]

BRIN, DAVID. 1950- .
Sundiver. Bantam, 1980 [2200s]

BRINCHMANN, ALEXANDER. 1888-1978. Pseudonym: Roy Roberts, q.v.

BRINGLE, MARY
The Footpath Murder. Doubleday, 1975; Hale, 1976

BRINK, CAROLINE
The Bellini Look. Bantam, 1976 [Venice, 1929]

BRINKWORTH, IAN. Pseudonym: Ian Brook, q.v.

BRINTON, HENRY. 1901-1977. Pseudonym: Alex Fraser, q.v. Ref: CA, CC. SC: John and Sally Strang, in at least those marked S. Set: Eng.
An Apple a Day. Hutchinson, 1958; Washburn, 1959
Apprentice to Fear; see An Ordinary Day
Can Death Be Sleep? Hutchinson, 1965
Coppers and Gold. Hutchinson, 1957; Macmillan, 1958 S
Death to Windward. Hutchinson, 1954 S
Drug on the Market. Hutchinson, 1956; Macmillan, 1957 S
Ill Wind. Hutchinson, 1957 S
Now Like to Die. Hutchinson, 1955
One Down and Two to Slay. Hutchinson, 1954. Also published as: Two to Slay. Arrow, 1959 S
An Ordinary Day. Hutchinson, 1959. U.S. title: Apprentice to Fear. Macmillan, 1961 S
Purple-6. Hutchinson, 1962; Walker, 1962
Rude Awakening. Hutchinson, 1961
Two to Slay; see One Down and Two to Slay

BRISBANE, COUTTS. Pseudonym of R. C(outts) Armour, q.v. All titles feature Sexton Blake and were published by Amalgamated Press.
Blind Man's Secret. 1936
The Case of the Three Absconding Swindlers. 1936
The Crime of Gunga Dass. 1936
Dead Man's Peak. 1933
The Death House. 1931
Dr. Ferraro's Frame-Up. 1933
The Fatal Talisman. 1932
The Gang's Deserter. 1930
The Masked Man of the Desert. 1937
The Middle of the Negro's Head. 1939
Murder in the Air. 1932
The Mystery of the Missing Doctor. 1938
The Mystery of the Rajah's Son. 1935
The Mystery of the Red Tower. 1940
The Mystery of the Tramp Steamer. 1933
The Nursing Home Crime. 1935
The Secret of the Balkan Heiress. 1936
The Secret of the Glen. 1935
The Secret of the Loch. 1933
The Secret of the Sanatorium. 1931
The Secret Temple. 1934
The Trafalgar Square Mystery. 1932
The Trail of the White Turban. 1936
The Trapper's Victim. 1930

BRISCO, PATTY [PATRICIA BRISCO MATTHEWS]. 1927- . Clayton (Hartley) Matthews, 1918- , q.v., collaborated with his wife on these titles.
The Crystal Window. Avon, 1973
Horror at Gull House. Belmont, 1973 [Calif.]
House of Candles. Manor, 1973
Mist of Evil. Manor, 1976

BRISTOL, PEGGY. See: Irving Shulman, 1913- .

BRISTOL, STEPHEN
Crime Photographer. French, 1950 (3-act play based on the character created by George Harmon Coxe, 1901- , q.v.)

BRISTOW, BOB
Marked! Dell, 1961
-Sin Street. Dell, 196?

BRISTOW, GWEN [MRS. BRUCE MANNING], 1903-1980, and BRUCE MANNING. Ref: CA, EM. See also: Owen Davis, 1874-1956. SC: Wade = W.
The Gutenberg Murders. Mystery League, 1931 W [New Or.]
The Invisible Host. Mystery League, 1930. Also published as: The Ninth Guest. Popular Library, 1975 [New Or.]
The Mardi Gras Murders. Mystery League, 1932 W [New Or.]
The Ninth Guest; see The Invisible Host
Two and Two Make Twenty-Two. Mystery League, 1932 [Miss.]

BRISTOWE, ANTHONY (LYNN). 1921- . Ref: CA.
The Tunnel. Belmont, 1965 [1900, Eng.]

BRITTON, KENNTH PHILLIPS and ROY HARGRAVE
Houseparty. French (NYC), 1930 (3-act play.)

BRITTON, SUMNER. 1902- . See: Maurice Beam.

BROAD, PETER
Death on the Beach. Cassell, 1959

BROADBRIDGE, HUGH
Moorland Terror. Butterworth, 1930

BROADHURST, GEORGE (HOWELLS). 1866-1952. See: Arthur Hornblow, 1865-1941?

BROADLEY, PHILIP
In the Key of Black. Hodder, 1963

BROCHET, JEAN ALEXANDRE. 1921-1963. Pseudonym: Jean Bruce, q.v.

BROCK, ALAN (ST. HILL). 1886- . Pseudonym: Peter Dewdney, q.v. Set: Eng.
After the Fact. Nicholson, 1935
The Browns of the Yard. Harrap, 1952
By Misadventure. Nicholson, 1934
A Casebook of Crime. Rockliff, 1948
Earth to Ashes. Nicholson, 1939
Further Evidence. Nicholson, 1934
Inquiries by the Yard. Harrap, 1950
Miss Hamblett's Ghost. Macdonald, 1946
Suspicion Was Aroused. Nicholson, 1936

BROCK, EDWIN. 1927- .
-The Little White God. Hutchinson, 1962

BROCK, LYNN. Pseudonym of Alister McAlister, 1877-1943. Other pseudonym: Anthony Wharton, q.v. Ref: CC, EM, MM, MP, TC. SC: Colonel Gore = G; Sgt. Venn = V. Set: Eng.
The Barrington Mystery; see The Deductions of Colonel Gore
Colonel Gore's Second Case. Collins, 1925; Harper, 1926 G
Colonel Gore's Third Case. Collins, 1927. U.S. title: The Kink. Harper, 1927 G
The Dagwort Coombe Murder. Collins, 1929. U.S. title: The Stoke Silver Case. Harper, 1929
The Deductions of Colonel Gore. Collins, 1924; Harper, 1925. Also published as: The Barrington Mystery. Collins, 1932 G
Fourfingers. Collins, 1939 V
The Kink; see Colonel Gore's Third Case
The Mendip Mystery. Collins, 1929. U.S. title: Murder at the Inn. Harper, 1929 G
Murder at the Inn; see The Mendip Mystery
Murder on the Bridge; see Q.E.D.
Nightmare. Collins, 1932
Q.E.D. Collins, 1930. U.S. title: Murder on the Bridge. Harper, 1930. Reprinted in England under the U.S. title: Collins, 1932 G
The Riddle of the Roost. Collins, 1939
The Silver Sickle Case. Collins, 1938 V
The Slip-Carriage Mystery. Collins, 1928; Harper, 1928 G
The Stoat. Collins, 1940 V
The Stoke Silver Case; see The Dagwort Coombe Murder

BROCK, ROSE. Pseudonym of Joseph Hansen, 1923- , q.v.
Long Leaf. Harper, 1974
Tarn House. Avon, 1971; Harrap, 1975 [Wis.]

BROCK, STUART. Pseudonym of Louis (Preston) Trimble, 1917- , q.v. Other pseudonym: Gerry Travis, q.v.
Bring Back Her Body. Ace, 1953 [Wash.]
Death Is My Lover. Mill, 1948 [Wash.]
Just Around the Coroner. Mill, 1948 [Seattle]
Killer's Choice. Graphic, 1956 [Wash.]

BROCKE, JULIAN. Pseudonym of Richard Hill Wilkinson, 1904- , q.v. Other pseudonyms: Eugene Hayford, E. Harrison Ott, Paul Pray, qq.v.
Thomas Shelton's Ghost. Drama Guild, 1936. (Play.)

BROCKETT, LINUS PIERPONT. 1820-1893.
-The Camp, the Battlefield, and the Hospital. National, 1866. Also published as: Scouts, Spies, and Heroes of the Great Civil War. Star, 1892, as by Captain Joseph Powers Hazelton. And as: Scouts, Spies, and Detectives of the Great Civil War. National Tribune, 1899, as by Hazelton ss

BRODE, ROBERT
The Clue of the Curious Cat. Empire, 1935 [Md.]

BRODERICK, GERRY P. See: Erwin N. Nistler.

BRODEUR, PAUL (ADRIAN, JR.). 1931- . Ref: CA.
-The Sick Fox. Little, 1963; Gollancz, 1963
The Stunt Man. Atheneum, 1970; Bodley, 1970 [Calif.]

BRODIE, GORDON. SC: John Borham, in at least those marked JB.
The Lady Had a Tiger. Hale, 1968 JB
The Poison of Poppies. Hale, 1968 JB
The Will to Kill. Hale, 1969
Who Called Diamonds? Hale, 1970 JB

BRODIE, JULIAN PAUL. 1908- . Joint pseudonym with Alan (Baer) Green, 1906-1975, q.v.: Roger Denbie, q.v.

BRODIE-INNES, JOHN WILLIAM. 1848- .
-The Devil's Mistress. Rider, 1915
The Golden Rope. Lane (London & NYC), 1919
The Tragedy of an Indiscretion. Lane (London & NYC), 1916

BRODY, MARC. Pseudonym of R(ichard) Wilkes-Hunter, 1906-   , q.v. Other pseudonyms: Tod Conrad, Alex Crane, qq.v. SC: Marc Brody, in most (all?) titles. These books were first published in Australia, probably all as Horwitz paperbacks, but detailed information is lacking.
  Baby, Your Type's Murder.
  Blonde at Bay. Horwitz, 1959
  Blueprints for a Blonde.
  Book Her for Murder.
  Dame on a Death Round.
  Hers Is a Hearse.
  High Tide Temptress.
  Hot Line for a Honey.
  Lady, Don't Shroud Me! Horwitz, 1958
  Late Final Blonde.
  Move On, Miss Mayhem.
  Murder Is a Maiden's Handicap.
  One Shot for Sadie.
  Penthouse Preview.
  Red Hot and Morgue Bound.
  Second Storey Sinner.
  Sinister Sister. Horwitz, 1959
  Siren on the Skids.
  Stop Press in Scarlet.
  Sugar, You're A Scoop!
  Teaser Set to Kill. Horwitz, 1958 [Fla.]
  Undercover Cutie.
  Write Off the Redhead.

BROEMEL, ROSE
  The Elusive Criminal. Murray, 1930

BROGAN, COLM. 1902-   . SC: Patrick Heron, in both titles. Set: Eng.
  The Ghost Walks. Skeffington, 1932
  The Plunge. Skeffington, 1933

BROGAN, DENIS WILLIAM. 1900-1974. Pseudonym: Maurice Barrington, q.v.

BROGAN, JAMES. Pseudonym of (John) Christopher (Glazebrook) Hodder-Williams, 1926-   , q.v.
  The Cummings Report. Hodder, 1958. Reprinted later as by Christopher Hodder-Williams.

BROINOWSKI, ALISON
  Take One Ambassador. Macmillan (London), 1973

BROME, ROBERT. 1917-   .
  The Black Cat. Eldridge, 1972 (1-act play based on a ss by Edgar A. Poe, 1809-1849, q.v.)
  The Fall of the House of Usher. Eldridge, 1971 (1-act play based on the ss by Edgar A. Poe, 1809-1849, q.v.)
  The Murders in the Rue Morgue. Eldridge, 1968 (1-act play based on the ss by Edgar A. Poe, 1809-1849, q.v.)
  The Purloined Letter. Eldridge, 1973 (1-act play based on the ss by Edgar A. Poe, 1809-1849, q.v.)
  The Spider. Northwestern, 1939 (1-act play.)
  The Spider's Web. Bugbee, 1940 (3-act play.)
  The Suicide Club. Eldridge, 1964 (1-act play based on the ss by Robert Louis Stevenson, 1850-1894, q.v.)
  The Unsuspected. Dramatic, 1962. (Play adapted from the novel by Charlotte Armstrong, 1905-1969, q.v.)

BROME, (HERBERT) VINCENT. 1910-   . Ref: CA.
  The Ambassador and the Spy; see The Embassy
  The Embassy. Cassell, 1972. U.S. title: The Ambassador and the Spy. Crown, 1973
  The Happy Hostage. Cassell, 1976

BROMIGE, IRIS (AMY EDNA). 1910-   .
  -A Haunted Landscape. Hodder, 1976
  -Rosevean. Hodder, 1962; Chilton-Musson, 1962

BROMLEY, GORDON. SC: Insp. Severn, in all titles.
  The Chance to Poison. Collins, 1973
  In the Absence of the Body. Collins, 1972
  A Midsummer Night's Crime. Hale, 1977 [theatre]

BRONSON, F(RANCIS) W(OOLSEY). 1901-1966. Born in Mpls.; graduate of Yale and editor of the "Yale Alumni Magazine" for almost 30 years.
  The Bulldog Has the Key. Farrar, 1949 [Conn., acad.]
  Nice People Don't Kill. Farrar, 1940 [New Eng.]
  The Uncas Island Murders. Farrar, 1942 [Conn.]

BRONSON-HOWARD, GEORGE (FITZALAN). 1833-1922. See also: Ethel Watts Mumford, 1878-1940. Ref: EM. SC: Yorke Norroy = YN.
  -Birds of Prey. Watt, 1918 [NYC]
  The Black Book. Watt, 1920 YN [NYC]
  The Devil's Chaplain. Watt, 1922; Paul, 1924
  An Enemy to Society. Doubleday, 1911; Laurie, 1911 [NYC]
  The Green-Eyed Monster. Detective Tales, 19?? (63 pp. mini-paperback.)
  Norroy, Diplomatic Agent. Saalfield, 1907 ss YN
  Slaves of the Lamp. Watt, 1917 YN

BRONTE, LOUISA. Pseudonym of Janet Louise Roberts, 1925-   , q.v. Other pseudonyms: Rebecca Danton, Janette Radcliffe, qq.v
  Casino Greystone. Ballantine, 1976 [New Eng.]
  Freedom Trail to Greystone. Ballantine, 1976 [New Eng.]
  Gathering at Greystone. Ballantine, 1976 [New Eng., 1812]
  Greystone Heritage. Ballantine, 1976 [New Eng.]
  Greystone Tavern. Ballantine, 1975 [New Eng., 1776]
  Her Demon Lover. Avon, 1973
  Lord Satan. Avon, 1972
  Moonlight at Greystone. Ballantine, 1976 [New Eng.]
  The Vallette Heritage. Jove, 1978
  The Van Rhyne Heritage. Jove, 1979

BROOCKS, SCHUYLER
  Murder Makes a Marriage. Mystery House, 1946

BROOK, IAN. Pseudonym of Ian Brinkworth.
  The Golden Bull. Cassell, 1968

BROOKE, EMMA (FRANCIS)
  The Confession of Stephen Whapshare. Hutchinson, 1898; Putnam, 1898

BROOKE, HUGH (FELIX CONRAD). 1902-   .
  -The Mad Shepherdess. Longmans, 1930
  Man Made Angry. Longmans, 1932; Long & Smith, 1932
  Miss Mitchell. Heinemann, 1934. U.S. title: The Web. Doubleday, 1934
  The Web; see Miss Mitchell

BROOKE, JUSTIN. Set: Eng.
  The Clue by the Golden Tooth. Modern, 193?
  Death at Dale's End. Modern, 1935
  Gangster's Isle. Modern, 1937
  The Limping Sailor. Modern, 193?
  Murder in the Temple. Modern, 193?
  The Mystery at Folly Mill. Modern, 193?
  The Secret of the Siding. Modern, 1935
  The Sinister Encounter. Modern, 1938
  Who Killed Mr. Fisk? Modern, 1935

BROOKER, BERTRAM. 1888-1955. Pseudonym: Huxley Herne, q.v.

BROOKER, CLAIRE
  Dark Mosaic. Arcadia, 1957

BROOKES, OWEN. Pseudonym.
  -Inheritance. Holt, 1980; Hutchinson, 1980
  The Widow of Ratchets. Holt, 1979; Fontana, 1980 [Eng.]

BROOKHOUSE, (JOHN) CHRISTOPHER. 1938-   . Ref: CA.
  Wintermute. Dutton, 1978 [Vt.]

BROOKMAN, LAURA LOU. 1898-   .
  Unknown Blond. Grosset, 1934

BROOKS, ANNE TEDLOCK
  White Camellias. Arcadia, 1960 [Eng.]

BROOKS, (WILLIAM) COLLIN. 1893-   . SC: O. Swete McTavish, in at least those marked OSM; Raeburn Steel, in at least those marked RS. Set: Eng.
  Account Paid. Hutchinson, 1930
  The Body Snatchers. Hutchinson, 1927 RS
  The Catspaws. Hutchinson, 1929
  Found Dead. Hutchinson, 1930 OSM
  Frame-Up. Hutchinson, 1935
  The Ghost Hunters. Hutchinson, 1928; Sears, 1928 RS
  Mr. Daddy—Detective. Hutchinson, 1933
  Mr. X. Hutchinson, 1927 RS
  O Sweet McTavish. Hutchinson, 1930 OSM
  Seven Hells. Hutchinson, 1929
  The Swimming Frog. Hutchinson, 1951
  Three Yards of Cord. Hutchinson, 1931 OSM

BROOKS, EDWY SEARLES. 1889-1965. Pseudonyms: Berkeley Gray, Victor Gunn, Carlton Ross, qq.v. Ref: CC, EM, TC. SC: Sexton Blake (with many other authors), in those titles listed without publisher (which was Amalgamated Press); Insp. William Beeke (The Grouser) = WB.
  The Black Dagger. 1933
  The Boarding-House Mystery. 1924
  The Brixham Manor Mystery. 1924
  The Case of the Sleeping Partner. 1924
  The Case of the Twin Detectives. 1916
  The Green Eyes. 1923
  The Grouser Investigates. Harrap, 1936 WB
  The House at Waterloo. 1923
  The House with the Double Moat. 1917
  The Human Bloodhound. 1924
  The Impersonators. 1926
  In the Night Watch. 1925
  The Midnight Lorry Crime. 1937
  Midst Balkan Perils. 1916
  The Mystery of Rodney's Cove. 1924
  On the Bed of the Ocean. 1922
  The Peril of the Prince! 1916
  The Red Spider. 1916
  The Riddle of the Body on the Road. 1941
  The Strange Case of the Antlered Man. Harrap, 1935 WB

BROOKS, MRS. F. See: Berkeley Gray.

BROOKS, HENRY S. 1830?-1910.
  A Catastrophe in Bohemia and other stories. Webster, 1893 ss, one criminous

BROOKS, HILDEGARD. 1875-   .
  Without a Warrant. Scribner, 1901 [Ga.]

BROOKS, JAMES J.
  Whiskey Drips: A Series of Interesting Sketches, Illustrating the Operations of the Whiskey Thieves in Their Evasions of the Law and Its Penalties. Evans, 1873. Also published as: The Adventures of a U.S. Detective. Souder, 1876 ss

BROOKS, KATE
  The Immaculate Murders. Manor, 1979
  Murder in the Laboratory. Manor, 1979
  The Secret of Killer Mountain Inn. Manor, 1978

BROOKS, LAURA FRANCES. Pseudonym of W(illiam) E(dward) D(aniel) Ross, 1912-   , q.v. Other pseudonyms: Rose Dana, Jan Daniels, Ellen Randolph, Clarissa Ross, Dan Ross, Dana Ross, Marilyn Ross, qq.v.
  The Old Evil House. Ace, 1975

BROOKS, LEONARD HAROLD.   -1950. Brother of Edwy Searles Brooks, 1889-1965, q.v. All titles feature Sexton Blake and were published by Amalgamated Press.
  The Affair of the Blackfriars Financier. 1920
  The Avenging Seven. 1920
  Fingerprints of Fate! 1922
  The Gnat. 1921
  The House of Ghosts. 1922
  The Mystery of Glyn Castle. 1923
  The Riddle of the Lascar's Head. 1926
  The Secret of Thurlston Towers. 1923

BROOKS, LIONEL. See: Berkeley Gray.

BROOKS, (AMY HELEN) PATRICIA. 1926-   . Ref: CA.
  Find the Tiger. Deane, 1961 (3-act play.)
  Missing Person. Steele's, 1963 (3-act play.)

BROOKS, VIVIAN COLLIN. 1922-   . Pseudonym: Osmington Mills, q.v.

BROOM, J. A.
  Wanton Fury. Paul, 1940

BROOME, ADAM. Pseudonym of Godfrey Warden James, 1888-   . Ref: CC. SC: Insp. Bramley = B (set in Eng.); Capt./Commissioner Denzil Grigson = DG, set in Afr., W.
  The Black Mamba. Bles, 1936 [Afr., W.]
  The Cambridge Murders. Bles, 1936 B [acad.]
  The Crocodile Club. Bles, 1935 DG
  Crowner's Quest. Benn, 1930 DG
  Dream Murder. Macdonald, 1946 DG
  Flame of the Forest. Bles, 1943 DG
  The Island of Death. Bles, 1932 DG
  The Oxford Murders. Bles, 1929 B [acad.]
  The Porro Palaver. Bles, 1928 [Afr., W.]

The Queen's Hall Murder. Bles, 1933 DG
The Red Queen Club. Bles, 1939
Snakes and Ladders. Bles, 1938 DG

BROPHY, JOHN. 1899-1965. Ref: CA, CC.
Behold the Judge. Collins, 1937
The Day They Robbed the Bank of England. Chatto, 1959 [1900, Eng.]
The Front Door Key. Heinemann, 1960
I Let Him Go. Cape, 1935
Solitude Island. Collins, 1941

BROSNAN, KATE
A Cry in the Night. Leisure, 1977

BROSTER, D(OROTHY) K(ATHLEEN). 1877-1950.
World Under Snow, with G. Forester. Heinemann, 1935

BROTHERS, (M.) JAY. 1931-   . Ref: CA.
Ox. Bobbs, 1975 [NYC]

BROTHERS, WILLIAM P.
Morocco Episode. Hillman-Curl pb, 1959 [Mor.]

BROUGHTON, F. LUSK
Harry Williams, the New York Detective. Ogilvie, 1887
Nemo, the Shadow Detective. Ogilvie, 1885
A Victim of Villainy. Street (Magnet)

BROUGHTON, MARY
Prisoners of Fear. Joseph, 1933

BROUN, DANIEL. Ref: CC. SC: Harry Egypt = HE.
Counterweight. Holt, 1962 [NYC]
Egypt's Choice. Holt, 1963; Gollancz, 1964 HE [Md.]
From 9 O'Clock to Jamaica Bay. Holt, 1964 [N.Y.]
The Subject of Harry Egypt. Holt, 1963; Gollancz, 1963 HE [NYC]

BROWN, ALEX (JOHN CHARLES). 1900-1962.
Green Lane; or, Murder at Moat Farm. Cape, 1930
The Hollow Mountain. Macmillan (London), 1939
A Time to Kill. Cape, 1930 (2 stories.)

BROWN, ALICE. 1857-1948.
The Mysteries of Ann. Macmillan, 1925

BROWN, ALYS
The Pearls of Pilolu. Eldon, 1933

BROWN, ANDREW CASSELS. 1875-   . Set: Eng.
Birds of Prey. Methuen, 1929
Dark Dealing. Methuen, 1930
Dr. Glazebrook's Revenge. Mills, 1928; Dodd, 1928
Josselin Takes a Hand. Mills, 1927; Dodd, 1927

BROWN, ANTONY. British scriptwriter, playwright, TV interviewer.
Slay Me Suddenly. Long, 1968; Walker, 1969 [Sp.]

BROWN, CARL L. 1919-   .
The Killer That's Dead! Vantage, 1977

BROWN, CARNABY. Set: Eng.
The Man on the Stairs. Boardman, 1957
The Small Change. Boardman, 1958; Roy, 1958

BROWN, CARTER. Pseudonym of Alan Geoffrey Yates, 1923-   , q.v. Other pseudonym: Caroline Farr, q.v. Ref: CA, TC. Earliest books were published as by Peter Carter-Brown (PC-B), then as by Peter Carter Brown (PCB), then as by Carter Brown. Uncorrelated rewrites and title changes probably exist in this list. SC: Larry Baker = LB; Danny Boyd, in at least those marked DB; Paul Donavan = PD; Mike Farrel, in at least those marked MF; Rick Holman = RH; Andy Kane, in at least those marked AK; Randy Roberts = RR; Mavis Seidlitz, in at least those marked MS; Al Wheeler, in at least those marked AW.
And the Undead Sing. Signet, 1974 MS [L.A.]
Angel! Horwitz, 1962; Signet, 1962 AW [Calif.]
The Angry Amazons. Horwitz, 1972; Signet, 1972 RR,DB [Calif.]
The Aseptic Murders. Horwitz, 1972; Signet, 1972 AW [Calif.]
Baby, You're Guilt-Edged. Horwitz-Transport, 1956, as by PCB

The Ballad of Loving Jenny. Horwitz, 1963. U.S. & British title: The White Bikini. Signet, 1963; Four Square, 1965 RH [L.A.]
Bella Donna Was Poison. Horwitz-Transport, 1957, as by PCB
Bid the Babe Bye-Bye. Horwitz-Transport, 1956, as by PCB
Bird in a Guilt-Edged Cage. Horwitz, 1963. U.S. & British title: The Guilt-Edged Cage. Signet, 1962; Four Square, 1963 (Rewritten reissue of: That's Piracy, My Pet, q.v.) AK [H. Kong]
The Black Lace Hangover. Horwitz, 1966; Signet, 1966; Four Square, 1969 DB [NYC]
Black Widow Weeps. Transport, 1953?, as by PC-B?
The Blonde. Horwitz-Transport?, 1958; Signet, 1958; Four Square, 1964 AW [Calif.]
Blonde, Bad and Beautiful. Horwitz-Transport, 1957?, as by PCB. (Rewritten and reissued as: The Hong Kong Caper, q.v.)
Blonde, Beautiful and—BLAM! Horwitz-Transport, 1956, as by PCB
Blonde on a Broomstick. Horwitz, 1966; Signet, 1966; Four Square, 1966 RH [Calif.]
Blonde on the Rocks. Horwitz, 1963; Signet, 1963; Four Square, 1964 RH [L.A.]
Blonde Verdict. Horwitz-Transport, 1956, as by PCB AW
The Body. Horwitz, 1961; Signet, 1958; Four Square, 1963 (Rewritten reissue of: No Law Against Angels, q.v.) AW [Calif.]
The Bombshell. Horwitz, 1960; Signet, 1960; Four Square, 1968 (Rewritten reissue of: Doll for the Big House, q.v.) AW
Booty for a Babe. Horwitz-Transport, 1956, as by PCB
The Born Loser. Horwitz, 1973; Signet, 1973 AW [Calif.]
The Brazen. Horwitz, 1960; Signet, 1960; Four Square, 1962 AW [Calif.]
The Bribe Was Beautiful. Horwitz-Transport, 1956, as by PCB
A Bullet for My Baby. Horwitz-Transport, 1955, as by PCB MS
The Bump and Grind Murders. Horwitz, 1965; Signet, 1964; Four Square, 1965 MS [L.A.]
Burden of Guilt. Horwitz, 1971; Signet, 1970 AW [Calif.]
Busted Wheeler. Horwitz, 1979; Belmont, 1979; Corgi, 1979 AW
Caress Before Killing. Horwitz-Transport, 1956, as by PCB
Catch Me a Phoenix! Horwitz, 1965; Signet, 1965; Four Square, 1966 DB [Eng.]
Charlie Sent Me! Horwitz, 1963; Signet, 1963; Four Square, 1965 (Rewritten reissue of: Swan Song for a Siren, q.v.) LB [NYC]
Charmer Chased. Horwitz-Transport, 1958?, as by PCB
Chinese Donavan. Horwitz, 1976; Signet, 1976 PD [H. Kong]
Chorine Makes a Killing. Horwitz-Transport, 1957, as by PCB AW
The Clown. Horwitz, 1973; Signet, 1972 AW [Calif.]
The Coffin Bird. Horwitz, 1971; Signet, 1970 DB [Syd.]
The Corpse. Horwitz, 1960; Signet, 1958; Four Square, 1963 (Rewritten reissue of: Death on the Downbeat, q.v.) AW
A Corpse for Christmas. Horwitz, 1965; Signet, 1965; Four Square, 1966 AW
The Coven. Horwitz, 1971; Signet, 1971 RH [L.A.]
The Creative Murders. Horwitz, 1971; Signet, 1971 AW [Calif.]
Curtains for a Chorine. Horwitz-Transport, 1955, as by PCB
Curves for a Coroner. Horwitz-Transport, 1955, as by PCB
Cutie Cashed His Chips. Horwitz-Transport, 1955, as by PCB (Rewritten and reissued as: The Million Dollar Babe, q.v.)
Cutie Takes the Count. Horwitz-Transport, 1958, as by PCB
Cutie Wins a Corpse. Horwitz-Transport, 1957?, as by PCB (Rewritten and reissued as: Graves, I Dig!, q.v.)
The Dame. Horwitz, 1959; Signet, 1959; Four Square, 1966 AW [Calif.]
The Dance of Death. Horwitz, 1964; Signet, 1964; Four Square, 1965 AW [Calif.]

Darling, You're Doomed. Horwitz-Transport, 1956, as by PCB
The Deadly Kitten. Horwitz, 1968; Signet, 1967 RH [L.A.]
Deadly Miss. Horwitz-Transport, 1958, as by PCB
Death of a Doll. Horwitz-Transport, 1956, as by PCB (Rewritten and reissued under the same title: Horwitz, 1960. U.S. title: The Ever-Loving Blues. Signet, 1961 RH [Fla.])
Death on the Downbeat. Horwitz-Transport, 1958, as by PCB (Rewritten and reissued as: The Corpse, q.v.)
Death to a Downbeat. Horwitz, 1980; Tower, 1980 DB
The Deep Cold Green. Horwitz, 1968; Signet, 1968 AW [Calif.]
Delilah Was Deadly. Horwitz-Transport, 1956, as by PCB
The Desired. Horwitz, 1959; Signet, 1960; Four Square, 1966 AW
Die Anytime, After Tuesday! Horwitz, 1969; Signet, 1969 RH [L.A.]
Doll for the Big House. Horwitz-Transport, 1957, as by PCB (Rewritten and reissued as: The Bombshell, q.v.)
Donavan. Horwitz, 1974; Signet, 1974 PD [Eng.]
Donavan's Day. Horwitz, 1975?; Signet, 1975 PD
Donavan's Delight. Horwitz, 1979; Belmont, 1979; Corgi, 1979 PD [Eng.]
Donna Died Laughing. Horwitz, 1956, as by PCB
The Dream Is Deadly. Horwitz, 1960; Signet, 1960; Four Square, 1962 DB [NYC]
The Dream Merchant. Horwitz, 1977; Signet, 1976 AW
The Dumdum Murder. Horwitz, 1962; Signet, 1962; Four Square, 1963 AW [Calif.]
The Early Boyd. Horwitz, 1975; Signet, 1975 DB
Eve—It's Extortion. Horwitz-Transport, 1957, as by PCB (Rewritten and reissued in Australia as: Walk Softly Witch!, q.v., and in the U.S. as: The Victim.)
The Eve of His Dying. Horwitz-Transport, 1956, as by PCB
The Ever-Loving Blues; see Death of a Doll
The Exotic. Horwitz, 1961; Signet, 1961; Four Square, 1962 AW [Calif.]
The Fabulous; see None But the Lethal Heart
Felon Angel; see Homicide Harem and Felon Angel
The Flagellator. Horwitz, 1969; Signet, 1969 RH [L.A.]
The Frame Is Beautiful. Transport, 1953, as by PC-B
Fraulein Is Feline. Transport, 1953, as by PC-B
The Girl from Outer Space. Horwitz, 1966; Signet, 1965; Four Square, 1966 RH [L.A.]
Girl in a Shroud. Horwitz, 1965; Signet, 1963; Four Square, 1964 AW [Calif.]
The Girl Who Was Possessed; see The Sinners
Goddess Gone Bad. Horwitz-Transport, 1958, as by PCB?
Good Morning, Mavis. Horwitz-Transport, 1957?, as by PCB MS
A Good Year for Dwarfs? Horwitz, 1971; Signet, 1970 RH [L.A.]
Graves, I Dig! Horwitz, 1960; Signet, 1960 (Rewritten reissue of: Cutie Wins a Corpse, q.v.) [Miami]
The Guilt-Edged Cage; see Bird in a Guilt-Edged Cage
Had I But Groaned. Horwitz, 1968; Signet, 1968. British title: The Witches. Four Square, 1969 LB [N.Y.]
The Hammer of Thor. Horwitz, 1967; Signet, 1965 AW [Calif.]
The Hang-Up Kid. Horwitz, 1970; Signet, 1970 RH [L.A.]
The Hellcat. Horwitz, 1962; Signet, 1962; Four Square, 1962 AW [Calif.]
Hi-Fi Fadeout. Horwitz-Transport, 1958, as by PCB?
Hi-Jack for a Jill. Horwitz-Transport, 1956, as by PCB
High Fashion in Homicide. Horwitz-Transport, 1958, as by PCB
Homicide Harem and Felon Angel. Horwitz, 1965
Homicide Hoyden. Horwitz-Transport?, 1954, as by PCB
Honey, Here's Your Hearse! Horwitz-Transport, 1955, as by PCB MS

The Hong Kong Caper. Horwitz, 1962; Signet, 1962; Four Square, 1963 (Rewritten reissue of: Blonde, Bad and Beautiful, q.v.) AK [H. Kong]
The Hoodlum Was a Honey. Horwitz-Transport, 1956, as by PCB
Hot Seat for a Honey; see Penthouse Passout
House of Sorcery. Horwitz, 1968; Signet, 1967; Four Square, 1968 DB [NYC]
Ice Cold in Ermine. Horwitz-Transport, 1958, as by PCB
The Ice-Cold Nude. Horwitz, 1962; Signet, 1962; Four Square, 1962 DB [Calif.]
The Invisible Flamini. Horwitz, 1972; Signet, 1971 RH [L.A.]
The Iron Maiden. Horwitz, 1975; Signet, 1975 LB
The Jade-Eyed Jinx. Horwitz, 1963. U.S. and British title: The Jade-Eyed Jungle. Signet, 1963; Four Square, 1964 RH [L.A.]
The Jade-Eyed Jungle; see The Jade-Eyed Jinx
The Killer Is Kissable. Horwitz-Transport?, 1954, as by PCB?
Kiss and Kill. Horwitz-Transport, 1955, as by PCB
Kiss Me Deadly. Horwitz-Transport, 1955, as by PCB
The Lady Has No Convictions. Horwitz-Transport, 1956, as by PCB
The Lady Is Available; see The Lady Is Not Available
The Lady Is Chased. Transport, 1953, as by PC-B
The Lady Is Not Available. Horwitz, 1963. U.S. & British title: The Lady Is Available. Signet, 1963; Four Square, 1964 AW [Calif.]
The Lady Is Transparent. Horwitz, 1962; Signet, 1962; Four Square, 1963 AW [Calif.]
Lament for a Lousy Lover. Horwitz, 1961; Signet, 1960; Four Square, 1968 MS,AW [L.A.]
Last Note for a Lovely. Horwitz-Transport, 1957, as by PCB
Lead Astray. Horwitz-Transport, 1955, as by PCB
Lethal in Love. Transport, 1953?, as by PC-B? Also published as: The Minx Is Murder. Horwitz-Transport, 1957, as by PCB
Lipstick Larceny. Horwitz-Transport, 1955, as by PCB
Long Time No Leola. Horwitz, 1967; Signet, 1967 RH [L.A.]
The Lover. Horwitz-Transport, 1958; Signet, 1959; Four Square, 1963 AW
Lover, Don't Come Back! Horwitz, 1962; Signet, 1962; Four Square, 1963 DB [Australia]
The Loving and the Dead. Horwitz, 1959; Signet, 1959; Four Square, 1966 MS
Luck Was No Lady. Horwitz-Transport, 1958?, as by PCB
Madam You're Mayhem. Horwitz-Transport, 1957, as by PCB
Maid for Murder. Transport, 1954, as by PCB
Manhattan Cowboy. Horwitz, 1973; Signet, 1973 DB [Calif.]
The Master. Horwitz, 1973; Signet, 1973 RH [L.A.]
Meet Murder, My Angel. Horwitz-Transport, 1956, as by PCB
The Million Dollar Babe. Horwitz, 1962; Signet, 1961 (Rewritten reissue of: Cutie Cashed His Chips, q.v.) MF [L.A.]
The Mini-Murders. Horwitz, 1968; Signet, 1968 DB [Calif.]
The Minx Is Murder; see Lethal in Love
Miss Called Murder. Horwitz-Transport, 1955, as by PCB
The Mistress. Horwitz-Transport?, 1958; Signet, 1959; Four Square, 1963 AW [Calif.]
Model for Murder. Horwitz, 1980; Tower, 1980 AW
Model of No Virtue. Horwitz-Transport, 1956, as by PCB
Moonshine Momma; see A Siren Signs Off
A Morgue Amour. Horwitz-Transport?, 1954, as by PCB?
Murder by Miss-Demeanour. Horwitz-Transport, 1956, as by PCB
Murder in the Family Way. Horwitz, 1972; Signet, 1971 RR [Calif.]
Murder in the Harem Club. Horwitz, 1962. U.S. and British title: Murder in the Key Club. Signet, 1962; Four Square, 1962 RH

Murder in the Key Club; see Murder in the Harem Club
Murder Is a Package Deal. Horwitz, 1964; Signet, 1964; Four Square, 1965 RH [L.A.]
Murder Is My Mistress. Associated General Publications, 1954, as by PC-B (Rewritten and reissued as: The Savage Salome, q.v.)
Murder Is So Nostalgic! Horwitz, 1973; Signet, 1972 MS [Calif.]
Murder Is the Message. Horwitz, 1970; Signet, 1969 DB [Calif.]
Murder on High. Horwitz, 1973; Signet, 1973 RR [Calif.]
Murder—Paris Fashion. Transport, 1954, as by PC-B
Murder Wears a Mantilla. Horwitz-Transport, 1957, as by PCB (Revised and reissued under the same title: Horwitz, 1963; Signet, 1962; Four Square, 1962 MS [Mex. City])
The Murderer Among Us. Horwitz, 1962. U.S. & British title: A Murderer Among Us. Signet, 1962; Four Square, 1964 RH [Conn.]
My Darling Is Deadpan. Horwitz-Transport, 1956, as by PCB
My Mermaid Murmurs Murder. Transport, 1953, as by PC-B
The Myopic Mermaid. Horwitz, 1962; Signet, 1961 (Rewritten reissue of: A Siren Signs Off, q.v.)
Negative in Blue. Horwitz, 1975; Signet, 1974 RH [L.A.]
Nemesis Wore Nylons. Transport, 1954, as by PC-B
The Never-Was Girl. Horwitz, 1964; Signet, 1964; Four Square, 1965 RH [L.A.]
Night Wheeler. Signet, 1974 AW [Calif.]
No Blonde Is an Island. Horwitz, 1965; Signet, 1965; Four Square, 1965 LB [S. Pac.]
No Body She Knows. Horwitz-Transport, 1958, as by PCB (Carter Brown Collectors' Series edition, Horwitz, 1960, also includes: Slaughter in Satin.)
No Future Fair Lady. Horwitz-Transport, 1958, as by PCB
No Halo for Hedy. Horwitz-Transport, 1956, as by PCB
No Harp for My Angel. Horwitz-Transport, 1956, as by PCB
No Law Against Angels. Horwitz-Transport, 1957, as by PCB (Rewritten and reissued as: The Body, q.v.)
No Tears from the Widow. Horwitz, 1966; Signet, 1966; Four Square, 1968 RH [L.A.]
None But the Lethal Heart. Horwitz, 1959; Signet, 1959; Four Square, 1967. Also published as: The Fabulous. Horwitz, 1961 MS [L.A.]
Nude—with a View. Horwitz, 1965; Signet, 1965; Four Square, 1966 RH
Nymph to the Slaughter. Horwitz, 1963; Signet, 1963; Four Square, 1964 DB [NYC]
Only the Very Rich? Horwitz, 1969; Signet, 1969 DB [Eng.]
The Passionate. Horwitz, 1959; Signet, 1959; Four Square, 1966 AW [Calif.]
The Passionate Pagan. Horwitz, 1963; Signet, 1963; Four Square, 1964 DB [NYC]
Penthouse Passout. Transport, 1953?, as by PC-B? Also published as: Hot Seat for a Honey. Horwitz-Transport, 1956, as by PCB
The Phantom Lady. Horwitz, 1980; Tower, 1980 RH [L.A.]
Phreak-Out! Horwitz, 1975; Signet, 1973 RH [L.A.]
The Pipes Are Calling. Signet, 1976 DB
Play Now—Kill Later! Horwitz, 1966; Signet, 1966 RH [L.A.]
The Plush-Lined Coffin. Horwitz, 1967; Signet, 1967; Four Square, 1968 AW [Calif.]
Poison Ivy; see Yogi Shrouds Yolanda and Poison Ivy
The Pornbroker. Horwitz, 1972; Signet, 1972 RH [L.A.]
Remember Maybelle? Horwitz, 1976; Signet, 1976 RH
Ride the Roller Coaster. Horwitz, 1975?; Signet, 1975 RH
The Rip-Off. Horwitz, 1980; Belmont, 1979; Corgi, 1979 DB
The Sad-Eyed Seductress; see The Seductress

The Savage Salome. Horwitz, 1961; Signet, 1961 (Rewritten reissue of: Murder Is My Mistress, q.v.) DB [NYC]
The Savage Sisters. Signet, 1976
The Scarlet Flush. Horwitz, 1963; Signet, 1963; Four Square, 1965 MF [L.A.]
The Seductress. Horwitz, 1961. U.S. & British title: The Sad-Eyed Seductress. Signet, 1961; Four Square, 1962 DB [Calif.]
See It Again, Sam. Horwitz, 1979; Belmont, 1979; Corgi, 1979 RH
Seidlitz and the Super-Spy. Horwitz, 1967; Signet, 1967. British title: The Super Spy. Four Square, 1969 MS [It.]
The Seven Sirens. Horwitz, 1972; Signet, 1972 RH [Can.]
The Sex Clinic. Horwitz, 1971; Signet, 1972 DB [Conn.]
Sex Trap. Horwitz, 1975; Signet, 1975 RR
Shady Lady. Transport, 1953?, as by PC-B?
Shamus, Your Slip Is Showing. Horwitz-Transport, 1955, as by PCB
Shroud for My Sugar. Horwitz-Transport, 1955, as by PCB
The Silken Nightmare. Horwitz, 1963; Signet, 1963; Four Square, 1964 DB [Ia.]
Sinfully Yours. Horwitz-Transport, 1958?, as by PCB
Sinner, You Slay Me! Horwitz-Transport, 1957, as by PCB
The Sinners. Horwitz, 1963. U.S. & British title: The Girl Who Was Possessed. Signet, 1963; Four Square, 1963 AW [Calif.]
A Siren Signs Off. Horwitz-Transport, 1958, as by PCB (Carter Brown Collectors' Series edition, Horwitz, 1960, also includes: Moonshine Momma.) (Rewritten and reissued as: The Myopic Mermaid, q.v.)
Slaughter in Satin; see No Body She Knows
So Deadly, Sinner! Horwitz, 1959. U.S. & British title: Walk Softly, Witch. Signet, 1959; Four Square, 1965 DB [NYC]
So Lovely She Lies. Horwitz-Transport, 1958, as by PCB
So Move the Body. Horwitz, 1973; Signet, 1973 DB [Calif.]
So What Killed the Vampire? Horwitz, 1966; Signet, 1966; Four Square, 1967 LB [Eng.]
Sob-Sister Cries Murder. Horwitz-Transport, 1955, as by PCB
The Sometime Wife. Horwitz, 1966; Signet, 1965; Four Square, 1966 DB
The Spanking Girls. Horwitz, 1979; Belmont, 1979; Corgi, 1979 AW
The Star-Crossed Lover. Signet, 1974 RH
The Strawberry Blonde Jungle. Horwitz, 1979; Belmont, 1979; Corgi, 1979 DB
The Streaked-Blond Slave. Horwitz, 1970; Signet, 1969 RH [L.A.]
Strictly for Felony. Horwitz-Transport, 1956, as by PCB
Strip Without Tease. Transport, 1953?, as by PC-B?
The Stripper. Horwitz, 1961; Signet, 1961; Four Square, 1962 AW [Calif.]
Stripper, You've Sinned. Horwitz-Transport, 1957?, as by PCB
Suddenly by Violence. Horwitz, 1959; Signet, 1959 DB [NYC]
The Super-Spy; see Seidlitz and the Super-Spy
Swan Song for a Siren. Horwitz-Transport, 1955, as by PCB (Rewritten and reissued as: Charlie Sent Me!, q.v.)
Sweetheart, This Is Homicide. Horwitz-Transport, 1956, as by PCB
The Swingers. Horwitz, 1980; Tower, 1980 RH
Target for Their Dark Desire. Horwitz, 1967; Signet, 1966; Four Square, 1968 AW [Calif.]
Tempt a Tigress. Horwitz-Transport, 1958?, as by PCB
The Temptress. Horwitz, 1960; Signet, 1960; Four Square, 1964 AW [Calif.]
Ten Grand Tallulah and Temptation. Horwitz-Transport, 1957, as by PCB
Terror Comes Creeping. Horwitz, 1959; Signet, 1959; Four Square, 1967 DB [New Eng.]
That's Piracy, My Pet. Horwitz-Transport, 1957?, as by PCB (Rewritten and reissued in Australia as: Bird in a Guilt-Edged Cage, q.v., and in the U.S. and Britain as: The Guilt-Edged Cage.)

The Tigress. Horwitz, 1961; Signet, 1961. British title: Wildcat. Four Square, 1962 AW [Calif.]
Tomorrow Is Murder. Horwitz, 1960; Signet, 1960 MS [L.A.]
Trouble Is a Dame. Transport, 1953?, as by PC-B?
True Son of the Beast! Signet, 1970 LB [Eng.]
The Two-Timing Blonde. Horwitz-Transport, 1955, as by PCB
The Unorthodox Corpse. Horwitz-Transport, 1957, as by PCB (Rewritten and reissued under the same title: Horwitz, 1961; Signet, 1961 AW [Calif.])
Until Temptation Do Us Part. Horwitz, 1967; Signet, 1967; Four Square, 1968 AW [Calif.]
The Up-Tight Blonde. Horwitz, 1970; Signet, 1969 AW [Calif.]
The Velvet Vixen; see The Vixen
Venus Unarmed. Transport, 1953, as by PC-B
The Victim! see Walk Softly Witch!
The Vixen. Horwitz, 1964. U.S. & British title: The Velvet Vixen. Signet, 1964; Four Square, 1965 AW [Calif.]
W.H.O.R.E. Horwitz, 1972; Signet, 1971 AW [Calif.]
Walk Softly, Witch; see So Deadly, Sinner! (This is a completely different book from the following entry.)
Walk Softly, Witch! Horwitz, 1959. U.S. title: The Victim. Signet, 1959 (Rewritten reissue of: Eve—It's Extortion, q.v.) AW [Calif.]
The Wanton. Horwitz, 1959; Signet, 1959; Four Square, 1968 AW [Calif.]
The Wayward; see The Wayward Wahine
The Wayward Wahine. Horwitz, 1960; Signet, 1960; Four Square, 1966. Also published as: The Wayward. Horwitz, 1962 DB
The Wench Is Wicked. Horwitz-Transport, 1955, as by PCB
Wheeler, Dealer! Horwitz, 1975; Signet, 1975 AW
Wheeler Fortune. Signet, 1974 AW [Calif.]
Where Did Charity Go? Horwitz, 1971; Signet, 1970 RH [L.A.]
The White Bikini; see The Ballad of Loving Jenny
Who Killed Dr. Sex? Horwitz, 1965; Signet, 1964; Four Square, 1965 RH
Widow Bewitched. Horwitz-Transport, 1958?, as by PCB
Wildcat; see The Tigress
The Wind-Up Doll. Horwitz, 1965; Signet, 1964; Four Square, 1965 RH [L.A.]
The Witches; see Had I But Groaned
Wreath for a Redhead. Horwitz-Transport, 1957, as by PCB
Wreath for Rebecca. Transport, 1953?, as by PC-B?
Yogi Shrouds Yolanda and Poison Ivy. Horwitz, 1965
Zelda. Horwitz, 1961; Signet, 1961; Four Square, 1962 RH [L.A.]

BROWN, CHARLES BROCKDEN. 1771-1910. These titles originally appeared anonymously. Ref: CC, DD, EM.
Arthur Mervyn; or, Memoirs of the Year 1793. H. Maxwell, 1799-1800 [Phil.]
Edgar Huntley; or, The Memoirs of a Sleepwalker. H. Maxwell, 1799; Colburn, 1831
Ormond; or, The Secret Witness. Caritat, 1799 [Phil.]
Wieland; or, The Transformation. Caritat, 1798; Colburn, 1811 [Pa.]

BROWN, CHARLES R. See: Arthur Morgan.

BROWN, CHRISTY. 1932-   .
Wild Grow the Lilies. Stein, 1976; Secker, 1976

BROWN, DEE A(LEXANDER). 1908-   . Ref: CA.
They Went Thataway. Putnam, 1960

BROWN, DOROTHY FOSTER
Grimm Death. Smith, 1946 [New Eng.]

BROWN, EDNA A(DELAIDE). 1875-1944.
That Affair at St. Peter's. Lothrop, 1920

BROWN, EDWARD. SC: Major Adrian Titterton, in at least those marked AT.
The Big Man. Harrap, 1965
A Penny To Spend. Harrap, 1966 AT
Vandersley. Harrap, 1967 AT

BROWN, ELIJAH. 1867-   . Pseudonym: Alan Raleigh, q.v.

BROWN, ELIZABETH (LOUISE). 1924-   .
Ref: CA.
The Candle of the Wicked. Zondervan, 1972

BROWN, ELWOOD (S.). Born and lives in California; magazine ss writer.
The Elephant Murders. Vantage, 1955

BROWN, FREDRIC (WILLIAM). 1906-1972. Ref: CA, CC, DD, EM, TC. SC: Ed and Am Hunter = H.
The Bloody Moonlight. Dutton, 1949. British title: Murder in the Moonlight. Boardman, 1950 H [Chi.]
The Case of the Dancing Sandwiches. Dell, 1951 (A novelet, published separately in Dell's short-lived 10¢ pb series.)
Compliments of a Fiend. Dutton, 1950; Boardman, 1951 H [Chi.]
The Dead Ringer. Dutton, 1948; Boardman, 1950 H [Ind.]
Death Has Many Doors. Dutton, 1951; Boardman, 1952 H [Chi.]
The Deep End. Dutton, 1952; Boardman, 1953
The Fabulous Clipjoint. Dutton, 1947; Boardman, 1949 H [Chi.]
The Far Cry. Dutton, 1951; Boardman, 1952 [New Mex.]
The Five-Day Nightmare. Dutton, 1963; Boardman, 1963 [Phoenix]
Here Comes a Candle. Dutton, 1950; Boardman, 1951 [Chi., Milw.]
His Name Was Death. Dutton, 1954; Boardman, 1955 [L.A.]
Knock Three-One-Two. Dutton, 1959; Boardman, 1959
The Late Lamented. Dutton, 1959; Boardman, 1959 H [Chi.]
The Lenient Beast. Dutton, 1956; Boardman, 1957 [Tuscon]
Madball. Dell, 1953; Muller, 1962
Mrs. Murphy's Underpants. Dutton, 1963; Boardman, 1965 H [Chi.]
Mostly Murder. Dutton, 1953; Boardman, 1954 ss
Murder Can Be Fun. Dutton, 1948; Boardman, 1951. Also published as: A Plot for Murder. Bantam, 1949 [NYC]
Murder in the Moonlight; see The Bloody Moonlight
The Murderers. Dutton, 1961; Boardman, 1962 [L.A.]
Night of the Jabberwock. Dutton, 1950; Boardman, 1951
Nightmares and Geezenstacks. Bantam, 1961 (A collection of short-shorts, some fantasy, some sf, some mystery, some all three.)
One for the Road. Dutton, 1958; Boardman, 1959 [Ariz.]
A Plot for Murder; see Murder Can Be Fun
The Screaming Mimi. Dutton, 1949; Boardman, 1950 [Chi.]
The Shaggy Dog and Other Murders. Dutton, 1963. British title: The Shaggy Dog and other stories. Boardman, 1964 ss
We All Killed Grandma. Dutton, 1952; Boardman, 1953
The Wench Is Dead. Dutton, 1955 [L.A.]

BROWN, GEORGE DOUGLAS. 1869-1902. Pseudonym: George Douglas, q.v.

BROWN, GERALD. SC: Duke McCale, in both titles.
Murder in Plain Sight. Phoenix, 1945
Murder on Beacon Hill. Phoenix, 1941 [Boston]

BROWN, HARRY JOE, JR.
Duffy. Dell, 1968 (Novelization of the movie.) [Fr.]

BROWN, HORACE. 1908-   . Pseudonym: Leslie Allen, q.v.
The Penthouse Killings. Newsstand, 1950 [NYC]

BROWN, J(OHN) E(DWARD). 1920-   . Advertising director for a group of magazines.
Incident at 125th Street. Doubleday, 1970 [NYC]

BROWN, JAMES AMBROSE. 1919-   .
The Assassins; see The Pact
The Pact. Putnam, 1966. Original title and publication probably: "The Assasins." Johannesburg, 1965.
The Snare. Macdonald, 1975

BROWN, JOHN
Death Gets a Place. Allen, 1951
Death in the Silver Ring. Background Books, 1948
Murder Each Way. Allen, 1953

BROWN, JOHN. 1924-   .
The Chancer. Macmillan (London), 1972

BROWN, JOY
Night of Terror. Harlequin, 1950 [NYC]

BROWN, L. ROCKWELL
Duel of Shadows. Vantage, 1979

BROWN, L. VIRGINIA
The Wade Inheritance. Pyramid, 1977

BROWN, LIONEL
This Year—Next Year. Deane, 1956 (3-act play.)

BROWN, LOIS ANN. Joint pseudonym with Barbara Levy, 1921-   , q.v.: Jessica Eliot, q.v.

BROWN, MARY. 1913-   . Pseudonym: Vanessa Blake, q.v.

BROWN, MARY MONROE
The Phantom Bride. Major, 1976

BROWN, MORNA DORIS MacTAGGART. 1907-   .
Pseudonym: Elizabeth Ferrars, q.v.

BROWN, PETER CARTER. Pseudonym of Alan Geoffrey Yates, 1923-   , q.v. See: Carter Brown. Other pseudonym: Caroline Farr, q.v.

BROWN, RAE
Darkness at Sunrise. Lenox, 1974

BROWN, RICHARD (BLAKE). 1902?-   .
The Blank Cheque. Fortune, 1934
Rococo Coffin. Fortune, 1936

BROWN, ROBERT CARLTON. 1886-1959. Ref: CC.
The Remarkable Adventures of Christopher Poe. Browne, 1913 ss
What Happened to Mary? Clode, 1913

BROWN, ROSEL GEORGE. 1926-1967. SC: Sibyl Sue Blue, in both titles.
Galactic Sibyl Sue Blue; see Sibyl Sue Blue
Sibyl Sue Blue. Doubleday, 1966. Also published as: Galactic Sibyl Sue Blue. Berkley, 1968
The Waters of Centaurus. Doubleday, 1970

BROWN, ROYAL
Escape. Dutton, 1938

BROWN, VERA
Reckless Lady. Edwards, 1946

BROWN, VINCENT
The Chief Constable. Chapman, 1912; Brentano's, 1912

BROWN, W(ILLIAM) M(acENERY). 1859-   .
The Queen's Bush. Bale, 1932 [Can.]

BROWN, W(ILLIAM) P(ERRY). 1847-1923.
Pseudonym: Nicholas Carter, q.v.
The Great Baruma Mystery. Henderson, 1904

BROWN, WALTER C. Ref: CC. SC: Det. Insp. Stephen Harper, in all titles.
Laughing Death. Lippincott, 1932
Murder at Mocking House. Lippincott, 1933
The Second Chance. Lippincott, 1929

BROWN, WENZELL. 1912-   . Ref: CA. SC: Peter Aswell = PA.
An Act of Passion. Monarch, 1962
The Big Rumble. Popular Library, 1955. Also published as: Jailbait Jungle. Belmont, 1962 [NYC]
Cry Kill. GM, 1959 [NYC]
Gang Girl. Avon, 1954
Hong Kong Aftermath. Smith, 1943 [H. Kong]

The Hoods Ride In. Pyramid, 1959 [NYC]
Jailbait Jungle; see The Big Rumble
The Murder Kick. GM, 1960; Muller pb, 1961 [NYC]
Murder Seeks an Agent. Five Star, 1945; Curzon, 1947 PA [NYC]
The Naked Hours. Popular Library, 1956 [NYC]
Possess and Conquer. Warner, 1975
Prison Girl. Pyramid, 1958
The Rum and Coca-Cola Murders. Saint Mystery Library, 1960 (Also contains a ss, "Calypsonian," by Samuel Selvon.) PA [Trin.]
Run, Chico, Run. GM, 1953; Fawcett (London), 1959 [NYC]
Teen-Age Mafia. GM, 1959
Teen-Age Terror. GM, 1958
The Wicked Streets. GM, 1957 [NYC]

BROWN, WHITNEY
And So to Eternity. Merit, 1954

BROWN, WILL(IAM) H(ERBERT). 1864-1929.
The Legacy of the Golden Key. Standard, 1914

BROWN, ZENITH JONES. 1898- . Pseudonyms: Leslie Ford, David Frome, qq.v.

BROWNE, BARUM. Joint pseudonym of Geoffrey Dennis and Hilary (Aiden) St. George Saunders, 1898-1951, q.v. Joint pseudonym of Saunders with John (Leslie) Palmer, 1885-1949, q.v.: Francis Beeding, q.v.
The Devil and X.Y.Z. Gollancz, 1931; Doubleday, 1931

BROWNE, COURTNEY. Pseudonym of Reginald David Stanley Courtney-Browne, 1915- .
The Ancient Pond. Hale, 1967; Harper, 1967 [Jap.]

BROWNE, COWDRAY
Oliver Quendon's First Case. Hutchinson, 1927

BROWNE, DOUGLAS G(ORDON). 1884-1963. Ref: CC. SC: Major Maurice Hemyock, in at least those marked MH; Insp. Thew, in at least those marked T; Harvey Tuke = HT. Set: Eng.
The Cotfold Conundrums. Methuen, 1933 T
The Dead Don't Bite. Methuen, 1933 MH
Death in Perpetuity. Macdonald, 1950 HT
Death in Seven Volumes. Macdonald, 1958 HT
Death Wears a Mask. Hutchinson, 1940; Macmillan, 1954 HT
The House of the Sword. Hutchinson, 1939
The Looking-Glass Murders. Methuen, 1935 MH
The May-Week Murders. Longmans, 1937 MH
Plan XVI. Methuen, 1934; Doubleday, 1934 T
Rustling End. Macdonald, 1948 HT
Sergeant Death. Macdonald, 1955 HT
Too Many Cousins. Macdonald, 1946; Macmillan, 1953 HT
Uncle William and other stories. Blackwood, 1930 ss, one about MH
What Beckoning Ghost. Macdonald, 1947 HT

BROWNE, ELEANORE
Murder by Appointment. Macaulay, 1934 [Fr.]

BROWNE, GEORGE WALDO. 1851-1930. Pseudonym: Nicholas Carter, q.v.

BROWNE, GERALD A(USTIN)
11 Harrowhouse. Arbor, 1972; Deutsch, 1973 [Eng.]
Green Ice. Delacorte, 1976; Hart-Davis, 1978 [Colom.]
Hazard. Arbor, 1973; Hart-Davis, 1974

BROWNE, HOWARD. 1908- . Pseudonym: John Evans, q.v. Ref: CA, EM. SC: Paul Pine (see also the John Evans entry) = PP.
The Taste of Ashes. Simon, 1957; Gollancz, 1958 PP [Ill.]
Thin Air. Simon, 1954; Gollancz, 1955 [N.Y.]

BROWNE, K(ENNETH) R(OBERT) G(ORDON). 1895- .
Following Ann. Cassell, 1925. U.S. title: The Cheerful Fraud. Putnam, 1925

BROWNE, NICHOLAS. Pseudonym: Nick Carter, q.v.

BROWNE, ROBERT GORE. 1893- . See: Robert Gore-Browne.

BROWNE, THOMAS ALEXANDER. 1826-1915. Pseudonym: Rolf Boldrewood, q.v.

BROWNER, JOHN
Death of a Punk. PB, 1980 [NYC]
-Who Killed the Snowman? PB, 1979

BROWNING, GARETH H. Pseudonym of George Henry Browning, 1887- .
The Black Ink Mystery. Hutchinson, 1927

BROWNING, GEORGE HENRY. 1887- . Pseudonym: Gareth H. Browning, q.v.

BROWNING, JOHN
If Your Cover Is Blown. Hale, 1970
A Quiet War. Hale, 1974
The Saffron Robe. Hale, 1970
The Sleeper. Hale, 1974

BROWNING, STERRY. Pseudonym of Leonard (Reginald) Gribble, 1908- , q.v. Other pseudonyms: Leo Grex, Louis Grey, Dexter Muir, qq.v. See also: Janet Green.
Crime at Cape Folly. Clerke, 1951
Sex Marks the Spot. Long, 1954

BROXHOLME, JOHN FRANKLIN. 1930- . Pseudonym: Duncan Kyle, q.v.

BROYLES, R. L.
The Man Who Could Read Cards. Manor, 1980

BRUCE, GEORGE. 1898-
Claim of the Fleshless Corpse. Dodge, 1937. British title: Corpse Without Flesh. Jenkins, 1938 [NYC, L.I.]
Corpse Without Flesh; see Claim of the Fleshless Corpse
Too Tough to Die. Caslon, 1936; Long, 1937 [NYC]

BRUCE, JEAN. Pseudonym of Jean Alexandre Brochet, 1921-1963. Ref: CC. SC: Hubert Bonisseur de la Bath, in all titles, except possibly "Corpses Galore."
Cold Spell. Corgi, 1967 (Translation of "Cinq Gars pour Singapore." Paris, 1957.)
Corpses Galore. Archer, 1951
Dead Silence. Corgi, 1967
Deep Freeze. Cassell, 1963 (Translation of "Tactique Artique." Paris, 1960.)
Double Take. Cassell, 1964 (Translation of "Rentre dans la Dans." Paris, 1961.)
Flash Point. Cassell, 1965 (Translation of "Moche Coup a Moscou." Paris, 1958.) [Moscow]
High Treason. Corgi, 1967 (Translation of "Trahison." Paris, 1965.)
Hot Line. Corgi, 1967. U.S. title: Trouble in Tokyo. Crest, 1965 (Translation of "A Tout Coeur a Tokie." Paris, 1958.) [Tokyo]
The Last Quarter Hour; see Live Wire
Live Wire. Corgi, 1965. U.S. title: The Last Quarter Hour. Crest, 1965 (Translation of "De Dernier Quart d'Heure." Paris, 1955.) [Buen. A.]
Photo Finish. Corgi, 1965 (Translation of "O.S.S.177 a l'Ecole." Paris, 1961.)
Pole Reaction. Cassell, 1965 (Translation of "O.S.S.177 Repond Toujours." Paris, 1953.)
Shock Tactics. Cassell, 1965 (Translation of "Ombres sur la Bosphore." Paris, 1954.)
Short Wave. Cassell, 1964 (Translation of "Affaire No. 1." Paris, 1954.)
Soft Sell. Corgi, 1965 (Translation of "Plan de Bataille pour O.S.S. 117." Paris, 1957.)
Strip Tease. Corgi, 1968 (Translation of "Strip Tease pour O.S.S. 117." Paris, 1962.)
Top Secret. Corgi, 1967
Trouble in Tokyo; see Hot Line

BRUCE, KENNEDY
The Fakir's Curse. Jenkins, 1931 [India]
The Poisoned Fang. Jenkins, 1930
The Sliding Death. Jenkins, 1933 [India]

BRUCE, LEO. Pseudonym of Rupert Croft-Cooke, 1903-1979. SC: Sgt. Beef = SB; Carolus Deene = CD. Set: Eng.
At Death's Door. H. Hamilton, 1955 CD
A Bone and a Hank of Hair. Davies, 1961; British Book Centre, 1961 CD
Case for Sergeant Beef. Nicholson, 1947; Academy Chicago, 1980 SB
Case for Three Detectives. Bles, 1936; Stokes, 1937 SB
Case with Four Clowns. Davies, 1939; Stokes, 1939 SB
Case with No Solution. Bles, 1939 SB
Case with Ropes and Rings. Nicholson, 1940; Academy Chicago, 1980 SB
Case Without a Corpse. Bles, 1937; Stokes, 1937 SB
Cold Blood. Gollancz, 1952; Academy Chicago, 1980 SB
Crack of Doom. Davies, 1963. U.S. title: Such Is Death. London House, 1963 CD
Dead for a Ducat. Davies, 1956 CD
Dead Man's Shoes. Davies, 1958 CD
Death at Hallows End. Allen, 1965; British Book Centre, 1966 CD
Death at St. Asprey's School. Allen, 1967 CD [acad.]
Death by the Lake. Allen, 1971 CD
Death in Albert Park. Allen, 1964; Scribner, 1979 CD
Death in the Middle Watch. Allen, 1974 CD
Death of a Bovver Boy. Allen, 1974 CD
Death of a Commuter. Allen, 1967 CD
Death of Cold. Davies, 1956 CD
Death on Allhallowe'en. Allen, 1970 CD
Death on Romney Marsh. Allen, 1968 CD
Death on the Black Sands. Allen, 1966 CD [Sp.]
Death with Blue Ribbon. Allen, 1969; London House, 1970 CD
Die All, Die Merrily. Davies, 1961; British Book Centre, 1961 CD
Furious Old Women. Davies, 1960 CD
Jack on the Gallows Tree. Davies, 1960; Academy Chicago, 1983 CD
A Louse for the Hangman. Davies, 1958 CD
Neck and Neck. Gollancz, 1951; Academy Chicago, 1980 SB
Nothing Like Blood. Davies, 1962 CD
Our Jubilee Is Death. Davies, 1959 CD
Such Is Death; see Crack of Doom

BRUCKER, MARGARETTA. 1883-1958.
Death in the Dormitory. Phoenix, 1937 [acad.]
Murder at Lover's Lake. Phoenix, 1943
Poison Party. Phoenix, 1938 [Mich.]

BRULLER, JEAN MARCEL. 1902- . Pseudonym: Vercors, q.v.

BRUN, T.
The Haunted Heart. Westhouse, 1946

BRUN, VINCENT. Pseudonym of Hans Flesch, 1897- .
The Blond Spider. Cape, 1939 [Vienna]

BRUNNER, BERNARD. Ph.D. in literature from U. of Chicago; in 1960's professor of English at De Paul University.
The Face of Night. Fell, 1967 [Chi.]

BRUNNER, JOHN (KILIAN HOUSTON). 1934- . Ref: CA. SC: Max Curfew, in at least those marked MC.
Black Is the Color. Pyramid, 1969
Blacklash; see A Plague on Both Your Causes
The Gaudy Shadows. Constable, 1970; Beagle, 1971
Good Men Do Nothing. Hodder, 1970; Pyramid, 1971 MC [Greece]
Honky in the Woodpile. Constable, 1971 MC
A Plague on Both Your Causes. Hodder, 1969. U.S. title: Blacklash. Pyramid, 1969 MC
Total Eclipse. Nicholson, 1975; Doubleday, 1974
Wear the Butcher's Medal. PB, 1965 [Ger.]

BRUSSEL, JAMES A(RNOLD). 1905-1982. Ref: CA.
Just Murder, Darling. Scribner, 1959 [N.Y.]

BRUTON, ERIC (MOORE). 1915- . Ref: CA, CC, TC. SC: Insp. George Judd = GJ. Set: Eng.
Death in Ten Point Bold. Jenkins, 1957
The Devil's Pawn. Boardman, 1962
Die, Darling, Die. Boardman, 1959
The Finsbury Mob. Boardman, 1964 GJ
The Fire Bug. Boardman, 1967 GJ
The Hold Out. Boardman, 1961
King Diamond. Boardman, 1961
The Laughing Policeman. Boardman, 1963 GJ
The Smithfield Slayer. Boardman, 1965 GJ
Violent Brothers. Boardman, 1960
The Wicked Saint. Boardman, 1965 GJ

BRYAN, FRANK. Oil geologist and lease trader in Texas.
The Long Shadow. Comet, 1954

BRYAN, JOHN. Pseudonym of Josephine Delves-Broughton, 1916- . SC: Richard Sarel, in all titles.
The Contessa Came Too. Faber, 1957 [It.]
The Difference to Me. Faber, 1957; British Book Centre, 1960
The Man Who Came Back. Faber, 1958; London House, 1959

BRYAN, MICHAEL. Pseudonym of Willis Kingsley Wing.
Intent to Kill. Dell, 1956; Eyre, 1956 [hosp., Montr.]
Murder in Majorca. Dell, 1957; Eyre, 1958 [Maj.]

BRYAN, SOFI O.
The Secret of the Priory. Dell, 1975

BRYANT, M(ARGUERITE) and G(EORGE) H. MacANALLY. See also: Marguerite Bryant.
Breakfast for Three. Methuen, 1930

BRYANT, MARGUERITE. See also: M(arguerite) Bryant.
The Adventures of Louis Dural. Brown Langham, 1905
Mrs. Fuller. Hurst, 1925; Duffield, 1925
The Redemption of Richard. Hurst, 1922. U.S. title: Richard. Duffield, 1922
Richard; see The Redemption of Richard

BRYANT, MATT. Born in Indiana; author of short magazine fiction.
Cue for Murder. Vanguard, 1954; Barker, 1956 [NYC]

BRYANT, PETER. Pseudonym of Peter (Bryan) George, 1924-1966, q.v. Other pseudonym: Bryan Peters, q.v.
Two Hours to Doom. Boardman, 1958. (Suppressed by British Intelligence under the Official Secrets Act.) U.S. title: Red Alert. Ace, 1958 [U.S.]

BRYANT, ROY
Clouds of Fear. Hammond, 1966

BRYANT, WILL. 1923- . Born in Arizona; illustrator, designer, novelist.
Blue Russell. Random, 1976; Secker, 1976 [West, 1899]

BRYCE, MRS. CHARLES. SC: Mr. Gimblet, in at least those marked G. Set: Eng.
The Ashiel Mystery. Bodley, 1915 G
The Long Spoon. Bodley, 1917
Mrs. Vanderstein's Jewels. Bodley, 1914 G

BRYCE, LLOYD (STEPHENS). 1851-1917.
Romance of an Alter Ego. Brentano's, 1889; Routledge, 1891. Also published as: An Extraordinary Experience; or, The Romance of an Alter Ego. Brentano's, 1891 [NYC]

BRYCE, ROBERT
The Colchicine Factor. Major, 1978

BRYDON, STANLEY
The Death Cap. Wright, 1962
Guns over the Border. Wright, 1962 [Ire.]
Harvest of Violence. Wright, 1960
Manhunt in Sicily. Wright, 1960 [Sic.]
Nightmare Incident. Wright, 1963
Penman's Progress. Wright, 1961
Saraband for a Smuggler. Wright, 1961

BRYERS, PAUL. 1945- . Ref: CA.
The Cat Trapper. Deutsch, 1978
Hollow Target. Duetsch, 1976. U.S. title: Target Plutex. Doubleday, 1976
Target Plutex; see Hollow Target

BRYKCZYNSKI, TERRY
Caged. Crown, 1980 [S.F.]

BRYSON, CHARLES. 1887- . Pseudonym: Charles Barry, q.v.

BRYSON, LEIGH. Pseudonym of Nancy Rutledge, q.v.
The Gloved Hand. Handi-Books, 1947 [Chi.]

BUCHAN, JOHN. 1875-1940. Ref: CC, EM, MC, MP, TC. SC: Richard Hannay = RH; Edward Leithen = EL; Duncan McCunn = DM.
Castle Gay. Hodder, 1930; Houghton, 1930 DM [Scot.]
-The Courts of Morning. Hodder, 1929; Houghton, 1929
-The Dancing Floor. Hodder, 1926; Houghton, 1926 EL
-The Gap in the Curtain. Hodder, 1932; Houghton, 1932 EL

Greenmantle. Hodder, 1916; Doran, 1917 RH
The House of the Four Winds. Hodder, 1935; Houghton, 1935 DM
Huntingtower. Hodder, 1922; Doran, 1922 [Scot.] DM
The Island of Sheep. Hodder, 1936. U.S. title: The Man from the Norlands. Houghton, 1936 RH
John Macnab. Hodder, 1925; Houghton, 1925 EL [Scot.]
The Man from the Norlands; see The Island of Sheep
Mr. Standfast. Hodder, 1919; Doran, 1919 RH
The Moon Endureth. Blackwood, 1912; Sturgis, 1912 ss, EL in one story
Mountain Meadow; see Sick Heart River
The Power-House. Blackwood, 1916; Doran, 1916 EL
-The Prince of the Captivity. Hodder, 1933; Houghton, 1933
The Runagates Club. Hodder, 1928; Houghton, 1928 ss, EL and RH each in one story
Sick Heart River. Hodder, 1941. U.S. title: Mountain Meadow. Houghton, 1941 EL [Can.]
The Thirty-Nine Steps. Blackwood, 1915; Doran, 1916 RH [Scot.]
The Three Hostages. Hodder, 1924; Houghton, 1924 RH
The Watcher by the Threshold. Blackwood, 1902; Doran, 1918 [Scot.]

BUCHAN, SINCLAIR
Singleton's Mill. Hodder, 1975

BUCHAN, STUART. 1942- . Ref: CA.
Fleeced. Putnam, 1975; Hale, 1976 [Mex.]

BUCHAN, WILLIAM (JAMES DE L'AIGLE). 1916- . Ref: CC.
-The Blue Pavilion. Duckworth, 1966; Morrow, 1966
Helen All Alone. Duckworth, 1961; Morrow, 1961

BUCHANAN. Pseudonym: Nicholas Carter, q.v.

BUCHANAN, BETTY JOAN. 1923- . Pseudonym: Joan Shepherd, q.v.

BUCHANAN, CARL
The Black Cloak Murders. Pearson, 1936 [N.C.]
Night of Horror. Mellifont, 1939
The Red Scorpion. Mellifont, 1939

BUCHANAN, EILEEN-MARIE DUELL. 1922- . Pseudonym: Rhona Petrie, q.v.

BUCHANAN, HUGH
The Masterful Voice. Hutchinson, 1927

BUCHANAN, JAMES DAVID. Film writer living in California.
The Professional. Constable, 1972; Coward, 1972 [Cuba]
Red Dog. GM, 1979 [Calif.]

BUCHANAN, MADELEINE SHARPS. -1940.
The Black Pearl Murders. McClurg, 1930
The Crimson Blade. Chelsea, 1926
Haunted Bells. Chelsea, 1929; Skeffington, 1930
The Poison Eye. Chelsea, 1928; Skeffington, 1930
Powdered Proof. Chelsea, 1927
The Subway Murder. McClurg, 1930

BUCHANAN, PATRICK. Joint pseudonym of Edwin (Raymond) Corley, 1931-1981, q.v., and Jack Murphy. Corley pseudonyms: David Harper, William Judson, qq.v. SC: Ben Shock and Charity Tucker, in all titles.
A Murder of Crows. Stein, 1970; Hale, 1973 [Ky.]
A Parliament of Owls. Stein, 1971; Hale, 1973 [Mass.]
A Requiem of Sharks. Dodd, 1973; H. Hamilton, 1975 [Miss.]
A Sounder of Swine. Dodd, 1974 [Eng.]

BUCHANAN, ROBERT (WILLIAM). 1841-1901.
Foxglove Manor. Chatto, 1884
Matt. Chatto, 1885; Appleton, 1885
-The Moment After. Heinemann, 1890; Munro, 1890

BUCHARD, ROBERT. 1931- . Ref: CA.
Thirty Seconds over New York. Morrow, 1970; Collins, 1970 (Translation of "Trente Secondes nur New York." Paris, 1969)

BUCK, CHARLES NEVILLE. 1879- .
Alias Red Ryan. Doubleday, 1923 [NYC]
A Gentleman in Pajamas. Century, 1924

Iron Will. Doubleday, 1927; Heinemann, 1927
The Key to Yesterday. Watt, 1910; Greening, 1912
Marked Men. Doubleday, 1929 [NYC]
Mountain Justice. Houghton, 1935 [Ky.]
Portuguese Silver. Century, 1925 [Cape Cod]
The Rogue's Badge. Doubleday, 1924; Heinemann, 1924

BUCK, HOWARD
-A Woman in Exchange. Macaulay, 1936

BUCK, PAUL. 1946- .
The Honeymoon Killers. Award, 1970; Sphere, 1970 (Novelization of the movie.)

BUCK, PEARL S(YDENSTRICKER). 1892-1973. Ref: CA.
Death in the Castle. Day, 1965; Methuen, 1966 [Eng.]

BUCKINGHAM, BRUCE. Joint pseudonym of Peter Lilley and Anthony Stansfeld. Ref: CC. SC: Don Pancho, in both titles, both set in Mex.
Broiled Alive. Joseph, 1957
Three Bad Nights. Joseph, 1956

BUCKINGHAM, DAVID. Pseudonym of David Hugh Villiers, a director of documentary films. SC: Sam Wharton, in both titles.
The Cliff Face. Macdonald, 1960
The Wind Tunnel. Macdonald, 1959

BUCKINGHAM, NANCY. Joint pseudonym of John Sawyer, 1919- , and Nancy Buckingham Sawyer, 1924- . He is an advertising executive turned full-time writer; she a medical social worker turned full-time writer. Other pseudonym: Erica Quest, q.v.
Call of Glengarron. Hale, 1969; Ace, 1968 [Scot.]
Cloud over Malverton. Hale, 1970; Ace, 1967
The Dark Summer. Hale, 1968; Ace, 1968
Heart of Marble. Hale, 1967. U.S. title: Storm in the Mountains. Ace, 1967 [Fr.]
The Hour Before Moonrise; see Victim of Love
The House Called Edenhythe. Hale, 1970; Hawthorn, 1972 [past, Eng.]
The Jade Dragon. Hale, 1976; Hawthorn, 1975 [Port., 1800s]
Kiss of Hot Sun. Hale, 1969
The Legend of Haverstock Manor; see Romantic Journey
-Marianne. Eyre, 1980
The Other Cathy. Eyre, 1978; Curley, 1981
Quest for Alexis. Hale, 1974; Hawthorn, 1973
Return to Vienna. Hale, 1973; Dell, 1971 [Vienna]
Romantic Journey. Hale, 1968. U.S. title: The Legend of Haverstock Manor. Ace, 1968
The Secret of the Ghostly Shroud; see Shroud of Silence
Shroud of Silence. Hale, 1970. U.S. title: The Secret of the Ghostly Shroud. Lancer, 1969
Storm in the Mountains; see Heart of Marble
Valley of the Ravens. Hale, 1975; Hawthorn, 1973
Victim of Love. Hale, 1967. U.S. title: The Hour Before Moonrise. Ace, 1967
Vienna Summer. Eyre, 1979; St. Martin's, 1979 [Vienna, 1897]

BUCKLEY, CHRISTOPHER
Rain Before Seven. Hodder, 1947
Royal Chase. Hodder, 1949

BUCKLEY, EDITH E.
The Snare of Circumstance. Little, 1910

BUCKLEY, R(OBERT) J(OHN)
The Master Spy. Ward, 1902 ss

BUCKLEY, WILLIAM F(RANK), JR. 1925- . Ref: CA. SC: Blackford Oakes, in all titles.
Saving the Queen. Doubleday, 1976; Allen, 1976 [Eng., 1940s]
Stained Glass. Doubleday, 1978; Penguin, 1979 [Ger., 1950]
Who's on First? Doubleday, 1980; Lane, 1980

BUCKMAN, PETER. 1941- . Ref: CA.
The Rothschild Conversion. Secker, 1979; McGraw, 1979

BUCKMASTER, HENRIETTA. Pseudonym of Henrietta Henkle Stephens, 1909-1983. Ref: CA.
    The Walking Trip. Harcourt, 1972; Gollancz, 1972

BUCKROSE, J. E. Pseudonym of Mrs. Annie Edith Foster Jameson, 1868-1931.
    The Good-Natured Lady. Hodder, 1927

BUDD, JACKSON. Pseudonym of William John Budd, 1898-   . Other pseudonym: Wallace Jackson, q.v
    A Convict Has Escaped. Joseph, 1941
    -The Dark Horseman. Joseph, 1939
    Daughter of Illusion. Low, 1934
    The Gallows Waits; see I Stood in the Shadow of the Black Cap
    The Gold Express. Low, 1947
    I Stood in the Shadow of the Black Cap. Low, 1932. U.S. title: The Gallows Waits. Putnam, 1932
    John Lisbon, Agent. Joseph, 1942
    Precious Company. Joseph, 1938
    -The Princely Quartet. Low, 1932
    The Story of Professor X. Stonevale, 1951
    -The Three Jolly Vagabonds. Low, 1935
    Tragedy in a Brick Box. Low, 1933
    -A Wife in Toledo. Low, 1938

BUDD, JOHN. Pseudonym: Julian Prescot, q.v.

BUDD, WILLIAM JOHN. 1898-   . Pseudonyms: Jackson Budd, Wallace Jackson, qq.v.

BUDE, JOHN. Pseudonym of Ernest Carpenter Elmore, 1901-1957. Ref: CC, TC. SC: Insp. Meredith, in at least those marked M; Insp. Sherwood, in at least those marked S. Set: Eng.
    Another Man's Shadow. Macdonald, 1957 M
    The Cheltenham Square Murder. Skeffington, 1937 M
    The Constable and the Lady. Macdonald, 1951 M
    The Cornish Coast Murder. Skeffington, 1935 M
    Dangerous Sunlight. Macdonald, 1948 M
    Death Deals a Double. Cassell, 1943 M
    Death in Ambush. Macdonald, 1945 M
    Death in White Pajamas. Cassell, 1944
    Death Knows No Calendar. Cassell, 1942 M
    Death Makes a Prophet. Macdonald, 1947 M
    Death of a Cad. Hale, 1940 M
    Death on Paper. Hale, 1940 M
    Death on the Riviera. Macdonald, 1952 M
    Death Steals the Show. Macdonald, 1950 M [theatre]
    A Glut of Red Herrings. Macdonald, 1949 M
    Hand on the Alibi. Skeffington, 1939 M
    The Lake District Murder. Skeffington, 1935 M
    Loss of a Head. Skeffington, 1938 M
    Murder in Montparnasse. Brown, 1949
    The Night the Fog Came Down. Macdonald, 1958; Washburn, 1958 S
    A Shift of Guilt. Macdonald, 1956 M
    Slow Vengeance. Hale, 1941 M
    So Much in the Dark. Macdonald, 1954 M
    The Sussex Downs Murder. Skeffington, 1936 M
    A Telegram from Le Touquet. Macdonald, 1956 M
    Trouble A-Brewing. Macdonald, 1946 M
    Twice Dead. Macdonald, 1953 M
    A Twist of the Rope. Macdonald, 1958 S
    Two Ends to the Town. Macdonald, 1955 M
    When the Case Was Opened. Macdonald, 1952 M

BUDRYS, ALGIS [ALGIRDAS JONAS BUDRYS]. 1931-   . Ref: CA.
    Who? Pyramid, 1958; Badger, 1960

BUELL, JOHN (EDWARD). 1927-   . Ref: CA, CC.
    The Chosen Girl; see The Pyx
    Four Days. Farrar, 1962; Macmillan (London), 1962 [Montr.]
    The Pyx. Farrar, 1959; Secker, 1960. Also published as: The Chosen Girl. Four Square, 1964 [Montr.]
    The Shrewsdale Exit. Farrar, 1972; Angus, 1973

BUFFER, JOE
    Skull. Pinnacle, 1975

BUHET, GIL. 1908-   .
    -The Grand Catch. Cape, 1957 (Translation of "Pierrot a la Belle Croche." Paris, 1956.)
    -The Honey Siege. Cape, 1953 (Translation of "Le Chevalier Pierrot." Paris, 1951.)
    -Mamizelle Bon Voyage. Cape, 1960
    -The Story Teller. Cape, 1955 (Translation of "La Romanciere." Paris, 1954.)

BULL, LOIS. 1900-   . Pseudonym: Melville Burt, q.v.
    Broadway Virgin. Macaulay, 1931; Queensway, 1936

BULLETT, GERALD (WILLIAM). 1893-1958. Pseudonym: Sebastian Fox, q.v. See also: J(ohn) B(oynton) Priestley, 1894-   . Ref: CC. Set: Eng.
    Judgment in Suspense. Dent, 1946 [acad.]
    The Jury. Dent, 1935; Knopf, 1935
    A Man of Forty. Dent, 1940; Knopf, 1940
    The Trouble at Number Seven. Joseph, 1952
    When the Cat's Away. Dent, 1940; Knopf, 1941

BULLEY, H. A.
    -The Seal of Confession. Greening, 1906

BULLIET, RICHARD (WILLIAMS). 1940-   . Pseudonym: Clarence J.-L. Jackson, q.v. Ref: CA.
    The Tomb of the Twelfth Imam. Harper, 1979 [Iran]

BULLIVANT, CECIL H(ENRY). 1882-   . Ref: EM. SC: Garnett Bell, in at least those marked GB. Set: Eng.
    -Because of the Woman. Pearson, 1922
    Blood Money. Long, 1924 GB
    -A Broken Honeymoon. Wright, 1931
    -The Call of the World. Wright, 1933
    The Dancing Spy. Odhams, 19??
    -A Daughter of Allah. Jarrolds, 1922
    -A Desert Wooing. Aldine, 1923
    -Destiny's Daughter. Wright, 1933
    -The Devil's Double. Wright, 1932
    -The Enchantress. Wright, 1932
    -Eyes of Desire. Wright, 1931
    -Fatal Power. Wright, 1934
    The Fringe of the Law. Wright, 1931
    Garnett Bell, Detective. Odhams, 1920 GB ss
    -The Great Alternative. Lloyds, 1921
    -The Hammer of God. Mellifont, 1935
    -Innocence. Jarrolds, 1923
    Jim the Penman. Mellifont, 1935
    Judge Not. Long, 1926
    A King of Crooks. Wright, 1932
    -Love's Great Surrender. Wright, 1932
    Millie Lynn, Shop Investigator. Odhams, 1920
    The Mysteries of Myra. Odhams, 19??
    -Quicksands of London. Aldine, 1917
    -The Rose of Algiers. Long, 1924
    -A Strong Man's Way. Odhams, 1919
    The Ticket-of-Leave Man. Mellifont, 1935
    -The Unbarred Door. Long, 1927
    -White Raiment. Wright, 1930
    Whose Wife? Jenkins, 1918
    The Wife Whom God Forgot. Odhams, 1919
    The Woman Always Wins; see The Woman Wins
    The Woman Wins. Pearson, 1919. Also published as: The Woman Always Wins. Hale, 1937

BULLOCK, LOTTE. 1918-
    Aquarius Angel. Macmillan (London), 1970

BULMER, (HENRY) KENNETH. 1921-   . Pseudonym: Ken Blake, q.v. Ref: CA.
    The Doomsday Men. Hale, 1968; Doubleday, 1968

BULWER-LYTTON, EDWARD (GEORGE EARLE). 1803-1873. Ref: CC, DD, MC.
    Alice; or, The Mysteries. Saunders, 1838; Harper, 1838
    Ernest Maltravers. Saunders, 1837; Harper, 1837
    Eugene Aram. Colburn, 1832; Harper, 1832. Also published as: The Strange Case of Eugene Aram. Collins, 1930
    Godolphin. Bentley, 1833; Carey, 1833
    Lucretia; or, The Children of the Night. Saunders, 1846; Harper, 1846
    Paul Clifford. Colburn, 1830
    Pelham; or, The Adventures of a Gentleman. Colburn, 1828; Collins and Haunay, 1828
    The Strange Case of Eugene Aram; see Eugene Aram
    A Strange Story. Low, 1862; Lippincott, 1879

BUMPUS, DORIS MARJORIE. 1905-   . Pseudonym: Marjorie Alan, q.v.
    -Pattern in Beads. Hale, 1944

BUNCE, FRANK (DAVID). 1907-   . Ref: CA.
    Rehearsal for Murder. Abelard (NYC & London), 1956
    So Young a Body. Simon, 1950; News of the World, 1952 [ship]

BUNCE, SYDNEY (GEORGE)
    No Sainted City. Angus, 1961
    Take This Life. Angus, 1960

BUNKER, EDWARD. 1933-   . Ref: CA.
    No Beast So Fierce. Norton, 1973. Also published as: Straight Time. Dell, 1978

BUNKER, JANE
    Diamond Cut Diamond. Bobbs, 1913 [Paris]

BUNN, THOMAS. 1944-   . Ref: CA.
    Closet Bones. Putnam, 1977 [N.Y.]

BUNNELL, RICHARD D(AY). Born in Conn,; later a Tucson rancher.
    Terror by Night. Naylor, 1957 [Ariz.]

BUNTLINE, NED. Pseudonym of Edward Zane Carroll Judson, 1821-1886.
    The Battle of Hate; or, Hearts Are Trumps. Brady, 1865
    The Convict; or, The Conspirator's Victim. Dick, 1863
    The Curse! Roberts, 1847
    The Death-Mystery. Brady, 1861
    Eldrida, the Red Rover's Daughter. Brady, 1860
    The Grossbeak Mansion. Brady, 1862
    Hilliare Henderson; or, The Secret Revealed. Brady, 1861
    The Mysteries and Miseries of New Orleans. Berford, 1848 [New Or.]
    The Mysteries and Miseries of New York. Judson, 1848 [NYC]
    The Naval Detective's Chase; or, Nick the Steepleclimber. Street, 1889
    Rose Seymour; or, The Ballet Girl's Revenge. Hilton, 1865
    Three Years After. Burgess, 1849
    The White Cruiser; or, The Fate of the Unheard-Of. Garrett, 1853
    The White Wizard; or, The Great Prophet of the Seminoles. Brady, 1858

BURANELLI, PROSPER. 1890-1960. Joint pseudonym with John Chipman Farrar, 1896-1974: John Prosper, q.v. Writer; editor of Movietone News; editor of many crossword puzzle books; lived in NYC. SC: Nick Morro = NM.
    Big Nick. Doubleday, 1931 MM [NYC]
    The Happy Nightmare. Crown, 1953
    News Reel Murder. Funk, 1940 NM [NYC]

BURBRIDGE, EDITH JOAN. 1919-   . Pseudonym: Joan Cockin, q.v.

BURCHELL, SIDNEY HERBERT
    The Grip of Fear. Hurst, 1906

BURDETT, CHARLES. 1815-   . Ref: EM.
    The Gambler; or, The Policeman's Story. Baker and Scribner, 1848
    Lilla Hart. Baker, 1946

BURDON, FREDERICK
    The Squire of Kilderman; or, The Snake Bracelet. Henderson

BURFORD, ROGER D'ESTE. 1904-   . Pseudonym: Roger East, q.v. Joint pseudonym with Oswell Blakeston, 1907-   , q.v.: "Simon", q.v.

BURGE, MILWARD RODON KENNEDY. 1894-1968. Pseudonyms: Evelyn Elder, Milward Kennedy, qq.v. Joint pseudonym with Archibald Gordon McDonell, 1895-1941, q.v.: Robert Milward Kennedy, q.v.

BURGE, REGINALD J.
    There Is a Destiny... Heath Cranton, 1917

BURGER, NEAL R. See: George E(dward) Simpson, 1944-   .

BURGER, ROSAYLMER. Pseudonym: C. H. Wallace, q.v. Joint pseudonym with Julia Perceval: Jessyca Paull, q.v.

BURGESS, ANTHONY. Pseudonym of John Anthony Burgess Wilson. Other pseudonym: Joseph Kell, q.v. Ref: CA, CC.
    A Clockwork Orange. Heinemann, 1962; Norton, 1962
    -The Doctor Is Sick. Heinemann, 1960; Norton, 1960
    Tremor of Intent. Heinemann, 1966; Norton, 1966 [Russ.]

BURGESS, ERIC (ALEXANDER). 1912-   . Ref: CA. SC: Harry Tong = HT. Set: Eng.
    Accident to Adeline. Joseph, 1952

Closely Confined. Hale, 1962 HT
Deadly Deceit. Hale, 1963 HT
Divided We Fall. Collins, 1959
Exit Pretty Poll. Hale, 1968 HT
A Killing Frost. Collins, 1961 HT
A Knife for Celeste. Joseph, 1949
The Malice of Monday. Joseph, 1950

BURGESS, (FRANK) GELETT. 1866-1951. See also: Anonymous. Ref: CC, EM, MP, TC.
Find the Woman. Bobbs, 1911 [NYC]
Ladies in Boxes. Alliance, 1942 [NYC]
A Murder at the Dome. Book Club of California, 1937 (26 pp.)
The Picaroons, with Will(iam Henry) Irwin, 1873-1948, q.v. McClure, 1904; Chatto, 1904 ss
Two O'Clock Courage. Bobbs, 1934; Nicholson, 1934 [Boston]
The White Cat. Bobbs, 1907; Chapman, 1908

BURGESS, HELEN STEERS. Pseudonym: Helen Steers, q.v.

BURGESS, WILLIAM WATSON. 1855- .
Life Sentence; or, Duty in Dealing with Crime. Badger, 1905

BURGOYNE, VICTORIA
Savaged. Futura, 1980

BURKE, MRS.
The Secret of the Cavern. Minerva, 1805

BURKE, CHARLES RUSSELL
-Thistle Sifters. Neely, 1898

BURKE, J(ACKSON) F(REDERICK). 1915- .
Ref: CA. SC: Samuel Moses Kelly = SK; Joe Streeter = JS.
Crazy Woman Blues. Dutton, 1978; Constable, 1979 JS [NYC]
Death Trick. Harper, 1975; Constable, 1976 SK [NYC]
The Kama Sutra Tango. Harper, 1977 JS [NYC]
Kelly Among the Nightingales. Dutton, 1979 SK [NYC]
Location Shots. Harper, 1974; Constable, 1974 SK [NYC]

BURKE, JAMES WAKEFIELD. 1916- . Ref: CA.
Three Day Pass—to Kill. World Wide, 1954 [Ger.]

BURKE, JOHN (FREDERICK). 1922- . Pseudonyms: Jonathan Burke, Robert Miall, Martin Sands, qq.v. Joint pseudonym with his wife: Harriet Esmond, q.v. Joint pseudonym with George Theiner, 1927- : Jonathan George, q.v. Ref: CA, TC. SC: Dr. Alexander Caspian = AC.
The Angry Silence. Hodder, 1961 (Novelization of the movie.)
-Another Chorus. Laurie, 1949
The Black Charade. Weidenfeld, 1977; Coward, 1977 AC [ca.1890, Eng.]
-Chastity House. Laurie, 1952
The Devil's Footsteps. Weidenfeld, 1976; Coward, 1976 AC [1888, Eng.]
-Expo 80. Cassell, 1972
Guilty Party. Elek, 1962 (Novelization of the play by George Ross and Campbell Singer.)
Ladygrove. Weidenfeld, 1978; Coward, 1978 AC [ca.1890, Eng.]
The Man Who Finally Died. Pan, 1963 (Novelization of the movie.)
-The Outward Walls. Laurie, 1952
The Poison Cupboard. Secker, 1956
Privilege. Pan, 1967; Avon, 1967 (Novelization of the movie.)
Strange Report. Hodder pb, 1970; Lancer, 1970 (Novelization of the TV series.)
-Swift Summer. Laurie, 1949
-These Haunted Streets. Laurie, 1950
The Trap. Pan, 1966 (Novelization of the movie.)

BURKE, JONATHAN. Pseudonym of John (Frederick) Burke, 1922- , q.v. Other pseudonyms: Robert Miall, Martin Sands, qq.v. Joint pseudonym with his wife: Harriet Esmond, q.v. Joint pseudonym with George Theiner, 1927- : Jonathan George, q.v. SC: Mike Merriman, in at least those marked MM.
Corpse to Copenhagen. Amalgamated, 1957 (Sexton Blake.)
Deadly Downbeat. Long, 1962 MM
Echo of Barbara. Long, 1959
Echo of Treason; see The Twisted Tongues
Fear by Instalments. Long, 1960 MM
Four Stars for Danger. Long, 1970

Goodbye, Gillian; see The Weekend Girls
Gossip to the Grave. Long, 1967. U.S. title: The Gossip Truth. Doubleday, 1968
The Gossip Truth; see Gossip to the Grave
Only the Ruthless Can Play. Long, 1965
Rob the Lady. Long, 1969
Someone Lying, Someone Dying. Long, 1968
Teach Yourself Treachery. Long, 1962
The Twisted Tongues. Long, 1964. U.S. title: Echo of Treason. Dodd, 1966
The Weekend Girls. Long, 1966; Doubleday, 1967. Also published as: Goodbye, Gillian. Ace, 196? Reprinted as by John Burke: Pan, 1968

BURKE, LEDA. Pseudonym of David Garnett, 1892-1981, q.v. Ref: CA.
Dope-Darling. Laurie, 1919

BURKE, LEE JOHN
The Cairo Counterplot. Hale, 1977 [Cairo]

BURKE, MARGARET ISABEL
When Duty Calls. Dorrance, 1966

BURKE, NOEL. Pseudonym of (Julia Clara Catherine) Dolores (Birk Olsen) Hitchens, 1907-1973, q.v. Other pseudonyms: Dolan Birkley, D. B. Olsen, qq.v.
The Shivering Bough. Dutton, 1942

BURKE, RICHARD. 1886- . Born in L.A.; a newspaperman. SC: Quinny Hite = QH.
Barbary Freight. Putnam, 1943; Boardman, 1945 [NYC]
Chinese Red. Putnam, 1942 QH [NYC]
The Dead Take No Bows. Houghton, 1941 QH [NYC]
The Fourth Star. Mystery House, 1946 QH [NYC]
The Frightened Pigeon. Putnam, 1944; Jarrolds, 1946 [Fr.]
Here Lies the Body. Putnam, 1942 QH [Conn.]
Murder on High Heels. Gateway, 1940 [L.I.]
The Red Gate. Ziff-Davis, 1947
Reluctant Hussy. Curl, 1946; Jarrolds, 1947
Sinister Street. Ziff-Davis, 1948 QH [NYC]

BURKE, SIMON
Death Is the Pay-Off. Scion, 1949

BURKE, STEWART
Key to Murder. French (London), 1978 (Play.)

BURKE, THOMAS. 1886-1945. Ref: CC, EM, MC, TC. SC: Quong Lee = QL.
Abduction. Jenkins, 1939
The Bloomsbury Wonder. Mandrake, 1929
Broken Blossoms. Richards, 1920 (A selection of ss from "Limehouse Nights", q.v.)
Dark Nights. Jenkins, 1944 (ss, including "The Bloomsbury Wonder," q.v.)
East of Mansion House. Cassell, 1928; Doran, 1926 ss
In Chinatown. Richards, 1921 (A selection of ss from "Limehouse Nights," q.v.)
Limehouse Nights. Richards, 1916; McBride, 1917 ss QL
More Limehouse Nights; see Whispering Windows
Murder at Elstree. Longmans, 1936
Night Pieces. Constable, 1935; Appleton, 1936 ss
The Pleasantries of Old Quong. Constable, 1931. U.S. title: A Tea-Shop in Limehouse. Little, 1931 ss QL
A Tea-Shop in Limehouse; see The Pleasantries of Old Quong
Whispering Windows. Richards, 1921. U.S. title: More Limehouse Nights. Doran, 1921 ss

BURKHARDT, EVE. 1899- . Joint pseudonyms with Robert Ferdinand Burkhardt, 1892-1947: Adam Bliss, Rex Jardin, qq.v.

BURKHARDT, ROBERT FERDINAND. 1892-1947. Joint pseudonyms with Eve Burkhardt, 1899- : Adam Bliss, Rex Jardin, qq.v.

BURKHOLDER, ED. Pseudonym: Robert Wallace, q.v.

BURKHOLZ, HERBERT. 1932- . Joint pseudonym with Clifford (Michael) Irving, 1930- , q.v.: John Luckless, q.v.
Mulligan's Seed. Harcourt, 1975

BURKS, ALLISON L.
Tight Rope. Duell, 1945; Heinemann, 1947 [Calif.]

BURLAND, HARRIS. See: J(ohn) B(urland) Harris-Burland, 1870- .

BURLEIGH, DONALD Q(UIMBY). 1894- .
The Kristiana Killers. Dutton, 1937 [Maine]

BURLEIGH, FLORENCE (S. HOWARD)
The Applewood Mystery. Fiction House, 1942

BURLEIGH, HILARY
Murder at Maison Manche. Hurst, 1948

BURLESON, CLYDE W. 1934- .
The Mexican Affair. Carlyle, 1979 [Mex.]
Operation: Evangeline. Carlyle, 1979

BURLEY, W(ILLIAM) J(OHN). 1914- .
Ref: CA, CC, TC. SC: Henry Pym = HP; Supt. Charles Wycliffe = CW. Set: Eng.
Charles and Elizabeth. Gollancz, 1979; Walker, 1981
Death in a Salubrious Place. Gollancz, 1973; Walker, 1973 CW
Death in Stanley Street. Gollancz, 1974; Walker, 1974 CW
Death in Willow Pattern. Gollancz, 1969; Walker, 1970 HP
Guilt Edged. Gollancz, 1971; Walker, 1972 CW
The Schoolmaster. Gollancz, 1977; Walker, 1977
A Taste of Power. Gollancz, 1966 HP [acad.]
Three-Toed Pussy. Gollancz, 1968 CW [Wales]
To Kill a Cat. Gollancz, 1970; Walker, 1970 CW
Wycliffe and the Pea-Green Boat. Gollancz, 1975; Walker, 1975 CW
Wycliffe and the Scapegoat. Gollancz, 1978; Walker, 1978 CW
Wycliffe and the Schoolgirls. Gollancz, 1976; Walker, 1976 CW
Wycliffe in Paul's Court. Gollancz, 1980; Doubleday, 1980 CW

"BURMAR." Pseudonym of Richard Marr.
The Smith Slayer. Gardner, 1939. Reprinted as by Richard Marr: Big Ben, 1940

BURMEISTER, JON. 1933- . Ref: CA.
The Glory Hunters. Joseph, 1979
The Hard Men. Joseph, 1978; St. Martin's, 1978
-The Protector Conclusion. Joseph, 1977; St. Martin's, 1977
Running Scared. Joseph, 1972; St. Martin's, 1973 [S. Afr.]
Someone Else's War. Joseph, 1973; St. Martin's, 1974 [Sp.]
The Weatherman Guy. Joseph, 1975; St. Martin's, 1975

BURNABY, NIGEL. Pseudonym of Harold Pincton Ellett, 1882- . SC: Chief Insp. Drewry = D. Set: Eng.
The Clue of the Green-Eyed Girl. Ward, 1935 D
The Forest Mystery. Ward, 1934
The Secret of Matchams. Ward, 1934
Two Deaths for a Penny. Ward, 1935 D

BURNE, GLEN. Joint pseudonym of Alan (Baer) Green, 1906-1975, q.v., and Gladys Elizabeth Blun Green, 1908- . Joint pseudonym of Alan (Baer) Green and Julian P. Brodie: Roger Denbie, q.v.
Murder to Music. Dodd, 1934 [NYC]

BURNETT, GEORGE (STANLEY). 1918- .
SC: Insp. Gulliver, in at least those marked G.
Dead Account. Hodder, 1966
The Finsbury Lot. Hodder, 1963
The Sheep and the Wolves. Hodder, 1962 G
Violent Security. Hodder, 1962 G

BURNETT, HALLIE (SOUTHGATE). 1908- .
Ref: CA.
Watch on the Wall. Morrow, 1965

BURNETT, W(ILLIAM) R(ILEY). 1899-1982. Pseudonym: John Monahan, q.v. See also: Ben Maddow, 1909- . Ref: CA, EM, MC, TC.

The Asphalt Jungle. Knopf, 1949; Macdonald, 1950 [Midwest]
Conant. Popular Library, 1961
The Cool Man. GM, 1968 [Calif.]
Dark Hazard. Harper, 1933; Heinemann, 1934 [Calif.]
High Sierra. Knopf, 1940; Heinemann, 1940 [Calif.]
Little Caesar. Dial, 1929; Cape, 1929 [Chi.]
Little Men, Big World. Knopf, 1951; Macdonald, 1952 [Midwest]
Nobody Lives Forever. Knopf, 1943; Heinemann, 1944 [L.A.]
The Quick Brown Fox. Knopf, 1942; Heinemann, 1943
Romelle. Knopf, 1946; Heinemann, 1947 [L.A.]
Round the Clock at Volari's. GM, 1961
The Silver Eagle. Dial, 1931; Heinemann, 1932 [Chi.]
Tomorrow's Another Day. Knopf, 1945; Heinemann, 1946
Underdog. Knopf, 1957; Macdonald, 1957
Vanity Row. Knopf, 1952; Macdonald, 1953
The Widow Barony. Macdonald, 1962 (U.S. title?)

BURNHAM, CLARA LOUISE (ROOT). 1854-1927.
Tobey's First Case. Houghton, 1926

BURNHAM, DAVID. 1907- . Ref: CC.
Last Act in Bermuda. Scribner, 1940 [Bermuda]

BURNHAM, GEORGE P(ICKERING). 1814-1902.
American Counterfeits. Holland, 1875 ss

BURNHAM, HELEN. SC: "One Week" Wimble, in both titles.
The Murder of Lalla Lee. McBride, 1931; Arrowsmith, 1931 [NYC]
The Telltale Telgram. McBride, 1932 [S.F.]

BURNING, MICHAEL and ALTHEA GREY
Dusty Death. Jenkins, 1949

BURNS, ALMA. 1917- . Pseudonym: Claire Dalton, q.v.
The Witches of Turnstone Bay. Zebra, 1977

BURNS, MARY LOVELAND
Murder at Crawford Notch. Humphries, 1944

BURNS, REX (RAOUL STEPHEN SEHLER). 1935- . Ref: CA, TC. SC: Gabriel Wager, in all titles.
The Alvarez Journal. Harper, 1975; Hale, 1976 [Denver]
Angle of Attack. Harper, 1979; Hale, 1980 [Denver]
The Farnsworth Score. Harper, 1977; Hale, 1978 [Colo.]
Speak for the Dead. Harper, 1978; Hale, 1980 [Denver]

BURNS, WILLIAM J., 1861-1932, and ISABEL (EGENTON) OSTRANDER, 1883-1924, q.v.
Pseudonyms of Isabel Ostrander: Robert Orr Chipperfield, David Fox, Douglas Grant, qq.v.
The Crevice. Watt, 1915. British title: The Lawton Mystery. Nash, 1917

BURR, ANNA (ROBESON BROWN). 1873-1941.
-Alain of Halfdene. Lippincott, 1895
The Bottom of the Matter. Appleton, 1935
The Great House in the Park. Duffield, 1924
-The House on Charles Street. Duffield, 1921
The House on Smith Square. Duffield, 1923
-The Jessop Bequest. Houghton, 1907
Palludia. Duffield, 1928; Melrose, 1929
West of the Moon. Duffield, 1926; Melrose, 1927
Wind in the East. Duffield, 1933
The Wrong Move. Macmillan, 1923; Brentano's (London), 1924

BURRAGE, A(LFRED) M(cLELLAND). 1889-1956.
Courtland's Crime. Long, 1928
Don't Break the Seal. Swan, 1946
-The Golden Barrier. Leng, 1925
-Poor Dear Esme. Newnes, 1925
Seeker to the Dead. Swan, 1942
-The Smokes of Spring. Long, 1926

BURRAGE, ALFRED S(HERRINGTON)
The Man with the Yellow Eyes; or, The Woman of Mystery. Henderson

BURRAGE, E(DWIN) HARCOURT. 1839-1916.
Ching Ching on the Trail. Lucas, 1892
The Fatal Nugget. Partridge, 1900
The Missing Million. Partridge, 1897
The Vanished Yacht. Nelson, 1898

BURREN, MICHAEL. See: George Marton, 1900- .

BURROUGHS, EDGAR RICE. 1875-1950. Ref: CA.
The Efficiency Expert. Charter, 1979 [Chi.]
The Girl from Farris's. Charter, 1979 [Chi.]
The Oakdale Affair. Burroughs, 1937

BURROWS, JULIE. SC: Supt. Bowman, in both titles. Set: Eng.
Like an Evening Gone. Macmillan (London), 1973
No Need for Violence. Cassell, 1970

BURT, K(ATHERINE) N(EWLIN). 1882-1977
Beggars All. Houghton, 1933
Captain Millett's Island. Macrae-Smith, 1944
Lady in the Tower. Macrae-Smith, 1946
-Rapture Beyond. Scribner, 1935
The Red Lady. Houghton, 1920; Constable, 1920 [N.C.]
-Safe Road. Macrae-Smith, 1938
Still Water. Macrae-Smith, 1948; Coker, 1951
-When Beggars Choose. Macrae-Smith, 1937

BURT, MELVILLE. Pseudonym of Lois Bull, 1900- , q.v.
The Granville Crypt Murders. Macaulay, 1936 [Eng.]
The Yellow Robe Murders. Macaulay, 1935

BURT, MICHAEL. 1900- . SC: Roger Poynings = RP.
The Case of the Angels' Trumpets. Ward, 1947 RP
The Case of the Fast Young Lady. Ward, 1942 RP
The Case of the Laughing Jesuit. Ward, 1948 RP
Catch-'Em-Alive-O! Chambers, 1938
The House of Sleep. Ward, 1945
Secret Orchards. Ward, 1938

BURTIS, THOMSON. 1896- .
Flying Blood. Fiction League, 1932 [Ohio]

BURTON, ANNE. Pseudonym of Sara Hutton Bowen-Judd, 1922- . Other pseudonyms: Mary Challis, Margaret Leek, Sara Woods, qq.v. SC: Richard Trenton, in both titles. Set: Eng.
The Dear Departed. Raven, 1980
Where There's a Will. Raven, 1980

BURTON, ANTHONY. 1933- . Ref: CA.
The Coventry Option. Putnam, 1976; Sphere, 1979 [Eng., WWII]

BURTON, CARL D. 1913- . Ref: CA.
-The Long Goodnight. Morrow, 1961 [South]

BURTON, EDMUND. Pseudonym of Edmund Burton Childs.
The Riddle of the Cloisters. Pendulum, 1946
The Royal Special, and other stories. Century, 1947 ss

BURTON, EDWARD J. 1917- . Pseudonym: Michael Carey, q.v.

BURTON, FREDERICK R(USSELL). 1861-1909. Pseudonym: Nicholas Carter, q.v.
A Seven Day's Mystery. Street (Magnet), 1900

BURTON, MAX
The Mound Hill Mystery. Fortuny's, 1938

BURTON, MILES. Pseudonym of Cecil John Charles Street, 1884-1961. Other pseudonym: John Rhode, q.v. SC: Inspector Arnold and Desmond Merrion, almost always together, in all titles except "The Hardway Diamonds Mystery" and "Murder at the Moorings." Set: Eng.
Accidents Do Happen; see Early Morning Murder
Beware Your Neighbor. Collins, 1951
Bones in the Brickfield. Collins, 1958
The Cat Jumps. Collins, 1946
The Charabanc Mystery. Collins, 1934
The Chinese Puzzle. Collins, 1957
The Clue of the Fourteen Keys; see Death at the Club
The Clue of the Silver Brush; see The Milk Churn Murder
The Clue of the Silver Cellar; see Where Is Barbara Prentice?
A Crime in Time. Collins, 1955
Dark Is the Tunnel; see Death in the Tunnel
Dead Stop. Collins, 1943
Death at Ash House; see This Undesirable Residence
Death at Low Tide. Collins, 1938
Death at the Club. Collins, 1937. U.S. title: The Clue of the Fourteen Keys. Doubleday, 1937
Death at the Crossroads. Collins, 1933
Death in a Duffle Coat. Collins, 1956
Death in Shallow Water. Collins, 1948
Death in the Tunnel. Collins, 1936. U.S. title: Dark Is the Tunnel. Doubleday, 1936 [train]
Death Leaves No Card. Collins, 1939
Death of Mr. Gantley. Collins, 1932
Death of Two Brothers. Collins, 1941
Death Paints a Picture. Collins, 1960
Death Takes a Detour. Collins, 1958
Death Takes a Flat. Collins, 1940. U.S. title: Vacancy with Corpse. Doubleday, 1941
Death Takes the Living. Collins, 1949. U.S. title: The Disappearing Parson. Doubleday, 1949
Death Visits Downspring; see Up the Garden Path
The Devereux Court Mystery. Collins, 1935
Devil's Reckoning. Collins, 1948; Doubleday, 1949
The Disappearing Parson; see Death Takes the Living
Early Morning Murder. Collins, 1945. U.S. title: Accidents Do Happen. Doubleday, 1946
Fate at the Fair. Collins, 1933
Found Drowned. Collins, 1956
Four-Ply Yarn. Collins, 1944. U.S. title: The Shadow on the Cliff. Doubleday, 1944
Ground for Suspicion. Collins, 1950
The Hardway Diamonds Mystery. Collins, 1930; Mystery League, 1930
Heir to Lucifer. Collins, 1947
Heir to Murder. Collins, 1953
Legacy of Death. Collins, 1960
Look Alive. Collins, 1949; Doubleday, 1950
The Man with the Tattooed Face; see Murder in Crown Passage
The Menace on the Downs. Collins, 1931
The Milk Churn Murder. Collins, 1935. U.S. title: The Clue of the Silver Brush. Doubleday, 1936
Mr. Babbacombe Dies. Collins, 1939
Mr. Westerby Missing. Collins, 1940; Doubleday, 1940
The Moth-Watch Murder. Collins, 1957
Murder at the Moorings. Collins, 1932; Sears, 1934
Murder in Absence. Collins, 1954 [ship]
Murder in Crown Passage. Collins, 1937. U.S. title: The Man with the Tattooed Face. Doubleday, 1937
Murder in the Coalhole. Collins, 1940. U.S. title: Written in Dust. Doubleday, 1940 [acad.]
Murder M.D. Collins, 1943. U.S. title: Who Killed the Doctor? Doubleday, 1943
Murder of a Chemist. Collins, 1936
Murder on Duty. Collins, 1952
Murder Out of School. Collins, 1951 [acad.]
Murder Unrecognized. Collins, 1955
The Mystery of High Eldersham; see The Secret of High Eldersham
Not a Leg to Stand On. Collins, 1945; Doubleday, 1945
The Platinum Cat. Collins, 1938; Doubleday, 1938
Return from the Dead. Collins, 1959
The Secret of High Eldersham. Collins, 1930; Mystery League, 1931. Also published as: The Mystery of High Eldersham. Collins, 1933
The Shadow on the Cliff; see Four-Ply Yarn
Situation Vacant. Collins, 1946
A Smell of Smoke. Collins, 1959
Something to Hide. Collins, 1953
This Undesirable Residence. Collins, 1942. U.S. title: Death at Ash House. Doubleday, 1942
The Three Corpse Trick. Collins, 1944
The Three Crimes. Collins, 1931
To Catch a Thief. Collins, 1934
Tragedy at the Thirteenth Hole. Collins, 1933
Unwanted Corpse. Collins, 1954
Up the Garden Path. Collins, 1941. U.S. title: Death Visits Downspring. Doubleday, 1941
Vacancy with Corpse; see Death Takes a Flat
A Village Afraid. Collins, 1950
Where Is Barbara Prentice? Collins, 1936. U.S. title: The Clue of the Silver Cellar. Doubleday, 1937
Who Killed the Doctor?; see Murder M.D.

A Will in the Way. Collins, 1947;
  Doubleday, 1947
Written in Dust; see Murder in the
  Coalhole

BURTON, MINA E.
  Ruling the Planets. Bentley, 1891; Harper, 1892

BUSBY, ROGER (CHARLES). 1941-   . Ref:
  CA, TC. SC: Det.-Insp. Leric = L.
  Deadlock. Collins, 1971 L
  The Frighteners. Collins, 1970 L
  Garvey's Code. Collins, 1978
  Main Line Kill, with Gerald Holtham.
    Cassell, 1968; Walker, 1968
  New Face in Hell. Collins, 1976
  Pattern of Violence. Collins, 1973 L
  A Reasonable Man. Collins, 1972 L
  Robbery Blue. Collins, 1969 L

BUSCHLEN, JOHN PRESTON. 1888-   . Pseudonym: Jack Preston, q.v.

BUSH, CHRISTOPHER. 1885-1973. Pseudonym:
  Michael Home, q.v. Ref: CA, CC, DD,
  EM, MP, TC. SC: Ludovic Travers, in
  all titles. Set: Eng.
  The Body in the Bonfire; see The Case
    of the Bonfire Body
  The Case of the Amateur Actor. Macdonald, 1955; Macmillan, 1956
  The Case of the April Fools. Cassell,
    1933; Morrow, 1933
  The Case of the Benevolent Bookie.
    Macdonald, 1955; Macmillan, 1956
  The Case of the Bonfire Body. Cassell,
    1936. U.S. title: The Body in the
    Bonfire. Holt, 1936
  The Case of the Burnt Bohemian. Macdonald, 1953; Macmillan, 1954
  The Case of the Careless Thief. Macdonald, 1959; Macmillan, 1960
  The Case of the Chinese Gong. Cassell,
    1935; Holt, 1935
  The Case of the Climbing Rat. Cassell,
    1940 [Fr.]
  The Case of the Corner Cottage. Macdonald, 1951; Macmillan, 1952
  The Case of the Corporal's Leave. Cassell, 1945
  The Case of the Counterfeit Colonel.
    Macdonald, 1952; Macmillan, 1953
  The Case of the Curious Client. Macdonald, 1947; Macmillan, 1948
  The Case of the Dead Man Gone. Macdonald, 1961; Macmillan, 1962
  The Case of the Dead Shepherd. Cassell,
    1934. U.S. title: The Tea Tray Murders. Morrow, 1934 [acad.]
  The Case of the Deadly Diamonds. Macdonald, 1967; Macmillan, 1968
  The Case of the Extra Grave. Macdonald,
    1961; Macmillan, 1962
  The Case of the Extra Man. Macdonald,
    1956; Macmillan, 1957
  The Case of the Fighting Soldier. Cassell, 1942
  The Case of the Flowery Corpse. Macdonald, 1956; Macmillan, 1957
  The Case of the Flying Ass. Cassell,
    1939
  The Case of the Fourth Detective. Macdonald, 1951
  The Case of the Frightened Mannequin;
    see The Case of the Happy Warrior
  The Case of the Good Employer. Macdonald, 1966; Macmillan, 1966
  The Case of the Grand Alliance. Macdonald, 1964; Macmillan, 1965
  The Case of the Green Felt Hat. Cassell, 1939; Holt, 1939
  The Case of the Hanging Rope. Cassell,
    1937. U.S. title: The Wedding Night
    Murder. Holt, 1937
  The Case of the Happy Warrior. Macdonald, 1950. U.S. title: The Case of
    the Frightened Mannequin. Macmillan,
    1951
  The Case of the Haven Hotel. Macdonald,
    1948
  The Case of the Heavenly Twin. Macdonald, 1963; Macmillan, 1964
  The Case of the Housekeeper's Hair.
    Macdonald, 1948; Macmillan, 1949
  The Case of the Jumbo Sandwich. Macdonald, 1965; Macmillan, 1966
  The Case of the Kidnapped Colonel. Cassell, 1942
  The Case of the Leaning Man. Cassell,
    1938. U.S. title: The Leaning Man.
    Holt, 1938
  The Case of the Magic Mirror. Cassell,
    1943
  The Case of the Missing Men. Macdonald,
    1946; Macmillan, 1947
  The Case of the Missing Minutes. Cassell, 1937. U.S. title: Eight
    O'Clock Alibi. Holt, 1937
  The Case of the Monday Murders. Cassell, 1936. U.S. title: Murder on
    Monday. Holt, 1936
  The Case of the Murdered Major. Cassell, 1941
  The Case of the 100% Alibis. Cassell,
    1934. U.S. title: The Kitchen Cake
    Murder. Morrow, 1934
  The Case of the Platinum Blonde. Cassell, 1944; Macmillan, 1949
  The Case of the Prodigal Daughter. Macdonald, 1968; Macmillan, 1969
  The Case of the Purloined Picture. Macdonald, 1949; Macmillan, 1951
  The Case of the Red Brunette. Macdonald, 1954; Macmillan, 1955
  The Case of the Running Man. Macdonald,
    1958; Macmillan, 1959
  The Case of the Running Mouse. Cassell,
    1944
  The Case of the Russian Cross. Macdonald, 1957; Macmillan, 1958
  The Case of the Sapphire Brooch. Macdonald, 1960; Macmillan, 1961
  The Case of the Second Chance. Macdonald, 1946; Macmillan, 1947
  The Case of the Seven Bells. Macdonald,
    1949; Macmillan, 1950
  The Case of the Silken Petticoat. Macdonald, 1953; Macmillan, 1954
  The Case of the Three Lost Letters.
    Macdonald, 1954; Macmillan, 1955
  The Case of the Three-Ring Puzzle. Macdonald, 1962; Macmillan, 1963
  The Case of the Three Strange Faces.
    Cassell, 1933. U.S. title: The Crank
    in the Corner. Morrow, 1933
  The Case of the Treble Twist. Macdonald, 1958. U.S. title: The Case of
    the Triple Twist. Macmillan, 1958
  The Case of the Triple Twist; see The
    Case of the Treble Twist
  The Case of the Tudor Queen. Cassell,
    1938; Holt, 1938
  The Case of the Unfortunate Village.
    Cassell, 1932
  The Crank in the Corner; see The Case
    of the Three Strange Faces
  Cut Throat. Heinemann, 1932; Morrow,
    1932
  Dancing Death. Heinemann, 1931; Doubleday, 1931
  Dead Man Twice. Heinemann, 1930;
    Doubleday, 1930
  Dead Man's Music. Heinemann, 1931;
    Doubleday, 1930
  The Death of Cosmo Revere; see Murder
    at Fenwold
  Eight O'Clock Alibi; see The Case of
    the Missing Minutes
  The Kitchen Cake Murder; see The Case
    of the 100% Alibis
  The Leaning Man; see The Case of the
    Leaning Man
  Murder at Fenwold. Heinemann, 1930.
    U.S. title: The Death of Cosmo
    Revere. Doubleday, 1930
  Murder on Monday; see The Case of the
    Monday Murders
  The Perfect Murder Case. Heinemann,
    1929; Doubleday, 1929
  The Plumley Inheritance. Jarrolds, 1926
  The Tea Tray Murders; see The Case of
    the Dead Shepherd
  The Wedding Night Murder; see The Case
    of the Hanging Rope

BUSNACH, WILLIAM (BERTRAND), 1832-1907,
  and HENRI CHABRILLAT
  Lecoq, the Detective's Daughter. Vizetelly, 1888 (Translation of "La
    Fille de M. Lecoq.")

BUSSELL, CHASE
  The Mountain Cabin Mystery. Dorrance,
    1935

BUTCHER, MARGARET
  Comet's Hair. Skeffington, 1939
  Destiny on Demand. Skeffington, 1938
  Hogdown Farm Mystery. Skeffington, 1950
  Vacant Possession. Skeffington, 1940

BUTLER, ELLIS PARKER. 1869-1937. Ref: EM.
  Philo Gubb, Correspondence School Detective. Houghton, 1919 ss

BUTLER, EWAN
  Conspiracy of Silence. Hodder, 1950
  Strange Sanctuary. Hodder, 1949

BUTLER, GEORGE (FRANK). 1857-1921.
  The Exploits of a Physician Detective.
    Clinic, 1908 ss

BUTLER, GERALD (ALFRED). 1907-   .
  Blow Hot, Blow Cold; see Choice of Two
    Women
  Choice of Two Women. Jarrolds, 1951.
    U.S. title: Blow Hot, Blow Cold.
    Rinehart, 1951
  Dark Rainbow; see Their Ranbow Had
    Black Edges
  Kiss the Blood Off My Hands. Nicholson,
    1940; Rinehart, 1946. Also published
    as: The Unafraid. Dell, 1948
  The Lurking Man; see Mad with Much
    Heart
  Mad with Much Heart. Jarrolds, 1945;
    Rinehart, 1946. Also published as:
    The Lurking Man. Lion, 1952
  Slippery Hitch. Jarrolds, 1948; Rinehart, 1949
  Their Rainbow Had Black Edges. Jarrolds, 1943. U.S. title: Dark Rainbow. Farrar, 1945
  There Is a Death, Elizabeth. Hale, 1972
  They Cracked Her Glass Slipper. Jarrolds, 1941
  The Unafraid; see Kiss the Blood Off
    My Hands

BUTLER, GWENDOLINE (WILLIAMS). 1922-   .
  Pseudonym: Jennie Melville, q.v. Ref:
  CA, CC, TC. SC: Sgt./Insp. John Coffin = JC; Insp./Supt. William Winter
  = WW. Set: Eng.
  The Brides of Friedberg. Macmillan
    (London), 1977. U.S. title: Meadowsweet. Coward, 1977 [Ger., 1800s]
  Coffin Following. Bles, 1968 JC
  Coffin for Baby. Bles, 1963; Walker,
    1963 JC
  A Coffin for Pandora. Macmillan (London), 1973. U.S. title: Sarsen Place.
    Coward, 1974 [Eng., 1800s]
  A Coffin for the Canary. Macmillan
    (London), 1974. U.S. title: Olivia.
    Coward, 1974 JC
  A Coffin from the Past. Bles, 1970 JC
  Coffin in Malta. Bles, 1964; Walker,
    1965 JC [Malta]
  Coffin in Oxford. Bles, 1962 JC
  Coffin Waiting. Bles, 1964; Walker,
    1963 JC
  Coffin's Dark Number. Bles, 1969 JC
  Dead in a Row. Bles, 1957 JC,WW
  Death Lives Next Door. Bles, 1960. U.S.
    title: Dine and Be Dead. Macmillan,
    1960 JC
  Dine and Be Dead; see Death Lives Next
    Door
  The Dull Dead. Bles, 1958; Walker, 1962
    JC,WW
  The Interloper. Bles, 1959
  Make Me a Murderer. Bles, 1961 JC
  Meadowsweet; see The Brides of Friedberg
  The Murdering Kind. Bles, 1958; Roy,
    1964 WW
  A Nameless Coffin. Bles, 1966; Walker,
    1967 JC
  Olivia; see A Coffin for the Canary
  Receipt for Murder. Bles, 1956
  The Red Staircase. Collins, 1980; Coward, 1979 [1917, Russ.]
  Sarsen Place; see A Coffin for Pandora
  The Vesey Inheritance. Macmillan (London), 1976; Coward, 1975 [1800s,
    Eng.]

BUTLER, IVAN. Pseudonym of Edward Ivan
  Oakley Beuttler. Ref: CA. See:
  (Thomas) Falkland L(itton) Cary;
  and: A(rthur) A(lexander) Malcolm)
  Thomson, 1884-   .

BUTLER, JOAN. Pseudonym of Robert William
  Alexander, 1905-1980.
  Rapid Fire. Paul, 1939
  Something Rich. Paul, 1937

BUTLER, K(ATHARINE) R(OSEMARY). 1925-   .
  Born in England; a teacher, secretary and journalist in South Africa.
  A Desert of Salt. Hodder, 1965; Mill,
    1964 [Afr.]
  The Evil Damp. Bles, 1966
  A Fall of Rock. Bles, 1967 [Rhod.]
  Kanaga. Bles, 1971
  Quirindi. Bles, 1970

BUTLER, LESLIE. SC: Horton and Jordan,
  in all titles.
  The Man Who Crawled Away. Hale, 1966
  Night and the Judgement. Hale, 1964
  Recover or Kill. Hale, 1965

BUTLER, MICHAEL, 1941-   , and DENNIS
  SHRYACK
  The Gauntlet. Warner, 1977; Star, 1977
    (Novelization of the movie.)

BUTLER, (RAYMOND) RAGAN. 1930-   . SC:
  Capt. George Nash, in both titles.
  Captain Nash and the Honour of England.
    Harwood, 1975; St. Martin's, 1977
    [ca.1770, Eng.]
  Captain Nash and the Wroth Inheritance.
    St. Martin's, 1976 [1771, Eng.]

BUTLER, RICHARD. 1925-   . Born in England; a teacher, first in England,
  and later in Australia.

The Buffalo Hook. Long, 1974
Fingernail Beach. Long, 1964 [Far East]
Lift-Off at Satan. Long, 1978; St. Martin's, 1979
More Dangerous Than the Moon; see South of Hell's Gates
Sharkbait. Long, 1970
South of Hell's Gates. Long, 1967. U.S. title: More Dangerous Than the Moon. Walker, 1968 [Tas.]

BUTLER, RICHARD. Pseudonym of Ted Allbeury, 1917-   , q.v. Other pseudonym: Patrick Kelly, q.v.
Italian Assets. Davies, 1976
Where All the Girls Are Sweeter. Davies, 1975

BUTLER, WALTER C. Pseudonym of Frederick Schiller Faust, 1892-1944. Other pseudonyms: Max Brand, Frederick Frost, qq.v.
Cross Over Nine. Macaulay, 1935
The Night Flower. Macaulay, 1936

BUTLER, WILLIAM. 1929-   . Born in Oregon.
-The Bone House. Owen, 1972
-The Butterfly Revolution. Owen, 1962; Putnam, 1967
-Cire Perdue. Owen, 1965
-A Danish Gambit. Owen, 1966
-The Experiment. Owen, 1961
-Man in a Net. Owen, 1971
Mr. Three. Owen, 1964; Putnam, 1966 [Afr.]
-The Ring in Meiji. Owen, 1965; Putnam, 1965
-Spying at the Fountain of Youth. Owen, 1968

BUTLER, WILLIAM VIVIAN. 1927-   . An advertising copywriter. SC: Commander George Gideon = GG (following J. J. Marric, q.v.); Richard Rollison = RR (following John Creasey, 1908-1973, q.v.).
Gideon's Force. Hodder, 1978 GG
The Toff and the Dead Man's Finger. Hodder, 1978 RR

BUTOR, MICHEL (MARIE FRANCOIS). 1926-   . Ref: CA, TC.
Passing Time. Calder, 1960; Simon, 1960 (Translation of "L'Emploi du Temps." Paris, 1956.)

BUTTENSHAW, DIANA (MARGUERITE)
-Chain of Command. Hodder, 1950
-Violence in Paradise. Hodder, 1957

BUTTERFIELD, W(ALTON), 1898-   , and L(EE) MORRISON
The Canary Murder Case. French (NYC), 1930 (3-act play based on the novel by S. S. Van Dine, q.v.)

BUTTERWORTH, FRANK NESTLE. Pseudonym: Peter Blundell, q.v.

BUTTERWORTH, MICHAEL. 1924-   . Pseudonym: Sara Kemp, q.v. Ref: CA.
The Black Look. Collins, 1972; Doubleday, 1972 [Paris]
Festival! Collins, 1976
Flowers for a Dead Witch. Collins, 1971; Doubleday, 1971
The Man in the Sopwith Camel. Collins, 1974; Doubleday, 1974
Remains to Be Seen. Collins, 1976; Doubleday, 1976
The Soundless Scream. Long, 1967; Doubleday, 1967 [Fr.]
The Uneasy Sun; see Vanishing Act
Vanishing Act. Collins, 1970. U.S. title: The Uneasy Sun. Doubleday, 1970 [Malta]
Villa on the Shore. Collins, 1973; Doubleday, 1974 [It.]
Walk Softly in Fear. Long, 1968
X Marks the Spot. Collins, 1978; Doubleday, 1978

BUTTERWORTH, WILLIAM EDMUND III. 1929-   . Pseudonym: Webb Beech, q.v.

BUXTON, ANNE. Pseudonyms: Anne Maybury, Katherine Troy, qq.v.

BUXTON, RAYMOND
No Gentle Lady. Modern Fiction, 1949

BYERS, BRUCE
Agent of the Id. Hale, 1974
All My Dead Men. Hale, 1973

BYERS, C(HARLES) A(LMA). 1879-   .
The Inverness Murder. Dial, 1935 [L.A.]

BYFIELD, BARBARA NINDE, 1930-   . Ref: CA. SC: Simon Bede and Helen Bullock, in all titles.
Forever Wilt Thou Die. Doubleday, 1976 [Mich.]
A Harder Thing Than Triumph. Doubleday, 1977 [Mass.]
A Parcel of Their Fortunes. Doubleday, 1979 [Mor.]
Solemn High Murder, with Frank L. Tedeschi. Doubleday, 1975; Davies, 1976 [NYC, church]

BYFORD-JONES, W(ILFRED)
Death by Order. Modern, 193?

BYRD, ELIZABETH. 1912-   . Ref: CA.
The Diamond. Macmillan (London), 1979
The Search for Maggie Hare. Macmillan (London), 1976; Avon, 1977

BYRNE, BEVERLY
Murder on the Menu. Leisure, 1980

BYRNE, (BRIAN OSWALD) DONN. 1889-1928.
The Hand of Ireland and other stories. Low, 1934; Appleton, 1935 ss, one criminous

BYRNE, M. ST. CLARE. See: Dorothy L(eigh) Sayers, 1893-1957.

BYRNE, MARY
Murder at the "Signal". Long, 1936

BYRNE, ROBERT. 1938-   . Ref: CA.
The Tunnel. Harcourt, 1977; Joseph, 1977

BYRNE, STUART JAMES. 1913-   . Pseudonym: Rothayne Amare, q.v.

BYROM, JAMES. Pseudonym of James Guy Bramwell, 1911-   . Ref: CA, CC. Set: Eng.
Or Be He Dead. Chatto, 1958
Take Only As Directed. Chatto, 1959
Thou Shouldst Be Living. Heinemann, 1964

BYRON, CHRISTOPHER
Foreign Matter. Doubleday, 1980 [Greece]

BYRON, JAMES
TNT for Two. Ace, 1956 [Oreg.]

C., R. B. Pseudonym of Charles Hull.
-Redeemed. Dillingham, 1894

CABALLERO, ANN (MALLORY). 1928-   . Ref: CA.
Stranger in the House. Coward, 1965

CABLE, BOYD. Pseudonym of Ernest Andrew Ewart, 1878-1943.
A Double Scoop. Hutchinson, 1924 [ship]
The Flying Courier. Wright, 1936

CABOT, ISABEL. Pseudonym of Isabel Capeto, q.v.
The Missing Witness. Avalon, 1961
Murder Is a House Guest. Avalon, 1962

CABOT, JOAN
Vail's Gate. Lenox, 1970

CADE, ALEXANDER. Pseudonym of Kenneth (Walter) Methold, 1931-   , q.v.
Turn Up a Stone. Bles, 1969

CADE, COULSON T.
-The Cornish Penny. Richards, 1922; Stokes, 1922

CADE, PAUL
Death Slams the Door. Modern Age, 1937 [Can.]

CADE, ROBIN. Pseudonym of Christopher Robin Nicole, 1930-   . Other pseudonym: Andrew York, q.v.
The Fear Dealers. Cassell, 1974; Simon, 1974 [Jap.]

CADELL, (VIOLET) ELIZABETH. 1903-   . Pseudonym: Harriet Ainsworth, q.v. Ref: CA.
Alice, Where Art Thou? Hodder, 1959
Canary Yellow. Hodder, 1965; Morrow, 1965
The Corner Shop. Hodder, 1966; Morrow, 1967
Crystal Clear; see Journey's Eve
Deck with Flowers. Hodder, 1973; Morrow, 1974
The Fox from His Lair. Hodder, 1965; Morrow, 1966
Game in Diamonds. Hodder, 1976; Morrow, 1976
-Journey's Eve. Hodder, 1953. U.S. title: Crystal Clear. Morrow, 1953
Parson's House. Hodder, 1977; Morrow, 1977
Return Match. Hodder, 1979; Morrow, 1979
Round Dozen. Hodder, 1978; Morrow, 1978
The Yellow Brick Road. Hodder, 1960; Morrow, 1960

CADETT, HERBERT
The Adventures of a Journalist. Sands, 1900 ss

CADMAN, JOHN
With Dead Bodies. Stockwell, 1957 ss

CAGNEY, PETER. Pseudonym of Bevis Winter, 1918-   , q.v. Other pseudonyms: Al Bocca, Gordon Shayne, qq.v. SC: Mike Strong, in all titles.
A Grave for Madam. Jenkins, 1961
Hear the Stripper Scream. Jenkins, 1960; Roy, 1962
No Diamonds for a Doll. Jenkins, 1960; Roy, 1961

CAIDIN, MARTIN. 1927-   . Ref: CA. SC: Steve Austin, in at least those marked SA.
Almost Midnight. Morrow, 1971; Bantam (London), 1974
Anytime, Anywhere. Dutton, 1969; Allen, 1970
Aquarius Mission. Corgi, 1978
-The Cape. Doubleday, 1971
Cyborg. Arbor, 1972; Allen, 1973 SA
Cyborg IV. Arbor, 1975; Allen, 1977 SA
Devil Take All. Dutton, 1966; Allen, 1968
Encounter Three; see The Mendelov Conspiracy
-Four Came Back. McKay, 1968
-The God Machine. Dutton, 1968
High Crystal. Arbor, 1974; Allen, 1975 SA
The Last Fathom. Meredith, 1967; Joseph, 1969
Maryjane Tonight at Angels Twelve. Doubleday, 1972 [Fla.]
The Mendelov Conspiracy. Meredith, 1969; Allen, 1971. Also published as: Encounter Three. Pinnacle, 1978 SA
-No Man's World. Dutton, 1967
Operation Nuke. Arbor, 1973; Allen, 1974 SA
Three Corners to Nowhere. Bantam, 1975; Corgi, 1975 [Carib.]

CAILLOU, ALAN. Pseudonym of Allan Lyle-Smythe, 1914-   . Ref: CA, TC. SC: Cabot Cain = CC; Mike Benasque = MB; Matthew Tobin = MT.
Afghan Assault. Pinnacle, 1972 MT [Afghan.]
Alien Virus. Davies, 1957. U.S. title: Cairo Cabal. Pinnacle, 1974 [Cairo]
Assault on Aimata. Avon, 1975 CC
Assault on Fellawi. Avon, 1972 CC [Mid. East]
Assault on Kolchak. Avon, 1969 CC [Brazil]
Assault on Loveless. Avon, 1969 CC [Lisbon]
Assault on Ming. Avon, 1970 CC [China]
Cairo Cabal; see Alien Virus
Congo War Cry. Pinnacle, 1972 MT [Bel. Congo]
Dead Sea Submarine. Pinnacle, 1971 MT [Mid. East]
Death Charge. Pinnacle, 1973 MT [Mex.]
Diamonds Wild. Avon, 1979 MB
The Garonsky Missile. Pinnacle, 1976 MT
A Journey to Orassia. Doubleday, 1965; Allen, 1966
Marseilles. PB, 1964 MB [Mars.]
The Mindanao Pearl. Pinnacle, 1973; Davies, 1959
The Plotters. Harper, 1960; Davies, 1960 MB [S. Am.]
Rogue's Gambit. Davies, 1955
Swamp War. Pinnacle, 1973 MT [Fla.]
Terror in Rio. Pinnacle, 1971 MT [Rio de J.]
Who'll Buy My Evil? PB, 1966 MB [Mid. East]

CAIN, JAMES M(ALLAHAN). 1892-1977. Ref: CA, CC, EM, MC, TC.
The Butterfly. Knopf, 1947. British publication in: Three of Hearts, q.v.
Career in C Major and other stories. Avon, 1943. British publication of title story in: Three of Hearts, q.v. Also published as: Everybody Does It (includes The Embezzler, q.v.). Signet, 1949 ss

Double Indemnity. Avon, 1943. British publication, and American republication, in: Three of a Kind, q.v. [Calif.]
The Embezzler. Avon, 1944. British publication, and American republication, in: Three of a Kind, q.v.
Everybody Does It; see Career in C Major and other stories
Galatea. Knopf, 1953; Hale, 1954 [Md.]
The Institute. Mason/Charter, 1976; Hale, 1977 [Wash. D.C.]
Jealous Woman. Avon, 1950; Hale, 1955, also contains the first British publication of Sinful Woman, q.v. [Reno]
Love's Lovely Counterfeit. Knopf, 1942. British publication in: Three of Hearts, q.v.
The Magician's Wife. Dial, 1965; Hale, 1966 [Md.]
Mignon. Dial, 1962; Hale, 1963
Mildred Pierce. Knopf, 1941; Hale, 1943 [Calif.]
The Moth. Knopf, 1948; Hale, 1950
Past All Dishonor. Knopf, 1946. British publication in: Three of Hearts, q.v. [Calif., 1860s]
The Postman Always Rings Twice. Knopf, 1934; Cape, 1934 [Calif.]
Rainbow's End. Mason/Charter, 1975; Allen, 1975 [Ohio]
The Root of His Evil. Avon, 1952; Hale, 1954. Also published as: Shameless. Avon, 1958
Serenade. Knopf, 1937; Cape, 1938 [Mex.]
Shameless; see The Root of His Evil
Sinful Woman. Avon, 1948; Hale, 1955, in Jealous Woman, q.v. [Reno]
Three of a Kind. Knopf, 1944; Hale, 1956 (Contents: Career in C Major, The Embezzler, and Double Indemnity, qq.v.)
Three of Hearts. Hale, 1949 (Contents: Love's Lovely Counterfeit, Past All Dishonor, and The Butterfly, qq.v.)

CAIN, PAUL. Pseudonym of George Sims, 1902-1966.
Fast One. Doubleday, 1933; Constable, 1936 [L.A.]
Seven Slayers. Saint Enterprises, 1946 ss

CAINE, (THOMAS HENRY) HALL. 1853-1931.
The Shadow of a Crime. Chatto, 1885; Harper, 1885

CAINE, HAMILTON T. Pseudonym of Stephen L. Smoke.
Carpenter, Detective. Charter, 1980 [Calif.]

CAINE, JEFFREY (ANDREW). 1944- . Joint pseudonym with Campbell Black, 1944- , q.v.: Jeffrey Campbell, q.v. Ref: CA.
The Cold Room. Allen, 1977; Knopf, 1977 [Berlin]
-Heathcliff. Allen, 1977; Knopf, 1978 [1800s, Eng.]

CAIRD, JANET (HINSHAW). 1913- . Ref: CA, CC, TC. Set: Scot., all titles.
In a Glass Darkly; see Murder Reflected
The Loch. Bles, 1968; Doubleday, 1969
Murder Reflected. Bles, 1965. U.S. title: In a Glass Darkly. Morrow, 1966
Murder Remote. Doubleday, 1973. Also published as: The Shrouded Way. Signet, 1973
Murder Scholastic. Bles, 1967; Doubleday, 1968 [acad.]
Perturbing Spirit. Bles, 1966; Doubleday, 1967
The Shrouded Way; see Murder Remote
-The Umbrella-Maker's Daughter. Macmillan (London), 1980; St. Martin's, 1980

CAIRNS, CICELY. -ca.1949. Ref: CC.
Murder Goes to Press. Constable, 1950; Macmillan, 1951

CAIRNS, COLLEEN
Great Gorme. Weybright, 1975

CAIRO, JACK
Cocksure Dame. Scion, 1952
Dames for Danger. Scion, 1953
You've Had Your Chance. Scion, 1950

CAKE, PATRICK. Pseudonym of Timothy L. Welch, 1935- , q.v. SC: Dion Quince = DQ (see also the Welch entry).
The Pro-Am Murders. Proteus, 1979 DQ [Calif.]

CALDE, MARK A(UGUSTINE). 1945- . Ref: CA.
Shadowboxer. Putnam, 1976; Hale, 1977 [Wash. D.C.]

CALDER, ROBERT. Pseudonym of a writer of 20 other books under his real name and pseudonyms. 1941- . Ref: CA.
The Dogs. Delacorte, 1976; Hodder, 1976

CALDERWOOD, CARMELITA, -1950, and JAMES HEARST
Bonesetter's Brawl. Dorrance, 1979 [1940s, hosp.]

CALDWELL, ALFRED BETTS. SC: Freddy Philpotts = FP.
Coffee for None. Mathews, 1934
Death Rattle. Doubleday, 1940 FP [Pa.]
No Tears Shed. Doubleday, 1937 FP [NYC]
Turquoise Hazard. Doubleday, 1936 FP [NYC]

CALDWELL, CELESTE
Thirteen Towers. Belmont, 1974

CALDWELL, FRED. Pseudonym of Wilbur Braun, 1896- , q.v. Other pseudonyms: Walter Blake, Bruce Brandon, Raymond Dumkey, Nan Fleming, Marsha Grable, Edwin F. Hornung, Jed Parish, Basil Ring, Orville Snap, Mortimer Sprague, Bert Stoner, qq.v.
Aunt Susie Shoots the Works! French (NYC), 1938 (3-act play.)

CALDWELL, GEORGE S.
Gristmill. H. Hamilton, 1975

CALDWELL, (JANET MIRIAM) TAYLOR (HOLLAND). 1900- .
The Late Clara Beame. Doubleday, 1963; Collins, 1964 [Conn.]
Wicked Angel. Reback, 1965; Coronet, 1966

CALEF, NOEL. 1907- .
Frantic. GM, 1961 (Translation of "Ascenseur pour l'Echafaud." Paris, 1956.) [Fr.]
The Snare. Souvenir, 1969 (Translation of "La Nasse." Paris, 1966.)

CALIN, ANNE
Decision at Dawn. Lancer, 1967
A Multitude of Shadows. Lancer, 1966

CALIN, HAL JASON. Born in N.Y.
Rocks and Ruin. Vanguard, 1954. Also published as: Payoff in Blood. Jonathan, 1955 [NYC]

CALL, WILLIAM TIMOTHY. 1856-1917.
Blackmail. (Author), 1915

CALLAGHAN, MORLEY (EDWARD). 1903- . Ref: CA.
-Strange Fugitive. Scribner, 1928

CALLAHAN, JAY
The Ace of Death. Dale, 1979 [N.J.]

CALLAHAN, ROBERT E(LMER)
Assassins in White. Vantage, 1955

CALLAHAN, ROD
Step Softly, Sweetheart. World, 1951

CALLAN, MICHAEL FEENEY
The Bronze Heist. Arrow, 1978 (Novelization of the BBC TV series "Target.")
Cinderella's Dead. Hale, 1978

CALLAND, MARY
The Billion-Dollar Hold-Up. Hale, 1969

CALLARD, MAURICE (FREDERICK THOMAS). 1912- . Ref: CA.
A Night in October. New Playwrights, 1980 (Play.)
Sweet Nelly. New Playwrights, 1972 (2-act play.)

CALLAS, THEO. Pseudonym of Shaun (Lloyd) McCarthy, 1928- , q.v. Other pseudonym: Desmond Cory, q.v.
The City of Kites. Muller, 1955; Walker, 1964 [Vienna]

CALLAWAY, SLOANE
The Crime at the Conquistador. Phoenix, 1938

CALLENDER, JULIAN. Pseudonym of Austin Lee, 1904-1965, q.v. Other pseudonym: John Austwick, q.v.
Corpse Too Many. Jenkins, 1965

CALLISON, BRIAN (RICHARD). 1934- . Ref: CA. SC: Brevet Cable = BC.
An Act of War; see A Frenzy of Merchantmen
A Flock of Ships. Collins, 1970; Putname, 1970
A Frenzy of Merchantmen. Collins, 1977. U.S. title: An Act of War. Dutton, 1977 BC
A Plague of Sailors. Collins, 1971; Putnam, 1971 BC
A Web of Salvage. Collins, 1973; Putnam, 1974

CALMER, NED. 1907- . Ref: CA.
The Avima Affair. Doubleday, 1973 [Wash. D.C., Carib.]
Madam Ambassador. Doubleday, 1975
The Peking Dimension. Doubleday, 1976

CALNAN, T(HOMAS) D(ANIEL). 1915- . Ref: CA.
The Reluctant Spy. Curtis, 1973

CALTHROP, DION (WILLIAM PALGRAVE) CLAYTON. 1878-1937. See also: (Chambers) Haldane (Cooke) MacFall, 1860-1928.
The Lavender Dagger. Hodder, 1931

CALVERT, WALTER
Justine; or, A Woman's Honour. Eden Remington, 1891

CALVIN, HENRY. Pseudonym of Clifford Hanley, 1922- , q.v.
Boka Lives! see The Chosen Instrument
The Chosen Instrument. Hutchinson, 1969. U.S. title: Boka Lives! Harper, 1969
The D.N.A. Business. Hutchinson, 1967
The Italian Gadget. Hutchinson, 1966 [Rome]
It's Different Abroad. Hutchinson, 1963; Harper, 1963 [Fr.]
Miranda Must Die. Hutchinson, 1968
A Nice Friendly Town. Hutchinson, 1967
The Poison Chasers. Hutchinson, 1971
The System. Hutchinson, 1962
Take Two Popes. Hutchinson, 1972

CAMACHO, GEORGE
Murder on the Brampton. Hale, 1978

CAMBARDS, MICHELLE
Guilty of Love. Mystique, 1979 (Translation of "Reviens, Juliana." Paris, 1970.)
Trial by Love. Mystique, 1980 (Translation of "Plaidoyer pour un Amour." Paris, 1966.)

CAMBRIDGE, ADA [ADA CAMBRIDGE CROSS]. 1844-1926.
At Midnight and other stories. Ward, 1897 ss, some criminous

CAMERON, CHARLOTTE (WALES-ALMY). -1946.
-Zenia: Spy in Togoland. Laurie, 1916 [Afr., W.]

CAMERON, DONALD CLOUGH. ca.1909- .
Born in Detroit; newspaperman turned freelance writer. SC: Abelard Voss = AV.
And So He Had to Die. Holt, 1941 AV [NYC]
Death at Her Elbow. Holt, 1940 [NYC]
Dig Another Grave. Mystery House, 1946 [NYC]
Grave Without Grass. Holt, 1940 AV [L.I.]
Murder's Coming. Holt, 1939 AV [Mass.]
White for a Shroud. Mystery House, 1947; Boardman, 1949 [Mich.]

CAMERON, ELEANOR ELFORD. 1910- . Ref: CA
Box for a Long Journey. Dell, 1973
The Curse of the Casa Del Monte. Dell, 1975 [Calif.]
House on the Beach. PB, 1972 [Calif.]
A Place of Mischief. Popular Library, 1972 [Cape Cod]
The Spider Stone. Dell, 1973
The Young Widow. Dell, 1974

CAMERON, EVELYN. SC: Sheriff Jack Thompson, in both titles, set in Tex.
Dead Man's Shoes. Doubleday, 1939
Malice Domestic. Doubleday, 1940

CAMERON, JOHN. Pseudonym of Archibald Gordon MacDonell, 1895-1941. Other pseudonym: Neil Gordon, q.v. Joint pseudonym with Milward Rodon Kennedy Burge, 1894-1968, q.v.: Robert Milward Kennedy, q.v.
Body Found Stabbed. Methuen, 1932
Seven Stabs. Gollancz, 1929; Doubleday, 1930

CAMERON, KATE. Pseudonym of (Elizabeth) Lorinda DuBreuil, 1924-1980, q.v. Other pseudonyms: Linda Hagen, Elizabeth Hanley, qq.v. Series: Holderly Hall, in at least those marked HH; Whispering Hills, in at least those marked WH.
  The Awakening Dream. Leisure, 1974 [Ind.] WH
  The Curse of Whispering Hills. Leisure, 1974 WH [1860s, Ind.]
  Deadly Nightshade. Leisure, 1975 HH [Tenn.]
  Echoes of Evil. Leisure, 1974 WH [Ind.]
  Evil at Whispering Hills. Leisure, 1973 WH [past, Ind.]
  Kiss Me, Kill Me. Belmont, 1979
  Legacy of Terror. Leisure, 1974 WH [Ind.]
  The Legend of Holderly Hall. Leisure, 1974 HH [Tenn.]
  Music from the Past. Leisure, 1975
  Portraits of the Past. Leisure, 1975 HH [Tenn.]
  Shadows of the Past. Leisure, 1974 HH [Tenn.]
  Shadows on the Moon. Leisure, 1974 WH [past, Ind.]
  Voices in the Fog. Leisure, 1975 HH [Tenn.]

CAMERON, KENNETH M. 1931- . Pseudonym: George Bartram, q.v.

CAMERON, LOU. 1924- . Ref: CA.
  The Amphorae Pirates. Random, 1970; Hodder, 1971 [It.]
  Angel's Flight. GM, 1960
  Barca. Berkley, 1974; Ellis, 1974 [N.J.]
  Before It's Too Late. GM, 1970
  Behind the Scarlet Door. GM, 1971
  The Block Busters. McKay, 1964 [NYC]
  The Closing Circle. Berkley, 1974; Ellis, 1975
  Code Seven. Berkley, 1977
  Devil in the Pines. Berkley, 1975
  The Dragon's Spine. Avon, 1968
  The Empty Quarter. GM, 1962
  File on a Missing Redhead. GM, 1968; Coronet, 1969 [Las Veg.]
  The Girl with the Dynamite Bangs. Lancer, 1973 [Brazil]
  The Outsider. Popular Library, 1969 (Novelization of the TV series.) [L.A.]
  The Sky Divers. GM, 1962
  -The Sky Riders. GM, 1976 (Novelization of the movie.)
  Tancredi. Berkley, 1975; Ellis, 1976 [N.J.]

CAMERON, MONTGOMERY
  The Ugly Woman. Vantage, 1966

CAMERON, (COURTNEY) OWEN. 1905- .
  Born in Oregon; settled in California; ss writer and novelist. SC: Deputy Sheriff Jake Brown = JB.
  The Antagonists. Doubleday, 1946
  The Butcher's Wife. Simon, 1954; Hammond, 1955 [Mont.]
  Catch a Tiger. Simon, 1952; Hammond, 1954 JB [Calif.]
  The Demon Stirs; see The Fire Trap
  The Fire Trap. Simon, 1957; Hammond, 1958. Also published as: The Demon Stirs. Dell, 1958 JB [Calif.]
  Man Hunt; see The Mountains Have No Shadow
  The Mountains Have No Shadow. Harper, 1952. British title: Man Hunt. Hammond, 1958
  The Owl and the Pussycat. Harper, 1949 [ship]
  The Silent One. Random, 1958; Hammond, 1960 [Calif.]

CAMERON, WILLIAM ERNEST. 1881- . Pseudonym: Mark Allerton, q.v.

CAMP, (CHARLES) WADSWORTH. 1879-1936. Ref: CC. SC: Garth = G.
  The Abandoned Room. Doubleday, 1917; Jarrolds, 1919
  The Communicating Door. Doubleday, 1923 ss, 3 about G
  -The Forbidden Years. Doubleday, 1930
  The Gray Mask. Doubleday, 1920 G [N.Y.]
  The House of Fear. Doubleday, 1916; Hodder, 1917. Also published as: The Last Warning. Readers Library, 1929
  The Last Warning; see The House of Fear
  Sinister Island. Dodd, 1915 [La.]

CAMP, WILLIAM. 1928- .
  The Jacobs Park Killings. Vanguard, 1978 [Calif.]
  Night Beat. Vanguard, 1968 [Calif.]

CAMPBELL, ALICE (ORMOND). 1887- .
  Born in Georgia; moved to England before beginning to write crime fiction. Ref: MP. SC: Insp. Headcorn = H; Tommy Rostetter = TR.
  The Bloodstained Toy. Collins, 1948 TR,H
  The Borrowed Cottage; see No Murder of Mine
  Child's Play. Collins, 1947. U.S. title: Veiled Murder. Random, 1949 (revised)
  The Click of the Gate. Collins, 1932; Farrar, 1931 TR [Paris]
  The Cockroach Sings. Collins, 1946. U.S. title: With Bated Breath. Random, 1946 H
  The Corpse Had Red Hair. Collins, 1950
  Death Framed in Silver. Collins, 1937 H
  Desire to Kill. Collins, 1934; Farrar, 1934 TR [Paris]
  A Door Closed Softly. Collins, 1939
  Flying Blind. Collins, 1938 TR
  Juggernaut. Hodder, 1928; Doubleday, 1928 [Fr.]
  Keep Away from Water! Collins, 1935; Farrar, 1935 [Fr.]
  Murder in Paris; see Spiderweb
  The Murder of Caroline Bundy. Collins, 1933; Farrar, 1932
  No Light Came On. Collins, 1942; Scribner, 1945 [Paris]
  No Murder of Mine. Collins, 1941; Scribner, 1941. Also published as: The Borrowed Cottage. H
  Ringed with Fire. Collins, 1943; Random, 1942
  Spiderweb. Hodder, 1930. U.S. title: Murder in Paris. Farrar, 1930 [Paris]
  They Hunted a Fox. Collins, 1940; Scribner, 1940 H
  Traveling Butcher. Collins, 1944
  Veiled Murder; see Child's Play
  Water Weed. Hodder, 1929; Farrar, 1929
  With Bated Breath; see The Cockroach Sings

CAMPBELL, ARMINE
  Getting Away with Murder. Vantage, 1976

CAMPBELL, COLIN. Pseudonym of Douglas Christie, 1894- , q.v. Other pseudonym: Lynn Durie, q.v.
  -Caught in the Machine. Rich, 1936
  -Fool's Fair. Hurst, 1932
  Murder on the Moors. Rich, 1934
  Murder up the Glen. Rich, 1933 [Scot.]
  Out of Wild Hills. Hurst, 1932
  The Red Glen. Rich, 1936

CAMPBELL, D(ONALD) FREDERICK. 1906- . See: B(urton) S(eely) Keirstead, 1907- .

CAMPBELL, SIR GILBERT (EDWARD). 1838-1899.
  A Fair Freelance. Routledge, 1891
  -From Shadow to Light. Ward, 1889
  The Mystery of Mandeville Square. Ward, 1888
  New Detective Stories. Ward, 1891 ss
  -The Romance of the Ruby. Ward, 1891. U.S. title: A Ruby Beyond Price. Minerva, 1891
  A Ruby Beyond Price; see The Romance of the Ruby
  The Vanishing Diamond. Ward, 1891
  Wild and Weird; or, Remarkable Stories of Russia. Ward, 1889 ss, some criminous [Russ.]

CAMPBELL, HARRIETTE R(USSELL). 1883- .
  Ref: CC, MP. Born in N.Y., the daughter of the state's attorney-general; married a Scotsman and settled in London. SC: Simon Brade = SB.
  Crime in Crystal. Harper, 1946 SB [Eng.]
  Magic Makes Murder. Harper, 1943 SB [Eng.]
  The Moor Fires Mystery. Harper, 1939; Heinemann, 1938 SB [Eng.]
  Murder Set to Music. Harper, 1941 SB [Eng.]
  The Porcelain Fish Mystery. Knopf, 1937. British title: The Porcelain Fish. Heinemann, 1937 SB [Eng.]
  The String Glove Mystery. Knopf, 1936; Heinemann, 1936 SB [Eng.]
  Three Lost Ladies. Heinemann, 1949
  Three Names for Murder. Harper, 1940; Collins, 1940 SB

CAMPBELL, HAZEL
  The Burqa. Long, 1930
  The Makra Mystery. Long, 1931
  Olga Knaresbrook, Detective. Long, 1933
  -The Secret Brotherhood. Long, 1929 [India]
  -The Servants of the Goddess. Long, 1928

CAMPBELL, JEFFREY. Joint pseudonym of Jeffrey (Andrew) Caine, 1944- , q.v., and Campbell Black, 1944- , q.v. Pseudonym of Campbell Black alone: Thomas Altman, q.v.
  The Homing. Putnam, 1980; Joseph, 1980 [N.Y.]

CAMPBELL, KAREN. Pseudonym of Betty Beaty, 1922- . Ref: CA.
  The Bells of St. Martin. Eyre, 1979
  The Brocken Spectre; see Suddenly, in the Air.
  Death Descending. Collins, 1976; Stein, 1977
  Suddenly, in the Air. Collins, 1969; Stein, 1969. Also published as: The Brocken Spectre. Fontana, 1972 [air.]
  Thunder on Sunday. Collins, 1972; Bobbs, 1972 [Hebrides]
  Wheel Fortune. Collins, 1973. U.S. title: The Wheel of Fortune. Bobbs, 1973
  The Wheel of Fortune; see Wheel Fortune

CAMPBELL, KEITH. Pseudonym of Keith Campbell West-Watson. SC: Mike Brett = MB.
  Born Beautiful. Macdonald, 1951 MB
  The Broken Branch. Rich, 1944
  Darling, Don't. Macdonald, 1950 MB
  Goodbye Gorgeous. Macdonald, 1947 MB
  The Last Journey. Rich, 1941
  Listen, Lovely. Macdonald, 1949 MB
  Pardon My Gun. Macdonald, 1954 MB
  That Was No Lady. Macdonald, 1942 MB

CAMPBELL, SIR MALCOLM. 1885-1948.
  Salute to the Gods. Cassell, 1934; Putnam, 1935
  -Thunder Ahead. Cassell, 1934

CAMPBELL, MARGARET. Pseudonym of Gabrielle Margaret Vere Campbell Long, 1886-1952. Other pseudonyms: Marjorie Bowen, George Preedy, Joseph Shearing, qq.v. For titles (re)published under the Margaret Campbell byline, see: Joseph Shearing.

CAMPBELL, MARGARET ELIZABETH BAIRD. Joint pseudonym of Johanna Frederika Jansen: Fred Bayard, q.v.

CAMPBELL, MARY E(LIZABETH). 1903- . Born in Ohio; obtained Ph.D. from Yale and became a member of the English department at Indiana U.
  Scandal Has Two Faces. Doubleday, 1943 [Ohio, acad.]
  The White Hand Murder Mystery. Renaissance, 1936

CAMPBELL, PATRICIA. 1901- .
  Cedarhaven. Macmillan, 1965 [Wash., 1859]

CAMPBELL, R. T. Pseudonym of Ruthven Todd, 1914- . Ref: CA, CC, MC. SC: Prof. John Stubbs = JS. Set: Eng.
  Adventure with a Goat. Westhouse, 1946 JS
  Apollo Wore a Wig. Westhouse, 1946
  Bodies in a Bookshop. Westhouse, 1946 JS
  The Death Cap. Westhouse, 1946 JS
  Death for Madame. Westhouse, 1946 JS
  Swing Low, Sweet Death. Westhouse, 1946 JS
  Take Thee a Sharp Knife. Westhouse, 1946 JS
  Unholy Dying. Westhouse, 1945 JS

CAMPBELL, R(OBERT) WRIGHT. 1927- . Ref: CA.
  Circus Couronne. Putnam, 1977 [Switz., 1914]
  Killer of Kings. Bobbs, 1979; Sidgwick, 1980 [L.A.]
  The Spy Who Sat and Waited. Putnam, 1975; Weidenfeld, 1975 [Scot.]

CAMPBELL, (JOHN) RAMSEY. 1946- . Ref: CA.
  The Doll Who Ate His Mother. Bobbs, 1976; Millington, 1978 [Eng.]

CAMPBELL, REGINALD (WILFRID). 1894-1950. See also: Peter Motte.
  The Abominable Twilight. Cassell, 1948
  The Admiralty Regrets—. Cassell, 1937
  The Bangkok Murders. Cassell, 1939 [Bangkok]
  Brainstorm. Cassell, 1950
  Coffin for a Murderer. Cassell, 1947
  Cruiser in Action. Cassell, 1940
  Death by Apparition. Cassell, 1949
  -Death in Tiger Valley. Hodder, 1931
  -Fear in the Forest. Hodder, 1932
  The Haunting of Kathleen Saunders. Cassell, 1938

-The King's Enemies. Chapman, 1927
Married into Murder. Cassell, 1951
Murder of My Wife. Cassell, 1952
Murder She Says!, with Peter Motte. Cassell, 1952
-Striped Majesty. Heinemann, 1947
-This Animal Is Dangerous. Hodder, 1934
-Uneasy Virtue. Chapman, 1926

CAMPBELL, RONALD
Marked for Murder. Hammond, 1958

CAMPBELL, SCOTT. Pseudonym of Frederick William Davis, 1858-1933. SC: Felix Boyd = FB.
The Adventures of Felix Boyd. Street (New Magnet #603), 1909 FB ss
A Battle of Wits. Street (Magnet #449), 190?
Below the Dead-Line. Street (Magnet #428), 1906 ss FB [NYC]
A Bid for Life. Street (Magnet #373), 190?
The Doctor's Secret; or, The Shadow on the Wall. Street (Magnet #170), 1901
Driven to the Wall; or, A Forced Confession. Street (Magnet #154), 1897
Exploits of a Private Detective. Street (New Magnet #591), 1909 ss FB
The Fate of Austin Craige. Street (Magnet #190), 190?
Felix Boyd's Final Problems. Street (New Magnet #627), 1909 ss FB
Felix Boyd's Revelations. Street (New Magnet #615), 1909 ss FB
The Honor of a Black Sheep. Street (Magnet #173), 190?
The Links in the Chain; or, Who Killed Judge Noble? Street (Magnet #167), 190?
The Lion of the Law; or, The Helena Street Puzzle. Street (Magnet #154), 190?
The Man Outside. Street (Magnet #181), 1901
On the Trail of "Big Finger". Street (Magnet #429), 1906 ss FB
A Plot for Millions; or, A Game of Cross Purposes. Street (Magnet #161), 1900
The Red Stain. Street (Magnet #404), 190?
The Reporter's Triumph; or, The Mystery of the Missing Bride. Street (Magnet) #164), 1900
Sealed Lips. Street (Magnet #195), 190?
A Supernatural Clue. Street (Magnet #185), 190?
The Tragedy of Ascot Mills. Street (Magnet #176), 190?
An Unexpected Move. Street (Magnet #355), 190?
Union Down; A Signal of Distress. Arena, 1893
Woman in Red. Street (Magnet #335), 190?

CAMPBELL, MRS. VERE [JOSEPHINE ELISABETH CAMPBELL]
The Crime of Keziah Keene. Ward, 1889
-The Master Schemer. Greening, 1909
-Of This Death. Ward, 1891

CAMPBELL, WALTER STANLEY. 1887-1957. Pseudonym: Stanley Vestal, q.v.

CAMPBELL, WILLIAM EDWARD MARCH. 1894-1954. Pseudonym: William March, q.v.

CAMPDEN, JOHN
The Hundredth Acre. Ward, 1906 [Paris]

CAMPERT, REMCO (WOUTER). 1929- .
The Gangster Girl. Hart-Davis, 1968 (Translation of "Het Gangstermeisje." Amsterdam, 1968.)

CAMPION, CYRIL (THERON). 1894- .
Ladies in Waiting. French (London), 1934 (3-act play.)
Madeleine. French (London), 1949 (2-act play.)

CAMPION, PETER. Set: Eng.
Diamonds Worth a Death or Two. Arco, 1955
Model for Murder. Arco, 1955

CAMPION, SARAH. Pseudonym of Mary Rose Coulton.
Unhandsome Corpse. Davies, 1938

CAMPTON, DAVID. 1924- . Ref: CA.
Laughter and Fear. Blackie, 1969 (Nine 1-act plays, some criminous.)
The Lunatic View. Studio Theatre, 1960 (Plays.)
Mutatis Mutandis. (Author), 1967

CANADAY, JOHN EDWIN. 1907- . Pseudonym: Matthew Head, q.v.

CANARY, GLEN
The Perfect Plot. Pinnacle, 1974
A Walk in the Jungle. Pinnacle, 1975

CANAWAY, W(ILLIAM) H(AMILTON). 1925- . Ref: CA.
The Solid Gold Buddha. Hutchinson, 1979
Trouble Trip. Panther, 1976
The Willow-Pattern War. Hutchinson, 1976

CANDY, EDWARD. Pseudonym of Barbara Alison Boodson Neville, 1925- . Ref: CA, CC, TC. SC: Insp. Burnivel = B.
Bones of Contention. Gollancz, 1954; Doubleday, 1983 B
Scene Changing. Gollancz, 1977
Which Doctor? Gollancz, 1953; Rinehart, 1954 B [hosp.]
Words for Murder Perhaps. Gollancz, 1971 [acad.]

CANE, BEVIS
-The Haunted Tower. Blackett, 1888
The Missing Man. Eglington, 1889

CANELSTEIN, HARRY
A Dull Tree. Vantage, 1970

CANFIELD, MIRIAM. Pseudonym of Dorothy Fletcher, q.v.
The Tuscany Madonna. Lancer, 1965 [Fr.]

CANLER, M. (LOUIS). 1797-1865.
Autobiography of a French Detective. Ward, 1862. U.S. title (?): Memoirs of a Veteran Detective. Munro, 1882 (Translation of "Memoires de Canlet, Ancien Chef du Service de Surete." Paris, 1862.) ss [Fr.]

CANNAN, JOANNA. Pseudonym of Joanna Maxwell Cannan Pullein-Thompson, 1898-1961. Ref: CC, TC. SC: Insp. Guy Northeast = GN; Insp. Ronald Price = RP. Set: Eng.
All Is Discovered. Gollancz, 1962 RP
And Be a Villain. Gollancz, 1958 RP
Body in the Beck. Gollancz, 1952 RP
Death at the Dog. Gollancz, 1940; Reynal, 1941 GN
Frightened Angels. Gollancz, 1936; Harper, 1936
A Hand to Burn. Hodder, 1936
-The Hills Sleep On. Hodder, 1935
Long Shadows. Gollancz, 1955 RP
Murder Included. Gollancz, 1950. U.S. title: Poisonous Relations. Morrow, 1950. Also published as: The Taste of Murder. Dell, 1951 RP
No Walls of Jasper. Benn, 1930; Doubleday, 1931
Orphan of Mars; see The Simple Pass On
Poisonous Relations; see Murder Included
The Simple Pass On. Benn, 1929. U.S. title: Orphan of Mars. Bobbs, 1930
The Taste of Murder; see Murder Included
They Rang Up the Police. Gollancz, 1939 GN
Under Proof. Hodder, 1934

CANNELL, CHARLES. Pseudonym of E(velyn) Charles (H.) Vivian, 1882-1947, q.v. Other pseudonym: Jack Mann, q.v.
-And the Devil. Lane, 1931
-Ash. Hutchinson, 1925
-Barker's Drift. Hutchinson, 1924
The Guarded Woman. Hutchinson, 1923
-The Guardian of the Cup. Hodder, 1925
-The Passionless Quest. Hodder, 1926

CANNELL, J(OHN) C(LUCAS)
100 Mysteries for Arm-Chair Detectives. Long, 1932 quiz ss

CANNING, VICTOR. 1911- . Ref: CA, CC, EM, TC. SC: Rex Carver = RC.
Bird of Prey; see Venetian Bird
Birdcage. Heinemann, 1978; Morrow, 1979
Black Flamingo. Hodder, 1962; Sloane, 1963 [Bel. Congo]
Burden of Proof; see Hidden Face
The Burning Eye. Hodder, 1960; Sloane, 1960
The Captives of Mora Island; see The Dragon Tree
Castle Minerva. Hodder, 1955. U.S. title: A Handful of Silver. Sloane, 1954 [Fr.]
The Chasm. Hodder, 1947; Mill, 1947 [It.]
A Delivery of Furies. Hodder, 1961; Sloane, 1961 [Carib.]
-The Doomsday Carrier. Heinemann, 1976; Morrow, 1977
Doubled in Diamonds. Heinemann, 1966; Morrow, 1967 RC
The Dragon Tree. Hodder, 1958; Sloane, 1958. Also published as: The Captives of Mora Island. Permabooks, 1959
Fall from Grace. Heinemann, 1980; Morrow, 1981
Family Plot; see The Rainbird Pattern
The Finger of Saturn. Heinemann, 1973; Morrow, 1974
Firecrest. Heinemann, 1971; Morrow, 1972
The Forbidden Road; see The Manasco Road
A Forest of Eyes. Hodder, 1950; Mill, 1950 [Yugos.]
The Golden Salamander. Hodder, 1949; Mill, 1949 [Afr., N.]
The Great Affair. Heinemann, 1970; Morrow, 1971
A Handful of Silver; see Castle Minerva
Hidden Face. Hodder, 1956. U.S. title: Burden of Proof. Sloane, 1956
His Bones Are Coral. Hodder, 1955. U.S. title: Twist of the Knife. Sloane, 1955 [Mid. East]
The House of the Seven Flies. Hodder, 1952; Mill, 1952 [Holl.]
The Kingsford Mark. Heinemann, 1975; Morrow, 1976
The Limbo Line. Heinemann, 1963; Sloane, 1964 [Fr.]
The Man from the Turkish Slave. Hodder, 1954; Sloane, 1954 [Brazil]
The Manasco Road. Hodder, 1957; Sloane, 1957. Also published as: The Forbidden Road. Permabocks, 1959 [Maj.]
The Mask of Memory. Heinemann, 1974; Morrow, 1975
The Melting Man. Heinemann, 1968; Morrow, 1969 RC [Fr.]
Oasis Nine; see Young Man on a Bicycle
Panther's Moon. Hodder, 1948; Mill, 1948 [Switz.]
The Python Project. Heinemann, 1967; Morrow, 1968 RC
Queen's Pawn. Heinemann, 1969; Morrow, 1970
The Rainbird Pattern. Heinemann, 1972; Morrow, 1973. Also published as: Family Plot. Award, 1976
The Satan Sampler. Heinemann, 1979; Morrow, 1980
The Scorpio Letters. Heinemann, 1964; Sloane, 1964 [Fr.]
Twist of the Knife; see His Bones Are Coral
Venetian Bird. Hodder, 1951. U.S. title: Bird of Prey. Mill, 1951 [Venice]
The Whip Hand. Heinemann, 1965; Sloane, 1965 RC
Young Man on a Bicycle. Hodder, 1958. U.S. title: Oasis Nine. Sloane, 1959 (4 novelets.)

CANNON, CURT. Pseudonym of Evan Hunter, 1926- , q.v. Other pseudonyms: Hunt Collins, Ezra Hannon, Ed McBain, Richard Marsten, qq.v. SC: Curt Cannon, in both titles.
I Like 'Em Tough. GM, 1958 ss [NYC]
I'm Cannon—for Hire. GM, 1958; Fawcett (London), 1959 [NYC]

CANNON, ELLIOTT. Pseudonym of Arthur Elliott-Cannon. Other pseudonym: Nicholas Forde, q.v. SC: Guy Fosse, in at least those marked GF.
The Big Chip. Hale, 1976 GF
Breakaway. Hale, 1973
Dead Reckoning. Hale, 1978
Dead-Ringer. Hale, 1980
Devil's Paradise. Hale, 1979
The Dumbo Dossier. Hale, 1975 GF
The Edge of Hate. Hale, 1979
Element of Risk. Hale, 1975
A Foe to Sleep. Hale, 1980
If You Can't Be Good. Hale, 1979
A Kind of Nightmare. Hale, 1975
A Nice Guy Like Me. Hale, 1977
A Piece of Action. Hale, 1973
A Sense of Danger. Hale, 1973
Stand By to Shoot. Hale, 1973
The Tin Soldier. Hale, 1978
The Treachery Trade. Hale, 1977
The V2 Virus. Hale, 1980

CANNON, FRANK
Hide in Hell. Vega, 1964
Satan in Malibu. Vega, 1963

CANON, JACK. Pseudonym: Nick Carter, q.v. SC: Mike Paradise in all titles.
An Angel for Paradise. Charter, 1979
A Hangman for Paradise. Charter, 1980
No Love for Paradise. Charter, 1979

CANYON, CLAUDIA. Pseudonym of Betty Anderson.
The Junior League Murders. Arcadia, 1954 [Wis.]

CAPEK, KAREL. 1890-1938. Ref: CA, CC.
Tales from Two Pockets. Faber, 1932; Macmillan, 1943 ss

CAPELLI, ACE
   Chicago Payoff. Gaywood, 1949 [Chi.]
   The Double Cross. Gaywood, 1950
   Frisco Hi-Jack. Gaywood, 1950 [S.F.]
   Get Me Headquarters. Kaye, 1949
   Never Turn Your Back. Gaywood, 1950
   This Man Is Death. Gaywood, 1949

CAPES, BERNARD (EDWARD JOSEPH). -1918. Ref: CC, MC. Set: Eng.
   Bag and Baggage. Constable, 1913 ss, some criminous
   The Fabulists. Mills, 1915 ss, some criminous
   Gilead Balm, Knight Errant. Unwin, 1911; Baker, 1911 ss
   The Great Skene Mystery. Methuen, 1907
   -The Green Parrot. Smith Elder, 1918
   The House of Many Voices. Unwin, 1911
   The Lake of Wine. Heinemann, 1898
   Loaves and Fishes. Methuen, 1906 ss
   The Mill of Silence. Long, 1902; Rand, 1897
   The Mystery of the Skeleton Key; see The Skeleton Key
   -Our Lady of Darkness. Blackwood, 1899; Dodd, 1899
   A Rogue's Tragedy. Methuen, 1906
   The Secret in the Hill. Elder, 1903
   The Skeleton Key. Collins, 1919. U.S. title: The Mystery of the Skeleton Key. Doran, 1918. Reprinted in Britain under the U.S. title: Collins, 1929
   The Vanishing Cheques. Daily Mail, 1904
   Why Did He Do It? Methuen, 1910; Brentano's, 1910
   The Will and the Way. Murray, 1910

CAPETO, ISABEL. Pseudonym: Isabel Cabot, q.v.
   A Few Drops of Murder. Arcadia, 1955 [Boston]

CAPIT, ELINE
   Run from the Sheep. Arcadia, 1955

CAPOCY, EDWARD J., SR.
   House of Death. Vantage, 1977

CAPON, (HARRY) PAUL. 1912-1969. Ref: CA, CC. SC: Arnold "Tiger" Wragge, in at least those marked AW.
   -Amongst Those Missing. Heinemann, 1959 [Guy.]
   Battered Caravanserai. Heinemann, 1942
   -Brother Cain. Heinemann, 1945
   Dead Man's Chest. Nicholson, 1947 AW
   Death at Singlestrand. Ward, 1951
   Death on a Wet Sunday. Ward, 1952
   Delay of Doom. Ward, 1952
   The Hosts of Midian. Nicholson, 1946 AW
   Image of a Murder. Boardman, 1949 AW
   -In All Simplicity. Heinemann, 1953
   Malice Domestic. Ward, 1954
   Margin of Terror. Ward, 1955
   The Murder of Jacob Canansey. Heinemann, 1947
   No Time for Death. Ward, 1951
   -O Clouds Unfold. Ward, 1948
   The Seventh Passenger. Ward, 1953
   Thirty Days Hath September. Ward, 1955
   -Threescore Years. Ward, 1950
   -Toby Scuffell. Ward, 1949

CAPOTE, TRUMAN. 1924-   . Ref: CA.
   In Cold Blood. Random, 1965; H. Hamilton, 1966
   Music for Chameleons. Random, 1980; H. Hamilton, 1981 sketches and ss, at least one criminous

"CAPSTAN." Pseudonym of Rex Hardinge, 1904-   , q.v.
   Black Magic. Wright, 1941
   Broadcast Murder. Mellifont, 1939 (64 pp.)
   Cap'n Luke, Filibuster. Wright, 1937
   Carver of the Swamp. Wright, 1938
   The Chinese Cabinet. Mellifont, 1941 (48 pp.)
   The Feud. Wright, 1950
   Forbidden Territory. Wright, 1949
   The Hole in the Mountain. Wright, 1939
   Inkosi-Carver Investigates. Wright, 1943 [Mali]
   Murder of a Musician. Brown Watson, 1949
   The Night Coach. Mellifont, 1938
   Operation Diamond. Wright, 1951
   The Polite Pirate. Wright, 1938
   The Problem in Ciphers. Wright, 1952

CARANE, MICHAEL
   Why Jane Matcham Disappeared. Ward, 1907

CARBALLIDO, EMILIO. 1925-   . Ref: CA.
   The Golden Thread, and other plays. U. of Texas, 1970 (Plays, one criminous.)

CARCO, FRANCIS. Pseudonym of Francis Carcopino-Tusoli, 1886-1958.
   The Noose of Sin. Cape, 1923. U.S. title: The Hounded Man. Seltzer, 1924 (Translation of "L'Homme Traque." Paris, 1922.) [Paris]

CARCOPINO-TUSOLI, FRANCIS. 1886-1958. Pseudonym: Francis Carco, q.v.

CARDEN, PERCY T(HEODORE)
   The Murder of Edwin Drood. Palmer, 1920; Putnam, 1920 (Completion of "The Mystery of Edwin Drood" by Charles Dickens, 1812-1870, q.v.)

CARDIFF, SARA. Joint pseudonym of Rebecca Kavalier, Louise DeCormier, and Gloria Kirchheimer.
   The Bonaparte Kiss. GM, 1979
   Fool's Apple. Random, 1971 [Mass.]
   The Inner Steps. Random, 1973 [NYC]
   The Severing Line. Random, 1974 [Vt.]
   The Speaking Stones. Coward, 1976 [Calif.]

CARDWELL, ANN. Pseudonym of Jean Powley.
   Crazy to Kill. Mystery House, 1941
   Murder at Calamity House. Arcadia, 1947

CARE, B.
   Lever's Folly. Drane, 1910

CAREW, CHARLES
   The Poacher's Wife. Ollier, 1849

CAREW, DUDLEY. 1903-1981(?)
   The Puppet's Part. Home, 1948

CAREW, HENRY
   -The Secret of the Sphinx. Hodder, 1923
   -The Vampire of the Andes. Hodder, 1925

CAREW, JACK
   The Secret of the Stargazer's Club. Aldine, 1926

CAREW, JEAN. Pseudonym of Jane (Irenita) Corby, 1899-   , q.v. Other pseudonyms: Joanne Holden, q.v., Laura Brighton.
   Samantha. Arcadia, 1966. Also published as: Terror at Bramble Tor. Magnum, 197?

CAREY, ALFRED EDWARD
   -Sealed Orders. Greening, 1909
   -Time's Hour Glass. Greening, 1914

CAREY, BASIL
   -Captain Christine. Jarrolds, 192
   The Dangerous Isles. Constable, 1926; Dial, 1927 [Indon.]
   Dead Man's Shadow. Constable, 1931. U.S. title(?): Isle of Desire. Clode, 1931 [S. Pac.]
   -The Dreaming God. Constable, 1927
   Gray Amber. Clode, 1930 (British title?)
   Isle of Desire; see Dead Man's Shadow
   Left for Dead. Jarrolds, 1934
   -Mountain Gold. Constable, 1929; Clode, 1930
   The Secret Enterprise. Jarrolds, 1932
   -The Secret of Ayanora. Hale, 1937
   -Secret Voyage. King, 1933 (British title?)

CAREY, BERNICE. 1910-   . Set: Calif., in all titles.
   The Beautiful Stranger. Doubleday, 1951
   The Body on the Sidewalk. Doubleday, 1950
   The Fatal Picnic. Doubleday, 1955
   The Frightened Widow; see Their Nearest and Dearest
   The Man Who Got Away with It. Doubleday, 1950
   The Missing Heiress. Doubleday, 1952
   The Reluctant Murderer. Doubleday, 1949
   Their Nearest and Dearest. Doubleday, 1953. Also published as: The Frightened Widow. Mercury, 1954, abridged
   The Three Widows. Doubleday, 1952

CAREY, CHARLES. Pseudonym of C(harles) C(arey) Waddell, 1868-1930, q.v.
   The Van Suyden Sapphires. Dodd, 1905. British title: The Motor Cracksman. Unwin, 1905

CAREY, CONSTANCE
   The Chekhov Proposal. Putnam, 1975 [Mass.]

CAREY, DONNELL
   Kisses Can Kill. Phantom, 1951

CAREY, DOUGLAS
   The Raven's Feathers. Graphic (Ottawa), 1930
   The Scorpion. Graphic (Ottawa), 1931

CAREY, ELIZABETH. Joint pseudonym with Marion Austin White Magoon, 1885-   : Carey Magoon, q.v.

CAREY, HELEN A. See: Douglas Stapleton, 1904-   .

CAREY, JOHN B.
   The Oddities of Short-Hand; or, The Coroner and His Friends. Excelsior, 1891 ss

CAREY, MICHAEL. Pseudonym of Edward J. Burton, 1917-   . Ref: CA.
   The Vice Net. Avon, 1958
   Vice Squad Cop. Avon, 1957 [NYC]

CAREY, ROSA NOUCHETTE. 1840-1890. Pseudonym: Le Voleur, q.v.
   -Barbara Heathcote's Trial. Bentley, 1883; Munro, 1885
   -The Search for Basil Lyndhurst. Bentley, 1889; Lovell, 1889

CAREY, WEBSTER. SC: Sheriff Buford Pusser (see also W. R. Morris).
   Walking Tall: Part 2. Bantam, 1975 (Novelization of the movie.) [Tenn.]

CAREY, WYMOND
   "No. 101." Putnam, 1905; Blackwood, 1906

CARFAX, CATHERINE. Pseudonym of Eleanor Fairburn, 1928-   . Ref: CA.
   The Locked Tower; see To Die a Little
   The Semper Inheritance. Hale, 1972
   A Silence with Voices. Macmillan (London), 1969
   The Sleeping Salamander. Macmillan (London), 1973; Stein, 1973 [Fr.]
   To Die a Little. Hale, 1974. U.S. title: The Locked Tower. GM, 1974

CARGILL, LESLIE. Ref: CC. SC: Major Mosson, in at least those marked M; Morrison Sharpe, in at least those marked MS. Set: Eng.
   Beyond the Frontiers. Jenkins, 1940
   Cherry's Choice. Pemberton, 1948
   Death Goes by Bus. Jenkins, 1936 MS
   Death Sets the Pace. Jenkins, 1950
   Death Walks in Scarlet. Jenkins, 1941
   Fortune's Apprentice. Jenkins, 1946
   Gestapo Gauntlet. Jenkins, 1939
   Heads You Lose. Jenkins, 1938 MS
   It Might Have Meant Murder. Jenkins, 1940 M
   The Lady Was Elusive. Jenkins, 1952 [Ger.]
   The Man from the Rhine. Jenkins, 1943
   The Man Who Wasn't Himself. Jenkins, 1947
   Matrimony Most Dangerous. Jenkins, 1949; Roy, 1958
   The Missing Background. Jenkins, 1942 M
   Motley Menace. Jenkins, 1949
   Murder in the Procession. Jenkins, 1937 M
   Next Door to Murder. Jenkins, 1948 M
   The Surprising Sanctuary. Jenkins, 1945
   Was It Montelli? Jenkins, 1947
   The Yellow Phantom. Fiction House, 1935

CARGILL, MORRIS. 1914-   . Joint pseudonym with John Hearne, 1926-   : John Morris, q.v.

CARHART, ARTHUR HAWTHORNE. 1892-   . Pseudonym: V. A. Van Sickle, q.v.

CARIN, MICHAEL. 1951-   .
   Five Hundred Keys. Deneau (Ottawa), 1980

CARKEET, DAVID. 1946-   . Ref: CA.
   Double Negative. Dial, 1980 [Ind.]

CARLE, C. E. Joint pseudonym with Dean M. Dorn: Michael Morgan, q.v.

CARLETON, COUSIN MAY. Pseudonym of May Agnes Fleming, 1840-1880, q.v. Other pseudonym: M(ay) A(gnes) Earlie, q.v.
   La Masque; or, The Midnight Queen. Brady, 1863

CARLETON, MARJORIE (CHALMERS). 1897-1964. Ref: CC. Writer of ss and radio scripts; composer; lived near Boston.
   The Bride Regrets. Morrow, 1950; Joseph, 1951 (Novel is based on an earlier play of the same title, published by Baker in 1944.) [New Eng.]
   Cry Wolf. Morrow, 1945. Also published as: The Demarest Inheritance. Pyramid, 196? [Boston]
   The Demarest Inheritance; see Cry Wolf
   Dread the Sunset. Morrow, 1962; Joseph, 1963. Also published as: Shadows on the Hill. Pyramid, 1966

The Night of the Good Children. Morrow,
  1957; Joseph, 1958. Also published
  as: One Night of Terror. Pyramid,
  1970
One Night of Terror; see The Night of
  the Good Children
Shadows on the Hill; see Dread the Sunset
The Swan Sang Once. Morrow, 1947; Joseph, 1948 [Mass.]
Their Dusty Hands. Brimmer, 1924
Vanished. Morrow, 1955 [Boston]

CARLETON, S. Pseudonym of Susan Carleton
  Jones, 1864- .
  The LaChance Mine Mystery. Little,
    1920; Duckworth, 1921 [Can.]

CARLING, JOHN R.
  -The Shadow of the Czar. Little, 1902;
    Ward, 1902
  -The Viking's Skull. Little, 1904; Ward,
    1904
  The Weird Picture. Little, 1905; Ward,
    1905 [Switz.]

CARLINO, LEWIS JOHN. 1932- . Ref: CA.
  The Brotherhood. Signet, 1968 (Noveli-
    zation of the movie.)
  The Mechanic. Signet, 1972 (Noveliza-
    tion of the movie.)

CARLISLE, D. M. Pseudonym of Dorothy
  Mary Cook, 1907- . Ref: CA.
  Althea's Falcon. Barker, 1974

CARLISLE, HELEN GRACE. 1898- .
  The Tiger Sniffs the Rose. Doubleday,
    1958

CARLISLE, HENRY (COFFIN). 1926- .
  The Contract. Bobbs, 1968

CARLISLE, RILLA. Pseudonym of Anne
  (Louise) Coulter Martens, 1906- ,
  q.v. Other pseudonyms: Jane Kendall,
  Ann Reynolds, qq.v.
  The Black Ghost. Dramatic, 1945
    (3-act play.)

CARLON, PATRICIA (BERNADETTE). Ref: CA.
  SC: Jefferson Shields, in at least
  those marked JS.
  Betray Me--If You Dare. Hodder, 1966
  Circle of Fear. Ward, 1961
  Crime of Silence. Ward, 1965
  Danger in the Dark. Ward, 1962
  Death by Demonstration. Hodder, 1970 JS
  Forty Pieces of Alloy. Hodder, 1968
    [Australia]
  Hush, It's a Game. Hodder, 1967
  The Price of an Orphan. Hodder, 1964
  The Running Woman. Hodder, 1966
  See Nothing--Say Nothing. Hodder, 1967;
    Walker, 1968
  The Souvenir. Hodder, 1970 JS
  The Unquiet Night. Hodder, 1965
  The Whispering Wall. Hodder, 1969
  Who Are You, Linda Condrick? Ward, 1962

CARLSON, NATALIE (SAVAGE). 1906- . Ref:
  CA.
  Old Murders Never Die. Arcadia, 1960

CARLTON, LEWIS. ca.1886- . All titles
  were published by Amalgamated Press
  and feature Sexton Blake.
  The Case of the Stranded Touring Com-
    pany. 1933
  The Monomark Mystery. 1928
  The Night Safe Mystery. 1932

CARLTON, LIEUT.
  The Arm of the Law. Street, ca.1900
  After the Bribe Takers. Street, ca.1900
  The Bank Note Plates. Street, ca.1900
  The Corridor of Death. Street, ca.1900
  A Counterfeiter's Wake. Street, ca.1900
  A Government Spy. Street, ca.1900
  The Haunt of the "Queen Makers."
    Street, ca.1900
  The Man in Mail. Street, ca.1900
  The Man in Stripes. Street, ca.1900
  The Man with a Gun. Street, ca.1900
  The Moonshiner's Dupe. Street, ca.1900
  The Pirate's Retreat. Street, ca.1900
  The Poisoned Arrow. Street, ca.1900

CARLTON, JOSEPH. Pseudonym of J(oseph)
  C(arl) McMullen, 1882- , q.v.
  See also: Robert C. Schimmel.
  Ladies in Danger. Baker, 1945 (3-act
    play.)

CARLTON, MITCHELL
  Hot Oil. Belmont, 1980 [Tex.]

CARLYLE, ANTHONY. Pseudonym of Gladys
  Alexandra Milton.
  Children of Chance. Mills, 1923;
    Houghton, 1923
  Cock Crow. Hodder, 1930

The Fugitive Millionaire; see The
  Tavern and the Arrows
The Law of Nemesis. Mills, 1924
The Tavern and the Arrows. Mills, 1922.
  U.S. title: The Fugitive Millionaire.
  Houghton, 1922
A Vow of Vengeance. Mellifont, 1940

CARMACK, JESSE
  The Tell-Tale Clock Mystery. Stokes,
    1937 [Tenn.]

CARMEL, KATHLEEN
  "S-S-S-Sh!" Nicholson, 1948

CARMICHAEL, ARCHIBALD
  Personal Adventures of a Detective.
    Morison, 1892 ss

CARMICHAEL, FRED(ERICK WALKER). 1924- .
  Ref: CA. All titles are plays, with
  the number of acts in parenthesis.
  All the Better to Kill You. French
    (NYC), 1968 (2)
  Any Number Can Die. French (NYC), 1965
    (3)
  The Best Laid Plans. French (NYC), 1966
    (2)
  Done to Death. French (NYC), 1971 (2)
  Double in Diamonds. French (NYC), 1967
    (2) [Bahamas]
  Exit the Body. French (NYC), 1962 (3)
    [New Eng.]
  Foiled by an Innocent Mind; or, The
    Curse of the Iron Horse. French
    (NYC), 1977
  Inside Lester. French (NYC), 1955 (3)
  The Night Is My Enemy. French (NYC),
    1956 (3) [Eng.]
  The Pen Is Deadlier. French (NYC), 1960
    (3) [L.A.]
  The Robin Hood Caper. French (NYC),
    1963 (3)
  Victoria's House. French (NYC), 1969
    (2)

CARMICHAEL, HARRY. Pseudonym of Leopold
  Horace Ognall, 1908-1979. Other pseu-
  donym: Hartley Howard, q.v. Ref:
  CA, CC, TC. SC: John Piper = JP,
  and/or Quinn = Q, in virtually all
  titles and certainly in those so
  marked. Set: Eng.
  Alibi. Collins, 1961; Macmillan, 1962
    JP,Q
  Candles for the Dead. Collins, 1973;
    Saturday Review Press, 1976 JP,Q
  The Condemned. Collins, 1967
  Confession. Collins, 1961
  The Dead of the Night. Collins, 1956
    JP,Q
  Deadly Night-Cap. Collins, 1953 JP,Q
  Death Counts Three. Collins, 1954. U.S.
    title: The Screaming Rabbit. Simon,
    1955 JP
  Death Leaves a Diary. Collins, 1952
    JP,Q
  Death Trap. Collins, 1970; McCall, 1971
    JP,Q
  Emergency Exit. Collins, 1957 JP
  False Evidence. Collins, 1976; Dutton,
    1977 JP,Q
  Flashback. Collins, 1964 JP,Q
  A Grave for Two. Collins, 1977 JP,Q
  Into Thin Air; see Put Out That Star
  James Knowland: Deceased. Collins, 1958
    JP,Q
  Justice Enough. Collins, 1956 JP,Q
  The Late Unlamented; see Requiem for
    Charles
  Life Cycle. Collins, 1978 JP,Q
  The Link. Collins, 1962 JP,Q
  Marked Man; see Stranglehold
  Money for Murder. Collins, 1955 JP,Q
  Most Deadly Hate. Collins, 1971; Sat-
    urday Review Press, 1974 JP,Q
  The Motive. Collins, 1974; Dutton, 1977
    JP,Q
  Murder by Proxy. Collins, 1967 JP,Q
  Naked to the Grave. Collins, 1972;
    Saturday Review Press, 1973 JP,Q
  Noose for a Lady. Collins, 1955 JP,Q
  Of Unsound Mind. Collins, 1962; Double-
    day, 1962 JP,Q
  ...Or Be He Dead. Collins, 1959;
    Doubleday, 1958 JP,Q
  Post Mortem. Collins, 1965; Doubleday,
    1966 JP,Q
  Put Out That Star. Collins, 1957. U.S.
    title: Into Thin Air. Doubleday, 1958
    JP,Q
  A Question of Time. Collins, 1958
  The Quiet Woman. Collins, 1971; Satur-
    day Review Press, 1972 JP,Q
  Remote Control. Collins, 1970; McCall,
    1971 JP,Q
  Requiem for Charles. Collins, 1960.
    U.S. title: The Late Unlamented.
    Doubleday, 1961 JP,Q
  Safe Secret. Collins, 1964; Macmillan,
    1965 JP,Q
  School for Murder. Collins, 1953 JP

The Screaming Rabbit; see Death Counts
  Three
The Seeds of Hate. Collins, 1960 JP,Q
A Slightly Bitter Taste. Collins, 1968
  Q
Stranglehold. Collins, 1959. U.S.
  title: Marked Man. Doubleday, 1959
  JP,Q
Suicide Clause. Collins, 1966 JP,Q
Too Late for Tears. Collins, 1973; Sat-
  urday Review Press, 1975 JP,Q
The Vanishing Trick. Collins, 1952 JP
Vendetta. Collins, 1963; Macmillan,
  1963 JP,Q
Why Kill Johnny? Collins, 1954 JP,Q

CARNAC, CAROL. Pseudonym of Edith Carol-
  ine Rivett, 1894-1958. Other pseudo-
  nym: E. C. R. Lorac, q.v. SC: Chief
  Insp. Julian Rivers = JL; Insp.
  Ryvet = R. Set: Eng.
  Affair at Helen's Court; see Long Sha-
    dows
  The Burning Question. Collins, 1957
  The Case of the First-Class Carriage.
    Davies, 1939 R
  Clue Sinister. Macdonald, 1967 JR
  Copy for Crime. Macdonald, 1950;
    Doubleday, 1951 JR
  Crossed Skis. Collins, 1952 JR
    [Austria]
  Death in the Diving Pool. Davies, 1940
    R
  Death of a Lady Killer. Collins, 1959
  A Double for Detection. Macdonald, 1945
    JR
  The Double Turn. Collins, 1956. U.S.
    title: The Late Miss Trimming.
    Doubleday, 1957 JR
  Impact of Evidence. Collins, 1954;
    Doubleday, 1954 JR [Wales]
  It's Her Own Funeral. Collins, 1951;
    Doubleday, 1952 JR
  The Late Miss Trimming; see The Double
    Turn
  Long Shadows. Collins, 1958. U.S.
    title: Affair at Helen's Court.
    Doubleday, 1958 JR
  The Missing Rope. Skeffington, 1937 R
  Murder Among Members. Collins, 1955 JR
  Murder As a Fine Art. Collins, 1953 JR
  Murder at Mornington. Skeffington, 1937
    R
  Over the Garden Wall. Macdonald, 1948;
    Doubleday, 1949 JR
  A Policeman at the Door. Collins, 1953;
    Doubleday, 1954 JR
  Rigging the Evidence. Collins, 1955 JR
  The Striped Suitcase. Macdonald, 1946;
    Doubleday, 1947 JR
  Triple Death. Butterworth, 1936 R
  Upstairs and Downstairs; see Upstairs,
    Downstairs
  Upstairs, Downstairs. Macdonald, 1950.
    U.S. title: Upstairs and Downstairs.
    Doubleday, 1950 JR
  When the Devil Was Sick. Davies, 1939 R

CARNAC, NICHOLAS. Pseudonym of F. H. M.
  Edwards.
  Tournament of Shadows. H. Hamilton,
    1978; Scribner, 1979

CARNAHAN, WALTER H(ERVEY). 1891- .
  Ref: CA.
  -Hoffman's Row. Bobbs, 1963

CARNEY, DANIEL. 1944- .
  The Whispering Death. College Press
    (Salisbury), 1969; Pan, 1972

CARNEY, (JOHN) OTIS. 1922- . Ref: CA.
  -The Paper Bullet. Morrow, 1966

CARNI, ROSS
  Against the F.B.I. Hamilton Stafford,
    1952
  Date for Homicide. Hamilton Stafford,
    1952
  Death Called China. Hamilton Stafford,
    1951
  No Time for Corpses. Hamilton Stafford,
    1952
  The Set-Up. Hamilton Stafford, 1952
  The Showdown. Hamilton Stafford, 1952

CAROL, J.
  Spin Your Crime. Warren, 1952

CAROL, ROBERT. Pseudonym of Camille Bour-
  geois.
  Ancestor. Paperback Library, 1969
  Gwenyth. Paperback Library, 1969
  The Gypsy's Curse. Award, 1971

CAROTHERS, A. J.
  Hero at Large. Ballantine, 1980. (No-
    velization of the movie.)

CARPENTER, CARLETON. 1926-   . Actor in 15 NYC shows, over 2000 radio and TV shows, and 14 films; song recordings earned him two gold records. SC: Chester Long = CL.
  Cat Got Your Tongue? Curtis, 1973 [Vt.]
  Deadhead. Curtis, 1974 CL [NYC]
  Games Murderers Play. Curtis, 1973 [NYC]
  Only Her Hairdresser Knew... Curtis, 1973 CL [NYC]
  Sleight of Hand. Popular Library, 1975 [Cape Cod]

CARPENTER, DON(ALD RICHARD). 1931-   . Ref: CA.
  Blade of Light. Barker, 1967; Harcourt, 1968

CARPENTER, EDWARD CHILDS. 1872?-1950. See: Reginald Wright Kauffman, 1877-1959; also: Helen (Alden) K(nipe) Carpenter; also: Laurence Gross, 1889-1965.

CARPENTER, GRANT
  The Night Tide. Fly, 1920

CARPENTER, HELEN (ALDEN) K(NIPE)
  Whistling in the Dark. Dodd, 1932 (Novelization of the play by Laurence Gross, 1889-1965, and Edward Childs Carpenter, 1872?-1950.) [NYC]

CARPENTER, MARGARET. 1893-   . Ref: CC.
  Experiment Perilous. Little, 1943; Harrap, 1943 [NYC]

CARPENTIER, CHARLES
  Flight One. Simon, 1972; Eyre, 1973

CARPOZI, GEORGE, JR. See: Daniel T. Chiodo.

CARR, A(LBERT) H. Z(OLOTKOFF). 1902-1971. Ref: CA, EM, TC.
  Finding Maubee. Putnam, 1970. British title: The Calypso Murders. Hale, 1973 [Carib.]

CARR, ANTONY (JOHN EDWIN)
  Candles in the Night. Cassell, 1956
  A Comedy of Terrors. Cassell, 1955
  The Girl in Green. Cassell, 1959
  The Man in Room 3. Cassell, 1958
  Strange Harmony. Earl, 1948

CARR, COMYNS. See: Robert Marshall.

CARR, GEORGE CHARLES
  The Towers of Urbandine. York, 1805

CARR, GLYN. Pseudonym of (Frank) Showell Styles, 1908-   , q.v. SC: Abercrombie Lewker, in all titles (and also in titles under the Styles byline).
  A Corpse at Camp Two. Bles, 1955 [Nepal]
  The Corpse in the Crevasse. Bles, 1952 [Austria]
  Death Finds a Foothold. Bles, 1961 [Wales]
  Death of a Weirdy. Bles, 1965 [Wales]
  Death on Milestone Buttress. Bles, 1951 [Wales]
  Death Under Snowdon. Bles, 1954 [Wales]
  Fat Man's Agony. Bles, 1969
  Holiday with Murder. Bles, 1960 [Maj.]
  The Ice-Axe Murders. Bles, 1958 [Fr.]
  Lewker in Norway. Bles, 1963 [Nor.]
  Lewker in Tirol. Bles, 1967 [Austria]
  Murder on the Matterhorn. Bles, 1951; Dutton, 1953 [Switz.]
  Swing Away, Climber. Bles, 1956; Washburn, 1959 [Wales]
  The Youth Hostel Murders. Bles, 1952; Dutton, 1953

CARR, JESS(E CROWE, JR.). 1930-   . Ref: CA.
  Moonshiners. Springwood, 1979

CARR, JOHN DICKSON. 1905-1977. Pseudonyms: Carr Dickson, Carter Dickson, Roger Fairbairn, qq.v. See also: Adrian Conan Doyle, 1911-1970; and: John Rhode. Ref: all except MM. SC: Henri Bencolin = HB; Dr. Gideon Fell = GF; Colonel March (also under the Carter Dickson byline) = CM; Sir Henry Merrivale (also under the Carter Dickson byline) = HM; Patrick Butler = PB; Jeff Marle = JM.
  The Arabian Nights Murder. Harper, 1936; H. Hamilton, 1936 GF [Eng.]
  Below Suspicion. Harper, 1949; H. Hamilton, 1950 GF,PB [Eng.]
  The Black Spectacles; see The Problem of the Green Capsule
  The Blind Barber. Harper, 1934; H. Hamilton, 1934 GF [ship]
  The Bride of Newgate. Harper, 1950; H. Hamilton, 1950 [Eng., 1815]
  The Burning Court. Harper, 1937; H. Hamilton, 1937 [Phil.]
  Captain Cut-Throat. Harper, 1955; H. Hamilton, 1955 [Fr., 1805]
  The Case of the Constant Suicides. Harper, 1941; H. Hamilton, 1941 GF [Scot.]
  Castle Skull. Harper, 1931; Severn, 1976 HB,JM [Ger.]
  The Corpse in the Waxworks. Harper, 1932. British title: The Waxworks Murder. H. Hamilton 1932 HB,JM [Paris]
  The Crooked Hinge. Harper, 1938; H. Hamilton, 1938 GF [Eng.]
  Dark of the Moon. Harper, 1967; H. Hamilton, 1968 GF [Charleston]
  The Dead Man's Knock. Harper, 1958; H. Hamilton, 1958 GF [Va., acad.]
  Deadly Hall. Harper, 1971; H. Hamilton, 1971 [New Or., 1927]
  Death Turns the Tables. Harper, 1941. British title: The Seat of the Scornful. H. Hamilton, 1942 GF [Eng.]
  Death-Watch. Harper, 1935; H. Hamilton, 1935 GF [Eng.]
  The Demoniacs. Harper, 1962; H. Hamilton, 1962 [Eng., 1757]
  The Devil in Velvet. Harper, 1951; H. Hamilton, 1951 [Eng., 1675]
  Dr. Fell, Detective, and other stories. Mercury, 1947 (Mixed ss and radio plays, five about GF.)
  The Door to Doom and Other Detections. Harper, 1980; H. Hamilton, 1981 (ss and radio plays, including 4 ss about HB, 1 radio play about GF, and 2 Sherlock Holmes parodies.)
  The Eight of Swords. Harper, 1934; H. Hamilton, 1934 GF [Eng.]
  The Emperor's Snuff-Box. Harper, 1942; H. Hamilton, 1943 [Eng.]
  Fire, Burn! Harper, 1957; H. Hamilton, 1957 [Eng., 1829]
  The Four False Weapons. Harper, 1937; H. Hamilton, 1938 HB,JM [Paris]
  The Ghosts' High Noon. Harper, 1969; H. Hamilton, 1970 [New Or., 1912]
  Hag's Nook. Harper, 1933; H. Hamilton, 1933 GF [Eng.]
  He Who Whispers. Harper, 1946; H. Hamilton, 1946 GF [Eng.]
  The Hollow Man; see The Three Coffins
  The House at Satan's Elbow. Harper, 1965; H. Hamilton, 1965 GF [Eng.]
  The Hungry Goblin. Harper, 1972; H. Hamilton, 1972 [Eng., 1869]
  In Spite of Thunder. Harper, 1960; H. Hamilton, 1960 GF [Geneva]
  It Walks by Night. Harper (NYC & London), 1930 HB,JM [Paris]
  The Lost Gallows. Harper (NYC & London), 1931 HB,JM [Eng.]
  The Mad Hatter Mystery. Harper, 1933; H. Hamilton, 1933 GF [Eng.]
  The Man Who Could Not Shudder. Harper, 1940; H. Hamilton, 1940 GF [Eng.]
  The Men Who Explained Miracles. Harper, 1963; H. Hamilton, 1964 (7 ss, 2 about CM, 2 about GF, and one about HM.)
  Most Secret. Harper, 1964; H. Hamilton, 1964 (Revision of "Devil Kinsmere," as by Roger Fairbairn, q.v.) [Eng., 1815]
  The Murder of Sir Edmund Godfrey. Harper, 1936; H. Hamilton, 1936 [Eng., 1678]
  The Nine Wrong Answers. Harper, 1952; H. Hamilton, 1952 [Eng.]
  Panic in Box C. Harper, 1966; H. Hamilton, 1966 GF [N.Y.]
  Papa La-Bas. Harper, 1968; H. Hamilton, 1969 [New Or., 1858]
  Patrick Butler for the Defense. Harper, 1956; H. Hamilton, 1956 PB [Eng.]
  Poison in Jest. Harper, 1932; H. Hamilton, 1932 JM [Pa.]
  The Problem of the Green Capsule. Harper, 1939. British title: The Black Spectacles. H. Hamilton, 1939 GF [Eng.]
  The Problem of the Wire Cage. Harper, 1939; H. Hamilton, 1940 GF [Eng.]
  Scandal at High Chimneys. Harper, 1959; H. Hamilton, 1959 [Eng., 1865]
  The Seat of the Scornful; see Death Turns the Tables
  The Sleeping Sphinx. Harper, 1947; H. Hamilton, 1947 GF [Eng.]
  The Third Bullet and other stories. Harper, 1954; H. Hamilton, 1954 (Contains the title novelet, published separately in England under the Carter Dickson byline, plus 6 ss, including 3 about GF and 1 about HM.)
  The Three Coffins. Harper, 1935. British title: The Hollow Man. H. Hamilton, 1935 GF [Eng.]
  Till Death Do Us Part. Harper, 1944; H. Hamilton, 1944 GF [Eng.]
  To Wake the Dead. Harper, 1938; H. Hamilton, 1938 GF [Eng.]
  The Waxworks Murder; see The Corpse in the Waxworks
  The Witch of the Low Tide. Harper, 1961; H. Hamilton, 1961 [Eng., 1907]

CARR, JOLYON
  Death Comes by Post. Jenkins, 1940
  Freedom for Two. Jenkins, 1939
  Masters of the Parachute Mail. Jenkins, 1940
  Murders in the Dispensary. Jenkins, 1938

CARR, JOSEPH BAKER. SC: Oceola Archer, in both titles.
  Death Whispers. Viking, 1933; Cassell, 1933 [Mass.]
  The Man with Bated Breath. Viking, 1934; Cassell, 1935 [Ga.]

CARR, KIRBY. SC: Mike Ross = MR.
  Don't Bet on Living, Alice! Major, 1975 MR [L.A.]
  The Girls Who Came to Murder. Canyon, 1974 MR
  The Impossible Spy. Major, 1976
  Let Me Kill You Sweetheart! Canyon, 1974 MR
  They're Coming to Kill You, Jane! Canyon, 1975 MR
  Who Killed You, Cindy Castle? Canyon, 1974 MR
  You Die Next, Jill Baby! Major, 1975 MR
  You're Hired; You're Dead. Major, 1975 MR

CARR, MARGARET. Pseudonyms: Martin Carroll, Carole Kerr, qq.v. Ref: CA, TC.
  Blindman's Bluff. Hale, 1976
  Blood Will Out. Hale, 1975
  Daggers Drawn. Hale, 1980
  Dare the Devil. Hale, 1976
  -An Innocent Abroad. Hale, 1979
  Out of the Past. Hale, 1976
  Sharendel. Hale, 1976
  Sitting Duck. Hale, 1972
  Too Close for Comfort. Hale, 1975
  Tread Warily at Midnight. Hale, 1971
  Twin Tragedy. Hale, 1977
  Wait for the Wake. Hale, 1974
  Who's the Target? Hale, 1974
  -The Witch of Wykham. Hale, 1978

CARR, PHILIPPA. Pseudonym of Eleanor Alice Burford Hibbert, 1906-   . Other pseudonyms: Elbur Ford, Victoria Holt, Kathleen Kellow, qq.v.
  The Lion Triumphant. Collins, 1974; Putnam, 1974 [Eng., 1500s]
  The Miracle at St. Bruno's. Collins, 1972; Putnam, 1972 [Eng., 1500s]
  The Witch from the Sea. Collins, 1975; Putnam, 1975 [Eng., 1800s]

CARR, RAY. Pseudonym of Emile Charles Victor Foucar, 1894-   .
  The Cluster of Gems. Skeffington, 1930
  -Love in Burma. Bles, 1928 [Burma]
  -Moonshine. Howe, 1932
  The Red Tiger. Skeffington, 1929 [Burma]

CARR, WILLIAM H(ENRY) A(LEXANDER). 1924-   . Ref: CA.
  Medical Examiner. Lancer, 1963

CARREL, FREDERIC
  -The Adventures of John Johns. Bliss Sands, 1897. U.S. title: John Johns. Kennerley, 1908
  John Johns; see The Adventures of John Johns
  The Methods of Mr. Ames. Laurie, 1908; Kennerley, 1908
  -The Realization of Justus Moran. Long, 1900

CARREL, MARK. Pseudonym of Lauran Bosworth Paine, 1916-   . Other pseudonyms: John Armour, Reg Batchelor, Kenneth Bedford, Frank Bosworth, Robert Clarke, Richard Dana, J. F. Drexler, Troy Howard, Jared Ingersol, John Kilgore, Hunter Liggett, J. K. Lucas, John Morgan, qq.v. SC: Andrew McCall, in at least those marked AM.
  Assignment for Trouble. Hale, 1974
  The Blood Pit. Hale, 1967 AM
  Case of the Hollow Man. Foulsham, 1958
  Case of the Innocent Witness. Foulsham, 1959 [Calif.]
  The Case of the Perfect Alibi. Foulsham, 1960
  Counsel for the Killer. Hale, 1972
  The Dark Edge of Violence. Hale, 1967 AM

The Emerald Heart. Hale, 1971 [L.A.]
Kill and Be Damned. Hale, 1970
Murder Without Motive. Hale, 1974
The Octopus' Shadow. Hale, 1974
One Last Time. Hale, 1973
Shadow of a Hawk. Hale, 1967
The Steel Mask. Hale, 1968
A Sword of Silk. Hale, 1967 AM
Tears of Blood. Hale, 1967 AM [Ohio]
The Underground Men. Hale, 1975

CARRICK, JOHN. Pseudonym of Hugh Provan Crosbie, 1912- . Ref: CA.
Beware the Shadows. Hale, 1967
Bond of Hate. Hale, 1966
Fairways and Foul. Hale, 1964
The Killer Conference. Hale, 1968
Mario. Hale, 1965
The Vulture. Hale, 1964
The Young and Deadly. Hale, 1969

CARRIER, WARREN (PENDLETON). 1918- . Ref: CA.
Bay of the Damned. Day, 1957; Cassell, 1958. Also published as: A Hell of a Murder. Avon, 1958 [Fla.]
A Hell of a Murder; see Bay of the Damned
The Hunt. New Directions, 1952; Owen, 1952
The Lost and the Damned. Berkley, 1957

CARRIGAN, NANCY. See: Richard Carrigan.

CARRIGAN, RICHARD and NANCY
The Siren Stars. Pyramid, 1971

CARRINGTON, ELAINE STERNE. 1892-1958.
The Crimson Goddess. Appleton, 1936 [L.I.]

CARRINGTON, GLENDA. Pseudonym of Karen Glenn.
Master of Greystone. Berkley, 1977

CARRINGTON, V. Pseudonym of Valerie Anne Hughes.
One Man's Awe. Barker, 1956

CARROLL, CHARLES
Chicago. PB, 1976 [Chi.]

CARROLL, JAMES P. 1943?- . Ref: CA.
Madonna Red. Little, 1976; Hodder, 1977 [Wash. D.C.]

CARROLL, LESLIE
The Blackmailer and the Blonde. Mitre, 1944 (32 pp.) [Chi.]
The Lamp Burns Blood. Mitre, 1944 (34 pp.)

CARROLL, LOREN. 1904-1978. Ref: CA.
Wild Onion. Dodd, 1930 [Chi.]

CARROLL, MARTIN. Pseudonym of Margaret Carr, 1935- , q.v. Other pseudonym: Carole Kerr, q.v.
Bait. Hale, 1970
Begotten Murder. Hale, 1967
Blood Vengeance. Hale, 1968
Dead Trouble. Hale, 1968
Goodbye Is Forever. Hale, 1968
Hear No Evil. Hale, 1971
Miranda Said Murder. Hale, 1970
Too Beautiful to Die. Hale, 1969

CARROLL, ROBERT. Pseudonym of Hollis Alpert, 1916- . Ref: CA.
A Disappearance. Dial, 1975. British title: The Budapest Tradeoff. Harwood, 1976 [1957-67, Europe]

CARROLL, ROBERT F(RANCIS)
Heat Lightning. French (NYC), 1949 (1-act play.)

CARROLL, THOMAS D. 1926-1975.
Grounds for Murder. Lancer, 1966
A Plastic Kind of Death. Lancer, 1968

CARRUTHERS, ANNIE
A Left-Handed Murder. Gale, 1892

CARRYL, CHARLES E. 1841-1920.
The River Syndicate. Harper (NYC & London), 1899 ss

CARSON, BART
Bread for the Dead. Hamilton Stafford, 1954
Cuban Heel. Hamilton Stafford, 1953
The Lady Is a Spitfire. Hamilton Stafford, 1953
The Late Demented. Hamilton Stafford, 1955
Murder Matinee. Hamilton Stafford, 1953
Phone for a Hearse. Hamilton Stafford, 1953
She Died Downtown. Hamilton Stafford, 1953

Ten Grand Story. Hamilton Stafford, 1951
There Could Be Trouble. Hamilton Stafford, 1954
Torment Was a Woman. Hamilton Stafford, 1953

CARSON, ROBERT. 1909-1983. Ref: CA.
The Golden Years Caper. Little, 1970; Allen, 1972 [L.A.]
The Quality of Mercy. Holt, 1954; Hale, 1955 [L.A.]

CARSTAIRS, HENRY. SC: Lydford Long, in all titles. Set: Eng.
Black Burying. Ward, 1945
Blackdrop Hall. Ward, 1950
Blood, M'Lud. Ward, 1948
Cruel Dart. Ward, 1947
Death's Duet. Ward, 1954
Drifting Death. Ward, 1944
Harpinger's Hunch. Ward, 1943
Lying Down Below. Ward, 1951
Oh, No, You Don't. Ward, 1952
Secretary of State for Death. Ward, 1946
When Three Makes Two. Ward, 1953
Who Lies Bleeding? Ward, 1949
The Winton Street Mystery. Ward, 1955

CARSTAIRS, JOHN PADDY. 1910- . SC: Garaway Trenton, in all titles.
The Concrete Kimono. Allen, 1965; Walker, 1965 [Afr.]
Gardenias Bruise Easily. Allen, 1958; British Book Centre, 1959 [Fr.]
No Thanks for the Shroud. Allen, 1967
No Wooden Overcoat. Allen, 1959 [Tangier]
Pardon My Gun. Allen, 1962
A Smell of Peardrops. Allen, 1966 [Tangier]
Touch a French Pom-Pom. Allen, 1960

CARSTARPHEN, FRANK E. See: Frances (Newbold) Noyes Hart, 1890-1943.

CARTER, ALBERTA SIMPSON. Pseudonym of Alfred Bercovici. Other pseudonym: Alberta Simpson, q.v.
An Adopted Face. Popular Library, 1975 [La.]
Fool's Proof. Popular Library, 1975

CARTER, ALLEN
A Perfect Demon! or, The Oak House Mystery. Alliance, 1888

CARTER, AMANDA
Write Me a Murder. Zebra, 1979

CARTER, ANGELA. 1940- . Ref: CA.
The Bloody Chamber and other stories. Gollancz, 1979. U.S. title: The Bloody Chamber. Harper, 1980 ss
The Passion of New Eve. Gollancz, 1977; Harcourt, 1977

CARTER, ARTHUR PHILIP
The Number. Dramatists, 1952 (3-act play.)

CARTER, BEATRIX
All Set for Murder. Kenyon-Deane, 1973 (3-act play.)

CARTER, DIANA
The Ghost Writer. Cassell, 1974; Macmillan, 1975

CARTER, EDITH. See: Winifred Carter.

CARTER, HERBERT
Never Look Back. Vantage, 1966

CARTER, JOHN
The Diamond Mercenaries. Futura, 1976 (Novelization of the movie.) [S.W. Afr.]
The Eagle's Nest. Futura, 1976; Berkley, 1978 (Novelization of "The New Avengers" TV series.)

CARTER, JOHN FRANKLIN. 1897-1967. Pseudonym: Diplomat, q.v.

CARTER, MAX
Call Me Killer! Avon, 1953 [NYC]

CARTER, NICHOLAS. House name, used by at least the following writers. The numbers are used with specific titles below to identify works by these authors. Where two or more numbers are used, a combining of several dime novel works, rather than a collaboration, should be inferred. Note that first names have not yet been identified for some of the authors. (1) Andrews; (2) A. L. Armagnac; (3) Babcock; (4) Ball; (5) William Perry Brown, q.v.; (6) George Waldo Browne,
1851-1930; (7) Buchanan; (8) Frederick R(ussell) Burton, 1861-1909, q.v.; (9) O. P. Caylor, (10) Stephen Chalmers, 1880-1935, q.v.; (11) Weldon J. Cobb; (12) William Wallace Cook, q.v.; (13) John Russell Coryell, 1851-1924, q.v.; (14) Frederick William Davis, 1858-1933, q.v.; (15) E. C. Derby, q.v.; (16) Frederic Van Rensselaer Dey, 1861-1922, q.v.; (17) Ferguson; (18) Walter Bertram Foster, 1869-1929, q.v.; (19) Charles Witherle Hooke, 1861-1929, q.v.; (20) Howard; (21) William Cadwalader Hudson, 1843-1915, q.v.; (22) George Charles Jenks, 1850-1929, q.v.; (23) W. L. or Joseph Larned; (24) Lincoln; (25) Charles Agnew MacLean, 1880-1928; (26) Makee; (27) St. George Henry Rathborne, 1854-1938, q.v.; (28) Rich; (29) Russell; (30) Eugene T. Sawyer, 1846-1924, q.v.; (31) Vincent E. Scott; (32) Samuel C. Spalding, (33) Splint; (34) Edward L. Stratemeyer, 1862-1930, q.v.; (35) Alfred B. Tozer; (36) Tyson; (37) R. F. Walsh; (38) Willard. The characterization of Nick Carter began well before the turn of the century and he appeared abundantly in dime novels, which are not listed here. Beginning with the Magnet (M) and New Magnet (NM) Libraries of Street and Smith, the Nicholas Carter byline and characterization appeared in book form. These book appearances, some of which were reprints of dime novels, are listed below. Separately listed, at the end of the entry, are several later American volumes and three British collections.

M-NM Libraries:
Accident or Murder? 1906 (16,20)
An Accidental Password. 1898 (8)
The Adder's Brood. 1917 (32)
The Adventures of Harrison Keith, Detective. 1899 ss
After the Verdict. 1914
Against Desperate Odds. 1904 (16)
Ahead of the Game. 1904 (11,34,35)
An Amazing Scoundrel. 1907 (16)
The American Marquis. 1887 in Secret Service Series; 1897 in M (13)
Among the Counterfeiters. 1898 (16)
Among the Nihilists. 1898 (8)
The Amphitheatre Plot. 1918 (32)
The Angel of Death. 1913 (32)
An Artful Schemer. 1908 (16)
As a Crook Sows. 1915 (22)
At Face Value. 1911 (16?)
At Mystery's Threshold. 1909 (14)
At Odds with Scotland Yard. 1898 (8)
At the Knife's Point. 1902 (9,34,35)
At Thompson's Ranch. 1898 (8)
An Australian Klondyke. 1897 (8)
The Babbington Case. 1913 (16)
Baffled, But Not Beaten. 1906 (16)
A Baffled Oath. 1905 (12)
Bandits of the Air. 1912 (19)
The Bank Draft Puzzle. 1907 (16,35)
A Bargain in Crime. 1907 (16,30)
The Barrel Mystery. 1903 (8)
A Battle for the Right. 1919
Behind a Mask. 1902 (16)
Behind a Throne. 1906 (16)
Behind Closed Doors. 1910
Behind the Black Mask. 1910
Beyond Pursuit. 1904 (19,34)
Birds of Prey. 1914 (14)
A Bite of an Apple, and other stories. 1899 ss (19)
A Blackmailer's Bluff. 1903 (19,21,37)
The Blind Man's Daughter. 1914 (14)
A Blindfold Mystery. 1909 (16)
The Blood-Red Badge. 1903 (8)
Blood Will Tell. 1918 (14)
The Bloodstone Terror. 1905 (16)
A Blow for Vengeance. 1903 (8)
The Blow of a Hammer and other stories. 1901 ss (11)
A Bogus Clew. 1901 (8)
Bolts from Blue Skies. 1914 (32)
A Bonded Villain. 1903 (9)
The Bottle with the Black Label. 1901 (11)
The Boulevard Mutes. 1905 (16)
The Broadway Cross. 1906 (16)
Broken Bars. 1916 (14)
A Broken Bond. 1919
Broken on Crime's Wheel. 1911 (35)
A Broken Trail. 1904 (35)
The Brotherhood of Death. 1907 (16)
Brought to Bay. 1900 (11,34)
Brought to the Mark. 1913
The Bullion Mystery. 1914 (22)
A Bundle of Clews. 1904 (9,30)
The Burden of Proof. 1916
The Buried Secret. 1912 (16?)
By an Unseen Hand. 1912 (32)
The Cab Driver's Secret. 1904 (9,35)
A Call in the Night. 1912 (32?)

C

Carter, Nicholas

A Call on the Phone. 1911 (16)
Called to Account. 1914 (28)
Captain Sparkle, Private. 1906 (16)
A Carnival of Crime. 1910 (16)
The Case of Many Clues. 1916 (32)
The Case of the Two Doctors. 1912
A Case Without a Clue. 1906 (16)
The Cashier's Secret. 1903 (9,19)
Caught in a Whirlpool. 1913
Caught in the Toils. 1897 (16)
The Certified Check. 1904 (12,15,35)
The Chain of Clues. 1907 (16,25)
The Chain of Evidence. 1903 (16)
A Chance Discovery. 1898 (16)
A Chase for Millions. 1911 (16)
A Chase in the Dark. 1907 (16,19,30)
Check No. 777. 1898 (8)
A Checkmated Scoundrel. 1903 (21)
A Cigarette Clew. 1905 (12)
Circumstantial Evidence. 1903 (21)
The Claws of the Tiger. 1902 (14)
The Clever Celestial. 1899 (8)
Clew Against Clew. 1918
Clew by Clew. 1912 (14)
The Cloak of Guilt. 1903 (8,34)
A Clue from the Unknown. 1916 (32)
The Clutch of Dread. 1913 (32)
Comrades of the Right Hand. 1911 (35)
The Confidence King. 1911 (16)
The Connecting Link. 1912 (14)
A Conspiracy of Rumors. 1916 (32)
Cornered at Last. 1913 (14)
The Council of Death. 1903 (21)
The Crescent Brotherhood. 1899 (35)
The Crime and the Motive. 1908 (16)
A Crime in Paradise. 1914 (32)
The Crime of a Century. 1912 (16)
The Crime of a Countess. 1888 in
  Secret Service Series; 1897 in M (13)
The Crime of the Camera. 1905 (16)
The Crime of the French Cafe and other
  stories. 1900 ss (19)
The Criminal Link. 1904 (16)
The Crimson Flash. 1912 (14)
The Crook's Blind. 1914 (14)
The Crook's Double. 1918 (14)
The Crossed Needles. 1918 (22)
Crossed Wires. 1900 (11)
The Crown Diamond. 1903 (8)
A Cry for Help. 1907 (16,38)
The Crystal Mystery. 1911 (16)
The Danger of Folly. 1915 (32)
The Day of Reckoning. 1913
The Dead Man's Accomplice. 1912 (16)
A Dead Man's Grip. 1899 (16)
The Dead Stranger. 1907
The Deadly Scarab. 1912 (32)
A Deal in Diamonds. 1902 (11)
Death at the Feast. 1909 (16)
The Death Circle. 1906 (16)
Death in Life. 1918 (32?)
The Deeper Game. 1914 (16)
The Demon's Eye. 1907 (16,38)
The Demons of the Night. 1907 (8,16)
A Deposit Vault Puzzle. 1898 (16)
A Desperate Chance. 1901 (14)
The Detective's Pretty Neighbor and
  other stories. 1899 ss
A Detective's Theory. 1904 (9,11)
The Devil's Son. 1911 (32)
Diamond Cut Diamond. 1913
The Diamond Mine Case. 1899 (8)
The Diamond Trail. 1905 (8)
The Disappearing Princess. 1910 (16)
A Disciple of Satan. 1909 (14)
Doctor Quartz, Magician. 1906 (16)
Doctor Quartz's Quick Move. 1906 (16)
The Doctor's Strategem. 1908 (14)
Dodging the Law. 1914
Done in the Dark. 1907 (16)
The Doom of the Reds. 1910 (16)
Doomed to Failure. 1913
The Door of Doubt. 1914
A Double-Handed Game. 1902 (16,34)
A Double Identity. 1913 (16)
A Double Mystery. 1913 (14?)
A Double Plot. 1909 (16)
The Double Shuffle Club. 1898 (8)
Down and Out. 1905 (16)
Driven from Cover. 1904 (16)
Driven to Desperation. 1905
A Duel of Brains. 1913 (32)
The Dumb Witness and other stories.
  1901 ss (11)
The Dynamite Trap. 1907 (6,16)
The Elevated Railroad Mystery and other
  stories. 1900 ss (19)
An Elusive Knave. 1911 (16)
Evidence by Telephone. 1898 (16)
The Evil Formula. 1916 (16)
The Face in the Shadow. 1911 (35)
A Fair Criminal. 1898 (8)
The False Claimant. 1908 (16)
A False Combination. 1902
A Fatal Margin. 1911 (16)
A Fatal Falsehood. 1911 (16)
The Fatal Hour. 1912 (16?)
The Fatal Prescription. 1903 (21)
A Fight for a Throne. 1907 (16,35)
A Fight for Right. 1914
A Fight with a Fiend. 1908 (16)

Fighting Against Millions. 1888 in
  Secret Service Series; 1897 in M (13)
The Finger of Suspicion. 1907 (16)
The Finish of a Rascal. 1913
The Fixed Alibi. 1914 (14)
Following a Chance Clew. 1904 (9,19,35)
For a Madman's Millions. 1911 (16)
For a Pawned Crown. 1917 (32)
For the Sake of Revenge. 1913
Found in the Jungle. 1917 (22)
Found on the Beach. 1898 (16)
The Four-Fingered Glove. 1905 (16)
The Four Hoodoo Charms. 1911 (16)
A Framework of Fate. 1900 (14)
From a Prison Cell. 1906 (16)
From Clue to Clue. 1916
From Peril to Peril. 1908 (16,31)
The Gambler's Syndicate. 1897 (16)
A Game of Craft. 1900 (30,35)
A Game of Plots. 1907 (16,35)
A Game Well Played. 1908 (9,16)
The Gargoni Girdle. 1915 (14)
Gideon Drexel's Millions and other sto-
  ries. 1899 ss (16)
The Gift of the Gods. 1911 (33)
The Girl in the Case. 1908 (16)
The Girl Prisoner. 1915 (32)
The Gloved Hand. 1914 (14)
The Grafters. 1914 (32)
A Great Conspiracy. 1903 (8)
The Great Diamond Sydnicate. 1910 (35)
The Great Enigma. 1888 in Secret Ser-
  vice Series; 1897 in M (16)
The Great Money Order Swindle. 1899
  (16)
The Great Opium Case. 1916
The Guilty Governor. 1903 (8)
The Hand That Won. 1908 (16,24)
Hand to Hand. 1908 (3,16,26)
The Handcuff Wizard. 1911 (23)
Harrison Keith and the Phantom Heiress.
  1909 (23)
Harrison Keith at Bay. 1909 (23)
Harrison Keith, Magician. 1909 (14)
Harrison Keith, Sleuth. 1907 (16)
Harrison Keith—Star Reporter. 1910
  (23)
Harrison Keith's Abduction Tangle. 1909
  (23)
Harrison Keith's Battle of Nerve. 1909
  (23)
Harrison Keith's Big Stakes. 1907 (24)
Harrison Keith's Cameo Case. 1909 (23)
Harrison Keith's Chance Clue. 1907 (24)
Harrison Keith's Chance Shot. 1908 (22)
Harrison Keith's Close Quarters. 1909
  (14)
Harrison Keith's Crooked Trail. 1908
  (18)
Harrison Keith's Cyclone Clue. 1910
  (23)
Harrison Keith's Danger. 1907 (30)
Harrison Keith's Death Compact. 1909
  (14)
Harrison Keith's Death Watch. 1910 (23)
Harrison Keith's Diamond Case. 1908
  (30)
Harrison Keith's Dilemma. 1907 (30)
Harrison Keith's Double Cross. 1909
  (14)
Harrison Keith's Double Mystery. 1908
  (22)
Harrison Keith's Drag Net. 1908 (18)
Harrison Keith's Dual Role. 1909 (14)
Harrison Keith's Fight for Life. 1908
  (18)
Harrison Keith's Greatest Task. 1907
  (18)
Harrison Keith's Green Diamond. 1909
  (23)
Harrison Keith's Haunted Client. 1909
  (23)
Harrison Keith's Labyrinth. 1910 (23)
Harrison Keith's Lucky Strike. 1909
  (22)
Harrison Keith's Mummy Mystery. 1909
  (23)
Harrison Keith's Mystic Letter. 1908
  (18)
Harrison Keith's Oath. 1907 (24)
Harrison Keith's Padlock Mystery. 1909
  (14)
Harrison Keith's Perilous Contract.
  1910 (by S. A. D. Cox.)
Harrison Keith's Poison Problem. 1910
Harrison Keith's Queer Clue. 1908 (22)
Harrison Keith's River Front Ruse. 1909
  (23)
Harrison Keith's River Mystery. 1910
  (23)
Harrison Keith's Sparkling Trail. 1909
  (23)
Harrison Keith's Strange Summons. 1908
  (18)
Harrison Keith's Struggle. 1907
Harrison Keith's Studio Crime. 1910
  (23)
Harrison Keith's Tact. 1908 (18)
Harrison Keith's Time Lock Case. 1908
  (18)
Harrison Keith's Triple Tragedy. 1909
  (14)

Harrison Keith's Triumph. 1907 (30)
Harrison Keith's Wager. 1910 (23)
Harrison Keith's Warning. 1907 (30)
Harrison Keith's Weird Partner. 1908
  (18)
Harrison Keith's Wireless Message. 1908
  (30)
The Hate That Kills. 1917 (14)
Heard in the Dark. 1903 (21)
The Heart of the Underworld. 1913
Held for Trial. 1900 (14)
Held in Suspense. 1915 (22)
A Herald Personal and other stories.
  1899 ss (19)
A Heritage of Trouble. 1914
Hidden Foes. 1919
The Hole in the Vault. 1903 (21)
The "Hot Air" Clew. 1904 (1,34)
Hounded to Death. 1902 (21)
The House Across the Street. 1913
The House of Doom. 1911 (27)
The House of the Yellow Door. 1911 (23)
The House of Whispers. 1912 (14)
The Human Fiend. 1907 (16,30)
A Hunter of Men. 1908 (16,19)
In Death's Grip. 1908 (16)
In Letters of Fire. 1901 (11)
In Queer Quarters. 1912
In Record Time. 1915 (2,15)
In Search of Himself. 1909 (16)
In Suspicion's Shadow. 1913 (29)
In the Face of Evidence. 1912 (27)
In the Gloom of Night. 1904 (16)
In the Grip of Fate. 1916 (32)
In the Lap of Danger. 1906 (30)
In the Nick of Time. 1912
In the Shadow of Fear. 1913
In the Toils of Fear. 1914 (22)
An Ingenious Strategem. 1904 (16)
Instinct at Fault. 1941 (16)
The International Crook League. 1913
  (14)
Into Nick Carter's Web. 1908 (16)
The Jeweled Mummy. 1911 (16)
The Just and the Unjust. 1914 (22)
Just One Slip. 1915 (22)
The Keeper of the Black Hounds. 1914
  (22)
The Key Ring Clew. 1905 (2)
King of the Underworld. 1911 (33)
The King's Prisoner. 1910 (16)
A Klondike Claim. 1897 (8)
Knaves in High Places. 1914
Knots in the Noose. 1913
The Kregoff Necklace. 1913 (16)
The Lady of Shadows. 1911 (16)
Lady Velvet. 1900
The Last Call. 1914 (16)
The Last Move in the Game. 1910 (18)
A Legacy of Hate. 1909 (9,16)
The "Limited" Hold-Up. 1906 (16)
A Live Wire Clue. 1911 (18)
The Living Mask. 1905
The Lost Chittendens. 1910 (16)
The Lure of Gold. 1906 (16)
Madame "Q". 1911 (23)
The Magic Necklace. 1916
Man Against Man. 1902 (16)
The Man and His Price. 1902 (8,12,35)
The Man at the Window. 1901 (14)
The Man from India. 1898 (8)
The Man from London. 1901 (11)
The Man in the Auto. 1911 (18)
The Man of Iron. 1907 (16)
The Man of Many Faces. 1916 (32)
The Man of Mystery. 1901 (30)
The Man of Riddles. 1914
The Man They Held Back. 1917 (22)
A Man to Be Feared. 1909 (16)
The Man Who Changed Faces. 1914 (2)
The Man Who Fainted. 1913
The Man Who Paid. 1914
The Man Who Stole Millions and other
  stories. 1900 ss (19)
The Man Who Vanished. 1899 (8,11)
The Man Who Was Cursed. 1906 (16)
The Man with a Crutch. 1912 (14)
The Man with a Double. 1912
The Man Without a Conscience. 1907 (16)
The Man Without a Will. 1916 (32)
Marked for Death. 1906 (16)
The Marked Hand. 1905
A Master Criminal. 1912 (14)
A Master of Deviltry. 1909 (16)
The Master Villain. 1904 (6,19,30)
A Masterly Trick. 1911 (33)
A Matter of Skill. 1911 (33)
A Maze of Motives. 1913
The Microbe of Crime. 1914 (14)
The Middle Link. 1915 (14)
The Midnight Message. 1913 (16)
A Million in Diamonds. 1912 (32)
A Millionaire Partner. 1898 (8)
A Millionaire's Mania. 1913 (23)
Millions at Stake and other stories.
  1901 ss (11,30,35)
The Mills of the Law. 1913 (32)
A Miscarriage of Justice. 1914 (32)
The Missing Cotton King. 1912 (8,16,35)
The Missing Deputy Chief. 1912 (32?)
A Missing Man. 1904 (9,19,30)

A Mixed-Up Mess. 1916 (14)
A Move in the Dark. 1902 (14)
A Moving Picture Mystery. 1913
The Murray Hill Mystery. 1901
The Mysterious Castle. 1911 (16)
The Mysterious Cavern. 1912 (16)
A Mysterious Foe. 1904 (8,21)
A Mysterious Game. 1903
A Mysterious "Graft". 1905 (12,14)
The Mysterious Mail Robbery. 1897 (16)
The Mystic Diagram. 1904 (16)
Nabob and Knave. 1908 (14,16)
A Nation's Peril. 1910 (16)
The Needy Nine. 1917 (14)
A Network of Crime. 1918 (14)
A New Serpent in Eden. 1915 (32)
Nick Carter and the Green Goods Men. 1899 (16)
Nick Carter and the Red Button. 1913 (16)
Nick Carter Down East. 1900 (8)
Nick Carter's Auto Trail. 1910 (16)
Nick Carter's Chance Clue. 1912 (16)
Nick Carter's Chinese Puzzle. 1907 (16)
Nick Carter's Cipher. 1908 (15,16)
Nick Carter's Clever Protege. 1899 (8,11)
Nick Carter's Clever Ruse. 1900 (14)
Nick Carter's Close Call. 1907 (16,30)
Nick Carter's Close Finish. 1912
Nick Carter's Convict Client. 1910 (35)
Nick Carter's Counterplot. 1912 (16)
Nick Carter's Death Warrant. 1902 (30,35)
Nick Carter's Double Catch. 1905 (16)
Nick Carter's Egyptian Clew. 1912 (12)
Nick Carter's Fall. 1906 (16)
Nick Carter's Girl Detective. 1900 (11)
Nick Carter's Intuition. 1911 (23?)
Nick Carter's Last Card. 1912 (16)
Nick Carter's Masterpiece. 1906 (16)
Nick Carter's Menace. 1912 (16)
Nick Carter's New Assistant. 1931 (16)
Nick Carter's Persistence. 1910 (5)
Nick Carter's Promise. 1908 (16,30)
Nick Carter's Retainer. 1900
Nick Carter's Roundup. 1911 (23)
Nick Carter's Star Pupils. 1900 (11)
Nick Carter's Subtle Foe. 1912 (16)
Nick Carter's Swim to Victory. 1909 (16)
Nick Carter's Treasure Chest Case. 1913 (14)
Nick Carter's Wildest Chase. 1910 (16)
Not on the Records. 1914
The Old Detective's Pupil. 1887 in Secret Service Series; 1898 in M (13)
On a Crimson Trail. 1912 (14)
On a Million-Dollar Trail. 1915 (31)
On the Eve of Triumph. 1913 (32)
On the Ragged Edge. 1914 (22)
The $100,000 Kiss. 1915 (32)
One Object in Life. 1914 (22)
One Shipwreck Too Many. 1915
One Step Too Far. 1910 (18)
Out for Vengeance. 1912 (14)
Out of Crime's Depths. 1909 (14)
Out of Death's Shadow. 1906 (30)
Out with the Tide. 1914 (22)
Outlaws of the Blue. 1917 (22)
Over the Edge of the World. 1916 (32)
Paid with Death. 1903 (14)
Partners in Peril. 1919
The Path of the Spendthrift. 1912
Pauline—A Mystery. 1911 (16)
Paying the Price. 1917 (14)
A Perilous Parole. 1914 (22)
The Photographer's Evidence. 1903 (8)
The Piano Box Mystery. 1888 in Secret Service Series; 1897 in M (16)
A Play for Millions. 1912 (16)
Played to a Finish. 1902 (14)
Playing a Bold Game. 1897 (16)
Playing a Lone Hand. 1904 (11)
Playing for a Fortune. 1905 (14)
A Plaything of Fate. 1909 (16)
Plea for Justice. 1913
A Plot for a Warship. 1912
A Plot for an Empire. 1911 (16)
The Plot That Failed. 1905
A Plot Uncovered. 1909 (16,35)
A Plot Within a Plot. 1906 (16)
A Plunge into Crime. 1908 (16)
Points to Crime. 1913 (16)
The Poisons of Exili. 1913 (14)
The Pressing Peril. 1917 (14)
The Pretty Stenographer Mystery. 1905 (26)
The Price of a Secret. 1901 (16)
The Price of Treachery. 1905 (16)
The Prince of Liars. 1908 (15,31)
A Prince of Rogues. 1901 (11)
A Princess of Crime. 1900 (11)
The Purple Spot. 1913 (14)
The Puzzle of the Five Pistols and other stories. 1899 ss (19)
The Queen of Diamonds. 1904 (9,30)
The Queen of Knaves and other stories. 1901 ss (16,35)

The Quest of "The Lost Hope." 1911 (35)
A Question of Time. 1911 (27)
A Race for Ten Thousand. 1902 (14)
A Race Track Gamble. 1903 (21,34)
The Rajah's Ruby. 1910 (16)
A Rascal of Quality. 1914 (22)
Rascals and Co. 1915 (32)
Reaping the Whirlwind. 1909 (14)
The Red God of Tragedy. 1914 (32)
The Red League. 1907 (16,30)
The Red Plague. 1916 (32)
The Red Signal. 1902 (14)
The Red Triangle. 1912 (16)
Repaid in Like Coin. 1913
A Riddle of Identities. 1913 (16)
A Ring of Dust. 1903 (8)
A Ring of Rascals. 1908 (16)
A Rogue of Quality. 1913 (32)
A Rogue Worth Trapping. 1914
The Rogue's Reach. 1912 (16?)
The Room of Mirrors. 1911 (16)
A Rope of Slender Threads. 1914 (32)
Round the World for a Quarter. 1916 (32)
A Royal Thief. 1905 (8,12)
The Ruby Pin. 1904 (8)
Run to Earth. 1902 (16)
The Sandal Wood Slipper. 1914 (1)
Satan's Apt Pupil. 1915 (22)
Saved by a Ruse. 1909 (16)
A Scientific Forger. 1904 (8,16,35)
Scoundrels Rampant. 1916
The Scourge of the Wizard. 1910
Scourged by Fear. 1915 (32)
A Scrap of Black Lace. 1901 (14)
The Sea Fox. 1919
The Seal of Death. 1903
The Seal of Silence. 1901 (11)
The Sealed Door. 1916 (32)
Sealed Orders. 1899 (16)
The Second Mr. Carstairs. 1911 (27)
The Secret of the Marble Mantle. 1920 (32)
The Secret Panel. 1904 (19,35)
The Senator's Plot. 1911 (16)
The Seven Schemers. 1912 (16)
A Sharper's Downfall. 1903 (21)
Shown on the Screen. 1911 (16)
The Sign of the Coin. 1913 (16)
The Sign of the Crossed Knives. 1899 (8)
The Sign of the Dagger. 1906 (16)
The Silent Guardian. 1907 (16,30)
The Silent Partner. 1908 (14,16)
The Silent Passenger. 1900 (14)
The Silver Hair Clue. 1912 (14)
A Skyline Message. 1914 (14)
The Slave of Crime. 1912
The Snare and the Game. 1908 (14)
Snarled Identities. 1918
The Soul Destroyers. 1915 (22)
The Spider's Parlor. 1913 (16)
A Spinner of Death. 1920 (32)
Spoilers and the Spoils. 1914
The Spoils of Chance. 1914 (14)
The Steel Casket and other stories. 1901 ss (30)
The Sting of the Adder. 1913 (32)
The Stolen Brain. 1916 (7,32)
The Stolen Race Horse. 1899 ss (19)
A Stolen Identity. 1888 in Secret Service Series; 1897 in M (16)
A Stolen Name. 1912 (16)
The Stolen Pay Train and other stories. 1899 ss (19)
The Streaked Peril. 1911 (16)
A Strike for Freedom. 1908 (16,34)
A Stroke of Policy. 1902 (21)
A Struggle with Destiny. 1914 (22)
A Submarine Trail. 1911 (18)
The Sultan's Pearls. 1917 (22)
The Sway of Sin. 1913
A Syndicate of Rascals. 1902 (11)
Talika, the Geisha Girl. 1910 (16)
A Tangled Case. 1905 (19,34,35)
Tangled in Crime. 1912 (16?)
A Tangled Skein. 1914 (32)
Tangled Threads. 1908 (14,16)
The Taxicab Riddle. 1912 (16)
The Tell-Tale Photographs. 1902 (14)
The Temple of Vice. 1909 (16)
The Terrible Thirteen. 1905 (16)
The Terrible Threat. 1904
A Test of Courage. 1915
The Thief in the Night. 1913
The Thief Who Was Robbed. 1914 (14)
A Threefold Disappearance. 1919 (32)
Through the Cellar Wall. 1906 (16)
A Titled Counterfeiter. 1888 in Secret Service Series; 1897 in M (13)
To the Ends of the Earth. 1915 (22)
Too Late to Talk. 1915
Tooth and Nail. 1912 (14)
The Toss of a Coin. 1902 (16,34)
The Toss of a Penny. 1904 (9,15)
A Tower of Strength. 1913
Toying with Fate. 1913
Tracked Across the Atlantic. 1897 (16)
The Trail of the Human Tiger. 1916 (16)
The Trail of the Catspaw. 1910

The Trail of the Fingerprints. 1914 (32)
The Trail of the Yoshiga. 1912
A Trap of Tangled Wire. 1908 (16,17)
Trapped by a Woman. 1906 (16)
Trapped in His Own Net. 1905 (16)
A Triple Crime. 1901 (11)
A Triple Identity. 1905 (16)
A Triple Knavery. 1912 (4)
The Triple Knock. 1911 (35)
A Trusted Rogue. 1902 (14)
The Turn of a Card. 1913 (16)
Twelve in a Grave. 1916 (32)
The Twelve Tin Boxes. 1899 (11)
The Twelve Wise Men. 1899 (8)
The Twin Mystery. 1903 (21)
Two Plus Two. 1899 (16)
Two Villains in One. 1902 (21)
The Unaccountable Crook. 1906 (16)
Under a Black Veil. 1905 (16)
Under False Colors. 1903 (8)
Under the Tiger's Claws. 1906 (16)
The Unfinished Letter. 1913 (16)
Unseen Foes. 1914 (14)
A Vain Sacrifice. 1912 (16?)
The Vampire's Trail. 1912 (18)
The Van Alstine Case. 1899 (8)
The Vanishing Emerald. 1911 (18)
The Vanishing Heiress. 1912 (16)
The Vial of Death. 1902 (16,34)
A Victim of Circumstances. 1900 (14)
A Victim of Deceit. 1905 (16)
A Villainous Scheme. 1905 (8,21)
A Voice from the Past. 1906 (30)
The Wages of Rascality. 1914 (10)
A Wall Street Haul. 1887 in Secret Service Series; 1897 in M (13)
Wanted: A Clew. 1914 (14)
Wanted by Two Clients. 1899 (8)
A War of Brains. 1911 (18)
The Way of the Wicked. 1911 (35)
A Weak-Kneed Rogue. 1911 (27)
Weaving the Web. 1902 (16)
Weighed in the Balance. 1913 (32)
A Weird Treasure. 1915 (32)
When a Man Yields. 1911 (23)
When a Rogue's in Power. 1913 (32)
When All Is Staked. 1913
When Brave Men Tremble. 1915 (22)
When Clews Are Hidden. 1913 (32)
When Destruction Threatens. 1914 (14)
When Honors Pall. 1915 (2)
When Jealousy Spurs. 1912
When Necessity Drives. 1911 (36)
When Rogues Conspire. 1916 (32)
When the Trap Was Sprung. 1908 (16)
When the Wicked Prosper. 1909 (16)
Where Peril Beckons. 1915 (22)
While the Fetters Were Forged. 1913
The Whirling Death. 1911 (27)
Whom the Gods Would Destroy. 1913 (32)
Wildfire. 1920 (32)
With Links of Steel. 1905 (16)
With Shackles of Fire. 1914 (32)
Without a Clue. 1908 (16)
The Wizard of the Cue. 1904 (9,34,35)
The Wolf Within. 1914 (16)
A Woman at Bay. 1909 (16)
The Woman in Black. 1912 (6)
The Woman of Evil. 1907 (16)
A Woman of Mystery. 1912 (16)
The Woman of Steel. 1907 (16,30)
A Woman's Hand. 1888 in Secret Service Series, as by John R. Coryell; 1897 in M (13)
Won by Magic. 1917 (22)
The Worst Case on Record. 1907 (34)
Written in Blood. 1912 (14)
The Yellow Brand. 1915 (32)
The Yellow Label. 1918 (22,32)

Vital Publications issued the following digest-size reprints from "Nick Carter Magazine," usually with a change in title. The original titles as well as the authors' real names are given below in parenthesis.

Death Has Green Eyes! 1946 (Richard Wormser) [NYC]
Empire of Crime. 1956 ("Crooks' Empire"; Richard Wormser) [NYC]
Murder Unlimited. 1945 ("Bid for a Railroad"; Richard Wormser)
Park Avenue Murder! 1946 ("Death on Park Avenue"; Richard Wormser) [NYC]
Rendezvous with a Dead Man. 1948 ("Murder on Skull Island"; John Chambliss)
The Yellow Disc Murder. 1948 ("Power"; T. C. McClary)

The following titles were published by juvenile fiction publisher Whitman; the stories were reprinted from dime novels.

Gideon Drexel's Millions. 1930
The Man Who Stole Millions. 1930
The Secret Agents of Brazil. 1930
The Stolen Pay Train. 1930
The Stolen Race Horse. 1930
A Triple Crime. 1930

These three collections of ss, presumably taken from American editions, were published by Pearson in England.
Final Exploits of Nick Carter.
Further Exploits of Nick Carter, Detective. 1920
New Exploits of Nick Carter.

And finally, this collection of six novelets.
Nick Carter, Detective. Macmillan, 1963

CARTER, NICK. House name; the real identities of the writers are shown in parenthesis with their works below. Although the Nick Carter dime novel characterization purports to continue in the books below, Carter has been transformed from a private detective into an oversexed superspy.
Agent Counter Agent. Award, 1973; Tandem, 1975 (by Ralph Eugene Hayes, q.v.) [Caracas]
The Amazon. Award, 1969; Tandem, 1969 (by Jon Messmann, q.v.) [Brazil]
Amsterdam. Award, 1968; Tandem, 1969 (by William L. Rohde, q.v.) [Amst.]
And Next the King. Charter, 1980 (by Steve Simmons) [Sp.]
The Arab Plague. Award, 1970. British title: The Slavemaster. Tandem, 1970 (by Jon Messmann, q.v.) [Saud. Arab.]
The Asian Mantrap. Charter, 1978 (by William Odell, q.v.) [Hanoi]
Assassin—Code Name Vulture. Award, 1974; Tandem, 1977 (by Ralph Eugene Hayes, q.v.) [Greece]
Assassination Brigade. Award, 1973; Tandem, 1974 (by Thomas Chastain, q.v.)
Assault on England. Award, 1972; Tandem, 1973 (by Ralph Eugene Hayes, q.v.) [Eng.]
Assignment: Intercept. Award, 1976; Star, 1978 (by Marilyn Granbeck, q.v.) [Mex.]
Assignment: Israel. Award, 1967; Tandem, 1968 (by Manning Lee Stokes, q.v.) [Isr.]
The Aztec Avenger. Award, 1974; Tandem, 1976 (by Saul Wernick, q.v.) [Mex.]
Beirut Incident. Award, 1974 (by Forrest V. Perrin, q.v.) [NYC]
Berlin. Award, 1969; Tandem, 1971 (by Jon Messmann, q.v.) [Berlin]
The Black Death. Award, 1970; Tandem, 1972 (by Manning Lee Stokes, q.v.) [Haiti]
The Bright Blue Death. Award, 1967; Tandem, 1968 (by Nicholas Browne) [Swed., Ger.]
A Bullet for Fidel. Award, 1965; Star, 1979 (by Valerie Moolman) [Cuba]
Butcher of Belgrade. Award, 1973; Tandem, 1964 (by Ralph Eugene Hayes, q.v.) [train]
The Cairo Mafia. Award, 1972; Tandem, 1972 (by Ralph Eugene Hayes, q.v.) [Cairo]
Cambodia. Award, 1970; Tandem, 1971 (by George Snyder) [Camb.]
Carnival for Killing. Award, 1969; Tandem, 1969 (by Jon Messmann, q.v.) [Rio de J.]
The Casbah Killers. Award, 1969; Tandem, 1970 (by Jon Messmann, q.v.) [Casa.]
Checkmate in Rio. Award, 1964; Digit, 1965 (by Valerie Moolman) [Rio de J.]
The China Doll. Award, 1964; Digit, 1965 (by Michael Avallone, q.v., and Valerie Moolman)
The Chinese Paymaster. Award, 1967; Tandem, 1968 (by Nicholas Browne)
The Cobra Kill. Award, 1969; Tandem, 1970 (by Manning Lee Stokes, q.v.) [Mal.]
The Code. Award, 1973; Tandem, 1975 (by Larry Powell, q.v.)
Code Name: Werewolf. Award, 1973; Tandem, 1973 (by Martin Cruz Smith, q.v.) [Madrid]
Counterfeit Agent. Award, 1975 (by Douglas Marland) [Eng., Switz.]
Danger Key. Award, 1966; Tandem, 1968 (by Lew Louderback) [Fla.]
Day of the Dingo. Charter, 1980 (by John Stevenson, q.v.) [Jap., Australia]
Deadly Doubles, Charter, 1978; Star, 1980 (by Lawrence Van Gelder)
Death Message: Oil 74-2. Award, 1976; Tandem, 1978 (by Dee Stuart, q.v., and Ansel Chapin) [Carib.]
Death Mission: Havana. Charter, 1980 (by Ron Felber, q.v.) [Wash. D.C., Havana]
Death of the Falcon. Award, 1974 (by Jim Bowser) [Wash. D.C.]
The Death Strain. Award, 1970; Tandem, 1971 (by Jon Messmann, q.v.) [NYC]

The Death's Head Conspiracy. Award, 1973 (by Robert Colby, q.v.)
The Defector. Award, 1969; Tandem, 1969 (by George Snyder) [H. Kong, China]
The Devil's Cockpit. Award, 1967; Tandem, 1968 (by Manning Lee Stokes, q.v.) [Buda.]
The Devil's Dozen. Award, 1973; Tandem, 1974 (by Martin Cruz Smith, q.v.)
Dr. Death. Award, 1975 (by Craig Nova) [Carib.]
The Doomsday Formula. Award, 1969; Tandem, 1970 (by Jon Messmann, q.v.) [Haw.]
The Doomsday Spore. Charter, 1979 (by George Warren, q.v.)
Double Identity. Award, 1967; Tandem, 1969 (by Manning Lee Stokes, q.v.) [India]
Dragon Flame. Award, 1966; Tandem, 1968 (by Manning Lee Stokes, q.v.) [H. Kong]
The Ebony Cross. Charter, 1978; Star, 1979 (by Jack Canon, q.v.) [Buda.]
Eight Card Stud. Charter, 1980 (by Robert E. Vardeman) [Las Veg.]
The Executioners. Award, 1970; Tandem, 1971 (by Jon Messmann, q.v.) [Australia]
The Eyes of the Tiger. Award, 1965; Mayflower, 1967 (by Manning Lee Stokes, q.v.) [Switz.]
The Fanatics of Al Asad. Award, 1976 (by Saul Wernick, q.v.) [NYC]
The Filthy Five. Award, 1967; Tandem, 1968 (by Manning Lee Stokes, q.v.) [P. Rico]
14 Seconds to Hell. Award, 1968; Tandem, 1969 (by Jon Messmann, q.v.) [China]
Fraulein Spy. Award, 1964; Digit, 1965 (by Valerie Moolman)
The Gallagher Plot. Award, 1976 (by Saul Wernick, q.v.) [Fr.]
The Golden Serpent. Award, 1967; Mayflower, 1968 (by Manning Lee Stokes, q.v.) [Mex.]
The Green Wolf Connection. Award, 1976 (by Dennis Lynds, q.v.) [Mid. East]
Hanoi. Award, 1966; Mayflower, 1968 (by Valerie Moolman) [Hanoi]
Hawaii. Charter, 1979; Star, 1982 (by Daniel C. Prince) [Haw.]
A High Yield in Death. Award, 1976 (by Jim Bowser) [Fla., Can.]
Hood of Death. Award, 1968; Tandem, 1970 (by William L. Rohde, q.v.) [Wash. D.C.]
Hour of the Wolf. Award, 1973; Tandem, 1975 (by Jeffrey M. Wallmann, q.v.) [Yugos.]
The Human Time Bomb. Award, 1969; Tandem, 1970 (by William L. Rohde, q.v.) [Colo.]
Ice Bomb Zero. Award, 1971; Tandem, 1972 (by George Snyder) [Arc.]
Ice Trap Terror. Award, 1974; Tandem, 1977 (by Jeffrey M. Wallmann, q.v.) [Nic.]
The Inca Death Squad. Award, 1972; Tandem, 1973 (by Martin Cruz Smith, q.v.) [Chile]
Istanbul. Award, 1965; Tandem, 1969 (by Manning Lee Stokes, q.v.) [Istan.]
The Jamaican Exchange. Charter, 1979 (by Leon Lazarus) [Jam.]
The Jerusalem File. Award, 1975; Star, 1978 (by Linda Stewart, q.v.) [Jerus.]
Jewel of Doom. Award, 1970 (by George Snyder) [Paris]
The Judas Spy. Award, 1968; Tandem, 1970 (by William L. Rohde, q.v.) [Djakarta]
The Katmandu Contract. Award, 1975; Tandem, 1977 (by James Fritzhand, q.v.) [Nepal]
A Korean Tiger. Award, 1967; Tandem, 1968 (by Manning Lee Stokes, q.v.) [Ger., Kor.]
The Kremlin File. Award, 1973; Tandem, 1976 (by W. T. Ballard, q.v.) [Fla.]
The Liquidator. Award, 1973; Tandem, 1974 (by Richard Hubbard, q.v.) [Greece]
The List. Award, 1976; Tandem, 1978 (by James Fritzhand, q.v.) [Burma]
The Living Death. Award, 1969; Tandem, 1970 (by Jon Messmann, q.v.)
Macao. Award, 1968; Tandem, 1968 (by Manning Lee Stokes, q.v.) [Macao]
The Man Who Sold Death. Award, 1974 (by Lawrence Van Gelder) [NYC, Fr.]
The Mark of Cosa Nostra. Award, 1971; Tandem, 1972 (by George Snyder) [It.]
Massacre in Milan. Award, 1974; Tandem, 1977 (by Al Hine) [Rome, Milan]
The Mind Killers. Award, 1970; Tandem, 1971 (by Jon Messmann, q.v.) [Wash. D.C.]

The Mind Poisoners. Award, 1966; Tandem, 1968 (by Lionel White, q.v., and Valerie Moolman) [Las Veg., S.F.]
Mission to Venice. Award, 1967; Tandem, 1970 (by Manning Lee Stokes, q.v.) [Venice]
Moscow. Award, 1970 (by George Snyder) [Moscow]
The Nichovev Plot. Award, 1976 (by Craig Nova) [Wash. D.C.]
Night of the Avenger. Award, 1973; Tandem, 1974 (by Chet Cunningham, q.v., and Daniel T. Streib, q.v.) [Wash. D.C.]
The Nowhere Weapon. Charter, 1979; Star, 1982 (by William Odell, q.v.) [Paris, Geneva]
The N3 Conspiracy. Award, 1974; Tandem, 1977 (by Dennis Lynds, q.v.) [Mozam.]
The Omega Terror. Award, 1972; Tandem, 1973 (by Ralph Eugene Hayes, q.v.) [Tangier]
Operation Che Guevara. Award, 1969; Tandem, 1970 (by Jon Messmann, q.v.) [Bolivia]
Operation Moon Rocket. Award, 1968; Tandem, 1968 (by Lew Louderback) [Fla.]
Operation Snake. Award, 1969; Tandem, 1970 (by Jon Messmann, q.v.) [Nepal]
Operation Starvation. Award, 1966; Tandem, 1968 (by Nicholas Browne) [Paris, China]
Our Agent in Rome Is Missing. Award, 1973; Tandem, 1976 (by Al Hine) [Rome]
The Pamplona Affair. Charter, 1978 (by Dee Stuart, q.v., and Ansel Chapin) [Sp.]
The Peking Dossier. Award, 1974 (by Linda Stewart, q.v.)
Peking/The Tulip Affair. Award, 1969; Tandem, 1973 (by Arnold Marmor) [Peking, H. Kong] (2 novelets)
The Pemex Chart. Charter, 1979 (by Dwight Vreeland Swain, 1915-   ) [Mex.]
Plot for the Fourth Reich. Award, 1977 (by Bob Latona) [Arg., Colom.]
Race of Death. Charter, 1978 (by David Hagberg, q.v.) [Belg.]
The Red Guard. Award, 1967; Tandem, 1968 (by Manning Lee Stokes, q.v.) [China, Tib.]
The Red Rays. Award, 1969; Tandem, 1969 (by Manning Lee Stokes, q.v.) [Peru]
The Red Rebellion. Award, 1970; Tandem, 1970 (by Jon Messmann, q.v.) [Calif.]
The Redolmo Affair. Charter, 1979 (by Jack Canon, q.v.) [Mex.]
Reich Four. Charter, 1979; Star, 1982 (by Frederick Vincent Huber, q.v.) [Ger.]
Revenge of the Generals. Charter, 1978; Star, 1979 (by Saul Wernick, q.v.) [Boston, Sp.]
Rhodesia. Award, 1968; Tandem, 1969 (by William L. Rohde, q.v.) [Rhod.]
Run, Spy, Run. Award, 1964; Tandem, 1969 (by Michael Avallone, q.v., and Valerie Moolman) [NYC, Eng.]
Safari for Spies. Award, 1964; Digit, 1965 (by Valerie Moolman) [Casa.]
Saigon. Award, 1964; Digit, 1965 (by Michael Avallone, q.v., and Valerie Moolman) [Saigon]
The Satan Trap. Charter, 1979; Star, 1982 (by Jack Canon, q.v.)
The Sea Trap. Award, 1969; Tandem, 1969 (by Jon Messmann, q.v.) [ship]
Seven Against Greece. Award, 1967; Tandem, 1968 (by Nicholas Browne) [Greece]
Sign of the Cobra. Award, 1974; Tandem, 1977 (by James Fritzhand, q.v.) [New Delhi]
The Sign of the Prayer Shawl. Award, 1976 (by David Hagberg, q.v.) [Jap.]
Six Bloody Summer Days. Award, 1975; Tandem, 1978 (by DeWitt S. Copp, q.v.) [Afr.]
The Slavemaster; see The Arab Plague
The Snake Flag Conspiracy. Award, 1976; Star, 1978 (by Saul Wernick, q.v.) [Boston]
The Spanish Connection. Award, 1973; Tandem, 1976 (by Bruce Cassiday, q.v.) [Sp.]
Spy Castle. Award, 1966; Tandem, 1968 (by Manning Lee Stokes, q.v.) [Eng.]
Strike Force Terror. Award, 1973; Tandem, 1973 (by Ralph Eugene Hayes, q.v.) [Turk.]
Strike of the Hawk. Charter, 1980 (by Joseph L. Gilmore, q.v.)
The Suicide Seat. Charter, 1980 (by George Warren, q.v.)
Target: Doomsday Island. Award, 1973; Tandem, 1974 (by Richard Hubbard, q.v.) [Bahamas]
Tarantula Strike. Charter, 1980 (by Dan Reardon)

Temple of Fear. Award, 1968; Tandem, 1969 (by Manning Lee Stokes, q.v.) [Tokyo]
Ten Times Dynamite. Charter, 1980 (by Frank Adduci, Jr.) [Fla., Brazil]
The Terrible Ones. Award, 1966; Mayflower, 1968 (by Valerie Moolman) [Haiti]
The 13th Spy. Award, 1965; Digit, 1965 (by Valerie Moolman) [Moscow]
Thunderstrike in Syria. Charter, 1979; Star, 1980 (by Joseph Rosenberger, q.v.) [Syr.]
Time Clock of Death. Award, 1970; Tandem, 1971 (by George Snyder) [Djakarta, Java]
Triple Cross. Award, 1976 (by Dennis Lynds, q.v.)
Tropical Deathpact. Charter, 1979; Star, 1982 (by Bob Stokesberry) [Cent. Am.]
Trouble in Paradise. Charter, 1978; Star, 1980 (by Robert Derek Steeley, q.v.) [Bahamas]
Turkish Bloodbath. Charter, 1980 (by Jerry Ahern) [Turk.]
The Turncoat. Award, 1976; Tandem, 1978 (by Leon Lazarus) [Beirut, Yugos.]
The Ultimate Code. Award, 1975 (by William Odell, q.v.) [Greece]
Under the Wall. Charter, 1978; Star, 1982 (by DeWitt S. Copp, q.v.) [Berlin]
Vatican Vendetta. Award, 1974; Tandem, 1977 (by Ralph Eugene Hayes, q.v., and George Snyder)
The Vulcan Disaster. Award, 1976 (by George Warren, q.v.) [Far East]
War from the Clouds. Charter, 1980 (by Joseph L. Gilmore, q.v.) [Carib.]
The Weapon of Night. Award, 1967; Mayflower, 1968 (by Valerie Moolman) [N.Y.]
Web of Spies. Award, 1966; Mayflower, 1967 (by Manning Lee Stokes, q.v.) [Sp.]
The Z Document. Award, 1975; Tandem, 1978 (by Homer Morris) [Ethio.]

CARTER, NOEL VREELAND
-The Lazarus Inheritance. Popular Library, 1976
This Band of Spirits. Signet, 1980

CARTER, WINIFRED
The Dead Return. Rivers, 1929
Marriage by Mistake. Modern, 193?
The Two Mrs. Camerons, with Edith Carter. King's Stone Press, 1936; Dramatists, 1937 (3-act play.)

CARTER, (P.) YOUNGMAN, 1904-1969. Ref: CC. Husband of Margery Allingham, 1904-1966, q.v.; continued her Albert Campion series with the following titles.
Mr. Campion's Falcon. Heinemann, 1970. U.S. title: Mr. Campion's Quarry. Morrow, 1971
Mr. Campion's Farthing. Heinemann, 1969; Morrow, 1969
Mr. Campion's Quarry; see Mr. Campion's Falcon

CARTER-BROWN, PETER. Pseudonym of Alan Geoffrey Yates, 1923-   , q.v. See: Carter Brown. Other pseudonym: Carolyn Farr, q.v.

CARTLEDGE, H(ORACE) A(VRON)
Peloton, Detective. Arnold, 1937

CARTLIDGE, ALICE
Murder at Moreby. Stockwell, 1935

CARTMILL, CLEVE. 1908-1964. See: George Sanders, 1906-1972.

CARTRELL, PIERRE
The Sin of Sister Betty. Continental, 1946 [N.Y.]

CARTWRIGHT, JUSTIN
Deep Six. Futura, 1977
Fighting Men. Futura, 1977 (Novelization of "The New Avengers" TV series)
The Horse of Darius. H. Hamilton, 1980; Macmillan, 1980 [Switz.]
The Revenge. Contemporary, 1978

CARVALHO, CLAIRE and BOYDEN SPARKES, 1890-1954.
Crime in Ink. Scribner, 1929 (Somewhat fictionalized true crime accounts.)

CARVER, MRS.
The Horrors of Oakendale Abbey. Minerva, 1797

CARVER, STEWART
Died o' Wednesday. Melrose, 1953

Sneeze on Monday. Melrose, 1951
Trouble on Tuesday. Melrose, 1952

CARVIC, HERON.   -1980. Ref: CA, CC, TC. SC: Miss Seeton, in all titles.
Miss Seeton, Bewitched. Bles, 1971. U.S. title: Witch Miss Seeton. Harper, 1971
Miss Seeton Draws the Line. Bles, 1969; Harper, 1970
Miss Seeton Sings. Davies, 1974; Harper, 1973 [Geneva]
Odds on Miss Seeton. Davies, 1976; Harper, 1975
Picture Miss Seeton. Bles, 1968; Harper, 1968
Witch Miss Seeton; see Miss Seeton Bewitched

CARY, (THOMAS) FALKLAND L(ITTON). See also: A. A. Thomson.
An Air for Murder, with Philip King, 1904-   , q.v. French (London), 1958 (3-act play.)
The Artist's Murder. Lewis, 1944 (3-act play.)
Burning Cold, with A. A. Thomson. French, 1943 (3-act play.)
Candied Peel. Lewis, 1944 (3-act play)
Danger Inside, with Ivan Butler (pseudonym of Edward Ivan Oakley Beuttler). French (London), 1960 (Play.)
Doctor—There's Danger. French, 1938 (3-act play.)
Knight's Move. French (London), 1949 (3-act play.)
Madam Tic-Tac, with Philip Weathers, 1908-   , q.v. French (London), 1951 (3-act play.)
Murder at the Varsity, with A. A. Thomson. French, 1942 (3-act play.)
Murder Out of Tune. Thornley, 1944; revised: French, 1953 (3-act play.)
Murder Party. Garamond, 1935 (3-act play.)
Open Verdict, with Philip Weathers, 1908-   , q.v. French, 1952 (3-act play.)
The Paper Chain, with Ivan Butler (pseudonym of Edward Ivan Oakley Beuttler). French (London), 1953 (3-act play.)
Pitfall. Stacey, 1955 (3-act play.)
The Proof of the Poison..., with Philip Weathers, 1908-   , q.v. French (London), 1963 (3-act play.)
The Shadow Witness with Philip Weathers, 1908-   , q.v. French (London), 1961 (2-act play.)

CARY, MORLAND. Pseudonym of Hugh Edward Cary Nevill.
Because Their Hearts Were Pure. Dramatists, 1952 (3-act play.)
Love Rides the Rails. Dramatists, 1940 (Play.)

CASBERG, MELVIN A. 1909-   . Ref: CA.
Death Stalks the Punjab. Strawberry Hill, 1980 [India]

CASE, DAVID. 1937-   . Born in NYC.
And Now the Screaming Starts; see Fengriffin
The Cell: Three Tales of Horror. Hill, 1969; Macdonald, 1969 (3 novelets.)
Fengriffin. Hill, 1970; Macdonald, 1971. Also published as: And Now the Screaming Starts. Macdonald, 1971
Wolf Tracks. Belmont, 1980 [Toronto]

CASE, FRANCES POWELL. Pseudonym: Frances Powell, q.v.

CASELEYR, CAMILLE AUGUST MARIE. 1909-   . Pseudonym: Jack Danvers, q.v.

CASEY, BERNARD L. See: Sharon (B.) Wagner, 1936-   .

CASEY, KEVIN. 1940-   . Ref: CA.
A Sense of Survival. Faber, 1974

CASEY, MERVIN
The Mutilators. Major, 1976

CASEY, PATRICK and TERENCE
-The Gay-Cat. Fly, 1921

CASEY, ROBERT. A former Jesuit priest; spent much of his life in the universities and parishes of Boston.
The Jesus Man. Evans, 1979 [Boston]

CASEY, ROBERT J. 1890-1962. Ref: MP. SC: Jim Sands = JS.
Cambodian Quest. Bobbs, 1931; Mathews, 1932 [Camb.]
Four Faces of Siva. Bobbs, 1929; Harrap, 1929 [Camb.]
Hot Ice. Greenberg, 1933; Mathews, 1933 JS

News Reel. Bobbs, 1932. British title: The Secret of the Dark Room. Mathews, 1932 JS
The Secret of the Bungalow. Bobbs, 1930; Mathews, 1931 JS
The Secret of the Dark Room; see News Reel
The Secret of Thirty-Seven Hardy Street. Bobbs, 1929; Mathews, 1930 JS
The Third Owl. Bobbs, 1934; Nicholson, 1934 JS [Ill.]
The Voice of the Lobster. Bobbs, 1930

CASEY, TERENCE. See: Patrick Casey.

CASHMAN, JOHN. Pseudonym of Timothy Francis Tothill Davis, 1941-   . Ref: CA.
The Cook General. Harper, 1974; H. Hamilton, 1975 [Eng., 1870s]
The Gentleman from Chicago. Harper, 1973; H. Hamilton, 1974 [Chi., 1800s]
Kid Glove Charlie. Harper, 1978; Hale, 1979 [Eng., 1870s]

CASLER, RONALD
Death List. Pinnacle, 1975

CASPARY, VERA. 1899-   . See also: Frederick Goldsmith; and: (William Cantwell) Frank (Thorpe) Vreeland, 1891-   . Ref: CA, EM, MC, TC.
Bedelia. Houghton, 1945; Eyre, 1945 [Conn.]
A Chosen Sparrow. Putnam, 1964; Allen, 1964
Death Wish; see The Weeping and the Laughter
Elizabeth X; see The Secret of Elizabeth
Evvie. Harper, 1960; Allen, 1960 [Chi.]
False Face. Allen, 1954
Final Portrait. Allen, 1971
The Husband. Harper, 1957; Allen, 1957 [Eng.]
Lady in Mink; see The Murder in the Stork Club
Laura. Houghton, 1943; Eyre, 1944 [NYC] (3-act play version, with George Sklar: Dramatists, 1945; English Theatre, 1952.)
The Man Who Loved His Wife. Putnam, 1966; Allen, 1966
The Murder in the Stork Club. Detective Book Club, 1946. British title: Lady in Mink. Gordon Martin, 1946 [NYC]
The Rosecrest Cell. Putnam, 1967; Allen, 1968
Ruth. Pockettes, 1972
The Secret of Elizabeth. PB, 1979. British title: Elizabeth X. Allen, 1978
Stranger Than Truth. Random, 1946; Eyre, 1947
Thelma. Little, 1952; Allen, 1953
The Weeping and the Laughter. Little, 1950. British title: Death Wish. Eyre, 1951 [L.A.]

CASS, ZOE. Pseudonym of Lois Dorothea Low, 1916-   . Other pseudonym: Lois Paxton, q.v. Ref: CA.
Island of the Seven Hills. Random, 1974; Cassell, 1975 [Malta]
The Silver Leopard. Random, 1976; Elek, 1978
A Twist in the Silk. Elek, 1980

CASSELLS, JOHN. Pseudonym of W(illiam) Murdoch Duncan, 1909-1975, q.v. Other pseudonyms: John Dallas, Neill Graham, Martin Locke, Peter Malloch, Lovat Marshall, qq.v. SC: Insp. Flagg, in at least those marked F; The Picaroon (Ludovic Saxon), in at least those marked P. Set: Eng.
Action of the Picaroon. Long, 1975 P
Again Inspector Flagg. Muller, 1956 F
The Audacious Picaroon. Long, 1967 P
The Avenging Picaroon. Muller, 1955 P
The Bastion of the Damned. Melrose, 1946
The Benevolent Picaroon. Long, 1965 P
Beware! the Picaroon. Muller, 1957 P
Blackfingers. Long, 1966 F
Blue Mask. Long, 1964 F
The Brothers of Benevolence. Long, 1962 F
Call for Superintendent Flagg. Long, 1968 F
Case for Inspector Flagg. Muller, 1954 F
Case 29. Long, 1958 F
The Castle of Sin. Melrose, 1949 F
Challenge for the Picaroon. Long, 1964 P
The Circle of Dust. Melrose, 1950 F
The Clue of the Purple Asters. Melrose, 1949 F
The Council of the Rat. Long, 1963 F
The Double-Crosser. Long, 1969
The Elusive Picaroon. Long, 1968 P
The Enforcer. Long, 1973 F
The Engaging Picaroon. Long, 1950 P

Enter Superintendent Flagg. Long, 1959 F
Enter the Picaroon. Long, 1958 F
The Enterprising Picaroon. Long, 1959 P
Exit Mr. Shane. Melrose, 1951 F
The Grafter. Long, 1970 F
Grey Face. Long, 1965 F
The Grey Ghost. Melrose, 1951 F
The Hatchet Man. Long, 1971 F
Inspector Flagg and the Scarlet Skeleton. Muller, 1955 F
Killer's Rope. Long, 1974 F
The League of Nameless Men. Melrose, 1948 F
The Mark of the Leech. Melrose, 1947
Master of the Dark. Melrose, 1948 F
Meet the Picaroon. Long, 1957 P
Murder Comes to Rothesay. Melrose, 1946 F
Night of the Picaroon. Long, 1969 P
The Picaroon Collects. Long, 1970 P
The Picaroon Gets the Run-Around. Long, 1976 P
The Picaroon Goes West. Long, 1962 P [Can.]
The Picaroon Laughs Last. Long, 1973 P
Plunder for the Picaroon. Long, 1966 P
Presenting Inspector Flagg. Muller, 1957 F
Prey for the Picaroon. Long, 1963 P
Problem for Superintendent Flagg. Long, 1961 F
Profit for the Picaroon. Long, 1972 P
Quest for Superintendent Flagg. Long, 1975 F
Quest for the Picaroon. Long, 1970 P
The Rattler. Melrose, 1952 F
The Room in Quiver Court. Long, 1967 F
Salute Inspector Flagg. Muller, 1953 F
Salute the Picaroon. Long, 1960 P
Score for Superintendent Flagg. Long, 1960 F
The Second Mrs. Locke. Melrose, 1952 F
The Sons of the Morning. Melrose, 1946
The Waters of Sadness. Melrose, 1950 F

CASSELS, LOUIS. 1922-1974. Ref: CA.
A Bad Investment. Pyramid, 1974 [Calif.]

CASSERA, NORA
The Blue Flower Mystery. Heath, 1930

CASSERLY, GORDON
The Elephant God. Allan, 1920; Putnam, 1921

CASSIDAY, BRUCE (BINGHAM). 1920- .
Pseudonyms: Carson Bingham, Nick Carter, Mary Anne Drew, Annie Laurie McAllister, Annie Laurie McMurdie, Michael Stratford, qq.v. Ref: CA.
SC: Cash Madigan = CM.
The Brass Shroud. Ace, 1958
The Buried Motive. Ace, 1957 CM [Mo.]
The Corpse in the Picture Window. Ace, 1961 [Conn.]
The Floater. Abelard (NYC & London), 1960 [Conn.]
The Girl in the Trunk. Ace, 1973 [Haw.]
Operation Goldkill. Award, 1967 [It.]
While Murder Waits. Graphic, 1957 CM [NYC]

CASSIDY, JOHN (RUFUS). 1922- . Ref: CA.
A Station in the Delta. Scribner, 1979 [Viet Nam]

CASSILIS, INA L(EON)
Between Midnight and Dawn. Vizetelly, 1885
Blind Justice. Aldine, 1926
Martyr or Criminal? Aldine, 1925

CASSILIS, ROBERT
Arrow of God. H. Hamilton, 1979
Winding Sheet. H. Hamilton, 1978

CASSILL, R(ONALD) V(ERLIN). 1919- .
Ref: CA.
-Doctor Cobb's Game. Geis, 1970
Dormitory Women. Lion, 1954 [acad.]
The Hungering Shame. Avon, 1956
-Lustful Summer. Avon, 1958
-Naked Morning. Avon, 1957
-A Taste of Sin. Ace, 1955
The Wife Next Door. GM, 1959
-The Wound of Love. Avon, 1956

CASSON, STANLEY. 1889-1944. Born in London; archeologist, expert on the Byzantine period, Fellow of New College (Oxford); author of scholarly works on sculpture, archeology and history.
Murder by Burial. H. Hamilton, 1938; Harper, 1938

CASTANG, VIOLA
The Invisible Cord. Allen, 1958
A Smell of Garbage. Hale, 1972

CASTIER, JULES
Rather Like. Jenkins, 1920; Lippincott, 1920 ss, at least one criminous

CASTILLOU, HENRY. 1921- .
The Night of the Rose. Redman, 1958 (Translation of "Le Nuit de la Rose." Paris, 1957.)

CASTLE, AGNES (SWEETMAN), -1922, and EGERTON CASTLE, 1858-1920.
Flower o' the Orange, and other stories. Methuen, 1908; Macmillan, 1908 ss, some criminous

CASTLE, BRENDA. Pseudonym: Georgina Ferrand, q.v.

CASTLE, DENNIS
The Fourth Gambler. Muller, 1964

CASTLE, EGERTON. 1858-1920. See: Agnes (Sweetman) Castle, -1922.

CASTLE, FRANK. Pseudonym: Steve Thurman, q.v. Born in New Mexico; graduate of U. of Oklahoma; magazine and book writer.
Dead—and Kicking. GM, 1956; Fawcett (London), 1957 [Calif.]
Hawaiian Eye. Dell, 1962. (Novelization of the TV series.) [Haw.]
Lovely and Lethal. GM, 1957; Red Seal, 1959 [Calif.]
Move Along, Stranger. GM, 1954; Fawcett (London), 1954
Murder in Red. GM, 1957; Fawcett (London), 1959 [N. Mex.]
Vengeance Under Law. GM, 1957
The Violent Hours. GM, 1956; Fawcett (London), 1956 [L.A.]

CASTLE, JOHN. Joint pseudonym of John William Garrod and Ronald Charles Payne.
Flight into Danger, with Arthur Hailey, 1920- ; Souvenir, 1958. U.S. title: Runway Zero-Eight. Doubleday, 1959 [Can.]
Runway Zero-Eight; see Flight into Danger
The Seventh Fury. Souvenir, 1961; Walker, 1963

CASTLE, MORT. 1946- . Ref: CA.
The Deadly Election. Major, 1976

CASTLETOWN, LORD [BERNARD EDWARD BARNABY FITZPATRICK]. 1849- .
A Bundle of Lies. Drane's, 1924 ss, some criminous

CASWELL, HELEN (RAYBURN). 1923- .
Ref: CA.
Never Wed an Old Man. Doubleday, 1975 [Ire.]

CATALAN, HENRI. Pseudonym of Henri Dupuy-Mazuel, 1885- . Ref: CC. SC:
Soeur Angele, in all titles.
The Embarrassed Ladies Affair; see Soeur Angele and the Embarrassed Ladies
The Ghosts of Chambord Affair; see Soeur Angele and the Ghosts and Chambord
Soeur Angele and the Bell Ringer's Niece. Sheed, 1957 [Fr.]
Soeur Angele and the Embarrassed Ladies. Sheed, 1955. Also published as: The Embarrassed Ladies Affair. Sheed, 1973 (Translation of "Le Cas de Soeur Angele." Paris, 1953.) [Paris]
Soeur Angele and the Ghosts of Chambord. Sheed, 1956. Also published as: The Ghosts of Chambord Affair. Sheed, 1973 (Translation of "Soeur Angele et les Fantomes de Chambord." Paris, 1953.) [Fr.]

CATHER, GEORGE P.
Dora's Device. Peterson, 1885

CATTO, MAX(WELL JEFFREY). 1909- .
Ref: CA. Pseudonym: Simon Kent, q.v.
-All or Nothing. Popular Library, 1956 (British title?)
The Banana Men. Heinemann, 1967; Simon, 1967
-The Empty Tiger. Joseph, 1977; St. Martin's, 1977
-The Killing Frost. Heinemann, 1950. Also published as: Trapeze. Four Square, 1959
Mister Midas. Joseph, 1976
-A Prize of Gold. Heinemann, 1953
Sam Casanova. Heinemann, 1973; Signet, 1977 [Paris]
The Tiger in the Bed. Heinemann, 1962; Morrow, 1963
Trapeze; see The Killing Frost

CAUDWELL, VERA
The Sole Condition. Long, 1926

CAULFIELD, MAX [MALACHY FRANCIS CAULFIELD]. 1915- . Ref: CA.
Bruce Lee Lives? Dell, 1976

CAULFIELD, RICHARD
Showdown. Arrow, 1950

CAUNTER, CYRIL F(RANCIS). 1899- .
Death to the Killer. Eldon, 1935
Ex-Gangster. Eldon, 1933

CAUSEY, JAMES O.
The Baby Doll Murders. GM, 1957; Fawcett (London), 1959
Frenzy. Crest, 1960 [Calif.]
Killer Take All! Graphic, 1957; Hale, 1960 [Calif.]

CAVANAGH, ARTHUR. 1926- . Born in N.Y., graduate of William and Mary College; has been actor, TV writer, and textbook editor.
The Children Are Gone. Simon, 1966; Heinemann, 1966 [NYC]

CAVE, EMMA
The Blood Bond. Heinemann, 1979; Harper, 1979
Little Angie. Deutsch, 1977; Coward, 1977

CAVE, HUGH B(ARNETT). 1910- . Ref: CA.
The Nebulon Horror. Dell, 1980
Run, Shadow, Run. Hale, 1968

CAVE, PETER (LESLIE). 1940- . Pseudonym: Peter Maxwell, q.v. See also: C. S. Cotelo.
The Crime Commandoes. Everest, 1976
Firefloood. Futura, 1980
Foxbat. Futura, 1978; Jove, 1979
Hostage. Futura, 1977 (Novelization of "The New Avengers" TV series.)
House of Cards. Futura, 1976; Berkley, 1978 (Novelization of "The New Avengers" TV series.)
Last of the Cybernauts. Futura, 1977 (Novelization of "The New Avengers" TV series.)
Siege. Hamlyn, 1980

CAVENDISH, CHARLES
The Lure. Collins, 1930 (Novelization of the film adapted from the play by Major J. S. Clair.)

CAVENEY, PHILIP (RICHARD). 1951- .
Ref: CA.
The Sins of Rachel Ellis. St. Martin's, 1978; Hale, 1979

CAVERHILL, WILLIAM MELVILLE. 1910- .
Pseudonym: Alan Melville, q.v.

CAWLEY, ROBERT
Friend or Foe? Sphere, 1977
Shockwave. Sphere, 1979

CAY, NOWELL
-A Foe in the Family. Digby, 1905
-In Hot Pursuit. Digby, 1906
The Presumption of Stanley Hay, M.P. Warne, 1901

CAYLOR, O. P. Pseudonym: Nicholas Carter, q.v.

CAYWOOD, MARK. Pseudonym.
Paradise Island. Bles, 1927. U.S. title: Rainbow Island. Viking, 1927
Rainbow Island; see Paradise Island
-Virginia's Quest. Gray, 1934

CEARLEY, J. B.
A Touch of Murder. Caravelle, 1968

CEARNACH, CONALL. See: Cearnach Conall.

CECIL, ALLAN
Turquoise Clues. Rich, 1949

CECIL, HENRY. Pseudonym of Henry Cecil Leon, 1902-1976. Ref: CC, EM, TC.
See also: Felicity Douglas. SC:
Colonel Brain and Ambrose Low = B&L;
Roger Thursby = RT. Set: Eng.
According to the Evidence. Chapman, 1954; Harper, 1954 B&L
Alibi for a Judge. Joseph, 1966; Harper, 1966
The Asking Price. Joseph, 1966; Harper, 1966
The Blackmailers; see No Fear or Favour
Brief Tales from the Bench. BBC, 1968; Simon, 1972 ss
Brothers in Law. Joseph, 1955; Harper, 1955. Play version, by Ted Willis, 1918- , q.v., and Henry Cecil: French (London), 1957 RT
-The Buttercup Spell. Joseph, 1971; British Book Centre, 1974
A Child Divided; see Fathers in Law

Daughters in Law. Joseph, 1961; Harper, 1961
Fathers in Law. Joseph, 1965. U.S. title: A Child Divided. Harper, 1965
Friends at Court. Joseph, 1956; Harper, 1956 RT
Full Circle. Chapman, 1948
Hunt the Slipper. Joseph, 1977
Independent Witness. Joseph, 1963; British Book Centre, 1974
Juror in Waiting. Joseph, 1970
The Long Arm; see Much in Evidence
Much in Evidence. Joseph, 1957. U.S. title: The Long Arm, Harper, 1957
Natural Causes. Chapman, 1953; British Book Centre, 1974
No Bail for the Judge. Chapman, 1952; Harper, 1952 B&L
No Fear or Favour. Joseph, 1968. U.S. title: The Blackmailers. Simon, 1969
The Painswick Line. Chapman, 1951; British Book Centre, 1974
Portrait of a Judge and other stories. Joseph, 1964; Harper, 1965 ss
Settled Out of Court. Joseph, 1959; Harper, 1959. Play version, by William Saroyan, 1908- , and Henry Cecil: French (London), 1962
Sober As a Judge. Joseph, 1958; Harper, 1959 RT
Tell You What I'll Do. Joseph, 1969; Simon, 1970
Truth with Her Boots On. Joseph, 1974
Unlawful Occasions. Joseph, 1962; British Book Centre, 1974
The Wanted Man. Joseph, 1972; British Book Centre, 1974
Ways and Means. Chapman, 1952; British Book Service, 1952
A Woman Named Anne. Joseph, 1967; Harper, 1967

CECIL, OLIVE
Behold the Body! Long, 1932
Four Women Went. Long, 1931
-Lighter of Candles. Nash, 1930
The Pepper-Pot Problem. Long, 1933

CELESTIN, JACK and JACK DE LEON, q.v.
The Man at Six. French, 1929 (3-act play).

CELLO, J.
Corruption's Tutor. Scion, 1953
Crisis. Scion, 1953
Duet to Corruption. Scion, 1953
A Guy Gets His. Scion, 1950
Jeanie with the Light Brown Corpse. Scion, 1952
Lights Out. Scion, 1953
Sin Has No Future. Scion, 1954
Sin Is Her Mantle. Scion, 1953
They Don't Live Long. Scion, 1951

CENNI, JOSEPH
Mafia Women. Tandem, 1974

CERF, CHRISTOPHER BENNETT. 1941- . Joint pseudonym with Michael E. Frith: I*n Fl*m*ng, q.v. Ref: CA.

CERRA, GERDA ANN
A Darker Heritage. Lancer, 1972

CERVUS, G. I. Pseudonym of William James Roe, 1843- .
-White Feathers. Lippincott, 1885

CHABER, M. E. Pseudonym of Kendall Foster Crossen, 1910-1981, q.v. Other pseudonyms: Bennett Barlay, Richard Foster, Christopher Monig, Clay Richards, qq.v. SC: Milo March, in all titles.
All the Way Home; see No Grave for March
As Old As Cain. Holt, 1954. Also published as: Take One for Murder. Bestseller, 1955 [Ohio]
The Bonded Dead. Holt, 1971; Hale, 1973 [Miami]
Born to Be Hanged. Holt, 1973 [Nev.]
The Day It Rained Diamonds. Holt, 1966; Macdonald, 1968 [L.A.]
Don't Get Caught; see Hangman's Harvest
The Flaming Man. Holt, 1969; Hale, 1970 [L.A.]
The Gallows Garden. Rinehart, 1958; Boardman, 1958. Also published as: The Lady Came to Kill. PB, 1959 [Carib.]
Green Grow the Graves. Holt, 1970; Hale, 1971
Hangman's Harvest. Holt, 1952. Also published as: Don't Get Caught. Popular Library, 1953 [Calif.]
A Hearse of Another Color. Rinehart, 1958; Boardman, 1959 [New Or.]
Jade for a Lady. Rinehart, 1962; Boardman, 1962 [H. Kong]
The Lady Came to Kill; see The Gallows Garden

A Lonely Walk. Rinehart, 1956; Boardman, 1957 [It.]
A Man in the Middle. Holt, 1967 [H. Kong]
The Man Inside. Holt, 1954; Eyre, 1955. Also published as: Now It's My Turn. Popular Library, 1954
No Grave for March. Holt, 1953; Eyre, 1954. Also published as: All the Way Down. Popular Library, 1953 [Berlin]
Now It's My Turn; see The Man Inside
Six Who Ran. Holt, 1964; Boardman, 1965 [Rio de J.]
So Dead the Rose. Rinehart, 1959; Boardman, 1960 [Berlin]
Softly in the Night. Holt, 1963; Boardman, 1963 [L.A.]
The Splintered Man. Rinehart, 1955; Boardman, 1957 [Berlin]
Take One for Murder; see As Old As Cain
Uneasy Lies the Dead. Holt, 1964; Boardman, 1964
Wanted: Dead Men. Holt, 1965; Boardman, 1966
Wild Midnight Falls. Holt, 1968 [Moscow]

CHABREY, F.
The Invisible Image. International, 1969

CHABRILLAT, HENRI. See: WILLIAM (BERTRAND) BUSNACH, 1832-1907.

CHACKO, DAVID. 1942- . Ref: CA.
Gage. St. Martin's, 1974; Panther, 1976 [Ohio]
Price. St. Martin's, 1973; Gollancz, 1974 [Ohio]

CHADWICK, CHARLES. 1874-1953.
The Cactus. Crowell, 1925 [N.Y., Mex.]
The Moving House of Foscaldo. Cassell, 1926 [Fr.]

CHADWICK, JOSELYN. Pseudonym of Joseph L. Chadwick, q.v. Other pseudonyms: John Conway, Jo Anne Creighton, John Creighton, qq.v.
Evil Is the Night. Avon, 1974
The Web of Evil. Avon, 1972

CHADWICK, JOSEPH L. Pseudonyms: Joselyn Chadwick, John Conway, Joe Anne Creighton, John Creighton, qq.v.
The Golden Frame. GM, 1955

CHADWICK, PAUL. Pseudonym: Brant House, q.v.

CHALKER, JACK L(AURENCE). 1944- .
-A Jungle of Stars. Ballantine, 1976

CHALLIS, MARY. Pseudonym of Sara Hutton Bowen-Judd, 1922- . Other pseudonyms: Anne Burton, Margaret Leek, Sara Woods, qq.v. SC: Jeremy Locke, in both titles, both set in Eng.
Burden of Proof. Raven, 1980
Crimes Past. Raven, 1980

CHALLIS, SIMON
Death on a Quiet Beach. Hale, 1968

CHALMERS, STEPHEN. 1880-1935. Pseudonym: Nicholas Carter, q.v. Ref: CC.
The Affair of the Gallows Tree. Doubleday, 1930; Selwyn, 1931 [Calif.]
Blood on the Heather. Doubleday, 1932; World's Work, 1935 [Scot.]
The Crime in Car 13. Doubleday, 1930 [train, 1913]
The Greater Punishment. Doubleday, 1920; Bale, 1923 [Scot.]
House of Two Green Eyes. Doubleday, 1928 [NYC]
The Vanishing Smuggler. Clode, 1909; Mills, 1910
The Whispering Ghost. Doubleday, 1932

CHAMBERLAIN, ANNE. 1917- .
The Tall, Dark Man. Bobbs, 1955; Hart-Davis, 1955 [Ohio]

CHAMBERLAIN, ELINOR. 1901- . Ref: CA
Appointment in Manila. Dodd, 1945; Eyre, 1949 [Manila]
Manila Hemp. Dodd, 1947
Mystery of the Moving Island. Lippincott, 1965
Snare for Witches. Dodd, 1948; Gollancz, 1949 [Mass., 1663]

CHAMBERLAIN, ESTHER and LUCIA. See also: Lucia Chamberlain.
The Coast of Chance. Bobbs, 1908 [S.F.]

CHAMBERLAIN, GEORGE AGNEW. 1879-1966.
The Great Van Suttart Mystery. Putnam, 1925 [NYC]
In Defense of Mrs. Mason. Bobbs, 1938 [L.I.]

Night at Lost End. Brewer, 1931 [Pa.]
The Red House. Bobbs, 1945 [N.J.]
The Silver Cord. Putnam, 1927

CHAMBERLAIN, LUCIA. See also: Esther Chamberlain.
The Other Side of the Door. Bobbs, 1909 [S.F., 1865]

CHAMBERLAIN, WILLIAM
Red January. Paperback Library, 1964 [1969, U.S.]

CHAMBERS, DANA. Pseudonym of Albert Leffingwell, 1895-1966, q.v. Other pseudonym: Giles Jackson, q.v. SC: Jim Steele = JS.
The Blonde Died First. Dial, 1941; Hale, 1943 JS [ship]
The Case of Caroline Animus. Dial, 1946; Hale, 1951. Also published as: Dear, Dead Women. Jonathan, 1948 JS [Miami]
Darling, This Is Death. Dial, 1945; Hale, 1951 [Miami]
Dear, Dead Women; see The Case of Caroline Animus
Death Against Venus. Dial, 1946; Hale, 1953 [N.Y.]
The Frightened Man. Dial, 1942; Hale, 1945 JS [NYC]
The Last Secret. Dial, 1943; Hale, 1949 JS [NYC]
Rope for an Ape. Dial, 1947; Hale, 1952 JS [NYC]
She'll Be Dead by Morning. Dial, 1940; Hale, 1941 JS [NYC]
Some Day I'll Kill You. Dial, 1939; Hale, 1939 JS [Conn.]
Too Like the Dead; see Too Like the Lightning
Too Like the Lightning. Dial, 1939; Hale, 1940. Also published as: Too Like the Dead. Bestseller, 1951 JS [NYC]

CHAMBERS, DEREK HYDE. Pseudonym: D. Herbert Hyde, q.v.

CHAMBERS, MARY (STROTHER). 1899- .
See: (Elwyn) Whitman Chambers, 1896- .

CHAMBERS, PETER. Pseudonym of Dennis (John Andrew) Phillips, 1924- , q.v. See also: W(illiam Arthur) Howard Baker, 1925- . SC: Mark Preston, in all titles. Set: Calif., in most (all?) titles, and certainly those so marked.
Always Take the Big Ones. Hale, 1965
The Bad Die Young. Hale, 1967; Roy, 1968 [Calif.]
The Beautiful Golden Frame. Hale, 1980
The Big Goodbye. Hale, 1962
The Blonde Wore Black. Hale, 1968; Roy, 1968
Dames Can Be Deadly. Hale, 1963; Abelard, 1963
The Day of the Big Dollar. Hale, 1979
The Deader They Fall. Hale, 1979
The Deep Blue Cradle. Hale, 1980
Don't Bother to Knock. Hale, 1966
Down-Beat Kill. Hale, 1963; Abelard, 1964 [Calif.]
Lady, This Is Murder. Hale, 1963
Lady, You're Killing Me. Hale, 1979
Murder Is for Keeps. Hale, 1961; Abelard, 1962 [Calif.]
No Gold When You Go. Hale, 1966
No Peace for the Wicked. Hale, 1968; Roy, 1968 [Calif.]
Nobody Lives Forever. Hale, 1964
Nothing Personal. Hale, 1980
Somebody Has to Lose. Hale, 1975
Speak Ill of the Dead. Hale, 1968; Roy, 1969 [Calif.]
They Call It Murder. Hale, 1973
This'll Kill You. Hale, 1964
Wreath for a Redhead. Hale, 1962; Abelard, 1962 [Calif.]
You're Better Off Dead. Hale, 1965

CHAMBERS, PHILIP. 1936- . TV and film scriptwriter. All titles feature Sexton Blake and were published by Amalgamated Press.
Bullets to Baghdad. 1960
Dangerous Playmate. 1962
Keep It a Secret. 1961
Lotus Leaves and Larceny. 1963
Moscow Manhunt. 1962 [Moscow]
Shot from the Dark. 1961

CHAMBERS, ROBERT. 1933- . Raised in Minnesota. SC: Hank Moody, in all titles, all set in NYC.
Divide by Seven. Bobbs, 1969. British title: The Lesser Evil. Hale, 1971
The Lesser Evil; see Divide by Seven
Moth in a Rag Shop. Bobbs, 1968; Hale, 1969. Also published as: Village East. Dell, 1970

The Neon Preacher. Mason/Charter, 1977
Village East; see Moth in a Rag Shop

CHAMBERS, ROBERT W(ILLIAM). 1865-1933.
Born in Brooklyn, lived in N.Y.
Magazine illustrator turned novelist,
particularly of historical romances.
The Dark Star. Appleton, 1917
The Flaming Jewel. Doran, 1922; Hodder,
1922 [N.Y.]
In Secret. Doran, 1919; Hodder, 1919
-The Laughing Girl. Appleton, 1918
Marie Halkett. Appleton, 1937; Unwin,
1925
The Moonlit Way. Appleton, 1919
The Mystery Lady. Grosset, 1925 ss
The Mystery of Choice. Appleton (NYC &
London), 1897
Secret Service Operator 13. Appleton,
1934. British title: Spy No. 13.
Allan, 1935 [1862, U.S.]
Spy No. 13; see Secret Service Operator
13
The Tracer of Lost Persons. Appleton,
1906; Murray, 1907 ss [NYC]

CHAMBERS, (ELWYN) WHITMAN. 1896-   .
Ref: MP.
Action at World's End. Dutton, 1945
[Mex.]
Bright Star of Danger. Doubleday, 1940
[Fla.]
Bring Me Another Murder. Dutton, 1942
[Calif.]
The Campanile Murders. Appleton, 1933
The Coast of Intrigue. Henkle, 1928.
British title: Contraband Coast.
Nelson, 1928 [S. Am.]
-The Come-On. Pyramid, 1953
Contraband Coast; see The Coast of In-
trigue
Dangerous Water. Doubleday, 1941. Also
published as: Deadly Lure. Jonathan,
1955 (abridged)
Dead Men Leave No Fingerprints. Double-
day, 1935; Cassell, 1935 [Calif.]
Deadly Lure; see Dangerous Water
Dog Eat Dog. Doubleday, 1938. British
title: Murder in the Mist. Cassell,
1938 [S.F.]
Dry Tortugas. Doubleday, 1940 [Carib.]
In Savage Surrender. Monarch, 1959
[Fla.]
-Manhandled. Monarch, 1960
Murder for a Wanton. Doubleday, 1934;
Melrose, 1936
Murder in the Mist; see Dog Eat Dog
Murder Lady; see Once Too Often
The Navy Murders. Dodd, 1932; Hutchin-
son, 1931, as by Mary (Strother)
Chambers (1899-   ) and Whitman
Chambers
Once Too Often. Doubleday, 1938. Bri-
tish title: Murder Lady. Cassell,
1938 [Calif.]
Thirteen Steps. Doubleday, 1935 [S.F.]
You Can't Get Away by Running. Double-
day, 1939; Cassell, 1939 [Mex.]

CHAMBERS, WILLIAM E. 1943-   . Ref: CA.
Death Toll. Popular Library, 1976
[New Eng.]
The Redemption Factor. Popular Library,
1980

CHAMIER, JOHN (EDWIN DesCHAMPS)
Cannonball. Cassell, 1966

CHAMPAGNE, PAUL M. 1936-   . Born and
raised in Canada; active in Canadian
politics.
A Fair Affair. Greywood, 1967

CHAMPION, JOAN
Incidental Murder. Macdonald, 1946

CHAMPION DE CRESPIGNY, ROSE.   -1935.
See: Mrs. Philip Champion De Crespigny.

CHAMPLIN, VIRGINIA. Pseudonym of Grace
Virginia Lord,   -1885.
Shadowed by a Detective; or, The Woman
in Wax. Ogilvie, 1885 [NYC]

CHANCE, JOHN NEWTON. 1911-   . Pseudo-
nym: J. Drummond, John Lymington,
qq.v. See also: Desmond Reid. Ref:
CC, TC. SC: Supt. Black, in at least
those marked B; Jonathan Blake, in at
least those marked JB; John Newton
Chance, in at least those marked JC;
Mr. DeHavilland, in at least those
marked D; Jason, in at least those
marked J; John Marsh, in at least
those marked JM. Set: Eng.
The Abel Coincidence. Hale, 1969 JB
The Affair at Dead End. Hale, 1966 JB
Affair with a Rich Girl. Hale, 1958
Alarm at Black Brake. Hale, 1960 D
Aunt Miranda's Murder. Macdonald, 1951;
Dodd, 1951

A Bad Dream of Death. Hale, 1972 JB
The Black Highway. Macdonald, 1947 D
The Brandy Pole. Macdonald, 1949 D
The Canterbury Kilgrims. Hale, 1974 JB
The Case of the Death Computer. Hale,
1967 JM
The Case of the Fear Makers. Hale, 1967
JM
The Cat Watchers. Hale, 1971 JB
Commission for Disaster. Hale, 1964
Coven Gibbet. Macdonald, 1958 D
The Crimes at Rillington Place. Hodder,
1961
Dead Man's Knock. Hale, 1957
Dead Man's Shoes. Hale, 1968 JB
The Dead Tale-Tellers. Hale, 1972 JB
Death of an Innocent. Gollancz, 1938
B,D
Death of a Wild Bird. Hale, 1968 JB
Death Stalks the Cobbled Square; see
Screaming Fog
Death Under Desolate. Hale, 1964
The Death Watch Ladies. Hale, 1980
The Death Woman. Hale, 1967 JB
The Devil Drives. Gollancz, 1936
The Devil in Greenlands. Gollancz, 1939
The Devil's Edge. Hale, 1975
The Double Death. Hale, 1966 JB
A Drop of Hot Gold. Hale, 1979
The Ducrow Folly. Hale, 1978
End of an Iron Man. Hale, 1978
The Eye in Attendance. Macdonald, 1946
JC
The Faces of a Bad Girl. Hale, 1971 JB
A Fall-Out of Thieves. Hale, 1976
The Farm Villains. Hale, 1973 JB
The Fatal Fascination. Hale, 1959
Fate of the Lying Jade. Hale, 1968 JB
The Forest Affair. Hale, 1963 D
The Frightened Fisherman. Hale, 1977
The Ghost of Truth. Gollancz, 1939 B
The Girl in the Crime Belt. Hale, 1974
JB
The Grab Operators. Hale, 1973 JB
The Guilty Witness. Hale, 1979
The Halloween Murders. Hale, 1968
Hill Fog. Hale, 1975 JB
The House of the Dead Ones. Hale, 1977
The Hurrican Drift. Hale, 1967 JB
The Ice Maidens. Hale, 1969 JB
Import of Evil. Hale, 1961
Involvement in Austria. Hale, 1969 JB
[Austria]
The Jason Affair. Macdonald, 1953. U.S.
title (text differs somewhat from
British): Up to Her Neck. Popular
Library, 1955 J
Jason and the Sleep Game. Macdonald,
1954 J
Jason Goes West. Macdonald, 1955 J
The Jason Murders. Macdonald, 1954 J
The Killer Reaction. Hale, 1969 JB
[Ger.]
The Killing Experiment. Hale, 1969 JB
The Knight and the Castle. Macdonald,
1946 D
Lady in a Frame. Hale, 1960
The Last Seven Hours. Macdonald, 1956
Last Train to Limbo. Hale, 1972 JB
The Little Crime. Hale, 1957
The Love-Hate Relationship. Hale, 1973
Maiden Possessed. Gollancz, 1937 D
The Man Behind Me. Hale, 1963
The Man in My Shoes. Macdonald, 1952
JC
The Man with No Face. Hale, 1959
Man with Three Witches. Hale, 1958
The Man with Two Heads. Hale, 1972 JB
Mantrap. Hale, 1968 JB
The Mask of Pursuit. Hale, 1967 JB
The Mayhem Madchen. Hale, 1980
The Mirror Train. Hale, 1970 JB
The Mists of Treason. Hale, 1970 JB
The Monstrous Regiment. Hale, 1975
Motive for a Kill. Hale, 1977
Murder in Oils. Gollancz, 1935
The Murder Makers. Hale, 1976
The Night of the Full Moon. Macdonald,
1950 D
The Night of the Settlement. Hale, 1961
The Randy Inheritance. Macdonald, 1953
The Red Knight. Macdonald, 1945; Mac-
millan, 1945 JC,B,D
Return to Death Valley. Hale, 1976
Rhapsody in Fear. Gollancz, 1937
A Ring of Liars. Hale, 1970 JB
The Rogue Aunt. Hale, 1968 JB
The Screaming Fog. Macdonald, 1944.
U.S. title: Death Stalks the Cobbled
Square. McBride, 1946 JC
A Shadow Called Janet. Macdonald, 1956
The Shadow of the Killer. Hale, 1974 JB
The Starfish Affair. Hale, 1974 JB
Stormlight. Hale, 1965 D
Thieves' Kitchen. Hale, 1979
The Three Masks of Death. Hale, 1970 JB
The Thug Executive. Hale, 1967 JM
Triangle of Fear. Hale, 1962
The Twopenny Box. Hale, 1962
Up to Her Neck; see The Jason Affair
Wheels in the Forest. Gollancz, 1935
D,B

A Wreath of Bones. Hale, 1971 JB

CHANCE, ROGER (JAMES FERGUSON)
Be Absolute for Death. Davies, 1964

CHANCE, SIMON
Death of a Tax Inspector. Staples, 1941

CHANCE, STEPHEN. Pseudonym of Philip Wil-
liam Turner, 1925-   . Ref: CA. SC:
Rev. Septimus Treloar, in all titles.
Set: Eng.
Septimus and the Danedyke Mystery. Bod-
ley, 1971; Nelson, 1973
Septimus and the Minister Ghost. Bod-
ley, 1972. U.S. title: Septimus and
the Minister Ghost Mystery. Nelson,
1974
Septimus and the Minister Ghost Mys-
tery; see Septimus and the Minister
Ghost
Septimus and the Spy Ring. Bodley, 1979
Septimus and the Stone of Offering.
Bodley, 1976. U.S. title: The Stone
of Offering. Nelson, 1977 [Wales]
The Stone of Offering; see Septimus and
the Stone of Offering

CHANCELLOR, JOHN. Pseudonym of Charles de
Balzac Rideaux, 1900-1971. Ref: CA.
SC: Capt. Frass, in at least those
marked F. Set: Eng.
-Another Man's Wife. Newnes, 1911
The Dark God. Hutchinson, 1927; Cen-
tury, 1928
-Desert Desire. Gramol, 1932
-The Farther Off from England. Cassell,
1969
Frass. Hutchinson, 1929 F
-Her Garden of Eden. Newnes, 1926
The Jersey Plunder. Cassell, 1970
-The Knave of Hearts. Gramol, 1937
The Ladder of Cards. Hutchinson, 1936
The Murder Syndicate. Eldon, 1949
Mystery at Angel's End. Long, 1930
The Mystery of Norman's Court. Hutchin-
son, 1923; Small, 1924
-The Prim Windows. Cape, 1967
The Return of Frass. Hutchinson, 1930 F
Stolen Gold. Hutchinson, 1932

CHANDLER, BRYN
The Coral Kill. Signet, 1978 [Bahamas]

CHANDLER, DAVID (LEON). Ref: CA.
The Aphrodite. Morrow, 1977; Cassell,
1978
The Gangsters. Morrow, 1975; Allen,
1975
The Glass Totem. Appleton, 1962 [NYC]
The Ramsden Case. Simon, 1967

CHANDLER, NOEL
Satan in High Heels. Belmont, 1963
(Novelization of the movie.)

CHANDLER, PETER. Pseudonym of L. M. D.
Fonzo and J. L. Kornbluth.
Bucks. Avon, 1980

CHANDLER, RAYMOND (THORNTON). 1888-1959.
Ref: CA, CC, DD, EM, MC, TC. SC:
Philip Marlowe = PM.
The Big Sleep. Knopf, 1939; H. Hamil-
ton, 1939 PM [Calif.]
The Blue Dahlia. Southern Illinois
University Press, 1976; Feffer, 1976
(Screenplay.)
Farewell, My Lovely. Knopf, 1940; H.
Hamilton, 1940 PM [Calif.]
Finger Man and other stories. Avon,
1946 (Three pulp novelets from the
1930s, later included in hardcover in
The Simple Art of Murder, q.v.)
Five Murderers. Avon, 1944 (Five pulp
stories, all but one included later
in hardcover in The Simple Art of
Murder, q.v.)
Five Sinister Characters. Avon, 1945
(Five pulp stories, all included la-
ter in hardcover in The Simple Art of
Murder, q.v.)
The High Window. Knopf, 1942; H. Hamil-
ton, 1943 PM [L.A.]
Killer in the Rain. Houghton, 1964; H.
Hamilton, 1964 (Eight pulp stories,
six in their first book appearances
and all adapted into the first four
PM novels.) [L.A.]
The Lady in the Lake. Knopf, 1943; H.
Hamilton, 1944 PM [Calif.]
The Little Sister. Houghton, 1949; H.
Hamilton, 1949. Also published as:
Marlowe. PB, 1969 PM [L.A.]
The Long Goodbye. Houghton, 1954; H.
Hamilton, 1953 PM [L.A.]
Marlowe; see The Little Sister
The Notebooks of Raymond Chandler and
English Summer, A Gothic Romance.
Ecco Press, 1976 (Nonfiction and
one story, heretofore unpublished.)

Pearls Are a Nuisance. H. Hamilton, 1953 (ss, none in first book appearance.)
Pick-Up on Noon Street; see The Simple Art of Murder
Playback. Houghton, 1958; H. Hamilton, 1958 PM [Calif.]
Red Wind. World, 1946 (Five pulp stories, none in first book appearance, and all but one later included in hardcover in The Simple Art of Murder, q.v.)
The Simple Art of Murder. Houghton, 1950; H. Hamilton, 1950 (Twelve pulp stories and an essay. The stories include all but one of the combined contents of Finger Man, Five Murderers, Five Sinister Characters, Red Wind and Spanish Blood, qq.v. However, this large collection was itself broken into three paperbacks, all issued by PB: Pick-Up on Noon Street, 1952; The Simple Art of Murder, 1953; and Trouble Is My Business, 1951.) [Calif.]
Smart-Aleck Kill. H. Hamilton, 1953 (ss, none in first book appearance.)
The Smell of Fear. H. Hamilton, 1965 (Another collection of pulp writings, but here including one story in its first book appearance.)
Spanish Blood. World, 1946 (Five pulp stories, none in first book appearance, and all included later in The Simple Art of Murder, q.v.)
Trouble Is My Business; see The Simple Art of Murder

CHANG, LEE. Pseudonym of Joseph Rosenberger, q.v., and, at least in the one indicated case, of another writer. Other Rosenberger pseudonym: Nick Carter, q.v. SC: Mace, in all titles (see also: C. K. Fong).
The Year of the Ape. Manor, 1978
The Year of the Boar. Manor, 1975 (by Leonard Levinson, 1935- , q.v.)
The Year of the Dragon. Manor, 1974
The Year of the Horse. Manor, 1974
The Year of the Rat. Manor, 1974
The Year of the Snake. Manor, 1974
The Year of the Tiger. Manor, 1973

CHANNING, B.
Dressed to Kill. World Distributors, 1952

CHANNING, MARK. SC: Colin Gray, in all titles.
-King Cobra. Hutchinson, 1933; Lippincott, 1934 [India]
-Nine Lives. Harrap, 1937; Lippincott, 1937 [India]
-White Python. Hutchinson, 1934; Lippincott, 1934 [Tibet]

CHANNON, E(THEL) M(ARY) [MRS. FRANCIS CHANNON]. 1875- . Set: Eng.
The Chimney Murder. Benn, 1929; Little, 1930
The Gilt-Edged Mystery. Benn, 1932
Golden Glory. Benn, 1931
The House with No Address. Benn, 1931
Twice Dead. Benn, 1930

CHANSLOR, ROY. 1899- .
Hazard. Simon, 1947
Lowdown. Farrar, 1931

CHANSLOR, (MARJORIE) TORREY (HOOD). 1899- . SC: Lutie and Amanda Beagle, in both titles.
Our First Murder. Stokes, 1940 [NYC]
Our Second Murder. Stokes, 1941 [NYC]

CHANTLER, DAVID T(HOMAS). 1925- . Ref: CA.
The Capablanca Opening. St. Martin's, 1977 [Cent. Am.]

CHAPIN, ANNA ALICE. 1880-1920. See: George C(harles) Jenkins, 1850-1929. Pseudonym (?): Harry Coverdale, q.v.

CHAPIN, ANSEL. Pseudonym: Nick Carter, q.v.

CHAPIN, CARL M(ATTISON). 1879-1938.
Three Died Beside the Marble Pool. Doubleday, 1936; World's Work, 1937 [Vt.]

CHAPLIN, PATRICE
By Flower and Dead Street, and The Love Apple. Duckworth, 1976

CHAPMAN, GEORGE WARREN VERNON. 1925- . Pseudonym: Vernon Warren, q.v.

CHAPMAN, H. E.
The Heseltine Mystery. Crowther, 1944

CHAPMAN, HESTER W(OLFERSTAN). 1899-1976.
Limmerston Hall. Cape, 1972; Coward, 1973 [1800s, Eng.]

CHAPMAN, JOHN (ROY). 1927- . See: Ray Cooney.

CHAPMAN, JOHN. 1947- .
Other Men's Lives. Hale, 1980

CHAPMAN, RAYMOND. 1924- . Pseudonym: Simon Nash, q.v.

CHAPMAN, ROBERT (ALEC MARK). 1916- . Reporter for a London newspaper. SC: Rex Banner, in at least those marked RB. Set: Eng.
Be My Ghost. Hale, 1963
Behind the Headlines. Laurie, 1955 RB
Crime on My Hands. Laurie, 1952 RB
Deep Secret. Rich, 1939
The Downward Path. Hale, 1959 RB
The Frozen Stiff. Laurie, 1956 RB
The Hot Half-Million. Hale, 1963
Murder for the Million. Laurie, 1953 RB
One Jump Ahead. Laurie, 1951 RB
The Seven Sisters. Crowther, 1945
Winter Wears a Shroud. Laurie, 1952 RB
Wish You Were Dead. Hale, 1960

CHAPPELL, MOLLIE
Murder Comes Home. Collins, 1967

CHARBONNEAU, LOUIS (HENRY). 1924- . Ref: CA.
And Hope to Die. Ace, 1970 [L.A.]
Intruder. Doubleday, 1979
From a Dark Place. Dell, 1974
The Lair. GM, 1979 [Mex.]
Night of Violence. Dodd, 1959. British title: The Trapped Ones. Barker, 1960
Nor All Your Tears. Dodd, 1959
The Trapped Ones; see Night of Violence

CHARLES, ERNEST F. SC: Dick Torreyton, in all titles.
Before the Wind. Nelson, 1938
Death Comes Ashore. Nelson, 1938
Death Crosses the Line. Nelson, 1937 [ship]

CHARLES, FRANKLIN. Joint pseudonym of Cleve F(ranklin) Adams, 1895-1949, q.v., and Robert Leslie Bellem, q.v. Other Adams pseudonym: John Spain, q.v.
The Vice Czar Murders. Funk, 1941

CHARLES, IONA. Joint pseudonym of Carolyn Nichols and Stanlee Coy.
Grenencourt. Popular Library, 1975 [past, Eng.]
When Only the Bougainvillea Blooms. Popular Library, 1975 [Vir. Is.]

CHARLES, JOHN
The Man Without a Mouth. Stockwell, 1935

CHARLES, MOIE and BARBARA TOY
The Murder at the Vicarage. French (London), 1950 (A play adapted from the novel by Agatha Christie, 1890-1976, q.v.)

CHARLES, ROBERT. Pseudonym of Robert Charles Smith, 1938- . Other pseudonym: Charles Leader, q.v. SC: Simon Larren, in at least those marked SL; Supt. Mark Nicolson, in at least those marked MN. Ref: CA.
Arctic Assignment. Hale, 1966 SL [Russ.]
The Arms of the Mantis. Hale, 1978
Assassins for Peace. Hale, 1967 SL
The Big Fish. Hale, 1969 SL
-The Burning. Hale, 1979
A Clash of Hawks. Hale, 1976; Pinnacle, 1975 [Mid. East]
Cobra Strike; see Venom of the Cobra
Dark Vendetta. Hale, 1964 SL [Far East]
Dead Before Midnight. Hale, 1975
The Faceless Fugitive. Hale, 1963
The Flight of the Raven. Hale, 1975; Pinnacle, 1975 MN [Fr.]
The Fourth Shadow. Hale, 1966 SL
The Hour of the Wolf. Hale, 1974; Pinnacle, 1975 MN
-A Lance for the Devil. Hale, 1980
Mission of Murder. Hale, 1965 SL
Nothing to Lose. Hale, 1963 SL
One Must Survive. Hale, 1964 SL
The Prey of the Falcon. Hale, 1977
The Scream of the Dove. Hale, 1976; Pinnacle, 1975 MN [ship]
Sea Vengeance. Hale, 1974; Pinnacle, 1976
The Snarl of the Lynx. Hale, 1977
Stamboul Intrigue. Hale, 1968; Roy, 1968 SL [Turk.]
Strikefast. Hale, 1969 SL
The Sun Virgin. Hale, 1974

This Side of Hell. Hale, 1965 [Afr.]
Three Days to Live. Hale, 1968; Roy, 1968 [Brazil]
The Venom of the Cobra. Hale, 1977. U.S. title: Cobra Strike. Pinnacle, 1980

CHARLES, THERESA. Joint pseudonym of Charles Swatridge and Irene Maude Mossop Swatridge. Pseudonym of Irene Swatridge alone: Jan Tempest, q.v. These titles were apparently published in England as romances and in the U.S. as gothics.
The Burning Beacon. Cassell, 1956; Lancer, 1966
Dark Legacy; see Happy Now I Go
Fairer Than She. Cassell, 1953; Dell, 1968
Happy Now I Go. Longmans, 1947. U.S. title: Dark Legacy. Dell, 1968
House on the Rocks. Hale, 1962; Paperback Library, 1966
Lady in the Mist; see Nurse Alice in Love
The Man for Me. Hale, 1965. U.S. title: The Shrouded Tower. Ace, 1966
Nurse Alice in Love. Hale, 1964. U.S. title: Lady in the Mist. Ace, 1966
Proud Citadel. Hale, 1967; Dell, 1967
Return to Terror; see Widower's Wife
The Shrouded Tower; see The Man for Me
Widower's Wife. Hale, 1963. U.S. title: Return to Terror. Paperback Library, 1966

CHARLES, WILL. Pseudonym of Charles Ray Willeford III, 1919- .
The Hombre from Sonora. Lenox, 1971

CHARLESTON, WALLY
The Hero Rat. Warner, 1975 [S.F.]

CHARLESWORTH, M. E. Pseudonym of Maud Ballington Charlesworth Booth, 1865-1948.
The Relentless Current. Putnam, 1912. Also published as: Was It Murder?; or, The Relentless Current. Putnam, 1912, as by Maud Ballington Booth

CHARLTON, JOHN. Pseudonym of Martin Woodhouse, 1932- , q.v.
The Remington Set. Macmillan (London), 1976

CHARLTON, MARJORY
Death of a Fashion Writer. Murray, 1940

CHARLTON, MARY
The Homicide. Minerva, 1805

CHARNWOOD, LORD. See: Godfrey R(athbone) Benson, 1864-1945.

CHARTERIS, LESLIE. 1907- . Name originally: Leslie Charles Bowyer Yin. Ref: all except MM. SC: Bill Kennedy = BK; Insp. Claude Eustace Teal, in Saint stories set in England, and in "Daredevil," = CT; Simon Templar (The Saint) = ST. Set: mostly Eng., unless indicated otherwise.
The Ace of Knaves. Hodder, 1937; Doubleday, 1937. Also published as: The Saint in Action. Sun Dial, 1938; and as: The Saint: Ace of Knaves. Avon, 1955 (Three ST novelets)
Alias the Saint. Hodder, 1931 (Three ST novelets, all included in the U.S. collection Wanted for Murder, q.v. Note that there are two U.S. paperbacks entitled Alias the Saint, one published by Bonded, 1945, the other by Avon, 1957; each contains only two stories from the British edition.)
Angels of Doom; see She Was a Lady
Arrest the Saint; see The First Saint Omnibus
The Avenging Saint; see Knight Templar
The Bandit. Ward, 1929; Doubleday, 1930
Boodle. Hodder, 1934. U.S. title: The Saint Intervenes. Doubleday, 1934 (14 ST ss. Note that some Avon paperback reprint editions are incomplete.)
The Brighter Buccaneer. Hodder, 1933; Doubleday, 1933. Also published as: The Saint—The Brighter Buccaneer. Avon, 1957 (ST ss. Note that the Avon reprint is incomplete.)
Call for the Saint. Hodder, 1948; Doubleday, 1948 (2 ST novelets.) [Chi., NYC]
Catch the Saint. Hodder, 1975; Doubleday, 1975 (2 ST novelets, adapted by Fleming Lee, 1933- , from original stories by Norman Worker.) [1930s, Phil.]
Concerning the Saint. Avon, 1958 (One of two reprints comprising tales omitted from Avon editions of ST ss volumes.)

Count on the Saint. Hodder, 1980; Doubleday, 1980 (Two ST stories developed by Graham Weaver from teleplay outlines by Donne Avenell.)
Daredevil. Ward, 1929; Doubleday, 1929 CT
Enter the Saint. Hodder, 1930; Doubleday, 1931 (3 ST novelets.)
Featuring the Saint. Hodder, 1931 (3 ST novelets, all included in the U.S. collection Wanted for Murder, q.v. Note that the Avon reprint entitled Featuring the Saint, 1958, contains only 2 novelets, but that the earlier reprint under this title, Bonded, 1945, contains all 3 stories.)
The First Saint Omnibus. Hodder, 1939; Doubleday, 1939. Also published as: Arrest the Saint! Permabooks, 1951 (A large collection taken from the many pre-1939 volumes of ST ss and novelets, each tale prefaced with extensive commentary by Charteris written especially for this omnibus.)
Follow the Saint. Hodder, 1939; Doubleday, 1938 (6 ST ss.)
Getaway. Hodder, 1932; Doubleday, 1933. Also published as: Saint's Getaway. Sun Dial, 1943 ST [Ger.]
The Happy Highwayman. Hodder, 1939; Doubleday, 1939. Also published as: The Saint—The Happy Highwayman. Avon, 1955 (9 ST ss. Note that the Avon reprint is incomplete.)
The Holy Terror. Hodder, 1932. U.S. title: The Saint vs. Scotland Yard. Doubleday, 1932 (3 ST novelets.)
Knight Templar. Hodder, 1930. U.S. title: The Avenging Saint. Doubleday, 1931 ST
Lady on a Train. Shaw, 1945 (Novelization of the movie.) [L.I.]
The Last Hero. Hodder, 1930; Doubleday, 1930. Also published as: The Saint Closes the Case. Sun Dial, 1941; and as: The Saint and the Last Hero. Avon, 1953 ST
Meet the Tiger. Ward, 1928; Doubleday, 1929. Also published as: The Saint Meets the Tiger. Sun Dial, 1940 ST
The Misfortunes of Mr. Teal. Hodder, 1934; Doubleday, 1934. Also published as: The Saint in England. Sun Dial, 1941 (3 ST novelets.)
Once More the Saint. Hodder, 1933. U.S. title: The Saint and Mr. Teal. Doubleday, 1933 (3 ST novelets.)
Paging the Saint. Jacobs, 1945 (Contains 2 stories from Wanted for Murder, q.v.)
Prelude for War. Hodder, 1938; Doubleday, 1938. Also published as: The Saint Plays with Fire. Triangle, 1942 ST
The Saint Abroad. Hodder, 1970; Doubleday, 1969 (2 ST short novels adapted by Fleming Lee, 1933- , from ST teleplays by Michael Pertwee, with final manuscript revision by Charteris.)
The Saint: Ace of Knaves; see The Ace of Knaves
The Saint and Mr. Teal; see Once More the Saint
The Saint and the Fiction Makers. Hodder, 1969; Doubleday, 1968 (Adapted by Fleming Lee, 1933- , from an ST teleplay by John Kruse, with final manuscript revision by Charteris.)
The Saint and the Hapsburg Necklace. Hodder, 1976; Doubleday, 1976 (By Christopher Short, q.v.) ST [Vienna, ca.1940]
The Saint and the Last Hero; see The Last Hero
The Saint and the People Importers. Hodder pb, 1971; Doubleday, 1971 (Adapted by Fleming Lee, 1933- , from his own ST teleplay, with final manuscript revision by Charteris.)
The Saint and the Sizzling Saboteur; see The Saint on Guard
The Saint and the Templar Treasure. Hodder, 1979; Doubleday, 1979 (Developed by Graham Weaver from an original outline by Donne Avenelle.) ST
The Saint Around the World. Hodder, 1957; Doubleday, 1956 (6 ST ss.)
The Saint at a Thieves' Picnic; see Thieves' Picnic
The Saint at Large. Sun Dial, 1943 (A collection of ST ss, all from the three prior ss volumes with some new introductory matter by Charteris.)
The Saint Bids Diamonds; see Thieves' Picnic
The Saint—The Brighter Buccaneer; see The Brighter Buccaneer

The Saint Cleans Up. Avon, 1959 (One of two reprints comprising tales omitted from Avon editions of ST ss volumes. The other is Concerning the Saint, q.v.)
The Saint Closes the Case; see The Last Hero
Saint Errant. Hodder, 1949; Doubleday, 1948 (9 ST ss.)
The Saint Goes On. Hodder, 1934; Doubleday, 1935 (3 ST novelets.)
The Saint Goes West. Hodder, 1942; Doubleday, 1942 (3 ST novelets. Note that most U.S. reprints contain only two of the three, whereas British paperback reprints are generally complete.) [Calif.]
The Saint—The Happy Highwayman; see The Happy Highwayman
The Saint in Action; see The Ace of Knaves
The Saint in England; see The Misfortunes of Mr. Teal
The Saint in Europe. Hodder, 1954; Doubleday, 1953 (7 ST ss.)
The Saint in Miami. Hodder, 1941; Doubleday, 1940 ST [Miami]
The Saint in New York. Hodder, 1935; Doubleday, 1935 ST [NYC]
The Saint in Pursuit. Hodder, 1971; Doubleday, 1970 (Based on an ST comic strip from 1959-60.) [Port.]
The Saint in Trouble. Coronet, 1978; Doubleday, 1978 (Two novelets adapted by Graham Weaver from original teleplays by Terence Feely and John Kruse.)
The Saint Intervenes; see Boodle
The Saint in the Sun. Hodder, 1964; Doubleday, 1963 (7 ST ss.)
The Saint Meets His Match; see She Was a Lady
The Saint Meets the Tiger; see Meet the Tiger
The Saint on Guard. Hodder, 1945; Doubleday, 1944 (2 ST novelets. Each was published by Avon in a separate reprint volume: the Avon title The Saint on Guard, 1958, contains only "The Black Market", while The Saint and the Sizzling Saboteur, 1956, contains only "The Sizzling Saboteur.") [NYC, Tex.]
The Saint on the Spanish Main. Hodder, 1956; Doubleday, 1955 (6 ST ss.) [Carib.]
The Saint on TV. Hodder, 1968; Doubleday, 1968 (2 ST novelets, adapted by Fleming Lee, 1933- , from teleplays, with final manuscript revision by Charteris.)
Saint Overboard. Hodder, 1936; Doubleday, 1936 ST [ship]
The Saint Plays with Fire; see Prelude for War
The Saint Returns. Hodder, 1969; Doubleday, 1968 (2 ST short novels adapted by Fleming Lee, 1933- , from teleplays, with final manuscript revision by Charteris.) [Ire.]
The Saint Sees It Through. Hodder, 1947; Doubleday, 1946 ST [NYC]
The Saint Steps In. Hodder, 1944; Doubleday, 1943 ST [U.S.]
The Saint to the Rescue. Hodder, 1961; Doubleday, 1959 (6 ST ss.) [Calif.]
The Saint: Two in One. Sun Dial, 1942 (The Ace of Knaves, and The Happy Highwayman, qq.v., bound together in one volume.)
The Saint vs. Scotland Yard; see The Holy Terror
The Saint—Wanted for Murder; see Wanted for Murder
Saint's Getaway; see Getaway
The Second Saint Omnibus. Hodder, 1952; Doubleday, 1951 (A collection taken from the volumes of ST ss and novelets published between 1939 and 1951, with extensive commentary by Charteris written especially for this volume.)
Send for the Saint. Hodder, 1977; Doubleday, 1978 (2 novelets adapted by Peter Bloxsam from teleplays.) ST
Senor Saint. Hodder, 1959; Doubleday, 1958 (4 ST ss.)
She Was a Lady. Hodder, 1931. U.S. title: Angels of Doom. Doubleday, 1932. Also published as: The Saint Meets His Match. Bonded, 1945 ST
Thanks to the Saint. Hodder, 1958; Doubleday, 1957 (6 ST ss.)
Thieves' Picnic. Hodder, 1937; Doubleday, 1937. Also published as: The Saint Bids Diamonds. Triangle, 1942 and as: The Saint at a Thieves' Picnic. Avon, 1951 ST [Sp.]
Trust the Saint. Hodder, 1962; Doubleday, 1962 (6 ST ss.)
Vendetta for the Saint. Hodder, 1965; Doubleday, 1964 ST [Sic.]

Wanted for Murder. Doubleday, 1931 (A volume of 6 ST novelets, including the complete contents of the two British collections entitled Alias the Saint, and Featuring the Saint, qq.v. The entire volume was also published as: The Saint—Wanted for Murder. Sun Dial, 1943. The 6 novelets were reprinted by Avon in three paperbacks of two tales each, these three volumes being confusingly titled: Alias the Saint, 1958; Featuring the Saint, 1958; and The Saint—Wanted for Murder, 1956.)
The White Rider. Ward, 1928; Doubleday, 1930 BK
X Esquire. Ward, 1927 BK

CHARYN, JEROME. 1937- . Ref: CA. SC: Isaac Sidel, in all titles, all set in NYC.
Blue Eyes. Simon, 1975
The Education of Patrick Silver. Arbor, 1976
Marilyn the Wild. Arbor, 1976
Secret Isaac. Arbor, 1978

CHASE, ALAN (LOUIS). 1929- . Ref: CA.
The Kidneyed Caper. Simon, 1960

CHASE, ALLAN. 1913- .
The Five Arrows. Random, 1944
Shadow of a Hero. Little, 1949

CHASE, ARTHUR M(INTURN). 1875-1947. SC: Lt. Dan Durkin = DD.
Danger in the Dark. Dodd, 1933; Eldon, 1934 [New Eng.]
Murder of a Missing Man. Dodd, 1934 DD [Tex.]
No Outlet. Dodd, 1940
The Party at the Penthouse. Dodd, 1932 DD [NYC]
Peril at the Spy Nest. Dodd, 1943 [L.I.]
Twenty Minutes to Kill. Dodd, 1936 DD [NYC]

CHASE, BORDEN. A screen writer.
Diamonds of Death. Hart, 1947

CHASE, JAMES HADLEY. Pseudonym of Rene Brabazon Raymond, 1906- . Other pseudonyms: James L. Docherty, Ambrose Grant, Raymond Marshall, qq.v. Ref: CC, EM, MC, TC. SC: Al Barney = AB; Dave Fenner = DF; Mark Girland = MG; Steve Harmas = SH; Vic Malloy = VM; Herman Radnitz = HR; Helga Rolfe = HR*; Lu Silk = LS; Frank Terrell = FT.
An Ace Up My Sleeve. Hale, 1971 HR*
Believe This...You'll Believe Anything. Hale, 1975
Believed Violent. Hale, 1968 MG, FT, HR, LS [Fla.]
Cade. Hale, 1966; PB, 1973
A Can of Worms. Hale, 1979
The Case of the Strangled Starlet; see Not Safe to Be Free
A Coffin from Hong Kong. Hale, 1962 [Calif.]
Come Easy—Go Easy. Hale, 1960; PB, 1974 [S.W.]
Consider Yourself Dead. Hale, 1978
Dead Ringer; see Safer Dead
The Dead Stay Dumb. Jarrolds, 1939. U.S. title: Kiss My Fist! Eton, 1952. Reprinted in U.S. under British title: PB, 1973 [U.S.]
Do Me a Favour, Drop Dead. Hale, 1976
The Doll's Bad News; see Twelve Chinks and a Woman
The Double Shuffle. Hale, 1952; Dutton, 1953 SH [Calif.]
An Ear to the Ground. Hale, 1968 AB, SH, FT [Fla.]
-Eve. Jarrolds, 1945 [L.A.]
The Fast Buck. Hale, 1952 [U.S.]
Figure It Out for Yourself. Hale, 1950; Duell, 1951. Also published as: The Marijuana Mob. Eton, 1952 VM [Calif.]
The Flesh of the Orchid. Jarrolds, 1948; PB, 1972 [U.S.]
Goldfish Have No Hiding Place. Hale, 1974
The Guilty Are Afraid. Hale, 1957; Signet, 1959 [Calif.]
Have a Change of Scene. Hale, 1973
Have This One on Me. Hale, 1967 MG [Prague]
I Hold the Four Aces. Hale, 1977 HR
I Would Rather Stay Poor. Hale, 1962; PB, 1974 [Calif.]
I'll Bury My Dead. Hale, 1953; Dutton, 1954 [U.S.]
I'll Get You for This. Jarrolds, 1946; Avon, 1951 [Calif.]
The Joker in the Deck. Hale, 1975 HR*
Just a Matter of Time. Hale, 1972
Just Another Sucker. Hale, 1961; PB, 1974 [Calif.]

Kiss My Fist!; see The Dead Stay Dumb
Knock, Knock! Who's There? Hale, 1973
Last Page. French (London), 1947 (3-act play.)
Lay Her Among the Lilies. Hale, 1950. U.S. title: Too Dangerous to Be Free. Duell, 1951 VM [Calif.]
Like a Hole in the Head. Hale, 1970
A Lotus for Miss Quon. Hale, 1961 [Saigon]
The Marijuana Mob; see Figure It Out for Yourself
Miss Callaghan Comes to Grief. Jarrolds, 1941
-Miss Shumway Waves a Wand. Jarrolds, 1944
My Laugh Comes Last. Hale, 1977
No Orchids for Miss Blandish. Jarrolds, 1939; Howell Soskin, 1942. Also published as: The Villain and the Virgin. Avon, 1948. Revised edition, under original title: Panther, 1961; Avon, 1961 DF [Kan.]
Not Safe to Be Free. Hale, 1958. U.S. title: The Case of the Strangled Starlet. Signet, 1958 [Fr.]
One Bright Summer Morning. Hale, 1963; PB, 1974 [Nev.]
Safer Dead. Hale, 1954. U.S. title: Dead Ringer. Ace, 1955 [Calif.]
Shock Treatment. Hale, 1959; Signet, 1959 SH [Calif.]
So What Happens to Me? Hale, 1974
The Soft Centre. Hale, 1964 FT [Fla.]
Strictly for Cash. Hale, 1951; PB, 1973 [Fla.]
Tell It to the Birds. Hale, 1963; PB, 1974 SH [Calif.]
There's a Hippie on the Highway. Hale, 1970 FT
There's Always a Price Tag. Hale, 1956; PB, 1973 SH [Calif.]
This Is for Real. Hale, 1965; Walker, 1967 MG,HR
This Way for a Shroud. Hale, 1953 [Calif.]
Tiger by the Tail. Hale, 1954
Too Dangerous to Be Free; see Lay Her Among the Lilies
Try This One for Size. Hale, 1980 [NYC]
Twelve Chinamen and a Woman; see Twelve Chinks and a Woman
Twelve Chinks and a Woman. Jarrolds, 1940; Howell Soskin, 1941. Also published, in revised form, as: Twelve Chinamen and a Woman. Novel Library, 1950; and as: The Doll's Bad News. Panther, 1970 DF [NYC]
The Villain and the Virgin; see No Orchids for Miss Blandish
The Vulture Is a Patient Bird. Hale, 1969
Want to Stay Alive? Hale, 1971
The Way the Cookie Crumbles. Hale, 1965; PB, 1974 PB [Fla.]
Well Now, My Pretty—. Hale, 1967; PB, 1972 FT [Fla.]
What's Better Than Money? Hale, 1960; PB, 1972 [L.A.]
The Whiff of Money. Hale, 1969; PB, 1972 MG,HR,LS [Ger.]
The World in My Pocket. Hale, 1959; Popular Library, 1962 [U.S.]
You Can Say That Again. Hale, 1980
You Have Yourself a Deal. Hale, 1966; Walker, 1968 MG [Fr.]
You Must Be Kidding. Hale, 1979
You Never Know with Women. Jarrolds, 1949; PB, 1972 [Calif.]
You're Dead Without Money. Hale, 1972 AB,HR
You're Lonely When You're Dead. Hale, 1949; Duell, 1950 VM [Calif.]
You've Got It Coming. Hale, 1955; PB, 1973 [Calif.]

CHASE, JOSEPHINE.   -1931.
Behind the Purple Mask. Penn, 1932 [Pa.]
The Blue Shadow Mystery. Penn, 1935 [Phil.]
The Golden Imp. Penn, 1933 [Pa.]
The Green Jade Necklace. Penn, 1931 [NYC]
The Mark of the Red Diamond. Penn, 1929 [Fla.]

CHASE, KIP. Pseudonym of Trevett Coburn Chase. SC: Justine Carmichael, in all titles.
Killer Be Killed. Hammond, 1963 [Mex.]
Murder Most Ingenious. Hammond, 1962
Where There's a Will. Hammond, 1961 [Calif.]

CHASE, MARY (COYLE). 1907-
Mrs. McThing. Oxford, 1952 (2-act play.)

CHASE, OLIVE
Countercrime, with Stanley Clayton. French (London), 1968 (Play.)
Driven to Murder, with Stanley Clayton. French (London), 1978 (Play.)
Party to Murder, with Stuart Burke. French (London), 1974 (Play.)
Person Unknown, with Stanley Clayton. French (London), 1965 (2-act play.)

CHASE, PHILIP. Pseudonym of Philip Friedman. SC: Aaron Eisenberg, in at least those marked AE.
Betrayal in Eden. Dell, 1976 [Ind. O.]
Deadly Crusade. Dell, 1976 AE [Mid. East]
Defame and Destroy. Dell, 1976
Merchants of Death. Dell, 1976 AE

CHASE, TREVETT COBURN. Pseudonym: Kip Chase, q.v.

CHASTAIN, THOMAS. Newspaper reporter and editor turned novelist. Pseudonym: Nick Carter, q.v. SC: Insp. Max Kauffman = MK; J. T. Spanner = JS.
The Christmas Bomber; see 911
Death Stalk. Award, 1971
High Voltage. Doubleday, 1979; Hale, 1980 MK [NYC]
911. Mason/Charter, 1976. British title: The Christmas Bomber. Cassell, 1976. Reprinted in Britain under the U.S. title: Corgi, 1977 MK [NYC]
Pandora's Box. Mason/Charter, 1974; Cassell, 1975 MK [NYC]
Spanner. Mason/Charter, 1977 MK,JS
Vital Statistics. Times Books, 1977 JS [NYC]

CHATER, ELIZABETH. Pseudonym: Lee Chaytor, q.v.

CHATER, GEORGE
Tracking Tranter. Jarrolds, 1922

CHATTERTON, E(DWARD) KEBLE. 1878-1944.
-Below the Surface. Hurst, 1934
Sea Spy. Hurst, 1937
Secret Ship. Hurst, 1939

CHAVETTE, EUGENE. Pseudonym of Eugene Vachette, 1827-1902. Ref: DD.
Mystery of Hotel Brichet. Bonner, 1894

CHAVIS, ROBERT
The Terror Package. Ace, 1957 [Ariz.]

CHAYES, SALLY
Jail Bait. Godwin, 1933

CHAYTOR, LEE. Pseudonym of Elizabeth Chater. In 1969 was Professor of English at San Diego State College.
A Course in Murder. Transition, 1969 [Calif., acad.]

CHAZE, (LEWIS) ELLIOT. Mississippi newspaperman, novelist, article and ss writer.
Black Wings Has My Angel. GM, 1953; Red Seal, 1957. Also published as: One for My Money. Berkley, 1962
One for My Money; see Black Wings Has My Angel
Wettermark. Scribner, 1969 [Miss.]

CHEAME, WILLIS
"When First We Practise." Long, 1936

CHEATHAM, LILLIAN. Wife of a doctor; lives in Columbia, South Carolina.
The Marriage Pact. Doubleday, 1974 [NYC, 1830]
Portrait of Emma. Doubleday, 1975 [Boston, 1700s]
The Secret of Saramount. Doubleday, 1978 [South, ca.1900]

CHELLIS, MARY DWINELL
Mystery of the Lodge. Lothrop, 1873

CHELTON, JOHN. Pseudonym of Paul Durst, 1921-   , q.v. Other pseudonym: Peter Bannon, q.v.
My Deadly Angel. GM, 1955 [Fla.]

CHERRELL, GWEN
The Madam. French (London), 1966 (Play.)

CHESBRO, GEORGE (CLARK). 1940-   . Ref: CA. SC: Dr. Robert Frederickson (Mongo) = RF.
An Affair of Sorcerers. Simon, 1979; Severn, 1980 RF [NYC]
City of Whispering Stone. Simon, 1978; Severn, 1981 RF [NYC]
King's Gambit. New English Library pb, 1976
Shadow of a Broken Man. Simon, 1977; Severn, 1981 RF [NYC]

CHESHAM, HENRY. Pseudonym of D(avid) E(rnest) Bingley, 1920-   , q.v. Other pseudonym: George Fallon, q.v.
Naples, or Die! Hale, 1966
Skyborne Sapper. Hale, 1966

CHESNEY, MICHAEL. SC: Colonel "Steel" Callaghan, in all titles. Set: Eng.
Callaghan Meets His Fate. Jenkins, 1939
Callaghan of Intelligence. Jenkins, 1938
"Steel" Callaghan. Jenkins, 1939

CHESNEY, WEATHERBY. Pseudonym of C(harles) J(ohn) Cutcliffe (Wright) Hyne, 1865-1944, q.v. Set: Eng.
The Adventures of a Solicitor. Bowden, 1898 ss, some criminous
The Adventures of an Engineer. Bowden, 1898 ss, some criminous
The Branded Prince. Methuen, 1902
The Cable-Man. Chatto, 1907
-The Claimant. Chatto, 1908
The Dilemma of Commander Brett. Bowden, 1899
-The Foundered Galleon. Methuen, 1902
-Four Red Nightcaps. Macqueen, 1900
-John Topp, Pirate. Methuen, 1901
The Mystery of a Bungalow. Methuen, 1904
-The Romance of a Queen. Chatto, 1908
The Tragedy of the Great Emerald. Methuen, 1904

CHESSMAN, CARYL (WHITTIER). 1921-1960. Ref: CA.
The Kid Was a Killer. GM, 1960; Muller pb, 1960

CHESTER, ALFRED. 1929?-1971.
The Exquisite Corpse. Simon, 1967; Deutsch, 1970

CHESTER, ANN
Slightly Imperfect. Arcadia, 1956 [NYC]

CHESTER, GEORGE RANDOLPH. 1869-1924. Ref: EM. SC: James Rufus Wallingford, in all titles.
Get-Rich-Quick Wallingford. Altemus, 1908; Richards, 1908 ss
The Son of Wallingford, with Lillian Eleanor Chester, 1888-   . Small, 1921
Wallingford and Blackie Daw. Bobbs, 1913; Hodder, 1918 ss
Wallingford in His Prime. Bobbs, 1913; Newnes, 1916 ss
Young Wallingford. Bobbs, 1910; Hodder, 1917 ss

CHESTER, GILBERT. Pseudonym of H(arry) H(ornsby) Clifford Gibbons, 1888-1958, q.v. With the one exception noted, all the following were published by Amalgamated Press and feature Sexton Blake.
The Abyssinian Mystery. 1935
The Beauty Parlor Murder. 1935
The Black-Out Crime. 1940
The Caravan Crime. 1934
The Case of the Bogus Prince. 1933
The Case of the Brass-Bound Chest. 1936
The Case of the Deportee. 1934
The Case of the Man on Leave. 1940
The Case of the Repatriated Prisoner. 1943
The Charity Fund Mystery. 1937
The Coronation Mystery. 1937
The Crime of Corporal Sherwood. 1941
The Crime on the Clyde. 1933
A Date with Danger. 1947
Death Walks In. Wright, 1938 (not Sexton Blake.)
The Depository Mystery. 1939
Doctor Sinister. 1943
Dr. Duvene's Crime. 1932
The Great Currency Racket. 1947
The Green Room Crime. 1930
The Hire Purchase Crime. 1938
The House in the Wood. 1945
The House on the Cliffs. 1937
The Man from Moscow. 1941
The Man from Norway. 1941
The Man They Couldn't Buy. 1944
The May Who Bailed Out. 1942
The Man Who Wouldn't Quit. 1944
The Monastery Mystery. 1939
The Murder on the Broads. 1932
Murder on the Marshes. 1931
Murder on the Pier. 1935
Murder to Music. 1933
The Mystery Gangster. 1931
The Mystery of the Condemned Cottage. 1939
The Mystery of the Confiscated Ship. 1945
The Mystery of the Crashed Air Liner. 1947
The Mystery of the Demobilized Soldier. 1944

The Mystery of the Double Burglary. 1946
The Mystery of the Greek Exile. 1936
The Mystery of the Hush-Hush Factory. 1941
The Mystery of the Kidnapped Munition Worker. 1943
The Mystery of the Old Curiosity Shop. 1936
The Mystery of the Underground Factory. 1942
The Palais de Danse Tragedy. 1932
The Paper Salvage Crime. 1942
Previously Reported Missing—Now? 1944
The Red Van Mystery. 1946
The Riddle of the Gas Meter. 1940
The Riddle of the Kidnapped Pensioner. 1944
The Riddle of the Missing Fire Watcher. 1941
The Riddle of the Murdered Fisherman. 1940
The Riddle of the Night Garage. 1949
The Savage Pirates. 1934
The Secret of the Farm. 1932
The Secret of the Snows. Dean, 1968
The Secret of the Steps. 1936
The Secret of Stillwater Mere. 1943
The Secret of the Sunken Ships. 1938
The Silk Stocking Murders. 1942
The Soldier Who Came Back. 1943
The Stage Door Crime. 1946
The Strange Case of the Footman's Crime. 1944
The Studio Crime. 1932
The Sword of Vengeance. 1945
The Taxi Man's Quest. 1936
The Tithe War Mystery. 1935
Under Police Observation. 1945
The Victim of the Combine. 1942

CHESTER, LILLIAN ELEANOR. 1888- .
See: George Randolph Chester, 1869-1924.

CHESTER, PETER. Pseudonym of Dennis (John Andrew) Phillips, 1924- , q.v. Other pseudonym: Peter Chambers, q.v. See also: W(illiam Arthur) Howard Baker, 1925- . SC: Johnny Preston, in at least those marked JP.
Blueprint for Larceny. Jenkins, 1964
Killing Comes Easy. Jenkins, 1958; Roy, 1959 JP
Murder Forestalled. Jenkins, 1960; Roy, 1961 JP [Calif.]
The Pay-Grab Murders. Jenkins, 1962
The Traitors. Jenkins, 1964

CHESTER, ROY
The Damocles Factor. Long, 1977
The Pillars of Hell. Long, 1979

CHESTER, S(AMUEL) BEACH. 1880- .
The Arsene Lepine—Herlock Soames Affair. Aspen, 1976

CHESTERTON, G(ILBERT) K(EITH). 1874-1936. Ref: all eight. SC: Father Brown = FB. Set: Eng.
The Club of Queer Trades. Harper (London & NYC), 1905 ss
The Ecstatic Thief; see Four Faultless Felons
The Father Brown Omnibus. Dodd, 1935 (This volume contains the entire contents of all five books of FB short stories. A new edition, Dodd, 1951, also includes one FB ss that is not in any of the earlier 5 volumes.)
Four Faultless Felons. Cassell, 1930; Dodd, 1930 (Four novelets. Note that prior to this collection there were two small Dodd volumes containing three of the quartet in book form: The Moderate Murderer and The Honest Quack, 1929, 68 pp; and The Ecstatic Thief, 1930, 68 pp.)
The Incredulity of Father Brown. Cassell, 1926; Dodd, 1926 FB ss
The Innocence of Father Brown. Cassell, 1911; Lane, 1911 ss FB
The Man Who Knew Too Much and other stories. Cassell, 1922; Harper, 1922 (The U.S. edition has 3 fewer ss than the British.) ss
The Man Who Was Thursday. Simpkin, 1908; Dodd, 1908
The Moderate Murderer and The Honest Quack; see Four Faultless Felons
The Paradoxes of Mr. Pond. Cassell, 1936; Dodd, 1937 ss
The Poet and the Lunatics. Cassell, 1929; Dodd, 1929 ss
The Scandal of Father Brown. Cassell, 1935; Dodd, 1935 ss FB
The Secret of Father Brown. Cassell, 1927; Harper, 1927 ss FB
The Wisdom of Father Brown. Cassell, 1914; Lane, 1915 ss FB

CHETTUR, S(ANKARA) K(RISHNA)
Bombay Murder. ca.1940 [Bombay]
The Cobras of Dhermasheri. Higginbotham, 1937 ss
Muffled Drums. Ganeson, 1927 ss

CHETWYND, BRIDGET. SC: Petunia Best and Max Frend, in at least those marked B&F.
Death Has Ten Thousand Doors. Hutchinson, 1951 B&F
Rubies, Emeralds and Diamonds. Hutchinson, 1952 B&F
-Uneasy Street. Hutchinson, 1952

CHEYWYND-HAYES, R(INALD HENRY GLYNN). 1919- . Ref: CA.
And Love Survived; see The Dark Man
Cold Terror. Tandem, 1973; Pyramid, 1975
The Dark Man. Sidgwick, 1964. U.S. title: And Love Survived. Zebra, 1979
-The Elemental. Fontana, 1974
-The Man from the Bomb. Spencer, 1959
-The Monster Club. New English Library pb, 1975
-The Night Ghouls. Fontana, 1975
Terror by Night. Tandem, 1974; Pyramid, 1976 ss
-The Unbidden. Tandem, 1971; Pyramid, 1975

CHEVALIER, HAAKON (MAURICE). 1902- .
Ref: CA.
For Us the Living. Knopf, 1949; Secker, 1949 [Calif., 1929-41]

CHEVALIER, PAUL. 1925-1981.
The Grudge. Hodder, 1980; St. Martin's, 1981 [WWII, Eng.]

CHEVIGNY, PAUL (G.) 1935- . Ref: CA.
Criminal Mischief. Pantheon, 1977; Gollancz, 1978 [NYC]

CHEVIOT, ANDREW
Trick, Trial and Triumph. Morison, 1891

CHEYNEY, JEANNE
The Secret of Giltham Hall. Chime, 1980 [Eng., 1600s]

CHEYNEY, PETER [REGINALD SOUTHOUSE CHEYNEY]. 1896-1951. See also: Gerald Verner. Ref: CC, DD, EM, MC, MP, TC. SC: Lemmy Caution = LC; Slim Callaghan = SC; Michael Kells = MK; Alonzo MacTavish = AM; Shaun O'Mara = SO; Everard Peter Quayle = EQ; Johnny Vallon = JV. Note: Cheyney appeared in numerous WWII pamphlets; these are grouped together at the end of the entry.
The Adventures of Julia and two other spy stories. Todd, 1954. U.S. title: The Killing Game. Belmont, 1975 (ss, all or most of which apparently appeared first in Britain in pamphlet form.)
Another Little Drink. Collins, 1940. U.S. title: A Trap for Bellamy. Dodd, 1941. Also published as: Premeditated Murder. Avon, 1943
The Best Stories of Peter Cheyney. Collins, 1954 ss
Callaghan; see Dangerous Curves
Calling Mr. Callaghan. Todd, 1953 (12 ss, at least some first published in pamphlet form.)
Can Ladies Kill? Collins, 1938 LC [S.F.]
The Case of the Dark Hero; see Dark Hero
Case of the Dark Wanton; see Dark Wanton
Cocktails and the Killer; see Ladies Won't Wait
The Counterspy Murders; see Dark Duet
The Curiosity of Etienne MacGregor. Locke, 1940 (Note that a later edition, Todd, 1952, is 43 pages longer and may contain new material.) Also published as: The Sweetheart of the Razors. Four Square, 1952
Dames Don't Care. Collins, 1937; Coward, 1938 LC [Calif.]
Dance Without Music. Collins, 1947; Dodd, 1948
Dangerous Curves. Collins, 1939. U.S. title: Callaghan. Belmont, 1973 SC
Dark Bahama. Collins, 1950; Dodd, 1951. Also published as: I'll Bring Her Back. Eton, 1952 JV [Bahamas]
Dark Duet. Collins, 1942; Dodd, 1943. Also published as: The Counterspy Murders. Avon, 1944
Dark Hero. Collins, 1946; Dodd, 1946. Also published as: The Case of the Dark Hero. Avon, 1947
Dark Interlude. Collins, 1947; Dodd, 1947. Also published as: The Terrible Night. Avon, 1959 SO,EQ [Fr.]
Dark Street. Collins, 1944; Dodd, 1944. Also published as: The Dark Street Murders. Avon, 1946 EQ
The Dark Street Murders; see Dark Street
Dark Wanton. Collins, 1948; Dodd, 1949. Also published as: Case of the Dark Wanton. Avon, 1958 EQ
Don't Get Me Wrong. Collins, 1939 LC [Mex. City, U.S.]
Farewell to the Admiral; see Sorry You've Been Troubled
Fast Work; see The Mystery Blues and other stories
G Man at the Yard. Poynings, 1946 LC
G Man at the Yard. Todd, 1953 (ss about LC, SC and MA, all or most of the tales having first been published in pamphlet form.)
He Walked in Her Sleep. Todd, 1946. U.S. title: MacTavish. Belmont, 1973 AM ss
I'll Bring Her Back; see Dark Bahama
I'll Say She Does! Collins, 1945; Dodd, 1946 LC [Fr.]
It Couldn't Matter Less. Collins, 1941; Arcadia, 1943. Also published as: Set-Up for Murder. Pyramid, 1950 SC
The Killing Game; see The Adventures of Julia and two other spy stories
Knave Takes Queen. Collins, 1939 ss
Ladies Won't Wait. Collins, 1951; Dodd, 1951. Also published as: Cocktails and the Killer. Avon, 1957 MK
Lady, Behave! Collins, 1950. U.S. title: Lady Beware. Dodd, 1950 JV
Lady Beware; see Lady, Behave!
The London Spy Murders; see The Stars Are Dark
MacTavish; see He Walked in Her Sleep
Making Crime Pay. Faber, 1944 (ss, articles and radio plays.)
The Man Nobody Saw; see You Can Call It a Day
Mr. Caution—Mr. Callaghan. Collins, 1941 ss LC,SC
Mistress Murder; see One of Those Things
The Mystery Blues and other stories. Todd, 1954. Also published as: Fast Work. Four Square, 1964 ss
Never a Dull Moment. Collins, 1942 LC
No Ordinary Cheyney. Faber, 1948 (ss and articles.)
One of Those Things. Collins, 1949; Dodd, 1950. Also published as: Mistress Murder. Avon, 1951
Poison Ivy. Collins, 1937 LC [U.S.]
Premeditated Murder; see Another Little Drink
Set-Up for Murder; see It Couldn't Matter Less
Sinister Errand. Collins, 1945; Dodd, 1945. Also published as: Sinister Murders. Avon, 1957 MK
Sinister Murders; see Sinister Errand
Sorry You've Been Troubled. Collins, 1942. U.S. title: Farewell to the Admiral. Dodd, 1943 SC
The Stars Are Dark. Collins, 1943; Dodd, 1943. Also published as: The London Spy Murders. Avon, 1944 EQ
The Sweetheart of the Razors; see The Curiosity of Etienne MacGregor
The Terrible Night; see Dark Interlude
They Never Say When. Collins, 1944; Dodd, 1945 SC
This Man Is Dangerous. Collins, 1936; Coward, 1938 LC
A Trap for Bellamy; see Another Little Drink
Try Anything Twice. Collins, 1948; Dodd, 1948. Also published as: Undressed to Kill. Avon, 1959
Undressed to Kill; see Try Anything Twice
Uneasy Terms. Collins, 1946; Dodd, 1947 SC
The Unscrupulous Mr. Callaghan. Handi-Books, 1943 SC (British title?)
The Urgent Hangman. Collins, 1938; Coward, 1939 SC
Velvet Johnnie and other stories. Collins, 1952 (ss, at least some of which were probably first published in pamphlets.)
You Can Always Duck. Collins, 1943 LC
You Can Call It a Day. Collins, 1949. U.S. title: The Man Nobody Saw. Dodd, 1949 JV
You Can't Hit a Woman and other stories. Collins, 1937 (ss, at least some later reprinted in pamphlets.)
You Can't Keep the Change. Collins, 1940; Dodd, 1944 SC
You'd Be Surprised. Collins, 1940 [Paris]
Your Deal, My Lovely. Collins, 1941 LC

Account Rendered. Polybooks, 1944
The Adventures of Alonzo MacTavish. Polybooks, 1943 AM

The Adventures of Julia. Poynings, 1945
Alonzo MacTavish Again. Polybooks, 1943 AM
Cocktail for Cupid and other stories. Bantam (London), 1948 ss
Cocktail Party and other stories. Bantam (London), 1948 ss
Dance Without Music. Polybooks, 1945
Date After Dark and other stories. Polybooks, 1944 ss
Dressed to Kill. Todd, 1952 (Contains biographical material and title story, published earlier as Night Club, q.v.)
Escape for Sandra. Poynings, 1945
Fast Work and other stories. Bantam (London), 1948 (This volume almost certainly differs from that with a similar title in the first section, for this has 48 pages and that has 188 pages.) ss
He Walked in Her Sleep and other stories. Polybooks, 1946 (This almost certainly differs from the volume with a similar title in the first section, since this has 62 pages and that has 187 pages.) ss
Information Received and other stories. Bantam (London), 1948 ss
Lady in Green and other stories. Bantam (London), 1947 ss
The Lady in Tears and other stories. Bantam (London), 1948 ss
Love with a Gun and other stories. Polybooks, 1943 (16 pp.); Polybooks, 1946 (62 pp.)
The Man with the Red Beard. Todd, 1943 (From: You Can't Hit a Woman and other stories, q.v.)
The Man with Two Wives and other stories. Polybooks, 1946 ss
A Matter of Luck and other stories. Bantam (London), 1947
The Murder of Alonzo. Polybooks, 1943 AM
Night Club. Poynings, 1945. See also: Dressed to Kill.
A Spot of Murder and other stories. Polybooks, 1946 ss
Time for Caution. Foster, 1946 LC
A Tough Spot for Cupid and other stories. Vallancey, 1945 ss
The Unhappy Lady and other stories. Bantam (London), 1948 ss
Vengeance with a Twist and other stories. Vallancey, 1946 ss
You Can't Trust Duchesses and other stories. Vallancey, 1946 ss

CHICHESTER, HUGH
The Mystery Man in the Tower. Burns, 1938

CHICHESTER, JOHN JAY. SC: Maxwell Sanderson = MS; Jimmy "Wiggly" Price = JP.
The Bigamist. Chelsea, 1925; Hutchinson, 1927 JP [NYC]
The House of the Moving Room. Chelsea, 1926; Hutchinson, 1926 JP [L.I.]
The King of Diamonds. Chelsea, 1930; Hutchinson, 1931 MS [N.Y.]
The Porcelain Mask. Chelsea, 1924; Jenkins, 1925
Rogues of Fortune. Chelsea, 1929; Hutchinson, 1930 MS [N.Y.]
Sanderson: Master Rogue. Chelsea, 1929; Hutchinson, 1930 MS [NYC]
Sanderson's Diamond Loot. Chelsea, 1935; Hutchinson, 1935 MS [NYC]
The Silent Cracksman. Chelsea, 1929; Hutchinson, 1929 MS [NYC]

CHIDSEY, DONALD BARR. 1902-1981. Ref: CA.
Nobody Heard the Shot. Bantam (L.A.) 1941

CHILCOT, HARRIET
Moreton Abbey; or, The Fatal Mystery. Baker, 1796

CHILD, NELLISE. SC: Jeremiah Irish, in both titles.
The Diamond Ransom Murders. Knopf, 1935; Collins, 1934 [L.A.]
Murder Comes Home. Knopf, 1933; Collins, 1933 [Calif.]

CHILD, RICHARD WASHBURN. 1881-1935. Ref: EM.
-The Blue Wall: A Story of Strangeness and Struggle. Houghton, 1912; Constable, 1912
Fresh Waters and other stories. Dutton, 1924; Hodder, 1925 ss
The Vanishing Men. Dutton, 1920 [NYC]
The Velvet Black. Dutton, 1921; Hodder, 1921 ss

CHILD, RODERICK. 1949- . Ref: CA.
The Carrington Assignment. Hale, 1968
Claustrophobia. Hale, 1971
Spy on Approval. Hale, 1969

CHILDERNESS, GEORGE. SC: Chet Phelps in both titles.
Murder in False Face. Phoenix, 1943
Too Many Murderers. Phoenix, 1944; Pemberton, 1946

CHILDERS, (ROBERT) ERSKINE. 1870-1922. Ref: CC, EM, MC, TC.
The Riddle of the Sands. Smith Elder, 1903; Dodd, 1915 [ship]

CHILDERS, JAMES SAXON. 1899- .
The Bookshop Mystery. Appleton, 1930

CHILDS, EDMUND BURTON. Pseudonym: Edmund Burton, q.v.

CHILDS, MARQUIS (WILLIAM). 1903- .
Ref: CA.
Taint of Innocence. Harper, 1967; Cassell, 1968 [Mid. East]

CHILDS, TIMOTHY. 1941- . Ref: CA.
Cold Turkey. Harper, 1979; Hale, 1981 [L.A.]

CHIMENTI, FRANCESCA
Night Falls Too Soon. Pyramid, 1972
The Silent Room. Pyramid, 1972 [N.Y., 1910]
The Web of Allyngrood. Doubleday, 1977. Also published as: The Web of Deception. Dell, 1979 [Eng., 1800s]
The Web of Deception; see The Web of Allyngrood

CHIODO, DANIEL J. and GEORGE CARPOZI, JR.
The Velvet Jungle. Playboy, 1979

CHIPPERFIELD, ROBERT ORR. Pseudonym of Isabel (Egenton) Ostrander, 1883-1924, q.v. Other pseudonyms: David Fox, Douglas Grant, qq.v. See also: William J. Burns, 1861-1932. SC: Barry O'Dell = BO.
Above Suspicion. McBride, 1923; Hurst, 1923 [N.Y.]
Bright Lights. McBride, 1924; Hurst, 1924 [NYC]
The Man in the Jury Box. McBride, 1921; Hurst, 1921 BO [NYC]
The Second Bullet. McBride, 1919; Skeffington, 1920
The Trigger of Conscience. McBride, 1921; Hurst, 1922 [New Eng.]
Unseen Hands. McBride, 1920; Hurst, 1920 BO [NYC]

CHITTENDEN, F(RANK) A(LBERT). 1910- .
Darkness over Hycroft. Gifford, 1947
The Four Cornered Story. Boardman, 1951
Strange Welcome. Boardman, 1949; Coward, 1949
The Uninvited. Boardman, 1954
The Widow in White. Gifford, 1949

CHITTENDEN, MARGARET. 1935- . Ref: CA.
The Face in the Mirror. Pinnacle, 1980 [past]
Findlay's Landing. Ace, 1975 [Wash.]
House of the Twilight Moon. Pinnacle, 1979
The Other Child. Pinnacle, 1979
Song of Dark Water. Pinnacle, 1978

CHITTY, SIR THOMAS WILLES. 1926- .
Pseudonym: Thomas Hinde, q.v.

CHIU, TONY
Port Arthur Chicken. Morrow, 1979; Collins, 1980. Also published as: Onyxx. Berkley, 1981; Fontana, 1982 [NYC]

CHODOROV, EDWARD. 1904- . Ref: CA.
Cue for Passion, with H. S. Kraft. French (NYC), 1941 (3-act play.)
Decision. French (NYC), 1946 (3-act play.)
Kind Lady. French (NYC), 1936 (Play based on the ss "The Silver Mask" from "All Souls' Night" by Hugh Walpole, 1884-1941, q.v.)

CHOLMONDELEY, MARY. 1859-1925. Ref: CC.
The Danvers Jewels. Bentley, 1887; Harper, 1890 (bound with "Sir Charles Danvers," as by "The Author of The Danvers Jewels")
-Prisoners. Hutchinson, 1906; Dodd, 1906

CHRISTIAN, JOHN. Pseudonym of Roger Dixon, 1930- . Ref: CA. SC: Richard Deutsch, in both titles.
Five Gates to Armageddon. Harwood-Smart, 1975; St. Martin's, 1975 [Jerus., 1985]
The Persian Death-Trap. Harwood, 1976 [Mid. East]

CHRISTIAN, KIT. Joint pseudonym of Delos Russell Thorson, 1906- , and Sara Winfree Thorson, 1906- .
Death and Bitters. Dutton, 1943 [Chi.]

CHRISTIAN, NICK. Pseudonym of Edward A. Pollitz, Jr., q.v.
Homicide Zone 4. Signet, 1978; New English Library pb, 1979 [NYC]
Intensive Fear. Signet, 1980 [NYC, hosp.]

CHRISTIANSEN, SIGURD (WESLEY). 1891-1948.
-Chaff Before the Wind. Liveright, 1934 (Translation of "Agner i Stormen." Oslo, 1933.)
Two Living and One Dead. Gollancz, 1932; Liveright, 1932 (Translation of "To Levende Og en Dod." Oslo, 1931.) [Nor.]

CHRISTIANSON, BARBARA
A Triumphant Defeat. Neely, 1901

CHRISTIE, AGATHA. 1890-1976. See also: Moie Charles, Leslie Darbon, G. R(oy) McRae, Michael Morton, Arnold Ridley, Gerald Verner, Frank Vosper. Ref: all eight. SC: Supt. Battle = B; Tuppence & Tommy Beresford = T&T; Jane Marple = JM; Hercule Poirot = HP; Parker Pyne = PP; Harley Quin = HQ; Colonel Race = R. Grouped separately at the end of the listing are some WWII pamphlets. Set: mostly Eng.
The ABC Murders. Collins, 1936; Dodd, 1936. Also published as: The Alphabet Murders. PB, 1966 HP
The Adventure of the Christmas Pudding. Collins, 1960 (6 ss, 5 with HP, 1 with JM. 5 of the 6 are spread throughout the U.S. collections entitled The Regatta Mystery, Three Blind Mice, The Under Dog, and Double Sin, qq.v. An earlier and shorter version of the 6th, "The Mystery of the Spanish Chest," appeared in The Regatta Mystery as "The Mystery of the Baghdad Chest.")
After the Funeral. Collins, 1953. U.S. title: Funerals Are Fatal. Dodd, 1953. Also published as: Murder at the Gallop. Fontana, 1963 HP
Afternoon at the Seaside. French, 1963 (1-act play.)
The Alphabet Murders; see The ABC Murders
And Then There Were None; see Ten Little Niggers
Appointment with Death. Collins, 1938; Dodd, 1938 HP (Also a play by this title, but without HP: French, 1956.) [Jerus.]
At Bertram's Hotel. Collins, 1965; Dodd, 1966 JM
The Big Four. Collins, 1927; Dodd, 1927 HP (A "novel" incorporating 10 HP ss.)
Black Coffee. Ashley, 1934; Baker, 1934 (Play.)
Blood Will Tell; see Mrs. McGinty's Dead
The Body in the Library. Collins, 1942; Dodd, 1942 JM
The Boomerang Clue; see Why Didn't They Ask Evans?
By the Pricking of My Thumbs. Collins, 1968; Dodd, 1968 T&T
Cards on the Table. Collins, 1936; Dodd, 1937 HP,SB,R
A Caribbean Mystery. Collins, 1964; Dodd, 1965 JM [Carib.]
The Case of the Moving Finger; see The Moving Finger
Cat Among the Pigeons. Collins, 1959; Dodd, 1960 HP [acad.]
The Clocks. Collins, 1963; Dodd, 1964 HP
Crooked House. Collins, 1949; Dodd, 1949
Curtain. Collins, 1975; Dodd, 1975 HP
Dead Man's Folly. Collins, 1956; Dodd, 1956 HP
Dead Man's Mirror; see Murder in the Mews
Death Comes As the End. Collins, 1945; Dodd, 1944 [Egypt, 2000 B.C.]
Death in the Air; see Death in the Clouds
Death in the Clouds. Collins, 1935. U.S. title: Death in the Air. Dodd, 1935 HP
Death on the Nile. Collins, 1937; Dodd, 1938 HP,R [Egypt]
Destination Unknown. Collins, 1954. U.S. title: So Many Steps to Death. Dodd, 1955
Double Sin and other stories. Dodd, 1961 (8 ss, 4 with HP, 2 with JM. Two of the 8 appear in the British collection The Adventure of the Christmas Pudding, and one in The Hound of Death, qq.v.; 3 appear later in Poirot's Early Cases, q.v.; 2 remain uncollected in Britain.)
Dumb Witness. Collins, 1937. U.S. title: Poirot Loses a Client. Dodd, 1937 HP

Easy to Kill; see Murder Is Easy
Elephants Can Remember. Collins, 1972; Dodd, 1972 HP
Endless Night. Collins, 1967; Dodd, 1968
Evil Under the Sun. Collins, 1941; Dodd, 1941 HP
Five Little Pigs. Collins, 1943. U.S. title: Murder in Retrospect. Dodd, 1942 HP
4.50 from Paddington. Collins, 1957. U.S. title: What Mrs. McGillicuddy Saw! Dodd, 1957. Also published as: Murder, She Said. Cardinal, 1961 JM
Funerals Are Fatal; see After the Funeral
Go Back for Murder. French, 1960 (A play based on the novel Five Little Pigs, q.v., but without HP.)
The Golden Ball and other stories. Dodd, 1971 (15 ss, none with a SC. 8 are from the British collection The Listerdale Mystery, 5 from The Hound of Death, qq.v.; 2 remain uncollected in Britain.)
Hallowe'en Party. Collins, 1969; Dodd, 1969 HP
Hercule Poirot's Christmas. Collins, 1938. U.S. title: Murder for Christmas. Dodd, 1939. Also published as: A Holiday for Murder. Avon, 1947 HP
Hercule Poirot's Early Cases; see Poirot's Early Cases
Hickory Dickory Death; see Hickory Dickory Dock
Hickory Dickory Dock. Collins, 1955. U.S. title: Hickory Dickory Death. Dodd, 1955 HP
A Holiday for Murder; see Hercule Poirot's Christmas
The Hollow. Collins, 1946; Dodd, 1946. Also published as: Murder After Hours. Dell, 1954 HP Also a play, without HP: French, 1952
The Hound of Death and other stories. Odhams, 1933 (12 ss, none with a series character. 6 appear in the U.S. collection The Witness for the Prosecution, 1 in Double Sin, and 5 in The Golden Ball and other stories, qq.v.)
The Incredible Theft; see Murder in the Mews
The Labours of Hercules. Collins, 1947; Dodd, 1947 (12 ss with HP.)
The Listerdale Mystery. Collins, 1934 (12 ss, none with a series character. 2 appear in the U.S. collection The Witness for the Prosecution, 1 in Surprise! Surprise!, qq.v.; the remaining story is uncollected in the U.S.)
Lord Edgeware Dies. Collins, 1933. U.S. title: Thirteen at Dinner. Dodd, 1933 HP
The Man in the Brown Suit. Lane, 1924; Dodd, 1924 R [S. Afr.]
The Mirror Crack'd; see The Mirror Crack'd from Side to Side
The Mirror Crack'd from Side to Side. Collins, 1962. U.S. title: The Mirror Crack'd. Dodd, 1963 JM
Miss Marple and the Thirteen Problems; see The Thirteen Problems
Miss Marple's Final Cases. Collins, 1979 (6 JM ss and 2 others.)
The Mousetrap; see Three Blind Mice
The Mousetrap and Other Plays. Dodd, 1978 (Plays.)
The Moving Finger. Collins, 1943; Dodd, 1942. Also published as: The Case of the Moving Finger. Avon, 1948 JM
Mr. Parker Pyne, Detective; see Parker Pyne Investigates
Mrs. McGinty's Dead. Collins, 1952; Dodd, 1952. Also published as: Blood Will Tell. Detective Book Club, 1952 HP
Murder After Hours; see The Hollow
Murder at Hazelmoor; see The Sittaford Mystery
Murder at the Gallop; see After the Funeral
The Murder at the Vicarage. Collins, 1930; Dodd, 1930 JM
Murder for Christmas; see Hercule Poirot's Christmas
Murder in Mesopotamia. Collins, 1936; Dodd, 1936 HP [Mesop.]
Murder in Retrospect; see Five Little Pigs
Murder in the Calais Coach; see Murder on the Orient Express
Murder in the Mews. Collins, 1937. U.S. title: Dead Man's Mirror. Dodd, 1937 (4 HP stories. 3 of these were later published separately as: The Incredible Theft. Mercury, 194?. Other U.S. paperback editions also contain only three of the four stories, whereas British paperback reprints are generally complete.)

Murder in Three Acts; see Three Act Tragedy
A Murder Is Announced. Collins, 1950; Dodd, 1950 JM
Murder Is Easy. Collins, 1939. U.S. title: Easy to Kill. Dodd, 1939 SB
The Murder of Roger Ackroyd. Collins, 1926; Dodd, 1926 HP
The Murder on the Links. Lane, 1923; Dodd, 1923 HP [Fr.]
Murder on the Nile. French, 1948 (A play based on the novel Death on the Nile, q.v., but without HP.) [Egypt]
Murder on the Orient Express. Collins, 1934. U.S. title: Murder in the Calais Coach. Dodd, 1934 HP [train]
Murder, She Said; see 4.50 from Paddington
Murder with Mirrors; see They Do It with Mirrors
The Mysterious Affair at Styles. Lane (London & NYC), 1920 HP
The Mysterious Mr. Quin. Collins, 1930; Dodd, 1930 (12 ss with HQ.)
The Mystery of the Blue Geranium, and other Tuesday Club Murders. Bantam (NYC), 1940 (ss taken from The Thirteen Problems, q.v.)
The Mystery of the Blue Train. Collins, 1928; Dodd, 1928 HP [Fr., train]
N or M? Collins, 1941; Dodd, 1941 T&T
Nemesis. Collins, 1971; Dodd, 1971 JM
One, Two, Buckle My Shoe. Collins, 1940. U.S. title: The Patriotic Murders. Dodd, 1941. Also published as: An Overdose of Death. Dell, 1953 HP
Ordeal by Innocence. Collins, 1958; Dodd, 1959
An Overdose of Death; see One, Two, Buckle My Shoe
The Pale Horse. Collins, 1961; Dodd, 1962
Parker Pyne Investigates. Collins, 1934. U.S. title: Mr. Parker Pyne: Detective. Dodd, 1934 (12 ss with PP)
Partners in Crime. Collins, 1929; Dodd, 1929 (17 ss about T&T, disguised as a novel, the second half of which was reprinted separately as: The Sunningdale Mystery. Collins, 1933.)
Passenger to Frankfurt. Collins, 1970; Dodd, 1970
The Patient. French, 1963 (1-act play)
The Patriotic Murders; see One, Two, Buckle My Shoe
Peril at End House. Collins, 1932; Dodd, 1932 HP
A Pocket Full of Rye. Collins, 1953; Dodd, 1954 JM
Poirot Investigates. Lane, 1924; Dodd, 1925 (The British edition has 11 HP ss; the American adds 3 more. Note that some U.S. paperback editions are incomplete.)
Poirot Loses a Client; see Dumb Witness
Poirot's Early Cases. Collins, 1974. U.S. title: Hercule Poirot's Early Cases. Dodd, 1974 (18 HP ss reshuffled from earlier collections.)
Postern of Fate. Collins, 1973; Dodd, 1973 T&T
The Rats. French, 1963 (1-act play.)
The Regatta Mystery. Dodd, 1939 (9 ss, 5 with HP, 2 with PP, 2 with JM, 1 supernatural. Several appeared in Britain in "raid library" pamphlets during WWII but three remain uncollected in hardcover British Christie volumes.)
Remembered Death; see Sparkling Cyanide
Sad Cypress. Collins, 1940; Dodd, 1940 HP
The Secret Adversary. Lane, 1922; Dodd, 1922 T&T
The Secret of Chimneys. Lane, 1925; Dodd, 1925
The Seven Dials Mystery. Collins, 1929; Dodd, 1929 SB
The Sittaford Mystery. Collins, 1931. U.S. title: Murder at Hazelmoor. Dodd, 1931
Sleeping Murder. Collins, 1976; Dodd, 1976 JM
So Many Steps to Death; see Destination Unknown
Sparkling Cyanide. Collins, 1945. U.S. title: Remembered Death. Dodd, 1945 R
Spider's Web. French, 1957 (Play.)
The Sunningdale Mystery; see Partners in Crime
Surprise! Surprise! Dodd, 1965 (A reshuffling of ss from earlier Christie hardcover collections.)
Taken at the Flood. Collins, 1948. U.S. title: There Is a Tide... Dodd, 1948 HP
Ten Little Indians; see Ten Little Niggers

Ten Little Niggers. Collins, 1939. U.S. title: And Then There Were None. Dodd, 1940. Also published as: Ten Little Indians. PB, 1965. Also a play under the original British title: French (London), 1944; and as Ten Little Indians. French (NYC), 1946
There Is a Tide...; see Taken at the Flood
They Came to Baghdad. Collins, 1951; Dodd, 1951 [Baghdad]
They Do It with Mirrors. Collins, 1952. U.S. title: Murder with Mirrors. Dodd, 1952 JM
Third Girl. Collins, 1966; Dodd, 1967 HP
Thirteen at Dinner; see Lord Edgware Dies
13 Clues for Miss Marple. Dodd, 1966 (A reshuffling of JM ss from prior hardcover Christie collections.)
13 for Luck! Collins, 1966; Dodd, 1961 (A reshuffling of ss from prior hardcover Christie collections.)
The Thirteen Problems. Collins, 1932. U.S. title: The Tuesday Club Murders. Dodd, 1933. Also published as: Miss Marple and the Thirteen Problems. Penguin, 1953 (13 ss about JM.)
Three Act Tragedy. Collins, 1935. U.S. title: Murder in Three Acts. Dodd, 1934 HP
Three Blind Mice. Dodd, 1950. Also published as: The Mousetrap. Dodd, 1960 (A "novelettization" of the famous Christie stage play, plus 8 ss, 3 with HP, 4 with JM, 1 with HQ. 5 of the 9 tales have not been collected in any British Christie volume.) The play was published separately as: The Mousetrap. French, 1954
Towards Zero. Collins, 1944; Dodd, 1944. Also as a play (with Gerald Verner, q.v.): French, 1957; Dramatists, 1957 SB
The Tuesday Club Murders; see The Thirteen Problems
Two Thrillers; see The Under Dog and other stories
The Under Dog and other stories. Dodd, 1951 (A novelet and 8 ss, all about HP, all subsequently appearing in Christie collections in Britain. The title novelet appeared in book form in Britain, bound together with "Blackman's Wood" by E. Phillips Oppenheim, q.v. Readers Library, 1929. This volume was reprinted as: Two Thrillers. London Daily Express Fiction Library, 1936.)
The Unexpected Guest. French, 1958 (A play.)
Verdict. French, 1958 (2-act play.)
What Mrs. McGillicuddy Saw! see 4.50 from Paddington
Why Didn't They Ask Evans? Collins, 1934. U.S. title: The Boomerang Clue. Dodd, 1935
The Witness for the Prosecution. Dodd, 1948 (9 ss, one with HP. All but the HP story are collected in Britain, 6 in The Hound of Death, 2 in The Listerdale Mystery, qq.v. The title story also as a play: French, 1954.)

The Crime in Cabin 66; see The Mystery of the Crime in Cabin 66
The Mystery of the Baghdad Chest. Bantam (London), 1943 (HP story from The Regatta Mystery, q.v.)
The Mystery of the Crime in Cabin 66. Bantam (London), 1943. Also published as: The Crime in Cabin 66. Vallancey, 1944 (HP story from The Regatta Mystery, q.v., where it is titled "Problem at Sea.")
Poirot and the Regatta Mystery. Bantam (London), 1943 (HP story, modified from the PP tale, "The Regatta Mystery," in the book of that title, q.v.)
Poirot Knows the Murderer. Polybooks, 1946 (3 HP stories reshuffled from earlier pamphlets: The Mystery of the Baghdad Chest; The Crime in Cabin 66; and Christmas Adventure
Poirot Lends a Hand. Polybooks, 1946 (3 HP stories, the first two as published in the pamphlets Problem at Pollensa Bay and Christmas Adventure, and Poirot and the Regatta Mystery, qq.v.; the third as published in the U.S. edition of Poirot Investigates, q.v.)
Poirot on Holiday. Polybooks, 1943 (2 HP stories contained in other pamphlets: The Regatta Mystery, and The Crime in Cabin 66.)

Problem at Pollensa Bay and Christmas
Adventure. Polybooks, 1943 (HP stories, the first modified from the PP tale of the same title in The Regatta Mystery, q.v., the second not previously published in book form.)
The Veiled Lady and The Mystery of the Baghdad Chest. Polybooks, 1944 (HP stories from the U.S. edition of Poirot Investigates and from The Regatta Mystery, qq.v.)

CHRISTIE, CAMPBELL. See: Dorothy Christie

CHRISTIE, DOROTHY and CAMPBELL
Grand National Night. French (London), 1947 (3-act play.)
Someone at the Door. French (London & NYC), 1936 (3-act play.)
The Touch of Fear. French (London), 1957 (3-act play.)

CHRISTIE, DOUGLAS. 1894- . Pseudonyms: Colin Campbell, Lynn Durie, qq.v.
-Isle of Confusion. Hurst, 1930
-Isle of Desire. Hurst, 1929
The Rajah's Casket. Hurst, 1933
-The Striking Force. Rich, 1934
-Terry of Tangistan. Hurst, 1932
Trouble on the Frontier. Rich, 1935
-Under Observation. Hurst, 1931
-"Yellow—Like Gold!" Hurst, 1931

CHRISTIE, KATE. Born in England; author of several novels and a work of non-fiction.
Child's Play. Macmillan (London), 1968; Harcourt, 1969

CHRISTIE, LOUIS
Better Than Weapons. Rich, 1935

CHRISTIE, STEPHEN. Pseudonym of D. S. C. Kuruppu. SC (with many other authors): Sexton Blake, in both titles.
Crash and Carry. Mayflower, 1967 [Cey.]
Slaughter in the Sun. Baker, 1969

CHRISTNER, D. W.
Epitaph for Emily. Zebra, 1979

CHRISTOPHER, EDGAR EARL. 1872- .
The Invisibles. Saalfield, 1903

CHRISTOPHER, JAY
Murder-Go-Round. Dramatic, 1976 (3-act play.)

CHRISTOPHER, JOHN. Pseudonym of (Christopher) Samuel Youd, 1922- , q.v. Other pseudonyms: Hilary Ford, Peter Graaf, Peter Nichols, qq.v.
The Caves of Night. Eyre, 1958; Simon, 1958 [Austria]
-The Little People. Hodder, 1967; Simon, 1967 [Ire.]
Pendulum. Hodder, 1968; Simon, 1968
A Scent of White Poppies. Eyre, 1959; Simon, 1959

CHRISTOPHER, MATTHEW F. 1917- . Ref: CA.
Look for the Body. Phoenix, 1952

CHRISTY, HELEN
Mr. Ace. Bart, 1946 (Novelization of the movie.)

CHURCH, GRANVILLE. Pseudonym of Granville Church People. Born in Boston.
Bombs Burst Once. Mill, 1941. Also published as: Wings over Panama. Adventure Novel Classic, 194? [Cent. Am.]
Race with the Sun. Mill, 1944 [Calif.]
Wings over Panama; see Bombs Burst Once

CHURCHER, W. R. M.
Benevolent Blackmail. Mortiboy's, 1930

CHURCHILL, EDWARD
Menace of Death. Dodge, 1937

CHURCHILL, LUANNA. Joint pseudonym of husband and wife writing team; has written radio plays, ss and novels, over 133 stories published under various pseudonyms.
Bride of the Unliving. Lenox, 1975; Remploy, 1975
Craven Castle. Lenox, 1972; Remploy, 1973
Death Rides a Black Steed. Lenox, 1975 [Ohio]
Glowering Gables. Lenox, 1974; Remploy, 1974
The Grinning Ghoul. Lenox, 1974; Remploy, 1974
Macabre Mansion. Lenox, 1973; Remploy, 1973
Moonlake Manor. Lenox, 1972

Shades and Shadows. Lenox, 1973; Remploy, 1974 [Fla.]
Shadow on the Moon. Lenox, 1974; Remploy, 1974
Witch Haven. Lenox, 1973; Remploy, 1974
Wraithwood. Lenox, 1973; Remploy, 1974

CHURCHWARD, JOHN
The Rainbow Deaths. New English Library, 1977

CHUTE, M(ARY) G(RACE). 1907- . Born, raised, and educated in Minnesota.
Sheriff Olson. Appleton, 1942 ss

CHUTE, NOELINE BULLOCK
Tea and Trickery. Bakers, 1970 (1-act play.)

CHUTE, VERNE. 1917- . Born in Calif.
Blackmail; see Wayward Angel
Flight of an Angel. Morrow, 1946; Museum Press, 1950 [Calif.]
Sweet and Deadly. Popular Library, 1952
Wayward Angel. Knopf, 1948. British title: Blackmail. Museum Press, 1951 [Calif., Mex.]

CICELLIS, KAY [CATHERINE-MATHILDA CICELLIS]. 1926- . Ref: CA.
-The Day the Fish Came Out. Bantam, 1967 (Novelization of the movie.)

CLAD, NOEL (CLOVIS). 1924-1962. Born in White Plains, N.Y.; educated in economics and served with the Marshall Plan Mission. Killed in plane crash.
The Mafia; see The Savage
The Savage. Simon, 1958; Gollancz, 1958. Also published as: The Mafia. Belmont, 1970
A Taste for Brilliants. Random, 1964; Hammond, 1965 [L.A.]

CLAIRE, MARVIN
The Drowning Wire. Ace, 1953 [Minn.]

CLANCY, AMBROSE. 1948- .
Blind Plot. Morrow, 1980; Macmillan (London), 1981 [Ire.]

CLANCY, EUGENE A.
Fast Money. Chelsea, 1926 [L.I.]
-Red Mountain, Limited. Chelsea, 1926; Hutchinson, 1927
Watched Out. Chelsea, 1925 [NYC]

CLANCY, LEO. Journalist living in London.
Fix. Secker, 1979; Knopf, 1979

CLANDON, HENRIETTA. Pseudonym of John (George) Hazlette Vahey, 1881- , q.v. Other pseudonyms: John Haslette, Anthony Lang, Vernon Loder, John Mowbray, Walter Proudfoot, qq.v. SC: Penny & Vincent Mercer = M; William Power = WP. Set: Eng.
Fog Off Weymouth. Bles, 1938 M
The Ghost Party. Bles, 1934
Good by Stealth. Bles, 1936 WP
Inquest. Bles, 1933
Power on the Scent. Bles, 1937 WP,M
Rope by Arrangement. Bles, 1935 WP,M
This Delicate Murder. Bles, 1936 WP

CLAPP, EVA CATHARINE
A Dark Secret. Laird, 1888

CLAPP, PATRICIA. 1912- . Ref: CA.
If a Body Meet a Body. Art Craft, 1963 (3-act play.)

CLAPPEN, JOHN. 1901- .
Snow in Essex. Eldon, 1933

CLAPPERTON, RICHARD. 1934- . Ref: CA. SC: Peter Fleck, in at least those marked PF.
No News on Monday. Constable, 1968. U.S. title: You're a Long Time Dead. Putnam, 1968 PF [Australia]
The Sentimental Kill. Constable, 1976 PF [Australia]
Victims Unknown. Constable, 1970
You're a Long Time Dead; see No News on Monday

CLARE, AUSTIN. Pseudonym of Wilhelmina Martha James.
The Conscience of Dr. Holt. Long, 1908
Out of the Net; or, The Change in Robert Holt. SPCK, 1899

CLARE, JOHN. Magazine and newspaper editor in Canada.
The Passionate Invaders. Doubleday, 1965 [Can.]

CLARE, MARGUERITE. Pseudonym of Mary Heppell.
-Barefoot Witch. Wright, 1968
-Blaze at Noon. Hale, 1966

-Candle of the Night. Wright, 1963
-Chariot of the Sun. Hale, 1965
-The Cintra Story. Wright, 1960
-Deadline for Loren. Wright, 1962
-Deep Is the Lake. Wright, 1967
Fear Treads Soft Shod. Wright, 1956
-Golden Enchantress. Wright, 1967
-The Lane of Darkness. Wright, 1949
The Mask of Danger. Wright, 1952
-Pierce the Gloom. Wright, 1958
-Pillar of Fire. Hale, 1964
-Smouldering Fire. Wright, 1959
Spin a Dark Web. Wright, 1961
-Star of the Goddess. Wright, 1968
-The Wild Secret. Wright, 1961

CLARE, T.
The Nine Club. Hutchinson, 1929

CLARETIE, JULES [ARSENE ARNAUD CLARETIE]. 1840-1913. Ref: CC.
The Crime of the Boulevard. Fenno, 1897 [Fr.]
For Jacques' Sake. Vizetelly, 1888

CLARK, AL C. Pseudonym of Donald Goines, 1935?-1974, q.v. SC: Kenyatta, in at least those marked K.
Crime Partners. Holloway, 1974 K
Cry Revenge! Holloway, 1974
Death List. Holloway, 1974 K
Kenyatta's Escape. Holloway, 1974 K
Kenyatta's Last Hit. Holloway, 1975 K

CLARK, AL W.
Graves Ghost. Art Craft, 1956 (Play.)
Hot Ice. Heuer, 1952 (2-act play.)
The Showboat Mystery. Banner, 1938 (3-act play.)
Tailspin Sammy. Eldridge, 1943 (3-act play.)
This Ghost Business. Heuer, 1946 (3-act play.)

CLARK, ALFRED ALEXANDER GORDON. 1900-1958. Pseudonym: Cyril Hare, q.v.

CLARK, CECILY
Ravensley Manor. PB, 1976 [Eng., 1800s]

CLARK, CHRISTOPHER. 1911- .
-The Unleashed Will. Little, 1947

CLARK, CURT. Pseudonym of Donald E(dwin) Westlake, 1933- , q.v. Other pseudonyms: Tucker Coe, Timothy J. Culver, Richard Stark, qq.v.
Anarchaos. Ace, 1967 [future]

CLARK, DALE. Pseudonym of Ronal Kayser. Novelist; author of some 400 magazine stories; creative writing teacher.
The Blonde, the Gangster and the Private Eye; see The Red Rods
Country Coffins. Bouregy, 1961
Death Wore Fins. Mystery House, 1959 [Calif.]
Focus on Murder. Lippincott, 1943
Mambo to Murder. Ace, 1955
The Narrow Cell. Lippincott, 1944 [Calif.]
The Red Rods. Messner, 1946. Also published as: The Blonde, the Gangster and the Private Eye. Avon, 1949 [Calif.]
A Run for the Money. Ace, 1956 [Calif.]

CLARK, DOROTHY PARK. 1899- . Ref: CA.
Just for the Bride. Doubleday, 1950 [Tenn.]
Poison Speaks Softly. Doubleday, 1947 [Ky.]
Roll, Jordan, Roll. Doubleday, 1947 [Ky.]

CLARK, DOUGLAS. ca.1920- . Publicist for a British pharmaceutical company. Pseudonym: James Ditton, q.v. SC: Insp./Supt. George Masters, in all titles. Set: Eng.
Deadly Pattern. Cassell, 1970; Stein, 1970
Death After Evensong. Cassell, 1969; Stein, 1970
Dread and Water. Gollancz, 1976
The Gimmel Flask. Gollancz, 1977; Dell, 1982
Golden Rain. Gollancz, 1980; Dell, 1982
Heberden's Seat. Gollancz, 1979
The Libertines. Gollancz, 1978
Nobody's Perfect. Cassell, 1969; Stein, 1969
Poacher's Bag. Gollancz, 1980
Premedicated Murder. Gollancz, 1975; Scribner, 1976
Sick to Death. Cassell, 1971; Stein, 1971
Sweet Poison. Cassell, 1970
Table D'Hote. Gollancz, 1977

CLARK, EDWARD C.
The Fatal Element. Empire, 1934 [Chi.]

CLARK, ELLERY H(ARDING). 1874-1949.
 The Carleton Case. Bobbs, 1910
 Loaded Dice. Bobbs, 1909

CLARK, ERIC. 1937-   . Ref: CA.
 Black Gambit. Hodder, 1978; Morrow, 1978 [Russ.]
 The Sleeper. Hodder, 1979; Atheneum, 1980

CLARK, EVERT and NICHOLAS (MORTON) HORROCK, 1936-   .
 Corsican Contract. Bantam (London), 1974

CLARK, FRANCES BETTY
 Darken the Moon. Blackwood, 1953
 Night on Penwith. Hammond, 1961

CLARK, GAIL. 1944-   . Raised in Pa., author of screenplays and TV commercials; lives in L.A. SC: Dulcie Bligh, in both titles, both set in Eng., ca.1810.
 The Baroness of Bow Street. Putnam, 1979
 Dulcie Bligh. Putnam, 1978

CLARK, LAURENCE (WALTER). 1914-   . Ref: CA.
 Murder of the Prime Minister. Veracity, 1965 [1812, Eng.]

CLARK, LYDIA BENSON. Pseudonym of Eloise Meaker, 1915-   . Other pseudonym: Amanda McAllister, q.v.
 Demon Cat. Zebra, 1975. Also published as: Seance for Susan. Zebra, 1977
 Seance for Susan; see Demon Cat
 Yesterday's Evil. Ace, 1974

CLARK, MABEL MARGARET COWIE. Pseudonym: Lesley Storm, q.v.

CLARK, MARIAN B(UXTON). Born in Cincinnati; has been merchandise manager for a department store.
 The Model Corpse. Hale, Cushman & Flint, 1942; Boardman, 1945 [Cin.]

CLARK, MARY HIGGINS. 1931-   . Ref: CA.
 The Cradle Will Fall. Simon, 1980; Collins, 1980 [hosp., N.J.]
 A Stranger Is Watching. Simon, 1978; Collins, 1978 [NYC]
 Where Are the Children? Simon, 1975; Talmy Franklin, 1975 [Cape Cod]

CLARK, PHILIP
 The Dark River. Simon, 1949; Wingate, 1950 [S.C.]
 Flight into Darkness. Simon, 1948 [W. Va.]

CLARK, ROBERT and GEORG ARMIN SHAFTEL
 Tune in Tonight. French (NYC), 1947 (3-act play.)

CLARK, ROSY LEE WINIFRED CECELIA. 1909-   . Pseudonym: Scott Finley, q.v.

CLARK, W(ESLEY) C(LARKE). 1907-   . Born in Cleveland; Ph.D. from U. of Pa.; for many years journalism professor at Syracuse University.
 Murder Goes to Bank Night. Hale, Cushman & Flint, 1940 [Pa.]

CLARK, WILLIAM (DONALDSON). 1916-   .
 Special Relationship. Heinemann, 1968; Houghton, 1969

CLARK, WILLIAM A(RTHUR). 1931-   . Ref: CA.
 The Girl on the Volkswagen Floor. Harper, 1971 (Novelized true crime.) [Ohio]

CLARKE, ANNA. 1919-   . Ref: CA, TC.
 The Darkened Room. Long, 1968
 The Deathless and the Dead. Collins, 1976. U.S. title: This Downhill Path. McKay, 1977
 The End of the Shadow. Chatto, 1972
 The Lady in Black. Collins, 1977; McKay, 1978 [Eng., 1882]
 Last Voyage. Collins, 1976
 Letter from the Dead. Collins, 1977; Doubleday, 1981
 A Mind to Murder. Chatto, 1971
 My Search for Ruth. Collins, 1975
 One of Us Must Die. Collins, 1978; Doubleday, 1980
 Plot Counter-Plot. Collins, 1974; Walker, 1975
 Poison Parsley. Collins, 1979
 The Poisoned Web. Collins, 1979
 This Downhill Path; see The Deathless and the Dead

CLARKE, COLIN
 Clash by Night. Heinemann, 1980

CLARKE, DONALD HENDERSON. 1887-1958.
 Confidential. Vanguard, 1936; Laurie, 1937
 Louis Beretti. Vanguard, 1929; Knopf (London), 1930
 Murderer's Holiday. Vanguard, 1940; Laurie, 1941 [NYC]

CLARKE, DUDLEY (WRANGEL). 1899-1974. Ref: CA.
 Golden Arrow. Hodder, 1955

CLARKE, EDWARD
 The Best Will Always Do. Standfast, 1973

CLARKE, IDA CLYDE (GALLAGHER). 1878-   .
 -Record No. 33. Appleton, 1915

CLARKE, JOHN BOYD
 Findings Is Keepings. Clode, 1927

CLARKE, JOSEPH CALVITT. 1888-   . Pseudonym: Richard Grant, q.v.

CLARKE, LAURENCE (AYSCOUGH)
 Bernard Treve's Boots. Hodder, 1920
 -The Borrowed Liner. Mills, 1916
 -The Call of the People. Hodder, 1926
 The Lady in the Blue Veil. Hodder, 1923
 The Mayfair Mystery. Hutchinson, 1927
 -Millions of Money. Hodder, 1925
 -Murray of the Scots Greys. Jarrolds, 1906
 -A Prince of India. Hodder, 1915
 -The Sport of Fate. Hodder, 1925

CLARKE, MARCUS (ANDREW HISLOP). 1846-1881.
 For the Term of His Natural Life; see His Natural Life
 Heavy Odds. Hutchinson, 1896; Lippincott, 1896
 His Natural Life. Robertson (Melbourne), 1874; Bentley, 1875; Harper, 1875. Also published as: For the Term of His Natural Life. Bentley (Melbourne), 1885; Bentley (London), 1889; Weeks, 1893. Abridged edition: Men in Chains. Penguin, 1944. 4-act play version: Bentley, 1886
 -Long Odds. Clarson (Melbourne), 1869
 Men in Chains; see His Natural Life
 -The Mystery of Major Molineux, and Human Repetends. Cameron (Melbourne), 1881 (2 stories.)
 -Sensational Tales. Cole (Sydney), 1886 ss

CLARKE, PERCY A. Pseudonym: Martin Frazer, q.v.

CLARKE, ROBERT. Pseudonym of Lauran Bosworth Paine, 1916-   . Other pseudonyms: John Armour, Reg Batchelor, Kenneth Bedford, Frank Bosworth, Mark Carrel, Richard Dana, J. F. Drexler, Troy Howard, Jared Ingersol, John Kilgore, Hunter Liggett, J. K. Lucas, John Morgan, qq.v. Ref: CC.
 The Case of the Gambler's Corpse. Hale, 1969
 Death of a Flower Child. Hale, 1970
 Murderers Are Silent. Hale, 1969 [Calif.]
 A Synonym for Murder. Hale, 1972 [L.A.]
 The Thirteenth Lover. Hale, 1970

CLARKE, T(HOMAS) E(RNEST) B(ENNETT). 1907-   . Ref: CA.
 The Man Who Seduced a Bank. Joseph, 1977
 -The Trail of the Serpent. Joseph, 1968
 Two and Two Make Five. Long, 1938
 The Wide Open Door. Joseph, 1966
 The Wrong Turning. Hale, 1971

CLARKE, T. KINGSTON
 Men v. Devils. Sands, 1901

CLARKE, WILLIAM JAMES. 1872-   . Pseudonym: G. F. Monkshood, q.v.

CLARKSON, L. Pseudonym of Louise Clarkson Whitelock, 1865-1928.
 The Shadow of John Wallace. White, 1884 [L.I.]

CLASON, CLYDE B. 1903-   . Born in Denver; an advertising copywriter in Chicago and trade paper editor before becoming full-time writer. Ref: MP. SC: Theocritus Lucius Westborough, in all titles.
 Blind Drifts. Doubleday, 1937 [Colo.]
 Clue to the Labyrinth; see Murder Gone Minoan
 The Death Angel. Doubleday, 1936; Heinemann, 1937 [Wis.]
 Dragon's Cave. Doubleday, 1939; Heinemann, 1940 [Chi.]
 The Fifth Tumbler. Doubleday, 1936; Heinemann, 1937 [Chi.]
 Green Shiver. Doubleday, 1941; Heinemann, 1948 [L.A.]
 The Man from Tibet. Doubleday, 1938; Heinemann, 1938 [Chi.]
 Murder Gone Minoan. Doubleday, 1939. British title: Clue to the Labyrinth. Heinemann, 1939 [Calif.]
 Poison Jasmine. Doubleday, 1940 [Calif.]
 The Purple Parrot. Doubleday, 1937; Heinemann, 1937 [Chi.]
 The Whispering Ear. Doubleday, 1938; Heinemann, 1939 [L.A.]

CLAUDE, M.
 Memoirs of Monsieur Claude. Munro, 1892 ss

CLAUDIA, SUSAN. Pseudonym of William Johnston, 1924-   , q.v.
 Clock and Bell. Doubleday, 1974 [Eng.]
 Madness at the Castle. Signet, 1966 [Calif.]
 Master of Foxhallow. Beagle, 1973 [Va.]
 Mrs. Barthelme's Madness. Putnam, 1976
 The Other Brother. Beagle, 1974
 The Searching Spectre. Signet, 1967
 The Silent Voice. Signet, 1967

CLAUSEN, CARL. 1885-   .
 The Gloyne Murder. Dodd, 1930 [NYC]
 Jaws of Circumstance. Dodd, 1931; Lane, 1931 [New Eng.]

CLAUSSE, SUZANNE
 Bride's Ransom. Mystique, 1980 (Translation of "Ombre Cherie." Paris, 1965.)
 Death's Dark Deceit. Mystique, 1980 (Translation of "Le Val d'Esperance." Paris, 1957.)
 Edge of Violence. Mystique, 1980 (Translation of "Un Sour sur la Grave." Paris, 1970.)
 Fly South to Danger. Mystique, 1980 (Translation of "Deux Noms sur la Sable." Paris, 1968.)
 The Haunting Image. Mystique, 1978 (Translation of "L'Obsedante Image." Paris, 1970.)
 Motive for Revenge. Mystique, 1980 (Translation of "L'Inoubliable Nuit." Paris, 1970.)
 Requiem for a Murder. Mystique, 1980 (Translation of "Telle Etait Deborah." Paris, 1977.)

CLAWSON, PETER. See: J(ohn) T(homas) Edson.

CLAY, BERTHA M. Pseudonym of Charlotte M(onica) Braeme, 1836-1884, q.v., and others.
 -Crime or Folly? Wright, 1939
 A Fair Mystery. Munro, 1885
 Her Hidden Past. Modern, 1935
 The Moat House Mystery. Wright, 1938
 -The Mysterious Mrs. Nutford. Modern, 1935
 -The Shadow of Tarleton Manor. Wright, 1943

CLAY, PATRICK
 Sgt. Hawk. Leisure, 1979

CLAY, ROBERT (KEATING)
 By Night. Blackwood, 1927; Lippincott, 1927

CLAYDON, STELLA
 Lesson in Murder. Long, 1960

CLAYFORD, JAMES
 Sideshow Girl. Crow (Toronto), 1950

CLAYMORE, TOD. Pseudonym of Hugh Clevely, q.v. See also: Edgar (Alfred) Jepson, 1863-1938. SC: Tod Claymore, in at least those marked TC.
 Appointment in New Orleans. Cassell, 1950 TC [New Or.]
 Dead Men Don't Answer. Cassell, 1954 TC [New Or.]
 Nest of Vipers. Cassell, 1948 TC
 Rendezvous on an Island. Cassell, 1957 TC
 Reunion in Florida. Cassell, 1952 TC [Fla.]
 -Speedwell. Cassell, 1946
 This Is What Happened; see You Remember the Case
 You Remember the Case. Nelson, 1939. U.S. title: This Is What Happened. Simon, 1939 TC
 What Else Could I Do? Cassell, 1948

CLAYTON, RICHARD HENRY MICHAEL. 1907-   . Pseudonym: William Haggard, q.v.

CLAYTON, STANLEY. See: Olive Chase.

CLEARY, C. P.
　Death in the Life Department. Metropolitan, 1947
　Flower-Bed Murder. Morris, 1945
　The Widow Wore White. Morris, 1946

CLEARY, DENIS J. and FRANK J. MAHER
　The Capricorn Run. New English Library, 1978; Playboy, 1979. Also published as: The Hook. Severn, 1980 [S. Afr.]
　The Hook; see The Capricorn Run
　Sahara Strike. New English Library pb, 1980 [Afr.]
　Wipe-Out! New English Library pb, 1980

CLEARY, JON (STEPHEN). 1917-　. Ref: CA, TC. SC: Scobie Malone = SM.
　The Climate of Courage. Collins, 1954. U.S. title: Naked in the Night. Popular Library, 1955
　Dust in the Sun; see Justin Bayard
　The Fall of an Eagle. Collins, 1965; Morrow, 1964
　A Flight of Chariots. Collins, 1964; Morrow, 1963
　Forests of the Night. Collins, 1963; Morrow, 1963
　Helga's Web. Collins, 1970; Morrow, 1970　SM [Syd.]
　The High Commissioner. Collins, 1966; Morrow, 1966　SM
　-High Road to China. Collins, 1970; Morrow, 1977 [China, 1920s]
　Just Let Me Be. Laurie, 1950 [Australia]
　Justin Bayard. Collins, 1955; Morrow, 1956. Also published as: Dust in the Sun. Four Square, 1960; Popular Library, 1957 [Australia]
　The Liberators; see Mask of the Andes
　The Long Pursuit. Collins, 1967; Morrow, 1967 [Sum.]
　The Long Shadow. Laurie, 1949
　-Man's Estate. Collins, 1972. U.S. title: The Ninth Marquess. Morrow, 1972
　Mask of the Andes. Collins, 1971. U.S. title: The Liberators. Morrow, 1971 [Bolivia]
　Naked in the Night; see The Climate of Courage
　The Ninth Marquess; see Man's Estate
　North from Thursday. Collins, 1960; Morrow, 1961
　Peter's Pence. Collins, 1974; Morrow, 1974 [It.]
　The Pulse of Danger. Collins, 1966; Morrow, 1966 [Tib.]
　Ransom. Collins, 1973; Morrow, 1973　SM
　The Safe House. Collins, 1975; Morrow, 1975
　Season of Doubt. Collins, 1968; Morrow, 1968 [Leb.]
　A Sound of Lightning. Collins, 1976; Morrow, 1976 [Mont.]
　These Small Glories. Angus, 1946
　Vortex. Collins, 1977; Morrow, 1978 [Mo.]
　You Can't See Around Corners. Angus, 1948; Scribner, 1947

CLEATON, IRENE
　The Outsider. Little, 1944 [Scot.]

CLEAVER, ANASTASIA
　Summerstorm. Ace, 1979 [Eng.]

CLEAVER, H(YLTON) R(EGINALD). 1891-1961. Ref: CA.
　Danger at Ringside. Hutchinson, 1952

CLEEVE, BRIAN (BRENDON TALBOT). 1921-　. Ref: CA, CC, TC. SC: Sean Ryan = SR.
　Assignment to Vengeance. Hammond, 1961 [Switz.]
　Birth of a Dark Soul. Jarrolds, 1953. U.S. title: The Night Winds. Houghton, 1954
　Counterspy; see Vote X for Treason
　Dark Blood, Dark Terror. Hammond, 1966; Random, 1965　SR
　Death of a Painted Lady. Hammond, 1962; Random, 1963 [Ire.]
　Death of a Wicked Servant. Hammond, 1963; Random, 1964 [Ire.]
　Escape from Prague; see Exit from Prague
　Exit from Prague. Corgi, 1970. U.S. title: Escape from Prague. Pinnacle, 1973 [Prague]
　The Judas Goat. Hammond, 1966. U.S. title: Vice Isn't Private. Random, 1966　SR
　The Night Winds; see Birth of a Dark Soul
　Tread Softly in This Place. Cassell, 1972; Day, 1972
　Vice Isn't Private; see The Judas Goat

Violent Death of a Bitter Englishman. Corgi, 1969; Random, 1967　SR
　Vote X for Treason. Collins, 1964; Random, 1965. Also published as: Counterspy. Lancer, 1966　SR [Ire.]
　You Must Never Go Back. Random, 1968 [It.]

CLEEVE, LUCAS. Pseudonym of Adelina Georgina Isabella Wolff Kingscote, -1908.
　Counsels of the Night. Unwin, 1906
　The World's Blackmail. White, 1900

CLEFT-ADDAMS, J(ULIA)
　The Secret Deed; see A Woman Always Knows
　The Wasp. Wright, 1932
　A Woman Always Knows. Hurst, 1925. U.S. title (?): The Secret Deed. McBride, 1926

CLEGG, THOMAS BAILEY. 1857-　.
　The Bishop's Scapegoat. Lane (London & NYC), 1908
　-Joan of the Hills. Lane (London & NYC), 1909
　-The Love Child. Lane, 1906
　-The Wilderness. Lane, 1907

CLEIFE, (KENNETH) PHILIP (HUBERT). 1906-　. SC: Martyn Finch, in at least those marked MF.
　The Pinchbeck Masterpiece. Macmillan (London), 1970. U.S. title: Tour de Force. Harper, 1971　MF [Sp.]
　The Slick and the Dead. Macmillan (London), 1972　MF
　Tour de Force; see The Pinchbeck Masterpiece
　The Zuss Imperative. Harwood-Smart, 1976

CLEM, EMERSON S.　A career-long educator in Minnesota.
　Which—Innocent or Guilty? Comet, 1955　ss

CLEMENS, BRIAN (HORACE). 1931-　. See also: Ted Hart.
　-The Edge of Darkness. French (London), 1978 (Play.)
　Shock! French (London), 1979 (Play.)

CLEMENS, NANCY. Pseudonym. See: Vance Randoll, 1892-　.

CLEMENS, SAMUEL LANGHORNE. 1835-1910. Pseudonym: Mark Twain, q.v.

CLEMENS, WILL(IAM) M(ONTGOMERY). 1860-1931.
　The Gilded Lady. Dillingham, 1903; Unwin, 1903

CLEMENT, DICK and IAN LA FRENAIS
　Going Straight. BBC, 1978 (Novelization of the TV series.)

CLEMENT, ERNEST C.　Pseudonym: Candace Connell, q.v.

CLEMENT, FRANK A.　SC: Supt. Mersey, in all titles. Set: Eng.
　No End of a Rogue. Longmans, 1936
　Picture Him Dead. Longmans, 1935
　Scandal at the Home Office. Longmans, 1937

CLEMENT, HAL. Pseudonym of Harry Clement Stubbs, 1922-　.
　From Outer Space; see Needle
　Iceworld. Gnome, 1953
　Needle. Doubleday, 1950; Gollancz, 1951. Also published as: From Outer Space. Avon, 1957

CLEMENT, HENRY.　SC: Slaughter = S (see also: Abel Kane).
　Any Old Port in a Storm. Popular Library, 1975 (Novelization of the "Columbo" TV series.) [Calif.]
　By Dawn's Early Light. Popular Library, 1975 (Novelization of the "Columbo" TV series.) [Calif.]
　Darling Lili. Signet, 1970 (Novelization of the movie.)
　Dillinger. Curtis, 1973 (Novelization of the movie.)
　-The Hearse. Pinnacle, 1980 (Novelization of the movie.)
　A Quiet Place in the Country. Signet, 1969 (Novelization of the movie.)
　Slaughter. Curtis, 1972 (Novelization of the movie.)　S

CLEMENTS, ABIGAIL
　Christabel's Room. GM, 1975 [Scot.]
　Highland Fire. GM, 1976 [Scot.]
　Mistress of the Moor. GM, 1974 [Scot., 1909]

CLEMENTS, CALVIN
　-Barge Girl. GM, 1953
　-Dark Night of Love. Popular Library, 1956
　Hell Ship to Kuma. GM, 1954 [ship]
　Satan Takes the Helm. GM, 1952 [ship]

CLEMENTS, COLIN (CAMPBELL). 1894-1948.
　See: Florence Ryerson, 1894-　.

CLEMENTS, E(ILEEN) H(ELEN). 1905-　.
　Ref: CA, CC, MP. SC: Alister Woodhead, in at least those marked AW.
　Back in Daylight. Hodder, 1957　AW
　Berry Green. Hodder, 1945　AW
　Chair-Lift. Hodder, 1955　AW
　Cherry Harvest. Hodder, 1943; Messner, 1944　AW
　Discord in the Air. Hodder, 1955　AW
　High Tension. Hodder, 1959　AW [Scot.]
　Honey for the Marshal. Hodder, 1960　AW
　Let Him Die. Hodder, 1939; Dutton, 1940　AW
　Let or Hindrance. Hale, 1963　AW
　Make Fame a Monster. Hodder, 1940
　A Note of Enchantment. Hodder, 1961　AW
　The Other Island. Hodder, 1956　AW [Wales]
　Over and Done For. Hodder, 1952
　Parcel of Fortune. Hodder, 1954
　Perhaps a Little Danger. Hodder, 1942; Dutton, 1942 [Scot.]
　Sea Change. Hodder, 1951
　Uncommon Cold. Hodder, 1958　AW
　Weathercock. Hodder, 1949　AW

CLEMOW, VALENTINE
　Chinese Chanty. Hurst, 1938

CLERC, MICHEL
　Deadly Payoff. Signet, 1979 (Translation of "Bakchich." Paris, 1976.)

CLERI, MARIO. Pseudonym of Mario Puzo, 1920-　, q.v.
　Six Graves to Munich. Banner, 1967 [Ger.]

CLERK, ERNIE
　Do You Like Tahiti? International, 1969

CLERY, WILLIAM EDWARD. Pseudonym: Austin Fryers, q.v. See also: Alfred Wilson Barrett, 1871-　.

CLEVELAND, CYNTHIA E(LOISE). 1845-　.
　-His Honor; or, Fate's Mysteries. American News, 1889

CLEVELAND, JOHN. Pseudonym of John Deane Hilton, 1855-　.
　Hustler Paul. Sidgwick, 1914

CLEVELAND, JOHN. Pseudonym of (Elizabeth) Adeline McElfresh, 1918-　, q.v. Other pseudonym: Jennifer Blair, q.v.
　Minus One Corpse. Arcadia, 1954

CLEVELY, HUGH. Pseudonym: Tod Claymore, q.v. See also: Edgar (Alfred) Jepson, 1863-1938. Ref: CC. SC: Maxwell Archer, in at least those marked MA; Sexton Blake (with many other authors) = SB; John Martinson = JM; Insp. Williams = W.
　Amateur Crook. Hutchinson, 1936　W
　Archer Plus Twenty. Cassell, 1938　MA
　Blood and Thunder. Cassell, 1951　MA
　Call the Yard! see Hell to Pay!
　Calling Whitehall 1212. Amalgamated, 1952　SB
　The Case of the Criminal's Daughter. Amalgamated, 1954　SB
　The Case of the Legion Deserter. Amalgamated, 1955　SB
　The Case of the Smuggled Currency. Amalgamated, 1953　SB
　The Case of the Three Survivors. Amalgamated, 1954　SB
　The Crime at 3 A.M. Amalgamated, 1954　SB
　Dark Eyes and Danger. Hutchinson, 1934
　Death's Counterfeit. Hutchinson, 1937　W
　Frazer Butts In. Hutchinson, 1929; Clode, 1931　W
　Further Outlook Unsettled. Hutchinson, 1932　W
　Gang Law. Hutchinson, 1931
　The Gang Smasher. Hutchinson, 1928; Clode, 1930　JM
　The Gang Smasher Again. Cassell, 1938　JM
　The Girl from Toronto. Amalgamated, 1953　SB
　The Heir of Tower House. Amalgamated, 1954　SB
　Hell to Pay! Hutchinson, 1930. U.S. title: Call the Yard! Doubleday, 1930　W
　The House of Evil. Amalgamated, 1955　SB
　More Trouble for Archer. Cassell, 1949　MA

Mr. Munt Carries On. Hutchinson, 1934
The Nightclub Mystery. Amalgamated, 1953 SB
No Peace for Archer. Cassell, 1947 MA
Not Nice People. Cassell, 1950 MA
Public Enemy. Cassell, 1953
Somebody Killed Kelvin. Cassell, 1953
The Strange Affair of the Widow's Diamonds. Amalgamated, 1955 SB
Three Wooden Overcoats. Cassell, 1939 MA
Turning Point; see The Wolf That Follows
The Wind Was Cold. Cassell, 1955; Morrow, 1956
The Wolf That Follows. Cassell, 1955. U.S. title: Turning Point. Morrow, 1955
The Wrong Murderer. Hutchinson, 1935
Zero the 14th. Cassell, 1937 MA

CLEWES, HOWARD (CHARLES VIVIAN). 1916- .
An Epitaph for Love. Macmillan (London), 1952; Doubleday, 1953
The Libertines; see Man on the Horse
The Long Memory. Macmillan (London), 1951; Doubleday, 1952
-Man on a Horse. Cape, 1964. U.S. title: The Libertines. Doubleday, 1964

CLIFFORD, CHARLES. Pseudonym: Robert Ames, q.v.

CLIFFORD, CHARLES L.
Sword of Allah; see While the Bells Rang
-Too Many Boats. Little, 1934; Heinemann, 1935
While the Bells Rang. Doubleday, 1941. British title: Sword of Allah. Heinemann, 1941 [Tex.]

CLIFFORD, FRANCIS. Pseudonym of Arthur Leonard Bell Thompson, 1917-1975. Ref: CA, TC.
Act of Mercy. H. Hamilton, 1959; Coward, 1960. Also published as: Guns of Darkness. Dell, 1962 [S. Afr.]
All Men Are Lonely Now. Hodder, 1967; Coward, 1967
Amigo, Amigo. Hodder, 1973; Coward, 1973 [Guat.]
Another Way of Dying. Hodder, 1968; Coward, 1969 [Sic.]
The Blind Side. Hodder, 1971; Coward, 1971
Drummer in the Dark. Hodder, 1976; Harcourt, 1976
Good-Bye and Amen; see The Grosvenor Square Goodbye
The Green Fields of Eden. Hodder, 1963; Coward, 1963 [Sp.]
The Grosvenor Square Goodbye. Hodder, 1974. U.S. title: Good-Bye and Amen. Harcourt, 1974
Guns of Darkness; see Act of Mercy
The Hunting-Ground. Hodder, 1964; Coward, 1964 [Carib.]
The Naked Spur. Hodder, 1966; Coward, 1966 [Leip.]
Overdue. H. Hamilton, 1957; Dutton, 1958 [Ariz.]
Spanish Duet. Coward, 1966 (Contains U.S. editions of Time Is an Ambush, and The Trembling Earth, qq.v.)
Ten Minutes on a June Morning. Hodder, 1977 ss, some criminous
The Third Side of the Coin. Hodder, 1965; Coward, 1965 [Sp.]
Time Is an Ambush. Hodder, 1962. U.S. edition in Spanish Duet, q.v. [Sp.]
-The Trembling Earth. H. Hamilton, 1955. U.S. edition in Spanish Duet, q.v. [Sp.]
A Wild Justice. Hodder, 1972; Coward, 1972 [Ire.]

CLIFFORD, GUY. Pseudonym of Arthur Guy Roberts, 1903- .
Michael Intervenes. Methuen, 1927

CLIFFORD, READ
Guard the Girl. Mills, 1939
Hunt the Evidence. Mills, 1938

CLIFT, DENNISON (HALLEY). 1885-1961.
The Spy in the Room. Mystery House, 1944 [Eng.]

CLIFTON, BUD. Pseudonym of David Derek Stacton, 1925-1968. Other pseudonym: David West, q.v.
-The Bad Girls. Pyramid, 1958
-D for Delinquent. Ace, 1958
Let Him Go Hang. Ace, 1961 [Ariz.]
The Murder Specialist. Ace, 1959 [Calif.]
-Muscle Boy. Ace, 1958
The Power Gods. Pyramid, 1959; Eyre, 1958

CLINE, C. TERRY (JR.). 1935- . Born in Birmingham, Ala.
Cross Currents. Doubleday, 1979; New English Library, 1980
Death Knell. Putnam, 1977; Collins, 1978

CLINE, LEONARD (LANSON). 1893-1929.
-The Dark Chamber. Viking, 1927

CLINTON, MAX
The Dead Were Strangers. Comyns, 1952
Don't Make Me Kill. Comyns, 1953
No Dame Wants to Die. Comyns, 1952
No Place for a Dame. Comyns, 1953
Red, Hot and Deadly. Comyns, 1953
So Long, Sucker. Comyns, 1953
Strictly Illegal. Comyns, 1952

CLINTON, DANIEL JOSEPH. 1900- . Pseudonym: Thomas Rourke, q.v.

CLINTON, DOROTHY RANDLE
The Maddening Scar. Christopher, 1962

CLINTON-BADDELEY, V(ICTOR VAUGHAN REYNOLDS GERAINT) C(LINTON). 1900-1970. Ref: CA, CC, TC. SC: Dr. Davie, in all titles, set in Eng.
Death's Bright Dart. Gollancz, 1967; Morrow, 1970 [acad.]
My Foe Outstretch'd Beneath the Tree. Gollancz, 1968; Morrow, 1968
No Case for the Police. Gollancz, 1970; Morrow, 1970
Only a Matter of Time. Gollancz, 1969; Morrow, 1970
To Study a Long Silence. Gollancz, 1972

CLIVE, MRS. ARCHER (CAROLINE WIGLEY CLIVE]. 1801-1873. See: Anonymous.

CLIVE, JOHN. 1933- . See also: J. D. Gilman. Ref: CA.
The Last Liberator. Hamlyn, 1980; Delacorte, 1980 [Holl., 1963]

CLOSE, ROBIN
The Boheme Combination. Joseph, 1973; Walker, 1974 [Rome]

CLOUSTON, J(OSEPH) STORER. 1870-1944. Ref: CC. SC: Ursula Dolling = UD; Francis Mandell-Essington = FM; F. T. Carrington = FC. Set: Eng.
-The Adventures of M. D'Haricot. Blackwood, 1902; Harper, 1902
After the Deed. Blackwood, 1929
Beastmark the Spy. Blackwood, 1941 FC
The Best Story Ever. Blackwood, 1932 FM
Carrington's Cases. Blackwood, 1920 ss FC
Colonel Dam. Blackwood, 1930 UD
Count Bunker. Blackwood, 1906; Brentano's, 1907 FM
-A Country Family. Murray, 1908
-The Duke. Arnold, 1900; Longmans, 1900
-Garmiscath. Blackwood, 1904
His First Offense. Mills, 1912. U.S. title: The Mystery of No. 47. Moffat, 1911
-The Jade's Progress. Lane, 1928
The Lunatic at Large. Blackwood, 1899; Appleton, 1900 FM
The Lunatic at Large Again. Nash, 1922; Dutton, 1923 FM
The Lunatic in Charge. Bodley, 1926; Dutton, 1926 FM
The Lunatic in Love; see Mr. Essington in Love
The Lunatic Still at Large. Nash, 1923; Dutton, 1924 FM
The Man from the Clouds. Blackwood, 1918; Doran, 1919
Mr. Essington in Love. Lane, 1927. U.S. title: The Lunatic in Love. Dutton, 1927 FM
The Mystery of No. 47; see His First Offense
Our Lady's Inn. Blackwood, 1903; Harper, 1903
-Our Member Mr. Muttlebury. Jenkins, 1935
Scotland Expects. Jenkins, 1936
-Scots Wha Ha'e. Jenkins, 1936
Simon. Blackwood, 1919; Doran, 1919 FC
The Spy in Black. Blackwood, 1917; Doran, 1918
The Two Strange Men. Nash, 1924
-The Virtuous Vamp. Blackwood, 1931 UD

CLOUTIER, HELEN (H.). 1909- .
Murder, Absolutely Murder. Chicago Paperback, 1962 [Mich.]

CLUGSTON, KATE [KATHERINE THATCHER CLUGSTON]. 1892- . Born in Indiana; degrees from Wells College and Radcliffe; author of plays, articles and radio sketches.

A Murderer in the House. Wyn, 1947. Also published as: Twist the Knife Slowly. Ace, 1952 [Mass.]

CLUNE, FRANK [FRANCIS PATRICK CLUNE]. 1893-1971. Ref: CA.
The Blue Mountains Murderer. Horwitz, 1959

CLUNE, M. A.
"Call in the Yard." Mitre, 1946
Masked Alibi. Rolls, 1945
Strange Heritage. Rolls, 1945

CLUTTON-BROCK, ALAN (FRANCIS). Ref: CC.
Murder at Liberty Hall. Lane, 1941; Macmillan, 1941 [acad.]

CLYDE, LEONARD WORSWICK. 1906- . Pseudonym: Peter Baron, q.v.

COATES, JOHN. 1912- . Born in England, educated at Cambridge; author also of a play.
Time for Tea. Methuen, 1948; Macmillan, 1950

COATES, ROBERT M(YRON). 1897-1973. Ref: CA.
The Hour After Midnight. Harcourt, 1947 ss, some criminous
The Night Before Dying; see Wisteria Cottage
Wisteria Cottage. Harcourt, 1948; Gollancz, 1949. Also published as: The Night Before Dying. Lion, 1955

COBB, (GEOFFREY) BELTON. 1892-1971. Ref: CA, CC, TC. SC: Insp. Cheviot Burmann, in at least those marked CB; Supt. Manning, in at least those marked M; Bryan Armitage, in at least those marked BA. Set: Eng.
Catch Me—If You Can. Allen, 1970 CB
Corpse at Casablanca. Allen, 1956; Abelard, 1956 CB [ship]
Corpse in the Cargo. Allen, 1961 CB
Corpse Incognito. Methuen, 1953 CB
Dead Girl's Shoes. Allen, 1964 CB
Death Defies the Doctor. Longmans, 1939 CB
Death in the 13th Dose. Longmans, 1946 CB
Death of a Peeping Tom. Allen, 1963 CB
Death with a Difference. Allen, 1960 CB
Detective in Distress. Methuen, 1953 CB
Don't Lie to the Police. Allen, 1960 CB
Double Detection. Longmans, 1945 CB
Doubly Dead. Allen, 1957 CB
Drink Alone and Die. Allen, 1956 CB
Early Morning Poison. Longmans, 1947 M
Fatal Dose. Longmans, 1937 CB
The Fatal Holiday. Longmans, 1938 CB
Food for Felony. Allen, 1969 BA
The Framing of Carol Woan. Longmans, 1948 M
Home Guard Mystery. Longmans, 1942
The Horrible Man in Heron's Wood. Allen, 1970 CB
I Fell Among Thieves. Allen, 1971
I Never Miss Twice. Allen, 1965 CB,BA
Inspector Burmann's Black-Out. Longmans, 1941 CB
Inspector Burmann's Busiest Day. Longmans, 1939 CB
Last Drop. Allen, 1965 CB
Like a Guilty Thing. Longmans, 1938; British Book Centre, 1959 CB
Lost Without Trace. Allen, 1967 CB
The Lunatic, the Lover. Methuen, 1950
The Missing Scapegoat. Allen, 1958 CB
Murder: Men Only. Allen, 1962 CB
Need a Body Tell? Allen, 1954 CB
Next Door to Death. Methuen, 1952 CB
No Alibi. Longmans, 1936 CB
No Charge for the Poison. Methuen, 1950 M
No Last Words. Longmans, 1949 M
No Mercy for Margaret. Methuen, 1952 CB
No Shame for the Devil. Allen, 1964 CB
Poisoner's Base. Allen, 1957; British Book Centre, 1958 CB
The Poisoner's Mistake. Longmans, 1936 CB
Quickly Dead. Longmans, 1937 CB
Scandal at Scotland Yard. Allen, 1969 BA
Search for Sergeant Baxter. Allen, 1961 CB
Secret Inquiry. Allen, 1968 BA,CB
The Secret of Superintendent Manning. Longmans, 1948 M
Security Secrets Sold Here. Allen, 1967 CB
Sergeant Ross in Disguise. Longmans, 1940
Silence Under Threat. Allen, 1968 CB
Some Must Watch. Allen, 1966 CB
Stolen Strychnine. Longmans, 1949 M
A Stone for His Head. Allen, 1966 CB
Suspicion in Triplicate. Allen, 1971 CB

The Willing Witness. Allen, 1955 CB
With Intent to Kill. Allen, 1958; British Book Centre, 1958 CB

COBB, CLAYTON W. Pseudonym of J. A. Patten.
The Mountaineer Detective. Street, 1889

COBB, ELIZABETH [MRS. ELIZABETH COBB CHAPMAN] and MARGARET CASE MORGAN
Murder in Your Home. Long & Smith, 1932 (20 short plays with a quiz after each.)

COBB, IRVIN S(HREWSBURY). 1876-1944. Ref: EM, MP. SC: Judge Priest, at least partially included in titles marked JP.
-Alias Ben Alibi. Doran, 1925
-Back Home. Doran, 1912 ss JP
-Down Yonder with Judge Priest. Long & Smith, 1932 ss JP
 The Escape of Mr. Trimm. Doran, 1913; Hodder, 1914 ss JP
 Faith, Hope and Charity. Bobbs, 1934 ss JP
 Judge Priest Turns Detective. Bobbs, 1937 JP [Ky.]
 Murder Day by Day. Bobbs, 1933; Cassell, 1934 [L.I.]
-Old Judge Priest. Doran, 1916 ss JP
-Snake Doctor and other stories. Doran, 1923 ss JP

COBB, IVO GEIKIE. 1887-   . Pseudonym: Anthony Weymouth, q.v.

COBB, MICHAEL. Pseudonym of Alfred Daniel Wintle.
-Coldharbour. Selwyn, 1939
-The Emancipation of Ambrose. Hurst, 1928
 Sholto Budd. Hurst, 1932
 Sir Peter's Arm. Chapman, 1929

COBB, SYLVANUS, JR. 1823-1887.
-The Armorer of Tyre. Lupton, 1893
-The Bandit of Syracuse. Bonner, 1891
-The Conspirator of Cordova. Bonner, 1896
-The Council of Ten. Street, 1900
-A Dark Plot. Ogilvie, 1891
-The Double Duel. Ogilvie, 1892
-The Earl's Ward. Gleason, 1852
-The Fortunes of Conrad. Bonner, 1866
-The Iron Cross; or, The Countess of Errol. Peterson, 1850
-Ivan the Serf. French, 1853
-The Juggler of Nankin; or, The Grandee's Plot. French, 185?
-Karl, the Lion. Street, 1891
-The King's Talisman; or, The Young Lion of Mt. Hor. Gleason, 1851
-The Lost Heir. Gleason, 1953
-Marco; or, The Female Smuggler. Gleason, 1857
-Orion, the Gold Beater. Cassell (NYC), 1888
-The Painter of Parma; or, The Magic of a Masterpiece. Cassell (NYC), 1889
-The Queen's Revenge. Lupton, 1892
-Red Hand. Laird, 1893
-The Robber Countess. Bonner, 1891
-Roderick of Kildare. Bonner, 1891
-Rollo of Normandy. Bonner, 1891
-The Royal Outlaw. Bonner, 1891
-The Scourge of Damascus. Bonner, 1891
-The Secrets of the Coast. Donohue, ca. 1897
-The Smuggler of King's Cove; or, The Old Chapel Mystery. Cassell (NYC), 1889
-The Spectre's Secret. Bonner, 1892

COBB, THOMAS. 1853-1932. SC: Insp. Bedison, in at least those marked B.
-The Amateur Emigrants. Rivers, 1907
 Andrew and His Wife. Mills, 1914
-The Anger of Olivia. Mills, 1910
-The Bishop's Gambit. Richards, 1901
-Brownie's Plot. Ward, 1889
-The Busy Whisper. Chapman, 1915
-Captain Marraday's Marriage. Lane (NYC & London), 1918
-Carpet Courtship. Lane, 1898
-A Change of Pace. Methuen, 1904
 The Chichester Intrigue. Lane (NYC & London), 1908
-The Choice of Theodora. Mills, 1911
-Collusion. Rivers, 1906
-The Composite Lady. Chapman, 1903
 Crime at Keeper's. Benn, 1930
 The Crime Without a Clue. Benn, 1929 B
 Death on the Cliff. Benn, 1932
-The Deception of Ursula. Paul, 1923
 The Disappearance of Mr. Derwent. Ward, 1894; Neely, 1896
-The Dissemblers. Lane, 1901
-Enter Bridget. Mills, 1910
-False Pretences. Nash, 1926
-For Value Received. Ward, 1890

-The Friendship of Veronica. Rivers, 1905
-The Future Mrs. Dering. Laurie, 1908
 Getting Rid of Anne. Nash, 1921
-A Giver in Secret. Laurie, 1911
-The Head of the Household. Chapman, 1902
-The Hillerway Letters. Chapman, 1917
 The House by the Common. Ward, 1891
-The Impossible Apollo. Lane (NYC & London), 1920
 Inspector Bedison and the Sunderland Case. Benn, 1931 B
 Inspector Bedison Risks It. Benn, 1931 B
-The Intriguers. Nash, 1903
-Joanna Sets to Work. Paul, 1925
-The Judgement of Helen. Lane (NYC & London), 1899
-Lady Gwendoline. Richards, 1902
-Lady Sylvia's Imposter. Mills, 1914
 The Late Mr. Beverly. Paul, 1924
-A Man of Sentiment. Richards, 1902
-Margaret Rutland. Mills, 1910
-A Marriage of Inconvenience. Mills, 1913
-Masterman's Mistake. Wells Gardner, 1913
 The Metal Box. Benn, 1933
-Miss Merewether's Money. Ward, 1892
-Mr. Burnside's Responsibility. Mills, 1909
-Mr. Passingham. Lane, 1899
-Mr. Preston's Daughter. Lane (NYC & London), 1920
-Mrs. Belfort's Strategem. Nash, 1904
-Mrs. Erricker's Reputation. Rivers, 1906. Also published as: Mrs. Pomeroy's Reputation. Lane, 1918
-Mrs. Latham's Extravagance. Chapman, 1915
 Mrs. Pomeroy's Reputation; see Mrs. Erricker's Reputation
-Mrs. Whiston's Party. Everett, 1909
-On Trust. Hurst, 1891
-One Who Passed By. Paul, 1924
-An Open Secret. Rand, 1898 (British title?)
-Pat. Chapman, 1916
-Peggy's Dilemma. Nash, 1923
-Phillida. Mills, 1911
-Priscilla to the Rescue. Nash, 1922
 The Sark Street Chapel Murder. Benn, 1930
-Scruples. Richards, 1900; Lane (NYC), 1900
-Second in the Field. Chapman, 1916
-A Sentimental Season. Laurie, 1907
-Severence. Lane (NYC & London) 1901
 The Silver Bag. Lane (NYC & London), 1919
-Sophy Bunce. Nash, 1905
-The Transformation of Timothy. Mills, 1913
-The Voice of Bethia. Mills, 1912
 Wedderburn's Will. Ward, 1892
-The Westlakes. Farran, 1892
-While Guy Was in France. Paul, 1918
 Who Closed the Casement? Benn, 1932 B
 Who Opened the Door? Benn, 1928

COBB, WELDON J. Pseudonym: Nicholas Carter, q.v.

COBBAN, J(AMES) MacLAREN. 1849-1903. SC: Mr. Townshend, in at least those marked T.
-The Angel of the Covenant. Methuen, 1898; Fenno, 1899
 The Avenger of Blood. Cassell, 1895
-The Burden of Israel. Chatto, 1893; Harper, 1893
-By Telegraph. SPCK, 1888
-The Cure of Souls. Chatto, 1879
 The Golden Tooth. Digby, 1901; Buckles, 1901 T
-The Green Turbans. Long, 1902; Burt, 1902
-Her Royal Highness's Love Affair. Pearson, 1897
 The Horned Cat; see Sir Ralph's Secret; or, The Horned Cat
-I'd Crowns Resign. Long, 1900
-The Iron Hand. Long, 1904
-The Last Alive. Richards, 1902
 Missing Partner; or, Tinty Vapours; see Tinted Vapours; or, A Nemesis
 A Nemesis; or, Tinted Vapours; see Tinted Vapours; or, A Nemesis
 Pursued by the Law. Long, 1899; Appleton, 1899 T
-The Reverend Gentleman. Methuen, 1891; Lovell, 1891
-A Royal Exchange. Appleton, 1901 (British title?)
 Sir Ralph's Secret; or, The Horned Cat. Warne, 1891. U.S. title: The Horned Cat. National Book, 1891
-A Soldier and a Gentleman. Long, 1904; Street, 1901
 The Terror by Night. Long, 1905

-Tinted Vapours; or, A Nemesis. Warne, 1885. Also published as: Missing Partner; or, Tinted Vapours. Warne, 1889. U.S. title: A Nemesis; or, Tinted Vapours. Lupton, 1892
-Wilt Thou Have This Woman? Methuen, 1897; Lippincott, 1897

COBDEN, GUY. SC: John Chadwick, in all titles. Set: Eng.
 I Saw Murder. Hale, 1962
 Murder for Her Birthday. Hale, 1960
 Murder for His Money. Hale, 1959
 Murder Inherited. Hale, 1961
 Murder Was My Neighbor. Rich, 1955
 Murder Was Their Medicine. Jarrolds, 1957
 My Guess Was Murder. Rich, 1956

COBNOR, JOHN
 The Four Answers. Cape, 1931

COBURN, ANDREW. 1932-   . Ref: CA.
 The Babysitter. Norton, 1979; Secker, 1980 [Boston]
 Off Duty. Norton, 1980; Secker, 1981 [Boston]
 The Trespassers. Houghton, 1974 [Mass.]

COBURN, SAMMY
 Brunettes Are No Better. Scion, 1952
 Don't Tempt Me. Scion, 1951
 Hot Cargo. Scion, 1950
 The Lady Pays. Scion, 1951
 Uneasy Street. Scion, 1950
 You Can't Die Here. Scion, 1950

COCHRAN, ALAN. Pseudonym.
 Two Plus Two. Doubleday, 1980 [L.A.]

COCHRAN, RUTH GILBERT. 1893-   . Born in Wash. D.C.; author of numerous series books for boys and girls, of magazine stories; was fiction editor for newspaper syndicate.
 Victoria Pruitt Comes to Town. Mystery House, 1941 [NYC]

COCHRANE, ELIZABETH J. 1867-1922. Pseudonym: Nellie Bly, q.v.

COCKAIN, FRANK
 The Draftsman. Futura, 1978
 The Inside Out Man. Futura, 1975

COCKBURN, FRANCIS CLAUD. 1904-1981. Pseudonym: James Helvick, q.v.

COCKIN, JOAN. Pseudonym of Edith Joan Burbridge, 1919-   . SC: Insp. Cam, in all titles. Set: Eng.
 Curiosity Killed the Cat. Hodder, 1947
 Deadly Ernest. Hodder, 1952
 Villainy at Vespers. Hodder, 1949

COCKING, RONALD
 Die with Me, Lady. Harlequin, 1953 [Can.]
 High Tide at Midnight. Hurst, 1950
 The House in Brook Street. Hurst, 1949
 Weep No More, Lady. Hurst, 1952 [Can.]

COCKRELL, FRANK and MARIAN (BROWN) COCKRELL, 1909-   , q.v.
 Dark Waters. World, 1944 [La.]

COCKRELL, MARIAN (BROWN). 1909-   . Ref: CA. See also: Frank Cockrell.
 Something Between. Harper, 1946

COCKSHUT, NAIDRA. Pseudonym: Naidra Gray, q.v.

COCKTON, HENRY. 1807-1853.
 Sylvester Sound, the Somnambulist. Clark, 1844; Burgess, 1844

CODY, C(HARLES) S. Pseudonym of Leslie Waller, 1923-   , q.v. Other pseudonym: Patrick Mann, q.v.
 Lie Like a Lady. Ace, 1955
 The Witching Night. World, 1952; Corgi, 1953

CODY, H(IRAM) A(LFRED). 1872-1948.
 The Long Patrol. Doran, 1912; Hodder, 1912 [Can.]
 Under Sealed Orders. Doran, 1917

CODY, JAMES P. Pseudonym of Peter Thomas Rohrbach, 1926-   . Ref: CA. SC: Brian Petersen, in all titles.
 A French Killing. Berkley, 1975
 Search and Destroy. Berkley, 1974 [Wash. D.C.]
 Top Secret Kill. Berkley, 1974 [Wash. D.C.]
 Your Daughter Will Die! Berkley, 1975

CODY, LIZA
  Dupe. Collins, 1980; Scribner, 1981

CODY, (EDWARD) MORRILL. 1901- .
  Passing Stranger. Macaulay, 1936

COE, CAPTAIN. Joint pseudonym of Edward Card Mitchell and Lincoln Springfield.
  The Coroner's Understudy. Arrowsmith, 1891

COE, CHARLES FRANCIS. 1890-1956. Ref: EM.
  About Two A.M. Cosmopolitan, 1931
  Ashes. Random, 1952
  G Man. Lippincott (Phil. and London), 1935
  Gunman. Gollancz, 1930 (U.S. title?)
  Hooch! Doubleday, 1929
  Knockout. Lippincott, 1936; Hutchinson, 1938
  Me—Gangster. Putnam (NYC & London), 1927
  The Other Half. Cosmopolitan, 1930
  Pressure. Random, 1951; Allen, 1952
  Ransom. Lippincott (Phil. & London), 1934
  The River Pirate. Putnam (NYC & London), 1928
  Swag. Putnam (NYC & London), 1928
  Triumph: The Undoing of Rafferty, Ward Heeler. Sears, 1929

COE, TUCKER. Pseudonym of Donald E(dwin) Westlake, 1933- , q.v. Other pseudonyms: Curt Clark, Timothy J. Culver, Richard Stark, qq.v. SC: Mitchell Tobin, in all titles.
  Don't Lie to Me. Random, 1972; Gollancz, 1974 [NYC]
  A Jade in Aries. Random, 1971; Gollancz, 1973 [NYC]
  Kinds of Love, Kinds of Death. Random, 1966; Souvenir, 1967 [NYC]
  Murder Among Children. Random, 1968; Souvenir, 1968 [NYC]
  Wax Apple. Random, 1970; Gollancz, 1973 [N.Y.]

COEN, FRANKLIN. Screenwriter.
  The Plunderers. Coward, 1980; Severn, 1981 [Paris, WWII]

COFFEY, BRIAN. Pseudonym of Dean R(ay) Koontz, 1945- , q.v. Other pseudonyms: David Axton, Deanna Dwyer, K. R. Dwyer, Leigh Nichols, Anthony North, qq.v. SC: Mike Tucker = MT.
  Blood Risk. Bobbs, 1973; Barker, 1974 MT
  The Face of Fear. Bobbs, 1977; Davies, 1978, as by K. R. Dwyer
  Surrounded. Bobbs, 1974; Barker, 1975 MT [L.A.]
  The Voice of the Night. Doubleday, 1980; Hale, 1981 [Calif.]
  The Wall of Masks. Bobbs, 1975 MT [Mex.]

COFFIN, CARLYN
  Dogwatch. Farrar, 1944 [Conn.]
  Mare's Nest. Farrar, 1941 [Md.]

COFFEY, FRANK
  -The Shaman. St. Martin's, 1980

COFFIN, GEOFFREY. Joint pseudonym of (Francis) Van Wyck Mason, 1897-1978, and Helen Brawner, 1902- . SC: Insp. Scott Stuart, in both titles.
  The Forgotten Fleet Mystery. Dodge, 1936; Jarrolds, 1943, as by Van Wyck Mason. Also published in the U.S. as by Mason: Arrow, 194?
  Murder in the Senate. Dodge, 1935; Hurst, 1936 [Wash. D.C.]

COFFIN, PETER. Pseudonym of Jonathan (Wyatt) Latimer, 1906-1983, q.v.
  The Search for My Great-Uncle's Head. Doubleday, 1937 [Mich.]

COFFMAN, VIRGINIA (EDITH). 1914- .
  Pseudonym: Victor Cross, q.v. Ref: CA. Lucifer Cove series = LC; Moura series = M.
  -The Affair at Alkali. Arcadia, 1960. British title: Nevada Gunslinger. Gresham, 1962
  The Alpine Coach. Dell, 1976; Souvenir, 1980
  The Beach House. Signet, 1970; Piatkus, 1982
  The Beckoning. Ace, 1965 [Ire.]
  Black Heather. Lancer, 1966 [Eng.]
  Call of the Flesh. Lancer, 1968
  The Candidate's Wife. Lancer, 1968
  Careen. Dell, 1977
  The Castle at Witch's Coven. Lancer, 1966
  Castle Barra. Paperback Library, 1966 [Fr.]
  Chalet Diabolique. Lancer, 1971 LC [Calif.]
  The Chinese Door. Lancer, 1967; Hale, 1971 [Haw.]
  The Cliffs of Dread. Lancer, 1972; Piatkus, 1981 [Ire.]
  The Curse of the Island Pool. Lancer, 1965 [Carib.]
  The Dark Beyond Moura; see The Dark Gondola
  The Dark Gondola. Ace, 1968. Also published as: The Dark Beyond Moura. Ace, 1977 M [Venice, 1790s]
  The Dark Palazzo. Arbor, 1973; Piatkus, 1980 [Venice, 1797]
  The Demon Tower. Signet, 1966 [It., past]
  The Devil's Mistress. Lancer, 1970 LC [Calif.]
  The Devil's Vicar. Ace, 1966. Revised edition: The Vicar of Moura. Ace, 1972 M [Eng.]
  The Devil's Virgin. Lancer, 1971 LC [Calif.]
  -Dinah Faire. Arbor, 1979; Souvenir, 1980
  Enemy of Love. Dell, 1976 [Carib.]
  The Evil at Queen's Priory. Lancer, 1973; Piatkus, 1980 [Eng.]
  A Fear of Heights. Lancer, 1973. Also published as: Legacy of Fear. Signet, 1980 [S.F.]
  A Few Fiends to Tea. Belmont, 1967 [Fr.]
  -Fire Dawn. Arbor, 1977; Piatkus, 1979 [Calif.]
  From Satan, with Love. Lancer, 1971 LC [Calif.]
  Garden of Shadows. Lancer, 1973
  -The Gaynor Women. Arbor, 1978; Souvenir, 1981 [Va., 1880s]
  A Haunted Place. Lancer, 1966; Milton House, 1975 [Fr.]
  The High Terrace. Lancer, 1966. British title: To Love a Dark Stranger. Hale, 1969 [S.F.]
  The Hounds of Hell. Belmont, 1967
  The House at Sandalwood. Arbor, 1974; Milton House, 1975 [Haw.]
  The House on the Moat. Lancer, 1972 [Eng., 1810]
  Hyde Place. Arbor, 1974 [S.F., ca. 1900]
  The Ice Forest. Dell, 1975
  Isle of the Undead. Lancer, 1969. British title: Voodoo Widow. Hale, 1970 [Carib.]
  Legacy of Fear; see A Fear of Heights
  The Looking-Glass. Dell, 1978 [Swed.]
  -Marsanne. Arbor, 1976; Souvenir, 1979 [Eng., ca.1820]
  Masque by Gaslight. Ace, 1970; Hale, 1971, as by Virginia C. DuVaul
  Masque of Satan. Lancer, 1971 LC [Calif.]
  The Master of Blue Mire. Dell, 1971; Milton House, 1975
  The Mist at Darkness. Signet, 1968 [Eng., 1821]
  Mistress Devon. Arbor, 1972 [Boston, ca.1850]
  Moura. Crown, 1959 M [Fr., 1815]
  Nevada Gunslinger; see The Affair at Alkali
  Night at Sea Abbey. Lancer, 1962; Piatkus, 1981
  Of Love and Intrigue. Signet, 1969
  One Man Too Many. Lancer, 1967
  -Pacific Cavalcade. Arbor, 1980
  Priestess of the Damned. Lancer, 1970 LC [Calif.]
  The Rest Is Silence. Lancer, 1967
  The Richest Girl in the World. Lancer, 1967
  The Secret of Shower Tree. Lancer, 1966. Also published as: Strange Secrets. Signet, 1976
  The Shadow Box. Lancer, 1967 [Fr.]
  The Small Tawny Cat. Lancer, 1967. Also published as: The Stalking Terror. Signet, 1977 [Paris]
  The Stalking Terror; see The Small Tawny Cat
  Strange Secrets; see The Secret of Shower Tree
  Survivor of Darkness. Lancer, 1973
  To Love a Dark Stranger; see The High Terrace
  The Vampyre of Moura. Ace, 1970 M [Fr., 1821]
  Veronique. Arbor, 1975; Souvenir, 1978 [Paris, 1790]
  The Vicar of Moura; see The Devil's Vicar
  The Villa Fountains. Belmont, 1968

COFYN, CORNELIUS. Joint pseudonym of Hilary (Aiden) St. George Saunders, 1898-1951, q.v., and John deVere Loder. Joint pseudonym of Saunders and John (Leslie) Palmer, 1885-1944, q.v.: Francis Beeding, q.v. Joint pseudonym of Saunders and Geoffrey Dennis: Barum Browne, q.v.
  The Death-Riders. Gollancz, 1935; Knopf, 1936

COGGIN, JOAN
  Dancing with Death. Hurst, 1949
  The Mystery of Orchard House. Hurst, 1947
  Who Killed the Curate? Hurst, 1944
  Why Did She Die? Hurst, 1947

COGGINS, PASCHAL HESTON. 1852-1917. Pseudonym: Sidney Marlow, q.v.

COGSWELL, GEORGIA
  Golden Obsession. Zebra, 1979

COHAN, GEORGE M(ICHAEL). 1879-1942.
  The Return of the Vagabond. French, 1940 (Play.)
  Seven Keys to Baldpate. French, 1914; Rees, 1914 (Play based on the novel by Earl Derr Biggers, 1884-1933, q.v.)
  The Tavern. French, 1933 (Play.)

COHANE, M. E.
  Murder One! Pinnacle, 1975 [NYC]

COHEN, ALFRED J. 1861-1928. Pseudonym: Alan Dale, q.v.

COHEN, ARTHUR A(LLEN). 1928- .
  Acts of Theft. Harcourt, 1980; Secker, 1980 [Mex.]

COHEN, BARNEY
  Coliseum. Dell, 1975 [Tex.]

COHEN, IRVING R.
  The Passover Commando. Crown, 1979 [S.F.]

COHEN, OCTAVUS ROY. 1891-1959. Ref: EM, MP, TC. SC: David Carroll = DC; Lt. Max Gold = MG; Jim Hanvey = JH; Lt. Marty Walsh = MW.
  The Backstage Mystery. Appleton, 1930. Also published as: Curtain at Eight. Grosset, 1933 JH
  A Bullet for My Love. Macmillan, 1950; Barker, 1951 MW [L.A.]
  -Cameos. Appleton, 1931 ss
  Child of Evil. Appleton, 1936
  The Corpse That Walked. GM, 1951; Red Seal, 1957
  The Crimson Alibi. Dodd, 1919; Nash, 1919 DC
  Curtain at Eight; see The Backstage Mystery
  Danger in Paradise. Macmillan, 1945; Hale, 1949 MG [NYC]
  Dangerous Lady. Macmillan, 1946; Barker, 1948
  -Detours. Little, 1927 ss, JH in one
  Don't Ever Love Me. Macmillan, 1947; Barker, 1948 MG [NYC]
  East of Broadway. Appleton, 1938
  Florian Slappey. Appleton, 1938 ss, one criminous
  Gray Dusk. Dodd, 1920; Nash, 1920 DC [S.C.]
  I Love You Again. Appleton, 1937. Also published as: There's Always Time to Die. Popular Library, 1946
  The Intruder; see Love Can Be Dangerous
  The Iron Chalice. Little, 1925; Cassell, 1926
  Jim Hanvey, Detective. Dodd, 1923; Nash, 1924 ss JH
  Lady in Armor. Appleton, 1941
  Lost Lady. GM, 1951; Fawcett (London), 1953 [L.A.]
  Love Can Be Dangerous. Macmillan, 1955; Barker, 1955. Also published as: The Intruder. Graphic, 1956 [L.A.]
  Love Has No Alibi. Macmillan, 1946; Hale, 1952 MG [NYC]
  The May Day Mystery. Appleton, 1929 JH [South, acad.]
  Midnight. Dodd, 1922; Nash, 1922 DC
  More Beautiful Than Murder. Macmillan, 1948; Barker, 1950 MW [L.A.]
  Murder in Season; see Romance in Crimson
  My Love Wears Black. Macmillan, 1948; Barker, 1949 MW [L.A.]
  The Other Woman, with J. U. Giesy. Macaulay, 1917; Gardner, 1920
  The Outer Gate. Little, 1927; Hodder, 1927
  Romance in Crimson. Appleton, 1940. Also published as: Murder in Season. Popular Library, 1946 [Va.]
  Romance in the First Degree. Macmillan, 1944; Hale, 1951
  Scrambled Yeggs. Appleton, 1934 JH ss
  Six Seconds of Darkness. Dodd, 1921; Nash, 1921 DC
  Sound of Revelry. Macmillan, 1943; Hale, 1945 [NYC]
  Star of Earth. Appleton, 1932 JH [L.A.]

Strange Honeymoon. Appleton, 1939
There's Always Time to Die; see I Love
   You Again
The Townsend Murder Mystery. Appleton,
   1933 (First radio play published in
   book form.)

COHEN, STANLEY. 1928-   . Ref: CA.
The Abduction; see Taking Gary Feldman
The Diane Game. Stein, 1973; Constable,
   1974 [S.F.]
Taking Gary Feldman. Putnam, 1970. British title: The Abduction. Constable,
   1971
330 Park. Putnam, 1977; New English Library, 1978 [NYC]

COHEN, SUSAN HANDLER. 1938-   . Pseudonym: Elizabeth St. Clair, q.v.

COHLER, DAVID KEITH. 1940-   . Ref: CA.
Gamemaker. Doubleday, 1980; Allen,
   1980. Also published as: Blood Sport.
   Star, 1981 [NYC]

COKE, PETER. 1913-   .
Midsummer Mink. French (London), 1965
   (Play.)

COLBRON, GRACE ISABEL. 1869-1948. SC:
   Joe Muller = JM (see also: Augusta
   Groner, 1850-   ).
The Club Car Mystery. Macaulay, 1928
   [Pa.]
Joe Muller, Detective, with Augusta
   Groner, 1850-   ). Duffield, 1910
   ss JM [Vienna]

COLBURN, LAURA. SC: Carol Gates, in all
   titles.
Death in a Small World. Zebra, 1979
   [NYC]
Death of a Prima Donna. Zebra, 1979
   [theatre]
Death Through the Mill. Zebra, 1979
   [Vt.]

COLBY, LYDIA
The Touch of Evil. Playboy, 1977
   [Calif.]

COLBY, ROBERT. Pseudonym: Nick Carter,
   q.v. Born in NYC; radio and TV an-
   nouncer for 15 years, then full-time
   writer.
Beautiful But Bad. Monarch, 1962
The Captain Must Die. GM, 1959; Muller
   pb, 1960 [Louisville]
The Deadly Desire. GM, 1959; Muller pb,
   1961 [L.A.]
Executive Wife. Monarch, 1964
The Faster She Runs. Monarch, 1963
In a Vanishing Room. Ace, 1961 [Calif.]
Kill Me a Fortune. Ace, 1961 [L.A.]
Kim. Monarch, 1962 [Miami]
Lament for Julie. Monarch, 1961 [Va.]
Make Mine Vengeance. Avon, 1959 [Fla.]
Murder Mistress. Ace, 1959 [Miami]
Murder Times Five. GM, 1972
The Quaking Widow. Ace, 1956 [Fla.]
Run for the Money. Avon, 1960 [L.A.]
Secret of the Second Door. GM, 1959;
   Muller pb, 1960 [NYC]
The Star Trap. GM, 1960 [L.A.]
These Lonely, These Dead. Pyramid, 1959
   [L.A.]

COLCORD, LINCOLN. 1883-1947.
The Drifting Diamond. Macmillan, 1912
The Game of Life and Death. Macmillan
   (NYC & London), 1914 ss, some cri-
   minous

COLE, BARRY. 1936-   . Ref: CA.
The Search for Rita. Methuen, 1970

COLE, BURT. 1930-   . Ref: CA.
Sahara Survival. Harper's Magazine
   Press, 1973 [Afr.]

COLE, DIANE
Murder at the White Tulip. Arcadia,
   1960 [Okla.]

COLE, G(EORGE) D(OUGLAS) H(OWARD), 1889-
   1959, and MARGARET (ISABEL POSTGATE)
   COLE, 1893-1980. Ref: all eight. SC:
   Everard Blatchington = EB; Dr. Benja-
   min Tancred = BT; Mrs. Elizabeth War-
   render = EW; Supt. Henry Wilson = HW.
   A number of pamphlets are grouped to-
   gether at the end of the entry. Set:
   Eng.
The Affair at Aliquid. Collins, 1933
The Berkshire Mystery; see Burglars in
   Bucks
Big Business Murder. Collins, 1935;
   Doubleday, 1935 HW
The Blatchington Tangle. Collins, 1926;
   Macmillan, 1926 HW,EB

The Brooklyn Murders. Collins, 1923;
   Seltzer, 1924 (The first HW novel,
   written by G.D.H. Cole alone.)
The Brothers Sackville. Collins, 1936;
   Macmillan, 1937 HW
Burglars in Bucks. Collins, 1930. U.S.
   title: The Berkshire Mystery. Brewer,
   1930 HW,EB
Corpse in Canonicals. Collins, 1930.
   U.S. title: The Corpse in the Con-
   stable's Garden. Morrow, 1931 HW
The Corpse in the Constable's Garden;
   see Corpse in Canonicals
Counterpoint Murder. Collins, 1940;
   Macmillan, 1941 HW
Dead Man's Watch. Collins, 1931;
   Doubleday, 1932 HW
Death in the Quarry. Collins, 1934;
   Doubleday, 1934 HW,EB
Death of a Millionaire. Collins, 1925;
   Macmillan, 1925 HW
Death of a Star. Collins, 1932; Double-
   day, 1933
Disgrace to the College. Hodder pb,
   1937 (A novelet.)
Double Blackmail. Collins, 1939; Mac-
   millan, 1939 HW
Dr. Tancred Begins. Collins, 1935;
   Doubleday, 1935 BT,HW
End of an Ancient Mariner. Collins,
   1933; Doubleday, 1934 HW
The Great Southern Mystery. Collins,
   1931. U.S. title: The Walking Corpse.
   Morrow, 1931 HW
Greek Tragedy. Collins, 1939; Macmil-
   lan, 1940 HW [Greece, ship]
Knife in the Dark. Collins, 1941; Mac-
   millan, 1942 EW [acad.]
Last Will and Testament. Collins, 1936;
   Doubleday, 1936 BT, HW in minor role
A Lesson in Crime. Collins, 1933 (11
   ss, 8 about HW, 1 about EW.)
The Man from the River. Collins, 1928;
   Macmillan, 1928 HW
The Missing Aunt. Collins, 1937; Mac-
   millan, 1938 HW
Mrs. Warrender's Profession. Collins,
   1938; Macmillan, 1939 ss EW
The Murder at Crome House. Collins,
   1927; Macmillan, 1927
The Murder at the Munition Works. Col-
   lins, 1940; Macmillan, 1940 HW
Murder in Four Parts. Collins, 1934
Off with Her Head! Collins, 1938; Mac-
   millan, 1939 HW [acad.]
Poison in the Garden Suburb. Collins,
   1929. U.S. title: Poison in a Garden
   Suburb. Payson, 1929 HW
Scandal at School. Collins, 1935. U.S.
   title: The Sleeping Death. Doubleday,
   1936 EB [acad.]
The Sleeping Death; see Scandal at
   School
Superintendent Wilson's Holiday. Col-
   lins, 1928; Payson, 1929 ss HW
Toper's End. Collins, 1942; Macmillan,
   1942 HW
The Walking Corpse; see The Great
   Southern Mystery
Wilson and Some Others. Collins, 1940
   ss, some about HW

Birthday Gifts and other stories. Poly-
   books, 1946 ss
The Bone of the Dinosaur. Bantam (Lon-
   don), 1943
Death in the Sun. Vallancey, 1945 (From
   Mrs. Warrender's Profession, q.v.)
Death in the Tankard. Polybooks, 1943
Death of a Bride. Vallancey, 1945 (From
   Mrs. Warrender's Profession, q.v.)
Fatal Beauty. Locke, 1948 (From Mrs.
   Warrender's Profession, q.v.)
In a Telephone Cabinet. Polybooks,
   1944 (From Superintendent Wilson's
   Holiday, q.v.)
In Peril of His Life. Locke, 1948 (From
   Mrs. Warrender's Profession, q.v.)
A Lesson in Crime and other stories.
   Polybooks, 1946 (From A Lesson in
   Crime, q.v.) ss
A Lesson in Crime, and The Motive.
   Polybooks, 1943 (From A Lesson in
   Crime, q.v.) ss
The Missing Baronet. Polybooks, 1943
   (From Superintendent Wilson's Holi-
   day, q.v.)
Murder in Broad Daylight, and Crime at
   Eslington Hall. Polybooks, 1943 (From
   Wilson and Some Others, q.v.) ss
The Oxford Mystery. Bantam (London),
   1943 (From Superintendent Wilson's
   Holiday, q.v.)
Strychnine Tonic, and A Dose of Cya-
   nide. Polybooks, 1943 ss
Superintendent Wakely's Mistake. Val-
   lancey, 1944 (From A Lesson in
   Crime, q.v.)
The Toys of Death. Locke, 1948 (From
   Mrs. Warrender's Profession, q.v.)
Wilson Calling. Vallancey, 1944 (From
   A Lesson in Crime, q.v.)

COLE, K(ATHARINE) S.
I'm Afraid I'll Live! Houghton, 1936;
   Heinemann, 1936 [Paris]

COLE, LOIS DWIGHT. 1902-1979. Pseudonym:
   Anne Eliot, q.v.

COLE, MARGARET (ISABEL POSTGATE). 1893-
   1980. See: G(eorge) D(ouglas) H(oward) Cole, 1889-1959.

COLE, R(OBERT) W(ILLIAM)
-The Artificial Girl. Greening, 1908
The Death Trap. Greening, 1907
-His Other Self. Greening, 1906

COLEMAN, CLARA
Nightmare in July. Horwitz, 1965; Lan-
   cer, 1967 [L.I.]
A Scent of Sandalwood. Lancer, 1966

COLEMAN, CLAYTON W.
Timbalier. Dell, 1969

COLEMAN, F. X. J. Ph.D. in philosophy
   from Johns Hopkins U.; prof. of
   philosophy at U. of Pittsburgh.
Philip, the Draftsman. Lippincott, 1970

COLERIDGE, GILBERT (JAMES DUKE).
   1859-   .
An Instinctive Criminal. Treherne, 1905

COLERIDGE, M(ARY) E(LIZABETH). 1861-1907.
-The Shadow on the Wall. Arnold, 1904

COLES, CYRIL HENRY. 1899-1965. Joint
   pseudonyms with Adelaide Frances Oke
   Manning, 1891-1959: Manning Coles,
   Francis Gaite, qq.v.

COLES, MANNING. Joint pseudonym of Ade-
   laide Frances Oke Manning, 1891-1959,
   and Cyril Henry Coles, 1899-1965.
   Other joint pseudonym: Francis Gaite,
   q.v. Note that, after Manning's
   death, Cyril Coles collaborated with
   Tom Hammerton on the last two Manning
   Coles titles ("The House at Pluck's
   Gutter" and "Search for a Sultan").
   Ref: CC, EM, MP, TC. SC: Tommy Ham-
   bledon = TH. Note that several titles
   published in the U.S. as by Manning
   Coles appeared in Britain under the
   Francis Gaite pseudonym, and are
   listed there herein.
Alias Uncle Hugo. Hodder, 1953; Double-
   day, 1952. Also published as: Opera-
   tion Manhunt. Jonathan, 1954 TH
   [Russ.]
All That Glitters; see Not for Export
Among Those Absent. Hodder, 1948;
   Doubleday, 1948 TH
The Basle Express. Hodder, 1956;
   Doubleday, 1956 TH [Austria]
Birdwatcher's Quarry; see The Three
   Beans
A Brother for Hugh. Hodder, 1947. U.S.
   title: With Intent to Deceive.
   Doubleday, 1947 TH
Concrete Crime; see Crime in Concrete
Crime in Concret. Hodder, 1960. U.S.
   title: Concrete Crime. Doubleday,
   1960 TH [Fr.]
Dangerous by Nature. Hodder, 1950;
   Doubleday, 1950 TH [Cent. Am.]
Death of an Ambassador. Hodder, 1957;
   Doubleday, 1957 TH [Fr.]
Diamonds to Amsterdam. Hodder, 1950;
   Doubleday, 1949 TH
Drink to Yesterday. Hodder, 1940;
   Knopf, 1941 TH [Ger., 1917]
The Fifth Man. Hodder, 1946; Doubleday,
   1946 TH
Green Hazard. Hodder, 1945; Doubleday,
   1946 TH [Berlin]
The House at Pluck's Gutter. Hodder,
   1963; Pyramid, 1968 TH
A Knife for the Juggler. Hodder, 1953;
   Doubleday, 1964. Also published as:
   The Vengeance Man. Pyramid, 1967 TH
   [Sp.]
Let the Tiger Die. Hodder, 1948;
   Doubleday, 1947 TH
The Man in the Green Hat. Hodder, 1955;
   Doubleday, 1955 TH [It.]
The Mystery of the Stolen Plans; see
   Not for Export
Night Train to Paris. Hodder, 1952;
   Doubleday, 1952 TH [Fr.]
No Entry. Hodder, 1958; Doubleday, 1958
   TH [Ger.]
Not for Export. Hodder, 1954. U.S.
   title: All That Glitters. Doubleday,
   1954. Also published as: The Mystery
   of the Stolen Plans. Berkley, 1960
   TH [Berlin]
Not Negotiable. Hodder, 1949; Double-
   day, 1949 TH [Belg.]
Nothing to Declare. Doubleday, 1960 ss
   TH

C

Now or Never. Hodder, 1951; Doubleday, 1951 TH [Ger.]
Operation Manhunt; see Alias Uncle Hugo
Pray Silence. Hodder, 1940. U.S. title: A Toast to Tomorrow. Doubleday, 1941 TH [Ger.]
Search for a Sultan. Hodder, 1961; Doubleday, 1961 TH
They Tell No Tales. Hodder, 1941; Doubleday, 1942 TH
This Fortress. Doubleday, 1942
The Three Beans. Hodder, 1957. U.S. title: Birdwatcher's Quarry. Doubleday, 1956 TH [Fr.]
A Toast to Tomorrow; see Pray Silence
The Vengeance Man; see A Knife for the Juggler
With Intent to Deceive; see A Brother for Hugh
Without Lawful Authority. Hodder, 1943; Doubleday, 1943 TH

COLIN, AUBREY. Ref: CC. SC: Insp. Bill Murray, in both titles. Set: Eng.
Death Comes to Dinner. Hammond, 1965
Hands of Death. Hammond, 1963

COLIZZI, GIUSEPPE. 1925-   . Active in films as scriptwriter and directorial assistant.
The Night Has Another Voice. Abelard (London & NYC), 1963 (Translation of "La Notte ha Un'altra Voce." Milan, 1958.)

COLLES, EDMUND
Fair Exchange. Jenkins, 1931
-A Fool and His Money. Jenkins, 1932

COLLETT, DOROTHY
The Whispering Leaves. Major, 1978

COLLEY, I(SOBEL) B.
Death in the Dimness. Hale, 1974

COLLIER, CONSTANCE. See: Phyllis Bottome.

COLLIER, JANE. Pseudonym of Zena Feldman Shumsky, 1926-   . Ref: CA.
Deadly Feast. Hale, 1978

COLLIER, JOHN (HENRY NOYES). 1901-   .
Ref: CA, EM, TC.
Fancies and Goodnights. Doubleday, 1951 ss

COLLIER, PETER. 1939-   . Ref: CA.
-Downriver. Holt, 1978

COLLIER, RICHARD (HUGHESON). 1924-   .
Ref: CA.
-Beautiful Friend. Pilot, 1947
The Lovely and the Damned. Pilot, 1949
Pay-Off in Calcutta. Pilot, 1948. U.S. title: Solitary Witness. Pellegrini, 1948 [Calcutta]
Solitary Witness; see Pay-Off in Calcutta

COLLIN, RAYMOND
-Locust in the Wind. Long, 1968
Night of the Eagles. Hammond, 1966

COLLIN, RICHARD OLIVER. 1940-   . Ref: CA.
Imbroglio. St. Martin's, 1980 [Rome]

COLLINGWOOD, CHARLES (CUMMINGS). 1917-   . Ref: CA.
The Defector. Harper, 1970; Hart-Davis, 1970 [Viet Nam]

COLLINS, CHARLES ALLSTON. 1828-1873.
At the Bar. Chapman, 1866
The Bar Sinister. Smith Elder, 1864
-Strethcairn. Low, 1864

COLLINS, COLIN
The Blinding Light. Greening, 1910
-Four Million a Year. Greening, 1911
The House of Silence. Lloyd, 1921
The Human Mole. Greening, 1909
Step by Step. Lloyd, 1921

COLLINS, CORNELIUS J.
Bitter Is the Fruit. Berkley, 1974

COLLINS, DALE. 1897-1956.
The Fifth Victim. Harrap, 1930
-Ordeal. Heinemann, 1924; Knopf, 1924 [ship]
Stolen or Strayed. Bookstall (Sydney), 1922
-Vulnerable. Benn, 1933; Bobbs, 1933

COLLINS, MRS. E. BURKE. Pseudonym of Mrs. Emma Augusta Brown Sharkey, 1858-   .
A Debt of Vengeance. Street, 1890
Lillian's Vow; or, The Mystery of Raleigh House. Munro, 1889

COLLINS, FRANK
Here's Why. Constable, 1938

COLLINS, FREDERICK LEWIS. 1882-1950.
Pseudonym: Frederick Lewis, q.v.

COLLINS, GILBERT. 1900-   . SC: Hugh Carding = HC. Set: Eng.
The Channel Million. Bles, 1932 HC [ship]
Chinese Red. Bles, 1932. U.S. title: Red Death. Holt, 1932 [China]
The Dead Walk. Bles, 1933 HC
Death Meets the King's Messenger. Bles, 1934; Doubleday, 1934 HC
The Haven of Unrest. Bles, 1936 HC
Horror Comes to Thripplands. Bles, 1930
The Mongolian Mystery. Ward, 1937
Murder at Brambles; see The Phantom Tourer
Mystery in St. James Square. Ward, 1937
The Phantom Tourer. Bles, 1931. U.S. title: Murder at Brambles. Holt, 1932 HC
Poison Pool. Bles, 1935 HC
Post-Mortem. Bles, 1930 HC
Red Death; see Chinese Red

COLLINS, HUNT. Pseudonym of Evan Hunter, 1926-   , q.v. Other pseudonyms: Curt Cannon, Ezra Hannon, Ed McBain, Richard Marsten, qq.v.
Cut Me In. Abelard, 1954; Boardman, 1960. Also published as: The Proposition. Pyramid, 1955 [NYC]

COLLINS, JACKIE
Lovehead. Allen, 1974

COLLINS, JAMES H(IRAM). 1873-   .
The Great Taxi-Cab Mystery. Lane, 1912 [NYC]

COLLINS, JOHN
Sheer Bluff. Jenkins, 1934

COLLINS, LARRY, 1929-   , and DOMINIQUE LAPIERRE, 1931-   . Ref: CA (both authors).
The Fifth Horseman. Simon, 1980; Granada, 1980

COLLINS, MABEL [MABEL COLLINS COOK]. 1851-1927.
Cobwebs. Tinsley, 1882 ss, some criminous

COLLINS, MARY (GARDEN). 1908-   .
Dead Center. Scribner, 1942 [S.F.]
Death Warmed Over. Scribner, 1947 [L.A.]
Dog Eat Dog. Scribner, 1949 [Calif.]
The Fog Comes. Scribner, 1941 [S.F.]
Only the Good. Scribner, 1942 [Calif.]
The Sister of Cain. Scribner, 1943 [S.F.]

COLLINS, MAX (ALLAN JR.). 1948-   .
Ref: CA. SC: Frank Nolan = FN; Quarry = Q.
Bait Money. Curtis, 1973; New English Library pb, 1976 FN [Ia.]
Blood Money. Curtis, 1973; New English Library pb, 1976 FN [Ia.]
The Broker. Berkley, 1976 Q
The Broker's Wife. Berkley, 1976 Q [Ia.]
The Dealer. Berkley, 1976 Q
The Slasher. Berkley, 1977 Q [Wis.]

COLLINS, MICHAEL. Pseudonym of Dennis Lynds, 1924-   , q.v. Other pseudonyms: William Arden, Nick Carter, John Crowe, Carl Dekker, Maxwell Grant, Mark Sadler, qq.v. SC: Dan Fortune, in all titles.
Act of Fear. Dodd, 1967; Joseph, 1968 [NYC]
The Blood-Red Dream. Dodd, 1976; Hale, 1977 [NYC]
Blue Death. Dodd, 1975; Hale, 1976
The Brass Rainbow. Dodd, 1969; Joseph, 1970 [NYC]
Night of the Toads. Dodd, 1970; Hale, 1972 [NYC]
The Nightrunners. Dodd, 1978; Hale, 1979 [Conn.]
Shadow of a Tiger. Dodd, 1972 [NYC]
The Silent Scream. Dodd, 1973; Hale, 1975 [NYC]
The Slasher. Dodd, 1980; Hale, 1981 [L.A.]
Walk a Black Wind. Dodd, 1971; Hale, 1973 [N.Y.]

COLLINS, MICHELLE. SC: Megan Marshall, in both titles.
Murder at Willow Run. Zebra, 1979 [N.Y.]
Premiere at Willow Run. Zebra, 1980 [N.Y., theatre]

COLLINS, (EDWARD JAMES) MORTIMER. 1827-1876.
Who Is the Heir? Maxwell, 1865

COLLINS, NORMAN (RICHARD). 1907-1982.
Ref: CA.
The Bat That Flits. Collins, 1952; Little, 1952
The Husband's Story. Collins, 1978; Atheneum, 1979

COLLINS, RANDALL. 1941-   . Ph.D. from Berkeley; author of several books in sociology field.
The Case of the Philosopher's Ring. Crown, 1978; Harvester, 1980 (Sherlock Holmes) [Eng., acad.]

COLLINS, THOMAS
Nightside. Manor, 1979 [N.Y.]

COLLINS, (WILLIAM) WILKIE. 1824-1889.
Ref: all except CA. See also: Tim J. Kelly, 1937-   ; Merritt Stone; and Dan Sutherland. No attempt has been made here to distinguish among Collins' fiction on the basis of criminous content. Set: Eng.
After Dark. Smith & Elder, 1856; Dick 1856 ss
Armadale. Smith & Elder, 1866; Harper, 1866
Basil. Bentley, 1852; Appleton, 1853. Also published as: The Crossed Path; or, Basil. Peterson, 1861
The Black Robe. Chatto, 1881; Belford, 1881
Blind Love. Chatto, 1890; Appleton, 1890 (Completed by Sir Walter Besant.)
The Crossed Path; or, Basil; see Basil
The Dead Secret. Bradbury, 1857; Miller, 1857 ss
The Evil Genius. Chatto, 1886; Harper, 1886
The Fallen Leaves. Chatto, 1879; Rose-Belford, 1879
The Frozen Deep. Bentley, 1874; Gill, 1875 ss
The Ghost's Touch and other stories. Harper, 1885 (ss, taken from other collections.)
The Guilty River. Arrowsmith, 1886; Harper, 1886
The Haunted Hotel. Chatto, 1878; Munro, 18?? [Venice]
Heart and Science. Chatto, 1883; Belford Clarke, 1883
Hide and Seek. Bentley, 1854; Dick, 1858
I Say "No". Chatto, 1884; Harper, 1884
Jezebel's Daughter. Chatto, 1880; Munro, 1880
The Law and the Lady. Chatto, 1875; Harper, 1875
The Legacy of Cain. Chatto, 1889; Lovell, 1888
Little Novels. Chatto, 1887
Man and Wife. Ellis, 1870; Harper, 1870
Miss or Mrs? Bentley, 1873; Peterson, 1872 ss
Mr. Wray's Cash Box; or, The Mask and the Mystery. Bentley, 1852. U.S. title: The Stolen Mask; or, The Mysterious Cash Box. Peterson, 1862
The Moonstone. Tinsley, 1868; Harper, 1868
My Lady's Money. Harper, 1878 (British title?)
My Miscellanies. Low, 1863; Harper, 1874
The New Magdalen. Bentley, 1873; Harper, 1873
No Name. Low, 1862; Harper, 1863
A Plot in Private Life, and other tales. Tauschnitz, 1859 (Stories from The Queen of Hearts, q.v.)
Poor Miss Finch. Bentley, 1872; Harper, 1872
The Queen of Hearts. Hurst, 1859; Harper, 1859 ss
A Rogue's Life. Bentley, 1879; Appleton, 1879
The Stolen Mask; or, The Mysterious Cash Box; see Mr. Wray's Cash Box; or, The Mask and the Mystery
Tales of Suspense. Folio Society, 1954 (ss taken from other collections.)
Tales of Terror and the Supernatural. Dover, 1972 (ss taken from earlier collections.)
The Two Destinies. Chatto, 1876; Harper, 1876
The Woman in White. Low, 1860; Harper, 1860
The Yellow Mask. Popular Library, 1967 (ss taken from earlier collections.)

COLLIS, E. T.
Murder by Warrant. Glen, 1898

COLLIS, LAURISTON
    The Mystery of Holly Tavern. Lippincott, 1873

COLLIS, LOUISE (EDITH). 1925-   . Ref: CA.
    The Great Flood. Macmillan (London), 1966

COLLIS, MAURICE (STEWART). 1889-   .
    Ref: CA.
    The Dark Door. Faber, 1940

COLLISON, WILSON. 1893-1941. Pseudonym: Willis Kent, q.v.
    Begins with Murder; see Save a Lady
    Dark Dame. Kendall, 1935
    Diary of Death. McBride, 1930 [NYC]
    Glittering Isle. Covici, 1936 [NYC]
    The Last Witness; see The Murder in the Brownstone House
    The Murder in the Brownstone House. McBride, 1929. British title: The Last Witness. Arrowsmith, 1931 [NYC]
    Murder in the Rain. McBride, 1930 [NYC]
    Red-Haired Alibi. McBride, 1932 [N.Y.]
    The Second Mrs. Lynton. Kendall, 1935 [NYC]
    Save a Lady. Kendall, 1935. British title: Begins with Murder. Long, 1936 [NYC]

COLOMBO, PAT
    Throw Back the Little Ones. Avon, 1963 [Rome]

COLSON, PERCY, 1873-   , and DOUGLAS HOARE
    Murder to Music. Gifford, 1945

COLTER, ELI(ZABETH). SC: Pat Campbell = PC.
    Cheer for the Dead. Mill, 1947; Boardman, 1949 PC [L.A.]
    The Gull Cove Murders. Mill, 1946; Pendulum, 1946 PC [Calif.]
    Rehearsal for the Funeral. Arcadia, 1953

COLTER, FRANK. SC: Death Squad, in both titles.
    Gang War. Belmont, 1975
    Killers for Hire. Belmont, 1975

COLTMAN-ALLEN, VIVIAN ERNEST. 1908-   .
    Pseudonym: Ernest Dudley, q.v.

COLTON, A. J. Pseudonym of Alfred Samuel Hook.
    The Coatine Case. Hale, 1953

COLTON, JOHN, 1889-1946, and CARLTON MILES
    Nine Pine Street. French (NYC), 1934 (3-act play.)

COLTON, MEL. Pseudonym of Hal Braham, q.v. Other pseudonym: Merrill Trask, q.v.
    The Big Fix. Ace, 1952
    Big Woman. Magazine Productions, 1953
    Double Take. Ace, 1953 [L.A.]
    Never Kill a Cop. Ace, 1953
    Point of No Escape. Ace, 1955

COLTRANE, JAMES. Pseudonym of James P(aul) Wohl, 1937-   , q.v.
    Talon. Bobbs, 1978; New English Library, 1978 [NYC]

COLVER, ANNE. 1908-   . Pseudonym: Colver Harris, q.v.

COLWALL, JAMES. Pseudonym of Gilbert Sheldon, 1870-   .
    The Coomsberrow Mystery. Cassell, 1890

COMBER, LEON. Graduate of London University's School of Oriental Studies; lived and worked for many years in Singapore and Hong Kong.
    The Strange Cases of Magistrate Pao. Tuttle, 1964 (ss, "translated and retold" by Comber from ancient sources.) [China, ca.1100]

COMBES, SHARON M.
    Caly. Zebra, 1980 [Maine]
    -So Little Time. Zebra, 1980

COMFORT, IRIS (TRACY). Ref: CA.
    Echoes of Evil. Doubleday, 1977

COMLEY, GERTRUDE. Set: Eng.
    -Fate's Pendulum. Eldon, 1934
    The Mansel Disappearance Mystery. Rivers, 1929
    Who Murdered Westaway? Rivers, 1932

COMMORDE, R.
    A Dame Is Snatched. Gray, 1952

COMO, LYNN. Set: U.S. in both titles.
    Man Hunt! Hamilton Stafford, 1952
    Stuttering Death. Hamilton Stafford, 1953

COMPORT, BRIAN. 1938-   .
    Mumsy, Nanny, Sonny, and Girly. Sphere, 1970; Lancer, 1970 (Novelization of the play by Maisie Mosco.)

COMPTON, D(AVID) G(UY). 1930-   . Pseudonym: Frances Lynch, q.v. See also: (David) Guy Compton. Ref: CA, CC.
    -The Palace. Hodder, 1969; Norton, 1969

COMPTON, (DAVID) GUY. 1930-   . Pseudonym: Frances Lynch, q.v. SC: Ben Anderson, in at least those marked BA. Set: Eng.
    And Murder Came Too. Long, 1966
    Dead on Cue. Long, 1964
    Disguise for a Dead Gentleman. Long, 1964 BA [acad.]
    High Tide for Hanging. Long, 1965
    Medium for Murder. Long, 1963 BA
    Too Many Murderers. Long, 1962

COMPTON, HERBERT (EASTWICK). 1853-1906.
    The Palace of Spies. Treherne, 1903
    To Defeat the Ends of Justice. Chatto, 1906
    The Undertaker's Field; or, Murder Will Out. Bachelor, 1904
    The Wilful Way. Chatto, 1903

COMPTON-RICKETT, ARTHUR. 1869-1937. See also: Patrick Leyton; and: Ernest (Henry) Short, 1875-1959. Ref: MP.
    The Railway Hotel Murder, with Ernest (Henry) Short. Jenkins, 1931

COMSTOCK, CAROLINE
    The Bandar-Log Murder. Barker, 1956

CONALL, CEARNACH. Pseudonym of Frederick William O'Connell, 1876-1929.
    The Fatal Move, and other stories. Gill, 1924 ss, some criminous

CONANT, PAUL. Raised in California; newspaperman in New Jersey.
    Dr. Gatskill's Blue Shoes. Wyn, 1952 [NYC]

CONAWAY, JAMES (ALLEY). 1941-   . Ref: CA.
    The Big Easy. Houghton, 1970; Faber, 1971 [New Or.]
    -World's End. Morrow, 1978 [La.]

CONAWAY, JIM C. SC: Jana Blake = JB.
    Angel Possessed. Belmont, 1974 [Jam.] JB
    Deadlier Than the Male. Belmont, 1977 JB
    They Do It with Mirrors. Belmont, 1977 JB [NYC]

CONDE, PHILLIP. SC: Dick Pemberty, in at least those marked DP; Irving Todd, in at least those marked IT. Set: Eng.
    The Case of the Crazy Pilot. Wright, 1938 DP
    The Corpse in the Clouds. Wright, 1937 IT
    Dead Reckoning. Wright, 1938 IT
    Death from the Air. Wright, 1936 DP
    Death Laughs Aloft. Wright, 1940 DP
    Death Loop. Wright, 1938 DP
    Death Takes the Joystick. Wright, 1937 IT
    The Devil Has Wings. Wright, 1937 DP
    The Ghost Plane. Wright, 1936
    Murder at 10,000 Feet. Wright, 1938 IT
    Murder in the Cockpit. Wright, 1936 IT
    Mystery of the Vanishing Aerodrome. Wright, 1939 DP
    The Phantom Pilot. Wright, 1936
    Pilot's Graveyard. Wright, 1937 DP
    Secret of the Scarlet Bomber. Wright, 1939 DP
    Skyway Vampire. Wright, 1938 IT
    Spawn of the Hawk. Wright, 1938 DP
    Visibility Nil. Wright, 1940
    Vultures of the Sky. Wright, 1935

CONDER, ARTHUR R(EIGNIER)
    The Seal of Silence. Smith Elder, 1901; Appleton, 1901

CONDON, FRANK, 1882-1940, and CHARLTON L(AWRENCE) EDHOLM
    The Dancing Doll. Barse, 1927; Long, 1928 [NYC]

CONDON, RICHARD (THOMAS). 1915-   .
    Ref: CA, TC. SC: Capt. Colin Huntington = CH.
    Arigato. Dial, 1972; Weidenfeld, 1972 CH
    Bandicoot. Dial, 1978; Hutchinson, 1978 CH
    Death of a Politician. Marek, 1978; Hutchinson, 1979 [NYC]
    The Ecstasy Business. Dial, 1967; Heinemann, 1967
    The Entwining. Marek, 1980; Hutchinson, 1981 [Wash. D.C., 1984]
    The Happy Thieves; see The Oldest Confession
    An Infinity of Mirrors. Random, 1964; Heinemann, 1967
    The Manchurian Candidate. McGraw, 1959; Joseph, 1960
    Mile High. Dial, 1969; Heinemann, 1969
    The Oldest Confession. Appleton, 1958; Longmans, 1959. Also published as: The Happy Thieves. Bantam, 1962
    The Whisper of the Axe. Dial, 1976; Weidenfeld, 1976
    Winter Kills. Dial, 1974; Weidenfeld, 1974

CONEY, MICHAEL G(REATREX). 1932-   .
    Ref: CA.
    -Hello Summer, Goodbye. Gollancz, 1975

CONGER, DONALD. Pseudonym of Donald C. Emerson.
    Closeout. Leisure, 1980

CONLY, ROBERT L. 1918-1973. Pseudonym: Robert C. O'Brien, q.v.

CONNABLE, ALFRED (B.). 1931-   . Ref: CA.
    Twelve Trains to Babylon. Little, 1971; MacGibbon, 1971 [NYC]

CONNELL, CANDACE. Pseudonym of Ernest C. Clement.
    Dark Legacy; see The Red Turrets of Orne
    Ellena. Zebra, 1975. Also published as: The House at Parson's Landing. Zebra, 1977
    The House at Parson's Landing; see Ellena
    The Red Turrets of Orne. Doubleday, 1979. Also published as: Dark Legacy. Dell, 1980

CONNELL, CHARLES
    Catt Among the Pigeons. Jenkins, 1950
    Meet Me at Philippi. Jenkins, 1948 [Rome, ca.50 B.C.]
    Most Delicious Poison. Jenkins, 1951 [Mid. East, ca.50 B.C.]

CONNELL, EDWIN
    I Had to Kill Her. Ballantine, 1966 [NYC]

CONNELL, RICHARD (EDWARD). 1893-1949. See also: Leo Brady, 1917-   .
    Ref: CC, EM.
    Ironies. Minton, 1930 ss, some criminous
    Mr. Braddy's Safe and other humorous tales. Chapman, 1922 ss, some criminous
    Murder at Sea. Minton, 1929; Jarrolds, 1929 [ship]
    Variety. Minton, 1925; Parsons, 1925 ss, at least one ("The Most Dangerous Game") criminous

CONNELL, VIVIAN. 1903-   .
    Monte Carlo Mission. GM, 1954 [Fr.]

CONNELLY, J. H.
    Neila Sen and My Casual Death. Lovell, 1890 (2 stories.)

CONNELLY, MARC(US COOK). 1890-   . Ref: CA.
    A Souvenir from Qam. Holt, 1965 [Mid. East]

CONNER, (PATRICK) REARDON. 1907-   .
    Ref: CA.
    I Am Death. Chapman, 1936. U.S. title: Time to Kill. Knopf, 1936 [Ire.]

CONNERS, BERNARD F. 1926-   . Ref: CA.
    Don't Embarrass the Bureau. Bobbs, 1972; Allen, 1973

CONNINGTON, J. J. Pseudonym of Alfred Walter Stewart, 1880-1947. Ref: CC, EM, MM, MP, TC. SC: Sir Clinton Driffield = CD; Mark Brand = MB; Supt. Ross = R. Set: Eng.
    The Boat-House Riddle. Gollancz, 1931; Little, 1931 CD

The Brandon Case; see The Ha-Ha Case
The Case with Nine Solutions. Gollancz, 1928; Little, 1929 CD
The Castleford Conundrum. Hodder, 1932; Little, 1932 CD
Common Sense Is All You Need. Hodder, 1947 CD
The Counsellor. Hodder, 1939; Little, 1939 MB
The Dangerfield Talisman. Benn, 1926; Little, 1927
Death at Swaythling Court. Benn, 1926; Little, 1926
The Eye in the Museum. Gollancz, 1929; Little, 1930 R
For Murder Will Speak. Hodder, 1938. U. S. title: Murder Will Speak. Little, 1938 CD
The Four Defenses. Hodder, 1940; Little, 1940 MB
Gold Brick Island; see Tom Tiddler's Island
Grim Vengeance; see Nemesis at Raynham Parva
The Ha-Ha Case. Hodder, 1934. U.S. title: The Brandon Case. Little, 1934 CD
In Whose Dim Shadow. Hodder, 1935. U.S. title: The Tau Cross Mystery. Little, 1935 CD
Jack-in-the-Box. Hodder, 1944; Little, 1944 CD
A Minor Operation. Hodder, 1937; Little, 1937 CD
Murder in the Maze. Benn, 1927; Little, 1927 CD
Murder Will Speak; see For Murder Will Speak
Mystery at Lynden Sands. Gollancz, 1928; Little, 1928 CD
Nemesis at Raynham Parva. Gollancz, 1929. U.S. title: Grim Vengeance. Little, 1929 CD
No Past Is Dead. Hodder, 1942; Little, 1942 CD
The Sweepstake Murders. Hodder, 1931; Little, 1932 CD
The Tau Cross Mystery; see In Whose Dim Shadow
Tom Tiddler's Island. Hodder, 1933. U.S. title: Gold Brick Island. Little, 1933
Tragedy at Ravensthorpe. Benn, 1927; Little, 1928 CD
Truth Comes Limping. Hodder, 1938; Little, 1938 CD
The Twenty-One Clues. Hodder, 1941; Little, 1941 CD
The Two Tickets Puzzle. Gollancz, 1930. U.S. title: The Two Ticket Puzzle. Little, 1930 R

CONNOLLY, COLM
The Pact. Deutsch, 1980

CONNOLLY, HENRY
The Finger of Death. Hutchinson, 1929

CONNOLLY, PAUL. Pseudonym of Tom [Thomas Grey] Wicker, 1926- , q.v.
Get Out of Town. GM, 1951; Fawcett (London), 1959
So Fair, So Evil. GM, 1955; Fawcett (London), 1958 [Ala.]
Tears Are for Angels. GM, 1952

CONNOLLY, R. P.
Dynamite! Scion, 1951
He Died Laughing. Scion, 1952

CONNOLLY, RAY. 1940- . Ref: CA.
Newsdeath. Collins, 1978; Atheneum, 1978

CONNOLLY, VIVIAN. 1925- . Pseudonym: Andrea Harris, q.v. Ref: CA.
The Fires of Ballymorris. Dell, 1975 [Ire.]
South Coast of Danger. Macfadden, 1973

CONNOR, KEVIN
New Departure. Jefferson House, 1962 [1800s]

CONNOR, RALPH. Pseudonym of Charles William Gordon, 1860-1937.
Corporal Cameron. Hodder, 1912. U.S. title: Corporal Cameron of the North West Mounted Police. Doran, 1912 [Can.]

CONNOR, SKID
My Grave Is for the Living. Grayling, 1950

CONOT, ROBERT E. 1929- . Ref: CA.
Ministers of Vengeance. Lippincott, 1964; Heinemann, 1965 [Calif., 1920s]

CONRAD, BARNABY, 1922- , and NIELS MORTENSEN. Ref: on Conrad: CA.
Endangered. Putnam, 1978; New English Library pb, 1980

CONRAD, BRENDA
Caribbean Conspiracy. Scribner, 1942
-Girl with a Golden Bar. Scribner, 1944
The Stars Give Warning. Scribner, 1941

CONRAD, CLIVE. Pseudonym of Frank King, 1892-1958, q.v. Set: Eng.
The Crime of His Life. Museum, 1951
Money's Worth of Murder. Museum, 1949
There Was a Little Man. Museum, 1948

CONRAD, JOSEPH [JOZEF TEODOR KONRAD KORZENIOWSKI]. 1857-1924. Ref: CA, CC, EM, MC.
The Nature of a Crime, with F(ord) M(adox) Hueffer [Joseph Leopold Ford Hermann Madox Hueffer, 1873-1939]. Duckworth, 1924; Doubleday, 1924, with "Ford Madox Ford"
The Secret Agent. Methuen, 1907; Harper, 1907
A Set of Six. Methuen, 1908; Doubleday, 1915 ss, one criminous
Under Western Eyes. Methuen, 1911; Harper, 1911

CONRAD, CAPT. THOMAS N(ELSON)
A Confederate Spy. Ogilvie, 1892

CONRAD, TOD. Pseudonym of R(ichard) Wilkes-Hunter, 1906- , q.v. Other pseudonyms: Marc Brody, Alex Crane, qq.v.
The Colonel and the Corpse. Webster, 1958
Kane and Miss Able. Webster, 1958
Rawhide Vixen. Webster, 1958

CONROY, A. L.
The Storefront Lawyers. Bantam, 1970 (Novelization of the TV series.)

CONROY, AL. Pseudonym of Marvin H(ubert) Albert, 1924- , q.v. Other pseudonyms: Mike Barone, Albert Conroy, Ian MacAlister, Nick Quarry, Anthony Rome, qq.v. SC: Johnny Morini, in all titles.
Blood Run. Lancer, 1973
Death Grip! Lancer, 1972 [Phil.]
Murder Mission! Lancer, 1973 [New Or.]
Soldato! Lancer, 1972 [Utah]
Strangle Hold! Lancer, 1973 [Fla.]

CONROY, ALBERT. Pseudonym of Marvin H(ubert) Albert, 1924- , q.v. Other pseudonyms: Mike Barone, Al Conroy, Ian MacAlister, Nick Quarry, Anthony Rome, qq.v.
The Chiselers. GM, 1953
Devil in Dungarees. Crest, 1960
The Looters. Crest, 1961 [Carib.]
The Mob Says Murder. GM, 1958; Fawcett (London), 1960
Mr. Lucky. Dell, 1960 (Novelization of the TV series.) [Calif.]
Murder in Room 13. GM, 1958; Fawcett (London), 1960
Nice Guys Finish Dead. GM, 1957; Fawcett (London), 1958
The Road's End. GM, 1952; Fawcett (London), 1958

CONSTABLE, LAWRENCE
House Without Windows. Milton House, 1973

CONSTANDUROS, MABEL
Murder at the Mugginses, with Michael Hagan. French (London & NYC), 1930 (Play).
On the Run, with Howard Agg, q.v. Hammond, 1943

CONSTANTINE, EDDIE
The God Player. Ellis, 1976 (Translation of "Le Proprietaire." Paris, 1975.)

CONSTANTINE, K. C. Pseudonym. SC: Mario Balzac, in all titles, set in Pa.
The Blank Page. Saturday Review Press, 1974 [acad.]
A Fix Like This. Saturday Review Press, 1975
The Man Who Liked to Look at Himself. Saturday Review Press, 1973
The Rocksburg Railroad Murders. Saturday Review Press, 1972

CONSTINER, (FRANCIS) MERLE
Hearse of a Different Color. Phoenix, 1952

CONTE, CHARLES
The Fear of Death. Hale, 1972
The Spanish Crown Affair. Hale, 1971

CONTE, MANFRED
Cassia. Collins, 1955. U.S. title: Jeopardy. Sloane, 1956 (Translation of "Cassia und der Abenteurer." Stuttgart, 1951.) [Fr.]

CONTENT, NIKKI
Hideaway. GM, 1953 [Mex.]

CONTY, J. P.
A Big Secret Suzuki. International Publishers, 1969

CONVERSE, FLORENCE. 1871- .
Into the Void. Little, 1926 [New Eng.]
Sphinx. Dutton, 1931; Dent, 1931

CONVERSE, FRANK H.
The Mystery of a Diamond. Lovell, 1890

CONWAY, HUGH. Pseudonym of F(rederick) J(ohn) Fargus, 1840-1885, q.v. Some titles published in the U.S. under the pseudonym appeared in England as by F. J. Fargus.
At What Cost, and other stories. Maxwell, 1885 ss
Bound by a Spell. Lovell, 1887 (British title?)
Bound Together. Remington, 1884; Holt, 1884 ss
Called Back. Arrowsmith, 1883; Holt, 1884
A Cardinal Sin. Eden, 1886; Holt, 1886
Daughter of the Stars and other tales. Munro, 1884 (British title?)
A Family Affair. Macmillan (London), 1885; Holt, 1885
Living or Dead. Macmillan (London), 1886; Holt, 1886
The Missing Will and other stories. Ogilvie, ca.1886 (British title?) ss
Somebody's Story. Field, 1886; Lovell, 1886

CONWAY, JOAN DITZEL. 1933- . Ref: CA.
Island of Fear. GM, 1972 [Chan. Is.]

CONWAY, JOHN. Pseudonym of Joseph Chadwick, q.v. Other pseudonyms: Joselyn Chadwick, Jo Anne Creighton, John Creighton, qq.v.
Hell Is My Destination. Monarch, 1959
Love in Suburbia. Monarch, 1961
Madigan's Women. Monarch, 1959
Requiem for a Chaser. Monarch, 1960
Sin in Time. Monarch, 1961
This Dark Desire. Monarch, 1960

CONWAY, JOHN W(ILLIAM). 1851- .
Something or Nothing. Christopher, 1928 [Kan.]

CONWAY, KEITH
Hammerhead Reef. Hale, 1971
The Naked Nemesis. Hale, 1970

CONWAY, LAURA. Pseudonym of Dorothy Phoebe Ansle. Other pseudonyms: Hebe Elsna, Lyndon Snow, qq.v. Works of this author appear to have been published in England as romances; those also published in the U.S. as gothics are listed below. Set: Eng.
The Abbot's House. Collins, 1969; Saturday Review Press, 1974 [Eng., past]
Dark Symmetry. Saturday Review Press, 1973 (British title, byline?)
Heiress Apparent. Collins, 1966; McCall, 1970
The Night of the Ruby. Collins, 1969; McCall, 1971
The Unforgotten. Collins, 1967; Saturday Review Press, 1972

CONWAY, NORMAN. SC: Adam Hunter, in both titles.
The Omega Operation. Canyon, 1974
Operation: Alpha Death. Canyon, 1975

CONWAY, PETER. Pseudonym of George Alexis Milkomanovich Milkomane, 1903- . Other pseudonyms: George Braddon, Alec Redwood, George Sava, qq.v.
-A Dark Side Also. Faber, 1940
Expert Witness. Macdonald, 1949
-Hands Without Healing. Macdonald, 1950
-His Hand Betrays. Dakers, 1953
-Miss Pegham. Dakers, 1951
-The Palindrome. Dakers, 1951
Revised Proof. Macdonald, 1947
-The Road Winds Back. Faber, 1942
-Still They Smile. Macdonald, 1946
Tapestry Odyssey. King, 1944
-Those That Have Eyes. Faber, 1943
-The Unwanted Child. Faber, 1941
-The Weather of My Fate. Macdonald, 1947

CONWAY, PETER. Pseudonym of Peter Claudius Gautier-Smith, 1929- . SC: Lucy Beck, in at least those marked LB.
Cradle Snatch. Hale, 1976
The Dancing Bear. Hale, 1978
The Devil to Pay. Hale, 1976
Escape to Danger. Hale, 1974 LB
Flight of Fear. Hale, 1976
Hostages to Fortune. Hale, 1975
Motive for Revenge. Hale, 1972 LB
Murder in Duplicate. Hale, 1975
Nut Case. Hale, 1980
One for the Road. Hale, 1979
The Padded Cell. Hale, 1973 LB
Pulling Strings. Hale, 1980
Repent at Leisure. Hale, 1980
Thirty Days to Live. Hale, 1979
Victims of Circumstance. Hale, 1977
A Word in Her Ear. Hale, 1977

CONYERS, DOROTHEA (SMYTH). 1873- .
Lady Elverton's Emeralds. Hutchinson, 1909

CONYN, CORNELIUS and JON C(HISHOLM) MARTEN
The Bali Ballet Murder. Harrap, 1961 [Bali]

COOK, BRUCE. 1932- . Ref: CA.
Sex Life. Evans, 1979 [Chi.]

COOK, DOROTHY MARY. 1907- . Pseudonym: D. M. Carlisle, q.v.

COOK, ELLA BOOKER. 1886- .
The Ghost of Windy Hill. Vantage, 1964

COOK, EUGENIA
The Forbidden Tower. Dell, 1973 [Ill.]

COOK, KENNETH. 1929- .
Bloodhouse. Heinemann, 1974; St. Martin's, 1974 [Syd.]
Chain of Darkness. Joseph, 1962
The Man Underground. Macmillan (London), 1977
Wake in Fright. Joseph, 1961; St. Martin's, 1962

COOK, (JOHN) LENNOX. 1923- . Operates a school of English in Cambridge, Eng.
The Manipulator. Joseph, 1978; Coward, 1978

COOK, MERCER B. Pseudonym of Robert (Harry) Turner, 1915-1980, q.v.
In Hot Blood. Challenge, 1966 [N.C.]

COOK, PETRONELLE MARGUERITE MARY. 1925- . Pseudonym: Margot Arnold, q.v.

COOK, ROBIN. 1940- .
Coma. Little, 1977; Macmillan (London), 1977 [Boston, hosp.]
Sphinx. Putnam, 1979; Macmillan (London), 1979 [Egypt]

COOK, SY
The Child and the Serpent. Seaview, 1980

COOK, THEODORE KENYON. 1897- .
The Catastrophe at Cliff Haven. Dorrance, 1940

COOK, THOMAS H. Book editor of "Atlanta" magazine, previously a professor of history.
Blood Innocents. Playboy, 1980 [NYC]
The Killing of the Fallow Deer. Playboy, 1979 [NYC]

COOK, W(ILLIAM) VICTOR. 1875- .
Ben Hassan's Secret. Aldine, 1922
By Order of the Dead. Aldine, 1923
Grey Fish. Chambers, 1919 ss, some criminous
The Search for Miss Sylvester. Aldine, 1922
Treason Under Seal. Harrap, 1934

COOK, WILFRED
-The Amateurs. Cresset, 1951
Man in the Dark. Cresset, 1959

COOK, WILLIAM WALLACE. 1867-1933. Pseudonym: Nicholas Carter, q.v.
-His Friend the Enemy. Dillingham, 1903
In the Web; or, An Artful Villain. Street, ca.1905
-A Quarter to Four; or, The Secret of Fortune Island. Dillingham, 1909
A Round Trip to the Year 2000. Street, 1925 [2000, U.S.]

COOKE, A(RTHUR) O(WENS). 1867-1930.
-Five Hundred Pounds Reward. Nelson, 1927

The Mellbridge Mystery. Arnold, 1926

COOKE, DAVID C(OXE). 1917- . Ref: CA. SC: Peter Rourke, in at least those marked PR.
c/o American Embassy. Dodd, 1967; Hale, 1968 PR [India]
The 14th Agent. Dodd, 1967; Hale, 1968 PR [H. Kong]
Night of the Tiger. Hale, 1970
Sleep with Nightmares. Hale, 1969 PR

COOKE, G(EOFFREY) WALTER. 1924- . A Londoner, formerly in the R.A.F., then in the automotive business. SC: Peter Mitchell, in all titles. Set: Eng.
Death Can Wait. Bles, 1957
Death Is the End. Bles, 1965
Death Takes a Dive. Bles, 1962

COOKE, GRACE MacGOWAN. 1863- .
The Man Behind the Mask. Stokes, 1927; Benn, 1928 [S.F.]

COOKE, H. O.
The Sign of the Dagger. Street (Magnet #371)

COOKE, JOHN ESTEN. 1830-1886.
Col. Ross of Piedmont; see The Maurice Mystery
Doctor Vandyke. Appleton, 1872
-The Heir of Greymount. Van Evrie, 1870
-Her Majesty the Queen. Lippincott, 1873
The Maurice Mystery. Appleton, 1885. Also published as: Col. Ross of Piedmont. Dillingham, 188?
-Mr. Grantley's Idea. Harper, 1879
Out of the Foam. Carleton, 1871

COOKE, JOSEPH COTTIN. Born in NYC; surveyor, reporter, freelance writer.
The Vera Gerard Case. Manthorne, 1937 [NYC]

COOKE, L. A. B.
War at the Gates. Bles, 1937

COOKE, M. E. Pseudonym of John Creasey, 1908-1973, q.v. Other pseudonyms: Gordon Ashe, Norman Deane, Robert Caine Frazer, Patrick Gill, Michael Halliday, Charles Hogarth, Brian Hope, Colin Hughes, Kyle Hunt, Abel Mann, Peter Manton, J. J. Marric, Richard Martin, Rodney Matheson, Anthony Morton, Jeremy York, qq.v. Some of the titles below may be juveniles or not crime fiction.
The Big Radium Mystery. Mellifont, 1936
The Black Heart. Gramol, 1935
The Casino Mystery. Mellifont, 1935
The Crime Gang. Mellifont, 1936
The Day of Terror. Mellifont, 1936
The Death Dive. Mellifont, 1935
The Dummy Robberies. Mellifont, 1936
Fire of Death. Fiction House, 1934
For Her Sister's Sake. Fiction House, 1938
The Hadfield Mystery. Mellifont, 1937
The Hypnotic Demon. Fiction House, 1936
The Moat Farm Mystery. Fiction House, 1936
The Mountain Terror. Mellifont, 1938
The Moving Eye. Mellifont, 1937
Number One's Last Crime. Fiction House, 1935
The Raven. Fiction House, 1937
The Secret Fortune. Fiction House, 1936
The Stolen Formula Mystery. Mellifont, 1935
The Successful Alibi. Mellifont, 1936
The Verrall Street Affair. Newnes, 1940

COOKE, MARJORIE BENTON. 1876-1920.
The Clutch of Circumstance. Doran, 1918; Skeffington, 1919 [Eng.]

COOKE, RACHEL E. Born in Indiana; writer of songs, ss, verse and novels.
Four Mad Monarchs. Vantage, 1954

COOKE, RUPERT CROFT-. 1903- . See: Rupert Croft-Cooke.

COOKE, W. BOURNE. 1869- .
The Horned Owl. Drane, 1905

COOKSON, CATHERINE (ANN McMULLEN). 1906- . Ref: CA. Pseudonym: Catherine Marchant, q.v. These titles are generally published in England as romances, but at least some appear in the U.S. as gothics. Set: Eng.
The Blind Miller. Macdonald, 1963; Signet, 1974
Colour Blind. Macdonald, 1953; Beagle, 1971, as by Catherine Marchant
The Devil and Mary Ann. Macdonald, 1958; Morrow, 1976
Fanny Bride. Macdonald, 1959; Bantam, 1976
Feathers in the Fire. Macdonald, 1971; Bantam, 1973
Fenwick Houses. Macdonald, 1960; Bantam, 1973
The Fifteen Streets. Macdonald, 1952; Bantam, 1973
The Gambling Man. Heinemann, 1975; Morrow, 1975
The Garment. Macdonald, 1962
The Glass Virgin. Macdonald, 1970; Bobbs, 1969
A Grand Man. Macdonald, 1954; Macmillan, 1955
Hannah Massey. Macdonald, 1964; Signet, 1973
The Invisible Cord. Heinemann, 1975; Dutton, 1975
The Invitation. Macdonald, 1970; Signet, 1974
Kate Hannigan. Macdonald, 1950; Bantam, 1972
Katie Mulholland. Macdonald, 1967; Bobbs, 1967
The Long Corridor. Macdonald, 1965; Beagle, 1971, as by Catherine Marchant
The Lord and Mary Ann. Macdonald, 1956; Morrow, 1975
Maggie Rowan. Macdonald, 1954; Beagle, 1971, as by Catherine Marchant
The Mallen Girl. Heinemann, 1974; Dutton, 1973
The Mallen Litter. Heinemann, 1974. U.S. title: The Mallen Lot. Dutton, 1974
The Mallen Lot; see The Mallen Litter
The Mallen Streak. Heinemann, 1973; Dutton, 1973
The Menagerie. Macdonald, 1958; Bantam, 1975
The Mists of Memory, as by Catherine Marchant. Lancer, 1967 (British title?)
The Nice Bloke. Macdonald, 1969
Pure As the Lily. Macdonald, 1972; Bobbs, 1973
Rooney. Macdonald, 1957; Bantam, 1976
Slinky Jane. Macdonald, 1959; Signet, 1976

COOKSON, GATHORNE
Murder Pays No Dividends. Muller, 1938

COOLIDGE, ERWIN L.
Gilt-Edge Tom, Conductor; or, The Pride of the Valley Route. Ogilvie, 1896
The Mountain Limited. Ogilvie, 1893 [train]
The Mystery of the Montauk Mills. Ogilvie, 1893

COOLIDGE-RASK, MARIE
London After Midnight. Grosset, 1928; Readers Library, 1928 (Novelization of the movie.)

COOM, CHARLES S(LEEMAN). 1851-1930?
The Baronet Rag-Picker. Clark, 1905

COOMBS, MURDO. Pseudonym of Frederick C(lyde) Davis, 1902-1977, q.v. Other pseudonyms: Stephen Ransome, Curtis Steele, qq.v.
A Moment of Need. Dutton, 1947 [NYC]

COONEY, CAROLINE B. 1947- . Ref: CA.
Rear-View Mirror. Random, 1980 [N.C.]

COONEY, MICHAEL. 1921- . Ref: CA. SC: Queen's Investigator, in both titles.
Doomsday England. Cassell, 1967; Walker, 1968
Ten Days to Oblivion. Cassell, 1968

COONEY, RAY and JOHN (ROY) CHAPMAN, 1927- .
My Giddy Aunt. English Theatre, 1970 (2-act play.)

COONS, MAURICE. Pseudonym: Armitage Trail, q.v.

COOPER, AGNES ROSEMARY. Joint pseudonym with Mary Elizabeth Phyllis Weller: Ramsay Bell, q.v.

COOPER, (EVELYN) BARBARA. 1915- . Graduate of Nottingham U. in economics and statistics; went to New Zealand in 1950. SC: Insp. Gibbon, in at least those marked G.
Drown Him Deep. Hale, 1966 G [N.Z.]
House of Masks. Hale, 1968
Target for Malice. Hale, 1964 G [N.Z.]
Who Is My Enemy? Hale, 1967

COOPER, BRIAN (NEWMAN). 1919- . Ref: CA, TC.

Genesis 38. Heinemann, 1965. U.S. title: The Murder of Mary Steers. Vanguard, 1966 [Eng., 1903]
Giselle; see A Path to the Bridge
Maria; see Where the Fresh Grass Grows
A Mission for Betty Smith. Heinemann, 1967. U.S. title: Monsoon Murder. Vanguard, 1968 [India]
Monsoon Murder; see A Mission for Betty Smith
The Murder of Mary Steers; see Genesis 38
A Path to the Bridge. Heinemann, 1958. U.S. title: Giselle. Vanguard, 1958
A Time to Retreat. Heinemann, 1963; Vanguard, 1963
A Touch of Thunder. Heinemann, 1961; Vanguard, 1962 [India]
The Van Langeren Girl. Heinemann, 1960; Vanguard, 1960 [India]
Where the Fresh Grass Grows. Heinemann, 1955. U.S. title: Maria. Vanguard, 1956

COOPER, BRYAN (ROBERT WRIGHT). 1932- . Ref: CA.
Wildcatters. Macdonald, 1976

COOPER, CHARLES. Pseudonym of Arnold Charles Cooper Lock.
The Turkish Spy. Stockwell, 1932 [Egypt]

COOPER, CLARENCE L.
-The Dark Messenger. Regency, 1962
-Weed. Regency, 1961

COOPER, COLIN (SYMONS). 1926- . Pseudonym: Daniel Benson, q.v.
Outcrop. Faber, 1969

COOPER, COURTNEY RILEY. 1886-1940.
Action in Diamonds. Penn, 1942 [Fla.]
-Caged. Little, 1930
The Challenge of the Bush. Little, 1929; Collins, 1930
-The Cross Cut. Little, 1921; Collins, 1922
-End of Steel. Farrar, 1931
-The Mystery of the Four Abreast. Collins, 1929 (U.S. title?) [West]
-Trigger Finger. Collins, 1930 (U.S. title?)
-The White Desert. Little, 1922; Hurst, 1923

COOPER, CRAIG. SC: Matt Savage, in at least those marked MS.
Blackmail Is Murder. Hale, 1968 MS
Catch and Squeeze. Hale, 1968; Roy, 1969 MS [U.S.]
Dame in Distress. Hale, 1968; Roy, 1968 MS [U.S.]
No Haloes for Hoods. Hale, 1969; Roy, 1969 [U.S.]
Run with the Fox. Hale, 1971
Running Scared. Hale, 1972
Snatch the Lady. Hale, 1970
Value for Murder. Hale, 1972
What's Funny About Murder. Hale, 1968; Roy, 1968 MS [U.S.]
Who Killed Honeybee? Hale, 1968; Roy, 1969 MS [U.S.]
You'll Die Laughing. Hale, 1968 MS

COOPER, DOMINIC (XAVIER). 1944- . Ref: CA.
The Dead of Winter. Chatto, 1975; St. Martin's, 1976

COOPER, EDMUND. 1926- . Ref: CA.
Prisoner of Fire. Hodder, 1974; Walker, 1975

COOPER, EDWARD H(ERBERT). 1867-1910.
Resolved to Be Rich. Duckworth, 1899; Duffield, 1906

COOPER, H(UGH) H(OMFRAY)
A Cave with Two Exits. Ross, 1969

COOPER, HENRY ST. JOHN
Dangerous Paths. Low, 1933
-The Golconda Necklace. Low, 1926
-The Splendid Love. Low, 1932
Toils of Silence. Low, 1935

COOPER, JAMES FENIMORE. 1789-1851. Ref: DD, MC, MP.
The Spy. Wiley, 1821; Whitakker, 1822
The Ways of the Hour. Putnam, 1850; Bentley, 1850

COOPER, JAMIE LEE. Ref: CA.
Grasshopper Summer. Bobbs, 1975 [Midwest]
The Great Dandelion. Bobbs, 1972

COOPER, JOHN
Canaries Sometimes Croak. World Distributors, 1952
Extortion Incorporated. World Distributors, 1952

COOPER, JOHN C. Pseudonym of John Croydon. Ref: CC. SC: Insp. James Dale, in at least those marked JD.
The Body Was of No Account. Boardman, 1957 JD
Death in Aberration. Boardman, 1958 JD
The Grip of the Strangler. Digit, 1958. U.S. title: The Haunted Strangler. Ace, 1959 (Novelization of the movie.)
The Haunted Strangler; see The Grip of the Strangler

COOPER, JOHN MURRAY. 1908- . Pseudonym: William Sutherland, q.v.

COOPER, KENNETH S.
Cipher Stories Puzzle Book. Copeland, 1928 (Puzzle ss.)

COOPER, LEONARD
The Accomplices. Cresset, 1960
Wanted at His Office. Barker, 1953

COOPER, LETTICE (ULPHA). 1897- . Ref: CA.
Tea on Sunday. Gollancz, 1973

COOPER, LOUISE (FIELD). 1905- .
In Memory of Sarah Bailey. New English Library pb, 1977

COOPER, LYNNA. Pseudonym of Gardner F(rancis) Fox, 1911- , q.v.
The Brittany Stones. Beagle, 1974
Folly Hall. Beagle, 1974
-Forgotten Love. Signet, 1979
-From Paris with Love. Signet, 1980
-Hearts in the Highlands. Signet, 1980
-Her Heart's Desire. Signet, 1976
-The Hired Wife. Signet, 1978
The Hour of the Harp. Saturday Review Press, 1975 [Ire., 1800s]
Moon Chapel. Beagle, 1973
-My Treasure, My Love. Signet, 1978
-An Offer of Marriage. Signet, 1976
-Portrait of Love. Signet, 1980
Stark Island. Avon, 1974 [Maine]
-Substitute Bride. Signet, 1977

COOPER, M(AE) K(LEIN)
Private Lies. Simon, 1979

COOPER, MARION
A Dress to Die In. Vantage, 1980

COOPER, MONTE
Death near the River. Holt, 1928 [Ark.]

COOPER, MORTON. 1925- .
Anything for Kicks. Avon, 1959
-Come Feed on Me. GM, 1953; Muller pb, 1954
-Delinquent! Avon, 1958
-The Flesh and Mr. Rawlie. GM, 1956; Fawcett (London), 1959. Also published as: The Flesh Traders. New English Library pb, 1970
The Flesh Traders; see The Flesh and Mr. Rawlie
-Ginny. Avon, 1959
-High School Confidential. Avon, 1958 (Novelization of the movie.)
The Innocent and Willing. GM, 1956; Fawcett (London), 1958. Also published as: No Angel. Paperback Library, 1963 [NYC]
No Angel; see The Innocent and Willing
Rich People. Evans, 1977; Allen, 1977
-The Ungilded Lily. GM, 1958
-Young and Wild. Avon, 1958 (Novelization of the movie.)

COOPER, PARLEY J(OSEPH). 1937- . Ref: CA.
-Dark Desires. PB, 1976; Sphere, 1977
The Devil Child. PB, 1972
The Inheritance. Popular Library, 1972 [Calif.]
Marianne's Kingdom. PB, 1972
Moonblood. PB, 1975 [Oreg.]
My Lady Evil. Simon, 1974 [Fr., ca. 1815]
Restaurant. Macmillan, 1979 [Calif.]
The Shuddering Fair One. PB, 1974 [Oreg.]
-Wreck. Ace, 1977; Magnum, 1978

COOPER, RODERICK
Blood on Blue Denim. Hale, 1977
No Place for a Tickle. Hale, 1975
Open Verdict. Hale, 1976
The Patsy Prize. Hale, 1976
The Tennyson Code. Hale, 1979

COOPER, WILL. 1929- . Ref: CA.
Death Has a Thousand Doors. Bobbs, 1976; Hale, 1979 [S.W.]

COOPERSMITH, JEROME. 1925- . Ref: CA.
Baker Street. Doubleday, 1966 (Play.)

COPE, HARLEY (FRANCIS). 1898- .
Death Stalks the Fleet. Lymanhouse, 1939 [L.A.]

COPEAU, JACQUES, 1879-1949, and JEAN CROUE
The Brothers Karamazov. Theatre Guild, 1927; Heinemann, 1927. (5-act play based on the novel by Fedor Mikhailovich Dostoevskii, 1821-1881, q.v.)

COPELAND, BILL [PAUL WILLIAM COPELAND]. 1917- . Ref: CA.
The File on Charlie. Pyramid, 1968

COPELAND, RICHARD. Pseudonym of Hugh (George) McLeave, 1923- , q.v. SC: Dr. Gregor Maclean = GM (see also the McLeave entry).
No Face in the Mirror. Macmillan (London), 1980; Walker, 1980, as by Hugh McLeave GM

COPELAND, WILLIAM. Writer for radio, TV, theatre, and film; film producer.
Five Hours from Isfahan. Putnam, 1975; Hart-Davis, 1976 [Iran, 1943]

COPP, A. E. See: S. J. Stutley.

COPP, DeWITT (S.). Pseudonym: Nick Carter, q.v. Teacher; freelance writer for radio, TV, films.
A Different Kind of Rain. Norton, 1978; Hale, 1979
The Pursuit of Agent M. Mill, 1961 [Czech.]

COPPEE, FRANCOIS (EDOUARD JOACHIM). 1842-1908.
The Guilty Man. Dillingham, 1911; Greening, 1912 (Translation of "Le Coupable." Paris, 1896.) [Fr., 1866]

COPPEL, ALEC. 1909?-1972. Ref: CA, TC.
The Gazebo. Dramatists, 1959 (Play.)
I Killed the Count. Heinemann, 1938. (Play.) Novel based on this play: Blackie, 1939
-The Last Parable. Barker, 1953
A Man About a Dog. Harrap, 1947. U.S. title: Over the Line. Doubleday, 1947. Also published as: Obsession. Corgi, 1953
Moment to Moment. GM, 1966 (Novelization of the movie.) [Fr.]
Mr. Denning Drives North. Harrap, 1950; Dutton, 1951
Obsession; see A Man About a Dog
Over the Line; see A Man About a Dog
Tweedledum and Tweedledee. Bles, 1967

COPPEL, ALFRED. 1921- . Pseudonym: A. C. Marin, q.v. Ref: CA.
The Dragon. Harcourt, 1977; Macmillan (London), 1977 [Eng.]
The Hastings Conspiracy. Holt, 1980; Macmillan (London), 1980
Thirty-Four East. Harcourt, 1974; Macmillan (London), 1974 [Mid. East]

COPPER, BASIL. 1924- . Ref: TC. SC: Mike Faraday = MF (set in L.A.); Solar Pons = SP (following August Derleth, 1909-1971, q.v.).
The Big Chill. Hale, 1972 MF
The Big Rip-Off. Hale, 1972 MF
The Breaking Point. Hale, 1973 MF
The Caligari Complex. Hale, 1980 MF
Crack in the Sidewalk. Hale, 1976 MF
The Curse of the Fleers. Harwood, 1976; St. Martin's, 1977
The Dark Mirror. Hale, 1966 MF
Dead File. Hale, 1970 MF
Death Squad. Hale, 1977 MF
Die Now, Live Later. Hale, 1968 MF
Don't Bleed on Me. Hale, 1968 MF
The Dossier of Solar Pons. Pinnacle, 1979; L.S.P. Books, 1980 ss SP [Eng., 1920s]
Feedback. Hale, 1974 MF
Flip-Side. Hale, 1980 MF
The Further Adventures of Solar Pons. Pinnacle, 1979; L.S.P. Books, 1980 ss SP [past, Eng.]
A Good Place to Die. Hale, 1975 MF
A Great Year for Dying. Hale, 1973 MF
The High Wall. Hale, 1975 MF
Impact. Hale, 1975 MF
The Lonely Place. Hale, 1976 MF
The Marble Orchard. Hale, 1969 MF
Murder One. Hale, 1978 MF
Necropolis. Arkham, 1980; Sphere, 1981 [Eng., 1800s]
Night Frost. Hale, 1966 MF
No Flowers for the General. Hale, 1967 MF

No Letters from the Grave. Hale, 1971 MF
A Quiet Room in Hell. Hale, 1979 MF
Ricochet. Hale, 1974 MF
Scratch on the Dark. Hale, 1967 MF
The Secret Files of Solar Pons. Pinnacle, 1979 ss SP [past, Eng.]
Shock-Wave. Hale, 1973 MF
Strong-Arm. Hale, 1972 MF
Tight Corner. Hale, 1976 MF
The Uncollected Cases of Solar Pons. Pinnacle, 1980 ss SP [past, Eng.]
A Voice from the Dead. Hale, 1974 MF
-Voices of Doom. Hale, 1980 ss
When Footsteps Echo. Hale, 1975; St. Martin's, 1975 ss
The Year of the Dragon. Hale, 1977 MF

COPPLESTONE, BENNET. Pseudonym of Frederick Harcourt Kitchin, 1867-1932, q.v. Ref: CC, MP. SC: Chief Insp. Dawson = D.
The Diversions of Dawson. Murray, 1923; Dutton, 1924 D ss
The Last of the Grenvilles. Murray, 1919; Dutton, 1920
The Lost Naval Papers. Murray, 1917; Dutton, 1917 D ss

CORA, JOHN LACEY
They Rubbed Him Out. Everybody's, 1944

CORAM, CHRISTOPHER. Pseudonym of Peter N(orman) Walker, 1936- , q.v. Other pseudonym: Nicholas Rhea, q.v. SC: Ross MacAllister, in at least those marked RM.
A Call to Danger. Hale, 1968
A Call to Die. Hale, 1969
Death in Ptarmigan Forest. Hale, 1970 RM
Death on the Motorway. Hale, 1973
Murder Beneath the Trees. Hale, 1977
Murder by the Lake. Hale, 1975 RM

CORBETT, MRS. GEORGE [ELIZABETH BURGOYNE CORBETT]. 1846- .
Adventures of a Lady Detective. Tudor, ca.1890 (Cited by Ellery Queen in "The Detective Short Story" and in "When the Sea Gives Up Its Dead," below, but not listed in either "The English Catalogue" or "British Museum Catalogue.") ss
The Adventures of an Ugly Girl. Collier, 1893 (British title?)
The Missing Note. Chapman, 1891
Mrs. Grundy's Victim. Tower, 1893
Secrets of a Private Enquiry Office. Routledge, 1891 ss
When the Sea Gives Up Its Dead. Tower, 1894

CORBETT, JAMES. Ref: CC.
Agent No. 5. Jenkins, 1945
The Air Killer. Jenkins, 1941
At Dawn I Die. Jenkins, 1949
The Body in the Bungalow. Jenkins, 1938
The Carteret Hotel Mystery. Jenkins, 1948; Roy, 1957
Dancing with Death. Jenkins, 1950
Death—by Appointment. Jenkins, 1945
Death Comes to Fanshawe. Jenkins, 1933
Death Is My Shadow. Jenkins, 1947
Death Makes a Date. Jenkins, 1950
The Death Pool. Jenkins, 1936
Gallows Wait. Jenkins, 1947
The Ghost Plane. Jenkins, 1939
Her Private Murder. Jenkins, 1932
Her Second Murder. Jenkins, 1940
The Hound of Death. Jenkins, 1944
The Lion's Mouth. Jenkins, 1941
The Man They Could Not Kill. Jenkins, 1935
The Man Who Saw the Devil. Jenkins, 1934
The Man with Nine Lives. Jenkins, 1938
The Merrivale Mystery. Jenkins, 1929; Mystery League, 1931
The Monster of Dagenham Hall. Jenkins, 1935
The Moon Killer. Jenkins, 1938
Murder at Night. Jenkins, 1940
Murder at Pringlehurst. Jenkins, 1933
Murder at Red Grange. Jenkins, 1931
Murder at the Palace. Jenkins, 1937
Murder Begets Murder. Jenkins, 1951
Murder Minus Motive. Jenkins, 1943
Murder While You Wait. Jenkins, 1937
No Other Killer. Jenkins, 1936
Red Dagger. Jenkins, 1934
Red Farm Mystery. Jenkins, 1935
Rendezvous with Danger. Jenkins, 1948
Rendezvous with Death. Jenkins, 1937
The Somerville Case. Jenkins, 1949
Vampire of the Skies. Jenkins, 1932
Wednesday at Noon. Jenkins, 1941
When Death Walks. Jenkins, 1941
The White Angel. Jenkins, 1931
Who Was the Killer? Jenkins, 1939
The Winterton Hotel Mystery. Jenkins, 1930

CORBIN, GARY. SC: Harry Reilly, in both titles.
Cosa Nostra Circus. Nite Time, 1964
The Last Time I Saw Mary. Jade, 1963

CORBY, JANE (IRENITA). 1899- . Pseudonyms: Jean Carew, Joanne Holden, qq.v., Laura Brighton.
As Deadly Does. Bouregy, 1961 [N.Y.]
Fall, Darkness, Fall!; see Peril at Stone House
Farewell to the Castle. Arcadia, 1967 [New Eng.]
Girl in the Tower. Arcadia, 1966
Peril at Stone House. Arcadia, 1969. Also published as: Fall, Darkness, Fall! Leisure, 1975, as by Laura Brighton
Riverwood. Arcadia, 1968
The Shadow and the Fear. Arcadia, 1968

CORCORAN, WILLIAM. 1901- . Born in Pa.; magazine editor.
The Dark Waters. Appleton, 1936; Hodder, 1936 [NYC]

CORDELL, ALEXANDER. Pseudonym of George Alexander Graber, 1914- . Ref: CA.
The Bright Cantonese. Gollancz, 1967. U.S. title: The Deadly Eurasian. Weybright, 1968 [China]
The Deadly Eurasian; see The Bright Cantonese
To Slay the Dreamer. Hodder, 1980; St. Martin's, 1980 [Sp.]

CORDELL, MELISSA
Bond of Evil. Manor, 1977
Shades of Peril. Manor, 1977

CORDER, ERIC. Pseudonym of Jerrold Mundis.
The Bite. Dell, 1975; Allen, 1976 [NYC]
Hellbottom. Allen, 1974

CORDER, R. E. Pseudonym of James Dunn.
Tales Told to the Magistrate. Melrose, 1925 ss

CORES, LUCY (MICHAELA). 1914- . Ref: CC. SC: Captain Andrew Torrent = AT.
Corpse de Ballet. Duell, 1944; Cassell, 1948 AT [NYC]
Let's Kill George. Duell, 1946; Cassell, 1950 [Conn.]
The Misty Curtain. Harper, 1964; Hale, 1965 [NYC]
Painted for the Kill. Duell, 1943; Cassell, 1946 AT [NYC]

COREY, FRANK
By Blood Alone. Berkley, 1961

COREY, HERBERT. 1872-1954
Crime at Cobb's House. Appleton, 1934; Methuen, 1935

COREY, JEAN
The Scar of Crime. Munro, 1891

CORIOLA. Pseudonym of Jane Gaillot.
Intrigue in Morocco. Mystique, 1980 (Translation of "La Troisieme Femme." Paris, 1953.) [Mor.]
Stranger at Midnight. Mystique, 1980 (Translation of "Le Voyageur de la Nuit." Paris, 1955.)

CORKILL, LOUIS
Fish Lane. Bobbs, 1951

CORLETT, WILLIAM
The Dark Side of the Moon. H. Hamilton, 1976

CORLEY, EDWIN (RAYMOND). 1931-1981. Pseudonyms: David Harper, William Judson, qq.v. Joint pseudonym with Jack Murphy: Patrick Buchanan, q.v. Ref: CA.
-Air Force One. Doubleday, 1978; Joseph, 1978 [air.]
The Jesus Factor. Stein, 1970; Joseph, 1971 [future, U.S.]
-Sargasso. Doubleday, 1977; Joseph, 1977

CORLISS, ALLENE. 1898- .
Error in Judgment. Bouregy, 1964
Unwelcome Visitor. Bouregy, 1962

CORMACK, BARTLETT. 1897?-1942.
The Racket. French (NYC), 1928 (3-act play.) [Chi.]

CORMIER, ROBERT
After the First Death. Pantheon, 1979; Gollancz, 1979

CORNE, M(OLLY) E. SC: Mac McIntyre, in all titles.

Death at a Masquerade. Mill, 1938. Also published as: Death Is No Lady. Black Knight, 1946 [Chi.]
Death at the Manor. Mill, 1938. Also published as: Death Hides a Mask. Arrow, 194? [Ohio]
Death Hides a Mask; see Death at the Manor
Death Is No Lady; see Death at a Masquerade
Jealousy Pulls the Trigger; see A Magnet for Murder
A Magnet for Murder. Mill, 1939. Also published as: Jealousy Pulls the Trigger. Double-Action Detective, 1943 [Chi.]

CORNELIUS, OLIVIA SMITH. 1882- .
The Eyes at the Window. Broadway, 1911
-The Persian Tassel. Neale, 1914

CORNELL, LOUIS. SC: Michael Joyce, in both titles.
Murder Case Number 33. Brentano's, 1932 [Okla.]
Poison Case Number 10. Brentano's, 1931 [NYC]

CORNISH, CONSTANCE. Broadway actress; wrote and acted for radio.
Dead of Winter. Simon, 1959; Cassell, 1961 [Vt.]

CORNWALLIS, KINAHAN. 1839-1917.
-Adrift with a Vengeance. Carleton, 1870
A Marvellous Coincidence; or, A Chain of Misadventures and Mysteries. Dillingham, 1891. Also published as: Two Strange Adventures; or, A Marvellous Coincidence. Neely, 1897
Two Strange Adventures; see A Marvellous Coincidence; or a Chain of Misadventures and Mysteries

CORNWELL, DAVID JOHN MOORE. 1931- . Pseudonym: John Le Carre, q.v.

CORNWELL, JOHN
The Super. Leisure, 1979

CORRADI, LOU
The Set-Up. GM, 1979

CORRADOT, JEANNE ELIZABETH MARIE JOSEPHINE. Pseudonym: Magali, q.v.

CORRELL, A. BOYD. See also: Philip MacDonald, 1899-1981. Newspaperman, writer for Walt Disney, author of magazine ss.
Murder Is an Art. Phoenix, 1950 [Calif.]

CORREN, GRACE. Pseudonym of Robert Hoskins, 1933- , q.v. Other pseudonyms: Susan Jennifer, Michael Kerr, qq.v.
The Attic Child. Pinnacle, 1979
Dark Island; see A Place on Dark Island
Dark Threshold. Popular Library, 1977
The Darkest Room. Lancer, 1969
Evil in the Family. Lancer, 1972
Mansion of Deadly Dreams. Popular Library, 1973
A Place on Dark Island. Lancer, 1971. Also published as: Dark Island. Belmont, ca.1973 [N.Y.]

CORREY, LEE. Pseudonym of George Harry Stine, 1928- . Ref: CA.
Star Driver. Ballantine, 1980 [Conn.]

CORRIE, JOE
Murder at the Play. French (London), 1948 (1-act play.)

CORRIGAN, MARK. Pseudonym of Norman Lee, 1905-1962. Other pseudonyms: Raymond Armstrong, Robertson Hobart, qq.v. Ref: CC, TC. SC: Mark Corrigan, in all titles.
All Brides Are Beautiful. Laurie, 1953
Baby Face. Laurie, 1952
Big Boys Don't Cry. Angus, 1956
The Big Squeeze. Angus, 1955 [Australia]
Bullets and Brown Eyes. Laurie, 1948
The Cruel Lady. Angus, 1957
Danger's Green Eyes. Angus, 1962 [Afr.]
Dumb As They Come. Angus, 1957 [Chi.]
The Girl from Moscow. Angus, 1959
The Golden Angel. Laurie, 1950
Honolulu Snatch. Angus, 1958 [Haw.]
I Like Danger. Laurie, 1954 [Midwest]
Lady from Tokyo. Angus, 1960 [Tokyo]
Lady of China Street. Laurie, 1952
Love for Sale. Laurie, 1954
Lovely Lady. Laurie, 1950
Madam and Eve. Laurie, 1955
Madame Sly. Laurie, 1951

Menace in Siam. Angus, 1958 [Bangkok]
The Naked Lady. Laurie, 1954
Riddle of Double Island. Angus, 1962 [Scot.]
The Riddle of the Spanish Circus. Angus, 1964 [Sp.]
Shanghai Jezebel. Laurie, 1951 [Shanghai]
Sin of Hong Kong. Angus, 1960 [H. Kong]
Singapore Downbeat. Angus, 1959 [Sing.]
Sinner Takes All. Laurie, 1949
Sweet and Deadly. Laurie, 1953
Sydney for Sin. Angus, 1956
The Wayward Blonde. Laurie, 1950
Who Do Women...? Angus, 1963

CORTAZAR, JULIO. 1914- . Ref: CA.
End of the Game, and other stories. Pantheon, 1967 (Translation from the Spanish.) ss, at least one criminous

CORY, DESMOND. Pseudonym of Shaun (Lloyd) McCarthy, 1928- , q.v. Other pseudonym: Theo Callas, q.v. Ref: CA, CC, TC. SC: Johnny Fedora, in at least those marked JF; Linda Gray, in at least those marked LG; Mr. Dee, in at least those marked D; Mr. Pilgrim, in at least those marked P.
Begin, Murderer! Muller, 1951 LG
Bennett. Macmillan (London), 1977; Doubleday, 1977 [Sp.]
A Bit of a Shunt Up the River. Doubleday, 1974
The Circe Complex. Macmillan (London), 1975; Doubleday, 1975 [Wales]
Deadfall. Muller, 1965; Walker, 1965 [Sp.]
Dead Man Falling. Muller, 1953. U.S. title: The Hitler Diamonds. Award, 1969 JF [Austria]
Dead Men Alive; see Height of Day
Even If You Run; see Take My Drum to England
Feramontov. Muller, 1966; Walker, 1966 JF [Sp.]
The Gestapo File; see This Traitor, Death
Hammerhead. Muller, 1963. U.S. title: Shockwave. Walker, 1964 JF [Madrid]
The Head. Muller, 1960 JF
Height of Day. Muller, 1955. U.S. title: Dead Men Alive. Award, 1969 JF [Afr.]
High Requiem. Muller, 1965; Award, 1969 JF
The Hitler Diamonds; see Dead Man Falling
Intrigue. Muller, 1954. U.S. title: Trieste. Award, 1968 JF [It.]
Johnny Goes East. Muller, 1958. U.S. title: Mountainhead. Award, 1968 JF [Tib.]
Johnny Goes North. Muller, 1956. U.S. title: The Swastika Hunt. Award, 1969 JF
Johnny Goes South. Muller, 1959; Walker, 1964. Also published as: Overload. New English Library pb, 1966 JF [Arg.]
Johnny Goes West. Muller, 1959; Walker, 1967 JF [S. Am.]
Lady Lost. Muller, 1953 LG
Mountainhead; see Johnny Goes East
The Name of the Game. Muller, 1964 D
The Nazi Assassins; see Secret Ministry
The Night Hawk. Hodder, 1969; Walker, 1969 [Sp.]
Overload; see Johnny Goes South
The Phoenix Sings. Muller, 1955
Pilgrim at the Gate. Muller, 1957; Washburn, 1958 P
Pilgrim on the Island. Muller, 1959; Walker, 1961 P [Ger.]
Secret Ministry. Muller, 1951. U.S. title: The Nazi Assassins. Award, 1970 JF
The Shaken Leaf. Muller, 1955 LG
Shockwave; see Hammerhead
Stranglehold. Muller, 1961 D
Sunburst. Hodder, 1971; Walker, 1971 JF [Sp.]
The Swastika Hunt; see Johnny Goes North
Take My Drum to England. Hodder, 1971. U.S. title: Even If You Run. Doubleday, 1972 [Sp.]
This Is Jezebel. Muller, 1952 LG
This Traitor, Death. Muller, 1952. U.S. title: The Gestapo File. Award, 1971 JF [Paris]
Timelock. Muller, 1967; Walker, 1967 JF [Sp.]
Trieste; see Intrigue
Undertow. Muller, 1962; Walker, 1963 JF [Sp.]

CORYELL, JOHN R(USSELL). 1851-1924. Pseudonyms: Nicholas Carter, Geraldine Fleming, qq.v.
A Woman's Hand; or, Detective's Wit Against Lawyer's Wiles. Street, 1890

COSGRAVE, PATRICK. 1941- . Ref: CA.
Cheyney's Law. Macmillan (London), 1977
The Three Colonels. Macmillan (London), 1979

COSSERY, ALBERT. 1913- .
The House of Certain Death. Hutchinson, 1947; New Directions, 1949 (Translation of "La Maison de la Mort Certaine." Paris, 1947.)

COSTELLO, PAUL. SC: Terence O'Hara, in at least those marked TO.
Blue Diamond. Cassell, 1962 TO
The Cat and the Fiddle. Cassell, 1961
The Long Silence. Hale, 1957 TO
Mortgage for Murder. Cassell, 1960 TO
The Red Beard. Hale, 1958 TO

COSTIGAN, LEE
Never Kill a Cop. PB, 1959
The New Breed. GM, 1962; Muller pb, 1963 (Novelization of the TV series.)

COTELO, C. S.
White Line Fever. Signet, 1975; New English Library pb, 1975, as by Peter (Leslie) Cave, 1940- , q.v.

COTLER, GORDON. 1923- . Pseudonym: Alex Gordon, q.v. Ref: CA.
The Bottletop Affair. Simon, 1959. Also published as: The Horizontal Lieutenant. Dell, 1962 [S. Pac.]
The Horizontal Lieutenant; see The Bottletop Affair
Mission in Black. Random, 1967; Heinemann, 1968 [Carib.]

COTTAR, GUY. Pseudonym of Clive Garsia.
Tenacity. Jarrolds, 1927

COTTE, JEAN LOUIS. 1923- .
The Trap. Abelard, 1961 (Translation of "L'Appat." Paris, 1958.)

COTTER, JOHN and JUDITH FRANKLE
-Nights with Sasquatch. Berkley, 1977

COTTERELL, BRIAN. Pseudonym of Aylward Edward Dingle, 1874-1947.
Sinister Eden. Harrap, 1934; Lippincott, 1934

COTTINGHAM, BARRY
-Forbidden by Law. Trischler, 1891
Kinsman to Death. Remington, 1893

COTTON, JERRY. House name.
In the Lion's Den. Three Star, 1965

COTTON, JOSE MARIO GARRY ORDONEZ EDMONDSON Y. 1922- . Pseudonym: Kelly P. Gast, q.v.

COTTON, R. T.
Mr. Carington. King, 1873

COTTON, WILL
The Night Was Made for Murder. Avon, 1959 [Boston]

COUGHLIN, HANORAH
-Strange Fates; or, Detta. Broadway, 1904

COUGHLIN, WILLIAM J(EREMIAH). 1924- .
Day of Wrath. Delacorte, 1980
The Destruction Committee. Harrap, 1971 [U.S.]
The Dividend Was Death. Jenkins, 1968
The Stalking Man. Delacorte, 1979; Magnum, 1981 [Midwest]
The Widow Wondered Why. Hammond, 1966

COULSON, FELICITY WINIFRED CARTER. 1907- . Pseudonym: Emery Bonett, q.v. Joint pseudonym with John Hubert Arthur Coulson, 1906- : John and Emery Bonett, q.v.

COULSON, JOHN HUBERT ARTHUR. 1906- Joint pseudonym with Felicity Winifred Carter Coulson, 1907- : John and Emery Bonett, q.v.

COULSON, JUANITA. 1933- . Ref: CA.
Door into Terror. Berkley, 1972
Fear Stalks the Bayou. Ballantine, 1976; Magnum, 1976 [New Or.]
The Secret of Seven Oaks. Berkley, 1972
Stone of Blood. Beagle, 1975 [Wis.]

COULSON, ROBERT STRATTON. 1928- . Ref: CA. Joint pseudonym with (Thomas Eu)Gene DeWeese, 1934- , q.v.: Thomas Stratton, q.v.

COULSON, THOMAS. 1886- .
The Queen of Spies. Constable, 1935 (Novelized biography of Louise de Bettignies.)

COULTER, H. G.
Death Comes to Casanova. Manthorne, 1945 [Calif.]

COULTER, STEPHEN. 1913- . Pseudonym: James Mayo, q.v. Ref: TC.
An Account to Render. Heinemann, 1970
Death in the Sun; see A Stranger Called the Blues
Embassy. Heinemann, 1969; Coward, 1969
-The Loved Enemy. Deutsch, 1952
Offshore! Heinemann, 1965; Morrow, 1966
Players in a Dark Game; see A Stranger Called the Blues
The Soyuz Affair. Hart-Davis, 1977
A Stranger Called the Blues. Heinemann, 1968. U.S. title: Players in a Dark Game. Morrow, 1968. Also published as: Death in the Sun. Pan, 1970
Threshold. Heinemann, 1964; Morrow, 1964

COULTON, MARY JANE. Pseudonym: Sarah Campion, q.v.

COUNSEL, FIRTH
Juvenile Jungle. Avon, 1958; Panther, 1962 (Novelization of the movie.)

COURAGE, JOHN. Pseudonym of Richard Goyne, 1902-1957, q.v. SC: William Brittain, in at least those marked WB; David Cane, in at least those marked DC. Set: Eng.
The Affair Ravel. Paul, 1948 WB [Fr.]
The Buccaneer's Parrot. Puzzle Books, 1933
A Corpse for Charlie. Paul, 1957
Death Goes to the Fair. Paul, 1937 DC
Death of a Gentleman. Paul, 1951
Death of a Village. Paul, 1954
Death on Tour. Paul, 1937 DC
The Dread Cave. Paul, 1952 WB
Four Doors to Death. Paul, 1936 DC
The House with a Past. Paul, 1955
International Commando. Paul, 1944
Lakeland Tragedy. Paul, 1947 WB
Made to Murder. Paul, 1957
Murder Run Riot. Paul, 1940
My Wife's Lover. Paul, 1953
Nightingales Never Sing. Paul, 1950 [Scot.]
No Moon Tonight. Paul, 1950
The Obliging Corpse. Paul, 1954
The Parker Case. Paul, 1958
Perhaps the Prodigal. Paul, 1953
Spooks Sometimes Sing. Paul, 1946
They All Came Back. Paul, 1945 DC
We the Unworthy. Paul, 1944
Who Screamed? Paul, 1939 DC
Why Murder Mrs. Hope? Paul, 1940 DC

COURNOS, JOHN. 1881-1966. Pseudonyms: John Courtney, Mark Gault, qq.v.

COURT, KATHERINE
But Don't Go Alone. Playboy, 1978 [Nepal]

COURT, S.
The Black Mask. Modern, 193?

COURTENEY, CECIL
Link by Link. Bevington, 1886
-Traced Through a Dream. Arrowsmith, 1887

COURTENEY, T(HOMAS) G.
The Fayolle Formula. Jenkins, 1934

COURTIER, S(IDNEY) H(OBSON). 1904-1974. Ref: CA, CC, EM, TC. SC: Insp. "Digger" Haig, in at least those marked DH; Insp./Supt. Ambrose Mahon, in at least those marked AM. Set: Australia.
Come Back to Murder. Hammond, 1957 AM
A Corpse at Least. Hammond, 1966 DH
A Corpse Won't Sing. Hammond, 1964 AM
Dead If I Remember. Hale, 1972
Death in Dream Time. Hammond, 1959 DH
Gently Dust the Corpse. Hammond, 1960. Also published as: Softly Dust the Corpse. Corgi, 1961
The Glass Spear. Dakers, 1952; Wyn, 1950 AM
Let the Man Die. Hammond, 1961 AM
Ligny's Lake. Hale, 1971; Simon, 1971
Listen to the Mocking Bird. Hale, 1974
Mimic a Murderer. Hammond, 1964 AM
Murder's Burning. Hammond, 1967; Random, 1968
No Obelisk for Emily. Jenkins, 1970 DH
Now Seek My Bones. Hammond, 1957 DH
One Cried Murder. Hammond, 1956; Rinehart, 1954 AM
The Ringnecker. Hammond, 1965 DH
See Who's Dying. Hammond, 1967
A Shroud for Unlac. Hammond, 1958 AM
Softly Dust the Corpse; see Gently Dust the Corpse
Some Village Borgia. Hale, 1971

Swing High, Sweet Murder. Hammond, 1962 DH
Who Dies for Me? Hammond, 1962
A Window in Chungking. Hale, 1975

COURTIS, GERALD
  The Big Noise. Hale, 1977
  The Spider Game. Hale, 1976

COURTNEY, JOHN. Pseudonym of John Cournos, 1881-1966. Other pseudonym: Mark Gault, q.v. Ref: CA.
  Grandmother Martin Is Murdered. Skeffington, 1930; Farrar, 1930, as by John Cournos

COURTNEY-BROWNE, REGINALD DAVID STANLEY. 1915- . Pseudonym: Courtney Browne, q.v.

COUSIN, MICHEL. Film director,
  Where Did the Girls Go? Stein, 1969 (Translation of "Detournement de Mineurs." Paris, 1967.)

COUSINS, E(DMUND) G(EORGE). 1893- .
  SC: Colonel Richard Barne, in at least those marked RB. Set: Eng.
  Any Kind of Danger. Benn, 1951
  Body Behind the Curtain. Gifford, 1966 RB
  -Come Like a Storm. Benn, 1950
  Death by Marriage. Gifford, 1959 RB
  Death by Treble Chance. Gifford, 1959 RB
  Death in a Quiet Place. Gifford, 1967 RB
  Dressed Up to Kill. Panther, 1961
  Fear of Mr. Taltry. Gifford, 1960 RB
  -Give Me That Man. Collins, 1955
  -Great Elk. Jenkins, 1956
  Harlot's House. Panther, 1960
  -Moab Is My Washpot. Benn, 1952. Also published as: Wine of War. Panther, 1959
  Murder in the Top Drawer. Gifford, 1964 RB
  Sapphire. Panther, 1959 (Novelization of the movie.)
  -To Comfort the Signora. Benn, 1951
  -Untimely Frost. Benn, 1953
  Weekend with Maxwell. Gifford, 1961 [Calif.]
  Wine of War; see Moab Is My Washpot

COUSINS, MARGARET. 1905- . Pseudonym: Avery Johns, q.v.

COUSSEAU, JACQUES
  The Death of Miss Cunningham. Faber, 1962 (Translation of "Les Singes." Paris, 1960.)

COVER, ARTHUR BYRON
  An East Wind Coming. Berkley, 1979

COVERACK, GILBERT. Pseudonym of J(ohn) Russell Warren, 1886- , q.v.
  SC: Insp. M'Guire = M (also under the J. Russell Warren byline).
  ATS Mystery. Hurst, 1943; Macmillan, 1944
  The Magpie Murder. Earl, 1947; Sheridan, 1942, as by J. Russell Warren M
  Time for a Murder. Hurst, 1941; Sheridan, 1941, as by J. Russell Warren M

COVERDALE, HARRY. Pseudonym (?) of Anna Alice Chapin, 1880-1920.
  The Seventh Shot. Chelsea, 1924; Skeffington, 1926 [NYC]
  The Unknown Seven. Chelsea, 1923; Unwin, 1924 [NYC]

COVERT, PAUL. 1941- . Ref: CA.
  Escape to Nowhere. McKay, 1976

COWAN, BERTHA MUZZY BOWEN SINCLAIR. 1874-1940. Pseudonym: B. M. Bower, q.v.

COWAN, G. K. Set: Wales, in both titles.
  The Cry in the Valley. Jenkins, 1934
  The Fanshaw Case. Jenkins, 1933

COWAN, SADA
  Bitter Justice. Doubleday, 1943; Gifford, 1946 [NYC]

COWDROY, JOAN. SC: Li Moh, in at least those marked LM; Chief Insp. Gorham, in at least those marked G. Set: Eng.
  Death Has No Tongue. Hutchinson, 1938 LM
  Disappearance. Hutchinson, 1934 LM
  The Flying Dagger Murder; see Watch Mr. Moh
  Framed Evidence. Hutchinson, 1936 G
  -The Mask. Hutchinson, 1928
  Merry-Go-Round. Hutchinson, 1940 LM
  Murder of Lydia. Hutchinson, 1933 LM
  Murder out of Court. Hutchinson, 1944 G
  Murder Unsuspected. Hutchinson, 1936 LM
  Mystery of Sett. Hutchinson, 1930
  Nine Green Bottles. Hutchinson, 1939
  Watch Mr. Moh. Hutchinson, 1931. U.S. title: The Flying Dagger Murder. McBride, 1932 LM

COWEN, FRANCES. 1915- . Pseudonym: Eleanor Hyde, q.v. Ref: CA, TC. Set: Eng.
  The Balcony. Gresham, 1962
  The Bitter Reason. Gresham, 1966
  The Curse of the Clodaghs. Hale, 1973; Ace, 1974 [Ire.]
  The Dangerous Child. Hale, 1975
  The Daylight Fear. Hale, 1969; Ace, 1973
  The Desperate Holiday. Gresham, 1962
  The Edge of Terror. Hale, 1970
  The Elusive Quest. Gresham, 1965
  The Fractured Silence. Hale, 1969
  The Gentle Obsession. Hale, 1968
  The Haunting of Helen Farley. Hale, 1976
  The Hounds of Carvello. Hale, 1970; Ace, 1973
  Lake of Darkness. Hale, 1971; Ace, 1974
  The Little Heiress. Gresham, 1961
  The Lost One. Hale, 1977
  The Medusa Connection. Hale, 1976
  The Nightmare Ends. Hale, 1970; Ace, 1972
  The One Between. Hale, 1967
  Scented Danger. Gresham, 1966
  The Secret of Weir House. Hale, 1975
  The Shadow of Polperro. Hale, 1969; Ace, 1973
  Shadow of Theale. Hale, 1974; Ace, 1974
  The Silent Pool. Hale, 1977
  Sinister Melody. Hale, 1976
  A Step in the Dark. Gresham, 1962
  The Unforgiving Moment. Hale, 1971
  The Village of Fear. Hale, 1975; Ace, 1974

COWEN, RON
  The Book of Murder. Dramatists, 1974 (1-act play.)

COWLES, JOHN CLIFFORD
  The Whispering Buddha. Hollyway, 1932

COX, A(NTHONY) B(ERKELEY). 1893-1970. Pseudonyms: Anthony Berkeley, Francis Iles, qq.v. Ref: see Anthony Berkeley.
  Mr. Priestley's Problem. Collins, 1927. U.S. title: The Amateur Crime. Doubleday, 1928

COX, ANNE. Pseudonym: Annabel Gray, q.v.

COX, ANNE-MARIE
  Danger at Hand. Chivers, 1976
  Fair Exchange. Chivers, 1976

COX, CONSTANCE. 1915- .
  Lady Audley's Secret. French (London), 1976 (Play based on the novel by M. E. Braddon, 1837-1915, q.v.)
  Lord Arthur Savile's Crime. French (London), 1963 (Play adapted from the story by Oscar Wilde, 1854-1900, q.v.)
  The Murder Game. French (London), 1976 (Play.)

COX, SIR EDMUND C(HARLES). 1856- .
  SC: John Carruthers = JC.
  The Achievements of John Carruthers. Constable, 1911 JC ss [India]
  The Exploits of Kesho Naik, Dacoit. Constable, 1912 ss [India]
  John Carruthers: Indian Policeman. Cassell, 1905 JC ss [India]

COX, H(ARRY) H(UBERT). See: Tom Gurr.

COX, IRVING E., JR.
  Murder Among Friends. Abelard, 1957; Nelson, 1957 [Calif.]

COX, RICHARD (HUBERT FRANCIS). 1931- . Ref: CA.
  Auction. Hutchinson, 1979. U.S. title: The Botticelli Madonna. McGraw, 1979
  The Botticelli Madonna; see Auction
  SAM 7. Hutchinson, 1977; Reader's Digest Press, 1977

COX, S. A. D. Pseudonym: Nicholas Carter, q.v.

COX, THOMAS R.
  Shadows of One Another. Exposition, 1971

COX, WILLIAM R(OBERT). 1901- . SC: Tom Kincaid = TK.
  Death Comes Early. Dell, 1961 [NYC]
  Death on Location. Signet, 1962 TK [Nev.]
  Hell to Pay. Signet, 1958 TK
  Hot Times. GM, 1973
  -The Lusty Men. Pyramid, 1957
  Make My Coffin Strong. GM, 1954; Fawcett (London), 1955
  Murder in Vegas. Signet, 1960 TK [Las Veg.]
  The Tycoon and the Tigress. GM, 1958 [L.A.]
  Way to Go, Doll Baby! Banner, 1967

COXE, GEORGE HARMON. 1901- . See also: Stephen Bristol. Ref: CA, CC, EM, MC, MP, TC. SC: Flash Casey = FC (see also: Paul Ayres); Sam Crombie = SC; Jack Fenner = JF; Max Hale = MH; Kent Murdock = KM.
  Alias the Dead. Knopf, 1943 [Conn.]
  Assignment in Guiana. Knopf, 1942; Macdonald, 1943 [Guiana]
  The Barotique Mystery. Knopf, 1936; Heinemann, 1937. Also published as: Murdock's Acid Test. Dell, 1947 KM [Carib.]
  The Big Gamble. Knopf, 1958; Hammond, 1960 KM [Boston]
  The Camera Clue. Knopf, 1937; Heinemann, 1938 KM [Boston]
  The Candid Imposter. Knopf, 1967; Hale, 1969 [Pan.]
  The Charred Witness. Knopf, 1942; Swan, 1949 KM,JF [Conn.]
  The Crimson Clue. Knopf, 1953; Hammond, 1955 KM [Boston]
  Dangerous Legacy. Knopf, 1946; Hammond, 1949 [Manila]
  Deadly Image. Knopf, 1964; Hammond, 1964 FC [Boston]
  Death at the Isthmus. Knopf, 1954; Hammond, 1956 [Pan.]
  Double Identity. Knopf, 1970; Hale, 1971 [Suri.]
  An Easy Way to Go. Knopf, 1969; Hale, 1969 KM [Boston]
  Error of Judgment. Knopf, 1961; Hammond, 1962. Also published as: One Murder Too Many. Pyramid, 1969 FC [Boston]
  Eye Witness. Knopf, 1950; Hammond, 1963 KM [Mass.]
  Fashioned for Murder. Knopf, 1947; Hammond, 1950 [NYC]
  Fenner. Knopf, 1971; Hale, 1973 JF,KM [Boston]
  The Fifth Key. Knopf, 1947; Hammond, 1950 KM [NYC]
  Flash Casey, Detective. Avon, 1946 (4 1930's pulp novelets with FC.)
  Focus on Murder. Knopf, 1954; Hammond, 1956 KM [Boston]
  Four Frightened Women. Knopf, 1939; Heinemann, 1939 KM,JF [Boston]
  The Frightened Fiancee. Knopf, 1950; Hammond, 1953 SC [Conn.]
  The Glass Triangle. Knopf, 1940 KM [Boston]
  The Groom Lay Dead. Knopf, 1944; Hammond, 1946 [N.Y.]
  The Hidden Key. Knopf, 1963; Hammond, 1964 KM [Boston]
  The Hollow Needle. Knopf, 1948; Hammond, 1951 KM [Boston]
  The Impetuous Mistress. Knopf, 1958; Hammond, 1959 SC [Conn.]
  Inland Passage. Knopf, 1949; Hammond, 1952 [ship]
  The Inside Man. Knopf, 1974; Hale, 1975 [Belize]
  The Jade Venus. Knopf, 1945; Hammond, 1947 KM [Boston]
  The Lady Is Afraid. Knopf, 1940; Heinemann, 1940 MH
  Lady Killer. Knopf, 1949; Hammond, 1952 KM [Boston]
  The Last Commandment. Knopf, 1960; Hammond, 1961 KM [Boston]
  Man on a Rope. Knopf, 1956; Hammond, 1958 [Guy.]
  The Man Who Died Too Soon. Knopf, 1962; Hammond, 1963 FC [Boston]
  The Man Who Died Twice. Knopf, 1951; Hammond, 1954 [Barbados]
  Mission of Fear. Knopf, 1962; Hammond, 1963 [Conn.]
  Moment of Violence. Knopf, 1961; Hammond, 1962 [Barbados]
  Mrs. Murdock Takes a Case. Knopf, 1941; Swan, 1949 KM [Boston]
  Murder for the Asking. Knopf, 1939; Heinemann, 1940 MH
  Murder for Two. Knopf, 1943; Hammond, 1944 FC [Boston]
  Murder in Havana. Knopf, 1943; Hammond, 1945 [Havana]
  Murder on Their Minds. Knopf, 1957; Hammond, 1958 KM [Boston]
  Murder with Pictures. Knopf, 1935; Heinemann, 1937 KM [Boston]
  Murdock's Acid Test; see The Barotique Mystery
  Never Bet Your Life. Knopf, 1952; Hammond, 1955 [Fla.]
  No Place for Murder. Knopf, 1975; Hale, 1976 JF [Boston]
  No Time to Kill. Knopf, 1941 [Boston]

One Hour to Kill. Knopf, 1963; Hammond, 1964 [Trin.]
One Minute Past Eight. Knopf, 1957; Hammond, 1959 [Caracas]
One Murder Too Many; see Error of Judgment
One Way Out. Knopf, 1960; Hammond, 1961 [New Or.]
The Reluctant Heiress. Knopf, 1965; Hammond, 1966 KM [Boston]
The Ring of Truth. Knopf, 1966; Hammond, 1967
Silent Are the Dead. Knopf, 1942 FC [Boston]
The Silent Witness. Knopf, 1973; Hale, 1974 JF,KM [Boston]
Slack Tide. Knopf, 1959; Hammond, 1960 [Conn.]
Suddenly a Widow. Knopf, 1956; Hammond, 1957 [Conn.]
Top Assignment. Knopf, 1955; Hammond, 1957
Uninvited Guest. Knopf, 1953; Hammond, 1956 [Barbados]
Venturous Lady. Knopf, 1948; Hammond, 1951
The Widow Had a Gun. Knopf, 1951; Hammond, 1954 KM [Boston]
With Intent to Kill. Knopf, 1965; Hammond, 1965 [Belize]
Woman at Bay. Knopf, 1945; Hammond, 1948 [Havana]
Woman with a Gun. Knopf, 1972; Hale, 1974 [Carib.]

COXE, KATHLEEN BUDDINGTON. Joint pseudonym of Amelia Reynolds Long, 1904-1978, q.v., and Edna McHugh. Other Long pseudonyms: Patrick Laing, Adrian Reynolds, Peter Reynolds, qq.v.
Murder Most Foul. Phoenix, 1946 [acad.]

COXE, VIRGINIA ROSALIE
The Embassy Ball. Neely, 1897

COXWELL, HENRY (TRACEY). 1819-1900.
A Knight of the Air; or, The Aerial Rivals. Digby, 1895

COY, STANLEE. Joint pseudonym with Carolyn Nichols: Iona Charles, q.v.

COYLE, JOHN B.
Man from the S.A.S. New Horizon, 1979

COZZENS, JAMES GOULD. 1903-1978. Ref: CA, CC.
The Just and the Unjust. Harcourt, 1942; Cape, 1943

CRABB, ARTHUR. Pseudonym. SC: Samuel Lyle, in both titles.
Ghosts. Century, 1921. British title: Mrs. Brown's Pearls. Page (London), 1921 [New Eng.]
Mrs. Brown's Pearls; see Ghosts
Samuel Lyle, Criminologist. Century, 1920 ss

CRABB, NED
Ralph; or, What's Eating the Folks in Fatchakulla County? Morrow, 1979 [Fla.]

CRABTREE, SIMON. SC: Hector Tumbler = HT, in both titles. Set: Eng.
Forgotten Memories. Jarrolds, 1941 ss, including 1 about HT
Hector Tumbler Investigates. Jarrolds, 1943 ss

CRADDOCK, CHARLES EGBERT. Pseudonym of Mary Noailles Murfree, 1850-1922.
The Mystery of Witch-Face Mountain, and other stories. Houghton, 1895 ss

CRADDOCK, IRVING
The Yazoo Mystery. Britton, 1919 [New Or.]

CRADOCK, PHYLLIS NAN SORTAIN. Pseudonym: Frances Dale, q.v.

CRAGG, E. H.
Almack, the Detective. London Literary Society, 1886

CRAIG, ALISA. Pseudonym of Charlotte (Matilda Hughes) MacLeod, 1922- q.v.
A Pint of Murder. Doubleday, 1980 [Can.]

CRAIG, BILL. 1930-   . Ref: CA.
Scobie in September. Hutchinson, 1971. U.S. title: September Can Be Dangerous in Edinburgh. Walker, 1971 [Scot.]

CRAIG, DAVID. Pseudonym of (Allan) James Tucker, 1929- , q.v. SC: Stephen Bellecroix and Sheila Roath, in at least those marked B&R; Roy Rickman, in at least those marked RR. Set: Eng.
The Albion Case. Macmillan (London), 1975
The Alias Man. Cape, 1968; Stein, 1968 RR [Eng., 1970s]
Bolthole. Macmillan (London), 1973. U.S. title: Knifeman. Stein, 1973
Contact Lost. Cape, 1970; Stein, 1970 RR [Eng., 1970s]
A Dead Liberty. Macmillan (London), 1974
Double Take. Macmillan (London), 1972; Stein, 1972
Faith, Hope and Death. Macmillan (London), 1976
Knifeman; see Bolthole
Message Ends. Cape, 1969; Stein, 1969 RR [Eng., 1970s]
The Squeeze. Stein, 1974 (British title?)
Up from the Grave. Macmillan (London), 1971
A Walk at Night. Macmillan (London), 1971; Stein, 1971 B&R
Whose Little Girl Are You? Macmillan (London), 1974
Young Men May Die. Cape, 1970; Stein, 1970 B&R

CRAIG, JOHN (ERNEST). 1921-   . Ref: CA.
Close Doesn't Count. Macmillan (Toronto), 1975; Macdonald, 1975
If You Want to See Your Wife Again. Putnam, 1971; Cassell, 1973 [Can.]
In Council Rooms Apart. Putnam, 1971 [Can.]
Superdude. Paperback Library, 1974

CRAIG, JONATHAN. Pseudonym of Frank E. Smith, 1919-   . Ref: CC. SC: Pete Selby = PS.
Alley Girl. Lion, 1954. Also published as: Renegade Cop. Berkley, 1959
The Case of the Beautiful Body. GM, 1957; Fawcett (London), 1958 PS [NYC]
Case of the Brazen Beauty. GM, 1966 PS [NYC]
Case of the Cold Coquette. GM, 1957; Fawcett (London), 1958 PS [NYC]
Case of the Laughing Virgin. GM, 1960 PS [NYC]
Case of the Nervous Nude. GM, 1959; Muller pb, 1960 PS [NYC]
Case of the Petticoat Murder. GM, 1958; Fawcett (London), 1960 PS [NYC]
Case of the Silent Stranger. GM, 1964 PS [NYC]
Case of the Village Tramp. GM, 1959; Muller pb, 1961 PS [NYC]
Come Night, Come Evil. GM, 1957; Red Seal, 1959
The Dead Darling. GM, 1955; Red Seal, 1958 PS [NYC]
Morgue for Venus. GM, 1956; Fawcett (London), 1957 PS [NYC]
Red-Headed Sinner. Croydon, 1953
Renegade Cop; see Alley Girl
So Young, So Wicked. GM, 1957; Fawcett (London), 1958 PS [N.Y.]

CRAIG, MARY. 1923-   . Byline also: Mary Francis (Craig) Shura, q.v. Ref: CA.
A Candle for the Dragon. Dell, 1973
The Cranes of Ibycus. Hawthorn, 1974. Also published as: Shadows of the Past. Manor, 1976 [West]
Mistress of Lost River; see Ten Thousand Several Doors
Shadows of the Past; see The Cranes of Ibycus
Ten Thousand Several Doors. Hawthorn, 1973. Also published as: Mistress of Lost River. Manor, 1966
Were He a Stranger. Dodd, 1978; Collins, 1979 [Calif.]

CRAIG, PETER. Pseudonym of Victor MacLure, 1887-1963, q.v.
Conspiracy Island. Harrap, 1933

CRAIG, PHILIP (R.). 1933-   . Ref: CA.
Gate of Ivory, Gate of Horn. Doubleday, 1969; Macmillan (London), 1970 [Swed.]

CRAIG, (CHARLES WILLIAM) THURLOW. 1901-   . SC: Lt. Bunjy Hearne, in at least those marked BH.
-Bitter Is the Harvest. Hutchinson, 1949
The Changed Face. Hutchinson, 1939 BH
-Ghost Mesa. Hutchinson, 1944
-Love Under Smoke. Hutchinson, 1937
Plague over London. Hutchinson, 1939 BH
-The River of Diamonds. Hutchinson, 1945
-The Swamp of Cardelli. Hutchinson, 1947
-West of Rio Grande. Hutchinson, 1948
White Girls Eastward. Hutchinson, 1938 BH

CRAIG, WILLIAM. 1929-   . Born in Mass.; M.A. in history from Columbia U.
The Strasbourg Legacy. Reader's Digest, 1975; Hodder, 1976 [Ger.]
The Tashkent Crisis. Dutton, 1971; Hodder, 1971

CRAIGIE, HAMILTON
Derring-Do. Detective Tales, 19?? (62 pp. mini-paperback.)

CRAIL, LOU
The Strange Legacy of Aunt Bettina. Manor, 1978

CRANBROOK, SHELDON
The King of the Peak. Wright, 1937
The Spider of Soho. Wright, 1937

CRANDALL, EDWARD
White Violets. Little, 1954 [New Eng.]

CRANDOLPH, AUGUSTUS JACOB
The Mysterious Hand; or, Subterranean Horrours! Newman, 1811

CRANE, ALEX. Pseudonym of R(ichard) Wilkes-Hunter, 1906-   , q.v. Other pseudonyms: Marc Brody, Tod Conrad, qq.v.
Bushman. Horwitz, 1959
One Night of Fear. Horwitz, 1959

CRANE, CAROLINE. 1930-   . Ref: CA.
The Girls Are Missing. Dodd, 1980; Hale, 1981 [N.Y.]
Summer Girl. Dodd, 1979 [L.I.]

CRANE, FRANCES. 1896-   . Ref: CC, EM, TC. SC: Pat and Jean Abbott, in at least those marked A.
The Amber Eyes. Random, 1962; Hammond, 1962 A [S.F.]
The Amethyst Spectacles. Random, 1944; Hammond, 1946 A [New Mex.]
The Applegreen Cat. Lippincott, 1943; Hammond, 1945 A [Eng.]
Black Cypress. Random, 1948; Hammond, 1950 A [Calif.]
Body Beneath a Mandarin Tree. Hammond, 1965 A
The Buttercup Case. Random, 1958; Hammond, 1958 A [La.]
The Cinnamon Murder. Random, 1946; Hammond, 1948 A [NYC]
The Coral Princess Murders. Random, 1954; Hammond, 1955 A [Tangier]
The Daffodil Blonde. Random, 1950; Hammond, 1951 A [Ky.]
Death in Lilac Time. Random, 1955; Hammond, 1955 A [Ky.]
Death in the Blue Hour; see Murder in Blue Street
Death-Wish Green. Random, 1960; Hammond, 1960 A [S.F.]
The Flying Red Horse. Random, 1949; Hammond, 1949 A [Dallas]
The Golden Box. Lippincott, 1942; Hammond, 1944 A [Ill.]
The Gray Stranger; see The Man in Gray
Horror on the Ruby X. Random, 1956; Hammond, 1956 A [New Mex.]
The Indigo Necklace. Random, 1945; Hammond, 1947. Also published as: The Indigo Necklace Murders. Bantam, 1949 A [New Or.]
The Indigo Necklace Murders; see The Indigo Necklace
The Man in Gray. Random, 1958. British title: The Gray Stranger. Hammond, 1958 A [S.F.]
Murder in Blue Street. Random, 1951. British title: Death in the Blue Hour. Hammond, 1952 A [Paris]
Murder in Bright Red. Random, 1953; Hammond, 1954 A
Murder on the Purple Water. Random, 1947; Hammond, 1949 A [Fla.]
The Pink Umbrella. Lippincott, 1943; Hammond, 1944. Also published as: The Pink Umbrella Murder. Popular Library, 1950 A [NYC]
The Pink Umbrella Murder; see The Pink Umbrella
The Polkadot Murder. Random, 1951; Hammond, 1952 A [New Mex.]
The Reluctant Sleuth. Hammond, 1961
The Shocking Pink Hat. Random, 1946; Hammond, 1948 A [S.F.]
13 White Tulips. Random, 1953; Hammond, 1953 A [S.F.]
Three Days in Hong Kong. Hammond, 1965 [H. Kong]
The Turquoise Shop. Lippincott, 1941; Hammond, 1943 A [New Mex.]
The Ultraviolet Widow. Random, 1956; Hammond, 1957 A [Mex.]
A Very Quiet Murder. Hammond, 1966
Worse Than a Crime. Hale, 1968
The Yellow Violet. Lippincott, 1942; Hammond, 1944 [S.F.]

CRANE, ROBERT. Pseudonym of Con(nie Leslie) Sellers (Jr.), 1922- , q.v. Ref: CA. SC: Ben Corbin, in at least those marked BC.
Operation Vengeance. Pyramid, 1965 BC [Tokyo]
Out of Time; see Time Running Out
The Paradise Trap. Pyramid, 1967 BC [Haw.]
The Sergeant and the Queen. Pyramid, 1964 BC [Kor.]
Sgt. Corbin's War. Pyramid, 1964 BC [Kor.]
Strikeback! Pyramid, 1965 [Kor.]
Time Running Out. Papillon, 1974. Also published as: Out of Time. Decade, 1980 BC [Tokyo]
Tongue of Treason. Pyramid, 1967 BC [Calif.]

CRANKSHAW, EDWARD. 1909- . Ref: CA.
The Creedy Case. Joseph, 1954

CRANSTON, CLAUDIA. 1886-1947. SC: Clarice Claremont, in both titles.
Murder Maritime. Lippincott, 1935 [ship]
The Murder on Fifth Avenue. Lippincott, 1934 [NYC]

CRANSTON, MAURICE (WILLIAM). 1920- . Ref: CA. SC: Insp. Mortimer Blunt, in both titles. Set: Eng.
Philosopher's Hemlock. Westhouse, 1946
Tomorrow We'll Be Sober. Westhouse, 1946

CRAUFORD, W(ILLIAM) H(AROLD) L(ANE). 1886- . SC: Detective Kellerway, in at least those marked K. Set: Eng.
And Then There Were Nine. Ward, 1945
Another Woman's Poison. Ward, 1954
The Bride Wears Black. Ward, 1948
The Cat Dies First. Ward, 1955
The Crimson Mask. Ward, 1932
A Date with Death. Ward, 1947
-The Dearly Beloved Wives. Ward, 1953
Drakmere Must Die. Ward, 1950
Elementary, My Dear Freddie. Ward, 1950
The Final Curtain. Ward, 1933
The Hawkmoor Mystery. Ward, 1932
-The Ivory Goddess. Ward, 1954
Joseph Proctor's Money. Ward, 1948
A Man's Shadow. Ward, 1951
The Missing Ace. Ward, 1931 K
Murder of a Dead Man. Ward, 1952
Murder to Music. Ward, 1936 K
One Man's Meat. Ward, 1952
The Ravenscroft Mystery. Ward, 1934
Smooth Killing. Ward, 1949
Till Murder Do Us Part. Ward, 1949
Where Is Jenny Willet? Ward, 1953

CRAWFORD, ALEXANDER
Outside the Law. Blackwood, 1914

CRAWFORD, E. M.
She Saw the Murderer. Stanley Smith, 1936

CRAWFORD, IAIN (PADRUIG). 1922- . Ref: CA.
Scare the Gentle Citizen. Hammond, 1966

CRAWFORD, JACK R(ANDALL). 1878-1968. Professor of Literature at Yale U.
The Philosper's Murder Case. Sears, 1931; Long, 1932 [NYC]

CRAWFORD, JAMES TEMPLE
The Hot Pick-Up. Arrow (New Zealand), 1978

CRAWFORD, LINK
The Ransom. Decade, 1980 [Calif.]

CRAWFORD, MAX. 1938- . Ref: CA.
The Bad Communist. Harcourt, 1979
Waltz Across Texas. Farrar, 1975 [Tex.]

CRAWFORD, OLIVER. Pseudonym of Oliver Kaufman, 1917- . Ref: CA.
The Execution. St. Martin's, 1978; Hamlyn pb, 1979 [L.A.]

CRAWFORD, PETRINA
Seed of Evil. Lancer, 1973 [Eng.]

CRAWFORD, ROBERT. Pseudonym of Hugh C(rauford) Rae, 1935- , q.v. Other pseudonyms: R. B. Houston, Stuart Stern, qq.v. SC: Arthur Salisbury & Frank Shearer, in at least those marked S&S.
The Badger's Daughter. Constable, 1971. Reprinted as by Hugh C. Rae: Sphere, 1974
Cockleburr. Constable, 1969; Putnam, 1970. Also published as: Pay As You Die. Berkley, 1971 S&S

Kiss the Boss Goodbye. Constable, 1970; Putnam, 1971. Reprinted as by Hugh C. Rae: Sphere, 1974 S&S
Pay As You Die; see Cockleburr
The Shroud Society. Constable, 1969; Putnam, 1969
Whip Hand. Constable, 1972. Reprinted as by Hugh C. Rae: Sphere, 1974

CRAWFORD, ROSEMARY A.
Image of Evil. Dell, 1971 [La.]

CRAWFORD, STANLEY (GOTTLIEB). 1937- . Ref: CA.
Gascoyne. Putnam, 1966; Cape, 1966

CRAWFORD, THELMAR WYCHE. 1905- .
Terror Wears a Feathered Cloak. Westminster, 1979

CRAWFORD, WALLACE
Nest of Vipers. Hale, 1969

CRAWFORD, WILLIAM (ELBERT). 1929- . Pseudonyms: Don Logan, Jim Peterson, Paul Ross, Steve Scott, qq.v. Ref: CA. SC: Colin Stryker = CS.
The Chinese Connection. Pinnacle, 1973 [Mex.]
Cop-Kill. Pinnacle, 1974 CS
Deadly Alliance. Pinnacle, 1975 CS
Drug Run. Pinnacle, 1974 CS
Stryker. Pinnacle, 1973 CS [New Mex.]

CRAWFURD, OSWALD (JOHN FREDERICK). 1834-1909. Ref: CC.
The League of the White Hand. Chapman, 1909
The Mystery of Myrtle Cottage. Chapman, 1908
The Revelations of Inspector Morgan. Chapman, 1906; Dodd, 1907 ss
Sylvia Arden. Kegan Paul, 1888; Lovell, 1889
-The Ways of the Millionaire. Chapman, 1908

CRAWLEY, J. COOPER. Pseudonym.
Investment in Crime. Boardman, 1957
My Rubies Are Blood Red. Boardman, 1957

CRAWLEY, RAYBURN. Pseudonym. SC: Ned Shackleton, in both titles.
-Chattering Gods. Harper, 1931 [Afr.]
-The Valley of Creeping Men. Harper, 1930 [Afr.]

CREASEY, JOHN. 1908-1973. Pseudonyms: Gordon Ashe, M. E. Cooke, Norman Deane, Robert Caine Frazer, Patrick Gill, Michael Halliday, Charles Hogarth, Brian Hope, Colin Hughes, Kyle Hunt, Abel Mann, Peter Manton, J. J. Marric, Richard Martin, Rodney Mattheson, Anthony Morton, Jeremy York, qq.v. Ref: CA, CC, DD, EM, MC, TC. SC: Commander George Gideon = GG (see also the J. J. Marric entry); Sexton Blake = SB (with many other authors); Richard Rollison (The Toff) = RR; Roger West = RW; Dr. Palfrey = P; Department Z = Z. Note: Some titles originally published under pseudonyms have been reprinted under the John Creasey byline; these reprints are omitted from the following list and will be found under the original byline. Also note: A number of paperback originals are grouped at the end of the listing. Finally, many early Creasey novels were revised for republication in the 1950s-1970s; these revisions are not noted in this or other Creasey lists. Set: mostly Eng.
Accident for Inspector West. Hodder, 1957. U.S. title: Hit and Run. Scribner, 1959 RW
Accuse the Toff. Long, 1943; Walker, 1975 RR
Alibi. Hodder, 1971; Scribner, 1971 RW
Battle for Inspector West. Paul, 1948 RW
A Beauty for Inspector West. Hodder, 1954. U.S. title: The Beauty Queen Killer. Harper, 1956. Also published as: So Young, So Cold, So Fair. Dell, 1958 RW
The Beauty Queen Killer; see A Beauty for Inspector West
The Black Spiders. Hodder, 1957; Popular Library, 1975 Z
The Blight. Hodder, 1968; Walker, 1968 P [Calif.]
The Blind Spot; see Inspector West at Bay
Break the Toff; see The Toff Down Under
A Bundle for the Toff. Hodder, 1967; Walker, 1968 RR
Call the Toff. Hodder, 1953; Walker, 1969 RR [Cape Town]
Carriers of Death. Melrose, 1937; Popular Library, 1972 Z

The Case Against Paul Raeburn; see Triumph for Inspector West
A Case for Inspector West. Evans, 1951. U.S. title: The Figure in the Dusk. Harper, 1952 RW
The Case of the Acid Throwers; see Inspector West at Bay
The Case of the Innocent Victims. Hodder, 1960; Scribner, 1966 RW
The Case of the Mad Inventor. Amalgamated, 1942 SB
The Case of the Murdered Financier. Amalgamated, 1937 SB
The Children of Despair; see The Children of Hate
The Children of Hate. Evans, 1952. U.S. title: The Killers of Innocence. Walker, 1971. Also published as: The Children of Despair. Jay, 1958 P
The Creepers; see Inspector West Cries Wolf
Dangerous Quest. Long, 1944; Walker, 1974 Z
Dark Harvest. Long, 1947; Walker, 1977 P
Dark Peril. Paul, 1944; Popular Library, 1975 Z
The Dawn of Darkness. Long, 1949 P
The Day of Disaster. Long, 1942 Z
Days of Danger. Melrose, 1937; Popular Library, 1972 Z
Dead or Alive. Evans, 1951; Popular Library, 1974 Z
Death by Night. Long, 1940; Popular Library, 1972 Z
Death in Cold Print. Hodder, 1961; Scribner, 1962 RW
Death in the Rising Sun. Long, 1945; Walker, 1976 P [China]
The Death Miser. Melrose, 1932 Z
Death of an Assassin; see A Prince for Inspector West
Death of a Postman; see Parcels for Inspector West
Death of a Racehorse. Hodder, 1959; Scribner, 1962 RW
Death Round the Corner. Melrose, 1935; Popular Library, 1972 Z
Death Stands By. Long, 1938; Popular Library, 1972 Z
The Department of Death. Evans, 1949; Popular Library, 1979 Z
The Depths. Hodder, 1963; Walker, 1967 P
The Dissemblers; see Puzzle for Inspector West
A Doll for the Toff. Hodder, 1963; Walker, 1965 RR
Doorway to Death; see Find Inspector West
Double for the Toff. Hodder, 1959; Walker, 1965 RR
The Drought. Hodder, 1959; Walker, 1967. Also published as: Dry Spell. Four Square, 1967 P [S.W.]
Dry Spell; see The Drought
The Enemy Within. Evans, 1950; Popular Library, 1977 Z
The Executioners. Hodder, 1967; Scribner, 1967 RW
The Extortioners. Hodder, 1974; Scribner, 1975 RW
The Famine. Hodder, 1967; Walker, 1968 P
Feathers for the Toff. Long, 1945; Walker, 1970 RR
The Figure in the Dusk; see A Case for Inspector West
Find Inspector West. Hodder, 1957. U.S. title: The Trouble at Saxby's. Harper, 1959. Also published as: Doorway to Death. Berkley, 1961 RW
First Came a Murder. Melrose, 1934; Popular Library, 1972 Z
The Flood. Hodder, 1956; Walker, 1969 P [Scot.]
Follow the Toff. Hodder, 1961; Walker, 1967 RR
Fool the Toff. Evans, 1950; Walker, 1966 RR
The Foothills of Fear. Hodder, 1961 [Ariz.]
The Gelignite Gang; see Inspector West Makes Haste
Gideon's Fear. Evans, 1966 (3-act play based on Gideon's Week by J. J. Marric, q.v.) GG
Give a Man a Gun; see A Gun for Inspector West
Go Away Death. Long, 1942; Popular Library, 1976 Z
Go Away to Murder; see Inspector West Leaves Town
The Great Air Swindle. Amalgamated, 1939 SB
A Gun for Inspector West. Hodder, 1953. U.S. title: Give a Man a Gun. Harper, 1954 RW
Hammer the Toff. Long, 1947 RR
Hang the Little Man. Hodder, 1963; Scribner, 1963 RW

Here Comes the Toff. Long, 1940; Walker, 1967 RR
Hit and Run; see Accident for Inspector West
Holiday for Inspector West. Paul, 1946 RW
The Hounds of Vengeance. Long, 1945 P [Algeria]
The House of the Bears. Long, 1947; Walker, 1975 P
Hunt the Toff. Evans, 1952; Walker, 1969 RR
The Inferno. Hodder, 1965; Walker, 1966 P
Inspector West Alone. Evans, 1950; Scribner, 1975 RW
Inspector West at Bay. Evans, 1952. U.S. title: The Blind Spot. Harper, 1954. Also published as: The Case of the Acid Throwers. Avon, 1955 RW
Inspector West at Home. Paul, 1944; Scribner, 1973 RW
Inspector West Cries Wolf. Evans, 1950. U.S. title: The Creepers. Harper, 1952 RW
Inspector West Kicks Off. Paul, 1949. U.S. title: Sport for Inspector West. Lancer, 1971 RW
Inspector West Leaves Town. Paul, 1943. U.S. title: Go Away to Murder. Lancer, 1972 RW
Inspector West Makes Haste. Hodder, 1955. U.S. title: The Gelignite Gang. Harper, 1956. Also published as: Night of the Watchman. Berkley, 196? And as: Murder Makes Haste. Lancer, 197? RW
Inspector West Regrets. Paul, 1945; Lancer, 1971 RW
Inspector West Takes Charge. Paul, 1942; Scribner, 1972 RW
The Insulators. Hodder, 1972; Walker, 1973 P
Introducing the Toff. Long, 1938 RR
The Island of Peril. Long, 1940; Popular Library, 1976 Z
The Kidnapped Child; see The Toff and the Kidnapped Child
Kill the Toff. Evans, 1950; Walker, 1966 RR
The Killers of Innocence; see The Children of Hate
The Killing Strike; see Strike for Death
A Kind of Prisoner. Hodder, 1954; Popular Library, 1975 Z
Kiss the Toff; see Make-Up for the Toff
A Knife for the Toff. Evans, 1951; Pyramid, 1964 RR
The League of Dark Men. Paul, 1947; Popular Library, 1975 Z
The League of Light. Evans, 1949 P
Leave It to the Toff. Hodder, 1963; Pyramid, 1965 RR
The Legion of the Lost. Long, 1943; Daye, 1944 P
Look Three Ways at Murder. Hodder, 1964; Scribner, 1965 RW
Make-Up for the Toff. Hodder, 1956; Walker, 1967. Also published as: Kiss the Toff. Lancer, 1971 RR
The Man from Fleet Street. Amalgamated, 1940 SB
The Man Who Shook the World. Evans, 1950 P
The Mark of the Crescent. Melrose, 1935; Popular Library, 1972 Z
A Mask for the Toff; see The Toff Goes Gay
The Masters of Bow Street. Hodder, 1974; Simon, 1974 [Eng.: 1739-1829]
Men, Maids and Murder. Melrose, 1933
Menace! Long, 1938; Popular Library, 1972 Z
The Mists of Fear. Hodder, 1955; Walker, 1977 P [Sp.]
Model for the Toff. Hodder, 1957; Pyramid, 1965 RR
The Mountain of the Blind. Hodder, 1960 [Afr.]
Murder, London-Australia. Hodder, 1965; Scribner, 1965 RW
Murder, London-Miami. Hodder, 1969; Scribner, 1969 RW
Murder, London-New York. Hodder, 1958; Scribner, 1961 RW [NYC]
Murder, London-South Africa. Hodder, 1966; Scribner 1966 RW
Murder Makes Haste; see Inspector West Makes Haste
Murder Must Wait. Long, 1939; Popular Library, 1972 Z
Murder on the Line. Hodder, 1960; Scribner, 1963 RW
Murder: One, Two, Three; see Two for Inspector West
Murder Out of the Past. Barrington Gray, 1953 RR
Murder Tips the Scales; see Two for Inspector West
Night of the Watchman; see Inspector West Makes Haste

No Darker Crime. Paul, 1943; Popular Library, 1976 Z
The Oasis. Hodder, 1969; Walker, 1970 P
Panic! Long, 1939; Popular Library, 1972 Z
Parcels for Inspector West. Hodder, 1956. U.S. title: Death of a Postman. Harper, 1957 RW
A Part for a Policeman. Hodder, 1970; Scribner, 1970 RW
The Peril Ahead. Paul, 1946; Popular Library, 1974 Z
The Perilous Country; see The Valley of Fear
The Plague of Silence. Hodder, 1958; Walker, 1968 P
Poison for the Toff; see The Toff on Ice
Policeman's Dread. Hodder, 1962; Scribner, 1964 RW
Prepare for Action. Paul, 1942; Popular Library, 1975 Z
A Prince for Inspector West. Hodder, 1956. U.S. title: Death of an Assassin. Scribner, 1960 RW [Milan]
Private Carter's Crime. Amalgamated, 1943 SB
The Prophet of Fire. Evans, 1951 P [Russ.]
Puzzle for Inspector West. Evans, 1951. U.S. title: The Dissemblers. Scribner, 1967 RW
Redhead. Hurst, 1934 Z
A Rocket for the Toff. Hodder, 1960; Pyramid, 1964 RR
Sabotage. Long, 1941; Popular Library, 1976 Z
Salute the Toff. Long, 1941; Walker, 1971 RR
The Scene of the Crime. Hodder, 1961; Scribner, 1963 RW
A Score for the Toff; see A Six for the Toff
Send Inspector West. Hodder, 1953. U.S. title: Send Superintendent West. Scribner, 1954 RW
Send Superintendent West; see Send Inspector West
Seven Times Seven. Melrose, 1932
Shadow of Doom. Long, 1946 P
A Sharp Rise in Crime. Hodder, 1978; Scribner, 1979 RW
A Six for the Toff. Hodder, 1955; Walker, 1969. Also published as: A Score for the Toff. Lancer, 1972 RR
The Sleep. Hodder, 1964; Walker, 1968 P [Rhod.]
The Smog. Hodder, 1970; Walker, 1971 P
The Sons of Satan. Long, 1948 P
So Young, So Cold, So Fair; see A Beauty for Inspector West
So Young to Burn. Hodder, 1968; Scribner, 1968 RW
A Splinter of Glass. Hodder, 1972; Scribner, 1972 RW
Sport for Inspector West; see Inspector West Kicks Off
Stars for the Toff. Hodder, 1968; Walker, 1968 RR
Strike for Death. Hodder, 1958. U.S. title: The Killing Strike. Scribner, 1961 RW
The Terror. Hodder, 1962; Walker, 1966 P
Terror for the Toff; see The Toff on the Farm
The Terror Trap. Melrose, 1936; Popular Library, 1972 Z
The Theft of Magna Carta. Hodder, 1973; Scribner, 1973 RW
Thunder in Europe. Melrose, 1936; Popular Library, 1972 Z
The Thunder-Maker. Hodder, 1976; Walker, 1976 P
The Toff. Evans, 1963 (3-act play) RR
The Toff Among the Millions. Long, 1943; Walker, 1976 RR
The Toff and Old Harry. Long, 1948; Walker, 1970 RR
The Toff and the Crooked Copper. Hodder, 1977 RR
The Toff and the Curate. Long, 1944; Walker, 1969. Also published as: The Toff and the Deadly Parson. Lancer, 1970 RR
The Toff and the Deadly Parson; see The Toff and the Curate
The Toff and the Deep Blue Sea. Hodder, 1955; Walker, 1967 RR [Fr.]
The Toff and the Fallen Angels. Hodder, 1970; Walker, 1970 RR
The Toff and the Golden Boy. Hodder, 1969; Walker, 1969 RR
The Toff and the Great Illusion. Long, 1944; Walker, 1967 RR
The Toff and the Kidnapped Child. Hodder, 1960; Walker, 1965. Also published as: The Kidnapped Child. Popular Library, 1972 RR
The Toff and the Lady. Long, 1946; Walker, 1975 RR

The Toff and the Runaway Bride. Hodder, 1959; Walker, 1964 RR
The Toff and the Sleepy Cowboy. Hodder, 1974; Walker, 1975 RR
The Toff and the Spider. Hodder, 1965; Walker, 1966 RR
The Toff and the Stolen Tresses. Hodder, 1958; Walker, 1965 RR
The Toff and the Teds. Hodder, 1961. U.S. title: The Toff and the Toughs. Walker, 1968 RR
The Toff and the Terrified Tax Man. Hodder, 1973; Walker, 1973 RR
The Toff and the Toughs; see The Toff and the Teds
The Toff and the Trip-Trip-Triplets. Hodder, 1972; Walker, 1972 RR
The Toff at Butlin's. Hodder, 1954; Walker, 1976 RR [Wales]
The Toff at the Fair. Hodder, 1954; Walker, 1968 RR
The Toff Breaks In. Long, 1940 RR
The Toff Down Under. Hodder, 1953; Walker, 1969. Also published as: Break the Toff. Lancer, 1970 RR [Australia]
The Toff Goes Gay. Evans, 1951. U.S. title: A Mask for the Toff. Walker, 1966 RR [Paris]
The Toff Goes On. Long, 1939 RR
The Toff Goes to Market. Long, 1942; Walker, 1967 RR
The Toff in New York. Hodder, 1956; Pyramid, 1964 RR [NYC]
The Toff in Town. Long, 1948; Walker, 1977 RR
The Toff in Wax. Hodder, 1966; Walker, 1966 RR
The Toff Is Back. Long, 1942; Walker, 1974 RR
The Toff on Board. Evans, 1949; Walker, 1973 RR [ship]
The Toff on Fire. Hodder, 1957; Walker, 1966 RR
The Toff on Ice. Long, 1947. U.S. title: Poison for the Toff. Pyramid, 1965 RR
The Toff on the Farm. Hodder, 1958; Walker, 1964. Also published as: Terror for the Toff. Pyramid, 1965 RR
The Toff on the Trail. Everybody's pb, 194? RR
The Toff Proceeds. Long, 1941; Walker, 1968 RR
The Toff Steps Out. Long, 1939 RR
The Toff Takes Shares. Long, 1948; Walker, 1972 RR
The Touch of Death. Hodder, 1954; Walker, 1969 P
Traitor's Doom. Long, 1942; Walker, 1970 P
Triumph for Inspector West. Paul, 1948. U.S. title: The Case Against Paul Raeburn. Harper, 1958 RW
The Trouble at Saxby's; see Find Inspector West
Two for Inspector West. Hodder, 1955. U.S. title: Murder: One, Two, Three. Scribner, 1960. Also published as: Murder Tips the Scales. Berkley, 1962 RW
The Unbegotten. Hodder, 1971; Walker, 1972 P
The Valley of Fear. Long, 1943. U.S. title: The Perilous Country. Walker, 1973. British reprint editions bear the same title as the U.S. edition. P
The Voiceless Ones. Hodder, 1973; Walker, 1974 P
Vote for the Toff. Hodder, 1971; Walker, 1971 RR
The Whirlwind. Hodder, 1979 P
The Wings of Peace. Long, 1948; Walker, 1978 P [India]

The Cinema Crimes. Pemberton, 1945
Dixon Hawke, Secret Agent. Thompson, 1939 (Dixon Hawke.)
Documents of Death. Mellifont, 1939
The Double Motive. Mellifont, 1938
The Doublecross of Death. Mellifont, 1938
The Fear of Felix Corder. Fleetway, 19??
The Hidden Hoard. Mellifont, 1939
John Brand, Fugitive. Fleetway, 19??
The Killer Squad. Newnes, 1936
The Men Who Died Laughing. Thompson, 1935
The Missing Hoard. Mellifont, 1938
Mottled Death. Thompson, 1939
Murder by Magic. Amalgamated, 1937
The Mysterious Mr. Rocco. Mellifont, 1937
Mystery at Manby House. Northern News, 1938
The Mystery of Blackmoor Prison. Mellifont, 1939
The Night of Dread. Fleetway, 19??
The Poison Gas Robberies. Mellifont, 1940

The Sacred Eye. Thompson, 1939
The Ship of Death. Thompson, 1939

CREBBIN, EDWARD HORACE. Pseudonym: Sea-Wrack, q.v.

CRECY, JEANNE. Pseudonym of Jeanne Williams, 1930- . Other pseudonym: Deirdre Rowan, q.v. Ref: CA.
Curse of the Wolfskin. Signet, 1975
The Evil Among Us. Signet, 1975 [Nor.]
Hands of Terror. Berkley, 1972
Lady Gift. Hale, 1973 (U.S. title?)
The Lightning Tree. Berkley, 1973
My Face Beneath the Stone. Signet, 1975 [Prague]
The Night Hunters. Signet, 1975 [La.]
The Winter Keeper. Signet, 1975 [Mont.]

CREED, DAVID. Pseudonym of James Shields Guthrie, 1931- . Ref: CA.
-Death Watch. Secker, 1979
The Scarab. Secker, 1980
Trial of Lobo Icheka. Macmillan (London), 1971

CREED, SIBYL
The Shot. Chatto, 1924; Doran, 1924

CREED, WILL. Pseudonym of William Long, 1922- . Other pseudonym: Peter Yates, q.v.
Death Comes Grinning. Five-Star, 1946; Edwards, 1947 [Pitt.]
Death Wears a Green Hat. Five-Star, 1946; Edwards, 1946 [NYC]

CREEKMORE, DONNA
The Coachman's Daughter. Dell, 1979
The Silver Shroud. Manor, 1978

CREIGHTON, JO ANNE. Pseudonym of Joseph L. Chadwick, q.v. Other pseudonyms: Joselyn Chadwick, John Conway, John Creighton, qq.v.
The Dark Side of Paradise. Popular Library, 1976
The Harlan Legacy. Popular Library, 1977
House of Fury. Curtis, 1973 [Arg.]
Inn of Evil. Popular Library, 1974 [Md.]
The Mask of Evil. Curtis, 1973 [Cey.]

CREIGHTON, JOHN. Pseudonym of Joseph L. Chadwick, q.v. Other pseudonyms: Joselyn Chadwick, John Conway, Jo Anne Creighton, qq.v.
The Blonde Cried Murder. Ace, 1961
Destroying Angel. Ace, 1956
Evil Is the Night. Ace, 1959 [Tucson]
A Half Interest in Murder. Ace, 1960 [L.A.]
Not So Evil as Eve. Ace, 1957 [Ariz.]
Stranglehold. Ace, 1959
Trial by Perjury. Ace, 1958
The Wayward Blonde. Ace, 1958

CRESSWELL, HENRY
Without Issue. Hurst, 1897

CRESSWELL, MAURICE
Murder in a Road Gang. Low, 1936 [Can.]

CREW-JONES, FLORENCE. See: Albert Boissiere, 1866- .

CRICHTON, CONSTANTINE HOTHAM
Tales of Love and Hate. Mills, 1922 ss, some criminous

CRICHTON, LOUISE
China Rose. Columbine, 1939
-Less Than the Dust. Columbine, 1939
Mandarin's Dagger. Columbine, 1939

CRICHTON, (JOHN) MICHAEL. 1942- . Pseudonyms: Jeffery Hudson, John Lange, qq.v. Ref: CA, TC.
The Great Train Robbery. Knopf, 1975; Cape, 1975 [1855, Eng.]

CRISP, FRANK (ROBSON). 1915- . Ref: CA.
-The Ape of London. Hodder, 1959
-By Whose Hand. Paul, 1951
-The Chandu Men. Paul, 1955
-Fazackerley's Millions. Paul, 1955
-The Manila Stranger. Long, 1957
-The Nail of Suspicion. Low, 1949
-The Night Callers. Long, 1960
The Voice from Yesterday. Paul, 1948
-Within This House. Paul, 1947

CRISP, JACK H. 1923- . SC: Special Operations Executive, in both titles.
Dragon Spoor. Simon & Pierre (Toronto), 1978; Futura, 1979
Final Act. Simon & Pierre (Toronto), 1978; Futura, 1979

CRISP, N(ORMAN) J(AMES). 1923- . Ref: CA. SC: Sidney Kenyon = SK.
The Gotland Deal. Weidenfeld, 1976; Viking, 1976 SK
The London Deal. Macdonald, 1978; St. Martin's, 1979 SK
The Odd Job Man. Macdonald, 1977; St. Martin's, 1979

CRISP, PETER A(LAN)
In the Shadow of the Dragon. Macmillan (London), 1961 [Sing.]

CRISP, QUENTIN. 1908- .
-Chog. Methuen (NYC), 1979; Eyre, 1979

CRISPIN, EDMUND. Pseudonym of Robert Bruce Montgomery, 1921-1978. Ref: CA, CC, DD, EM, MC, TC. SC: Gervase Fen, in all titles. Set: Eng.
Beware of the Trains. Gollancz, 1953; Walker, 1962 ss
Buried for Pleasure. Gollancz, 1948; Lippincott, 1949
The Case of the Gilded Fly. Gollancz, 1944. U.S. title: Obsequies at Oxford. Lippincott, 1945 [theatre, acad.]
Dead and Dumb; see Swan Song
Fen Country. Gollancz, 1979; Walker, 1980 ss
Frequent Hearses. Gollancz, 1950. U.S. title: Sudden Vengeance. Dodd, 1950
The Glimpses of the Moon. Gollancz, 1977; Walker, 1978
Holy Disorders. Gollancz, 1945; Lippincott, 1946
The Long Divorce. Gollancz, 1951; Dodd, 1951. Also published as: A Noose for Her. Mercury, 1952, abridged
Love Lies Bleeding. Gollancz, 1948; Lippincott, 1948 [acad.]
The Moving Toyshop. Gollancz, 1946; Lippincott, 1946
A Noose for Her; see The Long Divorce
Obsequies at Oxford; see The Case of the Gilded Fly
Sudden Vengeance; see Frequent Hearses
Swan Song. Gollancz, 1947. U.S. title: Dead and Dumb. Lippincott, 1947. Re-issued in the U.S. under the British title: Walker, 1980 [theatre]

CROCKETT, ANTHONY (JOHN SINCLAIR)
The Perimeter Fence. Hale, 1957
Toys of Desperation. Hale, 1960

CROCKETT, JAMES. Joint pseudonym of Cornelia Warriner and James A. MacPhail.
Lullaby with Lugers. Crown, 1946 [NYC]

CROCKETT, S(AMUEL) R(UTHERFORD). 1860-1914.
Deep Moat Grange. Hodder, 1908; Appleton, 1908
-The Firebrand. Macmillan (London), 1901; McClure, 1901
The Lady of the Hundred Dresses. Nash, 1911 ss

CROFT, D(ESMOND) W(ARRICK). 1894- .
-Frederick Lonton. Longmans (NYC & London), 1926

CROFT-COOKE, RUPERT. 1903-1979. Pseudonym: Leo Bruce, q.v. Ref: CA, CC, MP, TC.
Clash by Night. Eyre, 1962
Nasty Piece of Work. Eyre, 1973
Paper Albatross. Eyre, 1965; Abelard, 1968
Pharoah with His Waggons and other stories. Jarrolds, 1937 27 ss, 8 criminous
Release the Lions. Jarrolds, 1933; Dodd, 1934
Seven Thunders. Macmillan (London), 1956; St. Martin's, 1955
Thief. Eyre, 1960; Doubleday, 1961
Three in a Cell. Eyre, 1968

CROFTS, ANDREW
Crown Kidnap. Satellite, 1979

CROFTS, FREEMAN WILLS. 1879-1957. Ref: all except CA. SC: Insp. Joseph French = JF. Two wartime pamphlets are listed at the end of this entry.
The Affair at Little Wokeham. Hodder, 1943. U.S. title: Double Tragedy. Dodd, 1943 JF
Antidote to Venom. Hodder, 1938; Dodd, 1939 JF
Anything to Declare? Hodder, 1957 JF
The Box Office Murders. Collins, 1929. U.S. title: The Purple Sickle Murders. Harper, 1929 JF
The Cask. Collins, 1920; Seltzer, 1924 [Fr., 1910-12]
The Cheyne Mystery; see Inspector French and the Cheyne Mystery
Circumstantial Evidence; see James Tarrant, Adventurer
Cold-Blooded Murder; see Man Overboard
Crime at Guildford. Collins, 1935. U.S. title: The Crime at Nornes. Dodd, 1935 JF
The Crime at Nornes; see Crime at Guildford
Crime on the Solent; see Mystery on Southampton Water
Dark Journey; see French Strikes Oil
Death of a Train. Hodder, 1946; Dodd, 1947 JF
Death on the Way. Collins, 1932. U.S. title: Double Death. Harper, 1932 JF
Double Death; see Death on the Way
Double Tragedy; see The Affair at Little Wokeham
The End of Andrew Harrison. Hodder, 1938. U.S. title: The Futile Alibi. Dodd, 1938 JF
Enemy Unseen. Hodder, 1945; Dodd, 1945 JF [ship]
Fatal Venture. Hodder, 1939. U.S. title: Tragedy in the Hollow. Dodd, 1939 JF
Fear Comes to Chalfont. Hodder, 1942; Dodd, 1942 JF
Found Floating. Hodder, 1937; Dodd, 1937 JF
French Strikes Oil. Hodder, 1952. U.S. title: Dark Journey. Dodd, 1951 JF
The Futile Alibi; see The End of Andrew Harrison
Golden Ashes. Hodder, 1940; Dodd, 1940 JF
The Groote Park Murder. Collins, 1923; Seltzer, 1925 [Scot.]
The Hog's Back Mystery. Hodder, 1933. U.S. title: The Strange Case of Dr. Earle. Dodd, 1933 JF
Inspector French and the Cheyne Mystery. Collins, 1926. U.S. title: The Cheyne Mystery. Boni, 1926 JF
Inspector French and the Starvel Tragedy. Collins, 1927. U.S. title: The Starvel Hollow Tragedy. Harper, 1927 JF
Inspector French's Greatest Case. Collins, 1924; Seltzer, 1925 JF
James Tarrant, Adventurer. Hodder, 1941. U.S. title: Circumstantial Evidence. Dodd, 1941 JF
The Losing Game. Hodder, 1941. U.S. title: A Losing Game. Dodd, 1941 JF
The Loss of the Jane Vosper. Collins, 1936; Dodd, 1936 JF [ship]
Man Overboard! Collins, 1936; Dodd, 1936. Also published as: Cold-Blooded Murder. Avon, 1947, abridged JF
Many a Slip. Hodder, 1955 ss JF
Murderers Make Mistakes. Hodder, 1947 ss JF
Mystery in the Channel. Collins, 1931. U.S. title: Mystery in the English Channel. Harper, 1931 JF
Mystery in the English Channel; see Mystery in the Channel
The Mystery of the Sleeping Car Express, and other stories. Hodder, 1956 ss JF
Mystery on Southampton Water. Hodder, 1934. U.S. title: Crime on the Solent. Dodd, 1934 JF
The Pit-Prop Syndicate. Collins, 1922; Seltzer, 1925
The Ponson Case. Collins, 1921; Boni, 1927
The Purple Sickle Murders; see The Box Office Murders
The Sea Mystery. Collins, 1928; Harper, 1928 JF
Silence for the Murderer. Hodder, 1949; Dodd, 1948 JF
Sir John Magill's Last Journey. Collins, 1930; Harper, 1930 JF [Ire.]
The Starvel Hollow Tragedy; see Inspector French and the Starvel Tragedy
The Strange Case of Dr. Earle; see The Hog's Back Mystery
Sudden Death. Collins, 1932; Harper, 1932 JF
Tragedy in the Hollow; see Fatal Venture
The 12:30 from Croydon. Hodder, 1934. U.S. title: Wilful and Premeditated. Dodd, 1934 JF
Wilful and Premeditated; see The 12:30 from Croydon

The Hunt Ball Murder. Todd, 1943
Mr. Sefton, Murderer. Polybooks, 1944

CROLL, MAURICE
Little Miss David—and Goliath. Vantage, 1980

CROMARSH, H. RIPLEY. Pseudonym of Bryan Mary Angell, 1877- .
The Secret of the Moor Cottage. Small, 1906; Ward, 1907

CROMARTY, NOEL
   Ashes for the Living. Hodder, 1949
   The Blind Side. Hodder, 1951
   An Epitaph for Meredith. Hodder, 1953
   Neither Had I Rest. Hodder, 1949
   Rogue's Harvest. Hodder, 1950

CROMBIE, MICHAEL
   The Awakening of Theodore Wrenn. Gray, 1934
   The Frightened Girl. Mystery House, 1941 (British title?)
   The Gentleman Crook. Gramol, 1935
   The House of Horror. Gray, 193?
   Life Must Go On. Gray, 1936
   Murder!! Gramol, 1935
   The Sealed Room Murder. Gray, 1934

CROMIE, ALICE (HAMILTON). 1914-   . Ref: CA.
   Lucky to Be Alive? Simon, 1979; Collins, 1980 [Ill.]

CROMIE, ROBERT. 1856-1907. Ref: CC.
   -The Crack of Doom. Digby, 1895
   El Dorado. Ward, 1904. U.S. title: From the Cliffs of Croaghaun. Saalfield, 1904
   From the Cliffs of Croaghaun; see El Dorado
   The Lost Liner. Newnes, 1899
   The Romance of Poisons: Being Weird Episodes from Life. Jarrolds, 1903 ss

CROMMELIN, MAY [MARIA HENRIETTA DE LA CHEROIS CROMMELIN]
   Dead Men's Dollars. Arrowsmith, 1887

CROMWELL, A. G. E. SC: Rodney Wayne, in both titles. Set: Eng.
   Death in the Copse. Wright, 1940
   Murder in Flat 14. Wright, 1939

CROMWELL, ELSIE. Pseudonym of Elsie Lee, 1912-   , q.v. Joint pseudonym with Michael Sheridan: Lee Sheridan, q.v.
   The Governess. Paperback Library, 1969
   Ivorstone Manor. PB, 1970

CRONIN, A(RCHIBALD) J(OSEPH). 1896-1981. Ref: CA.
   Beyond This Place. Gollancz, 1953; Little, 1953

CRONIN, BERNARD CHARLES. 1884-   . Pseudonyms: Dennis Adair, Eric North, qq.v.

CRONIN, BRENDAN LEO. 1907-   . Pseudonyms: Michael Cronin, David Miles, qq.v.

CRONIN, GEORGE P. 1933-   .
   Answer from a Dead Man. Condor, 1978
   Death of a Delegate. Condor, 1978

CRONIN, MICHAEL. Pseudonym of Brendan Leo Cronin, 1907-   . Other pseudonym: David Miles, q.v. SC: Sam Harris, in at least those marked SH; James Hellier, in at least those marked JH; Richard Maidment ("The Pilgrim"), in at least those marked RM. Set: Eng.
   Ask for Trouble. Hale, 1969
   Begin with a Gun. Hale, 1960; Walker, 1961 RM
   The Big C. Hale, 1973 JH
   The Big Tickle. Hale, 1974 SH
   A Black Leather Case. Hale, 1971 SH
   -The Born Loser. Hale, 1980
   By His Own Hand. Hale, 1969
   Caribbean Kidnap. Hale, 1969 [Carib.]
   Climb the Wall. Museum, 1956; Washburn, 1957 RM
   The Con Game. Hale, 1972 SH
   Curtain Call. Hale, 1961 RM
   The Dangerous Lady. Hale, 1962
   Dead, and Done With. Hale, 1959
   Death in Transit. Hale, 1974
   Dead Loss. Hale, 1970 JH
   Duet for Death. Hale, 1973
   The Elusive Lady. Hale, 1957
   Emergency Exit. Hale, 1970 JH
   -Epitaph for a Lady. Hale, 1980
   Escape at Sunrise. Hale, 1972 JH
   The Fast Exit. Hale, 1962
   The Final Installment. Hale, 1976
   Fit to Kill. Hale, 1976
   The Girl on the Beach. Hale, 1967
   I Can Cope. Museum, 1955 RM
   The Intruder. Hale, 1966
   Jump the Gun. Hale, 1963
   The Killing Is Easy. Hale, 1975
   The Last Indictment. Hale, 1964
   Leave It to Me. Museum, 1953
   The Long Memory. Hale, 1971 JH
   The Loose End. Hale, 1971
   Loser Takes Nothing. Museum, 1955
   -The Macamba Project. Hale, 1977
   Man Alive. Hale, 1968 JH
   Man at Large. Hale, 1962
   Man on the Run. Hale, 1978
   Marked to Die. Hale, 1967
   The Marksman. Hale, 1974 [Mid. East]
   Murder Incidental. Hale, 1965
   Murder Mislaid. Hale, 1963
   The Night of the Party. Hale, 1957; Washburn, 1958
   No Sale. Ward, 1950
   Nobody Needs a Corpse. Hale, 1972 SH
   Pacific Pearl. Museum, 1954
   Paid in Full. Museum, 1953 RM
   A Pair of Knaves. Hale, 1977
   A Proper Carve-Up. Hale, 1970
   The Second Bounce. Hale, 1959
   The Spanish Lady. Hale, 1960
   Strictly Legitimate. Ward, 1951
   Strictly Private Business. Hale, 1975
   Sweet Water. Museum, 1957; Washburn, 1957 RM [Mex.]
   Unfinished Business. Hale, 1977
   The Unquiet Night. Hale, 1958
   You Never Learn. Museum, 1952
   You Pay Your Money. Museum, 1954

CROOKENDEN, ISAAC
   Fatal Secrets; or, Etherlinda de Salmoni. Lee, 1806 [Sic.]
   Horrible Revenge; or, The Monster of Italy! Harrild, 1808 [1500s, It.]
   The Memoirs of Villain; or, Singular Adventures of Joseph Saunders. Fisher, 1803
   The Mysterious Murder; or, The Usurper of Naples. Lee, 1806 [Naples]
   The Nocturnal Assassin; or, Spanish Jealousy. Lee, 1806
   The Revengeful Turk; or, Mystic Cavern. Fisher, 1802
   The Skeleton; or, Mysterious Discovery. Neil, 1805
   Spectre of the Turret; or, Guolto Castle. Harrild, 18??

CROOKER, HERBERT. SC: Clay Brooke, in at least those marked CB.
   The Crime in Washington Mews. Macaulay, 1931 CB [NYC]
   The Hollywood Murder Mystery. Macaulay, 1930; Long, 1930 CB [L.A.]
   -The Sweet Cheat. Macaulay, 1932

CROSBIE, HUGH PROVAN. 1912-   . Pseudonym: John Carrick, q.v.

CROSBIE, JOHN
   The Gun Runners. Low, 1936 [S. Afr.]
   -The Lion Men. Low, 1938

CROSBY, G(EORGE) S.
   -The Mystery; or, Platonic Love. Lippincott, 1875

CROSBY, JOHN
   Death by Proxy. Langdon, 1948

CROSBY, JOHN
   Contract on the President. Dell, 1973

CROSBY, JOHN (CAMPBELL). 1912-   . Ref: CA.
   An Affair of Strangers. Stein, 1975; Cape, 1975 [Fr.]
   The Company of Friends. Stein, 1977; Cape, 1977
   Dear Judgment. Stein, 1978; Cape, 1979 [La.]
   Nightfall. Stein, 1976. British title: Snake. Cape, 1977 [Maj.]
   Party of the Year. Stein, 1979; Cape, 1980 [NYC]
   Snake; see Nightfall

CROSBY, KINGSLAND
   The Strange Case of Eleanor Cuyler. Dodd, 1910 [NYC]

CROSBY, LEE. Pseudonym of Ware Torrey (Budlong), 1905-1967. Other pseudonyms: Meg Padget, Judith Ware, Joan Winslow, qq.v. Newspaperwoman, feature writer, editor, book columnist, foreign correspondent, ss writer. SC: Eric Hazard, in at least those marked EH.
   Bridge House. Belmont, 1965
   Doors to Death; see Too Many Doors
   Midsummer Night's Murder. Dutton, 1942 [Conn.]
   Night Attack. Dutton, 1943 [L.I.]
   Terror by Night. Dutton, 1938 EH
   Too Many Doors. Dutton, 1941. Also published as: Doors to Death. Thriller Novel Classic, 194? Revised edition: Belmont, 1965 EH [Conn.]

CROSLAND, T(HOMAS) W(ILLIAM) H(ODGSON). 1865-1924.
   The Rogue. Paul, 1926

CROSS, AMANDA. Pseudonym of Carolyn Gold Heilbrun, 1926-   . Ref: CA, CC, TC. SC: Kate Fansler, in all titles.
   In the Last Analysis. Macmillan, 1964; Gollancz, 1964 [NYC]
   The James Joyce Murder. Macmillan, 1967; Gollancz, 1967 [N.Y.]
   Poetic Justice. Knopf, 1970; Gollancz, 1970 [NYC, acad.]
   The Question of Max. Knopf, 1976; Gollancz, 1976
   The Theban Mysteries. Knopf, 1971; Gollancz, 1972 [NYC, acad.]

CROSS, (ALAN) BEVERLEY. 1931-   . Ref: CA.
   The Nightwalkers. Hart-Davis, 1956; Little, 1957 [Fr.]

CROSS, GENE
   Nitty-Gritty Affair. Ember, 1967

CROSS, GILBERT B. Pseudonym: Jon Winters, q.v.

CROSS, JAMES. Pseudonym of Hugh Jones Parry, 1916-   . Ref: CA.
   The Dark Road. Messner, 1959; Heinemann, 1960 [Ger.]
   The Grave of Heroes. GM, 1961; Heinemann, 1961 [Fr.]
   Root of Evil. Messner, 1957; Heinemann, 1958
   To Hell for Half-a-Crown. Random, 1967; Constable, 1968

CROSS, JOHN KEIR. 1914-1967. Ref: CA.
   The Other Passenger. Westhouse, 1944; Lippincott, 1946 ss

CROSS, LAURENCE. SC: Tommy Lumb and Peter Marsham in both titles. Set: Eng.
   The Dope Dealers. Jarrolds, 1928
   The White Chalet. Jarrolds, 1929

CROSS, MARK. Pseudonym of Archibald Thomas Pechey, 1876-1961. Other pseudonym: Valentine, q.v. SC: Daphne Wrayne and the Four Adjusters, in all titles (see also the Valentine entry). Set: Eng.
   The Best-Laid Schemes. Ward, 1955
   The Black Spider. Ward, 1953
   Challenge to the Four. Ward, 1939
   The Circle of Freedom. Ward, 1953
   Desperate Steps. Ward, 1957
   Find the Professor. Ward, 1940
   Foul Deeds Will Arise. Ward, 1958
   The Four at Bay. Ward, 1939
   The Four Get Going. Ward, 1938
   The Four Make Holiday. Ward, 1938
   The Four Strike Home. Ward, 1937
   The Green Circle. Ward, 1942
   The Grip of the Four. Ward, 1934
   The Hand of the Four. Ward, 1935
   How Was It Done? Ward, 1941
   In the Dead of Night. Ward, 1955
   It Couldn't Be Murder. Ward, 1940
   The Jaws of Darkness. Ward, 1952
   The Mark of the Four. Ward, 1936
   Missing from His Home. Ward, 1949
   Murder As Arranged. Ward, 1943
   Murder in Black. Ward, 1944
   Murder in the Air. Ward, 1943
   Murder in the Pool. Ward, 1941
   Murder Will Speak. Ward, 1954
   The Mystery of Gruden's Gap. Ward, 1942
   The Mystery of Joan Marryat. Ward, 1945
   The Mystery of the Corded Box. Ward, 1956
   Not Long to Live. Ward, 1959
   Once Too Often. Ward, 1960
   Once Upon a Crime. Ward, 1961
   On the Night of the 14th. Ward, 1950
   Other Than Natural Causes. Ward, 1949
   Over Thin Ice. Ward, 1958
   Perilous Hazard. Ward, 1961
   The Secret of the Grange. Ward, 1946
   The Shadow of the Four. Ward, 1934
   The Strange Affair at Greylands. Ward, 1948
   The Strange Case of Pamela Wilson. Ward, 1954
   Surprise for the Four. Ward, 1937
   Third Time Unlucky. Ward, 1959
   Wanted for Questioning. Ward, 1960
   The Way of the Four. Ward, 1936
   When Danger Threatens. Ward, 1959
   When Thieves Fall Out. Ward, 1956
   Who Killed Henry Wickenstrom. Ward, 1951

CROSS, MARY
   -False Witness. Oliphant, 1891
   -Under Sentence. Ward, 1890

CROSS, RALPH D(ONALD). 1931-   . Ref: CA.
   Denton's Army. Belmont, 1979
   The Key to Murder. Belmont, 1980

CROSS, SETON
   The Twelfth Crime. Newnes, 1916

CROSS, VICTOR. Pseudonym of Virginia (Edith) Coffman, 1914- , q.v.
Blood Sport. Award, 1966; Tandem, 1967

CROSSEN, KENDELL FOSTER. 1910-1981. Pseudonyms: Bennett Barlay, M. E. Chaber, Richard Foster, Christopher Monig, Clay Richards, qq.v. Ref: CA, CC, TC. SC: Jason Jones and Necessary Smith = J&S; Kim Locke = KL.
The Big Dive. Dutton, 1959; Eyre, 1959 KL [Eng.]
The Case of the Curious Heel (by Ken Crossen). Eerie Series, 1944 J&S [NYC]
The Case of the Phantom Fingerprints (by Ken Crossen). Eerie Series, 1945 J&S [NYC]
Murder Out of Mind (by Ken Crossen). Five Star, 1945
The Tortured Path. Dutton, 1957; Eyre, 1958 KL [China]

CROSSLEY, MAUDE. 1879- . SC: Guy Bannister, in at least those marked GB.
A Box of Secrets. Jenkins, 1933
The Crimson Feather, with Charles (Thomas) King, 1868- . Jenkins, 1926
Crookery Inn. Jenkins, 1931 GB
The Forbidden Hour, with Charles (Thomas) King, 1868- . Jenkins, 1925 GB
The Lilac Bride Mystery. Mellifont, 1933
Murder in the Vestry. Mellifont, 1935
Secrecy Street. Mellifont, 1933
Shackled. Mellifont, 1934

CROTHERS, RACHEL. 1878- .
Caught Wet. French (NYC), 1932 (3-act play.)

CROUCH, J. M.
Corpse from the Sky. Gulliver, 1950

CROUDACE, GLYNN. 1917- . Ref: CA.
-The Black Rose. Hale, 1968
Blackadder. Macmillan (London), 1969
-The Dark Tide. Hale, 1967
Motives for Murder. Central News Agency (South Africa), 1957
The Scarlet Bikini. Macmillan (London), 1970
-The Silver Grass. Hale, 1968

CROUE, JEAN. See: Jacques Copeau, 1879-1949.

CROUSE, RUSSEL. 1893- . See: Howard Lindsay, 1889-1968.

CROW, C(HARLES) P(ATRICK). 1938- . Ref: CA.
No More Monday Mornings. Viking, 1980 [N.Y.]

CROWCROFT, PETER. 1923- . Ref: CA.
That Man Bolt. PB, 1974 (Novelization of the movie.) [H. Kong]

CROWE, CECILY
Abbeygate. Coward, 1977 [Ire.]
Northwater. Holt, 1968 [New Eng.]
The Talisman. St. Martin's, 1979 [Scot.]
The Tower of Kilraven. Holt, 1965 [Ire.]

CROWE, JOHN. Pseudonym of Dennis Lynds, 1924- , q.v. Other pseudonyms: William Arden, Nick Carter, Michael Collins, Carl Dekker, Maxwell Grant, Mark Sadler, qq.v. SC: Lee Beckett, in all titles, all set in Calif.
Another Way to Die. Random, 1972
Bloodwater. Dodd, 1974
Close to Death. Dodd, 1979
Crooked Shadows. Dodd, 1975
A Touch of Darkness. Random, 1972
When They Kill Your Wife. Dodd, 1977

CROWE, PAT(RICK T.). 1869-1938.
Society's Prodigal. Crowe, 1906

CROWELL, WILL
Murder in Mocking Valley. Eerie Series, 1945 [Ohio]

CROWTHER, BRUCE. 1933- . Pseudonym: James Grant, q.v.
Dead Man's Cocktail. Hale, 1976; Walker, 1976
Sleeper; see Underkill
Underkill. Hale, 1976. U.S. title (?): Sleeper. Walker, 1977

CROWTHER, JOHN. 1939- .
Firebase. Constable, 1975; St. Martin's, 1976 [Viet Nam]

CROYDON, JOHN. Pseudonym: John C. Cooper, q.v.

CROYLAND, WILLIAM
Sinister Civility. Nash, 1924

CROZIER, ALFRED O(WEN). 1863-1939.
The Magnet. Funk, 1908 [NYC]

CROZIER, JOHN. SC: Falcon, in both titles. Set: Eng.
Kidnapped Again. Hutchinson, 1935
Murder in Public. Hutchinson, 1934; Houghton, 1935 [theatre]

CRUGER, JULIE GRINNELL. -1920.
Pseudonym: Julien Gordon, q.v.

CRUICKSHANK, CHARLES (GREIG). 1914- Ref: CA.
The Tang Murders. Hale, 1976
The V-Mann Papers. Hale, 1976

CRUMLEY, JAMES. 1939- . Ref: CA.
The Last Good Kiss. Random, 1978; Granada, 1979 [West]
The Wrong Case. Random, 1975; Hart-Davis, 1976 [West]

CRUMP, LOUISE (ESKRIGGE)
The Face of Fear. Longmans, 1954; Foulsham, 1956

CRUMP, PAUL. Born in Chicago; given a life sentence in Ill. for murder.
Burn, Killer, Burn. Johnson, 1962 [Chi.]

CRUNDEN, ALLEN B., 1878- , and ROBERT MORSE CRUNDEN, 1940- .
Chicago Winter's Tale. Vantage, 1960 [Chi., WWI]

CRUNDEN, ROBERT MORSE. 1940- . Ref: CA. See: Allen B. Crunden, 1878-

CRUZ, MARK. SC: Chester C. Tabor, in all titles.
Dead End. Manor, 1975
Dead Wrong. Manor, 1975
Kill Squad. Manor, 1975
Voyage of Death. Manor, 1975

CSIDA, JOE
Crime Is of the Essence. Five Star, 1946 [NYC]

CUDAHY, SHEILA. Editor, poet, translator.
The Trojan Gold. Harper, 1979 [NYC]

CULLEN, ANTHONY
Studd. Avon, 1972 [Afr.]

CULLEN, CARTER. Joint pseudonym of Mildred and Richard Macaulay.
The Deadly Chase. GM, 1957; Fawcett (London), 1958 [NYC]
Don't Get Caught. GM, 1951; Fawcett (London), 1959 [Calif.]

CULLEN, S(TEPHEN)
The Haunted Priory; or, The Fortunes of the House of Rayo. Bell, 1794; Carey, 1794

CULLEY, CHRISTOPHER
The Green Mountain Murders. Ward, 1937
The Texas Bank Murders. Eldon, 1938

CULLINAN, THOMAS (P.). TV writer and playwright.
The Besieged. Horizon, 1970
The Eighth Sacrament. Putnam, 1977; Hale, 1978 [Ohio]

CULLINGFORD, GUY. Pseudonym of C(onstance) Lindsay Taylor, 1907- , q.v. Set: Eng.
Brink of Disaster. Bles, 1964; Roy, 1966
Conjurer's Coffin. Hammond, 1954; Lippincott, 1954
Framed for Hanging. Hammond, 1956; Lippincott, 1956
If Wishes Were Hearses. Hammond, 1952; Lippincott, 1953
Post Mortem. Hammond, 1953; Lippincott, 1953
The Stylist. Bles, 1968
Third Party Risk. Bles, 1962
A Touch of Drama. Hammond, 1960
The Whipping Boys. Hammond, 1958

CULLUM, RIDGWELL. 1867-1943. SC: Sgt., Insp. Stanley Fyles, in at least those marked SF.
-The Brooding Wild. Chapman, 1905
-The Bull Moose. Chapman, 1931; Lippincott, 1931
-The Candy Man. Palmer, 1926. U.S. title: Child of the North. Doran, 1926
Child of the North; see The Candy Man
-The Compact. Chapman, 1926
-The Devil's Keg. Chapman, 1903. U.S. title: The Story of the Foss River Ranch. Page, 1903. Also published as: Foss River Ranch; or, The Devil's Keg. Newnes, 1927
-The Flaming Wilderness. Chapman, 1934; Lippincott, 1934
The Forfeit; see The Purchase Price
Foss River Ranch; or, The Devil's Keg; see The Devil's Keg
-The Golden Woman. Chapman, 1913; Jacobs, 1913
-The Heart of Unaga. Chapman, 1920; Putnam, 1920
-The Hound from the North. Chapman, 1904; Page, 1904
-In the Brooding Wild. Page, 1905 (British title?)
The Law Breakers. Chapman, 1914; Jacobs, 1914 SF [Can.]
The Law of the Gun. Chapman, 1918; Jacobs, 1918 SF [Can.]
-The Luck of the Kid. Palmer, 1923; Putnam, 1923
The Man from the Lias River; see The Saint of the Speedway
-The Man in the Twilight. Palmer, 1922; Putnam, 1923
-The Men Who Wrought. Chapman, 1916; Jacobs, 1916
-The Mystery of the Barren Lands. Cassell, 1928; Lippincott, 1928 [Can.]
-The Night Riders. Chapman, 1906; Jacobs, 1913
One Who Kills. Chapman, 1938; Lippincott, 1938
-The One-Way Trail. Chapman, 1911; Jacobs, 1911
-The Purchase Price. Chapman, 1917. U.S. title: The Forfeit. Jacobs, 1917
-The Riddle of Three-Way Creek. Palmer, 1925; Doran, 1925 [Can.]
-The Saint of the Speedway. Palmer, 1924; Doran, 1924. Also published as: The Man from the Lias River. Brown Watson, 1950
-Sheets in the Wind. Chapman, 1932; Lippincott, 1932
-The Sheriff of Dyke Hole. Chapman, 1909; Jacobs, 1909
-The Son of His Father. Chapman, 1915; Jacobs, 1915
The Story of the Foss River Ranch; see The Devil's Keg
-The Tiger of Cloud River. Cassell, 1929; Lippincott, 1929
-The Trail of the Axe. Chapman, 1910; Jacobs, 1910
-The Treasure of Big Waters. Cassell, 1930; Lippincott, 1930
-The Triumph of John Kars. Chapman, 1917; Jacobs, 1917
-The Twins of Suffering Creek. Chapman, 1912; Jacobs, 1912
-The Vampire of N'Gobi. Chapman, 1935; Lippincott, 1936
-The Watchers of the Plains. Chapman, 1908; Jacobs, 1909
-The Way of the Strong. Chapman, 1914; Jacobs, 1914
-The Wolf Pack. Palmer, 1927; Lippincott, 1927

CULPAN, MAURICE. 1918- . Ref: CC. SC: Chief Insp. Bill Houghton, in all titles. Set: Eng.
Bloody Success. Collins, 1969
In a Deadly Vein. Collins, 1967
The Minister of Injustice. Collins, 1966; Walker, 1966
A Nice Place to Die. Collins, 1965
The Vasiliko Affair. Collins, 1968

CULVER, TIMOTHY J. Pseudonym of Donald E(dwin) Westlake, 1933- , q.v. Other pseudonyms: Curt Clark, Tucker Coe, Richard Stark, qq.v.
-Ex Officio. Evans, 1970. Also published as: Power Play. Dell, 1971

CUMBERLAND, GERALD. Pseudonym of Charles Frederick Kenyon, 1879-1926.
The Cypress Chest. Richards, 1927
-Tales of a Cruel Country. Richards, 1919; Brentano's, 1919 ss

CUMBERLAND, MARTEN. 1892-1972. Pseudonym: Kevin O'Hara, q.v. Ref: CA, CC, TC. SC: Saturnin Dax, in at least those marked SD, which are set in Paris/France.
And Then Came Fear. Hurst, 1949; Doubleday, 1948 SD
And Worms Have Eaten Them. Hurst, 1948. U.S. title: Hate Will Find a Way. Doubleday, 1947 SD
Attention! Saturnin Dax. Hutchinson, 1962 SD
Bird of Prey. Gramol, 1937

Booked for Death. Hurst, 1952. U.S. title: Grave Consequences. Doubleday, 1952 SD
The Charge Is Murder. Hurst, 1953 SD
Confetti Can Be Red. Hurst, 1951. U.S. title: The House in the Forest. Doubleday, 1950 SD
The Crime School. Eldon, 1949 [Paris]
The Dark House. Gramol, 1935
Darkness As a Bride. Hurst, 1947
Devil's Snare. Gramol, 1935
The Dice Were Loaded. Hutchinson, 1965 SD
A Dilemma for Dax; see Hearsed in Death
Etched in Violence. Hurst, 1953 SD
Everything He Touched. Macdonald, 1945
Fade Out the Stars. Hurst, 1952; Doubleday, 1952 SD
Far Better Dead! Hutchinson, 1957 SD
The Frightened Brides. Hurst, 1954 SD
Grave Consequences; see Booked for Death
Hate Finds a Way. Hutchinson, 1964 SD
Hate for Sale. Hutchinson, 1957; British Book Centre, 1957 SD
Hate Will Find a Way; see And Worms Have Eaten Them
Hearsed in Death. Hurst, 1947. U.S. title: A Dilemma for Dax. Doubleday, 1946 SD
The House in the Forest; see Confetti Can Be Red
The Imposter. Gramol, 1935
The Knife Will Fall. Hurst, 1943; Doubleday, 1944 SD
Loaded Dice, with B. V. Shann. Methuen, 1926. Also published as by James Bevis: Gramol, 1933
A Lovely Corpse. Hurst, 1946 SD
Lying at Death's Door. Hurst, 1956 SD
The Man Who Covered Mirrors. Hurst, 1951; Doubleday, 1949 SD
Murder at Midnight, with B. V. Shann. Mellifont, 1935
Murmurs in the Rue Morgue. Hutchinson, 1959; British Book Centre, 1959 SD
No Sentiment in Murder. Hutchinson, 1966 SD
Nobody Is Safe; see Which of Us Is Safe?
Not Expected to Live. Hurst, 1945 SD
On the Danger List. Hurst, 1950 SD
One Foot in the Grave. Hurst, 1952 SD
Out of This World. Hutchinson, 1958; British Book Centre, 1959 SD
The Perilous Way. Jarrolds, 1926
Policeman's Nightmare. Hurst, 1950; Doubleday, 1949 SD
Postscript to a Death. Hutchinson, 1963 SD
Questionable Shape. Hurst, 1941 SD
Quislings over Paris. Hurst, 1942 SD
Remains to Be Seen. Hutchinson, 1960 SD
Shadowed. Mellifont, 1936
-The Sin of David. Selwyn, 1932
Someone Must Die. Hurst, 1940 SD
Steps in the Dark. Hurst, 1945; Doubleday, 1945 SD
The Testing of Tony. Macdonald, 1943
There Must Be Victims. Hutchinson, 1961 SD
Unto Death Utterly. Hurst, 1954 SD
Which of Us Is Safe? Hurst, 1953. U.S. title: Nobody Is Safe. Doubleday, 1953 SD [Buen. A.]

CUMBERLAND, STEWART C. Pseudonym of Charles Garner.
-A Fatal Affinity. Blackett, 1889
-Marked for a Victim: A Tale of Modern Black Magic. Ogilvie, 1889 (British title?)
-The Vasty Deep. Low, 1889

CUMMINGS, JACK. 1940-   .
The Venture. Charter House, 1978; Springwood, 1979

CUMMINGS, JOHN W., JR.
The Ultimate Game. Major, 1976

CUMMINGS, RAY(MOND KING). 1887-1957.
Tales of the Scientific Crime Club. Ferret Fantasy, 1979 ss

CUMMINGS, SCOTT
The Rexworth Mystery. Philadelphia Suburban, 1911

CUMMINS, R(OBERT) E(MMET). 1849-
A Perfect Score. Stratford, 1925

CUNNINGHAM, A(LBERT) B(ENJAMIN). 1888-1962. Pseudonym: Estil Dale, q.v. Ref: CC, MP. SC: Sheriff Jess Roden, in all titles, all (with one exception) set in Ky.
The Affair at the Boat Landing. Dutton, 1943
The Bancock Murder Case. Dutton, 1942
Blood Runs Cold; see The Hunter Is the Hunted

The Cane-Patch Mystery. Dutton, 1944; Swan, 1953
Death at "The Bottoms". Dutton, 1942
Death Haunts the Dark Lane. Dutton, 1948
Death of a Bullionaire. Dutton, 1946
The Death of a Worldly Woman. Dutton, 1948
Death Rides a Sorrel Horse. Dutton, 1946
Death Visits the Apple Hole. Dutton, 1945
The Great Yant Mystery. Dutton, 1943; Swan, 1959
The Hunter Is the Hunted. Dutton, 1950. Also published as: Blood Runs Cold. Mercury, 1954, abridged
The Killer Watches the Manhunt. Dutton, 1950; Boardman, 1951
Murder at Deer Lick. Dutton, 1939
Murder at the Schoolhouse. Dutton, 1940
Murder Before Midnight. Dutton, 1945
Murder Without Weapons. Dutton, 1949; Mellifont, 1955
One Man Must Die. Dutton, 1946
Skeleton in the Closet. Dutton, 1951
The Strange Death of Manny Square. Dutton, 1941
Strange Return. Dutton, 1952
Who Killed Pretty Becky Low? Dutton, 1951

CUNNINGHAM, CHET. 1928-   . Pseudonyms: Nick Carter, Cathy Cunningham, Lionel Derrick, Paul Richards, qq.v. Ref: CA.

CUNNINGHAM, CATHY. Pseudonym of Chet Cunningham, 1928-   . Other pseudonyms: Nick Carter, Lionel Derrick, Paul Richards, qq.v.
The Demons of Highpoint House. Popular Library, 1973 [Oreg., 1910]

CUNNINGHAM, E. V. Pseudonym of Howard (Melvin) Fast, 1914-   , q.v. Other pseudonym: Walter Ericson, q.v. SC: John Comaday and Larry Cohen = C&C; Harvey Krim = HK; Sgt. Masao Masuto = MM.
Alice. Doubleday, 1963; Deutsch, 1965 [N.J.]
The Assassin Who Gave Up His Gun. Morrow, 1969 [Eng.]
The Case of the One-Penny Orange. Holt, 1977; Deutsch, 1978 MM [L.A.]
The Case of the Poisoned Eclairs. Holt, 1979; Deutsch, 1980 MM [L.A.]
The Case of the Russian Diplomat. Holt, 1978; Deutsch, 1979 MM [L.A.]
Cynthia. Morrow, 1968; Deutsch, 1969 HK [NYC]
Helen. Doubleday, 1966; Deutsch, 1967
Lydia. Doubleday, 1964; Deutsch, 1965 HK [NYC]
Margie. Morrow, 1966; Deutsch, 1968 C&C [NYC]
Millie. Morrow, 1973; Deutsch, 1974 [L.A.]
Penelope. Doubleday, 1965; Deutsch, 1966 C&C [NYC]
Phyllis. Doubleday, 1962; Deutsch, 1963 [NYC]
Sally. Morrow, 1967; Deutsch, 1967 [NYC]
Samantha. Morrow, 1967; Deutsch, 1968 MM [L.A.]
Shirley. Doubleday, 1964; Deutsch, 1964 [NYC]
Sylvia. Doubleday, 1960; Deutsch, 1962

CUNNINGHAM, JERE (PEARSON). 1943-   .
Hunter's Blood. GM, 1977
The Visitor. St. Martin's, 1978; Hodder, 1979

CUNNINGHAM, LOUIS ARTHUR. 1900-1954.
Discords of the Deep. Quality, 1938 ss, some criminous
-Fog over Fundy. Penn, 1936
-The Sign of the Burning Ship. Penn, 1940

CUNNINGHAM, RICHARD. 1939-   . Ref: CA.
A Ceremony in the Lincoln Eclairs. Sheed Andrews, 1978; Arrow, 1980 [NYC]

CUNNINGHAM, SCOTT
After the Kill. Carousel, 1980

CUNNINGHAM, WILLIAM. 1901-1967. Born and educated in Oklahoma.
Pretty Boy. Vanguard, 1936. British title: Tough Guy. Long, 1938 [Okla.]

CUOMO, GEORGE (MICHAEL). 1929-   . Ref: CA.
-Among Thieves. Doubleday, 1968; Hodder, 1969

CURLE, RICHARD (HENRY PARNELL). 1883-1968.
Corruption. Bobbs, 1933; Constable, 1933 [L.I.]
Who Goes Home? Bobbs, 1935; Constable, 1935 [Eng.]

CURLEY, THOMAS
-It's a Wise Child. New Author's Guild, 1960; Barker, 1961. Also published as: The Crooked Road. Avon, 1962

CURRAN, DALE
-Dupree Blues. Knopf, 1948

CURRIE, BARTON (WOOD), 1878-   , and AUGUSTIN McHUGH
Officer 666. Fly, 1912; Paul, 1912 [NYC]

CURRIE, JOHN DESMOND. Joint pseudonym with Elizabeth Warner: Douglas Warner, q.v.

CURRIER, JAY L. Pseudonym of James Leal Henderson, 1913-   , q.v
Cargo of Fear. Messner, 1947 [Mex., Calif.]

CURRINGTON, O(WEN) J(OSIAH). 1924-   .
SC: Jack Lovel, in both titles.
A Bad Night's Work. Deutsch, 1974
Break-Out. Deutsch, 1978

CURRY, AVON. Pseudonym of Jean Bowden, 1925-   . Other pseudonym: Jennifer Bland, q.v. Ref: CA. SC: Jerome Aylwin, in at least those marked JA. Set: Eng.
Derry Down Death. Allen, 1960 JA
Dying High. Allen, 1961 JA
The Fetish Murders. Ace, 1973 (British title?)
The Girl in the Killer's Bed; see Shack-Up
Hunt for Danger. Milton House, 1974
A Place of Execution. Long, 1969
Shack-Up. Long, 1971. U.S. title: The Girl in tne Killer's Bed. Ace, 1972

CURRY, ELLSWORTH
The Happening. Bantam, 1967 (Novelization of the movie.)

CURRY, G. LEA
A Portrush Mystery. Baird, 1909 [Ire.]

CURRY, MARIAN STEARNS
Come Sweet Death. Cherry Tree, 1946

CURRY, THOMAS ALBERT. 1900-1976. Pseudonyms: John L. Benton, Albert Jeffers, qq.v.

CURTIES, CAPTAIN HENRY. 1860-   .
-The Blood Bond. White, 1910
Idina's Lover. Ouseley, 1912
Love and the Law. Jenkins, 1925
Out of the Shadows. Greening, 1908
A Queen's Error. White, 1911
The Queen's Gate Mystery. Rivers, 1908; Estes, 1908
The Scales of Chance. Constable, 1911
The Silver Shamrock. Greening, 1911
-Tears of Angels. Sisley's, 1907

CURTIES, T. J. HORSLEY
Ancient Records; or, The Abbey of St. Oswythe. Lane, 1801
The Monk of Udolpho. Hughes, 1807 [It.]
Saint Botolph's Priory; or, The Sable Mask. Hughes, 1806 [ca.1640, Eng.]

CURTIS, FREDERICK
Vivian Morgan's First Case. Western Mail, 19??

CURTIS, GEORGE and JOSEPHINE DENVER CURTIS
-Chivalry and the Gibbet. Devin-Adair, 1926

CURTIS, JACK
Banjo. Macmillan, 1971

CURTIS, JAMES. Pseudonym.
The Gilt Kid. Cape, 1936
There Ain't No Justice. Cape, 1937; Knopf, 1937
-They Drive by Night. Cape, 1938
What Immortal Hand. Nicholson, 1939
You're in the Racket, Too. Cape, 1937; Knopf, 1938

CURTIS, JEAN LOUIS. 1917-   .
Lucifer's Dream. Lehmann, 1952; Putnam, 1953 (Translation of "Gibier de Potence." Paris, 1949.)

CURTIS, JOSEPHINE DENVER. See: George Curtis.

CURTIS, JULIA ANN KEMBLE. 1764-1838.
    The Secret Avengers; or, The Rock of
      Glotzden. Minerva, 1815
    Sicilian Mysteries; or, The Fortress
      Del Vechii. Colburn, 1812 [Sic.]

CURTIS, MARJORIE. Pseudonym of Marjorie
    Mary Curtis Prebble, 1912-   .
    Ref: CA.
    Dew in the Morning. Hale, 1975

CURTIS, MIKE
    Midtown North. Leisure, 1976
    -Overdrive. Belmont, 1976
    The Savage Woman. Leisure, 1976

CURTIS, PETER. Pseudonym of Norah (Robin-
    son) Lofts, 1904-   , q.v. Other
    pseudonym: Juliet Astley, q.v.
    The Bride of Moat House; see Dead March
      in Three Keys
    Dead March in Three Keys. Davies, 1940.
      Reprinted as by Norah Lofts: Hodder,
      1970. U.S. title: No Question of Mur-
      der. Doubleday, 1959. Reprinted as:
      The Bride of Moat House. Dell, 1969
    The Devil's Own. Macdonald, 1960;
      Doubleday, 1960. Also published as:
      The Witches. Pan, 1966; and as: The
      Little Wax Doll, as by Norah Lofts.
      Hodder, 1971; Doubleday, 1970
    Lady Living Alone. Macdonald, 1945
    The Little Wax Doll; see The Devil's
      Own
    No Question of Murder; see Dead March
      in Three Keys
    The Witches; see The Devil's Own
    -You're Best Alone. Macdonald, 1943

CURTIS, RICHARD. SC: Dave Bolt (The Pro),
    in all titles.
    Death in the Crease. Warner, 1975
      [Montr.]
    Strike Zone. Warner, 1975
    The Suicide Squad. Warner, 1975
    The $3 Million Turn-Over. Warner, 1974

CURTIS, ROBERT
    Curiosities of Detection; or, The Sea-
      Coast Station and other tales. Ward,
      1862 ss
    The Irish Police Officer. Ward, 1861
      ss [Ire.]

CURTIS, ROGER (G.).   -ca.1936.
    The Children of Light. Hutchinson, 1935
    Corpses Can't Walk. Hutchinson, 1936
    The Green Pack. Hutchinson, 1933;
      Doubleday, 1933, as by Edgar Wallace
      and R. G. Curtis (Novelization of
      the play by Edgar Wallace, 1875-1932,
      q.v.)
    Invitation to Murder. Hutchinson, 1936
    The Man Who Changed His Name. Hutchin-
      son, 1934; Doubleday, 1934, as by
      Edgar Wallace and R. G. Curtis
      (Novelization of the play by Edgar
      Wallace, 1875-1932, q.v.)
    The Mouthpiece. Hutchinson, 1935;
      Dodge, 1936, as by Edgar Wallace and
      Robert Curtis (Novelization of the
      play by Edgar Wallace, 1875-1932,
      q.v.)
    Sanctuary Island. Hutchinson, 1936
      (Novelization of the play by Edgar
      Wallace, 1875-1932, q.v.)
    Smoky Cell. Hutchinson, 1935 (Noveli-
      zation of the play by Edgar Wallace,
      1875-1932, q.v.) [U.S.]
    The Table. Hutchinson, 1936 (Noveliza-
      tion of the play by Edgar Wallace,
      1875-1932, q.v.)

CURTIS, SPENCER
    A Picture of Murder. Hale, 1972
    Step into Murder. Hale, 1971

CURTIS, SUSANNAH
    The Monk's Retreat. Hurst, 1973

CURTIS, SYDNEY ALBERT
    The Evil That Men Do. Hale, 1977
    Nobody Shoots Forever. Hale, 1979
    The Violent Breed. Hale, 1978
    When Thieves Fall Out. Hale, 1976

CURTIS, WADE. Pseudonym of Jerry Eugene
    Pournelle, 1933-   . Ref: CA. SC:
    Paul Crane, in both titles.
    Red Dragon. Berkley, 1971 [L.A.]
    Red Heroin. Berkley, 1969 [Seattle]

CURTIS, WARDON ALLAN. 1867-1940.
    The Strange Adventures of Mr. Middle-
      ton. Stone, 1903 ss [Ill.]

CURTISS, E(LIZABETH) M(ANGAM). SC: Dr.
    Nathaniel Bunce, in both titles.
    Dead Dogs Bite. Simon, 1939 [Naples]
    Nine Doctors and a Madman. Simon, 1937;
      Jenkins, 1938 [hosp.]

CURTISS, PHILIP EVERETT. 1855-1964.
    Crater's Gold. Harper, 1919; Butter-
      worth, 1920
    The Gay Conspirators. Harper, 1924
      [Mass.]
    The Mysterious Mr. Pickering; see
      Wanted: A Fool
    Wanted: A Fool. Harper, 1920. British
      title: The Mysterious Mr. Pickering.
      Butterworth, 1921 [NYC]

CURTISS, URSULA (REILLY). 1923-   .
    Ref: CA, CC, EM, MC, TC.
    The Birthday Gift. Dodd, 1976. British
      title: Dig a Little Deeper. Macmillan
      (London), 1976 [Conn.]
    Catch a Killer; see The Noonday Devil
    Child's Play; see Out of the Dark
    Danger: Hospital Zone. Dodd, 1966;
      Hodder, 1967 [Albuq.]
    The Deadly Climate. Dodd, 1954; Eyre,
      1955 [Mass.]
    Dig a Little Deeper; see The Birthday
      Gift
    Don't Open the Door. Dodd, 1968; Hod-
      der, 1969 [Albuq.]
    The Face of the Tiger. Dodd, 1958;
      Eyre, 1960 [Conn.]
    The Forbidden Garden. Dodd, 1962; Eyre,
      1963. Also published as: Whatever
      Happened to Aunt Alice? Ace, 1969
      [New Mex.]
    The Hollow House; see The Second Sickle
    Hours to Kill. Dodd, 1961; Eyre, 1962
      [New Mex.]
    In Cold Pursuit. Dodd, 1977; Macmillan
      (London), 1978 [Mex.]
    The Iron Cobweb. Dodd, 1953; Eyre, 1953
      [Mass.]
    Letter of Intent. Dodd, 1971; Macmil-
      lan (London), 1972 [Conn.]
    The Menace Within. Dodd, 1979; Macmil-
      lan (London), 1979 [Albuq.]
    The Noonday Devil. Dodd, 1951; Eyre,
      1953. Also published as: Catch a
      Killer. PB, 1953 [Mass.]
    Out of the Dark. Dodd, 1964. British
      title: Child's Play. Eyre, 1965
      [S.W.]
    The Poisoned Orchard. Dodd, 1980; Mac-
      millan (London), 1980 [Albuq.]
    The Second Sickle. Dodd, 1950. British
      title: The Hollow House. Evans, 1951
      [Boston]
    So Dies the Dreamer. Dodd, 1960; Eyre,
      1960 [Mass.]
    The Stairway. Dodd, 1957; Eyre, 1958
      [Conn.]
    Voice Out of Darkness. Dodd, 1948;
      Evans, 1949 [Conn.]
    The Wasp. Dodd, 1963; Eyre, 1964
      [Conn.]
    Whatever Happened to Aunt Alice?; see
      The Forbidden Garden
    Widow's Web. Dodd, 1956; Eyre, 1956
      [Conn.]

CURTOIS, M(ARGARET) A(NNE)
    In Minden Town. Faber, 1926

CURWOOD, JAMES OLIVER. 1878-1927.
    Philipp Steele of the Royal Northwest
      Mounted Police. Bobbs, 1911; Everett,
      1912 [Can.]

CURZON, CLARE
    A Leaven of Malice. Collins, 1979

CURZON, COLIN. ca.1917-   . With the
    R.A.F. during WWII. SC: Mark Antony,
    in both titles. Set: Eng.
    The Body in the Barrage Balloon; or,
      Who Killed the Corpse? Hurst, 1941;
      Macmillan, 1942
    The Case of the Eighteenth Ostrich.
      Hurst, 1943; Macmillan, 1944

CUSACK, (ELLEN) DYMPHNA. 1902-   . Ref:
    CA.
    Say No to Death. Heinemann, 1951

CUSHING, E. LOUISE. SC: Insp. MacKay, in
    at least those marked M.
    Blood on My Rug. Arcadia, 1956 M
      [Can.]
    Murder Without Regret. Arcadia, 1954 M
    Murder's No Picnic. Arcadia, 1953;
      Wright, 1956
    The Unexpected Corpse. Arcadia, 1957 M

CUSHMAN, CLARISSA FAIRCHILD. 1889-1980.
    Ref: MP. Author of serials and roman-
    tic fiction.
    The Fatal Step. Little, 1953
    I Wanted to Murder. Farrar, 1940;
      Methuen, 1941 [N.Y.]

CUSHMAN, DAN. 1909-   . Ref: CA. SC:
    Crawford, in at least those marked C.
    -The Fabulous Finn. GM, 1954; Fawcett
      (London), 1955
    -The Forbidden Land. GM, 1958; Fawcett
      (London), 1959
    Jewel of the Java Sea. GM, 1951; Red
      Seal, 1957 [Borneo]
    -Jungle She. GM, 1953; Fawcett (London),
      1954
    Naked Ebony. GM, 1951; Fawcett (Lon-
      don), 1953 C
    Opium Flower. Bantam, 1963; Hammond,
      1964 [Far East]
    Port Orient. GM, 1955 [Far East]
    Savage Interlude. GM, 1952; Fawcett
      (London), 1953 C
    -Timberjack. GM, 1953; Fawcett (Lon-
      don), 1955
    -Tongking! Ace, 1954

CUSSLER, CLIVE (ERIC). 1931-   . Ref:
    CA. SC: Dirk Pitt = DP.
    Iceberg. Dodd, 1975; Sphere, 1976 DP
    Mayday! see The Mediterranean Caper
    The Mediterranean Caper. Pyramid, 1973.
      British title: Mayday! Sphere, 1977
    Raise the Titanic! Viking, 1976; Jo-
      seph, 1977 DP
    Vixen 03. Viking, 1978; Hodder, 1978
      DP [1988, U.S.]

CUTLER, ROLAND
    The Gates of Sagittarius. Dial, 1980
      [Havana, 1939]

D., A. E. Pseudonym of Alice Elizabeth
    Dracott.
    A Mystery at King's Grant. SPCK, 1896

D., E. A. B. Pseudonym of E. A. Bland.
    Constable 42Z. Religious Tract Soci-
    ety, 1888

D'ABBES, INGRAM and FENN SHERIE
    Murder in Motley. French (London), 1953
    (3-act play.)

DABBS, GEORGE H(ENRY) R(OQUE). 1846-1913.
    The Manor Inn. Deacon, 1899

DACRE, CHARLOTTE. 1782-   .
    Zofloya; or, The Moor. Longman, 1806;
      Arno, 1974 [1400s]

DA CRUZ, DANIEL (JR.). 1921-   . Ref: CA.
    SC: Jock Sergeant = JS; Ape Swain =
    AS.
    The Captive City. Ballantine, 1976 AS
      [Mid. East]
    Deep Kill. GM, 1974 JS
    Double Kill. GM, 1973; Coronet, 1973
      JS [Calif.]
    Fire Kill. GM, 1976; Coronet, 1976 JS
      [NYC]
    The Landfall Finesse. Ballantine, 1975
      AS [Mid. East]
    The Pipe Dream Finesse. Ballantine,
      1975 AS
    Sky Kill. GM, 1974; Coronet, 1976 JS
    Vulcan's Hammer. New American Library,
      1967 [Wash. D.C.]

DAEMER, WILL. Joint pseudonym of Robert
    Wade, 1920-   , q.v., and Bill Mil-
    ler, 1920-1961. Other joint pseudo-
    nyms: Whit Masterson, Wade Miller,
    Dale Wilmer, qq.v. See also: Bob
    Wade.
    The Case of the Lonely Lovers. Farrell,
      1951 [Calif.]

DAGLESS, THOMAS
    The Light in Dends Wood, and other sto-
      ries. Greening, 1903 ss, some cri-
      minous

DAGMAR. SC: Randy Kidd and Regina, in
    both titles.
    The Spy Who Came In from the Copa. Lan-
      cer, 1967
    The Spy with the Blue Kazoo. Lancer,
      1967

D'AGNEAU, MARCEL
    Eeny Meeny Miny Mole. Arlington, 1980
      [future]

DAHL, ROALD. 1916-   . Ref: CA, MC, TC.
    Kiss Kiss. Joseph, 1960; Knopf, 1960
      ss
    -More Tales of the Unexpected. Joseph,
      1980; Penguin, 1980 ss
    Someone Like You. Secker, 1954; Knopf,
      1953. Revised and expanded edition:
      Joseph, 1961 ss
    Switch Bitch. Joseph, 1974; Knopf, 1974
      ss, one criminous
    -Tales of the Unexpected. Joseph, 1979;
      Vintage, 1980 ss

DAHLGREN, MADELEINE VINTON. 1825-1898.
    The Woodley Lane Ghost and other sto-
      ries. Drexel Biddle, 1899 ss, some
      criminous

DAIGER, K(ATHERINE) S. SC: Insp. Everett Anderson, in both titles, set in Md.
  Fourth Degree. Macrae Smith, 1931; Harrap, 1932
  Murder on Ghost Tree Island. Macrae Smith, 1934; Harrap, 1934

DAINGERFIELD, FOXHALL (ALEXANDER). 1887-1933.
  Ghost House. Appleton, 1926 [La.]
  The House Across the Way. Appleton, 1928
  The Linden Walk Tragedy. Appleton, 1929 [South]
  The Silver Urn. Appleton, 1927
  That Gay Nineties Murder. Doubleday, 1928 [Ky., 1890]

DAINTON, WILLIE. Pseudonym.
  -Blind Quest. Nicholson, 1944
  The Matsu Dossier. Nicholson, 1948

DAKERS, ANDREW HERBERT. 1887- . Pseudonym: Andrew Stewart, q.v.

DALE, ADRIAN
  Murder Behind the Mask. French (London), 1977 (Play.)

DALE, ALAN. Pseudonym of Alfred J. Cohen, 1861-1928.
  Ned Bachman, the New Orleans Detective. Ogilvie, 1887 [New Or.]

DALE, CELIA (MARJORIE). 1912- . Ref: CA. Set: Eng.
  A Dark Corner. Macmillan (London), 1971
  The Deception; see Helping with Inquiries
  A Helping Hand. Macmillan (London), 1966; Walker, 1966
  Helping with Inquiries. Macmillan (London), 1979. U.S. title: The Deception. Harper, 1980

DALE, DARLEY. Pseudonym of Francesca Maria Steele, 1848- .
  -The Village Blacksmith. Hutchinson, 1892. U.S. title: Reuben Foreman, the Village Blacksmith. Bonner's, 1892

DALE, ESTIL. Pseudonym of A(lbert) B(enjamin) Cunningham, 1888-1962, q.v.
  The Last Survivor. Dutton, 1952

DALE, FRANCES. Pseudonym of Phyllis Nan Sortain Cradock.
  -Scorpion's Suicide. Hurst, 1942

DALE, HENRY
  Adventurous Exploits of the Younger Brothers. Street, 1890

DALE, JO ANNE
  Long Distance. Zebra, 1980 [Houston]

DALE, OLIVER
  A Bit of Red May. Allen, 1896
  Strange Stories of Strange People. Henry, 1894 ss, some criminous

DALE, VIRGINIA
  They Waited for the Night. Doubleday, 1939

DALE, WILLIAM
  John Doe—Murderer. Gateway, 1942; United Authors, 1946
  Outside the Law. Dodge, 1938
  The Terror of the Handless Corpse. Gateway, 1939

DALEY, JOSEPH A(NDREW). 1927- . Ref: CA.
  Spicy Lady. St. Martin's, 1973; Macdonald, 1974 [NYC, 1968]

DALEY, ROBERT (BLAKE). 1930- .
  To Kill a Cop. Crown, 1976 [NYC]

DALHEATH, DAVID
  The Shadow of the Cobra. Hale, 1975

DALL, JACK
  Death of a Revolutionist. Gateway, 1940. Also published as: Murder Moves On. Green Dragon, 194?, abridged [Eng.]

DALLAS, DUNCAN. SC: Paul Richards, in both titles.
  "I.L.F." Ouseley, 1909
  Paul Richards—Detective. Ouseley, 1908 ss

DALLAS, JOHN. Pseudonym of W(illiam) Murdoch Duncan, 1909-1975, q.v. Other pseudonyms: John Cassells, Neill Graham, Martin Locke, Peter Malloch, Lovat Marshall, qq.v.
  The Night of the Storm. Jenkins, 1961 [Can.]
  Red Ice. Hale, 1973

DALLAS, OSWALD (C. C.). See: Draycot (Montagu) Dell, 1888- .

DALLAS, RICHARD. Pseudonym of Nathan Winslow Williams, 1860-1924.
  A Master Hand. Putnam, 1903 [NYC]

DALMAINE, JAMES
  The Vengeance of Science. Stockwell, 1927

DALMAN, MAX. Set: Eng.
  Buried Once. Ward, 1946
  The Burnt Bones Mystery. Ward, 1940
  Death Before Day. Ward, 1942
  Death Disposes. Ward, 1945
  Death on May Morning. Ward, 1938
  Doctor Disappears. Ward, 1941
  The Elusive Nephew. Ward, 1948
  Herald of Death. Ward, 1943
  The Hidden Light. Ward, 1937
  Mask for Murder. Ward, 1940
  The Missing Grave. Ward, 1939
  Poison Unknown. Ward, 1939
  Third Alibi. Ward, 1942
  Three Strangers. Ward, 1937
  Vampire Abroad. Ward, 1938

DALMAS, HERBERT
  Exit Screaming. Walker, 1966 [acad.]
  The Fowler Formula. Doubleday, 1967; Gollancz, 1968 [Mass.]

D'ALPINS, MARCHIONESS
  The House of the Lost Court. Hodder, 1908

DALTON, CLAIRE. Pseudonym of Alma Burns, 1917- , q.v.
  The Second Life of Cecily Pride. Beagle, 1973

DALTON, EMMETT. 1871- .
  Beyond the Law. Ogilvie, 1916

DALTON, JOHN J.
  The Vindicator. Manor, 1979

DALTON, MORAY. Ref: CC. SC: Insp. Hugh Collier, in at least those marked HC. Set: Eng.
  The Art School Murders. Low, 1943
  The Belfry Murder. Low, 1933 HC
  The Belgrave Manor Crime. Low, 1935 HC
  The Black Death. Low, 1934
  The Black Wings. Jarrolds, 1927
  The Body in the Road. Low, 1931; Harper, 1930
  The Case of Alan Copeland. Low, 1937
  The Case of the Dark Stranger. Low, 1948 HC
  The Condamine Case. Low, 1947 HC
  Death at the Villa. Low, 1946
  Death in the Cup. Low, 1932
  Death in the Dark. Low, 1938 HC
  Death in the Forest. Low, 1939 HC
  Death of a Spinster. Low, 1951 HC
  The Edge of Doom. Low, 1934
  The Harvest of Tares. Low, 1933 HC
  The House of Fear. Low, 1951
  Inquest on Miriam. Low, 1949 HC
  The Kingsclere Mystery. Jarrolds, 1924
  The Longbridge Murders. Low, 1945 HC
  The Murder of Eve. Low, 1945
  The Mystery of the Kneeling Woman. Low, 1936 HC
  The Night of Fear. Low, 1931; Harper, 1931 HC
  One by One They Disappeared. Jarrolds, 1929; Harper, 1929 HC
  The Price of Silence. Low, 1939
  The Shadow on the Wall. Jarrolds, 1926
  The Strange Case of Harriet Hall. Low, 1936 HC
  The Stretton Darknesse Mystery. Jarrolds, 1927
  The Wife of Baal. Low, 1932 [It.]

DALTON, PAT
  Devil's End. PB, 1978

DALTON, PRISCILLA. Pseudonym of Michael (Angelo) Avallone (Jr.), 1924- , q.v. Other pseudonyms: Nick Carter, Mark Dane, Jean-Anne de Pre, Stuart Jason, Steve Michaels, Dorothea Nile, Dora Highland, Edwina Noone, Sidney Stuart, Max Walker, qq.v.
  The Darkening Willows. Paperback Library, 1965 [N.Y., ca.1910]
  90 Gramercy Park. Paperback Library, 1965 [NYC]
  The Silent, Silken Shadows. Paperback Library, 1965 [Conn.]

DALY, CARROLL JOHN. 1889-1958. Ref: EM, MC, TC. SC: Vee Brown, in at least those marked VB; Satan Hall, in at least those marked SH; Race Williams, in at least those marked RW.
  The Amateur Murderer. Washburn, 1933; Hutchinson, 1933 RW [Balt.]
  Better Corpses. Hale, 1940
  Death's Juggler; see The Mystery of the Smoking Gun
  Emperor of Evil. Stokes, 1937; Hutchinson, 1936 VB [NYC]
  The Hidden Hand. Clode, 1929; Hutchinson, 1930 RW [Fla.]
  The Legion of the Living Dead. Popular Publications (Toronto), 1947
  The Man in the Shadows. Clode, 1928; Hutchinson, 1929 [New Eng.]
  Mr. Strang. Stokes, 1936; Hale, 1937
  Murder at Our House. Museum, 1950
  Murder from the East. Stokes, 1935; Hutchinson, 1935 RW [NYC]
  Murder Won't Wait. Washburn, 1933; Hutchinson, 1934 VB [NYC]
  The Mystery of the Smoking Gun. Stokes, 1936. British title: Death's Juggler. Hutchinson, 1935 SH [NYC]
  Ready to Burn. Museum, 1951 SH [NYC]
  The Snarl of the Beast. Clode, 1927; Hutchinson, 1928 RW
  The Tag Murders. Clode, 1930; Hutchinson, 1931 RW
  Tainted Power. Clode, 1931; Hutchinson, 1931 RW [NYC]
  The Third Murderer. Farrar, 1931; Hutchinson, 1932 RW [NYC]
  The White Circle. Clode, 1926; Hutchinson, 1927 [NYC]

DALY, ELIZABETH. 1878-1967. Ref: CA, CC, EM, MP, TC. SC: Henry Gamadge, in all titles.
  And Dangerous to Know. Rinehart, 1949; Hammond, 1952 [NYC]
  Any Shape or Form. Farrar, 1945; Hammond, 1949
  Arrow Pointing Nowhere. Farrar, 1944; Hammond, 1946. Also published as: Murder Listens In. Bantam, 1949 [NYC]
  The Book of the Crime. Rinehart, 1951; Hammond, 1954 [NYC]
  The Book of the Dead. Farrar, 1944; Hammond, 1946 [NYC]
  The Book of the Lion. Rinehart, 1948; Hammond, 1951 [NYC]
  Deadly Nightshade. Farrar, 1940; Hammond, 1948 [Maine]
  Death and Letters. Rinehart, 1950; Hammond, 1953 [N.Y.]
  Evidence of Things Seen. Farrar, 1943; Hammond, 1946 [Conn.]
  The House Without a Door. Farrar, 1942; Hammond, 1945 [NYC]
  Murder Listens In; see Arrow Pointing Nowhere
  Murders in Volume 2. Farrar, 1941; Eyre, 1943 [NYC]
  Night Walk. Rinehart, 1947; Hammond, 1950 [N.Y.]
  Nothing Can Rescue Me. Farrar, 1943; Hammond, 1945
  Shroud for a Lady; see The Wrong Way Down
  Somewhere in the House. Rinehart, 1946; Hammond, 1949 [NYC]
  Unexpected Night. Farrar, 1940; Gollancz, 1940 [New Eng.]
  The Wrong Way Down. Rinehart, 1946; Hammond, 1950. Also published as: Shroud for a Lady. Bestseller, 1956 [NYC]

DALY, HAMLIN
  Case of the Cancelled Redhead. Falcon, ca.1952

DALY, TREVE. Pseudonym. See: Raymond Thompson, 1949- .

DALZELL, WILLIAM. See: Newt Mitzman.

D'AMATO, BARBARA. 1938- . Ref: CA.
  The Hands of Healing Murder. Charter, 1980 [Chi.]

DAMER, ANNE and JACK DENTON SCOTT, 1915- , q.v.
  Too Lively to Live. Doubleday, 1945 [Eng.]

DAMIEN, CHRISTINE. Pseudonym of Cynthia Kreke.
  Appleshaw. Ballantine, 1975 [Ky.]

DAMORE, LEO. 1929- . Ref: CA.
  Cache. Arbor, 1979; Curley, 1980

DAN, URI
  Carlos Must Die, with Peter Mann. Leisure, 1978
  The Eichmann Syndrome, with Edward Radley. Leisure, 1977
  The Face of Terror. Leisure, 1978
  Ultimatum: PU-94, with Peter Mann. Leisure, 1977

DANA, FRANCIS
  The Decoy. Lane, 1902

DANA, FREEMAN. Pseudonym of Phoebe Atwood Taylor, 1909-1976, q.v. Other pseudonym: Alice Tilton, q.v.
    Murder at the New York World's Fair. Random, 1938 [NYC]

DANA, MARVIN. 1867- .
    The Lake Mystery. McClurg, 1923 [Mass.]
    The Master Mind. Fly, 1913 (Novelization of the play by Daniel D. Carter.) [NYC]
    The Mystery of the Third Parrot. McClurg, 1924; Hodder, 1925 [NYC]
    Paid; see Within the Law
    Within the Law. Fly, 1913; Mills, 1913, as by Marvin Dana and Esme Forest. Also published as: Paid. Grosset, 1930 (Novelization of the play by Bayard Veiller, 1869-1943, q.v.) [NYC]

DANA, RICHARD. Pseudonym of Lauran Bosworth Paine, 1916- . Other pseudonyms: John Armour, Reg Batchelor, Kenneth Bedford, Frank Bosworth, Mark Carrel, Robert Clarke, J. F. Drexler, Troy Howard, Jared Ingersol, John Kilgore, Hunter Liggett, J. K. Lucas, John Morgan, qq.v.
    Death of a Millionaire. Hale, 1969 [Memphis]
    Death Was the Echo. Hale, 1975 [L.A.]
    Murder in Paradise. Hale, 1969 [S. Pac.]
    Murderer's Moon. Hale, 1969

DANA, ROSE. Pseudonym of W(illiam) E(dward) D(aniel) Ross, 1912- , q.v. Other pseudonyms: Laura Frances Brooks, Jan Daniels, Ellen Randolph, Clarissa Ross, Dan Ross, Dana Ross, Marilyn Ross, qq.v.
    Brooding Mist. Hale, 1967

DANBY, FRANK. Pseudonym of Julia Davis Frankau, 1864-1916.
    -The Sphinx's Lawyer. Heinemann, 1906; Stokes, 1906
    The Story Behind the Verdict. Cassell, 1915; Dodd, 1915 ss

DANBY, H. C.
    -Clang on the Anvil. Jarrolds, 1946
    -Sleeping Dogs Laugh. Jarrolds, 1948

DANE, CLEMENCE and HELEN (De GUERRY) SIMPSON, 1897-1940, q.v. Clemence Dane is the pseudonym of Winifred Ashton, 1888-1965. Ref: CC, MM, MP, TC. SC: Sir John Saumarez = JS. Set: Eng.
    Author Unknown; see Printer's Devil
    Enter Sir John. Hodder, 1928; Cosmopolitan, 1928 JS
    Printer's Devil. Hodder, 1930. U.S. title: Author Unknown. Cosmopolitan, 1930
    Re-Enter Sir John. Hodder, 1932; Farrar, 1932 JS

DANE, DANIEL. Pseudonym of Ernest S. Hanson.
    Vengeance Is Mine. Cassell (London & NYC), 1890. Also published as: Is She Not a Woman?; or, Vengeance Is Mine. Cassell (NYC), 1895

DANE, ELLIOTT
    Crime Takes the Count. Background, 1948

DANE, EVA
    A Lion by the Mane. Macdonald, 1977
    Shadows in the Fire. Macdonald, 1975
    The Vaaldorp Diamond. Macdonald, 1978

DANE, JOEL Y. Pseudonym of Joseph Francis Delaney, 1905- . SC: Sgt. Cass Harty, in all titles.
    The Cabana Murders. Doubleday, 1937 [L.I.]
    The Christmas Tree Murders. Doubleday, 1938 [NYC]
    Grasp at Straws. Doubleday, 1938 [NYC]
    Murder Cum Laude. Smith & Haas, 1935. British title: Murder in College. Bell, 1935 [NYC, acad.]
    Murder in College; see Murder Cum Laude

DANE, JOHN COLIN
    The Hidden House. Cassell, 1906

DANE, MARK. Pseudonym of Michael (Angelo) Avallone (Jr.), 1924- , q.v. Other pseudonyms: Nick Carter, Priscilla Dalton, Jean-Anne de Pre, Dora Highland, Stuart Jason, Steve Michaels, Dorothea Nile, Edwina Noone, Sidney Stuart, Max Walker, qq.v.
    Felicia. Belmont, 1964 (Novelization of the movie.) [P. Rico]

DANE, MARY. Pseudonym of Nigel Morland, 1905- , q.v. Other pseudonyms: John Donavan, Norman Forrest, Roger Garnett, Neal Shepherd, Vincent McCall, qq.v.
    Death Traps the Killer. Wright, 1938

DANIEL, F(ERDINAND) E(UGENE). 1839-1914.
    -The Strange Case of Dr. Bruno. Guarantee, 1906

DANIEL, GLYN (EDMUND). 1914- . Pseudonym: Dilwyn Rees, q.v. Ref: CA, CC, EM, TC. SC: Sir Richard Cherington, in the title below and that published as by Dilwyn Rees.
    Welcome Death. Gollancz, 1954; Dodd, 1955 [Wales]

DANIEL, ROBIN. Ref: CC.
    Death by Drowning. Gollancz, 1960; Walker, 1961

DANIEL, (WILLIAM) ROLAND. 1880-1969. Ref: TC. SC: Wu Fang, in at least those marked WF; Michael Grant, in at least those marked MG; John Hopkins, in at least those marked JH; Insp. Neville Langham, in at least those marked NL; Buddy Mustard, in at least those marked BM; Brian O'Malley, in at least those marked BO; Insp. Jack Pearson, in at least those marked JP; The Remover, in at least those marked R; Bill Saville, in at least those marked BS; Insp. John Walk, in at least those marked JW; Michael Wallace, in at least those marked MW. Set: Eng.
    Again the Remover. Wright, 1939 R,BS
    All Thugs Are Dangerous. Wright, 1958
    Amber Eyes. Wright, 1935
    Ann Turns Detective. Wright, 1932 JW
    The Arch-Criminal. Wright, 1933
    Arrested for Murder. Wright, 1950 BO
    The Arrow of Death. Wright, 1951 BM
    At the Silver Butterfly. Wright, 1938
    The Big Racket. Wright, 1955
    The Big Shot. Wright, 1962 BM
    The Big Squeal. Wright, 1940
    The Black Eagle. Wright, 1950
    The Black Market. Wright, 1943
    The Black Raven. Wright, 1939
    The Blackmailer. Wright, 1934 R,BS
    The Blonde Murder Case. Wright, 1939
    The Brown Murder Case. Shaylor, 1930 NL
    Brunettes Are Dangerous. Wright, 1960 MG
    The Buddha's Secret. Wright, 1937
    A Bunch of Crooks. Wright, 1946
    The Case of the Blackmailed King; see The Case of the King of Montavia
    The Case of the King of Montavia. Wright, 1953. Also published as: The Case of the Blackmailed King. Mellifont, 1955
    The Crackswoman. Wright, 1932 JP
    The Crawshay Jewel Mystery. Wright, 1941 BM
    The Crimson Shadow. Wright, 1935 JP
    Dangerous Mission. Wright, 1959
    Dangerous Moment. Wright, 1957
    Deadly Mission. Wright, 1961 BO
    A Dead Man Sings. Wright, 1949 BM
    Dead Man's Corner. Wright, 1932
    Dead Man's Vengeance. Shaylor, 1931 JW
    Death by the Lake. Wright, 1963 MG
    The Death House. Wright, 1941
    The Desert Crime. Wright, 1946
    The Devil Woman. Wright, 1964 BO
    The Doublecrosser. Wright, 1942
    A Double-Crossing Traitor. Wright, 1959
    The Dragon's Claw. Wright, 1934
    Evil Eyes. Wright, 1942
    Evil Shadows. Wright, 1944 BM
    The Female Spy. Wright, 1964 BO
    Frightened Eyes. Wright, 1956 MG
    The Gangster. Wright, 1932
    The Gangster's Daughter. Wright, 1965 BM
    The Gangster's Last Shot. Wright, 1939 JP
    The Girl by the Roadside. Wright, 1942
    The Girl in the Dark. Wright, 1945
    The Great Secret. Wright, 1958
    The Green Jade God. Wright, 1932
    The Hangman Waits. Wright, 1963 BM
    The Haughton Diamond Robbery. Wright, 1947
    Human Vultures. Wright, 1939 JW
    The Hunchback of Soho. Wright, 1943
    Husky Voice. Wright, 1932
    It Happened at Night. Wright, 1952
    The Jail-Breakers. Wright, 1934
    The Kenya Tragedy. Wright, 1948
    Kidnapped Wife. Wright, 1965
    The Kidnappers. Wright, 1959 MG
    The Killer. Wright, 1935
    Killers Must Die. Wright, 1955
    The Lady in Scarlet. Wright, 1947 BM
    The Lady Turned Traitor. Wright, 1961
    The Lady Was a Spy. Wright, 1962 MW
    The Langley Murder Case. Wright, 1938
    The Little Old Lady. Wright, 1950
    The 'Lo Sweeny Gang. Wright, 1935
    Lovely But Dangerous. Wright, 1960 MW
    The Man from Paris. Wright, 1958 BM
    The Man from Prison. Wright, 1949
    The Man Who Sold Secrets. Wright, 1948
    The Man Who Sought Trouble. Wright, 1935
    The Man with the Magnetic Eyes. Wright, 1938
    The Millionaire Crook. Wright, 1944
    The Missing Body. Wright, 1961 BM
    The Missing Heiress. Wright, 1942
    The Missing Lady. Wright, 1937 JW
    Mrs. Greystone—Murdered. Wright, 1947
    Murder at a Cottage. Wright, 1949 BM
    Murder at Little Malling. Wright, 1946 JP
    The Murder Gang. Wright, 1954 BM
    Murder Goes Free. Wright, 1954
    Murder in Dawson City. Wright, 1957
    Murder in Ocean Drive. Wright, 1964 MG
    Murder in Piccadilly. Wright, 1950
    Murder of a Bookmaker. Wright, 1953
    Murder of Guy Thorpe. Wright, 1956
    The Murphy Gang. Wright, 1934
    The Mystery of Mary Hamilton. Wright, 1932
    Night Club Murder. Wright, 1963 MW
    On the Run. Wright, 1955
    The Princess' Own. Wright, 1933
    The Prisoner. Wright, 1965 MW
    The Professor. Wright, 1944 BM
    Quicksilver. Wright, 1953
    Red-Headed Dames and Murder. Wright, 1960 MG
    Red Murchison. Wright, 1936
    The Remover. Wright, 1933 R,BS
    The Remover Returns. Wright, 1935 R,BS
    The Return of Wu Fang. Wright, 1937 WF
    The River Gang. Wright, 1938
    The Rosario Murder Case. Brentano's, 1930 JH,NL
    Ruby of a Thousand Dreams. Wright, 1933
    Sally of the Underworld. Wright, 1934
    Scarthroat. Wright, 1934; Godwin, 1935
    The Secret Hand. Wright, 1936
    The Secret Service Girl. Wright, 1966
    Shattered Hopes. Wright, 1941
    The Shooting of Sergius Leroy. Wright, 1932 JH
    The Signal. Wright, 1932
    Singapore Kate. Wright, 1943
    Slant Eye. Wright, 1940
    The Slayer. Wright, 1936
    Slick-Fingered Kate. Wright, 1936
    Snake Face. Wright, 1936
    The Snide Man. Wright, 1937
    The Society of the Spiders. Brentano's, 1928 BS
    The Son of Wu Fang. Wright, 1935 WF
    Special Agent. Wright, 1957
    Spencer Blair, G-Man. Wright, 1949
    The Spider's Web. Wright, 1943
    The Stedman Gang. Wright, 1936
    The Stolen Necklace. Wright, 1954
    The Stool Pigeon. Wright, 1936 JW
    The Stop-at-Nothing Man. Wright, 1950
    Suicide Can Be Murder. Wright, 1956
    This Woman Is Wanted. Wright, 1940
    Three Sundays to Live. Wright, 1952 BM
    "The Tipster." Wright, 1937
    Trouble at the Inn. Wright, 1953
    The Twenty-Two Windows. Wright, 1942
    The Undercover Girl. Wright, 1951
    White Eagle. Wright, 1933
    Women—Dope—and Murder. Wright, 1962 MG
    Wu Fang. Brentano's, 1929 WF,BS
    Wu Fang's Revenge. Wright, 1934 WF
    The Yellow Devil. Wright, 1932
    The "Z" Case. Wright, 1947

DANIELS, A(LBERT) FREDERICK
    Deadly Date. Kenyon, 1979 (1-act play.)

DANIELS, CORA LINN. 1852- .
    The Bronze Buddha. Little, 1899; Gay & Bird, 1899 [NYC]
    -Sardia. Lee, 1891

DANIELS, DOROTHY. 1915- . Pseudonyms: Danielle Dorsett, Angela Gray, Cynthia Kavanaugh, Suzanne Somers, Geraldine Thayer, Helen Gray Weston, qq.v. Ref: CA.
    Affair in Hong Kong. Pyramid, 1969 [H. Kong]
    Affair in Marakesh. Pyramid, 1968 [Mor.]
    The Apollo Fountain. Paperback Library, 1974
    The Attic Rope. Lancer, 1970 [past, La.]
    The Beaumont Tradition. Paperback Library, 1971 [Calif.]
    Bed of Ashes; see The Last of the Mansions
    The Bell. Paperback Library, 1971 [1892, Maine]
    Blackthorn. PB, 1975 [1903, Md.]
    Blue Devil Suite. Belmont, 1968

Bridal Black. Signet, 1980
The Caldwell Shadow. Paperback Library, 1973
Candle in the Sun. Lancer, 1968
The Carson Inheritance. Paperback Library, 1969 [N.Y.]
Castle Morvant. Paperback Library, 1972 [Calif., theatre]
Child of Darkness. PB, 1974; Curley, 1981 [1911, N.Y.]
Circle of Guilt. PB, 1976 [S.F., ca.1910]
Cliffside Castle. Lancer, 1965 [1890, N.Y.]
Conover's Folly. Paperback Library, 1971 [1890, Maine]
The Cormac Legend. Signet, 1979 [Ire.]
The Curse of Mallory Hall. GM, 1970; Coronet, 1972 [Va.]
Dance in Darkness. Lancer, 1965 [1890, N.Y.]
Danger Mansion; see Nurse at Danger Mansion
Dark Heritage. Signet, 1976
Dark Island. Paperback Library, 1972 [Haiti]
The Dark Stage. Paperback Library, 1970 [1892, New Or.]
Dark Villa. Lancer, 1967
Darkhaven. Paperback Library, 1965 [1890, N.Y.]
Diablo Manor. Paperback Library, 1971; Star, 1977 [Fla.]
Duet. Lancer, 1968
The Duncan Dynasty. Paperback Library, 1973
The Eagle's Nest. Lancer, 1967
Emerald Hill. Paperback Library, 1970 [Md.]
The Exorcism of Jenny Slade. PB, 1972 [N.Y.]
Ghost Song. PB, 1974 [New Or.]
The Guardian of Willow House. PB, 1975; Magna, 1977 [1915, N.Y.]
Hermitage Hill. Signet, 1978 [Maine]
Hills of Fire. Paperback Library, 1973
The House of Broken Dolls. Paperback Library, 1972
The House of Many Doors. Paperback Library, 1971 [Miss., past]
House of Silence. Signet, 1980
House of Stolen Memories. Lancer, 1967. Also published as: Mansion of Lost Memories. Lancer, 1969 [Conn., 1800s]
House of the Seven Courts. Lancer, 1967 [H. Kong]
The House on Circus Hill. Paperback Library, 1972 [1895, Ind.]
Illusion at Haven's Edge. PB, 1973; Magna, 1977 [Va.]
Image of a Ghost. Paperback Library, 1973 [Maine]
In the Shadows. Signet, 1978 [N.Y., past]
Island of Bitter Memories. Paperback Library, 1974
Island of Evil. Paperback Library, 1970 (Novelization of the "Strange Paradise" TV series.) [Carib.]
Jade Green. Paperback Library, 1973 [Can.]
Journey into Terror. Pyramid, 1970 [S.C., ca.1860]
Juniper Hill. PB, 1976 [S.F.]
Key Diablo. Paperback Library, 1971
Knight in Red Armor. Lancer, 1966
Lady of the Shadows. Paperback Library, 1968 [Conn., past]
The Lanier Riddle. Paperback Library, 1972 [1890, Ky.]
The Larrabee Heiress. Paperback Library, 1972 [L.A.]
The Last of the Mansions. Lancer, 1966. Also published as: Survivors of Darkness. Lancer, 1969. Original title: Bed of Ashes.
Legend of Death. Signet, 1980
The Leland Legacy. Pyramid, 1965 [1890, N.Y.]
The Lily Pond. Paperback Library, 1965 [Md.]
The Lonely Place. Signet, 1978
The Magic Ring. Warner, 1978 [It.]
The Man from Yesterday. Paperback Library, 1970 [N.Y., ca.1900]
Mansion of Lost Memories; see House of Stolen Memories
The Marble Angel; see The Marble Leaf
The Marble Hills. Warner, 1975
The Marble Leaf. Paperback Library, 1966. Also published as: The Marble Angel. Lancer, 1970 [N.Y., past]
Marriott Hall. Paperback Library, 1965 [1880, Maine]
The Maya Temple. Paperback Library, 1972 [Guat.]
-Meg. Signet, 1979
Midday Moon. Lancer, 1966
A Mirror of Shadows. Warner, 1977; Star, 1977 [Ire.]
The Mistress of Falcon Hill. Pyramid, 1965 [1867, La.]

Mostly by Moonlight. Lancer, 1963 [1871, Maine]
-Nicola. Belmont, 1980
Night Shade. PB, 1976 [Maine]
Night Shadow. Signet, 1979 [Ga., 1895]
Nightfall. PB, 1977 [Va.]
Nurse at Danger Mansion. Lancer, 1966. Also published as: Danger Mansion. Lancer, 19??
-Perrine. Warner, 1978
Poison Flower. PB, 1977 [1895, Vt.]
Portrait of a Witch. PB, 1976
The Possessed. PB, 1975 [1900, Maine]
The Possession of Tracy Corbin. Paperback Library, 1973
The Prisoner of Malville Hall. Paperback Library, 1973 [Maine]
The Purple and the Gold. Signet, 1980
The Raging Waters. Pyramid, 1966
Raxl, Voodoo Priestess. Paperback Library, 1970 (Novelization of the "Strange Paradise" TV series.) [Carib.]
The Sevier Secrets. Lancer, 1967
Shadow Glen. Paperback Library, 1965 [N.Y.]
Shadow of a Man. Popular Library, 1975 [La., 1890]
Shadows from the Past. Paperback Library, 1972 [1890, N.Y.]
Shadows of Tomorrow. Paperback Library, 1969
The Silent Halls of Ashenden. Paperback Library, 1973 [N.Y., past]
The Spanish Chapel. Belmont, 1972
The Stone House. Paperback Library, 1973
Strange Paradise. Paperback Library, 1969 (Novelization of the "Strange Paradise" TV series.) [Carib.]
The Summer House. Warner, 1976 [NYC, ca.1900]
Survivor of Darkness; see The Last of the Mansions
The Templeton Memoirs. Lancer, 1966 [1890, N.Y.]
This Ancient Evil. Lancer, 1966
The Tidemill. Popular Library, 1975 [Va., 1895]
The Tormented. Paperback Library, 1969 [La., 1883]
The Tower Room. Lancer, 1965
Traitor's Road. Lancer, 1967
Twilight at the Elms. Signet, 1976
The Two Worlds of Peggy Scott. PB, 1974; Magna, 1977 [Mass.]
The Unearthly. Lancer, 1970 [Ga., 1880]
The Unguarded. Lancer, 1965
The Unlamented. PB, 1975; Curley, 1981 [Maine]
Valley of Shadows. Signet, 1980
Veil of Treachery. Signet, 1979 [NYC, theatre]
The Vineyard Chapel. PB, 1976 [1918, Calif.]
Voice on the Wind. Paperback Library, 1969 [1895, New Eng.]
The Watcher in the Dark. Ballantine, 1973
A Web of Peril. Pyramid, 1970 [N.Y., past]
Whistle in the Wind. PB, 1976 [L.A., 1885]
Willow Weep. Pyramid, 1970
-The Wines of Cyprien. Pyramid, 1977
Witch's Castle. Paperback Library, 1971 [Maine]
Witch's Island. Paperback Library, 1972
A Woman in Silk and Shadows. Signet, 1977 [N.C.]
Yesterday's Evil. Signet, 1979 [Vt.]

DANIELS, HAROLD R(OBERT). 1919-   . Ref: CA.
The Accused. Dell, 1958; Deutsch, 1961 [Mass.]
For the Asking. GM, 1962; Muller pb, 1963
The Girl in 304. Dell, 1956 [Ga.]
House on Greenapple Road. Random, 1966; Deutsch, 1967 [Mass.]
In His Blood. Dell, 1955
The Snatch. Dell, 1977; Deutsch, 1960

DANIELS, J(EFFERY) R(OBERT). Trained in aeronautical engineering; an automotive journalist.
Crash Programme. Macmillan (London), 1973. U.S. title: First Flight. Coward, 1973
Firegold. Macmillan (London), 1975; Coward, 1976 [Indon.]
First Flight; see Crash Programme

DANIELS, JAN. Pseudonym of W(illiam) E(dward) D(aniel) Ross, 1912-   , q.v. Other pseudonyms: Laura Frances Brooks, Rose Dana, Ellen Randolph, Clarissa Ross, Dan Ross, Dana Ross, Marilyn Ross, qq.v
Bride for Arundel. Hale, 1966

DANIELS, MAX
Passport to Terror. Avon, 1960 [Rome]

DANIELS, NORMAN (A.). Birth name: Norman A. Danberg. Pseudonyms: Harrison Judd, Robert Wallace, qq.v. Ref: CA. SC: Bruce Baron = BB; Kelly Carvel = KC; John Keith = JK.
Arrest and Trial. Lancer, 1963 (Novelization of the TV series.) [L.A.]
The Baron of Hong Kong. Lancer, 1967 BB [H. Kong]
Baron's Mission to Peking. Lancer, 1968 BB [Peking]
The Captive. Avon, 1959 [NYC]
Chase. Berkley, 1974 (Novelization of the TV series.)
The Deadly Game. Avon, 1959 [NYC]
The Detectives. Lancer, 1962 (Novelization of the TV series.)
The Hunt Club. Pyramid, 1964 JK [Munich]
A Killing in the Market. Lancer, 1967
The Kono Diamond. Berkley, 1969
Lady for Sale. Avon, 1960 [Nev.]
License to Kill. Pyramid, 1972 KC [Urug.]
Lover, Let Me Live. Avon, 1960
The Magnetic Man. Berkley, 1968 (Novelization of "The Avengers" TV series.) [Eng.]
The Mausoleum Key. Gateway, 1942 [NYC]
Meet the Smiths. Berkley, 1971 (Novelization of the "Smith Family" TV series.)
The Missing Witness. Lancer, 1964 (Novelization of the "Arrest and Trial" TV series.)
Mistress on a Deathbed. Falcon, 1952
Moon Express. Berkley, 1969 (Novelization of "The Avengers" TV series.)
One Angry Man. Pyramid, 1971 KC [L.A.]
Operation K. Pyramid, 1965 JK
Operation N. Pyramid, 1966 JK [Beirut]
Operation S-L. Pyramid, 1971 JK [Sierra Leone]
Operation T. Pyramid, 1967 JK [Australia]
Operation VC. Pyramid, 1967 JK [Viet Nam]
Overkill. Pyramid, 1964 JK [Alb.]
The Rape of a Town. Pyramid, 1970 KC [Calif.]
The Secret War. Pyramid, 1964
Some Die Running. Avon, 1960 [Vienna]
Something Burning. GM, 1963; Muller pb, 1963
Spy Ghost. Pyramid, 1965 JK [Paris]
Spy Hunt. Pyramid, 1960 [Russ.]
Suddenly by Shotgun. GM, 1961

DANIELS, PAUL
The Transister Girls. Monarch, 1961 [Jap.]

DANIELS, PHILIP
Alibi of Guilt. Hale, 1980
Goldmine—London W.1. Hale, 1979
The Nice Quiet Girl. Hale, 1980
The Scarred Man. Hale, 1980

DANNAY, FREDERIC. 1905-1982. Joint pseudonyms with Manfred Bennington Lee, 1905-1971: Ellery Queen, Barnaby Ross, qq.v.

DANNE, MAX HALLAN
Premature Burial. Lancer, 1962 (Novelization of the movie.)

DANNETT, SYLVIA (G. L.). 1909-   . Ref: CA.
Defy the Tempest, with Edwin Bennett. Mesnner, 1944
The Door to the Tower. Lancer, 1966
Nor Iron Bars, with Edwin Bennett. Fortuny, 1940

DANNING, MELROD. Pseudonym of Sinclair Gluck, 1887-   , q.v.
The Majesty of the Law. Hodder, 1916

DANTON, REBECCA. Pseudonym of Janet Louise Roberts, 1925-   , q.v. Other pseudonyms: Louisa Bronte, Janette Radcliffe, qq.v.
Black Horse Tavern. Popular Library, 1972
-Fire Opals. Crest, 1977
Ship of Hate. Dell, 1977 [ship]
Sign of the Golden Goose. Popular Library, 1972

DANVERS, JACK. Pseudonym of Camille Auguste Marie Caseleyr, 1909-   . Ref: CA.
-The End of It All. Heinemann, 1962
-The Living Come First. Heinemann, 1961

DANVERS, MILTON. SC: Robert Spicer, in at least those marked RS. Set: Eng.
A Desperate Dilemma; or, An Unheard of Crime. Diprose, 1892 RS

The Detective's Honeymoon; or, The Doctor of the "Pinjarrah". Diprose, 1894 RS
The Doctor's Crime; or, Simply Horrible! Diprose, 1891 RS
The Fatal Finger Mark, Rose Courtenay's First Case. Diprose, 1895 RS
The Grantham Mystery; or, Confidence and Crime. Diprose, 1893 RS
The "Lone Cross Manor" Mystery; or, Hugh Darrill's Confession. Diprose, 1896
Mysterious Disappearance of a Bride; or, Who Was She? Diprose, 1895 RS
The Squire's Fatal Will; or, Twenty Years of Plot and Crime. Diprose, 1897

D'APERY, HELEN BURRELL GIBSON. 1842-1915. Pseudonym: Olive Harper, q.v.

DARBON, LESLIE
A Murder Is Announced. French (London), 1978 (Play based on the novel by Agatha Christie, 1890-1976, q.v.)
Time to Kill. French (London), 1979 (Play.)

DARBY, CATHERINE. Pseudonym of Maureen Peters, 1935- . Other pseudonym: Veronica Black, q.v.
Cobweb Across the Moon. Popular Library, 1978 [Eng.]
-A Dream of Fair Serpents. Popular Library, 1979
The Falcon and the Moon. Popular Library, 1976 [Eng., 1886]
A Falcon for a Witch. Popular Library, 1975 [Eng., ca.1910]
Falcon Rising. Popular Library, 1976 [Eng., 1818]
Falcon Royal. Popular Library, 1976 [Eng.]
Falcon Sunset. Popular Library, 1976 [Eng., 1916]
Falcon to the Lure. Popular Library, 1978 [Eng.]
The Falcon Tree. Popular Library, 1976 [1841, Eng.]
Falcon's Claw. Popular Library, 1978 [1399, Eng.]
The Flaunting Moon. Popular Library, 1977 [1644, Eng.]
Fortune for a Falcon. Popular Library, 1975 [Eng.]
Frost on the Moon. Popular Library, 1977
A Game of Falcons. Popular Library, 1975
The King's Falcon. Popular Library, 1975 [1644, Eng.]
Moon in Pisces. Popular Library, 1978
Season of the Falcon. Popular Library, 1976 [Eng.]
Seed of the Falcon. Popular Library, 1978 [Eng.]
Sing Me a Moon. Popular Library, 1977
Whisper down the Moon. Popular Library, 1977

DARBY, EMMA
A Conflict of Women. Hale, 1971; St. Martin's, 1972
-Into the Arena. Hale, 1969; St. Martin's, 1972

DARBY, J. N. Pseudonym of (Mary) Christine Noble Govan, 1898- , q.v. Other pseudonym: Mary Allerton, q.v.
Murder in the House with the Blue Eyes. Bobbs, 1939

DARBY, RUTH. SC: Peter and Janet Barron, in all titles.
Beauty Sleep. Doubleday, 1942 [L.I.]
Death Boards the Lazy Lady. Doubleday, 1939 [Carib.]
Death Conducts a Tour. Doubleday, 1940 [Havana]
If This Be Murder. Doubleday, 1941 [Mex.]
Murder with Orange Blossoms. Doubleday, 1943; Muller, 1947 [NYC]

D'ARCY, EDGAR
The Morton Mystery. Popular, 1880

D'ARCY, JACK. See: Robert Wallace, q.v.

DARD, F(REDERIC). Pseudonym: San Antonio, q.v.
The Man of the Avenue. International, 1969 (Translation of "L'Homme de l'Avenue." Paris, 1962.)

DARE, ALAN. Pseudonym of George Goodchild, 1888-1969, q.v. Other pseudonym: Jesse Templeton, q.v.
-Body and Soul. Jarrolds, 1929
-The Guarded Soul. Jenkins, 1928
-The Isle of Hate. Jenkins, 1924. Reprinted as by George Goodchild: Newnes, 1935

-Killigrew. Jenkins, 1922
-Out of the Desert. Jenkins, 1925. Reprinted as by George Goodchild: Newnes, 1934

DARE, MICHAEL
Murder Incognito. Partridge, 1947

DARGON. Pseudonym.
The Nameless Order. Lane, 1924

DARK, JAMES. Pseudonym of James Edmond MacDonnell, 1917- . Most if not all of the titles below were originally published by Horwitz in Australia under the author's real name. SC: Mark Hood, in at least those marked MH.
Assignment Hong Kong. Horwitz, 1966. U.S. title: Hong Kong Incident. Signet, 1966 MH [H. Kong]
Assignment Tokyo. Signet, 1966 MH (Australian title?) [Tokyo]
The Bamboo Bomb. Horwitz, 1965; Signet, 1965 MH [Far East]
Come Die with Me. Horwitz, 1965; Signet, 1965 MH [Bahamas]
Hong Kong Incident; see Assignment Hong Kong
The Invisibles. Horwitz, 1970; Signet, 1969 MH
Operation Ice Cap. Horwitz, 1970; Signet, 1969 MH [Arctic]
Operation Jackal. Horwitz, 1967
Operation Missat. Horwitz, 1966
Operation Octopus. Horwitz, 1970; Signet, 1968 MH
Operation Scuba. Signet, 1967 (Australian title?) MH [Jam.]
The Reluctant Assassin. Horwitz, 1970 MH
Sea Scrape. Signet, 1971 (Australian title?) MH [Switz.]
Spy from the Deep. Horwitz, 1966
Spy from the Grave. Horwitz, 1964 [It.]
Spying Blind. Horwitz, 1968; Signet, 1968 MH
The Sword of Genghis Khan. Horwitz, 1967; Signet, 1967 MH [Mong.]
The Throne of Satan. Signet, 1967 (Australian title?) MH

DARK, JOHNNY. Pseudonym of Victor (George Charles) Norwood, 1920- , q.v. Other pseudonyms: Mark Hampton, Hank Jenson, Nat Karta, Mark Shane, qq.v.
Dame on the Lam. Milestone, 1952
Fig Leaves for a Lady. Milestone, 1953
A Guy Must Live. Mlestone, 1954
Snake Walk. Scion, 1951
The Squeaker. Milestone, 1954
Venom. Milestone, 1953

DARK, REX. SC: Bartholomew Dane, in at least those marked BD.
The Channing Affair. Wright, 1937 BD
Dead Men Tell... Wright, 1937 BD
The Invisible Hand. Wright, 1937 BD
The Ming Vase Mystery. Wright, 1936 BD
Murder in Berkeley Square. Wright, 1938
The Prison Murder. Wright, 1939
Spy 222. Wright, 1940 BD
The Tremlow Murder Case. Wright, 1938
The Uranian Jewel Case. Wright, 1939 BD
The Wardour Street Mystery. Wright, 1936 BD

DARK, RICHARD. 1876- .
Dibchick. Moray, 1937

DARLINGTON, W(ILLIAM) A(UBREY CECIL). 1890-1979. Ref: CA.
Mr. Cronk's Cases. Jenkins, 1931 ss

DARNELL, HENRY FAULKNER. 1831-1917.
The Craze of Christian Englehart. Appleton, 1890

DARRELL, GRATIANA
The Haunted Looking Glass. Digby, 1897

DARRELL, STANLEY
Inquest—Eleven Thirty. Crowther, 1947

DARTEY, LEO. Pseudonym of Henriette Fechy.
Midnight Visitor. Mystique, 1979 (Translation of "La Visiteur de Minuit." Paris, 1963.)
Return to Foxdale. Mystique, 1980 (Translation of "La Colline aux Genets." Paris, 1964.)
A Stranger Threatens. Mystique, 1979 (Translation of "Les Yeux Verts." Paris, 1975.)

DARWENT, GEORGE
Mystery in the Snow. Rich, 1935

D'ASTOR, JEAN. Pseudonym of Jean-Francois Orsat.

The Coast of Fear. Mystique, 1980 (Translation of "La Princesse aux Maines Bleues." Paris, 1965.)
Fatal Choice. Mystique, 1980 (Translation of "Le Piege d'Or." Paris, 1962.)
The Sea Gull. Mystique, 1977 (Translation of "Le Goeland." Paris, 1969.)
Tower of Malecombe. Mystique, 1978 (Translation of "Quand le Diable S'en Mele." Paris, 1961.)

DATE, JOHN H.
Escape Route M6. Hale, 1977

DATESH, JOHN NICHOLAS. 1950- . Ref: CA.
The Janus Murder. Leisure, 1979
The Moscow Tape. Leisure, 1980 [Moscow]
The Nightmare Machine. Leisure, 1979

D'AUVERGNE, EDMUND B(ASIL FRANCIS)
No Choice. Long, 1925

DAVE, SHYAM. Joint pseudonym of Hugh Gantzer, 1931- , q.v., and Colleen Gantzer.
Ballots for Violence. Jaico, 1972
The Brain Drain Docket. Orient (Delhi), ca.1977
The Guru Docket. Orient (Delhi), ca. 1977
The Issac Docket. Orient (Delhi), ca. 1978
The Kumbh Docket. Jaico, 1972
The Stark Docket. Orient (Delhi), ca. 1979

DAVENPORT, DIANA
The Power Eaters. Morrow, 1979; Granada, 1979

DAVENPORT, FRANCINE. Pseudonym of Velma Tate, 1913- . Ref: CA.
The Secret of the Bayou. Ace, 1966 [La., past]

DAVENPORT, GWEN LEYS. 1910- . Joint pseudonym with Gustav J. Breuer: Michael Hardt, q.v. Ref: CA.

DAVENPORT, JOHN. 1908-1966. See: Dylan Thomas, 1914-1953.

DAVENTRY, LEONARD (JOHN). 1915- . Ref: CA.
-A Man of Double Deed. Gollancz, 1965; Doubleday, 1965 [2090]

DAVEY, JOCELYN. Pseudonym of Chaim Raphael, 1908- . Ref: CA, CA, TC. SC: Ambrose Usher, in all titles.
A Capitol Offense; see The Undoubted Deed
A Killing in Hats. Chatto, 1965
The Naked Villainy. Chatto, 1958; Knopf, 1958
A Touch of Stagefright. Chatto, 1960 [L.I.]
A Treasury Alarm. Chatto, 1976; Walker, 1981 [Boston]
The Undoubted Deed. Chatto, 1956. U.S. title: A Capitol Offense. Knopf, 1956 [Wash. D.C.]

DAVID, D(AVID) L(AWRENCE)
This Man Is a Spy. Rich, 1948

DAVID, K.
Born to Die. Warren, 1952
I Was Alone. Warren, 1952
It's Easier for Homicide. Warren, 1952
The Man Who Went Away. Warren, 1952
Now We Are Free. Warren, 1952

DAVID, MARIE DeSAFFRON. 1831-1885. Pseudonym: Raoul DeNavery, q.v.

DAVIDOV, LEN
The Zinger. Zebra, 1976

DAVIDSON, ANDREW
The Golden Lode. Hutchinson, 1956; Abelard, 1957
-The Wilderness Road. Jarrolds, 1958; Roy, 1959

DAVIDSON, ANGELA. See: Rebecca Noyes Winstead.

DAVIDSON, AVRAM. 1923- . See also: Ellery Queen. Ref: CA.
The Enquiries of Dr. Eszterhazy. Warner, 1975 ss

DAVIDSON, BASIL. 1914- . Ref: CA.
-Golden Horn. Cape, 1952

DAVIDSON, DAVID (ALBERT). 1908- . Ref: CA.
The Quest of Juror 19. Doubleday, 1971

DAVIDSON, DIANE. 1924- . Ref: CA.
-Feversham. Crown, 1969

DAVIDSON, HUGH COLEMAN. 1852- .
The Gargrave Mystery. Warne, 1889
The Queen of the Black Hand. Trischler, 1890

DAVIDSON, LIONEL. 1922- . Ref: CA, TC.
The Chelsea Murders. Cape, 1978. U.S. title: Murder Games. Coward, 1978.
A Long Way from Shiloh. Gollancz, 1966. U.S. title: The Menorah Men. Harper, 1966 [Mid. East]
Making Good Again. Cape, 1968; Harper, 1968 [Ger.]
The Menorah Men; see A Long Way from Shiloh
Murder Games; see The Chelsea Murders
Night of Wenceslas. Gollancz, 1960; Harper, 1960 [Czech.]
The Rose of Tibet. Gollancz, 1962; Harper, 1962 [Tib.]
The Sun Chemist. Cape, 1976; Knopf, 1976

DAVIDSON, MURIEL. Investigative reporter.
-Hot Spot. Marek, 1980
The Thursday Woman. Atheneum, 1979; NEL, 1979 [L.A.]

DAVIDSON, PAUL
The Katmandu Affair. Vantage, 1980 [Nepal]

DAVIDSON, T. L. Pseudonym of David Landsborough Thomson, 1901-1964. Ref: CC.
The Murder in the Laboratory. Methuen, 1929; Dutton, 1929 [acad.]

DAVIE-MARTIN, HUGH. Pseudonym of Hugh (Davie-Martin) McCutcheon, 1909- q.v.
The Girl in My Grave. Hale, 1976
The Pearl of Oyster Island. Hale, 1977
Spaniard's Leap. Hale, 1979

DAVIES. House name.
The Warehouse Murder. Amalgamated, 1930

DAVIES, A. A. T.
The Horses of Winter. Weidenfeld, 1967

DAVIES, ARTHUR LLEWELLYN. 1903-
Death Plays a Duet. Exposition, 1977

DAVIES, BETTY EVELYN. Pseudonym: Pauline Warwick, q.v.

DAVIES, EDWARD C.
The Maker of Frocks. Hodder, 1928

DAVIES, ERNEST. 1873- . Pseudonym: Oliver Martin, q.v.
-Dives and Son. Rivers, 1910
-The Moment. Rivers, 1911
The Widow's Necklace. Duckworth, 1913; Devin-Adair, 1913 [Scot.]

DAVIES, FREDRIC. Joint pseudonym of Ron Ellik, 1938-1968, and Frederic Langley.
The Cross of Gold Affair. Ace, 1968 (Novelization of "The Man from U.N.C.L.E." TV series.) [NYC]

DAVIES, G(EOFFREY) H(OWARD)
Justice by Proxy. Hale, 1967

DAVIES, GWYNNETH. Pseudonym of William Delligan.
The Portrait of Susan. Popular Library, 1977 [NYC]
The Terror at Dearcliff House. Popular Library, 1976 [Pa.]

DAVIES, HUGH SYKES. 1909- .
Full Fathom Five. Lane, 1956
No Man Pursues. Lane, 1950
The Papers of Andrew Melmoth. Methuen, 1960; Morrow, 1961

DAVIES, J(UNE) WYNDHAM. See: Elizabeth Addyman, 1900- .

DAVIES, JACK. 1913- .
Atlantic Incident; see North Sea Hijack
Esther, Ruth and Jennifer. Allen, 1979
The Hold-Up. Allen, 1977
North Sea Hijack. Star, 1980. U.S. title: Atlantic Incident. Jove, 1980 (Novelization of the movie.)

DAVIES, JOHN. ca.1914- . Once a schoolmaster, then in the military, then a journalist, and then an editor and freelance writer.
Mystery Flight. Ward, 1956
Sabotage at Sea. Ward, 1959
See Naples and Die. Ward, 1961 [Naples]

DAVIES, JOHN EVAN WESTON. Pseudonym: Berkley Mather, q.v.

DAVIES, KENDAL
Nine Bells. Hutchinson, 1947

DAVIES, L(ESLIE) P(URNELL). 1914- . Pseudonym: Leslie Vardre, q.v. Ref: CA, CC, TC. Set: Eng.
The Artificial Man. Jenkins, 1965; Doubleday, 1967
Assignment Abacus. Barrie, 1975; Doubleday, 1975 [Scot.]
Give Me Back Myself. Barrie, 1972; Doubleday, 1971
The Lampton Dreamers. Jenkins, 1966; Doubleday, 1967
The Land of Leys. Hale, 1980; Doubleday, 1979
Man Out of Nowhere. Jenkins, 1965. U.S. title: Who Is Lewis Pinder? Doubleday, 1966
The Paper Dolls. Jenkins, 1964; Doubleday, 1966
Possession. Hale, 1976; Doubleday, 1976
The Shadow Before. Barries, 1971; Doubleday, 1970
Stranger to Town. Jenkins, 1969; Doubleday, 1969
What Did I Do Tomorrow? Barrie, 1972; Doubleday, 1973
The White Room. Barrie, 1970; Doubleday, 1969
Who Is Lewis Pinder?; see Man Out of Nowhere

DAVIES, MARTIN
The Gold Machine. Pinnacle, 1979

DAVIES, MELISSA. Pseudonym of Gordon Winthrop Davis.
The Face of Chalk. Popular Library, 1977 [Calif.]

DAVIES, N. E.
Doctor Cockaigne. Methuen, 1930

DAVIES, RHYS. 1903-1978. Ref: CA.
Nobody Answered the Bell. Heinemann, 1971; Dodd, 1971

DAVIES, STAN GEBLER. See: Robin Moore.

D'AVIGDOR, ELIM HENRY. 1841-1895. Pseudonym: Wanderer, q.v.

DAVIOT, GORDON. Pseudonym of Elizabeth MacKintosh, 1896-1952. Other pseudonym: Josephine Tey, q.v. SC: Insp. Alan Grant = AG, whose cases are continued under the Josephine Tey by-line.
The Man in the Queue. Methuen, 1929; Dutton, 1929. Reprinted as by Josephone Tey: Macmillan, 1953. Also published as: Killer in the Crowd, as by Josephine Tey. Mercury, 1954, abridged AG

DAVIS, ANDREW JACKSON. 1826-1910.
Tale of a Physician; or, The Seeds and Fruits of Crime. White, 1869

DAVIS, BERRIE. 1922- . Ref: CA.
The Fourth Day of Fear. Putnam, 1973; Barker, 1974 [Fr.]
Trevena's Daughter. Dell, 1978 [Eng.]

DAVIS, BURTON. 1893- . Joint pseudonym with Clare Ogden Davis, 1892- : Lawrence Saunders, q.v.

DAVIS, CHARLES. 1923- . Ref: CA.
Two Weeks to Find a Killer. Carlton, 1966

DAVIS, CLARE OGDEN. 1892- . Joint pseudonym with Burton Davis, 1893- : Lawrence Saunders, q.v.

DAVIS, CLYDE BRION. 1894-1962. Ref: CA.
The Rebellion of Lee McGuire. Rinehart, 1944; Corgi, 1953

DAVIS, DOROTHY SALISBURY. 1916- . Ref: CA, CC, EM, TC. SC: Mrs. Norris = N; Julia Hayes = JH; Jasper Tully = JT.
Black Sheep, White Lamb. Scribner, 1963; Boardman, 1964 [N.Y.]
The Clay Hand. Scribner, 1950 [W. Va.]
A Death in the Life. Scribner, 1976; Gollancz, 1977 JH [NYC]
Death of an Old Sinner. Scribner, 1957; Secker, 1958 N,JT [NYC]
Enemy and Brother. Scribner, 1967; Hodder, 1967 [Greece]
A Gentle Murderer. Scribner, 1951 [NYC]
A Gentleman Called. Scribner, 1958; Secker, 1958 N,JT [NYC]
God Speed the Night, with Jerome Ross. Scribner, 1968; Hodder, 1969 [Fr.]
The Judas Cat. Scribner, 1949 [Midwest]
The Little Brothers. Scribner, 1973; Barker, 1974 [NYC]
Old Sinners Never Die. Scribner, 1959; Secker, 1960 N [Wash. D.C.]
The Pale Betrayer. Scribner, 1965; Hodder, 1967 [NYC]
Scarlet Night. Scribner, 1980; Gollancz, 1981 JH [NYC]
Shock Wave. Scribner, 1972; Barker, 1974 [Ill., acad.]
A Town of Masks. Scribner, 1952 [Midwest]
Where the Dark Streets Go. Scribner, 1969; Hodder, 1970 [NYC]

DAVIS, DUANE
Bedroom Bang Bang. Series 70, 1968

DAVIS, ELIZABETH. Pseudonym of Lou Ellen Davis, 1936- . Other pseudonym: Pat Bannister, q.v. Ref: CA.
Along Came a Spider. Signet, 1970
My Soul to Keep. Pyramid, 1970
Suffer a Witch to Die. Signet, 1969
There Was an Old Woman. Doubleday, 1971; Hale, 1972 [NYC]

DAVIS, FRANKLIN M(ILTON), JR., 1918-1981. Ref: CA. SC: Quinn Leland = QL.
Kiss the Tiger. Pyramid, 1961 QL [Far East]
The Naked and the Lost. Lion, 1954
Secret: Hong Kong. Pyramid, 1962 QL [H. Kong]
-Spearhead. Permabooks, 1958

DAVIS, FREDERICK C(LYDE). 1902-1977. Pseudonyms: Murdo Coombs, Stephen Ransome, Curtis Steele, qq.v. Ref: TC. SC: Cyrus Hatch = CH; Schyler Cole & Luke Speare = C&S.
Another Morgue Heard From. Doubleday, 1954. British title: Deadly Bedfellows, as by Stephen Ransome. Gollancz, 1955 C&S
Coffins for Three. Doubleday, 1938. British title: One Murder Too Many. Heinemann, 1938 CH [NYC]
Deadly Bedfellows; see Another Morgue Heard From
The Deadly Miss Ashley. Doubleday, 1950; Gollancz, 1950, as by Stephen Ransome C&S [NYC]
Deep Lay the Dead. Doubleday, 1942 [Pa.]
Detour to Oblivion. Doubleday, 1947 CH [NYC]
Drag the Dark. Doubleday, 1953; Gollancz, 1954, as by Stephen Ransome C&S [NYC]
Gone Tomorrow. Doubleday, 1948 CH [NYC]
The Graveyard Never Closes. Doubleday, 1940 CH [Pa.]
He Wouldn't Stay Dead. Doubleday, 1939; Heinemann, 1939 CH [NYC]
High Heel Homicide. Ace, 1961
Let the Skeletons Rattle. Doubleday, 1944 CH [Pa.]
Lilies in Her Garden Grew. Doubleday, 1951; Gollancz, 1951, as by Stephen Ransome C&S [NYC]
Murder Doesn't Always Out; see Poor, Poor Yorick
Night Drop. Doubleday, 1955; Gollancz, 1956, as by Stephen Ransome C&S [NYC]
One Murder Too Many; see Coffins for Three
Poor, Poor Yorick. Doubleday, 1939. British title: Murder Doesn't Always Out. Heinemann, 1939 CH [NYC]
Thursday's Blade. Doubleday, 1947 CH [NYC]
Tread Lightly, Angel. Doubleday, 1952; Gollancz, 1952, as by Stephen Ransome C&S [NYC]

DAVIS, FREDERICK WILLIAM. 1858-1933. Pseudonyms: Scott Campbell, Nicholas Carter, qq.v.

DAVIS, GEORGE. Ref: CC. SC: Simon Good, in all titles. Set: Eng.
The Crime in Threadneedle Street. Collins, 1968
Death of a Fire-Raiser. Collins, 1974
Friday Before Bank Holiday. Collins, 1964
The Killer Grew Tired. Collins, 1971
Roag's Syndicate. Chapman, 1960
Toledano. Chapman, 1962

DAVIS, GERRY. See; Kit Pedler.

DAVIS, GORDON. Pseudonym of (Everette) Howard Hunt, 1918- , q.v. Other pseudonyms: Robert Dietrich, David St. John, qq.v.
Counterfeit Kill. GM, 1963; Muller pb, 1964. Reprinted as by E. Howard Hunt: Pinnacle, 1975 [Wash. D.C.]

House Dick. GM, 1961; Muller pb, 1962. Also published as: Washington Payoff. Pinnacle, 1975, as by E. Howard Hunt [Wash. D.C.]
I Came to Kill. GM, 1953; Fawcett (London), 1955 [Havana]
Ring Around Rosy. GM, 1964 [Fla.]
Washington Payoff; see House Dick
Where Murder Waits. GM, 1965. Reprinted as by E. Howard Hunt: GM, 1973

DAVIS, GORDON
The Goering Treasure. Zebra, 1980

DAVIS, GORDON WINTHROP. Pseudonym: Melissa Davies, q.v.

DAVIS, GWEN
The Aristocrats. Playboy, 1977 [Calif.]
The Set. Playboy, 1978; New English Library, 1978

DAVIS, HAROLD A. See: Kenneth Robeson.

DAVIS, HARRY. Pseudonym of Roberta Elizabeth Sebenthal, 1917-   . Other pseudonym: Paul Kruger, q.v.
My Brother's Wife. Greenberg, 1956
Portrait of Rene. Greenberg, 1956

DAVIS, HELEN
"For So Little": The Story of a Crime. Swan, 1890 [Australia]

DAVIS, HOWARD CHARLES. 1909-   . Worked in a London bank; by 1964 had written 20 thrillers under his own name and one pseudonym. SC: Hugh Rudd, in at least those marked HR; Edward Tope, in at least those marked ET. Set: Eng.
And Murder Won. Long, 1969
The Big Heist. Long, 1964
The Child Witness. Jarrolds, 1957
Dangerous Twin. Long, 1967
Dead Man's Cross. Long, 1965
Death in the Scillies. Long, 1968
The Death of Laura. Hale, 1963
Desperate Night. Long, 1965
The Gunmen of Gozo. Long, 1970
The Man Who Wasn't Murdered. Jarrolds, 1955
Murder Out of Class. Ward, 1961
Murder Starts from Fishguard. Long, 1966 HR
The Night of the Funeral. Long, 1958
Perhaps to Kill. Hale, 1963 [Greece]
A Pistol for Miss Preedy. Jarrolds, 1956
Renegade from Russia. Long, 1959
The Selsey Gold. Hale, 1980
The Third Assassin. Long, 1959
The Tortured Boy. Ward, 1961 ET
Trouble in the Bank. Ward, 1960 ET
The Waxworks Spies. Ward, 1962 HR

DAVIS, J(AMES) FRANK. 1870-   .
The Chinese Label. Little, 1920 [San Antonio]

DAVIS, J. R.
The Right to Die. Belmont, 1976 [Conn.]

DAVIS, JOHN GORDON
-Years of the Hungry Tiger. Joseph, 1974; Doubleday, 1975 [H. Kong]

DAVIS, JULIA. 1900-   . Pseudonym: F. Draco, q.v.

DAVIS, KENN. See also: John Stanley, 1940-   . SC: Carver Bascombe, in both titles.
The Dark Side, with John Stanley, 1940-   . Avon, 1976 [S.F.]
The Forza Trap. Avon, 1979 [theatre, S.F.]

DAVIS, LAURIE
Where Vultures Reign. Hale, 1976

DAVIS, LAVINIA R(IKER). 1909-1961. SC: Nora Hughes (Blaine) and Larry Blaine = B.
Barren Heritage. Doubleday, 1946 [N.J.]
Evidence Unseen. Doubleday, 1945 B [N.J.]
Reference to Death. Doubleday, 1950 [Conn.]
Taste of Vengeance. Doubleday, 1947 B [Conn.]
Threat of Dragons. Doubleday, 1948; Cherry Tree, 1950 [Calif.]

DAVIS, LEOPOLD
Strange Occurrences. Davis, 1877 ss

DAVIS, LOU ELLEN. 1936-   . Pseudonyms: Pat Bannister, Elizabeth Davis, qq.v.

DAVIS, MAGGIE (HILL). Ref: CA.
Rommel's Gold. Lippincott, 1971; Barrie, 1972 [Tun.]

DAVIS, MARTHA WIRT. Pseudonym: Wirt Van Arsdale, q.v.

DAVIS, MEANS. SC: Matthew Higgins = MH.
The Chess Murders. Random, 1937
The Hospital Murders. Smith, 1934; Bell, 1934 MH [hosp.]
Murder Without Weapons. Smith, 1934; Bell, 1935 MH [hosp.]

DAVIS, MILDRED (B.). Ref: CA.
The Dark Place. Simon, 1955
The Invisible Border. Random, 1974; Hale, 1975 [L.I.]
Nightmare of Murder; see Walk into Yesterday
The Room Upstairs. Simon, 1948 [NYC]
Scorpion. Random, 1977; Hale, 1978 [Vir. Is.]
The Sound of Insects. Doubleday, 1966; Hodder, 1967 [NYC]
Strange Corner. Doubleday, 1967; Hodder, 1968 [Haw.]
Tell Them What's-Her-Name Called. Random, 1975; Hale, 1976 [acad.]
They Buried a Man. Simon, 1953
The Third Half. Doubleday, 1969; Hale, 1970 [Eng.]
Three Minutes to Midnight. Random, 1971; Hale, 1973
The Voice on the Telephone. Random, 1964
Walk into Yesterday. Doubleday, 1967. British title: Nightmare of Murder. Hale, 1969

DAVIS, NORBERT. Joint pseudonym with W(illis) T(odhunter) Ballard, 1903-   , q.v.: Harrison Hunt, q.v. SC: Doan and Carstairs = D&C.
Dead Little Rich Girl; see The Mouse in the Mountain
The Mouse in the Mountain. Morrow, 1943. Also published as: Dead Little Rich Girl. Handi-Books, 1945 D&C [Mex.]
Oh, Murderer Mine. Handi-Books, 1946 D&C
Rendezvous with Fear. Cherry Tree, 1944 (U.S. title?)
Sally's in the Alley. Morrow, 1943; Boardman, 1944 D&C [Calif.]

DAVIS, OLIVE BELL
-Exodus: 20. Pageant, 1959

DAVIS, OWEN. 1874-1956.
At 9:45. French (NYC), 1928. British title: 9:45. French (London), 1927 (Play).
The Donovan Affair. French (NYC & London), 1930 (Play).
The Haunted House. French (NYC), 1926 (Play).
Mr. & Mrs. North. French, 1941 (Play based on stories by Francis & Richard Lockridge, q.v.)
9:45; see At 9:45
The Ninth Guest. French (NYC), 1930 (Play based on the novel by Gwen Bristow, 1903-1980, and Bruce Manning, q.v.)
No Way Out. Dramatic, 1945 (3-act play)

DAVIS, PHIL
Nemesis. Avon, 1979

DAVIS, REGINALD. Set: Eng.
The Crowing Hen. Bles, 1936; Doubleday, 1936
Nine Days' Panic. Bles, 1937; Doubleday, 1938
Twelve Midnight. Bles, 1938

DAVIS, RICHARD HARDING. 1864-1916. Ref: CC, EM.
In the Fog. Russell, 1901; Ward, 1901 [Eng.]
-The Scarlet Car. Scribner, 1907
-The White Mice. Scribner, 1909

DAVIS, STEVE
Stalk the Killer. Vega, ca.1964

DAVIS, STRATFORD. Pseudonym of Maisie Sharman Bolton, 1915-   . Other pseudonym: Maisie Sharman, q.v. Ref: CA.
Death in Seven Hours. Melrose, 1952 [acad.]
His Father's Ghost. Abelard (London & NYC), 1963 [It.]
No Tears Are Shed. Melrose, 1952
One Man's Secret. Boardman, 1956
The Troubled Mind. Melrose, 1953

DAVIS, TECH. SC: Aubrey Nash, in all titles.
Full Fare for a Corpse. Doubleday, 1937 [train, Wyo.]
Murder on Alternate Tuesdays. Doubleday, 1938 [Conn.]
Terror on Compass Lake. Doubleday, 1935 [N.Y.]

DAVIS, TIMOTHY EDWARD TOTHILL. 1941-   . Pseudonym: John Cashman, q.v.

DAVIS, YORKE. Pseudonym.
The Green Cloak. Sturgis, 1910; Sidgwick, 1910

DAVIS, ZEKE
-Invited. Pageant, 1959

DAVIS-GOFF, ANNABEL. 1942-   . Ref: CA.
Night Tennis. Coward, 1978; Hutchinson, 1979

DAVISON, G(ILDEROY). 1892-   . SC: Twisted Face (Straussman) = TF; Peter Castle, in at least those marked PC. Set: Eng.
Death in the A.R.P. Jenkins, 1939
The Devil's Apprentice. Jenkins, 1933 TF
The Devil's Diamonds; or, Beauty and the Beast. Jenkins, 1938
A Dog Fight with Death. Jenkins, 1940 TF,PC
Exit Mr. Brent. Jenkins, 1936 PC
Jewel of Destiny. Jenkins, 1938
A Killer at Scotland Yard. Jenkins, 1933
The Lily-Pond Mystery. Jenkins, 1937
The Man with Half a Face. Jenkins, 1936 PC
The Man with the Twisted Face. Jenkins, 1931 TF,PC
Murder in a Muffler; or, Dead Man's Farm. Jenkins, 1937
The Mysterious Mr. Brent. Jenkins, 1935
Mystery of the Red-Haired Valet. Jenkins, 1934 PC
The Prince of Spies. Jenkins, 1932 TF,PC
Robin Hoodwinker, V.C. Jenkins, 1944
Satan's Satellite. Jenkins, 1945
A Traitor Unmasked. Jenkins, 1932 TF
Twisted Face Defends His Title. Jenkins, 1940 TF
Twisted Face Strikes Again. Jenkins, 1939 TF
Twisted Face, the Avenger. Jenkins, 1935 TF

DAVISON, GEOFFREY. 1927-   . SC: Stephen Fletcher, in at least those marked SF.
The Berlin Spy Trap. Hale, 1974 [Berlin]
The Chessboard Spies. Hale, 1969; Roy, 1969 SF [Turk.]
The Fallen Eagles. Hale, 1970
The Honourable Assassins. Hale, 1971
Nest of Spies. Hale, 1968 SF
No Names on Their Graves. Hale, 1978
Spy Puppets. Hale, 1973
The Spy Who Swopped Shoes. Hale, 1967 SF

DAVISON, JEAN (JEFFRIES). 1937-   . Ref: CA.
The Devil's Horseman. Doubleday, 1976 [Haiti]
Dreaming Witness. Berkley, 1978
The Golden Lure; see The Golden Torrent
The Golden Torret. Doubleday, 1978. Also published as: The Golden Lure. Dell, 1979

DAVISON, NORMA
Reivaulx Abbey. Ace, 1975

DAVY, COLIN (KAYSER). 1896-   . SC: David Sheridan, in at least those marked DS.
Agents of the League. Harrap, 1936 DS
Brown Paper Twice. Collins, 1939
-A Heritage in Trust. Hale, 1957
Mariella—Spy! Harrap, 1935 DS
The Twister's Double. Hale, 1954

DAWE, (WILLIAM) CARLTON. 1865-1935. Set: Eng. SC: Colonel Gantian (Leathermouth), in at least those marked G.
The Admiralty's Secret. Long, 1918
After Many Days. Ward, 1928
The Black Spider. Nash, 1911
-A Brush with Fate. Long, 1920
-Captain Castle. Smith Elder, 1897
-The Chief. Ward, 1933
-Cludia Pole. Hutchinson, 1901
-The Confessions of a Currency Girl. Ward, 1894
-The Confessions of Cleodora. Long, 1908
The Crackswoman. Ward, 1914
Crumpled Lilies. Ward, 1933 G
-The Demagague. Hodder, 1902
-The Desirable Woman. Ward, 1929
-Desperate Love. Ward, 1924
-The Emu's Head. Ward, 1893
-Euryale in London. Ward, 1922 ss

D

Fifteen Keys. Ward, 1932 G
Fishers of Men. Ward, 1930
-The Forbidden Shrine. Ward, 1926
The Girl from Nippon. Ward, 1915
-The Glare. Ward, 1926
-The Grand Duke. Hutchinson, 1905
The Green Killer. Ward, 1936 G
-Her Highness's Secretary. Nash, 1907
The Knightsbridge Affair. Ward, 1927
-Lammas Grove. Brown, 1904
The Law of the Knife. Ward, 1934 G
Lawless. Ward, 1932
Leathermouth. Ward, 1931 G
Leathermouth's Luck. Ward, 1934 G
-The Life Perilous. Hutchinson, 1907
Live Cartridge. Ward, 1937
The London Plot. Nash, 1908
-The Mighty Arm. Long, 1919
The Missing Clue. Ward, 1930
The Missing Treaty. Ward, 1934 G
-A Morganatic Marriage. Hutchinson, 1906
-Mount Desolation. Cassell, 1892
-The New Andromeda. Nash, 1909
-One Fair Enemy. Long, 1908
-Pacific Blue. Ward, 1928
The Plotters of Peking. Nash, 1907
-The Prime Minister and Mrs. Grantham. Nash, 1903
-The Redemption of Grace Milroy. Lane, 1916
A Royal Alliance. Ward, 1935 G
-A Saint in Mufti. Nash, 1910
The Shadow of Evil. Laurie, 1913
The Sign of the Glove. Ward, 1932 G
-Slings and Arrows. Ward, 1927
-A Strange Destiny. Ward, 1937
-Stranger Than Fiction. Ward, 1923
-Straws in the Wind. Hurst, 1901
-The Super-Barbarians. Lane, 1915
-A Tangled Marriage. Ward, 1921
-The Temptation of Selma. Ward, 1924
Tough Company. Ward, 1936 G
-Virginia. Ward, 1923
Wanted! Ward, 1931
Waste Lands. Ward, 1935 G
-The Way of a Maid. Ward, 1925
-The Winding Road. Ward, 1929
-The Woman, the Man, and the Monster. Stuyvesant Press, 1909 (British title?)
The Woman with the Yellow Eyes. Long, 1917
-The Yellow Man. Hutchinson, 1900

DAWE, JOHN STANLEY
Crime Takes Wings. Eldon, 1939

DAWSON, A(LEC) J(OHN). 1872-1951.
The Case Books of X 37. Richards, 1930 ss

DAWSON, CAROLYN BYRD
The Lady Wept Alone. Doubleday, 1940
Remind Me to Forget. Doubleday, 1942 [Mo.]

DAWSON, CLARE. 1937- .
Death in a Tranquil Place. Hale, 1979

DAWSON, CONINGSBY (WILLIAM). 1883-1959.
-The House of the Weeping Woman. Hodder, 1908 (U.S. title?)
Murder Point. Doran, 1910 [Can.]
The Vanishing Point. Cosmopolitan, 1922; Hutchinson, 1922

DAWSON, FORBES
A Sensational Trance. Downey, 1895

DAWSON, JAMES. Born in N.C.; reporter, editor; in public relations and advertising.
Hell Gate. McKay, 1967

DAWSON, JANIS
Mackenzie's Glen. Hale, 1975

DAWSON, MINNIE TWILIGHT. 1876-
The Stillwater Murder; or, A Society Crime. (Author), 1908

DAWSON, (FRANCIS) WARRINGTON. 1878-1962.
Adventure in the Night. Doubleday, 1924; Unwin, 1924
-The Crimson Pall. Bernard, 1927

DAWSON, WILLIAM JAMES. 1854-1928.
The Borrowdale Tragedy. Lane (London & NYC), 1920

DAX, ANTHONY. Pseudonym of (Alfred) John Hunter, 1891-1961. Other pseudonyms: John Addiscombe, L. H. Brenning, Anthony Drummond, Peter Meriton, qq.v.
The Man Behind. World's Work, 1937; Dutton, 1938, as by John Hunter

DAY, ALBERT A.
The Mysterious Beggar. Ogilvie, 1891; Gay & Bird, 1891

DAY, GINA. Pseudonym.
Tell No Tales. Hart-Davis, 1967; Stein, 1968

DAY, JULIAN
Design for Death. Hale, 1958

DAY, JULIUS E(DGAR). 1884-
Crooked Money. Barron, 1937

DAY, LILLIAN, 1893- , and NORBERT (LEWIS) LEDERER, 1888-1955. SC: Frederick Hunt, in both titles.
Death Comes on Friday. Cassell, 1937; Dutton, 1937 [NYC]
Murder in Time. Cassell, 1935; Furman, 1936 [NYC]

DAY, LULA M.
The Mystery of the Red Suitcase. Hip Books, 1946 (11 other titles by this author were announced but apparently none was published.)

DAY, PATIENCE. Pseudonym of Patience Zawadsky, 1927- , q.v.

DAY, VALENTINE
That Fatal Tree. Mayne, 1893

DAY, WILL B. SC: Steven Flagg, in both titles.
Bravo 9. Caravelle, 1967
The Man from M.O.D. Caravelle, 1968 [Ger.]

DAY-LEWIS, CECIL. 1904-1972. Pseudonym: Nicholas Blake, q.v.

DAYE, JOHN. Pseudonym of Major General Sir John Adye, 1857-1930, q.v.
Who Killed Lord Henry Rollestone? Jenkins, 1924

DAYLE, DEXTER
Claws of Fate. Fiction House, 1939
The Crooked Jacket. Fiction House, 1938
Dangerous Love. Fiction House, 1938
The Day of Vengeance. Fiction House, 1940
Death in the Theatre. Fiction House, 1935 [theatre]
Death to the Spy. Fiction House, 1939
Five Were Doomed. Fiction House, 1935
Kidnapped for a Million. Fiction House, 1935
Love's Ordeal. Fiction House, 1937
Murder in Mid-Air. Fiction House, 1935
The Purple Threat. Fiction House, 1935
The Torture Machine. Fiction House, 1935
The Towers of Terror. Fiction House, 1935

DAYMONT, J.
Pelota Murder. Gannet, 1954

DAYNE, J. BELFORD
In the Name of the Tzar. Blackwood, 1887; Harper, 1887
-Tribute to Satan. Blackwood, 1888

DeACTON, EUGENIA. Pseudonym of Alethea Brereton Lewis, 1749-1827.
The Nuns of the Desert; or, The Woodland Witches. Lane, 1805

DEAKIN, H(ILDA) L. See also: Grace Miller White. Set: Eng.
The Secret of the Cove. Methuen, 1930
The Shot That Killed Graeme Andrews. Nelson, 1931

DEAL, BABS H(ODGES). 1929- . Ref: CA.
The Crystal Mouse. Doubleday, 1973; New English Library, 1973
Fancy's Knell. Doubleday, 1966; Gollancz, 1967
Friendships, Secrets and Lies; see The Walls Came Tumbling Down
Waiting to Hear from William. Doubleday, 1975; New English Library, 1976 [N.Y.]
The Walls Came Tumbling Down. Doubleday, 1968; Cassell, 1968. Also published as: Friendships, Secrets and Lies. Crest, 1979 [Ala.]

DEAL, BORDEN. 1922- . Pseudonym: Lee Borden, q.v. Ref: CA.
-Adventure. Doubleday, 1978; New English Library, 1979
Killer in the House. Signet, 1957

DEAL, MASON. Pseudonym of Henry Ware Eliot, 1879-1947.
The Rumble Murders. Houghton, 1932

DEAN, AMBER. 1902- . Ref: CA, TC. SC: Albie Harris = AH.
August Incident. Doubleday, 1951 [N.Y.]
Be Home by Eleven. Putnam, 1973; Hale, 1974 [N.Y.]
The Blonde Is Dead; see Call Me Pandora
Bullet Proof. Doubleday, 1960 [N.Y.]
Call Me Pandora. Doubleday, 1946. Also published as: The Blonde Is Dead. Mystery Novel Classic, 194? AH [N.Y.]
Chanticleer's Muffled Crow. Doubleday, 1945 AH [N.Y.]
Collector's Item. Doubleday, 1953 [N.Y.]
Dead Man's Float. Doubleday, 1944 AH [N.Y.]
Deadly Contact. Doubleday, 1963; Hale, 1964 [Roch.]
The Devil Threw Dice. Doubleday, 1954 [N.Y.]
The Dower Chest. Putnam, 1970; Hale, 1972 [N.Y.]
Encounter with Evil. Doubleday, 1961 [Can.]
Foggy Foggy Dew. Doubleday, 1947 [N.Y.]
No Traveller Returns. Doubleday, 1948 AH [N.Y.]
Snipe Hunt. Doubleday, 1949 AH [NYC]
Something for the Birds. Doubleday, 1959 [N.Y.]
Ticket to Buffalo. Doubleday, 1951 [N.Y.]
Wrap It Up. Doubleday, 1946 AH [N.Y.]

DEAN, DENNIS
The Emerald Murder Case. Phoenix, 1939

DEAN, DUDLEY. Pseudonym of Dudley Dean MacGaughy. Other pseudonym: Owen Dudley, q.v.
Lila My Lovely. GM, 1960 [Calif.]

DEAN, ELIZABETH. Ref: MP. SC: Emma Marsh and Hank Fairbanks, in all titles.
Murder a Mile High. Doubleday, 1944; Boardman, 1948 [Colo.]
Murder Is a Collector's Item. Doubleday, 1939; Cassell, 1939 [Boston]
Murder Is a Serious Business. Doubleday, 1940; Swan, 1943 [Boston]

DEAN, GRAHAM M. 1904- .
The Front Page Mystery. Appleton, 1931
Gleaming Rails. Appleton, 1930

DEAN, GREGORY. Pseudonym of Jacob D. Posner, 1883- . SC: Dep. Commissioner Benjamin Simon, in all titles.
The Case of Marie Corwin. Covici, 1933; Nicholson, 1934 [NYC]
The Case of the Fifth Key. Covici, 1934; Nicholson, 1936 [NYC]
Murder on Stilts. Hillman-Curl, 1939 [N.Y.]

DEAN, HAYDON. Pseudonym of Harry Harding, 1885- , q.v.
The Caves of Blackscar. Nicholson, 1934

DEAN, HOWARD
-The Iron Hand. Abbey, 1898

DEAN, LYN. Pseudonym of Winifred Selina Garrett, 1909- .
Ask No Questions. Melrose, 1937
The Rope Waits. Melrose, 1937

DEAN, ROBERT GEORGE. Ref: MP. SC: Tony Hunter = TH; Pat Thompson = PT.
Affair at Lover's Leap. Doubleday, 1953. British title: Death at Lover's Leap. Boardman, 1954 TH [Maine]
The Body Was Quite Cold. Dutton, 1951 TH [Wash. D.C.]
The Case of Joshua Locke. Dutton, 1951 TH [Wash. D.C., Va.]
Death at Lover's Leap; see Affair at Lover's Leap
Layoff. Scribner, 1942 TH [Fla.]
A Murder by Marriage. Scribner, 1940 TH [Conn.]
Murder in Mink. Scribner, 1941 TH [Midwest]
Murder Makes a Merry Widow. Doubleday, 1938 TH [St. Louis]
Murder Most Opportune. Doubleday, 1939 [Tex.]
A Murder of Convenience. Doubleday, 1938 TH [NYC]
Murder on Margin. Doubleday, 1937 PT [NYC]
Murder Through the Looking Glass. Doubleday, 1940 TH [Midwest]
On Ice. Scribner, 1942 TH [NYC]
The Sutton Place Murders. Doubleday, 1936; Heinemann, 1936 PT [NYC]
Three Lights Went Out. Doubleday, 1936 PT
What Gentleman Strangles a Lady? Doubleday, 1936 PT [Conn.]

DEAN, SPENCER. Pseudonym of Prentice Winchell, 1895- . Other pseudonyms: Jay de Bekker, Stewart Sterling, Dexter St. Clair, Dexter St. Clare, qq.v. SC: Don Cadee, in all titles, all set in NYC.
Credit for a Murder. Doubleday, 1961; Boardman, 1962
Dishonor Among Thieves. Doubleday, 1958; Boardman, 1959
The Frightened Fingers. Washburn, 1954; Boardman, 1955
Marked Down for Murder. Doubleday, 1956; Boardman, 1957
The Merchant of Murder. Doubleday, 1959; Boardman, 1960
Murder After a Fashion. Doubleday, 1960; Boardman, 1961
Murder on Delivery. Doubleday, 1957; Boardman, 1958
Price Tag for Murder. Doubleday, 1959; Boardman, 1960
The Scent of Fear. Washburn, 1954; Boardman, 1956. Also published as: The Smell of Fear. Jonathan, 1956
The Smell of Fear; see The Scent of Fear

DeANDREA, WILLIAM L(OUIS). 1952- . Ref: CA.
The Hog Murders. Avon, 1979 [N.Y.]
Killed in the Ratings. Harcourt (NYC), 1978; Harcourt (London), 1979 [NYC]
The Lunatic Fringe. Evans, 1980 [NYC, 1896]

DEANE, DONALD. Set: Eng.
Hidden Clues. Hamilton, 1932
The Luck of Luce. Hamilton, 1931
The Mystery of the Fifth Tulip. Hamilton, 1930

DEANE, EDWIN S.
Bob Younger's Fate. Street, 1890

DEANE, HAMILTON and JOHN L(LOYD) BALDERSTON, 1889- .
Dracula. French (NYC), 1933 (3-act play based on the novel by Bram Stoker, 1847-1912, q.v.)

DEANE, JIM. SC: Nick Merlotti, in both titles.
The Great Pretender. Signet, 1974 [NYC]
Moon over Miami. Signet, 1975 [Miami]

DEANE, NORMAN. Pseudonym of John Creasey, 1908-1973, q.v. Other pseudonyms: Gordon Ashe, M. E. Cooke, Robert Caine Frazer, Patrick Gill, Michael Halliday, Charles Hogarth, Brian Hope, Colin Hughes, Kyle Hunt, Abel Mann, Peter Manton, J. J. Marric, Richard Martin, Rodney Mattheson, Anthony Morton, Jeremy York, qq.v. SC: Bruce Murdoch = BM; The Liberator = L. Reprinted in England as by John Creasey = *; reprinted there as by Michael Halliday = #. Set: Eng.
Come Home to Crime. Hurst, 1945 L *
Dangerous Journey. Hurst, 1939; McKay, 1974, as by John Creasey BM *
Death in the Spanish Sun. Hurst, 1954 # [Sp.]
Double for Murder. Hurst, 1951 [It.]
Gateway to Escape. Hurst, 1944 L
Golden Death. Hurst, 1952
I Am the Withered Man. Hurst, 1941; McKay, 1973, as by John Creasey BM
Incense of Death. Hurst, 1954 *
Intent to Murder. Hurst, 1948
Look at Murder. Hurst, 1952 [S. Afr.]
The Man I Didn't Kill. Hurst, 1950 #
Murder Ahead. Hurst, 1953 [S. Afr.]
No Hurry to Kill. Hurst, 1950
Play for Murder. Hurst, 1946
Return to Adventure. Hurst, 1943 L
Secret Errand. Hurst, 1943; McKay, 1974, as by John Creasey BM *
The Silent House. Hurst, 1947
Unknown Mission. Hurst, 1940; McKay, 1972, as by John Creasey BM
Where Is the Withered Man? Hurst, 1942; McKay, 1974, as by John Creasey BM
Why Murder? Hurst, 1948
The Withered Man. Hurst, 1940; McKay, 1974, as by John Creasey BM

DEANE, PHILIP. Born on the Greek island of Cephalonia; journalist, diplomat, TV host.
A Time for Treason. Longmans (Canada), 1966 [Wash. D.C.]

DEANE, SHIRLEY (JOAN). 1920- . Ref: CA.
No Tears for the Dead. Ward, 1968. U.S. title: Corpses in Corsica. Vanguard, 1969 [Cors.]

DEARDEN, HAROLD. See: Roland Pertwee, 1885-1963.

DEARDEN, HILDA DANVERS
The Blonde Madonna. Grayson, 1933
"In the King's Name—!" Hurst, 1932
The Mystery of the Skating Rink. Hurst, 1931
Revolt from Bondage. Grayson, 1935
Strange Rendezvous. Grayson, 1934
"This Road Is Dangerous!" Hurst, 1930
-The Trappings Are Gorgeous. Hale, 1937

DEARDEN, R(ICHARD) L(IONEL). 1883- .
Care of the Commander. Jenkins, 1939 [ship]

DEASY, MARY (MARGARET). 1914- . Ref: CA.
The Corioli Affair. Little, 1954; Heinemann, 1955 [South]
Devil's Bridge. Little, 1952; Heinemann, 1956

DEATH, J.
Death Dates a Dame. Gray, 1952
Deep Is My Grave. Gray, 1951

DEBANS, (JEAN BAPTISTE) CAMILLE. 1834- .
A Sheep in Wolf's Clothing. Nimmo, 1880; Lovell, 1884 (Translation from the French.)

DE BANZIE, ERIC. 1894- . Joint pseudonym with John Sellar Matheson Ressich, 1877- : Gregory Baxter, qq.v.

DE BEKKER, JAY. Pseudonym of Prentice Winchell, 1895- . Other pseudonyms: Spencer Dean, Dexter St. Clair, Dexter St. Clare, Stewart Sterling, qq.v.
Gutter Gang. Beacon, 1954
Keyhole Peeper. Beacon, 1955

DE BILIO, BETH. Lives in New York.
Vendetta Con Brio. Bobbs, 1973. Also published as: The Widow's Escort. Dell, 1979

DE BLASIS, CELESTE (NINETTE). 1946- . Ref: CA.
The Night Child. Coward, 1975 [1865, Maine]
Suffer a Sea Change. Coward, 1976 [Bermuda]

DE BORCHGRAVE, ARNAUD, 1926- , and ROBERT MOSS, 1946- . Ref on De Borchgrave: CA.
The Spike. Weidenfeld, 1980; Crown, 1980

DE BOSSCHERE, JOHN. 1878- .
-Marthe and the Madman. Covici, 1928 (Translation of "Marthe et L'Enrage." Paris, 1927.)

DE BRA, LEMUEL
Ways That Are Wary. Butterworth, 1924; Clode, 1925 ss, some criminous [S.F.]

DE BRAHM, JEANNE ICHORD ALCANTER. 1890- . Pseudonym: Jean Rosmer, q.v.

DE BREMONT, ANNA
The Black Opal. Jarrolds, 1918 [Fr.]

DEBRETT, HAL. Joint pseudonym of Davis Dresser, 1904-1977, and Kathleen Rollins Dresser. Other pseudonyms of Davis Dresser: Asa Baker, Brett Halliday, qq.v. Joint pseudonym with (Walter) Ryerson Johnson, 1901- q.v.: Matthew Blood, q.v.
Before I Wake. Dodd, 1949; Jarrolds, 1953. Reprinted as by Brett Halliday: Dell, 1955 [L.I.]
A Lonely Way to Die. Dodd, 1950; Jarrolds, 1954 [N.Y.]

DE BRUNE, (CHARLES FRANCIS) AIDAN. 1879- .
The Carson Loan Mystery. Cornstall (Sydney), 1926
The Dagger and Cord. Cornstall (Sydney), 1927
Shadow Crook. Angus (Sydney), 1930

DE CAIRE, EDWIN. Pseudonym of Edwin Alfred Williams. Ref: CC.
Death Among the Writers. Hodder, 1952
The Umgasi Diamonds. Hodder, 1954

DECKER, DUANE. 1910-1964.
The Devil's Punchbowl. Ace, 1960 [Mass.]

DECOIN, DIDIER. 1945- .
The Case Against Love. NAL, 1967 (Translation of "Le Proces d'Amour." Paris, 1966.)

DeCORMIER, LOUISE. Joint pseudonym with Rebecca Kavalier and Gloria Kirchheimer: Sara Cardiff, q.v.

DE CRESPIGNY, MRS. PHILIP CHAMPION [ROSE CHAMPION DE CRESPIGNY]. -1935. Set: Eng.
A Case for the C.I.D. Cassell, 1933
-The Coming of Aurora. Nash, 1909
The Dark Sea. Lane, 1927
The Eye of Nemesis. Cassell, 1931
-The Five of Spades. Mills, 1912
-From Behind the Arras. Unwin, 1902
-The Grey Domino. Nash, 1906
-Hester and I. Milles, 1915
-Malloy's Tryst. Mills, 1914
-The Mark. Mills, 1912
-The Mischief of a Glove. Unwin, 1903
The Missing Piece. Cassell, 1927
-My Cousin Cynthia, and others. Nash, 1908 ss
The Riddle of the Emeralds. Cassell, 1929
-The Rose Brocade. Nash, 1905
-The Spanish Prisoner. Nash, 1907
-Stories of Today and Yesterday. Mills, 1917 ss
Straws in the Wind. Cassell, 1928
Tangled Evidence. Cassell, 1924
-The Valley of Achor. Mills, 1910

DECREST, JACQUES. Pseudonym of Jacques Napoleon Faure-Biguet, 1893- . SC: M. Gilles, in at least those marked G.
Body on the Beach. Hammond, 1953 (Translation of "Le Rendez-Vous du Dimanche Soir." Paris, 1935.) G
Meet a Body. Hammond, 1953 (Translation of "Hasard." Paris, 1933.) G
The Missing Formula. Hammond, 1956 (Translation of "Les Trois Jeunes Filles de Vienne." Paris, 1934.) G

DE CROISSET, FRANCIS. See: Edgar (Alfred) Jepson, 1863-1938.

DEDINA, MICHEL. 1933- . Ref: CA.
The Harm in Trying. Muller, 1964
The Mink Steel. Muller, 1966

DEEGAN, JON J. Pseudonym of Robert George Sharp.
Beyond the Fourth Door. Hamilton Stafford, 1954 [future]
-Reconnoitre Krellig II. Hamilton Stafford, 1951
-Underworld of Zello. Hamilton Stafford, 1952

DEEMSTER, NICK
Run, Killer, Run. Mitre, 1946

DE FELITTA, FRANK (PAUL). 1921- . Ref: CA.
Audrey Rose. Putnam, 1975; Collins, 1976
Oktoberfest. Doubleday, 1973; Collins, 1974
Sea Trial. Avon, 1980; Gollancz, 1980

DE FILIPPO, EDUARDO
Three Plays. H. Hamilton, 1976 (3 plays, one criminous.)

DE FONTMELL, E. V. Pseudonym.
Honour Lost, All Lost. Scholartis, 1929

DE FORD, MIRIAM ALLEN. 1888-1975. Ref: CA, EM, MP, TC.
The Theme Is Murder. Abelard, 1967 ss

DE FOREST, J(OHN) W(ILLIAM). 1826-1906. Ref: EM.
-The Bloody Chasm. Appleton, 1881. Also published as: The Oddest of Courtships; or, The Bloody Chasm. Appleton, 1882
The Oddest of Courtships; see The Bloody Chase
-Playing the Mischief. Harper, 1875
Seacliffe; or, The Mystery of the Westervelts. Phillips, 1859
The Weatherel Affair. Sheldon, 1873

DE FORREST, BETTY
The Snows of Yesterday. Ace, 1973 [L.I.]

DE FRAGA, GEOFF. 1913- .
Murder at the Cookout. Cassell, 1968
Murder by Wash of Light. Rigby (Adelaide), 1970; Hale (London), 1971 [Australia]

DE GRAMONT, SANCHE. 1932- . Ref: CA.
Lives to Give. Putnam, 1971; Hodder, 1972

DEGRAS, HENRY ERNEST. 1910- . Pseudonym: Mary Benney, q.v.

DE GROOT, J. MORGAN
-The Affair on the Bridge. Blackwood, 1909
-The Bar Sinister. Blackwood, 1899
A Man of Iron. Long, 1901

DE HALSALLE, HENRY. 1872- . See also: R(ichard) D('Oyly) Hemingway, 1878- . SC: Olga von Kopf = OK.
The Life Story of Madame Zelle, the World's Most Beautiful Spy. Skeffington, 1918
A Secret Service Woman. Laurie, 1917 OK
A Woman Spy. Skeffington, 1918 OK [Russ.]

DE HAMEL, HERBERT
Many Thanks, Ben Hassett. Simpkin, 1915; Congreve, 1948 [Australia]

DE HAVILLAND, R(OBERT J.) L(ANGSTAFF)
The Forked Tongue. Vizetelly, 1885

DE HAVILLAND, SAUMAREZ
The Mystic Serpent. Iliffe, 1891
Ritherdon's Grange. Trischler, 1890
-Strange Clients, and other tales. Iliffe, 1890

DEIGHTON, LEN [LEONARD CYRIL DEIGHTON]. 1929- . Ref: CA, CC, EM, MC, TC. SC: nameless British agent known from the films as Harry Palmer = HP.
The Billion Dollar Brain. Cape, 1966; Putnam, 1966 HP
Catch a Falling Spy; see Twinkle, Twinkle, Little Spy
An Expensive Place to Die. Cape, 1967; Putnam, 1967 HP [Paris]
Funeral in Berlin. Cape, 1964; Putnam, 1965 HP
Horse Under Water. Cape, 1963; Putnam, 1968 HP
The Ipcress File. Hodder, 1962; Simon, 1963 HP
Spy Story. Cape, 1974; Harcourt, 1974 HP
SS-GB. Cape, 1978; Knopf, 1979 [1941, Eng.]
Twinkle, Twinkle, Little Spy. Cape, 1976. U.S. title: Catch a Falling Spy. Harcourt, 1976 HP
Yesterday's Spy. Cape, 1975; Harcourt, 1975 [Fr.]

DE JEAN, GEORGES. 1886- .
Who Killed Lord Brixham? Jenkins, 1937 [Fr.]

DE JEAN, LOUIS (LEON)
The Girl in Black Velvet. Macaulay, 1937

DEJEANS, ELIZABETH. -1928?
The Double House. Doubleday, 1924; Hutchinson, 1924 [L.A.]
The Moreton Mystery. Bobbs, 1920; Allen & Unwin, 1922 [NYC]
The Romance of a Million Dollars. Bobbs, 1922; Hutchinson, 1926 [NYC]
The Tiger's Coat. Bobbs, 1917; Butterworth, 1923

DE JONG, DOLA. 1911- . Ref: CA.
The Whirligig of Time. Doubleday, 1964

DEKKER, ANTHONY
Divers Diamonds. Collins, 1970
Temptation in a Private Zoo. Constable, 1969; Morrow, 1970

DEKKER, CARL. Pseudonym of John (Alfred Charles) Laffin, 1922- , q.v.
Other pseudonyms: Mark Napier, Dirk Sabre, qq.v.
Don't Bother to Knock. Calvert, 1954
Silence So Deadly. Calvert, 1953

DEKKER, CARL. Pseudonym of Dennis Lynds, 1924- , q.v. Other pseudonyms: William Arden, Nick Carter, Michael Collins, John Crowe, Maxwell Grant, Michael Sadler, qq.v.
Woman in Marble. Bobbs, 1972 [L.A.]

DEKKER, J.
Dolls and Dollars. Martin, 1948
Hex Marks the Spot. Martin, 1949
Manhunt in Manhattan. Martin, 1949 [NYC]
Shoot to Kill. Martin, 1949
The Siamese Cat. Martin, 1948
Singapore Set-Up. Martin, 1948 [Sing.]
Streetcar to Hell. Martin, 1949

DEKOBRA, MAURICE. Pseudonym of Ernest Maurice Tessier, 1885-1973. Ref: CA, CC. SC: Bradley Adams, in at least those marked BA.
The Bachelor's Widow; see Hell Is Sold Out

Blood and Caviar. Laurie, 1937 (Translation of "Le Fou de Bassan." Paris, 1935.)
-The Blue Parrot. Laurie, 1948 (Translation of "Le Perruche Bleue.")
Chinese Puzzle. Allen, 1956
-The Cloven-Footed Angel. Macaulay, 1932
-Confucius in a Tail-Coat. Laurie, 1935; Greenberg, 1935 (Translation of "Confucius en Pullover." Paris, 1934)
-Diamond Queen. Allen, 1965 (Translation of "L'Amazone de Pretaria.") [Trans., 1900]
-Double or Quits. Allen, 1962 (Translation of "Bouddha le Terrible." Paris, 1961.)
-Emigrants de Luxe. Laurie, 1943 (Translation of "Emigres de Luxe.")
-Flames of Velvet. Laurie, 1929. U.S. title: The Love Clinic. Payson, 1929 (Translation of "Flammes de Velours." Paris, 1927.)
The Golden-Eyed Venus. Allen, 1963 (Translation of "La Venus aux Yeux d'Or." Paris, 1962.)
-Hamydal, the Vagabond Philosopher. Laurie, 1937 (Translation of "Hamydal le Philosophe." Paris, 1918.)
The Hangman Never Waits. Allen, 1960 (Translation of "Le Bourreau n"attend Jamais." Paris, 1959.) [L.A.]
-Hell Is Sold Out. Laurie, 1948. U.S. title: The Bachelor's Widow. Ace, 1954
-His Chinese Concubine. Laurie, 1935 (Translation of "Madame Joli-Supplice." Paris, 1934.)
-Honeymoon in Shanghai. Laurie, 1946. U.S. title: Shanghai Honeymoon. Philosophical Library, 1946 (Translation of "Lune de Miel a Shanghai.") [Shanghai]
The Lady Is a Vamp. Allen, 1958 (Translation of "Vamp ou Vestale." Paris, 1957.) BA [L.A.]
-Love Calling. Laurie, 1933 (Translation of "La Volupte Eclairant le Monde." Paris, 1932.)
The Love Clinic; see Flames of Velvet
-The Madonna in Hollywood. Laurie, 1945 (Translation of "La Madone a Hollywood." Paris, 1943.) [L.A.]
The Madonna of the Sleeping Cars. Laurie, 1927; Payson, 1927 (Translation of "La Madone des Sleepings." Paris, 1925.)
The Man Who Died Twice. Allen, 1954 (Translation of "Les Vestales du Veau d'Or." Paris, 1948.)
-Midnight on the Place Pigalle. Laurie, 1932 (Translation of "Minuit—Place Pigalle." Paris, 1923.)
Operation Magali. Allen, 1952 (Translation of "Operation Magali." Paris, 1951.) [Fr.]
-Passion Lighting the World. Macaulay, 1933
-The Phantom Gondola. Laurie, 1928. U.S. title: The 13th Lover. Payson, 1928 (Translation of "La Gondola aux Chimeres." Paris, 1926.)
-Phryne; or, Love Is a Fine Art. Laurie, 1931 (Translation of "Le Geste de Phryne." Paris, 1930.)
Poison at Plessis. Allen, 1965 (Probably a translation of "La Pavane des Poisons." Paris, 1950.)
-Prince or Clown. Readers Library, 1928 (Translation of "Prince ou Pitre?" Paris, 1920.) [Paris]
-Princess Brinda. Laurie, 1935 (Translation of "La Prison des Reves." Paris, 1933.)
-The Romance of a Coward. Laurie, 1943 (Translation of "Le Roman d'un Lache." Paris, 1942.)
Serenade to the Hangman. Laurie, 1929; Payson, 1929 (Translation of "Serenade au Bourreau." Paris, 1928.)
The Seventh Wife of Prince Hassan. Allen, 1961 (Translation of "Les Sept Femmes du Prince Hassan.")
Shanghai Honeymoon; see Honeymoon in Shanghai
She Wore Pink Gloves. Allen, 1958 (Translation of "La Veuve aux Ganta Roses." Paris, 1956.) BA
-Some Tommies. Paul, 1919 (Translation of "Messieurs les Tommies." Paris, 1917.)
-Stars and Stripes. Laurie, 1936 (Translation of "Mimi Broadway." Paris, 1936.)
-The Street of Painted Lips. Laurie, 1934; Macaulay, 1934 (Translation of "La Rue des Bouches-Peintes.")
The 13th Lover; see The Phantom Gondola
-Venus on Wheels. Laurie, 1930; Macaulay, 1930 (Translation of "La Venus a Roulettes." Paris, 1925.)

The Widow with the Pink Gloves. Laurie, 1938 (Translation of "Fusille a l'Aube." Paris, 1937.)
-The Widow's Might. Allen, 1957 (Translation of "Les Lotus Dorment la Nuit." Paris, 1956.)
-Wings of Desire. Laurie, 1927; Macaulay, 1925 (Translation of "Mon Coeur au Ralenti." Paris, 1924.)

DE KREMER, JEAN RAYMOND. 1887-1964. Pseudonym: Jean Ray, q.v.

DELACORTE, PETER. 1943- . Ref: CA.
Games of Chance. Seaview, 1980

DE LAGUNA, FREDERICA (ANNIS). 1906- . Ref: CA.
The Arrow Points to Murder. Doubleday, 1937 [NYC]
Fog on the Mountain. Doubleday, 1938 [Alaska]

DELAMARE, GEORGE. 1886- .
The Midnight King. Henkle, 1927 (Translation of "La Roi de Minuit." Paris, 1926.) [Ger.]

DE LA MARE, WALTER (JOHN). 1873-1956.
The Riddle, and other stories. Selwyn, 1923; Knopf, 1923 ss

DELANCEY, ROGER
Murder Below Wall Street. Appleton (NYC & London), 1934 [NYC]

DELANE, BRIAN
Her Crooked Lover. Fiction House, 1935
Who Killed the Count? Fiction House, 1938

DELANEY, DENIS. Pseudonym of Peter (Morris) Green, 1924- , q.v.
Cat in Gloves. Gryphon, 1956

DELANEY, LAURENCE
The Triton Ultimatum. Crowell, 1977; New English Library, 1978

DELANEY, M.
Protection for a Lady. Milestone, 1953
She Had My Number. Milestone, 1953

DELANNOY, (H.) BURFORD. SC: Watson Ward, in at least those marked WW. Set: Eng.
Beaten to the Post. Digby, 1907
Between the Lines. Ward, 1901
Dead Man's Rooms. Ward, 1905 WW
Denzil's Device. Everett, 1904
The Flat Below. Rivers, 1931 WW
The Garden Court Mystery. Street, 1899 (Magnet #112) (British title?)
In Mid-Atlantic. Ward, 1904
The Margate Murder Mystery. Ward, 1902; Brentano's, 1901
The Midnight Special. Milne, 1902
The Missing Cyclist and other stories. Simpkin, 1898 ss
The Money Lender. Ward, 1907
M.R.C.S. Ward, 1903
Nineteen Thousand Pounds. Ward, 1901; Fenno, 1900
The Pound of Flesh. Digby, 1911
The Scales of Justice. Digby, 1908
A Studio Model. Digby, 1909
A Thespian Detective and other theatrical stories. Ellis, 1899 ss

DELANY, JOSEPH FRANCIS. 1905- . Pseudonym: Joel Y. Dane, q.v.

DE LARRABEITI, MICHAEL
The Bunce. Joseph, 1980; Doubleday, 1981

DE LA TORRE, LILLIAN [LILLIAN DE LA TORRE BUENO McCUE]. 1902- . Ref: CA, CC, DD, EM, MC, TC. SC: Dr. Sam: Johnson = SJ.
The Detections of Dr. Sam: Johnson. Doubleday, 1960 SJ ss [Eng., ca.1770]
Dr. Sam: Johnson, Detector. Knopf, 1946; Joseph, 1948 SJ ss [Eng., ca.1770]
Elizabeth Is Missing. Knopf, 1945; Joseph, 1947 [Eng., 1753]
Goodbye, Miss Lizzie Borden. Baker, 1948 (1-act play.)
The Heir of Douglas. Knopf, 1952; Joseph, 1953 [Scot., 1700s]
The Truth About Belle Gunness. GM, 1955; Muller, 1960

DE LAUER, MARJEL JEAN
The Mystery of the Phantom Billionaire. Ashley, 1972

DE LEON, JACK. See also: Jack Celestin.
The Man at Six. Collins, 1930 (Novelization of the play by Jack Celestin and Jack de Leon.)

DELF, T. W. H.
　The Man in the Check Suit. Jarrolds, 1897

DELF, THOMAS. 1810-1865. Pseudonym: Charles Martel, q.v.

DELFT, JAPHET
　The Drums of Kufu. Quartet, 1976

DELILLE, JOHN DOUGLAS
　Canon Lucifer. Gilber, 1887

DE LILLO, DON. 1936-　. Ref: CA.
　Running Dog. Knopf, 1978; Gollancz, 1979 [NYC]

DE L'ISLE, F. D. A. C.
　The Adventures of a Turf Detective. Everett, 1910　ss

DELL, AMEN. Born in NYC; active in the theatre.
　Johnny on the Spot. Mystery House, 1943 [NYC]

DELL, DRAYCOT (MONTAGU), 1888-　, and OSWALD (C. C.) DALLAS
　The Death Gang. Columbine, 193?

DELL, JEFFREY. 1899-　.
　The Hoffmann Episode. Cape, 1954
　Payment Deferred. French (London & NYC), 1934　(3-act play based on the novel by C. S. Forester, 1899-1966, q.v.)

DELLA, LEW
　Dark Angel. Milestone, 1953
　Fast and Loose. Milestone, 1953
　Ladies Sleep Alone. Archer, 19??; Kaywin, 1951
　Life Is Short. Milestone, 1953
　Love Comes Lethal. Milestone, 1953
　Risky! Milestone, 1954
　Shadows Sometimes Scream. Milestone, 1954
　Touch and Go. Milestone, 1954

DELLAR, H. J.
　Incident Closed. Quality, 1947

DELLBRIDGE, JOHN. 1887-　. SC: Rupert Hambledon, in at least those marked RH.
　The Lady in the Wood. Hurst, 1950　RH
　The Moles of Death. Diamond, 1927 [India]
　Searchlight on Hambledon. Hurst, 1947 RH
　Unfit to Plead. Hurst, 1949

DELLIGAN, WILLIAM. Pseudonym: Gwynneth Davies, q.v.

DELMAN, DAVID. 1924-　. Executive of a Philadelphia advertising agency. SC: Lt. Jacob Horowitz.
　He Who Digs a Grave. Doubleday, 1973; Hale, 1975
　The Nice Murderers. Morrow, 1977; Collins, 1977 [L.I.]
　One Man's Murder. McKay, 1975; Collins, 1975 [L.I.]
　Sudden Death. Doubleday, 1972; Collins, 1973 [N.Y.]
　A Week to Kill. Doubleday, 1972

DEL MAR, DON. 1904-　. Born in the Philippines; came to the U.S. in the 1930s.
　Blood Pearls of Sulu. Vantage, 1972 [Philip.]

DELMAS, LEON RENE. 1830-1904. Pseudonym: Rene De Pont-Jest, q.v.

DELMERE, F.
　Dead Man's Gang. Mellifont, 1934
　The Lion's Claws. Gramol, 1934

DELMONICO, ANDREA. Pseudonym of Eula Atwood Morrison, 1911-　. Ref: CA.
　Chateau Chaumond. Ace, 1968 [Wis.]
　Eyrie of an Eagle. Ace, 1969 [Wash.]

DEL REY, LESTER [RAMON FELIPE SAN JUAN MARIO SILVIO ENRICO ALVAREZ DEL REY]. 1915-　. Pseudonym: Erik van Lhin, q.v.

DELVES-BROUGHTON, JOSEPHINE. 1916-　. Pseudonym: John Bryan, q.v.

DELVING, MICHAEL. Pseudonym of Jay Williams, 1914-1978. Ref: CA, CC, TC. SC: Dave Cannon = DC; Bob Eddison = BE.
　Bored to Death. Scribner, 1975. British title: A Wave of Fatalities. Collins, 1975　DC　[Eng.]
　The China Expert. Scribner, 1977; Collins, 1976　[Eng.]
　The Devil Finds Work. Scribner, 1969; Collins, 1970　DC,BE　[Eng.]
　Die Like a Man. Scribner, 1970; Collins, 1970　DC　[Wales]
　No Sign of Life. Doubleday, 1979; Collins, 1978　DC　[Eng.]
　A Shadow of Himself. Scribner, 1972; Collins, 1972　BE　[Eng.]
　Smiling the Boy Fell Dead. Scribner, 1967; Macdonald, 1967　DC　[Eng.]
　A Wave of Fatalities; see Bored to Death

DEMAINE, CHRISTY
　A Matter of Revenge. Payboy, 1977

DE MAR, PAUL. Pseudonym of Pearl Foley, q.v.
　The Gnome Mine Mystery. Hamilton, 1933 [Can.]

DE MARCO, GORDON
　October Heat. Germinal, 1979　[S.F., 1934]

DEMAREST, ANNE. Pseudonym of Florence Demarest Foos Bond.
　Murder on Every Floor. Hillman-Curl, 1939 [NYC]
　-She Was His Secretary. Gramercy, 1939

DEMAREST, JUDITH H.
　The Model Murders. Carlyle, 1979

DEMAREST, PHYLLIS GORDON.　-1973.
　The House on Washington Place. Curtis, 1974 [NYC, 1860s]

DE MARIA, ROBERT. 1928-　. Ref: CA.
　Outbreak! Jove, 1978

DEMARIS, OVID. Pseudonym of Ovide E. Desmarais, 1919-　. Ref: CA, TC.
　Candyleg. GM, 1961; Muller pb, 1962. Also published as: Machine Gun McCain. GM, 1970; Coronet, 1970
　The Contract; see The Organization
　The Enforcer. GM, 1960
　The Extortionists. GM, 1960; Muller pb, 1961　[L.A.]
　The Gold-Plated Sewer. Avon, 1960 [L.A.]
　The Hoods Take Over. GM, 1957　[L.A.]
　The Long Night. Avon, 1959
　The Lusting Drive. GM, 1958; Muller pb, 1961
　Machine Gun McCain; see Candyleg
　The Organization. Tower, 1965. Also published as: The Contract. Belmont, 1970; Sphere, 1971
　The Overlord. Signet, 1972
　The Parasite. Berkley, 1963
　Ride the Gold Mare. GM, 1957　[L.A.]
　The Slasher. GM, 1959　[L.A.]

DE MARNE, DENIS. See: Ron Pember.

DE MARQUAND, ALIX
　House on Somber Lake. Lancer, 1968

DEMBO, SAMUEL
　The Amber Eyes of the Lion. Redman, 1963
　Kalahari Kill; see The Sands of Lilliput
　The Sands of Lilliput. Redman, 1963. U.S. title: Kalahari Kill. Mill, 1964 [Afr.]

DE MEXICO, N. R.
　Madman on a Drum. Cavalcade, 1944. Also published as: Strange Pursuit. Suspense Novel, 1951 [NYC]
　Marijuana Girl. Universal Publishing, 1951
　Strange Pursuit; see Madman on a Drum

DEMIJOHN, THOM. Joint pseudonym of Thomas M(ichael) Disch, 1940-　, q.v., and John Sladek, 1937-　, q.v.
　Black Alice. Doubleday, 1968; Allen, 1969 [Va.]

DE MILLE, JAMES. 1837-1880.
　The American Baron. Harper, 1872
　-Among the Brigands. Lee, 1872
　-A Castle in Spain. Harper, 1878 [Sp.]
　-A Comedy of Terrors. Osgood, 1872
　-Cord and Cheese. Harper, 1869
　The Cryptogram. Harper, 1871
　The Lady of the Ice. Appleton, 1870
　-The Living Link. Harper, 1874
　-An Open Question. Appleton, 1873
　-A Strange Manuscript Found in a Copper Cylinder. Harper, 1888; Chatto, 1888

DE MILLE, NELSON. 1943-　. Ref: CA. SC: Keller = K; Ryker = R (see also: Edson T. Hamill).
　The Agent of Death. Leisure, 1974　R [NYC]
　By the Waters of Babylon. Harcourt, 1978; Hart-Davis, 1978 [Mid. East]
　The Cannibal. Manor, 1975　K　[NYC]
　The Hammer of God. Leisure, 1974　R [NYC]
　Night of the Phoenix. Manor, 1975　K
　The Quest. Manor, 1975
　The Smack Man. Manor, 1975　K
　The Sniper. Leisure, 1974　R　[NYC]
　The Terrorists. Leisure, 1974　R　[NYC] (Written by Leonard Levinson, 1935-　, q.v.)

DEMING, RICHARD. 1915-　. Pseudonyms: Max Franklin, Emily Moor, qq.v. See also: Nick Marino, Ellery Queen. Ref: CA, TC.　SC: Manville Moon = MM; Matt Rudd = MR.
　Anything But Saintly. Permabooks, 1963 MR [Calif.]
　Body for Sale. PB, 1962
　The Careful Man. Allen, 1962
　Death of a Pusher. PB, 1964　MR [Calif.]
　Dragnet: The Case of the Courteous Killer. PB, 1958　(Novelization of the TV series.)　[L.A.]
　Dragnet: The Case of the Crime King. PB, 1959　(Novelization of the TV series.)　[L.A.]
　Edge of the Law. Berkley, 1960
　Fall Girl. Zenith, 1959. British title: Walk a Crooked Mile. Boardman, 1959
　The Gallows in My Garden. Rinehart, 1952; Boardman, 1953　MM
　Give the Girl a Gun; see Whistle Past the Graveyard
　The Greek God Affair. Pyramid, 1968 (Novelization of the "Mod Squad" TV series.)　[L.A.]
　A Groovy Way to Die. Pyramid, 1968 (Novelization of the "Mod Squad" TV series.)　[L.A.]
　Hand-Picked to Die; see Tweak the Devil's Nose
　The Hit. Pyramid, 1970　(Novelization of the "Mod Squad" TV series.)
　Hit and Run. PB, 1960　[N.Y.]
　Juvenile Delinquent. Boardman, 1958 MM
　Kiss and Kill. Zenith, 1960; Digit, 1961
　She'll Hate Me Tomorrow. Monarch, 1963
　The Sock-It-to-Em Murders. Pyramid, 1968 (Novelization of the "Mod Squad" TV series.)　[L.A.]
　Spy-In. Pyramid, 1969 (Novelization of the "Mod Squad" TV series.)　[L.A.]
　This Game of Murder. Monarch, 1964
　This Is My Night. Monarch, 1961 [L.A.]
　Tweak the Devil's Nose. Rinehart, 1953; Boardman, 1953. Also published as: Hand-Picked to Die. Jonathan, 1956　MM　[Midwest]
　Vice Cop. Belmont, 1961　MR
　Walk a Crooked Mile; see Fall Girl
　What's the Matter with Helen? Beagle, 1971　(Novelization of the movie.) [Ia., 1933]
　Whistle Past the Graveyard. Rinehart, 1954; Boardman, 1955. Also published as: Give the Girl a Gun. Jonathan, 1955　MM

DE MIRJIAN, ARTO, JR. 1931-　. Ref: CA.
　Not a Clue. Popular Library, 1974 [NYC]

DE MONTFORT, GUY. Pseudonym of Donald McIntosh Johnson, 1930-　. Ref: CA.
　All the Queen's Men. Hamlyn, 1980

DE MORGAN, WILLIAM FREND. 1839-1917.
　The Old Madhouse. Heinemann, 1919; Holt, 1919

DEMOUZON, (ALAIN). 1945-　. SC: Robert Flecheux = RF; Nicholas Placard = NP.
　Farewell, La Jolla. Peebles, 1980 (Translation of "Adieu, La Jolla." Paris, 1978.)　NP
　The First Born of Egypt. Peebles, 1979 (Translation of "Le Premier ne d'Egypte." Paris, 1979.)　RF
　Mouche. Peebles, 1979 (Translation from the French.)　RF　[Paris]
　A Rotten Deal. Peebles, 1980 (Translation from the French.)　NP

DEMPSEY, AL and ROBIN MOORE, q.v.
　The Red Falcons. Pinnacle, 1976; Sphere, 1978 [Conn.]

DE NAVERY, RAOUL. Pseudonym of Marie de Saffron David, 1831-1885.
　Idols; or, The Secret of the Rue Chaussee D'Antin. Benziger, 1882; Gill, 1890 (Translation from the French.)

DENBIE, ROGER. Joint pseudonym of Alan (Baer) Green, 1906-1975, q.v., and Julian Paul Brodie, 1908-   . Ref: CC. Joint pseudonym of Alan (Baer) Green and Gladys Elizabeth Green, 1908-   : Glen Burne, q.v. SC: Dr. Quentin Pace, in both titles.
  Death Cruises South. Morrow, 1934; Nicholson, 1934 [Bermuda]
  Death on the Limited. Morrow, 1933. British title: The Timetable Murder. Nicholson, 1934 [train]
  The Timetable Murder; see Death on the Limited

DENBOW, WILLIAM
  Chandler. Belmont, 1977 [NYC]

DENBY, EDWIN (ORR). 1903-1983.
  Mrs. W's Last Sandwich. Horizon, 1972. Also published as: Scream in a Cave. Popular Library, 1979 [Sp.]

DENEVI, MARCO. 1922-   .
  Rosa at Ten O'Clock. Holt, 1964 (Translation of "Rosaura a las Diez." Buenos Aires, 1957.) [Buen. A.]

DENHAM, BERTIE. 1927-   . Ref: CA.
  The Man Who Lost His Shadow. Macmillan (London), 1979; Scribner, 1979

DENHAM, LILLIAN (MARY). See: Edward Percy

DENHAM, REGINALD. 1894-1983. See also: Edward Percy. Ref: CA.
  Recipe for a Crime. Dramatists, 1962 (2-act play.)

DENHAM, THOMAS S(IDNEY). 1906-   .
  Background to Murder, and other stories. Mitre, 1943 ss
  The Grand National Mystery, and other tales. Mitre, 1944 ss

DENIS, JOHN
  Hostage Tower. Fontana, 1980 (Story outline by Alistair MacLean, 1923-   , q.v.)

DENISON, FRANK
  Tales of the Strong Room. Digby, 1899 ss

DENISON, MRS. MARY A(NDREWS). 1826-1911.
  A Brave Little Woman. Lupton, 1892 ss
  -Led to the Light. Claxton, 1867
  The Man in Blue; or, Which Did He Love? Street, 1889
  -Opposite the Jail. Hoyt, 1859
  -Out of Prison. Sheldon, 1864
  -Sequel to Opposite the Jail; or, On Trial for His Life. Bradley, 1883

DENISON, THOMAS STEWART. 1848-1911.
  My Invisible Partner. Rand, 1898; Syndicate, 1899

DENKER, HENRY. 1912-   . Ref: CA.
  -Error of Judgment. Simon, 1979; Macdonald, 1980
  -The Starmaker. Simon, 1977; Allen, 1977

DENMAN, PETER
  The Man Who Guided Missiles. Hale, 1973

DENNING, MARK. Pseudonym of John Stevenson, q.v. Other pseudonyms: Nick Carter, Bruno Rossi, qq.v. SC: John Marshall, in all titles.
  Beyond the Prize. Jove, 1978 [Ire.]
  Die Fast, Die Happy. Pyramid, 1976
  Shades of Gray. Pyramid, 1976

DENNIS, CHARLES. 1946-   . Ref: CA.
  The Next-to-Last Train Ride. Macmillan (London), 1974; St. Martin's, 1974
  The Periwinkle Assault. Futura, 1977
  Somebody Just Grabbed Annie. Macmillan (London), 1975; St. Martin's, 1975
  Stoned Cold Soldier. Bachman, 1973

DENNIS, EVE
  Death for Safety. Gifford, 1949

DENNIS, GEOFFREY POMEROY. 1892-1963. Joint pseudonym with Hilary (Aiden) St. George Saunders, 1898-1951, q.v.: Barum Browne, q.v.

DENNIS, RALPH. SC: Jim Hardman = JH, all set in Atlanta.
  Atlanta Deathwatch. Popular Library, 1974 JH
  The Buy Back Blues. Popular Library, 1977 JH
  The Charleston Knife's Back in Town. Popular Library, 1974 JH
  The Deadly Cotton Heart. Popular Library, 1976 JH
  Down Among the Jocks. Popular Library, 1974 JH
  The Golden Girl and All. Popular Library, 1974 JH
  Hump's First Case. Popular Library, 1977 JH
  The Last of the Armageddon Wars. Popular Library, 1977 JH
  Murder's Not an Odd Job. Popular Library, 1974 JH
  MacTaggart's War. Holt, 1979; Hodder, 1979 [Can., 1940]
  The One-Dollar Rip-Off. Popular Library, 1977 JH
  Pimp for the Dead. Popular Library, 1974 JH
  Working for the Man. Popular Library, 1974 JH

DENNIS, ROBERT C. 1920-   . Ref: CA. SC: Paul Reeder, in both titles.
  Conversations with a Corpse. Bobbs, 1974; Gollancz, 1974 [Calif.]
  The Sweat of Fear. Bobbs, 1973; Gollancz, 1973 [Calif.]

DENNISON, DULCIE WINIFRED CATHERINE. 1920-   . Pseudonym: Dulcie Gray, q.v.

DENNISTON, ELINORE. 1900-1978. Pseudonyms: Dennis Allan, Rae Foley, qq.v.

DENNY, ERNEST. 1869-
  The Happy Prodigal. French (NYC), 1930 (3-act play.)

DENNY, FELIX. Pseudonym: Dennis Barr, q.v.

DENT, JOHN CHARLES. 1841-1888. Ref: CC.
  The Gerrard Street Mystery and other weird tales. Rose (Toronto), 1888 ss

DENT, LESTER. 1905-1959. Pseudonym: Kenneth Robeson, q.v. Ref: TC. SC: Chance Malloy = CM.
  Cry at Dusk. GM, 1952
  Dead at the Take-Off. Doubleday, 1946; Cassell, 1948. Also published as: High Stakes. Ace, 1953 CM [air.]
  Hades and Hocus-Pocus. Pulp Press, 1979 (2 novelets)
  High Stakes; see Dead at the Take-Off
  Lady Afraid. Doubleday, 1948; Cassell, 1950 [Fla.]
  Lady in Peril. Ace, 1959 [Mo.]
  Lady So Silent. Cassell, 1951
  Lady to Kill. Doubleday, 1946; Cassell, 1949 CM [train]

DENT, ROXANNE
  Island of Fear. Avon, 1973

DENTON, RALPH
  Charlie Finds a Corpse. Yates, 1949

DENVER, PAUL. SC: Cannon = C (see also: Douglas Enefer, Richard Gallagher), novelizations of the TV series.
  Dead on Time. Five Star, 1973
  The Falling Blonde. Star, 1975 C
  The Golden Bullet. World Distributors, 1973 C
  The Last Laugh, and No Pictures for Cathy. Consul, 1965
  Striptease for Murder. Consul, 1965

DE POLNAY, PETER. 1906-   . Ref: CA.
  Blood and Water. Allen, 1975
  The Crow and the Cat. Allen, 1974; St. Martin's, 1975
  It's Cold Next Door. Allen, 1978
  A Life of Ease. Allen, 1971
  Make-Believe. Allen, 1980
  The Other Shore of Time. Allen, 1978

DE PONT-JEST, RENE. Pseudonym of Leon Rene Delmas, 1830-1904.
  Artist and Model; see The Divorced Princess
  The Case of Doctor Plemen. Spencer Blackett, 1888. U.S. title: Rhea; or, The Case of Dr. Plemen. Rand, 1889. Also published as: The Romance of a Pretty Girl. Brandus, 1891 (Translation of "Cas du Docteur Plemen." Paris, 1887.) [Paris]
  The Divorced Princess. Vickers, 1888. U.S. title: Artist and Model. Rand, 1889 (Translation of "Divorcee." Paris, 1885.)
  No. 13 Rue Marlot. Lee, 1880 (Translation of "Le No. 13 de la Rue Marlot." Paris, 1877.)
  Rhea; see The Case of Doctor Plemen
  The River of Pearls; or, The Red Spider. Page, 1899
  The Romance of a Pretty Girl; see The Case of Doctor Plemen

DE PRE, JEAN-ANNE. Pseudonym of Michael (Angelo) Avallone (Jr.), 1924-   , q.v. Other pseudonyms: Nick Carter, Priscilla Dalton, Mark Dane, Dora Highland, Stuart Jason, Steve Michaels, Dorothea Nile, Edwina Noone, Sidney Stuart, Max Walker, qq.v.
  Aquarius, My Evil. Popular Library, 1972 [NYC]
  Die, Jessica, Die. Popular Library, 1972 [1910, L.I.]
  A Sound of Dying Roses. Popular Library, 1971 [1871, Va.]
  The Third Woman. Popular Library, 1971; Sphere, 1973 [1912, NYC]
  Warlock's Woman. Popular Library, 1973

DEPTULA, WALTER (J., JR.). SC: Frank Arrow, in both titles.
  Naked Mistress. Curtis, 1974 [Haw., Mex.]
  Wine, Women...and Death. Curtis, 1974 [Haw.]

DE PUY [DE PUE], E(DWARD) SPENCE. 1872-   . SC: Sam Houston = SH.
  Dr. Nicholas Stone. Dillingham, 1905; Unwin, 1905
  The Hospital Homicides. Phoenix, 1937 SH [Calif., hosp.]
  The Long Knife. Doubleday, 1936 SH [Calif., hosp.]

DERBY, E. C. Pseudonym: Nicholas Carter, q.v.
  A Counterfeiter's Roguery. Street, ca.1900
  The Crossing of Clues. Street, ca.1900
  The Empty Mail Bags. Street, ca.1900
  Foiling a Counterfeiter. Street, ca.1900
  The Gold Maker's Secret. Street, ca.1900
  The Government's Man. Street, ca.1900
  In League with Counterfeiters. Street, ca.1900
  The Mail Robbers' Syndicate. Street, ca.1900
  The Man on the Couch. Street, ca.1900
  A Master Stroke. Street, ca.1900
  A Nihilist's Vengeance. Street, ca.1900
  The Outlaw's Oath. Street, ca.1900
  A Smuggler's Fate. Street, ca.1900
  The Test of Anarchy. Street, ca.1900

DERBY, MARK. Pseudonym of Harry Wilcox. Served extensively with the British military in the Far East.
  Afraid in the Dark; see Malayan Rose
  The Bad Step; see Out of Asia Alive
  The Big Water. Collins, 1953; Viking, 1953 [Mal.]
  The Dark. Collins, 1962
  Echo of a Bomb. Viking, 1957 (British title?) [China, Burma]
  Element of Risk. Collins, 1952; Viking, 1952
  Five Nights in Singapore. Collins, 1961 [Sing.]
  Ghost Blonde. Viking, 1960 (British title?) [Sing.]
  Malayan Rose. Collins, 1951. U.S. title: Afraid in the Dark. Viking, 1952 [Mal.]
  Out of Asia Alive. Collins, 1954. U.S. title: The Bad Step. Viking, 1954 [Far East]
  Sun in the Hunter's Eyes. Collins, 1958; Viking, 1958 [Sing.]
  The Sunlit Ambush. Collins, 1955; Viking, 1955 [Indon.]
  The Tigress. Collins, 1959. U.S. title: Womanhunt. Viking, 1959 [Mal.]
  Womanhunt; see The Tigress

DE RESZKE, DAVID
  Nine Dragon Man. Pyramid, 1975

D'ERIGNY, SIMONE
  The Mysterious Madame S. Lippincott, 1934 (Translation of "L'Estrange Volonte du Professuer Lorrain." Paris, 1933.) [Fr.]

DERING, JOAN (ROSALIND CORDELIA). 1917-   . Ref: CA, CC.
  -The Caravanners. Hodder, 1959
  Louise. Hodder, 1956; Washburn, 1957
  Marianne. Hodder, 1960
  -Mrs. Winterton's Rebellion. Hodder, 1958
  Not Proven. Hodder, 1966
  Number Two, North Steps. Hodder, 1965
  The Silent Witness. Hodder, 1962

DERLETH, AUGUST (WILLIAM). 1909-1971. Pseudonym: Tally Mason, q.v. Ref: CA, CC, EM, TC. SC: Judge Ephraim Peck = EP; Solar Pons = SP, set in Eng., 1930s.
  The Adventure of the Orient Express. Candlelight Press, 1965 SP

The Adventure of the Unique Dickensians. Mycroft, 1968 SP
The Adventures of Solar Pons; see In re Sherlock Holmes
The Casebook of Solar Pons. Mycroft, 1965 SP ss
The Chronicles of Solar Pons. Mycroft, 1973; Robson, 1975 SP ss
Death by Design. Arcadia, 1953 [Madison]
Death Stalks the Wakely Family; see Murder Stalks the Wakely Family
Fell Purpose. Arcadia, 1953 EP [Wis.]
In re Sherlock Holmes: The Adventures of Solar Pons. Mycroft, 1945. British title: The Adventures of Solar Pons. Robson, 1975. Also published as: Regarding Sherlock Holmes. Pinnacle, 1974 SP ss
The Man on All Fours. Loring, 1934; Newnes, 1936 EP [Wis.]
The Memoirs of Solar Pons. Mycroft, 1951 SP ss
Mischief in the Lane. Scribner, 1944; Muller, 1948 EP [Wis.]
Mr. Fairlie's Final Journey. Mycroft, 1968 SP
Murder Stalks the Wakely Family. Loring, 1934. British title: Death Stalks the Wakely Family. Newnes, 1937 EP [Wis.]
The Narracong Riddle. Scribner, 1940 EP [Madison]
No Future for Luana. Scribner, 1945; Muller, 1948 EP [Wis.]
A Praed Street Dossier. Mycroft, 1968 SP
Praed Street Papers. Candlelight Press, 1965 SP
Regarding Sherlock Holmes; see In re Sherlock Holmes
The Reminiscences of Solar Pons. Mycroft, 1961 SP ss
The Return of Solar Pons. Mycroft, 1958 SP ss
Sentence Deferred. Scribner, 1939; Heinemann, 1939 EP [Wis.]
The Seven Who Waited. Scribner, 1943; Muller, 1945 EP [Wis.]
Sign of Fear. Loring, 1935; Newnes, 1936 EP [Wis.]
Three Problems for Solar Pons. Mycroft, 1952 SP ss
The Three Straw Men. Candlelight Press, 1970
Three Who Died. Loring, 1935 EP [Wis.]

DE ROO, EDWARD
Go, Man, Go. Ace, 1959
The Little Caesars. Ace, 1961

DE ROUEN, REED. See: Robert McKew.

DERRICK, HENRY. See: George Douglas, pseudonym of Mrs. George Ferme.

DERRICK, LIONEL. Alternating pseudonym of Mark K. Roberts (odd-numbered titles) and Chet Cunningham, 1928- , q.v. (even-numbered titles). Other Cunningham pseudonyms: Nick Carter, Cathy Cunningham, qq.v. SC: Mark Hardin (The Penetrator), in all titles.
The Animal Game. Pinnacle, 1978 [Conn.]
Aryan Onslaught. Pinnacle, 1979
Baja Bandidos. Pinnacle, 1974 [Mex.]
Black Massacre. Pinnacle, 1980
Blood on the Strip. Pinnacle, 1973 [Las Veg.]
Bloody Boston. Pinnacle, 1976 [Boston]
Candidate's Blood. Pinnacle, 1980
Capitol Hell. Pinnacle, 1974 [Wash. D.C.]
Computer Kill. Pinnacle, 1979 [Chi.]
Countdown to Terror. Pinnacle, 1976 [NYC]
Cruise into Chaos. Pinnacle, 1980
Cryogenic Nightmare. Pinnacle, 1978 [Fla.]
Deadly Silence. Pinnacle, 1980
Death Ray Terror. Pinnacle, 1979
Deepsea Shootout. Pinnacle, 1976 [Bahamas, ship]
Demented Empire. Pinnacle, 1976 [Fla.]
Divine Death. Pinnacle, 1977 [Ga.]
Dixie Death Squad. Pinnacle, 1976
Dodge City Bombers. Pinnacle, 1975
Floating Death. Pinnacle, 1978 [Calif.]
Hawaiian Trackdown. Pinnacle, 1980 [Haw.]
The Hellbomb Flight. Pinnacle, 1975
High Disaster. Pinnacle, 1977 [Oreg.]
Hijacking Manhattan. Pinnacle, 1974 [NYC]
Mankill Sport. Pinnacle, 1976 [Can.]
Mardi Gras Massacre. Pinnacle, 1974 [New Or.]
Mexican Brown. Pinnacle, 1978 [Mex.]
The Northwest Contract. Pinnacle, 1975 [Seattle]
Oklahoma Firefight. Pinnacle, 1979 [Okla.]
Panama Power Play. Pinnacle, 1977 [Pan.]
The Quebec Connection. Pinnacle, 1976 [Can.]
The Radiation Hit. Pinnacle, 1977 [Colo.]
Satellite Slaughter. Pinnacle, 1979
Showbiz Wipeout. Pinnacle, 1979 [L.A.]
The Skyhigh Betrayers. Pinnacle, 1978
The Supergun Mission. Pinnacle, 1977 [Tex.]
The Target Is H. Pinnacle, 1973 [L.A.]
Terror in Taos. Pinnacle, 1975 [New Mex.]
Tokyo Purple. Pinnacle, 1974 [Tokyo]

DERWENT, ROBERT
The Algarve Affair. Hale, 1976

DE ST. JORRE, JOHN, 1936- , and BRIAN SHAKESPEARE. Ref for De St. Jorre: CA. Shakespeare has worked for the BBC, "The Economist," and the British Embassy in Paris.
The Patriot Game. Hodder, 1973; Houghton, 1973 [Ire.]

DE SAIX, TYLER. Pseudonym of H(enry) DeVere Stacpoole, 1863-1951, q.v. Set: Eng.
The Man Without a Head. Moffat, 1908
The Vulture's Prey. Unwin, 1909. Reprinted as by H. DeVere Stacpoole: Unwin, 1918

DE SAVALLO, DONA TERESA. Pseudonym of A(lice) M(uriel Livingston) Williamson, 1869- , q.v. See also: C(harles) N(orris) Williamson, 1859-1920.
The House of the Lost Court. McClure, 1908 (British title?)

DES CARS, GUY. 1911- . Born in Paris; journalist, playwright and novelist.
The Brute. Wingate, 1952; Greenberg, 1952 (Translation of "La Brute." Paris, 1951.) [Fr.]
-Chantal. Houghton, 1954. Also published as: Woman of Paris. Popular Library, 1955 (Translation of "L'Impure." Paris, 1946.)
-The Damned One. Pyramid, 1956
-A Strange Affection. Sidgwick, 1965 (Translation of "Cette Etrange Tendresse." Paris, 1960.)
-The Unclean. Wingate, 1953 (Translation of "La Corruptrice." Paris, 1952.)
Woman of Paris; see Chantal

DE SECARY, JEAN
Portrait of Love. Mystique, 1977 (Translation of "Rencontre a Tolede." Paris, 1973.)
Twist of Fate. Mystique, 1980 (Translation of "L'Angoissant Soupcon." Paris, 1962.)

DES LIGNERIS, FRANCOISE
Bijoux. Avon, 1963

DESMARAIS, OVIDE E. 1919- . Pseudonym: Ovid Demaris, q.v.

DESMOND, CLIVE
Intrigue. Hodder, 1919

DESMOND, COLIN
-The Secret of Stark Island. Pilgrim, 1928

DESMOND, EUGENIA
Shadow at Dunster Hall. Tower, 1965

DESMOND, HUGH. Ref: CC, TC. SC: Alan Fraser, in at least those marked AF. Set: Eng.
Appointment at Eight. Wright, 1957 AF
Blood Cries for Vengeance. Wright, 1948
Bluebeard's Wife. Wright, 1947
Bodies in a Cupboard. Wright, 1963 AF
Breath of Suspicion. Wright, 1954
Calling Alan Fraser. Wright, 1951 AF
The Case of the Blue Orchid. Wright, 1961 AF
A Clear Case of Murder. Wright, 1950 AF
Condemned. Wright, 1964 AF
Dark Deeds. Wright, 1952
The Dark Shadow. Wright, 1965 AF
Death at My Elbow. Wright, 1960
Death in the Shingle. Wright, 1948
Death Let Loose. Wright, 1956
The Death Parade. Wright, 1954 AF
Death Strikes at Dawn. Wright, 1943
Death Walks in Scarlet. Wright, 1948 AF
Deliver Us from Evil. Wright, 1953 AF
A Desperate Gamble. Wright, 1946
Destination—Death. Wright, 1955 AF
Doorway to Death. Wright, 1959 AF [Buen. A.]
The Edge of Horror. Wright, 1950 [W.I.]
Escape. Wright, 1968
Fanfare for Murder. Wright, 1961 AF
Fear Walks the Island. Wright, 1951
The Fuehrer Dies. Wright, 1944
Gallows' Fruit. Wright, 1949
The Hand of Vengeance. Wright, 1945 AF [Czech.]
The Hangman Waits. Wright, 1955
Highways of Death. Wright, 1940
His Reverence the Rogue. Wright, 1946
Horror at the Moated Mill. Wright, 1967 AF
Hostage to Death. Wright, 1964 AF
In Fear of the Night. Wright, 1960 AF
Intent to Kill. Hale, 1942
The Jacaranda Murders. Wright, 1951
The Lady Has Claws. Wright, 1966 AF
Lady in Peril. Wright, 1946
Lady, Where Are You? Wright, 1957 AF [S. Afr.]
Look upon the Prisoner. Wright, 1958
Mask of Terror. Wright, 1968 AF
The Misty Pathway. Wright, 1940
Murder at Midnight. Wright, 1962
Murder Is Justified. Wright, 1951
Murder on the Moor. Wright, 1967 AF
Murder Run Wild. Hale, 1941
Murder Strikes at Dawn. Wright, 1965 AF [S. Afr.]
Murderer's Bride. Wright, 1954
The Mystery Killer. Wright, 1943
Night of Terror. Wright, 1953
The Night of the Crime. Wright, 1953 AF
No Reprieve. Wright, 1957
Not Guilty, My Lord. Wright, 1965 AF
Overture to Death. Wright, 1947
A Pact with the Devil. Wright, 1952 AF
Poison Pen. Wright, 1958 AF
Put Out the Light. Wright, 1962
Reign of Terror. Wright, 1952
A Scream in the Night. Wright, 1955
The Secret of the Moat. Wright, 1940
The Secret Voice. Wright, 1942
She Met Murder. Wright, 1956 AF
The Silent Witness. Wright, 1963 AF [S. Afr.]
The Slasher. Wright, 1939
A Slight Case of Murder. Wright, 1963 AF
Someday I'll Kill You. Wright, 1964 AF
Stay of Execution. Wright, 1962 AF
Stella Shall Die. Wright, 1956
Stranger Than Fiction. Wright, 1961 AF
The Strangler. Wright, 1947
A Strong Dose of Poison. Wright, 1959
Suicide Fleet. Wright, 1959
Terror Walks by Night. Wright, 1944
They Lived with Death. Wright, 1945
Turn Back from Death. Wright, 1960 [Fr.]
The Viper's Sting. Wright, 1946 AF
We Walk with Death. Wright, 1968 AF
The Wicked Shall Flourish. Wright, 1959
A Wife in the Dark. Wright, 1948

DESMOND, RACHEL. See: Edmond Taillet.

DESPARD, LESLIE. Pseudonym of John Leslie Despard Howitt. Set: Eng.
The Amazing Adventures of Mr. Henry Button. Hodder, 1927
The Crime Without a Flaw. Nash, 1931
The Mystery of the Tower Room. Hodder, 1925

DESSART, GINA. 1912- .
Cry for the Lost. Harper, 1959 [S.W.]
The Last House. Harper, 1950; Hodder, 1951
A Man Died Here. Harper, 1947; Hodder, 1948 [Mass.]

DE STEFANO, ANTHONY. SC: Mondo, in at least those marked M.
Cocaine Kill. Manor, 1977 M
Dachau Treasure. Manor, 1977
The Hard Edge. Manor, 1978
A Minute to Pray, a Second to Die. Manor, 1977 M
Mondo. Manor, 1975 M
-The Sorceress. Manor, 1977

DE STEIGUER, WALTER. 1884- .
Jewels for a Shroud. Morrow, 1950; Locke, 1951 [NYC]

DETECTION CLUB
Ask a Policeman. Barker, 1933; Morrow, 1933
Double Death. Gollancz, 1939
The Floating Admiral. Hodder, 1931; Doubleday, 1932

DE TERAMOND, GUY. Pseudonym of Edmond Gautier Teramond, 1869- .
The Mystery of Lucien Delorme. Appleton, 1915 (Translation of "L'Homme Qui Voit a Travers les Murailles." Paris, 1913.) [Paris]

DE TOLEDANO, RALPH. 1916-
-Devil Take Him. Putnam, 1979

DETZER, KARL (WILLIAM). 1891-   .
    Ref: CA.
    The Broken Three. Bobbs, 1929 [Fr.]
    -Contrabando. Bobbs, 1936
    True Tales of the D.C.I. Bobbs, 1925 ss

DEUTSCH, ARTHUR V.
    Starett. Arbor, 1978 [NYC]

DEUTSCHMAN, DEBORAH. Poet.
    Signals. Seaview, 1978 [Calif.]

DEVANEY, ROBERT. Pseudonym: Sandra Abbott, q.v.

DEVERELL, WILLIAM (H.). 1937-   .
    Journalist, then lawyer; practices law in Vancouver.
    Needles. Little, 1979; Deutsch, 1979 [Van.]

DEVI, SHAKUNTALA
    Perfect Murder. Orient (Delhi), 1976

DE VILLIERS, DIRK
    The Wild Sound of Murder. Hale, 1978

DE VILLIERS, GERARD. 1929-   . Ref: CA.
    SC: Malko Linge, in all titles.
    The Angel of Vengeance. Pinnacle, 1974 (Translation of "L'Ange de Montevideo." Paris, 1973.)
    The Belfast Connection. Pinnacle, 1976 (Translation of (?): "Furie a Belfast." Paris, 1974.) [Belfast]
    Black Magic in New York. New English Library, 1970. U.S. title: Operation New York. Pinnacle, 1973 (Translation of "Magie Noire a New York." Paris, 1967.) [NYC]
    Checkpoint Charlie. Pinnacle, 1975 [Berlin]
    The Countess and the Spy. Pinnacle, 1974 (Translation of "Le Bol de la Comtesse Adler." Paris, 1971.) [Austria, Hung.]
    Death in Santiago. Pinnacle, 1976 (Translation of "L'Ordre Regne a Santiago." Paris, 1975.)
    Death on the River Kwai. Pinnacle, 1975 (Translation of "L'Or de la Riviere Kwai." Paris, 1968.) [Thai.]
    Hostage in Tokyo. Pinnacle, 1976 (Translation of " Les Ostages de Tokyo." Paris, 1975.) [Tokyo]
    Kill Kissinger. Pinnacle, 1974 (Translation of "Kill Kissinger." Paris, 1974.)
    The Man from Kabul. Pinnacle, 1973 (Translation of "L'Homme de Kabul." Paris, 1971.)
    Operation Apocalypse. New English Library, 1970 (Translation of "Operation Apocalypse." Paris, 1970.)
    Operation New York; see Black Magic in New York
    The Portuguese Defection. Pinnacle, 1976 (Translation of "Les Sorcies du Tage." Paris, 1975.) [Port.]
    Que Viva Guevara. Pinnacle, 1975 (Translation of "Que Viva Guevara." Paris, 1970.) [Venez.]
    Versus the C.I.A. New English Library, 1969; Pinnacle, 1974 (Translation of "Contra C.I.A." Paris, 1965.) [Iran]
    West of Jerusalem. New English Library, 1969; Pinnacle, 1973 (Translation of "A L'Ouest de Jerusalem." Paris, 1967.) [It.]

DE VINCENT, ELEANORA
    Tower Park. Popular Library, 1973 [New Eng.]

DEVINE, D(AVID) M(cDONALD). 1920-1981.
    Pseudonym: Dominic Devine, q.v.
    Ref: CA, CC, EM, TC.
    Death Is My Bridegroom. Collins, 1969; Walker, 1969 [acad.]
    The Devil at Your Elbow. Collins, 1966; Walker, 1967 [acad.]
    Doctors Also Die. Collins, 1962; Dodd, 1963 [Scot.]
    The Fifth Cord. Collins, 1967; Walker, 1967 [Scot.]
    His Own Appointed Day. Collins, 1965; Walker, 1966 [Scot.]
    My Brother's Killer. Collins, 1961; Dodd, 1962
    The Royston Affair. Collins, 1964; Dodd, 1965

DEVINE, DOMINIC. Pseudonym of D(avid) M(cDonald) Devine, 1920-1981, q.v.
    Dead Trouble. Collins, 1971; Doubleday, 1971
    Illegal Tender. Collins, 1970; Walker, 1970 [Scot.]
    The Sleeping Tiger. Collins, 1968; Walker, 1968
    Sunk Without Trace. Collins, 1978; St. Martin's, 1979

    Three Green Bottles. Collins, 1972; Doubleday, 1972

DEVINE, (VIRGINIA) STEWART
    Even in Death. Doubleday, 1950 [Va.]
    Listen for a Stranger. Doubleday, 1951 [Va.]

DEVON, NICOLA
    House of Illusion. Ace, 1969 [Eng.]

DE VOTO, BERNARD AUGUSTINE. 1897-1955.
    Pseudonym: John August, q.v.

DE VRIES, ANKE. 1936-   .
    The Secret of Belledonne Room 16. McGraw, 1979

DE VRIES, JULIEN. 1904-   .
    The Black Spear. World, 1933

DE WAAL, PHILIP (HENRY OVERBECK). -1942.
    The Mystery of the Green Garnet Murder. (no publisher), ca.1932

DEWAR, EVELYN
    A Dying Business. Bles, 1974
    Perfumes of Arabia. Bles, 1973; Walker, 1974 [Saud. Arab.]

DEWDNEY, PETER. Pseudonym of Alan (St. Hill) Brock, 1886-   , q.v.
    Arising from an Accident. Wright, 1939
    On Appeal. Wright, 1938

DeWEESE, (THOMAS EU)GENE. 1934-   .
    Joint pseudonym with Robert Stratton Coulson, 1918-   , q.v.: Thomas Stratton, q.v. Pseudonym of DeWeese alone: Jean DeWeese, q.v. Ref: CA.
    SC: Joe Karns = JK.
    Charles Fort Never Mentioned Wombats, with Robert (Stratton) Coulson, 1918-   . Doubleday, 1977; Hale, 1978 JK [Australia]
    Now You See It-Him-Them, with Robert (Stratton) Coulson, 1918-   . Doubleday, 1975; Hale, 1976 JK [acad.]
    The Wanting Factor. Playboy, 1980

DeWEESE, JEAN. Pseudonym of (Thomas Eu) Gene DeWeese, 1934-   , q.v. Joint pseudonym with Robert Stratton Coulson, 1918-   .: Thomas Stratton, q.v.
    The Carnelian Cat. Ballantine, 1975
    Cave of the Moaning Wind. Ballantine, 1976
    The Doll with Opal Eyes. Doubleday, 1976; Hale, 1977
    Hour of the Cat. Doubleday, 1980; Hale, 1980 [Ind.]
    The Moonstone Spirit. Ballantine, 1975
    Nightmare in Pewter. Doubleday, 1978 [Midwest]
    The Reimann Curse. Ballantine, 1975 [New Eng.]
    Web of Guilt. Ballantine, 1976 [acad.]

DEWES, SIMON. Pseudonym of John St. Clair Muriel, 1909-   .
    Cul-de-Sac. Rich, 1941
    Death Stalks the Waterway. Rich, 1946
    Panic in Pursuit. Rich, 1945

DEWEY, THOMAS B(LANCHARD). 1915-   .
    Pseudonym: Tom Brandt, q.v. Ref: CA, CC, EM, TC. SC: Singer Batts = SB; Mac = M; Pete Schofield = PS.
    And Where She Stops. Popular Library, 1957. British title: I.O.U. Murder. Boardman, 1958 PS [L.A.]
    As Good As Dead. Jefferson, 1946; Dakers, 1952 SB
    The Brave, Bad Girls. Simon, 1956; Boardman, 1957 M [Chi.]
    Can a Mermaid Kill. Tower, 1965 [Calif.]
    The Case of the Chased and the Unchaste. Random, 1959; Boardman, 1960 M [L.A.]
    The Case of the Murdered Model; see Prey for Me
    Dame in Danger; see Draw the Curtain Close
    Deadline. Simon, 1966; Boardman, 1967 M [Ill.]
    Death and Taxes. Putnam, 1967; Hale, 1969 M [Chi.]
    Death Turns Right; see The King Killers
    Don't Cry for Long. Simon, 1964; Boardman, 1965 M [Chi.]
    Draw the Curtain Close. Jefferson, 1947; Dakers, 1951. Also published as: Dame in Danger. Dell, 1958 M
    Every Bet's a Sure Thing. Simon, 1953; Dakers, 1953 M [L.A.]
    The Girl in the Punchbowl. Dell, 1964; Boardman, 1965 PS [Calif.]

    The Girl Who Never Was; see The Girl Who Wasn't There
    The Girl Who Wasn't There. Simon, 1960; Boardman, 1960. Also published as: The Girl Who Never Was. Mayflower, 1962 M [Chi.]
    The Girl with the Sweet Plump Knees. Dell, 1963; Boardman, 1963 PS [Calif.]
    Go, Honeylou. Dell, 1962; Boardman, 1962 PS [Calif.]
    Go to Sleep, Jeannie. Popular Library, 1959; Boardman, 1960 PS [L.A.]
    The Golden Hooligan. Dell, 1961. British title: Mexican Slayride. Boardman, 1961 PS [Mex.]
    Handle with Fear. Mill, 1951; Dakers, 1955 SB [Ill.]
    How Hard to Kill. Simon, 1962; Boardman, 1963 M [Chi.]
    Hue and Cry. Jefferson, 1944. British title: The Murder of Marion Mason. Dakers, 1951. Also published as: Room for Murder. Signet, 1950 SB [Ill.]
    Hunter at Large. Simon, 1961; Boardman, 1962
    I.O.U. Murder; see And Where She Stops
    The King Killers. Putnam, 1968. British title: Death Turns Right. Hale, 1969 M [Chi.]
    The Love-Death Thing. Simon, 1969 M [L.A.]
    The Mean Streets. Simon, 1955; Boardman, 1955 M [Chi.]
    Mexican Slayride; see The Golden Hooligan
    Mourning After. Mill, 1950; Dakers, 1953 SB
    The Murder of Marion Mason; see Hue and Cry
    My Love Is Violent. Popular Library, 1956; Consul, 1961 [West]
    Nude in Nevada. Dell, 1965; Boardman, 1966 PS [Nev.]
    Only on Tuesdays. Dell, 1964; Boardman, 1964 PS [L.A.]
    Portrait of a Dead Heiress. Simon, 1965; Boardman, 1966 M [Chi.]
    Prey for Me. Simon, 1954; Boardman, 1954. Also published as: The Case of the Murdered Model. Avon, 1955 M [Chi.]
    Room for Murder; see Hue and Cry
    A Sad Song Singing. Simon, 1963; Boardman, 1964 M
    A Season for Violence. GM, 1966
    The Taurus Trip. Simon, 1970 M [L.A.]
    Too Hot for Hawaii. Popular Library, 1960; Boardman, 1963 PS [Haw.]
    You've Got Him Cold. Simon, 1958; Boardman, 1959 M [Chi.]

DEWHURST, EILEEN
    After the Ball. Macmillan (London), 1976 [Fr.]
    Curtain Fall. Macmillan (London), 1977
    Death Came Smiling. Hale, 1975
    Drink This. Collins, 1980; Doubleday, 1981

DE WIL, ERNEST
    The Brookham Mystery. International, 1893

DE WITT, JACK
    Murder on Shark Island. Liveright, 1941 [Fla.]

DEXTER, BRUCE
    I'll Sing You the Death of Bill Brown. McGraw, 1963; Allen, 1964 [L.A.]

DEXTER, (NORMAN) COLIN. 1930-   . Ref: CA. SC: Insp. Morse, in all titles; set in Eng.
    Last Bus to Woodstock. Macmillan (London), 1975; St. Martin's, 1975
    Last Seen Wearing. Macmillan (London), 1976; St. Martin's, 1976
    Service of All the Dead. Macmillan (London), 1979; St. Martin's, 1980
    The Silent World of Nicholas Quinn. Macmillan (London), 1977; St. Martin's, 1977

DEXTER, LEE
    The Case of the Brooklyn Mobsters. Warren, 1949 [NYC]
    Detective Crime Stories. Warren, 1949 ss
    Police Detective Stories. Warren, 1949 ss

DEXTER, TED and CLIFFORD MAKINS, 1925-   . SC: Jack Stenton, in both titles.
    Deadly Putter. Allen (London & NYC), 1979
    Testkill. Allen, 1976

Author Index

DEY, FREDERIC MERRILL VAN RENSSELAER. 1861-1922. Pseudonyms: Nicholas Carter, Marmaduke Dey, Frederic Ormond, Varick Vanardy, qq.v.

DEY, MARMADUKE. Pseudonym of Frederic Merrill van Rensselaer Dey, 1861-1922. Other pseudonyms: Nicholas Carter, Frederic Ormond, Varick Vanardy, qq.v.
Muertalma; or, The Poisoned Pen. Street, 1890

DIAL, JEAN. 1937- . Ref: CA.
Deadly Lady. GM, 1980

DIAMOND, B.
Redheads Die Young. Spencer, 1950
Say It with Homicide. Spencer, 1952
Sister Sinister. Spencer, 1949
Such Men Are Dangerous. Spencer, 1951

DIAMOND, FRANK. SC: Ransome Dragoon & Vicky Gaines = D&G
Love Me to Death. Ace, 1955
Murder in Five Columns. Mystery House, 1944 D&G [NYC]
Murder Rides a Rocket. Mystery House, 1946; Equerry, 1947 D&G [NYC]
The Widow Maker. Ace, 1961 [NYC]

DIAMOND, STEPHEN (ARTHUR). 1946- . Ref: CA.
-Panama Red. Avon, 1979

DIAPOULOS, PETER and STEVEN LINAKIS
The Sixth Family. Bantam, 1977

DIBB, C. E.
The Bite. Hale, 1978
-Spotted Soldiers. Hale, 1978

DIBDIN, MICHAEL. 1947- . Ref: CA.
The Last Sherlock Holmes Story. Pantheon, 1978; Cape, 1978 (Sherlock Holmes.) [Eng., 1888]

DIBNER, MARTIN. 1911- . Ref: CA.
-A God for Tomorrow. Doubleday, 1961
Ransom Run. Doubleday, 1977; Hale, 1978 [Maine]

DICK, ALEXANDRA. Pseudonym of Sibyl Cicely Alexandra Dick Erikson. Other pseudonym: Frances Hay, q.v.
And Only Man. Hurst, 1944
Crime in the Close. Hale, 1955
Cross Purposes. Hurst, 1950
The Curate's Crime. Hurst, 1945; Boureguy, 1946, as by Sibyl Ericson
Death at the Golden Crown. Hale, 1956
The Innocence of Rosamond Prior. Hale, 1953
MacAlistair Looks On. Hurst, 1947 [Scot.]
No Sentiment. Hodder, 1939
An Old-Fashioned Christmas. Hurst, 1944
-One Is One. Hale, 1958
The Witch's Doing. Hurst, 1951

DICK, GEORGE
Fitch and His Fortunes. Stock, 1898

DICK, PHILIP K(ENDRED). 1928-1982. Ref: CA.
-Flow My Tears, the Policeman Said. Doubleday, 1974; Gollancz, 1974
-The Man Who Japed. Ace, 1956; Magnum, 1978
-A Maze of Death. Doubleday, 1970; Gollancz, 1972
-A Scanner Darkly. Doubleday, 1977; Gollancz, 1977

DICK, T. Pseudonym of Eric Richard Osler, 1900- .
Dark Before Dawn. Long, 1935

DICKENS, CHARLES (JOHN HUFFHAM). 1812-1870. See also: Percy T(heodore) Carden; Leon Garfield, 1921- ; Edwin Harris; and Eric Jones-Evans, 1898- . Ref: CC, DD, EM, MC, MP, TC.
Bleak House. Bradbury, 1853; Harper, 1853
Hunted Down. Hotten, 1871
The Mystery of Edwin Drood. Chapman, 1870; Fields, 1870

DICKENS, FRANK
A Curl Up and Die Day. Owen, 1980

DICKENS, MARY ANGELA. 1838-1896.
A Mist of Error. Collier, 1890

DICKENS, MONICA (ENID). 1915- . Ref: CA.
The Room Upstairs. Heinemann, 1966; Doubleday, 1966 [Cape Cod]

DICKENSON, FRED. Reporter and editor.
Kill 'Em with Kindness. Bell, 1950 [NYC]

DICKINSON, PETER. 1927- . Ref: CA, CC, EM, TC. SC: (Supt.) James Pibble = JP. Set: mostly Eng.
The Glass-Sided Ants' Nest; see Skin Deep
-The Green Gene. Hodder, 1973; Pantheon, 1973
King and Joker. Hodder, 1976; Pantheon, 1976
The Lively Dead. Hodder, 1975; Pantheon, 1975
The Lizard in the Cup. Hodder, 1972; Harper, 1972 JP [Greece]
The Old English Peep Show; see A Pride of Heroes
One Foot in the Grave. Hodder, 1979; Pantheon, 1980 JP
The Poison Oracle. Hodder, 1974; Pantheon, 1974 [Mid. East]
A Pride of Heroes. Hodder, 1969. U.S. title: The Old English Peep Show. Harper, 1969 JP
The Seals. Hodder, 1970. U.S. title: The Sinful Stones. Harper, 1970 JP [Hebrides]
The Sinful Stones; see The Seals
Skin Deep. Hodder, 1968. U.S. title: The Glass-Sided Ants' Nest. Harper, 1968 JP
Sleep and His Brother. Hodder, 1971; Harper, 1971 JP
Walking Dead. Hodder, 1977; Pantheon, 1978 [Carib.]

DICKINSON, WEED
Dead Man Talks Too Much. Lippincott (Philadelphia & London), 1937 [NYC]

DICKSON, ARTHUR (PARKINSON). 1888-1940?
Death Bids for Corners. Humphries, 1941

DICKSON, CARR. Pseudonym of John Dickson Carr, 1905-1977, q.v. Other pseudonyms: Carter Dickson, Roger Fairbairn, qq.v. See also: John Rhode; and: Adrian Conan Doyle, 1911-1970.
The Bowstring Murders. Morrow, 1933; Heinemann, 1934, as by Carter Dickson (All reprints as by Carter Dickson.) [Eng.]

DICKSON, CARTER. Pseudonym of John Dickson Carr, 1905-1977, q.v. Other pseudonyms: Carr Dickson, Roger Fairbairn, qq.v. See also: John Rhode; and: Adrian Conan Doyle, 1911-1970. SC: Sir Henry Merrivale = HM (see also John Dickson Carr entry).
And So to Murder. Morrow, 1940; Heinemann, 1941 HM [Eng.]
Behind the Crimson Blind. Morrow, 1952; Heinemann, 1952 HM [Tangier]
The Cavalier's Cup. Morrow, 1953; Heinemann, 1954 HM [Eng.]
Cross of Murder; see Seeing Is Believing
The Crossbow Murder; see The Judas Window
The Curse of the Bronze Lamp. Morrow, 1945. British title: Lord of the Sorcerers. Heinemann, 1946 HM [Eng.]
Death and the Gilded Man; see The Gilded Man
Death in Five Boxes. Morrow, 1938; Heinemann, 1938 HM [Eng.]
The Department of Queer Complaints. Morrow, 1940; Heinemann, 1940 (11 ss, 7 about Colonel March, 4 non-series. The 7 March stories were reprinted as: Scotland Yard: Department of Queer Complaints. Dell, 1944.) [Eng.]
Fear Is the Same. Morrow, 1956; Heinemann, 1956 [Eng., 1795]
The Gilded Man. Morrow, 1942; Heinemann, 1942. Also published as: Death and the Gilded Man. PB, 1947 HM [Eng.]
A Graveyard to Let. Morrow, 1949; Heinemann, 1950 HM [N.Y.]
He Wouldn't Kill Patience. Morrow, 1944; Heinemann, 1944 HM [Eng.]
The Judas Window. Morrow, 1938; Heinemann, 1938. Also published as: The Crossbow Murder. Berkley, 1964 HM [Eng.]
Lord of the Sorcerers; see The Curse of the Bronze Lamp
The Magic Lantern Murders; see The Punch and Judy Murders
Murder in the Atlantic; see Nine—and Death Makes Ten
Murder in the Submarine Zone; see Nine—and Death Makes Ten
My Late Wives. Morrow, 1946; Heinemann, 1947 HM [Eng.]
Night at the Mocking Widow. Morrow, 1950; Heinemann, 1951 HM [Eng.]
Nine—and Death Makes Ten. Morrow, 1940. British title: Murder in the Submarine Zone. Heinemann, 1940. Also published as: Murder in the Atlantic. World Distributors, 1959 HM [ship]
The Peacock Feather Murders. Morrow, 1937. British title: The Ten Teacups. Heinemann, 1937 HM [Eng.]
The Plague Court Murders. Morrow, 1934; Heinemann, 1935 HM [Eng.]
The Punch and Judy Murders. Morrow, 1937. British title: The Magic Lantern Murders. Heinemann, 1936 HM [Eng.]
The Reader Is Warned. Morrow, 1939; Heinemann, 1939 HM [Eng.]
The Red Widow Murders. Morrow, 1935; Heinemann, 1935 HM [Eng.]
Scotland Yard: Department of Queer Complaints; see The Department of Queer Complaints
Seeing Is Believing. Morrow, 1941; Heinemann, 1942. Also published as: Cross of Murder. World Distributors, 1959 HM [Eng.]
She Died a Lady. Morrow, 1943; Heinemann, 1943 HM [Eng.]
The Skeleton in the Clock. Morrow, 1948; Heinemann, 1949 HM [Eng.]
The Ten Teacups; see The Peacock Feather Murders
The Third Bullet. Hodder pb, 1937 (A paperback novelet about Colonel Marquis, a prototype of Colonel March. This novelet is included in hardcover in the collection of the same name as by John Dickson Carr, q.v.)
The Unicorn Murders. Morrow, 1935; Heinemann, 1936 HM [Paris]
The White Priory Murders. Morrow, 1934; Heinemann, 1935 HM [Eng.]

DICKSON, GRIERSON. SC: Supt. "Cissie" Marlow, in at least those marked CM. Set: Eng.
Design for Treason. Hutchinson, 1937 CM
The Devil's Torch. Hutchinson, 1936 CM
Gun Business. Hutchinson, 1935
Knight's Gambit. Hutchinson, 1950 CM
The Seven Screens. Hutchinson, 1950
Soho Racket. Hutchinson, 1935
Traitor's Market. Hutchinson, 1936 CM

DICKSON, JAMES GRIERSON. Pseudonym: Hilary King, q.v.

DIDELOT, (ROGER) FRANCIS. 1902- . Ref: CC. SC: Commissaire Orestes Bignon = OB; Inspector Lecain = L.
Death of the Deputy. Lippincott (Philadelphia & London), 1935 (Translation of "L'Assassin du Depute." Paris, 1934.) L [Paris]
Death on the Champs-Elysees. Macdonald, 1965 (Translation of "Bignon et la Verite." Paris, 1963.) OB [Paris]
The Many Ways of Death. Belmont, 1966 (Translation of "6 Heures d'Anguisse." Paris, 1955.) OB [air]
Murder in the Bath. Lippincott (Philadelphia & London), 1933 (Translation from the French.) L [Paris]
The Seventh Juror. Macdonald, 1960; Belmont, 1963 (Translation of "Le Septieme Jure." Paris, 1958.) [Fr.]
The Tenth Leper. Macdonald, 1962 (Translation of "Feu Sur le Mage!" Paris, 1956.) OB [Paris]
Warrant for Arrest. Macdonald, 1963 (Translation of "Mandat d'Arret." Paris, 1961.) OB [Paris]

DIEHL, ALICE M(ANGOLD). 1844-1912.
The Desborough Mystery. Digby, 1903
-Entrapped. Long, 1904
-A Mysterious Bohemian. Digby, 1908
-The Secret of Sir George Hartley. Digby, 1910

DIEHL, WILLIAM (FRANCIS JR.). 1924- . Born in NYC; graduate of U. of Mo., reporter, columnist and editor in Atlanta.
Sharky's Machine. Delacorte, 1978; Hutchinson, 1978 [Atlanta]

DIETRICH, ROBERT. Pseudonym of (Everette) Howard Hunt, 1918- , q.v. Other pseudonyms: Gordon Davis, David St. John, qq.v. SC: Steve Bentley = SB.
Angel Eyes. Dell, 1961 SB [Wash. D.C.]
Be My Victim. Dell, 1956 [Fla.]
The Cheat. Pyramid, 1954
Curtains for a Lover. Lancer, 1961 SB [Wash. D.C.]
End of a Stripper. Dell, 1959 SB [Wash. D.C.]
The House on Q Street. Dell, 1959 SB [Wash. D.C.]
Mistress to Murder. Dell, 1960 SB [Wash. D.C.]

Murder on Her Mind. Dell, 1960 SB
[Wash. D.C.]
Murder on the Rocks. Dell, 1957; Ward,
1958 SB [Wash. D.C.]
My Body. Lancer, 1962. Reprinted as by
E. Howard Hunt: Lancer, 1973 SB
[Nassau]
One for the Road. Pyramid, 1954 [Fla.]
Steve Bentley's Calypso Caper. Dell,
1961 SB [Virg. Is.]

DIETZ, LEW. 1907- . Ref: CA.
The Running Man. Avon, 1969

DIGNAM, C. B. Set: Eng.
Black Velvet. Hamilton, 1926
The Sons of Seven. Hamilton, 1928

DIKE, DONALD
The Bishop's Park Mystery. Cassell,
1926

DILKE, CHRISTOPHER (WENTWORTH). 1913-
-The Guardian. Hale, 1953

DILLARD, R(ICHARD) H(ENRY) W(ILDE).
1937- . Ref: CA.
The Book of Changes. Doubleday, 1974

DILLON, CATHERINE
Constantine Cay. Hodder, 1975; Signet,
1976
Rockfire. Hodder, 1977. U.S. title:
White Fires Burning. Signet, 1977
White Fires Burning; see Rockfire
-The White Khan. Hodder, 1978; Signet,
1978

DILLON, EILIS. 1920- . Ref: CA, CC.
SC: Inspector Mike Kenny = MK.
Death at Crane's Court. Faber, 1953;
Walker, 1963 MK [Ire.]
Death in the Quadrangle. Faber, 1956;
British Book Centre, 1962 MK
[Dub., acad.]
Sent to His Account. Faber, 1954; Bri-
tish Book Centre, 1961 [Ire.]

DILLON, JACK
A Great Day for Dying. GM, 1968; Coronet, 1968

DILLWYN, E(LIZABETH) A(MY).
A Burglary; or, Unconscious Influence.
Tinsley, 1883

DILNOT, FRANK (BUCKLAND). 1875-1946.
Scoundrel Mark. Blackwood, 1906

DILNOT, GEORGE. 1883-1951. See also:
Frank Froest. Ref: CC. SC: Horace
Augustus Elver = HE; Val Emery = VE;
Jim Strang = JS, Insp. Strickland =
S; Sexton Blake (with many other au-
thors) = SB. Set: Eng.
The Black Ace. Bles, 1929; Houghton,
1929 S
The Black Ace. Amalgamated, 1938 SB
The Case of the Missing Bridegroom.
Amalgamated, 1938 SB
Counter-Spy. Bles, 1942 JS
The Crime Reporter's Secret. Amalgam-
ated, 1937 SB
Crook's Castle. Bles, 1934; Houghton,
1934 HE
The Crooks' Game. Bles, 1927; Houghton,
1927 S
Fighting Fool. Bles, 1939 VE
The Great Mail Racket. Bles, 1936 HE
The Hat-Pin Murder. Bles, 1927. U.S.
title: Suspected. Clode, 1920
The Inside Track. Bles, 1935
The Lazy Detective. Bles, 1926
Murder at Scotland Yard. Bles, 1937 HE
Murder Masquerade. Bles, 1935 HE
The Real Detective. Bles, 1933
Rogues' March. Bles, 1934 ss
The Secret Service Man. Nash, 1916 JS
Sister Satan. Bles, 1933; Houghton,
1933
Suspected; see The Hat-Pin Murder
The Thousandth Case. Bles, 1932;
Houghton, 1933
Tiger Lily. Bles, 1939 VE

DILTZ, HANSON PENN
Dunleath Abbey; or, The Fatal Inheritance. Dillingham, 1889

DIMENT, ADAM. ca.1945- . Ref: TC. SC:
Philip McAlpine, in all titles. Set:
Eng.
The Bang Bang Birds. Joseph, 1968; Dut-
ton, 1968
The Dolly Dolly Spy. Joseph, 1967; Dut-
ton, 1967
The Great Spy Race. Joseph, 1968; Dut-
ton, 1968
Think Inc. Joseph, 1971

DIMMOCK, F(REDERICK) H(AYDN). 1895-1955.
The Clue of the Ivory Claw, with
Michael Poole (q.v.; pseudonym of
Reginald Heber Poole, 1885- ,
q.v.). Pearson, 1919
The Lost Trooper. Pearson, 1920
The Secret of Gaunt House, with Michael
Poole (as above). Pearson, 1931

DI MONA, JOSEPH. Ref: CA. SC: George
Williams = GW.
The Benedict Arnold Connection. Morrow,
1977; Joseph, 1978 GW
The Last Man at Arlington. Fields,
1973; Weidenfeld, 1974 GW
70 Sutton Place. Dodd, 1972
To the Eagle's Nest. Morrow, 1980;
Joseph, 1980 GW [Ger.]

DINELLI, MEL
The Man. Dramatists, 1950; English
Theatre Guild, 1954 (2-act play.)

DINES, MICHAEL. 1916- . Ref: CA. SC:
Johnny Manning = JM.
Abrams and Jones, Homicide. Hale, 1977
[NYC]
I Said I Was Sorry. Hale, 1979
Operation—Deadline. Ward, 1967 JM
Operation—Kill or Be Killed. Hale,
1969 JM
Operation—To Kill a Man. Ward, 1968 JM

DINGLE, AYLWARD EDWARD. 1874-1947. Pseudonym: Brian Cotterell, q.v.

DINGWALL, PETER. Pseudonym of Robin Forsythe, 1879- , q.v.
The Poison Duel. Methuen, 1934

DINNEEN, JOSEPH F(RANCIS). 1897- .
The Alternate Case. Little, 1959; Cas-
sell, 1960. Also published as: The
Biggest Holdup. Ace, 1961
The Anatomy of a Crime. Scribner, 1954;
Cassell, 1955
The Biggest Holdup; see The Alternate
Case
The Merry-Go-Round of Murder. Mystery
Novel of the Month, 194?

DINNER, WILLIAM and WILLIAM MORUM. Pseu-
donym of William Dinner: Surrey
Smith, q.v.
The Bluffing of Gaston Leroux. French
(London), 1949 (1-act play.)
Edwina Black; see The Late Edwina Black
Ladies' Bar. Deane, 1954 (1-act play.)
The Late Edwina Black. French (London),
1950. U.S. title: Edwina Black.
French (NYC), 1951 (3-act play.)
Too Soon for Daisies. Deane, 1964
(Play.)

DI PEGO, GERALD F(RANCIS). 1941- .
Ref: CA.
With a Vengeance. McGraw, 1977; Macmil-
lan (London), 1977

DIPLOMAT. Pseudonym of John Franklin
Carter, 1897-1967. Ref: CC, EM, MP.
SC: Dennis Tyler, in all titles.
The Brain Trust Murder. Coward, 1935
[Wash. D.C.]
The Corpse on the White House Lawn.
Covici, 1932; Hurst, 1933 [Wash.
D.C.]
Death in the Senate. Covici, 1933
[Wash. D.C.]
Murder in the Embassy. Cape & Smith,
1930; Harrap, 1931 [Wash. D.C.]
Murder in the State Department. Cape &
Smith, 1930 [Wash. D.C.]
Scandal in the Chancery. Cape & Smith,
1931 [Fr.]
Slow Death at Geneva. Coward, 1934
[Geneva]

DIPPER, ALAN. 1922- Ref: CA, CC.
The Colour of Darkness. Joseph, 1974
Drowning Day. Joseph, 1976
The Golden Virgin. Joseph, 1972; Walk-
er, 1973 [Scot.]
The Hard Trip. Joseph, 1970
The Paradise Formula. Morrow, 1970
The Wave Hangs Dark. Morrow, 1969

DIRCKX, JOHN H. 1938- . SC (following
R. Austin Freeman, 1862-1943; and
Norman Donaldson, 1922- , qq.v.):
Dr. John Thorndyke = JT.
Dr. Thorndyke's Dilemma. Aspen, 1974
JT [Eng.]

DISCH, THOMAS (MICHAEL). 1940- .
Pseudonym: Leonie Hargrave, q.v.
Joint pseudonyms with John Sladek,
1937- , q.v.: Thom Demijohn, Cas-
sandra Knye, qq.v. Ref: CA.
The Prisoner. Ace, 1969; Dobson, 1979
(Novelization of the TV series.)
[Eng.]

DISNEY, DORIS MILES. 1907-1976. Ref: CA,
CC, EM, TC. SC: Jeff DiMarco = JD;
David Madden = DM; Jim O'Neill = JO.
Appointment at Nine. Doubleday, 1947 JO
[New Eng.]
At Some Forgotten Door. Doubleday,
1966; Hale, 1967 [Conn., 1886]
Black Mail. Doubleday, 1958; Foulsham,
1960 DM [Conn.]
The Case of the Straw Man; see Straw
Man
The Chandler Policy. Putnam, 1971;
Hale, 1973 JD [Conn.]
A Compound for Death. Doubleday, 1943
JO [New Eng.]
Count the Ways. Doubleday, 1949 [Conn.]
Cry for Help. Doubleday, 1975; Hale,
1976 [Va.]
Dark Lady. Doubleday, 1960. British
title: Sinister Lady. Hale, 1962
[Conn.]
Dark Road. Doubleday, 1946; Nimmo,
1947. Also published as: Dead Stop.
Dell, 1956 JD [New Eng.]
The Day Miss Bessie Lewis Disappeared.
Doubleday, 1972; Hale, 1973 [Va.]
Dead Stop; see Dark Road
Death by Computer; see Do Not Fold,
Spindle or Mutilate
Death for My Beloved; see Enduring Old
Charms
The Departure of Mr. Gaudette. Double-
day, 1964. British title: Fateful
Departure. Hale, 1965
Did She Fall or Was She Pushed? Double-
day, 1959; Hale, 1962 JD [R.I.]
Do Not Fold, Spindle or Mutilate.
Doubleday, 1970. British title: Death
by Computer. Hale, 1971 [Va.]
Do Unto Others. Doubleday, 1953
[New Eng.]
Don't Go into the Woods Today. Double-
day, 1974 [New Eng.]
Driven to Kill; see The Last Straw
Enduring Old Charms. Doubleday, 1947.
Also published as: Death for My Be-
loved. Bestseller, 1949 [Mass.]
Family Skeleton. Doubleday, 1949 JD
[Conn.]
Fatal Choice; see Two Little Children
and How They Grew
Fateful Departure; see The Departure of
Mr. Gaudette
Find the Woman. Doubleday, 1962; Hale,
1964 JD [Conn.]
Fire at Will. Doubleday, 1950 JO
[Conn.]
Flame of Evil; see Night of Clear
Choice
The Halloween Murder; see Trick or
Treat
Heavy, Heavy Hangs. Doubleday, 1952
[New Eng.]
Here Lies. Doubleday, 1963; Hale, 1964
[Conn.]
The Hospitality of the House. Double-
day, 1964. British title: Unsuspected
Evil. Hale, 1965 [N.Y.]
The Last Straw. Doubleday, 1954. Bri-
tish title: Driven to Kill. Foulsham,
1957 JO [Conn.]
Look Back on Murder. Doubleday, 1951
[New Eng.]
The Magic Grandfather. Doubleday, 1966.
British title: Mask of Evil. Hale,
1967 [Conn.]
Mask of Evil; see The Magic Grandfather
Method in Madness. Doubleday, 1957.
British title: Quiet Violence. Foul-
sham, 1959. Also published as: Too
Innocent to Kill. Avon, 1959 JD
[Conn.]
Money for the Taking. Doubleday, 1968;
Hale, 1968
Mrs. Meeker's Money. Doubleday, 1961;
Hale, 1963 DM [Conn.]
Murder on a Tangent. Doubleday, 1945
JO [Conn.]
My Neighbor's Wife. Doubleday, 1957;
Foulsham, 1958 [Conn.]
Night of Clear Choice. Doubleday, 1967.
British title: Flame of Evil. Hale,
1968 [Conn.]
No Next of Kin. Doubleday, 1959; Foul-
sham, 1961
Only Couples Need Apply. Doubleday,
1973; Hale, 1974 [Conn.]
The Post Office Case; see Unappointed
Rounds
Prescription: Murder. Doubleday, 1953
[New Eng.]
Quiet Violence; see Method in Madness
Room for Murder. Doubleday, 1955; Foul-
sham, 1959 [Conn.]
Shadow of a Man. Doubleday, 1965; Hale,
1966 [Conn.]
Should Auld Acquaintance. Doubleday,
1962; Hale, 1963 [Conn.]
Sinister Lady; see Dark Lady
Sow the Wind; see Who Rides a Tiger

Straw Man. Doubleday, 1951. British title: The Case of the Straw Man. Foulsham, 1958 JD [Conn.]
Testimony by Silence. Doubleday, 1948 [Conn.]
That Which Is Crooked. Doubleday, 1948 [Conn., 1898-1946]
Three's a Crowd. Doubleday, 1971; Hale, 1972 [Va.]
Too Innocent to Kill; see Method in Madness
Trick or Treat. Doubleday, 1955. British title: The Halloween Murder. Foulsham, 1957 JD
Two Little Children and How They Grew. Doubleday, 1969. British title: Fatal Choice. Hale, 1970 [Conn.]
Unappointed Rounds. Doubleday, 1956. British title: The Post Office Case. Foulsham, 1957 DM [Conn.]
Unsuspected Evil; see The Hospitality of the House
Voice from the Grave. Doubleday, 1968; Hale, 1969 [Maine]
Who Rides a Tiger. Doubleday, 1946. British title: Sow the Wind. Nimmo, 1948 [Conn.]
Winifred. Doubleday, 1976 [Va.]

DISNEY, DOROTHY CAMERON. 1903- . Ref: CC, EM, MP, TC.
The Balcony. Random, 1940; Hale, 1941 [Md.]
Crimson Friday. Random, 1943; Hale, 1945
Death in the Back Seat. Random, 1936; Hale, 1937 [Conn.]
Explosion. Random, 1948 [Wash. D.C.]
The Golden Swan Murder. Random, 1939; Hale, 1940 [L.A.]
The Hangman's Tree. Random, 1949 [S.C.]
The 17th Letter. Random, 1945; Hale, 1948 [Can.]
Strawstack. Random, 1939; Hale, 1939. Also published as: Strawstack Murders. Dell, 1944 [Md.]
Strawstack Murders; see Strawstack
30 Days Hath September, with George Sessions Perry (1910-1956). Random, 1942; Hale, 1950 [Conn.]

DITTON, JAMES. Pseudonym of Douglas Clark, ca.1920- , q.v.
The Bigger They Are. Hale, 1973
Copley's Hunch. Gollancz, 1980 [WWII]
Escapemanship. Hale, 1975
You're Fairly Welcome. Hale, 1973

DIVEN, ROBERT JOSEPH. 1869- .
The Black Wolf Mystery. Century, 1931

DIVINE, A(RTHUR) D(URHAM). 1904- . Pseudonyms: David Divine, q.v., David Rame. Ref: CA.
Admiral's Million. Methuen, 1936 [Wales]
Dark Moon. Methuen, 1933
Escape from Spain. Methuen, 1936
Fire in the Ice. Blackwell, 1937
Graveyard Watch. Methuen, 1931
Lawless Voyage. Hodder pb, 1937
Pelican Island. Methuen, 1932
The Pub on the Pool. Collins, 1938
Sea Loot. Methuen, 1930; McBride, 1931
Seventy Fathom Treasure. Newnes, 1936
Slack Watch. Collins, 1939
Terror in the Thames. Collins, 1938 [ship]
They Blocked the Suez Canal. Methuen, 1935; Furman, 1936
Tunnel from Calais. Collins, 1942; Macmillan, 1943, as by David Rame
U-Boat in the Hebrides. Collins, 1940 [Hebrides]
Wings over the Atlantic. Lane, 1936

DIVINE, DAVID. Pseudonym of A(rthur) D(urham) Divine, 1904- , q.v. Other pseudonym: David Rame.
Atom at Spithead. Hale, 1953; Macmillan, 1953
-The Blunted Sword. Hutchinson, 1964
Boy on a Dolphin. Murray, 1955; Macmillan, 1955
-The Daughter of the Pangaran. Hutchinson, 1963; Little, 1963
-The Golden Fool. Murray, 1954; Macmillan, 1954

DIVOMLIKOFF, LAVR. Pseudonym.
The Traitor. Doubleday, 1973; Heinemann, 1974 (Translation of "Le Tretre." Paris, 1972.) [Greece]

DIX, BEULAH MARIE. 1876- .
Wedding Eve Murder. McBride, 1941

DIX, MAURICE B(UXTON). 1889-1956. SC: Supt. Simon Bullion, in at least those marked B; Tommy Malins, Anthony Mornington and George Hawkins, in at least those marked M&M&H; Insp. James Miller, in at least those marked JM; Sexton Blake (with many other authors) = SB. Set: Eng.
The Affair of the Smuggled Millions. Amalgamated, 1943 SB
Beacons of Death. Ward, 1937 M&M&H
The Dartmoor Mystery. Ward, 1935
Emily Coulton Dies. Ward, 1936
The Fixer. Ward, 1936
The Flame of the Khan. Ward, 1934
The Fleetwood Mansions Mystery. Ward, 1934 JM
The Golden Fluid. Ward, 1935 M&M&H
The Great Hush-Hush Mystery. Amalgamated, 1939 SB
The Kidnapped Scientist. Ward, 1937 M&M&H
A Lady Richly Left. Staples, 1951
The Masinglee Murders. Hale, 1947
Murder at Grassmere Abbey. Ward, 1933 JM
Murder Strikes Twice. Ward, 1939 B
The Night Assassin. Hale, 1941
Prologue to Murder. Ward, 1938
The Secret of the Dead Convict. Amalgamated, 1937 SB
The Secret of the Siegfried Line. Amalgamated, 1940 SB
The Third Degree. Gramol, 1936
This Is My Murder. Ward, 1938 B
The Treasure of Scarland. Ward, 1936
Twisted Evidence. Ward, 1933 M&M&H
The Victim of the Girl Spy. Amalgamated, 1936 SB

DIXON, CHARLES
A Fortune for the Taking. Hale, 1963
A Hand in Murder. Hale, 1962
Ministry Murder. Hale, 1961
Red Murder File. Hale, 1964
So Slender a Thread. Hale, 1962
A Trail to Treason. Hale, 1964

DIXON, H(ARRY) VERNOR. 1908- . Ref: CA.
Cry Blood. GM, 1956 [Calif.]
Deep Is the Pit. GM, 1952
Get out of Town. GM, 196?
The Hunger and the Hate. GM, 1955
Killer in Silk. GM, 1956; Fawcett (London), 1957 [S.F.]
A Lover for Cindy. GM, 1954; Fawcett (London), 1955 [Calif.]
-The Marriage Bed. Red Seal (U.S.), 1952
The Pleasure Seekers. Monarch, 1963 [Calif.]
The Rag Pickers. McKay, 1966; Hale, 1967
Something for Nothing. Harper, 1950; H. Hamilton, 1950 [Calif.]
To Hell Together. GM, 1951 [Calif.]
Too Rich to Die. GM, 1953; Fawcett (London), 1956
Up a Winding Stair. GM, 1953; Fawcett (London), 1954 [Calif.]

DIXON, J. EARLE
Killers in the Sun. Abelard (London), 1960; Abelard (NYC), 1961 [Sp.]

DIXON, PETER L(EE), 1932- , and LAIRD P. KOENIG, q.v. Ref on Dixon: CA.
The Children Are Watching. Ballantine, 1970; Longmans, 1971

DIXON, ROGER. 1930- . Pseudonym: John Christian, q.v.
Going to Jerusalem. Collins, 1977; Coward, 1977 [Jerus.]

DIXON, STEPHEN. 1936- . Ref: CA.
Too Late. Harper, 1978 [NYC]

DIXON, W(ILLMOTT) WILLMOTT. 1843- . Pseudonym: Thormanby, q.v.
The Adventures of Captain Mounsell. Everett, 1902
-The Rogue of Rye. Chatto, 1909

DOBBINS, PAUL H. 1916- .
Death in the Dunes. Phoenix, 1950 [Ariz.]
Death Trap. Phoenix, 1951 [S.W.]
Fatal Finale. Phoenix, 1949
Murder Moon. Murray & Gee, 1949

DOBBS, FRANK
Speech Day Murder. Hale, 1961

DOBNER, MAEVA (PARK). 1918- . Ref: CA.
The Gingerbread House. Dell, 1974 [N.Y.]
Heather. Dell, 1970 [N.Y.]
Sea Wind. Dell, 1976 [Ice.]
The Woman in the Maze. Dell, 1970

DOBSON, KENNETH AUSTIN. 1907- .
Mail Train. Hodder, 1946

DOBYNS, STEPHEN. 1941- . Ref: CA.
A Man of Little Evils. Atheneum, 1973 [Eng.]
Saratoga Longshot. Atheneum, 1976; Hale, 1978 [N.Y.]

DOCHERTY, JAMES L. Pseudonym of Rene Brabazon Raymond, 1906- . Other pseudonyms: James Hadley Chase, Ambrose Grant, Raymond Marshall, qq.v.
He Won't Need It Now. Rich, 1939

DODD, ALLEN ROBERT. 1887- . Pseudonym: Robert Allen, q.v.

DODGE, ALICE M. and MADELEINE SAPONOV
The Eye of the Peacock. Boureqy, 1966 [S.F.]

DODGE, CONSTANCE W(OODBURY). 1896- .
The Unrelenting. Doubleday, 1950 [N.H.]

DODGE, DAVID (FRANCIS). 1910- . Ref: CA, TC. SC: Al Colby = AC; John Abraham Lincoln = JL; Whit Whitney = WW.
Angel's Ransom. Random, 1956. British title: Ransom of the Angel. Joseph, 1957 [ship]
Bullets for the Bridegroom. Macmillan, 1944; Joseph, 1948 WW [Nev.]
Carambola. Little, 1961. British title: High Corniche. Joseph, 1961 [Sp.]
Death and Taxes. Macmillan, 1941; Joseph, 1947 WW [S.F.]
A Drug on the Market; see It Ain't Hay
Hatchetman; see Hooligan
High Corniche; see Carambola
Hooligan. Macmillan, 1969. British title: Hatchetman. Joseph, 1970 JL [H. Kong]
It Ain't Hay. Simon, 1946. British title: A Drug on the Market. Joseph, 1949 WW [S.F.]
The Lights of Skaro. Random, 1954; Joseph, 1954 [Balkans]
The Long Escape. Random, 1948; Joseph, 1950 AC [Chile]
Loo Loo's Legacy. Little, 1961; Joseph, 1961
Plunder of the Sun. Random, 1949; Joseph, 1950 AC [Chile]
Ransom of the Angel; see Angel's Ransom
The Red Tassel. Random, 1950; Joseph, 1951 AC [Bolivia]
Shear the Black Sheep. Macmillan, 1942; Joseph, 1949 WW [L.A.]
To Catch a Thief. Random, 1952; Joseph, 1953 [Fr.]
Troubleshooter. Macmillan, 1971; Joseph, 1972 JL [S. Afr.]

DODGE, LANGDON. Pseudonym of Victor Wolfson, 1910- , q.v.
Midsummer Madness. Doubleday, 1950 [New Eng.]

DODGE, LOUIS. 1870- .
Whispers. Scribner, 1920

DODGE, MARY LOUISE
Sticks and Stones. Manor, 1979 [Mich.]
Tamara. Paperback Library, 1969

DODGE, STEVE. Pseudonym of Stephen (David) Becker, 1927- , q.v.
Shanghai Incident. GM, 1955; Fawcett (London), 1956 (Later reprints are as by Stephen Becker.) [Shanghai]

DODS, MARCUS. 1874-1935.
The Bunker at the 5th. Hodge, 1925

DODSON, DANIEL B(OONE). 1918- . Ref: CA.
The Dance of Love. Mason, 1974; New English Library, 1975
The Man Who Ran Away. Dutton, 1961; Barker, 1961

DODSON, SAM. Ref: CA.
Majorca. GM, 1977; Futura, 1977 [Maj.]
Sausalito. GM, 1978 [Calif.]

DOE, JOHN. Pseudonym of Tiffany (Ellsworth) Thayer, 1902-1959, q.v.
Eye-Witness! Day, 1931; Hurst, 1931 [NYC]

DOGBERRY
Humours and Oddities of the London Police Courts. Leadenhall, 1894 ss

DOHERTY, EDWARD J. 1890-1975. Ref: CA.
  The Broadway Murders. Doubleday, 1929.
    Also published as: Murder on the
    Roof. Grosset, 193? [NYC]
  The Corpse Who Wouldn't Die (as by Ed
    Doherty). Mystery House, 1945
  Murder on the Roof; see The Broadway
    Murders

DOLAN, PATRICK
  Poison in the Blood. Hale, 1970

DOLBEY, ETHEL M. Joint pseudonym with
  Geoffrey May Dolbey: E. M. D. Hawthorne, q.v.

DOLBEY, GEOFFREY MAY. Joint pseudonym
  with Ethel M. Dolbey: E. M. D. Hawthorne, q.v.

DOLE, JEREMY (HASKELL). 1932-   . Ref:
  CA.
  Venus Disarmed. Crown, 1966

DOLINER, ROY. 1932-   . Ref: CA.
  On the Edge. Viking, 1978; Collins,
    1979 [NYC]
  The Orange Air. Scribner, 1961 [Cuba]
  Sandra Rifkin's Jewels. NAL, 1966
  The Thin Line. Crown, 1980 [Viet Nam,
    1963]

DOLINSKY, MEYER. 1923-   . Ref: CA.
  Hot Rod Gang Rumble. Avon, 1957
    (Novelization of the movie.)
  There Is No Silence. Hale, 1959

DOLLAND, JOHN. Pseudonym of H. F. Dolland Parsons.
  A Gentleman Hangs. Longmans, 1940; Macmillan, 1941

DOLPH, JACK. 1894-1962. Born in Portland,
  Oregon; race-horse trainer, radio
  network manager; radio producer, writer and actor. SC: Doc Connor, in
  all titles.
  Dead Angel. Doubleday, 1953; Boardman,
    1954 [NYC, Cuba]
  Hot Tip. Doubleday, 1951; Boardman,
    1952 [NYC]
  Murder Is Mutuel. Morrow, 1948; Boardman, 1950 [NYC]
  Murder Makes the Mare Go. Doubleday,
    1950 [NYC]
  Odds-On Murder. Morrow, 1948; Boardman, 1950 [NYC]

DOLPHIN, REX [REGINALD CHARLES DOLPHIN].
  SC (with many other authors): Sexton
    Blake = SB.
  The Devil to Pay. Amalgamated, 1961 SB
  Driven to Kill. Baker, 1969 SB
  Guilty Party. Amalgamated, 1959 SB
  Murder Goes Nap. Mayflower, 1966 SB
  Ride the Man Down. Mayflower, 1967
  Some Died Laughing! Amalgamated, 1960
    SB
  Stop Press—Homicide! Amalgamated, 1959
    SB
  The Trial of the Golden Girl. Mayflower, 1967; Macfadden, 1969 SB
  Trouble Is My Name. Amalgamated, 1961
    SB
  Walk in the Shadows. Amalgamated, 1959
    SB

DOLSON, HILDEGARDE. 1908-1981. Ref: CA,
  TC. SC: Lucy Ramsdale, in all
  titles, all set in Conn.
  Beauty Sleep. Lippincott, 1977; Hale,
    1979
  A Dying Fall. Lippincott, 1973; Curley,
    1979
  Please Omit Funeral. Lippincott, 1975
  To Spite Her Face. Lippincott, 1971;
    Curley, 1979

DOMENICA
  Island of Fear. Mystique, 1980 (Translation of "L'Homme de Majorque."
    Paris, 1970.)

DOMINIC, R. B. Joint pseudonym of Mary
  Jane Latsis, ca.1927-   , and Martha
  Henissart, ca.1929-   . Other joint
  pseudonym: Emma Lathen, q.v. SC:
  Ben Safford, in all titles.
  The Attending Physician. Harper, 1980;
    Macmillan (London), 1980 [Ohio]
  Epitaph for a Lobbyist. Doubleday,
    1974; Macmillan (London), 1974
    [Wash. D.C.]
  Murder in High Place. Doubleday, 1970;
    Macmillan (London), 1969 [Wash. D.C.]
  Murder out of Commission. Doubleday,
    1976; Macmillan (London), 1976
    [Ohio, Wash. D.C.]
  Murder out of Court; see There Is No
    Justice
  Murder, Sunny Side Up. Abelard, 1968
    [Wash. D.C.]

  There Is No Justice. Doubleday, 1971.
    British title: Murder out of Court.
    Macmillan (London), 1971 [Wash. D.C.]

DONAHUE, JACK or JACKSON. 1917-   . Ref:
  CA. SC: Harlan Cole = HC.
  The Confessor. World, 1964; Barker,
    1963 [Houston]
  Erase My Name. World, 1964; Barker,
    1964
  The Lady Loved Too Well. McGraw, 1978
    HC [Houston]
  Pray to the Hustlers' God. Reader's Digest, 1977 HC [Houston]

DONAHUE, MARILYN (CRAM)
  Sutter's Sands. Belmont, 1971 [Fla.]

DONALD, MILES. Born in England; taught at
  U. of Texas for 3 years; champion
  squash player; fiction writer and
  journalist.
  Boast. St. Martin's, 1980

DONALD, STUART
  The Uncertain Agent. Hale, 1970

DONALDSON, NORMAN. 1922-   . Ref: CA.
  SC (following R. Austin Freeman,
  1862-1943, q.v., and preceding John
  H. Dirckx, 1938-   , q.v.): Dr.
  John Thorndyke = JT.
  Goodbye, Dr. Thorndyke. Norris, 1972 JT
  [Eng., 1943]

DONALDSON, ROBERT and MICHAEL JOSEPH
  Wilderness. H. Hamilton, 1975

DONATI, SERGIO
  The Paper Tomb. Collins, 1958

DONAVAN, JOHN. Pseudonym of Nigel Morland, 1905-   , q.v. Other pseudonyms: Mary Dane, Norman Forrest,
  Roger Garnett, Vincent McCall, Neal
  Shepherd, qq.v. SC: Sgt. Johnny Lamb,
  at least in those marked JL. Set: Eng.
  The Case of the Beckoning Dead. Hale,
    1938; Hillman-Curl, 1938. Apparently
    reprinted as by Nigel Morland: Mystery Novel of the Month, 194? JL
  The Case of the Coloured Wind. Hodder,
    1939. U.S. title: The Case of the
    Violet Smoke. Mystery House, 1940 JL
  The Case of the Plastic Man. Hodder,
    1940. U.S. title: The Case of the
    Plastic Mask. Mystery House, 1941 JL
  The Case of the Plastic Mask; see The
    Case of the Plastic Man
  The Case of the Rusted Room. Hale,
    1937; Hillman-Curl, 1937 JL
  The Case of the Talking Dust. Hale,
    1938; Mystery House, 1941 JL
  The Case of the Violet Smoke; see The
    Case of the Coloured Wind
  The Dead Have No Friends. Home & Van
    Thal, 1952

DONCASTER, (FREDERICK) PATRICK. 1917-
  The Devil Held the Aces. Allen, 1944
  The Long Week. Allen, 1951
  A Sigh for a Drum-Beat. Earl, 1947;
    Dutton, 1948

DONG, EUGENE, M.D., and SPYROS ANDREOPOULOS, 1929-   .
  Heart Beat. Coward, 1978 [S.F.]

DONISTHORPE, G(LADYS) SHEILA. 1898-   .
  Fruit of the Tree. French (London),
    1958 (Play.)

DONNE, MAXIM. Pseudonym of Madelaine
  Duke, 1925-   , q.v.
  Claret, Sandwiches and Sin. Heinemann,
    1964; Doubleday, 1964, as by Madelaine Duke [1979]
  This Business of Bomborg. Heinemann,
    1967; Doubleday, 1969, as by Madelaine Duke

DONNEL, C. P(HILIP), JR. ca. 1907-   .
  Newspaperman in Va.; author of many
  ss.
  Murder-Go-Round. McKay, 1945; Boardman,
    1948 [Stock., Wash. D.C.]

DONNELLY, DESMOND (LOUIS). 1920-   .
  Ref: CA.
  The Nearing Storm. Hutchinson, 1968

DONNELLY, ELEANOR C(ECILIA). 1838-1917.
  The Fatal Diamonds. Benziger, 1897

DONOHUE, H(AROLD) E(DWARD) F(RANCIS)
  The Higher Animals. Viking, 1965;
    Deutsch, 1966 [Chi.]

DONOVAN, DICK. Pseudonym of J(oyce) E(mmerson Preston) Muddock, 1843-1934,
  q.v. Ref: DD, EM, MC, MP, TC. SC:
  Dick Donovan, in at least those
  marked DD. Set: Eng.
  The Adventures of Tyler Tatlock, Private Detective. Chatto, 1900 ss
  Caught at Last! Leaves from the Notebook of a Detective. Chatto, 1889
    ss DD
  The Chronicles of Michael Danevitch of
    the Russian Secret Service. Chatto,
    1897 ss
  The Crime of the Century: Being the
    Life Story of Richard Piggott. Long,
    1904
  Dark Deeds. Chatto, 1895 ss DD
  Deacon Brodie; or, Behind the Mask.
    Chatto, 1901
  A Detective's Triumphs. Chatto, 1891
    ss DD
  Eugene Vidocq: Soldier, Thief, Spy,
    Detective. Hutchinson, 1895
  The Fatal Ring. Hurst, 1905
  The Fatal Woman. White, 1911
  For Honour or Death. Ward, 1910
  Found and Fettered: A Series of Thrilling Detective Stories. Hutchinson,
    1894 ss DD
  From Clue to Capture: A Series of
    Thrilling Detective Stories. Hutchinson, 1893 ss DD
  From Information Received: Detective
    Stories. Chatto, 1892 ss DD
  A Gilded Serpent. Ward, 1908
  The Gold-Spinner. White, 1907
  The Great Turf Fraud, and Other Notorious Crimes. Mellifont, 1936 ss
  In the Face of Night. Long, 1908
  In the Grip of the Law. Chatto, 1892
    ss DD
  In the Queen's Service. Long, 1907
  Jim the Penman: The Life Story of One
    of the Most Astounding Criminals That
    Have Ever Lived. Newnes, 1901
  A Knight of Evil. White, 1905
  The Knutsford Mystery. White, 1906
  Lil of the Slums. Laurie, 1909
  Link by Link: Detective Stories.
    Chatto, 1893 ss DD
  The Man from Manchester. Chatto, 1890
  The Man-Hunter. Chatto, 1888; Lovell,
    1891 ss DD
  The Mystery of Jamaica Terrace. Chatto,
    1896
  The Naughty Maid of Mitcham. White,
    1910
  Out There: A Romance of Australia.
    Everett, 1922 [Australia]
  Preaching Jim; see The Sin of Preaching
    Jim
  The Records of Vincent Trill of the
    Detective Service. Chatto, 1899 ss
  The Rich Man's Wife, with E(rnest)
    W(ay) Elkington, 1872-   , q.v.
    Ham-Smith, 1912
  Riddles Read. Chatto, 1896 ss DD
  The Scarlet Seal: A Tale of the Borgias. Long, 1902 [It., ca.1500]
  Scarlet Sinners: Stories of Notorious
    Criminals and Crimes. Newnes, 1910 ss
  The Shadow of Evil. Everett, 1907
  The Sin of Preaching Jim. Everett,
    1908. Also published as: Preaching
    Jim. Aldine, 1919
  Startling Crimes and Notorious Criminals. Mellifont, 1936 ss
  Stories from the Note-Book of a Detective; see Tracked and Taken
  Suspicion Aroused. Chatto, 1893 ss DD
  Tales of Terror. Chatto, 1899 ss
  Tangled Destinies. Laurie, 1908
  Thurtell's Crime. Laurie, 1906
  Tracked and Taken: Detective Sketches.
    Chatto, 1890. U.S. title: Stories
    from the Note-Book of a Detective
    (2 volumes). Street, 1900 ss DD
  Tracked to Doom. Chatto, 1892 DD
  The Trap. White, 1911
  The Triumphs of Fabian Field: Criminologist. White, 1912 ss
  The Turning Wheel: A Story of the Charn
    Hall Inheritance. White, 1912
  Wanted! A Detective's Strange Adventures. Chatto, 1892 ss DD
  Who Poisoned Hetty Duncan? and other
    detective stories. Chatto, 1890 ss DD
  A Wild Beauty. White, 1908

DONOVAN, GENE
  The Ghoul Friend. Dramatic, 1960
    (3-act play.)

DONOVAN, LAURENCE. Pseudonym: Robert
  Wallace, q.v. See also: Kenneth
  Robeson.

DOODY, MARGARET (ANNE). 1939-   . Ref:
  CA.
  Aristotle Detective. Bodley, 1978; Harper, 1980 [Athens, 332 B.C.]

DOOLEY, H. H.
Last Rights. Doubleday, 1980 [NYC]

DOOLEY, ROGER (BURKE). 1920-   . Ref: CA.
Flashback. Doubleday, 1969 [L.A.]

DORAN, JAMES. 1837-1917.
-In the Depths of the First Degree: A Romance of the Battle of Bull Run. Peter Paul, 1898 [Va., 1862]

DORAN, MARIE
An Accusing Finger. French (NYC), 1929 (3-act play.)
Fast Colors. French (NYC), 1928 (3-act play.)

DORER, FRANCES. See: Nancy Dorer.

DORER, NANCY and FRANCES
The Cry of the Nighthawk. Manor, 1979
Deadman's Rest. Manor, 1978
-God of the Forest. Manor, 1978
Sentinel Point. Manor, 1978
You Will Like It Here. Manor, 1979 [Scot.]

DORIAN, PHILIP. Pseudonym of college instructor and long-time resident of Iowa.
The Streaker Murders. Dorrance, 1976 [Midwest]

DORIEN, RAY
The House of Dread. Paperback Library, 1968 [Scot.]

DORLAND, MICHAEL. 1948-   . Ref: CA.
The Double-Cross Circuit. Grosset, 1978 [Paris]

DORLING, HENRY TAPRELL. 1883-1968. Pseudonym: Taffrail, q.v.

DORN, DEAN M. Joint pseudonym with C. E. Carle: Michael Morgan, q.v.

DORRANCE, ETHEL (ARNOLD SMITH); 1880-   , and JAMES (FRENCH) DORRANCE, 1879-   , q.v.
Get Your Man. Macaulay, 1921. British title: Rawson of the Mounted. Cassell, 1927 [Can.]
-His Robe of Honor. Macaulay, 1916
-Lonesome Town. Macaulay, 1922
Rawson of the Mounted; see Get Your Man

DORRANCE, JAMES (FRENCH), 1879-   . See also: Ethel (Arnold Smith) Dorrance, 1880-   .
-Fighting Hearts. Macaulay, 1932; Wright, 1933
The Golden Alaskan. Macaulay, 1931; Skeffington, 1935
The Long Arm of the Mounted. Macaulay, 1926; Nelson, 1928 [Can.]
Never Fire First. Macaulay, 1924; Nicholson, 1936 [Can.]
The Rio Rustlers. Macaulay, 1928; Hurst, 1928

DORRELL, MIKE. SC: Dick Barton = DB (see also: Larry Pryce).
Mystery of the Missing Formula. Star, 1978 DB

DORRINGTON, ALBERT
Children of the Cloven Hoof. Mills, 1911 [Australia]
The Fatal Call. Methuen, 1929
The Half-God. Wright, 1933
The Radium Terrors. Nash, 1912; Doubleday, 1912
The Velvet Claw. Wright, 1932

DORSETT, DANIELLA. Pseudonym of Dorothy Daniels, 1915-   , q.v. Other pseudonyms: Angela Gray, Cynthia Kavanagh, Suzanne Somers, Geraldine Thayer, Helen Gray Weston, qq.v.
The Duelling Oaks. Pinnacle, 1972 [New Or., past]

DORTORT, DAVID
Burial of the Fruit. Crown, 1947

DORY, JOHN. Pseudonym.
The Casting of the Shadows. Stockwell, 1922
Grip Finds the Lady. Benn, 1932

DOSTOEVSKII, FEDOR MIKHAILOVICH. 1821-1881. See also: Rodney Ackland, 1908-   ; and: Marcel Dubois. Ref: EM, MC.
The Brothers Karamazov. Macmillan, 1912; Heinemann, 1912 (Translation of "Brat'ia Karamazovy.") [Russ.]
Crime and Punishment. Vizetelly, 1886; Crowell, 1886 [Russ.]

DOTY, WILLIAM LODEWICK. 1919-   . Ref: CA.
Button, Button. Our Sunday Visitor, 1979

DOUBLEDAY, ROMAN. Pseudonym of Lily Augusta Long, 1890-1927.
The Fullerton Case; see The Hemlock Avenue Mystery
The Green Tree Mystery. Appleton, 1917
The Hemlock Avenue Mystery. Little, 1908. British title: The Fullerton Case. Nash, 1920
The Red House on Rowan Street. Little, 1910
The Saintsbury Affair. Little, 1912

DOUBTFIRE, DIANNE (JOAN ABRAMS). 1918-   . Ref: CA.
Behind the Screen. Davies, 1969
Lust for Innocence. Davies, 1960; Morrow, 1960
Reason for Violence. Davies, 1961

DOUGALL, BERNARD. SC: Steve Borden, in both titles.
I Don't Scare Easy. Dodd, 1941 [NYC]
The Singing Corpse. Dodd, 1943; Boardman, 1944 [N.Y.]

DOUGALL, L(ILY). 1858-1923.
The Earthly Purgatory. Hutchinson, 1904. U.S. title: The Summit House Mystery. Funk, 1905 [Ga.]

DOUGHERTY, RICHARD. 1921-   . Ref: CA.
The Commissioner. Doubleday, 1963; Hart-Davis, 1963. Also published as: Madigan. PB, 1968

DOUGLAS, ALECK
The Murder Hole Road. Stockwell, 1940 [Ire.]

DOUGLAS, ARTHUR. Pseudonym of Douglas Arthur Moreton, 1928-   . SC: Mark Register, in all titles.
The Decoy Murders. Milton House, 1975
The Noah's Ark Murders. Milton House, 1974
The Special Murders. Milton House, 1974

DOUGLAS, BARBARA. Pseudonym of Barbara Ovstedal. Other pseudonyms: Rosalind Laker, Barbara Paul, qq.v.

DOUGLAS, BILL [WILLIAM]
Bloody Precinct. Belmont, 1960 [San Diego]

DOUGLAS, DAYLE
Haunted Harbor. Mystery House, 1943

DOUGLAS, ELLEN [ELLEN DOUGLAS WILLIAMSON] Ref: CA.
Moon of Violence. Avalon, 1960

DOUGLAS, FELICITY and HENRY CECIL, q.v., pseudonym of Henry Cecil Leon, 1902-1976.
According to the Evidence. French, 1967 (3-act play based on the Cecil novel.)

DOUGLAS, GAVIN. SC: Captain Samson, in at least those marked S.
Captain Samson, A.B. Collins, 1937; Putnam, 1937 S
-Last Night on Masada. Hale, 1979
The Obstinate Captain Samson. Collins, 1936; Putnam, 1937 S
Rough Passage. Collins, 1936. U.S. title: The Tall Man. Putnam, 1936 S [ship]
The Search for the Blue Sedan. Collins, 1938
The Struggle. Hale, 1951
A Tale of Pimlico. Hale, 1948
The Tall Man; see Rough Passage

DOUGLAS, GEORGE. Pseudonym of Mrs. George Ferme.
The Mystery of North Fortune, with Henry Derrick. Oliphant, 1893; Ogilvie, 1895

DOUGLAS, GEORGE. Pseudonym of George Douglas Brown, 1869-1902.
The House with the Green Shutters. Macqueen, 1901

DOUGLAS, GEORGE
The Case of the Greedy Rainmaker. Bouregy, 1963

DOUGLAS, GEORGE. Pseudonym of Douglas (George) Fisher, 1902-1981, q.v. Other pseudonym: George Fisher, q.v. SC: Insp. Hallan & Sgt. Spratt, in at least those marked H&S; Sgt./Insp. Brian "Bonny" Lee, in at least those marked BL. Set: Eng.

Crime Most Foul. Hale, 1971 H&S
Crime Without Reason. Hale, 1975 BL
Dead on Delivery. Hale, 1976
Dead on the Dot. Hale, 1974
Dead Reckoning. Hale, 1969 H&S
Death in Darkness. Hale, 1973 BL
Death in Duplicate. Hale, 1968 H&S
Death in Retreat. Hale, 1975
Death of a Big Shot. Hale, 1980
Death on the Doorstep. Hale, 1973 BL
Death Unheralded. Hale, 1967 H&S
Death Went Hunting. Hale, 1967 H&S
The Devil to Pay. Hale, 1969 H&S
Double Cross. Hale, 1979
End of the Line. Hale, 1977
Gunman at Large. Hale, 1968
Luckless Lady. Hale, 1976
Murder Unmourned. Hale, 1970 H&S
Odd Woman Out. Hale, 1966 H&S
One to Jump. Hale, 1972 H&S
Time to Die. Hale, 1971 H&S
Unholy Terror. Hale, 1978
Unwanted Witness. Hale, 1966 H&S

DOUGLAS, GRAEME
A Foreign Affair. Hale, 1980

DOUGLAS, HUDSON. Pseudonym of Robert Aitken, 1872-   , q.v.
The Lantern of Luck. Watt, 1909; Murray, 1910, as by Robert Aitken
A Million a Minute. Watt, 1908; Newnes, 1912
The Man in the Mirror. Watt, 1910; Robert Aitken, 1910, as by Robert Aitken
The White Blackbird. Little, 1912

DOUGLAS, J. B.
Propsy. London Literary Society, 1887

DOUGLAS, LAURA W.
The Case of the Copper Cat. Arcadia, 1960
The Mystery of Arrowhead Hill. Avalon, 1963
The Mystery of Crooknose. Avalon, 1963 [N.H.]

DOUGLAS, MALCOLM. Pseudonym of (Ronald) Douglas Sanderson, 1922-   , q.v. Other pseudonym: Martin Brett, q.v.
The Deadly Dames. GM, 1956; Consul, 1961
Murder Comes Calling. GM, 1958
Pure Sweet Hell. GM, 1957
Rain of Terror. GM, 1956; Fawcett (London), 1956

DOUGLAS, MARGARET
The Great Money-Mail Mystery. Gramol, 1935
Murder at the "Mike." Gramol, 1936

DOUGLAS, MARY K.
-Beloved Enemy. Fiction House, 1948
-Dangerous Course. Mellifont, 1941
-Dark House. Mellifont, 1939
-Fool's Bet. Mellifont, 1940
-The Gift Horse. Mellifont, 1937
-The Great Deception. Mellifont, 1935
-Heavy Stakes. Mellifont, 1938
One Thrilling Night. Fiction House, 1940
-The Outsider. Mellifont, 1939
Peril of the Course. Mellifont, 1936
-Rival Stables. Mellifont, 1940

DOUGLAS, ROBERT K(ENNAWAY). 1838-   .
See: L(illie) T(homas) Meade.

DOUGLAS, RONALD MacDONALD
-The Closed Door. Modern Age, 1941

DOUGLAS, ROY. Salesman, film producer and editor, cameraman and reporter.
Who Is Nemo? Harrap, 1937; Lippincott, 1937
Winner Take All. Mellifont, 1934

DOUGLAS, THEO. Pseudonym of Mrs. H. D. Everett.
-Behind a Mask. Harper (London), 1898
Carr of Discaur. Harper (London), 1899
-Iris. Blackwood, 1896; Harper (NYC), 1896
-A Legacy of Hate. Pearson, 1899
Three Mysteries. Everett, 1904 (3 stories.)

DOUGLAS, WILLIAM
Money to Burn. Arrowsmith, 1926

DOUGLAS-IRVINE, HELEN.   -1947. See: Helen Douglas Irvine.

DOUGLASS, DONALD McNUTT. 1899-1975. Ref: CA, CC. SC: Bolivar Manchenil, in all titles.
Many Brave Hearts. Harper, 1958; Eyre, 1959 [ship, Carib.]

DOUIE, MARJORIE
    The Pointing Man. Hutchinson, 1917; Dutton, 1920 [Burma]

DOUTHWAITE, L(OUIS) C(HARLES). 1878- . SC (with many other authors): Sexton Blake = SB. Set: Eng.
    The Army Defaulter's Secret. Amalgamated, 1943 SB
    The Clean-Up. Gramol, 1933
    Crime Limited. Gramol, 1933
    Crook Bait. Gramol, 1933
    -Diana of the Woods. Brentano's (London), 1929
    -Dimbleby's. Parsons, 1924
    The Eyes of Omar. Gramol, 1934
    Fear! Gramol, 1933
    -Fourflush Island. Brentano's (London), 1929
    The Ghost Trail. Amalgamated, 1932. Also published as: The Riddle of the Yukon. Amalgamated, 1940 SB [Can.]
    Horror House. Amalgamated, 1930 SB
    House of Torture. Mellifont, 1933
    The Killer. Gramol, 1933
    -The Luck of St. Boniface. Jarrolds, 1925
    The Man from Chicago. Gramol, 1934
    Murder Goes West. Nelson, 1946 [Can.]
    The Riddle of the Yukon; see The Ghost Trail
    The Scarlet Scarab. Gramol, 1933
    The Secret of Tso Feng. Gramol, 1933
    The Silent Terror. Gramol, 1933
    Sinister House. Mellifont, 1941
    The Terror of the Moat House. Gramol, 1933
    -The Third Robin Featherstone. Chambers, 1929
    -Warden of the North. Nelson, 1938 [Can.]
    -Waters of the North. Ducksworth, 1926 [Can.]
    -Yellerlegs. Chambers, 1930
    Zero Hour. Gramol, 1933

DOW, JOHN. ca.1903- . Born in Long Island; artist and editor.
    The Little Boy Laughed. Mystery House, 1945. Also published as: The Blonde Is Dead. Handi-Books, 1945

DOWDELL, DOROTHY (FLORENCE) KARNS. 1910- . Pseudonym: Amanda McAllister, q.v. Ref: CA.
    Hawk over Hollyhedge Manor. Avon, 1973 [Calif.]
    The House in Munich. Avon, 1975 [Munich]

DOWLING, RICHARD. 1846-1898.
    A Baffling Quest. Ward, 1891; Lovell, 1891
    -Below Bridge. Ward, 1895
    Catmur's Caves; or, The Quality of Mercy. Black, 1892; National Book, 1891
    The Crimson Chair, and other stories. Ward, 1891 ss, some criminous
    A Dark Intruder. Downey, 1895
    The Duke's Sweetheart. Tinsley, 1881
    -Fatal Bonds. Ward, 1886
    -The Fate of Luke Ormerod. Hurst, 1905
    -The Hidden Flame. Tinsley, 1885
    High-Water Mark. Munro, 1880 (British title?)
    -The Husband's Secret. Tinsley, 1881; Munro, 188?
    An Isle of Surrey. Ward, 1889
    -The Last Call. Tinsley, 1884
    -Miracle Gold. Ward, 1888; Lovell, 1888
    -My Darling's Ransom. Ogilvie, 1881 (British title?)
    The Mystery of Killard. Tinsley, 1879
    Old Corcoran's Money. Chatto, 1897
    -On the Embankment. Tinsley, 1884 ss
    -A Sapphire King, and other stories. Tinsley, 1882 ss
    The Skeleton Key. Ward, 1886
    -The Sport of Fate. Tinsley, 1880 ss
    -Sweet Inisfail. Tinsley, 1882; Munro, 1883
    -Tempest Driven. Tinsley, 1886; Appleton, 1887
    -Under St. Paul's. Tinsley, 1880; Munro, 1881
    The Weird Sisters. Tinsley, 1880
    While London Sleeps. Ward, 1895
    -With the Unhanged. Swan, 1887

DOWNES, DONALD. 1903- .
    The Easter Dinner. Rinehart, 1960
    Orders to Kill. Rinehart, 1958; Panther, 1960 [Fr.]
    A Red Rose for Maria. Rinehart, 1959; Panther, 1961 [It.]
    Rebecca's Pride. Harper, 1956; Eyre, 1956 [Carib.]
    Saba's Treasure. Harper, 1961; Eyre, 1963 [Carib.]

    The Scarlet Thread: Adventures in Wartime Espionage. British Book Centre, 1953; Verschoyle, 1953 [WWII]

DOWNES, QUENTIN. Pseudonym of Michael Harrison, 1907- , q.v. SC: Det. Insp. Abraham Kozminski, in all titles. Set: Eng.
    Heads I Win. Wingate, 1953; Roy, 1955
    No Smoke No Flame. Wingate, 1952; Roy, 1956
    They Hadn't a Clue. Arco, 1954

DOWNEY, EDMUND. 1856-1937.
    A House of Tears. Ward, 1886; Lovell, 1888

DOWNING, (GEORGE) TODD. 1902- . SC: Peter Bounty = PB; Hugh Rennert = HR.
    The Case of the Unconquered Sisters. Doubleday, 1936; Methuen, 1937 HR [Mex.]
    The Cat Screams. Doubleday, 1934; Methuen, 1935 HR [Mex.]
    Death Under the Moonflower. Doubleday, 1938 PB [Tex.]
    The Last Trumpet. Doubleday, 1937; Methuen, 1938 HR [Tex., Mex.]
    The Lazy Lawrence Murders. Doubleday, 1941 PB [Mex., train]
    Murder on the Tropic. Doubleday, 1935; Methuen, 1936 PB [Mex.]
    Murder on Tour. Putnam, 1933 HR [Tex., Mex.]
    Night over Mexico. Doubleday, 1937; Methuen, 1938 HR [Mex.]
    Vultures in the Sky. Doubleday, 1935; Methuen, 1936 HR [Mex., train]

DOWNING, WARWICK. 1931- . Ref: CA. SC: Joe Reddman, in all titles, all set in Denver.
    The Gambler, the Minstrel, and the Dance Hall Queen. Dutton, 1976
    The Mountains West of Town. Saturday Review, 1975
    The Player. Saturday Review, 1974

DOWNS, HUNTON (LEACHE). 1918- . Ref: CA.
    The Opium Stratagem. Bantam, 1973

DOWNS, SARAH ELIZABETH FORBUSH. 1843- . Pseudonym: Mrs. Georgie Sheldon, q.v.

DOWSETT, LORRIE
    The Master Mystery. Littledown, 1966
    -The Youth Hostel Mystery. Littledown, 1966

DOXEY, WILLIAM S(ANFORD JR.). 1935- . Ref: CA.
    Dead Wrong. Belmont, 1980
    Espionage. Belmont, 1979

DOYLE, (SIR) A(RTHUR) CONAN. 1859-1930. See also: Charles George, 1893- ; (John) Michael (Drinkrow) Hardwick, 1924- ; Tim J. Kelly, 1937- ; F(rederic) Andrew Leslie, 1927- ; Dennis Rosa; Wall Spence. Ref: all eight. SC: Sherlock Holmes = SH (see also series index).
    The Adventures of Sherlock Holmes. Newnes, 1892; Harper, 1892 ss SH
    The Black Doctor and other tales of terror and mystery. Doran, 1925 (Contains 8 ss from Round the Fire Stories, q.v., and 5 ss from other collections.)
    The Captain of the Polestar, and other stories. Longmans, 1890; Munro, 1894 ss, some criminous
    The Case-Book of Sherlock Holmes. Murray, 1927; Doran, 1927 ss SH
    Danger!, and other stories. Murray, 1918; Doran, 1919 ss, some criminous
    The Doings of Raffles Haw. Cassell, 1892; Lovell, 1891
    The Green Flag and other stories of war and sport. Smith, 1900; McClure, 1900 ss, some criminous
    His Last Bow. Murray, 1917; Doran, 1917 ss SH
    The Hound of the Baskervilles. Newnes, 1902; McClure, 1902 SH
    -The Last Galley. Smith, 1911; Doubleday, 1911
    The Memoirs of Sherlock Holmes. Newnes, 1894; Harper, 1894 ss SH
    My Friend the Murderer and other mysteries and adventures. Lovell, 1893 ss, some criminous
    Mysteries and Adventures. Scott, 1889 ss, some criminous
    The Mystery of Cloomber. Ward, 1889; Fenno, 1895
    The Return of Sherlock Holmes. Newnes, 1905; McClure, 1905 ss SH
    Round the Fire Stories. Smith Elder, 1908 ss, some criminous
    Round the Red Lamp. Methuen, 1894; Appleton, 1894 ss, some criminous
    The Sign of the Four. Blackett, 1890; Lippincott, 1890 SH
    A Study in Scarlet. Beeton's Christmas Annual, 1887; Lippincott, 1890 SH
    The Surgeon of Gaster Fell. Ivers, 1885; Westbrook, ca.1920
    Tales of Terror and Mystery. Murray, 1922 ss
    Tales of Terror and Mystery. Doubleday, 1977 ss (Same as previous title?)
    The Valley of Fear. Smith Elder, 1915; Doran, 1915 SH

DOYLE, ADRIAN (MALCOLM) CONAN, 1910-1970, and JOHN DICKSON CARR, 1905-1977, q.v. Ref for Doyle: CA. For Carr, see also pseudonyms: Carr Dickson, Carter Dickson, Roger Fairbairn. SC (following A. Conan Doyle, 1859-1930, q.v.): Sherlock Holmes = SH.
    The Exploits of Sherlock Holmes. Murray, 1954; Random, 1954. Reprinted in two volumes: The Exploits of Sherlock Holmes. Murray, 1963; and: More Exploits of Sherlock Holmes. Murray, 1964 SH

DOYLE, DR. C(HARLES) W(ILLIAM). 1852-1903.
    The Shadow of Quong Lung. Lippincott, 1900; Constable, 1900 ss [S.F.]

DOYLE, MONTE. 1926- .
    Signpost to Murder. French (London), 1963 (Play)

DOYLE, RICHARD. 1948- . Ref: CA.
    Imperial 109. Arlington, 1977

DRABBLE, J(OHN) F(REDERICK). 1906- .
    Death's Second Self. Sidgwick, 1971

DRABEK, JAN. 1935- . Ref: CA.
    The Lister Legacy. Beaufort, 1980

DRACHMAN, THEODORE S(OLOMON). 1904- . Ref: CA, CC.
    Addicted to Murder; see Something for the Birds
    Cry Plague! Ace, 1953
    Reason for Madness. Abelard (NYC & London), 1970 [N.Y.]
    Something for the Birds. Crown, 1958; Boardman, 1959. Also published as: Addicted to Murder. Avon, 196?

DRACO, F. Pseudonym of Julia Davis, 1904- . Ref: CA. SC: Lord and Lady (Ginger) Tintagel, in both titles.
    Cruise with Death. Rinehart, 1952 [ship]
    The Devil's Church. Rinehart, 1951 [Eng.]

DRACOTT, ALICE ELIZABETH. Pseudonym: A. E. D., q.v.

DRAGO, (HARRY) SINCLAIR. 1888-1979.
    -Women to Love. Amour, 1931; Melrose, 1932

DRAKE, ARNOLD
    The Steel Noose. Ace, 1954

DRAKE, BURGESS. See: H(enry) B(urgess) Drake.

DRAKE, DREXEL. Pseudonym of Charles H. Huff, 1887?-1959. SC: The Falcon, in all titles, all set in NYC.
    The Falcon Cuts In. Lippincott, 1937
    The Falcon Meets a Lady. Lippincott, 1938
    The Falcon's Prey. Lippincott, 1936; Harrap, 1937

DRAKE, FRANCIS
    Appointment in Peking. Hale, 1978 [Peking]
    A Chance to Die. Hale, 1976
    Come to Dust. Hale, 1980
    Death of the Dragon. Hale, 1976
    Double Identity. Hale, 1977 [H. Kong]

DRAKE, H(ENRY) B(URGESS)
    Chinese White. Falcon, 1950, as by Burgess Drake
    -Cursed Be the Treasure. Lane, 1926; Macy-Masius, 1928
    -The Shadowy Thing. Macy-Masius, 1928 (British title?)

DRAKE, MAURICE. 1875-1924.
    The Coming Back of Laurence Averil; see The Salving of a Derelict
    The Doom Window. Hodder, 1923; Dutton, 1925
    Galleon Gold. Hodder, 1924

Lethbridge of the Moor. Laurie, 1908; Kearney, 1908
The Mystery of the Mud Flats; see WO$_2$
The Ocean Sleuth. Methuen, 1915; Dutton, 1916
The Salving of a Derelict. Laurie, 1906. U.S. title: The Coming Back of Laurence Averil. Clode, 1915
WO$_2$. Methuen, 1913; Dutton, 1913. Also published as: The Mystery of the Mud Flats. Collins, 1930
Wrack. Duckworth, 1910

DRAMANN, ANN
The Last Victim. Tower, 1980 [Colo.]

DRAMOND, ALONZO E.
A Secret of the Midway Plaza. Byron S. Adams, 1890

DRAPER, ALFRED (ERNEST). 1924-   . Ref: CA.
The Death Penalty. Macmillan (London), 1972
Swansong for a Rare Bird. Macmillan (London), 1970; Coward, 1970

DRATLER, JAY J. 1911-   . Born in NYC; editorial adviser to publishers, translator, author of ss and novels, screen writer.
-All for a Woman. Popular Library, 1958
-Doctor Paradise. Popular Library, 1957
-Dream of a Woman. Popular Library, 1958
Ducks in Thunder. Reynal, 1940 [Austria]
The Judas Kiss. Holt, 1955. British title: Without Mercy. Hale, 1957 [L.A.]
The Pitfall. Crown, 1947 [L.A.]
Without Mercy; see The Judas Kiss

DRAX, PETER. Pseudonym of Eric Elrington Addis. Ref: MP. SC: Chief Insp. Thompson, in at least those marked T. Set: Eng.
Crime to Music; see Tune to a Corpse
Crime Within Crime; see Death by Two Hands
Death by Two Hands. Hutchinson, 1937. U.S. title: Crime Within Crime. Appleton, 1938 T
He Shot to Kill. Hutchinson, 1936
High Seas Murder. Hutchinson, 1939 [ship]
Murder by Chance. Hutchinson, 1936 T
Murder by Proxy. Hutchinson, 1937
Sing a Song of Murder. Hutchinson, 1944
Tune to a Corpse. Hutchinson, 1938. U.S. title: Crime to Music. Appleton, 1939 T

DRAYTON, RICKY. Pseudonym of Michael Barnes, q.v.
Anyone's Grief. Scion, 1951
Crime on My Hands. Scion, 1952
Death Comes Wholesale. Milestone, 1953
Eve Was No Lady. Scion, 1952
Get a Load o' Dis. Scion, 1952
Get That Man. Scion, 1952
Grin and Dare It. Milestone, 1953
The Heat's On. Scion, 1952
Hell and High Water. Scion, 1951
Hell's Belles. Milestone, 1953
The Howling Dog. Gannet, 1954
I Don't Die Easy. Scion, 1952
It Doesn't Add Up. Scion, 1952
It's Murder. Milestone, 1953
Make It Lethal. Milestone, 1954
The Midnight Male. Milestone, 1954
The Nude Was Framed. Milestone, 1953
One False Move. Milestone, 1954
Stay Dead, Sweetheart. Scion, 1951
Stick or Bust. Milestone, 1953
Stripped to Kill. Scion, 1952
Take It on the Lam. Scion, 1951
Too Late to Shout. Milestone, 1954
Troubled Night. Milestone, 1953

DREISER, THEODORE. 1871-1945. Ref: EM.
An American Tragedy. Boni, 1925; Constable, 1926

DRENNEN, RAYMOND
Murder Beat. Mystery House, 1956 [NYC]
You'll Die Now! Toby, 1953

DRESDEN, THOMAS
Queen's Ransom. Futura, 1979

DRESSER, DAVIS. 1904-1977. Pseudonyms: Asa Baker, Brett Halliday, qq.v. Joint pseudonym with Kathleen Rollins Dresser: Hal Debrett, q.v. Joint pseudonym with (Walter) Ryerson Johnson, 1901-   , q.v.: Matthew Blood, q.v.

DREW, JOHN H. 1949-   .
Edge of the Tightrope. Communication Creativity, 1979

DREW, MARY ANNE. Pseudonym of Bruce (Bingham) Cassiday, 1920-   , q.v. Other pseudonyms: Carson Bingham, Nick Carter, Annie Laurie McAllister, Annie Laurie McMurdie, Michael Stratford, qq.v.
The Diabolist. Avon, 1975 [Conn.]

DREW, PATRICIA. Byline used by Lloyd S. Kaye, and by Julia Perceval, q.v.
Deep in a Dark Country. Lancer, 1968
Who Is Melody? Belmont, 1968

DREW, SIDNEY. Pseudonym of Edgar Joyce Murray, 1878-   , q.v. SC (with many other authors): Sexton Blake, in all titles, published by Amalgamated.
The Fortnight of Fear. 1931
The Gangster's Deputy. 1930
The Mansion House Mystery. 1931

DREWE, MARCUS
The Barber of Littlewick. Jenkins, 1930

DREWRY, EDITH S(TEWART). Ref: DD.
A Death Ring. Moor, 1881
-On Dangerous Ground. White, 1883

DREXLER, J. F. Pseudonym of Lauran Bosworth Paine, 1916-   . Other pseudonyms: John Armour, Reg Batchelor, Kenneth Bedford, Frank Bosworth, Mark Carrel, Robert Clarke, Richard Dana, Troy Howard, Jared Ingersol, John Kilgore, Hunter Liggett, J. K. Lucas, John Morgan, qq.v.
The Anonymous Assassin. Hale, 1968
The Fire Ant. Hale, 1975
The Unsuspecting Victim. Hale, 1976

DRIN, MICHAEL
Signpost to Fear. Ward, 1964

DRISCOLL, PETER (JOHN). 1942-   . Ref: CA, TC.
The Barboza Credentials. Macdonald, 1976; Lippincott, 1976 [Mozam.]
In Connection with Kilshaw. Macdonald, 1974; Lippincott, 1974 [Ire.]
Pangolin. Macdonald, 1979; Lippincott, 1979 [Far East]
The While Lie Assignment. Macdonald, 1971; Lippincott, 1975 [Alb.]
The Wilby Conspiracy. Macdonald, 1973; Lippincott, 1972 [S. Afr.]

DRIVER, C(HARLES) J(ONATHAN). 1939-   . Ref: CA.
Elegy for a Revolutionary. Faber, 1969; Morrow, 1970

DROGE, EDWARD F., JR.
The Honor Legion. Signet, 1979 [NYC]
In the Highest Tradition. Atheneum, 1974; Secker, 1975 [NYC]

DRUCE, HUBERT
Henry Cassland. Melrose, 1911

DRUMMOND, A(NDREW) L(EWIS). 1844-   .
True Detective Stories. Dillingham, 1909 (Fictionalized true crime ss.)

DRUMMOND, ANTHONY. Pseudonym of (Alfred) John Hunter, 1891-1961, q.v. Other pseudonyms: John Addiscombe, L. H. Brenning, Anthony Dax, Peter Meriton, qq.v.
Blood Money. Gramol, 1935
The Devil's Signpost. Gramol, 1935
The Island of Dangerous Men. Gramol, 1937
The Scented Death. Unwin, 1924 [Russ.]

DRUMMOND, CHARLES. Pseudonym of Kenneth Giles, 1922-1972, q.v. Other pseudonym: Edmund McGirr, q.v. SC: Sgt. Reed, in all titles, set in Eng.
Death and the Leaping Ladies. Gollancz, 1968; Walker, 1969
A Death at the Bar. Gollancz, 1972; Walker, 1973
Death at the Furlong Post. Gollancz, 1967; Walker, 1968
The Odds on Death. Gollancz, 1969; Walker, 1970
Stab in the Back. Gollancz, 1970; Walker, 1970

DRUMMOND, HAMILTON. 1857-1935.
Gobelin Grange. Black, 1896 ss, some criminous
Room Five. Ward, 1904
-The Three Envelopes. Paul, 1912
-The Tournelles Plot. Paul, 1933

DRUMMOND, IVOR. Pseudonym of Roger (Erskine) Longrigg, 1929-   , q.v. Other pseudonym: Frank Parrish, q.v. SC: Jennifer Norrington, Alessandro di Ganzarello, and Coleridge Tucker III, in all titles.
The Diamonds of Loreta. Constable, 1980; St. Martin's, 1980 [Prague]
The Frog in the Moonflower. Macmillan (London), 1972; St. Martin's, 1973 [Afr., E.]
The Jaws of the Watchdog. Macmillan (London), 1973; St. Martin's, 1973
The Man with the Tiny Head. Macmillan (London), 1969; Harcourt, 1970
The Necklace of Skulls. Joseph, 1977; St. Martin's, 1977 [India]
The Power of the Bug. Macmillan (London), 1974; St. Martin's, 1974 [U.S.]
The Priests of the Abomination. Macmillan (London), 1970; Harcourt, 1971
A Stench of Poppies. Joseph, 1978; St. Martin's, 1978 [Turk.]
A Tank of Sacred Eels. Joseph, 1976; St. Martin's, 1976 [Mor.]

DRUMMOND, J. Pseudonym of John Newton Chance, 1911-   , q.v. Other pseudonym: John Lymington, q.v. SC (with many other authors): Sexton Blake, in all titles, published by Amalgamated Press. Set: Eng.
At Sixty Miles Per Hour. 1945
The Case of the "Dead" Spy. 1949
The Case of L.A.C. Dickson. 1950
The Case of the Man with No Name. 1951
The Case of the Two-Faced Swindler. 1955
The Essex Road Crime. 1944
Hated by All! 1951
The House in the Woods. 1950
The House on the Hill. 1945
The House on the River. 1952
The Manor House Menace. 1944
The Mystery of the Deserted Camp. 1948
The Mystery of the Five Guilty Men. 1954
The Mystery of the Haunted Square. 1950
The Mystery of the Sabotaged Jet. 1951
The Painted Dagger. 1944
The Riddle of the Leather Bottle. 1944
The Riddle of the Mummy Case. 1945
The Riddle of the Receiver's Hoard. 1949
The Secret of the Living Skeleton. 1949
The Secret of the Sixty Steps. 1950
The South Coast Mystery. 1949
The Teddy-Boy Mystery. 1955
The Town of Shadows. 1948
The Tragic Case of the Station Master's Legacy. 1944

DRUMMOND, JACK. 1923?-1978. Pseudonym: George Redder, q.v.

DRUMMOND, JOHN. 1900-1982.
Proof Positive. Duckworth, 1956

DRUMMOND, JUNE. 1923-   . Ref: CA, CC, TC.
Bang! Bang! You're Dead. Gollancz, 1973
The Black Unicorn. Gollancz, 1959
The Boon Companions. Gollancz, 1974. U.S. title: Drop Dead. Walker, 1976
Cable-Car. Gollancz, 1965; Holt, 1967 [Switz.]
Drop Dead; see The Boon Companions
Farewell Party. Gollancz, 1971; Dodd, 1973 [S. Afr.]
Funeral Urn. Gollancz, 1976; Walker, 1977
The Gantry Episode. Gollancz, 1968. U.S. title: Murder on a Bad Trip. Holt, 1968
I Saw Him Die. Gollancz, 1979
Murder on a Bad Trip; see The Gantry Episode
The Patriots. Gollancz, 1979
The People in Glass House. Gollancz, 1969; Simon, 1970
The Saboteurs. Gollancz, 1967; Holt, 1967 [S. Afr.]
Slowly the Poison. Gollancz, 1975; Walker, 1974 [S. Afr., 1911]
Such a Nice Family. Gollancz, 1980
Welcome, Proud Lady. Gollancz, 1964; Holt, 1968 [Cape Town]

DRUMMOND, WILLIAM
Gaslight. Arrow, 1967; Paperback Library, 1966 (Novelization of the play by Patrick Hamilton, 1904-1962, q.v.)
Life for Ruth. Corgi, 1962 (Novelization of the movie.)
Midnight Lace. Pan, 1960 (Novelization of the movie.)
Night Must Fall. Fontana, 1964; Signet, 1964 (Novelization of the movie.)
Victim. Corgi, 1961 (Novelization of the movie.)

DRURY, REV. SHELDON
    The Startling and Thrilling Narrative of the Dark and Terrible Deeds of Henry Madison, and His Associate and Accomplice, Miss Ella Stevens, Who Was Executed by the Vigilance Committee of San Francisco, on the 20th September Last. Barclay, 1957 [S.F.]

DRURY, W(ILLIAM) P(RICE). 1861-1949.
    Bearers of the Burden. Lawrence, 1899 ss, some criminous
    "Fightingcocks." Hutchinson, 1939

DRYER, BERNARD VICTOR
    The Image Makers. Harper, 1958; Hutchinson, 1959
    Murder in Port Afrique; see Port Afrique
    Port Afrique. Harper, 1949; Cassell, 1950. Also published as: Murder in Port Afrique. Avon, 1956 [Afr.]
    The Torch Bearers. Simon, 1968; Heinemann, 1968

DUANE, ALLAN
    The Hadrian Ransom. Putnam, 1979 [It.]

DUBOIS, MARCEL (GUSTAVE). 1891- .
    Crime and Punishment. Dramatic, 1960 (Play based on the novel by Fedor Mikhailovich Dostoevskii, 1821-1881, q.v.)

DU BOIS, THEODORA (McCORMICK). 1890- .
    Ref: CC, MP. Born in Brooklyn; author of ss, juveniles; involved in amateur and school dramatics. SC: Anne & Jeffrey McNeill = M.
    Armed with a New Terror. Houghton, 1936; Heinemann, 1937 M [N.Y.]
    The Body Goes Round and Round. Houghton, 1942 M
    The Case of the Perfumed Mouse. Doubleday, 1944; Boardman, 1946 M [Conn.]
    The Cavalier's Corpse. Doubleday, 1952; Boardman, 1953 M [Ire.]
    Death Comes to Tea. Houghton, 1940 M [New Eng.]
    Death Dines Out. Houghton, 1939; Readers Library, 1942 M [New Eng.]
    Death Is Late to Lunch. Houghton, 1941; Boardman, 1943 M [Conn.]
    Death Sails in a High Wind. Doubleday, 1945; Boardman, 1946 M [Conn.]
    Death Tears a Comic Strip. Houghton, 1939 M [NYC]
    Death Wears a White Coat. Houghton, 1938 M [New Eng.]
    The Devil and Destiny. Doubleday, 1948; Boardman, 1949 M [N.Y.]
    The Face of Hate. Doubleday, 1948 M [ship]
    The Footsteps. Doubleday, 1947; Boardman, 1949 M
    Fowl Play. Doubleday, 1951; Boardman, 1952 M [N.Y.]
    High Tension. Doubleday, 1950; Boardman, 1951 [NYC]
    It's Raining Violence. Doubleday, 1949; Boardman, 1950. Also published as: Money, Murder and the McNeills. Lancer, 1969 M [Conn.]
    The Late Bride. Washburn, 1965; Hale, 1966 [NYC]
    The Listener. Doubleday, 1953
    The McNeills Chase a Ghost. Houghton, 1941 M [New Eng.]
    Money, Murder and the McNeills; see It's Raining Violence
    Murder Strikes an Atomic Unit. Doubleday, 1946; Boardman, 1947 M [Conn.]
    Rogue's Coat. Doubleday, 1949 [Fla.]
    Seeing Red. Doubleday, 1954; Collins, 1955 M [N.Y.]
    Shannon Terror. Washburn, 1964 [Ire.]
    The Wild Duck Murders. Doubleday, 1943; Boardman, 1948 M [New Eng.]

DU BOIS, W.
    Pistols with Coffee. Newcoll, 1945

DU BOIS, WILLIAM. 1903- . Newspaperman and Broadway playwright. SC: Jack Jordan, in all titles.
    The Case of the Deadly Diary. Little, 1940. British title: The Deadly Diary. Macdonald, 1947 [NYC]
    The Case of the Frightened Fish. Little, 1940; Swan, 1947 [Bahamas]
    The Case of the Haunted Brides. Little, 1941; Swan, 1947 [Conn.]
    The Deadly Diary; see The Case of the Deadly Diary

DU BOISGOBEY, FORTUNE (HIPPOLYTE AUGUSTE). 1821-1891. Ref: CC, DD, EM, MC, MM, MP. Here listed are known English translations of this French author. No attempt has been made to distinguish among his works on the basis of criminous content.
    The Ace of Hearts. Munro, 1883; Vizetelly, 1889
    The Angel of the Bells. Munro, 1885; Aldine, 1877. Also published as: The Blue Veil; or, The Angel of the Belfry. Laird, 1889; Maxwell, 1886. And as: The Blue Veil; or, The Crime of the Tower. Lovell, 1889. And as: The Angel of the Chimes. Greening, 1903
    The Angel of the Chimes; see The Angel of the Bells
    Babiole, the Pretty Milliner. Munro, 1885
    Bertha's Secret. Lovell, 1888; Vizetelly, 1885
    The Blue Veil; or, The Angel of the Belfry; see The Angel of the Bells
    The Blue Veil; or, The Crime of the Tower; see The Angel of the Bells
    The Bride of a Day; see The Convict Colonel
    Cash on Delivery. Munro, 1887; Routledge, 1887
    The Cat's-Eye Ring, A Secret of Paris Life. Routledge (London & NYC), 1888 [Paris]
    Cecile's Fortune; see Merindol
    Chevalier Casse-Cou. DeWitt, 1875
    The Closed Door. Munro, 1886. British title: The Condemned Door. Routledge, 1887. Also published as: The Condemned Door; or, The Secret of Trigabon Castle. Lovell, 1884
    The Condemned Door; see The Closed Door
    The Condemned Door; or, The Secret of Trigabon Castle; see The Closed Door
    The Consequences of a Duel. Munro, 1885. Also published as: The Results of a Duel. Lovell, 1888; Vizetelly, 1888
    The Convict Colonel. Street, 1891; Vizetelly, 1887. Also published as: (?): The Bride of a Day. Routledge, 1887
    The Coral Pin. Munro, 1883; Vizetelly, 1886 [Paris]
    The Count's Millions. Street (Magnet #216)
    The Crime of the Opera House. Munro, 1881
    The Cry of Blood. Munro, 1886. British title: The Cry of Blood: A Story of Crime and Its Penalty. Maxwell, 1886
    The Day of Reckoning. Vizetelly, 1885 [Paris]
    The Detective's Crime. Donohue, ca.1897
    The Detective's Dilemma. Street, ca. 1888
    The Detective's Eye. Lovell, 1888. Also published as: Piedoche, A French Detective. Munro, 1884. And as: The Parisian Detective. Ivers, 1887
    The Detective's Triumph. Street, ca. 1888
    Doctor Villagos; or, The Nihilist Chief. Street, 1901; Pollard, 1889
    An Exchanged Identity. Street, ca.1897
    The Felon's Bequest. Maxwell, 1887
    Fernande's Choice. Vizetelly, 1887
    The Ferry Boat. Munro, 1882. Also published as: Love's Triumph: The Tragedy of the Ferry. Tousey, 1882. And as: Was It Murder? or, Who Is the Heir? McNally, 1883
    Fickle Heart. Maxwell, 1890
    A Fight for a Fortune. Donohue, ca. 1897; Vizetelly, 1886
    Fontenay, the Swordsman: A Military Novel. McNally, 1891
    The Golden Pig. Munro, 1882. British title: The Golden Pig; or, The Idol of Modern Paris. Vizetelly, 1886 [Paris]
    The Golden Trees. Claxton, 1896
    The Great Jewel Mystery. Donohue, ca. 1897
    The Half-Sister's Secret. Routledge, 1889
    The High Roller; or, Plunging and Honeyfugling on the Race Track: A Sporting Romance. Pollard, 1891
    His Great Revenge. Munro, 1882
    In the Serpent's Coils. Vizetelly, 1885
    The Iron Mask. Munro, 1884
    The Jailer's Pretty Wife; see The Pretty Jailer
    The Lost Casket. Putnam, 1881. Also published as: The Severed Hand. Munro, 1888; Vizetelly, 1885. And as: The Severed Hand; or, A Terrible Confession. Ogilvie, ca.1895
    The Lottery Ticket. Munro, 1885. Also published as: The Red Lottery Ticket. Lovell, 1888; Vizetelly, 1887
    Love's Triumph: The Tragedy of the Ferry; see The Ferry Boat
    Marie-Rose; or, The Mystery. Munro, 1883
    Married for Love. Routledge, 1888
    The Matapan Affair. Munro, 1880; Vizetelly, 1885. Also published as: The Matapan Jewels. Lotus Library (London), 1902
    The Matapan Jewels; see The Matapan Affair
    Merindol. Munro, 1884. British title: Cecile's Fortune. Vizetelly, 1 86
    The Millionaire's Fate. Donohue
    The Missing Rubies. Donohue, ca.1897
    The Mysterious Juror. Higgins, 1892
    The Mystery of an Omnibus. Munro, 1882. British title: An Omnibus Mystery (with: The Old Age of Lecoq, the Detective, q.v.). Vizetelly, 1885
    A Mystery Still. Boulevard Novels, 1888; Vizetelly, 1888
    The Nameless Man. Westbrook, ca.1920; Vizetelly, 1887
    An Ocean Knight; or, The Corsairs and Their Conquerors. Warne (London & NYC), 1891
    The Old Age of Lecoq, the Detective; see The Old Age of Monsieur Lecoq
    The Old Age of Monsieur Lecoq. Munro, 1888. British title: The Old Age of Lecoq, the Detective. Vizetelly (with An Omnibus Mystery, q.v.), 1885
    An Omnibus Mystery; see The Mystery of an Omnibus
    The Parisian Detective; see The Detective's Eye
    The Phantom Leg. Vizetelly, 1886
    Piedouche, A French Detective; see The Detective's Eye
    The Pretty Jailer. Munro, 1886. British title: The Jailer's Pretty Wife. Vizetelly, 1886
    The Prima Donna's Husband. Munro, 1885
    The Privateersman's Legacy. Munro, 1882
    A Railway Tragedy. Vizetelly, 1887
    The Red Band, The Adventures of a Young Girl During the Siege of Paris. Munro, 1887. British title: The Red Band; or, The Siege and the Commune. Maxwell, 1887
    The Red Camelia. Vizetelly, 1887
    The Red Lottery Ticket; see The Lottery Ticket
    The Results of a Duel; see The Consequences of a Duel
    The Robbery of the Orphans; or, JT's Inheritance. Munro, 1882
    Satan's Coach. Munro, 1883
    Saved from the Harem. Vizetelly, 1888
    The Sculptor's Daughter; see The Vitriol Thrower
    Sealed Lips. Munro, 1883
    The Severed Hand; see The Lost Casket
    The Steel Necklace. Street, 1891; Vizetelly, 1886
    The Temple of Death. Westbrook, ca.1920
    Thieving Fingers. Vizetelly, 1887
    The Thumb Stroke. Vizetelly, 1886
    The Vitriol Thrower. Tousey, 1884. Also published as: The Sculptor's Daughter. Munro, 1886
    Was It Murder? or, Who Is the Heir?; see The Ferry Boat
    Where's Zenobia?; see Zenobie Capitaine
    Who Died Last?; or, The Rightful Heir. Vizetelly, 1885
    The Youngest Soldier of the Grand Armee. Higgins, 1892
    Zenobie Capitaine. Munro, 1884. British title: Where's Zenobia? Vizetelly, 1888
    Zig-Zag the Clown; or, The Steel Gauntlets. Munro, 1885

DU BREUIL, (ELIZABETH) L(OR)INDA. 1924-1980. Pseudonyms: Kate Cameron, Linda Hagen, Elizabeth Hanley, qq.v. Ref:CA.
    Break a Leg. Zebra, 1980
    Crooked Letter. Belmont, 1979
    Deadly Party. Belmont, 1979
    Double Standard. Leisure, 1980
    Evil, Evil. Belmont, 1973
    Follow the Leader. Belmont, 1979
    The Legend of Molly Moor. Belmont, 1973 [Md., past]
    Mirror Image. Belmont, 1979 [New Or.]
    Nightmare Baby. Belmont, 1970
    The Secret. Lancer, 1972
    So Dear, So Deadly. Leisure, 1979
    Some Call It Perjury. Leisure, 1979

DU CAMP, ALWYN
    Twana. Mercantile (Clairwood, South Africa), 1969?

DU CANN, C(HARLES) G(ARFIELD) L(OTT). 1889- .
    The Secret Hand. Methuen, 1929

DUCHESS, THE. Pseudonym of Mrs. (Margaret Wolfe Hamilton) Hungerford, 1855-1897, q.v.
    The Haunted Chamber. Lovell, 1886
    -A Passive Crime, and other stories. Lovell, 1885 ss

DUDLEY, (HELEN) DOROTHY, 1895-   , and
   JUANITA SHERIDAN, q.v.
   What Dark Secret. Morrow, 1943 [Haw.]

DUDLEY, ERNEST. Pseudonym of Vivian Er-
   nest Coltman-Allen, 1908-   . Ref:
   CA. SC: Dr. Morelle, in at least
   those marked M. Set: Eng.
   The Adventures of Jimmy Strange. Long,
      1945 ss
   Alibi and Dr. Morelle. Hale, 1959 M
   The Blind Beak. Hale, 1954
   Callers for Dr. Morelle. Hale, 1957 M
   Confess to Dr. Morelle. Hale, 1959 M
   The Crooked Inn. Hodder, 1953
   The Crooked Straight. Hodder, 1948
   The Dark Bureau. Hodder, 1950
   Dr. Morelle, with Arthur Watkyn, q.v.
      Evans, 1954 M (Play.)
   Dr. Morelle and Destiny. Hale, 1958 M
   Dr. Morelle and the Doll. Hale, 1960 M
   Dr. Morelle and the Drummer Girl. Hod-
      der, 1950 M
   Dr. Morelle at Midnight. Hale, 1959 M
   Dr. Morelle Meets Murder and other new
      adventures. Findon, 1948 M ss
   Dr. Morelle Takes a Bow. Hale, 1957 M
   The Harassed Hero. Hodder, 1951
   Leatherface. Hale, 1958
   Look out for Lucifer! Long, 1951
   Meet Dr. Morelle. Long, 1943 M ss
   Meet Dr. Morelle Again. Long, 1944 M
   Menace for Dr. Morelle. Long, 1947 M
   The Mind of Dr. Morelle. Hale, 1958 M
   Mr. Walker Wants to Know. Wright, 1939
   Nightmare for Dr. Morelle. Hale, 1960 M
   Picaroon. Hale, 1952; Bobbs, 1953
      [1770s, Eng.]
   The Private Eye. Long, 1950
   To Love and to Perish. Hale, 1962
      [Wales]
   Two-Face. Long, 1951
   The Whistling Sands. Hodder, 1956

DUDLEY, FRANK. Pseudonym of Ward Greene,
   1892-1956, q.v.
   The Havana Hotel Murders. Houghton,
      1936; Bell, 1937 [Havana]
   King Cobra. Carrick, 1940
   Ride the Nightmare. Cape (NYC), 1930

DUDLEY, OWEN. Pseudonym of Dudley Owen
   McGaughy. Other pseudonym: Dudley
   Dean, q.v.
   The Deep End. Ace, 1956 [Calif.]
   Murder for Charity. Ace, 1957 [Calif.]
   Run If You Can. Ace, 1960 [Calif.]

DUDLEY, OWEN FRANCIS. 1882-1952.
   -The Coming of the Monster. Longmans,
      1936

DUDOWICZ, EDWARD
   The Thirty-Second Floor. Decade, 1980
      [NYC]

DUERRENMATT, FRIEDRICH. 1921-   . See
   also: James Yaffe, 1927-   . Ref:
   CA, CC, MC, TC. SC: Kommissar Hans
   Barlach = HB.
   A Dangerous Game. Cape, 1960. U.S.
      title: Traps. Knopf, 1960 (Transla-
      tion of "Die Panne." Zurich, 1956.)
   End of the Game; see The Judge and His
      Hangman
   The Judge and His Hangman. Jenkins,
      1954; Harper, 1955. Also published
      as: End of the Game. Warner, 1976
      (Translation of "Der Richter und Sein
      Henker." Einsiedeln, 1952.) HB
      [Switz.]
   The Pledge. Cape, 1959; Knopf, 1959
      (Translation of "Das Versprechen."
      Zurich, 1958.) [Switz.]
   The Quarry. Cape, 1962; New York Gra-
      phic Society, 1962 (Translation of
      "Der Verdacht." Einsiedeln, 1959.)
      HB
   Traps; see A Dangerous Game

DUFF, BELDON
   Ask No Questions. Doubleday, 1930
      [Conn.]
   The Central Park Murder. Doubleday,
      1929 [NYC]

DUFF, DAVID (SKENE). 1912-   .
   Castle Fell. Burke, 1950
   Loch Spy. Burke, 1948 [Scot.]
   Traitor's Pass. Staples, 1954; Roy,
      1955

DUFF, DOUGLAS V(ALDER). 1901-   .
   Peter Darington. Thames, 19?? ss

DUFF, JAMES P. SC: Johnny Phelan = JP.
   Dangerous to Know. Ace, 1959 [Las Veg.]
   Run from Death. Mystery House, 1957
      [Mex., L.A.]
   Some Die Young. Graphic, 1956 JP [L.A.]
   Who Dies There? Graphic, 1956 JP [L.A.]

DUFFIELD, ANNE. 1895-   .
   -The Grand Duchess. Pan, 1959

DUFFY, MAUREEN. 1933-   .
   Housespy. H. Hamilton, 1978

DUFFY, V(INCENT). See: M(orris) Ankrum.

DUGDALE, (ARTHUR) GILES
   Should a Corpse Tell? Earl, 1948

DUGGAN, DENISE. 1930-   . Pseudonym:
   Denise Egerton, q.v.

DUGGAN, FLOYD
   Pay-Off for a Dumb Dame. Barrington
      Gray, 1953

DUHART, WILLIAM H.
   The Deadly Pay-Off. GM, 1958; Fawcett
      (London), 1959 [Milw.]

DUKE, FRANCIS
   The Gold Cup Murder. New English Li-
      brary pb, 1973

DUKE, MADELAINE. 1925-   . Pseudonym:
   Maxim Donne, q.v. Ref: CA. SC: Norah
   North = NN. Set: Eng.
   The Bormann Receipt. Panther, 1977;
      Stein, 1978 [Vienna]
   Death at the Wedding. Joseph, 1976 NN
   Death of a Dandie Dinmont. Joseph, 1978
      NN
   Death of a Holy Murderer. Joseph, 1975
      NN

DUKE, WILL. Pseudonym of William Campbell
   Gault, 1910-   , q.v. Other pseudo-
   nym: Roney Scott, q.v.
   Fair Prey. Graphic, 1956; Boardman,
      1958 [L.A.]

DUKE, WINIFRED.   -1962. Ref: EM.
   Bastard Verdict. Jarrolds, 1931; Knopf,
      1934
   -The Black Mirror. Jarrolds, 1948
   -Blind Geese. Jarrolds, 1946
   -The Cherry-Fair. Hale, 1954
   Crookedshaws. Jarrolds, 1935
   -The Dancing of the Fox. Hale, 1956
   -Death and His Sweetheart. Jarrolds,
      1938
   -Dirge for a Dead Witch. Jarrolds, 1949
   -The Drove Road. Jarrolds, 1930
   Funeral March of a Marionette. Jar-
      rolds, 1945
   Heir to Kings; see The Laird
   -The Hour-Glass. Jarrolds, 1934
   -The House of Ogilvie. Long, 1922
   -The Laird. Long, 1925. U.S. title (?):
      Heir to Kings. Stokes, 1926
   -The Lost Cause. Hale, 1953
   -Madeleine Smith. Hodge, 1928
   Murder of Mr. Mallabee. Jarrolds, 1937
   -The Needful Journey. Jarrolds, 1950
   Room for a Ghost. Jarrolds, 1937
   -The Royal Ishmael. Jarrolds, 1943
   -Seven Women. Jarrolds, 1947
   -Shadows. Jarrolds, 1951
   -The Shears of Destiny. Jarrolds, 1942
   Skin for Skin. Gollancz, 1935; Little,
      1935
   -The Spider's Web. Jarrolds, 1945
   -Stubble. Jarrolds, 1935
   Tales of Hate. Hodge, 1927 (2 of 3
      stories criminous.)
   -The Unjust Jury. Jarrolds, 1941
   -A Web in Childhood. Hale, 1952
   -The Wild Flame. Long, 1923
   -Winter Pride. Hale, 1952

DUMAS, CHARLES ROBERT. S: Second Bureau,
   both titles.
   Second Bureau. Eldon, 1939 [Fr.]
   Spies Against Them. Eldon, 1940

DUMAS, CLAIRE. Pseudonym of Marthe Van
   Weddingen, 1924-   . Ref: CA.
   The Stranger. Ballantine, 1977 (Trans-
      lation of "L'Herbe Chaude." Paris,
      1975.)

DU MAURIER, ANGELA. 1904-   .
   Treveryan. Joseph, 1942; Doubleday,
      1942

DU MAURIER, DAPHNE. 1907-   . Ref: CA,
   EM, TC. See also: Diana Morgan.
   The Apple Tree. Gollancz, 1952. U.S.
      title: Kiss Me Again, Stranger.
      Doubleday, 1953. Also published as:
      The Birds and other stories. Penguin,
      1963 ss
   The Birds and other stories; see The
      Apple Tree
   The Blue Lenses and other stories; see
      The Breaking Point
   The Breaking Point. Gollancz, 1959;
      Doubleday, 1959. Also published as:
      The Blue Lenses and other stories.
      Penguin, 1970 ss
   Don't Look Now; see Not After Midnight
   Echoes from the Macabre. Gollancz,
      1976; Doubleday, 1977 (ss taken from
      previous collections.)
   The Flight of the Falcon. Gollancz,
      1965; Doubleday, 1965 [It.]
   The House on the Strand. Gollancz,
      1969; Doubleday, 1969
   Jamaica Inn. Gollancz, 1936; Doubleday,
      1936 [Eng., ca.1815]
   Kiss Me Again, Stranger; see The Apple
      Tree
   My Cousin Rachel. Gollancz, 1951;
      Doubleday, 1952
   Not After Midnight. Gollancz, 1971.
      U.S. title: Don't Look Now. Double-
      day, 1971 ss
   Rebecca. Gollancz, 1938; Doubleday,
      1938. 3-act play based on this novel:
      Gollancz, 1940; Dramatists, 1943
   The Scapegoat. Gollancz, 1957; Double-
      day, 1957 [Fr.]

DU MAURIER, GERALD. 1873-1934. See:
   H(erman) C(yril) McNeile, 1888-1937.

DUMKEY, RAYMOND. Pseudonym of Wilbur
   Braun, 1896-   , q.v. Other pseudo-
   nyms: Walter Blake, Bruce Brandon,
   Fred Caldwell, Nan Fleming, Marsha
   Grable, Edwin F. Hornung, Jed Parish,
   Basil Ring, Orville Snap, Mortimer
   Sprague, Bert Stoner, qq.v.
   The House Nobody Lived In. French
      (NYC), 1947 (3-act play.)

DUN, (MARIE DE) NERVAUD
   Point of Death. Hammond, 1954

DUNBAR, JOHN G.
   -A Way to Adventure, and two other sto-
      ries. Stockwell, 1942 ss

DUNCAN, ACTEA CAROLINE. 1913-   . Pseudonym: Carolyn Thomas, q.v.

DUNCAN, ALLAN. SC: Major Charles Douglas
   Ker(r)wood, in both titles.
   A Cabinet Minister Resigns. Hutchinson,
      1939
   An Official Secret. Hutchinson, 1937;
      Crowell, 1937 [Ger.]

DUNCAN, DAVID. 1913-   . Ref: CA.
   The Bramble Bush. Macmillan, 1948; Low,
      1949. Also published as: Sweet and
      Deadly. Mercury, 1949 [S.F.]
   The Madrone Tree. Macmillan, 1949;
      Gollancz, 1950. Also published as:
      Worse Than Murder. PB, 1954 [Calif.]
   -Remember the Shadows. McBride, 1944
   -The Serpent's Egg. Macmillan, 1950
   The Shade of Time. Random, 1946; Grey
      Walls, 1948 [Calif.]
   Sweet and Deadly; see The Bramble Bush
   Worse Than Murder; see The Madrone Tree

DUNCAN, FRANCIS. SC: Peter Justice, in at
   least those marked PJ; Mordecai Eur-
   ipides Tremaine, in at least those
   marked MT. Set: Eng.
   Behold a Fair Woman. Long, 1954 MT
   Dangerous Mr. X. Jenkins, 1939
   Fear Holds the Key. Jenkins, 1945
   The Hand of Justice. Jenkins, 1945 PJ
   In at the Death. Long, 1952 MT
   Justice Limited. Jenkins, 1941 PJ
   Justice Returns. Jenkins, 1940 PJ
   The League of Justice. Jenkins, 1937 PJ
   Ministers Too Are Mortal. Long, 1951
   Murder But Gently. Long, 1953
   Murder for Christmas. Long, 1949
   Murder Has a Motive. Long, 1947 MT
   Murder in Man. Jenkins, 1940
   Murderer's Bluff. Jenkins, 1948 MT
   Night Without End. Jenkins, 1943
   A Question of Time. Hale, 1959
   So Pretty a Problem. Long, 1950 MT
   The Sword of Justice. Jenkins, 1937 PJ
   They'll Never Find Out. Jenkins, 1944
      MT
   Tigers Fight Alone. Jenkins, 1938

DUNCAN, LEE. N.Y. freelance writer; graduate of U. of Mich.; author of numerous magazine articles and ss under various names, ghosted several
   books, wrote paperback novels.
   Fidel Castro Assassinated. Monarch,
      1961 [Cuba]

DUNCAN, LOIS [LOIS DUNCAN ARQUETTE].
   1934-   . Ref: CA.
   Five Were Missing. Signet, 1972
   Game of Danger. Dodd, 1962
   I Know What You Did Last Summer.
      Little, 1973
   Point of Violence. Doubleday, 1966;
      Hale, 1968 [Fla.]

DUNCAN, PETER
   The Tell-Tale Tart. GM, 1961; Muller
      pb, 1962

D

DUNCAN, ROBERT L(IPSCOMB). 1927-   .
Pseudonym: James Hall Roberts, q.v.
Ref: TC. Born in Oklahoma City; graduate of and teacher at U. of Okla.
Brimstone. Morrow, 1980; Joseph, 1980
The Day the Sun Fell. Morrow, 1970 [Jap.]
Dragons at the Gate. Morrow, 1975; Joseph, 1976 [Tokyo]
Fire Storm. Morrow, 1978; Joseph, 1979 [Jap.]
Temple Dogs. Morrow, 1977; Joseph, 1978 [Far East]

DUNCAN, RONALD (FREDERICK). 1914-   .
Ref: CA.
A Kettle of Fish. Allen, 1971 ss, one criminous

DUNCAN, W(ILLIAM) MURDOCH. 1909-1975.
Ref: CA, CC, TC. Pseudonyms: John Cassells, John Dallas, Neill Graham, Martin Locke, Peter Malloch, Lovat Marshall, qq.v. SC: The Dreamer (Supt. Donald Reamer) = D; Insp. Flagg (see also John Cassells entry) = F; Supt. Gaylord, in at least those marked G; Greensleeves series, at least those marked Gr; Mr. Gilly, in at least those marked MG; Insp. Laurie Hume, in at least those marked LH; Supt. Leslie, in at least those marked L; Supt. MacNeill, in at least those marked M. Set: Eng.
Again the Dreamer. Long, 1965 D
The Big Timer. Long, 1973
The Black Mitre. Melrose, 1951
The Blackbird Sings of Murder. Melrose, 1948
The Blood Red Leaf. Melrose, 1952
The Breath of Murder. Long, 1972
The Brothers of Judgement. Melrose, 1950
Case for the Dreamer. Long, 1966 D
Challenge for the Dreamer. Long, 1969 D
The Company of Sinners. Melrose, 1951
Cord for a Killer. Long, 1969
The Council of Comforters. Long, 1967 L
The Crime Master. Long, 1963 MG
The Cult of the Queer People. Melrose, 1949 Gr
Death and Mr. Gilly. Long, 1974 MG
Death Beckons Quietly. Melrose, 1946 F
Death Comes to Lady's Steps. Melrose, 1952
Death Stands Round the Corner. Rich, 1955 M
Death Wears a Silk Stocking. Melrose, 1945
The Deathmaster. Hutchinson, 1953
Detail for the Dreamer. Long, 1971 D
The Doctor Deals with Murder. Melrose, 1944
The Dreamer at Large. Long, 1972 D
The Dreamer Deals with Murder. Long, 1970 D
The Dreamer Intervenes. Long, 1968 D
The Green Knight. Long, 1964
The Green Triangle. Long, 1969 L
The Hooded Man. Long, 1960 G
The Hour of the Bishop. Long, 1964
The House in Spite Street. Long, 1961
The House of Wailing Winds. Long, 1965
The Joker Deals with Death. Long, 1958
Killer Keep. Melrose, 1946
A Knife in the Night. Rich, 1955 M
Laurels for the Dreamer. Long, 1975 D
Meet the Dreamer. Long, 1963 D
Murder at Marks Caris. Melrose, 1945
Murder Calls the Tune. Long, 1957 LH
The Murder Man. Long, 1959 LH
Murder of a Cop. Long, 1976 [Scot.]
Mystery on the Clyde. Melrose, 1945 Gr
The Nighthawk. Long, 1962 G
Pennies for His Eyes. Rich, 1956 M
Presenting the Dreamer. Long, 1966 D
Prey for the Dreamer. Long, 1974 D
Problem for the Dreamer. Long, 1967 D
The Puppets of Father Bouvard. Melrose, 1948
Redfingers. Long, 1962
Salute the Dreamer. Long, 1968 D
Straight Ahead for Danger. Melrose, 1946 Gr
The Tiled House Mystery. Melrose, 1947
The Whisperer. Long, 1970
The Whispering Man. Long, 1959 LH

DUNCOMBE, MRS. A.
The Village Gentleman, and The Attorney at Law. (London), 1808

DUNCOMBE, FRANCES (RIKER). 1900-   .
Ref: CA, CC.
Death of a Spinster. Scribner, 1958; Secker, 1958 [N.Y.]

DUNDAS, LAWRENCE [LAURENCE GEORGE DIONICIO DUNDAS]. SC: Andrew Salmond, in all titles.
He Liked Them Murderous. Hammond, 1964 [S. Am.]

A Spider at the Elvira. Hammond, 1949 [S. Am.]
The Strange Smell of Murder. Hammond, 1965 [S. Am.]

DUNDEE, ROBERT. Pseudonym of Robert R. Kirsch, 1922-1980. Ref: CA.
Inferno. Signet, 1962 [Calif.]
Pandora's Box. Signet, 1962

DUNLEAVY, STEVE
The Very First Lady. Simon, 1980 [1985, Wash. D.C.]

DUNLOP, AGNES MARY ROBERTSON. Pseudonym: Elizabeth Kyle, q.v.

DUNMORE, SPENCER (SAMBROOK). 1928-   Ref: CA.
-Means of Escape. Davies, 1978

DUNN, DETECTIVE. Pseudonym of Charles E(dward) Pearce, q.v.
The Beautiful Devil. Paul, 1923
A Queen of Crooks. Paul, 1924
The Red Mill Mystery. Paul, 1925

DUNN, DOROTHY. 1913-   . Born in Portland, Maine; teacher in St. Louis.
Murder's Web. Harper, 1950; Foulsham, 1951 [St. Louis]

DUNN, IRMA LARAWAY
A Slightly Disjointed Affair. Vantage, 1963

DUNN, J(OSEPH) ALLAN (ELPHINSTONE). 1872-1941.
-Dead Man's Gold. Hurst, 1921; Doubleday, 1920
The Death Gamble. Hamilton, 1932 [N.Y.]
The Dragon's Claw. Mellifont, 1940
The Elimination Syndicate. Pemberton, 1949
-The Girl of Ghost Mountain. Pearson, 1927; Small, 1921
The House on Doubloon Inlet. Earl, 1947 [S.C.]
-The Isle of the Drums. Hurst, 1923
-Long-Haired Bill. Hurst, 1927
-Luck and a Lady. Mellifont, 1942
The Man Trap. Hurst, 1922; Doubleday, 1921 [U.S.]
The Sign of the Skull. Hurst, 192?

DUNN, JAMES. Pseudonym: R. E. Corder, q.v.

DUNN, N. J.
The Vultures of Erin: A Tale of the Penal Laws. Kenedy, 1886 [Ire.]

DUNNE, BERNARD
Dead Man's Bluff. Hale, 1980

DUNNE, JOHN GREGORY. 1932-   . Ref: CA, TC.
True Confessions. Dutton, 1977; Weidenfeld, 1978 [L.A.]

DUNNE, LEE. 1934-   .
Ringleader. Simon, 1980; Molendinar, 1981 [Ire.]

DUNNE, THOMAS L.   Editor at NYC publishing house.
The Scourge. Coward, 1978; Sphere, 1980 [Atlanta]

DUNNETT, ALASTAIR MacTAVISH. 1908-   . Pseudonym: Alec Tavis, q.v. Ref: CA.
No Thanks to the Duke. Cape, 1978; Doubleday, 1981 [Scot.]

DUNNETT, DOROTHY. U.S. byline of Dorothy Halliday, 1923-   , q.v.

DUNNING, JOHN. 1942-   . Ref: CA.
The Holland Suggestions. Bobbs, 1975 [Colo.]
Looking for Ginger North. GM, 1980 [Calif.]

DUNNING, LAWRENCE. 1931-   . Ref: CA.
Keller's Bomb. Avon, 1978 [S.W.]
Neutron Two Is Critical. Avon, 1977

DUNSANY, LORD [EDWARD JOHN MORETON DRAX PLUNKETT]. 1878-1957. Ref: CA, CC, EM.
The Little Tales of Smethers, and other stories. Jarrolds, 1952 ss, some criminous

DUNTON, JAMES G(ERALD). 1899-   .
The Murders in Lovers' Lane. Small, 1927

DUPREE, MORRISON. Pseudonym of Sherlock Bronson Gass, 1878-1945.
A Tap on the Shoulder. Doubleday, 1929

DUPREY, RICHARD ALLEN. 1929-   . Pseudonym: Alan Fields, q.v.

DUPUY, ELIZA A(NN). 1814-1881.
-The Cancelled Will. Peterson, 1872; Halifax, 1878
-The Dethroned Heiress. Peterson, 1873
-Florence; or, The Fatal Vow. Stratton, 1852
-The Gipsy's Warning. Peterson, 1873
-The Hidden Sin. Harper, 1866
-How He Did It. Peterson, 1871. Also published as: Was He Guilty? Peterson, 1873
Was He Guilty?; see How He Did It
-Who Shall Be Victor? Peterson, 1872; Halifax, 1878

DUPUY, WILLIAM ATHERTON. 1876-1941.
Uncle Sam, Detective. Stokes, 1916 ss

DUPUY-MAZUEL, HENRI. 1885-   . Pseudonym: Henri Catalan, q.v.

DURAND, ALICE MARIE CELESTE FLEURY. 1842-1902. Pseudonym: Henry Greville, q.v.

DURAND, ROBERT
Lady in a Cage. Popular Library, 1964 (Novelization of the movie.)

DURAS, MARGUERITE
Ten-Thirty on a Summer Night. Calder, 1962; Grove, 1963 (Translation of "Dix Heures et Demie du Soir en Ete." Paris, 1960.) [Sp.]

DURBIN, CHARLES
The Patriot. Coward, 1971; Joseph, 1972
Vendetta. Coward, 1970; Joseph, 1971

DURBRIDGE, FRANCIS (HENRY). 1912-   . Joint pseudonym with James Douglas Rutherford McConnell, 1915-   : Paul Temple, q.v. Ref: CC, EM, TC. SC: Paul Temple (also under the Paul Temple byline) = PT; Tim Frazer = TF. Set: Eng.
Another Woman's Shoes. Hodder, 1965
Back Room Girl. Long, 1950
Bat out of Hell. Hodder, 1972
Beware of Johnny Washington. Long, 1951
The Case of the Twisted Scarf; see The Scarf
The Curzon Case. Coronet, 1972 PT
Dead to the World. Hodder, 1967
Design for Murder. Long, 1951
The Desperate People. Hodder, 1966
A Game of Murder. Hodder, 1975
The Geneva Mystery. Hodder pb, 1971 PT
The Gentle Hook. French, 19?? (Play.)
A Man Called Harry Brent. Hodder, 1970 (Novelization of the TV series.)
Murder with Love. French (London), 1977 (Play.)
My Friend Charles. Hodder, 1963
My Wife Melissa. Hodder, 1967
News of Paul Temple. Long, 1940 PT
The Other Man. Hodder, 1958 (Novelization of the TV serial.)
The Passenger. Hodder, 1977
Paul Temple and the Front Page Men. Long, 1939 PT (Adapted by Durbridge and Charles Hatton from the play by Durbridge.)
Paul Temple and the Harkdale Robbery. Hodder pb, 1970 PT
Paul Temple and the Kelby Affair. Hodder pb, 1970 PT
Paul Temple Intervenes. Long, 1944 PT
The Pig-Tail Murder. Hodder, 1969
Portrait of Alison. Hodder, 1962; Dodd, 1962
The Scarf. Hodder, 1960. U.S. title: The Case of the Twisted Scarf. Dodd, 1961
Send for Paul Temple. Long, 1938 PT
Send for Paul Temple Again! Long, 1948 PT
Suddenly at Home. French (London), 1973 (2-act play.)
Tim Frazer Again. Hodder, 1964 TF
Tim Frazer Gets the Message. Hodder, 1978 TF
A Time of Day. Hodder, 1959
The World of Tim Frazer. Hodder, 1962; Dodd, 1962 TF

DURHAM, DAVID. Pseudonym of Roy Vickers, 1888-1965, q.v. Other pseudonyms: Sefton Kyle, John Spencer, qq.v. SC: Insp. George Rason = GR (see also Vickers entry); Insp. J. Rason = JR (see also Vickers entry); James Segrove = JS (see also Vickers entry).
Against the Law. Jenkins, 1939
The Exploits of Fidelity Dove. Hodder, 1924. Reprinted as by Roy Vickers: Newnes, 1935 ss, GR in 9
The Forgotten Honeymoon. Jenkins, 1935

The Girl Who Dared. Jenkins, 1938
Hounded Down. Hodder, 1923. Reprinted as by Roy Vickers: Newnes, 1935 GR
The Pearl-Headed Pin. Hodder, 1925. Reprinted as by Roy Vickers: Newnes, 1935 JR
The Woman Accused. Hodder, 1923. Reprinted as by Roy Vickers: Newnes, 1936 JS

DURHAM, MARY. SC: Insp. York in at least those marked Y. Set: Eng.
Castle Mandragora. Gifford, 1950
Cornish Mystery. Crowther, 1946
Corpse Errant. Skeffington, 1949
Crime Insoluble. Crowther, 1947 Y
The Devil Was Sick. Gifford, 1952
Forked Lightning. Gifford, 1951
Hate Is My Livery. Gifford, 1945 Y
Keeps Death His Court. Crowther, 1946 Y
Murder by Multiplication. Skeffington, 1948 Y
Murder Hath Charms. Skeffington, 1948
Why Pick on Pickles? Crowther, 1945 Y

DURIE, LYNN. Pseudonym of Douglas Christie, 1894-   , q.v. Other pseudonym: Colin Campbell, q.v.
Paydirt. Ward, 1931
This Yellow Slave. Ward, 1933 [Saud. Arab.]
The Triall Case. Ward, 1932

DURIS, GENE
Real Endings. Manor, 1978

DURRANT, DIGBY. 1926-   . Ref: CA. SC: Hamish Oath = HO. Set: Eng.
Addle. Owen, 1980
Trunch. Bachman, 1978 HO
With My Little Eye. Gollancz, 1975; St. Martin's, 1978 HO

DURRANT, THEO. Byline on a collaborative novel by California members of the Mystery Writers of America, reportedly under the guidance of Anthony Boucher, q.v.
The Marble Forest. Knopf, 1951; Wingate, 1951. Also published as: The Big Fear. Popular Library, 1953 [Calif.]

DURRENMATT, FRIEDRICH. 1921-   . See: FRIEDRICH DUERRENMATT.

DURST, PAUL. 1921-   . Pseudonyms: Peter Bannon, John Chelton, qq.v. Ref: CA. SC: Michael Carmichael = MC.
Backlash. Cassell, 1967 MC
Badge of Infamy. Cassell, 1968 MC
Die, Damn You! Lion, 1952

DURSTON, P. E. H. Born in NYC; editor and writer of articles.
Mortissimo. Random, 1967; Macdonald, 1968 [Rome]

DU SOE, ROBERT C(OLEMAN). 1892-1958.
The Devil Thumbs a Ride. McBride, 1938 [Calif.]

DUSTON, MERLE
-The Wind in Our Hands. Harlo, 1966

DUTHOIT, EUNICE H.
Death Takes the Stump. Phoenix (London), 1946

DUTTON, CHARLES J(UDSON). 1888-1964. SC: John Bartley = JB; Harley Manners = HM.
Black Fog. Dodd, 1934; Hurst, 1934 HM [New Eng.]
The Circle of Death. Dodd, 1933; Hurst, 1933 HM
The Clutching Hand. Dodd, 1928 JB [Conn.]
The Crooked Cross. Dodd, 1926 JB [N.Y.]
Flying Clues. Dodd, 1927; Lane, 1927 JB [New Eng.]
The House by the Road. Dodd, 1924; Lane, 1924 JB [Vt.]
Murder in a Library. Dodd, 1931; Hurst, 1931 HM
Murder in the Dark. Brentano's (London), 1929 (U.S. title?)
Out of the Darkness. Dodd, 1922; Lane, 1922 JB [N.Y.]
Poison Unknown. Dodd, 1932. British title: The Vanishing Murderer. Hurst, 1932 HM
The Second Bullet. Dodd, 1925. British title: The Westwood Mystery. Hurst, 1926 JB [New Eng.]
The Shadow of Evil. Dodd, 1930; Hurst, 1930 HM
The Shadow on the Glass. Dodd, 1923; Jenkins, 1925 JB [R.I.]
Streaked with Crimson. Dodd, 1929 HM [New Eng.]
The Underwood Mystery. Dodd, 1921; Robinson & Birch, 1922 JB [New Eng.]
The Vanishing Murderer; see Poison Unknown
The Westwood Mystery; see The Second Bullet

DUTTON, JAMES S., JR.
Underground. Zebra, 1977

DUVAL, HENRI
The Devil in Her. Laurie, 1946
Mayfair Nights. Hamilton, 1946
Passion's Victim. Curzon, 1947
Search the Lady. Murray, 1946
She Vamped a Strangler. Curzon, 1946
Tortured Love. Curzon, 1946

DuVAUL, VIRGINIA C. Pseudonym of Virginia (Edith) Coffman, 1914-   , q.v. Other pseudonym: Victor Cross, q.v.

DWIGHT, OLIVIA. Pseudonym of Mary Hazard, 1928-   . Ref: CC.
Close His Eyes. Harper, 1961 [Midwest, acad.]

DWYER, DEANNA. Pseudonym of Dean R(ay) Koontz, 1945-   , q.v. Other pseudonyms: David Axton, Brian Coffey, K. R. Dwyer, Leigh Nichols, Anthony North, qq.v.
Children of the Storm. Lancer, 1972
Dance with the Devil. Lancer, 1973 [N.Y.]
The Dark of Summer. Lancer, 1972
The Demon Child. Lancer, 1971
Legacy of Terror. Lancer, 1971 [Pitt.]

DWYER, JAMES FRANCIS. 1874-1952.
Cold Eyes. Methuen, 1934

DWYER, K. R. Pseudonym of Dean R(ay) Koontz, 1945-   , q.v. Other pseudonyms: David Axton, Brian Coffey, Deanna Dwyer, Leigh Nichols, Anthony North, qq.v.
Chase. Random, 1972; Barker, 1974
Dragonfly. Random, 1975; Davies, 1977
Shattered. Random, 1973; Barker, 1974

DWYER-JOYCE, ALICE (LOUISE). 1913-   . Ref: CA.
-Cry the Soft Rain. Hale, 1972; St. Martin's, 1973
The Glitter-Dust. Hale, 1977; St. Martin's, 1978
Lachlan's Woman. Hale, 1979; St. Martin's, 1979
-The Moonlit Way. Hale, 1974; St. Martin's, 1974 [Ire.]
The Rainbow Glass. Hale, 1973; St. Martin's, 1973 [Ire.]
Reach for the Shadows. Hale, 1972; St. Martin's, 1973 [Ire.]
-The Storm of Wrath. Hale, 1977; St. Martin's, 1978
-The Strolling Players. Hale, 1975; St. Martin's, 1975

DYAN, JOHN
Exit—the Killer. Paul, ca.1938

DYAR, C. W. See: Charles Howard Montague, 1858-1889.

DYAR, HARRISON GRAY. 1866-1929.
-Diamonds Going and Coming. Stratford, 1926

DYE, CHARLES. 1927-1955
Prisoner in the Skull. Abelard (NYC), 1952; Abelard (London), 1960

DYE, WILLIAM H. Born in Pa.; reporter and feature writer in the Far East, bookseller, steelworker.
The Devil's Cameo. Exposition, 1956 [Cleve.]

DYER, CHARLES RAYMOND. 1928-   . Byline also: Raymond Dyer, q.v. Ref: CA.
Time, Murderer, Please. English Theatre Guild, 1962 (3-act play.)

DYER, GEORGE (BELL). 1903-1978. Ref: CA, CC, MP. S: Catalyst Club = CC.
Adriana. Scribner, 1939. British title: The Mystery at Martha's Vineyard. Heinemann, 1939 [Mass.]
The Catalyst Club. Scribner, 1936; Heinemann, 1937 CC [S.F.]
The Five Fragments. Houghton, 1932; Skeffington, 1933 [S.F.]
The Long Death. Scribner, 1937; Heinemann, 1938 CC [S.F.]
The Mystery of Martha's Vineyard; see Adriana
The People Ask Death. Scribner, 1940; Heinemann, 1940 CC [S.F.]
A Storm Is Rising. Houghton, 1934; Skeffington, 1934 [Pa.]
The Three-Cornered Wound. Houghton, 1931; Skeffington, 1932 [Calif.]

DYER, (CHARLES) RAYMOND. 1928-   . Byline also: Charles Raymond Dyer, q.v. Wanted—One Body! English Theatre, 1961 (3-act play.)

DYSON, JOHN
The Prime Minister's Boat Is Missing. Angus, 1974

E

"E.7". Pseudonym.
Romance of a Spy. Hurst, 1947

E., W. T. Pseudonym of W. T. Eady.
I.D.B.; or, The Adventures of Solomon Davis on the Diamond Fields and Elsewhere. Chapman, 1887 [S. Afr.]

EACHUS, IRV
Raid on the Bremerton. Viking, 1980 [L.A.]

EADES, M(AUD) L. SC: Winston Barrows = WB. Set: Eng.
The Crown Swindle. Jenkins, 1925 WB
In Another Man's Shoes. Jenkins, 1936
The Torrington Square Mystery. Jenkins, 1932 WB

EADIE, ARLTON.   -1935.
The Carnival of Death. Fiction House, 1935
The Crimson Query. Jarrolds, 1929
The Death Express. Fiction House, 1935
Her Lover's Peril. Fiction House, 1935
Heroine of the Desert. Fiction House, 1935
The League of the Lotus. Fiction House, 1935
Murder Manor. Fiction House, 1935
Murder on the Wing. Fiction House, 1935
The Murillo Mystery. Fiction House, 1935
The Phantom Lover. Fiction House, 1935
The Phantom of the Films. Fiction House, 1935
The Trail of the Cloven Hoof. Skeffington, 1935
-The Veiled Vampire. Fiction House, 1937

EADY, W. T. Pseud: W. T. E., q.v.

EAGLE, JOHN
The Hoodlums. Avon, 1953 [Chi.]

EAMES, D.
Say It with Violence. Bear Hudson, 1944

EAMES, ROWLAND A.
The Lady Is in Danger. Morris, 1947

EARL, LAWRENCE. 1915-   . Ref: CA.
Risk. Harrap, 1969

EARLIE, M(AY) A(GNES). Pseudonym of May Agnes (Early) Fleming, 1840-1880, q.v. Other pseudonym: Cousin May Carleton, q.v.
Eulalie; or, The Wife's Tragedy. Brady, 1866

EARLY, CHARLES. Writer for theatre, films and magazines.
The Tigers Are Hungry. Morrow, 1967; Rapp & Whiting, 1968

EARLY, ROBERT. 1940-   .
A Time of Madness. Graham (Rhodesia), 1977; Star, 1978 [Rhod.]

EAST, FRED. 1895-   . Pseudonym: Fred Orpet, q.v.

EAST, MICHAEL. Pseudonym of Morris L(anglo) West, 1916-   , q.v.
The Concubine; see McCreary Moves In
McCreary Moves In. Heinemann, 1958. U.S. title: The Concubine. Dell, 1958. Reprinted in Britain under the U.S. title: Four Square, 1967. Reprinted under this title as by Morris L. West: New English Library, 1973. Reprinted under original title as by Morris L. West: Heinemann, 1974 [Indon.]
The Naked Country. Heinemann, 1960; Dell, 1961. Reprinted as by Morris L. West: Heinemann, 1974

EAST, ROGER. Pseudonym of Roger d'Este Burford, 1904-   . Joint pseudonym with Oswell Blakeston, 1907-   , q.v.: "Simon", q.v. SC: Colin Knowles, in at least those marked CK.
The Bell Is Answered. Collins, 1934

Candidate for Lilies. Collins, 1934; Knopf, 1934
Detectives in Gum Boots. Collins, 1936 CK
Kingston Black. Collins, 1960
Murder Rehearsal. Collins, 1933; Knopf, 1934 CK
The Mystery of the Monkey-Gland Cocktail. Putnam (London & NYC), 1932
The Pearl Choker. Collins, 1954 [Venez.]
The Pin Men. Hodder, 1963
Twenty-Five Sanitary Inspectors. Collins, 1935 [W.I.]

EASTERLING, NARENA. Pseudonym: Renee Easterling, q.v.

EASTERLING, RENEE. Pseudonym of Narena Easterling.
A Strange Way Home. Pageant, 1952

EASTMAN, ELIZABETH. 1905- . Born on Cape Cod; teacher and ss writer.
The Mouse with Red Eyes. Farrar, 1948; Heinemann, 1950. Also published as: His Dead Wife. Lion, 1950 [NYC]

EASTMAN, ROBERT (E.). 1913- . Ref: CA.
Pendulum. Harcourt, 1979 [Cleve.]

EASTMAN, ROY O. 1883- .
The Mysteries of Blair House. Conjure House, 1948 [NYC]

EASTON, JOHN
Dog-Face. Allan, 1927. Revised edition: Eyre, 1937 [Tib.]
Ferrol Bond. Putnam (London & NYC), 1933 [India]
-Matheson Fever. Allan, 1928
-Old Granstock. Grayson, 1934
Red Sap. Putnam (London & NYC), 1930. Revised edition: Eyre, 1938 [Tib.]

EASTON, LAWRENCE
The Driven Flesh. Ace, 1955 [Ida.]

EASTON, M. G.
-The House by the Bridge. Lane, 1906

EASTON, MICHAEL
Solent Intrigue. Stockwell, 1969

EASTON, NAT. SC: Bill Banning = BB. Set: Eng.
Always the Wolf. Boardman, 1957 BB
Bill for Damages. Boardman, 1958; Roy, 1958 BB
A Book for Banning. Boardman, 1959; Roy, 1959 BB
Forgive Me, Lovely Lady. Boardman, 1961 BB
Frangipani. Boardman, 1958
Mistake Me Not. Boardman, 1958; Roy, 1959 BB
Moment on Ice. Boardman, 1960
Nothing for Nothing. Boardman, 1958
One Good Turn. Boardman, 1957 BB
Quick Tempo. Boardman, 1960 BB
Right for Trouble. Boardman, 1960 BB

EASTVALE, MARGARET
As the Sparks Fly. Crest, 1975 [Eng., 1800s]

EASTWICK, MRS. EGERTON
The Rubies of Rajmar; or, Mr. Charlecote's Daughters. Newnes, 1895

EASTWOOD, HELEN (BAKER). 1892- . Pseudonym: Oliver Baxter, q.v.
Fatal Ring of Light. Hale, 1976

EASTWOOD, JAMES. 1918- . Foreign correspondent and author of numerous TV and feature films. SC: Anna Zordan = AZ.
The Chinese Visitor. Cassell, 1965; Coward, 1965 AZ
Come Die with Me. Macmillan (London), 1970. U.S. title: Diamonds Are Deadly. McKay, 1969 AZ
-Deadline. Dakers, 1952 (Novelization of the movie.)
Diamonds Are Deadly; see Come Die with Me
Henry in a Silver Frame. Macmillan (London), 1972; McKay, 1972
Little Dragon from Peking. Cassell, 1967; Coward, 1967. Also published as: Seduce and Destroy. Pan, 1969; Dell, 1968 AZ
Murder Inc. Dakers, 1952 (Novelization of the movie.)
Seduce and Destroy; see Little Dragon from Peking

EATOCK, MARJORIE. 1927- . Ref: CA.
Haunted Heirloom. Popular Library, 1975 [Ill.]

The Ivory Tower. Curtis, 1972
Too Many Candles. Popular Library, 1979
The Wedding Journey. Dell, 1980

EATON, FRANCES U.
A Fearless Investigator. McClurg, 1896

EATON-BACK, MRS. B. Pseudonym: Derek Vane, q.v.

EBERHARD, FREDERICK G(EORGE). 1889- . Born in Indiana; received an M.D. from Northwestern U. SC: Chief of Police Sutherland = S.
The Microbe Murders. Macaulay, 1935 S [NYC]
The Secret of the Morgue. Macaulay, 1932
The Skeleton Talks. Macaulay, 1933
Super-Gangster. Macaulay, 1932 [N.Y.]
The 13th Murder. Macaulay, 1931 S [NYC]

EBERHARDT, WALTER F. 1891?-1935.
A Dagger in the Dark. Morrow, 1932 [NYC]
The Jig-Saw Puzzle Murder. Grosset, 1933 [NYC]

EBERHART, MIGNON G(OOD). 1899- . Ref: CA, CC, DD, EM, MP, TC. SC: Susan Dare = SD; Sarah Keate & Lance O'Leary = K&O; Sarah Keate = SK.
Another Man's Murder. Random, 1957; Collins, 1958 [Fla.]
Another Woman's House. Random, 1947; Collins, 1948 [N.Y.]
The Bayou Road. Random, 1979; Collins, 1979 [1863, New Or.]
Brief Return. Collins, 1939
Call After Midnight. Random, 1964; Collins, 1965 [NYC]
Casa Madrone. Random, 1980; Collins, 1980 [1906, S.F.]
The Cases of Susan Dare. Doubleday, 1934; Lane, 1935 ss SD
The Chiffon Scarf. Doubleday, 1939; Collins, 1940 [New Mex.]
The Crime at Honotassa; see The Cup, the Blade or the Gun
The Crimson Paw. Hammond, 1959 (Three novelets, two included in the U.S. collection Deadly Is the Diamond, q.v., the third uncollected in the U.S.)
The Cup, the Blade or the Gun. Random, 1961. British title: The Crime at Honotassa. Collins, 1962
Danger in the Dark. Doubleday, 1937. British title: Hand in Glove. Collins, 1937 [Ill.]
Danger Money. Random, 1975; Collins, 1975 [N.Y.]
The Dark Garden. Doubleday, 1933. British title: Death in the Fog. Lane, 1934 [Chi.]
Dead Men's Plans. Random, 1952; Collins, 1953 [Chi.]
Deadly Is the Diamond. Dell, 1951 (One of Dell's 10¢ pb series.)
Deadly Is the Diamond. Random, 1958 (Four novelets, one previously published in book form as above, two each collected in the British volumes Five of My Best, and The Crimson Paw, qq.v.)
Death in the Fog; see The Dark Garden
El Rancho Rio. Random, 1970; Collins, 1971 [Nev.]
Enemy in the House. Random, 1962; Collins, 1963 [Jam.]
Escape the Night. Random, 1944; Collins, 1945 [Calif.]
Fair Warning. Doubleday, 1936; Collins, 1936 [Ill.]
Family Fortune. Random, 1976; Collins, 1977 [ca.1860, W. Va.]
Five of My Best. Hammond, 1949 (Five novelets, two included in the U.S. collection Deadly Is the Diamond, q.v., the other three uncollected in the U.S.; one about S.D.)
Five Passengers from Lisbon. Random, 1946; Collins, 1946 [ship]
From This Dark Stairway. Doubleday, 1931; Heinemann, 1932 K&O [hosp.]
The Glass Slipper. Doubleday, 1938; Collins, 1938 [Chi., hosp.]
Hand in Glove; see Danger in the Dark
The Hangman's Whip. Doubleday, 1940; Collins, 1941 [Wis.]
Hasty Wedding. Doubleday, 1938; Collins, 1939 [Chi.]
The House by the Sea. Pockettes, 1972
House of Storm. Random, 1949; Collins, 1949 [Carib.]
The House on the Roof. Doubleday, 1935; Collins, 1935 [Chi.]
Hunt with the Hounds. Random, 1950; Collins, 1951 [Va.]
Jury of One. Random, 1960; Collins, 1961 [New Eng.]

Man Missing. Random, 1954; Collins, 1954 SK [West]
The Man Next Door. Random, 1943; Collins, 1944 [Wash. D.C.]
Melora. Random, 1959; Collins, 1960. Also published as: The Promise of Murder. Dell, 1961 [NYC]
Message from Hong Kong. Random, 1969; Collins, 1969
Murder by an Aristocrat. Doubleday, 1932. British title: Murder of My Patient. Lane, 1934 K&O
Murder in Waiting. Random, 1973; Collins, 1974 [Conn.]
Murder of My Patient; see Murder by an Aristocrat
The Mystery of Hunting's End. Doubleday, 1930; Heinemann, 1931 K&O [Neb.]
Never Look Back. Random, 1951; Collins, 1951 [NYC]
Nine O'Clock Tide. Random, 1978; Collins, 1978 [L.I.]
The Patient in Room 18. Doubleday, 1929; Heinemann, 1929 K&O [hosp.]
The Pattern. Doubleday, 1937; Collins, 1937. Also published as: Pattern of Murder. Popular Library, 1948 [Midwest]
Pattern of Murder; see The Pattern
Postmark Murder. Random, 1956; Collins, 1956 [Chi.]
The Promise of Murder; see Melora
R.S.V.P. Murder. Random, 1965; Collins, 1966 [NYC]
Run Scared. Random, 1963; Collins, 1964
Speak No Evil. Random, 1941; Collins, 1941 (This is an expanded version of Strangers in Flight, q.v.)
Strangers in Flight. Bantam (Los Angeles), 1941 (Expanded version: Speak No Evil, q.v.)
Two Little Rich Girls. Random, 1972; Collins, 1972 [NYC]
Unidentified Woman. Random, 1943; Collins, 1945 [Fla.]
The Unknown Quantity. Random, 1953; Collins, 1953 [N.Y.]
While the Patient Slept. Doubleday, 1930; Heinemann, 1930 K&O
The White Cockatoo. Doubleday, 1933; Lane, 1933 [Fr.]
The White Dress. Random, 1946; Collins, 1947 [Fla.]
Wings of Fear. Random, 1945; Collins, 1946 [Mex. City]
With This Ring. Random, 1941; Collins, 1942 [La.]
Witness at Large. Random, 1966; Collins, 1967 [L.I.]
Wolf in Man's Clothing. Random, 1942; Collins, 1943 SK [Mass.]
Woman on the Roof. Random, 1967; Collins, 1968 [NYC]

EBERSOHN, WESSEL (SCHALK). 1940- . Ref: CA.
A Lonely Place to Die. Gollancz, 1979; Pantheon, 1979 [S. Afr.]
-Store Up the Anger. Gollancz, 1980

EBERT, ARTHUR FRANK. 1902- . Pseudonym: Frank Arthur, q.v.

EBY, LOIS (CHRISTINE), 1908- . See also: next entry.
Nurse on Nightmare Island. Lancer, 1966

EBY, LOIS (CHRISTINE), 1908- , and JOHN C(HESTER) FLEMING, 1906-1964. Both born in Indiana; first cousins and jointly authors of novels, radio and screenplays. See also: previous entry.
Blood Runs Cold. Dutton, 1946 [L.A.]
The Case of the Malevolent Twin. Dutton, 1946. Also published as: The Case of the Wicked Twin. Mystery Novel Classic, 194? [Wyo.]
The Case of the Wicked Twin; see The Case of the Malevolent Twin
Death Begs the Question. Abelard, 1952; Abelard-Schuman (London), 1959 [L.A.]
Hell Hath No Fury. Dutton, 1947 [L.A.]
The Velvet Fleece. Dutton, 1947 [Calif.]

ECCLES, CHARLOTTE O'CONOR. -1911. Pseudonym: Hal Godfrey, q.v.

ECHARD, MARGARET
Before I Wake. Doubleday, 1943 [Calif.]
The Dark Fantastic. Doubleday, 1947
I Met Murder on the Way. Doubleday, 1965; Hale, 1967 [Ky.]
If This Be Treason. Doubleday, 1944 [Oreg.]
A Man Without Friends. Doubleday, 1940
Stand-In for Death. Doubleday, 1940 [L.A.]
Who Killed Frankie Leash? Curtis, 1973 [Calif.]

EDELMAN, MAURICE. 1911-1975. Ref: CA.
  A Call on Kuprin. Longmans, 1959; Lippincott, 1959 [Russ.]
  A Dream of Treason. Wingate, 1954; Lippincott, 1955
  The Fratricides. H. Hamilton, 1963; Random, 1963

EDELSTEIN, MORTIMER S. See: Marion K. Sanders, -1977.

EDEN, DOROTHY (ENID). 1912-1982. Pseudonym: Mary Paradise, q.v. Ref: CA, TC. Set: largely Eng.
  Afternoon for Lizards. Hodder, 1962. U.S. title: Bridge of Fear. Ace, 1966 [Australia]
  An Afternoon Walk. Hodder, 1971; Coward, 1971
  Bella. Hodder, 1964. U.S. title: Ravenscroft. Coward, 1965 [Eng., 1800s]
  The Bird in the Chimney. Hodder, 1963. U.S. title: Darkwater. Coward, 1964
  Bride by Candlelight. Macdonald, 1954; Ace, 1972 [N.Z.]
  Bridge of Fear; see Afternoon for Lizards
  The Brooding Lake; see Lamb to the Slaughter
  Cat's Prey. Macdonald, 1952; Ace, 1967 [N.Z.]
  Crow Hollow. Macdonald, 1950; Ace, 1967
  Darkwater; see The Bird in the Chimney
  Darling Clementine. Macdonald, 1955. U.S. title: Night of the Letter. Ace, 1967
  The Daughters of Ardmore Hall; see The Schoolmaster's Daughters
  The Deadly Travelers. Macdonald, 1959; Ace, 1966
  Death Is a Red Rose. Macdonald, 1956; Ace, 1970
  -The House in Hay Hill. Coronet, 1977; Crest, 1976 ss
  Lady of Mallow; see Samantha
  Lamb to the Slaughter. Macdonald, 1953. U.S. title: The Brooding Lake. Ace, 1966 [N.Z.]
  The Laughing Ghost. Macdonald, 1943; Ace, 1968
  -A Linnet Singing. Pockettes, 1972
  Listen to Danger. Macdonald, 1958; Ace, 1967
  The Marriage Chest. Hodder, 1965; Coward, 1966, as by Mary Paradise [Sp.]
  -The Millionaire's Daughter. Hodder, 1974; Crest, 1978
  -Never Call It Loving. Hodder, 1966; Crest, 1976
  Night of the Letter; see Darling Clementine
  The Pretty Ones. Macdonald, 1957; Ace, 1966
  Ravenscroft; see Bella
  Samantha. Hodder, 1960. U.S. title: Lady of Mallow. Coward, 1962 [Eng., 1800s]
  The Schoolmaster's Daughters. Macdonald, 1946. U.S. title: The Daughters of Ardmore Hall. Ace, 1968
  The Shadow Wife. Hodder, 1968; Coward, 1968 [Den.]
  -The Singing Shadows. Paul, 1940
  Sleep in the Woods. Hodder, 1960; Coward, 1961 [Eng., 1800s]
  The Sleeping Bride. Macdonald, 1959; Ace, 1969
  -Speak to Me of Love. Hodder, 1972; Crest, 1977
  -The Storrington Papers. Hodder, 1979; Coward, 1978
  Summer Sunday. Macdonald, 1946
  The Vines of Yarrabee. Hodder, 1969; Coward, 1969
  The Voice of the Dolls. Macdonald, 1950; Ace, 1971
  Waiting for Willa. Hodder, 1970; Coward, 1970 [Stock.]
  Walk into My Parlour. Macdonald, 1947
  We Are for the Dark. Macdonald, 1944
  Whistle for the Crows. Hodder, 1962; Ace, 1962 [Ire.]
  Winterwood. Hodder, 1967; Coward, 1967
  Yellow Is for Fear and other stories. Severn, 1977; Ace, 1968 ss

EDEN, FRANCIS I. S.
  The Ninth Life. Arcadia, 1969

EDEN, MATTHEW. Born in Canada; newspaper correspondent. SC: Mark Savage = MS.
  Conquest Before Autumn. Abelard, 1973 MS
  Countdown to Crisis. Hale, 1968 MS
  Dangerous Exchange. Hale, 1969 MS
  Document of the Last Nazi. H. Hamilton, 1979
  Flight of Hawks. Hale, 1969; Abelard, 1970 MS
  The Gilt-Edged Traitor. Abelard (London & NYC), 1972 MS
  The Man Who Fell. Hale, 1970

  The Murder of Lawrence of Arabia. New English Library, 1980; Crowell, 1980 [1930s, Saud. Arab.]

EDGAR, ALFRED. 1896-   . Pseudonym: Barre Lyndon, q.v. SC (with many other authors): Sexton Blake, in all titles, all published by Amalgamated Press. Set: Eng.
  The Cup Final Mystery. 1927
  Lawless Justice. 1922
  The Power of the Unknown. 1922
  The Secret of the Safe. 1923
  The Secret of the Tong; see The Sign in the Sky
  The Sign in the Sky. 1922. Also published as: The Secret of the Tong, as by H. Gregory. 1936

EDGAR, GEORGE. 1877-   .
  The Red Colonel. Mills, 1913; Appleton, 1913

EDGAR, JOSEPHINE. Pseudonym of Mary Mussi, 1907-   . At least some of these titles were published in England as romances and in the U.S. as gothics. Ref: CA. Set: Eng.
  The Dancer's Daughter. Collins, 1968; Dell, 1970 [Eng., past]
  The Dark Tower. Collins, 1966
  The Devil's Innocents. Collins, 1972; Dell, 1975
  Duchess. Macdonald, 1976
  The Lady of Wildersley. Macdonald, 1975; PB, 1977
  My Sister Sophie. Collins, 1964; PB, 1974
  Shadows in the Sun. Collins, 1957
  The Stranger at the Gate. Collins, 1973; PB, 1975
  Time of Dreaming. Collins, 1968; PB, 1974

EDGAR, KEITH. Born in Toronto; reporter and press photographer.
  Honduras Double Cross. Howard, 1944 [ship]
  I Hate You to Death. Howard, 1944 [NYC]
  The Incendiary Blonde. Howard, 1946

EDGAR, KEN. 1925-   . Ref: CA.
  Frogs at the Bottom of the Well. Playboy, 1976; Hamlyn, 1979

EDGAR, STANLEY WALTER
  Perchance to Kill. Bishop, 1979

EDGE, SPENCER
  A Maker of Ware. Cassell, 1913

EDGELEY, CYRIL. Pseudonym: Brian Rodney, q.v.

EDGINTON, MAY [MRS. HELEN MARION EDGINTON BAILEY]. 1883-1957.
  The Adventures of Napoleon Prince. Cassell (London & NYC), 1912 ss

EDGLEY, LESLIE. 1912-   . Pseudonym: Robert Bloomfield, q.v. Joint pseudonym with Mary Edgley: Brook Hastings, q.v.
  The Angry Heart. Doubleday, 1947; Barker, 1949. Also published as: Tracked Down. Ace, 1954 [L.A.]
  Diamonds Spell Death; see The Runaway Pigeon
  A Dirty Business. Putnam, 1969; Hale, 1970 [L.A.]
  False Face. Simon, 1947; Barker, 1948
  Fear No More. Simon, 1946; Barker 1948 [Calif.]
  Final Reckoning. Hale, 1971
  The Judas Goat. Doubleday, 1952; Barker, 1953 [L.A.]
  One Blonde Died; see The Runaway Pigeon
  The Runaway Pigeon. Doubleday, 1953. British title: Diamonds Spell Death. Barker, 1954. Also published as: One Blonde Died. Bestseller, 1954
  Tracked Down; see The Angry Heart

EDGLEY, MARY. Joint pseudonym with Leslie Edgley, 1912-   , q.v.: Brook Hastings, q.v.

EDHOLM, CHARLTON L(AWRENCE). See: Frank Condon, 1882-1940.

EDINGTONS, THE [ARLO CHANNING EDINGTON, 1890-1953, and CARMEN BALLEN EDINGTON, 1894-   ]. SC: Captain Smith, in at least those marked S.
  -Drum Madness, with Marianne Barrett. Cassell, 1934
  The House of the Vanishing Goblets. Century, 1930. British title: Murder to Music. Collins, 1930 S [L.A.]
  The Monk's Hood Murders. Cosmopolitan, 1931; Collins, 1931 S [L.A.]

  Murder to Music; see The House of the Vanishing Goblets
  The Studio Murder Mystery. Reilly & Lee, 1929; Collins, 1929 S [L.A.]

EDMISTON, HELEN (JEAN MARY). 1913-   . Pseudonym: Helen Robertson, q.v. Ref: CA, CC.
  The Shake-Up. Macdonald, 1962

EDMONDS, HARRY (MORETON SOUTHEY). 1891-   .
  Across the Frontiers. Ward, 1936
  The Clockmaker of Heidelberg; or, The Strange Affair of Hugh Brodie, Englishman. Macdonald, 1949
  The Death Ship; or, The Tragedy of the "Valmeira". Lane, 1933
  The East Coast Mystery. Lane, 1934
  The North Sea Mystery: A Story of Naval Intelligence Work. Ward, 1930
  The Orphans of Brandenburg. Ward, 1953
  -The Red Desert. Ward, 1931
  Red Invader. Ward, 1933
  The Riddle of the Straits. Ward, 1931
  The Rockets—Operation Manhattan. Macdonald, 1951
  The Trail of the Lonely River. Ward, 1934 [Russ.]
  Wind in the East. Ward, 1935

EDMUNDS, BRENT. SC: Pete Marvin, in all titles.
  Beware the Crimson Cord! Laurie, 1956 [Colo.]
  A Gun in My Back. Laurie, 1955
  Ride a Dead Horse. Laurie, 1955
  Spiders in the Night. Laurie, 1956

EDQVIST, DAGMAR. 1903-   .
  Black Sister. Doubleday, 1963; Joseph, 1963 (Translation of "Den Svarta Systern." Stockholm, 1961.)

EDSON, J(OHN) T(HOMAS), 1928-   , and PETER CLAWSON. Ref for Edson: CA.
  Blonde Genius. Corgi, 1973

EDWARD, MARIE ELAINE
  Amberleigh. Paperback Library, 1967
  Lenore. Paperback Library, 1966
  Terror Manor. Paperback Library, 1967

EDWARDS, ALEXANDER. Pseudonym of Leonore Fleischer. Other pseudonym: Mike Roote, q.v. See also: Philip Fenty.
  The Black Bird. Warner, 1975; Star, 1976 (Novelization of the movie.) [S.F.]
  The Last of Sheila. Paperback Library, 1973 (Novelization of the movie.) [Fr.]
  McQ. Paperback Library, 1974 (Novelization of the movie.) [Seattle]

EDWARDS, ANNE (JOSEPHSON). 1927-   . Ref: CA.
  Alexandrovitch Is Missing! see Miklos Alexandrovitch Is Missing
  Child of Night. Random, 1975 [Richmond]
  Haunted Summer. Coward, 1972; Hodder, 1973 [Switz.]
  Miklos Alexandrovitch Is Missing. Coward, 1970. British title: Alexandrovitch Is Missing! Hodder, 1970 [Paris]
  Raven Wings. Millington, 1977
  The Survivors. Holt, 1968; Allen, 1968 [Eng., Switz.]

EDWARDS, BLAIR
  Murder Blues. Modern Fiction, 1946

EDWARDS, CHARMAN. Pseudonym of Frederick Anthony Edwards, 1896-   . Other pseudonym: Julius Van Dyke, q.v. SC: Percy Aloysius Huff, in at least those marked PH. Set: Eng.
  -A Big, Strong Man! Low, 1923
  The Blue Macaw. Ward, 1935 PH
  Confetti for a Killing. Ward, 1937 PH
  -Derision. Ward, 1926
  -Dolly's Walk. Ward, 1950
  -Drama of Mr. Dilly. Hale, 1939
  -Drink No Deeper. Ward, 1933
  Fear Haunts the Roses. Ward, 1936 PH
  -Gabriel Sounds for Africa. Hale, 1938
  Give Me a Ship! Ward, 1928
  High Street. Ward, 1928
  No Coffins in China. Hale, 1937
  -Rainbrother. Ward, 1927
  -Sir Richard Penniless. Ward, 1928
  -Tall Pines in Paddington. Ward, 1949
  Ten Thirteen. Ward, 1936 PH
  Terror Ship. Ward, 1935 PH
  -Windfellow. Ward, 1925
  -The Yellow Wagon. Ward, 1932

EDWARDS, F. H. M. Pseudonym: Nicholas Carnac, q.v.

EDWARDS, FREDERICK ANTHONY. 1896-   .
    Pseudonyms: Charman Edwards, Julius
    Van Dyke, qq.v.

EDWARDS, GILLIAN M(ARY). 1918-   . Ref:
    CA.
    -Fatal Grace. Hale, 1978

EDWARDS, GRANT
    The Mystery of the Lyons Mail. Collins,
        1930 [Fr.]
    The Office Scandal. London Book Co.,
        1929

EDWARDS, H(ENRY) SUTHERLAND. 1828-1906.
    The Case of Reuben Malachi. Chapman,
        1886; Rand, 1886
    The Missing Man. Remington, 1885

EDWARDS, HARRY STILLWELL. 1855-1938.
    -The Marbeau Cousins. Rand, 1896
    Sons and Fathers. Rand, 1896

EDWARDS, HUGH. 1878-1952.
    All Night at Mr. Stanyhurst's. Cape,
        1933 [1783, Eng.]

EDWARDS, IRENE. Pseudonym: Elizabeth
    Barr, q.v.

EDWARDS, JAMES G. Pseudonym of James
    William MacQueen, 1900-   . Ref:
    MP. SC: Insp. Victor Bondurant =
    VB. Set: hosp.
    But the Patient Died. Doubleday, 1948;
        Cherry Tree, 1949 VB [Chi.]
    Death Among Doctors. Doubleday, 1942
        VB [Chi.]
    Death Elects a Mayor. Doubleday, 1939
        VB
    F Corridor. Doubleday, 1936 VB [Chi.]
    Murder at Leisure. Doubleday, 1937
        VB
    Murder in the Surgery. Doubleday, 1935
        VB [Chi.]
    The Odor of Bitter Almonds. Doubleday,
        1938 VB [Chi.]
    The Private Pavilion. Doubleday, 1935
        VB [Chi.]

EDWARDS, JANE (CAMPBELL). 1932-   . Ref:
    CA.
    The Houseboat Mystery. Bouregy, 1965

EDWARDS, LEE. Pseudonym of Edward J.
    Levy.
    Ask Me No Questions. French (NYC),
        1949 (3-act play.)

EDWARDS, MIKE
    Assassin. Berkley, 1976

EDWARDS, NORMAN. Set: Eng.
    Dilemma. Jenkins, 1936
    The Frightened Village. Jenkins, 1937

EDWARDS, PAUL. House name. Titles by Man-
    ning Lee Stokes, q.v. = #; titles by
    Robert Lory = *; titles by Paul Eiden
    = +. SC: John Eagle (The Expediter),
    in all titles.
    The Brain Scavengers. Pyramid, 1973;
        New English Library pb, 1976 #
    The Deadly Cyborgs. Pyramid, 1975 +
        [Tib.]
    The Death Devils. Pyramid, 1974 *
    The Fist of Fatima. Pyramid, 1975; New
        English Library pb, 1976 * [Libya]
    The Glyphs of Gold. Pyramid, 1974 *
    The Green Goddess. Pyramid, 1975 +
    The Holocaust Auction. Pyramid, 1975
        * [India]
    The Ice Goddess. Pyramid, 1974 +
        [Arctic]
    The Laughing Death. Pyramid, 1973; New
        English Library pb, 1976 * [Far
        East]
    Needles of Death. Pyramid, 1973; New
        English Library pb, 1976 # [Mong.]
    Operation Weatherkill. Pyramid, 1975 +
    Poppies of Death. Pyramid, 1975 +
    Silverskull. Pyramid, 1975 #
    Valley of Vultures. Pyramid, 1973; New
        English Library pb, 1976 # [Ecua.]

EDWARDS, RACHELLE
    The Captain's Lady. Hale, 1977; Zebra,
        1977 [Eng., past]
    -Devil's Bride. Hale, 1976; Crest, 1979
    -A Hasty Marriage. Crest, 1978 (British
        title?)
    -In the Shadow of Tyburn. Hale, 1980
    -Lord Heathbury's Revenge. Hale, 1979;
        Fawcett, 1980
    -Miranda's Folly. Hale, 1978; Crest,
        1979
    -The Outrageous Lady Caroline. Hale,
        1980
    -Reckless Masquerade. Hale, 1975
    The Secret of Monk's House. Hale, 1978
    -The Silken Net. Hale, 1978; Crest, 1979
    -The Smithfield Bargain. Hale, 1980

    -A Spy for Napoleon. Hale, 1977
    -The Thief of Hearts. Hale, 1973; Crest,
        1977
    -An Unequal Match. Hale, 1974
    -Wager for Love. Hale, 1979; Fawcett,
        1980

EDWARDS, REX
    Dixon of Dock Green. Pan, 1974 (7 ss
        from the BBC-TV series.)

EDWARDS, RICHARD KEMBLE
    The Mystery of the Miniature. Clark,
        1908

EDWARDS, SAMUEL. Pseudonym of Noel B(er-
    tram) Gerson, 1914-   , q.v. Other
    pseudonym: Leon Phillips, q.v.
    The Caves of Guernica. Praeger, 1975
    The Exploiters. Praeger, 1974; Heine-
        mann, 1975 [Mid. East]

EDWARDS, STAFFORD. ca.1900-   . Born in
    N.Y.; executive of electrical manu-
    facturing corporation.
    Money Order Murder. Vantage, 1963 [NYC]

EDWARDS, WALTER. Pseudonym of Walter
    Shute,   -ca.1940. Wrote (with
    many other authors): Sexton Blake, in
    all titles, which were published by
    Amalgamated Press. Set: Eng.
    The Ambush. 1931
    The Barber's Shop Crime. 1936
    The Case of the Murdered Pawn Broker.
        1935
    The Fatal Memoirs. 1934
    The Great Stores Crime. 1933
    The Great Stores Mystery. 1940
    The Hiker's Secret. 1933
    The Man in Brown. 1935
    The Murder on the Moor. 1932
    The Mystery of the Marchers. 1937
    The Newspaper Seller's Secret. 1938
    The Secret of the Cellar. 1939
    The Secret of the Identification Par-
        ade. 1936

EDWIN, MARIBEL. 1895-   .
    Sound Alibi. Ward, 1935; Hillman, 1938
    The Valiant Jester. Ward, 1930
    Windfall Harvest. Ward, 1931

EFFINGER, GEORGE ALEC. 1947-   . Ref:
    CA.
    Felicia. Berkley hb, 1976 [La.]

EGAN, LESLEY. Pseudonym of (Barbara) Eli-
    zabeth Linington, 1921-   , q.v.
    Other pseudonyms: Anne Blaisdell,
    Dell Shannon, qq.v. SC: Jesse Falken-
    stein = JF; Vic Varallo = VV. Set:
    L.A., in all titles.
    Against the Evidence. Harper, 1962;
        Gollancz, 1963 JF
    The Blind Search. Doubleday, 1977; Gol-
        lancz, 1977 JF
    The Borrowed Alibi. Harper, 1962; Gol-
        lancz, 1963 VV
    A Case for Appeal. Harper, 1961; Gol-
        lancz, 1962 JF,VV
    A Choice of Crimes. Doubleday, 1980;
        Gollancz, 1981 VV
    Detective's Due. Harper, 1965; Gol-
        lancz, 1966 VV
    A Dream Apart. Doubleday, 1978; Gol-
        lancz, 1978 VV
    The Hunters and the Hunted. Doubleday,
        1979; Gollancz, 1980 VV
    In the Death of a Man. Harper, 1970;
        Gollancz, 1970 JF
    Look Back on Death. Doubleday, 1978;
        Gollancz, 1979 JF
    Malicious Mischief. Harper, 1971; Gol-
        lancz, 1972 VV
    Motive in Shadow. Doubleday, 1980; Gol-
        lancz, 1980 JF
    My Name Is Death. Harper, 1964; Gol-
        lancz, 1964 JF
    The Nameless Ones. Harper, 1967; Gol-
        lancz, 1968 VV
    Paper Chase. Harper, 1972; Gollancz,
        1973 JF
    Run to Evil. Harper, 1963; Gollancz,
        1964 VV
    Scenes of Crime. Doubleday, 1976; Gol-
        lancz, 1976 VV
    A Serious Investigation. Harper, 1968;
        Gollancz, 1969 JF
    Some Avenger, Rise! Harper, 1966; Gol-
        lancz, 1967 JF
    The Wine of Violence. Harper, 1969;
        Gollancz, 1970 VV

EGERTON, DENISE. Pseudonym of Denise Dug-
    gan, 1930-   .
    Design for an Accident. Hodder, 1957;
        Washburn, 1958 [Fr.]
    The Hour of Truth. Hodder, 1959; Wash-
        burn, 1960 [Sp.]
    It Couldn't Be Caroline. Hodder, 1961

    A Man That I Love. Hodder, 1955
    No Thoroughfare. Hodder, 1954; Coward,
        1955

EGERTON, FRANCIS CHARLES GRANVILLE. Pseu-
    donym: Charles Granville, q.v.

EGERTON, J. KENILWORTH
    A Soul Laid Bare. Street, 1906 [NYC]

EGERTON-THOMAS, CHRISTOPHER
    A Taste of Conspiracy. Carlyle, 1978

EGGAR, ARTHUR
    The Hatanee. Murray, 1906 [Burma]

EGGLESTON, EDWARD. 1837-1902.
    The Mystery of Metropolisville. Judd,
        1873; Routledge, 1873

EGLETON, CLIVE (FREDERICK). 1927-   .
    Pseudonym: John Tarrant, q.v. Ref:
    CA, TC. SC: David Garnett = DG, in
    novels set in future Eng.
    Backfire. Hodder, 1979; Atheneum, 1979
    The Black Windmill; see Seven Days to a
        Killing
    The Bormann Brief; see The October Plot
    The Judas Mandate. Hodder, 1972; Cow-
        ard, 1972 DG
    Last Post for a Partisan. Hodder, 1971;
        Coward, 1971 DG
    The Mills Bomb. Hodder, 1978; Atheneum,
        1978
    The October Plot. Hodder, 1974. U.S.
        title: The Bormann Brief. Coward,
        1974 [WWII]
    A Piece of Resistance. Hodder, 1970;
        Coward, 1970 DG
    Seven Days to a Killing. Hodder, 1973;
        Coward, 1973. Also published as: The
        Black Windmill. Crest, 1974 [Paris]
    Skirmish. Hodder, 1975; Coward, 1975
    State Visit. Hodder, 1976

EHRENFELD, DAVID. See: Carol K. Mack.

EHRLICH, COLLIS
    Attack. Ballantine, 1980

EHRLICH, J(ACOB) W(ILBURN). 1900-1971.
    See: Brad Williams, 1918-   .

EHRLICH, JACK [JOHN GUNTHER EHRLICH].
    1930-   . Ref: CA. SC: Robert
    Flick, in at least those marked RF.
    Bloody Vengeance. PB, 1973
    Court Martial. Pyramid, 1959
    Cry, Baby. Dell, 1962 RF [N.Y.]
    The Drowning. PB, 1970; Hale, 1972
        [L.I.]
    The Girl Cage. Dell, 1967 RF
    Parole. Dell, 1960 RF
    Revenge. Dell, 1958
    Slow Burn. Dell, 1961 RF [N.Y.]

EHRLICH, MAX (SIMON). 1909-   . Ref: CA.
    The Bond; see Reincarnation in Venice
    Dead Letter; see First Train to Babylon
    Deep Is the Blue. Doubleday, 1963;
        Gollancz, 1964
    First Train to Babylon. Harper, 1955;
        Gollancz, 1955. Also published as:
        Dead Letter. Corgi, 1958. And as:
        The Naked Edge. Corgi, 1961
    The Naked Edge; see First Train to
        Babylon
    Reincarnation in Venice. Simon, 1979.
        British title: The Bond. Mayflower,
        1980 [Venice]
    The Reincarnation of Peter Proud.
        Bobbs, 1974; Allen, 1975
    Spin the Glass Web. Harper, 1952;
        Corgi, 1957 [NYC]
    The Takers. Harper, 1961; Gollancz,
        1961

EHRLICHMAN, JOHN (DANIEL). 1925-   .
    Ref: CA.
    -The Company. Simon, 1976; Collins, 1976
        [Wash. D.C.]
    -The Whole Truth. Simon, 1979; Collins,
        1979 [Wash. D.C.]

EHRMANN, MAX. 1872-1945.
    -A Fearsome Riddle. Bowen-Merrill, 1901;
        Stevens, 1901
    The Mystery of Madeline Le Blanc.
        Cooperative, 1900

EICHLER, ALFRED. 1908-   . Born in NYC;
    advertising copywriter. SC: Martin
    Ames = MA; Insp. Knickman = K.
    The Big Bruiser. Phoenix, 1941. British
        title: The Gentle Giant. Swan, 1943
    Bury in Haste. Arcadia, 1957 K [NYC]
    Death at the Mike. Lantern, 1946; Ham-
        mond, 1954 K,MA [NYC]
    Death of an Ad Man. Abelard, 1954. Bri-
        tish title: A Hearse for the Boss.
        Hammond, 1956 K,MA [NYC]

Death of an Artist. Arcadia, 1955; Hammond, 1955 K,MA [NYC]
Election by Murder. Lantern, 1947 MA [L.A.]
The Gentle Giant; see The Big Bruiser
A Hearse for the Boss; see Death of an Ad Man
Moment for Murder. Arcadia, 1956; Hammond, 1957 K [Conn.]
Murder in the Radio Department. Gold Label, 1943; Hammond, 1953 K,MA [NYC]
Murder Off Stage. Hammond, 1963 (U.S. title?)
Pipeline to Death. Hammond, 1962 (U.S. title?) MA

EIDEN, PAUL. Pseudonyms: Paul Edwards, Don Romano, qq.v.

EIKER, MATHILDE. 1893- . Pseudonym: March Evermay, q.v.

EINSTEIN, CHARLES. 1926- . Ref: CA.
The Blackjack Hijack. Random, 1976 [Las Veg.]
The Bloody Spur. Dell, 1953. Also published as: While the City Sleeps. Dell, 1956 [NYC]
-The Last Laugh. Dell, 1956
The Naked City. Dell, 1959; World Distributors, 1960 (ss version of TV scripts by Stirling Silliphant, 1918- , q.v.) [NYC]
No Time at All. Simon, 1957; Davies, 1958 [N.Y.]
While the City Sleeps; see The Bloody Spur
Wiretap! Dell, 1955

EISENBERG, HERSHEY (H.). 1927- . Ref: CA.
The Reinhard Action. Morrow, 1980

EISINGER, JO
The Walls Came Tumbling Down. Coward, 1943; Jarrolds, 1945 [NYC]

EISNER, SIMON. Pseudonym of C(yril) M. Kornbluth, 1923-1958. Other pseudonym: Jordan Park, q.v.
The Naked Storm. Lion, 1952

EKBERGH, IDA DIANA. Writer of articles for newspapers and periodicals.
The Mysterious Chinese Mandrake, and other stories. Pageant, 1954 ss

ELAND, CHARLES. Pseudonym of Charles Adolph von Rimanoczy, 1906- . SC: Mark Randall, in all titles.
The Desperate Search. Hale, 1971
Dossier Closed. Hale, 1970
The Gold Hijack. Hale, 1973

ELDER, EVELYN. Pseudonym of Milward Rodon Kennedy Burge, 1894-1968. Other pseudonym: Milward Kennedy, q.v. Joint pseudonym with Archibald Gordon Macdonell, 1895-1941, q.v.: Robert Milward Kennedy, q.v.
Angel in the Case. Methuen, 1932
Murder in Black and White. Methuen, 1931

ELDER, MARK. 1935- . Ref: CA.
-Jedcrow. GM, 1974
The Prometheus Operation. McGraw, 1980; Hale, 1981 [1945, U.S.]
Wolf Hunt. Ballantine, 1976 [Okla.]

ELDER, MICHAEL (AIKEN). 1931- . Ref: CA.
The Phantom in the Wings. Murray, 1957

ELDREDGE, GILBERT. SC: Thibault Parew and Chips Carpenter, in both titles.
Death for the Surgeon. Phoenix, 1939 [Calif.]
Murder in the Stratosphere. Phoenix, 1940 [Calif.]

ELDRIDGE, GEORGE DYRE. 1848-1928.
In the Potter's House. Doubleday, 1908; Methuen, 1908
The Millbank Case. Holt, 1905; Nash, 1907 [Maine]

ELDRIDGE, JIM
Down Payment on Death. Hale, 1972

ELDRIDGE, MARK
Lightning May Strike Anywhere. Vantage, 1968

ELDRIDGE, RUBY
The Legend of the Grey Castle. Vantage, 1969

ELDRIDGE, WILLIAM TILLINGHAST. 1881-1941.
Hilma. Dodd, 1907; Stevens, 1907
Meryl. Dodd, 1908; Stevens, 1908

ELEGANT, ROBERT S(AMPSON). 1928- . Ref: CA.
A Kind of Treason. Holt, 1966; Piatkus, 1980 [Viet Nam]

ELGIN, MARY. Pseudonym of Dorothy Mary Stewart, 1917-1965. Ref: CA.
Highland Masquerade; see Return to Glenshael
A Man from the Mist; see Visibility Nil
Return to Glenshael. Hodder, 1965. U.S. title: Highland Masquerade. Mill, 1966 [Scot.]
Visibility Nil. Hodder, 1964. U.S. title: A Man from the Mist. Mill, 1965 [Scot.]
The Wood and the Trees. Hodder, 1967; Mill, 1967

EL HAKIM, TEWFIK
Maze of Justice. Harvill, 1947 (Translation from the Arabic.) [Egypt]

ELIADE, MIRCEA. 1907- . Ref: CA.
-Two Tales of the Occult. Herder, 1970 (2 novelets) [India]

ELIADES, DAVID. Joint pseudonym with Robert Forrest-Webb, 1929- , q.v.: David Forrest, q.v.

ELIAS, ALBERT J. 1920- . Ref: CA.
The Bowman Test. Dell, 1977 [NYC]
The Sonora Mutation. Avon, 1978; Hamlyn, 1979 [Mex.]

ELIAS, DAVID. SC: Nell Bartlett, in at least those marked NB.
The Cause of the Screaming. Hammond, 1953 NB [U.S.]
Dress Up and Die. Hammond, 1955
The Gory Details. Hammond, 1954 NB [NYC]

ELIOT, ANNE. Pseudonym of Lois Dwight Cole, 1902-1979. Ref: CA.
The Dark Beneath the Pines. Hawthorn, 1974; Hale, 1976 [N.Y.]
Incident at Villa Rahmana. Hawthorn, 1972; Hale, 1975 [Mor.]
Return to Aylforth. Meredith, 1967 [Eng.]
Shadows Waiting. Meredith, 1969 [Fr.]
Stranger at Pembroke. Hawthorn, 1971 [Miss.]

ELIOT, MAJOR GEORGE F(IELDING). 1894-1971. Ref: CA. SC: Dan Fowler, in all titles.
Federal Bullets. Caslon, 1936; Cassell, 1936 [Kan. City]
The Navy Spy Murders. Dodge, 1937 [R.I.]
The Purple Legion. Caslon, 1936; Cassell, 1937

ELIOT, HENRY WARE. 1879-1947. Pseudonym: Mason Deal, q.v.

ELIOT, JESSICA. Pseudonym of Lois Ann Brown and Barbara Levy.
Home to the Highlands. Dell, 1980

ELKINGTON, E(RNEST) WAY. 1872- . See also: Dick Donovan.
-The Lucky Shot. Treherne, 1902
The Rugged Way. Drane, 1903
-The Two Forces. Long, 1907

ELLERBECK, ROSEMARY (ANNE L'ESTRANGE). Born in S. Afr., lived since childhood in England; editor and writer.
Hammersleigh. Corgi, 1977; McKay, 1976
Inclination to Murder. Hodder, 1965
Rose, Rose...Where Are You? Hale, 1978; Coward, 1978 [Fr.]

ELLERTON, EDWARD
A Fatal Resemblance. Lennon, 1885

ELLERY, JAN. SC: Adrienne Bishop = AB.
Death on the Circuit. Zebra, 1979 [Sp.]
Family Affairs. Zebra, 1979 [New Eng.]
High Strung. Zebra, 1980 AB
The Last Set. Zebra, 1979 AB

ELLETT, HAROLD PINCTON. 1882- . Pseudonym: Nigel Burnaby, q.v.

ELLIK, RONALD D. 1938-1968. Joint pseudonym with Frederic Langley: Frederic Davies, q.v.

ELLIN, STANLEY (BERNARD). 1916- . Ref: CA, CC, EM, MC, TC.
The Big Night; see Dreadful Summit
The Bind. Random, 1970. British title: The Man from Nowhere. Cape, 1970 [Miami]
The Blessington Method, and other strange tales. Random, 1964; Macdonald, 1965 ss
Dreadful Summit. Simon, 1948; Boardman, 1958. Also published as: The Big Night. Lion, 1950 [NYC]
The Eighth Circle. Random, 1958; Boardman, 1959 [NYC]
House of Cards. Random, 1967; Macdonald, 1967 [Paris]
The Key to Nicholas Street. Simon, 1952; Boardman, 1953
Kindly Dig Your Grave, and other wicked stories. Davis, 1975 ss
The Luxembourg Run. Random, 1977; Cape, 1978
The Man from Nowhere; see The Bind
Mirror, Mirror on the Wall. Random, 1972; Cape, 1973 [NYC]
Mystery Stories. Simon, 1956; Boardman, 1957. Also published as: Quiet Horror. Dell, 1959. And as: The Specialty of the House. Penguin, 1968 ss
The Panama Portrait. Random, 1962; Macdonald, 1963
Quiet Horror; see Mystery Stories
The Specialty of the House; see Mystery Stories
The Specialty of the House and other stories. Mysterious Press, 1979 (All ss from previous collections plus uncollected ss.)
Star Light, Star Bright. Random, 1979; Cape, 1979 [Miami]
Stronghold. Random, 1975; Cape, 1975 [N.Y.]
The Valentine Estate. Random, 1968; Macdonald, 1968
The Winter After This Summer. Random, 1960; Boardman, 1961

ELLINGER, GEOFFREY. SC: Roger Hartley = RH. Set: Eng.
Bars of Gold. Heritage, 1935
The Blasted Acre. Smith, 1936
The Lyddon House Mystery. Jenkins, 1928
The Return of Cardannesley. Heritage, 1934 RH
The Ricksha Clue. Jenkins, 1931 [China]
The Trap in the Tunnel. Jenkins, 1931 RH

ELLINGTON, RICHARD. ca.1914-1980. Ref: CA. SC: Steve Drake, in all titles.
Exit for a Dame. Morrow, 1951; Boardman, 1954 [NYC]
It's a Crime. Morrow, 1948; Cassell, 1956
Just Killing Time. Morrow, 1953; Boardman, 1954. Also published as: Shakedown. Bantam, 1955 [NYC]
Shakedown; see Just Killing Time
Shoot the Works. Morrow, 1948; Cassell, 1950 [NYC]
Stone Cold Dead. Morrow, 1950; Cassell, 1952 [Vir. Is.]

ELLIOT, JOHN MICHAEL
The Danube Convenant. Dell, 1977 [Austria]

ELLIOTT, BRUCE (WALTER GARDNER LIVELY STACEY). 1915?-1973. Ref: CA.
One Is a Lonely Number. Lion, 1952 [Ohio]
You'll Die Laughing. Five Star, 1945

ELLIOTT, FRANCIS PERRY. 1861-1924.
The Haunted Pajamas. Bobbs, 1911

ELLIOTT, GEORGE
The Case of the Missing Airmen. Swan, 1944 (Martin Speed.)
The Mystery of the Missing Corpses. Swan, 1945

ELLIOTT, JANE
Darkening Night. Popular Library, 1975

ELLIOTT, JANICE. 1931- . Ref: CA.
The Singing Head. Secker, 1968

ELLIOTT, PEERS
The Mystery of the Black Dagger. Hale, 1952
The Pay Out. Hale, 1940
The Silent Bullet. Hale, 1941 [Australia]
Trust the Police. Hale, 1939

ELLIOTT, R. C.
The Blackmailer. Hornsey, 1938
The Phantom Bat. Amalgamated, 1930 (Sexton Blake.)
Sabotage. Gray, 1956

ELLIOTT, ROBIN
The House of Dogs. Jenkins, 1948

ELLIOTT, SUMNER LOCKE. 1917- . Ref: CA.
Careful, He Might Hear You. Harper, 1962; Gollancz, 1963
The Man Who Got Away. Harper, 1972; Joseph, 1973

ELLIOTT, W. GERALD
    Nine Days' Blunder. Jenkins, 1933
    Treasure on the Broads. Jenkins, 1933

ELLIOTT, WILLIAM J(AMES). 1886-   .
    SC: Anthony England, in at least
        those marked AE; Royston Frere, in at
        least those marked RF; Ed Gunning, in
        at least those marked EG; Bren Hardy,
        in at least those marked BH.
    "And Worms Have Eaten Them..." Swan,
        1940
    Bren Hardy Again. Swan, 1945 BH
    Bren Hardy, Tough Dame. Swan, 1942 BH
        [U.S.]
    -The Demon of Desire. Swan, 1940
    Dope Devils. Swan, 1942 RF [NYC]
    False Pretenses. Mellifont, 1934
    Footprints in the Sand. Eldon, 1937
    Freak Racket. Swan, 1941 EG
    Gunning in England. Swan, 1946 EG
    Kissed Corpse. Swan, 1946
    -Lost Souls in Bohemia. Swan, 1941
    Mystery of Me...? Swan, 1944
    £1,000,000. Swan, 1949
    The Running Killer. Swan, 1946 RF
    Sheer Silk. Swan, 1946 AE
    Shot-Silk. Swan, 1943 AE
    "Silk!" Swan, 1942 AE
    The Silver Panther. Gramol, 1934
    Snatched Dame. Swan, 1942 EG [Chi.]
    Spun Silk. Swan, 1947 AE
    The Suicide Circle. Gramol, 1934
    Tough Ghosts. Swan, 1941 [U.S.]
    Triggers Are Trumps. Swan, 1942 EG
    The Wolf of Corsica. Mellifont, 1932
    The Yellow Fiend. Mellifont, 1932

ELLIOTT-CANNON, ARTHUR ELLIOTT.
    1919-   . Pseudonyms: Elliott Can-
    non, Nicholas Forde, qq.v.

ELLIS, DAVID
    Make Me a Widow. French (London), 1965
    (3-act play.)

ELLIS, EDWARD S(YLVESTER). 1840-1916.
    Pseudonym: J. G. Bethune, q.v.
    The Eye of the Sun. Rand, 1897; Weekly
        Telegraph Novels (abridged), n.d.
        [Eng.]
    The Heart of Oak Detective. Westbrook,
        n.d. [Tex.]

ELLIS, J. C.
    Black Fame. Hutchinson, 1926 ss
    Blackmailers & Co. Selwyn, 1929
    The Night of Mystery. Selwyn, 1928

ELLIS, J(OHN) BRECKENRIDGE. 1870-1956.
    The Mysterious Dr. Oliver. Macaulay,
        1929 [Calif.]
    The Red Box Clue. Revell, 1902
    The Third Diamond. Badger, 1913

ELLIS, JAMES J(OSEPH)
    A Bad Name; or, The Brand of Cain.
        Author's Cooperative, 1890

ELLIS, JULIE (M.). Pseudonyms: Susan Mar-
    ino, Susan Marvin, Susan Richard,
    qq.v.
    Eden. Simon, 1975
    Evil at Hillcrest. Avon, 1971
    The Girl in White. PB, 1976
    The Jeweled Dagger. Dell, 1973
    Kara. Dell, 1974
    -Long Dark Night of the Soul. PB, 1978
    The Magnolias. Simon, 1976
    Rendezvous in Vienna. Dell, 1976
        [Vienna]
    Savage Oaks. Simon, 1977
    Walk a Tightrope. Dell, 1975 [Maine]
    Walk into Darkness. Dell, 1973
    Wexford. PB, 1976 [1852, New Or.]

ELLIS, KENNETH. M.
    Dolores Divine, Guilty or Innocent?
        Grosset, 1931 [N.Y.]
    The Trial of Vivienne Ware. Grosset,
        1931

ELLIS, MEL(VIN RICHARD). 1912-   . Ref:
    CA.
    No Man for Murder. Holt, 1973 [South]

ELLIS, N. A. TEMPLE. See: N. A. Temple-
    Ellis, pseudonym of Neville Aldridge
    Holdaway, 1894-   .

ELLIS, RON(ALD WALTER). 1941-   . Ref:
    CA.
    Murder First Class. Hale, 1980

ELLIS, VIRGINIA
    Death Comes Like a Thief. Arcadia, 1952
        [Calif., acad.]

ELLIS, WILLIAM. 1918-   . Ref: CA.
    The Knife Edge. Macmillan (London),
        1972; Walker, 1973 [ship]
    No Will to Die. Walker, 1975

ELLIS, WILLIAM SENIOR. Joint pseudonym
    with Emeric Hulme-Beaman, q.v.: Ben
    Strong, q.v.

ELLISON, EARL
    The Big Deal. Spencer, 1952
    Blood of the Dragon. Hamilton Stafford,
        1948
    Corpses Don't Care. Curzon, 1946
    Corrupt City. Spencer, 1953
    Desert Intrigue. Hamilton Stafford,
        1949
    Design for Danger. Spencer, 1952
    Don't Mourn for Me. Spencer, 1953
    Framed. Spencer, 1953
    Gun Fever. Burrell, 1947
    Guns and Saddles. Hamilton Stafford,
        1948
    A Lady on Loan. Spencer, 1950
    Midnight Alibi. Spencer, 1952
    Miss Gloria Gets Wise. Spencer, 1949
    No Escape. Spencer, 1953
    Paid in Full. Spencer, 1953
    Rita Makes a Killing. Spencer, 1949
    Too Much Ambition. Spencer, 1953
    Too Smart to Live. Spencer, 1953
    Undercover Agent. Spencer, 1953
    Unwilling Guest. Spencer, 1952

ELLISON, HARLAN (JAY). 1934-   . Ref:
    CA.
    The Deadly Streets. Ace, 1958; Digit,
        1959
    Deathbird Stories. Harper, 1975; Mil-
        lington, 1977 ss, one criminous
    Gentleman Junkie and Other Stories of
        the Hung-Up Generation. Regency, 1961
        ss
    The Juvies. Ace, 1961
    Memos from Purgatory. Regency, 1961
    No Doors, No Windows. Pyramid, 1975 ss
    Rockabilly. GM, 1961; Muller pb, 1963
    Rumble. Pyramid, 1958

ELLSON, HAL
    Blood on the Ivy. Pyramid, 1971
    Duke. Scribner, 1949 [NYC]
    Games. Ace, 1967 (Novelization of the
        movie.)
    The Golden Spike. Ballantine, 1952.
        British title: Reefer Boy. Spearman,
        1955
    I'll Fix You. Popular Library, 1956
        [NYC]
    Jailbait Street. Monarch, 1959
    A Killer's Kiss. Hillman, 1959 [Mex.]
    The Knife. Lancer, 1961
    A Nest of Fear. Ace, 1961
    Nightmare Street. Belmont, 1964
    Reefer Boy; see The Golden Spike
    Rock. Ballantine, 1955
    Stairway to Nowhere. Ballantine, 1959
    Summer Street. Ballantine, 1953
    Tell Them Nothing. Ballantine, 1956 ss
    That Glover Woman. Award, 1967
    This Is It. Popular Library, 1956
    Tomboy. Scribner, 1950 [NYC]

ELMAN, RICHARD (M.). 1934-   . Ref: CA.
    The Breadfruit Lotteries. Methuen
        (NYC), 1980 [Jam.]

ELMONT, LOUISE
    The Egremont Mystery. Stockwell, 1953
        ss

ELSNA, HEBE. Pseudonym of Dorothy Phoebe
    Ansle. Other pseudonyms: Laura Con-
    way, Lyndon Snow, qq.v. Titles by
    this author were apparently published
    in England as romances; those also
    published in the U.S. as gothics are
    listed below.
    Cast a Long Shadow. Collins, 1976; Dut-
        ton, 1978, as by Laura Conway
        [Eng., 1905]
    The Cherished Ones. Collins, 1974. U.S.
        title (?): Don't Shut Me Out. Dutton,
        1977, as by Laura Conway
        [Eng., ca.1910]
    Dark Dream; see Distant Landscape
    Distant Landscape. Collins, 1975. U.S.
        title (?): Dark Dream. Dutton, 1976,
        as by Laura Conway
    Don't Shut Me Out; see The Cherished
        Ones
    Strange Visitor. Hale, 1956; Saturday
        Review Press, 1975, as by Laura Con-
        way
    Take Heed of Loving Me. Collins, 1970;
        Saturday Review Press, 1976, as by
        Laura Conway

ELSON, JANE
    The Romance of the Castle. Lane, 1800
        [Wales]

ELSTOW, T. FRANCIS
    A Human Vampire. Modern, 193?
    The Scarlet Gargoyle. Modern, 193?
    Yellow Fangs. Modern, 1938

ELSWORTHY, A(LEXANDER) L(OCKHART)
    -Burdock. Hutchinson, 1937
    Death Glides In. Hutchinson, 1935
        [Egypt]

ELTON, EDWARD
    The Murder Chase. Hutchinson, 1929
    -She Drew the Bolt. Hutchinson, 1928

ELTON, JAMES T.
    Assignment in Tokyo. Badger, 1960
    The Quest of the Seeker. Badger, 1958

ELVESTAD, SVEN (CHRISTOPHER SVENDSON).
    1894-1934. SC: Asbjorn Krag = Osborne
    Crag = AK.
    The Case of Robert Robertson. Lane,
        1930; Knopf, 1930 (Translation of
        "Faenomenet Robert Robertson." Oslo,
        1923, as by Stein Riverton.) [Den.]
    The Man Who Plundered the City.
        McBride, 1924 (Translation of "Man-
        den Som Vilde Plyndre Kristiania."
        Oslo, 1915, as by Stein Riverton.)
        AK [Nor.]
    The Mystery of the Abbe Montrose. Jar-
        rolds, 1924 (Translation of "Mon-
        trose." Oslo, 1917, as by Stein Ri-
        verton.) AK

ELVY, CLARA EVELYN
    The Magic of Chez Finnie. Stockwell,
        1967

ELWIN, MALCOLM. 1902-   .
    The Little Hangman. Macdonald, 1953

ELY, DAVID. Pseudonym of David Eli Lili-
    enthal, Jr., 1927-   . Ref: CA.
    Poor Devils. Houghton, 1970
    Seconds. Pantheon, 1963; Deutsch, 1964
        [NYC]
    Time Out. Delacorte, 1968; Secker, 1968
        ss
    The Tour. Delacorte, 1967; Secker, 1967
    Trot. Pantheon, 1963; Secker, 1963
        [Paris]

ELZINGA, KENNETH GERALD. 1946-   . Joint
    pseudonym with William Breit: Mar-
    shall Jevons, q.v.

EMERICK, LUCILLE. See also: Francis
    Swann.
    -The City Beyond. Holt, 1952
    The Web of Evil. Doubleday, 1948 [1887,
    Pa.]

EMERSON, (ALAN) DAVID. 1900-   . Ref:
    CA.
    A Murder in the Family. Hutchinson,
        1970 [1840, Eng.]

EMERSON, DONALD C. Pseudonym: Donald
    Conger, q.v.

EMERSON, JOHN. 1874-1956. See: Robert
    (Melville) Baker, 1868-1929.

EMERSON, P(ETER) H(ENRY). 1856-1936.
    The Blood Eagle, and other mystery
    tales. Melrose, 1925 ss

EMERY, CHARLES
    D Is for Danger. French (NYC), 1960
    (1-act play.)
    One of Us. French (NYC), 1947 (Play.)

EMERY, (RUSSELL) GUY. 1908-   .
    Front for Murder. Macrae-Smith, 1947;
    Boardman, 1948 [S.F.]

EMERY, J. INMAN
    The Luck of Udaipur. Jarrolds, 1925
    The Tiger of Baragunga. Jarrolds, 1924;
    Putnam, 1925 [India]

EMERY, SAMUEL
    At Nine Bells. Dutton, 1932; Paul, 1932
        [ship]
    The House That Whispered. Dutton, 1929;
    Paul, 1929 [Vt.]

EMMET, E(RIC) R(EVELL)
    The Great Detective Puzzle Book. Barnes
    (NYC & London), 1979 puzzle ss

EMSLEY, LLOYD
    False Freedom. Hale, 1971

ENDFIELD, MERCEDES. Pseudonym of Bela
    William von Block, 1922-   . Other
    pseudonyms: Jonathan Black, E. L.
    McGinnis, qq.v. S: Ms. Squad, in both
    titles.
    Lucky Pierre. Bantam, 1975
    On the Brink. Bantam, 1975

ENDICOTT, JOHN S.
    Crime Inc. Fiction League, 1932 [NYC]

ENDICOTT, STEPHEN. Pseudonym of W(alter) Adolphe Roberts, 1886-1962, q.v.
Mayor Harding of New York. Mohawk, 1931 [NYC]
-The Strange Career of Bishop Sterling. Meteor, 1932

ENDORE, GUY. 1900-1970. Ref: CA, CC.
Detour at Night. Simon, 1959. British title: Detour Through Devon. Gollancz, 1959
Detour Through Devon; see Detour at Night
The Man from Limbo. Farrar, 1930; Gollancz, 1931
Methinks the Lady—. Duell, 1945; Cresset, 1947. Also published as: Nightmare. Dell, 1956
Nightmare; see Methinks the Lady—
The Werewolf of Paris. Farrar, 1933; Long, 1934 [Paris, 1871]

ENEFER, DOUGLAS. SC: Sam Bawtry, in at least those marked SB; Cannon (novelizations of the TV series; see also: Paul Denver) = C; Dale Shand, in at least those marked DS.
The Avengers. Consul, 1963
The Dark Kiss. World Distributors, 1965; Leisure, 1973 DS [NYC]
The Days of Vengeance. World Distributors, 1961
The Deadline Dolly. Hale, 1970 DS
The Deadly Quiet. World Distributors, 1961; Leisure, 1973 DS [NYC]
Farewell, Little Sister. Corgi, 1978 C
The Gilded Kiss. Hale, 1969 DS
The Girl Chase. Hale, 1968 DS
Girl in a Million. Hale, 1970 SB
Girl in Arms. Hale, 1968 SB
Girl on the M6. Hale, 1973 SB
The Goodbye Blonde. Hale, 1980
Ice in the Sun. Hale, 1977
The Jade Green Judy. Hale, 1974
Lakeside Zero. Hale, 1973 SB
The Last Door. World Distributors, 1959
The Last Train to Rock Ferry. Hale, 1975 SB
The Long Chance. World Distributors, 1961; Leisure, 1973 DS [NYC]
The Long Hot Night. Hale, 1967 DS
A Long Way to Pitt Street. Hale, 1972 SB
Pacific North-West. Hale, 1975 DS
The Painted Death. Hale, 1966 DS
Pierhead 627. Hale, 1968 DS
Riverside 90. Hale, 1970; Roy, 1970 SB
Sammy. World Distributors, 1963
The Screaming Orchid. Hale, 1972 DS
Seven Nights at the Resort. Hale, 1976 DS
The Shining Trap. World Distributors, 1965
Shoot-Out. Corgi, 1979 C
The Sixth Raid. Hale, 1979
13 Steps to Lime Street. Hale, 1969 SB

ENGLAND, EDWARD HAROLD
Chateau Rocca. New Horizon, 1979

ENGLAND, GEORGE ALLAN. 1877-1936.
-Adventure Isle. Century, 1926
The Alibi. Small, 1916 [N.Y.]
-The Gift Supreme. Doran, 1916
The Greater Crime. Cassell, 1917 (U.S. title?) [NYC]
Pod, Bender & Co. McBride, 1916; Laurie, 1916

ENGLAND, JANE. Pseudonym of Vera Murdock Stuart Jervis, 1897- .
-Flight into Danger. Hurst, 1950
-House of Fears. Hurst, 1951
-Safe Conduct. Hurst, 1942
Trader's License. Hurst, 1936

ENGLANDER, SEYMOUR
The Remus Code. New Horizon, 1978

ENGLISH, ARNOLD
Edge of Violence. Vega, 196? [NYC]

ENGLISH, ERNEST I(VAN)
Killers Come Cheap. Hale, 1967
Who Needs Forever? Hale, 1974

ENGLISH, (EMMA) JEAN (MARTIN). 1937- . Ref: CA.
Dark Moonshine. Beagle, 1974
The Devices of Darkness. Doubleday, 1976; Hale, 1978
The Scarlet Tower. Beagle, 1974

ENGLISH, RICHARD. Pseudonym of Richard Murray, 1910-1957.
The Sugarplum Staircase. Simon, 1947 [NYC]

ENGSTRAND, STUART (DAVID). 1905-1955.
More Deaths Than One. Messner, 1955 [Calif.]
-The Sling and the Arrow. Creative Age, 1947 [Calif.]

ENRIGHT, RICHARD E(DWARD). 1871-1953.
The Borrowed Shield. Watt, 1925 [NYC]
Vultures of the Dark. Brentano's, 1924; Brentano's (London), 1926 [NYC]

ENSOR, (ALICK CHARLES) DAVID(SON). 1906- .
Verdict Afterwards. Jenkins, 1960

EPHESIAN. Pseudonym of Carl Eric Bechhofer Roberts, 1894-1949. See also: George Goodchild, 1888-1969. SC: A.B.C. Hawkes, in all titles. Set: Eng.
A.B.C. Investigates. Jarrolds, 1937 ss
A.B.C. Solves Five. Hodder, 1937 ss
A.B.C.'s Test Case. Jarrolds, 1936

EPPLEY, LOUISE and REBECCA GAYTON
Murder in the Cellar. Morrow, 1931; Grayson, 1932 [Pa.]

EPSTEIN, EDWARD JAY. 1935- . Ref: CA.
Cartel. Putnam, 1978; Arrow, 1979 [Iran, 1952-3]

EPSTEIN, EDWARD Z. See: Joe Morella.

ERBSTEIN, CHARLES E.
The Show-Up. Covici, 1926 ss

ERDMAN, PAUL E(MIL). 1932- . Ref: CA, TC.
The Billion Dollar Killing; see The Billion Dollar Sure Thing
The Billion Dollar Sure Thing. Scribner, 1973. British title: The Billion Dollar Killing. Hutchinson, 1973 [Switz.]
The Silver Bears. Scribner, 1974; Hutchinson, 1974

ERICKSON, NANCY WATSON
Splinters of Fear. Avon, 1960 [NYC]

ERICSON, LIZ
Deadly Advice. Zebra, 1979 [Calif.]

ERICSON, WALTER. Pseudonym of Howard (Melvin) Fast, 1914- , q.v. Other pseudonym: E. V. Cunningham, q.v.
Fallen Angel. Little, 1952. Also published as: The Darkness Within. Ace, 1953. And as: Mirage, as by Howard Fast. Crest, 1965 [NYC]

ERIKSON, SIBYL CICELY ALEXANDRA DICK. Pseudonyms: Alexandra Dick, Frances Hay, qq.v.

ERLANGER, MICHAEL. 1915- . In the textile business in N.C. and NYC.
Mindy Lindy May Surprise. Random, 1969

ERNST, PAUL. 1886- . Pseudonym: Kenneth Robeson (The Avenger series), q.v. SC: Shirley Leighton (Harper) and Bill Harper = H; Lt. Jim Ryan = JR.
The Bronze Mermaid. Mill, 1952; Cassell, 1954 JR [NYC]
Hangman's Hat. Mill, 1951; Muller, 1952 JR,H [NYC]
Lady, Get Your Gun. Mill, 1955. British title: A Rose from the Dead. Cassell, 1956 H [Miami]
A Rose from the Dead; see Lady, Get Your Gun
Short of Murder. Mystery House, 1959

ERSKINE, FIRTH. Joint pseudonym of Gladys Shaw Erskine, 1895- , and Ivan Eustace Firth, 1891- .
Naked Murder. Macaulay, 1933; Butterworth, 1935 [NYC]

ERSKINE, GLADYS SHAW. 1895- . Joint pseudonym with Ivan Eustace Firth, 1891- : Firth Erskine, q.v.

ERSKINE, LAURIE YORK. 1894-1976. Ref: CA.
The Coming of Cosgrove. Appleton, 1926
The Confidence Man. Appleton, 1925
The Laughing Rider. Appleton, 1924; Hodder, 1927

ERSKINE, MARGARET. Pseudonym of Margaret Wetherby Williams. Ref: CA, CC, DD, TC. SC: Insp. Septimus Finch, in all titles. Set: Eng.
And Being Dead. Bles, 1938. U.S. title: The Limping Man. Doubleday, 1939. Also published as: The Painted Mask. Ace, 1972
Besides the Wench Is Dead. Hodder, 1973; Doubleday, 1973
The Brood of Folly. Hodder, 1971; Doubleday, 1971
Caravan of Night; see I Knew MacBean
The Case of Mary Fielding. Hodder, 1970; Doubleday, 1970
Case with Three Husbands. Hodder, 1967; Doubleday, 1967
Dead by Now. Hammond, 1953; Doubleday, 1954
The Dead Don't Speak; see Fatal Relations
Death of Our Dear One. Hammond, 1952. U.S. title: Look Behind You, Lady. Doubleday, 1952. Also published as: Don't Look Behind You. Ace, 1972
The Disappearing Bridegroom. Hammond, 1950. U.S. title: The Silver Ladies. Doubleday, 1951
Don't Look Behind You; see Death of Our Dear One
The Ewe Lamb. Hodder, 1968; Doubleday, 1968
The Family at Tammerton; see Take a Dark Journey
Fatal Relations. Hammond, 1955. U.S. title: Old Mrs. Ommanney Is Dead. Doubleday, 1955. Also published as: The Dead Don't Speak. Detective Book Club, 1955
Give Up the Ghost. Hammond, 1949; Doubleday, 1949
A Graveyard Plot; see The House of the Enchantress
Harriet Farewell. Hodder, 1975; Doubleday, 1975
The House in Belmont Square. Hodder, 1963. U.S. title: No. 9 Belmont Square. Doubleday, 1963
The House in Hook Street. Hale, 1978; Doubleday, 1977
The House of the Enchantress. Hodder, 1959. U.S. title: A Graveyard Plot. Doubleday, 1959
I Knew MacBean. Hammond, 1948; Doubleday, 1948. Also published as: Caravan of Night. Ace, 1972
The Limping Man; see And Being Dead
Look Behind You, Lady; see Death of Our Dear One
No. 9 Belmont Square; see The House in Belmont Square
Old Mrs. Ommanney Is Dead; see Fatal Relations
The Painted Mask; see And Being Dead
The Silver Ladies; see The Disappearing Bridegroom
Sleep No More. Hodder, 1958; Ace, 1969
Take a Dark Journey. Hodder, 1965. U.S. title: The Family at Tammerton. Doubleday, 1966
The Voice of Murder. Hodder, 1956; Doubleday, 1956
The Voice of the House; see The Whispering House
The Whispering House. Hammond, 1947. U.S. title: The Voice of the House. Doubleday, 1947
The Woman at Belguardo. Hodder, 1961; Doubleday, 1961

ERVIN, MARI
Death in the Yew Alley. Phoenix, 1937. Also published as: If I Die—It's Murder. Green Dragon, 194?

ESCOTT, JONATHAN. 1922- . Pseudonym: Jack S. Scott, q.v.

ESCOTT-INMAN, H(ERBERT). See: H(erbert) Escott Inman.

ESHLEMAN, JOHN M(ORTON). ca.1914- .
Graduate of U. of California; newspaperman in S.F. SC: Lt. Larry Koharik, in both titles.
The Deadly Chase; see The Long Chase
Death of a Cheat; see The Long Window
The Long Chase. Washburn, 1954. Also published as: The Deadly Chase. Mercury, 1955 [S.F.]
The Long Window. Washburn, 1953. Also published as: Death of a Cheat. Mercury, 1955 [S.F.]

ESLER, ANTHONY (JAMES). 1934- . Ref: CA.
The Blade of Castlemayne. Morrow, 1974

ESMOND, HARRIET. Joint pseudonym of John (Frederick) Burke, 1922- , q.v., and his wife. Other pseudonyms: Jonathan Burke, Robert Miall, Martin Sands, qq.v. Joint pseudonym with George Theiner, 1927- : Jonathan George, q.v.
Darsham's Folly. Collins, 1974. U.S. title: Darsham's Tower. Delacorte, 1973 [past, Eng.]
Darsham's Tower; see Darsham's Folly
The Eye Stones. Collins, 1975; Delacorte, 1975 [1800s, Eng.]
The Florian Signet. Collins, 1977; GM, 1977

ESMOND, SIDNEY
The Dead Look Down. Hutchinson, 1945
The Evil Cross. Hutchinson, 1944

E

ESSER, ROBIN. 1933-   . Ref: CA.
The Peacock's Feather. Hutchinson, 1947
Sacrament of Death. Redman, 1950
The Secret Cargo. Hutchinson, 1945
Verboten. Hutchinson, 1940

ESSER, ROBIN. 1933-   . Ref: CA.
The Hot Potato. Joseph, 1969
The Paper Chase. Joseph, 1971

ESSEX, DAVID
Betrayed. Warren, 1948
Retribution. Warren, 1949
-Secret Betrothal. Warren, 1949
Star Detective. Warren, 1948

ESSEX, LOUIS. Pseudonym of Levi Isaacs.
The Crook of Crauford Court. Amalgamated Press, 1930 (Sexton Blake.)

ESSEX, RICHARD. Pseudonym of Richard (Henry) Starr, 1878-   , q.v. SC: Lessinger = L; John Slade = JS.
Assisted by Lessinger. Jenkins, 1939 L
The Girl in Black. Tallis, 1966 (Retitled reprint of ?) JS,L
Lessinger Comes Back. Jenkins, 1935 L,L
Lessinger Laughs Last. Jenkins, 1938 L
Marinova of the Secret Service. Jenkins, 1937 L
Murder in the Bank. Jenkins, 1936 L,JS
Slade of the Yard. Jenkins, 1932; McBride, 1933 L,JS
Slade Scores Again. Jenkins, 1933; McBride, 1933 L,JS

ESTABROOKS, G(EORGE) H(OBEN). 1896?-1973. Ref: CA. See: Richard (Orson) Lockridge, 1898-1982.

ESTES, CARROLL COX
Eavesdropping on Death. Arcadia, 1952 [Dallas]
Embrace of Death; see The Moon Gate
The Moon Gate. Doubleday, 1954; Barker, 1958. Also published as: Embrace of Death. Bestseller, 1955 [Dallas]
Unhappy New Year. Doubleday, 1953 [Tex.]

ESTEVEN, JOHN. Pseudonym of Samuel Shellabarger, 1888-1954. Other pseudonym: Peter Loring, q.v. Ref: CC. SC: Insp. Rae Norse = RN; Miles Le Breton = ML.
Assurance Double Sure. Hodder, 1939
Blind Man's Night. Hodder, 1938
By Night at Dinsmore. Doubleday, 1935; Harrap, 1935 ML [New Eng.]
The Door of Death. Century, 1928; Methuen, 1929 RN [New Eng.]
Graveyard Watch. Modern Age, 1938
Voodoo. Doubleday, 1930; Hutchinson, 1930 RN
While Murder Waits. Doubleday, 1937; Harrap, 1936 ML [Maine]

ESTEY, DALE. Canadian writer.
A Lost Tale. St. Martin's, 1980; Allen, 1980 [Isle of Man, WWII]

ESTLEMAN, LOREN D. 1952-   . Ref: CA. SC: Sherlock Holmes = SH.
Dr. Jekyll and Mr. Holmes. Doubleday, 1979; Penguin, 1981 SH [1890s, Eng.]
Motor City Blue. Houghton, 1980; Hale, 1982 [Det.]
The Oklahoma Punk. Major, 1976
Sherlock Holmes vs. Dracula; or, The Adventures of the Sanguinary Count. Doubleday, 1978; New English Library, 1978 SH [1890s, Eng.]

ESTOW, DANIEL. SC: William Schaefer, in both titles.
The Moment of Fiction. Carlyle, 1979
The Moment of Silence. Carlyle, 1980

ESTRIDGE, ROBIN. Pseudonym: Philip Loraine, q.v.

ETHAN, JOHN B. SC: Victor Grant, in all titles, all set in NYC.
The Black Gold Murders. Detective Book Club, 1959
Call Girls for Murder. PB, 1960
Murder on Wall Street. Mill, 1960

ETHERIDGE, A. I.
The Elvin Court Mystery. Stockwell, 1929

ETHERIDGE, CHRISTINA
The Cranshaw Inheritance. Jove, 1979

EUSTACE, ROBERT. Pseudonym of Eustace Robert Barton, 1854-1943. See also: L. T. Meade; Dorothy L(eigh) Sayers, 1893-1957; Gertrude Warden, with whom he collaborated. Ref: MM, MP, TC.
The Human Bacillus. Long, 1907

EUSTIS, HELEN. 1916-   . Ref: CC, EM, MC, TC.
The Fool Killer. Doubleday, 1954; Secker, 1955
The Horizontal Man. Harper, 1946; H. Hamilton, 1947 [New Eng., acad.]

EVANS, ALAN. Pseudonym of Alan Stoker, 1930-   . Ref: CA.
Bannon. Cassell, 1968
The Big Deal. Hale, 1971
The End of the Running. Cassell, 1966
Mantrap. Cassell, 1967
Vicious Circle. Hale, 1970

EVANS, ALBERT EUBULE. 1839-1896. Pseudonym: Roy Tellet, q.v.

EVANS, ALFRED JOHN. 1889-   .
All's Fair on Lake Garda. Hodder, 1958
The Escaping Club. Lane, 1921
The House of Anna. Hodder, 1953
The V2 Expert. Hodder, 1956
Who's the Guy? Hodder, 1940

EVANS, CICELY LOUISE. Pseudonym. Author of stories, a play, an earlier novel; lives in Canada.
Nemesis Wife. Doubleday, 1970 [Eng.]

EVANS, CONSTANCE MAY. 1890-   . Pseudonym: Mairi O'Nair, q.v.

EVANS, DEAN. Pseudonym of George Kull. Born in N.Y.; machinist in the missile industry on the west coast.
No Slightest Whisper. Abelard, 1955. Also published as: This Kill Is Mine. Graphic, 1956 [Reno]

EVANS, E. EVERETT. 1893-1958. SC: George Hanlon, in both titles.
-Alien Minds. Fantasy Press, 1955
Man of Many Minds. Fantasy Press, 1953 [future]

EVANS, VICE ADMIRAL E(DWARD) R(ATCLIFFE) G(ARTH) R(USSELL). 1880-1957.
Spanish Death. Jarrolds, 1933

EVANS, ELAINE
Black Autumn. Lancer, 1973
A Dark and Deadly Love. Lancer, 1972
Shadowland. Lancer, 1970 [Fla.]
Wintershade. Popular Library, 1974 [W. Va.]

EVANS, ERIC JONES. See: Eric Jones-Evans.

EVANS, (FRANCIS) FALLON. 1925-   . Ref: CA.
Pistols and Pedagogues. Sheed, 1963 [Chi., acad.]

EVANS, GENE
Murder on Queer Street. Brandon, 1968

EVANS, GEORGE BIRD. 1906-   . Joint pseudonyms with Kay Harris Evans, 1906-   : Brandon Bird, Harris Evans, qq.v. Ref: CA.

EVANS, GWYN(FIL ARTHUR). 1899-1938. SC: Sexton Blake (with many other authors) = SB (all such titles published by Amalgamated Press); Chester Brett, in at least those marked CB; Quentin Drex, in at least those marked QD; Bill Kellaway, in at least those marked BK; Double O'Day, in at least those marked DO. Set: Eng.
The Abandoned Car Crime. 1931 SB
The Barton Manor Mystery. 1925. Also published as: The Curse of the Santyres. 1937 SB
The Black Cap. 1934 SB
Bluebeard's Keys. Wright, 1937 DO
The Case of the Climbing Corpse. Wright, 1939 CB
The Case of the Crimson Conjurer. 1928 SB
The Case of the Jack of Clubs. 1928 SB
The Case of the Man Who Never Slept; see The Man Who Never Slept!
The Case of the Poisoned Pen. 1927 SB
Castle Sinister. Wright, 1936
The Clue of the Missing Link. Wright, 1938 CB
Coffins for Two. Wright, 1939 DO
The Crook of Fleet Street. 1926 SB
The Crystal Cell. 1931 SB
The Curse of the Santyres; see The Barton Manor Mystery
Death in the Jungle. 1933 SB
The Death Sign. 1931 SB
Death Speaking. Wright, 1934
Dr. Sinister. 1933 SB
The Fatal Friendship. 1933 SB
The Great Waxworks Crime. 1932 SB
The Hanging Judge. Wright, 1936
Hercules, Esq. Shaylor, 1930. U.S. title: Mr. Hercules. Dial, 1931 BK
His Majesty—the Crook. Wright, 1935 QD
The Homicide Club. Shaylor, 1931; Dial, 1932 BK
The Iron Mask. Wright, 1938 DO
King of the Underworld. 1928 SB
The Man from Dartmoor. 1932 SB
The Man Who Never Slept! 1925. Also published as: The Case of the Man Who Never Slept. 1936 SB
The Man with the Scarlet Skull, and other tales. Wright, 1935 ss
The Mission of Doom. 1930 SB
Mr. Hercules; see Hercules, Esq.
Murderers Meet. Wright, 1934
The Mysterious Miss Death. Wright, 1937 CB
The Mystery of Mitcham Common. 1928 SB
The Prisoners of Peru. 1927 SB
The Return of Hercules, Esq. Wright, 1937 BK
The Riddle of the Red Dragon. Wright, 1935
The Riddle of the Turkish Baths. 1931 SB
Rogue Royal. Wright, 1936 QD
Satan Ltd. Wright, 1935; Godwin, 1935 BK
The Sign of the Saracen. Wright, 1936
The Silent Jury. 1930 SB
Sinister Castle. 1932 SB
The Sleepless Man. Wright, 1940 DO
Steel Face. 1931 SB
The Triangle of Terror. Wright, 1938 CB

EVANS, HARRIS. Joint pseudonym of George Bird Evans, 1906-   , and Kay Harris Evans, 1906-   . Other joint pseudonym: Brandon Bird, q.v.
The Pink Carrara. Dodd, 1960; Allen, 1960

EVANS, HOWEL
The Actor's Knife. Jarrolds, 1930
Crabtree House. Richards, 1919
A Girl Alone. Richards, 1917; Putnam, 1918
The Murder Club. Jarrolds, 1924; Putnam, 1925
The Murder Trap. Richards, 1925
The Sixth Commandment. Jarrolds, 1925

EVANS, HUGH AUSTIN. Pseudonym: Hugh Austin, q.v.

EVANS, JACKSON
Death Haunts the Charnel Estate. Bear Hudson, 1946

EVANS, JOHN. Pseudonym of Howard Browne, 1908-   , q.v. SC: Paul Pine = PP (also under the Howard Browne byline).
Halo for Satan. Bobbs, 1948; Boardman, 1949 PP [Chi.]
Halo in Blood. Bobbs, 1946 PP [Chi.]
Halo in Brass. Bobbs, 1949; Foulsham, 1951 PP [Chi.]
If You Have Tears. Mystery House, 1947. Also published as: Lona. Lion, 1952 [Calif.]
Lona; see If You Have Tears
Weep Not Fair Lady. Harlequin, 1950 (Canadian title of ?)

EVANS, JOHN P. and JOHN B. MANNION
A Breach of Fate. GM, 1980 [Afr.]

EVANS, JONATHAN
Misfire. Joseph, 1980; Pinnacle, 1982 [Mid. East]

EVANS, JULIA RENDEL. 1913-   . Pseudonym: Polly Hobson, q.v.

EVANS, KAY HARRIS. 1906-   . Joint pseudonyms with George Bird Evans, 1906-   : Brandon Bird; Harris Evans, qq.v. Ref: CA.

EVANS, (CYRIL) KENNETH. 1917-   . Ref: CA.
Blueprint to Kill. Hale, 1975
No Cause for Dying. Hale, 1969
Oasis of Fear. Hale, 1968; Roy, 1968 [Cairo]
A Rich Way to Die. Hale, 1973
Shadows of Violence. Hale, 1971 [Tun.]

EVANS, KENNETH L. Film studio executive and screenwriter.
A Feast for Spiders. Crowell, 1979 [L.A.]

EVANS, MARGUERITE FLORENCE HELENE JERVIS. 1894-   . Pseudonym: Oliver Sandys, q.v.

EVANS, PETER. 1926-
Megadeath. New English Library pb, 1976

EVANS, PETER. 1933-   .
    Twisted Nerve. Sphere, 1969 (Novelization of the movie.)

EVANS, PHILIP. 1944-   .
    The Bodyguard Man. Hodder, 1973
    Next Time, You'll Wake Up Dead. Hodder, 1972

EVANS, SAM. Born in New Jersey; once professional boxer, then scrap dealer during WWII, then owner of national auto parts company.
    Love, Lust and Larceny. Leason, 1949

EVANS, STUART. 1934-   .
    The Caves of Alienation. Hutchinson, 1977

EVARTS, HAL G(EORGE). 1915-   . Ref: CA.
    The Turncoat. GM, 1961 [Tib.]

EVELYN, CHARLES
    I Am a Smuggler. Cassell, 1952
    The Return of Van Weik. Cassell, 1952

EVELYN, FRANCES and LANGFORD REED, 1889-1954, q.v.
    The Prime Minister's Pyjamas. Archer, 1933

EVELYN, JOHN MICHAEL. 1916-   . Pseudonym: Michael Underwood, q.v.

EVERETT, MRS. H. D. Pseudonym: Theo Douglas, q.v.

EVERETT, PETER. 1931-   .
    A Day of Dwarfs. Spearman, 1962
    The Fetch. Cape, 1966; Simon, 1967
    The Instrument. Hutchinson, 1962
    Negatives. Cape, 1964; Simon, 1965
    Visions of Heydrich. Allen, 1979

EVERETT-GREEN, E(VELYN). 1856-1932.
    -Adventurous Annie. Paul, 1916
    -The Back Number. Paul, 1926
    -Barbed Wire. Paul, 1914
    -Billy's Bargain. Paul, 1920
    -Blackladies. Hutchinson, 1914
    -Blue Mist and Mystery. Paul, 1928
    -The Boys of Red House. Melrose, 1902
    -The Chatterton Mystery. Clarke, 1896
    -The City of the Golden Gate. Paul, 1909
    -Claud the Charmer. Paul, 1927
    -Clive Lorimer's Marriage. Paul, 1911
    -Co-Heiresses. Paul, 1909
    -The Curse of Carlyon. Wright, 1931
    -Dare Lorimer's Heritage. Hutchinson, 1891
    -Dashing Dick's Daughter. Paul, 1916
    Duckworth's Diamonds. Paul, 1912
    -A Fiery Chariot. Hutchinson, 1900
    -The Heronstroke Mystery. Religious Tract Society, 1915
    -A Holiday in a Manor House; or, Who Solved the Mystery. Biggs, 1892
    -The Mystery of Alton Grange. Nelson, 1899
    -The Secret Chamber at Chad. Nelson, 1894
    -The Secret of Maxshelling. Shaw, 1902
    -The Secret of Wold Hall. Hutchinson, 1905; McClurg, 1905
    -The Squire's Heir; or, The Secret of Rochester's Will. Melrose, 1903
    -Temple's Trial; or, For Life or Death. Nelson, 1887

EVERITT, BRIDGET (MARY). 1924-   . Ref: CA.
    A Cold Front. Davies, 1972; Walker, 1973 [Cyprus]

EVERMAY, MARCH. Pseudonym of Mathilde Eiker, 1893-   . Ref: CC, MP. SC: Insp. Glover, in both titles.
    They Talked of Poison. Macmillan, 1938; Jarrolds, 1939
    This Death Was Murder. Macmillan, 1940; Jarrolds, 1940

EVERTON, FRANCIS. Pseudonym of Francis William Stokes, 1883-   . SC: Insp. George Annesley = GA; Det.-Insp. Allport = A. Set: Eng.
    The Dalehouse Murder. Collins, 1927; Bobbs, 1927 A
    The Hammer of Doom. Collins, 1928; Bobbs, 1929 A
    Insoluble. Collins, 1934
    Murder at Plenders. Collins, 1930. U.S. title: Murder Through the Window. Morrow, 1930 GA
    Murder May Pass Unpunished. Collins, 1936 GA,A
    Murder Through the Window; see Murder at Plenders
    The Young Vanish. Collins, 1932; Morrow, 1932 A

EWART, ERNEST ANDREW. 1878-1943. Pseudonym: Boyd Cable, q.v.

EWING, JULIANA HORATIA (GATTY). 1841-1885.
    Miscellanea. SPCK, 1896 ss, one criminous

EWINGS, MICHAEL. Pseudonym: Blair Stuart, q.v. Joint pseudonym with Colin Northway: Frank Ross, q.v.

EXBRAYAT, CHARLES. 1906-   .
    The Ravishing Idiot. Popular Library, 1965 (Translation of "Une Ravissante Idiote." Paris, 1962.) [Eng.]

EYERLY, JEANNETTE (HYDE). 1908-   . Ref: CA.
    The Leonardo Touch. Lippincott, 1976 [Wales]

EYERS, JOHN
    Special Branch: In at the Kill. Barker, 1976 (Novelization of the TV series.)

EYLES, ALFRED W. SC: Paul Chisholm, in at least those marked PC.
    Mirrored Murder. Fiction House, 1945
    Murder at Out-Patients. World's Work, 1948 PC
    Murder Brewing. World's Work, 1947 PC
    Murder in Hospital. World's Work, 1944 PC [hosp.]

EYLES, (MARGARET) LEONORA (PITCAIRN). 1889-1960. SC: Dr. Joan Marvin, in both titles. Set: Eng.
    Death of a Dog. Hutchinson, 1936
    They Wanted Him Dead! Hutchinson, 1936

EYRE, ARCHIBALD
    The Girl in Waiting. Luce, 1906; Ward, 1906

EYRE, JOHN R.
    Condemned to Death. Ouseley, 1908

EYRE, KATE
    A Step in the Dark. Cassell, 1894

EYRE, KATHERINE WIGMORE. 1901-1970. Ref: CA.
    Amy. Appleton, 1963; Hodder, 1964
    The Chinese Box. Appleton, 1959; Hodder, 1960 [S.F., 1880s]
    The Lute and the Glove. Appleton, 1955; Hodder, 1957
    Monk's Court. Appleton, 1966 [Eng.]
    The Sandalwood Fan. Meredith, 1968 [S.F., Haw.]

EYRE, MARIE. Pseudonym of Richard Hubbard,   -ca.1974. Other pseudonyms: Nick Carter, Regina Hubbard, Chris Stratton, qq.v.
    The Absence. Popular Library, 1973 [Ariz.]
    Blackgable Inn. Popular Library, 1971
    Bury Me Not at Sea. Popular Library, 1974
    Eyrie of the Fox. Popular Library, 1973
    The Girl in the Tiffany Dress. Popular Library, 1972 [Pitt., 1810]
    The Omen. Popular Library, 1973
    The Presence. Popular Library, 1972 [Conn.]
    Return to Gravesend. Popular Library, 1972 [La.]

F, INSPECTOR. Pseudonym of William Russell. Other pseudonym: Waters, q.v.
    Experiences of a Real Detective. Ward, 1862 ss
    Mrs. Waldegrave's Will and other tales. Ward, 1870 ss

F., E. M. Pseudonym of Mrs. E. M. Foster.
    The Duke of Clarence. Lane, 1795

FABER, CHRISTINE. Pseudonym.
    -A Fatal Resemblance. Kenedy, 1900
    The Guardian's Mystery; or, Rejected for Conscience's Sake. Kenedy, 1887
    -A Mother's Sacrifice; or, Who Was Guilty? Kenedy, 1891

FABER, DORIS
    Journey into Danger. Mystique, 1979 (Translation of "Coeurs, Volcans et Chrisanthemes." Paris, 1965.)

FABIAN, RUTH
    A Scent of Violets. Popular Library, 1974

FACOS, JAMES (FRANCIS). 1924-   . Ref: CA.
    The Silver Lady. Atheneum, 1972

FADIMAN, EDWIN, JR. 1925-   . Ref: CA.
    An Act of Violence. Signet, 1957
    The Glass Play Pen. Signet, 1956
    The One-Eyed King. Geis, 1971; Allen, 1972
    Who Will Watch the Watchers. Little, 1970; Allen, 1971

FAGAN, NORBERT
    The Crooked Mile. GM, 1953; Fawcett (London), 1955 [N.Y.]
    One Against the Odds. GM, 1954; Fawcett (London), 1955 [N.Y.]

FAGYAS (FEKETE), M(ARIA). Ref: CA.
    The Devil's Lieutenant. Putnam, 1970; Blond, 1970 [1909, Vienna]
    The Fifth Woman. Doubleday, 1963; Hodder, 1965 [Buda.]
    The Widowmaker. Doubleday, 1966; Cassell, 1967 [Hung.]

FAHERTY, ROBERT
    Better Than Dying. Doubleday, 1935; Gollancz, 1935

FAHRENKOPF, ANNE. Joint pseudonym with Ruth Fox (Hume), 1922-1980: Alexander Irving, q.v.

FAIR, A. A. Pseudonym of Erle Stanley Gardner, 1889-1970, q.v. Other pseudonyms: Carleton Kendrake, Charles J. Kenny, qq.v. SC: Donald Lam and Bertha Cool, in all titles. Set: Calif./L.A., unless otherwise indicated.
    All Grass Isn't Green. Morrow, 1970; Heinemann, 1970
    An Axe to Grind; see Give 'Em the Ax
    Bachelors Get Lonely. Morrow, 1961; Heinemann, 1962
    Bats Fly at Dusk. Morrow, 1942; Hale, 1951
    Bedrooms Have Windows. Morrow, 1949; Heinemann, 1956
    Beware the Curves. Morrow, 1956; Heinemann, 1957
    The Bigger They Come. Morrow, 1939. British title: Lam to the Slaughter. H. Hamilton, 1939
    Cats Prowl at Night. Morrow, 1943; Hale, 1949
    The Count of Nine. Morrow, 1958; Heinemann, 1959
    Crows Can't Count. Morrow, 1946; Heinemann, 1953
    Cut Thin to Win. Morrow, 1965; Heinemann, 1966
    Double or Quits. Morrow, 1941; Hale, 1949
    Fish or Cut Bait. Morrow, 1963; Heinemann, 1964
    Fools Die on Friday. Morrow, 1947; Heinemann, 1955
    Give 'Em the Ax. Morrow, 1944. British title: An Axe to Grind. Heinemann, 1951
    Gold Comes in Bricks. Morrow, 1940; Hale, 1942
    Kept Women Can't Quit. Morrow, 1960; Heinemann, 1961
    Lam to the Slaughter; see The Bigger They Come
    Owls Don't Blink. Morrow, 1942; Hale, 1951 [New Or.]
    Pass the Gravy. Morrow, 1959; Heinemann, 1960
    Shills Can't Cash Chips. Morrow, 1961. British title: Stop at the Red Light. Heinemann, 1962
    Some Slips Don't Show. Morrow, 1957; Heinemann, 1959 [S.F.]
    Some Women Won't Wait. Morrow, 1953; Heinemann, 1958 [Haw.]
    Spill the Jackpot! Morrow, 1941; Hale, 1948 [Las Veg.]
    Stop at the Red Light; see Shills Can't Cash Chips
    Top of the Heap. Morrow, 1952; Heinemann, 1957 [S.F.]
    Traps Need Fresh Bait. Morrow, 1967; Heinemann, 1968
    Try Anything Once. Morrow, 1962; Heinemann, 1963
    Turn on the Heat. Morrow, 1940; H. Hamilton, 1940
    Up for Grabs. Morrow, 1964; Heinemann, 1965
    Widows Wear Weeds. Morrow, 1966; Heinemann, 1966
    You Can Die Laughing. Morrow, 1957; Heinemann, 1958

FAIRBAIRN, DOUGLAS. 1926-   . Ref: CA.
    Shoot. Doubleday, 1973; Heinemann, 1974
    Street 8. Delacorte, 1977; Heinemann, 1977 [Miami]

FAIRBAIRN, ROGER. Pseudonym of John Dickson Carr, 1905-1977, q.v. Other pseudonyms: Carr Dickson, Carter Dickson, qq.v. See also: John Rhode; Adrian Conan Doyle, 1911-1970.
   Devil Kinsmere. Harper, 1934; H. Hamilton, 1934. Revised edition: Most Secret, as by John Dickson Carr. Harper, 1964; H. Hamilton, 1964 [Eng., 1670]

FAIRBANK, JANET AYER. 1878?-1951. See: Henry Kitchell Webster, 1875-1932.

FAIRBURN, ELEANOR. 1928- . Pseudonym: Catherine Carfax, q.v.

FAIRBURN, JAMES
   The Hit Man. New English Library pb, 1976

FAIRCHILD, WILLIAM. Ref: CA.
   The Sound of Murder. French (London), 1960 (3-act play.)
   The Swiss Arrangement. Macmillan (London), 1973; St. Martin's, 1974 [Switz.]

FAIRFAX, DENNIS
   The Masked Ball Murder. Jenkins, 1934

FAIRFAX, JANE
   The Commons Killing. Hale, 1978

FAIRFAX-BLAKEBOROUGH, J(OHN FREEMAN). 1883-1978? Set: Eng.
   Beating the Nobblers. Allan, 1933
   The Disappearance of Cropton. Allan, 1933
   -Gypsy's Luck, with Christopher Somers. Allan, 1932
   -A Last Gamble. Allan, 1936
   Nat Wedgewood, Jockey. Allan, 1933 ss
   Queen of the Gangsters. Allan, 1936
   -A Rank Outsider. Allan, 1933
   A Turf Mystery, with Rupert St. Cloud. Allan, 1934
   Warned Off. Allan, 1934
   Who Maimed Spurto? Allan, 1933

FAIRLAWN, JAMES
   The Nimrod Affair. Hale, 1978

FAIRLIE, GERARD. 1899- . Ref: MM, MP, TC. SC: Victor Caryll = VC; Bulldog Drummond (following H. C. McNeile, 1888-1937, q.v.; see also: Henry Reymond) = BD; Johnny Macall = JM; Mr. Malcolm = M. Set: Eng.
   Birds of Prey. Hodder, 1932
   Bulldog Drummond Attacks. Hodder, 1939; Gateway, 1940 BD
   Bulldog Drummond on Dartmoor. Hodder, 1938; Hillman-Curl, 1939 BD
   Bulldog Drummond Stands Fast. Hodder, 1947 BD
   Calling Bulldog Drummond. Hodder, 1951 BD
   Captain Bulldog Drummond. Hodder, 1945 BD
   Copper at Sea. Hodder, 1934
   Deadline for Macall. Hodder, 1956; Mill, 1956 JM
   Double the Bluff. Hodder, 1957 JM [Fr.]
   The Exquisite Lady. Hodder, 1929. U.S. title: Yellow Munro. Little, 1929
   Hands Off Bulldog Drummond. Hodder, 1949 BD
   Macall Gets Curious. Hodder, 1959 JM
   The Man Who Laughed. Hodder, 1928; Little, 1928 VC
   The Man with Talent. Hodder, 1931
   Men for Counters. Hodder, 1933 M
   Mr. Malcolm Presents. Hodder, 1932 M
   The Muster of the Vultures. Hodder, 1929; Little, 1929
   No Sleep for Macall. Hodder, 1955 JM [NYC]
   The Pianist Shoots First. Hodder, 1938
   Please Kill My Cousin. Hodder, 1961 JM
   The Reaper. Little, 1929 (British title?)
   The Return of the Black Gang. Hodder, 1954 BD
   The Rope Which Hangs. Hodder, 1932 (2 novelets.)
   Scissors Cut Paper. Hodder, 1927; Little, 1928 VC [Fr.]
   Shot in the Dark. Hodder, 1932; Doubleday, 1932 M
   Stone Blunts Scissors. Hodder, 1928; Little, 1929 VC
   Suspect. Hodder, 1930; Doubleday, 1930
   That Man Returns. Hodder, 1934 VC
   They Found Each Other. Hodder, 1946
   The Treasure Nets. Hodder, 1933
   Unfair Lady. Hodder, 1931
   Winner Take All. Hodder, 1953; Dodd, 1953 JM
   Yellow Munro; see The Exquisite Lady

FAIRMAN, PAUL W. 1916-1977. Pseudonyms: Ivar Jorgensen, Paulette Warren, qq.v. See also: Ellery Queen.
   Coffy. Lancer, 1973 (Novelization of the movie.)
   -The Cover Girls. Macfadden, 1970
   The Ghost of Graveyard Hill. Curtis, 1972
   The Glass Ladder. Handi-Books, 1950 [Chi.]
   -The Joy Wheel. Lion, 1954
   Pattern for Destruction. Macfadden, 1970
   -Playboy. Macfadden, 1970
   Search for a Dead Nympho. Lancer, 1967 [Chi.]
   That Girl. Popular Library, 1971 (Novelization of the TV series.) [Maine]
   To Catch a Crooked Girl. Pinnacle, 1971 [NYC]
   Terror by Night. Curtis, 1972
   -The World Grabbers. Monarch, 1964 (Novelization of the "One Step Beyond" TV series.)

FAIRWAY, SIDNEY. Pseudonym of Sidney Herbert Daukes, 1879- . Doctor in London. Ref: CC. Set: Eng.
   -A Cuckoo in Harley Street. Paul, 1932. U.S. title: Dr. Falke of Harley Street. Kinsey, 1933
   Dr. Falke of Harley Street; see A Cuckoo in Harley Street
   -Doctor Severin's Secret. Paul, 1943
   -The Doctor's Defence. Paul, 1931; Kinsey, 1932
   -He Loved Freedom. Paul, 1947
   -It Came to Pass. Paul, 1944
   -A Late Recovery. Paul, 1940
   The Long Tunnel. Paul, 1935; Doubleday, 1936 [acad.]
   Thanks to Dr. Molly. Paul, 1937
   The Yellow Viper. Paul, 1931

FAIRWEATHER, NANCY
   Shadows on the Moon. Belmont, 1978

FALCON, MARY LEE
   The Dungeon. Belmont, 1967

FALES, WILLIAM E. S.
   Bits of Broken China. Street, 1902; Henderson, 1902 ss, some criminous

FALK, DAVID G.
   Rick; or, The Recidiviste. Trischler, 1891

FALK, LEE (HARRISON). 1915- . Titles ghosted by Ron(ald Joseph) Goulart, 1933- , q.v., = *. SC: The Phantom, in all titles. Ref: CA.
   The Assassins. Avon, 1975
   The Curse of the Two-Headed Bull. Avon, 1975 [Afr.]
   The Goggle-Eyed Pirates. Avon, 1974 * [Afr.]
   The Golden Circle. Avon, 1973 * [NYC]
   The Hydra Monster. Avon, 1973 * [S.F.]
   The Island of Dogs. Avon, 1975 [Afr.]
   Killer's Town. Avon, 1973 [Afr.]
   The Mysterious Ambassador. Avon, 1973 [Afr.]
   The Mystery of the Sea Horse. Avon, 1973 * [Calif.]
   The Scorpion Menace. Avon, 1972 (Adapted by Basil Copper, 1924- , q.v.)
   The Slave Market of Mucar. Avon, 1972 [Mid. East]
   The Story of the Phantom. Avon, 1972 [Afr.]
   The Swamp Rats. Avon, 1974 [Afr.]
   The Vampires and the Witch. Avon, 1974 [Afr.]
   The Veiled Lady. Avon, 1973 * [Afr.]

FALKIRK, RICHARD. Pseudonym of Derek (William) Lambert, 1929- , q.v. SC: Edmund Blackstone = EB, most set in Eng., early 1800s.
   Beau Blackstone. Eyre, 1973; Stein, 1974 EB
   Blackstone. Eyre, 1972; Stein, 1973 EB
   Blackstone and the Scourge of Europe. Eyre, 1974; Stein, 1974 EB
   Blackstone on Broadway. Eyre, 1977 EB
   Blackstone's Fancy. Eyre, 1973; Stein, 1973 EB
   Blackstone Underground. Eyre, 1976 EB
   The Chill Factor. Joseph, 1971; Doubleday, 1971 [Isr.]
   The Twisted Wire. Corgi, 1972; Doubleday, 1971 [Isr.]

FALKNER, AMY S.
   -Bells of Doom. Mellifont, 1944
   -A Moorland Mystery. Mellifont, 1945

FALKNER, J(OHN) MEADE. 1858-1932. Ref: CC.
   The Lost Stradivarius. Blackwood, 1895
   The Nebuly Coat. Arnold, 1903

FALKNER, LEONARD. 1900-1977.
   M. Holt, 1931
   Murder off Broadway. Holt, 1930; Hamilton, 1930 [NYC]

FALKNER, W(ILLIAM) C. 1826-1889.
   The White Rose of Memphis. Carleton, 1881 [Memphis]

FALLON, GEORGE. Pseudonym of D(avid) E(rnest) Bingley, 1920- , q.v. Other pseudonym: Henry Chesham, q.v.
   Rendezvous in Rio. Hale, 1967 [Rio de J.]

FALLON, MARTIN. Pseudonym of Harry Patterson, 1929- , q.v. Other pseudonyms: James Graham, Jack Higgins, Hugh Marlowe, qq.v. SC: Paul Chavasse, in all titles.
   Dark Side of the Street. Long, 1967; GM, 1974, as by Jack Higgins. Reprinted in England as by Jack Higgins: Coronet, 1973
   A Fine Night for Dying. Long, 1969
   The Keys of Hell. Abelard (London & NYC), 1965. Reprinted as by Jack Higgins: Coronet, 1972; GM, 1976 [Alb.]
   Midnight Never Comes. Long, 1966; GM, 1975, as by Jack Higgins. Reprinted in Britain as by Jack Higgins: Coronet, 1973
   The Testament of Caspar Schultz. Abelard (London & NYC), 1962. Reprinted as by Jack Higgins: GM, 1978 [Ger.]
   Year of the Tiger. Abelard (London), 1963; Abelard (NYC), 1964 [Tib.]

FALLON, THOMAS
   The Last Warning. French, 1935 (Play based on the novel "The House of Fear" by Wadsworth Camp, 1879-1936, q.v.)

FALSTEIN, LOUIS. 1909- . Ref: CA.
   Slaughter Street. Lion, 1953; Panther, 1961 [NYC]
   Sole Survivor. Dell, 1954 [NYC]

FANE, ANTHONY
   The Wycliffe-Pepin Case. Poe, 1931

FANE, JULIAN (CHARLES). 1927- . Ref: CA.
   -Revolution Island. H. Hamilton, 1979

FANGER, HORST. 1919- .
   A Life for a Life. Ballantine, 1954; Hale, 1956 (Translation of "Wir Selber Sind das Rad." Darmstadt, 1952.) [Ger.]

FANTONI, BARRY. ca.1940- .
   Mike Dime. Hodder, 1940; Watts, 1941 [Phil., 1948]

FARAGO, LUCIEN
   An Easy Victim. Cape, 1957 (Translation of "Un Homme a Devorer." Paris, 1955.)

FARGUS, F(REDERICK) J(OHN). 1840-1885. Pseudonym: Hugh Conway, q.v.
   Carriston's Gift and other stories. Arrowsmith, 1884; Holt, 1885, as by Hugh Conway. Also published as: Dead Man's Face. Munro, 1885, as by Hugh Conway ss
   Circumstantial Evidence. Bailey, 1887; Ogilvie, 1885, as by Hugh Conway ss
   Dark Days. Arrowsmith, 1884. Also published as by Hugh Conway: Tauchnitz, 1885
   Dead Man's Face; see Carriston's Gift and other stories
   Paul Vargas, a Mystery, and other tales. Lovell, 1885, as by Hugh Conway (ss, taken from Carriston's Gift and other stories, q.v.)
   Slings and Arrows and other tales. Arrowsmith, 1885; Holt, 1885, as by Hugh Conway

FARHI, (MUSA) MORIS. 1935- . Ref: CA.
   The Pleasure of Your Death. Constable, 1972

FARJEON, B(ENJAMIN) L(EOPOLD). 1838-1903. Ref: DD, EM. Set: Eng.
   -The Amblers. Hutchinson, 1904
   -Basil and Annette. White, 1890; U.S. Book Co., 1890
   -The Bells of Penraven. Tinsley, 1879; Harper, 1879
   The Betrayal of John Fordham. Hutchinson, 1896; Fenno, 1896

-Blade-o'-Grass. Hutchinson, 1899
-The Blood White Rose. Trischler, 1889
The Clairvoyante. Hutchinson, 1905
Devlin the Barber. Ward, 1888; Arno, 1976
-Doctor Glennie's Daughter: A Story of Real Life. Hurst, 1889
For the Defense. Trischler, 1891; Lovell, 1891
Gautran; see The House of the White Shadows
The Golden Land; or, Links from Shore to Shore. Ward, 1886
Great Porter Square. Ward, 1885; Harper, 1885. Also published as: 119 Great Porter Square. Munro, 1881?
-Grif. Tinsley, 1870; DeWitt, 1871?
The House of the White Shadows. Tinsley, 1884. U.S. title: Gautran; or, The House of the White Shadows. Lovell, 1883
-In a Silver Sea. Ward, 1886
-Jessie Trim. Tinsley, 1874; Harper, 1875
The Last Tenant. Hutchinson, 1893; Cassell, 1893
-London's Heart. Tinsley, 1873; Harper, 1873
-Love's Harvest. Lovell, 1885 (British title?)
-Love's Victory. Tinsley, 1875; Harper, 1875
The March of Fate. White, 1893
The Mesmerists. Hutchinson, 1900
Miriam Rozella. White, 1898
-Miser Farebrother. Ward, 1888; Harper, 1887
-Mrs. Dimmock's Worries. Hutchinson, 1906
Mrs. Isaacs; see Solomon Isaacs
The Mystery of M. Felix. White, 1890; Lovell, 1890
The Mystery of Roaring Meg. Tinsley, 1878. U.S. title: The Widow Cherry; or, The Mystery of Roaring Meg. Carleton, 1878
The Mystery of the Royal Mail. Hutchinson, 1902
The Nine of Hearts. Ward, 1886; Harper, 1886
119 Great Porter Square; see Great Porter Square
The Peril of Richard Pardon. White, 1890; Harper, 1888
The Pride of Race. Hutchinson, 1901; Jacobs, 1901
Samuel Boyd of Catchpole Square: A Mystery. Hutchinson, 1899; New Amsterdam, 1899
A Secret Inheritance. Ward, 1887
-Self-Doomed. Farran, 1885; Harper, 1885
-The Shield of Love. Arrowsmith, 1891; Holt, 1891
-Solomon Isaacs. Carleton, 1877. Also published as: Mrs. Isaacs. Carleton, 1883 (British title?)
Something Occurred. Routledge (London & NYC), 1893
-A Strange Enchantment. White, 1889
Toilers of Babylon. Ward, 1888; Harper, 1889
The Tragedy of Featherstone. Ward, 1887
-A Very Young Couple. White, 1890; U.S. Book Co., 1890
The Widow Cherry; see The Mystery of Roaring Meg
-A Young Girl's Life. Ward, 1889

FARJEON, J(OSEPH) JEFFERSON. 1883-1955. Pseudonym: Anthony Swift, q.v. Ref: CC, MM, MP. SC: Ben the Tramp = B; Insp. Kendall = K. Set: Eng.
Adventure at Eighty. Macdonald, 1948
Adventure for Nine. Macdonald, 1951
The Appointed Date. Longmans, 1929; Dial, 1930
At the Green Dragon. Harrap, 1927. U.S. title: The Green Dragon. Dial, 1926
Aunt Sunday Sees It Through. Collins, 1940. U.S. title: Aunt Sunday Takes Command. Bobbs, 1940
Aunt Sunday Takes Command; see Aunt Sunday Sees It Through
Back to Victoria. Macdonald, 1947
Ben on the Job. Collins, 1952 B
Ben Sees It Through. Collins, 1932; Dial, 1933 B
Black Castle. Collins, 1944 [Balkans]
Bob Hits the Headlines. Bodley, 1954
The Caravan Adventure. Macdonald, 1955
Castle of Fear. Collins, 1954
Cause Unknown. Collins, 1950
The Crook's Shadow. Harrap, 1927; Dial, 1927
Dangerous Beauty. Collins, 1936 [Sudan]
Dark Lady. Collins, 1938
Dead Man's Heath. Collins, 1933. U.S. title: The Mystery of Dead Man's Heath. Dodd, 1934
Death in Fancy Dress; see The Fancy Dress Ball

Death in the Inkwell; see End of an Author
Death of a World. Collins, 1948
Detective Ben. Collins, 1936 B
The Disappearance of Uncle David. Collins, 1949
The Double Crime. Collins, 1953
End of an Author. Collins, 1938. U.S. title: Death in the Inkwell. Bobbs, 1942
Exit John Horton. Collins, 1939. U.S. title: Friday the 13th. Bobbs, 1940
-Facing Death. Quality, 1940 ss
The Fancy Dress Ball. Collins, 1934. U.S. title: Death in Fancy Dress. Bobbs, 1939
The 5.18 Mystery. Collins, 1929; Dial, 1929
Following Footsteps. Dial, 1930 (British title?)
Friday the 13th; see Exit John Horton
The Green Dragon; see At the Green Dragon
Greenmask. Collins, 1944; Bobbs, 1944 [Wales]
Holiday at Half-Mast. Collins, 1937
Holiday Express. Collins, 1935
The House of Disappearance. Harrap, 1928; Dial, 1927
The House of Shadows. Collins, 1943
The House on the Marsh; see The Mystery of the Creek
The House Opposite. Collins, 1931; Dial, 1931 B
The House over the Tunnel. Collins, 1951
The Impossible Guest. Macdonald, 1949
The Judge Sums Up. Collins, 1942; Bobbs, 1942
Little God Ben. Collins, 1935 B
The Master Criminal. Brentano's (London), 1924; Dial, 1924
Money Walks. Macdonald, 1953
Mountain Mystery. Collins, 1935
Murderer's Trail. Collins, 1931. U.S. title: Phantom Fingers. Dial, 1931 B
Mystery in White. Collins, 1937; Bobbs, 1938
The Mystery of Dead Man's Heath; see Dead Man's Heath
The Mystery of the Creek. Collins, 1933. U.S. title: The House on the Marsh. Dial, 1933
The Mystery on the Moor. Collins, 1930
Mystery Underground; see Underground
Number Nineteen. Collins, 1952 B
No. 17. Hodder, 1926; Dial, 1926 B
Old Man Mystery. Collins, 1933
The Oval Table. Collins, 1946
Peril in the Pyrenees. Collins, 1946 [Sp.]
The Person Called "Z". Collins, 1930; Dial, 1929
Phantom Fingers; see Murderer's Trail
Prelude to Crime. Collins, 1948
Room Number 6. Collins, 1941
Seven Dead. Collins, 1939; Bobbs, 1939 K
The Shadow of Thirteen. Collins, 1949
Shadows by the Sea. Harrap, 1928; Dial, 1928
Sinister Inn. Collins, 1934; Dodd, 1934 [Fr.]
-Sometimes Life's Funny. Methuen, 1933
The Third Victim. Collins, 1941
Thirteen Guests. Collins, 1936; Bobbs, 1938 K
Trunk Call. Collins, 1932. U.S. title: The Trunk Call Mystery. Dial, 1932
The Trunk Call Mystery; see Trunk Call
Underground. Collins, 1929; Dial, 1928. Also published as: Mystery Underground. Collins, 1932
Uninvited Guests. Brentano's (London), 1925; Dial, 1925
The Windmill Mystery. Collins, 1934
Yellow Devil. Collins, 1937
The "Z" Murders. Collins, 1932; Dial, 1932

The following are WWII pamphlets:
Down the Green Stairs and other stories. Todd, 1943 ss
The Invisible Companion and other stories. Todd, 16 pp.; Polybooks, 62 pp. 1946 ss
Midnight Adventure and other stories. Polybooks, 1946 ss
The Twist and other stories. Vallancey, 1944 ss
Waiting for the Police and other stories. Todd, 1943 ss

FARMER, BERNARD J(AMES). 1902- . Ref: CA, CC. SC: P. C. James Wigan, in all titles, set in Eng.
Death at the Cascades. Heinemann, 1953
Death of a Bookseller. Heinemann, 1956
Murder Next Year. Heinemann, 1959
Once, and Then the Funeral. Heinemann, 1958

FARMER, GEOFFREY NORTON
Quella. Rivers, 1914

FARMER, JOAN. 1914- .
Sedona. St. Martin's, 1979 [Eng., 1838]

FARMER, LUCY
The Chronicles of Cardewe Manor. Hutchinson, 1891

FARMER, PATRICIA. Pseudonym of Maureen Lines, q.v.
The Legend of Piper's Hole. Popular Library, 1973 [Eng.]

FARMER, PHILIP JOSE. 1918- . Ref: CA.
The Adventure of the Peerless Peer. Aspen, 1974 (Sherlock Holmes.) [1916, Afr.]
-The Image of the Beast. Essex, 1968

FARMLET, CHARLES
Fair in the Fearless Old Fashion. Tinsley, 1875

FARNCOMBE, FRANK E. See: Robert L. Hadfield.

FARNDALE, JOHN. Pseudonym of John Wilfred Harvey, 1889- .
The Nine Nicks. Methuen, 1930

FARNOL, (JOHN) JEFFERY. 1878-1952. Ref: CC. SC: Sgt. Jasper Shrig, in at least those marked JS, set ca.1818 in Eng.
-The Amateur Gentleman. Low, 1913; Little, 1913 JS
-Another Day. Low, 1929; Little, 1929
-Beltane the Smith. Low, 1915; Little, 1915
-Black Bartlemy's Treasure. Low, 1920; Little, 1920
-The Broad Highway. Low, 1910; Little, 1911
-Charmian, Lady Vibart. Low, 1932; Little, 1932
-The Chronicles of the Imp. Low, 1915
The Crooked Furrow. Low, 1937; Doubleday, 1938 JS
-The Definite Object. Low, 1917; Little, 1917
-The Fool Beloved. Low, 1949
-The Glad Summer. Low, 1951
-Gyfford of Weare. Low, 1928; Little, 1928
The Happy Harvest. Low, 1939; Doubleday, 1940 JS
Heritage Perilous. Low, 1946; McBride, 1947 JS
The High Adventure. Low, 1926; Little, 1926 JS
-The Honourable Mr. Tawnish. Low, 1913; Little, 1913
-The Jade of Destiny. Low, 1931; Little, 1931, as A Jade of Destiny
-John o' the Green. Low, 1935; Little, 1935
Justice by Midnight. Low, 1956
-The Lonely Road. Low, 1938; Doubleday, 1938
The Loring Mystery. Low, 1925; Little, 1925 JS
A Matter of Business and other stories. Low, 1940; Doubleday, 1940 ss, one about JS
-The Money Moon. Low, 1911; Dodd, 1911
Most Sacred of All; see My Lord of Wrybourne
Murder by Nail. Low, 1942. U.S. title: Valley of Night. Doubleday, 1942 JS
-My Lady Caprice. Stevens, 1907; Dodd, 1907
-My Lord of Wrybourne. Low, 1948. U.S. title: Most Sacred of All. McBride, 1948
The Ninth Earl. Low, 1950 JS
-Our Admirable Betty. Low, 1918; Little, 1925
-Over the Hills. Low, 1930; Little, 1930
-Peregrine's Progress. Low, 1922; Little, 1922 JS
-The "Piping Times." Low, 1945
-The Quest of Youth. Low, 1927; Little, 1927
The Shadow, and other stories. Low, 1929; Little, 1929 ss
-Sir John Dering. Low, 1923; Little, 1923
Valley of Night; see Murder by Nail
Waif of the River. Low, 1952 JS
-The Way Beyond. Low, 1933; Little, 1933
-Winds of Fortune. Low, 1934; Little, 1934

FARNSWORTH, MONA
The Castle That Whispered. Award, 1976 [Madeira]
Companion to Evil. Ace, 1971 [N. Mex.]

A Cross for Tomorrow. Pinnacle, 1972
[N. Mex.]
Dark Wood. Award, 1976 [Cape Cod]
Death by the Zodiac. Apollo, 1972
The Evil That Waited. Pinnacle, 1973
[1904, Mass.]
Footsteps That Follow. Manor, 1976
The Great Stone Heart. Pinnacle, 1971
[Sante Fe]
House of Deadly Calm. Apollo, 1970
The House of Whispering Death. Apollo,
1971
The Menace of Marble Hill. Manor, 1974
[Vt.]
Ransome Castle. Apollo, 1970
The Starcrossed Road. Pinnacle, 1973
The Three Sisters of No End House. Ace,
1972

FARR, CAROLINE. Pseudonym of Alan G(eoffrey) Yates, 1923-   , q.v. Other pseudonym: Carter Brown, q.v. Most of these titles were probably published in Australia by Horwitz, but complete information is lacking. In addition, this list probably contains uncorrelated title changes.
Brecon Castle. Signet, 1976
The Castle in Canada. Signet, 1972 [Can.]
A Castle in Spain; see Web of Horror
Castle of Terror. Horwitz, 1975; Signet, 1975 [Maine]
Castle on the Loch. Horwitz, 1979
Castle on the Rhine. Horwitz, 1979; Signet, 1979 [Ger.]
Chateau of Wolves. Signet, 1976
Dark Citadel. Horwitz, 1976; Signet, 1971 [Carib.]
Dark Mansion. Signet, 1974 [Can.]
Granite Folly. Horwitz, 1967; Signet, 1967 [Can.]
Heiress of Fear. Horwitz, 1978; Signet, 1978 [Can.]
Heiress to Corsair Keep. Horwitz, 1978; Signet, 1978 [Carib.]
The House at Landsdowne. Horwitz, 1977; Signet, 1977
House of Dark Illusions. Signet, 1973 [Can.]
House of Destiny. Signet, 1970
House of Secrets. Signet, 1973 [Calif.]
The House of Tombs. Horwitz, 1966; Signet, 1966 [Maine]
House of Treachery. Signet, 1977 [Cape Cod]
House of Valhalla. Signet, 1978 [Maine]
The House on the Cliffs. Signet, 1974 [Oreg.]
The Intruder. Horwitz, 1966
Island of Evil. Horwitz, 1978; Signet, 1979 [Haw.]
Mansion Malevolent. Signet, 1974 [Carib.]
Mansion of Evil. Signet, 1966 [Maine]
Mansion of Menace. Signet, 1976 [Carib.]
Mansion of Peril. Horwitz, 1966; Signet, 1975
The Possessed. Horwitz, 1973
Ravensnest. Signet, 1977
Room of Secrets. Horwitz, 1979; Signet, 1979
The Scream in the Storm. Horwitz, 1977; Signet, 1975
The Secret of Castle Ferrara. Signet, 1971
Secret at Ravenswood. Horwitz, 1980; Signet, 1980
The Secret of the Chateau. Signet, 1967
Sinister House. Horwitz, 1978; Signet, 1978 [Calif.]
So Near and Yet. Signet, 1967
Terror on Duncan Island. Signet, 1971 [Maine]
The Towers of Fear. Horwitz, 1977; Signet, 1972 [Maine]
Villa of Shadows. Horwitz, 1966
Web of Horror. Horwitz, 1966; Signet, 1966. Also published as: A Castle in Spain. Signet, 1967 [Sp.]
Witch's Hammer. Horwitz, 1967; Signet, 1967 [Maine]

FARR, FINIS (KING). 1904-1982. Ref: CA.
The Elephant Valley. Arlington, 1967 [Wash.]

FARR, JOHN. Pseudonym of Jack Webb, 1920-   , q.v.
The Deadly Combo. Ace, 1958 [L.A.]
Don't Feed the Animals. Abelard-Schuman, 1955. British title: The Zoo Murders. Foulsham, 1956. Also published as: Naked Fear. Jonathan, 1955
The Lady and the Snake. Ace, 1957 [Calif.]
Naked Fear; see Don't Feed the Animals
-She Shark. Ace, 1956
The Zoo Murders; see Don't Feed the Animals

FARR, SEBASTIAN. Pseudonym of Eric Walter Blom, 1888-1959.
Death on the Down Beat. Dent, 1941

FARRAN, ROY (ALEXANDER). 1921-   .
Never Had a Chance. Bles, 1967

FARRANT, SARAH. Pseudonym of Valerie Harris, 1930-   . Set: Eng.
The Curse of Pengrail Park. Hale, 1976. U.S. title: Sweet Jael. Playboy, 1978
The Lady of Chantry Glades. Hale, 1972; Beagle, 1974
Lady of Drawbridge Court. Hale, 1973; Beagle, 1974
Lady of Mariner's Mead. Hale, 1976. U.S. title (?): The Reluctant Paragon. Ballantine, 1976 [Eng., 1800s]
Lady of Monkswood Manor. Hale, 1972; Beagle, 1974
Lady of Rogan's Tower. Hale, 1974; Beagle, 1975 [past, Eng.]
Lady of Winston Park. Hale, 1972; Beagle, 1974
The Reluctant Paragon; see Lady of Mariner's Mead
Sweet Jael; see The Curse at Pengrail Park
The Tavern Wench. Hale, 1978; Doubleday, 1979
A Touch of Terror. Hale, 1980; St. Martin's, 1980 [Eng., 1860s]

FARRAR, HELEN. A schoolteacher.
Murder Goes to School. Ziff-Davis, 1948 [Calif., acad.]

FARRAR, HELEN GRAHAM
How Evil the Word. Avon, 1974 [Vir. Is.]

FARRAR, JOHN CHIPMAN. 1896-1974. Joint pseudonym with Prosper Buranelli, 1890-1960, q.v.: John Prosper, q.v. Ref: CA.

FARRAR, STEWART. SC: Insp. Elwyn Morgan = EM. Set: Eng.
Death in the Wrong Bed. Collins, 1963; Walker, 1964 EM
The Snake on 99. Collins, 1958; Washburn, 1959 EM
-The Twelve Maidens. Joseph, 1974; St. Martin's, 1974
Zero in the Gate. Collins, 1960; Walker, 1961 EM

FARRELL, DAVID. Pseudonym of Frederick E(screet) Smith, 1922-   , q.v.
The Other Cousin. Gresham, 1962. U.S. title: The Dark Cliffs. Paperback Library, 1966, as by Frederick E. Smith

FARRELL, HENRY. Pseudonym: Charles Henry, q.v. Born in Calif.; published numerous ss and novelets under a variety of pseudonyms; author of many TV and film scripts.
Death on the Sixth Day. Holt, 1961; Eyre, 1962
How Awful About Allan. Holt, 1963; Eyre, 1964
Such a Gorgeous Kid Like Me. Delacorte, 1967 [Calif.]
What Ever Happened to Baby Jane? Rinehart, 1960; Eyre, 1960 [L.A.]

FARRER, KATHERINE (DOROTHY). 1911-   .
Ref: CC, TC. SC: Insp. Richard Ringwood, in all titles.
The Cretan Counterfeit. Collins, 1954
Gownsman's Gallows. Hodder, 1957 [acad.]
The Missing Link. Collins, 1952

FARRERE, CLAUDE. Pseudonym of Frederic Charles Pierre Edouard Bargone, 1876-1957.
The House of the Secret. Dutton, 1923; Dent, 1923 (Translation of "La Maison des Hommes Vivants." Paris, 1911.) [Fr.]
The Man Who Killed. Brentano's, 1917 (Translation of "L'Homme Qui Assassina." Paris, 1907.) [Turk.]

FARRIMOND, JOHN. 1913-   . Ref: CA.
-Dust in My Throat. Harrap, 1963
-The Hollow Shell. Harrap, 1964
Kill Me a Priest. Harrap, 1965
Pick and Run. Harrap, 1966
-The Unending Track. Harrap, 1970

FARRINGTON, FIELDEN. 1909-   . Born in Indiana; newspaperman; radio announcer; writer of TV and radio scripts.
A Little Game. Walker, 1968; Macdonald, 1968 [L.I.]
The Strangers in 7-A. McKay, 1972 [NYC]

FARRINGTON, JOSEPH
The Hand. Jenkins, 1961 [Kenya]
Night Train to Mombasa. Jenkins, 1962 [Afr.]

FARRINGTON, JOSEPH J.
The Uncrowned Prince; or, The Mystery of the Yellow Manse. (New York), 1900

FARRIS, JOHN. 1936?-   . Ref: CA.
All Heads Turn When the Hunt Goes By. Playboy, 1978; Macdonald, 1978
The Captors. Trident, 1969; New English Library, 1971
The Corpse Next Door. Graphic, 1956
The Fury. Playboy, 1976; Macdonald, 1977
Happy Anniversary, Harrison High. PB, 1973
Sharp Practice. Simon, 1974; Weidenfeld, 1975 [Tenn.]
Shatter. Popular Library, 1982; Allen, 1980
The Trouble at Harrison High. PB, 1970
When Michael Calls. Trident, 1967; New English Library, 1970

FARROW, MORLEY
After Baxter's Death. Tinsley, 1870

FAST, HOWARD (MELVIN). 1914-   . Pseudonyms: E. V. Cunningham, Walter Ericson, qq.v. Ref: CA, TC.
The Winston Affair. Crown, 1959; Methuen, 1960

FAST, JONATHAN. Born in NYC; published numerous ss and written extensively for movies and TV.
The Inner Circle. Delacorte, 1979; Hale, 1980 [L.A.]
Mortal Gods. Harper, 1978 [2226]

FAST, JULIUS. 1919-   . Ref: CA.
And Then Murder; see Street of Fear
The Bright Face of Danger. Rinehart, 1946 [hosp.]
Down Through the Night; see Walk in Shadow
A Model for Murder. Rinehart, 1956; Hale, 1957 [NYC]
Street of Fear. Rinehart, 1958; Hale, 1959. Also published as: And Then Murder. Hillman, 1959 [NYC]
Walk in Shadow. Rinehart, 1947. Also published as: Down Through the Night. Crest, 1956 [NYC]
Watchful at Night. Farrar, 1945 [Mass.]

FAULEY, WILBUR FINLEY. 1872-1942. Byline sometimes: Wilbur Finley Fawley.
-After Midnight. Ogilvie, 1904
Burnt Earth. Carlyle, 1936 (3-act play)
Fires of Fate. Metropolitan, 1923
-Jenny Be Good. Britton, 1919
-Mesalliance. Macaulay, 1934
Queenie: The Adventures of a Nice Young Lady. Macaulay, 1921 [NYC]
-The Shuddering Castle. Green Circle, 1936

FAULKNER, ANNE IRVIN. 1906-   . Pseudonym: Nancy Faulkner, q.v.

FAULKNER, NANCY. Pseudonym of Anne Irvin Faulkner, 1906-   . Ref: CA.
The Jade Box. Popular Library, 1974
-Savannah. Popular Library, 1978
The Summer of the Fire Ship. Popular Library, 1976
Witch's Brew. Curtis, 1973

FAULKNER, WILLIAM. 1897-1962. Ref: CA, CC, EM, MC, TC. SC: Gavin Stevens = GS.
Intruder in the Dust. Random, 1948; Chatto, 1949 GS [Miss.]
Knight's Gambit. Random, 1949; Chatto, 1951 GS ss [Miss.]
Sanctuary. Cape & Smith, 1931; Chatto, 1931 [Miss.]

FAUR, MICHAEL P., JR.
A Friendly Place to Die. Signet, 1966; Tandem, 1967 [NYC]

FAURE-BIGUET, JACQUES NAPOLEON. 1893-   . Pseudonym: Jacques Decrest, q.v.

FAUST, FREDERICK SCHILLER. 1892-1944. Pseudonyms: Max Brand, Walter C. Butler, Frederick Frost, qq.v.

FAUST, RON
The Burning Sky. Playboy, 1978 [New Mex.]
Death Fires. GM, 1980 [Mex.]
The Long Count. GM, 1979 [S. Am.]

Tombs of Blue Ice. Bobbs, 1975; Hale, 1976 [Fr.]
The Wolf in the Clouds. Bobbs, 1977 [Colo.]

FAWCETT, EDGAR. 1847-1904.
-The Evil That Men Do. Belford, 1889
-A Hopeless Case. Houghton, 1880
-Loaded Dice. Tait, 1891
Rutherford. Funk, 1884; Hunt, 1887

FAWCETT, F(RANK) DUBREZ. 1891-1968. Pseudonyms: Griff, Spike Gordon (?), Ben Sarto, Elmer Eliot Saks, qq.v.
Journey to Genoa. Amalgamated, 1960 (Sexton Blake.)

FAWKES, F(RANK) A(TTFIELD)
Adventures of a Chemist. Simpkin, 1930 ss

FAWLEY, WILBUR FINLEY. See: Wilbur Finley Fauley, 1872-1942.

FAY, DOROTHY. Pseudonym of Anna Chandler Lindholm, 1870-   .
The Black Pearl of Passion. Galleon, 1936 [Calif.]

FAY, JUDITH. Pseudonym: Kate Nicholson, q.v.

FEAGLES, ANNA MacRAE. 1927-   . Pseudonym: Travis MacRae, q.v.

FEAKES, G. J.
Moonrakers and Mischief. Chapman, 1961; Washburn, 1962

FEAR, WILLIAM H(ENRY CHARLES)
The Killers. Digit, 1964 [Fr.]

FEARING, KENNETH (FLEXNER). 1902-1961. Ref: CC, EM, MC, TC.
The Big Clock. Harcourt, 1946; Bodley, 1947 [NYC]
The Crozart Story. Doubleday, 1960
Cry Killer! see Dagger of the Mind
Dagger of the Mind. Random, 1941; Lane, 1941. Also published as: Cry Killer! Avon, 1958
The Generous Heart. Harcourt, 1954; Bodley, 1955 [NYC]
The Loneliest Girl in the World. Harcourt, 1951; Bodley, 1952. Also published as: The Sound of Murder. Mercury, 1952 [NYC]
The Sound of Murder; see The Loneliest Girl in the World

FEARN, JOHN RUSSELL. 1908-1960. Pseudonyms: Hugo Blayn, Spike Gordon, Volsted Gribdan, Griff, Nat Karta, John Slate, qq.v.
-Slaves of Ijax. Kaner, 1947

FEARNLEY, JOHN BLAKEWAY
A Corpse to Bury. Jarrolds, 1956
Murder by Degrees. Hale, 1940

FEARON, DIANA. SC: Arabella Frant, in at least those marked AF.
Death Before Breakfast. Hale, 1959 AF
Murder-on-Thames. Hale, 1960 AF
Nairobi Nightmare. Hale, 1958 [Kenya]
A Rhino for Rosamund. Hale, 1959 [Afr.]

FECHER, CONSTANCE. 1911-   . See: Constance (Fecher) Heaven.

FECHY, HENRIETTE. Pseudonym: Leo Dartey, q.v.

FEDER, ROBERT ARTHUR. 1909-1969. Pseudonym: Robert Arthur, q.v.

FEEGEL, JOHN R(ICHARD). 1932-   . Ref: CA.
Autopsy. Avon, 1975
Death Sails the Bay. Avon, 1978 [Fla.]

FEELY, TERENCE
Who Killed Santa Claus? French (London), 1971 (2-act play.)

FEENY, ALFRED
By a Vanished Hand. Ward, 1906 ss, some criminous

FEIBLEMAN, PETER S. 1930-   . Raised in New Orleans; lived in and wrote about Spain for many years.
Charlie Boy. Little, 1980 [New Or.]

FEIFFER, JULES. 1929-   . Ref: CA.
Ackroyd. Simon, 1977; Hutchinson, 1978

FEILDING, DOROTHY. 1884-   . Pseudonym: A. Fielding, q.v.

FEIN, HARRY H.
-The Flying Chinaman. Knopf, 1938

FEIST, AUBREY (NOEL LYDSTON). 1903-   . Ref: CA.
Among Those Present. Evans, 1950 (1-act play.)
-The Black Cabinet. French (London), 1947 (1-act play.)
The Eyes of St. Emlyn. Long, 1938
Key Men. Melrose, 1937

FELBER, RON. Pseudonym: Nick Carter, q.v.
The Indian Point Conspiracy. Manor, 1977

FELDMAN, ANALTOLE FRANCE. Pseudonym: Robert Wallace, q.v.

FELIX, CHARLES. Pseudonym of John Retcliff (?). Ref: MC.
The Notting Hill Mystery. Saunders, 1865; Arno, 1976
-Ram Dass. Tinsley, 1875
-Velvet Lawn. Saunders, 1864

FELIX, CHRISTOPHER. See: George Marton, 1900-   .

FELTNER, BERT, JR. Born in Ky.; a professional in the U.S. military.
Death Comes Easy. Carlton, 1964

FEMLING, JEAN
Backyard. Harper, 1975 [Calif.]

FENADY, ANDREW J. 1928-   . Ref: CA.
SC: Sam Marlow, in both titles.
The Man with Bogart's Face. Regnery, 1977 [L.A.]
The Secret of Sam Marlow. Contemporary, 1980 [L.A.]

FENISONG, RUTH.   -1978. Ref: CC, TC.
SC: Capt. Gridley Nelson = GN
Bite the Hand. Doubleday, 1956. British title: The Blackmailer. Foulsham, 1958 GN [NYC]
The Blackmailer; see Bite the Hand
But Not Forgotten. Doubleday, 1960. British title: Sinister Assignment. Foulsham, 1960 GN [NYC]
The Butler Died in Brooklyn. Doubleday, 1943; Aldor, 1946 GN [NYC]
The Case of the Gloating Landlord; see The Schemers
Dead Weight. Doubleday, 1962; Hale, 1964 GN [NYC]
Dead Yesterday. Doubleday, 1951 GN [NYC]
Deadlock. Doubleday, 1952 GN [NYC]
Death Is a Gold Coin; see The Lost Caesar
Death Is a Lovely Lady; see Jenny Kissed Me
Death of the Party. Doubleday, 1958 GN [NYC]
Desperate Cure. Doubleday, 1946 [NYC]
The Drop of a Hat. Doubleday, 1970; Hale, 1971 [NYC]
Grim Rehearsal. Doubleday, 1950; Foulsham, 1951 GN [NYC]
Ill Wind. Doubleday, 1950; Foulsham, 1952 [Carib.]
Jenny Kissed Me. Doubleday, 1944. Also published as: Death Is a Lovely Lady. Popular Library, 1949 [Conn.]
The Lost Caesar. Doubleday, 1945; Aldor, 1946. Also published as: Death Is a Gold Coin. Popular Library, 1950 [NYC]
Miscast for Murder. Doubleday, 1954. Also published as: Too Lovely to Live. Bestseller, 1955 GN [NYC]
Murder Needs a Face. Doubleday, 1942 GN [NYC]
Murder Needs a Name. Doubleday, 1942; Swan, 1950 GN [NYC]
Murder Runs a Fever. Doubleday, 1943 GN [NYC]
The Schemers. Doubleday, 1957. British title: The Case of the Gloating Landlord. Foulsham, 1958 [It.]
Sinister Assignment; see But Not Forgotten
Snare for Sinners. Doubleday, 1949; Foulsham, 1951 [N.Y.]
Too Lovely to Live; see Miscast for Murder
Villainous Company. Doubleday, 1967; Hale, 1968 [New Eng.]
The Wench Is Dead. Doubleday, 1953 GN [L.I.]
Widows' Blackmail; see Widow's Plight
Widow's Plight. Doubleday, 1955. British title: Widows' Blackmail. Foulsham, 1957 [NYC]

FENN, CAROLINE K. Joint pseudonym with Julia McGrew: Fenn McGrew, q.v.

FENN, G(EORGE) MANVILLE. 1831-1909.
-The Adventures of Doc Lavington. Partridge, 1896
Aynsley's Case. Long, 1908

The Bag of Diamonds. Ward, 1887; Lovell, 1887
-Beneath the Sea. Crowell, 1896 (British title?)
-Bent, Not Broken. Tinsley, 1867
-The Black Bar. Low, 1893
Black Blood: A Peculiar Case. Lovell, 1888 (British title?)
Black Shadows. Chatto, 1902
Blind Policy. Long, 1904
-By Birth a Lady. Tinsley, 1871
-The Cankerworm: Being Episodes in a Woman's Life. Chatto, 1901
The Case of Ailsa Gray. White, 1896
The Chaplain's Craze; Being the Mystery of Findon Friars. Ward, 1886; Harper, 1886
-The Clerk of Portwick. Chapman, 1880
-Coming Home to Roost. White, 1904
-Commodore Junk. Cassell, 1888; Munro, 1889
Cormorant Crag: A Tale of the Smuggling Days. Partridge, 1895; Dodd, 1895
-A Country Squire: Being an Impossible Story. White, 1907
A Crimson Crime. Chatto, 1899
Cursed by a Fortune. White, 1896; Rand, 1897
The Dark House: A Knot Unravelled. Ward, 1885; Harper, 1885
Double Cunning: A Tale of a Transparent Mystery. Chapman, 1896
A Double Knot. Methuen, 1890; U.S. Book Co., 1891
-Dutch the Diver; or, A Man's Mistake. Cassell, 1883
-Fire Island: Being the Adventures of Uncertain Naturalists in an Unknown Track. Low, 1894
-A Fluttered Dovecote. Ward, 1890
-In an Alpine Valley. Hurst, 1894
In Jeopardy, and other stories of peril. Ward, 1889 ss
-It Came to Pass. White, 1903
-Jack the Rascal. Everett, 1909
-King of the Castle. Ward, 1892
-Lady Maude's Mania. Warne, 1890; U.S. Book Co., 1890
-The Lass That Loved a Soldier. Ward, 1889
-Mad: A Story of Dust and Ashes. Tinsley, 1868
-Mahme Nousie. Hurst, 1891
-The Man with a Shadow. Ward, 1888
-The Master of the Ceremonies. Ward, 1886
-Midnight Webs. Tinsley, 1872
-Morgan's Horror: A Romance of the "West Countree." Cassell (London), 1885; Cassell (NYC), 1888
The Mynns' Mystery. Warne, 1890; Lovell, 1889
-The New Mistress. Chatto, 1891
-Nic Revel. Chambers, 1898
-Nurse Elisia. Hurst, 1893; Cassell, 1892
-Of High Descent. Ward, 1889
-Off to the Wilds: Being the Adventures of Two Brothers. Low, 1881
-One Maid's Mischief. Ward, 1887; Appleton, 1888
Original Penny Christmas Readings. Routledge, 1866 ss, some criminous
-The Parson o' Dumford. Chapman, 1879; Cassell, 1883
-The Queen's Scarlet: Being the Adventures and Misadventures of Sir Richard Frayne. Cassell (London), 1895
-The Rajah of Dah. Chambers, 1891
-The Rosery Folk: A Country Tale. Chapman, 1884; Munro, 1884
-Running Amok: A Story of Adventure. Chatto, 1901
-Sappers and Miners; or, The Flood Beneath the Sea. White, 1896
-The Sapphire Cross. Tinsley, 1871
Sawn Off. Henry, 1891
-A Secret Quest. Taylor, 1893 (British title?)
-The Silver Canyon: A Tale of the Western Plains. Low, 1884
-Sir Hilton's Sin. White, 1908
-So Like a Woman. Chatto, 1905
-The Star-Gazers. Methuen, 1894
-The Story of Antony Grace; or, Some Shared Pages. Ward, 1888; Appleton, 1888
-Sweet Mace: A Sussex Legend of the Iron Times. Chapman, 1884; Cassell (NYC), 1885
-Thereby Hangs a Tale. Tinsley, 1876
-This Man's Wife. Ward, 1887; Lovell, 1887
-Three People's Secret: A Tale of the Faculty. Simpkin Marshall, 1889
-The Tiger Lily: A Story of Two Passions. Chatto, 1894; Cassell, 1895
-The Traitor's Gate and other stories. Digby Long, 1906 ss
-The Vibart Affair. Pearson, 1899
-The Vicar's People: A Story of a Stain. Chapman, 1881; Munro, 1881

-Webs in the Way. Tinsley, 1867
-The White Virgin. Chatto, 1894; Rand, 1896
Witness to the Deed. Chatto, 1893; Cassell, 1893
-A Woman Worth Winning. Chatto, 1898; Rand, 1898

FENN, LOUIS ANDERSON
The Killing Bottle Murder. Methuen, 1936

FENN, W(ILLIAM) W(ILTHEW). 1827?- .
After Sundown; or, The Palette and the Pen. Low, 1880 ss, some criminous
Half Hours of a Blind Man's Holiday; or, Summer and Winter Sketches in Black and White. Low, 1878 ss, some criminous
'Twixt the Lights. Drane, 1894 ss, some criminous

FENNELLY, PARKER (W.)
Cuckoos on the Hearth. Dramatists, 1942 (3-act play.)

FENNERTON, WILLIAM. Born in England; journalist and writer.
-Christmas Without Roddy. Hutchinson, 1965
Czech Mate. Elek, 1979
The Jensen Scenario. Elek, 1978 [Brus.]
The Lucifer Cell. Hodder, 1969; Atheneum, 1968
-Old Fox. Davies, 1972
The Potentate. Gollancz, 1963; Harper, 1961
-A Touch of Red. Hutchinson, 1966

FENTON, EDWARD. 1917- . Pseudonym: Edwina Follett, q.v. Ref: CA.
The Double Darkness. Doubleday, 1947 [Athens]

FENTON, JESSIE (M. CHASE). 1894- .
Down the Dark Street. Houghton, 1937; H. Hamilton, 1938

FENTON, NORMAN. 1895- .
Murder at Vista Point? Vantage, 1977

FENTON, PAT
This Little Angel Went to Hell. Caravelle, 1967

FENTY, PHILIP
Super Fly. Ballantine, 1972 (Novelization of the movie, actually written by Leonore Fleischer, q.v.)

FENWICK, E. P. [ELIZABETH FENWICK WAY]. 1920- . Byline also: Elizabeth Fenwick, q.v.
The Inconvenient Corpse. Farrar, 1943
Murder in Haste. Farrar, 1944 [NYC, acad.]
Two Names for Death. Farrar, 1945; Wells Gardner, 1949 [Boston]

FENWICK, ELIZA
Secrecy; or, The Ruin on the Rock. Lane, 1795

FENWICK, ELIZABETH [ELIZABETH FENWICK WAY]. 1920- . Byline also: E. P. Fenwick, q.v. Ref: TC.
Disturbance on Berry Hill. Atheneum, 1968; Gollancz, 1968
A Friend of Mary Rose. Harper, 1961; Gollancz, 1962
Goodbye, Aunt Elva. Atheneum, 1968; Gollancz, 1969 [New Eng.]
Impeccable People. Gollancz, 1971
The Last of Lysandra. Gollancz, 1973
A Long Way Down. Harper, 1959; Gollancz, 1959 [acad.]
The Make-Believe Man. Harper, 1963; Gollancz, 1964
A Night Run. Gollancz, 1961
The Passenger. Atheneum, 1967; Gollancz, 1967 [N.Y.]
Poor Harriet. Harper, 1957; Gollancz, 1958 [Conn.]
The Silent Cousin. Atheneum, 1966; Gollancz, 1962 [N.Y.]

FERGUSON. Pseudonym: Nicholas Carter, q.v.

FERGUSON, ANTHONY
The Big Snatch. Hale, 1971
A Game of Chance. Hale, 1970
A Running Man. Hale, 1969 [Afr., W.]

FERGUSON, AUSTIN. 1941- .
Jet Stream. Morrow, 1974; Hutchinson, 1975 [air]
Random Track; see Random Track to Peking
Random Track to Peking. Morrow, 1979. British title: Random Track. Hutchinson, 1980 [Russ.]

FERGUSON, CHRIS(TOPHER WILSON). 1944- . Ref: CA.
-The Molting Season. Harper, 1974

FERGUSON, JOHN (ALEXANDER). 1873- .
Ref: CC, MM, MP. SC: Francis MacNab = FM.
The Dark Geraldine. Lane (London & NYC), 1921 FM (A different character than in the other FM books?) [Scot.]
Death Comes to Perigord. Collins, 1931; Dodd, 1931 FM [Chan. Is.]
Death of Mr. Dodsley. Collins, 1937 FM
The Grouse Moor Murder; see The Grouse Moor Mystery
The Grouse Moor Mystery. Collins, 1934. U.S. title: The Grouse Moor Murder. Dodd, 1934 FM
The Man in the Dark. Lane, 1928; Dodd, 1928 FM
Murder on the Marsh. Lane, 1930; Dodd, 1930 FM
Night in Glengyle. Collins, 1933; Dodd, 1933 [Scot.]
The Secret Road. Bodley, 1925; Dodd, 1925 [India]
Stealthy Terror. Lane (London & NYC), 1918 [Berlin]
Terror on the Island. Collins, 1942; Vanguard, 1942 [Ger.]

FERGUSON, MARGARET
The Sign of the Ram. Hale, 1943; Blakiston, 1945

FERGUSON, PAMELA. 1943- . Ref: CA.
The Olympic Mission. Everest, 1976
The Pipe Dream. Everest, 1974

FERGUSON, RUBY (CONSTANCE ANNIE)
A Woman with a Secret. Hodder, 1965

FERGUSON, W(ILLIAM) B(LAIR) M(ORTON). 1881-1967. Pseudonym: William Morton, q.v. SC: Dan Cluer, in at least those marked DC.
The Big Take. Long, 1952
-Black Bread. Long, 1933
The Black Company. Jenkins, 1925; Chelsea, 1924 [N.Y.]
Boss of the Skeletons. Long, 1945
The Clue in the Glass. Jenkins, 1927. U.S. title: The Clew in the Glass. Chelsea, 1926 [U.S.]
Crackerjack. Long, 1936
Dog Fox. Long, 1938
Escape to Eternity. Long, 1944 DC [NYC]
The Island of Surprises. Long, 1935
London Lamb. Long, 1939
Other Folks' Money. Nelson, 1928
Phonies. Long, 1951
Prelude to Horror. Long, 1943
The Riddle of the Rose. Jenkins, 1929; McBride, 1929 [N.Y.]
Sally. Long, 1940
The Shayne Case. Long, 1947 DC [NYC]
Somewhere Off Borneo. Long, 1936
The Vanishing Men. Long, 1932
Wyoming Tragedy. Long, 1935 [Wyo.]

FERGUSON, W. HUMER
The Mystery of a Wheelbarrow. Scott, 1888

FERGUSSON, BERNARD (EDWARD). 1911-1980. Ref: CA.
The Rare Adventure. Collins, 1954; Rinehart, 1955

FERM, BETTY. 1926- . Ref: CA.
Edge of Beauty. Dell, 1974 [NYC]
Eventide. Dell, 1974
False Idols. Putnam, 1974 [N.Y.]
The Vengeance of Valdone. Dell, 1973 [Fr.]

FERME, MRS. GEORGE. Pseudonym: George Douglas, q.v.

FERNALD, CHESTER BAILEY. 1869-1938.
The Cat and the Cherub and other stories. Century, 1896 ss, at least one criminous
-Chinatown Stories. Heinemann, 1900 ss

FERNAND, ROLAND F.
The Case of the Sulky Girl. Dramatic, 1951 (3-act play based on the novel by Erle Stanley Gardner, 1889-1970, q.v.)

FERNANDES, J. R.
Yokohama Hood. Vantage, 1967 [Jap.]

FERNANDEZ, ALONZO
The Castle of Lugas. Jamaica, 1927 [Sp.]

FERNEE, HERBERT
The Narrow House. Christophers, 1948
Now, Gentlemen, Please. Faber, 1940
They Wetted His Head. Faber, 1943

FERRAND, GEORGINA. Pseudonym of Brenda Castle.
-Call Back Yesterday. Hale, 1977
Dangerous Inheritance. Hale, 1976; Beagle, 1974
Encounter in Athens. Hale, 1976 [Athens]
-The Gilded Cage. Hale, 1979
House of Glass. Hale, 1977; Beagle, 1975 [Venice, past]
-Land of Eucalyptus. Hale, 1980
-Reluctant Lover. Hale, 1980
-A Scent of Roses. Hale, 1978
-Shadows of the Past. Hale, 1977
-Summer Concerto. Hale, 1979
The Thickening Light. Hale, 1977; Beagle, 1974

FERRARS, ELIZABETH (XAVIA). U.S. byline: E. X. Ferrars. Pseudonym of Morna Doris MacTaggart Brown, 1907- . Ref: CA, CC, EM, TC. SC: Toby Dyke = TD; Virginia Freer, in at least those marked VF. Set: Eng.
Alibi for a Witch. Collins, 1952; Doubleday, 1952 [It.]
Alive and Dead. Collins, 1974; Doubleday, 1975
Always Say Die. Collins, 1956. U.S. title: We Haven't Seen Her Lately. Doubleday, 1956
Blood Flies Upwards. Collins, 1976; Collins, 1977
Breath of Suspicion. Collins, 1972
The Busy Body. Collins, 1962. U.S. title: Seeing Double. Doubleday, 1962
Cheat the Hangman; see Murder Among Friends
The Clock That Wouldn't Stop. Collins, 1952; Doubleday, 1952
Count the Cost; see Unreasonable Doubt
The Cup and the Lip. Collins, 1975; Doubleday, 1976
Death in Botanist's Bay. Hodder, 1941. U.S. title: Murder of a Suicide. Doubleday, 1941 TD
The Decayed Gentlewoman; see A Legal Fiction
Depart This Life; see A Tale of Two Murders
Designs on Life. Collins, 1980; Doubleday, 1980 ss
Don't Monkey with Murder. Hodder, 1942. U.S. title: The Shape of a Stain. Doubleday, 1942 TD
The Doubly Dead. Collins, 1963; Doubleday, 1963
Drowned Rat. Collins, 1975; Doubleday, 1975
Enough to Kill a Horse. Collins, 1955; Doubleday, 1955
Fear the Light. Collins, 1960; Doubleday, 1960
Foot in the Grave. Collins, 1973; Doubleday, 1972
Frog in the Throat. Collins, 1980; Doubleday, 1980 VF
Furnished for Murder. Collins, 1957
Give a Corpse a Bad Name. Hodder, 1940 TD
Hanged Man's House. Collins, 1974; Doubleday, 1974
Hunt the Tortoise. Collins, 1950; Doubleday, 1950
I, Said the Fly. Hodder, 1945; Doubleday, 1945
In at the Kill. Collins, 1978; Doubleday, 1979 [Scot.]
Kill or Cure; see Murder Moves In
Last Will and Testament. Collins, 1978; Doubleday, 1978 VF
A Legal Fiction. Collins, 1964. U.S. title: The Decayed Gentlewoman. Doubleday, 1963
The Lying Voices. Collins, 1954
The March Hare Murders. Collins, 1949; Doubleday, 1949
Milk of Human Kindness. Collins, 1950
Murder Among Friends. Collins, 1946. U.S. title: Cheat the Hangman. Doubleday, 1946
Murder in Time. Collins, 1953
Murder Moves In. Collins, 1956. U.S. title: Kill or Cure. Doubleday, 1956
Murder of a Suicide; see Death in Botanist's Bay
Murders Anonymous. Collins, 1977; Doubleday, 1978
Neck in a Noose; see Your Neck in a Noose
Ninth Life. Collins, 1965
No Peace for the Wicked. Collins, 1966; Harper, 1966
The Pretty Pink Shroud. Collins, 1977; Doubleday, 1977
Rehearsals for Murder; see Remove the Bodies
Remove the Bodies. Hodder, 1940. U.S. title: Rehearsals for Murder. Doubleday, 1941 TD
Seeing Double; see The Busy Body

The Seven Sleepers. Collins, 1970;
  Walker, 1970
The Shape of a Stain; see Don't Monkey
  with Murder
Skeleton Staff. Collins, 1969; Walker,
  1969 [Madeira]
Sleeping Dogs. Collins, 1960; Double-
  day, 1960
The Small World of Murder. Collins,
  1973; Doubleday, 1973
A Stranger and Afraid. Collins, 1971;
  Walker, 1971
The Swaying Pillars. Collins, 1968;
  Walker, 1969 [Afr.]
A Tale of Two Murders. Collins, 1959.
  U.S. title: Depart This Life.
  Doubleday, 1958
Unreasonable Doubt. Collins, 1958.
  U.S. title: Count the Cost. Double-
  day, 1957
The Wandering Widows. Collins, 1962;
  Doubleday, 1962 [Hebrides]
We Haven't Seen Her Lately; see Always
  Say Die
With Murder in Mind. Collins, 1948
Witness Before the Fact. Collins, 1979;
  Doubleday, 1980 [Madeira]
Your Neck in a Noose. Hodder, 1942.
  U.S. title: Neck in a Noose. Double-
  day, 1943 TD
Zero at the Bone. Collins, 1967;
  Walker, 1968

FERRARS, FRANCIS
  Jim Cummings; or, The Crime of the
    Frisco Express. RR Publishing, 1887.
    (Later rewritten and published as by
    A. Frank Pinkerton, q.v.)

FERREOL, MARCEL AUGUSTE. 1899-1974. Pseudonym: Marcel Achard. Ref: CA. See:
  Harry Kurnitz, 1907-1968.

FERRIS, JEAN ERSKINE
  House of Hate. Remploy, 1974

FERRIS, PAUL (FREDERICK). 1929-   . Ref:
  CA.
  The Detective. Weidenfeld, 1976. U.S.
    title: High Places. Coward, 1977
  High Places; see The Detective
  Talk to Me About England. Weidenfeld,
    1979; Coward, 1979

FERRIS, TOM. Pseudonym of Peter N(orman)
  Walker, 1936-   , q.v. Other pseudo-
  nyms: Christopher Coram, Nicholas
  Rhea, qq.v.
  Espionage for a Lady. Hale, 1969

FERRIS, WALLY
  Across 110th. Harper, 1970. British
    title: The Hunt. MacGibbon, 1971
    [NYC]

FESSIER, MICHAEL. 1905-   .
  Fully Dressed and in His Right Mind.
    Knopf, 1935; Gollancz, 1935 [S.F.]

FETHALAND, JOHN
  The Murder at Charters. Gollancz, 1939

FETTA, EMMA LOU. Newspaper reporter and
  foreign correspondent. SC: Lyle Curtis and Susan Yates, in at least
  those marked C&Y.
  Dressed to Kill. Doubleday, 1941
  Murder in Style. Doubleday, 1939 C&Y
    [NYC]
  Murder on the Face of It. Doubleday,
    1940 C&Y [NYC]

FETTER, ELIZABETH HEAD. 1904-1973. Pseudonym: Hannah Lees, q.v.

FFORDE, (ARTHUR) BROWNLOW. 1871-   .
  The Subaltern, the Policeman, and the
    Little Girl. Low, 1890
  The Trotter: A Poona Mystery. Low, 1890
    [India]

FIASCHETTI, MICHAEL
  You Gotta Be Rough. Doubleday, 1930.
    British title: The Man They Couldn't
    Escape. Selwyn, 1928 ss [NYC]

FICK, CARL. Motion picture scriptwriter
  and director.
  The Danziger Transcript. Putnam, 1971;
    Deutsch, 1973

FICKLING, FORREST E. 1925-   . Ref: CA.
  Joint pseudonym with Gloria Fickling:
  G. G. Fickling, q.v.

FICKLING, G. G. Joint pseudonym of
  Gloria Fickling and Forrest E. Fick-
  ling, 1925-   . SC: Honey West =
  HW; Erik March = EM.
  Blood and Honey. Pyramid, 1961 HW
    [NYC]
  Bombshell. Pyramid, 1964 HW [Fla.]

The Case of the Radioactive Redhead.
  Belmont, 1963 EM
The Crazy Mixed-Up Nude. Belmont, 1964
  EM
Dig a Dead Doll. Pyramid, 1960 HW
  [Mex.]
Girl on the Loose. Pyramid, 1958 HW
  [Calif.]
Girl on the Prowl. Pyramid, 1959 HW
  [L.A.]
A Gun for Honey. Pyramid, 1958 HW
  [Calif.]
Honey in the Flesh. Pyramid, 1959 HW
  [Calif.]
Honey on Her Tail. Pyramid, 1971 HW
  [Fr.]
Kiss for a Killer. Pyramid, 1960 HW
  [Calif.]
Naughty But Dead. Belmont, 1962 EM
  [L.A.]
Stiff as a Broad. Pyramid, 1971 HW,EM
  [S.F.]
This Girl for Hire. Pyramid, 1957 HW
  [Calif.]

FICKLING, GLORIA. Joint pseudonym with
  Forrest E. Fickling, 1925-   : G.
  G. Fickling, q.v.

FIDLER, HENRY J.
  Chronicles of Dennis Chetwynd. Hutchin-
    son, 1927 ss

FIEDLER, JEAN (NETTE FELDMAN). Ref: CA.
  Atone with Evil. Bantam (NYC & London),
    1976 [Mex.]

FIELD, HERBERT N.
  The Marsh Gang. Jarrolds, 1929
  The Needle. Jarrolds, 1929

FIELD, KATHERINE. SC: Det. Insp. Ross
  Paterson, in all titles, set in Eng.
  Disappearance of a Niece. Murray, 1941
  Murder to Follow. Jenkins, 1944
  The Two-Five to Mardon. Murray, 1942

FIELD, MEDORA. 1898-   . Ref: CC, MP.
  Blood on Her Shoe. Macmillan, 1942;
    Jarrolds, 1943 [Ga.]
  Who Killed Aunt Maggie? Macmillan,
    1939; Jarrolds, 1940 [Ga.]

FIELD, MOIRA. Ref: CC. SC: Det. Insp.
  Flower, in both titles, set in Eng.
  Foreign Body. Bles, 1950; Macmillan,
    1951
  Gunpowder Treason and Plot. Bles, 1951

FIELD, PENELOPE. Pseudonym of Dorothy
  (Dodds) Giberson, q.v.
  Someone Is Watching. Little, 1976;
    Prior, 1977 [Calif.]

FIELD, RUTH BAKER
  Wild Violets. Zebra, 1980

FIELD, TEMPLE. Pseudonym of Raoul Whit-
  field, 1898-1945, q.v.
  Five. Farrar, 1931 [air.]
  Killer's Carnival. Farrar, 1932 [NYC]

FIELDING, A. Pseudonym of Dorothy
  Feilding, 1884-   . Ref: CC, MM, MP,
  TC. SC: Insp. Pointer = P. (Note: A
  few U.S. titles have the byline A. E.
  Fielding.) Set: Eng.
  Black Cats Are Lucky. Collins, 1937;
    Kinsey, 1938, as by AEF P
  The Case of the Missing Diary. Collins,
    1935; Kinsey, 1936 P
  The Case of the Two Pearl Necklaces.
    Collins, 1936; Kinsey, 1936, as by
    AEF P
  The Cautley Conundrum. Collins, 1934.
    U.S. title: The Cautley Mystery.
    Kinsey, 1934 P
  The Cautley Mystery; see The Cautley
    Conundrum
  The Charteris Mystery. Collins, 1925;
    Knopf, 1925 P
  The Clifford Affair. Collins, 1927;
    Knopf, 1927. Also published as: The
    Clifford Mystery. Collins, 1933 P
  The Clifford Mystery; see The Clifford
    Affair
  The Cluny Problem. Collins, 1928;
    Knopf, 1929 P
  The Craig Poisoning Mystery. Collins,
    1930; Cosmopolitan, 1930 P
  Death of John Tait. Collins, 1932;
    Kinsey, 1932 P
  Deep Currents. Collins, 1924
  The Eames-Erskine Case. Collins, 1924;
    Knopf, 1925 P
  The Footsteps That Stopped. Collins,
    1926; Knopf, 1926 P
  Murder at the Nook. Collins, 1929;
    Knopf, 1930 P
  Murder in Suffolk. Collins, 1938; Kin-
    sey, 1938, as by AEF

The Mysterious Partner. Collins, 1929;
  Knopf, 1929 P
Mystery at the Rectory. Collins, 1936;
  Kinsey, 1937, as by AEF P
The Net Around Joan Ingilby. Collins,
  1928; Knopf, 1928 P
The Paper-Chase. Collins, 1934. U.S.
  title: The Paper-Chase Mystery. Kin-
  sey, 1935 P
The Paper-Chase Mystery; see The Paper
  Chase
Pointer to a Crime. Collins, 1944;
  Mystery House, 1945 P
Scarecrow. Collins, 1973; Kinsey, 1937,
  as by AEF P
The Tall House Mystery. Collins, 1933;
  Kinsey, 1933 P
Tragedy at Beechcroft. Collins, 1935;
  Kinsey, 1935 P
The Upfold Farm Mystery. Collins, 1931;
  Kinsey, 1932 P
The Wedding-Chest Mystery. Collins,
  1930; Kinsey, 1932 P
The Westwood Mystery. Collins, 1932;
  Kinsey, 1933 P

FIELDING, A. E. See: A. Fielding.

FIELDING, HOWARD. Pseudonym of Charles
  Witherle Hooke, 1861-1929.
  The Confederate; see Hidden Out
  Equal Partners. Dillingham, 1901 [NYC]
  Hidden Out. Chelsea, 1927. British
    title: The Confederate. Nelson, 1929
  The Housekeeper's Secret. (New York)
    1889
  Straight Crooks. Chelsea, 1927 [NYC]
  -The Victim of His Clothes. Ogilvie,
    1890

FIELDING, JOY. 1945-   . Ref: CA.
  Trance. Playboy, 1977; Hamlyn, 1979
    [Chile]
  The Transformation. Playboy, 1976
    [L.A.]

FIELDING, PETER
  Text for Murder. Evans, 1951

FIELDING, WILLIAM H. Pseudonym of Darwin
  L. Teilhet, 1904-1964, q.v. See also:
  Hildegarde Tolman Teilhet, 1906-   .
  Take Me As I Am. GM, 1952
  The Unpossessed. GM, 1951

FIELDS, ALAN. Pseudonym of Richard Allen
  Duprey, 1929-   . Ref: CA.
  V-J Day. Dell, 1978; Hamlyn, 1979
    [NYC, 1945]

FILER, TOM. 1925-   .
  -The Man on Watch. Harper, 1961; Hutch-
    inson, 1961 [ship]

FILGATE, (C.) MACARTNEY. Operates crea-
  tive design company in London. SC:
  Charlotte Eliot, in both titles.
  Bravo Charlie. Muller, 1979. U.S.
    title (?): Runway to Death. Walker,
    1980
  Delta November. Muller, 1979
  Runway to Death; see Bravo Charlie

FINCH, MATTHEW. Pseudonym of Morton Fink,
  1921-   . SC: a female private eye,
  in both titles. Ref: CA.
  Eye Spy. Dobson, 1975
  Eye with Mascara. Dobson, 1968

FINCH, PHILLIP
  Storm Front. Coward, 1977; Sphere, 1979

FINDLEY, FERGUSON. Pseudonym of Charles
  Weiser Frey, 1910-   . Born in Pa.;
  graduate of Naval Academy. SC: John-
  ny Malone = JM.
  Counterfeit Corpse. Ace, 1956 [New
    Eng.]
  Dead Ringer; see The Man in the Middle
  A Handful of Murder; see The Man in the
    Middle
  Killer Cop; see My Old Man's Badge
  The Man in the Middle. Duell, 1952.
    British title: A Handful of Murder.
    Reinhardt, 1955. Also published as:
    Dead Ringer. Bestseller, 1953 [NYC]
  Murder Makes Me Mad. Popular Library,
    1956 [NYC]
  My Old Man's Badge. Duell, 1950; Rein-
    hardt, 1950. Also published as:
    Killer Cop. Monarch, 1959 JM [NYC]
  Remember That Face!; see Waterfront
  Waterfront. Duell, 1951. British title:
    Remember That Face! Reinhardt, 1951
    JM [NYC]

FINDLEY, TIMOTHY. 1930-   . Ref: CA.
  The Butterfly Plague. Viking, 1969;
    Deutsch, 1970
  The Last of the Crazy People. Meredith,
    1967; Macdonald, 1967

FINE, PETER HEATH. 1938-   . Pseudonym: Peter Heath, q.v.
   Night Trains. Lippincott, 1979; New English Library, 1979, as by Peter Heath

FINK, MERTON. 1921-   . Pseudonym: Matthew Finch, q.v.

FINLAY, IAIN. Born in Australia; reporter and radio and TV journalist on location around the world.
   The Azanian Assignment. Harper, 1978; Futura, 1980 [1981, S. Afr.]

FINLEY, GLENNA [GLENNA FINLEY WHITE]. 1925-   . Ref: CA.
   Death Strikes Out. Arcadia, 1957 [NYC]

FINLEY, SCOTT. Pseudonym of Rosy Lee Winifred Cecelia Clark, 1909-   .
   The Case of the Black Sheep. Phoenix, 1950 [NYC]

FINN, EDMUND. 1819-1898
   The Hordern Mystery. McKinley (Melbourne), 1889
   A Priest's Secret; Under Seal of Confession. McKinley (Melbourne), 1888

FINN, JOAN LOCKWOOD
   Heritage of Evil. Belmont, 1968

FINNEGAN, ROBERT. Pseudonym of Paul William Ryan, 1906-1947. Ref: TC. SC: Dan Banion, in all titles.
   The Bandaged Nude. Simon, 1946; Boardman, 1949 [S.F.]
   The Lying Ladies. Simon, 1946; Bodley, 1949
   Many a Monster. Simon, 1948; Boardman, 1950 [S.F.]

FINNEY, JACK. Pseudonym of Walter Braden Finney, 1911-   . Ref: TC.
   Assault on a Queen. Simon, 1959; Eyre, 1960 [ship]
   Five Against the House. Doubleday, 1954; Eyre, 1954
   The House of Numbers. Dell, 1957; Eyre, 1957 [Calif.]
   The Night People. Doubleday, 1977 [Calif.]

FINNEY, R. C. SC: Insp. Bourne, in at least some of these titles.
   The Coleville Skeleton. Scion, 1950
   The Crimson Hand. Scion, 1949
   Death in the Mist. Burrell, 1947
   Death Takes a Ride. Scion, 1951
   Find the Lady. Scion, 1949
   The Haunted Rock. Century, 1948
   Honeymoon Murder. Burrell, 1947
   Lover's Feud. Scion, 1949
   Love's Prisoner. Scion, 1952
   Meet Inspector Bourne. Newcoll, 1945
   The "Scarlet Ship". Partridge, 1928
   The Secret Tunnel. Mellifont, 1937
   Talking Clues. Scion, 1949
   Three Point Murder. Scion, 1949

FINNEY, WALTER BRADEN. 1911-   . Pseudonym: Jack Finney, q.v.

FIRMSTONE, GEORGE W. H.
   The Mystery of Crowther Castle and other stories. Digby, 1890 ss

FIRTH, ANTHONY. 1937-1980. Ref: CA, CC, MC.
   Tall, Balding, Thirty-Five. Hutchinson, 1966; Harper, 1967. Also published as: The Limbo Affair. Lancer, 1968 [Ger.]

FIRTH, IVAN EUSTACE. 1891-   . Joint pseudonym with Gladys Shaw Erskine, 1895-   : Firth Erskine, q.v.

FIRTH, J. W.
   Crime Confessions. Spencer, 1948

FIRTH, N. WESLEY
   Concerto for Fear. Bear Hudson, 1945
   Dames Play Rough. Murray, 1946
   Gangster Pay-Off. Hughes, n.d.
   -Guns of Calliope. Fiction House, 1948
   Lady in Leicester Square. Brown Watson, 1946
   Manhattan Bombshell. Hamilton Stafford, 1946 [NYC]
   Murder for Sale. Bear Hudson, 1945
   Mystery Crime Cases. Spencer, 1948 ss
   -Outlawed Guns. Mitre, 1946
   Phantom Detective Cases. Spencer, 1948 ss
   Terror Stalks by Night. Bear Hudson, 1945
   This Is Murder, Lady! Mitre, 1945 ss
   Trouble Buster. Mitre, 1946
   When Shall I Sleep Again? Gifford, 1950
   The Woman of Danger. Modern Fiction, 1946

FIRTH, VIOLET MARY. 1890-1946. Pseudonym: Dion Fortune, q.v.

FISCHER, BRUNO. 1908-   . Pseudonym: Russell Gray, q.v. Ref: CA, TC. SC: Ben Helm = BH; Rick Train = RT.
   The Angels Fell. Dodd, 1950; Boardman, 1951. Also published as: The Flesh Was Cold. Signet, 1950 BH [N.Y.]
   The Bleeding Scissors. Ziff-Davis, 1948. British title: The Scarlet Scissors. Foulsham, 1950 [Conn.]
   Croaked the Raven; see Quoth the Raven
   The Dead Men Grin. McKay, 1945; Quality, 1947 BH [N.Y.]
   The Evil Days. Random, 1974; Hale, 1976 [N.Y.]
   The Fast Buck. GM, 1952; Red Seal, 1959 [NYC]
   The Fingered Man; see Quoth the Raven
   The Flesh Was Cold; see The Angels Fell
   Fools Walk In. GM, 1952; Red Seal, 1958
   The Girl Between. GM, 1960 [New Eng.]
   The Hornet's Nest. Morrow, 1944; Quality, 1947 RT [NYC]
   House of Flesh. GM, 1950; Red Seal, 1958
   Kill to Fit. Five Star, 1946; Instructive Arts, 1951 RT [New Eng.]
   Knee-Deep in Death. GM, 1956; Fawcett (London), 1957
   The Lady Kills. GM, 1951
   More Deaths Than One. Ziff-Davis, 1947; Foulsham, 1950 BH
   Murder in the Raw. GM, 1957; Fawcett (London), 1959 [N.Y.]
   The Paper Circle. Dodd, 1951; Boardman, 1952. Also published as: Stripped for Murder. Signet, 1953 BH [N.Y.]
   The Pigskin Bag. Ziff-Davis, 1946; Foulsham, 1951 [NYC]
   Quoth the Raven. Doubleday, 1944. British title: Croaked the Raven. Quality, 1947. Also published as: The Fingered Man. Ace, 1953 [NYC]
   The Restless Hands. Dodd, 1949; Foulsham, 1950 BH [N.Y.]
   Run for Your Life. GM, 1953; Fawcett (London), 1954 [N.Y.]
   The Scarlet Scissors; see The Bleeding Scissors
   Second-Hand Nude. GM, 1959; Muller pb, 1960 [NYC]
   The Silent Dust. Dodd, 1950; Boardman, 1951 BH [L.I.]
   So Much Blood. Greystone, 1939. Also published as: Stairway to Death. Pyramid, 1951 [NYC]
   So Wicked My Love. GM, 1954; Fawcett (London), 1957 [NYC]
   The Spider Lily. McKay, 1946; Quality, 1953 [N.Y.]
   Stairway to Death; see So Much Blood
   Stripped for Murder; see The Paper Circle

FISCHER, ERWIN. 1928-   . Born and living in Ger.; journalist, TV newscaster, editor, free-lance writer.
   The Berlin Indictment. World, 1971 (Translation of "Kameradenessen." Munich, 1970.) [Ger.]

FISCHER, MARJORIE. 1903?-1961.
   Embarrassment of Riches. Random, 1944

FISH, ROBERT L(LOYD). 1912-1981. Pseudonym: Robert L. Pike, q.v. See also: Jack London, 1876-1916. Ref: CA, CC, EM, TC. SC: Jose da Silva = JdS; Kek Huuygens = KH; Schlock Homes = SH; Carruthers, Simpson and Briggs = C&S&B.
   Always Kill a Stranger. Putnam, 1967 JdS [Rio de J.]
   Brazilian Sleigh Ride. Simon, 1965; Boardman, 1966 JdS [Brazil]
   The Bridge That Went Nowhere. Putnam, 1968; Long, 1970 JdS [Brazil]
   Death Cuts the Deck; see Rub-a-Dub-Dub
   The Diamond Bubble. Simon, 1965; Boardman, 1965 JdS [Rio de J.]
   The Fugitive. Simon, 1962; Boardman, 1963 JdS [Rio de J.]
   The Gold of Troy. Doubleday, 1980
   The Green Hell Treasure. Putnam, 1971 JdS [Barbados]
   A Gross Carriage of Justice. Doubleday, 1979 C&S&B [Eng.]
   A Handy Death, with Henry Rothblatt. Simon, 1973; Hale, 1975 [N.Y.]
   The Hochmann Miniatures. NAL, 1967 KH [Lisbon]
   The Incredible Schlock Homes. Simon, 1966 SH ss [Eng.]
   Isle of the Snakes. Simon, 1963; Boardman, 1964 JdS [Brazil]
   Kek Huuygens, Smuggler. Mysterious Press, 1976 ss KH
   The Memoirs of Schlock Homes. Bobbs, 1974 SH ss [Eng.]
   The Murder League. Simon, 1968; New English Library, 1970 C&S&B [Eng.]
   Pursuit. Doubleday, 1978; Macdonald, 1980
   Rub-a-Dub-Dub. Simon, 1971. Also published as: Death Cuts the Deck. Ace, 1972 C&S&B [ship]
   The Shrunken Head. Simon, 1963; Boardman, 1965 JdS [Brazil]
   Trials of O'Brien. Signet, 1965 (Novelization of the TV series.) [NYC]
   The Tricks of the Trade. Putnam, 1972; Hale, 1974 KH
   Trouble in Paradise. Doubleday, 1975 JdS [Brazil]
   The Wager. Putnam, 1974; Hale, 1976 KH
   Whirligig. World, 1970 KH
   The Xavier Affair. Putnam, 1969; Hale, 1974 JdS [Rio de J.]

FISHER, ALAN E.
   The Midnight Men. Hale, 1980

FISHER, DAVE. See: Joey.

FISHER, DAVID E(LIMELECH). 1932-   . Ref: CA.
   Crisis. Doubleday, 1971; Allen, 1971 [NYC]
   The Last Flying Tiger. Scribner, 1976; Allen, 1977 [Miami]

FISHER, DOUGLAS (GEORGE). 1902-1981. Pseudonym: George Douglas, q.v. Other byline: George Fisher, q.v. Ref: CC. SC: Jeff Tellford, in at least those marked JT. Set: Eng.
   Corpse in Community. Hodder, 1953
   Death at Pyford Hall. Hodder, 1952 JT
   Poison-Pen at Pyford. Hodder, 1951 JT
   What's Wrong at Pyford? Hodder, 1950 JT

FISHER, GEORGE. Full name: Douglas (George) Fisher, 1902-1981, q.v. Pseudonym: George Douglas, q.v.
   The Hostages. Hale, 1976
   Operation V.I.P. Hale, 1977

FISHER, GERARD
   Hospitality for Murder. Hale, 1959; Washburn, 1959
   It's Your Turn to Die. Hale, 1960

FISHER, GRAHAM. 1920-   . Journalist and writer of books about the Royal Family. SC: Mike King, in all titles.
   End of the Line. Macdonald, 1975
   Face of Danger. Macdonald, 1974
   Villain of the Piece. Macdonald, 1977

FISHER, LAINE. Pseudonym of James A(rch) Howard, 1922-   , q.v.
   Fare Prey. Ace, 1959 [train]

FISHER, LAWRENCE (V.). 1923-   . Ref: CA.
   Death by the Day. Berkley, 1961
   Die a Little Every Day. Random, 1963; Boardman, 1963

FISHER, NORMAN. 1910-1972. British publishing executive. SC: Nigel Morrison, in all titles.
   The Last Assignment. Triton, 1972; Walker, 1973 [Paris]
   Rise at Dawn. Triton, 1971; Walker, 1971 [Greece]
   Walk at a Steady Pace. Triton, 1970; Walker, 1971 [It.]

FISHER, RICHARD. 1899-   .
   -Crisis Comes to Mister Smith. Selwyn, 1939
   Indian Police. Selwyn, 1939 [India]
   -Out of Evil. Selwyn, 1928

FISHER, RUDOLPH. 1897-1934.
   The Conjure Man Dies. Covici, 1932 [NYC]

FISHER, STEVE [STEPHEN GOULD FISHER]. 1912-1980. Pseudonyms: Stephen Gould, Grant Lane, qq.v. Ref: EM, TC. SC: Sheridan Doome = SD (see also Stephen Gould entry)
   The Big Dream. Doubleday, 1970 [L.A.]
   The Hell-Black Night. Sherbourne, 1970 [S.F.]
   I Wake Up Screaming. Dodd, 1941; Hale, 1943. Revised edition: Bantam, 1960 [L.A.]
   Image of Hell. Dutton, 1961 [L.A.]
   Murder of the Pigboat Skipper. Hillman-Curl, 1937. Also published as: Murder on the S-23. Mystery Book of the Month, 194? SD
   Murder on the S-23; see Murder of the Pigboat Skipper
   The Night Before Murder. Hillman-Curl, 1939 [N.Y.]
   No House Limit. Dutton, 1958
   Satan's Angel. Macaulay, 1935

Saxon's Ghost. Sherbourne, 1969 [S.F.]
The Sheltering Night. GM, 1952
Take All You Can Get. Random, 1955 [Calif.]
Winter Kill. Dodd, 1946 [NYC]

FISHMAN, JACK. 1920- . Joint pseudonym with Douglas (William) Orgill, 1922- , q.v.: J. D. Gilman, q.v. Ref: CA.

FISHMAN, HAL. See: Barry Schiff.

FISHTER, J(ACOB) FRANZ. 1904- .
The Ambassador of Death. Macaulay, 1937 [Paris]

FISKE, DORSEY
Academic Murder. Cassell, 1980 [acad.]

FISON, PETER. Pseudonym: Milo Ainsworth, q.v.

FITT, MARY. Pseudonym of Kathleen Freeman, 1897-1959, q.v. Other pseudonym: Stuart Mary Wick, q.v. SC: Supt. Mallett, in at least those marked M. Set: Eng.
Aftermath of Murder; see Death and Mary Dazill
The Banquet Ceases. Macdonald, 1949 M
Bulls Like Death. Nicholson, 1937 [Berlin]
Case for the Defence. Macdonald, 1958; British Book Centre, 1958
Clues to Christabel. Joseph, 1944; Doubleday, 1944 M
Death and Mary Dazill. Joseph, 1941. U.S. title: Aftermath of Murder. Doubleday, 1941 M
Death and the Bright Day. Macdonald, 1948 M
Death and the Pleasant Voices. Joseph, 1946; Putnam, 1946 M
Death and the Shortest Day. Macdonald, 1952 M
Death at Dancing Stones. Nicholson, 1939 M
Death Finds a Target; see Death on Herons' Mere
Death on Herons' Mere. Joseph, 1941. U.S. title: Death Finds a Target. Doubleday, 1942 M
Death Starts a Rumour. Nicholson, 1940 M
Expected Death. Nicholson, 1938 M
A Fine and Private Place. Macdonald, 1947; Putnam, 1947 M
An Ill Wind. Macdonald, 1951 M
The Late Uncle Max. Macdonald, 1957 [Med. Is.]
Love from Elizabeth. Macdonald, 1954 M
The Man Who Shot Birds and other tales. Macdonald, 1954 M ss
Mizmaze. Joseph, 1959; British Book Centre, 1959 M
Murder Mars the Tour. Nicholson, 1936 [Austria]
Murder of a Mouse. Nicholson, 1939
The Night-Watchman's Friend. Macdonald, 1953
Pity for Pamela. Macdonald, 1950; Harper, 1951
Requiem for Robert. Joseph, 1942 M
Sky-Rocket. Nicholson, 1938 M
Sweet Poison. Macdonald, 1956 M
There Are More Ways of Killing... Joseph, 1960; British Book Centre, 1960
The Three Hunting Horns. Nicholson, 1937
Three Sisters Flew Home. Nicholson, 1936; Doubleday, 1936

FITTS, JAMES FRANKLIN. 1840-1890.
A Sharp Night's Work. Laird, 1888

FITZ, JEAN DeWITT. 1912- . Ref: CA.
The Devon Maze. Geron-X, 1969 [W. Va.]
Graven Image. Pyramid, 1975 [Ga.]
The Viper's Bite. Geron-X, 1969 [hosp.]

FITZGERALD, ARLENE J. Pseudonym: Monica Heath, q.v. Ref: CA.
Blackthorn. Popular Library, 1977 [Ire.]
The Devil's Gate. Popular Library, 1977 [Nev.]
House of Tragedy. Manor, 1973 [La.]
-Numbers for Lovers. Manor, 1974
Pamela's Palace. Manor, 1972 [Calif.]
-Satanic Sex. Manor, 1973

FITZGERALD, F(RANCIS) SCOTT (KEY). 1896-1940. Ref: EM.
The Mystery of the Raymond Mortgage. Random, 1960

FITZGERALD, KEVIN. 1902- . SC: Bernard Feston, in at least those marked BF.
Dangerous to Lean Out. Heinemann, 1960; Macmillan, 1961 BF [Athens]

It's Different in July. Heinemann, 1955 BF
It's Safe in England. Heinemann, 1949
Kill Him Gently, Nurse. Heinemann, 1966
Not So Quickly. Heinemann, 1948
Quiet Under the Sun. Heinemann, 1953; Little, 1954 BF [Sp.]
A Throne of Bayonets. Heinemann, 1952
Trouble in West Two. Heinemann, 1958

FITZGERALD, NIGEL. 1906- . Ref: CC, TC. SC: Insp./Supt. Duffy, in at least those marked D; Alan Russell, in at least those marked AR.
Affairs of Death. Collins, 1967 D [Ire.]
Black Welcome. Collins, 1961; Macmillan, 1962 D [Ire.]
The Candles Are All Out. Collins, 1960; Macmillan, 1961 AR [Ire.]
The Day of the Adder. Collins, 1963. U.S. title: Echo Answers Murder. Macmillan, 1965 D [Ire.]
Echo Answers Murder; see The Day of the Adder
Ghost in the Making. Collins, 1960 AR [Ire.]
The House Is Falling. Collins, 1955 D [Ire.]
Imagine a Man. Collins, 1956 D [It.]
Midsummer Malice. Collins, 1953; Macmillan, 1959 D,AR [Ire.]
The Rosy Pastor. Collins, 1954 D,AR [Ire.]
The Student Body. Collins, 1958 D [Ire.]
Suffer a Witch. Collins, 1958 D [Ire.]
This Won't Hurt You. Collins, 1959; Macmillan, 1960

FITZGERALD, PENELOPE. 1916- . Ref: CA.
The Golden Child. Duckworth, 1977; Scribner, 1979

FITZGERALD, PERCY (HETHERINGTON). 1834-1925.
Chronicles of the Bow Street Police-Office. Chapman, 1888 ss
The Night Mail. Maxwell, 1862 ss, some criminous

FITZGERALD, T(HOMAS) A. 1862- .
Fits and Starts. Gill, 1915; Herder, 1915 ss, some criminous

FITZGERALD, TOM
-Chocolate Charlie. Paperback Library, 1974
A Matter of Scents. Pyramid, 1974

FITZGIBBON, (ROBERT LOUIS) CONSTANTINE. 1919- . Ref: CA.
The Rat Report. Constable, 1980

FITZHAMON, LEWIN
The Rival Millionaires. Ward, 1904
The Vixen. Ward, 1915

FITZMAURICE, EUGENE
Circumstantial Evidence. Jove, 1978 [Phil.]
The Hawkeland Cache. Wyndham, 1980

FITZPATRICK, JANINE. Pseudonym of James Fritzhand. Other pseudonym: Nick Carter, q.v.
The Dreamwalker. PB, 1975 [NYC]
Serena. Warner, 1976 [Maine]

FITZSIMMONS, CORTLAND. 1893-1949. Ref: CC, MP. SC: Arthur Martinson = AM; Percy Peacock = PP; Ethel Thomas = ET.
The Bainbridge Murder. McBride, 1930; Eyre, 1930 AM [N.Y.]
Crimson Ice. Stokes, 1935 [Boston]
Death on the Diamond. Stokes, 1934
Death Rings a Bell. Lippincott, 1942; Boardman, 1943 PP [Cape Cod]
The Evil Men Do. Stokes, 1941; Boardman, 1942 ET [L.A.]
The Girl in the Cage, with John Mulholland (1898-1970). Stokes, 1939 [NYC]
The Manville Murders. McBride, 1930 AM [L.I.]
The Moving Finger. Stokes, 1937 ET [NYC]
Murder Is Swift; see One Man's Poison
Mystery at Hidden Harbor. Stokes, 1938; Lane, 1939 ET [L.I.]
No Witness! Stokes, 1932; Hutchinson, 1933 [L.I.]
One Man's Poison. Stokes, 1940. British title (?): Murder Is Swift. Boardman, 1944 [Calif.]
Red Rhapsody. Stokes, 1933
70,000 Witnesses. McBride, 1931
Sudden Silence. Stokes, 1938; Lane, 1939 [S.F.]
This—Is Murder!, with Gerald Adams. Stokes, 1941 [ship]

Tied for Murder. Lippincott, 1943; Boardman, 1945 PP [Calif.]
The Whispering Window. Stokes, 1936; Boardman, 1943 ET [NYC]

FITZSIMONS, CHRISTOPHER. Journalist, author of radio and TV dramas; public relations executive.
Early Warning. Hodder, 1978; Viking, 1979
Reflex Action. Hodder, 1980; Atheneum, 1980

FLAGG, JAMES MONTGOMERY. 1877-1960.
The Mystery of the Hated Man and Then Some. Doran, 1916 ss, at least one criminous

FLAGG, JOHN. Pseudonym of John Gearon, q.v. Ref: CC. SC: Hart Muldoon = HM.
Dear, Deadly Beloved. GM, 1954 HM [It.]
Death and the Naked Lady. GM, 1951; Muller, 1953 [ship]
Death's Lovely Mask. GM, 1951; Fawcett (London), 1960 HM [Venice]
The Lady and the Cheetah. GM, 1951; Fawcett (London), 1954 [It.]
Murder in Monaco. GM, 1957; Red Seal, 1959 HM [Fr.]
The Paradise Gun. GM, 1961; Muller pb, 1962 HM [Carib.]
The Persian Cat. GM, 1950 [Iran]
Woman of Cairo. GM, 1953; Muller, 1954 HM [Cairo]

FLAGG, JONAS and GEOFFREY GRAVES
Seven Days to Disaster. Major, 1976

FLAGG, W(ILLIAM) J(OSEPH). 1818-1898.
Wall Street and the Woods; or, Woman the Stronger. Baker, 1885

FLAHERTY, JOE
Fogarty and Co. Coward, 1973

FLAMMENBERG, LORENZ. Pseudonym of Karl Friedrich Kahlert, 1765-1813.
The Necromancer; or, The Tale of the Black Forest. Lane, 1794

FLANAGAN, T. J.
Harry Blount, the Detective; or, The Martin Mystery Solved. Ogilvie, 1891

FLANDERS, IAN
Golden Girl. Novel, 1965

FLANNERY, SEAN. Pseudonym of David Hagberg, 1942- , q.v. Other pseudonym: Nick Carter, q.v.
Eagles Fly. Charter, 1980
The Kremlin Conspiracy. Charter, 1979 [Moscow]

FLATAU, HERMIONE
Drama of Mount Street. Hurst, 1930

FLATTERY, M(AURICE) DOUGLAS. 1870-1925.
A Pair of Knaves and A Few Trumps. Abbey, 1900

FLAVIN, MARTIN. 1883-1967. Ref: CA.
Cameron Hill. Harper, 1957; Muller, 1958

FLEET, CHARLES
A Place Like Hessberg. Raven, 1980 [Neb.]

FLEETWOOD, HUGH (NIGEL). 1944- . Born in England; lived in Italy for some years.
An Artist and a Magician. H. Hamilton, 1977. U.S. title: Roman Magic. Atheneum, 1978 [Rome]
The Beast. H. Hamilton, 1978; Atheneum, 1979 ss, some criminous
A Conditional Sentence. H. Hamilton, 1974; PB, 1978
-Fictional Lives. H. Hamilton, 1980
Foreign Affairs. H. Hamilton, 1973; Stein, 1974 [Rome]
The Girl Who Passed for Normal. H. Hamilton, 1973; Stein, 1973 [Rome]
-The Godmother. H. Hamilton, 1979
The Order of Death. H. Hamilton, 1976; Simon, 1976 [NYC]
A Painter of Flowers. H. Hamilton, 1972; Viking, 1972
A Picture of Innocence. H. Hamilton, 1975; PB, 1979
The Redeemer. H. Hamilton, 1979; Atheneum, 1980
Roman Magic; see An Artist and a Magician

FLEISCHER, LEONORE. Pseudonyms: Alexander Edwards, Mike Roote, qq.v. See also: Philip Fenty.

FLEISCHMAN, A(LBERT) S(IDNEY). 1920-   .
    Ref: CA.   SC: Max Brindle = MB.
    Chinese Crimson; see Look Behind You,
        Lady
    Counterspy Express. Ace, 1954
    Danger in Paradise. GM, 1953; Jenkins,
        1964 [Bali]
    Look Behind You, Lady. GM, 1952; Faw-
        cett (London), 1953. Also published
        as: Chinese Crimson. Jenkins, 1962
        [Macao]
    Malay Manhunt; see Malay Woman
    Malay Woman. GM, 1954; Fawcett (Lon-
        don), 1955. Also published as: Malay
        Manhunt. Jenkins, 1966 [Mal.]
    Murder's No Accident. Phoenix, 1949
        MB [Shanghai]
    Shanghai Flame. GM, 1951; Fawcett (Lon-
        don), 1957 [Shanghai]
    The Straw Donkey Case. Phoenix, 1948
        MB [San Diego]
    The Venetian Blonde. GM, 1963; Muller
        pb, 1964 [Calif.]

FLEMING, BRANDON. 1889-   . Pseudonym:
    Gerald Anstruther, q.v. Set: Eng.
    The Beauty-Killer. White, 1920. U.S.
        title: The Crooked House. Clode, 1921
    The Crime Maker. White, 1923
    The Crooked House; see The Beauty-
        Killer
    Masks. Everett, 1913
    Pillory. White, 1921

FLEMING, E(DWARD) L(ASCELLES)
    Nazi Shadows. Williams, 1935

FLEMING, ETHYL
    Murder Takes a Honeymoon. Gateway, 1940
        [NYC]

FLEMING, GERALDINE. Pseudonym of John
    R(ussell) Coryell, 1851-1924, q.v.
    Other pseudonym: Nicholas Carter,
    q.v.
    -False. Lovell, 1888
    $5000 Reward; or, The Missing Bride.
        Munro, 1887
    -How He Won Her, and A False Friend.
        Munro, 1885
    -A Sinless Crime. Lovell, 1888
    -A Sister's Sacrifice. Munro, 1885
    -Sunlight and Gloom. Munro, 1885
    -A Terrible Secret. Munro, 1885

FLEMING, H(ORACE) K(INGSTON). 1901-   .
    Ref: CA.
    The Day They Kidnapped Queen Victoria.
        Frewin, 1969; St. Martin's, 1978
        [1867, Eng.]
    Eden Eden. Gollancz, 1949

FLEMING, IAN (LANCASTER). 1908-1964. Ref:
    CA, CC, EM, MC, TC. SC: James Bond,
    in all titles.
    Casino Royale. Cape, 1953; Macmillan,
        1953. Also published as: You Asked
        for It. Popular Library, 1955 [Fr.]
    Diamonds Are Forever. Cape, 1956; Mac-
        millan, 1956 [U.S.]
    Doctor No. Cape, 1958; Macmillan, 1958
        [Carib.]
    For Your Eyes Only. Cape, 1960; Viking,
        1960
    From Russia, with Love. Cape, 1957;
        Macmillan, 1957
    Goldfinger. Cape, 1959; Macmillan, 1959
    Live and Let Die. Cape, 1954; Macmil-
        lan, 1955 [U.S.]
    The Man with the Golden Gun. Cape,
        1965; NAL, 1965
    Moonraker. Cape, 1955; Macmillan, 1955.
        Also published as: Too Hot to Handle.
        Permabooks, 1957
    Octopussy; see Octopussy and The Living
        Daylights
    Octopussy and The Living Daylights.
        Cape, 1966. U.S. title: Octopussy.
        NAL, 1966 ss (Note that the paper-
        back edition, Signet, 1967, contains
        one additional story.)
    On Her Majesty's Secret Service. Cape,
        1963; NAL, 1963 [Switz.]
    The Spy Who Loved Me. Cape, 1962;
        Viking, 1962 [N.Y.]
    Thunderball. Cape, 1961; Viking, 1961
        [Bahamas]
    Too Hot to Handle; see Moonraker
    You Asked for It; see Casino Royale
    You Only Live Twice. Cape, 1964; NAL,
        1964 [Jap.]

FL*M*NG, I*N. Joint pseudonym of Chris-
    topher Bennett Cerf, 1941-   , and
    Michael K. Frith.
    Alligator. Vanitas, 1962 (A parody on
        the James Bond stories of Ian Flem-
        ing, 1908-1964, q.v.)

FLEMING, JANE. Pseudonym of Steve Smith.
    Hawthorn Wood. Berkley, 1975 [La.,
        past]

FLEMING, JOAN (MARGARET). 1908-1980. Ref:
    CA, CC, TC. SC: Nuri Iskirlak, in at
    least those marked NI. Set: Eng.
    Alas, Poor Father. Collins, 1972; Put-
        nam, 1973
    Be a Good Boy; see Grim Death and the
        Barrow Boys
    The Chill and the Kill. Collins, 1964;
        Washburn, 1964
    A Cup of Cold Poison; see The Man Who
        Looked Back
    A Daisy-Chain for Satan. Hutchinson,
        1950; Doubleday, 1951
    The Day of the Donkey Derby. Collins,
        1978; Putnam, 1978
    Death of a Sardine. Collins, 1963;
        Washburn, 1964 [Port.]
    The Deeds of Dr. Deadcert. Hutchinson,
        1955; Washburn, 1957. Also published
        as: The Merry Widower. H. Hamilton,
        1975
    Dirty Butter for Servants. H. Hamilton,
        1972
    Every Inch a Lady. Collins, 1977; Put-
        nam, 1977 [1950s, Eng.]
    The Gallows in My Garden. Hutchinson,
        1951
    The Good and the Bad. Hutchinson, 1953;
        Doubleday, 1953 [Paris]
    Grim Death and the Barrow Boys. Col-
        lins, 1971. U.S. title (?): Be a Good
        Boy. Putnam, 1971
    He Ought to Be Shot. Hutchinson, 1955;
        Doubleday, 1955
    Hell's Belle. Collins, 1968; Washburn,
        1969 [Paris]
    How to Live Dangerously. Collins, 1974;
        Putnam, 1975
    In the Red. Collins, 1961; Washburn,
        1961
    Kill or Cure. Collins, 1968; Washburn,
        1968
    Maiden's Prayer. Collins, 1957; Wash-
        burn, 1958
    Malice Matrimonial. Collins, 1959;
        Washburn, 1959
    The Man from Nowhere. Collins, 1960;
        Washburn, 1960
    The Man Who Looked Back. Hutchinson,
        1951; Doubleday, 1952. Also published
        as: A Cup of Cold Poison. H. Hamil-
        ton, 1969
    The Merry Widower; see The Deeds of Dr.
        Deadcert
    Midnight Hag. Collins, 1966; Washburn,
        1966
    Miss Bones. Collins, 1959; Washburn,
        1960
    No Bones About It. Collins, 1967;
        Washburn, 1967
    Nothing Is the Number When You Die.
        Collins, 1965; Washburn, 1965 NI
        [Turk.]
    Polly Put the Kettle On. Hutchinson,
        1952
    Screams from a Penny Dreadful. H. Ham-
        ilton, 1971 [ca.1850, Eng.]
    ...To Make an Underworld. Collins,
        1976; Putnam, 1976
    Too Late! Too Late! The Maiden Cried.
        H. Hamilton, 1975; Putnam, 1975
        [1800s, Eng.]
    Two Lovers Too Many. Hutchinson, 1949
    When I Grow Rich. Collins, 1962; Wash-
        burn, 1962 NI [Istan.]
    You Can't Believe Your Eyes. Collins,
        1957; Washburn, 1957
    You Won't Let Me Finish. Collins, 1973.
        U.S. title: You Won't Let Me Finnish.
        Putnam, 1974 [Helsinki]
    Young Man, I Think You're Dying. Col-
        lins, 1970; Putnam, 1970

FLEMING, JOHN C(HESTER). 1906-1964. See:
    Lois (Christine) Eby, 1908-   .

FLEMING, KEITH
    By the Night Express. Routledge, 1889

FLEMING, MAY AGNES (EARLY). 1840-1880.
    Pseudonyms: Cousin May Carleton,
    M(ay) A(gnes) Earlie, qq.v.
    The Actress's Daughter. Carleton, 1886;
        Milner, 1903
    -The Baronet's Bride; or, A Woman's
        Vengeance. Brady, 1868
    -The Dark Secret. Federal Book, 1875
    -Ermine; or, The Gipsy's Vow. Brady,
        1862
    -A Fateful Abduction; or, The Secret
        Sorrow. Dillingham, 1907
    The Heiress of Glen Gower; or, The
        Hidden Crime. Munro, 1892
    -Norine's Revenge, and Sir Noel's Heir.
        Carleton, 1875
    One Night's Mystery. Carleton, 1876;
        Low, 1876
    Sharing Her Crime. Carleton, 1882
    A Terrible Secret. Carleton, 1874; Low,
        1874
    -Who Wins?; or, The Secret of Monkshood
        Waste. Donohue, 1870

FLEMING, NAN. Pseudonym of Wilbur Braun,
    1896-   , q.v. Other pseudonyms:
    Walter Blake, Bruce Brandon, Fred
    Caldwell, Raymond Dumkey, Marsha
    Grable, Edwin F. Hornung, Jed Parish,
    Basil Ring, Orville Snap, Mortimer
    Sprague, Bert Stoner, qq.v.
    The Ghost Plane. French (NYC), 1948
        (3-act play.)

FLEMING, NICHOL. 1939-   . Son of author
    Peter Fleming, 1907-1971, q.v., and
    nephew of Ian Fleming, 1908-1964,
    q.v.
    Counter Paradise. Joseph, 1968; Coward,
        1968
    Czech Point. Joseph, 1970
    Hash. Joseph, 1971

FLEMING, OLIVER. Joint pseudonym of
    Philip MacDonald, 1899-1981, q.v.,
    and his father, Ronald MacDonald,
    1860-1933. Other Philip MacDonald
    pseudonyms: Martin Porlock, q.v.,
    Anthony Lawless.
    Ambrotox and Limping Dick. Ward, 1920
    The Spandau Quid. Palmer, 1923

FLEMING, (ROBERT) PETER. 1907-1971. Ref:
    CA.
    The Sixth Column. Hart-Davis, 1951;
        Scribner, 1951
    A Story to Tell. Cape, 1942; Scribner,
        1942 ss

FLEMING, ROBERT. 1891-   .
    And Death Drove On; see Night Freight
        Murders
    A Bullet in His Cap; see Night Freight
        Murders
    Murder Comes to Dinner; see Night
        Freight Murders
    Night Freight Murders. Smith & Durrell,
        1942. British title: Murder Comes to
        Dinner. Long, 1943. Also published
        as: A Bullet in His Cap. Handi-Books,
        1942. And as: And Death Drove On.
        Green Dragon, 194? [L.A.]

FLEMING, RUDD. 1908-   .
    Cradled in Murder. Simon, 1938; H. Ham-
        ilton, 1938 [New Or.]

FLEMING, THOMAS J(AMES). 1927-   . Ref:
    CA.
    A Cry of Whiteness. Morrow, 1967

FLEMING-ROBERTS, G. T. Pseudonym: Brant
    House, q.v.

FLESCH, HANS. 1897-   . Pseudonym: Vin-
    cent Brun, q.v.

FLETCHER, AARON. Pseudonym (?): Frank
    Scarpetta, q.v.
    The Card Game. Tower, 1980

FLETCHER, DAVID. Pseudonym of Dulan F.
    Barber, 1940-   . Ref: CA. SC:
    A. J. Raffles = AR (following E. W.
    Hornung, 1866-1921, q.v., and
    Barry Perowne, q.v.). Set: Eng.
    Accomplices. Macmillan (London), 1976
    Don't Whistle "MacBeth." Macmillan
        (London), 1976 [theatre]
    A Lovable Man. Macmillan (London),
        1974; Coward, 1975
    Only Children. Macmillan (London), 1977
    Raffles. Macmillan (London), 1977; Put-
        nam, 1977 ss AR
    A Respectable Woman. Macmillan (Lon-
        don), 1975; Coward, 1975

FLETCHER, DOROTHY. Pseudonym: Miriam Can-
    field, q.v.
    Beyond Recall. Lancer, 1971
    The Brand Inheritance. Lancer, 1973
        [N.Y.]
    Farewell to Vienna. Lancer, 1970
        [Vienna]
    House of Hate. Lancer, 1967
    The Late Contessa. Lancer, 1971 [It.]
    Meeting in Madrid. Lancer, 1970
        [Madrid]
    The Music Master. Lancer, 1971
        [Florence]
    Shadows on the Water. Beagle, 1972
    Still Waters. Paperback Library, 1970

FLETCHER, FRANCES
    The Murder Sonata. Leisure, 1980

FLETCHER, H(ARRY) L(UFT) V(ERNE).
    1902-   . Pseudonym: John Garden,
    q.v. Ref: CA.
    -The Devil Has the Best Tunes. Macdon-
        ald, 1947
    -Forest Inn. Macdonald, 1948
    -High Pastures. Macdonald, 1957
    -The Lonely Island. Macdonald, 1958
    Miss Agatha. Gardner, 1946. U.S. title:
        Miss Agatha Doubles for Death. Mess-
        ner, 1947 [Wales]

Miss Agatha Doubles for Death; see Miss Agatha
-The Reluctant Prodigal. Macdonald, 1958
-The Rising Sun. Macdonald, 1951
-The Storm. Macdonald, 1954
The Whip and the Tongue. Macdonald, 1949
-The Woman's House. Macdonald, 1944

FLETCHER, HENRY
The North Shore Mystery. Swan, 1899

FLETCHER, J(OSEPH) S(MITH). 1863-1935. Ref: all except CA. SC: Ronald Camberwell = RC; Paul Campenhaye = PC; Sgt. Charlesworth = C; Richard Goulburn = RG; Insp. Skarratt = S. Set: Eng.
The Adventures of Archer Dawe, Sleuth-Hound. Digby Long, 1909. Also published as: The Contents of the Coffin. Novel Library, 1928 ss
The Air-Ship. Digby Long, 1903 ss
The Amaranth Club. Ward, 1918; Knopf, 1926
The Ambitious Lady. Ward, 1923
And Sudden Death; see The Lynne Court Spinney
Andrewlina. Kegan Paul, 1889
The Annexation Society. Ward, 1916; Knopf, 1925
The Bartenstein Case. Long, 1913. U.S. title: The Bartenstein Mystery. Dial, 1927
The Bartenstein Mystery; see The Bartenstein Case
The Bedford Row Mystery. Hodder, 1925. U.S. title: The Strange Case of Mr. Henry Marchmont. Knopf, 1927
Behind the Monocle. Jarrolds, 1928; Doubleday, 1930 ss
Behind the Panel; see In the Mayor's Parlour
The Black House in Harley Street; see The Million-Dollar Diamond
The Borgia Cabinet. Jenkins, 1932; Knopf, 1930 C
The Borough Treasurer. Ward, 1919; Knopf, 1921
The Box Hill Murder. Jenkins, 1931; Knopf, 1929
The Burma Ruby. Benn, 1932; Dial, 1933 C
The Canterbury Mystery; see The Ravenswood Mystery
The Carrismore Ruby. Jarrolds, 1935 ss
The Cartwright Gardens Murder. Collins, 1924; Knopf, 1926
The Charing Cross Mystery. Jenkins, 1923; Putnam, 1923
The Chestermarke Instinct. Allen & Unwin, 1918; Knopf, 1921
The Clue of the Artificial Eye; see Paul Campenhaye, Specialist in Criminology
Cobweb Castle. Jenkins, 1928; Knopf, 1928
The Contents of the Coffin; see The Adventures of Archer Dawe, Sleuth-Hound
The Copper Box. Hodder, 1923; Doran, 1923 [Scot.]
Dead Man's Money; see Droonin' Watter
The Death That Lurks Unseen. Ward, 1899 ss
The Diamond Murders; see The Diamonds
The Diamonds. Digby Long, 1904. U.S. title: The Diamond Murders. Dodd, 1929
The Double Chance. Nash, 1928; Dodd, 1928
The Dressing-Room Murder. Jenkins, 1930; Knopf, 1931
Droonin' Watter. Allen & Unwin, 1919. U.S. title: Dead Man's Money. Knopf, 1930
The Ebony Box. Butterworth, 1934; Knopf, 1934 RC
The Eleventh Hour. Butterworth, 1935; Knopf, 1935 RC
Exterior to the Evidence. Hodder, 1920; Knopf, 1923
False Scent. Jenkins, 1924; Knopf, 1925
-Families Repaired. Allen & Unwin, 1916
The Fear of the Night. Routledge, 1903 ss
Find the Woman. Collins, 1933 ss
The Flamstock Mystery; see The Malachite Jar
The Golden Spur. Long, 1901; Dial, 1928 [Ire.]
The Great Brighton Mystery. Hodder, 1925; Knopf, 1926
Green Ink. Jenkins, 1926; Small Maynard, 1926 ss
The Green Rope. Jenkins, 1927; Knopf, 1927
The Guarded Room. Long, 1931; Clode, 1931
Hardican's Hollow. Everett, 1910; Doran, 1927

The Harvest Moon. Nash, 1908; Doran, 1927
The Heaven-Kissed Hill. Hodder, 1922; Doran, 1924
The Heaven-Sent Witness and other stories. Doubleday, 1930 (Contains 14 of the 27 ss in The Ivory God, q.v., and 7 of the ss in The Man in No. 3, q.v.)
The Herapath Property. Ward, 1920; Knopf, 1921
The House in Tuesday Market. Jenkins, 1930; Knopf, 1929
In the Mayor's Parlour. Bodley, 1922. Also published as: The Time-Worn Town. Collins, 1929; Knopf, 1924. And as: Behind the Panel. Collins, 1931
The Investigators. Long, 1902; Clode, 1930
The Ivory God. Murray, 1907 (14 of the 27 ss in this volume were included in The Heaven-Sent Witness, q.v.)
The Kang-He Vase. Collins, 1924; Knopf, 1926
The King Versus Wargrave. Ward, 1915; Knopf, 1924
The Lost Mr. Linthwaite. Hodder, 1920; Knopf, 1923
The Lynne Court Spinney. Ward, 1916. U.S. title: The Mystery of Lynne Court. Remington, 1923. Also published as: And Sudden Death. Hillman, 1938. And as: Pedigreed Murder Case. Detective Novel Classics, 194?
The Malachite Jar. Collins, 1930. Also published as: The Flamstock Mystery. Collins, 1932. The first 11 ss also reprinted separately as: The Manor House Mystery. Collins, 1933 ss
Malvery Hold. Ward, 1917. U.S. title: The Mystery of the Hushing Pool. Hillman, 1938
The Man in No. 3. Collins, 1931 (7 of the ss were included in The Heaven-Sent Witness, q.v.)
The Man in the Fur Coat. Collins, 1932 ss
The Manor House Mystery; see The Malachite Jar
The Mantle of Ishmael. Nash, 1909 RG
Many Engagements. Long, 1923 ss
Marchester Royal. Everett, 1909; Doran, 1926 S
The Markenmore Mystery. Jenkins, 1922; Knopf, 1923
The Marrendon Mystery, and other stories of crime and detection. Collins, 1930 ss
-The Marriage Lines. Nash, 1914
The Massingham Butterfly. Jenkins, 1926; Small Maynard, 1926 ss, PC in two
The Matheson Formula. Jenkins, 1930; Knopf, 1929
The Mazaroff Murder. Jenkins, 1923. U.S. title: The Mazaroff Mystery. Knopf, 1924
The Mazaroff Mystery; see The Mazaroff Murder
The Middle of Things. Ward, 1922; Knopf, 1922
The Middle Temple Murder. Ward, 1919; Knopf, 1919
The Mill House Murder; see Todmanhawe Grange
The Mill of Many Windows. Collins, 1925; Doran, 1925
The Million-Dollar Diamond. Jenkins, 1923. U.S. title: The Black House in Harley Street. Doubleday, 1928 RG
The Missing Chancellor; see The Stolen Budget
The Mortover Grange Affair; see The Mortover Grange Mystery
The Mortover Grange Mystery. Jenkins, 1926. U.S. title: The Mortover Grange Affair. Knopf, 1927
Murder in Wrides Park. Harrap, 1931; Knopf, 1931 RC
Murder in Four Degrees. Harrap, 1931; Knopf, 1931 RC
The Murder in Medora Mansions. Collins, 1933 ss
The Murder in the Pallant. Jenkins, 1927; Knopf, 1928
Murder in the Squire's Pew. Harrap, 1932; Knopf, 1932 RC
Murder of a Banker; see The Mystery of the London Banker
Murder of the Lawyer's Clerk; see Who Killed Alfred Snowe?
Murder of the Ninth Baronet. Harrap, 1932; Knopf, 1932 RC
Murder of the Only Witness. Harrap, 1933; Knopf, 1933 RC
Murder of the Secret Agent. Harrap, 1934; Knopf, 1934
The Mysterious Chinaman. Jenkins, 1924. U.S. title: The Rippling Ruby. Putnam, 1923
The Mystery of Lynne Court; see The Lynne Court Spinney

The Mystery of the Hushing Pool; see Malvery Hold
The Mystery of the London Banker. Harrap, 1933. U.S. title: Murder of a Banker. Knopf, 1933 RC
Old Lattimer's Legacy. Jarrolds, 1892; Clode, 1929
The Orange-Yellow Diamond. Newnes, 1920; Knopf, 1921
Paradise Court. Unwin, 1908; Doubleday, 1929
The Paradise Mystery; see The Wrychester Paradise
Pasquinado. Ward, 1898 ss, some criminous
The Passenger to Folkestone. Jenkins, 1927; Knopf, 1927
Paul Campenhaye, Specialist in Criminology. Ward, 1918. U.S. title: The Clue of the Artificial Eye. Hillman, 1939 ss PC
Pedigreed Murder Case; see The Lynne Court Spinney
The Perilous Crossways. Ward, 1917; Hillman, 1938
-Perris of the Cherry Trees. Nash, 1931; Doubleday, 1920
-The Queen of a Day. Unwin, 1907; Doubleday, 1929
The Ransom for London. Long, 1914; Dial, 1929
Ravensdene Court. Ward, 1922; Knopf, 1922
The Ravenswood Mystery. Collins, 1929. Also published as: The Canterbury Mystery. Collins, 1933
The Rayner-Slade Amalgamation. Allen & Unwin, 1917; Knopf, 1922
The Rippling Ruby; see The Mysterious Chinaman
The Root of All Evil. Hodder, 1921; Doran, 192?
Safe Number Sixty-Nine. International Pocket Library, 1931 ss
The Safety Pin. Jenkins, 1924; Putnam, 1924
Scarhaven Keep. Ward, 1920; Knopf, 1922
Sea Fog. Jenkins, 1925; Knopf, 1925
The Secret Cargo. Ward, 1913 PC
The Secret of Secrets. Clode, 1929 S (British title?)
The Secret of the Barbican. Hodder, 1924; Doran, 1925 ss
The Secret Way. Digby Long, 1903; Small Maynard, 1925
The Seven Days' Secret. Jarrolds, 1919; Clode, 1930
The Shadow of Ravenscliffe. Digby Long, 1914; Clode, 1928
The Solution of a Mystery. Harrap, 1932; Doubleday, 1932
The South Foreland Murder. Jenkins, 1930; Knopf, 1930
The Stolen Budget. Hodder, 1926. U.S. title: The Missing Chancellor. Knopf, 1927
The Strange Case of Mr. Henry Marchmont; see The Bedford Row Mystery
The Talleyrand Maxim. Ward, 1919; Knopf, 1920
The Three Days' Terror. Long, 1901; Clode, 1927
The Threshing Floor. Unwin, 1905
The Time-Worn Town; see In the Mayor's Parlour
Todmanhawe Grange. Butterworth, 1937. U.S. title: The Mill House Murder. Knopf, 1937 (Completed after JSF's death by Torquemada, q.v., pseudonym of Edward Powys Mathers, 1892-1939.) RC
The Valley of Headstrong Men. Hodder, 1919; Doran, 1924
-The Wheatstack. Nash, 1909 ss
Who Killed Alfred Snowe? Harrap, 1933. U.S. title: Murder of the Lawyer's Clerk. Knopf, 1933 RC
-The Winding Way. Kegan Paul, 1890
The Wolves and the Lamb. Ward, 1914; Knopf, 1925 S
The Wrist Mark. Jenkins, 1929; Knopf, 1928
The Wrychester Paradise. Ward, 1921. U.S. title: The Paradise Mystery. Knopf, 1922
The Yorkshire Moorland Murder. Jenkins, 1930; Knopf, 1930

FLETCHER, LUCILLE [LUCILLE FLETCHER WALLOP]. 1912- . See also: Allan Ullman. Ref: CA, CC, TC.
...And Presumed Dead. Random, 1963; Eyre, 1963 [Switz.]
Blindfold. Random, 1960; Eyre, 1960
Eighty Dollars to Stamford. Random, 1975; Hale, 1977
The Girl in Cabin B54. Random, 1968; Hodder, 1969 [ship]
Night Watch. Dramatists, 1972 (2-act play.)

Sorry Wrong Number, and The Hitchhiker. Dramatists, 1952 (2 plays.)
The Strange Blue Yawl. Random, 1964; Eyre, 1965 [Md.]

FLETCHER, MARY MANN
The Devil's Dress. Lancer, 1972
Devil's Instrument. Lancer, 1969
The House Called Whispering Winds. Beagle, 1974
The Scorpion of Chateau Laverria. Beagle, 1970 [La.]

FLETCHER, R(OBERT) J(AMES). 1877- .
SC: Gilbert Davison, in all titles. Set: Eng.
By Misadventure. Murray, 1930
Half Devil, Half Tiger, with Alex(ander) McLachlan. Murray, 1929
The Missing Doctor. Murray, 1930

FLETCHER, ROBERT HOWE. 1850-1936.
The Johnstown Stage, and other stories. Appleton, 1891. British title: The Mystery of a Studio and other stories. Lawrence, 1892 ss

FLETCHER, VERNE
Death and the Durlings. Swan, 1942

FLETT, ALFRED. Reporter and playwright in New Zealand and England.
Never Shake a Skeleton. Joseph, 1973; Walker, 1978 [Cairo]

FLIEGEL, DORIAN. 1945- .
The Fix. Houghton, 1978

FLINN, JOHN JOSEPH. 1851-1929.
The Mysterious Disappearance of Helen St. Vincent. Hazlitt, 1895

FLINT, ANNIE AUSTIN. 1866- .
The Breaking Point. Broadway, 1915

FLINT, JEREMY. See: Terence Reese, 1913- .

FLOOD, CHARLES BRACELEN. 1929- . Ref: CA.
Trouble at the Top. McGraw, 1972

FLOOD, ROBERT J.
The Hit Man. Manor, 1972; Allen, 1974

FLORA, FLETCHER. 1914-1968. See also: (Charles) Stuart Palmer, 1905-1968. Ref: CA, TC.
-The Brass Bed. Lion, 1956
-The Hotshot. Avon, 1956
The Irrepressible Peccadillo. Macmillan, 1962; Boardman, 1963
Killing Cousins. Macmillan, 1960; Cape, 1961
Leave Her to Hell! Avon, 1958
Let Me Kill You, Sweetheart! Avon, 1958
-Most Likely to Love. Monarch, 1960
-Park Avenue Tramp. GM, 1958; Fawcett (London), 1959 [NYC]
-The Seducer. Monarch, 1961
Skuldoggery. Belmont, 1967
-Strange Sisters. Lion, 1954
-Take Me Home. Monarch, 1959
-Wake Up with a Stranger. Signet, 1959
-Whispers of the Flesh. Signet, 1958

FLOREN, LEE. 1910- . Pseudonym: Stuart Jason, q.v. Ref: CA.

FLORES, JANIS. 1946- . Ref: CA.
Hawkshead. Doubleday, 1976 [1800s, Eng.]
Peregrine House. Doubleday, 1977

FLOWER, ELLIOTT. 1863-1920.
Policeman Flynn. Century, 1902 ss

FLOWER, PAT(RICIA MARY BRYSON). 1914-1978. Ref: CA, TC. SC: Insp. Swinton, in at least those marked S.
Cat's Cradle. Collins, 1973; Stein, 1978 [Australia]
Cobweb. Collins, 1972; Stein, 1978 [Australia]
Crisscross. Collins, 1976; Stein, 1977 [Syd.]
Fiends of the Family. Hale, 1966 S [Australia]
Goodbye, Sweet William. Angus, 1959 S [Australia]
Hell for Heather. Hale, 1962 S [Australia]
Hunt the Body. Hale, 1968
Odd Job. Collins, 1974; Stein, 1978
One Rose Less. Angus, 1961 S [Australia]
Shadow Show. Collins, 1976; Stein, 1978 [Australia]
Slyboots. Collins, 1974; Stein, 1978 [Australia]
Term of Terror. Hale, 1963 S [Australia]
Vanishing Point. Collins, 1975; Stein, 1977 [Australia]
Wax Flowers for Gloria. Angus, 1958 S [Australia]
A Wreath of Water-Lilies. Angus, 1960 S [Australia]

FLOWERDEW, HERBERT
-A Celibate's Wife. Lane (London & NYC), 1898
-In an Ancient Mirror. Unwin, 1897
Love and a Title. Greening, 1913
-Maynard's Wives. Nash, 1907
-Mrs. Gray's Past. Paul, 1913
The Realist. Lane (London & NYC), 1900. Also published as: The Room of Mirrors. Nash, 1912
-Retaliation. Constable, 1901
The Room of Mirrors; see The Realist
-The Second Elopement. Paul, 1910
The Seventh Postcard. Greening, 1914
-The Third Kiss. Nash, 1905
The Villa Mystery. Paul, 1912; Brentano's, 1912
-The Ways of Men. Unwin, 1908
-The Woman's View. Richards, 1903

FLOWERS, CHARLES. 1942- . Ref: CA.
It Never Rains in Los Angeles. Coward, 1970 [L.A.]

FLOYD, LESLIE
The Case of the Frantic Ladies. Harrap, 1938

FLOYD, LOUISE McKNIGHT
The Commencement Day Murders. Vantage, 1954

FLOYD, MORDIE
The Secret of Saraband. Bouregy, 1961 [Fla.]

FLYNN, BRIAN. 1885- . Ref: CC. An accountant in government service, lecturer in Elocution and Speech, an amateur actor. SC: Anthony Bathurst, in all titles. Set: Eng.
And Cauldron Bubble. Long, 1951
The Billiard-Room Mystery. Hamilton, 1927; Macrae-Smith, 1929
Black Agent. Long, 1950
Black Edged. Long, 1939; Macrae-Smith, 1939
The Case of Elymas the Sorcerer. Long, 1945
The Case of the Black Twenty-Two. Hamilton, 1928; Macrae-Smith, 1929
The Case of the Faithful Heart. Long, 1939
The Case of the Painted Ladies. Long, 1940
The Case of the Purple Calf. Long, 1934. U.S. title: The Ladder of Death. Macrae-Smith, 1935
Cold Evil. Long, 1938
Conspiracy at Angel. Long, 1947
The Creeping Jenny Mystery. Long, 1930. U.S. title: The Crime at the Crossways. Macrae-Smith, 1932
The Crime at the Crossways; see The Creeping Jenny Mystery
The Dice Are Dark. Long, 1956
The Doll's Done Dancing. Long, 1954
The Ebony Stag. Long, 1938
The Edge of Terror. Long, 1932
Exit Sir John. Long, 1947
Fear and Trembling. Long, 1936. U.S. title: The Somerset Murder Case. Mill, 1937
The Feet of Death. Long, 1954
The Five Red Fingers. Long, 1929; Mill, 1938
The Fortescue Candle. Long, 1936
Glittering Prizes. Long, 1942
The Grim Maiden. Long, 1944
The Hands of Justice. Long, 1957
The Horn. Long, 1934
Invisible Death. Hamilton, 1929
The Ladder of Death; see The Case of the Purple Calf
The League of Matthias. Long, 1934 [Antwerp]
Men for Pieces. Long, 1949
The Mirador Collection. Long, 1955
Murder En Route. Long, 1930; Macrae-Smith, 1932
The Murders Near Mapleton. Hamilton, 1929; Macrae-Smith, 1930
The Mystery of the Peacock's Eye. Hamilton, 1928; Macrae-Smith, 1930
The Nine Cuts. Long, 1958
The Orange Axe. Long, 1931
Out of the Dusk. Long, 1953
The Padded Door. Long, 1932
Reverse the Charges. Long, 1943
The Ring of Innocent. Long, 1952
The Running Nun. Long, 1952
The Saints Are Sinister. Long, 1958
The Seventh Sign. Long, 1952
The Shaking Spear. Long, 1955
The Sharp Quillet. Long, 1947
The Somerset Murder Case; see Fear and Trembling
The Spiked Lion. Long, 1933; Macrae-Smith, 1934
Such Bright Disguises. Long, 1941
The Sussex Cuckoo. Long, 1935
The Swinging Death. Long, 1948
They Never Came Back. Long, 1940
The Toy Lamb. Long, 1956
Tread Softly. Long, 1937; Mill, 1938
The Triple Bite. Long, 1931
Where There Was Smoke. Long, 1951
The Wife Who Disappeared. Long, 1957

FLYNN, J. M. Also uses byline: Jay Flynn, q.v.
Danger Zone. Belmont, 1977 [Mex.]
The Deadly Boodle. Ace, 1958 [Calif.]
Deep Six. Ace, 1961 [Calif.]
Drink with the Dead. Ace, 1959 [Calif.]
The Girl from Las Vegas. Ace, 1961 [Calif.]
The Hot Chariot. Ace, 1960 [Calif.]
One for the Death House. Ace, 1961 [Calif.]
Ring Around a Rogue. Ace, 1960 [S.F.]
The Screaming Cargo. Ace, 1962 [Mex.]
SurfSide 6. Dell, 1962 (Novelization of the TV series.) [Fla.]
Terror Tournament. Mystery House, 1959 [Calif.]
Warlock. PB, 1976 [Paris]

FLYNN, JAY. Also uses byline: J. M. Flynn, q.v. SC: Bannerman = B; McHugh, in at least those marked M.
The Action Man. Avon, 1961
Bannerman. Leisure, 1976 B [1916, Denver]
Blood on Frisco Bay. Leisure, 1976 [S.F.]
A Body for McHugh. Avon, 1960; Consul, 1961 M [S.F.]
Border Incident. Leisure, 1976 B
The Five Faces of Murder. Avon, 1962; Consul, 1965 M [S.F., Switz.]
It's Murder, McHugh. Avon, 1960; Consul, 1961 M [Mex.]
McHugh. Avon, 1959; Consul, 1961 M [S.F.]
Viva McHugh. Avon, 1960 M [Carib.]

FLYNN, T(HOMAS) T(HEODORE). 1902- .
It's Murder! Hector Kelly, 1950
Murder Caravan. Hector Kelly, 1950

FLYNN, WILLIAM J(AMES). 1867-1952.
The Barrel Mystery. McCann, 1919 [NYC]
Eagle's Eye. Prospect, 1919

FLYNT, JOSIAH. Pseudonym of Josiah Flynt Willard, 1869-1907. Ref: EM.
Notes of an Itinerant Policeman. Page, 1900
The Powers That Prey, with Francis Walton (pseudonym of Alfred Hodder, 1866-1907). McClure, 1900; Ward, 1901 ss
The Rise of Ruderick Clowd. Dodd, 1903; Richards, 1904

FOCKE, ERNEST. 1896- . Pseudonym: Ernest Paul, q.v.

FODEN, FREDERICK
-Denver Lil. Gray, 1953
-Hick Town Dame. Gray, 1953
Syndicate of Death. Warren, 1950

FOGARTY, MICHAEL. 1939- . Director of a small investments and insurance firm in London.
The Achilles Mandate. Davis-Poynter, 1975

FOGELSON, GENIA
Jewel: Undercover Cop. Holloway, 1980 [Calif.]

FOGERTY, J.
A Game at Chess; or, When Jew Meets Greek. Diprose, 1894 ss

FOKKER, NICOLAS. 1908- .
The Tamer. Harper (London), 1979 (Translation of "Dar Vaxer Inga Rosar i Sagspanet." Stockholm, 1973.)

FOLDER, LOUIS
Rocky Libido in San Francisco. Contact, 1962 [S.F.]

FOLDES, YOLANDA. 1903- .
Mind Your Own Murder. Hutchinson, 1948

FOLEY, HELEN
Come to Grief. Hodder, 1976

FOLEY, LORETTE
  Bury by Night. Hale, 1977 [Ire.]
  Dead for Danger. Hale, 1979 [Ire.]

FOLEY, PEARL. Pseudonym: Paul De Mar, q.v.
  The Octagon Crystal. Carrier & Isles, 1929; Brentano's (London), 1929
  The Yellow Circle. Lippincott (Philadelphia & London), 1937 [NYC]

FOLEY, RAE. Pseudonym of Elinore Denniston, 1900-1978. Other pseudonym: Dennis Allan, q.v. Ref: CA, CC, TC. SC: John Harland = JH; Hiram Potter = HP.
  An Ape in Velvet. Dodd, 1951; Boardman, 1952 JH [N.Y.]
  Back Door to Death. Dodd, 1963; Boardman, 1964. Also published as: Nightmare Honeymoon. Dell, 1976 HP [New Eng.]
  The Barclay Place. Dodd, 1975; Hale, 1976 [Conn.]
  Bones of Contention. Dodd, 1950. Also published as: The Other Woman. Dell, 1976 [New Eng.]
  The Brownstone House. Dodd, 1974. British title: Murder by Bequest. Hale, 1976 [NYC]
  A Calculated Risk. Dodd, 1970; Hale, 1972 HP [NYC]
  Call It Accident. Dodd, 1965; Hale, 1966 HP [Las Veg.]
  Curtain Call; see It's Murder, Mr. Potter
  Dangerous to Me. Dodd, 1959; Hammond, 1960 HP [Conn.]
  The Dark Hill. Dodd, 1975; Hale, 1976 [NYC]
  Dark Intent. Dodd, 1954; Boardman, 1955
  The Deadly Noose; see Repent at Leisure
  Death and Mr. Potter. Dodd, 1955; Boardman, 1955. Also published as: The Peacock Is a Bird of Prey. Dell, 1976 HP [NYC]
  Don't Kill, My Love; see Wake the Sleeping Wolf
  Fatal Lady. Dodd, 1964; Boardman, 1964 HP [NYC]
  Fear of a Stranger. Dodd, 1967; Hale, 1968 [Conn.]
  The First Mrs. Winston. Dodd, 1972; Chivers, 1974
  The Girl from Nowhere. Dodd, 1949 JH
  Girl on a High Wire. Dodd, 1969; Hale, 1971 [Vt.]
  The Girl Who Had Everything. Dodd, 1977; Hale, 1978 [NYC]
  The Hundredth Door. Dodd, 1950; Boardman, 1951 JH
  It's Murder, Mr. Potter. Dodd, 1961; Hammond, 1961. Also published as: Curtain Call. Dell, 1976 HP [NYC]
  The Last Gamble. Dodd, 1956; Boardman, 1957 HP [Conn.]
  Malice Domestic. Dodd, 1968; Hale, 1969
  The Man in the Shadow. Dodd, 1953; Boardman, 1954 [N.Y.]
  Murder by Bequest; see The Brownstone House
  Nightmare Honeymoon; see Back Door to Death
  Nightmare House. Dodd, 1968; Hale, 1969 [NYC]
  No Hiding Place. Dodd, 1969; Hale, 1970 [NYC]
  No Tears for the Dead. Dodd, 1948; Cherry Tree, 1949 [Conn.]
  Ominous Star. Dodd, 1971; Hale, 1973 [NYC]
  One O'Clock at the Gotham. Dodd, 1974; Hale, 1975
  The Other Woman; see Bones of Contention
  The Peacock Is a Bird of Prey; see Death and Mr. Potter
  Put Out the Light. Dodd, 1976; Hale, 1977 [New Eng.]
  Reckless Lady. Dodd, 1973; Hale, 1975
  Repent at Leisure. Dodd, 1962. British title: The Deadly Noose. Hammond, 1963 HP [Conn.]
  Run for Your Life. Dodd, 1957; Boardman, 1958 HP
  Scared to Death. Dodd, 1966; Hale, 1967
  The Shelton Conspiracy. Dodd, 1967; Hale, 1968 [Conn.]
  Sleep Without Morning. Dodd, 1972; Hale, 1974 [NYC, Ariz.]
  The Slippery Step. Dodd, 1977; Hale, 1978 [NYC]
  Suffer a Witch. Dodd, 1965; Hale, 1966
  This Woman Wanted. Dodd, 1971; Hale, 1972 [Calif.]
  Trust a Woman? Dodd, 1973 [NYC]
  Wake the Sleeping Wolf. Dodd, 1952; Boardman, 1953. Also published as: Don't Kill, My Love. Bestseller, 1953
  Where Helen Lies. Dodd, 1976; Hale, 1977

  Where Is Nancy Bostwick? Dodd, 1958; Boardman, 1958 HP [NYC]
  Wild Night. Dodd, 1966; Hale, 1967 [Fla.]

FOLLETT, EDWINA. Pseudonym of Edward Fenton.
  The Villa of the Scorpions. Popular Library, 1975 [It.]

FOLLETT, JAMES. 1939- . Trained as marine engineer; suspense and documentary TV scriptwriter.
  Churchill's Gold. Weidenfeld, 1980; Houghton, 1981 [ship, 1941]
  Crown Court. Barker, 1977; St. Martin's, 1978
  -The Doomsday Ultimatum. Weidenfeld, 1976
  -Ice. Weidenfeld, 1978; Stein, 1978
  U-700. Weidenfeld, 1979. U.S. title: The Wotan Warhead. Stein, 1979 [1941]
  The Wotan Warhead; see U-700

FOLLETT, KEN(NETH MARTIN). 1949- .
  Ref: CA. Pseudonym: Symon Myles, q.v. SC: Piers Roper = PR.
  The Bear Raid. Harwood, 1976 PR
  Eye of the Needle; see Storm Island
  The Key to Rebecca. H. Hamilton, 1980; Morrow, 1980 [1942, Egypt]
  The Shakeout. Harwood, 1975 PR
  Storm Island. Macdonald, 1978. U.S. title: Eye of the Needle. Arbor, 1978. Published in Britain under the U.S. title: Prior, 1979 [WWII, Eng.]
  Triple. Macdonald, 1979; Arbor, 1979

FOLLIOTT, DORIA
  Signpost to Murder. Popular Library, 1964 (Novelization of the movie.) [Eng.]

FONBLANQUE, ALBANY (DE GRENIER). 1829-1924.
  A Tangled Skein. Tinsley, 1862; Burnham, 1863
  Tom Rocket. Ward, 1860

FONG, C. K. SC: Mace (see also: Lee Chang) = M.
  The Year of the Cock. Manor, 1975 M

FONSECA, ESTHER HAVEN. 1900- .
  The Affair at the Grotto. Doubleday, 1939 [Wis.]
  Death Below the Dam. Doubleday, 1936 [Wis.]
  The Thirteenth Bed in the Ballroom. Doubleday, 1937 [Midwest]

FONTANA, DOROTHY C.
  The Questor Tapes. Ballantine, 1974 (Novelization of the TV movie.)

FONZO, L. M. D. Joint pseudonym with J. L. Kornbluth: Peter Chandler, q.v.

FOOTE, HORTON
  Baby, the Rain Must Fall. Popular Library, 1965 (Novelization of the movie.)
  The Chase. Rinehart, 1956. Play version: Dramatists, 1952

FOOTE, SHELBY. 1916- . Ref: CA.
  Follow Me Down. Dial, 1950; H. Hamilton, 1951 [Miss.]
  September September. Random, 1978 [Memphis, 1957]

FOOTE, T. VICARS
  My Weird Wooing. Trischler, 1889

FOOTE-SMITH, ELIZABETH. 1913- . Ref: CA. SC: Will Woodfield, in both titles.
  A Gentle Albatross. Putnam, 1976 [Midwest, acad.]
  Never Say Die. Putnam, 1977 [Ill.]

FOOTMAN, DAVID (JOHN). 1895- .
  Ref: CA.
  -The Mine in the Desert. Long, 1929
  -A Pretty Pass; or, Just a Little Careless. Morrow, 1933 (British title?)
  The Yellow Rock. Jenkins, 1929

FOOTMAN, ROBERT
  Once a Spy. Dodd, 1980 [Far East]

FOOTNER, (WILLIAM) HULBERT. 1879-1944.
  Ref: CC, EM, MM, MP, TC. SC: Madame Rosika Storey = RS; Amos Lee Mappin = AM.
  The Almost Perfect Murder. Lippincott, 1937; Collins, 1933 RS ss [NYC]
  Anybody's Pearls. Doubleday, 1930; Hodder, 1929 [Eng.]
  -A Backwoods Princess. Doran, 1926; Hodder, 1926

  -Cap'n Sue. Doubleday, 1928; Hodder, 1927
  The Casual Murderer. Lippincott, 1937; Collins, 1932 RS ss All but the title story reprinted as: The Kidnapping of Madame Storey. Collins, 1936
  -The Case of the Linda Belle. Hodder, 1925 (U.S. title?)
  Dangerous Cargo. Harper, 1934; Collins, 1934 RS [ship]
  The Dark Ships. Harper, 1937; Collins, 1937 [Md.]
  Dead Man's Hat. Harper, 1932; Collins, 1932 [NYC]
  The Death of a Celebrity. Harper, 1938; Collins, 1938 AM [NYC]
  Death of a Saboteur. Harper, 1943; Collins, 1944 AM [NYC]
  The Deaves Affair. Doran, 1922; Collins, 1922 [NYC]
  The Doctor Who Held Hands. Doubleday, 1929; Collins, 1929. Also published as: The Murderer's Challenge. Collins, 1932 RS [NYC]
  Easy to Kill. Harper, 1931; Collins, 1931 RS [R.I.]
  The Folded Paper Mystery; see The Mystery of the Folded Paper
  The Fugitive Sleuth. Hodder, 1918 (U.S. title?) [NYC]
  -The Fur-Bringers. McCann, 1920; Hodder, 1916
  The House with the Blue Door. Harper, 1942; Collins, 1943 AM [N.Y.]
  -The Huntress. McCann, 1922; Hodder, 1917
  The Island of Fear. Harper, 1936; Cassell, 1936 [Md.]
  -Jack Chanty. Doubleday, 1913; Hodder, 1917
  The Kidnapping of Madame Storey; see The Casual Murderer
  Madame Storey. Doran, 1926; Collins, 1926 ss RS [NYC]
  Murder in the Sun; see The Obeah Murders
  Murder of a Bad Man. Harper, 1936; Collins, 1935 [NYC]
  Murder Runs in the Family. Harper, 1934; Collins, 1934 [Conn.]
  The Murder That Had Everything. Harper, 1939; Collins, 1939 AM [NYC]
  The Murderer's Challenge; see The Doctor Who Held Hands
  Murderer's Vanity. Harper, 1940; Collins, 1941 AM [NYC]
  Mystery at Ramshackle House; see Ramshackle House
  The Mystery of the Folded Paper. Harper, 1930. British title: The Folded Paper Mystery. Collins, 1930 AM [NYC]
  The Nation's Missing Guest. Harper, 1939; Collins, 1939 AM [Wash. D.C.]
  The New Made Grave; see The Whip-Poor-Will Mystery
  The Obeah Murders. Harper, 1937. British title: Murder in the Sun. Collins, 1938 [W.I.]
  Officer! Doran, 1924; Collins, 1924 [NYC]
  On Swan River; see The Woman from Outside
  Orchids to Murder. Harper, 1945; Collins, 1945 AM [NYC]
  The Owl Taxi. Doran, 1921; Collins, 1922 [NYC]
  The Queen of Clubs. Doran, 1927; Collins, 1928 [NYC]
  Ramshackle House. Doran, 1922; Collins, 1923. Also published as: Mystery at Ramshackle House. Collins, 1932 [Md.]
  The Ring of Eyes. Harper, 1933; Collins, 1933 [NYC]
  Scarred Jungle. Harper, 1935; Cassell, 1935 [Brazil]
  -The Sealed Valley. Doubleday, 1914; Hodder, 1915
  A Self-Made Thief. Doubleday, 1929; Collins, 1929 [NYC]
  -The Shanty Sled. Doran, 1926; Hodder, 1925 [Can.]
  Sinfully Rich. Harper, 1940; Collins, 1940 [NYC]
  The Substitute Millionaire. Doran, 1919; Collins, 1921 [NYC]
  Thieves' Wit. Doran, 1918; Hodder, 1919 [NYC]
  Tortuous Trails. Collins, 1937 ss [Can.]
  Trial by Water. Farrar, 1931; Hodder, 1930 [La.]
  -Two on the Trail. Doubleday, 1911; Methuen, 1911
  The Under Dogs. Doran, 1925; Collins, 1925 RS [NYC]
  Unneutral Murder. Harper, 1944; Collins, 1944 AM [Lisbon]
  The Velvet Hand. Doubleday, 1928; Collins, 1928 RS ss
  The Viper. Collins, 1930 (Three stories, 2 from The Velvet Hand, q.v.)

The Whip-Poor-Will Mystery. Harper, 1935. British title: The New Made Grave. Collins, 1935 [Conn.]
-The Wild Bird. Doran, 1923; Hodder, 1923
Who Killed the Husband? Harper, 1941; Collins, 1941 AM [NYC]
-The Woman from Outside. McCann, 1921. British title: On Swan River. Hodder, 1919 [Can.]

FORAN, PHIL. See: Robert McLaughlin, 1925- .

FORAN, W(ILLIAM) ROBERT. 1882- .
Drums of Sacrifice. Hutchinson, 1934
-The Land of Fear. Hutchinson, 1937
-The Path of Ivory. Hutchinson, 1934
Roshanara of the Seven Cities. Hutchinson, 1933
Watchers in the Hills. Hutchinson, 1935

FORBAT, SANDOR. 1890- . Pseudonym: A. F. Witley, q.v.

FORBES, LADY ANGELA [SELINA BIANCA ST. CLAIR-ERSKINE]. 1876- .
Should She Have Spoken? Nash, 1923

FORBES, BRYAN. 1926- . Ref: CA.
Familiar Strangers. Hodder, 1979. U.S. title: Stranger. Doubleday, 1980

FORBES, COLIN. Pseudonym of Raymond H(arold) Sawkins, 1923- , q.v. Other pseudonyms: Jay Bernard, Richard Raine, qq.v.
Avalanche Express. Collins, 1977; Dutton, 1977 [train]
The Heights of Zervos. Collins, 1970; Dutton, 1971 [1941, Greece]
The Palermo Affair; see The Palermo Ambush
The Palermo Ambush. Collins, 1972. U.S. title: The Palermo Affair. Dutton, 1972
The Stone Leopard. Collins, 1975; Dutton, 1976 [Fr.]
Target Five. Collins, 1973; Dutton, 1973
Year of the Golden Ape. Collins, 1974; Dutton, 1974 [S.F., 1977]

FORBES, D. R.
Murder of an Unpopular Man. Bles, 1941

FORBES, DANIEL. Pseudonym of Michael Kenyon, 1931- , q.v.

FORBES, DELORIS FLORINE STANTON. 1923- . Pseudonyms: Stanton Forbes, Tobias Wells, qq.v. Joint pseudonym with Helen B. Rydell: Forbes Rydell, q.v.

FORBES, DIANA (R.)
The Man Behind the Tinted Glasses. Holden, 1924
Whose the Hand? Holden, 1925

FORBES, DONALD
The Eleventh Hour. Hutchinson, 1955; Roy, 1955

FORBES, EDMUND
Red Fate. Greening, 1901

FORBES, HAY
A Detective in Italy; or, The Mystery of Berwyn Kennedy. Ward, 1891

FORBES, J. D.
Murder...in Full View. Caravelle, 1968 [Calif.]

FORBES, MURRAY
Hollow Triumph. Ziff-Davis, 1946; Martin, 1946

FORBES, ROBERT ERSTONE. Pseudonym of Ralph Straus, 1882- , q.v.
The Transactions of Oliver Prince. Chapman, 1924 ss

FORBES, (JOAN) ROSITA (TORR). 1893- .
The Cavaliers of Death. Butterworth, 1930; Macaulay, 1930

FORBES, STANTON. Pseudonym of DeLoris Florine Stanton Forbes, 1923- .
Other pseudonym: Tobias Wells, q.v. Joint pseudonym with Helen B. Rydell: Forbes Rydell, q.v. Ref: CA, CC, EM, TC.
All for One and One for Death. Doubleday, 1971; Hale, 1972
Buried in So Sweet a Place. Doubleday, 1977; Hale, 1978 [Boston, 1918]
Bury Me in Gold Lame. Doubleday, 1974; Hale, 1975 [Conn.]
A Business of Bodies. Doubleday, 1966; Hale, 1967 [New Eng.]
But I Wouldn't Want to Die There. Doubleday, 1972; Hale, 1973
A Deadly Kind of Lonely. Doubleday, 1971; Hale, 1973 [Tex., 1934]
Encounter Darkness. Doubleday, 1967; Hale, 1968 [New Eng.]
Go to Thy Death Bed. Doubleday, 1968; Hale, 1969 [1891, N.C.]
Grieve for the Past. Doubleday, 1963; Gollancz, 1964 [Kan.]
If Laurel Shot Hardy the World Would End. Doubleday, 1970. British title: Murder Runs Riot. Hale, 1971
If Two of Them Are Dead. Doubleday, 1968; Hale, 1968 [Kan., 1930s]
The Last Will and Testament of Constance Cobble. Doubleday, 1980; Hale, 1980 [Carib.]
The Long Hate; see The Terrors of the Earth
Melody of Terror; see The Terrors of the Earth
Murder Runs Riot; see If Laurel Shot Hardy the World Would End
The Name's Death, Remember Me? Doubleday, 1969; Hale, 1970 [ship]
Relative to Death. Doubleday, 1965; Hale, 1966 [New Eng.]
The Sad, Sudden Death of My Fair Lady. Doubleday, 1971; Hale, 1971 [Chi., 1933]
She Was Only the Sheriff's Daughter. Doubleday, 1970; Hale, 1970 [Tex., 1940s]
Some Poisoned by Their Wives. Doubleday, 1974; Hale, 1975 [Tex.]
Terror Touches Me. Doubleday, 1966; Hale, 1966 [Ire.]
The Terrors of the Earth. Doubleday, 1964. British title: The Long Hate. Hale, 1966. Also published as: Melody of Terror. Pyramid, 1967 [Mass.]
Welcome, My Dear, to Belfry House. Doubleday, 1973; Hale, 1974 [Cape Cod]

FORBES, WILLIAM G. SC: Ben Bradley, in at least those marked BB.
Ben Bradley's Puzzle. Street (Magnet), 190? BB
Ben Bradley's Weirdest Case. Street (Magnet), 190? BB
Fighting an Unknown Power. Street (Magnet), 190?
Fight to a Finish. Street (Magnet), 190?
From Despair to Triumph. Street (Magnet), 1906
Into the Jaws of Death. Street (Magnet), 190?

FORBES-DENNIS, PHYLLIS. 1884-1963. Pseudonym: Phyllis Bottome, q.v.

FORD, BRYANT
Show Business. Dodd, 1939 [NYC]

FORD, COREY. 1902-1969. Pseudonym: John Riddell, q.v.

FORD, ELBUR. Pseudonym of Eleanor Burford Hibbert, 1906- . Other pseudonyms: Philippa Carr, Victoria Holt, Kathleen Kellow, qq.v.
The Bed Disturbed. Laurie, 1952
Evil in the House; see Such Bitter Business
Flesh and the Devil. Laurie, 1950
Poison in Pimlico. Laurie, 1950
Such Bitter Business. Heinemann, 1953. U.S. title: Evil in the House. Morrow, 1954

FORD, ELIZABETH. Pseudonym of Marjory Elizabeth Sarah Bidwell, -1977. Other pseudonym: Mary Anne Gibbs, q.v. Ref: CA.
The Amber Cat. Hurst, 1976
The Belvedere. Hurst, 1973
Butter Market House. Hurst, 1958
A Charming Couple. Hurst, 1975
The Cottage at Drimble. Hurst, 1957
A Country Holiday. Hurst, 1966. U.S. title: Dangerous Holiday. Ace, 1968
Dangerous Holiday; see A Country Holiday
The Day of the Storm. Hurst, 1971
The Empty Heart. Hurst, 1957
English Rose. Hurst, 1953
Fog. Chapman, 1933
Four Days in June. Hurst, 1951
The Green Beetle. Hurst, 1972
Heron's Nest. Hurst, 1960
A Holiday Arrangement. Hurst, 1963
The House with the Myrtle Trees. Lutterworth, 1942
The Irresponsibles. Hurst, 1946
Just Around the Corner. Hurst, 1952
Limelight in London. Hurst, 1970
Meeting in Spring. Hurst, 1954
Mountford Show. Hurst, 1948
No Room for Joanna. Hurst, 1964
One Fine Day. Hurst, 1954
Open Day at the Manor. Hurst, 1977
Outrageous Fortune. Hurst, 1955
Queen's Harbour. Hurst, 1944
So Deep Suspicion. Hurst, 1950
Spring Comes to the Crescent. Hurst, 1949
That Summer at Bacclesea. Hurst, 1956
The Turbulent Messiters. Hurst, 1967
A Week by the Sea. Hurst, 1962
Young Ann. Hurst, 1973
The Young Ladies' Room. Hurst, 1945

FORD, FLORENCE
Fear Is a Weapon. Hale, 1969
Laughter in the Night. Hale, 1964
The Ninth Candle. Collins, 1960 [New Eng.]
Play with Matches. Hale, 1966 [Bermuda]
Shadow on the House. Collins, 1958

FORD, FORD MADOX. 1873-1939. Name originally: Ford Madux Heuffer; changed legally. See: Joseph Conrad, 1957-1924.

FORD, GEORGE
'Gator. Award, 1976

FORD, HARRIET. 1868-1949. See also: Arthur Hornblow, 1865-1941?
The Argyle Case, with Harvey J(errold) O'Higgins, 1876-1929, q.v. French, 1927 (Play.)

FORD, HILARY. Pseudonym of (Christopher) Samuel Youd, 1922- , q.v. Other pseudonyms: John Christopher, Peter Graaf, Peter Nichols, qq.v.
Bella on the Roof. Longmans, 1965; Banner, 1967 [Ger.]
A Bride for Bedivere. H. Hamilton, 1976; Harper, 1977 [1800s, Eng.]
Castle Malindine. Macmillan (London), 1975; Harper, 1975 [Ire., 1860s]
-Felix Running. Eyre, 1959
-Felix Walking. Eyre, 1958
Sarnia. H. Hamilton, 1974; Doubleday, 1974

FORD, JAMES ALLAN. 1920- . Ref: CA.
A Judge of Men. Hodder, 1968

FORD, JEREMY
Murder Laughs Last. Bouregy, 1956; Ward, 1959

FORD, LESLIE. Pseudonym of Zenith Jones Brown, 1898- . Other pseudonyms: David Frome, q.v. Ref: CA, CC, EM, MP, TC. SC: Lt. Joseph Kelly = JK; Grace Latham = GL; Col. John Primrose = JP.
All for the Love of a Lady. Scribner, 1944. British title: Crack of Dawn. Collins, 1945 GL,JP [Wash. D.C.]
The Bahamas Murder Case. Scribner, 1952; Collins, 1952 [Bahamas]
Burn Forever. Farrar, 1935. British title: Mountain Madness. Hutchinson, 1935 [Tenn.]
By the Watchman's Clock. Farrar, 1932 [Md., acad.]
The Capital Crime; see The Murder of the Fifth Columnist
The Clue of the Judas Tree. Farrar, 1933 JK [Md.]
Crack of Dawn; see All for the Love of a Lady
Date with Death. Scribner, 1949. British title: Shot in the Dark. Collins, 1949 [Md.]
The Devil's Stronghold. Scribner, 1948; Collins, 1948 GL,JP [L.A.]
False to Any Man. Scribner, 1939. British title: Snow-White Murder. Collins, 1940 GL,JP [Va.]
Footsteps on the Stairs; see The Sound of Footsteps
The Girl from the Mimosa Club. Scribner, 1957; Collins, 1957 [Balt.]
Honolulu Murder Story; see Honolulu Story
Honolulu Murders; see Honolulu Story
Honolulu Story. Scribner, 1946. British title: Honolulu Murder Story. Collins, 1947. Also published as: Honolulu Murders. Popular Library, 1967 GL,JP [Haw.]
Ill Met by Moonlight. Farrar, 1937; Collins, 1937 GL,JP [Md.]
Invitation to Murder. Scribner, 1954; Collins, 1955 [R.I.]
The Lying Jade; see Washington Whispers Murder
Mountain Madness; see Burn Forever
Mr. Cromwell Is Dead; see Reno Rendezvous
Murder Comes to Eden. Scribner, 1955; Collins, 1956
Murder Down South; see Murder with Southern Hospitality

Murder in Maryland. Farrar, 1932;
    Hutchinson, 1933 JK [Md.]
Murder in the O.P.M. Scribner, 1942.
    British title: The Priority Murder.
    Collins, 1943 GL,JP [Wash. D.C.]
Murder Is the Pay-Off. Scribner, 1951;
    Collins, 1951
The Murder of the Fifth Columnist.
    Scribner, 1941. British title: The
    Capital Crime. Collins, 1941 GL,JP
    [Wash. D.C.]
Murder with Southern Hospitality.
    Scribner, 1942. British title: Murder
    Down South. Collins, 1943 [Miss.]
Old Lover's Ghost. Scribner, 1940 GL,JP
    [Wyo.]
The Philadelphia Murder Story. Scrib-
    ner, 1945; Collins, 1945 GL,JP
    [Phil.]
The Priority Murder; see Murder in the
    O.P.M.
Reno Rendezvous. Farrar, 1939. British
    title: Mr. Cromwell Is Dead. Collins,
    1939 GL,JP [Reno]
Road to Folly. Scribner, 1940; Collins,
    1941 [Charleston]
Shot in the Dark; see Date with Death
The Simple Way of Poison. Farrar, 1937;
    Collins, 1938 GL,JP [Wash. D.C.]
Siren in the Night. Scribner, 1943;
    Collins, 1944 GL,JP [S.F.]
Snow-White Murder; see False to Any Man
The Sound of Footsteps. Doubleday,
    1931. British title: Footsteps on the
    Stairs. Gollancz, 1931 [Wash. D.C.]
The Strangled Witness. Farrar, 1934
    JP [Wash. D.C.]
Three Bright Pebbles. Farrar, 1938;
    Collins, 1938 GL [Md.]
The Town Cried Murder. Scribner, 1939;
    Collins, 1939 [Va.]
Trial by Ambush. Scribner, 1962; Bri-
    tish title: Trial from Ambush. Col-
    lins, 1962 [Balt.]
Trial from Ambush; see Trial by Ambush
Washington Whispers Murder. Scribner,
    1953. British title: The Lying Jade.
    Collins, 1953 GL,JP [Wash. D.C.]
The Woman in Black. Scribner, 1947;
    Collins, 1948 GL,JP [Wash. D.C.]

FORD, MARY FORKER. 1905-   . Ref: CA.
The Dude Ranch Murders. Bouregy, 1965
Long Journey Home. Bouregy, 1966
Murder, Country Style. Bouregy, 1964
The Rosewell Heritage. Bouregy, 1968
Shadow of Murder. Bouregy, 1965 [Phil.]
The Silent Witness. Bouregy, 1964

FORD, PAUL LEICESTER. 1865-1902. Ref: CC.
The Great K & A Train Robbery. Dodd,
    1897; Low, 1897 [Ariz.]

FORDE, DON
Cocaine. Scion, 1950
Death Rides the Speedway. Warren, 1949
Highway to Hell. Scion, 1950

FORDE, NICHOLAS. Pseudonym of Arthur El-
    liott-Cannon, 1919- . Other pseu-
    donym: Elliott Cannon, q.v.
Engaged in Murder. Hale, 1977
Urgent Action. Hale, 1974
Urgent Delivery. Hale, 1975
Urgent Enquiry. Hale, 1973
Urgent Trip. Hale, 1979
Urgent Wedding. Hale, 1977

FORES, JOHN. 1914-   . Ref: CA.
The Abandoned Power. Hodder, 1970
Candidates for Glory. Hodder, 1968
The Desirable Dictator. Hodder, 1967
The Forgotten Place. Hodder, 1956;
    Coward, 1956
The Human Element; see No Mercy in the
    Sky
New Man in Lowuni. Hodder, 1961
No Mercy in the Sky. Hodder, 1957. U.S.
    title: The Human Element. Doubleday,
    1958
Overload of Hope. Hodder, 1966
The Secret Island. Hodder, 1959
The Springboard. Hodder, 1956
Water for the Fire. Hodder, 1969

FOREST, ESME. See: Marvin Dana, 1867- .

FORESTER, C(ECIL) S(COTT). 1899-1966.
    See also: Jeffrey Dell, 1899- .
    Ref: CA, CC, EM.
The Paid Piper. Methuen, 1924 ss, some
    criminous
Payment Deferred. Lane, 1926; Little,
    1942
Plain Murder. Lane, 1930; Dell, 1954

FORESTER, E(LSPETH) LASCELLES
'Ware Wolf! Cassell, 1928

FORFEX ET HESTA. Pseudonym of Bessie C.
    Morris and Anne B. Spear.
The Lost Key; or, The Mysterious Box.
    Grant, 1879

FORGIONE, LOUIS
The Men of Silence. Dutton, 1928; Dent,
    1929 [It.]

FORMA, WARREN. 1923-   . Ref: CA.
The Falling Man. Crowell, 1973

FORMAN, HENRY JAMES. 1879-1966. Ref: CA.
Guilt. Boni & Liveright, 1924 [NYC]
The Rembrandt Murder. Smith, 1931;
    Paul, 1931 [NYC]

FORMAN, JUSTUS MILES. 1875-1915.
The Six Rubies. Ward, 1914

FORREST, A(LFRED) E(DGAR). 1863-   .
Silent Guests. Covici, 1927 [Can.]

FORREST, DAVID. Joint pseudonym of Robert
    Forrest-Webb, 1929-   , and David
    Eliades. Other Forrest-Webb pseudo-
    nyms: Forrest Webb, Robert Trevelyan,
    qq.v.
The Great Dinosaur Robbery. Hodder,
    1970. U.S. title: One of Our Dino-
    saurs Is Missing. Avon, 1975 [NYC]

FORREST, ELIZABETH
The Garbage Boy. Hale, 1977

FORREST, GEORGE F.
Misfits. Harvey, 1905 ss, some crimin-
    ous

FORREST, NORMAN. Pseudonym of Nigel Mor-
    land, 1905-   , q.v. Other pseudo-
    nyms: Mary Dane, John Donavan, Roger
    Garnett, Vincent McCall, Neal Shep-
    herd, qq.v. SC: John Finnegan, in
    both titles. Set: Eng.
Death Took a Greek God. Harrap, 1937;
    Hillman-Curl, 1938
Death Took a Publisher. Harrap, 1936;
    Hillman-Curl, 1938

FORREST, RICHARD (STOCKTON). 1932-   .
    Pseudonym: Stockton Woods, q.v. SC:
    Lyon Wentworth = LW, all set in Conn.
A Child's Garden of Death. Bobbs, 1975;
    Hale, 1979 LW
The Death in the Willows. Holt, 1979;
    Hale, 1981 LW
Death Through the Looking Glass. Bobbs,
    1978; Hale, 1979 LW
The Killing Edge. Tower, 1980 [Conn.]
Who Killed Mr. Garland's Mistress?
    Pinnacle, 1974
The Wizard of Death. Bobbs, 1977; Hale,
    1978 LW

FORREST, WILLIAMS
The Huntress. GM, 1964
-Seed of Violence. Crest, 1957
Stigma. Crown, 1957. Also published as:
    Stigma for Valor. Crest, 1958 [Kor.]
Stigma for Valor; see Stigma
-The Woman with Claws. GM, 1956

FORREST, WILMA
Anne of Destiny House. GM, 1973
    [past, Scot.]
Last Hope House. GM, 1968 [1855, Ire.]
Shadow Mansion. GM, 1969

FORREST-WEBB, ROBERT. 1929-   . Joint
    pseudonym with David Eliades: David
    Forrest, q.v. Pseudonyms: Robert
    Trevelyan, Forrest Webb, qq.v.

FORRESTER, ANDREW, JR.
The Female Detective. Ward, 1864 ss
The Private Detective. Ward, 1865 ss;
    a partial reissue of earlier titles
Revelations of a Detective; see The
    Revelations of a Private Detective
The Revelations of a Private Detective.
    Ward, 1863. Also published as: Reve-
    lations of a Detective. Ward, 1868 ss
Secret Service; or, Recollections of a
    City Detective. Ward, 1864 ss
Tales by a Female Detective. Ward,
    1968 ss; a partial reissue of ear-
    lier titles

FORRESTER, IZOLA L(OUISE). 1878-   .
The Dangerous Inheritance; or, The
    Mystery of the Tittani Rubies.
    Houghton, 1920 [NYC]
The Secret of the Blue Macaw. Macrae,
    1936

FORRESTER, LARRY. 1924-   . Ref: CA.
-Battle of the April Storm. Harrap,
    1969; Day, 1970
Diamond Beach. Harrap, 1973; McKay,
    1974 [Afr.]
A Girl Called Fathom. Heinemann, 1967;
    GM, 1967

FORSTER, JOSEPH
-Studies in Black and Red. Ward, 1896 ss

FORSTER, MARGARET. 1938-   . Born in
    England; degree in history; author
    of many volumes of fiction and non-
    fiction; chief non-fiction reviewer
    for London newspaper.
The Bride of Lowther Fell. Secker,
    1980; Atheneum, 1981

FORSYTE, CHARLES. Pseudonym of husband
    and wife writing team. Ref: CC. SC:
    Insp. Richard Left = RL.
The Decoding of Edwin Drood. Gollancz,
    1980; Scribner, 1980 (Discussion of
    previous attempts to complete the
    novel by Charles Dickens, 1812-1870,
    q.v., with a new ending by this au-
    thor.) [1860s, Eng.]
Diplomatic Death. Cassell, 1961; Mor-
    row, 1961 RL [Istan.]
Dive into Danger; see Diving Death
Diving Death. Cassell, 1962. U.S.
    title: Dive into Danger. Morrow,
    1962 RL [Fr.]
Double Death. Cassell, 1965 RL
Murder with Minarets. Cassell, 1968
    [Turk.]

FORSYTH, FREDERICK. 1938-   . Ref: CA,
    TC.
The Day of the Jackal. Hutchinson,
    1971; Viking, 1971 [Fr.]
The Devil's Alternative. Hutchinson,
    1979; Viking, 1980
-The Dogs of War. Hutchinson, 1974;
    Viking, 1974
The Odessa File. Hutchinson, 1972;
    Viking, 1972 [Ger.]

FORSYTH, PHIL
The Man Who Feared. Jarrolds, 1927

FORSYTHE, ROBIN. 1879-   . Pseudonym:
    Peter Dingwall, q.v. SC: Anthony
    Vereker = AV. Set: Eng.
The Ginger Cat Mystery. Lane, 1935.
    U.S. title: Murder at Marston Manor.
    Appleton, 1935 AV
The Hounds of Justice. Lane, 1930 AV
Missing or Murdered. Lane, 1929 AV
Murder at Marston Manor; see The Gin-
    ger Cat Mystery
Murder on Paradise Island. World's
    Work, 1937 [S. Pac.]
The Pleasure Cruise Mystery. Lane,
    1933; Appleton, 1934 AV [ship]
The Polo Ground Mystery. Lane, 1932 AV
The Spirit Murder Mystery. Lane, 1936
    AV

FORTUNE, MRS. Pseudonym: W. W., q.v.

FORTUNE, DION. Pseudonym of Violet Mary
    Firth, 1890-1946.
The Secrets of Dr. Taverner. Douglas,
    1926; Llewellyn, 1962

FORVE, GUY
Ofanu. Carlyle, 1979

FOSBURGH, HUGH (WHITNEY). 1916-1976.
    Ref: CA.
-The Drowning Stone. Morrow, 1958; Cape,
    1959

FOSS, JOHN. Pseudonym of James Gordon,
    1912-   .
Flesh and Blood. Dobson, 1951 [Afr.,
    N.]
Plush and Guilt. Dobson, 1953

FOSTER, CHARLES FREEMAN. 1830-   . Pseu-
    donym: Hatherly Sealis, q.v.

FOSTER, DAVID SKAATS. 1852-1920.
-The Road to London. Franklin, 1914

FOSTER, DIRK
Blonde Bombshell. Gaywood, 1952
Don't Scare Me, Sister. Gaywood, 1952
Lady, Shed Your Head. Gaywood, 1952
Some Dames Die Young. Gaywood, 1952
Tough for You, Hazel. Gaywood, 1952

FOSTER, MRS. E. M. Pseudonym: E. M. F.,
    q.v.

FOSTER, GEORGE C(ECIL). 1893-   . Pseu-
    donym: Seaforth, q.v.
Cracksmen All. Jenkins, 1943
-Crocodile down the River. Jenkins, 1942
-Green Lipstick. Jenkins, 1940
Peace Among the Pelicans. Jenkins, 1949
Poindexter Crashes the Fifth Column.
    Jenkins, 1941
-Say It with Flowers. Jenkins, 1939

FOSTER, GLADYS S.
Two Tickets to Destruction. Exposition,
    1975

FOSTER, IRIS. Pseudonym of Richard Posner, 1944-   , q.v. Other pseudonyms: Beatrice Murray, Paul Todd, qq.v.
  The Crimson Moon. Lancer, 1973
  Deadly Sea, Deadly Sand. Lancer, 1972
  The Moorwood Legacy. Lancer, 1972 [L.I.]
  Nightshade. Lancer, 1973
  The Sabath Quest. Lancer, 1973 [Mass.]

FOSTER, J. MONK
  Passion's Aftermath. Digby, 1892

FOSTER, JAN
  Echo My Tears. Dial, 1948; Muller, 1952

FOSTER, JOHN. 1867-   .
  The Searchers. Hodder, 1919; Doran, 1920 [Scot.]

FOSTER, JOHN
  Dark Heritage. GM, 1955; Red Seal, 1959

FOSTER, MAXIMILIAN. 1872-1956.
  -Bubbles. Lippincott, 1929
  -Corrie Who? Small Maynard, 1908
  Crooked. Lippincott, 1928 [NYC]
  Humdrum House. Appleton, 1924 [New Eng.]
  -I Want to Be a Lady. Lippincott, 1926
  -Rich Man, Poor Man. Appleton, 1916
  The Trap. Appleton, 1920 [N.Y.]
  The Whistling Man. Appleton, 1913 [NYC]

FOSTER, R(EGINALD) FRANCIS. 1896-1975. SC: Anthony Ravenhill, in at least those marked AR. Set: Eng.
  Anthony Ravenhill, Crime Merchant. Jarrolds, 1926 AR
  The Body in the Shaft; see The Lift Murder
  The Chillery Court Mystery; see Something Wrong at Chillery
  Confession. Nash, 1927
  The Dark Night. Nash, 1930
  The Lift Murder. Jarrolds, 1924. U.S. title: The Body in the Shaft. Siebel, 1925 AR
  The Missing Gates. Jarrolds, 1924; Siebel, 1926 AR
  The Moat House Mystery. Nash, 1928; Macaulay, 1930 AR
  Murder from Beyond. Nash, 1930; Macaulay, 1930
  The Music Gallery Murder. Unwin, 1927 AR
  The Mystery at Chillery; see Something Wrong at Chillery
  The Secret of the White Thug. Amalgamated Press, 1929 (Sexton Blake.)
  Something Wrong at Chillery. Nash, 1931. U.S. title: The Mystery at Chillery. Fiction League, 1931. Also published as: The Chillery Court Mystery. Mellifont, 1936 AR

FOSTER, RICHARD. Pseudonym of Kendell Foster Crossen, 1910-1981, q.v. Other pseudonyms: Bennett Barlay, M. E. Chaber, Christopher Monig, Clay Richards, qq.v. SC: Chin Kwang Kham = CK; Pete Draco, in at least those marked PD.
  Bier for a Chaser. GM, 1959; Muller pb, 1960 PD [Fla.]
  Blonde and Beautiful. Popular Library, 1955 [Las Veg.]
  The Girl from Easy Street. Popular Library, 1952 [NYC]
  The Invisible Man Murders. Five Star, 1945 CK [L.A.]
  The Laughing Buddha Murders. Vulcan, 1944 CK [Cleve.]
  The Rest Must Die. GM, 1959; Muller pb, 1960
  Too Late for Mourning. GM, 1960; Muller pb, 1961 PD [Miami]

FOSTER, ROBERT FREDERICK. 1853-1948.
  Cab No. 44. Stokes, 1910 [NYC]

FOSTER, TONY
  Zig Zag...to Armageddon. Ermine, 1978

FOSTER, W(ALTER) BERT(RAM). 1869-1929. Pseudonym: Nicholas Carter, q.v.
  From Six to Six. Clode, 1927 [New Eng.]

FOUCAR, EMILE CHARLES VICTOR. 1894-   . Pseudonym: Ray Carr, q.v.

FOUGHT, CATHERINE ANNE
  Rabble's Curse. NAL, 1980; Sphere, 1981 [Vt.]

FOURNIER, PIERRE. 1916-   . Pseudonym: Pierre Gascar, q.v.

FOUTS, EDWARD LEE. 1902-   . Pseudonym: Edward Lee, q.v.

FOWLER, DENNIS
  The Ladies of Holderness. Berkley, 1976

FOWLER, KEITH
  All the Skeletons in All the Closets. Macaulay, 1934. British title: Skeletons in the Cupboard. Jarrolds, 1935 [NYC]

FOWLER, MARIE LOUISE
  The Toll. Field, 1938

FOWLER, SYDNEY. Pseudonym of Sydney Fowler Wright, 1874-1965. U.S. byline: S. Fowler Wright. Ref: CC, TC. SC: Prof. Blinkwell, in at least those marked B; Insp. Cauldron, in at least those marked IC; Insp. Cleveland, in at least those marked C; Mr. Jellipot, in at least those marked J. Set: Eng.
  The Adventure of the Blue Room. Rich, 1945 [1990]
  Arresting Delia. Jarrolds, 1933; Macaulay, 1933 C
  The Attic Murder. Butterworth, 1936 J
  The Bell Street Murders. Harrap, 1931; Macaulay, 1931 J,B
  A Bout with the Mildew Gang. Eyre, 1941 IC
  By Saturday. Lane, 1931 C
  The Case of Anne Bickerton; see The King Against Anne Bickerton
  Crime and Co.; see The Handprint Mystery
  Dinner in New York. Eyre, 1943 J
  The End of the Mildew Gang. Eyre, 1944 IC
  Four Callers in Razor Street. Jenkins, 1937 J
  The Hand-Print Mystery. Jarrolds, 1932. U.S. title: Crime and Co. Macaulay, 1931 C
  The Hanging of Constance Hillier. Jarrolds, 1931; Macaulay, 1932 C
  The Jordans Murder. Jenkins, 1938; Hillman-Curl, 1939 J
  The King Against Anne Bickerton. Harrap, 1930. U.S. title: The Case of Anne Bickerton. Boni & Liveright, 1930. Also published as: Rex v. Anne Bickerton. Penguin, 1947
  The Murder in Bethnel Square. Jenkins, 1938 J
  Post-Mortem Evidence. Butterworth, 1936 J
  The Rissole Mystery. Rich, 1941
  Second Bout with the Mildew Gang. Eyre, 1942 IC
  The Secret of the Screen. Jarrolds, 1933 B
  Three Witnesses. Butterworth, 1935
  Too Much for Mr. Jellipot. Eyre, 1945 J
  Was Murder Done? Butterworth, 1936
  Who Else But She? Jarrolds, 1934
  Who Murdered Reynard? Rich, 1947 B
  The Wills of Jane Kanwhistle. Jenkins, 1939 J
  With Cause Enough? Harvill, 1954 J

FOWLES, ANTHONY. SC: Richard Powell = RP.
  Double Feature. Allen, 1972; Simon, 1973 RP
  Dupe Negative. Allen, 1970; Simon, 1972 RP
  Pastime. Allen, 1974

FOWLES, FRANK. 1941-   .
  The Peruvian Contracts. Putnam, 1976

FOWLES, JOHN. 1926-   . Ref: CA.
  The Collector. Cape, 1963; Little, 1963

FOX, ANTHONY. Pseudonym of Anthony Fullerton.
  Kingfisher Scream. Joseph, 1980; Viking, 1980
  Threat Warning Red. Joseph, 1979

FOX, CLAYTON. 1919-   . Lives in Wash. End of a Big Wheel. Ace, 1962
  Never Forget, Never Forgive. Ace, 1961
  A Sweet Bait of Money. Manor, 1977 [S. Am.]

FOX, DAVID. Pseudonym of Isabel (Egenton) Ostrander, 1883-1924, q.v. Other pseudonyms: Robert Orr Chipperfield, Douglas Grant, qq.v. See also: William Burns, 1861-1932. SC: The Shadowers, Inc., in all titles. Note: In England these titles were published as by Robert Orr Chipperfield.
  The Doom Dealer. McBride, 1923; Hurst, 1925 [N.Y.]
  Ethel Opens the Door. McBride, 1922; Hurst, 1924 [NYC]
  The Handwriting on the Wall. McBride, 1924; Hurst, 1925 [NYC]
  The Man Who Convicted Himself. McBride, 1920; Hurst, 1923 [NYC]

FOX, GARDNER F(RANCIS). 1911-   . Pseudonym: Lynna Cooper, q.v. Ref: CA.
  One Wife's Ways. GM, 1963; Muller pb, 1963 [N.Y.]
  Terror over London. GM, 1957 [London, 1888]
  Witness This Woman. GM, 1959; Muller pb, 1961 [N.Y.]

FOX, GEORGE (RICHARD). 1934-   . Ref: CA.
  Without Music. Holt, 1971

FOX, GEORGE R.
  The Fangs of the Serpent. Minton Balch, 1924 [Chi.]

FOX, JAMES M. Pseudonym of Johannes Matthijs Willem Knipscheer. Other pseudonym: Grant Holmes, q.v. Ref: CA. SC: Steve Harvester = SH; Sgts. Jerry Long & Chuck Conley = L&C; John (and usually Suzy) Marshall = M.
  The Aleutian Blue Mink. Little, 1951; Home and Van Thal, 1952. Also published as: Fatal in Furs. Dell, 1952 M [L.A.]
  Bright Serpent. Little, 1953; Hammond, 1956. Also published as: Rites for a Killer. Jonathan, 1957 M [L.A.]
  Cell Car 54; see Free Ride
  Cheese from a Mousetrap. Davies, 1944 M [Ger.]
  Code Three. Little, 1953; Hammond, 1956. Also published as: Dead Shot. Major, 1979 L&C [L.A.]
  Dark Crusade. Little, 1954; Cassell, 1955, as by Grant Holmes SH [Paris]
  The Dead Canary; see Dead Pigeon
  Dead Pigeon. Hammond, 1967. U.S. title: The Dead Canary. Major, 1979 L&C
  Dead Shot; see Code Three
  Death Commits Bigamy. Coward, 1948; Home & Van Thal, 1950 M [L.A.]
  Don't Try Anything Funny. Davies, 1943 M
  Fatal in Furs; see The Aleutian Blue Mink
  Free Ride. Popular Library, 1957; Cassell, 1957. Also published as: Cell Car 54. Major, 1977 L&C
  The Gentle Hangman. Little, 1950; Home & Van Thal, 1951 M [L.A.]
  Hell on the Way. Davies, 1943 M
  The Inconvenient Bride. Coward, 1948; Home & Van Thal, 1951 M [L.A.]
  The Iron Virgin. Little, 1951; Hammond, 1954 M [L.A.]
  Journey into Danger. Cherry Tree, 1943 M
  The Lady Regrets. Coward, 1947; Davies, 1947 M [L.A.]
  Operation Dancing Dog. Walker, 1974 SH
  Rites for a Killer; see Bright Serpent
  Save Them for Violence. Monarch, 1959
  The Scarlet Slippers. Little, 1952; Hammond, 1955 M [L.A.]
  A Shroud for Mr. Bundy. Little, 1952; Hammond, 1955 M [L.A.]
  The Wheel Is Fixed. Little, 1951; Home & Van Thal, 1952 [Calif.]

FOX, JOSEPH, JR.
  Santa Maria; or, The Mysterious Pregnancy. Kearsley, 1797

FOX, LESLIE H.
  Design for Murder, and five other stories. Alliance (London), 1945 ss
  -The Heel of Achilles. Pan, 1961 ss
  -Twisted Tales. Alliance (London), 1946 ss
  The Vampire, and sixteen other stories. Alliance (London), 1945 ss, mostly criminous

FOX, MARION. 1885-   .
  Aunt Isabel's Lover. Lane, 1928
  The Mystery Keepers. Lane (London & NYC), 1919

FOX, PETER (F.). 1946-   . Has Ph.D. in mathematical physics; has done research in mathematics, physics, and computer simulation.
  Mantis. Macmillan (London), 1979; St. Martin's, 1980

FOX (HUME), RUTH. Joint pseudonym with Anne Fahrenkopf, 1922-1980: Alexander Irving, q.v.

FOX, SEBASTIAN. Pseudonym of Gerald (William) Bullett, 1893-1958, q.v. See also: J(ohn) B(oynton) Priestley, 1894-   . SC: George Lydney, in both titles, set in Eng.
  Odd Woman Out. Dent, 1958
  One Man's Poison. Chatto, 1956

FOX, COLONEL VICTOR J. Pseudonym of Robert Alexander Winston, 1907-1974. Ref: CA.
The Pentagon Case. Freedom Press, 1958; Blandford, 1959

FOX-DAVIES, A(RTHUR) C(HARLES). 1871-1928. SC: Ashley Tempest, in at least those marked AT. Set: Eng.
The Average Man. Routledge, 1907 AT
The Dangerville Inheritance. Lane (London & NYC), 1907 AT
The Duplicate Death. Long, 1910; Macaulay, 1910 AT
The Finances of Sir John Kynnersley. Lane (London & NYC), 1908 ss
The Mauleverer Murders. Lane (London & NYC), 1907 AT
The Testament of John Hastings. Long, 1911
The Troubles of Colonel Marwood. White, 1909
The Ultimate Conclusion. Long, 1912 AT

FOXALL, ARTHUR J.
-The Singing Soul. Christopher, 1932

FOXALL, P(ETER) A(UGUSTUS). SC: Insp. Frank Derben, in at least those marked FD.
Act of Terror. Hale, 1979
The Big-Timer. Hale, 1973
Confessions of a Convict. Hale, 1974
A Dishonest Way to Die. Hale, 1977
Dynasty of Doom. Hale, 1972; Drake, 1972
The Hell's Angel Kidnapping. Hale, 1978
Hostage of the Damned. Hale, 1979
Inspector Derben and the Widow Maker. Hale, 1977 FD
Inspector Derben's War. Hale, 1976 FD
The Murder Machine. Hale, 1976
No Life for a Loser. Hale, 1977
A Prayer for the Guilty. Hale, 1976
Scamp's Law. Hale, 1975
Sequel to Yesterday's Crime. Hale, 1979
Taming the Furies. Hale, 1978
Testament to Violence. Hale, 1980
To Kill a Call Girl. Hale, 1980
Vultures in the Smoke. Hale, 1972

FOXALL, RAYMOND (JEHOIADA CAMPBELL). 1916-   . Ref: CA. SC: Harry Adkins, in at least those marked HA; John Crispin, in at least those marked JC.
-The Amorous Rogue. Hale, 1978; Signet, 1977 JC [ca.1750, Eng.]
Brandy for the Parson. Hale, 1970; St. Martin's, 1974 HA [ca.1807, Eng.]
The Dark Forest. Hale, 1972; St. Martin's, 1974 HA [1807, Eng.]
-The Devil's Smile. Hale, 1960
-The Devil's Spawn. Hale, 1965
-Here Lies the Shadow. Hale, 1957
The Little Ferret. Hale, 1968; St. Martin's, 1974 HA [1807, Eng.]
-Noble Pirate. Hale, 1980; Signet, 1978 JC [ca.1750, Eng.]
The Silver Goblet. Hale, 1974; St. Martin's, 1974 HA [1808, Eng.]
-Society of the Dispossessed. Hale, 1978; Signet, 1976 JC [ca.1750, Eng.]
-Song for a Prince. Hale, 1959
-Squire Errant. Hale, 1968
-The Wicked Lord. Hale, 1962

FOXE, ALISON
Heirs to Kildrennan. Melrose, 1951
Winged Danger. Melrose, 1952

FOXX, JACK. Pseudonym of Bill Pronzini, 1943-   , q.v. Other pseudonym: Alex Saxon, q.v. SC: Dan Connell = DC.
Dead Run. Bobbs, 1975 DC [Mal.]
Freebooty. Bobbs, 1976 [S.F., 1863]
The Jade Figurine. Bobbs, 1972 DC [Sing.]
Wildfire. Bobbs, 1978 [Calif.]

FOY, KENNETH RUSSELL. 1922-   . Pseudonym: Keith Franklin, q.v.

FRALEY, OSCAR
The Director. Award, 1976
Four Against the Mob. Award, 1976

FRANCE, VICTOR. SC: Oliver Galt and Hugo Tower, in both titles.
The Carved Emerald. Selwyn, 1926
The Naked Five. Selwyn, 1927 [Fr.]

FRANCES, STEPHEN D(ANIEL). Also wrote under the Hank Janson byline, q.v. SC: John Gail, in at least those marked JG.
The Ambassador's Plot; see The Sad and Tender Flesh
Bad Boy. Consul, 1964
The Caress of Conquest. Mayflower, 1968; Award, 1970 JG
Cry for My Lovely. Mayflower, 1971
A Grave for Coyotes. Consul, 1965
Hate Is for the Hunted. Mayflower, 1968; Award, 1970 JG
The Illusionist. Mayflower, 1970
The Sad and Tender Flesh. Mayflower, 1966. U.S. title: The Ambassador's Plot. Award, 1970 JG [Paris]
The Sweet Shame of Fury. Mayflower, 1968
This Woman Is Death. Mayflower, 1965; Award, 1969 JG
To Love and Yet to Die. Mayflower, 1966; Award, 1970 JG [Sp.]

FRANCILLON, R(OBERT) E(DWARD). 1841-1919.
Romances of the Law. Chatto, 1889; Gebbie, 1889 (12 ss, including 2 from Romantic Stories of the Legal Profession, q.v.)
Romantic Stories of the Legal Profession. Low, 1883 7 ss

FRANCIS, BASIL (HOSKINS). 1906-   . Ref: CA, CC. SC: Insp. Ghent, in at least those marked G; Sgt. Paul Dean, in at least those marked PD. Set: Eng.
Death at the Bank. Constable, 1938 PD
Death for Safe Custody. Quality, 1944 PD
Death in Act IV. Jenkins, 1954 G [theatre]
Death on the Atoll. Quality, 1948 [Ind. O.]
Death on the Roof. Quality, 1946 PD,G [hosp.]
The Holiday Camp Murder. Constable, 1939 PD
Slender Margin. Constable, 1938 PD

FRANCIS, C. D. E. Pseudonym of Patrick John Fielding Howarth, 1916-   , q.v.
Portrait of a Killer. Hammond, 1956

FRANCIS, CAROLINE
Directors' Corridor. Hutchinson, 1936
It Couldn't Be Suicide. Hutchinson, 1936

FRANCIS, CHARLOTTE
The Truth Will Out. Eldridge, 1974 (2-act play.)

FRANCIS, DICK [RICHARD STANLEY FRANCIS]. 1920-   . Ref: CA, CC, EM, MC, TC. SC: Sid Halley = SH. Set: Eng.
Blood Sport. Joseph, 1967; Harper, 1968 [U.S.]
Bonecrack. Joseph, 1971; Harper, 1972
Dead Cert. Joseph, 1962; Holt, 1962
Enquiry. Joseph, 1969; Harper, 1970
Flying Finish. Joseph, 1966; Harper, 1967
For Kicks. Joseph, 1965; Harper, 1965
Forfeit. Joseph, 1969; Harper, 1969
High Stakes. Joseph, 1975; Harper, 1976
In the Frame. Joseph, 1976; Harper, 1977 [Australia]
Knock Down. Joseph, 1974; Harper, 1975
Nerve. Joseph, 1964; Harper, 1964
Odds Against. Joseph, 1965; Harper, 1966 SH
Rat Race. Joseph, 1970; Harper, 1971
Reflex. Joseph, 1980; Putnam, 1981
Risk. Joseph, 1977; Harper, 1978
Slay-Ride. Joseph, 1970; Harper, 1971 [Nor.]
Smokescreen. Joseph, 1972; Harper, 1973 [S. Afr.]
Trial Run. Joseph, 1978; Harper, 1979 [Moscow]
Whip Hand. Joseph, 1979; Harper, 1980 SH

FRANCIS, EMILY
Elena. Leisure, 1977 [Greece]

FRANCIS, RICHARD H. 1945-   . Ref: CA.
Blackpool Vanishes. Faber, 1980
Daggerman. Faber, 1980; Pantheon, 1980

FRANCIS, WILLIAM. Pseudonym of William Francis Urell. SC: Anthony Martin, in at least those marked AM.
Bury Me Not. Morrow, 1943; Boardman, 1950 AM [L.A.]
The Corrupters. Lion, 1953
Don't Dig Deeper. Lion, 1953
I.O.U.—Murder; see Rough on Rats
Kill or Cure. Morrow, 1942; Boardman, 1951
Rough on Rats. Morrow, 1942. Also published as: I.O.U.—Murder. Signet, 1951 AM [L.A.]

FRANK, E. Z.
-Counter Plot. Fiction House, 1948
-Dead City Round Up. Fiction House, 1949
-Six-Gun Judgment. Fiction House, 1949

FRANK, LEONHARD. 1882-1961.
The Cause of the Crime. Davies, 1928 (Translation of "Die Ursache." Leipzig, 1929.) [Ger.]

FRANK, PAT (HARRY HART). 1907-1964. Reporter and foreign correspondent.
An Affair of State. Lippincott, 1948; Dymock, 1951 [Buda.]
Forbidden Area. Lippincott, 1956. British title: Seven Days to Never. Constable, 1957
Seven Days to Never; see Forbidden Area

FRANK, THEODORE. Pseudonym of D(orothea) F(rances) Gardiner, 1879-   , q.v.
The Lifted Latch. Butterworth, 1929

FRANK, WALDO (DAVID). 1889-1967. Ref: CA, MP.
Chalk Face. Boni, 1924 [NYC]

FRANKAU, GILBERT. 1884-1952. Ref: CC, EM.
Air Ministry, Room 28; see Winter of Discontent
Concerning Peter Jackson and others. Hutchinson, 1931 ss, some criminous
Experiments in Crime. Hutchinson, 1937; Dutton, 1937 ss
The Lonely Man. Hutchinson, 1932; Dutton, 1933
Secret Services. Hutchinson, 1934 ss
Winter of Discontent. Hutchinson, 1941. U.S. title: Air Ministry, Room 28. Dutton, 1942

FRANKAU, JULIA. 1864-1916. Pseudonym: Frank Danby, q.v.

FRANKAU, PAMELA. 1908-1967. Ref: CA, CC.
Appointment with Death; see A Democrat Dies
Colonel Blessington. Bodley, 1969; Delacorte, 1969 (Completed by Diana Raymond.)
A Democrat Dies. Heinemann, 1939; Dutton, 1940

FRANKEL, SANDOR, 1943-   , and WEBSTER MEWS, a pseudonym. Ref on Frankel: CA.
The Aleph Solution. Stein, 1978; Melbourne, 1980

FRANKISH, H.
Dr. Cunliffe—Investigator. Heath, 1913 ss

FRANKLAND, EDWARD PERCY. 1884-   .
-The Half Brothers. Macdonald, 1947
-The Invaders. Redman, 1958
The Murders at Crossby. Dent, 1955 [900s, Eng.]
Mystery at Grimsdale. Low, 1929
-The Nymph at Bay. Low, 1930
The Swarthmoor Tragedy. Stockwell, 1922

FRANKLE, JUDITH. See: John Cotter.

FRANKLIN, CHARLES. Pseudonym of Frank (Hugh) Usher, 1909-1976, q.v. Other pseudonym: Frank Lester, q.v. SC: Insp. Jim Burgess, in at least those marked JB; Maxine Dangerfield, in at least those marked MD; Grant Garfield, in at least those marked GG.
The Bath of Acid. Hale, 1962 JB
Breathe No More. Hale, 1959 GG
Cocktails with a Stranger. Collins, 1947 GG
The Dangerous Ones. Hale, 1964 MD
Darling Murderess. Hale, 1957
Death in the East. Hale, 1967 MD
Death on My Shoulder. Hale, 1958 GG
Died in the Grass. Hale, 1971
The Escape. Hale, 1968 MD
Escape to Death. Collins, 1951 GG
Exit Without Permit. Collins, 1946 GG
Face the Music. Hale, 1957
Fear Runs Softly. Hale, 1961 GG [Fr.]
The Fortieth Victim. Hale, 1963
Gallows for a Fool. Collins, 1952 GG
Girl in Shadow. Collins, 1955 GG
Guilt for Innocence. Hale, 1959 JB
Guilty You Must Be. Hale, 1959 GG
A Handful of Sinners. Hale, 1960 GG
The Home Secretary Affair. Hale, 1971
The KGB Is Here. Hale, 1972
Kill Me and Live. Hale, 1961 JB
Maid for Murder. Collins, 1951 GG
The Mark of Kane. Collins, 1949 GG
Murder Before Dinner. Hale, 1963 JB
The Murder Column. Hale, 1970
Murder on My Hands. Hale, 1973
No Other Victim. Collins, 1952 GG
On the Day of the Shooting. Hale, 1965 MD
One Night to Kill. Collins, 1950 GG
Out of Time. Collins, 1956 GG
Perchance to Kill. Collins, 1954
Play with Death. Collins, 1953
Rope of Sand. Collins, 1948 GG

She'll Love You Dead. Collins, 1950 GG
Stop That Man. Collins, 1954 GG
Storm in an Inkpot. Collins, 1949 GG
The Stranger Came Back. Collins, 1953 GG
The Third Degree. Hale, 1970
The Trembling Thread. Collins, 1955
[Fr., Cent. Am.]

FRANKLIN, DONALD. S: Special Squad, in at least those marked SS.
Lethal Playground. New English Library pb, 1975 SS
Stray Bullet. New English Library pb, 1975
Two-Way Witness. New English Library pb, 1974 SS
The Velvet Hammer. New English Library pb, 1974 SS

FRANKLIN, EDGAR. Pseudonym of Edgar Franklin Stearns, 1879-   .
In and Out. Watt, 1917 [NYC]

FRANKLIN, EUGENE. Pseudonym of (Eugene) Franklin Bandy (Jr.), 1914-   , q.v. SC: Berkeley Barnes and Larry Howe, in all titles, all set in NYC.
The Bold House Murders. Stein, 1973; Hale, 1975
The Money Murders. Stein, 1972
Murder Trapp. Stein, 1971

FRANKLIN, GORDON
Smouldering Fire. Heath, 1923

FRANKLIN, HARRY
Crash. Hale, 1968
Don't Go to Ceuta. Chapman, 1970

FRANKLIN, JUNE. 1924-   .
The Sugar Man's Dead. Hale, 1972

FRANKLIN, KEITH. Pseudonym of Kenneth Russell Foy, 1922-   . Ref: CA.
Murder at Shirttail Flats. GM, 1968 [Calif.]

FRANKLIN, MAX. Pseudonym of Richard Deming, 1915-   , q.v. Other pseudonym: Emily Moor, q.v. See also: Nick Carter, Nick Marino, Ellery Queen. SC: Charlie's Angels = CA (novelizations of the TV series); Starsky and Hutch = S&H (novelizations of the TV series), all set in L.A.
Angels in Chains. Ballantine, 1977; Futura, 1977 CA
Angels on a String. Ballantine, 1977 CA
Angels on Ice. Ballantine, 1978; Futura, 1978 CA
Bounty Hunter. Ballantine, 1977; Futura, 1977 S&H
Charlie's Angels. Ballantine, 1977; Futura, 1977 CA
The Dark. Signet, 1978 [L.A.]
Death Ride. Ballantine, 1976; Futura, 1976 S&H
The Destructors. Ballantine, 1974 (Novelization of the movie.)
The 5th of November. Ballantine, 1975. British title: Hennessy. Futura, 1975 (Novelization of the movie.) [Eng.]
Good Guys Were Black. Signet, 1978 (Novelization of the movie.)
Hell Street. Rinehart, 1954
Hennessy; see The 5th of November
Justice Has No Sword. Rinehart, 1953; Boardman, 1954. Also published as: Murder Muscles In. Bestseller, 1956 [St. Louis]
Kill Huggy Bear. Ballantine, 1976; Barker, 1977 S&H
The Killing Kind. Ballantine, 1977; Futura, 1977 CA
Murder Muscles In; see Justice Has No Sword
Murder on Playboy Island. Ballantine, 1978; Futura, 1978 S&H
99 44/100 % Dead. Award, 1974; Tandem, 1974 (Novelization of the movie.)
The Psychic. Ballantine, 1977 S&H
The Set-Up. Ballantine, 1978; Futura, 1978 S&H
Starsky and Hutch. Ballantine, 1976; Futura, 1976 S&H
Terror on the Docks. Ballantine, 1977 S&H
Vegas. Ballantine, 1978 (Novelization of the TV series.) [Las Veg.]

FRANKLIN, STEVE. Pseudonym of Franklin Stevens, 1933-   . Ref: CA.
The Chickens in the Airshaft. Doubleday, 1972 [NYC]
The Malcontents. Doubleday, 1970 [Fr.]

FRANKS, THETTA Q(UAY)
Money in the Air. French (NYC), 1932 (3-act play.)

FRANZ. Pseudonym (?) of Edward Wyman.
The Felthams; or, Contrasts in Crime. Wyman, 1879

FRASER, ALEX. Pseudonym of Henry Brinton, 1901-   , q.v. SC: Insp. Noel Tracy, in at least those marked NT. Set: Eng.
Bury Their Dead. Bles, 1959; Roy, 1960 NT
Constables Don't Count. Bles, 1957; Roy, 1960 NT
The Dark Places. Bles, 1960
Death Is So Final. Bles, 1958; Roy, 1962
High Tension. Bles, 1959 NT
The Three Wives. Bles, 1957; Roy, 1958

FRASER, ANTHEA (MARY). 1930-   . Ref: CA. Set: Eng.
Breath of Brimstone. Corgi, 1978; Dodd, 1977
Home Through the Dark. Milton House, 1974; Dodd, 1976
Island in Waiting. Hale, 1979; St. Martin's, 1979 [Isle of Man]
Laura Possessed. Milton House, 1974; Dodd, 1974
The Stone. Hale, 1980; St. Martin's, 1980
Whistler's Lane. Milton House, 1975; Dodd, 1975

FRASER, ANTONIA (PAKENHAM). 1932-   . Ref: CA, TC. SC: Jemima Shore, in both titles.
Quiet As a Nun. Weidenfeld, 1977; Viking, 1977
The Wild Island. Weidenfeld, 1978; Norton, 1978 [Scot.]

FRASER, COLIN. 1935-   . Ref: CA. See: Philip Ridgeway.

FRASER, ELISE (PARKER). 1903-   . Ref: CA.
The Emerald Necklace. Van Kampen, 1950 [S.F.]
The Jade Elephant. Van Kampen, 1952
The Mystery of the Star Sapphire. Zondervan, 1961 [S.F.]

FRASER, FERRIN L.
The Screaming Portrait. Sears, 1928 [Eng.]

FRASER, GUY
A Plate of Ladies. Hale, 1979

FRASER, HERMIA (HARRIS). 1902-   .
One Touch of Murder. Arcadia, 1953

FRASER, J. MALCOLM. See: B(ertram) Fletcher Robinson.

FRASER, JAMES. Pseudonym of Alan White, 1924-   , q.v. Other pseudonym: Alec Whitney, q.v. SC: Insp. William Aveyard, in all titles, set in Eng.
Blood on a Window's Cross. Barrie, 1972
A Cock-Pit of Roses. Jenkins, 1969; Harcourt, 1970
Deadly Nightshade. Jenkins, 1970; Harcourt, 1970
Death in a Pheasant's Eye. Barrie, 1971; Walker, 1972
The Evergreen Death. Jenkins, 1968; Harcourt, 1969
The Five-Leafed Clover. Barrie, 1973
Hearts Ease in Death. Barrie, 1977; Doubleday, 1977
Who Steals My Name? Barrie, 1976; Doubleday, 1976
A Wreath of Lords and Ladies. Barrie, 1974; Doubleday, 1975

FRASER, JAMES BAILLIE. 1783-1856.
The Khan's Tale. Simms, 1850

FRASER, JEAN
Corpse with Camera. Hale, 1976
The Deadly Nightshade. Hale, 1973
Death on the Dordogne. Hale, 1976
Death on the Piazza. Hale, 1973
The Lone Vendetta. Hale, 1972

FRASER, JOHN
Death the Showman. Unwin, 1901

FRASER, JOHN. 1931-   . Ref: CA.
Clap Hands If You Believe in Fairies. Collins, 1969. U.S. title: The Babysitter. Putnam, 1969

FRASER, JOHN ARTHUR. Pseudonym: Hawkshaw, q.v.
The Cronin Mystery. Eagle, 1889

FRASER, ROBERT
The Fire Opal. Clode, 1911
Three Men and a Maid. Clode, 1907

FRASER, RON(ALD LESLIE)
The After-Dark. Ward, 1961

FRASER, STUART
The Night in George Square. Long, 1960

FRASER, T. A.
The Eye of Jinas and other stories. Fraser Asher, 1923 ss

FRASER, W(ILLIAM) A(LEXANDER). 1859-1933.
The Eye of a God and Other Tales of East and West. Doubleday, 1899 ss, some criminous

FRASER, W. J.
-A Living Skeleton. Neely, 1899

FRASER-SIMPSON, C(ICELY DEVENISH)
Count the Hours. Hutchinson, 1940
Danger Follows. Heinemann, 1929
Footsteps in the Night. Methuen, 1926; Dutton, 1927
The Swinging Shutter. Heinemann, 1927; Dutton, 1928

FRAY, AL. Pseudonym of Ralph Salaway.
And Kill Once More. Graphic, 1955 [Calif.]
Built for Trouble. Dell, 1958; Hale, 1960 [L.A.]
Come Back for More. Dell, 1958; Hale, 1960
The Dame's the Game. Popular Library, 1960 [L.A.]
The Dice Spelled Murder. Dell, 1957 [L.A.]

FRAYN, MICHAEL. 1933-   . Ref: CA.
The Russian Interpreter. Collins, 1966; Viking, 1966 [Moscow]

FRAZEE, (CHARLES) STEVE. 1909-   . Ref: CA.
Flight 409. Avon, 1969
Running Target. GM, 1957; Fawcett (London), 1958
The Sky Block. Rinehart, 1953; Bodley, 1955 [West]

FRAZER, ANDREW. Pseudonym of Stephen Marlowe, 1928-   , q.v. Name originally: Milton Lesser. Other pseudonyms: Jason Ridgway, C. H. Thames, qq.v. See also: Richard S(cott) Prather, 1921-   ; and also: Ellery Queen. SC: Duncan Pride, in both titles.
The Fall of Marty Moon. Avon, 1960 [NYC]
Find Eileen Hardin—Alive! Avon, 1959

FRAZER, MARTIN. Pseudonym of Percy A. Clarke. SC (with many other authors): Sexton Blake, in all Amalgamated Press titles. Set: Eng.
Acquitted! Wright, 1937
The Case of the Dope Dealers. Amalgamated, 1952
The Case of the Shot Looter. Amalgamated, 1941
The Crime at Crown Inn. Amalgamated, 1936
The Crook Ship. Wright, 1940
Dangerous Waters. Wright, 1951
The Fainting Lady. Wright, 1938
The Fatal V Sign. Amalgamated, 1942
The Four Jealous Men. Wright, 1938 [Sol. Is.]
The Mystery of the German Prisoner. Amalgamated, 1940
The Mystery of the Shadowed Footballer. Amalgamated, 1948
The Riddle of Dead Man's Mine. Amalgamated, 1937
Secret in Seven Fathoms. Wright, 1946
The Star in the Forest. Wright, 1940

FRAZER, ROBERT CAINE. Pseudonym of John Creasey, 1908-1973, q.v. Other pseudonyms: Gordon Ashe, M. E. Cooke, Norman Deane, Patrick Gill, Michael Halliday, Charles Hogarth, Brian Hope, Colin Hughes, Kyle Hunt, Abel Mann, Peter Manton, J. J. Marric, Richard Martin, Rodney Mattheson, Anthony Morton, Jeremy York, qq.v. SC: Mark Kilby, in all titles.
The Hollywood Hoax. PB, 1961; Collins, 1964 [L.A.]
Mark Kilby and the Manhattan Murders; see Mark Kilby Stands Alone
Mark Kilby and the Miami Mob. PB, 1960. British title: The Miami Mob, in the double volume: The Miami Mob and Mark Kilby Stands Alone. Collins, 1965 [Miami]
Mark Kilby and the Secret Syndicate. PB, 1960. British title: The Secret Syndicate. Collins, 1961 [Las Veg.]

Mark Kilby Solves a Murder. PB, 1959. British title: R.I.S.C. Collins, 1962. Also published as: The Timid Tycoon. Fontana, 1965 [NYC]
Mark Kilby Stands Alone. PB, 1962. British edition included in the double volume: The Miami Mob and Mark Kilby Stands Alone. Collins, 1965. Also published as: Mark Kilby and the Manhattan Murders. Fontana, 1966 [NYC]
Mark Kilby Takes a Risk. PB, 1962 [NYC]
The Miami Mob and Mark Kilby Stands Alone; see Mark Kilby and the Miami Mob, and Mark Kilby Stands Alone
R.I.S.C.; see Mark Kilby Solves a Murder
The Secret Syndicate; see Mark Kilby and the Secret Syndicate
The Timid Tycoon; see Mark Kilby Solves a Murder

FREDE, RICHARD. Pseudonym of Macdowell Frederics, 1934- , q.v.
Coming-Out Party. Random, 1969

FREDERICKS, ARNOLD. Pseudonym of Frederick Arnold Kummer, 1873-1943, q.v. SC: Richard Duvall = RD.
The Blue Lights. Watt, 1915; Simpkin, 1917 RD [Paris]
The Film of Fear. Watt, 1917; Hayes, 1921 RD [NYC]
The Ivory Snuff Box. Watt, 1912; Simpkin, 1916 RD
The Little Fortune. Watt, 1915; Simpkin, 1917 RD [NYC]
The Mark of the Rat. Sears, 1929; Paul, 1930 [Va.]
One Million Francs. Watt, 1912; Nash, 1920 RD [Paris]
The Spanish Lady. Sears, 1933

FREDERICKS, ERNEST JASON
Cry Flood! Ace, 1959. British title: Murder Matrix. Ward, 1960
Lost Friday; see Shakedown Hotel
Murder Matrix; see Cry Flood!
Shakedown Hotel. Ace, 1958. British title: Lost Friday. Hale, 1959 [Chi.]

FREDERICKS, HARRIET. Joint pseudonym of James Smock and Clyde Laurents.
The Dream Hunter. Beagle, 1974

FREDERICS, JOCKO. An "itinerant" lighthouse keeper.
Everybody's Ready to Die. Holt, 1966. British title: Ready to Die. Hale, 1968 [New Eng.]

FREDERICS, MACDOWELL. 1934- . Pseudonym: Richard Frede, q.v.
Black Work. Crowell, 1976
Emergency Procedure. Coward, 1970; Hale, 1971 [N.H.]

FREDMAN, (HENRY) JOHN. 1927- . Ref: CA. SC: Charles Dexter, in all titles. Set: Eng.
Epitaph to a Bad Cop. Hale, 1973; McKay, 1973
The False Joanna. Hutchinson, 1970; Bobbs, 1971
The Fourth Agency. Hutchinson, 1969; Bobbs, 1970

FREDMAN, MIKE. Creative director of London advertising agency. SC: Willie Halliday, in both titles. Set: Eng.
Kisses Leave No Fingerprints. Elek, 1979; St. Martin's, 1980
You Can Always Blame the Rain. Elek, 1978; St. Martin's, 1980

FREDRICS, GEORGE
Consider Yourself Dead. Powell, 1969 (2 novelets.)
Operation Nightmare. Powell, 1969 (2 novelets.)

FREEBORN, BRIAN (JAMES). 1939- . Ref: CA. SC: Harry Grant (alias Cain), in both titles.
Good Luck, Mr. Cain. Secker, 1976; St. Martin's, 1977
Ten Days, Mr. Cain. Secker, 1977; St. Martin's, 1978

FREEBORN, RICHARD (H.). 1926- . Ref: CA.
Russian Roulette. Cassell, 1979

FREED, DONALD. 1932- . Ref: CA.
The China Card. Arbor, 1980
The Killing of R.F.K. Dell, 1975; Sphere, 1977
The Spymaster. Arbor, 1980; Corgi, 1981

FREEDGOOD, MORTON. 1912- . Pseudonym: John Godey, q.v.

FREEDLAND, NATHANIEL. See: Paul Ross.

FREEDMAN, COLE. Pseudonym: Will Manson, q.v.

FREELING, NICOLAS. 1927- . Pseudonym: F. R. E. Nicolas, q.v. Ref: CA, CC, EM, MC, TC. SC: Henry Castang = HC; Inspector Van Der Valk = V; Arlette Van Der Valk (Davidson), as a secondary character in most of the Insp. Van Der Valk titles, and as a principal in those marked AV.
Aupres de ma Blonde; see A Long Silence
Because of the Cats. Gollancz, 1963; Harper, 1964 V [Holl.]
The Bugles Blowing; see What Are the Bugles Blowing For?
Castang's City. Heinemann, 1980; Pantheon, 1980 HC [Fr.]
Criminal Conversation. Gollancz, 1965; Harper, 1966 V [Amst.]
Death in Amsterdam; see Love in Amsterdam
Double Barrel. Gollancz, 1964; Harper, 1965 V [Holl.]
The Dresden Green. Gollancz, 1966; Harper, 1967 [Ger.]
A Dressing of Diamond. H. Hamilton, 1974; Harper, 1974 HC [Fr.]
Gadget. Heinemann, 1977; Coward, 1977 [Ger.]
Gun Before Butter. Gollancz, 1963. U.S. title: Question of Loyalty. Harper, 1964 V [Holl.]
The King of the Rainy Country. Gollancz, 1966; Harper, 1966 V
Lake Isle. Heinemann, 1976. U.S. title: Sabine. Harper, 1978 HC [Fr.]
A Long Silence. H. Hamilton, 1972. U.S. title: Aupres de ma Blonde. Harper, 1972 V,AV [Amst.]
Love in Amsterdam. Gollancz, 1962; Harper, 1963. Also published as: Death in Amsterdam. Ballantine, 1964 V [Amst.]
The Lovely Ladies; see Over the High Side
The Night Lords. Heinemann, 1978; Pantheon, 1978 HC [Fr.]
Over the High Side. H. Hamilton, 1971. U.S. title: The Lovely Ladies. Harper, 1971 V [Amst.]
Question of Loyalty; see Gun Before Butter
Sabine; see Lake Isle
Strike Out Where Not Applicable. Gollancz, 1967; Harper, 1968 V [Holl.]
This Is the Castle. Gollancz, 1968; Harper, 1968 [Fr.]
Tsing-Boum. H. Hamilton, 1969; Harper (spelled Tsing-Boom), 1969 V [Fr.]
What Are the Bugles Blowing For? Heineman, 1975. U.S. title: The Bugles Blowing. Harper, 1976 HC [Fr.]
The Widow. Heinemann, 1979; Pantheon, 1979 AV [Fr.]

FREEMAN, BARBARA
Mirror, Mirror on the Wall. Manor, 1978

FREEMAN, ELIZABETH WOODS. 1888- .
Murder Sets the Pace. Pageant, 1952 [Calif.]

FREEMAN, KATHLEEN. 1897-1959. Pseudonyms: Mary Fitt, Stuart Mary Wick, qq.v. Ref: CC, TC.
The Intruder, and other stories. Cape, 1926 ss, some criminous
Gown and Shroud. Macdonald, 1947 [acad.]

FREEMAN, LUCY (GREENBAUM). 1916- . Ref: CA. SC: Dr. William Ames, in all titles.
The Case on Cloud Nine. Arbor, 1975 [NYC]
The Dream. Arbor, 1971
The Psychiatrist Says Murder. Arbor, 1973 [NYC]

FREEMAN, MARTIN J(OSEPH). 1899- . Ref: CC. SC: Jerry Todd = JT.
The Case of the Blind Mouse. Dutton, 1935; Eldon, 1936 JT [Chi.]
Murder by Magic. Dutton, 1932
The Murder of a Midget. Dutton, 1931; Eldon, 1934 [Tex.]
The Scarf on the Scarecrow. Dutton, 1938 JT [Chi.]

FREEMAN, R(ICHARD) AUSTIN. 1862-1943. Joint pseudonym with John James Pitcairn, 1860-1936: Clifford Ashdown, q.v. Ref: all except CA. SC: Dr. John Thorndyke = JT (see also: Norman Donaldson, 1922- ; and: John H. Dirckx, 1938-). Set: Eng.
The Adventures of Dr. Thorndyke; see The Singing Bone
As a Thief in the Night. Hodder, 1928; Dodd, 1928 JT
The Blue Scarab; see Dr. Thorndyke's Case-Book
The Case of Oscar Brodski. Dodd, 1923 (Separate publication of one story from The Singing Bone, q.v.)
The Cat's Eye. Hodder, 1923; Dodd, 1927 JT
A Certain Dr. Thorndyke. Hodder, 1927; Dodd, 1928 JT
The D'Arblay Mystery. Hodder, 1926; Dodd, 1926 JT
Death at the Inn; see Felo De Se?
Dr. Thorndyke Intervenes. Hodder, 1933; Dodd, 1933 JT
Dr. Thorndyke Investigates. Univ. of London Press, 1930 (5 ss culled from earlier collections.)
The Dr. Thorndyke Omnibus; see The Famous Cases of Dr. Thorndyke
Dr. Thorndyke's Case-Book. Hodder, 1923. U.S. title: The Blue Scarab. Dodd, 1924 JT ss
Dr. Thorndyke's Cases; see John Thorndyke's Cases
Dr. Thorndyke's Discovery; see When Rogues Fall Out
The Exploits of Danby Croker. Duckworth, 1916 ss
The Eye of Osiris. Hodder, 1911. U.S. title: The Vanishing Man. Dodd, 1912 JT
The Famous Cases of Dr. Thorndyke. Hodder, 1929. U.S. title: The Dr. Thorndyke Omnibus. Dodd, 1932 (The British edition contains 37 out of the 40 Thorndyke ss, leaving out 3 from John Thorndyke's Cases, q.v. The U.S. edition has 38 of the 40, omitting the two that were originally included in The Great Portrait Mystery, q.v.) JT ss
Felo De Se? Hodder, 1937. U.S. title: Death at the Inn. Dodd, 1937 JT
-Flighty Phyllis. Hodder, 1928
For the Defence: Dr. Thorndyke. Hodder, 1934; Dodd, 1934 JT
The Great Portrait Mystery. Hodder, 1918 ss, two with JT
Helen Vardon's Confession. Hodder, 1922 JT
The Jacob Street Mystery. Hodder, 1942. U.S. title: The Unconscious Witness. Dodd, 1942 JT
John Thorndyke's Cases. Chatto, 1909. U.S. title: Dr. Thorndyke's Cases. Dodd, 1931 JT ss
The Magic Casket. Hodder, 1927; Dodd, 1927 JT ss
Mr. Polton Explains. Hodder, 1940; Dodd, 1940 JT
Mr. Pottermack's Oversight. Hodder, 1930; Dodd, 1930 JT
The Mystery of Angelina Frood. Hodder, 1924; Dodd, 1925 JT
The Mystery of 31, New Inn. Hodder, 1912; Winston, 1913 JT
The Penrose Mystery. Hodder, 1936; Dodd, 1936 JT
Pontifex, Son & Thorndyke. Hodder, 1931; Dodd, 1931 JT
The Puzzle Lock. Hodder, 1925; Dodd, 1926 JT ss
The Red Thumb Mark. Collingwood, 1907; Newton, 1911 JT
A Savant's Vendetta. Pearson, 1920. U.S. title: The Uttermost Farthing. Winston, 1914 ss
The Shadow of the Wolf. Hodder, 1925; Dodd, 1925 JT
A Silent Witness. Hodder, 1914; Winston, 1915 JT
The Singing Bone. Hodder, 1912; Dodd, 1923. Also published as: The Adventures of Dr. Thorndyke. Popular Library, 1947. One story published separately as: The Case of Oscar Brodski, q.v. JT ss
The Stoneware Monkey. Hodder, 1938; Dodd, 1939 JT
-The Surprising Adventures of Mr. Shuttlebury Cobb. Hodder, 1927
The Unconscious Witness; see The Jacob Street Mystery
The Uttermost Farthing; see A Savant's Vendetta
The Vanishing Man; see The Eye of Osiris
When Rogues Fall Out. Hodder, 1932. U.S. title: Dr. Thorndyke's Discovery. Dodd, 1932 JT

FREEMAN-HILTON, THOMAS. Ref: CC.
The Sayle Case. Gifford, 1946

FREEMANTLE, BRIAN (HARRY). 1936- . Ref: CA, TC. SC: Charlie Muffin = CM.
Charlie M.; see Charlie Muffin
Charlie Muffin. Cape, 1977. U.S. title: Charlie M. Doubleday, 1977. Reprinted in Britain under the U.S. title: Sphere, 1978 CM

Charlie Muffin U.S.A.; see Charlie Muffin's Uncle Sam
Charlie Muffin's Uncle Sam. Cape, 1980. U.S. title: Charlie Muffin U.S.A. Doubleday, 1980 CM [Fla.]
Clap Hands, Here Comes Charlie. Cape, 1978. U.S. title: Here Comes Charlie M. Doubleday, 1978 CM
Face Me When You Walk Away. Cape, 1974; Putnam, 1975 [Russ.]
Goodbye to an Old Friend. Cape, 1973; Putnam, 1973
Here Comes Charlie M; see Clap Hands, Here Comes Charlie
The Inscrutable Charlie Muffin. Cape, 1979; Doubleday, 1979 CM [H. Kong]
The Man Who Wanted Tomorrow. Cape, 1975; Stein, 1976
The November Man. Cape, 1976

FREESTONE, BASIL. 1910- .
-Crave Pity from the Wind. Dobson, 1962
-The Golden Drum. Quality, 1954

FREETHY, VERNON F.
Dangerous Homecoming. McKay, 1962

FREIHOFER, LOIS DIANE. 1933- . Pseudonym: Lois Barth, q.v.

FREIVALDS. JOHN. 1944- . Ref: CA.
The Famine Plot. Stein, 1978 [1980]

FREMLIN, CELIA. Pseudonym of Celia Margaret Goller, 1914- . Ref: CA, CC, TC. Set: Eng.
Appointment with Yesterday. Gollancz, 1972
By Horror Haunted. Gollancz, 1974 ss
Don't Go to Sleep in the Dark. Gollancz, 1970; Lippincott, 1970 ss
The Hours Before Dawn. Gollancz, 1958; Lippincott, 1959
The Jealous One. Gollancz, 1965; Lippincott, 1965
The Long Shadow. Gollancz, 1975; Doubleday, 1976
Possession. Gollancz, 1969; Lippincott, 1969
Prisoner's Base. Gollancz, 1967; Lippincott, 1967
Seven Lean Years. Gollancz, 1961. U.S. title: Wait for the Wedding. Lippincott, 1961
The Spider-Orchid. Gollancz, 1977; Doubleday, 1978
The Trouble Makers. Gollancz, 1963; Lippincott, 1963
Uncle Paul. Gollancz, 1959; Lippincott, 1960
Wait for the Wedding; see Seven Lean Years
With No Crying. Gollancz, 1980; Doubleday, 1981

FRENCH, ALICE. 1850-1934. Pseudonym: Octave Thanet, q.v.

FRENCH, E. T.
Never Smile at Children. Pyramid, 1959

FRENCH, FERGUS
Invitation to Die. Hale, 1970
Smouldering Fuse. Hale, 1970

FRENCH, H(ENRY) W(ILLARD). 1854?- .
Castle Foam; or, The Heir of Meerschaum. Lee, 1880

FRENCH, RICHARD P. Graduate of Yale; has degree in psycholinguistics; freelance journalist and book reviewer.
A Spy Is Forever. Tuttle, 1970 [Jap.]

FRETLAND, D. JOHN. 1943- . Born in Chi.; has degrees in chemistry and engages in biochemical research.
Morning of the Tiger. Exposition, 1969

FREUND. PHILIP. 1909- . Ref: CA.
The Beholder. Allen, 1961; British Book Centre, 1963 ss
The Devious Ways. Allen, 1962; London House, 1963
The Spymaster. Allen, 1965; Washburn, 1966 (4 stories.)

FREW, JAMES. See: Robin Moore.

FREWER, GLYN MERVYN LOUIS. 1931- .
Pseudonym: Mervyn Lewis, q.v.

FREY, CHARLES WEISER. 1910- . Pseudonym: Ferguson Findley, q.v.

FREYER, FREDERIC. Pseudonym of Bill S(anborn) Ballinger, 1912-1980, q.v. Other pseudonym: B. X. Sanborn, q.v.
The Black, Black Hearse. St. Martin's, 1955; Hale, 1960. Also published as: Case of the Black, Black Hearse. Avon, 1955 [Fr.]

FREYTAG, JOSEPH
The Mercenary. Pinnacle, 1977 [S.F.]

FREYTAG, JOSEPHINE
Amber Palace. PB, 1980 [N.Y., past]

FRIED, BARBARA. 1924- . Ref: CA.
Concerto in the Key of Death. Tower, 1980 [Mass.]

FRIEDMAN, BRUCE JAY. 1930- . Ref: CA.
The Dick. Knopf, 1970; Cape, 1971

FRIEDMAN, HAL [HAROLD]. 1942- . Ref: CA.
Tunnel. Morrow, 1979; Hamlyn, 1981 [NYC]

FRIEDMAN, PHILIP. 1944- . Pseudonym: Philip Chase, q.v.
Rage. Atheneum, 1972; Sphere, 1973 (Novelization of the movie). [Wyo.]
Termination Order. Dial, 1979; Hodder, 1980

FRIEDMAN, ROY. 1934-
The Insurrection of Hippolytus Brandenberg. Stein, 1968; Macmillan (London), 1968 [NYC]

FRIEDMAN, STUART. 1913- . Pseudonym: Elizabeth Erin Mande, q.v. Ref: CA.
The Bedside Corpse; see The Gray Eyes
Ex-Con; see Free Are the Dead
Free Are the Dead. Abelard, 1954. Also published as: Ex-Con. Pyramid, 1954
The Gray Eyes. Abelard, 1955. Also published as: The Bedside Corpse. Lion, 1957
Nikki. Monarch, 1959
-Ravaged. Monarch, 1962
-The Trouble with Ava. Monarch, 1961
-The Troubles of Doctor Cortland. Monarch, 1965
-The Way We Love. Monarch, 1960
The Woman and the Prowler. Avon, 1957

FRIEDRICH, OTTO (ALVA). 1929- . Ref: CA.
The Loner. Crown, 1964; Allen, 1965

FRIEL, ARTHUR O(LNEY). 1885-1959.
-King—of Kearsarge. Penn, 1921; Melrose, 1922
-The Pathless Trail. Harper, 1922
-Tiger River. Harper, 1923; Long, 1924

FRIEND, ED. Pseudonym of Richard (Edward) Wormser, 1908-1977, q.v.
The Corpse in the Castle. Lancer, 1970
The Infernal Light. Dell, 1966 (Novelization of the "Green Hornet" TV series.)
The Most Deadly Game. Lancer, 1970 (Novelization of the TV series.)

FRIEND, OSCAR J(EROME). 1897-1963. Pseudonym: Owen Fox Jerome, q.v.
Domes of Silence. Paul, 1929

FRIERSON, TOMMY R.
A Six-Letter Word for Death. Vantage, 1970

FRISBIE, CARL
At War with the Unknown. Street (New Magnet)
A Flash of Light. Street (New Magnet)
The Great Turf Mystery. Street (New Magnet)
Out of Satan's Grip. Street (New Magnet)
When Cold Steel Clashed. Street (New Magnet)

FRISCHAUER, PAUL. See: Allen Haden.

FRITCH, CHARLES E.
Negative of a Nude. Ace, 1959 [L.A.]

FRITH, MICHAEL K. Joint pseudonym with Christopher Bennett Cerf, 1941- : I*n Fl*m*ng, q.v.

FRITH, WALTER
The Sack of Monte Carlo. Arrowsmith, 1897; Harper, 1898 [Fr.]

FRITZHAND, JAMES. Pseudonyms: Nick Carter, Janine Fitzpatrick, qq.v.

FRIZELL, BERNARD
Timetable for the General. Collins, 1972. U.S. title: The Grand Defiance. Morrow, 1972

FROEST, FRANK. Ref: CC. Set: Eng.
The Crime Club, with George Dilnot, 1883-1951, q.v. Nash, 1915 ss
The Grell Mystery. Nash, 1913; Clode, 1914
The Maelstrom; see The Rogues' Syndicate
The Rogues' Syndicate, with George Dilnot, 1883-1951, q.v. Nash, 1916. U.S. title: The Maelstrom. Clode, 1916, as by Frank Froest alone

FROME, DAVID. Pseudonym of Zenith Jones Brown, 1898- . Other pseudonym: Leslie Ford, q.v. SC: Evan Pinkerton = EP; Major Gregory Lewis = GL. Set: Eng., in all except noted title.
Arsenic in Richmond; see Mr. Pinkerton Goes to Scotland Yard
The Black Envelope. Farrar, 1937. British title: The Guilt Is Plain. Longmans, 1938 EP
The Body in Bedford Square; see Mr. Pinkerton Grows a Beard
The Body in the Turl; see Mr. Pinkerton Finds a Body
The By-Pass Murder; see Two Against Scotland Yard
The Eel Pie Murders. Farrar, 1933. British title: The Eel Pie Mystery. Longmans, 1933 EP
The Eel Pie Mystery; see The Eel Pie Murders
The Guilt Is Plain; see The Black Envelope
The Hammersmith Murders. Doubleday, 1930; Methuen, 1930 EP
Homicide House. Rinehart, 1950. British title: Murder on the Square. Hale, 1951 EP
In at the Death. Longmans (New York), 1930; Skeffington, 1929
The Man from Scotland Yard. Farrar, 1932. British title: Mr. Simpson Finds a Body. Longmans, 1933 EP
Mr. Pinkerton and the Old Angel; see Mr. Pinkerton at the Old Angel
Mr. Pinkerton at the Old Angel. Farrar, 1939. British title: Mr. Pinkerton and the Old Angel. Longmans, 1939 EP
Mr. Pinkerton Finds a Body. Farrar, 1934. British title: The Body in the Turl. Longmans, 1935 EP
Mr. Pinkerton Goes to Scotland Yard. Farrar, 1934. British title: Arsenic in Richmond. Longmans, 1934 EP
Mr. Pinkerton Grows a Beard. Farrar, 1935. British title: The Body in Bedford Square. Longmans, 1935 EP
Mr. Pinkerton Has the Clue. Farrar, 1936; Longmans, 1936 EP
Mr. Pinkerton: Passage for One. Royce, 1945 (Originally published in the anthology "The Mystery Book." Farrar, 1939.) EP
Mr. Simpson Finds a Body; see The Man from Scotland Yard
The Murder of an Old Man. Methuen, 1929 GL
The Murder on the Sixth Hole; see The Strange Death of Martin Green
Murder on the Square; see Homicide House
Scotland Yard Can Wait! Farrar, 1933. British title: That's Your Man, Inspector! Longmans, 1934
The Strange Death of Martin Green. Doubleday, 1931. British title: The Murder on the Sixth Hole. Methuen, 1931 GL [Md.]
That's Your Man, Inspector!; see Scotland Yard Can Wait!
Two Against Scotland Yard. Farrar, 1931. British title: The By-Pass Murder. Longmans, 1932 EP

FROST, A. C.
High Dudgeon. Chatto, 1934

FROST, BARBARA [BARBARA FROST SHIRELY]. Born in NYC; was publicity manager for J. B. Lippincott Co. SC: Marka de Lancey = ML.
The Corpse Died Twice. Coward, 1951 ML [NYC]
The Corpse Said No. Coward, 1949 ML [NYC]
Innocent Bystander. Coward, 1955 ML
The Unwelcome Corpse. Coward, 1947 [NYC]

FROST, C. VERNON
The Crime on the Heath. Amalgamated, 1937 (Sexton Blake.)

FROST, CONRAD
Evidence Before Gabriel. Aldor, 1947

FROST, FREDERICK. Pseudonym of Frederick Schiller Faust, 1892-1944. Other pseudonyms: Max Brand, Walter C. Butler, qq.v. SC: Anthony Hamilton, in all titles.
The Bamboo Whistle. Macrae, 1937
Secret Agent Number One. Macrae, 1936; Harrap, 1937 [Fr.]
Spy Meets Spy. Macrae, 1937; Harrap, 1937

FROST, KELMAN (DALGETY)
    Death Registers at the Eagle Arms.
      Oberon, 194? [Scot.]
FROST, LESLEY. 1899-   . Ref: CA.
    Murder at Large. Coward, 1932 [L.I.]
FROST, WALTER ARCHER. 1876-1964.
    The Man Between. Doubleday, 1913
      [S. Afr.]
    The Marworth Mystery. Long, 1930 [N.Y.]
    No Questions Asked. Long, 1927
FROUD, P.
    Used in Evidence. Kangaroo, 1947 ss
FRUCHTER, NORMAN. 1937-   . Ref: CA.
    Single File. Knopf, 1970
FRUTTERO, C(ARLO) and LUCENTINI, FRANCO
    The Sunday Woman. Harcourt, 1973; Col-
      lins, 1974 (Translation of "La Donna
      della Domenica." Milan, 1972.) [It.]
FRY, ALAN. 1931-   . Ref: CA.
    -The Revenge of Annie Charlie. Double-
      day, 1973 [Can.]
FRY, CHRISTOPHER. 1907-   . Ref: CA.
    -The Lady's Not for Burning. Oxford,
      1949 (3-act play.)
FRY, PETE. Pseudonym of James Clifford
    King, 1914-   . Born in England;
    author of novels, radio plays, gen-
    eral nonfiction, articles for
    British periodicals; theatre journal-
    ist. SC: Pete Fry, in all titles.
    The Black Beret. Boardman, 1959; Roy,
      1959
    The Black Cotton Gloves. Long, 1970
    The Bright Green Waistcoat. Long,
      1967; Roy, 1967 [Ire.]
    The Brown Suede Jacket. Long, 1968;
      Roy, 1968 [Paris]
    The Green Scarf. Boardman, 1961
    The Grey Sombrero. Boardman, 1958; Roy,
      1958 [Tangier]
    The Long Overcoat. Boardman, 1957
      [Paris]
    The Orange Necktie. Boardman, 1968
    The Paint-Stained Flannels. Boardman,
      1965; Roy, 1966 [Sp.]
    The Purple Dressing Gown. Boardman,
      1960
    The Red Stockings. Boardman, 1962; Roy,
      1962
    The Scarlet Cloak. Boardman, 1958
    The Thick Blue Sweater. Boardman, 1964;
      Roy, 1964 [Fr.]
    The White Crash Helmet. Long, 1969;
      Roy, 1969
    The Yellow Trousers. Boardman, 1963;
      Roy, 1963 [Fr.]
FRYERS, AUSTIN. Pseudonym of William Ed-
    ward Clery. See also: Alfred Wilson
    Barrett, 1871-   .
    The Uncreated Man. Ouseley, 1912
FUENTOS, CARLOS. 1928-   . Ref: CA.
    The Hydra Head. Farrar, 1978; Secker,
      1978 (Translation of "La Cabeza de
      la Hidra." Mexico City, 1978.) [Mex.]
FUENTES, ROBERTO. See: Piers Anthony.
FULFORD, PAUL A.
    Who's Got the Bastard Pope? PaperJacks,
      1978
FULK, DAVID
    The Potman Spoke Sooth. Dramatic, 1977
      (1-act play.)
FULLER, ALBERT C(HARLES). See: Clyde
    North.
FULLER, ANNE and MARCUS ALLEN
    Blood on the Common. Dutton, 1933 [New
      Eng.]
    Blood on the Outer Shoal. Dutton, 1934
      [New Eng.]
FULLER, BLAIR. 1927-   . Ref: CA.
    A Far Place. Harper, 1957; Secker, 1957
FULLER, H(AROLD) E(DGAR)
    A Sickness of the Soul. Hale, 1971
FULLER, HECTOR. 1865-1934.
    -Roach & Co., Pirates, and other sto-
      ries. Bowen-Merrill, 1898 ss
FULLER, JAMES
    The Open Window. Dramatic, 1964 (Play
      based on the ss by Saki, pseudonym of
      Hector Hugh Munro, 1870-1916.)
FULLER, LESTER. 1908-   . Motion picture
    studio talent manager; director of
    feature films. See: Edwin Rolfe,
    1909-1954.

FULLER, MISS (ANNE).   -1790.
    Alan Fitz Osborne. Byrne, 1786
FULLER, PETER. 1943-   .
    The In-Between Spy. Hale, 1980
FULLER, ROGER. Pseudonym of Don(ald
    Fiske) Tracy, 1905-1976, q.v.
    All the Silent Voices. PB, 1964 (No-
      velization of "The Defenders" TV
      series.)
    Burke's Law; see Who Killed Beau Spar-
      row?
    Eve of Judgment. PB, 1965 (Novieliza-
      tion of "The Defenders" TV series.)
      [NYC]
    Fear in a Desert Town. PB, 1964 (No-
      velization of "The Fugitive" TV ser-
      ies.) [Ariz.]
    The Martini Murders; see Who Killed
      Madcap Millicent?
    On the Double. PB, 1961 (Novelization
      of the movie.)
    Ordeal. PB, 1964 (Novelization of "The
      Defenders" TV series.) [NYC]
    -The Timeless Serpent. PB, 196?
    Who Killed Beau Sparrow? Perma, 1964.
      British title: Burke's Law. Fontana,
      1965 (Novelization of the "Burke's
      Law" TV series.)
    Who Killed Madcap Millicent? PB, 1964.
      British title: The Martini Murders.
      Fontana, 1964 (Novelization of the
      "Burke's Law" TV series.)
FULLER, ROY (BROADBENT). 1912-   . Ref:
    CA, CC, MC, TC. Set: Eng.
    Fantasy and Fugue. Verschoyle, 1954;
      Macmillan, 1956
    The Second Curtain. Verschoyle, 1953;
      Macmillan, 1956
    With My Little Eye. Lehmann, 1948;
      Macmillan, 1957
FULLER, SAMUEL (MICHAEL). 1911-   .
    Ref: TC.
    Crown of India. Award, 1966
    The Dark Page. Duell, 1944. Also pub-
      lished as: Murder Makes a Deadline.
      Bestseller, 1952 [NYC]
    Dead Pigeon on Beethoven Street. Pyra-
      mid, 1974 (Novelization of the
      movie.) [Ger.]
    Murder Makes a Deadline; see The Dark
      Page
    The Naked Kiss. Belmont, 1964 (Noveli-
      zation of the movie.)
    144 Piccadilly. Baron, 1971; New Eng-
      lish Library, 1972
FULLER, TIMOTHY. 1914-   . Ref: CC, MP.
    SC: Jupiter Jones, in all titles.
    Harvard Has a Homicide. Little, 1936.
      British title: J for Jupiter. Col-
      lins, 1937 [Boston, acad.]
    J for Jupiter; see Harvard Has a Homi-
      cide
    Keep Cool, Mr. Jones. Little, 1950;
      Heinemann, 1951 [Mass.]
    Reunion with Murder. Little, 1941;
      Heinemann, 1947 [Boston]
    This Is Murder, Mr. Jones. Little,
      1943; Heinemann, 1944 [N.Y.]
    Three Thirds of a Ghost. Little, 1941;
      Heinemann, 1947 [Boston]
FULLER, VINCENT. Pseudonym.
    The Long Green Gaze. Huebsch, 1925
FULLER, WILLIAM.   SC: Brad Dolan = BD.
    Back Country. Dell, 1954 BD [Fla.]
    Brad Dolan's Blonde Cargo. Dell, 1957
      BD [Carib.]
    Brad Dolan's Miami Manhunt. Dell, 1958;
      World Distributors, 1959 BD [Miami]
    The Girl in the Frame. Dell, 1957; Four
      Square, 1967 BD [Fla.]
    Goat Island. Dell, 1954. Also published
      as: Local Talent. Dell, 1959 BD
      [Fla.]
    Local Talent; see Goat Island
    The Pace That Kills. Dell, 1956 [Fla.]
    Tight Squeeze. Dell, 1959; World Dis-
      tributors, 1960 BD [Cuba]
FULLERTON, ALEXANDER. Pseudonym: Anthony
    Fox, q.v.
FULTON, CHANDOS. 1839-1904.
    The Vidocq of New York. American News,
      1891 [NYC]
FURBER, DOUGLAS. Pseudonym of Michael
    Lewin, 1885-1961.
    Just Another Murder. Dakers, 1950
FUREY, MICHAEL. Pseudonym of Arthur Henry
    Sarsfield Ward, 1883-1959. Other
    pseudonym: Sax Rohmer, q.v.
    Wulfheim. Jarrolds, 1950; Bookfinger,
      1972, as by Sax Rohmer

FURMAN, A(BRAHAM) L(OEW). 1902-   .
    Chief Counsel. Macaulay, 1934
FURNESS, AUDREY. 1911-   .
    Clue to Danger. Mills, 1966
    Debt to Dishonour. Mills, 1969
    A Face in the Mirror. Hurst, 1961
    The Forbidden Cave. Macdonald, 1964
    House of Menace; see Letter to a Ghost
    In Search of Emily Crew. Mills, 1971
    Letter to a Ghost. Mills, 1962. U.S.
      title: House of Menace. Paperback
      Library, 1966
    Lonely Heritage. Mills, 1968
    The Long Road. Mills, 1962
    A Reason for Loving. Mills, 1964
    Return to Ballyrock. Mills, 1970
    The River of Marriage. Mills, 1969
    To Love Again. Mills, 1965
    The Young Accused. Mills, 1967
FURNIVALL, GORDON. Set: Eng.
    The Perfect Criminal. Jenkins, 1932
    The Tracker Tracked. Jenkins, 1928
FURST, ALAN. 1941-   . Ref: CA. SC:
    Roger Levin, in both titles.
    The Paris Drop. Doubleday, 1976
    Your Day in the Barrel. Atheneum, 1976
FUTRELLE, JACQUES. 1875-1912. Ref: CC,
    DD, EM, MC, MP, TC. SC: Prof. Augus-
    tus S. F. X. Van Dusen (The Thinking
    Machine) = AV.
    Best Thinking Machine Detective Sto-
      ries. Dover, 1973 (12 ss, 10 taken
      from The Thinking Machine and The
      Thinking Machine on the Case, qq.v.,
      the remaining 2 heretofore uncol-
      lected in book form.) AV
    Blind Man's Buff. Hodder, 1914 (U.S.
      title?)
    The Chase of the Golden Plate. Dodd,
      1906 AV
    The Diamond Master. Bobbs, 1909; Hol-
      den, 1912 (Contains 88-pp. novelet
      about AV.) [NYC]
    Elusive Isabel. Bobbs, 1909. British
      title: The Lady in the Case. Nelson,
      1910 [Wash. D.C.]
    Great Cases of the Thinking Machine.
      Dover (NYC & London), 1977 AV ss
    The High Hand. Bobbs, 1911. British
      title: The Master Hand. Hodder, 1914
    The Lady in the Case; see Elusive Isa-
      bel
    The Master Hand; see The High Hand
    My Lady's Garter. Rand, 1912; Hodder,
      1913
    The Problem of Cell 13; see The Think-
      ing Machine
    The Professor on the Case; see The
      Thinking Machine on the Case
    The Simple Case of Susan. Appleton,
      1908 (See also: "Lieutenant What's-
      His-Name," by May Futrelle, 1876-   .)
      [NYC]
    The Thinking Machine. Dodd, 1907; Chap-
      man, 1907. Also published as: The
      Problem of Cell 13. Dodd, 1918 AV ss
    The Thinking Machine on the Case.
      Appleton, 1908. British title: The
      Professor on the Case. Nelson, 1909
      AV ss
FUTRELLE, MAY (PEEL). 1876-   .
    Lieutenant What's-His-Name. Bobbs,
      1915; Newnes, 1916 (Elaborated from
      "The Simple Case of Susan," by her
      husband, Jacques Futrelle, 1875-
      1912, q.v.) [NYC]
    Secretary of Frivolous Affairs. Bobbs,
      1911; Gay, 1912 [Mass.]
FYHRLUND, ERIC
    Hasington. Manor, 1979
FYTTON, FRANCIS
    The Nation Within. Ambit, 1967; Pan-
      theon, 1969 [Paris, ca.1960]

G., M. E.
    -The Manoeuvres of Celeste. Beumar, 1912
      ss
GABBERT, FLORENCE SCOTT
    Shadow from the Past. Exposition, 1960
GABORIAU, EMILE. 1833-1873. Ref: all ex-
    cept CA. SC: Monsieur Lecoq, in at
    least those marked L. Set: Fr.
    An Adventuress of France; see The Mar-
      quise de Brinvilliers
    Baron Trigault's Vengeance; see The
      Count's Secret
    A Beautiful Scourge; see The Little Old
      Men of the Batignolles
    The Blackmailers; see File No. 113

G

The Catastrophe. Vizetelly, 1885
Caught in the Net; see The Slaves of Paris
The Champdoce Mystery; see The Slaves of Paris
A Chance Marriage; see Marriages of Adventure
The Clique of Gold. Osgood, 1874; Street, 1891. Also published as: The Gilded Clique. Lovell, 1884; Ward Lock, 1909 (Translation of "La Clique Doree." Paris, 1873.)
The Count's Millions; see The Count's Secret
The Count's Secret. Estes, 1881; Routledge, 1888 (A two-part novel, with Part I, "Pascal et Marguerite," published separately as: The Count's Millions. Scribner, 1913; Part II, "Lia d'Argeles," as: Baron Trigault's Vengeance. Scribner, 1913.) (Translation of "La Vie Infernale." Paris, 1870.)
Crime at Orcival; see The Mystery of Orcival
Dossier No. 113; see File No. 113
The Downward Path. Estes, 1883; Routledge, 1887 (Translation of "La Degringolade." Paris, 1872.)
File No. 113. Lovell, 1883; Routledge, 1887. Also published as: The Blackmailers. Lotus Library, 1907; Collins, 1929. And as: Dossier No. 113. Vizetelly, 1883. And as: File 113. Harvill, 1953 (A brief summary of the book was published as: Warrant No. 113; or, The Mystery of the Steel Safe. Crown, 1884.) (Translation of "Le Dossier No. 113." Paris, 1867.)
The Gilded Clique; see The Clique of Gold
The Honor of the Name; see Monsieur Lecoq
In Deadly Peril; see Within an Inch of His Life
In Peril of His Life; see Within an Inch of His Life
The Intrigues of a Prisoner. Vizetelly, 1885
The Lerouge Case; see The Widow Lerouge
The Little Old Man of the Batignolles. Munro, 1880 (Translation of "Le Petit Vieux de Batignolles." Paris, 1876.) (The French book contained the title novelet plus five stories. Various assortments of Gaboriau's ss were published as: Max's Marriage; or, the Viscount's Choice. Munro, 1880. And as: The Little Old Man of Batignolles and other stories. Vizetelly, 1884; Lovell, 1888. And as: A Thousand Francs Reward. Munro, 1887. And as: A Beautiful Scourge. Tousey, 1883.)
Marie de Brinvilliers; see The Marquise de Brinvilliers
The Marquise de Brinvilliers. Aldine, 1886. Also published as: Marie de Brinvilliers. Routledge, 1888. And as: An Adventuress of France. Robinson, 1921; Federation Press, 1926 (Translation of "Les Amours d'une Empoisonneuse." Paris, 1881.)
Marriage at a Venture; see Marriage of Adventure
Marriage of Adventure. Robins, 1921; Federation Press, 1925 (A two-part novel, with Part I, "M.J.D. de Saint-Roch, Amabassaduer Matrimoniel," published separately as: A Chance Marriage. Privately Printed, 1878. And as: Marriage at a Venture. Munro, 1879. Part II, "Promesses de Mariage," as: Promise of Marriage. Lovell, 1883. And as: Promises of Marriage. Munro, 1884.) (Translation of "Les Mariages d'Aventure." Paris, 1862.)
Max's Marriage; or, The Viscount's Choice; see The Little Old Man of the Batignolles
The Men of the Bureau. Munro, 1880 (Translation of "Les Gens de Burcau." Paris, 1862.)
Monsieur Lecoq. Estes, 1880; Routledge, 1887 (A two-part novel, with Part I, "L'Enquete," published separately as: Monsieur Lecoq: The Detective's Dilemma. Street, 1891; Ward, 1888. And as: Monsieur Lecoq. Scribner, 1900. Part II, "L'Honneur du Nom," as: Monsieur Lecoq: The Detective's Triumph. Street, 1891; Ward, 1888. And as: The Honor of the Name. Scribner, 1900; Hodder, 1920.) (Translation of "Monsieur Lecoq." Paris, 1868.) L
Monsieur Lecoq: The Detective's Dilemma; see Monsieur Lecoq
Monsieur Lecoq: The Detective's Triumph; see Monsieur Lecoq

The Mystery of Orcival. Holt, 1871; Routledge, 1887. Also published as: Crime at Orcival. Harvill, 1952, abridged (Translation of "Le Crime d'Orcival." Paris, 1867.) L
Other People's Money. Osgood, 1875; Routledge, 1888 (Translation of "L'Argent des Autres." Paris, 1873.)
Promise(s) of Marriage; see Marriages of Adventure
The Slaves of Paris. Estes, 1882; Routledge, 1887 (A two-part novel, with Part I, "Le Chantage," published separately as: Caught in the Net. Street, 1891. Part II, "Le Secret de Champdoce," as: The Champdoce Mystery. Street, 1891 (Translation of "Les Esclaves de Paris." Paris, 1868.) L
A Thousand Francs Reward; see The Little Old Man of the Batignolles
Warrant No. 113; or, The Mystery of the Steel Safe; see File No. 113
The Widow Lerouge. Osgood, 1873; Routledge, 1887. Also published as: The Lerouge Case. Federation Press, 1925 (Translation of "L'Affaire Lerouge." Paris, 1866.) L
Within an Inch of His Life. Osgood, 1874; Routledge, 1888. Also published as: In Peril of His Life. Lovell, 1883. And as: In Deadly Peril. Ward, 1884 (Translation of "La Corde au Cou." Paris, 1873.)
Written in Cipher. Aldine, 1894

GABRIEL, H. WILHELM
A Corpse for a Client. Arcadia, 1961

GADDA, CARLO EMILIO. 1893-1973. Ref: CC.
That Awful Mess on Via Merulana. Braziller, 1965; Secker, 1966 (Translation of "Quer Pasticciaccio Brutto de via Merulana." Milan, 1957.) [Rome, 1927]

GADHART, RINE
Too Tough to Die. Swan, 1942

GADNEY, REG. 1941- . Ref: CA, TC.
The Cage; see The Champagne Marxist
The Champagne Marxist. Hutchinson, 1977. U.S. title: The Cage. Coward, 1977
Drawn Blanc. Heinemann, 1970; Coward, 1971
-The Last Hours Before Dawn. Heinemann, 1975. U.S. title: Victoria. Coward, 1975
Seduction of a Tall Man. Heinemann, 1972
Something Worth Fighting For. Heinemann, 1974
Somewhere in England. Heinemann, 1971; St. Martin's, 1971
Victoria; see The Last Hours Before Dawn

GAFFNEY, MARGUERITE S.
Escape into Danger. Ermine, 1978

GAGE, EDWIN. 1943- . Ref: CA.
Phoenix No More. Harper, 1978 [Phoenix]

GAGE, NICHOLAS. Pseudonym of Nicholas Ngagoyeanes, 1939- . Ref: CA.
Bones of Contention. Berkley/Putnam, 1974 [NYC]

GAGE, WILLIAM H(ENRY), JR. 1915-1973. Ref: CA.
Appointment with Dishonor. Little, 1958; Hale, 1959 [Cyprus]

GAINES, AUDREY [AUDREY GAINES SCHULTZ]. SC: Chauncey O'Day = CO; Jeff Strange = JS.
No Crime Like the Present. Arcadia, 1952 JS [Wash. D.C.]
The Old Must Die. Crowell, 1939 CO [Va.]
Omit Flowers, Please. Messner, 1946 JS [Wash. D.C.]
The Voodoo Goat. Crowell, 1942 CO [Va.]
While the Wind Howled. Crowell, 1940 CO [Md.]

GAINES, ROBERT. Pseudonym of Rowland Sommerscales, 1912- . Ref: CC.
Against the Public Interest. Macdonald, 1959; Walker, 1964
The Cruel Deadline. Macdonald, 1960
Daybreak at Deest. Heinemann, 1951
Final Night. Heinemann, 1950; Doubleday, 1950
The Invisible Evil. Macdonald, 1963; Walker, 1963
A Kind of Justice. Heinemann, 1955
The Name Is Judas. Joseph, 1966
The Vain Ambitions. Heinemann, 1953

GAINFORT, JOHN
He's Dead All Right. French (NYC), 1949 (1-act play.)

GAINHAM, SARAH. Pseudonym of Sarah Rachel Stainer Ames, 1922- . Ref: CA, TC.
Appointment in Vienna; see The Mythmaker
The Cold Dark Night. Barker, 1957; Walker, 1961 [Berlin]
Maculan's Daughter. Macmillan (London), 1973; Putnam, 1974
The Mythmaker. Barker, 1957. U.S. title: Appointment in Vienna. Dutton, 1958 [Vienna, 1940]
Night Falls on the City. Collins, 1967; Holt, 1967
A Place in the Country. Weidenfeld, 1969; Holt, 1969
Private Worlds. Weidenfeld, 1971; Holt, 1971
The Silent Hostage. Eyre, 1960; Dutton, 1960 [Yugos.]
The Stone Roses. Eyre, 1959; Dutton, 1959 [Prague, 1948]
Takeover Bid. Weidenfeld, 1970; Holt, 1972 [Brus.]
Time Right Deadly. Barker, 1956; Walker, 1960 [Vienna]

GAINSLEY, SIDNEY
Love and Dr. Hawkins. Brown, 1945

GAIR, MALCOLM. Pseudonym of John Dick Scott. Ref: CC. SC: Mark Raeburn, in all titles.
The Bad Dream. Collins, 1960
The Burning of Troy. Collins, 1959; Doubleday, 1958
A Long Hard Look. Collins, 1958
Sapphires on Wednesday. Collins, 1957; Doubleday, 1958
The Schultz Money. Collins, 1960; Doubleday, 1960
Snow Job. Collins, 1962; Doubleday, 1962 [Switz.]

GAITE, FRANCIS. Joint pseudonym of Adelaide Frances Oke Manning, 1891-1959, and Cyril Henry Coles, 1899-1965. Other joint pseudonym: Manning Coles, q.v. All titles below published in the U.S. as by Manning Coles. SC: Charles and James Latimer = L.
Brief Candles. Hodder, 1954; Doubleday, 1954 L [Fr.]
Come and Go. Hodder, 1958; Doubleday, 1958 L [Fr.]
Duty Free. Hodder, 1959; Doubleday, 1959
A Family Matter. Hodder, 1956. U.S. title: Happy Returns. Doubleday, 1955 L [Fr.]
The Far Traveller. Hodder, 1957; Doubleday, 1956 [Ger.]
Happy Returns; see A Family Matter

GALCOM, G.
The Green Mandarin Mystery. Warren, 1950

GALE, ADELA
Angel Among Witches. Signet, 1969 [Austria]
Goddess of Terror. Signet, 1967
Harvest of Terror. Signet, 1969 [Maj.]

GALE, JOHN. Pseudonym of Richard Gaze, 1917- . Ref: CA, CC. Set: Eng.
Death by Chalk Face. Long, 1960
Death for Short; see The Short Reaction
The Short Reaction. Long, 1961. U.S. title: Death for Short. Macmillan, 1962
Spare Time for Murder. Long, 1960; Macmillan, 1961

GALL, SANDY. 1927- .
Gold Scoop. Collins, 1977

GALLACHER, TOM
Natural Causes. French (London), 1980 (2-act play.)

GALLAGHER, GALE. Joint pseudonym of Will(iam Charles) Oursler, 1913- q.v., and Margaret Scott. Other Oursler pseudonym: Nick Marino, q.v. SC: Gale Gallagher, in both titles.
Chord in Crimson. Coward, 1949; Boardman, 1950
I Found Him Dead. Coward, 1947 [NYC]

GALLAGHER, P. B.
Long Night. Zebra, 1979

GALLAGHER, PATRICIA. Ref: CA.
Answer to Heaven. Avon, 1964; Muller, 1962
The Fires of Brimstone. Avon, 1966
Shadows of Passion. Avon, 1971
Shannon. Avon, 1967
The Sons and the Daughters. Messner, 1961; Muller, 1961
Summer of Sighs. Avon, 1971
The Thicket. Avon, 1974

GALLAGHER, RICHARD
  The Doomsday Committee. Award, 1970 [NYC]
  Murder by Gemini. Lancer, 1971 (Novelization of the "Cannon" TV series.) [Wyo.]
  The One-Armed Murder. Lancer, 1971 (Novelization of "The Most Deadly Game" TV series.) [NYC]
  The Stewardess Strangler. Lancer, 1971 (Novelization of the "Cannon" TV series.) [NYC]

GALLANT, GLADYS S. Magazine and TV writer.
  Living Image. Doubleday, 1978 [NYC]

GALLETLEY, LEONARD
  -King's Justice. Williams, 1932
  The Yatton Murders. Williams, 1935

GALLICO, PAUL (WILLIAM). 1897-1976. Ref: CA. SC: Alexander Hero = AH; Hiram Holliday = HH.
  The Adventures of Hiram Holliday. Knopf, 1939; Joseph, 1939 ss HH
  The Boy Who Invented the Bubble Gun. Delacorte, 1974; Heinemann, 1974
  The Hand of Mary Constable. Doubleday, 1964; Heinemann, 1964 AH [NYC]
  The Secret Front. Knopf, 1944 HH
  Thief Is an Ugly Word. Dell 10¢ pb, 1951
  Too Many Ghosts. Doubleday, 1959; Joseph, 1961 AH [Eng.]
  Trial by Terror. Knopf, 1952; Joseph, 1952 [Buda.]
  The Zoo Gang. Coward, 1971; Heinemann, 1971 ss [Fr.]

GALLIE, MENNA (PATRICIA HUMPHREYS). 1920- . Ref: CA, CC.
  Strike for a Kingdom. Gollancz, 1959; Harper, 1959 [Wales]
  -Travels with a Duchess. Gollancz, 1968; Harper, 1968
  -You're Welcome to Ulster! Gollancz, 1970; Harper, 1970 [Ire.]

GALLIMORE, F. A.
  The Ebony Mirror. Methuen, 1933

GALLON, TOM. 1866-1914.
  Aunt Phipps. Hutchinson, 1905
  -Boden's Boy. Hutchinson, 1904
  -Brother Rogue and Brother Saint. Paul, 1909
  -The Charity Ghost. Hutchinson, 1902
  -Christmas at Poverty Castle. Nash, 1907
  -Comethup. Hutchinson, 1899
  The Dead Ingleby. Hutchinson, 1902
  Dead Man's Love. Ward, 1911; Brentano's, 1910
  -The Diamond Trail. Mills, 1916
  The Dream—and the Woman. Paul, 1909
  -Fortune A-Begging. Hurst, 1906
  The Girl Behind the Keys. Hutchinson, 1903 ss
  -The Golden Thread. Nash, 1904
  -The Great Gay Road. Long, 1910; Brentano's, 1912
  -The Idol of the Blind. Appleton, 1899 (British title?)
  -In a Little House. Hutchinson, 1903
  -"It Will Be All Right!" Hutchinson, 1914
  Jarwick the Prodigal. Ward, 1904
  -Judy—and the Philosopher. Hutchinson, 1907
  -Kiddy. Hutchinson, 1900; Valentine, 1900
  The Kingdom of Hate. Hutchinson, 1899; Appleton, 1899
  -The Lackey and the Lady. Hurst, 1908
  -The Lady in the Black Mask. Mills, 1917
  The Lady of the Cameo. Hutchinson, 1903
  -Lagden's Luck. Arrowsmith, 1905
  Levity Hicks. Long, 1912
  -The Man Hunt. Mills, 1916
  -The Man in Motley. Mills, 1915
  Meg the Lady. Hutchinson, 1905
  The Mystery of John Peppercorn. Hutchinson, 1902
  The Mystery of Roger Bullock. Paul, 1910
  -Peplow's Paper-Chase. Hutchinson, 1904
  -The Prince of Mischance. Hutchinson, 1897; Appleton, 1898
  -The Princess of Happy Chance. Hutchinson, 1915
  Rickerby's Folly. Methuen, 1901
  A Rogue in Love. Hutchinson, 1900
  -The Rogue's Heiress. Hutchinson, 1910; Dillingham, 1910
  -The Second Dandy Chater. Hutchinson, 1901; Dodd, 1901
  Tatterley. Hutchinson, 1897; Appleton, 1897
  Tinman. Ward, 1908; Small, 1907
  -The Touch of the Child, and other stories. Mills, 1918
  -Young Eve and Old Adam. Long, 1913

GALLOWAY, DAVID (DARRYL). 1937- . Ref: CA.
  Lamaar Ransom—Private Eye. Riverrun Press, 1979; Calder, 1979 [L.A., WWII]

GALLOWAY, LINDSAY
  Sutherland's Law. Pan, 1974 (ss based on the TV series.)

GALTON, RAY(MOND PERCY), 1930- , and ALAN (FRANCIS) SIMPSON, 1929- .
  The Spy with a Cold Nose. Dell, 1966; Arrow, 1967 (Novelization of the movie.) [Eng.]

GALWAY, ROBERT CONINGTON. Pseudonym of Philip (Donald) McCutchan, 1920- , q.v. SC: James Packard, in all titles. Ref: CC.
  Assignment Andalusia. Hale, 1965 [Sp.]
  Assignment Argentina. Hale, 1969 [Arg.]
  Assignment Death Squad. Hale, 1970
  Assignment Fenland. Hale, 1969
  Assignment Gaolbreak. Hale, 1968
  Assignment London. Hale, 1963
  Assignment Malta. Hale, 1966 [Malta]
  Assignment New York. Hale, 1963 [NYC]
  Assignment Sea Bed. Hale, 1969
  Assignment Sydney. Hale, 1970 [Syd.]
  The Negative Man. Hale, 1971
  The Timeless Sleep. Hale, 1963

GALWEY, G(EOFFREY) V(ALENTINE). 1912- . Ref: CC. SC: Insp. "Daddy" Bourne, in all titles.
  Full Fathom Five. Hodder, 1951
  The Lift and the Drop. Bodley, 1948
  Murder on Leave. Lane, 1946 [Scot.]

GAMBIER, JAMES W(ILLIAM). 1841- .
  -Swifter Than a Weaver's Shuttle. Sonnenschein, 1887

GAMBLE, FREDERICK (JOHN). 1904- . Ref: CA.
  The Frightened One. Barker, 1958
  -A Man and a Half. Barker, 1956
  -My Coat Is Travel-Stained. Barker, 1957

GAMMON, DAVID J. Set: Eng.
  The Getaway Gang. Archer, 1946
  Meet the Falcon. Archer, 1947

GANACHILLY, ALFRED
  The Whispering Dead. Methuen, 1919; Knopf, 1920 [Chile]

GANDLEY, KENNETH ROYCE. 1920- . Pseudonyms: Oliver Jacks, Kenneth Royce, qq.v.

GANDOLFI, SIMON
  The 100 Kilo Club. Wildwood, 1975

GANN, ERNEST K(ELLOGG). 1910- . Ref: CA.
  Of Good and Evil. Simon, 1963; Hodder, 1963 [S.F.]

GANNETT, JAMES
  Murder After Dark. Muller, 1956

GANNOLD, JOHN. Pseudonym of John (Franklin Coasten) Langdon, 1913- , q.v.
  The Fix. Hale, 1972
  The Night of the Fox. Hale, 1974

GANPAT. Pseudonym of Martin Louis Alan Gompertz, 1886-1951.
  -The Marches of Honour. Hodder, 1931
  The One-Eyed Knave. Hodder, 1936
  Out of Evil. Hodder, 1933
  -The Second Tigress. Hodder, 1933
  -The Snow Falcon. Hodder, 1935
  -Stella Nash. Blackwood, 1924; Houghton, 1924
  The Three R's. Hodder, 1930; Doubleday, 1931

GANT, JONATHAN. Pseudonym of Clifton Adams, 1919- , q.v.
  The Long Vendetta. Avalon, 1963
  Never Say No to a Killer. Ace, 1956

GANT, MATTHEW. Pseudonym of Arnold Hano, 1922- . Other pseudonym: Mike Heller, q.v. Ref: CA.
  Queen Street. Regency, 1963 [NYC]

GANT, NORMAN
  Burn. Lancer, 1970 (Novelization of the movie.)

GANTZER, COLLEEN. Joint pseudonym with Hugh Gantzer, 1931- , q.v.: Shyam Dave, q.v.

GANTZER, HUGH. 1931- . Joint pseudonym with Colleen Gantzer: Shyam Dave, q.v. Ref: CA.
  Operation Overkill. Orient (Delhi), ca. 1975
  The President's Ransom. Orient (Delhi), ca.1976
  The Thomas Document. Orient (Delhi), ca.1977

GAR, ROBIN
  The Avenger. Gramol, 1934
  The Big Boss. Fiction House, 1946
  The Dead Ones Don't Talk. Mellifont, 1933
  "Hate!" Mellifont, 1933
  Jade of Death. Gramol, 1934
  "Moon of Death!" Gramol, 1934
  Murder on the River. Mellifont, 1935
  The Mystery in Minchin Mews. Mellifont, 1946
  The Stolen Plans. Mellifont, 1934
  The Valley of Fear. Mellifont, 1935

GARBO, NORMAN. 1919- . Ref: CA.
  Cabal. Norton, 1979; Allen, 1979 [Mid. East, 1967]
  Confrontation, with Howard Goodkind. Harper, 1966 [Wash. D.C.]
  Spy. Norton, 1980; Allen, 1980

GARD, OLIVER
  The Seventh Chasm. Dodd, 1953; Boardman, 1954 [NYC]

GARDEN, JOHN. Pseudonym of H(arry) L(uft) V(erne) Fletcher, 1902- , q.v.
  All on a Summer's Day. Joseph, 1949
  Day of Reckoning; see Murder Isn't Private
  Death in the Village. Hale, 1967
  A Little Time to Stay. Joseph, 1953
  Murder Isn't Private. Joseph, 1950. U.S. title: Day of Reckoning. Lippincott, 1951
  6 to 10. Joseph, 1947

GARDENER, HELEN H(AMILTON CHENOWETH). 1853-1925.
  -A Thoughtless Yes. Belford, 1890 ss

GARDENHIRE, SAMUEL M(AJOR). 1855-1923.
  The Long Arm. Harper (NYC & London), 1906 ss
  The Silence of Mrs. Harrold. Harper (NYC & London), 1905

GARDINER, D(OROTHEA) F(RANCES). 1879- . Pseudonym: Theodore Frank, q.v.
  Another Night, Another Day. Constable, 1930
  The Beguiling Shore. Constable, 1930
  Murder at a Dog Show. Muller, 1935
  The Prison House. Constable, 1929

GARDINER, DOROTHY. 1894-1979. Ref: CA, TC. SC: Sheriff Moss Magill = MM; Mr. Watson = W.
  Beer for Psyche. Doubleday, 1946; Hurst, 1948
  The Case of the Hula Clock; see What Crime Is It?
  A Drink for Mr. Cherry. Doubleday, 1934. British title: Mr. Watson Intervenes. Hurst, 1935 W [West]
  Lion in Wait. Doubleday, 1963. British title: Lion? or Murder? Hammond, 1964 MM [Colo.]
  Lion? or Murder?; see Lion in Wait
  Mr. Watson Intervenes; see A Drink for Mr. Cherry
  The Seventh Mourner. Doubleday, 1958; Hammond, 1960 MM [Scot.]
  The Transatlantic Ghost. Doubleday, 1933; Harrap, 1933 W [Calif.]
  What Crime Is It? Doubleday, 1956. British title: The Case of the Hula Clock. Hammond, 1957 MM [NYC]

GARDINER, GORDON. 1874-1937.
  At the House of Dree. Low, 1928; Houghton, 1928 [Scot.]
  The Man with a Weak Heart. Low, 1932; Houghton, 1932
  The Pattern of Chance. Low, 1929; Houghton, 1930 [S. Afr.]
  The Reconnaissance. Chapman, 1914; Macmillan, 1914

GARDINER, HEATHER
  Money on Murder. Hutchinson, 1951
  Murder in Haste. Hutchinson, 1954; Roy, 1954 [Syd.]

GARDINER, LINDA
  -His Heritage. Paul, 1888
  Mrs. Wylde. Jarrolds, 1897
  -The Rev. Miles Latimer. Remington, 1885
  -The Sound of a Voice. Hurst, 1897
  -Sylvia in Flowerland. Seeley, 1899; Dutton, 1899

GARDINER, STEPHEN. 1925- . Ref: CA, CC.
  Death Is an Artist. Barker, 1958; Washburn, 1959

GARDINER, WAYNE J.
  The Man on the Left. Charter, 1980 [Ger.]

GARDNER, ALAN (HAROLD). 1925- . Ref: CA. SC: David Troy, in at least those marked MM.
  Assignment Tahiti. Muller, 1965 DT [Tahiti]
  The Escalator. Muller, 1963 DT
  The Hibernation of Ginger Scrubb. Muller, 1968
  The Man Who Was Too Much. Muller, 1967 DT
  Six-Day Week. Muller, 1966; Coward, 1966 DT [Rome]

GARDNER, ARTHUR R(OBERT) L(EE)
  Lower Underworld. Quality, 1942
  Tinker's Kitchen. Allen, 1932

GARDNER, CHARLES W.
  -The Doctor and the Devil; or, Midnight Adventures of Dr. Parkhurst. Gardner, 1894

GARDNER, CURTISS T.
  Bones Don't Lie. Mill, 1946. Also published as: The Fatal Cast. Graphic, 1954

GARDNER, ERLE STANLEY. 1889-1970. Pseudonyms: A. A. Fair, Carleton Kendrake, Charles J. Kenny, qq.v. See also: Roland F. Fernand, William McCleery. Ref: all except MM. SC: Perry Mason = PM; Doug Selby = DS; Terry Clane = TC; Sheriff Bill Eldon = BE; Gramps Wiggins = W. Set: generally L.A.
  The Amazing Adventures of Lester Leith. Davis, 1980 ss
  The Case of the Amorous Aunt. Morrow, 1963; Heinemann, 1969 PM
  The Case of the Angry Mourner. Morrow, 1951; Heinemann, 1958 PM [Calif.]
  The Case of the Backward Mule. Morrow, 1946; Heinemann, 1955 TC [S.F.]
  The Case of the Baited Hook. Morrow, 1940; Cassell, 1940 PM
  The Case of the Beautiful Beggar. Morrow, 1965; Heinemann, 1972 PM
  The Case of the Bigamous Spouse. Morrow, 1961; Heinemann, 1967 PM
  The Case of the Black-Eyed Blonde. Morrow, 1944; Cassell, 1948 PM
  The Case of the Blonde Bonanza. Morrow, 1962; Heinemann, 1967 PM
  The Case of the Borrowed Brunette. Morrow, 1946; Cassell, 1951 PM
  The Case of the Buried Clock. Morrow, 1943; Cassell, 1945 PM
  The Case of the Calendar Girl. Morrow, 1958; Heinemann, 1964 PM
  The Case of the Careless Cupid. Morrow, 1968; Heinemann, 1973 PM
  The Case of the Careless Kitten. Morrow, 1942; Cassell, 1944 PM
  The Case of the Caretaker's Cat. Morrow, 1935; Cassell, 1936 PM
  The Case of the Cautious Coquette. Morrow, 1949; Heinemann, 1955 PM (Note: The Dollar Mystery Guild edition includes two PM novelets, the Case of the Crimson Kiss, and The Case of the Crying Swallow.)
  The Case of the Counterfeit Eye. Morrow, 1935; Cassell, 1935 PM
  The Case of the Crimson Kiss. Morrow, 1970; Heinemann, 1975 (A collection containing the title novelet, with PM, and four stories with other characters.)
  The Case of the Crooked Candle. Morrow, 1944; Cassell, 1947 PM
  The Case of the Crying Swallow. Morrow, 1971; Heinemann, 1974 (A collection containing the title novelet, with PM, and three stories with other characters.)
  The Case of the Curious Bride. Morrow, 1935; Cassell, 1935 PM
  The Case of the Dangerous Dowager. Morrow, 1937; Cassell, 1937 PM
  The Case of the Daring Decoy. Morrow, 1957; Heinemann, 1963 PM
  The Case of the Daring Divorcee. Morrow, 1964; Heinemann, 1969 PM
  The Case of the Deadly Toy. Morrow, 1959; Heinemann, 1964 PM
  The Case of the Demure Defendant. Morrow, 1956; Heinemann, 1959 PM
  The Case of the Drowning Duck. Morrow, 1942; Cassell, 1944 PM
  The Case of the Drowsy Mosquito. Morrow, 1943; Cassell, 1946 PM
  The Case of the Dubious Bridegroom. Morrow, 1949; Heinemann, 1954 PM
  The Case of the Duplicate Daughter. Morrow, 1960; Heinemann, 1965 PM
  The Case of the Empty Tin. Morrow, 1941; Cassell, 1943 PM
  The Case of the Fabulous Fake. Morrow, 1969; Heinemann, 1974 PM
  The Case of the Fan-Dancer's Horse. Morrow, 1947; Heinemann, 1952 PM
  The Case of the Fenced-In Woman. Morrow, 1972; Heinemann, 1976 PM
  The Case of the Fiery Fingers. Morrow, 1951; Heinemann, 1957 PM
  The Case of the Foot-Loose Doll. Morrow, 1958; Heinemann, 1964 PM [Calif.]
  The Case of the Fugitive Nurse. Morrow, 1954; Heinemann, 1959 PM
  The Case of the Gilded Lily. Morrow, 1956; Heinemann, 1962 PM
  The Case of the Glamorous Ghost. Morrow, 1955; Heinemann, 1960 PM
  The Case of the Gold-Digger's Purse. Morrow, 1945; Cassell, 1948 PM
  The Case of the Green-Eyed Sister. Morrow, 1953; Heinemann, 1959 PM
  The Case of the Grinning Gorilla. Morrow, 1952; Heinemann, 1959 PM
  The Case of the Half-Wakened Wife. Mill, 1945; Cassell, 1949 PM
  The Case of the Haunted Husband. Morrow, 1941; Cassell, 1942 PM
  The Case of the Hesitant Hostess. Morrow, 1953; Heinemann, 1959 PM
  The Case of the Horrified Heirs. Morrow, 1964; Heinemann, 1971 PM
  The Case of the Howling Dog. Morrow, 1934; Cassell, 1935 PM
  The Case of the Ice-Cold Hands. Morrow, 1962; Heinemann, 1968 PM
  The Case of the Irate Witness. Morrow, 1972; Heinemann, 1975 (A collection containing the title story, with PM, and three stories with other characters.)
  The Case of the Lame Canary. Morrow, 1937; Cassell, 1937 PM
  The Case of the Lazy Lover. Morrow, 1947; Heinemann, 1954 PM
  The Case of the Lonely Heiress. Morrow, 1948; Heinemann, 1952 PM
  The Case of the Long-Legged Models. Morrow, 1958; Heinemann, 1963 PM
  The Case of the Lucky Legs. Morrow, 1934; Harrap, 1934 PM
  The Case of the Lucky Loser. Morrow, 1957; Heinemann, 1962 PM
  The Case of the Mischievous Doll. Morrow, 1963; Heinemann, 1968 PM
  The Case of the Moth-Eaten Mink. Morrow, 1952; Heinemann, 1958 PM
  The Case of the Murderer's Bride. Davis pb, 1969 (A collection of 7 ss and novelets.)
  The Case of the Musical Cow. Morrow, 1950; Heinemann, 1957 (A non-series police procedural.)
  The Case of the Mythical Monkeys. Morrow, 1959; Heinemann, 1965 PM
  The Case of the Negligent Nymph. Morrow, 1950; Heinemann, 1956 PM
  The Case of the Nervous Accomplice. Morrow, 1955; Heinemann, 1961 PM
  The Case of the One-Eyed Witness. Morrow, 1950; Heinemann, 1956 PM
  The Case of the Perjured Parrot. Morrow, 1939; Cassell, 1939 PM [Calif.]
  The Case of the Phantom Fortune. Morrow, 1964; Heinemann, 1971 PM
  The Case of the Postponed Murder. Morrow, 1973; Heinemann, 1977 PM
  The Case of the Queenly Contestant. Morrow, 1967; Heinemann, 1973 PM
  The Case of the Reluctant Model. Morrow, 1962; Heinemann, 1967 PM
  The Case of the Restless Redhead. Morrow, 1954; Heinemann, 1960 PM
  The Case of the Rolling Bones. Morrow, 1939; Cassell, 1940 PM
  The Case of the Runaway Corpse. Morrow, 1954; Heinemann, 1960 PM [Calif.]
  The Case of the Screaming Woman. Morrow, 1957; Heinemann, 1963 PM
  The Case of the Shapely Shadow. Morrow, 1960; Heinemann, 1966 PM
  The Case of the Shoplifter's Shoe. Morrow, 1938; Cassell, 1939 PM
  The Case of the Silent Partner. Morrow, 1940; Cassell, 1941 PM
  The Case of the Singing Skirt. Morrow, 1959; Heinemann, 1965 PM
  The Case of the Sleepwalker's Niece. Morrow, 1936; Cassell, 1936 PM
  The Case of the Smoking Chimney. Morrow, 1943; Cassell, 1945 W [Calif.]
  The Case of the Spurious Spinster. Morrow, 1961; Heinemann, 1966 PM
  The Case of the Stepdaughter's Secret. Morrow, 1963; Heinemann, 1968 PM
  The Case of the Stuttering Bishop. Morrow, 1936; Cassell, 1937 PM
  The Case of the Substitute Face. Morrow, 1938; Cassell, 1938 PM [S.F.]
  The Case of the Sulky Girl. Morrow, 1933; Harrap, 1934 PM
  The Case of the Sun Bather's Diary. Morrow, 1955; Heinemann, 1961 PM
  The Case of the Terrified Typist. Morrow, 1956; Heinemann, 1961 PM
  The Case of the Troubled Trustee. Morrow, 1965; Heinemann, 1971 PM
  The Case of the Turning Tide. Morrow, 1941; Cassell, 1942 W [Calif.]
  The Case of the Vagabond Virgin. Morrow, 1948; Heinemann, 1952 PM
  The Case of the Velvet Claws. Morrow, 1933; Harrap, 1933 PM
  The Case of the Waylaid Wolf. Morrow, 1959; Heinemann, 1965 PM
  The Case of the Worried Waitress. Morrow, 1966; Heinemann, 1972 PM
  The D.A. Breaks a Seal. Morrow, 1946; Cassell, 1950 DS [Calif.]
  The D.A. Breaks an Egg. Morrow, 1949; Heinemann, 1957 DS [Calif.]
  The D.A. Calls a Turn. Morrow, 1944; Cassell, 1947 DS [Calif.]
  The D.A. Calls It Murder. Morrow, 1937; Cassell, 1937 DS [Calif.]
  The D.A. Cooks a Goose. Morrow, 1942; Cassell, 1943 DS [Calif.]
  The D.A. Draws a Circle. Morrow, 1939; Cassell, 1940 DS [Calif.]
  The D.A. Goes to Trial. Morrow, 1940; Cassell, 1941 DS [Calif.]
  The D.A. Holds a Candle. Morrow, 1938; Cassell, 1939 DS [Calif.]
  The D.A. Takes a Chance. Morrow, 1948; Heinemann, 1956 DS [Calif.]
  Murder Up My Sleeve. Morrow, 1937; Cassell, 1938 TC [S.F.]
  Over the Hump. Gordon Martin (London), 1945 (A 92-page version of the novelet "Death Rides a Boxcar" included in the collection The Case of the Murderer's Bride, q.v.)
  Two Clues. Morrow, 1937; Cassell, 1951 (Two novelets about BE.) [Calif.]

GARDNER, JOHN (EDMUND). 1926- . Ref: CA, CC, MC, DC. SC: Herbie Kruger = HK; Prof. Moriarty = M; Boysie Oakes = BO; Derek Torry = DT. Set: mostly Eng.
  Air Apparent; see The Airline Pirates
  The Airline Pirates. Hodder, 1970. U.S. title: Air Apparent. Putnam, 1971 BO
  Amber Nine. Muller, 1966; Viking, 1966 BO
  The Assassination File. Corgi, 1974 ss
  -The Censor. New English Library, 1970
  A Complete State of Death. Cape, 1969; Viking, 1969. Also published as: The Stone Killer. Award, 1973 DT
  The Corner Men. Joseph, 1974; Doubleday, 1976 DT
  The Dancing Dodo. Hodder, 1978; Doubleday, 1978
  Founder Member. Joseph, 1969 BO
  The Garden of Weapons. Hodder, 1980; McGraw, 1981 HK
  Golgotha. Allen, 1980. U.S. title: The Last Trump. McGraw, 1980 [1990, Eng.]
  Hideaway. Corgi, 1968 ss, BO in two
  A Killer for a Song. Hodder, 1975 BO
  The Last Trump; see Golgotha
  The Liquidator. Muller, 1964; Viking, 1964 BO [Fr.]
  Madrigal. Muller, 1967; Viking, 1968 BO
  Moriarty; see The Return of Moriarty
  The Nostradamus Traitor. Hodder, 1979; Doubleday, 1979 HK
  The Return of Moriarty. Weidenfeld, 1974; Putnam, 1974. Also published as: Moriarty. Pan, 1976 M
  The Revenge of Moriarty. Weidenfeld, 1975; Putnam, 1976 M
  The Stone Killer; see A Complete State of Death
  To Run a Little Faster. Joseph, 1976
  Traitor's Exit. Muller, 1970 BO
  Understrike. Muller, 1965; Viking, 1965 BO [U.S.]
  The Werewolf Trace. Hodder, 1977; Doubleday, 1977

GARDNER, LEE. Pseudonym of Lee Gladson.
  Calina. Award, 1967

GARDNER, MAURICE B.
  -Horrors of Smiling Manor. Forum, 1962

GARDNER, S. A.
  Outwitted at Last. Carleton, 1878

GARDNER, WILLIAM HENRY. 1837- .
  The Curious Case of Gen. Delaney Smythe. Abbey, 1900

GARFIELD, BRIAN (FRANCIS WYNNE). 1939- . Pseudonyms: John Ives, Drew Mallory, Frank O'Brian, qq.v. See also: Donald E(dwin) Westlake, 1934- . Ref: CA, TC. SC: Paul Benjamin = PB; Sam Watchman = SW.

Death Sentence. Evans, 1975; Macmillan (London), 1976 PB [Chi.]
Death Wish. McKay, 1972; Hodder, 1973 PB
Deep Cover. Delacorte, 1971; Hodder, 1972
The Hit. Macmillan, 1970 [S.W.]
Hopscotch. Evans, 1975; Macmillan (London), 1975
Kolchak's Gold. McKay, 1973; Macmillan (London), 1974 [Russ.]
The Last Bridge. McKay, 1966
Line of Succession. Delacorte, 1972; Hodder, 1974
The Paladin. Simon, 1980; Macmillan (London), 1980 [Eng., WWII]
Recoil. Morrow, 1977; Macmillan (London), 1977
Relentless. World, 1972; Hodder, 1973 SW [Ariz.]
The Romanov Succession. Evans, 1974; Macmillan (London), 1974 [1941, Europe]
The Threepersons Hunt. Evans, 1974; Coronet, 1975 SW
Tripwire. McKay, 1973; Coronet, 1976 [1880s, West]
-The Villiers Touch. Delacorte, 1970
What of Terry Conniston? World, 1971; Coronet, 1976 [Ariz.]

GARFIELD, LEON, 1921- , and CHARLES (JOHN HUFFHAM) DICKENS, 1812-1870, q.v. Ref for Garfield: CA.
The Mystery of Edwin Drood. Deutsch, 1980; Pantheon, 1981

GARFORTH, JOHN. SC: Sexton Blake (with many other authors) = SB; novelizations of "The Avengers" TV series = A.
The Floating Game. Panther, 1967; Berkley, 1967 A
Heil Harris! Panther, 1967; Berkley, 1967 A
The Laugh Was on Lazarus. Panther, 1967; Berkley, 1967 A
The Passing of Gloria Munday. Panther, 1967; Berkley, 1967 A
Sexton Blake and the Demon God. Mirror Books, 1978 (Novelization of the TV serial.) SB
The Sixth Sense Is Death. Hodder pb, 1969 (Novelization of "The Champions" TV series.)
Sleep, and the City Trembles. Panther, 1969

GARIS, ROGER. 1901- .
Never Take Candy from a Stranger. Dell, 1961

GARLAND, BOB [ROBERT F. GARLAND]. Executive with Burlington Northern Railroad; lives in Minn.
Derfflinger. Manor, 1978

GARLAND, (MARY) ISABEL. 1903- . Joint pseudonym with Mindret Lord: Garland Lord, q.v. Daughter of American writer and Pulitzer Prize winner Hamlin Garland.
Abandon Hope. Mystery House, 1941. Also published as: Death Comes Courting. Mystery Novel of the Month, 1942 [Vt.]

GARLAND, JOHN
Crime of the Crossword. Columbine, 1939

GARLAND, NICHOLAS. Pseudonym of Herbert M. Katz.
Buy Back the Dawn. Marek, 1980; Fontana, 1981

GARLAND, RODNEY. Pseudonym of Adam Hegedus, 1910- .
-The Heart in Exile. Allen, 1953
-Hell and High Water. Allen, 1962
Sorcerer's Broth. Allen, 1966
The Troubled Midnight. Allen, 1954; Coward, 1955
-World Without Dreams. Allen, 1961

GARLAND, RUFUS CUMMINS
Zalea: A Psychological Episode and Tale of Love. Neale, 1900 [Wash. D.C.]

GARLINGTON, PHILIP. 1943- . Ref: CA.
Aces & Eights. Evans, 1975; Ellis, 1976 [S.F.]

GARNER, A. F.
Death for Love. Gnome, 1945

GARNER, CHARLES. Pseudonym: Stewart C. Cumberland, q.v.

GARNER, CRAIG C.
Inn-Side Murder. Carlyle, 1980

GARNER, DAVID
This Fell Sergeant. New English Library pb, 1974

GARNER, HUGH. 1913-1979. Ref: CA. SC: Insp. Walter McDumont, in all titles. Set: Can.
Death in Don Mills. McGraw, 1975
Murder Has Your Number. McGraw (Toronto), 1978
The Sin Sniper. PB (Canada), 1970. Also published as: Stone Cold Dead. PaperJacks, 1978
Stone Cold Dead; see The Sin Sniper

GARNER, WILLIAM. 1920- . Ref: CA. SC: Mick Jagger = MJ.
The Andra Fiasco. Collins, 1971. U.S. title: Strip Jack Naked. Bobbs, 1971 [Mid. East]
A Big Enough Wreath. Collins, 1974; Putnam, 1975 MJ
The Deep, Deep Freeze. Collins, 1968; Putnam, 1968 MJ
Ditto, Brother Rat! Collins, 1972
The Manipulators; see The PuppetMasters
The Mobius Trip. Hodder, 1979; Putnam, 1978
Overkill. Collins, 1966; NAL, 1966 MJ
The Puppet-Masters. Collins, 1970. U.S. title: The Manipulators. Bobbs, 1970
Strip Jack Naked; see The Andra Fiasco
The Us or Them War. Collins, 1969; Putnam, 1969 MJ

GARNETT, DAVID. 1892-1981. Pseudonym: Leda Burke, q.v.

GARNETT, ROGER. Pseudonym of Nigel Morland, 1905- , q.v. Other pseudonyms: Mary Dane, John Donavan, Norman Forrest, Vincent McCall, Neal Shepherd, qq.v. SC: R. I. Perkins, in at least those marked RP; Chief Insp. Jonathan Black, in at least those marked JB; John Yardley, in at least those marked JY. Set: Eng.
The Croaker. Wright, 1938 JB
Danger—Death at Work. Wright, 1939 JB
Death in Piccadilly. Wright, 1937 JB
Death Spoke Sweetly. Wright, 1946 JY
Dusky Death. Wright, 1948
Eve Finds the Killer. Martin & Reid, 1947 (16 pp.)
The Killing of Paris Norton. Wright, 1938 RP
A Man Died Talking. Wright, 1943 JB
Starr Bedford Dies. Wright, 1937 RP,JY

GARRATT, MARIE
And Then Look Down. Hurst, 1964. U.S. title: Dangerous Enchantment. Ace, 1966
Dangerous Enchantment; see And Then Look Down
Festival of Darkness; see Where No Fire Burns
Where No Fire Burns. Hurst, 1963. U.S. title: Festival of Darkness. Ace, 1966

GARRETT, RANDALL (PHILLIPS). 1927- . Joint pseudonym with Larry M(ark) Harris, 1933- , q.v.: Mark Phillips, q.v. SC: Lord Darcy, in both titles.
Murder and Magic. Ace, 1979 ss [Fr.]
Too Many Magicians. Doubleday, 1967; Macdonald, 1968 [Eng.]

GARRETT, ROBERT. SC: Alan Brett, in both titles.
Run Down: The World of Alan Brett. Joseph, 1970; Atheneum, 1972
Spiral: The World of Alan Brett. Joseph, 1971; Atheneum, 1972

GARRETT, TRUMAN. Pseudonym of Margaret (Haddican) Judd, 1906- , q.v.
Murder—First Edition. Arcadia, 1956

GARRETT, WILLIAM (A.). 1890-1967. Ref: CA. SC: James Drew = JD. Set: Eng.
Dr. Ricardo. Hutchinson, 1925; Appleton, 1925 JD
Friday to Monday. Hutchinson, 1923; Appleton, 1923 JD
From Dusk Till Dawn. Lane, 1929; Appleton, 1929
The Professional Guest. Lane, 1928; Appleton, 1928
The Secret of the Hills. Jarrolds, 1920. U.S. title: Treasure Royal. Appleton, 1926 JD [Scot.]
Treasure Royal; see The Secret of the Hills

GARRETT, WINIFRED SELINA. 1909- .
Pseudonym: Lyn Dean, q.v.

GARRIK, IVAN. Pseudonym of author and picture-frame designer; born in Chile and living in the U.S.
The Cave and the Beast. Vantage, 1966

GARRISON, CHARLES M. Pseudonym: Charles MacDaniel, q.v.

GARRISON, CHRISTIAN (BASCOM). 1942- .
Ref: CA.
Snake Doctor. Avon, 1980 [South]

GARRISON, JIM. 1921- . Lawyer and district attorney in New Orleans.
The Star Spangled Contract. McGraw, 1976; Allen, 1977

GARRITY. Pseudonym of David J(ames) Gerrity, 1923- , q.v.
Cry Me a Killer. GM, 1961; Muller pb, 1963
Dragon Hunt. Signet, 1967 [NYC]
The Hot Mods. Signet, 1969
Kiss Off the Dead. GM, 1960; Muller pb, 1961

GARROD, JOHN WILLIAM. Joint pseudonym with Ronald Charles Payne: John Castle, q.v.

GARROD, PAT
-Little Doll. Allen, 1963
Man in a Net. Allen, 1966

GARSIA, CLIVE. Pseudonym: Guy Cottar, q.v.

GARSTON, GUY. Pseudonym of Bernard John Hurren, 1907- .
The Champagne Mystery. Muller, 1935

GARTH, DAVID. 1908- .
-Angels Are Cowards. Dodd, 1934
Appointment with Danger; see The Road to Glenfairlie
Bermuda Calling. Putnam, 1944 [Bermuda]
Challenge for Three. Kinsey, 1938; Hale, 1939
Eastward in Eden. Kinsey, 1939; Hale, 1940
Fire on the Wind. Putnam (NYC), 1951; Putnam (London), 1952
Four Men and a Prayer. Kinsey, 1937
Gray Canaan. Putnam, 1947
A Love Like That. Kinsey, 1937
Manila Masquerade. Kinsey, 1942 ss
-Never Mind the Lady. Dodd, 1935
The Road to Glenfairlie. Kinsey, 1940; Hale, 1942. Also published as: Appointment with Danger. Popular Library, 1948
Three Roads to a Star. Putnam, 1955; Hale, 1956
Thunderbird. Kinsey, 1942; Paul, 1943 [Carib.]
Tiger Milk. Kinsey, 1941; Paul, 1942
The Tortured Angel. Putnam, 1948 [Fr.]
The Watch on the Bridge. Putnam, 1959

GARTH, ED. Both titles are novelizations of the "Matt Lincoln" TV series.
The Hostage. Lancer, 1971
The Revolutionist. Lancer, 1970

GARTLAND, HANNAH
The Globe Hollow Mystery. Dodd, 1923 [Conn.]
The House of Cards. Dodd, 1922; Jenkins, 1924 [NYC]

GARVE, ANDREW. Pseudonym of Paul Winterton, 1908- . Other pseudonyms: Roger Bax, Paul Somers, qq.v. Ref: CA, CC, EM, MC, TC. Set: mostly Eng.
The Ascent of D-13. Collins, 1969; Harper, 1969 [Turk.]
The Ashes of Loda. Collins, 1965; Harper, 1965 [Russ.]
Boomerang. Collins, 1970; Harper, 1970 [Australia]
By-Line for Murder; see A Press of Suspects
The Case of Robert Quarry. Collins, 1972; Harper, 1972
Counterstroke. Collins, 1978; Crowell, 1978
The Cuckoo Line Affair. Collins, 1953; Harper, 1953
Death and the Sky Above. Collins, 1953; Harper, 1954
The End of the Track. Collins, 1955; Harper, 1956
The Far Sands. Collins, 1961; Harper, 1960
The File on Lester. Collins, 1974. U.S. title: The Lester Affair. Harper, 1974
Fontego's Folly; see No Mask for Murder
Frame-Up. Collins, 1964; Harper, 1964
The Galloway Case. Collins, 1958; Harper, 1958

The Golden Deed. Collins, 1960; Harper, 1960
A Hero for Leanda. Collins, 1959; Harper, 1959 [ship]
Hide and Go Seek; see Murderer's Fen
A Hole in the Ground. Collins, 1952; Harper, 1952
Home to Roost. Collins, 1976; Crowell, 1976
The House of Soldiers. Collins, 1962; Harper, 1961 [Ire.]
The Late Bill Smith. Collins, 1971; Harper, 1971
The Lester Affair; see The File on Lester
The Long Short Cut. Collins, 1968; Harper, 1968
The Megstone Plot. Collins, 1956; Harper, 1957
Murder in Moscow. Collins, 1951. U.S. title: Murder Through the Looking Glass. Harper, 1952 [Moscow]
Murder Through the Looking Glass; see Murder in Moscow
Murderer's Fen. Collins, 1966. U.S. title: Hide and Go Seek. Harper, 1966
The Narrow Search. Collins, 1957; Harper, 1957
No Mask for Murder. Collins, 1950. U.S. title: Fontego's Folly. Harper, 1950
No Tears for Hilda. Collins, 1950; Harper, 1950
A Press of Suspects. Collins, 1951. U.S. title: By-Line for Murder. Harper, 1951
Prisoner's Friend. Collins, 1962; Harper, 1962
The Riddle of Samson. Collins, 1954; Harper, 1955
The Sea Monks. Collins, 1963; Harper, 1963
A Very Quiet Place. Collins, 1967; Harper, 1967

GARVICE, CHARLES. 1833-1920.
The Fatal Ruby. Hodder, 1909; Doran, 1909

GARVIN, RICHARD M(cCLELLAN), 1934- , and EDMUND G. ADDEO. Ref for Garvin: CA.
The FORTEC Conspiracy. Sherbourne, 1968 [Calif.]
The Talbott Agreement. Sherbourne, 1968 [China]

GASCAR, PIERRE. Pseudonym of Pierre Fournier, 1916- . Ref: CA.
Lambs of Fire. Braziller, 1965 (Translation of "Les Moutons de Feu." Paris, 1963.) [Paris]

GASCOIGNE, PETER. Pseudonym of Peter Townend, 1935- , q.v.
Zero Always Wins. Collins, 1961

GASH, JONATHAN. Pseudonym of John Grant, 1933- , an English doctor and amateur actor. SC: Lovejoy, in all titles. Set: Eng.
Gold by Gemini; see Gold from Gemini
Gold from Gemini. Collins, 1978. U.S. title: Gold by Gemini. Harper, 1979
The Grail Tree. Collins, 1979; Harper, 1980
The Judas Pair. Collins, 1977; Harper, 1977
Spend Game. Collins, 1980; Ticknor, 1981

GASK, ARTHUR (CECIL). 1872- . Ref: CC. SC: Gilbert Larose = GL.
The Beachy Head Murder. Jenkins, 1941 GL
Cloud the Smiter. Jenkins, 1926 GL [Australia]
Crime Upon Crime. Jenkins, 1952; Roy, 1957 GL
The Dark Highway. Jenkins, 1928 GL [Australia]
The Dark Mill Stream. Jenkins, 1947 GL
The Fall of a Dictator. Jenkins, 1939
Gentlemen of Crime. Jenkins, 1932; Macaulay, 1933 GL
The Grave-Digger of Monks Arden. Jenkins, 1938 GL
The Hangman's Knot. Jenkins, 1936 GL
The Hidden Door. Jenkins, 1934; Macaulay, 1935 GL
His Prey Was Man. Jenkins, 1942 GL
The House on the Fens. Jenkins, 1940 GL
The House on the Island. Jenkins, 1932 GL
The House with the High Wall. Jenkins, 1948 GL
The Judgment of Larose. Jenkins, 1934; Macaulay, 1935 GL
The Lonely House. Jenkins, 1929; Macaulay, 1931 GL [Australia]
The Man of Death. Jenkins, 1946 GL
Marauders by Night. Jenkins, 1951 GL
The Master Spy. Jenkins, 1937; Macaulay, 1937 GL
Murder in the Night; see The Red Paste Murders
The Mystery of Fell Castle. Jenkins, 1944 GL
Night and Fog. Jenkins, 1951
The Night of the Storm. Jenkins, 1937 GL
The Poisoned Goblet. Jenkins, 1935 GL
The Red Paste Murders. Jenkins, 1924. U.S. title: Murder in the Night. Macaulay, 1932 [Australia]
The Secret of the Garden. Jenkins, 1924 [Australia]
The Secret of the Sandhills. Jenkins, 1923 [Australia]
The Shadow of Larose. Jenkins, 1939 GL [Australia]
The Silent Dead. Jenkins, 1950 GL
The Storm Breaks. Jenkins, 1949 GL
The Tragedy of the Silver Moon. Jenkins, 1940 GL
The Unfolding Years. Jenkins, 1947 GL
The Vaults of Blackarden Castle. Jenkins, 1950 GL
The Vengeance of Larose. Jenkins, 1939 GL

GASKELL, MRS. E(LIZABETH) C(LEGHORN STEVENSON). 1810-1865. Ref: DD.
Stories of Mystery and Horror. Gollancz, 1978. U.S. title: Mrs. Gaskell's Tales of Mystery and Horror. Scribner, 1979 ss

GASKELL, JANE. 1941- . Ref: CA.
-A Sweet, Sweet Summer. Hodder, 1969

GASKIN, CATHERINE. 1929- . Ref: CA, TC.
Edge of Glass. Collins, 1967; Doubleday, 1967 [Ire.]
The File on Devlin. Collins, 1965; Doubleday, 1965
Fiona. Collins, 1970; Doubleday, 1970 [W.I.]
The Lynmara Legacy. Collins, 1975; Doubleday, 1976
The Property of a Gentleman. Collins, 1974; Doubleday, 1974
The Tilsit Inheritance. Collins, 1963; Doubleday, 1963

GASS, IRENE
A Mixture of Plays. Blackie, 1961 (Plays, some criminous.)

GASS, SHERLOCK BRONSON. 1878-1945. Pseudonym: Morrison Dupree, q.v.

GAST, KELLY P. Pseudonym of Jose Mario Garry Ordonez Edmondson y Cotton, 1922- .
Dil Dies Hard. Doubleday, 1975 [Wash., 1915]

GASTON, BILL [WILLIAM JAMES GASTON]. 1927- . SC: Roy MacLean, in at least those marked RM.
Dark Roots of Fear. Jenkins, 1969
Death Crag. Hammond, 1965 RM [Scot.]
The Death Dealers. Hammond, 1966 [Fr.]
Deep Green Death. Hammond, 1963 RM [Scot.]
Drifting Death. Hammond, 1964 RM [Scot.]
Shabby Eagles. Hale, 1973
-Winter and the "White Witch." Hale, 1979
-Winter of the Wildcat. Hale, 1977
Zero 08.00. Hammond, 1966

GATCHELL, CHARLES. 1851-1910. Pseudonym: Thorold King, q.v.

GATENBY, ROSEMARY. 1918- . Ref: CA.
Aim to Kill. Morrow, 1968; Hale, 1969 [Midwest]
Deadly Relations. Morrow, 1970; Hale, 1971 [N.Y.]
Evil Is As Evil Does. Mill, 1967; Hale, 1968 [NYC]
The Fugitive Affair. Dodd, 1976
Hanged for a Sheep. Dodd, 1973; Hale, 1974 [Midwest]
The Nightmare Chrysalis. Dodd, 1977; Hale, 1978 [Conn.]
The Season of Danger. Dodd, 1974 [Tex., N.Y.]
The Third Identity. Dodd, 1979; Hale, 1981
Whisper of Evil. Dodd, 1978 [Mex. City]

GATES, CLIFFORD
The Case of the Murdered Caretaker. Amalgamated Press, 1940 (Sexton Blake.)

GATES, H(ENRY) L(EYFORD). 1880-1937.
-Born to Sin. Macaulay, 1934
Death Counts Five. Watt, 1934 [Calif.]
-The Devil's Lady. Macaulay, 1933
-Even the Rich Girl. Macaulay, 1934
-High Road to Hell. Godwin, 1938
The House of Murder. Fiction League, 1930 [Fr.]
The Laughing Peril. Macaulay, 1933 [S.F.]
Murder in the Fog. Macaulay, 1932. British title: Murder in the Mist. Hurst, 1933 [S.F.]
Murder in the Mist; see Murder in the Fog
The Mystery of the Hope Diamond. International Copyright Bureau, 1921
The Mystery of the 7 Bad Men. Macaulay, 1933
-The Red Dancer of Moscow. Barse, 1928; Readers Library, 1928
The Scarlet Fan. Macaulay, 1932 [NYC]

GATES, NATALIE. Ref: CA.
Decoy in Diamonds. Putnam, 1971; Hale, 1973 [S. Afr.]
Hush Hush Johnson. Holt, 1967 [N.J.]

GATES, TUDOR. SC: Danny Scipio = DS (novelizations of the "Vendetta" TV series).
Ancora Scipio. Muller, 1970 DS
I Was Walking Down Below. Corgi, 1967
Mister Scipio. Corgi, 1968 DS
Scipio. Corgi, 1967 DS
Who Killed Agatha Christie? French (London), 1980 (Play.)

GATHORNE-HARDY, ROBERT. 1902- .
-The Wind and the Waterfall. Collins, 1938

GATTZDEN, MATT
Black Vendetta. Belmont, 1970
O.D. at Sweet Claude's. Belmont, 1970 [NYC]

GAULDEN, RAY. 1914- .
A Good Place to Die. Hale, 1965

GAULT, MARK. Pseudonym of John Cournos, 1881-1966. Other pseudonym: John Courtney, q.v.
The Face of Death. Methuen, 1933 [Florence]

GAULT, WILLIAM CAMPBELL. 1910- . Pseudonyms: Will Duke, Roney Scott, qq.v. Ref: CA, CC, EM, TC. SC: Brock (The Rock) Callahan = BC; Joe Puma = JP (see also Roney Scott entry).
The Bad Samaritan. Raven, 1980 BC [Calif.]
Blood on the Boards. Dutton, 1953; Boardman, 1954 [L.A.]
The Bloodstained Bokhara; see The Bloody Bokhara
The Bloody Bokhara. Dutton, 1952. British title: The Bloodstained Bokhara. Boardman, 1953 [Milw.]
The Cana Diversion. Raven, 1980 BC; JP in minor role [Calif.]
The Canvas Coffin. Dutton, 1953; Boardman, 1953 [L.A.]
Come Die with Me. Random, 1959; Boardman, 1961 BC [L.A.]
The Convertible Hearse. Random, 1957; Boardman, 1958 BC [L.A.]
County Kill. Simon, 1962; Boardman, 1963 BC [Calif.]
Day of the Ram. Random, 1956; Boardman, 1958 BC [L.A.]
Dead Hero. Dutton, 1963; Boardman, 1964 BC [L.A.]
Death Out of Focus. Random, 1959; Boardman, 1959 [L.A.]
Don't Call Tonight; see End of a Call Girl
Don't Cry for Me. Dutton, 1952; Boardman, 1952 [L.A.]
End of a Call Girl. Crest, 1958. British title: Don't Call Tonight. Boardman, 1960 JP
The Hundred-Dollar Girl. Dutton, 1961; Boardman, 1963 JP [L.A.]
Million Dollar Tramp. Crest, 1960; Boardman, 1962 JP [L.A.]
Murder in the Raw; see Ring Around Rosa
Night Lady. Crest, 1958; Boardman, 1960 JP [L.A.]
Ring Around Rosa. Dutton, 1955; Boardman, 1955. Also published as: Murder in the Raw. Dell, 1956 BC [L.A.]
Run, Killer, Run. Dutton, 1954; Boardman, 1955 [L.A.]
Square in the Middle. Random, 1956; Boardman, 1957 [L.A.]
The Sweet Blond Trap. Zenith, 1959
Sweet Wild Wench. Crest, 1959; Boardman, 1961 JP [L.A.]
Vein of Violence. Simon, 1961; Boardman, 1962 BC [L.A.]
The Wayward Widow. Crest, 1959; Boardman, 1960 JP [Calif.]

GAUNT, ARTHUR NETTLETON. Pseudonym: Arthur Nettleton, q.v.

GAUNT, JEFFREY. Pseudonym of Geo(rge) E(rnest) Rochester, q.v.
 The Haunted Man. Eldon, 1951

GAUNT, M. B. Pseudonym of Richard Henry Horsfield, 1872-1942.
 The Leases of Death. Long, 1937 [Can.]

GAUNT, MARY (ELIZABETH BAKEWELL). 1872-1942.
 The Mummy Moves. Laurie, 1910; Clode, 1925

GAUTIER, JEAN-JACQUES
 -The Bridge of Asses. Barker, 1953
 -Skin Deep. Barker, 1955
 Triple Mirror. Barker, 1951; Roy, 1954

GAUTIER-SMITH, PETER CLAUDIUS. 1929- . Pseudonym: Peter Conway, q.v.

GAVIN, BERNARD
 Ring of Fire. Allen, 1977
 Stones of Stavros. Allen, 1978

GAVIN, CATHERINE (IRVINE). 1907- . Ref: CA. SC: Jacques Brunel = JB.
 The Devil in Harbour. Hodder, 1968; Morrow, 1968
 -None Dare Call It Treason. Hodder, 1978; St. Martin's, 1978 JB [Fr., 1941]
 Traitor's Gate. Hodder, 1976; St. Martin's, 1977 JB

GAVIN, MARIAN
 -Jailer, My Jailer. Doubleday, 1964; Dent, 1964

GAVINE, WILLIAM
 Wings of Mystery. Collins, 1929

GAY, VIRGINIA
 The Rector. Doubleday, 1980

GAYE, PHOEBE FENWICK. 1905- .
 Treen and Wild Horses. Cassell, 1958; British Book Service, 1958

GAYET, CAROLINE
 By Love Forgotten. Mystique, 1977 (Translation of "L'Oubliee." Paris, 1972.)
 Dark Suspicion. Mystique, 1980 (Translation of "La Seconde Chimere." Paris, 1968.)
 Heart's Ransom. Mystique, 1979 (Translation of "Le Drame des Autres." Paris, 1975.)
 Prisoner of Lemnos. Mystique, 1979 (Translation of "Vacances a Lemnos." Paris, 1977.)
 Rendezvous in Tripoli. Mystique, 1977 (Translation of "Rendez-Vous a Tripoli." Paris, 1970.)
 To Stalk a Killer. Mystique, 1980 (Translation of "En Ete en Romagne." Paris, 1966.)
 Winter at Blackfont. Mystique, 1977 (Translation of "Noirefontaine." Paris, 1973.)

GAYLE, B.
 Rena. Vantage, 1977

GAYLE, NEWTON. Joint pseudonym of Maurice C. Guiness and Muna Lee de Munoz Marin, 1895- . SC: James Greer, in all titles.
 Death Follows a Formula. Scribner, 1935; Gollancz, 1935 [Eng.]
 Death in the Glass. Scribner, 1937; Gollancz, 1937 [NYC]
 Murder at 28:10. Scribner, 1936; Gollancz, 1936 [P. Rico]
 Murder in the Haunted Sentry-Box; see The Sentry-Box Murder
 The Sentry-Box Murder. Scribner, 1935. British title: Murder in the Haunted Sentry-Box. Gollancz, 1935 [P. Rico]
 Sinister Crag. Scribner, 1939; Gollancz, 1938 [Eng.]

GAYLORD, OTIS H.
 The Rise and Fall of Legs Diamond. Bantam, 1960 (Novelization of the movie.)

GAYTON, REBECCA. See: Louise Eppley.

GAZE, RICHARD. 1917- . Pseudonym: John Gale, q.v.

GEACH, CHRISTINE. 1930- . Pseudonym: Anne Loring, q.v.

GEARON, JOHN. Pseudonym: John Flagg, q.v.
 The Velvet Well. Duell, 1946; Pilot, 1947 [N.Y.]

GEBHARD, H. HARRIS. See: Leslie Horvitz.

GEDDES, PAUL. A lawyer in London. SC: Paul Venneker = PV.
 Code Name Hangman; see Hangman
 Hangman. Faber, 1977. St. Martin's, 1977. Also published as: Code Name Hangman. Penguin, 1979 PV [Fr.]
 The High Game. Joseph, 1968; Weybright, 1968 PV
 A November Wind. Joseph, 1970; Coward, 1971
 The Ottawa Allegation. Faber, 1973; Coward, 1973

GEE, MAURICE (GOUGH). 1931- . Ref: CA.
 In My Father's Den. Faber, 1972

GEHMAN, RICHARD (BOYD). 1921-1972. Ref: CA.
 Driven. McKay, 1954; Davies, 1956
 Each Life to Live. Red Seal (Fawcett), 1952
 The Had. Simon, 1965
 The Slander of Witches. Rinehart, 1955

GEIS, GILBERT L. Pseudonym: Gil Lawrence, q.v.

GELB, ALAN LLOYD. Lives in NYC.
 -The Janissary. Rawson, 1978; Hamlyn, 1980 [Balt.]

GELIEN, MODENA
 Walking Shadows. Accent, 1978

GELLER, ELI
 Window Episode. Mystery House, 1958

GELLER, MICHAEL. SC: Bud Dugan = BD.
 A Corpse for a Candidate. Belmont, 1980 BD [NYC]
 Disco Deathbeat. Belmont, 1980 BD
 -The Man Who Needed Action. Belmont, 1979
 Mayhem on the Coney Beat. Belmont, 1979 BD [NYC]

GELLER, STEPHEN
 Gad. Harper, 1979
 Pretty Poison; see She Let Him Continue
 She Let Him Continue. Dutton, 1966. Also published as: Pretty Poison. Ballantine, 1967

GELLIBRAND, EDWARD
 The End of a Cigarette. Long, 1924
 The Windblow Mystery. Hamilton, 1926

GELLIS, ROBERTA (LEAH JACOBS). 1927- . Ref: CA.
 Sing Witch, Sing Death. Bantam, 1975 [Eng., ca.1900]

GENET, JEAN. 1910- . Ref: CA.
 -The Balcony. Grove, 1958 (Translation of "Le Balcon." Paris, 1956.) (9-scene play.)

GEOGHEGAN, LAURENCE. Set: Eng.
 The Brackenridge Enigma. Methuen, 1929
 The Double Death Mystery. Mellifont, 1934
 The Subterranean Club. Hodder, 1932
 The Vagabond Sonata. Hodder, 1930

GEORGE, ALFRED K.
 Snow Among the Stars. Paul, 1938

GEORGE, BRIAN
 Atom of Doubt. Methuen, 1959

GEORGE, CHARLES. 1893- . Pseudonyms: Leland Price, Henry Rowland, Dorothy Sterling, qq.v. All titles are plays with number of acts in parenthesis.
 Bertha, the Bartender's Beautiful Baby. Dramatists, 1960 (1)
 Bertha, the Beautiful Typewriter Girl. Baker, 1939 (4)
 The Jeweled Hand. French (NYC), 1934 (1)
 Miss Information. Eldridge, 1932 (3)
 Murder in the Ferris-Wheel. Baker, 1936 (1)
 Sadie Socks the Saboteurs. Baker, 1942 (1)
 Sherlock Holmes. Baker, 1936 (3-act play based on "A Study in Scarlet" by A. Conan Doyle, 1859-1930, q.v.)
 The Thirteenth Day. Paine, 1931 (3)

GEORGE, DAVID ROBINSON
 Death Meets the Deadline. Vulcan, 1944 [NYC]

GEORGE, JONATHAN. Joint pseudonym of John (Frederick) Burke, 1922- , q.v., and George Theiner, 1927- . Other Burke pseudonyms: Jonathan Burke, Robert Miall, Martin Sands, qq.v. Joint pseudonym of Burke and his wife: Harriet Esmond, q.v.
 Dead Letters. Macmillan (London), 1972

The Kill Dog. Macmillan (London), 1970; Doubleday, 1970 [Prague]

GEORGE, PETER (BRYAN). 1924-1966. Pseudonyms: Peter Bryant, Bryan Peters, qq.v. Ref: CA.
 Come Blond, Came Murder. Boardman, 1952; Harlequin, 1952
 Commander-1. Heinemann, 1965; Delacorte, 1965 [China]
 Cool Murder. Boardman, 1958. Reprinted as by Bryan Peters: Mayflower, 1965 [Calif.]
 Dr. Strangelove. Corgi, 1963; Bantam, 1963
 The Final Steal. Boardman, 1962; Dell, 1965 [Utah]
 Pattern of Death. Boardman, 1954

GEORGE, SARA. 1947- . Ref: CA.
 Acid Drop. Macmillan (London), 1975; Atheneum, 1975
 Fatal Shadows. Macmillan (London), 1976
 Screen Test. Macmillan (London), 1979

GEORGE, THEODORE. Pseudonym of Theodore George Berk, born in Brooklyn, a public relations manager in industry. SC: Lt. Al Zimmerman, in both titles, both set in NYC.
 The Deadly Homecoming. Dodd, 1972; Hale, 1974
 The Murders on the Square. Dodd, 1971

GEORGE, VERNON. Pseudonym of George Shirra Gibb Vernon, 1885- .
 Hamish Munro's Experiment. Stockwell, 1935

GEORGE, W(ALTER) L(IONEL). 1882-1926.
 One of the Guilty. Harper, 1923; Chapman, 1923

GEORGIUS. Pseudonym of Georges Guibourg, 1897- .
 My Fair Lady. Staples, 1951; Roy, 1954

GERAHTY, DIGBY GEORGE. Pseudonym: Robert Standish, q.v.

GERARD, FRANCIS. 1905- . Ref: MP. SC: Commissioner Sanders (continuing the character created by Edgar Wallace, 1875-1932, q.v.) = S; Sir John Meredith, in at least those marked JM.
 Bare Bodkin. Macdonald, 1951 JM
 The Black Emperor. Rich, 1936 JM
 Concrete Castle. Rich, 1936. U.S. title: The Concrete Castle Murders. Holt, 1936 JM
 The Concrete Castle Murders; see Concrete Castle
 The Dictatorship of the Dove. Rich, 1936 JM
 Emerald Embassy. Rich, 1939 JM
 The Envoy of the Emperor. Macdonald, 1951
 Fatal Friday. Rich, 1937; Holt, 1937 JM
 -The Flail and the Fish. Macdonald, 1949
 Flight into Fear. Macdonald, 1948 JM
 Golden Guilt. Rich, 1938; Dutton, 1940 JM
 The Justice of Sanders. Rich, 1951 S [Afr.]
 The Law of the River. Rich, 1939; Dutton, 1940 S ss [Afr.]
 The Mark of the Moon. Macdonald, 1952; Popular Library, 1953 [Fr.]
 The Mind of John Meredith. Macdonald, 1946 JM
 Number 1-2-3. Rich, 1936. U.S. title: The 1-2-3 Murders. Holt, 1937 JM
 The 1-2-3 Murders; see Number 1-2-3
 The Prince of Paradise. Rich, 1938; Dutton, 1941 JM [Saud. Arab.]
 The Prisoner of the Pyramid. Macdonald, 1948 JM [Mex.]
 The Promise of the Phoenix. Macdonald, 1950 JM
 Red Rope. Rich, 1937; Dutton, 1939 JM
 The Return of Sanders of the River. Rich, 1938; Dutton, 1939 S ss [Afr.]
 Secret Sceptre. Rich, 1937; Dutton, 1939 JM
 Sinister Secret. Macdonald, 1952
 Sorcerer's Shaft. Macdonald, 1947 JM in very minor role
 Transparent Traitor. Macdonald, 1950 JM
 Wotan's Wedge. Rich, 1939

GERARD, LOUISE. 1878?-1970. Ref: CA.
 The Mystery of "Golden Lotus." Mills, 1919
 The Strange Young Man. Mills, 1931; Macaulay, 1931

GERARD, MORICE. Pseudonym of John Jessop Teague, 1856-1929.
 The Adventures of an Equerry. Cassell, 1905. Also published as: Under the Red Star; or, The Adventures of an Equerry. Cassell, 1911

G

The Adventures of Marmaduke Clegg. Hodder, 1917
-Beacon Fires. Hodder, 1915
-Black Gull Rock. Nelson, 1897
A Black Vintage. Digby, 1901
-The Broken Sword. Hodder, 1910
-Cast Out. Hurst, 1890
-Check to the King. Hodder, 1906
A Corner in Diamonds. Hodder, 1916
-The Countess of Zelle. Odhams, 1919
-Crenland Castle. Hodder, 1912
-The Crowning of Esther. Odhams, 1919
-Danes Abbey. Hodder, 1918
Dr. Manton. Long, 1907
-A Fair Prisoner. Partridge, 1912
-A Fair Refugee. Hodder, 1909
For England. Ward, 1902
-For France. Odhams, 1922
-Fortune's Wheel. Odhams, 1921
-A Gentleman of London. Nash, 1908
A Grey Fair. Holden, 1924
-The Grip of the Wolf. Marshall, 1900
-The Haunted Shore. Hodder, 1918
-The Heart of a Hero. Hodder, 1913
-A Heather Mixture. Hodder, 1914
A Heather Mystery. Odhams, 1919
-An Interrupted Wedding. Hodder, 1910
-John Montcalm. Long, 1908
-The King's Signet. Hodder, 1909
-The King Waits. Odhams, 1921
-The Last Link. Hodder, 1911
-The League of Life. Jarrolds, 1909
-A Lieutenant of the King. Cassell, 1904
Love in the Purple; see Purple Love
The Man of the Moment. Ward, 1900
The Man with the White Face. Ward, 1903
The Mystery Car. Hodder, 1913
-The New Order. Hodder, 1917
Night Wings. Hodder, 1915
-One of Marlborough's Captains. Hodder, 1912
-Prince Karl. Nelson, 1900
-Purple Love. Hodder, 1908. Also published as: Love in the Purple. Hodder, 1911
-The Prisoner. Nash, 1908
-Queen's Mate. Hodder, 1901
-The Red Seal. Cassell, 1906
-Rose of Blenheim. Hodder, 1907
The Secret of the Moor. Newnes, 1907
-The Shadow of Gilsland. Marshall, 1901
-The Silent Conquest. Century, 1911
-A Snow Heroine. Hodder, 1912
-The Tenant of the Grange. Cassell, 1903
-The Tide of Fortune. Hodder, 1916
Under the Red Star; or, The Adventures of an Equerry; see The Adventures of an Equerry
-The Unseen Barrier. Hodder, 1911
-The Unspoken Word. Hodder, 1910
-The Ward of Navarre. Odhams, 1921

GERLACH, ROBERT. See: James McDonald.

GERMESHAUSEN, ANNA LOUISE. 1906-1968.
Cats in Crime...and others. Luther Norris, 1970 ss

GEROULD, GORDON HALL. 1877-1953. Ref: CC.
A Midsummer Mystery. Appleton (NYC and London), 1925 [Wash. D.C.]

GERRARD, R. J. See: Randle McKay.

GERRARE, WIRT. Pseudonym of William Oliver Greener, 1862-   .
Phantasms. Roxburghe, 1895 ss
Rufin's Legacy. Hutchinson, 1892

GERRITY, DAVID J(AMES). 1923-   . Pseudonym: Garrity, q.v. Ref: CA. SC: Frank Cardolini, in all titles.
The Never Contract. Signet, 1975
The Numbers Man. Signet, 1977 [NYC]
The Plastic Man. Signet, 1976 [NYC]

GERRY, MARGARITA SPALDING. 1870-   .
The Sound of Water. Harper, 1914 [Maine]

GERSHE, LEONARD
Miss Pell Is Missing. French (London), 1963 (3-act play.)

GERSON, JACK
The Assassination Run. BBC, 1980 (Novelization of the TV serial.)
Man on the Crater's Edge. Hale, 1972
The Omega Factor. BBC, 1979 (Novelization of the TV series.)

GERSON, NOEL B(ERTRAM). 1914-   . Pseudonyms: Samuel Edwards, Leon Phillips, qq.v. Ref: CA.
All That Glitters. Doubleday, 1975; Heinemann, 1976, as by Samuel Edwards [H. Kong]
Neptune. Dodd, 1976
The Smugglers. Crowell, 1977; Piatkus, 1979
Special Agent. Dutton, 1976 [Conn.]

State Trooper. Doubleday, 1973; Barker, 1974 [Conn.]
Temptation to Steal. Doubleday, 1972

GERSTINE, JACK [JOHN]. 1915-   .
Play It Cool. Ace, 1959

GERVAIS, ALBERT. 1892-
The Ghosts of Sin-Chang. H. Hamilton, 1936 (Translation of "L'Ombre du Makoui." Paris, 1936.)

GEUMLEK, LOIS
The House in the Fog. Avon, 1974

GHEORGHIU, C(ONSTANTIN) VIRGIL. 1916-   .
Ref: CA.
-The Death of Kyralessa. Regnery, 1968 (Translation of "Le Meurtre de Kyralessa." Paris, 1966.)
The Immortals of the Mountain. Regnery, 1969 (Translation of "Les Immortels d'Agapia." Paris, 1964.) [Rum.]
-The Twenty-Fifth Hour. Knopf, 1950; Heinemann, 1950 (Translation of "La Vingt-Cinquieme Heure." Paris, 1949.)

GIANETTA, SAL
The Capac Legacy. Simon, 1975; Allen, 1975

GIBBON, CHARLES. 1843-1890. Ref: DD.
-Amoret. Maxwell, 1886
-Beyond Compare. Low, 1888
-Blood Money, and other stories. Chatto, 1889 ss
-The Braes of Yarrow. Low, 1881; Harper, 1881
-By Mead and Stream. Chatto, 1884; Harper, 1884
-Clare of Claresmede. Low, 1886; Harper, 1886
Dangerous Connexions. Maxwell, 1864
-The Dead Heart. Maxwell, 1865
-Fancy Free and other stories. Chatto, 1884 ss
-The Flower of the Forest. Chatto, 1882
-For Lack of Gold. Blackie, 1871; Munro, 1880
-Garvock. Maxwell, 1885
-The Golden Knot. Chatto, 1882; Harper, 1882
A Hard Knot. Chatto, 1885; Harper, 1885 (A plagiarized version of Emile Gaboriau's "L'Affaire Lerouge," q.v.)
-Heart's Delight. Chatto, 1885; Harper, 1885
-A Heart's Problem. Chatto, 1881; Harper, 1882
-In Cupid's Wars. White, 1884
-In Honour Bound. Chatto, 1874; Munro, 1880
-In Love and War. Chatto, 1877
-In Pastures Green and other stories. Chatto, 1880; Munro, 1883 ss
Lady Grace's Mistake. Modern, 193? (Original title?)
-Loving a Dream, and One of His Inventions. Chatto, 1884
-A Maiden Fair and other stories. Maxwell, 1885; Munro, 1883 ss
Margaret Carmichael; or, A Princess of Jutedom; see A Princess of Jutedom
-Of High Degree. Chatto, 1883; Harper, 1882
-A Princess of Jutedom. Ward, 1886. U.S. title: Margaret Carmichael; or, A Princess of Jutedom. New Amsterdam, 1896
-Queen of the Meadow. Chatto, 1880; Harper, 1880
-Robin Grey. Blackie, 1869; Munro, 1880
-The Shadow of Wrong. Maxwell, 1886
-A Strange Wooing. Ward, 1890. U.S. title: Was Ever Woman in This Humor Wooed? Lovell, 1890
Was Ever Woman in This Humor Wooed?; see A Strange Wooing
-What Will the World Say? Bentley, 1875; Munro, 1883

GIBBON, PERCEVAL. 1879-1926.
The Adventures of Miss Gregory. Dent, 1912; Putnam, 1913 ss
-The Dark Places. Methuen, 1926 ss
-Salvator. Blackwood, 1908; Doubleday, 1909
The Second Class Passenger, and other stories. Methuen, 1913 ss
-Souls in Bondage. Blackwood, 1904
-Those Who Smiled, and other stories. Cassell, 1920
Vrouw Grobelaar and Her Leading Cases; see The Vrouw Grobelaar's Leading Cases
The Vrouw Grobelaar's Leading Cases. Blackwood, 1905. U.S. title: Vrouw Grobelaar and Her Leading Cases. McClure, 1906 ss

GIBBONS, CROMWELL. 1893-   .
-The Bat Woman. World, 1938
Murder in Hollywood. Kemp, 1936 [L.A.]

GIBBONS, H(ARRY) H(ORNABY) CLIFFORD. 1888-1958. Pseudonym: Gilbert Chester, q.v. All titles below feature Sexton Blake and were published by Amalgamated Press.
The Affair of the Country Club. 1924
The Affair of the Cross-Roads. 1926
The Affair of the Diamond Star. 1925
The Affair of the Kidnapped Crook. 1927
The Ballot Box Mystery. 1929
The Case of the Bogus Bride! 1925
The Case of the Old Oak Chest. 1926
The Case of the Red Crimona's. 1925
The Case of the Silent Safe-Cutters. 1926
The Crook of Mayfair. 1925
The Excavator's Secret. 1926. Reprinted in 1938 as by Gilbert Chester
The Flaming Belt. 1929
The Fur Raiders. 1928. Reprinted in 1939 as by Gilbert Chester
The Great Revue Mystery. 1923
The Great Salvage Swindle. 1927
The King's Secret. 1924
Limited Liability. 1925
The Motor Show Mystery. 1929
The Mystery of the Four Rooms. 1927
The Mystery of the Mansion Fire. 1927
On the Night Express! 1925
The Riddle of the Garage. 1928
The Riddle of the Registry Office. 1925
The Riddle of the Runaway Cat. 1928
The Riddle of the West End Hairdresser. 1928. Reprinted in 1939 as by Gilbert Chester
The Secret Millionaire. 1924
The Secret of the Carpathians. 1924
The Secret of the Snows. 1927. Reprinted in 1938 as by Gilbert Chester
The Secret People. 1924
Solved in Thirty-Six Hours! 1923
The South Coast Mystery. 1926
The Third Key. 1924
Who Killed Carson? 1927
The Yellow Cat. 1925

GIBBONS, JAMES
The Green Jade Buddha. Swan, 1946

GIBBONS, SCOTT
Fool's Gamble. GM, 1980

GIBBS, ANGELICA
Murder Between Drinks. Morrow, 1932 [NYC]

GIBBS, GEORGE F(ORT). 1870-1942. Born in New Orleans; artist, portrait painter, on staff of "Saturday Evening Post."
Anything Can Happen. Appleton, 1936 [Wyo.]
The Black Stone. Appleton, 1919
The Castle Rock Mystery. Appleton, 1927 [Pa.]
-The Fire Within. Appleton, 1930
Foul Weather. Appleton, 1933 [ship]
The Golden Bough. Appleton, 1918. British title: Under the Golden Bough. Mellifont, 1944, abridged [Ger.]
Hunted. Appleton, 1937 [West]
Isle of Illusion. Sears, 1929; Hodder, 1929
The Joyous Conspirator. Sears, 1927; Hodder, 1929
The Maker of Opportunities. Appleton, 1912
The Medusa Emerald. Appleton, 1907
Out of the Dark. Appleton, 1934 [Pa.]
-Paradise Garden. Appleton, 1916
The Road to Bagdad. Appleton, 1938 [Mid. East]
The Secret Witness. Appleton, 1917
The Silent Battle. Appleton, 1913
The Silver Death. Appleton, 1939 [Ger.]
The Sleeper Wakes. Appleton, 1941
The Splendid Outcast. Appleton, 1920 [Fr.]
The Triangle Man. Appleton, 1939 [N.Y.]
Under the Golden Bough; see The Golden Bough
The Vagrant Duke. Appleton, 1921
The Vanishing Idol. Appleton, 1936 [China]
The Yellow Diamond. Appleton, 1935 [Afr.]
The Yellow Dove. Appleton, 1915 [Ger.]

GIBBS, HENRY (ST. JOHN CLAIR). 1909-1975. Pseudonym: Simon Harvester, q.v. Ref: CA, CC, TC.
At a Farthing's Rate. Jarrolds, 1943
The Bamboo Prison. Jarrolds, 1961
Blue Days and Fair. Jarrolds, 1946
Cape of Shadows. Jarrolds, 1954
Children's Overture. Jarrolds, 1947
Cream and Cider. Jarrolds, 1952
Disputed Barricade. Jarrolds, 1952
From All Blindness. Jarrolds, 1944
Know Then Thyself. Jarrolds, 1947
The Mortal Fire. Jarrolds, 1963

Not to the Swift. Jarrolds, 1944
The Six-Mile Face. Jarrolds, 1952
The Splendor and the Dust. Jarrolds, 1955
Taps, Colonel Roberts. Jarrolds, 1951
Ten-Thirty Sharp. Jarrolds, 1949
Thunder at Dawn. Jarrolds, 1957
The Tumult and the Shouting. Jarrolds, 1958
The Winds of Time. Jarrolds, 1956
Withered Garland. Jarrolds, 1950

GIBBS, MARY ANNE. Pseudonym of Marjory Elizabeth Sara Bidwell,   -1977. Other pseudonym: Elizabeth Ford, q.v.
The Amateur Governess. Hurst, 1964. U.S. title: The House of Ravensbourne. Pyramid, 1965 [Eng., 1897]
The House of Ravensbourne; see The Amateur Governess
-The Tempestuous Petticoat. Hurst, 1977; Mason/Charter, 1977

GIBBS, PHILIP (HAMILTON). 1877-1962.
The Ambassador's Wife. Hutchinson, 1956

GIBBS-SMITH, C(HARLES) H(ARVARD). 1909-   . Ref: CA. SC: Paul Harvard = PH.
The Caroline Affair; see Operation Caroline
Escape and Be Secret. Hutchinson, 1957 PH
Operation Caroline. Heinemann, 1953. U.S. title: The Caroline Affair. Viking, 1954 PH
-Yankee Poodle. Heinemann, 1955

GIBERSON, DOROTHY (DODDS). Pseudonym: Penelope Field, q.v. Ref: CA.
The Echoing Wave. Coward, 1960; Gresham, 1962

GIBNEY, SOMERVILLE
A Charge from the Grave. Ward, 1889
Sentenced! Chatto, 1890
The Trial of Parson Finch. Ward, 1891

GIBSON, GEORGE
Captain Incognito. Harrap, 1977

GIBSON, WALTER B(ROWN). 1897-   . Pseudonym: Maxwell Grant, q.v. Ref: EM, TC. SC: Lamont Cranston (The Shadow) = LC (see also Grant entry).
A Blonde for Murder. Atlas, 1948
Crime over Casco. [Maine] See: The Shadow: Crime over Casco and The Mother Goose Murders
The Freak Show Murders; see The Shadow: A Quarter of Eight and The Freak Show Murders
Looks That Kill! Atlas, 1948
The Mask of Mephisto. [New Or.] See: The Shadow
The Mother Goose Murders. [NYC] See: The Shadow: Crime over Casco and The Mother Goose Murders
Murder by Magic; see The Shadow
A Quarter of Eight. [NYC] See: The Shadow: A Quarter of Eight, and The Freak Show Murders
Return of the Shadow. Belmont, 1963 LC
The Shadow. Doubleday, 1975 (Contains two pulp novels: The Mask of Mephisto, and Murder by Magic.) LC
The Shadow: Crime over Casco and The Mother Goose Murders. Doubleday, 1979 (Two pulp LC novels.)
The Shadow: A Quarter of Eight and The Freak Show Murders. Doubleday, 1978 (Two pulp LC novels.)

GIBSON-JARVIE, CLODAGH. 1923-   . Ref: CA.
The Web. Weidenfeld, 1979. U.S. title: The Loom and the Web. St. Martin's, 1979

GIDDINGS, HARRY
Loser by a Head. Ace, 1957

GIDDY, ERIC CAWOOD GWYDDYN. 1895-   . Pseudonym: W. Kobold Knight, q.v.

GIDE, ANDRE (PAUL GUILLAUME). 1869-1951.
-The Immoralist. Knopf, 1930; Cassell, 1953 (Translation of "L'Immoraliste." Paris, 1902.)
-Isabelle. Crofts, 1947; Harrap, 1947 (Translation of "Isabelle." Paris, 1911.)
The Vatican Cellars; see The Vatican Swindle
-The Vatican Swindle. Knopf, 1925. British title: The Vatican Cellars. Cassell, 1914 (Translation of "Les Caves du Vatican." Paris, 1914.)

GIDLEY, WILL(IAM) S(ELDEN). 1852-   .
A Dicker in Souls, and other stories. Hazen, 1905 ss, some criminous

GIELGUD, VAL (HENRY). 1900-1981. Ref: CA, CC, EM, TC. SC: Antony Havilland, in at least those marked AH; Insp. Gregory Pellew and Viscount Clymping, in at least those marked P&C; Insp. Simon Spears, in at least those marked SS. Set: Eng.
And Died So? Collins, 1961 P&C
Beyond Dover. Hutchinson, 1940 ss
The Black Sambo Affair. Macmillan (London), 1972 P&C
The Broken Men. Constable, 1932; Houghton, 1933
The Candle-Holders. Macmillan (London), 1970 P&C
Cat. Collins, 1956; Random, 1957
Conduct of a Member. Collins, 1967 P&C
Confident Morning. Collins, 1943
Death of an Extra, with Holt Marvell (pseudonym of Eric Maschwitz, 1901-1969, q.v.). Rich, 1935 SS
Death at Broadcasting House, with Holt Marvel (pseudonym of Eric Maschwitz, 1901-1969, q.v.). Rich, 1934. U.S. title: London Calling. Doubleday, 1934 SS
Death in Budapest, with Holt Marvell (pseudonym of Eric Maschwitz, 1901-1969, q.v.). Rich, 1937 SS [Buda.]
Fall of a Sparrow. Collins, 1949. U.S. title: Stalking Horse. Morrow, 1950 AH
A Fearful Thing. Macmillan (London), 1975 P&C
The First Television Murder, with Eric Maschwitz, 1901-1969, q.v. Hutchinson, 1940
Gallows' Foot. Collins, 1958 P&C
The Goggle-Box Affair. Collins, 1963. U.S. title: Through a Glass Darkly. Scribner, 1963 P&C
Gravelhanger. Cassell, 1934. U.S. title: The Ruse of the Vanishing Women. Doubleday, 1934 AH
The High Jump. Collins, 1953. U.S. title: Ride for a Fall. Morrow, 1953
Imperial Treasure. Constable, 1931; Houghton, 1931
In Such a Night... Macmillan (London), 1974 P&C
London Calling; see Death at Broadcasting House
A Necessary End. Collins, 1969 P&C [ship]
Outrage in Manchukuo. Cassell, 1937 AH
Prinvest-London. Collins, 1965 P&C
The Red Account. Rich, 1938
Ride for a Fall; see The High Jump
The Ruse of the Vanished Women; see Gravelhanger
Special Delivery. Collins, 1950 AH
Stalking Horse; see Fall of a Sparrow
Through a Glass Darkly; see The Goggle-Box Affair
To Bed at Noon. Collins, 1960 P&C [Sic.]
Under London, with Holt Marvell (pseudonym of Eric Maschwitz, 1901-1969, q.v.). Rich, 1933

GIESY, J(OHN) U(LRICH), 1877-1947, and JUNIUS B. SMITH
The Mystery Woman. Whitman, 1929

GIFFORD, A(LICE) S(HERMAN)
A Romance of Hellerism. Neely, 1901 (3 novelets, at least one criminous.)

GIFFORD, LEE
Pieces of the Game. GM, 1960

GIFFORD, NICHOLAS
Long Distance—Wrong Number. Jenkins, 1962

GIFFORD, THOMAS (EUGENE). 1937-   . Ref: CA, TC.
The Cavanaugh Quest. Putnam, 1976; H. Hamilton, 1977 [Mpls.]
The Glendower Legacy. Putnam, 1978; H. Hamilton, 1979
Hollywood Gothic. Putnam, 1979; H. Hamilton, 1980 [L.A.]
The Man from Lisbon. McGraw, 1977; H. Hamilton, 1978 [Lisbon]
The Wind Chill Factor. Putnam, 1975; H. Hamilton, 1975

GIFT, THEO. Pseudonym of Theodora Havers Boulger,   -1889.
-Victims. Hurst, 1887; Holt, 1887

GIGGAL, KENNETH. 1927-   . Pseudonym: Angus Ross, q.v.

GILBART-SMITH, MARCUS MERVYN TOBIAS. 1899-   . Pseudonym: Hibbart Gilson, q.v.

GILBERT, ANNA. Pseudonym of Marguerite Lazarus, 1916-
A Family Likeness. Hodder, 1977; St. Martin's, 1978 [Eng., 1800s]
Flowers for Lilian. Hodder, 1980; St. Martin's, 1981 [Eng., 1800s]
Images of Rose. Hodder, 1974; Delacorte, 1974 [Eng., 1883]
The Leavetaking. Hodder, 1979; St. Martin's, 1980
The Look of Innocence. Hodder, 1975; St. Martin's, 1977 [Eng., 1800s]
-Remembering Louise. Hodder, 1978; St. Martin's, 1978

GILBERT, ANTHONY. Pseudonym of Lucy Beatrice Malleson, 1899-1973. Other pseudonyms: J. Kilmeny Keith, Anne Meredith, qq.v. Ref: CA, CC, DD, EM, MC, TC. SC: Arthur Crook = AC: Scott Egerton = SE: M. Dupuy = D. Set: Eng.
After the Verdict; see She Shall Die
And Death Came Too. Collins, 1956; Random, 1956 AC
The Bell of Death. Collins, 1939 AC
Black Death; see Footsteps Behind Me
The Black Stage. Collins, 1945; Smith & Durrell, 1946. Also published as: Murder Cheats the Bride. Bantam, 1948 AC
The Body on the Beam. Collins, 1932; Dodd, 1932 SE
By Hook or by Crook; see The Spinster's Secret
The Case Against Andrew Fane. Collins, 1931; Dodd, 1931
A Case for Mr. Crook; see Miss Pinnegar Disappears
The Case of the Tea-Cosy's Aunt. Collins, 1942. U.S. title: Death in the Blackout. Smith & Durrell, 1943 AC
The Clock in the Hatbox. Collins, 1939; Arcadia, 1943 AC
Courtier to Death. Collins, 1936. U.S. title: The Dover Train Mystery. Dial, 1936 D
Dark Death; see Footsteps Behind Me
Dear Dead Woman. Collins, 1940; Mystery House, 1942. Also published as: Death Takes a Redhead. Arrow, 1944 AC
Death Against the Clock. Collins, 1958; Random, 1958 AC
Death at Four Corners. Collins, 1929; Dial, 1929 SE
Death at the Door; see He Came by Night
Death Casts a Long Shadow; see Death Takes a Wife
Death in Fancy Dress. Collins, 1933
Death in the Blackout; see The Case of the Tea-Cosy's Aunt
Death in the Wrong Room. Collins, 1947; Barnes, 1947 AC
Death Knocks Three Times. Collins, 1949; Random, 1950 AC
Death Lifts the Latch; see Don't Open the Door!
Death Takes a Redhead; see Dear Dead Woman
Death Takes a Wife. Collins, 1959. U.S. title: Death Casts a Long Shadow. Random, 1959 AC
Death Wears a Mask. Collins, 1970. U.S. title: Mr. Crook Lifts the Mask. Random, 1970 AC
Death Won't Wait; see Snake in the Grass
Die in the Dark. Collins, 1947. U.S. title: The Missing Widow. Barnes, 1948 AC
Don't Open the Door! Collins, 1945. U.S. title: Death Lifts the Latch. Barnes, 1946 AC
The Dover Train Mystery; see Courtier to Death
The Fingerprint. Collins, 1964; Random, 1964 AC
Footsteps Behind Me. Collins, 1953. U.S. title: Black Death. Random, 1953. Also published as: Dark Death. Pyramid, 1963 AC
Give Death a Name. Collins, 1957 AC
He Came by Night. Collins, 1944. U.S. title: Death at the Door. Smith & Durrell, 1945 AC
The Innocent Bottle; see Lift Up the Lid
Is She Dead Too? Collins, 1955. U.S. title: A Question of Murder. Random, 1955 AC
Knock, Knock, Who's There? Collins, 1964. U.S. title: The Voice. Random, 1965 AC
Lady Killer. Collins, 1951 AC
Lift Up the Lid. Collins, 1948. U.S. title: The Innocent Bottle. Barnes, 1949 AC
The Long Shadow. Collins, 1932 SE
The Looking Glass Murder. Collins, 1966; Random, 1967 AC
The Man in the Button Boots. Collins, 1934; Holt, 1935 D
The Man Who Was Too Clever. Collins, 1935 SE
The Man Who Wasn't There. Collins, 1937 AC

Miss Pinnegar Disappears. Collins, 1952. U.S. title: A Case for Mr. Crook. Random, 1952 AC
Missing from Her Home. Collins, 1969; Random, 1969 AC
The Missing Widow; see Die in the Dark
Mr. Crook Lifts the Mask; see Death Wears a Mask
The Mouse Who Wouldn't Play Ball. Collins, 1943. U.S. title: 30 Days to Live. Smith & Durrell, 1944 AC
Murder Anonymous; see Night Encounter
Murder by Experts. Collins, 1936; Dial, 1937 AC
Murder Cheats the Bride; see The Black Stage
Murder Comes Home. Collins, 1950; Random, 1951 AC
Murder Has No Tongue. Collins, 1937 AC
Murder Is Cheap; see The Scarlet Button
The Murder of Mrs. Davenport. Collins, 1928; Dial, 1928 AC
Murder's a Waiting Game. Collins, 1972; Random, 1972 AC
The Musical Comedy Crime. Collins, 1933 SE
Mystery in the Woodshed; see Something Nasty in the Woodshed
The Mystery of the Open Window. Gollancz, 1929; Dodd, 1930 SE
The Mystery of the Woman in Red; see The Woman in Red
A Nice Cup of Tea. Collins, 1950. U.S. title: The Wrong Body. Random, 1951 AC
A Nice Little Killing. Collins, 1974; Random, 1974 AC
Night Encounter. Collins, 1968. U.S. title: Murder Anonymous. Random, 1968 AC
The Night of the Fog. Gollancz, 1930; Dodd, 1930 SE
No Dust in the Attic. Collins, 1962; Random, 1963 AC
An Old Lady Dies. Collins, 1934 SE
Out for the Kill. Collins, 1960; Random, 1960 AC
Passenger to Nowhere. Collins, 1965; Random, 1966 AC [Fr.]
Prelude to Murder; see Third Crime Lucky
A Question of Murder; see Is She Dead Now?
Riddle of a Lady. Collins, 1956; Random, 1957 AC
Ring for a Noose. Collins, 1963; Random, 1964 AC
The Scarlet Button. Collins, 1944; Smith & Durrell, 1945. Also published as: Murder Is Cheap. Bantam, 1949 AC
She Shall Die. Collins, 1961. U.S. title: After the Verdict. Random, 1961 AC
She Vanished in the Dawn; see The Vanishing Corpse
Snake in the Grass. Collins, 1954. U.S. title: Death Won't Wait. Random, 1954 AC
Something Nasty in the Woodshed. Collins, 1942. U.S. title: Mystery in the Woodshed. Smith & Durrell, 1942 AC
The Spinster's Secret. Collins, 1946. U.S. title: By Hook or by Crook. Barnes, 1947 AC
A Spy for Mr. Crook. Barnes, 1944 (British title?) AC
Tenant for the Tomb. Collins, 1971; Random, 1971 AC
Third Crime Lucky. Collins, 1959. U.S. title: Prelude to Murder. Random, 1959 AC
Thirty Days to Live; see The Mouse Who Wouldn't Play Ball
The Tragedy at Freyne. Collins, 1927; Dial, 1927 SE
Treason in My Breast. Collins, 1938 AC
Uncertain Death. Collins, 1961; Random, 1962 AC
The Vanishing Corpse. Collins, 1941. U.S. title: She Vanished in the Dawn. Arcadia, 1941 AC
The Visitor. Collins, 1967; Random, 1967 AC
The Voice; see Knock, Knock, Who's There?
The Woman in Red. Collins, 1941; Smith & Durrell, 1943. Also published as: The Mystery of the Woman in Red. Handi-Books, 1944 AC
The Wrong Body; see A Nice Cup of Tea

GILBERT, BERNARD. 1882-   .
-Tattershall Castle. Horncastle, 1913

GILBERT, ELLIOTT
Don't Push Me Around. Popular Library, 1955
The Vice Trap. Avon, 1958

GILBERT, HARRIETT. 1948-   . Ref: CA.
Given the Ammunition. Harper, 1976 (= Tide Race?)
Hotels with Empty Rooms. Hodder, 1973; Harper, 1973 [Fr.]
An Offense Against the Persons. Hodder, 1974; Harper, 1975
Tide Race. Constable, 1977

GILBERT, MICHAEL (FRANCIS). 1912-   . Ref: CA, CC, DD, EM, MC, TC. SC: Insp. Hazelrigg = H; Patrick Petrella = PP. Set: mostly Eng.
After the Fine Weather. Hodder, 1963; Harper, 1963 [Austria]
Amateur in Violence. Davis, 1973 PP in 4 ss, H in 3 ss
The Bargain. Constable, 1961 (Play.)
Be Shot for Sixpence. Hodder, 1956; Harper, 1956
Blood and Judgment. Hodder, 1959; Harper, 1959 PP
The Body of a Girl. Hodder, 1972; Harper, 1972
A Clean Kill. Constable, 1960 (Play.)
Close Quarters. Hodder, 1947; Walker, 1963 H [church]
The Country-House Burglar; see Sky High
The Crack in the Teacup. Hodder, 1966; Harper, 1966
The Danger Within; see Death in Captivity
Death Has Deep Roots. Hodder, 1951; Harper, 1951 H
Death in Captivity. Hodder, 1952. U.S. title: The Danger Within. Harper, 1952 [It., WWII]
Death of a Favorite Girl. Hodder, 1980. U.S. title: The Killing of Katie Steelstock. Harper, 1980
The Doors Open. Hodder, 1949; Walker, 1962 H
The Dust and the Heat. Hodder, 1967. U.S. title: Overdrive. Harper, 1968
The Empty House. Hodder, 1978; Harper, 1979
The Etruscan Net. Hodder, 1969. U.S. title: The Family Tomb. Harper, 1970 [Florence]
The Family Tomb; see The Etruscan Net
Fear to Tread. Hodder, 1953; Harper, 1953 H
Flash Point. Hodder, 1974; Harper, 1974
Game Without Rules. Hodder, 1968; Harper, 1967 ss
He Didn't Mind Danger; see They Never Looked Inside
The Killing of Katie Steelstock; see Death of a Favorite Girl
The Night of the Twelfth. Hodder, 1976; Harper, 1976 [acad.]
The Ninety-Second Tiger. Hodder, 1973; Harper, 1973 [Mid. East]
Overdrive; see The Dust and the Heat
Petrella at Q. Hodder, 1977; Harper, 1977 ss PP
The Shot in Question. Constable, 1963 (Play.)
Sky High. Hodder, 1955. U.S. title: The Country-House Burglar. Harper, 1955
Smallbone Deceased. Hodder, 1950; Harper, 1950 H
Stay of Execution. Hodder, 1971 ss, 2 with H
They Never Looked Inside. Hodder, 1948. U.S. title: He Didn't Mind Danger. Harper, 1949 H

GILBERT, NELSON RUST
The Affair at Pine Court. Lippincott, 1907 [N.Y.]

GILBERT, (WILLIAM) STEPHEN. 1912-   . Ref: CA.
Ratman's Notebooks. Joseph, 1968; Viking, 1969. Also published as: Willard. Lancer, 1971

GILBERT, W(ILLIAM) S(CHWENK). 1836-1911. Ref: CA.
Foggerty's Fairy and other tales. Routledge, 1890 ss, some criminous

GILBERT, WILLIAM. 1804-1890.
The Landlord of "The Sun." Bentley, 1871

GILCHRIST, R(OBERT) MURRAY. 1868-1917.
The Abbey Mystery. Ward, 1908
-Beggar's Manor. Heinemann, 1903
-The Chase. White, 1914
-The Courtesy Dame. Heinemann, 1900; Dodd, 1900
-Damosel Croft. Paul, 1912
-The First Born. Laurie, 1911
-The Gentle Thespians. Milne, 1908
-Good-Bye to Market. Moorlands, 1908 ss
-Hercules and the Marionettes. Bliss, 1894
-Honeysuckle Rogue. Westall, 1917
-The Labyrinth. Richards, 1902
-Lords and Ladies. Hurst, 1903 ss
-Passion the Plaything. Heinemann, 1890; Lovell, 1890
-Pretty Fanny's Way. Everett, 1909
-Roadknight. Holden, 1913
-The Rue Bargain. Richards, 1898
-The Secret Tontine. Long, 1912
-The Stone Dragon and Other Tragic Romances. Methuen, 1894 ss
-The Two Goodwins. Milne, 1908
Under Cover of Night. Long, 1914
-Weird Wedlock. Long, 1913
-Willowbrake. Methuen, 1898
-Willowford Woods. Ward, 1911

GILES, ELIZABETH. Pseudonym of John Robert Holt, 1926-   . Other pseudonym: Raymond Giles, q.v. Ref: CA.
As Darker Grows the Night. Lancer, 1972
Children of the Griffin. Lancer, 1971. British title: Night of the Griffin, as by Raymond Giles. New English Library pb, 1971
Night of the Griffin; see Children of the Griffin

GILES, FREDERICK R(EED). 1864-1898.
The Mysterious Mr. Jarvis. Rowland, 1892

GILES, GUY ELWYN. 1904-   . SC: Brice Kent, in both titles.
Target for Murder. Morrow, 1943 [Conn.]
3 Died Variously. Reynal, 1941 [N.Y.]

GILES, HERBERT A(LLEN). 1845-1935.
Historic China, and other sketches. de la Rue, 1882 ss, some criminous
Strange Stories from a Chinese Studio. de la Rue, 1880 ss

GILES, KENNETH. 1922-1972. Pseudonyms: Charles Drummond, Edmund McGirr, qq.v. Ref: CC, TC. SC: Insp. Harry James = HJ. Set: Eng.
The Big Greed. Gollancz, 1966
Death Among the Stars. Gollancz, 1968; Walker, 1969 HJ
Death and Mr. Prettyman. Gollancz, 1967; Walker, 1969 HJ
Death Cracks a Bottle. Gollancz, 1969; Walker, 1970 HJ
Death in Diamonds. Gollancz, 1967; Simon, 1968 HJ
A Death in the Church. Gollancz, 1970 HJ
A File on Death. Gollancz, 1973; Walker, 1973 HJ
Murder Pluperfect. Gollancz, 1970; Walker, 1970 HJ
Picture of Death; see A Provenance of Death
A Provenance of Death. Gollancz, 1966; Simon, 1967. Also published as: Picture of Death. Panther, 1970 HJ
Some Beasts No More. Gollancz, 1965; Walker, 1968 HJ

GILES, NORMAN. Pseudonym of Norman Robert McKeown, 1879-1947.
-Keerboskloof. Collins, 1929
-The Whips of Time. Collins, 1931

GILES, PETER
A Monster unto Many. Muller, 1980

GILES, RAYMOND. Pseudonym of John Robert Holt, 1926-   . Other pseudonym: Elizabeth Giles, q.v.
Shamus. Lancer, 1973 (Novelization of the movie.) [NYC]

GILFORD, C(HARLES) B(ERNARD). 1920-   . Ref: CA.
The Crooked Shamrock. Doubleday, 1969; Arlington, 1970 [Ire.]
Dead Man Out. Flagship, 1967 [Carib.]

GILL, B(ARBARA) M. Pseudonym. Set: Eng.
Death Drop. Hodder, 1979; Scribner, 1980 [acad.]
Suspect; see Victims
Target Westminster. Hale, 1977
Victims. Hodder, 1980. U.S. title: Suspect. Scribner, 1981 [hosp.]

GILL, BARTHOLOMEW. Pseudonym of Mark McGarrity, 1943-   , q.v. SC: Insp. McGarr, in all titles.
McGarr and the Politician's Wife. Scribner, 1977; Hale, 1978 [Ire.]
McGarr and the Sienese Conspiracy. Scribner, 1977; Hale, 1979 [It.]
McGarr at the Dublin Horse Show. Scribner, 1980; Hale, 1980 [Dub.]
McGarr on the Cliffs of Moher. Scribner, 1978; Hale, 1980 [Ire.]

GILL, ELIZABETH. SC: Benvenuto Brown, in all titles.
The Crime Coast; see Strange Holiday
Crime de Luxe. Cassell, 1933; Doubleday, 1933 [ship]
Strange Holiday. Cassell, 1931. U.S. title: The Crime Coast. Doubleday, 1931 [Fr.]
What Dread Hand? Cassell, 1932; Doubleday, 1932

GILL, HERBERT J.
The Second Knife. Houghton (London), 1935

GILL, JOHN. Pseudonym of John Russell Gillies, 1920- . Born in the S. Pac., lives in Spain; writer for magazines and French TV.
Kiki. Cape, 1979; Little, 1979 [Fr.]
The Last Heroes. Collins, 1973; Random, 1974
The Listener; see The Tenant
The Tenant. Collins, 1972. U.S. title: The Listener. Stein, 1972

GILL, JOSEPHINE (PAULINE ECKERT). 1921- . Ref: CC.
Dead of Summer. Doubleday, 1959; Macdonald, 1960 [N.Y.]
The House That Died. Doubleday, 1955; Collins, 1956

GILL, PATRICK. Pseudonym of John Creasey, 1908-1973, q.v. Other pseudonyms: Gordon Ashe, M. E. Cooke, Norman Deane, Robert Caine Frazer, Michael Halliday, Charles Hogarth, Brian Hope, Colin Hughes, Kyle Hunt, Abel Mann, Peter Manton, J. J. Marric, Richard Martin, Rodney Mattheson, Anthony Morton, Jeremy York, qq.v.
The Battle for the Cup. Mellifont, 1939
The Fighting Footballers. Mellifont, 1937
The Fighting Tramp. Mellifont, 1939
The Laughing Lightweight. Mellifont, 1937
The Mystery of the Centre-Forward. Mellifont, 1939
The Secret Super-Charger. Mellifont, 1940
The £10,000 Trophy Race. Mellifont, 1939

GILLA, ESKER N. Born in Cincinnati and teacher in Cincinnati public schools.
Cap and Gown for a Shroud. Vantage, 1960 [Cin., acad.]

GILLEN, MOLLIE. 1908- . Ref: CA.
A Star of Death. Bles, 1960

GILLER, NORMAN. See: Jimmy Greaves.

GILLES, DANIEL. 1917- .
-The Anthill. Chapman, 1962; Vanguard, 1963

GILLESPIE, ROBERT (B.). Lives in N.Y.; crossword puzzle editor for national newspaper syndication.
The Crossword Mystery. Raven, 1980; Constable, 1979 [NYC]
Little Sally Does It Again. Raven, 1980 [N.Y.]

GILLETTE, PAUL
The Chinese Godfather. GM, 1980 [S.F.]

GILLETTE, PAUL J. 1938- . Ref: CA.
The Cat O' Nine Tails. Award, 1971 (Novelization of the movie.)
Play Misty for Me. Award, 1971; Tandem, 1972 (Novelization of the movie.)

GILLETTE, WILLIAM (HOOKER). 1855-1937. See also: Cyrus Townsend Brady, 1861-1920; and: Tim J. Kelly, 1937- . Ref: CC, MP.
The Astounding Crime on Torrington Road. Harper, 1927; Cassell, 1928 [Boston]
-A Legal Wreck. Rockwood, 1888
The Painful Predicament of Sherlock Holmes. Abramson, 1955 (Play.)
The Red Owl. French, 1924 (Play.)
Secret Service. French, 1898 (Play.)
Sherlock Holmes. French, 1922 (2-act play.)

GILLIAM, EDWARD W(INSLOW). 1834-1925.
-Ravenswood. Neale, 1908

GILLIAN, MICHAEL
Warrant for a Wanton. Mill, 1952 [Chi.]

GILLIES, JOHN RUSSELL. 1920- . Pseudonym: John Gill, q.v.

GILLIS, JACKSON. Native of Pacific Northwest; prolific TV writer.
The Killers of Starfish. Lippincott, 1977; Hale, 1979 [Wash.]

GILLMORE, RUFUS (HAMILTON). 1879-1935.
The Alster Case. Appleton, 1914 [NYC]
The Ebony Bed Murder. Mystery League, 1932 [NYC]
The Mystery of the Second Shot. Appleton, 1912
The Opal Pin. Appleton, 1914 [Boston]

GILMAN, DOROTHY [DOROTHY GILMAN BUTTERS]. 1923- . Ref: CA, TC. SC: Mrs. Emily Pollifax = EP.
The Amazing Mrs. Pollifax. Doubleday, 1970; Hale, 1971 EP [Turk.]
The Clairvoyant Countess. Doubleday, 1975; Prior, 1976
The Elusive Mrs. Pollifax. Doubleday, 1971; Hale, 1973 EP [Bulg.]
Mrs. Pollifax on Safari. Doubleday, 1977; Hale, 1977 EP [Zambia]
Mrs. Pollifax, Spy; see The Unexpected Mrs. Pollifax
A Nun in the Closet. Doubleday, 1975. British title: A Nun in the Cupboard. Hale, 1976
A Nun in the Cupboard; see A Nun in the Closet
A Palm for Mrs. Pollifax. Doubleday, 1973; Hale, 1974 EP [Switz.]
The Tightrope Walker. Doubleday, 1979; Hale, 1980 [Maine]
Uncertain Voyage. Doubleday, 1967; Hale, 1968
The Unexpected Mrs. Pollifax. Doubleday, 1966; Hale, 1967. Also published as: Mrs. Pollifax, Spy. Tandem, 1971 EP [Mex., Alb.]

GILMAN, J. D. and JOHN CLIVE, 1933- , q.v. J. D. Gilman is the joint pseudonym of Jack Fishman, 1920- , and Douglas (William) Orgill, 1922- , q.v.
KG 200. Souvenir, 1977; Simon, 1977

GILMAN, JAMES. Pseudonym of Joseph (Lee) Gilmore, 1929- , q.v. Other pseudonym: Nick Carter, q.v.
Operation NAZI-U.S.A. Major, 1976

GILMER, J. LANCE. A S.F. newsman.
Hell Has No Exit. Holloway, 1976 [S.F.]
Hell Is Forever. Holloway, 1977 [S.F.]

GILMORE, CHRISTOPHER COOK
Atlantic City Proof. Simon, 1978 [N.J., ca.1928]

GILMORE, JOSEPH (LEE). 1929- . Pseudonyms: Nick Carter, James Gilman, qq.v. Ref: CA.
Rattlers. Signet, 1979; Hamlyn, 1979
Vendetta. Pinnacle, 1973

GILMOUR, H. B. 1939- . Ref: CA.
The Eyes of Laura Mars. Bantam, 1978; Corgi, 1978 (Novelization of the movie.)
Windows. PB, 1980; Coronet, 1981 (Novelization of the movie.)

GILMOUR, R.
-Bewitched. Mellifont, 1935
Death in the Ring. Mellifont, 1940
Double-Cross Murder. Mellifont, 1943
The Kukri Killer. Mellifont, 1945
The Missing Rajah. Mellifont, 1946
Wanted for Murder. Mellifont, 1939

GILRUTH, SUSAN. 1911- . SC: Liane Crawford and Insp. Hugh Gordon, in all titles.
A Corpse for Charybdis. Hodder, 1956 [ship]
Death in Ambush. Hale, 1952
Drown Her Remembrance. Hodder, 1961 [Maj.]
Postscript to Penelope. Hale, 1954
The Snake Is Living Yet. Hodder, 1963 [Tangier]
Sweet Revenge. Hale, 1951
To This Favour. Hodder, 1957

GILSON, HIBBART. Pseudonym of Marcus Mervyn Tobias Gilbart-Smith, 1899- .
The Unaccepted Death. Gill, 1928

GILTENE, JEAN. 1913- .
The Candid Killer. Muller, 1955 (Translation of "Trente ans de Frousse." Paris, 1954.)

GILZEAN, ELIZABETH (HOUGHTON BLANCHET) 1913- . Ref: CA.
Murder on Sundays. Hale, 1967

GIMPEL, ERICH. 1910- .
Spy for Germany. Hale, 1957. (Translation of "Spion fur Deutschland." Munich, 1956.) (Fictionalized true account.)

GINN, R(EGIS) C. K. Was officer in U.S. Air Force; teaches in California.
Tyger! Tyger! Macmillan, 1968

GINTY, E(LIZABETH) B(EALL)
Missouri Legend. Random, 1938 (3-act play.) [Mo.]

GIOVANNI, JOSE. 1923- .
The Break. Cape, 1960 (Translation of "Le Trou." Paris, 1957.)

GIPE, GEORGE. 1933- . Ref: CA.
Coney Island Quickstep. Crowell, 1977

GIRARD, BERNARD
Cool Jade. Dell, 1975 [S.F.]

GIRARD, HENRI GEORGES. 1917- . Pseudonym: Georges Arnaud, q.v.

GIRTIN, TOM [THOMAS GIRTIN]. 1913- . Ref: CA.
Unnatural Break. Hutchinson, 1959

GIVENS, CHARLES G(ARLAND). 1899-1964. SC: Jimmy Hastings, in at least those marked JH.
All Cats Are Grey. Bobbs, 1937; Long, 1938
Big Mike. Pyramid, 1953
-Devil Takes a Hill Town. Bobbs, 1939
The Jig-Time Murders. Bobbs, 1936 JH [South]
The Rose Petal Murders. Bobbs, 1935 JH [Midwest]

GIVENS, JOHN
A Friend in the Police. Harcourt, 1980 [Far East]
Sons of the Pioneers. Harcourt, 1977

GIVINS, ROBERT CARTWRIGHT. 1845-1915. Pseudonym: Snivig C. Trebor, q.v.

GLADSON, LESLIE. Pseudonym: Lee Gardner, q.v.

GLADSTONE, ARTHUR M. 1921- . Pseudonym: Margaret Sebastian, q.v.

GLAENZER, RICHARD B(UTLER). 1876-1937.
Spoofs. McBride, 1933 ss, at least one criminous

GLANVILLE, ALEC. Pseudonym of Alexander Haig Glanville Grieve, 1902- . SC: Insp. "Dusty" Muller and "Tiny" Meldrum = M&M.
The Body in the Trawl. Harrap, 1938 M&M
Death Goes Ashore. Harrap, 1936 M&M
Death in Our Wake. Harrap, 1937
Gunner's Island. Jenkins, 1949
Out of the Shadow. Jenkins, 1951; Roy, 1958

GLANVILLE, BRIAN (LESTER). 1931- . Ref: CA.
After Rome, Africa. Secker, 1959

GLANVILLE, ERNEST. 1856-1925.
A Fair Colonist. Chatto, 1894 [S. Afr.]

GLASKIN, G(ERALD) M(ARCUS). 1923- . Ref: CA.
The Man Who Didn't Count. Barrie, 1965; Delacorte, 1967 [Amst.]

GLASMON, KUBEC and JOHN BRIGHT
The Public Enemy. Grosset, 1931 (Novelization of the movie.) [Chi.]

GLASPELL, SUSAN. 1882-1948.
A Jury of Her Peers. Benn, 1927
Trifles. Benn, 1926; Shay, 1916 (1-act play version of A Jury of Her Peers, q.v.)

GLASSFORD, WILFRED. Pseudonym of Wilfred (Glassford) McNeilly, 1921- , q.v. Other pseudonyms: W(illiam) Howard Baker, William A. Ballinger, Errol Lecale, Desmond Reid, Peter Saxon, qq.v.
Alpha-Omega. New English Library pb, 1977

GLAZNER, JOSEPH MARK. 1945- . Ref: CA. SC: Billy Nevers, in all titles.
Dirty Money Can't Wash Both Hands at Once. Warner, 1980
Fast Money Shoots from the Hip. Warner, 1980; Hamlyn, 1980
Smart Money Doesn't Sing or Dance. Warner, 1979; Hamlyn, 1980

G

G

GLEIG, CHARLES. 1862-   . See also: Edwin W(illiam) Pugh, 1874-1930.
-The Edge of Honesty. Lane, 1898
The Nancy Manoeuvres. Brown Langham, 1907
-Reeds in the Wind. Brentano's (London), 1927

GLEMSER, BERNARD. 1908-   . Pseudonym: Geoffrey Napier, q.v.
Grand Opening. Little, 1976; Eyre, 1977 [Far East]

GLEN, ELSA
The Secret of Villa Vanesta. Collins, 1935 [Fr.]

GLENDINNING, RICHARD. 1917-   . Ref: CA.
-Carnival Girl. Popular Library, 1956
Mission to Murder. GM, 1954 [Ger.]
Retreat into Night. GM, 1954
Terror in the Sun. GM, 1952 [Fla.]
-Too Fast We Live. Popular Library, 1954
Who Evil Thinks. GM, 1952 [Fla.]

GLENN, KAREN. Pseudonym: Glenda Carrington, q.v.

GLESS, ELEANOR GREEN
Aunt Ivy Diddit. Chapman, 1948
Murder at Tall Tip. Avalon, 1964 [L.A.]

GLEW, D(ORIS) M(URIEL). 1899-   .
The Fourth Murder. Melrose, 1929

GLICK, CARL (CANNON). 1890-1971. Ref: CA.
Death Sits In. Washburn, 1954
The Devil's Host. Baker, 1934 (3-act play.)
The Laughing Buddha. Lothrop, 1937; Bell, 1937 [NYC]

GLIDDEN, FREDERICK DILLEY. 1908-1975. Pseudonym: Luke Short, q.v.

GLIDDEN, M(INNA MAUD) W(ESSELHOFT). SC: Carey Brent, in both titles.
Come Dwell with Death. Black Knight, 1946 (Retitled reprint of ?)
Death Strikes Home. Phoenix, 1937 [L.I.]
The Long Island Murders. Phoenix, 1937 [L.I.]

GLINTO, DARCY. Pseudonym of Harold Ernest Kelly, 1899-   . Other pseudonyms: Eugene Ascher, Gordon Holt, Buck Toler, qq.v.
Blue Blood Flows East. Robin Hood, 1947
Curtains for Carrie. Robin Hood, 1947
Dainty Was a Jane. Robin Hood, 1948
Dames Between Two. Robin Hood, 1948
"Dames Are Out." Robin Hood, 1953
Lady—Don't Turn Over. Wells Gardner, 1940
The Mannequin Doll. Robin Hood, 1948
No Come-Back from Connie. Robin Hood, 1948
No Mortgage on a Coffin. Robin Hood, 1941
One More Nice White Body. Robin Hood, 1950
Road Floozie. Robin Hood, 1950
She Gave Me Hell and... Robin Hood, 1950
"Snow" Vogue. Wells Gardner, 1941
Straight-Up Girl. Robin Hood, 1949
"You Took Me...Keep Me." Robin Hood, 1941

GLOAG, JOHN (EDWARDS). 1896-1981. Ref: CA. SC: Lionel Buckby = LB. Set: Eng.
-All England at Home. Cassell, 1949
Documents Marked "Secret." Cassell, 1938
In Camera. Cassell, 1945
Kind Uncle Buckby. Cassell, 1946 LB
Mr. Buckby Is Not at Home. Cassell, 1942 LB
Not in the Newspapers. Cassell, 1953
Ripe for Development. Cassell, 1936 LB
-Rising Suns. Cassell, 1964
-Slow. Cassell, 1954
Sweet Racket. Cassell, 1936
Unlawful Justice. Cassell, 1962
Unwilling Adventurer. Cassell, 1940 LB

GLOAG, JULIAN. 1930-   . Ref: CA.
Maundy. Secker, 1969; Simon, 1969
Our Mother's House. Secker, 1963; Simon, 1963
A Sentence of Life. Secker, 1966; Simon, 1966
Sleeping Dogs Lie. Secker, 1980; Dutton, 1980
A Woman of Character. Weidenfeld, 1973; Random, 1973

GLORE, CHARLES
Moonshine Mountain. Novel Books, 1964 (Novelization of the movie.)

GLOVER, ROBERT. 1913-   .
Lace in the Mews. Elek, 1956
Murderer's Maze. Elek, 1951
Things Happen. Elek, 1941

GLUCK, SINCLAIR. 1887-   . Born in Buffalo, N.Y.; educated in N.Y. and London; lived for some years in England. Pseudonym: Melrod Danning, q.v. SC: Paul Bernard = PB; Jack Clayton = JC; Ross McCoy = RM.
The Blind Fury. Dodd, 1930; Mills, 1930 RM [N.Y.]
Come and Kill Me. Mills, 1941 [NYC]
Death Comes to Dinner; see Shadow in the House
The Deeper Scar. Dodd, 1927; Mills, 1927 [S. Pac.]
A Delicate Case of Murder. Macmillan, 1937; Mills, 1937 [NYC]
The Dragon in Harness. Dodd, 1932; Mills, 1927 JC [Far East]
The Four Winds. Dodd, 1926; Mills, 1926 [NYC]
The Golden Panther; see The House of the Missing
The Great London Mystery. Mills, 1936 [Eng.]
The Green Blot. Dodd, 1925; Mills, 1925 [NYC]
Honourable Mister Death and other stories. World's Work, 1942 ss
The House of the Missing. Dodd, 1924. British title: The Golden Panther. Mills, 1923 JC [NYC]
The Last Trap. Dodd, 1928; Mills, 1928 PB
The Man Who Never Blundered. Dodd, 1929; Mills, 1928 RM [NYC]
Minus X. Mills, 1933 [NYC]
Red Emeralds. Mills, 1932 [Algiers]
Sea Shroud. Mills, 1934
Shadow in the House. Dodd, 1929. British title: Death Comes to Dinner. Mills, 1929 PB
Thieves' Honor. Dodd, 1925; Mills, 1924 [China]
The White Streak. Clode, 1924; Mills, 1924 [NYC]
The Wildcat. Dodd, 1932; Mills, 1931 [Ariz.]

GLUCKMAN, JANET and WOODY GREER
The Execution Exchange. Leisure, 1980

GLUT, DONALD F(RANK). 1944-   . Ref: CA. SC: Frankenstein, in all titles.
-Bones of Frankenstein. New English Library pb, 1977
-Frankenstein Lives Again. New English Library pb, 1977
-Frankenstein Meets Dracula. New English Library pb, 1977
-Terror of Frankenstein. New English Library pb, 1977

GLUYAS, CONSTANCE. 1920-   .
The House of Twyford Street. McKay, 1976; Magnum, 1978
Vantage Hall. Leisure, 1971

"G-MAN". Pseudonym. Set: U.S.
Call in the Feds. Hamilton Stafford, 1951
F.B.I. Showdown. Hamilton Stafford, 1952
F.B.I. Special Agent. Hamilton Stafford, 1952
Federal Agent. Hamilton Stafford, 1952

GOBER, DON. SC: James Rhodes, in all titles.
Black Cop. Holloway, 1974
Doomsday Squad. Holloway, 1975
Killer Cop. Holloway, 1975
Killing Ground! Holloway, 1976

GOBLE, (LLOYD) NEIL. 1933-   . Ref: CA.
Condition Green: Tokyo. Tuttle, 1966 [Tokyo]

GODDARD, ANTHEA. Born in Australia; former journalist and feature writer; wife of novelist Alan Scholefield, 1931-   , q.v.
-The Aztec Skull. Deutsch, 1976; Walker, 1977
A Time for Violence. Magnum, 1979; Walker, 1978
The Vienna Pursuit. Milton House, 1974; Walker, 1976 [Austria]

GODDARD, GLORIA. 1897-   . Pseudonym: Paul Palmer, q.v.

GODDARD, HARRY
The Silent Force. Popular Library, 1971 (Novelization of the TV series.)

GODDARD, HENRY. 1800-1883.
Memoirs of a Bow Street Runner. Museum, 1956; Morrow, 1957 (Fictionalized episodes of true crime.)

GODDARD, NORMAN. 1881-1917.
The Man with the Green Eyes. Amalgamated Press, 1917 (Sexton Blake.)

GODDEN, JON. 1906-   . Ref: CA.
Kitten with Blue Eyes. Chatto, 1971.
U.S. title: Mrs. Starr Lives Alone. Knopf, 1972

GODDEN, RUMER. 1907-   . See: Ruth Perry.

GODEY, JOHN. Pseudonym of Morton Freedgood, 1912-   . Ref: EM, TC. SC: Jack Albany = JA.
The Blonde Betrayer; see The Man in Question
The Blue Hour. Doubleday, 1948; Boardman, 1949. Also published as: Killer at His Back. Bestseller, 1955. And as: The Next to Die. Tandem, 1975 [NYC]
The Clay Assassin. Boardman, 1959
The Fifth House. Berkley, 1973; Boardman, 1960
The Gun and Mr. Smith. Doubleday, 1947; Coronet, 1976 [N.Y.]
Killer at His Back; see The Blue Hour
The Man in Question. Doubleday, 1951; Boardman, 1953. Also published as: The Blonde Betrayer. Bestseller, 1955 [NYC]
Never Put Off Till Tomorrow What You Can Kill Today. Random, 1970 JA [NYC]
The Next to Die; see The Blue Hour
The Reluctant Assassin. Hale, 1966
The Snake. Putnam, 1978; New English Library, 1978 [NYC]
The Taking of Pelham One Two Three. Putnam, 1973; Hodder, 1973 [NYC]
The Talisman. Putnam, 1976; Allen, 1977 [Wash. D.C.]
This Year's Death. Doubleday, 1953; Boardman, 1953 [NYC]
A Thrill a Minute with Jack Albany. Simon, 1967 JA [NYC]
The Three Worlds of Johnny Handsome. Random, 1972; Hodder, 1973

GODFREY, ELLEN. Lives in Canada; executive of Canadian publishing house.
The Case of the Cold Murderer. Musson, 1976
Murder Among the Well-To-Do. Porcepic, 1978

GODFREY, HAL. Pseudonym of Charlotte O'Conor Eccles,   -1911.
-The Rejuvenation of Mrs. Semaphore. Jarrolds, 1897; Page, 1898

GODFREY, LIONEL ROBERT HOLCOMBE. 1932-   . Pseudonyms: Elliot Kennedy, Scott Mitchell, qq.v.

GODFREY, PETER. 1917-   .
Death Under the Table. Scientific Pub. Co. (Cape Town), 1954 ss [S. Afr.]

GODLEY, ROBERT. 1908-   . Pseudonym: Franklin James, q.v.

GODWIN, JOHN. 1928-   . Ref: CA, CC.
Requiem for a Rat. Jenkins, 1963 [Syd.]

GODWIN, WILLIAM. 1756-1836. Ref: CC, DD, EM, MC, TC.
Things As They Are; or, The Adventures of Caleb Williams. Crosby, 1794; Rice, 1795. Variously reprinted as: Caleb Williams; and as: The Adventures of Caleb Williams.

GODWYN, MARJORIE
Let's Ask Aunt. Allan, 1936

GOENEY, WILLIAM M(ORTON). 1914-   . Ref: CA.
The Moment of Truth. Holt, 1959 [Calif.]

GOFF, GEORGINA
The Black Dog. Belmont, 1971 [Mich.]

GOFF, IVAN and BEN ROBERTS
Portrait in Black. French (NYC & London), 1948 (3-act play.)

GOFF, OLIVER
The Eye of the Peacock. Eyre, 1975 [S. Afr.]

GOINES, DONALD. 1935?-1974. Pseudonym: Al C. Clark, q.v.
Black Gangster. Holloway, 1972
Black Girl Lost. Holloway, 1973
Daddy Cool. Holloway, 1974

Dopefiend. Holloway, 1971 [Det.]
Eldorado Red. Holloway, 1974
Inner City Hoodlum. Holloway, 1975
  [L.A.]
Never Die Alone. Holloway, 1974
Street Players. Holloway, 1973
Swamp Man. Holloway, 1974
White Man's Justice: Black Man's Grief.
  Holloway, 1973
Whoreson. Holloway, 1972

GOLD, DON
  The Park. Harper, 1978 [NYC]

GOLD, G. See: Hank Janson.

GOLD, HERBERT. 1924- .
  Slave Trade. Arbor, 1979 [S.F.]

GOLDBERG, ABRAHAM
  The Syndicate That Failed. Vantage,
    1977

GOLDBERG, EDWARD. Pseudonym: "Goldey",
  q.v.

GOLDBERG, GERALD J(AY). 1929- . Ref:
  CA.
  -The Lynching of Orin Newfield. Dial,
    1970

GOLDBERG, HARRY. Pseudonym: Harry Grey,
  q.v.

GOLDBERG, MARSHALL. Surgeon and director
  of medical education at a hospital in
  Michigan; TV scriptwriter.
  The Anatomy Lesson. Putnam, 1974
    [Boston]
  The Chengtu Strain, with Kenneth Kay.
    Pinnacle, 1976
  The Karamanov Equations. World, 1972;
    MacGibbon, 1972 [Paris]

"GOLDEY". Pseudonym of Edward Goldberg.
  Tracked by a Woman; or, The Female
    Detective. Eagle, 1889

GOLDHURST, RICHARD. 1927- . Ref: CA.
  The Deceivers. Signet, 1965

GOLDIE, BERTHA (BARRE). 1871-1938.
  -Dahlia. Ward, 1937
  -The Discipline of Christine. Rivers,
    1904
  The Green Tablets; see The Green Tab-
    loids
  The Green Tabloids. Hodder, 1929. Also
    published as: The Green Tablets.
    Ward, 1939 [Fr.]
  The Hand of the Waverleys. Melrose,
    1928
  -Nightlights. Ward, 1936
  The Piper of Arristoun. Ward, 1935
  -Raven. Ward, 1936
  -The Signature. Ward, 1937
  -Vellum. Ward, 1935
  -The Village Never Knew. Ward, 1938
  -Whispering Galleries. Ward, 1940

GOLDIE, VALENTINE FRANCIS TAUBMAN. See:
  Valentine Francis Taubman-Goldie.

GOLDING, LOUIS. 1895-1958.
  The Doomington Wanderer. Gollancz, 1934
    ss, at least one criminous
  The Frightening Talent. Allen, 1973
  Luigi of Catanzaro. Archer, 1926
  Pale Blue Nightgown. Corvinus, 1936
  Pale Blue Nightgown. Hutchinson, 1944
    ss
  The Pursuer. Gollancz, 1936; Farrar,
    1936

GOLDING, MORTON JAY. 1925- . Pseudonyms: Stephanie Lloyd, Patricia Morton, qq.v.

GOLDMAN, JAMES (A.). 1927- . Ref: CA.
  The Man from Greek and Roman. Random,
    1974; Hutchinson, 1975

GOLDMAN, LAWRENCE (LOUIS). SC: Johnny
  Saturday = JS.
  Black Fire. Ace, 1956
  Dangerous Design. Arcadia, 1952
  Fall Guy for Murder. Dutton, 1943; Gif-
    ford, 1945 JS [Calif.]
  -The Heart Merchants. Paperback Library,
    196?
  Judd for the Defense. Paperback Li-
    brary, 1968 (Novelization of the TV
    series.)
  Judd for the Defense #2: The Secret
    Listeners. Paperback Library, 1968
    (Novelization of the TV series.)
    [Houston]
  Tiger by the Tail. McKay, 1946 JS
    [Calif.]
  Wolf Tone. Mill, 1948

GOLDMAN, RAYMOND LESLIE. 1895- . Sur-
  vived polio, deafness and diabetes to
  become radio and magazine writer;
  was living in Nashville. SC: Asaph
  Clume = AC.
  Death Plays Solitaire. Coward, 1939;
    Boardman, 1945 AC [Midwest]
  The Hartwell Case. Skeffington, 1929
    [Calif.]
  Judge Robinson Murdered! Coward, 1936;
    Boardman, 1937
  Murder Behind the Mike. Coward, 1942;
    Boardman, 1943 AC [Midwest]
  The Murder of Harvey Blake. Skeffing-
    ton, 1931 AC [L.A.]
  Murder Without Motive. Coward, 1938 AC
    [Midwest]
  Out on Bail. Coward, 1937; Cassell,
    1938
  The Purple Shells. Ziff-Davis, 1947;
    Boardman, 1948 AC
  The Snatch. Coward, 1940; Boardman,
    1945 AC [Midwest]

GOLDMAN, WILLIAM (W.). 1931- . Pseudonym: Harry Longbaugh, q.v. Ref: CA.
  Marathon Man. Delacorte, 1974; Mac-
    millan (London), 1975 [NYC]

GOLDSMITH, FREDERIC
  Murder in Mayfair. Allen, 1954 (Novel-
    ization of a ss by Vera Caspary,
    1899- , q.v.)
  The Smugglers. Allen, 1955

GOLDSMITH, GENE. Ref: CC.
  Layout for a Corpse. Mill, 1949; Board-
    man, 1950 [S.F.]
  Murder on His Mind. Mill, 1947; Qual-
    ity, 1954 [NYC]

GOLDSMITH, JOHN. 1947- .
  The Icing of Balthazar. Cassell, 1977

GOLDSMITH, LOUIS C.
  The Streamlined Dragon. World's Work,
    1948

GOLDSMITH, MARTIN M.
  Detour. Macaulay, 1939; Hurst, 1939
    [S.W.]
  Double Jeopardy. Macaulay, 1938; Hurst,
    1938 [N.Y.]
  Shadows at Noon. Ziff-Davis, 1943

GOLDSMITH, NORMAN
  The Atlantic City Murder Mystery.
    Macaulay, 1936 [N.J.]

GOLDSTEIN, ARTHUR D(AVID). 1937- .
  Ref: CA, TC. Pseudonym: Albert Ross,
  q.v. SC: Max Guttman, in all titles.
  Nobody's Sorry He Got Killed. Random,
    1976 [Calif.]
  A Person Shouldn't Die Like That. Ran-
    dom, 1972; Prior, 1977 [NYC]
  You're Never Too Old to Die. Random,
    1974; Prior, 1977 [Calif.]

GOLDSTEIN, WILLIAM (ISAAC). 1932- .
  Ref: CA. SC: Dr. Phibes, in both
  titles, which are movie noveliza-
  tions.
  Dr. Phibes. Award, 1971
  Dr. Phibes Rises Again. Award, 1972

GOLDSTON, ROBERT C(ONROY). 1927- .
  Pseudonym: James Stark, q.v. Ref: CA.
  The Catafalque. Rinehart, 1958 [Sp.]

GOLDSTONE, LAWRENCE ARTHUR. 1903- .
  Original name of: Lawrence Treat,
  q.v.
  -Run Far, Run Fast. Greystone, 1937

GOLDTHWAITE, EATON K(ENNETH). 1907- .
  Ref: CA. SC: Lt. Joseph Dickerson =
  JD.
  The Body Next Door; see You Did It
  Cat and Mouse. Duell, 1946. British
    title: Cat and Mouse Murder. Jar-
    rolds, 1950. Also published as: Date
    with Death. Bantam, 1947; Corgi, 1962
    JD
  Cat and Mouse Murder; see Cat and Mouse
  Cut for Partners. Duell, 1951. Also
    published as: The Scarlet Spade.
    Ace, 1952 [Las Veg.]
  Date with Death; see Cat and Mouse
  Death Springs the Trap; see You Did It
  Don't Mention My Name. Duell, 1942
    [N.Y.]
  The Marble Forest. Doubleday, 1971;
    Hale, 1973 [NYC]
  Once You Stop, You're Dead. Morrow,
    1968
  Root of Evil. Duell, 1948 JD [Boston]
  Scarecrow. Duell, 1945; Jarrolds, 1948
    JD [Conn.]
  The Scarlet Spade; see Cut for Partners
  The Sixpenny Dame. Dodd, 1953 [L.I.]

You Did It. Duell, 1943; Jarrolds,
  1945. Also published as: Death
  Springs the Trap. Death House, 1944.
  And as: The Body Next Door. Handi-
  Books, 1946 JD

GOLLER, CELIA MARGARET. 1914- . Pseudonym: Celia Fremlin, q.v.

GOLLER, NICHOLAS
  Tomorrow's Silence. Macmillan (London),
    1979; St. Martin's, 1980

GOLLIN, JAMES. Yale graduate living in
  Conn.; worked in insurance, advertising and public relations; has had
  lifelong interest in music; author of
  two volumes of nonfiction.
  The Philomel Foundation. St. Martin's,
    1980; Magnum, 1982

GOLLOMB, JOSEPH. 1881-1950. SC: Galt = G.
  The Curtain of Storm. Macmillan, 1933
    G [NYC]
  The Girl in the Fog. Boni, 1923; Long,
    1924 [Eng.]
  Master Manhunters. Macaulay, 1926
    (Novelized true crime accounts.)
  The Portrait Invisible. Macmillan,
    1928; Heinemann, 1928 G [NYC]
  The Subtle Trail. Macaulay, 1929;
    Heinemann, 1930 G [NYC]

GOLSWORTHY, ARNOLD. 1865- .
  A Cry in the Night. Greening, 1899
  Death and the Woman. Favourite, 1898
  -Hands in the Darkness. Pearson, 1899;
    Fenno, 1900
  -The New Master. Pearson, 1901

GOMBROWICZ, WITOLD. 1904-1969. Ref: CA.
  -Possessed. Boyars, 1980 (Originally
    published in Polish in 1973.)

GOMPERTZ, MARTIN LOUIS ALAN. 1886-1951.
  Pseudonym: "Ganpat", q.v.

GONZALES, JOHN. Pseudonym of Robert Ter-
  rall, 1914- , q.v. Other pseudo-
  nym: Robert Kyle, q.v. See also:
  Brett Halliday. SC: Harry Horne = HH.
  Death for Mr. Big. GM, 1951; Fawcett
    (London), 1953
  End of a JD. GM, 1960 HH
  Follow That Hearse! GM, 1963 HH [South]
  The Magnificent Moll. Red Seal (U.S.),
    1952
  Someone's Sleeping in My Bed. GM, 1962;
    Muller pb, 1963 HH

GOOCH, R(ICHARD) H(EATHCOTE)
  Her Ladyship's Jewels and What Became
    of Them. [Author], 1870s

GOODALL, CEDRIC
  The Black Chalice. Melrose, 1935; Mac-
    aulay, 1935
  Death by Appointment. Pemberton, 1950
  The Destroyer; or, Adventures of the
    Scorpion. Modern, 1935
  Hidden Death. Blackie, 1935
  The House of Death. Gramol, 1934
  The Prisoner of the Priory. Gramol,
    1934
  -The Unicorn. Modern, 1935
  Without Trace. Hamilton, 1938

GOODCHILD, GEORGE. 1888-1969. Pseudonyms:
  Alan Dare, Jesse Templeton, qq.v. See
  also next entry. Ref: CC. Born in
  Eng.; worked as journalist and in
  publishing house before becoming full
  time writer. SC: Insp. McLean, in at
  least those marked M; Q (John Tre-
  lawny) = Q; Nigel Rex, in at least
  those marked NR. Set: Eng.
  Ace High. Hodder, 1927 [Can.]
  Again McLean. Hodder, 1939 M ss
  The Alaskan. Lloyds, 1921
  The Barton Mystery. Jarrolds, 1916
    (Novelization of the play by Walter
    Hackett, 1876-1944, q.v.)
  Behind That Door. Ward, 1943
  The Black Orchid. Hodder, 1926
  Brave Interlude. Ward, 1942
  Call McLean. Hodder, 1937 M ss
  Captain Crash. Hayes, 1924
  Captain Sinister. Hodder, 1933
  Cauldron Bubble. Macdonald, 1946
  Chief Inspector McLean. Hodder, 1932 M
    ss
  The Clock Struck Seven. Hale, 1939
  -Colorado Jim; or, The Taming of Angela.
    Hayes, 1920; Watt, 1922
  Companion to Sirius. Rich, 1949 M
  The Compassionate Rogue. Jarrolds, 1920
  The Crimson Domino. Simpkin, 1919. Also
    published as by Jesse Templeton:
    Mellifont, 1933 ss
  Danger Below. Hodder pb, 1937
  The Danger Line. Jarrolds, 1958
  Dear Conspirator. Ward, 1948

Death on the Centre Court. Hodder, 1935; Green Circle, 1936 M
Double Acrostic. Jarrolds, 1954 M
-Down "Plug Street" Way, and other stories. Simpkin, 1918 ss
East of Singapore. Mellifont, 1946
The Efford Tangle. Rich, 1950 M
-The Elephant; or, The Man from Beyond. Hodder, 1929
The Emperor of Hallelujah Island. Hodder, 1930; Houghton, 1931
False Intruder. Jarrolds, 1960
Final Score. Ward, 1950
Find the Lady. Rich, 1955 M ss
Follow McLean. Jarrolds, 1961 M
-The Footlight's Call. Mellifont, 1945
For Reasons Unknown. Hodder, 1932
Forced Landing. Hodder, 1940
Forever McLean. Jarrolds, 1957 M ss
-The Girl at Pine Creek. Thomson, 1930
-The Girl Who Failed Him. Thomson, 1930
-The Great Alone. Simpkin, 1919 ss
Hail McLean! Hodder, 1945 M ss
Having No Hearts. Hodder, 1937 M
-The Homeward Trail. Newnes, 1935
How Now, McLean? Hodder, 1931 M ss
-Hurricane Tex. Hodder, 1925
Infamous Gentleman. Hale, 1938
Inspector McLean's Casebook. Rich, 1949 M ss
Inspector McLean's Holiday; see McLean Takes a Holiday
Jack O'Lantern. Hodder, 1929; Mystery League, 1930
-Jim Goes North. Hodder, 1926
-Klondyke Kit's Revenge. Jenkins, 1923
Knight Takes Queen. Newnes, 1935
Knock and Come In. Ward, 1935 NR
Known as Z.1. Ward, 1940
Lady Take Care. Ward, 1946
-The Land of Eldorado. Jarrolds, 1919
-The Last Cruise of the "Majestic". Simpkin, 1917
The Last Ditch. Mellifont, 1944
The Last Redoubt. Rich, 1952 M
The Last Secret. Rich, 1956 [Afr.]
Laurels for McLean. Jarrolds, 1964 M ss
Lead On, McLean! Hodder, 1936 M ss
McLean at the Golden Owl. Hodder, 1930 M ss
McLean Carries On. Rich, 1950 M ss
McLean Deduces. Hodder, 1940 M ss
McLean Disposes. Jarrolds, 1958 M ss
McLean Excels. Hodder, 1939 M ss
McLean Finds a Way. Hodder, 1936 M ss
McLean Incomparable. Hodder, 1938 M ss
McLean Intervenes. Hodder, 1939 M ss
McLean Investigates. Hodder, 1930 M ss
McLean Invincible. Jarrolds, 1963. M ss
McLean Keeps Going. Hodder, 1941 M ss
McLean Knows Best. Hodder, 1935 M ss
McLean Knows the Answers. Long, 1967 M ss
McLean: Non-Stop. Hodder, 1941 M ss
McLean of Scotland Yard. Hodder, 1929 M ss
McLean Plays a Hand. Ward, 1934 M
McLean Predominant. Rich, 1951 M ss
McLean Prevails. Ward, 1935 M ss
McLean Remembers! Hodder, 1936 M
McLean Scores Again. Jarrolds, 1959 M ss
McLean Sees It Through. Hodder, 1939 M
McLean Solves It. Rich, 1956 M ss
McLean Steps In. Rich, 1952 M M
McLean Takes a Holiday. Hodder, 1942. Revised edition: Inspector McLean's Holiday. Pan, 1951 M
McLean Takes Charge. Hodder, 1937 M ss
McLean Takes Over. Long, 1966 M ss
McLean the Magnificent. Hodder, 1940 M ss
McLean to the Dark Tower Came. Rich, 1951 M
Mad Mike. Chapman, 1934
The Man from the West. Thomson, 1929. Reprinted as by Jesse Templeton: Mellifont, 1933
The Man from the West, and other stories of adventure. Newnes, 1935 ss
-Man Peter. Ward, 1941
-The Man Who Wasn't. Jenkins, 1924 [Can.]
Mister Q33. Newnes, 1935 Q
The Monster of Grammont. Hodder, 1927; Mystery League, 1930 [Fr.]
-Mountain Gold. Hodder, 1933
A Murder Will Be Committed. Hale, 1937
-Mushalong. Hayes, 1934
Next of Kin. Jarrolds, 1957 M ss
No Exit. Newnes, 1936
Operator No. 19. Ward, 1937
-Petticoat Lane. Mellifont, 1932
The Public Defender; see The Splendid Crime
Q33. Odhams, 1933 Q [Ger.]
Q33—Spy Catcher. Newnes, 1937 Q ss
Quest of Nigel Rex. Ward, 1934 NR
The Rain on the Roof. Hodder, 1928
-Rivers to Cross. Ward, 1947
The Road to Marrakesh. Hodder, 1931; Houghton, 1932 [Mor.]

-Rough Going. Ward, 1936
Safety Last. Ward, 1944
Savage Encounter. Jarrolds, 1962 M
The Spanish Steps. Ward, 1951 [Rome]
The Splendid Crime. Hodder, 1930; Houghton, 1930. Also published as: The Public Defender. Grosset, 1931
The Square Deal. Modern, 193? [Can.]
-Steve. Hale, 1936
-Stout Cortez. Ward, 1949
-Summer Moon. Leng, 1936
-Tall Timber. Hodder, 1927; Watt, 1924
-The Taming of Nancy. Thomson, 1925
This Woman Is Wanted. Newnes, 1936
Tiger, Tiger. Jarrolds, 1959 M ss
The Triumph of McLean. Hodder, 1933; Houghton, 1933 M
Trooper O'Neill. Hayes, 1921; Watt, 1923 ss [Can.]
Trust McLean. Rich, 1954 M
Uncle Oscar's Niece. Hodder, 1944 M
Up, McLean! Hodder, 1940 M
-The Valley of Lies. Long, 1923
Watch McLean. Rich, 1955 M
Well Caught, McLean! Rich, 1953 M
-Wise Virgin. Mellifont, 1945
The Woollen Monkey. Lloyds, 1920
-Yellowstones. Ward, 1938
Yes, Inspector McLean. Hodder, 1934 M

GOODCHILD, GEORGE, 1888-1969, and (CARL ERIC) BECHHOFER ROBERTS, 1894-1949. See also: previous entry. Pseudonyms of George Goodchild: Alan Dare, Jesse Templeton, qq.v. Pseudonym of Roberts: Ephesian, q.v. Set: Eng.
The Dear Old Gentleman. Jarrolds, 1935; Harper, 1936
The Jury Disagree. Jarrolds, 1934; Macmillan, 1935
The Prisoner's Friend. Jarrolds, 1938
Tidings of Joy. Jarrolds, 1936
We Shot an Arrow. Gollancz, 1939

GOODE, BILL. Pseudonym of William F. Goodykoontz. Born in W. Va.; educated in law; sports and police reporter; covered congress for International News Service.
The Senator's Nude. Ziff-Davis, 1947 [Wash. D.C.]

GOODE, GEORGE W.
King Dan, the Factory Detective. Katahdin, 1896
The Post-Office Detective; or, A Mystery of the Mails. Street, 1888

GOODFIELD, (GWYNETH) JUNE. 1927- .
Ref: CA.
Courier to Peking. Hart-Davis, 1973; Dutton, 1973

GOODHART, HONOR (MAHON). See: Lionel (Peel) Yates.

GOODING, KATHLEEN
Belfriere. Wingate, 1976; Berkley, 1978

GOODIS, DAVID. 1917-1967. Ref: CA, CC.
Behold This Woman. Appleton, 1947
Black Friday. Lion, 1954
The Blonde on the Street Corner. Lion, 1954
The Burglar. Lion, 1953 [N.J.]
Cassidy's Girl. GM, 1951; Red Seal, 1958
The Dark Chase; see Nightfall
Dark Passage. Messner, 1946; Heinemann, 1947 [S.F.]
Down There. GM, 1956; Fawcett (London), 1958. Also published as: Shoot the Piano Player. Black Cat, 1962
Fire in the Flesh. GM, 1957; Fawcett (London), 1958 [Phil.]
The Moon in the Gutter. GM, 1953
Night Squad. GM, 1961; Fawcett (London), 1962
Nightfall. Messner, 1947; Heinemann, 1948. Also published as: The Dark Chase. Lion, 1953 [NYC]
Of Missing Persons. Morrow, 1950 [L.A.]
-Of Tender Sin. GM, 1952
Retreat from Oblivion. Dutton, 1939
Shoot the Piano Player; see Down There
Somebody's Done For. Banner, 1967
Street of No Return. GM, 1954; Red Seal, 1958
Street of the Lost. GM, 1952; Fawcett (London), 1959
The Wounded and the Slain. GM, 1955; Red Seal, 1959

GOODKIND, HOWARD. Publishing editor and executive. See: Norman Garbo, 1919- .

GOODMAN, E(DWARD) J(OHN). 1836-
The Fate of Herbert Wayne. Chatto, 1892
-His Other Self. Ward, 1889
The Only Witness: What Did She See? Trischler, 1891

-Paid in His Own Coin. Bentley, 1888
-Too Curious. Bentley, 1887; Lippincott, 1888

GOODMAN, G. S.
The Mysterious Abduction. Greening, 1908

GOODMAN, GEORGE (JEROME WALDO), 1930- , and WINTHROP KNOWLTON.
A Killing in the Market. Doubleday, 1958; Macdonald, 1958, as by Winthrop Goodman [NYC]

GOODMAN, JONATHAN. 1931- . Ref: CA. Set: Eng.
Criminal Tendencies. Long, 1964
Hello Cruel World, Goodbye. Long, 1964
Instead of Murder. Hammond, 1961
The Last Sentence. Hutchinson, 1978; St. Martin's, 1980

GOODMAN, WINTHROP. See: George (Jerome Waldo) Goodman, 1930- .

GOODNER, MARIE B. Pseudonym: Marye Adams, q.v.

GOODRICH, DAVID L(LOYD). 1930- . Ref: CA.
Paint Me a Million. Putnam, 1978 [NYC]

GOODRUM, CHARLES A(LVIN). 1923- . Ref: CA. SC: Edwin George, in both titles.
Carnage of the Realm. Crown, 1979. British title: Dead for a Penny. Gollancz, 1980 [Wash. D.C.]
Dead for a Penny; see Carnage of the Realm
Dewey Decimated. Crown, 1977; Curley, 1978 [Wash. D.C.]

GOODSPEED, EDGAR J(OHNSON). 1871-1962. Ref: CA.
The Curse in the Colophon. Willett Clark, 1935

GOODWIN, I(NGE DOROTHEA ROSI). 1923- .
Bury Me in Lead. Wingate, 1952

GOODWIN, JOHN. Pseudonym of Sidney (Floyd) Gowing, 1878- , q.v. SC: Det.-Sgt./Supt. Scarfe, in at least those marked S. Set: Eng.
Above the Law. Jenkins, 1936
The Avenger. Putnam, 1926 (British title?)
Blackmail. Amalgamated, 1910
Blood Money. Putnam (London), 1931; Sears, 1932
Dead Man's Treasure. Putnam (London), 1929. U.S. title: Let It Lie. Putnam (NYC), 1929
-Helen of London. Jenkins, 1923
The House of Marney. Jenkins, 1923. U.S. title: The Sign of the Serpent. Putnam (NYC), 1923
In Full Cry. Jenkins, 1941 S
Jennifer. Jenkins, 1934
The King's Elm Mystery. Jenkins, 1934
Let It Lie; see Dead Man's Treasure
Mafalda. Hodder, 1925
The Man with the Brooding Eyes; see Paid in Full
Paid in Full. Jenkins, 1921. U.S. title: The Man with the Brooding Eyes. Putnam, 1921
The Shadow Man. Putnam (London), 1932; Sears, 1932 S
The Sign of the Serpent; see The House of Marney
The Spider Woman. Jenkins, 1920
The Stronger Hand. Hodder, 1926
When Dead Men Tell Tales. Putnam, 1928 (British title?) [Scot.]
Without Mercy. Jenkins, 1920; Putnam, 1920

GOODWIN, JOHN C(UTHBERT). 1891-
Diamonds and Hearts. Hutchinson, 1927
-The Zig-Zag Man. Hutchinson, 1925

GOODWIN, RALPH A.
The Stoenberg Affair. Sully, 1913 [Ger.]

GOODYKOONTZ, WILLIAM F. Pseudonym: Bill Goode, q.v.

GORDON, A. C.
Solve-A-Crime. Foulsham, 1980 puzzle ss

GORDON, ALEX. Pseudonym of Gordon Cotler, 1923- , q.v.
The Cipher. Simon, 1961; Boardman, 1962 [NYC]

GORDON, ARTHUR. 1912- . Ref: CA.
Reprisal. Simon, 1950; H. Hamilton, 1950 [Ga.]

GORDON, CHARLES WILLIAM. 1860-1937. Pseudonym: Ralph Connor, q.v.

GORDON, DIANA. Pseudonym of Lucille Andrews. Other pseudonym: Joanna Marcus, q.v.
　A Few Days in Endel. Corgi, 1968; Ace, 1973. Reprinted as by Joanna Marcus: Barrie, 1978

GORDON, DONALD. Pseudonym of Donald Gordon Payne, 1924-　. Ref: CA.
　The Flight of the Bat. Hodder, 1963; Morrow, 1964
　The Golden Oyster. Hodder, 1967; Morrow, 1968
　Leap in the Dark. Hodder, 1970; Morrow, 1971

GORDON, ETHEL (EDISON). 1915-　. Ref: CA.
　The Birdwatcher. McKay, 1974; Barker, 1975 [Scot.]
　The Chaperone. Coward, 1973; Barker, 1974 [Fr.]
　The Freebody Heiress. McKay, 1975; Barker, 1974 [Vt.]
　Freer's Cove. Coward, 1972 [Maine]

GORDON, FRITZ. Joint pseudonym of Frederick Gordon Jarvis, Jr., 1930-　, and Robert F. Van Beever. Ref on Jarvis: CA. SC: Schuyler Townsend, in both titles.
　The Flight of the Bamboo Saucer. Award, 1967
　Tonight They Die to Mendelssohn. Award, 1968

GORDON, GILES (ALEXANDER ESME). 1940-　. Ref: CA.
　Girl with Red Hair. Hutchinson, 1974

GORDON, GORDON. 1906-　. See: The Gordons. Ref: CA.

GORDON, HAVA
　Dead on Arrival. Modern Fiction, 1953 [NYC]
　Devil's Coffin. Modern Fiction, 1953

GORDON, IAN (DOUGLAS FELLOWES). 1921-　. Ref: CA.
　After Innocence. Dell, 1955
　The Big Success. Dell, 1956; World Distributors, 1957
　The Burden of Guilt. Simon, 1951 [NYC]
　Deep Is My Desire; see The Whip Hand
　Harlem Is My Heaven; see The Night Thorn
　The Night Thorn. Dial, 1952. Also published as: Harlem Is My Heaven. Berkley, 1957
　The Whip Hand. Crown, 1954. Also published as: Deep Is My Desire. Popular Library, 1955

GORDON, JAMES. 1912-　. Pseudonym: John Foss, q.v.

GORDON, JAN. 1882-1944. Pseudonym: William Gore, q.v.

GORDON, JANE
　Mistress of Mount Fair. Lancer, 1965

GORDON, JOHN V.
　The Ethical Solution. North Country, 1976
　Missing, Presumed Dead. North Country, 1976

GORDON, JULIEN. Pseudonym of Julie Grinnell Cruger, 　-1920.
　-A Diplomat's Diary. Lippincott, 1890; Routledge, 1890

GORDON, KURTZ. Pseudonym of C. Gordon Kurtz, 1902-　, q.v. All titles are plays with number of acts given in parenthesis.
　The Black Ace. Fitzgerald, 1934
　The Bride's Bouquet. Dramatists, 1968 (3)
　Dressed to Kill. Baker, 1949 (3)
　Fair Exchange. Dramatists, 1959 (3)
　Murder Sails at Midnight. Baker, 1938 (3)
　Not for Sale. Baker, 1950 (3)

GORDON, LESLIE HOWARD
　The Camp of Fear. Hodder, 1920
　-The Gates of Tien T'ze. Hodder, 1920
　-The House of Night. Hodder, 1921; Small, 1921
　-The Land of Big Things. Hodder, 1918
　-The Little Brother of God. Hodder, 1919
　-The Little Lady of the Shot-Gun. Hodder, 1917

GORDON, MAX
　The Dead Say No. Warren, 1952
　I Never Killed. Warren, 1952
　Look Down for Mercy. Warren, 1952
　Why Squeal on Me? Warren, 1952

GORDON, MILDRED. 1912-1979. See also: The Gordons. Ref: CA.
　The Little Man Who Wasn't There. Doubleday, 1946 [Ariz.]

GORDON, NEIL. Pseudonym of Archibald Gordon Macdonell, 1895-1941. Other pseudonym: John Cameron, q.v. Joint pseudonym with Millward Rodon Kennedy Burge, 1894-1968, q.v.: Robert Milward Kennedy, q.v. Ref: CC, MP. SC: Peter Kerrigan = PK. Set: Eng.
　The Big Ben Alibi. Lane, 1930
　The Factory on the Cliff. Longmans, 1928. U.S. title: The New Gun Runners. Harcourt, 1928 [Scot.]
　Murder in Earl's Court. Lane, 1931　PK
　The New Gun Runners; see The Factory on the Cliff
　The Professor's Poison. Longmans, 1928; Harcourt, 1928
　The Shakespeare Murders. Barker, 1933; Holt, 1933　PK
　The Silent Murders. Longmans, 1929; Doubleday, 1930

GORDON, NOAH. 1926-　. Ref: CA.
　The Jerusalem Diamond. Random, 1979; Deutsch, 1979 [Isr.]

GORDON, PATRICIA. 1909-　. Ref: CA.
　Brief Suspicion. Evans, 1960 (3-act play.)

GORDON, PETER
　The Case of the Missing Bullion. Baker, 1969

GORDON, R(ICHARD) L(AURENCE)
　The River Gets Wider. Crowell, 1974; Hart-Davis, 1975

GORDON, RICHARD. Pseudonym of Gordon Ostlere, 1921-　. Born in London; a doctor and specialist in anesthetics, who became a full-time writer in 1952.
　Jack the Ripper; see The Private Life of Jack the Ripper
　The Medical Witness. Heinemann, 1971. U.S. title: Witness for the Crown. Simon, 1971
　The Private Life of Jack the Ripper. Collins, 1980. U.S. title: Jack the Ripper. Atheneum, 1980 [Eng., 1888]
　Witness for the Crown; see The Medical Witness

GORDON, RUSSELL
　Dead Level. Morrow, 1948. Also published as: She Posed for Death. Avon, 1950 [L.A.]

GORDON, SAMUEL. 1871-1927.
　The Avenger. Macaulay, 1921

GORDON, SPIKE. House name. Used by F(rank) Dubrez Fawcett, 1891-1968, q.v. Other Fawcett pseudonyms: Griff, Ben Sarto, Elmer Eliot Saks, qq.v. Also used by John Russell Fearn, 1908-1960, q.v. Other Fearn pseudonyms: Hugo Blayn, Volsted Gribban, Griff, Nat Karta, John Slate, qq.v.
　The Big Fix. Modern Fiction, 1953
　Doctor Samovar, Crook. Modern Fiction, 1953
　Don't Tempt the Hangman. Modern Fiction, 1953
　Don't Touch Me (by John Russell Fearn). Modern Fiction, 1953
　Gale Gallyon Takes a Hand. Modern Fiction, 1951
　I Don't Get It. Modern Fiction, 1953
　She Means Trouble. Modern Fiction, 1953
　Taken for Dollars. Modern Fiction, 1953
　Unhappy Hophead. Modern Fiction, 1953
　You Take the Rap. Modern Fiction, 1953
　You're No Lady. Modern Fiction, 1953

GORDON, WELCHE
　Jesse James, and His Band of Notorious Outlaws. Laird, 1890
　Jim the Penman. Laird, 1891

GORDONS, THE. Byline of Gordon Gordon, 1906-　, and Mildred Gordon, 1912-1979, q.v. Ref: EM, TC. SC: D. C. Randall (a cat) = DC; John Ripley = JR; Gail and Mitch = G&M.
　The Big Frame. Doubleday, 1957; Macdonald, 1957 [Calif.]
　Campaign Train. Doubleday, 1952; Wingate, 1952. Also published as: Murder Rides the Campaign Train. Bantam, 1956 [train]
　Captive. Doubleday, 1957; Macdonald, 1958　JR [Ariz.]
　Case File: FBI. Doubleday, 1953; Macdonald, 1954　JR [Chi.]
　The Case of the Talking Bug. Doubleday, 1955. British title: Playback. Macdonald, 1955 [Calif.]
　Catnapped: The Further Adventures of Undercover Cat. Doubleday, 1974; Macdonald, 1975　DC [L.A.]
　Experiment in Terror; see Operation Terror
　FBI Story. Doubleday, 1950; Corgi, 1957　JR [Chi.]
　The Informant. Doubleday, 1973; Macdonald, 1973　JR [L.A.]
　Journey with a Stranger; see Menace
　Make Haste to Live. Doubleday, 1950 [Ariz.]
　Menace. Doubleday, 1962. British title: Journey with a Stranger. Macdonald, 1963 [Far East]
　Murder Rides the Campaign Train; see Campaign Train
　Night After the Wedding. Doubleday, 1979; Macdonald, 1980　G&M
　Night Before the Wedding. Doubleday, 1969; Macdonald, 1969　G&M [L.A.]
　Operation Terror. Doubleday, 1961; Macdonald, 1961. Also published as: Experiment in Terror. Bantam, 1962　JR [L.A.]
　Ordeal. Doubleday, 1976; Macdonald, 1977 [Ariz.]
　Playback; see The Case of the Talking Bug
　Power Play. Doubleday, 1965; Macdonald, 1966 [Wash. D.C.]
　That Darn Cat; see Undercover Cat
　Tiger on My Back. Doubleday, 1960; Macdonald, 1960 [Mor.]
　Undercover Cat. Doubleday, 1963; Macdonald, 1964. Also published as: That Darn Cat. Bantam, 1966; Corgi, 1966　DC [L.A.]
　Undercover Cat Prowls Again. Doubleday, 1966; Macdonald, 1967　DC [L.A.]

GORE, MRS. [CATHERINE GRACE FRANCES MOODY]. 1799-1861.
　Craigallen Castle; or, The Stolen Will. Garrett, 1852

GORE, WILLIAM. Pseudonym of Jan Gordon, 1882-1944. SC: Insp. Penk = P. Set: Eng.
　Death in the Wheelbarrow. Harrap, 1935; Mystery House, 1940, as by Jan Gordon　P
　Murder Most Artistic. Harrap, 1937. U.S. title: The Mystery of the Painted Nude. Doubleday, 1938　P
　The Mystery of the Painted Nude; see Murder Most Artistic
　There's Death in the Churchyard. Harrap, 1934

GORE-BROWNE, ROBERT. 1893-　. Ref: CC. SC: Lucien Clay, in at least those marked LC. Set: Eng.
　By Way of Confession; see Death on Delivery
　-The Crater. Collins, 1925; Doran, 1926
　Death on Delivery. Collins, 1929. U.S. title: By Way of Confession. Doubleday, 1930　LC
　-An Imperfect Lover. Collins, 1928; Doubleday, 1929
　In Search of a Villain; see Murder of an M.P.
　Murder of an M.P. Collins, 1927. U.S. title: In Search of a Villain. Doubleday, 1928　LC

GORELL, LORD. 1884-　. Given name: Ronald Gorell Barnes, q.v. SC: Insp. Harry Farrant = HF; Insp. Maurice Hepburn = MH; Insp. Gordon Ross = GR; Evelyn Temple = ET (see also the Barnes entry). Set: Eng.
　D.E.Q. Murray, 1922　MH,ET?
　Devil's Drum. Murray, 1929　MH
　The Devouring Fire. Murray, 1928　HF
　Earl's End. Ward, 1951
　"He Who Fights..." Murray, 1928
　Let Not Thy Left Hand. Ward, 1949　GR
　Murder at Manor House. Ward, 1954　GR
　Murder at Mavering. Murray, 1943　MH
　Red Lilac. Murray, 1935　MH,HF,ET
　Venturers All. Murray, 1927
　Where There's a Head. Ward, 1952

GORES, JOE [JOSEPH N. GORES]. 1931-　. Ref: CA, TC. SC: Daniel Kearney Associates = DKA.
　Dead Skip. Random, 1972; Gollancz, 1973　DKA [S.F.]
　Final Notice. Random, 1973; Gollancz, 1974　DKA [S.F.]
　Gone, No Forwarding. Random, 1978; Gollancz, 1979　DKA [S.F.]
　Hammett. Putnam, 1975; Macdonald, 1976 [S.F., 1928]

Interface. Evans, 1974; Futura, 1977
  [S.F.]
A Time of Predators. Random, 1969;
  Allen, 1970 [S.F.]

GORING, ANNE
Morwenna. Macdonald, 1976; St. Martin's, 1976

GORON, M(ARIE) F(RANCOIS). 1847-1933.
The Red Nights of Paris. Dillingham, 1912 [Paris]
The Truth About the Case. Lippincott, 1907. British title: The World of Crime: True Detective Stories. Hurst, 1907 ss [Paris]
The World of Crime; see The Truth About the Case

GOSHGARIAN, GARY. A university English teacher; a certified scuba diver.
Atlantis Fire. Dial, 1980 [Greece]

GOSLING, PAULA. Born in Detroit, has worked in advertising, lives in England.
Fair Game; see A Running Duck
Loser's Blues. Macmillan (London), 1980. U.S. title: Solo Blues. Coward, 1981
A Running Duck. Macmillan (London), 1978. U.S. title (expanded and revised): Fair Game. Coward, 1978 [S.F.]
Solo Blues; see Loser's Blues
The Zero Trap. Macmillan (London), 1979; Coward, 1980 [Arctic]

GOSSELIN, LOUIS LEON THEODORE. 1857-1925.
Pseudonym: G. Lenotre, q.v.

GOTTFRIED, THEODORE MARK. 1928-   .
Pseudonyms: Harry Gregory, Katherine Tobias, qq.v.

GOTTLIEB, ANNIE. Book reviewer and article writer living in NYC. See: Jacques Sandulescu.

GOTTLIEB, NATHAN
Stinger. Jove, 1978 [N.J.]

GOTTLIEB, PAUL. 1936-   . Ref: CA.
Agency. Musson (Ontario), 1974; Hale, 1975

GOUD, ANNE. 1917-   . Pseudonym: Anne-Mariel, q.v.

GOUGH, GEORGE W(OOLEY). 1869-   .
-A Daughter of Kings. Skeffington, 1930
My Lady Vamp. Methuen, 1926
The Terror by Night. Blackwood, 1922 ss

GOULART, RON(ALD JOSEPH). 1933-   .
Pseudonym: Josephine Kains, q.v. See also: Kenneth Robeson. Ref: CA, TC. SC: John Easy = JE; Cleopatra Jones (in novelizations of movies) = CJ.
After Things Fell Apart. Ace, 1970; Arrow, 1975
Calling Dr. Patchwork. Daw, 1978
Capricorn One. GM, 1978
Cleopatra Jones. Paperback Library, 1973 CJ
Cleopatra Jones and the Casino of Gold. Paperback Library, 1975 CJ
The Enormous Hour Glass. Award, 1975
Ghost Breaker. Ace, 1971 ss [Calif.]
Ghosting. Raven, 1980 [Conn.]
Hawkshaw. Doubleday, 1972; Hale, 1973
If Dying Was All. Ace, 1971 JE [Calif.]
Odd Job No. 101, and other future crimes and intrigues. Scribner, 1975; Hale, 1976 ss [future]
One Grave Too Many. Ace, 1974 JE [Calif.]
The Same Lie Twice. Ace, 1973 JE [Calif.]
Skyrocket Steele. PB, 1980
Spacehawk, Inc. Daw, 1974
The Sword Swallower. Doubleday, 1968 [future]
Too Sweet to Die. Ace, 1972 JE [Calif.]
What's Become of Screwloose? and other inquiries. Scribner, 1971; Sidgwick, 1971 ss, criminous in part [future]

GOULD, ANTHONY
-The Faithful Achates. Judge, 1889
A Woman of Sorek. American News, 1889

GOULD, CHESTER. 1900-   . SC: Dick Tracy, in all titles, which are, with one exception noted, collected newspaper comic strips.
The Celebrated Cases of Dick Tracy, 1931-1951. Chelsea, 1970
Dick Tracy and the Woo Woo Sisters. Dell, 1947 (A novel, not a strip.)
Dick Tracy: The Thirties—Tommy Guns and Hard Times. Chelsea, 1978

The Exploits of Dick Tracy, Detective: The Case of the Brow. Rosdon, 1946
Pruneface. GM, 1975
Snowflake and Shaky. GM, 1975

GOULD, HEYWOOD. SC: Josh Krales = JK.
Deadline for Murder. Panther, 1977 (U.S. title?)
Glitterburn. St. Martin's, 1977 JK
One Dead Debutante. St. Martin's, 1975 JK [NYC]

GOULD, JAY REID. 1906-   . Ref: CA.
Running Tide. Dramatic, 1952 (1-act play.)

GOULD, MAGGY
The Dowry. Morrow, 1949; Wingate, 1950

GOULD, NAT(HANIEL). 1857-1919.
Chased by Fire; or, A Stable Mystery. Ogilvie, 1905 (British title?)
-A Dangerous Stable. Long, 1922
The Dark Horse. Routledge, 1899
-A Dead Certainty. Routledge, 1900
The Doctor's Double. Routledge, 1896
The Exploits of a Race-Course Detective. Long, 1927 ss
-The Jockey's Revenge. Long, 1909
A Lad of Mettle. Routledge, 1897
Landed at Last. Routledge, 1899
-A Racecourse Tragedy. Everett, 1901
A Stable Mystery, and other stories. Robinson, 1921 ss
-The Stolen Race. Long, 1909
-A Turf Conspiracy. Long, 1916
-Warned Off. Everett, 1901
Who Did It? Routledge, 1896 [Australia]

GOULD, STEPHEN. Pseudonym of Steve Fisher (Stephen Gould Fisher), 1912-1980, q.v. Other pseudonym: Grant Lane, q.v. SC: Sheridan Doome = SD (see also Fisher entry).
Homicide Johnny. Mystery House, 1940; Pemberton, 1946. Reprinted as by Steve Fisher: Popular Library, 1950 [Calif.]
Murder of the Admiral. Macaulay, 1936 SD [ship]

GOULDEN, PIERCE
The Compassionate Crook. Eldon, 1939
Death Rope Island. Eldon, 1934
The Golden Scarab. Eldon, 1939

GOULDING, EDMUND. 1891-   .
The Ryan Girl. French (NYC), 1946 (3-act play.)

GOUZE, ROGER
A Quiet Game of Bambu. Doubleday, 1964 (Translation of "La Partie de Bambu." Paris, 1963.) [Fr.]

GOVAN, (MARY) CHRISTINE NOBLE. 1898-   . Pseudonyms: Mary Allerton, J. N. Darby, qq.v. Ref: CA.
Murder on the Mountain. Houghton, 1937
Plantation Murder. Houghton, 1938 [S.C.]

GOVER, (JOHN) ROBERT. 1929-   . Ref: CA.
The Maniac Responsible. Grove, 1963; MacGibbon, 1964

GOWING, SIDNEY (FLOYD). 1878-   . Pseudonym: John Goodwin, q.v.
-Heather-Bells. Hodder, 1927
Held to Ransom. Jenkins, 1924
-Kim Ruff. Jenkins, 1925
-Sea Lavender. Hodder, 1925; Holt, 1925
Sealed Orders. Putnam (London), 1929; Putnam (NYC), 1929, as by John Goodwin

GOYDER, MARGOT. 1903-   . Joint pseudonym with Aune Neville Goyder Joske, 1893-   : Margot Neville, q.v.

GOYNE, RICHARD. 1902-1957. Pseudonym: John Courage, q.v. SC: Supt. "Tubby" Greene = TG; The Padre = P; Paul Templeton = PT. Set: Eng.
The Broken Circle. Federation, 1926
The Cinema Crime. Amalgamated, 1933 (Sexton Blake.)
-The Clock. Paul, 1950
The Courtway Case. Paul, 1951 P
The Crime Philosopher. Paul, 1945 P
Danger in Suburbia. Paul, 1939
The Dark Mind. Paul, 1948 P
The Darkened Room. Paul, 1952
Daughter of Darkness. Paul, 1953
Death by Desire. Paul, 1936; Macaulay, 1937 PT
Death in Harbour. Paul, 1937 PT
Destination Unknown. Paul, 1945
Fear Haunts the Fells. Paul, 1944 PT
The Fentons. Paul, 1956
Five Roads Inn. Paul, 1944 PT
Fugitive Men. Long, 1957
The Gravel Patch. Paul, 1953

The Great Fear. Aldine, 1927
Hanged I'll Be! Paul, 1936 PT
Harvest of Hate. Paul, 1952
In the Last Act. Aldine, 1927
Introducing the Super. Paul, 1955 TG
-The Invisible Verdict. Paul, 1950
The Last Shot and other stories. Federation, 1925 ss
The Kidnapper's Victim. Amalgamated, 1934 (Sexton Blake.)
The Lipstick Clue. Paul, 1954
The Man in the Trilby Hat. Paul, 1946
The Merrylees Mystery. Paul, 1939 PT
The Missing Minx. Paul, 1957 TG [Wales]
Murder at the Inn. Paul, 1935 PT
Murder Made Easy. Paul, 1944 PT
Murderer's Moon. Paul, 1949 PT
Overnight. Paul, 1953
Parisian Nights. Federation, 1925 (Novelization of the movie.)
Produce the Body. Paul, 1935 PT
Savarin's Shadow. Paul, 1947 P
Seven Were Suspect. Paul, 1938 PT
Strange Motives. Paul, 1934 PT
Suicide Squad. Paul, 1942
Traitor's Tide. Paul, 1948 P
Who Killed My Wife? Paul, 1940 PT
You Can't Kill Shadows. Paul, 1954

GRAAF, PETER. Pseudonym of (Christopher) Samuel Youd, 1922-   , q.v. Other pseudonyms: John Christopher, Hilary Ford, Peter Nichols, qq.v. SC: Joe Dust, in at least those marked JD. Set: Eng.
Daughter Fair. Joseph, 1958; Washburn, 1958 JD
Dust and the Curious Boy. Joseph, 1957. U.S. title: Give the Devil His Due. Mill, 1957 JD
Give the Devil His Due; see Dust and the Curious Boy
-The Gull's Kiss. Davies, 1962
The Sapphire Conference. Joseph, 1959; Washburn, 1959 JD [acad.]

GRABER, GEORGE ALEXANDER. 1914-   .
Pseudonym: Alexander Cordell, q.v.

GRABLE, MARSHA. Pseudonym of Wilbur Braun, 1896-   , q.v. Other pseudonyms: Walter Blake, Bruce Brandon, Fred Caldwell, Raymond Dumkey, Nan Fleming, Edwin F. Hornung, Jed Parish, Basil Ring, Orville Snap, Mortimer Sprague, Bert Stoner, qq.v.
What Price Murder? French (NYC), 1957 (1-act play.)

GRABO, CARL (HENRY). 1881-   . See: Herbert O(sborn) Yardley, 1889-

GRACE, ALICIA. Pseudonym of Irving A. Greenfield.
The Enchanted Circle. Lancer, 1968
Hawksbill Manor. Lancer, 1967 [W.I.]
The Head of Medusa. Lancer, 1967. Also published as: Hour of Evil. Belmont, 1973
Hour of Evil; see The Head of Medusa
The House at Swansea. Manor, 1976
House of the Darkest Death. Manor, 1976
Mass for a Dead Witch. Lancer, 1969
The Terrified Heart; see The Terrified Target
The Terrified Target. Lancer, 1966. Also published as: The Terrified Heart. Belmont, 1973
Wharf Sinister. Lancer, 1969 [NYC, ca.1860]

GRACE, ANITA. Pseudonym: Gail St. John, q.v.

GRADY, FRANK P.
Sergeant Death. Mussey, 1936 [N.Y.]

GRADY, JAMES (THOMAS). 1949-   . Ref: CA. SC: Richard Malcolm (The Condor), in both titles.
Shadow of the Condor. Putnam, 1975; Hodder, 1976 [Mont.]
Six Days of the Condor. Norton, 1974; Hodder, 1975. Also published as: Three Days of the Condor. Dell, 1975 [Wash. D.C.]
Three Days of the Condor; see Six Days of the Condor

GRADY, RONAN CALISTUS, JR. 1921-   .
Pseudonym: John Murphy, q.v.

GRAEME, BRUCE. Pseudonym of Graham Montague Jeffries, 1900- . Other pseudonyms: David Graeme, Roderic Hastings, qq.v. Ref: CA, CC, EM, MP, TC. SC: Blackshirt (Richard Verrell) = B (see also: Roderic Graeme); Insp. Auguste Jantry, in at least those marked AJ; Det. Sgt. Robert Mather = RM; Insps. Stevens & Allain, in at least those marked S&A; Theodore I. Terhune, in at least those marked TT; Lord Blackshirt (Anthony Verrell) = LB. Set: Eng.
The Accidental Clue. Hutchinson, 1957
Adventures of Blackshirt; see Blackshirt Again
Alias Blackshirt. Harrap, 1932; Dodd, 1932 B
Almost Without Murder. Hutchinson, 1963
Always Expect the Unexpected. Hutchinson, 1965
And a Bottle of Rum. Hutchinson, 1949 TT
Blackshirt. Unwin, 1925; Dodd, 1925 B ss
Blackshirt Again. Hutchinson, 1929. U.S. title: Adventures of Blackshirt. Dodd, 1929 B ss
Blackshirt, Counter-Spy. Hutchinson, 1938 B
Blackshirt Interferes. Hutchinson, 1939 B
Blackshirt Strikes Back. Hutchinson, 1940 B
Blackshirt Takes a Hand. Hutchinson, 1937 B
Blackshirt the Adventurer. Hutchinson, 1936 B
Blackshirt the Audacious. Hutchinson, 1935; Lippincott, 1936 B
Blind Date for a Private Eye. Hutchinson, 1969
Body Unknown. Hutchinson, 1939 S&A
Boomerang. Hutchinson, 1959
A Brief for O'Leary, and Two Other Episodes in His Career. Hutchinson, 1947 (3 novelets.)
Calling Lord Blackshirt. Hutchinson, 1943 LB
Cardyce for the Defence. Hutchinson, 1936
A Case for Solomon. Hutchinson, 1943 TT
A Case of Books. Hutchinson, 1946 TT
Cherchez la Femme. Hutchinson, 1951 AJ [Paris, 1800s]
The Coming of Carew. Hutchinson, 1945
The Corporal Died in Bed. Hutchinson, 1940 S&A
The "D" Notice. Hutchinson, 1974 RM
Dead Pigs at Hungry Farm. Hutchinson, 1951 TT
The Devil Was a Woman. Hutchinson, 1966
Disappearance of Roger Tremayne. Hutchinson, 1937
Double Trouble. Hutchinson, 1978 RM
Encore Allain! Hutchinson, 1941 S&A
Epilogue. Hutchinson, 1933; Lippincott, 1934 S alone
Fog for a Killer. Hutchinson, 1960
Gigins Court. Hutchinson, 1932
Hate Ship. Hutchinson, 1928; Dodd, 1928 [ship]
Holiday for a Spy. Hutchinson, 1963
House with Crooked Walls. Hutchinson, 1942 TT
Impeached! Hutchinson, 1933
The Imperfect Crime. Hutchinson, 1932; Lippincott, 1933 S&A [Fr.]
An International Affair. Hutchinson, 1934 S&A
Invitation to Mather. Hale, 1980 RM
John Jenkin, Public Enemy; see Public Enemy—No. 1
Just an Ordinary Case. Hutchinson, 1956
La Belle Laurine. Unwin, 1926. Revised edition: Laurine. Allan, 1935
The Lady Doth Protest. Hutchinson, 1971
Lady in Black. Hutchinson, 1952 AJ [Paris, 1800s]
Laurine; see La Belle Laurine
The Long Night. Hutchinson, 1958
Lord Blackshirt. Hutchinson, 1942 LB
Madame Spy. Allan, 1935
The Man from Michigan. Hutchinson, 1938. U.S. title: The Mystery of the Stolen Hats. Lippincott, 1939 S&A [Paris]
Mather Again. Hutchinson, 1979 RM
Mather Investigates. Hale, 1980 RM
Mr. Whimset Buys a Gun. Hutchinson, 1953
Much Ado About Something. Hutchinson, 1967
A Murder of Some Importance. Hutchinson, 1931; Lippincott, 1931 S&A
The Mystery of the Stolen Hats; see The Man from Michigan
Mystery on the Queen Mary. Hutchinson, 1937; Lippincott, 1938 S&A [ship]
Never Mix Business with Pleasure. Hutchinson, 1968
News Travels by Night. Hutchinson, 1943 S&A [Paris]
No Clues for Dexter. Hutchinson, 1948
Not Proven. Hutchinson, 1935 S&A
The Penance of Brother Alaric. Hutchinson, 1930
Poisoned Sleep. Hutchinson, 1939 S&A
Public Enemy—No. 1. Hutchinson, 1934. U.S. title: John Jenkin, Public Enemy. Lippincott, 1935
The Quiet Ones. Hutchinson, 1970 RM
Racing Yacht Mystery. Hutchinson, 1938 [ship]
The Return of Blackshirt. Unwin, 1927; Dodd, 1927 B ss
Satan's Mistress. Hutchinson, 1935 S&A
Seven Clues in Search of a Crime. Hutchinson, 1941 TT
The Snatch. Hutchinson, 1976 RM
So Sharp the Razor. Hutchinson, 1955
Some Geese Lay Golden Eggs. Hutchinson, 1968
Son of Blackshirt. Hutchinson, 1941 LB
Suspense. Hutchinson, 1953
Ten Trails to Tyburn. Hutchinson, 1944 TT
Thirteen in a Fog. Hutchinson, 1940
Through the Eyes of the Judge. Hutchinson, 1930; Lippincott, 1930
Tigers Have Claws. Hutchinson, 1949
Tomorrow's Yesterday. Hutchinson, 1972
The Trail of the White Knight. Harrap, 1926; Doran, 1927 [Hung.]
Trouble! Harrap, 1929; Lippincott, 1929
Two and Two Make Five. Hutchinson, 1973 RM
Two-Faced. Hutchinson, 1977 RM
The Undetective. Hutchinson, 1962; London House, 1963
Unsolved. Hutchinson, 1931; Lippincott, 1932
The Way Out. Hutchinson, 1954
Without Malice. Hutchinson, 1946
Work for the Hangman. Hutchinson, 1944 TT

GRAEME, DAVID. Pseudonym of Graham Montague Jeffries, 1900- . Other pseudonyms: Bruce Graeme, Roderic Hastings, qq.v. SC: Monsieur Blackshirt (Raoul de Rohan), an ancestor of Bruce Graeme's character = MB.
The Drums Beat Red. Harrap, 1963 [Haiti]
The Inn of the Thirteen Swords. Harrap, 1938 MB [Fr., ca.1600]
Monsieur Blackshirt. Harrap, 1933; Lippincott, 1933 MB [Fr., ca.1600]
The Sword of Monsieur Blackshirt. Harrap, 1936; Lippincott, 1936 MB [Fr., ca.1600]
The Vengeance of Monsieur Blackshirt. Harrap, 1934; Lippincott, 1935 MB [Fr., ca.1600]

GRAEME, RODERIC. Pseudonym of Roderic (Graeme) Jeffries, 1926- , q.v. Other pseudonyms: Peter Alding, Jeffrey Ashford, Graham Hastings, qq.v. SC: Blackshirt (Richard Verrell), continuing the character created by his father, Bruce Graeme, q.v., in all titles. Set: Eng.
The Amazing Mr. Blackshirt. Hutchinson, 1955
Blackshirt at Large. Long, 1966
Blackshirt Finds Trouble. Long, 1961 [Paris]
Blackshirt Helps Himself. Long, 1961
Blackshirt in Peril. Long, 1967
Blackshirt Meets the Lady. Long, 1956
Blackshirt on the Spot. Long, 1963
Blackshirt Passes By. Hutchinson, 1953
Blackshirt Saves the Day. Hutchinson, 1964
Blackshirt Sees It Through. Long, 1960
Blackshirt Sets the Pace. Long, 1959
Blackshirt Stirs Things Up. Long, 1969
Blackshirt Takes the Trail. Long, 1962
Blackshirt Wins the Trick. Hutchinson, 1953
Call for Blackshirt. Long, 1963
Concerning Blackshirt. Hutchinson, 1952
Danger for Blackshirt. Long, 1965
Double for Blackshirt. Long, 1958
Paging Blackshirt. Long, 1957
Salute to Blackshirt. Hutchinson, 1954

GRAEME-HOLDER, W.
The Decker. Lane, 1931 [N.Z.]

GRAFF, MAB
Clangor in the Bell Tower. Accent, 1978

GRAFFY, JOSEPH
The Man Who Was Not Himself. Hodder, 1958

GRAFTON, C(ORNELIUS) W(ARREN). 1909-1982. Born in China of missionary parents; graduate in journalism and law; practiced law in Louisville. SC: Gil Henry = GH.
Beyond a Reasonable Doubt. Rinehart, 1950; Heineman, 1951
The Rat Began to Gnaw the Rope. Farrar, 1943; Gollancz, 1944 GH
The Rope Began to Hang the Butcher. Farrar, 1944; Gollancz, 1945 GH

GRAFTON, SAMUEL. 1907- .
A Most Contagious Game. Doubleday, 1955; Hart-Davis, 1956 [NYC]

GRAHAM, ALAN
-Araminta and the River. Newnes, 1916
Follow the Little Pictures! Blackwood, 1920
The Golden Torrent. Hodder, 1922
Murder Disqualifies. Blackwood, 1922
-The Treasure on Camise. Paul, 1929
-The Voyage Home. Blackwood, 1921
Who Killed Gerald Cruden? Jenkins, 1925 [Wales]
Witch Temple. Paul, 1929

GRAHAM, ANTHONY. SC: Eric Marsden, in some titles including that marked EM; Frank Richmond, in at least those marked FR.
Act of Silence. Boardman, 1963
Behind the Arras. Boardman, 1964
The Deadly Lovers. Boardman, 1966 FR
The Death Business. Boardman, 1967 FR [L.A.]
The Desperate Witch. Boardman, 1962
Minus a Shamus. Boardman, 1955
No Sale for Haloes. Boardman, 1954
The Veetols. Boardman, 1965 EM

GRAHAM, BURTON. SC: Michael Evans, in both titles.
Spy or Die. Dent, 1972
The Spy Trap. Dent, 1971; Weybright, 1972

GRAHAM, DAVID
Grave of Sand. Hale, 1963
Operation Cleansweep. Hale, 1965

GRAHAM, JAMES. Pseudonym of Harry Patterson, 1929- , q.v. Other pseudonyms: Martin Fallon, Jack Higgins, Hugh Marlowe, qq.v.
Bloody Passage. Macmillan (London), 1974. U.S. title: The Run to Morning. Stein, 1974 [Libya]
A Game for Heroes. Macmillan (London), 1970; Doubleday, 1970 [Chan. Is.]
The Khufra Run. Macmillan (London), 1972; Doubleday, 1973 [Sp.]
The Run to Morning; see Bloody Passage
The Wrath of God. Macmillan (London), 1971; Doubleday, 1971 [Mex., 1922]

GRAHAM, JOHN ALEXANDER. 1941- . Ref: CA.
The Aldeburg Cezanne. Atlantic-Little, 1970 [NYC]
Arthur. Harper, 1969 [Mass.]
The Involvement of Arnold Wechsler. Atlantic-Little, 1971 [acad.]
Something in the Air. Atlantic-Little, 1970; H. Hamilton, 1970 [NYC]

GRAHAM, NANCY
-The Black Swan. Cassell, 1958
-The Purple Jacaranda. Cassell, 1958

GRAHAM, NEILL. Pseudonym of W(illiam) Murdoch Duncan, 1909-1975, q.v. Other pseudonyms: John Cassells, John Dallas, Martin Locke, Peter Malloch, Lovat Marshall, qq.v. SC: Mr. Sandyman, in at least those marked S; James "Solo" Malcolm, in at least those marked SM. Set: Eng.
Again, Mr. Sandyman. Jarrolds, 1952 S
The Amazing Mr. Sandyman. Jarrolds, 1952 S
Assignment, Murder. Long, 1974 SM
Blood on the Pavement. Long, 1970 SM
Candidate for a Coffin. Long, 1968 SM
Cop in a Tight Frame. Long, 1973 SM
Death of a Canary. Long, 1969 SM
Frame-Up. Long, 1972 SM
Graft Town. Long, 1963 SM
Hit Me Hard. Jarrolds, 1958 SM
Killers Are on Velvet. Long, 1960 SM
Label It Murder. Long, 1963 SM
Make Mine Murder. Long, 1962 SM
A Matter of Murder. Long, 1971 SM
Money for Murder. Long, 1966 SM
Motive for Murder. Long, 1977 SM
Murder, Double Murder. Long, 1971 SM
Murder Has Been Done. Long, 1967 SM
Murder in a Dark Room. Long, 1973 SM
Murder Is My Weakness. Long, 1961 SM
Murder Lies in Waiting. Long, 1969 SM
Murder Made Easy. Long, 1964 SM
Murder Makes a Date. Jarrolds, 1955; Roy, 1955 SM
Murder Makes It Certain. Long, 1967 SM
Murder Makes the News. Long, 1967 SM
Murder of a Black Cat. Long, 1964 SM
Murder on Demand. Long, 1966 SM

Murder on My Hands. Long, 1965 SM
Murder on the "Duchess." Long, 1961 SM
Murder on the List. Long, 1975 SM
Murder Rings the Bell. Jarrolds, 1959 SM
Murder Walks on Tiptoe. Melrose, 1951 S
Murder's Always Final. Long, 1965 SM
One for the Book. Long, 1970 SM
Passport to Murder. Melrose, 1949 S
Pay Off. Long, 1968 SM
Play It Solo. Jarrolds, 1955 SM
The Quest of Mr. Sandyman. Jarrolds, 1951 S
Salute Mr. Sandyman. Jarrolds, 1953 S
Salute to Murder. Long, 1958 SM
Say It with Murder. Jarrolds, 1956 SM
Search for a Missing Lady. Long, 1976 SM
The Symbol of the Cat. Melrose, 1948 S
The Temple of Slumber. Melrose, 1950
You Can't Call It Murder. Jarrolds, 1957 SM

GRAHAM, PAUL. See: Ted Willis, 1918- .

GRAHAM, PETER. Pseudonym of Kenneth (Joseph Robb) Langmaid, q.v.
Tiger Mark. Hamilton, 1928

GRAHAM, PETER
-The Atom-Busters. Foster, 1948
Behind the First Wall. Quality, 1946
The Doctor Detective. Foster, 1946
-Life Is No Bargain. Quality, 1948

GRAHAM, ROBERT. Pseudonym of Joe William Haldeman, 1943- . Ref: CA. Both titles in Attar series.
-Attar's Revenge. PB, 1975
-War of Nerves. PB, 1975

GRAHAM, ROSS
Death on a Smokeboat. Hurst, 1947

GRAHAM, SCOTT. Pseudonym of Hazelton Black.
-A Bolt from the Blue. Long, 1891
-By Bitter Experience. Partridge, 1906
-An Earl Without an Earldom. Partridge, 1908
The Golden Milestone. Wyman, 1885
-A Lost Inheritance. Partridge, 1912
The Sandcliff Mystery. Oliphant, 1891
-The Showman's Daughter. Hurst, 1897

GRAHAM, SEAN. 1920- . Ref: CA.
Hippo's Coup. Weidenfeld, 1968
A Surfeit of Sun. Weidenfeld, 1964; Doubleday, 1965

GRAHAM, SHEILAH
Gentleman-Crook. Rich, 1933

GRAHAM, VICTORIA
The Witchstone. Pyramid, 1974

GRAHAM, WHIDDEN. Ref: CC.
Crimson Hairs. Greenleaf, 1968

GRAHAM, (MATILDA) WINIFRED (MURIEL). SC: Miss Woolfe, in at least those marked W. Set: Eng.
The Frozen Death. Hutchinson, 1938
-Ghostly Strength. Hutchinson, 1936
Glenvirgin's Ghost. Hutchinson, 1938
-Hallowmass Abbey. Hutchinson, 1935
-Identity. Hutchinson, 1933
In Fear of a Woman. Hutchinson, 1925
The Last Laugh. Hutchinson, 1930 W
-The Life of a Nobody. Hutchinson, 1932
The Man Behind the Chair. Hutchinson, 1935
-Sacrifice & Co. Hutchinson, 1940
-A Spider Never Falls. Hutchinson, 1944
Unholy Matrimony. Hutchinson, 1927
-What Next? Hutchinson, 1945
-What Thinkest Thou, Simon? Hutchinson, 1936
Wolf-Net. Hutchinson, 1931 W
A Wolf of the Evenings. Hutchinson, 1930 W
World Without End. Rivers, 1907

GRAHAM, WINSTON (MAWDSLEY). 1909- . Ref: CA, DD, TC. Set: Eng.
After the Act. Hodder, 1965; Doubleday, 1966
Angell, Pearl and Little God. Collins, 1970; Doubleday, 1970
Bride to Vengeance; see The Little Walls
The Dangerous Pawn. Ward, 1937
The Forgotten Story. Ward, 1945
Fortune Is a Woman. Hodder, 1952; Doubleday, 1953
The Giant's Chair. Ward, 1938
Greek Fire. Hodder, 1958; Doubleday, 1958
The House with the Stained Glass Windows. Ward, 1934
Into the Fog. Ward, 1935
The Japanese Girl. Collins, 1971; Doubleday, 1972 ss
Keys of Chance. Ward, 1939
The Little Walls. Hodder, 1955; Doubleday, 1955. Also published as: Bridge to Vengeance. Bestseller, 1957, abridged
Marnie. Hodder, 1961; Doubleday, 1961
The Merciless Ladies. Ward, 1944
My Turn Next. Ward, 1942
Night Journey. Ward, 1941; Doubleday, 1968
Night Without Stars. Hodder, 1950; Doubleday, 1960 [Fr.]
No Exit. Ward, 1940
The Riddle of John Rowe. Ward, 1935
The Sleeping Partner. Hodder, 1956; Doubleday, 1956
Strangers Meeting. Ward, 1939
Take My Life. Ward, 1947; Doubleday, 1967
The Tumbled House. Hodder, 1959; Doubleday, 1960
The Walking Stick. Collins, 1967; Doubleday, 1967
Without Motive. Ward, 1936
Woman in the Mirror. Bodley, 1975; Doubleday, 1975 (Based in part on The Giant's Chair, q.v.) [Wales]
The Wreck of the Grey Cat. Doubleday, 1958 (British title?) [Eng., 1898]

GRAHAME, ARTHUR W.
-Rabbitfoot. Dorrance, 1967

GRAINGER, FRANCIS EDWARD. 1857-1927. Pseudonym: Headon Hill, q.v.

GRAINGER, TOM
The Injured. Playwrights, 1976 (3-act play.)

GRAM, DEWEY
Boulevard Nights. Warner, 1979 (Novelization of the movie.)

GRANBECK, MARILYN. 1927- . Pseudonyms: Ben Grant, Clayton Moore, qq.v. Joint pseudonyms with Arthur Moore, q.v.: Adam Hamilton, Van Saxon, qq.v. Ref: CA.
The Magician's Daughter. Manor, 1977

GRANBY, GEORGE
The Secret of Musterton House. Mills, 1929; Dutton, 1929

GRANDOWER, ELISSA. Pseudonym of Hillary (Baldwin) Waugh, 1920- , q.v. Other pseudonyms: H. Baldwin Taylor, Harry Walker, qq.v.
Blackbourne Hall. Doubleday, 1979; Gollancz, 1980, as by Hillary Waugh [ca.1910]
Rivergate House. Doubleday, 1980; Gollancz, 1981, as by Hillary Waugh [NYC, 1920s]
Seaview Manor. Doubleday, 1976; Gollancz, 1977, as by Hillary Waugh [Conn.]
The Secret Room of Morgate House. Doubleday, 1977; Gollancz, 1978, as by Hillary Waugh [Ill., 1896]
The Summer at Raven's Roost. Doubleday, 1976; Gollancz, 1978, as by Hillary Waugh

GRANGER, BILL
The November Man. GM, 1979; New English Library pb, 1981 [Edin.]
Public Murders. Jove, 1980; New English Library, 1981 [Chi.]
Sweeps. GM, 1980

GRANGER, HENRY FRANCIS
The Gray Gull. Garden City, 1924

GRANT, ALAN. Pseudonym of (Gilbert) Alan Kennington, 1906- , q.v.
It Walks the Woods. Nicholson, 1936. Reprinted as by Alan Kennington: Mellifont, 1944

GRANT, AMBROSE. Pseudonym of Rene Raymond, 1906- . Other pseudonyms: James Hadley Chase, James L. Docherty, Raymond Marshall, qq.v.
More Deadly Than the Male. Eyre, 1946. Reprinted as by James Hadley Chase: Panther, 1960

GRANT, BEN. Pseudonym of Marilyn Granbeck, 1927- . Other pseudonym: Clayton Moore, q.v. Joint pseudonyms with Arthur Moore, q.v.: Adam Hamilton, Van Saxon, qq.v.
Alice Dies Twice. Major, 1975
Hitchhike to Hell. Merit, 1963
Murder in the Raw. Merit, 1964
One for the Road. Merit, 1966

GRANT, CHARLES L. 1942- . Pseudonym: Deborah Lewis, q.v. Ref: CA.
The Hour of the Oxrun Dead. Doubleday, 1977 [New Eng.]
The Last Call of Mourning. Doubleday, 1979 [New Eng.]
The Sound of Midnight. Doubleday, 1978

GRANT, DAVID. Pseudonym of Craig Thomas, 1942- , q.v.
Emerald Decision. Joseph, 1980; Holt, 1980 [Eng., 1940]
Moscow 500. Joseph, 1979; Holt, 1979 [Moscow]

GRANT, DOUGLAS. Pseudonym of Isabel (Egenton) Ostrander, 1883-1924, q.v. Other pseudonyms: Robert Orr Chipperfield, David Fox, qq.v. See also: William J. Burns, 1861-1932.
Anything Once. Watt, 1920
Booty. Watt, 1919; Hurst, 1921
The Fifth Ace. Watt, 1918; Hurst, 1921. Also published as: The Red Glove. Grosset, 19??
The Red Glove; see The Fifth Ace
The Single Track. Watt, 1919; Hurst, 1922
Two-Gun Sue. McBride, 1922; Hurst, 1922

GRANT, DOUGLAS ALLEN
Monsieur Brunner. Butterworth, 1933

GRANT, (CHARLES) GRAHAM
The Diary of a Police Surgeon. Pearson, 1920 (Fictionalized episodes of true crime.)

GRANT, HILDA KAY. 1910- . Pseudonym: Jan Hilliard, q.v.

GRANT, JAMES. Pseudonym of Bruce Crowther, 1933- , q.v.
Don't Shoot the Pianist. Piatkus, 1980
Island of Gold. Muller, 1977; Walker, 1978 [Cors.]
The Left-Handed Shell. Muller, 1978
The Ransom Commando. Muller, 1978
The Rose Medallion. Muller, 1977
Tightrope. Muller, 1979
Victims. Piatkus, 1980

GRANT, JAMES EDWARD
The Green Shadow. Hartney, 1935

GRANT, JOAN (MARSHALL). 1907- .
The Laird and the Lady. Methuen, 1949. U.S. title: Castle Cloud. Ace, 1966

GRANT, JOHN. 1933- . Pseudonym: Jonathan Gash, q.v.

GRANT, MAXWELL
-Barrier Reef. Allen, 1980

GRANT, MAXWELL. House name under which were published the adventures of The Shadow. Most of the original Shadow stories in the pulps, as well as the stories about Norgil, were written by Walter B(rown) Gibson, 1897- , q.v. All Belmont titles, except that marked *, were written by Dennis Lynds, 1924- , q.v. Those from other publishers are reprints from 1930s and 1940s pulps. SC: Lamont Cranston (The Shadow) = LC; Norgil = N (also reprints from the pulp ss written by Gibson) = N.
The Black Master. Pyramid, 1974; New English Library pb 1975 LC [NYC]
Charg, Monster. Jove, 1977 LC [NYC]
The Creeping Death. Pyramid, 1977 LC
The Crime Cult. Pyramid, 1975 LC [NYC]
The Crime Oracle and The Teeth of the Dragon. Dover, 1975; Constable, 1975 (2 LC novels.)
Cry Shadow! Belmont, 1965 LC [NYC]
The Death Giver. Jove, 1978 LC [NYC]
The Death Tower. Bantam, 1969 LC [NYC]
Double Z. Pyramid, 1975 LC [NYC]
Eyes of the Shadow. Street, 1931 LC [NYC]
Fingers of Death. Jove, 1977 LC
Gangdom's Doom. Bantam, 1970 LC [Chi.]
The Ghost Makers. Bantam, 1970 LC [NYC]
Gray Fist. Pyramid, 1977 LC [NYC]
Green Eyes. Pyramid, 1977 LC [S.F.]
Grove of Doom. Grosset, 1966, in the Weird Adventures of the Shadow. Also published as by Walter B. Gibson: Tempo, 1969 LC [L.I.]
Hands in the Dark. Pyramid, 1975; New English Library pb, 1977 LC [NYC]
Hidden Death. Bantam, 1970 LC [NYC]
Kings of Crime. Pyramid, 1976 LC [NYC]
The Living Shadow. Street, 1931; New English Library pb, 1976 LC [NYC]
Mark of the Shadow. Belmont, 1966 LC
The Mobsmen on the Spot. Pyramid, 1974; New English Library pb, 1976 LC [NYC]
Mox. Pyramid, 1975 LC [NYC]

Murder by Moonlight. Grosset, 1966, in The Weird Adventures of the Shadow. Also published as by Walter B. Gibson: Tempo, 1969
Murder Trail. Jove, 1977 LC [NYC]
Night of the Shadow. Belmont, 1966 LC
Norgil: More Tales of Prestidigitection. Mysterious Press, 1979 ss N
Norgil the Magician. Mysterious Press, 1977 ss N
The Red Menace. Pyramid, 1975 LC [NYC]
Return of the Shadow. Belmont, 1963 LC * (Written by Walter B. Gibson.)
The Romanoff Jewels. Pyramid, 1975 LC [Moscow]
The Shadow and the Voice of Murder. Bantam (Los Angeles), 1945 LC
Shadow Beware. Belmont, 1965 LC [Eng.]
The Shadow—Destination Moon. Belmont, 1967 LC [West]
Shadow—Go Mad! Belmont, 1966 LC
The Shadow Laughs! Street, 1931 LC [NYC]
The Shadow Strikes. Belmont, 1964 LC [N.J.]
Shadowed Millions. Pyramid, 1976 LC [NYC]
The Shadow's Revenge. Belmont, 1965 LC [Afr.]
The Shadow's Shadow. Pyramid, 1977 LC [NYC]
The Silent Death. Jove, 1978 LC [NYC]
The Silent Seven. Pyramid, 1975 LC [NYC]
The Teeth of the Dragon; see The Crime Oracle
Voodoo Death. Grosset, 1966, in The Weird Adventures of the Shadow. Also published as by Walter B. Gibson: Tempo, 1969 LC [NYC]
The Wealth Seeker. Jove, 1978 LC [NYC]
The Weird Adventures of the Shadow; see the individual novels: The Grove of Doom, Murder by Moonlight, and Voodoo Death.
Zemba. Jove, 1977 LC [Paris]

GRANT, RICHARD. Pseudonym of Joseph Calvitt Clarke, 1888- . Set: Eng.
The Case of the Baronet's Memoirs. Long, 1960
Circle of Death. Paul, 1952
The Death Light. Long, 1959
Doom Candle. Paul, 1943
Five Ways to Die. Paul, 1946
Formula for Crime. Paul, 1956
Legacy of Danger. Paul, 1954 [Afr.]
Lives in a Box. Paul, 1951
Men in Knots. Paul, 1945
The Serpent Stirs. Paul, 1942
Shoot Your Enemies. Paul, 1948
The Silky Ones Sting. Paul, 1947
The Slaves of Ishtar. Paul, 1951
The Sniper Murders. Long, 1958
The Storm Gang. Paul, 1952
This Is Dynamite. Paul, 1955
The Threat of the Cloven Hand. Paul, 1950
Who Strikes by Night. Paul, 1944

GRANT, ROBERT. 1852-1940.
The Law-Breakers and other stories. Scribner, 1906 ss

GRANT, RODERICK. 1941- . Born in Scotland; reporter and editor before becoming full-time writer.
A Private Vendetta. Hale, 1978; Scribner, 1979 [Cyprus]
A Savage Freedom. Hale, 1978
The Stalking of Adrian Lawford. New English Library pb, 1974; Pyramid, 1975 [Scot.]

GRANTHAM, GERALD
Dope Runners. Popular Publications (Australia), 193?
Mystery of the S. S. Timor. Popular Publications (Australia), 193?

GRANTLAND, KEITH. Joint pseudonym of Charles Nutt, 1929-1967, and John (E.) Tomerlin, 1930- , q.v. Other Nutt pseudonym: Charles Beaumont, q.v.
Run from the Hunter. GM, 1957; Boardman, 1959 [Ala.]

GRANVILLE, AUSTYN
-The Shadow of Shame. Sergel, 1891

GRANVILLE, CHARLES. Pseudonym of Francis Charles Granville Egerton.
-A Broken Stirrup-Leather. Murray, 1888
-Mrs. John Foster. Heinemann, 1897
A Sapphire Ring. Murray, 1895
-Sir Hector's Watch. Murray, 1887

GRANVILLE, EDGAR
The Domino Plan. Bachman, 1975

GRATUS, JACK, 1935- , and T. PRESTON
Ref on Gratus: CA.

What the Peeper Saw. Signet, 1972 (Novelization of the movie.)

GRAVATT, GLENN
The Adventure of the Mysterious Lodger. Magico, 1979 (Sherlock Holmes.)

GRAVES, CHARLES (PATRICK RANKE). 1899- .
Dusk to Dawn. Hutchinson, 1946
-Five Survive. Hutchinson, 1944

GRAVES, EVELYN and GEORGE MONAHAN
Liquid Terror. Carlyle, 1979

GRAVES, GEOFFREY. See: Jonas Flagg.

GRAVES, RICHARD L(ATSHAW). 1928- .
Ref: CA. SC: Hugo Wolfram = HW.
The Black Gold of Malverde. Stein, 1973; Hart-Davis, 1974 HW [Carib.]
C.L.A.W. Stein, 1976
Cobalt 60. Stein, 1975 HW
The Platinum Bullet. Stein, 1974 HW
Quicksilver. Stein, 1976 HW [Guat.]

GRAY, ANGELA. Pseudonym of Dorothy Daniels, 1915- , q.v. Other pseudonyms: Danielle Dorsett, Cynthia Kavanaugh, Suzanne Somers, Geraldine Thayer, Helen Gray Weston, qq.v.
The Ashes of Falconwyck. Lancer, 1971
Blackwell's Ghost. Lancer, 1972
The Ghost Dancers. Lancer, 1971
The Golden Packet. Lancer, 1971
The Lattimore Arch. Lancer, 1971 [Wash. D.C., 1895]
Nightmare at Riverview. Lancer, 1973 [Ga., 1885]
Ravenswood Hall. Lancer, 1971
The Warlock's Daughter. Lancer, 1973

GRAY, ANNABEL. Pseudonym of Anne Cox.
The Mystic Number Seven. Simpkin, 1900

GRAY, ANTHONY
Dead Nigger. Methuen, 1929

GRAY, ANTHONY. Pseudonym of Hank Searls, 1922- , q.v.
The Perpetrators. Putnam, 1965; Souvenir, 1965

GRAY, BERKELEY. Pseudonym of Edwy Searles Brooks, 1889-1965, q.v. Other pseudonyms: Victor Gunn, Carlton Ross, qq.v. SC: Norman Conquest, in all titles except the one noted. Set: mostly Eng.
Alias Norman Conquest. Collins, 1945
The Big Brain. Collins, 1959 [Paris]
Blonde for Danger. Collins, 1943
Calamity Conquest. Collins, 1965 [Sp.]
Call Conquest for Danger. Collins, 1961
Castle Conquest. Collins, 1964
Cavalier Conquest. Collins, 1944
Conquest After Midnight. Collins, 1957
Conquest Calls the Tune. Hale, 1968 (Actually written by Mrs. F. Brooks and Lionel Brooks.)
Conquest Goes Home. Collins, 1957
Conquest Goes West. Collins, 1954
Conquest in California. Collins, 1958 [L.A.]
Conquest in Command. Collins, 1956
Conquest in Ireland. Hale, 1969. (Actually written by Lionel Brooks.) [Ire.]
Conquest in Scotland. Collins, 1951 [Scot.]
Conquest in the Underworld. Collins, 1962
Conquest Likes It Hot. Collins, 1965
Conquest Marches On. Collins, 1939
Conquest on the Run. Collins, 1960
Conquest Overboard. Collins, 1964
Conquest Takes All. Collins, 1940
The Conquest Touch. Collins, 1948
Convict 1066. Collins, 1940
Count Down for Conquest. Collins, 1963
Curtains for Conquest? Collins, 1966
Dare-Devil Conquest. Collins, 1950
Death on the Hit Parade. Collins, 1958
Duel Murder. Collins, 1949
Follow the Lady. Collins, 1954 [Yugos.]
The Gay Desperado. Collins, 1944
Get Ready to Die. Collins, 1961
The Half-Open Door. Collins, 1953
The House of the Lost. Collins, 1956 [Fr.]
Killer Conquest. Collins, 1947
The Lady Is Poison. Collins, 1952
Leave It to Conquest. Collins, 1939 [Wales]
Meet the Don. Collins, 1940
Miss Dynamite. Collins, 1939
Mr. Ball of Fire. Collins, 1946
Mr. Mortimer Gets the Jitters. Collins, 1938
Murder & Co. Collins, 1959
Nightmare House. Collins, 1960
Operation Conquest. Collins, 1951
Seven Dawns to Death. Collins, 1950

Six Feet of Dynamite. Collins, 1941 [Ger.]
Six to Kill. Collins, 1940
The Spot Marked X. Collins, 1948
Target for Conquest. Collins, 1953
Thank You, Mr. Conquest. Collins, 1941
Three Frightened Men. Amalgamated, 1938 (Sexton Blake.)
Turn Left for Danger. Collins, 1955
Vultures, Ltd. Collins, 1938

GRAY, CHARLES EDWARD
Murder Defies the Roman Emperor. Humphries, 1957

GRAY, CURME
Murder in Millenium VI. Shasta, 1951 [future]

GRAY, DOROTHEA
Murder of a Wanton. Lewis, 1947

GRAY, DULCIE. Pseudonym of Dulcie Winifred Catherine Dennison, 1920- .
Ref: CA, CC, TC. SC: Insp./Supt. Cardiff, in at least those marked C. Set: mostly Eng.
Baby Face. Barker, 1959 [S. Afr.]
Dark Calypso. Macdonald, 1979
Dead Give Away. Macdonald, 1974
Deadly Lampshade. Macdonald, 1971
The Devil Wore Scarlet. Macdonald, 1964
Died in the Red. Macdonald, 1968 C
Epitaph for a Dead Actor. Barker, 1960 C
For Richer for Richer. Macdonald, 1970 [Mor.]
Murder in Melbourne. Barker, 1958 [Melb.]
Murder in Mind. Macdonald, 1963
The Murder of Love. Macdonald, 1967
Murder on Honeymoon. Macdonald, 1969
Murder on a Saturday. Barker, 1961
Murder on the Stairs. Barker, 1957; British Book Centre, 1958
No Quarter for a Star. Macdonald, 1965
Ride on a Tiger. Macdonald, 1975
Stage Door Fright. Macdonald, 1977 ss
Understudy to Murder. Macdonald, 1972

GRAY, HARRIET. Pseudonym of Denise (Naomi) Robins, 1897- , q.v.
Bride of Doom. Rich, 1956

GRAY, HILARY
Frightened to Death. Hurst, 1950
Week-End with Death. Hurst, 1951

GRAY, JONATHAN. Pseudonym of Herbert Adams, 1874-1958, q.v. Set: Eng.
The Owl. Harrap, 1937; Lippincott, 1937
Safety Last. Muller, 1934

GRAY, JONATHAN. Pseudonym of Jack Taylor. Ref: CC.
Untimely Slain. Hutchinson, 1947 [acad.]

GRAY, MAXWELL
-Unconfessed. Long, 1911

GRAY, MICHAEL (WAUDE)
Minutes to Impact. Cassell, 1967

GRAY, NICHOLAS STUART. 1922- . Ref: CA.
Killer's Cookbook. Dobson, 1976

GRAY, OSCAR. Set: Eng.
The Bagshot Mystery. Selwyn, 1928; Macaulay, 1929
Three Shots. Selwyn, 1929

GRAY, RUSSELL. Pseudonym of Bruno Fischer, 1908- , q.v.
The Lustful Ape. Lion, 1950. Reprinted as by Bruno Fischer: GM, 1959; Red Seal, 1959

GRAY, SIMON (JAMES HALLIDAY). 1936- .
Pseudonym: Hamish Reade, q.v. Ref: CA.
Dutch Uncle. Faber, 1969 (2-act play.)
Stage Struck. Eyre, 1979; Seaver, 1981 (2-act play.)

GRAYDON, ROBERT MURRAY. -1937. Born in Pa., son of W(illiam) Murray Graydon, 1864-1946, q.v.; taken to live in England as a child. All titles below were published by Amalgamated Press and feature Sexton Blake.
The Masked Marauder. 1930
The Masquerader. 1919
The Mysterious Mr. Reece. 1917
The Mystery of the Mandarin's Idol. 1928

GRAYDON, W(ILLIAM) MURRAY. 1864-1946. Born in Pa.; full-time writer, first in the U.S., and later, for most of his life, in Eng. All titles below without publisher were published by Amalgamated Press and feature Sexton Blake. Set: Eng.
The Adventure of the Annamese Prince. 1925
The Adventure of the Rogue's Apprentice. 1927
The Affair of the Missing Witness. 1926
The Affair of the Three Gunmen. 1924
African Gold. 1920
An Amateur in Crime. 1924
The Arctic Trail. 1923
At the Shrine of the Buddha. 1921
Behind the Walls. 1926
Black Cargo. 1925
The Black Streak. 1920
The Blackshirt Mystery. 1926
The Blockade Runners. 1917
The Bloodhound's Revenge. 1926
The Bogus Tourist-Agency. 1929
A Breach of Trust. 1921
The Brigand's Secret. 1922
The Burglar of White Birches. 1927
By Order of the King! 1925
By the Terms of the Will. 1920
Carfax Baines: His Strange and Remarkable Exploits. Henderson ss
The Case for the Prosecution. 1921
The Case of the Adopted Daughter. 1923
The Case of the Bogus Treasure Hunt. 1926
The Case of the Cashiered Officer. 1916
The Case of the Fatal Taxi Cab. 1928
The Case of the Five Merchants. 1921
The Case of the Four Barons. 1923
The Case of the Human Ape. 1927
The Case of the Mill Owner's Son. 1921
The Case of the Murdered Mahout. 1929
The Case of the Mysterious Jockey. 1919
The Case of the Nabob's Son. 1925
The Case of the Society Blackmailer. 1925
The Case of the Suppressed Will. 1916
The Case of the Theatrical Profiteer. 1926
The Case of the Two Guardians. 1924
The Case of the Two Scapegraces. 1925
The Clause in the Will. 1926
Craft and Cunning. 1917
Crag Island; or, The Mystery of Val Stanlock. Partridge, 1904
The Crime in the Wood. 1924
The Crime of Convict 13. 1930
The Crook of Chinatown. 1927
The Cryptogram. Street, 1899
The Curious Case of the Crook's Memoirs. 1924
Dark Secrets. 1919
The Derelicts. 1922
The Desert of Doom. 1930
The Deserter of the Foreign Legion. 1928
The Doctor Who Wouldn't Tell. 1928
Down East. 1923
The Earl's Return. 1922
The Embassy Detective. 1917
Exiled to Siberia. Penn, 1900
The Feud of Fear. 1930
The Five Diamonds. 1919
Five Years After. 1919
The Four Trails. 1919
From Lake to Wilderness; or, The Cruise of the Yolande. Street, 1899
The Game Keeper's Secret. 1924
Gipsy or Gentleman? 1921
The Great Abduction Mystery. 1918
The Green Turban. 1921
The Hand That Hid in Darkness. 1920
Held in Trust! 1925
His Father's Crime. 1925
In Barracks and Wigwam. Street, 1900
In Double Disguise. 1924
In Fort and Prison; or, The Mystery of Larry Redmayne. Street, 1903
In Friendship's Guise. Street, 1899
In the Hand of the Riffs. 1924
In Triple Disguise. 1925
The Island Secret. Pilgrim, 1935
Lady Sharlow's Secret. 1922
The Lama's Secret. 1922
Lost in Cambodia. 1922
Lost in the Slave Land; or, The Mystery of the Sacred Lamp Rock. Partridge, 1902
The Man Who Came Back. 1929
The Man Who Drove On. 1927
The Masked Dictator. 1927
The Master of Charteris Towers; or, A Rank Imposter. Henderson
The Mystery of Monte Carlo. 1928
The Mystery of the Abandoned Cottage. 1924
The Mystery of the Docks. 1929
The Mystery of the Dover Road. 1923
The Mystery of the Golden Chalice. 1928
The Mystery of the Swamp. 1922
Next O' Kin. 1924
On Winding Waters. Partridge, 1902
One of the Flying Squad. 1921
The Ordeal of Alick Hillersdon. 1918
The Path of Fear. 1923
The Perils of Pekin. Shaw, 1904
Perils of Petrograd. 1917
The Priest's Secret. 1925
The Princess of the Purple Palace. McClure, 1901
The Prisoner of Ellis Island. 1924
The Prisoner of the Mountains. 1926
The Rajah's Fortress. Street, 1900
The Record of the Case. 1919
The Reformation of Royce Remington. 1918
The Riddle of Crocodile Creek. 1928
The Rogue of Afghanistan. 1928
Rogues of the Desert. 1927
Salvage of the Sea. 1919
The Secret of the Flames. 1929
The Secret of the Past. 1917
The Secret of the Russian Refugees. 1928
The Secret of the Two Blackmailed Men. 1928
The Secret of the Vampire Actress. 1929
Sexton Blake in Silesia. 1922
Shadowed Lives. 1920
A Sheep in Wolf's Clothing. 1919
The Shield of the Law. 1923
The Shipwrecked Detective. 1926
The Sign of the Serpent. 1921
The Sixth Victim. 1929
The Taming of Neville Ibbetson. 1922
Ten Day's Leave. 1918
Their Great Adventure. 1916
Thirty Years After. 1921
The Three Trails. 1917
The Trader's Daughter. 1922
The Trail of Death. 1927
The Traitor Dragoon. Aldine, 1897
The Vanishing Death. 1929
The Vengeance of Three. 1920
Wanted. 1927
Where the Trail Ended. 1917
The White Death. 1926
The White King of Africa; or, The Mystery of the Ancient Fort. Street, 1899
With Cossack and Convict. Jarrolds, 1903
Within Fourteen Days. 1921
The Yacht of Mystery. 1926
The Yellow Face. 1921

GRAYLAND, V(ALERIE) MERLE (SPANNER). Pseudonyms: Lee Belvedere, Valerie Subond, qq.v. Ref: CA. SC: Hoani Mata, probably in all titles.
The Dead Men of Eden. Hale, 1962
The Grave-Digger's Apprentice. Hale, 1964
Jest of Darkness. Hale, 1965
Night of the Reaper. Hale, 1963

GRAYSON, ELIZABETH
By Demons Possessed. Manor, 1973
Macabre Manor. Manor, 1974
A Token of Evil. Manor, 1974

GRAYSON, PAULINE
Pyrrha: A Story of Two Crimes. American News, 1889. Also published as: Run to Earth; or, The Story of Two Crimes. Donohue, 189?
Run to Earth; see Pyrrha
-The Social Evil; or, The Woman Lalarge. Ogilvie, 1893

GRAYSON, RICHARD. Pseudonym of Richard Grindal, an official with the Scotch Whisky Trade Association, in London. SC: John Bryant, in at least those marked JB; Insp. Gautier = G.
Dead Soo Soon. Hammond, 1960 JB
Death in Melting. Hammond, 1957 JB
Madman's Whisper. Hammond, 1958 JB
The Monterant Affair. Gollancz, 1980; St. Martin's, 1980 G [Paris, ca. 1900]
Murder Red-Handed. Long, 1965
The Murders at Impasse Louvain. Gollancz, 1978; St. Martin's, 1979 G [Paris, ca.1900]
Play the Roman Fool and Die. Long, 1970
The Spiral Path. Hammond, 1955 JB
Spy in Camera. Long, 1968
A Taste of Death. Hale, 1973

GRAYSON, RUPERT. SC: Gunston Cotton = GC. (Note that all U.S. titles give the series character in full, Gunston, whereas British titles shorten it to Gun.)
Death Rides the Forest. Nash, 1921; Dutton, 1930 GC
Escape with Gun Cotton. Grayson, 1934 GC [Fin.]
Gun Cotton: A Romance of Secret Service. Nash, 1929. U.S. title: Gunston Cotton: Secret Service Agent. Dutton, 1936 GC
Gun Cotton—Ace High. Grayson, 1937 GC
Gun Cotton—Adventure Nine. Grayson, 1937 GC [NYC]
Gun Cotton—Adventurer. Grayson, 1933; Dutton, 1937 GC
Gun Cotton at Blind Man's Hood. Grayson, 1938 GC
Gun Cotton Goes to Russia. Grayson, 1936 GC [Russ.]
Gun Cotton in Hollywood. Grayson, 1936 GC [L.A.]
Gun Cotton in Mexico. Grayson, 1937; Dutton, 1940 GC [Mex.]
Gun Cotton—Murder at the Bank. Grayson, 1939 GC
Gun Cotton—Outside the Law. Grayson, 1936 GC
Gun Cotton, Secret Agent. Grayson, 1934 GC [S. Afr.]
Gun Cotton—Secret Airman. Grayson, 1939; Dutton, 1939 GC
Gunston Cotton: Secret Service Agent; see Gun Cotton: A Romance of Secret Service
Introducing Mr. Robinson. Eldon, 1940
Scarlet Livery. Nash, 1928
Secret Agent in Africa. Dutton, 1939 GC (British title?) [Afr.]

GRAYSON, RUTH (KING). 1926- . Ref: CA.
Thieves' Highway. Hale, 1973 [Ger.]
Yesterday's Poison. Hale, 1975

GRAYSTONE, JOHN
The Bradfield Case. Stockwell, 1943

GREATOREX, CLIFFORD W(ILLEY). 1896- .
The Secret of the Diamonds. Fiction House, 1935

GREATOREX, WILFRED. 1921- . Ref: CA.
Crossover. Weidenfeld, 1976. U.S. title: Three Potato, Four. Coward, 1977
Quicksand. Weidenfeld, 1979
Three Potato, Four; see Crossover

GREAVES, JIMMY and NORMAN GILLER
The Final. Barker, 1979

GREAVES, RICHARD. Pseudonym of Peter Simonds, 1906- .
The Case of Constable Shields. Dorrance, 1940

GRECCO, JOHNNY
Call Her Savage. Kaye, 1953
"Emma Slasky." Kaye, 1953
Mexican Deadline. Gaywood, 1950
Million Dollar Snatch. Gaywood, 1952
Send Another Coffin. Gaywood, 1950
She's No Lady. Kaye, 1953

GREELEY, ANDREW (MORAN). 1928- . Ref: CA.
Death in April. McGraw, 1980 [Chi.]

GREEN, MRS. See: W. G. Wills, 1828-1891.

GREEN, ALAN (BAER). 1906-1975. Joint pseudonym with Gladys Elizabeth Blun Green, 1908- : Glen Burne, q.v. Joint pseudonym with Julian P. Brodie: Roger Denbie, q.v. Ref: CA. SC: John Hugo, in both titles.
They Died Laughing. Simon, 1952; Panther, 1957 [N.H.]
What a Body! Simon, 1949; Redman, 1950 [Fla.]

GREEN, ANNA KATHARINE. 1846-1935. Ref: all except CA. SC: Ebenezer Gryce = EG; Violet Strange = VS; Caleb Sweetwater = CS.
Agatha Webb. Putnam, 1899; Ward, 1900 CS
The Amethyst Box. Bobbs, 1905; Chatto, 1905
Behind Closed Doors. Putnam, 1888; Routledge, 1888 EG [NYC]
The Chief Legatee. Authors, 1906. British title: A Woman of Mystery. Collier (London), 1909 [Conn.]
The Circular Study. McClure, 1900; Ward, 1902 EG [NYC]
Cynthia Wakeham's Money. Putnam, 1892; Ward, 1904 [N.Y.]
Dark Hollow. Dodd, 1914; Nash, 1914
A Difficult Problem and other stories. Lupton, 1900; Ward, 1903 ss, one with EG
The Doctor, His Wife, and the Clock. Putnam, 1895; Unwin, 1895 EG ss
Doctor Izard. Putnam, 1895; Cassell, 1895 [Mass.]
The Filigree Ball. Bobbs, 1903; Unwin, 1904 [Wash. D.C.]
The Forsaken Inn. Bonner, 1890; Routledge, 1890 [N.Y.]
The Golden Slipper and Other Problems for Violet Strange. Putnam, 1915 ss VS

Hand and Ring. Putnam, 1883; Ward, 1884
    EG [N.Y.]
The House in the Mist. Bobbs, 1905
    (Contains the title novel and 2 ss.)
    [Pa.]
The House of the Whispering Pines.
    Putnam, 1910; Nash, 1910 CS [N.Y.]
Initials Only. Dodd, 1911; Nash, 1912
    EG,CS [NYC]
The Leavenworth Case. Putnam, 1878;
    Routledge, 1884 EG [NYC]
Lost Man's Lane. Putnam, 1898 EG [N.Y.]
Marked "Personal". Putnam, 1893; Ward,
    1904 [NYC]
Masterpieces of Mystery. Dodd, 1913.
    Also published as: Room Number 3 and
    other stories. Dodd, 1919 ss
A Matter of Millions. Bonner, 1890;
    Routledge, 1890 EG [NYC]
The Mayor's Wife. Bobbs, 1907; London
    Daily Mail, 1909 [West]
The Mill Mystery. Putnam, 1886; Rout-
    ledge, 1886
The Millionaire Baby. Bobbs, 1905;
    Chatto, 1905 [N.Y.]
Miss Hurd: An Enigma. Putnam, 1894
    [N.Y.]
The Mystery of the Hasty Arrow. Dodd,
    1917 EG,CS [NYC]
The Old Stone House and other stories.
    Putnam, 1891 ss
One of My Sons. Putnam, 1901; Ward,
    1904 EG
-Risifi's Daughter. Putnam, 1887
Room Number 3 and other stories; see
    Masterpieces of Mystery
7 to 12. Putnam, 1887; Routledge, 1887
The Step on the Stair. Dodd, 1923;
    Lane, 1923 [N.Y.]
A Strange Disappearance. Putnam, 1880;
    Routledge, 1884 EG [NYC]
The Sword of Damocles. Putnam, 1881;
    Ward, 1884 [N.Y.]
That Affair Next Door. Putnam, 1897;
    Nash, 1903 EG [NYC]
Three Thousand Dollars. Badger, 1910
    [NYC]
To the Minute and Scarlet and Black:
    Two of Life's Perplexities. Putnam,
    1916
The Woman in the Alcove. Bobbs, 1906;
    Chatto, 1906 CS
A Woman of Mystery; see The Chief
    Legatee
XYZ. Putnam, 1883; Ward, 1883 ss
    [Mass.]

GREEN, CHALMERS
    The Scarlet Venus. GM, 1952; Fawcett
    (London), 1959 [Mich.]

GREEN, CHARLES. Pseudonym: Robert Wal-
    lace, q.v.

GREEN, DANIEL DAVID
    Hangman's Noose. Stockwell, 1954

GREEN, EDITH PINERO. 1929-   . Ref: CA.
    SC: Dearborn V. Pinch = DP.
    The Death Trap. Dell, 1975
    The Mark of Lucifer. Dell, 1974
    Rotten Apples. Dutton, 1977; Curley,
    1980 DP [L.I.]
    Sneaks. Dutton, 1979; Curley, 1981
    DP [Fla.]
    A Woman's Honor. Dell, 1977

GREEN, F(REDERICK) L(AWRENCE). 1902-1953.
    Born in England; studied law and
    lived for many years in Ire.
    Ambush for the Hunter. Joseph, 1952;
    Random, 1953
    -Clouds in the Wind. Joseph, 1950;
    Coward, 1951
    -A Flask for the Journey. Joseph, 1945;
    Reynal, 1948
    -A Fragment of Glass. Joseph, 1947
    -Give Us the World. Joseph, 1941
    The Magician. Joseph, 1951; Coward,
    1951
    Mist on the Waters. Joseph, 1948; Har-
    court, 1949 [Belfast]
    Odd Man Out. Joseph, 1945; Reynal, 1947
    [Belfast]
    On the Edge of the Sea. Joseph, 1944
    On the Night of the Fire. Joseph, 1939;
    Macmillan, 1939
    -A Song for the Angels. Joseph, 1943
    -The Sound of Winter. Joseph, 1940

GREEN, GERALD. 1922-   . Ref: CA.
    Faking It; or, The Wrong Hungarian.
    Trident, 1971 [Paris]
    The Hostage Heart. Playboy, 1976;
    Allen, 1976 [hosp.]

GREEN, GLADYS ELIZABETH BLUM. 1908-
    Joint pseudonym with Alan (Baer)
    Green, 1906-1975, q.v.: Glen Burne,
    q.v.

GREEN, GLINT. Pseudonym of Margaret (Ann)
    Peterson, 1883-1933, q.v. SC: Insp.
    Wield, in all titles.
    Beauty—A Snare. Hutchinson, 1933
    Devil Spider. Hutchinson, 1932
    Poison Death. Hutchinson, 1933
    Strands of Red...Hair! Hutchinson, 1931

GREEN, HELEN
    -Mr. Jackson. Dodge, 1909

GREEN, JANET. Pseudonym of Victoria
    McCormick, 1914-   .
    Gently Does It. Dramatists, 1954
    (2-act play.)
    Murder Mistaken, with Leonard (Regin-
    ald) Gribble, 1908-   , q.v. Allen,
    1953 (Novelization of Janet Green's
    play.)
    My Turn Now. Triton, 1971

GREEN, JULIEN (HARTRIDGE). 1900-   .
    Ref: CA.
    The Dark Journey. Heinemann, 1929;
    Harper, 1929 (Translation of "Levia-
    than." Paris, 1929.)

GREEN, MAURY. 1916-   . Ref: CA.
    The Delphi Calculus. Dell, 1978 [1981,
    U.S.]

GREEN, PETER (MORRIS). 1924-   . Pseudo-
    nym: Denis Delaney, q.v. Ref: CA.
    Habeas Corpus and other stories. H.
    Hamilton, 1962; World, 1963 ss

GREEN, MRS. SARAH
    The Carthusian Friar; or, The Mysteries
    of Montanville. Sherwood, 1814

GREEN, STAGG
    -Commando Escape. Hammond, 1943
    Fortress of the Maquis. Hammond, 1944

GREEN, STEPHEN
    Missing from Home. Redman, 1962

GREEN, THOMAS J. Author of magazine ar-
    ticles, screenplays and plays.
    The Flowered Box. Beaufort, 1980
    [Boston]

GREEN, WILLIAM CHILD
    Abbot of Montserrat; or, The Pool of
    Blood. Newman, 1826; Arno, 1977
    Alibeg the Tempter. Newman, 1831
    The Prophecy of Duncannon; or, The
    Dwarf and the Seer. Emans, 1824

GREEN, WILLIAM M(ARK). 1929-   . Ref:
    CA.
    Avery's Fortune. Bobbs, 1972; Hale,
    1973 [ship]
    The Man Who Called Himself Devlin.
    Bobbs, 1978 [Mid. East]
    The Plutonium Heist; see Spencer's Bag
    The Salisbury Manuscript. Bobbs, 1973;
    Hale, 1975
    See How They Run. Bobbs, 1975 [NYC]
    Spencer's Bag. Simon, 1971. British
    title: The Plutonium Heist. Hale,
    1973

GREENAN, RUSSELL H(ENRY). Born and educa-
    ted in NYC; lived most of adult life
    in Boston and Fr.
    The Bric-a-Brac Man. Random, 1976
    [Boston]
    Heart of Gold. Random, 1975 [Boston]
    It Happened in Boston. Random, 1968
    [Boston]
    Keepers. St. Martin's, 1979
    Nightmare. Random, 1970. British title:
    Nightmare in Colour. Joseph, 1971
    [NYC]
    Nightmare in Colour; see Nightmare
    The Queen of America. Random, 1972
    [Boston]
    The Secret Life of Algernon Pendleton.
    Random, 1973 [New Eng.]

GREENAWAY, GLADYS. 1901-   . Ref: CA.
    -The Affair at Little Todsham. Hurst,
    1964
    -Coffee in the Morning. Hurst, 1967
    -Devil in the Wind. Hurst, 1966
    -Feather Your Nest. Hurst, 1967
    -Follow a Shadow. Hale, 1961
    -Follow My Leader. Hurst, 1966
    -No Looking Back. Hurst, 1963
    -Shadows on the Sand. Hurst, 1958
    -Sing Softly, Stranger. Hurst, 1963
    -Spring Came Late. Hale, 1961
    -View of the Mountain. Hurst, 1959
    -Week of Suspense. Hurst, 1962

GREENBAUM, LEONARD. 1930-   . Ref: CA.
    Out of Shape. Harper, 1969; Gollancz,
    1970 [Mich., acad.]

GREENBERG, DAVE. 1943-   .
    Play It to a Bust. Hawthorn, 1975;
    Futura, 1977

GREENBERG, JOANNE (GOLDENBERG). 1932-   .
    Ref: CA.
    High Crimes and Misdemeanors. Holt,
    1980 ss

GREENBURG, DAN. 1936-   . Ref: CA.
    Love Kills. Harcourt, 1978; Secker,
    1978 [NYC]
    Philly. Simon, 1969; Secker, 1970
    [Chi.]

GREENE, A(LVIN) C(ARL). 1923-   .
    Ref: CA.
    The Santa Claus Bank Robbery. Knopf,
    1972 [Tex.]

GREENE, E(LIZABETH RUSSELL) PLUNKETT.
    1899-   . See: R(ussell George Her-
    bert Plunkett) Greene, 1901-   .

GREENE, FRANCES NIMMO. 1850-1921.
    The Devil to Pay. Scribner, 1918
    Into the Night. Crowell, 1909;
    Methuen, 1910
    -One Clear Call. Scribner, 1915

GREENE, GRAHAM. 1904-   . Ref: CA, CC,
    EM, MC, TC. Set: many Eng.
    The Basement Room and other stories.
    Cresset, 1935 ss
    Brighton Rock. Heinemann, 1938; Viking,
    1938
    A Burnt-Out Case. Heinemann, 1961;
    Viking, 1961 [Bel. Congo]
    The Comedians. Bodley, 1966; Viking,
    1966 [Haiti]
    The Confidential Agent. Heinemann,
    1939; Viking, 1939
    -Doctor Fischer of Geneva; or, The Bomb
    Party. Bodley, 1980; Simon, 1980
    The End of the Affair. Heinemann, 1951;
    Viking, 1951
    England Made Me. Heinemann, 1935;
    Doubleday, 1935. Also published as:
    The Shipwrecked. Viking, 1953
    A Gun for Sale. Heinemann, 1936. U.S.
    title: This Gun for Hire. Doubleday,
    1936
    The Heart of the Matter. Heinemann,
    1948; Viking, 1948 [Afr., W.]
    The Honorary Consul. Bodley, 1973;
    Simon, 1973 [Arg.]
    The Human Factor. Bodley, 1978; Simon,
    1978
    It's a Battlefield. Heinemann, 1934;
    Doubleday, 1934. Revised edition:
    Heinemann, 1948; Viking, 1952
    The Labyrinthine Ways; see The Power
    and the Glory
    Loser Takes All. Heinemann, 1955;
    Viking, 1957
    The Man Within. Heinemann, 1929;
    Doubleday, 1929
    The Ministry of Fear. Heinemann, 1943;
    Viking, 1943
    The Name of Action. Heinemann, 1930;
    Doubleday, 1931
    Nineteen Stories. Heinemann, 1947;
    Viking, 1949 (Includes 8 ss from
    The Basement Room, q.v.)
    Orient Express; see Stamboul Train
    Our Man in Havana. Heinemann, 1958;
    Viking, 1958 [Havana]
    The Potting Shed. French (London &
    NYC), 1957 (3-act play.)
    The Power and the Glory. Heinemann,
    1940. U.S. title: The Labyrinthine
    Ways. Viking, 1940. Reprinted as:
    The Power and the Glory. Viking, 1946
    The Quiet American. Heinemann, 1955;
    Viking, 1956
    The Return of A. J. Raffles. Bodley,
    1975; Simon, 1976 (Play, continuing
    the character created by E. W. Hor-
    nung, 1866-1921, q.v.)
    Rumour at Nightfall. Heinemann, 1931;
    Doubleday, 1932
    A Sense of Reality. Bodley, 1963;
    Viking, 1963 ss
    Shades of Greene. Bodley, 1975 (Col-
    lects ss dramatized in a British TV
    series: 7 from May We Borrow Your
    Husband?, 2 from A Sense of Reality,
    9 from Twenty-One Stories, qq.v.)
    The Shipwrecked; see England Made Me
    Stamboul Train. Heinemann, 1932. U.S.
    title: Orient Express. Doubleday,
    1933 [train]
    The Third Man and The Fallen Idol.
    Heinemann, 1950. U.S. title: The
    Third Man. Viking, 1950 (The Fallen
    Idol does not appear in the U.S. edi-
    tion but is included under its ori-
    ginal title, The Basement Room, in
    Nineteen Stories, q.v.) [Vienna]
    This Gun for Hire; see A Gun for Sale
    Travels with My Aunt. Bodley, 1969;
    Viking, 1970

Twenty-One Stories. Heinemann, 1954; Viking, 1962 (Revision of Nineteen Stories, q.v., with 2 tales removed from the earlier edition and 4 new ss added.)

GREENE, HARRIS (CARL). 1921-   . Ref: CA.
The Athens Affair; see FSO-1
Cancelled Accounts. Doubleday, 1972; New English Library, 1973 [Switz.]
The Flags at Doney. Doubleday, 1964 [It., 1956]
FSO-1. Doubleday, 1977; New English Library, 1977. Also published as: The Athens Affair. New English Library pb, 1979 [Athens]
-The "Mozart" Leaves at Nine. Doubleday, 1961; Heinemann, 1961 [Austria]

GREENE, JOSIAH E(NSIGN). 1911-1955.
The Laughing Loon. Morrow, 1939 [Minn.]
Madmen Die Alone. Morrow, 1938 [hosp.]

GREENE, L. PATRICK. Name originally: Louis Montague Greene. SC: Dynamite Drury, in at least those marked DD; Sgt. Lancey, in at least those marked L; Aubrey St. John Major, in at least those marked AM. Set: S. Afr., in most titles, certainly those marked *.
Black Tide Rising. Harrap, 1936 AM
The Devil's Kloof. Hamilton, 1928 AM
Drums Call the Major. Harrap, 1938 AM *
Dynamite Drury. Selwyn, 1929 DD *
Dynamite Drury Again. Jarrolds, 1930 DD
Dynamite Drury Patrols. Devonshire, 1946 DD
Escape from Liberty. Hamilton, 1939 AM *
Face Value. Hamilton, 1939 AM *
The Flame. Hamilton, 1930 *
Forbidden Valley. Hamilton, 1932 AM *
Just Vengeance. Hamilton, 1934 AM *
The Lake of the Dead. Hamilton, 1935 AM
Major Adventures. Heinemann, 1928 AM *
Major Developments. Hamilton, 1931 AM *
The Major—Diamond Buyer. Hamilton, 1926; Doubleday, 1924 AM *
Major Exploits. Selwyn, 1930 AM *
Major Hazards. Hamilton, 1932 AM *
The Major—Knight Errant. Heinemann, 1929 AM *
Major Occasions. Hamilton, 1931 AM *
Murder Beacon, with Walter S(idney) Masterman, 1876-   , q.v. Low, 1932
The Point of a Thousand Spears. Hamilton, 1934 L,AM
The Red Idol. Hamilton, 1928 AM *
Sergeant Lancey Carries On. Hamilton, 1933 L *
Sergeant Lancey Reports. Hamilton, 1931 L *
Sergeant Lancey Tells the Tale. Devonshire, 1947 L
The Splendid Exile. Hamilton, 1935 AM *
Swordsman of Fortune. Mellifont, 1943
White Man's Stride. Selwyn, 1929 ss AM

GREENE, R(USSELL GEORGE HUBERT PLUNKET), 1901-   , and E(LIZABETH RUSSELL) PLUNKET GREENE, 1899-   .
Eleven-Thirty Till Twelve. Secker, 1934
-Where Ignorance Is Bliss. Murray, 1932

GREENE, WARD. 1892-1956. Pseudonym: Frank Dudley, q.v.
Death in the Deep South. Stackpole, 1936; Cassell, 1937 [South]

GREENE, WILL
The Riot Act. Dramatists, 1963 (3-act play.)

GREENER, WILLIAM OLIVER. 1862-   . Pseudonym: Wirt Gerrare, q.v.
The Exploits of Jo Salis, a British Spy. Hurst, 1905
A Secret Agent in Port Arthur. Constable, 1905

GREENFIELD, GEORGE
-At Bay. Cassell, 1955
-Desert Episode. Macmillan (London), 1945
-This World Is Wide Enough. Laurie, 1948

GREENFIELD, IRVING A. 1928-   . Pseudonym: Alicia Grace, q.v. Ref: CA.
Barracuda. Arbor, 1978
Clove Crest. Belmont, 1969. Reprinted as by Alicia Grace: Manor, 1978
Doesn't Everyone. Manor, 1977
-The Face of Him. Manor, 1976
High Terror. Popular Library, 1978 [Paris]
Julius Caesar Is Alive and Well. Manor, 1977
Tagget. Arbor, 1979
-Waters of Death. Manor, 1977
-Who Knows? Manor, 1977

GREENFIELD, JOHN
Death in the Library. Kangaroo, 1944

GREENFIELD, RICHARD PIERCE
One Shot. Manor, 1977

GREENHAM, G(EORGE) H(EPBURN)
Scotland Yard Experiences. Routledge, 1904 ss

GREENING, ARTHUR
The Curse of Kali. Jarrolds, 1922

GREENLAND, FRANCIS (LOFFAN). 1924-   .
The Misericordia Drop. Davis-Poynter, 1976
Shade Against the Sun. Hale, 1980

GREENLAND, WILLIAM KINGSCOTE. Pseudonym: W. Scott King, q.v.

GREENLEAF, SAUL G.
The Three Knaves. Fenno, 1912 [Eng.]

GREENLEAF, STEPHEN (HOWELL). 1942-   . Ref: CA. SC: John Tanner, in both titles.
Death Bed. Dial, 1980 [S.F.]
Grave Error. Dial, 1979; New English Library, 1981 [S.F.]

GREENLEAVES, WINIFRED
The Trout Inn Tragedy. Collins, 1929. U.S. title: The Trout Inn Mystery. Dial, 1929

GREENLEE, SAM. 1930-   . Ref: CA.
Baghdad Blues. Bantam, 1976 [Baghdad]
The Spook Who Sat by the Door. Baron, 1969; Allison, 1969 [Chi.]

GREENOUGH, MRS. (SARA DANA LORING). 1827-1885.
In Extremis. Roberts, 1872
Treason at Home. Newby, 1865; Peterson, 187?

GREENWALD, NANCY. Hollywood movie and TV writer.
Lady Cat. Crown, 1980 [S.F.]

GREENWOOD, DUNCAN. 1919-   . Ref: CA.
Murder Delayed. French (London), 1961 (3-act play.)

GREENWOOD, EDWIN. British stage and screen director and producer.
Dark Understudy. Hale, 1940
The Deadly Dowager; see Skin and Bone
The Fair Devil; see Pins and Needles
French Farce. Skeffington, 1936; Doubleday, 1937 [Paris]
-Miracle in the Drawing Room. Skeffington, 1935; Doubleday, 1936
Old Goat. Heinemann, 1937
Pins and Needles. Skeffington, 1935. U.S. title: The Fair Devil. Doubleday, 1935
Skin and Bone. Skeffington, 1935. U.S. title: The Deadly Dowager. Doubleday, 1935

GREENWOOD, WALTER. 1903-1974. Ref: CA.
Only Mugs Work. Hutchinson, 1938

GREER, BEN. 1948-   . Ref: CA.
Halloween. Macmillan, 1978 [South]

GREER, WOODY. See: Janet Gluckman.

GREET, MRS. (DORA VICTORIA)
Mrs. Greet's Story of the Golden Owl. Leadenhall, 1892

GREGG, CECIL FREEMAN. 1898-   . Ref: CC, MP. SC: Insp. Cuthbert Higgins = CH; Henry Prince = HP. Set: Eng.
Accidental Murder. Methuen, 1952 CH
Airtight Alibi. Methuen, 1956
The Body Behind the Bar. Methuen, 1932 CH
The Body in the Safe; see The Murdered Manservant
The Brazen Confession. Hutchinson, 1930. U.S. title: I Have Killed a Man! Dial, 1931 CH
The Chief Constable. Methuen, 1955 CH
Danger at Cliff House. Methuen, 1935; Dial, 1936 CH
Danger in the Dark. Methuen, 1939 CH
Dead on Time. Methuen, 1956 CH
The Double Solution. Hutchinson, 1931; Dial, 1932 CH
The Duke's Last Trick. Methuen, 1933 CH
The Execution of Diamond Deutsch. Methuen, 1934. U.S. title: Murder in the Park. Dial, 1935 CH
Exit Harlequin. Methuen, 1946 CH
Expert Evidence, Rex v. Marfelt. Methuen, 1938
The Fatal Error. Methuen, 1940 CH
Finlay of the Sentinel. Methuen, 1957
From Information Received. Methuen, 1950 CH
Henry Prince in Action. Methuen, 1936 HP
I Have Killed a Man!; see The Brazen Confession
Inspector Higgins Goes Fishing. Methuen, 1951 CH
Inspector Higgins Hurries. Hutchinson, 1932; Dial, 1932 CH
Inspector Higgins Sees It Through. Methuen, 1934; Appleton, 1934 CH
Justice! Methuen, 1941
The Man with a Monocle. Methuen, 1948 CH
Melander's Millions. Methuen, 1944 CH
Murder at Midnight. Methuen, 1947 CH
Murder in the Park; see The Execution of Diamond Deutsch
The Murder of Estelle Cantor; see The Ten Black Pearls
The Murder on the Bus. Hutchinson, 1930; Dial, 1930 CH
The Murdered Manservant. Hutchinson, 1928. U.S. title: The Body in the Safe. Dial, 1930 CH
Mystery at Moor Street. Methuen, 1938 CH
Night Flight to Zurich. Methuen, 1954 CH
The Obvious Solution. Methuen, 1958 CH
The Old Manor. Methuen, 1945; McNaughton, 1946 CH
Professional Jealousy. Methuen, 1960 CH
The Return of Henry Prince. Methuen, 1943 HP
The Rutland Mystery. Hutchinson, 1931; Dial, 1931 CH
Sufficient Rope. Methuen, 1953 CH
The Ten Black Pearls. Methuen, 1935. U.S. title: The Murder of Estelle Cantor. Dial, 1936 HP
The Three Daggers. Hutchinson, 1929; Dial, 1929 CH
Tragedy at Wembley. Methuen, 1936; Dial, 1936 CH
Two Died at Three. Methuen, 1943; Mystery House, 1944 CH
The Ugly Customer. Methuen, 1949 CH
The Vandor Mystery. Methuen, 1942 CH
Who Dialled 999? Methuen, 1939 CH
The Wrong House. Methuen, 1937 CH

GREGOR, MANFRED. 1929-   .
-Town Without Pity. Random, 1961; Heinemann, 1961 (Translation of "Das Urteil." Vienna, 1960.) [Ger.]

GREGOR, PAUL
Jump into the Sun. Berkley, 1961 (Translation of "Le Saut dans Soleil." Paris, 1960.) [Brazil]

GREGORY, LADY (ISABELLA AUGUSTA PERSSE). 1852-1932.
Selected Plays. Putnam (London), 1962; Hill, 1963 (Plays, some criminous.)

GREGORY, DAN
Three Must Die! Graphic, 1956

GREGORY, F(RANKLIN) L(ONG). 1905-   .
The Cipher of Death. Harper (London & NYC), 1934 [NYC]
Murder at Four Dot Ranch. World's Work, 1936
-The White Wolf. Random, 1941

GREGORY, H. Pseudonym. See: Alfred Edgar, 1896-   ; Reginald H(eber) Poole, 1885-   .

GREGORY, HARRY. Pseudonym of Theodore Mark Gottfried, 1928-   . Other pseudonym: Katherine Tobias, q.v.
The Man from MOTHER. PB, 1967

GREGORY, HYLTON. Pseudonym. See: Harry Egbert Hill.

GREGORY, JACKSON. 1882-1943. SC: Paul Savoy = PS.
A Case for Mr. Paul Savoy. Scribner, 1933. British title: The Second Case of Mr. Paul Savoy. Hodder, 1933 PS [S.F.]
The Emerald Murder Trap. Scribner, 1934. British title: The Third Case of Mr. Paul Savoy. Hodder, 1934 PS [Calif.]
The First Case of Mr. Paul Savoy; see The House of the Opal
The House of the Opal. Scribner, 1932. British title: The First Case of Mr. Paul Savoy. Hodder, 1933 PS [Calif.]
Ladyfingers. Scribner, 1920; Melrose, 1921 [S.F.]
Mystery at Spanish Hacienda. Dodd, 1929. British title: Rapidan. Hodder, 1929
Rapidan; see Mystery at Spanish Hacienda
The Second Case of Mr. Paul Savoy; see A Case for Mr. Paul Savoy
The Third Case of Mr. Paul Savoy; see The Emerald Murder Trap

GREGORY, JAMES
    Children of the Reich. Leisure, 1980

GREGORY, MASON. Joint pseudonym of Doris
    Meek and Adrienne Jones, 1915- .
    Other joint pseudonym: Gregory Mason,
    q.v.
    If Two of Them Are Dead. Arcadia, 1953

GREGORY, SACHA. Pseudonym.
    Yellowleaf. Heinemann, 1919; Lippin-
    cott, 1919

GREGORY, STEPHAN. Pseudonym of Don(ald
    Eugene) Pendleton, 1927-   , q.v.
    Frame Up. Vega, 1962 [Calif.]

GREIG, IAN (BAXTER). SC: Insp. Swinton,
    in all titles. Set: Eng.
    Baxter's Second Death. Benn, 1932;
        Kinsey, 1933
    False Scent. Benn, 1933
    The King's Club Murder. Benn, 1930.
        U.S. title: The Silver King Mystery.
        Holt, 1930
    Murder at Lintercombe. Benn, 1931
    The Silver King Mystery; see The King's
        Club Murder
    The Tragedy of the Chinese Mine. Benn,
        1930; Holt, 1931

GREIG, MAYSIE. 1902-1971. Pseudonyms:
    Jennifer Ames, q.v., Mary Douglas
    Warren. Ref: CA.
    Cloak and Dagger Lover. Collins, 1955.
        U.S. title: Moon over the Water.
        Arcadia, 1956, as by Mary Douglas
        Warren
    Moon over the Water; see Cloak and
        Dagger Lover
    Whispers in the Sun. Collins, 1949;
        Random, 1949

GRESHAM, ELIZABETH (FENNER). 1904- .
    Pseudonym: Robin Grey, q.v. Ref: CA.
    SC: Jenny Gilette (Lewis) and
    Hunter Lewis = L (see also Grey en-
    try).
    Daughter of Darkness. Popular Library,
        1977
    Lucifer Was Tall. Popular Library, 1976
        [Boston]
    Pawn in Jeopardy. Popular Library, 1977
        [NYC]
    Prisoner's Base. Popular Library, 1979
        [New Eng.]
    Puzzle in Paisley. Curtis, 1972 L
        [Cape Cod]
    Puzzle in Parchment. Curtis, 1973 L
        [N.H., acad.]
    Puzzle in Parquet. Curtis, 1973 L
        [N.Y.]
    Puzzle in Patchwork. Curtis, 1973 L
    -The Sickly Flame. Popular Library, 1977

GRESHAM, WILLIAM LINDSAY. 1909-1962.
    Nightmare Alley. Rinehart, 1946; Heine-
        mann, 1947

GRETH, LeROMA (ESHBACH). All titles are
    plays; number of acts in parenthesis.
    The Dancing Ghost. Baker, 1961 (3)
    The Ghost from Outer Space. Baker, 1958
        (1)
    The Ghost of Cemetery Ridge. Baker,
        1962 (3)
    The Happy Hunting Ground. Baker, 1959
        (3)
    Nightmare! Dramatic, 1961 (3)
    Washington Never Slept Here. Art Craft,
        1960 (3)

GREVILLE, HENRY. Pseudonym of Alice Marie
    Celeste Fleury Durand, 1842-1902.
    Un Mystere (A Mystery). Donohue, 1890.
        Also published as: The Beaurand Mys-
        tery. Mershon, 1900 (Translation of
        "Un Mystere." Paris, 1890.) [Fr.]

GREW, WILLIAM. Pseudonym of William
    O'Farrell, 1904-1962, q.v.
    Doubles in Death. Doubleday, 1953 [NYC]
    Murder Has Many Faces. Graphic, 1955
        [Mex.]

GREX, LEO. Pseudonym of Leonard (Regin-
    ald) Gribble, 1908-   , q.v. Other
    pseudonyms: Sterry Browning, Louis
    Grey, Dexter Muir, qq.v. See also:
    Janet Green. SC: Paul Irving, in at
    least those marked PI; Phil Sander-
    son, in at least those marked PS.
    Set: Eng.
    Ace of Danger. Hutchinson, 1952 PI
    The Black-Out Murders. Harrap, 1940
    The Brass Knuckle. Long, 1964
    The Carlent Manor Crime. Hutchinson,
        1939. Reprinted as by Leonard Grib-
        ble: Cherry Tree, 1946 PI
    Crooked Sixpence. Harrap, 1949
    Crooner's Swan Song. Hutchinson, 1935
    Death Throws No Shadow. Hale, 1976
    Die—As in Murder. Hale, 1974

The Hard Kill. Long, 1969 PS
Kill Now—Pay Later. Long, 1971
King Spiv. Harrap, 1948
Larceny in Her Heart. Long, 1959
The Lonely Inn Mystery. Hutchinson,
    1933 PI
The Madison Murder. Hutchinson, 1933 PI
The Man from Manhattan. Hutchinson,
    1934; Doubleday, 1935
Mix Me a Murder. Hale, 1978
Murder in the Sanctuary. Hutchinson,
    1934 PI
The Nightborn. Hutchinson, 1931
The Stalag Mites. Harrap, 1947
Stolen Death. Hutchinson, 1936 PI
Terror Wears a Smile. Long, 1962
Thanks for the Felony. Long, 1958
The Tragedy at Draythorpe. Hutchinson,
    1931 PI
Transatlantic Trouble. Hutchinson,
    1937. Reprinted as by Leonard Grib-
    ble: Cherry Tree, 1946
Violent Keepsake. Long, 1967 PS

GREY, A. F. Pseudonym of Adeline Phyllis
    Neal, 1894-1977.
    Momentary Stoppage. Gollancz, 1942

GREY, ALTHEA. See: Michael Burning.

GREY, ANTHONY. 1938-   . Ref: CA.
    The Bulgarian Exchange. Joseph, 1976;
        Dial, 1977 [Bulg.]
    The Chinese Assassin. Joseph, 1978;
        Holt, 1979
    Some Put Their Trust in Chariots.
        Joseph, 1973

GREY, DOUGLAS
    The Tracking of K.K. Chelsea, 1925;
        Skeffington, 1926 [N.Y.]

GREY, HARRY. Pseudonym of Harry Goldberg.
    Call Me Duke. Crown, 1955
    The Hoods. Crown, 1952
    Portrait of a Mobster. Signet, 1958
        [NYC, 1920s]

GREY, LOUIS. Pseudonym of Leonard (Regin-
    ald) Gribble, 1908-   , q.v. Other
    pseudonyms: Sterry Browning, Leo
    Grex, Dexter Muir, qq.v. See also:
    Janet Green.
    The Signet of Death. Nicholson, 1934.
        Reprinted as by Dexter Muir: Jenkins,
        1946

GREY, MAXWELL. Pseudonym of Mary Gleed
    Tuttiett,   -1923.
    -An Innocent Imposter and other stories.
        Appleton, 1893 ss

GREY, NAIDRA. Pseudonym of Naidra Cocks-
    hut.
    Dark Sun, Pale Shadows. Putnam, 1973.
        British title: The Quinta Affair.
        Macmillan (London), 1974 [Port.]
    Foxglove Summer. Putnam, 1976; Davies,
        1977 [Eng.]
    The Quinta Affair; see Dark Sun, Pale
        Shadows

GREY, ROBIN. Pseudonym of Elizabeth (Fen-
    ner) Gresham, 1904-   , q.v. SC:
    Jenny Gilette (Lewis) and Hunter
    Lewis, in both titles (see also
    Gresham entry).
    Puzzle in Pewter. Duell, 1947. Reprint-
        ed as by Elizabeth Gresham: Curtis
        1973 [Va.]
    Puzzle in Porcelain. Duell, 1945. Re-
        printed as by Elizabeth Gresham:
        Curtis, 1973 [Va.]

GREY, SCARLET. Pseudonym.
    -Golden Hooves. Columbine, 1939
    Jock MacKay, Crook. Columbine, 1939

GREY, STEPHEN
    Dead on Time. Dramatic, 1964 (3-act
        play.)

GRIBBEN, JAMES. 1915-   . Pseudonym:
    Vincent James, q.v.

GRIBBLE, DOROTHY ROSE
    The Cask of Amontillado. Plantagenet,
        1977 (1-act play based on the ss by
        Edgar A. Poe, 1809-1849, q.v.)

GRIBBLE, LEONARD (REGINALD). 1908-   .
    Pseudonyms: Sterry Browning, Leo
    Grex, Louis Grey, Dexter Muir, qq.v.
    See also: Janet Green. Ref: all ex-
    cept MC. SC: Supt. Anthony Slade, in
    at least those marked AS. Set: Eng.
    Alias the Victim. Hale, 1971 AS
    The Arsenal Stadium Mystery. Harrap,
        1939. Revised edition: Jenkins, 1950
        AS
    Atomic Murder. Harrap, 1947; Ziff-
        Davis, 1947 AS

The Case-Book of Anthony Slade. Qual-
    ity, 1937 AS ss
The Case of the Malverne Diamonds. Har-
    rap, 1936; Greenberg, 1937 AS
The Case of the Marsden Rubies. Harrap,
    1929; Doubleday, 1930 AS
Crime on Her Hands. Hale, 1977
The Death Chime. Harrap, 1934
Death Needs No Alibi. Hale, 1979
Death Pays the Piper. Jenkins, 1956;
    Roy, 1958 AS
A Diplomat Dies. Jenkins, 1969 AS
Don't Argue with Death. Jenkins, 1959;
    Roy, 1959 AS
The Frightened Chameleon. Jenkins,
    1951; Roy, 1957 AS
The Gillespie Suicide Mystery. Harrap,
    1929. U.S. title: The Terrace Suicide
    Mystery. Doubleday, 1929 AS
The Glass Alibi. Jenkins, 1952; Roy,
    1956 AS
The Grand Modena Murder. Harrap, 1930;
    Doubleday, 1931 AS
Hangman's Moon. Allen, 1950 AS
Heads You Die. Jenkins, 1964 AS
The Inverted Crime. Jenkins, 1954 AS
Is This Revenge? Harrap, 1931. U.S.
    title: The Serpentine Murder. Dodd,
    1932 AS
Midsummer Slay Ride. Hale, 1976
Murder Out of Season. Jenkins, 1952 AS
Mystery at Tudor Arches. Harrap, 1935
    AS
Mystery Manor. Goulden, 1951
Programmed for Death. Hale, 1973
The Riddle of the Ravens. Harrap, 1934
    AS
Riley of the Special Branch. Harrap,
    1936 AS
Sally of Scotland Yard, with Geraldine
    Laws. Allen, 1954
The Secret of Tangles. Harrap, 1933;
    Lippincott, 1934 AS
The Serpentine Murder; see Is This Re-
    venge?
She Died Laughing. Jenkins, 1953 AS
    [Fr.]
Stand-In for Murder. Jenkins, 1957;
    Roy, 1958 AS
The Stolen Home Secretary. Harrap,
    1932. U.S. title: The Stolen States-
    man. Dodd, 1932 AS
The Stolen Statesman; see The Stolen
    Home Secretary
Strip-Tease Macabre. Jenkins, 1967 AS
Superintendent Slade Investigates.
    Jenkins, 1956; Roy, 1957 AS ss
The Terrace Suicide Mystery; see The
    Gillespie Suicide Mystery
They Kidnapped Stanley Matthews. Jen-
    kins, 1950 AS
Tragedy in E Flat. Harrap, 1938; Hill-
    man-Curl, 1939 AS
The Velvet Mask and other stories.
    Allen, 1952 ss
The Violent Dark. Jenkins, 1965 AS
Wantons Die Hard. Jenkins, 1961; Roy,
    1961 AS
Who Killed Oliver Cromwell? Harrap,
    1937; Greenberg, 1938 AS
The Yellow Bungalow Mystery. Harrap,
    1933 AS
You Can't Die Tomorrow. Hale, 1975

GRIBBON, WILLIAM LANCASTER. 1879-1940.
    Pseudonym: Talbot Mundy, q.v.

GRIBDAN, VOLSTED. Pseudonym of John Rus-
    sell Fearn, 1908-1960, q.v. Other
    pseudonyms: Hugo Blayn, Spike Gordon,
    Griff, Nat Karta, John Slate, qq.v.
    SC: Adam Quirke, in both titles.
    The Lonely Astronomer. Scion, 1954
    The Master Must Die. Scion, 1953

GRIEG, JAN
    The Sign of the Flying Fox. Vantage,
        1976

GRIEG, MICHAEL. 1922-   . Ref: CA.
    A Fire in His Hand. Doubleday, 1963
        [NYC]

GRIERSON, EDWARD (DOBBYN). 1914-1975.
    Ref: CA, CC, DD, MC, TC. Set: Eng.
    A Crime of One's Own. Chatto, 1967;
        Putnam, 1967
    The Massingham Affair. Chatto, 1962;
        Doubleday, 1963 [Eng., 1890s]
    Reputation for a Song. Chatto, 1952;
        Knopf, 1953
    The Second Man. Chatto, 1956; Knopf,
        1956

GRIERSON, FRANCIS (DURHAM). 1888-1972.
    Ref: CA, CC, MM, MP. SC: Supt. Andrew
    Ash = AA; Chief Det. Insp. George
    Muir = GM; Det. Insp. Sims and Prof.
    Wells = S&W; Richard Furling = RF;
    Commissaire Patras = P. Set: Eng.
    The Acrefield Mystery. Butterworth,
        1938

Blackmail in Red. Hale, 1954 AA
The Blind Frog. Hale, 1955 AA
The Blue Bucket Mystery. Bles, 1929; Clode, 1930 S&W
Boomerang Murder. Hutchinson, 1951 GM
The Buddha of Fleet Street. Hutchinson, 1949 AA,GM
The Cabaret Crime. Butterworth, 1938 GM
A Covenant with Death. Butterworth, 1938 GM
The Coward's Club. Butterworth, 1937 P
The Crimson Cat. Eyre, 1944 GM
Death on Deposit. Butterworth, 1935 S&W
The Double Thumb. Hodder, 1925 S&W ss
The Empty House. Butterworth, 1933; Appleton, 1934
Entertaining Murder. Eyre, 1945 GM
The Green Diamond Mystery. Collins, 1929 [Paris]
Green Evil. Hale, 1958 AA
He Had It Coming to Him. Eyre, 1948 AA,GM
The Heart in the Box. Butterworth, 1936 P [Paris]
The Ink Street Murder. Butterworth, 1940 GM
The Jackdaw Mystery. Collins, 1931 [Paris]
Judas C.I.D. Hale, 1954 AA
The Lady of Despair. Collins, 1930 P
The Limping Man. Hodder, 1924; Clode, 1926 S&W
The Lost Pearl. Hodder, 1925; Clode, 1926 S&W
The Mad Hatter Murder. Eyre, 1941 GM
Madame Shadow. Hutchinson, 1952 AA,GM [Paris]
The Man from Madagascar. Butterworth, 1937 P [Paris]
The Monkhurst Murder. Collins, 1933 RF
Murder at Lancaster Gate. Butterworth, 1934 S&W
Murder at the Wedding; see The Yellow Rat
Murder in Black. Butterworth, 1935; Appleton, 1935 S&W
Murder in Mortimer Square. Collins, 1932 RF
Murder in the Gardne; see The Zoo Murder
The Mysterious Mademoiselle. Collins, 1930 S&W [Fr.]
Mystery in Red. Collins, 1931
The Mystery of the Golden Angel. Collins, 1933 RF
The Mystery of the Two-Faced Man. Butterworth, 1939 GM
No Wreaths for the Duchess. Hutchinson, 1948 AA,GM
Out of the Ashes. Eyre, 1946 AA
The Red Cobra. Hale, 1960 AA
Secret Judges. Hodder, 1925 S&W
The Sign of the Nine. Hale, 1956 AA
The Smiling Death. Bles, 1927; Clode, 1927 S&W
The Strange Case of Edgar Heriot. Hutchinson, 1950 GM
Thrice Judas. Eyre, 1942 GM
Traitor's Cross. Hutchinson, 1952 AA,GM
The White Camellia. Bles, 1929; Clode, 1929 S&W
The Yellow Rat. Collins, 1929. Also published as: Murder at the Wedding. Collins, 1932 S&W
The Zoo Murder. Bles, 1926. U.S. title: The Murder in the Garden. Clode, 1927 S&W [Paris]

GRIEVE, ALEXANDER HAIG GLANVILLE. 1902-   . Pseudonym: Alec Glanville, q.v.

GRIFF. House name. Those written by F(rank) Dubrez Fawcett, 1891-1968, q.v., marked *. Other Fawcett pseudonyms: Spike Gordon, Elmer Eliot Saks, Ben Sarto, qq.v. Those written by Ernest L(ionel) McKeag, , q.v., marked #. Other McKeag pseudonyms: Mark Grimshaw, Ramon Lacroix, qq.v. That written by John Russell Fearn, 1908-1960, q.v., marked +. Other Fearn pseudonyms: Hugo Blayn, Spike Gordon, Volsted Gribdan, Nat Karta, John Slate, qq.v.
Back-Alley Blond. Modern Fiction, 1952 *
Brooklyn Moll Shoots Bedmate. Modern Fiction, 1951 [NYC]
Bullets for Snoopers. Modern Fiction, 1953
Cage of Corruption. Modern Fiction, 1953
Caribbean Cutie. Modern Fiction, 1953
The City of Lost Women. Modern Fiction, 1953
Come and Get Me. Modern Fiction, 1949 #
Crooked Coffins. Modern Fiction, 1952 *
Curves Can Cast Shadows. Modern Fiction, 1953
Dames Don't Forget. Modern Fiction, 195?
Dared by a Dame. Modern Fiction, 1953
Dead Bones Tell Tales. Modern Fiction, 1953
Demon Barber of Broadway. Modern Fiction, 1953 [NYC]
Devil's Daughter. Modern Fiction, 1952
Dope Is for Dopes. Modern Fiction, 1949 #
The Doped and the Damned. Modern Fiction, 1953
Eastern Men—Chicago Women. Modern Fiction, 1951
From Dance Hall to Opium Den. Modern Fiction, 1950 *
Good-Bye Tomorrow. Modern Fiction, 1951
Hank Tries the Sidewalk. Modern Fiction, 1953
Hell-Bomb Floozies. Modern Fiction, 1951
Hi-Jack That Dame. Modern Fiction, 1950
Hot-Shot Rita. Modern Fiction, 1951 *
I Don't Get It. Modern Fiction, 1953
I Spit on Your Grave. Modern Fiction, 195?
Kiss Tomorrow Goodbye. Modern Fiction, 1952
Liquid Death. Modern Fiction, 1953 +
Main Street Morgue. Modern Fiction, 1953
Midnight Hostess. Modern Fiction, 1955
Molls Mean Murder. Modern Fiction, 1949
Murder by Contract. Modern Fiction, 1951
Night Patrol. Modern Fiction, 1953
Only Mugs Die Young. Modern Fiction, 1949 #
Played the Hard Way. Modern Fiction, 1954
Poisonous Angel. Modern Fiction, 1953
The Quick and the Dead. Modern Fiction, 1953
Rackets Incorporated. Modern Fiction, 1949 #
Rub-Out Specialty. Modern Fiction, 1949 #
She Had It Coming—. Modern Fiction, 1951
She Paid 'Em Off. Modern Fiction, 1951
Shoot to Live. Modern Fiction, 1953
The Silver Key. Modern Fiction, 1953
Some Rats Have Two Legs. Modern Fiction, 1950 *
Stiffs Can't Squeal. Modern Fiction, 1950
That Room in Camden Town. Modern Fiction, 1952 *
Too Tough to Live. Modern Fiction, 1952
Trading with Bodies. Modern Fiction, 1950
Vice Queens on Broadway. Modern Fiction, 1951 [NYC]
You Pay the Price. Modern Fiction, 1952

GRIFFIN, A. M.
The Man Who Called Too Soon. Gifford, 1945
Nurse Lester's First Case. Gifford, 1947

GRIFFIN, (EDITHA) ACEITUNA. 1876-   .
-Amber and Jade. Longmans, 1928
Commandments Six and Eight. Low, 1936
-Conscience. Murray, 1931
Delia's Dilemma. Pawling, 1934
-Genesta. Murray, 1930
-Lady Sarah's Deed of Gift. Blackwood, 1906
Motive for Murder, with Joy Griffin. Low, 1935
-Mrs. Vannock. Nash, 1907
-Pearl and Plain. Longmans, 1927
The Punt Murder. Low, 1936
-A Servant of the King. Blackwood, 1906
Sweets and Sinners. Low, 1937
-The Tavistocks. Laurie, 1908
"Where There Is a Will..." Low, 1939

GRIFFIN, ANNE J. Pseudonym of Arthur J. Griffin, 1921-   . Other pseudonyms: Susan James, q.v. Ref: CA.
Ocean of Fear. Avon, 1974 [L.I.]
The Spirit of Brynmaster Oaks. Avon, 1974 [L.I.]

GRIFFIN, ARTHUR J. 1921-   . Pseudonyms: Anne J. Griffin, Susan James, qq.v.

GRIFFIN, FRANK
Appointment with My Lady. Westhouse, 1946
Danger at Midnight. Mellifont, 1948
Death After Dark. Fiction House, 1947
Death Takes a Hand. Bear Hudson, 1945
Killer's Progress. Pendulum, 1947
October Day. Secker, 1939
A Rope for Christmas. Yates, 1951
She Deserved to Die. Yates, 1951
Strumpet's Fool. Westhouse, 1947

GRIFFIN, GERALD. 1803-1840.
The Collegians. Saunders, 1829; Harper, 1829

GRIFFIN, GERALD G(EHRIG). 1933-   . See also: Robin Moore.
The Corruptors. Condor, 1977

GRIFFIN, JOHN. Pseudonym of Michael John Clay, 1934-   . SC: Richard Raven, in all titles.
Anarchists' Moon. Hale, 1977
The Antarctic Convergence. Hale, 1979 [Antarctic]
The Camelot Conundrum. Hale, 1979
Circle of Darkness. Hale, 1976
The Florentine Madonna. Hale, 1979 [Florence]
The Midas Operation. Hale, 1976
The Ring of Kerry. Hale, 1978 [Ire.]
St. Catherine's Wheel. Hale, 1978
Seeds of Destruction. Hale, 1977
Standing into Danger. Hale, 1976

GRIFFIN, JOY. See: (Editha) Aceituna Griffin, 1876-   .

GRIFFIN, LEROY F. [LAROY FREESE GRIFFIN]. 1844-1916.
The Abduction of Princess Chriemhild. Weed, 1898

GRIFFIN, ROBERT J. SC: Coopersmith, in all titles.
-Coopersmith. Pyramid, 1968
-Coopersmith's Dolls. Pyramid, 1969
-Genghis Coopersmith. Pyramid, 1972
-King Coopersmith. Pyramid, 1971

GRIFFIN, SAMUEL FRANKLIN
Betencourt Five. Gold Side, 1971
Little Squaw Big Hurry. Gold Side, 1971
The Willfreud Curse. Gold Side, 1972

GRIFFITH, MRS. and MRS. E. G. Pseudonym: Jason Griffith, q.v.

GRIFFITH, GEORGE (CHETWYND). 1859-1906.
Brothers of the Chain. White, 1900
A Conquest of Fortune. White, 1906
-A Criminal Croesus. Long, 1904
Denver's Double. White, 1901
-The Great Syndicate. White, 1908
His Beautiful Client. White, 1906
-His Better Half. White, 1905
The Justice of Revenge. White, 1901
Knaves of Diamonds. Pearson, 1899 ss
A Mayfair Magician. White, 1905
The White Witch of Mayfair. White, 1902
-The World Masters. Long, 1903

GRIFFITH, (RICHARD) GLYN. 1892-   .
Fire over Baghdad. Long, 1939 [Baghdad]
-Hangman's Tale. Long, 1933

GRIFFITH, JASON. Joint pseudonym of Mr. & Mrs. E. G. Griffith.
The Monkey Wrench. Stratford, 1933

GRIFFITHS, (MAJOR) ARTHUR (GEORGE FREDERICK). 1838-1908. Ref: CC, DD, MC. Set: Eng.
Agony Terrace: Some Secrets of the Cynosure Club. White, 1907 ss
The Bank Robbers; see Fast and Loose
-Before the British Raj: A Story of Military Adventure in India. Everett, 1903 [India]
-A Bid for Empire: A Story of Love and Adventure in Modern Egypt. Digby Long, 1902 [Egypt]
The Brand of the Broad Arrow. Pearson, 1900
Criminals I Have Known. Chapman, 1895 ss
-A Duchess in Difficulties: A Story of Modern Manners. White, 1902
Fast and Loose. Chapman, 1885; Munro, 1886. Also published as: The Bank Robbers; or, Fast and Loose. Munro, 1894
Forbidden by Law. Jarrolds, 1897
Ford's Folly, Ltd. Macqueen, 1900
A Girl of Grit: A Story of the Intelligence Department. Milne, 1898; Fenno, 1899
The House in Spring Gardens. Nash, 1906
In Tight Places: Some Experiences of an Amateur Detective. Jarrolds, 1900 ss
The Lezaire Mystery. Mellifont, 1937
Locked Up. Blackwood, 1887
My Peril in a Pullman Car and other tales. Drane, 1893 ss
No. 99. Chapman, 1885; Munro, 1885. New edition, with another story, "Blue Blood": Macqueen, 1901
The Passenger from Calais. Nash, 1905; Page, 1906
The Prison Princess: A Romance of Millbank Penitentiary. Cassell, 1893
The Rome Express. Milne, 1896; Page, 1907 [Fr.]

A Royal Rascal: Episodes in the Career of Colonel Sir Theophilus St. Clair, K.C.B. Unwin, 1905 ss
A Set of Flats. Milne, 1901
-The Silver Spoon: The Adventures of a Young Gentleman in Society. White, 1903
-A Son of Mars. Remington, 1900
Tales of a Government Official. White, 1902 ss
-The Thin Red Line. Chapman, 1886
Thrice Captive. White, 1908
-Viscount Lacklands: A Tale of Modern Mammon. Remington, 1881; Munro, 1883
-A Wayward Woman. Smith Elder, 1879; Harper, 1880
-Winnifred's Way. White, 1905
A Woman of Business. Long, 1904
The Wrong Road; see The Wrong Road by Hook or Crook
The Wrong Road by Hook or Crook. Blackwood, 1888. Also published as: The Wrong Road. Milne, 1903

GRIFFITHS, PETER. 1944- .
-Final Approach. Hale, 1977; St. Martin's, 1977
-The Thirty-Ninth Victim. Hale, 1979

GRIMES, LEE. 1920- . Ref: CA.
-The Ax of Atlantis. Warner, 1975
The Eye of Shiva. Warner, 1974
McIver's Secret. Berkley, 1976

GRIMSEY, LEN
-The Amsterdam Connection. Hale, 1978 [Amst.]

GRIMSHAW, BEATRICE (ETHEL). 1871-1953.
The Beach of Terror, and other stories. Cassell, 1931 ss
The Mystery of Tumbling Reef. Cassell, 1932; Houghton, 1932 [S. Pac.]
-The Sands of Oro. Hurst, 1924; Doubleday, 1924
South Sea Sarah, and Murder in Paradise. New Century Press (Sydney), 1920 (2 novels) [S. Pac.]
-The Terrible Island. Hurst, 1920
-The Wreck of the Redwing. Hurst, 1927; Holt, 1927

GRIMSHAW, MARK. Pseudonym of Ernest L(ionel) McKeag, 1896- , q.v. Other pseudonyms: Griff, Ramon Lacroix, qq.v.
Colwyn Dane—the Outlawed Detective. Amalgamated, 1937
The Sign of the Grinning Dragon. Amalgamated, 1938

GRINDAL, RICHARD. Pseudonym: Richard Grayson, q.v.

GRISEWOOD, HARMON (JOSEPH GERARD). 1906- . Ref: CA.
-The Last Cab on the Rank. Macdonald, 1964
-The Recess. Macdonald, 1963

GRISEWOOD, R(OBERT) NORMAN. 1876- .
-The Venture. Fenno, 1911

GRISON, GEORGES. 1841-1928.
Dispatch and Secrecy. Vizetelly, 1888

GRISSOM, FAY. Pseudonym of Fay Grissom (Shulman) Stanley, 1925- , q.v.
Portrait in Jigsaw. Popular Library, 1975

GRISWOLD, GEORGE. Pseudonym of Robert George Dean, q.v. SC: Mr. Groode, in all titles.
A Checkmate by the Colonel. Dutton, 1953; Eyre, 1954 [NYC]
A Gambit for Mr. Groode. Dutton, 1952; Eyre, 1953
The Pinned Man. Little, 1955; Eyre, 1956 [Switz.]
Red Pawns. Dutton, 1954; Eyre, 1955 [Leb.]

GRISWOLD, LATTA. 1876-1931.
The Inn at the Red Oak. Shores, 1917

GROC, LEON. 1882- .
The Bus That Vanished. Macaulay, 1928 (Translation of "L'Autobus Evanoui." Paris, 1914.) [Paris]
The House of Death. Readers Library, 1921 (Translation of "La Maison des Morts." Paris, 19??)

GROGAN, EMMETT. 1942-1978. Ref: CA.
Final Score. Holt, 1976; Heinemann, 1977 [NYC]

GROGAN, WALTER E.
The Curse of the Fultons. Everett, 1907
The 10.12 Express. Sisley's, 1908

GRONER, AUGUSTA. 1850- . See also: Grace Isabel Colbron, 1869-1948, translator of Groner's work and sometimes billed as her collaborator. SC: Joe Muller (see also the Colbron entry), in all titles.
The Lady in Blue, with Grace Isabel Colbron. Duffield, 1922 [Austria]
The Man with the Black Cord. Duffield, 1911; Chatto, 1911 [Austria]
Mene Tekel: A Tale of Strange Happenings. Duffield, 1912 [Mid. East]

GROOM, K(ATHLEEN) C(LARICE)
The Folly of Fear. Hurst, 1947
Phantom Fortune. Hurst, 1948
The Recoil. Hutchinson, 1952

GROOM, (ARTHUR JOHN) PELHAM. SC: Peter Mohune, in at least those marked PM.
"Defend the Rock." Jarrolds, 1945
The Devil Fish. Ward, 1955
The Fourth Seal. Jarrolds, 1948 PM
High Adventure. Ace (London), 1938
The Little Hanging Men. Jarrolds, 1946 PM
Mohune's Nine Lives; see What Are Your Angels Now?
-The Purple Twilight. Laurie, 1948 PM
Sabotage Unlimited. Hamilton, 1938 PM
Temperamental Journey. Jarrolds, 1947 [ship]
What Are Your Angels Now? Jarrolds, 1943. U.S. title: Mohune's Nine Lives. Books, Inc., 1944 PM
Whistling Wires. Melrose, 1935

GROOM, MRS. SIDNEY
Detective Sylvia Shale. Hurst, 1923

GROOME, FRANCIS HINDES. 1851-1902.
-Kriegspiel: The War Game. Ward (London & NYC), 1896

GROPPER, MILTON HERBERT, 1897-1955, and EDNA SHERRY, -1967, q.v.
Grounds for Indecency. Macaulay, 1931
Is No One Innocent? Cosmopolitan, 1930 [NYC]

GROSS, LAURENCE, 1889-1965, and EDWARD CHILDS CARPENTER, 1872?-1950. See also: Helen (Alden) K(nipe) Carpenter.
Whistling in the Dark. French (NYC & London), 1933 (Play.)

GROSS, MARK S(TANISLAUS). 1889- .
To the Dark Tower. Kenedy, 1922 [Chi.]

GROSS, SHELLY (HARVEY). 1921- . Ref: CA.
Havana X. Arbor, 1978; Piatkus, 1980 [Havana]

GROSS, TUDOR
The Adventures of Kerlock Shomes and Dr. Warsaw. Magico, 1980

GROSSBACH, ROBERT. 1941- . Ref: CA.
...And Justice for All. Ballantine, 1979; Corgi, 1980 (Novelization of the movie.) [Balt.]
The Cheap Detective. Warner, 1978 (Novelization of the movie.) [S.F., 1940]

GROSSE, KARL FREIDRICH AUGUST. 1768-1847.
Horrid Mysteries. Lane, 1796

GROSSO, SONNY. See: Philip Rosenberg, 1942- .

GROTE, WILLIAM
Cain's Girl Friend. Ace, 1957 [L.A.]

GROVE, MARJORIE. SC: Maxine Reynolds, in all titles.
You'll Die, Darling. Zebra, 1979 [L.A.]
You'll Die Laughing. Zebra, 1978 [Eng.]
You'll Die Today. Zebra, 1979 [L.A.]
You'll Die Tomorrow. Zebra, 1978 [W.I.]
You'll Die Tonight. Zebra, 1979 [NYC]
You'll Die When You Hear This. Zebra, 1978 [L.A.]
You'll Die Yesterday. Zebra, 1979

GROVE, WALT
-Down. Dell, 1953; World Distributors, 1961
Hell-Bent for Danger. GM, 1950
The Man Who Said No. GM, 1950; Fawcett (London), 1954 [NYC]

GROVES, REGINALD. 1908- . Ref: CA.
The Mystery of Victor Grayson. Pendulum, 1946

GROVES, W(ILLIAM) E.
Bride of the Wolf. Pearson, 1939
The Scarlet Mask. Leng, 1938
The Schemer. Leng, 1936
The Secret of the Spectre's Nest. Fiction House, 1945

GRUBB, DAVIS (ALEXANDER). 1919-1980. Ref: CA.
Fools' Parade. World, 1969
The Golden Sickle. World, 1968
The Night of the Hunter. Harper, 1953; H. Hamilton, 1954
One Foot in the Grave; see Twelve Tales of Suspense and the Supernatural
-Shadow of My Brother. Holt, 1966; Hutchinson, 1966
Twelve Tales of Suspense and the Supernatural. Scribner, 1964. British title: One Foot in the Grave. Arrow, 1966
The Watchman. Scribner, 1961; Joseph, 1962 [W. Va.]

GRUBER, FRANK. 1904-1969. Pseudonyms: Stephen Acre, Charles K. Boston, John K. Vedder, qq.v. Ref: CA, CC, EM, MP, TC. SC: Otis Beagle = OB (see also Charles K. Boston entry); Johnny Fletcher & Sam Cragg = F&C; Simon Lash = SL; Oliver Quade = OQ.
Beagle Scented Murder. Rinehart, 1956. Also published as: Market for Murder. Penguin (New American Library), 1947 OB
Brass Knuckles. Sherbourne, 1966 OQ ss
Bridge of Sand. Dutton, 1963; Boardman, 1964 [Mid. East]
Brothers of Silence. Dutton, 1962; Boardman, 1962
The Buffalo Box. Farrar, 1942; Nicholson, 1944 SL [L.A.]
The Corpse Moved Upstairs; see The Mighty Blockhead
Die Like a Dog; see The Hungry Dog
The Etruscan Bull. Dutton, 1969; Hale, 1970 [It.]
The Fourth Letter. Rinehart, 1947 [Ia.]
The French Key. Farrar, 1940; Hale, 1941. Also published as: The French Key Mystery. Avon, 1942. And as: Once over Deadly. Jonathan, 1956, abridged F&C [NYC]
The Gamecock Murders; see The Scarlet Feather
The Gift Horse. Farrar, 1942; Nicholson, 1943 F&C [NYC]
The Gold Gap. Dutton, 1968; Hale, 1968 [Chi.]
The Greek Affair. Dutton, 1964; Boardman, 1965 [Greece]
The Honest Dealer. Rinehart, 1947 F&C [Las Veg.]
The Hungry Dog. Farrar, 1941; Nicholson, 1950. Also published as: Die Like a Dog. Jonathan, 1953 F&C [Mo.]
A Job of Murder; see The Leather Duke
The Laughing Fox. Farrar, 1940; Nicholson, 1942 F&C [Midwest]
The Leather Duke. Rinehart, 1949; Pemberton, 1950. Also published as: A Job of Murder. Signet, 1950 F&C [Chi.]
The Limping Goose. Rinehart, 1954; Barker, 1955. Also published as: Murder One. Belmont, 1973 F&C [NYC]
Little Hercules. Dutton, 1965; Boardman, 1966
The Lock and the Key. Rinehart, 1948; World's Work, 1950. Also published as: Too Tough to Die. Jonathan, 1954; and as: Run, Thief, Run. Crest, 1955 [L.A.]
The Lonesome Badger. Rinehart, 1954. Also published as: Mood for Murder. Graphic, 1956 OB [L.A.]
The Long Arm of Murder; see Murder '97
Market for Murder; see Beagle Scented Murder
The Mighty Blockhead. Farrar, 1942; Nicholson, 1948. Also published as: The Corpse Moved Upstairs. Belmont, 1964 F&C [NYC]
Mood for Murder; see The Lonesome Badger
Murder '97. Rinehart, 1948; Barker, 1956. Also published as: The Long Arm of Murder. Jonathan, 1956 SL [L.A.]
Murder One; see The Limping Goose
The Navy Colt. Farrar, 1941; Nicholson, 1942 F&C [Chi.]
Once over Deadly; see The French Key
Run, Fool, Run. Dutton, 1966; Hale, 1967 [L.A.]
Run, Thief, Run; see The Lock and the Key
The Scarlet Feather. Rinehart, 1948; Cherry Tree, 1951. Also published as: The Gamecock Murders. Signet, 1949 F&C [Chi.]
The Silver Tombstone. Farrar, 1945; Nicholson, 1949. Also published as: The Silver Tombstone Mystery. Signet, 1959 F&C [Calif.]

The Silver Tombstone Mystery; see The
    Silver Tombstone
Simon Lash, Detective; see Simon Lash,
    Private Detective
Simon Lash, Private Detective. Farrar,
    1941. British title: Simon Lash,
    Detective. Nicholson, 1943 SL [L.A.]
The Spanish Prisoner. Dutton, 1969;
    Hale, 1970 [Sp.]
Swing Low, Swing Dead. Belmont, 1964
    F&C [NYC]
The Talking Clock. Farrar, 1941; Nich-
    olson, 1942 F&C [N.Y.]
Too Tough to Die; see The Lock and the
    Key
Twenty Plus Two. Dutton, 1961; Board-
    man, 1961
The Twilight Man. Dutton, 1967; Hale,
    1967 [Calif.]
The Whispering Master. Rinehart, 1947
    F&C [NYC]

GRUBER, HELMUT. 1928-   . Ref: CA.
    The Temptation of Adam. Everest, 1979

GRUPPE, HENRY. Naval officer, retired to
    work with the Agency for Internation-
    al Development.
    The Truxton Cipher. Simon, 1973; Gol-
        lancz, 1974 [ship]

GUENTER, C. H. Pseudonym of K. H. Gun-
    ther. SC: Robert Urban, apparently in
    all titles, which are translated from
    the German.
    Days of Vengeance. Manor, 1979
    Dead Drop in Havana. Manor, 1978
        [Havana]
    Dead in Aqaba. Manor, 1978 [Mid. East]
    Hunter of Men. Pinnacle, 1975
    A Swindler Named Zefano. Manor, 1979
    To Know Is to Die. Manor, 1977
    Web of Silence. Manor, 1977

GUEST, FRANCIS HAROLD. 1901-   . Pseudo-
    nym: James Spenser, q.v.

GUIBOURG, GEORGES. 1897-   . Pseudonym:
    Georgius, q.v.

GUIGO, ERNEST PHILIP. Pseudonym: E.
    Carleton Holt, q.v.

GUIL, J. and J(EAN) BANCAL. J. Guil is
    the pseudonym of Jean Guillemonat.
    One Crime Too Many. Staples, 1953 [Fr.]

GUILD, NICHOLAS (M.). 1944-   . Ref: CA.
    SC: Ray Guinness = RG.
    The Lost and Found Man. Harper's Maga-
        zine Press, 1975; Hale, 1977 [Switz.]
    Old Acquaintance. Seaview, 1979 RG
        [S.C.]
    The Summer Soldier. Seaview, 1978;
        Magnum, 1979 RG

GUILDFORD, JOHN. Pseudonym of Bluebell
    Matilda Hunter, 1887-   .
    Big Ben Looks On! Grayson, 1933
    Death Dams the Tide. Grayson, 1932

GUILLAUD, SUZANNE. Pseudonym: Marianne
    Andrau, q.v.

GUILLEMONAT, JEAN. Pseudonym: J. Guil,
    q.v.

GUINESS, MAURICE C. Joint pseudonym with
    Muna Lee de Munoz Marin, 1895-   :
    Newton Gayle, q.v.

GUINN, WILLIAM
    Death Lies Deep. GM, 1955 [Colo.]

GUINNESS, K(ATHERINE) D(ORIS). Ref: CC.
    Fisherman's End. Macdonald, 1958
        [Ire.]

GUIRDHAM, ARTHUR. 1905-   . Ref: CA.
    -I-A Stranger. Quality, 1949
    -The Lights Were Going Out. Quality,
        1944

GUISE, STANLEY
    The Falcon Mystery. Long, 1930
    The Green Cat. Long, 1940

GULL, C(YRIL ARTHUR EDWARD) RANGER.
    1876-1923. Pseudonym: Guy Thorne,
    q.v. Oxford graduate; journalist be-
    fore becoming full-time writer.
    Set: Eng.
    The Adventures of Mr. Topham, Comedian.
        Greening, 1903
    The Air Pirates. Hurst, 1919; Harcourt,
        1920
    Black Honey. Greening, 1913
    -The Bridge Players. White, 1908
    -The Chain Invisible. Laurie, 1907
    Cinema City. Hurst, 1927; Harcourt,
        1923
    -The Creggan Peerage. Long, 1916

-The Enemies of England. Laurie, 1914
-A Gentleman from Portland. Laurie, 1909
-The Glad Eye. Greening, 1912 (Noveli-
    zation of the play by Jose Levy.)
-The Harvest of Love. Long, 1905
-House of Torment: Memoirs of the Life
    of Mr. John Commendone. Greening,
    1911
The Hypocrite. Greening, 1898
The Iron Box. Hurst, 1923
The Lost Judge. White, 1914
-Miss Malevolent. Greening, 1899
-The Monstrous Enemy. Laurie, 1915
Murder Limited. Laurie, 1913
The Parrot Faced Man. White, 1912
-The Path of a Hundred Deaths. Fiction
    Lover's Library, 1913
-The Patron Saint and other stories.
    White, 1908 ss
-The Price of Pity. White, 1905
The Ravenscroft Affair; see The Ravens-
    croft Horror
The Ravenscroft Horror. Laurie, 1917.
    U.S. title: The Ravenscroft Affair,
    as by Guy Thorne. Clode, 1924
-The Reins of Chance. White, 1910
Retribution. Laurie, 1909
Rogues Ltd. Goodship, 1922
The Snare of the Fowler. Jarrolds, 1917
A Story of the Stage. White, 1905
The Terror by Night. White, 1909
-When Satan Ruled. Greening, 1914
-Wings of Love. Greening, 1912
The Woman in the Case. Greening, 1909

GULLIVER, HAL [HAROLD S. GULLIVER].
    1935-   . Ref: CA.
    Kill with Style. Scribner, 1974 [W.I.]

GULLIVER, SAM. Educated in economics in
    London; with a Swiss consortium in
    Geneva.
    The Vulcan Bulletins. Hodder, 1974;
        Simon, 1973

GULYASHKI, ANDREI. 1914-   . Born in
    Bulgaria; bestselling Bulgarian
    author.
    The Zakhov Mission. Cassell, 1968;
        Doubleday, 1969 (Translation of
        "Prikliucheniiata na Avakum Zakhov."
        Sofia, 1963.) [Bulg.]

GUMLEY, F. W. Set: Eng.
    Crime in the Crypt. Swan, 1943
    Death Behind the Door. Mitre, 1944
    Death Calls the Tune. Mitre, 1945
    Death Goes Touring. Mitre, 1945
    Death on Delivery. Mitre, 1944
    The Death Seance. Mitre, 1945
    Death Stills the Brush. Mitre, 1946
    Death Visits the Parish. Mitre, 1945
    Diary of Death. Mellifont, 1942
    The Football Racketeers. Mellifont,
        1944
    The Ghoul Goalie. Pan, 1945
    The Hoodoo Half-Back. Mellifont, 1942
    The House of Fatal Mirrors. Grafton,
        1944
    The Lurking Death. Mitre, 1944
    Murder in the Museum. Mellifont, 1944
    Mystery at Horseshoe Island. Gordon,
        1947
    The Phantom Footballer. Millifont, 1939
    The Phantom Greyhound. Pan, 1946
    The Toast Is Death! Mitre, 1945

GUNN, JAMES (EDWARD)
    Deadlier Than the Male. Duell, 1942
        [S.F.]

GUNN, JAMES (EDWIN). 1923-   . Ref: CA.
    The Magicians. Scribner, 1976

GUNN, JOHN. 1922-   .
    The Wild Abyss. Hale, 1972

GUNN, ROBERT A(LEXANDER). 1844-   .
    Bruce Douglas, A Man of the People.
        Mayhew, 1909

GUNN, VICTOR. Pseudonym of Edwy Searles
    Brooks, 1889-1965, q.v. Other pseudo-
    nyms: Berkeley Gray, Carlton Ross,
    qq.v. SC: Bill "Ironsides" Cromwell
    of Scotland Yard, in all titles. Set:
    Eng.
    Alias the Hangman. Collins, 1950
    All Change for Murder. Collins, 1962
        [It.]
    The Black Cap Murder. Collins, 1965
    The Body in the Boot. Collins, 1963
    The Body Vanishes. Collins, 1952
    The Borgia Head Mystery. Collins, 1951
    Castle Dangerous. Collins, 1957
    The Crippled Canary. Collins, 1954
    The Crooked Staircase. Collins, 1954
    Dead in a Ditch. Collins, 1959
    The Dead Man Laughs. Collins, 1944
    Dead Man's Warning. Collins, 1949
    Dead Men's Bells. Collins, 1956
    Death at Traitor's Gate. Collins, 1960

Death Comes Laughing. Collins, 1952
Death on Bodmin Moor. Collins, 1960
Death on Shivering Sand. Collins, 1946
    [Wales]
Death's Doorway. Collins, 1941
Devil in the Maze. Collins, 1961
Footsteps of Death. Collins, 1939
The Golden Monkey. Collins, 1957
Ironsides' Lone Hand. Collins, 1941
Ironsides of the Yard. Collins, 1940
Ironsides on the Spot. Collins, 1948
Ironsides Sees Red. Collins, 1957 (3
    novelets.)
Ironsides Smashes Through. Collins,
    1940
Ironsides Smells Blood. Collins, 1946
    (3 novelets.)
The Laughing Grave. Collins, 1955
Mad Hatter's Rock. Collins, 1942
Murder at the Motel. Collins, 1964
Murder on Ice. Collins, 1951
Murder on Whispering Sands. Collins,
    1965
Murder with a Kiss. Collins, 1963
The Next One to Die. Collins, 1959
Nice Day for a Murder. Collins, 1945
The Painted Dog. Collins, 1955
The Petticoat Lane Murders. Collins,
    1966
Road to Murder. Collins, 1949
The 64 Thousand Murder. Collins, 1958
Sweet Smelling Death. Collins, 1961
Three Dates with Death. Collins, 1947
The Treble Chance Murder. Collins, 1958
The Whistling Key. Collins, 1953

GUNN, VIRGINIA S.
    The Wayward Season. Doubleday, 1980

GUNTER, ARCHIBALD CLAVERING. 1847-1907.
-Adrienne de Portalis. Home, 1900
-The Adventures of Dr. Burton. Home,
    1905
-Ballyho Bey; or, The Power of Women.
    Hurst (NYC), 1897; Routledge, 1897
Baron Montez of Panama and Paris. Home,
    1893; Routledge, 1893
-Billy Hamilton. Home, 1898; Routledge,
    1898
-Bob Covington. Home, 1897; Routledge,
    1897
-The Changing Pulse of Madame Touraine.
    Home, 1905
The City of Whispers. Home, 1902;
    French, 1902 [Fr.]
-The Conscience of a King. Home, 1903;
    French, 1903
-Deacon and Actress. White, 1902 (U.S.
    title?)
-The Deacon's Second Wind. Home, 1901;
    Routledge, 1901
Doctor Burton. Ward, 1907 (3 novel-
    ets.) (U.S. title?)
-Doctor Burton's Success. Ward, 1908
    (U.S. title?) [NYC]
Don Belasco of Key West. Home, 1896;
    Routledge, 1897 [Fla.]
The Empty Hotel. Ward, 1902 (U.S.
    title?)
-The Fighting Troubadour. Home, 1899;
    Routledge, 1899
-The First of the English. Home, 1894;
    Routledge, 1895
-Her Senator. Home, 1896; Routledge,
    1896
-Jack Curzon. Home, 1898; Routledge,
    1899
-The King's Stockbroker. Home, 1894;
    Routledge, 1906
-The Ladies' Juggernaut. Home, 1895;
    Routledge, 1895
-A Lost American. Home, 1898; Rout-
    ledge, 1898
M. S. Bradford, Special. Home, 1899;
    Routledge, 1899
-The Man Behind the Door. Home, 1904;
    French, 1904
A Manufacturer's Daughter; or, Tangled
    Flags; see Tangled Flags
-Miss Dividends. Home, 1892; Routledge,
    1892
-Miss Nobody of Nowhere. Hurst (NYC),
    1888; Routledge, 1890
-Mr. Barnes of New York. Welch, 1887;
    Vizetelly, 1887
-Mr. Barnes, American. Dodd, 1907;
    Stevens, 1907
Mr. Potter of Texas. Home, 1888;
    French, 1888
-My Japanese Prince. Home, 1904; French,
    1904
-Phil Conway. Home, 1903; French, 1904
-The Power of Woman. Home, 1897; Rout-
    ledge, 1897 (Contains both Susan
    Turnbull and Ballyho Bey, qq.v.)
-A Prince in the Garret. Home, 1905;
    French, 1905
-Prince Karl. Dillingham, 1907; Ward,
    1907
The Princess of Copper. Home, 1900
-A Princess of Paris. Home, 1894; Rout-
    ledge, 1894

-The Shadow of a Vendetta. Ward, 1908
  (U.S. title?)
 The Spy Company. Hurst (NYC), 1900;
  French, 1903
 The Surprises of an Empty Hotel. Home,
  1902; Routledge, 1902
-Susan Turnbull; or, The Power of Woman.
  Hurst (NYC), 1897; Routledge, 1897
-The Sword in the Air. Ward, 1904 (U.S.
  title?)
-Tangled Flags. Home, 1900; Routledge,
  1900. Also published as: A Manufac-
  turer's Daughter; or, Tangled Flags.
  White, 1902
 That Frenchman! Home, 1889; Routledge,
  1889 [Fr.]
-Twixt Sword and Glove. French, 1906
  (U.S. title?)

GUNTER, MRS. ARCHIBALD CLAVERING. See:
 Richard Henry Savage, 1846-1903.

GUNTHER, JOHN. 1901-1970.
 The Bright Nemesis. Bobbs, 1932;
  Secker, 1932

GUNTHER, MAX, 1927-   , and DR. RICHARD
 A. LERNER. Ref on Gunther: CA.
-Epidemic 9. Morrow, 1980 [N.J.]

GUNTON, ERIC
 Trouble Ahead. Popular Publications
  (Australia), 193?

GURDON, J(OHN) E(VERARD). 1898-   .
-Banners Yellow. Newnes, 1938
 Feeding the Wind. Chapman, 1924
 The Monkey Trick. Newnes, 1936 ss
-Over and Above. Collins, 1919

GURNEY, PETER
 Queer Things at Queechy. Crowther,
  1946

GURR, DAVID. 1936-   .
 Troika. Macdonald, 1979; Methuen (U.S.)
  1979

GURR, TOM and H(ARRY) H(UBERT) COX
 Obsessions. Muller, 1958

GUTHRIE, A(LFRED) B(ERTRAM), JR.
 1901-   . Ref: CA. SC: Sheriff Chick
 Charleston = CC.
 The Genuine Article. Houghton, 1977 CC
  [Mont.]
 Murders at Moon Dance. Dutton, 1943.
  Also published as: Trouble at Moon
  Dance. Popular Library, 1951 [West]
 No Second Wind. Houghton, 1980 CC
  [Mont.]
 Trouble at Moon Dance; see Murders at
  Moon Dance
 Wild Pitch. Houghton, 1973 CC [Mont.]

GUTHRIE, JAMES SHIELDS. 1931-   . Pseudonym: David Creed, q.v.

GUTTERIDGE, (THOMAS GORDON) LINDSAY.
 1923-   . Ref: CA. SC: Mathew Dilke,
 in all titles.
 Cold War in a Country Garden. Cape,
  1971; Putnam, 1971
 Fratricide Is a Gas. Cape, 1975
 Killer Pine. Cape, 1973; Putnam, 1973
  [West]

GWINN, WILLIAM R. Pseudonym: William
 Randall, q.v.

GWYNNE, ESTELLE
 The Fulfilling of the Law. Epworth,
  1924

GWYNNE, P. N. Pseudonym.
 Firmly by the Tail. Putnam, 1976 [Afr.]

H., I.
 Phantoms of the Cloister; or, The Mys-
  terious Manuscript. Minerva, 1795
  [Eng., ca.1420]

HAAF, BEVERLY T.
 The Crystal Pawns. Popular Library,
  1973 [N.J.]

HAAS, BEN(JAMIN LEOPOLD). 1926-1977. Ref:
 CA. Pseudonym: Richard Meade, q.v.
 Daisy Canfield. Simon, 1973; Davies,
  1973 [N.C.]

HAAS, CHARLIE, 1952-   , and TIM HUNTER,
 1947-   . Ref on each author: CA.
 The Soul Hit. Harper, 1977; Hale, 1978
  [Calif.]

HAAS, JOSEPH L. 1929-1971.
 Vendetta. Regnery, 1975 [Chi.]

HAASE, JOHN. 1923-   . Ref: CA.
-The Noon Balloon to Rangoon. Simon,
  1967

HABBERTON, JOHN. 1842-1921.
 The Bowsham Puzzle. Funk, 1884; Ward,
  1884

HABE, HANS. Pseudonym of Jean Bekessy,
 1911-1977. Ref: CA.
 Agent of the Devil. Harrap, 1958. U.S.
  title: The Devil's Agent. Fell, 1958
  (Translation of "In Namen des Teu-
  fels." Vienna, 1956.)
 The Devil's Agent; see Agent of the
  Devil
 The Poisoned Stream. Harrap, 1969;
  McGraw, 1969 [Rome]

HABERSHAM, ELIZABETH
 Island of Deceit. Pinnacle, 1977
  [S.C., 1890s]

HACKER, SHYRLE. 1910-   . Ref: CA.
 Whispers in the Dark. Major, 1976

HACKETT, WALTER. 1876-1944. See also:
 Louise Jordan Miln, 1864-1933; and:
 George Goodchild, 1888-1969.
 The Barton Mystery. French (London &
  NYC), 1930 (4-act play.)
 The Fugitives. French (London), 1937
  (3-act play.)
 The Gay Adventures. French (London &
  NYC), 1933 (3-act play.)
 Hyde Park Corner. French (London &
  NYC), 1935 (3-act play.)
 Intrigue. French (London & NYC), 1935
  (3-act play.)
 Road House. French (London & NYC), 1933
  (3-act play.)
 77, Park Lane. French (London & NYC),
  1929 (3-act play.)

HACKETT, WALTER ANTHONY. 1909-   .
 Decision. Baker, 1950 (1-act play.)

HACKFORTH-JONES, (FRANK) GILBERT.
 1900-   . Ref: CA. SC: Paul Decker,
 in at least those marked PD; Joe Gar-
 ton, in at least those marked JG;
 Earl of Millington, in at least those
 marked EM.
 All Stations to Malta. Hodder, 1971 PD
 Chinese Poison. Hodder, 1969 PD
 Crack of Doom. Hodder, 1961
 Danger Below. Hodder, 1963 JG
 Dangerous Trade. Hodder, 1952
 Death of an Admiral. Hodder, 1956
 An Explosive Situation. Hodder, 1973 PD
 Fight to a Finish. Hodder, 1968
 Fish Out of Water. Hodder, 1954
-The Greatest Fool. Hodder, 1948
 I am the Captain. Hodder, 1963 JG
-Life on the Ocean Wave. Hodder, 1960
-No Less Renowned. Blackwood, 1939 ss
-One Man's Wars. Hodder, 1964
 One-One-One. Hodder, 1942 ss
 The Price Was High. Hodder, 1946 EM
 The Questing Hound. Hodder, 1947 EM
 Redoubtable Dexter. Hodder, 1975 PD
 Rough Passage. Hodder, 1946 EM
 Second-in-Command. Hodder, 1974 PD
 Security Risk. Hodder, 1970
 Shadow of the Rock. Hodder, 1973 PD
 Sixteen Bells. Hodder, 1946 ss EM
 The Sole Survivor. Hodder, 1953
 The Stern Chase. Hodder, 1966
 Storm in Harbour. Hodder, 1965
 Submarine Flotilla. Hodder, 1940 EM
-Sweethearts and Wives. Hodder, 1949
  (Novelization of the play by Gilbert
  Hackforth-Jones and Margaret Hack-
  forth-Jones.)
-Warrior's Playtime. Hodder, 1967
 The Worst Enemy. Hodder, 1950
 Yellow Peril. Hodder, 1972

HACKFORTH-JONES, MARGARET. See: (Frank)
 Gilbert Hackforth-Jones, 1900-   .

HACKSTAFF, RICHARD
 Tracked by a Pin. Street (Magnet)

HADATH, JOHN EDWARD GUNBY. 1880?-1954.
 Pseudonym: Shepherd Pearson, q.v.

HADDAD, C(AROLYN) A. SC: David Haham =
 DH.
 The Academic Factor. Harper, 1980
  [Bulg.]
 Bloody September. Harper, 1976 DH
 The Moroccan. Harper, 1975; Allen, 1977
  [Isr.]
 Operation Apricot. Harper, 1978 DH
  [Isr.]

HADDON, CHRISTOPHER. Pseudonym of John
 (Leslie) Palmer, 1885-1944, q.v.
 Joint pseudonym with Hilary (Aiden)
 St. George Saunders, 1898-1951, q.v.:
 Francis Beeding, q.v.

 Under the Long Barrow. Gollancz, 1939.
  U.S. title: The Man in the Purple
  Gown. Dodd, 1939, as by John Palmer

HADDOW, DENIS. Ref: CC.
 Hanged by a Thread. Hutchinson, 1947

HADEN, ALLEN
 My Enemy—My Wife. Putnam, 1951 (Novelization of a story by Paul Frischauer.)

HADFIELD, ROBERT L. and FRANK E. FARN-
 COMBE
-Red Radio. Jenkins, 1927
 Ruled by Radio. Jenkins, 1925

HADLEY, HAROLD
 Come See Them Die. Messner, 1934

HADLEY, MARTIN
 He Died Twice. Columbine, 1940

HAEDRICH, MARCEL. Pseudonym. 1913-   .
 Crack in the Mirror. Allen, 1960; Dell,
  1961 (Translation of "Drame dans un
  Miroir." Paris, 1958.) [Paris]

HAGAN, ARTHUR P.
 The Day the Bookies Took a Bath. Sherbourne, 1971

HAGBERG, DAVID. 1942-   . Pseudonyms:
 Nick Carter, Sean Flannery, qq.v.
 The Capsule. Dell, 1976

HAGEN, LINDA. Pseudonym of (Elizabeth)
 Lorinda DuBreuil, 1924-1980, q.v.
 Other pseudonyms: Kate Cameron,
 Elizabeth Hanley, qq.v.
 In the Eye of the Law. Belmont, 1979

HAGEN, MIRIAM-ANN. Sister of Aaron Marc
 Stein, 1906-   , q.v. SC: Hortense
 Clinton, in all titles.
 Dig Me Later. Doubleday, 1949 [Can.]
 Murder—But Natch. Doubleday, 1951
  [ship]
 Plant Me Now. Doubleday, 1947 [train]

HAGENBACH, KEITH
 The Fox Potential. Allen, 1980

HAGER, JEAN. 1932-   . Pseudonyms: Amanda McAllister, Sara North, qq.v.

HAGERTY, HARRY J.
 The Jasmine Trail. Lothrop, 1936
  [Mass.]

HAGGARD, (SIR) H(ENRY) RIDER. 1856-1925.
 Ref: CC.
 Mr. Meeson's Will. Blackett, 1888;
  Harper, 1888

HAGGARD, PAUL. Pseudonym of Stephen Long-
 street, 1907-   , q.v. Other pseudo-
 nym: Henri Weiner, q.v. SC: Mike War-
 lock, in all titles, all set in NYC.
 Dead Is the Door-Nail. Lippincott, 1937
 Death Talks Shop. Hillman-Curl, 1938
 Death Walks on Cat Feet. Hillman-Curl,
  1938
 Poison from a Wealthy Widow. Hillman-
  Curl, 1938

HAGGARD, RAYMOND (GORDON RIDER).
 1921-   .
 Miss Ivory White. Collins, 1970; Dell,
  1972

HAGGARD, WILLIAM. Pseudonym of Richard
 Henry Michael Clayton, 1907-   .
 Ref: CA, CC, EM, MC, TC. SC: Col.
 Charles Russell = CR; Paul Martiny
 = PM. Set: many in Eng.
 The Antagonists. Cassell, 1964; Wash-
  burn, 1964 CR
 The Arena. Cassell, 1961; Washburn,
  1961 CR
 The Bitter Harvest. Cassell, 1971. U.S.
  title: Too Many Enemies. Walker, 1971
  CR
 Closed Circuit. Cassell, 1960; Wash-
  burn, 1960
 The Conspirators. Cassell, 1967;
  Walker, 1968 CR
 A Cool Day for Killing. Cassell, 1968;
  Walker, 1968 CR
 The Doubtful Disciple. Cassell, 1969
 The Hard Sell. Cassell, 1965; Washburn,
  1966 CR [It.]
 The Hardliners. Cassell, 1970; Walker,
  1971 CR
 The High Wire. Cassell, 1963; Washburn,
  1963 CR
 The Kinsmen. Cassell, 1974; Walker,
  1974 PM
 The Median Line. Cassell, 1979; Walker,
  1981 CR [Mid. East]

The Notch on the Knife; see The Old
   Masters
The Old Masters. Cassell, 1973. U.S.
   title: The Notch on the Knife.
   Walker, 1973 CR [Balkans]
The Poison People. Cassell, 1978;
   Walker, 1979 CR
The Powder Barrel. Cassell, 1965; Wash-
   burn, 1965 CR [Mid. East]
The Power House. Cassell, 1966; Wash-
   burn, 1967 CR
The Protectors. Cassell, 1972; Walker,
   1972 PM [Cyprus]
The Scorpion's Tale. Cassell, 1975;
   Walker, 1975 CR [Sp.]
Slow Burner. Cassell, 1958; Little,
   1958 CR
The Telemann Touch. Cassell, 1958;
   Little, 1958 [W.I.]
Too Many Enemies; see The Bitter Har-
   vest
The Unquiet Sleep. Cassell, 1962; Wash-
   burn, 1962 CR
Venetian Blind. Cassell, 1959; Wash-
   burn, 1959 CR
Visa to Limbo. Cassell, 1978; Walker,
   1979 CR [Isr.]
Yesterday's Enemy. Cassell, 1976;
   Walker, 1976 CR [Switz.]

HAGUE, JOHN. Pseudonym.
   Fillets on the Menu. Hutchinson, 1933

HAIBLUM, ISIDORE. 1935-   . NYC-born
   science fiction writer. SC: Dunjer =
   D.
   Interworld. Dell, 1977; Penguin, 1980 D
   Nightmare Express. GM, 1979
   Outerworld. Dell, 1979   D

HAIG, ALEC. Pseudonym. SC: Alec Haig, in
   all titles.
   Flight from Montego Bay. Dodd, 1972;
      Heinemann, 1972
   Peruvian Printout. Dodd, 1970; Heine-
      mann, 1974
   Sign On for Tokyo. Dodd, 1968; Heine-
      mann, 1968

HAIG, ROBERT
   The Antrobus Trust. Macmillan (Lon-
      don), 1976

HAILEY, ARTHUR. 1920-   . See: John
   Castle; and: William A. Miles. Ref:
   CA.

HAINES, WILLIAM WISTER. 1908-   . Ref:
   CA.
   Target. Little, 1964 [Fr., 1944]

HAINING, PETER. 1940-   . Ref: CA.
   The Hero. New English Library, 1973

HAKE, THOMAS ST. EDMUND
   Within Sound of the Weir. Cassell, 1891

HALDANE, EMMA
   Maluti Murder. Eldon, 1933

HALDEMAN, JOE WILLIAM. 1943-   . Pseudonym: Robert Graham, q.v.

HALDIMON, MADELAINE. See: J. A. Knipe.

HALE, ARLENE. 1924-   . Pseudonym: Lynn
   Williams, q.v. Ref: CA.
   -A Glimpse of Paradise. Little, 1974;
      Prior, 1975
   Island of Mystery. Little, 1977; Prior,
      1978
   One More Bridge to Cross. Little, 1975;
      Prior, 1976
   The Other Side of the World. Little,
      1976; Prior, 1977
   Where the Heart Is. Little, 1974

HALE, CHRISTOPHER. Pseudonym of Frances
   Moyer Ross Stevens, 1895-1948. Ref:
   MP. SC: Lt. Bill French = BF.
   Dead of Winter. Doubleday, 1941. Bri-
      tish title (?): Going, Going, Gone.
      Boardman, 1950 BF [Mich.]
   Deadly Ditto. Doubleday, 1948; Board-
      man, 1949 BF [Mich.]
   Exit Screaming. Doubleday, 1942; Board-
      man, 1943 BF [Mich.]
   Ghost River. Doubleday, 1937; Boardman,
      1947 [West]
   Going, Going, Gone; see Dead of Winter
   Hangman's Tie. Doubleday, 1943; Board-
      man, 1946 BF [Mich.]
   He's Late This Morning. Doubleday,
      1949; Boardman, 1951 BF [Fla.]
   Midsummer Nightmare. Doubleday, 1945;
      Boardman, 1948 BF [Mich.]
   Murder in Tow. Doubleday, 1943; Board-
      man, 1944 BF [Fla.]
   Murder on Display. Doubleday, 1939;
      Boardman, 1947 BF [Mich.]
   Rumor Hath It. Doubleday, 1945; Board-
      man, 1947 BF [Mich.]

Smoke Screen. Harcourt, 1935; Boardman, 1948 BF [Mich.]
Stormy Night. Doubleday, 1937; Heinemann, 1937 BF [Mich.]
Witch Wood. Doubleday, 1940; Boardman,
   1946 BF [Mich.]

HALE, EDGAR. SC: Montague Migglewade =
   MM; Insp. Michael Regan = MR. Set:
   Eng.
   Blue Murder. Ward, 1948 MM
   Coffee for One. Ward, 1949 MM
   Death Came Back. Ward, 1948 MR
   Death Dealt the Cards. Ward, 1947 MR
   Devil's Tears. Ward, 1946 MR
   Never Shoot a Lady. Ward, 1947 MR
   So the Lady Died. Ward, 1949 MR

HALE, JENNIFER. Pseudonym of Frank Ellis
   Smith, 1918-   . Ref: CA.
   Beyond the Dark. Berkley, 1978 [Fla.]
   House of Strangers. Prestige, 1972
      [Fla.]
   The House on Key Diablo. Beagle, 1974
      [Fla.]
   Portrait of Evil. Ballantine, 1975
   Ravensridge. Lancer, 1971 [Va.]

HALE, JOHN (BARRY). 1926-   .
   The Fort. Quartet, 1973
   Lovers and Heretics. Gollancz, 1976;
      Dial, 1978

HALE, JULIAN ANTHONY STUART. 1940-   .
   Pseudonym: Anthony Stuart, q.v.

HALE, MRS. MARICE RUTLEDGE GIBSON.
   1884-   . Pseudonym: Maryse Rutledge, q.v.

HALE, MARTIN. Oxford graduate in history;
   reporter and magazine staff writer.
   The Empire on Arumac. Cape, 1966
      [Peru]
   The Fourth Reich. Cape, 1965

HALEGUA, LILLIAN
   The Hanging. Owen, 1970

HALES, A(LFRED) G(REENWOOD). 1870-1936.
   -Abner Crane's Vengeance. Long, 1932
   Marozia. Unwin, 1908 ss, some crimin-
      ous
   The Mystery of Wo-Sing. Long, 1924

HALIDOM, M. Y. Pseudonym.
   The Poison Ring. Greening, 1912 [It.]
   A Son of Desolation. Greening, 1909
   -The Woman in Black. Greening, 1906

HALIFAX, CLIFFORD. Ref: MP. See: L(illie)
   T(homas) Meade.

HALIFAX, ROBERT
   The Grip of Gold. Digby, 1907
   -The House of Horror. Digby, 1911
   The Jewels of Death. Newnes, 1911

HALIGON, RICHARD
   The Flying Porcupine. Futura, 1980

HALKET, ROBERTSON
   Documentary Evidence. Nicholson, 1936
   Where Every Prospect Pleases. Benn,
      1933

HALL, ADAM. Pseudonym of Elleston Trevor,
   1920-   , q.v. Name originally: Tre-
   vor Dudley Smith, q.v. Other pseudo-
   nyms: Mansell Black, Howard North,
   Simon Rattray, Warwick Scott, Caesar
   Smith, qq.v. SC: Quiller = Q.
   The Berlin Memorandum. Collins, 1965.
      U.S. title: The Quiller Memorandum.
      Simon, 1965 Q [Berlin]
   The Kobra Manifesto. Collins, 1976;
      Doubleday, 1976 Q
   The Mandarin Cypher. Collins, 1975;
      Doubleday, 1975 Q [H. Kong]
   The 9th Directive. Heinemann, 1966;
      Simon, 1966 Q [Bangkok]
   The Quiller Memorandum; see The Berlin
      Memorandum
   The Scorpion Signal. Collins, 1979;
      Doubleday, 1980 Q [Moscow]
   The Sinkiang Executive. Collins, 1978;
      Doubleday, 1978 Q [Russ.]
   The Striker Portfolio. Heinemann, 1969;
      Simon, 1969 Q [Ger.]
   The Tango Briefing. Collins, 1973;
      Doubleday, 1973 Q [Afr.]
   The Volcanoes of San Domingo. Collins,
      1963; Simon, 1964 [S. Am.]
   The Warsaw Document. Heinemann, 1971;
      Doubleday, 1970 Q [Warsaw]

HALL, ANDREW. 1935-   . Ref: CA.
   Frost. Cassell, 1966; Putnam, 1967
   Man in Aspic. Cassell, 1965
   Safe Behind Bars. Cassell, 1968

HALL, ANGUS. 1932-   . Ref: CA, CC.
   -The Come-Uppance of Arthur Hearne.
      Hammond, 1967
   Devilday; see Qualtrough
   -The Gentle Sex. Sphere, 1972
   -The High-Bouncing Lover. Hammond, 1966
   -The Late Boy Wonder. Jenkins, 1969;
      Ace, 1970
   -Live Like a Hero. Hammond, 1967
   A Long Way to Fall. Allen, 1971
   Madhouse; see Qualtrough
   On the Run. Harrap, 1974
   Qualtrough. Jenkins, 1968. Also pub-
      lished as: Devilday. Sphere, 1969;
      Ace, 1971. And as: Madhouse. Award,
      1974
   The Rigoletto Murder. Hale, 1978
   -The Scars of Dracula. Sphere, 1971;
      Beagle, 1971
   -To Play the Devil. Sphere, 1971

HALL, DOUGLAS. 1929-   .
   The Brittle Thread. Zondervan, 1968
   The Girl in 906. Zondervan, 1970
   The Kirsty Affair. Zondervan, 1972
   The Long Way Down. Zondervan, 1971

HALL, EDITH MACOMBER
   The Black Trail. Greaves, 1911 ss, some
      criminous

HALL, F. CAMERON
   A Country Tragedy. Neely, 1898

HALL, F. H. 1926-   . Ref: CA.
   In the Lamb White Days. Bobbs, 1975
      [Mich.]

HALL, GEOFFREY HOLIDAY. Ref: CC.
   The End Is Known. Simon, 1949; Heine-
      mann, 1950 [NYC]
   The Watcher at the Door. Simon, 1954
      [Vienna]

HALL, GIMONE. 1940-   . Ref: CA.
   The Blue Taper. Macfadden, 1970 [La.]
   Devil's Walk. Macfadden, 1972
   The Juliet Room. Manor, 1974 [Pa.]
   The Silver Strand. Dell, 1974 [Eng.]
   Witch's Suckling. Macfadden, 1970 [NYC]

HALL, HOLWORTHY. Pseudonym of Harold
   Everett Porter, 1887-1936.
   What He Least Expected. Bobbs, 1917

HALL, HOWARD. See: Charles E. Blaney,
   1865?-1944.

HALL, JAY
   Evidently Murdered. Dorrance, 1943

HALL, JENNI(FER ANTOINETTE). 1939-   .
   -Ask Agamemnon. Cassell, 1964; Atheneum,
      1964. Also published as: Goodbye
      Gemini. Sphere, 1970
   -The Diamond Trip. New English Library,
      1971
   Goodbye Gemini; see Ask Agamemnon
   -Mr. Capon. Cassell, 1965; Harcourt,
      1965

HALL, LELAND. 1883-1957.
   Sinister House. Houghton, 1919

HALL, MARJORY [MARJORY HALL YEAKLEY].
   1908-   . Ref: CA.
   Mystery at October House. Westminster,
      1977
   Rosamunda. Dell, 1974

HALL, MICHAEL
   Once Upon a Crime. Falcon, 1947 [Ger.]

HALL, OAKLEY M(AXWELL). 1920-   . Pseu-
   donym: Jason Manor, q.v. Ref: CA.
   A Game for Eagles. Morrow, 1970
   Murder City. Farrar, 1949; Barker,
      1950. Canadian title: Wanton City.
      Harlequin, 1951 [Calif.]
   -So Many Doors. Random, 1950 [Calif.]
   Wanton City; see Murder City

HALL, PATRICK. 1932-   . Ref: CA.
   The Power Sellers. Putnam, 1969

HALL, RICHARD
   The Butterscotch Prince. Pyramid, 1975

HALL, RICHARD S. S.
   Betrayal into Darkness. Vantage, 1967

HALL, ROBERT LEE. 1941-   . Ref: CA.
   Exit Sherlock Holmes. Scribner, 1977;
      Murray, 1977 (Sherlock Holmes.)
      [Eng., 1903]
   The King Edward Plot. McGraw, 1980
      [Eng., 1906]

HALL, ROGER (WOLCOTT). 1919-   . Ref:
   CA.
   19. Norton, 1970

HALL, STEPHANIE. Pseudonym of William J. Smith.
Queen of Coins. Popular Library, 1975
Whisper in the Dust. Popular Library, 1976 [N.Y.]
The Witch of Murray Hill. Popular Library, 1974

HALL, STEVE(N PETER)
Rape of the Nicollet Mall Mannequin. Con Brio, 1978 [Mpls.]

HALL, WARNER
Even Jericho. Macrae-Smith, 1944

HALL, WHYTE. Pseudonym of Augustus Alfred Rayner, 1894-   . Set: Eng.
Crime and a Clock. Harrap, 1936
Death and the Golden Image. Harrap, 1936
Death of the Doctor's Wife. Quality, 1939
Method of Murder. Wells Gardner, 1946

HALLAHAN, WILLIAM H(ENRY). Born in Brooklyn; has degrees in journalism and English from Temple U.
Catch Me, Kill Me. Bobbs, 1977; Gollancz, 1978 [NYC]
The Dead of Winter. Bobbs, 1972; Sphere, 1979 [NYC]
Keeper of the Children. Morrow, 1978; Gollancz, 1979 [Phil.]
The Ross Forgery. Bobbs, 1973; Gollancz, 1977
The Search for Joseph Tully. Bobbs, 1974; Macmillan (London), 1975 [NYC]

HALLAS, RICHARD. Pseudonym of Eric Mowbray Knight, 1897-1943.
You Play the Black and the Red Comes Up. McBride, 1938 [L.A.]

HALLATT, WILLIAM
Suppression. Skeffington, 1930 [Fr.]

HALLERAN, E(UGENE) E(DWARD). 1905-   . Ref: CA.
Thirteen Toy Pistols. McKay, 1945 [N.J.]

HALLEY, LAURENCE. Born in England; living in NYC in 1978.
Simultaneous Equations. Cape, 1975; St. Martin's, 1978

HALLIDAY, BRETT. Pseudonym of Davis Dresser, 1904-1977. Other pseudonym: Asa Baker, q.v. Joint pseudonym with Kathleen Rollins Dresser: Hal Debrett, q.v. Joint pseudonym with (Walter) Ryerson Johnson, 1901-   , q.v.: Matthew Blood, q.v. See also: James Reach, 1909?-1970. Beginning about 1958, most books under the Halliday byline were ghosted by other authors: those by (Walter) Ryerson Johnson, 1901-   , q.v., are marked *; those by Robert Terrall, 1914-   , q.v., are marked #. Ref: CA, CC, EM, MP, TC. SC: Michael Shayne, in all titles.
Armed...Dangerous... Dell, 1966 [NYC] #
At the Point of a .38. Dell, 1974 [Miami] #
The Blonde Cried Murder. Torquil/Dodd, 1956; Jarrolds, 1957 [Miami]
Blood on Biscayne Bay. Ziff-Davis, 1946; Jarrolds, 1950 [Miami]
Blood on the Black Market. Dodd, 1943. In Britain contained in: Michael Shayne Takes a Hand. Jarrolds, 1944. Revised edition: Heads You Lose. Torquil/Dodd, 1958 [Miami]
Blood on the Stars. Dodd, 1948. British title: Murder Is a Habit. Jarrolds, 1951 [Miami]
Blue Murder. Dell, 1973 [Miami] #
Bodies Are Where You Find Them. Holt, 1941. In Britain contained in: Michael Shayne Investigates. Jarrolds, 1943 [Miami]
The Body Came Back. Torquil/Dodd, 1963 [Miami]
Call for Michael Shayne. Dodd, 1949; Jarrolds, 1951 [Miami]
The Careless Corpse. Torquil/Dodd, 1961 [Miami]
The Case of the Walking Corpse; see The Corpse Came Calling
Caught Dead. Dell, 1972 [Venez.] #
The Corpse Came Calling. Dodd, 1942. In Britain contained in: Michael Shayne Investigates. Jarrolds, 1943. Also published as: The Case of the Walking Corpse. Handi-Books, 1943 [Miami]
The Corpse That Never Was. Torquil/Dodd, 1963 [Miami]
Count Backwards to Zero. Dell, 1971 #
Counterfeit Wife. Ziff-Davis, 1947; Jarrolds, 1950 [Miami]

Date with a Dead Man. Torquil/Dodd, 1959; Long, 1960 (Expansion of the novelet "Dead Man's Diary", included in Michael Shayne's Triple Mystery, q.v.) [Miami]
Dead Man's Diary; see Michael Shayne's Triple Mystery
Death Has Three Lives. Torquil/Dodd, 1955; Jarrolds, 1955 [Miami]
Die Like a Dog. Torquil/Dodd, 1959; Long, 1961 [Miami]
Dinner at Dupre's; see Michael Shayne's Triple Mystery
Dividend on Death. Holt, 1939; Jarrolds, 1941 [Miami]
Dolls Are Deadly. Torquil/Dodd, 1960 [Miami] *
Fit to Kill. Torquil/Dodd, 1958; Long, 1959 [Miami] #
Fourth Down to Death. Dell, 1970 [Miami] #
Framed in Blood. Dodd, 1951; Jarrolds, 1953 [Miami]
Guilty As Hell. Dell, 1967 [Miami] #
Heads You Lose; see Blood on the Black Market
The Homicidal Virgin. Torquil/Dodd, 1960
I Come to Kill You. Dell, 1971 [Miami] #
In a Deadly Vein; see Murder Wears a Mummer's Mask
Kill All the Young Girls. Dell, 1973 [Miami] #
Killers from the Keys. Torquil/Dodd, 1961 [Miami] *
Lady, Be Bad. Dell, 1969 [Fla.] #
The Lady Came by Night; see One Night with Nora
Last Seen Hitchhiking. Dell, 1974 [Fla.] #
Marked for Murder. Dodd, 1945; Jarrolds, 1950 [Miami]
Mermaid on the Rocks. Dell, 1967 [Fla.] #
Michael Shayne Investigates. Jarrolds, 1943. Contains: Bodies Are Where You Find Them, and The Corpse Came Calling, qq.v.
Michael Shayne Takes a Hand. Jarrolds, 1944. Contains: Murder Wears a Mummer's Mask, and Blood on the Black Market, qq.v.
Michael Shayne's 50th Case. Torquil/Dodd, 1964 [Fla.]
Michael Shayne's Long Chance. Dodd, 1944; Jarrolds, 1945 [New Or.]
Michael Shayne's Triple Mystery. Ziff-Davis, 1948 (Three novelets: Dead Man's Diary, A Taste for Cognac, and Dinner at Dupre's. A Dell reprint combined #1 and #3 in 1950; a later Dell reprint, 1959, combined #1 and #2. #2, A Taste for Cognac, was reprinted separately as a Dell 10¢ paperback in 1951. #1 was later expanded into the novel Date with a Dead Man, q.v.)
Million Dollar Handle. Dell, 1976 [Miami] #
Murder and the Married Virgin. Dodd, 1944; Jarrolds, 1946 [New Or.]
Murder and the Wanton Bride. Torquil/Dodd, 1958; Long, 1959 [Miami]
Murder by Proxy. Torquil/Dodd, 1962; Mayflower, 1968
Murder in Haste. Torquil/Dodd, 1961; Mayflower, 1963 [Miami] #
Murder Is a Habit; see Blood on the Stars
Murder Is My Business. Dodd, 1945; Jarrolds, 1945 [Tex.]
Murder Spins the Wheel. Dell, 1966 [Miami] #
Murder Takes No Holiday. Torquil/Dodd, 1960 [Miami] #
Murder Wears a Mummer's Mask. Dodd, 1943. In Britain contained in: Michain Shayne Takes a Hand. Jarrolds, 1944. Also published as: In a Deadly Vein. Dell, 1956 [Colo.]
Never Kill a Client. Torquil/Dodd, 1962 [Miami]
Nice Fillies Finish Last. Dell, 1965 [Miami]
One Night with Nora. Torquil/Dodd, 1953. British title: The Lady Came by Night. Jarrolds, 1954 [Miami]
Pay-Off in Blood. Torquil/Dodd, 1962 [Miami]
The Private Practice of Michael Shayne. Holt, 1940; Jarrolds, 1941 [Miami]
A Redhead for Mike Shayne. Torquil/Dodd, 1964
She Woke to Darkness. Torquil/Dodd, 1954; Jarrolds, 1955 [NYC]
Shoot the Works. Torquil/Dodd, 1957; Long, 1958 [Miami]
Shoot to Kill. Torquil/Dodd, 1964
Six Seconds to Kill. Dell, 1970 [Miami] #

So Lush, So Deadly. Dell, 1968 [Miami] #
Stranger in Town. Torquil/Dodd, 1955; Jarrolds, 1956 [Fla.]
Target: Mike Shayne. Torquil/Dodd, 1959; Long, 1960 [Miami] #
A Taste for Cognac; see Michael Shayne's Triple Mystery
A Taste for Violence. Dodd, 1949; Jarrolds, 1952 [Ky.]
This Is It, Michael Shayne. Dodd, 1950; Jarrolds, 1952 [Miami]
Tickets for Death. Holt, 1941, Jarrolds, 1942 [Fla.]
Too Friendly, Too Dead. Torquil/Dodd, 1963; Mayflower, 1964 [Miami]
The Uncomplaining Corpses. Holt, 1940; Jarrolds, 1942 [Miami]
Violence Is Golden. Dell, 1968 [Carib.] #
The Violent World of Michael Shayne. Dell, 1965 [Wash. D.C.]
Weep for a Blonde. Torquil/Dodd, 1957; Long, 1958 [Miami]
What Really Happened. Dodd, 1952; Jarrolds, 1953 [Miami]
When Dorinda Dances. Dodd, 1951; Jarrolds, 1953 [Miami]
Win Some, Lose Some. Dell, 1976 [Miami] #

HALLIDAY, DOROTHY. U.S. byline: Dorothy Dunnett. Ref: CA, CC. SC: Johnson Johnson, in all titles.
Dolly and the Cookie Bird. Cassell, 1970. U.S. title: Murder in the Round. Houghton, 1970. Reprinted in the U.S. under the British title: Vantage, 1982 [Sp.]
Dolly and the Doctor Bird. Cassell, 1971. U.S. title: Match for a Murderer. Houghton, 1971. Reprinted in the U.S. under the British title: Vantage, 1982 [Bahamas]
Dolly and the Nanny Bird. Joseph, 1976; Knopf, 1982
Dolly and the Singing Bird. Cassell, 1968. U.S. title: The Photogenic Soprano. Houghton, 1968. Reprinted in the U.S. under the British title: Vantage, 1982 [Scot.]
Dolly and the Starry Bird. Cassell, 1972. U.S. title: Murder in Focus. Houghton, 1973. Reprinted in the U.S. under the British title: Vantage, 1982
Match for a Murderer; see Dolly and the Doctor Bird
Murder in Focus; see Dolly and the Starry Bird
Murder in the Round; see Dolly and the Cookie Bird
The Photogenic Soprano; see Dolly and the Singing Bird

HALLIDAY, FRED. 1937-   . Ref: CA. SC: Stanley Delphond, in all titles
A Case of Indelicate Champagne. Pinnacle, 1977. Also published as: A Slight Case of Champagne, in the omnibus: Murder in the Kitchen. Pinnacle, 1979 [Eng.]
The Chocolate Mousse Murders. Pinnacle, 1974 [NYC]
Murder in the Kitchen; see A Case of Indelicate Champagne
The Raspberry Tart Affair. Pinnacle, 1976
A Slight Case of Champagne; see A Case of Indelicate Champagne

HALLIDAY, LEONARD. 1917-   .
The Devil's Door. Hammond, 1959 [It.]
The Smiling Spider. Hammond, 1955 [Austria]
Stay of Execution. Hammond, 1964
Top Secret. Hammond, 1957

HALLIDAY, MICHAEL. Pseudonym of John Creasey, 1908-1973, q.v. Other pseudonyms: Gordon Ashe, M. E. Cooke, Norman Deane, Robert Caine Frazer, Patrick Gill, Charles Hogarth, Brian Hope, Colin Hughes, Kyle Hunt, Abel Mann, Peter Manton, J. J. Marric, Richard Martin, Rodney Mattheson, Anthony Morton, Jeremy York, qq.v. Some titles originally published under the Norman Deane byline, where they are listed herein, were reprinted as by Michael Halliday. SC: Dr. Emmanuel Cellini = EC; Martin & Richard Fane = F. Set: Eng.
As Empty As Hate. Hodder, 1972; World, 1972, as by Kyle Hunt EC
As Lonely as the Damned. Hodder, 1971; World, 1972, as by Kyle Hunt EC
As Merry as Hell. Hodder, 1973; Stein, 1974, as by Kyle Hunt EC
Cat and Mouse. Hodder, 1955. U.S. title: Hilda, Take Heed, as by Jeremy York. Scribner, 1957

H

Halloway, Vance
  Come Here and Die; see Death of a Stranger
  Crime with Many Voices. Paul, 1945
  Cruel as a Cat. Hodder, 1968; Macmillan, 1969, as by Kyle Hunt EC
  Cunning as a Fox. Hodder, 1965; Macmillan, 1965, as by Kyle Hunt EC
  Death of a Stranger. Hodder, 1957. U.S. title: Come Here and Die, as by Jeremy York. Scribner, 1959
  Death Out of Darkness. Hodder, 1954; World, 1971, as by John Creasey [Afr.]
  Dine with Murder. Evans, 1950
  The Dying Witnesses. Evans, 1949
  The Edge of Terror. Hodder, 1961; Macmillan, 1963, as by Jeremy York
  First a Murder. Paul, 1948; McKay, 1972, as by Jeremy York
  Five to Kill. Paul, 1943
  Foul Play Suspected. Paul, 1942
  Four Find Danger. Cassell, 1937
  The Girl with the Leopard-Skin Bag; see How Many to Kill?
  Go Ahead with Murder. Hodder, 1960 U.S. title: Two for the Money, as by Jeremy York. Doubleday, 1962 [Fr.]
  Guilt of Innocence. Hodder, 1964
  Hate to Kill. Hodder, 1962
  Heir to Murder. Paul, 1940
  Hilda, Take Heed; see Cat and Mouse
  How Many to Kill? Hodder, 1960. U.S. title: The Girl with the Leopard-Skin Bag. Scribner, 1961
  The Lame Dog Murder. Evans, 1952; World, 1972, as by John Creasey F
  Lend a Hand to Murder. Paul, 1947
  The Man I Killed. Hodder, 1961; Macmillan, 1963, as by Jeremy York
  Man on the Run. Hodder, 1953; World, 1972, as by John Creasey F
  The Man Who Was Not Himself. Hodder, 1976; Stein, 1977, as by Kyle Hunt EC
  Missing; see Missing from Home
  Missing from Home. Hodder, 1959. U.S. title: Missing, as by Jeremy York. Scribner, 1960
  Murder Assured. Hodder, 1958
  Murder at End House. Hodder, 1955
  Murder at King's Kitchen. Paul, 1943
  Murder by the Way. Paul, 1941
  Murder Come Home. Paul, 1940
  Murder in the Stars. Hodder, 1953
  Murder Makes Murder. Paul, 1946
  Murder Week-End. Evans, 1950 [Fr.]
  Mystery Motive. Paul, 1947; McKay, 1974, as by Jeremy York
  No Crime More Cruel. Paul, 1944
  No End to Danger. Paul, 1948
  Out of the Shadows. Hodder, 1954; World, 1971, as by John Creasey
  A Period of Evil. Hodder, 1970; World, 1971, as by Kyle Hunt EC
  Quarrel with Murder. Evans, 1951
  The Quiet Fear. Hodder, 1963; Macmillan, 1968, as by Jeremy York
  Runaway. Hodder, 1957; World, 1971, as by John Creasey
  Sly as a Serpent. Hodder, 1967; Macmillan, 1967, as by Kyle Hunt EC
  Take a Body. Evans, 1951; World, 1972, as by John Creasey F
  Thicker Than Water. Hodder, 1959; Doubleday, 1962, as by Jeremy York
  This Man Did I Kill? Hodder, 1974; Stein, 1974, as by Kyle Hunt EC
  Three for Adventure. Cassell, 1937
  Too Good to Be True. Hodder, 1969; Macmillan, 1969, as by Kyle Hunt EC
  Two for the Money; see Go Ahead with Murder
  Two Meet Trouble. Cassell, 1938
  Who Died at the Grange? Paul, 1942
  Who Killed Rebecca? Paul, 1949
  Who Said Murder? Paul, 1944
  Who Saw Him Die? Paul, 1941
  Wicked as the Devil. Hodder, 1966; Macmillan, 1966, as by Kyle Hunt EC

HALLOWAY, VANCE. See: J(oseph) C(lare) McMullen, 1882- .

HALLS, GERALDINE (MARY JAY). 1919- . Pseudonym: Charlotte Jay, q.v. Ref: CA, CC, TC.
  The Voice of the Crab. Constable, 1974; Harper, 1974, as by Charlotte Jay [New Guinea]

HALLUMS, JAMES
  Bodysnatch. Futura, 1980
  Underground. Futura, 1979

HALPERN, JAY
  The Jade Unicorn. Macmillan, 1979 [NYC]

HALPERN, OSCAR SAUL. 1932- . Pseudonym: Oscar Saul, q.v.

HALPIN, MARY D. Pseudonym: Christina Blake, q.v.

HALSE, A. W.
  -The White Crusaders. Jenkins, 1935

HALSEY, FORREST. 1878-
  -The Bawlerout. FitzGerald, 1912
  -The Shadow on the Hearth. American, 1914
  The Stain. Browne, 1913
  -A Term of Silence. FitzGerald, 1913

HALSEY, HARLAN PAGE. 1937-1898. Pseudonyms: Old Sleuth, Tony Pastor, Judson R. Taylor, qq.v.
  -Annie Wallace; or, The Exile of Penang. Miller, 1857
  The Chosen Man; or, The Mystery of the Secret Service. Street, 1888
  -Her Great Surprise. Parlor Car, 1893
  -A Lady Bachelor. Parlor Car, 1892
  The Masked Detective. Street, 1888
  Van, the Government Detective; or, The Base Metal Coiners. Street, 1888; Aldine, 18??, as by Judson R. Taylor

HALSEY, HELEN NORWOOD
  The Child Witness. Neely, 1898

HALSTEAD, ADA L. Pseudonym of Mrs. Laura Eugenia Newhall, 1861- .
  Adopted; or, The Serpent Bracelet. Golden Era, 1886
  -After the Night Has Passed. Laird, 1896
  The Bride of Infelice. Bancroft, 1892
  The Death Trust. [Author], 1889. Also published as: Hazel Verne; or, The Death Trust. [Author], 1889
  Hazel Verne; or, The Death Trust; see The Death Trust

HALSTEAD, JOHN. SC: Insp. Todd, in at least those marked T. Set: Eng.
  The Black Arab. Paul, 1933
  The Black Fear. Paul, 1935 T
  The Black Flame. Paul, 1936
  The Black Hate. Paul, 1937 T
  The Black Nat. Paul, 1932
  The Black Templar. Paul, 1934 T

HALSTEAD, THAYER
  The Godfather Must Live. Dell, 1974

HAMBLEDON, PHYLLIS. Pseudonym of Phyllis MacVean, 1892- . Other pseudonym: Philippa Vane, q.v. SC: Insp. "Tubby" Hall, in at least those marked TH. Set: Eng.
  Death of an Uncle. Hale, 1962
  I Know a Secret. Laurie, 1951
  Invitation to Terror. Laurie, 1950
  Keys for the Criminal. Hale, 1958 TH
  The Listening Boy. Laurie, 1951
  Murder and Miss Ming. Hale, 1959 TH
  Murder's No Picnic. Hale, 1961 [Fr.]
  Passports to Murder. Hale, 1959

HAMBLETT, CHARLES
  The Crazy Kill. Sidgwick, 1956

HAMEL, FELIX JOHN. Pseudonym: Lionel J. F. Hexham, q.v.

HAMILL, DENIS
  Stomping Ground. Delacorte, 1980 [NYC]

HAMILL, DESMOND
  -Bitter Orange. Hutchinson, 1979; Morrow, 1980

HAMILL, EDSON T. SC: Ryker, in all titles (see also: Nelson De Mille, 1943-).
  The Child Killer. Leisure, 1975 [NYC]
  Motive for Murder. Leisure, 1975
  The Sadist. Leisure, 1975 [NYC]
  The Slasher. Leisure, 1976 [NYC]

HAMILL, PETE. 1935- . Ref: CA. SC: Sam Briscoe, in both titles.
  The Deadly Piece. Bantam (NYC & London), 1979 [NYC]
  Dirty Laundry. Bantam (NYC), 1978; Bantam (London), 1979

HAMILL, STUART. 1899- . Born in Phil.; news writer, feature writer and editor on newspapers; playwright and actor.
  China Kill. Harlo, 1974

HAMILTON, ADAM. Joint pseudonym of Marilyn Granbeck, 1927- , q.v., and Arthur Moore, q.v. Other joint pseudonym: Van Saxon, q.v. Other Granbeck pseudonyms: Ben Grant, Clayton Moore, qq.v. For Arthur Moore, see also: Don Hoyt. SC: Barrington Hewes-Bradford (The Peacemaker), in all titles.
  The Wyss Pursuit. Berkley, 1975
  The Xander Pursuit. Berkley, 1974
  The Yashar Pursuit. Berkley, 1974 [Mid. East]
  The Zaharan Pursuit. Berkley, 1974

HAMILTON, ALEX (JOHN). 1939- .
  As If She Were Mine. New Authors, 1962
  Beam of Malice. Hutchinson, 1966; McKay, 1967 ss
  The Dead Needle. Hutchinson, 1969
  Flies on the Wall. Hutchinson, 1972 ss
  Town Parole. Hutchinson, 1964
  Wild Track. Hutchinson, 1963

HAMILTON, ALISTAIR. Pseudonym of Tasman Beattie, 1930- , q.v.
  The Halo Jump. Hamlyn, 1979

HAMILTON, (ARTHUR DOUGLAS) BRUCE. 1900- . Ref: CC, EM. Set: Eng.
  The Brighton Murder Trial: Rex v. Rhodes. Boriswood, 1937
  Dead Reckoning; see Middle Class Murder
  Hanging Judge; see Let Him Have Judgment
  Hue and Cry. Collins, 1931
  Let Him Have Judgment. Cresset, 1948. U.S. title: Hanging Judge. Harper, 1948
  Middle Class Murder. Methuen, 1936. U.S. title: Dead Reckoning. Simon, 1937
  Pro: An English Tragedy. Cresset, 1946
  So Sad, So Fresh. Cresset, 1952
  The Spring Term. Methuen, 1933
  To Be Hanged. Faber, 1930; Doubleday, 1930
  Too Much of Water. Cresset, 1958; Perennial, 1983 [ship]
  Traitor's Way. Cresset, 1938; Bobbs, 1939

HAMILTON, CARSON C(RANDALL). 1900- . Has Ph.D. from U. of Pittsburgh; taught composition and literature at Michigan State U.
  Jeff Utter. Exposition, 1964

HAMILTON, CHARLES HAROLD ST. JOHN. 1876-1961. Pseudonym: Peter Todd, q.v.

HAMILTON, CLARE. Pseudonym of Bettyclare Hamilton Lawless, 1915- . Ref: CA.
  Twilight Forest. Pyramid, 1973 [S.F.]

HAMILTON, DONALD (BENGTSSON). 1916- . Ref: CA, CC, EM, TC. SC: Matt Helm = MH.
  The Ambushers. GM, 1963; Coronet, 1967 MH [S.W.]
  Assassins Have Starry Eyes; see Assignment: Murder
  Assignment: Murder. Dell, 1956. Also published as: Assassins Have Starry Eyes. GM, 1966 [N. Mex.]
  The Betrayers. GM, 1966; Coronet, 1968 MH [Haw.]
  Date with Darkness. Rinehart, 1947; Wingate, 1951
  Death of a Citizen. GM, 1960; Muller, 1960 MH [S.W.]
  The Devastators. GM, 1965; Coronet, 1967 MH [Scot.]
  The Interlopers. GM, 1969; Coronet, 1969 MH [Can.]
  The Intimidators. GM, 1974; Coronet, 1974 MH [Carib.]
  The Intriguers. GM, 1973; Coronet, 1973 MH [S.W.]
  Line of Fire. Dell, 1955; Wingate, 1956
  The Menacers. GM, 1968; Hodder, 1968 MH [Mex.]
  The Mona Intercept. GM, 1980 [Carib.]
  Murder Twice Told. Rinehart, 1950; Wingate, 1952 (2 novelets.)
  Murderer's Row. GM, 1962; Muller, 1963 MH [Wash. D.C.]
  Night Walker. Dell, 1954. British title: Rough Company. Wingate, 1954 [Md.]
  The Poisoners. GM, 1971; Coronet, 1971 MH
  The Ravagers. GM, 1964 MH [Can.]
  The Removers. GM, 1961; Muller, 1962 MH [Reno]
  The Retaliators. GM, 1976; Coronet, 1979 MH [Mex.]
  Rough Company; see Night Walker
  The Shadowers. GM, 1964; Muller, 1964 MH
  The Silencers. GM, 1962; Hodder pb, 1966 MH [N. Mex.]
  The Steel Mirror. Rinehart, 1948; Wingate, 1948 [Colo.]
  The Terminators. GM, 1975; Coronet, 1976 MH [Nor.]
  The Terrorizers. GM, 1977 MH [Can.]
  The Wrecking Crew. GM, 1960; Muller, 1961 MH [Swed.]

HAMILTON, EDMOND. 1904-1977. Ref: CA.
  Murder in the Clinic. Newcoll, 1946 (2 stories.)

HAMILTON, ELAINE. SC: Insp. Reynolds, in at least those marked R. Set: Eng.
  The Casino Mystery. Ward, 1936 R [Fr.]
  The Chelsea Mystery. Paul, 1932 R

The Green Death. Paul, 1932 R
Murder Before Tuesday. Ward, 1937 R
Murder in the Fog. Paul, 1931 R
Peril at Midnight. Ward, 1934 R
The Silent Bell. Paul, 1933
Some Unknown Hand. Paul, 1930. U.S. title: The Westminster Mystery. Century, 1931 R
Tragedy in the Dark. Ward, 1935 R
The Westminster Mystery; see Some Unknown Hand

HAMILTON, (LORD) ERNEST (WILLIAM). 1858-1939. Ref: CC.
The Four Tragedies of Memworth. Gollancz, 1928
The Perils of Josephine. Unwin, 1899; Stone, 1899

HAMILTON, (LORD) FREDERIC SPENCER. 1856-1928. Ref: CC, MP. SC: P. J. Davenant, in all titles. Set: Eng.
The Beginnings of Mr. P. J. Davenant. Hodder, 1917 ss
The Education of Mr. P. J. Davenant. Nash, 1916 ss
The Holiday Adventures of Mr. P. J. Davenant. Nash, 1915 ss
-More About P. J., the Secret Service Boy. Nelson, 1923 ss
Nine Holiday Adventures of Mr. P. J. Davenant in the Year 1915. Newnes, 1916 (A revised edition of The Holiday Adventures of Mr. P. J. Davenant, q.v.)
-P. J., the Secret Service Boy. Nelson, 1922 ss
Some Further Adventures of Mr. P. J. Davenant. Nash, 1915 ss

HAMILTON, HENRIETTA. 1920-   . Born in Scotland; graduate of Oxford in modern languages. SC: Sally and Johnny Heldar, in all titles.
Answer in the Negative. Hodder, 1959
At Night to Die. Hodder, 1959 [Scot.]
Death at One Below. Hodder, 1957
The Two Hundred Ghost. Hodder, 1956

HAMILTON, HENRY. 1853?-1918. See: Cecil Raleigh.

HAMILTON, IAN. 1935-   . Born in Melb.; advertising copywriter and TV commercial writer. SC: Pete Heysen, in all titles.
The Creeping Vicar; see The Man with the Brown Paper Face
The Man with the Brown Paper Face. Constable, 1967. U.S. title: The Creeping Vicar. Lippincott, 1967 [Australia]
Never Die in Honolulu. Mayflower, 1969; Lippincott, 1969 [Haw.]
The Persecutor. Constable, 1965; Lippincott, 1965 [Syd.]
The Thrill Machine. Collins, 1972 [Syd.]

HAMILTON, J. LINDSAY. Set: Eng.
The Black Asp. Jenkins, 1931
The Gorgon. Jenkins, 1930

HAMILTON, JESSICA
Elizabeth. Random, 1976; Harrap, 1976

HAMILTON, MARY AGNES. 1884-1966.
Life Sentence. H. Hamilton, 1935. U.S. title: Sentenced to Life. Houghton, 1935
Murder in the House of Commons. H. Hamilton, 1931; Houghton, 1931
Sentenced to Life; see Life Sentence
-Special Providence: A Tale of 1917. Allen & Unwin, 1930. U.S. title: Three Against Fate: A Tale of 1917. Houghton, 1930 [1917]
Three Against Fate; see Special Providence

HAMILTON, MICHAEL
Teeth for the Brigadier. Sphere, 1976

HAMILTON, MOLLIE. Pseudonym of M(ary) M(argaret) Kaye, 1911-   , q.v.

HAMILTON, (ANTHONY WALTER) PATRICK. 1904-1962. Ref: CC, EM, TC. SC: Ernest Ralph Gorse, in at least those marked EG. Set: Eng.
Angel Street; see Gas Light
Gas Light. Constable, 1939. U.S. title: Angel Street. French, 1942 (3-act play.)
Hangover Square; or, The Man with Two Minds. Constable, 1941; Random, 1942
-The Man Upstairs. Constable, 1954 (Play.)
Mr. Stimpson and Mr. Gorse. Constable, 1953 EG
Money with Menaces, and To the Public Danger. Constable, 1939 (2 radio plays.)
Rope. Constable, 1929. U.S. title: Rope's End. Smith, 1930 (Play.)
Rope's End; see Rope
Unknown Assailant. Constable, 1955 EG
The West Pier. Constable, 1951; Doubleday, 1952 EG

HAMILTON, ROGER
Living's a Dying Game. Hale, 1969
Mosquitoes Don't Kill. Hale, 1971
The Rules Don't Apply. Hale, 1968

HAMLEY, MAJOR GENERAL W(ILLIAM) G(EORGE). 1815-1893.
Guilty, or Not Guilty? Blackwood, 1878

HAMMETT, (SAMUEL) DASHIELL. 1894-1961. Ref: all eight. SC: Secret Agent X-9 = SA; The Continental Op = CO; Sam Spade = SS.
The Adventures of Sam Spade and other stories. Bestseller, 1944 (7 stories, 3 about SS. The complete collection was reprinted as: They Can Only Hang You Once. Mercury, 1949. The 3 SS stories and 2 of the other 4 were reprinted as: A Man Called Spade. Dell, 1945.) [S.F.]
The Big Knockover (novelet about CO); see $106,000 Blood Money
The Big Knockover. Random, 1966. British title: The Dashiell Hammett Story Omnibus. Cassell, 1966 (A collection, with introduction by Lillian Hellman, containing 7 CO ss, a chapter from Hammett's unfinished novel, and the CO novelet The Big Knockover, for further data on which see: $106,000 Blood Money. This collection was split for paperback reprint into two separate volumes, confusingly titled The Big Knockover, Dell, 1967, and The Continental Op, Dell, 1967.)
The Big Knockover (partial paperback reprint of hardcover collection of the same title); see The Big Knockover
Blood Money; see $106,000 Blood Money
The Continental Op. Bestseller, 1945 (4 ss about CO.) [S.F.]
The Continental Op (partial paperback reprint of hardcover collection The Big Knockover); see The Big Knockover
The Continental Op. Random, 1974; Macmillan (London), 1975 (A collection of 7 CO ss taken from earlier collections, with an introduction by Steven Marcus.)
The Creeping Siamese. Jonathan, 1950 (6 ss, 3 about CO.) [S.F.]
The Dain Curse. Knopf, 1929; Cassell, 1929 CO [Calif.]
The Dashiell Hammett Omnibus. Cassell, 1950 (Contains all 5 major novels plus 4 ss about CO.)
The Dashiell Hammett Story Omnibus; see The Big Knockover
Dead Yellow Women. Jonathan, 1947 (6 ss, 4 about CO.) [S.F.]
The Glass Key. Knopf, 1931; Cassell, 1931
Hammett Homicides. Bestseller, 1946 (6 ss, 4 about CO.) [S.F.]
The Maltese Falcon. Knopf, 1930; Cassell, 1930 SS [S.F.]
A Man Called Spade; see The Adventures of Sam Spade and other stories
A Man Named Thin. Mercury, 1962 (8 ss, 1 about CO.) [S.F.]
Nightmare Town. Mercury, 1948 (4 ss, 2 about CO.)
$106,000 Blood Money. Bestseller, 1943. Also published as: Blood Money. World, 1943; and as: The Big Knockover. Jonathan, 1948. Also included as the title story in the hardcover collection The Big Knockover, q.v. (Note: This novelet was originally published in two parts in "Black Mask", February and May 1927, the first part titled "The Big Knockover" and the second "$106,000 Blood Money.")
Red Harvest. Knopf, 1929; Cassell, 1929 CO [Calif.]
The Return of the Continental Op. Jonathan, 1945 (5 ss about CO.) [S.F.]
Secret Agent X-9. McKay, 1934 SA
Secret Agent X-9: Book Two. McKay, 1934 SA
They Can Only Hang You Once; see The Adventures of Sam Spade and other stories
The Thin Man. Knopf, 1934; Barker, 1934 [NYC]
Woman in the Dark. Jonathan, 1951 (7 ss, 3 about CO.) [S.F.]

HAMMIL, JOEL
Limbo. Arbor, 1980 [Calif.]

HAMMOCK, CLAUDE STUART. 1876-   .
Why Murder the Judge? Macmillan, 1930 [NYC]

HAMMOND, CLEMENT MILTON. See: Charles Howard Montague, 1858-1889.

HAMMOND, GERALD. 1926-   .
Dead Game. Macmillan (London), 1979
The Loose Screw. Hodder, 1966
Mud in His Eye. Hodder, 1967
The Reward Game. Macmillan (London), 1980; St. Martin's, 1980 [Scot.]

HAMMOND, LAWRENCE. 1925-   . Ref: CA.
A Life to Lose. Allen, 1966 [Cors.]

HAMMOND, MARC
Fathom. Futura, 1978; Jove, 1979
Killer Mountain. Futura, 1980
-The Theseus Code. Futura, 1979

HAMMOND, (DR.) WILLIAM A(LEXANDER). 1828-1900, and CLARA HAMMOND LANZA, 1859-   . Ref: CC.
Tales in Eccentric Life. Appleton, 1886 ss

HAMMOND-INNES, RALPH. 1913-   . See: (Ralph) Hammond Innes.

HAMPTON, JAY
The Coven. Pinnacle, 1978

HAMPTON, MARK. Pseudonym of Victor (George Charles) Norwood, 1920-   , q.v. Other pseudonyms: Johnny Dark, Nat Karta, Hank Janson, Mark Shane, qq.v.
I Don't Scare Easy. Scion, 1952
Killer Take All. Scion, 1953
Raw Deal for Dames. Scion, 1952
That's Her Problem. Scion, 1952

HAMPTON, RUTH
The Girl in the Wall. Moody, 1978

HANCOCK, FRANCES DEAN. Pseudonym of Jeanne Judson, 1890-1981, q.v.
Legacy of Fear. Avalon, 1969

HANCOCK, HARRIE I(RVING). 1868-1922.
Blackmail: A Central Office Problem. Street, 1899
Detective Johnson of New Orleans: A Tale of Love and Crime. Ogilvie, 1891 [New Or.]
His Evil Eye: or, Sybil's Trials. Ogilvie, 1891
Inspector Henderson, the Central Office Detective. Ogilvie, 1892

HANCOCK, SIBYL. 1940-   . Ref: CA.
Mosshaven. Beagle, 1973

HANDLEY, ALAN
Kiss Your Elbow. McKay, 1948. Also published as: Terror in Times Square. Pyramid, 1950 [NYC]

HANDLEY, ALFRED
Death in Still Water. Hale, 1980
The Scorpion Trap. Hale, 1980

HANDLEY, LEONARD (MOURANT H.). 1890-   .
-Luxury Tour. Long, 1941
Remote Journey. Long, 1939
-There Was No Island. Long, 1942

HANING, BOB [JAMES ROBERT HANING]. 1928-   . Ref: CA.
Turkey-Track Rampage. Lenox, 1974. Also published as: Rampage. Belmont, 1975

HANKINS, ARTHUR P(RESTON). 1880-1932. Pseudonym: Emart Kinsburn, q.v.
-Cole of Spyglass Mountain. Dodd, 1923 [Calif.]
Judy the Torch. Chelsea, 1928

HANKINS, R(OBERT) M(AXWELL). 1905-   .
-Ace-in-the-Hole Haggerty. Macrae, 1945; Hodder, 1948

HANKINSON, CHARLES JAMES. 1866-1959. Pseudonym: Clive Holland, q.v.

HANLEY, CLIFFORD. 1922-   . Pseudonym: Henry Calvin, q.v. Ref: CA, CC.
Prissy. Collins, 1978

HANLEY, ELIZABETH. Pseudonym of (Elizabeth) Lorinda DuBreuil, 1924-1980, q.v. Other pseudonyms: Kate Cameron, Linda Hagen, qq.v.
Guilty As Charged. Belmont, 1979 [Ill.; 1930s]

HANLEY, JACK
The Violated One. Zenith, 1960

HANLEY, WILLIAM
    Leaving Mt. Venus. Ballantine, 1977

HANNA, DAVID. 1917-   . Ref: CA.
    The Vacant Throne. Belmont, 1979 [Rome]

HANNA, FRANCES NICHOLS. Pseudonym: Fan
    Nichols, q.v.

HANNAH, BARRY
    Nightwatchman. Viking, 1973

HANNAY, J(AMES) F(REDERICK) W(YNNE).
    1906-
    Flight of an Angel. Methuen, 1932
    Gin and Ginger. Methuen, 1931 [ship]
    Murder and Me. Hutchinson, 1937
    The Thirteenth Floor. Methuen, 1931
        [Tex.]
    Three Alibis. Hutchinson, 1938
    When the Wicked Man... Methuen, 1934

HANNAY, JAMES OWEN. 1865-1950. Pseudonym:
    George A. Birmingham, q.v.

HANNON, EZRA. Pseudonym of Evan Hunter,
    1926-   , q.v. Other pseudonyms:
    Curt Cannon, Richard Marsten, Ed
    McBain, qq.v.
    Doors. Stein, 1975; Macmillan (London),
        1976 [NYC]

HANO, ARNOLD. 1922-   . Pseudonyms:
    Matthew Gant, Mike Heller, qq.v.

HANSARD, RENE
    The Silver Fox. Morrow, 1938; Heine-
        mann, 1938

HANSEN, JOSEPH. 1923-   . Pseudonym:
    Rose Brock, q.v. Ref: CA, TC. SC:
    Dave Brandstetter = DB.
    Death Claims. Harper, 1973; Harrap,
        1973 DB [L.A.]
    Fadeout. Harper, 1970; Harrap, 1972
        DB [Calif.]
    The Man Everybody Was Afraid Of. Holt,
        1978; Faber, 1978 DB [Calif.]
    Pretty Boy Dead. Major, 1977
    Skinflick. Holt, 1979; Faber, 1980 DB
        [Calif.]
    Stranger to Himself. Major, 1977
    Troublemaker. Harper, 1975; Harrap,
        1975 DB [Calif.]

HANSEN, ROBERT. 1883-1957. Pseudonym:
    Jens Anker, q.v.

HANSEN, ROBERT P(OWELL)
    Back to the Wall. Mill, 1957; Boardman,
        1958 [Vt.]
    Dead Pigeon. Mill, 1951; Barker, 1953
        [Calif.]
    Deadly Purpose. Mill, 1958; Boardman,
        1959 [Calif.]
    Mark Three for Murder. Mill, 1957;
        Boardman, 1957 [Vt.]
    Murder Is Where You Find It. Mill,
        1956; Boardman, 1957 [Calif.]
    There's Always a Payoff. Mill, 1959;
        Boardman, 1960 [Calif.]
    Trouble Comes Double. Mill, 1954;
        Barker, 1955 [Calif.]
    Walk a Crooked Mile. Mill, 1955; Board-
        man, 1955 [Calif.]

HANSEN, VERN
    -Claws of the Night. Digit, 1963
    -Creatures of the Night. Digit, 1963
    -The Grip of Fear. Digit, 1964
    Murder with Menaces. Digit, 1962
    -The Twisters. Digit, 1963
    The Whisper of Death. Digit, 1963 [NYC]

HANSHEW, HAZEL PHILLIPS. See also: Thomas
    W. Hanshew, 1857-1914; and: Mary E.
    Hanshew. SC: Hamilton Cleek, in both
    titles (and under Thomas W. Hanshew
    and Mary E. Hanshew bylines).
    Murder in the Hotel. Long, 1932
    The Riddle of the Winged Death. Long,
        1931

HANSHEW, MARY E. and THOMAS W. HANSHEW,
    1857-1914. SC: Hamilton Cleek, in all
    titles; see also Hazel Phillips Han-
    shew and Thomas W. Hanshew bylines).
    The Amber Junk. Hutchinson, 1924. U.S.
        title: The Riddle of the Amber Ship.
        Doubleday, 1924 (Actually written by
        Hazel Phillips Hanshew.)
    The Frozen Flame. Simpkin, 1920. U.S.
        title: The Riddle of the Frozen
        Flame. Doubleday, 1920 (Actually
        written by Hazel Phillips Hanshew.)
    The House of Discord. Hutchinson, 1922.
        U.S. title: The Riddle of the Spin-
        ning Wheel. Doubleday, 1922 (Actu-
        ally written by Hazel Phillips Han-
        shew.)
    The House of the Seven Keys. Hutchin-
        son, 1925 (Actually written by Hazel
        Phillips Hanshew.)
    The Riddle of the Amber Ship; see The
        Amber Junk
    The Riddle of the Frozen Flame; see The
        Frozen Flame
    The Riddle of the Mysterious Light.
        Doubleday, 1921 (Actually written by
        Hazel Phillips Hanshew.)
    The Riddle of the Spinning Wheel; see
        The House of Discord

HANSHEW, THOMAS W. 1857-1914. Ref: CC,
    EM, MP, TC. SC: Hamilton Cleek = HC
    (see also Hazel Phillips Hanshew, and
    Mary E. Hanshew entries).
    Beautiful But Dangerous; or, The Heir
        of Shadowdene. Street, 1891
    Cleek of Scotland Yard. Cassell, 1914
        Doubleday, 1914 (An episodic novel
        incorporating several HC ss.)
    Cleek, the Man of the Forty Faces.
        Cassell (London & NYC), 1913 (An
        episodic novel constituting a revised
        edition of The Man of the Forty
        Faces, q.v.) HC
    Cleek, the Master Detective; see The
        Man of the Forty Faces
    Cleek's Government Cases; see Cleek's
        Greatest Riddles
    Cleek's Greatest Riddles. Simpkin,
        1916. U.S. title: Cleek's Government
        Cases. Doubleday, 1917 (An episodic
        novel incorporating several HC ss.)
    Fate and the Man. Cassell, 1910
    The Great Ruby. Ward, 1905
    The Hoxton Mystery; see The World's
        Finger
    The Mallison Mystery. Ward, 1903
    The Man of the Forty Faces. Cassell,
        1910. U.S. title: Cleek, the Master
        Detective. Doubleday, 1918 HC ss
    The Riddle of the Night. Simpkin, 1916;
        Doubleday, 1915 (Actually written by
        Mary E. Hanshew and Hazel Phillips
        Hanshew based on notes by Thomas W.
        Hanshew.) HC
    The Riddle of the Purple Emperor, with
        Mary E. Hanshew. Simpkin, 1918;
        Doubleday, 1919 (Actually written by
        Mary E. Hanshew and Hazel Phillips
        Hanshew.) HC
    The Shadow of a Dead Man. Ward, 1906
    The World's Finger. Ward, 1901; Irwin,
        1901. Also published as: The Hoxton
        Mystery. Ogilvie, 1905

HANSOM, MARK
    The Beasts of Brahm. Wright, 1937
    The Ghost of Gaston Revere. Wright,
        1935
    Master of Souls. Wright, 1937
    The Shadow on the House. Wright, 1934;
        Godwin, 193?
    Sorcerer's Chessman. Wright, 1939
    The Wizard of Berner's Abbey. Wright,
        1935

HANSON, ERNEST S. Pseudonym: Daniel
    Dane, q.v.

HANSON, JAMES W. Born in S. Dak.; newspa-
    per reporter and editor in Fla.
    Brother Berserk. Vantage, 1969 [Mex.]

HANSON, V. J.
    Death and Little Girl Blue. Amalgama-
        ted, 1962   (Sexton Blake.)

HANSON, VIC J.
    The End of the Kill. Hale, 1980

HANSON, VIRGINIA (L.). 1905-1968. SC:
    Adam Drew and Katherine (Kay) Cor-
    nish, in all titles.
    Casual Slaughters. Doubleday, 1939
        [Wis.]
    Death Walks the Post. Doubleday, 1938
        [Midwest]
    Mystery for Mary. Doubleday, 1942
        [N.J.]

HARBAGE, ALFRED BENNETT. 1901-1976. Pseu-
    donym: Thomas Kyd, q.v.

HARBAUGH, THOMAS CHALMERS. 1849-1924.
    Pseudonym: Captain Howard Holmes,
    q.v.

HARBEN, WILL(IAM) N(ATHANIEL). 1858-1919.
    The Caruthers Affair. Neely (NYC & Lon-
        don), 1898 [NYC]
    From Clue to Climax. Street, 1902
    The North Walk Mystery. Street, 1899

HARBINSON, W(ILLIAM) A(LLEN). 1941-
    Ref: CA.
    Death of an Idol. Horwitz, 1969
    Genesis. Corgi, 1980; Dell, 1982
    -Instruments of Death. Corgi, 1973
    No Limit for Charlie. Panther, 1977
    The Oil Heist. Corgi, 1978
    The Running Man. Horwitz, 1967; Award,
        1970

HARBORD, GORDON. See: Jack Roffey.

HARCOURT, F(REDERICK) C. VERNON.
    1845-   .
    Bolts and Bars. Digby, 1905 ss
    The Devil's Derelicts. Digby, 1905 ss

HARCOURT, PALMA. Ref: CA.
    Agents of Influence. Collins, 1978;
        Walker, 1978 [H. Kong]
    At High Risk. Collins, 1977; Walker,
        1978 [Paris]
    Climate for Conspiracy. Collins, 1974
    Dance for Diplomats. Collins, 1976
    A Fair Exchange. Collins, 1975; McKay,
        1976
    A Sleep of Spies. Collins, 1979
    Tomorrow's Treason. Collins, 1980

HARDIE, D(AVID) W(ILLIAM) F(ERGUSON).
    1906-   . SC: Det.-Insp. Elwyn
    Hughes, in all titles. Set: Eng.
    The Case of the Praying Evangelist.
        Nicholson, 1950
    A Grave for Miss Carling. Nicholson,
        1952
    The Iron Egg. Nicholson, 1947
    The Riddle of the Cambrian Venus.
        Nicholson, 1949 [Wales]

HARDIN, PETER. Pseudonym of Louis Charles
    Vaczek, 1913-   . Ref: CA.
    The Frightened Dove. Scribner, 1951;
        Heinemann, 1952 [Montr.]
    The Hidden Grave. Harper, 1955; Muller,
        1956 [Ohio]

HARDIN, ROBERT. 1934-   . Ref: CA.
    Amateur Hour. Bobbs, 1977 [S.F.]

HARDING, ALBERT
    Death on Raven's Scar. Staples, 1953

HARDING, ANTHONY
    Arms for the Love of Allah. Hutchinson,
        1939

HARDING, D. E.
    How Briggs Died. Harrap, 1940

HARDING, ERIC
    Behold! the Executioner! Hutchinson,
        1939
    Pray for the Dawn. Low, 1946

HARDING, GEORGE. 1923-
    -Dragon's Gap. Hale, 1967
    -The Gun Merchants. Hale, 1969
    -North of Bushman's Rock. Hale, 1965
    -The Skytrap. Macmillan (London), 1972

HARDING, HARRY. 1885-   . Pseudonym:
    Haydon Dean, q.v.
    The Beckoning Finger. Methuen, 1926
    -The Hawk of Rede. Hodder, 1922

HARDING, JOHN WILLIAM. 1864-   .
    A Conjurer of Phantoms. Neely, 1898

HARDING, RICHARD
    Appointment in Tenerife. Hurst, 1966
        [Can. Is.]
    -Gay Deception. Hale, 1967

HARDING, RONALD S. L.
    The Black Bottle. Fiction House, 1935
    Castle of Fear. Fiction House, 1938
    The Demon of Hong Kong. Mowl, 1934
        [H. Kong]
    The Library of Death. Modern, 1938
    The Murder Maniac. Fiction House, 1935
    "One Dreadful Night." Modern, 1935
    Strange Fate. Fiction House, 1937

HARDING, WILLIAM HENRY. 1945-   . Ref:
    CA.
    Rainbow. Holt, 1979; Joseph, 1979
        [N.Y., 1925]

HARDINGE, GEORGE. Pseudonym: George Mil-
    ner, q.v.

HARDINGE, REX. 1904-   . Name original-
    ly: Charles Wrexe Hardinge. Born in
    India; came to Eng. as a youth; set
    many stories in India and Afr. Pseu-
    donym: "Capstan." All titles below
    listed without publisher were pub-
    lished by Amalgamated Press and
    feature Sexton Blake.
    Beyond the Skyline. Eldon, 1933
    The Black-Hill Murder Case. 1933
    The Blazing Launch Murder. 1934
    The Body on the Beach. 1937
    By Whose Hand? 1956
    The Case of the African Emigrant. 1948
    The Case of the African Hoodoo. 1953
    The Case of the African Trader. 1949
    The Case of the Black Magician. 1935
    The Case of the Chinese Courier. 1949
    The Case of the Crime Reporter. 1949
    The Case of the Frightened Girl. 1951
    The Case of the Green Caravan. 1951

The Case of the Kidnapped Specialist.
   1938
The Case of the Missing Musician. 1939
The Case of the Murdered Postman. 1938
The Case of the Secret Agent. 1949
The Case of the Stolen Mine. 1948
Consider Your Verdict; see The Mystery
   of the Devil Mask
The Crime in Carson's Shack. 1935
The Crooked Gambler.
Dangerous Money. 1938
The Ex-Serviceman's Secret. 1936
The Fatal Car. 1930
Found—Adventure. Jenkins, 1938
The Gargoyle of Polgelly. 1948
The Headmaster's Secret. 1951
The Ivory Tusk. 1933
The Legacy of Hate. 1949
The Lodging-House Mystery. 1954
The Man from Chun King. 1946
The Man from Holland. 1934
The Man from Mongolia. 1947
The Man from Space. 1952
The Man from the Jungle. 1940
The Man They Could Not Convict. 1937
The Man with Five Enemies. 1955
The Masked Slayer. 1932
The Midnight Mystery. 1929
The Mission of Menace. 1930
The Mission of Vengeance. 1931
The Motor Show Mystery. 1936
The Murder at Hermit's Cottage. 1936
Murder on the Boat Express. 1936
Murder on the Veld. Wright, 1954
The Mystery of the African Expedition.
   1937
The Mystery of the African Farm. 1939
The Mystery of the African Mine. 1936
The Mystery of the Body on the Cliff.
   1953
The Mystery of the Devil Mask. 1949.
   Reprinted in revised version as:
   Consider Your Verdict. 1959
The Mystery of the Forbidden Territory.
   1950
The Mystery of the Murdered Chef. 1934
The Mystery of the Outlawed Black. 1955
The Mystery of the Reunion Dinner. 1932
The Observer Corps Mystery. 1940
One of Seven. 1941
The Police Station Mystery. 1939
The Prisoner of the Manor. 1952
The Problem in Ciphers. Wright, 1952
The Radio Crook. 1931
The Riddle of the Crooked Gambler. 1952
The Riddle of the Highwayman's Stone.
   1948
The Riddle of the Invisible Menace.
   1954
The Riddle of the Sealed Room. 1948
Safari with Fear! 1959
The Secret of the African Settler. 1948
The Secret of the African Trader. 1932
The Secret of the Dental Surgeon. 1937
The Secret of the Desert. 1951
The Secret of the Fated Family. 1953
The Secret of the Jungle. 1947
The Secret of the Man Who Died. 1955
The Secret of the Sale Room. 1936
The Secret of the Sheba. Wright, 1954
The Secret of the Smuggler's Cove. 1935
The Secret of the Veld. 1947
"Three Rounds Rapid—". Skeffington,
   1936
The Tragedy of the Bromleigh's. 1949
The Tragedy of Windyridge. 1950
The Victim of the Devil's Bowl. 1954
The Voyage of Fear. 1954
With Criminal Instinct. 1950
The Yellow Terror. 1947

HARDT, MICHAEL. Joint pseudonym of Gwen
   Leys Davenport, 1910-   , and Gustav
   J. Breuer.
   A Stranger and Afraid. Bobbs, 1943
   [Austria]

HARDWICK, (JOHN) MICHAEL (DRINKROW),
   1924-   . Ref: CA, CC.
   Four More Sherlock Holmes Plays, with
   Mollie Hardwick, q.v. Murray, 1973
   (Plays featuring Sherlock Holmes and
   based on the stories by A. Conan
   Doyle, 1859-1930, q.v.)
   Four Sherlock Holmes Plays, with Mollie
   Hardwick, q.v. Murray, 1964 (Plays
   featuring Sherlock Holmes and based
   on stories by A. Conan Doyle, 1859-
   1930, q.v.)
   The Game's Afoot, with Mollie Hardwick,
   q.v. Murray, 1969 (Plays featuring the
   Sherlock Holmes stories by A. Conan
   Doyle, 1859-1930, q.v.)
   Prisoner of the Devil. Proteus, 1979;
   Proteus (NYC), 1980 (Sherlock
   Holmes) [Eng., 1895]
   The Private Life of Sherlock Holmes,
   with Mollie Hardwick, q.v. Mayflower
   1970; Bantam, 1971 (Novelization of
   the movie.) (Sherlock Holmes)
   -Regency Rake. Joseph, 1979
   -Regency Revenge. Joseph, 1980

-Regency Royal. Joseph, 1978; Coward,
   1978

HARDWICK, MOLLIE. Ref: CA. See also:
   (John) Michael (Drinkrow) Hardwick,
   1924-   .
   Juliet Bravo. Pan, 1980 (ss based on
   the TV series.)

HARDWICK, RICHARD (HOLMES, JR.).
   1923-   . Ref: CA.
   Hawk. Belmont, 1966 (Novelization of
   the TV series.) [NYC]
   The Plotters. Doubleday, 1965; Hale,
   1966 [South]
   The Season to Be Deadly. Doubleday,
   1966; Hale, 1967 [South]

HARDY, A(RTHUR) S(TEFFENS). Pseudonym of
   Arthur Joseph Steffens, 1873-   .
   All titles were published by Amalgam-
   ated Press and feature Sexton Blake.
   The Bookmaker's Crime. 1935
   The Case of the Mystery Champion. 1928
   The Crimson Mask. 1919
   The Crook of Newmarket. 1931
   The Mystery of the Championship Belt.
   1926
   The Secret of the Mine. 1919
   Sexton Blake's Vow. 1918
   The Team of Crooks. 1927
   The Touring Company Crime. 1935
   The Trainer's Secret. 1925
   Traitor and Spy. 1917
   Who Killed Trainer Lincoln? 1930

HARDY, ARTHUR SHERBURNE. 1847-1930. Ref:
   EM.
   Diane and Her Friends. Houghton, 1914
   ss [Fr.]
   No. 13, Rue du Bon Diable. Houghton,
   1917 [Fr.]

HARDY, IZA DUFFUS
   -A Broken Faith. Hurst, 1879
   -Hearts or Diamonds. White, 1885
   -His Silence. Digby, 1907
   -The Lesser Evil. Chatto, 1901
   MacGilleroy's Millions. Simpkin, 1900
   The Mystery of a Moonlight Tryst.
   Digby, 1908
   A New Othello. Jarrolds, 1980
   The Silent Watchers. Digby, 1910
   The Strange Disappearance of John
   Haversham. Digby, 1909
   -A Trap of Fate. Digby, 1906
   The Westhorpe Mystery. White, 1886

HARDY, J(OCELYN) L(EE). 1894-   .
   Everything Is Thunder. Lane, 1935;
   Doubleday, 1935
   I Escape. Allied News, 1938
   Never in Vain. Collins, 1936; Double-
   day, 1936
   Pawn in the Game. Collins, 1939
   Recoil. Collins, 1936; Doubleday, 1936
   The Stroke of Eight. Collins, 1938

HARDY, LINDSAY. Born in Australia; TV
   writer there and in Hollywood; later
   living in NYC. SC: Gregory Keen, in
   at least those marked GK.
   The Faceless Ones. Hale, 1956 (U.S.
   title?)
   The Nightshade Ring. Appleton, 1954;
   Hale, 1955 GK [Macao]
   Requiem for a Redhead. Appleton, 1953
   GK [Eng.]
   Show No Mercy. Popular Library, 1955

HARDY, ROBERT. Pseudonym. 1917-   .
   A Winter's Tale. Chatto, 1959

HARDY, ROBIN
   The Education of Don Juan. Wyndham,
   1979; Macmillan (London), 1980
   -The Wicker Man, with Anthony (Joshua)
   Shaffer, 1926-   , q.v. Crown,
   1978; Hamlyn, 1979

HARDY, RONALD (HAROLD). 1919-   . Ref:
   CA.
   The Face of Jalanath. Putnam, 1973

HARDY, WILLIAM M(ARION). 1922-   . Ref:
   CA.
   The Case of the Missing Co-Ed; see A
   Little Sin
   Lady Killer. Dodd, 1957; H. Hamilton,
   1957 [acad.]
   A Little Sin. Dodd, 1958; H. Hamilton,
   1959. Also published as: The Case of
   the Missing Co-Ed. Dell, 1960 [N.C.]
   A Time of Killing. Dodd, 1962; H. Ham-
   ilton, 1963

HARE, ARNOLD. 1921-   . A don at Salis-
   bury U. in England.
   The Man Who Never Laughed. Allen, 1963;
   Norton, 1963

HARE, CYRIL. Pseudonym of Alfred Alexan-
   der Gordon Clark, 1900-1958. Ref: CC,
   EM, MC, TC. SC: Insp. Mallett = M;
   Francis Pettigrew = FP. Set: Eng.
   Best Detective Stories of Cyril Hare.
   Faber, 1959; Walker, 1961 ss
   The Christmas Murder; see An English
   Murder
   Death Is No Sportsman. Faber, 1938 M
   Death Walks the Woods; see That Yew
   Tree's Shade
   An English Murder. Faber, 1951; Little,
   1951. Also published as: The Christ-
   mas Murder. Mercury, 1951
   He Should Have Died Hereafter. Faber,
   1958. U.S. title: Untimely Death.
   Macmillan, 1958 M,FP
   Suicide Excepted. Faber, 1939; Mac-
   millan, 1954 M
   Tenant for Death. Faber, 1937; Dodd,
   1937 M
   That Yew Tree's Shade. Faber, 1954.
   U.S. title: Death Walks the Woods.
   Little, 1954 FP
   Tragedy at Law. Faber, 1942; Harcourt,
   1943 M,FP
   Untimely Death; see He Should Have Died
   Hereafter
   When the Wind Blows. Faber, 1949. U.S.
   title: The Wind Blows Death. Little,
   1950 FP
   The Wind Blows Death; see When the Wind
   Blows
   With a Bare Bodkin. Faber, 1946 M,FP

HARE, ROBERT. Pseudonym of Robert Hare
   Hutchinson, 1887-   , q.v. Set: Eng.
   The Crime in the Crystal; see Spectral
   Evidence
   The Doctor's First Murder. Hurst, 1933;
   Longmans, 1933
   The Hand of the Chimpanzee. Hurst,
   1934; Longmans, 1934
   Spectral Evidence. Hurst, 1932. U.S.
   title: The Crime in the Crystal.
   Longmans, 1933

HARE, WALTER BEN. 1870-1950. All titles
   are plays; number of acts given in
   parenthesis.
   And Billy Disappeared. Baker, 1919 (4)
   And Home Came Ted. Denison, 1917 (3)
   Assisted by Sadie. Denison, 1919 (4)
   Aunt What's-Her-Name! Baker, 1922 (3)
   The Dutch Detective. Baker, 1914 (3)
   The Gold Bug. Denison, 1920 (Based
   in part on the ss by Edgar A. Poe,
   1809-1849, q.v.)
   Has Anyone Seen Jean? Baker, 1927 (3)

HARGRAVE, LEONIE. Pseudonym of Thomas
   M(ichael) Disch, 1940-   , q.v.
   Joint pseudonym with John (Thomas)
   Sladek, 1937-   , q.v.: Thom Demi-
   john, q.v.
   -Clara Reeve. Knopf, 1975; Hutchinson,
   1975 [Eng., 1800s]

HARGRAVE, ROY. See: Kenneth Phillips
   Britton.

HARINGTON, DONALD. 1935-   . Ref: CA.
   Some Other Place, the Right Place.
   Little, 1972; Cape, 1973

HARKER, CHARLES R.
   A Singular Sinner. Abbey, 1900

HARKINS, STERLING
   The Butcherknife Killings. Brandon,
   1974

HARKNETT, TERRY. 1936-   . Pseudonyms:
   Joseph Hedges, William Pine, Thomas
   H. Stone, William Terry, qq.v. Ref:
   CA. SC: Chief Supt. John Crown = JC;
   Steve Wayne, in at least those marked
   SW.
   The Benevolent Blackmailer. Hale, 1962
   SW
   Crown: Bamboo Shoot-Out. Futura, 1975
   JC [China]
   Crown: Macao Mayhem. Futura, 1974 JC
   [Macao]
   Crown: The Sweet and Sour Kill. Futura,
   1974; Pinnacle, 1974 JC
   Dead Little Rich Girl. Hale, 1963 SW
   Death of an Aunt. Hammond, 1967 SW
   The Evil Money. Hale, 1964 SW
   Invitation to a Funeral. Hale, 1963 SW
   The Man Who Did Not Die. Hale, 1964 SW
   -Promotion Tour. New English Library pb,
   1972
   The Scratch on the Surface. Hale, 1962
   SW
   The Softcover Kill. Hale, 1971 SW
   The Two-Way Frame. Hammond, 1967 SW
   The Upmarket Affair. Hale, 1973

HARLAND, HENRY. 1861-1905. Pseudonym:
   Sidney Luska, q.v.

HARLEY, MRS. M.
    The Castle of Mowbray. Stalker, 1788
    Priory of St. Bernard; see Saint Bernard's Priory
    Saint Bernard's Priory. [Author], 1786. Also published as: Priory of St. Bernard. Lane, 1789

HARLING, ROBERT. 1910- . Ref: CC, TC.
    The Dark Saviour. Chatto, 1952; Harper, 1953
    The Endless Colonnade. Chatto, 1958; Putnam, 1959 [It.]
    The Enormous Shadow. Chatto, 1955; Harper, 1956
    The Hollow Sunday. Chatto, 1967
    The Paper Palace. Chatto, 1951; Harper, 1951

HARMAN, NEAL. S: Protection Ltd., in at least those marked P.
    The Case of the Wounded Mastiff. Barker, 1947 P
    -Crown Colony. Barker, 1939
    Death and the Archdeacon. Barker, 1949 P
    Peace and Peter Lamont. Barker, 1950
    -Rebellion. Barker, 1937
    Yours Truly, Angus MacIvor. Barker, 1952

HARMON, MARGARET. 1906- .
    The Mistress of Corey's Landing. Zebra, 1980

HARNAN, TERRY. Pseudonym: Eric Traviss Hull, q.v. Ref: CA.
    Signal for Danger. Doubleday, 1946

HARNETT, CHARLES B. See: Larry T. Maxim.

HARPER, DAVID. Pseudonym of Edwin (Raymond) Corley, 1931-1981. Other pseudonym: William Judson, q.v. Joint pseudonym with Jack Murphy: Patrick Buchanan, q.v.
    The Hanged Men. Dodd, 1976; H. Hamilton, 1977 [N.Y.]
    Hijacked. Dodd, 1970; Souvenir, 1971. Also published as: Skyjacked. Bantam, 1971; Corgi, 1972 [air.]
    The Patchwork Man. Dodd, 1975; Prior, 1975
    Skyjacked; see Hijacked

HARPER, E. M.
    The Assassin. Berkley, 1960

HARPER, HARRY
    File No. 115; or, A Man of Steel. Ogilvie, 1886

HARPER, HARRY
    The Sign of the Knotted String. Mellifont, 1944

HARPER, HENRY G.
    The Silent Stranger. Street, ca.1900

HARPER, HENRY HOWARD. 1871- .
    -The Devil's Nest. (Boston), 1923

HARPER, LYNETTE
    The House of the Unicorn. Hale, 1976
    -Lord of the Falcons. Hale, 1978
    -Moonlight Can Betray. Hale, 1976
    -Strange Heritage. Hale, 1971

HARPER, OLIVE. Pseudonym of Helen Burrell Gibson D'Apery, 1842-1915.
    The Burglar and the Lady. Ogilvie, 1912
    -Caught in Mid-Ocean. Ogilvie, 1911 [ship]
    The Chinatown Trunk Mystery. Ogilvie, 1909
    The Convict's Sweetheart. Ogilvie, 1909
    The Creole Slave's Revenge. Ogilvie, 1908
    A Desperate Chance. Ogilvie, 1903
    -The Gambler of the West. Ogilvie, 1906
    Jack Sheppard, the Bandit King. Ogilvie, 1908
    -King of Bigamists. Ogilvie, 1909
    Millionaire and the Policeman's Wife. Ogilvie, 1908
    A Millionaire's Revenge. Ogilvie, 1906
    On Trial for His Life. Ogilvie, 1908
    The Opium Smugglers of Frisco; or, The Crimes of a Beautiful Opium Fiend. Ogilvie, 1908 [S.F.]
    Queen of the Secret Seven. Ogilvie, 1909
    -Shadow Behind the Throne. Ogilvie, 1908
    -A Slave of the Mill. Ogilvie, 1905
    Wanted by the Police. Ogilvie, 1909

HARPER, RICHARD
    Death to the Dancing Masters. GM, 1980 [Ariz.]

HARPER, RICHARD J.
    The Dragonhead Deal. Warner, 1975 [ship]

HARPER, STEPHEN (DENNIS). 1924- . Ref: CA.
    A Necessary End. Collins, 1975. U.S. title: Mirror Image. Doubleday, 1976 [Sp.]

HARRADEN, BEATRICE. 1864-1935.
    Search Will Find It Out. Mills, 1928

HARRAGAN, STEVE. SC: Steve Harragan, in all titles.
    The Bigamy Kiss. Universal, 1952
    Carney's Burlesque. Universal, 1953
    Cuban Heel. Universal, 1953
    Dope Doll. Universal, 1952
    Kiss of the Damned. Universal, 1952
    The Queer Sisters. Universal, 1953
    The Shayne Dame. Universal, 1953
    Side-Show Girl. Universal, 1952
    Sin is a Redhead. Universal, 1952
    Smuggled Sin. Universal, 1952
    Three Bad Girls. Universal, 1953

HARRELL, J.
    Death Comes to the Hermit. Pan, 1946 ss

HARRINGTON, DENIS J.
    The Silent Pursuit. Major, 1976

HARRINGTON, JOSEPH (JAMES). 1903- . Ref: CC, EM, TC. SC: Lt. Kerrigan, in all titles.
    Blind Spot. Lippincott, 1966; Hale, 1967 [NYC]
    The Last Doorbell. Lippincott, 1969; Hale, 1970 [NYC]
    The Last Known Address. Lippincott, 1965; Hale, 1966 [NYC]

HARRINGTON, JOYCE. Ref: TC.
    No One Knows My Name. St. Martin's, 1980; Macmillan (London), 1981 [Mich.]

HARRINGTON, R(OBERT) E(DWARD)
    Death of a Patriot. Putnam, 1979; Secker, 1979 [Wash. D.C.]
    Quintain. Putnam, 1977; Secker, 1977 [L.A.]
    The Seven of Swords. Putnam, 1976; Secker, 1976 [Calif.]

HARRINGTON, WILLIAM. 1931- . Ref: CA.
    The Gospel of Death; see The Power
    The Jupiter Crisis. McKay, 1971
    Mister Target. Delacorte, 1973; Joseph, 1974
    Partners. Seaview, 1980
    -The Power. Bobbs, 1964. British title: The Gospel of Death. Joseph, 1966
    Scorpio 5. Coward, 1975 [Fla.]
    The Search for Elizabeth Brandt. McKay, 1969 [Ger., 1938-1945]
    Trial. McKay, 1970; Barrie, 1970 [Cleve.]
    Which the Justice, Which the Thief. Bobbs, 1963; Joseph, 1965 [Ohio]
    -Yoshar the Soldier. Bobbs, 1966; Eyre, 1967

HARRIS, A. L.
    The Fatal Request. Street (Magnet #253)

HARRIS, ALFRED. 1928- . Joint pseudonym with Arthur Moore, q.v.: Gwen Addison, q.v. Ref: CA.
    Baroni. Putnam, 1975 [Calif.]
    The Joseph File. Putnam, 1974

HARRIS, ANDREA. House name. At least two were written by Vivian Connolly, 1925- , q.v. The title marked * is by Irma (Ruth Roden) Walker, 1921- , q.v. Other Walker pseudonym: Ira Walker, q.v.
    Byzantine Encounter. Playboy, 1979
    An Irish Affair (by VC). Playboy, 1978 [Ire.]
    A Scream Away. Playboy, 1979
    Windfall. Playboy, 1979 *

HARRIS, CHARLES. 1913- .
    Death of a Barrow Boy. Phoenix (London), 1952
    Three Ha-Pence to the Angel. Phoenix (London), 1950

HARRIS, CHARLIE AVERY
    Black and Deadly. Holloway, 1977
    Con Man. Holloway, 1978 [NYC]
    Mocking Gangster. Holloway, 1976

HARRIS, COLVER. Pseudonym of Anne Colver, 1908- . Ref: CA. SC: Timothy Fowler, in all titles.
    Going to St. Ives. Macrae Smith, 1936 [Balt.]
    Hide and Go Seek. Minton Balch, 1933 [NYC]
    Murder by Proxy; see Murder in Amber
    Murder in Amber. Hillman-Curl, 1938. Also published as (?): Murder by Proxy. Mystery Novel of the Month, 194? [ship]

HARRIS, EDWIN
    John Jasper's Gatehouse. Mackays, 1931 (A sequel to The Mystery of Edwin Drood by Charles Dickens, 1812-1970, q.v.)

HARRIS, ELMER BANEY
    Johnny Belinda. Dramatists, 1961 (3-act play.)

HARRIS, EVELYN
    Against the Flame. Hale, 1977
    Down Among the Dead Men. Hale, 1979
    Medium for Murder. Hale, 1980
    Night Scream. Hale, 1978

HARRIS, H. B.
    The Seven Elms Mystery. Stockwell, 1937

HARRIS, HERBERT. 1911- . Ref: CA, EM, TC.
    The Angry Battalion. Star, 1976 (Novelization of the "Hawaii Five-0" TV series.) [Haw.]
    Who Kill to Live. Jenkins, 1962

HARRIS, HYDE. See: Timothy (Hyde) Harris, 1946- .

HARRIS, JOEL CHANDLER. 1848-1908. Ref: CA.
    On the Wings of Occasions. Doubleday, 1900; Murray, 1900. Also published as: The Kidnapping of Lincoln and Other War Detective Stories. Doubleday, 1909 ss

HARRIS, JOHN. 1916- . Pseudonym: Mark Hebden, q.v. Ref: CA.
    Adventure's End; see Road to the Coast
    The Claws of Mercy. Hurst, 1955
    Close to the Wind; see Getaway
    The Courtney Entry. Hutchinson, 1971; Doubleday, 1970
    Covenant with Death. Hutchinson, 1961; Sloane, 1961 [WWI]
    The Cross of Lazzaro. Hutchinson, 1965; Morrow, 1965
    Getaway. Hurst, 1956. U.S. title: Close to the Wind. Sloane. 1956
    Hallelujah Corner. Hurst, 1952
    The Jade Wind; see The Mercenaries
    A Kind of Courage. Hutchinson, 1972
    Light Cavalry Action. Hutchinson, 1967; Morrow, 1967
    The Lonely Voyage. Hurst, 1951
    The Mercenaries. Hutchinson, 1969. U.S. title: The Jade Wind. Doubleday, 1969
    The Mustering of the Hawks. Hutchinson, 1972
    The Old Trade of Killing. Hutchinson, 1966; Morrow, 1966 [Afr.]
    The Professionals. Hutchinson, 1973
    Ride Out the Storm. Hutchinson, 1975
    Right of Reply. Hutchinson, 1968; Coward, 1968
    Road to the Coast. Hutchinson, 1959. U.S. title: Adventure's End. Sloane, 1959
    The Sea Shall Not Have Them. Hurst, 1953. U.S. title: The Undaunted. Sloane, 1953
    The Sleeping Mountain. Hutchinson, 1958; Sloane, 1958
    Smiling Willie and the Tiger. Hutchinson, 1974
    The Spring of Malice. Hutchinson, 1962; Sloane, 1962 [Fr.]
    Sunset at Sheba. Hutchinson, 1960; Sloane, 1960 [S. Afr., 1914]
    The Undaunted; see The Sea Shall Not Have Them
    The Unforgiving Wind. Hutchinson, 1963; Sloane, 1964 [Arctic]
    Vardy. Hutchinson, 1964; Sloane, 1965
    The Victors. Hutchinson, 1975

HARRIS, JOHN NORMAN. 1915- .
    The Weird World of Wes Beattie. Harper, 1963; Faber, 1964 [Can.]

HARRIS, JOHN WYNDHAM PARKES LUCAS BEYNON. 1903-1969. Pseudonym: John Beynon, q.v.

HARRIS, LARRY M(ARK). 1933- . Pseudonym: Laurence M. Janifer, q.v. Joint pseudonym with Randall (Phillips) Garrett, 1927- , q.v.: Mark Phillips, q.v. Ref: CA.
    The Pickled Poodles. Random, 1960; Boardman, 1961 (Novel based on the series character John J. Malone created by Craig Rice, 1908-1957, q.v.) [Chi.]
    The Protector. Random, 1961; Boardman, 1962 [NYC]

HARRIS, LEONARD. 1929-   . Ref: CA.
    Don't Be No Hero. Crown, 1978; Hamlyn,
        1979 [Mass.]
    The Masada Plan. Crown, 1976; Joseph,
        1977

HARRIS, MacDONALD. Pseudonym of Donald
    William Heiney, 1921-   . Ref: CA.
    The Treasure of Sainte-Foy. Atheneum,
        1980; Gollancz, 1980 [Fr.]

HARRIS, MARILYN [MARILYN HARRIS SPRINGER]. 1931-   .
    Bledding Sorrow. Putnam, 1976 [Eng.]
    The Conjurers. Random, 1974; Panther,
        1977

HARRIS, MAX F.
    A Country Killing. Leisure, 1980

HARRIS, MURIEL
    The Scornful Man. Cape, 1932. U.S.
        title: The Clinic of Dr. Aicadre.
        Harper, 1932

HARRIS, DETECTIVE NICK [NICHOLAS BOILVIN
    HARRIS]
    In the Shadows. Times Mirror, 1923 ss
        [L.A.]

HARRIS, (WILLIAM) PETER. 1923-   .
    Cry Hold! Long, 1970
    The Final Set. Long, 1965
    Letters of Discredit. Long, 1964
        [S. Afr.]
    What Became of Alex Bretherton? Long,
        1967

HARRIS, RANDOLPH
    The Black Connection. Holloway, 1974
    Trickshot. Holloway, 1974

HARRIS, REX [REGINALD DUCKETT HARRIS].
    1904-   .
    A Hand in Diamonds. Constable, 1961

HARRIS, RICHARD. 1926-   . For many
    years a reporter for "The New Yorker"; author of numerous nonfiction
    books.
    Enemies. Marek, 1979; Hutchinson, 1979

HARRIS, ROGER
    The L.S.D. Dossier. Compact, 1966
        (Nick Allard) [Cent. Am.]

HARRIS, ROSEMARY (JEANNE). 1923-   .
    Ref: CA, TC.
    All My Enemies. Faber, 1967; Simon,
        1973
    The Double Snare. Faber, 1974; Simon,
        1975 [It.]
    The Nice Girl's Story. Faber, 1968.
        U.S. title: Nor Evil Dreams. Simon,
        1973
    Nor Evil Dreams; see The Nice Girl's
        Story
    Three Candles for the Dark. Faber, 1976
        [Vt.]
    A Wicked Pack of Cards. Faber, 1969;
        Walker, 1970

HARRIS, THOMAS. 1940-   . Born in Miss.;
    press reporter and editor.
    Black Sunday. Putnam, 1975; Hodder,
        1975 [New Or.]

HARRIS, TIMOTHY (HYDE). 1946-   . Pseudonym: Hyde Harris. Ref: CA. SC:
    Thomas Kyd = TK.
    Good Night and Goodbye. Delacorte,
        1979; Pan, 1981 TK [L.A.]
    Heat Wave. Dell, 1979 (Novelization of
        the movie.) [L.A.]
    Kyd for Hire. Dell, 1978; Gollancz,
        1977, as by Hyde Harris. Reprinted in
        Britain under the U.S. byline: Pan,
        1981 TK
    Steelyard Blues. Bantam, 1972 (Novelization of the movie.)

HARRIS, VALERIE. 1930-   . Pseudonym:
    Sarah Farrant, q.v.

HARRIS, VIVIAN BEYNON
    -Confusion at Campden Trig. Museum, 1948
    -One Thing Constant. Museum, 1949
    -Song for a Siren. Museum, 1951

HARRIS, WALTER. 1925-   .
    To Catch a Rat. Barker, 1977; Berkley,
        1978 (Novelization of "The New Avengers" TV series.)

HARRIS-BURLAND, J(OHN) B(URLAND).
    1870-   . Set: Eng.
    Baldragon. Chapman, 1914
    The Black Motor-Car. Richards, 1906;
        Dillingham, 1905, as by Harris Burland
    The Broken Law. Richards, 1906; Cupples, 1908
    The Brown Book. Long, 1923
    The Curse of Cloud. Chapman, 1914
    -Dacobra; or, The White Priests of
        Ahriman. Everett, 1903
    The Disc. Greening, 1909 [Wales]
    -The Financier. Greening, 1906; Dillingham, 1906, as by Harris Burland
    -The Gold Worshippers. Greening, 1907;
        Dillingham, 1906
    The Grey Cat. Chapman, 1913
    The Hidden Hour. Long, 1925
    The House of the Soul. Chapman, 1909
    -Life's Golden Web. Newnes, 1912
    Lord of Irongray. Greening, 1911
    Love the Criminal. Greening, 1907;
        Cupples, 1908
    The Poison League. Bale, 1921
    -The Red Moon. Long, 1923
    -The Secret of Enoch Seal. Chapman, 1910
    The Shadow of Malreward. Chapman, 1911;
        Knopf, 1919
    -Sunk Island. Newnes, 1911
    The Torhaven Mystery. Chapman, 1910
    The White Rook. Chapman, 1917; Knopf,
        1918
    Workers in Darkness. Greening, 1908

HARRISON, BARBARA. 1941-   . Ref: CA.
    A Cold Night's Death. Award, 1973
        (Novelization of the TV movie.)

HARRISON, BRUCE. Pseudonym of Edgar Pangborn, 1909-1976, q.v.
    A-100. Dutton, 1930 [NYC]

HARRISON, MRS. BURTON [CONSTANCE CARY
    HARRISON]. 1843-1920.
    The Carcellini Emerald, with other
        tales. Stone, 1899; Richards, 1899
        ss, some criminous

HARRISON, CHIP. Pseudonym of Lawrence
    Block, 1938-   , q.v. Other pseudonym: Paul Kavanagh, q.v. SC: Leo
    Haig, in both titles.
    Make Out with Murder. GM, 1974 [NYC]
    The Topless Tulip Caper. GM, 1975 [NYC]

HARRISON, E(RNEST) J(OHN). 1873-   .
    -Rasprava. Bles, 1924
    The Red Camarilla. Allen, 1923

HARRISON, EDWIN. Pseudonym of Eric Alan
    Ballard. All titles below were published by Amalgamated Press and feature Sexton Blake.
    Diamonds Can Be Trouble. 1958
    The Fatal Hour. 1958 [Sp.]
    Killer's Playground. 1959
    Witness to Murder. 1959

HARRISON, F(ANNIE) HEWITT. 1878-   .
    The White Cowl. Burney, 1937

HARRISON, HARRY (MAX). 1925-   . Ref:
    CA. SC: Slippery Jim Di Griz = JD;
    Tony Hawkin = TH.
    Montezuma's Revenge. Doubleday, 1972
        TH [Mex.]
    The QEII Is Missing. Futura, 1980;
        Pinnacle, 1982 [ship]
    Queen Victoria's Revenge. Doubleday,
        1974; Severn House, 1977 TH
    The Stainless Steel Rat. Pyramid, 1961;
        Sphere, 1973 JD
    The Stainless Steel Rat Saves the
        World. Putnam, 1972; Faber, 1973 JD
    The Stainless Steel Rat Wants You.
        Bantam, 1979; Joseph, 1978 JD
    The Stainless Steel Rat's Revenge.
        Walker, 1970; Faber, 1971 JD

HARRISON, J. E.
    The Kara Yerta Tragedy. Scott, 1889

HARRISON, JIM [JAMES THOMAS HARRISON].
    1937-   . Ref: CA.
    A Good Day to Die. Simon, 1973; Allen,
        1975

HARRISON, JOEL
    -Bloody Wednesday. Major, 1978

HARRISON, LEWIS. Pseudonym of Lewis H.
    Watson.
    -Not to the Swift. Welch, 1891
    -A Strange Infatuation. Rand, 1890

HARRISON, MICHAEL. 1907-   . Pseudonym:
    Quentin Downes, q.v. Ref: EM, TC.
    The Darkened Room. Home & Van Thal,
        1952
    The Exploits of the Chevalier Dupin.
        Mycroft, 1968. British title: Murder
        in the Rue Royale. Stacey, 1972 (The
        U.S. edition contains 7, the British
        edition 13, ss based on the character
        C. Auguste Dupin, created by Edgar A.
        Poe, 1809-1849, q.v.) [Paris, 1800s]
    I, Sherlock Holmes. Dutton, 1977
        (Sherlock Holmes.) [Eng., 1881-1891]
    Murder in the Rue Royale; see The Exploits of the Chevalier Dupin

HARRISON, RICHARD (MOTTE). 1901-   .
    Pseudonym: Peter Motte, q.v. See
    also: Reginald (Wilfrid) Campbell,
    1894-1950. Ref: CC. SC: Chief Insp.
    William Bastion, in at least those
    marked WB. Set: Eng.
    Aftermath of Murder. Jarrolds, 1942
    Black Widow. Jarrolds, 1946 WB
    Bootlaces for Bastion. Jarrolds, 1947
        WB
    Brickbats for Bastion. Jarrolds, 1948
        WB
    The Circle of Von Boden. Jarrolds, 1944
    The Dog It Was. Jarrolds, 1940
    Foul Deeds Will Rise. Long, 1958
    Murder-on-Sea. Jarrolds, 1949 WB
    Our Doom Is Gone. Jarrolds, 1951
    Rope over Jezebel. Jarrolds, 1950 WB
    The Shuttle of Hate. Jarrolds, 1942
    Suburban Sarabanda. Jarrolds, 1952
    The Utmost Ebb. Jarrolds, 1944

HARRISON, W. G. A.   Pseudonym: A. G. Wilson, q.v.

HARRISON, WHIT. Pseudonym of Harry (Benjamin) Whittington, 1915-   , q.v.
    Body and Passion. Original Novels, 1952
    Swamp Kill. Phantom, 1952
    Violent Night. Phantom, 1952

HARRISON, WILLIAM (J.). 1933-   . Born in
    Dallas; has M.A. from Vanderbilt and
    in 1969 was in English department at
    U. of Arkansas.
    Hell's Full. Manor, 1977
    In a Wild Sanctuary. Morrow, 1969; Gollancz, 1970 [Chi., acad.]

HART, CAROLYN G(IMPEL). 1936-   . Ref:
    CA.
    Flee from the Past. Bantam (NYC & London), 1975 [Pa.]
    A Settling of Accounts. Doubleday,
        1976; Hale, 1978 [Eng.]

HART, FRANCES (NEWBOLD) NOYES. 1890-1943.
    Ref: all except CA.
    The Bellamy Trial. Doubleday, 1927;
        Heinemann, 1927. Play version, with
        Frank E. Carstarphen: French (NYC &
        London), 1932
    Contact and other stories. Doubleday,
        1923 ss, some mildly criminous
    The Crooked Lane. Doubleday, 1934;
        Heinemann, 1934 [Wash. D.C.]
    Hide in the Dark. Doubleday, 1929;
        Heinemann, 1929 [Md.]

HART, FRANK
    When Passions Rule. Digby, 1897

HART, GEORGE
    Harvest of Death. Mitre, 1972
    The Punch and Judy Murders. Golden
        Eagle, 1977

HART, I(NNES) R(UTH) G(RAY). 1889-   .
    Adjustments. Benn, 1931
    Coloured Glass. Rich, 1933
    The Dead Hand. Benn, 1929
    The Double Image. Benn, 1928
    Facets. Benn, 1930
    Forests of the Night. Benn, 1930
    Frontier of Fear. Benn, 1928. U.S.
        title (?): Torture Island. Simon,
        1928
    Like Water. Benn, 1931
    Torture Island; see Frontier of Fear

HART, JANET
    File for Death. Boardman, 1965 [U.S.,
        acad.]
    Who's Been Sleeping in My Grave? Boardman, 1966 [Ky.]

HART, JON
    Death Raid. Chelsea, 1980
    Guerilla Attack. Chelsea, 1980
    High Slaughter. Chelsea, 1980
    Triangle of Death. Chelsea, 1980

HART, L. H. Set: Eng.
    Court of Last Resort. Macdonald, 1943
    Murder at Cost Price. Swan, 1947
    Venus Died at Dawn. Macdonald, 1947
    You'll End Up Dead. Macdonald, 1945

HART, NORMAN PHILLIP
    An Inspector Answers. French (NYC),
        1975 (1-act play.)

HART, STAN
    The Martha's Vineyard Affair. Dell,
        1980 [Mass.]

HART, TED. S: Titles adapted from the
    stories by Brian (Horace) Clemens,
    1931-   , q.v., for the TV series
    = T.
    Hunter's Walk. Severn, 1976 (Novelization of the TV series.)

More Stories from Thriller. Fontana, 1975   ss   T
Thriller. Fontana, 1974   ss   T

HART, TOM
They Call It Murder. Quartet (London & NYC), 1977

HART-DAVIS, DUFF. 1936-   . Ref: CA. SC: Sam Sholto, in at least those marked SS.
The Gold of St. Matthew. Constable, 1970. U.S. title: The Gold-Trackers. Doubleday, 1970   SS
The Gold-Trackers; see The Gold of St. Matthew
The Heights of Rimring. Cape, 1980; Atheneum, 1981   [Nepal]
The Megacull. Constable, 1968
Spider in the Morning. Constable, 1972; Doubleday, 1972   SS

HARTE, MRS. (EDITH) BAGOT
Wrongly Condemned. Jarrolds, 1896

HARTENFELS, JEROME. 1933-   . Born in Ger., educated in Eng., returned to live in Munich.
Doctor Death. Hill, 1970; Calder, 1971   [Eng.]

HARTER, WALTER L.
The Nice Young Man. Holt, 1962. British title: Deadly Reunion. Boardman, 1965

HARTLEY, JOHN. 1839-1915.
A Rolling Stone. Nicholson, 1878

HARTLEY, NORMAN. Reporter and foreign correspondent.
Quicksilver. Collins, 1979; Atheneum, 1979
The Viking Process. Collins, 1976; Simon, 1976

HARTLEY, OLGA
The Malaret Mystery. Methuen, 1925; Small, 1926
-The Witch of Chelsea. Methuen, 1930

HARTMAN, JAN. Joint pseudonym with Lorie Hartman: Susannah Lawrence, q.v.

HARTMAN, LEE FOSTER. 1879-1941.
The White Sapphire. Harper, 1914

HARTMAN, LORIE. Joint pseudonym with Jan Hartman: Susannah Lawrence, q.v.

HARTMANN, HELMUT HENRY. 1931-   . Pseudonym: H(enry) Seymour, q.v.

HARTMANN, MICHAEL. 1944-   . Ref: CA. SC: Ben Dryden, in at least those marked BD.
Days of Thunder. Heinemann, 1980; St. Martin's, 1980   BD   [Afr.]
Game for Vultures. Heinemann, 1975   [Rhod.]
The Hunted; see Shadow of the Leopard
Leap for the Sun. Heinemann, 1976; St. Martin's, 1977   [Afr.]
Shadow of the Leopard. Heinemann, 1978. U.S. title: The Hunted. St. Martin's, 1979   BD   [S. Afr.]

HARTSHORNE. Pseudonym of Richard H. Blum.
Codename, Starlight. Hale, 1978
The Mexican Assassin. Hale, 1977; Scribner, 1978   (The U.S. edition differs from the British.)   [Mex.]

HARVESTER, SIMON. Pseudonym of Henry (St. John Clair) Gibbs, 1909-1975, q.v. SC: Roger Fleming, in at least those marked RF; Malcolm Kenton, in at least those marked MK; Heron Murmur, in at least those marked HM; Dorian Silk, in at least those marked DS.
Arrival in Suspicion. Jarrolds, 1953
Assassins Road. Jarrolds, 1965; Walker, 1965   DS   [Mid. East]
The Bamboo Screen. Jarrolds, 1955; Walker, 1968   MK   [Far East]
Battle Road. Jarrolds, 1967; Walker, 1967   DS   [Thai., Viet Nam]
A Breastplate for Aaron. Rich, 1949   RF   [Egypt]
Cat's Cradle. Jarrolds, 1952
The Chinese Hammer. Jarrolds, 1960; Walker, 1961   HM   [Tib.]
The Copper Butterfly. Jarrolds, 1957; Walker, 1962   MK   [Jap.]
A Corner of the Playground. Jarrolds, 1973
Delay in Danger. Jarrolds, 1954
Dragon Road. Jarrolds, 1956; Walker, 1969   MK   [Thai., Burma]
Epitaph for Lemmings. Rich, 1943; Macmillan, 1944   RF
Flight in Darkness. Jarrolds, 1964; Walker, 1965
The Flying Horse; see Troika
Forgotten Road. Hutchinson, 1974; Walker, 1974   DS
The Golden Fear. Jarrolds, 1957   MK   [Indon.]
Good Men and True. Rich, 1949
An Hour Before Zero. Jarrolds, 1959
A Lantern for Diogenes. Rich, 1946
Let Them Pray. Rich, 1942   RF
Lucifer at Sunset. Jarrolds, 1953
Maybe a Trumpet. Rich, 1945   RF
Moonstone Jungle. Jarrolds, 1961   [Cey.]
Moscow Road. Jarrolds, 1970; Walker, 1971   DS   [Moscow]
Nameless Road. Jarrolds, 1969; Walker, 1970   DS   [Mong.]
Obols for Charon. Jarrolds, 1951   RF
The Paradise Men. Jarrolds, 1956   MK   [New Guinea]
Red Road. Jarrolds, 1963; Walker, 1964   DS   [Russ.]
Sahara Road. Jarrolds, 1972; Walker, 1972   DS   [Afr.]
The Sequins Lost Their Lustre. Rich, 1948
Shadows in a Hidden Land. Jarrolds, 1966; Walker, 1966   [China]
Sheep May Safely Graze. Rich, 1950   RF
Siberian Road. Hutchinson, 1976; Walker, 1976   DS   [Russ.]
Silk Road. Jarrolds, 1962; Walker, 1963   DS   [Afghan.]
Spiders' Web. Jarrolds, 1953
Tiger in the North. Jarrolds, 1955; Walker, 1963   [Far East]
Traitors' Gate. Jarrolds, 1952
Treacherous Road. Jarrolds, 1966; Walker, 1967   DS   [Yem.]
Troika. Jarrolds, 1962. U.S. title: The Flying Red Horse. Walker, 1964   HM   [Kor.]
Unsung Road. Jarrolds, 1960; Walker, 1961   DS   [Iran]
The Vessel May Carry Explosives. Jarrolds, 1951   RF
Whatsoever Things Are True. Rich, 1947
Witch Hunt. Jarrolds, 1951
The Yesterday Walkers. Jarrolds, 1958   [Mal.]
Zion Road. Jarrolds, 1968; Walker, 1968   DS   [Isr.]

HARVEY, ANNIE JANE TENNANT.   -1898. Pseudonym: Andree Hope, q.v.

HARVEY, JACK. See: Milton M(ichael) Raison, 1903-1982.

HARVEY, JOHN. 1938-   . SC: Scott Mitchell, in at least those marked SM.
Amphetamines and Pearls. Sphere, 1976   SM
Frame. Magnum, 1979
The Geranium Kiss. Sphere, 1976   SM
Junkyard Angel. Sphere, 1977   SM
Neon Madman. Sphere, 1977

HARVEY, JOHN HENRY. Pseudonyms: John H. Barrington, Operator 1384, qq.v.

HARVEY, JOHN WILFRED. 1889-   . Pseudonym: John Farndale, q.v.

HARVEY, MARION. 1900-   . SC: Graydon McKelvie, in at least those marked GM.
Alias the Eagle; see The Clue of the Clock
The Arden Mystery. Brentano's (London), 1925   (U.S. title?)
The Clue of the Clock. Clode, 1929. British title: Alias the Eagle. Brentano's (London), 1928   [NYC]
The Dragon of Lung Wang. Clode, 1928; Wright, 1934   GM   [NYC]
The House of Seclusion. Small, 1925; Wright, 1935   GM   [NYC]
The Inner Circle. Longmans (NYC), 1930   (3-act play.)
The Mystery of the Hidden Room. Clode, 1922; Brentano's (London), 1923   GM   [NYC]
The Vengeance of the Ivory Skull. Clode, 1923; Wright, 1935   GM   [Rio de J.]

HARVEY, WILLIAM C(LUNIE). 1900-   .
Death's Treasure Hunt. Eldon, 1933
Murder Abroad. Eldon, 1933

HARVEY, WILLIAM F(RYER). 1885-1937. SC: Athelstan Digby = AD.
The Arm of Mrs. Egan and other strange stories. Dent, 1951; Dutton, 1952   ss
-The Beast with Five Fingers. Dent, 1928; Dutton, 1928   ss
-Caprimulgus. Constable, 1936
-Midnight House and other tales. Dent, 1910   ss
-Midnight Tales. Dent, 1946   ss
The Misadventures of Athelstan Digby. Swarthmore, 1920   ss   AD
-Moods and Tenses. Blackwell, 1933   ss
-Mr. Murray and the Boocooks. Nelson, 1938
The Mysterious Mr. Badman. Pawling, 1934   AD

HARWOOD, CAROLINE
The Castle of Vivaldi; or, The Mysterious Injunction. Minerva, 1810

HARWOOD, RONALD. 1934-   . Ref: CA.
The Genoa Ferry. Secker, 1976; Mason/Charter, 1977   [Mid. East]
The Guilt Merchants. Cape, 1963; Holt, 1969   [S. Am.]

HASLETTE, JOHN. Pseudonym of John (George) Hazlette Vahey, 1881-   , q.v. Other pseudonyms: Henrietta Clandon, Anthony Lang, Vernon Loder, John Mowbray, Walter Proudfoot, qq.v.
-The Carven Ball. Digby, 1910
-Desmond Rourke, Irishman. Low, 1911; Appleton, 1911
-Johnnie Madison. Smith Elder, 1914
The Man Who Pulled the Strings. Nash, 1916
-The Mesh. Low, 1912
-The Passion of the President. Everett, 1909
-The Shadow of Salvador. Heath Cranston, 1913

HASLUCK, ALEXANDRA
Of Ladies Dead. Angus (Sydney), 1970   (ss of historical mystery.)

HASLUCK, NICHOLAS (P.). 1942-   . Practices law in western Australia.
The Blue Guitar. Macmillan (London), 1980
Quarantine. Macmillan (London), 1978; Holt, 1979

HASTINGS, BEVERLY
Don't Talk to Strangers. Jove, 1980

HASTINGS, BROOK. Joint pseudonym of Leslie Edgley, 1912-   , q.v., and Mary Edgley. Other pseudonym of Leslie Edgley: Robert Bloomfield, q.v.
The Demon Within. Doubleday, 1953; Boardman, 1954   [Calif.]

HASTINGS, CHARLOTTE
Bonaventure. French (London), 1950. U.S. title: The High Ground. French (NYC), 1951   (3-act play.)

HASTINGS, D(OROTHY) G(RACE). 1911-   .
Death at the Depot. Harper, 1944   [Vt.]

HASTINGS, GEORGE
-His Royal Highness. Brandus, 1891
-Mrs. Jonathan Abroad. Argonaut, 1890
Philip Henson M.D. Brandus, 1891; Ward, 1892. Also published as: A Tale of the Town; or, Philip Henson, M.D. Iver, 1894   [NYC]
A Tale of the Town; see Philip Henson M.D.

HASTINGS, GRAHAM. Pseudonym of Roderic (Graeme) Jeffries, 1926-   , q.v. Other pseudonyms: Peter Alding, Jeffrey Ashford, Roderic Graeme, qq.v.
Deadly Game. Hale, 1961
Twice Checked. Hale, 1959

HASTINGS, HARRINGTON. Joint pseudonym of Florence Shepherd and John Marsh, 1907-   , q.v.
Criminal Square. Hutchinson, 1929
-The War Dog Stirs. Hutchinson, 1930

HASTINGS, MACDONALD. 1909-   . Ref: CA, CC, EM, TC. SC: Montague Cork in all titles. Set: Eng.
Cork and the Serpent. Joseph, 1955
Cork in Bottle. Joseph, 1953; Knopf, 1954
Cork in the Doghouse. Joseph, 1957; Knopf, 1958
Cork on Location; see Cork on the Telly
Cork on the Telly. Joseph, 1966. U.S. title: Cork on Location. Walker, 1967
Cork on the Water. Joseph, 1951; Randon, 1951. Also published as: Fish and Kill. Mercury, 1952, abridged   [Scot.]
Fish and Kill; see Cork on the Water

HASTINGS, MICHAEL
They Killed a Spy. Harrap, 1940

HASTINGS, MICHAEL. 1937-   .
The Castle of Vengeance. Macdonald, 1971
The Citadel of the Bats. Macdonald, 1962
The Coast of No Return. Methuen, 1953
Dangerous Oasis. Macdonald, 1968
Death Across the Tamagash. Macdonald, 1965   [Cent. Am.]
Death in Deep Green. Methuen, 1952
Desert Convoy. Macdonald, 1975
The Digger of the Pit. Methuen, 1955
Dragon Island. Macdonald, 1974
Fire Mountain. Macdonald, 1970

The Green Silence. Macdonald, 1966
[S. Pac.]
An Hour-Glass to Eternity. Macdonald, 1959
Killer Road. Macdonald, 1972
The Killing in Black and White. Macdonald, 1969
The Man Who Came Back. Macdonald, 1957
The Port of Lost Cargoes. Macdonald, 1963
The Puma Quest. Macdonald, 1979
The Rising Sea. Macdonald, 1962
River of Fate. Macdonald, 1976
The Sands of Khali. Macdonald, 1964 [Saud. Arab.]
Satan's Bay. Macdonald, 1978 [New Guinea]
The Snake and the Arrow. Macdonald, 1967 [Brazil]
Tiger Reef. Macdonald, 1973
The Trader of Skull Island. Macdonald, 1977
Twelve on Endurance. Macdonald, 1958
Veiled Isis. Macdonald, 1960 [Egypt]
The Voyage of the "San Marcos." Macdonald, 1960

HASTINGS, MICHAEL (GERALD TAILOR). 1938- . A London playwright.
The Frauds. Allen, 1960
The Game. Allen, 1957
The Nightcomers. Pan, 1973; Delacorte, 1972 (Novelization of the movie.)

HASTINGS, PHYLLIS (DORA HODGE). 1913- .
An Act of Darkness. Hale, 1969. U.S. title: The House on Malador Street. Putnam, 1970 [Eng., 1890s]
The Conservatory. Hale, 1973; PB, 1974 [Eng., 1871]
-The Death-Scented Flower. Hale, 1977
Field of the Forty Footsteps. Hale, 1978; St. Martin's, 1979 [Fr., ca.1795]
The Harlot's Daughter; see Their Flowers Were Always Black
House of the Twelve Caesars. Hale, 1975; Berkley, 1976
The House on Malador Street; see An Act of Darkness
-The Image Maker. Hale, 1976
-Running Thursday. Hale, 1980
-The Stratford Affair. Hale, 1978
-The Swan River Story. Hale, 1968
-Their Flowers Were Always Black. Hale, 1967. Also published as: The Harlot's Daughter. New English Library pb, 1967
-When the Gallows Is High. Hale, 1971

HASTINGS, RODERIC. Pseudonym of Graham Montague Jeffries, 1900- . Other pseudonyms: Bruce Graeme, David Graeme, qq.v.
Naked Tide. Avon, 1958 (British title?)

HASTINGS, ROSLYN. See also: Kate Klein.
Dead Wrong. Avalon, 1963
Mind over Murder. Avalon, 1960
Where There's a Will. Avalon, 1960

HASTINGS, W(ELLS) S(OUTHWORTH). 1878-1923.
The Man in the Brown Derby. Bobbs, 1911 [NYC]
The Professor's Mystery, with Brian Hooker. Bobbs, 1911

HASTY, JOHN EUGENE. 1897- .
Angel with Dirty Wings. GM, 1961; Muller pb, 1962 [Calif.]
Man Without a Face. Dodd, 1958; Long, 1960
Some Mischief Still. GM, 1962; Muller pb, 1963

HATCH, (ALDEN) DENISON. 1935- . Ref: CA.
The Fingered City. Eriksson, 1973; New English Library, 1975

HATCH, ERIC (STOWE). 1901-1973. Ref: CA.
-Crockett's Woman. GM, 1951; Fawcett, (London), 1953
-The Golden Woman. GM, 1952; Fawcett (London), 1959

HATCH, MARY R. P(LATT). 1848-1935.
The Bank Tragedy. Welch Fracker, 1890 [Conn.]
The Berkeley Street Mystery. Page, 1928 [Boston]
The Missing Man. Lee & Shepard, 1893 [N.H.]
The Strange Disappearance of Eugene Comstocks. Dillingham, 1895 [Maine]
The Upland Mystery. Laird, 1887

HATCH, RICHARD W(ARREN). 1898- .
Delayed Action. Rich, 1951

HATHAWAY, ANN
The Man in the Monkey Suit. Godwin, 1933

HATHAWAY, MAVIS. Pseudonym of Ira Avery, 1914- .
A Silence of Nightingales. Popular Library, 1977 [It.]
Son of Nightingales. Popular Library, 1977

HATHWAY, ALAN. See: Kenneth Robeson.

HATTON, CHARLES. See: Ted Willis, 1918-

HATTON, JOSEPH. 1841-1907. Set: Eng.
The Abbey Murder. Blackett, 1888; Lovell, 1888
-Against the Stream. Skeet, 1866
-The Banishment of Jessop Blythe. Hutchinson, 1895; Lippincott, 1895
-Behind a Mask. Dicks, 1886
-By Order of the Czar. Hutchinson, 1890; Lovell, 1890. A play by this title: Hutchinson, 1904
-Captured by Cannibals. Hodder, 1888; Pott, 1889
-Christopher Henrick. Bradbury, 1869; Putnam, 1869
-Clytie. Chapman, 1874; Lovell, 1876
-Cruel London. Chapman, 1878; Lovell, 1883
-The Dagger and the Cross. Hutchinson, 1897; Fenno, 1897
A Daughter of France; see When Greek Meets Greek
The Gay World. Hurst, 1877
-In Male Attire. Hutchinson, 1900
-In the Lap of Fortune. Chapman, 1873
John Needham's Double. Maxwell, 1885; Harper, 1885
-A Modern Ulysses. Chapman, 1883; U.S. Book Co., 1892
The Old House at Sandwich. Low, 1887; Appleton, 1887
The Park Lane Mystery. Arrowsmith, 1887
-The Princess Mazaroff. Hutchinson, 1891; Lovell, 1891
-Provincial Papers. Kent, 1861 ss
-The Queen of Bohemia. Beccles, 1877; Harper, 1882
The Tallants of Barton. Tinsley, 1867
-Three Recruits, and the Girls They Left Behind Them. Hurst, 1880; Harper, 1880
-Tom Chester's Sweetheart. Hutchinson, 1895
Under the Great Seal. Hutchinson, 1893; Cassell (NYC), 1893
-The Valley of Poppies. Chapman, 1871
-The Vicar. Hutchinson, 1898; Lippincott, 1898
A Vision of Beauty. Hutchinson, 1902; Burt, 1902
-When Greek Meets Greek. Hutchinson, 1895; Lippincott, 1896. Also published as: A Daughter of France. Hutchinson, 1896
When Rogues Fall Out. Pearson, 1899; Lippincott, 1899

HAUBOLD, CLEVE (ERNST). 1930- .
The Man on the Tower. French (NYC), 1967 (1-act play.)

HAUCK, DARBY
The Death Cry. Shores, 1917

HAUCK, LOUISE PLATT. 1883-1943. Pseudonyms: Lane Archer, Louise Landon, qq.v.
The Mystery of Tumult Rock. Burton, 1920

HAUGHEY, THOMAS BRACE. Lives in Texas; director of an evangelical missionary society. SC: Geoffrey Weston, in all titles, all set in Eng.
The Case of the Frozen Scream. Bethany, 1979
The Case of the Invisible Thief. Bethany, 1978
The Case of the Kidnapped Shadow. Bethany, 1980
The Case of the Maltese Treasure. Bethany, 1979

HAWK, JOHN. 1893- . SC: Mortimer Sark, in at least those marked MS.
The Family Skeleton. Skeffington, 1933
The House of Sudden Sleep. Skeffington, 1930; Mystery League, 1930 [Conn.]
It Was Locked; see The Locked Door
The Locked Door. Skeffington, 1929. U.S. title: It Was Locked. Farrar, 1930
The Lone Lodge Mystery. Hodder, 1926; Doran, 1926 MS
The Mid-Ocean Tragedy. Hodder, 1927; Doran, 1927 MS [ship]
Murder at Arondale Farm. Skeffington, 1931; Farrar, 1932
The Murder of a Mystery Writer. Skeffington, 1929; Doubleday, 1929 MS
The Serpent-Headed Stick. Hodder, 1926; Doran, 1927 MS
The Titanic Hotel Mystery. Skeffington, 1928; Doubleday, 1928 MS

HAWKER, BESSY
Overlooked. Wells Gardner, 1898

HAWKES, F. A.
Adventures of a Chemist. 1930 ss

HAWKES, ROBERT. Pseudonym of Marc Olden, q.v. SC: John Bolt, in all titles.
The Beauty Kill. Signet, 1975
Corsican Death. Signet, 1975
The Death List. Signet, 1974; Star, 1975
Death of a Courier. Signet, 1974
Death Song. Signet, 1975
The Delgado Killings. Signet, 1974
Kill for It. Signet, 1975 [NYC]
Kill the Dragon. Signet, 1974
NARC. Lancer, 1973 [NYC]

HAWKEY, RAYMOND
Side-Effect. Cape, 1979; Ballantine, 1979
Wild Card, with Roger Bingham. Cape, 1974; Stein, 1974 [U.S., future]

HAWKINS, SIR ANTHONY HOPE. 1863-1933. Pseudonym: Anthony Hope, q.v. See also: Robert Marshall.

HAWKINS, DEAN
Headsman's Holiday. Mystery House, 1946 [South]
In Memory of Murder. Doubleday, 1937 [South]
Skull Mountain. Doubleday, 1941
Walls of Silence. Doubleday, 1943 [South]

HAWKINS, EDWARD H. 1934- . Ref: CA.
Prisoners of Devil's Claw. Apollo, 1971
Wellspring. Echo House, 1969 [Colo.]

HAWKINS, FRANK N., JR.
Ritter's Gold. Signet, 1980 [Greece]

HAWKINS, JOHN, 1910-1978, and WARD HAWKINS, 1912- .
Broken River. Dutton, 1944; World's Work, 1948
Death Watch. Dodd, 1958; Eyre, 1959 (2 novelets.)
Devil on His Trail. Dutton, 1944
The Floods of Fear. Dodd, 1954; Eyre, 1957. Also published as: A Girl, a Man, and a River. Popular Library, 1957
A Girl, a Man, and a River; see The Floods of Fear
If I Kill Him; see We Will Meet Again
Pilebuck. Dutton, 1943. Also published as: Secret Command. Adventure Novel Classic, 194?
Secret Command; see Pilebuck
Violent City. Dodd, 1957; Eyre, 1959 [Wash.]
We Will Meet Again. Dial, 1940. Also published as: If I Kill Him. Handi-Books, 1945, abridged

HAWKINS, ODIE. 1937- . Ref: CA.
Chicago Hustle. Holloway, 1977 [Chi.]

HAWKINS, WARD. 1912- . See: John Hawkins, 1910-1978.

HAWKINS, WILLARD E. 1887- .
The Cowled Menace. Sears, 1930 [West]

HAWKSHAW. Pseudonym of John Arthur Fraser, q.v.
The Benwell Mystery. Continental, 1891
Blinkey Morgan, the Detective's Foe. Eagle, 1888
Escaped from Sing Sing. Eagle, 1888
The Fatal Chair; see Kemmler
Kemmler; or, The Fatal Chair. Eagle, 1890. Also published as: The Fatal Chair. Donohue, 189?
Shadowed from Europe. Eagle, 1889. Also published as: The Story of a Dark Crime; or, Shadowed from Europe. Donohue, 189?
The Story of a Dark Crime; see Shadowed from Europe
The Swamps of Death. Donohue, 189?
A Wayward Girl's Fate. Eagle, 1890

HAWKWOOD, ALLAN. Pseudonym of H(enry) James O'Brien) Bedford-Jones, 1887-1949, q.v.
-John Solomon, Incognito. Hurst, 1925

HAWTHORN, E. M. D. Joint pseudonym of

Ethel M. Dolbey and Geoffrey May Dolbey.
    Quietly She Lies. H. Hamilton, 1953; Harper, 1953

HAWTHORNE, JULIAN. 1846-1934. Ref: CC, EM, MP. SC: Insp. Byrnes = B.
    An American Monte Cristo. Allen, 1893 (U.S. title?)
    An American Penman. Cassell, 1887; Cassell (London), 1888 B [NYC]
    Another's Crime. Cassell, 1888; Cassell (London), 1889 B [NYC]
    -Beatrix Randolph. Osgood, 1884; Chatto, 1884
    -Bressant. Appleton, 1873; King, 1873
    -Constance, and Calbot's Rival. Appleton, 1889 ss
    David Poindexter's Disappearance, and other tales. Appleton, 1888; Chatto, 1888 ss (British edition has 2 additional ss.)
    -A Dream and a Forgetting. Belford, 1888; Chatto, 1888
    -Dust. Houghton, 1882; Chatto, 1883
    A Fool of Nature. Scribner, 1896; Downey, 1896
    -Fortune's Fool. Osgood, 1883; Chatto, 1883
    Garth. Appleton, 1877; Bentley, 1877
    -The Golden Fleece. Lippincott, 1896 [Calif.]
    The Great Bank Robbery. Cassell, 1887; Cassell (London), 1888 B [NYC]
    John Parmelee's Curse. Cassell (NYC & London), 1886
    -The Laughing Mill and other stories. Macmillan (London), 1879 ss (U.S. title?)
    -Love Is a Spirit. Harper, 1896
    -Love—or a Name. Ticknor, 1885; Chatto, 1885
    A Messenger from the Unknown. Collier, 1892
    -Miss Cadogna. Chatto, 1885 (U.S. title?)
    Mr. Dunton's Invention, and other stories; see Six Cent Sam's
    -Mrs. Gainsborough's Diamonds. Appleton, 1878; Chatto, 1879
    -Noble Blood. Appleton, 1885
    -Pauline. U.S. Book Co., 1890
    Prince Saroni's Wife. Funk, 1884; Chatto, 1882 ss
    -Sebastian Strome. Appleton, 1880; Bentley, 1879
    Section 558; or, The Fatal Letter. Cassell (NYC & London), 1888 B [NYC]
    Six Cent Sam's. Price, 1893. Also published as: Mr. Dunton's Invention, and other stories. Merriam, 1896 ss
    A Tragic Mystery. Cassell, 1887; Cassell (London), 1888 B [NYC]
    The Trial of Gideon, and Countess Almara's Murder. Funk, 1886 (2 stories.)

HAWTHORNE, NATHANIEL. 1804-1864.
    Dr. Grimshawe's Secret. Osgood, 1882; Longmans, 1883
    Twice-Told Tales. American Stationers, 1837 ss

HAWTHORNE, VIOLET. Pseudonym of Christopher Rainone.
    Diary of Evil. Lancer, 1973 [L.I.]
    Identical Strangers. Ballantine, 1975
    Sweet Deadly Passion. Ballantine, 1976 [L.I.]

HAWTON, HECTOR. 1901- . Pseudonym: John Sylvester, q.v. Ref: CA, CC. SC: Asmun Hill, in at least those marked AH. Set: Eng.
    The Case of the Crazy Atom. Ward, 1948
    Deadly Nightcap. Ward, 1949 AH
    Death of a Witch. Ward, 1952
    Frozen Fire. Amalgamated, 1935
    The Green Scorpion. Ward, 1957
    Murder at H.Q. Ward, 1945 AH
    Murder by Mathematics. Ward, 1948 [acad.]
    Murder Cave. Amalgamated, 1934
    Murder Most Foul. Ward, 1946 AH
    The Nine Singing Apes. Ward, 1949 AH
    -Operation Superman. Ward, 1951
    Rope for the Judge. Ward, 1954 AH
    The Skeletons in the Cupboard. Ward, 1955
    The Tower of Darkness. Hodder, 1949; Roy, 1951
    Unnatural Causes. Ward, 1947 AH

HAY, FRANCES. Pseudonym of Sibyl Cicely Alexandra Dick Erikson. Other pseudonym: Alexandra Dick, q.v.
    Barbary Kate. Jenkins, 1964
    The Lady with a Rose. Jenkins, 1960
    There Was No Moon. Jenkins, 1957 [Crete]
    Traitor's Island. Jenkins, 1956

HAY, JAMES, JR. 1881-1936. Ref: MP. SC: Jefferson Hastings, in at least those marked JH.
    The Bellamy Case. Dodd, 1925 JH [South]
    The Hidden Woman. Dodd, 1929
    The Melwood Mystery. Dodd, 1920 JH [Wash. D.C.]
    Mrs. Marden's Ordeal. Little, 1918
    "No Clue!" Dodd, 1920; Jenkins, 1923 JH [Va.]
    That Washington Affair. Dodd, 1926; Jenkins, 1927 [Wash. D.C.]
    The Unlighted House. Dodd, 1921; Jenkins, 1922 [Wash. D.C.]
    The Winning Clue. Dodd, 1919; Jenkins, 1920 [N.C.]

HAY, L(INDSAY) F(ITZGERALD). SC: Archibald Beldrum and Nigel Blair, in all titles. Set: Eng.
    It Wasn't a Nightmare. Hutchinson, 1937; Macmillan, 1937
    No Mean Tartar. Hutchinson, 1938
    The Terrible Hand. Hutchinson, 1937

HAY, M(AVIS) DORIEL. Set: Eng.
    Death on the Cherwell. Skeffington, 1935
    Murder Underground. Skeffington, 1934
    The Santa Klaus Murder. Skeffington, 1936

HAY, MARIE. Pseudonym of Agnes Blanche Marie von Hindeburg, 1873- .
    The Evil Vanguard. Putnam (London), 1923

HAY, MARY CECIL. 1840?-1886.
    -Among the Ruins and other stories. Harper, 1882; Griffith, 1891 ss
    -The Arundel Motto. Harper, 1877; Blackett, 1877
    -Back to the Old Home. Harper, 1878
    -Bid Me Discourse. Harper, 1883; Hurst, 1883 ss
    -Brenda Yorke, and other tales. Munro, 1879; Hurst, 1875
    -A Dark Inheritance. Harper, 1878
    -Dorothy's Venture. Harper, 1882; Hurst, 1882
    -For Her Dear Sake. Harper, 1880; Hurst, 1880
    Hidden Perils. Harper, 1876; Hurst, 1874
    -Into the Shade, and other stories. Harper, 1881 ss
    -Lester's Secret. Harper, 1886; Hurst, 1885
    Missing! and other tales. Harper, 1880; Hurst, 1881 ss
    -Nora's Love Test. Harper, 1877; Hurst, 1876
    Old Myddelton's Money. Harper, 1875; Hurst, 1874
    -A Shadow on the Threshold. Harper, 1878
    -The Sorrow of a Secret. Harper, 1879
    -The Squire's Legacy. Harper, 1876; Hurst, 1875
    Under the Will, and other tales. Hurst, 1878 (U.S. title?) ss
    -Victor and Vanquished. Harper, 1876; Hurst, 1874
    -A Wicked Girl. Harper, 1886; Hurst, 1886 ss

HAY, W(ILLIAM) LAING. 1892- .
    Who Cut the Colonel's Throat? Longmans (London), 1931

HAY, WILLIAM (GOSSE). 1875-1945.
    The Escape of the Notorious Sir William Heans, and The Mystery of Mr. Daunt. Allen & Unwin, 1918
    The Mystery of Alfred Doubt. Allen & Unwin, 1937

HAYCOX, ERNEST. 1899-1950.
    Murder on the Frontier. Little, 1952 ss [West]
    Rough Air. Doubleday, 1934

HAYES, JOSEPH (ARNOLD). 1918- . Ref: CA, TC.
    Calculated Risk. French (NYC), 1963 (Play based on another play, "Any Other Business," by George Ross and Campbell Singer.)
    The Deep End. Viking, 1967; Allen, 1967
    The Desperate Hours. Random, 1954; Deutsch, 1954. A play: Random, 1955; revised edition: French (NYC & London), 1956 [Indianapolis]
    Don't Go Away Mad. Random, 1962; Allen, 1964
    The Hours After Midnight. Random, 1958; Deutsch, 1959
    Like Any Other Fugitive. Dial, 1971; Deutsch, 1972
    The Long Dark Night. Putnam, 1974; Deutsch, 1974 [New Eng.]
    Missing...and Presumed Dead. NAL, 1976; Deutsch, 1977
    The Third Day. McGraw, 1964; Allen, 1965 [Conn.]
    -Winner's Circle. Delacorte, 1980 [Ky.]

HAYES, LEAL
    The Challoners of Bristol. Belmont, 1973 [R.I., 1811]
    Dark Legend. Belmont, 1973 [Scot.]
    Harlequin House. Ace, 1967 [S.C., 1869]

HAYES, MARY-ROSE. 1939- . Ref: CA.
    The Caller. Pinnacle, 1979; Fontana, 1979

HAYES, MILTON
    -Bad Men Make Good Wives. Hurst, 1930
    Cling of the Clay. Hodder, 1925; Adelphi, 1925

HAYES, RALPH (EUGENE). 1927- . SC: Agent of Cominsec (Taggart) = A; Check Force (Alexander Chane and Vladimir Karlov) = CF; Mark Stoner = MS; John Yard (The Hunter) = JY.
    The Big Fall. Zebra, 1979
    The Bloody Monday Conspiracy. Belmont, 1974 A
    Clouds of War. Manor, 1975 CF
    The Deadly Prey. Leisure, 1975 JY [N.Y.]
    The Death Makers Conspiracy. Belmont, 1975 A [Far East]
    The Doomsday Conspiracy. Belmont, 1974 A
    The Golden God. Manor, 1976; New English Library, 1978 MS
    The Hellfire Conspiracy. Belmont, 1974 A
    The Hostages of Hell. Zebra, 1979
    King's Ransom. Manor, 1978 MS [Arg.]
    Night of the Jackals. Leisure, 1975 JY [Afr.]
    The Nightmare Conspiracy. Belmont, 1974 A [Afr.]
    Nightmare Island. Manor, 1975 CF
    100 Megaton Kill. Manor, 1975 CF
    The Peking Plot. Manor, 1975 CF
    The Satan Stone. Manor, 1976 MS
    Scavenger Kill. Leisure, 1975 JY [Kenya]
    Seeds of Doom. Manor, 1976 CF
    Sheryl. Belmont, 1980
    A Taste of Blood. Leisure, 1975 JY [Afr., E.]
    Track of the Beast. Leisure, 1975 JY [Uganda]
    The Turkish Mafia Conspiracy. Belmont, 1974 A [Istan.]
    Vengeance Is Mine. Manor, 1978

HAYES, ROY. Lives in L.A.; formerly in advertising.
    The Hungarian Game. Simon, 1973; Secker, 1973 [Calif.]

HAYES, WILLIAM EDWARD. 1897- . SC: Arthur Halstead, in all titles.
    Before the Cock Crowed. Doubleday, 1937 [Md.]
    Black Chronicle. Doubleday, 1938 [Md.]
    The Black Doll. Doubleday, 1936 [Md.]

HAYFORD, EUGENE. Pseudonym of Richard Hill Wilkinson, 1904- , q.v. Other pseudonyms: Julian Brocke, E. Harrison Ott, Paul Pray, qq.v.
    One Horrible Night. Drama Guild, 1939 (3-act play.)

HAYLES, BRIAN
    Goldhawk. New English Library pb, 1979

HAYLES, KENNETH
    The Death-Masque. Hale, 1962; Roy, 1963
    The Long Reach. Hale, 1956
    The Purple Sheba. Hale, 1959
    Trader Brook. Hale, 1957
    Volcano. Hale, 1958

HAYMON, MARK
    Dreams Die Hard. Hale, 1979
    The Nice Lady. Hale, 1979

HAYMON, S. T.
    Death and the Pregnant Virgin. Constable, 1980; St. Martin's, 1980

HAYNES, ANNIE. -1929. SC: Insp. Furnival, in at least those marked F; Insp. Stoddart, in at least those marked S. Set: Eng.
    The Abbey Court Murder. Bodley, 1923 F
    The Blue Diamond. Bodley, 1925
    The Bungalow Mystery. Bodley, 1923
    The Crime at Tattenham Corner. Bodley, 1929 S
    The Crow's Inn Tragedy. Bodley, 1927; Dodd, 1927 F
    The Crystal Beads Murder. Bodley, 1930 S
    The House in Charlton Crescent. Bodley, 1926 F
    The Man with the Dark Beard. Bodley, 1928
    The Master of the Priory. Bodley, 1927
    The Secret of Greylands. Bodley, 1924; Watt, 1925

Who Killed Charmian Karslake? Bodley, 1929; Dodd, 1930 S
The Witness on the Roof. Bodley, 1925

HAYNES, BRIAN. See: Tom Keene.

HAYS, H(OFFMAN) R(EYNOLDS). 1904-1980. Ref: CA.
Lie Down in Darkness. Reynal, 1944; Hale, 1948
Stranger on the Highway. Little, 1943; Hale, 1947 [Ind.]

HAYS, LEE. Pseudonym: Sarah Nichols, q.v.
-Black Christmas. Popular Library, 1976
Harry-O. Popular Library, 1975 (Novelization of the TV series.) [San Diego]
Harry-O #2. Popular Library, 1976. British title: The High Cost of Living. Severn, 1978 [L.A.]
The High Cost of Living; see Harry-O #2
Murder by the Book. Popular Library, 1976 (Novelization of the "Columbo" TV series.)
Nakia. Popular Library, 1974 (Novelization of the TV series.) [S.W.]

HAYS, PETER. 1927-   . Pseudonym: Ian Jefferies, q.v.

HAYS, SUE BROWN. Lived in Louisiana and Mississippi; advertising copywriter; residing in New Or. in 1946.
Go Down, Death. Scribner, 1946; Hammond, 1948 [Miss.]

HAYSOM, DERRICK
The Espionage Infection. Hale, 1978
Ice Trap. Hale, 1977

HAYTHORNE, JOHN
None of Us Cared for Kate. Cassell, 1968; Dutton, 1968 [Far East]

HAYWARD, C. F. R.
The Mentons: Was It a Crime? Donnelley, 1887

HAYWARD, DAVID
The Provo Link. Hale, 1979

HAYWARD, RICHARD. Pseudonym (?) of Baynard H(ardwick) Kendrick, 1894-1977, q.v.
The Soft Arms of Death. GM, 1955; Fawcett (London), 1955 [Charleston]
Trapped. GM, 1952 [Calif.]

HAYWARD, WILLIAM STEPHENS. See also: Anonymous.
Eulalie; or, The Red and White Roses. Clarke, 1874
-Hunted to Death; or, Life in Two Hemispheres. (London), 1862
John Hazel's Vengeance. Maxwell, 1800 ss
Love Against the World. Clarke, 1875
The Stolen Will. Maxwell, 1881 ss

HAYWOOD, JOHN CAMPBELL
Driftwood and other tales. United States Review, 1905 ss, some criminous

HAYWORTH, EVELYNE. Pseudonym of Evan Lee Heyman. Other pseudonym: Joy Ann Blackwood, q.v.
The Evil at Bayou Laforche. Popular Library, 1972 [La.]
Haggard's Manor. Popular Library, 1973

HAZARD, FORRESTER. Pseudonym of Alexander (Hazard) Williams, 1894-1952, q.v.
The Hex Murder. Lippincott, 1936 [NYC]

HAZARD, LAURENCE
The Andean Murders. Barker, 1960

HAZELTINE, HORACE. Pseudonym of Charles Stokes Wayne, 1858-   .
The Sable Lorcha. McClurg, 1912

HAZELTON, CAPTAIN JOSEPH POWERS. Pseudonym of Linus Pierpont Brockett, 1820-1893, q.v.

HAZO, SAMUEL (JOHN). 1928-   . Ref: CA.
The Very Fall of the Sun. Hudson Review, 1976

HAZZARD, MARY. 1928-   . Pseudonym: Olivia Dwight, q.v.

HEAD, ANN. Pseudonym of Anne Christenson Morse, 1915-   . Ref: CA.
Always in August. Doubleday, 1961; Hurst, 1964 [S.C.]
Everybody Adored Cara. Doubleday, 1963; Hurst, 1964 [New Eng.]

HEAD, HELEN SMITH
Death Below Zero. Comet, 1954 [Alaska]

HEAD, (JOANNE) LEE. 1931-   . Ref: CA. SC: Lexey Jane Pelazoni, in both titles.
The Crystal Clear Case. Putnam, 1977 [N. Mex.]
The Terrarium. Putnam, 1976 [Dallas]

HEAD, MATTHEW. Pseudonym of John Edwin Canaday, 1907-   . Ref: CA, CC, EM, TC. SC: Dr. Mary Finney = MF.
The Accomplice. Simon, 1947 (Kan. City, 1935; Paris, 1934]
Another Man's Life. Simon, 1953
The Cabinda Affair. Simon, 1949; Heinemann, 1950 MF [Afr., W.]
The Congo Venus. Simon, 1950; Garland (London), 1976 MF [Bel. Congo]
The Devil in the Bush. Simon, 1945 MF [Bel. Congo]
Murder at the Flea Club. Simon, 1955; Heinemann, 1957 MF [Paris]
The Smell of Money. Simon, 1943 [Calif.]

HEADLAM, CUTHBERT (MORLEY). 1876-   . Pseudonym: B. B., q.v.
Knight Reluctant. Murray, 1934

HEAL, ANTHONY. From 1958 to 1970 a detective with the London Metropolitan Police.
The Decimate Decision. Allen, 1979. U.S. title: Man in the Middle. Scribner, 1980

HEALD, TIM(OTHY VILLIERS). 1944-   . Ref: CA, TC. SC: Simon Bognor = SB. Set: Eng.
Blue Blood Will Out. Hutchinson, 1974; Stein, 1974 SB
Deadline. Hutchinson, 1975; Stein, 1975 SB
Jealous in Honour: Volume 1 of The Authorized Biography of John Steed. Weidenfeld, 1977 (John Steed is the main character in "The Avengers" and "The New Avengers" TV series.)
Just Desserts. Hutchinson, 1977; Scribner, 1979 SB
Let Sleeping Dogs Lie. Hutchinson, 1976; Stein, 1976 SB
Unbecoming Habits. Hutchinson, 1973; Stein, 1973 SB

HEALEY, BEN(JAMIN JAMES). 1908-   . Pseudonyms: Jeremy Sturrock, q.v., J. G. Jeffreys. Was artist and designer in the British film industry. SC: Harcourt d'Espinal, in at least those marked HE; Paul Hedley, in at least those marked PH.
The Blanket of the Dark. Hale, 1976 PH [Wales]
Death in Three Masks. Hale, 1967. U.S. title: The Terrible Pictures. Harper, 1967 PH [Fr.]
The Horstmann Inheritance. Hale, 1975 HE
The Millstone Men. Hale, 1966 PH
Murder Without Crime. Hale, 1968 PH
The Red Head Herring. Hale, 1969
The Snapdragon Murders. Hale, 1978
The Stone Baby. Hale, 1974; Lippincott, 1973 HE [Venice]
The Terrible Pictures; see Death in Three Masks
The Trouble with Penelope. Hale, 1972 PH
The Vespucci Papers. Hale, 1972; Lippincott, 1972 HE [Venice]
Waiting for a Tiger. Hale, 1965; Harper, 1965 PH [Fr.]

HEALEY, EVELYN. See also: Anne Hocking.
The Braydon Mystery. Long, 1963
Death in Cold Storage. Long, 1965 [Tib.]
Let X Equal Murder. Long, 1961

HEALY, EUGENE P. SC: Paul Craine, in both titles, both set in NYC.
Craine's First Case. Holt, 1938; Hale, 1939
Mr. Sandeman Loses His Life. Holt, 1940

HEAPS, LEO. 1922?-   .
The Quebec Plot. Davies, 1978

HEARD, H(ENRY) F(ITZGERALD). 1889-1971. Ref: CA, CC, EM, MC, TC. SC: Mr. Mycroft = M.
The Black Fox. Cassell, 1950 [1870s]
Doppelgangers. Vanguard, 1947; Cassell, 1948 [1997]
The Great Fog and other weird tales. Vanguard, 1944; Cassell, 1947 ss, some criminous
The Lost Cavern and other tales of the fantastic. Vanguard, 1948; Cassell, 1949 ss, some criminous
Murder by Reflection. Vanguard, 1942; Cassell, 1945 [NYC]
The Notched Hairpin. Vanguard, 1949; Cassell, 1951 M [Eng.]
Reply Paid. Vanguard, 1942 M [Calif.]
A Taste for Honey. Vanguard, 1941; Cassell, 1942. Also published as: A Taste for Murder. Avon, 1955 M [Eng.]
A Taste for Murder; see A Taste for Honey

HEARD, NATHAN C(LIFF). 1936-   . Ref: CA.
-To Reach a Dream. Dial, 1972
When Shadows Fall. Playboy, 1977

HEARNDEN, BERYL. Joint pseudonym with Eva Balfour: Hearnden Balfour, q.v.

HEARNE, JOHN. 1926-   . Joint pseudonym with Morris Cargill, 1914-   : John Morris, q.v.

HEARST, JAMES. College English teacher in Iowa; author of nine books of poetry. See: Carmelita Calderwood,   -1950.

HEATH, CATHERINE. 1924-   .
-Stone Walls. Cape, 1973
The Vulture. Cape, 1974

HEATH, ELIZABETH ALDEN. Pseudonym of Edith Austin Holton, 1881-   .
The Affair at Tideways. Crowell, 1932 [New Eng.]

HEATH, ERIC. SC: Wade Anthony = WA; Cornelius Clift, Jr. = CC.
Death Takes a Dive. Hillman-Curl, 1938 CC [L.A.]
Murder in the Museum. Hillman-Curl, 1939 CC
Murder of a Mystery Writer. Arcadia, 1955 WA [Calif.] (Rewritten version of Death Takes a Dive, q.v.)
The Murder Pool. Arcadia, 1954 WA

HEATH, MONICA. Pseudonym of Arlene J. Fitzgerald, q.v.
Calderwood. Signet, 1975 [La.]
Castlereagh. Signet, 1978 [Jam.]
Chateau of Shadows. Signet, 1973
Clancumara's Keep. Signet, 1978 [Ire.]
Clerycastle. Signet, 1969 [Ire.]
Dunleary. Signet, 1967 [Ire.]
Duncraig. Signet, 1974
Falconlough. Signet, 1966 [Calif.]
Hawk Shadow. Playboy, 1980 [Calif.]
House of the Strange Woman. Signet, 1977 [Calif., 1800s]
The Legend of Blackhurst. Signet, 1976 [La.]
The Legend of Crownpoint. Signet, 1974 [Calif.]
Marshwood. Signet, 1977 [La.]
Mistress of Ravenstone. Signet, 1973 [Ire.]
Raneslough. Signet, 1976 [Ire.]
Return to Clerycastle. Signet, 1970 [Oreg.]
The Secret Citadel. Signet, 1975 [Calif.]
The Secret of the Vineyard. Signet, 1970 [Calif.]
Secrets Can Be Fatal. Signet, 1967 [Nev.]
Woman in Black. Signet, 1974

HEATH, PERCY
Slightly Scarlet. World Wide, 1930; Readers Library, 1930 (Novelization of the movie.)

HEATH, PETER. Pseudonym of Peter Heath Fine, 1938-   , q.v. SC: Jason Starr and Adam Cyber, in all titles.
Assassins for Tomorrow. Lancer, 1967 [Mex.]
Men Who Die Twice. Lancer, 1968
The Mind Brothers. Lancer, 1967

HEATH, ROY A(UBREY) K(ELVIN)
The Murderer. Allison, 1978

HEATH, THOMAS EDWARD
Tales in Prose and Verse. King, 1906 ss, at least one criminous

HEATH, W(ILLIAM) L(EDBETTER). 1924-   .
Blood on the River. Long, 1961
The Good Old Days. McCall, 1971
Ill Wind. Harper, 1957; H. Hamilton, 1957
Violent Saturday. Harper, 1955; H. Hamilton, 1955 [Tenn.]

HEATH-MILLER, MAVIS
-Always Say Goodbye. Collins, 1969

HEATTER, BASIL. 1918-   . Born on L.I., the son of radio commentator Gabriel Heatter; was advertising copywriter;

in 1970s living on a boat off Fla. and racing and chartering. SC: Timothy Devlin = TD.
Act of Violence. Lion, 1954 [N.H.]
Any Man's Girl. GM, 1961; Muller pb, 1962
-The Better Part of Valor. Doubleday, 1964
Devlin's Triangle. Pinnacle, 1976 TD [Carib.]
The Golden Stag. Pinnacle, 1976 TD [Boston]
Harry and the Bikini Bandits. GM, 1971
The Mutilators. GM, 1962; Muller pb, 1962 [Fr.]
The Naked Island. Trident, 1968; Hale, 1970 [Bahamas]
-Sailor's Luck. Lion, 1953
The Scarred Man. GM, 1973 [Fla.]
Virgin Cay. GM, 1963; Muller pb, 1964

HEAVEN, CONSTANCE (FECHER). 1911- . Pseudonym: Christina Merlin, q.v. Ref: CA.
Castle of Eagles. Heinemann, 1974; Coward, 1974 [Vienna, 1847]
The Fires of Glenlochy. Heinemann, 1976; Coward, 1976 [Scot., 1700s]
-Lord of Ravensley. Heinemann, 1978; Coward, 1978
The Place of Stones. Heinemann, 1975; Coward, 1975 [Fr.]
-The Queen and the Gypsy. Heinemann, 1977; Coward, 1977

HEBACH, LOUISE
The Murder of Bishop Conrad. Fortuny's, 1940 [NYC]

HEBDEN, MARK. Pseudonym of John Harris, 1916- , q.v. SC: Colonel Mostyn, in at least those marked M; Insp. Clovis Pel = CP.
The Dark Side of the Island. Joseph, 1973; Harcourt, 1973 [Hebrides]
Death Set to Music. H. Hamilton (London & NYC), 1979 CP [Fr.]
The Errant Knights. Harrap, 1968; Harcourt, 1968 [Sp.]
The Eyewitness. Harrap, 1966; Harcourt, 1967 [Paris]
Grave Journey; see Portrait in a Dusty Frame
A Killer for the Chairman. Joseph, 1972; Harcourt, 1972 [China]
The League of 89. H. Hamilton, 1977
Mask of Violence. Joseph, 1971; Harcourt, 1970 M [Ger.]
Pel and the Faceless Corpse. H. Hamilton (London & NYC), 1979 CP [Fr.]
Pel Under Pressure. H. Hamilton, 1980 CP [Fr.]
Portrait in a Dusty Frame. Harrap, 1969. U.S. title: Grave Journey. Harcourt, 1970 [Peru]
A Pride of Dolphins. Joseph, 1974; Harcourt, 1974 M [ship]
What Changed Charley Farthing. Harrap, 1965

HEBERDEN, M(ARY) V(IOLET). 1906- . Pseudonym: Charles L. Leonard, q.v. Ref: CC. SC: Desmond Shannon = DS; Rick Vanner = RV.
Aces, Eights, and Murder. Doubleday, 1941 DS [NYC]
The Case of the Eight Brothers. Doubleday, 1948; Cherry Tree, 1949 DS [NYC]
Death on the Door Mat. Doubleday, 1939 DS [NYC]
Drinks on the Victim. Doubleday, 1947 DS [N.J.]
Engaged to Murder. Doubleday, 1949 RV [Buen. A.]
Exit This Way. Doubleday, 1950; Hale, 1954. Also published as: You'll Fry Tomorrow. Bestseller, 1955 DS [NYC]
Fugitive from Murder. Doubleday, 1940 DS [NYC]
Ghosts Can't Kill; see That's the Spirit
The Lobster Pick Murder. Doubleday, 1941 DS [N.Y.]
Murder Cancels All Debts. Doubleday, 1946; Edwards, 1947 RV
Murder Follows Desmond Shannon. Doubleday, 1942; Hale, 1949 DS [W.I.]
Murder Goes Astray. Doubleday, 1943; Hale, 1951 DS [N.J.]
Murder Makes a Racket. Doubleday, 1942 DS [NYC]
Murder of a Stuffed Man. Doubleday, 1944 DS [NYC]
Murder Unlimited. Doubleday, 1953; Hale, 1954 DS [NYC]
The Sleeping Witness. Doubleday, 1951; Hale, 1955 RV [NYC]
Subscription to Murder. Doubleday, 1940 DS [NYC]
That's the Spirit. Doubleday, 1950. British title: Ghosts Can't Kill. Clerke, 1951 DS [Conn.]
They Can't All Be Guilty. Doubleday, 1947 DS [N.Y.]
To What Dread End. Doubleday, 1944; Hale, 1952 [Eng.]
Tragic Target. Doubleday, 1952; Hale, 1953 DS [Conn.]
Vicious Pattern. Doubleday, 1945; Hale, 1952 DS [Conn.]
You'll Fry Tomorrow; see Exit This Way

HECHT, BEN. 1894-1964. Ref: EM.
Actor's Blood. Covici, 1936 ss
Broken Necks and other stories. Haldeman-Julius, 1924. Expanded edition: Covici, 1926 ss
The Champion from Far Away. Covici, 1931 ss, some criminous
The Collected Stories of Ben Hecht. Crown, 1945; Hammond, 1950. (A selection of 8 largely criminous tales from this collection published as: Concerning a Woman of Sin and other stories. Avon, 1947.) ss
Concerning a Woman of Sin and other stories; see The Collected Stories of Ben Hecht
Count Bruga. Boni, 1926 [NYC]
The Florentine Dagger. Boni, 1923; Heinemann, 1924 [NYC]
Hollywood Mystery!; see I Hate Actors!
I Hate Actors! Crown, 1944. Also published as: Hollywood Mystery! Bart, 1946 [L.A.]
Ladies and Gentlemen, with Charles C. MacArthur. French, 1941 (3-act play)
The Sensualists. Messner, 1959; Blond, 1960
A Thousand and One Afternoons in Chicago. Covici, 1922 ss [Chi.]
1001 Afternoons in New York. PM, 1941 ss [NYC]

HECKSTALL-SMITH, ANTHONY. 1904- . Ref: CC.
The Man with Yellow Shoes. Wingate, 1957; Roy, 1958 [Cairo]
Murder on the Brain. Wingate, 1958; Roy, 1958
Where There Are Vultures. Wingate, 1958; Roy, 1959 [Fr.]

HECTOR, ANNIE FRENCH. 1825-1902. Pseudonym: Mrs. Alexander, q.v.

HECTOR, BARBARA
-As the Stars Fade. Swan, 1947
-No Through Road. Swan, 1942
The Victim's Niece. Swan, 1946

HEDDLE, ETHEL F(ORSTER)
-A Mystery of St. Rule's. Blackie, 1902 [acad.]

HEDDON, JAMES
Love and Bullets. Charter, 1979; Futura, 1979 (Novelization of the movie.)

HEDGES, JOSEPH. Pseudonym of Terry Harknett, 1936- , q.v. Other pseudonyms: William Pine, Thomas H. Stone, William Terry, qq.v. SC: John Stark, in all titles.
Angel of Destruction. Sphere, 1977
Arms for Oblivion. Sphere, 1973; Pyramid, 1975
The Chauffer-Driven Pyre. Sphere, 1976
The Chinese Coffin. Sphere, 1975; Pyramid, 1975
Corpse on Ice. Sphere, 1975; Pyramid, 1975
Funeral Rites. Sphere, 1973; Pyramid, 1974
The Gates of Death. Sphere, 1976
The Gold Plated Hearse. Sphere, 1974; Pyramid, 1975 [Ger.]
Mexican Mourning. Sphere, 1975 [Mex.]
The Mile Deep Grave. Sphere, 1975
Rainbow Coloured Shroud. Sphere, 1974; Pyramid, 1975
The Stainless Steel Wreath. Sphere, 1975

HEDGES, SID(NEY) G(EORGE). 1897-1974. Ref: CA.
The Channel Tunnel Mystery. Jenkins, 1931
Diamond Duel. Jenins, 1935 [Cairo]
The Malta Mystery. Jenkins, 1932 [Malta]
Mediterranean Mystery. Mellifont, 1940
Plague Panic. Jenkins, 1934
The Venetian Swimmer Mystery. Jenkins, 1933 [Venice]
The Weir Boyd Mystery. Jenkins, 1930

HEDLEY, FRANK. Pseudonym of C(larence) Hedley Barker, q.v. Other pseudonym: Seafarer, q.v.
Cavalier of Crime. Harrap, 1937; Lippincott, 1937

HEED, RUFUS
Ghosts Never Die. Vantage, 1954

HEFFERNAN, DEAN
Murder at Sunset Gables. Duffield, 1932 [Midwest]

HEFFERNAN, WILLIAM (A.). 1937- . Ref: CA.
Broderick. Crown, 1980 [NYC, 1920s]

HEGEDUS, ADAM. 1910- . Pseudonym: Rodney Garland, q.v.

HEGGY, JOE P.
The Grab. Hamilton Stafford, 1953
Make It Nylons. Hamilton Stafford, 1953
Poison Ivy. Hamilton Stafford, 1953
The Trouble with Women. Hamilton Stafford, 1954

HEGNER, WILLIAM. 1928- . Ref: CA.
-The Adopters. PB, 1974

HEHL, EILEEN
Lilac Mansion. Zebra, 1980

HEILBRUN, CAROLYN GOLD. 1926- . Pseudonym: Amanda Cross, q.v.

HEIMER, MEL(VIN LYTTON). 1915-1971. Ref: CA.
The Empty Man. McCall, 1971

HEINECKE, HAZEL JOAN
And the Winds Blew. Comet, 1957 [L.A.]

HEINEY, DONALD WILLIAM. 1921- . Pseudonym: MacDonald Harris, q.v.

HEITNER, IRIS. Pseudonym: Robert James, q.v.

HELD, PETER. Pseudonym of John Holbrook Vance, 1917- , q.v. Byline also: Jack Vance, q.v. Other pseudonym: Alan Wade, q.v. See also: Ellery Queen.
Take My Face. Mystery House, 1957 [S.F.]

HELDMAN, GLADYS M.
The Harmonetics Investigation. Crown, 1979

HELEY, VERONICA
Cry for Kit. Hale, 1976
Death for Deborah. Hale, 1978
Fear for Francis. Hale, 1977
Scream for Sarah. Hale, 1975
Sue for Mercy. Hale, 1974

HELITZER, FLORENCE (SAPERSTEIN). 1928- . Ref: CA.
Hans, Who Goes There? Harper, 1964

HELLER, FRANK. Pseudonym of Martin Gunnar Serner, 1866-1947. SC: Mr. Collin = C.
The Chinese Coats; see The Emperor's Old Clothes
The Emperor's Old Clothes. Crowell, 1923. British title: The Chinese Coats. Jarrolds, 1924 [Copen.]
The Grand Duke's Finances. Crowell, 1924; Jarrolds, 1925
Lead Me into Temptation. Crowell, 1927
The London Adventures of Mr. Collin. Crowell, 1924. British title: The Perilous Transactions of Mr. Collin. Lane, 1924 ss C [Eng.]
The Marriage of Yussuf Khan. Crowell, 1923; Hutchinson, 1924
Mr. Collin Is Ruined. Crowell, 1925 C [Rome]
The Perilous Transactions of Mr. Collin; see The London Adventures of Mr. Collin
The Strange Adventures of Mr. Collin. Crowell, 1926 ss C
The Thousand and Second Night. Crowell, 1925; Williams & Norgate, 1926 ss [Mid. East]

HELLER, LARRY. Pseudonym of Lorenz Heller, q.v. Other pseudonyms: Larry Holden, Frederick Lorenz, qq.v.
Body of the Crime. Pyramid, 1962
I Get What I Want. Popular Library, 1956

HELLER, LORENZ. Pseudonyms: Larry Heller, Larry Holden, Frederick Lorenz, qq.v.
Murder in Makeup. Messner, 1937 [NYC]

HELLER, MIKE. Pseudonym of Arnold Hano, 1922- . Other pseudonym: Matthew Gant, q.v.
So I'm a Heel. GM, 1957; Red Seal, 1958 [Calif.]

HELLINGER, MARK. 1903-1947.
The Ten Million. Farrar, 1934; Bodley, 1935   ss, some criminous
HELM, JEANETTE
The House of the Purple Stairs. Jenkins, 1925 [N.Y.]
Without Clues. Boni, 1923; Brentano's (London), 1924 [N.Y.]
HELM, PETER (JAMES). 1916-   . Ref: CA. SC: Martin Ridgway, in all titles.
Dead Man's Fingers. Long, 1960. U.S. title: A Walk into Murder. Scribner, 1960
Death Has a Thousand Entrances. Long, 1962 [Amst.]
The Man with No Bones. Long, 1966
A Walk into Murder; see Dead Men's Fingers
HELMORE, THOMAS
Affair at Quala. Simon, 1964; Cape, 1965 [S.F.]
HELSETH, HENRY EDWARD. 1912-   .
The Brothers Brannigan. Signet, 1961 (Novelization of the TV series.)
The Chair for Martin Rome. Dodd, 1947; Laurie, 1952
The Devil's Behind You. Harper, 1942
This Man Dawson. Signet, 1962 (Novelization of the TV series.)
The Yellow Angels. Harper, 1940
HELVICK, JAMES. Pseudonym of Francis Claud Cockburn, 1904-1981. Ref: CA.
Beat the Devil. Boardman, 1953; Lippincott, 1951
The Horses. McGibbon, 1961; Walker, 1963
HELWIG, DAVID (GORDON). 1938-   . Ref: CA.
The Day Before Tomorrow. Oberon, 1971. Also published as: Message from a Spy. PaperJacks, 1975
HELY, ELIZABETH. Pseudonym of Elizabeth Hely Younger, 1913-   . Wife of William Younger, 1917-1962 (= William Mole, q.v.). SC: Antoine Cirret, in at least those marked AC.
Dominant Third. Heinemann, 1959. U.S. title: I'll Be Judge, I'll Be Jury. Scribner, 1959 AC [Paris]
I'll Be Judge, I'll Be Jury; see Dominant Third
The Long Shot. Heinemann, 1963 [Austria]
A Mark of Displeasure. Heinemann, 1961; Scribner, 1960 AC [Edin.]
Package Deal. Hale, 1965
HEMING, BRACEBRIDGE
Where Angels Fear... Hamilton, 1938
HEMINGWAY, JOAN (1951-   ), and PAUL BONNECARRERE, 1925?-1977, q.v.
Rosebud. Ellis, 1974; Morrow, 1974 (Translation of "Rosebud." Paris, 1973.)
HEMINGWAY, KENNETH
Murder Flight. Quality, 1954
HEMINGWAY, R(ICHARD) D('OYLY), 1878-   , and HENRY DE HALSALLE, 1872-   , q.v.
Three Gentlemen from New Caledonia. Paul, 1915; Putnam, 1915
HEMPSTEAD, JUNIUS L(ACKLAND). 1842-   .
Thompson the Detective. Abbey, 1902
HEMYNG, (SAMUEL) BRACEBRIDGE. 1841-1901. Ref: EM.
-The Bondage of Brandon. Maxwell, 1881
A Brighton Mystery; or, The Disappearance of Captain Jarvice. Diprose, 1894
Called to the Bar. Clarke, 1867
Contesting the County, and other tales. Clarke, 1868 ss
Curious Crimes. Clarke, 1871 ss
The Danger Signal and other tales. Ward, 1868 ss
-Dead Heat; or, Neck in Neck. Clarke, 1887
-The Demon Jockey; or, A Run of Luck. Clarke, 1887
-The Favorite Scratched; or, The Spider and the Fly. Clarke, 1869
-Gaspar Trenchard. Maxwell, 1864
-Held in Thrall. Clarke, 1869
In the Force; or, Revelations of a Private Policeman. Maxwell, 1880 ss
On the Line and Danger Signal. Diprose, 1881 ss, some criminous
-On the Rank; or, The Adventures of a Cabman. Maxwell, 1880 ss
-On the Road: Tales Told by a Commercial Traveler. Routledge, 1868 ss
-The Orange Girl. Maxwell, 1865

-River Secrets. Maxwell, 1880 ss
-Secrets of the Dead-Letter Office. Clarke, 1866 ss
Secrets of the River. Berger, 1870 ss
Secrets of the Turf; or, How I Won the Derby. Clarke, 1868 ss
-The Sharks of Society. Diprose, 1888
-The Stockbroker's Wife, and other sensational tales. Maxwell, 1885 ss
-Strange Journeys. Maxwell, 1880 ss
-Telegraph Secrets. Clarke, 1866 ss
-The Toilers of the Thames. Clarke, 1860
-Too Sharp by Half; or, The Man Who Made Millions. Clarke, 1871
Tried for His Life; or, A Mysterious Case and other stories. Diprose, 1885 ss
The Women of London. Vickers, 1884
The Women of Paris. Vickers, 1884 [Paris]
HENAGHAN, JIM. 1919-   . Pseudonym: Archie O'Neill, q.v. Ref: CA. SC: Jeff Pride = JP (see also O'Neill entry).
Azor! St. Martin's, 1977 JP [Sp.]
HENDERSON, CECIL
Too Many Clues. Modern, 193?
HENDERSON, DONALD (LANDELS). 1905-   . Pseudonym: D. H. Landels, q.v. Ref: CC. Set: Eng.
Goodbye to Murder. Constable, 1946
Mr. Bowling Buys a Newspaper. Constable, 1943; Random, 1944
Murderer at Large. Paul, 1936
Procession—to Prison. Paul, 1937
The Trial of Lizzie Borden and other radio plays. Hurst, 1946 (Plays.)
HENDERSON, JAMES. 1934-   . Ref: CA.
Copperhead. Knopf, 1971; Collins, 1972 [Can.]
HENDERSON, JAMES LEAL. 1913-   . Pseudonym: Jay L. Currier, q.v.
-Whirlpool. Prentice-Hall, 1947
HENDERSON, LAURENCE. 1928-   . Ref: CA. SC: Det. Sgt. Arthur Milton, in all titles. Set: Eng.
Cage Until Tame. Harrap, 1972; St. Martin's, 1972
Major Enquiry. Harrap, 1976; St. Martin's, 1976
Sitting Target. Harrap, 1970; St. Martin's, 1972
With Intent. Harrap, 1968; St. Martin's, 1971
HENDERSON, WILLIAM
Clues; or, Leaves from a Chief Constable's Note Book. Oliphant, 1889; White and Allen, 1890 ss
Detective Stories. Heywood, 1891 ss
HENDRYX, JAMES B(EARDSLEY). 1880-1963. These are largely if not completely Northwest, Northwest Mounted Police, or frontier stories. SC: Black John, in at least those marked BJ; Corporal Downey, in at least those marked D; Connie Morgan, in at least those marked CM. Set: Can., in nearly all titles and certainly the BJ and D books.
At the Foot of the Rainbow. Putnam, 1924
Badmen on Halfaday Creek. Doubleday, 1950; Hammond, 1956 ss BJ,D
Beyond the Outposts. Hutchinson, 1924 (U.S. title?)
Black John of Halfaday Creek. Doubleday, 1939; Jarrolds, 1939 ss BJ
Blood of the North. Doubleday, 1938; Jarrolds, 1938
Blood on the Yukon Trail. Doubleday, 1930 D
Connie Morgan Hits the Trail. Doubleday, 1929 CM
Connie Morgan in Alaska. Putnam, 1916; Jarrolds, 1919 CM [Alaska]
Connie Morgan in Barren Lands. Jarrolds, 1934 (U.S. title?) CM
Connie Morgan in the Arctic. Putnam, 1936; Jarrolds, 1936 CM
Connie Morgan in the Cattle Country. Putnam, 1923; Jarrolds, 1927 CM
Connie Morgan in the Fur Country. Putnam, 1921; Jarrolds, 1928 CM
Connie Morgan in the Lumber Camps. Putnam, 1919; Jarrolds, 1928 CM
Connie Morgan, Prospector. Jarrolds, 1930 (U.S. title?) CM
Connie Morgan with the Forest Rangers. Putnam, 1925; Jarrolds, 1926 CM
Connie Morgan with the Mounted. Putnam, 1918; Jarrolds, 1924 CM
Corporal Downey Takes the Trail. Doubleday, 1931; Jarrolds, 1932 D,BJ
Courage of the North. Doubleday, 1946; Hammond, 1954

The Czar of Halfaday Creek. Doubleday, 1940; Hammond, 1955 ss BJ
Death Heads North; see Grubstake Gold
Devil's Gold. Jarrolds, 1940 (U.S. title?) D
Downey of the Mounted. Putnam, 1926; Hutchinson, 1926 D
Edge of Beyond. Doubleday, 1939
Frozen Inlet Post. Doubleday, 1927; Hutchinson, 1927
Gambler's Choice. Carlton, 1941; Museum, 1943 D
Gold and Guns on Halfaday Creek. Carlton, 1942; Hale, 1953 ss BJ
Gold—and the Mounted. Doubleday, 1928; Hutchinson, 1928 [Can.]
The Gold Girl. Putnam, 1920
Gold Is Where You Find It. Doubleday, 1953; Hammond, 1957
Good Men and Bad. Doubleday, 1954; Hammond, 1958
Grubstake Gold. Doubleday, 1936; Jarrolds, 1937. Also published as: Death Heads North. Adventure Novel Classic, 194?
The Gun-Brand. Putnam, 1917; Jarrolds, 1921
Hard Rock Man. Carlton, 1940; Hale, 1941 BJ
Intrigue on Halfaday Creek. Doubleday, 1953 ss BJ
It Happened on Halfaday Creek. Doubleday, 1944 ss BJ,D
Justice on Halfaday Creek. Doubleday, 1949; Museum, 1954 ss BJ
Law and Order on Halfaday Creek. Carlton, 1941; Hale, 1954 ss BJ
The Long Chase; see On the Rim of the Arctic
Man of the North. Doubleday, 1929; Hutchinson, 1930
Murder in the Outlands. Doubleday, 1949; Museum, 1953 D
Murder on Halfaday Creek. Doubleday, 1951 ss BJ
New Rivers Calling. Doubleday, 1943; Hale, 1952
North. Putnam, 1923
Oak and Iron. Putnam, 1925; Hutchinson, 1925
On the Rim of the Arctic. Doubleday, 1948; Museum, 1952. Also published as: The Long Chase. Dell, 1955
Outlaws of Halfaday Creek. Doubleday, 1935; Jarrolds, 1935 ss BJ
Prairie Flowers. Putnam, 1920; Jarrolds, 1923
The Promise. Putnam, 1915
Raw Gold. Doubleday, 1933; Jarrolds, 1933 D
The Saga of Halfaday Creek. Doubleday, 1947; Hammond, 1955 ss BJ
Skullduggery on Halfaday Creek. Doubleday, 1946; Hammond, 1953 ss BJ
Snowdrift. Putnam, 1922
Sourdough Gold. Doubleday, 1952; Hammond, 1957 BJ
The Stampeders. Doubleday, 1951; Hammond, 1956
Strange Doings on Halfaday Creek. Doubleday, 1943; Hale, 1952 ss BJ
Terror on Halfaday Creek. Consul, 1963 (U.S. title?)
The Texan. Putnam, 1918; Jarrolds, 1922
The Way of the North. Doubleday, 1945; Edwards, 1946 BJ
Without Gloves. Putnam, 1924; Hutchinson, 1924
The Yukon Kid. Doubleday, 1934· Jarrolds, 1934 D

HENISSART, MARTHA. ca.1929-   . An economist with the U.N. and the U.S. government. Joint pseudonyms with Mary Jane Latsis, ca.1927-   : R. B. Dominic, Emma Lathen, qq.v.

HENISSART, PAUL (HENRI). 1923-   . Ref: CA.
Margin of Error. Hutchinson, 1980; Simon, 1980
Narrow Exit. Hutchinson, 1974; Simon, 1973 [Tun.]
Winter Quarry. Hutchinson, 1976. U.S. title: The Winter Spy. Simon, 1977
The Winter Spy; see Winter Quarry

HENKIN, HARMON. ca.1940-1980.
Crisscross. Putnam, 1976 [Wash. D.C.]

HENLE, THEDA O. 1918-   . Ref: CA.
Death Files for Congress. Vanguard, 1971

HENN, HENRY
-The Assessor. Manor, 1978
Atherwood Terminal. Manor, 1979
China Alley. Manor, 1979
Death Switch. Manor, 1980
The Papa San Files. Manor, 1977

HENNEKER, PHILIP
   And One Must Die. Hale, 1965
   Don't Be Afraid of the Dark. Hale, 1965
   Too Late for Tears. Hale, 1966

HENNESSEY, (JOHN) DAVID. 1847-
   -An Australian Bush Track. Low, 1896.
      Also published as: The Bush Track.
      Hodder, 1913 [Australia]
   The Bush Track; see An Australian Bush
      Track
   The Caves of Shend. Hodder, 1915
      [Australia]
   -Cords of Vanity. Hodder, 1920
   -The Dis-Honourable. Low, 1896
   -A Lost Identity. Warne, 1899
   -The Outlaw. Hodder, 1913
   -The Tail of Gold. Hodder, 1914
      Wynnum. Low, 1896

HENOT, GEORGES. 1848-1918. Pseudonym:
   Georges Ohnet, q.v.

HENRIQUEZ, RICHARD A.
   Four Way Proof. Phoenix, 1951 [NYC]

HENRY, CHARLES
   Bainbridge Holme. Remington, 1881

HENRY, CHARLES. Pseudonym of Henry Farrell, q.v.
   The Hostage. Random, 1959. British
      title: Moving Day. Secker, 1960. Also
      published as: Ride with Terror, as by
      Henry Farrell. New English Library,
      1972

HENRY, CLAY. SC: Matt Archer, in at
   least those marked MA.
   Devils Burn Too. Boardman, 1963
   Not Dead Enough. Boardman, 1965
   Nude on the Rocks. Boardman, 1965 MA
   The Third Twin. Boardman, 1966
   Welcome Home, Lily Glow. Boardman, 1960
      MA [Mich.]

HENRY, JACK
   Flannelfoot, Phantom Crook. Hutchinson,
      1949
   Lucifer and Partner. Modern, 1950

HENRY, JOAN. Pseudonym.
   -Yield to the Night. Doubleday, 1954;
      Gollancz, 1954

HENRY, MARGARET
   -The Householders. Cassell, 1964
   Unlucky Dip. Cassell, 1960

HENRY, MICHAEL
   Murder on the Old Jail. Hamilton, 1938
      [Ire.]

HENRY, O. Pseudonym of William Sydney
   Porter, 1862-1910. Some criminous
   tales are scattered through the short
   story collections listed below.
   Ref: CA, EM, MC.
   Cabbages and Kings. McClure, 1904
   Cops and Robbers. Bestseller, 1948 (A
      collection of criminous ss taken from
      the other collections.)
   The Four Million. McClure, 1906; Hodder, 1916
   The Gentle Grafter. McClure, 1908
   Heart of the West. McClure, 1907; Nash,
      1912
   Roads of Destiny. Doubleday, 1909
   Rolling Stones. Doubleday, 1912; Hodder, 1916
   Sixes and Sevens. Doubleday, 1911; Hodder, 1916
   Strictly Business. Doubleday, 1910
   The Trimmed Lamp. McClure, 1907; Hodder, 1915
   The Voice of the City. McClure, 1908;
      Hodder, 1916
   Waifs and Strays. Doubleday, 1917; Hodder, 1920
   Whirligigs. Doubleday, 1910; Hodder, 1916

HENRY, VERA. Ref: CA.
   Mystery of Cedar Valley. Bouregy, 1964

HENSHAW, (WILLIAM) KEITH
   Kath. Collins, 1964
   Sea Vermin. Collins, 1963

HENSHAW, NANCY ELY
   Worse and More of It. Vantage, 1959

HENSHAW, NEVIL (GRATIOT). 1880- .
   -The Painted Woods. Bobbs, 1924

HENSLEY, JOE L. [JOSEPH LOUIS HENSLEY].
   1926- . Attorney, judge and legislator in Ind. SC: Donald Robak = DR.
   Set: Ind., in all titles.
   The Color of Hate. Ace, 1960
   Deliver Us to Evil. Doubleday, 1971 DR
   A Killing in Gold. Doubleday, 1978;
      Gollancz, 1979 DR
   Legislative Body. Doubleday, 1972 DR
   Minor Murders. Doubleday, 1979 DR
   The Poison Summer. Doubleday, 1974
   Rivertown Risk. Doubleday, 1977
   Song of Corpus Juris. Doubleday, 1974
      DR

HENTY, G(EORGE) A(LFRED). 1832-1902.
   -Colonel Thorndyke's Secret. Chatto,
      1898; Mershon, 1901
   -Condemned As a Nihilist. Blackie, 1893;
      Scribner, 1892
   -The Curse of Carne's Hold. Blackett,
      1889; Lovell, 1889
   -Dorothy's Double. Chatto, 1894; Rand,
      1895
   -A Hidden Foe. Low, 1891; U.S. Book Co.,
      1890
   -The Lost Heir. Bowden, 1899; New Amsterdam, 1900
   -A Search for a Secret. Tinsley, 1867

HEPPELL, MARY. Pseudonym: Marguerite
   Clare, q.v.

HEPWORTH, GEORGE H(UGHES). 1833-1902.
   The Queerest Man Alive, and other stories. Fenno, 1897 ss, some criminous

HERBER, WILLIAM (EDWARD). 1920- .
   Born in Ind.; executive in display
   advertising in Chi. SC: Jimmy Rehm =
   JR.
   The Almost Dead. Lippincott, 1957;
      Foulsham, 1958 [Paris]
   Death Paints a Portrait. Lippincott,
      1958; Foulsham, 1959 [Chi.]
   King-Sized Murder. Lippincott, 1954;
      Foulsham, 1955. Also published as:
      Some Die Slow. Bantam, 1956 JR
      [Chi.]
   Live Bait for Murder. Lippincott, 1955;
      Foulsham, 1956 JR [La.]
   Some Die Slow; see King-Sized Murder

HERBERT, A(LAN) P(ATRICK). 1890-1971.
   Ref: CA, CC.
   The House by the River. Methuen, 1920;
      Knopf, 1921

HERBERT, BENSON. 1912- .
   Murder by Telephone. Newcoll, 1945
   The Parcel Post Murder. Cole, 1943
   -Strange Romance. Cole, 1943
   They Don't Always Hang Murderers. Cole,
      1942

HERBERT, CYRIL
   The Clue of the Six Kissing Girls.
      Mitre, 1946
   How Dark Are the Dunes. Mitre, 1946
   How Slow the Snooth. Mitre, 1946
   Justice Peeps over the Handkerchief.
      Mitre, 1946
   The Man Who Was Ten Years Late for
      Breakfast. Mitre, 1946
   Midnight Minute. Mitre, 1946

HERBERT, FRANK (PATRICK). 1920- .
   Ref: CA.
   The Dragon in the Sea. Doubleday,
      1956; Gollancz, 1960. Also published
      as: 21st Century Sub. Avon, 1956;
      and as: Under Pressure. Ballantine,
      1974 [2000s]

HERBERT, (EDWARD) IVOR (MONTGOMERY).
   1925- . Ref: CA.
   The Filly. Heinemann, 1977

HERBERT, JAMES. 1943- . Ref: CA.
   -The Dark. New English Library, 1980;
      Signet, 1980
   -The Fluke. New English Library, 1977;
      Signet, 1978
   -The Fog. New English Library, 1975;
      Signet, 1975
   -The Lair. New English Library, 1979;
      Signet, 1979
   -The Rats. New English Library, 1974;
      Signet, 1975
   -The Spear. New English Library, 1979;
      Signet, 1980
   -The Survivor. New English Library,
      1976; Signet, 1977

HERBERT, NAN
   -The Enemy Within. Hale, 1978
   Flight of the Shadows. Hale, 1976;
      Zebra, 1979
   The Shadow over Heldon Hall. Hale,
      1976; Zebra, 1978

HERBRAND, JAN(ICE McRORIE). 1931- .
   Ref: CA.
   The Altheimer Inheritance. Paperback
      Library, 1973
   The Dangerous House. Warner, 1975
      [Wash.]
   Lost Heritage. Paperback Library, 1972

HERCHENBACH, WILHELM. 1818-1889.
   The Coiner's Cave. Gill, 1887

HERD, TRAVIS
   Death of a Convict. Hale, 1960
   Fast Shuffle. Hale, 1961
   Guilty Party. Hale, 1961
   Snake's Picnic. Hale, 1960

HERE, R. A.
   Case of Doctor Tracey. Cranley, 1934

HERFORD, OLIVER. 1863-1935. See: Cleveland Moffett, 1863-1926.

HERING, HENRY A(UGUSTUS). 1864- .
   The Burglars' Club. Cassell, 1906;
      Dodge, 1906. Revised edition, with 6
      new stories: Cassell, 1910 ss

HERLIN, HANS. 1925- .
   Friends. Heinemann, 1975. U.S. title:
      Commemorations. St. Martin's, 1975
      (Translation of "Freunde." Munich,
      1974.)

HERMAN, HENRY. 1832-1894. See also: Henry
   Arthur Jones, 1851-1929; and: David
   Christie Murray, 1847-1907.
   The Crime of a Christmas Toy. Ward,
      1893
   A Dead Man's Story, and other tales.
      Warne, 1894 ss
   The Great Becklewaithe Mystery. Simpkin, 1896
   Hearts of Gold and Hearts of Steel.
      Newnes, 1893
   A King in Bohemia. Remington, 1894
   Lady Turpin. Beeton's, 1895
   -A Leading Lady. Chatto, 1891
   -The Postman's Daughter, and other
      tales. Warne, 1894 ss
   Scarlet Fortune. Trischler, 1891
   The Silver King's Vengeance, and other
      stories. Digby, 1907 ss
   The Sword of Fate. Greening, 1899
   Woman, the Mystery. Ward, 1894

HERMAN, J. B.
   Black Sabbat. Major, 1979
   Grandmother's House. Manor, 1980

HERMAN, LOUIS. 1905- . See: William
   Targ, 1907- .

HERMANN, WALTER. Pseudonym of Walter
   (Herman) Wager, 1924- , q.v. Other
   pseudonym: John Tiger, q.v.
   Operation Intrigue. Avon, 1956
   [Wash. D.C.]

HERNE, HUXLEY. Pseudonym of Bertram
   Brooker, 1888-1955.
   The Tangled Miracle. Nelson, 1936

HERNON, G. D.
   Louisa; or, The Black Tower. Gordon,
      1805

HERON, E. and H. See: K(atherine O'Brien) Prichard.

HERON, JAMES
   The Cat's Paw. Futura, 1977

HERON-MAXWELL, BEATRICE
   The Adventures of a Lady Pearl Broker.
      New Century, 1899 ss

HERRICK, MARIAN J. and J. TRUMBELL ROGERS
   When Last Seen... Manor, 1978

HERRIES, NORMAN
   Death Has Two Faces. Ace, 1955
   My Private Hangman. Ace, 1956 [Las
      Veg.]

HERRING, PAUL
   -Dragon's Silk. Cassell, 1908
   The Midnight Murder; see The Murder of
      Margot Midnight
   The Murder of Margot Midnight. Low,
      1932. U.S. title: The Midnight Murder. Lippincott, 1932
   -The Wrong Mr. Chamberlain and other
      stories. Arrowsmith, 1904 ss

HERRING, PETER L.
   The Murder Business. Major, 1976

HERRINGTON, LEE. Writer of pulp fiction.
   Carry My Coffin Slowly. Simon, 1951

HERRIOT, DENYS G.
   The Last of Mrs. Cheyney. Collins,
      1930 (Adapted from the play by
      Frederick Lonsdale, 1881-1954.)

HERRON, SHAUN. 1912- . Ref: CA, TC.
   SC: Miro = M.
   -The Bird in Last Year's Nest. Evans,
      1974; Cape, 1974
   The Hound and the Fox and the Harper.
      Random, 1970. British title: The Miro
      Papers. Hale, 1972 M [Ire.]
   Miro. Random, 1969; Hale, 1971 M [Can.]

The Miro Papers; see The Hound and the Fox and the Harper
Through the Dark and Hairy Wood. Random, 1972; Cape, 1973 M [Ire.]
The Whore-Mother. Evans, 1973; Cape, 1973 [Ire.]

HERSCHOLT, WOLFE. Pseudonym.
X-Ray Menace. Transport, ca.1941

HERSEY, JOHN (RICHARD). 1914- . Ref: CA.
The Walnut Door. Knopf, 1977; Macmillan (London), 1978

HERSHATTER, RICHARD L(AWRENCE). 1923- SC: Rand Stannard, in all titles.
Fallout for a Spy. Ace, 1969
The Spy Who Hated Licorice. Signet, 1966
The Spy Who Hated Fudge. Ace, 1970

HERSHMAN, MORRIS. 1920- . Pseudonyms: Evelyn Bond, Jess Wilcox, qq.v. Ref: CA.
Guilty Witness. Belmont, 1964 [NYC]
Target for Terror. Belmont, 1967 [Eng.]

HERST, ROGER
Status 1SQ. Futura, 1980

HERTZ, GEORGE
The Foreign Harry Complot. Hale, 1972

HERVEY, HARRY (CLAY). 1900-1951.
The Black Parrot. Century (NYC & London), 1923 [Far East]
Caravans by Night. Century, 1922; Butterworth, 1925
Red Ending. Liveright, 1929; Allen, 1952
Red Hotel. Jarrolds, 1932

HERVEY, MAURICE H.
-Amyas Egerton, Cavalier. Arrowsmith, 1896; Harper, 1896
Dartmoor. Arrowsmith, 1896; Stokes, 1895
-David Dimsdale, M.D. Redway, 1897
Dead Man's Court. Arrowsmith, 1895; Stokes, 1895
Dr. Somerville's Crime. Arrowsmith, 1901
-Eric the Archer. Arnold, 1895
-The Reef of Gold. Arnold, 1894

HERVEY, MICHAEL. 1920- . Ref: CA.
All in Good Crime. Hampton, 1953
Appointment with Death. Newcoll, 1945
Better Luck Next Crime. Forsyte, 1945
The Body in the Drum Mystery. Modern, 1951
The Book of Master Crimes. Mitre, 1945
Brooklyn Angel. Hamilton Stafford, 1947 [NYC]
The Case of the Missing Hand. Hampton, 1945 (2 stories.)
Corpse Parade. Hampton, 1946
Creeps Medley. Hampton, 1946 ss, some criminous
Crime a la Carte. Hampton, 1953
Crime Medley. Hampton, 1945
Cut Price Murder. Everybody's, 1944
Dames Spell Trouble. Bear, 1944 ss
Dark Waterfront. Hamilton Stafford, 1947
Death at My Heels, and other stories. Mitre, 1945 ss, some criminous
Death Tolls the Bell. Mitre, 1944
The Devil and Miss Thrace, and other stories. Pan, 1945 ss
Dumb Witness. Hampton, 1946 ss
G Is for Ghoul. Hampton, 1946 ss
Ghost Voice. Hampton, 1946
Gold Digger, and fourteen other short stories. Alliance, 1945 ss
Horror Medley. Hampton, 1945 ss, some criminous
Imperfect Alibi. Mitre, 1944 ss
Insufficient Evidence. Century, 1946
Laughter in the Ranks. Alliance, 1945 ss
Make Mine Murder. Hampton, 1948 (1-act play.)
Murder at the Movies. Mitre, 1944 ss
Murder by Installment. Everybody's, 1944
Murder Medley. Hampton, 1945 ss
Murder Thy Neighbor. Hampton, 1946
No Crime Like the Present. Mitre, 1944
No Excuse for Murder. Hampton, 1946
No More Love. Hampton, 1945
No Peace for the Living. Hampton, 1947 (Play.)
The Queer Looking Box, and other stories. Everybody's, 1944 ss, some criminous
Save Your Pity. Mitre, 1943
The Silver Death. Hampton, 1944
Suspicion. Hampton, 1946 ss
Toughs Afloat. Alliance, 1946
Toughs Ashore. Alliance, 1947
Travel the Hard Way. Mitre, 1944

The Walking Dead. Hampton, 1949
Wanted: Dead or Alive. Hampton, 1948 (1-act play.)
Wide Boy! Hampton, 1945 ss
Wide Girl. Hampton, 1945

HERZOG, ARTHUR. 1927- . Ref: CA.
Aries Rising. Marek, 1980; Heinemann, 1981 [Carib.]

HERZOG, DOROTHY
Undercover Woman. Macaulay, 1937; Brown Watson, 1950 [NYC]

HESKY, OLGA. -1974. Ref: CA. SC: Insp. Tami Shimoni = TS.
The Different Night. Long, 1970; Random, 1971 TS [Isr.]
Life Sentence. Doubleday, 1972 [Eng.]
The Sequin Syndicate. Long, 1969; Dodd, 1969 TS [Tel Aviv]
The Serpent's Smile. Long, 1966; Dodd, 1967 TS [Tel Aviv]
Time for Treason. Long, 1967; Dodd, 1968 TS [Tel Aviv]

HESLOP, HAROLD. 1898- .
The Crime of Peter Ropner. Fortune, 1934

HESS, KAMELLE
Darkness at Indian Key. Manor, 1978
The Fallen Staircase. Manor, 1978
Shadows at Noon. Manor, 1978
Shadows of Fear. Manor, 1979
-Wild Wave. Manor, 1979

HESSE, ALICE
The Guests at the Villa. Exposition, 1977
Terror in Taormina. Exposition, 1978

HETH, EDWARD HARRIS. 1909-1963.
-Any Number Can Play. Harper, 1945. Also published as: The Big Bet. Bantam, 1948

HEWENS, FRANK E(DGAR). 1912- . Ref: CA.
The Murder of the Dainty-Footed Model. Macmillan, 1968

HEWITT, C. P. Pseudonym: Peter Twist, q.v.

HEWITT, E. L.
Dangerous Edge. Hutchinson, 1939

HEWITT, KATHLEEN (DOUGLAS). 1893- . Pseudonym: Dorothea Martin, q.v. Born in India of missionary parents; English author and playwright.
-Comedian. Nicholson, 1934
-Decoration. Nicholson, 1935
-Fetish. Elkin Mathews, 1933
-Go Find a Shadow. Jarrolds, 1937
-The Golden Milestone. Jarrolds, 1939
-Harmony in Autumn. Jarrolds, 1955
-The House by the Canal. Jarrolds, 1938
-Lady Gone Astray. Jarrolds, 1939
-Mardi. Douglas, 1932
The Mice Are Not Amused. Jarrolds, 1942; Mystery House, 1943
Murder in the Ballroom. Jarrolds, 1948
-No Time to Play. Jarrolds, 1945
-One Man's Woman. Jarrolds, 1954
-A Pattern in Yellow. Douglas, 1932
-Plenty Under the Counter. Jarrolds, 1943
-Return to the River. Jarrolds, 1936
Stand-In for Danger. Jarrolds, 1940
-Still the World Is Young. Jarrolds, 1951
-Strange Salvation. Elkin Mathews, 1934
-Thanks for the Apple. Jarrolds, 1947
-Three Rainbows. Jarrolds, 1952

HEWLETT, WILLIAM
The Breaking Point. Skeffington, 1936
-The Child at the Window. Secker, 1915
The Crimson Claw. Allan, 1936
-Introducing William Allison. Secker, 1916
-Is and Was. Skeffington, 1936
-The Pear-Tree. Skeffington, 1938
The Plot-Maker. Duckworth, 1917
-Simpson of Snells. Skeffington, 1918
-Telling the Truth. Secker, 1913
-Uncle's Advice. Secker, 1913
-White Stacks. Hurst, 1923
-Windswept Farm. Routledge, 1918

HEXHAM, LIONEL J. F. Pseudonym of Felix John Hamel.
Harry Roughton; or, Reminiscences of a Revenue Officer. Simpkin, 1859. Also published as by Felix John Hamel: Singer, 1882

HEXT, HARRINGTON. Pseudonym of Eden Phillpotts, 1862-1960, q.v.
The Monster. Macmillan, 1925

Number 87. Butterworth, 1922; Macmillan, 1922
The Thing at Their Heels. Butterworth, 1923; Macmillan, 1923
Who Killed Cock Robin?; see Who Killed Diana?
Who Killed Diana? Butterworth, 1924. U.S. title: Who Killed Cock Robin? Macmillan, 1924

HEYER, GEORGETTE. 1902-1974. Ref: All except MM. SC: Insp. Hemingway = H; Supt. Hannasyde (with Hemingway, as a sergeant, in a supporting role) = H*. Set: Eng.
Behold, Here's Poison! Hodder, 1936; Doubleday, 1936 H*
A Blunt Instrument. Hodder, 1938; Doubleday, 1938 H*
Death in the Stocks. Longmans, 1935. U.S. title: Merely Murder. Doubleday, 1935 H*
Detection Unlimited. Heinemann, 1953; Dutton, 1969 H
Duplicate Death. Heinemann, 1951; Dutton, 1969 H
Envious Casca. Hodder, 1941; Doubleday, 1941 H
Footsteps in the Dark. Longmans, 1932
Merely Murder; see Death in the Stocks
No Wind of Blame. Hodder, 1939; Doubleday, 1939 H
Penhallow. Heinemann, 1942; Doubleday, 1943
They Found Him Dead. Hodder, 1937; Doubleday, 1937 H*
The Unfinished Clue. Longmans, 1934; Doubleday, 1937
Why Shoot a Butler? Longmans, 1933; Doubleday, 1936

HEYES, DOUGLAS. ca.1921- . Born in L.A.; has written for stage and radio.
Goodbye Stranger; see The Kiss-Off
The Kiss-Off. Simon, 1951. British title: Goodbye Stranger. Redman, 1952 [L.A.]
The 12th of Never. Random, 1963; Boardman, 1964

HEYGATE, BARBARA
The Crime of Vera Seymour; see "Unless a Child Is Born—"
The Sabbath Slayer. Pearson, 1939
-Thou Shalt Not Kill. Pearson, 1937
-"Unless a Child Is Born—". Pearson, 1939. Also published as: The Crime of Vera Seymour. Pearson, 1940

HEYM, STEFAN. 1913- . Ref: CA.
Hostages. Putnam (NYC), 1942; Putnam (London), 1943 [Prague]

HEYMAN, EVAN LEE. Pseudonyms: Joy Ann Blackwood, Evelyne Hayworth, qq.v.
Cain's Hundred. Popular Library, 1961 (Novelization of the TV series.)
Dead Heat on a Merry-Go-Round. Avon, 1966 (Novelization of the movie.) [L.A.]
Miami Undercover. Popular Library, 1961 (Novelization of the TV series.) [Miami]
The Thomas Crown Affair. Avon, 1968; Hodder pb, 1968 (Novelization of the movie.) [Boston]

HEYWARD, DOROTHY [MRS. DuBOSE HEYWARD]. 1890-1961.
The Pulitzer Prize Murders. Farrar, 1932 [L.I.]

HIBBERT, ELEANOR ALICE BURFORD. 1906- . Pseudonyms: Philippa Carr, Elbur Ford, Victoria Holt, Kathleen Kellow, qq.v.

HICHENS, ROBERT (SMYTHE). 1864-1950. Ref: CC.
After the Verdict. Methuen, 1924; Doran, 1924
Doctor Artz. Hutchinson, 1929
The Paradine Case. Benn, 1933; Doubleday, 1933
The Power to Kill. Benn, 1934; Doubleday, 1934
Secret Information. Hurst, 1938; Doubleday, 1938
-The Sixth of October. Cassell, 1936; Doubleday, 1936
That Which Is Hidden. Cassell, 1939; Doubleday, 1940

HICKERSON, HAROLD. See: Maxwell Anderson, 1888-1959.

HICKEY, T(HEODOSIA) F(RANCES) W(YNNE)
The Corpse in the Church. Methuen, 1930
The Hand; or, Mystery at Number Ten. Heinemann, 1937
-The Unexpected Adventure. Heinemann, 1935

HICKMAN, HAL
    The Bachelor Party. Lippincott, 1977;
        H. Hamilton, 1977 [S. Afr.]
HICKMAN, J. M.
    Death on the Run. Brown Watson, 1954
    Missing Witness. Brown Watson, 1955
    Nine O'Clock Curtains. Brown Watson,
        1954
    Tide of Death. Brown Watson, 1954
HICKMAN, W(ILLIAM) T(HEODORE)
    The Nick of Time. Maxwell, 1887
HICKOK, FRANCES
    An Eye for an Eye. Hale, Cushman and
        Flint, 1929; Paul, 1930 [Midwest]
HIGGIN, L(OUIS)
    Lyona Grimswood, Spinster. Pearson,
        1900
HIGGINS, GEORGE V(INCENT). 1939-   .
        Ref: CA, TC.
    Cogan's Trade. Knopf, 1974; Secker,
        1974 [Boston]
    The Digger's Game. Knopf, 1973; Secker,
        1973 [Boston]
    -Dreamland. Little, 1977; Secker, 1977
    The Friends of Eddie Coyle. Knopf,
        1972; Secker, 1972 [Boston]
    The Judgment of Deke Hunter. Little,
        1976; Secker, 1976 [Boston]
    Kennedy for the Defense. Knopf, 1980;
        Secker, 1980 [Boston]
HIGGINS, JACK. Pseudonym of Harry Patter-
        son, 1929-   , q.v. Other pseudo-
        nyms: Martin Fallon, James Graham,
        Hugh Marlowe, qq.v. Note that numer-
        ous titles originally published under
        other bylines have later been re-
        printed as by Jack Higgins.
    Day of Judgement. Collins, 1978; Holt,
        1979 [Ger., 1963]
    The Eagle Has Landed. Collins, 1975;
        Holt, 1975 [Ger., 1943]
    East of Desolation. Hodder, 1968;
        Doubleday, 1969 [Green.]
    In the Hour Before Midnight. Hodder,
        1969; Doubleday, 1969. Also published
        as: The Sicilian Heritage. Lancer,
        1970 [Sic.]
    The Last Place God Made. Collins, 1971;
        Holt, 1972 [Brazil, 1930s]
    Night Judgment at Sinos. Hodder, 1970;
        Doubleday, 1971 [Greece]
    A Prayer for the Dying. Collins, 1973;
        Holt, 1974
    The Savage Day. Collins, 1972; Holt,
        1972 [Ire.]
    The Sicilian Heritage; see In the Hour
        Before Midnight
    Solo. Collins, 1980; Stein, 1980
    -Storm Warning. Collins, 1976; Holt,
        1976
HIGGINS, MARGARET
    The Changeling. Ace, 1973; Barker, 1974
        [Eng.]
    A Doctor for the Dead. Ace, 1974
    Unholy Sanctuary. Ace, 1971; Barker,
        1974 [Eng.]
    A Witch Alone. Ace, 1972; Barker, 1975
        [Eng.]
HIGGINSON, HAROLD WYNYARD. 1887-   .
    The Murder by the Arch. Crowell, 1931
        [NYC]
HIGH, BERNARD G(EORGE)
    Ambush. Brown, 1976 (1-act play.)
HIGHLAND, DORA. Pseudonym of Michael
        (Angelo) Avallone (Jr.),   ,
        q.v. Other pseudonyms: Nick Carter,
        Priscilla Dalton, Mark Dane, Jean-
        Anne de Pre, Stuart Jason, Steve
        Michaels, Dorothea Nile, Edwina
        Noone, Sidney Stuart, Max Walker,
        qq.v.
    Death is a Dark Man. Popular Library,
        1974 [Conn.]
    One Five Three Oakland Street. Popular
        Library, 1973 [N.Y.]
HIGHSMITH, (MARY) PATRICIA (PLAUGMAN).
        1921-   . Ref: CA, CC, EM, MC, TC.
        SC = Tom Ripley = TR.
    The Animal-Lover's Book of Beastly Mur-
        der. Heinemann, 1975 ss
    The Blunderer. Coward, 1954; Cresset,
        1956. Also published as: Lament for a
        Lover. Popular Library, 1946 [NYC]
    The Boy Who Followed Ripley. Lippin-
        cott, 1980; Heinemann, 1980 TR [Fr.]
    The Cry of the Owl. Harper, 1962;
        Heinemann, 1963 [Pa.]
    Deep Water. Harper, 1957; Heinemann,
        1958 [Mass.]
    A Dog's Ransom. Knopf, 1972; Heinemann,
        1972 [NYC]
    -Edith's Diary. Simon, 1977; Heinemann,
        1977
    Eleven; see The Snail-Watcher and other
        stories
    A Game for the Living. Harper, 1958;
        Heinemann, 1959 [Mex. City]
    The Glass Cell. Doubleday, 1964; Heine-
        mann, 1965 [N.Y.]
    Lament for a Lover; see The Blunderer
    Little Tales of Misogyny. Heinemann,
        1977 ss
    Ripley Under Ground. Doubleday, 1970;
        Heinemann, 1970 TR [Fr.]
    Ripley's Game. Knopf, 1974; Heinemann,
        1974 TR [Fr.]
    Slowly, Slowly in the Wind. Heinemann,
        1979 ss
    The Snail-Watcher and other stories.
        Doubleday, 1970. British title:
        Eleven. Heinemann, 1970 ss
    The Story-Teller. Doubleday, 1965. Bri-
        tish title: A Suspension of Mercy.
        Heinemann, 1965 [Eng.]
    Strangers on a Train. Harper, 1950;
        Cresset, 1950 [train]
    A Suspension of Mercy; see The Story-
        Teller
    The Talented Mr. Ripley. Coward, 1955;
        Cresset, 1957 TR [It.]
    This Sweet Sickness. Harper, 1960;
        Heinemann, 1961 [N.Y.]
    Those Who Walk Away. Doubleday, 1967;
        Heinemann, 1967 [Venice]
    The Tremor of Forgery. Doubleday, 1969;
        Heinemann, 1969
    The Two Faces of January. Doubleday,
        1964; Heinemann, 1964 [Athens,
        Crete]
HILAIRE, FRANK. Lives in Calif.
    Traficante. St. Martin's, 1980
HILARION. Pseudonym of Campbell MacKel-
        lar.
    Grafin Rimsky and other tales. Reming-
        ton, 1892 3 stories, 1 criminous
HILDICK, (EDMUND) WALLACE. 1925-   .
        Ref: CA, TC.
    Bracknell's Law. H. Hamilton, 1976;
        Harper, 1975 [U.S.]
    The Loop. H. Hamilton, 1977
    Vandals. H. Hamilton, 1977 [L.I.]
    The Weirdown Experiment. H. Hamilton,
        1976; Harper, 1976
HILL, ALBERT FAY. See: David Campbell
        Hill.
HILL, AMY HOSKIN
    Murder on the Mountain. Arcadia, 1961
        [Colo.]
HILL, ANDREA
    Counterfeit Heiress. Gresham, 1968
    Dangerous Sanctuary. Gresham, 1970
    Jewel Island. Gresham, 1967
    Lost Encounter. Gresham, 1966
    Night Hath Eyes. Hale, 1971
    Strange Nocturne. Hale, 1970
    Web of Obsession. Gresham, 1969
HILL, ARCHIE
    Cage of Shadows. Hutchinson, 1973
    -A Corridor of Mirrors. Hutchinson, 1975
HILL, BENETT
    Diamond Crime Detective. Warren, 1950
HILL, BRIAN MERRIKIN. 1896-   . Pseudo-
        nym: Marcus Magill, q.v.
HILL, CHRISTOPHER. 1928-   . Actor and
        writer in Australia and his native
        Eng.
    Jackdaw. Collins, 1975; Holt, 1976
        [Fr.]
    Scorpion. Collins, 1974; St. Martin's,
        1974
HILL, DAVID CAMPBELL and ALBERT FAY HILL
    The Deadly Messiah. Atheneum, 1976
        [Ky.]
HILL, FREDERICK TREVOR. 1866-1930.
    The Accomplice. Harper, 1905
    The Case and Exceptions. Stokes, 1900
        ss
    The Minority. Stokes, 1902; Richards,
        1902
    Tales Out of Court. Stokes, 1920 ss
    The Thirteenth Juror. Century, 1913
    The Web. Doubleday, 1903; Heinemann,
        1903
HILL, H. HAVERSTOCK. Pseudonym of J(ames)
        M(organ) Walsh, 1897-1952, q.v. Other
        pseudonyms: Stephen Maddock, George
        M. White, qq.v.
    -Anne of the Flying Gap. Hodder, 1926
    -Golden Harvest. Hodder, 1929
    -The Golden Isle. Hodder, 1928
    -Spoil of the Desert. Hodder, 1927

HILL, HARRY EGBERT. All titles below pub-
        lished by Amalgamated Press and fea-
        ture Sexton Blake.
    The Actor's Secret. 1923
    The Blackmailed Baronet. 1926. Re-
        printed as: The Mystery of the Black-
        mailed Baronet, as by Hylton Gregory.
        1937
    The Case of the Rajah's Son. 1922
    The Curse of Kali; see The Shrine of
        Kali
    The Golden Goddess. 1922
    The Great Museum Mystery. 1924
    The Hunchback of Hatton Garden! 1925
    The Idol's Eye. 1921
    In Darkest Madras. 1923
    The Loot of Nana Sahib. 1924
    The Mill Pond Mystery. 1922
    The Mystery of the Blackmailed Baronet;
        see The Blackmailed Baronet
    The Rajah of Ghanapore. 1922
    The Riddle of the Amber Room. 1927. Re-
        printed as: The Sign of the Black
        Feather, as by Hylton Gregory. 1939
    The Shrine of Kali. 1924. Reprinted as:
        The Curse of Kali, as by Hylton Greg-
        ory. 1935
    The Sign of the Black Feather; see The
        Riddle of the Amber Room
HILL, HEADON. Pseudonym of Francis Edward
        Grainger, 1857-1927. Ref: DD, EM. SC:
        Sebastian Zambra, in at least those
        marked SZ.
    Aboard the American Duchess. Putnam,
        1902 (British title?)
    The Avengers. Ward, 1906; Dodge, 1907
    The Broken Seal. Ward, 1917
    By a Hair's Breadth. Cassell, 1897;
        Dodd, 1897
    Caged!: The Romance of a Lunatic Asy-
        lum. Ward, 1900
    The Cliff-Path Mystery. Ward, 1913
    Clues from a Detective's Camera. Arrow-
        smith, 1893 ss SZ
    The Comlyn Alibi. Ward, 1915
    Coronation Mysteries and other stories.
        Digby, 1902 ss
    The Cottage in the Chime. Ward, 1913
    The Crimson Honeymoon. Ward, 1914
    The Divinations of Kala Persad and
        other stories. Ward, 1895 ss SZ
    The Duke Decides. Cassell, 1903; Wes-
        sels, 1903
    The Duplicate Duke. Ward, 1920
    The Embassy Case. Ward, 1915
    The Epsom Mystery: A Race with Ruin;
        see A Race with Ruin
    Foes of Justice. Ward, 1910. U.S.
        title: The Monksglade Mystery. Fenno,
        1910
    The Golden Temptress. Jenkins, 1924
    The Great Bluff. Ward, 1925
    The Green Shade. Ward, 1924
    Guile. Ward, 1920
    Guilty Gold. Pearson, 1896
    The Hate of Man. Cassell, 1908
    Her Grace at Bay. Cassell, 1906
    Her Splendid Sin. Ward, 1908
    The Hour-Glass Mystery. Ward, 1913
    The Jesmond Mystery. Ward, 1919
    The Kiss of the Enemy. Cassell, 1904
    Links in the Chain. Long, 1909
    The Mammoth Mansions Mystery. Ward,
        1926
    The Man from Egypt. Ward, 1917
    Millions of Mischief: The Story of a
        Great Secret. Ward, 1905; Trans-
        atlantic, 1904
    The Monksglade Mystery; see Foes of
        Justice
    My Lord the Felon. Ward, 1912
    The Narrowing Circle. Jenkins, 1924 SZ
    The One Who Saw. Cassell, 1905; Victor-
        ia, 1905
    The Peer and His Plunder. Ward, 1922
    The Peril of the Prince: A Romance of
        Modern Anarchism. Pearson, 1901
    Perils of the Red Box. Ward, 1904 ss
    The Plunder Ship. Pearson, 1900
    The Queen of Night. Ward, 1896
    A Race with Ruin. Ward, 1904. U.S.
        title: The Epsom Mystery: A Race with
        Ruin. Fenno, 1908
    Radford Shone. Ward, 1908 ss
    -The Rajah's Second Wife. Warwick, 1894
    The Red Rain Mystery. Ward, 1925
    A Rogue in Ambush. Ward, 1911
    Seaward for the Foe. Ward, 1903 (2
        novelets.)
    The Sentence of the Court. Pearson,
        1901
    The Shadow of the Bear. Pearson, 1899
    Sir Vincent's Patient. Ward, 1914
    The Skeleton Finger. Ward, 1924
    Spectre Gold: A Romance of the Klon-
        dyke. Cassell, 1898 [Can.]
    The Spies of the Wight. Pearson, 1899
    The Split Peas. Paul, 1914
    Spriggs the Cracksman. Ogilvie, 1895
        (British title?)
    Storm-Wrack. Paul, 1926
    The Thread of Proof. Paul, 1912 ss

Tracked Down. Pearson, 1902
A Traitor's Wooing. Ward, 1909; Kearney, 1909
Troubled Waters. Paul, 1909
Unmasked at Last. Ward, 1906; Fenno, 1907
Zambra the Detective: Some Clues from His Notebook. Chatto, 1894 ss SZ
The Zone of Fire. Pearson, 1897

HILL, JOHN
Treason-Felony. Chatto, 1892

HILL, JOHN
The Dope Ring. Methuen, 1931

HILL, JOHN A(LEXANDER). 1858-1916.
Stories of the Railroad. Doubleday, 1899 ss, some criminous

HILL, K(ATE) F. Pseudonym of Mrs. Lucy A. Baer, ca.1844-1925.
The Mysterious Case; or, Tracing a Crime. Street, 1889; Ward, 1890
The Mystery of a Madstone; or, The Commercial Traveller Detective. Street, 1889
Sarah Brown, Detective; or, The Mystery of the Pavilion. Westbrook, 19??
The Twin Detectives; or, The Robbers of the Tomb. Street, 1888

HILL, KATHARINE. SC: Lorna Donahue, in both titles, both set in Conn.
Case for Equity. Dutton, 1945
Case of the Absent Corpse. Mystery Novel Classic, 194? (Retitled reprint of ?)
Dear Dead Mother-in-Law. Dutton, 1944

HILL, LAWRENCE. SC: Insp. Macsporran, in both titles.
Corpse Without Boots. Collins, 1940
Dagger Drawn. Collins, 1939 [Scot.]

HILL, MONICA. Pseudonym of Agnes Monica Baker, 1899-   .
Smooth Runs the Water. Hutchinson, 1936

HILL, NEWTON
The Body Drank Coffee. Hale, 1951

HILL, PAMELA. 1920-   . Ref: CA.
The Devil of Aske. Hodder, 1972; St. Martin's, 1973 [Eng., 1700s]
The Heatherton Heritage; see The Incumbent
The Incumbent. Hodder, 1974. U.S. title: The Heatherton Heritage. St. Martin's, 1976
The Malvie Inheritance. Hodder, 1973; St. Martin's, 1974
Whitton's Folly. Hodder, 1975; St. Martin's, 1975 [Scot.]

HILL, PETER. BBC TV scriptwriter; formerly a police officer for some years. SC: Commander Allan Dice = AD; Chief Insp. Robert Staunton = RS. Set: Eng.
The Enthusiast. Davies, 1978; Houghton, 1979 RS [Wales]
The Fanatics. Davies, 1977; Scribner, 1978 AD
The Hunters. Davies, 1976; Scribner, 1976 RS
The Liars. Davies, 1977; Houghton, 1978 RS
The Savages. Heinemann, 1980 RS
The Washermen. Davies, 1979 AD

HILL, R. LANCE. 1943-   . Ref: CA.
The Evil That Men Do. Times, 1978; Hodder, 1979 [Guat.]
King of White Lady. Putnam, 1975; Souvenir, 1976
Nails. Lester & Orpen (Toronto), 1974; Souvenir, 1975

HILL, REGINALD (CHARLES). 1936-   .
Ref: CA, TC. Pseudonym: Patrick Ruell, q.v. SC: Supt. Andrew Dalziel, in at least those marked AD. Set: Eng.
An Advancement of Learning. Collins, 1971 AD [acad.]
Another Death in Venice. Collins, 1976 [Venice]
An April Shroud. Collins, 1975
A Clubbable Woman. Collins, 1970 AD
A Fairly Dangerous Thing. Collins, 1972
Fell of Dark. Collins, 1971 AD
A Killing Kindness. Collins, 1980; Pantheon, 1981 AD
Pascoe's Ghost and Other Brief Chronicles of Crime. Collins, 1979 ss
A Pinch of Snuff. Collins, 1978; Harper, 1978 AD
Ruling Passion. Collins, 1973; Harper, 1977 AD
The Spy's Wife. Collins, 1980; Pantheon, 1980
A Very Good Hater. Collins, 1974

HILL, SAM
The Nodding Towers. Vantage, 1966

HILL, SUSAN (ELIZABETH). 1942-   .
Ref: CA.
I'm King of the Castle. H. Hamilton, 1970; Viking, 1970

HILL, VINCENT
Amber to Red. Hodder, 1952
The Cunning Enemy. Hodder, 1957
Lady from Hamburg. Hodder, 1954
The Soft Guy. Hodder, 1953

HILL, WARREN
The Crystal Skull. Jarrolds, 1930
That Which Is Crooked. Jarrolds, 1930
The Thumb-Mark. Jarrolds, 1929
Yellow Will Out! Jarrolds, 1929

HILL, WELDON. Pseudonym of William Ralph Scott, 1918-   . Ref: CA.
A Man Could Get Killed That Way. McKay, 1967

HILLARY, MAX
A Deadly Errand; see Hunted Down
Hunted Down. Ward, 1885; Marquis, 1885. Also published as: A Deadly Errand. Ward, 1886
-Once for All. Low, 1885

HILLCOAT, CHARLES H.
A Mystery of the Suez Canal. Bryce, 1896

HILLDRUP, ROBERT P.
To Die for a Golden Leaf. Manor, 1980 [South]

HILLER, GUY PEMBER. See: Guy Pember-Hiller.

HILLERMAN, TONY [ANTHONY GROVE HILLERMAN]. 1925-   . Ref: CA, CC, TC. SC: Joe Leaphorn - JL.
The Blessing Way. Harper, 1970; Macmillan (London), 1970 JL [Ariz.]
The Fly on the Wall. Harper, 1971
Dance Hall of the Dead. Harper, 1973 JL [N. Mex.]
Listening Woman. Harper, 1978; Macmillan (London), 1979 JL [Ariz.]
People of Darkness. Harper, 1980 [N. Mex.]

HILLGARTH, ALAN (HUGH). 1898-   .
Change for Heaven. Chapman, 1929. U.S. title: What Price Paradise? Houghton, 1929 [Fla.]
-Davy Jones. Nicholson, 1936
The Passionate Trail. Hutchinson, 1925
-The Prince and the Perjurer. Chapman, 1924
-The War Maker. Nelson, 1926
What Price Paradise?; see Change for Heaven

HILLIARD, A(LEC) R(OWLEY). 1908-   .
SC: Judge Manfred, in both titles.
Justice Be Damned. Farrar, 1941; Cassell, 1944
Outlaw Island. Farrar, 1942; Cassell, 1947

HILLIARD, JAN. Pseudonym of Hilda Kay Grant, 1910-   . Ref: CA.
Morgan's Castle. Abelard, 1964 [N.Y.]

HILLIARD, MAURICE. 1931-   . Born in Eng.; TV producer in Australia before returning to Eng.
The Witchfinder. Heinemann, 1974; Coward, 1974

HILLIERS, ASHTON. Pseudonym of Henry Marriage Wallis.
The Walbury Case. Methuen, 1923

HILLMAN, RALF RIDGWAY.   -1940.
The Houseboat Enigma. Dorrance, 1937

HILLS, WILLIAM MURRAY
Out of the East. Heath Cranton, 1915

HILLYARD, WILLIAM HEARD
Recollections of a Physician; or, Episodes of Life During Thirty Years of Practice. Ward, 1861 ss
Reginald Vernon; or, The Fatal Likeness. Routledge, 1888

HILTON, CHRISTOPHER
A Cemetery in Munich. Hale, 1979
Dead End. Hale, 1978

HILTON, JAMES. 1900-1954. Pseudonym: Glen Trevor, q.v.

HILTON, JOHN BUXTON. 1921-   . Ref: CA, CC, TC. SC: Insp. Thomas Brunt = TB; Supt. Simon Kenworthy = SK. Set: Eng.
The Anathema Stone. Collins, 1980; St. Martin's, 1980 SK
Dead-Nettle. Macmillan (London), 1977; St. Martin's, 1977 TB [1904, Eng.]
Death in Midwinter. Cassell, 1969; Walker, 1969 SK
Death of an Alderman. Cassell, 1968; Walker, 1968 SK
Gamekeeper's Gallows. Macmillan (London), 1976; St. Martin's, 1977 TB [1877, Eng.]
Hangman's Tide. Macmillan (London), 1975; St. Martin's, 1975 SK
No Birds Sang. Macmillan (London), 1975; St. Martin's, 1978 SK
Rescue from the Rose. Macmillan (London), 1976; St. Martin's, 1976 TB [1911, Eng.]
Some Run Crooked. Macmillan (London), 1978; St. Martin's, 1978 SK [1958, Eng.]

HILTON, JOHN DEANE. 1855-   . Pseudonym: John Cleveland, q.v.

HILTON, JOSEPH
-Angels in the Gutter. GM, 1955
-Beyond Mombasa. Avon, 1957
Cry Baby Killer. Avon, 1958 (Novelization of the movie.)
Ship of the Damned. Lancer, 1972 [ship]
-That French Girl. GM, 1953

HILTON, JOSEPH. SC: Bart Gould = BG; series continued under Joseph Milton byline, q.v.
President's Agent. Lancer, 1963 BG [Cent. Am.]

HIMES, CHESTER (BOMAR). 1909-   . Ref: CA, MC, TC. SC: Grave Digger Jones & Coffin Ed Johnson = J&J. Set: NYC, all titles.
All Shot Up. Avon, 1960; Panther, 1969 J&J
The Big Gold Dream. Avon, 1960; Panther, 1968 J&J
Blind Man with a Pistol. Morrow, 1969; Hodder, 1969. Also published as: Hot Day Hot Night. Dell, 1970 J&J
Come Back, Charleston Blue; see The Heat's On
Cotton Comes to Harlem. Putnam, 1965; Muller, 1965 J&J
The Crazy Kill. Avon, 1959; Panther, 1968 J&J
For Love of Imabelle. GM, 1957. Also published as: A Rage in Harlem. Avon, 1965; Panther, 1969 J&J
The Heat's On. Putnam, 1966; Muller, 1966. Also published as: Come Back, Charleston Blue. Berkley, 1970 J&J
Hot Day Hot Night; see Blind Man with a Pistol
A Rage in Harlem; see For Love of Imabelle
The Real Cool Killers. Avon, 1959; Panther, 1969 J&J
Run Man Run. Putnam, 1966; Muller, 1967

HIMMEL, RICHARD. Born and living in Chicago; interior designer and painter. SC: Johnny Maguire, in at least those marked JM.
Beyond Desire. GM, 1952 [Chi.]
The Chinese Keyhole. GM, 1951; Jenkins, 1968 JM
Cry of the Flesh. GM, 1955 JM
I Have Gloria Kirby. GM, 1951; Fawcett (London), 1953 JM [Chi.]
I'll Find You. GM, 1950; Fawcett (London), 1958. Also published as: It's Murder, Maguire. Jenkins, 1962 JM [Fla.]
It's Murder, Maguire; see I'll Find You
Lions at Night. Delacorte, 1979
The Name's Maguire. Jenkins, 1963 JM (U.S. title?)
The Rich and the Damned. GM, 1958; Fawcett (London), 1960 JM [Chi.]
The Shame. Avon, 1959
The Sharp Edge. GM, 1952
The Twenty-Third Web. Random, 1977 [Chi.]
Two Deaths Must Die. GM, 1954; Red Seal, 1957 JM [Calif.]

HINCKLEY, JULIAN. 1905-   .
Murder by Schedule. Golden Willow, 1946

HINCKS, CYRIL MALCOLM. 1881-1954.
The Throne of Peril. Amalgamated Press, 1930 (Sexton Blake)

HIND, C(HARLES) LEWIS. 1862-1927.
-The Enchanted Stone. Black, 1898; Dodd, 1899

HINDE, THOMAS. Pseudonym of Sir Thomas Wiles Chitty, 1926-   . Ref: CA.
Agent. Hodder, 1974
Bird. Hodder, 1970

The Day the Call Came. Hodder, 1964;
Vanguard, 1965
Games of Chance. Hodder, 1965; Vanguard, 1967

HINDS, ROY W.
The Man Called Eighty-Eight. McBride, 1930
The Treasure of Caricar. Altemus, 1927; Long, 1930
The Tunnel to Doom. Chelsea, 1927; Long, 1929 [N.W.]

HINE, AL. 1915- . Ref: CA. Pseudonym: Nick Carter, q.v.
Juggernaut. Bantam, 1974; Corgi, 1974 (Novelization of the movie.)

HINES, JEANNE
The Keys to Queenscourt. Popular Library, 1976
The Legend of Witchwynd. Popular Library, 1976 [New Or.]
Scarecrow House. Popular Library, 1976
The Slashed Portrait. Dell, 1973 [South]
Talons of the Hawk. Dell, 1975 [Mex.]
The Third Wife. Popular Library, 1977 [Mex.]

HINKEL, M. L.
Edge of Despair. Manor, 1978

HINKEMEYER, MICHAEL T(HOMAS). 1940- . Ref: CA.
The Creator. Pinnacle, 1978
The Dark Below. GM, 1974. Also published as: Sea Cliff. PB, 1979 [L.I.]
The Fields of Eden. Putnam, 1977; Futura, 1980 [Minn.]
Sea Cliff; see The Dark Below
Summer Solstice. Berkley hb, 1976; Futura, 1980 [Minn.]

HINKLE, VERNON
Music to Murder By. Belmont, 1978

HINTZE, NAOMI A(GANS). 1909- . Ref: CA.
Aloha Means Goodbye. Random, 1972. British title: Hawaii for Danger. Hale, 1973 [Haw.]
Cry Witch. Random, 1975; Collins, 1976 [Maj.]
Hawaii for Danger; see Aloha Means Goodbye
The House with the Watching Eyes; see You'll Like My Mother
Listen, Please Listen. Random, 1973; Hale, 1975 [Conn.]
The Stone Carnation. Random, 1971; Hale, 1973 [Va.]
You'll Like My Mother. Putnam, 1969. British title: The House with the Watching Eyes. Hale, 1970 [Ohio]

HINXMAN, MARGARET
End of a Good Woman. Collins, 1976
One-Way Cemetery. Collins, 1977

HIPKINS, CHARLES HAMMOND. 1893- . Pseudonym: Carl Talbot, q.v.

HIRAI, TARO. 1894- . Pseudonym: Edogawa Rampo, q.v.

HIRD, FRANK. 1873-
The Bannantyne Sapphires. Paul, 1930
-Chained. Chapman, 1927
Clipped Hedges. Paul, 1932
The Deeper Stain. Bell, 1909
-The Fourth Road. Paul, 1934
The Golden Crystal. Paul, 1933
-King Fritz's A.D.C. Bell, 1901
The Lustre Jug. Paul, 1931
The Secret Terror. Nash, 1926

HIRSCH, LEE. Pseudonym of Leon David Hirsch, 1881- . New Jersey newspaperman; city clerk in Trenton for 15 years.
Murder Steals the Show. Fell, 1946 [N.J.]

HIRSCH, LEON DAVID. 1881- . Pseudonym: Lee Hirsch, q.v.

HIRSCHBERG, CORNELIUS. 1901- . Ref: CA, CC, TC.
Florentine Finish. Harper, 1963; Gollancz, 1964 [NYC]

HIRSCHFELD, BURT. 1923- .
Bonnie and Clyde. Lancer, 1967; Hodder pb, 1967 (Novelization of the movie.) [1932, S.W.]
"Father Pig." Arbor, 1972; Allen, 1977
Gas. Curtis, 1970 (Novelization of the movie.)
Key West. Morrow, 1979; Corgi, 1980 [Fla.]
The Masters Affair. Arbor, 1971; Allen, 1973
Provincetown. Brodart, 1966; Allen, 1978
Secrets. Simon, 1975; Allen, 1976 [N.Y.]

HIRSCHHORN, RICHARD (CLARK). 1933- .
Ref: CA.
-A Pride of Healers. Morrow, 1977 [Boston]
Target Mayflower. Harcourt, 1977. British title: The Von Eyssen Deception. Joseph, 1978 [1944, New Eng.]
The Von Eyssen Deception; see Target Mayflower

HISCOCK, LESLIE. 1902- . Pseudonym: Patrick Marsh, q.v.

HISCOCK, ROBIN. 1929- .
The Killer Wind. Barker, 1958
The Last Run South. Longmans, 1956; Knopf, 1958
The Send-Off. Heinemann, 1967

HISCOTT, LESLIE
The Bishop's Move. Macdonald, 1961
The Margravine. Macdonald, 1966

HITCHCOCK, ALFRED (JOSEPH). 1899-1980.
Ref: EM, MP.
Rope. Dell, 1948 (Novelization, actually written by Don Ward, 1911- , q.v., of the movie directed by Hitchcock and based on the play by Patrick Hamilton, 1904-1962, q.v.) [NYC]

HITCHCOCK, RAYMOND (JOHN). 1922- .
Ref: CA.
Attack the Lusitania! Joseph, 1979; St. Martin's, 1980 [1915]
The Canaris Legacy; see Sea Wrack
Sea Wrack. Joseph, 1980. U.S. title: The Canaris Legacy. St. Martin's, 1980 [1940, Fr.]

HITCHENS, (HU)BERT (ALLEN) and (JULIA CLARA CATHERINE) DOLORES (BIRK OLSEN) HITCHENS, 1907-1973, q.v. Pseudonyms of Dolores Hitchens: Dolan Birkley, Noel Burke, D. B. Olsen, qq.v. Ref: CC. SC: John Farrel = JF; Collins & McKechnie = C&M.
End of the Line. Doubleday, 1957; Boardman, 1958 JF [Calif.]
F.O.B. Murder. Doubleday, 1955; Boardman, 1957 C&M [L.A.]
The Grudge. Doubleday, 1963; Boardman, 1964 JF [Calif.]
The Man Who Followed Women. Doubleday, 1959; Boardman, 1960 C&M [Calif.]
One-Way Ticket. Doubleday, 1956; Boardman, 1958 [L.A.]

HITCHENS, (JULIA CLARA CATHERINE) DOLORES (BIRK OLSEN). 1907-1973. See also: (Hu)Bert (Allen) Hitchens. Pseudonyms: Dolan Birkley, Noel Burke, D. B. Olsen, qq.v. Ref: CA, CC, TC. SC: Jim Sader, in at least those marked JS.
The Abductor. Simon, 1962; Boardman, 1962 [Calif.]
The Bank with the Bamboo Door. Simon, 1965; Boardman, 1965 [Calif.]
The Baxter Letters. Putnam, 1971; Hale, 1973 [NYC]
Beat Back the Tide. Doubleday, 1954; Macdonald, 1955. Also published as: The Fatal Affair. Bestseller, 1956, abridged [Calif.]
Cabin of Fear; see Postscript to Nightmare
A Collection of Strangers. Putnam, 1969; Macdonald, 1971 [Calif.]
The Fatal Flirt; see Beat Back the Tide
Fools' Gold. Doubleday, 1958; Boardman, 1958 [L.A.]
Footsteps in the Night. Doubleday, 1961; Boardman, 1961 [Calif.]
In a House Unknown. Doubleday, 1973; Hale, 1974 [La.]
The Man Who Cried All the Way Home. Simon, 1966; Hale, 1967 [Calif.]
Nets to Catch the Wind. Doubleday, 1952. Also published as: Widows Won't Wait. Dell, 1954 [Calif.]
Postscript to Nightmare. Putnam, 1967. British title: Cabin of Fear. Joseph, 1968 [Calif.]
Sleep with Slander. Doubleday, 1960; Boardman, 1961 JS [L.A.]
Sleep with Strangers. Doubleday, 1955; Macdonald, 1956 JS [L.A.]
Stairway to an Empty Room. Doubleday, 1951 [L.A.]
Terror Lurks in Darkness. Doubleday, 1953 [Calif.]
The Watcher. Doubleday, 1959; Boardman, 1959 [Calif.]
Widows Won't Wait; see Nets to Catch the Wind

HITTLEMAN, CARL K.
36 Hours. Popular Library, 1965 (Novelization of the movie.) [Ger.]

HIVELY, MILDRED ENGLISH
The Moday Mystery. Vantage, 1966

HJORTSBERG, WILLIAM (REINHOLD). 1941- . Ref: CA.
Falling Angel. Harcourt, 1978; Hutchinson, 1979 [NYC]

HOAR, PETER
Murder at Midnight. French (London), 1961 (3-act play based on "Design for Murder" by George Batson, 1918-1977, q.v.)

HOARE, DOUGLAS. See: Percy Colson, 1873- .

HOARE, HUGH ALAN
Now and for Ever. Hale, 1973

HOBART, DONALD BAYNE
The Adventure Trail. Nelson, 1929 (U.S. title?)
The Cell Murder Mystery. Fiction League, 1931
The Clue of the Leather Noose. Whitman, 1929 [N.J.]
Double Shuffle. Clode, 1928
Homicide Honeymoon. Arcadia, 1959
Hunchback House. Whitman, 1929

HOBART, ROBERTSON. Pseudonym of Norman Lee, 1905-1962, q.v. Other pseudonyms: Raymond Armstrong, Mark Corrigan, qq.v. SC: Grant Vickary, in at least those marked GV.
Blood on the Lake. Hale, 1961 [Australia]
The Case of the Shaven Blonde. Hale, 1959 GV
Dangerous Cargoes. Hale, 1960 GV [Australia]
Death of a Love. Hale, 1961

HOBBS, MARC J.
The Memoirs of J. (Paddy) MacDowell. Vantage, 1970

HOBBS, ROE R(AYMOND). 1871-1933.
-The Gates of Flame. Neale, 1908

HOBDAY, WILLIAM ALFRED
-Accessory After the Fact. Clark, 1911

HOBHOUSE, ADAM
The Hangover Murders. Knopf, 1935 [L.I.]

HOBHOUSE, CHRISTINA. 1941- . Ref: CA.
A Well-Told Lie. Macmillan (London), 1972; Knopf, 1973

HOBSON, CORALIE VON WERNER. 1891- .
Pseudonym: Sarah Salt, q.v.

HOBSON, FRANCIS. Ref: CC.
Death on a Back Bench. Eyre, 1959; Harper, 1959

HOBSON, HANK. Pseudonym of Harry Hobson, 1908- . Other pseudonym: Hank Janson, q.v. Ref: CA, CC. SC: Brad Ford, in all titles. Set: Eng.
Beyond Tolerance. Cassell, 1960
The Big Twist. Cassell, 1959
Death Makes a Claim. Cassell, 1958
The Gallant Affair. Cassell, 1957
The Mission House Murder. Cassell, 1959

HOBSON, HARRY. 1908- . Pseudonyms: Hank Hobson, Hank Janson, qq.v.

HOBSON, POLLY. Pseudonym of Julie Rendel Evans, 1913- . Ref: CA, CC. SC: Insp. Basil, in at least those marked B. Set: Eng.
Murder Won't Out. Jenkins, 1964 B
The Mystery House. Benn, 1963
A Terrible Thing Has Happened to Miss Dupont; see Titty's Dead
The Three Graces. Constable, 1970; British Book Centre, 1971 B
Titty's Dead. Constable, 1968. U.S. title: A Terrible Thing Has Happened to Miss Dupont. McCall, 1970 B

HOCH, EDWARD D(ENTINGER). 1930- . See also: Ellery Queen. Ref: CA, EM, TC. SC: Simon Ark = SA; Carl Crader and Earl Jazine = C&J; Nick Velvet = NV.
City of Brass, and other Simon Ark stories. Leisure, 1971 SA ss [N.Y.]
The Fellowship of the Hand. Walker, 1973; Hale, 1976 C&J
The Frankenstein Factory. Warner, 1975; Hale, 1976 C&J [2100s]

The Judges of Hades, and other Simon
  Ark stories. Leisure, 1971 ss SA
The Shattered Raven. Lancer, 1969;
  Hale, 1970 [NYC]
The Spy and the Thief. Davis pb, 1971
  ss, half about NV
The Thefts of Nick Velvet. Mysterious
  Press, 1978 ss NV
The Transvection Machine. Walker, 1971-
  Hale, 1974 C&J [2100s]

HOCHSTEIN, PETER
  The Fatal Fetish. Berkley, 1977 [NYC]

HOCKER, GEORG. 1860-   .
  The Tell-Tale Watch. Bonners, 1895
    (Translation of "Der Lebende Hat
    Recht.")

HOCKING ANNE. Pseudonym of Mona (Naomi
    Anne) Messer, 189?-   , q.v. SC:
    Insp. William Austen, in at least
    those marked WA. Set: Eng.
  All My Pretty Chickens. (Publisher and
    date unknown.) U.S. title: Death
    Loves a Shining Mark. Doubleday, 1943
    WA [Cairo]
  And No One Wept. Allen, 1954 WA
  As I Was Going to St. Ives. Paul, 1937
  At "The Cedars". Bles, 1949 WA
  The Best Laid Plans. Bles, 1952;
    Doubleday, 1950 WA
  Candidates for Murder. Long, 1961 WA
  Cat's Paw. Paul, 1933
  Deadly Is the Evil Tongue; see Old Mrs.
    Fitzgerald
  Death Among the Tulips. Allen, 1953 WA
  Death at the Wedding. Bles, 1946 WA
  Death Disturbs Mr. Jefferson. Bles,
    1951; Doubleday, 1950 WA
  Death Duel. Paul, 1933
  Death Loves a Shining Mark; see All My
    Pretty Chickens
  Epitaph for a Nurse. Allen, 1958. U.S.
    title: A Victim Must Be Found.
    Doubleday, 1959 WA
  The Evil That Men Do. Allen, 1953 WA
  The Finishing Touch; see Prussian Blue
  He Had to Die. Long, 1946 WA
  The House of En-Dor. Paul, 1936
  The Hunt Is Up. Paul, 1934
  Ill Deeds Done. Bles, 1938
  Killing Kin; see Mediterranean Murder
  The Little Victims Play. Bles, 1938
  Mediterranean Murder. Evans, 1951. U.S.
    title: Killing Kin. Doubleday, 1951
    WA [Sp., ship]
  Miss Milverton. Bles, 1941. U.S.
    title: Poison Is a Bitter Brew.
    Doubleday, 1942 WA
  Murder at Mid-Day. Allen, 1956 WA
  Murder Cries Out. Long, 1968 (Com-
    pleted by Evelyn Healey, q.v.) WA
  Night's Candles. Bles, 1941 [Cyprus]
  Nile Green. Bles, 1943 WA [Cairo]
  Old Mrs. Fitzgerald. Bles, 1939. U.S.
    title: Deadly Is the Evil Tongue.
    Doubleday, 1940 WA
  One Shall Be Taken. Bles, 1942 WA
  Poison in Paradise. Allen, 1955;
    Doubleday, 1955 WA
  Poison Is a Bitter Brew; see Miss Mil-
    verton
  Poisoned Chalice. Long, 1959 WA
  Prussian Blue. Bles, 1947. U.S. title:
    The Finishing Touch. Doubleday, 1948
    WA
  A Reason for Murder. Allen, 1955 WA
  Relative Murder. Allen, 1957 WA
  The Simple Way of Poison. Allen, 1957;
    Washburn, 1957 WA
  Six Green Bottles. Bles, 1943 WA
  So Many Doors. Bles, 1939 [Cyprus]
  Stranglehold. Paul, 1936
  There's Death in the Cup. Evans, 1952
  The Thin-Spun Thread. Long, 1960 WA
  To Cease Upon the Midnight. Long, 1959
    WA
  A Victim Must Be Found; see Epitaph for
    a Nurse
  The Vultures Gather. Bles, 1945 WA
  Walk into My Parlour. Paul, 1934
  What a Tangled Web. Paul, 1937
  The Wicked Flee. Bles, 1940 WA
  Without the Option. Paul, 1935

HOCKING, JOSEPH. 1860-1937.
  -"And Shall Trelawney Die?" Bowden, 1897
  The Case of Miss Dunstable. Hodder,
    1923
  The Secret of Trescobell. Ward, 1931
  The Sign of the Triangle. Ward, 1929
  -The Weapons of Mystery. Routledge, 1890

HOCKING, MARY (EUNICE). 1921-   . Ref:
    CA.
  Ask No Question. Chatto, 1967; Morrow,
    1967 [Switz.]
  The Bright Day. Chatto, 1975

HOCKING, SILAS (KITTO). 1850-1935.
  Adventures of Latimer Field, Curate.
    Warne, 1903 ss
  -The Beautiful Alien. Low, 1916
  Gripped. Warne, 1902
  His Own Accuser. Low, 1917
  -The Mystery Man. Low, 1930
  The Scarlet Clue. Warne, 1904
  -The Sinister Shadow. Low, 1926

HODDER, ALFRED. 1866-1907. Pseudonym:
    Francis Walton. See: Josiah Flynt.

HODDER, (WILLIAM) REGINALD. See also:
    R. Andom; and: Edgar Turner.
  -The Doubting of Joseph Brereton. Ward
    1903
  -Vampire. Rider, 1913

HODDER-WILLIAMS, (JOHN) CHRISTOPHER
    (GLAZEBROOK). 1926-   . Pseudonym:
    James Brogan, q.v. Ref: CA. Set: Eng
  Chain Reaction. Hodder, 1959; Double-
    day, 1959
  -The Egg-Shaped Thing. Hodder, 1967
  Final Approach. Hodder, 1960; Double-
    day, 1960
  The Higher They Fly. Hodder, 1963;
    Putnam, 1964
  -The Main Experiment. Hodder, 1964;
    Putnam, 1965
  -98.4. Hodder, 1969
  Turbulence. Hodder, 1961

HODDINOTT, DEREK
  Jigsaw. New Playwrights, 1975 (2-act
    play.)
  Murder in Style. New Playwrights, 1980
    (Play.)

HODEL, MICHAEL P. and SEAN M. WRIGHT.
    Hodel is a radio writer and news di-
    rector. Wright is a Sherlockian and
    lectures on the subject around the
    U.S.
  Enter the Lion. Hawthorn, 1979; Dent,
    1980 (Mycroft—and Sherlock—
    Holmes.) [1875, Eng.]

HODGE, CHARLES
  -The House of the Winds. Faber, 1948
  -The Raven's Causeway. Faber, 1946

HODGE, JANE AIKEN. 1917-   . Ref: CA.
  The Adventurers. Doubleday, 1965;
    Hodder, 1966
  Greek Wedding. Doubleday, 1970; Hodder,
    1970
  Here Comes a Candle. Doubleday, 1967;
    Hodder, 1967. Also published as: The
    Master of Penrose. Dell, 1968
    [Mass., 1812]
  Last Act. Coward, 1979; Hodder, 1979
  Marry in Haste. Doubleday, 1970; Hod-
    der, 1969
  The Master of Penrose; see Here Comes
    Candle
  Maulever Hall. Doubleday, 1964; Hale,
    1964 [Eng., past]
  One Way to Venice. Coward, 1975; Hod-
    der, 1974 [Venice]
  Savannah Purchase. Doubleday, 1971;
    Hodder, 1971
  Strangers in Company. Coward, 1973;
    Hodder, 1973 [Greece]
  Watch the Wall, My Darling. Doubleday
    1966; Hodder, 1967
  The Winding Stair. Doubleday, 1969;
    Hodder, 1968 [1806, Port.]

HODGES, A. NOEL
  The Bancaster Mystery. Eyre, 1932

HODGES, ARTHUR. 1864-1949.
  -Along the Road. Butterworth, 1936
  The Body in the Car. Butterworth, 1932
    [Paris]
  The Embassy Murder. Butterworth, 1931
    [Paris]
  -The Glittering Hour. Hurst, 1933
  -Madame Lucien. Butterworth, 1930
  -The Man of Substance. Hurst, 1931
  -The Multi-Millionaire. Butterworth,
    1937

HODGES, CARL G. 1902-1964. Ref: CA.
  Crime on My Hands. Suspense, 1951
  Murder by the Pack. Ace, 1953 [Chi.]
  Naked Villainy. Farrell, 1951 [Chi.]

HODGES, DORIS MARJORIE. 1915-   . Pseu-
    donym: Charlotte Hunt, q.v.

HODGES, HORACE, 1865-   , and T. WIGNEY
    PERCYVAL
  "Grumpy." French (NYC & London), 1921
    (4-act play.)

HODGKIN, M(ARION DeKAY) R(OUS). 1917-   .
    Ref: CC.
  Dead Indeed. Gollancz, 1955; Macmillan,
    1956 [NYC]

Student Body. Gollancz, 1950; Scribner,
  1949 [acad.]

HODGKINSON, IVAN TATTERSALL. 1891-   .
  Pseudonym: Ivan Tattersall, q.v.

HODGSON, WILLIAM HOPE. 1877-1918. Ref:
    EM, TC.
  Captain Gault. Nash, 1917; McBride,
    1918 ss
  Carnacki, the Ghost Finder. Nash, 1913;
    Mycroft, 1947 ss (The U.S. edition
    contains 3 ss not in the British.)
  Carnacki, the Ghost Finder, and a Poem.
    Reynolds, 1910 (14 pp.)

HOFFE, ARTHUR
  Something Evil. Avon, 1968

HOFFECKER, DOUGLAS M(EADE). Graduate of
    Yale and NYC businessman.
  The Wall Street Murders. Fortuny's,
    1936 [NYC]

HOFFENBERG, JACK. 1906-1977. Ref: CA.
  The Desperate Adversaries. Crown, 1975
    [L.A.]
  17 Ben Gurion. Putnam, 1977 [Isr.]

HOFFMAN, JAMES A.
  A Good Day to Die. Milestone, 1954

HOFFMAN, KURT. Pseudonym.
  Blackmarket Brains. Transport, ca.1941

HOFFMAN, LOUISE
  Conspiracy of Love. Hale, 1971
  Fear Among the Shadows. Hale, 1969;
    Ace, 1974 [L.A.]
  House of Intrigue. Hale, 1970; Dell,
    1972
  The Impossible Dream. Hale, 1973. U.S.
    title: To Dream of Evil. Ace, 1975
  A Quiet Passion. Hale, 1974; St. Mar-
    tin's, 1975
  Passing Stranger. Hale, 1974; St. Mar-
    tin's, 1974
  To Dream of Evil; see The Impossible
    Dream
  The Unknown Woman. Hale, 1968
  Woman Out of Nowhere. Hale, 1968

HOFFMAN, WILLIAM. 1925-   . Ref: CA.
  A Walk to the River. Doubleday, 1970;
    Hale, 1972 [Va.]

HOGAN, JAMES P.
  Inherit the Stars. Del Rey, 1977
    [future]

HOGAN, MICHAEL. See: Mabel Constanduros.

HOGAN, ROBERT J. 1897-1963. SC: G-8, in
    all titles, which are first book pub-
    lications of 1930s pulp magazine
    stories.
  Aces of the White Death. Berkley, 1970
    [Ger.]
  The Bat Staffel. Berkley, 1969 [Ger.]
  Bombs from the Murder Wolves. Berkley,
    1971
  Fangs of the Sky Leopard. Berkley, 1971
  Flight from the Grave. Berkley, 1971
    [Haiti]
  The Mark of the Vulture. Berkley, 1971
  Purple Aces. Berkley, 1970
  Vultures of the White Death. Berkley,
    1971 [Ger.]

HOGARTH, CHARLES. Joint pseudonym of John
    Creasey, 1908-1973, q.v., and Ivor
    Ian Bowen, 1908-   . Other Creasey
    pseudonyms: Gordon Ashe, M. E. Cooke,
    Norman Deane, Robert Caine Frazer,
    Patrick Gill, Michael Halliday, Brian
    Hope, Colin Hughes, Kyle Hunt, Abel
    Mann, Peter Manton, J. J. Marric,
    Richard Martin, Rodney Mattheson,
    Anthony Morton, Jeremy York, qq.v.
  Murder on Largo Island. Selwyn, 1944

HOGARTH, EMMETT. Joint pseudonym of
    Mitchell A. Wilson, 1913-1973, q.v.,
    and Abraham Lincoln Polonsky,
    1910-   .
  The Goose Is Cooked. Simon, 1940. Also
    published as: Death by Remote Con-
    trol. Detective Novel Classics, 194?
    [NYC]

HOGARTH, GRACE WESTON ALLEN. 1905-   .
    Ref: CA. Joint pseudonym with Alice
    Mary Norton, 1912?-   , q.v.: Allen
    Weston, q.v.

HOGG, DANIEL
  Murder at the Microphone. Quality, 1949

HOGG, GIL. Lawyer from New Zealand, with a large British corporation.
 A Smell of Fraud. Cassell, 1976; St. Martin's, 1976

HOGSTRAND, OLLE (EDVARD). 1933- . Reporter for the National Swedish News Agency; author of a mystery series for Radio Sweden. SC: Chief Insp. Lars Kollin, in all titles.
 The Debt. Pantheon, 1975; Hale, 1976 (Translation of "Skulden." Stockholm, 1973.) [Swed.]
 The Gambler. Pantheon, 1974; Hale, 1976 (Translation of "Spelarna." Stockholm, 1972.) [Swed.]
 On the Prime Minister's Account. Pantheon, 1972; Gollancz, 1972 (Translation of "Maskerat Brott." Stockholm, 1971.) [Stock.]

HOGUE, WILBUR OWINGS. 1910?-1952. Pseudonym: Carl Shannon, q.v.

HOHN, GEORGE K.
 The Bleak Strand. Dorrance, 1972

HOKLIN, LONN. See: Dan Oran.

HOLBROOK, J(AMES). 1812-1864.
 Ten Years Among the Mail Bags; or, Notes from the Diary of a Special Agent of the Post-Office Department. Cowperthwait, 1855 ss

HOLBROOK, MARION
 Crime Wind. Dodd, 1945 [S. Am.]
 Death Writes an Ad; see Suitable for Framing
 Suitable for Framing. Dodd, 1941; Cassell, 1946. Also published as: Death Writes an Ad. Mystery Novel Classic, 1943, abridged [NYC]
 Wanted: A Murderess. Dodd, 1943; Cassell, 1948 [New Eng.]

HOLCOMBE, W(ILLIAM) H(ENRY), M.D. 1825-1893.
 A Mystery of New Orleans. Lippincott, 1890 [New Or.]

HOLDAWAY, NEVILLE ALDRIDGE. 1894- .
 Pseudonym: N. A. Temple-Ellis, q.v.

HOLDEN, ANNE
 Death After School. Hale, 1968
 -The Empty Hills. Hale, 1967
 The Girl on the Beach. Macmillan (London), 1973; Delacorte, 1973 [Calif.]
 The Witnesses. Macmillan (London), 1971; Harper, 1971

HOLDEN, DENIS
 Menace from the East. Long, 1938

HOLDEN, GENEVIEVE. Pseudonym of Genevieve Long Pou, 1919- . Long-time resident of Atlanta. SC: Lt. Al White = AW.
 Deadlier Than the Male. Doubleday, 1961 [New Or.]
 Don't Go in Alone. Doubleday, 1965; Hale, 1966 [Atlanta]
 Down a Dark Alley. Doubleday, 1976 [Atlanta]
 Killer Loose! Doubleday, 1953 AW [South]
 Something's Happened to Kate. Doubleday, 1958 AW [South]
 Sound an Alarm. Doubleday, 1954 AW [South]
 The Velvet Target. Doubleday, 1956; Muller, 1957 AW [South]

HOLDEN, HELENE P.
 Satan, My Love. Curtis, 1974

HOLDEN, J. RAILTON. SC: "Spider" Stockwell, in at least those marked SS.
 Death Flies High. Newnes, 1935 SS
 Desert Squadron. Newnes, 1937
 Doomed Flight. Newnes, 1937
 The Hornet's Nest. Hamilton, 1933
 Night Hawk. Newnes, 1938
 Spider Flies Again. Newnes, 1937 SS [Egypt]
 Suez Patrol. Newnes, 1936 [Egypt]
 Suez Side Ace. Newnes, 1938 [Egypt]
 The Vanished Squadron. Newnes, 1936
 Winged Death. Newnes, 1935
 Wings of Revolution. Hamilton, 1934

HOLDEN, JOANNE. Pseudonym of Jane (Irenita) Corby, q.v. Other pseudonym: Jean Carew.
 Dangerous Legacy. Arcadia, 1966

HOLDEN, LARRY. Pseudonym of Lorenz Heller, q.v. Other pseudonyms: Larry Heller, Frederick Lorenz, qq.v.
 Crime Cop. Pyramid, 1959
 Dead Wrong. Pyramid, 1957 [Newark]
 Hide-Out. Eton, 1953 [Fla.]

HOLDEN, R(ICHARD) C(ORT)
 Snow Fury. Dodd, 1955

HOLDEN, RAYMOND P(ECKHAM). 1894- .
 Pseudonym: Richard Peckham, q.v.
 Ref: CA.
 Death on the Border. Holt, 1937 [Tex.]
 The Penthouse Murders. Doubleday, 1931 [NYC]

HOLDER, W. GRAEME. See: W. Graeme-Holder.

HOLDER, WILLIAM
 The Case of the Dead Divorcee. Signet, 1958 [Vt.]

HOLDING, ELISABETH SANXAY. 1889-1955.
 Ref: CC, EM, MP, TC. SC: Lt. Levy = L.
 The Blank Wall. Simon, 1947 L [L.I.]
 Dark Power. Vanguard, 1930
 The Death Wish. Dodd, 1934; Nicholson, 1935 [L.I.]
 The Girl Who Had to Die. Dodd, 1940 [L.I.]
 Hostess to Murder; see Speak of the Devil
 The Innocent Mrs. Duff. Simon, 1946
 Kill Joy. Duell, 1942. Also published as: Murder Is a Kill-Joy. Dell, 1946
 Lady Killer. Duell, 1942 [ship]
 Miasma. Dutton, 1929 [hosp.]
 Murder Is a Kill-Joy; see Kill Joy
 Net of Cobwebs. Simon, 1945; Corgi, 1952
 No Harm Intended; see The Obstinate Murderer
 The Obstinate Murderer. Dodd, 1938. British title: No Harm Intended. Lane, 1939
 The Old Battle Ax. Simon, 1943 [L.I.]
 The Party Was the Pay-Off; see Too Many Bottles
 Speak of the Devil. Duell, 1941. Also published as: Hostess to Murder. Mystery Novel Classic, 1943 [Carib.]
 The Strange Crime in Bermuda. Dodd, 1937; Lane, 1938 [Bermuda]
 Too Many Bottles. Simon, 1951; Muller, 1953. Also published as: The Party Was the Pay-Off. Mercury, 1952 L [L.I.]
 Trial by Murder; see Who's Afraid?
 The Unfinished Crime. Dodd, 1935; Newnes, 1936 [N.Y.]
 The Virgin Huntress. Simon, 1951 [N.Y.]
 Who's Afraid? Duell, 1940. Also published as: Trial by Murder. Thriller Novel Classic, 194?
 Widow's Mite. Simon, 1953; Muller, 1954 L [New Eng.]

HOLICKER, CHARLOTTE
 A Name My Own. Dell, 1974

HOLLAND, CLIVE. Pseudonym of Charles James Hankinson, 1866-1959.
 The Hidden Submarine; or, The Plot That Failed. Scott, 1917

HOLLAND, EDITH. 1898- . Pseudonym: Ruth Holland, q.v.

HOLLAND, HESTER
 -A Man Must Live. Butterworth, 1938
 -Week-Ends for Harry. Hurst, 1947

HOLLAND, ISABELLE. 1920- . Ref: CA.
 Cecily. Lippincott, 1967
 Counterpoint. Rawson, 1980; Collins, 1981 [N.Y.]
 Darcourt. Weybright, 1976; Collins, 1977 [S.C.]
 The DeMaury Papers. Rawson, 1977; Collins, 1978 [Eng.]
 Grenelle. Rawson, 1976; Collins 1978 [Va., acad.]
 Kilgaren. Weybright, 1974; Collins, 1975 [Carib.]
 The Marchington Inheritance. Rawson, 1979; Collins, 1980 [NYC]
 Moncrieff. Weybright, 1975. British title: The Standish Place. Collins, 1976 [NYC]
 The Standish Place; see Moncrieff
 Tower Abbey. Rawson, 1978; Collins, 1979 [N.Y.]
 Trelawny. Weybright, 1974. British title: Trelawny's Fell. Collins, 1976 [New Eng.]
 Trelawny's Fell; see Trelawny

HOLLAND, LILLIE
 The Eighteenth Summer. Lancer, 1973

HOLLAND, MARTY
 Blonde Baggage; see Fallen Angel
 Fallen Angel. Dutton, 1945; Davies, 1946. Also published as: Blonde Baggage. Novel Library, 1950 [Calif.]
 The Glass Heart. Messner, 1946; Davies, 1946. Also published as: Her Private Passions. Avon, 1948 [L.A.]
 Her Private Passions; see The Glass Heart

HOLLAND, NORMAN (NORWOOD). 1927- .
 Ref: CA.
 Three Prize Plays. New Playwrights, 1976 (3 plays, 1 criminous)

HOLLAND, REBECCA. Pseudonym of Ruby Horansky.
 Danger on Cue. Raven, 1980 [Conn., theatre]
 Shadows on the Bay. Popular Library, 1977

HOLLAND, ROBERT. 1940- . Ref: CA.
 The Hunter. Stein, 1971; Hale, 1974 [N.Y.]

HOLLAND, RUPERT SARGENT. 1878-1952.
 Crooked Lanes. Jacobs, 1923
 The House of Delusion. Jacobs, 1922 [Phil.]
 How Murder Speaks. Sears, 1933 [Pa.]
 The Man in the Moonlight. Jacobs, 1920; Paul, 1925
 Minot's Folly. Macrae, 1925 [Maine]
 The Mystery of the "Opal". Jacobs, 1924; Paul, 1924 [Maine]
 -Neptune's Son. Jacobs, 1919
 The Panelled Room. Jacobs, 1921 [Phil.]
 -Peter Cotterell's Treasure. Lippincott, 1922
 -A Race for a Fortune. Lippincott, 1931

HOLLAND, RUTH and J(OHN) B(OYNTON) PRIESTLEY, 1894- , q.v. Ruth Holland is the pseudonym of Edith Holland, 1898- .
 Dangerous Corner. H. Hamilton, 1932; Doubleday, 1933 (Novelization of the play by J. B. Priestley, q.v.)

HOLLAND, SHEILA. 1937- . Ref: CA.
 The Masque. Zebra, 1979

HOLLES, ROBERT (OWENS). 1926- . Ref: CA.
 Spawn. H. Hamilton, 1978; Doubleday, 1978

HOLLEY, HELEN. Born in Ohio; later living in Fla.; author of articles and ss. SC: Tessie Venable, in both titles.
 Blood on the Beach. Mystery House, 1946 [Fla.]
 Dead Run. Mystery House, 1947

HOLLINGSWORTH, LEONARD. SC: Insp./Supt. Adams, in all titles. Set: Eng.
 The Body on the Bus. Murray, 1930
 Dead Man's Alibi. Murray, 1933
 Death Leaves Us Naked. Murray, 1931

HOLLIS, JIM. Joint pseudonym of Hollis Spurgeon Summers, 1915- , and James Francis Anthony Rourke, 1922- .
 Teach You a Lesson. Harper, 1955; Foulsham, 1956. Also published as: The Case of the Bludgeoned Teacher. Avon, 1956 [acad.]

HOLLOWAY (McELDOWNEY), ELIZABETH HUGHES
 Cobweb House. Dutton, 1931 [Miss.]

HOLLOWAY, M.
 Three Keys to Murder. Fiction House, 1950

HOLLOWAY, TERESA BRAGUNIER. 1906- .
 Pseudonym: Elizabeth Beatty, q.v.

HOLLY, J. HUNTER. Pseudonym of Joan Carol Holly, 1932- . Ref: CA.
 The Assassination Affair. Ace, 1967 (Novelization of "The Man from UNCLE" TV series.)

HOLLY, JOAN CAROL. 1932- . Pseudonym: J. Hunter Holly, q.v.

HOLMAN, (CLARENCE) HUGH. 1914-1981. Pseudonym: Clarence Hunt, q.v. Ref: CA, TC. SC: Sheriff Macready = M. All books set in S.C.
 Another Man's Poison. Mill, 1947; Foulsham, 1950 M
 Death Like Thunder. Phoenix, 1942 [acad.]
 Slay the Murderer. Mill, 1946; Foulsham, 1950 M
 Trout in the Milk. Mill, 1945; Boardman, 1951 M
 Up This Crooked Way. Mill, 1946; Foulsham, 1951 M

HOLMAN, RUSSELL. See: Arthur (John Arbuthnott) Stringer, 1874-1950.

HOLME, TIMOTHY. An Englishman living in Venice.
   The Neapolitan Streak. Macmillan (London), 1980; Coward, 1980 [Naples]

HOLMES, AUBREY
   The Wake of a Lawyer. Houston American, 1960 [Houston]

HOLMES, BETH. Pseudonym.
   The Whipping Boy. Marek, 1978

HOLMES, DARRELL FORSYTHE, JR.
   Implied Immunity. Vantage, 1963

HOLMES, DAVID C(HARLES). 1919-   . Ref: CA.
   The Velvet Ape. Mystery House, 1957

HOLMES, GORDON. Pseudonym of Louis Tracy, 1863-1928, q.v., jointly in part with M(atthew) P(hipps) Shiel, 1865-1947, q.v. SC: Insp. Furneaux = F (see also Louis Tracy entry). Set: Eng.
   The Arncliffe Puzzle. Laurie, 1906; Clode, 1906. Revised edition: Jarrolds, 1932, as by Louis Tracy
   By Force of Circumstances. Mills, 1910; Clode, 1909. Reprinted as by Louis Tracy: Jarrolds, 1932 F
   The de Bercy Affair; see The Feldisham Mystery
   The Feldisham Mystery. Amalgamated, 1911. U.S. title: The de Bercy Affair. Clode, 1910 F
   The House 'Round the Corner. Ward, 1914; Clode, 1919
   The Late Tenant. Cassell, 1907; Clode, 1906. Also published as by Louis Tracy: Jarrolds, 1932

HOLMES, GRANT. Pseudonym of Johannes Matthijs Willem Knipscheer. Other pseudonym: James M. Fox, q.v.
   Surabaya. Cassell, 1956 [Indon.]

HOLMES, H. H. Pseudonym of William Anthony Parker White, 1911-1968. Other pseudonym: Anthony Boucher, q.v. See also: Theo Durrant. SC: Sister Ursula, in both titles, both set in L.A.
   Nine Times Nine. Duell, 1940. Subsequently reprinted as by Anthony Boucher.
   Rocket to the Morgue. Duell, 1942. Subsequently reprinted as by Anthony Boucher.

HOLMES, CAPTAIN HOWARD. Pseudonym of Thomas Chalmers Harbaugh, 1849-1924.
   The Never-Fail Detective. Westbrook, 1920s

HOLMES, J. GIBB
   -Ghosts' Gloom. Sonnenschein, 1889

HOLMES, MRS. M(ICHAEL) A(NGELO)
   Woman Against Woman. Ogilvie, 1885
   A Woman's Vengeance. Lovell, 1886

HOLMES, MRS. M. E.
   Her Fatal Sin. Laird, 1886
   The Tragedy of Redmount. Laird, 1886

HOLMES, MRS. MARY J(ANE). 1825-1907.
   Chateau d'Or. Carleton, 1880; Low, 1880

HOLMES, PAUL A(LLEN). 1901-   . Ref: CA.
   Murder Buttoned Up. Dutton, 1948

HOLMES, ROBERT
   Fear Comes to Euston Road. Hale, 1941

HOLMES, SAMUEL
   Fade into Murder. Langdon, 1947

HOLMGREN, FLORENCE (MARIETTA) DEPPE. 1908-1968.
   The Mystery of Bent Cove. Bouregy, 1966

HOLSTEIN, ANTHONY FREDERICK. Pseudonym.
   The Assassin of Saint Glenroy; or, The Axis of Life. Minerva, 1810
   Love, Mystery, and Misery! Minerva, 1810

HOLT, ALLISON
   Bier for a Hussy. Phoenix, 1943. Also published as: Death for a Hussy. Red Dagger, 1946, abridged [N.J.]

HOLT, BARRY
   The Mowbray Mystery. Stockwell, 1933

HOLT, DEBEN. Pseudonym.
   Circle of Shadows. Gifford, 1957
   Sinner Takes All. Gifford, 1948

HOLT, E. CARLETON. Pseudonym of Ernest Philip Guigo.
   Mystery at Arden Court. Stockwell, 1954

HOLT, GAVIN. Pseudonym of (Percival) Charles Rodda, 1891-   , q.v. Other pseudonyms: Gardner Low, q.v. Joint pseudonym with Eric Ambler, 1909-   , q.v.: Eliot Reed, q.v. SC: Prof. Luther Bastion, in at least those marked LB; Insp. Joel Saber, in at least those marked JS; Sherrett York, in at least those marked SY. Set: Eng.
   Begonia Walk. Hodder, 1946. U.S. title: Send No Flowers. Howell Soskin, 1947 JS
   Black Bullets. Hodder, 1935 LB
   Dark Lady. Hodder, 1933 LB
   The Dark Street. Hodder, 1942 [Ger.]
   Death Takes the Stage. Hodder, 1934; Little, 1934 LB [theatre]
   Drums Beat at Night. Hodder, 1932 LB
   Dusk at Penarder. Hodder, 1956
   The Emerald Spider. Hodder, 1935 LB
   Eyes in the Night. Hutchinson, 1927
   The Garden of Silent Beasts. Hodder, 1931 LB
   Garlands for Sylvia. Hodder, 1958
   Give a Man Rope. Hodder, 1942 JS
   The Golden Witch. Hodder, 1933 LB
   Green for Danger. Gollancz, 1939 JS
   Green Talons. Hodder, 1930; Bobbs, 1931 LB
   Irina. Hale, 1965 [Balkans]
   Ivory Ladies. Hodder, 1937 SY
   Ladies in Ermine. Hodder, 1947 JS
   Mark of the Paw. Hodder, 1933 LB
   Murder at Marble Arch. Hodder, 1931 LB
   Murder Train. Hodder, 1936 SY
   No Curtains for Cora. Hodder, 1950 [theatre]
   Pattern of Guilt. Hodder, 1960; Walker, 1962
   The Praying Monkey; see The White-Faced Man
   Red Eagle. Hodder, 1932 LB
   -Redemption Range. Gryphon, 1952
   Send No Flowers; see Begonia Walk
   Six Minutes Past Twelve. Hodder, 1928 LB
   Sole Survivor. Hale, 1969 [It.]
   Steel Shutters. Hodder, 1936 LB
   Storm. Hodder, 1931; Swain, 1933, as by Charles Rodda
   Swing It, Death. Gollancz, 1940 JS
   Take Away the Lady. Hodder, 1954 (Novelization of the TV play.)
   The Theme Is Murder. Gollancz, 1938; Simon, 1939 JS
   Tonight Is for Death. Hodder, 1952
   Trafalgar Square. Hodder, 1934 LB
   Trail of the Skull. Hodder, 1931 LB
   Valse Caprice. Hodder, 1932 LB
   The White-Faced Man. Hodder, 1929. U.S. title: The Praying Monkey. Dial, 1930 LB

HOLT, GLENN
   Aussie Lawman. Major, 1976

HOLT, GORDON. Pseudonym of Harold Ernest Kelly, 1899-   . Other pseudonyms: Eugene Ascher, Darcy Glinto, Buck Toler, qq.v.
   The Stables to £1,000,000. Hector Kelly, 1948

HOLT, HARRISON JEWELL
   Midnight at Mears House. Dodd, 1912; Simpkin, 1916 [Maine]

HOLT, HENRY. Crime reporter for London newspapers before becoming full-time writer. SC: Insp. Silver, in at least those marked S; Mike Logan, in at least those marked ML.
   The Ace of Spades. Harrap, 1930; Dial 1930
   Call Out the Flying Squad!; see Gallows Grange
   Calling All Cars. Collins, 1934. U.S. title: The Sinister Shadow. Doubleday, 1934 S
   Calling Scotland Yard. Hale, 1944 S
   Don't Shoot, Darling. Hale, 1961; Roy, 1963 ML,S
   Gallows Grange. Harrap, 1933. U.S. title: Call Out the Flying Squad! Doubleday, 1933 S
   The Man Who Forgot. Hale, 1943
   The Mayfair Murder; see The Mayfair Mystery
   The Mayfair Mystery. Harrap, 1929. U.S. title: The Mayfair Murder. Dial, 1929 S
   The Midnight Mail. Harrap, 1931; Doubleday, 1931 S
   Mink and Murder. Hale, 1958
   Motley and Murder. Hale, 1945 S
   Murder at the Bookstall. Collins, 1934 S
   Murder, My Sweet. Museum, 1950 S
   Murder of a Film Star. Collins, 1940
   Murderer's Luck. Harrap, 1932; Doubleday, 1932 S
   The Mystery of the Smiling Doll. Collins, 1939
   The Necklace of Death. Harrap, 1931; Doubleday, 1931 S
   No Lilies. Hale, 1947 ML
   No Medals for Murder. Museum, 1954
   The Scarlet Messenger. Collins, 1933; Doubleday, 1933 S
   The Sinister Shadow; see Calling All Cars
   There Has Been a Murder. Collins, 1936 S
   Tiger of Mayfair. Collins, 1935 S
   Unknown Terror. Collins, 1935
   Wanted for Murder. Collins, 1938
   The Whispering Man. Collins, 1938
   The Wolf; see The Wolf's Claw
   The Wolf's Claw. Harrap, 1932. U.S. title: The Wolf. Doubleday, 1932 S
   A Wreath for the Lady. Hale, 1959 ML,S

HOLT, JOHN ROBERT. 1926-   . Pseudonyms: Elizabeth Giles, Raymond Giles, qq.v.

HOLT, LEE
   The House of the Third Sense. Hodder, 1923

HOLT, RICHARD
   Money from Rome. Mayflower, 1965

HOLT, THOMAS LITTLETON
   John Horsleydown; or, The Confessions of a Thief. Ward, 1860 ss

HOLT, VICTORIA. Pseudonym of Eleanor Alice Burford Hibbert, 1906-   . Other pseudonyms: Philippa Carr, Elbur Ford, Kathleen Kellow, qq.v. See also: Mildred C(hristophe) Kuner, 1922-   . Set: Eng. Ref: CA, CC, EM.
   Bride of Pendorric. Collins, 1963; Doubleday, 1963
   The Curse of the Kings. Collins, 1973; Doubleday, 1973
   -The Devil on Horseback. Collins, 1977; Doubleday, 1977
   The House of a Thousand Lanterns. Collins, 1974; Doubleday, 1974
   The King of the Castle. Collins, 1968; Doubleday, 1968 [Fr.]
   Kirkland Revels. Collins, 1962; Doubleday, 1962
   The Legend of the Seventh Virgin. Collins, 1965; Doubleday, 1965
   Lord of the Far Island. Collins, 1975; Doubleday, 1975 [Eng., ca.1900]
   The Mask of the Enchantress. Collins, 1980; Doubleday, 1980
   Menfreya. Collins, 1966. U.S. title: Menfreya in the Morning. Doubleday, 1966
   Menfreya in the Morning; see Menfreya
   Mistress of Mellyn. Collins, 1961; Doubleday, 1960
   On the Night of the Seventh Moon. Collins, 1973; Doubleday, 1973
   The Pride of the Peacock. Collins, 1976; Doubleday, 1976
   The Secret Woman. Collins, 1971; Doubleday, 1970 [Eng., 1800s]
   The Shadow of the Lynx. Collins, 1972; Doubleday, 1971
   The Shivering Sands. Collins, 1969; Doubleday, 1969
   -The Spring of the Tiger. Collins, 1979; Doubleday, 1979

HOLT, WILL
   Savage Snow. Signet, 1980 [Boston]

HOLT-WHITE, W(ILLIAM EDWARD BRADDON), 1878-   .
   The Crime Club; see The Prime Minister's Secret
   -The Man Who Stole the Earth. Unwin, 1909
   The Prime Minister's Secret. Unwin, 1910. U.S. title: The Crime Club. Macaulay, 1910
   The Super Spy. Melrose, 1916
   -The Woman Who Saved the World. Everett, 1914
   -The World Stood Still. Everett, 1912

HOLTHAM, GERALD. See: Roger (Charles) Busby, 1941-   .

HOLTON, EDITH AUSTIN. 1881-   . Pseudonym: Elizabeth Alden Heath, q.v.

HOLTON, LEONARD. Pseudonym of Leonard (Patrick O'Connor) Wibberley, 1915-   , q.v. Ref: CA, EM, TC. SC: Father Joseph Bredder, in all titles.
   A Corner of Paradise. St. Martin's, 1977 [L.A., acad.]
   Deliver Us from Wolves. Dodd, 1963 [Port.]
   The Devil to Play. Dodd, 1974   [L.A.]
   Flowers by Request. Dodd, 1964   [L.A.]
   The Mirror of Hell. Dodd, 1972   [L.A.]
   Out of the Depths. Dodd, 1966; Hammond, 1967 [L.A.]
   A Pact with Satan. Dodd, 1960; Hale, 1961 [L.A.]
   A Problem in Angels. Dodd, 1970 [L.A.]
   The Saint Maker. Dodd, 1959; Hale, 1960 [L.A.]
   Secret of the Doubting Saint. Dodd, 1961 [L.A.]
   A Touch of Jonah. Dodd, 1968 [ship]

HOLZER, HANS W. 1920-   . Ref: CA. SC: Randy Knowles, in all titles.
   The Alchemy Deception. Award, 1973
   Psychic Detective: The Unicorn. Manor, 1976 [Eng.]
   The Red Chindvit Conspiracy. Award, 1970 [S.F.]

HOME, BERNARD
   Passport to Death. Hutchinson, 1937
   Rogue Haven. Hutchinson, 1938

HOME, MICHAEL. Pseudonym of Christopher Bush, 1885-1973, q.v.
   -The Auber File. Methuen, 1953
   -City of the Soul. Methuen, 1943
   -The Cypress Road. Methuen, 1945
   -The Harvest Is Past. Rich, 1937
   -The House of Shade. Methuen, 1942; Morrow, 1942 [Afr., N.]
   -July at Fritham. Rich, 1938
   No Snow at Laching. Methuen, 1949
   -The Questing Man. Rich, 1936
   -The Soundless Years. Methuen, 1951
   -The Strange Prisoner. Methuen, 1947
   -That Was Yesterday. Methuen, 1955

HOME-GALL, EDWARD R(EGINALD). 1899-   .
   The Haunted Ice-Rink. New Arts, 1946

HOME-GALL, WILLIAM BENJAMIN. 1861-1936. Born in H. Kong; lived for a time in Texas, then in England.
   State Secrets. Amalgamated Press, 1921 (Sexton Blake.)

HOMERSHAM, B(ASIL) H(ENRY). 1902-   . Pseudonym: Basil Manningham, q.v.
   Arsenic on the Menu. Paul, 1936
   Murder of an M.P. Paul, 1935

HOMES, GEOFFREY. Pseudonym of Daniel (Geoffrey Homes) Mainwaring, 1902-1977, q.v. Ref: CC, EM, MP, TC. SC: Robin Bishop = RB; Humphrey Campbell = HC; Jose Manuel Madero = JM.
   Build My Gallows High. Morrow, 1946 [Nev.]
   The Case of the Mexican Knife; see The Street of the Crying Woman
   The Case of the Unhappy Angels; see The Six Silver Handles
   Dead As a Dummy; see The Hill of the Terrified Monk
   The Doctor Died at Dusk. Morrow, 1936 RB [Calif.]
   Finders Keepers. Morrow, 1940 HC [Calif.]
   Forty Whacks. Morrow, 1941. Also published as: Stiffs Don't Vote. Bantam, 1947 HC [Calif.]
   The Hill of the Terrified Monk. Morrow, 1943. Also published as: Dead As a Dummy. Bantam, 1949 JM [Tucson]
   The Man Who Didn't Exist. Morrow, 1937; Eyre, 1939 RB [Calif.]
   The Man Who Murdered Goliath. Morrow, 1938; Eyre, 1940 RB [Calif.]
   The Man Who Murdered Himself. Morrow, 1936; Lane, 1936 RB [Calif.]
   No Hands on the Clock. Morrow, 1939 HC [Reno]
   Seven Died; see The Street of the Crying Woman
   Six Silver Handles. Morrow, 1944; Cherry Tree, 1946. Also published as: The Case of the Unhappy Angels. Bantam, 1950 HC [Calif.]
   Stiffs Don't Vote; see Forty Whacks
   The Street of the Crying Woman. Morrow, 1942. British title: Seven Died. Cherry Tree, 1943. Also published as: The Case of the Mexican Knife. Bantam, 1948 JM [Mex.]
   Then There Were Three. Morrow, 1938; Cherry Tree, 1945 RB,HC [Calif.]

HOMEWOOD, HARRY
   A Matter of Size. O'Hara, 1975

HONE, JOSEPH. 1937-   . Ref: CA. SC: Peter Marlow = PM.
   The Flowers of the Forest. Secker, 1980. U.S. title: The Oxford Gambit. Random, 1980 PM
   The Oxford Gambit; see The Flowers of the Forest
   The Paris Trap. Secker, 1977
   The Private Sector. H. Hamilton, 1971; Dutton, 1972 PM [Cairo]
   The Sixth Directorate. Secker, 1975; Dutton, 1975 PM

HONEYCOMBE, GORDON. 1936-   . Ref: CA.
   Adam's Tale. Hutchinson, 1974
   Dragon Under the Hill. Hutchinson, 1972; Simon, 1972
   Neither the Sea Nor the Sand. Hutchinson, 1969; Weybright, 1970 [Scot.]

HONEYMAN, WILLIAM CRAWFORD. Pseudonym: James M'Govan, q.v.

HONIG, DONALD. 1931-   . Ref: CA.
   Divide the Night. Regency, 1961
   I Should Have Sold Petunias. Jove, 1977
   -Judgment Night. Belmont, 1971
   Marching Home. St. Martin's, 1980
   The Operator; see Sidewalk Caesar
   The Severith Style. Scribner, 1972 [NYC]
   Sidewalk Caesar. Pyramid, 1958. Also published as: The Operator. Belmont, 1971

HONIG, LOUIS. 1911-1977. Ref: CA.
   For Your Eyes Only: Read and Destroy. Charles (L.A.), 1972 [Viet Nam]

HOOD, CHRISTOPHER
   The Mullenthorpe Thing. Chatto, 1971

HOOD, MARGARET PAGE. 1892-   . Ref: CA. SC: Gil Donan = GD. Set: Maine, all titles.
   The Bell on Lonely. Coward, 1959 GD
   Drown the Wind. Coward, 1961 GD
   In the Dark Night. Coward, 1957. Also published as: The Murders on Fox Island. Dell, 1960 GD
   The Murders on Fox Island; see In the Dark Night
   The Scarlet Thread. Coward, 1956 GD
   The Silent Women. Coward, 1954 GD
   The Sin Mark. Coward, 1963

HOOD, STEPHEN. Pseudonym of Jack Lewis, q.v. Other pseudonym: Lewis Jackson, q.v.
   The Crook from Chicago. Amalgamated Press, 1931 (Sexton Blake.)

HOOK, ALFRED SAMUEL. Pseudonym: A. J. Colton, q.v.

HOOKE, CHARLES WITHERLE. 1861-1929. Pseudonyms: Nicholas Carter, Howard Fielding, qq.v.

HOOKE, NINA WARNER. 1907-   . Ref: CA.
   Darkness I Leave You. Hale, 1956
   Deadly Record. Hale, 1958. Play version: French (London), 1965
   Not in the Contract. French (London), 1961 (1-act play.)

HOOKER, G(WENDA) DALTON
   Smith's Odyssey. Angus, 1962

HOOPER, C(YRUS) LAURON. 1863-   .
   A Cloverdale Skeleton. Alden, 1889

HOOPES, CLEMENT R. 1906-1979. Ref: CA.
   Angry Dust. Devin-Adair, 1967

HOPE, ANDREE. Pseudonym of Annie Jane Tennant Harvey,   -1898.
   The Secret of Wardale Court and other stories. Wilsons, 1894 ss, title ss criminous
   The Vyvyans; or, The Murder in the Rue Bellechasse. Chapman, 1893; Rand, 1893

HOPE, ANTHONY. Pseudonym of Sir Anthony Hope Hawkins, 1863-1933. See also: Robert Marshall.
   Beaumaroy Home from the Wars. Methuen, 1919. U.S. title: The Secret of the Tower. Appleton, 1919

HOPE, BRIAN. Pseudonym of John Creasey, 1908-1973, q.v. Other pseudonyms: Gordon Ashe, M. E. Cooke, Norman Deane, Robert Caine Frazer, Patrick Gill, Michael Halliday, Charles Hogarth, Colin Hughes, Kyle Hunt, Abel Mann, Peter Manton, J. J. Marric, Richard Martin, Rodney Mattheson, Anthony Morton, Jeremy York, qq.v.
   Four Motives for Murder. Newnes, 1938

HOPE, CAMILLA. Pseudonym of Grace E. Thompson.
   -Curiously Planned. Long, 1928
   Long Shadows. Long, 1928; Fiction Library, 1929
   -Moon of Joy. Long, 1927

HOPE, CHARLES (EVELYN) GRAHAM. 1900-1971. Ref: CA. Pseudonym: Anthony Pelham, q.v.
   The Second Plan. Hodder, 1938 [Russ.]

HOPE, COLIN. Set: Eng.
   Air Gold. Hamilton, 1935
   The Air Peril. Hamilton, 1937
   Death in the Fens. Hamilton, 1935
   A Ghost from the Past. Fiction House, 1936
   The Harne Grange Mystery. Mellifont, 1935
   The House in the Way. Modern, 1935
   The Mystery at Crowstone. Hamilton, 1936
   "No Honour—". Hamilton, 1935
   The Phantom Killer. Fiction House, 1935
   The Prince of Trouble. Hamilton, 1936
   Vengeance in the Air. Mellifont, 1940

HOPE, FIELDING. 1897-   . See also: John Angus.
   The Guinea Pig's Tail. Selwyn, 1934. U.S. title: Marie Arnaud, Spy. Macaulay, 1934
   Marie Arnaud, Spy; see The Guinea Pig's Tail
   The Mystery of the House of Commons. Selwyn, 1929; Dial, 1930

HOPE, FRANCES ESSEX THEODORA. Pseudonym: Essex Smith, q.v.

HOPE, HENRY. Pseudonym: Henry Andover, q.v.

HOPE, MARK. Pseudonym of Eustace Clare Grenville Murray, 1824-1881.
   Dark and Light Stories. Chapman, 1879 ss, some criminous

HOPE, (WILLIAM EDWARD) STANTON. 1889-1961. Born in London; world traveler; wrote widely on technical matters and much fiction; established a school of journalism in Australia. All titles below were published by Amalgamated Press and feature Sexton Blake.
   The Amazing Affair of the Shipyard Sabotage. 1940
   The Case of the Missing Ships. 1935
   The Case of the Monta Grandee Diamonds. 1945
   The Cruise of Terror. 1932
   The Death Ship. 1931
   The Dockyard Mystery. 1936
   In the Grip of the Gestapo. 1940
   The Mystery of the Engraved Skull. 1954
   The Secret at Sixty-Six Fathoms. 1938
   The Sign of the Blue Triangle. 1942
   The Stolen Submarine. 1937
   The Terror of Thunder Creek. 1936
   The Victim of the Red Mask. 1931; Red Mask, 194?

HOPE-SIMPSON, JACYNTH. 1930-   . Ref: CA.
   -The Unravish'd Bride. Putnam (London), 1963

HOPKINS, A. T. Pseudonym of Annette Turngren, 1902-1980. Ref: CA.
   Have a Lovely Funeral. Rinehart, 1954 [Minn.]

HOPKINS, JOHN (RICHARD). 1931-   . Ref: CA.
   This Story of Yours. Penguin, 1969 (3-act play.)

HOPKINS, (HECTOR) KENNETH. 1914-   . Pseudonym: Christopher Adams, q.v. Ref: CA, CC. SC: Dr. William Blow and Prof. Gideon Manciple = B&M; Gerry Lee = GL. Set: Eng.
   Body Blow. Macdonald, 1962; Holt, 1962 B&M
   Campus Corpse. Macdonald, 1963 GL [Tex., acad.]
   Dead Against My Principles. Macdonald, 1960; Holt, 1962 B&M
   The Forty-First Passenger. Macdonald, 1958 GL
   The Girl Who Died. Macdonald, 1955 GL
   Pierce with a Pin. Macdonald, 1960 GL
   She Died Because... Macdonald, 1957; Holt, 1964 B&M

HOPKINS, LINTON C(OOKE). 1872-1943.
    Born in Atlanta and practised law
    there.
    Black Buck. Little, 1931 [Ga.]
    The Candle. Green Circle, 1937; Joseph
        1936 [Atlanta]

HOPKINS, NEVIL MONROE. 1873-1945. SC:
    Mason Brant, in both titles.
    The Investigation at Holman Square; see
        The Strange Cases of Mason Brant
    The Racoon Lake Mystery. Lippincott,
        1917 [Maine]
    The Strange Cases of Mason Brant. Lip-
        pincott, 1916 (ss; one of the three
        stories was published separately as:
        The Investigation at Holman Square.
        Modern, 193?

HOPKINS, R(OBERT) THURSTON. 1883-   .
    See: Clarice Mayne.
    Valentine Vaughan Omnibus. Grafton,
        1947 ss

HOPKINS, ROBERT (S.). Pseudonym: Robert
    Rostand, q.v.
    The Raid on the Villa Joyosa. Putnam,
        1973; Barker, 1975 [Sp.]

HOPKINS, SEWARD W.
    A Baffled Imposter. Henderson, 189?
    -On a False Charge. Bonner's, 1895

HOPKINS, STANLEY, JR. SC: Peter Marrell,
    in both titles.
    Murder by Inches. Harcourt, 1943 [L.I.]
    The Parchment Key. Harcourt, 1944
        [L.I.]

HOPKINS, TIGHE. 1856-1919.
    The Silent Gate. Hurst, 1900

HOPKINSON, HENRY THOMAS. 1905-   . Ref:
    CA. Pseudonym: Thomas Pembroke. See:
    Mileson (Denis James) Horton,
    1899-   .

HOPLEY, GEORGE. Pseudonym of Cornell
    (George Hopley) Woolrich, 1903-1968,
    q.v. Other pseudonym: William Irish,
    q.v.
    Fright. Rinehart, 1950; Foulsham, 1950
        [NYC, 1915-16]
    Night Has a Thousand Eyes. Farrar,
        1945; Penguin, 1949. Reprinted as by
        William Irish: Dell, 1953. Reprinted
        as by Cornell Woolrich: Paperback
        Library, 1967

HOPPE, JOANNE. 1932-   . Ref: CA.
    The Lesson Is Murder. Harcourt, 1977
        [acad.]

HOPPER, JAMES (MARIE), 1876-1956, and
    FRED(ERICK) R(ITCHIE) BECHDOLT,
    1874-1950, q.v.
    9009. McClure, 1908; Heinemann, 1909

HOPWOOD, AVERY. 1884-1928. See: Mary
    Roberts Rinehart, 1876-1958.

HOPWOOD, JIM
    Death Rides the Rails. Manor, 1980

HORAN, JAMES D(AVID). 1914-1981. Ref: CA.
    The New Vigilantes. Crown, 1975 [NYC]

HORAN, KEITH
    The Squid. Barnardo, ca.1945

HORANSKY, RUBY. Pseudonym: Rebecca
    Holland, q.v.

HORLER, SYDNEY. 1888-1954. Ref: CC, EM,
    MP, TC. SC: The "Ace" (Justin March)
    = A; Sir Harker Bellamy = HB; Brett
    Carstairs = BC*; "Bunny" Chipstead =
    BC; Insp. H. Emp = HE; Sir Brian
    Fordinghame = BF; Martin Huish = MH;
    Sir William Kirby = WK; Sir Charles
    Knightley = CK; Gerald Lissendale =
    GL; Chief Constable George Meatyard =
    GM; Nighthawk (Gerald Frost) = N;
    Sebastian Quin = SQ; Peter Scarlett =
    PS; Tiger Standish = TS; Baron Vesel-
    offsky = BV; Paul Vivanti = PV; Ro-
    bert Wynnton = RW. Set: Eng.
    Adventure Calling! Hodder, 1931
    Beauty and the Policeman and other sto-
        ries. Hutchinson, 1933 ss, one about
        WK
    The Black Heart. Hodder, 1927; Double-
        day, 1928
    The Blade Is Bright. Eyre, 1952 GL
    The Blanco Case. Quality, 1950 [Eng,
        1876]
    The Breed of the Beverleys. Odhams,
        1921
    A Bullet for the Countess. Quality,
        1945 [Gib.]
    The Cage. Hale, 1953
    Cavalier of Chance. Hodder, 1931. U.S.
        title: Peril. Mystery League, 1930
    The Charlatan; see The Formula
    Checkmate. Hodder, 1930 [Fr.]
    Chipstead of the Lone Hand. Hodder,
        1928; Holt, 1929 BC
    The Closed Door. Pilot, 1948 GL
    Corridors of Fear. Quality, 1947
    The Curse of Doone. Hodder, 1928;
        Mystery League, 1930
    Danger Preferred. Hodder, 1942
    Danger's Bright Eyes. Hodder, 1930;
        Harper, 1932
    Dark Danger. Arcadia, 1945 (British
        title?)
    The Dark Hostess. Eyre, 1955
    Dark Journey. Hodder, 1938
    The Dark Night. Hodder, 1953 A
    Death at Court Lady. Collins, 1936 CK
    Death of a Spy. Museum, 1953
    The Destroyer and The Red-Haired Death.
        Hodder, 1938 (Two novelets, one
        about HB.)
    The Devil and the Deep; see The House
        in Greek Street
    The Devil Comes to Bolobyn. Percival
        Marshall, 1951
    Dying to Live and other stories. Hutch-
        inson, 1935 ss
    The Enemy Within the Gates. Hodder,
        1940 BC
    Enter the Ace. Hodder, 1941 A
    The Evil Chateau. Hodder, 1930; Knopf,
        1931 [Fr.]
    The Evil Messenger. Hodder, 1938 SQ,MH
    Exit the Disguiser. Hodder, 1948 TS
    The Face of Stone. Barker, 1952
    False-Face. Hodder, 1926; Doran, 1926
        BV,BF
    The False Purple; see Princess After
        Dark
    Fear Walked Behind. Hale, 1942 SQ
    The Formula. Long, 1933. U.S. title:
        The Charlatan. Little, 1934
    A Gentleman for the Gallows. Hodder,
        1938; Hillman-Curl, 1938
    Gentleman-in-Waiting. Benn, 1932
    The Great Adventure and Out of a Dark
        Sky. Hale, 1946 (Two novelets.)
    The Grim Game. Collins, 1936; Little,
        1936 TS,HB [Fr.]
    Harlequin of Death. Long, 1933; Little,
        1933
    Heart Cut Diamond. Hodder, 1929
    Hell's Brew. Hodder, 1952 A
    Here Is an S.O.S. Hodder, 1939 GM (A
        later edition, Hodder, 1942, has only
        43 pp.)
    The Hidden Hand. Collins, 1937
    The High Game. Redman, 1950
    High Hazard. Hodder, 1943
    High Stakes. Collins, 1932; Little,
        1935 BF
    Horror's Head. Hodder, 1932 HE
    The Hostage. Quality, 1943
    The House in Greek Street. Hodder,
        1935 (Four ss. A later edition,
        Crowther, 1946, contains the title ss
        and two others, "The Devil and the
        Deep" and "Knight at Arms", the lat-
        ter not appearing in the 1935 edi-
        tion.) 1 ss about SQ; 3 about HB
    The House of Jackals. Hodder, 1951 TS
    The House of Secrets. Hodder, 1926;
        Doran, 1927
    The House of the Uneasy Dead. Barker,
        1950
    The House with the Light. Hodder, 1948
    Huntress of Death. Hodder, 1933
    In the Dark. Hodder, 1927. U.S. title:
        A Life for Sale. Doubleday, 1928 BC
    Instruments of Darkness. Hodder, 1937
    Knaves & Co. Collins, 1938 ss, 2 about
        SQ
    Knight at Arms; see The House in Greek
        Street
    Lady of the Night. Hodder, 1929; Knopf,
        1930
    The Lady with the Limp. Hodder, 1944
        TS,HB
    The Lessing Murder Case. Collins, 1935
        WK
    A Life for Sale; see In the Dark
    Lord of Terror. Collins, 1935; Hillman-
        Curl, 1937 RV
    Love, the Sportsman. Hodder, 1923. Also
        published as: The Man with Two Faces.
        Collins, 1934
    The Man from Scotland Yard. Hutchinson,
        1934
    The Man in the Cloak. Eyre, 1951 RW
    The Man in the Hood. Redman, 1955
    The Man in the Shadows. Hale, 1955
    The Man in White. Staples, 1942
    A Man of Affairs. Pilot, 1949
    The Man of Evil. Barker, 1951 [Eng.,
        1600s]
    The Man Who Did Not Hang. Quality, 1948
    The Man Who Died Twice. Hodder, 1939.
        Play version: Nelson, 1941
    The Man Who Loved Spiders. Barker, 1948
        GM
    -The Man Who Mislaid the War. Muller,
        1943 (3-act play.)
    The Man Who Preferred Cocktails. Crow-
        ther, 1943
    The Man Who Shook the Earth. Hutchin-
        son, 1933 ss, one about CK
    The Man Who Used Perfume. Wingate, 1952
        RW
    The Man Who Walked with Death. Hodder,
        1931; Knopf, 1931 BC*
    The Man with Dry Hands. Eyre, 1944
    The Man with Two Faces; see Love, the
        Sportsman
    Master of Venom. Hodder, 1949 HE
    The Menace. Collins, 1933; Little, 1933
    Miss Mystery. Hodder, 1928; Little,
        1935 BV
    The Mocking Face of Murder. Hale, 1952
    Murder for Sale. Vallancey, 1945
        (16 pp.)
    Murder Is So Simple. Eyre, 1943
    The Murder Mask. Readers Library, 1930
        BF
    Murderer at Large. Hodder, 1952 HE
    My Lady Dangerous. Collins, 1932; Har-
        per, 1933 HB
    The Mystery Mission. Poynings, 1944
        (31 pp.)
    The Mystery Mission and other stories.
        Hodder, 1931 ss
    The Mystery of Mr. X. Foulsham, 1951
    The Mystery of No. 1. Hodder, 1925.
        U.S. title: The Order of the Octopus.
        Doran, 1926 PV
    The Mystery of the Seven Cafes. Hodder,
        1935 TS,HB
    Nap on Nighthawk. Hodder, 1950 N
    The Night of Reckoning. Eyre, 1942
    Nighthawk Mops Up. Hodder, 1944 N
    Nighthawk Strikes to Kill. Hodder, 1941
        N
    Nighthawk Swears Vengeance. Hodder,
        1954 N
    The Order of the Octopus; see The Mys-
        tery of No. 1
    Out of a Dark Sky; see Great Adventure
    Peril; see Cavalier of Chance
    -The Phantom Forward. Hodder, 1939
    The Prince of Plunder. Hodder, 1934;
        Little, 1934 BF
    Princess After Dark. Hodder, 1931. U.S.
        title: The False Purple. Mystery
        League, 1932 [Fr.]
    The Red-Haired Death; see The Destroyer
    The Return of Nighthawk. Hodder, 1940 N
    Ring Up Nighthawk. Hodder, 1947 N
    Scarlett Gets the Kidnapper. Foulsham,
        1951 PS
    Scarlett—Special Branch. Foulsham,
        1950 PS
    The Screaming Skull and other stories.
        Hodder, 1930 ss, 2 about HB, 1 about
        SQ
    The Secret Agent. Collins, 1934; Lit-
        tle, 1934 BC
    The Secret Hand. Barker, 1954
    The Secret Service Man. Hodder, 1929;
        Knopf, 1930 MH,GL
    Sinister Street. Vallancey, 1944
        (Taken from The Mystery Mission and
        other stories, q.v.)
    S.O.S. Hutchinson, 1934
    The Spy. Hodder, 1931 BC*
    The Stroke Sinister and other stories.
        Hutchinson, 1935 ss, one about MH
    -The Temptation of Mary Gordon. Newnes,
        1931
    Terror Comes to Twelvetrees. Eyre, 1945
    Terror on Tip-Toe. Hodder, 1939
    These Men and Women. Museum, 1951
    They Called Him Nighthawk. Hodder, 1937
        N
    They Thought He Was Dead. Hodder, 1949
        TS
    The 13th Hour. Readers Library, 1928
        (Novelization of the movie.)
    Tiger Standish. Long, 1932; Doubleday,
        1933 TS,HB
    Tiger Standish Comes Back. Hutchinson,
        1934 TS,HB
    Tiger Standish Does His Stuff. Hodder,
        1941 TS (2 novelets.)
    Tiger Standish Has a Party. Todd, 1943
        (16 pp.) TS
    Tiger Standish Steps on It. Hodder,
        1940 TS,HB
    Tiger Standish Takes the Field. Hodder,
        1939 TS,HB
    The Traitor. Collins, 1936; Little,
        1936
    The Vampire. Hutchinson, 1935; Book-
        finger, 1974
    Virus X. Quality, 1945 PV
    Vivanti. Hodder, 1927; Doran, 1927 PV
    Vivanti Returns. Hodder, 1931 PV
    The Web. Redman, 1951
    -Whilst the Crowd Roared. Archer, 1949
    Wolves of the Night. Readers Library,
        1931
    The Worst Man in the World. Hodder,
        1929 PV

HORN, HOLLOWAY. 1886-   .
    The Intruder. Collins, 1929
    The Murder at Linpara. Collins, 1931
        [Far East]
    The Neglected Fire. Collins, 1923
    The Purple Claw. Muller, 1935

HORNBLOW, ARTHUR. 1865-1941?
    The Argyle Case. Harper (NYC & London),
        1913 (Novelization of the play by
        Harriet Ford, 1868-1949, q.v., and
        Harvey O'Higgins, 1876-1929, q.v.)
        [NYC]
    Find the Woman; see The Third Degree
    -The Lion and the Mouse. Dillingham,
        1906 (Novelization of the play by
        Charles Klein.)
    The Mask. Dillingham, 1913 [S. Afr.]
    -The Price. Dillingham, 1914 (Noveliza-
        tion of the play by George Broad-
        hurst, 1866-1952.)
    The Profligate. Dillingham, 1908; Un-
        win, 1908 [NYC]
    The Third Degree, with Charles Klein.
        Dillingham, 1909. British title:
        Find the Woman; or, The Third Degree.
        Bird, 1912
    -The Watch Dog. Dillingham, 1915

HORNBY, JOHN WILKINSON. 1913-   . Ref:
        CA.
    Alpine Crack-Up. Hamilton Stafford,
        1952
    Death Pays Dividends. Hamilton Staf-
        ford, 1951
    Die Quickly, Brother. Hamilton Staf-
        ford, 1951
    Here Today—Dead Tomorrow. Hamilton
        Stafford, 1951

HORNE, GEOFFREY. 1916-   . Pseudonym:
        Gil North, q.v.
    -Land of No Escape. Hutchinson, 1958
    -The Man Who Was Chief. Chapman, 1960
    -The Portuguese Diamonds. Chapman, 1961
    -Winter. Hutchinson, 1957

HORNER, DAVID
    The Devil's Quill. Heinemann, 1959

HORNIBROOK, J(OHN) LAWRENCE
    The Shadow of a Life. Swan, 1888

HORNIMAN, ROY. 1874-1930.
    Israel Rank. Chatto, 1907

HORNUNG, E(RNEST) W(ILLIAM). 1866-1921.
        SC: Raffles = R.
    The Amateur Cracksman. Methuen, 1899;
        Scribner, 1899. Also published as:
        Raffles, the Amateur Cracksman. Nash,
        1906 R ss
    At Large. Scribner, 1902 (British
        title?)
    The Belle of Toorak. Richards, 1900.
        U.S. title: The Shadow of a Man.
        Scribner, 1901
    The Black Mask. Richards, 1901. U.S.
        title: Raffles: Further Adventures of
        the Amateur Cracksman. Scribner, 1901
        R ss
    -The Boss of Taroomba. Bliss, 1894;
        Scribner, 1900
    -A Bride from the Bush. Smith & Elder,
        1890; U.S. Book Co., as by "A New
        Writer", 1890
    The Camera Fiend. Unwin, 1911; Scrib-
        ner, 1911
    The Crime Doctor. Nash, 1914; Bobbs,
        1914 ss
    Dead Men Tell No Tales. Methuen, 1899;
        Scribner, 1899
    Denis Dent. Isbister, 1903; Stokes,
        1904
    -Irralie's Bushranger. New Vagabond Li-
        brary, 1896; Scribner, 1896
    Mr. Justice Raffles. Smith & Elder,
        1909; Scribner, 1909 R
    -My Lord Duke. Cassell, 1897; Scribner,
        1897
    Old Offenders and a Few Old Scores.
        Murray, 1923 ss
    Peccavi. Richards, 1900; Scribner, 1900
    Raffles: Further Adventures of the Ama-
        teur Cracksman; see The Black Mask
    Raffles, the Amateur Cracksman; see The
        Amateur Cracksman
    The Rogue's March. Cassell, 1896;
        Scribner, 1896
    The Shadow of a Man; see The Belle of
        Toorak
    The Shadow of a Rope. Chatto, 1902;
        Scribner, 1902
    Some Persons Unknown. Cassell, 1898;
        Scribner, 1898 ss
    Stingaree. Chatto, 1905; Scribner, 1905
        ss
    A Thief in the Night. Chatto, 1905;
        Scribner, 1905 R ss
    The Thousandth Woman. Nash, 1913;
        Bobbs, 1913

    -Tiny Luttrell. Cassell (London & NYC),
        1893
    -Under Two Skies. A. & C. Black, 1892
    -Witching Hill. Hodder, 1913; Scribner,
        1913 ss
    -Young Blood. Cassell, 1898; Scribner,
        1898

HORNUNG, EDWIN F. Pseudonym of Wilbur
        Braun, 1896-   , q.v. Other pseudo-
        nyms: Walter Blake, Bruce Brandon,
        Fred Caldwell, Raymond Dumkey, Nan
        Fleming, Marsha Grable, Jed Parish,
        Basil Ring, Orville Snap; Mortimer
        Sprague, Bert Stoner, qq.v.
    Your Time Is Up. French, 1949 (3-act
        play.)

HORROCK, NICHOLAS (MORTON). 1936-   .
        Ref: CA. See: Evert Clark.

HORSEFIELD, L(ESLIE) G(RAHAM)
    Murder at No. 3. Swan, 1950
    Mystery at Vellum. Scion, 1949

HORSFIELD, RICHARD HENRY. 1872-1942.
        Pseudonym: M. B. Gaunt, q.v.

HORSTMAN, THOMAS
    The Kessler Alliance. Belmont, 1980
        [Munich]

HORTON, GEORGE. 1852-1942.
    The Edge of Hazard. Bobbs, 1906
        [Far East]
    -A Fair Brigand. Stone, 1899; Ward,
        1900
    -A Fair Insurgent. Ward, 1906 (U.S.
        title?)
    -Like Another Helen. Bobbs, 1901;
        Stevens & Brown, 1901
    -The Long Straight Road. Bowen-Merrill,
        1902; Stevens & Brown, 1902
    -Miss Schuyler's Alias. Badger, 1913
    The Monk's Treasure. Bobbs, 1905; Ward,
        1907 [Greece]
    -The Temptation of Father Anthony.
        McClure, 1901
    -The Unspeakable Turk. McClure, 1900

HORTON, MILESON (DENIS JAMES), 1899-   ,
        and THOMAS PEMBROKE (pseudonym of
        Henry Thomas Hopkinson, 1905-   ).
    Photocrimes. Barker, 1936 (Illustrated
        puzzle ss.)

HORVITZ, LESLIE and H. HARRIS GEBHARD
    The Compton Effect. Signet, 1980;
        Sphere, 1981 [NYC, hosp.]

HOSEGOOD, LEWIS. 1920-   .
    The Minotaur Garden. Heinemann, 1972;
        Delacorte, 1972

HOSEGOOD, WILLIAM. 1920-   .
    The Time-Torn Man. Heinemann, 1973

HOSKEN, ALICE CECIL SEYMOUR. Pseudonym:
        Coralie Stanton, q.v.

HOSKEN, CLIFFORD (JAMES WHEELER). 1882-
        1950. Pseudonym: Richard Keverne,
        q.v. Ref: CC, MP, TC. Set: Eng.
    Missing from His Home. Putnam (London),
        1932. Reprinted as by Richard Kev-
        erne: Penguin, 1939
    The Pretender. Harrap, 1930
    The Shadow Syndicate. Harrap, 1930;
        Dial, 1929

HOSKEN, (ERNEST CHARLES) HEATH. 1875-
        See: Coralie Stanton.

HOSKINS, BERTHA LADD
    The Double Fortune. Neale, 1909

HOSKINS, ROBERT. 1933-   . Pseudonyms:
        Grace Corren, Susan Jennifer, Michael
        Kerr, qq.v. Ref: CA.
    Survival Run. Pinnacle, 1980 (Noveli-
        zation of the movie.)

HOSSENT, HARRY. 1916-   . Pseudonym:
        David Savage, q.v. Ref: CA. SC: Max
        Heald, in all titles.
    The Fear Business. Long, 1967 [Bulg.]
    Memory of Treason. Long, 1961 [Sp.]
    No End to Fear. Long, 1959 [Switz.]
    Run for Your Death. Long, 1965 [Yugos.]
    Spies Die at Dawn. Long, 1958
    Spies Have No Friends. Long, 1963

HOSTER, GRACE (MADELEINE JOHNSON).
        1893-
    Goodbye, Dear Elizabeth. Farrar, 1943;
        Hammond, 1948 [acad.]
    Trial by Murder. Farrar, 1944; Hammond,
        1952

HOSTOVSKY, EGON. 1908-1973. Czech diplo-
        mat.
    The Midnight Patient. Appleton, 1954;
        Heinemann, 1955
    Missing. Viking, 1952; Secker, 1952
        (Translated from the Czech.) [Prague]
    -The Plot. Doubleday, 1961; Cassell,
        1961
    -Three Nights. Cassell, 1964

HOTCHKISS, C(HAUNSEY) C(RAFTS). 1852-
        1920.
    The Ivory Ball. Watt, 1920
    -Mavde Baxter. Watt, 1911
    The Red Paper. Watt, 1912
    -The Spur of Danger. Watt, 1915

HOTCHNER, A(ARON) E(DWARD). 1920-   .
        Ref: CA.
    The Dangerous American. Random, 1958;
        Weidenfeld, 1959 [It.]
    Treasure. Random, 1970; Hodder, 1971

HOUGH, (HELEN) CHARLOTTE (WOODYATT).
        1924-   . Ref: CA.
    The Bassington Murder. Elek, 1980; St.
        Martin's, 1980

HOUGH, JOHN (T.), JR. 1946-   . Ref: CA.
    The Guardian. Little, 1975

HOUGH, S(TANLEY) B(ENNETT). 1917-   .
        Pseudonym: Bennett Stanley, q.v. Ref:
        CA, CC, TC. SC: Insp. Brentford, in
        at least those marked B. Set: Eng.
    The Bronze Perseus. Secker, 1959;
        Walker, 1962. Also published as: The
        Tender Killer. Avon, 1963; Ian Henry,
        1975
    Dear Daughter Dead. Gollancz, 1965;
        Walker, 1966 B
    Extinction Bomber. Bodley, 1956
    Fear Fortune, Father. Gollancz, 1974 B
    Frontier Incident. Hodder, 1951; Crow-
        ell, 1952
    Mission in Guemo. Hodder, 1953; Walker,
        1964 [Cent. Am.]
    Moment of Decision. Hodder, 1952
    -The Primitives. Hodder, 1954
    Sweet Sister Seduced. Gollancz, 1968 B
    The Tender Killer; see The Bronze Per-
        seus

HOUGHTON, CLAUDE. Pseudonym of Claude
        Houghton Oldfield, 1889-1961.
    -All Change, Humanity! Collins, 1942
    -At the End of a Road. Hutchinson, 1953
    -The Big Trail. Readers Library, 1931
        (Novelization of the movie.)
    Birthmark. Collins, 1950
    -Captain of the Guard. Readers Library,
        1930 (Novelization of the movie.)
    -The Clock Ticks. Hutchinson, 1954
    The Enigma of Conrad Stone. Collins,
        1952
    A Hair Divides. Butterworth, 1930;
        Doubleday, 1931
    I Am Jonathan Scrivener. Butterworth,
        1930; Simon, 1930
    -The Last Command. Readers Library,
        1929 (Novelization of the movie.)
    -The Man Who Could Still Laugh. Todd,
        1943 (16 pp.)
    -More Lives Than One. Hutchinson, 1957
    The Passing of Third Floor Back.
        Queensway, 1935
    -Passport to Paradise. Collins, 1944
    -The Quarrel. Collins, 1948
    The Riddle of Helena. Holden, 1927
    -The Sins of the Fathers. Readers Li-
        brary, 1930 (Novelization of the
        movie.)
    -Six Lives and a Book. Collins, 1943
    -Some Rise by Sin. Hutchinson, 1956
    Transformation Scene. Collins, 1946

HOUGRON, JEAN. 1923-   .
    A Question of Character. Hutchinson,
        1957; Farrar, 1958. Also published
        as: Trapped. Dell, 1959 (Translation
        of "Je Reviendrai a Kandara." Paris,
        1955.) [Fr.]

HOULT, NORAH. 1898-
    A Death Occurred. Hutchinson, 1954
    -Frozen Ground. Heinemann, 1952
    -The Last Days of Miss Jenkinson. Hutch-
        inson, 1962
    Scene for Death. Heinemann, 1943
    -There Were No Windows. Heinemann, 1944

HOUSE, BRANT. House name. Unless other-
        wise indicated, titles below are
        by Paul Chadwick. All titles are in
        the Secret Agent X series.
    Brand of the Metal Maiden (by G. T.
        Fleming-Roberts). R.W. Classic, 1974
    City of the Living Dead. Corinth, 1966
    Curse of the Mandarin's Fan (by G. T.
        Fleming-Roberts). Corinth, 1966
        [S.F.]

The Death-Torch Terror. Corinth, 1966
Octopus of Crime. Corinth, 1966
Servants of the Skull (by Emile C. Tepperman). Corinth, 1966
The Sinister Scourge. Corinth, 1966
The Torture Trust. Corinth, 1966

HOUSE, RON
  Bullshot Crummond. French (NYC), 1974 (2-act play.)

HOUSEHOLD, GEOFFREY (EDWARD WEST). 1900- . Ref: CA, CC, EM, MC, TC. SC: Roger Taine = RT.
  Arabesque. Chatto, 1948; Little, 1948 [Mid. East]
  The Brides of Solomon and other stories. Joseph, 1958; Little, 1958 ss
  The Courtesy of Death. Joseph, 1967; Little, 1967
  Dance of the Dwarfs. Joseph, 1968; Little, 1968
  Doom's Caravan. Joseph, 1971; Little, 1971 [Mid. East]
  -The Europe That Was. David, 1979; St. Martin's, 1979 ss
  Fellow Passenger. Joseph, 1955; Little, 1955. Also published as: Hang the Man High. Bestseller, 1957, abridged
  Hang the Man High; see Fellow Passenger
  The High Place. Joseph, 1950; Little, 1950 [Syr.]
  Hostage: London. Joseph, 1977; Little, 1977
  The Last Two Weeks of Georges Rivac. Joseph, 1978; Little, 1978
  The Lives and Times of Bernardo Brown. Joseph, 1973; Little, 1974 [Buch.]
  Man Hunt; see Rogue Male
  Olura. Joseph, 1965; Little, 1965 [Sp.]
  Red Anger. Joseph, 1975; Little, 1975
  Rogue Male. Chatto, 1939; Little, 1939. Also published as: Man Hunt. Triangle, 1942 RT
  A Rough Shoot. Joseph, 1951; Little, 1951 ss
  Sabres on the Sand. Joseph, 1966; Little, 1966 ss
  The Salvation of Pisco Gabar and other stories. Chatto, 1938; Little, 1940 (The U.S. edition has two more stories than the British.) ss
  -The Sending. Joseph, 1980; Little, 1980
  Tales of Adventurers. Joseph, 1952; Little, 1952 ss
  Thing to Love. Joseph, 1963; Little, 1963
  The Third Hour. Chatto, 1937; Little, 1938
  The Three Sentinels. Joseph, 1972; Little, 1972 [S. Am.]
  A Time to Kill. Joseph, 1952; Little, 1951 RT
  Watcher in the Shadows. Joseph, 1960; Little, 1960

HOUSER, LIONEL
  Lake of Fire. Kendall, 1933; Jarrolds, 1934 [Calif.]

HOUSMAN, LAURENCE. 1865-1959.
  Odd Pairs. Cape, 1925 ss, some criminous

HOUSTON, BILLIE. One of the Houston Sisters, a vaudeville act.
  Twice Round the Clock. Hutchinson, 1935

HOUSTON, DAVID
  Shadows on the Moon. Leisure, 1978 [Calif.]

HOUSTON, JAMES D. 1933- . Ref: CA.
  Continental Drift. Knopf, 1978 [Calif.]

HOUSTON, MARGARET BELLA.   -1966.
  -The Witch Man. Hutchinson, 1922; Small, 1922
  Yonder. Allen, 1955; Crown, 1955 [Fla.]

HOUSTON, R. B. Pseudonym of Hugh C(rauford) Rae, 1935- , q.v. Other pseudonyms: Robert Crawford, Stuart Stern, qq.v.
  Two for the Grave. Hale, 1972

HOUSTON, ROBERT
  Monday, Tuesday, Wednesday! Avon, 1978

HOVICK, ROSE LOUISE. 1914-1970. Pseudonym: Gypsy Rose Lee, q.v.

HOW, BRIEN
  Recoil. Hale, 1962

HOWARD. Pseudonym: Nicholas Carter.

HOWARD, CLARK. 1934- . Born in Tenn., grew up in Chi.
  The Doomsday Squad. Weybright, 1970; Allen, 1971

The Hunters. Dial, 1976 [Calif.]
The Killings. Dial, 1973; Souvenir, 1974 [Calif.]
Last Contract. Pinnacle, 1973
The Last Great Death Stunt. Berkley, 1977
Mark the Sparrow. Dial, 1975; Souvenir, 1976 [Calif.]
-A Movement Toward Eden. Moore, 1969
Summit Kill. Pinnacle, 1975

HOWARD, COLIN. Pseudonym of (Colin) Howard Shaw, 1934- . Teacher at Harrow in England.
  Killing No Murder. Hale, 1972; Scribner, 1981, as by Howard Shaw

HOWARD, GEORGE (FITZALAN) BRONSON. 1883-1922. See: George (Fitzalan) Bronson-Howard.

HOWARD, HARTLEY. Pseudonym of Leopold Horace Ognall, 1908-1979. Other pseudonym: Harry Carmichael, q.v. SC: Glenn Bowman, in at least those marked GB; Philip Scott, in at least those marked PS.
  The Armitage Secret. Collins, 1959 GB
  Assignment K; see Department K
  The Big Snatch. Collins, 1958 GB
  Bowman at a Venture. Collins, 1954 GB [NYC]
  Bowman on Broadway. Collins, 1954 GB
  Bowman Strikes Again. Collins, 1953 GB
  The Bowman Touch. Collins, 1956 GB [NYC]
  Count-Down. Collins, 1962 GB [NYC]
  Counterfeit. Collins, 1966
  Cry on My Shoulder. Collins, 1970 GB [NYC]
  Dead Drunk. Collins, 1974 GB
  Deadline. Collins, 1959 GB [NYC]
  Death of Cecilia. Collins, 1952 GB [NYC]
  Department K. Collins, 1964. U.S. title: Assignment K. Pyramid, 1968 PS
  Double Finesse. Collins, 1962
  Epitaph for Joanna. Collins, 1972 GB
  Extortion. Collins, 1960 GB [NYC]
  The Eye of the Hurricane. Collins, 1968 PS
  Fall Guy. Collins, 1960 GB [NYC]
  A Hearse for Cinderella. Collins, 1956 GB
  Highway to Murder. Collins, 1973 GB
  I'm No Hero. Collins, 1961 GB [NYC]
  Key to the Morgue. Collins, 1957 GB [NYC]
  The Last Appointment. Collins, 1951 GB [NYC]
  The Last Deception. Collins, 1951 GB [NYC]
  The Last Vanity. Collins, 1952 GB [NYC]
  The Long Night. Collins, 1957 GB [NYC]
  Million Dollar Snapshot. Collins, 1971 GB
  Murder One. Collins, 1971 GB
  Nice Day for a Funeral. Collins, 1972 GB
  No Target for Bowman. Collins, 1955 GB [NYC]
  One-Way Ticket. Collins, 1978 GB
  The Other Side of the Door. Collins, 1953 GB
  Out of the Fire. Collins, 1965
  Payoff. Collins, 1976 GB [NYC]
  Portrait of a Beautiful Harlot. Collins, 1966 GB [NYC]
  Room 37. Collins, 1970 GB [Ia.]
  Routine Investigation. Collins, 1967 GB [Mex.]
  The Sealed Envelope. Collins, 1979 GB
  The Secret of Simon Cornell. Collins, 1969 GB [Rome, Malta]
  Sleep for the Wicked. Collins, 1955 GB [Del.]
  Sleep, My Pretty One. Collins, 1958 GB
  The Stretton Case. Collins, 1963
  Time Bomb. Collins, 1961 GB [NYC]
  Treble Cross. Collins, 1975 GB

HOWARD, HERBERT EDMUND. 1900- . Pseudonym: R. Philmore, q.v.

HOWARD, JAMES A(RCH). 1922- . Ref: CA. Pseudonym: Laine Fisher, q.v. SC: Steve Ashe = SA.
  Blow Out My Torch. Popular Library, 1956; Digit, 1964 SA
  The Bullet-Proof Martyr. Dutton, 1961 [Ill.]
  Die on Easy Street. Popular Library, 1957; Digit, 1964 SA [L.A.]
  I Like It Tough. Popular Library, 1955; Digit, 1964 SA
  I'll Get You Yet. Popular Library, 1954; Digit, 1964 SA
  Murder in Mind. Dutton, 1960 [Calif.]
  Murder Takes a Wife. Dutton, 1958 [Tex.]

HOWARD, JOHN FREDERICK
  Bolt. Vantage, 1978

HOWARD, KEBLE. Pseudonym of John Keble Bell, 1875-1928.
  The Cheerful Knave. Unwin, 1927

HOWARD, KENT
  Go South, Go Crazy. Cooper, 1952
  Shooting Made Easy. Cooper, 1952
  Kearny Died Twice. Cooper, 1952
  Small Time Crooks. Cooper, 1952

HOWARD, LEIGH. Pseudonym of Leon Alexander Lee Howard, 1914-1979? Journalist and newspaper editor in London.
  Blind Date. Longmans, 1955; Simon, 1958. Also published as: Chance Meeting. Avon, 1960

HOWARD, LEON ALEXANDER LEE. 1914-1979? Pseudonym: Leigh Howard, q.v.

HOWARD, LESLEY
  Invitation to Paradise. Coward, 1974 [Med. Is.]

HOWARD, LINDEN. Pseudonym of Audrie Manley-Tucker.
  The Devil's Lady. Millington, 1980; St. Martin's, 1980
  Foxglove Country. Millington, 1978; St. Martin's, 1977 [Wales]

HOWARD, LOUIS G. REDMOND. See: L(ouis) G. Redmond-Howard.

HOWARD, TROY. Pseudonym of Lauran Bosworth Paine, 1916- . Other pseudonyms: John Armour, Reg Batchelor, Kenneth Bedford, Frank Bosworth, Mark Carrel, Robert Clarke, Richard Dana, J. F. Drexler, Jared Ingersol, John Kilgore, Hunter Liggett, J. K. Lucas, John Morgan, qq.v.
  The Black Light. Hale, 1968

HOWARD, VECHEL. Pseudonym of Howard Rigsby, 1909- , q.v. SC: Johnny Church, in both titles.
  Murder on Her Mind. GM, 1959; Muller pb, 1960 [Mex.]
  Murder with Love. GM, 1959; Muller pb, 1960 [Las Veg.]

HOWARD, VINCE
  Rendezvous in Rio. Nite Time, 1964 [Rio de J.]

HOWARD, WENDELL
  The Last Refuge of a Scoundrel and other stories. Exposition, 1952 ss

HOWARTH, CAROLINE M. Conn. resident.
  Eyes in the Night. Pageant, 1953 [Conn.]

HOWARTH, DAVID (ARMINE). 1912- . Ref: CA.
  Group Flashing Two. Hale, 1952
  One Night in Styria. Hale, 1953
  Thieves' Hole. Rinehart, 1954 (British title?) [Scot.]

HOWARTH, PATRICK (JOHN FIELDING). 1916- . Pseudonym: C. D. E. Francis, q.v.
  The Dying Ukrainian. Bodley, 1953

HOWATCH, SUSAN (STURT). 1940- . Ref: CA. Set: Eng.
  April's Grave. H. Hamilton, 1973; Ace, 1969
  Call in the Night. H. Hamilton, 1972; Ace, 1967
  Cashelmara. H. Hamilton, 1974; Simon, 1974
  The Dark Shore. H. Hamilton, 1972; Ace, 1965
  The Devil on Lammas Night. H. Hamilton, 1973; Ace, 1970
  Penmarric. H. Hamilton, 1971; Simon, 1971
  The Shrouded Walls. H. Hamilton, 1972; Ace, 1968
  The Waiting Sands. H. Hamilton, 1972; Ace, 1966 [Scot.]

HOWE, ARTHUR
  I Wanted the Killer. Vega, 1963

HOWE, EDGAR WATSON. 1853-1937.
  The Mystery of the Locks. Osgood, 1885

HOWE, FANNY
  Legacy of Lanshore. Berkely, 1973 [Maine]

HOWE, GEORGE (LOCKE). 1898-1977. Ref: CA.
  Call It Treason. Viking, 1949; Hart-Davis, 1950. Also published as: Decision Before Dawn. Digit, 1958

HOWE, J(OHN) M.
  Accessory for Murder. Zebra, 1980 [NYC]
HOWE, MURIEL. Pseudonym of Muriel
    Smithies. Ref: CA.
  The Affair at Falconers. Macdonald, 1957
  Pendragon. Macdonald, 1958
HOWE, RUSSELL WARREN. 1925-   . Ref: CA.
  Behold the City. Secker, 1953
  -The Light and the Shadows. Secker, 1952
    ss
HOWELL, JEAN
  The Weapon. Decade, 1980
HOWELL, PATRICIA HAGAN. 1939-   . Ref:
    CA.
  Winds of Terror. Avon, 1975 [Ala.]
HOWES, ROYCE (BUCKNAM). 1901-1973. Ref:
    CA. SC: Capt. Ben Lucias = BL.
  The Callao Clue. Doubleday, 1936 [ship]
  The Case of the Copy-Hook Killing. Dutton, 1945   BL [Mich.]
  Death Dupes a Lady. Doubleday, 1937 BL
    [Mich.]
  Death on the Bridge. Doubleday, 1935
    [ship]
  Death Rides a Hobby. Doubleday, 1939
    BL [Mich.]
  Murder at Maneuvers. Doubleday, 1938 BL
  The Nasty Name Murders. Doubleday, 1939
    BL [ship]
  Night of the Garter Murder. Doubleday,
    1937 BL [Det.]
HOWIE, EDITH. Magazine ss writer living
    in Minn. in the 1940s.
  The Band Played Murder. Mill, 1946;
    Boardman, 1948
  Cry Murder. Mill, 1944; Boardman, 1950
    [Midwest]
  Murder at Stone House. Farrar, 1942;
    Boardman, 1945 [N.J.]
  Murder for Christmas. Farrar, 1941;
    Boardman, 1942 [N.Y.]
  Murder for Tea. Farrar, 1941, in the
    threesome "Three Prize Murders";
    Boardman, 1942 [Midwest]
  Murder's So Permanent. Farrar, 1942;
    Boardman, 1944
  No Face to Murder. Mill, 1946; Boardman, 1946 [Mo., church]
HOWITT, JOHN LESLIE DESPARD. Pseudonym:
    Leslie Despard, q.v.
HOWLETT, JOHN (REGINALD). 1940-   . Ref:
    CA.
  The Christmas Spy. Hutchinson, 1975;
    Harcourt, 1975 [It.]
  -Maximum Credible Accident. Hutchinson,
    1980
  Tango November. Hutchinson, 1976;
    Atheneum, 1977 [Sic.]
HOXIE, WALTER PALMER. Pseudonym: Alton
    Hurlba, q.v.
HOYLE, FRED. 1915-   . Ref: CA.
  Ossian's Ride. Heinemann, 1959; Harper,
    1959
  The Westminster Disaster, with Geoffrey
    Hoyle, 1942-   . Heinemann, 1978;
    Harper, 1978
HOYLE, GEOFFREY. 1942-   . See: Fred
    Hoyle, 1915-   .
HOYLE, TREVOR
  The Sexless Spy. Sphere, 1977
  -The Svengali Plot. Sphere, 1978
HOYNE, THOMAS TEMPLE. 1875-1946.
  Intrigue on the Upper Level. Reilly,
    1934 [Chi., future]
HOYT, DON and ART(HUR) MOORE, q.v. Joint
    pseudonyms of Arthur Moore and Marilyn Granbeck, 1927-   , q.v.: Adam
    Hamilton, Van Saxon, qq.v.
  Death Is a Drag. Powell, 1970
HOYT, EDWIN PALMER (JR.). 1923-   . Ref:
    CA.
  -The Ghost Lane. Luce, 1971
  A Matter of Conscience. Duell, 1966
HOYT, PAUL
  Murderer's Wench. Hale, 1936
HOYT, RICHARD. 1941-   . Has been reporter, intelligence agent, and, more
    recently, teacher in Portland.
  Decoys. Evans, 1980; Hale, 1982
    [Seattle]
HOYT, VICTOR B.
  Spin a Coin for Murder. Milestone, 1954

HRABEL, BAHUMIL. 1914-   .
  The Death of Mr. Balishberger. Doubleday, 1974 (Translation of "Automat
    Svet.") ss
HUBBARD, GEORGE. 1884-   . See: Lilian
    Bennet-Thompson, 1883-1942.
HUBBARD, MARGARET ANN. 1909-   . Ref:
    CA.
  Murder at St. Dennis. Bruce, 1952
    [S. Dak., hosp.]
  Murder Takes the Veil. Bruce, 1950
    [La., acad.]
  Sister Simon's Murder Case. Bruce, 1959
    [Midwest]
  Step Softly on My Grave. Bruce, 1966
    [Midwest]
HUBBARD, P(HILIP) M(AITLAND). 1910-1980.
    Ref: CA, CC, TC. Set: many in Eng.
  The Causeway. Macmillan (London), 1976;
    Doubleday, 1978 [Scot.]
  Cold Waters. Bles, 1970; Atheneum, 1969
  The Country of Again; see The Custom of
    the Country
  The Custom of the Country. Bles, 1969.
    U.S. title: The Country of Again.
    Atheneum, 1969 [Pak.]
  The Dancing Man. Macmillan (London),
    1971; Atheneum, 1971 [Wales]
  Flush As May. Joseph, 1963; London
    House, 1963
  The Graveyard. Macmillan (London),
    1975; Atheneum, 1975 [Scot.]
  High Tide. Macmillan (London), 1971;
    Atheneum, 1970
  A Hive of Glass. Joseph, 1965; Atheneum, 1965
  The Holm Oaks. Joseph, 1965; Atheneum,
    1966
  Kill Claudio. Macmillan (London), 1979;
    Doubleday, 1979
  Picture of Millie. Joseph, 1964; London House, 1964
  The Quiet River. Macmillan (London),
    1978; Doubleday, 1978
  A Rooted Sorrow. Macmillan (London),
    1973; Atheneum, 1973
  A Thirsty Evil. Macmillan (London),
    1974; Atheneum, 1974
  The Tower. Bles, 1968; Atheneum, 1967
  The Whisper in the Glen. Macmillan
    (London), 1972; Atheneum, 1972
    [Scot.]
HUBBARD, REGINA. Pseudonym of Richard
    Hubbard, -ca.1974, q.v. Other
    pseudonyms: Nick Carter, Marie Eyre,
    Chris Stratton, qq.v.
  The Curse of Nightwind. Popular Library, 1975 [L.I.]
HUBBARD, RICHARD.   -ca.1974. Pseudonyms: Nick Carter, Marie Eyre, Regina
    Hubbard, Chris Stratton, qq.v.
  Close-Up of a Killing; see Retake
  Daughter of Despair. Dell, 1972 [L.I.]
  -East Hampton. Curtis, 1973
  Retake. Signet, 1969. British title:
    Close-Up of a Killing. New English
    Library pb, 1970
  The Silence. Popular Library, 1971
HUBBELL, WALTER. 1851-   .
  The Great Amherst Mystery. Brentano's,
    1888; Routledge, 1888
HUBELL, LOIS W. Pseudonym: Ned Hubell,
    q.v.
HUBELL, NED. Pseudonym of Lois W. Hubell.
  The Adventures of Creighton Holmes.
    Popular Library, 1979 ss [Eng.,
    1930s]
HUBER, BERTRAND
  Death and the Dowager. Appleton, 1934.
    British title: Murder with Gloves.
    Hale, 1936 [Eng.]
HUBER, FREDERIC VINCENT
  Tandem Rush. Dell, 1978
HUBER, LOUIS J(OSEPH). 1907-   .
  Six Minute Sketches. Northwestern, 1950
    (Plays, some criminous.)
  Who's Guilty. Northwestern, 1938
    (Plays.)
HUBERT, TORD. 1933-   . Swedish journalist.
  The Trap. Gollancz, 1976; McKay, 1977
    (Translation of "Fallan." Stockholm,
    1974.) [Swed.]
HUBLER, RICHARD G(IBSON). 1912-   . Ref:
    CA.
  The Chase. Coward, 1952 [Calif.]
  The Pass. Coward, 1955

HUCH, RICARDA (OCTAVIA). 1864-1947.
  The Deruga Trial. Macaulay, 1929; Gerald Howe, 1930 (Translation of "Der
    Fall Deruga." Berlin, 1917.)
    [Munich]
HUDIBERG, EDWARD
  Killer's Game. Lion, 1956 [NYC]
HUDSON, CHRISTOPHER. 1946-   . Literary
    editor, screenwriter, editorial writer and reviewer in London.
  The Final Act. Joseph, 1980; Holt, 1980
    [Chile]
HUDSON, JAMES. 1937-   . See: Gayle
    Rivers.
HUDSON, JEFFERY. Pseudonym of (John) Michael Crichton, 1942-   , q.v. Other
    pseudonym: John Lange, q.v.
  A Case of Need. NAL, 1968; Heinemann,
    1968 [Boston]
HUDSON, JOHN PAUL and WARREN WEXLER
  Superstar Murder. Insider Press, 1976
HUDSON, LAURA HOPE
  The Cruel Legacy. Lancer, 1969
HUDSON, NICK
  The Very Wicked. Berkley, 1960
HUDSON, W(ILLIAM) C(ADWALADER). 1843-
    1915. Pseudonyms: Nicholas Carter,
    Barclay North, qq.v.
  -An American Cavalier. Cassell (NYC),
    1897
  The Dugdale Millions. Cassell (NYC),
    1891. Reprinted as by Barclay
    North: Cassell (NYC), 1892 [NYC]
  J. P. Dunbar: A Story of Wall Street.
    Dodge, 1906 [NYC]
  Jack Gordon, Knight Errant, Gotham,
    1883. Cassell (NYC), 1890; Cassell (London), 1890, as by Barclay
    North [NYC]
  The Man with a Thumb. Cassell (NYC),
    1891. Reprinted as by Barclay North:
    Street, 1899 [NYC]
  On the Rack. Cassell (NYC), 1891. Reprinted as by Barclay North: Street,
    1899
  -Should She Have Left Him? Cassell
    (NYC), 1894. Reprinted as by Barclay
    North: Street, 1900
  -Vivier of Vivier, Longman & Company,
    Bankers. Cassell (NYC & London),
    1890. Reprinted as by Barclay North:
    Street, 1899
HUESTON, ETHEL. 1887-   .
  Idle Island. Bobbs, 1927; Hutchinson,
    1927
HUFF, AFTON PATRICIA (WALKER). 1928-
    Ref: CA.
  The Key to Hawthorn Heath. Berkley,
    1972 [Scot.]
HUFF, CHARLES H. 1887?-1959. Pseudonym:
    Drexel Drake, q.v.
HUFF, T(OM) E. 1938?-   . Pseudonyms:
    Edwina Marlow, Beatrice Parker,
    Katherine St. Clair, qq.v. Ref: CA.
  Meet a Dark Stranger. Hawthorn, 1974.
    Also published as: Whisper in the
    Darkness. Dell, 1977 [Eng.]
  Midnight at Mallyncourt. Berkley/Putnam, 1975
  Nine Buck's Row. Hawthorn, 1973
    [Eng., ca.1890]
  Whisper in the Darkness; see Meet a
    Dark Stranger
HUFFMAN, LAURIE (NELL ALFORD). 1916-
    Ref: CA.
  A House Behind the Mint. Doubleday,
    1969 [S.F., 1870s]
HUFFORD, SUSAN. 1940-   . Ref: CA.
  Cove's End. Popular Library, 1977
    [Maine]
  A Delicate Deceit. Popular Library,
    1976 [Mont.]
  The Devil's Sonata. Popular Library,
    1976
  Melody of Malice. Popular Library, 1979
  Midnight Sailing. Popular Library, 1975
    [ship]
  Satan's Sunset. Popular Library, 1977
  Skin Deep. Popular Library, 1978
  Trial of Innocence. Popular Library,
    1978 [Eng.]
HUGGINS, ROY. 1914-   . Graduate of
    UCLA; personnel expert turned writer.
    SC: Stuart Bailey = SB.
  The Double Take. Morrow, 1946; Cassell,
    1947 SB [L.A.]

Lovely Lady, Pity Me. Duell, 1949 [L.A.]
77 Sunset Strip. Dell, 1959 (3 novelets of the TV series based on Huggins' character.) SB [L.A.]
Too Late for Tears. Morrow, 1947; Cassell, 1950 [L.A.]

HUGHES, ALFRED
Leaves from the Note Book of a Chief of Police. Virtue, 1865? ss

HUGHES, BABETTE (PLECHNER). 1906- . Born and resident in Seattle; graduate of U. of Wash.; wife of playwright Glenn (Arthur) Hughes, 1894-1964, q.v., author of numerous 1-act plays.
Murder in Church. Appleton, 1934 [L.A., church]
Murder in the Zoo. Appleton, 1932; Benn, 1932 [acad.]

HUGHES, BEATRIX
The Mystery of St. Martin's Copse. Heath, 1929

HUGHES, (JOHN) CLEDWYN. 1920- . Ref: CA.
The Inn Closes for Christmas. Pilot, 1947. U.S. title: He Dared Not Look Behind. Wyn, 1947

HUGHES, COLIN. Pseudonym of John Creasey, 1908-1973, q.v. Other pseudonyms: Gordon Ashe, M. E. Cooke, Norman Deane, Robert Caine Frazer, Patrick Gill, Michael Halliday, Charles Hogarth, Brian Hope, Kyle Hunt, Abel Mann, Peter Manton, J. J. Marric, Richard Martin, Rodney Mattheson, Anthony Morton, Jeremy York, qq.v.
Triple Murder. Newnes, 1940

HUGHES, DENIS T.
The Aeroplane Mystery. Warren, 1948
-Beautiful Schemer. Hamilton Stafford, 1949
The Case of the River Smugglers. Warren, 1949
The Hidden Gang. Warren, 1948
-Istanbul Elopement. Hamilton Stafford, 1950 [Istan.]
Murder by Telecopter. Warren, 1950

HUGHES, DOROTHY B(ELLE FLANAGAN). 1904- . Ref: CA, CC, EM, MP, TC. SC: Insp. Tobin = T.
The Bamboo Blonde. Duell, 1941 [L.A.]
The Blackbirder. Duell, 1943; Nicholson, 1968 [Sante Fe]
The Body on the Bench; see The Davidian Report
The Candy Kid. Duell, 1950 [Tex.]
The Cross-Eyed Bear. Duell, 1940; Nicholson, 1943. Also published as: The Cross-Eyed Bear Murders. Dell, 1944 T [NYC]
The Cross-Eyed Bear Murders; see The Cross-Eyed Bear
The Davidian Report. Duell, 1952. Also published as: The Body on the Bench. Dell, 1955 [L.A.]
The Delicate Ape. Duell, 1944 [NYC]
Dread Journey. Duell, 1945; Nicholson, 1948
The Expendable Man. Random, 1963; Deutsch, 1964 [Phoenix]
The Fallen Sparrow. Duell, 1942; Nicholson, 1943 T [NYC]
In a Lonely Place. Duell, 1947; Nicholson, 1950 [L.A.]
Johnnie. Duell, 1944; Nicholson, 1946 [NYC]
Kiss for a Killer; see The Scarlet Imperial
Ride the Pink Horse. Duell, 1946; Bantam (London), 1979 [Sante Fe]
The Scarlet Imperial. Mystery Book Club, 1946. Also published as: Kiss for a Killer. Jonathan, 1954
The So Blue Marble. Duell, 1940; Bantam (London), 1979 T [NYC]

HUGHES, GLENN (ARTHUR). 1894-1964.
Fresh Air. Row-Peterson, 1946 (3-act play.)
Green Fire. French (NYC), 1932 (3-act play.) [1990]
The Green Scarab. Row-Peterson, 1945 (3-act play.)
Knock on Wood. Baker, 1949 (3-act play.)
Midnight. Row-Peterson, 1941 (3-act play.)
Suspense. Row-Peterson, 1942 (3-act play.)

HUGHES, KEN(NETH GRAHAM). 1922- . Ref: CA.
High Wray. Gifford, 1952

-The Long Echo. Constable, 1955

HUGHES, MICHAEL. 1940- .
The Sleeper Awakes. Allen, 1980

HUGHES, RODNEY
The Dragon Keepers. Popular Library, 1974

HUGHES, RUPERT. 1872-1956.
The Amiable Crimes of Dirk Memling. Appleton (NYC & London), 1913
-His Fabulous Fortune. Jarrolds, 1943
Ladies' Man. Harper, 1930; Hurst, 1930 [NYC]

HUGHES, VALERIE ANNE. Pseudonym: V. Carrington, q.v.

HUGHES, WILLIAM. SC: George Willis, in at least those marked GW.
Aces High. Barker, 1976 (Novelization of the movie.)
Blind Terror. Sphere, 1971. U.S. title: See No Evil. Award, 1971 (Novelization of the movie.)
Connecting Rooms. Tandem, 1970; Award, 1969 (Novelization of the movie.)
Deathsport. Sphere, 1978 (Novelization of the movie.)
Inside Out. Tandem, 1975; Award, 1976 (Novelization of the movie.) [Berlin]
Odds on Gold. Magread, 1980 GW
Secret Ceremony. Sphere, 1968; Award, 1968 (Novelization of the movie.)
See No Evil; see Blind Terror
Split on Red. Magread, 1979; Wyndham, 1979 GW

HUGHES, WILLIAM THOMAS MAINWARING. 1893- . Pseudonym: Main Waring, q.v.

HUGHESTON, JOSEPHINE. See: (Mabel) Dana Lyon, 1897- .

HUGHSTON, DANA. Pseudonym.
You Stand Accused. Hillman-Curl, 1937

HUGI, MAURICE G. 1904-1947. SC: Martin Speed, in at least those marked MS.
The Convict's Hoard. Swan, 1947 MS
He Died Thrice. Swan, 1947
Martin Speed Versus "The Snatcher." Swan, 1946 MS
Murder Begets Murder. Swan, 1947
The Tin Bath Murder. Swan, 1947 MS

HUGILL, ROBERT
Peril in Provence. Barrington Gray, 1953 [Fr.]
Said the Spider to the Fly. Hale, 1979

HULL, CHARLES. Pseudonym: C. R. B., q.v.

HULL, ERIC TRAVISS. Pseudonym of Terry Harnan, 1920- , q.v.
Murder Lays a Golden Egg. Doubleday, 1944; Westhouse, 1946

HULL, HELEN (ROSE). 1888?-1971. Ref: CA, CC.
Close Her Pale Blue Eyes. Dodd, 1963 [NYC]
A Tapping on the Wall. Dodd, 1960; Collins, 1961 [acad.]

HULL, RICHARD. Pseudonym of Richard Henry Sampson, 1896-1973. Ref: CC, DD, EM, MM, MP, TC. SC: Insp. Fenby = F. Set: Eng.
And Death Came Too. Collins, 1939; Messner, 1942
Beyond Reasonable Doubt; see Excellent Intentions
Excellent Intentions. Faber, 1938. U.S. title: Beyond Reasonable Doubt. Messner, 1941 F
The Ghost It Was. Faber, 1937; Putnam, 1937
Invitation to an Inquest. Collins, 1950
Keep It Quiet. Faber, 1935; Putnam, 1935
Last First. Collins, 1947 [Scot.]
Left-Handed Death. Collins, 1946
The Martineau Murders. Collins, 1953
A Matter of Nerves. Collins, 1950
Murder by Invitation; see My Own Murderer
Murder Isn't Easy. Faber, 1936; Putnam, 1936
The Murder of My Aunt. Faber, 1934; Minton Balch, 1934
The Murderers of Monty. Faber, 1937; Putnam, 1937 F
My Own Murderer. Collins, 1940; Messner, 1940. Also published as: Murder by Invitation. Mystery Novel of the Month, 1941
The Unfortunate Murderer. Collins, 1941; Messner, 1942
Until She Was Dead. Collins, 1949

HULME-BEAMAN, EMERIC. Joint pseudonym with William Senior Ellis: Ben Strong, q.v. SC: Ozmar, in at least those marked O.
The Experiment of Doctor Nevill. Long, 1900
The Faith That Kills. Hurst, 1899
Ozmar the Mystic. Sands, 1896 O
The Prince's Diamond. Hutchinson, 1898 O

HULTMAN, HELEN JOAN. 1891- . SC: Tim Asher = TA.
Death at Windward Hill. Fiction League, 1931 TA [Midwest]
Find the Woman. Doubleday, 1929 TA, in minor role [Midwest]
Murder in Odd Sizes. Hangman's House, 194? (Retitled reprint of ?)
Murder in the French Room. Mystery League, 1931
Murder on Route 40. Phoenix, 1940. Also published as: Murder Rings Twice. Fingerprint, ca.1940 [Ohio]
Murder Rings Twice; see Murder on Route 40
Ready for Death. Phoenix, 1939 [Pa.]
This Murderous Shaft. Phoenix, 1946 [Ia.]

HUMBLOT, PIERRE. 1928- . Pseudonym: Fred Kassak, q.v.

HUME, CYRIL, 1900-1966, and RICHARD MAIBAUM
Ransom. French (NYC), 1963 (Play.)

HUME, DAVID. Pseudonym of J(ohn) V(ictor) Turner, 1900-1945, q.v. Other pseudonym: Nicholas Brady, q.v. SC: Mick Cardby, in at least those marked MC; Tony Carter, in at least those marked TC; Det. Insp. Sanderson = S.
Below the Belt. Collins, 1934 MC
Bring 'Em Back Dead! Collins, 1936; Appleton, 1936 MC [Fr.]
Bullets Bite Deep. Putnam (London), 1932 MC
Call in the Yard. Collins, 1935 ss S
Cemetery First Stop! Collins, 1937 MC
Come Back for the Body. Collins, 1945 MC
Corpses Never Argue. Collins, 1938 MC
The Crime Combine. Collins, 1936 ss S
Crime Unlimited. Collins, 1933; McBride, 1933 MC
Dangerous Mr. Dell. Collins, 1935; Appleton, 1935 MC
Death Before Honour. Collins, 1939 MC
Destiny in My Name. Collins, 1942 MC
Dishonour Among Thieves. Collins, 1943 MC
Eternity, Here I Come! Collins, 1940 MC
Five Aces. Collins, 1940
The Foursquare Murder; see Murders Form Fours
The Gaol Gates Are Open. Collins, 1935. U.S. title: The Jail Gates Are Open. Appleton, 1935 MC
Get Out the Cuffs. Collins, 1943 MC
Good-Bye to Life. Collins, 1938 MC
Halfway to Horror. Collins, 1937 MC
Heading for a Wreath. Collins, 1946 MC
Heads You Lose. Collins, 1939 MC
Invitation to the Grave. Collins, 1940
The Jail Gates Are Open; see The Gaol Gates Are Open
Make Way for the Mourners. Collins, 1939 MC
Meet the Dragon. Collins, 1936 MC
Mick Cardby Works Overtime. Collins, 1944 MC
Murders Form Fours. Putnam (London), 1933. U.S. title: The Foursquare Murder. McBride, 1933 MC
Never Say Live! Collins, 1942 TC
Requiem for Rogues. Collins, 1942 TC
The Return of Mick Cardby. Collins, 1941 MC
Stand Up and Fight. Collins, 1941
They Called Him Death. Collins, 1934; Appleton, 1935 MC
They Never Came Back. Collins, 1945 MC
Toast to a Corpse. Collins, 1944 MC
Too Dangerous to Live. Collins, 1934 MC
You'll Catch Your Death. Collins, 1940 TC

HUME, DORIS
Dark Purpose. Popular Library, 1960

HUME, FERGUS(ON WRIGHT). 1859-1932. Ref: CC, DD, EM, MC, MP, EM. SC: Octavus Fanks, in at least those marked OF. Set: Eng.
Across the Footlights. White, 1912
-Aladdin in London. Black, 1892; Houghton, 1892
The Amethyst Cross. Cassell, 1908
Answered: A Spy Story. White, 1915
-The Best of Her Sex. Allen, 1894

Bishop Pendle; or, The Bishop's Secret; see The Bishop's Secret
The Bishop's Secret. Long, 1900. U.S. title: Bishop Pendle; or, The Bishop's Secret. Rand, 1900
The Black Carnation. Gale & Polden, 1892; U.S. Book Co., 1892
The Black Image. Ward, 1918
The Black Patch. Long, 1906
The Blue Talisman. Laurie, 1912; Clode, 1925
The Caravan Mystery. Hurst, 1926
The Carbuncle Clue. Warne, 1896 OF
The Caretaker. Ward, 1916
The Chinese Jar. Low, 1893 OF
Claude Duval of Ninety-Five: A Romance of the Road. Digby Long, 1897; Dillingham, 1897
The Clock Struck One. Warne, 1898
A Coin of Edward VII. Digby Long, 1903; Dillingham, 1903
Crazy-Quilt. Ward, 1919
A Creature of the Night. Low, 1891; Lovell, 1891 [It.]
The Crime of the Crystal. Digby Long, 1901
The Crime of the 'Liza Jane.' Ward, 1895
The Crimson Cryptogram. Long, 1900; Buckles, 1912
The Crowned Skull. Laurie, 1908. U.S. title (?): The Red Skull. Dodge, 1908
The Curse. Laurie, 1915
The Dancer in Red. Digby, 1906 ss
The Dark Avenue. Ward, 1920
The Devil-Stick. Downey, 1898
The Devil's Ace. Everett, 1909
The Disappearing Eye. Digby Long, 1909; Dillingham, 1909
Dowker-Detective. Seaside, 1892 (British title?)
The Dwarf's Chamber and other stories. Ward, 1896 ss
The Fatal Song. White, 1905
The Fever of Life. Low, 1892; Lovell, 1891
Flies in the Web. White, 1908
For the Defense. Rand, 1898 (British title?)
The 4 P.M. Express. White, 1914
From Thief to Detective. Street (Magnet #241).   (British title?)
The Gates of Dawn. Low, 1894; Neely, 1894
-The Gentleman Who Vanished. White, 1890. U.S. title: The Man Who Vanished. Liberty Book Co., 1892
The Girl from Malta. Hansom Cab Co., 1889; Lovell, 1889
The Golden Wang-Ho. Long, 1901. U.S. title: The Secret of the Chinese Jar. Westbrook, 1928
The Green Mummy. Long, 1908; Dillingham, 1908
The Grey Doctor. Ward, 1917
The Guilty House. White, 1903
Hagar of the Pawn-Shop. Skeffington, 1898; Buckles, 1898 ss
-The Harlequin Opal. Allen, 1893; Rand, 1893 [Mex.]
Heart of Ice. Hurst, 1918
High Water Mark. White, 1911
The Hurton Treasure Mystery. Mellifont, 1937
The Indian Bangle. Low, 1899
In Queer Street. White, 1913
The Jade Eye. Long, 1903
The Jew's House. Ward, 1911
Jonah's Luck. White, 1906
The Lady from Nowhere. Chatto, 1900
Lady Jezebel. Pearson, 1898
Lady Jim of Curzon Street. Laurie, 1905; Dillingham, 1906
The Last Straw. Hutchinson, 1932
The Lone Inn. Jarrolds, 1894; Cassell (NYC), 1895
The Lonely Church. Long, 1904
The Lonely Subaltern. White, 1910
The Lost Parchment. Ward, 1914; Dillingham, 1914
Madame Midas. Hansom Cab Co., 1888; Munro, 1888 [Australia]
The Man Who Vanished; see The Gentleman Who Vanished
The Man with a Secret. White, 1890
The Mandarin's Fan. Digby Long, 1904; Dillingham, 1904 [China]
A Marriage Mystery: Told from Three Points of View. Digby Long, 1896
The Masquerade Mystery. Digby Long, 1895
The Master-Mind. Hurst, 1919
A Midnight Mystery. Gale & Polden, 1894
The Mikado Jewel. Everett, 1910
The Millionaire Mystery. Chatto, 1901; Buckles, 1901
The Miser's Will. Treherne, 1903
Miss Mephistopheles. White, 1890; Lovell, 1890 (A sequel to Madame Midas, q.v.)
Monsieur Judas. Blackett, 1891 OF
The Moth-Woman. Hurst, 1923
Mother Mandarin. White, 1912
The Mystery of a Hansom Cab. (Hume), 1886; Munro, 1888 [Melb.]
The Mystery of a Motor Cab. Everett, 1908
The Mystery of Landy Court. Jarrolds, 1894
The Mystery of the Shadow. Cassell, 1906; Dodge, 1906
The Mystery Queen. Ward, 1912; Dillingham, 1912
Next Door. Ward, 1918
Not Wanted. White, 1914
The Opal Serpent. Long, 1905; Dillingham, 1905
The Other Person. White, 1920
The Pagan's Cup. Digby Long, 1902; Dillingham, 1902
The Peacock of Jewels. Digby Long, 1910; Dillingham, 1910
The Piccadilly Puzzle. White, 1889; Lovell, with 2 additional stories, 1889
The Pink Shop. White, 1911
The Purple Fern. Everett, 1907
The Rainbow Feather. Digby Long, 1898; Dillingham, 1898
The Rectory Governess. White, 1911
The Red Bicycle. Ward, 1916
The Red-Headed Man. Digby Long, 1899
Red Money. Ward, 1912; Dillingham, 1911
The Red Skull; see The Crowned Skull
The Red Window. Digby Long, 1904; Dillingham, 1904
The Sacred Herb. Long, 1908; Dillingham, 1908
The Scarlet Bat. White, 1905
The Sealed Message. Digby Long, 1908; Dillingham, 1907
The Secret of the Chinese Jar; see The Golden Wang-Ho
The Secret Passage. Long, 1905; Dillingham, 1905
Seen in the Shadow. White, 1913
Shylock of the River. Digby Long, 1900
The Silent House; see The Silent House in Pimlico
The Silent House in Pimlico. Long, 1899. U.S. title: The Silent House. Doscher, 1907
The Silent Signal. Ward, 1917
The Silver Bullet. Long, 1903
The Singing Head. Hurst, 1920
The Solitary Farm. Ward, 1909; Dillingham, 1909
A Speck of the Motley. Innes, 1893
The Spider. Ward, 1910
The Steel Crown. Digby Long, 1911; Dillingham, 1911
The Third Volume. Cassell (NYC), 1895 (British title?)
The Thirteenth Guest. Ward, 1913
Three. Ward, 1921
The Tombstone Treasure. Daffodil Library, 1897
The Top Dog. White, 1909
Tracked by Fate. Street (Magnet #225). (British title?)
Tracked by a Tattoo. Warne, 1896
A Traitor in London. Long, 1900; Buckles, 1900
A Trick of Time. Hurst, 1922
The Turnpike House. Long, 1902
The Unexpected. Odhams, 1921
The Unwilling Bride. Ogilvie, 1895 (British title?)
The Vanishing of Tera. White, 1900
The Wheeling Light. Chatto, 1904
The Whispering Lane. Hurst, 1924; Small, 1925
The White Prior. Warne, 1895
-Whom God Hath Joined: A Question of Marriage. White, 1891
Woman: The Sphinx. Long, 1901
A Woman's Burden. Jarrolds, 1901
The Woman Who Held On. Ward, 1920
The Wooden Hand. White, 1905
The Yellow Holly. Digby Long, 1903; Dillingham, 1903
The Yellow Hunchback. White, 1907

HUME, ROBERT W.
My Lodger's Legacy; or, The History of a Recluse. Funk, 1886

HUMES, LARRY R.
Bridge to Nowhere. Leisure, 1980

HUMMEL, GEORGE F(REDERICK). 1882-1952.
Summer Lightning. Liveright, 1929 [It.]

HUMPHREY, HARRY E. See: Bernard J. McOwen.

HUMPHREYS, ELIZA MARGARET J. GOLLAN. 1860-1938. Pseudonym: Rita, q.v.

HUMPHREYS, RAY. Reporter, then chief investigator for a D.A.'s office.
Hunch. Loring, 1934. British title: Death Hunch. Newnes, 1936 [West]

HUNGERFORD, MARGARET WOLFE HAMILTON. 1855-1897. Pseudonym: The Duchess, q.v.
The Red House Mystery. Chatto, 1893. U.S. title: The Red House, by "The Duchess". Rand, 1894

HUNT, CHARLOTTE. Pseudonym of Doris Marjorie Hodges, 1915-   . Ref: CA. SC: Dr. Paul Holton = PH.
Chambered Tomb. Ace, 1975 PH
The Cup of Thanatos. Ace, 1968 PH
Gemini Revenged. Ace, 1973 [Eng.]
The Gilded Sarcophagus. Ace, 1967 PH [Eng.]
The Lotus Vellum. Ace, 1970 PH [Eng.]
The Thirteenth Treasure. Ace, 1972 PH
A Touch of Myrrh. Ace, 1974 PH
Tremayne's Wife. Ace, 1974
A Wreath for Jenny's Grave. Ace, 1975

HUNT, CLARENCE. Pseudonym of (Clarence) Hugh Holman, 1914-1981. q.v.
Small Town Corpse. Phoenix, 1951 [S.C.]

HUNT, E(VERETTE) HOWARD. 1918-   . See: (Everette) Howard Hunt, 1918-   .

HUNT, (MARY) EVE(LYN)
The Danger Game. Hale, 1967
Girl on the Run. Hale, 1966

HUNT, HARRISON. Joint pseudonym of W(illis) T(odhunter) Ballard, 1903-1980, q.v., and Norbert Davis, q.v. Other Ballard pseudonyms: P. D. Ballard, Neil MacNeil, John Shepherd, qq.v.
Murder Picks the Jury. Curl, 1947

HUNT, (EVERETTE) HOWARD. 1918-   . By-line sometimes: E. Howard Hunt. Pseudonyms: Gordon Davis, Robert Dietrich, David St. John, qq.v. Many books originally published pseudonymously were reprinted as by Howard Hunt. Ref: CA, EM.
The Berlin Ending. Putnam, 1973
-Bimini Run. Farrar, 1949
Cruel Is the Night; see Maelstrom
Dark Encounter. GM, 1950
The Hargrave Deception. Stein, 1980
The Judas Hour. GM, 1951; Fawcett (London), 1953
Lovers Are Losers. GM, 1953 [L.A.]
Maelstrom. Farrar, 1948. Also published as: Cruel Is the Night. Berkley, 1955
The Violent Ones. GM, 1950; Fawcett (London), 1958 [Paris]
Whisper Her Name. GM, 1952; Fawcett (London), 1958

HUNT, KATHERINE CHANDLER. Pseudonym: Chandler Nash, q.v.

HUNT, KYLE. Pseudonym of John Creasey, 1908-1973, q.v. Other pseudonyms: Gordon Ashe, M. E. Cooke, Norman Deane, Robert Caine Frazer, Patrick Gill, Michael Halliday, Charles Hogarth, Brian Hope, Colin Hughes, Abel Mann, Peter Manton, J. J. Marric, Richard Martin, Rodney Matheson, Anthony Morton, Jeremy York, qq.v. Note: The Dr. Cellini series was published in England as by Michael Halliday and is listed in this bibliography under that byline.
Kill a Wicked Man. Barker, 1958; Simon, 1957
Kill My Love. Boardman, 1959; Simon, 1958
Kill Once, Kill Twice. Barker, 1957; Simon, 1956
To Kill a Killer. Boardman, 1960; Random, 1960

HUNT, MARY VINCENT
Cast a Green Shadow. Avalon, 1961
The Mystery of Daria Kane. Avalon, 1960 [L.A.]

HUNT, PETER. Joint pseudonym of George Worthing Yates, q.v., and Charles Hunt Marshall. SC: Alan Miller, in all titles.
Murder Among the Nudists. Vanguard, 1934 [Conn.]
Murder for Breakfast. Vanguard, 1934 [Conn.]
Murders at Scandal House. Appleton, 1933 [N.Y.]

HUNT, R. MARTIN
X-On. Vantage, 1979

HUNT, (ISOBEL) VIOLET. 1866-1942.
-The House of Many Mirrors. Paul, 1915
-The Last Ditch. Paul, 1918
-More Tales of the Uneasy. Heinemann, 1925 ss
-Tales of the Uneasy. Heinemann, 1911 ss

HUNT, (JOSEPH) WRAY (ANGUS). 1899-   .
  The Hayes Hall Affair. Fenland, 1932
HUNTER, ALAN (JAMES HERBERT). 1922-   .
  Ref: CA, CC, EM, TC. SC: Insp./Supt.
  Gently, in all titles. Set: Eng.
  Gently at a Gallop. Cassell, 1971
  Gently by the Shore. Cassell, 1956;
    Rinehart, 1956
  Gently Coloured. Cassell, 1969
  Gently Confidential. Cassell, 1967
  Gently Does It. Cassell, 1955; Rine-
    hart, 1955
  Gently Down the Stream. Cassell, 1957;
    Roy, 1960
  Gently Floating. Cassell, 1963; Berk-
    ley, 1964
  Gently French. Cassell, 1973
  Gently Go Man. Cassell, 1961; Berkley,
    1964
  Gently in the Highlands; see Gently
    North-West
  Gently in the Sun. Cassell, 1959; Berk-
    ley, 1964
  Gently in Trees. Cassell, 1974. U.S.
    title: Gently Through the Woods. Mac-
    millan, 1975
  Gently Instrumental. Cassell, 1977
  Gently North-West. Cassell, 1967. U.S.
    title: Gently in the Highlands. Mac-
    millan, 1975 [Scot.]
  Gently Sahib. Cassell, 1964
  Gently Through the Mill. Cassell, 1958;
    St. Martin's, 1971, in an omnibus,
    Gently in an Omnibus, which also con-
    tains Gently Does It and Gently in
    the Sun, qq.v. (British edition of
    Gently in an Omnibus: Cassell, 1966.)
  Gently Through the Woods; see Gently in
    Trees
  Gently to a Sleep. Cassell, 1978
  Gently to the Summit. Cassell, 1961;
    Berkley, 1965 [Wales]
  Gently Where the Birds Are. Cassell,
    1976
  Gently Where the Roads Go. Cassell,
    1962; St. Martin's, 1972, in an omni-
    bus: Gently in Another Omnibus (also:
    Cassell, 1969), in which are also:
    Gently Go Man, and Gently Floating,
    qq.v.
  Gently with Love. Cassell, 1975 [Scot.]
  Gently with the Innocents. Cassell,
    1970; Macmillan, 1974
  Gently with the Ladies. Cassell, 1965;
    Macmillan, 1974
  Gently with the Painters. Cassell,
    1960; Macmillan, 1976
  The Honfleur Decision. Constable, 1980;
    Walker, 1981 [Fr.]
  Landed Gently. Cassell, 1957; British
    Book Service, 1957
  Vivienne—Gently Where She Lay. Cas-
    sell, 1972

HUNTER, BLUEBELL MATILDA. 1887-   .
  Pseudonym: John Guildford, q.v.

HUNTER, CLAUDE
  Murders While You Wait. Alliance (Lon-
    don), 1945 ss

HUNTER, CLEMENTINE. Pseudonym of Helen
  Mary Keynes, 1892-   , q.v.
  Queens Have Died Young and Fair. Hutch-
    inson, 1947

HUNTER, EVAN. 1926-   . Pseudonyms: Curt
  Cannon, Hunt Collins, Ezra Hannon, Ed
  McBain, Richard Marsten, qq.v. Ref:
  CA, CC, EM, MC, TC. Name originally:
  Salvatore A. Lombino.
  The Big Fix. Falcon, 1952. Also pub-
    lished as: So Nude, So Dead, as by
    Richard Marsten. Crest, 1956 [NYC]
  The Blackboard Jungle. Simon, 1954;
    Constable, 1955
  Don't Crowd Me. Popular Library, 1953;
    World Distributors, 1960. Also pub-
    lished as: The Paradise Party. Four
    Square, 1968
  Every Little Crook and Nanny. Double-
    day, 1972; Constable, 1972 [N.Y.]
  The Evil Sleep! Falcon, 1952
  Happy New Year, Herbie and other sto-
    ries. Simon, 1963; Constable, 1965 ss
  A Horse's Head. Delacorte, 1967; Con-
    stable, 1968
  The Jungle Kids. PB, 1956 (12 ss, of
    which 6 were included in The Last
    Spin, q.v.)
  The Last Spin and other stories. Con-
    stable, 1960 (15 ss, including 6
    from The Jungle Kids, q.v.)
  A Matter of Conviction. Simon, 1959;
    Constable, 1959. Also published as:
    The Young Savages. PB, 1966 [NYC]
  Nobody Knew They Were There. Doubleday,
    1971; Constable, 1971
  The Paradise Party; see Don't Crowd Me
  So Nude, So Dead; see The Big Fix

  The Young Savages; see A Matter of Con-
    viction

HUNTER, HARRIET
  A Case for Punishment. Hale, 1967
  Inclination to Murder. Hale, 1966

HUNTER, JACK D(AYTON). 1921-   . Ref: CA.
  The Expendable Spy. Dutton, 1965; Mul-
    ler, 1966 [Ger., 1945]
  One of Us Works for Them. Dutton, 1967;
    Muller, 1968 [Ger.]
  Spies, Inc. Dutton, 1969; Muller, 1970
    [Pa.]
  The Terror Alliance. Leisure, 1980

HUNTER, JAMES H(OGG). 1890-   . Ref: CA.
  Banners of Blood. Evangelical Pub.,
    1947 [Isr.]
  The Mystery of Mar Saba. Evangelical
    Pub., 1940

HUNTER, (ALFRED) JOHN. 1891-1961. Pseu-
  donyms: John Addiscombe, L. H. Bren-
  ning, Anthony Dax, Anthony Drummond,
  Peter Meriton, qq.v. SC (with many
  other authors): Sexton Blake, in all
  titles without publisher (which is
  Amalgamated Press). Set: Eng.
  The Affair of the Spiv's Secret. 1948
  Barred from the West End. 1944
  The Case of the American Tourists. 1948
  The Case of the Bronze Statue. 1942
  The Case of the Crooked Skipper. 1951
  The Case of the Defaulting Sailor. 1946
  The Case of the Deserted War Bride.
    1945
  The Case of the Doped Favourite. 1952
  The Case of the Double Event. 1947
  The Case of the Fatal Film. 1935
  The Case of the French Raiders. 1942
  The Case of the Girl on Remand. 1952
  The Case of the Stolen Ransom. 1954
  The Crime on the French Frontier. 1954
  The Crime on the Promenade. 1937
  Crook Cargo. 1936
  The Curse of the Track. 1948
  Dead Man's Gate. Cassell, 1931
  Dead Man's Island. Newnes, 1932
  -Desperado. Cassell, 1932
  Destination Unknown. 1953
  The Devil of Danehurst. 1943
  Fourteen Years After! 1946
  Gangster's Girl. 1956
  The Great Airport Racket. 1945
  The House of Darkness. 1940
  It Happened in Melgrove Square. 1951
  The Man Behind. Cherry Tree, 1942
  The Man from the Far East. 1944
  The Man Who Turned King's Evidence.
    1938
  The Monopoly Menace. 1943
  Murder in the Air. 1955
  The Mysterious Mr. Maynard. 1940
  The Mystery of Moat Farm. 1946
  The Mystery of the American Envoy. 1942
  The Mystery of the New Tenant. 1951
  The Mystery of the Red Chateau. 1945
  The Mystery of the Vanished Trainer.
    1955
  The Prisoner of Lost Island. 1937
  Raiders Passed! 1941
  The Riddle of the Black Racketeers.
    1942
  The Riddle of the Italian Prisoner.
    1944
  The Riddle of the Lost Ship. 1939
  The Riddle of the Smiling Man. 1947
  The Riddle of the Uncensored Letter.
    1942
  The Secret of the Demolition Worker.
    1942
  The Secret of the Grave. 1941
  The Secret of the Hold. 1938
  Sergeant Gray's Crime. 1945
  Silent Witness. 1957
  The Spiv's Mistake. 1952
  The Thieves of Alexandria. 1953
  The Three Crows. Cassell, 1928
  Three Die at Midnight. 1934
  Thunder Island. Newnes, 1924
  The Trail of the Dope Chief. 1936
  The Victim of the Crooked Hypnotist.
    1952
  Warned Off! 1947
  When the Gunmen Came. Cassell, 1930
  When the Jury Disagreeed! 1950
  The White Phantom. Cassell, 1934; Smith
    & Haas, 1935 [ship]
  The Wimbledon Common Trap. 1946
  Witness to the Crime. 1950
  The Woman on the Spot. 1953

HUNTER, P(ETER) HAY. 1854-1910.
  -John Armiger's Revenge. Oliphant, 1897;
    Bradley, 1897
  The Silver Bullet. Oliphant, 1894

HUNTER, STEPHEN. 1946-   .
  The Master Sniper. Morrow, 1980;
    Heinemann, 1980 [WWII]

HUNTER, TIM. 1947-   . See: Charlie
  Haas, 1952-   .

HUNTING, (HENRY) GARDNER. 1872-1958.
  A Hand in the Game. Holt, 1911

HUNTINGDON, JOHN. Pseudonym of Gerald
  William Phillips, 1884-   .
  The Seven Black Chessmen. Holt, 1928;
    Gerald Howe, 1928

HUNTSBERRY, WILLIAM E(MERY). 1916-   .
  Ref: CA.
  Dangerous Harbour; see Harbor of the
    Little Boats
  Harbor of the Little Boats. Rinehart,
    1958. British title: Dangerous Har-
    bour. Hammond, 1960 [Haw.]
  Oscar Mooney's Head. Holt, 1961. Bri-
    tish title: Whose Head? Hammond, 1961
    [Haw.]
  Whose Head?; see Oscar Mooney's Head

HUNVALD, HENRY. Pseudonym of Henry H.
  Gross.
  The Masterpiece of Nice Mr. Breen.
    World, 1972 [N.J.]

HURD, DOUGLAS (RICHARD). 1930-   . Ref:
  CA. SC: Harvey, in at least those
  marked H.
  -Scotch on the Rocks, with Andrew Os-
    mond, 1938-   , q.v. Collins, 1971
  Send Him Victorious, with Andrew Os-
    mond, 1938-   , q.v. Collins, 1968;
    Macmillan, 1969 [Eng., 1975] H
  The Smile on the Face of the Tiger,
    with Andrew Osmond, 1938-   , q.v.
    Collins, 1969; Macmillan, 1970 H
    [Far East]
  Truth Game. Collins, 1972; St. Mar-
    tin's, 1972
  Vote to Kill. Collins, 1975

HURD, FLORENCE. 1918-   . Ref: CA.
  Curse of the Moors. Manor, 1975 [Eng.,
    past]
  The Gorgon's Head. Macfadden, 1971
  House of Shadows. GM, 1973 [La.]
  The House on Russian Hill. Signet, 1977
    [S.F., 1800s]
  The House on Trevor Street. Manor, 1972
  Legacy. Avon, 1977
  -Love's Fiery Dagger. Popular Library,
    1978
  Moorsend Manor. Manor, 1973
  Night Wind at Northriding. Signet, 1977
  Nightmare at Mountain Aerie. Manor,
    1974 [Calif.]
  The Possessed. Belmont, 1970
  Rommany. Avon, 1976 [Eng.]
  Seance for the Dead. Macfadden, 1972
  The Secret of Awen Castle. Avon, 1974
    [Eng., past]
  The Secret of Canfield House. GM, 1966;
    Coronet, 1972 [N.H.]
  The Secret of Hayworth Hall. Avon, 1975
  -Shadows of the Heart. Avon, 1980
  Storm House. Manor, 1973
  Tamarind. GM, 19??
  Terror at Seacliff Pines. Manor, 1976
  Voyage of the Secret Duchess. Avon,
    1975
  Wade House. Signet, 1967
  The Witches' Pond. Macfadden, 1972

HURLBA, ALTON. Pseudonym of Walter Palmer
  Hoxie.
  -Eugenia. Welles, 1888. British title:
    A Friend's Victim. Routledge, 1889

HURLBUT, EDWARD H.
  Lanagan, Amateur Detective. Sturgis,
    1913 ss [S.F.]

HURLEY, GENE
  Have You Seen This Man? Bobbs, 1944
    [NYC]

HURLEY, JOHN JEROME. 1930-   . Pseudonym: S. S. Rafferty, q.v.

HURLEY, T. P.
  The Avenging Eagle. Morrow, 1946

HURRELL, F(RANCIS) G(ORDON). 1885-   .
  John Lillibud. Rich, 1934; Kendall,
    1935

HURREN, BERNARD JOHN. 1907-   . Pseudonym: Guy Garston, q.v.

HURRY, ALFRED
  The Ace of Diamonds. Jarrolds, 1927
  Mayfair Lou. Jarrolds, 1928

HURST, EDWARD H(ARRY). 1868-   .
  Mystery Island. Page, 1907; Hurst, 1908
    [Fla.]

HURST, HEATHER SMITH
    Dark Is My Destiny. Bouregy, 1971
    [Wales]

HURST, J. H.
    Four Plus One. Martin, 1946

HURST, KATHRYN
    The Destruction of Eva. Manor, 1978

HURST, NORMAN
    The Ivory Queen. Milne, 1899

HURT, FREDA (MARY ELIZABETH). 1911- .
        Ref: CA. SC: Insp. Herbert Broom,
        in at least those marked HB. Set:
        Eng.
    Acquainted with Murder. Hale, 1962 HB
    The Body at Busman's Hollow. Macdonald, 1959
    A Cause for Malice. Hale, 1966 HB
    Cold and Unhonoured. Hale, 1964 HB
    Dangerous Visit. Hale, 1971
    Dark Design. Hale, 1972
    Death and the Bridegroom. Hale, 1963 HB
    Death and the Dark Daughter. Hale, 1966
    Death by Bequest. Macdonald, 1960 HB
    Death in the Mist. Hale, 1969
    Fatal Fortune. Hale, 1975
    Return to Terror. Hale, 1974
    Seven Year Secret. Hale, 1968
    So Dark a Shadow. Hale, 1967; Paperback Library, 1969
    Sweet Death. Macdonald, 1961 HB
    A Witch at the Funeral. Hale, 1970

HURWOOD, BERNHARDT J. 1926- . Ref: CA.
    Born Innocent. Ace, 1975 (Novelization of the movie.)
    Rip-Off! GM, 1972 [NYC]

HUSLIG, JO
    Goddess of Evil. Vantage, 1975

HUSTON, FRAN. Pseudonym of Ron S. Miller
    1936- . Ref: CA.
    The Rich Get It All. Doubleday, 1973;
    Macmillan (London), 1974 [L.A.]

HUSTON, H(OWARD) C(HAUNCEY). SC: Det.
    Chief Charles A. Baker, in both
    titles, both set in Wash. D.C.
    The Blind Saw Murder. Macmillan, 1954;
    Hodder, 1955
    With Murder for Some. Macmillan, 1953;
    Hodder, 1954

HUSTON, JOHN. 1906- . See: Ben Maddow, 1909- .

HUTCH, OLD. See: Old Hutch.

HUTCHESON, J(OHN) C(ONROY)
    -Caught in a Trap. Newby, 1870

HUTCHINSON, FRANK(LIN ISAAC)
    Out of the Past. Beck, 1934
    The Wise Thrush. Beck, 1934

HUTCHINSON, HORACE (or HORATIO) G(ORDON).
        1859-1932. Set: Eng.
    The Crime and the Confessor. Murray, 1928
    -The Eight of Diamonds. Hutchinson, 1914
    -Fairway Island. Cassell, 1892
    The Fate of Osmund Brett. Hutchinson, 1924
    The Foreign Secretary Who Vanished. Hutchinson, 1927
    -The Fortnightly Club. Murray, 1922
    -Glencairly Castle. Smith Eldor, 1904
    The Greenwell's Glory Case. Hutchinson, 1924
    The Lost Golfer. Murray, 1930 [Scot.]
    -Mr. Punt of Chelsea. Murray, 1924
    Murder in Monk's Wood. Murray, 1927
    The Mystery of the Summer-House. Hutchinson, 1925; Doran, 1919
    -A Prideful Woman. Hutchinson, 1926
    -That Fiddler Fellow. Arnold, 1891
    The Twins Murder Case. Murray, 1930
    Two Moods of a Man. Smith Eldor, 1905; Putnam, 1905
    -What Should a Man Do? Hutchinson, 1926

HUTCHINSON, ROBERT HARE. 1887- . Pseudonym: Robert Hare, q.v.
    The Fourth Challenge. Hurst, 1932

HUTCHISON, GRAHAM SETON. 1890-1946. Pseudonym: Graham Seton, q.v.

HUTTEN, BETTINA VON. 1874- . See:
    Von Hutten, Bettina.

HUTTER, A. D. Psychoanalyst and English professor.
    The Death Mechanic. Signet, 1980; NAL (London), 1981 [Calif.]

HUTTON, BRETT
    The Green Death and other stories. Bantam (L.A.), 1940 ss

HUTTON, J(OY) F(ERRIS). He graduated from U. of Calif.; ss writer.
    Dead Man Friday; see Too Good to Be True
    The Dolphin Mystery; see Too Good to Be True
    Too Good to Be True. Simon, 1948. British title: The Dolphin Mystery. Foulsham, 1949. Also published as: Dead Man Friday. Ace, 1953 [L.A.]

HUTTON, JOHN. 1928- . Teacher in Eng.
        29 Herriott Street. Bodley, 1979; St. Martin's, 1980

HUTTON, MALCOLM. Was in the British Civil Service.
    Jenny Nobody. Hale, 1979

HUTTON, MICHAEL CLAYTON
    Power Without Glory. Dramatists, 1948;
    French (London), 1950 (3-act play.)

HUTTON, W. R.
    Broadway Racket. Hamilton & Co., 1946 [NYC]
    Death at the Drome. Fiction House, 1948
    Death at the Golden Cockerel. Fiction House, 1947
    Death of a Wide-Boy. Fiction House, 1948
    Murder in Transit. Fiction House, 1949
    Not a Dog's Chance. Fiction House, 1947
    Valley of Death. Hamilton & Co., 1949

HUXLEY, ALDOUS (LEONARD). 1894-1963. Ref: CA, MC.
    The Gioconda Smile. Chatto, 1948. U.S. title: Mortal Coils. Harper, 1948 (3-act play based on the ss, below.)
    Mortal Coils; see The Gioconda Smile
    Mortal Coils. Chatto, 1922; Doran, 1922 (ss, including Huxley's famous and probably only crime story, "The Gioconda Smile.")

HUXLEY, DAVID
    The Seven-Year Friend. Bakers, 1971 (1-act play.)

HUXLEY, ELSPETH (JOCELYN GRANT).
        1907- . Ref: CA, CC, EM, MP, TC.
        SC: Supt. Vachell = V.
    The African Poison Murders; see Death of an Aryan
    Death of an Aryan. Methuen, 1939. U.S. title: The African Poison Murders. Harper, 1940 V [Afr., E.]
    The Incident at the Merry Hippo; see The Merry Hippo
    A Man from Nowhere. Chatto, 1964; Morrow, 1965
    The Merry Hippo. Chatto, 1963. U.S. title: The Incident at the Merry Hippo. Morrow, 1964 [Afr.]
    Murder at Government House. Methuen, 1937; Harper, 1937 V [Afr., W.]
    Murder on Safari. Methuen, 1938; Harper, 1938 V [Afr.]

HYAMS, EDWARD (SOLOMON). 1910-1975. Ref: CA.
    -The Death Lottery. Longmans, 1971
    The Final Agenda. Allen Lane, 1973

HYATT, BETTY HALE
    Ivy Halls. Arcadia, 1966
    The Jade Pagoda. Doubleday, 1980
    The Vesper Bells. Arcadia, 1967

HYATT, STANLEY PORTAL. 1877-1914.
    -Black Sheep. Laurie, 1909
    Fallen Among Thieves. Laurie, 1913
    -The Land of Promises. Laurie, 1913
    -The Law of the Bolo. Laurie, 1910; Estes, 1910
    -The Maker of Mischief. Laurie, 1911
    -The Mammoth. Laurie, 1916
    -A Man from the Past. Laurie, 1915
    -Marcus Hay. Constable, 1907
    The Markham Affair. Clode, 1925 (British title?)
    -The Way of the Cardines. Laurie, 1913

HYDE, AUSTIN
    Killer on the Line. Paxton, 1945
    Murders by Moonlight. Paxton, 1945

HYDE, CHRISTOPHER. 1949- . Born in Ottawa; writer and producer with Canadian Broadcasting Corporation for 10 years.
    The Wave. Doubleday, 1979; Hodder, 1980 [Wash., Can.]

HYDE, CYNTHIA
    The House of Sinister Shadows. Avon, 1972

HYDE, D. HERBERT. Pseudonym of Derek Hyde Chambers.
    Dressed to Kill. Amalgamated, 1959 (Sexton Blake.)

HYDE, ELEANOR. Pseudonym of Frances Cowen, 1915- , q.v.
    -Tudor Murder. Hale, 1977

HYDE, THEODORE. Pseudonym. Set: Eng.
    After the Execution. Eyre, 1934
    Murder in Whitehall. Murray, 1942

HYDER, ALAN
    -Black-Girl, White-Lady. Barker, 1934
    Prelude to Blue Mountains. Barker, 1936; Kendall, 1936
    Vampires Overhead. Allan, 1935

HYLAND, (HENRY) STANLEY. 1914- . Ref: CA, CC, TC.
    Green Grow the Tresses-O. Gollancz, 1965; Bobbs, 1967
    Top Bloody Secret. Gollancz, 1969; Bobbs, 1969
    Who Goes Hang? Gollancz, 1958; Dodd, 1959 (The U.S. edition is significantly shorter than the British.)

HYLTON, SARA
    Caprice. Hutchinson, 1980; St. Martin's, 1980 [Eng., 1900]

HYMAN, ANN. 1936- . Ref: CA.
    The Lansing Legacy. McKay, 1974; Millington, 1975

HYMERS, JOHN
    Utter Death. Gifford, 1952; Detective Book Club, 1953 [Egypt]

HYND, ALAN. 1908-1974. Ref: CA.
    'Til Death Do Us Part. Paperback Library, 1962

HYND, NOEL. Born in NYC, the son of Alan Hynd, 1908-1974, q.v.; raised in Conn., educated at U. of Pa.; crime reporter.
    False Flags. Dial, 1979; Allen, 1979 [Eng.]
    Revenge. Dial, 1976; Allen, 1976 [Fr.]
    The Sandler Inquiry. Dial, 1977; Allen, 1978 [NYC]

HYNE, C(HARLES) J(OHN) CUTCLIFFE (WRIGHT). 1865-1944. Pseudonym: Weatherby Chesney, q.v. Ref: CC, EM. SC: Captain Owen Kettle, in at least those marked OK.
    -Absent Friends. Ward, 1933
    -Admiral Teach. Methuen, 1931
    -Adventures of Captain Kettle. Pearson, 1898; Doubleday, 1898 OK
    -Beneath Your Very Boots. Digby, 1889
    -Captain Kettle, Ambassador. Ward, 1932 OK
    -Captain Kettle, K.C.B. Pearson, 1903. U.S. title (?): More Adventures of Captain Kettle, K.C.B. Federal, 1903 OK
    -Captain Kettle on the War-Path. Methuen, 1916 OK
    -Captain Kettle's Bit. Hodder, 1918 OK
    -The Captured Cruiser; or, Two Years from Land. Blackie, 1893
    -Currie, Curtis & Co., Crammers. Remington, 1890
    -The Derelict. Lewis, 1901 (Contains 13 of the 17 ss appearing in Mr. Horrocks, Purser, q.v., including all but one of the 6 Mr. Horrocks ss—missing is "The Looting of the Specie-Room.")
    Empire of the World. Everett, 1910
    The Escape Agents. Laurie, 1911 ss, some about OK
    -The Filabusters. Hutchinson, 1900; Stokes, 1900
    -Firemen Hot. Methuen, 1914
    -Further Adventures of Captain Kettle. Pearson, 1899. U.S. title: A Master of Fortune. Dillingham, 1901 ss OK
    -The Glass Dagger. New Amsterdam, 1899 (British title?)
    Honour of Thieves. Chatto, 1895; Fenno, 1899. Also published as: The Little Red Captain. Pearson, 1902 OK
    -Ivory Valley. Ward, 1938 OK
    Kate Meredith, Financier. Cassell, 1907; Empire, 1906 [Afr., W.]
    The Little Red Captain; see Honour of Thieves
    -McTodd. Macmillan (London & NYC), 1903

The Marriage of Captain Kettle; see The
    Marriage of Kettle
The Marriage of Kettle. Heinemann,
    1912. U.S. title: The Marriage of
    Captain Kettle. Bobbs, 1912 OK
A Master of Fortune; see Further Adven-
    tures of Captain Kettle
-A Matrimonial Mixture. Ward, 1891
Mr. Horrocks, Purser. Methuen, 1902 ss
    (See also: The Derelict.)
-Mr. Kettle, Third Mate. Ward, 1931 OK
More Adventures of Captain Kettle, K.C.
    B.; see Captain Kettle K.C.B.
The "Paradise" Coal-Boat, and other
    tales. Bowden, 1897 ss, including
    one about OK
-President Kettle. Nash, 1929 OK
The Recipe for Diamonds. Heinemann,
    1893; Appleton, 1893
-Red Herrings. Methuen, 1918
-The Rev. Captain Kettle. Harrap, 1925
    OK
-Steamboatmen. Penguin, 1943 ss
-Stinson's Reef. Blackie, 1899
-Thompson's Progress. Richards, 1902;
    Macmillan, 1903
-The Trials of Commander McTurk. Murray,
    1906; Dutton, 1906
-West Highland Spirits. Ward, 1932
-The Wild-Catters. Sunday School Union,
    1895
-Wishing Smith. Hale, 1939

HYTHE, GABRIEL. Pseudonym. Set: Eng.
    Death of a Goblin. Macdonald, 1960
    Death of a Puppet. Macdonald, 1959
    Death of a Scapegoat. Macdonald, 1961

IAMS, JACK [SAMUEL H. IAMS, JR.].
    1910-   . Ref: CC, EM, TC. SC: Rocky
    Rockwell = RR.
    The Body Missed the Boat. Morrow, 1947;
        Rich, 1949 [Bel. Congo]
    A Corpse of the Old School. Gollancz,
        1955 [acad., Ohio]
    Death Draws the Line. Morrow, 1949;
        Rich, 1951 [NYC]
    Do Not Murder Before Christmas. Morrow,
        1949 RR
    Girl Meets Body. Morrow, 1947; Rich,
        1950 [N.J.]
    Into Thin Air. Morrow, 1952; Gollancz,
        1953 [NYC]
    A Shot of Murder. Morrow, 1950; Gol-
        lancz, 1952 RR [Pol.]
    What Rhymes with Murder? Morrow, 1950;
        Gollancz, 1951 RR

IANNUZZI, JOHN N(ICHOLAS). 1935-   .
    Ref: CA, TC.
    Courthouse. Doubleday, 1975
    Part 35. Baron, 1970 [NYC]
    Sicilian Defense. Baron, 1972; Allen,
        1973
    -What's Happening? Barnes, 1963; Yose-
        loff, 1963

ILE, TASMAN. Pseudonym of Alan Palamoun-
    tain.
    Shanghai Nights. [Author], 1929
        [Shanghai]

ILES, BERT. Pseudonym of Z(ola) H(elen
    Girdey) Ross, 1912-   , q.v. Other
    pseudonym: Helen Arre, q.v.
    Murder in Mink. Arcadia, 1956 [Seattle]

ILES, FRANCIS. Pseudonym of A(nthony)
    B(erkeley) Cox, 1893-1970, q.v. Other
    pseudonym: Anthony Berkeley, q.v.
    Set: Eng.
    -As for the Woman. Jarrolds, 1939;
        Doubleday, 1939
    Before the Fact. Gollancz, 1932; Dou-
        bleday, 1932. Revised edition: Pan,
        1958
    Malice Aforethought. Gollancz, 1931;
        Harper, 1931

ILLING, CHRIS
    The Commitment. Vantage, 1980

IMBER, HUGH
    The House of the Apricots. Heffer, 1934
        [Fr.]
    On Helle's Wave. Hodder, 1930
    -The Spine. Hodder, 1929

IMBERT-TERRY, SIR HENRY (MACHU). 1854-
    1938. SC: Det. Insp. Du Cas, in at
    least those marked D. Set: Eng.
    Acid. Skeffington, 1928 D
    Clay. Skeffington, 1931 D
    Doom. Skeffington, 1929
    Nightshade. Skeffington, 1930
    Weeds. Skeffington, 1933 D

INCE, DOROTHEA
    In Those Dark Woods. Bell, 1937 [acad.]

INCHBALD, RALPH (MORDAUNT ELLIOT).
    1902-   . SC: Colonel Paternoster,
    in all titles. Set: Eng.
    Colonel Paternoster. Hodder, 1951
    The Five Inns. Hodder, 1952
    September Story. Hodder, 1955

IND, ALLISON. 1903-1974. Ref: CA.
    The Sino-Variant. McKay, 1969 [Eng.]

ING, DEAN
    Soft Targets. Ace, 1979 [1980-1]

INGATE, MARY. 1912-   . Ref: CA. SC: Ann
    Hales, in at least those marked AH.
    Set: Eng.
    Remembrance of Miranda; see The Sound
        of the Weir
    The Sound of the Weir. Macmillan (Lon-
        don), 1974; Dodd, 1974. Also pub-
        lished as: Remembrance of Miranda.
        Dell, 1977 AH
    This Water Laps Gently. Macmillan (Lon-
        don), 1977 AH
    A Tomb of Flowers. Macmillan (London),
        1979

INGERSOL, JARED. Pseudonym of Lauran Bos-
    worth Paine, 1916-   . Other pseudo-
    nyms: John Armour, Reg Batchelor,
    Kenneth Bedford, Frank Bosworth, Mark
    Carrel, Robert Clarke, Richard Dana,
    J. F. Drexler, Troy Howard, John Kil-
    gore, Hunter Liggett, J. K. Lucas,
    John Morgan, qq.v.
    The Beautiful Murder. Hale, 1970
    Diamond Fingers. Hale, 1974
    A Fine Day for Murder. Hale, 1974
    A Game Called Murder. Hale, 1969
        [P. Rico]
    The Golden Gloves. Hale, 1973
    The Jade Eye. Hale, 1970
    The Killer's Conscience. Hale, 1971
    The Man Who Made Roubles. Hale, 1972
    The Man Who Stole Heaven. Hale, 1971
    The Money Murder. Hale, 1971
    The Night of the Crisis. Hale, 1968
    The Non-Murder. Hale, 1972
    A Rose Can Kill. Hale, 1969 [L.A.]
    The Steel Garrotte. Hale, 1970
    The Witchcraft Murder. Hale, 1975

INGHAM, DANIEL. Pseudonym of Isobel
    (Mary) Lambot, 1926-   , q.v.
    Contract for Death. Hale, 1972

INGHAM, H(ENRY) LLOYD
    Bury Me Deep. Hammond, 1963

INGHAM, RICHARD (ARNISON). 1935-   .
    Yoris. Allison, 1974

INGRAHAM, CAPTAIN
    The Dancing Star. Donohue, 189?

INGRAM, ELEANOR M(ARIE). 1886-1921.
    -The Game and the Candle. Bobbs, 1909.
        British title: John Allard; or, The
        Game and the Candle. Laurie, 1912
    John Allard; see The Game and the
        Candle
    -Stanton Wins. Bobbs, 1911
    -The Twice American. Lippincott, 1917
    -The Unafraid. Lippincott, 1913

INGRAM, GEORGE. Pseudonym. Set: Eng.
    -Cockney Cavalcade. Archer, 1935
    The Muffled Man. Archer, 1936
    "Stir." Archer, 1933
    "Stir" Train. Archer, 1935
    -Welded Lives. Duckworth, 1939

INGRAM, GRACE
    Gilded Spurs. Collins, 1978; Stein,
        1978

INGRAM, (ARCHIBALD) KENNETH. 1882-1965.
    Set: Eng.
    The Ambart Trial. Quality, 1938
    Death Comes at Night. Allan, 1933;
        Sears, 1934
    -"It Is Expedient..." Bles, 1935
    -Return of Yesterday. Quality, 1942
    The Steep Steps. Allan, 1931
    -Storm in a Sanctuary. Benn, 1954
    -The Window. Ouseley, 1922

INGRAMS, RICHARD REID. 1937-   . Joint
    pseudonym with Andrew Osmond,
    1938-   , q.v.: Philip Reid, q.v.

INMAN, H(ERBERT) ESCOTT
    -The Mill Lass of Idderleigh. Warne,
        1908
    Nancy Lee, Mill Lass. Amalgamated,
        1909
    The Quest of Douglas Holms. Warne,
        1908
    What Shall It Profit? Amalgamated,
        1910

INMAN, PHILIP (ALBERT). 1892-   .
    -The Silent Loom. Bles, 1930 ss

INMAN, ROBERT (ANTHONY). 1931-   . Ref:
    CA.
    The Torturer's Horse. Bobbs, 1965

INNES, (RALPH) HAMMOND. 1913-   . Ref:
    CA, TC. Some of these titles are pro-
    bably more nearly adventure than
    crime fiction.
    Air Bridge. Collins, 1951; Knopf, 1952
        [Ger.]
    Air Disaster. Jenkins, 1937
    All Roads Lead to Friday. Jenkins, 1939
    The Angry Mountain. Collins, 1950;
        Harper, 1951 [It.]
    Atlantic Fury. Collins, 1962; Knopf,
        1962 [Can.]
    Attack Alarm. Collins, 1941; Macmillan,
        1942
    The Blue Ice. Collins, 1948; Harper,
        1949 [Nor.]
    Campbell's Kingdom. Collins, 1952;
        Knopf, 1952
    Dead and Alive. Collins, 1946
    The Doomed Oasis. Collins, 1960; Knopf,
        1960 [Saud. Arab.]
    The Doppelganger. Jenkins, 1936
    Fire in the Snow; see The Lonely Skier
    Gale Warning; see Maddon's Rock
    The Golden Soak. Collins, 1973; Knopf,
        1973 [Australia]
    The Killer Mine. Collins, 1947; Harper,
        1948. Also published as: Run by
        Night. Bantam, 1951
    The Land God Gave to Cain. Collins,
        1958; Knopf, 1958 [Can.]
    Levkas Man. Collins, 1971; Knopf, 1971
        [Greece]
    The Lonely Skier. Collins, 1947. U.S.
        title: Fire in the Snow. Harper, 1947
        [It.]
    Maddon's Rock. Collins, 1948. U.S.
        title: Gale Warning. Harper, 1948
        [ship]
    The Mary Deare. Collins, 1956. U.S.
        title: The Wreck of the Mary Deare.
        Knopf, 1956 [ship]
    The Naked Land; see The Strange Land
    North Star. Collins, 1974; Knopf, 1975
    Run by Night; see The Killer Mine
    Sabotage Broadcast. Jenkins, 1938
        [Scot.]
    Solomon's Seal. Collins, 1980; Knopf,
        1980 [New Guinea]
    The Strange Land. Collins, 1954. U.S.
        title: The Naked Land. Knopf, 1954
        [Mor.]
    The Strode Venturer. Collins, 1965;
        Knopf, 1965 [Ind. O.]
    The Survivors; see The White South
    Trapped; see Wreckers Must Breathe
    The Trojan Horse. Collins, 1940
    The White South. Collins, 1949. U.S.
        title: The Survivors. Harper, 1950
        [Antarctica]
    The Wreck of the Mary Deare; see The
        Mary Deare
    Wreckers Must Breathe. Collins, 1940.
        U.S. title: Trapped. Putnam, 1940

INNES, MICHAEL. Pseudonym of J(ohn)
    I(nnes) M(ackintosh) Stewart,
    1906-   , q.v. Ref: all except MM.
    SC: John Appleby = JA; Charles Honey-
    bath = CH. Set: Eng.
    The Ampersand Papers. Gollancz, 1978;
        Dodd, 1979 JA
    Appleby at Allington. Gollancz, 1968.
        U.S. title: Death by Water. Dodd,
        1968 JA
    The Appleby File. Gollancz, 1975; Dodd,
        1976 JA ss
    Appleby on Ararat. Gollancz, 1941;
        Dodd, 1941 JA [S. Pac.]
    Appleby Plays Chicken. Gollancz, 1957.
        U.S. title: Death on a Quiet Day.
        Dodd, 1957 JA
    Appleby Talking. Gollancz, 1954. U.S.
        title: Dead Man's Shoes. Dodd, 1954
        JA ss
    Appleby Talks Again. Gollancz, 1956;
        Dodd, 1957 JA ss
    Appleby's Answer. Gollancz, 1973; Dodd,
        1973 JA
    Appleby's End. Gollancz, 1945; Dodd,
        1945 JA
    Appleby's Other Story. Gollancz, 1974;
        Dodd, 1974 JA
    An Awkward Lie. Gollancz, 1971; Dodd,
        1971 JA
    The Bloody Wood. Gollancz, 1966; Dodd,
        1966 JA
    Candleshoe; see Christmas at Candleshoe
    The Case of Sonia Wayward; see The New
        Sonia Wayward
    The Case of the Journeying Boy; see The
        Journeying Boy
    A Change of Heir. Gollancz, 1966; Dodd,
        1966

Christmas at Candleshoe. Gollancz, 1953; Dodd, 1953. Also published as: Candleshoe. Penguin, 1978
A Comedy of Terrors; see There Came Both Mist and Snow
A Connoisseur's Case. Gollancz, 1962. U.S. title: The Crabtree Affair. Dodd, 1962 JA
The Crabtree Affair; see A Connoisseur's Case
The Daffodil Affair. Gollancz, 1942; Dodd, 1942 JA
Dead Man's Shoes; see Appleby Talking
Death at the Chase. Gollancz, 1970; Dodd, 1970 JA
Death at the President's Lodging. Gollancz, 1936. U.S. title: Seven Suspects. Dodd, 1937 JA [acad.]
Death by Moonlight; see The Man from the Sea
Death by Water; see Appleby at Allington
Death on a Quiet Day; see Appleby Plays Chicken
A Family Affair. Gollancz, 1969. U.S. title: Picture of Guilt. Dodd, 1969 JA
From London Far. Gollancz, 1946. U.S. title: The Unsuspected Chasm. Dodd, 1946
The "Gay Phoenix." Gollancz, 1976; Dodd, 1977 JA
Going It Alone. Gollancz, 1980; Dodd, 1980
Hamlet, Revenge! Gollancz, 1937; Dodd, 1937 JA
Hare Sitting Up. Gollancz, 1959; Dodd, 1959 JA
Honeybath's Haven. Gollancz, 1977; Dodd, 1978 CH
The Journeying Boy. Gollancz, 1949. U.S. title: The Case of the Journeying Boy. Dodd, 1949
Lament for a Maker. Gollancz, 1938; Dodd, 1938 JA [Scot.]
The Long Farewell. Gollancz, 1958; Dodd, 1958 JA
The Man from the Sea. Gollancz, 1955; Dodd, 1955. Also published as: Death by Moonlight. Avon, 1957
Money from Holme. Gollancz, 1964; Dodd, 1965
Murder is an Art; see A Private View
The Mysterious Commission. Gollancz, 1974; Dodd, 1975 CH
The New Sonia Wayward. Gollancz, 1960. U.S. title: The Case of Sonia Wayward. Dodd, 1960
A Night of Errors. Gollancz, 1948; Dodd, 1947 JA
Old Hall, New Hall. Gollancz, 1956. U.S. title: A Question of Queens. Dodd, 1956 JA [acad.]
One-Man Show; see A Private View
The Open House. Gollancz, 1972; Dodd, 1972 JA
Operation Pax. Gollancz, 1951. U.S. title: The Paper Thunderbolt. Dodd, 1951 JA
The Paper Thunderbolt; see Operation Pax
Picture of Guilt; see A Family Affair
A Private View. Gollancz, 1952. U.S. title: One-Man Show. Dodd, 1952. Also published as: Murder Is an Art. Avon, 1959 JA
A Question of Queens; see Old Hall, New Hall
The Secret Vanguard. Gollancz, 1940 Dodd, 1941 JA
Seven Suspects; see Death at the President's Lodging
Silence Observed. Gollancz, 1961; Dodd, 1961 JA
The Spider Strikes; see Stop Press
Stop Press. Gollancz, 1939. U.S. title: The Spider Strikes. Dodd, 1939 JA
There Came Both Mist and Snow. Gollancz, 1940. U.S. title: A Comedy of Terrors. Dodd, 1940 JA
The Unsuspected Chasm; see From London Far
The Weight of the Evidence. Gollancz, 1944; Dodd, 1943 JA [acad.]
What Happened at Hazelwood. Gollancz, 1946; Dodd, 1946

INNES, MURRAY M.
Cosgrove: Detective. Stockwell, 1938 ss

INNOCENTI, PAUL-CLAUDE. See: Jean Bazal.

IONESCO, EUGENE. 1912- . Ref: CA.
The Killer and other plays. Grove, 1960; Calder, 1963 (4 plays; title play criminous.)

IONS, EDMUND S. Pseudonym: Edmund Aubrey, q.v.

IRALDI, JAMES C.
The Problem of the Purple Maculas. Norris, 1968 (Sherlock Holmes pastiche)

IRELAND, DAVID. 1927- . Ref: CA.
The Chantic Bird. Heinemann, 1968; Scribner, 1968

IRELAND, (SAMUEL) WILLIAM HENRY. 1777-1835.
Gondez the Monk. Earle, 1805 [1200s]
Rimualdo; or, The Castle of Badajos. Longman, 1800

IRISH, WILLIAM. Pseudonym of Cornell (George Hopley) Woolrich, 1903-1968, q.v. Other pseudonym: George Hopley, q.v.
After-Dinner Story. Lippincott, 1944; Hutchinson, 1947. Also published as: Six Times Death. Popular Library, 1948 ss
And So to Death; see I Wouldn't Be in Your Shoes
The Blue Ribbon. Lippincott, 1949; Hutchinson, 1951. Also published as: Dilemma of the Dead Lady. Graphic, 1950 (which omits 2 ss from the hardcover edition) ss
Bluebeard's Seventh Wife. Popular Library, 1952 ss
Borrowed Crime. Avon, 1946 ss
The Dancing Detective. Lippincott, 1946; Hutchinson, 1948 ss
Dead Man Blues. Lippincott, 1948; Hutchinson, 1950 ss
Deadline at Dawn. Lippincott, 1944; Hutchinson, 1947 [NYC]
Deadly Night Call; see Somebody on the Phone
Dilemma of the Dead Lady; see The Blue Ribbon
Eyes That Watch You. Rinehart, 1952 ss
I Married a Dead Man. Lippincott, 1948; Hutchinson, 1950
I Wouldn't Be in Your Shoes. Lippincott, 1943; Hutchinson, 1945. Also published as: And So to Death. Jonathan, 1947. And as: Nightmare. Reader's Choice Library, 1950. (Both of these paperback editions omit two ss from the original hardcover.) ss
If I Should Die Before I Wake. Avon, 1945 ss
Marihuana. Dell 10¢ pb, 1951 (Separate publication of a story first collected in After-Dinner Story, q.v.)
The Night I Died; see Somebody on the Phone
Nightmare; see I Wouldn't Be in Your Shoes
Phantom Lady. Lippincott, 1942; Hale, 1945 [NYC]
Six Nights of Mystery. Popular Library, 1950 ss
Six Times Death; see After-Dinner Story
Somebody on the Phone. Lippincott, 1950. British title: The Night I Died. Hutchinson, 1951. Also published as: Deadly Night Call. Graphic, 1951, with two ss omitted. ss
Strangler's Serenade. Rinehart, 1951; Hale, 1952 [Mass.]
Waltz into Darkness. Lippincott, 1947; Hutchinson, 1948 [New Or.]
You'll Never See Me Again. Dell 10¢ pb, 1951 (Separate publication of a novelet later collected in Nightwebs, as by Cornell Woolrich, q.v.)

IRONSIDE, JOHN. Pseudonym of Euphemia Margaret Tait. SC: Det. Insp. John Freeman, in at least those marked JF. Set: Eng.
Blackmail. Mellifont, 1938
The Call-Box Mystery. Methuen, 1923. U.S. title: The Phone Booth Mystery. Holt, 1924
-Chris: A Love Story. Hodder, 1926
The Crime and the Casket. Mellifont, 1945
-Forged in Strong Fires. Methuen, 1912; Little, 1911
Jack of Clubs. Nelson, 1931
Lady Pamela's Pearls. Hodder, 1927
The Marten Mystery. Arrowsmith, 1933 JF
The Phone Booth Mystery; see The Call-Box Mystery
The Red Symbol. Nash, 1911; Little, 1910 JF

IRVINE, HELEN DOUGLAS. -1947.
Mirror of a Dead Lady. Longmans, 1940
77 Willow Road; see Sweet Is the Rose
Sweet Is the Rose. Longmans, 1944. U.S. title: 77 Willow Road. Doubleday, 1945

IRVINE, PATRICIA McCUNE
The Port of No Return. Major, 1976

IRVINE, R(OBERT) R(ALSTONE). 1936- . Ref: CA. SC: Bob Christopher, in at least those marked BC.
The Face Out Front. Popular Library, 1977
Freeze Frame. Popular Library, 1976 BC [L.A.]
Horizontal Hold. Popular Library, 1978 BC [L.A.]
Jump Cut. Popular Library, 1974 BC [L.A.]

IRVING, ALEXANDER. Joint pseudonym of Ruth Fox (Hume), 1922-1980, and Anne Fahrenkopf, 1932- : Dr. Anthony Post = AP. Ref for Fox: CA. SC: Dr. Anthony Post = AP.
Bitter Ending. Dodd, 1946 AP [acad.]
Deadline. Dodd, 1947 [N.Y.]
Symphony in Two Time. Dodd, 1948 AP

IRVING, CLIFFORD (MICHAEL). 1930- . Joint pseudonym with Herbert Burkholz, 1932- : John Luckless, q.v. Ref: CA.
The Losers. Coward, 1957; Heinemann, 1959
The Thirty-Eighth Floor. McGraw, 1965; Heinemann, 1965
-The Valley. McGraw, 1961; Heinemann, 1962

IRVING, CLIVE. 1933- . Ref: CA.
Axis. H. Hamilton, 1980; Atheneum, 1980

IRVING, PETER HENRY (HOWY). 1914- .
-Fully Ripe. Hurst, 1944
-Green for a Season. Hurst, 1947
The Inner Room. Evans, 1952
An Italian Called Mario. Evans, 1954
-The Lady and the Unicorn. Evans, 1953
-One Way Street. Hurst, 1948
-Roger Quinney. Hurst, 1949
-The Triumphal Chariot. Hurst, 1945

IRVING-JAMES, T(HOMAS)
Deserted by the Devil. Hale, 1971
Dinner After Death. Hale, 1964 [Fr.]
A Glimpse of Evil. Hale, 1967

IRWIN, F. WILMOT
Black Terror. Fiction House, 1935
A Continental Conspiracy. Mellifont, 1935
A Cup-Tie Mystery. Mellifont, 1933
Death Makes a Date. Fiction House, 1943
Death Visits the Cinema. Fiction House, 1945
Horror Hall. Fiction House, 1938
Murder Makes Merry. Fiction House, 1944
Murder Mission. Fiction House, 1944
Murder on the Mountain! Fiction House, 1935
The Mystery of Moor Manor. Mellifont, 1934
Terror Tower. Fiction House, 1935
The Third Shot. Fiction House, 1937
The Tragic Quest. Mellifont, 1941

IRWIN, FRANCES
-The Winter Killing. Hale, 1977

IRWIN, H(ARVEY) S(AMUEL)
Helena. Dillingham, 1899

IRWIN, INEZ HAYNES. 1873-1970. SC: Patrick O'Brien, in all titles.
A Body Rolled Downstairs. Random, 1938; Heinemann, 1938 [Boston, Cape Cod]
Many Murders. Random, 1941; Swan, 1950 [Boston, Cape Cod]
Murder in Fancy Dress; see Murder Masquerade
Murder Masquerade. Smith & Haas, 1935. British title: Murder in Fancy Dress. Heinemann, 1935 [Boston, Cape Cod]
The Poison Cross Mystery. Smith & Haas, 1936; Heinemann, 1936 [Boston, Cape Cod]
The Women Swore Revenge. Random, 1946; Boardman, 1948 [Cape Cod]

IRWIN, JUDY
Murderous Welcome. Hale, 1967; Roy, 1967

IRWIN, THEODORE D. 1907- . Ref: CA.
Collusion. Godwin, 1932 [NYC]

IRWIN, WALLACE (ADMAH). 1876-1959. Born in N.Y., raised in Colo.; brother of Will(iam Henry) Irwin, 1873-1948, q.v.; magazine and newspaper editor and writer, mostly in N.Y.
The Julius Caesar Murder Case. Appleton, 1935 [It., ca.50 B.C.]

IRWIN, WILL(IAM HENRY). 1873-1948. Brother of Wallace (Admah) Irwin, 1876-1959, q.v.; born in N.Y., raised in Colo. See also: (Frank) Gelett Burgess, 1866-1951.

The Confessions of a Con Man. Huebsch, 1909
The House of Mystery. Century, 1910 [NYC]
The Red Button. Bobbs, 1912 [NYC]

ISAACS, MRS.
Glenmore Abbey; or, The Lady of the Rock. Lane, 1805

ISAACS, LEVI. Pseudonym: Louis Essex, q.v.

ISAACS, SUSAN. 1943- . Ref: CA.
Compromising Positions. Times, 1978; Lane, 1978 [L.I.]

ISELY, REYMOURE KEITH. Broadcasting executive and radio actor turned farmer in Can.
A Strange Code of Justice. Bobbs, 1974 [West]

ISHAM, FREDERIC S(TEWART). 1866-1922.
-Half a Chance. Bobbs, 1909
-A Man and His Money. Bobbs, 1912
The Social Buccaneer. Bobbs, 1910; Everett, 1911

ISLAY, NICHOLAS. Pseudonym of Andrew (Nicholas) Murray, 1880-1929, q.v., SC: Sydney Vane, in both titles, both set in Eng.
A Brace of Rogues. Murray, 1920
The Selicombe Murder. Murray, 1920

ISOM, LOUISE and FELICIA (LEIGH) METCALFE, 1899- .
Monkey Business. Art Craft, 1950 (3-act play.)

ISRAEL, CHARLES E(DWARD). 1920- . Ref: CA.
The Hostages. Simon, 1966; Macmillan (London), 1966
The Mark. Simon, 1958; Macmillan (London), 1958
Shadows on a Wall. Simon, 1965; Macmillan (London), 1965

ISRAEL, J. LEON. Pseudonym: Peter Israel, q.v.

ISRAEL, PETER. Pseudonym of J. Leon Israel. Director of publishing companies in Paris and then in NYC.
SC: B. F. Cage, in all titles.
The French Kiss. Crowell, 1976; Hodder, 1977 [Paris]
Hush Money. Crowell, 1974; Hodder, 1975 [L.A.]
The Stiff Upper Lip. Crowell, 1978; Hodder, 1979 [Paris]

I-TING, WANG
Thirty Famous Chinese Stories. Commercial, 1934 ss, at least one criminous

IVES, JOHN. Pseudonym of Brian (Francis Wynne) Garfield, 1939- , q.v.
Other pseudonyms: Drew Mallory, Frank O'Brian, qq.v.
Fear; see Fear in a Handful of Dust
Fear in a Handful of Dust. Dutton, 1978. British title: Fear. Macmillan (London), 1978 [Ariz.]
The Marchand Woman. Dutton, 1979; Macmillan (London), 1980 [P. Rico]

J., R. C.
The Tragedy of Captain Harrison; or, The Brownlow Street Mystery. Nutt, 1890

JACK, JEREMIAH
The Parajacker. Warner, 1974
-Train Wreck! Manor, 1975

JACKMAN, STUART (BROOKE). 1922- .
Ref: CA, TC.
Guns Covered with Flowers. Faber, 1973
Operation Catcher. H. Hamilton, 1980.
U.S. title: Sandcatcher. Atheneum, 1980 [Yem., 1944]
Sandcatcher; see Operation Catcher Slingshot. Faber, 1974

JACKS, JEFF. SC: Shep Stone, in both titles.
Find the Don's Daughter. GM, 1974
Murder on the Wild Side. GM, 1972 [NYC]

JACKS, OLIVER. Pseudonym of Kenneth Royce Gandley, 1920- . Other pseudonym: Kenneth Royce, q.v.

Assassination Day. Hodder, 1976; Stein, 1976
Autumn Heroes. Hodder, 1977; St. Martin's, 1978 [Kenya]
Man on a Short Leash. Hodder, 1974; Stein, 1974

JACKSON, ACE
There's Danger, Miss Minden! Brown Watson, 1949

JACKSON, BASIL. 1920- . Ref: CA.
Supersonic. Norton, 1975

JACKSON, BLYDEN. 1910- . Ref: CA.
Operation Burning Candle. Third Press, 1973 [NYC]
Totem. Third Press, 1975

JACKSON, BRUCE. 1936- .
The Programmer. Doubleday, 1979 [N.Y.]

JACKSON, CHARLES ROSS. 1867-1915. SC: Quintus Oakes = QO.
Quintus Oakes. Dillingham, 1904; Unwin, 1904 QO [N.Y.]
-The Sheriff of Wasco. Dillingham, 1907
The Third Degree. Dillingham, 1903; Unwin, 1903 QO

JACKSON, CLARENCE J.-L. Pseudonym of Richard (Williams) Bulliet, 1940- , q.v.
Kicked to Death by a Camel. Harper, 1973 [Afr.]

JACKSON, EILEEN
Autumn Lace. Walker, 1976; Hale, 1978 [Wales, 1800s]

JACKSON, EVERATT. Pseudonym of Margaret Elizabeth Muggeson, 1942- . Ref: CA.
The Road to Hell. Hale, 1975

JACKSON, FELIX. Born in Hamburg; music and drama critic, then playwright and film writer in Europe; film and TV writer/producer then in the U.S.
So Help Me God. Viking, 1955; Cassell, 1957 [NYC]

JACKSON, FREDERICK. 1886-1953.
The Bishop Misbehaves. French (NYC & London), 1935 (3-act play.)
The Cat Will Mew. Jarrolds, 1932
The Diamond Necklace. Whitman, 1929 (British title?)
A Full House. French, 1922 (3-act play.)
-Intimate Relations. Jarrolds, 1930
-Into This Universe. Jarrolds, 1929
Pantoufle. Jarrolds, 1934; Knopf, 1935

JACKSON, GILES. Pseudonym of Albert Leffingwell, 1895-1946, q.v. Other pseudonym: Dana Chambers, q.v. SC: Nile Boyd, in both titles.
Blood on the Blonde; see Witch's Moon
Court of Shadows. Dial, 1943; Museum, 1945 [NYC]
Witch's Moon. Dial, 1941; Museum, 1943. Also published as: Blood on the Blonde, as by Dana Chambers. Jonathan, 1952, abridged [New Eng.]

JACKSON, JOAN
Murder Makes Me Laugh. Aldor, 1947

JACKSON, JON A(NTHONY). 1938- . Ref: CA. SC: Sgt. Mulheisen, in both titles, both set in Det.
The Blind Pig. Random, 1979; Hale, 1980
The Diehard. Random, 1977; Hale, 1978

JACKSON, KEN. SC: Jud Blade, in both titles, both set in Okla.
The Cutting Edge. Simon, 1970
The Sticking Point. Simon, 1971

JACKSON, LEWIS. Pseudonym of Jack Lewis, q.v. Other pseudonym: Stephen Hood, q.v. All titles below were published by Amalgamated Press and feature Sexton Blake. Set: Eng.
According to Plan. 1947
The Case of the Biscay Pirate. 1944
The Case of the Discharged Policeman. 1949
The Case of the Doped Heavyweight. 1948
The Case of the Fatal Souvenir. 1946
The Case of the Fighting Padre. 1947
The Case of the Five Fugitives. 1944
The Case of the Five Red Herrings. 1945
The Case of John Muir of Merchant Navy. 1942
The Case of the Missing Stoker. 1942
The Case of the Night Lorry Driver. 1946
The Case of the "Suspect" Watchmaker. 1943

The Crime on the Cliff. 1947
The Death of Mrs. Preedy. 1949
Down East! 1946
The Man from Arnheim. 1945
The Man from Persia. 1951
The Man Who Left Home. 1949
The Man Who Went Wrong. 1948
The Night of the 23rd. 1947
On Compassionate Leave. 1945
The Riddle of the Film Star's Jewels. 1947
The Riddle of the Ruins. 1944
The Riddle of the Workman Squire. 1945
The Tallyman's Fate. 1945
The Tenant of No. 13. 1946
The Woman with a "Record." 1946

JACKSON, MARR. Set: Eng.
A Dram of Poison. Bell, 1938
Escape into Murder. Cassell, 1939

JACKSON, MARY E.
The Spy of Osawatomie; or, The Mysterious Companions of Old John Brown. Bryan, 1881

JACKSON, O(LIVE) T.
Aftermath. Leisure, 1979
Dark Love, Dark Magic. Lancer, 1969 [Calif.]

JACKSON, RALPH
Violent Night. Ace, 1955

JACKSON, SHIRLEY. 1920-1965. See also: F. Andrew Leslie, 1927- ; and: Hugh Callingham Wheeler, 1912- . Ref: CA, TC.
The Bird's Nest. Farrar, 1954; Joseph, 1955. Also published as: Lizzie. Signet, 1957 ss
Come Along with Me. Viking, 1968; Joseph, 1969 ss
Hangsaman. Farrar, 1951; Gollancz, 1951
The Haunting of Hill House. Viking, 1959; Joseph, 1960
Lizzie; see The Bird's Nest
The Lottery. Farrar, 1949; Gollancz, 1950 ss
The Road Through the Wall. Farrar, 1949
The Sundial. Farrar, 1958; Joseph, 1958
We Have Always Lived in the Castle. Viking, 1962; Joseph, 1963

JACKSON, WALLACE. Pseudonym of William John Budd, 1898- . Other pseudonym: Jackson Budd, q.v. SC: Insp. Clancy Martin = CM; Archibald Penny = AP. Set: Eng.
The Diamonds of Death. Low, 1936; Hopkins, 1937 CM
The Extraordinary Case of Mr. Bell. Low, 1935; Hopkins, 1936 AP
The Sinister Madonna. Low, 1937; Hopkins, 1937 CM
Two Knocks for Death. Low, 1934; Hopkins, 1935 CM
The Zadda Street Affair. Low, 1934 AP

JACKSON, WILFRID S(CARBOROUGH). 1871- .
Nine Points of the Law. Lane (London & NYC), 1903

JACOB, PIERS ANTHONY DILLINGHAM. 1934- .
Pseudonym: Piers Anthony, q.v.

JACOBS, T(HOMAS) C(URTIS) H(ICKS). Pseudonym of Jacques Pendower, 1899-1976, q.v. SC: Chief Insp. Barnard, in at least those marked B; Det. Supt. John Bellamy, in at least those marked JB; Temple Fortune, in at least those marked TF; Mike Seton, in at least those marked MS; Jim Malone, in at least those marked JM. Set: Eng.
Appointment with the Hangman. Paul, 1936; Macaulay, 1936
Ashes in the Cellar. Hale, 1966 TF
The Black Box. Paul, 1946 B
The Black Devil. Hale, 1969 TF [Fr.]
Black Trinity. Long, 1959 JB
Blood and Sun-Tan. Paul, 1952 TF
Broken Alibi. Paul, 1957; Roy, 1957 JB
The Broken Knife. Paul, 1941 B
The Bronkhurst Case. Paul, 1931. U.S. title: Documents of Murder. Macaulay, 1933
Brother Spy. Paul, 1940 B
Cause for Suspicion. Paul, 1956 [Fr.]
The Curse of Khatra. Paul, 1947 JB
Danger Money. Hale, 1963 TF
Dangerous Fortune. Paul, 1949 TF
Deadly Race. Long, 1958 TF [Sp.]
Death in the Mews. Paul, 1955 TF,B
Death of a Scoundrel. Hale, 1967 TF
Documents of Murder; see The Bronkhurst Case
The Elusive Mr. Drago. Hale, 1965 MS [Fr.]
Final Payment. Hale, 1965 TF
Good Knight, Sailor. Paul, 1954 TF [Fr.]

The Grenson Murder Case. Paul, 1943 JB
House of Horror. Hale, 1969 TF
Identity Unknown. Paul, 1938 B
The Kestrel House Mystery. Paul, 1932; Macaulay, 1933 B
Lady, What's Your Game? Paul, 1952 TF [Fr.]
The Laughing Men. Hodder, 1937 B
Let Him Stay Dead. Hale, 1961 JM [Fr.]
Lock the Door, Mademoiselle. Paul, 1951 TF [Fr.]
Murder Market. Hale, 1962 TF
No Sleep for Elsa. Paul, 1953 TF
The Red Eyes of Kali. Paul, 1950 TF,B
The Red Net. Hale, 1962 JM [Fr.]
Results of an Accident. Paul, 1955 JB
Reward for Treason. Paul, 1944 B
Scorpion's Trail. Paul, 1932; Macaulay, 1934 B
The Secret Power. Hale, 1963 [Venice]
Security Risk. Hale, 1972
Silent Terror. Paul, 1936; Macaulay, 1937 B
Sinister Quest. Paul, 1934; Macaulay, 1934 B
Sweet Poison. Hale, 1966 TF
Target for Terror. Hale, 1961 MS,TF [Paris, Tun.]
The Tattooed Man. Hale, 1961
The Terror of Torlands. Paul, 1930
The 13th Chime. Paul, 1935; Macaulay, 1935 B
Traitor Spy. Paul, 1939 B
Wild Week-End. Hale, 1967 TF
With What Motive? Paul, 1948 JB
The Woman Who Waited. Paul, 1954 [Sp.]
Women Are Like That. Hale, 1960 TF,JB

JACOBS, W(ILLIAM) W(YMARK). 1863-1943. Ref: CC, EM.
The Lady of the Barge. Harper (London), 1902; Dodd, 1902 ss, some criminous
Sea Whispers. Hodder, 1926 ss, at least two criminous

JACOBSEN, JULIUS
-The Revelations of a Police Court Interpreter. Whitaker, 1866

JACOBSSON, PER. 1894-1963. Joint pseudonym with Vernon Barlett, 1894-   : Peter Oldfeld, q.v.

JACOLLIOT, J. L(OUIS). 1837-1890.
The Froler Case. Bonner's, 1893. Also published as: The Sign of the Dagger; or, The Froler Case. Street, 1904

JACQUEMARD, YVES. 1943-   . Joint pseudonym with Jean-Michel Senecal, 1943-   : Jacquemard-Senecal, q.v.

JACQUEMARD-SENECAL. Joint pseudonym of Yves Jacquemard, 1943-   , and Jean-Michel Senecal, 1943-   . Jacquemard was born in Algeria; studied French literature. Senecal was born in France; studied interior decor and publicity. Together they have written more than 20 plays.
The Body Vanishes. Collins, 1980; Dodd, 1980 (Translation of "Le Crime de la Maison Grun." Paris, 1976.) [Fr.]
The Eleventh Little Indian; see The Eleventh Little Nigger
The Eleventh Little Nigger. Collins, 1979. U.S. title: The Eleventh Little Indian. Dodd, 1979 (Translation of "Le Onquieme Petit Negro." Paris, 1977.) [Fr.]

JACQUES, NORBERT. 1880-1954.
Dr. Mabuse, Master of Mystery. Allen & Unwin, 1923 (Translation of "Doktor Mabuse." Berlin, 1920.) [Ger.]

JAEDIKER, KERMIT. Born in NYC; crime reporter and newspaper rewriter in NYC.
Hero's Lust. Lion, 1953
Tall, Dark and Dead. Mystery House, 1947 [NYC]

JAFFE, MICHAEL
Death Goes to a Party. Phoenix, 1942 [NYC]

JAFFE, SUSAN. Executive of pb publishing house.
The Other Anne Fletcher. NAL, 1980 [NYC]

JAFFEE, IRVING. See: Mary Jaffee

JAFFEE, MARY and IRVING. Ref for Mary Jaffee: CA.
Beyond Baker Street. Pontine, 1973 ss (Sherlock Holmes.)

JAGODA, ROBERT. 1923-   . Ref: CA.
A Friend in Deed. Norton, 1977 [N.Y.]

JAHN, (JOSEPH) MICHAEL. 1943-   . Ref: CA.
The Deadliest Game. Popular Library, 1976 (Novelization of the "Rockford Files" TV series.)
Killer on the Heights. GM, 1977 [NYC]
The Quark Maneuver. Ballantine, 1977 [NYC]
Shearwater. Hamlyn, 1980
Switch. Berkley, 1976; Star, 1976 (Novelization of the TV series.) [L.A.]
Switch #2. Berkley, 1976 (Novelization of the TV series.)
The Unfortunate Replacement. Popular Library, 1975 (Novelization of the "Rockford Files" TV series.)

JAKES, JOHN (WILLIAM). 1932-   . Pseudonyms: Alan Payne, Rachel Ann Payne, Jay Scotland, qq.v. See also: William Ard, 1922-1960. Ref: CA. SC: Johnny Havoc = JH.
The Devil Has Four Faces. Mystery House, 1958
Gonzaga's Woman. Universal, 1953
The Imposter. Mystery House, 1959
Johnny Havoc. Belmont, 1960 JH
Johnny Havoc and the Doll Who Had "It." Belmont, 1963 JH
Johnny Havoc Meets Zelda. Belmont, 1962 JH
Making It Big. Belmont, 1968 JH
A Night for Treason. Mystery House, 1956

JAMES, POLICE CAPTAIN. Pseudonym.
Little Lightning, the Shadow Detective; or, The Twenty-Third Street Mystery. Street, 1888
The Revenue Detective. Street, 1889

JAMES, BARBARA
Beauty That Must Die. Hodder, 1961; Ace, 1967
Bright Deadly Summer. Hodder, 1962; Ace, 1966

JAMES, BRENI [BRENI JAMES PEVEHOUSE]. Born in Denver, living in S.F. in 1960's; ss writer. Ref: CC. SC: Sgt. Gunnar Matson, in both titles, both set in S.F.
Night of the Kill. Simon, 1961; Hammond, 1963
The Shake-Up. Simon, 1964

JAMES, DON(ALD H.). 1905-   . Ref: CA.
Dark Hunger. Monarch, 1963

JAMES, DONALD. 1931-   . Joint pseudonym with Tony Barwick, 1934-   : James Barwick, q.v.
Shadow of the Wolf, with Tony Barwick, 1934-   . Collins, 1978; Coward, 1979, as by James Barwick [Eng., 1941]
A Spy at Evening. Collins, 1977; GM, 1981

JAMES, ELLEN BILES. 1877-   .
Out of the Night. Pageant, 1961

JAMES, FLORENCE ALICE PRICE. 1857-1929. Pseudonym: Florence Warden, q.v.

JAMES, FRANKIE-LEE. Pseudonym: Saliee O'Brien, q.v.

JAMES, FRANKLIN. Pseudonym of Robert Godley, 1908-   .
Killer in the Kitchen. Lantern Press, 1947 [Chi.]

JAMES, G(EORGE) P(AYNE) R(AINSFORD). 1801?-1860.
The Castle of Ehrenstein. Smith Elder, 1847; Harper, 1847

JAMES, GODFREY WARDEN. 1888-   . Pseudonym: Adam Broome, q.v.

JAMES, HALLAM
Fair-Isle Jumper Mystery. James, 1944 [Wales]

JAMES, HENRY. 1843-1916. See also: Michael (Scudamore) Redgrave, 1908-   ; and: William Archibald, 1924-1970. Ref: CA, CC.
The Other House. Macmillan, 1896; Heinemann, 1896
The Turn of the Screw. Macmillan, 1898; in Two Magics: Heinemann, 1898
Two Magics; see The Turn of the Screw

JAMES, HENRY COLBERT
The Girl from Taiping. Jarrolds, 1954
Gold Is Where You Find It. Harrap, 1949
The Green Opal. Jarrolds, 1953
The Madness of Charlie Pierce. Jarrolds, 1952

JAMES, JOHN
Blind Chance. Evans, 1961 (1-act play.)
Nightmare's End. Kenyon House, 1963 (Play.)

JAMES, LAURENCE. Pseudonym: Klaus Netzen, q.v.

JAMES, LEIGH. Pseudonym. 1918-   . Former Foreign Service officer, living in Wash. D.C.; a lawyer in banking.
The Caliph Intrigue. Dodd, 1979 [Wash. D.C.]
The Capitol Hill Affair. Weybright, 1968 [Wash. D.C.]
The Chameleon File. Weybright, 1967; Jenkins, 1968
The Push-Button Spy. Prentice-Hall, 1970
Triple Mirror. Mason, 1973 [Va.]

JAMES, MARGARET. Pseudonym of Pamela Bennetts, 1922-   , q.v.

JAMES, MARYL
Brandy on the Rocks. Lancer, 1967 [Fr.]

JAMES, MAX
Death Is Where You Meet It. Hamilton & Co., 1952 [U.S.]

JAMES, P(HYLLIS) D(OROTHY). 1920-   . Ref: CA, CC, EM, TC. SC: Adam Dalgliesh = AD. Set: Eng.
The Black Tower. Faber, 1975; Scribner, 1975 AD
Cover Her Face. Faber, 1962; Scribner, 1966 AD
Death of an Expert Witness. Faber, 1977; Scribner, 1977 AD
Innocent Blood. Faber, 1980; Scribner, 1980
A Mind to Murder. Faber, 1963; Scribner, 1967 AD
Shroud for a Nightingale. Faber, 1971; Scribner, 1971 AD [acad.]
Unnatural Causes. Faber, 1967; Scribner, 1967 AD
An Unsuitable Job for a Woman. Faber, 1972; Scribner, 1973 AD

JAMES, PAUL
What Became of Eugene Ridgewood? Carleton, 1883

JAMES, REBECCA (SALSBURY)
The House Is Dark. Doubleday, 1976; New English Library, 1977 [Conn.]
Storm's End. Doubleday, 1974; New English Library, 1975 [N.Y.]

JAMES, ROBERT. Pseudonym of Iris Heitner.
Board Stiff. Doubleday, 1951 [ship]
Death Wears Pink Shoes. Doubleday, 1952 [NYC]

JAMES, STUART
Jack the Ripper. Monarch, 1960 (Novelization of the movie.)
The Stranglers of Bombay. Monarch, 1960 (Novelization of the movie.) [Bombay]

JAMES, SUSAN. Pseudonym of Arthur J. Griffin, 1921-   . Other pseudonym: Anne J. Griffin, q.v.
The Hypnotist of Hilary Mansion. PB, 1977

JAMES, VINCENT. Pseudonym of James Gribben, 1915-   .
Island of the Pit. Benn, 1955; Messner, 1956
The Long Ride Out. Benn, 1957; Putnam, 1958
Morgan's Wife. Quality, 1949
Red Sky. Quality, 1953

JAMES, WILHELMINA MARTHA. Pseudonym: Austin Clare, q.v.

JAMESON, MRS. ANNIE EDITH FOSTER. 1868-1931. Pseudonym: J. E. Buckrose, q.v.

JAMESON, (MARGARET) STORM. 1891-   . Ref: CA.
Before the Crossing. Macmillan (London & NYC), 1947

JAMIESON, LELAND (SHATTUCK). 1904-1941. SC: Dan Gregory, in both titles, both set in the Carib.
G-Men on Murder Island. Swan, 1947
Murder Island. Melrose, 1935; Greenberg, 1936

JAMISON, AMELIA
The Lairds of Turriff Hall. Popular Library, 1974 [Scot.]

JANE, FRED(ERICK) T(HOMAS). 1865-1916.
  Ever Mohun. Macqueen, 1901
  -The Incubated Girl. Tower, 1896
  -The Lordship, the Passen, and We.
    Innes, 1897
  -A Royal Bluejacket. Low, 1908
  -To Venus in Five Seconds. Innes, 1897
  -The Violet Flame. Ward, 1899

JANEWAY, HARRIET
  This Passionate Land. Signet, 1979
    [South, 1850s]

JANIFER, LAURENCE M. Pseudonym of Larry
  M(ark) Harris, 1933-   , q.v. Joint
  pseudonym with Randall (Phillips)
  Garrett, 1927-   , q.v.: Mark
  Phillips, q.v.
  The Final Fear. Belmont, 1967 [NYC]
  The Woman Without a Name. Signet, 1966
    [Eng.]
  You Can't Escape. Lancer, 1967 [NYC]

JANIS, ELSIE, 1889-1956, and MARGUERITE
  ASPINWALL
  Counter Currents. Putnam (NYC & London), 1926

JANNEY, SAM(UEL MacPHERSON). 1892-   .
  The Amateur Detective. Baker, 1933
    (Play.)

JANSEN, JOHANNA FREDERIKA. Joint pseudonym with Margaret Elizabeth Baird
  Campbell: Fred Bayard, q.v.

JANSEN, LAURA MAY
  Bride of the Shadows. Lancer, 1967
    [New Eng.]

JANSON, HANK. House name. Used by Stephen
  D(aniel) Frances, q.v., who was probably the original author. Also used
  by Harry Hobson, 1908-   , q.v. Other
  pseudonym of Hobson: Hank Hobson, q.v.
  Also used by Victor (George Charles)
  Norwood, 1920-   , q.v. Other Norwood
  pseudonyms: Johnny Dark, Mark Hampton,
  Nat Karta, qq.v. SC: Hank Janson, in
  at least those marked HJ. Note that
  at least those titles published by
  Gold Star are copyrighted by G. Gold
  and D. Warburton.
  Abomination. Roberts, 1965
  The Affairs of Paula. Gold Star, 1965
    HJ [Chi.]
  Amorous Captive. Moring, 1958
  Angel Astray. Roberts, 1962
  Angel, Shoot to Kill. Frances, 1949
  Auctioned. New Fiction Press, 1952
  Avenging Nymph. Moring, 1958
  Baby, Don't Dare Squeal. Frances, 1951
  Backlash of Infamy. Roberts, 1965
  Bad Girl. Turton, 1959
  Beauty and the Beat. Roberts, 1962
  Becky. Gold Star, 1965
  Beloved Traitor. Roberts, 1960
  Bid for Beauty. Roberts, 1966
  The Big H. Roberts, 1966
  Blonde on the Spot. Gaywood, 1949
  Blood Bath. Roberts, 1962
  Brand Image. Roberts, 1963
  Brazen Seductress. Gold Star, 1963 HJ
  Break for a Lovely. Roberts, 1961
  The Bride Wore Weeds. Gaywood, 1950
  Broads Don't Scare Easy. New Fiction, 1951
  Casinopoly. Roberts, 1968
  Catch Me a Renegade. Roberts, 1965
  Chicago Chick. Roberts, 1962 [Chi.]
  Cold Dead Coed. Gold Star, 1964 HJ
  Come Quickly, Honey. Roberts, 1960
  Conflict. New Fiction Press, 1952
  Contraband. Moring, 1955
  Cool Sugar. Roberts, 1960
  Counter-Feat. Roberts, 1962
  Crime Beat Crisis. Roberts, 1964
  Crime on My Hands. Roberts, 1962
  Crowns Can Kill. Roberts, 1961
  Cutie on Call. Roberts, 1960
  Darling Delinquent. Roberts, 1966
  Dateline Darlene. Roberts, 1963
  Dateline Debbie. Roberts, 1963
  Dateline Diane. Roberts, 1963
  Daughter of Shame. Roberts, 1963
  Dead Certainty. Roberts, 1966
  Deadly Mission. Moring, 1955
  Death Wore a Petticoat. Francis, 1951
  Delicious Danger. Roberts, 1961
  Desert Fury. New Fiction, 1953
  Design for Dupes. Roberts, 1964
  Destination Dames. Roberts, 1961
  Devil and the Deep. Roberts, 1965
  Devil's Highway. Moring, 1956
  Dig Those Heels. Roberts, 1962
  Doctor Fix. Roberts, 1964
  Don't Dare Me, Sugar. Gaywood, 1950
  Don't Mourn Me, Toots. Frances, 1951
  Don't Scare Easy. Moring, 1958
  Double Take. Roberts, 1964
  Downtown Doll. Roberts, 1961
  Ecstasy. Roberts, 1960
  Escalation. Roberts, 1966
  Escape. Moring, 1956
  Exclusive. Roberts, 1962
  The Exotic Seductress. Gold Star, 1964
    HJ
  Expectant Nymph. Gold Star, 1964 HJ
  Fan Fare. Roberts, 1964
  Fanny. Gold Star, 1964 HJ
  Fast Buck. Roberts, 1963
  F.E.U.D. Roberts, 1966
  The Filly Wore Red. New Fiction, 1952
  Fireball. Roberts, 1961
  Flashpoint. Roberts, 1965
  Flight from Fear. Moring, 1958
  Flower of Desire. Roberts, 1964
  48 Hours. Moring, 1955
  Frails Can Be So Tough. New Fiction, 1951
  Framed. Moring, 1955
  Furtive Flame. Roberts, 1965
  A Girl in Hand. Roberts, 1964
  Go with a Jerk. Roberts, 1963
  Grape Vine. Roberts, 1962
  Gun Moll for Hire. Frances, 1948
  Gunsmoke in Her Eyes. Frances, 1949
  Hate. Moring, 1958
  Heartache. Roberts, 1963
  Helldorado. Roberts, 1966
  Hell's Angel. Moring, 1956; Gold Star, 1964 HJ
  Hell's Belles. Roberts, 1961
  Her Weapon Is Passion. Gold Star, 1964
    HJ
  Hilary's Terms. Roberts, 1963
  Honey for Me. Roberts, 1962
  Honey Take My Gun. Frances, 1949
  Hot House. Gold Star, 1964 HJ
  Hot Line. Roberts, 1963
  Hotsy, You'll Be Chilled. Frances, 1951
  I for Intrigue. Roberts, 1963
  Invasion. Moring, 1959
  It's Always Eve That Weeps. Frances, 1951
  It's Bedtime, Baby! Gold Star, 1964 HJ
  Jack Spot. Moring, 1959
  The Jane with Green Eyes. Gaywood, 1950
  Janson, Go Home. Roberts, 1961
  Jazz Jungle. Roberts, 1965
  Junk Market. Roberts, 1965
  Kill Her If You Can. New Fiction, 1952
  Kill Her with Passion. Gold Star, 1963
    HJ
  Kill Me for Kicks. Roberts, 1962
  Kill This Man. Moring, 1958
  Krush. Roberts, 1966
  The Lady Has a Scar. Gaywood, 1950
  Lady, Lie Low. Roberts, 1961
  Lady, Mind That Corpse. Frances, 1948;
    Checker, 1949
  Lady, Toll the Bell. Gaywood, 1950
  Ladybirds Are In. Roberts, 1967
  Lake Loot. Roberts, 1964
  The Last Lady. Roberts, 1964
  Late Night Revel. Roberts, 1961
  Like Crazy. Roberts, 1962
  Like Lethal. Roberts, 1962
  Like Poison. Roberts, 1962
  Lilies for My Lovely. Frances, 1949
  Limbo Lover. Roberts, 1964
  Liquor Is Quicker. Roberts, 1966
  Lola Brought Her Wreath. Gaywood, 1950
  Lose This Gun. Moring, 1958
  The Love Makers. Roberts, 1963
  The Love Secretaries. Roberts, 1964
  Lover. Gold Star, 1963 HJ
  Lust for Vengeance. Roberts, 1965
  Make Mine Mink. Roberts, 1966
  Master Mind. Roberts, 1961
  Mayfair Slayride. Roberts, 1966
  Menace. Moring, 1955
  Milady Took the Rap. New Fiction, 1951
  Missile Mob. Roberts, 1965
  Mistress of Fear. Moring, 1958
  Model in Mayhem. Roberts, 1965
  Murder. New Fiction, 1952
  Nefarious Quest. Roberts, 1966
  Nerve Centre. Roberts, 1963
  A Nice Way to Die. Gold Star, 1963
    HJ [Chi.]
  No Regrets for Clara. Frances, 1949
  Nymph in the Night. Roberts, 1962
  A Nympho Named Silvia. Gold Star, 1965
    HJ
  One Man in His Time. New Fiction, 1953
  Outcast. Roberts, 1961
  Passion Pact. Roberts, 1963
  Passionate Playmate. Gold Star, 1964 HJ
  Passionate Waif. Roberts, 1960
  Pattern of Rape. Roberts, 1964
  Physical Attraction. Roberts, 1967
  Play It Casual. Roberts, 1962
  Playgirl. Roberts, 1963
  Prey for a Newshawk. Roberts, 1961
  Quiet Waits the Grave. Roberts, 1960
  Rave for a Roughneck. Roberts, 1962
  Reluctant Hostess. Roberts, 1961
  Ripe for Rapture. Roberts, 1960
  Riviera Showdown. Roberts, 1967
  Roxy by Proxy. Roberts, 1965
  Run for Lover. Roberts, 1961
  Sadie, Don't Cry Now. New Fiction, 1952
  Same Difference. Roberts, 1968
  Savage Sequel. Roberts, 1962
  Say It with Candy. Roberts, 1965
  Scent from Heaven. Roberts, 1961
  Second String. Roberts, 1963
  Secret Session. Roberts, 1960
  Sentence for Sin. Roberts, 1960
  Sex Angle. Roberts, 1964
  The Sexy Vixen. Gold Star, 1964 HJ
  She Sleeps to Conquer. Roberts, 1961
  Short-Term Wife. Roberts, 1961
  Silken Snare. Moring, 1959
  Sister, Don't Hate Me. Frances, 1951
  Situation, Grave! Moring, 1958
  Skirts Bring Me Sorrow. New Fiction, 1952
  Slay-Ride for Cutie. Frances, 1949
  Smart Girls Don't Talk. Frances, 1949
  Soft Cargo. Roberts, 1964
  Some Look Better Dead. Frances, 1950
  Square One. Roberts, 1964
  Strange Ritual. Roberts, 1963
  Suddenly It's Sin. Roberts, 1961
  Sugar and Vice. Moring, 1958
  Sultry Avenger. Moring, 1959
  Sweet Talk. Roberts, 1965
  Sweetheart, Here's Your Grave! Frances, 1949
  Sweetie, Hold Me Tight. Frances, 1952
  Tail Sting. Roberts, 1965
  Take This—Sweetie. Roberts, 1962
  Tension. Frances, 1952
  That Brain Again. Roberts, 1964
  This Dame Dies Soon. Frances, 1951.
    Also published as: Too Soon to Die.
    Moring, 1962
  This Hood for Hire. Roberts, 1960
  This Woman Is Death. Frances, 1948
  Tigress. Roberts, 1964
  Tomorrow and a Day. Moring, 1955
  Too Soon to Die; see This Dame Dies
    Soon
  Top Ten. Roberts, 1964
  Torment for Trixy. Gaywood, 1950
  Torrid Temptress. Turton, 1959
  Twist for Two. Roberts, 1962
  Uncommon Market. Roberts, 1962
  Uncover Agent. Roberts, 1962
  The Unseen Assassin. Moring, 1956
  V for Vitality. Roberts, 1963
  Vagabond Vamp. Roberts, 1962
  Venus Makes Three. Roberts, 1961
  Visit from a Broad. Roberts, 1963
  Voodoo Violence. Roberts, 1964
  Way Out Wanton. Roberts, 1962
  When Dames Get Tough. Ward & Hitchon, 1946
  Whiplash. New Fiction, 1952
  Why Should Sylvia? Roberts, 1965
  Wild Girl. Turton, 1959
  Will-Power. Roberts, 1964
  Women Hate Till Death. New Fiction, 1951
  The Young Wolves. Roberts, 1968
  Zero Take All. Roberts, 1967

JANSSON, ROBERT
  Meet You in Munich. Barker, 1975
  News Caper. Macmillan (London), 1978

JAPRISOT, SEBASTIEN. Pseudonym of Jean
  Baptiste Rossi, 1931-   . Ref: CC,
  MC, TC.
  Goodbye, Friend. Simon, 1969; Souvenir,
    1969 (Translation of "Adieu L'Ami."
    Paris, 1968.) [Paris]
  The Lady in the Car with Glasses and a
    Gun. Simon, 1967; Souvenir, 1968
    (Translation of "La Dame dans l'Auto
    avec les Lunettes et un Fusil." Paris, 1966.) [Fr.]
  One Deadly Summer. Harcourt, 1980;
    Secker, 1980 (Translation of "L'Ete
    Meurtrier." Paris, 1978.) [Fr.]
  The Sleeping Car Murders; see The 10:30
    from Marseilles
  The 10:30 from Marseilles. Doubleday,
    1963; Souvenir, 1964. Also published
    as: The Sleeping Car Murders. PB,
    1967 (Translation of "Compartiment
    Tueurs." Paris, 1962.) [Fr., train]
  Trap for Cinderella. Simon, 1964; Souvenir, 1965 (Translation of "Piege
    pour Cendrillon." Paris, 1962.) [Fr.]

JAQUES, EDWARD TYRRELL. Pseudonym:
  Christian Tearle, q.v.

JARDIN, REX. Joint pseudonym of Robert
  Ferdinand Burkhardt, 1892-1947, and
  Eve Burkhardt, 1899-   . Other joint
  pseudonym: Adam Bliss, q.v.
  The Devil's Mansion. Fiction League,
    1931 [Can.]

JARDINE, JACK OWEN. 1931-   . Pseudonym: Larry Maddock, q.v.

JARDINE, WARWICK. Pseudonym of Francis
  Alister Warwick, son of Sydney Warwick, q.v. All titles here were published by Amalgamated Press and feature Sexton Blake. Set: Eng.

The British Museum Mystery. 1934
A Case for M.I.5. 1950
The Case of the Murdered Wedding Guest. 1936
The Cloakroom Murder. 1934
The Crime in Park Lane. 1933
Crook's Loot. 1932
Death Her Destination. 1961
Doomed Men. 1932. Revised version: 1940
The Great Dumping Mystery. 1932
The Hailey Street Murder. 1933
The Lift Shaft Crime. 1938
The Madman of the Marshes. 1949
The Man from Algiers. 1948
The Man from Tokyo. 1933
The Man with a Grievance. 1952
The Mystery of the Arab Agent. 1953
The Mystery of the Unknown Victim. 1933
The Old Man of the Moors. 1950
The Pavement Artist Mystery. 1937
The Pleasure Cruise Murder. 1933
The Riddle of the Green Cylinder. 1955
The Riddle of the Ranch. 1939
The Seaside Cafe Crime. 1936
The Seaside Crime. 1936
The Secret of Capri. 1950
The Secret of the Glacier. 1935
The Secret of the Sudan. 1933
The Secret of the Surgery. 1939
The Stolen Test-Tube. 1935
The 13th Code. 1939
Top Secret No. 1. 1951
The Victim of the Cult. 1937

JARRETT, CORA (HARDY). 1877- . Pseudonym: Faraday Keene, q.v. Ref: EM, MP, TC.
The Ginkgo Tree. Farrar, 1935; Barker, 1935
Night over Fitch's Pond. Houghton, 1933; Barker, 1933

JARVIE, CLODAGH GIBSON. 1923- .
He Would Provoke Death. Boardman, 1959; Roy, 1959
Variation on a Theme of Murder. Simpkin, 1948
Vicious Circuit. Boardman, 1957 [Fr.]

JARVIS, EDWARD
The Big Fix. Hale, 1969; Roy, 1970

JARVIS, FRED(ERICK) G(ORDON, JR.). 1930- . Joint pseudonym with Robert F. Van Beever: Fritz Gordon, q.v. Ref: CA.
Murder at the Met. Coward, 1971 [NYC, theatre]

JARVIS, H(ENRY) W(OOD)
The House of Silence. Muller, 1959

JASON, STUART. House name. Those titles by Lee Floren, 1910- , are marked *. Those by Michael (Angelo) Avallone, 1924- , q.v., are marked #. Avallone pseudonyms: Nick Carter, Priscilla Dalton, Mark Dane, Jean-Anne de Pre, Dora Highland, Steve Michaels, Dorothea Nile, Edwina Noone, Sidney Stuart, Max Walker, qq.v. SC: The Butcher, in all titles.
African Contract. Pinnacle, 1975 [S. Afr.]
Appointment in Iran. Pinnacle, 1977 [NYC, Iran]
Blood Debt. Pinnacle, 1972 [Mor.]
Blood Vengeance. Pinnacle, 1975 [Afr.]
Come Watch Him Die. Pinnacle, 1971
The Corporate Caper. Pinnacle, 1977 [Wash. D.C., NYC]
The Cubano Caper. Pinnacle, 1976
Deadly Deal. Pinnacle, 1973
The Deadly Doctor. Pinnacle, 1974 *
Death Race. Pinnacle, 1973 [Can.]
Fire Bomb. Pinnacle, 1973
Grecian Bloodbath. Pinnacle, 1976 [Greece]
The Hollywood Assassin. Pinnacle, 1976 [L.A.]
Instant Dead. Pinnacle, 1976 [Rome]
The Judas Judge. Pinnacle, 1979 [NYC] #
Keepers of Death. Pinnacle, 1971
Kill Gently, But Sure. Pinnacle, 1975
Kill Quick or Die. Pinnacle, 1970
Kill Them Silently. Pinnacle, 1980 #
Kill Time. Pinnacle, 1973
Killer's Cargo. Pinnacle, 1974
Mayday over Manhattan. Pinnacle, 1976 [NYC]
Sealed with Blood. Pinnacle, 1973 [NYC, Isr.]
Slaughter in September. Pinnacle, 1980 [S.W.] #
Suicide in San Juan. Pinnacle, 1975 [P. Rico]
The Terror Truckers. Pinnacle, 1977
The U.N. Affair. Pinnacle, 1976 [NYC]
Valley of Death. Pinnacle, 1974 [Calif.] *
Venetian Vendetta. Pinnacle, 1977 [Venice]

JAUNIERE, CLAUDE. Pseudonym: Claudette Jauniere, q.v.

JAUNIERE, CLAUDETTE. Pseudonym of Claude Jauniere, under which byline all titles below were originally published in France.
Conspiracy to Kill. Mystique, 1979 (Translation of "Piege Pour Deux Couers." Paris, 1962.)
The Law of Love. Mystique, 1977 (Translation of "Orages." Paris, 1967.)
Lost Honeymoon. Mystique, 1979 (Translation of "Lune de Miel." Paris, 1953.)
Passage to Jamaica. Mystique, 1980 (Translation of "Le Vent du Soir." Paris, 1967.)
Proper Age for Love. Mystique, 1977 (Translation of "L'Age de L'Amour." Paris, 1970.)
The Whims of Fate. Mystique, 1977 (Translation of "Les Caprices du Destin." Paris, 1972.)

JAVITS, HANK
Who Killed Uncle? Decade, 1980

JAVOR, F(RANK) A.
The Rim-World Legacy. Signet, 1967 [future]

JAY, CHARLOTTE. Pseudonym of Geraldine (Mary Jay) Halls, 1919- , q.v.
See also: Geraldine Mary Jay.
Arms for Adonis. Collins, 1960; Harper, 1961 [Leb.]
Beat Not the Bones. Collins, 1952; Harper, 1953 [New Guinea]
The Fugitive Eye. Collins, 1953; Harper, 1954
A Hank of Hair. Heinemann, 1964; Harper, 1954
The Knife Is Feminine. Collins, 1951
The Man Who Walked Away. Collins, 1958. U.S. title: The Stepfather. Harper, 1958
The Stepfather; see The Man Who Walked Away
The Yellow Turban. Collins, 1955; Harper, 1955 [Pak.]

JAY, GERALDINE MARY. Byline of Geraldine (Mary Jay) Halls, 1919- , q.v.
Pseudonym: Charlotte Jay, q.v.
The Feast of the Dead. Hale, 1956. U.S. title: The Brink of Silence. Harper, 1957, as by Charlotte Jay [New Guinea]

JAY, HARRIETT. 1857-1932. Pseudonym: Charles Marlowe. See: Robert (William) Buchanan, 1841-1901.

JAY, SIMON. Pseudonym of Colin James Alexander, 1920- . Ref: CA, CC.
Death of a Skin-Diver. Collins, 1964; Doubleday, 1964 [N.Z.]
Sleepers Can Kill. Collins, 1968; Doubleday, 1968 [N.Z.]

JAY, MRS. W. L. M. Pseudonym of Julia Louisa Matilda Curtiss Woodruff, 1833-1909.
Holden with the Cords. Ward, 1874; Dutton, 1874

JAY, WILLA. Pseudonym of William Johnston, 1924- , q.v. Other pseudonym: Susan Claudia, q.v.
A Fear in Borzano. Lancer, 1967 [It.]

JAYE, PETER
The Body's Name Was Jones. Ward, 1961

JEALOUS, GEORGE S(AMUEL)
How I Found a Five-Pound Note and What Became of It. Cassell, 1881 ss

JEAN, (MARIE JOSEPH) ALBERT. 1892- . See: Maurice Renard, 1875-1939.

JEBB, BERTHA [MRS. GLADWIN JEBB]
Some Unconventional People. Blackwood, 1896 ss, some criminous

JEFFERIES, IAN. Pseudonym of Peter Hays, 1927- . SC: Sgt. Craig, in at least those marked C.
-Dignity and Purity. Cape, 1960 C
-House-Surgeon. Cape, 1966
-It Wasn't Me! Cape, 1961 C
-Thirteen Days. Cape, 1959 C

JEFFERIS, BARBARA (TARLTON). 1917- . Ref: CA.
Beloved Lady. Sloane, 1955; Dent, 1956
Contango Day; see Undercurrent
Half Angel. Sloane, 1959; Dent, 1960
One Black Summer. Morrow, 1967; Hart-Davis, 1968 [Australia]
Solo for Several Players. Sloane, 1961; Dent, 1961
Undercurrent. Sloane, 1953. British title: Contango Day. Dent, 1954
The Wild Grapes. Sloane, 1963; Joseph, 1963

JEFFERS, ALBERT. Pseudonym of Thomas Albert Curry, 1900-1976. Other pseudonym: John L. Benton, q.v. Ref: CA.
Screen for Murder. Mystery House, 1941. Also published as: Design for Dying. Bleak House, 194?, abridged [N.Y.]

JEFFERS, H(ARRY) PAUL. 1934- . Ref: CA.
The Adventure of the Stalwart Companions. Harper, 1978; Cassell, 1979 (Sherlock Holmes.) [NYC, 1880]

JEFFERSON, BEATRICE (W.). Born in Louisville; wife of an Atlanta attorney; a painter.
Small Town Murder. Dutton, 1941 [S.C.]

JEFFERSON, PAUL. Foreign correspondent; former Grand Prix racer.
The Cuban Heel. Macmillan, 1969

JEFFERSON, ROLAND S., M.D.
The School on 103rd Street. Vantage, 1978

JEFFERY, C. E.
The Vicar's Secret. Murray, 1912

JEFFERY, RANSOM, 1943- , and JOHN KEEBLE, 1944- . Ref for each author: CA.
Mine. Grossman, 1974 [Ia.]

JEFFREYS, J. G. Pseudonym of Ben(jamin James) Healey, 1908- , q.v., used for U.S. editions of books published in England as by Jeremy Sturrock, q.v.

JEFFRIES, GRAHAM MONTAGUE. 1900- .
Pseudonyms: Bruce Graeme, David Graeme, Roderic Hastings, qq.v.

JEFFRIES, RODERIC (GRAEME). 1926- .
Pseudonyms: Peter Alding, Jeffrey Ashford, Roderic Graeme, Graham Hastings, qq.v. Ref: CA, CC, EM, TC. SC: Insp. Alvarez = A. Set: Eng.
The Benefits of Death. Collins, 1963; Dodd, 1964
Dead Against the Lawyers. Collins, 1965; Dodd, 1966
Dead Man's Bluff. Collins, 1970
A Deadly Marriage. Collins, 1967
Death in the Coverts. Collins, 1966
An Embarrassing Death. Collins, 1964; Dodd, 1965
Evidence of the Accused. Collins, 1961; London House, 1963
Exhibit No. Thirteen. Collins, 1962
Just Desserts. Collins, 1980 A [Maj.]
Mistakenly in Mallorca. Collins, 1974 A [Maj.]
Murder Begets Murder. Collins, 1979; St. Martin's, 1979 A [Maj.]
A Traitor's Crime. Collins, 1968
Troubled Deaths. Collins, 1977; St. Martin's, 1978 A [Maj.]
Two-Faced Death. Collins, 1976 A [Maj.]

JELLETT, DR. H(ENRY). 1872-1948. See: Ngaio Marsh, 1899-1982.

JELLEY, SYMMES M. Pseudonym: Le Jemlys, q.v.

JENKINS, CECIL. 1927- . Ref: CC.
Message from Sirius. Collins, 1961; Dodd, 1961

JENKINS, (JOHN) EDWARD. 1838-1910.
The Captain's Cabin. Mullan, 1877
A Week of Passion. Remington, 1884; Harper, 1885

JENKINS, (MARGARET) ELIZABETH (HEALD). 1905- . Ref: CA.
Dr. Gully. Joseph, 1972. U.S. title: Dr. Gully's Secret. Coward, 1972
Dr. Gully's Secret; see Dr. Gully
Harriet. Gollancz, 1934; Doubleday, 1934. Also published as: Murder by Neglect. Four Square, 1964
Murder by Neglect; see Harriet

JENKINS, GEOFFREY. 1920- . Ref: CA. SC: Commander Geoffrey Peace, in at least those marked GP.
A Bridge of Magpies. Collins, 1974; Putnam, 1975 [Afr.]
A Cleft of Stars. Collins, 1973; Putnam, 1973
The Disappearing Island; see A Grue of Ice

A Grue of Ice. Collins, 1962; Viking, 1962. Also published as: The Disappearing Island. Avon, 1964 [ship]
The Hollow Sea; see Scend of the Sea
Hunter-Killer. Collins, 1966; Putnam, 1967 GP
The River of Diamonds. Collins, 1964; Viking, 1964 [S. Afr.]
Scend of the Sea. Collins, 1971. U.S. title: The Hollow Sea. Putnam, 1972
A Twist of Sand. Collins, 1959; Viking, 1960 GP [S. W. Afr.]
The Watering Place of Good Peace. Collins, 1960

JENKINS, GEORGE B.
Ten Dangerous Hours. Detective Tales, 19?? (64 pp. mini-paperback.)

JENKINS, HERBERT (GEORGE). 1876-1923. Ref: CC. SC: Malcolm Sage, in all titles. Set: Eng.
John Dene of Toronto. Jenkins, 1920; Doran, 1919
Malcolm Sage, Detective. Jenkins, 1921; Doran, 1921 ss
The Stiffsons, and other stories. Jenkins, 1928 ss, including one about MS

JENKINS, JENNIFER. Pseudonym: Robert Boyle, q.v.

JENKINS, JERRY (BRUCE). 1949-   . Ref: CA. SC: Margo Franklin and Philip Spence, in all titles.
Hilary. Moody, 1980
Karlyn. Moody, 1980
Margo. Moody, 1979

JENKINS, (JOHN) ROBIN. 1912-   . Ref: CA.
-Some Kind of Grace. Macdonald, 1960

JENKINS, WILL(IAM) F(ITZGERALD). 1896-1975. Pseudonym: Murray Leinster, q.v. Ref: CA.
Destroy the U.S.A.; see The Murder of the U.S.A.
The Man Who Feared. Gateway, 1942 [NYC]
The Murder of the U.S.A. Crown, 1946. Also published as: Destroy the U.S.A. Ambassador (Toronto), 1946

JENKINSON, ARTHUR
-God's Winepress. Warne, 1896

JENKS, GEORGE C(HARLES). 1850-1929. Pseudonym: Nicholas Carter, q.v.
-The Climax. Fly, 1909 (Novelization of the play by Edward Locke, 1869-1945.)
The Deserters, with Anna Alice Chapin, 1880-1920, q.v. Fly, 1911
Stop Thief!, with Carlyle Moore, 1875-   . Fly, 1913 (Novelization of the play by Carlyle Moore, q.v.)

JENKS, KATHLEEN. Pseudonym: Jennifer Stephens, q.v.

JENNIFER, SUSAN. Pseudonym of Robert Hoskins, 1933-   . Other pseudonyms: Grace Corren, Michael Kerr, qq.v.
Country of the Kind. Avon, 1975
The House of Counted Hatreds. Avon, 1973. Also published as by Grace Corren: Pinnacle, 1980

JENNINGS, G. L.
Murders at the Lakes. Mortiboys, 1936

JENNINGS, HOWARD. See: Robin Moore.

JENSEN, RUBY JEAN
The Girl Who Didn't Die. Warner, 1975
The House at River's Bend. Dell, 1975
The House That Samael Built. Paperback Library, 1974 [South]
Satan's Sister. Major, 1978
Seventh All Hallows' Eve. Paperback Library, 1974

JENSON, MARTIN
The Echo on the Stairs. New English Library pb, 1977
An Odour of Decay. New English Library pb, 1975
Village of Fear. New English Library pb, 1974

JEPSON, EDGAR (ALFRED). 1863-1938. Ref: CC, MP. Set: Eng.
An Accidental Don Juan. Jenkins, 1935
Alice Devine; see Garthoyle Gardens
Arsene Lupin, with Maurice Leblanc, 1864-1941, q.v. Mills, 1909; Doubleday, 1909 (Novelization of the play by Maurice LeBlanc and Francis de Croisset.)
Barradine Detects. Jenkins, 1937 ss
The Buried Rubies. Jenkins, 1925; Siebel, 1926
Captain Sentimental and other stories. Mills, 1911 ss, some criminous
The Cuirass of Diamonds. Jenkins, 1928; Macy-Masius, 1929
The Dangerous Twins. Jenkins, 1935
-The Dictator's Daughter. Cassell, 1902
The Emerald Tiger; see The Splendid Adventures of Hannibal Tod
-Esther Lawes. Hutchinson, 1916
The Four Green Fish. Jenkins, 1939
-The Four Philanthropists. Unwin, 1907; Authors & Newspapers Assn., 1907
The Garden at No. 19; see No. 19
Garthoyle Gardens. Hutchinson, 1913. U.S. title: Alice Devine. Bobbs, 1916
Gentle Binns. Jenkins, 1931
The Gillingham Rubies. Hutchinson, 1915
The Girl's Head. Greening, 1910. Also published as: Tracked by the Ogpu. Eric Grant, 1937
The Grinning Avenger. Jenkins, 1934 [U.S.]
The House on the Mall. Hutchinson, 1912; Dillingham, 1911
-A Hundred Thousand Guineas. Jenkins, 1931
-James Whitaker's Dukedom. Hutchinson, 1914. U.S. title: Whitaker's Dukedom. Bobbs, 1914
Kitty Brown's Princes. Jenkins, 1936
-The Knight Errant. Jenkins, 1936
-L.2002. Hutchinson, 1918
-The Lady Noggs, Peeress. Unwin, 1906
The Loudwater Mystery. Odhams, 1919; Knopf, 1920
Lucy and the Dark Gods. Jenkins, 1936
The Man Who Came Back. Hutchinson, 1915
The Man with the Amber Eyes, with Hugh Clevely, q.v. Jenkins, 1928
-Man, Woman and Sin. Readers Library, 1928
The Murder in Romney Marsh. Jenkins, 1929
The Murder of Augustin Dench. Jenkins, 1938
The Mystery of the Myrtles. Hutchinson, 1909
The Night Hawk. Hutchinson, 1916
-No. 19. Mills, 1910. U.S. title: The Garden at No. 19. Wessels, 1910
An Obstinate Girl. Jenkins, 1934
-Peter Intervenes. Jenkins, 1926
The Pocket Hercules. Jenkins, 1938
-A Prince in Petrograd. Odhams, 1921
-A Professional Prince. Hutchinson, 1917; Reynolds, 1917
The Secret Square. Jenkins, 1933
-The Sentimental Warrior. Richards, 1902
The Smuggled Masterpiece. Jenkins, 1923
The Splendid Adventure of Hannibal Tod. Jenkins, 1927. U.S. title: The Emerald Tiger. Macy-Masius, 1928
The Sweepstakes Winner. Jenkins, 1933
The Theft of the Crown Jewels. Jenkins, 1937
Tracked by the Ogpu; see The Girl's Head
-The Tragedies of Mr. Pip. Jenkins, 1926
The Triumph of Tinker. Hodder, 1906 ss, some criminous
-The Whiskered Footman. Jenkins, 1922

JEPSON, SELWYN. 1899-   . Ref: CC, EM, MP, TC. SC: Eve Gill = EG; Ian MacArthur = IM. Set: Eng.
The Angry Millionaire. Macmillan (London), 1969; Harper, 1968
The Assassin. Collins, 1956; Lippincott, 1956
The Black Italian. Collins, 1954; Doubleday, 1954 EG
The Death Gong. Harrap, 1927; Watt, 1927 [Tun.]
Fear in the Wind. Allen, 1964 EG [Fr.]
The Golden Dart. Macdonald, 1949; Doubleday, 1949 EG
Golden-Eyes. Harrap, 1924. U.S. title: The Sutton Papers. Dial, 1924
Heads or Tails, with Michael Joseph. Jarrolds, 1933 ss
The Hungry Spider. Macdonald, 1951; Doubleday, 1950 EG
I Met Murder. Hodder, 1930; Harper, 1930
Keep Murder Quiet. Joseph, 1940; Doubleday, 1941
Killer by Proxy; see Man Running
-The King's Red-Haired Girl. Hutchinson, 1923
The Laughing Fish. Hart-Davis, 1960. U.S. title: Verdict in Question. Doubleday, 1960 EG
Letter to a Dead Girl. Macmillan (London), 1971
-Love—and Helen. Harrap, 1928; Watt, 1928
Love in Peril. Mellifont, 1934
Man Dead. Collins, 1951; Doubleday, 1951
Man Running. Macdonald, 1948. U.S. title: Outrun the Constable. Doubleday, 1948. Also published as: Killer by Proxy. Bantam, 1950 EG
Manchu Jade; see The Qualified Adventurer
The Mystery of the Rabbit's Paw; see Rabbit's Paw
A Noise in the Night. Hart-Davis, 1957; Lippincott, 1957 [Paris]
Outrun the Constable; see Man Running
Puppets of Fate. Hutchinson, 1922
The Qualified Adventurer. Hutchinson, 1922; Harcourt, 1922. Also published as: Manchu Jade. Mellifont, 1935 IM
Rabbit's Paw. Hodder, 1932. U.S. title: The Mystery of the Rabbit's Paw. Harper, 1932
-Riviera Love Story. Mellifont, 1948
Rogues and Diamonds. Harrap, 1925; Dial, 1925
Snaggletooth. Harrap, 1926
The Sutton Papers; see Golden-Eyes
-Tempering Steel. Mellifont, 1949
-That Fellow MacArthur. Hutchinson, 1923 IM
The Third Possibility. Allen, 1965
Tiger Dawn. Hodder, 1929
Verdict in Question; see The Laughing Fish
-The Wise Fool. Mellifont, 1934

JEROME, GILBERT. Pseudonym.
The Filibuster's Warning. Street, ca.1900
The Loaded Orange. Street (Magnet #263)

JEROME, JUDSON (BLAIR). 1927-   . Ref: CA.
The Fell of Dark. Houghton, 1966

JEROME, OWEN FOX. Pseudonym of Oscar J(erome) Friend, 1897-1963, q.v. SC: Philip MacCray = PM.
The Corpse Awaits. Mystery House, 1946; Wells Gardner, 1948. Canadian title: Night at Club Bagdad. Harlequin, 1950 [NYC]
Double Life; see Murder as Usual
The Five Assassins. Mystery House, 1958 PM [L.A.]
The Golf Club Murder. Clode, 1929. British title: The Golf-Course Murder. Hutchinson, 1928
The Golf-Course Murder; see The Golf Club Murder
The Hand of Horror. Clode, 1927; Skeffington, 1929 PM
Leave Everything to Me. Mystery House, 1959 PM
Murder As Usual. Gateway, 1942 [NYC]
The Murder at Avalon Arms. Clode, 1931; Hutchinson, 1930 PM [Chi.]
Night at Club Bagdad; see The Corpse Awaits
The Red Kite Clue. Clode, 1928; Skeffington, 1929 PM [Chi.]

JERROLD, IANTHE (BRIDGMAN). 1897-   .
Dead Man's Quarry. Chapman, 1930
-Seaside Comedy. Chapman, 1934
The Studio Crime. Chapman, 1929
-Summer's Day. Chapman, 1933

JERVIS, VERA MURDOCK STUART. 1897-   . Pseudonym: Jane England, q.v.

JESMER, ELAINE. 1939-   . Ref: CA.
-Number One with a Bullet. Farrar, 1974; Weidenfeld, 1974

JESSE, F(RYNIWYD) TENNYSON. 1889?-1958. Pseudonym: Beamish Tinker, q.v. Ref: CC, EM, MC, MP, TC.
A Pin to See the Peepshow. Heinemann, 1934; Doubleday, 1934
The Solange Stories. Heinemann, 1931; Macmillan, 1931 ss

JESSOP, GEORGE H. See: (James) Brander Matthews, 1852-1929.

JESSUP, HENRY WYNANS. 1864-1934.
-Abimelech Pott, the Don Quixote of the Bar. Neale, 1928
The Van Beck Will. Neale, 1928 [NYC]

JESSUP, RICHARD. 1925-1982. Pseudonym: Richard Telfair, q.v. Ref: CC.
Cry Passion. Dell, 1956 [Ga.]
The Cunning and the Haunted. GM, 1954
The Deadly Duo. Dell, 1959; Boardman, 1961 [Fr.]
Lowdown. Dell, 1958; Secker, 1958 [NYC]
The Man in Charge. Secker, 1957 (U.S. title?)
Night Boat to Paris. Dell, 1956; WDL, 1960 [Fr.]
Port Angelique. GM, 1961
A Rage to Die. GM, 1955
Wolf Cop. GM, 1961; Muller pb, 1963
The Young Don't Cry. GM, 1957; Red Seal, 1959

JEVONS, MARSHALL. Joint pseudonym of William Breit and Kenneth Gerald Elzinga, 1941-   . Ref for Elzinga: CA. Both authors are professors of economics at the U. of Va.
  Murder at the Margin. Horton, 1978; Melbourne, 1979 [Vir. Is.]

JEWELL, DEREK. 1927-   . Ref: CA.
  Come In Number One, Your Time Is Up. Macmillan (London), 1971; Doubleday, 1971
  Sellout. Macmillan (London), 1973

JEWELL, ROBERT
  The Mystery of Orleton House. Blackwood, 1876

JOB, THOMAS. 1900-   .
  Uncle Harry. French (NYC), 1942; French (London), 1945 (3-act play.)

JOBSON, HAMILTON. 1914-1981. Ref: CA, TC. SC: Insp./Supt. Anders, in all titles. Set: Eng.
  Contract with a Killer. Long, 1974
  The Evidence You Will Hear. Collins, 1975; Scribner, 1975
  Exit to Violence. Collins, 1979
  The House with Blind Eyes. Long, 1971
  Judge Me Tomorrow. Collins, 1978
  Naked to My Enemy. Long, 1970
  The Sand Pit. Long, 1972
  The Shadow That Caught Fire. Long, 1972; Scribner, 1976
  The Silent Cry. Long, 1970
  Smile and Be a Villain. Long, 1969; Abelard-Schuman, 1971
  Therefore I Killed Him. Long, 1968
  To Die a Little. Collins, 1978
  Waiting for Thursday. Collins, 1977; St. Martin's, 1978

JOCELYN, MRS. ROBERT [ADA MARIA JENYNS JOCELYN RODEN]. 1860-   .
  -A Big Stake. White, 1892; Lippincott, 1892
  The Criton Hunt Mystery. Hurst, 1890
  -A Dangerous Brute. Hutchinson, 1895
  -A Distracting Guest. White, 1889
  -Drawn Blank. White, 1892; Lippincott, 1892
  -For One Season Only. White, 1893
  -Henry Massinger. White, 1899
  -Juanita Carrington. Digby, 1896
  Lady Mary's Experiences. White, 1897
  -The M.F.H.'s Daughter. White, 1890
  -Miss Rayburn's Diamonds. White, 1898
  -£100,000 Versus Ghosts. White, 1888
  One of the Bevans; or, Only a Horse Dealer; see Only a Horse Dealer
  -Only a Flirt. White, 1897
  -Only a Horst Dealer. White, 1893. U.S. title: One of the Bevans; or, Only a Horse Dealer. Lippincott, 1893
  -Only a Love Story. Hutchinson, 1897
  -Pamela's Honeymoon. Hutchinson, 1894
  -A Regular Fraud. White, 1896
  -Run to Ground. Hutchinson, 1893
  -The Sea of Fortune. Digby, 1901

JOEY (BLACK) and DAVE FISHER. SC: Joey, in all titles.
  Hit #29. Playboy, 1974
  Joey Collects. Charter, 1980 [Las Veg.]
  Joey Kills. PB, 1975

JOHN, E. H.
  -Breach of Reason. Gifford, 1953

JOHN, HENDRIX. Pseudonym.
  The Carnellian Circle. Atheneum, 1975 [Russ.]

JOHN, KATHERINE. See: Romilly John.

JOHN, OWEN. 1918-   . Born in Wales. SC: Haggai Godin, in at least those marked HG.
  A Beam of Black Light. Joseph, 1968; Paperback Library, 1969 HG [Russ.]
  -The Controller. Hale, 1978
  Dead on Time. Joseph, 1969; Paperback Library, 1969 HG [Mid. East]
  The Diamond Dress. Cassell, 1970
  The Disinformer. Joseph, 1967; Paperback Library, 1968 HG [Can.]
  -Festival. Hale, 1978
  Getaway. Coronet, 1976
  -McGregor's Island. Hale, 1979
  Sabotage. Cassell, 1973; Dutton, 1973 HG [Wales]
  The Shadow in the Sea. Cassell, 1972; Dutton, 1972 HG [Russ.]
  Thirty Days Hath September. Joseph, 1966; Dutton, 1967 HG [It.]

JOHN, ROMILLY and KATHERINE
  Death by Request. Faber, 1935

JOHNS, AVERY. Pseudonym of Margaret Cousin, 1905-   . Ref: CA.
  Traffic with Evil. Doubleday, 1962 [L.I.]

JOHNS, DEREK
  -The Beatrice Mystery. Secker, 1980

JOHNS, FOSTER. Pseudonym of Gilbert Vivian Seldes, 1893-1970. Ref: CA.
  The Square Emerald. Day, 1928 [NYC]
  The Victory Murders. Day, 1927; Harrap, 1927

JOHNS, GILBERT. Pseudonym of James Stagg, q.v. Both titles below were published by Amalgamated Press and feature Sexton Blake.
  Thief of Clubs. 1961
  Vote for Violence. 1961

JOHNS, LARRY
  Czechmate. Hale, 1980
  Power Play. Hale, 1980
  Thunder Island. Hale, 1980

JOHNS, RICHARD. Pseudonym of Montague Slater, 1902-   .
  Man with a Background of Flames. Dobson, 1954; Roy, 1954

JOHNS, VERONICA PARKER. 1907-   . Ref: EM. SC: Webster Flagg = WF; Agatha Welch (Prentice) = AW.
  Hush, Gabriel! Duell, 1940 AW [Vir. Is.]
  Murder by the Day. Doubleday, 1953 WF [NYC]
  Servant's Problem. Doubleday, 1958 WF [NYC]
  Shady Doings. Duell, 1941 AW [Conn.]
  The Singing Widow. Duell, 1941 [Va.]

JOHNS, W(ILLIAM) E(ARL). 1893-1968. Ref: CA. SC: "Steeley" Delaroy, in at least those marked SD. Set: Eng.
  Blue Blood Runs Red. Newnes, 1936
  Desert Night. Hamilton, 1938
  The Man Who Lost His Way. Macdonald, 1959
  The Murder at Castle Deeping. Hamilton, 1938. Revised edition: Latimer, 1951 SD
  Murder by Air. Newnes, 1937. Revised edition: Latimer, 1951 SD
  No Motive for Murder. Hodder, 1958; Washburn, 1959 [Fr.]
  The Raid. Hamilton, 1935
  -Sinister Service. Oxford, 1942
  Sky Fever, and other stories. Latimer, 1953
  Sky High. Newnes, 1936. Revised edition: Latimer, 1951
  The Spy Flyers. Hamilton, 1933
  Steeley Flies Again. Newnes, 1936. Revised edition: Latimer, 1951 SD
  The Unknown Quantity. Hamilton, 1940
  Wings of Romance. Newnes, 1939. Revised edition: Latimer, 1951 SD

JOHNSON, ADRIAN. See: Elizabeth Johnson.

JOHNSON, B. B. Pseudonym. SC: Richard Spade, in at least those marked RS.
  Bad Day for a Black Brother. Paperback Library, 1970 RS [N.Y.]
  Black Is Beautiful. Paperback Library, 1970; Hamlyn, 1980 RS
  Blues for a Black Sister. Paperback Library, 1971
  Death of a Blue-Eyed Soul Brother. Paperback Library, 1970; Hamlyn, 1980 RS [L.A.]
  That's Where the Cat's At, Baby. Paperback Library, 1970 RS [Ohio]

JOHNSON, BILL
  Dirty Work at the Crossroads. French, 1942 (3-act play.)
  Ghost Road. French, 1950 (3-act play.)

JOHNSON, CRANE. 1921-   .
  Dracula. Dramatists, 1976 (2-act play based on the novel by Bram Stoker, 1847-1912, q.v.)

JOHNSON, DIANE. 1934-   . Ref: CA.
  The Shadow Knows. Knopf, 1974; Bodley, 1975 [Calif.]

JOHNSON, DONALD McINTOSH. 1903-   . Pseudonym: Guy De Montfort, q.v.

JOHNSON, DOROTHY
  The Death of a Spinster. Longmans, 1931
  -Doris. Jarrolds, 1925
  Private Inquiries. Longmans, 1932
  -To Meet Mr. Stanley. Longmans, 1926

JOHNSON, DUFF. SC: Gutsy Morgan, in at least those marked GM.
  The Chiseller. Hamilton Stafford, 1951 GM [U.S.]
  The Come Back. Hamilton Stafford, 1952
  Come Out Fighting. Hamilton Stafford, 1951
  The Dead Don't Rise. Hamilton Stafford, 1951
  Dynamite on Wheels. Hamilton Stafford, 1952
  One-Time Champ. Hamilton Stafford, 1951
  Operator from Chicago. Hamilton Stafford, 1950
  Racing Crazy. Hamilton Stafford, 1952
  Rocky Mountain. Hamilton Stafford, 1951 GM
  Sucker Punch. Hamilton Stafford, 1950

JOHNSON, E(MIL) RICHARD. 1937-   . Ref: CA, CC, TC. SC: Tony Lonto = TL.
  Cage Five Is Going to Break. Harper, 1970; Macmillan (London), 1971 [South]
  The Cardinalli Contract. Pyramid, 1975 [Chi.]
  Case Load—Maximum. Harper, 1971
  The God Keepers. Harper, 1970; Macmillan (London), 1971 [L.A.]
  The Inside Man. Harper, 1969; Macmillan (London), 1970 TL
  The Judas. Harper, 1971 [Kan. City]
  Mongo's Back in Town. Harper, 1969; Macmillan (London), 1970 [Midwest]
  Silver Street. Harper, 1968. British title: The Silver Street Killer. Hale, 1969 TL
  The Silver Street Killer; see Silver Street

JOHNSON, EDGAR. 1901-   . Ref: CA.
  The Praying Mantis. Stackpole, 1937; Cassell, 1938

JOHNSON, ELIZABETH and ADRIAN
  The Game of the Golden Ball. Macaulay, 1910

JOHNSON, EVELYN (DAVIES), 1904-   , and GRETTA PALMER, 1905-   .
  Murder. Covici Friede, 1928. British title: Murder and Mystery. Richards, 1929 (Short crime puzzles.)

JOHNSON, EVELYN KIMBALL
  Tangles Unravelled; A Realistic Melodrama Spiced with Comedy. Ogilvie, 1884

JOHNSON, (MRS.) F. BARRETT
  Rocks and Romance. Ogilvie, 1889

JOHNSON, GEORGE CLAYTON and JACK GOLDEN RUSSELL
  Ocean's 11. Cardinal, 1960 (Novelization of the movie.)

JOHNSON, GERALD WHITE. ca.1891-1980. Pseudonym: Charles North, q.v.

JOHNSON, GRACE (CECELIA TRACY) and HAROLD (NELS) JOHNSON. Husband and wife; he taught at Youngstown U. and she was listed in the first edition of "Who's Who of American Women."
  The Broken Rosary. Bruce, 1959 [Ohio]
  Roman Collar Detective. Bruce, 1953 [Ohio]

JOHNSON, HAROLD (NELS). See: Grace (Cecelia Tracy) Johnson.

JOHNSON, HENRY. Pseudonym: Muirhead Robertson, q.v.

JOHNSON, HENRY T. 1858-1930.
  The Ape Man. Modern, 193?
  -The Devil's Advocate. Mascot, 1916
  -A Fairy of the Film. Mascot, 1919
  The Murder Link. Modern, 1938
  -A Princess in Mufti. Mascot, 1919
  When London Sleeps. Modern, 1938
  -The World of Sin. Mascot, 1914

JOHNSON, J.
  What Befell a Bristol Trader. Drane, 1903

JOHNSON, JAMES L(EONARD). 1927-   . Ref: CA. SC: Sebastian = S.
  All the King's Men; see The Death of Kings
  Code Name Sebastian. Lippincott, 1967 S [Isr.]
  The Death of Kings. Doubleday, 1974. Also published as: All the King's Men. Harvest, 1981
  A Handful of Dominoes. Lippincott, 1970 S [Ger.]
  The Nine Lives of Alphonse. Lippincott, 1968 S [Fla.]
  A Piece of the Moon Is Missing. Holman, 1974 S [Arctic]

JOHNSON, KEN
  Blue Sunshine. Sphere, 1977; Dale, 1978 (Novelization of the movie.) [NYC]

JOHNSON, LEE. Pseudonym of Lilian Beatrice Johnson.
  Heads for Death. Gifford, 1966 [Can.]
  Keep It Simple. Gifford, 1963
  The Medallion. Gifford, 1962
  Murder Began Yesterday. Gifford, 1966 [Can.]

JOHNSON, LILIAN BEATRICE. Pseudonym: Lee Johnson, q.v.

JOHNSON, MAURICE C.
  Damning Trifles. Knopf, 1932 [Chi.]

JOHNSON, MENDAL W(ILLIAM). 1928-1976. Ref: CA.
  Let's Go Play at the Adams'. Crowell, 1974; Hart-Davis, 1974 [Md.]

JOHNSON, MIKE
  The Clone People. French, 19?? (Play.)

JOHNSON, OWEN (McMAHON). 1878-1952. Ref: CC, EM.
  Max Fargus. Barker & Taylor, 1906 [NYC]
  Murder in Any Degree. Century, 1913 ss, 2 criminous
  The Sixty-First Second. Stokes, 1913; Heinemann, 1913 [NYC]

JOHNSON, PAMELA HANSFORD. 1912-1981. Joint pseudonym with Neil Stewart: Nap Lombard, q.v. Ref: CA.

JOHNSON, PHILIP. 1900-   . All titles are plays; number of acts in parenthesis.
  After the Verdict. French (London), 1960 (1)
  Dark Brown. French (London), 1946 (1)
  Green for Danger. French (London), 1959 (1)
  The Late Miss Cordell. French (London), 1944 (1)
  Master Dudley. French (London), 1947 (1)
  Missing from Home. French (London), 1955 (1)
  The Samaritan. French (London), 1962 (1)
  Who Lies There? French (London), 1948 (1)

JOHNSON, PHILIP (EDWARD). 1911-   .
  Hung Until Dead. Phoenix, 1940 [N.Y.]

JOHNSON, (WALTER) RYERSON. 1901-   . Pseudonym: Robert Wallace. Joint pseudonym with Davis Dresser, 1904-1977, q.v.: Matthew Blood, q.v. See also: Brett Halliday; and: Kenneth Robeson.
  Lady in Dread. GM, 1955 [Ill.]
  Naked in the Streets. Red Seal (U.S.), 1952

JOHNSON, SANDY
  The CUPPI. Delacorte, 1979; Hodder, 1980 [NYC]

JOHNSON, STANLEY (PATRICK). 1940-   . Ref: CA.
  The Doomsday Deposit. Heinemann, 1980; Dutton, 1980 [China]
  God Bless America. Doubleday, 1974 (British title?) [1976]
  Gold Drain. Heinemann, 1967
  Panther Jones for President. Heinemann, 1968. U.S. title: The Presidential Plot. Simon, 1968 [Wash. D.C.]
  The Presidential Plot; see Panther Jones for President
  The Urbane Guerilla. Macmillan (London), 1975

JOHNSON, T(HOMAS) M(ARVIN). 1889-   . See: Judson (Pentecost) Philips, 1903-   .

JOHNSON, W. BOLINGBROKE. Pseudonym of Morris Gilbert Bishop, 1893-1973. Ref: CA, CC.
  The Widening Stain. Knopf, 1942; Lane, 1943 [acad.]

JOHNSON, WILHELMINA
  The Ranger of the Tomb; or, Gipsy's Prophecy. Lloyd, 1847

JOHNSON, WILLIAM OSCAR
  The Zero Factor. PB, 1980; Star, 1980

JOHNSON, ZOE. Set: Eng.
  At the Sign of the Clove and Hoof. Bles, 1937
  Mourning After. Bles, 1939

JOHNSTON, CHRISTOPHER N(ICHOLSON). Pseudonym of Christopher Nicholson Johnston Sands, 1857-1934.
  Major Owen, and other tales. Blackwood 1909 ss, some criminous

JOHNSTON, CLINT
  The Kabaka. Avon, 1970

JOHNSTON, DENNIS. See: Ernest Toller, 1893-1939.

JOHNSTON, FRANK (NORMAN HOWARD). 1900-   . Set: Eng.
  Disqualified. Wright, 1935
  The Dope Specialist. Long, 1943
  Easy Money: The Amazing Adventures of Tony Denton, the Raffles of the Turf. Wright, 1935
  The Fellowship of Five. Long, 1932
  Highway Robber's Derby. Long, 1933
  Li Kwang's Dagger. Wright, 1936
  Million Dollar Gamble. Long, 1946
  The Mystery Tipster. Wright, 1934
  Prince of Turf Crooks. Long, 1952
  Spider Joe. Wright, 1937
  The Strangest Grand National. Long, 1947
  The Trodmore Turf Mystery. Long, 1944
  The Turf Crook. Long, 1937
  Turf Racketeers. Long, 1933
  A Weird Legacy. Wright, 1936

JOHNSTON, GEORGE H(ENRY). 1912-1970.
  The Darkness Outside. Collins, 1959
  Death Takes Small Bites. Gollancz, 1948; Dodd, 1951 [Burma]

JOHNSTON, GRACE L. KEITH. Pseudonym: Leslie Keith, q.v.

JOHNSTON, GUNNAR. SC: Silber, in at least those marked S.
  The Claws of the Scorpion. Rider, 1935 S
  -Perilous Discovery. Duckworth, 1938
  The Two Kings. Rider, 1936 S

JOHNSTON, J(AMES) WESLEY. 1847?-1936.
  The Mystery of Miriam. Turner, 1904; Richards, 1904

JOHNSTON, MADELEINE. SC: Noah Bradshaw, in both titles.
  Comets Have Long Tails. Doubleday, 1938; Eyre, 1939
  Death Casts a Lure. Doubleday, 1938 [Can.]

JOHNSTON, MYRTLE. 1909-   . Born in Dublin; author of several novels.
  A Robin Redbreast in a Cage. Heinemann, 1950; Houghton, 1951

JOHNSTON, NORMA. Pseudonym: Nicole St. John, q.v.

JOHNSTON, OWEN DEAN, JR.
  The Death of the Good Samaritan. Dorrance, 1978

JOHNSTON, RAY(MOND) R. (CAREW)
  Maud Blackstone, the Millionaire's Daughter. Henneberry, 1901

JOHNSTON, RONALD. 1926-   . Ref: CA. SC: James Bruce, in at least those marked JB.
  The Angry Ocean. Collins, 1968; Harcourt, 1969 JB [ship]
  The Black Camels; see The Black Camels of Qashran
  The Black Camels of Qashran. Collins, 1970. U.S. title: The Black Camels. Harcourt, 1969 [Mid. East]
  Collision Ahead; see Disaster at Dungeness
  Danger at Bravo Key; see Red Sky in the Morning
  Disaster at Dungeness. Collins, 1964. U.S. title: Collision Ahead. Doubleday, 1965 JB
  The Eye of the Needle. Collins, 1975
  Paradise Smith. Collins, 1972; Harcourt, 1972
  Red Sky in the Morning. Collins, 1965. U.S. title: Danger at Bravo Key. Doubleday, 1965 [Carib.]
  The Stowaway. Collins, 1966; Harcourt, 1966 [ship]
  The Wrecking of Offshore Five. Collins, 1967; Harcourt, 1968

JOHNSTON, VELDA. Raised in Calif.; living in NYC and L.I.; ss writer.
  Along a Dark Path. Dodd, 1967; Milton House, 1974 [N.Y.]
  Castle Perilous; see I Came to a Castle
  Circle of Evil; see The People on the Hill
  Deveron Hall. Dodd, 1976; Prior, 1977 [Scot.]
  The Etruscan Smile. Dodd, 1977; Allen, 1980 [It.]
  The Face in the Shadows. Dodd, 1971; Hale, 1973 [NYC]
  The Frenchman. Dodd, 1976; Prior, 1977
  The Hour Before Midnight. Dodd, 1978; Allen, 1981 [Eng.]
  House Above Hollywood. Dodd, 1968; Milton House, 1974 [L.A.]
  The House on the Left Bank. Dodd, 1975 [Paris, 1870]
  A Howling in the Woods. Dodd, 1968; Hale, 1969 [Nev.]
  I Came to a Castle. Dodd, 1969. British title: Castle Perilous. Hale, 1971 [Sp.]
  I Came to the Highlands. Dodd, 1974; Milton House, 1975
  The Late Mrs. Fonsell. Dodd, 1972; Milton House, 1974
  The Light in the Swamp. Dodd, 1970; Hale, 1972 [L.I.]
  Masquerade in Venice. Dodd, 1973; Milton House, 1974 [Venice, 1880]
  The Mourning Trees. Dodd, 1972; Milton House, 1974 [Calif.]
  The People from the Sea. Dodd, 1979; Prior, 1981 [L.I.]
  The People on the Hill. Dodd, 1971. British title: Circle of Evil. Hale, 1972 [NYC]
  The Phantom Cottage. Dodd, 1970; Hale, 1971 [Cape Cod]
  A Presence in an Empty Room. Dodd, 1980 [Maine]
  A Room with Dark Mirrors. Dodd, 1975; Prior, 1976 [Paris]
  The Silver Dolphin. Dodd, 1979; Prior, 1981 [L.I., 1840s]
  The Stone Maiden. Dodd, 1980 [NYC]
  The White Pavilion. Dodd, 1973; Milton House, 1974 [Fla.]

JOHNSTON, WILLIAM (ANDREW). 1871-1929.
  An Accidental Accomplice. Doubleday, 1928 [NYC]
  The Affair in Duplex 9B. Doran, 1927 [NYC]
  The Apartment Next Door. Little, 1919; Jarrolds, 1923
  The House of Whispers. Little, 1918; Jarrolds, 1922 [NYC]
  The Innocent Murderers, with Paul West. Duffield, 1910 [acad.]
  The Mystery in the Ritsmore. Little, 1920; Jarrolds, 1924 [NYC]
  The Tragedy at the Beach Club. Little, 1922; Jarrolds, 1924 [L.I.]
  The Waddington Cipher. Doubleday, 1923; Paul, 1925 [N.Y.]
  The Yellow Letter. Bobbs, 1911; Greening, 1912 [NYC]

JOHNSTON, WILLIAM. 1924-   . Pseudonyms: Susan Claudia, Willa Jay, qq.v. Ref: CA. SC: Maxwell Smart = MS (in novelizations of the "Get Smart" TV series).
  And Loving It! Tempo, 1967 MS [Calif.]
  Angel, Angel, Down We Go. Lancer, 1969 (Novelization of the movie.)
  Asylum. Bantam, 1972 (Novelization of the movie.)
  Barney. Random, 1970 [NYC]
  Banyon. Paperback Library, 1971 (Novelization of the TV series.) [L.A., 1937]
  Captain Nice. Tempo, 1967 (Novelization of the TV series.)
  Dick Tracy. Tempo, 1970 (Novelization of the comic strip.)
  Get Smart! Tempo, 1965 MS [NYC]
  Get Smart Once Again! Tempo, 1966 MS [Wash. D.C.]
  Home Is Where the Quick Is. Pinnacle, 1971 (Novelization of the "Mod Squad" TV series.)
  Klute. Paperback Library, 1971; Sphere, 1971 (Novelization of the movie.)
  The Marriage Cage. Stuart, 1960 [NYC]
  Max Smart and the Ghastly Ghost Affair. Tempo, 1969 MS
  Max Smart and the Perilous Pellets. Tempo, 1966 MS
  Max Smart Loses Control. Tempo, 1968 MS
  Max Smart—The Spy Who Went Out to the Cold. Tempo, 1968 MS
  Missed It by That Much. Tempo, 1967 MS [Afr.]
  My Friend Tony. Lancer, 1968 (Novelization of the movie.)
  Sorry, Chief. Tempo, 1966 MS [ship]
  Then Came Bronson. Pyramid, 1970 (Novelization of the TV series.)

JOHNSTONE, C(ATHERINE) L(AURA). 1838-1923.
  Tyrants of Today; or, The Secret Society. Tinsley, 1883

JOHNSTONE, WILLIAM W.
  The Last of the Dog Team. Zebra, 1980

JONES, ADRIENNE. 1915-   . Joint pseudonyms with Doris Meek: Mason Gregory, Gregory Mason, qq.v. Ref: CA.

JONES, ALICE. 1853-1933.
-Bubbles We Buy. Turner, 1903; Richards, 1903. Also published as: Isabel Broderick—"Bubbles We Buy". Lane, 1904
-Gabriel Praed's Castle. Turner, 1904; Richards, 1904
 Isabel Broderick—"Bubbles We Buy"; see Bubbles We Buy
-Marcus Holbeach's Daughter. Appleton, 1912

JONES, ARTHUR E. Ref: CC. SC: Felix Holliday, in all titles.
 It Makes You Think. Long, 1958
 Too Dead to Talk. Hutchinson, 1957
 You Know the Way It Is. Hutchinson, 1956

JONES, (MALCOLM HENRY) BRADSHAW. 1904-   . Oil company executive; operated family firm of silversmiths; retired to Channel Islands. SC: Claude Ravel, in at least those marked CR. Set: Eng.
 But Ill He Lived. Long, 1968
 The Crooked Phoenix. Long, 1963 CR
 The Deadly Trade. Long, 1967 CR
 Death Deals in Diamonds. Long, 1965; Walker, 1966
 Death on a Pale Horse. Long, 1964 CR
 A Den of Savage Men. Long, 1967 CR
 The Embers of Hate. Long, 1966 CR
 The Hamlet Problem. Long, 1962 CR
 Layers of Deceit. Long, 1969; Bobbs, 1970 [Fr.]
 Murder Has No Friends. Long, 1966; Bobbs, 1968
 Private Vendetta. Long, 1964 CR
 The Shadowless Men. Long, 1970
 Taint of Plague. Long, 1970
 Testament of Evil. Long, 1966 CR [Fr.]
 Tiger from the Shadows. Long, 1963 CR
 To Catch a Shadow. Long, 1969; Bobbs, 1970

JONES, BRIAN. 1930-   .
 Dangerous Maze. Hale, 1979

JONES, C. DAVENPORT
 An Excellent Mystery. Sonnenschein, 1886

JONES, C. ROBERT
 Marked for Murder. Baker, 1969 (1-act play.)

JONES, CHARLES REED. SC: Leighton Swift = LS.
 The King Murder. Dutton, 1929 LS [NYC]
 The Rum Row Murders. Macaulay, 1931 [Boston]
 The Torch Murder. Dutton, 1930 LS [NYC]
 The Van Norton Murders. Macaulay, 1931 LS [L.I.]

JONES, CLARA AUGUSTA. Pseudonyms: Clara Augusta, Hero Strong, qq.v.

JONES, CRAIG. 1945-   . Ref: CA.
 Blood Secrets. Harper, 1978; H. Hamilton, 1979

JONES, ELWYN. 1923-   . Ref: CA. SC: Supt. Charles Barlow = CB. Set: Eng.
 The Barlow Casebook, with John Lloyd. Barker, 1973 ss CB
 Barlow Comes to Judgement. Barker, 1974; St. Martin's, 1976 CB
 Barlow Down Under. Weidenfeld, 1977 CB
 Barlow Exposed. Weidenfeld, 1976; St. Martin's, 1977 CB
 Barlow in Charge. Barker, 1973 CB
 Dick Barton, Special Agent. Barker, 1977 (3 novelets based on the radio series.)
 The Ripper File, with John Lloyd. Barker, 1975 CB
 Softly, Softly. Longman, 1976 (5 scripts from the BBC TV series.)

JONES, EMMA GARRISON. 1838-1898.
 A Terrible Crime. Street, 1903

JONES, EUGENE
 Who Killed Gregory? Stokes, 1928. British title: The Last Clue. Selwyn, 1931 [L.I.]

JONES, G. WAYMAN. House name.
 Alias Mr. Death. Fiction League, 1932

JONES, GEORGE E.
 Trap. Graphic, 1955 [L.A.]

JONES, GLYN. 1905-   . Ref: CA.
-The Blue Bed. Cape, 1937; Dutton, 1938
 Thriller of the Year. French (London), 1968 (3-act play.)

JONES, GREGORY
 Prowl Cop. Ace, 1956

JONES, H(ENRY DAVID) LLEWELLIN. 1890-   . SC: Fraser Todd, in both titles, both set in Eng.
 The Case Is Altered. Hamilton, 1929
 Under the Shadow. Hamilton, 1928

JONES, HANNAH MARIA [HANNAH MARIA JONES LOWNDES].   -1859?
-A Child of Mystery; or, The Cottager's Daughter. Tallis, 1837
 Elinor Clare; or, The Haunted Oak; see The Gipsey Chief
-Emily Moreland; or, the Mail of the Valley. Virtue, 1829
-The Forged Note; or, Julian and Marianne. Jacques, 1824
 The Gipsey Chief; or, The Haunted Oak. Virtue, 1840. Also published as: Elinor Clare; or, The Haunted Oak. Milner, 1868
 The Gipsey Girl; or, The Heir of Hazel Dell. Tallis, 1836
-The Gipsey Mother; or, The Miseries of Enforced Marriage. Virtue, 1833
-Gretna Green; or, The Elopement of Miss D—— with a Gallant Son of Mars. Tallis, 1821
-Katharine Beresford; or, The Shade and Sunshine of Woman's Life. M'Gowan, 1852
-The Outlaw's Bride. Virtue, 1838
-Rosaline Woodbridge; or, The Midnight Visit. Virtue, 1827
-The Scottish Chieftains; or, The Perils of Love and War. Virtue, 1831 [Scot.]
-The Strangers of the Glen; or, The Travellers Benighted. Virtue, 1827
-Trials of Love; or, Woman's Reward. M'Gowan, 1849
-The Victim of Fashion; or, A Treacherous Friend. Virtue, 1836
-Village Scandal; or, The Gossip's Tale. Emans, 1835
-The Wedding Ring; or, Married and Single. Virtue, 1824

JONES, HENRY ARTHUR, 1851-1929, and HENRY HERMAN, 1832-1894, q.v.
 The Silver King. French, 1907 (5-act play.)

JONES, HENRY JAMES O'BRIEN BEDFORD. 1887-1949. See: H(enry James O'Brien) Bedford-Jones.

JONES, HOWARD. 1906-   .
-Beware the Hunter! Cape, 1961; Duell, 1963

JONES, INIGO. Pseudonym.
 The Albatross Murders. Mystery House, 1941
 The Clue of the Hungry Corpse. Arcadia, 1939 [NYC]

JONES, J. G.
 The Secret of the Bucket Shop. Amalgamated, 1924 (Sexton Blake.)

JONES, JACK. 1924-   . Ref: CA.
 Journey into Death. GM, 1955 [China]

JONES, JAMES. 1921-1977. Ref: CA.
 A Touch of Danger. Doubleday, 1973; Collins, 1973 [Greece]

JONES, JENNIFER. Has been realtor, magazine manager, vaudeville singer. SC: Daisy Jane Mott, in all titles, all set in N.Y.
 Dirge for a Dog. Doubleday, 1939
 Murder al Fresco. Doubleday, 1939
 Murder-on-Hudson. Crowell, 1937

JONES, JOHN HANDEL
 C.I.G. Lewis, 1977

JONES, KEN
 Etched in Murder. Zenith, 1959

JONES, KIT O'BRIEN
 To the Dark Tower Came. Popular Library, 1976 [Ire., 1840s]

JONES, L(AWRENCE) E(VELYN). 1885-   . See: James M(atthew) Barrie, 1860-1937.

JONES, L. Q.
 The Brotherhood of Satan. Award, 1971 (Novelization of the movie.)

JONES, M. SHERIDAN
 Flames of Vengeance. Wright, 1935
 A Million to Burn. Wright, 1934
 Pay to Bearer. Wright, 1934
 The Shanghai Lily. Wright, 1935
 Storm Tossed. Wright, 1934

JONES, MADISON (PERCY, JR.). 1925-   . Ref: CA.
 A Cry in Absence. Crown, 1971; Deutsch, 1972 [South]

JONES, MARY TUPPER
 The System's Hand. Mid-West, 1920

JONES, MERVYN. 1922-   . Ref: CA.
 A Short Time to Live. Deutsch, 1980; St. Martin's, 1981

JONES, (MAY)NARD (BENEDICT). 1904-1972. Ref: CA.
 The Case of the Hanging Lady. Dodd, 1938 [Wash.]
 I'll Take What's Mine. GM, 1954
 Ride the Dark Storm. GM, 1955 [Wash.]

JONES, NOEL. 1939-   . Pseudonym: Patrick Aalben, q.v.

JONES, PHILIP (MITCHELL). 1919-   . Born and living in Australia.
 The Fifth Defector. Heinemann, 1967
 Johnny Lost. Heinemann, 1965; Holt, 1966 [Australia]
 La Bora. Angus, 1961
 The Month of the Pearl. Heinemann, 1964; Holt, 1965 [Rome]

JONES, ROBERT PAGE. See also: Dan(iel T. Streib. Born in Ga.; advertising agency executive in S.F.
 The Heisters. Monarch, 1963 [S.W.]
 The Man Who Killed Hitler. Jove, 1980 [Berlin, WWII]
 Wine of the Generals. Jove, 1978

JONES, ROBERT GERALLT
 Triptych. Lewis, 1977

JONES, SUSAN CARLETON. 1864-   . Pseudonym: S. Carleton, q.v.

JONES, TERRY. See: Michael Palin.

JONES, TRISTAN. 1924-   .
 Dutch Treat. Andrews, 1979; Bodley, 1980 [Holl., 1940]

JONES, (CHARLES) VICTOR. 1919-   . Ref: CA.
 Monument of Terror. Stuart, 1969 [Ger.]

JONES, W(ILFRED) BYFORD. See: W(ilfred) Byford-Jones.

JONES, WILLIAM J.
 Real Estate Skeleton Caper. Vantage, 1975

JONES-EVANS, ERIC. 1898-   . Ref: CA.
-The Black Bag. French (London), 1957 (1-act play.)
 Death of a Lawyer. Wilson, 1962 (3-act play based on "Bleak House" by Charles Dickens, 1812-1870, q.v.)
 John Jasper's Secret. French (London), 1951 (4-act play based on "The Mystery of Edwin Drood" by Charles Dickens, 1812-1870, q.v.)
 Suicide Isn't Murder. French (London), 1951 (Play.)

JONTOS, RICHARD
 Alpha-1 Conspiracy. Springwood, 1979

JOPSON, MARION
 A Fist in the Sky. Hale, 1970

JORDAN, DAVID. Pseudonym of "a well-known merchant banker." SC: Tom Kane and Condon, in both titles.
 Black Account. Joseph, 1975 [Afr.]
 Nile Green. Joseph, 1973; Day, 1974

JONES, ELIZABETH (GARVER). 1867-1947.
 After the Verdict. Appleton, 1939 [NYC]
 The Blue Circle. Century, 1922; Hodder, 1925
 The Devil and the Deep Blue Sea. Century, 1929; Hutchinson, 1929 [L.I.]
 The Life of the Party. Appleton, 1936; Long, 1936 [L.I.]
 Miss Blake's Husband. Century, 1926; Hutchinson, 1927
 The Night Club Mystery. Century, 1930; Hutchinson, 1930 [NYC]
 Page Mr. Pomeroy. Appleton, 1934; Long, 1934 [New Eng.]
-Red Riding Hood. Century, 1925; Hodder, 1926
 The Trap. Appleton, 1937 [Mass.]

JORDAN, F. P.
 Double Dealing. Beck, 1932

JORDAN, HOPE DAHLE
 Take Me to My Friend. Lothrop, 1962

JORDAN, J. A.
 Death in the Wind. Mellifont, 1935
 The Death Singer. Mellifont, 1939
 The Devil's Eye. Mellifont, 1942
 The Grey Mask Gang. Mellifont, 1938
-Guilty Hands. Pemberton, 1945
 The Gunboat Mystery. Mellifont, 1937
 The Haunting Shadow. Mellifont, 1938
-The Love Test. Mellifont, 1935
 Matched with Mystery. Fiction House, 1940
 The Murder Mask. Mellifont, 1942
 The Murder Trap. Mellifont, 1940
 Night Club Murder. Mellifont, 1939
-Out to Win. Mellifont, 1940
 Sterne of the Secret Service. Aldine, 1931

JORDAN, KEELING
 The Miramar Seduction. NAL, 1980

JORDAN, LEONARD. Pseudonym of Leonard
  Levinson, 1935-   . Other pseudo-
  nyms: Robert Novak, Philip Rawls,
  Bruno Rossi, qq.v. See also: Lee
  Chang; and: Nelson De Mille, 1943-   .
  Operation: Perfidia. Warner, 1975
  [Fla.]

JORDAN, ROBERT FURNEAUX. 1905-1978. Pseudonym: Robert Player, q.v.

JORGENSEN, H. R(AYMOND). 1898-   .
  The Red Lacquer Case. World, 1933
  [Eng.]

JORGENSEN, IVAR. Pseudonym of Paul W.
  Fairman, 1916-1977, q.v. Other pseudonym: Paulette Warren, q.v. See
  also: Ellery Queen.
  Rest in Agony. Monarch, 1963. Also published as: The Diabolist. Lancer,
  1972, by Paul W. Fairman

JORGENSON, GEORGE E(LLINGTON). See: Nora
  Jorgenson.

JORGENSON, NORA and GEORGE E(LLINGTON)
  JORGENSON
  The Circle of Vengeance. Appleton, 1930
  [Ill.]

JOSCELYN, ARCHIE (LYNN). 1899-   . Pseudonyms: A. A. Archer, Evelyn McKenna,
  qq.v.
  The Golden Bowl. World, 1931. Also published as: Eric Hearle, Detective.
  World, 1934

JOSEPH, ALAN. SC: Logan, in both titles.
  Killers at Sea. Belmont, 1970 [S.C.]
  Logan. Belmont, 1970 [ship]

JOSEPH, DON
  Skinnerball!!! in Pursuit of T.H.E.M.
  Vantage, 1978

JOSEPH, GEORGE (ISRAEL). 1912-   . Born
  in Glasgow; educated in law in N.Z.;
  barrister in England and N.Z.; autho
  of hundreds of magazine ss.
  Before I Die. Boardman, 1959
  The Curtain Has Lace Fringes. Muller,
  1954
  The Insider. Boardman, 1963
  Leave It to Me. Popular Library, 1955
  (British title?)
  Lie Fallow My Acre. Jenkins, 1957
  Murder in Paradise. Boardman, 1958
  Needle in a Haystack. Boardman, 1957
  [Cors.]
  Swan Song for a Thrush. Boardman, 1957
  Take Any City. Hale, 1970
  This Is for Keeps. Popular Library,
  1958 (British title?)
  Three Strangers. Boardman, 1956
  Venom in the Cup. Boardman, 1958
  When the Rainbow Is Pale. Hale, 1962

JOSEPH, MARIE
  Footsteps in the Park. Macdonald, 1978

JOSEPH, MICHAEL. See: Selwyn Jepson,
  1899-   .

JOSEPH, MICHAEL. See: Robert Donaldson.

JOSEPH, ROBERT. 1912-   . Graduate of
  Yale; magazine editor, wrote documen-
  tary films for the War Department;
  drama editor for a magazine in 1940s.
  Berlin at Midnight. Greenberg, 1948
  [Berlin]

JOSEPH-RENAUD, JEAN. See: Jean-Joseph
  Renaud.

JOSEY, ALEX A.
  Accident. [Author], 1930s

JOSKE, AUNE NEVILLE GOYDER. 1893-   .
  Joint pseudonym with Margot Goyder,
  1903-   : Margot Neville, q.v.

JOST, JOHN
  This Is Harry Flynn. Angus, 1974

JOURDAIN, ELEANOR F. See: Charlotte Anne
  Elizabeth Moberly.

JOURNET, TERENCE
  The Deathwishers. Hale, 1967
  The Godkillers. Hale, 1968
  A Troupe of Star-Crossed Killers. Hale,
  1973
  Victim. Hale, 1974

JOY, WILLIAM "TED". See: Warren B. Murphy, 1933-   .

JOYCE, CYRIL
  A Crime to Fit the Punishment. Hale,
  1977

Death of a Left-Handed Woman. Hale,
  1980
The Elimination Process. Hale, 1976
Has Anybody Here Seen Abby? Hale, 1978
A Hitch in Time. Hale, 1980
Incidental Murder. Hale, 1979
The Information Man. Hale, 1976
Run a Golden Mile. Hale, 1978
Seize a Passing Stranger. Hale, 1978
Sentence Suspended. Hale, 1979
Twice a Victim. Hale, 1977
Twist of Hate. Hale, 1976
A Web to Catch a Spider. Hale, 1975

JOYCE, T. ROBERT
  S.P.Y.S. PB, 1974; Sphere, 1974
  (Novelization of the movie.) [Paris]

JUDD, A. M.
  Pharaoh's Turquoise. White, 1905
  The White Vampire. Long, 1914

JUDD, HARRISON. Pseudonym of Norman (A.)
  Daniels, q.v. Other pseudonym: Robert Wallace, q.v.
  Shadow of a Doubt. GM, 1961; Muller pb,
  1962 [L.A.]

JUDD, MARGARET (HADDICAN). 1906-   .
  Ref: CA. Pseudonym: Truman Garrett,
  q.v.
  Gospel of Death. Arcadia, 1960
  Husband of the Corpse. Arcadia, 1958
  Murder Is a Best Seller. Arcadia, 1959
  [Vt.]
  Murder Makes Its Mark. Arcadia, 1961

JUDE, CHRISTOPHER
  The Case of Dan Morris. Low, 1939
  The Moorlands Murder. Low, 1938
  The Terror of the Shape. Low, 1937
  [Afr.]

JUDGE, JAMES P.
  Square Crooks. Readers Library, 1928;
  Longmans (NYC), 1927. 3-act play
  version: French (London), 1928

JUDGE, S(IDNEY) W(ALTER)
  The Mystery of the Elms. Stockwell,
  1944

JUDSON, EDWARD ZANE CARROLL. 1821-1866.
  Pseudonym: Ned Buntline, q.v.

JUDSON, JEANNE. 1890-1981. Pseudonym:
  Frances Dean Hancock, q.v.
  The Island Heirs. Avalon, 1958
  The Legacy of Redfern. Bouregy, 1968
  A Strange Case for Dr. Rolland. Avalon,
  1962
  Treasure of Wycliffe House. Bouregy,
  1967

JUDSON, WILLIAM. Pseudonym of Edwin (Ray-
  mond) Corley, 1931-1981, q.v. Other
  pseudonym: David Harper, q.v. Joint
  pseudonym with Jack Murphy: Patrick
  Buchanan, q.v.
  Alice and Me. Fields, 1973; Talmy
  Franklin, 1973 [NYC]
  Kilman's Landing. Mason, 1976 [Miss.]

JUSTIN, DEREK
  Shard's Rock. Elek, 1966

JUTA, HENRY (HUBERT). 1857-1939.
  Off the Track. Hutchinson, 1925

JUTE, ANDRE. 1945-   . Born in S. Afr.,
  educated there and in Australia.
  Reverse Negative. Norton, 1979; Secker,
  1980

KAFKA, F. L. See: Robin Moore.

KAGEY, RUDOLF HORNADAY. 1904-1946. Pseudonym: Kurt Steel, q.v.

KAHLER, HUGH (TORBERT) McNAIR. 1883-1969.
  Bright Danger. Triangle, 1942
  -Daniel P. Wack, "Dumb-Bell". Lloyd's,
  1922
  -Hills Were Higher Then. Farrar, 1931 ss
  -Local Talent. Lloyd's, 1921
  The White Rook. Chelsea, 1927

KAHLERT, KARL FRIEDRICH. 1765-1813. Pseudonym: Lorenz Flammenberg, q.v.

KAHN, ALEC
  -The Menace of X. Newnes, 1936

KAHN, JAMES
  Diagnosis: Murder. Carlyle, 1980

KAHN, STEVE [STEPHEN]. 1940-   . Ref:
  CA.
  New York, N. Y. 10022. PB, 1979; Coro-
  net, 1980 [NYC]

KAIL, ROBERT
  Swastika. Belmont, 1979 [Ger., WWII]

KAINS, JOSEPHINE. Pseudonym of Ron(ald
  Joseph) Goulart, 1933-   , q.v.
  See also: Kenneth Robeson. SC: Terry
  Spring, in all titles.
  The Curse of the Golden Skull. Zebra,
  1978 [Carib.]
  The Devil Mask Mystery. Zebra, 1978
  [Mass.]
  The Green Lama Mystery. Zebra, 1979
  [S.F.]
  The Laughing Dragon Mystery. Zebra,
  1980 [S.F.]
  The Whispering Cat Mystery. Zebra, 1979
  [New Or.]
  The Witch's Tower Mystery. Zebra, 1979
  [Conn.]

KALB, MARVIN (L.), 1930-   , and TED
  KOPPEL, 1940(?)-   . Ref on each
  author: CA.
  In the National Interest. Simon, 1977;
  Bodley, 1978 [Mid. East]

KALEDIN, VICTOR K. 1887-   .
  Flash D 13. Coward, 1930; Cassell, 1931
  ss [Russ.]

KALLEN, LUCILLE. Ref: CA. SC: C. B.
  Greenfield, in both titles.
  Introducing C. B. Greenfield. Crown,
  1979; Collins, 1979 [N.Y.]
  The Tanglewood Murder. Wyndham, 1980;
  Collins, 1980 [Mass.]

KAMARCK, LAWRENCE. 1927-   . Ref: CA.
  The Bellringer. Random, 1969 [New Eng.]
  The Dinosaur. Random, 1968; Dent, 1970
  [NYC]
  Informed Sources. Dial, 1979; Fontana,
  1981 [Wash. D.C.]
  The Zinsser Implant. Dial, 1979 [NYC]

KAMINSKY, HOWARD. 1940-   . Ref: CA.
  Joint pseudonym with Susan Stanwood:
  Brooks Stanwood, q.v.

KAMINSKY, STUART M(ELVIN). 1934-   .
  Ref: CA. SC: Toby Peters, in all
  titles.
  Bullet for a Star. St. Martin's, 1977;
  Curley, 1978 [L.A., 1940]
  The Howard Hughes Affair. St. Martin's,
  1979; Severn, 1980 [L.A., 1942]
  Murder on the Yellow Brick Road. St.
  Martin's, 1978; Curley, 1979 [L.A.,
  ca.1940]
  Never Cross a Vampire. St. Martin's,
  1980 [L.A., 1942]
  You Bet Your Life. St. Martin's, 1979
  [Chi., ca.1940]

KAMM, (JAN) DORINDA. 1952-   . Ref: CA.
  Cliff's Head. Lenox, 1972; Remploy,
  1974
  The Devil's Doorstep. Lenox, 1972; Rem-
  ploy, 1974
  Drearloch. Zebra, 1978
  The Secret of Marly Stones. Zebra, 1977
  [Wales]
  Shadow Game. Zebra, 1979

KAMPF, HAROLD B. 1916-   . Pseudonym:
  H. B. Kaye, q.v.

KANE, ABEL. SC: Slaughter = S (see also:
  Henry Clement).
  Slaughter's Big Rip-Off. Curtis, 1973
  S (Novelization of the movie.)
  [L.A.]

KANE, BOB
  Batman. Signet, 1966 ss

KANE, FRANK. 1912-1968. Pseudonym: Frank
  Boyd, q.v. Ref: CA, CC, TC. SC: Mick-
  ey Denton = MD; Johnny Liddell = JL.
  About Face. Mystery House, 1947. Also
  published as: Death About Face. Han-
  di-Books, 1948; and as: The Fatal
  Foursome. Dell, 1958 JL [L.A.]
  Bare Trap. Washburn, 1952 JL [L.A.]
  Barely Seen. Dell, 1964; Mayflower,
  1964 JL [NYC]
  Bullet Proof. Washburn, 1951; May-
  flower, 1964 JL [NYC]
  The Conspirators. Dell, 1962 [ship]
  Crime of Their Life. Dell, 1962; May-
  flower, 1964 JL [ship]
  Dead Rite. Dell, 1962; Mayflower, 1968
  JL,MD [L.A.]
  Dead Weight. Washburn, 1951 JL [NYC]
  Death About Face; see About Face
  Due or Die. Dell, 1961; Mayflower, 1963
  JL [Nev.]

Kane, Henry

Esprit de Corpse. Dell, 1965 JL [Calif.]
The Fatal Foursome; see About Face
Fatal Undertaking. Dell, 1964; Mayflower, 1965 JL [NYC]
Final Curtain. Dell, 1964; Mayflower, 1964 JL [NYC]
Grave Danger. Washburn, 1954 JL [NYC]
Green Light for Death. Washburn, 1949; Mayflower, 1966 JL [NYC]
The Guilt-Edged Frame. Dell, 1964 JL [S.F.]
Hearse Class Male. Dell, 1963; Mayflower, 1969 JL [NYC]
Johnny Come Lately. Dell, 1963; Mayflower, 1964 JL [NYC]
Johnny Liddell's Morgue. Dell, 1956; WDL, 1958 ss JL [NYC]
Juke Box King. Dell, 1959 MD [NYC]
Key Witness. Dell, 1956 [NYC]
The Line-Up. Dell, 1959; WDL, 1960 (Novelization of the TV series.) [S.F.]
The Living End. Dell, 1957 JL
Liz. Beacon, 1958
Maid in Paris. Dell, 1966 JL [Paris]
Margin for Terror. Dell, 1967 JL [NYC]
The Mourning After. Dell, 1961 JL [L.A.]
Poisons Unknown. Washburn, 1953 JL [La.]
A Real Gone Guy. Rinehart, 1956; Boardman, 1957 JL [NYC]
Red Hot Ice. Washburn, 1955; Boardman, 1956 JL
Ring-a-Ding-Ding. Dell, 1963; Mayflower, 1964 JL [NYC]
A Short Bier. Dell, 1960; Mayflower, 1964 JL [NYC]
Slay Ride. Washburn, 1950 JL [NYC]
Stacked Deck. Dell, 1961; Mayflower, 1964 ss JL [NYC]
Syndicate Girl. Dell, 1958
Time to Prey. Dell, 1960; Mayflower, 1964 JL [NYC]
Trigger Mortis. Rinehart, 1958 JL [NYC]
Two to Tangle. Dell, 1965 JL [NYC]

KANE, HENRY. 1918- . Pseudonym: Anthony McCall, q.v. Ref: CC, EM, TC. SC: Peter Chambers = PC; McGregor = M; Marla Trent = MT.

Armchair in Hell. Simon, 1948; Boardman, 1949 PC [NYC]
The Avenger. Atheneum, 1975
Better Wed Than Dead; see Unholy Trio
-The Bomb Job. Lancer, 1970 PC [NYC]
The Case of the Murdered Madame. Avon, 1955. British title: Triple Terror. Boardman, 1958 PC [NYC]
Come Kill with Me. Lancer, 1972 PC
Conceal and Disguise. Macmillan, 1966; Boardman, 1966 M [NYC]
A Corpse for Christmas. Lippincott, 1951; Boardman, 1952. Also published as: The Deadly Doll. Zenith, 1959. And as: Homicide at Yuletide. Signet, 1966 PC [NYC]
The Crumpled Cup. Signet, 1963; Boardman, 1961 [N.J.]
The Dangling Man; see Fistful of Death
Dead in Bed. Lancer, 1961; Boardman, 1963 PC [NYC]
The Deadly Doll; see A Corpse for Christmas
The Deadly Finger. Popular Library, 1957. British title: The Finger. Boardman, 1957 [NYC]
Death for Sale. Dell, 1957. Revised edition: Sleep Without Dreams. Lancer, 1970; Boardman, 1958 [NYC]
Death Is the Last Lover. Avon, 1959. British title: Nirvana Can Also Mean Death. Boardman, 1959 PC [NYC]
Death of a Dastard. Signet, 1963; Boardman, 1962 PC [NYC]
Death of a Flack. Signet, 1961; Boardman, 1961 PC [NYC]
Death of a Hooker. Avon, 1963; Boardman, 1961 PC [NYC]
Death on the Double. Avon, 1957; Boardman, 1958 (Two novelets.) PC [NYC]
Decision. Dial, 1973
The Devil to Pay; see Unholy Trio
Dirty Gertie. Belmont, 1965; Boardman, 1963. Also published as: To Die or Not to Die. Belmont, 1974 [NYC]
-Don't Call Me Madame. Lancer, 1969 PC [NYC]
Don't Go Away Dead. Lancer, 1970 PC
Edge of Panic. Simon, 1950; Boardman, 1951
-The Escort Job. Lancer, 1972 PC [NYC]
The Finger; see The Deadly Finger
Fistful of Death. Avon, 1958. British title: The Dangling Man. Boardman, 1959 PC [NYC]
Frenzy of Evil. Dell, 1966; Boardman, 1966 [L.I.]
The Glow Job. Lancer, 1971 PC
A Halo for Nobody. Simon, 1947; Boardman, 1950. Also published as: Martinis and Murder. Avon, 1956 PC [NYC]
Hang by Your Neck. Simon, 1949; Boardman, 1950 PC [NYC]
Homicide at Yuletide; see A Corpse for Christmas
Kill for the Millions. Lancer, 1972 PC
Killer's Kiss; see Kisses of Death
Kiss! Kiss! Kiss! Kiss! Lancer, 1970 (Four novelets, two from Report for a Corpse, and one each from The Case of the Murdered Madame and Death on the Double, qq.v.) PC
Kisses of Death. Belmont, 1962. British title: Killer's Kiss. Boardman, 1962 PC,MT
Laughter Came Screaming. Avon, 1954; Boardman, 1953. Also published as: A Mask for Murder. Avon, 1957
Laughter in the Alehouse. Macmillan, 1968 M [NYC]
Lust of Power. Atheneum, 1975
Martinis and Murder; see A Halo for Nobody
A Mask for Murder; see Laughter Came Screaming
The Midnight Man. Macmillan, 1965. British title: Other Sins Only Speak. Boardman, 1965 M [NYC]
The Moonlighter. Geis, 1971; Hale, 1972 [NYC]
Murder for the Millions; see Never Give a Millionaire an Even Break
Murder of a Park Avenue Playgirl; see Report for a Corpse
My Business Is Murder. Avon, 1954 (Two novelets, both included in the British edition of Trinity in Violence, q.v.) PC [NYC]
My Darlin' Evangeline. Dell, 1961. British title: The Perfect Crime. Boardman, 1961. Reprinted under the British title: Belmont, 1967 [Fla.]
The Name Is Chambers. Pyramid, 1957 (Six stories, including two from Trinity in Violence and one each from Report for a Corpse and The Case of the Murdered Madame, qq.v.) PC
The Narrowing Lust; see Too French and Too Deadly
Never Give a Millionaire an Even Break. Lancer, 1963. British title: Murder for the Millions. Boardman, 1964 PC [NYC]
Nirvana Can Also Mean Death; see Death Is the Last Lover
Nobody Loves a Loser. Belmont, 1963; Boardman, 1964. Also published as: Who Dies There? Lancer, 1969 PC [NYC]
Other Sins Only Speak; see The Midnight Man
The Perfect Crime; see My Darlin' Evangeline
Peter Gunn. Dell, 1960 (Novelization of the TV series.) [L.A.]
Prey by Dawn; see Two Must Die
Private Eyeful. Pyramid, 1959; Boardman, 1960 MT [NYC]
Report for a Corpse. Simon, 1948; Boardman, 1951. Also published as: Murder of the Park Avenue Playgirl. Avon, 1957 (Six stories and novelets, one later reprinted in The Name Is Chambers, q.v.) PC [NYC]
Run for Doom. Signet, 1962; Boardman, 1960 [N.J.]
The Schack Job. Lancer, 1969 PC [NYC]
Sleep Without Dreams; see Death for Sale
Snatch an Eye. Perma, 1964; Boardman, 1963 PC [NYC]
Sweet Charlie; see Who Killed Sweet Sue?
The Tail Job. Lancer, 1971 PC
To Die or Not to Die; see Dirty Gertie
Too French and Too Deadly. Avon, 1955. British title: The Narrowing Lust. Boardman, 1956 (Reprinted, complete, under the British title, in The Locked Room Reader, edited by Hans Stefan Santesson. Random, 1968.) PC
Trilogy in Jeopardy. Boardman, 1955 (Contains 3 novelets, two of which are in the U.S. title Trinity in Violence, q.v.) PC
Trinity in Violence. Avon, 1955 (Contains "Far Cry", "Slaughter on Sunday" and "Skip a Beat.") British edition: Boardman, 1954 (Contains: "The Big Touch", "Loose End" and "Far Cry"; the first two of these are collected in the U.S. as My Business Is Murder, q.v.) PC [NYC]
Triple Terror; see The Case of the Murdered Madame
The Tripoli Documents. Simon, 1976; Hamlyn, 1979 [Mid. East]
Two Must Die. Tower, 1963. British title: Prey by Dawn. Boardman, 1965 [N.Y.]
Unholy Trio. PB, 1967. British title: The Devil to Pay. Boardman, 1966. Also published as: Better Wed Than Dead. Lancer, 1970 PC [NYC]
Until You Are Dead. Simon, 1951; Boardman, 1952 PC [NYC]
-The Violator. Warner, 1974
-The Virility Factor. McKay, 1972
Who Dies There?; see Nobody Loves a Loser
Who Killed Sweet Sue? Avon, 1956. British title: Sweet Charlie. Boardman, 1957 PC [NYC]

KANE, KASPAR
The Gleaming Blade. Whitman, n.d.

KANE, MARK
Fit to Kill. Hale, 1972
Reluctant Transgressor. Hale, 1967
Sucker Trap. Hale, 1968; Roy, 1968 [U.S.]
Walk of the Devil. Hale, 1968

KANE, WILLIAM R(ENO). 1885- . See: Mason Wright.

KANER, HYMAN
An Alibi Too Much. Kaner, 1946
The Cynic's Desperate Mission. Kaner, 1946
Fire-Watcher's Night. Kaner, 1944 ss, some criminous
Hot Swag. Kaner, 1945 ss, some criminous
A Lady Screams. Kaner, 1946
The Naked Foot. Kaner, 1946 ss, some criminous
Ordeal by Moonlight. Kaner, 1947 ss
-Squaring the Triangle, and other short stories. Kaner, 1944 ss
The Terror Catches Up. Kaner, 1946 ss, some criminous

KANTOR, HAL. 1924- . Byline also: Harry Kantor, q.v. Ref: CA.
Blown Away. Morrow, 1980 [NYC, 1915-1948]
The Vegas Trap. Pinnacle, 1970

KANTOR, HARRY. 1924- . Byline also: Hal Kantor, q.v.
The Town That Saw No Evil. Major, 1977 [Ariz.]

KANTOR, MacKINLAY. 1904-1977. Ref: CA, CC, EM.
Author's Choice. Coward, 1944 ss, some criminous
It's About Crime. Signet, 1960 ss
Signal Thirty-Two. Random, 1950 [NYC]

KAPLAN, ANDREW
The Hour of the Assassins. Dell, 1980

KAPLAN, ARTHUR. 1925- . Ref: CA.
A Killing for Charity. Coward, 1976 [NYC]

KAPLAN, BARRY JAY. 1943- . Pseudonym: Bettina Kingsley, q.v. See also: Nicholas Meyer, 1945- .

KAPLAN, H(AROLD) J. 1918- .
-The Spirit and the Pride. Harper, 1951. British title: Anywhere Else. Secker, 1951

KAPLAN, HOWARD. 1950- . Ref: CA.
The Chopin Express. Dutton, 1978; Magnum, 1981 [Moscow]
The Damascus Cover. Dutton, 1977; Hodder, 1978 [Damascus]

KARIG, WALTER. 1898-1956. Pseudonym: Keats Patrick. q.v.

KARK, NINA MARY MABEY. 1925- . Pseudonym: Nina Bawden, q.v.

KARLOVA, IRINA
Broomstick. Hurst, 1946
Dreadful Hollow. Hurst, 1942; Vanguard, 1942
The Empty House. Hurst, 1944

KARLSON, HANS. Pseudonym.
Atomic Death. Associated General, ca. 1941

KARMAN, MAL. 1944- . Ref: CA.
The Foxbat Spiral. Dell, 1980

KARNEY, JACK. 1911- . SC: Jim Breen, in at least those marked JB.
Cop. Holt, 1951 [NYC]
Cry, Brother, Cry. Popular Library, 1959 [NYC]
Cut Me In. Pyramid, 1959 [NYC]
The Knave of Diamonds. Ace, 1959 JB [NYC]
Knock 'Em Dead. Ace, 1955 [NYC]

Layout for Murder. Berkley, 1960 JB [NYC]
The Ragged Edge. Morrow, 1946. Revised edition: Tough Town. Pyramid, 1951 [NYC]
Some Like It Tough. Monarch, 1959
There Goes Shorty Higgins. Morrow, 1945
Tough Town; see The Ragged Edge
Work of Darkness. Putnam, 1956
-Yield to the Night. Monarch, 1960

KARP, DAVID. 1922-   . Pseudonym: Wallace Ware, q.v. Ref: CA.
-All Honorable Men. Knopf, 1956; Gollancz, 1956
The Big Feeling. Lion, 1952
The Brotherhood of Velvet. Lion, 1952 [Wash. D.C.]
Cry Flesh. Lion, 1953. Also published as: The Girl on Crown Street. Lion, 1956
Enter Sleeping. Harcourt, 1960. British title: The Sleep-Walkers. Gollancz, 1960
Escape to Nowhere; see One
The Girl on Crown Street; see Cry Flesh
Hardman. Lion, 1953
-The Last Believers. Harcourt, 1964; Cape, 1965
One. Vanguard, 1953; Gollancz, 1954. Also published as: Escape to Nowhere. Lion, 1955 [acad.]
The Sleep-Walkers; see Enter Sleeping

KARR, LEE [LEONA C. KARR]
The Housesitter. Avon, 1980 [Denver]

KARSLAND, COLLIS. See: Veva Carsland.

KARSLAND, VEVA and COLLIS
The Witness Box; or, The Murder of Mr. A. B. C. Trischler, 1890

KARTA, NAT. House name. Used by Victor (George Charles) Norwood, 1920-   , q.v. Other pseudonyms: Johnny Dark, Mark Hampton, Hank Janson, Mark Shane, qq.v. Also used by John Russell Fearn, 1908-1960, q.v., for the title marked *, which has the same character, Insp. Garth, as in titles under Fearn's pseudonym, Hugo Blayn, q.v. Other Fearn pseudonyms: Spike Gordon, Volsted Gribdan, Griff, John Slate, qq.v.
Big Top Dame. Scion, 1952
Brother Rat. Scion, 1952
Climax. Scion, 1953
The Concrete Nymph. Scion, 1954
Eat Me If You Must. Muir Watson, 1949
The Elusive Corpse. Scion, 1954
Foolish Cargo. Scion, 1954
The Foolish Virgin. Thorpe, 1950
The Foolish Virgin Returns. Scion, 1953
The Foolish Virgin Says No! Scion, 1953
Jealousy. Scion, 1953
Love Me, Hurt Me. Scion, 1953
Payoff. Scion, 1953
Sinister Lovely. Scion, 1953
Some Dame. Scion, 1953
The Trap. Scion, 1954
Uneasy Alibi. Scion, 1954
Vision Sinister. Dragon, 1954 *
We the Condemned. Scion, 1953

KASPER, ROY CHARLES
Love Spy, Love. Caravelle, 1968 [Saigon]

KASSAK, FRED. Pseudonym of Pierre Humblot, 1928-   .
Come Kill with Me. Bobbs, 1976 (Translation of "Voulez-Vous Tuer Avec Moi?" Paris, 1970.) [Fr.]

KASTLE, HERBERT D(AVID). 1924-   . Ref: CA. SC: Sgt. Edmund Roersch = ER.
Countdown to Murder. Crest, 1961; Mayflower, 1978 [NYC]
Cross-Country. Delacorte, 1975; Allen, 1975 ER
Death Squad. Delacorte, 1977; Allen, 1978. Also published as: Hit Squad. Mayflower, 1979 ER [NYC]
The Gang. Dell, 1976; Allen, 1977 ER
Hit Squad; see Death Squad
Hot Prowl. GM, 1965; Mayflower, 1977 [NYC]
Miami Golden Boy. Geis, 1969; Allen, 1970 [Miami]
The Millionaires. Delacorte, 1972; Allen, 1973
Sunset People. Jove, 1980; Allen, 1980 [L.A.]

KASTNER, ERICH. 1899-1942?
The Missing Miniature. Cape, 1936; Knopf, 1937 (Translation of "Die Verschwundene Miniatur." Berlin, 1936.) [Ger.]

KATCHA, VAHE. Pseudonym of Vaha Katchadourian, 1928-   . Ref: CA.
Don't Look Down. Hart-Davis, 1962 (Translation of "Ne te Retourne Pas, Kipian." Paris, 1958.) [Leb.]

KATCHADOURIAN, VAHA. 1928-   . Pseudonym: Vahe Katcha, q.v.

KATCHER, LEO. Newspaper editor and reporter; writer of magazine fiction and non-fiction; film writer.
The Blind Cave. Viking, 1966 [Greece]
Hard Man. Macmillan, 1957
Hot Pursuit. Atheneum, 1971
The Money People. Doubleday, 1961
Now Is the Time. Macmillan, 1964 [Calif.]

KATHRENS, VAUGHAN. Ref: CC.
Benny Went First. Melrose, 1950
Hit and Run. Melrose, 1951
The Lady Makes News. Melrose, 1952
Violent End. Melrose, 1953

KATZ, HERBERT M. Pseudonym: Nicholas Garland, q.v.

KATZ, ROBERT. 1933-   . Ref: CA.
The Cassandra Crossing. Ballantine, 1977; Pan, 1977 (Novelization of the movie.)
The Spoils of Ararat. Houghton, 1978; Sphere, 1979 [Turk.]
Ziggurat. Houghton, 1977; Eyre, 1978 [Swed.]

KATZ, WILLIAM. 1940-   . Ref: CA.
Death Dreams. Ballantine, 1979; Arrow, 1979
Ghostflight. Dell, 1980; Severn, 1981
North Star Crusade. Putnam, 1976; Arrow, 1977

KATZENBERGER, FRANCES I(SABELLA). 1861-1938.
The Three Verdicts. Editor Publishing, 1898

KAUFFMAN, (RAY) FRANKLIN
The Coconut Wireless. Macmillan, 1948

KAUFFMAN, REGINALD WRIGHT. 1877-1959. SC: Frances Baird, in at least those marked FB.
-The Azure Rose. Macaulay, 1919; Laurie, 1918
Beg Pardon, Sir! Penn, 1929 [Eng.]
Blind Man. Duffield, 1927; Hurst, 1926
-The Chasm, with Edward Childs Carpenter, 1872?-1950. Appleton, 1903
-The Dark House in Florissant. Altemus, 1927
-The Free Lovers. Macaulay, 1925; Laurie, 1925
Jarvis; see Jarvis of Harvard
-Jarvis of Harvard. Page, 1901. Also published as: Jarvis. St. Botolph Society, 1923
-Jim. Moffat, 1915. British title: Jim Trent. Laurie, 1929
Jim Trent; see Jim
-The Mark of the Beast. Macaulay, 1916; Gardner, 1919
Miss Frances Baird, Detective. Page, 1906 FB [N.Y.]
Money to Burn. Chelsea, 1924; Hurst, 1927 [Carib.]
My Heart and Stephanie. Page, 1910; Pitman, 1910 FB
-The Ranger of the Susquehannock. Penn, 1924
Share and Share Alike. Chelsea, 1925; Hurst, 1926 [NYC]
The Spider's Web. Moffat, 1913 [NYC]
-The Things That Are Caesar's. Appleton, 1902

KAUFFMANN, LANE. 1921-   . Ref: CA, CC.
The Perfectionist. Lippincott, 1954; Macmillan (London), 1955
Waldo. Lippincott, 1960; Gollancz, 1962 [Fla.]

KAUFMAN, GEORGE S(IMON). 1889-1961. See: Alexander (Humphreys) Woollcott, 1887-1943.

KAUFMAN, LEONARD
The Lower Part of the Sky. Farrar, 1948. Also published as: Juvenile Delinquents. Avon, 1952

KAUFMAN, LOUIS. 1916-   . Pseudonym: Dan Keller, q.v.

KAUFMAN, MICHAEL
The Container. Hale, 1979

KAUFMAN, MICHAEL T.
The Gun. Award, 1974 (Novelization of the movie.)

The Nickel Ride. Award, 1974; Tandem, 1974 (Novelization of the movie.)

KAUFMAN, OLIVER. 1917-   . Pseudonym: Oliver Crawford, q.v.

KAUFMAN, PAMELA
Pandora. Avon, 1977 [Calif.]

KAUFMAN, WOLFE. 1905-1970. Ref: CA.
I Hate Blondes. Simon, 1946 [NYC]

KAVALIER, REBECCA. Joint pseudonym with Louise DeCormier and Gloria Kirchheimer: Sara Cardiff, q.v.

KAVANAGH, DAN. Pseudonym of Julian Barnes, 1946-   .
Duffy. Cape, 1980

KAVANAGH, PAUL. Pseudonym of Lawrence Block, 1938-   , q.v. Other pseudonym: Chip Harrison, q.v. See also: William (Thomas) Ard, 1922-1960.
Not Comin' Home to You. Putnam, 1974; Hodder, 1976
Such Men Are Dangerous. Macmillan, 1969; Hodder, 1971
The Triumph of Evil. World, 1971; Hodder, 1972

KAVANAUGH, CYNTHIA. Pseudonym of Dorothy Daniels, 1915-   , q.v. Other pseudonyms: Daniella Dorsett, Angela Gray, Suzanne Somers, Geraldine Thayer, Helen Gray Weston, qq.v.
Bride of Lenore. Pyramid, 1966 [1891, Va.]
The Deception. Pyramid, 1966 [Switz.]

KAY, CAMERON
Thieves Fall Out. GM, 1953; Red Seal, 1953 [Cairo]

KAY, GEORGE
Secret Life of Mr. Beauty. New Horizon, 1979

KAY, KENNETH (EDMOND). 1915-   . Ref: CA.
Trouble in the Air. Eyre, 1959 [West]

KAY, KENNETH. See: Marshall Goldberg.

KAYE, H. B. Pseudonym of Harold B. Kampf, 1916-   .
Death Is a Black Camel. Hammond, 1952
The Grave Can Wait. Gifford, 1950
The Hungry Heart. Gifford, 1949
The Man in My Chair. Gifford, 1948
Red Rafferty. Gifford, 1949
This Man Is a Stranger. Gifford, 1949
A Touch of the Sun. Quality, 1952
You Only Die Once. Gifford, 1950

KAYE, H. R. Pseudonym of Hugh Randolph Knox, 1942-   .
The Dark Mansion. Brandon, 1968
Two Gay Sleuths. Brandon, 1968

KAYE, M(ARY) M(ARGARET). 1909-   . Pseudonym: Mollie Kaye, q.v. Ref: CA.
Death in Zanzibar; see The House of Shade
Death Walked in Berlin. Staples, 1955 [Berlin]
Death Walked in Cyprus. Staples, 1956 [Cyprus]
Death Walked in Kashmir. Staples, 1953 [India]
The House of Shade. Longmans, 1959; Coward, 1959. Revised edition: Death in Zanzibar. St. Martin's, 1983 [Zanz.]
It's Later Than You Think; see Later Than You Think
Later Than You Think. Longmans, 1958; Coward, 1959, as by Mollie Hamilton. Also published as: It's Later Than You Think. WDL, 1960 [Kenya]
Night on the Island. Longmans, 1960
Trade Wind. Longmans, 1963; Coward, 1964

KAYE, MARVIN (NATHAN). 1938-   . Ref: CA. SC: Marty Gold = MG; Hilary Quayle = HQ.
Bullets for Macbeth. Saturday Review, 1976; Hale, 1978 HQ [Nashv.]
The Grand Ole Opry Murders. Saturday Review, 1974 HQ [Nashv.]
The Laurel and Hardy Murders. Dutton, 1977; Curley, 1978 HQ [NYC]
A Lively Game of Death. Saturday Review, 1972; Barker, 1974 HQ [NYC]
My Brother, the Druggist. Doubleday, 1979 MG [NYC]
My Son, the Druggist. Doubleday, 1977 MG [NYC]

KAYE, MICHAEL W.
Devil's Brew. Paul, 1912

KAYE, MOLLIE. Pseudonym of M(ary) M(argaret) Kaye, 1909-   , q.v.
  Six Bars at Seven. Hutchinson, 1940

KAYLIN, WALTER
  Another Time, Another Woman. GM, 1963

KAYSER, RONAL. Pseudonym: Dale Clark, q.v.

KEANE, CHRISTOPHER
  The Crossing. Arbor, 1978 [ship, 1945]
  The Heir. Morrow, 1977; Hamlyn, 1979 [ship]
  The Maximus Zone. Pyramid, 1975

KEAREY, CHARLES. 1916-   . Ref: CA.
  -Last Plane from Uli. Collins, 1972; Holt, 1972

KEARNEY, SELSKAR
  The False Finger Tip. Maunsel, 1921

KEATE, E(DITH) M(URRAY). SC: Sgt./Insp./Supt. Margetson, in at least those marked M. Set: Eng.
  Demon Again. Eldon, 1937 M
  Demon of the Air. Eldon, 1936 M
  -A Garden of the Gods. Rivers, 1914
  The Jackanapes Jacket. Low, 1931 M
  The Mystery of Nelson's Coat. Eldon, 1936
  A Wild-Cat Scheme. Rivers, 1930 M

KEATING, H(ENRY) R(EYMOND) F(ITZWALTER). 1926-   . Ref: CA, CC, EM, MC, TC. SC: Insp. Ganesh Ghote = GG.
  Bats Fly Up for Inspector Ghote. Collins, 1974; Doubleday, 1974 GG [India]
  Death and the Visiting Fireman. Gollancz, 1959; Doubleday, 1973
  Death of a Fat God. Collins, 1963; Dutton, 1966 [theatre]
  The Dog It Was That Died. Gollancz, 1962 [Ire.]
  Filmi, Filmi, Inspector Ghote. Collins, 1976; Doubleday, 1977 GG [India]
  Inspector Ghote Breaks an Egg. Collins, 1970; Doubleday, 1971 GG [India]
  Inspector Ghote Caught in Meshes. Collins, 1967; Dutton, 1968 GG [India]
  Inspector Ghote Draws a Line. Collins, 1979; Doubleday, 1979 GG [India]
  Inspector Ghote Goes by Train. Collins, 1971; Doubleday, 1972 GG [India]
  Inspector Ghote Hunts the Peacock. Collins, 1968; Dutton, 1968 GG [Eng.]
  Inspector Ghote Plays a Joker. Collins, 1969; Dutton, 1969 GG [Bombay]
  Inspector Ghote Trusts the Heart. Collins, 1972; Doubleday, 1973 GG [India]
  Inspector Ghote's Good Crusade. Collins, 1966; Dutton, 1966 GG [India]
  Is Skin Deep, Is Fatal. Collins, 1965; Dutton, 1965
  -A Long Walk to Wimbledon. Macmillan (London), 1978
  The Murder of the Maharajah. Collins, 1980; Doubleday, 1980 [India, 1930]
  The Perfect Murder. Collins, 1964; Dutton, 1965 GG [India]
  A Remarkable Case of Burglary. Collins, 1975; Doubleday, 1976 [Eng., 1871]
  A Rush on the Ultimate. Gollancz, 1961
  -The Strong Man. Heinemann, 1971
  Zen There Was Murder. Gollancz, 1960

KEATING, HENRY
  Murder by Death. Warner, 1976 (Novelization of the movie.) [S.F.]

KEATING, JOSEPH. 1871-1934.
  The Exploited Woman. Palmer, 1923
  The Fairfax Mystery. Wright, 1935

KEATOR, MAUDE C(OLE)
  The Eyes Through the Tree. Appleton, 1930

KECK, MAUDE and OLIVE ORBISON. Pseudonym: Keck Orbison, q.v.
  Behind the Devil Screen. Ives Washburn, 1928; Long, 1929, as by Keck Orbison [China]
  Thursday Island. Ives Washburn, 1932

KECKHUT, JOHN
  The Dublin Pawn. Norton, 1977

KEDDIE, HENRIETTA. 1827-1914. Pseudonym: Sarah Tytler, q.v.

KEEBLE, JOHN. 1944-   . See also: Ransom Jeffery. Ref: CA.
  Yellowfish. Harper, 1980 [N.W.]

KEECK, GERTRUDE C.
  The Charter Lane Mystery. Mitre, 1967
  -The Record of Jeffrye Cranfield. Mitre, 1963

KEECH, (JOHN) SCOTT. 1936-   .
  Ciphered. Harper, 1980 [acad.]

KEEGAN, WILLIAM. 1938-   . Born in London; a journalist.
  A Real Killing. Weidenfeld, 1977; St. Martin's, 1977

KEELER, HARRY STEPHEN. 1890-1967. Ref: CC, EM, MP, TC. SC: Angus MacWhorter = AM; Tuddleton Trotter = TT.
  The Ace of Spades Murder; see The Case of the Jeweled Ragpicker
  The Amazing Web. Dutton, 1930; Ward, 1929 [Chi.]
  Behind That Mask. Ward, 1933 (Earliest book edition of a story that Keeler later expanded into a two-volume novel published in the U.S. as Finger! Finger! and Behind That Mask, qq.v.) [Chi.]
  Behind That Mask. Dutton, 1938 (Second of the two volumes expanded by Keeler from the original British edition of Behind That Mask, q.v. The first book of the two-volume novel is Finger! Finger!, q.v.)
  The Barking Clock; see The Case of the Barking Clock
  The Black Satchel; see The Matilda Hunter Murder
  The Blue Spectacles; see The Spectacles of Mr. Cagliostro
  The Book with the Orange Leaves. Dutton, 1942; Ward, 1943
  The Bottle with the Green Wax Seal. Dutton, 1942 (Third and final novel in the sequence whose first two volumes were The Portrait of Jirjohn Cobb and Cleopatra's Tears, qq.v.)
  The Box from Japan. Dutton, 1932; Ward, 1933 [Chi., 1942]
  By Third Degree; see The Sharkskin Book
  The Case of the Barking Clock. Phoenix, 1947. British title: The Barking Clock. Ward, 1951 (The British edition is 5-8000 words longer than the U.S.) TT
  The Case of the Canny Killer. Phoenix, 1946. British title: Murder in the Mills. Ward, 1946
  The Case of the Ivory Arrow. Phoenix, 1945. British title: The Search for X-Y-Z. Ward, 1943 (The British edition is substantially longer than the U.S.) [Wis.]
  The Case of the Jeweled Ragpicker. Phoenix, 1948. British title: The Ace of Spades Murder. Ward, 1949 (The British edition is longer than the American.) AM [Chi.]
  The Case of the Lavender Gripsack. Phoenix, 1944. British title: The Lavender Gripsack. Ward, 1941 (Fourth and final volume in the sequence whose first three volumes were The Man with the Magic Eardrums, The Man with the Crimson Box, and The Man with the Wooden Spectacles, qq.v.) [Chi.]
  The Case of the Mysterious Moll. Phoenix, 1945. British title: The Iron Ring. Ward, 1944 (The British edition is probably longer than the U.S.) [Nev.]
  The Case of the 16 Beans. Phoenix, 1944. British title: The 16 Beans. Ward, 1945 [NYC]
  The Case of the Transposed Legs. Phoenix, 1948; Ward, 1951
  The Case of the Two Strange Ladies. Phoenix, 1943. British title: The Two Strange Ladies. Ward, 1945
  The Chameleon. Dutton, 1939 (Second of the two volumes expanded by Keeler from the original British edition of The Mysterious Mr. I, q.v. The first of the two U.S. volumes is also entitled The Mysterious Mr. I, q.v.) [Ill.]
  Cheung, Detective; see Y. Cheung, Business Detective
  Cleopatra's Tears. Dutton, 1940; Ward, 1940 (Volume two of the sequence of novels that began with The Portrait of Jirjohn Cobb, q.v., and concluded with The Bottle with the Green Wax Seal, q.v.)
  The Crilly Court Mystery; see The Face of the Man from Saturn
  The Crimson Box; see The Man with the Crimson Box
  The Defrauded Yeggman. Dutton, 1937 (The first book of the two-volume American edition of Keeler's Vagabond Nights, whose parts are scattered over three U.S. and two British titles. For details, see Vagabond Nights, below.) [Tex.]
  The Face of the Man from Saturn. Dutton, 1933. British title: The Crilly Court Mystery. Ward, 1933 [Chi.]
  The Fiddling Cracksman; see The Mystery of the Fiddling Cracksman
  Find Actor Hart; see The Portrait of Jirjohn Cobb
  Find the Clock. Dutton, 1927; Hutchinson, 1925 [Chi.]
  Finger! Finger! Dutton, 1938 (The first of two volumes expanded by Keeler from the original British edition of Behind That Mask, q.v. The second book of the two-volume U.S. edition is also titled Behind That Mask, q.v.) [Chi.]
  The Five Silver Buddhas. Dutton, 1935; Ward, 1935 [Chi.]
  The Fourth King. Dutton, 1930; Ward, 1929 [Chi.]
  The Green Jade Hand. Dutton, 1930; Ward, 1930 (The British edition is cut down from the American.) [Chi.]
  The Iron Ring; see The Case of the Mysterious Moll
  The Lavender Gripsack; see The Case of the Lavender Gripsack
  The Magic Eardrums; see The Man with the Magic Eardrums
  The Man with the Crimson Box. Dutton, 1940. British title: The Crimson Box. Ward, 1940 (Second book in the four-volume sequence that began with The Man with the Magic Eardrums, q.v., and went on to include The Man with the Wooden Spectacles and The Case of the Lavender Gripsack, qq.v.) [Chi.]
  The Man with the Magic Eardrums. Dutton, 1939. British title: The Magic Eardrums. Ward, 1939 (First book in the four-volume sequence that went on to include The Man with the Crimson Box, The Man with the Wooden Spectacles and The Case of the Lavender Gripsack, qq.v.)
  The Man with the Wooden Spectacles. Dutton, 1941. British title: The Wooden Spectacles. Ward, 1941 (Third book of the four-volume sequence that began with The Man with the Magic Eardrums and The Man with the Crimson Box, qq.v, and concluded with The Case of the Lavender Gripsack, q.v.) [Chi.]
  The Marceau Case. Dutton, 1936; Ward, 1936 (First book of the trilogy that went on the include X. Jones of Scotland Yard and The Wonderful Scheme of Mr. Christopher Thorne, qq.v.)
  The Matilda Hunter Murder. Dutton, 1931. British title: The Black Satchel. Ward, 1931 (The British edition is heavily cut.) TT [Chi.]
  The Monocled Monster. Ward, 1947 [Chi.]
  Murder in the Mills; see The Case of the Canny Killer
  The Murder of London Lew. Ward, 1952 [Ark.]
  The Murdered Mathematician. Ward, 1949 [Chi.]
  The Mysterious Mr. I. Ward, 1937 (Earliest book edition of a story that Keeler later expanded into a two-volume novel published in the U.S. as The Mysterious Mr. I and The Chameleon, qq.v.) [Chi.]
  The Mysterious Mr. I. Dutton, 1938 (First of the two volumes expanded by Keeler from the original British edition of The Mysterious Mr. I. The second of the two U.S. volumes is The Chameleon, q.v.)
  The Mystery of the Fiddling Cracksman. Dutton, 1934. British title: The Fiddling Cracksman. Ward, 1934 [Chi., St. Louis]
  The Peacock Fan. Dutton, 1941; Ward, 1942
  The Portrait of Jirjohn Cobb. Dutton, 1940. British title: Find Actor Hart. Ward, 1939 (First of the three-volume sequence that continued with Cleopatra's Tears, and concluded with The Bottle with the Green Wax Seal, qq.v.)
  The Riddle of the Traveling Skull. Dutton, 1934. British title: The Traveling Skull. Ward, 1934 [Chi.]
  The Riddle of the Yellow Zuri. Dutton, 1930. British title: The Tiger Snake. Ward, 1931 [Chi.]
  The Search for X-Y-Z; see The Case of the Ivory Arrow
  The Sharkskin Book. Dutton, 1941. British title: By Third Degree. Ward, 1948 [Chi.]
  Sing Sing Nights. Dutton, 1928; Hutchinson, 1927 [N.Y.]
  The 16 Beans; see The Case of the 16 Beans
  The Skull of the Waltzing Clown. Dutton, 1935 (For details of the English equivalent of this title, see Vagabond Nights, below.) [Chi.]

The Spectacles of Mr. Cagliostro. Dutton, 1929; Hutchinson, 1926. Also published as: The Blue Spectacles. Ward, 1931 [Chi.]
Stand By—London Calling! Ward, 1953 AM
The Steeltown Strangler. Ward, 1950
The Strange Will. Ward, 1949 [N.Y.]
Ten Hours. Ward, 1934 (The one-volume British edition of Keeler's Vagabond Nights, whose parts are scattered over three U.S. and two British titles. For details, see Vagabond Nights, below.)
10 Hours. Dutton, 1937 (Volume 2 of the two-volume American edition of Vagabond Nights, whose parts are scattered over three U.S. and two English titles. For details, see Vagabond Nights, below.) [Tex.]
Thieves' Nights. Dutton, 1929; Ward, 1930 [Chi.]
The Tiger Snake; see The Riddle of the Yellow Zuri
The Traveling Skull; see The Riddle of the Traveling Skull
The Two Strange Ladies; see The Case of the Two Strange Ladies
Under Twelve Stars; see The Washington Square Enigma
Vagabond Nights. (This was Keeler's overall title for a 180,000 word novel built on the same principle of three prisoners telling their stories as was the earlier Sing Sing Nights. The British version of this book was published first, and in a single volume, under the title Ten Hours, q.v. The American version is a two-volume novel, The Defrauded Yeggman and 10 Hours, qq.v. But between the British and American publications Keeler had expanded the tale of the first prisoner in the British version into a complete novel, The Skull of the Waltzing Clown, q.v., which was published only in the U.S. since a precis of the story had already appeared in England in Ten Hours. Finally, after the U.S. two-volume publication of Vagabond Nights as The Defrauded Yeggman and 10 Hours, Keeler expanded the tale of the first prisoner in the American edition—a tale totally different from the corresponding tale in the British edition—into a novel, When Thief Meets Thief, q.v., that was published in England since a precis had already appeared in the U.S. as part of The Defrauded Yeggman!)
The Vanishing Gold Truck. Dutton, 1941; Ward, 1942 AM
The Voice of the Seven Sparrows. Dutton, 1928; Hutchinson, 1924 [Chi., New Or.]
The Washington Square Enigma. Dutton, 1933. British title: Under Twelve Stars. Ward, 1933 [Chi.]
When Thief Meets Thief. Ward, 1938 (For details on the American equivalent of this novel, see Vagabond Nights, above.) [S. Am., Haw.]
The Wonderful Scheme; see The Wonderful Scheme of Mr. Christopher Thorne
The Wonderful Scheme of Mr. Christopher Thorne. Dutton, 1936. British title: The Wonderful Scheme. Ward, 1937 (Third book of the trilogy whose first two volumes were The Marceau Case and X. Jones of Scotland Yard, qq.v.
The Wooden Spectacles; see The Man with the Wooden Spectacles
X. Jones; see X. Jones of Scotland Yard
X. Jones of Scotland Yard. Dutton, 1936. British title: X Jones. Ward, 1936 (Second volume of the trilogy that began with The Marceau Case and ended with The Wonderful Scheme of Mr. Christopher Thorne, qq.v.)
Y. Cheung, Business Detective. Dutton, 1939. British title: Cheung, Detective. Ward, 1938 [Indianapolis]

KEELEY, EDMUND (LEROY). 1928- . Ref: CA.
The Imposter. Doubleday, 1970

KEENAN, JAMES
Run, Mann, Run! Major, 1975

KEENAN, WILLIAM. SC: John Marne, in all titles.
Lonely Mosaic. Hale, 1967
Mosaic of Death. Hale, 1969
Murder in Melancholy. Hale, 1971

KEENE, DAY.   -ca.1969. Ref: CC, TC. SC: Johnny Aloha = JA; Les Ferron = LF.
-About Doctor Ferrel. GM, 1952; Fawcett (London), 1958

The Big Kiss-Off. Graphic, 1954 [La.]
The Brimstone Bed. Avon, 1960 [Fla.]
Bring Him Back Dead. GM, 1956. Revised edition: Lancer, 1963 [La.]
Bye, Baby Bunting. Holt, 1963; Allen, 1963 [NYC]
Carnival of Death. Macfadden, 1965 [L.A.]
-Chautauqua, with Dwight Vincent. Putnam, 1960; Allen, 1961
-Chicago 11. Dell, 1966
The Dangling Carrot. Ace, 1955
Dead Dolls Don't Talk. Crest, 1959; Muller, 1963 [L.A.]
Dead in Bed. Pyramid, 1959 JA [Calif.]
Death House Doll. Ace, 1954
Evidence Most Blind; see Framed in Guilt
Farewell to Passion. Hanro, 1951. Also published as: The Passion Murders. Avon, 1955
Flight by Night. Ace, 1956; Red Seal, 1960 [Cent. Am.]
Framed in Guilt. Mill, 1949. British title: Evidence Most Blind. Hennel Locke, 1949 [L.A.]
-His Father's Wife. Pyramid, 1954
Home Is the Sailor. GM, 1952
Homicidal Lady. Graphic, 1954 [Fla.]
Hunt the Killer. Phantom, 1952 [Fla.]
If the Coffin Fits. Graphic, 1952 [S.W.]
It's a Sin to Kill. Avon, 1958
Joy House. Lion, 1954; Consul, 1964 [Chi.]
-Live Again, Love Again. Signet, 1970
Love Me—and Die! Phantom, 1951 [L.A.]
Miami 59. Dell, 1960; Mayflower, 1966 [Miami]
Moran's Woman. Zenith, 1959
Mrs. Homicide. Ace, 1953 [NYC]
Murder on the Side. GM, 1956; Fawcett (London), 1956 [Chi.]
My Flesh Is Sweet. Lion, 1951
Naked Fury. Phantom, 1952
Notorious. GM, 1954; Fawcett (London), 1955 LF [La.]
Passage to Samoa. GM, 1958; Fawcett (London), 1960 [ship]
The Passion Murders; see Farewell to Passion
Payola. Pyramid, 1960 JA [L.A.]
Seed of Doubt. Simon, 1961; Allen, 1962
Sleep with the Devil. Lion, 1954 LF
So Dead My Lovely. Pyramid, 1959 [L.A.]
-Southern Daughter. Macfadden, 1967
Strange Witness. Graphic, 1953 [Chi.]
Take a Step to Murder. GM, 1959; Muller pb, 1960 [Calif.]
There Was a Crooked Man. GM, 1954; Fawcett (London), 1955. Revised edition: Lancer, 1963
This Is Murder, Mr. Herbert and other stories. Avon, 1948 ss
To Kiss, or Kill. GM, 1952; Fawcett (London), 1953 [Chi.]
-Too Black for Heaven. Croydon, 1959
Too Hot to Hold. GM, 1959; Muller pb, 1960 [NYC]
Wake Up to Murder. Phantom, 1952 [Fla.]
Who Has Wilma Lathrop? GM, 1955; Jenkins, 1966 [Chi.]
-Wild Girl. Macfadden, 1970

KEENE, FARADAY. Pseudonym of Cora (Hardy) Jarrett, 1877-   , q.v.
Pattern in Black and Red. Houghton, 1934; Barker, 1934, as by Cora Jarrett [South]
Peccadilloes. Day, 1929; Noel Douglas, 1930 ss

KEENE, ROSWELL W.
The Blue Diamond. Abbey, 1902

KEENE, TOM and BRIAN HAYNES
Spyship. Lane, 1980; Marek, 1980

KEENER, JOYCE
Borderline. Ace, 1979 [Mex.]

KEEPING, TEMPEST
-Diamond Mountain. Eldon, 1935

KEIFETZ, NORMAN
-Welcome Sundays. Putnam, 1979 [Atlanta]

KEINZLEY, FRANCES. 1922-   . Ref: CA, CC.
The Cottage at Chapelyard. Bobbs, 1975
Illusion. Allen, 1970; Stein, 1970 [ship]
A Time to Prey. Allen, 1969; Stein, 1970 [N.Z.]

KEIRSTEAD, B(URTON) S(EELY), 1907-   , and D(ONALD) FREDERICK CAMPBELL, 1906-   . Ref: CA (for Keirstead), CC.
The Brownsville Murders. Macmillan, 1933 [Can.]

KEITH, CARLTON. Pseudonym of Keith Carlton Robertson, 1914-   . Ref: CA. SC: Jeff Green = JG.
The Crayfish Dinner. Doubleday, 1966. British title: The Elusive Epicure. Hale, 1968 JG [Pa.]
The Diamond-Studded Typewriter. Macmillan, 1958; Heinemann, 1960. Also published as: A Gem of a Murder. Dell, 1959 JG [NYC]
The Elusive Epicure; see The Crayfish Dinner
A Gem of a Murder; see The Diamond-Studded Typewriter
The Hiding Place. Doubleday, 1965; Hale, 1966 [N.J.]
The Missing Book-Keeper; see A Taste of Sangria
Missing, Presumed Dead. Doubleday, 1961 JG [N.J.]
Rich Uncle. Doubleday, 1963; Hale, 1965 JG [Pa.]
A Taste of Sangria. Doubleday, 1968. British title: The Missing Book-Keeper. Hale, 1969 JG

KEITH, DAVID. Pseudonym of Francis Steegmuller, 1906-   , q.v. Ref: CA, CC, MC, MP. SC: Ted S. Weaver = TW.
Blue Harpsichord. Dodd, 1949; Collins, 1950. Reprinted as by Francis Steegmuller: Dolphin, 1961 [NYC]
A Matter of Accent. Dodd, 1943 TW [NYC]
A Matter of Iodine. Dodd, 1940; Cassell, 1940 TW [Fr.]

KEITH, J. KILMENY. Pseudonym of Lucy Beatrice Malleson, 1899-1973. Other pseudonyms: Anthony Gilbert, Anne Meredith, qq.v.
The Man Who Was London. Collins, 1925
-The Sword of Harlequin. Collins, 1927

KEITH, LESLIE. Pseudonym of Grace L. Keith Johnston.
-A Pleasant Rogue. Hurst, 1902

KELL, JOSEPH. Pseudonym of John Anthony Burgess Wilson, 1917-   . Other pseudonym: Anthony Burgess, q.v.
-One Hand Clapping. Davies, 1961; Knopf, 1972, as by Anthony Burgess

KELLAND, CLARENCE BUDINGTON. 1881-1964. Ref: CC, TC. SC: Scattergood Baines = SB.
The Artless Heiress. Dodd, 1948
The Case of the Nameless Corpse. Harper, 1956; Hale, 1958 [Can.]
The Cat's Paw. Harper, 1934
Conflict. Harper, 1922; Hodder, 1928
Contraband. Harper, 1923; Hodder, 1928
Counterfeit Gentleman. Dodd, 1960; Hale, 1961
Dangerous Angel. Harper, 1953; Hale, 1955 [S.F., 1870s]
Death Keeps a Secret. Harper, 1956; Hale, 1957 [N. Nex.]
Double Treasure. Harper, 1946; Macdonald, 1949
The Great Mail Robbery. Harper, 1951; Museum, 1954 [NYC]
The Key Man. Harper, 1952; Hale, 1954
-Knuckles. Harper, 1928; Hodder, 1928
The Lady and the Giant. Dodd, 1959; Hale, 1960 [N.Y., 1869]
Mark of Treachery. Dodd, 1961 [Pa.]
The Monitor Affair. Dodd, 1960; Hale, 1961
Murder for a Million. World's Work, 1947 (U.S. title?)
Murder Makes an Entrance. Harper, 1955; Hale, 1956 [L.A.]
No Escape. Museum, 1951 (U.S. title?)
Party Man. Dodd, 1962
-Scattergood Baines. Harper, 1921; Hodder, 1942 SB
-Scattergood Baines Pulls the Strings. Harper, 1941 SB ss
-Scattergood Returns. Harper, 1940 SB ss
The Sinister Strangers. Dodd, 1961 [Wyo.]
Stolen Goods. Harper, 1950; Museum, 1951 [NYC]
Where There's Smoke. Harper, 1959; Hale, 1960 [NYC]

KELLER, BEVERLY (LOU). Ref: CA.
The Baghdad Defections. Bobbs, 1973 [Leb.]

KELLER, DAN. Pseudonym of Louis Kaufman, 1916-   .
Flee the Night in Anger. Popular Library, 1954
One Way Street. Hale, 1960

KELLER, DAVID H(ENRY). 1880-1966. American science fiction/fantasy writer, physician and psychiatrist.
Wolf Hollow Bubbles. ARRA Printers, 1933

K

KELLER, H(ARRY) A. 1894- . Editor of mystery and detective story magazines.
Death Sits In. Brentano's, 1932 [NYC]

KELLEY, J(AMES) D(OUGLAS) JERROLD. 1847-1922.
A Desperate Chance. Scribner, 1886

KELLEY, K(EITH) P(ATRICK)
The Plot. Caravelle, 1967

KELLEY, LAMAR
That's No Way to Die. Pyramid, 1970 [Fla.]

KELLEY, LEO P(ATRICK). 1928- .
Deadlocked! GM, 1973 [N.Y.]

KELLEY, MARTHA MOTT. See: Q. Patrick.

KELLEY, THOMAS P.
Tapestry Triangle. Associated Weekly Newspapers, 1946

KELLEY, WILLIAM. 1929- .
The Tyree Legend. Simon, 1979 [N.Y.]

KELLIHER, DAN T. Newspaper reporter and feature writer in Kansas City. Joint pseudonym with W. G. Secrist: Kelliher Secrist, q.v.

KELLOW, KATHLEEN. Pseudonym of Eleanor Alice Burford Hibbert, 1906- . Other pseudonyms: Philippa Carr, Elbur Ford, Victoria Holt, qq.v.
-Call of the Blood. Hale, 1956
-Danse Macabre. Hale, 1952
-It Began in Vauxhall Gardens. Hale, 1955
-Lilith. Hale, 1954
-Milady Charlotte. Hale, 1959
-Rooms at Mrs. Oliver's. Hale, 1952
-The World's a Stage. Hale, 1960

KELLY, ANTHONY PAUL
Three Faces East. French (NYC), 1935 (3-act play.)

KELLY, BILL. SC: Pepperoni Hero, in all titles.
Peanut Butter & Jelly Is Not for Kids. Zebra, 1975
Sandwiches Are Not My Business. Zebra, 1975
Tuna Is Not for Eating. Zebra, 1975 [Mex.]

KELLY, F. J.
The Gates of Brass. Monarch, 1963

KELLY, FLORENCE FINCH. 1858-1939.
The Delafield Affair. McClurg, 1908
The Fate of Felix Brand. Winston, 1913
-Frances. Sanfred, 1889
-On the Inside. Sanford, 1890
-With Hoops of Steel. Bowen-Merrill, 1900; Stevens, 1900

KELLY, GEORGE
The Price of Diamonds. Harris, 1979

KELLY, HAROLD ERNEST. 1899- . Pseudonyms: Eugene Ascher, Darcy Glinto, Gordon Holt, Buck Toler, qq.v.

KELLY, ISABELLA
The Abbey of St. Asaph. Lane, 1795; Arno, 1977
The Baron's Daughter. Bell, 1802
Madeline; or, The Castle of Montgomery. Lane, 1794
The Ruins of Avondale Priory. Minerva, 1796

KELLY, JOHN. 1921- . Ref: CA.
The Wooden Wolf. Dutton, 1976; Macdonald, 1977

KELLY, JUDITH (SAGE). 1908-1957. Born in Toronto; graduate of Vassar; lived in Mass.
A Diplomatic Incident. Houghton, 1949; Gollancz, 1950 [Wash. D.C.]

KELLY, MARY. 1927- . Ref: CA, CC, TC. SC: Insp. Brett Nightingale = BN; Nicholson = N. Set: Eng.
The Christmas Egg. Secker, 1958; Holt, 1966 BN
A Cold Coming. Secker, 1956; Walker, 1968 BN
Dead Corse. Joseph, 1966; Holt, 1967
Dead Man's Riddle. Secker, 1957; Walker, 1967 BN [acad., Edin.]
The Dead of Summer; see Due to a Death
Due to a Death. Joseph, 1962. U.S. title: The Dead of Summer. Mill, 1963 N
March to the Gallows. Joseph, 1964; Holt, 1965
The Spoilt Kill. Joseph, 1961; British Book Centre, 1961 N
That Girl in the Alley. Macmillan (London), 1974; Walker, 1974 [Eng., 1936]
The Twenty-Fifth Hour. Macmillan (London), 1971; Walker, 1972 [Fr.]
Write on Both Sides of the Paper. Joseph, 1969; London House, 1970 [Scot.]

KELLY, PATRICK. Pseudonym of Ted Allbeury, 1917- , q.v. Other pseudonym: Richard Butler, q.v.
Codeword Cromwell. Granada, 1980

KELLY, ROD
Just for the Bread. Hale, 1976

KELLY, TIM J. 1937- .
The Burning Man. French (NYC), 1962 (2-act play.)
"The Butler Did It." Baker, 1977 (3-act play.)
Creeps by Night. Baker, 1973 (1-act play.)
Egad, the Woman in White. French (NYC), 1975 (2-act play based on the novel by Wilkie Collins, 1824-1889, q.v.)
Frankenstein. French (NYC), 1974 (2-act play based on the novel by M. W. Shelley, 1797-1851, q.v.)
Hawkshaw the Detective. Pioneer, 1976 (2-act play.)
The Hound of the Baskervilles. French (NYC), 1976 (2-act play based on the novel by A. Conan Doyle, 1859-1930, q.v.) (Sherlock Holmes.)
Lizzie Borden of Fall River. Pioneer, 1976 (2-act play.)
Loco-Motion, Commotion, Dr. Gorilla and Me. Baker, 1977 (2-act play.)
Merry Murders at Montmarie. Performance, 1971 (Play.)
No Opera at the Op'ry House. Dramatic, 1972 (Play.)
Sherlock Holmes. Pioneer, 1977 (2-act adaptation of the play by William Gillette, 1855-1937, q.v.) (Sherlock Holmes.)

KELLY, VINCE
The Greedy Ones. Angus, 1958
The Shadow: From Frank Fahy. Mayflower, 1967

KELLY, W(ILLIAM) P(ATRICK). 1848- .
-The Cuban Treasure Island. Routledge, 1903
-Doctor Baxter's Invention. Greening, 1912
-The Dolomite Cavern; or, Light in the Darkness. Greening, 1899
The Harrington Street Mystery. Simpkin, 1915
-The House at Norwood. Arrowsmith, 1914
-Schoolboys Three. Downey, 1895

KELSEY, VERA. Ref: CC. SC: Lt. Diego = D.
The Bride Dined Alone. Doubleday, 1943 [L.I.]
Fear Came First. Doubleday, 1945 [Seattle]
The Owl Sang Three Times. Doubleday, 1941 D [Rio de J.]
Satan Has Six Fingers. Doubleday, 1943 D [Rio de J.]
Whisper Murder! Doubleday, 1946 [Minn.]

KELSTON, ROBERT
Kill One, Kill Two. Ace, 1958
Murder's End. Graphic, 1956 [Calif.]

KELTON, GERALD
-Dolores. Eldon, 1934
Wheels Beneath. Rich, 1935

KEMAL, YASHAR. 1922- .
The Lords of Akchasaz. Harvill, 1979 (Translation of "Demirciler Carsisi Cinayeti." Istanbul, 1974.)

KEMELMAN, HARRY. 1908- . Ref: CA, CC, EM, TC. SC: Rabbi David Small = DS.
Friday the Rabbi Slept Late. Crown, 1964; Hutchinson 1965 DS [Mass.]
Monday the Rabbi Took Off. Putnam, 1972; Hutchinson, 1972 DS [Isr.]
The Nine Mile Walk. Putnam, 1967; Hutchinson, 1968 ss
Saturday the Rabbi Went Hungry. Crown, 1966; Hutchinson 1967 DS [Mass.]
Sunday the Rabbi Stayed Home. Putnam, 1969; Hutchinson, 1969 DS [Mass.]
Thursday the Rabbi Walked Out. Morrow, 1978; Hutchinson, 1979 DS [Mass.]
Tuesday the Rabbi Saw Red. Fields, 1974; Hutchinson, 1974 DS [Mass., acad.]
Wednesday the Rabbi Got Wet. Morrow, 1976; Hutchinson, 1976 DS [Mass.]

KEMP, HAROLD (CURRY). 1896- . SC: Insp. Jimmy Brent, in at least those marked JB. Set: Eng.
As the Devil Burned. Hammond, 1949
Dead Snakes' Venom. Hammond, 1948
Death of a Dwarf. Bles, 1955
Heat Not a Furnace. Hammond, 1952 JB
Mark of a Witch. Bles, 1959 JB
Murder Humane. Hammond, 1947 JB
Red for Murder. Bles, 1957 JB

KEMP, SARAH. Pseudonym of Michael Butterworth, 1924- , q.v.
Goodbye, Pussy. Collins, 1979. U.S. title: Over the Edge. Doubleday, 1979

KEMPLEY, WALTER. Born in Ia.; TV writer ("The Tonight Show" and others) and producer ("The Merv Griffin Show").
The Invaders. Saturday Review, 1976 [Viet Nam]
The Probability Factor. Saturday Review, 1972 [Neb.]

KENDALL, CAROL (SEEGER). 1917- . Ref: CA.
The Baby-Snatcher. Lane, 1952
The Black Seven. Harper, 1946; Lane, 1950
The Other Side of the Tunnel. Abelard, 1957; Lane, 1956

KENDALL, JANE. Pseudonym of Anne (Louise) Coulter Martens, 1906- , q.v. Other pseudonyms: Rilla Carlisle, Ann Reynolds, qq.v.
The Girl with Two Faces. Dramatic, 1944 (3-act play.)

KENDALL, KATHRYA
Black Terrace. Arcadia, 1955
Death Rides the Storm. Arcadia, 1958 [Wash.]

KENDALL, RALPH S(ELWOOD). 1878- .
Benton of the Royal Mounted. Lane (NYC), 1918; Lane (London), 1919 [Can.]
The Luck of the Mounted. Lane (NYC & London), 1920 [Can.]

KENDRAKE, CARLETON. Pseudonym of Erle Stanley Gardner, 1889-1970, q.v. Other pseudonyms: A. A. Fair, Charles J. Kenny, qq.v.
The Clew of the Forgotten Murder. Morrow, 1935; Cassell, 1935 (Reprinted extensively, usually as The Clue of the Forgotten Murder, as by Erle Stanley Gardner.)

KENDRICK, BAYNARD (HARDWICK). 1894-1977. Ref: CA, CC, EM, MP, TC. Pseudonym (?): Richard Hayward, q.v. SC: Capt. Duncan Maclain = DM; Miles Standish Rice = MR.
The Aluminum Turtle. Dodd, 1960. British title: The Spear Gun Murders. Hale, 1961 DM [Fla.]
Blind Allies. Morrow, 1954 DM [NYC]
Blind Man's Bluff. Little, 1943; Methuen, 1944 DM [NYC]
Blood on Lake Louisa. Greenberg, 1934; Methuen, 1937 [Fla.]
Clear and Present Danger. Doubleday, 1958; Hale, 1959 DM [NYC]
Death Beyond the Go-Thru. Doubleday, 1938 SR [Fla.]
Death Knell. Morrow, 1945; Methuen, 1946 DM [NYC]
The Eleven of Diamonds. Greenberg, 1936; Methuen, 1937 SR [Miami]
Eyes in the Night; see The Odor of Violets
Flight from a Firing Wall. Simon, 1966; Hale, 1968 [Fla.]
Frankincense and Murder. Dodd, 1961; Hale, 1962 DM [NYC]
Hot Red Money. Dodd, 1959; Hale, 1962 [NYC]
The Iron Spiders. Greenberg, 1936; Methuen, 1938. Also published as: The Iron Spiders Murder. Dell, 1944 SR [Fla.]
The Iron Spiders Murder; see The Iron Spiders
The Last Express. Doubleday, 1937; Methuen, 1938 DM [NYC]
Make Mine Maclain. Morrow, 1947 (Three novelets.) DM
The Murderer Who Wanted More. Dell 10¢ pb, 1951 (Separate publication of one of the three novelets from Make Mine Maclain, q.v.) DM
Odor of Violets. Little, 1941; Methuen, 1941. Also published as: Eyes in the Night. Grosset, 1942 DM [Conn.]
Out of Control. Morrow, 1945; Methuen, 1947 DM [Tenn.]

Reservations for Death. Morrow, 1957;
   Hale, 1958 DM [NYC]
The Spear Gun Murders; see The Aluminum
   Turtle
The Tunnel. Scribner, 1949
The Whistling Hangman. Doubleday, 1937;
   Hale, 1959 DM [NYC]
You Die Today. Morrow, 1952; Hale,
   1958 DM [NYC]

KENDRICK, TERRY. Pseudonym of May Terry.
   One Too Many. Dorrance, 1977

KENEALLY, THOMAS (MICHAEL). 1935-   .
      Ref: CA.
   The Chant of Jimmie Blacksmith. Angus,
      1972; Viking, 1972
   The Fear. Cassell, 1965
   The Place at Whitten. Cassell, 1964;
      Walker, 1965 [Australia]
   The Survivor. Angus, 1969; Viking, 1970
      [Australia]
   A Victim of the Aurora. Collins, 1977;
      Harcourt, 1978 [Antarctic, 1910]

KENEALY, ARABELLA
   Belinda's Beaux and other stories.
      Bliss, 1897 ss, some criminous
   -King Edward Intervenes. Long, 1910

KENLEY, PETER
   -Surregar's Raft. Earl, 1948

KENNAWAY, JAMES (PEBLES EWING). 1928-
      1968. Ref: CA.
   The Mind Benders. Pan, 1963; Atheneum,
      1963

KENNEALLY, G. P.
   Nobody Wins. Manor, 1978 [S.F.]

KENNEDY, ADAM. Pseudonym: John Redgate,
      q.v. Born in Ind.; painter, actor and
      screenwriter.
   The Domino Principle. Viking, 1975;
      New English Library, 1976
   Love Song. Viking, 1976; New English
      Library, 1977

KENNEDY, BART. 1861-1930.
   The Wandering Romanoff. Burleigh, 1898

KENNEDY, ELLIOT. Pseudonym of Lionel Rob-
      ert Holcombe Godfrey, 1932-   .
      Other pseudonym: Scott Mitchell, q.v.
      Set: U.S.
   The Big Loser. Hale, 1972; Drake, 1972
   Bullets Are Final. Hale, 1973
   The Dead Sleep Late. Hale, 1975
   Never Say Dead. Hale, 1974
   No Love in a Bullet. Hale, 1976
   That Fatal Feeling. Hale, 1974

KENNEDY, HARVEY J. Born in Knoxville,
      Tenn.; lawyer, judge and legislator
      in Ga.
   Murder and the Shocking Miss Williams.
      Vantage, 1957

KENNEDY, HOWARD ANGUS. 1861-1938.
   Unsought Adventure. Carrier, 1929

KENNEDY, JAY RICHARD
   The Chairman. World, 1970 [China]

KENNEDY, JOHN (BOYD). 1921-   .
   Paper Chase. Abelard-Schuman, 1956
      [Manila]

KENNEDY, JOHN DE N(AVARRE). 1888-   .
   Crime in Reverse. Nelson, 1939
   In the Shadow of the Cheka. Nelson,
      1935; Macaulay, 1935
   The Rain of Death. Nelson, 1945 [Ger.]

KENNEDY, LUDOVIC (HENRY COVERLEY).
      1919-   . Ref: CA.
   Murder Story. Evans, 1955 (3-act
      play.)

KENNEDY, MILWARD. Pseudonym of Milward
      Rodon Kennedy Burge, 1894-1968. Other
      pseudonym: Evelyn Elder, q.v. Joint
      pseudonym with Archibald Gordon
      Macdonell, 1895-1941, q.v.: Robert
      Milward Kennedy, q.v. Ref: CC, EM,
      MC, MP, TC. SC: Sir George Bull = GB;
      Insp. Cornford = C. Set: Eng.
   Bull's Eye. Gollancz, 1933; Kinsey,
      1933 GB
   Corpse Guard Parade. Gollancz, 1929;
      Doubleday, 1930 C
   Corpse in Cold Storage. Gollancz, 1934;
      Kinsey, 1934 GB
   The Corpse on the Mat. Gollancz, 1929.
      U.S. title: The Man Who Rang the
      Bell, as by Robert Milward Kennedy.
      Doubleday, 1929 C
   Death in a Deck-Chair. Gollancz, 1930;
      Doubleday, 1931
   Death to the Rescue. Gollancz, 1931
   Escape to Quebec. Gollancz, 1946 [Can.]

Half-Mast Murder. Gollancz, 1930;
   Doubleday, 1930
I'll Be Judge, I'll Be Jury. Gollancz,
   1937
It Began in New York. Gollancz, 1943
   [NYC]
The Man Who Rang the Bell; see The
   Corpse on the Mat
The Murderer of Sleep. Gollancz, 1932;
   Kinsey, 1933
Poison in the Parish. Gollancz, 1935
The Scornful Corpse; see Sic Transit
   Gloria
Sic Transit Gloria. Gollancz, 1936.
   U.S. title: The Scornful Corpse.
   Dodd, 1936
The Top Boot. Hale, 1950
Two's Company. Hale, 1952

KENNEDY, NANCY
   -Head in the Highlands. Manor, 1978
   Shadow of the Cliff. Manor, 1972
   A Village Tale. Manor, 1978 [Oreg.]

KENNEDY, NANCY MacDOUGALL
   Winter Reckoning. Popular Library, 1979

KENNEDY, ROBERT MILWARD. Joint pseudonym
      of Milward Rodon Kennedy Burge, 1894-
      1968, and Archibald Gordon Macdonell,
      1895-1941. Other Burge pseudonyms:
      Evelyn Elder, Milward Kennedy, qq.v.
      Other Macdonell pseudonyms: John Cam-
      eron, Neil Gordon, qq.v.
   The Bleston Mystery. Gollancz, 1928;
      Doubleday, 1929

KENNEDY, STETSON. 1916-   . Ref: CA.
   Passage to Violence. Lion, 1954

KENNEDY, VAN G.
   The Penalty Is Death! Fiction House,
      1946

KENNEDY, WILLIAM. 1928-   . Ref: CA.
   Legs. Coward, 1975; Cape, 1976 [U.S.,
      1920s]

KENNINGTON, (GILBERT) ALAN. 1906-   .
      Educated at Oxford and in Ger.; no-
      velist and playwright. Set: Eng.
   All Fall Down. Jarrolds, 1950. U.S.
      title: Young Man with a Scythe. Mac-
      millan, 1951
   A Bagful of Bones. Jarrolds, 1942
      [acad.]
   Blood Velvet. Jarrolds, 1954
   Death of a Shrew. Jarrolds, 1937
   -Desirable Alien. Locker, 1947
   Flying Visitor. Jarrolds, 1946
   -Fritzi. Dickson, 1932
   The Golden Horse. Hale, 1958
   Hemlock Galore. Hale, 1974
   The Lost One. Jarrolds, 1955
   -Love on the Set. Mellifont, 1938
   Murder, M.A. Jarrolds, 1941
   The Night Has Eyes. Jarrolds, 1939
   See How They Run. Dickson, 1934
   She Died Young. Jarrolds, 1938
   Since There's No Help. Jarrolds, 1948
   Young Man with a Scythe; see All Fall
      Down

KENNY, CHARLES J. Pseudonym of Erle
      Stanley Gardner, 1889-1970, q.v.
      Other pseudonyms: A. A. Fair, Carle-
      ton Kendrake, qq.v.
   This Is Murder. Morrow, 1935; Methuen,
      1936 (Extensively reprinted as by
      Erle Stanley Gardner.)

KENNY, PAUL. Joint pseudonym of Jean Li-
      bert and Gaston Vandenpanhuise.
   The Tanagra Affair. International, 1969
      (Translation from the French.)
      [Athens]

KENRICK, DOUGLAS
   Death in a Tokyo Family. Hale, 1979
      [Tokyo]

KENRICK, TONY. 1935-   . Ref: CA, TC.
   The Chicago Girl. Joseph, 1977; Putnam,
      1976 [NYC]
   The 81st Site. Granada, 1980; NAL, 1980
      [Ger.]
   The Kidnap Kid. Joseph, 1975. U.S.
      title: Stealing Lillian. McKay, 1975
   The Nighttime Guy. Hart-Davis, 1979;
      Morrow, 1979 [NYC]
   The Only Good Body's a Dead One. Cape,
      1970; Simon, 1971 [Nice]
   The Seven Day Soldiers. Joseph, 1976;
      Regnery, 1976
   Stealing Lillian; see The Kidnap Kid
   A Tough One to Lose. Joseph, 1972;
      Bobbs, 1972 [S.F.]
   Two Lucky People. Joseph, 1978
   Two for the Price of One. Joseph, 1974;
      Bobbs, 1974

KENSCH, OTTO
   Death Is a Habit. Transport, ca.1941

KENT, ARTHUR (WILLIAM CHARLES). 1925-   .
      Ref: CA. SC (with many other au-
      thors): Sexton Blake = SB.
   Action of the Tiger. Consul, 1961
   Black Sunday. Hale, 1965
   Broken Doll. Digit, 1961
   Corpse to Cuba. Mayflower, 1966; Mac-
      fadden, 1967 SB [Cuba]
   Inclining to Crime. Amalgamated, 1956
      SB
   Plant Poppies on My Grave. Digit, 1966;
      Avon, 1967
   Red-Red-Red. Compact, 1966
   Special Edition—Murder. Amalgamated,
      1957 SB
   Stairway to Murder. Amalgamated, 1958
      SB
   Wake Up Screaming! Amalgamated, 1958 SB
   The Weak and the Strong. Amalgamated,
      1962 SB

KENT, DAVID. Pseudonym of Herman Hoffman
      Birney, 1891-1958. Born in Colo.;
      amateur archaeologist. SC: Jason
      Burr, in both titles.
   Jason Burr's First Case. Random, 1941
   A Knife Is Silent. Random, 1947

KENT, EDWARD
   A Lawful Crime. Leadenhall, 1899

KENT, ELIZABETH. Pseudonym.
   The House Opposite. Putnam (NYC & Lon-
      don), 1902 [NYC]
   Who? Putnam (NYC & London), 1912 [Eng.]

KENT, FORTUNE. Pseudonym of John Toombs.
   The House at Canterbury. PB, 1975
      [Calif.]
   House of Masques. Ballantine, 1975
   The Isle of the Seventh Sentry. PB,
      1974
   The Opal Legacy. Ballantine, 1975
      [Mich.]

KENT, GRAEME. 1933-   .
   Deadly Company. Hale, 1966
   The Foreign Squad. Hale, 1967
   Gypsy's Warning. Hale, 1968
   The Lurking Policeman. Hale, 1969
   -The Monkey Game. Muller, 1964
   Nelson's Blood. Hale, 1966
   Who Needs Enemies? Hale, 1970

KENT, LARRY
   Requiem for a Redhead. Cleveland, 19??

KENT, MARIANNE
   Philip Mordant's Ward. Warne, 1888

KENT, MARTIN
   -The Flying Hooligans. Low, 1936
   The Flying Kidnappers. Low, 1937
   The Hanging Rope. Eldon, 1944
   A Spy for England. Eldon, 1940

KENT, MARY. With Michael Kent, q.v.,
      author of about 1500 ss.

KENT, MICHAEL. See: Mary Kent.
   The Armitage Case, with Mary Kent.
      Crowther, 1943
   Hail, Victor, Hail! Staples, 1946

KENT, NORA. 1899-   . Ref: CA.
   A Hint of Murder. Macdonald, 1967
      [Ire.]

KENT, OLIVER
   -Her Heart's Gift. Dillingham, 1913
   -Her Right Divine. Dillingham, 1913

KENT, SIMON. Pseudonym of Max(well
      Jeffrey) Catto, 1909-   , q.v.
   The Lions at the Kill. Hutchinson, 1959
      [Fr.]

KENT, WILLIS. Pseudonym of Wilson Colli-
      son, 1893-1941, q.v.
   A Woman in Purple Pajamas. McBride,
      1931 [N.Y.]

KENTISH, MRS.
   The Maid of the Village; or, The Far-
      mer's Daughter of the Woodlands.
      Emans, 1835

KENWOOD, CLIVE
   The Film Studio Murder. World's Work,
      1937

KENYON, CAMILLA. 1876-   .
   Dark Harvest. Grayson, 1933

KENYON, CHARLES FREDERICK. 1879-1926.
   Pseudonym: Gerald Cumberland, q.v.

KENYON, LARRY. Pseudonym of Lou Louder-
      back. SC: Don Miles, in all titles.

Challenge at Le Mans. Avon, 1967 [Fr.]
Countdown at Monaco. Avon, 1967 [Fr.]
The Devil's Ring. Avon, 1967
Revenge at Indy. Avon, 1967 [Indianapolis]

KENYON, MICHAEL. 1931-   . Pseudonym: Daniel Forbes. Ref: CA, CC, TC. SC: Supt. O'Malley, in at least those marked S.
Deep Pocket. Collins, 1978. U.S. title: The Molehill File. Coward, 1978
Green Grass. Macmillan (London), 1969
May You Die in Ireland. Collins, 1965; Morrow, 1965 [Ire.]
Mr. Big. Collins, 1975; Coward, 1975, as by Daniel Forbes
The Molehill File; see Deep Pocket
The 100,000 Welcomes. Collins, 1970; Coward, 1970 O [Ire.]
Out of Season. Collins, 1968
The Rapist. Collins, 1977; Coward, 1977, as by Daniel Forbes O [Ire.]
The Shooting of Dan McGrew. Collins, 1972; McKay, 1975 O [Ire.]
A Sorry State. Collins, 1974; McKay, 1974 O [Philip.]
The Trouble with Series Three; see The Whole Hog
The Whole Hog. Collins, 1967. U.S. title: The Trouble with Series Three. Morrow, 1967 [Ill., acad.]

KEPPEL, CHARLOTTE. Pseudonym of Ursula Torday, 1888-   . Other pseudonyms: Paula Allardyce, Charity Blackstock, qqv., Lee Blackstock.
I Could Be Good to You. Hutchinson, 1980; St. Martin's, 1980
Loving Sands, Deadly Sands; see Madam, You Must Die
Madam, You Must Die. Hodder, 1975. U.S. title: Loving Sands, Deadly Sands. Delacorte, 1974 [1798, Eng.]
My Name Is Clary Brown; see When I Say Goodbye, I'm Clary Brown
The Villains. Piatkus, 1980
When I Say Goodbye, I'm Clary Brown. Hodder, 1977. U.S. title: My Name Is Clary Brown. Random, 1976 [Eng., 1700s]

KER, ANNE
Adeline Saint Julian; or, The Midnight Hour. Kerby, 1800 [1632]
Edric the Forester; or, The Mysteries of the Haunted Chamber. Clements, 1844 [1066]

KERKOW, HERBERT. Pseudonym of Val Lewton.
The Fateful Star Murder. Mohawk, 1931

KERNAHAN, (JOHN) COULSON. 1858-1943.
The Apples of Sin. Ward, 1898; Page, 1901 (Taken from A Book of Strange Sins, q.v.)
A Book of Strange Sins. Ward, 1893; Altemus, 1895 ss
Captain Shannon. Ward, 1897; Dodd, 1896
-A Dead Man's Diary. Ward, 1890; Ogilvie, 1905
The Dumpling: A Detective Love Story of a Great Labour Rising. Cassell, 1906; Dodge, 1907
The Jackal. Ward, 1905
-The Lonely God. Ward, 1897; Page, 1901 ss
-The Man of No Sorrows. Cassell (London), 1911; Cassell (NYC), 1912
Scoundrels & Co. Ward, 1901; Stone, 1899
A Strange Sin. Ward, 1898; Page, 1901 (Taken from A Book of Strange Sins, q.v.)

KERNAHAN, MRS. COULSON [MARY JANE HICKLING GWYNNE KERNAHAN]. 1857-   .
The Affair of Maltravers. Mellifont, 1949
-An Artist's Model. White, 1906
The Avenging of Ruthanna. Long, 1900
-A Beautiful Savage. White, 1904
The Blue Diamond. Everett, 1914
A Case for the Courts. White, 1907
-The Chance Child. Everett, 1914
-Devastation. Long, 1904
The Disappearance of the Duke. White, 1907
-A Fair Sinner. Everett, 1913
The Fate of Felix. Long, 1905
-Frank Redland, Recruit. Long, 1899
The Fraud. Hodder, 1907
-The Gate of Sinners. Everett, 1908
The Go-Between. Everett, 1912
The Graven Image. Milne, 1909
-The Hired Girl. Everett, 1912
-The House of Blight. Everett, 1912
The Mummy's Hand. Mellifont, 1937
The Mystery of Magdalen. Long, 1906
The Mystery of Mere Hall. Everett, 1912
-No Vindication. Long, 1901

-Quixote of Magdalen. Everett, 1909
-The Sinnings of Seraphine. Long, 1906
-The Soul of Phyllis Fabian. Mellifont, 1935
The Stolen Man. Everett, 1915
The Temptation of Gideon Holt. Epworth, 1923
-The Thirteenth Man. Everett, 1910; Dillingham, 1910
The Trap. Everett, 1917
-Trewinnot of Guy's. Long, 1898
-Two Legacies. Ward, 1886
-Under Seal of the Confessional. Everett, 1910
-An Unwise Virgin. Long, 1903
-The Vagrant Bride. Everett, 1911
A Village Mystery. White, 1905
-The Whip of the Will. Epworth, 1927
-The Whisperer. White, 1905
-The Wireless Call. Epworth, 1930
-The Woman Who Understood. Everett, 1916

KERNER, BEN. See: Tom Van Dycke.

KERR, BEN. Pseudonym of William (Thomas) Ard, 1922-1960. Other pseudonyms: Mike Moran, Thomas Wills, qq.v.
The Blonde and Johnny Malloy. Popular Library, 1958
Club 17. Popular Library, 1957
Damned If He Does. Popular Library, 1956 [Fla.]
Down I Go. Popular Library, 1955
I Fear You Not. Popular Library, 1956; Digit, 1960
Shakedown. Holt, 1952 [Fla.]

KERR, CAROLE. Pseudonym of Margaret Carr, 1935-   , q.v. Other pseudonym: Martin Carroll, q.v.
Shadow of the Hunter. Hale, 1975

KERR, ELIZA
The Mystery of Grange Drayton. Wesleyan Methodist, 1884
The Secret of Ashton Manor House. Wesleyan Methodist, 1884

KERR, GEOFFREY. 1895-   .
Under the Influence. Joseph, 1953; Lippincott, 1954

KERR, JAMES. 1923-   .
Emergency Room. Delacorte, 1975 [L.A., hosp.]

KERR, MICHAEL
Benjamin Seven. Secker, 1975

KERR, MICHAEL. Pseudonym of Robert Hoskins, 1933-   , q.v. Other pseudonyms: Grace Corren, Susan Jennifer, qq.v.
The Gemini Run. Charter, 1979

KERR, ORPHEUS C. Pseudonym of Robert Henry Newell, 1836-1901.
The Cloven Foot: Being an Adaptation of the English Novel, "The Mystery of Edwin Drood". Carleton, 1870. British title: The Mystery of Mr. E. Drood. Hotten, 1871

KERR, ROBERT. Pseudonym. 1899-   . Ref: CA.
The Stuart Legacy. Stein, 1973 [Scot., 1800s]

KERR, SOPHIE. 1880-1965.
-The Blue Envelope. Doubleday, 1917; Wayfarer's Library, 1919
-The Man Who Knew the Date. Rinehart, 1951; Allen, 1952

KERRIGAN, JOHN
The Phoenix Assault. Arrow, 1980; Signet, 1980 [Berlin, 1945]

KERRIGAN, M.
Once Upon a Crime. Milestone, 1953
Suddenly a Shroud. Milestone, 1954

KERSEY, JOHN. Pseudonym of Thurman Warriner, q.v. Other pseudonym: Simon Troy, q.v.
Night of the Wolf. Cassell, 1968

KERSH, GERALD. 1911-1968. Ref: CA, CC, EM, TC.
-The Angel and the Cuckoo. Heinemann, 1967; NAL, 1966
-An Ape, a Dog and a Serpent. Heinemann, 1945
-Battle of the Singing Men. Everybody's, 1944 ss
-Brain and Ten Fingers. Heinemann, 1943
-The Brazen Bull. Heinemann, 1952
-The Brighton Monster and others. Heinemann, 1953 ss
-Brock. Heinemann, 1969
-Clean, Bright and Slightly Oiled. Heinemann, 1946 ss

-Clock Without Hands. Heinemann, 1949
-The Great Wash. Heinemann, 1953. U.S. title: The Secret Masters. Ballantine, 1953
-Guttersnipe. Heinemann, 1954 ss
-The Horrible Dummy and other stories. Heinemann, 1944 ss
-The Hospitality of Miss Tolliver and other stories. Heinemann, 1965 ss
-The Implacable Hunter. Heinemann, 1961
-Jews Without Jehovah. Wishart, 1934
-A Long Cool Day in Hell. Heinemann, 1965
-Men Without Bones and other stories. Heinemann, 1955; Paperback Library, 1962 (British edition has 22 ss; U.S. edition has 13.)
-More Than Once Upon a Time. Heinemann, 1964 ss
-Neither Man Nor Dog. Heinemann, 1946 ss
Night and the City. Joseph, 1938; Simon, 1946
-Nightshade & Damnations. Coronet, 1969; GM, 1968 ss
Prelude to a Certain Midnight. Heinemann, 1947; Doubleday, 1947
-Sad Road to the Sea. Heinemann, 1947
The Secret Masters; see The Great Wash
-The Song of the Flea. Heinemann, 1948; Doubleday, 1948
-The Terribly Wild Flowers. Heinemann, 1962
-The Ugly Face of Love and other stories. Heinemann, 1960 ss

KERSHAW, JOHN. 1931-   .
Death by Arrangement. Hale, 1976
A Meeting in Casa. Hale, 1973

KESSEL, JOSEPH (ELIE). 1898-1979. Ref: CA.
The Bernan Affair. St. Martin's, 1965 (Translation of "L'Affaire Bernan." Paris, 1960.) [Paris, 1921]

KESSELRING, JOSEPH (OTTO). 1902-1967.
Arsenic and Old Lace. Random, 1941; English Theatre Guild, 1948 (Play.)

KETCHUM, PHILIP. 1902-   . Born and educated in Colo.; in social work for 10 years before turning to writing and moving to Calif.
Death at Dusk. Phoenix, 1938. Also published as: Kill at Dusk. Red Dagger, 1946
Death in the Library. Crowell, 1937
Death in the Night. Phoenix, 1939. Also published as: Good Night for Murder. Dagger House, 1946
Good Night for Murder; see Death in the Night
Kill at Dusk; see Death at Dusk
-The Stalkers. Berkley, 1961

KETTERER, BERNADINE
The Manderley Mystery. Eldon, 1937

KETTERING, RALPH T.
The Clutching Claw. Dramatists, 1938 (3-act play.)

KEVERN, BARBARA. Pseudonym of Donald Lee Shepherd, 1932-   . Ref: CA.
Dark Eden. PB, 1973 [Va.]
Darkness Falling. Pinnacle, 1974 [Wash.]
The Devil's Vineyard. Pinnacle, 1975
The Key. Beagle, 1974 [Wash.]

KEVERNE, RICHARD. Pseudonym of Clifford (James Wheeler) Hosken, 1882-1950, q.v. SC: Simon Artifex = SA; Insp. Mace = M; Franklin Parry and Leonard Harris = P&H. Set: Eng.
Artifex Intervenes. Constable, 1934 (3 novelets.) SA
At the Blue Gates. Constable, 1932; Doubleday, 1932
The Black Cripple. Collins, 1941
Carteret's Cure. Constable, 1926; Houghton, 1926
Coroner's Verdict: Accident; see The Lady in No. 4
Crook Stuff. Constable, 1935 ss, 3 with SA
Crooks and Vagabonds. Collins, 1941 ss
The Fleet Hall Inheritance. Constable, 1931; Harper, 1931
The Havering Plot. Constable, 1928; Harper, 1929
He Laughed at Murder. Constable, 1934; Holt, 1935
The Lady in No. 4. Collins, 1944. U.S. title: Coroner's Verdict: Accident. McKay, 1945
The Man in the Red Hat. Constable, 1930; Harper, 1930
Menace. Constable, 1933 P&H
More Crook Stuff. Constable, 1938 ss, one with SA
Open Verdict. Constable, 1940 M

The Sanfield Scandal. Constable, 1929; Harper, 1929
The Strange Case of William Cook; see William Cook—Antique Dealer
White Gas. Constable, 1937 M
William Cook—Antique Dealer. Constable, 1928. U.S. title: The Strange Case of William Cook. Harper, 1928 P&H

KEY, SEAN A.
The Mark of Cain. Dell, 1980 [Carib.]

KEY, (SAM)UEL (WHITTELL). 1874-   . SC: Prof. Arnold Rhymer, in both titles.
The Broken Fang. Hodder, 1920 ss
Yellow Death. Books Limited, 1921

KEYES, FRANCES PARKINSON. 1885-1970. Ref: CA.
Dinner at Antoine's. Messner, 1948; Eyre, 1949
The Gold Slippers; see Victorine
The Letter from Spain; see Station Wagon in Spain
The Royal Box. Messner, 1954; Eyre, 1954
Station Wagon in Spain. Farrar, 1959. British title: The Letter from Spain. Eyre, 1959 [Sp.]
Victorine. Messner, 1958. British title: The Gold Slippers. Eyre, 1958

KEYES, MICHAEL
The Dead Parrot. Doubleday, 1933. British title: The Murder Cruise. Harrap, 1934 [ship]

KEYNES, HELEN M(ARY). 1892-   . Pseudonym: Clementine Hunter, q.v.
Murder in Rosemary Lane. Melrose, 1936
Who Killed Jefferson Broome? Melrose, 1937

KEYSTONE, OLIVER. Pseudonym of James M. Mantinband. SC: Paul Plush, in all titles.
Arsenic for the Teacher. Phoenix, 1950 [NYC]
Deep As the Grave. Phoenix, 1950
Major Crime. Phoenix, 1948 [Ger.]

KEYWORTH, HENRY
The Black Market Murders. Kangaroo, 1944
Death in Gelly Wood. Kangaroo, 1944
Death in the Signal Box. Kangaroo, 1946
Killer by Night. Kangaroo, 1944

KEZER, GLENN
The Queen Is Dead. Jove, 1979

KIDDE, JANET. Pseudonym of George Volk.
The Prophetess. Jove, 1978 [NYC]

KIDDY, MAURICE G(EORGE). 1894-   . SC: Stonewall Steevens, in at least those marked SS. Set: Eng.
The Devil's Dagger. Hutchinson, 1928 [Russ.]
The House of Faith. Hutchinson, 1928
The Jade Hatpin. Hutchinson, 1933 SS
Killing No Murder. Hutchinson, 1931 SS
The Orange Ray. Hutchinson, 1934
Stonewall Steevens Investigates. Hutchinson, 1933 SS
-The Watcher in the Wood. Hutchinson, 1929

KIEFER, WARREN (DAVID). 1929-   . Ref: CA.
The Kidnappers. Harper, 1977 [Arg.]
The Lingala Code. Random, 1972 [Bel. Congo]
The Pontius Pilate Papers. Harper, 1976; H. Hamilton, 1976

KIELLAND, AXEL (ZETLITZ). 1907-   .
Dangerous Honeymoon. Collins, 1946; Little, 1946 (Translation of "Farlig Smekmanad." Stockholm, 1945.) [Ger.]
Live Dangerously. Collins, 1944. U.S. title: Shape of Danger. Little, 1945 (Translation of "Lev Farligt." Stockholm, 1943.) [Nor.]
Shape of Danger; see Live Dangerously

KIELY, BENEDICT. 1919-   . Ref: CA.
-The Cards of the Gambler. Methuen, 1953

KIENZLE, WILLIAM X(AVIER). 1928-   .
Ref: CA. SC: Father Bob Koesler, in both titles, both set in Det.
Death Wears a Red Hat. Andrews, 1980; Hodder, 1981
The Rosary Murders. Andrews, 1979; Hodder, 1979

KIERAN, JAMES
Come Murder Me. GM, 1951 [NYC]

KIESCHNER, SIDNEY. 1906-   . Pseudonym: Sidney Kingsley, q.v.

KILGORE, AXEL. SC: Hank Frost (The Mercenary), in all titles.
Fourth Reich Death Squad. Zebra, 1980
The Killer Genesis. Zebra, 1980 (Cent. Am.)
The Slaughter Run. Zebra, 1980 (Cent. Am.)

KILGORE, JOHN. Pseudonym of Lauran Bosworth Paine, 1916-   . Other pseudonyms: John Armour, Reg Batchelor, Kenneth Bedford, Frank Bosworth, Mark Carrel, Robert Clarke, Richard Dana, J. F. Drexler, Troy Howard, Jared Ingersol, Hunter Liggett, J. K. Lucas, John Morgan, qq.v.
Murder to Music. Hale, 1972
Some Die Young. Hale, 1970

KILLICK, BRIAN
The Camelot Club. H. Hamilton, 1977

KILLORAN, GERALDINE
The Stones of Strendleigh. Ace, 1974
Willough Haven. Ace, 1976 [Ariz.]

KILLOUGH, (KAREN) LEE. 1942-   . Ref: CA.
The Doppelganger Gambit. Ballantine, 1979 [future]

KILPATRICK, FLORENCE. SC: Elizabeth, in both titles.
Elizabeth Finds the Body. Jenkins, 1949
Elizabeth the Sleuth. Jenkins, 1946

KILPATRICK, SARAH
Wake All the Dead. Doubleday, 1970; White Lion, 1974 [Eng.]

KILVINGTON, EDWIN. SC: Crispin Quane, in both titles. Set: Eng.
Mystery in Glass. Houghton (London), 1931
Window in the Dark. Houghton (London), 1932

KIM, DON 'O
Password. Angus, 1975

KIMBERLEY, HUGH
Wreath for a Dead Angel. Clerke, 1951

KIMBRO, JEAN. Pseudonym of John M. Kimbro, 1929-   . Other pseudonyms: Kym Allyson, Ann Ashton, Charlotte Bramwell, Kathryn Kimbrough, qq.v.
Twilight Return. Ballantine, 1976 [Fr.]

KIMBRO, JOHN M. 1929-   . Pseudonyms: Kym Allyson, Ann Ashton, Charlotte Bramwell, Jean Kimbro, Kathryn Kimbrough, qq.v.

KIMBROUGH, KATHRYN. Pseudonym of John M. Kimbro, 1929-   . Other pseudonyms: Kym Allyson, Ann Ashton, Charlotte Bramwell, Jean Kimbro, qq.v. S: Phenwick Women = P.
Ann, the Gentle. Popular Library, 1978 P
Augusta, the First. Popular Library, 1975 P [Maine, 1742]
Augusta, the Second. Popular Library, 1979 P
Barbara, the Valiant. Popular Library, 1977 P
The Broken Sphinx. Popular Library, 1972
Carol, the Pursued. Popular Library, 1979 P
The Children of Houndstooth. Popular Library, 1972
Dorothy, the Terrified. Popular Library, 1977 P [South, 1863]
Evelyn, the Ambitious. Popular Library, 1978 P
Harriet, the Haunted. Popular Library, 1976 P
The Heiress to Wolfskill. Popular Library, 1973
The House on Windswept Ridge. Popular Library, 1971; Sphere, 1973
Ilene, the Superstitious. Popular Library, 1977 P
Isabelle, the Frantic. Popular Library, 1978 P
Jane, the Courageous. Popular Library, 1975 P [1771, Maine]
Johanna, the Unpredictable. Popular Library, 1976 P [Eng., 1834]
Joyce, the Beloved. Popular Library, 1979 P
Kate, the Curious. Popular Library, 1976 P
Kathrine, the Returned. Popular Library, 1980 P [Boston, 1900]
Louise, the Restless. Popular Library, 1978 P
Marcia, the Innocent. Popular Library, 1976 P [Eng., 1845]
Margaret, the Faithful. Popular Library, 1975 P [1783, Maine]
Millijoy, the Determined. Popular Library, 1977 P
Nancy, the Daring. Popular Library, 1976 P
Nellie, the Obvious. Popular Library, 1978 P
Olga, the Disillusioned. Popular Library, 1980 P
Ophelia, the Anxious. Popular Library, 1977 P
Patricia, the Beautiful. Popular Library, 1975 P
Peggy, the Concerned. Popular Library, 1980 P
The Phantom Flame of Wind House. Popular Library, 1973
Phyllis, the Cautious. Popular Library, 1980 P
Polly, the Worried. Popular Library, 1979 P
Rachel, the Possessed. Popular Library, 1975 P
Rebecca, the Mysterious. Popular Library, 1975 [1822, Mass.] P
Ruth, the Unsuspecting. Popular Library, 1977 P
The Shadow over Pleasant Heath. Popular Library, 1974 [Eng.]
A Shriek in the Midnight Tower. Popular Library, 1975 [La.]
The Spectre of Dolphin Cove. Popular Library, 1973 [N.C.]
Susannah, the Righteous. Popular Library, 1975 P
Thanesworth House. Popular Library, 1972 [Miss, 1800s]
The Three Sisters of Briarwick. Popular Library, 1973
The Twisted Cameo. Popular Library, 1971; Sphere, 1973 [Denver]
Unseen Torment. Popular Library, 1974 [Colo.]
Ursala, the Proud. Popular Library, 1980 P
Yvonne, the Confident. Popular Library, 1979 P

KIMMINS, ANTHONY (MARTIN). 1901-1964.
Lugs O'Leary. Heinemann, 1960

KINDER, KATHLEEN [KATHLEEN JILL KINDER POTTER]. 1932-   . Ref: CA.
The Raven and the Dove. Collins, 1979; St. Martin's, 1980 [Eng., 1876]

KINDON, THOMAS. Ref: CC.
Murder in the Moor. Methuen, 1929; Dutton, 1929

KING, ALBERT. 1924-   . Pseudonym: Paul Muller, q.v.

KING, ALFRED FITZMAURICE. Pseudonym of Frederick Langbridge.
The Clerical Cracksman. Simpkin, 1889

KING, ALICE. 1839-1894.
A Strange Tangle. Maxwell, 1888

KING, ALISON. Pseudonym of Teri Martini, 1930-   . Ref: CA.
The Dreamer, Lost in Terror. Popular Library, 1976 [Eng.]

KING, (WILLIAM BENJAMIN) BASIL. 1859-1928.
The Break of Day. Harper, 1930

KING, BRADLEY. See: Talbot Mundy.

KING, BRUCE.   -1976. Pseudonym: Zolar, q.v.

KING, C(HARLES) DALY. 1895-1963. Ref: CC, EM, MC, TC. SC: Michael Lord = ML; Dr. L. Rees Pons = LP.
Arrogant Alibi. Appleton, 1939; Collins, 1938 ML,LP [Conn.]
Bermuda Burial. Funk, 1941; Collins, 1940 ML [Bermuda]
Careless Corpse. Collins, 1937 ML,LP [N.Y.]
The Curious Mr. Tarrant. Dover, 1977; Collins, 1935 ss
Obelists at Sea. Knopf, 1933; Heritage, 1932 LP [ship]
Obelists en Route. Collins, 1934 ML,LP [train]
Obelists Fly High. H. Smith, 1935; Collins, 1935 ML,LP [air.]

KING, CHRISTOPHER
-Operation Mora. Hale, 1974

KING, (JAMES) CLIFFORD. 1914-   . Pseudonym: Pete Fry, q.v.
Bitter Springs. Convoy, 1950 (Novelization of the movie.)

End in Sight. Hutchinson, 1956
A Place to Hide. Hart-Davis, 1951
Two Shadows Pass. Hart-Davis, 1952

KING, FRANCIS (HENRY). 1923-   . Ref: CA.
-An Air That Kills. Home, 1948
-The Brighton Belle and other stories. Longmans, 1968 ss
-The Custom House. Longmans, 1961; Doubleday, 1962 [Jap.]
-A Domestic Animal. Longmans, 1969
-The Japanese Umbrella and other stories. Longmans, 1964 ss
-The Last of the Pleasure Gardens. Longmans, 1965
The Needle. Hutchinson, 1975; Mason/Charter, 1976
-Never Again. Home, 1947
-So Hurt and Humiliated and other stories. Longmans, 1959 ss
-To the Dark Tower. Home, 1946
-The Waves Behind the Boat. Longmans, 1967
-The Widow. Longmans, 1957

KING, FRANK. 1892-1958. Pseudonym: Clive Conrad, q.v. SC: The Dormouse, in at least those marked D; Dr. Frank King, in at least those marked FK; Insp./Supt. Gloom, in at least those marked G; Clarence Knight, in at least those marked CK. Set: Eng.
The Big Blackmail. Hale, 1954 D
Candidates for Murder. Hale, 1945
The Case of the Frightened Brother. Hale, 1959 D
The Case of the Painted Girl. Jarrolds, 1931 G
The Case of the Strange Beauties. Hale, 1952 D
The Case of the Vanishing Artist. Hale, 1956 G
The Catastrophe Club. Hale, 1947 D
Crooks' Caravan. Hale, 1955 D
Crooks' Cross. Hale, 1943 D [Ger.]
Death Changes His Mind. Hale, 1953 FK
Death Has a Double. Hale, 1955 FK
Death of a Cloven Hoof. Hale, 1951 FK
Death of a Halo. Hale, 1950 FK
Dictator of Death. Jarrolds, 1935
The Dormouse Has Nine Lives. Hale, 1938 D
The Dormouse—Peacemaker. Hale, 1938 D
The Dormouse—Undertaker. Hale, 1937 D
Dough for the Dormouse. Hale, 1939 D
The Empty Flat. Hale, 1957 D
Enter the Dormouse. Hale, 1936 D
Gestapo Dormouse. Hale, 1944 D
The Ghoul. Bles, 1928; Watt, 1929 CK
Green Gold. Jarrolds, 1933 G
Greenface. Jarrolds, 1929 CK
The House of Sleep. Jarrolds, 1934
The Midnight Sleep. Hale, 1941
Molly on the Spot. Hale, 1940 ss
Mr. Balkram's Band. Jarrolds, 1934
Night at Krumlin Castle. Jarrolds, 1932
Only Half the Doctor Died. Hale, 1954
Operation Halter. Hale, 1948 D
Operation Honeymoon. Hale, 1950 D
The Owl. Jarrolds, 1930; Watt, 1930 CK
Sinister Light. Hale, 1946 D
The Smiling Mask. Jarrolds, 1935
Terror at Staups House. Bles, 1927; Watt, 1929
That Charming Crook. Hale, 1958 D
They Vanish at Night. Hale, 1941 D
This Doll Is Dangerous. Hale, 1940 D
The Two Who Talked. Hale, 1958 D
What Price Doubloons? Hale, 1942 D

KING, FRANK(LIN). 1936- .
Down and Dirty. Marek, 1978 [NYC]
Night Vision. Marek, 1979; Sphere, 1980 [NYC]
Raya. Marek, 1980 [Cairo, 1942]

KING, GRAHAM. 1930-   . TV writer, poet and song writer in London.
Killtest. Arrow, 1978; St. Martin's, 1978

KING, HAROLD. 1945-   . Ref: CA.
Closing Ceremonies. Coward, 1979; Piatkus, 1980
Four Days. Bobbs, 1976; Sphere, 1977 [U.S., 1953]
Paradigm Red. Bobbs, 1975; Sphere, 1978. Also published as: Red Alert. PB, 1977 [N. Mex.]
Red Alert; see Paradigm Red
The Taskmaster. Coward, 1977; Sphere, 1979

KING, HILARY. Pseudonym of James Grierson Dickson. All titles below feature Sexton Blake and were published by Amalgamated Press.
The Big Circus Mystery. 1953
The Crime at the Fair. 1953
The Man from Dieppe. 1952
The Mystery of the Lost Loot. 1951
On the 11:40 Down. 1951
Partners in Crime. 1951

KING, IRENE, 1943-   , and CARYL THURMAN, 1938-   .
She's a Cop, Ain't She?, with W. Ware Lynch. Dial, 1975 [NYC]

KING, LOUIS
Cornered. Ace, 1958

KING, LOUISE W(OOSTER). Ref: CA.
The Rochemer Hag. Doubleday, 1967 [Eng., 1800s]

KING, O. B.
Five Million in Cash. Doubleday, 1932; Jarrolds, 1933 [NYC]

KING, PHILIP. 1904-   . See also: (Thomas) Falkland L(itton) Cary.
Dark Lucy, with Parnell Bradbury, 1904-   . French (London), 1971 (3-act play.)
Elementary, My Dear, with (Bertram) John Boland, 1913-1976, q.v. French (London), 1975 (Play.)
"How Are You, Johnnie?" French (London), 1963 (3-act play.)
Murder in Company, with (Bertram) John Boland, 1913-1976, q.v. French (London), 1973 (Play.)
Who Says Murder?, with (Bertram) John Boland, 1913-1976, q.v. French (London), 1975 (Play.)

KING, R(ICHARD) ASHE. 1839-1932.
-Love's Legacy. Ward, 1890

KING, R. RALEIGH
-The Clever Ones. Palmer, 1932
Gilbert the Ghost. Palmer, 1930
Joan in Jeopardy. Palmer, 1929

KING, RUFUS (FREDERICK). 1893-1966. Ref: CC, EM, MP, TC. SC: Stuff Driscoll = SD; Lt. Valcour = V.
The Case of the Constant God. Doubleday, 1936; Methuen, 1938 V [N.Y.]
The Case of the Dowager's Etchings. Doubleday, 1944; Methuen, 1946. Also published as: Never Walk Alone. Popular Library, 1951
The Case of the Redoubled Cross. Doubleday, 1949 [Fla.]
Crime of Violence. Doubleday, 1937; Methuen, 1938 V [NYC]
The Deadly Dove. Doubleday, 1945 [N.Y.]
Design in Evil. Doubleday, 1942 [ship]
Diagnosis: Murder. Doubleday, 1941; Methuen, 1942 ss [Ohio]
Duenna to a Murder. Doubleday, 1951; Methuen, 1951 [S.C.]
The Faces of Danger. Doubleday, 1964 ss SD [Fla.]
The Fatal Kiss Mystery. Doubleday, 1928 [N.Y.]
Holiday Homicide. Doubleday, 1940; Methuen, 1941 [NYC]
I Want a Policeman!, with Milton Lazarus. Dramatists, 1937 (2-act play.)
Invitation to a Murder. French (NYC), 1934 (3-act play.)
The Lesser Antilles Case. Doubleday, 1934. Also published as: Murder Challenges Valcour. Dell, 1944 V [ship]
Lethal Lady. Doubleday, 1947 [New Eng.]
Malice in Wonderland. Doubleday, 1958 ss SD [Fla.]
Murder by Latitude. Doubleday, 1930; Heinemann, 1931 V [ship]
Murder by the Clock. Doubleday, 1929; Chapman, 1929 V [NYC]
Murder Challenges Valcour; see The Lesser Antilles Case
Murder DeLuxe; see Mystery DeLuxe
Murder in the Willett Family. Doubleday, 1931 V [N.Y.]
Murder Masks Miami. Doubleday, 1939; Methuen, 1939 V [Miami]
Murder on the Yacht. Doubleday, 1932; H. Hamilton, 1932 V [ship]
A Murderer in This House; see Somewhere in This House
Museum Piece No. 13. Doubleday, 1946. Also published as: Secret Beyond the Door. Triangle, 1947
Mystery DeLuxe. Doran, 1927. British title: Murder DeLuxe. Parsons, 1927 [ship]
Never Walk Alone; see The Case of the Dowager's Etchings
Profile of a Murder. Harcourt, 1935 V [N.Y.]
Secret Beyond the Door; see Museum Piece No. 13
Somewhere in This House. Doubleday, 1930. British title: A Woman Is Dead. Chapman, 1929. Also published as: A Murderer in This House. Detective Novel Classic, 1945, abridged V [N.Y.]
The Steps to Murder. Doubleday, 1960 ss SD
Valcour Meets Murder. Doubleday, 1932 V [N.Y.]
A Variety of Weapons. Doubleday, 1943 [N.Y.]
A Woman Is Dead; see Somewhere in This House

KING, SHERRY. See: (Raymond) Sherwood King, 1904-   .

KING, (RAYMOND) SHERWOOD. 1904-   . Born in Yonkers, N.Y.; graduate of Marquette U.; in advertising and sales work, a newspaper contributor in Chicago.
Between Murders. Appleton, 1935, as by Sherry King. British title: Death Carries a Cane. Cherry Tree, 1941 [Chi.]
Death Carries a Cane; see Between Murders
If I Die Before I Wake. Simon, 1938; World's Work, 1938. Also published as: The Lady from Shanghai. World's Work, 1947 [L.I.]
The Lady from Shanghai; see If I Die Before I Wake

KING, STEPHEN. 1947-   . Ref: CA.
The Dead Zone. Viking, 1979; Macdonald, 1979
-Firestarter. Phantasia, 1980; Macdonald, 1980

KING, T. STANLEYAN. SC: Dixon Brett, in at least those marked DB; Scarsdale Waring, in at least those marked SW.
Black Magic. Mellifont, 1934 SW
The Call of Death. Mellifont, 1934 SW
The Fatal Image. Mellifont, 1940
The Headless Ghost. Mellifont, 1932
The Kidnapped Prince. Mellifont, 1932
The Missing Mayor. Aldine, 1926 DB
The Monk's Croft Mystery. Mellifont, 1933
The Motor Horn Mystery. Mellifont, 1932
The Mummy's Curse. Mellifont, 1933
Slayer of Souls. Mellifont, 1932
Vampire City. Mellifont, 1935 SW
Viola's Dilemma. Mellifont, 1932
Who Killed Stephen Tennant? Aldine, 1926
The Yellow Wolf. Aldine, 1926 DB

KING, TERRY JOHNSON. 1929-1978. Ref: CA.
The Neutron Beam Murder. Abelard (NYC & London), 1965
The Noose of Red Beads. Abelard (NYC), 1968; Abelard (London), 1969 [Miami, Bahamas]

KING, THOROLD. Pseudonym of Charles Gatchell, 1851-1910.
Hashish. McClurg, 1886

KING, W. SCOTT. Pseudonym of William Kingscote Greenland.
Behind the Granite Gateway. Hodder, 1902
-Hidden Paths. Epworth, 1920

KINGERY, DON
Death Must Wait. GM, 1956
-Paula. Dell, 1959
-Swamp Fire. Popular Library, 1957

KINGSBURY, MYRA
Beware the Bog. Ballantine, 1975 [Eng.]
Island of Fog. Ballantine, 1974 [Md.]

KINGSCOTE, ADELINE GEORGINA ISABELLA WOLFF.   -1908. Pseudonym: Lucas Cleeve, q.v.

KINGSLEY, BETTINA. Pseudonym of Barry Jay Kaplan.
The Black Angel. PB, 1974 [1933, Cape Cod]
Blind Chance. Dell, 1974 [Fla.]
The Captive. Dell, 1974
Darwick Castle. Dell, 1974
Daughter of Mars. Berkely, 1977
The House on the Drive. Dell, 1975; New English Library pb, 1977
Mistress of Destiny. Dell, 1974
Stages of Terror. Popular Library, 1972
The Stand In. Dell, 1973

KINGSLEY, GERRY
The Cat and the Canary. Sphere, 1977; Dale, 1978 (Novelization of the movie.)

KINGSLEY, MICHAEL J. 1917?-1972. Ref: CA.
Black Man, White Man, Dead Man. Random, 1970 [Ky.]
Branches of Evil; see Shadow over Elveron

Shadow over Elveron. Random, 1963. Also published as: Branches of Evil. Macfadden, 1964 [Ind.]

KINGSLEY, SIDNEY. Pseudonym of Sidney Kieschner, 1906-   . Ref: CA.
 Darkness at Noon. Random, 1951 (3-act play based on the novel by Arthur Koestler, 1905-   , q.v.)
 Dead End. Random, 1936 (3-act play.)
 Detective Story. Random, 1949 (3-act play.) [NYC]

KINGSLEY-SMITH, TERENCE. 1940-   . Ref: CA.
 The Forsaken. PB, 1975 [Kan., 1930s]

KINGSTON, CHARLES. Pseudonym of Charles Kingston O'Mahoney. SC: Insp. Wake, in at least those marked W. Set: Eng.
 The Brighton Beach Mystery. Ward, 1936 W
 Burning Conscience. Ward, 1938
 The Circle of Guilt. Ward, 1937 W
 Death Came Back. Paul, 1944 W
 The Delacott Mystery. Ward, 1941
 Fear Followed On. Paul, 1945 W
 The Great London Mystery. Lane, 1931
 The Guilty House. Lane, 1928; Dutton, 1929
 The Highgate Mystery. Lane, 1928
 I Accuse. Mellifont, 1939
 The Infallible System. Lane, 1929 [Fr.]
 A Miscarriage of Justice. Paul, 1925
 Murder in Disguise. Ward, 1938 W
 Murder in Piccadilly. Ward, 1936 W
 Murder Tunes In. Ward, 1942
 Mystery in the Mist. Ward, 1942
 Poison in Kensington. Ward, 1934
 The Portland Place Mystery. Paul, 1925
 The Rigdale Puzzle. Ward, 1937 W
 The Secret Barrier. Ward, 1939
 The Shadow of Monte Carlo and other stories. Richards, 1931 ss [Fr.]
 Six Under Suspicion. Ward, 1940
 Slander Villa. Ward, 1939
 -Stolen Virtue. Paul, 1921
 -Vain Pride. Ward, 1941

KINGSTON, KEEDY
 The Great Pimlico Mystery. Diprose, 1896

KINLAY, ALVIN
 Killers Cannot Live. Micron, 1961 [S.F.]

KINNELL, GALWAY. 1927-   . Ref: CA.
 Black Light. Houghton, 1966; Hart-Davis, 1967

KINNEY, JAMIE. Joint pseudonym with Stephen Soitos: Andre Sax, q.v.

KINNEY, THOMAS. Pseudonym of Curtis Thomas.
 Devil Take the Foremost. Doubleday, 1947 [N.Y.]

KINSBURN, EMART. Pseudonym of Arthur P(reston) Hankins, 1880-1932, q.v.
 Tong Men and a Million. Chelsea, 1927 [S.F.]
 The Wizard's Spyglass. Chelsea, 1926 [Calif.]

KINSLEY, PETER. English newspaperman.
 Pimpernel 60. Joseph, 1968; Dutton, 1968 [Alb.]
 The Vatchman Switch. Hale, 1980

KIPLEY, JOSEPH
 The Ice Pond Mystery. Laird, 1889

KIPPAX, PETER
 Goring's First Case. Joseph, 1936

KIRBY, ARTHUR. Pseudonym of Arthur (George) MacLean, q.v. Both titles below feature Sexton Blake and were published by Amalgamated Press.
 High Summer Homicide. 1962
 Man on the Run! 1960

KIRBY, DALLAS. SC: Victor Garrison, in at least those marked VG.
 Carnival of Death. Swan, 1942 [U.S.]
 Death at My Heels. Swan, 1942 [Calif.]
 Death Man. Swan, 1943 [U.S.]
 Victor. Swan, 1942 VG [Fr.]
 Victor Versus Verhasst. Swan, 1943 VG

KIRBY, R.
 East Side Assignment. Hamilton Stafford, 1950
 Newshound's Nemesis. Hamilton Stafford, 1949
 Why Call It Homicide? Hamilton Stafford, 1950

KIRCHHEIMER, GLORIA. Joint pseudonym with Rebecca Kavalier and Louise DeCormier: Sara Cardiff, q.v.

KIRK, LAURENCE. Pseudonym of Eric Andrew Simson, 1895-   .
 -Dangerous Cross-Roads. Hutchinson, 1928
 The Farm at Paranao; see The Farm at Sante Fe
 The Farm at Sante Fe. Heinemann, 1935. U.S. title: The Farm at Paranao. Doubleday, 1935 [Brazil]
 -Flight Errant. Hutchinson, 1929
 -The Gale of the World. Cassell, 1948
 -Halfway to Paradise. Blackwood, 1951
 -Matrimonial Causes. Cassell, 1949 ss
 Mushrooms on Toast. Heinemannn, 1938 ss, some criminous
 -One More River. Hutchinson, 1929
 -Red Herrings Ltd. Cassell, 1940
 Rings on Her Finger. Heinemann, 1936; Doubleday, 1936
 -Treasure on Earth. Heinemann, 1937
 Whispering Tongues. Heinemann, 1934; Doubleday, 1934

KIRK, LYDIA. ca.1898-   . Wife of Adm. Alan G. Kirk, U.S. Ambassador to Belgium, Soviet Union, and Nationalist China; living in NYC ca.1970.
 The Cuernavaca Question. Doubleday, 1974 [Mex.]
 The Embassy Madonna. Doubleday, 1971 [Belg.]
 The Man on the Raffles Verandah. Doubleday, 1969 [Sing.]

KIRK, MICHAEL. Pseudonym of Bill Knox, 1928-   , q.v. Other pseudonyms: Robert MacLeod, q.v., Noah Webster.

KIRK, PHILIP. SC: Butler = B.
 The Hydra Conspiracy. Leisure, 1979 B
 Killer Satellites. Leisure, 1980
 Love Me to Death. Leisure, 1980
 The Slayboys. Leisure, 1979 B
 Smart Bombs. Leisure, 1979 B

KIRK, RUSSELL (AMOS). 1918-   . Ref: CA.
 -Lord of the Hollow Dark. St. Martin's, 1979 [Edin.]
 Lost Lake; see The Surly Sullen Bell
 Old House of Fear. Fleet, 1961; Gollancz, 1962 [Hebrides]
 The Surly Sullen Bell. Fleet, 1962. Also published as: Lost Lake. Paperback Library, 1966 ss

KIRKBRIDE, RONALD (DE LEVINGTON). 1912-   . Ref: CA.
 -Jenny Wren. Angus, 1957
 Katrina. Allen, 1970
 -Only the Unafraid. Barker, 1953
 The Secret Journey. Barker, 1965
 The Short Night. Barker, 1968

KIRKPATRICK, JOHN (ALEXANDER). 1895-   All titles are plays, with number of acts given in parenthesis.
 "Come Away, Death." Baker, 1962 (3)
 The Cop on the Corner. French, 1963 (1)
 Eight Women—and a Ghost. French, 1963 (3)
 Gory Story. French, 1965 (1)
 A Home for Stray Cats. French, 1969 (3)
 Lady-Killers, or "How to Murder Your Husband." French, 1949 (1)
 The Mind of a Killer. French, 1960 (1)
 The Mother of Jack the Ripper. French, 1963 (1)
 Nellie Was a Lady. French, 1964 (1)
 Story of a Dead Woman. French, 1939 (1)
 Terror Walks Tonight. French, 1969 (1)
 The Woman at Dead Oaks. French, 1961 (3)

KIRKWOOD, JAMES. 1930-   . Ref: CA.
 P.S. Your Cat Is Dead. Stein, 1972; Quartet, 1974 [NYC]
 Some Kind of Hero. Crowell, 1975

KIRSCH, JONATHAN. Editor of "New West" magazine.
 Bad Moon Rising. Signet, 1978 [Calif., 1960s]
 Lovers in a Winter Circle. Signet, 1978

KIRSCH, ROBERT R. 1922-1980. Pseudonym: Robert Dundee, q.v.

KIRST, HANS HELLMUT. 1914-   . Ref: CA, TC. SC: Supt. Konstantin Keller = KK.
 The Adventures of Private Faust; see Who's in Charge Here?
 Affairs of the Generals; see Twilight of the Generals
 Brothers in Arms. Collins, 1965; Harper, 1967 (Translation of "Kameraden." Munich, 1961.)
 Camp 7 Last Stop. Collins, 1969. U.S. title: Last Stop Camp 7. Coward, 1969 (Translation of "Letzte Station Camp 7." Munich, 1966.)
 Damned to Success; see A Time for Scandal
 Death Plays the Last Card. Fontana, 1968. U.S. title: The Last Card. Pyramid, 1967 (Translation of "Die Letzte Karte Spielte der Tod." Munich, 1955.)
 Everything Has Its Price; see A Time for Payment
 -The Fox of Maulen. Collins, 1968. U.S. title: The Wolves. Coward, 1968 (Translation of "Die Wolfe." Munich, 1967.)
 Hero in the Tower. Collins, 1972; Coward, 1972 (Translation of "Held im Turm." Munich, 1970.) [Fr., 1940]
 The Last Card; see Death Plays the Last Card
 Last Stop Camp 7; see Camp 7 Last Stop
 -The Lieutenant Must Be Mad. Harrap, 1951 (Translation of "Wir Nannten Ihn Galgenstrick." Munich, 1950.)
 The Night of the Generals. Collins, 1963; Harper, 1963 (Translation of "Die Nacht der Generale." Munich, 1962.) [Ger., 1940s]
 The Nights of the Long Knives. Collins, 1976; Coward, 1976 (Translation of "Die Nachte der Langer Messer." Hamburg, 1975.) [Ger., 1933-9]
 No Fatherland; see Undercover Man
 The Officer Party. Collins, 1962; Doubleday, 1963 (Translation of "Fabrik der Offiziere." Munich, 1960.)
 -Party Games. Collins, 1980; Simon, 1980 (Translation of "08/15 in der Partei." Munich, 1979.)
 Soldiers' Revolt; see The 20th of July
 A Time for Payment. Collins, 1976. U.S. title: Everything Has Its Price. Coward, 1976 (Translation of "Alles Hat Seinen Preis." Hamburg, 1974.) KK [Munich]
 A Time for Scandal. Collins, 1973. U.S. title: Damned to Success. Coward, 1973 (Translation of "Verdammt zum Erfolg." Munich, 1971.) KK [Munich]
 A Time for Truth. Collins, 1974; Coward, 1974 (Translation of "Verurteilt zur Wahrheit." Munich, 1972.) KK [Munich]
 -The 20th of July. Collins, 1966. U.S. title: Soldiers' Revolt. Harper, 1966 (Translation of "Aufstand der Soldaten." Munich, 1965.)
 -Twilight of the Generals. Collins, 1979. U.S. title: Affairs of the Generals. Coward, 1979 (Translation of "Generalsaffaren." Munich, 1977.) [Berlin, 1938]
 Undercover Man. Collins, 1970. U.S. title: No Fatherland. Coward, 1970 (Translation of "Kein Vaterland." Munich, 1968.)
 -Who's in Charge Here? Collins, 1971. U.S. title: The Adventures of Private Faust. Coward, 1971 (Translation of "Faustrecht." Munich, 1969.)

KISTLER, MARY
 The Jarrah Tree. Doubleday, 1977; Souvenir, 1978
 The Night of the Tiger. Lancer, 1972 [Tex.]
 A Stranger at My Door. Doubleday, 1979; Hale, 1980

KITCHIN, C(LIFFORD) H(ENRY) B(ENN). 1895-1967. Ref: CC, EM, MC, TC. SC: Malcolm Warren, in all titles. Set: Eng.
 The Cornish Fox. Secker, 1949
 Crime at Christmas. Woolf, 1934; Harcourt, 1935
 Death of His Uncle. Constable, 1939
 Death of My Aunt. Woolf, 1929; Harcourt, 1935

KITCHIN, FREDERICK HARCOURT. 1867-1932. Pseudonym: Bennet Copplestone, q.v.
 Dead Men's Tales. Blackwood, 1926; Houghton, 1926, as by Bennet Copplestone ss

KLAINER, ALBERT S. Joint pseudonym with Jo-Ann (Showstack) Klainer, q.v.: L. T. Peters, q.v.

KLAINER, JO-ANN (SHOWSTACK) and ALBERT S. KLAINER. Joint pseudonym: L. T. Peters, q.v. Husband and wife; she is a consultant in medical communications; he is an infectious disease expert and professor of medicine in NYC.
 The Judas Gene. Marek, 1980 [NYC]

KLASNE, WILLIAM. 1933-   .
    Street Cops. Prentice, 1980 [Chi.]

KLAUSNER, LAWRENCE DAVID
    One Million Carats. Carlyle, 1979

KLEIN, CHARLES. See: Arthur Hornblow, 1865-1941?

KLEIN, DAVE. Sportswriter.
    Blind Side. Charter, 1980

KLEIN, ERNST. 1876-   .
    The Blackmailer. Avon, 1952 [Eng.]
    The Stolen Bride. Nisbet, 1930

KLEIN, KATE
    Plain Unvarnished Murder, with Roslyn S. Hastings, q.v. Arcadia, 1959
    The Seaway Tombstone. Arcadia, 1961

KLEIN, NORMAN. 1897-1948. Newspaperman in Chicago and NYC.
    The Destroying Angel. Farrar, 1933 [N.Y.]
    No! No! the Woman! Farrar, 1932 [NYC]
    Terror by Night. Farrar, 1935 [L.I.]

KLINGER, HENRY.   -1980. Ref: CC, TC. SC: Lt. Shomri Shomar, in all titles.
    Essence of Murder. Permabooks, 1963 [NYC]
    Lust for Murder. Trident, 1966 [Isr.]
    Murder off Broadway. Permabooks, 1962 [NYC]
    Wanton for Murder. Permabooks, 1961 [NYC]

KLINGSBERG, HARRY (M.)
    Doowinkle, D.A. Dial, 1940 ss

KLOP, THOMAS
    Harmattan. Bobbs, 1975 [Nig.]

KLOSE, KEVIN, 1940-   , and PHILIP A(LGIE) McCOMBS, 1944-   . Ref on Klose: CA.
    The Typhoon Shipments. Norton, 1974

KLUGE, P(AUL) F(REDERICK). 1942-   .
    Ref: CA.
    The Day That I Die. Bobbs, 1976 [Micronesia]
    Eddie and the Cruisers. Viking, 1980

KNAPP, G(EORGE) L(EONARD). 1872-   .
    The Face of Air. Lane (NYC & London), 1912
    The Scales of Justice. Lippincott, 1910

KNAPP, GREGORY CROMWELL. Film-maker and scriptwriter, resident in Tokyo.
    Stranglehold. Little, 1973 [Jap.]

KNEBEL, FLETCHER. 1911-   . Ref: CA.
    The Bottom Line. Doubleday, 1974; Hodder, 1975
    Convention, with Charles W. Bailey II, 1929-   . Harper, 1964; Weidenfeld, 1964 [Chi.]
    Dark Horse. Doubleday, 1972; Hodder, 1973 [Wash. D.C.]
    Dave Sulkin Cares! Doubleday, 1978 [Haw.]
    Night of Camp David. Harper, 1965; Weidenfeld, 1965
    Seven Days in May, with Charles W. Bailey II, 1929-   . Harper, 1962; Weidenfeld, 1962 [Wash. D.C.]
    Trespass. Doubleday, 1969; Allen, 1969 [N.J.]
    Vanished. Doubleday, 1968; Allen, 1968
    The Zinzin Road. Harper, 1966; Allen, 1967

KNERR, MICHAEL E.
    The Violent Lady. Monarch, 1963

KNEVELS, GERTRUDE. 1881-1962.
    By Candle-Light. Appleton, 1926 [N.Y.]
    Death on the Clock. Doubleday, 1940
    The Diamond Rose Mystery. Appleton, 1928 [N.Y.]
    Octagon House. Appleton, 1925
    Out of the Dark. Penn, 1932

KNICKMEYER, STEVE. 1944-   . Ref: CA. SC: Steve Cranmer, in both titles, both set in Okla.
    Cranmer. Random, 1978; Hamlyn, 1980
    Straight. Random, 1976; Harwood, 1977

KNIGHT, ADAM. Pseudonym of Lawrence Lariar, 1908-1981, q.v. Other pseudonyms: Michael Lawrence, Michael Stark, qq.v. SC: Steve Conacher, in at least those marked SC.
    Girl Running. Signet, 1956 SC [Paris]
    I'll Kill You Next! Appleton, 1954 SC [NYC]
    Kiss and Kill. Crown, 1953 SC
    Knife at My Back. Crown, 1952 SC [N.Y.]

    Murder for Madame. Crown, 1951 SC [NYC]
    Stone Cold Blonde. Crown, 1951 SC [NYC]
    Sugar Shannon. Belmont, 1960
    The Sunburned Corpse. Crown, 1952 SC [ship, P. Rico]
    Triple Slay. Signet, 1959 SC [NYC]

KNIGHT, ALANNA
    Castle Clodha. Hurst, 1972; Avon, 1972
    Lament for Lost Lovers. Hurst, 1973; Avon, 1973 [Scot.]
    Legend of the Loch. Hurst, 1969; Lancer, 1970 [Scot.]
    The October Witch. Hurst, 1971; Lancer, 1971 [Scot.]
    This Outward Angel. Lancer, 1972
    The White Rose. Hurst, 1973; Avon, 1973 [Scot.]
    The Wicked Wynsleys. Leisure, 1977

KNIGHT, BERNARD. 1931-   . Pseudonym: Bernard Picton, q.v.

KNIGHT, CLIFFORD (REYNOLDS). 1886-   . Ref: MP. Born in Kansas; educated in Kansas and at U. of Mich.; newspaper editor in Kansas City, freelance writer in Calif. SC: Huntoon Rogers = HR.
    The Affair at Palm Springs. Dodd, 1938 HR [Calif.]
    The Affair in Death Valley. Dodd, 1940 HR [Calif.]
    The Affair of the Black Sombrero. Dodd, 1939 HR [Mex.]
    The Affair of the Circus Queen. Dodd, 1940 HR [Manila]
    The Affair of the Corpse Escort. McKay, 1946 HR [L.A.]
    The Affair of the Crimson Gull. Dodd, 1941 HR [Calif.]
    The Affair of the Dead Stranger. Dodd, 1944 HR [Calif.]
    The Affair of the Fainting Butler. Dodd, 1943 HR [L.A.]
    The Affair of the Ginger Lei. Dodd, 1938 HR [Haw.]
    The Affair of the Golden Buzzard. McKay, 1946 HR [Calif.]
    The Affair of the Heavenly Voice. Dodd, 1937; Hale, 1938 HR [Calif.]
    The Affair of the Jade Monkey. Dodd, 1943 HR [Calif.]
    The Affair of the Limping Sailor. Dodd, 1942 HR [Calif.]
    The Affair of the Scarlet Crab. Dodd, 1937; Gollancz, 1937 HR [ship]
    The Affair of the Sixth Button. McKay, 1947 HR [Calif.]
    The Affair of the Skiing Clown. Dodd, 1941 HR [Calif.]
    The Affair of the Splintered Heart. Dodd, 1942 HR [Haw.]
    The Affair on the Painted Desert. Dodd, 1939 HR [Ariz.]
    Dark Abyss. Dutton, 1949 [Calif.]
    The Dark Road. Dutton, 1951 [Calif.]
    Death and Little Brother. Dutton, 1952 [Calif.]
    Death of a Big Shot. Dutton, 1951 [N. Mex.]
    Hangman's Choice. Dutton, 1949 [Calif.]
    The Yellow Cat. Dutton, 1950 [Calif.]

KNIGHT, DAVID. Pseudonym of Richard S(cott) Prather, 1921-   , q.v. Other pseudonym: Douglas Ring, q.v. SC: Shell Scott = SS (continued under the Prather byline).
    Case No. 561: Dragnet; see Dragnet: Case No. 561
    Dragnet: Case No. 561. PB, 1956. British title: Case No. 561: Dragnet. WDL, 1957 (Novelization of the TV series.) [L.A.]
    Pattern for Murder. Graphic, 1952. Also published as: The Scrambled Yeggs, as by Richard S. Prather. GM, 1958; Muller pb, 1961 SS
    The Scrambled Yeggs; see Pattern for Murder

KNIGHT, EDWARD FREDERICK. 1852-1925.
    A Desperate Voyage. Milne, 1898
    -Save Me from My Friends. Longmans, 1891
    The Threatening Eye. Vizetelly, 1885

KNIGHT, ERIC MOWBRAY. 1897-1943. Pseudonym: Richard Hallas, q.v.

KNIGHT, FRANK [FRANCIS EDGAR KNIGHT]. 1905-
    -Captains of the "Calabar". Ward, 1961
    -Pekoe Reef. Ward, 1962
    -The Sea's Fool. Ward, 1960

KNIGHT, H.
    The Mystery of Stephen Claverton & Co. Routledge, 1894

KNIGHT, KATHLEEN MOORE. Pseudonym: Alan Amos, q.v. Ref: CC, MP. SC: Margot Blair = MB; Elisha Macomber = EM.
    Acts of Black Night. Doubleday, 1938 EM [Cape Cod]
    Akin to Murder. Doubleday, 1953; Hammond, 1955 EM [Cape Cod]
    Bait for Murder. Doubleday, 1948; Hammond, 1952 EM [Cape Cod]
    The Bass Derby Murder. Doubleday, 1949; Hammond, 1953 EM [Cape Cod]
    Beauty Is a Beast. Doubleday, 1959; Hammond, 1960 EM [Cape Cod]
    Bells for the Dead. Doubleday, 1942; Cherry Tree, 1943 [Guat.]
    Birds of Ill Omen. Doubleday, 1948; Hammond, 1951 [Mex.]
    The Blue Horse of Taxco. Doubleday, 1947; Hammond, 1950 [Mex.]
    The Case of the Tainted Token; see The Tainted Token
    The Clue of the Poor Man's Shilling. Doubleday, 1936. British title: The Poor Man's Shilling. Hammond, 1947 EM [Cape Cod]
    A Cry in the Jungle. Hammond, 1958 (U.S. title?)
    Death Blew Out the Match. Doubleday, 1935; Heinemann, 1935 EM [Cape Cod]
    Death Came Dancing. Doubleday, 1940; Cherry Tree, 1946 EM [Pan.]
    Death Goes to a Reunion. Doubleday, 1952; Hammond, 1954 EM [Cape Cod]
    Death Wears a Veil; see Seven Were Veiled
    Design in Diamonds. Doubleday, 1944; Hammond, 1945 MB [Mex.]
    Dying Echo. Doubleday, 1949; Hammond, 1952 [Mex.]
    Exit a Star. Doubleday, 1941; Cherry Tree, 1943 MB [NYC]
    Footbridge to Death. Doubleday, 1947; Hammond, 1949 EM [Cape Cod]
    High Rendezvous. Doubleday, 1954; Hammond, 1956 [Switz.]
    Intrigue for Empire. Doubleday, 1944; Hammond, 1946. Also published as: Murder for Empire. Thriller Novel Classic, 194?, abridged [Mex.]
    Invitation to Vengeance. Doubleday, 1960; Hammond, 1961 [It.]
    Murder for Empire; see Intrigue for Empire
    Murder Greets Jean Holton; see The Wheel That Turned
    The Poor Man's Shilling; see The Clue of the Poor Man's Shilling
    Port of Seven Strangers. Doubleday, 1945; Hammond, 1948 [Mex.]
    Rendezvous with the Past. Doubleday, 1940; Cherry Tree, 1951 MB [Conn.]
    The Robineau Look. Doubleday, 1955. British title: The Robineau Murders. Hammond, 1956 [Ala.]
    The Robineau Murders; see The Robineau Look
    Seven Were Suspect; see Seven Were Veiled
    Seven Were Veiled. Doubleday, 1937. British title: Seven Were Suspect. Cherry Tree, 1942. Also published as: Death Wears a Veil. Novel Books, 194? EM [Cape Cod]
    The Silent Partner. Doubleday, 1950; Hammond, 1953 [Fla.]
    Stream Sinister. Doubleday, 1945; Hammond, 1948 [Mex.]
    The Tainted Token. Doubleday, 1938; Cherry Tree, 1942. Also published as: The Case of the Tainted Token. Mystery Novel Classic, 1943 EM [Pan.]
    Terror by Twilight. Doubleday, 1942; Cherry Tree, 1943 MB [Mass.]
    They're Going to Kill Me. Doubleday, 1955; Hammond, 1957 [Boston]
    Three of Diamonds. Doubleday, 1953; Hammond, 1955 EM [Cape Cod]
    Trademark of a Traitor. Doubleday, 1943; Hammond, 1945 [Pan.]
    The Trouble at Turkey Hill. Doubleday, 1946; Hammond, 1949 EM [Cape Cod]
    Valse Macabre. Doubleday, 1952; Hammond, 1955 EM [Cape Cod]
    The Wheel That Turned. Doubleday, 1936. Also published as: Murder Greets Jean Holton. Thriller Novel Classic, 194? EM [Cape Cod]

KNIGHT, LEONARD A(LFRED). 1895-   . SC: Jerry Scant, in at least those marked JS. Set: Eng.
    The Astounding Dr. Yell. Low, 1950
    The Brazen Head. Low, 1948
    Close the Frontier. Low, 1939
    Conqueror's Road. Low, 1945
    Contraband. Low, 1949
    The Creaking Tree Mystery. Low, 1931 JS
    The Creeping Death. Low, 1933 JS
    The Dancing Stones. Low, 1946
    Dangerous Knowledge. Low, 1950
    Deadman's Bay. Low, 1930 JS
    Death Stands Near. Low, 1936

High Treason. Gryphon, 1954
Judgment Rock. Low, 1947
Man Hunt. Low, 1930
The Morlo. Gryphon, 1956
Murder by Experiment. Low, 1935 JS
Night Express Murder. Low, 1936
One Way Down. Gryphon, 1956
The Pawn. Low, 1931 [Port.]
The Paying Guest. Low, 1951
Redbeard. Low, 1935
The Riddle of Nap's Hollow. Low, 1932
Rider in the Sky. Gryphon, 1953
The S. S. Mystery. Low, 1938
The Solander Box Mystery. Low, 1940 JS
Spanish Cove. Low, 1945
Spring Cruise. Low, 1934
Super-Cinema Murder. Low, 1937
The Valley of Green Shadows. Gryphon, 1955
The Viking Feast Mystery. Low, 1951

KNIGHT, MALCOLM
  Kiss of Death. Merit (Chi.), 1960

KNIGHT, MAXWELL. Schoolmaster and journalist in Eng.
  Crime Cargo. Allan, 1934 [ship]
  Gunman's Holiday. Allan, 1935

KNIGHT, STEPHEN. 1951- . Ref: CA.
  Requiem at Rogano. Eyre, 1979. U.S. title: Rogano. Doubleday, 1979 [Eng., 1902]

KNIGHT, W. KOBOLD. Pseudonym of Eric Cawood Gwyddyn Giddy, 1895-
  The Doctor of Souls. Cassell, 1927

KNIPE, EMILIE BENSON. 1870-1958. Pseudonym: Therese Benson, q.v.

KNIPE, J. A. and MADELAINE HALDIMON
  Murder Now and Again. Tower, 1980 [N.Y.]

KNIPSCHEER, JOHANNES MATTHIJS WILLEM. Pseudonym: James M. Fox, q.v.

KNOBLOCK, K(ENNETH) T(HOMAS). 1898- .
  Murder in the Mind. Harper, 1932 [La.]
  Take Up the Bodies. Harper, 1935 [La.]
  There's Been Murder Done. Harper, 1931; Selwyn, 1931 [New Or.]

KNOTT, FREDERICK (M. P.). 1918- . Ref: EM.
  Dial "M" for Murder. Random, 1953; French (London), 1955 (Play.)
  Wait Until Dark. Dramatists, 1967; French (London), 1968 (Play.)
  Write Me a Murder. Dramatists, 1962; French (London), 1963 (Play.)

KNOTTS, RAYMOND. Born in Illinois; newspaper editor and columnist in Chi. SC: Jim Hale, in both titles.
  And the Deep Blue Sea. Farrar, 1944; Paul, 1944, as by Gordon Volk [Fla.]
  Meeting by Moonlight. Doubleday, 1946 [Pa.]

KNOWLAND, HELEN (DAVIS HERRICK)
  Madame Baltimore. Dodd, 1949. Also published as: Baltimore Madame. Mercury, 1954 [Wash. D.C.]

KNOWLER, JOHN. 1932-1979.
  Divinitas. Cape, 1969. Also published as: Seeds of Corruption. Corgi, 1971
  Seeds of Corruption; see Divinitas
  The Singing Lizard. Cape, 1967; Farrar, 1967
  The Trap. Cape, 1964; Knopf, 1965

KNOWLES, MABEL WINIFRED. 1875-1949. Pseudonym: Lester Lurgan, q.v.

KNOWLES, WILLIAM. Pseudonyms: Clyde Allison, Clyde Ames, qq.v.

KNOWLTON, EDWARD ROGERS. 1909- . Pseudonym: Kerk Rogers, q.v.
  The Codfish Watch. Lenox, 1970

KNOWLTON, ROBERT A(LMY). 1914-1968. Ref: CA.
  Court of Crows. Gollancz, 1961; Harper, 1961

KNOWLTON, WINTHROP. See: George (Jerome Waldo) Goodman, 1930- .

KNOX, ALEXANDER. 1907- . Ref: CA.
  Raider's Moon. Macmillan (London), 1975; St. Martin's, 1976 [Eng., ca. 1790]

KNOX, BILL [WILLIAM KNOX]. 1928- .
  Pseudonyms: Robert MacLeod, q.v., Michael Kirk, Noah Webster. Ref: CA, CC, TC. SC: Colin Thane & Phil Moss = T&M; Webb Carrick = WC.
  Blacklight. Long, 1967; Doubleday, 1967 WC [Scot.]
  Blueback. Long, 1969; Doubleday, 1969 WC [Scot.]
  Bombship. Hutchinson, 1980; Doubleday, 1980 WC [Scot.]
  Children of the Mist. Long, 1970. U.S. title: Who Shot the Bull? Doubleday, 1970 T&M [Scot.]
  The Cockatoo Crime. Long, 1958 [Scot.]
  Deadline for a Dream. Long, 1957. U.S. title: In at the Kill. Doubleday, 1961 T&M [Glasgow]
  Death Calls the Shots. Long, 1961
  Death Department. Long, 1959 T&M [Glasgow]
  The Deep Fall. Long, 1966. U.S. title: The Ghost Car. Doubleday, 1966 T&M [Scot.]
  Devilweed. Long, 1966; Doubleday, 1966 WC [Hebrides]
  Die for Big Betsy. Long, 1961 [Glasgow]
  Draw Batons! Long, 1973; Doubleday, 1973 T&M [Glasgow]
  Figurehead; see The Klondyker
  The Ghost Car; see The Deep Fall
  The Grey Sentinels; see Sanctuary Isle
  Hellspout. Long, 1976; Doubleday, 1976 WC [Scot.]
  In at the Kill; see Deadline for a Dream
  Justice on the Rocks. Long, 1967; Doubleday, 1967 T&M [Glasgow]
  The Killing Game; see The Man in the Bottle
  The Klondyker. Long, 1968. U.S. title: Figurehead. Doubleday, 1968 WC [Scot.]
  Leave It to the Hangman. Long, 1960; Doubleday, 1960 T&M [Glasgow]
  Little Drops of Blood. Long, 1962; Doubleday, 1962 T&M [Glasgow]
  Live Bait. Long, 1978; Doubleday, 1979 T&M [Scot.]
  The Man in the Bottle. Long, 1963. U.S. title: The Killing Game. Doubleday, 1963 T&M [Scot.]
  Pilot Error. Long, 1977; Doubleday, 1977 T&M [Scot.]
  Rally to Kill. Long, 1975; Doubleday, 1975 T&M [Glasgow]
  Sanctuary Isle. Long, 1962. U.S. title: The Grey Sentinels. Doubleday, 1963 T&M [Scot.]
  The Scavengers. Long, 1964; Doubleday, 1964 WC [Scot.]
  Seafire. Long, 1970; Doubleday, 1971 WC [Scot.]
  Stormtide. Long, 1972; Doubleday, 1973 WC [Scot.]
  The Tallyman. Long, 1969; Doubleday, 1969 T&M [Glasgow]
  The Taste of Proof. Long, 1965; Doubleday, 1965 T&M [Glasgow]
  To Kill a Witch. Long, 1971; Doubleday, 1972 T&M [Glasgow]
  The View from Daniel Pike, with Edward Boyd, q.v. Arrow, 1974; St. Martin's, 1974 ss [Scot.]
  Whitewater. Long, 1974; Doubleday, 1974 WC [Scot.]
  Who Shot the Bull?; see Children of the Mist
  Witchrock. Long, 1977; Doubleday, 1978 WC [Scot.]

KNOX, E(DMUND GEORGE) V(ALPY). 1881- .
  Here's Misery. Methuen, 1931 ss, one criminous
  This Other Eden. Methuen, 1929 ss, one criminous

KNOX, HUGH RANDOLPH. 1942- . Pseudonym: H. R. Kaye, q.v.

KNOX, OLIVER. Nephew of Ronald A(rbuthnott) Knox, 1888-1957, q.v.
  Asylum. Collins, 1977

KNOX, RONALD A(RBUTHNOTT). 1888-1957.
  Ref: all except CA. SC: Miles Bredon = MB. Set: Eng.
  The Body in the Silo. Hodder, 1933. U.S. title: Settled Out of Court. Dutton, 1934 MB
  Double Cross Purposes. Hodder, 1937 MB [Scot.]
  The Footsteps in the Lock. Methuen, 1928 MB
  Settled Out of Court; see The Body in the Silo
  Still Dead. Hodder, 1934; Dutton, 1934 MB [Scot.]
  The Three Taps. Methuen, 1927; Simon, 1927 MB
  The Viaduct Murder. Methuen, 1925; Simon, 1926

KNOX, TIMOTHY
  Death in the State House. Houghton, 1934

KNYE, CASSANDRA. Joint pseudonym of Thomas M(ichael) Disch, 1940- , q.v., and John (Thomas) Sladek, 1937- , q.v. Other joint pseudonym: Thom Demijohn, q.v.
  The Castle and the Key. Paperback Library, 1967 (by Sladek alone.)
  The House That Fear Built. Paperback Library, 1966 [Mex.]

KOBRYN, A(LLEN) P(AUL). 1949- . Ref: CA.
  -Poseidon's Shadow. Rawson, 1979

KOCH, C(HRISTOPHER) J. 1932- .
  The Year of Living Dangerously. Joseph, 1978

KOCH, ERIC. 1919- . Ref: CA.
  Good Night, Little Spy. Godalming, 1979

KOEHLER, MARGARET HUDSON. Pseudonym: Russell Mead, q.v.

KOEHLER, ROBERT PORTNER. 1905- .
  SC: Avery Gregg and Tony Ellis = G&E; Pecos Appleby = PA; Al Branson = AB.
  The Blue Parakeet Murders. Phoenix, 1948 G&E [Cent. Am.]
  The Case of the Dead Cadet. Phoenix, 1938 [acad.]
  Corpse in the Wind. Phoenix, 1944
  The Doctor's Murder Case. Phoenix, 1939 [New Eng.]
  Here Come the Dead. Phoenix, 1942 PA [N. Mex.]
  The Hooded Vulture Murders. Phoenix, 1947 G&E [Mex.]
  Journey to Murder; see Salute to Murder
  Murder Expert. Phoenix, 1945 AB [L.A.]
  Murder in the Green Sedan. Phoenix, 1942. Also published as (?): Murder Wore Green. Hangman's House, 194? PA [L.A.]
  Murder Wore Green; see Murder in the Green Sedan
  Puppets of Chance. Sears, 1933 [Fr.]
  The Road House Murders. Phoenix, 1946; Boardman, 1948 G&E [N. Mex.]
  Salute to Murder. Phoenix, 1944. Also published as: Journey to Murder. Adventure Novel Classic, 194? [Cent. Am.]
  Sing a Song of Murder. Phoenix, 1941 PA [N. Mex.]
  Steps to Murder. Phoenix, 1943; Boardman, 1944 AB [L.A.]
  Tread Gently, Death. Phoenix, 1945 AB [Va.]

KOENIG, LAIRD (P.). See also: Peter L(ee) Dixon, 1932- . Ref: CA.
  The Little Girl Who Lives Down the Lane. Coward, 1974; Souvenir, 1974
  The Neighbor. Avon, 1978 [NYC]

KOESTLER, ARTHUR. 1905-1983. Ref: CA.
  Darkness at Noon. Cape, 1940; Macmillan, 1941. Play version: see Sidney Kingsley, 1906- .

KOLARZ, HENRY
  Kalahari. Popular Library, 1979 (Translated from the German.) [Afr.]

KOLB, KEN(NETH). 1926- . Ref: CA.
  The Couch Trip. Random, 1970 [L.A.]
  Night Crossing. Playboy, 1974

KOLBE, JOHN A.
  The Riddle of the Keys. Fiction House, 1937
  Vampires of Vengeance. Fiction House, 1935

KONING, HANS. Pseudonym of Hans Koningsberger, 1921- . Born in Holland; in British Army in WWII, novelist, reporter, playwright in U.S. since 1951.
  The Petersburg-Cannes Express. Harcourt, 1975; H. Hamilton, 1975 [train, 1900]

KONINGSBERGER, HANS. 1921- . Pseudonym: Hans Koning, q.v.

KONRAD, JAMES
  Target Amin. Sphere, 1977

KONVITZ, JEFFREY. 1944- . Ref: CA.
  The Sentinel. Simon, 1974; Secker, 1974

KOONCE, CHARLES
  The Weeping Willow Murders. Burton, 1934

KOONTZ, DEAN R(AY). 1945- . Pseudonyms: David Axton, Brian Coffey, Deanna Dwyer, K. R. Dwyer, Leigh Nichols, Anthony North, qq.v.
  After the Last Race. Atheneum, 1974 [Pa.]
  Night Chills. Atheneum, 1976; Allen, 1977 [Maine, 1977]
  The Vision. Putnam, 1977; Corgi, 1980 [Calif.]
  -A Werewolf Among Us. Ballantine, 1973
  Whispers. Putnam, 1980 [L.A.]

KOOTZ, (SAMUEL MELVIN). 1898-1982. Graduate in law from U. of Va.; advertising executive for films; art dealer and champion of abstract expressionism. SC: Jason Emory, in both titles.
  Puzzle in Paint. Crown, 1943 [NYC]
  Puzzle in Petticoats. Crown, 1944 [NYC]

KOPERWAS, SAM. 1948- . Ref: CA.
  Hot Stuff. Dutton, 1978

KOPPEL, TED. 1940?- . See: Marvin (L.) Kalb, 1930- .

KORMAN, KEITH. 1956- . Ref: CA.
  Swan Dive. Random, 1980

KORNBLUTH, C(YRIL) M. 1923-1958. Pseudonyms: Simon Eisner, Jordan Park, qq.v. Ref: CA.
  The Syndic. Doubleday, 1953; Sphere, 1968
  Takeoff. Doubleday, 1952

KORNBLUTH, J. L. Joint pseudonym with L. M. D. Fonzo: Peter Chandler, q.v.

KOROTKIN, JUDITH. 1931- . Ref: CA.
  Spotlight. Popular Library, 1974

KOSINSKI, JERZY (NIKODEM). 1933- . Ref: CA.
  Cockpit. Houghton, 1975; Hutchinson, 1975

KOSKI, DOMINIC. See: Virgil (Joseph) Scott, 1914- .

KOSNER, ALICE
  My Sister Ophelia. Berkley, 1975 [N.C.]

KOSTA, VICTOR. Pseudonym of Georges Simenon, 1903- , q.v.

KOTZWINKLE, WILLIAM. 1938- . Ref: CA.
  Fata Morgana. Knopf, 1977; Hutchinson, 1977 [Paris, 1861]
  Herr Nightingale and the Satin Woman. Knopf, 1978; Hutchinson, 1979

KOVALSKY, J. B.
  The Early Days of August. Caravelle, 1967
  The Runner Is Red. Caravelle, 1967

KOWET, DON. 1937- . Ref: CA.
  The 7th Game. Dell, 1977

KOZHEVNIKOV, VADIM
  Shield and Sword. MacGibbon, 1971 (Translation of "Shchit i Mech." Moscow, 1966.)

KOZLOFF, CHARLES
  The Ondine. St. Martin's, 1980; Allen, 1980 [N.J.]

KRAFT, H. S. See: E. Chodorov.

KRAMER, KARL. Pseudonym of Edward A. Morris. Born in R.I.; a pilot living in NYC.
  -Action Along the Humboldt. Ace, 1956
  The Deadly September. Monarch, 1960
  -Fair Game. Popular Library, 1955
  A Flame Too Hot. Monarch, 1964
  Kiss Me Quick. Monarch, 1959 [NYC]
  Not for a Curse. Monarch, 1959

KRASLOW, DAVID, 1926- , and R(OBERT) S. BOYD, 1928- . Ref for Kraslow: CA.
  A Certain Evil. Little, 1965; Barker, 1966

KRASNA, NORMAN
  Who Was That Lady I Saw You With? Random, 1958 (2-act play.)

KRASNER, WILLIAM. 1917- . Ref: CA, CC. SC: Sam Birge, in all titles.
  The Gambler. Harper, 1950; Corgi, 1951
  North of Welfare. Harper, 1954; Constable, 1955
  The Stag Party. Harper, 1957
  Walk the Dark Streets. Harper, 1949; Corgi, 1952

KRASNEY, SAMUEL A. 1922- . Ref: CA. SC: Lt. Ben Krahmer = BK; Lt. Abe Larson = AL.
  Death Cries in the Street. Rinehart, 1955; Muller, 1956 AL [NYC]
  Design for Dying. Ace, 1958 AL [NYC]
  Homicide Call. Morrow, 1962; Allen, 1963 AL [NYC]
  Homicide West. Morrow, 1961; Allen, 1962 AL [NYC2
  A Mania for Blondes. Ace, 1961 BK [Phil.]
  Morals Squad. Ace, 1959; WDL, 1960 BK [Phil.]
  The Rapist. Ace, 1959

KRAUSE, KATHALYN
  The Blue Key. Belmont, 1980
  Mellona. Belmont, 1979

KREKE, CYNTHIA. Pseudonym: Christine Damien, q.v.

KREPPS, ROBERT W(ILSON). 1919-1980. Pseudonym: Beatrice Brandon, q.v. Ref: CA.
  -Gamble My Last Game. Macmillan, 1958; Panther, 1961

KRINKEL, M. J.
  Good Night, Kathy. Evans, 1960 (Play.)

KROLL, HARRY HARRISON. 1888-1967.
  The Ghosts of Slave Driver's Bend. Bobbs, 1937; Lane, 1938

KROMER, TOM
  Waiting for Nothing. Knopf, 1935; Cassell, 1935

KRONE, CHESTER. Joint pseudonym with Phillip Breen: Wynn L. Morgan, q.v.
  Blood Wrath. Playboy, 1980 [NYC]

KRONEMULLER, HILDA. 1906(?)- . Pseudonym: Hilda Lawrence, q.v.

KROPP, LLOYD (EDWARD). Ref: CA.
  Who Is Mary Stark? Doubleday, 1974

KRUGER, HARDY. 1928- . Ref: CA.
  The Upside Down Tree. Allen, 1977; Citadel, 1977 (Translation of "Wer Stehend Stirbt, Lebt Laenger." German, 1973.)

KRUGER, PAUL. Pseudonym of Roberta Elizabeth Sebenthal, 1917- . Other pseudonym: Harry Davis, q.v. Ref: CA. SC: Phil Kramer = PK.
  The Bronze Claws. Simon, 1972 PK [Colo.]
  A Bullet for a Blonde. Dell, 1958
  The Cold Ones. Simon, 1972 PK [Colo.]
  Dig Her a Grave. Ace, 1960
  The Finish Line. Simon, 1968; Hale, 1971 [Wis.]
  If the Shroud Fits. Simon, 1969; Hale, 1971 PK [Colo.]
  Message from Marise. GM, 1963; Muller pb, 1964 [La.]
  Weave a Wicked Web. Simon, 1967; Hale, 1971 PK [Colo.]
  Weep for Willow Green. Simon, 1966; Hale, 1970 PK [Minn.]

KRUGER, (CHARLES) RAYNE. Ref: CA.
  The Even Keel. Longmans, 1955
  Ferguson. Longmans, 1956; Appleton, 1957
  My Name Is Celia. Longmans, 1954; Macmillan, 1955
  The Spectacle. Longmans, 1953; Macmillan, 1954
  Tanker. Longmans, 1952
  Young Villain with Wings. Longmans, 1953

KRULL, FELIX. Pseudonym of Stanley White, 1913- . Other pseudonym: James Dillon White, q.v.
  The Village Pub Murders. Ward, 1962

KRUMGOLD, JOSEPH (QUINCY). 1908-1980. Ref: CA, EM.
  Thanks to Murder. Vanguard, 1935; Gollancz, 1935

KUEHL, WILLIAM A.
  Night Fright. Bakers, 1966 (1-act play.)

KUETHER, EDITH LYMAN. 1915- . Pseudonym: Margaret Malcolm, q.v.

KUHN, GEORGE R.
  Comic Tragedy. Vantage, 1968

KUHNS, WILLIAM. 1943- . Ref: CA.
  The Reunion. Morrow, 1973; Cassell, 1973

KULL, GEORGE. Pseudonym: Dean Evans, q.v.

KULLAR, A.
  The Alpertol Affair. Orient (Delhi), ca.1976
  Shadow of the Dragon. Orient (Delhi), ca.1975

KUMMER, FREDERIC ARNOLD. 1873-1943. Pseudonym: Arnold Fredericks, q.v. SC: Judge Henry Tyson = HT.
  -The Brute. Watt, 1912
  The Clue of the Twisted Face; see The Twisted Face
  Death at Eight Bells. Lothrop, 1937; Hutchinson, 1937 [Wash. D.C.]
  Design for Murder. Lothrop, 1936; Hutchinson, 1936 [Wash. D.C.]
  -Forbidden Wine. Sears, 1931; Hutchinson, 1931
  -Gentlemen in Hades. Sears, 1930; Long, 1932
  The Green God. Watt, 1911 [Eng.]
  -Ladies in Hades. Sears, 1928; Hamilton, 1928
  -A Lost Paradise. Watt, 1914
  Manhattan Masquerade. Sears, 1934 [NYC]
  -The Painted Woman. Watt, 1917
  -Plaster Saints. Macaulay, 1922
  The Road to Fortune. Doran, 1925; Hodder, 1926
  The Scarecrow Murders. Dodd, 1938; Hutchinson, 1938 HT [Md.]
  -A Song of Sixpence. Watt, 1913
  The Twisted Face. Dodd, 1938; Hutchinson, 1938. Also published as: The Clue of the Twisted Face. Mystery Novel of the Month, 194? HT [Md.]
  The Web. Century, 1919 [Eng.]

KUNER, MILDRED C(HRISTOPHE). 1922- .
  Mistress of Mellyn. Dramatic, 1961 (3-act play based on the novel by Victoria Holt, q.v.)

KUNICZAK, W(IESLAW) S(TANISLAW). 1930- . Ref: CA.
  The Sempinski Affair. Doubleday, 1969; Hart-Davis, 1970

KUNST, EARLE
  The Mystery of Evangeline Fairfax. Metropolitan, 1910 [Colo.]

KURLAND, MICHAEL (J.). 1938- . Ref: CA. Pseudonym: Jennifer Plum, q.v.
  The Infernal Device. Signet, 1979; New English Library, 1979 (Sherlock Holmes) [ca.1890, Eng.]
  The Last President, with S. W. Barton (pseudonym of Barton Whaley). Morrow, 1980
  Mission: Police Action. Pyramid, 1969
  Mission: Tank War. Pyramid, 1968
  Mission: Third Force. Pyramid, 1967
  A Plague of Spies. Pyramid, 1969
  Psi Hunt. Berkley, 1980 [future, U.S.]

KURNITZ, HARRY. 1907-1968. Pseudonym: Marco Page, q.v. Ref: CA, CC, EM, MP, TC.
  Invasion of Privacy. Random, 1955; Eyre, 1956 [NYC]
  Reclining Figure. Random, 1955 (Play based on the author's novel of the same title, published as by Marco Page, q.v.)
  A Shot in the Dark. Random, 1962 (Play based on "L'Idiote", by Marcel Achard, pseudonym of Marcel Auguste Ferreol, 1899-1974.)

KURTZ, C. GORDON. 1902- . Pseudonym: Kurtz Gordon, q.v.
  Haunted. Bugbee, 1931 (3-act play.)

KURUPPU, D. S. C. Pseudonym: Stephen Christie, q.v.

KUTAK, ROSEMARY. 1908- . SC: Dr. Marc Castleman, in both titles.
  Darkness of Slumber. Lippincott, 1944
  I Am the Cat. Farrar, 1948

KUTCH, ARCHIE
  Young Sleuth's Victory; or, A Detective's Adventure. Ogilvie, 1885

KUTCHIN, VICTOR. 1851-1939.
  The Strange Case of John R. Graham. Dean, 1929 [Wis.]

KUTTNER, HENRY. 1914-1958. Pseudonym: Lewis Padgett, q.v. Ref: CC. SC: Dr. Michael Gray = MG.
  Man Drowning. Harper, 1952; Four Square, 1961 [Ariz.]

Murder of a Mistress. Permabooks, 1957 MG
Murder of a Wife. Permabooks, 1958 MG [S.F.]
The Murder of Ann Avery. Permabooks, 1956 MG [S.F.]
The Murder of Eleanor Pope. Permabooks, 1956 MG [S.F.]

KUTTNER, PAUL
The Man Who Lost Everything. Sterling, 1976 [NYC]

KWITNEY, JONATHAN. 1941-   . Ref: CA.
Shakedown. Putnam, 1977 [NYC]

KYD, THOMAS. Pseudonym of Alfred Bennett Harbage, 1901-1976. Ref: CA, CC, EM, TC. SC: Sam Phelan = SP.
Blood Is a Beggar. Lippincott, 1946; Hammond, 1949 SP [acad., Phil.]
Blood of Vintage. Lippincott, 1947; Hammond, 1950 SP [Phil.]
Blood on the Bosom Devine. Lippincott, 1948 SP [Phil.]
Cover His Face. Lippincott, 1949 [Eng.]

KYLE, DUNCAN. Pseudonym of John Franklin Broxholme, 1930-   . Ref: CA.
Black Camelot. Collins, 1978; St. Martin's, 1978 [1944]
A Cage of Ice. Collins, 1970; St. Martin's, 1971 [Russ.]
Flight into Fear. Collins, 1972; St. Martin's, 1972
Green River High. Collins, 1979; St. Martin's, 1980 [Borneo]
In Deep. Collins, 1976. U.S. title: Whiteout! St. Martin's, 1976. Also published in England under the U.S. title: Fontana, 1977 [Green.]
A Raft of Swords. Collins, 1974. U.S. title: The Suvarov Adventure. St. Martin's, 1974 [Can.]
The Suvarov Adventure; see A Raft of Swords
Terror's Cradle. Collins, 1975; St. Martin's, 1974
Whiteout!; see In Deep

KYLE, ELISABETH. Pseudonym of Agnes Mary Robertson Dunlop. Ref: CA.
-All the Nice Girls. Davies, 1976
-Broken Glass. Davies, 1940
-The Burning Hill. Davies, 1977
-But We Are Exiles. Davies, 1942
-Carolina House. Davies, 1955
-Carp Country. Davies, 1946
-Conor Sands. Davies, 1952
-Douce. Davies, 1950
-Down the Water. Davies, 1975
-Free As Air. Davies, 1974
-The Heron Tree. Davies, 1973
-High Season. Davies, 1968
-Lost Karim. Davies, 1948
Love Is for the Living. Davies, 1966; Holt, 1967 [Belg.]
Mally Lee. Davies, 1947; Doubleday, 1947. Also published as: The Second Mally Lee. Ace, 1967 [Scot.]
-A Man of Talent. Davies, 1948
Mirror Dance. Davies, 1970; Holt, 1971 [Copen.]
-The Other Miss Evans. Davies, 1968
-The Pleasure Dome. Davies, 1958
Queen's Evidence. Davies, 1969
-The Regent's Candlesticks. Davies, 1954
Return to the Alcazar. Davies, 1962
The Scent of Danger. Davies, 1971; Holt, 1972
The Second Mally Lee; see Mally Lee
-The Silver Pineapple. Davies, 1972
-The Skater's Waltz. Davies, 1944
-The Stark Inheritance. Davies, 1978
-A Summer Scandal. Davies, 1979
-The "Tontine Bell". Davies, 1951
-The White Lady. Davies, 1941

KYLE, ELLA JANE
Old Gumber's Mill. Ben Hur Press, 1928

KYLE, ROBERT. Pseudonym of Robert Terrall, 1914-   , q.v. Other pseudonym: John Gonzales, q.v. See also: Brett Halliday. SC: Ben Gates = BG.
Ben Gates Is Hot. Dell, 1964 BG
Blackmail, Inc. Dell, 1958 BG [NYC]
The Crooked City. Dell, 1954
The Golden Urge. Dell, 1954
Kill Now, Pay Later. Dell, 1960 BG [N.Y.]
Model for Murder. Dell, 1959 BG [NYC]
Nice Guys Finish Last. Dell, 1955 [Maine]
Some Like It Cool. Dell, 1962 BG [NYC]
A Tiger in the Night. Dell, 1955

KYLE, SEFTON. Pseudonym of Roy Vickers, 1888-1965, q.v. Other pseudonyms: David Durham, John Spencer, qq.v. SC: Insp. J. Rason, in at least those titles marked R (see also David Durham and Roy Vickers entries). Set: Eng.
The Bloomsbury Treasure. Jenkins, 1932
The Body in the Safe. Jenkins, 1937 R
Dead Man's Dower. Jenkins, 1925
The Durand Case. Jenkins, 1936
During His Majesty's Pleasure. Jenkins, 1938 R
The Girl Known As D 13. Jenkins, 1940
Guilty, But——. Jenkins, 1927
The Hawk. Jenkins, 1930; Dial, 1930, as by Roy Vickers R
The Judge's Dilemma. Jenkins, 1939
The Life He Stole. Jenkins, 1934 R
Love Was Married. Jenkins, 1943
The Man in the Shadow. Jenkins, 1924 R
The Man Without a Name. Jenkins, 1935
-Miss X. Jenkins, 1939
Missing! Jenkins, 1938
The Notorious Miss Walters. Jenkins, 1937
Number Seventy-Three. Jenkins, 1936
The Price of Silence. Jenkins, 1942
Red Hair. Jenkins, 1933 R
The Shadow over Fairholme. Jenkins, 1940
Silence. Jenkins, 1935 R
The Vengeance of Mrs. Danvers, Jenkins, 1932

KYTLE, RAY(MOND). 1941-   . Ref: CA.
Fire and Ice. McKay, 1975 [future]
Last Voyage. Dell, 1979. British title: Sea Stalk. Panther, 1980 [ship]
Meltdown. McKay, 1976; Panther, 1978
Sea Stalk; see Last Voyage

LA BERN, ARTHUR (JOSEPH). 1909-   . Ref: TC. Set: Eng.
The Big Money-Box. Kimber, 1960
Brighton Belle. Allen, 1963
Frenzy; see Goodbye Piccadilly, Farewell Leicester Square
Goodbye Piccadilly, Farewell Leicester Square. Allen, 1966; Stein, 1967. Also published as: Frenzy. Pan, 1972; Stein, 1972
It Always Rains on Sunday. Nicholson, 1945
-It Was Christmas Every Day. Jarrolds, 1952
It Will Be Warmer When It Snows. Allen, 1966
A Nice Class of People. Allen, 1969
Night Darkens the Streets. Nicholson, 1947
Nightmare. Allen, 1975
-Pennygreen Street. Jarrolds, 1950

LABORDE, JEAN. 1918-   . Born in France; reporter, especially covering murder trials.
The Dominici Affair. Morrow, 1974; Collins, 1974 (Translation of "Un Matin d'ete a Lurs." Paris, 1952.) (Fictionalized true crime.) [Fr.]
A Fair Trial. Doubleday, 1969. British title: The Falcon and the Dove. Bodley, 1962 (Translation of "Les Bonnes Causes." Paris, 1960.)
The Falcon and the Dove; see A Fair Trial
A Privileged Character. Doubleday, 1963 (Probably translation of "Un Homme a Part Entiere." Paris, 1961.) [Fr.]

LACHLAN, EDYTHE. Pseudonym: Rinalda Roberts, q.v.

LA COSTE, GUY ROBERT. Joint pseudonym with Eadfrid A. Bingham: Guy Berton, q.v.

LA COUR, TAGE
The Murder of Santa Claus. [Author] (Denmark), 1954

LACROIX, JEAN PAUL. 1914-   .
The Innocent Gunman. Elek, 1957 (Translation of "Le Gangster aux Etoiles." Paris, 1954.) [Paris]

LACROIX, RAMON. Pseudonym of Ernest L(ionel) McKeag, 1896-   . Other pseudonyms: Griff, Mark Grimshaw, qq.v.
-Danger for Love. Modern Fiction, 1947
-Hotel for Scandal. Modern Fiction, 1947
-Illicit Cargo. Modern Fiction, 1947
Murder at Le Touquet. Modern Fiction, 1947

LACRUZ, MARIO
The Suspect. Methuen, 1956 (Translation of "El Inocente." Barcelona, 1953.)

LACY, ED. Pseudonym of Leonard S. Zinberg, 1911-1968. Ref: EM, TC. SC: Lee Hayes = LH; Toussaint M. Moore = TM; Dave Wintino = DW.
Be Careful How You Live. Harper, 1959; Boardman, 1959. Also published as: Dead End. Pyramid, 1960 [NYC]
The Best That Ever Did It. Harper, 1955; Hutchinson, 1957. Also published as: Visa to Death. Permabooks, 1956 [NYC]
The Big Bust. Pyramid, 1969; New English Library pb, 1970
The Big Fix. Pyramid, 1960; Boardman, 1961
Blonde Bait. Zenith, 1959
Breathe No More, My Lady. Avon, 1958 [NYC]
Bugged for Murder. Avon, 1961 [NYC]
Dead End; see Be Careful How You Live
A Deadly Affair. Hillman, 1960 [NYC]
Death in Passing; see Sin in Their Blood
Devil for the Witch. Boardman, 1958 (U.S. title?) [L.I.]
Double Trouble. Lancer, 1967; Boardman, 1965 DW
Enter Without Desire. Avon, 1954 [NYC]
The Freeloaders. Berkley, 1961; Boardman, 1962
Go for the Body. Avon, 1954; Boardman, 1959 [Paris]
Harlem Underground. Pyramid, 1965 LH [NYC]
In Black & Whitey. Lancer, 1967 LH [NYC]
Lead with Your Left. Harper, 1957; Boardman, 1957 DW [NYC]
The Men from the Boys. Harper, 1956; Boardman, 1960 [NYC]
Moment of Untruth. Lancer, 1964; Boardman, 1965 TM [Mex.]
The Napalm Bugle. Pyramid, 1968 [Calif.]
Pity the Honest. Macfadden, 1965; Boardman, 1964 [N.Y.]
Room to Swing. Harper, 1957; Boardman, 1958 TM [Ohio]
The Sex Castle. Paperback Library, 1963; Digit, 1965. Also published as: Shoot It Again. Paperback Library, 1969 [Fr.]
Shakedown for Murder. Avon, 1958
Shoot It Again; see The Sex Castle
Sin in Their Blood. Eton, 1952. British title: Death in Passing. Boardman, 1959
South Pacific Affair. Belmont, 1961
Strip for Violence. Eton, 1953 [NYC]
Two Hot to Handle. Paperback Library, 1963; Digit, 1966 (2 novelets.)
Visa to Death; see The Best That Ever Did It
The Woman Aroused. Avon, 1951; Hale, 1969

LADLINE, ROBERT. SC: J. A. (Rem) Remington, in at least those marked JR. Set: Eng.
A Devil in Downing Street. Jenkins, 1937 JR
The Man Who Made a King. Jenkins, 1936
The Quest of the Vanishing Star. Jenkins, 1932
The Shoe Fits. Jenkins, 1936 JR
Sinister Craft. Jenkins, 1939 JR
The Sky's the Limit. Jenkins, 1937 JR
Stop That Man! Jenkins, 1940 JR
They Stuck at Nothing. Jenkins, 1935
When Fools Endanger Us. Jenkins, 1938 JR
When the Police Failed. Jenkins, 1933
The Wolf Swept Down. Jenkins, 1935

LADOUX, GEORGES (EMILE). 1875-1933.
The Kaiser's Blonde Spy. Hutchinson, 1934

LADY, FREDERICK
The City of Fear. Wright, 1933
The Master of Money. Jarrolds, 1931
A Million Pounds Reward. Jarrolds, 1929

LAFFEATY, CHRISTINA. 1932-   .
The Reluctant Bride. Hale, 1966. U.S. title: Mistress of Tara. Paperback Library, 1967

LAFFIN, JOHN (ALFRED CHARLES). 1922-   .
Pseudonyms: Carl Dekker, Mark Napier, Dirk Sabre, qq.v. Ref: CA.
Crime on My Hands. Horwitz, 1958
The Dancer of San Jose. Horwitz, 1958
Death by Ballot. King, 1954
Death Has My Number. Horwitz, 1957
The Devil's Emissary. Horwitz, 1958
-Devil's Goad. Dent, 1970

I'll Die Tonight. Horwitz, 1957
Jungle Manhunt. Horwitz, 1955
Murder in Paradise. Horwitz, 1958
Murder on Flight 354. King, 1956
My Brother's Executioner. Horwitz, 1957
Temptress on Trial. Horwitz, 1958
They Voted Me to Die. Horwitz, 1957
-The Walking Wounded. Amalgamated, 1963

LAFLIN, JACK. SC: Gregory Hiller, in at least those marked GH; Peter Winston = PW (see also: Peter Winston).
The Flaw. Belmont, 1964
The Reluctant Spy. Belmont, 1966 GH [Russ.]
A Silent Kind of War. Belmont, 1965; Digit, 1966 GH [Haw.]
The Spy in White Gloves. Belmont, 1965 GH [S. Am.]
The Spy Who Didn't. Belmont, 1966 GH [L.I.]
The Spy Who Loved America. Belmont, 1964 GH [NYC]
The Temple at Ilumquh. Award, 1970 PW [Mid. East]

LA FORCE, BEATRICE
The Sound of Hasty Footsteps. Bouregy, 1963

LAFORE, LAURENCE (DAVIS). 1917- . Ref: CA.
Nine Seven Juliet. Doubleday, 1968 [Ia.]

LAFOREST, SERGE. Pseudonym.
The Intruder. International, 1969 (Translation from the French.) [Alaska]

LA FOUNTAINE, GEORGE. 1934- . Ref: CA.
Flashpoint. Coward, 1976; Mayflower, 1977 [Tex.]
The Scott-Dunlap Ring. Coward, 1978; Mayflower, 1979 [U.S., 1870s]
Two Minute Warning. Coward, 1975; Mayflower, 1977 [L.A.]

LA FRANCE, MARSTON. 1927?- . Born in N.Y.; a farmer in N.Y. in 1950s.
Miami Murder-Go-Round. World, 1951 [Miami]

LA FRENAIS, IAN. See: Dick Clement.

LA GARDE, HENRY. Graduate of Cambridge; served with the War Office and the Foreign Office in Eng.
Tide Waits for No Man. Robertson, 1952 [Chan. Is.]

LAIDLAW, ROSS
The Lion Is Rampant. Molendinar, 1979

LAINE, ANNABEL
The Reluctant Heiress. Collins, 1978; Doubleday, 1978 [Eng., ca.1820]

LAING, ALEXANDER (KINNAN). 1903-1976. Ref: CA, CC, MP. SC: Dr. Scarlett = S. See also: Thomas Painter.
The Cadaver of Gideon Wyck. Farrar, 1934; Butterworth, 1934 [Maine]
Dr. Scarlett. Farrar, 1936; Rich, 1937 S [Far East]
The Methods of Dr. Scarlett. Farrar, 1937; Cassell, 1938 S

LAING, JANET
Before the Wind. Dent, 1918; Dutton, 1918
-The Borderlanders. Dent, 1904
The Honeycombers. Hodder, 1922
-The Moment More. Hodder, 1924
The Villa Jane. Hodder, 1929; Century, 1929
-The Wizard's Aunt. Dent, 1903

LAING, KENNETH. Pseudonym of Kenneth (Joseph Robb) Langmaid, q.v. SC: "Rolling" Stone, in at least those marked RS. Set: Eng.
The House of Darkness. Diamond, 1927
The Malignant Snowman. Jenkins, 1950 RS
The Midnight Walkers. Jenkins, 1951 RS
No Man's Laughter. Jenkins, 1950 RS
The Pay Off. Jenkins, 1951
The Red Horsemen. Jenkins, 1930
The Shadow People. Jenkins, 1952; Roy, 1956 RS

LAING, PATRICK. Pseudonym of Amelia Reynolds Long, 1904-1978, q.v. Other pseudonyms: Adrian Reynolds, Peter Reynolds, qq.v. Joint pseudonym with Edna McHugh: Kathleen Buddington Coxe, q.v. SC: Patrick Laing, in all titles.
A Brief Case of Murder. Phoenix, 1949 [Va.]
If I Should Murder. Pheonix, 1945 [Pa.]
The Lady Is Dead. Phoenix, 1951 [acad.]
Murder from the Mind. Phoenix, 1946
The Shadow of Murder. Phoenix, 1957
Stone Dead. Phoenix, 1945; Wells Gardner, 1947

LAIT, JACK [JAQUIN L. LAIT]. 1882-1954. SC: Polack Annie = PA.
The Beast of the City. Grosset, 1932 (Novelization of the movie.) [NYC]
The Big House. Grosset, 1930 (Novelization of the movie.)
Gangster Girl. Grosset, 1930 PA [NYC]
Put on the Spot. Grosset, 1930 PA [Chi.]

LAIT, ROBERT. 1921- . Ref: CA.
A Chance to Kill. Macmillan (London), 1968
Once Too Often. Hale, 1980
Switched Out. MacGibbon, 1970

LAKE, JAMES (THOMAS)
The Day They Hijacked Death. Boardman, 1963
Down Among the Dead Men. Boardman, 1961

LAKE, JANE
The Silent Scream. Major, 1976 [N.W.]

LAKE, JOE BARRY. Pseudonym: Joe Barry, q.v.

LAKE, PETER A. -ca.1976. Neurosurgeon, medical education director in Calif.; technical adviser to "Marcus Welby, M.D." TV series.
Leffert's Disease. Bobbs, 1976; Allen, 1977 [NYC]

LAKER, ROSALIND. Pseudonym of Barbara Ovstedal, 1925- . Other pseudonyms: Barbara Paul, q.v., Barbara Douglas.
Fair Winds of Love. Hale, 1974; Doubleday, 1980, as by Barbara Douglas
The Smuggler's Bride. Hale, 1976; Doubleday, 1975 [Eng., 1809]

LAKIN, RICHARD
Angel Take Care. Hodder, 1947 [Switz.]
The Body Fell on Berlin. Hodder, 1943; Putnam, 1943

LAMARRE, JOSEPH
-The Passion of the Beast. Stratford, 1928

LAMB, ANTONIA (BLICK). 1943- . Ref: CA.
The Greenhouse. Pyramid, 1966 [NYC]
Greystones. Pyramid, 1966 [R.I.]
Lady in Shadows. Lancer, 1966
Remember the Summer We Lived at the Pad. Lancer, 1973

LAMB, J. J. SC: Zack Rolfe, in all titles.
The Chinese Straight. Ballantine, 1976 [Calif.]
Losers Take All. Carlyle, 1979
A Nickel Jackpot. Ballantine, 1976 [Las Veg.]

LAMB, LYNTON (HAROLD). 1907-1977. Ref: CA, CC. SC: Supt. Quill and Insp. Glover, in all titles. Set: Eng.
Death of a Dissenter. Gollancz, 1969
Man in a Mist. Gollancz, 1974
Picture Frame. Gollancz, 1972
Worse Than Death. Gollancz, 1971

LAMB, MAX and HARRY SANFORD
The Last Nazi. Belmont, 1980

LAMBE, G(EORGE)
The Mysteries of Ferney Castle. Colburn, 1810 [Eng., 1600s]

LAMBERT, DEREK (WILLIAM). 1929- . Pseudonym: Richard Falkirk, q.v. Ref: CA.
Angels in the Snow. Joseph, 1969; Coward, 1969
I, Said the Spy. Arlington, 1980; Elliott, 1980
-The Memory Man. Arlington, 1979
The Red House. Joseph, 1972; Coward, 1972 [Wash. D.C.]
Rough Cut; see Touch the Lion's Paw
The Saint Peter's Plot. Arlington, 1978; Bantam, 1979
Touch the Lion's Paw. Arlington, 1975; Saturday Review Press, 1975. Also published as: Rough Cut. Bantam, 1980
The Yermakov Transfer. Arlington, 1974; Saturday Review Press, 1974 [Russ., train]

LAMBERT, DUDLEY. See: Rosa Lambert.

LAMBERT, ELISABETH
The Sleeping House Party. Coward, 1951; Joseph, 1951

LAMBERT, ERIC. 1918-1966. Ref: CA.
-The Ballarat. Muller, 1962
-The Dark Backward. Muller, 1958
Diggers Die Hard. Fleetway, 1958
-Dolphin. Muller, 1963
-The Drip Dry Man. Muller, 1963
-Glory Thrown In. Muller, 1959
Hiroshima Reef. Muller, 1967; Norton, 1967
-Kelly. Muller, 1964
-The Long White Night. Muller, 1965
The Rehabilitated Man. Muller, 1960
-A Short Walk to the Stars. Muller, 1964
-The Tender Conspiracy. Muller, 1965
-The Twenty Thousand Thieves. Muller, 1952
-The Veterans. Muller, 1954
-Waterman. Muller, 1956

LAMBERT, GERARD B(ARNES). 1886-1967.
Murder in Newport. Scribner, 1938 [R.I.]

LAMBERT, LEE
Blonde for Danger. Hale, 1980
The Guaymas Assignment. Hale, 1979

LAMBERT, LESLIE HARRISON. 1883-1940. Pseudonym: A. J. Alan, q.v.

LAMBERT, R. F.
The Crooked Men Came. Pendulum, 1946

LAMBERT, ROBERT. 1930- .
A Piece of the Moon. Saturday Review Press, 1975 [Calif.]

LAMBERT, ROSA and DUDLEY. SC: Glyn Morgan, in all titles.
Crime in Quarantine. Nelson, 1938 [Fr.]
Death Goes to Brussels; see Monsieur Faux-Pas
The Mediterranean Murder. Wishart, 1930 [Fr.]
Monsieur Faux-Pas. Wishart, 1928. Also published as: Death Goes to Brussels. Nelson, 1937 [Brus.]
The Mystery of the Golden Wings. Nelson, 1935; Macaulay, 1936 GM

LAMBIRTH, F. EDWIN
The Rivard House. Leisure, 1980 [Calif.]

LAMBOT, ISOBEL (MARY). 1926- . Pseudonyms: Daniel Ingham, Mary Turner, qq.v. Ref: CA. Set: Eng.
Come Back and Die. Hale, 1972
Danger Merchant. Hale, 1968
Dangerous Refuge. Hale, 1966
Deadly Return. Hale, 1966
Grip of Fear. Hale, 1974
The Identity Trap. Hale, 1978
Killer's Laughter. Hale, 1968
Let the Witness Die. Hale, 1969
Past Tense. Hale, 1979
Point of Death. Hale, 1969
The Queen Dies First. Hale, 1968
Shroud of Canvas. Hale, 1967
A Taste of Murder. Hale, 1966; Ace, 1972
Watcher on the Shore. Hale, 1972

LAMENSDORF, LEONARD. 1930- . Ref: CA.
In the Blood. Dell, 1974
The Paper Coffin. Dell, 1973

LAMONT, C. SKENE
The Glenbeg Mystery. Stockwell, 1977

LAMONT, STEWART
The Third Angle. Long, 1978

LAMPEN, C(HARLES) DUDLEY. 1859-1943.
The Dead Prior. Stock, 1896

LAMPP, JAMES W.
The Unicorn Caper. Leisure, 1980

LAMSON, DAVID (ALBERT)
Whirlpool. Scribner, 1937 [Wash.]

LANCASTER, GRAHAM. Head of a public relations firm in Eng.
The Nuclear Letters. Eyre, 1979; Atheneum, 1979
Seward's Folly. Eyre, 1980

LANCASTER, PAUL
The Disappearance of Norman Langdale. Paul, 1929
The Executioner's Axe. Paul, 1930
The Jolly Roger Mystery. Paul, 1930

LANCE, LESLIE. Pseudonym of Charles John Swatridge. Joint pseudonym with Irene Maude Mossop Swatridge: Theresa Charles, q.v.
The Bride of Emersham. Pyramid, 1967 (British title?)

Dark Stranger. Low, 1946
The House in the Woods. Ace, 1973
(British title?)

LAND, JANE. Joint pseudonym of Kathryn
Kilby Borland, 1916-   , and Helen
Ross Smith Speicher, 1915-   . Other
joint pseudonym: Alice Abbott, q.v.
Irena. Doubleday, 1979; Hale, 1980
These Tigers' Hearts. Doubleday, 1978;
Hale, 1979
To Walk the Night. Ballantine, 1976
[N.Y.]

LAND, MYRICK (EBBEN). 1922-   . Ref: CA.
The Dream Buyers. Norton, 1980 [Reno]
Last Flight. Norton, 1975
Quicksand. Harper, 1969; Gollancz, 1970
[L.A.]
The Search; see Search the Dark Woods
Search the Dark Woods. Funk, 1955. Also
published as: The Search. Dell, 1959

LANDAU, MARK ALEKSANDROVICH. 1886-1957.
Pseudonym: Mark Aldanov, q.v.

LANDELS, D. H. Pseudonym of Donald (Lan-
dels) Henderson, 1905-   , q.v.
The Announcer. Hurst, 1944. U.S. title:
A Voice Like Velvet. Random, 1948, as
by Donald Henderson
The Headmaster. Hurst, 1947 [acad.]
His Lordship the Judge. Paul, 1936
-A Man of Character. Hurst, 1944
Teddington Tragedy. Paul, 1935
-Uncle Xavier. Hurst, 1947
-The Understudy. Hurst, 1945
A Voice Like Velvet; see The Announcer

LANDERS, GUNNARD (WILLIAM). 1944-   .
Ref: CA.
The Hunting Party; see The Hunting
Shack
The Hunting Shack. Arbor, 1979. British
title: The Hunting Party. Arrow, 1981
[Wis.]
Rite of Passage. Arbor, 1980

LANDON, CHRISTOPHER (GUY). 1911-   .
Ref: CC. Set: Eng.
Dead Men Rise Up Never. Heinemann,
1963; Sloane, 1963
A Flag in the City. Heinemann, 1953;
Macmillan, 1954 [Iran]
Hornets' Nest. Heinemann, 1956
Ice-Cold in Alex. Heinemann, 1957;
Sloane, 1957
The Mirror Room. Heinemann, 1960; White
Lion, 1972
The Shadow of Time. Heinemann, 1957.
U.S. title: Unseen Enemy. Doubleday,
1957
Stone Cold Dead in the Market. Heine-
mann, 1955
Unseen Enemy; see The Shadow of Time

LANDON, EDWIN J.
Suspicion. Long, 1931

LANDON, HERMAN. 1882-1960. SC: The Grey
Phantom = GP; The Picaroon = P.
(Note that Gray in all U.S. titles is
spelled Grey in British titles.)
The Back-Seat Murder. Liveright, 1931;
Jarrolds, 1931
Buy My Silence! Cassell, 1929 P (4
stories.)
Death on the Air. Liveright, 1929; Jar-
rolds, 1929 [NYC]
The Elusive Picaroon. Cassell, 1932 P
(6 stories.) [Eng.]
The Forbidden Door. Dial, 1927; Hutch-
inson, 1927 [N.H.]
Gray Magic. Watt, 1925. British title:
The Grey Phantom's Triumph. Hutchin-
son, 1927 GP [Maine]
The Gray Phantom. Watt, 1921; Long,
1923 GP [NYC]
The Gray Phantom's Return. Watt, 1922;
Long, 1926 GP [NYC]
Gray Terror. Watt, 1923; Long, 1925 GP
[NYC]
The Green Shadow. Dial, 1928; Cassell,
1927 P [NYC]
The Grey Phantom's Triumph; see Gray
Magic
Hands Unseen. Watt, 1924; Hutchinson,
1926 GP [Conn.]
Haunting Fingers. Jarrolds, 1930
Murder Mansion. Liveright, 1928. Bri-
tish title: Mystery Mansion. Cassell,
1928 [Eng.]
Mystery Mansion; see Murder Mansion
The Owl's Warning. Liveright, 1932;
Jarrolds, 1932 [Maine]
The Picaroon and the Burglar Tools.
Thacker (Bombay), 1944 P
The Picaroon Does Justice. Cassell,
1928 P (5 stories.) [Eng.]
The Picaroon in Pursuit. Cassell, 1932
P

The Picaroon: Knight Errant. Cassell,
1933 P (3 stories.) [Eng.]
The Picaroon Resumes Practice. Cassell,
1931 P (3 stories.) [Eng.]
The Room Under the Stairs. Watt, 1923;
Hutchinson, 1925 [NYC]
The Silver Chest. Jarrolds, 1932 [NYC]
Three Brass Elephants. Liveright, 1930.
British title: Whispering Shadows.
Jarrolds, 1930 [NYC]
The Trailing of the Picaroon. Cassell,
1930 P (3 stories.) [Eng.]
The Voice in the Closet. Liveright,
1930 [NYC]
Whispering Shadows; see Three Brass
Elephants

LANDON, HILARY. SC: Timothy Drewer, in at
least those marked TD. Set: Eng.
Circle Round a Corpse. Gifford, 1948 TD
Exit Sir Toby Belch. Gifford, 1950
Murder at Morning Prayers. Gifford,
1947 TD

LANDON, LOUISE. Pseudonym of Louise Platt
Hauck, 1883-1943, q.v. Other pseudo-
nym: Lane Archer, q.v.
The Green Light. Penn, 1931; Paul, 1931
The Strange Death of a Doctor. Penn,
1933; Paul, 1933

LANE, ANDREW
Forgive the Executioner. New English
Library pb, 1978
The Ulsterman. New English Library pb,
1979

LANE, GRANT. Pseudonym of Stephen Gould
Fisher, 1912-1980. See also: Steve
Fisher. Other pseudonym: Stephen
Gould, q.v.
Spend the Night. Phoenix, 1935

LANE, GRET. (Given name probably Margar-
et.) SC: John Barrin, in at least
those marked JB; Insp. Hook, in at
least those marked H; Kate Marsh, in
at least those marked KM. Set: Eng.
The Cancelled Score Mystery. Jenkins,
1929
The Curlew Coombe Mystery. Jenkins,
1930 KM,JB
Death in Mermaid Lane. Jenkins, 1940
KM,JB
Death Prowls the Cove. Jenkins, 1942
KM,JB
Death Visits the Summer-House. Jenkins,
1939 KM,JB
Found on the Road. Jenkins, 1926
The Guest with the Scythe. Jenkins,
1943 KM,JB
The Hotel Cremona Mystery. Jenkins,
1932 KM,JB
The Lantern House Affair. Jenkins, 1931
KM
The Red Mirror Mystery. Jenkins, 1938 H
The Stolen Scar. Jenkins, 1925 [Ida.]
Three Died That Night. Jenkins, 1937 H
The Unknown Enemy. Jenkins, 1933 KM,JB

LANE, J(OHN) RUSSELL
-The House Between the Trees. Clark,
1909

LANE, JEREMY. 1893-1963. SC: Whitney
Wheat = WW.
Death to Drumbeat. Phoenix, 1944 WW
Kill Him Tonight. Phoenix, 1946 WW
[N.Y.]
The Left Hand of God. Washburn, 1929
Like a Man. Washburn, 1928; Allan, 1936
[Tex.]
Murder Menagerie. Phoenix, 1946 WW
[N.Y.]
Murder Spoils Everything. Phoenix, 1949
WW [N.Y.]

LANE, KENDALL
Gambit. GM, 1966 (Novelization of the
movie.) [Mid. East]

LANE, KENNETH WESTMACOTT. 1893-   .
Pseudonym: Keith West, q.v.

LANG, ANDREW. 1844-1912. Pseudonym: A.
Huge Longway, q.v.
The Disentanglers. Longmans, 1902 ss
The Mark of Cain. Scribner, 1886; Ar-
rowsmith, 1886
Old Friends. Longmans (NYC & London),
1890 (Parodies, one criminous.)

LANG, ANTHONY. Pseudonym of John (George)
Hazlette Vahey, 1881-   , q.v. Other
pseudonyms: Henrietta Clandon, John
Haslette, Vernon Loder, John Mowbray,
Walter Proudfoot, qq.v. Set: Eng.
The Case with Three Threads. Melrose,
1928
The Crime. Melrose, 1927
The Daring Diana. Melrose, 1929
Evidence. Melrose, 1930

Fly Country. Melrose, 1928

LANG, BRAD. SC: Fred Crockett, in all
titles.
Brand of Fear. Leisure, 1976 [Mich.]
Crockett on the Loose. Leisure, 1975
[Det., acad.]
The Perdition Express. Leisure, 1976
[Mich.]

LANG, HARRY. On staff of L.A. "Examiner"
in 1940s as crime reporter.
The Corpse on the Hearth. Macrae Smith,
1946; Boardman, 1946 [S.F.]

LANG, HILARY
-The House of Mystery. Mellifont, 1947

LANG, JACK
The Biter. Mayflower, 1968. U.S. title:
The Photo Game. Belmont, 1971

LANG, JOHN. 1817-1864.
Botany Bay. Tegg, 1859. Also published
as: Clever Criminals; or, Recollec-
tions of Botany Bay. Ward, 1878 ss
[Australia]
Clever Criminals; see Botany Bay
The Secret Police; or, Plot and Pas-
sion. Ward, 1859 ss

LANG, MARIA. Pseudonym of Dagmar Lange,
1914-   . SC: Christer Wick, in all
titles.
Death Awaits Thee. Hodder, 1967
(Translation of "Se, Doden pa dig
Vantar." Stockholm, 1955.) [Stock.,
theatre]
No More Murders. Hodder, 1967 (Trans-
lation of "Inte Flera Mord." Stock-
holm, 1951.) [Swed.]
A Wreath for the Bride. Hodder, 1966;
Regnery, 1968 (Translation of "Kung
Liljekonvalj av Dungen." Stockholm,
1957.) [Swed.]

LANG, THEO. Pseudonym: Peter Piper, q.v.
The House in Gowderdale. Macdonald,
1947

LANGBRIDGE, FREDERICK. Pseudonym: Alfred
Fitzmaurice King, q.v.

LANGDON, GEE. 1907-   .
Clue from the Past. Hale, 1973

LANGDON, JOHN (FRANKLIN COASTEN).
1913-   . Pseudonym: John Gannold,
q.v. Ref: CA.
Vicious Circuit. Macmillan, 1953
[Manila]

LANGE, JOHN. Pseudonym of (John) Michael
Crichton, 1942-   , q.v. Other pseu-
donym: Jeffery Hudson, q.v.
Binary. Knopf, 1972; Heinemann, 1972
Drug of Choice. Signet, 1970. British
title: Overkill. Sphere, 1972
[Nassau]
Easy Go. Signet, 1968; Sphere, 1972
[Egypt]
Grave Descend. Signet, 1970 [Jam.]
The Last Tomb. Bantam, 1974 [Egypt]
Odds On. Signet, 1966 [Sp.]
Overkill; see Drug of Choice
Scratch One. Signet, 1967 [Fr.]
The Venom Business. World, 1969 [Eng.]
Zero Cool. Signet, 1969; Sphere, 1972
[Sp.]

LANGE, OLIVER. Pseudonym. 1927-   .
Ref: CA.
Incident at La Junta. Stein, 1973
[Mex.]
Red Snow. Seaview, 1978; Davies, 1978
[N. Mex.]

LANGELAAN, GEORGE. 1908-   .
Turncoat. Hale, 1967

LANGHAM, JAMES R. SC: Samuel G. Abbott,
in both titles.
A Pocket Full of Clues. Simon, 1941;
Hale, 1943, as A Pocketful of Clues
[L.A.]
Sing a Song of Homicide. Simon, 1940.
British title: Sing a Song of Murder.
Hale, 1942 [L.A.]
Sing a Song of Murder; see Sing a Song
of Homicide

LANGLEY, BOB [ROBERT]. 1936-   . Ref:
CA.
Death Stalk. Joseph, 1977; Doubleday,
1978
Traverse of the Gods. Joseph, 1980;
Morrow, 1980 [Switz., 1944]
The War of the Running Fox. Joseph,
1978; Scribner, 1979 [Rhod.]
Warlords. Joseph, 1979; Morrow, 1981

LANGLEY, FREDERIC. Joint pseudonym with
   Ronald D. Ellik, 1938-1968: Frederic
   Davies, q.v.
LANGLEY, LEE. Pseudonym of Sarah Langley,
   1927- . Ref: CC. Graduate in
   journalism; occupational therapist at
   NYC hospital in 1960s. SC: Lt. Chris-
   topher Jensen, in both titles.
   Dead Center. Doubleday, 1968; Hale,
      1969 [acad.]
   Osiris Died in Autumn. Doubleday, 1964.
      British title: Twilight of Death.
      Hale, 1965 [N.Y.]
   Twilight of Death; see Osiris Died in
      Autumn
LANGLEY, NOEL (AUBREY). 1911-1980. Ref:
   CA.
   Tales of Mystery and Revenge. Barker,
      1950 ss
LANGLEY, SARAH. 1927- . Pseudonym: Lee
   Langley, q.v.
LANGLOIS, DORA
   In the Shadow of Pa-Menkh. Low, 1908
LANGMAID, KENNETH (JOSEPH ROBB). Pseudo-
   nym: Kenneth Laing, q.v.
   Mystery Cruise. Hale, 1958
LANGSLOW, JANE. See: Margaret R(ivers)
   Larminie, 1885- .
LANGTON, JANE (GILLSON). 1922- . Ref:
   CA. SC: Homer Kelly, in all titles.
   Dark Nantucket Noon. Harper, 1975
      [Mass.]
   The Memorial Hall Murder. Harper, 1978
      [Boston, acad.]
   The Minuteman Murder; see The Transcen-
      dental Murder
   The Transcendental Murder. Harper,
      1964. Also published as: The Minute-
      man Murder. Dell, 1976 [Mass.]
LANHAM, EDWIN (MOULTRIE). 1904-1979. Ref:
   CA, CC. SC: Lt. Gray = G; Frank
   Luther = FL; Lt. Madigan = M.
   The Case of the Missing Corpse; see
      Death of a Corinthian
   Death in the Wind. Harcourt, 1956;
      Boardman, 1957 G [Conn.]
   Death of a Corinthian. Harcourt, 1953;
      Boardman, 1954. Also published as:
      The Case of the Missing Corpse. Best-
      seller, 1955 G [Conn.]
   Double Jeopardy. Harcourt, 1959; Gol-
      lancz, 1959
   Headline for Murder; see Slug It Slay
   Headlined for Murder; see Slug It Slay
   It Shouldn't Happen to a Dog. Boardman,
      1947
   Monkey on a Chain. Harcourt, 1963; Gol-
      lancz, 1963 [NYC]
   Murder on My Street. Harcourt, 1958;
      Gollancz, 1958 FL
   No Hiding Place. Harcourt, 1962; Gol-
      lancz, 1962 FL [NYC]
   One Murder Too Many. Harcourt, 1952;
      Boardman, 1953 M [ship]
   Passage to Danger. Harcourt, 1962;
      Gollancz, 1962 [ship]
   Politics Is Murder. Harcourt, 1947 M
      [NYC]
   Six Black Camels. Harcourt, 1961; Gol-
      lancz, 1961 [Conn.]
   Slug It Slay. Harcourt, 1946; Boardman,
      1948. Also published as: Headlined
      for Murder. Bantam, 1948. And as:
      Headline for Murder. Boardman, 1950
      M [NYC]
LANNING, GEORGE (WILLIAM, JR.). 1925- .
   Ref: CA.
   The Pedestal. Harper, 1966; Joseph,
      1967 [Ohio]
LANSDALE, NINA
   The White Island. Arbor, 1975 [Sp.]
LANSDELL, SARAH
   Manfredi, Baron St. Osmund. Lane, 1796
   The Tower; or, The Romance of Ruthyne.
      Smith, 1798
LANSDOWNE, ANDREW
   -A Life's Reminiscences of Scotland Yard.
      Leadenhall, 1890; Scribner, 1890
LANTRY, MIKE. Pseudonym of Edwin Charles
   Tubb, 1919- . See also: Arthur
   (George) McLean.
   Assignment New York. Spencer, 1955
      [NYC]
LANZA, CLARA, 1858- , and JAMES C.
   HARVEY. For Lanza, see also: (Dr.)
   William A(lexander) Hammond, 1828-
   1900.
   Scarabaeus. Lovell, 1892

LAPATINE, KENNETH A.
   The Trials and Tribulations of Aaron
      Amsted. Walker, 1974
LAPIERRE, DOMINIQUE. 1931- . See:
   Larry Collins, 1929- .
LA PLANTE, JERRY. SC: Vance Garde (The
   Chameleon), in all titles.
   Garde Save the World. Zebra, 1979
   In Garde We Trust. Zebra, 1979
   The Wrath of Garde. Zebra, 1979
LA POINTE, DIANE
   Flames over the Castle. Ace, 1975
      [Calif.]
   The Picture of Death. Ace, 1975
LARANY, DANIEL
   The Big Red Sun. Prentice-Hall, 1971
      (Translation of "Le Grand Soleil
      Rouge." Paris, 1969.)
LARBALESTIER, P(HILIP) G(EORGE). SC:
   Insp. Michael Farrant, in at least
   those marked MF. Set: Eng.
   Black Shrouds the Bride. Gifford, 1951
      MF
   Darling, Don't Be Dumb. Gifford, 1950
      MF
   Death Casts No Shadow. Gifford, 1951
      MF
   Officer, That's Your Man. Gifford, 1947
      ss
   The Singing Sword. Gifford, 1954
   The Yellow Card Mystery. Gifford, 1950
LARIAR, LAWRENCE. 1908-1981. Pseudonyms:
   Adam Knight, Michael Lawrence,
   Michael Stark, qq.v. Ref: CA. SC:
   Homer Bull = HB.
   The Day I Died. Appleton, 1952 [Fla.]
   Death Is Confidential. Hillman, 1959
      [NYC]
   Death Is the Host; see Death Paints the
      Picture
   Death Paints the Picture. Phoenix,
      1943. Also published as: Death Is the
      Host. Crime Novel Selection, 1943 HB
      [N.Y.]
   Friday for Death. Crown, 1949; Board-
      man, 1950 [NYC]
   The Girl with the Frightened Eyes.
      Dodd, 1945; Cassell, 1950 HB [NYC]
   He Died Laughing. Phoenix, 1943; Board-
      man, 1946 HB [L.A.]
   The Man with the Lumpy Nose. Dodd, 1944
      HB [NYC]
   Win, Place and Die! Appleton, 1953
      [L.I.]
   You Can't Catch Me. Crown, 1951
LARKIN, R(OCHELLE) T. 1935- . Ref: CA.
   SC: The Donna, in all titles.
   For Godmother and Country. Lancer, 1972
      [Wash. D.C.]
   The Godmother. Lancer, 1971 [NYC]
   Honor Thy Godmother. Lancer, 1972
      [Sic.]
LARKING, CUTHBERT. 1842-1910.
   -Of the Deepest Dye. Hurst, 1897
LARMINIE, MARGARET R(IVERS), 1885-
   and JANE LANGSLOW
   Gory Knight. Longmans, 1937
LARNED, W. L. or JOSEPH. Pseudonym:
   Nicholas Carter, q.v.
LARNER, CELIA
   -Miranda. Milton House, 1973
   Summer's Lease. Milton House, 1974
LA ROCHE, K. ALISON
   Dear Dead Professor. Phoenix, 1944
      [acad.]
LaROSA, LINDA J., 1951- , and BARRY
   TANENBAUM, 1944- . LaRosa is a
   NYC freelance writer. Tanenbaum was
   born in NYC, is photo magazine edi-
   tor.
   The Random Factor. Doubleday, 1978;
      Gollancz, 1979 [NYC]
LARSEN, GAYLORD D. Media specialist at
   Calif. college; has been film produ-
   cer and editor, and in advertising.
   The Kilbourne Connection. Bethany, 1980
      [Calif.]
LARSON, CHARLES. 1922- . Ref: CA. SC:
   Nils-Frederik Blixen, in all titles.
   Matthew's Hand. Doubleday, 1974; Gol-
      lancz, 1978 [Calif.]
   Muir's Blood. Doubleday, 1976; Gol-
      lancz, 1978 [L.A.]
   Someone's Death. Lippincott, 1973
      [L.A.]

LARSON, RUSSELL W. 1908?- .
   Death Stalks a Marriage. Bellevue
      Books, 1956
LARTEGUY, JEAN. 1920- .
   Presumed Dead. Allen, 1974 (Transla-
      tion of "Enquete sur un Crucifie."
      Paris, 1973.)
LASCELLES, ESME
   The Italian Maze. Milton House, 1973
LASH, JENNIFER
   Get Down There and Die. Harvester, 1977
LA SPINA, (FANNY) GREYE (BRAGG). 1880-
   1969. Ref: CA.
   -Invaders from the Dark. Arkham, 1960.
      Also published as: Shadow of Evil.
      Paperback Library, 1966
LAST, JACK. All titles are plays; number
   of acts given in parenthesis.
   The Advancement of Mr. Simpkin. Baker,
      1954 (3)
   "Any Body for Tennis?" Deane, 1968 (2)
   Coffee for One. Deane, 1955 (1)
   Make It Murder. Deane, 1955 (3)
   Mr. Mason. Deane, 1955 (3)
LATEY, JOHN
   Love-Clouds. "Fun" Office, 1887
   The River of Life. "Fun" Office, 1886
LATHAM, AARON. 1943- . Ref: CA.
   Orchids for Mother. Little, 1977
      [Wash. D.C., Isr.]
LATHAM, ALISON. Joint pseudonym with
   Esther Latham: Murray Latham, q.v.
LATHAM, EDYTHE
   -The Seasons of God. Doubleday, 1963
LATHAM, ESTHER. Joint pseudonym with
   Alison Latham: Murray Latham, q.v.
LATHAM, JEAN LEE. 1902- . Ref: CA.
   The Arms of the Law. Dramatic, 1940
      (3-act play.)
   The Ghosts of Rhodes Manor. Dramatists,
      1939 (3-act play.)
   The House Without a Key. Dramatic, 1942
      (3-act play based on the novel by
      Earl Derr Biggers, 1884-1933, q.v.)
   The Nightmare. French (NYC), 1953
      (3-act play.)
LATHAM, LORRAINE. 1948- . Ref: CA.
   Identity Crisis. Morrow, 1975 [Eng.]
LATHAM, MURRAY. Joint pseudonym of Alison
   Latham and Esther Latham. Set: Eng.
   Enjoy Such Liberty. Hutchinson, 1943
   Even from the Law. Hutchinson, 1946
   Flight Without Wings. Hutchinson, 1950
   River in the Dark. Hutchinson, 1945
   Some Names Are Dangerous. Hutchinson,
      1948
LATHEN, EMMA. Joint pseudonym of Mary
   Jane Latsis, ca.1927- , and Martha
   Henissart, ca.1929- . Other joint
   pseudonym: R. B. Dominic, q.v. Ref:
   CC, EM, MC, TC. SC: John Putnam
   Thatcher, in all titles.
   Accounting for Murder. Macmillan, 1964;
      Gollancz, 1965 [NYC]
   Ashes to Ashes. Simon, 1971; Gollancz,
      1971 [NYC]
   Banking on Death. Macmillan, 1961; Gol-
      lancz, 1962 [N.Y.]
   By Hook or by Crook. Simon, 1975; Gol-
      lancz, 1975 [NYC]
   Come to Dust. Simon, 1968; Gollancz,
      1969 [acad., N.H.]
   Death Shall Overcome. Macmillan, 1966;
      Gollancz, 1967 [NYC]
   Double, Double, Oil and Trouble. Simon,
      1978; Gollancz, 1979
   The Longer the Thread. Simon, 1971;
      Gollancz, 1972 [P. Rico]
   Murder Against the Grain. Macmillan,
      1967; Gollancz, 1967 [NYC]
   Murder Makes the Wheels Go Round. Mac-
      mialln, 1966; Gollancz, 1966 [Det.]
   Murder to Go. Simon, 1969; Gollancz,
      1970 [N.J.]
   Murder Without Icing. Simon, 1972; Gol-
      lancz, 1973 [NYC]
   Pick Up Sticks. Simon, 1970; Gollancz,
      1971 [New Eng.]
   A Place for Murder. Macmillan, 1963;
      Gollancz, 1963 [Conn.]
   A Stitch in Time. Macmillan, 1968; Gol-
      lancz, 1968 [L.I.]
   Sweet and Low. Simon, 1974; Gollancz,
      1974 [N.Y.]
   When in Greece. Simon, 1969; Gollancz,
      1969 [Greece]

LATHOM, FRANCIS. 1777-1832.
   The Fatal Vow; or, St. Michael's Monastery. Crosby, 1807
   Italian Mysteries; or, More Secrets Than One. Newman, 1820 [It.]
   The Midnight Bell. Symonds, 1798; Folio, 1968
   Mystery. Symonds, 1800
   Mystic Events; or, The Vision of the Tapestry. Newman, 1830
   The Unknown; or, The Northern Gallery. Lane, 1808 [Eng., ca.1530]

LATHROP, GEORGE PARSONS. 1851-1898. Born in Honolulu; newspaper and periodical editor and novelist.
   In the Distance. Osgood, 1882 [N.H., acad.]
   Would You Kill Him? Harper, 1890; Douglas, 1889 [N.Y.]

LATIMER, JOHN. 1937- . Born in Can.
   Border of Darkness. Doubleday, 1972; Milton House, 1973 [Ger.]
   Kelpie's Burn. Musson, 1976

LATIMER, JONATHAN (WYATT). 1906-1983. Ref: CC, EM. MC, MP, TC. Pseudonym: Peter Coffin, q.v. SC: Bill Crane = BC.
   Black Is the Fashion for Dying. Random, 1959. British title: The Mink-Lined Coffin. Methuen, 1960
   The Dead Don't Care. Doubleday, 1938; Methuen, 1938 BC [Fla.]
   The Fifth Grave. Popular Library, 1950. British title: Solomon's Vineyard. Methuen, 1941
   Headed for a Hearse. Doubleday, 1935; Methuen, 1936. Also published as: The Westland Case. Sun Dial, 1938 BC [Chi.]
   The Lady in the Morgue. Doubleday, 1936; Methuen, 1937 BC [Chi.]
   The Mink-Lined Coffin; see Black Is the Fashion for Dying
   Murder in the Madhouse. Doubleday, 1935; Hurst, 1935 BC [N.Y.]
   Red Gardenias. Doubleday, 1939; Methuen, 1939. Also published as: Some Dames Are Deadly. Jonathan, 1955 BC
   Sinners and Shrouds. Simon, 1955; Methuen, 1956 [Chi.]
   Solomon's Vineyard; see The Fifth Grave
   Some Dames Are Deadly; see Red Gardenias
   The Westland Case; see Headed for a Hearse

LATIMER, RUPERT. Pseudonym of Algernon Victor Mills, 1905- .
   Death in Real Life. Macdonald, 1943
   Murder After Christmas. Macdonald, 1944

LATONA, BOB. Pseudonym: Nick Carter, q.v.

LATOUCHE, HARRIET
   Tarot Cards in Thessaly. New Horizon, 1980

LA TOURRETTE, JACQUELINE. 1926- . Ref: CA.
   An Ancient Rage. Dell, 1978
   -A Cruel Heart. Dell, 1977
   The Joseph Stone. Leisure, 1971 [Ire.]
   The Madonna Creek Witch. Dell, 1973 [Ariz., 1800s]
   A Matter of Sixpence. Dell, 1972
   The Pompeii Scroll. Delacorte, 1975. Also published as: Pompeii Splendor. Dell, 1977 [It.]
   Pompeii Splendor; see The Pompeii Scroll
   The Previous Lady. Dell, 1974 [Eng.]
   Shadows in Umbria. Putnam, 1979 [It.]

LATSIS, MARY JANE. ca.1927- . A lawyer. Joint pseudonyms with Martha Henissart, ca.1929- : R. B. Dominic, Emma Lathen, qq.v.

LATTA, GORDON. 1904- . SC: Arnholt, in all titles. Set: Eng.
   Arnholt Makes His Bow. Benn, 1931. U.S. title: The Toni Diamonds. Dial, 1931
   Exit Arnholt. Bles, 1935
   Re-Enter Arnholt. Benn, 1932
   The Toni Diamonds; see Arnholt Makes His Bow

LATTER, SIMON. Both titles are novelizations of "The Girl from UNCLE" TV series.
   The Global Globules Affair. Souvenir pb, 1967
   The Golden Boats of Taradata Affair. Souvenir pb, 1967

LAUBEN, PHILIP. Retired U.S. Air Force officer living in Tenn.
   Boogie Was a Gent. Hale, 1975
   The Krazny Connection. Hale, 1978
   Shall We Send Flowers? Hale, 1976

LAUDER, WILLIAM
   The Uncanny. Arrow, 1977

LAUFERTY, LILIAN. 1887-1958.
   The Crimson Thread. Simon, 1942; Jarrolds, 1943 [L.I.]
   The Hungry House. Simon, 1943; Jarrolds, 1944 [Conn.]

LAUMER, (JOHN) KEITH. 1925- . Ref: CA. Novelizations of "The Avengers" TV series = A; novelizations of "The Invaders" TV series = I.
   The Afrit Affair. Berkley, 1968 A [Eng.]
   Deadfall. Doubleday, 1971; Hale, 1974. Also published as: Fat Chance. PB, 1975; New English Library pb, 1975 [L.A., 1948]
   The Drowned Queen. Berkley, 1968 A [ship]
   Enemies from Beyond. Pyramid, 1967 I
   Fat Chance; see Deadfall
   The Gold Bomb. Berkley, 1968 A [Eng.]
   The Invaders. Pyramid, 1967. British title: The Meteor Men, as by Anthony LeBaron. Corgi, 1968
   The Meteor Men; see The Invaders

LAUNAY, DROO [ANDREW JOSEPH LAUNAY]. 1930- . Ref: CA. SC: Adam Flute, in all titles. Set: Eng.
   A Corpse in Camera. Boardman, 1963
   Death and Still Life. Boardman, 1964
   The New Shining White Murder. Boardman, 1962
   The Scream. Boardman, 1965
   She Modelled Her Coffin. Boardman, 1961
   The Two-Way Mirror. Boardman, 1964

LAURENCE, JOHN. Pseudonym of John Laurence Pritchard, 1885- . Set: Eng.
   The Double Cross Inn. Long, 1929
   The Fanshawe Court Mystery. Hodder, 1925
   The Gold Treasure Mystery. Low, 1938
   The Great Aeroplane Mystery. Low, 1935
   The Honeymoon Mystery. Long, 1929
   The Linkram Jewels. Jenkins, 1924
   Murder in the Stratosphere. Low, 1938
   The Mysteries of Ryeburn Manor. Long, 1930
   Mystery from the Air. Low, 1934
   Mystery Money. Long, 1930
   The Perfect Alibi. Jenkins, 1926
   The Pursuing Shadow. Hodder, 1927
   The Riddle of Wraye. Low, 1936
   The Secret of Sheen. Long, 1927; International Fiction Library, 1929
   The Whiteoaks Murder. Low, 1937

LAURENCE, ROSS
   The Fast Buck. Ace, 1953 [Chi.]

LAURENS, MARSHALL
   The Z Effect. PB, 1974

LAURENSON, R(OBERT) M(ARK). SC: Marc Jordan, in at least those marked MJ.
   Better Off Dead. Arcadia, 1955; Foulsham, 1956
   The Case of the Six Bullets. Phoenix, 1949; Foulsham, 1950 MJ
   The Railroad Murder Case. Phoenix, 1948; Foulsham, 1950 MJ

LAURENT-CELY, JACQUES. 1919- . Pseudonym: Cecil Saint-Laurent, q.v.

LAURENTS, CLYDE. Joint pseudonym with James Smock: Harriet Fredericks, q.v.

LAURIA, FRANK (JONATHAN). 1935- . Ref: CA. SC: Dr. Owen Orient, in all titles.
   Dr. Orient. Bantam, 1970
   Lady Sativa. Curtis, 1973
   The Seth Papers. Ballantine, 1979

LAURISTON, VICTOR. 1881- .
   The Twenty-First Burr. Doran, 1922

LAVERY, EMMET (GODFREY). 1902- .
   Murder in a Nunnery. French, 1944 (Play based on the novel by Eric Shepherd, 1892- , q.v.)

LAW, JANICE [JANICE LAW TRECKER]. 1941- . SC: Anna Peters, in all titles. Ref: CA.
   The Big Payoff. Houghton, 1976; Hale, 1978
   Gemini Trip. Houghton, 1977; Hale, 1978 [Paris]
   The Shadow of the Palms. Houghton, 1980; Hale, 1981 [Fla.]
   Under Orion. Houghton, 1978; Hale, 1979

LAW, MARJORIE J. Pseudonym of Marjorie Jean Liddelow.
   Death in the Spring. Cassell, 1965

LAWLESS, ANTHONY. Pseudonym of Philip MacDonald, 1899-1981, q.v. Other pseudonym: Martin Porlock, q.v. Joint pseudonym with Ronald MacDonald, 1860-1933: Oliver Fleming, q.v.

LAWLESS, BETTYCLARE HAMILTON. 1915- . Pseudonym: Clare Hamilton, q.v.

LAWRENCE, ALFRED
   Cade's County. Popular Library, 1972 (Novelization of the TV series.)
   Columbo. Popular Library, 1972; Wingate, 1976 (Novelization of the TV series.) [L.A.]
   The Dean's Death. Popular Library, 1975; Wingate, 1977 (Novelization of the "Columbo" TV series.) [L.A., acad.]

LAWRENCE, DAVID. Pseudonym of David Henry St. Lawrence Morris, 1920- . SC: Danny Leather, in both titles.
   Dead Orchid. Ward, 1958
   Death Has Two Hands. Ward, 1958

LAWRENCE, GIL. Pseudonym of Gilbert L. Geis.
   Fury with Legs. Pyramid, 1958
   The Woman Racket. Pyramid, 1959

LAWRENCE, H(ENRY) L(IONEL). 1908- . Ref: CA.
   The Children of Light. Macdonald, 1960
   The Sparta Medallion. Macdonald, 1961

LAWRENCE, HADLEY
   The Intruder. Micron, 1961 [Russ.]

LAWRENCE, HILDA. Pseudonym of Hilda Kronemiller, 1906(?)- . Ref: EM, TC. SC: Mark East = ME.
   The Bleeding House; see Duet of Death
   Blood Upon the Snow. Simon, 1944; Chapman, 1946 ME [New Eng.]
   Composition for Four Hands; see Duet of Death
   The Deadly Pavilion; see The Pavilion
   Death Has Four Hands; see Duet of Death
   Death of a Doll. Simon, 1947; Chapman, 1948 ME [NYC]
   Duet in Death; see Duet of Death
   Duet of Death. Simon, 1949; Chapman, 1949. Also published as: Duet in Death. Ace, 1963 (Two novelets, Composition for Four Hands and The House. The former was reprinted separately as: Death Has Four Hands. Bestseller, 1950. The latter was reprinted separately as: The Bleeding House. Bestseller, 1950.)
   The Pavilion. Simon, 1946; Chapman, 1948. Also published as: The Deadly Pavilion. PB, 1948 [South]
   A Time to Die. Simon, 1945; Chapman, 1947 ME [New Eng.]

LAWRENCE, JAMES D. SC: Angela Harpe, in all titles.
   The Dream Girl Caper. Pyramid, 1975
   The Emerald Oil Caper. Pyramid, 1975
   The Gilded Snatch Caper. Pyramid, 1975
   The Godmother Caper. Pyramid, 1975

LAWRENCE, JOSEPH I(VERS)
   Tower of Terror. Macaulay, 1933 [NYC]

LAWRENCE, LARS. Pseudonym of Philip Edward Stevenson.
   The Hoax. International, 1961; Calder, 1961

LAWRENCE, MARGERY (H.). -1969. Ref: CC. SC: Miles Pennoyer = MP.
   -Autumn Rose. Hale, 1971
   -Bride of Darkness. Hale, 1967; Ace, 1969
   -The Bridge of Wonder. Hale, 1939
   -Cardboard Castle. Hale, 1951
   -The Crooked Smile. Jarrolds, 1935
   -Drums of Youth. Hurst, 1929
   -Emma of Alkistan. Hale, 1953
   -Evil Harvest. Hale, 1954
   Fine Feathers. Curtiss, 1928 (British title)
   -The Floating Cafe, and other stories. Jarrolds, 1936 ss
   -Green Archer. Hale, 1962
   The Green Bough. Hale, 1968
   Madame Holle. Jarrolds, 1934
   The Madonna of the Seven Moons. Hurst, 1931; Bobbs, 1933
   Master of Shadows. Hale, 1959 ss MP
   Miss Brandt: Adventuress. Hutchinson, 1923 (3 novelets.)

-Nights of the Round Table. Hutchinson, 1926 ss
Number Seven Queer Street. Hale, 1945; Mycroft, 1969 ss MP
-Over My Shoulder. Hale, 1968
-Snapdragon. Hurst, 1931 ss
-Spanish Interlude. Hale, 1959
-Step Light, Lady. Hale, 1942
-Strange Caravan. Hale, 1941
-The Unforgettable Heart. Hale, 1963
-The Yellow Triangle. Hale, 1965

LAWRENCE, MARY MARGARET. 1920-   . Ref: CA.
Seven Thunders. Dell, 1974

LAWRENCE, MICHAEL. Pseudonym of Lawrence Lariar, 1908-1981, q.v. Other pseudonyms: Adam Knight, Michael Stark, qq.v. SC: Johnny Amsterdam, in both titles.
I Like It Cool. Popular Library, 1960
Naked and Alone. Popular Library, 1953

LAWRENCE, RAYMOND and KATHARINE MOUNT
-Liers in Wait. Humphries, 1956

LAWRENCE, REGINALD
The Legend of Lizzie. Dramatic, 1959 (2-act play.)

LAWRENCE, ROBERT JACKSON
Murder in Mayfair. Comet, 1958

LAWRENCE, SUSANNAH. Pseudonym of Lorie and Jan Hartman.
The Daughters of Music. Popular Library, 1973 [NYC]

LAWS, GERALDINE. See: Leonard (Reginald) Gribble, 1908-   .

LAWSON, STEVE
Scorpio. Pyramid, 1975 [L.A.]

LAWSON, W. B. SC: The Dalton Boys = DB; Jesse James = JJ.
Bob Ford, the Slayer of Jesse James; or, The Dramatic Life and Death of a Noted Desperado. Street, 1898 JJ
The Dalton Boys and the M.K. and T. Robbery. Street, 1899 DB
The Dalton Boys in California; or, A Bold Hold-Up at Ceres. Street, 1893 DB [Calif.]
Frank James in St. Louis; or, The Mysteries of a Great City. Street, 1898 [St. Louis]
The Hatfield-McCoy Feud. Street, 1898
Jesse James at Coney Island; or, The Wall Street Banker's Secret. Street, 1898 JJ [NYC]
Jesse James at Long Branch. Street, 1898 JJ
Jesse James' Double; or, The Man from Missouri. Street, 1898 JJ
Jesse James in New York; or, A Plot Against a Millionaire. Street, 1898 JJ [NYC]
Jesse James' Oath; or, Tracked to Death. Street, 1898 JJ
The Red Canyon Mystery. Street, 1902

LAYARD, G(EORGE) S(OMES). 1857-1925.
The Amateur Criminal. Allan, 1925 ss

LAYHEW, JANE. Born in Can., living in Montreal in 1940s.
Rx for Murder. Lippincott, 1946 [Van.]

LAYLAND-BARRATT, FRANCES.   -1953.
Lycanthia. Jenkins, 1935

LAYMON, RICHARD. 1947-   . Ref: CA.
The Cellar. Warner, 1980

LAYTON, FRANK GEORGE. 1872-1941.
"Hanged by the Neck." Nicholson, 1935

LAZARUS, LEON. Pseudonym: Nick Carter, q.v.

LAZARUS, MARGUERITE. 1916-   . Pseudonym: Anna Gilbert, q.v.

LAZARUS, MILTON. See: Rufus (Frederick) King, 1893-1966.

LEA, G(EORGE) F(RANCIS) PERCIVALE. 1907-   . Ref: CC.
A Detective Unawares. Hurst, 1928

LEA, HUGH. Set: Eng.
The Ghosts of Perranprah. Hodder, 1937
The Mine of Ill Omen. Hodder, 1939

LEA, TIMOTHY
Confessions of a Private Dick. Futura, 1975

LEACH, CHRISTOPHER. 1925-   . Born in London; painter, poet, novelist, author of children's books.
The Send-Off. Chatto, 1973; Scribner, 1974

LEACH, DOUGLAS
The Big Boys. Hale, 1969
The Man on the Marsh. Hale, 1969
Three for a Killing. Hale, 1971

LEACH, JOAN
Sheltered. Vantage, 1977

LEACOCK, STEPHEN (BUTLER). 1869-1944. Ref: CA.
Frenzied Fiction. Lane (NYC), 1918 ss, at least one criminous
Further Foolishness. Lane (NYC), 1916 ss, at least one criminous
Nonsense Novels. Lane (NYC), 1911 ss, at least one criminous

LEADER, CHARLES. Pseudonym of Robert Charles Smith, 1938-   . Other pseudonym: Robert Charles, q.v. SC: Ric McAdden, in at least those marked RM; Mike McCall, in at least those marked MM; Paul Mason, in at least those marked PM; David Chan, in at least those marked DC.
The Angry Darkness. Hale, 1968
Cargo to Saigon. Hale, 1969 RM [Saigon]
Death of a Marine. Hale, 1970 MM
The Double M Man. Hale, 1969 MM
The Dragon Roars. Hale, 1970
Frontiers of Violence. Hale, 1966 PM
The Golden Lure. Hale, 1967 RM
Kingdom of Darkness. Hale, 1978
Murder in Marrakech. Hale, 1966 [Mor.]
Nightmare on the Nile. Hale, 1967 [Egypt]
Salesman of Death. Hale, 1971 MM
-Scavengers at War. Hale, 1974
Strangler's Moon. Hale, 1968 PM
A Wreath for Miss Wong. Hale, 1976
A Wreath from Bangkok. Hale, 1975 DC
A Wreath of Cherry Blossom. Hale, 1977
A Wreath of Poppies. Hale, 1975 DC

LEADER, MARY (BARTELT). Ref: CA.
Triad. Coward, 1973; Hodder, 1973

LEADERMAN, GEORGE. Pseudonym of Richard Blundell Robinson, 1905-   . Set: Eng.
Death in Pursuit. Hurst, 1935
The Door Was Violence. Hurst, 1935

LEAHY, W(ILLIAM) A(UGUSTINE). 1867-   .
The Incendiary. Rand, 1897

LEAMAN, ADELE
The Green Bag. Skeffington, 1932

LEAN, FLORENCE MARRYAT CHURCH. 1837-1899. Pseudonym: Florence Marryat, q.v.

LEARMONTH, DAVID. SC: Silas Wortenheimer, in at least those marked SW.
-After the Battle. Hutchinson, 1933
Checkmate and Stalemate; see Red Mammon
-The Empty Glass. Hutchinson, 1931
-Galloping Gold. Hutchinson, 1926
Red Mammon. Hutchinson, 1928. Also published as: Checkmate and Stalemate. Hutchinson pb, 1939 SW
Tainted Turf. Hutchinson, 1927 SW
-Tic-Tac. Hutchinson, 1930

LEAROYD, C(YRIL) G(EORGE)
Physicians' Fare. Arnold, 1939; Longmans, 1939 ss, some criminous

LEARY, FRANCIS (W.)
This Dark Monarchy. Dutton, 1949; Evans, 1950

LEASOR, (THOMAS) JAMES. 1923-   . Ref: CA, JL, TC. SC: Dr. Jason Love = JL; the owner of Aristo Autos = AA.
The Chinese Widow.
Code Name Nimrod; see The Unknown Warrior
Host of Extras. Heinemann, 1973 JL
Love-All. Heinemann, 1971 JL
Love and the Land Beyond. Heinemann, 1979 JL
Never Had a Spanner on Her. Heinemann, 1970 AA [Egypt]
Passport to a Pilgrim. Heinemann, 1968; Doubleday, 1969 JL [Damascus]
Passport in Suspense. Heinemann, 1967. U.S. title: The Yang Meridian. Putnam, 1968 JL
Passport to Oblivion. Heinemann, 1964; Lippincott, 1965. Also published as: Where the Spies Are. Signet, 1965; Pan, 1965 JL
Passport to Peril. Heinemann, 1966. U.S. title: Spylight. Lippincott, 1966 JL [Pak.]
Spylight; see Passport to Peril
They Don't Make Them Like That Any More. Heinemann, 1969; Doubleday, 1970 AA
-The Unknown Warrior. Heinemann, 1980. U.S. title: Code Name Nimrod. Houghton, 1981 [WWII]
A Week of Love. Heinemann, 1969 JL ss
Where the Spies Are; see Passport to Oblivion
The Yang Meridian; see Passport to Suspense

LEATHER, EDWIN (HARTLEY CAMERON). 1919-   . Ref: CA. SC: Rupert Conway, in all titles.
The Duveen Letter. Macmillan (London), 1980; Doubleday, 1980
The Mozart Score. Macmillan (London), 1979; Doubleday, 1979
The Vienna Elephant. Macmillan (London), 1978; Dodd, 1977 [Vienna]

LE BAILLY, PIERRE
Watch of Evil. Exposition, 1964; Hodder, 1967 (Translation of "Les Bons Sentiments." Paris, 1958.)

LeBARON, ANTHONY. Pseudonym of (John) Keith Laumer, 1925-   , q.v.

LE BAS, MARY
Castle Walk. Nelson, 1934
-Second Thoughts. Nelson, 1935

LEBHAR, BERTRAM
The Black Eye Snapshot. Street, 1912 [NYC]
The Snapshot Chap. Street, 1910

LEBHERZ, RICHARD
The Altars of the Heart. Barrie, 1957; Grove, 1957
The Man in the White Raincoat. Hogarth, 1961; London House, 1961
The Nazi Overcoat. Panther, 1967

LEBLANC, MAURICE (MARIE EMILE). 1864-1941. Ref: all except CA. SC: Arsene Lupin = AL (see also: Edgar Jepson, 1863-1938). Set: Fr.
The Arrest of Arsene Lupin; see Arsene Lupin Versus Holmlock Shears
Arsene Lupin, Gentleman Burglar; see The Exploits of Arsene Lupin
Arsene Lupin Intervenes; see Jim Barnett Intervenes
Arsene Lupin, Super Sleuth; see The Girl with the Green Eyes
Arsene Lupin Versus Herlock Sholmes; see Arsene Lupin Versus Holmlock Shears
Arsene Lupin Versus Holmlock Shears. Richards, 1909. U.S. title: The Blonde Lady. Doubleday, 1910. Also published as: Arsene Lupin Versus Herlock Sholmes. Donohue, 1910. And as: The Arrest of Arsene Lupin. Nash, 1911. And as: Sherlock Holmes Versus Arsene Lupin: The Case of the Golden Blonde. Atomic, 1946. And as: The Fair Haired Lady (Translation of "Arsene Lupin contre Herlock Sholmes." Paris, 1908.) AL (Two novelets.)
The Blonde Lady; see Arsene Lupin Versus Holmlock Shears
The Bomb-Shell. Hurst, 1916. U.S. title: The Woman of Mystery. Macaulay, 1916 (Translation of "L'Eclat d'Obus." Paris, 1916.)
The Candlestick with Seven Branches. Hurst, 1925. U.S. title: Memoirs of Arsene Lupin. Macaulay, 1925 (Translation of "La Comtesse de Cagliostro." Paris, 1924.) AL
Coffin Island. Hurst, 1920. U.S. title: The Secret of Sarek. Macaulay, 1920 (Translation of "L'Ile aux Trents Cercuils." Paris, 1920.) AL
The Confessions of Arsene Lupin. Mills, 1912; Doubleday, 1913 (Translation of "Les Confidences d'Arsene Lupin." Paris, 1913.) AL ss
The Crystal Stopper. Hurst, 1913; Doubleday, 1913 (Translation of "Le Bouchon de Cristal." Paris, 1912.) AL
Dorothy the Rope Dancer. Hurst, 1923. U.S. title: The Secret Tomb. Macaulay, 1923 (Translation of "Dorothee, Danseuse de Corde." Paris, 1923.)
The Double Smile. Skeffington, 1933. U.S. title: The Woman with Two Smiles. Macaulay, 1933 (Translation of "La Femme aux Deux Sourires." Paris, 1933.) AL
The Eight Strokes of the Clock. Cassell, 1922; Macaulay, 1922 (Translation of "Les Huits Coups de l"Horloge." Paris, 1922.) AL ss

813. Mills, 1910; Doubleday, 1910 (Translation of "813." Paris, 1910.) AL
The Exploits of Arsene Lupin. Cassell, 1909; Harper, 1907. Also published as: The Seven of Hearts. Cassell, 1908. And as: (The Extraordinary Adventures of) Arsene Lupin, Gentleman Burglar. Donohue, 1910 (Translation of "Arsene Lupin, Gentleman-Cambrioleur." Paris, 1907.) AL ss
The Extraordinary Adventures of Arsene Lupin, Gentleman Burglar; see The Exploits of Arsene Lupin
The Fair-Haired Lady; see Arsene Lupin Versus Holmlock Shears
From Midnight to Morning. Hurst, 1933; Macaulay, 1933 (Translation of "De Minuit a Sept Heures." Paris, 1932.)
The Frontier. Mills, 1912; Doran, 1912 (Translation of "La Frontiere." Paris, 1911.)
The Girl with the Green Eyes. Hurst, 1927. U.S. title: Arsene Lupin, Super-Sleuth. Macaulay, 1927 (Translation of "La Demoiselle aux Yeux Verts." Paris, 1927.) AL
The Golden Triangle. Hurst, 1917; Macaulay, 1917 (Translation of "La Triangle d'Or." Paris, 1918.) AL
The Hollow Needle. Nash, 1911; Doubleday, 1910 (Translation of "L'Aiguille Creuse." Paris, 1909.) AL
Jim Barnett Intervenes. Mills, 1928. U.S. title: Arsene Lupin Intervenes. Macaulay, 1929 (Translation of "L'Agence Barnett et Cie." Paris, 1928.) AL ss
Man of Miracles. Skeffington, 1932; Macaulay, 1931 (Translastion of "Prince de Jericho." Paris, 1930.)
The Melamare Mystery. Mills, 1929; Macaulay, 1930 (Translation of "La Demeure Mysterieuse." Paris, 1929.) AL
Memoirs of Arsene Lupin; see The Candlestick with Seven Branches
The Return of Arsene Lupin. Skeffington, 1933; Macaulay 1933 (Translation of "Victor, de la Brigade Mondaine." Paris, 1933.) AL
The Secret of Sarek; see Coffin Island
The Secret Tomb; see Dorothy the Rope Dancer
The Seven of Hearts; see The Exploits of Arsene Lupin
Sherlock Holmes Versus Arsene Lupin; see Arsene Lupin Versus Holmlock Shears
The Teeth of the Tiger. Hurst, 1915; Doubleday, 1914 (Translation of "Les Dents du Tigre." Paris, 1921.) AL
-The Tremendous Event. Hurst, 1924; Macaulay, 1922 (Translation of "Le Formidable Evenement." Paris, 1921.)
-Wanton Venus. Long, 1935; Macaulay, 1935 (Translation of "L'Image de la Femme Nue." Paris, 1934.)
The Woman of Mystery; see The Double Smile
The Woman with Two Smiles; see The Double Smile

LE BRETON, AUGUSTE. Pseudonym of Auguste Montfort, 1913-   . Ref: CA.
The Law of the Streets. Collins, 1957 (Translation of "Le Loi des Rues." Paris, 1955.)
Rififi in New York. Stein, 1968 (Translation of "Du Rififi a New York." Paris, 1967.) [NYC]

LECALE, ERROL. Pseudonym of Wilfred (Glassford) McNeilly, 1921-   , q.v. Other pseudonyms: W(illiam) Howard Baker, William A. Ballinger, William Glassford, Desmond Reid, Peter Saxon, qq.v. S: Specialist = S.
Castledoom. New English Library pb, 1974   S
The Death Box. New English Library pb, 1974   S
The Severed Hand. New English Library pb, 1974   S
The Tigerman of Terrahpur. New English Library pb, 1973   S
Zombie. New English Library pb, 1975

LE CARRE, JOHN. Pseudonym of David John Moore Cornwell, 1931-   . Ref: CA, CC, EM, MC, TC. SC: George Smiley = GS. Set: Eng.
Call for the Dead. Gollancz, 1961; Walker, 1962. Also published as: The Deadly Affair. Penguin, 1968; Signet, 1968   GS
The Deadly Affair; see Call for the Dead
The Honourable Schoolboy. Hodder, 1977; Knopf, 1977   GS   [H. Kong]
The Looking Glass War. Heinemann, 1965; Coward, 1965   GS

A Murder of Quality. Gollancz, 1962; Walker, 1962   GS   [acad.]
A Small Town in Germany. Heinemann, 1968; Coward, 1968
Smiley's People. Hodder, 1980; Knopf, 1980   GS
The Spy Who Came in from the Cold. Gollancz, 1963; Coward, 1964   GS
Tinker, Tailor, Soldier, Spy. Hodder, 1974; Knopf, 1974   GS

LECHMERE, DAVID
In Deadly Peril. Ouseley, 1908 [Scot.]

LECOMBER, BRIAN. 1945-   . Ref: CA.
Dead Weight. Hodder, 1976; Delacorte, 1976
Turn Killer. Hodder, 1975; Stein, 1975

LEDERER, MIRA
The Adriatic Formula. Leisure, 1980

LEDERER, NORBERT (LEWIS). 1888-1955. See: Lillian Day, 1893-   .

LEDIG, ALMA. See: Ernestine Malan.

LEDIG, GERT. 1921-   .
The Brutal Years. Weidenfeld, 1959 (Translation of "Faustrecht." Munich, 1957.)

LEDWIDGE, (WILLIAM) BERNARD (JOHN). 1915-   . Ref: CA.
Frontiers. Weidenfeld, 1979; St. Martin's, 1979

LEE, AUSTIN. 1904-1965. Pseudonyms: John Austwick, Julian Callender, qq.v. Ref: CA, TC. SC: Miss Hogg, in all titles. Set: Eng.
Call in Miss Hogg. Cape, 1956
Miss Hogg and the Bronte Murders. Cape, 1956
Miss Hogg and the Covent Garden Murders. Cape, 1960
Miss Hogg and the Dead Dean. Cape, 1958
Miss Hogg and the Missing Sisters. Cape, 1961
Miss Hogg and the Squash Club Murder. Cape, 1957
Miss Hogg Flies High. Cape, 1958
Miss Hogg's Last Case. Cape, 1963
Sheep's Clothing. Cape, 1955

LEE, BABS. Pseudonym of Marion van der Veer Lee, 1914-   . SC: Argus Steele, in all titles.
Measured for Murder, with Clare Castler Saunders, q.v. Scribner, 1944; Muller, 1945 [NYC]
A Model Is Murdered. Scribner, 1942 [NYC]
Passport to Oblivion. Scribner, 1943 [Port.]

LEE, BRETON
The Pit of Death. Fiction House, 1935

LEE, DORIAN
-The Bad Companions. Long, 1955
-The Captive Years. Long, 1951
-Crooked Paths. Swan, 1943
-Cut the Cards, Lady. Long, 1952
-Dark Star Rising. Long, 1947
-The Fledgling. Long, 1952
-Green Bracken. Long, 1952
-Home to Our Valley. Long, 1956
-Lover Come Home. Long, 1950
-Luke's Summer. Long, 1951
-Prisoner Go Free. Long, 1954
-Sandover Goes Gay. Swan, 1946
-Snakes Have Fangs. Long, 1946
-Strange Partner. Long, 1948
-Uncertain Treasure. Swan, 1947
-Wild Apple Orchard. Long, 1954

LEE, EDWARD. Pseudonym of Edward Lee Fouts, 1902-   . SC: Red Blake, in both titles.
Death Goes Fishing; see A Fish for Murder
A Fish for Murder. Doubleday, 1944; Hurst, 1947. Also published as: Death Goes Fishing. Thriller Novel Classic, 1944, abridged. And as: Lust to Kill. Jonathan, 1955 [L.A.]
Lust to Kill; see A Fish for Murder
The Needle's Eye. Doubleday, 1941 [L.A.]

LEE, ELSIE. 1912-   . Pseudonym: Elsie Cromwell, q.v. Joint pseudonym with Michael Sheridan: Lee Sheridan, q.v. SC: Sam Benedict (who also appears in books by Howard L. Oleck, 1911-   , and Brad Williams, 1918-   , qq.v.) = SB. Ref: CA.
Barrow Sinister. Dell, 1969. British title: Romantic Assignment. Hale, 1974
The Blood Red Oscar. Lancer, 1962
Clouds over Vallenti. Lancer, 1965; Hale, 1972   [It.]
A Comedy of Terrors. Lancer, 1964 (Novelization of the movie.)
The Curse of Carranca. Lancer, 1966. British title: The Second Romance. Hale, 1974
Dark Moon, Lost Lady. Lancer, 1966; Hale, 1973 [Ger.]
Diplomatic Lover. Dell, 1971
Doctor's Office. Lancer, 1968
The Drifting Sands. Lancer, 1966 [Mid. East]
An Eligible Connection. Dell, 1975; Chivers, 1974
Fulfillment. Lancer, 1969
Mansion of the Golden Windows. Lancer, 1966 [Scot.]
The Masque of the Red Death. Lancer, 1964 (Novelization of the movie.)
Muscle Beach Party. Lancer, 1964 (Novelization of the movie.)
Mystery Castle; see Satan's Coast
-The Nabob's Widow. Delacorte, 1976
The Passions of Medora Graeme. Arbor, 1972
Prior Betrothal. Arbor, 1973; Hale, 1976
Romance on the Rhine; see Sinister Abbey
Romantic Assignment; see Barrow Sinister
Sam Benedict: Cast the First Stone. Lancer, 1963 (Novelization of the TV series; the cover of the book attributes it to Norman Daniels, q.v.)   SB [S.F.]
Satan's Coast. Lancer, 1969. British title: Mystery Castle. Hale, 1973 [Port.]
Season of Evil. Lancer, 1965. British title: Two Hearts Apart, as by Jane Gordon. Hale, 1971
The Second Romance; see The Curse of Carranca
The Second Season. Dell, 1973
Silence Is Golden. Dell, 1971 [Eng., 1860s]
Sinister Abbey. Lancer, 1967. British title: Romance on the Rhine. Hale, 1974 [Ger.]
The Spy at the Villa Miranda. Lancer, 1967. British title: The Unhappy Parting. Hale, 1973
Star-Crossed Love. Dell, 1972
Star of Danger. Dell, 1971
Two Hearts Apart; see Season of Evil
The Unhappy Parting; see The Spy at the Villa Miranda
The Wicked Guardian. Dell, 1973; Sphere, 1979
Wingarden. Arbor, 1971 [Va.]

LEE, FLEMING. 1933-   . See: Leslie Charteris, 1907-   . Ref: CA.

LEE, GERALD
Murder and Music. Talbot, 1943

LEE, GYPSY ROSE. Stage name of Rose Louise Hovick, 1914-1970. The books signed by her were actually written by Georgiana Ann Randolph Craig, 1908-1957 (pseudonyms: Craig Rice, Daphne Sanders, Michael Venning, qq.v.). SC: Gypsy Rose Lee, in both titles. Ref: CC, MC.
The G-String Murders. Simon, 1941. British title: The Strip-Tease Murders. Lane, 1943. Also published as: Lady of Burlesque. Tower, 1942 [NYC, theatre]

Lady of Burlesque; see The G-String Murders
Mother Finds a Body. Simon, 1942; Lane, 1944 [Tex.]
The Strip-Tease Murders; see The G-String Murders

LEE, H. FLETCHER. See: Olive Lethbridge.

LEE, H. H.
-Fun Fair. Swan, 1942
Racket Busters, Incorporated. Swan, 1946
Snappy Vendetta. Swan, 1944

LEE, HERBERT PATRICK
Hell's Harbour. Melrose, 1936

LEE, JENNETTE (BARBOUR PERRY). 1860-1951. SC: Millicent Newberry, in all titles.
Dead Right. Scribner, 1925; Hurst, 1925 [NYC]
The Green Jacket. Scribner, 1917; Skeffington, 1918
The Mysterious Office. Scribner, 1922; Hurst, 1922

LEE, JOHN (DARRELL). 1931-   . Ref: CA. SC: Brian Douglas = BD.
Assignment in Algeria. Walker, 1971. British title: The Killing Wind. Long, 1972 [Algeria]   BD

244 / Lee, John W.

Caught in the Act. Morrow, 1968; Long, 1969 BD [Madrid]
The Killing Wind; see Assignment in Algeria
-Lago. Doubleday, 1980 [WWII, It.]
The Ninth Man. Doubleday, 1976; Cassell, 1976 [1942, Wash. D.C.]
The Thirteenth Hour. Doubleday, 1978; Cassell, 1979 [1944, Berlin]

LEE, JOHN W. Set: Eng.
Background to Death. Pictorial Art, 1945
Death by the Radio. Mitre, 1946
One from Five. Halle, 1946

LEE, LEONARD
The Twisted Mirror. Ziff-Davis, 1947

LEE, LINDA. 1947- . Ref: CA.
One by One. Simon, 1977; New English Library, 1979 [NYC]

LEE, MANFRED BENNINGTON. 1905-1971. Joint pseudonyms with Frederic Dannay, 1905-1982: Ellery Queen, Barnaby Ross, qq.v.

LEE, MARION BEVERIDGE
The Man with the Rake. Abbey, 1901

LEE, MARION VAN DER VEER. 1914- .
Pseudonym: Babs Lee, q.v.

LEE, MAUREEN
The Visitor. French (London), 1977 (Play.)

LEE, MELISSA
Shadows of Reddoch's Landing. Belmont, 1972

LEE, NOEL
Danger in Numbers. Wright, 1944
Fear Without End. Wright, 1949
Papers Mean Peril. Wright, 1942

LEE, NORMA. SC: Norma "Nicky" Lee (The Beautiful Gunner), in all titles.
Another Woman's Man. Laurie, 1954
The Beautiful Gunner. Laurie, 1953 [NYC]
The Broadway Jungle. Laurie, 1954 [NYC]
Lover—Say It with Mink! Laurie, 1953 [NYC]

LEE, NORMAN
The "Four Winds" Mystery. Mitre, 1946
Peril at Journey's End. Foster, 1947

LEE, NORMAN. 1905-1962. Pseudonyms: Raymond Armstrong, Mark Corrigan, Robertson Hobart, qq.v.

LEE, PETER
Mystery o' Sunny Fowt; and Fotchin Relief. Clegg, 1906 (Two stories.)

LEE, SOPHIE. 1750-1824.
The Recess; or, A Tale of Other Times. Cadell, 1785

LEE, SUSAN and SONDRA TILL ROBINSON, 1931- . Ref for Robinson: CA.
Dear John. Marek, 1980

LEE, SUSAN RICHMOND. Pseudonym: Curtis Yorke, q.v.

LEE, THOMAS
The Old Bull Inn of Silver Street, Edmonton. Lee, 1887 [Can.]

LEE, THORNE. Pseudonym of Thornton Shiveley. Born in Neb.; in 1950s living in Calif. and instructing in English and speech at a junior college; actor; writer under another name.
The Monster of Lazy Hook. Duell, 1949 [Calif.]
Summer Shock. Abelard, 1956 [Oreg.]

LEECH, AUDREY
Pawn of Evil. Pyramid, 1971
The Terror of Stormcastle. Paperback Library, 1973
The Witches of Omen. Pyramid, 1971

LEEK, MARGARET. Pseudonym of Sara Hutton Bowen-Judd, 1922- . Other pseudonyms: Anne Burton, Mary Challis, Sara Woods, qq.v. SC: Stephen Marryat, in both titles, set in Eng.
The Healthy Grave. Raven, 1980
We Must Have a Trial. Raven, 1980

LEES, DAN. 1927- . Ref: CA. SC: Jeff Plummer = JP. Set: Eng.
Elizabeth R.I.P. Constable, 1974; St. Martin's, 1975 JP
Mayhem in Morton Episcopi. Hale, 1980
Our Man in Morton Episcopi. Hale, 1979

The Rainbow Conspiracy. Constable, 1971; Walker, 1972 JP
Rape of a Quiet Town. Constable, 1973; Walker, 1973 JP
Zodiac. Constable, 1972; Walker, 1973 JP [Fr.]

LEES, HANNAH. Pseudonym of Elizabeth Head Fetter, 1904-1973. Ref: CA.
The Dark Device. Harper, 1947; Murray, 1949 [NYC]
Death in the Doll's House, with Lawrence P(aul) Bachmann, 1912- q.v. Random, 1943; Murray, 1944 [hosp.]
Prescription for Murder. Random, 1941; Murray, 1943 [hosp.]

LEES, HAROLD P(ERCY)
Ten Thousand Passports to Hell. Hale, 1968
This Way to Evil. Hale, 1971
The Violence of Hate. Hale, 1970

LEETE-HODGE, LORNIE
Dangerous Guest. Chivers, 1976

LE FANU, JOSEPH SHERIDAN. 1814-1873. Ref: CC, DD, EM, MC, MM, TC. Set: Eng.
All in the Dark. Bentley, 1866; Harper, 1862
Checkmate. Hurst, 1871; Evans, 1871
-Chronicles of Golden Friars. Bentley, 1871
The Evil Guest. Downey, 1894
Ghost Stories and Mysteries. Dover, 1975 ss, taken from earlier collections
Guy Deverell. Bentley, 1865; Harper, 1866
Haunted Lives. Tinsley, 1868
The House by the Church-Yard. Bentley, 1863
In a Glass Darkly. Bentley, 1872 ss
A Lost Name. Bentley, 1868
Madam Crowl's Ghost, and other tales of mystery. Bell, 1923 ss
The Rose and the Key. Chapman, 1871; Dover, 1983
-The Tenants of Malory. Tinsley, 1867; Harper, 1867
Uncle Silas. Bentley, 1864; Munro, 1878
-The Watcher and other weird stories. Downey, 1894 ss
Willing to Die. Hurst, 1873
Wylder's Hand. Bentley, 1864; Carleton, 1865
The Wyvern Mystery. Tinsley, 1869

LEFEVRE, C.
Murder in Marseilles. Brown Watson, 1953 [Mars.]

LEFEVRE, EDWIN. 1871-1943.
The Plunderers. Harper, 1916 ss

LEFFINGWELL, ALBERT. 1895-1946. Pseudonym: Dana Chambers, Giles Jackson, qq.v.
Nine Against New York. Holt, 1941 [NYC]

LEFFINGWELL, ALSOP
The Mystery of Bar Harbor. Dillingham, 1887 [Maine]

LEFFLAND, ELLA. 1931- . Ref: CA.
-Mrs. Munck. Houghton, 1970; H. Hamilton, 1971 [S.F.]

LEGARET, JEAN. 1913-1976. Ref: CA.
Tightrope. Little, 1970 (Translation of "Le Conde." Paris, 1967.) [Paris]

LEGGE, F.
The Spectre Chief; or, The Blood-Stained Banner. Bailey, 1800

LEGGETT, H. W.
-The Man Who Came Back. Gramol, 1935
-The Second Mrs. Savenage. Gramol, 1936
Under Suspicion. Hamilton, 1935

LEGGETT, WILLIAM. 1801-1939. See: Anonymous.

LEHMAN, ERNEST PAUL. 1915- . Ref: CA.
The French Atlantic Affair. Atheneum, 1977; Macmillan (London), 1977

LEHMANN, R(UDOLF) C(HAMBERS). 1856-1929. Graduate of Cambridge; trained in law; on staff of "Punch" and edited London newspaper; served in Parliament; wrote books on politics and the law. SC: Picklock Holes, in both titles, set in Eng.
The Adventures of Picklock Holes. Bradbury Agnew, 1901; Aspen, 1975 ss
The Return of Picklock Holes. Magico, 1980

LE HURAY, C. P.
Death for a Holiday. Big Ben, 1946 [Chan. Is.]

LEIGH, HILARY
Greystones. Pyramid, 1966

LEIGH, JAMES. 1937- .
The Ludi Victor. Bodley, 1981; Coward, 1980

LEIGH, LOIS (E.) AUSTEN. See: Lois (E.) Austen-Leigh.

LEIGH, SUSANNAH
Dark Labyrinth. GM, 1975 [Nepal]

LEIGH, VERONICA
The Boris Story. Manor, 1976
The Cat of Nine Tales. Manor, 1976
Dark Seed, Dark Flower. Manor, 1974
The Heston House Horror. Manor, 1977
Voodoo Drums. Manor, 1975

LEIGHTON, FLORENCE. Pseudonym of Florence Leighton Pfalzgraf, 1902- .
As Strange a Maze. Archer, 1935

LEIGHTON, MARIE (FLORA BARBARA) CONNOR. 18??-1941. Ref: MP. Set: Eng.
The Amazing Verdict. Richards, 1904
-Beauty's Queen. White, 1884
Black Silence. Ward, 1913
The Bride of Dutton Market. Ward, 1911
Builders of Ships. Ward, 1911
Convict 413L. Ward, 1910
Convict 99, with Robert Leighton, 1859-1933. Richards, 1898
Convict 100. Ward, 1920
Dark Peril. Hodder, 1916
Deep Waters. Ward, 1909
-The Duchess Grace. Ward, 1918
Ducks and Drakes. Ward, 1913
Every Man Has His Price. Ward, 1917
An Eye for an Eye. Ward, 1909
-The Fires of Love. Ward, 1915
-For Love or Money. Ward, 1922
The Gates of Sorrow. Ward, 1915
Geraldine Walton—Woman! Ward, 1914
The Girl of the Yellow Diamonds. Pearson, 1920
Greed. Ward, 1911
Guilty or Innocent? Ward, 1918
The Hand of the Unseen. Ward, 1918
The Harvest of Sin. Bowden, 1898
Her Convict Husband. Ward, 1913
-Her Fate and His. Ward, 1921
-Her Heart's Awakening. Chapman, 1893
-Her Ladyship's Silence. Cassell, 1907
-Her Marriage Lines. Ward, 1912
Hidden Hands. Newnes, 1918
Human Nature. Ward, 1916
-Husband and Wife. White, 1888
In God's Good Time. Richards, 1903
In the Grip of a Lie. Long, 1916
In the Plotter's Web. Mellifont, 1937
In the Shadow of Guilt, with Robert Leighton, 1859-1933. Richards, 1901; Brentano's, 1901
Joan Mar, Detective. Ward, 1910
Justice! Ward, 1910
-The Lady of Balmerino. Trischler, 1891
Lucile Dare, Detective. Ward, 1919
The Man Who Knew All. Long, 1916
A Marked Woman. Hodder, 1916
Michael Dred, Detective; with Robert Leighton, 1859-1933. Richards, 1899; Brentano's, 1899
The Missing Miss Randolph. Ward, 1912
"Money." Ward, 1909
The Money Spider. Mellifont, 1936
-A Morganatic Marriage. White, 1885
The Mystery of the Three Fingers. Long, 1916
-A Napoleon of the Press. Hodder, 1900
The Opal Heart. Ward, 1920
Put Yourself in Her Place. Ward, 1908
Red Gold. Ward, 1919
The Red Painted Box. Macqueen, 1897
Sealed Lips. Ward, 1906
-The Shame of Silence. Long, 1917
-The Silence of Dr. Duveen. Mellifont, 1937
The Silent Clue. Ward, 1921
The Silver Stair. Ward, 1914
-The Stolen Honeymoon. Odhams, 1921
The Story of a Great Sin. Ward, 1916
-The Triangle. Ward, 1912
-The Triumph of Manhood. Chapman, 1889
Two Black Pearls. White, 1886
-Under the Broad Arrow. Hodder, 1914
Vengeance Is Mine. Ward, 1917
-Was She Worth It? Aldine, 1922
The Way of Sinners. Ward, 1916
Who Killed Lord Luxmore?, with Robert Leighton, 1859-1933. Pearson, 1929
-The Woman Bars the Way. Gramol, 1933

LEIGHTON, ROBERT. 1859-1933. See: Marie (Flora Barbara) Connor Leighton, 18??-1941.

LEIGHTON, TOM
  Night of the Sphinx. Dell, 1979
    [Egypt, 1936]
  The Phoenix Formula. Dell, 1980
LEIGHTON, WING
  -Whistle Me over the Water. Hurst, 1944
LEINSTER, MURRAY. Pseudonym of Will(iam)
    F(itzgerald) Jenkins, 1896-1975, q.v.
  Doctor to the Stars. Pyramid, 1964
    (3 novelets, 2 criminous.) [future]
  Guns for Achin. Wright, 1936
  Murder in the Family. Hamilton, 1935
  Murder Madness. Brewer, 1931
  Murder Will Out. Hamilton, 1932 [NYC]
  No Clues. Wright, 1935
  Scalps. Brewer, 1930. British title:
    Wings of Chance. Hamilton, 1935
    [Ariz.]
  Wanted Dead or Alive! Wright, 1950
  Wings of Chance; see Scalps
LEITCH, JAMES
  The Lawyer's Purpose. Maxwell, 1865
LEITE, GEORGE THURSTON. 1920-   . Joint
    pseudonym with Jody Scott, 1923-   :
    Thurston Scott, q.v.
LEITFRED, ROBERT H. SC: Simon Crole, in
    all titles.
  The Corpse That Spoke. Green Circle,
    1936; Harrap, 1937 [Calif.]
  Death Cancels the Evidence. Green
    Circle, 1938. Also published as: Mur-
    der Is My Racket. Tech Mysteries,
    194? [Calif.]
  The Man Who Was Murdered Twice. Green
    Circle, 1937 [S.F.]
  Murder Is My Racket; see Death Cancels
    the Evidence
LE JEMLYS. Pseudonym of Symmes W. Jelley.
  Lawyer Manton of Chicago. Eagle, 1888
    [Chi.]
  A Millionaire's Folly; or, The Beauti-
    ful Unknown. Ogilvie, 1888
  The Scarlet Handkerchief. Laird, 1889
  Shadowed to Europe. Belford, 1885
LEJEUNE, ANTHONY. Pseudonym of Edward
    Anthony Thompson, 1928-   . Ref:
    TC. SC: Adam Gifford, in at least
    those marked AG. Set: Eng.
  Crowded and Dangerous. Macdonald, 1959
  The Dark Trade. Macdonald, 1965;
    Doubleday, 1966. Also published as:
    Death of a Pornographer. Lancer, 1967
    AG
  Death of a Pornographer; see The Dark
    Trade
  Duel in the Shadows. Macdonald, 1962 AG
  Glint of Spears. Macdonald, 1963
    [Bel. Congo]
  Mr. Diabolo. Macdonald, 1960
  News of Murder. Macdonald, 1961 AG
LELCHUK, ALAN. 1938-   . Ref: CA.
  Shrinking. Little, 1978
LEM, STANISLAW. 1921-   . Ref: CA.
  The Chain of Chance. Harcourt, 1978;
    Secker, 1978 (Translation of "Ka-
    tar." Poland, 1976.) [It., Fr.]
  The Investigation. Seabury, 1974
    (Translation of "Sledztwo." Krakow,
    1959.)
LEMARCHAND, ELIZABETH (WHARTON).
    1906-   . Ref: CA, CC, TC. SC:
    Insp./Supt. Tom Wharton, in all
    titles. Set: Eng.
  The Affacombe Affair. Hart-Davis, 1968
  Alibi for a Corpse. Hart-Davis, 1969
  Buried in the Past. Hart-Davis, 1974;
    Walker, 1975
  Change for the Worse. Piatkus, 1980;
    Walker, 1981
  Cyanide with Compliments. MacGibbon,
    1972; Walker, 1973
  Death of an Old Girl. Hart-Davis, 1967;
    Award, 1970 [acad.]
  Death on Doomsday. Hart-Davis, 1971;
    Walker, 1975
  Let or Hindrance. Hart-Davis, 1973.
    U.S. title: No Vacation from Murder.
    Walker, 1974
  No Vacation from Murder; see Let or
    Hindrance
  Step in the Dark. Hart-Davis, 1976;
    Walker, 1977
  Suddenly While Gardening. Hart-Davis,
    1978; Walker, 1978
  Unhappy Returns. Hart-Davis, 1977;
    Walker, 1978
LE MAY, ALAN. 1899-1964.
  One of Us Is a Murderer. Doubleday,
    1930; Jarrolds, 1930 [S. Am.]

LEMIEUX, KENNETH. 1923-   . Pseudonym:
    Kenneth Orvis, q.v.
LEMMON, LAURA ELIZABETH. 1917-   . Pseu-
    donym: Lee Wilson, q.v.
LENEHAN, J(OHN) C(HRISTOPHER). Ref: CC.
    SC: Insp. Kilby, in at least those
    marked K; Charlie Ryan, in at least
    those marked CR. Set: Eng.
  Boston Belle Meets Murder. Jenkins,
    1935 CR
  Carnival of Death. Jenkins, 1934
  Deadly Decree. Jenkins, 1936
  Death Dances Thrice. Jenkins, 1933 CR
  Driven to Death. Jenkins, 1944 CR
  Guilty But Not Insane. Jenkins, 1938 CR
  The Joyful Jays. Jenkins, 1941
  The Mansfield Mystery. Jenkins, 1932 K
  The Marked Pistol. Jenkins, 1929
  The Masked Blackmailer. Jenkins, 1933
    CR
  One Murder Too Many. Jenkins, 1943
  The Silecroft Case. Jenkins, 1931 K
  The Tunnel Mystery. Jenkins, 1929; Mys-
    tery League, 1931 K
LENNON, JOHN. 1940-1980.
  A Spaniard in the Works. Cape, 1965;
    Simon, 1965 ss, at least one
    (Sherlockian parody) criminous
LENNOX, GILBERT
  X14. Nelson, 1931
LENNOX, JOHN
  The Paper Doll. Quality, 1949
LENOTRE, G. Pseudonym of Louis Leon
    Theodore Gosselin, 1857-1925.
  -The Woman Without a Name. Collins,
    1923 (Translation of "La Femme sans
    Nom." Paris, 1922.)
LENTON, ANTHONY. SC: Graham Darren, in
    both titles.
  Murder Beat. Hale, 1971
  Murder City. Hale, 1972
LENTON, DUDLEY
  The Blue Mandarin. Modern, 1938 [China]
  Crooks of Paris. Modern, 1938 [Paris]
  The Desert Trail. Modern, 193?
  In Lands of Terror. Modern, 193?
  The League of Five. Modern, 1935
  The Mystery of the Ironworks. Modern,
    193?
  The Spy in the Navy. Modern, 193?
  The Tiger of Karan. Modern, 1938
LEOKUM, LEONARD and PAUL POSNICK
  -Weather War. Pinnacle, 1978; Sphere,
    1979
LEON, HENRY CECIL. 1902-1976. Pseudonym:
    Henry Cecil, q.v.
LEONARD, A. B. Pseudonym of Earl Augus-
    tus Aldrich, 1886-   .
  The Judson Murder Case. Clode, 1933;
    Butterworth, 1933 [Mass.]
LEONARD, CHARLES L. Pseudonym of M(ary)
    V(iolet) Heberden, 1906-   , q.v.
    SC: Paul Kilgerrin, in all titles.
  Assignment to Death; see The Fanatic of
    Fez
  Deadline for Destruction. Doubleday,
    1942 [Va.]
  Expert in Murder. Doubleday, 1945
    [Afr.]
  The Fanatic of Fez. Doubleday, 1943.
    Also published as: Assignment to
    Death. Thriller Novel Classic, 194?,
    abridged [Mor.]
  The Fourth Funeral. Doubleday, 1948;
    Museum, 1951 [Brazil]
  Pursuit in Peru. Doubleday, 1946;
    Museum, 1948 [Peru]
  Search for a Scientist. Doubleday,
    1947; Museum, 1951 [Mars.]
  The Secret of the Spa. Doubleday, 1944
    [N.J.]
  Secrets for Sale. Doubleday, 1950
    [Wash. D.C.]
  Sinister Shelter. Doubleday, 1949;
    Museum, 1951 [Buen. A.]
  The Stolen Squadron. Doubleday, 1942
    [Conn.]
  Treachery in Trieste. Doubleday, 1951
    [It., Yugos.]
LEONARD, CONSTANCE (BRINK). 1923-   .
    Ref: CA.
  Hostage in Illyria. Dodd, 1976 [Yugos.]
  The Other Maritha. Dodd, 1972; Milton
    House, 1974 [N.H.]
  Steps to Nowhere. Dodd, 1974; Milton
    House, 1974 [Sp.]

LEONARD, ELMORE. 1925-   . SC: Frank
    Ryan, in at least those marked FR.
  The Big Bounce. GM, 1969; Hale, 1969
  City Primeval. Arbor, 1980 [Det.]
  Fifty-Two Pickup. Delacorte, 1974;
    Secker, 1974 [Det.]
  The Hunted. Delacorte, 1977; Secker,
    1978 [Isr.]
  The Moonshine War. Doubleday, 1969;
    Hale, 1970 [Ky.]
  Mr. Majestyk. Dell, 1974 (Novelization
    of the movie.)
  Ryan's Rule; see Swag
  Swag. Delacorte, 1976. Also published
    as: Ryan's Rule. Dell, 1978 FR
    [Det.]
  The Switch. Bantam, 1978; Secker, 1979
    [Det.]
  Unknown Man No. 89. Delacorte, 1977;
    Secker, 1977 FR [Det.]
  -Valdez Is Coming. GM, 1970; Hale, 1969
LEONARD, FRANK (G.). 1935?-1974. Ref: CA.
  Box 100. Harper, 1972 [NYC]
LEONARD, GEORGE (BURR). 1923-   . Ref:
    CA.
  Beyond Control. Macmillan, 1975
    [NYC, hosp.]
LEONARD, PHYLLIS G(RUBBS). 1924-   .
    Ref: CA.
  Phantom of the Sacred Well. McKay, 1976
    [Guat., 1879]
  Prey of the Eagle. McKay, 1974 [Mex.]
LEOPOLD, CHRISTOPHER. Educated in Dublin
    and Oxford; freelance journalist and
    corporate consultant.
  Casablack. H. Hamilton, 1978; Double-
    day, 1979 [Casa., 1942]
LE PELLEY, GUERNSEY. 1910-   .
  Absolutely Murder. Baker, 1955 (3-act
    play.)
  Ghost Wanted. Row, 1942 (3-act play.)
L'EPINE, CHARLES. Pseudonym.
  The Devil in a Domino. Greening, 1897
  The Lady of the Leopard. Greening, 1899
LEPPANEN, GEORGE CHARLES
  The Intelligence Quotient. Vantage,
    1979
LEQUEUX, WILLIAM (TUFNELL). 1864-1927.
    Ref: CC, EM, MC, MM, MP, TC. Set: Eng.
  The Amazing Count. Ward, 1929
  Annette of the Argonne. Hurst, 1916
  As We Forgave Them. White, 1904
  At the Sign of the Sword. Jack, 1915
  Behind the Bronze Door; see The Bronze
    Face
  Behind the German Lines. London Mail,
    1917 [Ger.]
  Behind the Throne. Methuen, 1905
  Beryl of the Biplane. Pearson, 1917 ss
  The Black Owl. Ward, 1926
  Blackmailed. Nash, 1927
  Bleke, the Butler. Jarrolds, 1924 ss
  The Blue Bungalow. Hurst, 1925
  Bolo the Super-Spy. Odhams, 1918
  The Bomb-Makers. Jarrolds, 1917 ss
  The Bond of Black. White, 1899; Dil-
    lingham, 1899
  The Breath of Suspicion. Long, 1917
  The Broadcast Mystery. Holden, 1925
  The Broken Thread. Ward, 1916
  The Bronze Face. Ward, 1923. U.S.
    title: Behind the Bronze Door. Macau-
    lay, 1923
  The Catspaw. Lloyds, 1918
  The Chameleon. Hodder, 1927. U.S.
    title: Poison Shadows. Macaulay, 1927
  "Cinders" of Harley Street. Ward, 1916
    ss
  Cipher Six. Hodder, 1919
  The Closed Book. Methuen, 1904; Smart
    Set, 1904
  Concerning This Woman. Newnes, 1928
  Confessions of a Ladies' Man. Hutchin-
    son, 1905 ss
  The Count's Chauffer. Nash, 1907 ss
  The Court of Honour. White, 1901 [Fr.]
  The Crime Code; see Double Nought
  The Crimes Club. Nash, 1927 ss
  The Crinkled Crown. Ward, 1929; Macau-
    lay, 1929
  The Crooked Way. Methuen, 1908
  The Crystal Claw. Hodder, 1924; Macau-
    lay, 1924
  The Czar's Spy. Hodder, 1905; Smart
    Set, 1905
  The Dangerous Game; see Hidden Hands
  The Day of Temptation. White, 1899;
    Dillingham, 1899
  The Death-Doctor. Hurst, 1912
  The Devil's Carnival. Hurst, 1917
  Devil's Dice. White, 1897; Rand, 1897
  The Doctor of Pimlico. Cassell, 1919;
    Macaulay, 1920
  Donovan of Whitehall. Pearson, 1917 ss

Double Nought. Hodder, 1927. U.S. title: The Crime Code. Macaulay, 1928
The Double Shadow. Hodder, 1915
The Elusive Four. Cassell, 1921 ss
England's Peril. White, 1899
An Eye for an Eye. White, 1900
The Factotum and other stories. Ward, 1931 ss
The Fatal Face. Hurst, 1926
Fatal Fingers. Cassell, 1912
Fatal Thirteen. Paul, 1909
The Fifth Finger. Paul, 1921; Moffat, 1921
Fine Feathers. Paul, 1924
The Forbidden Word. Odhams, 1919
The Four Faces. Paul, 1914; Brentano's, 1914
Further Secrets of Potsdam. London Mail, 1917 ss
The Gamblers. Hutchinson, 1901
The Gay Triangle. Jarrolds, 1922 ss
The German Spy. Newnes, 1914 ss
-The German Spy System from Within. Hodder, 1915
The Golden Face. Cassell, 1922; Macaulay, 1922
The Golden Three. Ward, 1930; Fiction League, 1931
The Great Court Scandal. White, 1907
The Great God Gold; see Treasure of Israel
The Great Plot. Hodder, 1907
The Green Ray; see The Mystery of the Green Ray
Guilty Bonds. Routledge, 1891; Fenno, 1895
The Hand of Allah. Cassell, 1914. Also published as: The Riddle of the Ring. Federation Press, 1927
The Heart of a Princess. Ward, 1920
Her Majesty's Minister. Hodder, 1901; Dodd, 1901
Her Royal Highness. Hodder, 1914
Hidden Hands. Hodder, 1926. U.S. title: The Dangerous Game. Macaulay, 1926
The Hotel X. Ward, 1919 ss
The House of Evil. Ward, 1927
The House of the Wicked. Hurst, 1906
The House of Whispers. Nash, 1909; Brentano's, 1910
The Hunchback of Westminster. Methuen, 1904
Hushed Up! Nash, 1911
Hushed Up at German Headquarters. London Mail, 1917 ss
The Idol of the Town. White, 1904
If Sinners Entice Thee. White, 1898; Dillingham, 1899
In Secret. Odhams, 1921 ss
In White Raiment. White, 1900
The Indiscretions of a Lady's Maid. Nash, 1911 ss
The Intriguers. Hodder, 1920; Macaulay, 1921
The King's Incognito. Odhams, 1919
The Lady in the Car. Nash, 1908; Lippincott, 1908 ss
The Lady-in-Waiting. Ward, 1921
-Landru: His Secret Love Affairs. Paul, 1922
The Lawless Hand. Hurst, 1927; Macaulay, 1928
The Letter E. Cassell, 1926. U.S. title: The Tattoo Mystery. Macaulay, 1927
The Little Blue Goddess. Ward, 1918
The Looker-On. White, 1908
The Lost Million. Nash, 1913
The Luck of the Secret Service. Pearson, 1921 ss
The Lure of Love. Ward, 1919
Lying Lips. Paul, 1910
Mademoiselle of Monte Carlo. Cassell, 1921; Macaulay, 1921
-A Madonna of the Music Halls. White, 1897. Also published as: A Secret Sin; or, The Madonna of the Music Halls. Gardner, 1913
The Maker of Secrets. Ward, 1914
The Man About Town. Long, 1916
The Man from Downing Street. Hurst, 1904
The Marked Man. Ward, 1925
The Mask. Long, 1905
The Minister of Evil. Cassell, 1918
The Money-Spider. Cassell, 1911; Badger, 1911
More Mysteries of a Great City; see Mysteries of a Great City
More Secrets of Potsdam. London Mail, 1917 ss [Ger.]
Mysteries. Ward, 1913 ss
Mysteries of a Great City. Hodder, 1920. Reprinted in paperback in two volumes: Mysteries of a Great City, and More Mysteries of a Great City, both Mellifont, 1934 ss
The Mysterious Mr. Miller. Hodder, 1906
The Mysterious Three. Ward, 1915
The Mystery of a Motor-Car. Hodder, 1906
The Mystery of Mademoiselle. Hodder, 1926
The Mystery of Nine. Nash, 1912
The Mystery of the Green Ray. Hodder, 1915. Also published as: The Green Ray. Hodder, 1916
No Greater Love. Ward, 1917
No. 7, Saville Square. Ward, 1920
Number 70, Berlin. Hodder, 1916
Of Royal Blood. Hutchinson, 1900
The Office Secret. Ward, 1927
The Open Verdict. Hodder, 1921
The Pauper of Park Lane. Cassell, 1908; Cupples, 1908
The Peril of Helen Marklove and other stories. Jarrolds, 1928 ss
The Place of the Dragons. Ward, 1916
Poison Shadows; see The Chameleon
The Power of the Borgias. Odhams, 1921 (Novelization of the movie.)
The Price of Power. Hurst, 1913
The Rainbow Mystery. Hodder, 1917 ss
Rasputin the Rascal Monk. Hurst, 1917
Rasputinism in London. Cassell, 1919
The Rat Trap. Ward, 1928; Macaulay, 1930
The Red Hat. London Daily Mail, 1904
The Red Room. Cassell, 1909; Little, 1911
The Red Widow; or, The Death-Dealers of London. Cassell, 1920
Revelations of the Secret Service. White, 1913
The Riddle of the Ring; see The Hand of Allah
The Room of Secrets. Ward, 1913
Sant of the Secret Service. Odhams, 1918
The Scandal-Monger. Ward, 1917 ss
The Scarlet Sign. Ward, 1926
The Secret Formula. Ward, 1928
The Secret Life of the Ex-Tsaritza. Odhams, 1918
The Secret of the Square. White, 1907
A Secret Service; see Strange Tales of a Nihilist
The Secret Shame of the Kaiser. Hurst, 1919
A Secret Sin; or, A Madonna of the Music Halls; see A Madonna of the Music Halls
The Secret Telephone. Jarrolds, 1921; McCann, 1920 ss
Secrets of Monte Carlo. White, 1899; Dillingham, 1920 ss
The Secrets of Potsdam. London Daily Mail, 1917 ss
Secrets of the Foreign Office. Hutchinson, 1903 ss
Secrets of the White Tsar. Odhams, 1919
The Seven Secrets. Hutchinson, 1903
The Sign of Silence. Ward, 1915
The Sign of the Seven Sins. Lippincott, 1901 (British title?)
The Sign of the Stranger. White, 1904
Sins of the City. White, 1905
The Sister Disciple. Hurst, 1918
Society Intrigues I Have Known. Odhams, 1920 ss
Sons of Satan. White, 1914
The Spider's Eye. Cassell, 1905
Spies of the Kaiser. Hurst, 1909 ss
The Spy Hunter. Pearson, 1916
The Sting. Hodder, 1928; Macaulay, 1928
Stolen Souls. Tower, 1895; Stokes, 1895 ss
The Stolen Statesman. Skeffington, 1918
Stolen Sweets. Nash, 1908
Strange Tales of a Nihilist. Ward, 1892; Cassell (NYC), 1892. Also published as: A Secret Service: Being Strange Tales of a Nihilist. Ward, 1896 ss [Russ.]
The Stretton Street Affair. Cassell, 1924; Macaulay, 1922
The Tattoo Mystery; see The Letter E
The Temptress. Tower, 1895; Stokes, 1895
The Terror of the Air. Lloyds, 1920 [air.]
This House to Let. Hodder, 1921
Three Glass Eyes. Treherne, 1903
Three Knots. Ward, 1922
The Tickencote Treasure. Newnes, 1903
Tracked by Wireless. Paul, 1922; Moffatt, 1922 ss
Treasure of Israel. Nash, 1910. U.S. title: The Great God Gold. Badger, 1910
Twice Tried. Hurst, 1928
Two in a Tangle. Hodder, 1917
The Under-Secretary. Hutchinson, 1902
-The Unknown Tomorrow. White, 1910
The Unnamed. Hodder, 1902
The Valley of the Shadow. Methuen, 1905
The Valrose Mystery. Ward, 1925
The Veiled Man. White, 1899
The Voice from the Void. Cassell, 1922; Macaulay, 1923
The Way to Win. Marshall, 1916
Whatsoever a Man Soweth. White, 1906
Where the Desert Ends. Cassell, 1923
The White Glove. Nash, 1915
The White Lie. Ward, 1914
Whither Thou Goest. Lloyds, 1920
Who Giveth This Woman? Hodder, 1905
Whoso Findeth a Wife. White, 1897; Rand, 1898
Whosoever Loveth: Being the Secret of a Lady's Maid. Hutchinson, 1907
Wiles of the Wicked. White, 1900
Without Trace. Nash, 1912
The Woman at Kensington. Cassell, 1906
The Woman in the Way. Nash, 1908
A Woman's Debt. Ward, 1924
The Yellow Ribbon. Hodder, 1918
The Young Archduchess. Ward, 1922; Moffat, 1922
The Zeppelin Destroyer. Hodder, 1916

LERMINA, JULES (HYPPOLYTE). 1839-1915.
The Chase. Nimmo, 1880
Three Exploits of M. Parent. Osgood, 1894 (3 novelets.)

LERNER, DR. RICHARD. See: Max Gunther, 1927-   .

LE ROS, CHRISTIAN
Christmas Day and How It Was Spent. Routledge, 1854

LEROUX, ETIENNE. Pseudonym of Stephanus Petrus Daniel Leroux, 1922-   . Ref: CA. SC: Sgt./Capt. Demosthenes H. deGoede, in both titles, both set in S. Afr.
One for the Devil. Allen, 1969; Houghton, 1968 (Translation of "Een vir Azazel." Cape Town, 1964.)
The Third Eye. Allen, 1969; Houghton, 1969 (Translation of "Die Derde Oog." Cape Town, 1966.)

LEROUX, GASTON. 1868-1927. Ref: CC, DD, EM, MM, MP, TC. SC: Cheri-Bibi, in at least those marked CB; Joseph Rouletabille, in at least those marked JR. Set: Fr.
The Adventures of a Coquette. Laurie, 1926
The Amazing Adventures of Carolus Herbert. Mills, 1922 (Translation of "Le Capitaine Hyx." Paris, 1920.)
Balaoo. Hurst, 1913 (Translation of "Balaoo." Paris, 1912.)
-The Bride of the Sun. Hodder, 1916; McBride Nast, 1915 (Translation of "L'Epouse du Soleil." Paris, 1913.) [Peru]
The Burgled Heart. Long, 1925. U.S. title: The New Terror. Macaulay, 1926 (Translation of "Le Coeur Cambriole." Paris, 1922.)
Cheri-Bibi and Cecily. Laurie, 1923. U.S. title: Missing Men. Macaulay, 1923 (Translation of "Cheri-Bibi et Cecily." Paris, 1921.) CB
Cheri-Bibi, Mystery Man. Long, 1924. U.S. title: The Dark Road. Macaulay, 1924 (Translation of "Fatalitas." Paris, 1921.) CB
The Dancing Girl. Long, 1924. U.S. title: Nomads of the Night. Macaulay, 1925 CB
The Dark Road; see Cheri-Bibi, Mystery Man
The Double Life. Laurie, 1916; Kearney, 1909
The Floating Prison. Laurie, 1922. U.S. title: Wolves of the Sea. Macaulay, 1923 (Translation of "Les Cages Flotantes." Paris, 1921.) CB [ship]
The Haunted Chair. Dutton, 1931 (Translation of "Le Lauteril Nante." Paris, 1911.)
The Kiss That Killed. Macaulay, 1934 (Translation of "La Poupee Sangiante." Paris, 1924.) [Paris]
Lady Helena; or, The Mysterious Lady. Laurie, 1931; Dutton, 1931 (Translation of "Lady Helena." Paris, 1929.)
The Machine to Kill. Macaulay, 1935 (Translation of "La Machine a Assassiner." Paris, 1923.)
The Man of a Hundred Faces; see The Man of a Hundred Masks
The Man of a Hundred Masks. Cassell, 1930. U.S. title: The Man of a Hundred Faces. Macaulay, 1930 (Translation of "Mister Flow." Paris, 1927.)
The Man Who Came Back from the Dead. Nash, 1916 (Translation of "L'Homme qui Revient de Loin." Paris, 1917.)
The Man with the Black Feather. Hurst, 1912; Small, 1912
The Masked Man. Long, 1927; Macaulay, 1929
The Midnight Lady. Long, 1930
The Missing Archduke. Long, 1931
Missing Men; see Cheri-Bibi and Cecily
Murder in the Bedroom; see The Mystery of the Yellow Room
The Mystery of the Yellow Room. London

Daily Mail, 1908; Brentano's, 1908. Also published as: Murder in the Bedroom. Brussel, 1945 (Translation of "Le Mystere de la Chambre Jaune." Paris, 1908.) JR
The New Idol. Long, 1928; Macaulay, 1929 (Translation of "Le Coup d'etat de Cheri-Bibi." Paris, 1925.) CB
The New Terror; see The Burgled Heart
Nomads of the Night; see The Dancing Girl
The Octopus of Paris; see The Sleuth Hounds
The Perfume of the Lady in Black. London Daily Mail, 1909; Brentano's, 1909 (Translation of "Le Parfum de la Dame en Noir." Paris, 1909.) JR
The Phantom Clue; see The Slave Bangle
The Phantom of the Opera. Mills, 1911; Bobbs, 1911 (Translation of "Le Fantome de L'Opera." Paris, 1910.)
The Secret of the Night. Nash, 1914; Macaulay, 1914 JR
The Slave Bangle. Long, 1925. U.S. title: The Phantom Clue. Macaulay, 1926 JR
The Sleuth Hound. Long, 1926. U.S. title: The Octopus of Paris. Macaulay, 1927 JR
The Son of Three Fathers. Long, 1927; Macaulay, 1928 (Translation of "Le Fils de Trois Peres." Paris, 1926.)
The Veiled Prisoner. Mills, 1923
Wolves of the Sea; see The Floating Prison

LEROUX, STEPHANUS PETRUS DANIEL. 1922- . Pseudonym: Etienne Leroux, q.v.

LEROY, AMELIE CLAIRE. 1851- . Pseudonym: Esme Stuart, q.v.

LEROY, HOWARD. Pseudonym: Will Manson, q.v.
The Keeper. Flagship, 1968

LESLIE, ALEEN. 1908- . Ref: CA.
The Windfall. World, 1970

LESLIE, DESMOND. 1921- . Ref: CA.
The Amazing Mr. Lutterworth. Wingate, 1958
Angels Weep! Laurie, 1948
-Careless Lives. Macdonald, 1945
Hold Back the Night. Owen, 1956
-Pardon My Return. Macdonald, 1946

LESLIE, EDWARD. Pseudonym of Leslie Edward Sellicks, 1902- .
The Red Slayer. Jenkins, 1929
The Seventh Entanglement. Jenkins, 1930
-White Man's Prestige. Warne, 1939

LESLIE, F(REDERIC) ANDREW. 1927- . Ref: CA.
The Haunting of Hill House. Dramatists, 1964 (3-act play based on the novel by Shirley Jackson, 1920-1965, q.v.)
The Hound of the Baskervilles. Dramatists, 1977 (2-act play based on the novel by A. Conan Doyle, 1859-1930, q.v.) (Sherlock Holmes.)
The Spiral Staircase. Dramatists, 1962 (2-act play adapted from the screenplay by Mel Dinelli of the novel by Ethel Lina White, 1887-1944, q.v.)

LESLIE, FRANCIS. SC: Jimmy Langry, in at least those marked JL. Set: Eng.
The Second Stroke. Hurst, 1949
Study of Death. Hurst, 1943 JL
Who Keeps the Keys? Hurst, 1948 JL

LESLIE, JEAN. SC: Peter Ponsonby = PP.
Blood on My Shoes; see Shoes for My Love
The Darling Sin. Doubleday, 1951; Hodder, 1952 [Calif.]
A Hair of the Dog. Doubleday, 1947 [L.A.]
The Intimate Journal of Warren Winslow. Doubleday, 1952; Hodder, 1953 [Calif.]
The Man Who Held Five Aces. Doubleday, 1949; Hodder, 1950 [Calif.]
One Cried Murder. Doubleday, 1945; Edwards, 1946 PP [Calif., acad.]
Shoes for My Love. Doubleday, 1948. Also published as: Blood on My Shoes. Bestseller, 1951 [S.F.]
Three-Cornered Murder. Doubleday, 1947; Hodder, 1948 PP [Calif.]
Two Faced Murder. Doubleday, 1946; Edwards, 1946 PP [Calif., acad.]

LESLIE, JOSEPHINE
The Devil and Mrs. Devine. PB, 1974; Millington, 1975

LESLIE, MIRIAM
Cavanaugh Keep. Lancer, 1968 [Scot.]

LESLIE, NORMAN. SC: Jumbo Rutherford, in at least those marked JR
Death Comes by Air. Nelson, 1937
Death Comes to Kenya. Ward, 1948 [Kenya]
How Bad Can They Be? Barker, 1955
The Kiwi Club. Ward, 1939 JR
The Man with the Glass Eye. Ward, 1948
Prelude to Murder. Barker, 1954
Raid over England. Ward, 1938 JR
Shadow over Europe. Ward, 1947
Widows Can Be Dangerous. Barker, 1958
Winged Victory. Nelson, 1931

LESLIE, PETER. 1922- . Trained as a geologist; journalist, editor and publicist in Eng. Pseudonym: Patrick McNee, q.v. SC: Father Hayes, in 3 titles, including those marked FH.
The Autumn Accelerator. Four Square, 1969 (Novelization of "The Invaders" TV series.)
-The Bastard Brigade. New English Library pb, 1970
-The Betrayers. Manor, 1978
-The Bitter Enders. New English Library pb, 1972 (Novelization of the movie.)
-The Bombers. New English Library pb, 1972
The Cornish Pixie Affair. Four Square, 1967 (Novelization of "The Girl from UNCLE" TV series.)
The Diving Dames Affair. Four Square, 1967; Ace, 1967 (Novelization of "The Man from UNCLE" TV series.) [Brazil]
-The Extremists. New English Library pb, 1970
-The Fakers. New English Library pb, 1971
Father Hayes. Zebra, 1976 FH
The Finger in the Sky Affair. Four Square, 1966; Ace, 1970 (Novelization of "The Man from UNCLE" TV series.) [Nice]
-The Four Letter Crowd. New English Library pb, 1971
The Frighteners. Four Square, 1968 (Novelization of the "Daktari" TV series.)
The Gay Deceiver. MacGibbon, 1967; Stein, 1967
Hell for Tomorrow. Consul, 1965; Macfadden, 1966 (Novelization of the "Secret Agent" TV series.) [Fr.]
The Holy Spirit. Zebra, 1977 FH
-Killer Corps. New English Library pb, 1971
The Mogul Men. Corgi, 1967
The Night of the Tribolites. Four Square, 1968 (Novelization of "The Invaders" TV series.)
-The Plastic Magicians. New English Library pb, 1970
The Radioactive Camel Affair. Four Square, 1966; Ace, 1966 (Novelization of "The Man from UNCLE" TV series.) [Afr.]
The Splintered Sunglasses Affair. Four Square, 1968; Ace, 1968 (Novelization of "The Man from UNCLE" TV series.) [It.]
-Storm Squad. New English Library pb, 1971
The Unfair Fare Affair. Four Square, 1968; Ace, 1969 (Novelization of "The Man from UNCLE" TV series.)

LESLIE, THANE
Yu-Malu, the Dragon Princess. Wright, 1967

LESLIE, WARREN. 1927- . Born in NYC; department store executive in Tex. during 1960s.
Love or Whatever It Is. McGraw, 1960; Four Square, 1962 [Mass.]

LESLIE-MELVILLE, BETTY
That Nairobi Affair. Doubleday, 1975 [Kenya]

LESSER, MILTON. 1928- . Name legally changed to Stephen Marlowe, q.v. Pseudonyms: Andrew Fraser, Jason Ridgway, C. H. Thames, qq.v. See also: Richard S(cott) Prather, 1921- ; and: Ellery Queen.

LESTER, BURT
Striptease for Murder. Triphammer, 1973

LESTER, E(DWARD) C(ASTELLAIN). SC: Nathaniel Moody, in both titles. Set: Eng.
The Guy Fawkes Murder. Long, 1936
The Murder of Martin Fotherill. Long, 1937

LESTER, FRANK. Pseudonym of Frank (Hugh) Usher, 1909-1976. Other pseudonym: Charles Franklin, q.v. SC: Geoffrey Slade, in at least those marked GS. Set: Eng.
The Bamboo Girl. Hale, 1961
The Corpse Wore Rubies. Hale, 1958 GS
Death and the South Wind. Hale, 1958 GS
Death in Sunlight. Hale, 1965
Death of a Frightened Traveller. Hale, 1959
Death of a Pale Man. Hale, 1960
Finch Takes to Crime. Hale, 1963
Fly Me a Killer. Hale, 1962
The Golden Murder. Hale, 1959 GS
Hide My Body. Hale, 1961
Lead Me to the Gallows. Hale, 1962

LESTER, MARK. Pseudonym of Martin (James) Russell, 1934- , q.v.
Terror Trade. Hale, 1976

LESTER, TERI. All titles probably first published in Australia by Horwitz.
Episode in Rome. Signet, 1967 [Rome]
Hawaiian Cruise. Signet, 1967
Island Mystery. Signet, 1967
The Ouija Board. Horwitz, 1969; Signet, 1969
Tania. Signet, 1968

LESTER, VINCENT. Set: Eng.
Crook's Crossing. Butterworth, 1935
Justice by Accident. Butterworth, 1936

LETHBRIDGE, OLIVE
The Black Parrot. Hurst, 1931 (Novelization of the play by H. Fletcher Lee.)

LETHBRIDGE, SYBIL CAMPBELL
-The Crime of Jane Dacre. Methuen, 1926

LETHERBY, JACK
Murder Lays the Odds. Ward, 1953
The Outsider. Ward, 1953

LETT, GORDON
The Many-Headed Monster. Hodder, 1957
Rossano. Hodder, 1955

LETTON, JENNETTE (DOWLING). Playwright; active on radio, TV, and stage; living in rural N.J. in 1960s.
Allegra's Child. Macrae Smith, 1969 [Pa.]
The Brass Bound Book. Milton House, 1975 (U.S. title?)
Cragsmoor. Macrae Smith, 1966 [Maine]
Don't Cry Little Sister. Macrae Smith, 1971
The Haunting of Cliffside. Walker, 1975 [N.H.]
Hilltop; see Jenny and I
Incident at Hendon. Macrae Smith, 1967 [Conn.]
Jenny and I. Macrae Smith, 1963; Hale, 1964. Also published as: Hilltop. Paperback Library, 1968 [N.H.]

LEVEL, MAURICE. 1875-1926.
Crises: Tales of Mystery and Horror. Erskine Macdonald, 1920. U.S. title: Tales of Mystery and Horror. McBride, 1920. Also published as: Grand Guignol Stories. Philpot, 1922 ss
Grand Guignol Stories; see Crises: Tales of Mystery and Horror
The Grip of Fear. Richards, 1909; Kennerley, 1909
The Shadow. Philpot, 1923. U.S. title: Those Who Return. McBride, 1923 (Translation of "L'Ombre." Paris, 1921.) [Fr.]
Tales of Mystery and Horror; see Crises: Tales of Mystery and Horror
Those Who Return; see The Shadow

LEVENE, PHILIP. 1926- . SC: Ambrose West = AW.
Ambrose in London. Hale, 1959 AW
Ambrose in Paris. Hale, 1960 AW [Paris]
Kill Two Birds. French (London), 1963 (3-act play.)
Murder When Necessary. Evans, 1958 (3-act play.)

LEVERAGE, (CARL) HENRY. 1885- . See also: Kate L. McLaurin.
-The Ice Pilot. Doubleday, 1921
The Phantom Alibi. Chelsea, 1926 [Pa.]
The Purple Limited. Chelsea, 1927
Where Dead Men Wait. Moffat, 1920
Whispering Wires. Moffat, 1918 [NYC]
The White Cipher. Moffat, 1919

LEVEY, ROBERT A.
Dictators Die Hard. Mystery House, 1959 [Cent. Am.]
Murder in Lima. Avon, 1957 [Lima]

LEVI, PETER (CHAD TIGAR). 1931- . Ref: CA.
    The Head in the Soup. Constable, 1979; Raven, 1980 [1972, Eng.]

LEVI, URI
    The Assassin. Doubleday, 1968

LEVICK, J. D.
    Tangled Web. Jarrolds, 1946

LEVIEN, MARION
    Odds on Murder. Dorrance, 1974

LEVIN, IRA. 1929- . Ref: CA, CC, EM, TC.
    The Boys from Brazil. Random, 1976; Joseph, 1976
    Deathtrap. Random, 1979; French (London), 1980 (Play.) [Conn.]
    Dr. Cook's Garden. Dramatists, 1968 (Play.)
    A Kiss Before Dying. Simon, 1953; Joseph, 1954 [acad.]
    -Rosemary's Baby. Random, 1967; Joseph, 1967
    -The Stepford Wives. Random, 1972; Joseph, 1972
    Veronica's Room. Random, 1974; Joseph, 1975 (Play.)

LEVIN, MEYER. 1905-1981. Ref: CA, MC.
    Compulsion. Simon, 1956; Muller, 1957 [Chi.]

LEVINE, LARRY
    Snowbird. GM, 1977; Hamlyn, 1978
    The Treasure. GM, 1979 [Mex.]

LEVINE, LAWRENCE
    New York One. Zebra, 1979 [NYC]

LEVINE, SIDNEY. See: Robin Moore.

LEVINE, WILLIAM. 1881- . Pseudonym: Will Levinrew, q.v.

LEVINREW, WILL. Pseudonym of William Levine, 1881- . SC: Prof. Herman Brierly = HB.
    Death Points a Finger. Mystery League, 1933 HB
    For Sale—Murder. Mystery League, 1932 [Newark]
    Murder from the Grave. McBride, 1930; Cassell, 1931 HB [NYC]
    Murder on the Palisades. McBride, 1930; Gollancz, 1930. Also published as: The Wheelchair Corpse. Bart, 1945 HB [N.J.]
    The Poison Plague. McBride, 1929; Cassell, 1930 HB
    The Wheelchair Corpse; see Murder on the Palisades

LEVINSON, LEONARD. 1935- . Pseudonyms: Leonard Jordan, Robert Novak, Philip Rawls, Bruno Rossi, qq.v. See also: Lee Chang, Nelson De Mille, 1943- . Ref: CA.

LEVINSON, RICHARD. 1934- . See: William Link.

LEVINSON, SAUL
    Murder Is Dangerous. Phoenix, 1949 [Tex.]
    Red-Hot Murder. Phoenix, 1949 [Tex.]

LEVISON, ERIC. SC: Dr. Edward Lester, in all titles, all set in Jacksonville.
    Ashes of Evidence. Bobbs, 1921
    The Eye Witness. Bobbs, 1921; Page (London), 1921
    Hidden Eyes. Bobbs, 1920

LE VOLEUR. Pseudonym of Rosa Nouchette Carey, 1840-1909, q.v.
    By Order of the Brotherhood. Jarrolds, 1895; Macmillan, 1895 [Russ.]
    The Champington Mystery. Digby, 1900
    -For Love of a Bedouin Maid. Hutchinson, 1897; Rand, 1897
    -In the Tsar's Dominions. Hutchinson, 1899 [Russ.]

LEVON, FRED. Pseudonym of L. Fred Ayvazian, 1919- . Ref: CA.
    The Manx Cat. World, 1970; Hale, 1972 [Boston]
    Much Ado About Murder. Dodd, 1955; Boardman, 1957 [NYC]

LEVY, BARBARA. 1921- . Joint pseudonym with Lois Ann Brown: Jessica Eliot, q.v. Born in NYC; a journalist in Paris before returning to NYC.
    The Missing Matisse. Doubleday, 1968 [Fr.]
    Place of Judgment. Doubleday, 1965
    The Shining Mischief. Putnam, 1971 [Fr.]

LEVY, D. LAWRENCE
    The Potomac Conspiracy. Major, 1976 [Wash. D.C.]

LEVY, EDWARD J. Pseudonym: Lee Edwards, q.v.

LEVY, JOSE. See: C(yril Arthur Edward) Ranger Gull, 1876-1923.

LEVY, JOSEPH
    Operation Damascus. Manor, 1976 [Damascus]

LEWELLEN, T(HEODORE) C(HARLES). 1940- . Ref: CA.
    The Billikin Courier. Random, 1968 [Calif.]

LEWIN, ALBERT. 1894-1968. Born in NYC; movie producer and director.
    The Unaltered Cat. Scribner, 1967; Harvill, 1967 [NYC]

LEWIN, MICHAEL. 1885-1961. Pseudonym: Douglas Furber, q.v.

LEWIN, MICHAEL Z(INN). 1942- . Ref: CA, TC. SC: Albert Samson = AS.
    Ask the Right Question. Putnam, 1971; H. Hamilton, 1972 [Indianapolis] AS
    The Enemies Within. Knopf, 1974; H. Hamilton, 1974 [Ind.] AS
    The Next Man. Warner, 1976; Coronet, 1977 (Novelization of the movie.)
    Night Cover. Knopf, 1976; H. Hamilton, 1976 AS (in minor role) [Indianapolis]
    Outside In. Knopf, 1980; Magnum, 1981 [Indianapolis]
    The Silent Salesman. Knopf, 1978; H. Hamilton, 1978 AS [Indianapolis]
    The Way We Die Now. Putnam, 1973; H. Hamilton, 1974 AS [Indianapolis]

LEWIS, ALETHEA BRERETON. 1749-1827. Pseudonym: Eugenia DeActon, q.v.

LEWIS, ALFRED HENRY. 1857-1914. Ref: EM.
    The Apaches of New York. Dillingham, 1912 ss [NYC]
    The Boss, and How He Came to Rule New York. Barnes, 1903 [NYC]
    Confessions of a Detective. Barnes, 1906 ss [NYC]

LEWIS, ARTHUR H. 1906- . Ref: CA.
    Children's Party. Trident, 1972
    Copper Beeches. Trident, 1971 [Phil.]

LEWIS, CANELLA. Pseudonym of Jonathan Richards.
    The Music of Aquarius. Berkley, 1977 [Fr.]
    Sensitive Encounter. Berkley, 1977 [Eng.]

LEWIS, CECIL DAY. 1904-1972. Pseudonym: Nicholas Blake, q.v.

LEWIS, COLIN
    The Golden Grin. Hamlyn, 1980

LEWIS, DAVID. SC: Steve Savage, in both titles.
    The Andromeda Assignment. Pinnacle, 1976 [Nor.]
    The Omega Assignment. Pinnacle, 1976

LEWIS, DEBORAH. Pseudonym of Charles L. Grant, 1942- , q.v.
    The Eve of the Hound. Zebra, 1977
    Kirkwood Fires. Zebra, 1978
    The Lady in the Tapestry. Zebra, 1977 [Scot.]
    Voices Out of Time. Zebra, 1977 [Scot.]
    The Wind at Winter's End. Zebra, 1979

LEWIS, EDWARD
    A Screw Loose. Paxton, 1960 (3-scene play.)

LEWIS, ELLIOTT. Ref: CA. SC: Bennett, in both titles.
    Dirty Linen. Pinnacle, 1980
    Two Heads Are Better. Pinnacle, 1980

LEWIS, FLORENCE JAY
    The Climax. Books Inc., 1944 (Novelization of the movie.) [Vienna]

LEWIS, FREDERICK. Pseudonym of Frederick Lewis Collins, 1882-1950.
    The Strange Case of Mary Page. Clode, 1916

LEWIS, GITA. See: Henrietta Martin.

LEWIS, H.
    The Mystery of Lady Chetwynd's Spectre. Henderson

LEWIS, MRS. HARRIET
    The Hampton Mystery. Henderson

LEWIS, H. H.
    By Whose Hand? Mellifont, 19??
    -Pearls and Perjury. Coker, 1950

LEWIS, HERSHELL G. Pseudonym of Michael Murphy, 1930- .
    Two Thousand Maniacs! Novel Books, 1964 (Novelization of the movie.)

LEWIS, HILDA (WINIFRED). 1896-1974. Ref: CA.
    The Case of the Little Doctor; see Said Dr. Spendlove
    Said Dr. Spendlove. Jarrolds, 1940. U.S. title: The Case of the Little Doctor. Random, 1949
    Strange Story. Jarrolds, 1945; Random, 1947

LEWIS, IRWIN. 1916- . SC: Horace Clarke, in both titles.
    -The Day New York Trembled. Avon, 1967 [NYC]
    -The Day They Invaded New York. Avon, 1964 [NYC]

LEWIS, JACK. Pseudonyms: Stephen Hood, Lewis Jackson, qq.v. All titles below feature Sexton Blake and were published by Amalgamated Press.
    The Affair of the Oriental Doctor. 1920
    The Affair of the World's Champion. 1920
    The Case of the Bendigo Heirlooms. 1922
    The Case of the Transatlantic Flyers. 1919
    The Chink in the Armour. 1919
    The Fallen Star. 1922
    The False Alibi. 1920
    The House of Fear. 1923
    The Jewels of Wu Ling. 1920
    The Kestrel Syndicate. 1919
    The Kestrel's Claw. 1920
    Kestrel's Conspiracy. 1921
    The Lady of Ravensedge. 1921
    The Mystery of X04. 1920
    The Red Heart of the Incas. 1919

LEWIS, JACK
    Blood Money. Headline, 1960
    A Night for Evil. Challenge, 1967 [Fla.]

LEWIS, JAMES
    The Canary That Died. JMC Publications, 1975
    Shadows of Death. JMC Publications, 1976

LEWIS, JANET [JANET LEWIS WINTERS]. 1899- . Ref: CA.
    The Trial of Soren Qvist. Doubleday, 1947; Gollancz, 1947

LEWIS, JULIUS WARREN. 1833-1920. Pseudonym: Leon Lewis, q.v.

LEWIS, JUNE R(OSEMARIE)
    The Witch's Mark. Hale, 1975

LEWIS, KEN
    Look Out Behind You. Ace, 1957

LEWIS, LANGE. Pseudonym of Jane Beynon, 1915- , q.v. SC: Lt./Insp. Richard Tuck, in all titles.
    The Birthday Murder. Bobbs, 1945; Bodley, 1951 [L.A.]
    Death Among Friends; see Murder Among Friends
    Juliet Dies Twice. Bobbs, 1943; Bodley, 1948 [L.A., acad.]
    Meat for Murder. Bobbs, 1943; Bodley, 1950 [L.A.]
    Murder Among Friends. Bobbs, 1942. British title: Death Among Friends. Bodley, 1950 [L.A., acad.]
    The Passionate Victims. Bobbs, 1952; Bodley, 1953

LEWIS, LEON. Pseudonym of Julius Warren Lewis, 1833-1920.
    -The Diamond Seeker of Brazil. Bonner's, 1891
    The Man of Mystery; or, Where Is Ben Stobie? Weeks, 1894

LEWIS, MARGO
    Concept for Murder. Decade, 1980 [L.A.]

LEWIS, MARY CHRISTIANNA MILNE. 1907- . Pseudonyms: Mary Ann Ashe, Christianna Brand, China Thompson, qq.v.

LEWIS, MATTHEW GREGORY. 1775-1818. Ref: CC, EM.
    Adelgitha; or, The Fruits of a Single Error. Hughes, 1806; Longworth, 1808 (5-act play.)
    Ambrosio; or, The Monk; see The Monk

The Castle of Lindenburg; or, The History of Raymond and Agnes. Fisher, 1798
The Castle Spectre. Bell, 1798; (Boston), 1798 (5-act play.)
Feudal Tyrants; or, The Counts of Carlsheim and Sargans. Hughes, 1806
The Monk. Bell, 1796; Moore, 1845. Also published as: Ambrosio; or, The Monk. Bell, 1798
One O'Clock; or, The Knight and the Wood Daemon. Lowndes, 1811; Longworth, 1813 (3-act play.)
-Rosario, the Female Monk. Laird, 1891 (British title?)

LEWIS, MAYNAH
The Unforgiven. Collins, 1974; Ace, 1976

LEWIS, MERVYN. Pseudonym of Glyn Mervyn Louis Frewer, 1931- .
Death of Gold. Hale, 1970

LEWIS, MICHAEL (ARTHUR). 1890-1970. SC: Sgt. Hobbs, in at least those marked H. Ref: CA.
The Brand of the Beast. Allen, 1925; Dial, 1925 H
The Crime of Herbert Wratislaus. Jenkins, 1931
The Island of Disaster. Allen, 1926 H
Roman Gold. Allen, 1927; Houghton, 1928
The Three Amateurs. Allen, 1929; Houghton, 1929

LEWIS, NORMAN. 1903- . Ref: CA.
Darkness Visible. Cape, 1960; Pantheon, 1960
The Day of the Fox. Cape, 1955; Rinehart, 1955
Dragon Tree Island; see The Tenth Year of the Ship
Every Man's Brother. Heinemann, 1967; Morrow, 1968 [Wales]
Flight from a Dark Equator. Collins, 1972; Putnam, 1972 [S. Am.]
-Samara. Cape, 1949
The Sicilian Specialist. Collins, 1975; Random, 1974
-A Single Pilgrim. Cape, 1953; Rinehart, 1954
A Small War Made to Order. Collins, 1966; Harcourt, 1966 [Cuba]
-The Tenth Year of the Ship. Collins, 1962; Harcourt, 1962. Also published as: Dragon Tree Island. Fontana, 1964
-The Volcanoes Above Us. Cape, 1957; Pantheon, 1957
-Within the Labyrinth. Cape, 1950

LEWIS, NORMAN. 1918- .
The German Company. Collins, 1979

LEWIS, RICHARD
Spiders. Hamlyn, 1978

LEWIS, (JOHN) ROY(STON). 1933- . Ref: CA, TC. SC: Insp. Crow, in at least those marked C. Set: Eng.
Blood Money. Collins, 1973 C
A Certain Blindness. Collins, 1980; St. Martin's, 1981
A Distant Banner. Collins, 1976 [Wales]
Double Take. Collins, 1975
Error of Judgment. Collins, 1971 C [acad.]
The Fenokee Project. Collins, 1971 [Can.]
A Fool for a Client. Collins, 1972
An Inevitable Fatality. Collins, 1978
A Lover Too Many. Collins, 1969; World, 1971 C
Nothing But Foxes. Collins, 1977; St. Martin's, 1979 C
Of Singular Purpose. Collins, 1973 [Scot.]
A Part of Virtue. Collins, 1975 C
A Question of Degree. Collins, 1974 C
A Secret Singing. Collins, 1972 C
An Uncertain Sound. Collins, 1978; St. Martin's, 1980
A Violent Death. Collins, 1979
Witness My Death. Collins, 1976 [Wales]
A Wolf by the Ears. Collins, 1970; World, 1972 C

LEWIS, ROY HARLEY. With his wife, operates an antiquarian book search service in London; writer for film, theatre and TV.
A Cracking of Spines. Hale, 1980; Walker, 1982

LEWIS, TED [EDWARD]. 1940- . Has worked in advertising, as an animation specialist in TV and films. SC: Jack Carter = JC.
All the Way Home and All the Night Through. New Authors, 1965
-Billy Rags. Joseph, 1973
Boldt. Joseph, 1976; Jove, 1980 [U.S.]
G.B.H. Sphere, 1980. U.S. title: Grievous Bodily Harm. Jove, 1980
Get Carter; see Jack's Return Home
Grievous Bodily Harm; see G.B.H.
Jack Carter and the Law; see Jack Carter's Law
Jack Carter and the Mafia Pigeon. Joseph, 1977 JC
Jack Carter's Law. Joseph, 1974. U.S. title: Jack Carter and the Law. Knopf, 1975 JC
Jack's Return Home. Joseph, 1970; Doubleday, 1970. Also published as: Get Carter. Pan, 1971; Popular Library, 1971 JC
Plender. Joseph, 1971

LEWIS, W(ALTER) R(EGINALD) SUNDERLAND. 1861- .
Cubwood. Lane, 1924; Boni, 1926

LEWTON, VAL. Pseudonym: Herbert Kerkow, q.v.

LEY, ALICE CHETWYND. 1915- . Ref: CA.
At Dark of the Moon. Hale, 1977; Ballantine, 1978 [Eng., 1804]
Beloved Diana; see Tenant of Chesdene Manor
Letters for a Spy. Hale, 1970. U.S. title: The Sentimental Spy. Ballantine, 1977 [Eng., ca.1800]
The Sentimental Spy; see Letters for a Spy
Tenant of Chesdene Manor. Hale, 1974. U.S. title: Beloved Diana. Ballantine, 1977 [Eng., ca.1820]

LEY, ARTHUR GORDON. 1911-1968. Pseudonym: Ray Luther, q.v.

LEYFORD, HENRY. Pseudonym.
Murder Moon. Macaulay, 1933 [Fr.]

LEYS, JOHN K(IRKWOOD). 1846-1909.
At the Sign of the Golden Horn. Newnes, 1898
The Black Terror. Low, 1899; Page, 1900
A Broken Fetter. Digby, 1905
Children of Mammon. Digby, 1908
A Desperate Game. Digby, 1906
Held in the Toils. Ward, 1904
The House-Boat Mystery. Ward, 1905
The Lawyer's Secret. Warne, 1897
The Missing Bridegroom. Digby, 1908
The Prisoner's Secret. Ward, 1904
A Sore Temptation. Chatto, 1901
A Suburban Vendetta. Pearson, 1900
Under a Mask. Bentley, 1897
Underground. Greening, 1909
A Wolf in Sheep's Clothing. Ward, 1905

LEYTON, PATRICK. SC: Eng.
The Barronwell Mystery. Paul, 1929
By Foul Means. Paul, 1928; International Fiction, 1929
The Crime at Grandison Hall. Paul, 1929
The Crime with Ten Solutions. Jenkins, 1935
The Delmayne Mystery. Jenkins, 1928
Exit Silas Danvers. Jenkins, 1932
Foul Play at Lentwood. Jenkins, 1935
Gentlemen of the Jury, with Arthur Compton-Rickett, 1869-1937, q.v. Jenkins, 1927
Grim Inheritance. Jenkins, 1941
Harvest of Hate. Jenkins, 1948
Haunted Abbey. Jenkins, 1936
The Inevitable Crime. Jenkins, 1926
The Island of Atonement. Selwyn, 1928
The Man Who Knew. Jenkins, 1925; Small, 1926
Murder Will Out. Jenkins, 1930
The Ordeal of Mark Bannister, with Arthur Compton-Rickett, 1869-1937, q.v. Jenkins, 1930
Outside the Law. Jenkins, 1927
Silent Death. Jenkins, 1940
Treasure of Greyladies. Jenkins, 1934
Within Twenty-Four Hours. Jenkins, 1931

LIBBEY, LAURA JEAN. 1862-1924.
Aleta's Terrible Secret; or, The Strange Mystery of a Wedding Eve. Westbrook, 190?
The Crime of Hallowe'en; or, The Heiress of Graystone Hall. Munro, 1891
Little Rosebud's Lovers; or, A Cruel Revenge. Munro, 1888
Parted by Fate; or, The Mystery of Black-Tor Lighthouse. Bonner, 1890

LIBBY, ALFRED F.
The Long Fast Ride. Vantage, 1966 [Calif.]

LIBERT, JEAN. Joint pseudonym with Gaston Vandenpanhuise: Paul Kenny, q.v.

LICHFIELD, RICHARD
Diana K.C. Henry Walker, 1930

LIDDELOW, MARJORIE JEAN. Pseudonym: Marjorie J. Law, q.v.

LIDDON, E(LOISE) S. 1897- . SC: Peggy Fairfield, in both books.
The Riddle of the Florentine Folio. Doubleday, 1935
The Riddle of the Russian Princess. Doubleday, 1934 [L.I.]

LIDDY, G(EORGE) GORDON (BATTLE). 1930- . Lawyer; FBI agent and supervisor; author of anti-crime legislation; mastermind of Watergate break-in.
Out of Control. St. Martin's, 1979; Severn, 1980

LIE, JONAS. 1899-1945.
The Devil's Birthday. Cassirer, 1940 (Translation of "Natten til Fandens." Oslo, 1934, as by Max Mauser.)

LIEBELER, JEAN MAYER. ca.1900- . Born in Mont.; graduate of U. of Minn.; worked for Mpls. Art Institute and a hospital service association before moving to the N.W. in the 1940s.
You, the Jury. Farrar, 1944; Skeffington, 1946, as by Virginia Mather [N.Y.]

LIEBERMAN, HERBERT (HENRY). 1933- . Ref: CA.
City of the Dead. Simon, 1976; Hutchinson, 1976 [NYC]
The Climate of Hell. Simon, 1978; Hutchinson, 1978 [Parag.]
Crawlspace. McKay, 1971; Hutchinson, 1972
The Eighth Square. McKay, 1973; Hutchinson, 1973

LIEBLING, HOWARD. 1928- .
The Trial of Billy Jack. B. J. Enterprises, 1974 (Novelization of the movie.)

LIFSON, DAVID S. 1908- . Resident of NYC; authority on Yiddish Theatre; professor of humanities, Fulbright scholar, theatrical producer and director, playwright.
Headless Victory. Barnes, 1978; Yoseloff, 1978 [Mass.]

LIGGETT, HUNTER. Pseudonym of Lauran Bosworth Paine, 1916- . Other pseudonyms: John Armour, Reg Batchelor, Kenneth Bedford, Frank Bosworth, Mark Carrel, Robert Clarke, Richard Dana, J. F. Drexler, Troy Howard, Jared Ingersol, John Kilgore, J. K. Lucas, John Morgan, qq.v.
Murder for Money. Hale, 1969
The Murder Maze. Hale, 1969
The Unknown Murderer. Hale, 1975
The Victim Died Twice. Hale, 1969

LILIENTHAL, DAVID ELI, JR. 1927- . Pseudonym: David Ely, q.v.

LILLEY, PETER. Joint pseudonym with Anthony Stansfeld: Bruce Buckingham, q.v.

LILLEY, TOM [THOMAS WILLIAM LILLEY]. 1924- . SC: Ralph Carter, in both titles.
The K Section. Macmillan (London), 1972
The Officer from Special Branch; see The Projects Section
The Projects Section. Macmillan (London), 1970. U.S. title: The Officer from Special Branch. Doubleday, 1971 [Mal.]

LILLIE, ARTHUR
The Cobra Diamond. Ward, 1890
-An Indian Wizard. Simpkin, 1887

LILLIE, HELEN. 1915- . Ref: CA.
Call Down the Sky. Hurst, 1973
The Listening Silence. Hurst, 1970; Hawthorn, 1974 [Scot.]

LILLINGSTON, CLAUDE. 1881- .
His Patients Died. Blackwood, 1936 [hosp.]

LILLO, GEORGE. 1693-1739.
Fatal Curiosity. Gray, 1737 (3-act play.)

LILLY, JEAN. SC: Bruce Perkins = BP.
Death in B-Minor. Dutton, 1934; Cassell, 1935 BP [L.I.]
Death Thumbs a Ride. Dutton, 1940 BP [N.Y.]
False Face. Dutton, 1929 BP [acad.]
The Seven Sisters. Dutton, 1928; Dent, 1929 [N.Y.]

LIMNELIUS, GEORGE. Pseudonym of Lewis (George) Robinson, 1886-   , q.v. Set: Eng.
   The Medbury Fort Murder. Benn, 1929; Doubleday, 1929
   Tell No Tales. Bles, 1931

LINAKIS, STEVEN. 1923-   . See also: Peter Diapolous.
   The Killing Ground. McKay, 1970 [L.I.]

LINARES, LOUISA-MARIA
   Fatal Legacy. Mystique, 1979 (Translation of "Ne Dis Pas Le Que J'Ai Fait Hier." Paris, 1971.)
   Web of Fear. Mystique, 1979 (Translation of "Huit Heures, Jean, Dix Heures, Paul." Paris, 1968.)

LINCOLN. Pseudonym: Nicholas Carter, q.v.

LINCOLN, FREEMAN. See: Joseph C(rosby) Lincoln, 1870-1944.

LINCOLN, JOSEPH C(ROSBY). 1870-1944.
   Blair's Attic, with Freeman Lincoln. Coward, 1929; Cassell, 1930
   Extricating Obadiah. Appleton, 1917
   Out of the Fog. Appleton, 1940 [Cape Cod]
   The Owley Inn, with Freeman Lincoln. Coward, 1939; Cassell, 1940 [Cape Cod]
   Storm Girl. Appleton, 1937

LINCOLN, NATALIE SUMNER. 1881-1935. Ref: MP. SC: Insp. Mitchell, in at least those marked M; Detective Ferguson, in at least those marked F.
   The Blue Car Mystery. Appleton, 1926 M [Wash. D.C.]
   C.O.D. Appleton, 1915
   The Cat's Paw. Appleton, 1922 M [Wash. D.C.]
   The Dancing Silhouette. Appleton, 1927 M [Wash. D.C.]
   The Fifth Latchkey. Appleton, 1929 [Md.]
   I Spy. Appleton, 1916 M [Wash. D.C.]
   The Lost Despatch. Appleton, 1913 [Wash. D.C., 1865]
   The Man Inside. Appleton, 1914 [Wash. D.C.]
   Marked "Cancelled". Appleton, 1930 [Wash. D.C.]
   The Meredith Mystery. Appleton, 1923 M [Va.]
   The Missing Initial. Appleton, 1925 M [Wash. D.C.]
   The Moving Finger. Appleton, 1918 M [Va.]
   The Nameless Man. Appleton, 1917 M [Wash. D.C.]
   The Official Chaperone. Appleton, 1915 [Wash. D.C.]
   P.P.C. Appleton, 1927 M [Wash. D.C.]
   The Red Seal. Appleton, 1920 F [Wash. D.C.]
   The Secret of Mohawk Pond. Appleton, 1928 [Conn.]
   13 Thirteenth Street. Appleton, 1932 [Wash. D.C.]
   The Thirteenth Letter. Appleton, 1924 [Md.]
   The Three Strings. Appleton, 1918 M [Wash. D.C.]
   The Trevor Case. Appleton, 1912 [Wash. D.C.]
   The Unseen Ear. Appleton, 1921 F [Wash. D.C.]

LINCOLN, PETER. Pseudonym: Thomas St. Martin, q.v.

LINCOLN, VICTORIA (ENDICOTT). 1904-1981. Ref: CA.
   The Swan Island Murders. Farrar, 1930; Cassell, 1931 [Can.]

LINDALL, EDWARD. Pseudonym of Edward Ernest Smith, 1915-   . Born in Australia; newspaperman in England and Australia.
   A Day for Angels. Constable, 1975
   Death and the Maiden. Constable, 1973
   -The Fires of Kiwai. Heinemann, 1968
   A Gathering of Eagles. Collins, 1970
   The Killers of Karawala. Hutchinson, 1961; Morrow, 1962 [Australia]
   -A Kind of Justice. Hutchinson, 1964; Morrow, 1964
   A Lively Form of Death. Constable, 1972
   No Place to Hide. Hutchinson, 1959. U.S. title: The Paper Ghost. Morrow, 1961
   -Northward the Coast. Heinemann, 1966
   The Paper Ghost; see No Place to Hide
   Search for Tomorrow. Constable, 1974
   Springs of Violence. Hutchinson, 1963; Morrow, 1963
   -Stranger Among Friends. Hutchinson, 1956

   -A Time Too Soon. Heinemann, 1967; Morrow, 1967

LINDAU, RUDOLPH. 1829-1900.
   Liquidated and The Seer. Appleton, 1878 (Two stories.)

LINDBLAD, JOHN
   Zap Day. PB (Canada), 1971 [Can.]

LINDEN, CATHERINE
   Kiss...But Never Tell. Pinnacle, 1980

LINDHOLM, ANNA CHANDLER. 1870-   . Pseudonym: Dorothy Fay, q.v.

LINDLEY, ERICA. Pseudonym of Aileen Quigley, 1930-   . Ref: CA.
   Belladonna. Signet, 1978
   The Brackenroyd Inheritance. Signet, 1975; Millington, 1976 [1800s, Eng.]
   The Devil in Crystal. Signet, 1977; Millington, 1979 [Eng.]

LINDOP, AUDREY ERSKINE [MRS. DUDLEY LESLIE]. 1920-   . Novelist and screenwriter in Eng.
   -Details of Jeremy Stratton. Heinemann, 1955. U.S. title: The Outer Ring. Appleton, 1955
   I Start Counting. Collins, 1966; Doubleday, 1966
   I Thank a Fool. Collins, 1958. U.S. title: Mist over Talla. Doubleday, 1957
   Journey into Stone. Macmillan (London), 1973; Doubleday, 1972
   Mist over Talla; see I Thank a Fool
   -Nicola. Collins, 1964; Doubleday, 1959
   The Outer Ring; see Details of Jeremy Stratton
   The Self-Appointed Saint. Macmillan (London), 1975; Doubleday, 1975
   Sight Unseen. Collins, 1969; Doubleday, 1969
   The Tall Headlines. Heinemann, 1950; Macmillan, 1950

LINDQUIST, DONALD. 1930-   . Ref: CA.
   Berlin Tunnel 21. Avon, 1978; Magnum, 1979 [Berlin]
   -The Street. Dutton, 1979

LINDSAY, C(HARLES) McDONALD
   Betrayed!!; or, What Might Come to Pass. Drane, 1928
   Murder at Constantia. Jenkins, 1932

LINDSAY, DAVID T. SC: Insp. John Jay "Jailbird" Jackson, in at least those marked JJ. Set: Eng.
   -Air Bandits. Jenkins, 1937
   Another Case for Inspector Jackson. Hamilton, 1937 JJ
   The Black Fetish. Hamilton, 1937
   -The Flying Armada. Hamilton, 1938
   -The Flying Crusader. Hamilton, 1937
   -The Green Ray. Hamilton, 1937
   Inspector Jackson Goes North. Hamilton, 1939 JJ
   Inspector Jackson Investigates. Hamilton, 1936 JJ
   The Man Nobody Knew. Hamilton, 1938 JJ
   Masked Judgment. Hamilton, 1937
   Mystery of the Tumbling V. Hamilton, 1940
   The Ninth Plague. Hamilton, 1936
   Stranglehold. Hamilton, 1936
   The Temple of the Flaming God. Hamilton, 1938
   The Two Red Capsules. Hamilton, 1936
   Wings over Africa. Hamilton, 1936 [Afr.]
   Wings over the Amazon. Hamilton, 1937 [Brazil]

LINDSAY, HOWARD. 1889-1968. See: Damon Runyon, 1880-1946. Ref: CA.
   Remains to Be Seen, with Russel Crouse, 1893-   . Random, 1951 (3-act play.)

LINDSAY, JOSEPHINE
   A House Is Just a House. Mayflower, 1967. U.S. title: Shadow of the House. Belmont, 1973

LINDSAY, KATHLEEN. 1903-   .
   -After the Wedding. Jenkins, 1943
   -Another Woman's Love. Jenkins, 1950
   -Beware of the Dawn. Hurst, 1959
   -Brave Heart of Youth. Jenkins, 1944
   -Danger Zone. Jenkins, 1936
   -Dangerous Madonna. Jenkins, 1938
   -Dangerous to Know. Hutchinson, 1956
   -Dark Destiny. Jenkins, 1937
   -The Devil's Dominion. Hutchinson, 1956
   -Enchantress of the Nile. Hurst, 1965
   -Fair Intruder. Jenkins, 1942
   -For Ever You'll Be Mine. Hurst, 1958
   -Glamour Girl. Jenkins, 1942
   -The Glorious Masquerade. Jenkins, 1937

   The Green Domino. Alexander-Ouseley, 1928
   -Harvest of Deceit. Long, 1934
   -He Should Have Been King. Hutchinson, 1954
   -Heaven Will Be Ours. Jenkins, 1948
   -Here in Eden. Hutchinson, 1951
   His Crooked Highness. Jenkins, 1938
   -If Love Be Ours. Jenkins, 1948
   -Incomparable Doll. Hurst, 1967
   -Into Temptation. Jenkins, 1949
   -It Happened at the Cape. Jenkins, 1931
   -A Lady for Botany Bay. Hurst, 1961
   -Lady Make-Believe. Jenkins, 1941
   -Less Than the Dust. Hurst, 1963
   -Lilli Marlene. Jenkins, 1950
   -Love Not Denied. Jenkins, 1946
   -Love's Atonement. Hurst, 1963
   -Loyal Lady. Hurst, 1965
   -Madonna of Hell. Hutchinson, 1954
   -The Moonlight Path. Jenkins, 1940
   -My Dear Heart. Hurst, 1970
   The Mystery at Greystones. Jenkins, 1932
   -'Neath the Southern Cross. Jenkins, 1931
   -Paulette. Hurst, 1962
   -Queen of the Mirage. Hurst, 1966
   Rebel Lady. Jenkins, 1939
   -Render unto Caesar. Hurst, 1969
   -The Road to Ballarat. Hurst, 1968
   -Rustle of Spring. Hurst, 1967
   -She Was My Beloved. Hurst, 1968
   -So Near to Love. Hutchinson, 1951
   -Song of the Dawn. Hurst, 1965
   -The Splendor Falls. Hutchinson, 1952
   Storm Maiden. Jenkins, 1939
   -Stormy Paradise. Hurst, 1957
   Suspense. Jenkins, 1940 [Malta]
   -Take This My Heart. Jenkins, 1947
   -Theodora. Hurst, 1964
   -There Is No Yesterday. Hurst, 1962
   -This Man Is Mine. Jenkins, 1947
   -Tomorrow We Die. Hutchinson, 1953
   -Treachery. Jenkins, 1937
   -Virginia. Hurst, 1969
   -Wind of Desire. Long, 1933
   -Winsome Lass. Hurst, 1960

LINDSAY, PHILIP. 1906-   .
   The Shadow of the Red Barn. Hutchinson, 1952

LINDSAY, R(OBERT) HOWARD. 1910-   . Born in Ontario; radio broadcast director in Canada.
   Fowl Murder. Little, 1941

LINDSEY, DAWN. Pseudonym.
   The Duchess of Videl. Doubleday, 1978

LINEBARGER, PAUL MYRON ANTHONY. 1913-1966. Pseudonym: Carmichael Smith, q.v.

LINES, MAUREEN. Pseudonym: Patricia Farmer, q.v.

LINGO, ADA E.
   Murder in Texas. Houghton, 1935 [Tex.]

LININGTON, (BARBARA) ELIZABETH. 1921-   . Pseudonyms: Anne Blaisdell, Lesley Egan, Dell Shannon, qg.v. (Note: Several novels published in the U.S. as by Dell Shannon have appeared in England as by Barbara Elizabeth Linington.) Ref: CA, CC, EM, MC, TC. SC: Ivor Maddox, in all titles, which are published in England as by Anne Blaisdell. Set: L.A., in all titles.
   Consequence of Crime. Doubleday, 1980; Gollancz, 1981
   Crime by Chance. Lippincott, 1973; Gollancz, 1974
   Date with Death. Harper, 1966; Gollancz, 1966
   Greenmask! Harper, 1964; Gollancz, 1965
   No Evil Angel. Harper, 1964; Gollancz, 1965
   No Villain Need Be. Doubleday, 1979; Gollancz, 1979
   Perchance of Death. Doubleday, 1977; Gollancz, 1978
   Policeman's Lot. Harper, 1968; Gollancz, 1969
   Practice to Deceive. Harper, 1971; Gollancz, 1971
   Something Wrong. Harper, 1967; Gollancz, 1968

LINK, WILLIAM, 1933-   , and RICHARD LEVINSON, 1934-   . Ref for each author: CA.
   Prescription: Murder. French (NYC), 1963 (3-act play.)

LINKLATER, ERIC (ROBERT RUSSELL). 1899-1974. Ref: CA.
   Mr. Byculla. Hart-Davis, 1950; Harcourt, 1951

LINKLATER, JOSEPH LANE. Pseudonym of Alex Watkins. SC: Silas Booth, in at least those marked SB. (Note: The usual by-line on these books is J. Lane Linklater, but a few are as by Joseph Linklater.)
...And She Had a Little Knife. Mill, 1948. British title: She Had a Little Knife. Foulsham, 1950 SB [L.A.]
The Bishop's Cap. Mill, 1948. British title: The "Bishop's Cap" Murder. Foulsham, 1949 SB [L.A.]
The "Bishop's Cap" Murder; see The Bishop's Cap
Black Opal. Mill, 1947; Boardman, 1949 SB [L.A.]
The Green Glove. Mystery House, 1959; Ward, 1960
Odd Woman Out. Bouregy, 1955; Ward, 1959 SB [L.A.]
Shadow for a Lady. Mill, 1947; Boardman, 1948 SB [L.A.]
She Had a Little Knife; see ...And She Had a Little Knife
A Tisket, a Casket. Mystery House, 1959 SB [L.A.]

LINN, EDWARD
The Adversaries. Saturday Review Press, 1973

LINNELL, GERTRUDE (BALDWIN).   -1933.
The Black Ghost of the Highway. Longmans, 1931 [Balkans]

LINTON, ADELIN SUMNER BRIGGS. 1899-   .
Pseudonym: Aldin Vinton, q.v.

LINTON, DUKE
Big-Time Racketeer. Scion, 1951
Bury Me Deep. Scion, 1950
Call Me Al. Scion, 1952
Crazy to Kill. Scion, 1950
Dames Die Too. Scion, 1950
The Dark Brings Death. Scion, 1951
Daughter of the Sidewalk. Scion, 1953
Deadline. Scion, 1954
Enough Rope. Scion, 1950
Give Me the Lowdown. Scion, 1953
Hold Everything. Scion, 1953
How Dead Can You Be? Scion, 1952
Keep Moving, Bud. Scion, 1952
Kill and Desire. Scion, 1950
Killer Bait. Scion, 1953
Lend Me a Rod. Scion, 1951
Sinner. Scion, 1953
Sin's Half Mile. Scion, 1953
So Dead, So Sweet. Scion, 1953
Strip Tease Angel. Scion, 1953
The Swinging Corpse. Scion, 1954
That Dame Sal. Scion, 1952
They've Got Me Again. Scion, 1952
Too Late for Death. Scion, 1950
Too Many Yesterdays. Scion, 1951
Was She Poison? Scion, 1953
What Do I Care? Scion, 1952
Who's Sorry Now? Scion, 1953

LINZEE, DAVID (AUGUSTINE ANTHONY). 1952-   . Ref: CA. SC: Sarah Saber & Chris Rockwell = S&R.
Belgravia. Seaview, 1979; Hale, 1982 S&R
Death in Connecticut. McKay, 1977 [Conn., 1971]
Discretion. Seaview, 1978; Hale, 1981 S&R [Rome]

LION, LEON M. See: Marian Bower.

LIPEZ, RICHARD. 1938-   . See: Peter Stein, 1932-   .

LIPKE, KAY [KATHERINE BELLOWS LIPKE]
Rain on the Roof. Dial, 1931; Methuen, 1932 [Calif.]

LIPMAN, CLAYRE,   -1979, and MICHEL LIPMAN
House of Evil. Lion, 1954; Banner, 1959

LIPMAN, MICHEL. See: Clayre Lipman,   -1979.

LIPMAN, WILLIAM (R.)
Yonder Grow the Daisies. Washburn, 1929

LIPPARD, GEORGE. 1822-1854.
The Ladye Annabel. Zieber, 1843. Also published as: The Mysteries of Florence. Peterson, 1864 [Florence]
The Mysteries of Florence; see The Ladye Annabel
The Quaker City; or, The Monks of Monk-Hall. Zieber, 1845 [Phil.]

LIPPINCOTT, BEVERLY
Born to Evil. Major, 1976

LIPPINCOTT, DAVID (McCORD). 1925-   .
Ref: CA.
The Blood of October. Signet, 1977; Allen, 1978
E Pluribus Bang! Viking, 1970; Joseph, 1971 [future, Wash. D.C.]
Salt Mine. Viking, 1979; Allen, 1979 [Moscow]
Savage Ransom. Rawson, 1978; Allen, 1978 [Conn.]
Tremor Violet. Putnam, 1975; Allen, 1976
The Voice of Armageddon. Putnam, 1974; Hodder, 1975

LIPPINCOTT, NORMAN
Murder at Glen Athol. Doubleday, 1935; World's Work, 1935 [Pa.]

LIPSKY, ELEAZAR. 1911-   . Graduate of Columbia U. and Columbia Law School; assistant D.A. for New York County for some years, subsequently specializing in civil law.
Day of Judgment; see Lincoln McKeever
The Devil's Daughter. Meredith, 1969 [Calif., 1880s]
The Hoodlum; see The Kiss of Death
The Kiss of Death. Penguin (NYC), 1947; Penguin (London), 1949. Also published as: The Hoodlum. Lion, 1953 [NYC]
Lincoln McKeever. Appleton, 1953; Deutsch, 1954. Also published as: Day of Judgment. Corgi, 1955 [N. Mex., 1890s]
Murder One. Doubleday, 1948 [NYC]
The People Against O'Hara. Doubleday, 1950; Wingate, 1951
The Scientists. Appleton, 1959; Longmans, 1959

LIPSYTE, MARJORIE (RUBIN). 1932-   .
Ref: CA.
Hot Type. Doubleday, 1980 [NYC]

LISSENDEN, GEORGE B.
-The Revolt. Cranton, 1928
-The Seeress. Cranton, 1927
A Woman's Prerogative. Stockwell, 1930

LISTER, STEPHEN. Pseudonym.
Delorme in Deep Water. Davies, 1958 [Fr.]

LITCHFIELD, CECIL
Bags of Blackmail. Pawling, 1934

LITCHMAN, FRANK. ca.1918-1981. Pseudonym: Ursula Nightingale, q.v.

LITSEY, EDWIN CARLILE. 1874-   .
The Beast. Mystery House, 1959

LITTELL, BLAINE. Newspaper reporter and feature writer; network TV news writer, producer, correspondent.
The Dolorosa Deal. Saturday Review Press, 1973; Collins, 1973 [Jerus.]

LITTELL, ROBERT. 1935-   . Has been general editor for "Newsweek."
The Debriefing. Harper, 1979; Hutchinson, 1979
The Defection of A. J. Lewinter. Houghton, 1973; Hodder, 1973
Mother Russia. Harcourt, 1978; Hutchinson, 1978 [Moscow]
-The October Circle. Houghton, 1973; Hodder, 1974 [Bulg.]
Sweet Reason. Houghton, 1974; Hodder, 1974

LITTLE, CLARKE
"Outlaws" or "When the Devil Drives." Ward, 1902 ss

LITTLE, CONSTANCE and GWENYTH. (Note: The byline on all English titles is Conyth Little, except for the starred one, which is signed in Eng. as in the U.S.) Ref: CC, DD, MP, TC.
The Black Coat. Doubleday, 1948; Collins, 1949 [NYC]
Black Corridors. Doubleday, 1940; Collins, 1941 [hosp.]
The Black Curl. Doubleday, 1953 [NYC]
The Black Dream. Doubleday, 1952; Collins, 1953
The Black Express; see Great Black Kanba
The Black Eye. Doubleday, 1945; Collins, 1946
The Black Gloves. Doubleday, 1939; Collins, 1940 [N.J.]
The Black Goatee. Doubleday, 1947; Collins, 1947
The Black-Headed Pin. Doubleday, 1938; Davies, 1939 * [N.J.]
The Black Honeymoon. Doubleday, 1944; Collins, 1944
The Black House. Doubleday, 1950; Collins, 1950 [NYC]
The Black Iris. Doubleday, 1953; Collins, 1953
The Black Lady; see The Black Rustle
The Black Paw. Doubleday, 1941; Collins, 1941
The Black Piano. Doubleday, 1948; Collins, 1948 [N.J.]
The Black Rustle. Doubleday, 1943. British title: The Black Lady. Collins, 1944
The Black Shrouds. Doubleday, 1941; Collins, 1942 [NYC]
The Black Smith. Doubleday, 1950; Collins, 1951
The Black Stocking. Doubleday, 1946; Collins, 1947 [hosp.]
The Black Thumb. Doubleday, 1942; Collins, 1943 [hosp.]
The Blackout. Doubleday, 1951; Collins, 1952 [Calif.]
Great Black Kanba. Doubleday, 1944. British title: The Black Express. Collins, 1945 [Australia]
The Grey Mist Murders. Doubleday, 1938 [ship]

LITTLE, CONYTH. See: Constance and Gwenyth Little.

LITTLE, GWENYTH. See: Constance and Gwenyth Little.

LITTLE, PAUL H. 1915-   . Pseudonyms: Paula Minton, Hugo Paul, qq.v.

LITTLE, PHILIP
Who Was He? Street (Magnet #367)

LITTLECHILD, JOHN GEORGE
The Reminiscences of Chief-Inspector Littlechild. Leadenhall, 1894 ss

LITTLEFIELD, ANNE
Which Mrs. Bennett? Doubleday, 1959 [Mass.]

LITVINOFF, EMANUEL
Blood on the Snow. Joseph, 1975 [Russ., ca.1920]
A Death out of Season. Joseph, 1973; Scribner, 1974
The Face of Terror. Joseph, 1978; Morrow, 1978

LITVINOFF, IVY. 1889?-1977. Ref: CA, TC.
His Master's Voice: A Detective Story. Heinemann, 1930. U.S. title: Moscow Mystery. Coward, 1943. Revised edition: Gollancz, 1973 [Moscow]

LITWAK, LEO (EZRA). 1924-   . Ref: CA.
Waiting for the News. Doubleday, 1969; MacGibbon, 1971 [Det., 1939-43]

LITZINGER, BOYD (A., JR.). 1929-   .
Ref: CA.
Watch It, Dr. Adrian. Putnam, 1977 [Eng.]

LIVINGSTON, ARMSTRONG. 1885-   . SC: Jimmy Treynor = JT; Peter Creighton = PC.
The Case of the Walking Corpse. Lucom, 1945
The Doublecross. Henkle, 1929; Skeffington, 1929 JT [L.I.]
The Guilty Accuser. Chelsea, 1928; Jarrolds, 1928 PC [N.Y.]
In Cold Blood. Bobbs, 1931; Skeffington, 1932 JT [Midwest]
Light Fingered Ladies. Chelsea, 1927; Jarrolds, 1928 PC [NYC]
Magic for Murder. Cavalcade, 1945; Skeffington, 1936 [Maine]
The Monk of Hambledon. Henkle, 1928 PC [New Eng.]
The Monster in the Pool. Bobbs, 1929; Skeffington, 1930 JT
Murder Is Easy! Speller, 1936; Skeffington, 1933
The Murder Trap. Bobbs, 1930; Skeffington, 1932 JT
The Mystery of the Twin Rubies. Moffat, 1922; Paul, 1923
Night of Crime. Sovereign House, 1938 JT [L.I.]
On the Right Wrists. Chelsea, 1925; Jarrolds, 1927 PC [N.Y.]
Trackless Death. Bobbs, 1930; Skeffington, 1930 PC [Conn.]

LIVINGSTON, KENNETH. Pseudonym of Kenneth Livingston Stewart, 1894-   . Ref: CC.
The Cloze Papers. Rich, 1936
The Dodd Cases. Methuen, 1933; Doubleday, 1934 ss

LIVINGSTON, M. JAY. Pseudonym of Myron Jabez Livingston, Jr., 1934-   .
Ref: CA.
-The Prodigy. Coward, 1978 [Cleve.]

LIVINGSTON, MYRON JABEZ, JR. 1934-   .
Pseudonym: M. Jay Livingston, q.v.

LIVINGSTON, WALTER. 1895-
The Mystery of Burnleigh Manor. Mystery League, 1930 [Eng.]
The Mystery of Villa Sineste. Mystery League, 1931 [It.]

LIVINGSTONE, ALICE
A Sealed Book. Sunday Circle, 1904; Fenno, 1906

LLEWELLYN, RICHARD. Pseudonym of Richard David Vivian Llewellyn Lloyd, 1906-   . Ref: CA. SC: Edmund Trothe = ET. Set: Eng.
But We Didn't Get the Fox. Joseph, 1970; Doubleday, 1970 ET
The End of the Rug. Joseph, 1969; Doubleday, 1968 ET
The Night Is a Child. Joseph, 1974; Doubleday, 1974 ET
Poison Pen. French (London), 1938 (3-act play.)
-Tell Me Now, and Again. Joseph, 1977; Doubleday, 1978
White Horse to Banbury Cross. Joseph, 1972; Doubleday, 1970 ET

LLOYD, A.
Death Stalks the Dykes. Hale, 1979
The Falcon's Nest. Hale, 1977

LLOYD, HERBERT
-Children of Chance. Andrews, 1893
A Lawyer's Secret. Andrews, 1896 ss

LLOYD, JACK (BATES). Born in Okla.; has lived mostly in Texas and N. Mex.
The Key Without a Lock. Vantage, 1964

LLOYD, JOHN. See also: Elwyn Jones, 1923-   . Set: Eng., both titles.
Death at Roman Farm. Hale, 1968
Until They Are Dead. Hale, 1967

LLOYD, LAVENDER. 1924-   .
The Linton Memorial. Longmans, 1957

LLOYD, NELSON (McALLISTER). 1873-1933.
The Robberies Co., Ltd. Scribner, 1906 [NYC]

LLOYD, RICHARD DAVID VIVIAN LLEWELLYN. 1906-   . Pseudonym: Richard Llewellyn, q.v.

LLOYD, STEPHANIE. Pseudonym of Morton Jay Golding, 1925-   . Other pseudonym: Patricia Morton, q.v.
Graveswood. Paperback Library, 1966

LLOYD, TOM
Champion and Crook. Aldine, 1929
'Gainst Chink and Gunman. Aldine, 1931
Samson's Surrender. Aldine, 1927

LLOYD, VICTOR (HENRY)
Don't Tie Me Down. Angus (Sydney), 1961; Angus (London), 1962 [Australia]
-The Hidden Enemy. Angus (London), 1957

LLOYD, WALLACE. Pseudonym of James Algie.
Bergen Worth. Unwin, 1901 [Chi.]
-Houses of Glass. Dillingham, 1898

LOBAN, ETHEL H(ARRIS). 1892-   .
The Calloused Eye. Doubleday, 1931 [Colo.]
Signed in Yellow. Doubleday, 1930 [Mich.]

LOBAUGH, ELMA K(LINEDORF). 1907-   .
Pseudonym: Kenneth Lowe, q.v.
I Am Afraid. Doubleday, 1949 [Ill.]
Shadows in Succession. Doubleday, 1946 [New Or.]
She Never Reached the Top. Doubleday, 1945 [Ill.]

LOBELL, G(RISELDA) G. 1916-   . See: N(athan) D(avid) Lobell, 1911-   .

LOBELL, N(ATHAN) D(AVID), 1911-   , and G(RISELDA) G. LOBELL, 1916-   . He was born in NYC; graduate of Columbia Law School; joined Securities and Exchange Commission in 1937. She was also born in NYC; attended Barnard and Columbia Law School.
The Shadow and the Blot. Harper, 1949 [NYC]

LOBO, GEORGE EDMUND. Pseudonym: Oliver Sherry, q.v.

LOCK, ARNOLD CHARLES COOPER. Pseudonym: Charles Cooper, q.v.

LOCK, SANFORD
Mail for McNair. Hutchinson, 1940

LOCKE, D(OROTHY) M(ARY)
Fatal Fragrance. Cassell, 1950

LOCKE, DOUGLAS
Death Lives in the Mansion; see The House of Two Wives
The Drawstring. Lancer, 1966 [S.W.]
The House of Two Wives. Lancer, 1967. Also published as: Death Lives in the Mansion. Lancer, 1969 [New Or.]

LOCKE, EDWARD. 1869-1945. See: George C(harles) Jenks, 1850-1929.

LOCKE, G(LADYS) E(DSON). 1887-   . SC: Insp. Burton, in at least those marked B; Mercedes Quero, in at least those marked MQ.
The Fenwood Murders. Long, 1931
The Golden Lotus. Page, 1927; Harrap, 1927
Grey Gables. Long, 1929
The House on the Downs. Page, 1925 B
The Purple Mist. Page, 1924 B
The Ravensdale Mystery. Page, 1935 [Eng.]
The Red Cavalier. Page, 1922 B,MQ
The Redmaynes. Page, 1928; Long, 1929 [Eng.]
-Ronald o' the Moors. Four Seas, 1919
The Scarlet Macaw. Page, 1923 B
That Affair at Portstead Manor. Sherman, 1914 MQ [Eng.]

LOCKE, MARTIN. Pseudonym of W(illiam) Murdoch Duncan, 1909-1975, q.v. Other pseudonyms: John Cassells, John Dallas, Neill Graham, Peter Malloch, Lovat Marshall, qq.v.
The Vengeance of Mortimer Daly. Ward, 1961

LOCKE, ROBERT DONALD
A Taste of Brass. Dell, 1957 [L.A.]

LOCKE, W(ILLIAM) J(OHN). 1863-1930.
The Joyous Adventures of Aristide Pujol. Lane (London & NYC), 1912 ss [Fr.]

LOCKHART, JOHN G(ILBERT). 1891-   .
East All the Way. Benn, 1928; Appleton, 1928
That Followed After. Benn, 1929

LOCKRIDGE, FRANCES (LOUISE DAVIS), 1896-1963, and RICHARD (ORSON) LOCKRIDGE, 1898-1982. See also: Richard Lockridge; and: Richard and Frances Lockridge; and: Owen Davis, 1874-1956. Ref: CA, CC, EM, MP, TC. British byline on those titles below marked FR: Francis Richards. SC: Mr. & Mrs. (Pam & Jerry) North = N; Bill Weigand = BW (BW also appears in every N novel except "Murder by the Book"); Nathan Shapiro = NS (see also the Richard Lockridge entry); Bernard Simmons = BS (see also the Richard Lockridge entry); Paul Lane = PL; Capt./Insp. Merton Heimrich = MH (see also the Richard Lockridge entry, and the Richard and Frances Lockridge entry).
And Left for Dead. Lippincott, 1962; Hutchinson, 1962 BS [NYC]
Call It Coincidence; see Murder and Blueberry Pie
Case of the Murdered Redhead; see The Faceless Adversary
Catch as Catch Can. Lippincott, 1958; Long, 1960, by FR [NYC]
Curtain for a Jester. Lippincott, 1953 N [NYC]
Dead As a Dinosaur. Lippincott, 1952; Hutchinson, 1956 N [NYC]
Death Has a Small Voice. Lippincott, 1953; Hutchinson, 1954 N [NYC]
Death of a Tall Man. Lippincott, 1946; Hutchinson, 1949 N,MH [NYC]
Death of an Angel. Lippincott, 1955; Hutchinson, 1957. Also published as: Mr. & Mrs. North and the Poisoned Playboy. Avon, 1957 N [NYC]
Death on the Aisle. Lippincott, 1942; Hutchinson, 1948 N [NYC]
Death Takes a Bow. Lippincott, 1943; Hutchinson, 1945 N [NYC]
The Devious Ones. Lippincott, 1964. British title: Four Hours to Fear. Long, 1965, by FR BS [NYC]
The Dishonest Murderer. Lippincott, 1949; Hutchinson, 1951 N [NYC]
The Drill Is Death. Lippincott, 1961; Long, 1963, by FR NS [NYC, acad.]
The Faceless Adversary. Lippincott, 1956. Also published as: Case of the Murdered Redhead. Avon, 1957 NS [NYC]
Four Hours to Fear; see The Devious Ones
The Golden Man. Lippincott, 1960; Hutchinson, 1961 [Conn.]
Hanged for a Sheep. Lippincott, 1942; Hutchinson, 1944 N [NYC]
The Innocent House. Lippincott, 1959; Long, 1961, by FR
The Judge Is Reversed. Lippincott, 1960; Hutchinson, 1961 N [NYC]
A Key to Death. Lippincott, 1954 N [NYC]
Killing the Goose. Lippincott, 1944; Hutchinson, 1947 N [NYC]
The Long Skeleton. Lippincott, 1958; Hutchinson, 1960 N [NYC]
Mr. & Mrs. North and the Poisoned Playboy; see Death of an Angel
Mr. & Mrs. North Meet Murder; see The Norths Meet Murder
Murder and Blueberry Pie. Lippincott, 1959. British title: Call It Coincidence. Long, 1962, by FR NS [NYC]
Murder by the Book. Lippincott, 1963; Hutchinson, 1964 N [Fla.]
Murder Comes First. Lippincott, 1951 N [NYC]
Murder Has Its Points. Lippincott, 1961; Hutchinson, 1962 N [NYC]
Murder in a Hurry. Lippincott, 1950; Hutchinson, 1952 N [NYC]
Murder Is Served. Lippincott, 1948; Hutchinson, 1950 N [NYC]
Murder Is Suggested. Lippincott, 1959; Hutchinson, 1961 N [NYC]
Murder Out of Turn. Stokes, 1941; Joseph, 1941 N [N.Y.]
Murder Within Murder. Lippincott, 1946; Hutchinson, 1949 N [NYC]
Night of Shadows. Lippincott, 1962; Long, 1964, by FR PL [NYC]
The Norths Meet Murder. Stokes, 1940; Joseph, 1940. Also published as: Mr. & Mrs. North Meet Murder. Avon, 1952 N [NYC]
Payoff for the Banker. Lippincott, 1945; Hutchinson, 1946 N [NYC]
A Pinch of Poison. Stokes, 1941; Hutchinson, 1948 N [N.Y.]
Quest for the Bogeyman. Lippincott, 1964; Hutchinson, 1965 PL [NYC]
The Tangled Cord. Lippincott, 1957; Hutchinson, 1959 BW,NS [N.Y.]
The Ticking Clock. Lippincott, 1962; Hutchinson, 1963 [N.Y.]
Untidy Murder. Lippincott, 1947 N [NYC]
Voyage into Violence. Lippincott, 1956; Hutchinson, 1959 N [ship]

LOCKRIDGE, RICHARD (ORSON). 1898-1982.
See also: Frances and Richard Lockridge; and: Richard and Frances Lockridge. SC: Capt./Insp. Merton Heimrich = MH (see also Frances and Richard Lockridge; and: Richard and Frances Lockridge); Bernard Simmons = BS (see also Frances and Richard Lockridge); Nathan Shapiro = NS (see also Frances and Richard Lockridge).
Dead Run. Lippincott, 1976; Long, 1977 MH [N.Y.]
Death in a Sunny Place. Lippincott, 1971; Long, 1973 [N.C.]
Death in the Mind, with G(eorge) H. Estabrooks, 1896?-1973. Dutton, 1945
Death on the Hour. Lippincott, 1974; Long, 1975 BS [NYC]
Die Laughing. Lippincott, 1969; Long, 1970, by Francis Richards NS [NYC]
Inspector's Holiday. Lippincott, 1971; Long, 1972 MH [ship]
A Matter of Taste. Lippincott, 1949; Hutchinson, 1951 [NYC]
Murder Can't Wait. Lippincott, 1964; Long, 1965, by Francis Richards MH,NS [N.Y.]
Murder for Art's Sake. Lippincott, 1967; Long, 1968, by Francis Richards NS [NYC]
Murder in False-Face. Lippincott, 1968; Hutchinson, 1969 [Conn.]
Murder Roundabout. Lippincott, 1966; Long, 1967, by Francis Richards MH [N.Y.]
Not I, Said the Sparrow. Lippincott, 1973; Long, 1974 MH [N.Y.]
The Old Die Young. Lippincott, 1980; Hale, 1981 NS [NYC, theatre]
Or Was He Pushed? Lippincott, 1975; Long, 1976 NS [NYC]
A Plate of Red Herrings. Lippincott, 1968; Long, 1969, by Francis Richards BS [NYC]
Preach No More. Lippincott, 1971; Long, 1972 NS [NYC]
A Risky Way to Kill. Lippincott, 1969; Long, 1970, by Francis Richards MH [N.Y.]
Something Up a Sleeve. Lippincott, 1972; Long, 1973 BS [NYC]

Squire of Death. Lippincott, 1965;
  Long, 1966, by Francis Richards BS
  [NYC]
A Streak of Light. Lippincott, 1976;
  Long, 1978 NS [NYC]
The Tenth Life. Lippincott, 1977; Long,
  1979 MH [N.Y.]
Troubled Journey. Lippincott, 1970;
  Hutchinson, 1971 [Fla.]
Twice Retired. Lippincott, 1970; Long,
  1971 BS [NYC, acad.]
With Option to Die. Lippincott, 1967;
  Long, 1968, by Francis Richards MH
  [N.Y.]
Write Murder Down. Lippincott, 1972;
  Long, 1974 NS [NYC]

LOCKRIDGE, RICHARD (ORSON), 1898-1982,
  and FRANCES (LOUISE DAVIS) LOCKRIDGE,
  1896-1963. See also: Frances and
  Richard Lockridge; and: Richard Lockridge. SC: Capt./Insp. Merton Heimrich, in all titles (see also: Frances and Richard Lockridge; and Richard Lockridge). British byline on all
  titles marked FR: Francis Richards.
Accent on Murder. Lippincott, 1958;
  Long, 1960, by FR [N.Y.]
Burnt Offering. Lippincott, 1955;
  Hutchinson, 1957, by FR [N.Y.]
A Client Is Cancelled. Lippincott,
  1951; Hutchinson, 1955 [N.Y.]
Death and the Gentle Bull. Lippincott,
  1954; Hutchinson, 1956. Also pub-
  lished as: Killer in the Straw. Mer-
  cury, 1955 [N.Y.]
Death by Association. Lippincott, 1952;
  Hutchinson, 1957. Also published as:
  Trial by Terror. Mercury, 1954 [Fla.]
The Distant Clue. Lippincott, 1963;
  Long, 1964, by FR [N.Y.]
First Come, First Kill. Lippincott,
  1962; Long, 1963, by FR [N.Y.]
Foggy, Foggy Death. Lippincott, 1950;
  Hutchinson, 1953 [N.Y.]
I Want to Go Home. Lippincott, 1948
Killer in the Straw; see Death and the
  Gentle Bull
Let Dead Enough Alone. Lippincott,
  1956; Hutchinson, 1958, by FR [N.Y.]
No Dignity in Death; see —With One
  Stone
Practise to Deceive. Lippincott, 1957;
  Hutchinson, 1959, by FR [N.Y.]
Show Red for Danger. Lippincott, 1960;
  Long, 1961 by FR [N.Y.]
Spin Your Web, Lady! Lippincott, 1949;
  Hutchinson, 1952 [N.Y.]
Stand Up and Die. Lippincott, 1953;
  Hutchinson, 1953 [N.Y.]
Think of Death. Lippincott, 1947 [N.Y.]
Trial by Terror; see Death by Associa-
  tion
—With One Stone. Lippincott, 1961.
  British title: No Dignity in Death.
  Long, 1962, by FR [N.Y.]

LOCKWOOD, DAVID
Death Has Scarlet Candles. Hodder, 1949
Night & Green Ginger. Hodder, 1951

LOCKWOOD, ETHEL
The Haunted Hammock. Lenox Hill, 1973;
  Remploy, 1973
Mistress of the Manor. Manor, 1977

LOCKWOOD, MARY. 1934-   . Ref: CA.
-The Accessory. Random, 1968; Macdonald,
  1969

LOCKWOOD, P(HILIP) H.
A Modern Man-Hunt. Stock, 1904 ss

LODER, JOHN deVERE. Joint pseudonym with
  Hilary Aiden St. George Saunders,
  1898-1951, q.v.: Cornelius Cofyn,
  q.v.

LODER, VERNON. Pseudonym of John (George)
  Hazlette Vahey, 1881-   , q.v. Other
  pseudonyms: Henrietta Clandon, John
  Haslette, Anthony Lang, John Mowbray,
  Walter Proudfoot, qq.v. SC: Insp.
  Brews = B; Insp. Chace = C; Donald
  Cairn = DC. Set: Eng.
Between Twelve and One; see Whose Hand?
The Button in the Plate. Collins, 1938
The Case of the Dead Doctor. Collins,
  1935
Chose Your Weapon. Collins, 1937
The Deaf-Mute Murders. Collins, 1936
Death at the Horse Show. Collins, 1935
  C
Death at the Wheel. Collins, 1933
Death in the Thicket. Collins, 1932
Death of an Editor. Collins, 1931; Mor-
  row, 1931 B
The Death Pool; see The Essex Murders
The Essex Murders. Collins, 1930. U.S.
  title: The Death Pool. Morrow, 1931 B
Kill in the Ring. Collins, 1938
The Little Man Murders. Collins, 1936

The Men with the Double Faces. Collins,
  1937 DC
Murder from Three Angles. Collins, 1934
  C
The Mystery at Stowe. Collins, 1928
Red Stain. Collins, 1931; Morrow, 1932
Ship of Secrets. Collins, 1936 [ship]
The Shop Window Murders. Collins, 1930;
  Morrow, 1930
Suspicion. Collins, 1933
Two Dead. Collins, 1934
The Vase Mystery. Collins, 1929
Whose Hand? Collins, 1929. U.S. title:
  Between Twelve and One. Morrow, 1929
A Wolf in the Fold. Collins, 1938 DC

LODGE, MRS.
-The Daringfords. Digby, 1900
-George Elvaston. Tinsley, 1883
-Lady Ottoline. Tinsley, 1881
The Mystery of Bloomsbury Crescent.
  Digby, 1896
The Mystery of Monkswood. Digby, 1899
-A Son of the Gods. Digby, 1898
-Under a Ban. Munro, 1884 (British
  title?)

LODWICK, JOHN. 1916-1959.
Brother Death. Heinemann, 1948; Duell,
  1951
The Destroyer; see Peal of Ordnance
First Steps Inside the Zoo. Heinemann,
  1950. U.S. title: The Man Dormant.
  Duell, 1950 [Fr.]
-Just a Song at Twilight. Heinemann,
  1949
Love Bade Me Welcome. Heinemann, 1952;
  Roy, 1953
The Man Dormant; see First Steps Inside
  the Zoo
-Peal of Ordnance. Methuen, 1947. Also
  published as: The Destroyer. Digit,
  1958
-Somewhere in the Heart. Heinemann, 1948
Somewhere a Voice Is Calling. Heine-
  mann, 1953; Roy, 1953 [Sp.]
-Stamp Me Mortal. Heinemann, 1950
-Twenty East of Greenwich. Heinemann,
  1947

LOEWENGARD, HEIDI HUBERTA FREYBE.
  1914-1981. Pseudonym: Martha Albrand,
  q.v.

LOFTS, NORAH (ROBINSON). 1904-   . Pseu-
  donyms: Juliet Astley, Peter Curtis,
  qq.v. Ref: CA, CC, TC.
Charlotte. Hodder, 1972
Checkmate. Corgi, 1975; Crest, 1978
The Golden Fleece; see Michael and All
  Angels
Michael and All Angels. Joseph, 1943.
  U.S. title: The Golden Fleece. Knopf,
  1944

LOGAN, CAROLYNNE and MALCOLM
One of These Seven. Mystery House,
  1946; Quality, 1948 [NYC]

LOGAN, DON. Pseudonym of William (Elbert)
  Crawford, 1929-   , q.v. Other pseu-
  donyms: Roger Brandt, Jim Peterson,
  Paul Ross, Steve Scott, qq.v.
The Rapist. PB, 1975

LOGAN, GUY H. B.
The Eternal Moment. Paul, 1932

LOGAN, MALCOLM. See: Carolynne Logan.

LOGUE, JOHN. 1933-   .
Follow the Leader. Crown, 1979
  [Atlanta]

LOMAS, GEOFFREY R(OBERT). 1950-   . Ref:
  CA.
Hostages. Scribner, 1979 [Eng.]

LOMAS, JOHN (E. W.)
The Man with the Scar. Heinemann, 1926;
  Houghton, 1926

LOMAX, W(ILLIAM) J(OSEPH). 1863-   .
-The Ambassador's Kiss. Nash, 1925
The Riddle of the Book-Mark. Nash, 1926

LOMBARD, LOUIS. 1861-1927.
-The Vicious Virtuoso. Neely, 1898

LOMBARD, NAP. Joint pseudonym of Pamela
  Hansford Johnson, 1912-1981, and
  Neil Stewart. Set: Eng.
The Grinning Pig; see Murder's a Swine
Murder's a Swine. Hutchinson, 1943.
  U.S. title: The Grinning Pig. Simon,
  1943
Tidy Death. Cassell, 1940

LOMBARDI, CYNTHIA
-Lighting Seven Candles. Appleton, 1926
  [It.]

LONDON, JACK. 1876-1916. Ref: CC.
The Assassination Bureau, Ltd. McGraw-
  Hill, 1963; Deutsch, 1963 (Completed
  by Robert L. Fish, 1912-1981, q.v.)

LONG, AMELIA REYNOLDS. 1904-1978. Pseudo-
  nyms: Patrick Laing, Adrian Reynolds,
  Peter Reynolds, qq.v. Joint pseudonym
  with Edna McHugh: Kathleen Buddington
  Coxe, q.v. SC: "Peter" Piper, in at
  least those marked PP; Steve Carter,
  in at least those marked SC; Edward
  Trelawny, in at least those marked
  ET.
The Carter Kidnapping Case; see Invi-
  tation to Death
The Corpse at the Quill Club. Phoenix,
  1940; Grafton, 1945 PP [Pa.]
The Corpse Came Back. Phoenix, 1949
Death Has a Will. Phoenix, 1944; Swan,
  1950 SC
Death Looks Down. Ziff-Davis, 1945
  ET,PP [Phil., acad.]
Death Wears a Scarab. Phoenix, 1943;
  Quality, 1946 SC
Four Feet in the Grave. Phoenix, 1941
  PP
The House with Green Shutters. Phoenix,
  1950 SC
Invitation to Death. Phoenix, 1940.
  British title (?): The Carter Kidnap-
  ping Case. Pemberton, 1944 ET
It's Death, My Darling! Mystery House,
  1948 PP [La.]
The Lady Saw Red. Phoenix, 1951
Murder by Magic. Phoenix, 1947; Graf-
  ton, 1956 SC
Murder by Scripture. Phoenix, 1942 PP
  [New Or.]
Murder by Treason. Phoenix, 1944; Pem-
  berton, 1948 SC
Murder Goes South. Phoenix, 1942 PP
  [La.]
Murder Times Three. Phoenix, 1940;
  Foulsham, 1950 ET
Murder to Type. Phoenix, 1943 SC
Once Acquitted. Phoenix, 1945; Quality,
  1947 SC [Pa.]
The Shakespeare Murders. Phoenix, 1939;
  Grafton, 1945 ET [acad.]
Symphony in Murder. Ziff-Davis, 1944;
  Quality, 1953 ET [Phil.]
The Triple Cross Murders. Ziff-Davis,
  1943; Gardner, 1947 ET [Phil.]

LONG, DEREK. Both titles below were published by Amalgamated Press and feature Sexton Blake.
The Case of Lord Greyburn's Son. 1946
The Mystery of the Italian Ruins. 1950

LONG, ERNEST LAURIE. 1886- ,   . SC: Liz-
  zie Collins, in at least those marked
  LC; Captain Flynn, in at least those
  marked F. At least many of the books
  are probably more sea adventure than
  crime fiction.
Abaft 'Midships. Ward, 1949
Anchor's Aweigh. Ward, 1940
As They Rise. Ward, 1934
The Blindness of Flynn. Ward, 1959 F
Buoyed Cables. Ward, 1941
Cabine de Luxe. Ward, 1961
Captain Flynn. Ward, 1939 F
Captain Flynn Ret'd. Ward, 1950 F
Captain Flynn, Sheriff. Ward, 1962 F
Carried Away. Ward, 1945
A Chief in Embryo. Ward, 1953
Clear Round. Ward, 1946
Coolie Tramp. Ward, 1956
The Crew of L.C. 454. Ward, 1947
Crime Cruise. Ward, 1957
A Cumsha Cruise. Ward, 1937
A Curtailed Voyage. Ward, 1957
Deep Channels. Ward, 1943
Dope Ship. Ward, 1954
Double Banked. Ward, 1940
Flat Aback. Ward, 1954
Flynn, A.B. Ward, 1936 F
Flynn of the "Martagon." Eldon, 1934 F
Flynn's Sampler. Ward, 1945 F
The Fortunes of Flynn. Ward, 1938 F
Foul Hawsers. Ward, 1935
Four in a Fairlead. Ward, 1950
The Gabbart Destiny. Ward, 1956
The Galleys of St. John. Ward, 1945
Gauges Steady. Ward, 1946
The Ghost of the Dunsany. Ward, 1941
Gold Ballast. Ward, 1952
The Good Ship Rajah. Ward, 1961
The Haven of St. Garth. Ward, 1951
High Noon to High Noon. Ward, 1959
Hunslett's Yard. Ward, 1962
In Full Commission. Ward, 1964
Lieutenant Flynn, R.N. Ward, 1948 F
Live Lumber. Ward, 1937
Loot Curran, R.N. Ward, 1963
The Luggar Audace. Ward, 1956
Lumber Ship. Ward, 1949
Madam Captain. Ward, 1958
The Masters of Kaolina. Ward, 1959
On Schedule. Ward, 1935

Open Roadsteads. Ward, 1963
Opium Clipper. Ward, 1942
Ould Flynn. Ward, 1953 LC
Port of Destination. Eldon, 1933 LC
Purser's Mate. Ward, 1938 LC
River Passage. Ward, 1956
A Saga of the Cliffs. Ward, 1944
The Sailor and the Widow. Ward, 1957
The Schooner "Sybil". Ward, 1936
Sea Dust. Ward, 1938
Sea Range. Ward, 1939
Seconds and Thirds. Ward, 1936
Son of Flynn. Ward, 1940
Storm Canvas. Ward, 1939
The Strong Room of the Sutro. Ward, 1948
Surgeons Adrift. Ward, 1960
Trawl Adrift. Ward, 1958
The Trials of the Phideas. Ward, 1944
Two Little Ships. Ward, 1935
Unhappy Ship. Ward, 1951 LC
The Vengeance of Flynn. Ward, 1942 F
'Way Loft. Ward, 1947
Young Flynn. Ward, 1937

LONG, FRANK BELKNAP. 1903- . Pseudonym: Lyda Belknap Long, q.v.
The Horror Expert. Belmont, 1961
John Carstairs, Space Detective. Fell, 1949; Cherry Tree, 1951 ss [future]
So Dark a Heritage. Lancer, 1966

LONG, FRANK CARLETON
-The Duke of Arcanum. Laird, 1894
-The Lady of the Lens. Crandall, 1891

LONG, FREDA M(ARGARET)
-The Heir of Frinton Park. Hale, 1978
-The Master of Frinton Park. Hale, 1977
-Mischief at Frinton Park. Hale, 1978

LONG, GABRIELLE MARGARET VERE CAMPBELL. 1886-1952. Pseudonyms: Marjorie Bowen, George R. Preedy, Joseph Shearing, qq.v., Margaret Campbell.

LONG, GEORGE
Fortune's Wheel. Greening, 1905
Hand and Land. Drane, 1906
-In the Days of Marlborough. Greening, 1908
A Just Fate. Greening, 1907
-Two Lives in Parenthesis. Drane, 1906
-Valhalla. Drane, 1906

LONG, HARMAN. SC: Franklyn Keen, in at least those marked FK.
The Corpse Can't Walk. Rich, 1950
The Golden Cat. Rich, 1947 FK [Paris]
Master of Evil. Rich, 1946
Seven to Die. Rich, 1946 FK
Silverface. Rich, 1948
Silverface Surrenders. Rich, 1949

LONG, JULIUS (W.). 1907-1955. Magazine writer.
Keep the Coffins Coming. Messner, 1947. Also published as: Murder in Her Big Blue Eyes. Avon, 1950

LONG, LILY AUGUSTA. 1890-1927. Pseudonym: Roman Doubleday, q.v.

LONG, LYDA BELKNAP. Pseudonym of Frank Belknap Long, 1903- , q.v.
Crucible of Evil. Avon, 1974 [New Or.]
Fire of the Witches. Popular Library, 1971
House of the Deadly Nightshade. Beagle, 1972 [Charleston]
Legacy of Evil. Beagle, 1973 [Mass.]
The Lemoyne Heritage. Zebra, 1977 [New Or.]
The Shape of Fear. Beagle, 1971
To the Dark Tower. Lancer, 1969
The Witch Tree. Lancer, 1971

LONG, MANNING. 1906- . SC: Liz Parrott, in at least those marked LP.
Bury the Hatchet. Duell, 1944; Hammond, 1949 LP [N.Y.]
Dull Thud. Duell, 1947; Hammond, 1950 LP [NYC]
False Alarm. Duell, 1943. Also published as: Invitation to Murder. Arrow, 1944 LP [NYC]
Here's Blood in Your Eye. Duell, 1941; Hammond, 1946. Also published as: Modeled in Murder. Best Novel Selection, 1943
Invitation to Murder; see False Alarm
Modeled in Murder; see Here's Blood in Your Eye
Savage Breast. Duell, 1948; Hammond, 1951 LP [NYC]
Short Shrift. Duell, 1945; Hammond, 1949 LP [Va.]
Vicious Circle. Duell, 1942; Hammond, 1946 LP [N.Y.]

LONG, MAX (FREEDOM). 1890- . SC: Komako Koa, in all titles, all set in Haw.
Death Goes Native. Lippincott, 1941
The Lava Flow Murders. Lippincott, 1940
Murder Between Dark and Dark. Lippincott, 1939; Hutchinson, 1940

LONG, PATRICK. SC: Martyn Cale, in both titles.
Eagle Six. Everest, 1975
Heil Britannia. Everest, 1973

LONG, WILLIAM. 1922- . Pseudonyms: Will Creed, Peter Yates, qq.v.

LONGBAUGH, HARRY. Pseudonym of William (W.) Goldman, 1931- , q.v.
No Way to Treat a Lady. GM, 1964; Muller pb, 1964. Reprinted as by William Goldman: Harcourt, 1968; Coronet, 1968 [NYC]

LONGMAN, M. E. Set: Eng.
I Was Murdered. Wright, 1936
The Phantom Millionaire. Wright, 1935
Terror Island. Wright, 1934; Godwin, 1934

LONGMATE, NORMAN (RICHARD). 1925- . Ref: CA, CC. SC: Insp./Supt. Bradbury and Sgt. Raymond, in all titles. Set: Eng.
Death in Office. Hale, 1961
Death Won't Wash. Cassell, 1957
A Head for Death. Cassell, 1958 [acad.]
Strip Death Naked. Cassell, 1959
Vote for Death. Cassell, 1960

LONGO, LUCAS
The Family on Vendetta Street. Doubleday, 1968 [NYC]

LONGRIGG, ROGER (ERSKINE). 1929- . Pseudonyms: Ivor Drummond, Frank Parrish, qq.v.
-The Desperate Criminals. Macmillan (London), 1971

LONGSTREET, STEPHEN. 1907- . Pseudonyms: Paul Haggard, Henri Weiner, qq.v. Ref: CA.
The Ambassador. Avon, 1978; Allen, 1979
The Crime. Simon, 1959 [Md.]

LONGSTRETH, T(HOMAS) MORRIS. 1886- . Ref: CA.
In Scarlet and Plain Clothes. Macmillan, 1933
Murder at Belle Butte, with Henry Vernon. Century, 1931 ss [Can.]
-The Silent Five. Century, 1924
Sons of the Mounted Police. Century, 1928 ss [Can.]
-Trial by Wilderness. Appleton, 1940

LONGWAY, A. HUGE. Pseudonym of Andrew Lang, 1844-1912, q.v.
Much Darker Days. Longmans, 1884 (Parody of "Dark Days" by Hugh Conway, q.v.)

LONSDALE, FREDERICK. 1881-1954. See: Denys G. Herriot.

LOOKABEE, EMMITT. Pseudonym.
A Twist of Yarn. Pageant, 1966

LOOMIS, NOEL (MILLER). 1905-1969. Ref: CA.
Murder Goes to Press. Phoenix, 1937 [Mpls.]

LORAC, E. C. R. Pseudonym of Edith Caroline Rivett, 1894-1958. Other pseudonym: Carol Carnac, q.v. Ref: CC, EM, MP, TC. SC: Insp./Supt. MacDonald = M. Set: Eng.
Accident by Design. Collins, 1950; Doubleday, 1951 M
The Affair at Thor's Head. Low, 1932 M
And Then Put Out the Light; see Policemen in the Precinct
Ask a Policeman. Collins, 1955 M
Bats in the Belfry. Collins, 1937; Macaulay, 1937 M
Black Beadle. Collins, 1939 M
Case in the Clinic. Collins, 1941 M
The Case of Colonel Marchand. Low, 1933; Macaulay, 1933 M
Checkmate to Murder. Collins, 1944; Arcadia, 1944 M
Crime Counter Crime. Collins, 1936 M
Crook o' Lune. Collins, 1953. U.S. title: Shepherd's Crook. Doubleday, 1953 M
Dangerous Domicile. Collins, 1957 M
Death at Dyke's Corner. Collins, 1940 M
Death Before Dinner. Collins, 1948. U.S. title: A Screen for Murder. Doubleday, 1948 M
Death Came Softly. Collins, 1943; Mystery House, 1943 M
Death in Triplicate. Collins, 1958. U.S. title: People Will Talk. Doubleday, 1958
Death of an Author. Low, 1935; Macaulay, 1937
Death on the Oxford Road. Low, 1933 M
The Devil and the C.I.D. Collins, 1938 M
Dishonour Among Thieves. Collins, 1959. U.S. title: The Last Escape. Doubleday, 1959 M
The Dog It Was That Died. Collins, 1952; Doubleday, 1952 M
Fell Murder. Collins, 1944 M
Fire in the Thatch. Collins, 1946; Mystery House, 1946 M
The Greenwell Mystery. Low, 1932; Macaulay, 1934 M
I Could Murder Her; see Murder of a Martinet
John Brown's Body. Collins, 1939 M
Let Well Alone. Collins, 1954 M
Murder by Matchlight. Collins, 1945; Mystery House, 1946 M
Murder in Chelsea. Low, 1934; Macaulay, 1935 M
Murder in St. John's Wood. Low, 1934; Macaulay, 1934 M
Murder in the Mill-Race. Collins, 1952. U.S. title: Speak Justly of the Dead. Doubleday, 1953 M
Murder in Vienna. Collins, 1956 M [Vienna]
Murder of a Martinet. Collins, 1951. U.S. title: I Could Murder Her. Doubleday, 1951 M
Murder on a Monument. Collins, 1958 M [Rome]
The Murder on the Burrows. Low, 1931; Macaulay, 1932 M
Murderer's Mistake; see The Theft of the Iron Dogs
The Organ Speaks. Low, 1935 M
A Pall for a Painter. Collins, 1936 M
Part for a Poisoner. Collins, 1948. U.S. title: Place for a Poisoner. Doubleday, 1949 M
People Will Talk; see Death in Triplicate
Picture of Death. Collins, 1957 M
Place for a Poisoner; see Part for a Poisoner
Policemen in the Precinct. Collins, 1949. U.S. title: And Then Put Out the Light. Doubleday, 1950 M
Post After Post-Mortem. Collins, 1936 M
Relative to Poison. Collins, 1947; Doubleday, 1948 M
Rope's End—Rogue's End. Collins, 1942 M
A Screen for Murder; see Death Before Dinner
Shepherd's Crook; see Crook o' Lune
Shroud of Darkness. Collins, 1954; Doubleday, 1954 M
The Sixteenth Stair. Collins, 1942 M
Slippery Staircase. Collins, 1938 M
Speak Justly of the Dead; see Murder in the Mill-Race
Still Waters. Collins, 1949 M
The Theft of the Iron Dogs. Collins, 1946. U.S. title: Murderer's Mistake. Mystery House, 1947 M
These Names Make Clues. Collins, 1937 M
Tryst for a Tragedy. Collins, 1940 M

LORAINE, PHILIP. Pseudonym of Robin Estridge. Ref: CC, TC.
And to My Beloved Husband—; see White Lie the Dead
The Angel of Death. Hodder, 1961; Mill, 1961 [It.]
Ask the Rattlesnake. Collins, 1975. U.S. title: Wrong Man in the Mirror. Random, 1975 [L.A.]
The Break in the Circle. Hodder, 1951; Mill, 1951. Also published as: Outside the Law. PB, 1953
Day of the Arrow. Collins, 1964; Mill, 1964. Also published as: The Eye of the Devil. Fontana, 1966; and as: 13. Lancer, 1966 [Fr.]
The Dead Men of Sestos. Collins, 1968; Random, 1968 [Greece]
The Dublin Nightmare. Hodder, 1952. U.S. title: Nightmare in Dublin. Mill, 1952 [Dub.]
Exit with Intent. Hodder, 1950 [theatre]
The Eye of the Devil; see Day of the Arrow
Lions' Ransom. Collins, 1980
A Mafia Kiss. Collins, 1968; Random, 1969 [It.]
Nightmare in Dublin; see The Dublin Nightmare
Outside the Law; see The Break in the Circle
Photographs Have Been Sent to Your Wife. Collins, 1971; Random, 1971

13; see Day of the Arrow
Voices in an Empty Room. Collins, 1973; Random, 1974 [S.F.]
White Lie the Dead. Hodder, 1950. U.S. title: And to My Beloved Husband—. Mill, 1950
W.I.L. One to Curtis. Collins, 1967; Random, 1967
Wrong Man in the Mirror; see Ask the Rattlesnake

LORD, DANIEL A(LOYSIUS). 1888-1955.
-Murder in the Sacristy. Queen's Work, 1941

LORD, GABRIELLE
Fortress. Aurora (Sydney), 1980; St. Martin's, 1981 [Australia]

LORD, GARLAND. Joint pseudonym of (Mary) Isabel Garland, 1903- , q.v., and Mindred Lord.
Murder, Plain and Fancy. Doubleday, 1943 [Wis.]
Murder with Love. Morrow, 1943
Murder's Little Helper. Doubleday, 1941 [NYC]
She Never Grew Old. Doubleday, 1942 [Conn.]

LORD, GRACE VIRGINIA. -1885. Pseudonym: Virginia Champlin, q.v.

LORD, GRAHAM (JOHN). 1943- . Ref: CA.
God and All His Angels. H. Hamilton, 1976; Viking, 1977 [Eng., future]
Marshmallow Pie. Macmillan (London), 1970; Coward, 1970
The Spider and the Fly. H. Hamilton, 1974; Viking, 1975

LORD, JEREMY. Pseudonym of Ben Ray Redman, 1896-1961. SC: Colonel Winston Creevy, in both titles. Ref: CA, MP.
The Bannerman Case. Doubleday, 1935; Hurst, 1936 [Eng.]
Sixty-Nine Diamonds. Doubleday, 1940; Hurst, 1940 [Calif.]

LORD, MINDRET. Joint pseudonym with (Mary) Isabel Garland, 1903- , q.v.: Garland Lord, q.v.

LORDAHL, JO ANN
Those Subtle Weeds. Ace, 1974 [Fla.]

LORE, PHILLIPS. Pseudonym of Terence Lore Smith, q.v. SC: Leo Roi, in all titles.
The Looking Glass Murders. Playboy, 1980 [Chi.]
Murder Behind Closed Doors. Playboy, 1980 [Chi.]
Who Killed the Pie Man? Saturday Review Press, 1975 [Ill.]

LORENA
Identity Unknown. Mystique, 1979 (Translation of "La Masque et L'Amour." Paris, 1974.)

LORENZ, FREDERICK. Pseudonym of Lorenz Heller, q.v. Other pseudonyms: Larry Heller, Larry Holden, qq.v.
Hot. Lion, 1956
Night Never Ends. Lion, 1954
A Party Every Night. Lion, 1956
A Rage at Sea. Lion, 1953 [ship]
Ruby. Lion, 1956
The Savage Chase. Lion, 1954

LORIMER, GEORGE C(LAUDE). 1838-1904.
-The Master of Millions. Revell, 1903

LORIMER, GEORGE HORACE. 1868-1937.
The False Gods. Appleton, 1906 [Boston]

LORIMER, GRAEME, 1903- , and SARAH (MOSS) LORIMER, 1906- .
Acquittal. Little, 1938; Cape, 1938 [Chi.]

LORIMER, NORMA (OCTAVIA). 1864-1948.
A Mender of Images. Hutchinson, 1920; Brentano's, 1921

LORIMER, SARAH (MOSS). 1906- . See: Graeme Lorimer, 1903- .

LORING, ANN. 1915- . Ref: CA.
The Mark of Satan. Award, 1969 [NYC]
The 13th Doll. Award, 1970 [L.I.]

LORING, PETER. Pseudonym of Samuel Shellabarger, 1888-1954. Other pseudonym: John Esteven, q.v.
-Grief Before Night. Macrae-Smith, 1938; Hodder, 1939
He Travels Alone; see Miss Rolling Stone

-Miss Rolling Stone. Macrae-Smith, 1939. British title: He Travels Alone. Hodder, 1939

LORIOT, NOELLE. Pseudonym: Laurence Oriol, q.v.

LORRAINE, JOHN. Pseudonym.
Men of Career. Crown, 1960

LORRIMER, CLAIRE. Pseudonym of Patricia Denise Robins (Clark), 1921- . Daughter of Denise (Naomi) Robins, 1897- , q.v.
Relentless Storm. Arlington, 1979; Avon, 1975
The Secret of Quarry House. Avon, 1976
The Shadow Falls. Avon, 1974
A Voice in the Dark. Souvenir, 1967; Avon, 1968 [Florence]

LORY, ROBERT. 1936- . Pseudonym: Paul Edwards, q.v. Ref: CA.
The Curse of Leo. Pinnacle, 1974
Gemini Smile, Gemini Kill. Pinnacle, 1975
The Green Flames of Aries. Pinnacle, 1974
The Revenge of Taurus. Pinnacle, 1974

LOTT, S(TANLEY) MAKEPEACE. SC: Stephen Ringway, in both titles. Set: Eng.
The Judge Will Call It Murder. Rich, 1951
Twopence for a Rat's Tail. Rich, 1947

LOTTMAN, EILEEN (SHUBB). 1927- . Pseudonym: Maud Willis, q.v. Ref: CA.
The Hemlock Tree. Popular Library, 1975 [L.I.]

LOUDERBACK, LEW. Pseudonyms: Nick Carter, Larry Kenyon, qq.v.

LOUGHEAD, FLORA HAINES (APPONYI). 1855- .
-The Abandoned Claim. Houghton, 1881; Watt, 1891
-The Black Curtain. Houghton, 1898; Duckworth, 1899
The Man Who Was Guilty. Houghton, 1886 [S.F.]

LOUIS, EDWARD
His Lordship the Crook. Skeffington, 1932

LOVATT, WILLIAM F.
The Curse of Kama. Houghton (London), 1932

LOVE, EDMUND G(EORGE). 1912- . Ref: CA.
Set-Up. Doubleday, 1980. British title: Set a Trap. Hale, 1981

LOVEGROVE, PETER
The Von Stahmer Jigsaw. Cassell, 1980

LOVELL, B. E. 1920- . SC: Edge Hannegan, in both titles.
...And Incidentally, Murder! Bouregy, 1952 [S.F.]
A Rage to Kill. Ace, 1957 [S.F.]

LOVELL, MARC. Pseudonym of Mark McShane, 1930- , q.v. SC: Jason Smart = JG.
And They Say You Can't Buy Happiness. Hale, 1979
The Blind Hypnotist. Doubleday, 1976 JG [Eng.]
Dreamers in a Haunted House. Doubleday, 1975; Hale, 1976
An Enquiry into the Existence of Vampires. Doubleday, 1974. British title: Vampire in the Shadows. Hale, 1976 [Eng.]
Fog Sinister. Manor, 1977 [Eng.]
The Ghost of Megan. Doubleday, 1968. Also published as: Memory of Megan. Ace, 1970 [Wales]
The Guardian Spectre. Manor, 1977 [Can.]
Hand over Mind. Doubleday, 1979; Hale, 1980 [Can.]
The Imitation Thieves. Doubleday, 1971 [Can.]
Memory of Megan; see The Ghost of Megan
A Presence in the House. Doubleday, 1972 [Can.]
The Second Vanetti Affair. Doubleday, 1977; Hale, 1979 JG
Shadows and Dark Places. Hale, 1980
The Spy Game. Doubleday, 1980; Hale, 1981
Vampire in the Shadows; see An Enquiry into the Existence of Vampires
A Voice from the Living. Doubleday, 1978 [Eng.]

LOVESEY, PETER (HARMER). 1936- . Ref: CA, CC, EM, TC. SC: Sgt. Cribb and Constable Thackeray, in all titles. Set: Eng., ca.1880, all titles.
Abracadaver. Macmillan (London), 1972; Dodd, 1972
A Case of Spirits. Macmillan (London), 1975; Dodd, 1975
The Detective Wore Silk Drawers. Macmillan (London), 1971; Dodd, 1971
Invitation to a Dynamite Party. Macmillan (London), 1974. U.S. title: The Tick of Death. Dodd, 1974
Mad Hatter's Holiday. Macmillan (London), 1973; Dodd, 1973
Swing, Swing Together. Macmillan (London), 1976; Dodd, 1976
The Tick of Death; see Invitation to a Dynamite Party
Waxwork. Macmillan (London), 1978; Pantheon, 1978
Wobble to Death. Macmillan (London), 1970; Dodd, 1970

LOVESMITH, JANET
Inherit the Shadows. Popular Library, 1971
Legacy of Fear. Popular Library, 1971 [Mass.]
The Lock. Popular Library, 1972

LOW, DOROTHY MACKIE. Pseudonym of Lois Dorothea Low, 1916- . Other pseudonyms: Zoe Cass, Lois Paxton, qq.v. Ref: CA.
-Dear Liar. Hurst, 1963
-A House in the Country. Hurst, 1968
-The Intruder. Hurst, 1965
Isle for a Stranger. Hurst, 1962; Ace, 1968
-A Ripple on the Water. Hurst, 1964
To Burgundy and Back. Hurst, 1970; Ace, 1973

LOW, GARDNER. Pseudonym of (Percival) Charles Rodda, 1891- , q.v. Other pseudonym: Gavin Holt, q.v. Joint pseudonym with Eric Ambler, 1909- , q.v.: Eliot Reed, q.v.
Invitation to Kill. Gollancz, 1937; Putnam, 1973 [NYC]

LOW, LOIS DOROTHEA. 1916- . Pseudonyms: Dorothy Mackie Low, Zoe Cass, Lois Paxton, qq.v.

LOW, WERNER A.
Peace Bridge. Vantage, 1975

LOWDEN, DESMOND (SCOTT). 1937- . Ref: CA.
Bandersnatch. Eyre, 1969; Holt, 1969
Bellman and True. Eyre, 1975; Holt, 1975
The Boondocks. Eyre, 1972; Holt, 1973
Boudapesti 3. Macmillan (London), 1979; Holt, 1979 [Athens]

LOWE, F(REDERICK) J(AMES)
Blood Money. Stockwell, 1957
The Killer from the Grave. Stockwell, 1959

LOWE, KENNETH. Pseudonym of Elma K(linedorf) Lobaugh, 1907- , q.v.
The Catalyst. Doubleday, 1958; Boardman, 1959 [Midwest]
Haze of Evil. Doubleday, 1953 [Ind.]
No Tears for Shirley Minton. Doubleday, 1955; Boardman, 1957 [Midwest]

LOWE, MARJORIE G(RIFFITHS). 1909- . Ref: CA.
Jess. Macdonald, 1961. U.S. title: The Sudden Lady. Putnam, 1961
Paking for the Moon. Macmillan (London), 1963
The Sudden Lady; see Jess

LOWELL, J. R. Joint pseudonym of Jan and Robert Lowell.
Daughter of Darkness. Delacorte, 1972; Souvenir, 1973
Secrets. New English Library, 1976

LOWELL, JAN. Joint pseudonym with Robert Lowell: J. R. Lowell, q.v.

LOWELL, ROBERT. Joint pseudonym with Jan Lowell: J. R. Lowell, q.v.

LOWING, ANNE. Pseudonym of Christine Geach, 1930- . Ref: CA.
Black Midnight. Hale, 1968
The Captain's Pawn. Hale, 1975
The Denbigh Affair. Hale, 1967
The Gossamer Thread. Hale, 1972
The Masked Ball. Hale, 1967
Melyonen. Hale, 1973
The Napoleon Ring. Hale, 1975
Shadow on the Wind. Hale, 1960
Yasmin. Hale, 1969

LOWIS, CECIL CHAMPAIN. 1866-1948.
　The Ava Mining Syndicate. Greening, 1908
　The District Bungalow. Cape, 1927; Doubleday, 1928 [Burma]
　-The Dripping Tamarinds. Laurie, 1933
　Four Blind Mice. Lane (London & NYC), 1920 [Burma]
　-The Grass Spinster. Cape, 1925
　Green Sandals. Cape, 1926; Doran, 1927
　The Green Tunnel. Dickson, 1935
　-The Huntress. Cape, 1929
　-In the Hag's Hands. Laurie, 1931
　-The Machinations of the Myo-ok. Methuen, 1903
　-The Penal Settlement. Cape, 1928
　-Prodigal's Portion. Dickson, 1936
　-The Runagate. Cape, 1924
　-Snags and Shallows. Lane (London), 1922
　-The Treasury-Officer's Wooing. Macmillan (London), 1899

LOWNDES, MARIE BELLOC. 1868-1947. Ref: CC, DD, EM, MC, MP, TC. Set: Eng.
　Afterwards; see Bread of Deceit
　And Call It Accident. Hutchinson, 1939; Longmans, 1936
　Another Man's Wife. Heinemann, 1934; Longmans, 1934
　Before the Storm. Longmans, 1941 (British title?)
　-Bread of Deceit. Hutchinson, 1925. U.S. title: Afterwards. Doubleday, 1925 ss
　The Chianti Flask. Heinemann, 1935; Longmans, 1935
　The Chink in the Armour. Methuen, 1912; Scribner, 1912. Also published as: The House of Peril. Readers Library, 1935 [Fr.]
　The Christine Diamond. Hutchinson, 1940; Longmans, 1940
　Cressida: No Mystery. Heinemann, 1928; Knopf, 1930
　-The Empress Eugenie. Longmans, 1938 (3-act play.)
　The End of Her Honeymoon. Methuen, 1914; Scribner, 1913 [Paris]
　The Fortune of Bridget Malone; see The Marriage-Broker
　The Gentleman Anonymous; see Out of the War?
　Good Old Anna. Hutchinson, 1915; Doran, 1916
　-The Heart of Penelope. Heinemann, 1904
　The House by the Sea. Hutchinson, 1937. U.S. title: Vanderlyn's Adventure. Cape & Smith, 1931
　The House of Peril; see The Chink in the Armour
　The Injured Lover. Hutchinson, 1939. U.S. title: The Second Key. Longman's, 1936
　Jenny Newstead. Heinemann, 1932; Putnam, 1932
　-The Key. Benn, 1930 (3-act play.)
　-A Labour of Hercules. Todd, 1943 (16 pp. pamphlet.)
　Letty Lynton. Heinemann, 1931; Cape & Smith, 1931
　Lizzie Borden: A Study in Conjecture. Hutchinson, 1940; Longmans, 1939 [Mass., 1890s]
　The Lodger. Methuen, 1913; Scribner, 1913
　The Lonely House. Hutchinson, 1920; Doran, 1920
　Love and Hatred. Chapman, 1917; Doran, 1917
　-Love Is a Flame. Benn, 1932
　-Love's Revenge. Readers Library, 1909
　The Marriage-Broker. Heinemann, 1937. U.S. title: The Fortune of Bridget Malone. Longmans, 1937
　Motive. Hutchinson, 1938. U.S. title (?): Why It Happened. Longmans, 1938
　One of Those Ways. Heinemann, 1929; Knopf, 1929
　-Out of the War? Chapman, 1918. Also published as: The Gentleman Anonymous. Allan, 1934
　-The Philosophy of the Marquise. Richards, 1899
　-The Price of Admiralty. Newnes, 1915
　-The Reason Why. Benn, 1932
　Reckless Angel. Longmans, 1939 (British title?)
　The Second Key; see The Injured Lover
　-Some Men and Women. Hutchinson, 1925; Doubleday, 1928 ss
　The Story of Ivy. Heinemann, 1927; Doubleday, 1928
　The Terriford Mystery. Hutchinson, 1924; Doubleday, 1924
　"Thou Shalt Not Kill." Hutchinson, 1927
　The Uttermost Farthing. Heinemann, 1908; Kennerley, 1910 [Fr.]
　Vanderlyn's Adventure; see The House by the Sea
　What Really Happened. Hutchinson, 1926; Doubleday, 1926. Play version: Benn, 1932
　When No Man Pursueth. Heinemann, 1910; Kennerley, 1911
　Who Rides on a Tiger. Heinemann, 1936; Longmans, 1935
　-Why Be Lonely?, with F. S. Lowndes. Benn, 1931 (Play.)
　Why It Happened; see Motive
　-Why They Married. Heinemann, 1923
　With All John's Love. Benn, 1930 (3-act play.)

LOWRY, BRIDGET
　Burden's End. Methuen, 1930

LUARD, NICHOLAS (LAMBERT). 1937- . Pseudonym: James McVean, q.v. Ref: CA.
　The Dirty Area. H. Hamilton, 1979. U.S. title: The Shadow Spy. Harcourt, 1979 [Tangier]
　The Orion Lion. Secker, 1976; Harcourt, 1977 [Fr.]
　The Robespierre Serial. Weidenfeld, 1975; Harcourt, 1975 [Sp.]
　The Shadow Spy; see The Dirty Area
　Traveling Horseman. Weidenfeld, 1975
　The Warm and Golden War. Secker, 1967; Pantheon, 1968 [Hung.]

LUCAROTTI, JOHN
　Operation Patch. Tandem, 1976

LUCAS, (JOHN) CARY
　Unfinished Business. Simon, 1947 [Mex. City]

LUCAS, J. K. Pseudonym of Lauran Bosworth Paine, 1916- . Other pseudonym: John Armour, Reg Batchelor, Kenneth Bedford, Frank Bosworth, Mark Carrel, Robert Clarke, Richard Dana, J. F. Drexler, Troy Howard, Jared Ingersol, John Kilgore, Hunter Liggett, John Morgan, qq.v.
　The Born Survivor. Hale, 1971
　Haight Is the Killer. Hale, 1969

LUCAS, NETLEY (EVELYN). 1903- . A criminologist.
　The Red Stranger. Paul, 1927 [Paris]

LUCAS, NORMAN. SC: Supt. Bill Rowlands, in all titles. Set: Eng.
　Corner in Crime. Jenkins, 1952; Roy, 1957
　The Red Dice. Jenkins, 1952
　Situations Vacant. Jenkins, 1956
　Testament of Death. Jenkins, 1953

LUCAS, VICTOR
　Murder at the Festival. Evans, 1962 (1-act play.)
　Search by Night. Evans, 1960 (1-act play.)

LUCE, HELEN
　In the Midst of Death. Macmillan (London), 1980

LUCENO, JAMES
　Head Hunters. Ballantine, 1980 [S. Am.]

LUCENTINI, FRANCO. See: C(arlo) Fruttero.

LUCK, PETER. Set: Eng.
　Crime Legitimate. Jenkins, 1937
　Infallible Witness. Jenkins, 1932
　The Killing of Ezra Burgoyne. Jenkins, 1929
　Terror by Night. Jenkins, 1934
　The Transome Murder Mystery. Jenkins, 1930
　Two Shots. Jenkins, 1931
　Under the Fourth—? Jenkins, 1927
　Who Killed Robin Cockland? Jenkins, 1933
　The Wingrave Case. Jenkins, 1935
　The Wrong Number. Jenkins, 1926

LUCKLESS, JOHN. Joint pseudonym of Clifford (Michael) Irving, 1930- , q.v., and Herbert Burkholz, 1932- .
　The Death Freak. Summit, 1978; Joseph, 1979

LUDDECKE, WERNER J(ORG). 1911- .
　Morituri. GM, 1965
　Thursday at Dawn. Doubleday, 1965; Allen, 1966 [Fr.]

LUDERS-KNEGTMANS, ANNEKE. Pseudonym: Adrienne Mans, q.v.

LUDLAM, HARRY. 1926- .
　The Coming of Jonathan Smith. Long, 1964

LUDLUM, JEAN KATE
　Under a Cloud. Bonner, 1891

LUDLUM, ROBERT. 1927- . Pseudonyms: Jonathan Ryder, Michael Shepherd, qq.v. Ref: CA, TC.
　The Bourne Identity. Marek, 1980; Granada, 1980
　The Chancellor Manuscript. Dial, 1977; Hart-Davis, 1977 [Wash. D.C.]
　The Gemini Contenders. Dial, 1976; Hart-Davis, 1976
　The Holcroft Covenant. Marek, 1978; Hart-Davis, 1978
　The Matarese Circle. Marek, 1979; Granada, 1979
　The Matlock Paper. Dial, 1973; Hart-Davis, 1973 [Conn.]
　The Osterman Weekend. World, 1972; Hart-Davis, 1972 [N.Y.]
　The Rhinemann Exchange. Dial, 1974; Hart-Davis, 1975 [WWII]
　The Scarlatti Inheritance. World, 1971; Hart-Davis, 1971 [1918-1944]

LUDWIG, BORIS. Pseudonym.
　Jaws of Doom. Associated General, ca.1941
　Whistle of Doom. Transport, 1941

LUDWIG, JERRY. 1934- . Ref: CA.
　Little Boy Lost. Delacorte, 1977; Magnum, 1979 [L.A.]

LUEHRMANN, ADELE
　The Curious Case of Marie Dupont. Century, 1916 [NYC]
　The Other Brown. Century, 1917 [NYC]
　The Triple Mystery. Dodd, 1920

LUGER, HANS
　Appointment with Desire. Scion, 1953
　The Bigger They Are. Scion, 1952
　Black Fedora. Scion, 1952
　Come Out with Your Hands Up. Scion, 1952
　Double or Quits. Scion, 1952
　Handle with Care. Scion, 1952
　Harvest for Harpies. Scion, 1953
　Killers End. Scion, 1952
　Lady—This Is It! Scion, 1950
　Leave It to Me. Scion, 1952
　Line Up. Scion, 1953
　The Marble Heart. Scion, 1954
　Midnight Sister. Scion, 1953
　One-Way Ticket. Scion, 1952
　Prelude to Passion. Scion, 1954
　Six Foot Deep. Scion, 1950
　This Side Up. Scion, 1952
　You Don't Say! Scion, 1951

LUHRS, VICTOR. 1912- .
　The Longbow Murder. Norton, 1941 [Eng., 1100s]

LUIGI, BELLI. Pseudonym.
　Death Has No Weight. Transport, ca.1941

LUKAS, SUSAN RIES
　Stereopticon. Stein, 1975

LUKE, THOMAS. Pseudonym of Graham Masterton, 1946- , q.v.
　The Hell Candidate. PB, 1980

LUKENS, JOHN
　-Adders Abounding. Hodder, 1954
　-The Bright Promise. Hodder, 1958
　-Mine Is the Power. Hodder, 1951

LUND, JAMES. Pseudonym of a British Member of Parliament.
　The Ultimate. Calder, 1976; Riverrun Press, 1978

LUND, T(RYGVE). 1886- . SC: Dick Weston, in at least those marked DW.
　The Murder of Dave Brandon. Laurie, 1931 DW [Can.]
　Robbery at Portage Bend. Laurie, 1933; Kendall, 1933 DW [Can.]
　-Steele Bey's Revenge. Laurie, 1934
　-Up North. Laurie, 1929
　The Vanished Prospector. Laurie, 1937
　Weston of the North-West Mounted Police; see Weston of the Royal North-West Mounted Police
　Weston of the Royal North-West Mounted Police. Laurie, 1928. Also published as: Weston of the North-West Mounted Police. Mellifont, 1938 DW [Can.]

LUNN, ARNOLD (HENRY MOORE). 1888- .
　"Within the Precincts of the Prison." Hutchinson, 1932

LUNN, PETER (NORTHCOTE). 1914- .
　Evil in High Places. Methuen, 1947 [Switz.]

LUNN-ROCKLIFFE, PAUL
　The Fake. Stockwell, 1973

LUPTON, LEONARD
   Murder Without Tears. Graphic, 1957
   [N.Y.]

LURGAN, LESTER. Pseudonym of Mabel Winifred Knowles, 1875-1949.
   The League of the Triangle. Greening, 1911
   -The Wrestler on the Shore. Everett, 1913

LUSKA, SIDNEY. Pseudonym of Henry Harland, 1861-1905.
   -As It Was Written. Cassell (London & NYC), 1885

LUSTGARTEN, EDGAR (MARCUS). 1907-1979. Ref: CA, CC, EM, MC, TC. Set: Eng.
   Blondie Iscariot. Museum, 1949; Scribner, 1948
   A Case to Answer. Eyre, 1947. U.S. title: One More Unfortunate. Scribner, 1947
   Game for Three Losers. Museum, 1952; Scribner, 1952
   I'll Never Leave You. Hart-Davis, 1971
   One More Unfortunate; see A Case to Answer
   Turn the Light Out As You Go. Elek, 1978

LUTHER, MARK LEE, 1872- , and LILLIAN C. FORD. SC: Arthur Raneleigh, in both titles, both set in L.A.
   Card 13. Bobbs, 1930
   The Saranoff Murder. Bobbs, 1930

LUTHER, RAY. Pseudonym of Arthur Gordon Ley, 1911-1968. Ref: CA.
   Intermind. Banner, 1967; Dobson, 1969, as by Arthur Sellings [Turk.]

LUTTRELL, WANDA
   The House of Elnora Garland. Belmont, 1971

LUTZ, JOHN (THOMAS). 1939- . Ref: CA, TC.
   Bonegrinder. Putnam, 1977; Hale, 1979 [Mo.]
   Buyer Beware. Putnam, 1976; Hale, 1977 [Fla.]
   Jericho Man. Morrow, 1980 [NYC]
   Lazarus Man. Morrow, 1979; New English Library pb, 1980
   The Truth of the Matter. PB, 1971 [Mo.]

LYALL, GAVIN (TUDOR). 1932- . Ref: CA, EM, TC.
   Blame the Dead. Hodder, 1972; Viking, 1973 [Nor.]
   Judas Country. Hodder, 1975; Viking, 1975 [Mid. East.]
   Midnight Plus One. Hodder, 1965; Scribner, 1965 [Fr.]
   The Most Dangerous Game. Hodder, 1964; Scribner, 1963 [Fin.]
   The Secret Servant. Hodder, 1980; Viking, 1980
   Shooting Script. Hodder, 1966; Scribner, 1966 [Carib.]
   Venus with Pistol. Hodder, 1969; Scribner, 1969
   The Wrong Side of the Sky. Hodder, 1961; Scribner, 1961 [Afr.]

LYDAY, DAVID PAUL
   Come Die for Me. Popular Library, 1977

LYDECKER, J. J.
   Half Moon Street. Muller, 1975

LYDSTON, G(EORGE) FRANK. 1858-1923.
   Poker Jim, Gentleman and other tales and sketches. Monarch, 1907 ss, some criminous

LYELL, WILLIAM DARLING. 1860- .
   In the Eye of the Law. Hodge, 1898
   The House in Queen Anne Square. Blackwood, 1920; Putnam, 1921 [Scot.]
   The Justice-Clerk. Hodge, 1923

LYLE, DOUGLAS
   The Inquisitors. Harrap, 1954

LYLE-SMYTHE, ALLAN. 1914- . Pseudonym: Alan Caillou, q.v.

LYMINGTON, JOHN. Pseudonym of John Newton Chance, 1911- , q.v. Other pseudonym: J. Drummond, q.v.
   -Give Daddy the Knife, Darling. Hodder, 1969
   The Laxham Haunting. Hodder, 1976
   -The Nowhere Place. Hodder, 1969

LYNCH, DAN
   Four-Time Loser. GM, 1962

LYNCH, FRANCES. Pseudonym of D(avid) G(uy) Compton, 1930- , q.v. Byline also: Guy Compton, q.v.
   Candle at Midnight; see Twice Ten Thousand Miles
   A Dangerous Magic. Souvenir, 1978; St. Martin's, 1978 [Scot., ca.1910]
   -The Fine and Handsome Captain. Souvenir, 1975; St. Martin's, 1975
   In the House of Dark Music. Hodder, 1979
   Stranger at the Wedding. Souvenir, 1977; St. Martin's, 1977 [It.]
   Twice Ten Thousand Miles. Souvenir, 1974; St. Martin's, 1974. Also published as: Candle at Midnight. Dell, 1977

LYNCH, J.
   Face to Face. Aldine, 1894 [N.Y.]

LYNCH, LAWRENCE L. Pseudonym of Emma Murdoch Van Deventer. Ref: EM. Titles published in Eng. under the author's real name are starred. SC: Neil Bathurst, in at least those marked NB; Carl Masters, in at least those marked CM; Madeline Payne, in at least those marked MP; Van Vernet, in at least those marked VV.
   Against Odds. Rand, 1894; Ward, 1894 * CM [Chi.]
   A Blind Lead. Laird, 1912; Ward, 1912 *
   The Danger Line. Ward, 1903 [NYC]
   Dangerous Ground; or, The Rival Detectives. Loyd, 1885. British title: The Rival Detectives; or, Dangerous Ground. Ward, 1887 VV
   A Dead Man's Step. Rand, 1893; Ward, 1893 *
   The Detective's Daughter; or, Madeline Payne; see Madeline Payne, the Detective's Daughter
   The Diamond Coterie. Loyd, 1882; Routledge, 1887 NB
   The Doverfields' Diamonds. Ward, 1907 *
   High Stakes. Laird, 1899; Ward, 1901
   The Last Stroke. Laird, 1896; Ward, 1897 [Ill.]
   The Lost Witness; or, The Mystery of Leah Paget. Laird, 1890; Ward, 1890 [NYC]
   Madeline Payne, the Detective's Daughter. Loyd, 1884. British title: The Detective's Daughter; or, Madeline Payne. Ward, 1887 * MP
   Man and Master. Laird, 1908; Ward, 1909 CM
   Moina; see Moina; or, Against the Mighty
   Moina; or, Against the Mighty. Laird, 1891. British title: Moina. Ward, 1891 MP
   A Mountain Mystery; or, The Outlaws of the Rockies. Loyd, 1886 VV [West]
   No Proof. Rand, 1895; Ward, 1895 *
   Out of the Labyrinth. Loyd, 1885; Ward, 1887 NB
   The Rival Detectives; or, Dangerous Ground; see Dangerous Ground
   A Sealed Verdict. Long, 1910 [Chi.]
   Shadowed by Three. Donnelly, 1879; Ward, 1884 NB
   A Slender Clue; or, The Mystery of Mardi Graz. Laird, 1891; Ward, 1891 *
   Under Fate's Wheel. Laird, 1900; Ward, 1900 *
   The Unseen Hand. Ward, 1896 *
   The Woman Who Dared. Ward, 1902
   A Woman's Tragedy; or, The Detective's Task. Ward, 1904 CM [Wyo.]

LYNCH, MIRIAM. Pseudonym of Mary Wallace, q.v. Other pseudonym: Claire Vincent, q.v. SC: Nell Willard = NW.
   Amber Twilight. Belmont, 1967
   Bells of Widows Bay. Pinnacle, 1971 [New Eng.]
   Blacktower. Paperback Library, 1966; New English Library pb, 1967 [New Eng., 1900]
   The Brides of Lucifer. Lancer, 1973
   Creighton's Castle. Ballantine, 1975 [Conn., 1920s]
   A Crime for Christmas. Arcadia, 1959
   Daughters of Cain. Lancer, 1970
   The Deadly Rose. Belmont, 1969 [New Eng.]
   The Devil's Mirror. PB, 1973
   Doctor Garrett's Girl. Dell, 1970
   The Doomsday Bells. Lancer, 1968
   An Echo of Weeping. Lancer, 1971
   From Secret Places. PB, 1973 [New Eng.]
   Gateway to the Grave. Arcadia, 1958
   Graymists. Paperback Library, 1967
   Grow Cold Along with Me. Arcadia, 1958
   Hate Thy Neighbor. PB, 1973
   A Heritage of Danger. Bouregy, 1964
   House of Evil. Bouregy, 1966
   House of Yesteryear. Beagle, 1974
   Journey into Twilight. Lancer, 1970
   The Light in the Tower. Curtis, 1973
   The Lonely Toys. Lancer, 1971
   The Mark of the Rope. Avon, 1972
   A Meeting with Murder. Arcadia, 1956
   Moon of Darkness. Belmont, 1969
   The Night of the Moonrose. Paperback Library, 1966 [1892]
   The Nightmare Dance. Popular Library, 1972
   Nightmare's Morning. Pinnacle, 1971
   Pale Hand of Danger. Bouregy, 1962
   Poor Roger Is Dead. Arcadia, 1957
   Riverwood. Lancer, 1971
   The Road to Midnight. Paperback Library, 1966 [U.S., 1888]
   The Secret of Lucifer's Island. Paperback Library, 1967 [New Eng.]
   The Silken Web. Bouregy, 1961 [Fla.]
   A Summer for Witches. Bouregy, 1962
   Time to Kill. Zebra, 1979 NW
   Twilight for Taurus. Berkley, 1976
   Unwilling Rebel. Pyramid, 1975
   Where Evil Waits. Beagle, 1976 [New Eng., 1782]
   Where Shadows Lie. Pinnacle, 1972 [Mass.]
   -Winter in a Dark Land. Dell, 1976
   The Witches of Windlake. Popular Library, 1971
   Witches' Holiday. Lancer, 1971 [U.S., ca.1900]
   The Witch's Song. Lancer, 1972
   You'll Be the Death of Me. Zebra, 1979 NW
   Your Casket Awaits, Madame. Arcadia, 1957

LYNCH, TERRY W(AYMAN). 1940- . See: Charles N(orman) Whaley, 1940- .

LYNCH, W. WARE. See: Irene King, 1943- .

LYNDE, FRANCIS. 1856-1930. Ref: CC, EM.
   Blind Man's Buff. Scribner, 1928
   The Grafters. Bobbs, 1904 [West]
   The Price. Scribner, 1911
   Scientific Sprague. Scribner, 1912 ss
   Stranded in Arcady. Scribner, 1917
   -The Wreckers. Scribner, 1920
   Young Blood. Scribner, 1929

LYNDON, BARRE. Pseudonym of Alfred Edgar, 1896- , q.v. See also: Jimmy Sangster, 1927- .
   The Amazing Dr. Clitterhouse. H. Hamilton, 1936; Random, 1937 (3-act play.)
   The Man in Half Moon Street. H. Hamilton, 1939 (Play.)
   They Came by Night. H. Hamilton, 1937 (5-scene play.)

LYNDS, DENNIS. 1924- . Pseudonyms: William Arden, Nick Carter, Michael Collins, John Crowe, Carl Dekker, Maxwell Grant, Mark Sadler, qq.v. Ref: CA, EM, TC.
   Charlie Chan Returns. Bantam (NYC & London), 1974 (Novelization of unproduced screenplay featuring the character created by Earl Derr Biggers, 1884-1933, q.v.) [NYC]
   Crossfire. PB, 1975 (Novelization of the "Swat" TV series.) [Calif.]

LYNN, DAVID
   Barney Christopher. Kangaroo, 1945
   Death of an Undertaker. Kangaroo, 1943
   -The Misadventures of Mr. Larkin. Staples, 1942
   Murder in the Bazaar. Kangaroo, 1945
   Zombie. Kangaroo, 1945 ss

LYNN, ERNEST
   The Yellow Stub. White House, 1926

LYNN, JACK. 1927- .
   The Professor. Dell, 1971; Allison, 1971 [NYC]
   The Turncoat. Delacorte, 1976; Robson, 1976

LYNN, KAY
   Dark Shadows. Hutchinson, 1935
   Laughing Mountains. Hutchinson, 1934; Dutton, 1936

LYNN, MARGARET. Pseudonym of Gladys Starkey Battye, 1915- . Textile designer, hotel proprietor in Eng.
   A Light in the Window. Hodder, 1967; Doubleday, 1968
   Mrs. Maitland's Affair; see Stranger by Night
   Stranger by Night. Hodder, 1963. U.S. title: Mrs. Maitland's Affair. Doubleday, 1963
   Sunday Evening. Hodder, 1969; Doubleday, 1971
   Sweet Epitaph. Hodder, 1971; Doubleday, 1972

To See a Stranger. Hodder, 1961; Doubleday, 1962
Whisper of Darkness. Hodder, 1965; Paperback Library, 1966

LYNNE, JAMES BROOM. 1920-   . Pseudonym: James Quartermain, q.v. Ref: CA.
Jet Race. Allen, 1978; Putnam, 1978
Rogue Diamond. Joseph, 1980; Atheneum, 1980
Verdict. Allen, 1976

LYNRAVN, N(ORMAN) S(OREN). See: L(incoln) W(illiam) Martin.

LYNWOOD, LESLIE J.
Lester Grayling, K.C. Bale, 1921 ss

LYNX, J. J. ca.1900-   . Born in Berlin; newspaper correspondent.
The Prince of Thieves. Cassell, 1963; Atheneum, 1964 [ca.1900]

LYON, (MABEL) DANA. 1897-1982. Californian, born in Ger. SC: Hilda Trenton = HT.
The Bathtub Murder, with Josephine Hugheston. Williams, 1933 [Calif.]
The Frightened Child. Harper, 1948. Also published as: House on Telegraph Hill. Mercury, 1951 [Calif.]
House on Telegraph Hill; see The Frightened Child
I'll Be Glad When You're Dead. Royce, 1945 [Calif.]
It's My Own Funeral. Farrar, 1944; Hammond, 1948 [Calif.]
The Lost One. Harper, 1958; Gollancz, 1958 [Calif.]
Spin the Web Tight. Ace, 1963 HT [Calif.]
The Tentacles. Harper, 1950 HT [Calif.]
The Trusting Victim. Ace, 1964

LYON, CAPT. E(DMUND) D(AVID)
The Signora. Remington, 1883

LYON, EDNA WRIGHT
The Unfinished Murder. Humphries, 1935

LYON, HARRIS MERTON. 1883-1916.
Graphics. Reed, 1913 ss, some criminous

LYON, WINSTON. SC: Batman = B.
Batman vs. the Fearsome Foursome. Signet, 1966 B (Novelization of the movie.)
Batman vs. Three Villains of Doom. Signet, 1966; Four Square, 1966 B (Novelization of the TV series.)
Criminal Court. PB, 1966 [NYC]

LYONS, ARTHUR (JR.). 1946-   . Ref: CA. SC: Jacob Ashe, in all titles.
All God's Children. Mason/Charter, 1975; Robson, 1977 [L.A.]
Castles Burning. Holt, 1980 [L.A.]
The Dead Are Discreet. Mason/Charter, 1974; Robson, 1977 [L.A.]
Dead Ringer. Mason/Charter, 1977
The Killing Floor. Mason/Charter, 1976; Houghton (London), 1979 [Calif.]

LYONS, AUGUSTA WALLACE. 1922-   . Ref: CA.
Murder at Prospect, Kentucky. Putnam, 1977 [Ky.]
Season of Doubt. Signet, 1961

LYONS, DELPHINE. Pseudonym of Evelyn E. Smith, 1927-   .
The Depths of Yesterday. Lancer, 1966
Flower of Evil. Pyramid, 1965 [NYC, past]
House of Four Windows. Lancer, 1965
Phantom at Lost Lake. Lancer, 1970
Valley of Shadows. Lancer, 1968

LYONS, ELENA
The Haunting of Abbotsgarth. Piatkus, 1980 [Eng., 1900]

LYONS, IVAN. 1934-   . See: Nan Lyons, 1935-   .

LYONS, NAN, 1935-   , and IVAN LYONS, 1934-   . Ref: CA.
-Champagne Blues. Simon, 1979; Cape, 1979 [Paris]
Someone Is Killing the Great Chefs of Europe. Harcourt, 1976; Cape, 1976

LYONS, SOPHIE [SOPHIE VAN ELKAN LYONS BURKE].
The Amazing Adventures of Sophie Lyons. Ogilvie, 1913

LYPE, E. J. ANDERS. Pseudonym: E. J. Anders, q.v.

LYS, CHRISTIAN. Pseudonym of Percy (James) Brebner, 1864-1922, q.v.
-The Black Card. Lawrence, 1899
-The Doctor's Idol. Warne, 1893
-The Dunthorpes of Westleigh. Downey, 1896
-The Fortress of Yadasara. Warne, 1899; Fenno, 1907. Also published as: The Knight of the Silver Star, as by Percy Brebner. Warne, 1925
The Hepsworth Millions. Warne, 1898
The Knight of the Silver Star; see The Fortress of Yadasara
-A London Cobweb. Trischler, 1892
The Mystery of Ladyplace. Warne, 1900
-Suspicion. Ward, 1889

LYSAGHT, ELIZABETH J.
-The Gold of Ophir. Ward, 1890
-Sealed Orders. Bentley, 1886
-The Veiled Picture; or, The Wizard's Legacy. Simpkin, 1890

LYTTLE, ANDREW (NELSON), 1902-   . Ref: CA.
The Long Night. Bobbs, 1936; Eyre, 1937
A Name for Evil. Bobbs, 1947

McAFEE, PAUL K.
Discord in Harmony. Lenox Hill, 1973

MacALISTER, IAN. Pseudonym of Marvin H(ubert) Albert, 1924-   , q.v. Other pseudonyms: Mike Barone, Al Conroy, Albert Conroy, Nick Quarry, Anthony Rome, qq.v.
Driscoll's Diamonds. GM, 1973; Coronet, 1974 [Mid. East]
Skylark Mission. GM, 1973; Coronet, 1974 [New Guinea, 1941]
Strike Force 7. GM, 1974; Coronet, 1975
Valley of the Assassins. GM, 1975; Coronet, 1976 [Saud. Arab.]

McALLISTER, ALISTER. 1877-1943. Pseudonym: Lynn Brock, q.v.

McALLISTER, AMANDA. House name. Used by Jean Hager, 1932-   . Other Hager pseudonyms: Sara North, q.v. Also used by Eloise Meaker, 1915-   . Other Meaker pseudonym: Lydia Benson Clark, q.v. Also used by Dorothy (Florence Karns) Dowdell, 1910-   , q.v.
Death Comes to a Party. Playboy, 1977
Look over Your Shoulder. Playboy, 1977 (By EM.)
No Need for Fear. Playboy, 1976
Pretty Enough to Kill. Playboy, 1976 (By DD.)
Terror in the Sunlight. Playboy, 1977
Trust No One at All. Playboy, 1976
Waiting for Caroline. Playboy, 1976 (By EM.)

McALLISTER, ANNIE LAURIE. Pseudonym of Bruce (Bingham) Cassiday, 1920-   , q.v. Other pseudonyms: Carson Bingham, Nick Carter, Mary Anne Drew, Annie Laurie McMurdie, Michael Stratford, qq.v.
House of Vengeance. Berkley, 1976 [Calif.]
Queen of the Looking-Glass. Berkley, 1978

MacANALLY, G(EORGE) H. See: M(arguerite) Bryant.

MACARDLE, DOROTHY. 1889-
Dark Enchantment. Davies, 1953; Doubleday, 1953 [Fr.]
-Earth-Bound. Harrigan, 1924 ss
-Fantastic Summer. Davies, 1946. U.S. title: The Unforeseen. Doubleday, 1946
-The Seed Was Kind. Davies, 1944
-Uneasy Freehold. Davies, 1941. U.S. title: The Uninvited. Doubleday, 1942
The Unforeseen; see Fantastic Summer
The Uninvited; see Uneasy Freehold

MacARTHUR, CHARLES C. See: Ben Hecht, 1894-1964.

MacARTHUR, D(AVID) WILSON. 1903-   . Pseudonym: David Wilson, q.v. SC: Alec Sinclair, in at least those marked AS. Ref: CA.
Convict Captain. Collins, 1939
Death at Slack Water. Ward, 1962
Harry Hogbin. Ward, 1961
Landfall. Nelrose, 1933 AS [Scot.]
-Lola of the Isles. Cassell, 1926
The Mystery of the "David M". Melrose, 1932 AS [Scot.]
The Past Dies Hard. Ward, 1965
The Quest of the "Stormalong". Melrose, 1934

A Rhino in the Kitchen. Ward, 1964
-The Road from Chilanga. Jarrolds, 1957
-Simba Bwana. Hurst, 1956
-Yellow Stockings. Cassell, 1925
-The Young Chevalier. Collins, 1946

MACAULAY, MILDRED. Joint pseudonym with Richard Macaulay: Carter Cullen, q.v.

MACAULAY, PAULINE
The Astrakhan Coat. French (London), 1968 (2-act play.)

MACAULAY, RICHARD. Joint pseudonym with Mildred Macaulay: Carter Cullen, q.v.

MACAULAY, ROSE. 1881-1958. Ref: CA.
Mystery at Geneva. Collins, 1922; Boni, 1923 [Geneva]

McAULIFFE, FRANK. Pseudonym: Frank Malachy, q.v. SC: Augustus Mandrell = AM (each title has 4 novelets).
The Bag Man. Zebra, 1979
For Murder I Charge More. Ballantine, 1971 AM
Of All the Bloody Cheek. Ballantine, 1965; New English Library, 1971 AM
Rather a Vicious Gentleman. Ballantine, 1968 AM

McBAIN, ED. Pseudonym of Evan Hunter, 1926-   , q.v. Other pseudonyms: Curt Cannon, Hunt Collins, Ezra Hannon, Richard Marsten, qq.v. See also: Craig Rice. SC: the men of the 87th Precinct = P, which is located in a city like NYC.
Ax. Simon, 1964; H. Hamilton, 1964 P
Blood Relatives. Random, 1975; H. Hamilton, 1976 P
Bread. Random, 1974; H. Hamilton, 1974 P
Calypso. Viking, 1979; H. Hamilton, 1979 P
The Con Man. Permabooks, 1957; Boardman, 1960 P
Cop Hater. Permabooks, 1956; Boardman, 1958 P
Doll. Delacorte, 1965; H. Hamilton, 1966 P
Eighty Million Eyes. Delacorte, 1966; H. Hamilton, 1966 (3 P novelets.)
The Empty Hours. Simon, 1962; Boardman, 1963 (3 P novelets.)
Fuzz. Doubleday, 1968; H. Hamilton, 1968 P
Ghosts. Viking, 1980; H. Hamilton, 1980 P
Give the Boys a Great Big Hand. Simon, 1960; Boardman, 1962 P
Goldilocks. Arbor, 1977; H. Hamilton, 1978 [Fla.]
Guns. Random, 1976; H. Hamilton, 1977 [NYC]
Hail, Hail, the Gang's All Here! Doubleday, 1971; H. Hamilton, 1971 P
Hail to the Chief. Random, 1973; H. Hamilton, 1973 P
He Who Hesitates. Delacorte, 1965; H. Hamilton, 1965 P
The Heckler. Simon, 1960; Boardman, 1962 P
Jigsaw. Doubleday, 1970; H. Hamilton, 1970 P
Killer's Choice. Permabooks, 1958; Boardman, 1960 P
Killer's Payoff. Permabooks, 1958; Boardman, 1960 P
Killer's Wedge. Simon, 1959; Boardman, 1961 P
King's Ransom. Simon, 1959; Boardman, 1961 P
Lady Killer. Permabooks, 1958; Boardman, 1961 P
Lady, Lady, I Did It! Simon, 1961; Boardman, 1963 P
Let's Hear It for the Deaf Man. Doubleday, 1973; H. Hamilton, 1973 P
Like Love. Simon, 1962; H. Hamilton, 1964 P
Long Time No See. Random, 1977; H. Hamilton, 1977 P
The Mugger. Permabooks, 1956; Boardman, 1959 P
The Pusher. Permabooks, 1956; Boardman, 1959 P
Sadie When She Died. Doubleday, 1972; H. Hamilton, 1972 P
See Them Die. Simon, 1960; Boardman, 1963 P
The Sentries. Simon, 1965; H. Hamilton, 1965 [Fla.]
Shotgun. Doubleday, 1969; H. Hamilton, 1969 P
So Long As You Both Shall Live. Random, 1976; H. Hamilton, 1976 P
Ten Plus One. Simon, 1963; H. Hamilton, 1964 P
'Til Death. Simon, 1959; Boardman, 1961 P

Where There's Smoke. Random, 1975; H. Hamilton, 1975

McBRIEN, JAMES
The Revolt of Abbe Lee. Monarch, 1964

McCABE, CAMERON. Pseudonym of Ernest (William Julius) Borneman, 1915- , q.v.
The Face on the Cutting Room Floor. Gollancz, 1937; Gregg, 1981

McCABE, EUGENE
Victims. Gollancz, 1976

McCAFFREY, ANNE (INEZ). 1926- . American fantasy writer living in Ire.
The Kitternan Legacy. Dell, 1975; Millington, 1976 [Ire.]
The Mark of Merlin. Dell, 1971; Millington, 1977
Ring of Fear. Dell, 1971; Millington, 1979

McCAGUE, JAMES (P.). 1909- . Ref: CA.
-The Big Ivy. Crown, 1955
-The Fortune Road. Harper, 1965
-To Be a Hero. Crown, 1962

McCAIG, DONALD. Pseudonym: Steven Ashley, q.v.

McCAIN, GEORGE NOX. 1856-1934.
The Crimson Dice. Jordan, 1903; Isbister, 1903

McCALL, ANTHONY. Pseudonym of Henry Kane, 1918- , q.v.
Holocaust. Trident, 1967 [Wash. D.C.]
Operation Delta. Trident, 1966; Joseph, 1967

McCALL, JOHN J.
Downbeat on a Debutante. Consul, 1964 [Calif.]

McCALL, K. T.
Angel Hold Fire. Atlas, 1958
Babes Up in Arms. Atlas, 1958
Black Lace Blackmail. Atlas, 1958
Caviar to Kill. Atlas, 1958
Dame on the Make. Atlas, 1958
Dance with Me Deadly. Horwitz, 1957
Deadly But Delectable. Horwitz, 1957
The Lady's a Decoy. Horwitz, 1957
M'amselle It's Murder. Horwitz, 1957
Million Dollar Mayhem. Atlas, 1958
A Redhead for Free. Horwitz, 1957

McCALL, VINCENT. Pseudonym of Nigel Morland, 1905- , q.v. Other pseudonyms: Mary Dane, John Donavan, Norman Forrest, Roger Garnett, Neal Shepherd, qq.v.
Eleven Thrilling Mysteries. Martin, 1945 ss
Smash and Grab. Martin, 1946

McCALLUM, NEIL 1916- . Ref: CA.
A Scream in the Sky. Cassell, 1964

McCANDLESS, ANTHONY
-Leap in the Dark. Collins, 1980; St. Martin's, 1980

McCANN, THOMAS. Born in Glasgow; author of non-crime novels under another name.
Come Out, Come Out, Whoever You Are. Collins, 1971

McCARDELL, ROY L(ARCOM). 1870- .
The Diamond from the Sky. Dillingham, 1916

MacCARGO, J. T. All titles are novelizations of the "Mannix" TV series.
The Faces of Murder. Belmont, 1975 [L.A.]
A Fine Day for Dying. Belmont, 1975
Round Trip to Nowhere. Belmont, 1975
A Walk on the Blind Side. Belmont, 1975

McCARRY, CHARLES. 1930- . Ref: CA, TC. SC: Paul Christopher = PC.
-The Better Angels. Dutton, 1979; Hutchinson, 1979 PC [U.S., 1990s]
The Miernik Dossier. Saturday Review Press, 1973; Hutchinson, 1974 PC
The Secret Lovers. Dutton, 1977; Hutchinson, 1977 PC [1960, Europe]
The Tears of Autumn. Saturday Review Press, 1975; Hutchinson, 1975 PC

McCARTHY, DAVID (EDGAR). 1925- . Ref: CA.
Killing at the Big Tree. Doubleday, 1960; Heinemann, 1961 [South]

McCARTHY, DUDLEY
The Fate of O'Loughlin. McGraw (Sydney), 1979; Macdonald, 1980 [New Guinea]

McCARTHY, EDWARD V., JR. 1924- . Ref: CA.
The Pied Piper of Helfenstein. Doubleday, 1975; Hale, 1976

McCARTHY, JAMES REMINGTON. 1900- .
Special Agent. Bobbs, 1938 [Wash. D.C.]

McCARTHY, JANE
The Dark Deception. Remploy, 1975

McCARTHY, JUSTIN. 1830-1912.
-The Dictator. Chatto, 1883; Harper, 1893
The Riddle Ring. Chatto, 1896; Appleton, 1896

McCARTHY, JUSTIN HUNTLY. 1860-1936.
Doom! Chatto, 1886; Harper, 1886
Red Diamonds. Chatto, 1893; Appleton, 1894

McCARTHY, MARY (THERESE). 1912- .
Cannibals and Missionaries. Harcourt, 1979; Weidenfeld, 1979 [Holl., 1975]

McCARTHY, SHAUN (LLOYD). 1928- . Pseudonyms: Theo Callas, Desmond Cory, qq.v.
Lucky Ham. Macmillan (London), 1977

McCARTHY, WILSON. 1930- .
The Detail. Hutchinson, 1973
The Fourth Man. Hutchinson, 1975

McCARTNEY, P.
Who Sups with the Devil? New English Library pb, 1975

McCARY, REED
Kiss and Kill. Avon, 1957
The Vice Merchants. Harlequin, 1954

McCHESNEY, MARY F. Pseudonym: Joe Rayter, q.v.

McCLEAN, J. SLOAN
The Aerie. Nash, 1975 [Can.]

McCLEERY, WILLIAM. SC: Perry Mason (following Erle Stanley Gardner, 1889-1970, q.v.) = PM.
A Case for Mason. French (NYC), 1967 (2-act play.) PM

McCLELLAND, DIANE MARGARET. 1931- .
Pseudonym: Diane Pearson, q.v.

McCLINTOCK, ALLERDYCE. Pseudonym.
The Case of the Three Broken Necks. Jenkins, 1965 [hosp.]

McCLOY, HELEN (WORRELL CLARKSON). 1904- . Ref: CA, CC, EM, MP, TC. SC: Basil Willing = BW; Miguel Urizan = MU.
Alias Basil Willing. Random, 1951; Gollancz, 1951 BW [NYC]
Before I Die. Dodd, 1963; Gollancz, 1963 [NYC]
Better Off Dead. Dell 10¢ pb, 1951
Burn This. Dodd, 1980; Gollancz, 1980 [Boston]
A Change of Heart. Dodd, 1973; Gollancz, 1973 [L.I.]
The Changeling Conspiracy. Dodd, 1976. British title: Cruel As the Grave. Gollancz, 1977 [Conn.]
Cruel As the Grave; see The Changeling Conspiracy
Cue for Murder. Morrow, 1942 BW [NYC]
Dance of Death. Morrow, 1938. British title: Design for Dying. Heinemann, 1938 BW [NYC]
The Deadly Truth. Morrow, 1941; H. Hamilton, 1942 BW [L.I.]
Design for Dying; see Dance of Death
Do Not Disturb. Morrow, 1943 [NYC]
The Further Side of Fear. Dodd, 1967; Gollancz, 1967 [Eng.]
The Goblin Market. Morrow, 1943; Hale, 1951 MU,BW [Carib.]
He Never Came Back; see Unfinished Crime
The Imposter. Dodd, 1977; Gollancz, 1978 [Mass.]
The Long Body. Random, 1955; Gollancz, 1955 BW [Conn.]
The Man in the Moonlight. Morrow, 1940; H. Hamilton, 1940 BW [NYC, acad.]
Minotaur Country. Dodd, 1975; Gollancz, 1975
Mr. Splitfoot. Dodd, 1968; Gollancz, 1969 BW [N.Y.]
The One That Got Away. Morrow, 1945; Gollancz, 1954 BW [Scot.]
Panic. Morrow, 1944; Gollancz, 1972
A Question of Time. Dodd, 1971; Gollancz, 1971 [Boston]
She Walks Alone. Random, 1948; Coker, 1950. Also published as: Wish You Were Dead. Bestseller, 1958 MU [ship]
The Singing Diamonds. Dodd, 1965. British title: Surprise, Surprise. Gollancz, 1965 ss, 2 about BW
The Slayer and the Slain. Random, 1957; Gollancz, 1958 [Va.]
The Sleepwalker. Dodd, 1974; Gollancz, 1974 [Boston]
The Smoking Mirror. Dodd, 1979; Gollancz, 1979 [Fr., 1940]
Surprise, Surprise; see The Singing Diamonds
Through a Glass, Darkly. Random, 1950; Gollancz, 1951 BW [N.Y., acad.]
Two-Thirds of a Ghost. Random, 1956; Gollancz, 1957 BW [NYC]
Unfinished Crime. Random, 1954. British title: He Never Came Back. Gollancz, 1954 [NYC]
Who's Calling. Morrow, 1942; Nicholson, 1948 BW
Wish You Were Dead; see She Walks Alone

McCLURE, JAMES (HOWE). 1939- . Ref: CA, TC. SC: Lt. Kramer and Sgt. Zondi = K&Z, which are set in S. Afr.
The Blood of an Englishman. Macmillan (London), 1980; Harper, 1981 K&Z
The Caterpillar Cop. Gollancz, 1972; Harper, 1973 K&Z
Four and Twenty Virgins. Gollancz, 1973
The Gooseberry Fool. Gollancz, 1974; Harper, 1974 K&Z
Rogue Eagle. Macmillan (London), 1976; Harper, 1976 [S. Afr.]
Snake. Gollancz, 1975; Harper, 1976 K&Z
The Steam Pig. Gollancz, 1971; Harper, 1972 K&Z
The Sunday Hangman. Macmillan (London), 1977; Harper, 1977 K&Z

MacCLURE, VICTOR. 1887-1963. Pseudonym: Peter Craig, q.v. Ref: CC. SC: Insp. Archie Burford = AB. Set: Eng.
The Clue of the Dead Goldfish. Harrap, 1933; Lippincott, 1934 AB
The Counterfeit Murders. Harrap, 1932 AB
The "Crying Pig" Murder. Harrap, 1929; Morrow, 1930
Death Behind the Door. Harrap, 1933; Houghton, 1933 AB
Death on the Set. Harrap, 1934; Lippincott, 1935 AB
The Diva's Emeralds. Harrap, 1937 AB
Hi-Spy-Kick-the-Can. Harrap, 1936 AB
The House of Dearth. Hodder, 1937 [Scot.]
-If They Fall—. Harrap, 1935
-Nicolette of the Quarter. Unwin, 1923

McCOMB, KATHERINE (WOODS). 1895- . Ref: CA.
A Day for Murder. Bouregy, 1963
Death in the Downpour. Arcadia, 1960

McCOMBIE, J. A. S.
Mandate for Murder. Manor, 1978

McCOMBS, PHILIP A(LGIE). 1944- . Ref: CA. See: Kevin Klose, 1940- .

McCOMBS, R(ALPH) L. F. 1897- .
Clue in Two Flats. Mystery House, 1940; Eldon, 1942 [Cin.]

McCONAUGHY, J. W.
-The Boss, with Edward Sheldon. Fly, 1911; Palmer, 1913
The Typhoon. Fly, 1912

McCONNAUGHEY, JAMES (PARKER). 1908- .
Three for the Money. Sloane, 1954; Hammond, 1955 [Ohio]

McCONNELL, JAMES DOUGLAS RUTHERFORD. 1915- . Pseudonym: Douglas Rutherford, q.v. Joint pseudonym with Francis (Henry) Durbridge, 1912- , q.v.: Paul Temple, q.v.

McCONNELL, JEAN
Wine in a Venetian Goblet. Kenyon-Deane, 1968 (1-act play.)

McCONNELL, MALCOLM
Clinton Is Assigned. PB, 1978; Hamlyn, 1979 [Mor.]

McCONNOR, VINCENT. Writer of ss; radio and TV scriptwriter.
The French Doll. Hill & Wang, 1965; Gollancz, 1966 [Paris]
The Provence Puzzle. Macmillan, 1980 [Fr.]

McCORMICK, JIM [JAMES PHILLIP McCORMICK]. 1920- .
   Last Seen Alive. Doubleday, 1979 [Ger.]

McCORMICK, LOIS ELIZABETH
   The Circle. Zebra, 1978

MacCORMICK, PAT
   -The Grave Gives Up. Exposition, 1964 ss

McCORMICK, VICTORIA. 1914- . Pseudonym: Janet Green, q.v.

McCOY, ANDREW
   -The Insurrectionist. Secker, 1979

McCOY, HORACE. 1897-1955. Ref: TC.
   Corruption City. Dell, 1959; WDL, 1961
   I Should Have Stayed Home. Barker, 1938
   Kiss Tomorrow Goodbye. Random, 1948; Barker, 1949
   No Pockets in a Shroud. Signet, 1948; Barker, 1937
   -Scalpel. Appleton, 1952; Barker, 1953
   They Shoot Horses, Don't They? Simon, 1935; Barker, 1935. New edition, including screenplay of movie version: Avon, 1969 [L.A.]

McCOY, NATHANIEL P.
   The Gold Makers. White, 1911

McCOY, PAUL S(TEVENS). 1908- . All titles plays; number of acts in parenthesis.
   The Ghost of Roaring Pines. Paine, 1939 (3)
   Lights Out. Heuer, 1941 (3)
   Stranger in the Night. Heuer, 1945
   The Vanishing Goddess. Northwestern, 1954 (3)
   Wednesday Midnight. Denison, 1939 (1)

McCOY, TRENT
   I'll Come Quietly. Cooper, 1952
   Order a Coffin Now. Hamilton Stafford, 1951
   Quinton Clyde, Private Investigator. Baker, 1952
   Wake the Sleeping Wolf. Hamilton Stafford, 1952

McCRACKEN, MIKE
   Black Death. Hamilton Stafford, 1952
   The Black Hammer. Hamilton Stafford, 1952
   Killer in Canvas Jeans. Hamilton Stafford, 1952
   -The Spahis. Hamilton Stafford, 1953

McCRAE, ELIZABETH
   House of the Whispering Winds. Signet, 1966 [Switz.]
   The Intrusion. Signet, 1967
   A Sudden Darkness. Signet, 1968
   A Well-Furnished Life. Signet, 1967

McCREADY, JACK. Pseudonym of Talmage Powell, 1920- , q.v. See also: Ellery Queen.
   The Raper. Monarch, 1962

McCRETTON, MICHAEL
   Beauty Can Kill. Vega, 1962 [NYC]

McCRUM, ROBERT. 1953- . Ref: CA.
   In the Secret State. H. Hamilton, 1980; Simon, 1980

McCUE, LILLIAN BUENO. 1902- . Pseudonym: Lillian de la Torre, q.v.

McCULLEY, JOHNSTON. 1883-1958. Pseudonym: Harrington Strong, q.v. SC: The Avenging Twins (Paul and Peter Selbon) = AT; Black Star = BS; The Crimson Clown (Dalton Prouse) = CC; The Spider (John Warwick) = S; The Thunderbolt (John Flatchley) = T.
   Alias the Thunderbolt. Chelsea, 1927; Cassell, 1930 T
   The Avenging Twins. Chelsea, 1927; Hutchinson, 1927 AT
   The Avenging Twins Collect. Chelsea, 1927 AT
   -Black Grandee. Hale, 1955
   The Black Star. Chelsea, 1921; Hutchinson, 1924 BS
   Black Star Again; see Black Star's Revenge
   Black Star's Campaign. Chelsea, 1924; Hutchinson, 1925 BS
   Black Star's Return. Chelsea, 1926; Hutchinson, 1927 BS
   Black Star's Revenge. Chelsea, 19??. British title: Black Star Again. Hutchinson, 1934 BS
   -The Blocked Trail. Watt, 1932; Hutchinson, 1933
   Broadway Bab. Watt, 1919; Hutchinson, 1926
   The Crimson Clown. Chelsea, 1928; Cassell, 1927 (4 CC novelets)
   The Crimson Clown Again. Chelsea, 192?; Cassell, 1928 (4 CC novelets.)
   The Demon. Chelsea, 1925
   -The Devil's Doubloons. Hutchinson, 1955
   The Masked Woman. Watt, 1920; Jenkins, 1925
   The Rollicking Rogue. Arcadia, 1941; Hutchinson, 1939
   The Scarlet Scourge. Chelsea, 1925 [NYC]
   The Spider's Debt. Chelsea, 1930; Hutchinson, 1930 S
   The Spider's Den. Chelsea, 1925 S
   The Spider's Fury. Chelsea, 1930; Hutchinson, 1931 S
   The Thunderbolt Collects. Lloyd, 1921 T
   The Thunderbolt's Jest. Chelsea, 1927 T
   A White Man's Chance. Watt, 1927; Hutchinson, 1927

McCULLOUGH, ANDREW
   Rough Cut. Morrow, 1976; Mayflower, 1978

McCULLOUGH, ESTHER MORGAN. Editor, novelist, patron of the arts; living in Vt. in 1950s.
   The Five Devils of Kilmainham. Taylor, 1955; Hodder, 1957 [Ire.]

McCULLOUGH, ROSE
   A Basket of Summer Fruit. Vantage, 1970

McCULLY, (ETHEL) WALBRIDGE. 1896-1980. SC: D. A. Carey Galbreath = CG.
   Blood on Nassau's Moon. Doubleday, 1945 [Nassau]
   Death Rides Tandem. Doubleday, 1942 CG [NYC]
   Doctors Beware! Doubleday, 1943 CG [N.Y., hosp.]

McCURTIN, PETER. SC: The Assassin (Robert Briganti) = A; The Death Dealer (Jim Rainey) = DD; The Marksman (Phillip Magellan) = M (see also: Frank Scarpetta).
   Ambush at Derati Wells. Belmont, 1977; New English Library, 1978 DD
   Battle Pay. Belmont, 1978 DD [Haiti]
   Body Count. Belmont, 1977 DD [New Guinea]
   Boston Bust Out. Dell, 1973; Mayflower, 1975 A [Boston]
   Cosa Nostra. Belmont, 1971; New English Library pb, 1972 [Maine]
   The Deadliest Game. Belmont, 1976; New English Library pb, 1978 DD [Buen. A.]
   Death Hunt. Belmont, 1973 M [NYC]
   -Escape from Devil's Island. Belmont, 1972
   The Exterminator. Manor, 1980 [NYC]
   First Blood. Belmont, 1977; New English Library, 1978 DD
   The Guns of Palembang. Belmont, 1977; New English Library, 1978 DD [Indon.]
   Loanshark. Belmont, 1979
   Mafioso. Belmont, 1970; New English Library pb, 1971 [NYC]
   Manhattan Massacre. Dell, 1973; Mayflower, 1975 A [NYC]
   The Massacre at Umtali. Belmont, 1976 DD [Rhod.]
   Minnesota Strip. Belmont, 1979 [NYC]
   New Orleans Holocaust. Dell, 1973; Mayflower, 1975 A [New Or.]
   Omerta. Leisure, 1972 [NYC]
   Operation Hong Kong. Belmont, 1977; New English Library, 1978 DD [H. Kong]
   The Pleasure Principle. Leisure, 1974
   Spoils of War. Belmont, 1976; New English Library, 1978 DD [Leb.]
   The Sun Dance Murders. Belmont, 1970 [Ariz.]
   The Syndicate. Belmont, 1972
   Vendetta. Belmont, 1973 M [Calif.]

McCUTCHAN, PHILIP (DONALD). 1920- . Pseudonym: Robert Conington Galway, q.v. Ref: CA, TC. SC: Commander Esmonde Shaw, in at least those marked ES; Simon Shard = SS.
   The All-Purpose Bodies. Harrap, 1969; Day, 1970 ES [Australia]
   Blackmail North. Hodder, 1978 SS
   Blood Run East. Hodder, 1976 SS
   Bluebolt One. Harrap, 1962; Berkley, 1965 ES [Afr., W.]
   -Bowering's Breakwater. Harrap, 1964
   The Bright Red Business Men. Harrap, 1969; Day, 1969 ES
   Call for Simon Shard. Harrap, 1974 SS
   Coach North. Harrap, 1974; Walker, 1975 [Scot.]
   Corpse. Hodder, 1980 ES
   The Day of the Coastwatch. Harrap, 1968
   The Dead Line. Harrap, 1966; Berkley, 1966 ES [U.S.]
   The Eros Affair. Hodder, 1977 SS
   -The German Helmet. Harrap, 1972
   Gibraltar Road. Harrap, 1960; Berkley, 1965 ES [Gib.]
   Half a Bag of Stringer. Harrap, 1970
   Hartinger's Mouse. Harrap, 1970 ES
   Hopkinson and the Devil of Hate. Harrap, 1961
   -The Kid. Harrap, 1958
   Leave the Dead Behind Us. Harrap, 1962
   The Man from Moscow. Harrap, 1963; Day, 1965 ES [Russ.]
   -Man, Let's Go On. Harrap, 1970
   -Marley's Empire. Harrap, 1963
   Moscow Coach. Harrap, 1964; Day, 1966 ES [Russ.]
   The Oil Bastards. Harrap, 1972
   Poulter's Passage. Harrap, 1967
   Redcap. Harrap, 1961; Berkley, 1965 ES [ship]
   The Screaming Red Balloons. Harrap, 1968; Day, 1968 ES [Brazil]
   Skyprobe. Harrap, 1966; Day, 1967 ES
   Sladd's Evil. Harrap, 1965; Day, 1967 [Tun.]
   -Storm South. Harrap, 1959
   Sunstrike. Hodder, 1979 ES
   This Drakotny—. Harrap, 1971 ES
   A Time for Survival. Harrap, 1966
   A Very Big Bang. Hodder, 1975 SS
   Warmaster. Harrap, 1963; Day, 1964 ES
   -Whistle and I'll Come. Harrap, 1957

McCUTCHEON, GEORGE BARR. 1866-1928. Ref: EM. SC: Anderson Crow = AC.
   Anderson Crow, Detective. Dodd, 1920 ss AC
   -Castle Craneycross. Stone, 1902; Richards, 1903
   The Daughter of Anderson Crow. Dodd, 1907; Hodder, 1907 AC [N.Y.]

McCUTCHEON, HUGH (DAVIE-MARTIN). 1909- . Pseudonym: Hugh Davie-Martin, q.v. Ref: CA, CC. SC: Jimmy Carroll, in at least those marked JC; Anthony Howard, in at least those marked AH; Richard Logan, in at least those marked RL; Insp. McKeller, in at least those marked M.
   And the Moon Was Full; see Killer's Moon
   The Angel of Light. Rich, 1951. U.S. title: Murder at the Angel. Dutton, 1952 AH,M
   The Black Attendant. Long, 1966 JC [Fr.]
   Brand for the Burning. Long, 1969
   The Cargo of Death. Hale, 1980
   Comes the Blind Fury. Long, 1959
   Cover Her Face. Rich, 1954 AH,M
   The Deadly One. Long, 1962
   A Hot Wind from Hell. Long, 1968 JC
   Instrument of Vengeance. Long, 1975
   Killer's Moon. Long, 1966. U.S. title: And the Moon Was Full. Doubleday, 1967 [Scot.]
   Murder at the Angel; see The Angel of Light
   Night Watch. Long, 1978
   None Shall Sleep Tonight. Rich, 1953; Dutton, 1953 M
   Prey for the Nightingale. Rich, 1953
   Red Sky at Night. Long, 1972; Walker, 1972 [Scot.]
   The Scorpion's Nest. Long, 1967 JC
   Something Wicked. Long, 1970 JC
   Suddenly, in Vienna. Long, 1963 RL [Vienna]
   To Dusty Death. Long, 1960 RL,M
   Treasure of the Sun. Long, 1964 JC [Sp.]
   Yet She Must Die. Long, 1962; Doubleday, 1962 [Tangier]

MacDANIEL, CHARLES. Pseudonym of Charles M. Garrison.
   Murder on the Moon. Vantage, 1968

McDANIEL, DAVID (EDWARD). 1939-1977. Ref: CA. Starred titles are novelizations of "The Man from UNCLE" TV series.
   The Dagger Affair. Ace, 1965; Four Square, 1966 * [Calif.]
   The Hollow Crown Affair. Ace, 1969 *
   The Monster Wheel Affair. Ace, 1967; Four Square, 1967 *
   The Prisoner #2. Ace, 1970 (Novelization of the TV series.)
   The Rainbow Affair. Ace, 1967 * [Eng.]
   The Utopia Affair. Ace, 1968 * [Australia]
   The Vampire Affair. Ace, 1966; Four Square, 1966 * [Rum.]

McDERMID, FINLAY. Born and living in Calif.; graduate of Stanford U.; movie story editor and TV script writer.

Ghost Wanted. Simon, 1943. Also published as: Kiss the Blonde Goodbye. Bestseller, 1948 [L.A.]
Kiss the Blonde Goodbye; see Ghost Wanted
See No Evil. Simon, 1959; Boardman, 1959 [Calif.]

MacDERMOTT, P. L.
Julius Vernon; or, A Strange Case of Circumstantial Evidence. Ward, 1892
The Last King of Yewle. Ward, 1893; Cassell (NYC), 1893

MacDONALD, DONALD. SC: Tommy Briggs, in all titles.
Briggs Investigates. Hale, 1968
No Judges' Rules. Hale, 1969
The Organizer. Hale, 1970
The Ryan Affair. Hale, 1970
Two Bullets for Briggs. Hale, 1971
Two Kinds of Murder. Hale, 1971

MacDONALD, ELIZABETH. 1926- . Ref: CA.
The House at Gray Eagle. Scribner, 1976 [Colo., 1904]

McDONALD, EVA (ROSE). Ref: CA.
-Cromwell's Spy. Hale, 1976
-Cry Treason Thrice. Hale, 1977
-The Deadly Dagger. Hale, 1977
-King in Jeopardy. Hale, 1976

McDONALD, FRANK J(AMES). 1941- . Ref: CA.
Provenance. Little, 1979; Macdonald, 1980

MacDONALD, GEORGE A(LEXANDER). 1869-1936.
The Light Side of the Law. Cassell, 1910 ss

McDONALD, GREGORY. 1937- . Ref: CA, TC. SC: Irwin M. Fletcher (Fletch) = F; Francis Xavier Flynn = FF.
Confess Fletch. Avon, 1976; Gollancz, 1977 F,FF [Boston]
Fletch. Bobbs, 1974; Gollancz, 1976 F [Calif.]
Fletch's Fortune. Avon, 1978; Gollancz, 1979 F [Va.]
Flynn. Avon, 1977; Gollancz, 1978 FF [Boston]
-Running Scared. Obolensky, 1964; Gollancz, 1977 [Mass.]
Snatched; see Who Took Toby Rinaldi?
Who Took Toby Rinaldi? Putnam, 1980. British title: Snatched. Gollancz, 1980 [S.F.]

MacDONALD, HAZEL CHRISTIE
Death Walks Softly. Phoenix, 1950 [N.Y.]

McDONALD, HUGH. See: Robin Moore.

McDONALD, HUGH C.
The Grey Mask Murders. DeVoras, 1941

McDONALD, HUGH C(HISHOLM). 1913- .
Ref: CA. SC: Paul Williams: PW.
The Auditorium Affair. Hale, 1973
Five Signs from Ruby. Pyramid, 1976 PW
The Hour of the Blue Fox. Pyramid, 1975 PW
Letter from Kiev. Pyramid, 1977 PW

McDONALD, JAMES, DAVID VOS and ROBERT GERLACH
Something's Afoot. French, 1975 (Play.)

MACDONALD, JOHN. Pseudonym of Kenneth Millar, 1915-1983, q.v. Other pseudonyms: John Ross Macdonald, Ross Macdonald, qq.v. SC: Lew Archer, in the title below and continued under the JRM and RM bylines.
The Moving Target. Knopf, 1949; Cassell, 1951. Also published as: Harper, as by Ross Macdonald. PB, 1966 [L.A.]

MacDONALD, JOHN D(ANN). 1916- . Ref: CA, CC, EM, MC, TC. SC: Travis McGee = TM.
All These Condemned. GM, 1954 [N.Y.]
April Evil. Dell, 1956; Hale, 1957 [Fla.]
Area of Suspicion. Dell, 1954; Hale, 1956. Revised edition: GM, 1961 [Fla.]
The Beach Girls. GM, 1959; Muller, 1964 [Fla.]
Border Town Girl. Popular Library, 1956. British title: Five Star Fugitive. Hale, 1970 (2 novelets.)
The Brass Cupcake. GM, 1950; Muller, 1955 [Fla.]
Bright Orange for the Shroud. GM, 1965; Hale, 1967 TM
A Bullet for Cinderella. Dell, 1955; Hale, 1960. Also published as: On the Make. Dell, 1960

Cape Fear; see The Executioners
Clemmie. GM, 1958
The Crossroads. Simon, 1959; Hale, 1961 [Ga.]
Cry Hard, Cry Fast. Popular Library, 1955; Hale, 1969
The Damned. GM, 1952; Muller, 1964 [Mex.]
Darker Than Amber. GM, 1966; Hale, 1968 TM [Fla.]
Dead Low Tide. GM, 1953; Fawcett (London), 1955 [Fla.]
A Deadly Shade of Gold. GM, 1965; Hale, 1967 TM
Deadly Welcome. Dell, 1959; Hale, 1961 [Fla.]
Death Trap. Dell, 1957; Hale, 1958 [Ill.]
The Deceivers. Dell, 1958
The Deep Blue Good-By. GM, 1964; Hale, 1965 TM
The Dreadful Lemon Sky. Lippincott, 1974; Hale, 1976 TM
Dress Her in Indigo. GM, 1969; Hale, 1971 TM [Mex.]
The Drowner. GM, 1963; Hale, 1964 [Fla.]
The Empty Copper Sea. Lippincott, 1978; Hale, 1979 TM
The Empty Trap. Popular Library, 1957; Magnum, 1980 [Mex.]
The End of the Night. Simon, 1960; Hale, 1964
End of the Tiger and other stories. GM, 1966; Hale, 1967 ss
The Executioners. Simon, 1958; Hale, 1959. Also published as: Cape Fear. Crest, 1962
Five Star Fugitive; see Border Town Girl
A Flash of Green. Simon, 1962; Hale, 1971 [Fla.]
The Girl in the Plain Brown Wrapper. GM, 1968; Hale, 1969 TM [Fla.]
The Girl, the Gold Watch & Everything. GM, 1962; Coronet, 1965 [Fla.]
The Green Ripper. Lippincott, 1979; Hale, 1980 TM
Hurricane; see Murder in the Wind
Judge Me Not. GM, 1951; Muller, 1964 [N.Y.]
A Key to the Suite. GM, 1962; Hale, 1968
The Last One Left. Doubleday, 1967; Hale, 1968
The Long Lavender Look. GM, 1970; Fawcett (London), 1970 TM [Fla.]
A Man of Affairs. Dell, 1957; Hale, 1959 [Bahamas]
Man-Trap; see Soft Touch
Murder for the Bride. GM, 1951; Fawcett (London), 1954 [New Or.]
Murder in the Wind. Dell, 1956. British title: Hurricane. Hale, 1957 [Fla.]
The Neon Jungle. GM, 1953; Fawcett (London), 1954
Nightmare in Pink. GM, 1964; Hale, 1966 TM [NYC]
On the Make; see A Bullet for Cinderella
On the Run. GM, 1963; Hale, 1965
One Fearful Yellow Eye. GM, 1966; Hale, 1968 TM [Chi.]
One Monday We Killed Them All. GM, 1961; Hale, 1963
The Only Girl in the Game. GM, 1960; Hale, 1962 [Las Veg.]
Pale Gray for Guilt. GM, 1968; Hale, 1969 TM [Fla.]
The Price of Murder. Dell, 1957; Hale, 1958
A Purple Place for Dying. GM, 1964; Hale, 1966 TM [S.W.]
The Quick Red Fox. GM, 1964; Hale, 1966 TM
The Scarlet Ruse. GM, 1973; Hale, 1975 TM [Fla.]
Seven. GM, 1971; Hale, 1974 ss, some criminous
Slam the Big Door. GM, 1960; Hale, 1961 [Fla.]
Soft Touch. Dell, 1958; Hale, 1960. Also published as: Man-Trap. Pan, 1961
A Tan and Sandy Silence. GM, 1972; Hale, 1973 TM [Fla.]
The Turquoise Lament. Lippincott, 1973; Hale, 1975 TM
Weep for Me. GM, 1951; Muller, 1964
Where Is Janice Gantry? GM, 1961; Hale, 1963 [Fla.]
You Kill Me; see You Live Once
You Live Once. Popular Library, 1956; Hale, 1976. Also published as: You Kill Me. GM, 1961 [Midwest]

MACDONALD, JOHN ROSS. Pseudonym of Kenneth Millar, 1915-1983, q.v. Other pseudonyms: John Macdonald, Ross Macdonald, qq.v. SC: Lew Archer = LA (originated under the John Macdonald byline, continued as by John Ross Macdonald, and finally as by Ross Macdonald).
The Drowning Pool. Knopf, 1950; Cassell, 1952, as by John Macdonald LA
Experience with Evil; see Meet Me at the Morgue
Find a Victim. Knopf, 1954; Cassell, 1955 LA [Calif.]
The Ivory Grin. Knopf, 1952; Cassell, 1953. Also published as: Marked for Murder. PB, 1953 LA
Marked for Murder; see The Ivory Grin
Meet Me at the Morgue. Knopf, 1953. British title: Experience with Evil. Cassell, 1954 [L.A.]
The Name Is Archer. Bantam, 1955 LA ss [Calif.]
The Way Some People Die. Knopf, 1951; Cassell, 1953 LA [L.A.]

MacDONALD, PHILIP. 1899-1981. Pseudonyms: Martin Porlock, q.v., Anthony Lawless. Joint pseudonym with Ronald MacDonald, 1860-1933: Oliver Fleming, q.v. Ref: all eight. SC: Colonel Anthony Gethryn = AG; Supt. Arnold Pike, as supporting character in most AG novels and by himself in that title marked AP. Set: Eng.
The Choice. Collins, 1931. U.S. title: The Polferry Riddle. Doubleday, 1931. Also published as: The Polferry Mystery. Collins, 1932 AG
The Crime Conductor. Collins, 1932; Doubleday, 1931 AG [theatre]
The Dark Wheel, with A. Boyd Correll, q.v. Collins, 1948; Morrow, 1948. Also published as: Sweet and Deadly. Zenith, 1959 [NYC]
Death and Chicanery. Jenkins, 1963; Doubleday, 1962 ss
Death on My Left. Collins, 1933; Doubleday, 1933
Fingers of Fear. Collins, 1953. U.S. title: Something to Hide. Doubleday, 1952 ss, AG in one
Guest in the House. Jenkins, 1956; Doubleday, 1955. Also published as: No Time for Terror. Bestseller, 1956 [Calif.]
Harbour. Collins, 1931; Doubleday, 1931, as by Anthony Lawless
The Link. Collins, 1930; Doubleday, 1930 AG
The List of Adrian Messenger. Jenkins, 1960; Doubleday, 1959 AG
The Man Out of the Rain. Jenkins, 1957; Doubleday, 1955 ss
The Maze. Collins, 1932. U.S. title: Persons Unknown. Doubleday 1931 AG
Menace; see R.I.P.
Murder Gone Mad. Collins, 1931; Doubleday, 1931 AP
No Time for Terror; see Guest in the House
The Noose. Collins, 1930; Dial, 1930 AG
The Nursemaid Who Disappeared. Collins, 1938. U.S. title: Warrant for X. Doubleday, 1938 AG
Persons Unknown; see The Maze
The Polferry Mystery; see The Choice
The Polferry Riddle; see The Choice
The Rasp. Collins, 1924; Dial, 1925 AG
R.I.P. Collins, 1933. U.S. title: Menace. Doubleday, 1933
Rope to Spare. Collins, 1932; Doubleday, 1932 AG
Rynox. Collins, 1930. U.S. title: The Rynox Murder Mystery. Doubleday, 1931. Also published as: The Rynox Mystery. Collins, 1933. And as: The Rynox Murder. Avon, 1968
The Rynox Murder; see Rynox
The Rynox Murder Mystery; see Rynox
Something to Hide; see Fingers of Fear
Sweet and Deadly; see The Dark Wheel
Warrant for X; see The Nursemaid Who Disappeared
The White Crow. Collins, 1928; Dial, 1928 AG
The Wraith. Collins, 1931; Doubleday, 1931 AG

MacDONALD, RONALD. 1860-1933. Joint pseudonym with Philip MacDonald, 1899-1981, q.v.: Oliver Fleming, q.v.

MACDONALD, ROSS. Pseudonym of Kenneth Millar, 1915-1983, q.v. Other pseudonyms: John Macdonald, John Ross Macdonald, qq.v. Ref: CA, CC, EM, MC, TC. SC: Lew Archer = LA (begun under the John Macdonald byline and continued as by John Ross Macdonald, and finally as Ross Macdonald. Titles marked * were published in Britain as by John Ross Macdonald. All titles are presently published as by Ross Macdonald, as reprints of all earlier titles.
The Barbarous Coast. Knopf, 1956; Caswell, 1957 * LA [L.A.]

Black Money. Knopf, 1966; Collins, 1966 LA [Calif.]
The Blue Hammer. Knopf, 1976; Collins, 1976 LA [Calif.]
The Chill. Knopf, 1964; Collins, 1964 LA [Calif., acad.]
The Doomsters. Knopf, 1958; Collins, 1958 * LA [Calif.]
The Far Side of the Dollar. Knopf, 1965; Collins, 1965 LA [Calif.]
The Ferguson Affair. Knopf, 1960; Collins, 1961 [L.A.]
The Galton Case. Knopf, 1959; Cassell, 1960 * LA [Calif.]
The Goodbye Look. Knopf, 1969; Collins, 1969 LA [Calif.]
The Instant Enemy. Knopf, 1968; Collins, 1968 LA [L.A.]
Lew Archer, Private Investigator. Mysterious Press, 1977 ss (Collects all LA ss.)
Sleeping Beauty. Knopf, 1973; Collins, 1973 LA [Calif.]
The Underground Man. Knopf, 1971; Collins, 1971 LA [Calif.]
The Wycherly Woman. Knopf, 1961; Collins, 1962 LA [Calif.]
The Zebra-Striped Hearse. Knopf, 1962; Collins, 1963 LA [Calif.]

MacDONALD, (ALLEN) WILLIAM COLT. 1891- . Born in Mich.; lived most of his life in the West; prolific author of westerns. SC: Gregory Quist (in western detective stories) = GQ.
Action at Arcanum. Lippincott, 1958; Hodder, 1961 GQ [Ariz.]
Blind Cartridges. Doubleday, 1951; Hodder, 1954
The Commanche Scalp. Lippincott, 1955; Hodder, 1958 GQ
Destination Danger. Lippincott, 1955; Hodder, 1957 GQ
The Devil's Drum. Lippincott, 1956; Hodder, 1962 GQ
The Gloved Saskia. Avalon, 1964; Hodder, 1965 [Calif.]
Law and Order, Unlimited. Doubleday, 1953; Hodder, 1955 GQ
Mascarada Pass. Doubleday, 1954; Hodder, 1957 GQ
The Osage Bow. Hodder, 1964 (U.S. title?) GQ
Tombstone for a Troubleshooter. Lippincott, 1960; Hodder, 1961 GQ

MACDONELL, ARCHIBALD GORDON. 1895-1941. Pseudonyms: John Cameron, Neil Gordon, qq.v. Joint pseudonym with Milward Rodon Kennedy Burge, 1894-1968, q.v.: Robert Milward Kennedy, q.v.

McDONELL, GORDON. 1905- . Born in Eng.; has spent many years in the U.S.
Burning Secret. Hart-Davis, 1959
The Clocktower. Harrap, 1952; Little, 1951
Intruder from the Sea. Harrap, 1953; Little, 1953 [L.A.]
Jump for Glory. Harrap, 1936; Green Circle, 1937
My Sister, Good Night. Harrap, 1948; Little, 1948 [L.A.]
The Reprieve of Roger Maine. Chatto, 1962; Prentice-Hall, 1961 [Calif.]
Silver Bugle. Harrap, 1938
They Won't Believe Me. Harrap, 1947
Wind Without Rain. Chatto, 1963

McDONELL, MARGARET
Althea. Doubleday, 1951 [Calif.]

McDONNELL, H. KEVIN. Set: Eng.
The Terror of Toynham Hall. Modern, 193?
The Vanishing Clue. Modern, 1938
The Vengeance of Five. Modern, 1938

MacDONNELL, JAMES EDMOND. 1917- .
Pseudonym: James Dark, q.v.

McDOUGALD, ROMAN. 1907?-1960. SC: Philip Cabot = PC.
The Blushing Monkey. Simon, 1953; Boardman, 1953 PC [NYC]
The Deaths of Lora Karen. Simon, 1944 PC [NYC]
Lady Without Mercy. Simon, 1948; Boardman, 1955
Purgatory Street. Simon, 1946
The Whistling Legs. Simon, 1945 PC [NYC]
The Woman Under the Mountain. Simon, 1950; Boardman, 1951

MacDOUGALL, JAMES K. Professor of English in Indiana. SC: David Stuart, in both titles.
Death and the Maiden. Bobbs, 1978; Hale, 1979 [Ohio]
Weasel Hunt. Bobbs, 1977; Hale, 1979 [Cleve.]

MacDOUGALL, (SAMUEL) MICHAEL. 1906- .
Danger in the Cards. Ziff-Davis, 1943

McDOUGALL, MURDOCH C(HRISTIE)
Chase the Snowman. Boardman, 1957 [Hamb.]
Soft as Silk. Boardman, 1957

MacDOUGALL, RUTH DOAN. 1939- . Ref: CA.
The Cost of Living. Putnam, 1971 [New Eng.]
One Minus One. Avon, 1972

McDOWELL, (ROBERT) EMMETT. 1914-1975. Byline also: Robert Emmett McDowell, q.v. SC: Jonathan Knox, in at least those marked JK.
Bloodline to Murder. Ace, 1960 JK [Louisville]
In at the Kill. Ace, 1960 JK [Louisville]
Stamped for Death. Ace, 1958 JK [Louisville]
Switcheroo. Ace, 1954
Three for the Gallows. Ace, 1958 (Three novelets, one with JK.) [Louisville]

McDOWELL, MICHAEL. 1950- . Joint pseudonym with Dennis Schuetz: Nathan Aldyne, q.v. Ref: CA.
Cold Moon over Babylon. Avon, 1980 [Fla.]
Gilded Needles. Avon, 1980 [NYC, 1882]

McDOWELL, ROBERT EMMETT. 1914-1975. Byline also: (Robert) Emmett McDowell, q.v. Ref: CA.
The Hound's Tooth. Mill, 1965; Cassell, 1967 [Ky.]
Portrait of a Victim. Bouregy, 1964

MacDUFF, DAVID. 1905- . Born in Scotland, educated there and at U. of Calif.; press agent and newspaperman.
Murder Strikes Three. Modern Age, 1937 [acad.]

McDUFF, E. M.
Murder in the Theatre. Lothian (Adelaide), 1947 [theatre]

McELFRESH, (ELIZABETH) ADELINE. 1918- .
Pseudonyms: Jennifer Blair, John Cleveland, qq.v. Ref: CA.
-Charlotte Wade. Arcadia, 1952
Keep Back the Dark. Phoenix, 1950 [Ind.]
Murder with Roses. Phoenix, 1950; Foulsham, 1953
My Heart Went Dead. Phoenix, 1949
Shattered Halo. Avalon, 1956; Ward, 1960

McELROY, HUGH (FRANCIS). SC: Insp. William Brewer, in all titles. Set: Eng.
The Curtain of the Dark. Chapman, 1944
The House of Malory. Chapman, 1948
The Silver Venus. Chapman, 1942
Unkindly Cup. Chapman, 1946

McELROY, JOSEPH (PRINCE). 1930- . Ref: CA.
Lookout Cartridge. Knopf, 1974

McELWAIN, MIRANDA
The Penguin Island Murders. Quality, 1954

McENERY, JOHN
A Black Inheritance. Greening, 1909
The Vision of the Foam. Greening, 1907

McEVOY, HUGH
Jones, A., Finds the Body. Gifford, 1946 [hosp.]

McEVOY, MARJORIE (HARTE). Ref: CA.
-Brazilian Stardust. Arcadia, 1967
Calabrian Summer. Doubleday, 1980 [WWII, It.]
Castle Doom; see The White Costello
The Chinese Box. Lenox, 1973
Dark Heritage; see Dusky Cactus
Dusky Cactus. Jenkins, 1968. U.S. title: Dark Heritage
Eaglescliffe; see My Love Johnny
Echoes from the Past. Doubleday, 1979
Enchanted Isle. Lenox, 1971
The Grenfell Legacy. Jenkins, 1968; Pyramid, 1968
The Hermitage Bell. Lenox, 1972
-Moon over the Danube. Jenkins, 1966
My Love Johnny. Hale, 1971. U.S. title: Eaglescliffe. Lenox, 1971
No Castle of Dreams. Jenkins, 1960; Lenox, 1972
Peril at Polvellyn. Lenox, 1972 [Eng., 1800s]
The Queen of Spades. Ballantine, 1975 [Sp.]
Ravensmount. Beagle, 1974
-A Red, Red Rose. Jenkins, 1960
Softly Treads Danger. Jenkins, 1963; Lenox, 1967
The White Costello. Jenkins, 1969. U.S. title: Castle Doom. Lenox, 1970 [Sic.]
Who Walks by Moonlight? Jenkins, 1966; Lenox, 1973
The Wych Stone. Beagle, 1974

McFADDEN, G(ERTRUDE) V(IOLET)
-The Bridegroom. Lane (London), 1928
The Honest Lawyer. Lane (London & NYC), 1916
-Maumbury Rings. Hodder, 1920; Doran, 1921
-Narcissus in the Way. Lane (London), 1922
The Preventive Man. Lane (London & NYC), 1920 [Eng., 1829]
-The Roman Way. Lane (London), 1925
Sheriff's Deputy. Lane (London), 1924
-So Speed We. Lane (London), 1926
The Trusty Servant. Lane (London & NYC), 1920
The Turning Sword. Lane (London), 1923 [Eng., ca.1815]

MacFADYEN, VIRGINIA
Bittern Point. Boni, 1924 [Conn.]
-Windows Facing West. Boni, 1924; Paul, 1925

MacFALL, (CHAMBERS) HALDANE (COOKE), 1860-1928, and DION (WILLIAM PALGRAVE) CLAYTON CALTHROP, 1878-1937, q.v.
Rouge. Brown, 1906

McFARLANE, ARTHUR E(MERSON). 1876- .
Behind the Bolted Door? Dodd, 1916; Nash, 1916 [NYC]

McFARLANE, LESLIE. SC: Michael Brent, in both titles.
The Murder Tree. Dutton, 1931; Paul, 1932 [Mass.]
Streets of Shadow. Dutton, 1930; Paul, 1931 [Montr.]

MacFARLANE, PETER CLARK. 1871-1924.
-The Centurion's Story. Revell, 1910
-The Crack in the Bell. Doubleday, 1918
-The Quest of the Yellow Pearl. Revell, 1909
-Those Who Have Come Back. Little, 1914 ss

McFATHER, NELLE. 1936- . Ref: CA.
Dark Refuge. Ace, 1976
Ecstasy's Captive. Belmont, 1979
Mistress of Shades. Manor, 1977
The Red Jaguar. Ace, 1974
Whispering Island. Ace, 1974

McFERRAN, JOYCE
Death Takes Over. Hale, 1967

McGARRITY, MARK. 1943- . Pseudonym: Bartholomew Gill, q.v. Ref: CA.
-A Passing Advantage. Rawson, 1980 [Ger.]

McGAUGHY, DUDLEY DEAN. Pseudonyms: Dudley Dean, Owen Dudley, Dean Owen, qq.v.

McGAW, J. W.
For Gain Not Glory. Hale, 1970

McGERR, PATRICIA. 1917- . Ref: CA, CC, TC. SC: Selena Mead = SM.
Catch Me If You Can. Doubleday, 1948; Collins, 1949 [Colo.]
Dangerous Landing. Dell, 1975
Daughter of Darkness. Popular Library, 1974
Death in a Million Living Rooms. Doubleday, 1951. British title: Die Laughing. Collins, 1952 [NYC]
Die Laughing; see Death in a Million Living Rooms
Fatal in My Fashion. Doubleday, 1954; Collins, 1955
Follow, As the Night. Doubleday, 1950. British title: Your Loving Victim. Collins, 1951 [NYC]
For Richer, for Poorer, Till Death. Luce, 1969; Hale, 1971 [Conn.]
Is There a Traitor in the House? Doubleday, 1964; Collins, 1965 SM [Wash. D.C.]
Legacy of Danger. Luce, 1970 SM [Wash. D.C.]
Murder Is Absurd. Doubleday, 1967; Gollancz, 1967 [Md.]

Pick Your Victim. Doubleday, 1946; Collins, 1947 [Wash. D.C.]
Save the Witness. Doubleday, 1949; Collins, 1950 [ship]
The Seven Deadly Sisters. Doubleday, 1947; Collins, 1948 [NYC]
Stranger with My Face. Luce, 1968; Hale, 1970
Your Loving Victim; see Follow, As the Night

McGHEE, BILL
Cut and Run. Hammond, 1962

McGHEE, EDWARD. See also: Robin Moore.
The Last Caesar. Pinnacle, 1980 [Wash. D.C.]

McGIBENY, DONALD
Slag. Bobbs, 1922
.38 Caliber. Bobbs, 1920

McGILL, GORDON. 1943- .
War Story. Joseph, 1979; Delacorte, 1980 [WWII, Berlin]

McGILL, NANCY
The Cave of the Moon. Ace, 1979

McGINITY, JAMES PATRICK
Whirlpools. Stockwell, 1925 ss, some criminous

McGINLEY, PATRICK
Bogmail. Martin Brian, 1978; Ticknor, 1981 [Ire.]

McGINNIS, E. L. Pseudonym of Bela (William) Von Block, 1927- . Other pseudonyms: Jonathan Black, Mercedes Endfield, qq.v.
The Strasburg Collection. Belmont, 1969 [It.]

McGIRR, EDMUND. Pseudonym of Kenneth Giles, 1922-1972, q.v. Other pseudonym: Charles Drummond, q.v. SC: Jim Piron, in all titles.
Bardel's Murder. Gollancz, 1973; Walker, 1974
Death Pays the Wages. Gollancz, 1970
An Entry of Death. Gollancz, 1969; Walker, 1969 [Wales]
The Funeral Was in Spain. Gollancz, 1966 [Sp.]
A Hearse with Horses. Gollancz, 1967
Here Lies My Wife. Gollancz, 1967
The Lead-Lined Coffin. Gollancz, 1968
A Murderous Journey. Gollancz, 1974; Walker, 1975 [NYC]
No Better Fiend. Gollancz, 1971; Walker, 1971

McGIVERN, MAUREEN. See: William P(eter) McGivern, 1927-1982.

McGIVERN, WILLIAM P(ETER). 1927-1982. Pseudonym: Bill Peters, q.v. Ref: CA, CC, EM, MC, TC.
The Big Heat. Dodd, 1952; H. Hamilton, 1953 [Phil.]
But Death Runs Faster. Dodd, 1948; Boardman, 1949. Also published as: The Whispering Corpse. PB, 1950 [Chi.]
The Caper of the Golden Bulls. Dodd, 1966; Collins, 1967 [Sp.]
Caprifoil. Dodd, 1972; Collins, 1973
Chicago-7; see The Seven File
A Choice of Assassins. Dodd, 1963; Collins, 1964 [Sp.]
The Crooked Frame. Dodd, 1952 [NYC]
The Darkest Hour. Dodd, 1955; Collins, 1956. Also published as: Waterfront Cop. PB, 1956 [NYC]
Heaven Ran Last. Dodd, 1949; Digit, 1958 [Chi.]
Killer on the Turnpike. PB, 1961 ss
Lie Down, I Want to Talk to You. Dodd, 1967; Collins, 1968 [NYC]
Margin of Terror. Dodd, 1953; Collins, 1955 [Rome]
Night Extra. Dodd, 1957; Collins, 1958
Night of the Juggler. Putnam, 1975; Collins, 1975
Odds Against Tomorrow. Dodd, 1957; Collins, 1958
A Pride of Place. Dodd, 1962 [Pa.]
Reprisal. Dodd, 1973; Collins, 1974 [L.A.]
The Road to the Snail. Dodd, 1961
Rogue Cop. Dodd, 1954; Collins, 1955
Savage Streets. Dodd, 1959; Collins, 1960 [L.I.]
-The Seeing, with Maureen McGivern. Tower, 1980
The Seven File. Dodd, 1956; Collins, 1957. Also published as: Chicago-7. Sphere, 1970 [NYC]
Seven Lies South. Dodd, 1960; Collins, 1961
Shield for Murder. Dodd, 1951 [Phil.]
Very Cold for May. Dodd, 1950 [Chi.]
Waterfront Cop; see The Darkest Hour
The Whispering Corpse; see But Death Runs Faster

McGLOIN, JOSEPH THADDEUS. 1917- .
Pseudonym: Thaddeus O'Finn, q.v.

M'GOVAN, JAMES. Pseudonym of William Crawford Honeyman. Set: Edin., in all titles. SC: James M'Govan, in all titles.
Brought to Bay; or, Experiences of a City Detective. Menzies, 1878 ss
Criminals Caught; or, Records of a City Detective. Jenkins, 1921 ss
Hunted Down; or, Recollections of a City Detective. Menzies, 1878 ss
The Invisible Pickpocket; or, Records of a City Detective. Jenkins, 1922 ss
Solved Mysteries; or, Revelations of a City Detective. Menzies, 1888 ss
Strange Clues; or, Chronicles of a City Detective. Menzies, 1881 ss
Traced and Tracked; or, Memoirs of a City Detective. Menzies, 1884 ss

McGOVERN, JAMES. 1923- . Ref: CA.
The Berlin Couriers. Abelard, 1960 [Berlin]
Fraulein. Crown, 1956; Calder, 1957
No Ruined Castles. Putnam, 1957; Calder, 1958

MacGOWAN, ALICE, 1858- , and PERRY NEWBERRY, 1870-1938. SC: Jerry Boyne, in all titles.
The Million Dollar Suitcase. Stokes, 1922; Hutchinson, 1923 [S.F.]
The Mystery Woman. Stokes, 1924; Hutchinson, 1924 [S.F.]
The Seventh Passenger. Stokes, 1926; Hutchinson, 1928 [S.F.]
Shaken Down. Stokes, 1925; Hutchinson, 1925 [S.F.]
Who Is This Man? Stokes, 1927; Hutchinson, 1927 [Calif.]

MacGOWAN, JONATHAN
-The Charge Is Rape. Hale, 1978
-Death at the Games. Hale, 1980

McGRADY, MIKE. 1933- . See: Harvey Aronson. Ref: CA.

MacGRATH, HAROLD. 1871-1932. SC: Cutty Clay, in at least those marked CC.
-The Adventures of Kathlyn. Bobbs, 1914
-The Best Man. Bobbs, 1907 ss
The Blue Rajah Murder. Doubleday, 1930; Long, 1930 [N.Y.]
-Captain Wardlaw's Kitbags. Garden City, 1923
The Carpet from Bagdad. Bobbs, 1911 [Cairo]
-The Cellini Plaque. Doubleday, 1925; Curtis Brown, 1925 [It.]
The Changing Road. Doubleday, 1928; Long, 1928
Deuces Wild. Bobbs, 1914
The Drums of Jeopardy. Doubleday, 1920; Hodder, 1923 CC [NYC]
-The Enchanted Hat. Bobbs, 1908
-Enchantment. Bobbs, 1905 ss
The Girl in His House. Harper, 1918
The Green Complex. Doubleday, 1930; Long, 1930 [Paris]
The Green Stone. Doubleday, 1924; Curtis Brown, 1924 [NYC, N.C.]
-The Luck of the Irish. Bobbs, 1917
-The Man on the Box. Bobbs, 1904; Hodder, 1914
The Man with Three Names. Doubleday, 1920; Hutchinson, 1920
The Million Dollar Mystery. Grosset, 1915 (Novelization of the movie.)
The Pagan Madonna. Doubleday, 1921
Pidgin Island. Bobbs, 1914
The Private Wire to Washington. Harper, 1919
The Voice in the Fog. Bobbs, 1915
The Wolves of Chaos. Doubleday, 1929; Long, 1929 CC [Paris]
The World Outside. Doubleday, 1923; Long, 1924 [NYC]
The Yellow Typhoon. Harper, 1919; Hodder, 1923

McGRATH, MANDA
East of Singapore. Wright, 1935
-Footlights. Wright, 1935
The Girl from Scotland Yard. Wright, 1935
-The Last Ditch. Wright, 1934
Outside the Law. Wright, 1935
-Wise Virgin. Wright, 1934

McGRAW, LEE
Hatchett. Ballantine, 1976 [Chi.]

McGREEVEY, JOHN
The Informer. Dramatic, 1949 (1-act play based on the novel by Liam O'Flaherty, 1896- , q.v.)
Seeds of Suspicion. Dramatic, 1952 (1-act play based on a story, "Suspicion," by Dorothy L. Sayers, 1893-1957, q.v.)
The Thursday Murders. Dramatic, 1951 (3-act play adapted from the novel, "The Thursday Turkey Murders", by Craig Rice, q.v.)

MacGREGOR, BILL
The Uncertain Trumpet. Hale, 1980

MacGREGOR, DUNCAN
Lady Christ. Stockwell, 1901

MacGREGOR, JAMES MURDOCH. 1925- .
Pseudonym: J. T. McIntosh, q.v.

McGREW, FENN. Joint pseudonym of Julia McGrew and Caroline K. Fenn. SC: Lt. Charles Hillary = CH.
Made for Murder. Rinehart, 1954 CH
Murder by Mail. Rinehart, 1951 [Ohio]
Taste of Death. Rinehart, 1953 CH [Columbus, acad.]

McGREW, JULIA. Joint pseudonym with Caroline K. Fenn: Fenn McGrew, q.v.

McGUIRE, ATHA
Homicide Hussy. GM, 1955

McGUIRE, FRANCES MARGARET (CHEADLE). Ref: CA.
-September Comes In. Heinemann, 1961
Time in the End. Heinemann, 1963

McGUIRE, NICHOLAS. Pseudonym of Nicholas Melides, 1912- , q.v.
Mosquito Serenade. Paladin, 1950

McGUIRE, PATRICK O. Pseudonym.
Fiesta for Murder. Hammond, 1962 [Sp.]
A Time for Murder. Hammond, 1955

McGUIRE, (DOMINIC) PAUL. 1903(?)- .
Ref: CC, EM, TC. SC: Insp./Supt. Fillinger, in at least those marked F; Chief Insp. Cummings, in at least those marked C. Set: Eng.
The Black Rose Murder; see Murder in Bostall
Born to Be Hanged. Skeffington, 1935
Burial Service. Heinemann, 1938. U.S. title: A Funeral in Eden. Morrow, 1938 [S. Pac.]
Cry Aloud for Murder. Heinemann 1937
Daylight Murder. Skeffington, 1935. U.S. title: Murder at High Noon. Doubleday, 1935 C,F
Death Fugue. Skeffington, 1933 F
Death Tolls the Bell; see The Tower Mystery
Enter Three Witches; see The Spanish Steps
A Funeral in Eden; see Burial Service
Murder at High Noon; see Daylight Murder
Murder by the Law. Skeffington, 1932 F
Murder in Bostall. Skeffington, 1931. U.S. title: The Black Rose Murder. Brentano's, 1932 C
Murder in Haste. Skeffington, 1934 C,F
Prologue to the Gallows. Skeffington, 1936
7.30 Victoria. Skeffington, 1935 C
The Spanish Steps. Heinemann, 1940. U.S. title: Enter Three Witches. Morrow, 1940 [Rome]
There Sits Death. Skeffington, 1933 F
Three Dead Men. Skeffington, 1931; Brentano's, 1932 C
Threepence to Marble Arch. Skeffington, 1936
The Tower Mystery. Skeffington, 1932. U.S. title: Death Tolls the Bell. Coward, 1933 F
W.1. Heinemann, 1937

McGURK, SLATER. Pseudonym of Arthur Joseph Roth, 1925- . Ref: CA.
The Big Dig. Macmillan, 1968; Hale, 1968 [L.I.]
The Copenhagen Affair; see The Denmark Bus
The Denmark Bus. Walker, 1966. Also published as: The Copenhagen Affair. Lancer, 1968
The Grand Central Murders. Macmillan, 1964; Hammond, 1965 [NYC]

McGUYER, NADINE
To Ravish Rani. Manor, 1979

McHALE, TOM. 1941-1982. Ref: CA.
Alinsky's Diamond. Lippincott, 1974 [Fr.]

The Lady from Boston. Doubleday, 1978
[Vt.]

MacHARDY, CHARLES
Blowdown. Collins, 1978

MacHARG, WILLIAM (BRIGGS). 1872-1951.
Ref: EM.
The Affairs of O'Malley. Dial, 1940.
Also published as: Smart Guy. Popular
Library, 1951 ss [NYC]
The Blind Man's Eyes, with Edwin Balmer, 1883-1959, q.v. Little, 1916;
Nash, 1916 [Chi.]
The Indian Drum, with Edwin Balmer,
1883-1959, q.v. Little, 1917; Paul,
1919 [Chi.]
Smart Guy; see The Affairs of O'Malley
The Surakarta, with Edwin Balmer, 1883-
1959, q.v. Small, 1913

McHENRY, JAMES. 1785-1845.
The Spectre of the Forest; or, Annals
of the Housatonic. Bliss, 1823;
Newman, 1824 [New Eng.]

McHUGH, AUGUSTIN. See: Barton (Wood) Currie, 1878-   .

McHUGH, EDNA. Joint pseudonym with Amelia
Reynolds Long, 1904-1978, q.v.: Kathleen Buddington Coxe, q.v. Ref: CA.

McHUGH, FRANCES Y(OULIN)
Bluethorne. Arcadia, 1966 [Conn.,
ca.1910]
The China Shepherdess. Arcadia, 1966
The Dropped Living Room. Lenox Hill,
1972
Emerald Mountain. Lenox Hill, 1970
The Frightened Bowerbird. Arcadia, 1968
The Ghost Wore Black. Lenox Hill, 1970
High on a Wall. Arcadia, 1967
The Hyacinth Spell. Lenox Hill, 1972
Love Like an Arrow. Lenox Hill, 1972;
Remploy, 1973
The Missing Grandfather. Arcadia, 1968
The Pale Pink House. Arcadia, 1967
The Rocking Chair. Arcadia, 1969
Saratoga Mire. Lenox Hill, 1970
Shadow Acres. Arcadia, 1967
Shadow over Mount Sharon. Arcadia, 1968
[Mass.]
Summer Velvet. Lenox Hill, 1972
Vow of Love. Lenox Hill, 1972
Window on the Seine. Arcadia, 1969

McILVANNEY, WILLIAM. 1936-   . Ref: CA.
Laidlaw. Hodder, 1977; Pantheon, 1977
[Glasgow]

MacILWAIN, DAVID. 1921-   . Pseudonyms:
Charles Eric Maine, Richard Rayner,
qq.v.

McINERNY, RALPH (MATTHEW). 1929-   .
Ref: CA. SC: Father Roger Dowling =
RD, all set in Ill.
Bishop as Pawn. Vanguard, 1978; Curley,
1979 RD
Her Death of Cold. Vanguard, 1977;
Hale, 1979 RD
Lying Three. Vanguard, 1979; Hale, 1980
RD
Romanesque. Harper, 1978; Hale, 1979
[Rome]
Second Vespers. Vanguard, 1980; Hale,
1981 RD
The Seventh Station. Vanguard, 1977;
Hale, 1979 RD

MacINNES, HAMISH
Death Reel. Hodder, 1976

MacINNES, HELEN. 1907-   . Ref: CA, CC,
EM, TC.
Above Suspicion. Little, 1941; Harrap,
1941 [Austria]
Agent in Place. Harcourt, 1976; Collins, 1976 [Fr.]
Assignment in Brittany. Little, 1942;
Harrap, 1942 [Fr.]
Decision at Delphi. Harcourt, 1960;
Collins, 1961 [Greece]
The Double Image. Harcourt, 1966; Collins, 1967 [Greece]
The Hidden Target. Harcourt, 1980; Collins, 1981
Horizon. Little, 1946; Harrap, 1945
[Austria]
I and My True Love. Harcourt, 1953;
Collins, 1953 [Wash. D.C.]
Message from Malaga. Harcourt, 1971;
Collins, 1972 [Sp.]
Neither Five Nor Three. Harcourt, 1951;
Collins, 1951 [NYC]
North from Rome. Harcourt, 1958; Collins, 1958 [It.]
Pray for a Brave Heart. Harcourt, 1955;
Collins, 1955 [Switz.]
Prelude to Terror. Harcourt, 1978; Collins, 1978 [Austria]

The Salzburg Connection. Harcourt,
1968; Collins, 1969 [Austria]
The Snare of the Hunter. Harcourt,
1974; Collins, 1974 [Czech.]
The Unconquerable; see While Still We
Live
The Venetian Affair. Harcourt, 1963;
Collins, 1964 [Venice]
While Still We Live. Little, 1944. British title: The Unconquerable. Harrap, 1944 [Pol.]

McINTIRE, MARGUERITE (GERTRUDE PEARMAN)
Old-Fashioned Murder. Farrar, 1941
[N.H.]

McINTIRE, WEBB KYLE
-Cider Row. Exposition, 1961

McINTOSH, J. T. Pseudonym of James Murdoch MacGregor, 1925-   . Ref: CA.
SC: Ambrose and Dominique Frayne, in
both titles. Set: Eng.
A Coat of Blackmail. Muller, 1970;
Doubleday, 1971
Take a Pair of Private Eyes. Muller,
1968; Doubleday, 1968 (Novelization
of a TV play by Peter O'Donnell,
1920-   , q.v.)

McINTOSH, KINN HAMILTON. 1930-   .
Pseudonym: Catherine Aird, q.v.

MacINTYRE, JOHN (THOMAS). 1871-1951.
Pseudonym: Kerry O'Neil, q.v. Ref:
CC, MP. SC: Ashton Kirk = AK.
Ashton-Kirk: Criminologist. Penn, 1918;
Robinson, 1921 AK
Ashton-Kirk: Investigator. Penn, 1910;
Robinson, 1921 AK
Ashton-Kirk: Secret Agent. Penn, 1912;
Palmer, 1916. Also published as:
Secret Agent: Ashton-Kirk. Robinson,
1921 AK
Ashton-Kirk: Special Detective. Penn,
1912. British title: Special Detective: Ashton-Kirk. Robinson, 1922 AK
In the Dead of Night. Lippincott, 1908;
Ward, 1909 [NYC]
In the Toils. Penn, 1898 (5-act play.)
The Museum Murder. Doubleday, 1929;
Bles, 1930 [NYC]
-The Ragged Edge. McClure, 1902
Secret Agent: Ashton-Kirk; see Ashton-
Kirk: Secret Agent
-Signing Off. Farrar, 1938
"Slag." Scribner, 1927
Special Detective: Ashton-Kirk; see
Ashton-Kirk: Special Detective
Steps Going Down. Farrar, 1936
-The Street Singer. Penn, 1908

MacISAAC, FRED(ERICK JOHN). 1886-1940.
Born in Mass.; playwright and novelist.
The Dealer of Death. Methuen, 1938
Death Rides the Deep. Methuen, 1938
[ship]
Don't Let Him Burn! Methuen, 1938 [NYC]
False-Face. Methuen, 1939
The Hole in the Wall. Waterson, 1927
[NYC]
Hot Gold. Methuen, 1938
The Mental Marvel. McClurg, 1930
Millions for Murder. Methuen, 1938
The Murder Special. Methuen, 1938
Tin Hats. Chelsea, 1926
The Vanishing Professor. Waterson,
1927; Methuen, 1939 [NYC]
The Wild Man of Cape Cod. Methuen, 1938
[Cape Cod]
The Winged Murderer. Methuen, 1939
The Yellow Shop. Hurst, 1928

MacIVERS, DONALD
The Cult of Killers. Leisure, 1976

MacIVERS, SARAH
Cry of the Wind. Belmont, 1974 [La.,
1800s]
The Curse of Ravenswood. Macfadden,
1973
Night Without End. Belmont, 1975
[La., 1870]

MACKAIL, DENIS (GEORGE). 1892-   .
Ref: CC.
-According to Gibson. Heinemann, 1923;
Houghton, 1923 ss
The "Majestic" Mystery. Heinemann,
1924; Houghton, 1924

MacKAY, ALISTAIR McCOLL. 1931-   . Ref:
CA.
The Triad Conspiracy. Bantam (NYC &
London), 1978 [Eng.]

MacKAY, AMANDA. Born in Va.; living in
Durham, N.C.
Death Is Academic. McKay, 1976; Hale,
1980 [N.C., acad.]

McKAY, HERBERT. 1881-   .
A Camouflage Revolution. Wells Gardner,
1929. Also published as: The Mystery
of White Fell Gill. James, 1947

MACKAY, HUGH LEWIS. 1897-1963. Pseudonym:
Hugh Matheson, q.v.

McKAY, KELVIN. Pseudonym of Charles Stanley Strong, 1906-1962. Other pseudonym: Charles Stoddard, q.v.
Murder at Barclay House. Phoenix, 1937

McKAY, KENNETH R.
Shadow of the Knife. Playboy, 1978

McKAY, RANDLE and R. J. GERRARD. For
McKay, see also: Lassiter Wren.
The "Intelligence" Game of Secret Service Cases and Problems. McBride,
1935 puzzle ss

McKEAG, ERNEST L(IONEL). 1896-   . Pseudonyms: Griff, Mark Grimshaw, Ramon
Lacroix, qq.v.
Green Eyes Are Dangerous. Jonathan
(London), 1947
The Man from the Gallows. Modern, 193?
The Sign of the Spider. Fiction House,
1939
A Traitor in the Fleet. Wright, 1939

McKEAND, GEO(RGE)
Lady Glenroy; or, The Mystery in the
Moonlight. Blackwood, 1893

McKECHNIE, N(EIL) K(ENNETH). 1873-   .
The Saddleroom Murder. Penn, 1937
[Can.]

McKELLAR, CAMPBELL. Pseudonym: Hilarion,
q.v.

McKELVEY, J.
Walk with Me into Darkness. Vantage,
1979 ss

McKELWAY, ST. CLAIR. 1905-1980. Ref: CA.
The Edinburgh Caper. Holt, 1962; Gollancz, 1963 [Edin.]

McKENNA, EVELYN. Pseudonym of Archie
(Lynn) Joscelyn, 1899-   . Other
pseudonym: A. A. Archer, q.v.
Castle Midnight. Arcadia, 1966

McKENNA, MARTHE. 1892-1969. SC: Clive
Granville, in at least those marked
CG.
Arms and the Spy. Jarrolds, 1942
Double Spy. Jarrolds, 1938
Drums Never Beat. Jarrolds, 1936
Hunt the Spy. Jarrolds, 1939
Lancer Spy. Jarrolds, 1937 CG
Nightfighter Spy. Jarrolds, 1943 [Ger.]
Set a Spy. Jarrolds, 1937
The Spy in Khaki. Jarrolds, 1941 CG
A Spy Was Born. Jarrolds, 1935;
McBride, 1935
Spying Blind. Jarrolds, 1939
Three Spies for Glory. Jarrolds, 1950
Watch Across the Channel. Jarrolds,
1944
What's Past Is Prologue. Jarrolds, 1951

McKENNA, STEPHEN. 1888-1967. Ref: CA.
The Datchley Inheritance. Ward, 1929;
Dodd, 1929
Pandora's Box and other stories. Ward,
1932 ss
Tales of Intrigue and Revenge. Hutchinson, 1924; Little, 1925 ss
While of Sound Mind. Hutchinson, 1936

McKENNEY, KENNETH. 1929-   . Ref: CA.
The Fire Cloud. Simon, 1979; Macdonald,
1980

McKENZIE, A(DELBERT) R(OLAND). 1907-   .
Death Gets a Head. Phoenix, 1942

MacKENZIE, ANDREW (CARR). 1911-   . SC:
Supt. Brannigan, in the titles
marked B, and others. Set: Eng.
Always Fight Back. Boardman, 1955
A Grave Is Waiting. Boardman, 1957
The House at the Estuary. Ward, 1948
A Man from the Past. Boardman, 1958
The Man Who Wanted to Die. Ward, 1951 B
The Missile. Boardman, 1959
Point of a Gun. Ward, 1951
The Reaching Hand. Boardman, 1957
Search in the Dark. Ward, 1948
Shadow of a Spy. Boardman, 1958
Shadows on the River. Ward, 1949
Splash of Red. Ward, 1949 B
Three Hours to Hang. Boardman, 1955
Voice from the Cell. Hale, 1961
Week of Suspense. Hale, 1962
Whisper If You Dare! Ward, 1950 B

MACKENZIE, ANNA MARIE (WIGHT)
  Dusseldorf; or, The Fratricide. Lane, 1798 [Ger.]
  Mysteries Elucidated. Lane, 1795

MacKENZIE, (ANTHONY EDWARD MONTAGU) COMPTON. 1883-1972. Ref: CA. SC: Commander Roger Waterlow = RW.
  Extremes Meet. Cassell, 1928; Doubleday, 1928 RW
  The Three Couriers. Cassell, 1929; Doubleday, 1929 RW
  Water on the Brain. Cassell, 1933; Doubleday, 1933

MacKENZIE, DONALD. 1908-   . Ref: CA, TC. SC: Henry Chalice and Crying Eddie = C&E; John Raven = JR. Set: Eng. in part.
  The Chalice Caper; see Sleep Is for the Rich
  Cool Sleeps Balaban. Collins, 1964; Houghton, 1964
  Dangerous Silence. Collins, 1960; Houghton, 1960
  Dead Straight. Hodder, 1969; Houghton, 1969
  Death Is a Friend. Hodder, 1967; Houghton, 1967 C&E
  Deep, Dark and Dead. Macmillan (London), 1978
  Double Exposure. Collins, 1963; Houghton, 1963. Also published as: I, Spy. Avon, 1964 [Ger.]
  The Genial Stranger. Collins, 1962; Houghton, 1962
  I, Spy; see Double Exposure
  The Juryman. Elek, 1957; Houghton, 1958
  Knife Edge. Houghton, 1961 [Fr.]
  The Kyle Contract. Hodder, 1971; Houghton, 1970 [Calif.]
  The Lonely Side of the River. Hodder, 1965; Houghton, 1965
  Manhunt; see Nowhere to Go
  Moment of Danger; see Scent of Danger
  Night Boat from Puerto Vedra. Hodder, 1970; Houghton, 1970 [Cent. Am.]
  Nowhere to Go. Elek, 1956. U.S. title: Manhunt. Houghton, 1957
  Postscript to a Dead Letter. Macmillan (London), 1973; Houghton, 1973 [Fr.]
  The Quiet Killer; see Three Minus Two
  Raven After Dark; see Raven Feathers His Nest
  Raven and the Kamikaze. Macmillan (London), 1977; Houghton, 1977 JR
  Raven and the Paperhangers. Macmillan (London), 1980; Houghton, 1980 JR [Fr.]
  Raven and the Ratcatcher. Macmillan (London), 1977; Houghton, 1977 JR
  Raven Feathers His Nest. Macmillan (London), 1979. U.S. title (?): Raven After Dark. Houghton, 1979 JR
  Raven in Flight. Macmillan (London), 1976; Houghton, 1976 JR [Sp.]
  Raven Settles a Score. Macmillan (London), 1979; Houghton, 1979 JR
  Salute from a Dead Man. Hodder, 1966; Houghton, 1966 C&E
  Scent of Danger. Collins, 1958; Houghton, 1958. Also published as: Moment of Danger. Pan, 1959; Dell, 1959
  Sleep Is for the Rich. Hodder (London), 1971; Houghton, 1971. Also published as: The Chalice Caper. Mayflower, 1974 C&E
  The Spreewald Collection. Macmillan (London), 1975; Houghton, 1975 [Lisbon]
  Three Minus Two. Hodder, 1968. U.S. title: The Quiet Killer. Houghton, 1968
  Zaleski's Percentage. Macmillan (London), 1974; Houghton, 1974 JR

McKENZIE, DONALD J.
  Detective Against Detective. Street (Magnet)
  Face to Face. Street (Magnet)
  A Past Master of Crime; or, Detective Bush's Clever Work. Street (Magnet), 1899
  The Reporter Detective. Street (Magnet), 1900
  Under His Thumb. Street, 1889
  The Wall Street Wonder. Street (Magnet) [NYC]
  The Working Man Detective; or, A Crime Against the Poor. Street (Magnet), 1899

MacKENZIE, J. ALEXANDER. SC: Joshua Bain, in all titles.
  The Jordan Intercept. Bethany, 1980
  The Omega Document. Bethany, 1979 [L.A.]
  The Rahab Link. Bethany, 1980 [Calif.]

MacKENZIE, JEANNE
  -All for the Apple. Hutchinson, 1948
  The Deadly Game. Hutchinson, 1939
  -The Homeward Tide. Hutchinson, 1935
  -Linda Walked Alone. Hutchinson, 1944
  -The Wayward Heart. Hutchinson, 1951

MacKENZIE, NIGEL. SC: Det. Insp. Charles Tremayne, in at least those marked CT. Set: Eng.
  Bandit's Moon. Wright, 1952
  Blood on the Snow. Wright, 1966
  The Case of the Glass Slipper. Wright, 1962
  Consider Your Verdict. Wright, 1952
  Could It Be Murder? Wright, 1948
  The Dark Night. Wright, 1950 [S. Afr.]
  The Dark Road. Wright, 1961
  Day of Judgment. Wright, 1956
  Death for a Traitor. Wright, 1948
  Death Holds His Court. Wright, 1960 [S. Afr.]
  Death in the Smog. Wright, 1963
  Death Takes a Holiday. Wright, 1966
  Fear Stalks the City. Wright, 1965 [Paris]
  Footprints of Death. Wright, 1957
  The Ghost Walks. Wright, 1949
  The Horror in the Dark. Wright, 1962
  The House of Horror. Wright, 1959
  In Great Danger. Wright, 1959 [Russ.]
  Killer at Large. Wright, 1961 CT
  Killing's No Murder. Wright, 1968
  Missing—A Lady. Wright, 1964
  Missing, Believed Dead. Wright, 1968
  Murder for Two. Wright, 1951
  The Murder in Cardigan Square. Wright, 1954
  Murder in the Rain Forest. Wright, 1952
  Murder over Karmak. Wright, 1949
  Murder Round the Corner. Wright, 1968
  Night of Fear. Wright, 1964 CT
  No Escape from Murder. Wright, 1964
  Pyramid of Death. Wright, 1953
  Queue Here for Murder. Wright, 1961
  Race Toward Death. Wright, 1963 CT
  The Red Light. Wright, 1950
  Seven Days to Death. Wright, 1959 [Tib.]
  Strange Happening. Wright, 1967 [Rhod.]
  Three Steps to Murder. Wright, 1965 [Australia]

MACKENZIE, SCOBIE. 1906-   . Set: Eng.
  Doctor Fram. Eyre, 1933; Dutton, 1933
  Three Dead, One Hurt. Eyre, 1934

MacKENZIE, SUSAN
  Death Has Many Doors. Lancer, 1968

MacKENZIE, W(ILLIAM) A(NDREW). 1870-   . SC: Sir Nigel Lacaita, in at least those marked NL. Set: Eng.
  The Bite of the Leech. Holden, 1914 NL
  The Black Butterfly. Ward, 1907 NL
  The Drexel Dream. Chatto, 1904 NL
  Flower o' the Peach. Ward, 1916
  -The Glittering Road. Ward, 1903
  His Majesty's Peacock. Richards, 1904 NL
  -In the House of the Eye. Ward, 1907
  -The Red Star of Night. Constable, 1911

MACKENZIE-LAMB, ERIC
  Labyrinth. Morrow, 1979; Hamlyn, 1980 [Fla.]

MacKEOWN, M. J. J.
  The Rale McCoy. Duffy, 1930; French (NYC), 1931 (3-act play.)

McKEOWN, NORMAN ROBERT. 1879-1947. Pseudonym: Norman Giles, q.v.

MacKERSEY, IAN
  -Long Night's Journey. Hale, 1974

McKEW, ROBERT and REED de ROUEN
  Death List. Dell, 1979; Futura, 1979

MACKEY, MARY. 1945-   . Ref: CA.
  -McCarthy's List. Doubleday, 1979; Eyre, 1980

MACKIE, JOHN. 1862-1939.
  -The Bush Mystery; or, The Lost Explorer. Nisbet, 1912
  -The Man Who Forgot. Jarrolds, 1901

McKIMMEY, JAMES. 1923-   . Ref: CA.
  Blue Mascara Tears. Ballantine, 1965; Boardman, 1966 [S.F.]
  A Circle in the Water. Morrow, 1965; Muller, 1966
  Cornered! Dell, 1960; Boardman, 1965 [Midwest]
  The Hot Fire. Hale, 1969
  The Long Ride. Dell, 1961; Boardman, 1963 [West]
  The Man with the Gloved Hand. Random, 1972; Hale, 1974 [Nev.]
  Never Be Caught. Boardman, 1966 (3 novelets.)
  The Perfect Victim. Dell, 1958; Boardman, 1965 [Midwest]
  Run If You're Guilty. Lippincott, 1963; Boardman, 1964 [Calif.]
  The Satyr. Monarch, 196?
  Squeeze Play. Dell, 1962; Boardman, 1965 [Calif.]
  24 Hours to Kill. Dell, 1961; Boardman, 1963
  Winner Take All. Dell, 1959; Boardman, 1963 [Calif.]
  The Wrong Ones. Dell, 1961; Boardman, 1964

MACKIN, MRS. MARIE
  The Mystery of the Marbletons. Abbey, 1900

MacKINLAY, (MALCOLM) STERLING. 1876-   .
  The Enemy Agent. Long, 1932

McKINLEY, F(RANCES) BURKS. 1907-   .
  Death Sails the Nile. Stratford, 1933 [Egypt]

MacKINNON, ALLAN. Ref: CC. SC: Mike Darroch = MD; Det. Insp. Duncan MacCallum = DM; Don Kendrick = DK.
  Assignment in Iraq. Collins, 1960; Doubleday, 1960 MD [Baghdad]
  Cormorant's Isle. Long, 1962; Doubleday, 1962 [Scot.]
  Danger by My Side. Collins, 1950
  Dead on Departure. Long, 1964. U.S. title: Report from Argyll. Doubleday, 1964 DK [Scot.]
  House of Darkness. Collins, 1947; Doubleday, 1947 DM [Scot.]
  Man Overboard; see No Wreath from Manuela
  Map of Mistrust. Collins, 1948; Doubleday, 1948 [Scot.]
  Money on the Black; see Nine Days' Murder
  Murder, Repeat Murder. Collins, 1952; Doubleday, 1952
  Nine Days' Murder. Collins, 1945. U.S. title: Money on the Black. Doubleday, 1946 DM
  No Wreath from Manuela. Long, 1965. U.S. title: Man Overboard. Doubleday, 1965 DK [ship]
  Red-Winged Angel. Collins, 1958. U.S. title: Summons from Baghdad. Doubleday, 1958 MD [Baghdad]
  Report from Argyll; see Dead on Departure
  Summons from Baghdad; see Red-Winged Angel

MACKINNON, CHARLES ROY. 1924-   . Pseudonym: Graham Montrose, q.v.

MacKINNON, CLARK K.
  The Flame Lily. Dakers, 1954
  Leopard Valley. Long, 1963
  Lost Hyena. Long, 1962 [Rhod.]

MacKINTOSH, ELIZABETH. 1896-1952. Pseudonyms: Gordon Daviot, Josephine Tey, qq.v.

MacKINTOSH, IAN. 1940-   . SC: Tim Blackgrove, in at least those marked TB. Ref: CA.
  The Brave Cannot Yield. Hale, 1970
  Count Not the Cost. Hale, 1968
  A Drug Called Power. Hale, 1968 TB
  The Man from Destiny. Hale, 1969
  The Sandbaggers. Corgi, 1978 (Novelization of the TV series.)
  A Slaying in September. Hale, 1967 TB [Antwerp]
  Wilde Alliance. Sphere, 1978 (Novelization of the TV series.)

MacKINTOSH, MAY. Born in Scot., later living in Sp. Pseudonym: Regina Ross, q.v. SC: Laurie Grant and Stewart Noble = G&N.
  Appointment in Andalusia. Collins, 1972; Delacorte, 1972 G&N [Sp.]
  Assignment in Andorra; see A King and Two Queens
  Balloon Girl; see Roman Adventure
  Dark Paradise; see The Sicilian Affair
  The Double Dealers. Collins, 1975. U.S. title: Highland Fling. Delacorte, 1975 [Scot.]
  Highland Fling; see The Double Dealers
  A King and Two Queens. Collins, 1973. U.S. title: Assignment in Andorra. Delacorte, 1973 G&N [Sp.]
  Roman Adventure. Collins, 1976. U.S. title: Balloon Girl. St. Martin's, 1977 [Rome]
  The Sicilian Affair. Collins, 1974; Delacorte, 1974. Also published as: Dark Paradise. Dell, 1978 G&N [Sic.]

McKNIGHT, BOB. 1906- . Mining engineer, pilot and horseracing handicapper before semi-retiring to Fla.
The Bikini Bombshell. Ace, 1959 [Fla.]
Downwind. Ace, 1957 [Sante Fe]
Drop Dead, Please. Ace, 1961 [Fla.]
The Flying Eye. Ace, 1961 [Fla.]
Homicide Handicap. Ace, 1963 [Fla.]
Kiss the Babe Goodbye. Ace, 1960 [Fla.]
Murder Mutuel. Ace, 1958 [Fla.]
Running Scared. Ace, 1960
Secret Sinners. Merit, 1960
A Slice of Death. Ace, 1960 [Fla.]
A Stone Around Her Neck. Ace, 1962 [Fla.]
Swamp Sanctuary. Ace, 1959 [Fla.]

McKNIGHT, CAROLYN
Gravetide. St. Martin's, 1980 [Eng., 1800s]
The House in the Shadows. St. Martin's, 1979; Hale, 1980 [N.Y.]

MacKNUTT, M. G.
Death on the Cuff. Phoenix, 1951

McLACHLAN, ALEX(ANDER). See: R(obert) J(ames) Fletcher, 1877- .

McLACHLAN, IAN. 1938- . Ref: CA.
The Seventh Hexagram. Dial, 1976; Hodder, 1977 [H. Kong]

McLACHLIN, DONALD
No Case for the Crown. Sidgwick, 1972

McLAREN, CHRISTABEL
The Divine Gift. Longmans, 1929

MACLAREN, DEANNA
-Dagger in the Sleeve. Allen, 1979

McLAREN, JACK. 1887-1954.
The Crystal Skull. Allan, 1936
-The Devil of the Depths. Allan, 1935
-A Diver Went Down. Mandrake, 1929
-Stories of Fear. Pendulum, 1947 ss

McLAREN, MORAY. Ref: CC.
-A Dinner with the Dead. Serif, 1947 ss
-Escape and Return. Chapman, 1947
The Pursuit. Jarrolds, 1959

MacLAREN-ROSS, J(ULIAN)
-Better Than a Kick in the Pants. Lawson, 1945 ss
-Bitten by the Tarantula. Wingate, 1945
The Doomsday Book. H. Hamilton, 1961; Obolensky, 1961
-The Funny Bone. Elek, 1956
-My Name Is Love. Times Press, 1964
-The Nine Men of Soho. Wingate, 1946 ss
-Of Love and Hunger. Wingate, 1947
-The Stuff to Give the Troops. Cape, 1944 ss
Until the Day She Dies. H. Hamilton, 1960

McLARTY, NANCY
Chain of Death. Doubleday, 1962 [Guat.]

McLAUGHLIN, ROBERT. 1925- .
Nothing to Report, with Phil Foran. Little, 1975 [NYC]
Pending Investigation. Berkley, 1977 [NYC]

McLAUGHLIN, ROBERT J.
A Horsehair Santa Claus and other stories. Christopher, 1931 ss

McLAUGHLIN, W(ILLIAM) R(AFFAN) D(AVIDSON). 1908- . Ref: CA.
Syndicate of Evil. Hale, 1965 [Far East]

McLAURIN, KATE L.
Whispering Wires. Baker, 1934 (3-act play based on the novel by Henry Leverage, 1885- , q.v.)

MacLEAN, ALISTAIR (STUART). 1922- . Pseudonym: Ian Stuart, q.v. Ref: CA, TC. SC: Capt. Mallory = M.
Athabasca. Collins, 1980; Doubleday, 1980 [Alaska]
Bear Island. Collins, 1971; Doubleday, 1971 [Arctic]
Breakheart Pass. Collins, 1974; Doubleday, 1974 [train, 1870s, West]
Caravan to Vaccares. Collins, 1970; Doubleday, 1970 [Fr.]
Circus. Collins, 1975; Doubleday, 1975
Fear Is the Key. Collins, 1961; Doubleday, 1961 [Fla.]
Force 10 from Navarone. Collins, 1968; Doubleday, 1968 M [Yugos., WWII]
The Golden Gate. Collins, 1976; Doubleday, 1976 [S.F.]
The Golden Rendezvous. Collins, 1962; Doubleday, 1962 [ship]
Goodbye California. Collins, 1977; Doubleday, 1978 [Calif.]
The Guns of Navarone. Collins, 1957; Doubleday, 1957 [Turk., WWII] M
Ice Station Zebra. Collins, 1963; Doubleday, 1963 [Arctic]
The Last Frontier. Collins, 1959. U.S. title: The Secret Ways. Doubleday, 1959 [Czech.]
Night Without End. Collins, 1960; Doubleday, 1960 [Green.]
Puppet on a Chain. Collins, 1969; Doubleday, 1969 [Amst.]
Seawitch. Collins, 1977; Doubleday, 1977
The Secret Ways; see The Last Frontier
South by Java Head. Collins, 1958; Doubleday, 1958 [ship]
The Way to Dusty Death. Collins, 1973; Doubleday, 1973 [Fr.]
When Eight Bells Toll. Collins, 1966; Doubleday, 1966 [ship]
Where Eagles Fly. Collins, 1967; Doubleday, 1967 [Ger.]

McLEAN, ALLAN CAMPBELL. 1922- . Ref: CA, CC. SC: Insp. Neil MacLeod, in at least those marked NM. Set: Eng.
The Carpet-Slipper Murder. Ward, 1956; Washburn, 1957 NM
Deadly Honeymoon. Ward, 1958
Death on All Hallows. Ward, 1958; Washburn, 1958 NM
Murder by Invitation. Ward, 1959 NM
Stand-In for Murder. Ward, 1960

MacLEAN, ARTHUR (GEORGE). Pseudonym: Arthur Kirby, q.v. See also: Desmond Reid. All titles below feature Sexton Blake and, where not otherwise indicated, were published by Amalgamated Press.
Bargain in Blood. 1962
Broken Toy. 1956
Canvas Jungle. 1956
Dark Frontier. 1956
Deadline for Danger. 1957
Fatal Curtain. 1958
Find Me a Killer! 1957. Also published as: Slaying on the 16th Floor. Mayflower, 1965
The House on the Bay. 1958
The Man Who Killed Me; see Redhead for Danger
Mask of Fury. 1957
Mission to Mexico. 1960 [Mex.]
Night Beat. 1956
Pursuit to Algeria. 1961 [Algeria]
Redhead for Danger. 1958. Also published as: The Man Who Killed Me. 1962
The Savage Squeeze. Mayflower, 1965
Slaying on the 16th Floor; see Find Me a Killer!
Touch of Evil. 1959 (Written by E. C. Tubb, 1919- , q.v.; revised by MacLean.)

MacLEAN, CHARLES AGNEW. 1880-1928. Pseudonym: Nicholas Carter, q.v.

MacLEAN, JANE. 1935- . Ref: CA.
Deadfall. Dutton, 1979; Hale, 1981 [Mex.]

MacLEAN, KATHERINE. 1925- . Ref: CA.
The Man in the Bird Cage. Ace, 1970
Missing Man. Berkley, 1975

MacLEAN, ROBINSON. Born in Idaho; magazine writer, author of biography of Haile Selassie.
The Baited Blonde. Mill, 1949; Barker, 1950 [Mid. East]

McLEAVE, HUGH (GEORGE). 1923- . Pseudonym: Richard Copeland, q.v. SC: Dr. Gregor Maclean (see also Copeland entry) = GM. Set: Eng.
A Borderline Case. Gollancz, 1979; Scribner, 1979 [Pak.]
Double Exposure. Gollancz, 1980; Scribner, 1979 [Russ.]
Only Gentlemen Can Play. Barker, 1975; Harcourt, 1974
A Question of Negligence. Collins, 1973; Harcourt, 1970 GM
The Steel Balloon. Muller, 1964
The Sword and the Scales. Davies, 1967; World, 1968
Vodka on Ice. Harcourt, 1969

McLEISH, DOUGAL. Set: Can., both titles.
The Traitor Game. Houghton, 1968
The Valentine Victim. Houghton, 1968

McLEISH, RODERICK. 1926- . Ref: CA.
The Man Who Wasn't There. Random, 1976. British title: Carnaby Rex. Weidenfeld, 1976 [Wash. D.C.]

McLENDON, JAMES. ca.1942-1982.
Deathwork. Lippincott, 1977; H. Hamilton, 1978 [Fla.]
Eddie Macon's Run. Viking, 1980 [Tex.]

MacLEOD, ADAM GORDON. SC: Sir William Burrill = WB. Set: Eng.
The Case of Matthew Crake. Harrap, 1932; Dial, 1933 WB
The Cathra Mystery. Harrap, 1926; Dial, 1926
Death Stalked the Fells. Harrap, 1937 WB
The Marloe Mansions Murder. Harrap, 1928; Dial, 1928 WB

MacLEOD, ANGUS. 1906- . Ref: CC.
Blessed Among Women. Dobson, 1965; Roy, 1967 [Scot.]
The Eighth Seal. Dobson, 1962; Roy, 1962 [Scot.]
The Tough and the Tender. Dobson, 1960; Roy, 1960 [Scot.]

MacLEOD, CHARLOTTE (MATILDA HUGHES). 1922- . Ref: CA. Pseudonym: Alisa Craig, q.v. SC: Prof. Peter Shandy = PS; Sarah Kelling = SK.
The Family Vault. Doubleday, 1979; Collins, 1980 SK [Boston]
The Luck Runs Out. Doubleday, 1979; Collins, 1981 PS [Mass., acad.]
Mystery of the White Knight. Avalon, 1964
Next Door to Danger. Avalon, 1965
Rest You Merry. Doubleday, 1978; Collins, 1979 PS [Mass., acad.]
The Withdrawing Room. Doubleday, 1980; Collins, 1981 SK [Boston]

McLEOD, KEN
A Body for a Blonde. Harlequin, 1954

MacLEOD, ROBERT. Pseudonym of Bill Knox, 1928- , q.v. Other pseudonyms: Michael Kirk, Noah Webster. SC: Talos Cord = TC; Jonathan Gaunt = JG; Andrew Laird = AL.
All Other Perils. Long, 1974; Doubleday, 1975, as by Michael Kirk AL [Maj.]
A Burial in Portugal. Long, 1973; Doubleday, 1973, as by Noah Webster JG [Port.]
Cargo Risk. Hutchinson, 1980; Doubleday, 1980, as by Michael Kirk AL [Fr.]
Cave of Bats. Long, 1964; Holt, 1966 TC [Burma]
Dragonship. Long, 1976; Doubleday, 1977, as by Michael Kirk AL [Copen.]
Drum of Power. Long, 1964. U.S. title: The Drum of Ungara, as by Bill Knox. Doubleday, 1963 [Afr.]
The Drum of Ungara; see Drum of Power
Flickering Death; see A Property in Cyprus
An Incident in Iceland. Long, 1979; Doubleday, 1979, as by Noah Webster JG [Ice.]
The Iron Sanctuary; see Lake of Fury
Isle of Dragons. Long, 1967 TC [Borneo]
A Killing in Malta. Long, 1972; Doubleday, 1972, as by Noah Webster JG [Malta]
Lake of Fury. Long, 1966. U.S. title: The Iron Sanctuary. Holt, 1968 TC [Afr., E.]
Nest of Vultures. Long, 1973 TC
Path of Ghosts. Long, 1971; McCall, 1971 TC
A Pay-Off in Switzerland. Long, 1977; Doubleday, 1977, as by Noah Webster JG [Switz.]
Place of Mists. Long, 1969; McCall, 1970 TC [Mid. East]
A Property in Cyprus. Long, 1970. U.S. title: Flickering Death, as by Noah Webster. Doubleday, 1970 JG [Cyprus]
Salvage Job. Long, 1978; Doubleday, 1979, as by Michael Kirk AL [Port.]
A Witchdance in Bavaria. Long, 1975; Doubleday, 1976, as by Noah Webster JG [Munich]

MacLEOD, RUTH. 1903- . Ref: CA.
Hawks of Glenaerie. Manor, 1974
Mendocino Menace. Avon, 1973 [Calif.]
Murder on Vacation. Avalon, 1962

M'LEVY, JAMES
At War with Society; or, Tales of the Outcasts. Cameron, 1870 ss
Casebook of a Victorian Detective. Canongate, 1975 ss, taken from The Sliding Scale of Life, and from Curiosities of Crime in Edinburgh, qq.v.

Curiosities of Crime in Edinburgh. Kay, 1861; Nimmo, 1861; Vicker, 1861 ss (All three British firms seem to have issued the book in the same year.) [Edin.]
The Mysteries of the City; or, Under the Surface of Society. Cameron, 186? ss
Romances of Crime; or, The Disclosures of a Detective. Griffin, 1869 ss
The Sliding Scale of Life; or, Thirty Years' Observations of Falling Men and Women in Edinburgh. Houlston, 1861 ss [Edin.]

McLOUGHLIN, MAURICE
Brush with a Body. French (London), 1963 (3-act play.)

McLOUGHLIN, ROY
The Yank in Fleet Street. Methuen, 1939

McMAHON, BRIAN PATRICK. Fighter pilot and career U.S. Air Force officer; son of Thomas Patrick McMahon, q.v.

McMAHON, ROBERT. Pseudonym of Robert Weverka, 1926-   , q.v. See: Leo Bergson.

McMAHON, THOMAS PATRICK. Police justice in N.Y.; consultant to food manufacturer and director of chain of supermarkets.
Cornered at Six, with Brian Patrick McMahon. Simon, 1972
The Hubschmann Effect. Simon, 1973. British title: The Little Victims. Constable, 1974 [N.Y.]
The Issue of the Bishop's Blood. Doubleday, 1972; Collins, 1973
Jink. Simon, 1971 [Fla.]
The Little Victims; see The Hubschmann Effect
Mayday, with Brian Patrick McMahon. Simon, 1973 [Jap.]

McMANIS, J. ALLEN
The Hooded Asp. Wetzel, 1928 [L.A.]

McMANUS, CHRIS
-The Deep-Sea Tow. Harrap, 1954
-The "Hades Belle." Harrap, 1955
-Whisky Johnny. Harrap, 1956

McMANUS, LESLIE
Operation Backlash. New English Library, 1977; Playboy, 1979 [WWII, Greece]

McMANUS, YVONNE. 1931-   . Ref: CA.
Bequeath Them No Tumbled House. Doubleday, 1977
-With Fate Conspire. Dell, 1974 [Calif.]

McMIKLE, BARBARA
The Secret of the Weeping Monk. Bantam, 1975

McMILLAN, ELSIE MILLS
The Devil's Bell. Canyon, 1974

MacMILLAN, GEORGETTE
The Woman in Mauve. Chelsea, 1925

McMORDIE, TABOR (L.)
By Executive Arrangement. McGraw (NYC & London), 1979

McMORROW, THOMAS. 1886-   .
The Sandalwood Fan. Sears, 1928 [NYC]
The Sinister History of Ambrose Hinkle. Sears, 1929 [NYC]

McMULLEN, J(OSEPH) C(ARL). 1882-   .
Pseudonym: Joseph Carlton, q.v. See also: Robert C(arl) Schimmel, 1895-   . All titles are plays; number of acts in parenthesis.
Apartment 13, with Vance Holloway (pseudonym). Baker, 1948 (3)
The Dead of Night. Barker, 1928 (3)
The Ghost in the Green Gown. Fitzgerald, 1938 (1)
The House of the Flashing Light; or, The Devil's Eye. Baker, 1929 (3)
Ring Around Rosie. Fitzgerald, 1932 (3)

McMULLEN, MARY. 1920-   . Ref: CC, EM, TC.
But Nellie Was So Nice. Doubleday, 1979; Collins, 1981 [NYC]
A Country Kind of Death. Doubleday, 1975; Hale, 1976 [Conn.]
A Dangerous Funeral. Doubleday, 1977; Hale, 1979 [Cape Cod]
Death by Bequest. Doubleday, 1977; Penguin, 1978 [Phil.]
Death of Miss X; see Strangle Hold
The Doom Campaign. Doubleday, 1974; Hale, 1976 [NYC]

Funny, Jonas, You Don't Look Dead. Doubleday, 1976; Hale, 1978 [Phil.]
The Man with Fifty Complaints. Doubleday, 1978; Hale, 1980 [N.J.]
My Cousin Death. Doubleday, 1980; Collins, 1981 [Ire.]
The Pimlico Plot. Doubleday, 1975; Hale, 1977 [Eng.]
Prudence Be Damned. Doubleday, 1978; Hale, 1979 [NYC]
Something of the Night. Doubleday, 1980; Collins, 1982 [Eng.]
Strangle Hold. Harper, 1951. British title: Death of Miss X. Collins, 1952 [NYC]
Welcome to the Grave. Doubleday, 1979; Collins, 1980 [Conn.]

McMURDIE, ANNIE LAURIE. Pseudonym of Bruce (Bingham) Cassiday, 1920-   , q.v. Other pseudonyms: Carson Bingham, Nick Carter, Mary Anne Drew, Annie Laurie McAllister, Michael Stratford, qq.v.
Nightmare Hall. Lancer, 1973 [L.A.]

McNAB, OLIVER
Horror Story. Houghton, 1979; Lane, 1980 [N.H.]

McNALLY, TERRENCE. 1939-   . Ref: CA.
The Ritz, and other plays. Dodd, 1976 (Plays, one criminous.)

MacNALTY, A(RTHUR) SALUSBURY. 1880-1969. Ref: CA.
The Mystery of Captain Burnaby. Pawling, 1934

McNAMARA, ED. 1911-   . Born in NYC, living in Conn. in 1950s; free-lance writer and employed in classified department of NYC newspaper.
Once Over Deadly. Abelard (NYC & London), 1958 [N.Y.]

McNAMARA, LENA B(ROOKE). 1891-   . Pseudonym: Evalina Mack, q.v. Portrait painter and teacher.
The Penance Was Death. Bruce, 1964
Pilgrim's End. Ace, 1967 [Va.]

McNAMARA, MICHAEL M. 1940-1979. Ref: CA.
-The Dancing Floor. Crown, 1978; Allen, 1979
The Sovereign Solution. Crown, 1979; Allen, 1980

MacNAUGHT, THOMAS P.
The Recollections of a Glasgow Detective Officer. Simpkin, 1887 ss [Glasgow]
Thrilling Detective Stories. Simpkin, 1891 ss

MACNAUGHTON, RICHARD. Pseudonym of Richard Young,   -1972.
The Preparatory School Murder. Fenland, 1934 [acad.]

MACNAUGHTON, BRIAN. 1935-   .
Guilty Until Proven Guilty. Carlyle, 1979
The Poacher. Carlyle, 1978

McNEAR, ROBERT
Carpet of Death. Hale, 1976

McNEE, PATRICK. Pseudonym of Peter Leslie, 1922-   , q.v.
Dead Duck. Hodder pb, 1966 (Based on "The Avengers" TV series.)
Deadline. Hodder pb, 1965 (Based on "The Avengers" TV series.)

McNEIL, JOHN. Computer consultant in Eng.
The Consultant. Weidenfeld, 1978; Coward, 1978
Spy Game. Weidenfeld, 1980; Coward, 1980

MacNEIL, NEIL. Pseudonym of W(illis) T(odhunter) Ballard, 1903-1980, q.v. Other pseudonyms: P. D. Ballard, John Shepherd, qq.v. Joint pseudonym with Norbert Davis, q.v.: Harrison Hunt, q.v. SC: Tony Costaine and Bert McCall, in all titles.
The Death Ride. GM, 1960; Muller pb, 1962 [Calif.]
Death Takes an Option. GM, 1958; Fawcett (London), 1960 [S.W.]
Hot Dam. GM, 1960; Muller pb, 1960 [N.Y.]
Mexican Slay Ride. GM, 1962; Muller pb, 1963 [Mex.]
The Spy Catchers. GM, 1963 [Calif.]
Third on a Seesaw. GM, 1959; Muller pb, 1961 [Pa.]
Two Guns for Hire. GM, 1959; Muller pb, 1960 [L.A.]

McNEILE, H(ERMAN) C(YRIL). 1888-1937. Ref: EM, MC, MP, TC. This author's works have appeared as by H. C. McNeile and/or Sapper, and are collectively listed here. Note that a number of McNeile ss were published separately in booklet form in the U.S.; these are listed separately at the end of this entry. SC: Hugh "Bulldog" Drummond = BD (see also: Gerard Fairlie, 1899-   ; and: Henry Reymond); Jim Maitland = JM; Ronald Standish = RS. Set: Eng.
Ask for Ronald Standish. Hodder, 1936 RS ss
The Black Gang. Hodder, 1922; Doran, 1922 BD
Bulldog Drummond. Hodder, 1920; Doran, 1920. 4-act play version, with Gerald Du Maurier, 1873-1934: French (London & NYC), 1925 BD
Bulldog Drummond and the Female of the Species; see The Female of the Species
Bulldog Drummond at Bay. Hodder, 1935; Doubleday, 1935 BD,RS
Bulldog Drummond Meets a Murderess; see The Female of the Species
Bulldog Drummond Returns; see The Return of Bulldog Drummond
Bulldog Drummond Strikes Back; see Knock-Out
Bulldog Drummond's Third Round; see The Third Round
Challenge. Hodder, 1937; Doubleday, 1937 BD,RS
The Dinner Club. Hodder, 1923; Doran, 1923 ss
The Female of the Species. Hodder, 1928; Doubleday, 1928. Also published as: Bulldog Drummond and the Female of the Species. Sun Dial, 1943. And as: Bulldog Drummond Meets a Murderess. Thriller Novel Classic, 194? BD
The Final Count. Hodder, 1926; Doran, 1926 BD
The Finger of Fate. Hodder, 1930; Doubleday, 1931 ss
Guardians of the Treasure; see The Island of Terror
-The Human Touch. Hodder, 1918; Doran, 1918 ss
The Island of Terror. Hodder, 1931. U.S. title: Guardians of the Treasure. Doubleday, 1931 JM
-Jim Brent. Hodder, 1926
Jim Maitland. Hodder, 1923; Doran, 1924 JM
Knock-Out. Hodder, 1933. U.S. title: Bulldog Drummond Strikes Back. Doubleday, 1933 BD
-The Lieutenant and Others. Hodder, 1915 ss
The Man in Ratcatcher, and other stories. Hodder, 1921; Doran, 1921 ss
Men, Women and Guns. Hodder, 1916; Doran, 1916 ss, one criminous
Michael Cassidy, Sergeant; see Sergeant Michael Cassidy, R.E.
-Mufti. Hodder, 1919; Doran, 1919 ss
-No Man's Land. Hodder, 1917; Doran, 1917 ss
-Out of the Blue. Hodder, 1925; Doran, 1925 ss
The Return of Bulldog Drummond. Hodder, 1932. U.S. title: Bulldog Drummond Returns. Doubleday, 1932 BD
Ronald Standish. Hodder, 1933 RS
-The Saving Clause. Hodder, 1927 ss
-Sergeant Michael Cassidy, R.E. Hodder, 1915. U.S. title: Michael Cassidy, Sergeant. Doran, 1916 ss
-Shorty Bill. Hodder, 1926 ss, taken from No Man's Land, and The Human Touch, qq.v.
Temple Tower. Hodder, 1929; Doubleday, 1929 BD
The Third Round. Hodder, 1924. U.S. title: Bulldog Drummond's Third Round. Doran, 1924 BD
Tiny Carteret. Hodder, 1930; Doubleday, 1930 RS
-When Carruthers Laughed. Hodder, 1934 ss
-Word of Honour. Hodder, 1926; Doran, 1926 ss

The criminous content of these ss has not been confirmed:
An Act of Providence. Doran, 1927
Billie Finds the Answer. Doran, 1927
The Brides of Mertonbridge Hall. Doubleday, 1932
Bulton's Revenge. Doran, 1924
The Diamond Hair Slide. Doran, 1927
Dilemma. Doran, 1927
The Ducking of Herbert Polton, and Coincidence. Doran, 1924
The Eleventh Hour. Doran, 1926
The Fatal Second. Doran, 1916
The Great Magor Diamond, and The Creaking Door. Doubleday, 1931
The Haunted Rectory. Doubleday, 1931

The Hidden Witness. Doubleday, 1929
A Hundred Per Cent. Doran, 1927
The Loyalty of Peter Drayton, and Mrs. Peter Skeffington's Revenge. Doran, 1926
The Man in Yellow, and The Empty House. Doubleday, 1933
Mark Danver's Sin, and The Madman of Coral Reef Lighthouse. Doran, 1923
A Matter of Tar. Doubleday, 1932
The Message. Doran, 1926
The Missing Chauffeur. Doubleday, 1931
Molly's Aunt at Angmering. Doran, 1923
The Motor-Gun. Doran, 1916
A Native Superstition. Doran, 1925
Once Bit, Twice Hit. Doran, 1927
The Other Side of the Wall. Doran, 1925
Peter Cornish's Revenge. Doran, 1923
The Professor's Christmas Party, and A Student of the Obvious. Doran, 1925
A Question of Identity. Doran, 1925
A Question of Mud. Doubleday, 1929
Relative Values. Doran, 1927
The Rout of the Oliver Samuelsons. Doran, 1926
The Rubber Stamp, and A Matter of Voice. Doran, 1926
The Saving Clause. Doran, 1926
A Scrap of Paper. Doran, 1924
The Taming of Sydney Marsham. Doran, 1926
That Bullet Hole Has a History! Doran, 1924
Three of a Kind, and The Haunting of Jack Burnham. Doran, 1926
The Truce of the Bear. Doran, 1918
Uncle James's Golf Match. Hodder, 1932
The Undoing of Mrs. Cransby. Doubleday, 1928
The Valley of the Shadow. Doran, 1924
When Carruthers Laughed. Doran, 1925
Who Was This Woman?, Two Photographs, and The King of Hearts. Doran, 1925
Word of Honour. Doran, 1926

McNEILL, GEORGE. Pseudonym: Jennifer Reddoch, q.v.

McNEILLE, JOHN. Pseudonym: Ian Niall, q.v.

McNEILLY, WILFRED (GLASSFORD). 1921-   . Pseudonyms: W(illiam) Howard Baker, William A. Ballinger, William Glassford, Errol Lecale, Desmond Reid, Peter Saxon, qq.v. SC (with many other authors): Sexton Blake = SB. Ref: CA.   Set: Eng.
The Break Out. Mayflower, 1965 SB
The Case of the Muckrakers. Mayflower, 1966; Macfadden, 1967 SB
The Case of the Stag at Bay. Mayflower, 1965 SB [Scot.]
Come Dark, Come Evil. Amalgamated, 1962 SB
Death in the Top Twenty. Mayflower, 1965 SB
Killer Pack. Amalgamated, 1962 SB
Land of the Free. Mayflower, 1966
No Way Out. Consul, 1966; Mayflower, 1966 (Novelization of the "Secret Agent" TV series.)
Terror Loch. Amalgamated, 1962 SB
Wanted for Questioning. Mayflower, 1965 SB
The War Runners. New English Library, 1970

MACOMBER, DARIA. Joint pseudonym of Ferdinan Stevenson and Patricia Colbert Robinson, 1923-   .
Bury Her Deep; see A Clearing in the Fog
A Clearing in the Fog. World, 1970. British title (?): Bury Her Deep. Hale, 1971 [Charleston]
Hunter, Hunter, Get Your Gun; see Return to Octavia
Return to Octavia. NAL, 1967. British title: Hunter, Hunter, Get Your Gun. Hodder, 1966 [South]

MACONECHY, J(OANNA)
Four Extra Daughters. Chatto, 1932
James Ballingray, Murderer. Collins, 1925
The Secret Journal of Charles Dunbar. Collins, 1923
Vanishing Shadows. Chatto, 1930

McOWEN, BERNARD J.
The Blue Ghost, with J. P. Riewerts. French (NYC), 1932 (Play.)
The Skull, with Harry E. Humphrey. Dramatists, 1938 (3-act play.)

McPARTLAND, JOHN. 1911-195?
Affair in Tokyo. GM, 1954 [Tokyo]
Big Red's Daughter. GM, 1953 [Calif.]
Danger for Breakfast. GM, 1956; Fawcett (London), 1957 [Tokyo]
The Face of Evil. GM, 1954; Fawcett (London), 1955 [Calif.]
I'll See You in Hell. GM, 1956; Red Seal, 1958 [Ark.]
The Kingdom of Johnny Cool. GM, 1959; Muller pb, 1960
The Last Night. GM, 1959; Muller pb, 1960 [Calif.]
Love Me Now. GM, 1952; Muller, 1957
No Down Payment. Simon, 1957; Macdonald, 1958
Ripe Fruit. GM, 1958; Fawcett (London), 1959 [Calif.]
Tokyo Doll. GM, 1953; Fawcett (London), 1954 [Tokyo]
The Wild Party. GM, 1956; Red Seal, 1959 [L.A.]

MacPHAIL, JAMES A. Joint pseudonym with Cornelia Warriner: James Crockett, q.v.

McPHELLAMY, STEPHEN
Murder Without Alibis. Quality, 1947

MacPHERSON, JOHN F.
-A Yankee Napoleon. Long, 1907
-Yetta the Magnificent. Long, 1908

MacPHERSON, MALCOLM (COOK). 1943-   . Ref: CA.
Protege. Dutton, 1980 [Afr., It.]

MacQUADE, MIKE
Who's for Dying. Hale, 1961

MacQUEEN, JAMES WILLIAM. 1900-   . Pseudonym: James G. Edwards, q.v.

McQUINN, DONALD E. Raised in Tex., later living in Wash.; was in Marine Intelligence in Saigon.
Targets. Macmillan, 1980 [Saigon, 1969]

McRAE, G. R(OY)
The Passing of Mr. Quinn. London Book Co., 1929 (Novelization of the film based on an Agatha Christie ss.)

MACRAE, TRAVIS. Pseudonym of Anita MacRae Feagles, 1926-   . Ref: CA. SC: Jim and Kate Harris = H.
Death in View. Holt, 1960; Hammond, 1961 H [N.Y.]
Multiple Murder; see Twenty Per Cent
Trial by Slander. Rinehart, 1960; Hammond, 1962 H [N.Y.]
Twenty Per Cent. Holt, 1961. British title: Multiple Murder. Hammond, 1962 H [N.Y.]

McREAY, ERNEST L.
Murder at Eight Bells. Columbine, 1939

MacROSS, ROSS. Joint pseudonym of James Reach, 1909?-1970, q.v., and Tom (Barnard) Taggart, q.v. Other Reach pseudonyms, used for plays: Hilda Manning, John Reed, Pete Williams, qq.v.
The Beautiful and Dead. GM, 1954

McROYD, ALLAN. SC: Insp. Franklin Brady, in all titles.
Death in Costume. Greystone, 1940 [L.I.]
The Double Shadow Murders. Greystone, 1939 [NYC]
The Golden Goose Murders. Greystone, 1938 [NYC]

McSHANE, MARK. 1930-   . Pseudonym: Marc Lovell, q.v. Ref: CA, CC, TC. SC: Det. Sgt. Norman Pink, in at least those marked NP; Myra Savage = MS.
The Crimson Madness of Little Doom. Hale, 1967; Doubleday, 1966
The Girl Nobody Knows. Hale, 1966; Doubleday, 1965 NP
The Hostage Game. Zebra, 1979
Ill Met by a Fish Shop on George Street. Hodder, 1969; Doubleday, 1968 [Australia]
Lashed But Not Leashed. Hale, 1978; Doubleday, 1976
The Man Who Left Well Enough. McCall, 1971
Night's Evil. Hale, 1966; Doubleday, 1966 NP [Scot.]
The Passing of Evil. Cassell, 1961
Seance; see Seance on a Wet Afternoon
Seance for Two. Hale, 1974; Doubleday, 1972 MS
Seance on a Wet Afternoon. Cassell, 1961. U.S. title: Seance. Doubleday, 1962 MS
The Singular Case of the Multiple Dead. Hodder, 1970; Putnam, 1969
The Straight and Crooked. Long, 1960
Untimely Ripped. Cassell, 1962; Doubleday, 1963
The Way to Nowhere. Hale, 1967 NP

MacSWAN, NORMAN
-The Inn with the Wooden Door. Cassell, 1958

MacTYRE, PAUL. Pseudonym of Robert James Adams, 1924-   . Ref: CC.
Bar Sinister. Hodder, 1964
-Fish on a Hook. Hodder, 1963

McVEAN, JAMES. Pseudonym of Nicholas Luard, 1937-   , q.v.
Bloodspoor. Macdonald, 1977; Dial, 1978
White Falcon. Macdonald, 1979

MacVEAN, PHYLLIS. 1892-   . Pseudonyms: Phyllis Hambledon, Philippa Vane, qq.v.

MacVEIGH, SUE. Pseudonym of Elizabeth Custer Nearing, 1898-   . Ref: CC, MP. SC: Capt. Andy MacVeigh and his wife Sue, in all titles.
The Corpse and the Three Ex-Husbands. Houghton, 1941 [Mich.]
Grand Central Murder. Houghton, 1939 [NYC]
Murder Under Construction. Houghton, 1939 [N.Y.]
Streamlined Murder. Houghton, 1940 [train]

MacVICAR, ANGUS. 1908-   . Starred titles are 1-act plays. Ref: CA, CC. SC: Rev. P. J. MacFarlane, in at least those marked PM; Bruce McLintock, in at least those marked BM.
The Canisbay Conspiracy. Long, 1966 [Scot.]
The Cavern. Paul, 1936
Crime's Masquerader. Paul, 1938
The Crooked Finger. Paul, 1937
The Crouching Spy. Paul, 1941 PM [Scot.]
The Dancing Horse. Long, 1961
Death by the Mistletoe. Paul, 1934 [Scot.]
Death on the Machar. Paul, 1947 [Scot.]
Duel in Glenfinnan. Long, 1969 [Scot.]
11 for Danger. Paul, 1939 [Scot.]
Escort to Adventure. Paul, 1952 [Scot.]
-Final Proof. Brown, 1958 *
Flowering Death. Paul, 1937
Fugitive's Road. Paul, 1949
The Golden Venus Affair. Long, 1972 BM
The Grey Shepherds. Long, 1964 [Scot.]
Greybreek. Long, 1947
The Hammers of Fingal. Long, 1963 [Scot.]
The Killings on Kersivay. Long, 1962 [Hebrides]
Maniac. Long, 1969
-Mercy Flight. Brown, 1959 *
Murder at the Open. Long, 1965 [Scot.]
Night on the Killer Reef. Long, 1967 [Scot.]
-The Other Man. Pemberton, 1947
The Painted Doll Affair. Long, 1973 BM
The Purple Rock. Paul, 1933 PM [Scot.]
The Screaming Gull. Paul, 1935 [Scot.]
The Singing Spider. Paul, 1938 [Scot.]
-Storm Tide. Brown, 1960 *
-Stranger at Christmas. Brown, 1964 *
Strangers from the Sea. Paul, 1939
The Temple Falls. Paul, 1935 PM [Scot.]
The Ten Green Brothers. Paul, 1936 [Scot.]
-Under Suspicion. Brown, 1962 *

McWATTERS, GEORGE S.
Detectives of Europe and America; or, Life in the Secret Service; see Knots Untied; or, Ways and Byways in the Hidden Live of American Detectives
Forgers and Confidence Men; or, The Secrets of the Detective Service Revealed. Laird, 1892 ss
The Gambler's Wax Finger and other startling detective experiences. Laird, 1892 ss
Knots Untied; or, Ways and Byways in the Hidden Life of American Detectives. Burr, 1871. Also published as: Detectives in Europe and America; or, Life in the Secret Service. Burr, 1877 ss

M—, Mr. Pseudonym of Charles Welch Mason, 1866-   .
The Chest of Opium. Beeman, 1896
The Shen's Pigtail, and Other Cues of Anglo-China Life. Unwin, 1894 ss

MAARTENS, MAARTEN. Pseudonym of Joost Marius Williem van der Poorten Schwartz, 1858-1915. See also: Anonymous ("The Black Box Murder"). Ref: MP.
The Sin of Joost Avelingh. Remington, 1889; Lovell, 1890 [Holl.]

MAAS, PETER. 1929- . Ref: CA.
 Made in America. Viking, 1979; H. Hamilton, 1980 [NYC]

MAAS, VIRGINIA (HARGRAVE). 1913- .
 Ref: CA.
 Castle Craggs. Manor, 1979

MAASS, EDGAR. 1896- .
 A Lady at Bay. Scribner, 1953 [Paris, 1672]

MAASS, JOACHIM. 1901-1972. Ref: CA.
 Gabrielle; see The Gouffe Case
 The Gouffe Case. Barrie, 1960; Harper, 1960. Also published as: Gabrielle. Corgi, 1964 (Translation of "Der Fall Gouffe." Vienna, 1958.) [Paris, 1889]
 The Magic Year. Barrie, 1964 (Translation of "Der Magische Jahr." Vienna, 1957.)

MABLEY, F. HARVEY
 The Scarlet Scarab. Murray, 1921

MACAO, MARSHALL
 The Kak-Abdullah Conspiracy. Freeway, 1973; Freeway (London), 1974 [Afr.]
 Mark of the Vulture. Freeway, 1974
 New York Necromancy. Freeway, 1974 [NYC]
 The Rape of Sun Lee Fong. Freeway, 1973; Freeway (London), 1974 [Burma]
 Red Plague in Bolivia. Freeway (U.S. & London), 1974 [Bolivia]
 Return of the Opium Wars. Freeway, 1973; Freeway (London), 1974 [China]
 Son of the Flying Tiger. Freeway, 1973; Freeway (London), 1974

MACCABEE, JOHN
 Day One. Bantam, 1978

MACE, GUSTAVE. 1835-1904.
 My First Crime. Vizetelly, 1886 (Translation of "Mon Premier Crime." Paris, 1885.) (See also: R. Millar.)

MACE, HELEN
 And Death Came Too. Hammond, 1961 [Australia]
 Death of a Golden Goose. Hammond, 1965
 House of Hate. Hammond, 1958
 Murder Among Those Present. Hammond, 1957 [Tas.]

MACE, MERLDA. SC: Christine Andersen = CA.
 Blondes Don't Cry. Messner, 1945 CA [Wash. D.C.]
 Headlong for Murder. Messner, 1943 CA [Conn.]
 Motto for Murder. Messner, 1943 [N.Y.]

MACHARD, ALFRED. 1887- .
 The Wolf Man. Clode, 1925; Butterworth, 1925 [Paris]

MACHEN, ARTHUR. Pseudonym of Arthur Llewellyn Jones, 1863-1947. Ref: CA, CC, EM, MC.
 The Three Imposters. Lane, 1895; Roberts, 1895

MACHLIN, MILT. See: Robin Moore.

MACHRAY, ROBERT. 1857- .
 The Ambassador's Glove. Long, 1904
 A Blow over the Heart. Chatto, 1902
 The Disappearance of Lady Diana. Everett, 1909
 -Grace O'Malley, Princess and Pirate. Cassell, 1898; Stokes, 1898
 Her Honour. Chatto, 1907
 Her Secret Life. White, 1913
 The Mystery of Lincoln's Inn. Chatto, 1903; Munro, 1903
 The Mystery of the Middle Temple. Everett, 1908
 The Private Detective. Chatto, 1906
 Sentenced to Death. Chatto, 1910
 -Sir Hector. Constable, 1901
 The Stanhope Gate Mystery. White, 1915
 The Woman Wins. Chatto, 1911

MACIAS, GABRIEL
 Detective Reynold's Hardest Case; or, An Ocean Chase. Street (Magnet), 1900

MACK, CAROL K. and DAVID W. EHRENFELD.
 Mack is a NYC playwright. Ehrenfeld, M.D., Ph.D., is biology professor at Rutgers U., teaches and does research on ecology.
 The Chameleon Variant. Dial, 1980 [Conn.]

MACK, EVALINA. Pseudonym of Lena B(rooke) McNamara, 1891- , q.v. Ref: CA.
 Corpse in the Cove. Arcadia, 1955
 Death Among the Sands. Arcadia, 1957

Death of a Portrait. Arcadia, 1952 [Va.]
Murder in Miniature. Arcadia, 1959

MACK, JOHNNY
 Body in the Boathouse. Paget, 1949
 Fall Guy. Paget, 1949
 Faust of the F.B.I. Hamilton Stafford, 1953
 Payoff. Paget, 1949
 Shakedown. Paget, 1949
 Shamus. Paget, 1949

MACK, THOMAS
 The Spectre Bullet. Gernsback, 1932

MACK, W. GAZLEY
 The Kidnapper, and Railway Line Murder. Stockwell, 1944

MACK, W(ALTER) H(AWLEY). 1906- .
 -Mr. Birdsall Breezes Through. Hillman-Curl, 1937

MACK, WILLARD. 1878-1934.
 Kick-In. French, 1925. (Play; for novelization, see: D. Torbett.)

MACKLIN, MARK
 The Thin Edge of Mania. Ace, 1956 [Miami]

MACKWORTH, JOHN (DOLBEN). 1887- .
 The Axe Is Laid. Longmans (London & NYC), 1925
 Broadcast. Longmans (London & NYC), 1925

MADDEN, ANNE WAKEFIELD
 The Amberley Diamonds. Beagle, 1973 [Eng., 1800s]

MADDEN, CECIL. See: Macgregor Urquhart.

MADDEN, (JERRY) DAVID. 1933- . Ref: CA.
 -Pleasure-Dome. Bobbs, 1979

MADDEN, E(DWARD) S(TANISLAUS). Ref: CA.
 Craig's Spur. Heinemann, 1961; Vanguard, 1961 [Australia]

MADDEROM, GARY. 1937- . Ref: CA.
 The Four Chambered Villain. Macmillan, 1971
 The Jewels That Got Away. Curtis, 1973 [NYC]

MADDOCK, LARRY. Pseudonym of Jack Owen Jardine, 1931- . Ref: CA. SC: Hannibal Fortune and Webley, in all titles.
 The Emerald Elephant Gambit. Ace, 1967
 The Flying Saucer Gambit. Ace, 1966 [2500s]
 The Golden Goddess Gambit. Ace, 1967 [2500s]
 The Time Trap Gambit. Ace, 1969

MADDOCK, LUCIE (LACOSTE)
 Fantine Avenel. Cornhill, 1922

MADDOCK, STEPHEN. Pseudonym of J(ames) M(organ) Walsh, 1897-1952, q.v. Other pseudonym: H. Haverstock Hill, q.v. SC: Insp. Slane, in at least those marked S; Timothy Terrel, in at least those marked TT. Set: Eng.
 Close Shave. Collins, 1952
 Conspirators at Large. Collins, 1937 TT
 Conspirators in Capri. Collins, 1935 TT [It.]
 Conspirators Three. Collins, 1936 TT
 Danger After Dark. Collins, 1934 TT
 Date with a Spy. Collins, 1941 TT
 Doorway to Danger. Collins, 1938 TT [Vienna]
 Drums Beat at Dusk. Collins, 1943 TT
 East of Piccadilly. Collins, 1948 S
 Exit Only. Collins, 1947 S
 The Eye at the Keyhole. Collins, 1935 TT
 Forbidden Frontiers. Collins, 1936 TT
 Gentlemen of the Night. Collins, 1934 TT [Naples, Malta]
 I'll Never Like Friday Again. Collins, 1945 TT
 Keep Your Fingers Crossed. Collins, 1949
 Lamp-Post 592. Collins, 1938 TT
 Overture to Trouble. Collins, 1946 TT
 Private Line. Collins, 1950 S
 Public Mischief. Collins, 1951
 Something on the Stairs. Collins, 1944 TT
 Spades at Midnight. Collins, 1940 TT
 Spies Along the Severn. Collins, 1939 TT
 Step Aside to Death. Collins, 1942
 The White Siren. Collins, 1934 TT
 A Woman of Destiny. Collins, 1933 TT

MADDOW, BEN, 1909- , and JOHN HUSTON, 1906- .
 The Asphalt Jungle. Southern Illinois University, 1980 [Screenplay based on the novel by W. R. Burnett, 1899-1982, q.v.)

MADDUX, BERTON J. 1871-1952.
 The Veil Withdrawn. Dillingham, 1910

MADELEY, JOAN
 The Shining Head. Hale, 1955

MADISON, REX
 The Black Inquisitor. Mellifont, 1943

MADISON, RICK
 Hit the Jackpot. Spencer, 1952
 The Lady Gets Wise. Spencer, 1952
 Save Your Tears. Spencer, 1953
 Set Up for Danger. Spencer, 1952
 Star Witness. Spencer, 1953
 Stranger Beware. Spencer, 1952
 Terror Rides the West Wind. Spencer, 1951

MADREYHIJO, L.
 A Phonographic Mystery. Remington, 1890

MADSEN, AXEL. 1930- . Ref: CA.
 Borderlines. Macmillan, 1975 [Mex.]

MADSEN, DAVID (LAWRENCE). 1929- . Ref: CA.
 Black Plumes. Simon, 1980 (Edgar Allan Poe) [N.Y., 1835-1852]

MAGALI. Pseudonym of Jeanne Elisabeth Marie Josephine Corradot.
 Captive in Paradise. Mystique, 1980 (Translation of "Un Amour Sauvage." Paris, 1967.)
 Caught by Fate. Mystique, 1980 (Translation of "Un Sourire d'Homme." Paris, 1966.)
 The Deadly Pawn. Mystique, 1980 (Translation of "L'Invitee du Week-End." Paris, 1976.)
 In Search of Sybil. Mystique, 1977 (Translation of "Sybil et le Baron des Neiges." Paris, 1961.)
 Loss of Innocence. Mystique, 1978 (Translation of "Le Dechirant Retour." Paris, 1976.)
 The Master of Palowar. Mystique, 1977 (Translation of "Le Miraculeux Voyage." Paris, 1963.)
 Maze of the Past. Mystique, 1980 (Translation of "Un Baiser Pour Cecelia." Paris, 1967.)
 The Moment of Truth. Mystique, 1977 (Translation of "L'Heure de Verite." Paris, 1975.)
 Night of the Storm. Mystique, 1979 (Translation of "Rencontre dans la Brume." Paris, 1975.)
 A Question of Guilt. Mystique, 1980 (Translation of "Un Jour, Tu Sauras..." Paris, 1959.)
 Vanishing Bride. Mystique, 1977 (Translation of "A Quoi Pensais-tu, Marion?" Paris, 1969.)

MAGARSHACK, DAVID. 1899- . Ref: CA. SC: Supt. Mooney, in all titles. Set: Eng.
 Big Ben Strikes Eleven. Constable, 1934
 Death Cuts a Caper. Constable, 1935; Holt, 1935
 Three Dead. Constable, 1937

MAGEE, BRYAN (EDGAR). 1930- . Ref: CA.
 To Live in Danger. Hutchinson, 1960 [Austria]

MAGGIO, JOE. 1938- . Ref: CA.
 Company Man. Putnam, 1972 [Bel. Congo]

MAGGS, DEREK
 Reporting Murder. Fiction House, 1945

MAGILL, MARCUS. Pseudonym of Brian Merrikin Hill, 1896- . Ref: CA, CC. Set: Eng.
 Death-in-the-Box. Knopf (London), 1929; Lippincott, 1930
 I Like a Good Murder. Knopf (London), 1930; Lippincott, 1930
 Murder in Full Flight. Hutchinson, 1932; Lippincott, 1933
 Murder Out of Tune. Hutchinson, 1931; Lippincott, 1931
 Who Shall Hang? Knopf (London), 1929; Lippincott, 1929

MAGNAY, SIR WILLIAM. 1855-1917.
 -The Amazing Duke. Unwin, 1907
 The Black Lake. Paul, 1915
 The Cloak of Darkness. Ward, 1915
 Count Zarka. Ward, 1903; Page, 1903
 The Duke's Dilemma. Long, 1906

The Fall of a Star. Macmillan (London), 1897
-Fauconberg. Ward, 1905
The Fruit of Indiscretion. Paul, 1913
The Heiress of the Season. Smith, Elder, 1899; Appleton, 1899
The Hunt Ball Mystery. Ward, 1918; Brentano's, 1918
The Long Hand. Paul, 1912
-The Man of the Hour. Ward, 1902
The Man-Trap. Smith, Elder, 1900
The Master Spirit. Ward, 1906; Little, 1906
The Mystery of the Unicorn. Ward, 1907
Paul Burdon. Paul, 1912
The Pitfall. Ward, 1908
The Players. Hodder, 1913
-A Poached Peerage. Ward, 1909
The Powers of Mischief. Ward, 1909
The Price of Delusion. Paul, 1914
The Pride of Life. Smith, Elder, 1899
-A Prince of Lovers. Ward, 1905; Little, 1905
The Red Chancellor. Ward, 1901; Brentano's, 1901
The Red Stain. Ward, 1908
Rogues in Arcady. Ward, 1912

MAGNUS, GEORGE G.
-Two in the Dark. Ouseley, 1908

MAGNUSON, JAMES. 1941- .
The Rundown. Dial, 1977

MAGNUSON, TEODORE. Lives in Wash.
A Small Gust of Wind. Bobbs, 1980; Allen, 1981 [Saigon]

MAGOON, CAREY. Joint pseudonym of Elizabeth Carey and Marian Austin Waite Magoon, 1885- .
I Smell the Devil. Farrar, 1943; Cassell, 1949 [Mich., acad.]

MAGOON, MARIAN AUSTIN WAITE. 1885- . Joint pseudonym with Elizabeth Carey: Carey Magoon, q.v.

MAGOWAN, RONALD. SC: Shane Mackenzie, in at least those marked SM.
Barracuda. Hale, 1972 SM
Cage of Violence. Hale, 1976
Fox in the Sea. Hale, 1975 SM
Funeral for a Commissar. Hale, 1970; Roy, 1970 SM
Monopoly to Murder. Hale, 1968 SM
No Flowers on My Grave. Hale, 1977

MAGUIRE, MICHAEL. 1945- . Ref: CA. SC: Simon Drake, in all titles. Set: Eng.
Scratchproof. Allen, 1976; St. Martin's, 1977
Shot Silk. Wingate, 1975
Slaughter Horse. Wingate, 1975

MAGUIRE, P. P.
A Certain Dr. Mellor. Browne & Nolan, 1946

MAHANNAH, FLOYD
The Broken Angel. Macrae Smith, 1957; Boardman, 1959 [Calif.]
The Broken Body; see The Golden Goose
The Golden Goose. Duell, 1951; Boardman, 1952. Also published as: The Broken Body. Signet, 1952 [Calif.]
The Golden Widow. Macrae Smith, 1956; Boardman, 1957
No Luck for a Lady; see The Yellow Hearse
Stopover for Murder. Macrae Smith, 1953; Boardman, 1954 [Calif.]
The Yellow Hearse. Duell, 1950; Boardman, 1951. Also published as: No Luck for a Lady. Signet, 1951 [Calif.]

MAHER, FRANK J. See: Denis J. Cleary.

MAHNER-MONS, HANS. Pseudonym: Hans Possendorf, q.v.

MAHONEY, GENE
Anatomy of an Arsonist. Condor, 1978

MAI, DENYSE
Shadowed by Danger. Mystique, 1979 (Translation of "Un Jour a Portofino." Paris, 1976.)

MAIBAUM, RICHARD. Ref: CA. See: Cyril Hume, 1900-1966.

MAILER, NORMAN. 1923- . Ref: CA.
The Executioner's Song. Little, 1979; Hutchinson, 1979 [Utah]

MAIMANE, ARTHUR
Victims. Allison, 1976

MAINE, CHARLES ERIC. Pseudonym of David McIlwain, 1921- . Other pseudonym: Richard Rayner, q.v. Ref: CA.
Count-Down. Hodder, 1959. U.S. title: Fire Past the Future. Ballantine, 1960 [future]
Fire Past the Future; see Count-Down
The Isotope Man. Hodder, 1957; Lippincott, 1957

MAINWARING, DANIEL (GEOFFREY HOMES). 1902-1977. Pseudonym: Geoffrey Homes, q.v.
One Against the Earth. Long & Smith, 1933 [Calif.]

MAINWARING, MARION. Ref: CA, CC.
Murder at Midyears. Macmillan, 1953; Gollancz, 1954 [New Eng., acad.]
Murder in Pastiche. Macmillan, 1954; Gollancz, 1955 [ship]

MAINWARING, MICHAEL. 1943- .
The Emissary. Allison, 1974

MAIR, ALISTAIR. 1924- . Ref: CA.
The Douglas Affair. Heinemann, 1966; Morrow, 1966 [Scot.]
Where the East Wind Blows. Heinemann, 1972

MAIR, GEORGE B(ROWN). 1914- . Ref: CA. SC: David Grant = DG.
Black Champagne. Jarrolds, 1968; Berkley, 1969 DG
Crimson Jade. Jarrolds, 1971 DG
The Day Krushchev Panicked. Cassell, 1961; Random, 1962
Death's Foot Forward. Jarrolds, 1963; Random, 1964 DG [Moscow]
The Girl from Peking. Jarrolds, 1967; Berkley, 1968 DG [Far East]
Goddesses Never Die. Jarrolds, 1969 DG
The Jade Cat. Pyramid, 1974 [S.F.]
Kisses from Satan. Jarrolds, 1966; Berkley, 1968 DG [Switz.]
Live, Love, and Cry. Jarrolds, 1965; Berkley, 1968 DG [Scot.]
Miss Turquoise. Jarrolds, 1964; Random, 1965 DG [Afr.]
Paradise Spells Danger. Jarrolds, 1973 DG
A Wreath of Camellias. Jarrolds, 1970 DG

MAIR, JOHN. Ref: MC.
Never Come Back. Gollancz, 1941; Little, 1941

MAIS, S(TUART) P(ETRE) B(RODIE). 1885-1975. Ref: CA.
Black Spider. Hutchinson, 1941
-Caper Sauce. Hutchinson, 1948
-Colour Blind. Richards, 1920
Come Love, Come Death. Hutchinson, 1951
-Interlude. Chapman, 1917
Men in Blue Glasses. Hutchinson, 1940
-Old King Cole. Cassell, 1938
Quest Sinister. Richards, 1922
-Rebellion. Richards, 1917
The Three-Coloured Pencil. Eyre, 1937
Who Dies? Hutchinson, 1949 [acad.]

MAITLAND, JAMES A.
The Lawyer's Story; or, The Orphan's Wrongs. Pearson, 1853
-Sartoroe: A Tale of Norway. Peterson, 1858 [Norway]

MAITLAND, OSCAR
The Society Detective. Street, 1889

MAKAGON, THOMAS K.
All Killers Aren't Ugly. Vega, 1963

MAKEE. Pseudonym: Nicholas Carter, q.v.

MAKIN, WILLIAM J(AMES). 1894- . SC: Det. Insp. Evans, in at least those marked E; Det. Insp. Graves, in at least those marked G. Set: Eng.
The Adventure of Red Head of the Red Sea. Jarrolds, 1933. Also published as: Red Head of the Red Sea. Newnes, 1937
The Covent Garden Murder; see Murder at Covent Garden
The Expoits of Jonathan Jow. Pearson, 1936
The Four Brains. Eldon, 1934
Gipsy in Evening Dress. Eldon, 1935 G
Murder at Covent Garden. Jarrolds, 1930. Also published as: The Covent Garden Murder. Newnes, 1938 E
Murder at Full Moon. Eldon, 1937 G
The Price of Exile. First Novel Library, 1922
Queer Mr. Quell. Hodder, 1937; McBride, 1938
Red Head of the Red Sea; see The Adventures of Red Head of the Red Sea
Red Mask. Hamilton, 1935 E

Red Sea Spy. Jarrolds, 1936
Syncopated Love. Jarrolds, 1930

MAKINS, CLIFFORD. 1925- . See: Ted Dexter.

MAKRIS, JOHN N.
Nightshade. Ace, 1953 [Calif.]

MALACHY, FRANK. Pseudonym of Frank McAuliffe, q.v.
Hot Town. Permabooks, 1956

MALAN, ERNESTINE and ALMA K. LEDIG
Cobwebs and Clues. Dorrance, 1944 [New Eng.]

MALCOLM, DAVID
A Fiend Incarnate. Tait, 1895
Fifty Thousand Dollars Ransom. Tait, 1896

MALCOLM, JEAN (EILEEN). Born in Sumatra, came to Scot. as a child; Cambridge graduate; worked in British Civil Service, later a fiction and women's magazine editor in London.
Discourse with Shadows. Doubleday, 1958; Gollancz, 1958 [Frank., 1945]

MALCOLM, MARGARET. Pseudonym of Edith Lyman Kuether, 1915- . Ref: CA.
Headless Beings. Doubleday, 1973 [Scot.]

MALCOLM-SMITH, GEORGE. 1901- . Living in Conn. in 1950s; edited an insurance company periodical.
Come Out, Come Out. Doubleday, 1965. British title: Dividend of Death. Hale, 1966 [Mass.]
Dividend of Death; see Come Out, Come Out
If a Body Meet a Body. Doubleday, 1959; Hale, 1961
The Lady Finger. Doubleday, 1962 [Boston]
Mugs, Molls and Dr. Harvey; see The Square Peg
The Square Peg. Doubleday, 1952. Also published as: Mugs, Molls and Dr. Harvey. Graphic, 1955 [NYC]
The Trouble with Fidelity. Doubleday, 1957; Hale, 1959

MALGAMUKAR, MANOHAR
Spy in Amber. Hind Pocket Books (Delhi), 1971

MALIM, BARBARA. SC: Simon Chard, in at least those marked SC. Set: Eng.
By That Sin. Archer, 1935
Death by Misadventure. Murray, 1934; Macmillan, 1934
Missing from Monte Carlo. Walker, 1929
Murder on Holiday. Murray, 1937 SC
Seven Looked On. Butterworth, 1939 SC
"To This End." Walker, 1927

MALINA, FRED
Murder over Broadway. Phoenix, 1948 [NYC]
Some Like 'Em Shot. Mill, 1949 [Miami]

MALING, ARTHUR (GORDON). 1923- . Ref: CA, TC. SC: Brock Potter = BP.
Bent Man. Harper, 1975; Prior, 1976 [Chi.]
Decoy. Harper, 1969; Joseph, 1971 [Mex.]
Dingdong. Harper, 1974
Go-Between. Harper, 1970; British title: Lambert's Son. Joseph, 1972 [Chi.]
The Koberg Link. Harper, 1979; Gollancz, 1980 BP [NYC]
Lambert's Son; see Go-Between
Loophole. Harper, 1971 [Chi.]
Lucky Devil. Harper, 1978; Gollancz, 1979 BP [Salt Lake City]
The Rheingold Route. Harper, 1979; Gollancz, 1979 [Eng.]
Ripoff. Harper, 1976; Hale, 1977 BP
Schroeder's Game. Harper, 1977; Gollancz, 1977 BP [Phoenix]
The Snowman. Harper, 1973

MALLANDAINE, CATHERINE E.
The Shadow of the Cliff. Christian Knowledge, 1900

MALLANSON, TODD
Ladykiller. Weidenfeld, 1980

MALLARY, AMOS
The Eight Penny Spy. Hale, 1971

MALLAY, MIRIAM
The Web. Vantage, 1977

MALLESON, LUCY BEATRICE. 1899-1973. Pseudonyms: Anthony Gilbert, J. Kilmeny Keith, Anne Meredith, qq.v.

MALLET, ANNE
　House on Eagle Ledge. Belmont, 1974

MALLET, JACQUELINE
　They Can't Hang Me! Comyns, 1947; Harper, 1974

MALLET, LYNDON. SC: Taffin, in both titles.
　Taffin. New English Library pb, 1980
　Taffin's First Law. New English Library, 1980

MALLETT, RICHARD. 1910-   . Newspaper and magazine editor in Eng.
　Watson's Revenge. Aspen, 1974   ss

MALLETTE, GERTRUDE E(THEL). 1887-   .
　Mystery in Blue. Doubleday, 1945

MALLEY, LOUIS
　Horns for the Devil. Appleton, 1951. Also published as: Shadow of the Mafia. Monarch, 1958
　Shadow of the Mafia; see Horns for the Devil
　Shakedown Strip; see Stool Pigeon
　Stool Pigeon. Avon, 1953. Also published as: Shakedown Strip. Avon, 1960 [NYC]
　Tiger in the Streets. Ace, 1957

MALLOCH, PETER. Pseudonym of W(illiam) Murdoch Duncan, 1909-1975, q.v. Other pseudonyms: John Cassells, John Dallas, Neill Graham, Martin Locke, Lovat Marshall, qq.v. SC: Dave Norton, in at least those marked DN.
　The Adjuster. Long, 1970
　Anchor Island. Long, 1962
　Backwash. Long, 1969
　The Big Deal. Long, 1977
　The Big Killing. Long, 1974
　The Big Steal. Long, 1966
　Blood Money. Long, 1962
　Blood on Pale Fingers. Long, 1969 DN
　Break-Through. Long, 1963 [Glasgow]
　Cop-Lover. Long, 1964 [Toronto]
　Death Whispers Softly. Long, 1968
　The Delinquents. Long, 1974
　Die, My Beloved. Long, 1967
　11.20 Glasgow Central. Rich, 1955 [Glasgow]
　Fly Away Death. Long, 1958
　Fugitive's Road. Long, 1963 [Scot.]
　The Grab. Long, 1970
　Hardiman's Landing. Long, 1960 [Montr.]
　Johnny Blood. Long, 1967
　Kickback. Long, 1973
　Killer's Blade. Long, 1975
　Lady of No Compassion. Long, 1966 [Glasgow]
　Murder of a Student. Long, 1968
　Murder of the Man Next Door. Long, 1966
　My Shadow. Long, 1959
　The Nicholas Snatch. Long, 1964
　The Slugger. Long, 1971 DN
　The Sniper. Long, 1965
　Sweet Lady Death. Rich, 1956
　Tread Softly, Death. Rich, 1957
　Two with a Gun. Long, 1971
　Walk In, Death. Rich, 1957 [Scot.]
　Write-Off. Long, 1972

MALLORY, ARTHUR. SC: Dr. Kirke Montgomery = KM.
　Apperson's Folly. Chelsea, 1930 KM [N.Y.]
　The Black Valley Murders. Chelsea, 1930 KM [N.Y.]
　Doctor Krook. Chelsea, 1929
　The Fiery Serpent. Chelsea, 1929
　The House of Carson. Chelsea, 1927
　Mysteries of Black Valley. Chelsea, 1930 KM [N.Y.]

MALLORY, DREW. Pseudonym of Brian (Francis Wynne) Garfield, 1939-   , q.v. Other pseudonyms: John Ives, Frank O'Brian, q.v. See also: Donald E(dwin) Westlake, 1934-   .
　Target Manhattan. Putnam, 1975 [NYC]

MALLORY, KATE
　Sarton Kell. Morrow, 1977

MALLORY, PETER
　Deadly Harvest. Hamlyn, 1979

MALLORY, ROOSEVELT. SC: Radcliff, in all titles.
　Double Trouble. Holloway, 1975
　Harlem Hit. Holloway, 1973 [NYC]
　New Jersey Showdown. Holloway, 1976 [N.J.]
　San Francisco Vendetta. Holloway, 1974 [S.F.]

MALM, DOROTHEA. 1915-   .
　Claire: Memoirs of a Governess. Putnam, 1956; Davies, 1957
　Every Third Thought. Doubleday, 1962; Davies, 1962
　On a Fated Night. Doubleday, 1965; Davies, 1966 [Paris]
　The Paper Mistress. Coward, 1959; Davies, 1960
　To The Castle. Appleton, 1957; Davies, 1955 [Fr.]
　The Woman Question. Appleton, 1957; Davies, 1957

MALMAR, McKNIGHT
　Fog Is a Shroud. Hurst, 1950
　Never Say Die. Hurst, 1944; Coward, 1943 [L.I.]
　The Past Won't Die. Hurst, 1948

MALMBERG, CARL. 1904-   . Pseudonym: Timothy Trent, q.v.

MALO, VINCENT GASPARD
　And Why Not? Barker, 1958; Abelard, 1959 [Paris]
　Murder on the Mistral. Barker, 1957; Abelard, 1958 [Mars.]

MALONEY, RALPH (LISTON). 1927-1973. Ref: CA.
　The Nixon Recession Caper. Norton, 1972 [N.Y.]

MALOT, HECTOR (HENRI). 1830-1907.
　-Baccarat; or, The Gambler's Career. Fox, 1891
　-Doctor Claude. Vizetelly, 1880 (Translation of "Le Docteur Claude." Paris, 1879.)
　-The Woman in the Case. Laird, 1899

MALTZ, ALBERT. 1908-   . See: Malvin (Daniel) Wald, 1927-   .

MALZBERG, BARRY (NORMAN). 1939-   .
　Pseudonyms: Mike Barry, Lee W. Mason, qq.v. See also: Bill Pronzini, 1943-   .

MANCERON, GENEVIEVE
　The Deadlier Sex. Dell, 1961 (Translation of "La Biche." Paris, 1957.) [Fr.]

MANCHESTER, IVY
　Pinecastle. Curtis, 1973

MANCHESTER, WILLIAM (RAYMOND). 1922-   Ref: CA.
　Beard the Lion. Mill, 1958; Cassell, 1959. Also published as: Cairo Intrigue. PB, 1959 [Cairo]
　Cairo Intrigue; see Beard the Lion
　The City of Anger. Ballantine, 1953
　Shadow of the Monsoon. Doubleday, 1956; Cassell, 1956

MANCINI, ANTHONY. 1939-   . Ref: CA. SC: Minnie Santangelo, in both titles, both set in NYC.
　Minnie Santangelo and the Evil Eye. Coward, 1977
　Minnie Santangelo's Mortal Sin. Coward, 1975

MANDE, ELIZABETH ERIN. Pseudonym of Stuart Friedman, 1913-   , q.v.
　The Phantom Room. Popular Library, 1971
　The Spirit of Melissa Norgate. Pyramid, 1972
　The Tower of the Dark Light. Popular Library, 1973

MANDEL, PAUL and SHEILA
　The Black Ship. Random, 1968; Hutchinson, 1969 [Holl., 1943]

MANDEL, SHEILA. See: Paul Mandel.

MANDELKAU, JAMIE
　The Leo Wyoming Caper. Putnam, 1977 [Tex.]

MANDEVILLE, COLIN
　Last Days of New York. Springwood, 1980 [NYC]

MANDEVILLE, D. E.
　Hot Line—Capricorn. Hale, 1972

MANDINO, OG. 1923-   . Ref: CA.
　-The Christ Commission. Lippincott, 1980 [Jerus., 36 A.D.]

MANER, WILLIAM. Ref: CC.
　Die of a Rose. Doubleday, 1970 [Va., acad.]
　The Image Killer. Doubleday, 1968; Hale, 1970 [N.C.]
　There Goes the Bride. Hale, 1973

MANGAT RAI, EDWARD NIRMAL. 1915-   .
　The Lalru Murders. Hind Pocket Books (Delhi), 1973

MANGIONE, JERRE (GERLANDO). 1909-   .
　Ref: CA.
　Night Search. Crown, 1965. British title: To Walk the Night. Muller, 1967

MANKIEWICZ, DON M(ARTIN). 1922-   .
　Ref: CA.
　It Only Hurts a Minute. Putnam, 1966; Deutsch, 1968
　See How They Run. Knopf, 1951
　Trial. Harper, 1955; Deutsch, 1955 [Calif.]

MANKOWITZ, WOLF. 1924-   . Ref: CA.
　Abracadabra. Macmillan (London), 1980
　Raspberry Reich. Macmillan (London), 1979

MANKTELOW, BETTINE
　Death Walked In. French (London), 1979 (Play.)
　They Call It Murder. French (London), 1977 (Play.)

MANLEY-TUCKER, AUDRIE. Pseudonym: Linden Howard, q.v.

MANLY, A(NGIE) STEWART
　Secrets of a Dark Plot in New York Society. Rhodes, 1893. Also published as: Kidnapped; or, Secrets of a Great Mystery. Rhodes, 1899 [NYC]

MANLY, MARLINE. Pseudonym of St. George (Henry) Rathborne, 1854-1938, q.v. Other pseudonym: Doctor Mark Merrick, q.v.
　Old Specie, the Treasury Detective; or, The Harbor Lights of New York. Street (Magnet), 189? [NYC]
　The Poker King; or, A Cool Million at Stake. Street, 1890
　Rube Burrows League; or, The Swamp Angels of Alabama. Street, 1891 [Ala.]
　The Vestibule Limited Mystery. Street (Magnet), 189?

MANN, ABBY
　Kojak. PB, 1974 (Novelization of the TV series.)

MANN, ABEL. Pseudonym of John Creasey, 1908-1973, q.v. Other pseudonyms: Gordon Ashe, M. E. Cooke, Norman Deane, Robert Caine Frazer, Patrick Gill, Michael Halliday, Charles Hogarth, Brian Hope, Colin Hughes, Kyle Hunt, Peter Manton, J. J. Marric, Richard Martin, Rodney Matheson, Anthony Morton, Jeremy York, qq.v.
　Danger Woman. PB, 1966 [Eng.]

MANN, (FRANCIS) ANTHONY. 1914-   . Ref: CA.
　Tiara. Bodley, 1973

MANN, E(RNEST) L.
　The Chislehurst Mystery. Eyre, 1938

MANN, EDWARD ANDREW. 1932-   . Ref: CA.
　The Portals. Simon, 1974; Sidgwick, 1975 [L.A.]

MANN, JACK. Pseudonym of E(velyn) Charles (H.) Vivian, 1882-1947, q.v. Other pseudonym: Charles Cannell, q.v. SC: Rex Coulson = RC; Gregory George Gordon Green = Gs. Set: Eng.
　Coulson Alone. Wright, 1936 RC
　Coulson Goes South. Wright, 1933 RC
　The Dead Man's Chest. Wright, 1934; Godwin, 1935 RC
　Detective Coulson. Wright, 1936 RC
　Egyptian Nights. Wright, 1934 RC [Egypt]
　Gees' First Case. Wright, 1936; Bookfinger, 1970 Gs
　The Glass Too Many. Wright, 1940; Bookfinger, 1973 Gs
　Grey Shapes. Wright, 1937; Bookfinger, 1970 Gs
　Her Ways Are Death. Wright, 1941 Gs
　The Kleinert Case. Wright, 1938 Gs
　Maker of Shadows. Wright, 1938; Bookfinger, 1977 Gs
　Nightmare Farm. Wright, 1937; Bookfinger, 1975 Gs
　The Ninth Life. Wright, 1939; Bookfinger, 1970 Gs
　Reckless Coulson. Wright, 1933 RC

MANN, JESSICA. Ref: CA, TC. SC: Thea Crawford = TC. Set: Eng.
　Captive Audience. Macmillan (London), 1975; McKay, 1975 TC [acad.]

A Charitable End. Collins, 1971; McKay, 1971 [Edin.]
The Eighth Deadly Sin. Macmillan (London), 1976
Mrs. Knox's Profession. Macmillan (London), 1972; McKay, 1972
The Only Security. Macmillan (London), 1973. U.S. title: Troublecross. McKay, 1973 TC [acad.]
The Sticking Place. Macmillan (London), 1974; McKay, 1974
The Sting of Death. Macmillan (London), 1978
Troublecross; see The Only Security

MANN, JOSEPHINE. Pseudonym of Josephine (Mary Wedderburn) Pullein-Thompson, q.v.
A Place with Two Faces. Coronet, 1972; PB, 1974

MANN, LEONARD. 1895-   . Ref: CC.
A Murder in Sydney. Cape, 1937; Doubleday, 1937 [Sydney]

MANN, PATRICK. Pseudonym of Leslie Waller, 1923-   , q.v. Other pseudonym: C. S. Cody, q.v.
Dog Day Afternoon. Delacorte, 1973; Hart-Davis, 1975 [NYC]
Steal Big. St. Martin's, 1981; Hart-Davis, 1978 [Eng.]
-The Vacancy. Putnam, 1973; Hart-Davis, 1975

MANN, PETER. See: Uri Dan.

MANN, RODERICK
Nothing to Declare. Jenkins, 1957

MANNERS, ALEXANDRA. Pseudonym of Anne Rundle, q.v. Other pseudonym: Joanne Marshall, q.v.
Candles in the Wood. Millington, 1975; Putnam, 1974
The Singing Swans. Putnam, 1975 [Scot., 1800s]
The Stone Maiden. Millington, 1974; Putnam, 1973 [Scot., ca.1905]

MANNERS, DAVID X. 1912-   .
Dead to the World. McKay, 1947 [NYC]
Memory of a Scream. Mystery House, 1946 [N.Y.]

MANNERS, GORDON
Murders at the Crab Apple Cafe. Jenkins, 1933

MANNIN, ETHEL (EDITH). 1900-   . Ref: CA.
Mission to Beirut. Hutchinson, 1973 [Beirut]

MANNING, ADELAIDE FRANCES OKE. 1891-1959. Joint pseudonyms with Cyril Henry Coles, 1899-1965: Manning Coles, Francis Gaite, qq.v.

MANNING, ARTHUR
-The Short Madness. Hale, 1960
Tainted Money. Hale, 1963
-We Never Die in the Winter. Jenkins, 1958

MANNING, BRUCE. See: Gwen Bristow, 1903-1980.

MANNING, HILDA. Pseudonym of James Reach, 1909?-1970, q.v. Other pseudonyms: John Rand, Pete Williams, qq.v. Joint pseudonym with Tom (Barnard) Taggart, q.v.: Ross MacRoss, q.v.
Dangerous Ladies. French, 1942 (3-act play.)
Detective in Spite of Himself. French, 1950 (3-act play.)

MANNING, JAMES C.
Blue Invective. Bobbs, 1973

MANNING, MARY
The Last Chronicles of Ballyfungus. Little, 1978; Routledge, 1978

MANNINGHAM, BASIL. Pseudonym of B(asil) H(enry) Homersham, 1902-   , q.v.
Motive for Murder. Hale, 1939

MANNION, JOHN B. See: John P. Evans.

MANNON, M. M. Joint pseudonym of Martha Mannon and Mary Ellen Mannon. SC: Sheriff George White = GW.
The Corpse in the Elevator. Arcadia, 1956 [Calif.]
Here Lies Blood. Bobbs, 1942 GW [Calif.]
Murder on the Program. Bobbs, 1944 GW [Calif.]

MANNON, MARTHA. Joint pseudonym with Mary Ellen Mannon: M. M. Mannon, q.v.

MANNON, MARY ELLEN. Joint pseudonym with Martha Mannon: M. M. Mannon, q.v.

MANOR, JASON. Pseudonym of Oakley M(axwell) Hall, 1920-   , q.v. SC: Steve Summers = SS.
The Girl in the Red Jaguar; see The Red Jaguar
No Halo for Me; see The Pawns of Fear
The Pawns of Fear. Viking, 1955; Secker, 1955. Also published as: No Halo for Me. Popular Library, 1956 SS [Calif.]
The Red Jaguar. Viking, 1954; Secker, 1955. Also published as: The Girl in the Red Jaguar. Popular Library, 1955 SS [Calif.]
Too Dead to Run. Viking, 1953; Secker, 1954 [Calif.]
The Tramplers. Viking, 1956; Secker, 1956 [Calif.]

MANOUSSI, JEAN. See: Louise Jordan Miln, 1864-1933.

MANS, ADRIENNE. Pseudonym of Anneke Luders-Knegtmans.
On the Shores of Night. Walker, 1967; Harrap, 1968 (Translation of "An den Ufern der Nacht.")

MANSFIELD, ELIZABETH. Pseudonym of Paula Schwartz, 1925-   .
My Lord Murderer. Berkley, 1978
The Phantom Lover. Berkley, 1979

MANSFIELD, PAUL H. 1922-   . Ref: CC. Born in Trinidad; photographer, hotel proprietor.
Final Exposure. Collins, 1957; Macmillan, 1958 [Carib.]

MANSON, WILL. House name. SC: Black, in at least those marked B.
The Chinese Conundrum. Caravelle, 1967 (By Howard LeRoy.) B [H. Kong]
The Dangerous One. Caravelle, 1968 B
The Deadly Game. Caravelle, 1967 [Fla.]
The Duke. Caravelle, 1968 [NYC]
The Mathematician. Caravelle, 1967 (By Cole Freedman.)
A Man Called Black. Caravelle, 1967 B [N.Y.]
A Talent for Violence. Tower, 1970 [N.Y.]
A Very Black Deed. Caravelle, 1968 B [Wash. D.C.]

MANTELL, LAURIE [MRS. LORRAINE MANTELL]. 1917?-   . SC: Sgt. Steve Arrow, in all titles, all set in N.Z.
Murder and Chips. Gollancz, 1980; Walker, 1982
Murder in Fancydress. Gollancz, 1978; Walker, 1981
A Murder or Three. Gollancz, 1980; Walker, 1981

MANTINBAND, JAMES M. Pseudonym: Oliver Keystone, q.v.

MANTLE. BEATRICE
In the House of Another. Century, 1920 [West]

MANTON, PETER. Pseudonym of John Creasey, 1908-1973, q.v. Other pseudonyms: Gordon Ashe, M. E. Cooke, Norman Deane, Robert Caine Frazer, Patrick Gill, Michael Halliday, Charles Hogarth, Brian Hope, Colin Hughes, Kyle Hunt, Abel Mann, J. J. Marric, Richard Martin, Rodney Matheson, Anthony Morton, Jeremy York, qq.v. Set: Eng.
The Charity Murders. Wright, 1954
The Circle of Justice. Wright, 1938
The Crime Syndicate. Wright, 1939
The Crooked Killer. Wright, 1954
Death Looks On. Wright, 1939
The Greyvale School Mystery. Low, 1937 [acad.]
The Midget Marvel. Mellifont, 1940
Murder in the Highlands. Wright, 1939 [Scot.]
Murder Manor. Wright, 1937
No Escape from Murder. Wright, 1952
Policeman's Triumph. Wright, 1948
Stand by for Danger. Wright, 1937
Thief in the Night. Wright, 1950
Three Days Terror. Wright, 1938

MANTZ, LEW
Hijacker's Morgue. Hamilton Stafford, 1952
The Snatch. Hamilton Stafford, 1952
Trapped. Hamilton Stafford, 1952

MANVILLE, (ARNOLD) ROGER. 1909-   . Ref: CA.
The Dreamers. Gollancz, 1958; Simon, 1958
The Passion. Heinemann, 1960

MANVILLE, W(ILLIAM) H(ENRY). 1930-   . Pseudonym: Henry Williams, q.v. Ref: CA.
Goodbye. Simon, 1977; H. Hamilton, 1977

MAPPLE, NELSON
-Bye-Bye, Blackbeard! Hurst, 1937
-The Haunted Suit. Hurst, 1939
High Explosive. Hurst, 1938
-Midsummer Mischief. Hurst, 1937

MARA, BERNARD
A Bullet for My Lady. GM, 1955; Fawcett (London), 1956 [Eng.]
French for Murder. GM, 1954 [Paris]
This Gun for Gloria. GM, 1956 [Paris]

MARAIS, MARC
Duel for a Dark Lady. New English Library pb, 1975

MARASCO, ROBERT
Burnt Offerings. Delacorte, 1973; Hodder, 1973 [NYC]
Child's Play. French, 1970 (6-scene play.)
Parlor Games. Delacorte, 1979; Hodder, 1980 [N.Y.]

MARBLE, M(ARGARET) S(HARP). 1913-   .
Die by Inches. Rinehart, 1947; Barker, 1948 [L.A.]
Everybody Makes Mistakes. Rinehart, 1946; Barker, 1947 [L.A.]
-The Lady Forgot. Harper, 1947 [L.A.]

MARCH, JERMYN. Pseudonym of Dorothy Anna Webb. Set: Eng.
The Dago. Hurst, 1928. U.S. title: The Scarlet Thumb. Henkle, 1929
Dear Traitor. Hurst, 1925
The Man Behind the Face. Hurst, 1927
Rust of Murder. Hurst, 1924; Watt, 1925
The Scarlet Thumb; see The Dago

MARCH, LINDSAY. Lives in N.J. with her husband and daughter.
These Cliffs Are Dangerous. Simon, 1973; H. Hamilton, 1973 [Eng.]

MARCH, MAXWELL. Set: Eng.
The Man of Dangerous Secrets; see Other Man's Danger
Other Man's Danger. Collins, 1933. U.S. title: The Man of Dangerous Secrets. Doubleday, 1933
Rogue's Holiday. Collins, 1935; Doubleday, 1935
The Shadow in the House. Collins, 1936; Doubleday, 1936

MARCH, WILLIAM. Pseudonym of William Edward March Campbell, 1894-1954.
The Bad Seed. Rinehart, 1954; H. Hamilton, 1954

MARCHANT, BESSIE. 1862-1941.
-A Dangerous Mission. Blackie, 1918
-From the Scourge of the Tongue. Melrose, 1901
-The Gold-Marked Charm. Blackie, 1918
-Joyce Harrington's Trust. Blackie, 1916
-A Mysterious Inheritance. Blackie, 1915
-The Mystery of the Silver Run. Wells Gardner, 1907
-The Secret of the Everglades. Blackie, 1902; Mershon, 1915 [Fla.]

MARCHANT, CATHERINE. Pseudonym of Catherine (Ann McMullen) Cookson, 1906-   , q.v. Set: Eng.
Evil at Roger's Cross; see The Iron Facade
The Fen Tiger. Macdonald, 1963. U.S. title: The House on the Fens. Lancer, 1965. Reprinted in the U.S. under the British title: Morrow, 1979
Heritage of Folly. Macdonald, 1962; Lancer, 1965
House of Men. Macdonald, 1963; Lancer, 1965
The House on the Fens; see The Fen Tiger
The Iron Facade. Heinemann, 1976. U.S. title: Evil at Roger's Cross. Lancer, 1966
-Miss Martha Mary Crawford. Heinemann, 1975; Morrow, 1976

MARCHANT, SIR HERBERT
His Excellency Regrets... Kimber, 1980

MARCHANT, M. A.
Rudolph and Adelaide; or, The Fort of St. Fernandos. Sherwood, 1811

MARCHANT, WILLIAM. 1923-   . Ref: CA.
  Firebird. Crown, 1980; Allen, 1981
  [Phil.]

MARCHETTI, VICTOR
  The Rope-Dancer. Grosset, 1971; Allen,
  1972

MARCHMONT, ARTHUR W(ILLIAM). 1852-1923.
  -At the Call of Honour. Cassell, 1910
  -Because of Misella. Cassell, 1916
  By Hand Unseen. Ward, 1922
  -By Right of Sword. Hutchinson, 1897;
  Grosset, 1897
  -By Snare of Love. Ward, 1904; Stokes,
  1903
  By Wit of Woman. Ward, 1906; Stokes,
  1906
  The Case of Lady Broadstone. Hodder,
  1910; Empire Book Co., 1908
  -A Courier of Fortune. Ward, 1905;
  Stokes, 1904
  A Dash for a Throne. Hutchinson, 1899;
  New Amsterdam, 1899 [Ger.]
  Dorothy Marlow; or, A Heritage of Per-
  il. Rand, 1900. Also published as:
  The Heritage of Peril. New Amsterdam,
  1901 (British title?)
  The Eagrave Square Mystery. Hodder,
  1912
  -Elfa. Hodder, 1911
  Face to Face with Death. Ogilvie, 1905
  (British title?)
  -The Faith-Healer. Hurst, 1924
  -For Love or Crown. Hutchinson, 1901;
  Stokes, 1901
  -The Greatest Gift. Hutchinson, 1899;
  Buckles, 1900
  -The Heir to the Throne. Ward, 1914
  -Her Sentinel. Cassell, 1916
  The Heritage of Peril; see Dorothy Mar-
  low; or, A Heritage of Peril
  -"His Majesty." Skeffington, 1920
  -An Imperial Marriage. Ward, 1909;
  Dodge, 1909
  In the Cause of Freedom. Ward, 1907;
  Stokes, 1907 [Pol.]
  -In the Name of a Woman. Longmans, 1901;
  Stokes, 1900
  -In the Name of the People. Ward, 1911
  -Isa. London Daily Mail, 1911
  -The Lady Passenger. Hodder, 1915
  The Little Anarchist. Ward, 1907
  Madeline Power. Oliphant Anderson,
  1891; Lippincott, 1900
  The Man Who Was Dead. Cassell, 1907;
  Stokes, 1908
  The Man Without Memory. Ward, 1919
  -A Millionaire Girl. Cassell, 1908
  A Millionaire Mystery. Ward, 1924
  Miser Hoadley's Secret. Methuen, 1904;
  New Amsterdam, 1902
  A Moment's Error; or, The Mystery of
  Mortimer Strange. Methuen, 1904;
  Rand, 1898. Also published as: The
  Mystery of Mortimer Strange; or, A
  Moment's Error. Rand, 1907
  -My Lady of the Yellow Domino. Hodder,
  1914
  My Lost Self. Cassell, 1908; Cupples,
  1908 [Sic.]
  The Mystery of Mortimer Strange; see A
  Moment's Error; or, The Mystery of
  Mortimer Strange
  The Old Mill Mystery. Taylor, 1892
  (British title?)
  Parson Thring's Secret. London Daily
  Mail, 1910; Cassell (NYC), 1895
  -The Price of Freedom; or, In the Grip
  of Hate. New Amsterdam, 1903 (Bri-
  tish title?)
  Prince Punnie. Ward, 1923
  -The Queen's Advocate. Ward, 1904;
  Stokes, 1904
  -The Ruby Heart of Kishgar. Hodder, 1912
  -Sarita, the Carlist. Hutchinson, 1902;
  Stokes, 1902
  Sir Gregory's Silence. Cassell, 1909
  -Sir Jaffray's Wife. Warne, 1895; Rand,
  1898
  A Tight Corner. Cassell, 1915
  -Under the Black Eagle. Ward, 1913
  -The Unguarded Hour. Cassell, 1918
  -When I Was Czar. Ward, 1903; Stokes,
  1903
  -When Love Called. Hodder, 1913
  -When the Empire Crashed. Ward, 1920
  -Who? London Daily Mail, 1911

MARCIN, MAX. 1879-1948. Ref: EM.
  Are You My Wife? Moffat, 1910. British
  title: The Wife He Never Saw. Nash,
  1911
  -Cheating Cheaters. French, 1932 (4-act
  play.)
  The Nightcap, with Guy Bolton, 1884- .
  (3-act play.)
  -The Substitute Prisoner. Moffat, 1911
  The Wife He Never Saw; see Are You My
  Wife?

MARCOTT, JAMES. Pseudonym of Duane R.
  Schermerhorn.
  Hard to Kill. GM, 1975 [Montr.]

MARCUS, A(RTHUR) A. SC: Pete Hunter, in
  all titles.
  Make Way for Murder. Graphic, 1955
  [NYC]
  Post-Mark Homicide; see The Widow Gay
  Walk the Bloody Boulevard. Graphic,
  1951
  The Widow Gay. McKay, 1948. Also pub-
  lished as: Post-Mark Homicide. Graph-
  ic, 1953

MARCUS, CARL. Intelligence agent.
  Mark Castle—Cable Address: Roma. Publishers Export Co., 1966 [Rome]

MARCUS, JOANNA. Pseudonym of Lucilla Andrews. Other pseudonym: Diana Gordon,
  q.v.
  Marsh Blood. Hutchinson, 1980

MARCUS, MORTON. 1936-   . Ref: CA.
  The Brezhnev Memo. Dell, 1980

MARDER, IRVING. Ref: CC.
  The Paris Bit. Collins, 1967; Dodd,
  1968 [Paris]

MAREAN, BEATRICE
  The Tragedies of Oak Hurst. Donohue,
  1891

MARFIELD, DWIGHT (STEELE) 1868-1955. SC:
  Gail McGurk = GM; Dudley Brent = DB;
  Major Krim = K; Inspector Skane = S.
  The Ghost on the Balcony. Dutton, 1939
  K [Calif.]
  The Man with a Paper Skull. Dutton,
  1932 S,GM,DB [NYC]
  The Mandarin's Sapphire. Dutton, 1938
  S [N.Y.]
  Mystery of King Cobra. Dutton, 1933
  DB,S,K [NYC]
  Mystery of the East Wind. Dutton, 1930
  DB,GM,S [NYC]
  The Sword in the Pool. Dutton, 1932
  DB,GM,S [NYC]

MARGOLIN, PHILLIP
  The Heartstone. PB, 1978 [U.S., 1960]

MARIE, JEANNE. Pseudonym of Marie Bea-
  trice Wilson, 1922-   . Ref: CA.
  Arrow of Terror. Lenox Hill, 1973; Rem-
  ploy, 1974
  Black for a Bride. Lenox Hill, 1973;
  Remploy, 1974
  Wait for Me, Wendy. Lenox Hill, 1974;
  Remploy, 1974

MARIN, A. C. Pseudonym of Alfred Coppel,
  1921-   , q.v.
  The Clash of Distant Thunder. Harcourt,
  1968; Heinemann, 1969
  Rise with the Wind. Harcourt, 1969;
  Heinemann, 1969 [Cent. Am.]
  A Storm of Spears. Harcourt, 1971;
  Hale, 1973 [Calif., acad.]

MARIN, MUNA LEE DE MUNOZ. Joint pseudonym
  with Maurice C. Guiness: Newton
  Gayle, q.v.

MARINER, DAVID. Pseudonym of David Mac-
  Leod Smith, 1920-   . Ref: CA.
  The Beaufort Dossier. Hale, 1973;
  Zebra, 1974
  The Chatham Rats. Hale, 1969. U.S.
  title: Operation Scorpio. Pinnacle,
  1975 [WWII]
  Countdown 1000; see A Shackleton Called
  Sheila
  Devil's Bread. Hale, 1969. U.S. title:
  The Yaroslav Incident. Zebra, 1974
  The Last Bridge; see A White Lie and No
  Glory
  Operation Scorpio; see The Chatham Rats
  A Shackleton Called Sheila. Hale, 1970.
  U.S. title: Countdown 1000. Pinnacle,
  1974
  Sinister Charade. Hale, 1979
  Symbol of Vengeance. Hale, 1975
  A White Lie and No Glory. Hale, 1971.
  U.S. title: The Last Bridge. Pin-
  nacle, 1974
  The Yaroslav Incident; see Devil's
  Bread

MARINER-SCARRITT, ELIZABETH
  Quid Est. Abbey, 1902

MARINO, NICK. Pseudonym of Will(iam
  Charles) Oursler, 1913-   , q.v.
  Joint pseudonym with Margaret Scott:
  Gale Gallagher, q.v. SC: Mike Mac-
  auley, in both titles.

City Limits. Pyramid, 1958; Digit,
  1958 (Written by Richard Deming,
  1915-   , q.v., from an outline by
  Oursler.) [Midwest]
One Way Street. Holt, 1952 [Midwest]

MARINO, SUSAN. Pseudonym of Julie (M.)
  Ellis, q.v. Other pseudonyms: Susan
  Marvin, Susan Richard, qq.v.
  Vendetta Castle. Avon, 1971

MARIO, QUEENA. 1896-1951. Metropolitan
  Opera star, later teacher and writer
  in Conn.
  Death Drops Delilah. Dutton, 1944
  [Conn.]
  Murder in the Opera House. Dutton, 1934
  [NYC, theatre]
  Murder Meets Mephisto. Dutton, 1942
  [NYC]

MARION, ELIZABETH. 1916-   . Born in
  Wash.
  The Keys to the House. Crowell, 1944;
  Hale, 1948 [Wash.]

MARION, FRANCES. 1886-1973. Ref: CA.
  The Secret Six. Grosset, 1931 (Novelization of the movie.)

MARK, GEOFFREY. 1928-   .
  The Veils of Fear. Long, 1960

MARKALL, WILL
  While There Is Life. Gollancz, 1930

MARKEY, MORRIS
  Unhurrying Chase. Pony, 1946

MARKHAM, ROBERT. Pseudonym of Kingsley
  (William) Amis, 1922-   , q.v.
  SC: James Bond (continuation of the
  character created by Ian Fleming,
  1908-1964, q.v.) = JB.
  Colonel Sun. Cape, 1968; Harper, 1968
  JB [Greece]

MARKHAM, VIRGIL. 1899-   . Ref: CC, MP.
  SC: Myles Rusby = MR.
  The Black Door. Knopf, 1930. British
  title: Shock! Collins, 1930 [Eng.]
  The Dead Are Prowling. Collins, 1934
  [Vt.]
  The Deadly Jest. Collins, 1935 MR
  [Eng.]
  Death in the Dusk. Knopf (NYC & Lon-
  don), 1928 [Wales]
  The Devil Drives. Knopf, 1932; Collins,
  1932 [Eng.]
  Inspector Rusby's Finale. Farrar, 1933;
  Collins, 1933 MR [Eng.]
  Red Warning. Farrar, 1933. British
  title: Song of Doom. Collins, 1932
  [Fr.]
  -The Scamp. Macmillan, 1926; Parsons,
  1926 [Eng., ca.1720]
  Shock!; see The Black Door
  Snatch. Collins, 1936 [Eng.]
  Song of Doom; see Red Warning

MARKO, ZEKIAL
  Scratch at Thief. GM, 1961. Also pub-
  lished as: Once a Thief. GM, 1965
  [S.F.]

MARKS, ALAN
  The Antenna Syndrome. Belmont, 1979
  -Skyraiders. Belmont, 1979

MARKS, HANNAH K.
  Triad. PB, 1980 [Calif.]

MARKS, PERCY. 1891-1956.
  Knave of Diamonds. Reynal, 1943

MARKS, PETER
  Collector's Choice. Random, 1972; H.
  Hamilton, 1972

MARKSMAN, H. CARSON
  The Lust of Treasure. Allan, 1934

MARKSON, DAVID (MERRILL). 1927-   . Ref:
  CA. SC: Harry Fannin, in at least
  those marked HF.
  Epitaph for a Dead Beat. Dell, 1961
  HF [NYC]
  Epitaph for a Tramp. Dell, 1959. Also
  published as: Fannin. Belmont, 1971
  HF [NYC]
  Fannin; see Epitaph for a Tramp
  Going Down. Holt, 1970 [Mex.]
  Miss Doll, Go Home. Dell, 1965 HF

MARKSTEIN, GEORGE. Military correspondent, then feature writer, story consultant, script editor, and series
  creator for British TV.
  Chance Awakening. Souvenir, 1977; Ballantine hc, 1978
  The Cooler. Souvenir, 1974; Doubleday,
  1974 [Eng., 1944]

The Goering Testament. Bodley, 1978; Ballantine hc, 1979
The Man from Yesterday. Souvenir, 1976
Traitor; see Traitor for a Cause
Traitor for a Cause. Bodley, 1979. U.S. title: Traitor. Ballantine, 1981

MARLAND, DOUGLAS. Pseudonym: Nick Carter, q.v.

MARLER, MICHAEL
Code Name: Mamba. Hale, 1979

MARLETT, MELBA (BALMAT). 1909-   . SC: Sarah O'Brien = SO.
Another Day Toward Dying. Doubleday, 1943. British title: Witness in Peril. Cherry Tree, 1948 SO
Death Has a Thousand Doors. Doubleday, 1941 SO
Death Is in the Garden. Doubleday, 1951
The Devil Builds a Chapel. Doubleday, 1942 [Ohio]
Escape While I Can. Doubleday, 1944 [Mich.]
The Frightened Ones. Doubleday, 1956 ss
Tomorrow Will Be Monday. Doubleday, 1946
Witness in Peril; see Another Day Toward Dying

MARLOW, EDWINA. Pseudonym of T(om) E. Huff, 1938?-   , q.v. Other pseudonyms: Beatrice Parker, Katherine St. Clair, qq.v.
Danger at Dahlkari. Putnam, 1975 [India, 1800s]
Falconridge. Ace, 1969 [Eng., 1800s]
The Lady of Lyon House. Ace, 1970 [Eng., 1800s]
The Master of Phoenix Hall. Ace, 1968 [Eng., 1888]
Midnight at Mallycourt. Berkley/Putnam, 1975 [Eng., 1800s]
When Emmalyn Remembers. Ace, 1970

MARLOW, SIDNEY. Pseudonym of Paschal Heston Coggins, 1852-1917.
-Harry Ambler; or, The Stolen Deed. Penn, 1890. Also published as: Harry Ambler and How He Saved the Homestead. Penn, 1893
Harry Ambler and How He Saved the Homestead; see Harry Ambler
-The Moncasket Mystery and How Tom Hardy Solved It. Penn, 1912

MARLOWE, ANN. Born in Canada; wife of Stephen Marlowe, 1928-   , q.v.
Thunder in the Kerk. Dodd, 1979; New English Library, 1979 [Holl.]
The Winnowing Winds. Dodd, 1978; New English Library, 1978 [Switz.]

MARLOWE, CHARLES. Pseudonym of Harriett Jay, 1857-1932. See: Robert (William) Buchanan, 1841-1901.

MARLOWE, DAN J(AMES). 1914-   . Ref: CA, EM, TC. SC: Earl Drake = ED; Johnny Killain = JK.
Backfire. Berkley, 1961
Death Deep Down. GM, 1965 [NYC]
Doom Service. Avon, 1960 JK [NYC]
Doorway to Death. Avon, 1959; Digit, 1959 JK [NYC]
The Fatal Frails. Avon, 1960 JK [NYC]
Flashpoint. GM, 1970. Also published as: Operation Flashpoint. GM, 1972; Coronet, 1972 ED [NYC]
Four for the Money. GM, 1966 [Nev.]
Killer with a Key. Avon, 1959 JK [NYC]
The Name of the Game Is Death. GM, 1962; Muller pb, 1963. Also published as: Operation Overkill. Coronet, 1973 ED [Fla.]
Never Live Twice. GM, 1964 [Fla.]
One Endless Hour. GM, 1969; Gold Lion, 1973. Also published as: Operation Endless Hour. Coronet, 1975 ED
Operation Breakthrough. GM, 1971; Coronet, 1972 ED
Operation Checkmate. GM, 1972; Coronet, 1973 ED [Formosa]
Operation Counterpunch. GM, 1976 ED [San Antonio]
Operation Deathmaker. GM, 1975; Coronet, 1977 ED [L.A.]
Operation Drumfire. GM, 1972; Coronet, 1972 ED [Calif.]
Operation Endless Hour; see One Endless Hour
Operation Fireball. GM, 1969; Coronet, 1972 ED
Operation Flashpoint; see Flashpoint
Operation Hammerlock. GM, 1974; Coronet, 1975 ED [Mex.]
Operation Overkill; see The Name of the Game Is Death
Operation Stranglehold. GM, 1973; Coronet, 1974 ED [Sp.]

Operation Whiplash. GM, 1973; Coronet, 1974 ED [Fla.]
The Raven Is a Blood Red Bird, with William Odell, q.v. GM, 1967 [Athens]
Route of the Red Gold. GM, 1967 [Carib.]
Shake a Crooked Town. Avon, 1961 JK [N.Y.]
Strongarm. GM, 1963
The Vengeance Man. GM, 1966 [S.C.]

MARLOWE, DEREK. 1938-   . Ref: CA, TC.
A Dandy in Aspic. Gollancz, 1966; Putnam, 1966 (U.S. and British texts differ considerably.)
The Disappearance; see Echoes of Celandine
Do You Remember England? Cape, 1972; Viking, 1972
Echoes of Celandine. Cape, 1970; Viking, 1970. Also published as: The Disappearance. Penguin, 1977
Nightshade. Cape, 1975; Viking, 1976 [Haiti]
Somebody's Sister. Cape, 1974; Viking, 1974 [S.F.]

MARLOWE, FRANCIS. SC: "Doc" Summers, in at least those marked DS.
Adventure Mysterious. Gray, 1934
-The Brig Jane May. Jarrolds, 1911
The Crime of Philip Garrison. Gray, 1935 DS
Crooked Business. Gramol, 1933
Crooked Company. Gramol, 1933
The Hatton Garden Mystery. Gray, 1934 DS
In Pursuit of a Million. Gray, 1936 DS
The Man Who Lost an Hour. Aldine, 1926
The Secret of the Sandhills. Low, 1907
Seven Red-Headed Men. Gramol, 1934
The Son-in-Law Syndicate. Gramol, 1934
-The Sunset Express. Nelson, 1925

MARLOWE, GREG. SC: Greg Marlowe, in all titles.
Behind the Enemy. Hamilton Stafford, 1952
Burma Battle. Hamilton Stafford, 1953 [Burma]
Death-Mask of War. Hamilton Stafford, 1952
Espionage! Hamilton Stafford, 1953 [Can.]

MARLOWE, HUGH. Pseudonym of Harry Patterson, 1929-   , q.v. Other pseudonyms: Martin Fallon, James Graham, Jack Higgins, qq.v.
A Candle for the Dead. Abelard (London & NYC), 1966. Also published as: The Violent Enemy, as by Jack Higgins. Hodder pb, 1969
Passage by Night. Abelard (London & NYC), 1964. Reprinted as by Jack Higgins: GM, 1977 [Carib.]
Seven Pillars to Hell. Abelard (London & NYC), 1963 [Saud. Arab.]
The Violent Enemy (as by Jack Higgins); see A Candle for the Dead

MARLOWE, PIERS. British writer of crime features for newspapers and magazines. SC: Supt. Frank Drury and Insp. Bill Hazard, in at least those marked D&H. Ref: CC. Set: Eng.
Cash My Chips, Croupier. Hale, 1969
The Dead Don't Scare. Gifford, 1963 D&H
Demon in the Blood. Paul, 1955
The Double Thirteen. Low, 1947
Hire Me a Hearse. Hale, 1968 D&H
Killer in the Shade. Hale, 1973
A Knife for Your Heart. Gifford, 1966 D&H
Loaded Dice. Low, 1949
The Men in Her Death. Gifford, 1964 D&H
Promise to Kill. Gifford, 1965 D&H

MARLOWE, REX
All or Nothing. Spencer, 1953
Big Time Girl. Spencer, 1952
Bullets Speak Louder. Spencer, 1950
Homicide Dragnet. Spencer, 1952
Identity Unknown. Spencer, 1952
Perilous Assignment. Spencer, 1952
Vengeance Is Mine. Spencer, 1950

MARLOWE, STEPHEN. 1928-   . Name originally: Milton Lesser. Pseudonyms: Andrew Frazer, Jason Ridgway, C. H. Thames, qq.v. See also: Richard S(cott) Prather, 1921-   ; and: Ellery Queen. Ref: CA, TC. SC: Chester Drum = CD.
Blonde Bait. Avon, 1959
Catch the Brass Ring. Ace, 1954 [NYC]
The Cawthorn Journals. Prentice-Hall, 1975; Allen, 1976. Also published as: Too Many Chiefs. New English Library pb, 1977 [Mex.]
Come Over, Red Rover. Macmillan, 1968

Danger Is My Line. GM, 1960; Muller pb, 1961 CD [Ice.]
Dead on Arrival. Ace, 1956
Death Is My Comrade. GM, 1960; Muller pb, 1961 CD [Russ.]
Drum Beat—Berlin. GM, 1964 CD [Berlin]
Drum Beat—Dominique. GM, 1965 CD [Paris]
Drum Beat—Erica. GM, 1967 CD
Drum Beat—Madrid. GM, 1966 CD [Madrid]
Drum Beat—Marianne. GM, 1968 CD [Yugos.]
Francesca. GM, 1963; Muller pb, 1963 CD [Switz.]
Homicide Is My Game. GM, 1959; Muller pb, 1960 CD [Wash. D.C.]
Jeopardy Is My Job. GM, 1962; Muller pb, 1963 CD [Sp.]
Killers Are My Meat. GM, 1957; Fawcett (London), 1958 CD [India]
The Man with No Shadow. Prentice-Hall, 1974; Allen, 1974
Manhunt Is My Mission. GM, 1961; Muller pb, 1962 CD [Saud. Arab.]
Mecca for Murder. GM, 1956; Fawcett (London), 1957 CD [Wash. D.C.]
Model for Murder. Graphic, 1955 [NYC]
Murder Is My Dish. GM, 1957 CD [S. Am.]
Passport to Peril. Crest, 1959 [Vienna]
Peril Is My Pay. GM, 1960; Muller pb, 1961 CD [Rome]
The Search for Bruno Heidler. Macmillan, 1966; Boardman, 1967 [Fr.]
The Second Longest Night. GM, 1955; Fawcett (London), 1958 CD
The Summit. Geis, 1970 [Switz.]
Terror Is My Trade. GM, 1958; Muller pb, 1960 CD
Too Many Chiefs; see The Cawthorn Journals
Translation. Prentice-Hall, 1976; Allen, 1977 [Conn.]
Trouble Is My Name. GM, 1957; Fawcett (London), 1958 CD [Ger.]
Turn Left for Murder. Ace, 1955 [NYC]
The Valkyrie Encounter. Putnam, 1978; New English Library, 1978 [Berlin, 1944]
Violence Is My Business. GM, 1958; Fawcett (London), 1959 CD [Wash. D.C.]

MARMOR, ARNOLD. Pseudonym: Nick Carter, q.v.

MARNAN, BASIL
-A Daughter of the Veldt. Heinemann, 1901; Holt, 1901
A Fair Freebooter. Cassell, 1902
-The Resident Magistrate. Hurst, 1902

MARQUAND, JOHN P(HILLIPS). 1893-1960. Ref: CA, CC, DD, EM, MP, TC. SC: Mr. Moto = M.
Don't Ask Questions. Hale, 1941
It's Loaded, Mr. Bauer. Hale, 1949 [S. Am.]
Last Laugh, Mr. Moto. Little, 1942; Hale, 1943 M [Carib.]
The Last of Mr. Moto; see Stopover: Tokyo
-Ming Yellow. Little, 1935; Dickson, 1935
Mr. Moto Is So Sorry. Little, 1938; Hale, 1939 M
Mr. Moto Takes a Hand; see No Hero
No Hero. Little, 1935. British title: Mr. Moto Takes a Hand. Hale, 1940. Also published as: Your Turn, Mr. Moto. Berkley, 1963 M [Far East]
Right You Are, Mr. Moto; see Stopover: Tokyo
Stopover: Tokyo. Little, 1957; Collins, 1957. Also published as: The Last of Mr. Moto. Berkley, 1963. And as: Right You Are, Mr. Moto. Popular Library, 1977 M [Tokyo]
Thank You, Mr. Moto. Little, 1936; Jenkins, 1937 M [Peking]
Think Fast, Mr. Moto. Little, 1937; Hale, 1938 M [Haw.]
Your Turn, Mr. Moto; see No Hero

MARQUIS, DON(ALD R. P.). 1878-1937. Ref: CA.
The Cruise of the Jasper B. Appleton (NYC & London), 1916

MARQUIS, MAX
The Traitor Machine. Hamlyn, 1980

MARR, R.
Death at Salterton Court. Everybody's, 1945

MARR, RICHARD. Pseudonym: "Burmar", q.v.

MARRIC, J. J. Pseudonym of John Creasey, 1908-1973. Other pseudonyms: Gordon Ashe, M. E. Cooke, Norman Deane, Robert Caine Frazer, Patrick Gill, Michael Halliday, Charles Hogarth, Brian Hope, Colin Hughes, Kyle Hunt,

MARRINER, BRIAN
Abel Mann, Peter Manton, Richard Martin, Rodney Mattheson, Anthony Morton, Jeremy York, qq.v. SC: Commander George Gideon, in all titles (see also: William Vivian Butler, 1927-   ; and the John Creasey entry). Set: Eng.
Gideon of Scotland Yard; see Gideon's Day
Gideon's Art. Hodder, 1971; Harper, 1971
Gideon's Badge. Hodder, 1966; Harper, 1965
Gideon's Day. Hodder, 1955; Harper, 1955. Also published as: Gideon of Scotland Yard. Berkley, 1958
Gideon's Drive. Hodder, 1976; Harper, 1976
Gideon's Fire. Hodder, 1961; Harper, 1961
Gideon's Fog. Hodder, 1975; Harper, 1975
Gideon's Lot. Hodder, 1965; Harper, 1964
Gideon's March. Hodder, 1962; Harper, 1962
Gideon's Men. Hodder, 1972; Harper, 1972
Gideon's Month. Hodder, 1958; Harper, 1958
Gideon's Night. Hodder, 1957; Harper, 1957
Gideon's Power. Hodder, 1969; Harper, 1969
Gideon's Press. Hodder, 1973; Harper, 1973
Gideon's Ride. Hodder, 1963; Harper, 1963
Gideon's Risk. Hodder, 1960; Harper, 1960
Gideon's River. Hodder, 1968; Harper, 1968
Gideon's Sport. Hodder, 1970; Harper, 1970
Gideon's Staff. Hodder, 1959; Harper, 1959
Gideon's Vote. Hodder, 1964; Harper, 1964
Gideon's Week. Hodder, 1956; Harper, 1956. Also published as: Seven Days to Death. Pyramid, 1958
Gideon's Wrath. Hodder, 1967; Harper, 1967
Seven Days to Death; see Gideon's Week

MARRINER, BRIAN
A Splinter of Ice. Hale, 1975

MARRIOTT, CRITTENDEN. 1867-1932.
Via Berlin. Shores, 1917

MARRIOTT, H(ERBERT) P(HILIP) FITZGERALD
-The Iron Detective of Germany. Ballantyne, 1908 [future]

MARRIOTT, JAMES WILLIAM. 1884-1953. Pseudonym: Roger Wray, q.v.

MARRIOTT, TAM. See: Adele Blood.

MARRIOTT-WATSON, H(ENRY) B(RERETON).
See: H(enry) B(rereton) Marriott Watson, 1863-1921.

MARRYAT, FLORENCE. Pseudonym of Mrs. Florence Marryat Church Lean, 1837-1899.
Blindfold. White, 1890; Lovell, 1890
-The Blood of the Vampire. Hutchinson, 1897
-Driven to Bay. White, 1887; Munro, 1887
-A Fatal Silence. Farran, 1891; Hovenden, 1891
The Hampstead Mystery. White, 1894
-In the Name of Liberty. Digby, 1897
-Iris the Avenger. Hutchinson, 1894
-The Lost Diamonds, with Charles Ogilvie. Ludgate Monthly, 1891
On Circumstantial Evidence. White, 1889; Lovell, 1889
-The Poison of Asps. Appleton, 1871 (British title?)
-The Root of All Evil. Tinsley, 1880; Munro, 1891
-A Scarlet Sin. Blackett, 1890; Lovell, 1890

MARS, ALASTAIR. 1915-   .
Arctic Submarine. Elek, 1955
Atomic Submarine. Elek, 1957. U.S. title: Fire in Anger. Mill, 1958
Fire in Anger; see Atomic Submarine
Submarine at Bay. Elek, 1956

MARSDEN, ANTONY. Pseudonym of Graham Sutton. SC: Insp. Buck, in at least those marked B; Jim Beverley, in at least those marked JB. Set: Eng.
Death on the Downs. Jarrolds, 1929 B
Death Strikes from the Rear. Low, 1934 B
The Man in the Sandhills. Jarrolds, 1927; Boni, 1927 JB
The Mercenary. Jarrolds, 1931
The Moonstone Mystery. Jarrolds, 1928 JB
The Mycroft Murder Case. Low, 1935
Salter's Folly. Jarrolds, 1927
The Six-Hour Mystery. Jarrolds, 1929
Swooning Venus. Low, 1932
Thieves' Justice. Jarrolds, 1929

MARSDEN, JOHN PENNINGTON
Job Lot Sketches and Stories. Hallowell, 1892 ss, one criminous

MARSH, ANNE
Room 12a. Pearson, 1939

MARSH, CHARLES L(EONARD). 1854?-1930.
A Gentleman Juror. Rand, 1899

MARSH, JAMES J. Pseudonym of Joseph R. Marshall. Reporter, magazine writer and editor; in public-relations.
The Peking Switch. McKay, 1972

MARSH, JEAN. Pseudonym of Evelyn Marshall, 1897-   . Ref: CA. Set: Eng.
Death Among the Stars. Long, 1955
Death at Peak Hour. Long, 1957
Death Stalks the Bride. Long, 1943
Death Visits the Circus. Long, 1953
Identity Unwanted. Long, 1951
Murder Next Door. Long, 1933
The Pattern Is Murder. Long, 1953
The Shore House Mystery. Hamilton, 1929

MARSH, JOHN. 1907-   . Joint pseudonym with Florence Shepherd: Harrington Hastings, q.v. Ref: CA. SC: Ray Felton, in at least those marked RF; Simon Luck, in at least those marked SL. Set: Eng.
-Body Made Alive: A Study in the Macabre. Stanley Smith, 1936
The Brain of Paul Menoloff. Robertson, 1953
By the World Condemned. Amalgamated, 1949
City of Fear. Gifford, 1958 RF
The Cruise of the Carefree. Ward, 1955
Girl in a Net. Hale, 1962 SL
-A Glimpse of Paradise. Boardman, 1944
The Golden Teddybear. Boardman, 1965
Hate Thy Neighbor. Hale, 1969
The Hidden Answer. Gifford, 1956
House of Echoes. Gifford, 1956
-Lonely Pathway. Paul, 1933
-Maiden Armour. Paul, 1932
-Many Parts. Swan, 1946
Master of High Beck. Hale, 1969
Monk's Hollow. Gifford, 1968; Ace, 1969
Murderer's Maze. Gifford, 1957 RF
Not My Murder. Gifford, 1967
Operation Snatch. Gifford, 1958 RF [Scot.]
The Reluctant Executioner. Hale, 1959 SL
-Return They Must. Paul, 1933
The Secret of the Seven Sisters. Ward, 1950
Shipwrecked Schoolship. Swan, 1949
Small and Deadly. Hale, 1960 RF
Two Mrs. Farrells. Boardman, 1946
-The Wrong That Was Done. Leng, 1935

MARSH, (EDITH) NGAIO. 1899-1982. Ref: all except MM. SC: Insp./Supt. Roderick Alleyn, in all titles. Set: Eng.
Artists in Crime. Bles, 1938; Furman, 1938
Black As He's Painted. Collins, 1974; Little, 1974
The Bride of Death; see Spinsters in Jeopardy
Clutch of Constables. Collins, 1968; Little, 1969 [ship]
Colour Scheme. Collins, 1943; Little, 1943 [N.Z.]
Dead Water. Collins, 1964; Little, 1963
Death and the Dancing Footman. Collins, 1942; Little, 1941
Death at the Bar. Collins, 1940; Little, 1940
Death at the Dolphin. Collins, 1967. U.S. title: Killer Dolphin. Little, 1966
Death in a White Tie. Bles, 1938; Furman, 1938
Death in Ecstasy. Bles, 1936; Sheridan, 1941
Death of a Fool; see Off with His Head
Death of a Peer; see Surfeit of Lampreys
Died in the Wool. Collins, 1945; Little, 1945 [N.Z.]
Enter a Murderer. Bles, 1935; PB, 1941
False Scent. Collins, 1960; Little, 1959
Final Curtain. Collins, 1947; Little, 1947
Grave Mistake. Collins, 1978; Little, 1978
Hand in Glove. Collins, 1962; Little, 1962
Killer Dolphin; see Death at the Dolphin
Last Ditch. Collins, 1977; Little, 1977
A Man Lay Dead. Bles, 1934; Sheridan, 1942
Night at the Vulcan; see Opening Night
The Nursing-Home Murder, with Dr. H(enry) Jellett, 1872-1948. Bles, 1935; Sheridan, 1941 [hosp.]
Off with His Head. Collins, 1957. U.S. title: Death of a Fool. Little, 1956
Opening Night. Collins, 1951. U.S. title: Night at the Vulcan. Little, 1951 [theatre]
Overture to Death. Collins, 1939; Furman, 1939
Photo-Finish. Collins, 1980; Little, 1980 [N.Z.]
Scales of Justice. Collins, 1955; Little, 1955
Singing in the Shrouds. Collins, 1959; Little, 1958 [ship]
Spinsters in Jeopardy. Collins, 1954; Little, 1953. Also published as: The Bride of Death. Mercury, 1955 [Fr.]
Surfeit of Lampreys. Collins, 1941. U.S. title: Death of a Peer. Little, 1940
Swing, Brother, Swing. Collins, 1949. U.S. title: A Wreath for Rivera. Little, 1949. Reprinted in the U.S. under the British title: PB, 1951
Tied up in Tinsel. Collins, 1972; Little, 1972
Vintage Murder. Bles, 1937; Sheridan, 1940 [N.Z., theatre]
When in Rome. Collins, 1970; Little, 1971 [Rome]
A Wreath for Rivera; see Swing, Brother, Swing

MARSH, PATRICK. Pseudonym of Leslie Hiscock, 1902-   .
Breakdown. Longmans (London), 1952; Longmans (NYC), 1953

MARSH, REBECCA. Pseudonym of William Arthur Neubauer, 1916-   . Ref: CA.
The Emerald Ring. Arcadia, 1964
Footsteps to Romance. Arcadia, 1966
Lady Detective. Arcadia, 1960

MARSH, RICHARD. 1867-1915. SC: Augustus Champnell, in at least those marked AC; Judith Lee, in at least those marked JL. Set: Eng.
-Ada Vernham, Actress. Long, 1900; Page, 1900
The Adventures of Augustus Short. Treherne, 1902 ss, some slightly criminous
The Adventures of Judith Lee. Methuen, 1916 ss JL
Amusement Only. Hurst, 1901 ss
The Ape and the Diamond; see The Devil's Diamond
-Apron-Strings. Long, 1920
An Aristocratic Detective. Bell, 1900 AC, in first four stories
The Beetle. Skeffington, 1897; Mansfield, 1898 AC
Between the Dark and the Daylight. Long, 1902
Both Sides of the Veil. Methuen, 1901 ss
A Case of Identity; see The Twickenham Peerage
The Chase of the Ruby. Skeffington, 1900
-Coming of Age. Long, 1916
The Coward Behind the Curtain. Methuen, 1908
The Crime and the Criminal. Ward, 1897
Curios: Some Strange Adventures of Two Bachelors. Long, 1898 ss
Cuthbert Grahame's Will; see A Duel
The Dagger of Fate. Westbrook, 1922 (British title?)
The Datchet Diamonds. Ward, 1898
-The Deacon's Daughter. Long, 1917
The Death Whistle. Treherne, 1903. U.S. title: The Whistle of Fate. Street, 1906
The Devil's Diamond. Henry, 1893. U.S. title: The Ape and the Diamond. Street, ca.1928
-A Drama of the Telephone and other tales. Digby Long, 1911 ss
A Duel. Methuen, 1904. Also published as: Cuthbert Grahame's Will. Pearson, 1930
-The Flying Girl. Ward, 1915
Frivolities. Bowden, 1899. Also published as: The Purse Which Was Found and other stories. Pearson, 1918 ss
The Garden of Mystery. Long, 1906
Garnered. Methuen, 1904 ss, one criminous

The Girl and the Miracle. Methuen, 1907
The Girl in the Blue Dress. Long, 1909 ss
The Goddess: A Demon. White, 1900
The Great Temptation. Unwin, 1916; Brentano's, 1916
-A Hero of Romance. Ward, 1900
-His Love or His Life. Chatto, 1915
The House of Mystery. White, 1898
If It Please You. Methuen, 1913 ss, some criminous
In Full Cry. White, 1899; Street, 1928
In the Service of Love. Methuen, 1904
The Interrupted Kiss. Cassell, 1909
-The Joss: A Reversion. White, 1901
Judith Lee: Some Pages from Her Life. Methuen, 1912 ss JL
Justice—Suspended. Chatto, 1913
Live Men's Shoes. Methuen, 1910
-Love in Fetters. Cassell, 1915
The Lovely Mrs. Blake. Cassell, 1910
A Man with Nine Lives. Ward, 1915
Margot—and Her Judges. Chatto, 1914
The Marquis of Putney. Methuen, 1905
Marvels and Mysteries. Methuen, 1900 ss
A Master of Deception. Cassell, 1913
-A Metamorphosis. Methuen, 1903
-Miss Arnott's Marriage. Long, 1904
-Molly's Husband. Cassell, 1914
Mrs. Musgrave—and Her Husband. Pioneer, 1894; Appleton, 1895
The Mystery of Philip Bennion's Death. Ward, 1897. Also published as: Philip Bennion's Death. Ward, 1899
On the Jury. Methuen, 1918
Outwitted. Long, 1919
Philip Bennion's Death; see The Mystery of Philip Bennion's Death
The Purse Which Was Found and other stories; see Frivolities
-The Romance of a Maid of Honour. Long, 1907
A Royal Indiscretion. Methuen, 1909
The Seen and the Unseen. Methuen, 1900; New Amsterdam, 1900 AC
A Strange Wooing; see The Strange Wooing of Mary Bowler
The Strange Wooing of Mary Bowler. Pearson, 1895. U.S. title: A Strange Wooing. Street, 1929
-The Surprising Husband. Methuen, 1908
The Twickenham Peerage. Methuen, 1902. U.S. title: A Case of Identity. Street, 19??
-Twin Sisters. Cassell, 1911
-Violet Forster's Lover. Cassell, 1912
Who Killed Lady Poynder? Appleton, 1907 (British title?)
The Whistle of Fate; see The Death Whistle
The Woman in the Car. Unwin, 1914
The Woman with One Hand, and Mr. Ely's Engagement. Bowden, 1899 (Two novelets.)

MARSH, ROBERT W.
-MacLaren's Men. Belmont, 1979

MARSHALL, ARCHIBALD. Pseudonym of Arthur Hammond Marshall, 1866-1934. See also: Horace Annesley Vachell, 1861-1955. Ref: EM. Set: Eng.
Big Peter. Collins, 1922; Dodd, 1922
The House of Merrilees. Rivers, 1905; Turner, 1905
The Mystery of Redmarsh Farm. Paul, 1911; Dodd, 1925
Nothing Hid. Collins, 1934; Houghton, 1935
The Terrors and other stories. Methuen, 1913 ss, some criminous

MARSHALL, ARTHUR HAMMOND. 1866-1934. Pseudonym: Archibald Marshall, q.v.

MARSHALL, BRUCE. 1899- . Ref: CA.
The Accounting. Houghton, 1958 [Paris, 1933]
The Month of the Falling Leaves. Constable, 1963; Doubleday, 1963 [Pol.]
-Operation Iscariot. Constable, 1974

MARSHALL, GEORGE HUNT. Joint pseudonym with George Worthing Yates, q.v.: Peter Hunt, q.v.

MARSHALL, EDISON (TESLA). 1894-1967. Ref: CA.
The Death Bell. Garden City, 1924 [Scot.]

MARSHALL, (DAVID) EDWARD. 1870-1933.
-The Middle Wall. Dillingham, 1904

MARSHALL, EVELYN. 1897- . Pseudonym: Jean Marsh, q.v.

MARSHALL, MRS. FRANCIS BRIDGES. Pseudonym: Alan St. Aubyn, q.v.

MARSHALL, HAMILTON
For Very Life. Chapman, 1871

MARSHALL, HURST
Enter Two Murderers. Longmans, 1937

MARSHALL, IAN. Set: Eng.
The Strange Case of Vintrix Polbarton. Nelson, 1929
The Vengeance of Kali. Nelson, 1930

MARSHALL, JOANNE. Pseudonym of Anne Rundle, q.v. Other pseudonym: Alexandra Manners, q.v.
Follow a Shadow. Collins, 1974; Putnam, 1974 [Sp.]
Last Act. Collins, 1976; Putnam, 1976
The Peacock Bed. Collins, 1978; St. Martin's, 1978

MARSHALL, JOSEPH R. Pseudonym: James J. Marsh, q.v.

MARSHALL, LOVAT. Pseudonym of W(illiam) Murdoch Duncan, 1909-1975, q.v. Other pseudonyms: John Cassells, John Dallas, Neill Graham, Martin Locke, Peter Malloch, qq.v. SC: Sugar Kane, in all titles. Set: Eng.
Blood on the Blotter. Hale, 1968
Date with Murder. Hale, 1973
The Dead Are Dangerous. Hale, 1966
The Dead Are Silent. Hale, 1966
Death Casts a Shadow. Hale, 1972
Death Is For Ever. Hale, 1969
Death Strikes in Darkness. Hale, 1965
Key to Murder. Hale, 1975
Ladies Can Be Dangerous. Hale, 1964
Loose Lady Death. Hale, 1973
Moment for Murder. Hale, 1972
Money Means Murder. Hale, 1968
Murder in Triplicate. Hale, 1963
Murder Is the Reason. Hale, 1964
Murder Mission. Hale, 1975
Murder of a Lady. Hale, 1967
Murder to Order. Hale, 1975
Murder Town. Hale, 1974
Murder's Just for Cops. Hale, 1971
Murder's Out of Season. Hale, 1970
The Strangler. Hale, 1974
Sugar Cuts the Corners. Long, 1957
Sugar for the Lady. Hurst, 1955
Sugar on the Carpet. Hurst, 1956
Sugar on the Cuff. Hale, 1960
Sugar on the Kill. Hale, 1961
Sugar on the Loose. Hale, 1962
Sugar on the Prowl. Hale, 1962
Sugar on the Target. Long, 1958

MARSHALL, MARGUERITE MOOERS. 1887-1964.
Murder Without Morals. Clifford Lewis, 1947

MARSHALL, RAYMOND. Pseudonym of Rene Brabazon Raymond, 1906- . Other pseudonyms: James Hadley Chase, James L. Docherty, Ambrose Grant, qq.v. Most of the titles below were subsequently reprinted as by James Hadley Chase. SC: Martin "Brick Top" Corridon = MC; Don Micklem = DM.
Blondes' Requiem. Jarrolds, 1945; Crown, 1946 [U.S.]
But a Short Time to Live. Jarrolds, 1951
Hit and Run. Hale, 1958 [U.S.]
In a Vain Shadow. Jarrolds, 1951
Just the Way It Is. Jarrolds, 1944 [U.S.]
Lady, Here's Your Wreath. Jarrolds, 1940 [U.S.]
Make the Corpse Walk. Jarrolds, 1946
Mallory. Jarrolds, 1950 MC
Mission to Siena. Hale, 1955 DM [It.]
Mission to Venice. Hale, 1954 DM [Venice]
Never Trust a Woman. Harlequin, 1957 (Retitled Canadian edition of ?)
No Business of Mine. Jarrolds, 1947
The Paw in the Bottle. Jarrolds, 1949
The Pickup. Harlequin, 1955 (Retitled Canadian edition of ?)
Ruthless. Harlequin, 1955 (Retitled Canadian edition of ?)
The Sucker Punch. Jarrolds, 1954 [Calif.]
The Things Men Do. Jarrolds, 1953
Trusted Like the Fox. Jarrolds, 1948
The Wary Transgressor. Jarrolds, 1952 [It.]
Why Pick on Me? Jarrolds, 1951 MC
You Find Him—I'll Fix Him. Hale, 1956 [Naples]

MARSHALL, ROBERT, 1863-1910, ANTHONY HOPE, q.v., and COMYNS CARR. Anthony Hope is the pseudonym of Sir Anthony Hope Hawkins, 1863-1933.
Gruesome Grange; or, The Banished Earl. Sphere, 1906 (Musical play.)

MARSHALL, SIDNEY
Some Like It Hot. Morrow, 1941 [Chi.]

MARSHALL, WILLIAM (LEONARD). 1944- Born in Australia, living in Eng.; journalist, scriptwriter, playwright. SC: Insp. Harry Peiffer = HP, all set in H. Kong.
-The Age of Death. Macmillan (London), 1970; Viking, 1971
-The Fire Circle. Macmillan (London), 1969
Gelignite. H. Hamilton, 1976; Holt, 1977 HP
The Hatchet Man. H. Hamilton, 1976; Holt, 1977 HP
-The Middle Kingdom. Macmillan (London), 1971
-Shanghai. H. Hamilton, 1979 [Shanghai]
Skulduggery. H. Hamilton, 1979; Holt, 1980 HP
Thin Air. H. Hamilton, 1977; Holt, 1978 HP
Yellowthread Street. H. Hamilton, 1975; Holt, 1976 HP

MARSLAND, AMY (LOUISE). 1924- . Ref: CA.
Cache-Cache. Doubleday, 1980; Hale, 1981 [Fr.]

MARSON, G(ERALD) F(RANCIS)
Ghosts, Ghouls and Gallows. Rider, 1946 ss

MARSTEN, RICHARD. Pseudonym of Evan Hunter, 1926- , q.v. Other pseudonyms: Curt Cannon, Hunt Collins, Ezra Hannon, Ed McBain, qq.v.
Big Man. PB, 1959; Penguin, 1978, as by Ed McBain [NYC]
Death of a Nurse; see Murder in the Navy
Even the Wicked. Permabooks, 1958; Penguin, 1980, as by Ed McBain [Mass.]
Murder in the Navy. GM, 1955. Also published as: Death of a Nurse, as by Ed McBain. PB, 1968; Coronet, 1972 [Va.]
Runaway Black. GM, 1954; Red Seal, 1957. Reprinted as by Ed McBain: PB, 1968; Coronet, 1971 [NYC]
The Spiked Heel. Holt, 1956; Constable, 1957
Vanishing Ladies. Permabooks, 1957; Boardman, 1961. Reprinted as by Ed McBain: Penguin, 1982

MARTEL, CHARLES. Pseudonym of Thomas Delf, 1810-1865.
The Detective's Note-Book. Ward, 1860 ss
Diary of an Ex-Detective. Ward, 1860 ss

MARTEN, JACQUELINE
Let the Crags Comb out Her Dainty Hair. Popular Library, 1975 [Eng., ca.1810]

MARTEN, JON C(HISHOLM). See: Cornelius Conyn.

MARTENS, ANNE (LOUISE) COULTER. 1906- . Pseudonyms: Rilla Carlisle, Jane Kendall, Anne Reynolds, qq.v.
Phantom of the High School. Dramatic, 1955 (3-act play.) [acad.]
The Right Kind of House. Dramatic, 1963 (1-act play based on a story by Henry Slesar, 1927- , q.v.)

MARTENS, PAUL. Pseudonym of Stephen Southwold, 1887-1964, q.v. Other pseudonym: Neil Bell, q.v.
-Death Rocks the Cradle. Collins, 1933
The Truth About My Father. Collins, 1934. Reprinted as by Neil Bell: Collins, 1936

MARTENSON, JAN
Death Calls on the Witches. Godalming, 1979 (Translation of "Haxhammaren." Stockholm, 1975.)

MARTIN, A(RCHIBALD) E(DWARD). 1885- . Ref: CC, DD. SC: Linley = L.
The Bridal Bed Murders. Simon, 1954. British title: The Chinese Bed Mysteries. Reinhardt, 1955 L [Australia]
The Chinese Bed Mysteries; see The Bridal Bed Murders
The Curious Crime. Doubleday, 1952; Muller, 1953 [Australia]
Death in the Limelight. Simon, 1946; Reinhardt, 1956 [Syd.]
The Outsiders. Simon, 1945; Nimmo, 1948 L [Eng.]
Sinners Never Die. Simon, 1944; Nimmo, 1947 [Australia, 1895]

MARTIN, A. RICHARD. SC: Branders Noble, in both titles. Set: Eng.
The Cassiodore Case. Methuen, 1927; McBride, 1928

The Death of the Claimant. Methuen, 1929; McBride, 1929

MARTIN, ABSALOM
Kastle Krags. Duffield, 1922 [Fla.]

MARTIN, AYLWIN LEE. SC: Matt Hughes, in at least those marked MH.
-Black Blood. Low, 1929
The Crimson Frame. GM, 1952 MH [L.A.]
Death for a Hussy. Graphic, 1952 MH
Death on a Ferris Wheel. GM, 1951; Fawcett (London), 1954 MH [L.A.]
Fear Comes Calling. GM, 1952 MH [L.A.]
-Mad Interlude. Low, 1930

MARTIN, CARL (L.). 1892-   . Born in Ind.; lived for many years in Ark.
Delta Deputies. Greenwich, 1959 ss [La.]

MARTIN, CAROLINE
The Blue Ridge Mystery. Weed, 1897

MARTIN, DAVID
Murder at the Wedding. Star, 1979 (Novelization of the TV serial.)

MARTIN, DESMOND
Death When You Want It. Hale, 1974
No Hero. Boardman, 1957
Prescription for Death. Hale, 1972
Wine, Women, and Murder. Boardman, 1955

MARTIN, DON
"Shed No Tears." Murray & Gee, 1948. Also published as: Blonde Menace. Red Circle, 1949

MARTIN, DOROTHEA. Pseudonym of Kathleen (Douglas) Hewitt, 1893-   , q.v.
Black Sunshine. Mathews, 1933

MARTIN, DWIGHT.   -ca.1979. A news periodical Asia expert.
The Triad Imperative. Congdon, 1980; Hamlyn, 1982

MARTIN, ED
To Hell with the Law. Columbine, 1939

MARTIN, ETHEL BOWYER
Nightmare House. Ace, 1975

MARTIN, FRANCIS
Ace in the Hole. Hamilton Stafford, 1954
Blood on the Sand. Hamilton Stafford, 1954

MARTIN, H(ECTOR) P(AULIN)
Encore to Murder. Skeffington, 1939
Time for Murder. Skeffington, 1938

MARTIN, HANSJORG. 1920-   . Born in Leipzig, journalist and playwright; author of more than a dozen thrillers in Germany.
Sleeping Girls Don't Lie. St. Martin's, 1976 (Translation of "Kein Schnaps fur Tamara." Germany, 1966.) [Ger., 1951]

MARTIN, HELEN R(IEMENSNYDER). 1868-1939.
The House on the Marsh. Dodd, 1936 [Pa.]

MARTIN, HENRIETTE and GITA LEWIS
The Naked Eye. Greenberg, 1950; Jarrolds, 1951

MARTIN, IAN KENNEDY. 1936-   . Ref: CA.
SC: Jack Regan = JR.
Billions. Heinemann, 1979; Atheneum, 1980 [Can.]
The Deal of the Century; see Regan and the Deal of the Century
The Manhattan File; see Regan and the Manhattan File
Regan. Barker, 1975; Holt, 1975. Also published as: The Sweeney. Futura, 1975 JR
Regan and the Deal of the Century. Barker, 1977. U.S. title: The Deal of the Century. Holt, 1977 JR
Regan and the Manhattan File. Barker, 1975. U.S. title: The Manhattan File. Holt, 1976 JR [NYC]
Rekill. Heinemann, 1977; Putnam, 1977 [Alb.]
The Sweeney; see Regan

MARTIN, JAMES E. 1936-   . High school teacher turned policeman and investigator in Ohio.
The 95 File. Simon, 1973; Collins, 1973 [Ohio]

MARTIN, KAY. Born in Chicago, author of some 72 books, living in Calif. in 1970s.
Vanessa. Putnam, 1974 [Eng.]

MARTIN, L(INCOLN) W(ILLIAM) and N(ORMAN) S(OREN) LYNRAVN
Murder on Mount Capita. Angus (Sydney), 1944; Quality (London), 1946 [Australia]

MARTIN, LANE
Bait. C. Warren, 1951
Chicago Rod. C. Warren, 1951
Verdict. C. Warren, 1951

MARTIN, NELL COLUMBIA BOYER. 1890-   .
Pseudonym: Columbia Boyer, q.v.

MARTIN, OLIVER. Pseudonym of Ernest Davies, 1873-   , q.v. SC: Timothy Cullinan, in at least those marked TC. Set: Eng.
The Iron Door. Hodder, 1923 TC
The Mermaid. Faber, 1926 TC
-Middle Distance. Benn, 1929

MARTIN, PHILIP. SC: John Kline, in both titles, which are novelizations of the "Kline" TV series.
Gangsters. Sphere, 1977
Gangsters #2. Sphere, 1977

MARTIN, RALPH
The Man Who Haunted Himself. Award, 1970; Tandem, 1970 (Novelization of the movie, adapted from "The Case of Mr. Pelham," by Anthony Armstrong, q.v.)

MARTIN, RICHARD. Pseudonym of John Creasey, 1908-1973, q.v. Other pseudonyms: Gordon Ashe, M. E. Cooke, Norman Deane, Robert Caine Frazer, Patrick Gill, Michael Halliday, Charles Hogarth, Brian Hope, Colin Hughes, Kyle Hunt, Abel Mann, Peter Manton, J. J. Marric, Rodney Mattheson, Anthony Morton, Jeremy York, qq.v.
Adrian and Jonathan. Hodder, 1954
Keys to Crime. Earl, 1947
Vote for Murder. Earl, 1948

MARTIN, ROBERT (LEE). 1908-1976. Ref: CA. Pseudonym: Lee Roberts, q.v. SC: Jim Bennett, in at least those marked JB.
Bargain for Death. Curtis, 1972; Hale, 1964 JB
Catch a Killer. Dodd, 1956; Hale, 1958 JB [Columbus]
A Coffin for Two. Curtis, 1972; Hale, 1962 JB [Ohio]
Dark Dream. Dodd, 1951; Muller, 1954 JB [Ohio]
The Echoing Shore. Dodd, 1955; Muller, 1956. Also published as: The Tough Die Hard. Bantam, 1957 [Mich.]
Hand-Picked for Murder. Dodd, 1957; Hale, 1958 JB [Ohio]
Just a Corpse at Twilight. Dodd, 1955; Muller, 1957
A Key to the Morgue. Dodd, 1958; Hale, 1960 JB [Cleve.]
Killer Among Us. Dodd, 1958; Hale, 1959 JB
She, Me, and Murder. Curtis, 1971; Hale, 1962 JB
Sleep, My Love. Dodd, 1953; Muller, 1955 JB [Cleve.]
Tears for the Bride. Dodd, 1954; Muller, 1955 JB [Ohio]
To Have and to Kill. Dodd, 1960; Hale, 1961 JB [Ohio]
The Tough Die Hard; see The Echoing Shore
The Widow and the Web. Dodd, 1954; Muller, 1956 JB

MARTIN, ROBERT BERNARD. 1918-   . Pseudonym: Robert Bernard, q.v.

MARTIN, SHANE. Pseudonym of George H(enry) Johnston, 1912-1970, q.v. SC: Prof. Ronald Challis, in all titles.
The Man Made of Tin. Collins, 1958
Mourner's Voyage; see A Wake for Mourning
The Myth Is Murder. Collins, 1959. U.S. title: The Third Statue. Morrow, 1959 [Greece]
The Saracen Shadow. Collins, 1957 [Fr.]
The Third Statue; see The Myth Is Murder
Twelve Girls in the Garden. Collins, 1957; Morrow, 1957
A Wake for Mourning. Collins, 1962. U.S. title: Mourner's Voyage. Doubleday, 1963 [ship]

MARTIN, STUART. 1882-   . Ref: CC.
-Babe Jardine. Selwyn, 1927
Capital Punishment. Hutchinson, 1931
The Fifteen Cells. Selwyn, 1927; Harper, 1928 ss
The Green Ghost. Selwyn, 1928

The Hangman's Guests. Hutchinson, 1931; Harper, 1931 ss
-Inheritance. Ouseley, 1912
The Mystery of Clough Mills. Mascot, 1920
Only Seven Were Hanged. Harper, 1929 (British title?)
-Pirates of the Main. Pearson, 1924
-Princess of Paradise. Selwyn, 1928
-The Surf Queen. Hurst, 1925
The Trial of Scotland Yard. Hutchinson, 1930; Harper, 1930 ss

MARTIN, THOM(AS FRANCIS). 1934-   .
Ref: CA.
Naked When We Die. Monarch, 1963

MARTIN, THOMAS HECTOR. 1913-   . Pseudonyms: Peter Saxon, Martin Thomas, qq.v.

MARTIN, TROY KENNEDY
The Italian Job, with Ken(neth) Wlaschin, q.v. Sphere, 1969; Signet, 1969 (Novelization of the movie.)
Z Cars. Trust, 1963 (Novelization of the TV series.)

MARTIN, WILLIAM. 1950-   .
Pack Bay. Crown, 1980 [Boston]

MARTINEZ, AL. 1929-   . Ref: CA.
Jigsaw John. Tarcher, 1975 [L.A.]

MARTINEZ, S(ALLY) A. 1938-   . Ref: CA.
Target for Terror. Major, 1976 [L.A.]

MARTING, RUTH LENORE. 1907-   . Pseudonym: Hilea Bailey, q.v.

MARTINI, TERI. 1930-   . Pseudonym: Alison King, q.v.

MARTOFF, NICKOLI. 1922-   . Pseudonym: Nick Mayo, q.v.

MARTON, GEORGE. 1900-   . Ref: CA.
Alarum. Allen, 1977
Catch Me a Spy, with Tibor Meray. Allen, 1971; Harper, 1969
The Janus Pope. Allen, 1980; Dell, 1979
The Obelisk Conspiracy, with Michael Burren. Allen, 1975; Stuart, 1976 [Fr.]
The Raven Never More, with Tibor Meray. Spearman, 1966
Three-Cornered Cover, with Christopher Felix (pseudonym). Allen, 1973; Holt, 1972

MARTYN, DON. Pseudonym of Barbara Martyn Borbolla.
House of Shadows. Hale, 1969
Nightmare Fiesta. Hale, 1967
No Guest at the Villa. Hale, 1971
Only at Sunset. Hale, 1970
Operation Castanets. Hale, 1966
Sinister Legacy. Hale, 1968 [Sp.]
Treachery at Guadamonte. Hale, 1965

MARTYN, FREDERIC
A Burglar in Baulk. Pearson, 1910
A Holiday in Gaol. Methuen, 1911; Macmillan, 1911
The Reminiscences of a Rogue. Routledge, 1908

MARTYN, OLIVER. Pseudonym of Herbert Oliver White, 1885-   . Professor at Irish university; writer.
The Body in the Pound. Eldon, 1933. U.S. title: The Man They Couldn't Hang. Morrow, 1933

MARTYN, WYNDHAM. 1875-   . Born in Eng., educated in mining engineering; spent most of adult life in U.S. SC: Christopher Bond = CB; Anthony Trent = AT.
-All the World to Nothing. Low, 1913; Little, 1912
Anthony Trent: Avenger. Jenkins, 1928 AT
Anthony Trent, Master Criminal. Jenkins, 1922; Moffat, 1918 AT [NYC]
The Bathurst Complex. Jenkins, 1924. U.S. title: The Murder in Beacon Street. McBride, 1930 [Boston]
The Blue Ridge Crime. Jenkins, 1937 AT
Cairo Crisis. Jenkins, 1945 CB [Cairo]
Capture. Jenkins, 1940 CB
Christopher Bond, Adventurer. Jenkins, 1933 CB
The Chromium Cat. Jenkins, 1952 CB [L.A.]
Criminals All. Jenkins, 1935 AT
Death by the Lake. Jenkins, 1934 AT [Can.]
The Death Fear. Jenkins, 1929; McBride, 1929 AT [U.S.]
The Denmede Mystery. Jenkins, 1936 CB

The Ghost City Killings. Jenkins, 1940 AT
The Great Ling Plot. Jenkins, 1933 AT
The Headland House Affair. Jenkins, 1941 AT
The House of Secrets. Jenkins, 1936 AT
The Last Scourge. Jenkins, 1946 AT [N.Y.]
The Man Outside. Dodd, 1910
Manhunt in Murder. Jenkins, 1950; Roy, 1958 AT
The Marrowby Myth. Jenkins, 1938 CB
Men Without Faces. Jenkins, 1943 AT [U.S.]
The Murder in Beacon Street; see The Bathurst Complex
Murder Island. Jenkins, 1929; McBride, 1929 AT [Maine]
Murder Walks the Deck. Jenkins, 1938 AT [ship]
The Mysterious Mr. Garland. Jenkins, 1923 AT
Nightmare Castle. Jenkins, 1935 AT
Noonday Devils. Jenkins, 1939 CB
The Old Manor Crime. Jenkins, 1937 AT
The Recluse of Fifth Avenue. Jenkins, 1925; McBride, 1929 [NYC]
The Return of Anthony Trent. Jenkins, 1923; Barse, 1925 AT [L.I.]
The Scarlett Murder. Jenkins, 1931 AT [N.J.]
The Secret of the Silver Car. Jenkins, 1922; Moffat, 1920 AT
Shadow Agent. Jenkins, 1941 CB
The Social Storming. Jenkins, 1930
The Spies of Peace. Jenkins, 1934 CB
Stones of Enchantment. Jenkins, 1948 AT [Belg. Congo]
Trent Fights Again. Jenkins, 1939 AT
Trent of the Lone Hand. Jenkins, 1927 AT
The Trent Trail. Jenkins, 1930; McBride, 1930 AT
The Triumphant Prodigal. Jenkins, 1928 [NYC]
Under Cover. Jarrolds, 1914; Little, 1914 (Novelization of the play by Roi Cooper Megrue, 1883-1927, q.v.)

MARVELL, ANDREW
Minimum Man; or, Time to Be Gone. Gollancz, 1938

MARVELL, HOLT. Pseudonym of Eric Maschwitz, 1901-1969, q.v. See also: Val (Henry) Gielgud, 1900-1981.

MARVIN, DWIGHT EDWARDS. 1851-1940.
-Prof. Slagg of London. Broadway, 1908

MARVIN, SUSAN. Pseudonym of Julie (M.) Ellis, q.v. Other pseudonyms: Susan Marino, Susan Richard, qq.v.
Chalet Bougy-Villars. Zebra, 1975 [Switz.]
Chateau in the Shadows. Dell, 1969 [Can.]
The Secret of Chateau Laval. Avon, 1973
The Secret of the Villa Como. Lancer, 1966 [It.]
Summer of Fear. Dell, 1971 [Fr.]
Where Is Holly Carleton? Beagle, 1974

MARY, JULES. 1851-1922.
The Mendon Mystery. Vizetelly, 1888

MASCHWITZ, ERIC. 1901-1969. Pseudonym: Holt Marvell. See: Val (Henry) Gielgud, 1900-1981.
Little Red Monkey, with Bevis Winter, 1918- , q.v. Jenkins, 1953 (Novelization of Maschwitz's TV play.)

MASCOTT, TRINA
The Wife Who Ran Away. Dell, 1975 [Calif.]

MASH, MAURICE H. B. Joint pseudonym with Willan George Bosworth, 1904- : Maurice Worth, q.v.

MASIELLO, JOSEPH
Family Trouble. Emporium, 1974 [Boston]

MASKE, JOHN. SC: Duncan Cainsforth = DC; Jeremy Flack = JF; Clarence E. Hemingway = CH.
The Cherbourg Mystery. Rich, 1934 JF,CH [Fr.]
The Dinard Mystery. Rich, 1933 DC
Ghost of a Cardinal. Rich, 1935 JF,CH
The Saint-Malo Mystery. Rich, 1933 JF,DC [Fr.]

MASON, A(LFRED) E(DWARD) W(OODLEY). 1865-1948. Ref: all except CA. SC: Insp. Hanaud = H.
The Affair at the Semiramis Hotel; see The Four Corners of the World
At the Villa Rose. Hodder, 1910; Scribner, 1910. 4-act play version: Hodder, 1928 H [Fr.]
Blanche de Maletroit. Capper, 1894 (1-act play based on the story "The Sire de Maletroit's Door" by Robert Louis Stevenson, 1850-1894, q.v.)
The Clock; see The Four Corners of the World
Dilemmas. Hodder, 1934; Doubleday, 1935 ss
Ensign Knightley and other stories. Constable, 1901; Stokes, 1901 ss, some criminous
The Four Corners of the World. Hodder, 1917; Scribner, 1917 ss (Two stories in this collection were also published separately as little books: The Affair at the Semiramis Hotel. Scribner, 1917, 77 pp., is an H story; The Clock, Paget, 1910, 12 pp., is not.
The House in Lordship Lane. Hodder, 1946; Dodd, 1946 H
The House of the Arrow. Hodder, 1924; Doran, 1924 H [Fr.]
No Other Tiger. Hodder, 1927; Doran, 1927 [Fr.]
The Prisoner in the Opal. Hodder, 1928; Doubleday, 1928 H [Fr.]
-Running Water. Hodder, 1907; Century, 1907
The Sapphire. Hodder, 1933; Doubleday, 1933 [India]
The Secret Fear. Doubleday, 1940 (22 pp.)
The Summons. Hodder, 1920; Doran, 1920
They Wouldn't Be Chessmen. Hodder, 1935; Doubleday, 1935 H [Fr.]
-The Watchers. Arrowsmith, 1899; Stokes, 1899
The Winding Stair. Hodder, 1923; Doran, 1923 [Afr.]
The Witness for the Defence. Hodder, 1913; Scribner, 1914. 4-act play version: French, 1913

MASON, ALEXANDER
Losers Keepers. Tower, 1980 [Afr.]
The Mexican Connection. Leisure, 1977

MASON, ARTHUR CHARLES. 1879- . Pseudonym: Mason Scrope, q.v.

MASON, BENJAMIN FRANKLIN. 1852-1927.
Through War to Peace. Pacific Press, 1891 (Sequel to title below.)
The Village Mystery; or, The Spectres of St. Argyle. Whiting, 1887

MASON, BEVERLY. Pseudonym: Mary Bishop, q.v.

MASON, BURNHAM F.
The Stroke of a Knife. Street (Magnet)

MASON, CAROLINE ATWATER. 1853-1939.
-The Mystery of Miss Motte. Page, 1909

MASON, CHARLES. Pseudonym: S. C. Mason, q.v.

MASON, (SYDNEY) CHARLES. 1911- .
Death in Regatta Week. Long, 1960

MASON, CHARLES WELCH. 1866- . Pseudonym: Mr. M—., q.v.

MASON, CLIFFORD
When Love Was Not Enough. Playboy, 1980 [NYC]

MASON, COLIN. 1926- .
Hostage. Macmillan (London), 1973; Walker, 1973 [Mid. East]

MASON, DAVID
The Blitzlicht Passage. Pyramid, 1976

MASON, EDITH HELEN. 1895- . Pseudonym: Hilary Mason, q.v.

MASON, GREGORY. Joint pseudonym of Doris Meek and Adrienne Jones, 1915- . Other joint pseudonym: Mason Gregory, q.v.
With Soul So Dead. Arcadia, 1956 [Calif.]

MASON, HILARY. Pseudonym of Edith Helen Mason, 1895- .
Tread Warily. Paul, 1937

MASON, HOWARD. Pseudonym of Jennifer Ramage.
Body Below. Joseph, 1955
Fit As a Filly; see Photo Finish
Photo Finish. Joseph, 1954. U.S. title: Fit As a Filly. Morrow, 1954
Proud Adversary. Joseph, 1951 [Fr.]
The Red Bishop. Joseph, 1953; Mill, 1954 [Ger.]

MASON, JOHN WILLIAM
Hot Blood—Cold Blood. Hale, 1958

Jail Bait. Hale, 1959
The Saboteurs. Hale, 1955
The Tiger's Back. Hale, 1957

MASON, LEE W. Pseudonym of Barry (Norman) Malzberg, 1939- . Other pseudonym: Mike Barry, q.v. See also: Bill Pronzini, 1943- .
Lady of a Thousand Sorrows. Playboy, 1977

MASON, LEONIE
Murder by Accident. Temple, 1947

MASON, MICHAEL. 1939-
71 Hours. Coward, 1972

MASON, PAULE. Born in Switz.; teacher, actress, radio reporter; living in L.A. in late 1960s.
The Dark Mirror; see Here Lies Georgia Linz
Here Lies Georgia Linz. World, 1968. British title: The Dark Mirror. Collins, 1967
The Man in the Garden. McKay, 1969. British title: The Shadow. Collins, 1969
The Shadow; see The Man in the Garden

MASON, PHILIP. 1906- . Pseudonym: Philip Woodruff, q.v.

MASON, RAYMOND [CLARENCE RAY MASON]
And Two Shall Meet. GM, 1954; Red Seal, 1958
Forever Is Today. GM, 1955; Fawcett (London), 1958
-Love After Five. GM, 1956
Someone and Felicia Warwick. GM, 1962; Muller pb, 1963 [Calif.]

MASON, ROBERT
And the Shouting Dies. Hurst, 1940
Arab Agent. Hurst, 1944
-Cairo Communique. Hurst, 1942 ss
Courage for Sale. Hurst, 1939
-More News from Middle East. Hurst, 1943 [Mid. East]
Murder to Measure. Pawling, 1934
-No Easy Way Out. Jarrolds, 1952
The Slaying Squad. Hurst, 1934
-Tandra. Hurst, 1945
-The Tender Leaves. Jarrolds, 1950
-There Is a Green Hill. Hurst, 1946
Three Cheers for Treason! Hurst, 1940

MASON, S. C. Pseudonym of Charles Mason. SC: Derek Glover = DG.
'Bloody Murder'. Bell, 1937
-The Gold of Gabria. Warne, 1950
The Man on the Spot. Bles, 1938 DG
Murder at Bador. Bell, 1938 DG
Murder on Manoeuvres. Bell, 1937

MASON, SARA ELIZABETH. 1911- . SC: Sheriff Bill Davies = BD.
The Crimson Feather. Doubleday, 1945; Gordon Martin, 1946 BD [Ala.]
The House That Hate Built. Doubleday, 1944 [Ala.]
Murder Rents a Room. Doubleday, 1943 BD [Ala.]
The Whip. Morrow, 1948; Corgi, 1952

MASON, TALLY. Pseudonym of August (William) Derleth, 1909-1971, q.v.
Consider Your Verdict. Stackpole, 1937 ss, in quiz form

MASON, (FRANCIS) VAN WYCK. 1897-1978. Joint pseudonym with Helen Brawner, 1902- : Geoffrey Coffin, q.v.
Ref: CA, CC, EM, MP, TC. SC: Capt./Maj./Col. Hugh North = HN.
The Branded Spy Murders. Doubleday, 1932; Eldon, 1936 HN
The Bucharest Ballerina Murders. Stokes, 1940; Jarrolds, 1941 HN [Buch.]
The Budapest Parade Murders. Doubleday, 1935; Eldon, 1935 HN [Buda.]
The Cairo Garter Murders. Doubleday, 1938; Jarrolds, 1938 HN [Cairo]
The Castle Island Case. Reynal, 1937; Jarrolds, 1938. Revised edition, with HN added: The Multi-Million-Dollar Murders. Cardinal, 1960; Hale, 1961 [Bermuda]
The China Sea Murders; see The Shanghai Bund Murders
Dardanelles Derelict. Doubleday, 1949; Barker, 1950 HN [Turk.]
The Deadly Orbit Mission. Doubleday, 1968; Hale, 1968 HN [Tangier]
The Fort Terror Murders. Doubleday, 1931; Eldon, 1936 HN [Philip.]
The Gracious Lily Affair. Doubleday, 1957; Hale, 1958 HN [Bermuda]
Himalayan Assignment. Doubleday, 1952; Hale, 1953 HN [Tib.]

The Hong Kong Airbase Murders. Doubleday, 1937; Jarrolds, 1940 HN [H. Kong]
Maracaibo Mission. Doubleday, 1965; Hale, 1966 HN [Venez.]
The Multi-Million-Dollar Murders; see The Castle Island Case
The Rio Casino Intrigue. Reynal, 1941; Jarrolds, 1942 HN [Rio de J.]
Saigon Singer. Doubleday, 1946; Barker, 1948 HN [Saigon]
Secret Mission to Bangkok. Doubleday, 1960; Hale, 1961 HN [Bangkok]
Seeds of Murder. Doubleday, 1930; Eldon, 1937 HN [L.I.]
The Seven Seas Murders. Doubleday, 1936; Eldon, 1937 (4 HN novelets.)
The Shanghai Bund Murders. Doubleday, 1933; Eldon, 1934. Revised edition: The China Sea Murders. PB, 1975; Consul, 1961 HN [Shanghai]
The Singapore Exile Murders. Doubleday, 1939; Jarrolds, 1939 HN [Sing.]
Spider House. Mystery League, 1932; Hale, 1959
The Sulu Sea Murders. Doubleday, 1933; Eldon, 1936. Revised edition: PB, 1958 HN [Far East]
Trouble in Burma. Doubleday, 1962; Hale, 1963 HN [Burma]
Two Tickets to Tangier. Doubleday, 1955; Hale, 1956 HN [Tangier]
The Vesper Service Murders. Doubleday, 1931; Eldon, 1935 HN [Mass.]
The Washington Legation Murders. Doubleday, 1935; Eldon, 1937 HN [Wash. D.C.]
The Yellow Arrow Murders. Doubleday, 1932; Eldon, 1935 HN [Cuba]
Zanzibar Intrigue. Doubleday, 1963; Hale, 1964 HN [Zanz.]

MASSEY, CHARLOTTE
The Bride of Invercoe. Macdonald, 1976; PB, 1978 [Scot., 1800s]
Polmarran Tower. Macdonald, 1975; PB, 1977 [Eng., 1830]

MASSEY, MORRELL. SC: Thornton Zane, in both titles.
Left Hand Left. Penn, 1932; Hutchinson, 1932 [Pa.]
Through the Lens. Penn, 1933 [NYC]

MASSEY, RUTH
The Crime in the Boulevard Raspail. Nelson, 1932. U.S. title: Death in the Wind. Nelson (NYC), 1932 [Fr.]

MASSIE, CHRIS. Pseudonym.
-The Confessions of a Vagabond. Low, 1931
-Corridor of Mirrors. Faber, 1941
Death Goes Hunting. Faber, 1953
-Escape from Julia. Faber, 1947
Falcon Road; see Hallelujah Chorus
Farewell, Pretty Ladies. Random, 1942 (British title?)
-Flood Light. Low, 1932
The Green Circle; see The Green Orb
The Green Orb. Faber, 1943. U.S. title: The Green Circle. Random, 1943
-The Incredible Truth. Random, 1958
-Lady. Heinemann, 1925
The Love Letters; see Pity My Simplicity
-My Love Is Stone. Faber, 1949
-The Other House. Secker, 1938
-Peccavi. Chapman, 1929
-Penny Whipp. Secker, 1939
Pity My Simplicity. Faber, 1944. U.S. title: The Love Letters. Random, 1944
-Portrait of a Beautiful Woman. Low, 1944
-They Being Dead Yet Speak. Chapman, 1929
-The Undivided Light. Faber, 1952
-When My Ship Comes Home. Faber, 1959

MASSON, RENE. 1922-   .
The Bottle Organ. Wingate, 1962 (Translation of "L'Orgue a Bouteilles." Paris, 1950.)
Cage of Darkness; see Sicily Street
Green Oranges. Knopf, 1953 (Translation of "Oranges Vertes." Paris, 1953.)
Landru; see Number One
Number One. Hutchinson, 1964. U.S. title: Landru. Doubleday, 1965 (Translation of "Les Roses de Gambais." Paris, 1962.)
Sicily Street. Wingate, 1961. U.S. title: Cage of Darkness. Knopf, 1951 (Translation of "Les Gamins du Roi du Sicile." Paris, 1950.)

MASSON, RICHARD
Creatures. Futura, 1979

MASTERMAN, J(OHN) C(ECIL). 1891-1977.
Ref: CA, CC, MC. SC: Ernst Brandel = EB. Set: Eng.
Bits and Pieces. Hodder, 1961 (ss, including a Sherlock Holmes pastiche and 2 about EB.)
The Case of the Four Friends. Hodder, 1957 EB
An Oxford Tragedy. Gollancz, 1933; Dover, 1981 EB [acad.]

MASTERMAN, MARGARET. 1910-   .
Death of a Friend. Nicholson, 1938
-Gentleman's Daughters. Nicholson, 1931
-The Grandmother. Nicholson, 1934

MASTERMAN, WALTER S(IDNEY). 1876-   .
See also: L. Patrick Greene. Ref: CC, MM, MP. SC: Sir Arthur Sinclair, in at least those marked AS; Dick Seldon, in at least those marked DS. Set: Eng.
The Avenger Strikes. Jarrolds, 1936; Dutton, 1937 AS
Back from the Grave. Jarrolds, 1940 AS
The Baddington Horror. Jarrolds, 1934; Dutton, 1934 AS
Blood on the Floor; see 2 L.O.
The Bloodhounds Bay. Jarrolds, 1936; Dutton, 1936 DS
The Border Line. Jarrolds, 1936; Dutton, 1937 DS
The Crime of the Reckaviles; see The Curse of the Reckaviles
The Curse of Cantire. Jarrolds, 1939 AS
The Curse of the Reckaviles. Methuen, 1927; Dutton, 1927. Also published as: The Crime of the Reckaviles. Methuen, 1934 AS
The Death Coins. Jarrolds, 1940 AS
Death Turns Traitor. Methuen, 1935; Dutton, 1936 AS
The Flying Beast. Jarrolds, 1932; Dutton, 1932 AS
The Green Toad. Gollancz, 1928; Dutton, 1929
The Hooded Monster. Jarrolds, 1939
The Hunted Man. Jarrolds, 1938; Dutton, 1938 AS
The Man Without a Head. Jarrolds, 1942
The Mystery of Fifty-Two. Jarrolds, 1931; Dutton, 1931 AS
The Nameless Crime. Jarrolds, 1932; Dutton, 1932 AS
The Perjured Alibi. Methuen, 1935; Dutton, 1935
The Rose of Death. Methuen, 1934; Dutton, 1936 AS
The Secret of the Downs. Jarrolds, 1938; Dutton, 1939 AS
The Silver Leopard. Jarrolds, 1941 AS
The Tangle. Jarrolds, 1931
2 L.O. Gollancz, 1928; Dutton, 1928. Also published as: Blood on the Floor. Newnes, 1935 AS
The Wrong Letter. Methuen, 1926; Dutton, 1926 AS
The Wrong Verdict. Jarrolds, 1937; Dutton, 1938 AS
The Yellow Mistletoe. Jarrolds, 1930; Dutton, 1930 AS

MASTERS, ANTHONY. 1940-   . Pseudonym: Richard Tate, q.v. Ref: CA.
The Syndicate. Joseph, 1971

MASTERS, JOHN. 1914-   .
The Breaking Strain. Joseph, 1967; Delacorte, 1967
The Himalayan Concerto. Joseph, 1976; Doubleday, 1976

MASTERS, SIMON
Target: The Men They Were Once. BBC, 1977 (Novelization of TV series.)

MASTERS, W(ILLIAM) W(ALTER). 1894-   .
Murder in the Mirror. Longmans, 1931

MASTERSON, LINDA
Summerhaven. Zebra, 1979

MASTERSON, WHIT. Joint pseudonym of Robert Wade, 1920-   , q.v., and Bill Miller, 1920-1961. Ref: CC. This byline continued by Wade alone after Miller's death. Other joint pseudonyms: Will Daemer, Wade Miller, Dale Wilmer, qq.v. See also: Bob Wade.
All Through the Night. Dodd, 1955; Allen, 1956. Also published as: A Cry in the Night. Bantam, 1956; Corgi, 1958 [Calif.]
Badge of Evil. Dodd, 1956; Allen, 1956. Also published as: Touch of Evil. Bantam, 1958 [Calif.]
A Cry in the Night; see All Through the Night
The Dark Fantastic. Dodd, 1959; Allen, 1960 [Mex.]
Dead, She Was Beautiful. Dodd, 1955; Allen, 1955 [Calif.]
The Death of Me Yet. Dodd, 1970; Hale, 1972 [Calif.]
Evil Come, Evil Go. Dodd, 1961; Allen, 1961 [Calif.]
The Gravy Train. Dodd, 1971; Hale, 1972. Also published as: The Great Train Hijack. Pinnacle, 1976
The Great Train Hijack; see The Gravy Train
A Hammer in His Hand. Dodd, 1960; Allen, 1960 [Calif.]
Hunter of the Blood. Dodd, 1977; Hale, 1978 [Calif., It.]
Killer with a Badge; see 711—Officer Needs Help
The Last One Kills. Dodd, 1969; Hale, 1972 [Mex.]
The Man on a Nylon String. Dodd, 1963; Allen, 1963 [Switz.]
The Man with Two Clocks. Dodd, 1974; Hale, 1975
Play Like You're Dead. Dodd, 1967; Hale, 1969 [Calif.]
711—Officer Needs Help. Dodd, 1965. British title: Killer with a Badge. Allen, 1966. Also published as: Warning Shot. Popular Library, 1967 [Calif.]
A Shadow in the Wild. Dodd, 1957; Allen, 1957 [Calif.]
The Slow Gallows. Dodd, 1979; Hale, 1979 [San Diego]
Touch of Evil; see Badge of Evil
The Undertaker Wind. Dodd, 1973; Hale, 1974 [N. Mex.]
Warning Shot; see 711—Officer Needs Help
Why She Cries, I Do Not Know. Dodd, 1972; Hale, 1974 [Calif.]

MASUR, HAROLD Q. 1909-   . See also: Helen Traubel. Ref: CA, CC, EM, TC. SC: Scott Jordan = SJ.
The Attorney. Random, 1973; Souvenir, 1974 [NYC]
The Big Money. Simon, 1954; Boardman, 1955 SJ [NYC]
Bury Me Deep. Simon, 1947; Boardman, 1961 SJ [NYC]
The Last Breath; see The Last Gamble
The Last Gamble. Simon, 1958. British title: The Last Breath. Boardman, 1958. Also published as: Murder on Broadway. Dell, 1959 SJ [NYC]
The Legacy Lenders. Random, 1967; Boardman, 1967 SJ [NYC]
Make a Killing. Random, 1964; Boardman, 1964 SJ [NYC]
Murder on Broadway; see The Last Gamble
The Name Is Jordan. Pyramid, 1962 SJ ss [NYC]
Send Another Hearse. Random, 1960; Boardman, 1960 SJ [NYC]
So Rich, So Lovely, and So Dead. Simon, 1952; Boardman, 1953 SJ [NYC]
Suddenly a Corpse. Simon, 1949; Boardman, 1950 SJ [NYC]
Tall, Dark, and Deadly. Simon, 1956; Boardman, 1957 SJ [NYC]
You Can't Live Forever. Simon, 1951; Boardman, 1951 SJ [NYC]

MATCHA, JACK. 1919-   . Ref: CA.
Ask for Lois. Monarch, 1962
-Gambler's Girl. Athena, 1962
Prowler in the Night. GM, 1959; Digit, 1959 [L.A.]

MATHER, ARTHUR (R.)
Easy Money. Hodder, 1979; Dell, 1982
The Mind Breaker. Hodder, 1980; Delacorte, 1980

MATHER, BERKELY. Pseudonym of John Evan Weston Davies. Ref: CC, TC. SC: Peter Feltham = PF; Idewald Rees = IR; James Wainwright = JW.
The Achilles Affair. Collins, 1959; Scribner, 1959 PF
The Break; see The Break in the Line
The Break in the Line. Collins, 1970. U.S. title: The Break. Scribner, 1970 JW [Tib.]
Geth Straker. Fontana, 1962 (Based on the TV series.) ss [It.]
The Gold of Malabar. Collins, 1966; Scribner, 1967 [India]
The Pass Beyond Kashmir. Collins, 1960; Scribner, 1960 IR [India]
The Road and the Star. Collins, 1965; Scribner, 1965
Snowline. Collins, 1973; Scribner, 1973 IR [India]
The Springers. Collins, 1968. U.S. title: A Spy for a Spy. Scribner, 1968 JW
A Spy for a Spy; see The Springers
The Terminators. Collins, 1971; Scribner, 1971 IR [India]
-The White Dacoit. Collins, 1974; Scribner, 1974 [India]

With Extreme Prejudice. Collins, 1975;
   Scribner, 1976 PF [Cyprus]
MATHER, VIRGINIA. Pseudonym of Jean Mayer
   Liebeler, ca.1900-   , q.v.
MATHERS, EDWARD POWYS. 1892-1939. Pseudo-
   nym: Torquemada, q.v.
MATHERS, HELEN B(UCKINGHAM). 1853-1920.
   Ref: DD.
   Blind Justice. Ward, 1890. U.S. title:
      Hedri; or, Blind Justice. Lovell,
      1889
   -Eyre's Acquittal. Bentley, 1884;
      Lovell, 1883
   -Found Out. Warne, 1885; Munro, 1885
   Hedri; see Blind Justice
   -The Juggler and the Soul. Skeffington,
      1896
   Land o' the Leal. Bentley, 1878; Munro,
      1878
   Love, the Thief. Paul, 1909
   Murder or Manslaughter. Routledge,
      1885; Munro, 1885
   The Mystery of No. 13. White, 1891;
      U.S. Book Co., 1890
   -Story of a Sin. Routledge, 1882; Munro,
      1883
MATHESON, HUGH. Pseudonym of Hugh Lewis
   Mackay, 1897-1963. SC: Geoffrey
   Branscombe, in both titles.
   The Balance of Fear. Gibbs, 1961
   The Third Force. Wingate, 1959; Wash-
      burn, 1960
MATHESON, JEAN (CHISHOLM). Set: Eng.
   The Dire Departed. Hodder, 1958
   So Difficult to Die. Collins, 1957
MATHESON, RICHARD (BURTON). 1926-   .
   Ref: CA.
   Fury on Sunday. Lion, 1953
   -Hell House. Viking, 1971; Cape, 1973
   Ride the Nightmare. Ballantine, 1959;
      Consul, 1961 [L.A.]
   Someone Is Bleeding. Lion, 1953 [L.A.]
   -A Stir of Echoes. Lippincott, 1958;
      Cassell, 1958 [Calif.]
MATHESON, SYLVIA ANNE. 1918-   . Pseudo-
   nym: Max Mundy, q.v.
MATHEWS, D(ONNA) L(ORRAINE). 1922-   .
   The Fatal Amateur. Rinehart, 1959;
      Jenkins, 1960
   The Late Unlamented; see A Very Welcome
      Death
   The Reach of Fear. Rinehart, 1958;
      Jenkins, 1959
   A Very Welcome Death. Holt, 1961. Bri-
      tish title: The Late Unlamented.
      Jenkins, 1961
MATHEWS, FRANCES (H. SHORTT). See: Vere
   (Dawson) Shortt, 1872-1915.
MATHEWS, FRANCES AYMAR. 1865?-1925.
   The Flame Dancer. Dillingham, 1908;
      Unwin, 1908
   A Little Tragedy at Tien-Tsin. Cooke,
      1904 ss
   The Staircase of Surprise. Appleton,
      1905 [China]
MATHEWS, NIEVES (M.). 1917-   .
   She Died Without Lights. Hodder, 1956
MATHEWSON, JOHN
   Running Scared. Hale, 1978
MATHEWSON, JOSEPH
   Alicia's Trump. Avon, 1980 [NYC]
MATHIESON, THEODORE. 1913-   . Ref: CA.
   The Devil and Ben Franklin. Simon, 1961
      [Phil., 1734]
   The Great "Detectives". Simon, 1960 ss
      [past]
MATRANGA, FRANCES C.
   Land of Shadows. Manor, 1977
MATSCHAT, CECILE HULSE. 1895?-1976. Ref:
   CA. SC: Andrea Reid (Ramsay) and
   David Ramsay, in both titles.
   Murder at the Black Crook. Farrar,
      1943; Cassell, 1945 [La.]
   Murder in Okefenokee. Farrar, 1941
      [Ga.]
MATSUMOTO, SEICHO. 1909-   . Prize-win-
   ning and prolific Japanese mystery
   writer.
   Points and Lines. Kodansha (U.S.),
      1970; Kodansha (U.K.), 1978 (Trans-
      lation of "Ten to Sen." Tokyo,
      1957.) [Jap.]

MATTHESON, RODNEY. Pseudonym of John
   Creasey, 1908-1973, q.v. Other pseu-
   donyms: Gordon Ashe, M. E. Cooke,
   Norman Deane, Robert Caine Frazer,
   Patrick Gill, Michael Halliday,
   Charles Hogarth, Brian Hope, Colin
   Hughes, Kyle Hunt, Abel Mann, Peter
   Manton, J. J. Marric, Richard Martin,
   Anthony Morton, Jeremy York, qq.v.
   The Dark Shadow. Fiction House, 193?
   The Secret of Ferrars. Fiction House,
      193?
MATTHEW, CHARLES
   Bazi Bazoum; or, A Strange Detective;
      see Mabel Seymour; or, A Strange De-
      tective
   The Inspector's Puzzle; or, Trapped at
      the Last Turn. Street (Magnet), 1899
   Mabel Seymour; or, A Strange Detective.
      Street, 1891. British title (?): Bazi
      Bazoum; or, A Strange Detective.
      Ward, 1889
MATTHEWS, ADELAIDE, 1886-   , and MARTHA
   M. STANLEY
   The Wasp's Nest. French (NYC), 1929
      (3-act play.)
MATTHEWS, ANTHONY. Pseudonym of Dudley
   Barker, 1910-   . Used as byline on
   some titles published in England as
   by another Barker pseudonym: Lionel
   Black, q.v.
MATTHEWS, (JAMES) BRANDER. 1852-1929.
   Ref: CC, MP.
   His Father's Son. Harper, 1898; Long-
      mans, 1895
   The Last Meeting. Scribner, 1885;
      Unwin, 1885 [NYC]
   -A Tale of Twenty-Five Hours, with
      George H. Jessop. Appleton, 1892
   Tales of Fantasy and Fact. Harper, 1896
      ss
   With My Friends. Longmans, 1891 ss,
      some criminous
MATTHEWS, CLAYTON (HARTLEY). 1918-
   Ref: CA. See also: Patty Brisco;
   and also: Arthur Moore.
   The Big Score. Brandon, 1973
   Dive into Death. Powell, 1969 ss
   Faithless. Monarch, 1962
   Hagar's Castle. Powell, 1969 ss
   Hong Kong. PB, 1976 [H. Kong]
   The Mendoza File. Powell, 1970
   The Negotiator. Pyramid, 1975
   Nylon Nightmare. Powell, 1970 [S.W.]
   A Rage of Desire. Monarch, 1960
MATTHEWS, CLYDE. 1917-   . Ref: CA.
   The Ides of March Conspiracy. Arbor,
      1979 [NYC, Wash. D.C., 1980s]
MATTHEWS, PATRICIA. 1927-   . See: Patty
   Brisco. Ref: CA.
MATTHEWS, T(HOMAS) S(TANLEY). 1901-   .
   Ref: CA.
   To the Gallows I Must Go. Knopf, 1931;
      H. Hamilton, 1931. Also published as:
      Darling, I Hate You. Popular Li-
      brary, 1953
MATTHEY, A. Pseudonym of Arthur Arnould.
   The Virgin Widow. Vizetelly, 1887
      (Translated from the French.)
MATTHISON, A(RTHUR) LL(EWELYN). 1869-   .
   Death in the Cemetery. Madison, 1938
MATURIN, CHARLES ROBERT. 1780-1824.
   Pseudonym: Dennis Jasper Murphy, q.v.
   Bertram; or, The Castle of Saint Aldo-
      brand. Murray, 1816; Longworth, 1816
      (Play.)
   Melmoth: The Wanderer. Constable, 1820;
      Wells, 1821
MAUGHAM, ROBERT CECIL ROMER. 1916-1981.
   Pseudonym: Robin Maugham, q.v.
MAUGHAM, ROBIN. Pseudonym of Robert Cecil
   Romer Maugham, 1916-1981. Ref: CA,
   CC, TC.
   -The Barrier. Allen, 1973
   The Dividing Line. Allen, 1979
   The Intruder; see Line on Ginger
   -Line on Ginger. Chapman, 1949; Har-
      court, 1950. Also published as: The
      Intruder. New English Library, 1968
   The Link: A Victorian Mystery. Heine-
      mann, 1969; McGraw, 1969
   The Man with Two Shadows. Longmans,
      1958; Harper, 1959 [Mid. East]
   -November Reef. Longmans, 1962; Monarch,
      1964
   -Testament: Cairo, 1898. DeHarrington,
      1972 (31 pp. ss.)

MAUGHAM, W(ILLIAM) SOMERSET. 1874-1965.
   See also: Rodney Ackland, 1908-   .
   Ref: CA, CC, DD, EM, MC, TC.
   Ah King. Heinemann, 1933; Doubleday,
      1933 ss, one criminous [Mal.]
   Ashenden; or, The British Agent. Heine-
      mann, 1928; Doubleday, 1928 ss
MAURICE, ARTHUR B(ARTLETT). 1873-1946.
   The Riddle of the Rovers. Dodd, 1942
      [NYC]
MAURICE, MICHAEL. Pseudonym of Conrad
   Arthur Skinner, 1889-   .
   The Final Sentence. Chapman, 1926
   -Frail Ghost. Low, 1935
   -The Last House. Low, 1933
   The Long Way Round. Unwin, 1925. U.S.
      title (?): The Permanent Eclipse.
      Frank-Maurice, 1926
   -Luther Wing. Low, 1930
   -Marooned. Low, 1932
   The Permanent Eclipse; see The Long Way
      Round
MAUSER, MAX. See: Jonas Lie, 1899-1945.
MAVITY, NANCY BARR. 1890-   . Crime
   journalist for Calif. newspaper; li-
   ving in Oakland in the 1930s. SC:
   Peter Piper = PP.
   The Body on the Floor. Doubleday, 1929;
      Collins, 1930 PP [Calif.]
   The Case of the Missing Sandals.
      Doubleday, 1930; Collins, 1931 PP
      [Calif.]
   The Fate of Jane McKenzie. Doubleday,
      1933; Collins, 1933 PP [Calif.]
   He Didn't Mind Hanging; see The Man Who
      Didn't Mind Hanging
   The Man Who Didn't Mind Hanging.
      Doubleday, 1932. British title: He
      Didn't Mind Hanging. Collins, 1932
      PP [S.F.]
   The Other Bullet. Doubleday, 1930; Col-
      lins, 1931 PP [Calif.]
   The State vs. Elna Jepson. Doubleday,
      1937
   The Tule Marsh Murder. Doubleday, 1929;
      Collins, 1930 PP [Calif.]
MAXFIELD, HENRY S.
   Another Spring. Little, 1974
   Legacy of a Spy. Harper, 1958; Heine-
      mann, 1958 [Switz.]
MAXIM, LARRY T. and CHARLES B. HARNETT
   No Time to Live. Arbo, 1953
MAXON, P. B.
   The Waltz of Death. Mystery House,
      1941
MAXWELL, ALLAN. Pseudonym of William
   J(ohn) Bayfield, 1871-1958, q.v.
   Other pseudonym: Allan Blair, q.v.
   The Priest's Secret. Amalgamated, 1936
      (Sexton Blake.)
MAXWELL, BRIGID. 1916-   .
   The Case of the Six Mistresses. Harrap,
      1955
MAXWELL, C. F.
   Plan 79. Gifford, 1947
MAXWELL, GERALD. 1862-   .
   -The Fear of Life. Blackwell, 1908
   The Last Lord Avanley. Mills, 1909
MAXWELL, HELEN K.
   The Girl in a Mask. Little, 1971
      [Conn.]
   Leave It to Amanda. Little, 1972
   The Livingston Heirs. Little, 1973
MAXWELL, HERBERT
   -The Quest of the Crooked. Digby Long,
      1907
   The Three Judges. Digby Long, 1908
      ss, mostly criminous
   The Unclaimed Million. Ward, 1904
MAXWELL, PATRICIA (ANNE PONDER). 1942-   .
   Ref: CA.
   The Bewitching Grace. Popular Library,
      1974 [La.]
   Bride of a Stranger. GM, 1974
   The Court of the Thorn Tree. Popular
      Library, 1974
   Dark Masquerade. GM, 1974 [La.]
   Night of the Candles. GM, 1979
   Plantation Inn. GM, 1971 [La.]
   The Secret of Mirror House. GM, 1970
      [South, ca.1870]
   The Stranger at Plantation Inn. GM,
      1971 [La.]

MAXWELL, PETER. Pseudonym of Peter (Leslie) Cave, 1940-   , q.v.
-The Insanity Machine. Hamlyn, 1978
Killfactor Five. Hamlyn, 1979

MAXWELL, RICHARD. Born in Tex.; law school graduate, assistant D.A. in Tex.
The Minus Man. Putnam, 1975 [Tex.]

MAXWELL, VICKY. Pseudonym of Anne(tte Isobel) Worboys, q.v.
Chosen Child. Collins, 1973
Flight to the Villa Mistra. Collins, 1973
-High Hostage. Collins, 1976
-The Other Side of Summer. Collins, 1977
The Way of the Tamarisk. Collins, 1974; Delacorte, 1975, as by Anne Worboys [ship, It.]

MAXWELL, W(ILLIAM) B(ABINGTON). 1866-1938.
Jacob's Ladder, and other stories. Hutchinson, 1937 ss, some criminous
Like Shadows on the Wall. Hutchinson, 1929 ss

MAY, GEOFFREY. Joint pseudonym with Ethel M. Dolbey: E. M. D. Hawthorn, q.v.

MAY, HENRY BAK
The Doctor Didn't Prescribe Murder. Exposition, 1957

MAY, JANIS SUSAN
-The Avenging Maid. Dell, 1980
Where Shadows Linger. Dell, 1980

MAY, ROBERT HAROLD
7 Murders. Macaulay, 1932

MAYBURY, ANNE. Pseudonym of Anne Buxton. Other pseudonym: Katherine Troy, q.v. The titles below were mostly published in the U.S. as gothics, but apparently in Eng. as romances.
Beloved Enemy. Collins, 1957
The Brides of Bellenmore; see My Dearest Elizabeth
Bridge to the Moon. Collins, 1960
Dark Star. Collins, 1978; Random, 1977 [Scot.]
Dear Lost Love. Collins, 1957
Follow Your Heart. Collins, 1955
Forbidden. Collins, 1956
Gabriella; see I Am Gabriella!
The Gay of Heart. Collins, 1959
Green Fire. Collins, 1963; Ace, 1966
I Am Gabriella! Collins, 1962; Ace, 1966. Also published as: Gabriella. Fontana, 1979 [Fr.]
Jessamy Court. Collins, 1975; Random, 1974
Jessica. Collins, 1965
The Jeweled Daughter. Collins, 1976; Random, 1976 [H. Kong]
The Midnight Dancers. Collins, 1974; Random, 1973 [Afr., N.]
The Minerva Stone. Hodder, 1968; Holt, 1968
The Moonlit Door. Hodder, 1967; Holt, 1967 [Fr.]
My Dearest Elizabeth. Collins, 1964. U.S. title: The Brides of Bellenmore. Ace, 1964
My Love Has a Secret. Collins, 1958
The Night My Enemy. Collins, 1962; Ace, 1967
The Other Juliet. Collins, 1955
The Pavilion at Monkshood. Collins, 1966; Ace, 1966
Radiance. Collins, 1980; Random, 1979
The Rebel Heart. Collins, 1959
Ride a White Dolphin. Hodder, 1971; Random, 1971
Shadow of a Stranger. Collins, 1960; Ace, 1966
The Stars Cannot Tell. Collins, 1958
Stay Until Tomorrow. Collins, 1961; Ace, 1967
The Terracotta Palace. Hodder, 1971; Random, 1970 [Rome]
Walk in the Paradise Garden. Collins, 1973; Random, 1972 [Greece]

MAYDWELL, W. D.
Convict International. Mellifont, 1941
The Dart Board Mystery. Mellifont, 1940
Death in the Tote Box. Mellifont, 1941
The Football Pools Mystery. Mellifont, 1940
The Football Racket. Mellifont, 1940
The Greyhound Murder Mystery. Mellifont, 1940
The Soccer League Scandal. Mellifont, 1941

MAYER, EDWARD E. and ROBIN MOORE, q.v. Robin Moore is the pseudonym of Robert Lowell Moore, Jr., 1925-   . Ref: CA.
The Cobra Team. Condor, 1979 [Cuba]

MAYER, MARTIN (PRAGER). 1928-   . Ref: CA.
Trigger Points. Harper, 1979; Gollancz, 1980

MAYER, ROBERT. 1939-   .
The Execution. Viking, 1979 [Utah]

MAYFAIR, FRANKLIN. Pseudonym of Felix Mendelsohn, Jr., 1906-   . Ref: CA.
Over My Dead Body. Book Co., 1965 [Calif.]

MAYFIELD, SERENA
The Lonely Terror. PB, 1973 [Fla.]
Stranger in the House. PB, 1972 [L.I.]

MAYHEW, G. A.
Murder at Daybreak. Vantage, 1975

MAYHEW, MARGARET
The Cry of the Owl; see The Owlers
The Master of Aysgarth. H. Hamilton, 1976; Doubleday, 1976 [Eng., 1832]
The Owlers. H. Hamilton, 1977. U.S. title: The Cry of the Owl. Doubleday, 1977 [Eng., 1700s]

MAYHEW, VIC
The Bomb Makers. PaperJacks, 1978. British title (?): Plutonium. Arrow, 1979

MAYLON, B. J.
The Corpse with Knee Action. Phoenix, 1940 [S.F.]

MAYNARD, LAWRENCE M. ca.1905-   . Magazine writer; novel below was written while he was serving a term in a state penetentiary; born in Calif.
The Pig Is Fat. Farrar, 1930; Gollancz, 1930

MAYNE, CLARICE and R(OBERT) THURSTON HOPKINS, 1883-   , q.v.
The Amber Girl. Palmer, 1923

MAYNE, ETHEL COLBURN. 187?-1941.
-Blindman. Chapman, 1917
-The Clearer Vision. Unwin, 1898 ss
-Come In. Chapman, 1917
-The Fourth Ship. Chapman, 1908
-Inner Circle. Constable, 1925 ss
-Jessie Vandeleur. Allen, 1902
-Nine of Hearts. Constable, 1923 ss
-One of Our Grandmothers. Chapman, 1916
-Things That No One Tells. Chapman, 1910 ss

MAYNE, WILLIAM (JAMES CARTER). 1928-   . Ref: CA.
-Ravensgill. Dutton, 1970; H. Hamilton, 1970

MAYO, GAEL
It's Locked in with You. Hutchinson, 1968

MAYO, ISABELLA FYVIE. 1843-1914.
The Mystery of Allan Grale. Bentley, 1885; Harper, 1886

MAYO, JAMES. Pseudonym of Stephen Coulter, 1913-   , q.v. SC: Charles Hood, in at least those marked CH.
Asking for It. Heinemann, 1971 CH
Hammerhead. Heinemann, 1964; Morrow, 1964 CH [Fr.]
Let Sleeping Girls Lie. Heinemann, 1965; Morrow, 1966 CH [It.]
The Man Above Suspicion. Heinemann, 1969 CH
Once in a Lifetime. Heinemann, 1968. U.S. title: Sergeant Death. Morrow, 1968 CH [Teheran]
The Quickness of the Hand. Deutsch, 1952
Rebound. Heinemann, 1961
A Season of Nerves. Heinemann, 1962
Sergeant Death; see Once in a Lifetime
Shamelady. Heinemann, 1966; Morrow, 1966 CH

MAYO, JOHN OLIVER
Deadly Knighthood. Hodder, 1938
-Death Says Good-Morning. Hodder, 1937
-On Target. Hodder, 1943

MAYO, KATHERINE. 1868?-1940.
Mounted Justice. Houghton, 1922 (ss of fictionalized true crime.) [Pa.]
The Standard-Bearers. Houghton, 1918 ss

MAYO, NICK. Pseudonym of Nickoli Martoff, 1922-   . Ref: CA.
The Benefit. Stein, 1980 [L.A.]

MAYOR, DOROTHY
It's an Ill Wind. Mill, 1947 [Maine]
Last Call for Lissa. Mill, 1958 [New Eng.]

MAYOR, F(LORA) M(acDONALD). 1872-   .
The Room Opposite, and other tales of mystery and imagination. Longmans, 1935 ss

MAYSE, ARTHUR
The Desperate Search. Morrow, 1952; Harrap, 1953
Morgan's Mountain. Morrow, 1960; Harrap, 1961
Perilous Passage. Morrow, 1949; Muller, 1952

MAYSON, WALTER H(ENRY). 1835-1904.
The Stolen Fiddle. Warne, 1897

MAZ. Pseudonym of Alfred Leonardus Mazure.
-The Adventures of Dick Boss. Literary Press, 1948
Cash on Destruction. Spearman, 1962
-Pigeon Parade. Spearman, 1961
-Priscilla Darling. Muller, 1963

MAZURE, ALFRED LEONARDUS. Pseudonym: Maz, q.v.

MAZZARO, ED. SC: Bruno Farrell, in at least those marked BF, set in Chi. in the 1920s.
Bootleg Angel. New English Library pb, 1977; Dale, 1978 BF
Chicago Deadline. New English Library pb, 1978; Dale, 1978 BF
One Death in the Red. New English Library pb, 1976; Dale, 1979 BF
Pawn to King's Cross. New English Library, 1978

MEAD, MATT. Pseudonym of Ross Richards, q.v. See also: Desmond Reid.
Star Crossed. Mayflower, 1967; Macfadden, 1969 (Sexton Blake.)

MEAD, ROBERT DOUGLAS. 1928-1983. Ref: CA.
You'll Never Take Me. Doubleday, 1978 [Minn.]

MEAD, RUSSELL. Pseudonym of Margaret Hudson Koehler.
The Moses Bottle. Raven, 1980 [Cape Cod]

MEAD, (EDWARD) SHEPHERD. 1914-   . Ref: CA.
How to Succeed at Business Spying by Trying. Simon, 1968; Harrap, 1969 [Mich.]

MEADE, DOROTHY COLE
Death over Her Shoulder. Scribner, 1939 [Mal.]
Fatal Shadows. Long & Smith, 1933 [Mal.]
The Shadow of a Hair. Hamilton, 1939

MEADE, EVERARD. 1914-   . Ref: CA.
Murder Squad. Major, 1978 [It.]
The President's Team. Major, 1976

MEADE, L(ILLIE) T(HOMAS). Pseudonym of Elizabeth Thomasina Meade Smith, 1854-1914. Ref: CC, DD, EM, MM, MP, TC. Note: Robert Eustace, coauthor of some titles below, is the pseudonym of Robert Eustace Barton, 1868-1943. Set: Eng.
The Adventures of Miranda. Long, 1904
-At the Back of the World. Hurst, 1904
-The Blue Diamond. Chatto, 1903
The Brotherhood of the Seven Kings, with Robert Eustace. Ward, 1899 ss
The Chateau of Mystery. Everett, 1907
-The Cleverest Woman in England. Nisbet, 1898
Confessions of a Court Milner. Long, 1902
A Double Revenge. Digby, 1902
Dr. Rumsey's Patient, with Clifford Halifax. Chatto, 1896; International News, 1896
-The Fountain of Beauty. Long, 1909
From the Hand of the Hunter. Long, 1906
The Gold Star Line, with Robert Eustace. Ward, 1899; New Amsterdam, 189? ss
A Golden Shadow. Ward, 1906
-Her Happy Face. Ward, 1914
The Home of Silence. Sisley's, 1907 [Ire.]
The House of Black Magic. White, 1912
-In an Iron Grip. Chatto, 1894

The Lost Square, with Robert Eustace. Ward, 1902 ss
-The Maid Indomitable. Ward, 1916
-A Maid of Mystery. White, 1904
A Master of Mysteries, with Robert Eustace. Ward, 1898 ss
-The Medicine Lady. Cassell (London & NYC), 1892
Micah Faraday, Adventurer. Ward, 1910 ss
The Necklace of Parmona. Ward, 1909
On the Brink of a Chasm. Chatto, 1898; Buckles, 1899
The Oracle of Maddox Street. Ward, 1904 ss
A Race with the Sun, with Clifford Halifax. Ward, 1901 ss
The Red Ruth. Laurie, 1907
A Ring of Rubies. Innes, 1892; Cassell, 1892
The Sanctuary Club, with Robert Eustace. Ward, 1900 ss
The Secret of the Dead. White, 1901
Silenced. Ward, 1904 ss
A Son of Ishmael. White, 1896; New Amsterdam, 1896
The Sorceress of the Strand. Ward, 1903 ss
Stories from the Diary of a Doctor, with Clifford Halifax. Newnes, 1894; Lippincott, 1895 ss
Stories from the Diary of a Doctor: Second Series, with Clifford Halifax. Sands, 1896 ss
This Troublesome World, with Clifford Halifax. Chatto, 1893; Macmillan, 1893
Twenty-Four Hours. White, 1911
Under the Dragon Throne, with Robert K(ennaway) Douglas, 1838- . Gardner, 1897 ss
The Voice of the Charmer. Chatto, 1895
Where the Shoe Pinches, with Clifford Halifax. Chambers, 1900 ss

MEADE, RICHARD. Pseudonym of Ben(jamin Leopold) Haas, 1926-1977, q.v. SC: John Allison, in both titles.
Beyond the Danube; see The Danube Runs Red
The Danube Runs Red. Random, 1968. British title: Beyond the Danube. Davies, 1967 [Austria]
The Lost Fraulein. Random, 1970. British title: A Score of Arms. Davies, 1969 [Afr.]
A Score of Arms; see The Lost Fraulein

MEADOW, HERB
Uncertain Glory. Grosset, 1944 (Novelization of the movie.) [Fr.]

MEADOWS, ALICE MAUD. -1913.
Blind Man's Buff. Everett, 1907
-Cut by Society. Digby, 1906
Days of Doubt. Ward, 1901
-The Dukedom of Portsea. Laurie, 1909
The Extreme Penalty. Digby, 1906
The Eye of Fate. Ward, 1899
-A Ghost from the Past. Laurie, 1911
-Her Soul's Desire. Laurie, 1910
-The House at the Corner. Laurie, 1908
I Charge You Both. Digby, 1905
-The Infatuation of Marcella. Digby, 1909
-An Innocent Sinner. Digby, 1910
A Million of Money. Sisley, 1907; Brentano's, 1907
-The Moth and the Flame. Milne, 1908
The Odd Trick. Long, 1908
-One Life Between. Ward, 1901
Out from the Night. Ward, 1899
-The Romance of a Madhouse. Arrowsmith, 1891
-Three Lovers and One Lass. Digby, 1908
-A Ticket-of-Leave Girl. Digby, 1911
-When the Heart Is Young. Digby, 1895
-The Wicked World. Laurie, 1910

MEADOWS, CATHERINE. Set: Eng.
Doctor Moon; see Henbane
Friday Market. Gollancz, 1938; Macmillan, 1938
Henbane. Gollancz, 1934. U.S. title: Doctor Moon. Putnam, 1935

MEADOWS, FELTON
The Death Dealers. Mellifont, 1939

MEAGHER, GEORGE E(DWARD). 1895- .
Tomorrow's Horizon. Dorrance, 1947 [China]

MEAGHER, JOSEPH W(ILLIAM)
Miss Bantling Is Missing. Macdonald, 1958

MEAKER, ELOISE. 1915- . Pseudonyms: Lydia Benson Clark, Amanda McAllister, qq.v.

MEAKER, MARIJANE. 1932- . Pseudonym: Vin Packer, q.v.

MEANS, MARY. Joint pseudonym with Theodore Saunders: Denis Scott, q.v.

MEARSON, LYON. 1888-1966.
Footsteps in the Dark. Macaulay, 1927; Hutchinson, 1928 [NYC]
Phantom Fingers. Macaulay, 1927; Hutchinson, 1929 [NYC]
The Whisper on the Stairs. Macaulay, 1924; Hutchinson, 1924 [NYC]

MECHEM, KIRKE. 1889- .
A Frame for Murder. Doubleday, 1936 [Kan.]

MECHEM, PHILIP. 1892-1969.
And Not for Love. Duell, 1942. Also published as: Murders I've Seen. Croydon, 1945, abridged [Colo.]
The Columbine Cabin Murders. Scribner, 1932 [Colo.]
Murders I've Seen; see And Not for Love

MEDUSA, K.
I Spy. Scion, 1951
Lowdown on G Men. Scion, 1951
They Kill by Night. Scion, 1952

MEE, HUAN. Pseudonym.
-A Beauty Spot. Gale, 1894 ss
A Diplomatic Woman. Sands, 1900; Harper, 1900 ss
The Jewel of Death. Ward, 1902
Solving the Unsolvable. Ferret, 1980 ss
Weaving the Web. Ward, 1902
-Wheels Within Wheels. Ward, 1901

MEEK, DORIS. Joint pseudonyms with Adrienne Jones, 1915- : Mason Gregory, Gregory Mason, qq.v.

MEEKER, ARTHUR, JR. 1902- .
-Strange Capers. Covici, 1931; Paul, 1931

MEFFORD, W. H.
The Games of 80. Belmont, 1980 [Moscow]

MEGAHY, COOPER
Cash and Carry. Futura, 1977
The Hustlers. Futura, 1976

MEGAW, ARTHUR STANLEY. 1872- . Pseudonym: Arthur Stanley, q.v.

MEGGS, BROWN (MOORE). 1930- . Ref: CA, TC.
The Matter of Paradise. Random, 1975; Collins, 1976
Saturday Games. Random, 1974; Collins, 1975 [L.A.]

MEGRUE, ROI COOPER. 1883-1927. See also: Richard Parker.
Under Cover. French, 1918; Bickers, 1914 (4-act play; for novelization see: Wyndham Martyn, 1875- .)

MEIK, VIVIAN. 1895-
The Curse of Red Shiva. Philip Allan, 1936; Hillman-Curl, 1938
Devil's Drums. Philip Allan, 1933 ss

MEIRING, DESMOND. Pseudonym of Desmond Charles Rice, 1924- . Ref: CA.
The President Plan. Constable, 1974

MEISELS, ANDREW
Six Other Days. Pyramid, 1973 [Isr.]

MEISER, EDITH. Pseudonym (?): Xantippe, q.v.

MEISSNER, HANS (OTTO). 1909- . Ref: CA.
Duel in the Snow. Davies, 1970; Morrow, 1972 (Translation of "Alatna." Gutersloh, 1964.)

MELCHIOR, IB (JORGEN). 1917- . Ref: CA.
The Haigerloch Project. Harper, 1977; Souvenir, 1977 [Ger., 1945]
The Marcus Device. Harper, 1980 [Calif.]
Order of Battle. Harper, 1972; Souvenir, 1973 [Ger., WWII]
Sleeper Agent. Harper, 1975; Souvenir, 1976 [Europe, WWII]
The Watchdogs of Abaddon. Harper, 1979; Souvenir, 1979 [L.A.]

MELDRUM, JAMES. Pseudonym of James (William) Mitchell, 1926- , q.v. Other pseudonym: James Munro, q.v.
The Semenov Impulse. Weidenfeld, 1975; St. Martin's, 1976

MELIDES, NICHOLAS. 1912- . Pseudonym: Nicholas McGuire, q.v.

-Buns from the Gutter. Paladin, 1951

MELTON, WILLIAM. 1920- . Ref: CA.
Nine Lives to Pompeii. McKay, 1974; Weidenfeld, 1974 [It.]

MELVILLE, ALAN. Pseudonym of William Melville Caverhill, 1910- . Ref: CC.
The Danube Flows Red. Skeffington, 1937 [Buda.]
Death of Anton. Skeffington, 1936
Quick Curtain. Skeffington, 1934
The Vicar in Hell. Skeffington, 1935
Warning to Critics. Skeffington, 1936
Week-End at Thrackley. Skeffington, 1934

MELVILLE, ANNABELLE (McCONNELL). 1910- . Ref: CA.
Rue the Reservoir. Bruce, 1956 [N.Y.]

MELVILLE, JAMES. 1931- . SC: Supt. Tetsuo Otani, in all titles.
The Chrysanthemum Chain. Secker, 1980; St. Martin's, 1982 [Jap.]
The Wages of Zen. Secker, 1979; Methuen (U.S.), 1981

MELVILLE, JENNIE. Pseudonym of Gwendoline (Williams) Butler, 1922- , q.v. SC: Charmian Daniels, in at least those marked CD. Set: Eng.
Axwater. Macmillan (London), 1978. U.S. title: Tarot's Tower. Simon, 1978
Burning Is a Substitute for Loving. Joseph, 1963; London House, 1964 CD
Come Home and Be Killed. Joseph, 1962; London House, 1964 CD
A Different Kind of Summer. Hodder, 1967 CD
Dragon's Eye. Macmillan (London), 1977; Simon, 1976
The Hunter in the Shadows. Hodder, 1969; McKay, 1970
Ironwood. Hodder, 1972; McKay, 1972
Murderers' Houses. Joseph, 1964 CD
Nell Alone. Joseph, 1966 CD
A New Kind of Killer; see A New Kind of Killer, an Old Kind of Death
A New Kind of Killer, an Old Kind of Death. Hodder, 1970. U.S. title: A New Kind of Killer. McKay, 1971 CD [acad.]
Nun's Castle. Hodder, 1974; McKay, 1973 [Wales]
Raven's Forge. Macmillan (London), 1975; McKay, 1975 [Eng., 1800s, theatre]
The Summer Assassin. Hodder, 1971
Tarot's Tower; see Axminster
There Lies Your Love. Joseph, 1965 CD

MELVILLE-ROSS, ANTONY. SC: Trelawney, in both titles.
Blindfold. Collins, 1978; Harper, 1978
Two Faces of Nemesis. Collins, 1979

MENDELSOHN, FELIX, JR. 1906- . Pseudonym: Franklin Mayfair, q.v.

MENDES, CATULLE. 1841-1909.
Number 56, and other stories. Laurie, 1928 (Translation of "Rue des Filles-Dieu, 56." Paris, 1895.) 4 ss, of which the first is criminous

MENDENHALL, KITTY
Angeltread. Manor, 1978

MENEGAS, PETER. 1942- .
The Great Victorian Mystery; or, The Nun of Calais. Arlington, 1978

MERAK, A. J.
-Blood on My Shadow. Spencer, 1956
-Dark Conflict. Spencer, 1959
-Intrigue. Spencer, 1955
-The Savage City. Spencer, 1961
This Time Forever. Spencer, 1957

MERAY, TIBOR. See: George Marton, 1900-

MERCER, CECIL WILLIAM. 1885-1960. Pseudonym: Dornford Yates, q.v.

MERCER, IAN
Curs in Clover. Earl, 1948
Epitaph for a Blonde. Boardman, 1959
The Green Windmill. Crowther, 1945
Journey into Darkness. Boardman, 1958
A Man Gets into His Tomb. Earl, 1948 [Fr.]
Mission to Majorca. Boardman, 1958 [Maj.]

MEREDITH, ANNE. Pseudonym of Lucy Beatrice Malleson, 1899-1973. Other pseudonyms: Anthony Gilbert, J. Kilmeny Keith, qq.v.
The Coward. Gollancz, 1934
Home Is the Heart; see There's Always Tomorrow

Portrait of a Murderer. Gollancz, 1933; Reynal, 1934
There's Always Tomorrow. Faber, 1941. U.S. title: Home Is the Heart. Howell Soskin, 1942

MEREDITH, DAVID WILLIAM. Pseudonym of Earl Schenck Miers, 1910-1972. Ref: CA.
The Christmas Card Murders. Knopf, 1951 [N.J.]

MEREDITH, K(ENNETH) LINCOLN
The Golden Chalice. Boardman, 1958 [It.]

MEREDITH, PETER. Pseudonym of Brian Arthur Worthington-Stuart. Other pseudonym: Brian Stuart, q.v.
Checkmate. Ward, 1950
-The City of Shadows. Warne, 1952
The Crocodile Man. Ward, 1951 [Afr., W.]
The Denzil Emeralds. Ward, 1954
Floodwater. Ward, 1950
Invitation to a Ball. Ward, 1949
Oasis. Ward, 1951
Sands of the Desert. Ward, 1953

MEREDITH, RICHARD C(ARLTON). 1937- . Ref: CA.
The Awakening. St. Martin's, 1979

MERITON, PETER. Pseudonym of (Alfred) John Hunter, 1891-1961, q.v. Other pseudonyms: John Addiscombe, L. H. Brenning, Anthony Dax, Anthony Drummond, qq.v. SC: Bill Langley = BL; Capt. Dack = D. Set: Eng.
The Affair of the Fraternizing Soldier. Amalgamated, 1946 (Sexton Blake.)
After Darvray Died. Hurst, 1938 BL
Captain Dack. Hurst, 1939 D
Conspiracy. Hurst, 1945 D
The Man from Madrid. Amalgamated, 1943 (Sexton Blake.)
Plunder. Hurst, 1948 D
Three Die at Midnight. Hurst, 1937; Dutton, 1937, as by John Hunter BL

MERITT, PAUL. -1895.
The Golden Plough. French (London & NYC), 1878? (4-act play.)
-The Hidden Million. Munro, 1883

MERIVALE, BERNARD. 1882-1939. See: Arnold Ridley, 1896- . And also: Ruth Alexander.

MERLAND, OLIVER. All titles below feature Sexton Blake and were published by Amalgamated Press.
The Branded Spy. 1919
The Case of Larachi the Lascar. 1924
The Case of the Man in Black. 1923
The Case of the Nameless Man. 1920
The Face in the Film. 1923

MERLE, ROBERT (JEAN GEORGES). 1908- . Ref: CA.
The Day of the Dolphin. Simon, 1969; Weidenfeld, 1969 (Translation of "Un Animal doue de Raison." Paris, 1967.) [Fla.]

MERLIN, CHRISTINA. Pseudonym of Constance (Fecher) Heaven, 1911- , q.v.
The Spy Concerto. Hale, 1980; St. Martin's, 1980

MERRETT, CHARLES H(ENRY)
Hidden Lives. Long, 1929
Sacrifice. Garamond, 1935 (1-act play.)

MERRICK, CHARLES
The Stolen Heiress. Hodder, 1938

MERRICK, GORDON. 1916- . Ref: CA.
Between Darkness and Day; see The Vallency Tradition
The Eye of One; see The Hot Season
The Hot Season. Morrow, 1958. British title: The Eye of One. Hale, 1959
-The Vallency Tradition. Messner, 1955. British title: Between Darkness and Day. Hale, 1957

MERRICK, LEONARD. 1864-1939.
The Call from the Past, and other stories. Nelson, 1910 ss, some criminous
Mr. Bazalgette's Agent. Routledge, 1888

MERRICK, DOCTOR MARK. Pseudonym of St. George (Henry) Rathborne, 1854-1938, q.v. Other pseudonyms: Marline Manly, q.v.
The Great Travers Case. Street, 1890 [NYC]

MERRICK, MOLLIE. Born in S.F.; reporter, feature writer, music critic, and Hollywood columnist. SC: Red Hanlon, in both titles.
Mysterious Mr. Frame. Washburn, 1938 [S.F.]
Upper Case. Washburn, 1936 [NYC]

MERRICK, WILLIAM. 1916-1969. Ref: CA.
The Packard Case. Random, 1961; Gollancz, 1961 [Paris]

MERRILEES, FRANCIS
The Pit. Macdonald, 1945

MERRILL, JAMES MILFORD. 1847-1936. Pseudonym: Morris Redwing, q.v.

MERRILL, P. J. Pseudonym of Holly Roth, 1916-1964, q.v. Other pseudonym: K. G. Ballard, q.v.
The Slender Thread. Harcourt, 1959; Macdonald, 1960 [Vt.]

MERRIMAN, HENRY SETON. Pseudonym of Hugh Stowell Scott, 1862-1903.
Suspense. Bentley, 1890; Dodd, 1899
With Edged Tools. Smith, 1894; Harper, 1894

MERRIMAN, PAT
Night Call. Hutchinson, 1939

MERRITT, A(BRAHAM). 1884-1943. Newspaper editor.
Burn, Witch, Burn! Liveright, 1933; Methuen, 1934
Creep, Shadow! Doubleday, 1934. British title: Creep, Shadow, Creep! Methuen, 1935
Creep, Shadow, Creep! see Creep, Shadow!
Seven Footprints to Satan. Boni, 1928; Richards, 1928 [NYC]

MERSEREAU, JOHN. 1898- . Born in Mich., raised and educated in Calif.; screenwriter.
The Corpse Comes Ashore. Lippincott, 1941 [Carib.]
Murder Loves Company. Lippincott, 1940 [S.F.]

MERTZ, BARBARA LOUISE GROSS. 1927- . Pseudonyms: Barbara Michaels, Elizabeth Peters, qq.v.

MERTZ, STEPHEN. Pseudonym: Stephen Brett, q.v.

MERWIN, BANNISTER
The Girl and the Bill. Dodd, 1909 [Chi.]

MERWIN, SAM(UEL KIMBALL), JR. 1910- . Pseudonym: Elizabeth Deare Bennett, q.v. SC: Amy Brewster = AB.
The Big Frame. Handi-Books, 1943
The Creeping Shadow. GM, 1952
Death in the Sunday Supplement. Gateway, 1942 [NYC]
Killer to Come. Abelard (NYC), 1953; Abelard (London), 1959 [future]
Knife in My Back. Mystery House, 1945; Quality, 1947 AB [Boston]
A Matter of Policy. Mystery House, 1946; Quality, 1952 AB [NYC]
Message from a Corpse. Mystery House, 1945; Quality, 1947 AB [NYC]
Murder in Miniatures. Doubleday, 1940 [NYC]
The Sex War; see The White Widows
-The White Widows. Doubleday, 1953. Also published as: The Sex War. Beacon, 1960

MERWIN, SAMUEL. 1874-1936.
Lady Can Do. Houghton, 1929

MESERVEY, RUSS
Masquerade into Madness. GM, 1953; Red Seal, 1957 [Maine]

MESSENGER, ELIZABETH (MARGERY ESSON). 1908- . Ref: CA, CC.
Dive Deep for Death. Hale, 1959 [N.Z.]
Golden Dawns the Sun. Hale, 1962
Growing Evil. Hale, 1964
A Heap of Trouble. Hale, 1963
Light on Murder. Hale, 1960 [N.Z.]
Material Witness. Hale, 1959 [N.Z.]
Murder Stalks the Bay. Hale, 1958 [N.Z.]
Publicity for Murder. Hale, 1961
The Tail of the 'Dozing Cat'. Hale, 1965
Uncertain Quest. Hale, 1965 [N.Z.]
The Wrong Way to Die. Hale, 1961
You Won't Need a Coat. Hale, 1964

MESSER, MONA (NAOMI ANNE HOCKING). 189?- . Pseudonym: Anne Hocking, q.v. Ref: CC, MP, TC.
A Castle for Sale. Methuen, 1930; Dial, 1930
Mouse Trap. Jarrolds, 1931; Putnam, 1931 [Fr.]

MESSICK, HANK [HENRY HICKS MESSICK]. 1922- . Ref: CA.
Syndicate Wife. Belmont, 1975

MESSMANN, JON. Pseudonyms: Nick Carter, Claudette Nicole, Paul Richards, qq.v. SC: Jefferson Boone (The Handyman) = JB; Ben Martin (The Revenger) = BM.
A Bullet for the Bride. Pyramid, 1972 [Fla.]
City for Sale. Signet, 1975 BM
The Deadly Deep. Signet, 1976
Fire in the Streets. Signet, 1974 BM
Game of Terror. New English Library pb, 1977 (U.S. title?)
The Inheritors. Pyramid, 1975 JB [Sp.]
Jefferson Boone, Handyman. Pyramid, 1974 JB
Jogger's Moon. Signet, 1980. British title: To Kill a Jogger. Hamlyn, 1980 [NYC]
Killers at Sea. Belmont, 1970
The Moneta Papers. Pyramid, 1973; New English Library pb, 1977 JB [It.]
Murder Today, Money Tomorrow. Pyramid, 1973 JB
Phone Call. Signet, 1979 (Novelization of the movie.)
A Promise for Death. Signet, 1975 BM [NYC]
Ransom! Pyramid, 1975 JB
The Revenger. Signet, 1973 BM [NYC]
The Stiletto Signature. Signet, 1974 BM [NYC]
The Swiss Secret. Pyramid, 1974 JB
To Kill a Jogger; see Jogger's Moon
The Vendetta Contract. Signet, 1975 BM

METCALFE, EDITH
-The Handle of Sin. Ward, 1917
Pyramids of Snow. Ward, 1903

METCALFE, FELICIA (LEIGH). 1889- . See also: Louise Isom.
All Night Long. Baker, 1929 (Play.)
Are You Mr. Butterworth? Row, 1938 (3-act play.)
Aunt Cathie's Cat. Heuer, 1943 (3-act play.)
Man Overboard! Art Craft, 1960 (3-act play.)
The Skeleton Walks! Heuer, 1945 (Play.)
Three Fingers in the Door. Heuer, 1949 (3-act play.)

METCALFE, HERBERT. Principal of an English salesmanship school.
The Amazing Dr. Khan. Church, 1966
The Packet of Death. Church, 1967

METCALFE, JOHN. 1891-1965.
-'Arms'-Length. Constable, 1930; Scribner, 1930
The Smoking Leg and other stories. Jarrolds, 1925; Doubleday, 1926 ss
Spring Darkness. Constable, 1928

METCALFE, SUSAN
Challenge of Evil. Regency, 1977

METCALFE, WHITAKER
Two Weeks Before Murder. Arcadia, 1959 [Fla.]

METHLEY, VIOLET M(ARY)
The Last Enemy. Blackie, 1936

METHOLD, KENNETH (WALTER). 1931- . Ref: CA. Pseudonym: Alexander Cade, q.v. Set: Eng.
All Suspect. Macdonald, 1960
The Man on His Shoulder. Macdonald, 1962

MEWS, WEBSTER. See: Sandor Frankel, 1943- .

MEWSHAW, MICHAEL. 1943- . Ref: CA.
-Land Without Shadow. Doubleday, 1979

MEYER, BILL
Ultimatum. Signet, 1966

MEYER, CHARLES
The Power of Gold. Warne, 1895
Shadows of Life. Warne, 1894 ss

MEYER, LAWRENCE (ROBERT). 1941- . Ref: CA.
A Capitol Crime. Viking, 1977; Collins, 1977 [Wash. D.C.]
False Front. Viking, 1979; Collins, 1979 [Wash. D.C.]

MEYER, LYNN
   Paperback Thriller. Random, 1975; Deutsch, 1976 [Boston]

MEYER, NICHOLAS. 1945- . Ref: CA, TC. SC: Sherlock Holmes = SH.
   Black Orchid, with Barry Jay Kaplan, 1943- . Dial, 1977; Corgi, 1978
   The Seven-Per-Cent Solution. Dutton, 1974; Hodder, 1975 SH [ca.1890]
   Target Practice. Harcourt, 1974; Hodder, 1975 [L.A.]
   The West End Horror. Dutton, 1976; Hodder, 1976 SH [Eng., ca.1890]

MEYERS, ALFRED. 1906-1963. Born in Oreg., graduate of Notre Dame, singer in opera and popular choruses; ss writer.
   Murder Ends the Song. Reynal, 1941; Rich, 1941 [Oreg.]

MEYERS, MANNY. 1930-
   The Last Mystery of Edgar Allan Poe. Lippincott, 1978 (Edgar Allan Poe.) [NYC, 1846-7]

MEYERS, MARTIN. SC: Patrick Hardy, in all titles.
   Hung up to Die. Popular Library, 1976
   Kiss and Kill. Popular Library, 1975 [NYC]
   Red Is for Murder. Popular Library, 1976
   Reunion for Death. Popular Library, 1976
   Spy and Die. Popular Library, 1976

MEYERS, RICHARD S. See: Richard Sapir, 1936- .

MEYERS, ROY LETHBRIDGE. 1910-1974. Ref: CA.
   The Man They Couldn't Kill. Blackfriars, 1944

MEYERSTEIN, E(DWARD) H(ARRY) W(ILLIAM). 1889-1952.
   The Pageant, and other stories. Sidney Press, 1934 ss, some criminous

MEYNELL, LAURENCE (WALTER). 1899- . Ref: CA, CC, TC. SC: George Stanhope Berkley, in at least those marked GB; Hooky Heffern(m)an, in at least those marked HH. Set: Eng.
   The Abandoned Doll. Collins, 1960
   And Be a Villain. Nicholson, 1939
   Asking for Trouble. Ward, 1931
   Bluefeather. Harrap, 1928; Appleton, 1928 GB
   -Break for Summer. H. Hamilton, 1965
   The Breaking Point. Collins, 1957
   The Bright Face of Danger. Collins, 1948
   Camouflage. Harrap, 1930. U.S. title: The Mystery at Newton Ferry. Lippincott, 1930
   -Consummate Rose. Hutchinson, 1931
   The Creaking Chair. Collins, 1941
   The Curious Crime of Miss Julia Blossom. Macmillan (London), 1970
   -The Dancers in the Reeds. H. Hamilton, 1963
   The Dandy. Nicholson, 1938
   Danger Round the Corner. Collins, 1952 HH [S. Afr.]
   The Dark Square. Collins, 1941 [Balkans]
   Death by Arrangement. Macmillan (London), 1972; McKay, 1972 HH
   Death of a Philanderer. Collins, 1968; Doubleday, 1969
   Death's Eye. Harrap, 1929. U.S. title: The Shadow and the Stone. Appleton, 1929
   Die by the Book. Collins, 1966 [Switz.]
   Don't Stop for Hooky Hefferman. Macmillan (London), 1975; Stein, 1977 HH
   The Door in the Wall. Nicholson, 1937; Harper, 1937
   Double Fault. Collins, 1965
   The Echo in the Cave. Collins, 1949
   -The Empty Saddle. H. Hamilton, 1965
   -The End of the Long Hot Summer. Hale, 1972
   The Evil Hour. Collins, 1947
   The Fairly Innocent Little Man. Macmillan (London), 1974; Stein, 1978 HH
   The Fatal Flaw. Macmillan (London), 1973; Stein, 1978 HH
   -The Footpath. Hale, 1975
   -The Fortunate Miss East. Hale, 1973
   The Frightened Man. Collins, 1952 HH
   The Gentlemen Go By; see Watch the Wall
   Give Me the Knife. Collins, 1954
   His Aunt Came Late. Nicholson, 1939
   Hooky and the Crock of Gold. Macmillan (London), 1975 HH
   Hooky and the Prancing Horse. Macmillan (London), 1980
   Hooky and the Villainous Chauffeur. Macmillan (London), 1979 HH
   Hooky Gets the Wooden Spoon. Macmillan (London), 1977; Stein, 1977 HH
   The House in Marsh Road. Collins, 1960
   The House in the Hills. Nicholson, 1937; Harper, 1938
   The House on the Cliff. Hutchinson, 1932; Lippincott, 1932
   The Hut. Nicholson, 1938
   The Lady on Platform One. Collins, 1950
   A Little Matter of Arson. Macmillan (London), 1972 HH
   The Lost Half Hour. Macmillan (London), 1976; Stein, 1977 HH
   The Man No One Knew. Collins, 1951
   The Mauve Front Door. Collins, 1967
   More Deadly Than the Male. Collins, 1964
   The Mystery of Newton Ferry; see Camouflage
   Odds on Bluefeather. Harrap, 1934; Lippincott, 1935 GB
   Of Malicious Intent. Collins, 1969
   "On the Night of the 18th..." Nicholson, 1936; Harper, 1936
   One Step from Murder. Collins, 1958
   Paid in Full. Harrap, 1933. U.S. title: So Many Doors. Lippincott, 1933
   Papersnake. Macmillan (London), 1978 HH
   Party of Eight. Collins, 1950
   The Pit in the Garden. Collins, 1961
   Saturday Out. Collins, 1956; Walker, 1962
   -Scoop. H. Hamilton, 1964
   The Shadow and the Stone; see Death's Eye
   -Shadow in the Sun. H. Hamilton, 1966
   -The Shelter. Hale, 1970
   Sleep of the Unjust. Collins, 1963
   So Many Doors; see Paid in Full
   Storm Against the Wall. Hutchinson, 1931; Lippincott, 1931
   Strange Landing. Collins, 1946
   -The Suspect Scientist. H. Hamilton, 1966
   Third Time Unlucky! Harrap, 1935
   The Thirteen Trumpeters. Macmillan (London), 1973; Stein, 1978 HH
   Too Clever by Half. Collins, 1953 HH
   -A View from the Terrace. Hale, 1972
   Virgin Luck. Collins, 1963; Simon, 1964
   Watch the Wall. Harrap, 1933. U.S. title: The Gentlemen Go By. Lippincott, 1934
   Where Is She Now? Collins, 1955
   The Woman in Number Five. Hale, 1974

MEYNELL, MARY
   Week-End at Green Trees. Bles, 1955

MEYRICK, GORDON
   Body on the Pavement. Eldon, 1942; Mystery House, 1945
   Danger at My Heels. Crowther, 1943
   The Ghost Hunters. Crowther, 1947 ss
   The Green Phantom. Eldon, 1941
   Pennyworth of Murder. Eldon, 1943

MIALL, DERWENT
   Disclosures of a Press Agent. Greening, 1912 ss
   The Powers of Darkness. Ward, 1905
   Solving a Mystery. Henderson, 1906
   The Strange Case of Vincent Hume. Everett, 1906
   A Threefold Threat. Ward, 1917

MIALL, ROBERT. Pseudonym of John (Frederick) Burke, 1922- , q.v. Other pseudonyms: Jonathan Burke, Martin Sands, qq.v. Joint pseudonym with his wife: Harriet Esmond, q.v. SC: Jason King = JK (novelizations of the TV series).
   The Adventurer. Pan, 1973
   Jason King. Pan, 1972 JK
   Kill Jason King. Pan, 1972 JK
   The Protectors. Pan, 1973

MICHAEL, DAVID J. 1944- . Ref: CA.
   Death Tour. Bobbs, 1978; New English Library, 1980

MICHAELS, ALAN. "Author of over 250 books under a number of pseudonyms."
   Diamonds. St. Martin's, 1980 [NYC]

MICHAELS, BARBARA. Pseudonym of Barbara Louise Gross Mertz, 1927- . Other pseudonym: Elizabeth Peters, q.v. Ref: CA, TC.
   Ammie, Come Home. Meredith, 1968; Jenkins, 1969 [Wash. D.C.]
   The Crying Child. Dodd, 1971; Souvenir, 1971
   The Dark on the Other Side. Dodd, 1970; Souvenir, 1973
   Greygallows. Dodd, 1972; Souvenir, 1974
   House of Many Shadows. Dodd, 1974; Souvenir, 1976 [Pa.]
   The Master of Blacktower. Appleton, 1966; Jenkins, 1967
   Mystery on the Moors; see Sons of the Wolf
   Patriot's Dream. Dodd, 1976; Souvenir, 1978 [Va.]
   Prince of Darkness. Meredith, 1969; Coronet, 1971 [Md.]
   The Sea King's Daughter. Dodd, 1975; Souvenir, 1977 [Greece]
   Sons of the Wolf. Meredith, 1967; Jenkins, 1968. Also published as: Mystery on the Moors. Paperback Library, 1968 [Eng.]
   Wait for What Will Come. Dodd, 1978; Souvenir, 1980 [Eng.]
   The Walker in Shadows. Dodd, 1979; Souvenir, 1981 [Md.]
   Wings of the Falcon. Dodd, 1977; Souvenir, 1979 [It., 1860]
   Witch. Dodd, 1973; Souvenir, 1975 [Va.]
   The Wizard's Daughter. Dodd, 1980; Souvenir, 1981 [Eng., 1857]

MICHAELS, BILL. See: Lewis Orde.

MICHAELS, ELENA
   Death and the I Ching. Potter, 1980

MICHAELS, JAN. SC: Darby Castle, in both titles.
   Death on the Late Show. Zebra, 1979
   Sing a Song of Murder. Zebra, 1978

MICHAELS, STEVE. Pseudonym of Michael (Angelo) Avallone (Jr.), 1924- , q.v. Other pseudonyms: Nick Carter, Priscilla Dalton, Mark Dane, Jean-Anne de Pre, Dora Highland, Stuart Jason, Dorothea Nile, Edwina Noone, Sidney Stuart, Max Walker, qq.v.
   The Main Attraction. Belmont, 1963 (Novelization of the movie.)

MICHEAUX, OSCAR. 1884-1951.
   -The Case of Mrs. Wingate. Book Supply, 1944
   -The Forged Note. Western Book Supply, 1915
   -The Story of Dorothy Stanfield. Book Supply, 1946
   -The Wind from Nowhere. Book Supply, 1941

MICHEL, M(ILTON) SCOTT. 1916- . Ref: CA, MC. Pseudonym: Milton Scott, q.v. SC: Dr. Alexander Cornell = AC (see also Scott entry); Wood Jason = WJ.
   The Black Key. Mystery House, 1946 AC
   House in Harlem; see Sweet Murder
   Murder in the Consulting Room; see The Psychiatric Murders
   The Murder of Me. Fell, 1961 (3-act play.)
   The Psychiatric Murders. Mystery House, 1946. British title: Murder in the Consulting Room. Hammond, 1954 [NYC]
   Sinister Warning; see The X-Ray Murders
   Sweet Murder. Coward, 1943; Hammond, 1945. Canadian title: House in Harlem. Harlequin, 1950 WJ [NYC]
   The X-Ray Murders. Coward, 1942; Hammond, 1945. Canadian title: Sinister Warning. Harlequin, 1950 WJ [NYC]

MICHELSON, BENNETT
   The Perfect Weapon. Tower, 1980

MICHELSON, MIRIAM. 1870-1942.
   A Yellow Journalist. Appleton, 1905 ss [S.F.]

MIDDLEMISS, JEAN
   -At the Altar Steps. Digby, 1910
   -Baiting the Trap. Chapman, 1874
   -Blanche Coningham's Surrender. White, 1898
   -By Fair Means. White, 1884
   -Count Remeny. Long, 1905
   -Dandy. Tinsley, 1881
   -An Evil Angel. Digby, 1908
   -The Falkners of Greenhurst. Digby, 1904
   -Fallen from Favour. Digby, 1902
   -A Felon's Daughter. Digby, 1906
   -Four in Hand. Tinsley, 1881
   -A Girl in a Thousand. Chapman, 1885
   -His Lawful Wife. Digby, 1901
   -How I Became Eminent. Eden, 1892
   Hush Money. Digby, 1895
   -In Storm and Strife. Digby, 1899
   -Innocence at Play. Tinsley, 1880
   -Lady Muriel's Secret. Munro, 1884 (British title?)
   -Lil. Hurst, 1872
   -The Loadstone of Love. White, 1886
   -Loves Old and New. Digby, 1908
   -Mignon's Peril. Digby, 1909
   -Mr. Dorillon. Chatto, 1876
   -The Mysterious Mrs. Nutford. Aldine, 1896

The Mystery of Clement Dunraven. Digby, 1894
-Nelly Jocelyn, Widow. White, 1887
-Patty's Partner. Tinsley, 1882
-Poisoned Arrows. White, 1884
The Queen Wasp. Digby, 1900
-Ruth Anstey. Digby, 1904
-Sackcloth and Broadcloth. Tinsley, 1880
-Sealed by a Kiss. Tinsley, 1880
-She's Fooling Thee! Aldine, 1895
-Silvermead. Munro, 1884 (British title?)
-Touch and Go. Chatto, 1877
-Two False Moves. White, 1890
-Vaia's Lord. Sonnenschein, 1888
-A Veneered Scamp. Long, 1906
-Vengeance Is Mine. Aldine, 1895
-A Wheel of Fire. Digby, 1901
-Wild Georgie. Chapman, 1873
-A Woman's Calvary. Digby, 1903
-The Yellow Badge. Digby, 1899

MIDDLEMISS, ROBERT (WILLIAM). 1938- . Ref: CA.
The Lofoten Run. GM, 1979
The Parrot Man. GM, 1977 [Brazil]

MIDDLETON, ELIZABETH. Pseudonym: Elizabeth Antill, q.v.

MIDDLETON, J(ESSE) E(DGAR). 1872-1960.
The Clever Ones. Nelson, 1936
-Green Plush. Methuen, 1932

MIDDLETON, TED
Operation Tokyo. Avon, 1956; Boardman, 1958 [Tokyo]

MIDGLEY, JOHN. 1931- .
The Chill Wind of Freedom. Hale, 1978
Donovan. Chivers, 1974
Nimrod. Hale, 1979
The Resurrection Game. Hale, 1980
Yesterday's Man. Hale, 1976

MIEHE, ULF. 1940- . German suspense fiction writer and film director.
A Dead One in Berlin. Bantam, 1976 (Translation of "Ich Hab Noch einen Toten in Berlin." Berlin, 1973.) [Berlin]
Puma. Weidenfeld, 1978; St. Martin's, 1978 (Translation of "Puma." Munich, 1976.) [Ger.]

MIERS, EARL SCHENCK. 1910-1972. Pseudonym: David William Meredith, q.v.

MIGLIS, JOHN. 1950- . Ref: CA.
Masterwork. Lippincott, 1980 [Amst.]
Not a Bad Man. Morrow, 1978

MIKES, GEORGE. 1912- . Ref: CA.
The Spy Who Died of Boredom. Deutsch, 1973; Harper, 1974

MIKOLOWSKI, KEN
Little Mysteries. Toothpaste Press, 1979 (Illustrated criminous poems.)

MILBROOK, JOHN
A Bridgeport Dagger. Lane, 1930

MILBURN, ELLEN
Wings of Darkness. Belmont, 1975 [La., ca.1860]

MILES, DAVID. Pseudonym of Brendan Leo Cronin, 1907- . Other pseudonym: Michael Cronin, q.v.
Inside Out. Hale, 1960
Nice and Easy. Hale, 1961
Over the Edge. Hale, 1964
Split down the Middle. Hale, 1962

MILES, DENNIS. 1927- .
Pattern of Chalk. New Authors, 1966 [acad.]

MILES, JOHN. Pseudonym of John Miles Bickham, 1930- . Other pseudonym: Jack Bickham, q.v.
The Blackmailer. Bobbs, 1974 [Ohio]
Dally with a Deadly Doll. Ace, 1961 [Okla.]
The Night Hunters. Bobbs, 1973; Hale, 1975 [Okla.]
Operation Nightfall, with Tom Morris. Bobbs, 1975; Souvenir, 1976
The Silver Bullet Gang. Bobbs, 1974; Hale, 1976

MILES, RICHARD. Pseudonym of Gerald Perreau-Saussine, 1938- .
-Angel Loves Nobody. Pyramid, 1974
-The Moonbathers. Pyramid, 1974
-That Cold Day in the Park. Pyramid, 1974

MILES, STELLA. Ref: CC.
Murder at the Arab Stud. Jenkins, 1951
Murder Knows No Master. Jenkins, 1952
Prescription for Murder. Jenkins, 1954
Saddled with Murder. Jenkins, 1953

MILES, WILLIAM A.
Shadow of Suspicion. Dramatic, 1961 (3-act play adapted from a teleplay by Arthur Hailey, 1920-   , q.v.)

MILFORD, FRED C.
In Crime's Disguise. Trischler, 1890
55 Guineas Reward. Field, 1886
-Lost! A Day. Field, 1886

MILKOMANE, GEORGE ALEXIS MILKOMANOVICH. 1903-   . Pseudonyms: George Braddon, Peter Conway, Alec Redwood, George Sava, qq.v.

MILLAR, FLORENCE N. SC: Chief Insp. Douglas Grant, in at least those marked DG.
Fishing Is Dangerous. Gifford, 1946 DG
Grant's Overture. Gifford, 1946 DG
-The Lone Kiwi. Dawson, 1948

MILLAR, JEFF(ERY LYNN). 1942-   . Ref: CA.
Private Sector. Dial, 1979; Macmillan (London), 1980

MILLAR, KENNETH. 1915-1983. Pseudonyms: John Macdonald, John Ross Macdonald, Ross Macdonald, qq.v. All titles are presently published as by Ross Macdonald. SC (in subordinate roles): Chet Gordon = CG.
Blue City. Knopf, 1947; Cassell, 1949
The Dark Tunnel. Dodd, 1944. Also published as: I Die Slowly. Lion, 1955 CG [Mich., acad.]
I Die Slowly; see The Dark Tunnel
Night Train; see Trouble Follows Me
The Three Roads. Knopf, 1948; Cassell, 1950 [Calif.]
Trouble Follows Me. Dodd, 1946. Also published as: Night Train. Lion, 1955 CG

MILLAR, MARGARET (ELLIS STURM). 1915-   . Ref: CA, CC, DD, EM, MC, TC. SC: Dr. Paul Prye = PP; Insp. Sands = S; Tom Aragon = TA.
An Air That Kills. Random, 1957. British title: The Soft Talkers. Gollancz, 1957 [Can.]
Ask for Me Tomorrow. Random, 1976; Gollancz, 1977 TA [Mex.]
Beast in View. Random, 1955; Gollancz, 1955 [L.A.]
Beyond This Point Are Monsters. Random, 1970; Gollancz, 1971 [Calif.]
-The Cannibal Heart. Random, 1949; H. Hamilton, 1950
The Devil Loves Me. Doubleday, 1942 PP,S [Toronto]
Do Evil in Return. Random, 1950; Museum, 1952
-Experiment in Springtime. Random, 1947
The Fiend. Random, 1964; Gollancz, 1964 [Calif.]
Fire Will Freeze. Random, 1944 [Can.]
How Like an Angel. Random, 1962; Gollancz, 1962 [Calif.]
The Invisible Worm. Doubleday, 1941; Long, 1943 PP
The Iron Gates. Random, 1945. British title: Taste of Fears. Hale, 1950 S [Toronto]
The Listening Walls. Random, 1959; Gollancz, 1959 [Calif., Mex. City]
The Lively Corpse; see Rose's Last Summer
The Murder of Miranda. Random, 1979; Gollancz, 1980 TA [Calif.]
Rose's Last Summer. Random, 1952; Museum, 1954. Also published as: The Lively Corpse. Dell, 1956 [Calif.]
The Soft Talkers; see An Air That Kills
A Stranger in My Grave. Random, 1960; Gollancz, 1960 [L.A.]
Taste of Fears; see The Iron Gates
Vanish in an Instant. Random, 1952; Museum, 1953 [Mich.]
Wall of Eyes. Random, 1943 S [Toronto]
The Weak-Eyed Bat. Doubleday, 1942 PP [Can.]

MILLAR, R.
Half a Corpse. Eyre, 1935 (Based on "My First Crime" by Gustave Mace, 1835-1904, q.v.) [Paris]

MILLARD, JOE [JOSEPH JOHN MILLARD]. 1908-   . Ref: CA.
The Hunted. Award, 1974 (Novelization of the "Hec Ramsey" TV series.)
The Hunting Party. Award, 1971; Tandem, 1971 (Novelization of the movie.)
Mansion of Evil. GM, 1950

Thunderbolt and Lightfoot. Award, 1974; Tandem, 1974 (Novelization of the movie.) [Mont.]
The Wickedest Man. GM, 1954; Muller pb, 1960

MILLARD, OSCAR (E.). Born in London and later living in Calif.; ss, motion picture and TV writer.
A Missing Person. McKay, 1972 [L.A.]

MILLER, AGNES
The Colfax Book-Plate. Century, 1926; Benn, 1927 [NYC]
The Obole of Paradise. Hutchinson, 1930

MILLER, ALAN
The Phantoms of a Physician. Grayson, 1935 ss

MILLER, MRS ALEX(ANDER) McVEIGH. 1858-   .
-The Bride of the Tomb. Lovell, 1888
-Countess Vera; or, The Oath of Vengeance. Munro, 1883
The Mystery of Suicide Place. Westbrook, 19??
-Nina's Peril. U.S. Book Co., 1891
-Queenie's Terrible Secret; or, A Young Girl's Strange Fate. Munro, 1883
-Sworn to Silence; or, Aline Rodney's Secret. Munro, 1890

MILLER, ALICE DUER. 1874-1942. See also: Florence Ryerson, 1894-   .
Death Sentence. Dodd, 1935; Allan, 1936
Manslaughter. Dodd, 1921; Parsons, 1922

MILLER, BEN E. SC: Cory Barnett, in both titles.
Death Deal. Powell, 1969
The Set-Up. Powell, 1969 [NYC]

MILLER, BILL. 1920-1961. Joint pseudonym with Robert Wade, 1920-   , q.v.: Will Daemer, Whit Masterson, Wade Miller, Dale Wilmer, qq.v. See also: Bob Wade.

MILLER, D(OROTHY) B(LANCHE)
The Unpardonable Crime. Houghton (London), 1935

MILLER, DENIS. 1935-   .
The Chinese Jade Affair. Milton House, 1973
Diplomatic Taffic. New English Library, 1978

MILLER, ELIZABETH YORK
The Blue Paroquet. Brentano's (London), 1928
The Macowen Murder. Gramol, 1935
The Mark of Yekel. Bles, 1927
Marked Dangerous. Wright, 1935

MILLER, FLOYD C. 1912-   . Ref: CA.
The Savage Streets. Popular Library, 1956 [NYC]

MILLER, FRANK S.
Knock on Any Head. Vega, 1962

MILLER, G. W.
Fettered by Fate. Digby, 1899

MILLER, HELEN TOPPING. 1884-1960.
Who Is This Girl? Appleton, 1941

MILLER, HUGH. 1937-   . Ref: CA.
-Ambulance. New English Library, 1975; St. Martin's, 1976
-The Dissector. New English Library, 1976
Double Deal. New English Library pb, 1974
The Drop Out. New English Library pb, 1973
Feedback. New English Library pb, 1974
-King Pin. New English Library, 1974
The Mourning Brooch. New English Library, 1978 (Novelization of the TV play.) [Glasgow]
The Open City. New English Library, 1973
-The Rejuvenators. New English Library, 1978
-The Saviour. New English Library, 1977
Short Circuit. New English Library pb, 1974
-A Soft Breeze from Hell. New English Library pb, 1976
Terminal Three. Futura, 1978

MILLER, JOHN. Pseudonym of Joseph Samachson, 1906-1980. Ref: CA.
Murder of a Professor. Putnam, 1937; Hale, 1937 [acad.]

MILLER, LANORA (WELZENBACK). 1932-   .
     Ref: CA.
  The Devil's Due. Ace, 1975
  The House on Wolf Trail. Ace, 1976
  Quickthorn. Ace, 1975 [Eng.]

MILLER, LAURITZ (P.). Far East correspondent, then magazine editor in Calif.
  Operation Godiva. Tuttle, 1971 [Tokyo]

MILLER, LEE and LYNDE MILLER
  'Sno Haven. Banner, 1953 (3-act play.)

MILLER, LYNDE. See: Lee Miller.

MILLER, MARC. Pseudonym of Marc(eil Genee Kolstad) Baker, 1911-   , q.v.
  Death at the Easel. Arcadia, 1956 [Calif.]
  Death Is a Liar. Arcadia, 1959
  The Plaid Shroud. Arcadia, 1957 [S.F.]
  Room, Board and Death. Arcadia, 1960 [S.F.]

MILLER, MERLE. 1919-   . Ref: CA.
  A Secret Understanding. Viking, 1956; Heinemann, 1957 [N.Y.]

MILLER, NATHAN. Born in NYC; magazine writer.
  X's Page. Exposition, 1952

MILLER, ORMAN L. 1893-   .
  The Mystery of the Horse with the Wrong Harness. Vantage, 1975

MILLER, RON S. 1936-   . Pseudonym: Fran Huston, q.v.

MILLER, SIGMUND (STEPHEN). 1917-   .
     Pseudonym: Stephanie Blackwood, q.v.
     Ref: CA.
  -One Bright Day. Dramatists, 1952 (3-act play.)
  The Snow Leopard. GM, 1961; Ward, 1959 [Amst.]
  -That's the Way the Money Goes. Crown, 1962

MILLER, VICTOR B. Novelizations of the "Kojak" TV series = K.
  Death Is Not a Passing Grade. PB, 1975. British title: Marked for Murder. Star, 1976 K [NYC]
  Fernanda. PB, 1976 [NYC]
  Girl in the River. PB, 1975; Star, 1975 K [NYC]
  Gun Business. PB, 1975; Wingate, 1978 K [NYC]
  Hide the Children. Ballantine, 1978 [N.Y.]
  Marked for Murder; see Death Is Not a Passing Grade
  Requiem for a Cop. PB, 1974; Wingate, 1976 K [NYC]
  Siege. PB, 1974 K [NYC]
  Take-Over. PB, 1975 K [NYC]
  Therapy in Dynamite. PB, 1975 K [NYC]
  The Trade-Off. PB, 1975 K [NYC]
  A Very Deadly Game. PB, 1975 K [NYC]

MILLER, WADE. Joint pseudonym of Robert Wade, 1920-   , q.v., and Bill Miller, 1920-1961. Other joint pseudonyms: Will Daemer, Whit Masterson, Dale Wilmer, qq.v. See also: Bob Wade. Ref: EM, MC, TC. SC: Max Thursday = MT; Lt. Austin Clapp, in the MT novels and one other marked AC.
  The Big Guy. GM, 1953; Red Seal, 1958 [L.A.]
  Branded Woman. GM, 1952; Fawcett (London), 1954 [Mex.]
  Calamity Fair. Farrar, 1950 MT [San Diego]
  Deadly Weapon. Farrar, 1946; Low, 1947 AC [San Diego]
  Devil May Care. GM, 1950; Fawcett (London), 1957 [Mex.]
  Devil on Two Sticks. Farrar, 1949. Also published as: Killer's Choice. Signet, 1950 [San Diego]
  Fatal Step. Farrar, 1948; Low, 1949 MT [San Diego]
  The Girl from Midnight. GM, 1962 [Calif.]
  Guilty Bystander. Farrar, 1947; Low, 1948 MT [San Diego]
  The Killer. GM, 1951; Fawcett (London), 1957
  Killer's Choice; see Devil on Two Sticks
  Kiss Her Goodbye. Lion, 1956; Allen, 1957 [Calif.]
  Kitten with a Whip. GM, 1959; Muller, 1960 [Calif.]
  Mad Baxter. GM, 1955; Fawcett (London), 1956 [Sard.]
  Murder Charge. Farrar, 1950 MT [San Diego]
  Nightmare Cruise. Ace, 1961. British title: The Sargasso People. Allen, 1961 [ship]
  The Sargasso People; see Nightmare Cruise
  Shoot to Kill. Farrar, 1951; Allen, 1953 MT [San Diego]
  Sinner Take All. GM, 1960; Muller pb, 1961 [Mex.]
  South of the Sun. GM, 1953; Red Seal, 1953 [Mex.]
  Stolen Woman. GM, 1950; Fawcett (London), 1958 [Mex.]
  The Tiger's Wife. GM, 1951; Red Seal, 1958 [L.A.]
  Uneasy Street. Farrar, 1948; Low, 1949 MT [San Diego]

MILLER, WALTER A. 1910-   . Born in Minn.; living in Kan. City in 1950s.
  Scum in the Pot. Comet, 1958

MILLER, WARREN
  The Banker's Millions. Street (Magnet)
  The Confession of a Thug. Street (Magnet)
  The Crimson Glove. Street (Magnet)
  The Deed of a Night. Street (Magnet)
  In Terror's Grasp. Street (Magnet)
  The Man Who Made Diamonds. Street (Magnet)
  A Midnight Vigil. Street (Magnet)
  The Missing Bullet. Street (Magnet)
  The Power of a Villain. Street (Magnet)
  The Price of Protection. Street (Magnet)
  The Sleepless Eye. Street (Magnet)
  An Unfortunate Rogue. Street (Magnet)

MILLET, F(RANCIS) D(AVIS). 1846-1912.
  A Capillary Crime and other stories. Harper, 1892 ss

MILLHAUSER, BERTRAM
  Whatever Goes Up. Doubleday, 1945 [Calif.]

MILLHISER, MARLYS (JOY). 1938-   . Ref: CA.
  Michael's Wife. Putnam, 1972 [Ariz.]
  Nella Waits. Putnam, 1974 [Ia.]
  Willing Hostage. Putnam, 1976 [West]

MILLIGAN, SPIKE. Pseudonym of Terence Alan Milligan, q.v.
  More Goon Show Scripts. Woburn, 1973; St. Martin's, 1975 (Plays, some criminous.)

MILLIGAN, TERENCE ALAN. 1918-   . Pseudonym: Spike Milligan, q.v.

MILLIN, SARAH GERTRUDE. 1889-1968.
  Three Men Die. Chatto, 1934; Harper, 1934

MILLINGTON, FRANCES (RYAN). 1899-1977. Ref: CA.
  The Crime Across the Way. Phoenix, 1937 [L.A.]

MILLS, ALGERNON VICTOR. 1905-   . Pseudonym: Rupert Latimer, q.v.

MILLS, ARTHUR (HOBART). 1887-   .
  -The Ant Heap. Hutchinson, 1934
  The Apache Girl. Collins, 1930 [Paris]
  Black Royalty. Collins, 1933 [Afr.]
  The Blue Spider. Collins, 1929 [Far East]
  Brighton Alibi. Collins, 1936
  The Broken Sword. Collins, 1938
  Cafe in Montparnasse. Collins, 1936 [Paris]
  The Danger Game. Hutchinson, 1926
  Don't Touch the Body. Collins, 1947
  Escapade. Collins, 1931 [China]
  French Girl. Collins, 1937
  Gentleman of Rio. Collins, 1933 [Brazil]
  The Gold Cat. Hutchinson, 1925
  Intrigue Island. Collins, 1930 [Far East]
  Jewel Thief. Collins, 1939
  The Jockey Died First. Staples, 1953
  Judgment of Death. Collins, 1932
  Last Seen Alive. Evans, 1951
  Live Bait. Hutchinson, 1927
  The Maliday Mystery. Staples, 1954
  Modern Cameos. Hutchinson, 1928 ss
  One Man's Secret. Collins, 1932
  Paris Agent. Collins, 1935 [Paris]
  -Pillars of Salt. Duckworth, 1922
  -The Primrose Path. Duckworth, 1923 ss
  Pursued. Collins, 1929 [S. Am.]
  Shroud of Snow. Evans, 1950
  Stowaway. Collins, 1931 [H. Kong]
  -Ursula Vanet. Bale, 1921
  White Negro. Collins, 1940
  -White Snake. Hutchinson, 1928
  The Yellow Dragon. Hutchinson, 1924
  Your Number Is Up. Evans, 1952

MILLS, CARLEY. 1897-1962. Ref: CA.
  A Nearness of Evil. Coward, 1961

MILLS, FRANCES MARY
  The Castle of Villeroy. Shury, 1801

MILLS, HARRY
  A Daughter of Satan. Katahdin, 1896
  His Downward Path. Ogilvie, 1895
  The Massbank Murder. Ogilvie, 1896
  The Woman Stealer. Katahdin, 1896

MILLS, HUGH (TRAVERS). Pseudonym: Hugh Travers, q.v. Ref: CC.
  -The Early Doors. Cresset, 1966
  -The House by the Lake. Evans, 1956 (Play.)
  In Pursuit of Evil. Triton, 1966; Lippincott, 1967 [It.]

MILLS, JAMES (SPENCER). 1932-   .
  One Just Man. Simon, 1974; Sphere, 1976 [NYC]
  The Panic in Needle Park. Farrar, 1966; Sphere, 1971 [NYC]
  The Prosecutor. Farrar, 1969; Allen, 1970 [NYC]
  Report to the Commissioner. Farrar, 1972; Barrie, 1972
  The Seventh Power. Dutton, 1976; Sphere, 1978 [NYC]
  The Truth About Peter Harley. Dutton, 1979 [Thai.]

MILLS, JOHN. 1930-   . Ref: CA.
  The October Men. Oberon (Ottawa), 1973

MILLS, (WILLIAM) MERVYN. 1906-   . Ref: CA.
  The Long Haul. Macmillan (London), 1956; St. Martin's, 1956

MILLS, OSMINGTON. Pseudonym of Vivian Collin Brooks, 1922-   . Ref: CC. SC: Insp./Supt. Baker, in at least those marked B; Patrick C. Shirley and Insp. Rip Irving, in at least those marked S&I. Set: Eng.
  At One Fell Swoop. Bles, 1963; Roy, 1965 B
  The Case of the Flying Fifteen. Bles, 1956 B
  Death Enters the Lists. Bles, 1967; Roy, 1967 S&I
  Dusty Death. Bles, 1965; Roy, 1966 S&I
  Enemies of the Bride. Bles, 1966; Roy, 1967 S&I
  Ghost of a Clue. Bles, 1970
  Headlines Make Murder. Bles, 1962
  Many a Slip. Bles, 1969 S&I
  The Misguided Missile. Bles, 1958 B
  No Match for the Law. Bles, 1957 B
  Stairway to Murder. Bles, 1959 B
  Sundry Fell Designs. Bles, 1968; Roy, 1968
  Traitor Betrayed. Bles, 1964; Roy, 1966 B
  Trial by Ordeal. Bles, 1961; Roy, 1961 B
  Unlucky Break. Bles, 1955; Roy, 1957 B

MILLS, ROBERT E.
  Under the Eye of Night. Leisure, 1980

MILLS, RUTH. Pseudonym of Ruth (Townsend Mills) Teague, 1896-   , q.v.
  Leading Lady. Kendall, 1936 [Midwest]

MILLS, (HARRY ROLAND) WOOSNAM. SC: John Howden = JH; John Melrose = JM. Set: Eng.
  Biting Fortune. Nelson, 1939 JM
  Blind Reckoning. Hodder, 1951 JH
  Dark Encounter. Nelson, 1938 JM
  Dusty Coinage. Hodder, 1953 JH
  French Hazard. Hodder, 1942 JH
  Grim Chancery. Nelson, 1937 JM
  Knaves Rampant. Nelson, 1938 JM
  Phantom Scarlet. Hodder, 1940
  Shadow Crusade. Hodder, 1941 JH [Amst.]
  Tarnished Gold. Hodder, 1951

MILLSON, JULIE
  The Face of the Foe. Hale, 1970
  The Night Has Red Eyes. Hale, 1970

MILLWARD, EDWARD J. SC: Insp. Gil Flicker = GF. Set: Eng.
  The Aero Clubs Mystery. Harrap, 1939 GF
  The Body Lies. Harrap, 1936 GF
  The Copper Bottle. Methuen, 1929; Dutton, 1929 [Wales]
  The House of Wraith. Harrap, 1935; Houghton, 1935

MILN, H. CRICHTON.   -1957.
  The Case of the Rival Race Gangs. Amalgamated Press, 1924 (Sexton Blake.)

MILN, LOUISE JORDAN. 1864-1933.
  The Invisible Foe. Jarrolds, 1918;
    Stokes, 1920 (Novelization of the
    play by Walter Hackett, 1876-1944.)
  Mr. Wu. Cassell, 1918; Stokes, 1920
    (Adapted from the play by Harry M.
    Vernon, 1878-   , and Harold Owens,
    1872-   .)
  The Purple Mask. Hodder, 1918; Stokes,
    1918 (Adapted from the play "Le
    Chevalier au Masque" by Paul Armont
    and Jean Manoussi.) [Paris, 1803]

MILNE, A(LAN) A(LEXANDER). 1882-1956. See
  also: Ruth Sergel. Ref: all except
  DD. Set: Eng.
  Four Days' Wonder. Methuen, 1933; Dut-
    ton, 1933
  The Fourth Wall. French (London), 1929.
    U.S. title: The Perfect Alibi. French
    (NYC), 1929   (Play.)
  The Perfect Alibi; see The Fourth Wall
  The Red House Mystery. Methuen, 1922;
    Dutton, 1922
  A Table Near the Band, and other sto-
    ries. Methuen, 1950; Dutton, 1950
    ss, two criminous

MILNE, SHIRLEY. Born in Malawi. SC: Det.
  Sgt. Steytler = S.
  Beware the Lurking Scorpion. Hale,
    1966; London House, 1967 [Afr.]
  False Witness. Hale, 1964 S [S. Afr.]
  The Hammer of Justice. Hale, 1963 S
  Stiff Silk. Hale, 1962 S

MILNER, GEORGE. Pseudonym of George
  Hardinge.
  The Crime Against Marcella. Hodder,
    1963
  A Dying Fall. H. Hamilton, 1957
  A Leavetaking. Hodder, 1966; Dodd, 1966
  -The Scarlet Fountains. Collins, 1956
  Shark Among Herrings. Collins, 1954
  Stately Homicide. Collins, 1953
  Your Money and Your Life. H. Hamilton,
    1957

MILTON, DAVID SCOTT. 1934-   . Ref: CA.
  Kabbalah. Harcourt, 1980
  Paradise Road. Atheneum, 1974; Ellis,
    1974

MILTON, GLADYS ALEXANDRA. Pseudonym:
  Anthony Carlyle, q.v.

MILTON, HENRY A.
  The President Is Missing! Banner, 1967

MILTON, JOSEPH. SC: Bart Gould, in all
  titles (see also: Joseph Hilton).
  Assignment: Assassination. Lancer,
    1964. Also published as: The Running
    Spy. Lancer, 1967
  Baron Sinister. Lancer, 1965 [Vienna]
  The Big Blue Death. Lancer, 1965
  The Death Makers. Lancer, 1966   [H.
    Kong]
  The Man Who Bombed the World. Lancer,
    1966
  Operation: World War Three. Lancer,
    1966
  The Running Spy; see Assignment: As-
    sassination
  Worldbreaker. Lancer, 1964

MINCHIN, DEVON (GEORGE). 1919-   .
  The Money Movers. Angus (Sydney), 1972

MINICK, MICHAEL. 1945-   . Ref: CA.
  The Kung Fu Avengers. Bantam (NYC &
    London), 1975 [NYC]

MINNEY, R(UBEIGH) J(AMES). 1895-   .
  Ref: CA. See: Juliet (Evangeline
  Glyn) Rhys-Williams, 1898-   .

MINOT, GEORGE E(VANS). 1898-   .
  Murder Will Out. Marshall Jones, 1928
    (Somewhat "novelized" true crime
    accounts.)

MINTON, PAULA. Pseudonym of Paul H.
  Little, 1915-   . Other pseudonym:
  Hugo Paul, q.v. Ref: CA.
  The Dark of Memory. Lancer, 1967. Also
    published as: The Loom of Terror.
    Lancer, 1968
  Engraved in Evil. Lancer, 1965 [Switz.]
  Fog Hides the Fury. Lancer, 1966 [S.F.]
  The Girl from Nowhere. Major, 1975
  Hand of the Imposter. Lancer, 1965
    [Austria]
  The Loom of Terror; see The Dark of
    Memory
  The Mask of Medusa. Major, 1975
  Orphan of the Shadows. Lancer, 1965
    [Fr.]
  Portrait of Terror. Belmont, 1967
  Secret Melody. Lancer, 1964 [Fr.]
  Shadow of a Witch. Belmont, 1967
  Thunder over the Reefs. Lancer, 1967

MIRKARIMI, JAVAD
  One Love Is Too Many for an Agent.
    Vantage, 1979

MIRON, CHARLES
  Airport Cop. Manor, 1974
  The Celluloid Caper. Manor, 1979
  Death Flight. Manor, 1975
  House of Three Eagles. Manor, 1978
  Murder on the Eighteenth Hole. Manor,
    1978
  Ten Million Dollar Girl. Manor, 1978
  To Kill a Snowman. Manor, 1978
  Twilight Strangler. Manor, 1975
  The $2,000,000 Blueprint. Manor, 1978

MITCHAM, GILROY. Pseudonym of William
  (Simpson) Newton, 1923-   , q.v.
  SC: Nick Marshall = NM. Set: Eng.
  The Dead Reckoning. Dobson, 1960; Roy,
    1960 NM
  The Full Stop. Dobson, 1957; Roy, 1957
    NM
  The Man from Bar Harbour. Dobson, 1958;
    Roy, 1958 NM
  Uncertain Judgement. Dobson, 1961; Roy,
    1962

MITCHELL, DODSON L(OMAX), 1868-1939, and
  CLYDE NORTH
  In Times Square. French (NYC), 1932
    (3-act play.) [NYC]

MITCHELL, EDMUND. 1861-1917.
  -The Despoilers. Cassell, 1904
  Plotters of Paris. Hutchinson, 1900
    [Paris]
  -The Temple of Death. Hutchinson, 1894

MITCHELL, EDWARD CARD. Joint pseudonym
  with Lincoln Springfield: Captain
  Coe, q.v.

MITCHELL, GLADYS (MAUDE WINIFRED).
  1901-   . Pseudonym: Malcolm Torrie,
  q.v. Ref: CA, CC, DD, EM, MP, TC.
  SC: Mrs. Adela Beatrice Lestrange
  Bradley, in all titles. Set: Eng.
  Adders on the Heath. Joseph, 1963;
    London House, 1963
  Brazen Tongue. Joseph, 1940
  Come Away, Death. Joseph, 1937
  Convent on Styx. Joseph, 1975
  The Croaking Raven. Joseph, 1966
  Dance to Your Daddy. Joseph, 1969
  The Dancing Druids. Joseph, 1948
  Dead Men's Morris. Joseph, 1936
  Death and the Maiden. Joseph, 1947
  Death at the Opera. Grayson, 1934. U.S.
    title: Death in the Wet. Macrae-
    Smith, 1934 [theatre]
  Death in the Wet; see Death at the
    Opera
  Death of a Delft Blue. Joseph, 1964;
    London House, 1964
  The Devil at Saxon Wall. Grayson, 1935
  The Devil's Elbow. Joseph, 1951
  The Echoing Strangers. Joseph, 1952
  Faintley Speaking. Joseph, 1954
  Fault in the Structure. Joseph, 1977
  Gory Dew. Joseph, 1970
  Groaning Spinney. Joseph, 1950
  Hangman's Curfew. Joseph, 1941
  A Hearse in May-Day. Joseph, 1972
  Here Comes a Chopper. Joseph, 1946
  A Javelin for Jonah. Joseph, 1974
  Lament for Leto. Joseph, 1971
  Late, Late in the Evening. Joseph, 1976
  Laurels Are Poison. Joseph, 1942
    [acad.]
  The Longer Bodies. Gollancz, 1930
  The Man Who Grew Tomatoes. Joseph,
    1959; London House, 1959
  Merlin's Furlong. Joseph, 1953
  Mingled with Venom. Joseph, 1978
  The Mudflats of the Dead. Joseph, 1979
  The Murder of Busy Lizzie. Joseph, 1973
  My Bones Will Keep. Joseph, 1962; Bri-
    tish Book Centre, 1962
  My Father Sleeps. Joseph, 1944
  The Mystery of a Butcher's Shop. Gol-
    lancz, 1929; Dial, 1930
  Nest of Vipers. Joseph, 1979
  The Nodding Canaries. Joseph, 1961
  Noonday and Night. Joseph, 1977
  Pageant of Murder. Joseph, 1965; London
    House, 1965
  Printer's Error. Joseph, 1939
  The Rising of the Moon. Joseph, 1945
  St. Peter's Finger. Joseph, 1938
  The Saltmarsh Murders. Gollancz, 1932;
    Macrae-Smith, 1933
  Say It with Flowers. Joseph, 1960; Lon-
    don House, 1960
  Skeleton Island. Joseph, 1967
  Speedy Death. Gollancz, 1929; Dial,
    1929
  Spotted Hemlock. Joseph, 1958; British
    Book Centre, 1958 [acad.]
  Sunset over Soho. Joseph, 1943
  Three Quick and Five Dead. Joseph, 1968
  Tom Brown's Body. Joseph, 1949

  Twelve Horses and the Hangman's Noose.
    Joseph, 1956; British Book Centre,
    1958
  The Twenty-Third Man. Joseph, 1957
    [It.]
  Uncoffin'd Clay. Joseph, 1980
  Watson's Choice. Joseph, 1955; McKay,
    1976
  When Last I Died. Joseph, 1941; Knopf,
    1942
  The Whispering Knights. Joseph, 1980
  Winking at the Brim. Joseph, 1974;
    McKay, 1977 [Scot.]
  The Worsted Viper. Joseph, 1943
  Wraiths and Changelings. Joseph, 1978

MITCHELL, HUTTON
  The Deviations of Diana. Philpot, 1923
  The Fourth Man. Selwyn, 1931

MITCHELL, IAN
  Dove of War. Hale, 1980
  The Kabul Contract. Hale, 1978
  The Old Gold Road. Hale, 1977

MITCHELL, ISAAC. 1759-1812.
  The Asylum; or, Alonzo and Melissa.
    Nelson, 1811 [Charleston]

MITCHELL, JAMES (WILLIAM). 1926-   .
  Pseudonyms: James Meldrum, James
  Munro, qq.v. Ref: CA. SC: David Cal-
  lan, in at least those marked DC.
  -Among Arabian Sands. Davies, 1963
  Callan; see A Magnum for Schneider
  Death and Bright Water. H. Hamilton,
    1974; Morrow, 1974 DC [Greece]
  Here's a Villain! Davies, 1957. U.S.
    title: The Lady Is Waiting. Morrow,
    1958
  -Ilion Like a Mist. Cassell, 1969. Also
    published as: Venus in Plastic.
    Corgi, 1970
  The Lady Is Waiting; see Here's a Vil-
    lain!
  A Magnum for Schneider. Jenkins, 1969.
    U.S. title: A Red File for Callan.
    Simon, 1971. Also published as:
    Callan. Corgi, 1974 DC
  A Red File for Callan; see A Magnum for
    Schneider
  Russian Roulette. H. Hamilton, 1973;
    Morrow, 1973 DC
  Smear Job. H. Hamilton, 1975; Putnam,
    1977 DC
  -Steady, Boys, Steady. Davies, 1960
  Venus in Plastic; see Ilion Like a Mist
  A Way Back. Davies, 1959; Morrow, 1960,
    as The Way Back
  -The Winners. Cassell, 1970

MITCHELL, LEBBEUS. 1879-   . Ref: CC.
  The Parachute Murder. Macaulay, 1933
    [NYC]

MITCHELL, NORMA. See: Wilbur Daniel
  Steele, 1886-1970.

MITCHELL, RONALD ELWY. 1905-   . Born in
  London, educated there and at Yale;
  prof. at U. of Wis. in 1940s.
  -Design for November. Harper, 1947
    [acad.]

MITCHELL, S(ILAS) WEIR. 1829-1914.
  The Adventures of Francois. Century,
    1898; Macmillan (London), 1898
  The Autobiography of a Quack, and The
    Case of George Dedlow. Century, 1900
  -A Diplomatic Adventure. Century, 1906

MITCHELL, SCOTT. Pseudonym of Lionel
  Robert Holcombe Godfrey, 1932-   .
  Other pseudonym: Elliot Kennedy, q.v.
  SC: Brock Devlin, in at least those
  marked BD. Set: generally U.S.
  Come, Sweet Death. Hammond, 1967 BD
  Dead on Arrival. Hale, 1974
  Deadly Persuasion. Hammond, 1964 BD
  Death's Busy Crossroads. Hale, 1975
  Double Bluff. Jenkins, 1968 BD
  The Girl in the Wet-Look Bikini. Hale,
    1973 BD
  A Haven for the Damned. Hale, 1971 BD
  A Knife-Edged Thing. Cassell, 1969 BD
  The Lonely Shroud. Hammond, 1964 BD
    [L.A.]
  Nice Guys Don't Win. Hale, 1974 BD
  Obsession. Hale, 1976
  Over My Dead Body. Hale, 1974
  Rage in Babylon. Hale, 1972 BD
  Sables Spell Trouble. Hammond, 1963 BD
  Some Dames Play Rough. Hammond, 1963 BD
  You'll Never Get to Heaven. Hale, 1972
    BD

MITCHELL, WILL
  The Goldfish Murders. GM, 1950; Red
    Seal, 1958 [NYC]

MITCHELSON, AUSTIN and NICHOLAS UTECHIN,
q.v. SC: Sherlock Holmes, in both
titles.
The Earthquake Machine. Belmont, 1976
[Eng., 1906]
Hellbirds. Belmont, 1976 [Eng., ca.
1905]

MITCHELTREE, TOM
Terror in Room 201. Tower, 1980 [Oreg.]

MITFORD, BERTRAM. 1855-1914. Set: generally Afr.
-Aletta. White, 1900
-Averno. Ward, 1913
-A Border Scourge. Long, 1910
The Curses of Clement Waynflete. Ward, 1894
-Dorrien of Cranston. Hurst, 1903
-A Duel Resurrection. Ward, 1910
-The Expiation of Wynne Palliser. Ward, 1896
-The Fire Trumpet. Blackett, 1889
Fordham's Feud. Ward, 1897
-Forging the Blades. Nash, 1908
A Frontier Mystery. White, 1905
-Golden Face. Trischler, 1892
-The Gun-Runner. Chatto, 1899; Fenno, 1898
-Harley Greenoak's Charge. Chatto, 1906
-Haviland's Chum. Chatto, 1903
The Heath Hover Mystery. Ward, 1911
-In the Whirl of the Rising. Methuen, 1904
-The Induna's Wife. White, 1898
-An Island of Eden. Ward, 1913
-John Ames, Native Commissioner. White, 1900
-The King's Assegai. Chatto, 1894; Fenno, 1894
-A Legacy of the Granite Hills. Long, 1909
-The Luck of Gerard Ridgeley. Chatto, 1894
-Ravenshaw of Rietholine. Ward, 1910
-The Red Derelict. Methuen, 1904
-Renshaw Fanning's Quest. Chatto, 1894
-The River of Unrest. Ward, 1912
-The Ruby Sword. White, 1899
-Seaford's Snake. Ward, 1912
-A Secret of the Lebombo. Hurst, 1905
-Selmin of Selmingfold. Ward, 1912
The Sign of the Spider. Methuen, 1896; Dodd, 1896
-The Sirdar's Oath. White, 1904
-The Triumph of Hilary Blackland. Chatto, 1901
-Tween Snow and Fire. Heinemann, 1892; Cassell (NYC), 1892
A Veldt Official. Ward, 1895 [S. Afr.]
A Veldt Vendetta. Ward, 1903 [S. Afr.]
-The Weird of Deadly Hollow. Sutton, 1891
-The White Hand and the Black. Long, 1907
-The White Shield. Cassell, 1895; Stokes, 1895
-The Word of the Sorceress. Hutchinson, 1902

MITFORD, C. GUISE
The Dual Identity. Long, 1915
The Hidden Mask. Greening, 1914
-His Dainty Whim. Hutchinson, 1902
-In Camera. Long, 1916
-Izelle of the Dunes. Long, 1907
-Love in Lilac-Land. Long, 1910
The Paxton Plot. Long, 1908
-The Spell of the Snow. Pearson, 1900
-The Wooing of Martha. Nash, 1911

MITTON, G(ERALDINE) E(DITH)
The Green Moth, with J(ames) G(eorge) Scott, 1851- . Murray, 1922 [Burma]
The Judge's Daughters. Nash, 1921

MITZMAN, NEWT and WILLIAM DALZELL
Books and Crooks. Dramatic, 1953 (3-act play.)
In 25 Words—or Death. French (NYC), 1955 (3-act play.)

MIZZEN, MATT. Pseudonym of Henry Llewellyn Williams, 1842- .
Binnacle Jack; or, The Cavern of Death. De Witt, 18??
Delaware Dick; or, The Chase of the Whip. De Witt, 18??
The Flying Arrow; or, The Pirate's Revenge. De Witt, 18??

MOAN, TERENCE. 1947- . Ref: CA.
The Deadly Frost. Rawson, 1979

MOBERLY, CHARLOTTE ANNE ELIZABETH, 1846-1937, and ELEANOR F(RANCES) JOURDAIN
-An Adventure. Macmillan (London), 1911

MOBERLY, L(UCY) G(ERTRUDE). 1860- .
-Fingers of Fate. Ward, 1929
-In a Fair Ground. Ward, 1931

-A Leap in the Dark. Mills, 1925
-A Mystery Chain. Ward, 1932
-A Tangled Web. Ward, 1908

MOCKLER, GRETCHEN
Roanleigh. Signet, 1966

MODELL, MIRRIAM. 1908- . Pseudonym: Evelyn Piper, q.v.

MOFFAT, GWEN. 1924- . Ref: CA, TC. SC: Melinda Pink = MP.
The Corpse Road. Gollancz, 1974
Deviant Death. Gollancz, 1973
Hard Option. Gollancz, 1975
Lady with a Cool Eye. Gollancz, 1973 MP
Miss Pink at the Edge of the World. Gollancz, 1975; Scribner, 1975 MP [Scot.]
Over the Sea to Death. Gollancz, 1976; Scribner, 1976 MP [Scot.]
Persons Unknown. Gollancz, 1978 MP [Wales]
A Short Time to Live. Gollancz, 1976 MP

MOFFATT, JAMES. 1870-1944.
A Tangled Web. Hodder, 1929

MOFFATT, JAMES. SC: Silas Manners, in at least those marked SM; Johnny Canuck, in at least those marked JC.
Blood Is a Personal Thing. Compact, 1965
Blue Line Murder. Compact, 1965; Leisure, 1970 JC
The Cambri Plot; see The Sleeping Bomb
Course of Villainy. Compact, 1966
-The Courtyard. New English Library pb, 1970
Curtain of Hate. Compact, 1966
The Eighth Veil. Compact, 1965
The Girl from H.A.R.D. New English Library, 1973
Justice for a Dead Spy. New English Library pb, 1971 SM
The Naked Light. New English Library pb, 1970
Perfect Assignment. New English Library pb, 1975 (Girl from H.A.R.D. series)
The Sleeping Bomb. New English Library pb, 1970. U.S. title: The Cambri Plot. Tower, 1973 SM
Terror-Go-Round. Compact, 1966
Time for Sleeping. Compact, 1965; Leisure, 1970 JC
The Twisted Thread. Compact, 1966
Virginia Box and the "Unsatisfied". New English Library pb, 1974 (Girl from H.A.R.D. series.)

MOFFETT, CLEVELAND (LANGSTON). 1863-1926. Ref: CC, EM, MP. SC: Paul Coquenil = PC.
The Bishop's Purse, with Oliver Herford, 1863-1935. Appleton, 1913 [Eng.]
The Master Mind. Appleton, 1927 PC [Paris]
The Mysterious Card. Small, 1912
Possessed. McCann, 1920
The Seine Mystery. Dodd, 1925; Melrose, 1924 [Paris]
Through the Wall. Appleton, 1909; Melrose, 1910 PC [Paris]
True Detective Stories from the Archives of the Pinkertons. Doubleday, 1897 ss

MOISEIWITSCH, MAURICE
-Bring Me My Bow. Muller, 1942
-Comrade Souvarin. Muller, 1945
-Mr. Penny. Muller, 1938
-Mr. Penny at War. Angus, 1942
-Mr. Penny Comes Down Heads. Angus, 1945 ss
Post-Mortem. Marlowe, 1947
She, the Accused. Heinemann, 1956
-A Sky-Blue Life. Heinemann, 1956
-The Sleeping Tiger. Heinemann, 1955
Woolf Sarason, Special Agent. Muller, 1941
-Yesterday's Enemy. Corgi, 1959 (Novelization of the play by Peter N. Newman.)

MOLE, WILLIAM. Pseudonym of William Antony Younger, 1917-1962. Ref: CC. SC: Casson Duker = CD.
Goodbye Is Not Worthwhile. Eyre, 1956 CD [Barbados]
The Hammersmith Maggot. Eyre, 1955. U.S. title: Small Venom. Dodd, 1956. Also published as: Shadow of a Killer. Dell, 1959 CD
The Lobster Guerillas. Eyre, 1953
Shadow of a Killer; see The Hammersmith Maggot
Skin Trap. Eyre, 1957. U.S. title: You Pay for Pity. Dodd, 1958 CD
Small Venom; see The Hammersmith Maggot
-Trample an Empire. Eyre, 1952
You Pay for Pity; see Skin Trap

MOLL, ELICK. 1907- . Ref: CA.
Night Without Sleep. Little, 1950; Davies, 1951

MOLLOY, J(OSEPH) FITZGERALD. 1858-1908.
An Excellent Knave. Hutchinson, 1893; Lovell, 1892
His Wife's Soul. Hutchinson, 1893. U.S title: Sweet Is Revenge. Taylor, 1891. Also published in England as: Sweet Is Revenge; or, His Wife's Soul. Hutchinson, 1895
How Came He Dead? Lovell, 1890 (British title?)
-It Is No Wonder. Hurst, 1882
-A Justified Sinner. Downey, 1897
-Merely Players. Tinsley, 1881
-A Modern Magician. Ward, 1887; Lovell, 1888
Sweet Is Revenge; see His Wife's Soul
-That Villain, Romeo! Ward, 1886
-What Has Thou Done? Hurst, 1883; Harper, 1883

MOLNAR, LOUIS. See: Charles Saxby.

MOLONY, J(OHN) CHARTRES. 1877- .
Savinelli. Methuen, 1930; Dial, 1930

MOLYNEAUX, C. B.
Death Called Twice. Pemberton, 1949
Murder in a Madhouse. Pemberton, 1946
The Poison Cocktail Murders. Pemberton, 1944

MONAHAN, GEORGE. See: Evelyn Graves.

MONAHAN, JOHN. Pseudonym of W(illiam) R(iley) Burnett, 1899-1982, q.v.
Big Stan. GM, 1953; Fawcett (London), 1955 [Midwest]

MONDOL, PROF. 1924- .
Operation Tibet. Vantage, 1979 [Tib.]

MONETTE, PAUL
Taking Care of Mrs. Carroll. Little, 1978 [New Eng.]

MONIG, CHRISTOPHER. Pseudonym of Kendell Foster Crossen, 1910-1981, q.v. Other pseudonyms: Bennett Barlay, M. E. Chaber, Richard Foster, Clay Richards, qq.v. SC: Brian Brett, in all titles.
Abra-Cadaver. Dutton, 1958; Boardman, 1958
The Burned Man. Dutton, 1956; Boardman, 1957. Also published as: Don't Count the Corpses. Dell, 1958
Don't Count the Corpses; see The Burned Man
The Lonely Graves. Dutton, 1960; Boardman, 1961
Once Upon a Crime. Dutton, 1959; Boardman, 1960 [Johan.]

MONIGLE, MARTHA
The Doll Castle. Ballantine, 1975

MONK, ELLIOT. See: Beatrice Baskerville

MONKSHOOD, G. F. Pseudonym of William James Clarke, 1872- .
My Lady Ruby and John Basileon, Chief of Police. Greening, 1899 (2 stories.)

MONMOUTH, JACK. Pseudonym of William Leonard Pember. SC: Tom Langley, in at least those marked TL. Set: Eng.
The Donovan Case. Jarrolds, 1955 TL
Lightning over Mayfair. Hale, 1958 TL
Lonely, Lovely Lady. Jarrolds, 1956 TL
Not Ready to Die. Hale, 1960
Sleepy-Eyed Blonde. Hale, 1957 TL

MONNOW, PETER. Pseudonym of Glynn Croudace, 1917- , q.v.
Fire Opal. Jenkins, 1968
The Hooded Skull. Hale, 1972
The Killing of Alquin Judd. Jenkins, 1969

MONRO, GAVIN. Pseudonym of Gertrude Monro-Higgs, 1905- . Ref: CA. Set: Eng.
A Bent for Blackmail. Hale, 1967
Marked with a Cross. Hale, 1968
Trip to Eternity. Hale, 1970
Who Killed Amanda? Hale, 1967

MONRO-HIGGS, GERTRUDE. 1905- . Pseudonym: Gavin Monro, q.v.

MONROE, ROY. Pseudonym. 1913- .
The Judge Speaks. Exposition, 1958

MONSARRAT, NICHOLAS (JOHN TURNEY). 1910-1979. Ref: CA.
Castle Garac. Pan, 1968; Knopf, 1955 [Fr.]

The Nylon Pirates. Cassell, 1960;
  Sloane, 1960
The Ship That Died of Shame, and other
  stories. Cassell, 1959; Sloane, 1959
  ss
Smith & Jones. Cassell, 1963; Sloane,
  1963
Something to Hide. Cassell, 1965; Morrow, 1966
-The Time Before This. Cassell, 1962;
  Sloane, 1962

MONSKY, MARK. 1941- . Ref: CA.
  Looking Out for #1. Simon, 1975 [NYC]

MONTAGU, IRVING
  Absolutely True. Allen, 1893

MONTAGUE, CHARLES HOWARD. 1859-1889.
  The Countess Muta. Belford, 1889;
    Routledge, 1890
  -The Doctor's Mistake; or, What Myrta
    Saw, with Clement Milton Hammond.
    T. Downey, 1888
  The Face of Rosenfel. Burt, 1888
  -The Romance of Lilies. Harris, 1886
  Two Strokes of the Bell. Harris, 1886
  Written in Red, with C. W. Dyar. Cassell (NYC), 1890 [Boston]

MONTAGUE, EDWARD
  The Castle of Berry Pomeroy. Minerva,
    1806
  The Demon of Sicily. Hughes, 1806
    [Sic.]

MONTAGUE, J. J. SC: Shauna Bishop, in all
  titles.
  The Chinese Kiss. Canyon, 1974
  The Cong Kiss. Canyon, 1974
  The French Kiss. Canyon, 1974

MONTAGUE, JEFFREY. SC: John Jeremy, in
  both titles. Set: Eng.
  John Jeremy—Cracksman. Allan, 1936
  The Mandarin's Pearl. Quality, 1942

MONTAGUE, JOSEPH
  Whose Millions? Chelsea, 1925 [NYC]

MONTANA, RON
  The Cathedral Option. Zebra, 1978
  -Sign of the Thunderbird. Manor, 1977

MONTANDON, PAT. Ref: CA.
  The Intruders. Coward, 1975 [S.F.]

MONTANO, PABLO
  The Collection. Arlington, 1970

MONTANYE, C(ARLETON) S(TEVENS). 1892-
  1948. Pseudonym: Robert Wallace, q.v.
  Moons in Gold. Lippincott, 1936; Harrap, 1937

MONTEILHET, HUBERT. 1928- . Ref: CC,
  TC.
  Andromache; or, The Inadvertent Murder.
    Simon, 1970; Hodder, 1971 (Translation of "Andromac our le Meurtre par
    Inadvertance." Paris, 1968.) [Fr.]
  Cupid's Executioners. Simon, 1967; Hodder, 1967 (Translation of "Les Bourreaux de Cupidon." Paris, 1966.)
  Dead Copy; see Murder at the Frankfurt
    Book Fair
  Murder at Leisure. Simon, 1971; Hodder,
    1972 (Translation of "Meurtre a
    Loisir." Paris, 1969.)
  Murder at the Frankfurt Book Fair.
    Doubleday, 1976. British title: Dead
    Copy. Macdonald, 1976 (Translation
    of "Mourir a Francfort." Paris,
    1975.) [Frank.]
  A Perfect Crime, or Two. Simon, 1971
    Translation of "De Quelques Crimes
    Parfaits." Paris, 1969.)
  Phoenix from the Ashes; see Return from
    the Ashes
  Praying Mantis; see The Praying Mantises
  The Praying Mantises. Simon, 1962. British title: Praying Mantis. H. Hamilton, 1962 (Translation of "Les Mantes Religieuses." Paris, 1960.)
  The Prisoner of Love. Simon, 1965;
    Chapman, 1966 (Translation of "Le
    Forcat de l'Amour." Paris, 1965.)
    [Paris]
  Return from the Ashes. Simon, 1963.
    British title: Phoenix from the
    Ashes. H. Hamilton, 1963 (Translation of "Le Retour des Cendres."
    Paris, 1961.) [Fr.]
  The Road to Hell. Simon, 1964; Chapman,
    1965 (Translation of "Les Paves du
    Diable." Paris, 1963.) [Fr.]

MONTFORT, AUGUSTE. 1913- . Pseudonym:
  Auguste Le Breton, q.v.

MONTGOMERIE, JAMES
  Implosion. Baker, 1974

MONTGOMERY, IONE. SC: Christopher Gibson,
  in both titles.
  Death Won a Prize. Doubleday, 1941;
    Cherry Tree (abridged), 1944 [Wash.]
  The Golden Dress. Doubleday, 1940;
    Boardman, 1944 [Midwest]

MONTGOMERY, MARY. -1975.
  Somebody Knew. Arcadia, 1961

MONTGOMERY, ROBERT BRUCE. 1921-1978.
  Pseudonym: Edmund Crispin, q.v.

MONTROSE, DAVID. SC: Russell Teed, in at
  least those marked RT.
  The Body on Mount Royal. Harlequin,
    1953
  The Crime on Cote des Neiges. Collins
    pb (Toronto), 1951 RT
  -Gambling with Fire. Hale, 1969
  Murder over Dorval. Collins pb (Toronto), 1952 RT

MONTROSE, GRAHAM. Pseudonym of Charles
  Roy Mackinnon, 1924- . Ref: CA.
  SC: Angel Brown, in all titles. Set:
  Eng.
  Angel Abroad. Hale, 1969
  Angel and the Nero. Hale, 1971
  Angel and the Red Admiral. Hale, 1972
  Angel at Arms. Hale, 1971
  Angel in Paradise. Hale, 1970
  Angel of Death. Hale, 1968
  Angel of No Mercy. Hale, 1968
  Angel of Vengeance. Hale, 1970
  Ask an Angel. Hale, 1970
  Fanfare for Angel. Hale, 1971
  A Matter of Motive. Hale, 1969
  Send for Angel. Hale, 1970
  Where Angel Treads. Hale, 1969

MONTROSS, DAVID. Pseudonym of Jean Louise
  Backus, 1914- . Ref: CA. SC: Remsen, in all titles.
  Fellow-Traveler. Doubleday, 1965; Hale,
    1966
  Traitor's Wife. Doubleday, 1962; Gollancz, 1962
  Troika. Doubleday, 1963; Gollancz,
    1963. Also published as: Who Is Elissa Sheldon? Paperback Library, 1967
  Who Is Elissa Sheldon?; see Troika

MOODEY, MORTHA LIVINGSTON
  -Alan Thorne. Lothrop, 1889
  The Tragedy of Brinkwater. Cassell
    (NYC), 1887; Cassell (London), 1888

MOODIE, EDWIN
  The Great Shakes. Museum, 1956

MOODY, ALAN B. 1900-1944.
  The House in Ralston Place. Gem, 1926

MOODY, LAURENCE. 1907- .
  Some Must Die. Hale, 1964

MOODY, RON
  The Devil You Don't. Robson, 1980

MOOLMAN, VALERIE. Pseudonym: Nick Carter,
  q.v.

MOONEY, JAMES. See also: John W. Postgate.
  The Trail of the Barrow; or, The Brother's Revenge. Ogilvie, 1888 [Eng.]

MOOR, EMILY. Pseudonym of Richard Deming,
  1915- , q.v. Other pseudonym: Max
  Franklin, q.v. See also: Nick Marino;
  and: Ellery Queen.
  The Shadowed Porch. Beagle, 1972

MOORCOCK, MICHAEL (JOHN). 1939- .
  Pseudonyms: Bill Barclay, Desmond
  Reid, qq.v. Ref: CA. SC: Jerry Cornelius, in all titles
  The Chinese Agent. Hutchinson, 1970;
    Macmillan, 1970 (Revision, with
    change in protagonist, of "Somewhere
    in the Night," as by Bill Barclay,
    q.v.)
  A Cure for Cancer. Allison, 1970; Holt,
    1971
  The English Assassin. Allison, 1972;
    Harper, 1974
  The Russian Intelligence. Savoy, 1980
    (Revision, with change in protagonist, of "Printer's Devil," as by Bill
    Barclay, q.v.)

MOORE, AMES
  Royce of the Royal Mounted. Harlequin,
    1950 [Can.]

MOORE, ANDREW. Pseudonym of Frederick
  Moore Binder, 1920- . Ref: CA.
  The Serbian Assignment. Apollo, 1971

MOORE, ARTHUR
  The Gay Deceivers. Methuen, 1899

MOORE, ARTHUR and CLAYTON (HARTLEY) MATTHEWS, 1918- , q.v. For Moore, see
  also: Don Hoyt. Joint pseudonyms of
  Arthur Moore and Marilyn Granbeck,
  1927- , q.v.: Adam Hamilton, Van
  Saxon, qq.v. Joint pseudonym of Arthur Moore and Alfred Harris,
  1928- , q.v.: Gwen Addison, q.v.
  For Clayton Matthews, see also: Patty
  Brisco.
  Las Vegas. PB, 1974; Futura, 1975
    [Las Veg.]

MOORE, AUSTIN. Pseudonym of (Charles)
  Augustus (Carlow) Muir, 1892- ,
  q.v. Set: Eng.
  Birds of the Night. Hodder, 1930;
    Smith, 1931. Reprinted as by Augustus
    Muir: Methuen, 1937
  The House of Lies. Hodder, 1932;
    Doubleday, 1932. Revised and published as by Augustus Muir: Methuen,
    1939

MOORE, BRIAN. 1921- . Ref: CA.
  The Executioners. Harlequin, 1951
  The Revolution Script. Holt, 1971;
    Cape, 1971 [Montr.]
  Wreath for a Redhead. Harlequin, 1951

MOORE, C(ATHERINE) L(UCILE). 1911- .
  Doomsday Morning. Doubleday, 1957;
    World, 1960 [future]

MOORE, CARLYLE. 1875- . See also:
  George C(harles) Jenks, 1850-1929.
  Listening In. French (NYC & London),
    1928 (3-act play.)
  Stop Thief! French (NYC), 1917 (Play.)

MOORE, CHARLES K.
  A Case of Blackmail. Arrowsmith, 1900

MOORE, CHET
  Knifed in the Back. Vantage, 1980

MOORE, CLAYTON. Pseudonym of Marilyn
  Granbeck, 1927- , q.v. Other pseudonym: Ben Grant, q.v. Joint pseudonyms with Arthur Moore, q.v.: Adam
  Hamilton, Van Saxon, qq.v.
  The Corrupters. Berkley, 1974
  End of Peckoning. Berkley, 1974

MOORE, DONALD. 1923- .
  Highway of Fear. Hodder, 1961

MOORE, DONALD L(LOYD)
  Mirrors of the Apocalypse. Springwood,
    1978; Charter, 1978

MOORE, DORIN(N)E
  Bride of the Dark Castle; see Castle
    Hohenfels
  Castle Hohenfels. Zebra, 1975. Also
    published as: Bride of the Dark
    Castle. Zebra, 1976
  The Caverns of Falkenhorst. Berkley,
    1973 [Ger.]
  Flight from Eden Key. Berkley, 1974
  A Legacy of Emeralds. Berkley, 1972
    [Austria]
  The Legend of Monk's Court. Beagle,
    1974
  Masquerade at Monfalcone. Berkley, 1974
    [It.]
  Miranda's Curse. Berkley, 1973

MOORE, DORIS LANGLEY (LEVY). 1903- .
  Ref: CA.
  -All Done by Kindness. Cassell, 1951;
    Lippincott, 1953
  -My Caravaggio Style. Cassell, 1959;
    Lippincott, 1959

MOORE, EDWARD
  Flight 685 Is Overdue. Ace, 1960

MOORE, EMMA
  Shallow Runs the River. Belmont, 1967
    [Wash.]

MOORE, F(RANK) FRANKFORT. 1855-1931.
  -"I Forbid the Banns." Hutchinson, 1893;
    Street, 1901

MOORE, FREDERICK FERDINAND. 1877- .
  The Devil's Admiral. Doubleday, 1913;
    Richards, 1913

MOORE, GEORGE
  Grasville Abbey. Robinson, 1797; Arno,
    1974

MOORE, H(ARRY) F. S. Ref: CC. SC: Casey
  Peters = CP.
  Death at 7:10. Doubleday, 1943 [NYC]
  Murder Goes Rolling Along. Doubleday,
    1942 CP [N.C.]

Shed a Bitter Tear. Doubleday, 1944
  CP [Atlanta]

MOORE, IRVING. See: Lillian Bergquist.

MOORE, ISABEL
  Chateau Sinister. Lancer, 1971 [Fr.]

MOORE, JOHN. 1729-1802.
  Zeluco. Strahan, 1789; West, 1792
    [Sic.]

MOORE, LEO
  Cold Waters. Decade, 1980 [Ariz.]

MOORE, MARY GALBRAITH. 1930-   . Pseudonym: Helena Osborne, q.v.

MOORE, PHILIPS
  Death Drives the Lead Car. Arcadia, 1961 [L.A.]
  Once Upon a Friday. Tower, 1965. Also published as: The Psycho. Tower, 1969
  The Psycho; see Once Upon a Friday

MOORE, RICHARD A. Newsman, later press secretary for U.S. senator. SC: Bob Whitfield, in both titles.
  Death in the Past. Raven, 1980 [Atlanta]
  Death of a Source. Raven, 1980 [Atlanta]

MOORE, ROBERT LOWELL, JR. 1925-   .
  Pseudonym: Robin Moore, q.v.

MOORE, ROBIN. Pseudonym of Robert Lowell Moore, Jr., 1925-   . Ref: CA. See also: Al Dempsey; Edward E. Mayer; Frank Schuler. SC: Tim Kyle, in at least those marked TK.
  -Aloha. Manor, 1977
  -The Banksters. Pinnacle, 1977
  The Big Paddle, with Sidney Levine. Arbor, 1978; Melbourne, 1979. Also published as: Fast Shuffle. Arrow, 1981 [Okla., 1933]
  The Black Sea Caper, with Hugh McDonald. Condor, 1978. British title: The Black Sea Connection. Severn, 1981
  The Black Sea Connection; see The Black Sea Caper
  -Caribbean Caper. Manor, 1978 [Carib.]
  The Chinese Ultimatum, with Edward McGhee. Pinnacle, 1976; Sphere, 1978 [Wash. D.C.]
  -Combat Pay. Manor, 1977
  Court-Martial, with Henry Rothblatt. Doubleday, 1971; Harrap, 1972
  The Death Disciple, with Gerald G(ehrig) Griffin, 1933-   , q.v. Condor, 1978
  -Death Never Forgets. Manor, 1978
  -Diamond Spitfire, with James Frew. Condor, 1978 [Bahamas]
  Diamonds and Blood. Manor, 1978
  Dubai. Doubleday, 1976; Barrie, 1976 [Mid. East]
  -The Edge of the Pond, with Ronald Van Duren. Manor, 1978
  The Establishment, with Harold Shumate. Manor, 1977
  The Family Man, with Milt Machlin. Pyramid, 1974; Panther, 1977
  Fast Shuffle; see The Big Paddle
  The Fifth Estate. Doubleday, 1973; Allen, 1973
  French Connection II, with Milt Machlin. Dell, 1975; Futura, 1975 (Novelization of the movie.) [Mars.]
  The Gold Connection, with Julian Askin. Condor, 1979
  The Italian Connection, with Al Dempsey. Pinnacle, 1975; Severn, 1981 TK [It.]
  The Kaufman Snatch. Manor, 1976
  The Khaki Mafia, with June Collins. Crown, 1971
  The London Connection; see The London Switch
  The London Switch, with Al Dempsey. Pinnacle, 1974. British title: The London Connection. Severn, 1979 TK [Eng.]
  -The Narrow Road, with F. L. Kafka. Manor, 1978
  The New York Connection; see The Set-Up
  Only the Hyenas Laughed, with Neville H. Romain. Manor, 1978; Sphere, 1980 [Afr.]
  Our Missile's Missing, with Stan Gebler Davies. Condor, 1977; Piatkus, 1980
  Phase of Darkness, with Al Dempsey. Third Press, 1974; New English Library, 1975 [Afr.]
  Search and Destroy. Condor, 1978
  The Set-Up, with Milt Machlin. Pyramid, 1975; Coronet, 1977. Also published as: The New York Connection. Severn, 1979 [NYC]

The Terminal Connection. Ace, 1976; Sphere, 1977
The Trinity Implosion, with Lewis Perdue. Manor, 1978

MOORE, RUTH. 1903-   . Ref: CA.
  -Lizzie and Caroline. Morrow, 1972

MOORE, WINNIE FIELDS. 1890-   .
  Wings of Destiny. Wetzel, 1930 ss

MOORHOUSE, FRANK
  Tales of Mystery and Romance. Angus, 1977 ss

MOORHOUSE, HERBERT JOSEPH. 1882-   .
  Pseudonym: Hopkins Moorhouse, q.v.

MOORHOUSE, HOPKINS. Pseudonym of Herbert Joseph Moorhouse, 1882-   . SC: Addison Kent = AK.
  -Every Man for Himself. Hodder, 1920
  The Gauntlet of Alceste. Musson (Toronto), 1921; Hodder, 1922; McCann, 1922 AK [N.Y.]
  The Golden Scarab. Hodder, 1926 AK [N.Y.]

MORALES, PABLO. SC: Pedro Moreno, in both titles.
  Big Deal in Veragua. Leisure, 1979
  Victim for Hire. Leisure, 1979 [Mex. City]

MORAN, MIKE. Pseudonym of William (Thomas) Ard, 1922-1960, q.v. Other pseudonyms: Ben Kerr, Thomas Wills, qq.v.
  Double Cross. Popular Library, 1953

MORAND, PAUL. 1888-1976. Ref: CA.
  East India and Company. Boni, 1927 ss, some criminous

MORAY, HELGA
  Trenfell Castle. Zebra, 1977

MORDEN, T. R.
  Steps in Mystery. Smith, 1935

MOREL, DIGHTON. Pseudonym of Kenneth Lewis Warner, 1918-   . Ref: CA.
  Moonlight Red. Secker, 1960

MORELLA, JANE
  Dark Memories. Lancer, 1971 [Vt.]

MORELLA, JOE and EDWARD Z. EPSTEIN
  The Ince Affair. Signet, 1978 [Calif., 1924]

MORELLI, SPIKE
  Coffin for a Cutie. Harborough, 1952
  Deal Me Out. Harborough, 1952
  Death for a Doll. Leisure, 195? (British title?)
  Give It to Me Straight. Harborough, 1953
  More Than Kisses, Baby. Harborough, 1952
  No Place for Me. Harborough, 1953
  Take It and Like It. Archer, 1951 [U.S.]
  This Way for Hell. Leisure, 1952 (British title?)
  You'll Never Get Me. Archer, 1950

MORETON, DOUGLAS ARTHUR. 1928-   . Pseudonym: Arthur Douglas, q.v.

MORETTE, EDGAR
  The Sturgis Wager. Stokes, 1899 [NYC]

MORFORD, HENRY. 1823-1881. See: Anonymous

MORGAN, AL(BERT). 1920-   .
  The Essential Man. Playboy, 1977

MORGAN, ALLAN. House name. SC: Mark Blood, in all titles.
  Blood. Award, 1974; Tandem, 1974
  The Cat Cay Warrant. Award, 1974
  The Spandau Warrant. Award, 1974; Tandem, 1974

MORGAN, ARTHUR and CHARLES R. BROWN
  The Disintegrator. Digby, 1891

MORGAN, BRYAN (STANFORD). 1923-1976. Ref: CA.
  The Business at Blanche Capel. H. Hamilton, 1953; Little, 1953

MORGAN, CLARINDA
  Devil's Cavern. Lancer, 1969 [Ire.]

MORGAN, DAN. 1925-   . Ref: CA.
  The Richest Corpse in Show Business. Compact, 1966

MORGAN, DEAN. SC: Rogue Ransome, in at least those marked RR; Rostron Outfit, in at least those marked RO.

Assassin Trail. Hamilton Stafford, 1952
Assignment to Sante Fe. Hamilton Stafford, 1952 [Sante Fe]
Contract for a Homicide. Hamilton Stafford, 1952
Desperate Justice. Hamilton Stafford, 1952
Four Guns to Carson City. Hamilton Stafford, 1952 [Nev.]
Four of a Kind. Hamilton Stafford, 1951
Green Hell Rampage. Hamilton Stafford, 1952
Murder on Coney Island. Hamilton Stafford, 1952 [NYC]
Nevada Alibi. Hamilton Stafford, 1952 [Nev.]
Rogue Ransom—Manhunter. Hamilton Stafford, 1952 RR
Rogue Ransom—Racket Buster. Hamilton Stafford, 1952 RR
Rogue Ransom—Triggerman. Hamilton Stafford, 1952 RR
The Rostron Outfit. Hamilton Stafford, 1951 RO
Rostron Outfit in Chicago. Hamilton Stafford, 1952 RO [Chi.]
Rostron Outfit in Mexico. Hamilton Stafford, 1952 RO [Mex.]
Rostron Outfit in Rio. Hamilton Stafford, 1952 RO [Rio de J.]
Rostron Outfit to Texas. Hamilton Stafford, 1952 RO [Tex.]
Rostron Outfit—Undercover Agents. Hamilton Stafford, 1952 RO

MORGAN, DIANA. 1913-   .
  My Cousin Rachel. French (London), 1979 (Play based on the novel by Daphne Du Maurier, 1907-   , q.v.)
  Time to Kill. Evans, 1961 (3-act play)

MORGAN, ELAINE
  License to Murder. French (London), 1963 (2-act play.)

MORGAN, GEOFFREY. 1916-   . Ref: CA. SC: Ricky Straight, in at least those marked RS. Set: Eng.
  Heavenly Body. Robertson, 1953 RS
  Murderer's Moon. Jenkins, 1942
  No Crest for the Wicked. Robertson, 1952 RS

MORGAN, JASON
  Death Is a Swinger. Lancer, 1971

MORGAN, JOHN. Pseudonym of Lauran Bosworth Paine, 1916-   . Other pseudonyms: John Armour, Reg Batchelor, Kenneth Bedford, Frank Bosworth, Mark Carrel, Robert Clarke, Richard Dana, J. F. Drexler, Troy Howard, Jared Ingersol, John Kilgore, Hunter Liggett, J. K. Lucas, qq.v.
  Death to Comrade X. Hale, 1969 [L.A.]
  The Ivory Penguin. Hale, 1974
  The Killer's Manual. Hale, 1972
  The Midnight Murder. Hale, 1971
  Murderer's Don't Smile. Hale, 1969
  The Nicest Corpse. Hale, 1970
  The Perfect Frame. Hale, 1970
  Spy in the Tunnel. Hale, 1969
  To Kill a Hero. Hale, 1969

MORGAN, JOHNNY [JOHN GLANFIL MORGAN]
  Involved. Heinemann, 1967
  -Nothing Barred. Secker, 1965

MORGAN, LORNA NICHOLL. Set: Eng.
  Another Little Murder. Macdonald, 1947
  The Death Box. Macdonald, 1946
  Murder in Devil's Hollow. World's Work, 1944
  Talking of Murder. Harrap, 1945

MORGAN, MAYBETH. Pseudonym of Peter Ronal.
  Darkness at Bromley Hall. Ace, 1975 [Barbados]

MORGAN, MICHAEL. Joint pseudonym of C.E. Carle and Dean M. Dorn. Carle: born in Kan.; newspaper reporter turned press agent in Calif., then movie publicist. Dorn: born in Wis.; freelance movie publicist. SC: Bill Ryan = BR.
  The Blonde Body; see Nine More Lives
  Decoy. Ace, 1953 BR [L.A.]
  -His Kind of Woman. Pyramid, 1954
  Nine More Lives. Random, 1947. Also published as: The Blonde Body. Lion, 1949 BR [L.A.]

MORGAN, MURRAY C(ROMWELL). 1916-   .
  Pseudonym: Cromwell Murray, q.v. Reporter and newspaper editor, then news editor for CBS, then radio editor for "Time" magazine.
  The Viewless Winds. Dutton, 1949

MORGAN, PATRICK. Pseudonym of George Snyder. SC: Bill Cartwright (Operation Hang Ten series), in all titles.
  Beach Queen Blowout. Macfadden, 1971
  Cute and Deadly Surf Twins. Macfadden, 1970
  Deadly Group Down Under. Macfadden, 1970 [Australia]
  Death Car Surfside. Macfadden, 1972 [Calif.]
  Freaked Out Stranger. Manor, 1973
  The Girl in the Telltale Bikini. Macfadden, 1971 [Australia]
  Hang Dead Hawaiian Style. Macfadden, 1969 [Haw.]
  Scarlet Surf at Makaha. Macfadden, 1970 [Haw.]
  Too Mini Murders. Macfadden, 1969 [L.A.]
  Topless Dancer Hangup. Macfadden, 1971

MORGAN, ROBERT
  The Golden Hoard. Pinnacle, 1975 [It.]

MORGAN, ROBERTS
  Spotlight on a Simple Case; or, Wiggins, Who Was That Horse I Saw with You Last Night? Cedar Tree, 1959 (Sherlock Holmes.)

MORGAN, STANLEY
  Sky-Jacked. Allen, 1976
  Too Rich to Live. Hamlyn, 1980; GM, 1979 [Fla.]

MORGAN, THOMAS CHRISTOPHER. 1914-   . Pseudonym: John Muir, q.v.

MORGAN, WESLEY
  The Enforcer. Warner, 1976; Star, 1977 (Novelization of the movie.) [S.F.]

MORGAN, WYNN L. Joint pseudonym of Chester Krone, q.v., and Phillip Breen.
  The Ice Man. Dell, 1979; New English Library pb, 1981 [NYC]

MORGULAS, JERROLD
  The Torquemada Principle. Rawson, 1980 [Ger., 1938]

MORICE, ANNE. Pseudonym of Felicity Shaw, 1918-   . Ref: CA, TC. SC: Tessa Crichton, in all titles. Set: Eng.
  Death and the Dutiful Daughter. Macmillan (London), 1973; St. Martin's, 1974
  Death in the Grand Manor. Macmillan (London), 1970
  Death in the Round. Macmillan (London), 1980; St. Martin's, 1980
  Death of a Gay Dog. Macmillan (London), 1971
  Death of a Heavenly Twin. Macmillan (London), 1974; St. Martin's, 1974
  Death of a Wedding Guest. Macmillan (London), 1976; St. Martin's, 1976
  Killing with Kindness. Macmillan (London), 1974; St. Martin's, 1975
  Murder by Proxy. Macmillan (London), 1978; St. Martin's, 1978
  Murder in Married Life. Macmillan (London), 1971
  Murder in Mimicry. Macmillan (London), 1977; St. Martin's, 1977 [Wash. D.C., theatre]
  Murder in Outline. Macmillan (London), 1979; St. Martin's, 1979 [theatre, acad.]
  Murder on French Leave. Macmillan (London), 1972
  Nursery Tea and Poison. Macmillan (London), 1975; St. Martin's, 1976
  Scared to Death. Macmillan (London), 1977; St. Martin's, 1978

MORLAND, CATHERINE. Pseudonym of John D. Schubert, q.v.
  The Legacy of Winterwyck. Pinnacle, 1976 [N.Y., 1842]

MORLAND, NIGEL. 1905-   . Pseudonyms: Mary Dane, John Donavan, Norman Forrest, Roger Garnett, Vincent McCall, Neil Shepherd, qq.v. Ref: CA, CC, EM, MP, TC. SC: Det. Insp. Rory Luccan = RL; Mrs. Palmyra Pym = PP; Chief Insp. Andy McMurdo = AM; Steven Malone = SM. Set: Eng.
  The Big Killing. Foster, 1946 (63 pp.)
  Blood on the Stars. Low, 1951 AM
  A Bullet for Midas. Cassell, 1958 PP
  Call Him Early for the Murder. Cassell, 1952 PP
  The Careless Hangman; see The Clue of the Careless Hangman
  The Case of the Innocent Wife. Arrow, 1947 (31 pp.)
  The Case Without a Clue. Cassell, 1938; Farrar, 1938 PP
  The Clue in the Mirror. Cassell, 1937; Farrar, 1938 PP
  The Clue of the Bricklayer's Aunt. Cassell, 1937 PP
  The Clue of the Careless Hangman. Cassell, 1940. U.S. title: The Careless Hangman. Farrar, 1941 PP
  A Coffin for the Body. Cassell, 1943 PP
  The Concrete Maze. Cassell, 1960 PP [Shanghai]
  Corpse in the Circus. Vallancey, 1945 (16 pp.)
  Corpse in the Circus and other stories. Polybooks, 1946 (62 pp.) ss
  The Corpse on the Flying Trapeze. Cassell, 1941; Farrar, 1941 PP
  The Corpse Was No Lady. Low, 1950 AM
  The Dear, Dead Girls. Cassell, 1961 PP
  Death and the Golden Boy. Cassell, 1958 PP
  Death for Sale. Hale, 1957 AM
  Death Takes a Star. Todd, 1943 (16 pp.)
  Death Takes an Editor. Aldor, 1949 SM
  Death to the Ladies. Hale, 1959 AM?
  Death When She Wakes. Evans, 1951 RL
  Death's Sweet Music; see Exit to Music and other stories
  Dressed to Kill. Cassell, 1947 PP
  Dumb Alibi. M B Books, 194?
  Exit to Music and other stories. Bonde, 1947. Also published as: Death's Sweet Music. Century, 1947, abridged ss
  -Fish Are So Trusting. Century, 1948
  A Girl Died Singing. Evans, 1952 RL
  A Gun for a God. Cassell, 1940. U.S. title: Murder in Wardour Street. Farrar, 1940 PP
  The Hatchet Murders. Arrow, 1947
  He Hanged His Mother on Monday. Low, 1951 AM
  How Many Coupons for a Shroud? Laird, 1946 (34 pp.) ss
  A Knife for the Killer. Cassell, 1939. U.S. title: Murder at Radio City. Farrar, 1939 PP
  The Laboratory Murder and other stories. Polybooks, 1944 (16 pp.) ss
  The Lady Had a Gun. Cassell, 1951 PP
  Look in Any Doorway. Cassell, 1957 PP
  Mrs. Pym and other stories. Ellis, 1976 ss PP
  Mrs. Pym of Scotland Yard. Vallancey, 1946 PP ss
  The Moon Murders. Cassell, 1935 PP
  The Moon Was Made for Murder. Low, 1953 AM
  Murder at Radio City; see A Knife for the Killer
  Murder in Wardour Street; see A Gun for a God
  Murder Runs Wild. Halle, 1946
  No Coupons for a Shroud. Low, 1949 AM
  The Phantom Gunman. Cassell, 1935 PP
  A Rope for the Hanging. Cassell, 1938; Farrar, 1939 PP
  She Didn't Like Dying. Low, 1948 AM
  Sing a Song of Cyanide. Cassell, 1953 PP [Shanghai]
  So Quiet a Death. Cassell, 1960 PP
  The Sooper's Cases. Todd, 1943 (16 pp.)
  Strangely She Died. Jenkins, 1946 SM
  The Street of the Leopard. Cassell, 1936 PP
  26 Three-Minute Thrillers. Arrow, 1947 (32 pp.) ss
  Two Dead Charwomen. Low, 1949 AM

MORLEY, CHARLES
  The Confessions of an Old Burglar. Newnes, 1900 ss

MORLEY, CHRISTOPHER (DARLINGTON). 1890-1957. Ref: CC, MP.
  The Haunted Bookshop. Doubleday, 1919; Chapman, 1920 [NYC]
  Tales from a Rolltop Desk. Doubleday, 1921; Curtis Brown, 1921 ss

MORLEY, ELLEN
  Intrigue in Rome. Manor, 1978 [Rome]
  Sinister Isle of Love. Manor, 1977 [Greece]

MORLEY, F(RANK) V(IGOR). 1899-1980. Ref: CA, CC.
  Dwelly Lane. Eyre, 1952. U.S. title: Death in Dwelly Lane. Harper, 1952

MORLEY, G. T.
  Deeds of Darkness; or, The Unnatural Uncle. Tipper, 1805 [1500s]

MORNINGSTAR, LILLIAN
  Hour of Death. Phoenix, 1950

MOROSO, JOHN A(NTONIO). 1874-1957. SC: James Tierney = JT.
  The City of Silent Men; see The Quarry
  The Listening Man. Appleton, 1924 ss JT [N.J.]
  The People Against Nancy Preston. Holt, 1921; Methuen, 1922 JT [NYC]
  The Quarry. Little, 1913. British title: The City of Silent Men. Low, 1922 [N.Y.]

MORRAH, DERMOT (MICHAEL MacGREGOR). 1896-1974. Ref: CA, CC.
  The Mummy Case. Faber, 1933. U.S. title: The Mummy Case Mystery. Harper, 1933 [acad.]

MORRELL, DAVID. 1943-   . Ref: CA.
  First Blood. Evans, 1972; Barrie, 1972 [Ky.]
  Testament. Evans, 1975; Chatto, 1976
  The Totem. Evans, 1979; Pan, 1981 [Wyo.]

MORRIS, ANTHONY P(ASCHEL). 1849-1921. SC: Mark Magic, in at least those marked MM.
  Burnt Powder; or, The Young Army Detective. Novelist Publishing, 1883
  The Cipher Detective; or, Mark Magic on a New Trail. Westbrook, 19?? MM
  Electro Pete, the Man of Fire; or, The Wharf Rats of Locust Point. Westbrook, 19??
  The Head Hunter; or, Mark Magic in the Mines. Westbrook, 19?? MM
  Mark Magic, the Detective; or, A Story of a Beautiful Woman's Strange Career. Westbrook, 19?? MM

MORRIS, ARTHUR
  The Dealer in Death and other stories. Cotton, 1897 ss

MORRIS, BESSIE C. Joint pseudonym with Anne B. Spear. See Forfex et Hesta, q.v.

MORRIS, CHARLES (SMITH). 1833-1922. Pseudonym: C. E. Tripp, q.v.
  Cap Colt, the Quaker Detective. Westbrook, 19??
  The Detective's Crime; or, The Van Peltz Diamonds. Rand, 1887
  The Pinkerton Ferret; or, Three Against One. Westbrook, 19??
  The Stolen Letter; or, Frank Sharp, the Washington Detective. Rand, 1887 [Wash. D.C.]

MORRIS, DAVID HENRY ST. LAWRENCE. 1920-   . Pseudonym: David Lawrence, q.v.

MORRIS, EDWARD
  The Five Fowlers. Bles, 1953 [Scot.]
  The Plume of Smoke. Bles, 1952
  The Small Hotel. Bles, 1953

MORRIS, EDWARD A. Pseudonym: Karl Kramer, q.v.

MORRIS, GOODALL VARNE
  Gold of Vala. Fontana, 1970

MORRIS, GOUVERNEUR
  Yellow Men and Gold. Dodd, 1911; Nash, 1911

MORRIS, GWENDOLEN SUTHERLAND. Pseudonym: Morris Sutherland, q.v.

MORRIS, HOMER. Pseudonym: Nick Carter, q.v.

MORRIS, IRA (VICTOR). 1903-   . Ref: CA.
  Kidnap. Dobson, 1974

MORRIS, JEAN. 1924-   . Pseudonym: Kenneth O'Hara, q.v.
  Man and Two Gods. Cassell, 1953; Viking, 1954

MORRIS, JIM. 1940-   .
  The Sheriff of Purgatory. Doubleday, 1979 [Ark., 1996]

MORRIS, JOE ALEX. 1904-   . Ref: CA.
  The Bird Watcher. McKay, 1966; Cassell, 1968

MORRIS, JOHN. Joint pseudonym of John Hearne, 1926-   , and Morris Cargill, 1914-   . SC: Robin McKay, in all titles.
  The Candywine Development. Collins, 1970; Citadel, 1971 [Jam.]
  The Checkerboard Caper. Citadel, 1975 [Jam.]
  Fever Grass. Collins, 1969; Putnam, 1969 [Jam.]

MORRIS, R. A. V. Ref: CC.
  The Lyttleton Case. Collins, 1922

MORRIS, T(HOMAS) B(ADEN). 1900-   . Ref: CA. SC: Insp. Headley, in at least those marked H.

Blind Bargain. Hale, 1957
Crash into Murder. Hale, 1961
The Crime of Mildred Bentham. French, 1955 (Play)
The Crooked Tree. Deane, 1963; Baker, 1963 (Play)
Death Among the Orchids. Hale, 1959 H
Deserted Night. Evans, 1961 (Play)
The Horns of Truth. Hale, 1972
Mandrakes in the Cupboard. Hale, 1960 H
Mine Enemy My Friend. Miller, 1960 (Play)
The Muddy Leaf Mystery. Hale, 1971
Murder on the Loire. Hale, 1964
Murder Without Men. French, 1948 (Play)
Nightmare Chessboard. French, 1959 (Play)
Orchids with Murder. Hale, 1966 H
The Papyrus Murder. Hale, 1958 H
Return of a Traitor. Hale, 1962
Shadows on Abu Simbel. Hale, 1967
Simple Justice. French, 1949 (Play)
So Many Dangers. Hale, 1960
Storm in the Sand. Hale, 1965
Third Time Unlucky. Hale, 1973
Two Aunts and a Grandmother. French, 1946 (Play)
Undying Serpent. Hale, 1970
Wild Justice. Hale, 1965 [Paris]
-The Woman and the Wheel. Muller, 1953

MORRIS, TOM. See: John Miles.

MORRIS, W(ALTER) F(REDERICK). 1892-   .
 Bretherton: Khaki or Field Grey? Bles, 1929. U.S. title: "G.B." Dodd, 1929
 The Channel Mystery. Joseph, 1939
 "G.B"; see Bretherton
 The Hold-Up. Bles, 1933
 No Turning Back. Joseph, 1937
 -Pagan. Bles, 1931
 Something to His Advantage. Bles, 1935

MORRIS, W. R. SC: Sheriff Buford Pusser = BP (see also: Webster Carey).
 The Twelfth of August. Bantam, 1974 (Novelization of the movie.) BP [Tenn.]

MORRISON, ALEXANDER
 The Crookshaven Murder. Houghton, 1927

MORRISON, ARTHUR. 1863-1945. Ref: all except CA. SC: Martin Hewitt = MH. Set: Eng.
 Adventures of Martin Hewitt. Ward, 1896 MH ss
 Chronicles of Martin Hewitt. Ward, 1895; Appleton, 1896 MH ss
 The Dorrington Deed-Box. Ward, 1897 ss
 The Green Diamond; see The Green Eye of Goona
 The Green Eye of Goona. Nash, 1904. U.S. title: The Green Diamond. Page, 1904 ss
 The Hole in the Wall. Methuen, 1902; McClure, 1902 [ca.1850]
 Martin Hewitt, Investigator. Ward, 1894; Harper, 1894 MH ss
 The Red Triangle. Nash, 1903; Page, 1903 MH ss

MORRISON, DAVID
 A Matter of Record. Bakers, 1958 (1-act play.)

MORRISON, EMMELINE
 Red Poppies. Hutchinson, 1928; Curtiss, 1930
 -A Tale Untold. Hutchinson, 1956

MORRISON, EULA ATWOOD. 1911-   . Pseudonym: Andrea Delmonico, q.v.

MORRISON, HUGO
 The Low Road. Methuen, 1930

MORRISON, JAMES W. R.
 Operation Steal. Hale, 1972

MORRISON, L(EE). See: W(alton) Butterfield, 1898-   .

MORRISON, MORAG D(APHNE)
 The Maiden Flight That Never Was. Stockwell, 1976

MORRISON, ROBERTA. Pseudonym of Jean Francis Webb, 1910-   , q.v.
 Tree of Evil. Paperback Library, 1966 [Haw.]

MORRISON, T(HOMAS) J(AMES). 1906-   .
 Pseudonym: Alan Muir, q.v.
 The Queen of Spades. Collins, 1935

MORRISON, (JAMES) WOODS
 Road End. Putnam, 1927

MORRISSEY, J(AMES) L(AWRENCE). Set: Eng.
 Design for Blackmail. Hutchinson, 1935
 The Double Problem. Burns, 1932
 High Doom. Hutchinson, 1933
 Necktie for Norman. Gifford, 1949
 Off with His Head. Gifford, 1947
 Poison Is Queen. Gifford, 1949

MORROW, SUSAN.   -1975. Lived in NYC.
 Dancing with a Tiger. Doubleday, 1968; Hale, 1969 [NYC]
 The Insiders. Doubleday, 1967; Hale, 1967 [New Or.]
 The Moonlighters. Doubleday, 1966; Hale, 1967 [South]
 Murder May Follow. Doubleday, 1959; Collins, 1960 [S.F.]
 The Rules of the Game. Doubleday, 1964; Hale, 1964 [Calif.]
 A Season of Evil. Doubleday, 1969 [Vir. Is.]

MORROW, WILLIAM C(HAMBERS). 1853-1923.
 The Ape, the Idiot and Other People. Lippincott, 1897; Richards, 1898 ss, some criminous
 Blood-Money. Walker, 1882 [Calif.]
 -A Man; His Mark. Lippincott, 1900; Richards, 1900

MORSE, ANNE CHRISTENSON. 1915-   . Pseudonym: Ann Head, q.v.

MORSE, ELIZABETH
 The Emerald Buddha. Dutton, 1935 [Bangkok]

MORSE, F(LORENCE) V(OLPE). 1887-
 Black Eagles Are Flying. Doubleday, 1943 [Ohio]

MORTENSEN, NIELS. See: Barnaby Conrad, 1922-   .

MORTIMER, JOHN (CLIFFORD). 1923-   .
 Ref: CA. SC: Rumpole, in all titles which include his name, which are ss taken from the TV series. Set: Eng.
 Five Plays. Methuen, 1970 (Plays, one criminous.)
 Rumpole. Lane, 1980 (Combines previous Rumpole titles.)
 Rumpole of the Bailey. Penguin (London), 1978; Penguin (NYC), 1980
 Rumpole's Return. Penguin (London), 1980; Penguin (NYC), 1982
 Three Plays. Elek, 1958; Grove, 1958 (Plays, two criminous.)
 The Trials of Rumpole. Penguin (London), 1979; Penguin (NYC), 1981

MORTIMER, PETER. Pseudonym (?) of Dorothy James Roberts, 1903-   .
 If a Body Kill a Body. Mystery House, 1946

MORTLOCK, BILL. Pseudonym of English solicitor.
 A Planned Coincidence. Gollancz, 1963; Macmillan, 1964

MORTON, ALEXANDER
 Detective Stories. Hedderwick, 1926 ss

MORTON, ANTHONY. Pseudonym of John Creasey, 1908-1973, q.v. Other pseudonyms: Gordon Ashe, M. E. Cooke, Norman Deane, Robert Caine Frazer, Patrick Gill, Michael Halliday, Charles Hogarth, Brian Hope, Colin Hughes, Kyle Hunt, Abel Mann, Peter Manton, J. J. Marric, Richard Martin, Rodney Matheson, Jeremy York, qq.v. SC: John Mannering (The Baron) = JM. Set: Eng.
 Affair for the Baron. Hodder, 1967; Walker, 1968 JM [U.S.]
 Alias Blue Mask; see Alias the Baron
 Alias the Baron. Low, 1939. U.S. title: Alias Blue Mask. Lippincott, 1939 JM
 Attack the Baron. Low, 1951 JM
 Bad for the Baron. Hodder, 1962. U.S. title: The Baron and the Stolen Legacy. Scribner, 1967 JM
 The Baron Again. Low, 1938. U.S. title: Salute Blue Mask. Lippincott, 1939 JM
 The Baron and the Arrogant Artist. Hodder, 1972; Walker, 1973 JM
 The Baron and the Beggar. Low, 1947; Duell, 1950 JM
 The Baron and the Chinese Puzzle. Hodder, 1965; Scribner, 1966 JM [H. Kong]
 The Baron and the Missing Old Masters. Hodder, 1968; Walker, 1969 JM
 The Baron and the Mogul Swords; see A Sword for the Baron
 The Baron and the Stolen Legacy; see Bad for the Baron
 The Baron and the Unfinished Portrait. Hodder, 1969; Walker, 1970 JM
 The Baron at Bay. Low, 1938. U.S. title: Blue Mask at Bay. Lippincott, 1938 JM
 The Baron at Large. Low, 1939. U.S. title: Challenge Blue Mask! Lippincott, 1939. Reprinted under the British title: Walker, 1975 JM
 The Baron Branches Out; see A Branch for the Baron
 The Baron Comes Back. Low, 1943 JM
 The Baron Goes A-Buying. Hodder, 1971; Walker, 1972 JM
 The Baron Goes East. Low, 1953 JM [India]
 The Baron Goes Fast. Hodder, 1954; Walker, 1972 JM
 The Baron in France. Hodder, 1953; Walker, 1976 JM [Fr.]
 The Baron—King Maker. Hodder, 1975; Walker, 1975 JM
 The Baron on Board. Hodder, 1964; Walker, 1968 JM [ship]
 The Baron Returns. Harrap, 1937. U.S. title: The Return of Blue Mask. Lippincott, 1937 JM
 Black for the Baron. Hodder, 1959. U.S. title: If Anything Happens to Hester. Doubleday, 1962 JM
 Blame the Baron. Low, 1949; Duell 1951 JM
 Blood Red; see Red Eye for the Baron
 Blue Mask at Bay; see The Baron at Bay
 Blue Mask Strikes Again; see Versus the Baron
 Blue Mask Victorious; see Call for the Baron
 Books for the Baron. Low, 1949; Duell, 1952 JM
 A Branch for the Baron. Hodder, 1961. U.S. title: The Baron Branches Out. Scribner, 1967 JM [Boston]
 Burgle the Baron. Hodder, 1973; Walker, 1974 JM
 Call for the Baron. Low, 1940. U.S. title: Blue Mask Victorious. Lippincott, 1940 JM
 Career for the Baron. Low, 1946; Duell, 1950 JM
 A Case for the Baron. Low, 1945; Duell, 1949 JM
 Challenge Blue Mask!; see The Baron at Large
 Cry for the Baron. Low, 1950; Walker, 1970 JM
 Danger for the Baron. Hodder, 1953; Walker, 1974 JM
 Deaf, Dumb and Blonde; see Nest-Egg for the Baron
 The Double Frame; see Frame the Baron
 Frame the Baron. Hodder, 1957. U.S. title: The Double Frame. Doubleday, 1961 JM
 Help from the Baron. Hodder, 1955; Walker, 1977 JM
 Hide the Baron. Hodder, 1956; Walker, 1978 JM
 If Anything Happens to Hester; see Black for the Baron
 Introducing Mr. Brandon. Low, 1944
 Last Laugh for the Baron. Hodder, 1970; Walker, 1971 JM
 Love for the Baron. Hodder, 1979 JM
 The Man in the Blue Mask; see Meet the Baron
 Meet the Baron. Harrap, 1937. U.S. title: The Man in the Blue Mask. Lippincott, 1937 JM
 Mr. Quentin Investigates. Low, 1943
 Nest-Egg for the Baron. Hodder, 1954. U.S. title: Deaf, Dumb and Blonde. Doubleday, 1961 JM
 Red Eye for the Baron. Hodder, 1958. U.S. title: Blood Red. Doubleday, 1960 JM
 The Return of Blue Mask; see The Baron Returns
 Reward for the Baron. Low, 1945 JM
 A Rope for the Baron. Low, 1948; Duell, 1949 JM
 Salute Blue Mask; see The Baron Again
 Salute for the Baron. Hodder, 1960; Walker, 1973 JM
 Shadow for the Baron. Low, 1951 JM
 Sport for the Baron. Hodder, 1966; Walker, 1969 JM [Australia]
 A Sword for the Baron. Hodder, 1963. U.S. title: The Baron and the Mogul Swords. Scribner, 1966 JM
 Trap the Baron. Low, 1950; Walker, 1971 JM
 Versus the Baron. Low, 1940. U.S. title: Blue Mask Strikes Again. Lippincott, 1940 JM
 Warn the Baron. Low, 1952 JM

MORTON, GUY (MAINWARING). 1896-   . Pseudonym: Peter Traill, q.v. SC: Konrad Roque, in at least those marked KR. Set: Eng.
 Ashes of Murder. Skeffington, 1935; Greenberg, 1936

Black Gold. Brentano's (London), 1924; Small, 1924
The Black Robe. Hodder, 1927; Minton, 1927
The Burleigh Murders. Skeffington, 1936
The Forbidden Road. Hodder, 1928
King of the World; or, The Pommeray Case. Hodder, 1927
Mystery at Hardacres. Skeffington, 1936
The Mystery at Hermit's End. Skeffington, 1932
The Perrin Murder Case. Skeffington, 1930; Greenberg, 1934 KR [NYC]
The Ragged Robin Murders. Skeffington, 1935; Greenberg, 1937 KR
The Scarlet Thumb Print. Skeffington, 1931 KR
The Silver-Voiced Murder. Skeffington, 1933
The 3-7-9 Murder. Skeffington, 1934
Zola's Thirteen. Skeffington, 1929

MORTON, MICHAEL. 1864-1931. See: Victoria Morton.

MORTON, PATRICIA. Pseudonym of Morton Jay Golding, 1925- . Other pseudonym: Stephanie Lloyd, q.v. Ref: CA.
Caves of Fear. Lancer, 1968
A Child of Value. Lancer, 1966
Destiny's Child. Belmont, 1967 [Fr.]
A Gathering of Moondust. Lancer, 1965
In the Province of Darkness. Banner, 1967 [Eng., 1800s]

MORTON, T. C. ST. C. and LADBROKE (LIONEL DAY) BLACK, 1877-1940, q.v.
All Square with Fate. Nicholson, 1932

MORTON, VICTORIA
The Whirlpool. Dutton, 1916
The Yellow Ticket. Fly, 1914 (Novelization of the play by Michael Morton, 1864-1931.) [Russ.]

MORTON, WILLIAM. Pseudonym of W(illiam) B(lair) M(orton) Ferguson, 1881-1967, q.v. SC: "Biff" Corrigan, in at least those marked BC.
The Case of Casper Gault. Hurst, 1932
Little Lost Lady. Hurst, 1931. U.S. title: The Murder of Christine Wilmerding, as by W. B. M. Ferguson. Liveright, 1932 [N.Y.]
Masquerade. Nelson, 1928; Chelsea, 1927 BC [N.Y.]
The Murder of Christine Wilmerding; see Little Lost Lady
The Murderer. Hurst, 1932. U.S. title: The Pilditch Puzzle, as by W. B. M. Ferguson. Liveright, 1932 BC [NYC]
The Mystery of the Human Bookcase. Hurst, 1931 Mason, 1931 BC [NYC]
The Pilditch Puzzle; see The Murderer

MOSCO, MAISIE. See: Brian Comfort.

MOSELEY, DANA. Born in Omaha, living in L.A. in 1950s; scriptwriter.
Dead of Summer. Abelard, 1953; Bodley, 1955 [Midwest]

MOSER, MAURICE and CHARLES F. RIDEAL
Stories from Scotland Yard. Routledge, 1890. U.S. title: True Detective Stories. Lovell, 1890 ss

MOSHER, J(OHN) S.
Liar Dice. Simon, 1939 [China]

MOSLER, BLANCHE Y.
Horror at the Hacienda. Avon, 1973 [N. Mex.]

MOSLEY, LEONARD O(SWALD). 1911- .
So I Killed Her. Joseph, 1936; Doubleday, 1937 [N.Y.]

MOSLEY, NICHOLAS. 1923- . Ref: CA.
Assassins. Hodder, 1966; Coward, 1967

MOSS, BARON
Chains. Bachman, 1978

MOSS, JACK
The Arson Job. Manor, 1979

MOSS, ROBERT. 1946- . See: Arnaud De Borchgrave, 1926- .

MOSS, ROSE. 1937- . Ref: CA.
The Terrorist. Harvester, 1979

MOSS, (IVAN) WILLIAM STANLEY. 1921- .
Bats with Baby Faces. Boardman, 1951; Harlequin, 1952 [Mid. East]

MOTT, MARIE MURPHY
The Cape Jasmine Murder. Vantage, 1963

MOTTA, LUIGI. 1881- .
Flames on the Bosphorus. Odhams, 1920 (Translation of "Fiamme sul Bosforo." Milan, 1913.)

MOTTE, PETER. Pseudonym of Richard (Motte) Harrison, 1901- , q.v. See also: Reginald (Wilfrid) Campbell, 1894-1950. Set: Eng.
A Dog's Death, with Reginald W(ilfrid) Campbell, 1894-1950. Cassell, 1953
Fall of the Curtain. Cassell, 1958
Fell Clutch. Cassell, 1956
The House at Hag's Curtain. Cassell, 1958
Phoenix from the Gutter. Cassell, 1956
The Village Called Death. Cassell, 1955

MOTTRAM, R(ALPH) H(ALE). 1883-1971. Ref: CA.
The Headless Hound and other stories. Chatto, 1931 ss, some criminous

MOULE, MARGARET
The Thirteenth Brydain. Jarrolds, 1897

MOULTON, H(UGH LAURENCE) FLETCHER. 1876-
-A Certain Liveliness. Arrowsmith, 1928
The Girl He Left Behind Him. Arrowsmith, 1927
-The Man in the Turkish Bath. Longmans, 1941
-The Unofficial Executor. Cassell, 1934
Urgent Private Affairs. Arrowsmith, 1930
Without the Law. Arrowsmith, 1926

MOUNCE, DAVID R. SC: Paul Fox, in both titles.
Operation Cuttlefish. Pyramid, 1972 [Carib.]
The Shield Project. Pyramid, 1971 [Can.]

MOUNT, KATHARINE. See: Raymond Laurence.

MOUNTENEY-JEPHSON, R(ICHARD). 1842- .
Blackmail. Routledge, 1885

MOUNTJOY, HENRY
The Minister of Police. Bobbs, 1912 [Fr., 1700s]

MOWATT, IAN. 1948- . Ref: CA.
Just Shaeffer, or Storms in the Troubled Heir. Harcourt, 1973; Hutchinson, 1974

MOWBRAY, JOHN. Pseudonym of John (George) Haslette Vahey, 1881- , q.v. Other pseudonyms: Henrietta Clandon, John Haslette, Anthony Lang, Vernon Loder, Walter Proudfoot, qq.v.
Call the Yard. Skeffington, 1931
The Frontier Mystery. Collins, 1940
The Megeve Mystery. Collins, 1941
On Secret Service. Collins, 1939
The Radio Mystery. Collins, 1941
-The Way of the Weasel. Partridge, 1922

MOWERY, WILLIAM BYRON. 1899-1957. On faculty at U. of Ill., then became full time writer, with more than 450 published stories.
The Black Automatic. Little, 1937 [Can.]
The Long Arm of the Mounted. Whittlesey, 1948 ss [Can.]
The Phantom Canoe. Little, 1935
Sagas of the Mounted Police. Bouregy, 1953. Also published as: Tales of the Mounted Police. Airmont, 1962 ss [Can.]
Tales of the Mounted Police; see Sagas of the Mounted Police

MOYES, PATRICIA. 1923- . Ref: CA, CC, EM, TC. SC: Henry and Emmy Tibbett, in all titles.
Angel Death. Collins, 1980; Holt, 1981 [Carib.]
Black Widower. Collins, 1975; Holt, 1975 [Wash. D.C.]
The Coconut Killings; see To Kill a Coconut
The Curious Affair of the Third Dog. Collins, 1973; Holt, 1973
Dead Men Don't Ski. Collins, 1959; Holt, 1960 [It.]
Death and the Dutch Uncle. Collins, 1968; Holt, 1968 [Holl.]
Death on the Agenda. Collins, 1962; Holt, 1962 [Geneva]
Down Among the Dead Men; see The Sunken Sailor
Falling Star. Collins, 1964; Holt, 1964
Johnny Under Ground. Collins, 1965; Holt, 1966
Many Deadly Returns; see Who Saw Her Die?
Murder a la Mode. Collins, 1963; Holt, 1963
Murder Fantastical. Collins, 1967; Holt, 1967
Season of Snows and Sins. Collins, 1971; Holt, 1971 [Switz.]
The Sunken Sailor. Collins, 1961. U.S. title: Down Among the Dead Men. Holt, 1961
To Kill a Coconut. Collins, 1977. U.S. title: The Coconut Killings. Holt, 1977 [Carib.]
Who Is Simon Warwick? Collins, 1978; Holt, 1979
Who Saw Her Die? Collins, 1970. U.S. title: Many Deadly Returns. Holt, 1970

MOYZISCH, L(UDWIG) C(ARL)
Operation Cicero. Coward, 1950; Wingate, 1950 (Translation of "Der Fall Cicero." Frankfurt, 1950.) [Turk.]

MUAT, PAGAN
Murder's No Picnic. Gifford, 1947

MUDDOCK, J(OYCE) E(MMERSON PRESTON). 1843-1934. Pseudonym: Dick Donovan, q.v.
-From the Bosom of the Deep. Swan, 1886
Whose Was the Hand? Digby, 1901

MUGGERIDGE, MALCOLM. 1903- .
Affairs of the Heart. H. Hamilton, 1949; Walker, 1961

MUGGESON, MARGARET ELIZABETH. 1942-
Pseudonym: Everatt Jackson, q.v.

MUIR, ALAN. Pseudonym of Thomas James Morrison, 1906- .
Death Comes on Derby Day. Jarrolds, 1939

MUIR, (CHARLES) AUGUSTUS (CARLOW). 1892- . Pseudonym: Austin Moore, q.v. Ref: CA, CC.
The Ace of Danger; see The Black Pavilion
Beginning the Adventure. Methuen, 1932. U.S. title: The Dark Adventure. Putnam, 1933
The Black Pavilion. Methuen, 1926. U.S. title: The Ace of Danger. Bobbs, 1927 [Scot.]
The Blue Bonnet. Methuen, 1926; Bobbs, 1926 [Scot.]
The Bronze Door. Methuen, 1936
-Candlelight in Avalon. Bles, 1954
Castles in the Air. Methuen, 1938
The Crimson Crescent. Methuen, 1935
The Dark Adventure; see Beginning the Adventure
The Green Lantern. Methuen, 1933
The Man Who Stole the Crown Jewels. Methuen, 1937
Raphael, M.D. Methuen, 1935 ss
The Red Carnation. Methuen, 1937 [Paris]
The Riddle of Garth. Methuen, 1933
The Sands of Fear. Methuen, 1940
Satyr Mask. Methuen, 1936 [Scot.]
The Shadow on the Left. Methuen, 1928; Bobbs, 1928 [Scot.]
The Silent Partner. Methuen, 1929; Bobbs, 1930
The Third Warning. Methuen, 1925; Bobbs, 1925 [Scot.]

MUIR, D(OROTHY) ERSKINE (SHEEPSHANKS). 1889- . SC: Insp. Woods, in both titles. Set: Eng.
Five to Five. Blackie, 1934
In Muffled Night. Methuen, 1933

MUIR, DENNIS
Death Defies the Doctor. Phoenix, 1944 [New Guinea]

MUIR, DEXTER. Pseudonym of Leonard (Reginald) Gribble, 1908- , q.v. Other pseudonyms: Sterry Browning, Leo Grex, Louis Grey, qq.v. See also: Janet Green. Set: Eng.
The Pilgrims Meet Murder. Jenkins, 1948
Rosemary for Death. Jenkins, 1952
The Speckled Swan. Jenkins, 1949

MUIR, JEAN. 1906-1973. Ref: CA.
The Smiling Medusa. Dodd, 1969; Hale, 1971 [Greece]
Stranger, Tread Light. Dodd, 1971; Hale, 1973 [Mex.]

MUIR, JOHN. Pseudonym of Thomas Christopher Morgan, 1914- .
Creatures of Satan. Hutchinson, 1956
Crook's Turning. Hutchinson, 1958
The Devil's Post Office. Hutchinson, 1955

MUIR, P. P. and E(DWARD) D(EVEREUX) H(AMILTON) TOLLEMACHE
Green Wounds. Boardman, 1947
-Mirage. Boardman, 1945

MUIR, THOMAS. SC: Roger Crammond, in at least those marked RC.
   Death Below Zero. Hutchinson, 1950 RC
   Death in Reserve. Hutchinson, 1948 RC
   Death in Soundings. Hutchinson, 1955 RC [Carib.]
   Death on the Loch. Hutchinson, 1949 RC [Scot.]
   Death on the Agenda. Hutchinson, 1953 RC
   Death on the Trooper. Hutchinson, 1948 RC
   Death Under Virgo. Hutchinson, 1952 RC [Scot.]
   Death Without Question. Hutchinson, 1951 RC
   Trouble Aboard. Hutchinson, 1957

MUKERJI, DHAN GOPAL. 1890-1936. Born in India, educated there and in the U.S., where he became a lecturer, poet and playwright.
   The Secret Listeners of the East. Dutton, 1926 [India]

MULHOLLAND, JOHN. 1898-1970. Ref: CA. See: Cortland Fitzsimmons, 1893-1949.

MULHOLLAND, P. H.
   The Calypso Murders. Avon, 1957 [Carib.]

MULKEEN, THOMAS P(ATRICK). 1923-   . Ref. CA. SC: Clem Talbot, in both titles.
   Honor Thy Godfather. Stein, 1973 [NYC]
   My Killer Doesn't Understand Me. Stein, 1973 [NYC]

MULLALLY, FREDERIC. 1920-   . Ref: CA. SC: Bob Sullivan, in at least those marked BS.
   The Assassins. Barker, 1964; Walker, 1965
   -Clancy. Hart-Davis, 1971
   Danse Macabre. Secker, 1959. U.S. title: Marianne. Viking, 1960 BS
   The Deadly Payoff. Allen, 1978
   -Hitler Has Won. Macmillan (London), 1975
   The Malta Conspiracy. Hart-Davis, 1972 BS [Malta]
   Man with Tin Trumpet. Barker, 1961
   Marianne; see Danse Macabre
   The Munich Involvement. Barker, 1968 BS [Munich]
   No Other Hunger. Barker, 1966; McKay 1966
   -Oh, Wicked Wanda. Sphere, 1970
   -The Prizewinner. Barker, 1967
   Split Scene. Barker, 1963
   -Venus Afflicted. Hart-Davis, 1973

MULLEN, CLARENCE. 1907-   . SC: Tony Lantz and Eddie Wright, in both titles.
   A Good Place for Murder. Phoenix, 1948 [N.Y.]
   Thereby Hangs a Corpse. Mystery House, 1946 [NYC]

MULLER, MARCIA. 1944-   . Ref: CA.
   Edwin of the Iron Shoes. McKay, 1977 [S.F.]

MULLER, MARY
   Flagdown. Souvenir, 1974

MULLER, PAUL. Pseudonym of Albert King, 1924-   . SC: Paul Muller, in all titles.
   Danger—Dame at Work. Hale, 1968; Roy, 1968 [U.S.]
   Don't Push Your Luck. Hale, 1970
   Finders, Losers—. Hale, 1968
   The Friendly Fiends. Hale, 1972
   Goodbye, Shirley. Hale, 1969
   The Hasty Heiress. Hale, 1968; Roy, 1969 [U.S.]
   The Lady Is Lethal. Hale, 1968; Roy, 1968 [U.S.]
   Make Mine Mayhem. Hale, 1967
   Slay Time. Hale, 1968; Roy, 1969 [U.S.]
   Some Dames Don't. Hale, 1970
   This Is Murder. Hale, 1971
   A Viper in Her Bosom. Hale, 1975
   Why Pick on Me? Hale, 1969
   The Wistful Wanton. Hale, 1971
   You Kill Me! Hale, 1967

MULVIHILL, WILLIAM (PATRICK). 1923-   . Ref: CA.
   I've Got Viktor Schalkenburg. Berkley, 1974
   The Mantrackers. Signet, 1960

MUMFORD, ETHEL WATTS. 1878-1940.
   All in the Night's Work, with George (Fitzalan) Bronson-Howard, 1883-1922, q.v. Garden City, 1924
   -Dupes. Putnam, 1901
   Out of the Ashes. Moffat, 1913 [NYC]

MUNCH, ANDREAS. 1881-1884.
   -The Maid from Norway. Chatto, 1878 (Translation of "Pigen fra Norge." Oslo, 1861.)

MUNDIS, HESTER JANE. 1938-   .
   Mercy at the Manor Manor. Parallax, 1967

MUNDIS, JERROLD. Pseudonym: Eric Corder, q.v.

MUNDY, MAX. Pseudonym of Sylvia Anne Matheson Schofield, 1918-   . Ref: CA. SC: Russell Jones = RJ.
   Death Cries Ole. Long, 1966 RJ [Sp.]
   Death Is a Tiger. Long, 1960 [Pak.]
   Dig for a Corpse. Long, 1962
   Pagan Pagoda. Long, 1965 RJ [Burma]

MUNDY, TALBOT. Pseudonym of William Lancaster Gribbon, 1879-1940. SC: Jimgrim (James Schuyler Grim) = J; Chullunder Ghose, in at least those marked CG; Cotswold Ommony, in at least those marked CO; Athelstan King, in at least those marked AK. (Note: Differentiating among Mundy's fiction by criminous content, even within series like the Jimgrim books, is very difficult. Some listed titles are more occult or occult adventure. Those most criminous are marked *.)
   Affair in Araby; see The King in Check
   -Black Light. Hutchinson, 1930; Bobbs, 1930 [India]
   C.I.D. Hutchinson, 1932; Century, 1932 CG [India]
   -Caesar Dies. Hutchinson, 1934; Centaur, 1973
   Caves of Terror. Hutchinson, 1932 AK
   Cock o' the North; see Gup Bahadur
   The Devil's Guard; see Ramsden
   Diamonds See in the Dark. Hutchinson, 1937
   East and West. Appleton, 1937 (British title?) [India]
   -The Eye of Zeitoon. Hutchinson, 1920; Bobbs, 1920
   Full Moon; see There Was a Door
   The Gunga Sahib. Hutchinson, 1933; Appleton, 1934 CG [India]
   -Guns of the Gods. Hutchinson, 1921; Bobbs, 1921 [India]
   -Gup Bahadur. Hutchinson, 1929. U.S. title: Cock o' the North. Bobbs, 1929 [India]
   -Her Reputation, with Bradley King. Bobbs, 1923 (British title?)
   The Hundred Days. Hutchinson, 1930; Century, 1931 J *
   -The Ivory Trail. Constable, 1920; Bobbs, 1919. Also published as: Trek East. Universal, 1953 [Afr.]
   Jimgrim. Hutchinson, 1931; Century, 1931. Also published as: Jimgrim Sahib. Universal, 1953 J,CG
   Jimgrim and Allah's Peace. Hutchinson, 1933; Appleton, 1936 J * [Mid. East]
   Jimgrim Sahib; see Jimgrim
   Jungle Jest. Hutchinson, 1931; Century, 1932 CO [India]
   The King in Check. Hutchinson, 1933; Appleton, 1934. Also published as: Affair in Araby. Universal, 1953 J * [Mid. East]
   -King of the Khyber Rifles. Constable, 1917; Bobbs, 1916 AK
   The Lion of Petra. Hutchinson, 1932; Appleton, 1933 J *
   The Lost Trooper. Hutchinson, 1931 J *
   The Marriage of Meldrum Strange. Hutchinson, 1930
   The Mystery of Khufu's Tomb. Hutchinson, 1933; Appleton, 1935 J [Egypt]
   The Nine Unknown. Hutchinson, 1924; Bobbs, 1924 J,AK,CG [India]
   Old Ugly Face. Hutchinson, 1939; Appleton, 1940 J [Tib.]
   Om. The Secret of Ahbor Valley. Hutchinson, 1924; Bobbs, 1924 CO [India]
   Ramsden. Hutchinson, 1926. U.S. title: The Devil's Guard. Bobbs, 1926 J [Tib.]
   The Red Flame of Erinpura. Hutchinson, 1934 CG
   The Seventeen Thieves of El-Kabil. Hutchinson, 1935 J *
   There Was a Door. Hutchinson, 1935. U.S. title: Full Moon. Appleton, 1935 [India]
   The Thunder Dragon Gate. Hutchinson, 1937; Appleton, 1937 J [Tib.]
   -Told in the East. Bobbs, 1920 (British title?) (3 novelets.) [India]
   Trek East; see The Ivory Trail
   -The Valiant View. Hutchinson, 1939 ss
   -When Trails Were New. Hutchinson, 1932
   -The Winds of the World. Cassell, 1916; Bobbs, 1917 [India]
   The Woman Ayisha. Hutchinson, 1930 J *

MUNRO, DENNIS
   Death Defies the Doctor. Green Dragon, 194?

MUNRO, HECTOR HUGH. 1870-1916. Pseudonym: Saki. See: James Fuller.

MUNRO, HUGH (MACFARLANE). Ref: CA, CC. SC: Clutha = C.
   The Brain Robbers. Hale, 1967 C [theatre, Edin.]
   A Clue for Clutha. Macdonald, 1960 C [Scot.]
   Clutha and the Lady. Hale, 1973 C
   Clutha Plays a Hunch. Macdonald, 1959; Washburn, 1959 C [Glasgow]
   Evil Innocence. Hale, 1976 C
   Get Clutha. Hale, 1974 C
   -Tribal Town. Macdonald, 1964
   Who Told Clutha. Macdonald, 1958; Washburn, 1958 C [Glasgow]

MUNRO, JAMES. Pseudonym of James (William) Mitchell, 1926-   , q.v. Other pseudonym: James Meldrum, q.v. SC: John Craig, in all titles.
   Die Rich, Die Happy. Hammond, 1965; Knopf, 1966
   The Innocent Bystanders. Jenkins, 1969; Knopf, 1970 [Turk.]
   The Man Who Sold Death. Hammond, 1964; Knopf, 1965 [Fr.]
   The Money That Money Can't Buy. Hammond, 1967; Knopf, 1968

MUNRO, NEIL. 1864-1930.
   The Lost Pibroch and Other Sheiling Stories. Blackwood, 1896 ss, some criminous

MUNSLOW, BRUCE (JAMES)
   Deep Sand. Hodder, 1955
   Joker Takes Queen. Long, 1965; Holt, 1966
   No Safe Road. Long, 1959; Walker, 1962 [Egypt]
   The Secret of the Little Flea. World's Work, 1961
   Spider Run Alive. Long, 1961

MURARI, TIMERI
   The Oblivion Tapes. Berkley, 1978; Magnum, 1979

MURDOCH, GRAHAM. See: Dave Smith.

MURFI, LIDIE
   The Magnolia Curse. PB, 1973 [Miss.]

MURFREE, MARY NOAILLES. 1850-1922. Pseudonym: Charles Egbert Craddock, q.v.

MURIEL, JOHN ST. CLAIR. 1909-   . Pseudonym: Simon Dewes, q.v.

MURPHY, AGATHA
   Hush-Hush Murder. Vantage, 1978

MURPHY, D(AVID) J(OHN). 1905-   .
   Inspector Malone Sails In. Selwyn, 1947

MURPHY, DENNIS JASPER. Pseudonym of Charles Robert Maturin, 1780-1824, q.v.
   The Fatal Revenge; or, The Family of Montorio. Longmans, 1807; Arno, 1974 [1670]

MURPHY, JAMES F., JR. 1932-   .
   Quonsett. Rawson, 1978 [Cape Cod]

MURPHY, JOHN. Pseudonym of Ronan Calistus Grady, Jr., 1921-   . Ref: CA.
   The El Greco Puzzle. Scribner, 1974 [Sp.]
   The Gunrunners. Macmillan, 1966; H. Hamilton, 1966
   The Long Reconnaissance. Doubleday, 1970 [Fla.]
   Pay on the Way Out. Scribner, 1975; Hale, 1977 [Sp.]

MURPHY, KEN. 1935-   .
   The Wind in His Fists. Chatto, 1969

MURPHY, MARGUERITE. 1892-   .
   Borrowed Alibi. Avalon, 1961 [Midwest]
   Dangerous Legacy. Avalon, 1962 [Calif.]

MURPHY, MICHAEL. 1930-   . Pseudonym: Hershell G. Lewis, q.v.

MURPHY, ROBERT (WILLIAM). 1902-1971. See also: Helen (Newington) Wills, 1906-   . Ref: CA.
   Murder in Waiting. Scribner, 1938

MURPHY, ROBERT FRANKLIN
   The Girl Factory. Zebra, 1975; New English Library pb, 1976. Also published as: The Man Made Woman. Zebra, 1976

King's Mate. Zebra, 1975; New English
   Library pb, 1976
The Man Made Woman; see The Girl Fac-
   tory

MURPHY, TOM [THOMAS BASIL MURPHY, JR.].
   1935-   .
   Aspen Incident. St. Martin's, 1978
      [Colo.]
   Auction! Signet, 1980
   Ballet! NAL, 1978; Cassell, 1978

MURPHY, WARREN B. 1933-   . See also:
   Richard Sapir, 1936-   . Ref: CA.
   SC: Ed Razoni and William Jackson =
   R&J; Remo Williams (The Destroyer) =
   RW (see also Sapir entry). Note that
   some titles originally published as
   by Sapir & Murphy are being reprinted
   as by Murphy alone (RW series).
   Atlantic City, with Frank Stevens. Pin-
      nacle, 1979; Sphere, 1980 [N.J.]
   Bay City Blast. Pinnacle, 1979; Corgi,
      1981, as by Sapir & Murphy   RW [N.J.]
   City in Heat. Pinnacle, 1973 R&J [NYC]
   Dangerous Games. Pinnacle, 1980 (Writ-
      ten with Robert J. Randisi, q.v.)
      RW [Moscow]
   Dead End Street. Pinnacle, 1973 R&J
      [NYC]
   Down and Dirty. Pinnacle, 1974   R&J
      [NYC]
   Firing Line. Pinnacle, 1980 RW [NYC]
   Leonardo's Law. Carlyle, 1978 [Conn.]
   Lynch Town. Pinnacle, 1974 R&J [NYC]
   The Missing Link. Pinnacle, 1980   RW
   On the Dead Run. Pinnacle, 1975   R&J
      [NYC]
   One Night Stand. Pinnacle, 1973   R&J
      [NYC]
   Subways Are for Killing. Pinnacle, 1973
   Timber line. Pinnacle, 1980 (Written
      with William "Ted" Joy.) RW [Brazil]

MURRAY, ANDREW (NICHOLAS). 1880-1929.
   Pseudonym: Nicholas Islay, q.v. All
   titles below feature Sexton Blake and
   were published by Amalgamated Press.
   Across the Divide. 1919
   The Admiral's Secret. 1920
   The Adventure of the Speed Mad Camden.
      1928
   Ambergris! 1921
   The Barrier Reef Mystery. 1917
   The Bathchair Mystery. 1919
   The Beachcomber. 1920
   Beyond the Law. 1922
   The Black Bat. 1917
   The Black Chrysanthemum. 1916
   The Black Opal Mine. 1921
   Blood-Brotherhood. 1920
   The Broken Trail. 1919
   The Case of the Amber Crown. 1923
   The Case of the Burmese Dagger. 1919
   The Case of the Cinema Star. 1921
   The Case of the Cotton Beetle. 1923
   The Case of the Master Organizer. 1923
   The Case of the Mystery Millionaire.
      1921
   The Case of the Paralyzed Man. 1922
   The Case of the Seaside Crooks. 1919
   The Case of the Two Brothers. 1918
   The Case of the Uncut Gems. 1922
   The Case of the Undischarged Bankrupt.
      1921
   The Case of the Un-Named Film. 1922
   The Case of the Woman in Black. 1922
   The Catspaw. 1917
   The Changeling. 1920
   The City of Apes. 1921
   A Convict by Proxy. 1919
   The Crook's Double. 1923
   The Ex-Soldier Employment Swindle. 1919
   The Fatal Fortune. 1939 (Reprint of
      unidentified earlier title.)
   The First-Born Son. 1919
   The Golden Belts. 1916
   The Great Explosion. 1922
   The Half-Caste. 1917
   The Head Hunter's Secret. 1920
   The Hidden Message. 1921
   His Excellency's Secret. 1916
   Ill Gotten Gains. 1915
   In the Midnight Express. 1920
   Loot! 1919
   The Luck of the Darrells. 1918
   The Man Behind the Curtain. 1923
   The Mandarin's Seal. 1919
   The Man from Kura-Kura. 1920
   The Man in the Grey Cowl. 1921
   Marooned! 1921
   The Missing Ships. 1918
   The Mosque of the Mahdi. 1918
   The Motor Coach Mystery. 1919
   The Mystery of the Clock. 1922
   The Mystery of the Hundred Chests. 1921
   The Mystery of the Thousand Peaks. 1920
   "North of 55°." 1923
   Outcasts. 1919
   The Oyster-Bed Mystery. 1923
   The Palzer Experiment. 1920
   The Prisoner of the Kremlin. 1922
   The Rajah's Revenge. 1915
   The Red Crescent. 1919
   The Secret of Draker's Folly. 1917
   The Secret of the Glacier. 1920
   The Secret of the Green Lagoon. 1928
   The Secret of the Hulk. 1918
   The Secret of the Hunger Desert. 1920
   Settler or Slaver. 1919
   The Sheikh's Son. 1920
   The Station Master's Secret. 1919
   Tinker's Lone Hand. 1921
   Vengeance. 1917
   Victims of Villainy. 1916

MURRAY, ANDREW
   The Lady of the Guns. Murray, 1920

MURRAY, AUDREY ALISON
   The Blanket. Deutsch, 1957; Vanguard,
      1958

MURRAY, BEATRICE. Pseudonym of Richard
   Posner, 1944-   , q.v. Other pseudo-
   nyms: Iris Foster, Paul Todd, qq.v.
   The Dark Sonata. Dell, 1971

MURRAY, CHARLES T(HEODORE). 1843-1924.
   Sub Rosa. Carleton, 1880

MURRAY, CROMWELL. Pseudonym of Murray
   C(romwell) Morgan, 1916-   , q.v.
   Day of the Dead. McKay, 1946 [Mex.]

MURRAY, DAVID CHRISTIE. 1847-1907. Ref:
   EM.
   -The Bishop's Amazement. Downey, 1896
   -The Bishop's Bible, with Henry Herman,
      1832-1894, q.v. Chatto, 1890;
      Lovell, 1890
   -A Bit of Human Nature; and, The "Live-
      ly Fanny." Chatto, 1885 ss
   -Bob Martin's Little Girl. Chatto, 1892;
      Taylor, 1892
   The Brangwyn Mystery. Long, 1906
   -By the Gate of the Sea. Chatto, 1883;
      Harper, 1883
   -A Capful o'Nails. Chatto, 1896
   -The Church of Humanity. Chatto, 1901
   -Coals of Fire and other stories. Chat-
      to, 1882; Munro, 1883 ss
   -Cynic Fortune. Chatto, 1886; Harper,
      1886
   A Dangerous Catspaw, with Henry Murray.
      Longmans, 1889; Harper, 1889
   -Despair's Last Journey. Chatto, 1901
   -First Person Singular. Chatto, 1886;
      Harper, 1885
   He Fell Among Thieves, with Henry Her-
      man, 1832-1894, q.v. Macmillan
      (London), 1891; Lovell, 1891
   -Hearts. Chatto, 1883; Harper, 1883
   -His Father's Honour. Ward, 1909
   -His Own Ghost. Chatto, 1902
      In Direst Peril. Chatto, 1894; Harper,
      1894
      In His Grip. Long, 1907
   The Investigations of John Pym. White,
      1895 ss
   -John Vale's Guardian. Macmillan (Lon-
      don), 1890
   -Joseph's Coat. Chatto, 1881; Munro,
      1881
   -A Life's Atonement. Griffith, 1880;
      Harper, 1881
   -The Martyred Fool. Smith, 1895; Harper,
      1895
   -A Model Father. Grant, 1883; Harper,
      1882
   -Mount Despair, and other stories. Chat-
      to, 1895 ss
   -Old Blazer's Hero. Chatto, 1887;
      Lovell, 1888
   -One Traveller Returns, with Henry Her-
      man, 1832-1894, q.v. Chatto, 1887;
      Lovell, 1888
   -Only a Shadow, with Henry Herman, 1832-
      1894, q.v. Griffith, 1891
      Paul Jones's Alias, with Henry Herman,
      1832-1894, q.v. Chatto, 1894 ss
   -The Penniless Millionaire. Long, 1907
   -The Queen's Scarf. Blackett, 1889
      A Race for Millions. Chatto, 1898
   -Rainbow Gold. Smith, 1885; Munro, 1885
   -A Rising Star. Hutchinson, 1894; Col-
      lier, 1894
      A Rogue's Conscience. Downey, 1897;
      Buckles, 1899
   -Schwartz. Macmillan (London), 1889 ss
   -Sweetbriar in Town, and other tales,
      with Henry Herman, 1832-1894, q.v.
      Munro, 1889 (British title?) ss
   -Tales in Prose and Verse. Chatto, 1898
      ss
   -This Little World. Chatto, 1897; Apple-
      ton, 1898
      Time's Revenges. Chatto, 1893; Harper,
      1892
   -V.C. Chatto, 1904
   -Val Strange. Chatto, 1883; Harper, 1882
   -Verona's Father. Chatto, 1903
      A Wasted Crime. Chatto, 1893; Harper,
      1893

-The Way of the World. Chatto, 1884;
   Harper, 1884
-The Weaker Vessel. Macmillan (London),
   1888; Harper, 1889
-Wild Darrie, with Henry Herman, 1832-
   1894, q.v. Longmans, 1889; Munro,
   1889
-A Woman in Armour. Long, 1908
-Young Mrs. Barter's Repentence. Munro,
   1888 (British title?)

MURRAY, EDGAR JOYCE. 1878-   . Pseudo-
   nym: Sidney Drew, q.v. All titles
   below feature Sexton Blake and were
   published by Amalgamated Press.
The Affair of the Phantom Car. 1925
The Calcroft Case. 1926
The Case of the Crimson Wizard. 1922
The Case of the Lone Plantation. 1926
The City of Masks. 1926
The Great Circus Mystery. 1924
The Legacy of Doom. 1925
The Mansion of Shadows. 1923
The Menace of the Silent Death. 1926
The Palace of Terror. 1927
The Pride of the Stable. 1921
The Riddle of the Golden Fingers. 1927
The Tangle of Terror. 1926

MURRAY, EDWARD
   The Four Liars. Butterworth, 1940

MURRAY, EUSTACE CLARE GRENVILLE. 1824-
   1881. Pseudonym: Mark Hope, q.v.

MURRAY, FIONA
   Invitation to Danger. Hale, 1965 [N.Z.]
   A Nice Day for Murder. Hale, 1971

MURRAY, HELEN
   Ski Lift to Love. Tiara, 1980

MURRAY, INSPECTOR. Pseudonym of Alexander
   Duke Bailie.
   Joseph Prickett, the Scotland Yard De-
      tective. Laird, 1889
   The League of Guilt; or, A Great Detec-
      tive's Greatest Case. Ogilvie, 1892

MURRAY, LIEUTENANT M. M. Pseudonym of
   Maturin M. Ballou, 1820-1895.
   The Arkansas Ranger; or, The Story of a
      Dark Crime. Donohue [Ark.]
   The Dog Detective and His Young Master.
      Street, 1888
   Held for Ransom. Street, 1889
   Life for a Life. Laird, 1887
   Masked Lady; or, The Fortunes of a
      Dragoon. Street, 1889
   Mezzoni, the Brigand; or, The King of
      the Mountains. Street, 1889

MURRAY, MARIAN
   Fruits of Deception. Avalon, 1965

MURRAY, MAX. 1901-1956. Ref: CC, TC.
   Born in Australia; newspaper reporter
   in that country, the U.S., and Eng.;
   scriptwriter and editor for BBC dur-
   ing WWII; married to Maysie Greig,
   1902-1971, q.v.
   Breakfast with a Corpse. Joseph, 1956.
      U.S. title: A Corpse for Breakfast.
      Washburn, 1957 [Fr.]
   A Corpse for Breakfast; see Breakfast
      with a Corpse
   The Doctor and the Corpse. Joseph,
      1953; Farrar, 1952 [Sing., ship]
   Good Luck to the Corpse. Joseph, 1953;
      Farrar, 1951 [Fr.]
   The King and the Corpse. Joseph, 1949;
      Farrar, 1948 [Fr.]
   The Neat Little Corpse. Joseph, 1951;
      Farrar, 1950 [Jam.]
   No Duty on a Corpse. Joseph, 1950. U.S.
      title: The Queen and the Corpse. Far-
      rar, 1949 [ship]
   The Queen and the Corpse; see No Duty
      on a Corpse
   The Right Honourable Corpse. Joseph,
      1952; Farrar, 1951 [Australia]
   Royal Bed for a Corpse. Joseph, 1955;
      Washburn, 1955
   The Sunshine Corpse. Joseph, 1954
      [Fla.]
   Twilight at Dawn. Joseph, 1957
   The Voice of the Corpse. Joseph, 1948;
      Farrar, 1947
   Wait for the Corpse. Joseph, 1957;
      Washburn, 1957

MURRAY, PATRICIA HAGAN. See: Florence
   Stevenson.

MURRAY, PAUL (COOPER). 1920-   .
   The Free Agent. Holt, 1952 [Eng.]

MURRAY, RICHARD. 1910-1957. Pseudonym:
   Richard English, q.v.

MURRAY, SINCLAIR. Pseudonym of (Edward) Alan Sullivan, 1868-1947, q.v.
-Antidote. Murray, 1932
-The Broken Marriage. Murray, 1928; Dutton, 1929
-Cornish Interlude. Murray, 1932
The Crucible. Bles, 1925
-Double Lives. Murray, 1929
-The Golden Foundling. Murray, 1931
-The Money Spinners. Low, 1936
-The Obstinate Virgin. Low, 1934
-Queer Partners. Murray, 1930
-What Fools Men Are! Low, 1933
Whispering Lodge. Murray, 1927
-With Love from Rachel. Low, 1937

MURRAY, W(ILLIAM) H(UTCHINSON). 1913- . Ref: CA.
Appointment in Tibet; see Five Frontiers
Dark Rose the Phoenix. Secker, 1965; McKay, 1965 [Fr.]
Five Frontiers. Dent, 1958. U.S. title: Appointment in Tibet. Putnam, 1959 [Tib.]
Maelstrom. Secker, 1962
-The Spurs of Troodos. Dent, 1960

MURRAY, WILLIAM. 1926- . Magazine writer, with homes in both Calif. and It.
The Killing Touch. Dutton, 1974 [L.A.]
The Mouth of the Wolf. Little, 1977; Magnum, 1978 [Rome]

MUSE, PATRICIA (ALICE). 1923- . Ref: CA.
The Belle Claudine. Bouregy, 1971
Eight Candles Glowing. Ballantine, 1976 [Fla.]
Sound of Rain. Bouregy, 1971

MUSSI, MARY. 1907- . Pseudonym: Josephine Edgar, q.v.

MUSTO, BARRY. 1930- .
Codename—Bastille. Hale, 1972
The Fatal Flaw. Hale, 1970
The Lawrence Barclay File. Hale, 1969
No Way Out. Hale, 1973
Storm Centre. Hale, 1970
The Weighted Scales. Hale, 1973

MUZZEY, VIRGINIA REYNOLDS
A Quiet Murder. Dorrance, 1973

MUZZY, ALICE M.
-Three Fair Philanthropists. Abbey, 1901

MYERS, BARRIE
Evil Ever After. Popular Library, 1972 (Substantially the same book as "The Shadow on Spanish Swamp," by Genevieve St. John, q.v.) [Ariz.]
Nightfall. Popular Library, 1971 [Fr. Ant.]
The Oblivious Host. Popular Library, 1973
Who Rides the Tiger. Popular Library, 1971

MYERS, GEORGE L.
Aboard "The American Duchess." Putnam, 1900 (Plagiarization of "The Queen of Night," by Headon Hill, q.v.)

MYERS, ISABEL BRIGGS. SC: Peter Jerningham, in both titles.
Give Me Death. Stokes, 1934; Gollancz, 1935
Murder Yet to Come. Stokes, 1930; Gollancz, 1930 [Pa.]

MYERS, MARY RUTH. 1947- . Ref: CA.
A Journey to Cuzco. Coward, 1979 [Peru]

MYERS, PHINEAS BARTON. 1888- .
Hollywood Murder. Exposition, 1958 [L.A.]

MYGATT, GERALD. 1887- .
Nightmare. Penn, 1929 [N.Y.]

MYKEL, A. W. Lives in N.J.
The Wind-Chime Legacy. St. Martin's, 1980; Severn, 1981

MYLES, SYMON. Pseudonym of Ken(neth Martin) Follett, 1949- , q.v. SC: "Apples" Carstairs, in both titles.
The Big Apple; see The Big Needle
The Big Black. Everest, 1974
The Big Needle. Everest, 1974. U.S. title: The Big Apple. Zebra, 1975

MYRER, ANTON. 1922- . Ref: CA.
The Intruder. Little, 1965; Heinemann, 1966

NABARRO, DERRICK. 1921- .
-The Chariot of Desire. Cassell, 1956
-North from Singapore. Cassell, 1956 [China]
The Rod of Anger. Cassell, 1953; Sloane, 1953. Also published as: Too Hard to Handle. Eagle, 1955
-The Seeds of Destruction. Cassell, 1954
Too Hard to Handle; see The Rod of Anger

NABOKOFF-SIRIN, VLADIMIR (VLADIMIROVICH). Also known as: Vladimir Nabokov. 1899-1977. Ref: CA.
Despair. Long, 1937. Reprinted as by Vladimir Nabokov: Weidenfeld, 1966; Putnam, 1966

NAHUM, LUCIEN
Shadow 81. Doubleday, 1975; New English Library, 1976

NAISMITH, MARION (OVEREND). 1922- . Ref: CA.
A Dream of Unicorns. Hurst, 1968; Dell, 1975
-Prelude to Darkness. Hurst, 1965; Signet, 1975

NAKAGAWA, KARL S.
The Rendezvous of Mysteries. Dorrance, 1928 [Calif.]

NAMES, LARRY D.
Twice Dead. Leisure, 1978

NAPIER, GEOFFREY. Pseudonym of Bernard Glemser, 1908- , q.v.
A Dear Hungarian Friend. Macdonald, 1966. U.S. title: A Very Special Agent. Funk, 1967 [NYC]
A Very Special Agent; see A Dear Hungarian Friend
The Wrong Box. Dell, 1966 (Novelization of the movie based on the novel by Robert Louis Stevenson, 1850-1894, q.v.)

NAPIER, MARK. Pseudonym of John (Alfred Charles) Laffin, 1922- , q.v. Other pseudonyms: Carl Dekker, Dirk Sabre, qq.v.
Doorways to Danger. Abelard, 1966

NAPIER, MARY. Pseudonym of Mary Patricia Wright, 1932- . Ref: CA.
Blind Chance. Collins, 1980. U.S. title (?): The Waiting. Bantam, 1980

NAPIER, MELISSA
Castle of Dark Evil. Avon, 1972
Child of Satan. PB, 1973 [N.Y.]
The Haunted Woman. Popular Library, 1971
House by the Bridge. Avon, 1972
House in White Mist. Avon, 1972
House of Dark Laughter. Avon, 1972
House of Rising Water. Avon, 1972
Mermaid of Dark Mountain. Avon, 1972
The Possession of Elizabeth Calder. PB, 1973 [N.J.]

NARCEJAC, THOMAS. Pseudonym of Pierre Ayraud, 1908- . See: Pierre (Prosper) Boileau, 1906- .

NASH, ANNE. 1890- . Ref: CC. SC: Mark Tudor = MT.
Cabbages and Crime. Doubleday, 1945; Hammond, 1948 [Calif.]
Death by Design. Doubleday, 1944; Hammond, 1954 MT [Calif.]
Said with Flowers. Doubleday, 1943; Hammond, 1953 MT [Calif.]
Unhappy Rendezvous. Doubleday, 1946; Hammond, 1950 [Calif.]

NASH, CHANDLER. Pseudonym of Katherine Chandler Hunt. Born in Can., living in Calif. in late 1950s.
Murder Is My Shadow. Macmillan, 1959; Hale, 1960 [Mex.]

NASH, FRANK. 1912- .
The House Cried Murder. Phoenix, 1952

NASH, N(ATHAN) RICHARD. 1913- . Pseudonym: N. Richard Nusbaum, q.v.
East Wind, Rain. Atheneum, 1977; Allen, 1977 [Haw., 1941]
Handful of Fire. French (NYC), 1959 (3-act play)
-The Last Magic. Atheneum, 1978; Allen, 1979
The Young and Fair. Dramatists, 1949 (3-act play)

NASH, SIMON. Pseudonym of Raymond Chapman, 1924- . Ref: CA, CC. SC: Insp. Montero and Adam Ludlow, in all titles. Set: Eng.
Dead of a Counterplot. Bles, 1962 [acad.]
Dead Woman's Ditch. Bles, 1964; Roy, 1966
Death over Deep Water. Bles, 1963; Roy, 1965 [ship]
Killed by Scandal. Bles, 1962; Roy, 1964
Unhallowed Murder. Bles, 1966; Roy, 1966 [church]

NASIELSKI, ADAM
The Ace of Spades. Macdonald, 1939 (Translation from the Polish: Warsaw, 1939.) [Pol.]

NASON, LEONARD H(ASTINGS). 1895- .
Born in Mass.
Contact Mercury. Doubleday, 1946 [Paris]
The Man in the White Slicker. Doubleday, 1929

NATHENSON, JOSEPH. Pseudonym: Cheryl St. John, q.v.
Radnitz. Manor, 1979
See Naples and Die. Manor, 1979 [Naples]

NAUGHTON, EDMUND. 1926- .
A Case in Madrid. Curtis, 1973 [Madrid]
The Maximum Game. Warner, 1975
McCabe. Macmillan, 1959; Deutsch, 1960. Also published as: McCabe and Mrs. Miller. Fontana, 1971
McCabe and Mrs. Miller; see McCabe

NAZEL, JOSEPH. 1944- . SC: Black = B; Iceman (Henry Highland West) = I.
Billion Dollar Death. Holloway, 1974 I
The Black Exorcist. Holloway, 1974
Black Fury. Holloway, 1976
The Black Gestapo. Holloway, 1975
Black Is Black. Pinnacle, 1974 B
Black Prophet. Holloway, 1976
Black Uprising. Holloway, 1976
Canadian Kill. Holloway, 1974 I
Death for Hire. Holloway, 1975
Dr. Feel Good. Holloway, 1978
The Golden Shaft. Holloway, 1974 I
My Name Is Black! Pinnacle, 1973 B
The Shakedown. Holloway, 1975 I
Slick Revenge. Holloway, 1978
Spider's Web. Holloway, 1978
Spinning Target. Holloway, 1974 I
Sunday Fix. Holloway, 1974 I

NEAL, ADELINE PHYLLIS. 1894-1977. Pseudonym: A. F. Grey, q.v.

NEAL, JOHN. 1793-1876.
Logan. Carey, 1822; Newman, 1823
Rachel Dyer. Shirley, 1828

NEARING, ELIZABETH CUSTER. 1898- .
Pseudonym: Sue MacVeigh, q.v.

NEBEL, (LOUIS) FREDERICK. 1903-1967. Ref: TC.
-Fifty Roads to Town. Little, 1936; Cape, 1936 [Maine]
Six Deadly Dames. Avon, 1950 ss
Sleepers East. Little, 1933; Collins, 1934 [train]

NED, NEVADA. Pseudonym of E. O. Tilburn. Other pseudonym: Dr. N. T. Oliver, q.v.
Convict 72. Eagle, 1888
The Great Bank Mystery. Laird, 1901
The King of Gold; or, The Mystery of the Lost Mine. Eagle, 1888
Mexican Bill, the Cowboy Detective. Laird, 1889
The Mystery of Dagget's Bank. Laird, 1896

NEEBEL, RICHARD. SC: Erik Chatham, in both titles.
The Halo Solution. Charter, 1979 [Afr.]
The Yunnan Terminus. Charter, 1980 [China]

NEELEY, DETA P(ETERSON). 1902- .
A Candidate for Hell. Meador, 1939
Murder at Sunset Rock. Meador, 1944
Through Devil's Gate, with Nathan Glen Neeley. Meador, 1941

NEELEY, NATHAN GLEN. See: Deta P(eterson) Neeley, 1902- .

NEELY, ESTHER (JANE)
The Moon Cat. Pyramid, 1977

NEELY, RICHARD. Advertising executive turned full-time writer.
The Damned Innocents. Ace, 1971. Also published as: Dirty Hands. Signet, 1976
Death to My Beloved. Signet, 1969 [NYC]

Dirty Hands; see The Damned Innocents
The Japanese Mistress. Saturday Review Press, 1972 [Calif.]
Lies. Putnam, 1978 [Calif.]
A Madness of the Heart. Crowell, 1976; Constable, 1978 [NYC]
No Certain Life. Jove, 1978 [L.A.]
The Obligation. Dell, 1979
The Plastic Nightmare. Ace, 1969; Hale, 1971 [Calif.]
The Ridgway Women. Crowell, 1975; Constable, 1976 [Calif.]
The Sexton Women. Putnam, 1972; Barker, 1974 [S.F.]
The Smith Conspiracy. Signet, 1972 [Calif.]
The Walter Syndrome. McCall, 1970; Souvenir, 1971 [NYC, 1938]
While Love Lay Sleeping. Ace, 1969; Hale, 1970 [NYC]

NEGULESCO, BRIAN. Pseudonym.
The Woman from A.U.N.T. Exposition, 1970

NEIDER, CHARLES. 1915- . Ref: CA.
The Authentic Death of Hendry Jones. Harper, 1956; Muller, 1957 [S.W.]

NEIDIG, WILLIAM J(ONATHAN). 1870-1955.
The Fire Flingers. Dodd, 1919 [Ill.]

NEIL, JOHN
-The Eye of the Gods. Gramol, 1933
Lord of the Gallows. Mowl, 1934

NEILAN, SARAH. Ref: CA.
An Air of Glory. Hodder, 1977; Morrow, 1977 [past]
The Braganza Pursuit. Hodder, 1976; Dutton, 1976 [Brazil, 1800s]

NEILL, ROBERT
The Devil's Door. Hutchinson, 1979; St. Martin's, 1980

NEILSON, MARGUERITE [JULIA MARGUERITE HUNTER MACHEE NEILSON TOMPKINS]. 1909- . Ref: CA.
The Bride of Alderburn. Wingate, 1976; Berkley, 1977 [past]
The Dark Path. Wingate, 1976; Manor, 1978 [past]

NEIMAN, IRVING GAYNOR
Murder Once Removed. Dramatists, 1972 (3-act play.)

NELMS, HENNING. 1900- . Pseudonym: Hake Talbot, q.v.

NELSON, C(HOLMONDELEY) M. 1903- . Ref: CA.
Barren Harvest. Doubleday, 1949 [Eng.]

NELSON, COUTTS
What Old Father Thames Said. Tinsley, 1876

NELSON, HUGH LAWRENCE. 1907- . Ref: CC. SC: Jim Dunn = JD; Steve Johnson = SJ.
The Copper Lady. Rinehart, 1947; Barker, 1949 SJ [S.F.]
Dark Echo. Rinehart, 1949; Barker, 1949 SJ [Colo.]
Dead Giveaway. Rinehart, 1950; Barker, 1951 SJ [S.F.]
The Fence. Rinehart, 1953 JD [Colo.]
Fountain of Death. Rinehart, 1948; Barker, 1949 SJ [S.F.]
Gold in Every Grave. Rinehart, 1951; Barker, 1953 JD [Colo.]
Island of Escape. Rinehart, 1948 [Calif.]
Kill with Care. Rinehart, 1953 JD [Colo.]
Murder Comes High. Rinehart, 1950; Barker, 1952 JD [Colo.]
Ring the Bell at Zero. Rinehart, 1949; Barker, 1950 JD [Colo.]
The Season for Murder. Rinehart, 1952; Benn, 1956 JD [Colo.]
The Sleep Is Deep. Rinehart, 1952; Benn, 1955 JD [Colo.]
Suspect. Rinehart, 1954 JD [Colo.]
The Title Is Murder. Rinehart, 1947; Barker, 1947 SJ [S.F.]

NELSON, JACK. See: Clyde North.

NELSON, JACK A.
The Parajacker. Paperback Library, 1974

NELSON, KENT. 1942- .
The Straight Man. Creative Arts, 1978

NELSON, MARK. Pseudonym.
The Crusoe Test. Macmillan (London), 1976; St. Martin's, 1976 [ship]

NELSON, MICHAEL HARRINGTON. 1921- .
Pseudonym: Henry Stratton, q.v.

NELSON, MILDRED
The Dark Stone. Pyramid, 1972 [S.F.]
The Island. PB, 1973 [Fla.]

NELSON, MOLLY
Terror in Exton. Modern Fiction, 1946

NELSON, WALTER (HENRY). 1928- . Ref: CA.
The Minstrel Code. Secker, 1979. U.S. title: The Siege of Buckingham Palace. Little, 1980 [Eng., ca.1985]

NEMEC, DAVID. 1938- . Ref: CA.
Bright Lights, Dark Rooms. Doubleday, 1980; Severn, 1981

NEPEAN, EDITH (BELLIS)
-Dangerous Diversion! Paul, 1932
-Midnight Surrender. Paul, 1953
-Moonlight Madness. Paul, 1926
-Perilous Waters. Paul, 1943
Secret Lover. Paul, 1937

NESBIT, E(DITH) [EDITH NESBIT BLAND]. 1858-1924. Ref: CC.
Dormant. Methuen, 1911
-Fear. Paul, 1910
-Grim Tales. Innes, 1893 ss
The House with No Address. Newnes, 1914; Doubleday, 1909
-The Red House. Methuen, 1902; Harper, 1902
-The Secret of Kyriels. Hurst, 1899
Something Wrong. Innes, 1893 ss
Thirteen Ways Home. Treherne, 1901 ss, at least one criminous
To the Adventurous. Hutchinson, 1923 ss, some criminous

NESS, TOM T. Pseudonym of Thomas L. Thienes.
Short of Murder. Phoenix, 1948 [Boston]

NESSEN, RON. 1934- .
-The First Lady. Playboy, 1979 [Wash. D.C., P. Rico]

NESTORIEN, ARTHUR. Pseudonym.
In Sin or Folly? Digby, 1893

NETTELL, RICHARD (GEOFFREY). 1907- . Ref: CA.
Girl in Blue Pants. Hodder, 1967

NETTLETON, ARTHUR. Pseudonym of Arthur Nettleton Gaunt.
Sinister Secret. Fiction House, 1937

NETTON, BUDLEIGH. SC: Derek Carrington, in at least those marked DC.
Death Rides the Range. Low, 1938
Desert Shadows. Low, 1939 DC
Guns in the Desert. Low, 1937 DC

NETTSON, KLAUS. U.S. byline of Klaus Netzen, q.v.

NETZEN, KLAUS. Byline on U.S. editions: Klaus Nettson. SC: The Killers = K.
The Churchill Mission; see The Winston Churchill Murder
Death Valley. Mayflower, 1976 K
The Fatal Friends. Mayflower, 1975; Pinnacle, 1974 K
Mission into Auschwitz; see Night and Fog
Night and Fog. Mayflower, 1974. U.S. title: Mission into Auschwitz. Pinnacle, 1974 K
Pearl of Blood. Mayflower, 1975; Pinnacle, 1975 K
Silent Enemy. Mayflower, 1976 K
To Win and to Lose. Mayflower, 1974; Pinnacle, 1974 [Paris, 1974]
The Winston Churchill Murder. Mayflower, 1974. U.S. title: The Churchill Mission. Zebra, 1974

NEUBAUER, WILLIAM ARTHUR. 1916- .
Pseudonym: Rebecca Marsh, q.v.

NEUMAN, FREDRIC (JAY). 1934- . Ref: CA.
The Seclusion Room. Viking, 1978; Gollancz, 1979 [hosp.]

NEUMANN, ROBERT. 1897-1975. Ref: CA.
The Inquest. Hutchinson, 1944; Dutton, 1945 [Austria]

NEVILL, HUGH EDWARD CARY. Pseudonym: Morland Cary, q.v.

NEVILLE, BARBARA ALISON BOODSON. 1925- . Pseudonym: Edward Candy, q.v.

NEVILLE, MARGOT. Joint pseudonym of Margot Goyder, 1903- , and Anne Neville Goyder Joske, 1893- . Ref: CC, TC. SC: Insp. Grogan, in at least those marked G.
Come See Me Die. Bles, 1963 G
Come, Thick Night. Bles, 1951. U.S. title: Divining Rod for Murder. Doubleday, 1952 [Australia]
Confession of Murder. Bles, 1960 G [Australia]
Divining Rod for Murder; see Come, Thick Night
Drop Dead. Bles, 1962 G [Australia]
The Flame of Murder. Bles, 1958 G [Australia]
The Hateful Voyage. Bles, 1956 [ship]
Head on the Sill. Bles, 1966 G
Ladies in the Dark. Bles, 1965 G
Lena Hates Men; see Murder in Rockwater
Murder and Gardenias. Bles, 1955 G
Murder and Poor Jenny. Bles, 1954 G [Sydney]
Murder Before Marriage. Bles, 1951; Doubleday, 1951 G [Australia]
Murder Beyond the Pale. Bles, 1961 G
Murder in a Blue Moon. Bles, 1948; Doubleday, 1949 G [Australia]
Murder in Rockwater. Bles, 1944. U.S. title: Lena Hates Men. Arcadia, 1953 G [Sydney]
Murder of a Nymph. Bles, 1949; Doubleday, 1950 G [Australia]
Murder of Olympia. Bles, 1956 G [Melb.]
Murder of the Well-Beloved. Bles, 1953; Doubleday, 1953 G [Australia]
Murder to Welcome Her. Bles, 1957 G
My Bad Boy. Bles, 1964 G [Sydney]
The Seagull Said Murder. Bles, 1952 G [Australia]
Sweet Night for Murder. Bles, 1959 G [Australia]

NEVINS, FRANCIS M(ICHAEL), JR. 1943- . Ref: CA, EM, TC. SC: Loren Mensing, in both titles.
Corrupt and Ensnare. Putnam, 1978; Hale, 1979
Publish and Perish. Putnam, 1975; Hale, 1977

NEW, CHRISTOPHER
Goodbye Chairman Mao. Coward, 1979; New English Library, 1979

NEW, CLARENCE HERBERT. 1862-1933.
The Unseen Hand. Doubleday, 1918 ss

NEW, WILLIAM SLOANE
The Night in Which All Cats Are Gray. Swamp Press, 1980

NEWALL, JOHN
Nature's Nobility. Charing Cross, 1879

NEWBERRY, PERRY. 1870-1938. See: Alice MacGowan, 1858- .

NEWCOMB, KERRY, 1946- , and FRANK SCHAEFER, 1936- . Ref: CA, each author
Pandora Man. Morrow, 1979; Hamlyn, 1980 [Tex.]

NEWCOME, L(OUIS) A.
Capture of the Paddy Ryan Gang of Burglars. Newcome, 1887
The Post Office Burglars of the Shawangunk Mountains. Newcome, 1886

NEWELL, AUDREY. SC: Patrick Michael Doyle, in both titles.
Murder Is Not Mute. Macrae-Smith, 1940
Who Killed Cavelotti? Century, 1930 [NYC]

NEWELL, ROBERT HENRY. 1836-1901. Pseudonym: Orpheus C. Kerr, q.v.

NEWELL, ROSEMARY. 1922- . Ref: CA.
Star House. Popular Library, 1973 [Suri.]

NEWHAFER, RICHARD (L.). 1922- . Ref: CA. See: Gilbert A(lexander) Ralston, 1912- .

NEWHALL, MRS. LAURA EUGENIA. 1861- .
Pseudonym: Ada L. Halstead, q.v.

NEWKIRK, CLYDE C. 1870-1938. Pseudonym: Newton Newkirk, q.v.

NEWKIRK, NEWTON. Pseudonym of Clyde C. Newkirk, 1870-1938.
Stealthy Steve, the Six-Eyed Sleuth: His Quest of the Big Blue Diamond. Luce, 1904

NEWLAND, N. M.
Walk to Your Grave. Phoenix, 1951 [L.A.]

NEWMAN, BERNARD (CHARLES). 1897-1968.
Pseudonym: Don Betteridge, q.v. Ref: CA, CC, TC. SC: Sgt./Insp. Marshall, in at least those marked M; Papa Pontivy, in at least those marked PP. Set: Eng.
Black Market. Gollancz, 1942 PP
Centre Court Murder. Gollancz, 1951
Cup Final Murder. Gollancz, 1950
Dead Man Murder. Gollancz, 1946 PP
Death at Lord's. Gollancz, 1952
Death of a Harlot. Laurie, 1934; Godwin, 1935
Death to the Fifth Column. Gollancz, 1941 PP
Death to the Spy. Gollancz, 1939 PP [Cors.]
Death Under Gibraltar. Gollancz, 1938 [Gib.]
Double Menace. Hale, 1954 PP
Draw the Dragon's Teeth. Hale, 1967
Evil Phoenix. Hale, 1966
The Flying Saucer. Gollancz, 1948; Macmillan, 1950
German Spy. Gollancz, 1936; Hillman-Curl, 1936
The Jail-Breakers. Hale, 1968
Lady Doctor—Woman Spy. Hutchinson, 1937
Maginot Line Murder. Gollancz, 1939. U.S. title: Papa Pontivy and the Maginot Murder. Holt, 1940 PP [Fr.]
Moscow Murder. Gollancz, 1948 PP [Moscow]
The Mussolini Murder Plot. Hutchinson, 1936; Hillman-Curl, 1939 M [It.]
Operation Barbarossa. Hale, 1956 PP
The Otan Plot. Hale, 1957 PP [Paris]
Papa Pontivy and the Maginot Murder; see Maginot Line Murder
The Red Spider Web. Latimer House, 1947
Second Front—First Spy. Gollancz, 1944 PP
Secret Servant. Gollancz, 1935; Hillman-Curl, 1936 M
Secret Weapon. Gollancz, 1941 PP
Shoot! Gollancz, 1949
Siegfried Spy. Gollancz, 1940 PP
Silver Greyhound. Hale, 1960
Spy. Gollancz, 1935; Appleton, 1935 M
The Spy at No. 10. Hale, 1965 PP
Spy Catchers. Gollancz, 1945 PP in 4 of 31 ss
The Spy in the Brown Derby. Gollancz, 1945 PP [L.A.]
Taken at the Flood. Hale, 1958
This Is Your Life. Hale, 1963 PP
The Travelling Executioners. Hale, 1964
The Wishful Think. Hale, 1954

NEWMAN, G(ORDON) F. Ref: CA. SC: Insp. Terry Sneed, in at least those marked TS. Set: Eng.
-The Abduction. New English Library, 1972
A Detective's Tale. Sphere, 1977
The Guvnor. Hart-Davis, 1977. U.S. title: Trade-Off. Dell, 1979 [NYC]
The List. Secker, 1979
-The Player and the Guest. New English Library, 1972
The Price. New English Library, 1974. Also published as: You Flash Bastard. Sphere, 1978 TS
A Prisoner's Tale. Sphere, 1977
Rogue Cop; see Sir, You Bastard
Sir, You Bastard. Allen, 1970; Simon, 1971. Also published as: Rogue Cop. Lancer, 1973 TS
The Split. New English Library, 1972
-3 Professional Ladies. New English Library, 1973
Trade-Off; see The Guvnor
A Villain's Tale. Sphere, 1977
You Flash Bastard; see The Price
You Nice Bastard. New English Library, 1972 TS

NEWMAN, MARGARET (EDITH). 1926-   .
Pseudonym: Anne Betteridge, q.v.
Murder to Music. Long, 1959

NEWMAN, PETER N. See: Maurice Moiseiwitsch.

NEWMAN, ROBERT (HOWARD). 1909-   . Ref: CA.
The Enchanter. Houghton, 1962

NEWMAN, RONALD M.
The Man with the Million Pounds. Hutchinson, 1923

NEWMAN, TERENCE [TERRY NEWMAN]. 1927-   .
Ref: CA.
Aftermath of Murder. Blackfriars, 1947
-Along for the Ride. Cassell, 1961
-From a High Tower. Cassell, 1965
-"The Independent." Cassell, 1959
-No More a Brother. Cassell, 1958
The Raphael "Resurrection". Eyre, 1954

NEWNHAM-DAVIS, LT. COL. N(ATHANIEL). 1854-1917.
"Baby" Wilkinson's V.C. and other stories. Downey, 1899 ss
-Jadoo. Downey, 1898
-Three Men and a God, and other stories. Downey, 1896 ss

NEWTON, (WILFRID) DOUGLAS. 1884-1951.
-The Beggar, and other stories. Washbourne, 1933 ss
-Black Finger. Mellifont, 1940
-The Brute. Cassell, 1928; Appleton, 1924
The Crime Specialist. Mellifont, 1942
Dark Pathway. Cassell, 1938
Double Crossed. Appleton (London & NYC), 1922 [Can.]
-Dr. Odin. Cassell, 1933
-Eyes of Men. Cassell, 1928
Falcon of the Foreign Office. Mellifont, 1940
The Golden Cat. Cassell, 1930
-I, Savaran! Cassell, 1937
-Infinite Morning. Cassell, 1938
The Jade-Green Garter. Cassell, 1929
Laughing Gangster. Pemberton, 1948
-The Lover Who Lost Himself. Gramol, 1933
-Marie Vee. Cassell, 1924
Marked Woman. Eldon, 1949
Of Six Suspects. Mitre, 1944
-Over the Top. Pearson, 1917 ss
-Phillip and the Flappers. Pearson, 1918
-Phillip in Particular. Simpkin, 1916
The Red Judas. Cassell, 1934 [Hung.]
-Savaran and the Great Sand. Cassell, 1939
-The Sixth Director. Fiction House, 1943
Sookey. Cassell, 1925; Dodd, 1926
The War Cache. Low, 1918; Appleton, 1918
-The Witch of Nun. Cassell, 1936

NEWTON, ELIZABETH. Pseudonym: Gillan Vase, q.v.

NEWTON, MACDONALD. Pseudonym of William (Simpson) Newton, 1923-   , q.v. Other pseudonym: Gilroy Mitcham, q.v.
To Have and to Hold. Boardman, 1963

NEWTON, MIKE. SC: Jon Steel, in both titles.
The Ripper. Publisher's, 1978
The Satan Ring. Publisher's, 1978

NEWTON, WATSON JAMES. 1846-1913.
Cupid and the Creeds. Neale, 1900

NEWTON, WILLIAM (SIMPSON). 1923-   .
Pseudonyms: Gilroy Mitcham, Macdonald Newton, qq.v. Ref: CA.
If the Price Is Right. Hale, 1979
The Night We Get Rich. Hale, 1979
Nothing Is for Free. Hale, 1980
A Slice of the Cake. Hale, 1978
The Smell of Money. Hale, 1980
Someone Has to Take the Fall. Hale, 1979
You Can Deal Me In. Hale, 1980

NGAGOYEANES, NICHOLAS. 1939-   . Pseudonym: Nicholas Gage, q.v.

NIALL, IAN. Pseudonym of John McNeillie.
The Village Policeman. Heinemann, 1971 [Wales]

NIALL, MICHAEL. Pseudonym of Howard Breslin. Ref: CA.
Bad Day at Black Rock. GM, 1954; Fawcett (London), 1955 [S.W.]
Run Like a Thief. Mill, 1962; Boardman, 1963 [NYC]

NICCOLLS, T. A.
-The Perilous Quest. Appleton, 1927

NICHOLAS, J. W.
At Midnight's Chime. Arrowsmith, 1889
The House of Mystery. Arrowsmith, 1891
-The Household of Hertz. Arrowsmith, 1903
-The Story of Clovelly's Wife. Arrowsmith, 1893 ss
-The Two Crosses. Arrowsmith, 1887
-The White Bird, and other stories. Stockwell, 1923 ss

NICHOLAS, JEROME. SC: Bill Anstruther, in at least those marked BA.
The Asbestos Mask. Hodder, 1948 BA [Sing.]
Deirdre. Hodder, 1952 BA
Salute to Tomorrow. Hodder, 1949
Whispering Steel. Hodder, 1949 BA
The Widow's Peak. Hodder, 1946 BA

NICHOLAS, ROBERT. Ref: CC.
The White Shroud. Collins, 1961 [acad.]

NICHOLS, AELETA
The Third Child. Pyramid, 1971 [N.Y.]

NICHOLS, (JOHN) BEVERLEY. 1899-   . Ref: CA, CC, TC. SC: Horatio Green, in all titles. Set: Eng.
Death to Slow Music. Hutchinson, 1956; Dutton, 1956
The Moonflower. Hutchinson, 1955. U.S. title: The Moonflower Murder. Dutton, 1955
The Moonflower Murder; see The Moonflower
Murder by Request. Hutchinson, 1960; Dutton, 1960
No Man's Street. Hutchinson, 1954; Dutton, 1954
The Rich Die Hard. Hutchinson, 1957; Dutton, 1958

NICHOLS, CAROLYN. Joint pseudonym with Stanlee Coy: Iona Charles, q.v.

NICHOLS, FAN. Pseudonym of Frances Nichols Hanna. Born in S. Dak., later moved to NYC; magazine writer.
Angel Face. Popular Library, 1955 [NYC]
Ask for Linda. Popular Library, 1953
Be Silent, Love. Simon, 1960; Boardman, 1961. Also published as: The Girl in the Death Seat. Ace, 1961
The Caged. GM, 1957; Fawcett (London), 1959
Count Me In. Popular Library, 1953
-Deadline for Lovers. Godwin, 1938
-Devil Take Her. Popular Library, 1954
The Girl in the Death Seat; see Be Silent, Love
He Walks by Night. Popular Library, 1957
Hideaway. Berkley, 1959
-I Know My Love. Popular Library, 1958
-I'll Never Let You Go. Popular Library, 1955
The Loner. Simon, 1956; Boardman, 1957 [NYC]
-Love Me Now. Monarch, 1958
One by One. Arco, 1951
-Pawn. Godwin, 1938
Possess Me Not. Fell, 1946; Allen, 1948
-Scandal. Godwin, 1937

NICHOLS, LEIGH. Pseudonym of Dean R(ay) Koontz, 1945-   , q.v. Other pseudonyms: David Axton, Brian Coffey, Deanna Dwyer, K. R. Dwyer, Anthony North, qq.v.
The Key to Midnight. PB, 1979; Magnum, 1980 [Jap.]

NICHOLS, PETER. Pseudonym of (Christopher) Samuel Youd, 1922-   , q.v. Other pseudonyms: John Christopher, Hilary Ford, Peter Graaf, qq.v.
Patchwork of Death. Hale, 1967; Holt, 1965

NICHOLS, SARAH. Pseudonym of Lee Hays, q.v. Wyndham Saga series = W.
Charity. Popular Library, 1979 W
The Clouded Moon. Popular Library, 1975
Elspeth. Popular Library, 1979 W
Fleur. Popular Library, 1977 W
Grave's Company. Popular Library, 1975
House of Rancour. Popular Library, 1974 [Eng., 1800s]
The Moon Dancers. Curtis, 1973
Nell. Popular Library, 1977 W
Rachel. Popular Library, 1977 W [Pa., ca.1770]
Rosemary for Remembrance. Popular Library, 1978
Satan's Spring. Popular Library, 1974
Serpent's Tooth. Popular Library, 1978
Silsby. Popular Library, 1977 W [Eng., 1600s]
The Sunless Day. Popular Library, 1975 [Pa.]
That Dark Inn. Curtis, 1973 [Pa.]
Tracey. Popular Library, 1977 W
Valerie. Popular Library, 1977 W
The Very Dead of Winter. Popular Library, 1977
Widow's Walk. Curtis, 1972 [Maine]

NICHOLSON, JOHN. Pseudonym of Norman Howe Parcell.
Costello—Psychic Investigator. Stockwell, 1954 ss

NICHOLSON, KATE. Pseudonym of Judith Fay.
Hook, Line and Sinker. Bles, 1966

NICHOLSON, MARGARET BEDA LARMINIE.
1924-   . Pseudonym: Margaret Yorke,
q.v.

NICHOLSON, MEREDITH. 1866-1947.
The House of a Thousand Candles. Bobbs,
1905; Daily Mail, 1908 [Ind.]
The Port of Missing Men. Bobbs, 1907;
Gay & Bird, 1907
The Siege of the Seven Suitors. Houghton, 1910; Constable, 1910 [N.Y.]

NICHOLSON, MICHAEL. 1937-   .
The Partridge Kite. Hart-Davis, 1978;
Holt, 1978
Red Joker. Granada, 1980

NICHOLSON, RENTON. 1809-1861.
Dombey and Daughter. Farris, 1847

NICKOLAY, MICHAEL
Brother and Sister. Lippincott, 1979
[NYC]

NICOLAI, CHARLES. SC: John Nolan, in all
titles.
Death at Chestnut Hill. Hammond, 1955
A Killer Is Loose. Hammond, 1954 [NYC]
Murder in the Fine Arts. Hammond, 1964
[S.F.]

NICOLAS, F. R. E. Pseudonym of Nicolas
Freeling, 1927-   , q.v.
Valparaiso. Gollancz, 1964; Harper,
1965, as by Nicolas Freeling

NICOLAYSEN, BRUCE. 1934-   . Ref: CA.
Perilous Passage. Playboy, 1976. British title: The Passage. Sphere, 1979

NICOLE, CHRISTOPHER ROBIN. 1930-   .
Pseudonyms: Robin Cade, Andrew York,
qq.v.

NICOLE, CLAUDE
The Cliffs of Death. Arcadia, 1968
[Ire.]

NICOLE, CLAUDETTE. Pseudonym of Jon Messmann, q.v. Other pseudonym: Nick Carter, q.v.
Bloodroots Manor. GM, 1970 [Ky.]
The Chinese Letter. Popular Library,
1973
Circle of Secrets. GM, 1972 [Ga.]
The Dark Mill. GM, 1972 [Maine]
Dark Whispers. Pyramid, 1975 [Ire.]
The Haunted Heart. Pyramid, 1972
[Oreg.]
The Haunting of Drumroe. GM, 1971; Gold
Lion, 1973 [Ire.]
The House at Hawk's End. GM, 1971; Gold
Lion, 1974 [Can.]
The Mistress of Orion Hall. GM, 1970;
Coronet, 1971 [Cyprus]
The Secret of Harbor House. Pyramid,
1975
When the Wind Cries. Pyramid, 1976
[La.]

NICOLE, CLAUDIA
Moonwater. Paperback Library, 1971

NICOLET, C(HARLES) C(ATHCART). 1900-1943.
Death of a Bridge Expert. Simon, 1932;
Gollancz, 1933 [NYC]

NICOLSON, J(OHN) U(RBAN). 1885-   .
Fingers of Fear. Covici, 1937 [N.Y.]

NIELSEN, HELEN (BERNICE). 1918-   .
Ref: CA, CC, EM, TC. SC: Simon Drake
= SD.
After Midnight. Morrow, 1966; Gollancz,
1967 SD [Calif.]
Borrow the Night. Morrow, 1956; Gollancz, 1956. Also published as: Seven
Days Before Dying. Dell, 1958 [L.A.]
The Brink of Murder. Gollancz, 1976 SD
The Crime Is Murder. Morrow, 1956; Gollancz, 1957 [Mich.]
The Darkest Hour. Morrow, 1969; Gollancz, 1969 SD [Calif.]
Dead on the Level; see Gold Coast Nocturne
Detour. Washburn, 1953. Also published
as: Detour to Death. Dell, 1955
[S.W.]
Detour to Death; see Detour
False Witness. Ballantine, 1959 [Oslo]
The Fifth Caller. Morrow, 1959; Gollancz, 1959 [Calif.]
Gold Coast Nocturne. Washburn, 1951.
British title: Murder by Proxy. Gollancz, 1952. Also published as: Dead
on the Level. Dell, 1954 SD [Chi.]
A Killer in the Street. Morrow, 1967;
Gollancz, 1967 SD [Tucson]
The Kind Man. Washburn, 1951; Gollancz,
1952 [Calif.]
Murder by Proxy; see Gold Coast Nocturne

Obit Delayed. Washburn, 1952; Gollancz,
1953
Seven Days Before Dying; see Borrow the
Night
The Severed Key. Gollancz, 1973 SD
Shot on Location. Morrow, 1971; Gollancz, 1971
Sing Me a Murder. Morrow, 1960; Gollancz, 1961 [Calif.]
Stranger in the Dark. Washburn, 1955;
Gollancz, 1956 [Copen.]
Verdict Suspended. Morrow, 1964; Gollancz, 1965 [Calif.]
Woman Missing and other stories. Ace,
1961 ss
The Woman on the Roof. Washburn, 1954;
Gollancz, 1955 [L.A.]

NIELSEN, TORBEN. 1918-   .
A Gallowsbird's Song. Collins, 1976.
U.S. title: An Unsuccessful Man.
Harper, 1976 (Translation of "Galgesangen." Copenhagen, 1973.) [Copen.]
19 Red Roses. Collins, 1978 (Translation of "Nitten Rode Roser." Copenhagen, 1973.)
An Unsuccessful Man; see A Gallowsbird's Song

NIELSEN, VIRGINIA [VIRGINIA NIELSEN
McCALL]. 1909-   . Ref: CA.
Dangerous Dream. Avalon, 1961 [Calif.]
The Mystery of Fyfe House. Avalon, 1962
[Calif.]

NIESEWAND, PETER. 1944-1983. Ref: CA.
A Member of the Club. Secker, 1979;
Dutton, 1979 [S. Afr.]
The Underground Connection. Secker,
1978

NIGHTINGALE, URSULA. House name.
Bitters Wood. Popular Library, 1973
(Written by Frank P. Litchman,
ca.1918-1981.) [Maine]
Dawn Comes Soon. Curtis, 1973 [S.C.]
Deviltower. Popular Library, 1971
Moonhaunt. Popular Library, 1972

NILE, DOROTHEA. Pseudonym of Michael (Angelo) Avallone (Jr.), 1924-   .
Other pseudonyms: Nick Carter, Priscilla Dalton, Mark Dane, Jean-Anne
De Pre, Dora Highland, Stuart Jason,
Steve Michaels, Edwina Noone, Sidney
Stuart, Max Walker, qq.v.
The Evil Men Do. Tower, 1966 [NYC,
past]
Mistress of Farrondale. Tower, 1966
[N.Y., ca.1880]
Terror at Deepcliff. Tower, 1966 [Boston, past]
The Third Shadow. Avon, 1973
The Vampire Cameo. Lancer, 1968 [Rum.]

NISBET, HELEN C.
The Raven's Beak. Hale, 1979

NISBET, HUME. 1849-1921?
-Ashes. Author's Cooperative, 1890. Also
published as: Wasted Fires. Methuen,
1902
"Bail Up!" Chatto, 1890
-The Black Drop. Trischler, 1891
Children of Hermes. Hurst, 1901
[S. Pac.]
-A Colonial King. White, 1905
Comrades of the Black Cross. White,
1899
-A Crafty Foe. White, 1901
-A Desert Bride. White, 1894
-The Divers. Black, 1892
-Doctor Bernard St. Vincent. Ward, 1889
-A Dream of Freedom. White, 1902
-For Liberty. White, 1898
-The Haunted Station, and other stories.
White, 1894 ss
-Her Loving Slave. Digby, 1894
-Hunting for Gold; or, Adventures in the
Klondyke. White, 1897
-In Sheep's Clothing. White, 1900
-A Losing Game. White, 1901
-My Love Noel. White, 1896
-Paths of the Dead. Long, 1899
-The Queen's Desire. White, 1893
-The Rebel Chief. White, 1896
The Revenge of Valerie. White, 1900
A Singular Crime. White, 1894
-Stories Weird and Wonderful. White,
1900 ss
-The Swampers. White, 1897
-A Sweet Sinner. White, 1897
Wasted Fires; see Ashes

NISOT, E. H. See: (Mavis) Elizabeth
(Hocking) Nisot, 1893-   .

NISOT, (MAVIS) ELIZABETH (HOCKING).
1893-   . Daughter of Joseph Hocking, 1860-1937, q.v. SC: Commissaire
Payran, in at least those marked P,
which are set in Geneva.

Alixe Derring. Paul, 1934
Extenuating Circumstances. Paul, 1937
False Witness. Paul, 1938 P
Hazardous Holiday. Paul, 1936 P
Shortly Before Midnight. Paul, 1934
[Fr.]
The Sleepless Men. Doubleday, 1959, as
by E. H. Nisot [NYC]
Twelve to Dine. Paul, 1935 P
Unnatural Deeds. Paul, 1939 P

NISTLER, ERWIN N. and GERRY P. BRODERICK
Roadside Night. Pyramid, 1951

NITSUA, BENJAMIN. Pseudonym of Benjamin
Fish Austin, 1850-1932.
The Mystery of Ashton Hall. Austin,
1910

NIVEN, LARRY [LAURENCE VAN COTT NIVEN].
1938-   . Ref: CA. SC: Gil Hamilton,
in both titles.
The Long Arm of Gil Hamilton. Ballantine, 1976 [2124]
The Patchwork Girl. Ace, 1980 [future]

NIXON, ALAN. 1937-   . Born in Eng.,
raised and educated in Glasgow, later
living in It.; variously employed,
including as a medical journalist.
SC: Lawrence Maver, in both titles.
The Attack on Vienna. Bodley, 1971; St.
Martin's, 1972
Item 7. Bodley, 1970; Simon, 1971 [It.]

NIXON, ALLAN. 1918-   . Ref: CA. See
also: Don Romano. SC: Tony Garrity =
TG.
Garrity; see Get Garrity
Get Garrity. Avon, 1969. British title:
Garrity. New English Library pb, 1970
TG
Go for Garrity. Avon, 1970 TG
Good Night, Garrity. Avon, 1969; New
English Library pb, 1971 TG [L.A.]
The Scavengers. Avon, 1969; New English
Library pb, 1970

NIZZA, PAUL
The Adventures of the Five Puce Map
Tacks. Fibonacci, 1976

NOBLE, EDWARD. 1857-1941.
Fisherman's Gat. Blackwood, 1906. U.S.
title: The Issue. Doubleday, 1907
The Issue; see Fisherman's Gat
Shadows from the Thames. Pearson, 1900
ss

NOEL, DENISE
Affair of Hearts. Mystique, 1977
(Translation of "Incorrigible Jalouse." Paris, 1963.)
Bitter Honey. Mystique, 1980 (Translation of "Le Miel Amer." Paris, 1958.)
Blind Obsession. Mystique, 1980
(Translation of "Le Chemin de
L'Espoir." Paris, 1960.)
Death of a Stranger. Mystique, 1980
(Translation of "Une Double Vie."
Paris, 1976.)
House of Secrets. Mystique, 1977, HEL,
1976 (Translation of "La Maison des
Secrets." Paris, 1961.)
Love's Rebel. Mystique, 1977 (Translation of "La Revoltee." Paris, 1971.)
Night Intruder. Mystique, 1980 (Translation of "La Belle Vagabonde."
Paris, 1974.)
Prisoner of the Past. Mystique, 1979
(Translation of "De Fiel de Miel."
Paris, 1968.)
To Love Again. Mystique, 1979 (Translation of "Pour un Nouvel Ete."
Paris, 1968.)
Traitor's Mask. Mystique, 1979 (Translation of "Faux Visage." Paris,
1974.)
Treacherous Mission. Mystique, 1980
(Translation of "Re Rendenz-Vous de
Maquelonne." Paris, 1964.)
Two Faces of Love. Mystique, 1979
(Translation of "La Belle at Son
Riflet." Paris, 1967.)

NOEL, JEFFREY. SC: Johnny Perfect, in
both titles.
The Trouble with Crime. Sphere, 1976
The Trouble with Guns. Sphere, 1976

NOEL, L. Pseudonym of Leonard Noel Barker, 1882-   .
-Bars of Steel. Paul, 1929
-The Cardboard Hero. Paul, 1930
-Crescent Moon. Paul, 1947
-Flame of Folly. Paul, 1933
-Forbidden Frontiers. Paul, 1937
-Isle of Innocence. Paul, 1928
Lady All Alone. Paul, 1936
Mystery Street. Paul, 1930
-One Last Chance. Paul, 1933
-The Silver Shadow. Paul, 1944

-Star of Evil. Paul, 1931
-Uneasy Years. Paul, 1931
-The Veil of Islam. Paul, 1927

NOEL, STERLING. 1903-   . Born in Calif.; a newspaperman.
  Chain of Death; see Hydra-Head
  Death Do Us Part. Boardman, 1959 (U.S. title?)
  Empire of Evil. Avon, 1961 [NYC]
  Few Die Well. Farrar, 1953; Hale, 1954 [N.J.]
  House of Secrets. Deutsch, 1956 (U.S. title?)
  Hydra-Head. Boardman, 1955. Also published as: Chain of Death. Corgi, 1958 (U.S. title?)
  I Killed Stalin. Farrar, 1951; Hale, 1952 [1959]
  I See Red. Ace, 1955
  Intrigue in Paris; see Storm over Paris
  Prelude to Murder. Avon, 1959 [Fr.]
  Run for Your Life! Avon, 1959
  Storm over Paris. Farrar, 1955. Also published as: Intrigue in Paris. Avon, 1957 [Paris]
  -We Who Survived. Avon, 1959

NOICE, TONY
  The Ship to Shore Murder. Dramatic, 1974 (1-act play.)

NOLAN, FREDERICK (W.). 1931-   .
  The Algonquin Project; see The Oshawa Project
  Brass Target; see The Oshawa Project
  Kill Petrosino! Barker, 1975
  The Mittenwald Syndicate. Cassell, 1976; Morrow, 1976 [Ger., 1945]
  No Place to Be a Cop. Barker, 1974
  The Oshawa Project. Barker, 1974. U.S. title: The Algonquin Project. Morrow, 1974. Also published as: Brass Target. Jove, 1979 [1946]
  The Ritter Double-Cross. Barker, 1974; Morrow, 1975 [Ger.]
  White Nights, Red Dawn. Hutchinson, 1981; Macmillan, 1980 [Russ., 1915]

NOLAN, JAMES VINCENT
  Meet Mike Desmond. Grafton, 1946
  Murder Strikes Twice. Grafton, 1945
  Murder Walks Alone. Grafton, 1945

NOLAN, JEANNETTE COVERT. 1897-1974. Ref: CA, CC. SC: Lace White, in at least those marked LW.
  A Fearful Way to Die. Washburn, 1956; Muller, 1957 LW
  Final Appearance. Duell, 1943 LW
  "I Can't Die Here." Messner, 1945 LW
  Murder Will Out; see Profile in Gilt
  Profile in Gilt. Funk, 1941. Also published as: Murder Will Out. Detective Novel Classics, 194?
  Sudden Squall. Washburn, 1955; Muller, 1956 LW [Ky.]
  Where Secrecy Begins. Long, 1938

NOLAN, JOHN R.
  Make It Look Like an Accident. Vantage, 1977

NOLAN, WILLIAM F(RANCIS). 1928-   . Ref: CA, EM, TC. SC: Bart Challis = BC.
  Death Is for Losers. Sherbourne, 1968 BC [L.A.]
  Impact-20. Paperback Library, 1963 ss, some criminous
  Space for Hire. Lancer, 1971 [future]
  The White Cad Cross-Up. Sherbourne, 1969 BC [L.A.]

NONWEILER, ARVILLE
  Murder on the Pike. Phoenix, 1944 [Wis.]

NOONE, CARL
  Even the Rainbow's Bent. New English Library pb, 1977
  Mind over Murder. New English Library pb, 1976
  Sweet Cyanide. New English Library pb, 1976

NOONE, EDWINA. Pseudonym of Michael (Angelo) Avallone (Jr.), 1924-   , q.v. Other pseudonyms: Nick Carter, Priscilla Dalton, Mark Dane, Jean-Anne de Pre, Dora Highland, Stuart Jason, Steve Michaels, Dorothea Nile, Sidney Stuart, Max Walker, qq.v.
  The Cloisonne Vase. Curtis, 1970
  Corridor of Whispers. Ace, 1965 [Pa., 1800s]
  The Craghold Creatures. Beagle, 1972 [Pa.]
  The Craghold Crypt. Curtis, 1973 [Pa.]
  The Craghold Curse. Beagle, 1972 [Pa.]
  The Craghold Legacy. Beagle, 1971 [Pa.]
  Dark Cypress. Ace, 1965 [New Eng., past]
  Daughter of Darkness. Signet, 1966 [Eng., 1890s]
  Heirloom of Tragedy. Lancer, 1965 [N.Y., past]
  Seacliffe. Signet, 1968 [Maine, past]
  The Second Secret. Belmont, 1966 [N.J., 1860s]
  The Victorian Crown. Belmont, 1966 [W. Va., ca.1870]

NOONE, JOHN. 1936-   .
  The Man with the Chocolate Egg. H. Hamilton, 1966; Grove, 1967

NORDEN, ERIC
  The Ultimate Solution. Paperback Library, 1973 [NYC]

NORDHOFF, JAMES J.
  Eastwind/Westwind. Morrow, 1980

NORDSTROM, FRANCES
  Lady Bug. French (NYC), 1935 (3-act play.)

NORHAM, GERALD
  Dead Branch. Hale, 1975
  The Exporters. Hale, 1972
  Gallows March. Hale, 1971
  A Question of Coercion. Hale, 1972
  Somewhere Quiet. Hale, 1980

NORMAN, AMES. 1920-   . Pseudonym: Norma Ames, q.v.

NORMAN, BARRY. Reporter, columnist and feature writer in Johannesburg, Salisbury, and London. SC: Paul Baker, in at least those marked PB.
  The Hounds of Sparta. Allen, 1968 PB
  The Matter of Mandrake. Allen, 1967; Walker, 1968 [Sp.] PB
  To Nick a Good Body. Quartet, 1978

NORMAN, BRUCE. SC: James Mallaby, in at least those marked JM. Set: Eng.
  The Black Pawn. Arrowsmith, 1927; Dial, 1927 JM
  -"Late of London Wall..." Arrowsmith, 1931
  -The Luck of Jocelyn Pinner, R. N. Arrowsmith, 1931
  The Thousand Hands. Arrowsmith, 1926; Dial, 1927 JM

NORMAN, EARL. SC: Burns Bannion, in all titles.
  Kill Me in Atami. Berkley, 1962 [Jap.]
  Kill Me in Shimbashi. Berkley, 1959 [Tokyo]
  Kill Me in Shinjuku. Berkley, 1961 [Tokyo]
  Kill Me in Tokyo. Berkley, 1958 [Tokyo]
  Kill Me in Yokohama. Berkley, 1960 [Jap.]
  Kill Me in Yoshiwara. Berkley, 1961 [Tokyo]
  Kill Me on the Ginza. Berkley, 1962 [Tokyo]

NORMAN, ELIZABETH
  Castle Cloud. Avon, 1977 [Eng., 1850]
  If the Reaper Ride. Avon, 1978 [Eng., ca.1850]
  Sleep, My Love. Avon, 1980

NORMAN, FRANK. 1930-1980. Ref: CA. SC: Ed Nelson, in both titles. Set: Eng.
  The Dead Butler Caper. Macdonald, 1978; St. Martin's, 1979
  Too Many Crooks Spoil the Caper. Macdonald, 1979; St. Martin's, 1980

NORMAN, JAMES. Pseudonym of James Norman Schmidt, 1912-   . Ref: CA, TC. SC: Gimiendo Hernandez Quinto, in all titles, all set in China.
  An Inch of Time. Morrow, 1944; Joseph, 1945
  Murder, Chop Chop. Morrow, 1942; Joseph, 1943
  The Nightwalkers. Ziff-Davis, 1946; Joseph, 1948

NORMAN, JOHN. SC: Martin Speed, in all titles.
  The Case of the Four Pages. Swan, 1946
  The Concert Party Murders. Swan, 1945
  The Express Train Murder. Swan, 1946
  The Mystery of the Aztec Chain. Swan, 1946

NORMAN, NESTA
  -Her Dangerous Memory. Shenstone, 1949
  Terror Love! Shenstone, 1949

NORMAN, YVONNE
  The Treasure of Seacliff Manor. Avalon, 1977

NORO, FRED
  Do No Evil. International, 1969 [Paris]

NORRIS, CAROLYN BRIMLEY
  Island of Silence. Popular Library, 1976

NORRIS, KATHLEEN (THOMPSON). 1880-1966. Ref: CA.
  The Black Flemings. Doubleday, 1926; Murray, 1926. Also published as: Gabrielle. Paperback Library, 1965 [Mass.]
  Gabrielle; see The Black Flemings
  Mystery House. Doubleday, 1939 [Calif.]
  The Mystery of Pine Point. Murray, 1936 (U.S. title?)
  Romance at Hillyard House; see The Secrets of Hillyard House
  The Secret of the Marshbanks. Doubleday, 1940; Murray, 1940 [Calif.]
  The Secrets of Hillyard House. Doubleday, 1947. British title: Romance at Hillyard House. Murray, 1948

NORRIS, STANLEY
  For His Friend's Honor. Street, 1900

NORRIS, W(ILLIAM) E(DWARD). 1847-1925.
  -The Baffled Conspirators. Blackett, 1890; Lovell, 1890
  -Jack's Father, and other stories. Methuen, 1891; Lovell, 1891 (The U.S. edition contains only 3 of the 7 ss in the British edition; the others are in: Mysterious Mrs. Wilkinson and other stories. Lovell, 1891.) ss
  Mysterious Mrs. Wilkinson and other stories; see Jack's Father, and other stories
  Not Guilty. Constable, 1910; Brentano's, 1910
  -The Rogue. Bentley, 1888; Holt, 1888
  -Troubled Tranton. Constable, 1915; Brentano's, 1916

NORSWORTHY, GEORGE. SC: Martin Crow, in at least those marked MC. Set: Eng.
  Casino. Low, 1934
  Crime at the Villa Gloria. Low, 1936; Greenberg, 1936 MC
  Dames-Errant. Low, 1935
  -The Hartness Millions. Low, 1936
  A House-Party Mystery. Low, 1935 MC
  Murder at Mulberry Cottage. Low, 1937
  Murder in Sussex. Hutchinson, 1940

NORTH, ANTHONY. Pseudonym of Dean R(ay) Koontz, 1945-   , q.v. Other pseudonyms: David Axton, Brian Coffey, Deanna Dwyer, K. R. Dwyer, Leigh Nichols, qq.v.
  Strike Deep. Dial, 1974

NORTH, BARCLAY. Pseudonym of W(illiam) C(adwalader) Hudson, 1843-1915, q.v.
  The Diamond Button: Whose Was It? Cassell (NYC), 1889; Cassell (London), 1890
  520%; or, The Great Franklin Syndicate. Street, 1900
  Linked to Crime. Street (Magnet)
  The Stevedore Mystery. Street (Magnet), 1900

NORTH, CHARLES. Pseudonym of Gerald White Johnson, ca.1891-1980.
  Beware of the Dog! Morrow, 1939. British title: Out of the Dog House. Cassell, 1940

NORTH, CLYDE, ALBERT C(HARLES) FULLER, and JACK NELSON
  Remote Control. French, 1931 (3-act play.)

NORTH, ELIZABETH. 1932-   .
  Enough Blue Sky. Gollancz, 1977

NORTH, ERIC. Pseudonym of Bernard Charles Cronin, 1884-   . Other pseudonym: Dennis Adair, q.v.
  A Chip on My Shoulder. Dobson, 1955; Roy, 1956
  The Name Is Smith. Dobson, 1957; Roy, 1957 [Melb.]
  Nobody Stops Me. Dobson, 1960; Roy, 1960 [Australia]

NORTH, GIL. Pseudonym of Geoffrey Horne, 1916-   , q.v. Ref: CA, CC, TC. SC: Sgt. Caleb Cluff = CC. Set: Eng.
  The Confounding of Sergeant Cluff. Chapman, 1966 CC
  A Corpse for Kofi Katt. Hale, 1978
  The Methods of Sergeant Cluff. Chapman, 1961 CC
  More Deaths for Sergeant Cluff. Chapman, 1963 CC
  No Choice for Sergeant Cluff. Eyre, 1971 CC
  The Procrastination of Sergeant Cluff. Eyre, 1969 CC

Sergeant Cluff and the Day of Reckoning. Chapman, 1967 CC
Sergeant Cluff and the Madmen. Chapman, 1964 (Two novelets.) CC
Sergeant Cluff and the Price of Pity. Chapman, 1965 CC
Sergeant Cluff Goes Fishing. Chapman, 1962 CC
Sergeant Cluff Rings True. Eyre, 1972 CC
Sergeant Cluff Stands Firm. Chapman, 1960 CC

NORTH, HOWARD. Pseudonym of Elleston Trevor, 1920- , q.v. Name originally: Trevor Dudley Smith, q.v. Other pseudonyms: Mansell Black, Adam Hall, Simon Rattray, Warwick Scott, Caesar Smith, qq.v.
Expressway. Collins, 1973; Simon, 1973 [N.J.]

NORTH, JESSICA. Pseudonym. Born in U.S., has lived mostly abroad, more recently in Mex.; lecturer in anthropology turned writer of books, ss and essays.
The High Valley. Random, 1973; Heinemann, 1974 [Mex.]
The Legend of the Thirteenth Pilgrim. Coward, 1969 [It.]
River Rising. Random, 1975 [Can.]

NORTH, SAM
209 Thriller Road. New English Library, 1979; St. Martin's, 1980

NORTH, SARA. House name. Used by Jean Hager, 1932- . Other Hager pseudonym: Amanda McAllister, q.v. Also used by Barbara Thomas Bonham, 1926- .
Evil Side of Eden. Playboy, 1976
Jasmine for My Grave (by BTM). Playboy, 1978 [San Antonio]
A Message from Julie. Playboy, 1977
Shadow of the Tamaracks. Playboy, 1979

NORTH, WILLIAM. 1869- . Pseudonym: Ralph Rodd, q.v.

NORTHMAN, PETER
Red Boxes. Skeffington, 1948

NORTHWAY, COLIN. Joint pseudonym with Michael Ewings: Frank Ross, q.v.

NORTON, ALICE MARY. 1912?- . Pseudonym: Andre Norton, q.v. Joint pseudonym with Grace Allen Hogarth, 1905- : Allen Weston, q.v.

NORTON, ANDRE. Pseudonym of Alice Mary Norton, 1912?- . Joint pseudonym with Grace Allen Hogarth, 1905- : Allen Weston, q.v. Ref: CA.
Iron Butterflies. GM, 1980
The Opal-Eyed Fan. Dutton, 1977 [Fla., ca.1850]
Snow Shadow. Crest, 1979 [Md.]
Velvet Shadows. GM, 1977
The White Jade Fox. Dutton, 1975; Wingate, 1976

NORTON, (FRANK R.) BROWNING, 1909- and CHARLES A. LANDOLF. Ref for Norton: CA.
I Prefer Murder. Graphic, 1956

NORTON, OLIVE (MARION CLAYDON). 1913-
The Corpse-Bird Cries. Cassell, 1971 [Wales]
Dead on Prediction. Cassell, 1970
Now Lying Dead. Cassell, 1967
A School for Liars. Cassell, 1966
The Speight Street Angle. Corgi, 1968

NORTON, PATRICIA
Daughter of Evil. Lancer, 1973

NORWAY, G(EORGE)
-Adventures of Johnnie Pascoe. Nisbet, 1889
-Bessie Kitson. National Society's Depository, 1896
-The Brand of Cain. Ward, 1888
-A Dangerous Conspirator. Jarrolds, 1897
Falsely Accused. Digby, 1900
In False Attire. Digby, 1902
-Mignonette. National Society Depository, 1903
-Riverslea. National Society Depository, 1900
-Tregarthen. Hurst, 1896

NORWAY, NEVIL SHUTE. 1899-1960. Pseudonym: Nevil Shute, q.v.

NORWOOD, ELLIOTT
Audit in Death. Hale, 1970 [Afr.]
Bullets in the Bush. Hale, 1969 [Afr.]

NORWOOD, HAYDEN (EUGENE). 1907- .
Death Down East. Phoenix, 1941 [Maine]
-They Met at Mrs. Bloxom's. Rodale, 1938

NORWOOD, JOHN. Pseudonym of Delbert Raymond Stark, 1919- .
No Time to Laugh. Ward, 1956

NORWOOD, JOSEPH
Breaking the Shell. Burke, 1923

NORWOOD, VICTOR (GEORGE CHARLES). 1920- . Pseudonyms: Shane V. Baxter, Johnny Dark, Mark Hampton, Hank Janson, Nat Karta, qq.v. SC: Jacare, in at least those marked J.
-The Caves of Death. Scion, 1951 J
-Cry of the Beast. Scion, 1952 J
Hell's Wenches. (U.S.), 1963
-The Island of Creeping Death. Scion, 1952 J
Journey into Fear. Hale, 1965
The Long Way Home. 1967
Night of the Black Horror. Badger, 1962
-The Skull of Kanaima. Scion, 1952 J
-The Temple of the Dead. Scion, 1951 J
-The Untamed. Scion, 1951 J
Valley of the Damned. 1968

NOTLEY, F(RANCES) E(LIZA) M(ILLETT). 1820- .
Beneath the Wheels. Tinsley, 1870

NOTLEY, JOHN (FRANKE). 1911- .
Corruption in Cantock. Jarrolds, 1941. U.S. title: Murder Has an Echo. Mystery House, 1945
-Hotel Geneva. Jarrolds, 1942
Murder Has an Echo; see Corruption in Cantock

NOTTINGHAM, POPPY
Hatred's Web. Ace, 1974 [La.]
Shadow of a Cat. Ace, 1974
Wasted Pride. Avon, 1978 [Australia]
Without a Grave. Ace, 1975

NOVA, CRAIG. Pseudonym: Nick Carter, q.v.

NOVAK, ROBERT. SC: Joe Blaze, in all titles.
The Big Payoff. Belmont, 1974 [NYC]
The Concrete Cage. Belmont, 1974 [NYC]
The Thrill Killers. Belmont, 1974 (Written by Leonard Levinson, 1935- , q.v.) [NYC]

NOVELLO, IVOR. 1893-1951. See: Phyllis Bottome, 1884-1963.

NOY, JOHN. 1892- . SC: Rufus Deville, in at least those marked RD.
Gangsters of the Air. Hamilton, 1938 RD
The Great Airways Plot. Hamilton, 1938 RD
The Mystery of the Crested Falcon. Hamilton, 1939 RD
The Pirate Airship. Hamilton, 1932
Red Devil of the Air Police. Hamilton, 1937 RD

NOYES, STANLEY. 1924- . Ref: CA.
Shadowbox. Macmillan, 1970 [N. Mex.]

NUELLE, HELEN S(HERMAN). 1923- . Ref: CA.
Evil Lives Here. Avalon, 1973
The Haunting of Bally Moran. Manor, 1976
Land Where Our Fathers Died. Manor, 1978
The Shadows of Amanda. Dell, 1976
The Sins of the Past. Manor, 1977

NUETZEL, CHARLES (ALEXANDER). 1934- . Ref: CA.
Murder Times 4. Powell, 1969 [L.A.]
Softly As I Kill You. Powell, 1969 [L.A.]

NULL, GARY. 1945- . Ref: CA. Both titles are in the Secret Circle series.
Cuban Expedition. Pyramid, 1974 [Cuba]
Operation Royal Family. Pyramid, 1975

NUSBAUM, N. RICHARD. Pseudonym of N(athan) Richard Nash, 1913- , q.v.
Incognito. French (NYC), 1941 (Play.)

NUTT, CHARLES. 1929-1967. Pseudonym: Charles Beaumont, q.v.

NUTTALL, ANTHONY
The Chinese Doll Affair. Hale, 1973
The Hot End of the Stick. Hale, 1971
It Adds Up to Trouble. Hale, 1972
A Pistol at My Head. Hale, 1972
The Ventilated Head. Hale, 1974

NUTTALL, JEFF. 1933- . Ref: CA.
Snipe's Spinster. Calder, 1975

NYLAND, GENTRY
Mr. South Burned His Mouth. Morrow, 1941. British title: Run for Your Money. Long, 1941. Also published as: Hot Bullets for Love. Double Action Detective Novel, 1943 [NYC]

NYSON, J. E.
Death Calls at Scotland Yard. Blackfriars, 1946

OAKES, PHILIP (BARLOW). 1928- . Ref: CA.
Experiment at Proto. Deutsch, 1973; Coward, 1973

OAKLEY, JOHN. See also: Nancy Oakley.
The Blackmailer. Ward, 1902
The Great Craneboro' Conspiracy. Ward, 1907
That Wilmslow Girl! Aldine, 1895

OAKLEY, NANCY and JOHN OAKLEY, q.v. Set: Eng.
The Clevedon Case. Jenkins, 1923; Lippincott, 1924
The Lint House Mystery. Jenkins, 1925

OAKROYD, SIMON
Maybe He's Dead. Belmont, 1971 [NYC]

O'BRIAN, FRANK. Pseudonym of Brian (Francis Wynne) Garfield, 1939- , q.v. Other pseudonyms: John Ives, Drew Mallory, qq.v.
The Rimfire Murders. Bouregy, 1962

O'BRIEN, EDNA. 1932- . Ref: CA.
Johnny, I Hardly Knew You. Weidenfeld, 1977. U.S. title: I Hardly Knew You. Doubleday, 1978

O'BRIEN, FITZ-JAMES. 1828-1862.
What Was It? and other stories. Ward, 1889 ss

O'BRIEN, FLANN. Pseudonym of Brian O'Nolan, 1911-1966. Ref: CA.
The Third Policeman. MacGibbon, 1967; Walker, 1967 [Ire.]

O'BRIEN, HOWARD VINCENT. 1888-1947.
Four-and-Twenty Blackbirds. Doubleday, 1928; Hodder, 1928 [Fr.]

O'BRIEN, LEE. Pseudonym of Candace Ward, 1948- . Ref: CA.
Sweet William Is Dead. Popular Library, 1975 [Mass.]
When She Wakes. Popular Library, 1975

O'BRIEN, MORROUGH
The League of the Ring and Torn Apart. Ireland's Own Library, 1914 ss

O'BRIEN, ROBERT C. Pseudonym of Robert L. Conly, 1918-1973. Ref: CA.
A Report from Group 17. Atheneum, 1972; Gollancz, 1973 [Wash. D.C.]

O'BRIEN, SALIEE. Pseudonym of Frankie-Lee James.
Beelfontaine. Berkley, 1974
The Bride of Gaylord Hall. Berkley, 1972
Heiress to Evil. Beagle, 1974
Night of the Scorpion. Berkley, 1976 [Calif.]
Shadow of the Caravan. PB, 1974 [Calif., 1862]

O'BRINE, (PADRAIC) MANNING. 1915- . TV script writer. SC: Michael the O'Kelly, in at least those marked MO; Mills = M.
Corpse to Cairo. Hammond, 1952 MO [Cairo]
Crambo. Joseph, 1970
Dagger Before Me. Hammond, 1957 MO
Dead As a Dodo; see Dodos Don't Duck
Deadly Interlude. Hammond, 1954 MO
Dodos Don't Duck. Hammond, 1953. Also published as: Dead As a Dodo. Corgi, 1954 MO
The Hungry Killer. Hammond, 1955 MO
Killers Must Eat. Hammond, 1951 MO [Rome]
Mills. Jenkins, 1969; Lippincott, 1969 M [It.]
No Earth for Foxes. Barrie, 1974; Delacorte, 1975 M
Pale Moon Rising. Futura, 1978; St. Martin's, 1978 [Fr., 1942]
Passport to Treason. Hammond, 1955 MO

OBSTFELD, RAYMOND. SC: Harry Gould, in both titles.
   The Dead-End Option. Charter, 1980 [Calif.]
   The Goulden Fleece. Charter, 1979 [L.A.]

O'CALLAGHAN, DMITRI
   The Scavengers. Paperback Library, 1963 (Novelization of the movie.) [H. Kong]

O'CALLAGHAN, MAXINE
   Death Is Forever. Raven, 1980 [L.A.]

OCKLEY, G. T. [MRS. C. E. THOMPSON]
   The Devil on Board. Heath Cranston, 1937 [ship]
   -The Man Under the Window. Houghton (London), 1935
   -The Tempestuous Wooer. Houghton (London), 1936

O'CONNELL, FREDERICK WILLIAM. 1876-1929. Pseudonym: Cearnach Conall, q.v.

O'CONNELL, T. J.
   Dead Man's Hoard. Mitre, 1946
   The Tyson Murder Case. Mitre, 1946

O'CONNOR, DERMOT
   The Eye of the Eagle. Long, 1971
   The Restless Quiet. Long, 1971
   The Slender Chance. Long, 1973 [Mid. East]

O'CONNOR, JOHN M(ARSHALL). 1909- .
   Anonymous Footsteps. Cheshire, 1932

O'CONNOR, MICHAEL P(ATRICK). See: G(ranville) P(ratt) Willis.

O'CONNOR, RAMONCITA SAYER
   Murder Won't Wait. Arcadia, 1953 [Calif.]

O'CONNOR, RICHARD. 1915-1975. Pseudonyms: Frank Archer, Patrick Wayland, qq.v.

OCORK, SHANNON. Sports photographer, later full-time writer in NYC.
   Sports Freak. St. Martin's, 1980 [N.Y.]

ODELL, WILLIAM C. Pseudonym: Nick Carter, q.v. See also: Dan J(ames) Marlowe, 1914- .
   The Leather Albatross. Apollo, 1972

ODLUM, JEROME. 1905-1954.
   Each Dawn I Die. Bobbs, 1938
   The Mirabilis Diamond. Scribner, 1945 [L.A.]
   The Morgue Is Always Open. Scribner, 1944 [NYC]
   Night and No Moon. Howell Soskin, 1942
   Nine Lives Are Not Enough. Sheridan, 1940; Boardman, 1944 [Mpls.]

O'DONNELL, ELLIOTT. 1872-1965. Ref: CA.
   Caravan of Crime. Grafton, 1946 ss, some criminous
   -The Dead Riders. Rider, 1952; Paperback Library, 1967
   The Devil in the Pulpit. Archer, 1932
   Haunted and Hunted. Grafton, 1946 ss, some criminous
   -Jennie Barlowe, Adventuress. Greening, 1906
   Murder at Hide and Seek. Eldon, 1945

O'DONNELL, LILLIAN (UDVARDY). 1926- .
Ref: CA, TC. SC: Mici Anhalt = MA; Norah Mulcahaney = NM.
   Aftershock. Putnam, 1977; Hale, 1979 MA [NYC]
   Babes in the Woods. Abelard (NYC & London), 1965 [N.J.]
   The Baby Merchants. Putnam, 1975; Bantam (London), 1976 NM [NYC]
   Death Blanks the Screen. Arcadia, 1961 [NYC]
   Death of a Player. Abelard (NYC & London), 1964 [NYC]
   Death on the Grass. Arcadia, 1960
   Death Schuss. Abelard (NYC & London), 1963 [Can.]
   Dial 577 R-A-P-E. Putnam, 1974; Barker, 1974 NM [NYC]
   Dive into Darkness. Abelard (NYC & London), 1971
   Don't Wear Your Wedding Ring. Putnam, 1973; Barker, 1974 NM [NYC]
   The Face of the Crime. Abelard (NYC & London), 1968 [NYC]
   Falling Star. Putnam, 1979; Hale, 1981 MA [NYC]
   Leisure Dying. Putnam, 1976 NM [NYC]
   Murder Under the Sun. Abelard (NYC & London), 1964 [San Juan]
   No Business Being a Cop. Putnam, 1978; Hale, 1980 NM [NYC]
   The Phone Calls. Putnam, 1972; Hodder, 1972
   The Sleeping Beauty Murders. Abelard (NYC & London), 1967
   The Tachi Tree. Abelard (NYC & London), 1968 [Carib.]
   Wicked Designs. Putnam, 1980 MA [NYC]

O'DONNELL, MARGARET
   -The Beehive. Eyre, 1980

O'DONNELL, PETER. 1920- . See also: J. T. McIntosh. Ref: TC. SC: Modesty Blaise, in all titles.
   Black Pearl and the Vikings. Star, 1978 (Comic strip.)
   Dragon's Claw. Souvenir, 1978
   I, Lucifer. Souvenir, 1967; Doubleday, 1967
   The Impossible Virgin. Souvenir, 1971; Doubleday, 1971
   In the Beginning. Star, 1978 (Comic strip.)
   Last Day in Limbo. Souvenir, 1976
   Modesty Blaise. Souvenir, 1965; Doubleday, 1965
   Modesty Blaise: The Black Pearl. Wyndham, 1978 (Comic strips.)
   Pieces of Modesty. Pan, 1972 ss
   Sabre-Tooth. Souvenir, 1966; Doubleday, 1966
   The Silver Mistress. Souvenir, 1973
   A Taste for Death. Souvenir, 1969; Doubleday, 1969

O'DONNELL, CAPTAIN SIMON
   The Great Diamond Robbery. Ogilvie, 1895
   The Runaway Wife; or, Love and Vengeance. Laird, 1889 [Chi.]

O'DRISCOLL, MICHAEL
   Flood's First Case. Mitre, 1946

O'DUFFY, EIMAR (ULTAN). 1893-1935. Set: Eng.
   The Bird Cage. Bles, 1932; Kinsey, 1933
   Head of a Girl. Bles, 1935
   The Secret Enemy. Bles, 1932

OELLRICHS, INEZ (HILDEGARD). 1907- .
Ref: MP. SC: Matt Winters, in at least those marked MW.
   And Die She Did. Doubleday, 1945; Hammond, 1953 MW
   Death in a Chilly Corner. Hammond, 1964 MW
   Death of a White Witch. Doubleday, 1949; Hammond, 1953 MW
   The Kettel Mill Mystery. Doubleday, 1939; Davies, 1940 MW
   The Man Who Didn't Answer. Doubleday, 1939; Davies, 1939 MW
   Murder Comes at Night. Doubleday, 1940; Hammond, 1951 MW
   Murder Helps. McKay, 1947 MW
   Murder Makes Us Gay. Doubleday, 1941; Hammond, 1952

OEMLER, MARIE CONWAY. 1879-1932.
   A Woman Named Smith. Century, 1919; Heinemann, 1920

O'FARRELL, BRIAN
   Mystery on the River. Blackwell, 1936

O'FARRELL, WILLIAM. 1904-1962. Pseudonym: William Grew, q.v.
   Brandy for a Hero. Duell, 1948 [NYC]
   Causeway to the Past. Duell, 1950; Corgi, 1954 [Charleston]
   The Devil His Due. Doubleday, 1955; Hale, 1955 [NYC]
   The Golden Key. Lancer, 1962 [Calif.]
   Grow Young and Die. Doubleday, 1952; Dakers, 1954 [Fr.]
   Gypsy, Go Home. GM, 1961 [Calif.]
   Harpoon of Death; see The Snakes of St. Cyr
   Lovely in Death; see The Snakes of St. Cyr
   Repeat Performance. Houghton, 1942; Allen, 1948. Revised edition: Pennant, 1954 [NYC]
   The Secret Fear; see Walk the Dark Bridge
   The Snakes of St. Cyr. Duell, 1951. British title: Harpoon of Death. Dakers, 1953. Also published as: Lovely in Death. Bestseller, 1955, abridged [Fr.]
   These Arrows Point to Death. Duell, 1951; Foulsham, 1952
   Thin Edge of Violence. Duell, 1949 [NYC]
   The Ugly Woman. Duell, 1948 [NYC]
   Walk the Dark Bridge. Doubleday, 1952. British title: The Secret Fear. Corgi, 1954 [NYC]
   Wetback. Dell, 1956 [Tex.]

OFFORD, LENORE GLEN. 1905- . Ref: CA, CC, EM, TC. SC: Bill & Coco Hastings = H; Todd McKinnon = TM.
   And Turned to Clay; see My True Love Lies
   Clues to Burn. Duell, 1942; Grayson, 1943 H [Ida.]
   The Glass Mask. Duell, 1944; Jarrolds, 1946 TM [Calif.]
   Murder Before Breakfast; see Murder on Russian Hill
   Murder on Russian Hill. Macrae Smith, 1938. British title: Murder Before Breakfast. Jarrolds, 1938 H [S.F.]
   My True Love Lies. Duell, 1947. British title: And Turned to Clay. Jarrolds, 1950 [S.F.]
   The 9 Dark Hours. Duell, 1941; Eldon, 1941 [S.F.]
   Skeleton Key. Duell, 1943; Eldon, 1944 TM [S.F.]
   The Smiling Tiger. Duell, 1949; Jarrolds, 1951 TM [Calif.]
   Walking Shadow. Simon, 1959; Ward, 1961 TM [Oreg.]

OFFUTT, ANDREW (JEFFERSON). 1934- .
Ref: CA.
   Operation: Super Ms. Berkley, 1974 [Fr.]

O'FINN, THADDEUS. Pseudonym of Joseph Thaddeus McGloin, 1917- . Ref: CA.
   Happy Holiday! Rinehart, 1950 [Wis.]

O'FLAHERTY, LIAM. 1896- . Ref: CA.
   The Assassin. Cape, 1928; Harcourt, 1928
   The Informer. Cape, 1925; Knopf, 1925 [Ire.]

O'FLAHERTY, LOUISE. 1920- . Ref: CA.
   The House of the Lost Woman. Pyramid, 1974
   A Tear in the Silk. Pyramid, 1976

O'FLANAGAN, DENIS
   Everything Happens to Joe. Nimmo, 1947

O'FRANCIS, MARY. Pseudonym: Margaret Blount, q.v.

OGAN, GEORGE (F.). 1912- . See also: Margaret (E. Nettles) Ogan, 1923-1979. SC: Johnny Bordelon, in both titles, both set in New Or.
   Murder in the Wind. Raven, 1980
   To Kill a Judge. Raven, 1980

OGAN, MARGARET (E. NETTLES), 1923-1979, and GEORGE (F.) OGAN, 1912- , q.v. Ref: CA.
   The Fortenberry Rites. Major, 1976

OGBURN, DOROTHY (STEVENS). 1890- .
   Death on the Mountain. Little, 1931 [N.C.]
   Ra-Ta-Plan—! Little, 1930; Nash, 1931 [South]
   The Will and the Deed. Dodd, 1935 [N.Y.]

OGILVIE, ELISABETH (MAY). 1917- .
Ref: CA.
   Bellwood. McGraw-Hill, 1969 [Maine]
   A Dancer in Yellow. McGraw-Hill, 1979 [Maine]
   The Devil in Tartan. McGraw-Hill, 1980 [Scot.]
   The Dreaming Summer. McGraw-Hill, 1976 [Maine]
   The Face of Innocence. McGraw-Hill, 1970 [New Eng.]
   Where the Lost Aprils Are. McGraw-Hill, 1975
   The Witch Door. McGraw-Hill, 1959; Allen, 1961

OGILVIE, FRANCES
   Green Bondage. Farrar, 1931; Nicholson, 1932

OGNALL, LEOPOLD HORACE. 1908-1979. Pseudonyms: Harry Carmichael, Hartley Howard, qq.v.

O'GRADY, ANNE. Ref: CA.
   Operation Midas. Davies, 1973; Harper, 1975

O'GRADY, LESLIE
   The Artist's Daughter. St. Martin's, 1979; Souvenir, 1980 [Eng., 1800s]

O'GRADY, ROHAN. Pseudonym of June O'Grady Skinner, 1922- . Ref: CA.
   Bleak November. Dial, 1970; Joseph, 1971 [Can.]
   Let's Kill Uncle. Macmillan, 1963; Longmans, 1964
   The Master of Montrolfe Hall; see Pippin's Journal

Author Index

O'Houlihan's Jest. Macmillan, 1961; Gollancz, 1961 [Ire.]
Pippin's Journal. Macmillan, 1962; Gollancz, 1962. Also published as: The Master of Montrolfe Hall. Ace, 1965 [Eng.]

O'HANLON, JAMES D. SC: Jason Cordry, in all titles.
As Good As Murdered. Random, 1940; Cherry Tree, 1941 [L.A.]
Murder at Coney Island. Phoenix, 1939 [NYC]
Murder at Horsethief. Phoenix, 1941; Boardman, 1943 [Ariz.]
Murder at Malibu. Phoenix, 1937 [L.A.]
Murder at 300 to 1. Phoenix, 1938; Long, 1939 [Calif.]

O'HARA, BORIS
The St. Valentine's Day Massacre. Dell, 1967 (Novelization of the movie.)

O'HARA, KENNETH. Pseudonym of Jean Morris, 1928- , q.v. Ref: CC, MC. Radio and TV scriptwriter; radio, film and TV director. SC: Dr. Alun Barry, in at least those marked AB. Set: Eng.
The Bird-Cage. Gollancz, 1968; Random, 1969
The Company of St. George. Gollancz, 1972
The Delta Knife. Gollancz, 1976
Double Cross Purposes. Cassell, 1962
The Ghost of Thomas Penry. Gollancz, 1977
The Searchers of the Dead. Gollancz, 1979 [Wales]
Sleeping Dogs Lying. Cassell, 1960; Macmillan, 1962 AB
Underhandover. Cassell, 1961; Macmillan, 1963
Unknown Man, Seen in Profile. Gollancz, 1967
A View to a Death. Cassell, 1958 AB

O'HARA, KEVIN. Pseudonym of Marten Cumberland, 1892-1972, q.v. SC: Chico Brett, in all titles. Set: Eng.
Always Tell the Sleuth. Hurst, 1953
And Here Is the Noose! Long, 1959
The Customer's Always Wrong. Hurst, 1951
Danger: Women at Work! Long, 1958
Don't Neglect the Body. Long, 1964
Don't Tell the Police. Long, 1963
Exit and Curtain. Hurst, 1952
If Anything Should Happen. Long, 1962
It Leaves Them Cold. Hurst, 1954
It's Your Funeral. Long, 1966
Keep Your Fingers Crossed. Hurst, 1955
The Pace That Kills. Hurst, 1955
Sing, Clubman, Sing! Hurst, 1952
Taking Life Easy. Long, 1961
Well, I'll Be Hanged! Long, 1958
Women Like to Know. Jarrolds, 1957

O'HARA, PATRICK
The Wohldorf Shipment. Arlington, 1978
The Yangtze Run. Arlington, 1977

O'HARA FAMILY, THE. Joint pseudonym of John Banim, 1798-1842, and Michael Banim, 1796-1874.
The Ghost-Hunter and His Family. Carey, 1833

O'HIGGINS, HARVEY J(ERROLD). 1876-1929. See also: Harriet Ford, 1868-1949; and: Arthur Hornblow, 1865-1941? Ref: CC, EM.
The Adventures of Detective Barney. Century, 1915 ss [NYC]
Detective Duff Unravels It. Liveright, 1929 ss [NYC]
The Dummy, with Harriet Ford, 1868-1949. French, 1925 (4-act play.)

OHNET, GEORGES. Pseudonym of Georges Henot, 1848-1918.
Antoinette; or, The Marl-Pit Mystery; see The Great Marl-Pit
A Debt of Hatred. Cassell (NYC), 1891
-Doctor Rameau. Chatto, 1889; Rand, 1889 (Translation of "Le Docteur Rameau." Paris, 1889.)
The Great Marl-Pit. Remington, 1886. U.S. title: Antoinette; or, The Marl-Pit Mystery. Lippincott, 1889. Also published as: The Marl-Pit Mystery. Vizetelly, 1889 (Translation of "Le Grande Marniere." Paris, 1885.) [Fr.]
-In Deep Abyss. Greening, 1904; Funk, 1901 (Translation of "Au Fond du Gouffre." Paris, 1899.)
The Marl-Pit Mystery; see The Great Marl-Pit
The Poison Dealer. Laurie, 1906 [Paris]
-A Weird Gift. Chatto, 1890; Munro, 1890 (Translation of "L'Ame de Pierre." Paris, 1890.)

The Woman of Mystery. Chatto, 1903 [Fr.]

O'KEEFE, BOB
Diamonds Can Be Dangerous. Spearhead (Pretoria), 1953
Gold Without Glitter. Central News Agency (South Africa), 1957

OKUN, LAWRENCE E(UGENE). 1929- . Ref: CA.
On the 8th Day. Celestial Arts, 1980

OLAY, LIONEL
The Dark Corners of the Night. Signet, 1960

OLBRICH, FRENY. SC: Frank Desouza, in all titles, all set in Bombay.
Desouza in Stardust. Heinemann, 1979
Desouza Pays the Price. Heinemann, 1978
Sweet and Deadly. Heinemann, 1979

OLD HUTCH. Pseudonym of O. L. Adams.
The Detective's Clew; or, The Tragedy of Elm Grove. Street, 1888. Also published as by O. L. Adams: Street, 189?

OLD SLEUTH. Pseudonym of Harlan Page Halsey, 1837-1898, q.v. Other pseudonyms: Tony Pastor, Judson R. Taylor, qq.v. SC: Old Sleuth, in at least those marked OS.
Aggravating Joe, the Prince of Mischief. Ogilvie, 1894
Allie Baird, the Settler's Son. Parlor Car, 1897
Almon Mitchell's Double. Royal, ca.1897
An Amazing Wizard. Ogilvie, 1898
The American Detective in Russia. Munro, 1892 [Russ.]
The American Monte Cristo. Royal, ca.1897
The American Thug. Munro, 1897
Amzi, the Detective. Ogilvie, 1896
Archie the Tumbler. Ogilvie, 1895
Arkie, the Runaway. Ogilvie, 1895
Arlie Bright. Ogilvie, 1896
The Autobiography of a Bottle of Bourbon. Munro, ca.1891
The Bank Robbers. Royal, ca.1897
A Beautiful Blackmailer. Royal, ca.1908
A Beautiful Fugitive. Parlor Car, 1898
Bertie Bland, the Detective. Ogilvie, 1895
The Bicycle Detective; see Bicycle Jim
Bicycle Jim. Ogilvie, 1895. Also published as: The Bicycle Detective. Ogilvie
Billy Mischief, a Regular Trained Detective. Royal, ca.1908
Billy Preston. Parlor Car, 1897
Billy, the Tramp. Ogilvie, 1895
Black Jess, the Outlaw. Royal, ca.1908
The Boy Detective. Munro, 1894
A Boy Fugitive. Ogilvie, 1896
Breezy Frank. Ogilvie, 1897
Bruce Angelo, the City Detective. Street, 1887
Cad Metti, the Female Detective. Ogilvie, 1895
Carroll Moore. Ogilvie, 1897
The Central Park Mystery. Ogilvie, 1898
The Chief of the Counterfeiters. Westbrook, 1920s
A Clever Detective. Ogilvie, 1894
Clew by Clew. Munro, 1894
A Close Call. Parlor Car, 1897
Clyde, the Resolute Detective. Parlor Car, 1897
Coal Tom. Ogilvie, 1894
The Confessions of an Imp. Munro, ca. 1892
The Cowboy Detective. Ogilvie, 1895
Creco the Swordsman. Ogilvie, 1895
Creston, the Detective. Parlor Car, 1897
Criminals Run Down. Royal, ca.1897
Crusoe Harry. Ogilvie, 1896
A Cute Boy Detective. Ogilvie, 1895
A Daring Conspiracy. Royal, ca.1897
Daring Maddie. Ogilvie, 1898
A Dashing Fugitive. Parlor Car, 1897
Days and Nights of Peril. Ogilvie, 1897
Dead Straight. Parlor Car, 1897
Desmond Dare. Parlor Car, 1897
A Desperate Chance. Parlor Car, 1897
Detective Archie. Munro, 1895
Detective Dale. Parlor Car, 1898
Detective Gay. Ogilvie, 1896
Detective Hanley. Ogilvie, 1896
Detective Kennedy. Ogilvie, 1896
Detective Murdock, the Silent. Royal, ca.1908
Detective Payne. Ogilvie, 1899
Detective Payne's Shadow. Ogilvie
Detective Thrash. Royal, ca.1908
The Detective Trio. Ogilvie, 1895
A Detective's Daughter. Ogilvie, 1898
A Detective's Enigma. Ogilvie, 1897
Dick, the Boy Detective. Ogilvie

The "Dock Rats" of New York. Westbrook, 1908 [NYC]
The Doom of the Demon Band. Westbrook, 1908
A Double Crime. Munro, 1897
Dudie Dunne. Ogilvie, 1895
The Duke of Omaha. Ogilvie, 1895
An Eastern Vendetta. Royal, ca.1897
The Ex-Pugilist Detective. Ogilvie, 1895
A Famous Boy. Parlor Car, 1897
The Fastest Boy in New York. Munro, 1892 [NYC]
The Female Detective. Ogilvie, 1905
A Female Ventriloquist. Ogilvie, 1896
Fighting for a Fortune. Royal, ca.1897
Fighting His Way. Royal, ca.1897
A Final Triumph. Ogilvie
Fire-Bomb Jack. Ogilvie, 1898
The Floating Head. Westbrook, 1920s
Flyaway Ned. Ogilvie, 1895
From Death to Life. Royal, ca.1897
Funny Bob. Ogilvie, 1894
Gentleman Thorne. Royal, ca.1908
The Giant Athlete. Munro, 1896
The Giant Detective Among the Cowboys. Westbrook, 1908
The Giant Detective Among the Italian Brigands. Royal, ca.1897 [It.]
The Giant Detective in France. Munro, 1892 [Fr.]
Gipsy Reno, the Detective. Ogilvie, 1896
Gipsy Rose, the Female Detective. Ogilvie, 1898
The Girl Champion. Royal, ca.1897
A Golden Legacy. Ogilvie, 1896
Grant McKenzie. Ogilvie, 1897
The Great Bank Robbery. Royal, ca.1908
Great Billy. Ogilvie, 1894
A Great Boy. Ogilvie, 1897
A Great Capture. Parlor Car, 1897
The Great Indian Scout Detective. Royal, ca.1897
The Great River Mystery. Westbrook, 1909
The Gypsy Detective. Munro, 1892
The Haunting Shadow. Royal, ca.1897
The Headless Mystery. Royal, ca.1897
Headless Girl of the North River. Westbrook, 1920s
Henry Broch, Old Sleuth's Assistant. Royal, ca.1908 OS
His Greatest "Shadow". Ogilvie, 1896
In the Russian Secret Service. Westbrook, 1909
The Irish Detective. Munro, 1892
Iron Burgess, the Government Detective. Royal, ca.1908
The Italian Bandit. Royal, ca.1897
Jack and Jill. Parlor Car, 1898
Jack Breakaway. Ogilvie, 1896
Jack the Juggler. Ogilvie, 1895
Jack the Juggler's Ordeal. Ogilvie
Jack the Juggler's Trial. Ogilvie, 1896
Jolly Jess. Ogilvie, 1896
Kefton, the Detective. Ogilvie, 1895
The Kidnapped Heiress. Royal, ca.1908
The King of Fun. Ogilvie, 1896
The King of the Detectives. Munro, 1891
The King's Detective. Parlor Car, 1898
Kingsley the Detective. Ogilvie, 1897
The Lady Detective. Munro, 1892
A Lady Shadower. Parlor Car, 1897
The League of Counterfeiters. Westbrook, 1908
A League of Three. Ogilvie
Life in New York. Ogilvie, 1897 [NYC]
The Little Colonel. Ogilvie, 1895
A Little Cowboy. Ogilvie, 1895
A Little Cowboy in New York. Ogilvie [NYC]
Little Dead-Sure. Ogilvie, 1895
A Little Giant. Ogilvie, 1895
The Little Miner. Ogilvie, 1896
Lively Luke. Parlor Car, 1897
The Lone House by the Sea. Westbrook, 1920s
Lorie. Ogilvie, 1896
Lure of the Black Pool. Westbrook, 1912
Magic Dick, a Boy Detective. Ogilvie, 1894
Malcolm the Wonder. Ogilvie, 1896
A Man of Mystery. Ogilvie
The Man Who Vanished. Ottenheimer, 189?
The Manordale Mystery. Ogilvie, 1898
The Man-Trapper. Munro, 1894
Marie, the Dancing Girl. Parlor Car, 1897
A Marvelous Escape. Ogilvie, 1898
The Mechanic's Son. Ogilvie, 1896
A Midnight Quest. Westbrook, 1908
A Million in Diamonds. Westbrook, 1920s
A Million in Jewels. Munro, 1896
Mura, the Western Detective. Munro, 1891
Murray, the Detective. Ogilvie
The Mysteries of New York. Royal, ca. 1897 [NYC]
The Mysterious Yankee. Royal, ca.1908

The Mystery of New York Bay. Royal, ca.1897
A Mystery of One Night. Ogilvie, 1898
The New York Detective. Munro, 1892
Night and Morning. Ogilvie
Nimble Ike, the Detective. Ogilvie
Nimble Ike, the Trick Ventriloquist. Ogilvie, 1894
Nimble Ike's Mystery. Ogilvie, 1896
Nimble Ike's Romance. Ogilvie
Norval, the Detective. Ogilvie, 1895
Old Electricity, the Lightning Detective. Munro, 1892
Old Ironsides Among the Italian Brigands. Royal, ca.1908 [It.]
The Old Miser's Mystery. Royal, ca.1897
The Old Miser's Ward. Ogilvie
Old Sleuth, the Avenger. Westbrook, 1920s OS
Old Sleuth, the Detective. Munro, 1891 OS
Old Sleuth to the Rescue. Westbrook, 1920s OS
Old Sleuth's Greatest Case. Westbrook, 1920s OS
Old Sleuth's Triumph. Munro, 1892 OS
Old Sleuth's Winning Hand. Westbrook, 1920s OS
Old Sleuth's Wonderful Revelation. Royal, ca.1908 OS
Old Terrible. Royal, ca.1908
The Omnipotent Avenger. Royal, ca.1897
On the Wing. Ogilvie, 1897
On Their Track. Royal, ca.1897
A One Night Mystery. Ogilvie, 1898 ss
Only a Photograph. Ogilvie, 1899
Oscar. Parlor Car, 1897
Pawnee Tom. Ogilvie, 1896
The Phantom of Meadow Creek. Westbrook, 1920s
The Phantom Wreck. Munro, 1899
Plot and Counterplot. Royal, ca.1897
Plucky Bob. Ogilvie, 1896
A Plucky Girl. Ogilvie, 1897
Preston Jayne. Ogilvie
The Prince of Ventriloquists. Ogilvie, 1895
A Puzzling Shadow. Ogilvie, 1895
Queen of the Highway. Ogilvie, 1905
Ramsey, the Detective. Parlor Car, 1898
Ray's Adventure. Royal, ca.1908
Red Cecil, the Detective. Ogilvie, 1898
A Remarkable Feat. Parlor Car, 1898
A Remarkable "Shadow". Parlor Car, 1897
Resolute Jack. Ogilvie, 1895
The River Detective and the Wharf Rat's Game. Westbrook, 1920s
The River Tragedy. Westbrook, 1920s
Romance of a Salvation Army Girl. Ogilvie, 1894
The Runaway. Ogilvie
Seth Bond. Parlor Car, 1898
The Shadow Detective. Munro, 1891
Shadowed by 2. Westbrook, 1908
Shadowed to His Doom. Westbrook, 1908
The Sheik's Capture. Royal, ca.1897
A Single Clue. Ogilvie
Snap and Jenny. Ogilvie
A Startling Discovery. Royal, ca.1908
A Straight Clue. Ogilvie, 1897
A Straight-Out Detective. Ogilvie, 1894
"Straight to the Mark". Ogilvie, 1897
A Struggle to Win. Parlor Car, 1898
A Successful "Shadow". Parlor Car, 1898
The Surprise of His Life. Royal, ca.1897
A Ten Day Mystery. Ogilvie, 1897
A Terrible Youth. Ogilvie, 1896
The Terror in the Night. Westbrook, 1920s
The Three Boy Detectives. Parlor Car, 1895
Three Little Tramps. Ogilvie, 1894
Thrifty Abe. Parlor Car, 1898
A Thrilling Mystery. Munro, 1895
Tom, the Young Explorer. Parlor Car, 1898
Tracked by a Female Detective. Westbrook, 1920s
Tracked by a Woman. Munro, 1904
Tracked on a Wheel. Ogilvie, 1896
A Tragic Mystery. Royal, ca.1897
A Tragic Quest. Ogilvie, 1899
Tragedy and Strategy. Royal, ca.1897
Trapped by a Female Detective. Westbrook, 1920s
Trapping the Moonshiners. Westbrook, 1920s
Tricks and Triumphs. Ogilvie, 1896
True Blue, the Detective. Ogilvie, 1894
The Twin Athletes. Parlor Car, 1898
The Twin Ventriloquists. Ogilvie, 1895
The Two Conspirators. Ogilvie, 1896
Two Wonderful Detectives. Ogilvie, 1898
The Ubiquitous Yank. Munro, 1891
Under a Veil. Ogilvie, 1897
Under Sentence of Death. Royal, ca.1897
Variety Jack. Royal, ca.1908
Vavel, the Wonderful Trasure Seeker. Ogilvie, 1894

The "Veiled Beauty". Westbrook, 1920s
The Ventriloquist Detective. Ogilvie
Weaver Webb. Ogilvie, 1896
A Weird Courtship. Ogilvie
A Weird Sea Mystery. Ogilvie
The West Point Lieutenant. Ogilvie
The West Shore Mystery. Munro, 1891
Winning a Princess. Ogilvie
Witch of Manhattan. Ogilvie [NYC]
The Wizard Detective. Royal, ca.1908
The Wizard Tramp. Parlor Car, 1897
The Woman of Death. Westbrook, 1908
Wonder Jack. Ogilvie, 1894
A Wonderful Detective. Ogilvie, 1895
Woodchuck Jerry, the Country Detective. Ogilvie
Woodchuck Jerry. Ogilvie, 1894
Yankey Rue, the Ex-Pugilist Detective. Ogilvie, 1894
A Young Alladin. Ogilvie, 1898
Young Chauncey. Ogilvie, 1898
Young Dash. Ogilvie, 1897
The Young Engineer. Ogilvie, 1896
Young Gingers. Ogilvie, 1895
Young Harold. Ogilvie, 1898
The Young Magician. Royal, 1905
Young Vigilance. Ogilvie, 1897
Zantelli. Ogilvie, 1897

OLD SPICER. Pseudonym.
A Dead Witness. Street (Magnet)
A Desperate Game. Street (Magnet)
A High Class Swindler. Street (Magnet)
In the Shadow. Street (Magnet)
A Matter of Thousands. Street (Magnet)
On the Brink of Ruin. Street (Magnet)
The Palace of Chance. Street (Magnet)
A Question of Evidence. Street (Magnet)
The Shadow of Guilt. Street (Magnet)
The Sport of Fate. Street (Magnet)
The Stolen Jewels. Street (Magnet)
The Tattooed Wrist. Street (Magnet), 1896
The Three Finger Marks. Street (Magnet)
Tightening of the Coils. Street (Magnet)

OLDE, NICHOLAS
The Incredible Adventures of Rowland Hern. Heinemann, 1928 ss

OLDEN, MARC. Pseudonym: Robert Hawkes, q.v. SC: Hawthorne Albert Harker = HH; Robert Sand = RS.
Black Samurai. Signet, 1974 RS
Cocaine. Signet, 1975
Dead and Paid For. Signet, 1976 HH
The Deadly Pearl. Signet, 1974 RS
The Golden Kill. Signet, 1974
-Gossip. GM, 1979; Hamlyn, 1979 [NYC]
The Harker File. Signet, 1976 HH
The Informant. Signet, 1978; New English Library pb, 1979 [NYC]
The Inquisition. Signet, 1974
The Katana. Signet, 1975
Kill the Reporter. Signet, 1978 HH
Killer Warrior. Signet, 1974
Poe Must Die. Charter, 1978; Hamlyn, 1978 (Edgar Allan Poe.) [NYC, 1840]
Sword of Allah. Signet, 1975
They've Killed Anna. Signet, 1977 HH [Nev.]
The Warlock. Signet, 1975
Wellington's. Signet, 1977

OLDFELD, PETER. Joint pseudonym of Per Jacobsson, 1894-1963, and Vernon Bartlett, 1894-   . Ref on Bartlett: CA.
The Alchemy Murder. Washburn, 1929; Constable, 1929
The Death of a Diplomat. Washburn, 1928; Constable, 1928 [Geneva]

OLDFIELD, CLAUDE HOUGHTON. 1889-1961. Pseudonym: Claude Houghton, q.v.

OLDREY, JOHN
The Devil's Henchmen. Methuen, 1926

OLDSEY, BERNARD (STANLEY). 1924-   . Ref: CA.
The Spanish Season. Harcourt, 1970 [Sp.]

O'LEARY, ED. See: Aron Spilken, 1939-   .

OLECK, HOWARD L(EONER). 1911-   . Ref: CA. SC: Sam Benedict, who also appears in books by Elsie Lee and Brad Williams, 1918-   , qq.v.
A Singular Fury. World, 1968 [S.F.]

OLESKER, HARRY. 1923?-1969. Ref: CC. Born in N.J.; radio and TV script writer.
Exit Dying. Random, 1959; Boardman, 1961 [NYC]
Impact. Random, 1961; Boardman, 1961 [NYC]
Now Will You Try for Murder? Simon, 1958; Boardman, 1959 [NYC]

OLESKER, J. BRADFORD. 1949-   . Born in Chi.
No Place Like Home. Putnam, 1976; Allen, 1978 [Chi.]
The Siege of Superport. Putnam, 1978; Sphere, 1980

OLIPHANT, MRS. MARGARET (OLIPHANT WILSON). 1828-1897.
-The Duke's Daughters, and, The Fugitives. Blackwood, 1890
Mystery of Blencarrow; see The Mystery of Mrs. Blencarrow
The Mystery of Mrs. Blencarrow. Blackett, 1890. U.S. title: Mystery of Blencarrow. Donohue, 1894
-Stories of the Seen and the Unseen. Blackwood, 1902; Roberts, 1889 ss

OLIVER, ANTHONY. 1923-   . Ref: CA.
The Pew Group. Heinemann, 1980; Doubleday, 1981

OLIVER, EDWIN. 1867-   .
A Rogue's Progress. Treherne, 1903

OLIVER, GAIL. Pseudonym of Marian Gallagher Scott, 1892-   . Other pseudonym: Katherine Wolffe, q.v.
The Moon Saw Murder. Macmillan, 1937; Bles, 1938

OLIVER, GEORGE. 1873-1961. Name originally: Oliver Onions, q.v.

OLIVER, JOHN
Detection in a Topper. Herbert Joseph, 1936

OLIVER, LAETITIA SELWYN
The Expiation of Lady Anne. Drane, 1905

OLIVER, LIONEL
-Mexican Adventure. Eldon, 1935 [Mex.]
Mongolian Interlude. Eldon, 1936 [Mong.]

OLIVER, DR. N. T. Pseudonym of E. O. Tilburn. Other pseudonym: Nevada Ned, q.v.
-Almeda. Rand, 1889
The Confession of Lorraine Herschel. Laird, 1896. Also published as: A Desperate Deed. Laird, 1900
A Desperate Deed; see The Confession of Lorraine Herschel
-Dr. Wilbur's Note Book. Rand, 1889
-The Fateful Hand; or, Saved by Lightning. Laird, 1896
An Unconscious Crime. Laird, 1891
The Whitechapel Mystery. Eagle, 1889
-A Woman of Nerve. Laird, 1900

OLIVY, D. J.
Never Ask a Policeman. Gollancz, 1970; Coward, 1970

OLMSTEAD, EDWIN
-Nightly She Sings. Knopf, 1937. British title: Clip-Joint. Constable, 1938

OLMSTED, HOWARD J.
The Hot Diary. Ace, 1960 [N.Y.]

OLMSTED, LORENA ANN. 1890-   . Ref: CA.
Cover of Darkness. Avalon, 1961
Dangerous Memory. Avalon, 1974
Death Walked In. Avalon, 1960
Footsteps of the Cat. Avalon, 1963
Setup for Murder. Avalon, 1962
To Love a Stranger. Avalon, 1964

OLSEN, D. B. Pseudonym of (Julia Clara Catharine) Dolores B(irk Olsen) Hitchens, 1907-1973, q.v. Other pseudonyms: Dolan Birkley, Noel Burke, qq.v. SC: Rachel and Jennifer Murdock = M; Lt. Stephen Mayhew = SM; Prof. A. Pennyfeather = P.
The Alarm of the Black Cat. Doubleday, 1942 M
Bring the Bride a Shroud. Doubleday, 1945; Aldor, 1945 P [Calif.]
The Cat and Capricorn. Doubleday, 1951 M [Calif.]
The Cat Saw Murder. Doubleday, 1939; Heinemann, 1940 M,SM
The Cat Walk. Doubleday, 1953 M [L.A.]
The Cat Wears a Mask. Doubleday, 1949 M [Ariz.]
The Cat Wears a Noose. Doubleday, 1944 M,SM [L.A.]
Cat's Claw. Doubleday, 1943 M,SM [L.A.]
Cat's Don't Need Coffins. Doubleday, 1946; Aldor, 1946 M,SM [Calif.]
Cat's Don't Smile. Doubleday, 1945; Aldor, 1948 M [Calif.]
Cats Have Tall Shadows. Ziff-Davis, 1948 M [Oreg.]
Catspaw for Murder. Doubleday, 1943 M,SM [Calif.]

The Clue in the Clay. Phoenix, 1938 SM
 [S.F.]
Dead Babes in the Wood; see Enrollment
 Cancelled
Death Cuts a Silhouette. Doubleday,
 1939 [Calif.]
Death Walks on Cat Feet. Doubleday,
 1956 M [L.A.]
Death Wears Cat's Eyes. Doubleday, 1950
 M [L.A.]
Devious Design. Doubleday, 1948 P
 [N.Y.]
Enrollment Cancelled. Doubleday, 1952.
 Also published as: Dead Babes in the
 Wood. Dell, 1954 P [acad., Calif.]
Gallows for the Groom. Doubleday, 1947
 P [L.A.]
Love Me in Death. Doubleday, 1951 P
 [Calif.]
Night of the Bowstring. Hale, 1963
 (U.S. title?)
Something About Midnight. Doubleday,
 1950 P [Calif.]
The Ticking Heart. Doubleday, 1940 SM
 [Calif.]
Widows Ought to Weep. Ziff-Davis, 1947
 [Calif.]

OLSEN, JACK. 1925- . Journalist, cor-
 respondent for "Time" magazine, edi-
 tor of "Sports Illustrated"; living
 in Wash.
 Massy's Game. Playboy, 1976
 Night Watch. Times, 1979
 The Secret of Fire 5. Random, 1977;
 Hale, 1978

OLSON, DONALD
 Beware, Sweet Maggie. Pyramid, 1977
 If I Don't Tell. Putnam, 1976 [Ohio]
 Sleep Before Evening. St. Martin's,
 1979

O'MAHONEY, CHARLES KINGSTON. Pseudonym:
 Charles Kingston, q.v.

O'MALLEY, FRANK. Pseudonym of Frank
 O'Rourke, 1916- , q.v.
 The Best Go First. Random, 1950; Benn,
 1955 [Tex.]

O'MALLEY, LADY MARY DOLLING SAUNDERS.
 1889-1974. Pseudonym: Ann Bridge,
 q.v.

O'MALLEY, PATRICK. SC: Harrigan & Hoef-
 fler, in all titles.
 The Affair of Chief Strongheart. Mill,
 1964 [N. Dak.]
 The Affair of John Donne. Mill, 1964
 [Calif.]
 The Affair of Jolie Madame. Mill, 1963;
 Hale, 1965 [Calif.]
 The Affair of Swan Lake. Mill, 1962
 [Minn.]
 The Affair of the Blue Pig. Mill, 1965
 [Calif.]
 The Affair of the Bumbling Briton.
 Mill, 1965 [Calif.]
 The Affair of the Red Mosaic. Mill,
 1961 [N. Mex.]

O'MANT, HEDLEY PERCIVAL ANGELO. 1899-
 1965. Pseudonym: Hedley Scott, q.v.

O'MEARA, WALTER (ANDREW). 1897- . Ref:
 CA.
 Minnesota Gothic. Holt, 1956. Also published as: Castle Danger. Macfadden,
 1966 [Minn.]

OMRE, ARTHUR. Pseudonym of Ole Arthur
 Juel Antonisen, 1887-1967.
 Flight. Appleton, 1940 (Translation
 of "Flukten." Oslo, 1936.)

O'NAIR, MAIRI. Pseudonym of Constance May
 Evans, 1890- . Ref: CA.
 Beautiful Crook. Mills, 1937
 Dangerous Lady. Mills, 1934
 The Girl with the X-Ray Eyes. Mills,
 1935 ss
 Jennifer Disappears. Mills, 1935
 Judy Ashbane, Police Decoy. Mills, 1944
 Mystery at Butlin's. Mills, 1960

O'NEIL, KERRY. Pseudonym of John T(homas)
 MacIntyre, 1871-1951, q.v. SC: Jerry
 Mooney = JM.
 Death at Dakar. Doubleday, 1942 [Sen.]
 Death Strikes at Heron House. Farrar,
 1944 JM [Phil.]
 Mooney Moves Around. Reynal, 1939 JM
 [Phil.]
 Ninth Floor: Middle City Tower. Farrar,
 1943 JM [Phil.]

O'NEIL, RUSSELL
 The Alcatraz Incident. McKay, 1971
 Don't Call Back. French (NYC), 1975.
 Novel based on this 2-act play: Dell,
 1978

 The Homecoming. Dell, 1980

O'NEIL, WILL(IAM DANIEL III). 1938- .
 Ref: CA.
 The Libyan Kill. Norton, 1980

O'NEILL, ARCHIE. Pseudonym of Jim Hena-
 ghan, 1919- , q.v. SC: Jeff Pride,
 in all titles (see also Henaghan
 entry).
 The Da Vinci Rose. Bantam, 1973 [Isr.]
 The Duplicate Stiff. Bantam, 1974
 The Ginzberg Circle. Bantam, 1974
 High Bid for Murder. Bantam, 1974
 [Eng.]

O'NEILL, DESMOND. Ref: CC.
 Life Has No Price. Gollancz, 1959;
 Dodd, 1960 [Ire.]

O'NEILL, EDWARD A(LOYSIUS)
 The Rotterdam Delivery. Coward, 1975;
 Gollancz, 1976 [ship]

O'NEILL, JAMES
 Garrison Tales from Tonquin. Copeland,
 1895 ss, some criminous

O'NEILL, JAMES
 The Molly Maquires. GM, 1969 (Novelization of the movie.)

O'NEILL, JOHN. 1869- .
 Souls in Hell. Brown, 1924. British
 title: As We Sow. Methuen 1926

O'NEILL-BARNA, ANNE
 Wentworth Hall. Popular Library, 1974

ONIONS, OLIVER. 1873-1961. Name later le-
 gally changed to: George Oliver. Ref:
 CC.
 A Case in Camera. Arrowsmith, 1920;
 Macmillan, 1921
 In Accordance with the Evidence.
 Secker, 1912; Luce, 1913 [acad.]

O'NOLAN, BRIAN. 1911-1966. Pseudonym:
 Flann O'Brien, q.v-

ONYEAMA, DILLIBE. 1951- .
 Female Target. Satellite, 1979
 Juju. Satellite, 1977
 Secret Society. Satellite, 1978

OPERATOR 1384. Pseudonym of John Henry
 Harvey. Other pseudonym: John H. Bar-
 rington, q.v.
 The Black Arab. Rich, 1937
 The Catacombs of Death. Hutchinson,
 1936
 The Devil's Diplomats. Hutchinson, 1935
 Jackals of the Secret Service. Rich,
 1938 [Mid. East]
 -Queen of the Riffs. Lane, 1937
 The Scourge of the Desert. Rich, 1936
 -Spies and Rebels. Rich, 1939
 -The White Tuareg. Rich, 1936

OPPENHEIM, E(DWARD) PHILLIPS. 1866-1946.
 Pseudonym: Anthony Partridge, q.v.
 Ref: CC, EM, MC, MM, MP, TC. SC: Gen.
 Besserley = B; Charles Lyson = CL;
 Peter Ruff = PR; Mr. Sabin = S.
 Set: Eng.
 Aaron Rodd, Diviner. Hodder, 1920;
 Little, 1927 ss
 The Adventures of Mr. Joseph P. Cray.
 Hodder, 1925; Little, 1927 ss
 Advice Limited. Hodder, 1935; Little,
 1936 ss
 The Amazing Judgment. Downey, 1897
 The Amazing Partnership. Cassell, 1914;
 Little, 1932, in the omnibus "Shud-
 ders and Thrills" ss
 The Amazing Quest of Mr. Ernest Bliss.
 Hodder, 1922. U.S. title: The Curious
 Quest. Little, 1919
 Ambrose Lavendale, Diplomat. Hodder,
 1920 ss
 An Amiable Charlatan; see The Game of
 Liberty
 And Still I Cheat the Gallows. Hodder,
 1938 ss
 Anna, the Adventuress. Ward, 1904;
 Little, 1904
 As a Man Lives. Ward, 1898; Little,
 1908. Also published as: The Yellow
 House. Doscher, 1908
 Ask Miss Mott. Hodder, 1936; Little,
 1937 ss
 The Avenger; see Conspirators
 The Bank Manager. Hodder, 1934. U.S.
 title: The Man Without Nerves.
 Little, 1934
 The Battle of Basinghall Street. Hod-
 der, 1935; Little, 1935
 Berenice. Ward, 1910; Little, 1907
 The Betrayal. Ward, 1904; Dodd, 1904
 The Bird of Paradise. Hodder, 1936.
 U.S. title: Floating Peril. Little,
 1936 [ship]

The Black Box. Hodder, 1917; Grosset,
 1915 (Novelization of the movie.)
Blackman's Wood. Readers Library, 1929
 (With "Underdog" by Agatha Christie,
 1890-1976, q.v.)
The Box with Broken Seals; see The
 Strange Case of Mr. Jocelyn Thew
Burglars Must Dine. Todd, 1943 (From
 Ask Miss Mott, q.v.)
The Channay Syndicate. Hodder, 1927;
 Little, 1927 ss
Chronicles of Melhampton. Hodder, 1928
 ss
The Cinema Murder; see The Other
 Romilly
The Colossus of Arcadia. Hodder, 1938;
 Little, 1938 [Fr.]
Conspirators. Ward, 1907. U.S. title:
 The Avenger. Little, 1908
The Court of St. Simon (by Anthony
 Partridge); see Seeing Life
Crooks in the Sunshine. Hodder, 1932;
 Little, 1933 ss [Fr.]
Curious Happenings to the Rooke Lega-
 tees. Hodder, 1937; Little, 1938 ss
The Curious Quest; see The Amazing
 Quest of Mr. Ernest Bliss
A Daughter of Astrea. Arrowsmith, 1898;
 Doscher, 1909
A Daughter of the Marionis. Ward, 1895.
 U.S. title: To Win the Love He
 Sought. Doscher, 1910. Reprinted un-
 der the British title: Little, 1920
 [It.]
The Devil's Paw. Hodder, 1921; Little,
 1920
The Double Four. Cassell, 1911. U.S.
 title: Peter Ruff and the Double
 Four. Little, 1912 ss PR (See
 also: Peter Ruff.)
The Double Life of Mr. Alfred Burton.
 Methuen, 1914; Little, 1913
The Double Traitor. Hodder, 1918; Lit-
 tle, 1915
The Dumb Gods Speak. Hodder, 1937; Lit-
 tle, 1937 [Fr.]
Enoch Strone; see Master of Men
Envoy Extraordinary. Hodder, 1937; Lit-
 tle, 1937
The Evil Shepherd. Hodder, 1923; Lit-
 tle, 1922
The Ex-Detective. Hodder, 1933; Little,
 1933 ss
The Ex-Duke. Hodder, 1927. U.S. title:
 The Interloper. Little, 1926
Exit a Dictator. Hodder, 1939; Little,
 1939
Expiation. Maxwell, 1887
The Exploits of Pudgy Pete & Co. Hod-
 der, 1928 ss
The Falling Star. Hodder, 1911. U.S.
 title: The Moving Finger. Little,
 1911
False Evidence. Ward (London), 1896;
 Ward (NYC), 1897
Floating Peril; see The Bird of Para-
 dise
For the Queen. Ward, 1912; Little, 1913
 ss
The Fortunate Wayfarer. Hodder, 1928;
 Little, 1928
Gabriel Samara. Hodder, 1925. U.S.
 title: Gabriel Samara, Peacemaker.
 Little, 1925
Gabriel Samara, Peacemaker; see Gabriel
 Samara
The Gallows of Chance. Hodder, 1934;
 Little, 1934
The Game of Liberty. Cassell, 1915.
 U.S. title: An Amiable Charlatan.
 Little, 1916 ss
Gangsters' Glory; see Inspector Dickins
 Retires
General Besserley's Puzzle Box. Hodder,
 1935; Little, 1935 ss B [Fr.]
General Besserley's Second Puzzle Box.
 Hodder, 1939; Little, 1940 ss B [Fr.]
The Glenlitten Murder. Hodder, 1929;
 Little, 1929
The Golden Beast. Hodder, 1926; Little,
 1926
The Golden Web; see The Plunderers
The Governors. Ward, 1908; Little, 1909
The Grassleyes Mystery. Hodder, 1940;
 Little, 1940 [Fr.]
The Great Awakening. Ward, 1902. U.S.
 title: A Sleeping Memory. Dillingham,
 1902
The Great Bear. Todd, 1943 (16 pp.)
The Great Impersonation. Hodder, 1920;
 Little, 1920
The Great Prince Shan. Hodder, 1922;
 Little, 1922
The Great Secret; see The Secret
Harvey Garrard's Crime. Hodder, 1927;
 Little, 1927
Havoc. Hodder, 1912; Little, 1911
The Hillman. Methuen, 1917; Little,
 1917
His Father's Crime; see The Mystery of
 Mr. Bernard Brown

The Honourable Algernon Knox, Detective. Hodder, 1920 s
The Human Chase. Hodder, 1929; Little, 1932, in the omnibus "Shudders and Thrills" ss
The Illustrious Prince. Hodder, 1910; Little, 1910
The Inevitable Millionaires. Hodder, 1923; Little, 1925
Inspector Dickins Retires. Hodder, 1931. U.S. title: Gangsters' Glory. Little, 1931 ss
The Interloper; see The Ex-Duke
Jacob's Ladder. Hodder, 1921; Little, 1921
Jeanne of the Marshes. Ward, 1909; Little, 1909
Jennerton & Co. Hodder, 1929; Little, 1931, in the omnibus "Clowns and Criminals" ss
Jeremiah and the Princess. Hodder, 1933; Little, 1933
Judy of Bunter's Buildings. Hodder, 1936. U.S. title: The Magnificent Hoax. Little, 1936
The Kingdom of the Blind. Hodder, 1917; Little, 1916
Last Train Out. Hodder, 1941; Little, 1940 [Vienna]
The Light Beyond. Hodder, 1928; Little, 1928
The Lighted Way. Hodder, 1912; Little, 1912
The Lion and the Lamb. Hodder, 1930; Little, 1930
The Little Gentleman from Okehampstead. Hodder, 1926 ss
The Long Arm. Ward, 1909. U.S. title: The Long Arm of Mannister. Little, 1908 ss
The Long Arm of Mannister; see The Long Arm
The Lost Ambassador; see The Missing Delora
A Lost Leader. Ward, 1906; Little, 1906
Madame. Hodder, 1927. U.S. title: Madame and Her Twelve Virgins. Little, 1927 [Fr.]
Madame and Her Twelve Virgins; see Madame
The Magnificent Hoax; see Judy of Bunter's Buildings
A Maker of History. Ward, 1905; Little, 1906 [Fr.]
The Malefactor; see Mr. Wingrave, Millionaire
The Man and His Kingdom. Ward, 1899; Lippincott, 1900 [S. Am.]
The Man from Sing Sing; see Moran Chambers Smiled
The Man Who Changed His Plea. Hodder, 1942; Little, 1942
The Man Who Thought He Was a Pauper. Polybooks, 1943 (16 pp.)
The Man Without Nerves; see The Bank Manager
The Master Mummer. Ward, 1905; Little, 1904
Master of Men. Methuen, 1901. U.S. title: Enoch Strone. Dillingham, 1902
Matorni's Vineyard. Hodder, 1929; Little, 1928 [Fr.]
The Mayor on Horseback. Little, 1937
Michael's Evil Deeds. Hodder, 1924; Little, 1923 ss
The Milan Grill Room. Hodder, 1940; Little, 1941 ss CL
The Million Pound Deposit. Hodder, 1930; Little, 1930
A Millionaire of Yesterday. Ward, 1900; Lippincott, 1900
The Mischief-Maker. Hodder, 1913; Little, 1912 [Fr.]
Miss Brown of X.Y.O. Hodder, 1927; Little, 1927
The Missing Delora. Methuen, 1910. U.S. title: The Lost Ambassador. Little, 1910 [Fr.]
The Missioner. Ward, 1908; Little, 1907
Mr. Billingham, the Marquis and Madelon. Hodder, 1927; Little, 1929 ss [Fr.]
Mr. Grex of Monte Carlo. Methuen, 1915; Little, 1915 [Fr.]
Mr. Laxworthy's Adventures. Cassell, 1913 ss [Fr.]
Mr. Lessingham Goes Home. Hodder, 1919. U.S. title: The Zeppelin's Passenger. Little, 1918
Mr. Marx's Secret. Ward, 1909; Westbrook, 1912
Mr. Mirakel. Hodder, 1943; Little, 1943
Mr. Wingrave, Millionaire. Ward, 1906. U.S. title: The Malefactor. Little, 1907
The Modern Prometheus. Unwin, 1896; Neely, 1897
A Monk of Cruta. Beeton's Christmas Annual, 1894; Neely, 1894. Also published as: The Tragedy of Andrea. Ogilvie, 1906

Moran Chambers Smiled. Hodder, 1932. U.S. title: The Man from Sing Sing. Little, 1932
The Moving Finger; see The Falling Star
Murder at Monte Carlo. Hodder, 1933; Little, 1933 [Fr.]
Mysteries of the Riviera. Cassell, 1916 ss [Fr.]
Mysterious Mr. Sabin. Ward, 1898; Little, 1905 S
The Mystery of Mr. Bernard Brown. Bentley, 1896; Little, 1910. Also published as: The New Tenant. Collier, 1912. And as: His Father's Crime. Street, 1929
The Mystery Road. Hodder, 1924; Little, 1923 [Fr.]
The New Tenant; see The Mystery of Mr. Bernard Brown
Nicholas Goade, Detective. Hodder, 1927; Little, 1929 ss
Nobody's Man. Hodder, 1922; Little, 1921
The Ostrekoff Jewels. Hodder, 1932; Little, 1932
The Other Romilly. Hodder, 1918. U.S. title: The Cinema Murder. Little, 1917 [NYC]
The Passionate Quest. Hodder, 1924; Little, 1924
The Pawns Count. Hodder, 1918; Little, 1918
The Peer and the Woman. Ward, 1895; Taylor, 1892
A People's Man. Methuen, 1915; Little, 1914
Peter Ruff. Hodder, 1912. U.S. title: Recalled by the Double-Four. Little, 1912, in Peter Ruff and the Double Four ss PR
Peter Ruff and the Double-Four; see The Double Four
The Plunderers. Hodder, 1912. U.S. title: The Golden Web. Little, 1910, as by Anthony Partridge. Reprinted in Britain under the U.S. title: Lloyds, 1918
The Postmaster of Market Deignton. Routledge, 1897
A Prince of Sinners. Ward, 1903; Little, 1903
Prodigals of Monte Carlo. Hodder, 1926; Little, 1926 [Fr.]
The Profiteers. Hodder, 1921; Little, 1921
A Pulpit in the Grill Room. Hodder, 1938; Little, 1939 ss CL
Recalled by the Double-Four; see Peter Ruff
The Secret. Ward, 1907. U.S. title: The Great Secret. Little, 1908
Seeing Life. Lloyd's, 1919. U.S. title: The Court of St. Simon, as by Anthony Partridge. Little, 1912 [Paris]
The Seven Conundrums. Hodder, 1924; Little, 1923 ss
The Shy Plutocrat. Hodder, 1941; Little, 1941
Simple Peter Cradd. Hodder, 1931; Little, 1931
Sinners Beware. Hodder, 1932; Little, 1932 ss [Fr.]
Sir Adam Disappeared. Hodder, 1939; Little, 1939
Slane's Long Shots. Hodder, 1930; Little, 1930 ss
A Sleeping Memory; see The Great Awakening
The Spy Paramount. Hodder, 1935; Little, 1935
The Spymaster. Hodder, 1938; Little, 1938
Stolen Idols. Hodder, 1925; Little, 1925
The Strange Boarders of Palace Crescent. Hodder, 1935; Little, 1934
The Strange Case of Mr. Jocelyn Thew. Hodder, 1919. U.S. title: The Box with the Broken Seals. Little, 1919 [ship]
The Stranger's Gate. Hodder, 1940; Little, 1939 [Balkans]
The Survivor. Ward, 1901; Brentano's, 1901
The Temptation of Tavernake. Hodder, 1913. U.S. title: The Tempting of Tavernake. Little, 1912
The Tempting of Tavernake; see The Temptation of Tavernake
The Terrible Hobby of Sir Joseph Londe, Bt. Hodder, 1924; Little, 1927 ss
Those Other Days. Ward, 1912; Little, 1913 ss
To Win the Love He Sought; see A Daughter of the Marionis
The Tragedy of Andrea; see A Monk of Cruta
The Traitors. Ward, 1902; Dodd, 1903
The Treasure House of Martin Hews. Hodder, 1929; Little, 1929
Up the Ladder of Gold. Hodder, 1931; Little, 1931 [Fr.]

The Vanished Messenger. Methuen, 1916; Little, 1914
The Vindicator. Little, 1907 (British title?)
The Way of These Women. Methuen, 1914; Little, 1913
What Happened to Forester. Hodder, 1929; Little, 1930 ss
The Wicked Marquis. Hodder, 1919; Little, 1919
The World's Great Snare. Ward, 1896; Lippincott, 1896
The Wrath to Come. Hodder, 1925; Little, 1924 [Fr., 1950]
The Yellow Crayon. Ward, 1903; Dodd, 1903 S
The Yellow House; see As a Man Lives
The Zeppelin's Passenger; see Mr. Lessingham Goes Home

ORAM, JOHN. Pseudonym of John Oram Thomas. Both titles are novelizations of the "Man from UNCLE" TV series.
The Copenhagen Affair. Ace, 1965; Four Square, 1966 [Copen.]
The Stone-Cold Dead in the Market Affair. Ace, 1970; Four Square, 1966 [Eng.]

ORAN, DAN and LONN HOKLIN. Oran is a Wash. D.C. lawyer and law professor.
Z Warning. Ballantine hb, 1979; Futura, 1979 [Wash. D.C.]

ORBISON, KECK. Joint pseudonym of Maud Keck, q.v., and Olive Orbison.
The Key to the Case. Washburn, 1929. British title: The Crested Key. Long, 1929 [Manila]

ORBISON, OLIVE. Joint pseudonym with Maud Keck, q.v.: Keck Orbison, q.v.

ORCUTT, WILLIAM DANA. 1870-1953.
-The Balance. Stokes, 1922

ORCZY, BARONESS (EMMUSKA) [EMMA MAGDALENA ROSALIA MARIA JOSIFA BARBARA, BARONESS ORCZY]. 1865-1947. Ref: all eight. SC: The Old Man in the Corner = OM. Set: Eng.
The Case of Miss Elliott. Unwin, 1905 ss OM
Castles in the Air. Cassell, 1921; Doran, 1922 ss [Fr.]
The Celestial City. Hodder, 1926; Doran, 1926
Lady Molly of Scotland Yard. Cassell, 1910; Arno, 1976 ss
The Man in Gray. Cassell, 1918; Doran, 1918 ss [Fr., ca.1810]
The Man in the Corner; see The Old Man in the Corner
-The Miser of Maida Vale. Doran, 1925 (British title?)
The Old Man in the Corner. Greening, 1909. U.S. title: The Man in the Corner. Dodd, 1909 ss OM
The Old Man in the Corner Unravels the Mystery of the Fulton Gardens Mystery, and The Moorland Tragedy. Doran, 1925 ss OM
The Old Man in the Corner Unravels the Mystery of the Khaki Tunic. Doran, 1923 OM
The Old Man in the Corner Unravels the Mystery of the Pearl Necklace, and The Tragedy in Bishop's Road. Doran, 1924 ss OM
The Old Man in the Corner Unravels the Mystery of the Russian Prince, and of Dog's Tooth Cliff. Doran, 1924 ss OM
The Old Man in the Corner Unravels the Mystery of the White Carnation, and The Montmartre Hat. Doran, 1925 ss OM
Skin o' My Tooth. Hodder, 1928; Doubleday, 1928 ss
Unraveled Knots. Hutchinson, 1925; Doran, 1926 OM ss (9 of the 13 ss in this volume were previously published in the U.S. in the 5 Doran booklets identified above.)

ORDE, LEWIS and BILL MICHAELS. Orde: born in Eng.; U.S. citizen. Michaels: journalist and writer/analyst in industry.
The Night They Stole Manhattan. Putnam, 1980; Dent, 1980 [NYC]

ORDE-POWLETT, NIGEL (AMYAS). 1900-
SC: Anthony Rillington, in both titles. Set: Eng.
The Cast of Death. Benn, 1932; Houghton, 1932
Driven Death. Benn, 1933

ORDWAY, PETER. 1916- .
Conspiracy of Vipers. Davies, 1961; British Book Service, 1961
The Face in the Shadows. Wyn, 1952
High Kill; see The Teak Forest

Night of Reckoning. Hale, 1967; Simon, 1965 [Sp.]
-Object of the Exercise. Hale, 1977
The Teak Forest. Boardman, 1958; Also published as: High Kill. World Distributors, 1960 [S. Am.]

O'REILLY, MARY BOYLE. 1873-1937.
The Black Fan. Reilly, 1928

ORFORD, ELLEN
The Bride of Raven Island. Curtis, 1974
The Maze. Curtis, 1973 [Maine]
The Sutter House. Popular Library, 1975

ORGAN, PERRY
The House on Cheyne Walk. Heinemann, 1975; Coward, 1975

ORGILL, DOUGLAS (WILLIAM). 1922- .
Ref: CA. Joint pseudonym with Jack Fishman, 1920- : J. D. Gilman, q.v. SC: William Mallett = WM.
The Astrid Factor. Davies, 1968; Walker, 1968 [It.]
The Cautious Assassin; see Ride a Tiger
The Days of Darkness. Davies, 1965. U.S. title: Man in the Dark. Morrow, 1965 [Fr.]
The Death Bringers. Davies, 1962. U.S. title: Journey into Violence. Morrow, 1963 WM [It.]
The Jasius Pursuit. Macmillan (London), 1973; St. Martin's, 1973 [Fr.]
Journey into Violence; see The Death Bringers
Man in the Dark; see The Days of Darkness
Ride a Tiger. Davies, 1963. U.S. title: The Cautious Assassin. Morrow, 1964. Reprinted in Britain under the U.S. title: Corgi, 1965 WM [Carib.]

ORIOL, LAURENCE. Pseudonym of Noelle Loriot.
A Murder to Make You Grow Up Little Girl. Macdonald, 1968; World, 1972 (Translation of "Un Meurte, ca fait Grandir." Paris, 1967.)
Short Circuit. Macdonald, 1967; World, 1968 (Translation of "L'Interne de Service." Paris, 1966.)

ORMEROD, ROGER. 1920- . Ref: CA, TC. SC: David Mallin, in at least those marked DM. Set: Eng.
The Amnesia Trap. Hale, 1979 DM
The Bright Face of Danger. Hale, 1979 DM
Cart Before the Hearse. Hale, 1980 DM
The Colour of Fear. Hale, 1976 DM
A Dip into Murder. Hale, 1978 DM
Double Take. Hale, 1980
Full Fury. Hale, 1975 DM
A Glimpse of Death. Hale, 1976 DM
More Dead Than Alive. Hale, 1980
Sealed with a Loving Kill. Hale, 1976 DM
The Silence of the Night. Hale, 1974 DM
A Spoonful of Luger. Hale, 1975 DM
This Murder Comes to Mind. Hale, 1977
Time to Kill. Hale, 1974 DM
Too Late for the Funeral. Hale, 1977 DM
The Weight of Evidence. Hale, 1978 DM

ORMHAUG, ELLA GRIFFITHS. 1926- . Pseudonym: Julia Westerham, q.v.

ORMOND, FREDERIC. Pseudonym of Frederic Merrill Van Rensselaer Dey, 1861-1922. Other pseudonyms: Nicholas Carter, Marmaduke Dey, Varick Vanardy, qq.v.
The Three Keys. Watt, 1909 [NYC]

ORNSTIEN, ALFRED
The Secret of the Ashes. Hutchinson, 1926

O'ROURKE, FRANK. 1916- . Pseudonym: Frank O'Malley, q.v. Born in Colo.; author of books and magazine ss; rare book collector.
The Abduction of Virginia Lee. Lippincott, 1970
High Dive. Random, 1954 [Mex.]
Latigo. Random, 1953; Panther, 1960
The Man Who Found His Way. Morrow, 1957; Panther, 1960 [N. Mex., 1927]
A Private Anger, and Flight and Pursuit. Morrow, 1963 [Calif.]
P's Progress. Morrow, 1966 [Calif.]
Window in the Dark. Morrow, 1960

ORPET, FRED. Pseudonym of Fred East, 1895- .
Murder's No Accident. Arcadia, 1954 [S.F.]

ORR, CLIFFORD. 1899-1951. Born in Maine, graduate of Dartmouth; editor of "The New Yorker."
The Dartmouth Murders. Farrar, 1929; Hamilton, 1931 [N.H., acad.]
The Wailing Rock Murders. Farrar, 1932; Cassell, 1933 [Maine]

ORR, MARY [MARY ORR DENHAM]. Ref: CA.
The Tejera Secrets. Dial, 1974 [Carib.]

ORR, MYRON DAVID
White Gold. Capper, 1936

ORSAT, JEAN-FRANCOIS. Pseudonym: Jean D'Astor, q.v.

ORTON, JOE. Pseudonym of John Kingsley Orton, 1933-1967. Ref: CA.
Crimes of Passion. Methuen, 1967 (2 plays.)
Loot. Methuen, 1967; Grove, 1968 (2-act play.)

ORTON, JOHN KINGSLEY. 1923-1967. Pseudonym: Joe Orton, q.v.

ORUM, POUL. 1919- . Ref: TC. SC: Insp. Jonas Morck, in both titles.
Nothing But the Truth. Gollancz, 1976; Pantheon, 1976 [Den.]
Scapegoat; see The Whipping Boy
The Whipping Boy. Gollancz, 1975. U.S. title: Scapegoat. Pantheon, 1975 (Translation of "Syndebuk." Copenhagen, 1972.) [Den.]

ORVIS, KENNETH. Pseudonym of Kenneth Lemieux, 1923- . Born and educated in Montr.; professional hockey player turned newspaperman and writer for TV and business publications. SC: Adam Breck, in at least those marked AB.
-Cry Hallelujah! Dobson, 1970
The Damned and the Destroyed. Dobson, 1962; Belmont, 1966 [Montr.]
The Disinherited. Hale, 1974 [N.Y.]
The Doomsday List. Hale, 1974 AB
Into a Dark Mirror. Dobson, 1971 [Fr.]
Night Without Darkness. Chatto, 1965; Coward, 1966 AB [Bulg.]

OSBORN, DAVID. 1923- .
The French Decision. Granada, 1980; Doubleday, 1980 [Fr.]
-The Glass Tower. Hodder, 1971
Open Season. Heinemann, 1974; Dial, 1974 [Mich.]

OSBORNE, BERESFORD
Bushido. Futura, 1980; Charter, 1981
The Disciples of Nemesis. Hale, 1977
The Receivers. Hale, 1977

OSBORNE, DOROTHY
Fog Island. Berkley, 1975 [Maine]
Whispering Willows. Popular Library, 1973

OSBORNE, GEOFFREY. 1930- . SC: James Dingle and Glyn Jones, in at least those marked D&J.
Balance of Fear. Hale, 1968 D&J
Checkmate for China. Hale, 1969 D&J
Death's No Antidote. Hale, 1971 D&J
The Power Bug. Hale, 1968 D&J
A Time for Vengeance. Hale, 1974
Traitor's Gate. Hale, 1969 D&J [Russ.]

OSBORNE, HELENA. Pseudonym of Mary Galbraith Moore, 1930- . Has degree in history from Oxford; diplomat in British Foreign Service.
The Arcadian Affair. Hodder, 1969. U.S. title: The Yellow Gold of Tiryns. Coward, 1969 [Greece]
The Joker. Hodder, 1979; Coward, 1979
My Enemy's Friend; see Pay-Day
Pay-Day. Hodder, 1972. U.S. title: My Enemy's Friend. Coward, 1972 [Leb.]
White Poppy. Hodder, 1977; Coward, 1977 [Afghan.]
The Yellow Gold of Tiryns; see The Arcadian Affair

OSBORNE, LOUISE
Keys of Hell. Popular Library, 1975 [Can.]
Rite of the Damned. Popular Library, 1977
The Saturn Stone. Popular Library, 1977
The Witches' Ladder. Popular Library, 1979

OSBORNE, MARK. Pseudonym of John William Bobin, -1935, q.v. Other pseudonym: John Ascott, q.v. All titles feature Sexton Blake and were published by Amalgamated Press.
The Boarding House Mystery. 1931
The Case of the Crook Iron Master. 1934
The Consulting Room Crime. 1932. Revised and reprinted as: The Consulting Room Mystery. 1940
The Consulting Room Mystery; see The Consulting Room Crime
Dead Man's Bay. 1932
The Dog Track Murder. 1934
The Great Art-Gallery Crime. 1934
The Kennels Crime. 1932
The Mystery of the Lost Legionnaire. 1933
The Stables Crime. 1933

OSBORNE, WILLIAM HAMILTON. 1873-1942. SC: William Murgatroyd = WM.
The Blue Buckle. McBride, 1914; Hodder, 1915 [NYC]
The Boomerang. McBride, 1915 [NYC]
The Catspaw. Dodd, 1911; Hodder, 1916 [NYC]
-The Girl of Lost Island. Hodder, 1916 (U.S. title?)
The Red Mouse. Dodd, 1909; Hodder, 1916 WM [NYC]
The Running Fight. Dodd, 1910 WM [NYC]

OSBOURNE, LLOYD. 1868-1947. See also: Robert Louis Stevenson, 1850-1894.
The Grierson Mystery. Heinemann, 1928. U.S. title: Not to Be Opened. Cosmopolitan, 1928
-The Kingdoms of the World. Methuen, 1911. U.S. title: A Person of Some Importance. Bobbs, 1911
Not to Be Opened; see The Grierson Mystery
Peril. Heinemann, 1929; Doubleday, 1929 [NYC]
A Person of Some Importance; see The Kingdoms of the World
The Under-World. Appleton, 1907 (Play.)

OSGOOD, LUCIAN AUSTIN
Murder in the Tomb. Unique Mystery Novels, 1937

OSLER, ERIC RICHARD. 1900- . Pseudonym: T. Dick, q.v.

OSMOND, ANDREW. 1938- . Joint pseudonym with Richard Reid Ingrams, 1937- : Philip Reid, q.v. See also: Douglas (Richard) Hurd, 1930- . Ref: CA.
-Saladin! Hutchinson, 1975

OSTLERE, GORDON. 1921- . Pseudonym: Richard Gordon, q.v.

OSTRANDER, ISABEL (EGENTON). 1883-1924. See also: William J. Burns, 1861-1932. Pseudonyms: Robert Orr Chipperfield, David Fox, Douglas Grant, qq.v. Ref: CC, DD, MM, MP. SC: Timothy McCarty = TM.
Annihilation. McBride, 1924; Hurst, 1923 TM [NYC]
Ashes to Ashes. McBride, 1919; Hurst, 1921 [N.Y.]
At One-Thirty. Watt, 1915; Simpkin, 1916
The Black Joker. McBride, 1925; Hurst, 1926
The Braddigan Murder; see The Sleeping Cop
The Clue in the Air. Watt, 1917; Skeffington, 1920 TM [NYC]
The Crimson Blotter. McBride, 1921; Hurst, 1921 [NYC]
Dust to Dust. McBride, 1924; Hurst, 1924 [NYC]
The Heritage of Cain. Watt, 1916; Hurst, 1922 [N.Y.]
How Many Cards? McBride, 1920; Hurst, 1922 TM [NYC]
Impulse; see Liberation
Island of Intrigue. McBride, 1918; Hurst, 1919 [Cape Cod]
Liberation. McBride, 1924. British title: Impulse. Hurst, 1925 [N.Y.]
McCarty, Incog. McBride, 1922; Hurst, 1923 TM [Cape Cod]
The Mathematics of Guilt. McBride, 1926; Hurst, 1927 [N.Y.]
The Neglected Clue. McBride, 1925; Hurst, 1925
The Sleeping Cat. McBride, 1926; Hurst, 1926 [N.Y.]
The Sleeping Cop, with Christopher (B.) Booth, q.v. Chelsea, 1927. British title: The Braddigan Murder. Hutchinson, 1928 [NYC]
Suspense. McBride, 1918; Skeffington, 1919 [N.Y.]
The Tattooed Arm. McBride, 1922; Hurst, 1922 [L.I.]
The Twenty-Six Clues. Watt, 1919; Hurst, 1921 TM [NYC]

OSTRANDER, KATE
Dance with a Ghost. Berkley, 1976
The Doom of Glendour. Saturday Review Press, 1975 [Scot.]
Foxfire Cove. Berkley, 1975 [Md.]

The Ghosts of Ballyduff. Popular Library, 1972 [Ire.]
The Image Seller. Popular Library, 1974 [NYC, 1800s]
Ring of Darkness. Berkley, 1974
The Sea Tower. Popular Library, 1974 [Ire.]
The Specter of the Dunes. Popular Library, 1974 [Va.]

O'SULLIVAN, J(AMES) B(RENDAN). 1919-   .
SC: Steve Silk, in at least those marked SS.
Backlash. Ward, 1960   SS   [Ire.]
Casket of Death. Grafton, 1946   ss
Cherry in the Wine Glass. Grafton, 1945
Choke Chain. Ward, 1958   SS
Cold Chisel. Ward, 1960   [Ire.]
Death Came Late. Pillar, 1945   SS
The Death Card. Pillar, 1945   SS
Death on Ice. Pillar, 1946   SS
The Death Seat. Ward, 1957
Death Stalks the Stadium. Pillar, 1946   SS
Disordered Death. Ward, 1957
Don't Hang Me Too High. Laurie, 1954; Mill, 1954   SS   [U.S.]
Double Negative. Ward, 1962
Gate Fever. Ward, 1959   SS
Guilt Edged. Ward, 1959
Hue and Cry. Ward, 1961
I Die Possessed. Laurie, 1953; Mill, 1953   [U.S.]
It Could Happen to You. Pillar, 1946
The Long Spoon. Ward, 1956   SS
Lunge Wire. Ward, 1965
Make My Coffin Big. Ward, 1964   SS
Murder Proof. Ward, 1968
Nerve Beat. Laurie, 1953   SS
Pick Up. Ward, 1964
Raid. Ward, 1958   SS
Someone Walked over My Grave. Laurie, 1954   SS
The Stuffed Man. Laurie, 1955   SS
There Is One S.O.S. Ward, 1961   [Ire.]
The Third Horseman. Mellifont, 1946

O'SULLIVAN, VINCENT. 1872-1940.
A Book of Bargains. Smithers, 1896   ss
Sentiment, and other stories. Duckworth, 1913   ss, some criminous

OTIS, G. H.
Bourbon Street. Lion, 1953 [New Or.]
Hot Cargo. Lion, 1953

O'TOOLE, GEORGE
An Agent on the Other Side. McKay, 1973; Barker, 1974
The Cosgrove Report. Rawson, 1979 [Wash. D.C., 1868]

OTT, E. HARRISON. Pseudonym of Richard Hill Wilkinson, 1904-   , q.v. Other pseudonyms: Julian Brocke, Eugene Hayford, Paul Pray, qq.v.
Mystery of "Crazy Canyon" Ranch. Drama Guild, 1940 (Play.)

OTTOLENGUI, RODRIGUES. 1861-1937. Ref: CC. SC: John Barnes = JB; Robert Leroy Mitchell = RM.
An Artist in Crime. Putnam, 1892   JB,RM [NYC]
A Conflict of Evidence. Putnam, 1893; Ward, 1904   JB,RM [N.H.]
The Crime of the Century. Putnam, 1896 JB,RM [NYC]
Final Proof; or, The Value of Evidence. Putnam, 1898   ss   JB,RM [NYC]
A Modern Wizard. Putnam, 1894

OTTUM, BOB
See the Kid Run. Simon, 1978; Allen, 1979 [NYC]
The Tuesday Blade. Simon, 1976; Heinemann, 1977 [NYC]

OURSLER, (CHARLES) FULTON. 1893-1952.
Pseudonym: Anthony Abbot, q.v. See also: Anonymous ("Dark Masquerade"); and: Grace (Perkins) Oursler, 1900-1955.
The Spider, with Lowell Brentano (1895-1950). French, 1926 (Play.)
The Wager, and The House at Fernwood. Pony, 1946 (Two novelets.)

OURSLER, GRACE (PERKINS). 1900-1955.
The Spider. Grosset, 1929 (Novelization of the play by Fulton Oursler, 1893-1952, q.v., and Lowell Brentano, 1895-1950.)

OURSLER, WILL(IAM CHARLES). 1913-   .
Pseudonym: Nick Marino, q.v. Joint pseudonym with Margaret Scott: Gale Gallagher, q.v. Ref: CA. SC: Philip Strong & James Matthews = S&M.
Bullets for a Blonde; see Departure Delayed

Departure Delayed. Simon, 1947. Also published as: Bullets for a Blonde. Bestseller, 1949   [NYC]
Folio on Florence White. Simon, 1942; Art & Educational Publishers, 1947 S&M [NYC]
Murder Memo to the Commissioner: The Carl Houston Case. Simon, 1950
The Trial of Vincent Doon. Simon, 1941; Museum, 1943   S&M [NYC]

OUSELEY, JOHN MULVY. See: Sidney Warwick.

OUTERBRIDGE, HENRY
Captain Jack. Century, 1928   ss

OVALOV, LEV S(ERGEYEVICH). 1905-   .
Comrade Spy. Award, 1975 (Translated from the Russian.) [Moscow]

OVERGARD, WILLIAM
Pieces of a Hero. Pyramid, 1973

OVERHOLSER, STEPHEN. 1944-   . Ref: CA.
Molly and the Confidence Man. Doubleday, 1975 [West]

OVERTON, ROBERT
A Chase Round the World. Warne, 1900
-Dangerous Days. Routledge, 1905
-Decoyed Across the Seas. Warne, 1907

OVSTEDAL, BARBARA. 1925-   . Pseudonyms: Rosalind Laker, Barbara Paul, qq.v., Barbara Douglas.

OWEN, THE BROTHERS
Biggle's Wharf. Ward, 1875

OWEN, DEAN. Pseudonym of Dudley Dean McGaughy.
Hec Ramsey. Award, 1973 (Novelization of the TV series.)
A Killer's Bargain. Manor, 1973

OWEN, ERIC R.
Dr. Zollinoff's Revenge. Modern, 193?

OWEN, GEORGE W(ASHINGTON).   -1916.
-The Leech Club; or, The Mysteries of the Catskills. Lee, 1874

OWEN, H(ARRY) COLLINSON. 1882-1956.
The Adventures of Antoine. Hodder, 1919 ss [Paris]
-Hector Duval. Cassell, 1929
The Riverton Wagers. Cassell, 1931
The Rockingham Diamond. Hodder, 1923

OWEN, HANS C.
Ways of Death. Green Circle, 1937. Reprinted as (?): Fit to Kill. Hangman's House, 194? [New Eng., acad.]

OWEN, (WILLIAM) HAROLD. 1872-   . Ref: CA. See: Louise Jordan Miln, 1864-1933.

OWEN, J(OHN) L(AWTON)
The Great Jekyll Diamond. Roxburghe, 1897

OWEN, JAMES
Deferred Payment. Rivers, 1930
-Forty Years On. Rivers, 1928

OWEN, PHILIP. Pseudonym of Judson (Pentecost) Philips, 1903-   , q.v. Other pseudonym: Hugh Pentecost, q.v.
Mystery at a Country Inn. Berkshire, 1979; Hale, 1981 [Conn.]

OWEN, RAY
Date with Doom. Hale, 1971
End of the Road. Hale, 1972
The Fall Guy. Hale, 1969
Find Tracey George. Hale, 1968
Flight from Fear. Hale, 1969
Mask of Shadows. Hale, 1972
Seek and Destroy. Hale, 1970
So Deadly a Web. Hale, 1971
Who Cries for a Loser? Hale, 1969

OWEN, RICHARD. 1942-   . SC: David Morgan, in both titles.
The Eye of the Gods. Dutton, 1978 [Venez.]
Nightmare. St. Martin's, 1979 [Cent. Am.]

OWEN, WENDY
-There Goes Davey Cohen. Hutchinson, 1966
Whatever Happened to Ruby? Owen, 1968

OXFORD, JANE
Die for Love. Ward, 1961

OZAKI, MILTON K. 1913-   . Pseudonym: Robert O. Saber, q.v. Ref: CC. SC: Prof. Caldwell & Lt. Phelan, in at least those marked C&P.

Case of the Cop's Wife. GM, 1958; Fawcett (London), 1960 [Chi.]
Case of the Deadly Kiss. GM, 1957
The Cuckoo Clock. Ziff-Davis, 1946. Also published as: Too Many Women. Handi-Books, 1950   C&P
The Deadly Pickup. Graphic, 1953
Dressed to Kill. Graphic, 1954 [Chi.]
The Dummy Murder Case. Graphic, 1951 C&P [Chi.]
A Fiend in Need. Ziff-Davis, 1947   C&P [Chi.]
Inquest. GM, 1960; Muller pb, 1961 [Wis.]
Maid for Murder. Ace, 1955
Murder Doll. Berkley, 1959
Never Say Die. Ace, 1956 [Chi.]
Too Many Women; see The Cuckoo Clock
Wake Up and Scream. GM, 1959; Muller pb, 1961 [Wis.]

P., F. H.
The Castle of Caithness. Minerva, 1802

PACE, ERIC. 1936-   . Ref: CA.
Any War Will Do. Random, 1973; Deutsch, 1974
Nightingale. Random, 1979; Collins, 1980 [Teheran]
Saberlegs. World, 1970; Deutsch, 1971 [Mid. East]

PACE, TOM [THOMAS C. PACE, SR.]. Born in Fla., graduated from Georgia Tech; works for aircraft firm. SC: Ben Garden = BG.
Afternoon of a Loser. Harper, 1969; Gollancz, 1970 [Fla.]
Fisherman's Luck. Harper, 1971; White Lion, 1973   BG [Fla.]
The Treasure Hunt. Harper, 1970   BG [Fla.]

PACKARD, FRANK (LUCIUS). 1877-1942. Ref: CC, EM, MP, TC. SC: Jimmie Dale = JD.
The Adventures of Jimmie Dale. Doran, 1917; Cassell, 1918   JD [NYC]
The Big Shot. Doubleday, 1929; Hodder, 1929 [NYC]
Broken Waters. Doran, 1925; Hodder, 1927
The Devil's Mantle. Doran, 1927; Hodder, 1928 [ship]
Doors of the Night. Doran, 1922; Hodder, 1922 [NYC]
The Dragon's Jaws. Doubleday, 1937; Hodder, 1937 [China]
The Four Stragglers. Doran, 1923; Hodder, 1923 [Fla.]
From Now On. Doran, 1919 [Calif.]
The Further Adventures of Jimmie Dale. Doran, 1919; Hodder, 1926   JD [NYC]
The Gold Skull Murders. Doubleday, 1931; Hodder, 1931 [Mal.]
The Hidden Door. Doubleday, 1933; Hodder, 1933 [Can.]
Jimmie Dale and the Blue Envelope Murder. Doubleday, 1930; Hodder, 1930 JD [NYC]
Jimmie Dale and the Missing Hour. Doubleday, 1935; Hodder, 1935   JD [NYC]
Jimmie Dale and the Phantom Clue. Doran, 1922; Hodder, 1923   JD [NYC]
The Locked Book. Doran, 1924; Hodder, 1924 [Far East]
The Miracle Man. Doran, 1914; Hodder, 1914 [Maine]
More Knaves Than One. Doubleday, 1938; Hodder, 1938   ss   [Far East]
-The Night Operator. Doran, 1919   ss
Pawned. Doran, 1921; Hodder, 1921 [NYC]
The Purple Ball. Doubleday, 1933; Hodder, 1934 [Far East]
The Red Ledger. Doran, 1926; Hodder, 1926 [NYC]
-Running Special. Doran, 1925; Hodder, 1926   ss
Shanghai Jim. Doubleday, 1928; Hodder, 1928 (Four stories.) [Far East]
The Sin That Was His. Doran, 1917; Hodder, 1926 [Can.]
The Slave Junk; see Two Stolen Idols
Tiger Claws. Doubleday, 1928; Hodder, 1929 [NYC]
Two Stolen Idols. Doran, 1927. British title (?): The Slave Junk. Hodder, 1927 [Far East]
The White Moll. Doran, 1920; Hodder, 1920 [NYC]
The Wire Devils. Doran, 1918 [West]

PACKER, BERNARD J(ULES). 1934-   . Ref: CA.
Caro. Dutton, 1975. British title: Doctor Caro. Heinemann, 1977 [S. Am.]

PACKER, JOY (PETERSON). 1905-1977. Ref: CA.
　The Dark Curtain. Eyre, 1977
　The Man in the Mews. Eyre, 1964; Dutton, 1965

PACKER, PETER. 1908- .
　-The Love Thieves. Holt, 1962; Barker, 1962

PACKER, VIN. Pseudonym of Marijane Meaker.
　Alone at Night. GM, 1963; Muller pb, 1963 [N.Y.]
　Come Destroy Me. GM, 1954; Digit, 1958 [Vt.]
　The Damnation of Adam Blessing. GM, 1960; Muller pb, 1962
　Dark Don't Catch Me. GM, 1956
　Dark Intruder. GM, 1952; Red Seal, 1958
　Don't Rely on Gemini. Delacorte, 1969; Macmillan (London), 1970
　The Evil Friendship. GM, 1958
　5:45 to Suburbia. GM, 1958; Red Seal, 1959
　The Girl on the Best Seller List. GM, 1960; Muller pb, 1961 [N.Y.]
　The Hare in March. Signet, 1966
　Intimate Victims. GM, 1962; Muller pb, 1963
　Look Back to Love. GM, 1953; Red Seal, 1958
　Something in the Shadows. GM, 1961; Muller pb, 1962 [N.J.]
　-Spring Fire. GM, 1952; Sphere, 1969
　3-Day Terror. GM, 1957 [South]
　The Thrill Kids. GM, 1955
　The Twisted Ones. GM, 1959; Red Seal, 1959
　Whisper His Sin. GM, 1954; Red Seal, 1959 [Va.]
　The Young and Violent. GM, 1956 [NYC]

PADDON, (WILLIAM) WREFORD. 1917- .
　A Corpse in the Coupe. Hammond, 1951
　Solo for No Voices. Boardman, 1955

PADGET, MEG. Pseudonym of Ware Torrey (Budlong), 1905-1967. Other pseudonyms: Lee Crosby, Judith Ware, Joan Winslow, qq.v.
　House of Strangers. Lancer, 1965 [Md.]

PADGETT, LEWIS. Pseudonym of Henry Kuttner, 1914-1958, q.v.
　The Brass Ring. Duell, 1946; Low, 1947. Also published as: Murder in Brass. Bantam, 1947 [N.Y.]
　The Day He Died. Duell, 1947 [NYC]
　Murder in Brass; see The Brass Ring

PAEON, DR. JUPITER. Pseudonym.
　The Dead Man's Secret; or, The Adventures of a Medical Student. Munro, 1885

PAGANO, JO. 1906- .
　The Condemned. Prentice-Hall, 1947. Also published as: Die Screaming. Zenith, 1958 [Calif.]

PAGE, ALAIN
　So Late, Monsieur Calone. International, 1969 [Vienna]

PAGE, EMMA. Pseudonym of Honoria Tirbutt. Ref: TC. Set: Eng.
　Add a Pinch of Cyanide; see A Fortnight by the Sea
　Element of Chance. Collins, 1975
　Family and Friends. Collins, 1972
　A Fortnight by the Sea. Collins, 1973. U.S. title: Add a Pinch of Cyanide. Walker, 1973
　In Loving Memory. Collins, 1970
　Missing Woman. Hale, 1980

PAGE, EVELYN. 1902- . Ref: CA. Joint pseudonym with Dorothy Blair, 1903- : Roger Scarlett, q.v.

PAGE, JAKE. Pseudonym of James Keena Page, Jr., 1936- . Ref: CA.
　Shoot the Moon. Bobbs, 1979; Hale, 1980 [Ariz.]

PAGE, JAMES KEENA, JR. 1936- . Pseudonym: Jake Page, q.v.

PAGE, MARCO. Pseudonym of Harry Kurnitz, 1907-1968, q.v.
　Fast Company. Dodd, 1938; Heinemann, 1938 [NYC]
　Reclining Figure. Random, 1952; Eyre, 1952 [Calif.]
　The Shadowy Third. Dodd, 1946. British title: Suspects All. Cherry Tree, 1948. Reprinted as by Harry Kurnitz: Paperback Library, 1964 [NYC]
　Suspects All; see The Shadowy Third

PAGE, MARTIN. 1938- . Ref: CA.
　The Pilate Plot. Coward, 1978; Heinemann, 1979

PAGE, MICHAEL F(ITZGERALD). 1922- .
　The Innocent Bystander. Hale, 1957
　Spare the Vanquished. Hale, 1952

PAGE, NORVELL W. 1904-1961. Pseudonym: Grant Stockbridge, q.v.

PAGE, SPIDER
　Legend in Blue Steel. Python, 1979 [NYC]

PAGE, STANLEY HART. Born in N.J.; a newspaperman in that state. SC: Christopher Hand, in all titles.
　Fool's Gold. Knopf, 1933; Paul, 1934 [NYC]
　Murder Flies the Atlantic. King, 1933 [air.]
　The Resurrection Murder Case. Knopf, 1932; Paul, 1933 [N.Y.]
　Sinister Cargo. Knopf, 1932; Paul, 1933 [NYC]
　The Tragic Curtain. Dial, 1935 [NYC]

PAGE, THOMAS. 1942- . Pseudonym: Thomas P. Martin, q.v. Ref: CA.
　Signet Active. Times, 1978; Hamlyn, 1980. Also published as: Skyfire. Hamlyn, 1982

PAHLOW, GERTRUDE (CURTIS BROWN). 1881-1937.
　Somebody Shot the Captain. Skeffington, 1930. U.S. title: Murder in the Morning. Clode, 1931 [NYC]

PAIER, ROBERT
　The Pied Piper. Geis, 1979

PAIGE, LESLIE. Pseudonym of Norman Rubington.
　A House Possessed. Belmont, 1974
　Queen of Hearts. Belmont, 1974
　She Walks in Shadow. Belmont, 1974

PAIN, BARRY (ERIC ODELL). 1864-1928. Ref: CC, EM, MP.
　-Confessions of Alphonse. Laurie, 1917
　Deals. Hodder, 1904 ss
　The Death of Maurice. Skeffington, 1920
　The Luck of Norman Dale, with James Blyth, 1864-1915, q.v. Nash, 1908
　The Memoirs of Constantine Dix. Unwin, 1905 ss
　One Kind and Another. Secker, 1914; Stokes, 1915 ss
　The Problem Club. Collins, 1919 ss
　-Stories in Grey. Laurie, 1911 ss
　Stories in the Dark. Richards, 1901 ss

PAIN, MARGARET CAMERON
　The de Marigny Affair. Stockwell, 1974

PAINE, ALBERT B(IGELOW). 1861-1937.
　The Mystery of Evelin Delorme. Arena, 1894

PAINE, LAURAN BOSWORTH. 1916- . Pseudonyms: John Armour, Reg Batchelor, Kenneth Bedford, Frank Bosworth, Mark Carrel, Robert Clarke, Richard Dana, J. F. Drexler, Troy Howard, Jared Ingersol, John Kilgore, Hunter Liggett, J. K. Lucas, John Morgan, qq.v. Ref: CA.

PAINTER, THOMAS and ALEXANDER (KINNAN) LAING, 1903-1976, q.v.
　The Motives of Nicholas Holtz. Farrar, 1936. British title: The Glass Centipede. Butterworth, 1936

PALAMOUNTAIN, ALAN. Pseudonym: Tasman Ile, q.v.

PALERMO, ANTHONY J(AMES)
　Who? Vantage, 1964

PALESCANDOLO, FRANK. Pseudonym: Frank Paley, q.v.

PALEY, FRANK. Pseudonym of Frank Palescandolo.
　Rumble on the Docks. Crown, 1953

PALIN, MICHAEL and TERRY JONES
　Ripping Yarns. Eyre, 1978; Pantheon, 1979 (3 plays, some criminous.)

PALLEN, CONDE B(ENOIST). 1858-1929.
　The King's Coil. Manhattanville, 1928

PALMER, BRUCE (HAMILTON). 1932- . Ref: CA.
　Blind Man's Mark. Simon, 1959. Also published as: The Shattered Affair. Avon, 1960 [Fr.]
　Flesh and Blood. Simon, 1960 [Fr.]
　-Hecatomb. Simon, 1965
　The Shattered Affair; see Blind Man's Mark

PALMER, EVA PEARL
　Rival Claimants. Day Library, 1895

PALMER, GRETTA. 1905- . See: Evelyn (Davies) Johnson, 1904- .

PALMER, JOHN
　The Haunted Cavern. Crosby, 1796; Keatinge, 1796 [Scot., ca.1450]
　The Mystery of the Black Tower. Lane, 1796 [1300s]

PALMER, JOHN. Pseudonym of Edgar John Palmer Watts, 1904- . SC: Guy Plante and Freye Matthews, in at least those marked P&M.
　Above and Below. Hodder, 1967 P&M [ship]
　The Caves of Claro. Hodder, 1964
　Cretan Cipher. Hodder, 1965 [Crete]
　So Much for Gennaro. Hodder, 1968 P&M

PALMER, JOHN (LESLIE). 1885-1944. Pseudonym: Christopher Haddon, q.v. Joint pseudonym with Hilary (Aiden) St. George Saunders, 1898-1951, q.v.: Francis Beeding, q.v.
　Mandragora. Gollancz, 1940. U.S. title: The Man with Two Names. Dodd, 1940

PALMER, LILI
　-A Time to Embrace. Macmillan, 1980; Weidenfeld, 1980 (Translation of "Umarmen Hat Seine Zeit." Switzerland, 1979.)

PALMER, LUCILE [MRS. ALFRED H. THOMPSON]. Poet; known for Hollywood Horoscopes.
　Cat-Eye. Sargent, 1949 [L.A.]

PALMER, MADELYN. 1910- . Pseudonym: Geoffrey Peters, q.v. Ref: CA.
　Dead Fellah. Cape, 1961

PALMER, P. K. SC: Jedediah Killinger III, in both titles.
　The Rainbow/Seagreen Case. Pinnacle, 1974
　The Turquoise/Yellow Case. Pinnacle, 1974 [Calif.]

PALMER, PAUL. Pseudonym of Gloria Goddard, 1897- .
　Murder from Heaven. Phoenix, 1939 [NYC]

PALMER, ROSE
　Orion Was Rising. Signet, 1970 [N.H.]

PALMER, (CHARLES) STUART. 1905-1968. Pseudonym: Jay Stewart, q.v. Ref: CC, DD, EM, MP, TC. SC: Hildegarde Withers = HW; Howie Rook = HR.
　Ace of Jades. Mohawk, 1931 [NYC]
　The Adventure of the Marked Man, and one other. Aspen, 1973 2 ss (Sherlock Holmes.) [Eng., 1890s]
　At One Fell Swoop; see The Green Ace
　Cold Poison. Mill, 1954. British title: Exit Laughing. Collins, 1954 HW [L.A.]
　Death in Grease Paint; see Unhappy Hooligan
　Exit Laughing; see Cold Poison
　Four Lost Ladies. Mill, 1949; Collins, 1950 HW [NYC]
　The Green Ace. Mill, 1950. British title: At One Fell Swoop. Collins, 1951 HW [NYC]
　Hildegarde Withers Makes the Scene, with Fletcher Flora, 1914-1968, q.v. Random, 1969 HW [S.F.]
　Miss Withers Regrets. Doubleday, 1947; Collins, 1948 HW [L.I.]
　The Monkey Murder, and other Hildegarde Withers stories. Bestseller, 1950 HW ss
　Murder on the Blackboard. Brentano's, 1932; Eldon, 1934 HW [NYC]
　Murder on Wheels. Brentano's, 1932; Long, 1932 HW [NYC]
　Nipped in the Bud. Mill, 1951; Collins, 1952. Also published as: Trap for a Redhead. Bestseller, 1955 HW [NYC]
　No Flowers by Request; see Omit Flowers
　Omit Flowers. Doubleday, 1937. British title: No Flowers by Request. Collins, 1937 [Calif.]
　The Penguin Pool Murder. Brentano's, 1931; Long, 1932 HW [NYC]
　People vs. Withers and Malone, with Craig Rice, q.v. Simon, 1963 HW (Also features Craig Rice's series character John J. Malone.) ss
　The Puzzle of the Blue Banderilla. Doubleday, 1937; Collins, 1937 HW [Mex. City]

The Puzzle of the Briar Pipe; see The
  Puzzle of the Red Stallion
The Puzzle of the Happy Hooligan.
  Doubleday, 1941; Collins, 1941 HW
  [L.A.]
The Puzzle of the Pepper Tree. Double-
  day, 1933; Jarrolds, 1934 HW [Calif.]
The Puzzle of the Red Stallion. Double-
  day, 1936. British title: The Puzzle
  of the Briar Pipe. Collins, 1936 HW
  [NYC]
The Puzzle of the Silver Persian.
  Doubleday, 1934; Collins, 1935 HW
  [Eng.]
The Riddles of Hildegarde Withers. Jon-
  athan, 1947 HW ss
Rook Takes Knight. Random, 1968 HR
  [L.A.]
Trap for a Redhead; see Nipped in the
  Bud
Unhappy Hooligan. Harper, 1956. British
  title: Death in Grease Paint. Col-
  lins, 1956 HR [Calif.]

PALMER, WILL
  The Tester. Hale, 1980
  Three Doors to Darkness. Hale, 1979
  Vengeance Is Also Mine. Hale, 1980

PALMTAG, DINAH
  Starling Street. Dell, 1973 [Fla.]

PAMELY, C(ARL) D(OUGLAS)
  Tales of Mystery and Terror. Stockwell,
  1926

PANBOURNE, OLIVER. Pseudonym of Howard
  Rockey, 1886-1934.
  The Varanoff Tradition. Macrae-Smith,
  1926 [NYC]

PANCOAST, CHALMERS L(OWELL). 1880-   .
  -Cub. Devin-Adair, 1928
  Pass the Aspirin. Pancoast, 1945 ss,
  some criminous

PANETTA, GEORGE (JOSEPH)
  Comic Strip. French (NYC), 1958
  (3-act play.)

PANGBORN, EDGAR. 1909-1976. Pseudonym:
  Bruce Harrison, q.v. Ref: CA.
  The Trial of Callista Blake. St. Mar-
  tin's, 1962; Davies, 1962

PANGBORN, FREDERIC W(ERDEN). 1855-1934.
  -Alice; or, The Wages of Sin. Dilling-
  ham, 1883
  -Perdida; A Round Unvarnished Tale
  Truthfully Delivered. Wright, 1889

PANSHIN, ALEXEI. 1940-   . Ref: CA. SC:
  Anthony Villiers, in all titles.
  -Masque World. Ace, 1969
  -Star Well. Ace, 1968
  -The Thurb Revolution. Ace, 1968

PAPE, GORDON, 1937-   , and TONY ASPLER,
  1939-   . Ref (both authors): CA.
  Chain Reaction. Viking, 1978; Barrie,
  1979 [Montr.]
  The Scorpion Sanction. Viking, 1980
  [Egypt, future]

PAPE, RICHARD (BERNARD). 1916-   .
  No Time to Die. Elek, 1962

PARADIS, VINCENT A. SC: Tut Claw, in both
  titles.
  The Castilian Caper. Manor, 1978
  The Cocaine Caper. Manor, 1978 [Mex.]

PARADISE, LUKE
  The Corpse Wore Nylon. Scion, 1950
  Scar on a Corpse. Scion, 1950

PARADISE, MARY. Pseudonym of Dorothy
  (Enid) Eden, 1912-1982, q.v.
  Face of an Angel. Hale, 1961; Ace, 1966
  [It.]
  Shadow of a Witch. Hale, 1962; Ace,
  1966

PARADISE, VIOLA (ISABEL). 1887-   .
  A Girl Died Laughing. Harper, 1935;
  Heinemann, 1935 [NYC]

PARAMORE, EDWARD E., JR.
  Set a Thief. French (NYC), 1927 (3-act
  play.)

PARCELL, NORMAN HOWE. Pseudonym: John
  Nicholson, q.v.

PARGETER, EDITH (MARY). 1913-   . Pseu-
  donym: Ellis Peters, q.v. Ref: CA,
  CC, TC. SC: the Felse family = F
  (continued in books under the Ellis
  Peters byline).
  The Assize of the Dying. Heinemann,
  1958; Doubleday, 1958 (2 novelets.)
  Fallen into the Pit. Heinemann, 1951 F

PARIS, MATTHEW
  Mystery. Avon, 1973 [NYC]

PARISH, DAVID MONROE
  The House of Rhinestad. Pageant, 1965

PARISH, JAMES
  Distinguished Gathering. French (London
  & NYC), 1936 (3-act play.)
  Mrs. Inspector Jones. French (London),
  1951 (3-act play.)

PARISH, JED. Pseudonym of Wilbur Braun,
  1896-   , q.v. Other pseudonyms:
  Walter Blake, Bruce Brandon, Fred
  Caldwell, Raymond Dumkey, Nan Flem-
  ing, Marsha Grable, Edwin F. Hornung,
  Basil Ring, Orville Snap, Mortimer
  Sprague, Bert Stoner, qq.v.
  Mystery, Mayhem, and Murder! Bakers,
  1954 (3-act play.)

PARK, HUGH
  Death Flies Low. Stockwell, 1942

PARK, J. A.
  Strange Occupation. Fortune, 1933. U.S.
  title: Dangerous Escapade. Greenberg,
  1935

PARK, JACQUELINE
  Charlie's Back in Town. Popular Library, 1975

PARK, JORDAN. Pseudonym of C(yril) M.
  Kornbluth, 1923-1958, q.v. Other
  pseudonym: Simon Eisner, q.v.
  The Man of Cold Rages. Pyramid, 1958

PARK, MALCOLM
  The Honest Rogue. Macdonald, 1947

PARK, OWEN
  The Chinatown Connection. Pinnacle,
  1977 [S.F.]

PARKE, F. G. Pseudonym.
  First Night Murder. Dial, 1931; Paul,
  1932 [NYC]

PARKER, BEATRICE. Pseudonym of T(om) E.
  Huff, 1938?-   , q.v. Other pseudo-
  nyms: Edwina Marlow, Katherine St.
  Clair, qq.v.
  Betrayal at Blackcrest. Dell, 1971
  [Eng.]
  Come to Castlemoor. Dell, 1970 [Eng.,
  1800s]
  Jamintha. Dell, 1975
  Stranger by the Lake. Dell, 1971
  Wherever Lynn Goes. Dell, 1975

PARKER, BOB
  Crooked Cop. Manor, 1973

PARKER, CLAIRE
  The Rookies. Bantam, 1973 (Novelization of the TV series.)

PARKER, GAY
  Dead in the Eye of the Law. Warne, 1892
  Mr. Perkins of New Jersey; or, The Stolen Bonds. Routledge, 1888; Ogilvie,
  1888

PARKER, HERBERT
  -The Cuckoo Woman. Anglo-Eastern, 1922
  The Midnight Lady. Anglo-Eastern, 1922

PARKER, (PERMELIA) JANE MARSH. 1836-1913.
  The Midnight Cry. Dodd, 1886

PARKER, KEN(NETH FULLER)
  Television Plays. Northwestern, 1954
  (Plays, some criminous.)
  There's Always a Murder. French (NYC),
  1946 (3-act play.)

PARKER, LEE. SC: Donovan, in all titles.
  The Assassination Is Set for July 4.
  Award, 1974
  Blue Print for Execution. Award, 1974
  The Guns of Mazatlan. Award, 1975

PARKER, M. M.
  Big Phil's Kid. Meredith, 1969

PARKER, MAUDE. 189?-1959. SC: Jim Little,
  in at least those marked JL.
  Along Came a Spider. Hodder, 1957 [NYC]
  Blood Will Tell; see The Intriguer
  Death Do Us Part. Hodder, 1960 [L.I.]
  Death Makes a Deal. Hodder, 1961 [Tex.]
  Final Crossroads; see Murder in Jackson
  Hole
  The Intriguer. Rinehart, 1952. British
  title: Blood Will Tell. Hodder, 1952
  JL [L.I.]
  Invisible Red. Rinehart, 1953; Hodder,
  1954

Murder in Jackson Hole. Rinehart, 1955.
  British title (?): Final Crossroads.
  Hodder, 1955 JL [Wyo.]
Which Mrs. Torr? Rinehart, 1951; Hod-
  der, 1952 JL [Colo.]

PARKER, MICHAEL. 1941-   .
  North Slope. Macmillan (London), 1980

PARKER, NORMAN
  Don't Cry, Little Girl. Whitmore, 1970

PARKER, PERCY SPURLARK. 1940-   . Ref:
  CA.
  Good Girls Don't Get Murdered. Scrib-
  ner, 1974

PARKER, RICHARD. 1915-   . Ref: CA.
  Boy on a Chain. Davies, 1964. U.S.
  title: Killer. Doubleday, 1964 [Tas.]
  -Draughts in the Sun. Collins, 1955
  -Fiddler's Place. Davies, 1961
  The Gingerbread Man. Collins, 1953;
  Scribner, 1954 [Scot.]
  Harm Intended. Secker, 1957; Scribner,
  1956
  Killer; see Boy on a Chain
  A Kind of Misfortune. Collins, 1954;
  Scribner, 1955
  Only Some Had Guns. Collins, 1952
  -The Sword of Ganelon. Collins, 1957

PARKER, RICHARD
  Three Knots. Macaulay, 1924
  -Under Fire. Macaulay, 1916 (Noveliza-
  tion of the play by Roi Cooper
  Megrue, 1883-1927, q.v.)
  -The Whip. Macaulay, 1913 (Novelization
  of the play by Cecil Raleigh, q.v.)

PARKER, ROBERT (BOGARDUS). 1906-1955.
  Ref: TC.
  Headquarters Budapest. Farrar, 1944
  [Buda.]
  Passport to Peril. Rinehart, 1951; Hod-
  der, 1952 [Hung.]
  Ticket to Oblivion. Rinehart, 1950;
  Macmillan (London), 1951 [Fr.]

PARKER, ROBERT B(ROWN). 1932-   . Ref:
  CA. SC: Spenser = S.
  God Save the Child. Houghton, 1974;
  Deutsch, 1975 S [Boston]
  The Godwulf Manuscript. Houghton, 1974;
  Deutsch, 1974 S [Boston, acad.]
  The Judas Goat. Houghton, 1978; Curley,
  1978 S
  Looking for Rachel Wallace. Delacorte,
  1980 S [Boston]
  Mortal Stakes. Houghton, 1975; Deutsch,
  1976 S [Boston]
  Promised Land. Houghton, 1976; Deutsch,
  1977 S [Cape Cod]
  Wilderness. Delacorte, 1979; Deutsch,
  1980 [Maine]

PARKES, (GRAHAM) ROGER. 1933-   . See
  also: Edward Boyd. Ref: CA.
  Death-Mask. Constable, 1970
  The Fourth Monkey. Collins, 1978 [Afr.]
  The Guardians. Constable, 1973; St.
  Martin's, 1974
  Line of Fire. Constable, 1971

PARKHIRST, DOUGLASS F.
  Early Frost. French (NYC), 1955 (1-act
  play.)

PARKHURST, JANE
  -The Southern Moon. Jove, 1979; Hamlyn,
  1980 [Ga., 1800s]

PARKMAN, SYDNEY M(ULLER). 1895-   .
  The Accidental Adventurer. Hodder, 1931
  Account Closed. Hodder, 1932
  The Acting Second Mate. Hodder, 1935.
  U.S. title: Out from Shanghai. Har-
  per, 1935
  Captain Bowker. Hodder, 1946
  The Cuban Legacy. Hodder, 1940
  East of Singapore. Hodder, 1931; Macrae
  Smith, 1932
  The Facts About Floyd. Hodder, 1938
  The Island Feud. Hodder, 1937
  Night-Action! Hodder, 1936; Harper,
  1936
  Out from Shanghai; see The Acting
  Second Mate
  The Passing of Tony Blount. Hodder,
  1939
  Plunder Bar. Hodder, 1934
  -The Reef Pearlers. U. of London Press,
  1937
  Seven Days' Hard. Hodder, 1938
  -Ship Ashore. Hodder, 1936; Harper, 1937
  Sunk Without Trace. Hodder, 1933
  The Tide Watchers. Hodder, 1937
  -The Trail of the Shadow. U. of London
  Press, 1937
  Uncharted. Hodder, 1935. U.S. title:
  The Uncharted Island. Harper, 1936
  The Uncharted Island; see Uncharted

PARMER, CHARLES (B.)
  Murder at the Kentucky Derby. Doubleday, 1942 [Ky.]

PARMER, ENRIQUE
  Maple Hall Mystery: A Romance. Author's Publishing, 1880

PARNELL, J. J. and BETTY BARON
  Code Word Christmas Tree. Vantage, 1976

PARRISH, BARNEY
  Big Night at Mrs. Maria's. Playboy, 1977; New English Library pb, 1977

PARRISH, FRANK. Pseudonym of Roger (Erskine) Longrigg, 1929-   , q.v. Other pseudonym: Ivor Drummond, q.v. SC: Dan Mallett, in both titles. Set: Eng.
  Fire in the Barley. Constable, 1977; Dodd, 1979
  Sting of the Honeybee. Constable, 1978; Dodd, 1979

PARRISH, RANDALL. 1858-1923.
  The Air Pilot. McClurg, 1913
  The Case and the Girl. Knopf, 1922; Paul, 1923 [Chi.]
  -Comrades of Peril. McClurg, 1919
  -"Contraband." McClurg, 1916; Curtis Brown, 1916
  Gift of the Desert. McClurg, 1922; Unwin, 1923
  The Mystery of the Silver Dagger. Doran, 1920; Hodder, 1920
  The Strange Case of Cavendish. Doran, 1918; Hodder, 1919 [Colo.]

PARRY, HUGH JONES. 1916-   . Pseudonym: James Cross, q.v.

PARRY, JAMES. 1943-   . Born in Chi., graduate of Harvard; co-founder of an advertising agency.
  The Discovery. Crowell, 1978; Macdonald, 1979

PARRY, MICHEL
  Supernatural Solution. Panther, 1976

PARSONS, ANTHONY. 1893-1963. All titles listed without publisher feature Sexton Blake and were issued by Amalgamated Press.
  The Affair of the Missing Parachutist. 1947
  The "Allah's Eye" Conspiracy. 1938
  The Bad Man of Cairo. 1951
  The Blackmailed Refugee. 1945
  Calling Whitehall 1212. 1943
  The Car Park Mystery. 1954
  The Case of the Banned Film. 1952
  The Case of the Blackmailed Prince. 1952
  The Case of the Crook Rajah. 1939
  The Case of the Dangra Millions. 1949
  The Case of the Frightened Man. 1955
  The Case of the Indian Dancer. 1951
  The Case of the Indian Millionaire. 1944
  The Case of the Indian Watcher. 1955
  The Case of the Japanese Contract. 1952
  The Case of the Missing D.F.C. 1943
  The Case of the Missing G.I. Bride. 1946
  The Case of the Missing Major. 1940
  The Case of the Missing Scientist. 1952
  The Case of the Missing Surgeon. 1949
  The Case of the Nameless Millionaire. 1953
  The Case of the Prince's Diary. 1953
  The Case of the Prince's Prisoners. 1946
  The Case of the Renegade Naval Officer. 1944
  The Case of the Second Crime. 1954
  The Case of the Secret Road. 1943
  The Case of the Sinister Farm. 1954
  The Case of the Six O'Clock Scream. 1955
  The Case of the Spanish Legatee. 1945
  The Case of the Spiv's Secret. 1950
  The Case of the Stolen Evidence. 1945
  The Case of the Swindler's "Stooge." 1946
  The Case of the Unknown Heir. 1953
  The Case of the Wicked Three. 1954
  The Clue of the Stolen Rupees. 1941
  The Crime of the Cashiered Major. 1943
  Crook's Deputy. 1953
  The Crooks of Tunis. 1955
  Death by the Nile. Wright, 1955 [Egypt]
  Death of a Governor. Wright, 1954
  Death on the Mall. Wright, 1947
  The Euston Road Mystery. 1947
  The Great Dollar Fraud. 1950
  The Harem Mystery. 1939
  Hotel Homicide. 1956
  The House with Steel Shutters. 1942
  The Income Tax Conspiracy. 1948
  Living in Fear. 1950
  The Loot of France. 1945
  The Loot of Pakistan. 1948
  The Man from China. 1940
  The Man from Kenya. 1947
  The Man from Maybrick Road. 1954
  The Man from Occupied France. 1941
  The Man Who Backed Out! 1948
  The Man Who Had to Quit. 1946
  The Man Without a Passport. 1952
  The Millionaire's Nest Egg. 1951
  Murder at the Red Cockatoo. Wright, 1955
  Murder at the Stadium. Pyramid (London),
  The Mystery of Avenue Road. 1948
  The Mystery of the Bankrupt Estate. 1946
  The Mystery of the Blitzed Tower. 1951
  The Mystery of the Bombed Monastery. 1944
  The Mystery of the Cairo Express. 1944
  The Mystery of the Crooked Gift. 1950
  The Mystery of the Free Frenchmen. 1940
  The Mystery of the Girl in Green. 1951
  The Mystery of the Indian Relic. 1944
  The Mystery of the Mason's Arms. 1952
  The Mystery of the One-Day Alibi. 1948
  The Mystery of the Red Cockatoo. 1948
  The Mystery of the Stolen Despatches. 1942
  The Mystery of the 250,000 Rupees. 1946
  The Mystery of the Whitehall Bomb. 1947
  No Alibi for Murder. Wright, 1951 [India]
  On the Stroke of Nine. 1941
  The Plot of the Yellow Emperor. 1942
  The Prisoner in the Hold. 1955
  Retired from the Yard. 1951
  The Riddle of Big Ben. 1938
  The Riddle of Cubicle 7. 1943
  The Riddle of the Burmese Curse. 1947
  The Riddle of the Captured Quisling. 1942
  The Riddle of the Disguised Crook. 1943
  The Riddle of the Escaped P.O.W. 1947
  The Riddle of the Gambling Den. 1945
  The Riddle of the Indian Alibi. 1946
  The Riddle of the Prince's Stooge. 1950
  The Riddle of the Rajah's Curios. 1949
  The Riddle of the Russian Bride. 1948
  The Secret of Oil Creek. 1940
  The Secret of the Burma Road. 1942
  The Secret of the Castle Ruins. 1954
  The Secret of the Golden Horse. 1939
  The Secret of the Indian Lawyer. 1953
  The Secret of the Moroccan Bazaar. 1954
  The Secret of the Roman Temple. 1955
  The Secret of the Ten Bales. 1937
  The Stowaway of the S. S. Wanderer. 1942
  Terror at Tree Tops. 1948
  Those on the List. 1950
  The Trail of the Missing Scientist. 1955

PARSONS, CORNELIA MITCHELL
  A Secret of the Sea. Ogilvie, 1896 [N.H.]

PARSONS, H. F. DOLLAND. Pseudonym: John Dolland, q.v.

PARSONS, LUKE
  Clough Plays Murder. Jarrolds, 1942

PARSONS, MRS. (ELIZA PHELP).   -1811.
  Castle of Wolfenbach. Minerva, 1793; Folio, 1968 [Ger.]
  The Mysterious Warning. Lane, 1796; Holden, 1928 [Ger.]

PARTRIDGE, ANTHONY. Pseudonym of E(dward) Phillips Oppenheim, 1866-1946, q.v.
  The Black Watcher; see The Kingdom of Earth
  The Distributors; see The Ghosts of Society
  The Ghosts of Society. Hodder, 1908. U.S. title: The Distributors. McClure, 1908
  The Kingdom of Earth. Mills, 1909; Little, 1909. Also published as: The Black Watcher, as by E. Phillips Oppenheim. Hodder, 1912
  Passers-By. Ward, 1911; Little, 1910

PARVIN, BRIAN
  Dead Wood. Hale, 1980
  The Deadly Dyke. Hale, 1979
  Death in the Past. Hale, 1980

PASSINGHAM, W(ILLIAM) J(OHN). 1897-   . SC (with many other authors): Sexton Blake = SB.
  Angels in Aldgate. Long, 1933
  The Case of the Ace Accomplice. Amalgamated, 1953 SB
  The Mystery of Theyne Manor. Mellifont, 1937
  The World Championship Mystery. Amalgamated, 1953 SB

PASTOR, TONY. Pseudonym of Harlan Page Halsey, 1837-1898, q.v. Other pseudonym: Old Sleuth, Judson R. Taylor, qq.v.
  Fritz, the German Detective. Ogilvie, 1882 [NYC]
  -Night Scenes in New York. American News, 1876 [NYC]
  O'Neil McDarragh, the Detective. American News, 1877
  The Swordsman of Warsaw; or, Ralpho of the Iron Arm. Street, 1889
  Tom and Jerry; or, The Double Detectives. Street, 1889

PATCH, DAN E. L. 1886-   .
  -Aamon Always. Bica, 1940
  -Behind the Veil. Zondervan, 1947
  The Hour Struck. Zondervan, 1945
  -Moon over Willow Run. Zondervan, 1943
  Past Finding Out. Bica, 1939

PATER, ROGER
  Mystic Voices. Burns, 1923 ss

PATERNOSTER, (GEORGE) SIDNEY. 1866-   . SC: Randolph Mannering = RM. Set: Eng.
  -Children of Earth. Long, 1905
  The Cruise of the Motor-Boat Conqueror. Page, 1906 (British title?) RM
  -The Folly of the Wise. Long, 1907
  -The Great Gift. Lane, 1917
  -Gutter Tragedies. Trehearne, 1903 ss
  The Hand of the Spoiler. Hodder, 1908. U.S. title: The Master Criminal. Empire, 1907
  The Lady of the Blue Motor. Long, 1907; Page, 1907
  The Master Criminal; see The Hand of the Spoiler
  The Motor Pirate. Chatto, 1903; Page, 1904 RM
  -The Orphan-Monger. Milne, 1908

PATERSON, (JAMES EDMUND) NEIL. 1916-   .
  Man on the Tight Rope. Hodder, 1953; Random, 1953 [Czech.]

PATON, RAYMOND
  The Autobiography of a Blackguard. Hutchinson, 1923; Houghton, 1924

PATRICK, ANDREW
  Beyond the Law. Berkley, 1977 (Novelization of the "Baretta" TV series.) [L.A.]

PATRICK, CHANN
  The House of Retrogression. Jacobsen, 1932

PATRICK, JOHN. 1905-   . Ref: CA.
  Everybody Loves Opal. Dramatists, 1961 (Play.)
  Scandal Point. Dramatists, 1969 (3-act play.)

PATRICK, KEATS. Pseudonym of Walter Karig, 1898-1956.
  Death Is a Tory. Bobbs, 1935; Melrose, 1936. Also published as: The Pool of Death. Best Detective, 1942, abridged [Wash. D.C.]

PATRICK, Q. Pseudonym of Richard Wilson Webb, 1901-   , with Mary Louise (White) Aswell, q.v., with Martha Mott Kelley, alone, and with Hugh Callingham Wheeler, 1912-   , q.v. Other joint pseudonyms of Webb and Wheeler: Patrick Quentin, Jonathan Stagge, qq.v. Ref: CC, EM, MC, MP, TC. Unless otherwise specified below, titles are by Wheeler and Webb. SC: Timothy Trant = TT.
  Cottage Sinister. Swain, 1931; Longmans, 1932 (Written by Webb and Kelley.) [Eng.]
  Danger Next Door. Cassell, 1951 [NYC]
  Darker Grows the Valley; see The Grindle Nightmare
  Death and the Maiden. Simon, 1939; Cassell, 1939 TT [acad., N.Y.]
  Death for Dear Clara. Simon, 1937; Cassell, 1937 TT [NYC]
  Death Goes to School. Smith & Haas, 1936; Cassell, 1936 [Eng., acad.]
  Death in Bermuda; see Return to the Scene
  Death in the Dovecote; see Murder at the Women's City Club
  File on Claudia Cragge. Morrow, 1938; Jarrolds, 1938 (Crime File #4.) TT
  File on Fenton and Farr. Morrow, 1937; Jarrolds, 1938 (Crime File #3.)
  The Grindle Nightmare. Hartney, 1935. British title: Darker Grows the Valley. Cassell, 1935 (Written by Webb and Aswell.) [New Eng.]

Murder at Cambridge. Farrar, 1933. British title: Murder at the 'Varsity. Longmans, 1933. (Written by Webb alone.) [Eng., acad.]
Murder at the 'Varsity; see Murder at Cambridge
Murder at the Women's City Club. Swain, 1932. British title: Death in the Dovecote. Cassell, 1934 (Written by Webb and Kelley.)
Return to the Scene. Simon, 1941. British title: Death in Bermuda. Cassell, 1941 [Bermuda]
S. S. Murder. Farrar, 1933; Cassell, 1933 (Written by Webb and Aswell.) [ship]

PATRICK, VICTOR
Three to Make Murder. Mystery House, 1947

PATRICK, VINCENT. 1935- . Ref: CA.
The Pope of Greenwich Village. Seaview, 1979; Deutsch, 1980 [NYC]

PATTEE, FRED LEWIS. 1863-1950.
-The House of the Black Ring. Holt, 1905

PATTEN, BRIAN. 1946- . Ref: CA.
-Mr. Moon's Last Case. Allen, 1975; Scribner, 1975

PATTEN, GILBERT. 1866-1945. Pseudonym: Burt L. Standish, q.v.

PATTERSON, ARTHUR M. [ARTHUR WILLIS PATTERSON]. 1888- .
The Heaviest Pipe. Jacobs, 1921 [Maine]

PATTERSON, HARRY. 1929- . Pseudonyms: Martin Fallon, James Graham, Jack Higgins, Hugh Marlowe, qq.v. Ref: CA. SC: Nick Miller, in at least those marked NM
Brought in Dead. Long, 1967 NM
Comes the Dark Stranger. Long, 1962
Cry of the Hunter. Long, 1960 [Ire.]
The Dark Side of the Island. Long, 1963; GM, 1977, as by Jack Higgins [Greece]
The Graveyard Shift. Long, 1965 NM
Hell Is Always Today. Long, 1968. Reprinted as by Jack Higgins: Arrow, 1977
Hell Is Too Crowded. Long, 1962; GM, 1976, as by Jack Higgins. Reprinted in Britain as by Jack Higgins: Coronet, 1977
The Iron Tiger. Long, 1966; GM, 1974, as by Jack Higgins. Reprinted in Britain as by Jack Higgins: Coronet, 1973
Pay the Devil. Barrie, 1963
A Phoenix in the Blood. Barrie, 1964
Sad Wind from the Sea. Long, 1959 [Far East]
The Thousand Faces of Night. Long, 1961
Thunder at Noon. Long, 1964 [Mex.]
To Catch a King. Hutchinson, 1979; Stein, 1979 [Lisbon, 1940]
Toll for the Brave. Long, 1971; GM, 1976, as by Jack Higgins. Reprinted in Britain as by Jack Higgins: Arrow, 1977
The Valhalla Exchange. Hutchinson, 1976; Stein, 1976 [Austria, 1944]
Wrath of the Lion. Long, 1964; GM, 1977, as by Jack Higgins. Reprinted in Britain as by Jack Higgins: Coronet, 1976

PATTERSON, (ISABELLA) INNIS. SC: Sebald Craft, in both titles.
The Eppworth Case. Farrar, 1930 [N.Y.]
The Standish Gaunt Case. Farrar, 1931 [NYC]

PATTERSON, J. T.
What Next?; or, The Honest Thief. Transylvania, 1899

PATTERSON, JAMES. 1947- . Copywriter for NYC advertising agency.
The Jericho Commandment. Crown, 1979; Hamlyn, 1980 [Moscow]
The Season of the Machete. Ballantine, 1977; Secker, 1978
The Thomas Berryman Number. Little, 1976; Secker, 1977 [Nashv.]

PATTERSON, JOHN M(cREADY)
Doubly Dead. Hale, 1969; Doubleday, 1969 [Chan. Is.]

PATTERSON, RICHARD NORTH. 1947- . Ref: CA.
The Lasko Tangent. Norton, 1979; Hale, 1980

PATTERSON, ROBERT
Gold Is the Color of Blood. Ballantine pb, 1960; Muller, 1961
-Man with a Past. Muller, 1963

PATTINSON, JAMES. 1915- . SC: Harvey Landon, in at least those marked HL.
Across the Narrow Seas. Harrap, 1960
The Angry Island. Hale, 1968 [W.I.]
Away with Murder. Hale, 1972
Blind Date. Hale, 1978
Busman's Holiday. Hale, 1980
Contact Mr. Delgado. Harrap, 1959 HL [ship]
Cordley's Castle. Hale, 1974
The Courier Job. Hale, 1979
Crusader's Cross. Hale, 1975
The Deadly Shore. Hale, 1970
Feast of the Scorpion. Hale, 1975
Final Run. Hale, 1977
Find the Diamonds. Hale, 1969
A Fortune in the Sky. Hale, 1973
Freedman. Hale, 1975
The Golden Reef. Hale, 1969
The Haunted Sea. Hale, 1974
The Honeymoon Caper. Hale, 1976
The Last Stronghold. Hale, 1968 HL [S. Am.]
The Levantine Trade. Hale, 1980
The Liberators. Harrap, 1961 HL
The Marakano Formula. Hale, 1973
The Murmansk Assignment. Hale, 1971
The Mystery of the Gregory Kotovsky. Harrap, 1958. U.S. title: The Silent Voyage. McDowell, 1959 [ship]
The No-Risk Operation. Hale, 1977
Ocean Prize. Hale, 1972
On Desperate Seas. Harrap, 1961
The Petronov Plan. Hale, 1974; Zebra, 1974 [Brazil]
The Plague Makers. Hale, 1969
The Rashevski Ikon. Hale, 1979
A Real Killing. Hale, 1976
Red Exit. Hale, 1979
The Rodriguez Affair. Hale, 1970
Sea Fury. Hale, 1971
Search Warrant. Hale, 1973
The Silent Voyage; see The Mystery of the Gregory Kotovsky
The Sinister Stars. Hale, 1971
Something of Value. Hale, 1978
The Spanish Hawk. Hale, 1977
The Spayde Conspiracy. Hale, 1980
Special Delivery. Hale, 1976
Three Hundred Grand. Hale, 1970
A Walking Shadow. Hale, 1976
Watching Brief. Hale, 1971
Weed. Hale, 1972
Whispering Death. Hale, 1969
Wild Justice. Harrap, 1960

PATTISON, RUTH. Pseudonym: Ruth Abbey, q.v.
The Shadow Between. Hale, 1970; Ace, 1974, as by Ruth Abbey

PATTON, CLIFF
The Omni Strain. Zebra, 1980

PATTON, DAVID KNOX
Murder on the Pacific. Dodd, 1940 [ship]

PAUL, BARBARA. Pseudonym of Barbara Ovstedal, 1925- . Other pseudonyms: Rosalind Laker, q.v., Barbara Douglas.
The Curse of Halewood. Macdonald, 1976. U.S. title: Devil's Fire, Love's Revenge. St. Martin's, 1976 [Ire.]
Devil's Fire, Love's Revenge; see The Curse of Halewood
An Exercise for Madmen. Berkley, 1978
First Gravedigger. Doubleday, 1980
The Fourth Wall. Doubleday, 1979 [NYC, theatre]
The Frenchwoman. Macdonald, 1977; St. Martin's, 1977
Liars and Tyrants and People Who Turn Blue. Doubleday, 1980
The Seventeenth Stair. Macdonald, 1975; St. Martin's, 1975 [Fr.]
To Love a Stranger. St. Martin's, 1979
A Wild Cry of Love. Macdonald, 1978

PAUL, CHARLOTTE [CHARLOTTE PAUL REESE]. 1916- . Ref: CA.
A Child Is Missing. Putnam, 1978; Mayflower, 1979 [Wash.]
-The Image. Warner, 1980; Coronet, 1981

PAUL, ELLIOT (HAROLD). 1891-1958. Pseudonym: Brett Rutledge, q.v. Ref: CC, EM, MC, MP, TC. SC: Homer Evans, in all titles.
The Black and the Red. Random, 1956 [Las Veg.]
The Black Gardenia. Random, 1952 [L.A.]
Fracas in the Foothills. Random, 1940 [Mont.]
Hugger-Mugger in the Louvre. Random, 1940; Nicholson, 1949 [Paris]
I'll Hate Myself in the Morning, and Summer in December. Random, 1945; Nicholson, 1949 (2 short novels, one about HE.)
Mayhem in B-Flat. Random, 1940; Corgi, 1951 [Paris]
Murder on the Left Bank. Random, 1951; Corgi, 1951 [Paris]
The Mysterious Mickey Finn; or, Murder at the Cafe du Dome. Modern Age, 1939; Penguin, 1953 [Paris]
Waylaid in Boston. Random, 1953 [Boston]

PAUL, ERNEST. Pseudonym of Ernest Focke, 1896- . SC: George Barclay, in all titles.
Curtains for Komespi. Hale, 1968
The Golden Fleece. Hale, 1969
Jewels in Jeopardy. Hale, 1967
The Komespi Affair. Hale, 1968
The Reluctant Cloak and Dagger Man. Hale, 1971
The Silent Murders. Hale, 1969

PAUL, GENE
The Big Make; see Little Killer
Little Killer. Lion, 1952. Also published as: The Big Make. Lion, 1957 [Newark]
Naked in the Dark. Lion, 1953

PAUL, HUGO. Pseudonym of Paul H. Little, 1915- . Other pseudonym: Paula Minton, q.v.
Rich, Hip and Deadly. Lancer, 1966
The Smashers. Lancer, 1964

PAUL, JOHN
Murder by Appointment. Skeffington, 1952
Oil by Murder. Skeffington, 1953

PAUL, PHYLLIS
-A Cage for the Nightingale. Heinemann, 1957
-Camilla. Heinemann, 1949
-Constancy. Heinemann, 1951
Echo of Guilt; see Pulled Down
An Invisible Darkness. Heinemann, 1967
-The Lion of Cooling Bay. Heinemann, 1953
A Little Treachery. Heinemann, 1962; Norton, 1962
Pulled Down. Heinemann, 1964; Norton, 1965. Also published as: Echo of Guilt. Lancer, 1966
-Rox Hall Illuminated. Heinemann, 1956
Twice Lost. Heinemann, 1960; Norton, 1960

PAULEY, BARBARA ANNE. 1925- . Ref: CA.
Blood Kin. Doubleday, 1972
Voices Long Hushed. Doubleday, 1976 [Miss., 1880s]

PAULL, H(ARRY) M(AJOR). 1854-1934.
Bluff! Hodder, 1928

PAULL, JESSICA. Joint pseudonym of Julia Perceval and Rosaylmer Burger. Pseudonym of Rosaylmer Burger: C. H. Wallace, q.v. For Perceval, see also: Patricia Drew. SC: Tracy Larrimore and Mike Thompson, in all titles.
Destination: Terror. Award, 1968
Passport to Danger. Award, 1968
Rendezvous with Death. Award, 1969

PAULSEN, GARY. 1939- . Ref: CA.
The Death Specialists. Major, 1976
The Implosion Effect. Major, 1976
The Sweeper. Raven, 1980 [Chi.]

PAVEY, L(EONARD) A(RTHUR). 1888- .
-Forward from Youth. Grayson, 1936

PAWLEY, E.
Death Was Her Escort. Streamlined, 1947

PAXTON, LOIS. Pseudonym of Lois Dorothea Low, 1916- . Other pseudonyms: Zoe Cass, Dorothy Mackie Low, qq.v.
The Man Who Died Twice. Hurst, 1968; Ace, 1970
The Quiet Sound of Fear. Hurst, 1971; Hawthorn, 1971
Who Goes There? Hurst, 1972; Ace, 1974

PAYES, RACHEL (RUTH) C(OSGROVE). 1922- . Pseudonym: E. L. Arch, q.v. Ref: CA. SC: Forsythia Brown, in at least those marked FB.
The Black Swan. Berkley, 1978
-Bride of Fury. Playboy, 1980 [Eng., ca.1890]
Curiosity Killed Kitty. Avalon, 1962
Death Sleeps Lightly. Avalon, 1960
Devil's Court. Berkley, 1974 [Eng., 1720]
Forbidden Island. Berkley, 1973
Forsythia Finds Murder. Avalon, 1960 FB

The House of Tarot. Berkley, 1975
Malverne Hall. Ace, 1970
Memoirs of Murder. Avalon, 1964 FB
The Mystery of Echo Caverns. Avalon, 1966
O Charitable Death. Doubleday, 1968; Hale, 1968
The Sapphire Legacy. Berkley, 1978

PAYN, JAMES. 1830-1898. Ref: CC, EM.
-Another's Burden. Downey, 1897
-At Her Mercy. Chapman, 1872; Harper, 1874
-The Bateman Household. Hall, 1860
 A Beggar on Horseback; or, A County Family; see A County Family
-Bentinck's Tutor. Low, 1868
-The Best of Husbands. Bentley, 1874; Harper, 1874
-A Bitter Reckoning. Munro, 1885 (British title?)
-Blondel Parva. Bradbury, 1868
-Bred in the Bone. Harper, 1871 (British title?)
-The Burnt Million. Chatto, 1890; Lovell, 1889
 By Proxy. Chatto, 1878; Harper, 1878
-The Canon's Ward. Chatto, 1884; Harper, 1884
-Carlyon's Year. Bradbury, 1868; Harper, 1967
-Cecil's Tryst. Tinsley, 1872; Harper, 1872
-The Clyffards of Clyffe. Hurst, 1866; Peterson, 1871?
 A Confidential Agent. Chatto, 1880; Harper, 1880
-A County Family. Tinsley, 1869. U.S. title: A Beggar on Horseback; or, A County Family. Harper, 1869
 The Disappearance of George Driffell. Smith, 1896
-The Eavesdropper. Smith, 1888; Harper, 1888
-Fallen Fortunes. Tinsley, 1876; Appleton, 1876
 The Family Scapegrace; see Richard Arbour; or, The Family Scapegrace
-For Cash Only. Chatto, 1882; Harper, 1882
 Found Dead. Tinsley, 1869; Harper, 1869
-From Exile. Chatto, 1881; Harper, 1881
 Glow-Worm Tales. Chatto, 1887; Harper, 1887 ss, one or two criminous
-A Grape from a Thorn. Smith, 1881; Harper, 1881
-Gwendoline's Harvest. Tinsley, 1870; Harper, 1870
-Halves, a novel (and other tales). Tinsley, 1876; Harper, 1876 ss
-The Heir of the Ages. Smith, 1886; Harper, 1886
-In Market Overt. Cox, 1895; Lippincott, 1895
-Kit. Chatto, 1883; Harper, 1882
-Less Black Than We're Painted. Chatto, 1878; Harper, 1878
-Like Father, Like Son. Tinsley, 1871
 Lost Sir Massingberd. Low, 1864; Peterson, 1870
-The Luck of the Darrells. Longmans, 1885; Harper, 1885
-A Marine Residence, and other stories. Chapman, 1871 ss
-Married Beneath Him. Macmillan (London), 1864; Peterson, 187?
-Maxims by a Man of the World. Tinsley, 1869
-Mirk Abbey. Hurst, 1866
-A Modern Dick Whittington; or, A Patron of Letters. Cassell, 1892; Taylor, 1892
-Murphy's Master, and other stories. Tinsley, 1873; Harper, 1873 ss
 The Mystery of Mirbridge. Chatto, 1888; Harper, 1888
-Not Wooed, But Won. Chapman, 1871
-One of the Family. Harper, 1868 (British title?)
-A Perfect Treasure. Tinsley, 1869
-A Prince of the Blood. Ward, 1888; Harper, 1888
 Richard Arbour; or, The Family Scapegrace. Edmonston, 1861. Also published as: The Family Scapegrace; or, Richard Arbour. Chapman, 1872
-Stories and Sketches. Smith, 1857 ss
-A Stumble on the Threshold. Cox, 1892; Appleton, 1892
-Sunny Stories, and Some Shady Ones. Chatto, 1891; Lovell, 1891 ss, some criminous
-The Talk of the Town. Smith, 1885; Harper, 1884
-Thicker Than Water. Longmans (London), 1883; Harper, 1883
-A Trying Patient. Chatto, 1893 ss
 Two Hundred Pounds Reward, and other tales. Chapman, 1879 ss, some criminous
-Under One Roof. Chatto, 1879; Harper, 1879

-Walter's Word. Tinsley, 1875; Harper, 1875
-What He Cost Her. Chatto, 1877; Harper, 1877
 A Woman's Vengeance. Bentley, 1872; Harper, 1872
-The Word and the Will. Chatto, 1890; Lovell, 1890

PAYNE, ALAN. Pseudonym of John (William) Jakes, 1932- , q.v. Other pseudonyms: Rachel Ann Payne, Jay Scotland, qq.v. See also: William (Thomas) Ard, 1922-1960.
 This'll Slay You. Ace, 1958 [Fla.]

PAYNE, DONALD GORDON. 1924- . Pseudonym: Donald Gordon, q.v.

PAYNE, EVELYN
 Held Open for Death. Arcadia, 1958

PAYNE, GEORGE
 Oonah; or, The Story of a Crime. Ward, 1884

PAYNE, HAROLD. Pseudonym of George C. Kelly, -1895.
 The Gilded Fly. Price, 1892

PAYNE, LAURENCE. 1919- . Ref: CA, CC. SC: Chief Insp. Sam Birkett, in at least those marked SB. Set: Eng.
 Birds in the Belfry. Hodder, 1966; Lippincott, 1967
 Deep and Crisp and Even. Hodder, 1964 SB
 The First Body; see The Nose on My Face
 The Nose on My Face. Hodder, 1961; Macmillan, 1962. Also published as: The First Body. Avon, 1964 SB
 Spy for Sale. Hodder, 1969; Doubleday, 1970
 Too Small for His Shoes. Hodder, 1962; Macmillan, 1963 SB

PAYNE, RACHEL ANN. Pseudonym of John (William) Jakes, 1932- , q.v. Other pseudonyms: Alan Payne, Jay Scotland, qq.v. See also: William (Thomas) Ard, 1922-1960.
 Ghostwind. Paperback Library, 1966

PAYNE, RONALD CHARLES. Joint pseudonym with John William Garrod: John Castle, q.v.

PAYNE, WILL. 1865-1954.
-The Losing Game. Dillingham, 1910
 Overlook House. Dodd, 1921 [New Eng.]
 The Scarred Chin. Dodd, 1920 [Chi.]

PAYNTER, T(HOMAS) C(AMBORNE). 1901- .
-Cannon Law. Longmans, 1928
 They Sailed on a Friday. Longmans, 1928

PEACOCK, DENNIS (MAX CORNELIUS WOODRUFFE). 1899- .
 The Perilous Secret. Hutchinson, 1929
 The Secret of the Mere. Hutchinson, 1931
 A Thief by Night. Hutchinson, 1929

PEACOCK, F(ERDINAND) M(ANSEL)
 A Military Crime. Gale, 1891

PEACOCK, THOMAS LOVE. 1785-1866.
 Crotchet Castle. Hookham, 1831
 Nightmare Abbey. Hookham, 1818; Carey, 1819

PEARCE, CHARLES E(DWARD). Pseudonym: Detective Dunn, q.v.
-The Ball of Fortune. Blackie, 1883
 The Bungalow Under the Lake. Paul, 1910
-Corinthian Jack. Paul, 1920
 The Crimson Mascot. Paul, 1914
 The Eyes of Alicia. Paul, 1913
-A Foe in the Shadow. Paul, 1919
-The Last of the Darrells. Aldine, 1925
-Love Besieged. Paul, 1909; McClurg, 1911
-Madame Flirt. Paul, 1922
 The Mystery of Judith. Lloyd, 1923
 The Mystery of the Furlined Cloak. Lloyd, 1921
-Red Revenge. Paul, 1911
 The Secret of Room No. 13. Lloyd, 1922
-The Soul of a Shop Girl. Aldine, 1915
-A Star of the East. Paul, 1912
 The Tanglewood Mystery. Aldine, 1926

PEARCE, DICK [RICHARD ELMO PEARCE]. 1909- . Ref: CA.
 The Darby Trial. Lippincott, 1954

PEARL, JACK [JACQUES BAIN PEARL]. 1923- . Ref: CA.
 The Cops. Pinnacle, 1972
 A Jury of His Peers. Prentice-Hall, 1975

 Lepke. PB, 1975 (Novelization of the movie.) [NYC]
 Our Man Flint. PB, 1965 (Novelization of the movie.)
 The Plot to Kill the President. Pinnacle, 1972
 Robin and the 7 Hoods. PB, 1964 (Novelization of the movie.)
 A Time to Kill...A Time to Die. Norton, 1971; Hale, 1974 [Colo.]
 Victims. Trident, 1973; Hale, 1974 [NYC]

PEARLMAN, GILBERT
 The Adventures of Sherlock Holmes' Smarter Brother. Ballantine, 1975; Futura, 1977 (Novelization of the movie.) (Sherlock Holmes.)

PEARSALL, RONALD. 1927- . Ref: CA.
 The Belvedere. Weidenfeld, 1977; Dial, 1977

PEARSON, ANN. SC: Maggie Courtney, in all titles.
 Cat Got Your Tongue? Zebra, 1980
 Murder by Degrees. Zebra, 1979 [Miss., acad.]
 A Stitch in Time. Zebra, 1979

PEARSON, D(AVID) A. G.
 The Golden Stone. Methuen, 1929; Dutton, 1929 [Switz.]

PEARSON, DIANE. Pseudonym of Diane Margaret McClelland, 1931- .
 The Loom of Tancred. Hale, 1967. U.S. title: Bride of Tancred. Bantam, 1967 [Eng., 1800s]

PEARSON, EDMUND (LESTER). 1880-1937.
 The Adventure of the Lost Manuscripts. Aspen, 1974
 Sherlock Holmes and the Drood Mystery. Aspen, 1973 (Sherlock Holmes.)

PEARSON, PETER. 1913- .
 Postscript for Malpas. Macmillan (London), 1975; Dodd, 1976 [Scot., 1985]

PEARSON, ROBERT E.
 The Fat Boy Must Die. Vega, 1963

PEARSON, SHEPHERD. Pseudonym of John Edward Gunby Hadath, 1880?-1954.
 The Second Count. Gifford, 1944

PEARSON, WILLIAM. 1922- .
 The Beautiful Frame. Simon, 1953; Reinhardt, 1954
 Hunt the Man; see Hunt the Man Down
 Hunt the Man Down. Simon, 1956. British title: Hunt the Man. Ward, 1957

PEART, JANE
 Night of the Darkest Moon. Lancer, 1973

PEATTIE, ELIA W(ILKINSON). 1862-1935.
 The Judge. Rand, 1891

PECHEY, ARCHIBALD THOMAS. 1876-1961. Pseudonyms: Mark Cross, Valentine, qq.v.

PECK, LEONARD. 1906- . Pseudonym: Leonard Brain, q.v. British civil servant; author of articles, ss and plays.
 Touch Pitch. Long, 1967 [Fr.]

PECK, (LADY) WINIFRED (FRANCES KNOX) 1882-1962.
 Arrest the Bishop? Faber, 1949
 The Warrielaw Jewel. Faber, 1933; Dutton, 1933 [Scot.]

PECKHAM, RICHARD. Pseudonym of Raymond P(eckham) Holden, 1894-1972, q.v.
 Murder in Strange Houses. Minton, 1929; Eyre, 1930 [NYC]

PEDDIE, JAMES
 Dangerous Dilemmas. Crown, 18?? ss
 Secrets of a Private Enquiry Office. Clarke, 1881 ss

PEDEN, WILLIAM HARWOOD. 1913- . Ref: CA.
 Twilight at Monticello. Houghton, 1973 [Va., acad.]

PEDLER, JOHN BRANFROST SIMPSON. Pseudonym: Dominic Torr, q.v.

PEDLER, KIT [CHRISTOPHER MAGNUS HOWARD PEDLER], 1927- , and GERRY DAVIS
 Brainwrack. Souvenir, 1974; PB, 1975

PEDRICK, GALE
 Meet the Rev. Low, 1947

PEEBLES, NILES N. SC: Ross McKellar, in both titles, both set in NYC.
Blood Brother, Blood Brother. Pyramid, 1969
See the Red Blood Run. Pyramid, 1968

PEEL, COLIN D(UDLEY). 1936-   . Born in Eng., has lived for some years in N.Z.
Adapted to Stress. Hale, 1973
Bitter Autumn. Hale, 1973
Cold Route to Freedom. Hale, 1975
Flameout. Hale, 1976; St. Martin's, 1978 [West]
Glimpse of Forever. Hale, 1980
Hell Seed. Hale, 1978; St. Martin's, 1979
Nightdive. Hale, 1977; St. Martin's, 1978 [S. Pac.]
On a Still Night. Hale, 1975
One Sword Less. Hale, 1973

PEEL, FREDERICK. 1888-   . Joint pseudonym with Charles Siddle, 1892-   : Rufus Slingsby, q.v.

PEEPLES, SAMUEL A(NTHONY). 1917-   . TV scriptwriter, film commentator.
The Man Who Died Twice. Putnam, 1976 [L.A., 1922]

PEERS, ROSS. See: David Thurlow.

PEI, MARIO A(NDREW). 1901-1978. Ref: CA.
-The Sparrows of Paris. Philosophical, 1958

PELHAM, ANTHONY. Pseudonym of Charles Evelyn Graham Hope.
The Fortress of Ashes. Hodder, 1936 [Tib.]
-Summons to Adventure. Hodder, 1937

PELL, FRANKLYN. Pseudonym of Frank E. Pelligrin.
Hangman's Hill. Dodd, 1946 [Fr.]

PELL, ROBERT
-That Winslow Woman. Playboy, 1977

PELLEY, WILLIAM DUDLEY. 1890-1965.
The Blue Lamp. Fiction League, 1931 [Vt.]

PELLIGRIN, FRANK E. Pseudonym: Franklyn Pell, q.v.

PELTRET, EDOUARD H. See: George M(ilton) Savage, 1904-   .

PEMBER, RON and DENIS DE MARNE
Jack the Ripper. French (London), 1976 (2-act play.)

PEMBER, WILLIAM LEONARD. Pseudonym: Jack Monmouth, q.v.

PEMBER-HILLER, GUY
Run Corpse, Run. Double Action Detective Novel, 1943; Swan, 1946 [N.Y.]

PEMBERTON, MARGARET. 1943-   . Ref: CA.
The Guilty Secret. Hale, 1979; St. Martin's, 1979 [Port.]
The Mystery of Saligo Bay. Macdonald, 1976
Rendezvous with Danger. Macdonald, 1974; Berkley, 1975
Shadows over Silver Sands. Futura, 1975; Berkley, 1976
-Tapestry of Fear. Hale, 1979
-Vengeance in the Sun. Hale, 1979

PEMBERTON, MAX. 1863-1950. Ref: CC, EM, TC. SC: Capt. Black, in at least those marked B.
The Adventures of Captain Jack. Mills, 1909
Aladdin in London; see The Lodestar
A Bagman in Jewels. Skeffington, 1919 ss, all but one criminous
Behind the Curtain. Nash, 1916
Captain Black. Cassell, 1911; Doran, 1911 B
-A Daughter of the States. Dodd, 1904 (British title?)
The Diamond Ship. Cassell, 1907; Appleton, 1907
The Diary of a Scoundrel. Ward, 1891
-Doctor Xavier. Hodder, 1903; Appleton, 1903
Dolores and Some Others. Mills, 1931 ss, some criminous
-Feo. Hodder, 1900; Dodd, 1900
-The Fortunate Prisoner. Hodder, 1909; Dillingham, 1909
-The Garden of Swords. Cassell, 1899; Dodd, 1899
A Gentleman's Gentleman. Innes, 1896; Harper, 1896
The Giant's Gate. Cassell, 1901; Stokes, 1901
The Gold Wolf. Ward, 1903; Dodd, 1903
-The Great White Army. Cassell, 1915
-Her Wedding Night. Jenkins, 1918 ss
-The House of Fortune. Nash, 1912
-The Hundred Days. Cassell, 1905; Appleton, 1905
-I Crown Thee King. Methuen, 1902
The Iron Pirate. Cassell, 1893; Rand, 1897 B
Jewel Mysteries from a Dealer's Notebook; see Jewel Mysteries I Have Known
Jewel Mysteries I Have Known. Ward, 1894. U.S. title: Jewel Mysteries from a Dealer's Notebook. Fenno, 1904 ss
John Dighton, Mystery Millionaire. Cassell, 1923
-Kronstadt. Cassell, 1898; Appleton, 1898
-The Lady Evelyn. Hodder, 1906; Authors & Newspapers, 1906
-Leila and Her Lover. Ward, 1913
-The Lodestar. Ward, 1907; Authors & Newspapers, 1907. Also published as: Aladdin of London; or, Lodestar. Empire, 1907
-Love the Harvester. Methuen, 1908; Dodd, 1900
-Lucienne, with Isabelle & Horizon of God. Mills, 1925
-The Man of Silver Mount. Cassell, 1918
The Man Who Drove the Car. Nash, 1910
-Mid the Thick Arrows. Hodder, 1905
-Millionaire's Island. Cassell, 1913
The Mystery of the Green Heart. Methuen, 1910; Dodd, 1910
-Night Lights. Mills, 1929 ss
The Phantom Army. Pearson, 1898; Appleton, 1898
-A Puritan's Wife. Cassell, 1895; Dodd, 1896
-Queen of the Jesters. Pearson, 1897; Dodd, 1897
-Red Morn. Cassell, 1904
-The Sea Wolves. Cassell, 1894; Harper, 1894
-The Shadow on the Sea. Westbrook, 1907 (British title?)
-The Show Girl. Cassell, 1909; Winston, 1909
The Signors of the Night. Pearson, 1899; Dodd, 1899 ss
-The Summer Book. Mills, 1911 ss
Two Women. Methuen, 1914
Wheels of Anarchy. Cassell, 1908
White Motley. Cassell, 1913; Sturgis, 1911
-White Walls. Ward, 1910
-A Woman of Kronstadt. Readers Library, 1941
-A Woman Who Knew. Hutchinson, 1922 ss

PEMBERTON, MAX JOSEPH
-An Adventurer from the East. Mills, 1925
The Bottles of Scented Sweets. Mills, 1926
-Hindoo Khan. Mills, 1922
Kidnapper of Women. Mills, 1927
The Mystery of a Millionaire. Mills, 1924
-Under the Red Flag. Mills, 1923

PEMBROKE, PETER
The Cuban Connection. Hale, 1980

PEMBROKE, THOMAS. See: Mileson Horton.

PENDEXTER, HUGH. 1875-1940.
Tiberius Smith. Harper (NYC & London), 1907 ss

PENDLETON, DON(ALD EUGENE). 1927-   . Ref: TC. Pseudonym: Stephan Gregory, q.v. SC: Mack Bolan (The Executioner), in all titles (see also: Jim Peterson).
Acapulco Rampage. Pinnacle, 1976; Corgi, 1977 [Mex.]
Arizona Ambush. Pinnacle, 1977; Corgi, 1978 [Ariz.]
Assault on Soho. Pinnacle, 1971; Corgi, 1973 [Eng.]
Battle Mask. Pinnacle, 1970; Sphere, 1973 [Calif.]
Boston Blitz. Pinnacle, 1972; Corgi, 1974 [Boston]
California Hit. Pinnacle, 1972; Corgi, 1974 [S.F.]
Canadian Crisis. Pinnacle, 1975; Corgi, 1977 [Montr.]
Caribbean Kill. Pinnacle, 1972; Corgi, 1973 [P. Rico]
Chicago Wipeout. Pinnacle, 1971; Corgi, 1973 [Chi.]
Cleveland Pipeline. Pinnacle, 1977; Corgi, 1978 [Cleve.]
Colorado Kill-Zone. Pinnacle, 1976; Corgi, 1977 [Colo.]
Command Strike. Pinnacle, 1977; Corgi, 1978 [NYC]
Continental Contract. Pinnacle, 1971; Sphere, 1973 [Fr.]
Death Squad. Pinnacle, 1969; Sphere, 1973 [L.A.]
Detroit Deathwatch. Pinnacle, 1974; Corgi, 1976 [Det.]
Dixie Convoy. Pinnacle, 1976; Corgi, 1978 [Atlanta]
Firebase Seattle. Pinnacle, 1975; Corgi, 1976 [Seattle]
Friday's Feast. Pinnacle, 1979; Corgi, 1981 [Balt.]
Hawaiian Hellground. Pinnacle, 1975; Corgi, 1976 [Haw.]
Jersey Guns. Pinnacle, 1974; Corgi, 1975 [N.J.]
Miami Massacre. Pinnacle, 1970; Corgi, 1973 [Miami]
Monday's Mob. Pinnacle, 1978; Corgi, 1979 [Ill.]
New Orleans Knockout. Pinnacle, 1974; Corgi, 1976 [New Or.]
Nightmare in New York. Pinnacle, 1971; Corgi, 1973 [NYC]
Panic in Philly. Pinnacle, 1973; Corgi, 1975 [Phil.]
St. Louis Showdown. Pinnacle, 1975; Corgi, 1977 [St. Louis]
San Diego Siege. Pinnacle, 1972; Corgi, 1974 [San Diego]
Satan's Sabbath. Pinnacle, 1980; Corgi, 1981 [NYC]
Savage Fire. Pinnacle, 1977; Corgi, 1978 [Mass.]
Tennessee Smash. Pinnacle, 1978; Corgi, 1978 [Nashv.]
Terrible Tuesday. Pinnacle, 1979; Corgi, 1979 [Calif.]
Texas Storm. Pinnacle, 1974; Corgi, 1975 [Tex.]
Thermal Thursday. Pinnacle, 1979; Corgi, 1980 [Fla.]
Vegas Vendetta. Pinnacle, 1971; Corgi, 1973 [Las Veg.]
War Against the Mafia. Pinnacle, 1969; Sphere, 1973 [Mass.]
Washington I.O.U. Pinnacle, 1972; Corgi, 1974 [Wash. D.C.]
Wednesday's Wrath. Pinnacle, 1979; Corgi, 1979 [N. Mex.]

PENDLETON, TOM. Pseudonym of Edmund van Zandt, ca.1919-   . Lawyer, active in oil businesses, banker, in Tex.
Hodak. McGraw, 1969; Joseph, 1970 [S. Am.]

PENDOWER, JACQUES. 1899-1976. Pseudonym: T.C.H. Jacobs, q.v. Ref: CA, CC, EM, TC. SC: Slade McGinty, in at least those marked SM.
Anxious Lady. Hale, 1960 [Sp.]
Betrayed; see The Widow from Spain
Cause for Alarm. Hale, 1971
The Dark Avenue. Hale, 1955
Date with Fear. Hale, 1974
Death on the Moor. Hale, 1962
Diamonds for Danger. Hale, 1970
Double Diamond. Hale, 1974
The Golden Statuette. Hale, 1969
Hunted Woman. Ward, 1955
The Long Shadow. Hale, 1959
Master Spy. Hale, 1964 SM
Mission in Tunis. Hale, 1958; Paperback Library, 1967 [Tun.]
Operation Carlo. Hale, 1963 SM [It.]
Out of This World. Hale, 1966
The Perfect Wife. Hale, 1962 SM
She Came by Night. Hale, 1971
Sinister Talent. Hale, 1964 SM [It.]
Spy Business. Hale, 1965
Traitor's Island. Hale, 1967 SM [Greece]
A Trap for Fools. Hale, 1968 [Venice]
Try Anything Once. Hale, 1967
The Widow from Spain. Hale, 1961. U.S. title: Betrayed. Paperback Library, 1967 [Fr.]

PENFIELD, CORNELIA. 1892-1938.
After the Deacon Was Murdered. Putnam, 1933 [Conn.]
After the Widow Changed Her Mind. Putnam, 1933 [Conn.]

PENLEY, NORMAN
-The Girl in the Green Beret. Modern, 1935
-The Loveless Isle. Modern, 1935
Miss Melbourn's Million. Modern, 193?

PENMARE, WILLIAM. Pseudonym of (Mavis) Elizabeth (Hocking) Nisot, 1893-   , q.v.
The Black Swan. Hodder, 1928
The Man Who Could Stop War. Hodder, 1929
The Scorpion. Hodder, 1929 [Switz.]

PENN, H. See: V. Andrews.

PENNANT-REA, RUPERT
  Gold Foil. Bodley, 1978

PENNY, F(ANNY) E(MILY FARR).   -1939.
  -Chowra's Revenge. Hutchinson, 1937
  -Dark Corners. Chatto, 1908
    The Elusive Bachelor. Hutchinson, 1935
  -The Familiar Stranger. Hutchinson, 1936
  -A Forest Officer. Methuen, 1900
  -The Inevitable Law. Chatto, 1907
  -Jackals and Others. Mills, 1939
  -The Lady of the Rifle. Hodder, 1932
  -Living Dangerously. Hodder, 1925
    The Malabar Magician. Chatto, 1912
      [India]
  -Missing! Chatto, 1917
    Pulling the Strings. Hodder, 1927
      [India]
    Sacrifice. Chatto, 1910
    A Spell of the Devil. Hutchinson, 1935
      [India]

PENNY, RUPERT. Pseudonym of Ernest Basil
  Charles Thornett. SC: Insp. Edward
  Beale, in all titles. Set: Eng.
    The Lucky Policeman. Collins, 1938
    Policeman in Armour. Collins, 1937
    Policeman's Evidence. Collins, 1938
    Policeman's Holiday. Collins, 1937
    Sealed-Room Murder. Collins, 1941
    She Had to Have Gas. Collins, 1939
    Sweet Poison. Collins, 1940
    The Talkative Policeman. Collins, 1936

PENOYRE, MARY [MARY PENOYRE MORGAN].
  1940-   .
    Breach of Security. Barker, 1974
    Let Him Go, Let Him Tarry. Barker, 1975

PENROSE, MARGARET. Ref: CA.
    Death on the Files. Long, 1961
    The Fatal Fifth. Long, 1963

PENTECOST, HUGH. Pseudonym of Judson
  (Pentecost) Philips, 1903-   , q.v.
  Other pseudonym: Philip Owen, q.v.
  SC: Luke Bradley = LB; Pierre Cham-
  brun = PC; George Crowder = GC; John
  Jericho = JJ; Lt. Pascal = P; Julian
  Quist = JQ; Grant Simon = GS; Dr.
  John Smith = JS.
    Around Dark Corners. Dodd, 1970 GC ss
      [New Eng.]
    The Assassins. Dodd, 1955 [NYC, ca.
      1860]
    Bargain with Death. Dodd, 1974; Hale,
      1976 PC [NYC]
    The Beautiful Dead. Dodd, 1973; Hale,
      1975 JQ [NYC]
    Beware Young Lovers. Dodd, 1980; Hale,
      1981 PC [NYC]
    Birthday, Deathday. Dodd, 1972; Hale,
      1975 PC [NYC]
    The Brass Chills. Dodd, 1943; Hale,
      1944 LB [S. Pac.]
    Cancelled in Red. Dodd, 1939; Heine-
      mann, 1939 LB [NYC]
    The Cannibal Who Overate. Dodd, 1962;
      Boardman, 1963 PC [NYC]
    Cat and Mouse. Royce, 1945
    The Champagne Killer. Dodd, 1972; Hale,
      1974 JQ [NYC]
    Chinese Nightmare. Dell 10¢ pb, 1951
      [China]
    Choice of Violence. Dodd, 1961; Board-
      man, 1962 GC [Conn.]
    The Creeping Hours. Dodd, 1966; Board-
      man, 1967 JJ,P [NYC]
    The Day the Children Vanished. PB,
      1976; Hale, 1977 [New Eng.]
    The Dead Man's Tale. Royce, 1945
    Dead Woman of the Year. Dodd, 1967;
      Macdonald, 1968 JJ,P [NYC]
    The Deadly Friend. Dodd, 1961; Board-
      man, 1962 [Mass.]
    The Deadly Joke. Dodd, 1971; Hale, 1972
      PC [NYC]
    Deadly Trap. Dodd, 1978; Hale, 1979 JQ
      [N.Y.]
    Death After Breakfast. Dodd, 1978;
      Hale, 1979 PC [NYC]
    Death Mask. Dodd, 1980; Hale, 1981 JQ
      [NYC]
    Death Wears a Copper Necktie and other
      stories. Edward, 1946 ss
    Die After Dark. Dodd, 1976; Hale, 1977
      JQ [L.I.]
    Don't Drop Dead Tomorrow. Dodd, 1971;
      Hale, 1973 JQ [NYC]
    The Evil That Men Do. Dodd, 1966;
      Boardman, 1966 PC [NYC]
    The Fourteen Dilemma. Dodd, 1976; Hale,
      1977 PC [NYC]
    The Gilded Nightmare. Dodd, 1968; Gol-
      lancz, 1969 PC [NYC]
    Girl Watcher's Funeral. Dodd, 1969;
      Gollancz, 1970 PC [NYC]
    The Girl with Six Fingers. Dodd, 1969;
      Gollancz, 1970 JJ [Conn.]
    The Golden Trap. Dodd, 1967; Macdonald,
      1968 PC [NYC]

    Hide Her from Every Eye. Dodd, 1966;
      Boardman, 1966 JJ [Conn.]
    The Homicidal Horse. Dodd, 1979; Hale,
      1980 JQ [L.I.]
    Honeymoon with Death. Dodd, 1975; Hale,
      1976 JQ [N.Y.]
    I'll Sing at Your Funeral. Dodd, 1942;
      Hale, 1945 LB [NYC]
    The Judas Freak. Dodd, 1974; Hale, 1976
      JQ [NYC]
    The Kingdom of Death. Dodd, 1960;
      Boardman, 1961 [NYC]
    Lt. Pascal's Tastes in Homicide. Dodd,
      1954; Boardman, 1955 (3 novelets.)
      P
    The Lonely Target. Dodd, 1959; Board-
      man, 1960 GS,P [NYC]
    Memory of Murder. Ziff-Davis, 1947
      (4 novelets.) JS; LB in one
    Murder As Usual. Dodd, 1977; Hale, 1978
      [New Eng.]
    The Obituary Club. Dodd, 1958; Board-
      man, 1959 GS,P [NYC]
    Only the Rich Die Young. Dodd, 1964;
      Boardman, 1964 P [NYC]
    A Plague of Violence. Dodd, 1970; Hale,
      1972 JJ [Conn.]
    Random Killer. Dodd, 1979; Hale, 1980
      PC [NYC]
    Shadow of Madness. Dodd, 1950 JS
    The Shape of Fear. Dodd, 1964; Board-
      man, 1964 PC [NYC]
    Sniper. Dodd, 1965; Boardman, 1966 JJ
      [Conn.]
    The Steel Palace. Dodd, 1977; Hale,
      1978 JQ [N.J.]
    The Tarnished Angel. Dodd, 1963; Board-
      man, 1963 [Conn.]
    Time of Terror. Dodd, 1975 PC [NYC]
    The 24th Horse. Dodd, 1940; Hale, 1951
      LB [NYC]
    Walking Dead Man. Dodd, 1973; Hale,
      1975 PC [NYC]
    Where the Snow Was Red. Dodd, 1949;
      Hale, 1951 JS [Vt.]

PENTELOW, JOHN NIX. 1872-1931. Titles below were published by Amalgamated
  Press and feature Sexton Blake.
    The Cleopatra Needle Mystery. 1927
    Missing in Mexico. 1925
    The Three Masked Men. 1927

PEOPLE, GRANVILLE CHURCH. Pseudonym:
  Granville Church, q.v.

PEPPER, JOAN ALEXANDER WETHERELL.
  1920-   . Pseudonym: Joan Alexander,
  q.v.

PERCEVAL, JULIA. Joint pseudonym with
  Rosaylmer Burger, q.v.: Jessyca
  Paull, q.v. See also: Patricia Drew.

PERCY, CATHERINE. Pseudonym of "a famous
  mystery writer."
    Death Is Skin Deep. Abelard, 1953 [NYC]

PERCY, DOUGLAS C(ECIL). 1914-   . Ref:
  CA.
    Hidden Valley. Zondervan, 1951 [Afr.]

PERCY, EDWARD. Pseudonym of Edward Percy
  Smith, 1891-1968.
    Ladies in Retirement, with Reginald
      Denham, 1894-1983. English Theatre
      Guild, 1940; Century, 1940 (3-act
      play.)
    The Lost Hat. Year Book Press, 1936;
      Baker, 1936 (1-act play.)
    The Man with Expensive Tastes, with
      Lilian (Mary) Denham. English Thea-
      tre, 1955 (3-act play.)
    Play with Fire. English Theatre Guild,
      1942. Also published as: The Shop at
      Sly Corner. English Theatre Guild,
      1946; Dramatists Play Service, 1949
      (3-act play.)
    The Shop at Sly Corner; see Play with
      Fire
    Suspect, with Reginald Denham,
      1894-1983. Secker, 1937; Dramatists
      Play Service, 1940 (3-act play.)
    Trunk Crime, with Reginald Denham,
      1894-1983. Dramatists Play Service,
      1940 (3-act play.)

PERCYVAL, T. WIGNEY. See: Horace Hodges.

PERDUE, LEWIS. See: Robin Moore.

PERDUE, VIRGINIA. 1899-1945. Ref: CC.
  SC: Eleanora Burke = EB.
    Alarum and Excursion. Doubleday, 1944;
      Jarrolds, 1947 [Calif.]
    The Case of the Foster Father. Double-
      day, 1942; Jarrolds, 1946 EB [L.A.]
    The Case of the Grieving Monkey.
      Doubleday, 1941 EB [L.A.]
    He Fell Down Dead. Doubleday, 1943;
      Jarrolds, 1944 [L.A.]

    The Singing Clock. Doubleday, 1941;
      Jarrolds, 1945 [Chi.]

PEREIRA, MICHAEL (NICHOLAS O'DONNELL).
  1928-   .
    An Angel Came Down. Bles, 1966
    Brought to Bay. Bles, 1974
    An Echo from Silence. Hale, 1968
    Equal Antagonism. Collins, 1975
    The Fifth Answer. Bles, 1969
    Masquerade. Collins, 1973
    Pigeon's Blood. Bles, 1970
    -A River Grown Deep. Hutchinson, 1959
    Second Cousin Twice Removed. Collins,
      1974
    The Singing Millionaire. Collins, 1972
      [Mars.]
    Stranger in the Land. Bles, 1967
    When One Door Shuts. Bles, 1969

PERELLI, M.
    Blind Murder. Scion, 1952
    Blonde for Danger. Scion, 1952
    Body Ran Home. Locker, 1950
    A Dame Doles Death. Scion, 1953
    Nothing to Hide. Scion, 1952
    She Sure Slipped. Scion, 1952
    Some Dames Don't. Scion, 1952
    Take It Easy. Milestone, 1953
    Two Dames Too Many. Scion, 1952

PERELMAN, S(IDNEY) J(OSEPH). 1904-   .
  Ref: CA.
    The Ill-Tempered Clavicord. Simon,
      1952; Reinhardt, 1953 ss, some
      criminous
    Keep It Crisp. Random, 1946; Heinemann,
      1947 ss, some criminous

PERKINS, FREDERICK B(EECHER). 1828-1899.
    Scrope; or, The Lost Library. Roberts,
      1874

PERKINS, KENNETH. 1890-1951.
    -Gold. Stokes, 1929; Hutchinson, 1930
    The Horror of the Juvenal Manse; see
      Voodoo'd
    The Mark of the Moccasin; see The Moc-
      casin Murders
    The Moccasin Murders. King, 1931. Bri-
      tish title: The Mark of the Moccasin.
      Paul, 1929 [Tex.]
    -Queen of the Night. McClurg, 1925
    Voodoo'd. Harper, 1931. British title:
      The Horror of the Juvenal Manse.
      Hutchinson, 1931 [New Or.]

PEROWNE, BARRY. Pseudonym of Philip
  Atkey, 1908-   , q.v. SC: Sexton
  Blake (with many other authors) =
  SB; J. R. (Rick) Leroy = JL; A. J.
  Raffles (following E. W. Hornung,
  1866-1921, q.v.) = AR. Set: Eng.
    All Exits Blocked; see Gibraltar Pri-
      soner
    The A.R.P. Mystery. Amalgamated, 1939
      AR
    Arrest These Men! Cassell, 1932 JL
    Ask No Mercy. Cassell, 1937
    Blonde Without Escort. Cassell, 1940
    Enemy of Women. Cassell, 1934
    Gibraltar Prisoner. Cassell, 1942. U.S.
      title: All Exits Blocked. Mystery
      House, 1942 [Gib.]
    The Girl on Zero. Cassell, 1939
    I'm No Murderer. Cassell, 1938; Hill-
      man-Curl, 1939 JL
    Ladies in Retreat. Cassell, 1935
    Raffles After Dark. Cassell, 1933. U.S.
      title: The Return of Raffles. Day,
      1933 AR
    Raffles and the Key Man. Lippincott,
      1940 AR,JL
    Raffles' Crime in Gibraltar. Amalgama-
      ted, 1937 AR,SB U.S. title: They
      Hang Them in Gibraltar. Hillman-Curl,
      1939 AR,JL (SB not in U.S. edition.)
      [Gib.]
    Raffles in Pursuit. Cassell, 1934 AR
      (4 novelets.)
    Raffles of the Albany. H. Hamilton,
      1976; St. Martin's, 1977 ss AR
      [Eng., ca.1900]
    Raffles of the M.C.C. Macmillan (Lon-
      don), 1979; St. Martin's, 1979 ss
      AR [Eng., 1905]
    Raffles Revisited. Harper, 1974; H.
      Hamilton, 1975 AR ss
    Raffles Under Sentence. Cassell, 1936
      AR (4 novelets.)
    Raffles vs. Sexton Blake. Amalgamated,
      1937 AR,SB
    The Return of Raffles; see Raffles
      After Dark
    Rogues' Island; see The Tilted Moon
    She Married Raffles. Cassell, 1936 AR
    A Singular Conspiracy. Bobbs, 1974
      [Paris, 1844]
    Ten Words of Poison; see The Whispering
      Cracksman
    They Hang Them in Gibraltar; see Raf-
      fles' Crime in Gibraltar

The Tilted Moon. Cassell, 1949. U.S. title: Rogues' Island. Mill, 1950 [Sp.]
The Whispering Cracksman. Cassell, 1940. U.S. title: Ten Words of Poison. Arcadia, 1941

PERRAULT, E(RNEST) G.
Spoil! Doubleday, 1975; Collins, 1976 [Arctic]
The Twelfth Mile. Doubleday, 1972; Collins, 1973

PERRAULT, GILLES. 1931- .
Dossier 51. Weidenfeld, 1971; Morrow, 1971 (Translation of "Le Dossier 51." Paris, 1969.)

PERREAU-SAUSSINE, GERALD. 1938- .
Pseudonym: Richard Miles, q.v.

PERRELLI, NICK
At Dead of Night. Milestone, 1954
A Dame Dies Greedy. Milestone, 1953
Dead on Time. Milestone, 1954
Rita Takes a Ride. Tempest, 1950
Sweet and Low. Milestone, 1954
Terror in Tokyo. Tempest, 1950 [Tokyo]
Virgins Die Lonely. Tempest, 1949
Virgin's Vendetta. Tempest, 1950
Who Told the Belle? Scion, 1953

PERRETT, GEOFFREY. 1940- . Ref: CA.
Executive Privilege. Coward, 1974 [Wash. D.C.]

PERRIN, FORREST V. Pseudonym: Nick Carter, q.v.
The Don. Award, 1971 [NYC]

PERRIN, ROBERT. 1939- . Journalist with BBC in London.
Jewels. Routledge, 1977; Stein, 1979 [Dublin, 1907]

PERRING, DOUGLAS
The Apostles of Violence. Hale, 1957

PERROT, IRENE
Freedom from Fear. Stockwell, 1975

PERRY, ANNE. 1938- . Ref: CA. SC: Charlotte Ellison (Pitt) and Insp. Thomas Pitt, in both titles.
Callander Square. Hale, 1980; St. Martin's, 1980 [ca.1882, Eng.]
The Cater Street Hangman. Hale, 1979; St. Martin's, 1979 [1881, Eng.]

PERRY, CHARLES E.
The Gables Mystery. Modern, 193?
In Satan's Bonds. Modern, 1935
Under the Spell of the Orient. Modern, 193?

PERRY, FRANK
The Mystery of the Girl in Blue. Dodge, 1938 [hosp.]

PERRY, GEORGE SESSIONS. 1910-1956. See: Dorothy Cameron Disney, 1903- .

PERRY, JAMES D(eWOLFF). 1895- .
Murder Walks the Corridors. Macmillan, 1937. British title: Corridors of Fear. Constable, 1937 [hosp.]

PERRY, PATRICIA
Deadly Memorial. Hale, 1973

PERRY, RITCHIE (JOHN ALLEN). 1942- .
Pseudonym: John Allen, q.v. SC: Philis, in all titles.
Bishop's Pawn. Collins, 1979; Pantheon, 1979
Dead End. Collins, 1977
Dutch Courage. Collins, 1978; Ballantine, 1982 [Holl.]
The Fall Guy. Collins, 1972; Houghton, 1972 [Brazil]
Grand Slam. Collins, 1980; Pantheon, 1980
A Hard Man to Kill; see Nowhere Man
Holiday with a Vengeance. Collins, 1974; Houghton, 1975 [Bahamas]
Nowhere Man. Collins, 1973. U.S. title: A Hard Man to Kill. Houghton, 1973
One Good Death Deserves Another. Collins, 1976; Houghton, 1977 [Brazil]
Ticket to Ride. Collins, 1973; Houghton, 1974
Your Money and Your Wife. Collins, 1975; Houghton, 1976 [Nor.]

PERRY, ROBIN. 1917- .
Welcome for a Hero. Livingston, 1975 [Wash. D.C., 1962]

PERRY, ROLAND 1946- .
Programme for a Puppet. Allen, 1979; Crown, 1980

PERRY, RUTH. 1892- .
The Greengage Summer. Dramatic, 1970 (3-act play based on a story by Rumer Godden, 1907- .)

PERRY, TYLINE. Set, both titles: Colo.
The Never Summer Mystery. King, 1932
The Owner Lies Dead. Covici, 1930; Gollancz, 1930

PERRY, V(ERONICA) M(ARGARET)
Murder Wears a Friendly Face. Hale, 1979

PERRY, WILL. Pseudonym of William John Weatherby. Ref: CA.
Death of an Informer. Pyramid, 1973; Robson, 1977, as by W. J. Weatherby
Home in the Dark. Pyramid, 1976; Robson, 1977, as by W. J. Weatherby [NYC]
The Kremlin Watcher. Dodd, 1978; Hale, 1978, as by W. J. Weatherby [NYC]
Murder at the U.N. Dodd, 1976; Robson, 1977, as by W. J. Weatherby [NYC]

PERSICO, JOSEPH E(DWARD). 1930- . Ref: CA.
The Spiderweb. Crown, 1979; Futura, 1981 [Ger., ca.1946]

PERTWEE, MICHAEL (HENRY ROLAND). 1916- .
Deadly Poison, with Roland Pertwee, 1885-1963, q.v. French, 1955 (Play.)
Night Was Our Friend. English Theatre, 1950 (2-act play.)

PERTWEE, ROLAND. 1885-1963. See also: Michael (Henry Roland) Pertwee, 1916- . Ref: CA, CC. Set: Eng.
-The Camelion's Dish. Davies, 1940
A Chalk Stream Killing. Jenkins, 1939
Death in a Domino. Houghton, 1932 (British title?)
Dirty Work. English Theatre Guild, 1954 (Play.)
-The Eagle and the Wren. Cassell, 1923
Expert Evidence. English Theatre Guild, 1946 (Play.)
Four Winds. Nicholson, 1935; Little, 1935
Gentlemen March; see The Romance of Nikko Cheyne
Hell's Loose; see The Million Pound Cipher
Interference. Cassell, 1927; Houghton, 1927. Play version: French, 1929
-It Means Mischief, with John Hastings Turner, 1892-1956. Heinemann, 1932
-May We Come Through? and other stories. Davies, 1940 ss
Men of Affairs. Knopf, 1922 (British title?)
The Million Pound Cipher. Heinemann, 1929. U.S. title: Hell's Loose. Houghton, 1929. Also published as: MW-XX.3. Heinemann, 1929
-Morosco. Nicholson, 1934
MW-XX.3; see The Million Pound Cipher
-No Such Word. Nicholson, 1934
Pink String and Sealing Wax. English Theatre, 1945; French (NYC), 1945 (3-act play.)
-A Prince of Romance. Heinemann, 1932
-Pursuit. Heinemann, 1930; Houghton, 1930
-Rivers to Cross. Cassell, 1926; Houghton, 1927
-The Romance of Nikko Cheyne. Cassell, 1927. U.S. title: Gentleman March. Houghton, 1927
-Royal Heritage. Houghton, 1931 (British title?)
-A South Sea Bubble. Cassell, 1924. U.S. title: Treasure Trail. Knopf, 1924
Such an Enmity. Nicholson, 1936; Little, 1936 [Fr.]
To Kill a Cat, with Harold Dearden. English Theatre Guild, 1939; Century, 1939 (3-act play.)
The Transactions of Lord Louis Lewis. Murray, 1917; Dodd, 1918 ss
Treasure Trail; see A South Sea Bubble

PERUTZ, LEO. 1884-1957. Ref: CC.
The Master of the Day of Judgment. Boni, 1930; Mathews, 1929 (Translation of "Der Meister des Jungsten Tages." Munich, 1923.)

PESKETT, S. JOHN. 1906- .
Murders at Turbot Towers. Butterworth, 1937

PETER, JOHN (DESMOND). 1921- . Born in S. Afr., educated there and at Cambridge; author of books of literary criticism; living and teaching at university in Can. in late 1960s.
Runaway. Doubleday, 1969 [S. Afr.]

PETERS, ALAN
-By Their Deeds. Heath, 1946
The Secret Formula. Heath, 1932
Who Killed the Doctors? Heath, 1933; Loring, 1934

PETERS, BILL. Pseudonym of William P(eter) McGivern, 1924-1982, q.v.
Blondes Die Young. Dodd, 1952; Foulsham, 1956 [Chi.]

PETERS, BRYAN. Pseudonym of Peter (Bryan) George, 1924-1966, q.v. Other pseudonym: Peter Bryant, q.v. SC: Anthony Brandon, in at least those marked AB.
The Big H. Boardman, 1961; Holt, 1963 AB [L.A.]
Hong Kong Kill. Boardman, 1958; Washburn, 1959 AB [H. Kong]
-Sons of Nippon. Digit, 1961
-Starbuck. Digit, 1957

PETERS, ELIZABETH. Pseudonym of Barbara Louise Gross Mertz, 1927- . Other pseudonym: Barbara Michaels, q.v. SC: Vicky Bliss = VB; Jacqueline Kirby = JK.
Borrower of the Night. Dodd, 1973; Cassell, 1974 VB [Ger.]
The Camelot Caper. Meredith, 1969; Cassell, 1976 [Eng.]
Crocodile on the Sandbank. Dodd, 1975; Cassell, 1976
The Dead Sea Cipher. Dodd, 1970; Cassell, 1975 [Mid. East]
Devil-May-Care. Dodd, 1977; Cassell, 1978 [Va.]
Ghost in Green Velvet; see Legend in Green Velvet
The Jackal's Head. Meredith, 1968; Jenkins, 1969 [Egypt]
Legend in Green Velvet. Dodd, 1976. British title: Ghost in Green Velvet. Cassell, 1977 [Scot.]
The Love Talker. Dodd, 1980; Souvenir, 1981 [Md.]
The Murders of Richard III. Dodd, 1974 JK [Eng.]
The Night of Four Hundred Rabbits. Dodd, 1971. British title: Shadows in the Moonlight. Coronet, 1975 [Mex.]
The Seventh Sinner. Dodd, 1972; Coronet, 1975 JK [Rome]
Shadows in the Moonlight; see The Night of Four Hundred Rabbits
Street of the Five Moons. Dodd, 1978 VB [Rome]
Summer of the Dragon. Dodd, 1979; Souvenir, 1980 [Ariz.]

PETERS, ELLIS. Pseudonym of Edith (Mary) Pargeter, 1913- , q.v. SC: Brother Cadfael = C, all set in 12th century Eng.; one or more members of the Felse family: Insp. George Felse, wife Bunty, son Dominic = F (see also Edith Pargeter entry). Set: Eng.
Black Is the Colour of My True Love's Heart. Collins, 1967; Morrow, 1967 F
City of Gold and Shadows. Macmillan (London), 1973; Morrow, 1974 F [Wales]
Death and the Joyful Woman. Collins, 1961; Doubleday, 1961 F
Death Mask. Collins, 1959; Doubleday, 1960
Death to the Landlords! Macmillan (London), 1972; Morrow, 1972 F [India]
Flight of a Witch. Collins, 1964 F
Funeral of Figaro. Collins, 1962; Morrow, 1964 [theatre]
The Grass-Widow's Tale. Collins, 1968; Morrow, 1968 F
The Horn of Roland. Macmillan (London), 1974; Morrow, 1974 [Austria]
The House of Green Turf. Collins, 1969; Morrow, 1969 F [Austria]
The Knocker on Death's Door. Macmillan (London), 1970; Morrow, 1971 F
Monk's Hood. Macmillan (London), 1980; Morrow, 1981 C
A Morbid Taste for Bones. Macmillan (London), 1977; Morrow, 1978 C
Mourning Raga. Macmillan (London), 1969; Morrow, 1970 F [New Delhi]
Never Pick Up Hitchhikers! Macmillan (London), 1976; Morrow, 1976
A Nice Derangement of Epitaphs. Collins, 1965. U.S. title: Who Lies Here? Morrow, 1965 F
One Corpse Too Many. Macmillan (London), 1979; Morrow, 1980 C
The Piper on the Mountain. Collins, 1966; Morrow, 1966 F [Czech.]
Rainbow's End. Macmillan (London), 1979; Morrow, 1979 F
Where There's a Will; see The Will and the Deed
Who Lies Here?; see A Nice Derangement of Epitaphs

The Will and the Deed. Collins, 1960.
U.S. title: Where There's a Will.
Doubleday, 1960. Reprinted in the
U.S. under the British title: Avon,
1966 [Austria]

PETERS, GEOFFREY. Pseudonym of Madelyn
Palmer, 1910-   , q.v. SC: Insp.
Trevor Nicholls, in all titles.
The Chill of a Corpse. Ward, 1968
The Claw of a Cat. Ward, 1964
The Eye of a Serpent. Ward, 1964
The Flick of a Fin. Ward, 1967
The Mark of a Buoy. Ward, 1967
[Australia]
The Twist of a Stick. Ward, 1966
[Australia]
The Whirl of a Bird. Ward, 1965

PETERS, HEATHER
House of Secrets. Avon, 1972

PETERS, L. T.   Joint pseudonym of Albert
S. Klainer and Jo-Ann Klainer, q.v.
The Eleventh Plague. Simon, 1973;
Secker, 1974. Reprinted under the
authors' real names: Pinnacle, 1975

PETERS, LUDOVIC. Pseudonym of Peter (Lud-
wig) Brent, 1931-   , q.v. SC: Ian
Firth, in at least those marked IF.
Set: Eng.
Cry Vengeance. Abelard (London & NYC),
1961 [Balkans]
Double Take. Hodder, 1968
Fall of Terror. Hodder, 1968
The Killing Game. Hodder, 1969
Out by the River. Hodder, 1964; Walker,
1965 IF
Riot '71. Hodder, 1967; Walker, 1967 IF
A Snatch of Music. Abelard (London &
NYC), 1962 IF
Tarakian. Abelard (London), 1964 IF; Abe-
lard (NYC), 1964 IF [Paris]
Two After Malic. Hodder, 1965; Walker,
1966 IF
Two Sets to Murder. Hodder, 1963; Cow-
ard, 1964 IF

PETERS, MAUREEN. 1935-   . Pseudonyms:
Veronica Black, Catherine Darby,
qq.v.

PETERS, OTHELLO
Satan's Daughters. Zebra, 1975. Also
published as: Whispers from the Dark
Side of Tomorrow. Zebra, 1977

PETERS, RON. SC: Stash Koval, in both
titles.
The Big Stash. Curtis, 1972 [NYC]
Stash Spots a Murder. Curtis, 1973
[NYC]

PETERSEN, HERMAN. 1893-   . SC: Doc
Miller = M.
The D.A.'s Daughter. Duell, 1943
[New Eng.]
Murder in the Making. McBride, 1940 M
Murder R.F.D. Duell, 1942 M
Old Bones. Duell, 1943; Swan, 1950 M

PETERSEN, JAN. 1907-   .
Gestapo Trial. Gollancz, 1939

PETERSON, AGNES EMELIE
The Eyes of Tlaloc. Row, 1936 (3-act
play.)

PETERSON, BERNARD. Pseudonym.
The Peripheral Spy. Collins, 1979; Putnam, 1980

PETERSON, JAMES
Arrivederci, Baby! Dell, 1966 (Novelization of the movie.)

PETERSON, JIM. Pseudonym of William (Elbert) Crawford, 1929-   , q.v. Other
pseudonyms: Roger Brandt, Paul Ross,
Steve Scott, qq.v. SC: Mack Bolan
(The Executioner), in the title below
and those by Don(ald Eugene) Pendleton, 1927-   , q.v.
Sicilian Slaughter. Pinnacle, 1973;
Corgi, 1973 [Sic.]

PETERSON, MARGARET (ANN). 1883-1933.
Pseudonym: Glint Green, q.v. Set:
Eng.
-Blind Eyes. Melrose, 1914
-Butterfly Wings. Hurst, 1916
-Dear, Lovely One! Benn, 1930
The Death Drum. Hurst, 1919
Death in Goblin Waters. Hutchinson,
1934
Every Cloud; see Poor Delights
The Eye of Isis. Hutchinson, 1931
Fatal Shadows. Hurst, 1917
-Fate and the Watcher. Hurst, 1917
Fear Shadowed. Hutchinson, 1927
The Feet of Death. Hutchinson, 1927

-The First Stone. Hurst, 1923
Green Stones of Evil. Melrose, 1921
Guilty, My Lord. Hutchinson, 1928
-Life—and a Fortnight. Benn, 1929
-Like a Rose. Benn, 1928
-Love Is Enough. Hurst, 1921
-Love's Burden. Hurst, 1918
-Love's Service. Hutchinson, 1932
Moonflowers. Hutchinson, 1926
-Ninon. Cassell, 1922
-Pamela and Her Lion Man. Hutchinson,
1926
-Passionate Particles. Benn, 1927
-The Pitiful Rebellion. Hurst, 1925
The Question. Benn, 1928
-Scarlet Blossoms. Hutchinson, 1927
-The Scent of the Rose. Cassell, 1923
-The Sword-Points of Love. Hurst, 1919
-Twice Broken. Hutchinson, 1933
-Twinkleface, the Merry Elf. Hutchinson,
1926
The Unknown Hand. Hurst, 1924

PETERSUNNE, RODDY RON. Pseudonym.
Safer Than Life. Vantage, 1979

PETERZEN, ELISABET. 1938-   .
Till Life Us Do Part. Wingate, 1970
(Translation of "Aktenskaps Brott."
Stockholm, 1969.)

PETRIE, GLEN
The Branch Bearers. Macmillan (London),
1973; Stein, 1973 [Eng., ca.1860]
-The Coming Out Party. Macmillan (London), 1972
-A Form of Release. Macmillan (London),
1971

PETRIE, RHONA. Pseudonym of Eileen-Marie
Duell Buchanan, 1922-   . Ref: CA,
CC, TC. SC: Insp. Marcus MacLurg, in
at least those marked MM; Nassim
Pride, in at least those marked NP.
Set: Eng.
Come Hell and High Water. Gollancz,
1970 ss
Dead Loss. Gollancz, 1966 MM
Death in Deakins Wood. Gollancz, 1963;
Dodd, 1964 MM
Despatch of a Dove. Gollancz, 1969 NP
Foreign Bodies. Gollancz, 1967 NP
MacLurg Goes West. Gollancz, 1968 MM
Murder by Precedent. Gollancz, 1964   MM
Running Deep. Gollancz, 1965   MM
Thorne in the Flesh. Gollancz, 1971

PETTEE, F(LORENCE) M(AE). 1888-   .
The Palgrave Mummy. Payson, 1929;
Skeffington, 1929
White Dominoes. Reilly, 1921

PETTERSSON, JULIUS. 1889-1925. Pseudonym: Julius Regis, q.v.

PETTIT, MIKE
The Axman Agenda. Dell, 1980; Sphere,
1982 [N.J.]

PETTIT, PAUL. 1911-   .
The Drug-Run. Barker, 1960
The Spaniard. Valentine, 1953; Harper,
1954

PETTRIDGE, WILLIAM. Pseudonym: Warwick
Simpson, q.v.

PETTY, BARBARA
Bad Blood. Dell, 1979
Thrill. Dell, 1977

PEVERETT, ALLAN
Death Stalks in Kenya. Stockwell, 1957
[Kenya]
The Lurking Terror. Stockwell, 1960

PEYRE, JOSEPH. 1892-1968.
A Matador Dies. Bles, 1937 (Translation of "Sang et Lumieres." Paris,
1935.)

PEYROU, MANUEL
Thunder of the Roses. Herder, 1972
(Translation of "El Estruendo de las
Rosas.")

PFALZGRAF, FLORENCE LEIGHTON. 1902-   .
Pseudonym: Florence Leighton, q.v.

PFLAUM, MELANIE (LOWENTHAL). 1909-   .
Ref: CA.
-Bolero. Heinemann, 1956; St. Martin's,
1957
The Insiders. Cassell, 1963
-Windfall. Cassell, 1962; British Book
Service, 1962

PHELAN, JIM [JAMES LEO PHELAN]. 1895-   .
Lifer. Davies, 1938
Murder by Numbers. Methuen, 1941

PHELPS, PAULINE and MARION SHORT, q.v.
The Ryerson Mystery. French (NYC), 1933
(3-act play.)

PHILIP, ALEX(ANDER) J(OHN). 1879-   .
Complete Change. Collins, 1926

PHILIP, J. C.
Memoirs of an Aberdeen Detective. Rose-
mont, 1903 ss

PHILIPS, (JOHN) AUSTIN (DRURY). 1875-
1947.
-The Boy at the Bank. Mills, 1928
-The Girl out in Corsica. Hutchinson,
1927 [Cors.]
The Man in the Night Mail Train. Hutch-
inson, 1927
-The Real Thing. Paul, 1933
-Somewhere in Sark. Selwyn, 1935
The Unknown Goddess. Hutchinson, 1929
-Were They Justified? Hutchinson, 1925

PHILIPS, GEORGE NORMAN. 1888?-   . A
surveyor. Pseudonym: Anthony Skene,
q.v. All titles below were published
by Amalgamated Press and feature
Sexton Blake. Set: Eng.
The Affair of the Seven Warnings. 1926
The Albino's Double. 1922
The Amazing Affair of the Renegade
Prince. 1925
The Case of the Crook M.P. 1929
The Case of the Rejuvenated Million-
aire. 1928. Reprinted in 1939 as by
Anthony Skene.
The Gangster's Revenge. 1930
The Giant City Swindle. 1927. Reprinted
in 1938 as by Anthony Skene.
The Man Who Squealed. 1929
The Mystery of the Shot P.C. 1928. Re-
printed in 1940 as by Anthony Skene.
The Mystery of the Swanley Viaduct.
1925. Reprinted in 1937 as by Anthony
Skene.
The Radium Profiteer. 1929
The Riddle of the Three Marked Men.
1930
The Roumanian Envoy. 1921
Victim of the Waterway. 1929

PHILIPS, JUDSON (PENTECOST). 1903-   .
Pseudonyms: Philip Owen, Hugh Pente-
cost, qq.v. Ref: CA, CC, EM, MP, TC.
SC: Coyle & Donovan = C&D; Carole
Trevor and Max Blythe = T&B; Peter
Styles = PS.
Backlash. Dodd, 1976; Gollancz, 1977
PS [Conn.]
The Black Glass City. Dodd, 1965; Gol-
lancz, 1965 PS [Conn.]
The Dead Can't Love. Dodd, 1963; Gol-
lancz, 1963 PS [NYC]
A Dead Ending. Dodd, 1962; Gollancz,
1963 [NYC]
Death Delivers a Postcard. Washburn,
1939; Hurst, 1940 T&B [L.I.]
Death Is a Dirty Trick. Dodd, 1980;
Hale, 1981 PS [NYC]
The Death Syndicate. Washburn, 1938;
Hurst, 1939 T&B [NYC]
Escape a Killer. Dodd, 1971; Gollancz,
1972 PS [Conn.]
Five Roads to Death. Dodd, 1977; Gol-
lancz, 1978 PS [NYC]
The Fourteenth Trump. Dodd, 1942; Hale,
1951 C&D [NYC]
Hot Summer Killing. Dodd, 1968; Gol-
lancz, 1969 PS [NYC]
Killer on the Catwalk. Dodd, 1959;
Gollancz, 1960 [NYC]
The Larkspur Conspiracy. Dodd, 1973;
Gollancz, 1974 PS [NYC]
The Laughter Trap. Dodd, 1964; Gol-
lancz, 1965 PS [Vt.]
A Murder Arranged. Dodd, 1978; Gol-
lancz, 1979 [New Eng.]
Murder Clear, Track Fast. Dodd, 1961;
Gollancz, 1962 [N.Y.]
Murder in Marble. Dodd, 1940; Hale,
1949 [Vt.]
Nightmare at Dawn. Dodd, 1970; Gol-
lancz, 1971 PS [Conn., acad.]
Odds on the Hot Seat. Dodd, 1941; Hale,
1946 C&D [NYC]
The Power Killers. Dodd, 1974; Gol-
lancz, 1975 PS [NYC, Conn.]
Red War, with Thomas M(arvin) John-
son, 1889-   . Doubleday, 1936
Thursday's Folly. Dodd, 1967; Gollancz,
1968 PS [Vt.]
The Twisted People. Dodd, 1965; Gol-
lancz, 1965 PS [Conn.]
The Vanishing Senator. Dodd, 1972; Gol-
lancz, 1973 PS
Walk a Crooked Mile. Dodd, 1975; Gol-
lancz, 1976 PS [NYC]
Whisper Town. Dodd, 1960; Gollancz,
1961
Why Murder? Dodd, 1979; Hale, 1980 PS
[NYC]
Wings of Madness. Dodd, 1966; Gol-
lancz, 1967 PS [Conn.]

PHILIPS, PAGE
    At Bay. Macaulay, 1914; Hodder, 1916
        (Novelization of the play by George
        Scarborough, q.v.) [Wash. D.C.]
PHILLIFENT, JOHN T(HOMAS). 1916-1976.
        Starred titles are novelizations of
        "Man from UNCLE" TV series.
    The Corfu Affair. Four Square, 1967;
        Ace, 1969 *
    The Lonely Man. Boardman, 1965
    The Mad Scientist Affair. Four Square,
        1966; Ace, 1966 * [Ire.]
    The Power Cube Affair. Four Square,
        1968; Ace, 1968 * [Eng.]
PHILLIPS, CAREY
    The Cape Cod Caper. Transition, 1969
        [Cape Cod]
PHILLIPS, CLYDE B.
    The Driver. Ballantine, 1978 (Noveli-
        zation of the movie.)
    Someone Killed Her Husband. Jove,
        1978; Futura, 1979 [NYC]
PHILLIPS, CONRAD. Set: Eng.
    Alone in the Grass. Barker, 1954
    The Barber's Wife. Barker, 1953
    Cry of the Dingo. Barker, 1956 ss
    Dolls with Sad Faces. Barker, 1957;
        Roy, 1957
    The Empty Cot. Barker, 1958
    Shadow Play. Barker, 1954
    The Siren and the Centaur. Langdon,
        1947
    Sunny Draper. Barker, 1956
    The Unrepentent. Barker, 1958; Roy,
        1958
    Walk in the Dark. Barker, 1955
PHILLIPS, DAVID ATLEE. 1922-   . Ref:
        CA.
    The Carlos Contract. Macmillan, 1978
PHILLIPS, DAVID GRAHAM. 1867-1911.
    The Master Rogue. McClure, 1903; Rich-
        ards, 1904 [NYC]
PHILLIPS, DENNIS (JOHN ANDREW). 1924-   .
    Pseudonyms: Peter Chambers, Peter
    Chester, qq.v. See also: W(illiam
    Arthur) Howard Baker, 1925-   .
    Ref: CA, CC.
    Revenge Incorporated. Hale, 1970
PHILLIPS, DERYCK. 1914-   .
    Design for Destruction. Whiting, 1966
PHILLIPS, GERALD WILLIAM. 1884-   .
    Pseudonym: John Huntingdon, q.v.
PHILLIPS, GORDON
    High Explosive. Nisbet, 1925; Dodd,
        1926
PHILLIPS, H(ENRY) LAWRENCE. 1868-   .
    Set: Eng.
    The Detective's Dilemma. Nelson, 1932
    -A Friendless Millionaire. Nelson, 1928
    The House of Secrets. Nelson, 1931
    The Moor Barn Mystery. Butterworth,
        1935
    The Park Mystery. Nelson, 1933
    The Tangle. Nelson, 1931
PHILLIPS, JAMES ATLEE. 1915-   . Pseudo-
        nym: Philip Atlee, q.v. Ref: TC. SC:
        Joe Gall = JG (see also Atlee entry).
    The Case of the Shivering Chorus Girls.
        Coward, 1942; Bodley Head, 1950 [NYC]
    The Deadly Mermaid. Dell, 1954 [Haiti]
    Pagoda. Macmillan, 1951; World's Work,
        1953 JG [Far East]
    Suitable for Framing. Macmillan, 1949;
        Bodley, 1952 [Mex.]
PHILLIPS, JEAN
    Day of Dark Memory. Lancer, 1970
    Greenwood. Lancer, 1965 [South, ca.
        1865]
    Hermit's Island. Lancer, 1967 [Maine]
    House of Darkness. Avon, 1971 [Mex.]
PHILLIPS, LEON. Pseudonym of Noel B(er-
        tram) Gerson, 1914-   , q.v. Other
        pseudonym: Samuel Edwards, q.v.
    Split Bamboo. Doubleday, 1966 [China]
PHILLIPS, LEON
    Fire in His Hand. Hale, 1979
    The Phoenix Reaction. Hale, 1980
PHILLIPS, MARK. Joint pseudonym of Larry
        M(ark) Harris, 1933-   , q.v., and
        Randall (Phillips) Garrett,
        1927-   , q.v. Other pseudonym of
        Larry M(ark) Harris: Laurence M. Jan-
        ifer, q.v. SC: Kenneth Malone, in all
        titles.

Brain Twister. Pyramid, 1962 [future]
The Impossibles. Pyramid, 1963 [1972,
    NYC]
Supermind. Pyramid, 1963 [1973]

PHILLIPS, MIKE
    The Payoff. Leisure, 1980
PHILLIPS, RUSSELL R.
    Death Smiles. Macaulay, 1936 [N.Y.]
PHILLIPS, STELLA. 1927-   . Ref: CA.
    SC: Insp. Matthew Furnival, in at
    least those marked MF. Set: Eng.
    Dear Brother, Here Departed. Hale, 1975
    Death in Arcady. Hale, 1969 MF
    Death in Sheep's Clothing. Hale, 1971;
        Walker, 1983 MF
    Death Makes the Scene. Hale, 1970 MF
    Down to Death. Hale, 1967 MF
    The Hidden Wrath. Hale, 1968; Walker,
        1982 MF
    Yet She Must Die. Hale, 1973
PHILLIPS, STEVEN. 1947-   . Ref: CA.
    Resisting Arrest. Doubleday, 1980; Mac-
        millan (London), 1980 [NYC]
PHILLIPS, WATTS. 1825-1874.
    The Hooded Snake: A story of the Secret
        Police. Ward, 1860
    Not Guilty. DeWitt, 187? (4-act play.)
    On the Jury. DeWitt, 187? (4-act play.)
    The Wentworth Mystery. Dicks, 18??
PHILLPOTTS, EDEN. 1862-1960. Pseudonym:
    Harrington Hext, q.v. Ref: CA, CC,
    EM, MC, MP, TC. SC: John Ringrose,
    in at least those marked JR; Avis
    Bryden = AB. Set: Eng.
    Address Unknown. Hutchinson, 1949
    -The American Prisoner. Methuen, 1904;
        Macmillan, 1903
    The Anniversary Murder; see Physician,
        Heal Thyself
    Awake Deborah! Methuen, 1940; Macmil-
        lan, 1941
    Black, White, and Brindled. Richards,
        1923; Macmillan, 1923 ss, some cri-
        minous
    Bred in the Bone. Hutchinson, 1932;
        Macmillan, 1933 AB
    -The Bronze Venus. Richards, 1921
    The Captain's Curio. Hutchinson, 1933;
        Macmillan, 1933
    The Changeling. Hutchinson, 1944
    A Close Call. Hutchinson, 1936; Macmil-
        lan, 1936
    A Clue from the Stars. Hutchinson,
        1932; Macmillan, 1932
    A Deed Without a Name. Hutchinson,
        1941; Macmillan, 1942
    Dilemma. Hutchinson, 1949
    Doubloons; see The Sinews of War
    The End of a Life. Arrowsmith, 1891
    The End of Count Rollo. Todd, 1943
        (From Peacock House and other mys-
        teries, q.v.)
    The End of Count Rollo and other sto-
        ries. Polybooks, 1946 (ss, extracted
        from Peacock House and other myster-
        ies, q.v.)
    Fancy Free. Methuen, 1901 ss, one
        criminous
    -A Fight to a Finish. Cassell, 1911
    Flower of the Gods. Hutchinson, 1942;
        Macmillan, 1943
    "Found Drowned". Hutchinson, 1931; Mac-
        millan, 1931
    George and Georgina. Hutchinson, 1952
    Ghostwater. Methuen, 1941; Macmillan,
        1941
    The Grey Room. Hurst, 1921; Macmillan,
        1921
    The Hidden Hand. Hutchinson, 1952
    -His Brother's Keeper. Hutchinson, 1952
    Jig-Saw; see The Marylebone Miser
    The Judge's Chair. Murray, 1914 ss
    The Jury. Hutchinson, 1927; Macmillan,
        1927
    Loup-Garou! Sands, 1899 ss, some cri-
        minous
    Lycanthrope, the Mystery of Sir William
        Wolf. Butterworth, 1937; Macmillan,
        1938
    The Marylebone Miser. Hutchinson, 1926.
        U.S. title: Jig-Saw. Macmillan, 1926
        JR
    The Master of Merripit. Ward, 1914
    Miser's Money. Heinemann, 1920; Macmil-
        lan, 1920
    Mr. Digweed & Mr. Lumb. Hutchinson,
        1933; Macmillan, 1934
    Monkshood. Methuen, 1939; Macmillan,
        1939
    My Adventure in the Flying Scotsman.
        Hogg, 1888; Aspen, 1976
    -Once Upon a Time. Hutchinson, 1936 ss
    Peacock House and other mysteries.
        Hutchinson, 1926; Macmillan, 1927 ss
    Physician, Heal Thyself! Hutchinson,
        1935. U.S. title: The Anniversary

    Murder. Dutton, 1936
    Portrait of a Scoundrel. Murray, 1938;
        Macmillan, 1938
    -Quartet. Hutchinson, 1946
    The Red Redmaynes. Hutchinson, 1923;
        Macmillan, 1922
    A Shadow Passes. Hutchinson, 1933; Mac-
        millan, 1934 AB
    The Sinews of War, with (Enoch) Arnold
        Bennett, 1867-1931, q.v. Laurie,
        1906. U.S. title: The Doubloons.
        McClure, 1906
    The Statue, with (Enoch) Arnold Ben-
        nett, 1867-1931, q.v. Cassell, 1908;
        Moffat Yard, 1908
    Tales of the Tenements. Murray, 1910;
        Lane, 1910 ss, some criminous
    There Was an Old Man. Hutchinson, 1959
    There Was an Old Woman. Hutchinson,
        1947
    They Were Seven. Hutchinson, 1944; Mac-
        millan, 1945
    The Three Knaves. Macmillan (London),
        1912
    -Through a Glass Darkly. Hutchinson,
        1951
    A Tiger's Cub. Arrowsmith, 1892
    The Transit of the Red Dragon, and
        other tales. Arrowsmith, 1903
        (3 novelets.)
    The Unlucky Number. Newnes, 1906 ss
    A Voice from the Dark. Hutchinson,
        1925; Macmillan, 1925 JR
    The Wife of Elias. Hutchinson, 1935;
        Dutton, 1937
    Witch's Cauldron. Hutchinson, 1933;
        Macmillan, 1933 AB
PHILMORE, R. Pseudonym of Herbert Edmund
    Howard, 1900-   . SC: Insp. Garnett
    = G; Swan = S. Set: Eng.
    Death in Arms. Collins, 1939 G
    The Good Books. Gollancz, 1936 S
    Journey Downstairs. Gollancz, 1934;
        Doubleday, 1934 S
    No Mourning in the Family. Collins,
        1937 S
    Procession of Two. Collins, 1940 G
    Riot Act. Gollancz, 1935 S
    Short List. Collins, 1938 S
PHIPPS, SARAH E.
    The Old House by the Sea. Neely, 1901
PHRAILE, LORIMER
    I Am Being Poisoned. Swan, 1947
PICANO, FELICE. 1944-   . Ref: CA.
    The Lure. Delacorte, 1979; New English
        Library, 1981 [NYC]
PICARD, SAM. SC: John Scott, in all
    titles.
    Dead Man Running. Award, 1971
    The Man Who Never Was. Award, 1971
    The Notebooks. Award, 1969; Tandem,
        1970 [Wash. D.C.]
PICI, J. R.
    The Phoney Hitman. Major, 1977
PICKERING, EDITH
    Murder of a Headmistress. Longmans,
        1937
PICKERING, R(OBERT) E(ASTON). 1934-   .
    Ref: CA, CC.
    Himself Again. Gollancz, 1966. U.S.
        title: The Uncommitted Man. Farrar,
        1967 [Vienna, Buda.]
PICKERING, YORKE
    -The Dancing Water. Gifford, 1944
    -No Sweet Aspersion. Gifford, 1946
    A Shadow Passes. Gifford, 1949
PICKERSGILL, JOSHUA
    The Three Brothers. Stockdale, 1803
PICTON, BERNARD. Pseudonym of Bernard
    Knight, 1931-   . Ref: CA. Set: Eng.
    The Expert. Sphere, 1976 (Novelization
        of the BBC TV series.)
    The Lately Deceased. Jenkins, 1963
    Mistress Murder. Hale, 1966
    Policeman's Progress. Hale, 1969
    Russian Roulette. Hale, 1968
    The Thread of Evidence. Hale, 1965
    Tiger at Bay. Hale, 1970
PIDGIN, CHARLES FELTON. 1844-1923. Ref:
    EM. SC: Quincy Adams Sawyer = QS.
    The Chronicles of Quincy Adams Sawyer,
        Detective, with J(ohn) M. Taylor,
        1888-   . Page, 1912 QS ss
    The Further Adventures of Quincy Adams
        Sawyer. Page, 1909 QS
    The Hidden Man. Mayhew, 1906 [Mass.]
PIERCE, GILBERT A(SHVILLE). 1841-1901.
    A Dangerous Woman. Donnelly, 1884

PIERCE, JOHN LEONARD, JR. 1921- .
    Pseudonym: John Bramlett, q.v.

PIERCE, NOEL. 1907- .
    Messenger from Munich. Coward, 1973
    Praetorius Point. Coward, 1978

PIERCE, RICHARD
    Run, Traitor, Run. Lancer, 1968 [Rome]

PIERSON, ELEANOR. 1903- . Wife of a
    President of the U.S. Export-Import
    Bank.
    The Defense Rests. Howell Soskin, 1942.
    Also published as: Murder Without
    Clues. Mystery Novel Classic, 1943
    [Wash. D.C.]
    The Good Neighbor Murder. Howell Soskin, 1941 [Rio de J.]
    Murder Without Clues; see The Defense
    Rests

PIERSON, ERNEST DeLANCEY
    -A Bargain in Souls. Laird, 1892. Also
    published as: An Uncle from India.
    Laird, 1897
    -The Black Ball. Belford, 1889
    A Dangerous Quest. Street (Magnet)
    A Hidden Clue. Street (Magnet)
    The Lady of the Lilacs. Street (Magnet)
    The Missing Cashier. Street (Magnet)
    The Portland Place Mystery. Street
    (Magnet)
    The Secret of the Diamond. Street (Magnet)
    The Secret of the Marionettes. National
    Book Co., 1892
    -The Shadow of the Bars. Belford, 1888
    -A Slave of Circumstances. Belford, 1888
    Stairs of Sand. Street (Magnet)
    An Uncle from India; see A Bargain in
    Souls
    -A Vagabond's Honor. Belford, 1889

PIERSON, TOBY W.
    The Yellow Fetish. Vantage, 1979

PIFER, DRURY L. Born in S. Afr. of American parents; naval aviator and helicopter pilot; living in Calif. in 1970.
    Circle of Women. Doubleday, 1970;
    Secker, 1970

PIGGOTT, WILLIAM CHARTER. 1870-1943.
    Pseudonym: Hubert Wales, q.v.

PIKE, ROBERT L. Pseudonym of Robert
    L(loyd) Fish, 1912-1981, q.v. See
    also: Jack London, 1876-1916. SC:
    Lt. Clancy = C; Lt. Jim Reardon = JR.
    Bank Job. Doubleday, 1974; Hale, 1975
    JR [S.F.]
    Bullitt; see Mute Witness
    Deadline 2 A.M. Doubleday, 1976; Hale,
    1977 JR [S.F.]
    The Gremlin's Grampa. Doubleday, 1972
    JR [S.F.]
    Mute Witness. Doubleday, 1963; Deutsch,
    1965. Also published as: Bullitt.
    Avon, 1968; Penguin, 1969 C [NYC]
    Police Blotter. Doubleday, 1965;
    Deutsch, 1966 C [NYC]
    The Quarry. Doubleday, 1964 C [NYC]
    Reardon. Doubleday, 1970 JR [S.F.]

PILCHER, ROSAMUNDE. 1924- . Ref: CA.
    Under Gemini. Collins, 1977; St. Martin's, 1976

PILEGGI, NICHOLAS
    Blye, Private Eye. Playboy, 1976

PILGRIM, CHAD
    The Silent Slain. Abelard (NYC & London), 1958 [New Eng., acad.]

PILKINGTON, MRS. (MARY HOPKINS). 1766-1839.
    The Accusing Spirit; or, DeCourcy and
    Eglantine. Lane, 1802

PILPEL, ROBERT H(ARRY). 1943- . Ref:
    CA.
    High Anxiety. Ace, 1977; Arrow, 1978
    (Novelization of the movie.)
    [Calif.]
    To the Honor of the Fleet. Atheneum,
    1979; Weidenfeld, 1980 [ship, 1912]

PIM, SHEILA. 1909- . Ref: CC.
    A Brush with Death. Hodder, 1950
    Common or Garden Crime. Hodder, 1945
    [Ire.]
    Creeping Venom. Hodder, 1946
    A Hive of Suspects. Hodder, 1952; British Book Centre, 1953
    -Other People's Business. Hodder, 1957
    -The Sheltered Garden. Hodder, 1964

PINCHER, (HENRY) CHAPMAN. 1914- .
    Ref: CA.
    Dirty Tricks. Sidgwick, 1980; Stein,
    1981
    The Eye of the Tornado. Joseph, 1976
    The Four Horses. Joseph, 1978
    The Giantkiller. Weidenfeld, 1967
    Not with a Bang. Weidenfeld, 1965
    The Penthouse Conspirators. Joseph,
    1970
    The Skeleton at the Villa Wolkonsky.
    Joseph, 1975

PINCHOT, ANN
    The Twisted Cross. Paperback Library,
    1964

PINE, WILLIAM. Pseudonym of Terry Harknett, 1936- , q.v. Other pseudonyms: Joseph Hedges, Thomas H. Stone,
    William Terry, qq.v.
    The Protectors. Constable, 1967

PINGET, ROBERT. 1919- . Ref: CA.
    The Inquisitory. Calder, 1966; Grove,
    1967 (Translation of "L'Inquisitoire." Paris, 1962.)
    Recurrent Melody. Calder, 1975 (Translation of "Passacaille." Paris,
    1969.)

PINK, HAL. SC: Sgt./Insp. Docker, in at
    least those marked D. Set: Eng.
    The Black Sombrero Mystery. Hutchinson,
    1940
    The Cossack Mystery. Mellifont, 1934
    The Fellowship of the Feather. Mellifont, 1933
    The Gas Mask Gang. Mellifont, 1933
    The Green Triangle Mystery. Hutchinson,
    1938 D
    -The Heritage of Kid McCleod. Mellifont,
    1932
    -Jean of the Lazy J Ranch. Mellifont,
    1932
    The Masked Terror. Mellifont, 1933
    -The Rattlesnake. Mellifont, 1934
    The Rodeo Murder Mystery. Hutchinson,
    1941 D
    The Secret Service Mystery. Mellifont,
    1936
    The Strelsen Castle Mystery. Hutchinson, 1939
    The Test Match Mystery. Hutchinson,
    1940 D

PINKERTON, A. FRANK. Byline sometimes:
    Frank Pinkerton. Pseudonym: Detective
    Patrick Ryan, q.v.
    Cornered at Last; see Five Thousand
    Dollars Reward
    The Crime of the Midnight Express; see
    Dyke Darrel, the Railroad Detective
    Dyke Darrel, the Railroad Detective;
    or, The Crime of the Midnight Express. Laird, 1886. British title:
    The Crime of the Midnight Express.
    Routledge, 1887. Also published as:
    A Race for Life. Laird, 1898 [Chi.]
    Five Thousand Dollars Reward; or, Cornered at Last. Laird, 1886. British
    title: Cornered at Last. Routledge,
    1887
    The Great Adams Express Robbery; see
    Jim Cummings
    Jim Cummings; or, The Great Adams Express Robbery. Laird, 1887. British
    title: The Great Adams Express Robbery. Routledge, 1887 [Chi.]
    Marked for Life; or, The Gambler's
    Fate. Laird, 1887 [Chi.]
    A Race for Life; see Dyke Darrel, the
    Railroad Detective
    Saved at the Scaffold; or, Nic Brown,
    the Chicago Detective. Laird, 1888
    [Chi.]
    The Whitechapel Murders; or, An American Detective in London. Laird, 1889
    [Eng.]

PINKERTON, ALLAN. 1819-1884. Ref: EM.
    Bank-Robbers and the Detectives. Carleton, 1883
    Bucholz and the Detectives. Carleton,
    1880
    The Burglar's Fate and the Detectives.
    Carleton, 1883
    Claude Melnotte As a Detective, and
    other stories. Keen, 1875 ss
    Criminal Reminiscences and Detective
    Sketches. Carleton, 1879 ss
    The Detective and the Somnambulist.
    Keen, 1875. Also published as: The
    Somnambulist and the Detective.
    Carleton, 1884
    A Double Life and the Detectives.
    Carleton, 1884
    The Expressman and the Detective. Keen,
    1874
    The Gypsies and the Detectives. Carleton, 1879
    Mississippi Outlaws and the Detectives.
    Carleton, 1879 (3 novelets.)
    The Model Town and the Detectives.
    Carleton, 1876
    The Molly Maguires and the Detectives.
    Carleton, 1877
    Professional Thieves and the Detective.
    Carleton, 1881
    The Rail-Road Forger and the Detectives. Carleton, 1881
    The Somnambulist and the Detective; see
    The Detective and the Somnambulist
    The Spiritualists and the Detectives.
    Carleton, 1877
    Strikers, Communists, Tramps and Detectives. Carleton, 1878

PINKERTON, FRANK. See: A. Frank Pinkerton

PINKERTON, MYRON
    The Creole's Crime; see A Woman's Revenge
    The Rokewood Tragedy; see The Stolen
    Will
    The Stolen Will; or, The Rokewood Tragedy. Laird, 1887. British title: The
    Rokewood Tragedy. Routledge, 1887
    A Woman's Revenge; or, The Creole's
    Crime. Laird, 1887. British title:
    The Creole's Crime. Routledge, 1887
    [New Or.]

PINKHAM, WALTER. In U.S. Army for 20
    years, involved with data processing/
    computers in Army and industry.
    The Second Oldest Profession. Vantage,
    1979 [Ger.]

PINSENT, ELLEN F(RANCES PARKER).
    1866- .
    Jenny's Case. Swan, 1892

PINTORO, JOHN. 1947- . Ref: CA.
    The Summoning. Avon, 1979

PIPER, EVELYN. Pseudonym of Merriam
    Modell, 1908- . Ref: TC.
    Bunny Lake Is Missing. Harper, 1957;
    Secker, 1958
    Death of a Nymph; see The Motive
    Hanno's Doll. Atheneum, 1961; Secker,
    1962
    The Innocent. Simon, 1949; Boardman,
    1951 [NYC]
    The Lady and Her Doctor. Doubleday,
    1956
    The Motive. Simon, 1950; Boardman,
    1951. Also published as: Death of a
    Nymph. Mercury, 1951 [NYC]
    The Naked Murderer. Atheneum, 1962
    [NYC]
    The Nanny. Atheneum, 1964; Secker, 1965
    [NYC]
    The Plot. Simon, 1951; Boardman, 1952
    [S.C.]
    The Stand-In. Washburn, 1970 [Eng.]

PIPER, H(ENRY) BEAM. 1904-1964. Born in
    Pa., employed on Pennsylvania Railroad; science fiction writer.
    Murder in the Gunroom. Knopf, 1953

PIPER, PETER. Pseudonym of Theo Lang,
    q.v. Newspaperman. SC: Insp. Gray,
    in at least those marked G.
    The Corpse That Came Back; see Death in
    the Canongate
    Death Came in Straw. Hurst, 1945
    Death in the Canongate. Hodder, 1952.
    U.S. title: The Corpse That Came
    Back. Random, 1954 G [Edin.]
    Margot Leck. Hurst, 1947 [Eng., 1880s]
    Murder After the Blitz. Hurst, 1943 G
    The Woman Delia. Hodder, 1957

PIRIE, DAVID (TARBAT). 1946- . Ref:
    CA.
    Mystery Story. Muller, 1980

PIRKIS, C(ATHERINE) L(OUISA). -1910.
    Ref: MP.
    A Dateless Bargain. Hurst, 1887; Appleton, 1887
    The Experiences of Loveday Brooke, Lady
    Detective. Hutchinson, 1894 ss

PITCAIRN, JOHN JAMES. 1860-1936. Joint
    pseudonym with R(ichard) Austin Freeman, 1862-1943, q.v.: Clifford Ashdown, q.v.

PITMAN, WILLIAM DENT
    The Quincunx Case. Turner, 1904; Richards, 1904

PITT, FRANKLIN
    Brothers of the Thin Wire. Street, 1915

PITT, INGRID
    Cuckoo Run. Futura, 1980

PITT, ROXANE
The Month of the Evil Moon. Bachman, 1977 [Sing.]

PITTINGER, VIRGINIA
Wait Until Midnight. Playboy, 1978

PITTS, DENIS (TREWIN). 1930- . Ref: CA.
The Predator. Mason/Charter, 1976; Hale, 1977
Rogue Hercules. Atheneum, 1978; Hodder, 1977 [Afr., E.]
Target Manhattan; see This City Is Ours
This City Is Ours. Mason/Charter, 1975. British title: Target Manhattan. Hodder, 1976 [NYC]

PLAGEMANN, BENTZ. 1913- . Ref: CA.
The Boxwood Maze. Saturday Review Press, 1972 [N.Y.]
Wolfe's Cloister. Saturday Review Press, 1974 [Pa.]

PLAIN, JOSEPHINE. SC: Colin Anstruther, in all titles.
The Pazenger Problem. Butterworth, 1936
The Secret of the Sandbanks. Butterworth, 1934
The Secret of the Snows. Butterworth, 1935 [Switz.]

PLANTZ, DONALD. Born in N.Y.; variously employed as newspaperman, free-lance writer, operator of advertising agency.
Marked for Death. Monarch, 1964 [Carib.]

PLATER, ALAN (FREDERICK). 1935- . Ref: CA.
You and Me. Blackie, 1973 (Plays, one criminous.)

PLATT, CHARLES. See: Lilian Bamburg.

PLATT, CHARLES. 1944- .
Sweet Evil. Berkley, 1977

PLATT, EDWARD. Pseudonym: Paul Trent, q.v.

PLATT, KIN. 1911- . Ref: CA. SC: Max Roper = MR.
The Body Beautiful Murder. Random, 1976; Hale, 1977 MR [L.A.]
Dead As They Come. Random, 1972; Hale, 1974 [NYC]
The Giant Kill. Random, 1974; Hale, 1975 MR [L.A.]
The Kissing Gourami. Random, 1970; Hale, 1973 MR [L.A.]
Match Point for Murder. Random, 1975 MR [L.A.]
A Pride of Women; see The Princess Stakes Murder
The Princess Stakes Murder. Random, 1973. British title: A Pride of Women. Hale, 1974. Reprinted in Britain under the U.S. title: Hale, 1977 MR [Calif.]
The Pushbutton Butterfly. Random, 1970; Hale, 1971 MR [Calif.]
The Screwball King Murder. Random, 1978 MR [L.A.]

PLATT, ROBERT. 1894- .
The Swaying Corpse. Phoenix, 1941 [NYC]

PLAYER, ROBERT. Pseudonym of Robert Furneaux Jordan, 1905-1978. Ref: MC, TC. Set: Eng.
The Homicidal Colonel. Gollancz, 1970
The Ingenious Mr. Stone. Gollancz, 1945; Rinehart, 1946
Let's Talk of Graves, of Worms, and Epitaphs. Gollancz, 1975
The Month of the Mangled Models. Gollancz, 1977 [Eng., 1800s]
Oh! Where Are Bloody Mary's Earrings? Gollancz, 1972; Harper, 1973

PLAYFAIR, JOCELYN
Murder Without Mystery. Hodder, 1939

PLEASANTS, W. SHEPARD
The Stingaree Murders. Mystery League, 1932 [ship]

PLEYDELL, GEORGE. Pseudonym of George Pleydell Bancroft, 1868-1956.
The Ware Case. Methuen, 1913; Doran, 1913

PLOMER, WILLIAM (CHARLES FRANKLYN). 1903-1973. Ref: CA.
The Case Is Altered. Woolf, 1932; Farrar, 1932

PLOMLEY, ROY
Murder Without Malice. Evans, 1955 (1-act play.)
Two Bottles of Relish. French (London), 1961 (1-act play based on the story by Lord Dunsany, 1878-1957, q.v.)

PLUM, JENNIFER. Pseudonym of Michael (J.) Kurland, 1938- , q.v.
The Secret of Benjamin Square. Belmont, 1972 [Eng., 1800s]

PLUM, MARY. SC: John Smith = JS.
The Broken Vase Mystery; see Murder at the World's Fair
Dead Man's Secret. Harper, 1931; Eyre, 1931 JS [Ill.]
The Killing of Judge McFarlane. Harper, 1930; Eyre, 1930 JS [Chi.]
Murder at the Hunting Club. Harper, 1932; Eyre, 1932 JS [Mich.]
Murder at the World's Fair. Harper, 1933. British title: The Broken Vase Mystery. Eyre, 1933 JS [Chi.]
Murder of a Redhaired Man. Arcadia, 1952; Eyre, 1951 [Wash. D.C.]
State Department Cat. Doubleday, 1945; Eyre, 1946 [Wash. D.C.]
Susanna, Don't You Cry! Doubleday, 1946 [Ia.]

PLUMMER, T(HOMAS) ARTHUR. Pseudonym: Michael Sarne, q.v. SC: Det. Insp. Andrew Frampton, in at least those marked AF. Set: Eng.
The Ace of Death. Paul, 1930
Alias—The Crimson Snake. Paul, 1933
The Barush Mystery. Paul, 1946 AF
The Black Rat. Paul, 1955 AF
The Black Ribbon Murders. Paul, 1940 AF
The Bonfire Murder; see Was the Mayor Murdered?
"Brent"—of Bleak House. Paul, 1948
The Broken Trust. Thomson, 1929
Condemned to Live. Paul, 1957 AF
Cornered. Leng, 1938
Creaking Gallows. Paul, 1934
Crime at Crooked Gables. Paul, 1941 AF
Death Haunts the Repertory. Paul, 1950 [theatre]
The Death Letter. Paul, 1951
Death on Danger Hill. Paul, 1931
The Death Symbol. Paul, 1937 AF
Death Takes a Hand. Paul, 1934
The Devil's Tea-Party. Paul, 1942 AF
The Dumb Witness. Paul, 1936; Macaulay, 1936 AF
The Elusive Killer. Long, 1958 AF
Five Were Murdered. Paul, 1938 AF
The Fool of the "Yard". Paul, 1942 AF
Frampton—of "The Yard"! Paul, 1935; Maculay, 1935 AF
Frampton Sees Red. Paul, 1953 AF
-The Girl in a Hurry. Thomson, 1932
Haunting Lights. Paul, 1932
-Her Own Affair. Leng, 1939
The Hospital Thief. Long, 1959 AF
The House in Sinister Lane. Paul, 1931
Hunted! Paul, 1948 AF
The "J for Jennie" Murders. Paul, 1945 AF
Lonely Hollow Mystery. Paul, 1933
-Lying Lips. Leng, 1938
The Man They Feared. Paul, 1937 AF
The Man They Put Away. Paul, 1938 AF
The Man Who Changed His Face. Paul, 1943 AF
The Man with the Crooked Arm. Paul, 1945 AF
-Margaret Benson's View. Leng, 1934
Melody of Death. Paul, 1940 AF
Murder at Brownhill. Long, 1946 AF
Murder at Lantern Corner. Long, 1957 AF
Murder at Marlington. Paul, 1951
Murder—by an Idiot. Paul, 1944 AF
The Murder House. Paul, 1930
Murder in the Surgery. Paul, 1955 AF
Murder in the Village. Paul, 1945 AF
Murder in Windy Coppice. Paul, 1954 AF
Murder Limps By. Paul, 1943 AF
The Murder of Doctor Grey. Paul, 1950 AF
Murder Through Room 45. Paul, 1952 AF
The Muse Theatre Murder. Paul, 1939 AF [theatre]
Pagan Joe. Paul, 1956 AF
The Pierced Ear Murders. Paul, 1947 AF
A Scream at Midnight. Paul, 1954 AF
Shadowed by the C.I.D. Paul, 1932 AF
Shot at Night. Paul, 1934 AF
The Silent Four. Paul, 1947 AF
Simon Takes "the Rap". Paul, 1944 AF
The Spider Man. Long, 1961 AF
Staring Eyes! Paul, 1935
The Starry Eyed Murder. Paul, 1952
The Strangler. Paul, 1945 AF
Strychnine for One. Paul, 1949 AF
Two Men from the East. Paul, 1939 AF
The Vestry Murder. Long, 1959 AF
Was the Mayor Murdered? Paul, 1936. U.S. title: The Bonfire Murder. Macaulay, 1937 AF
The Westlade Murders. Paul, 1953 AF
Where Was Trail Murdered? Paul, 1956 AF
Who Fired the Factory? Paul, 1947 AF
The Yellow Disc Murders. Paul, 1950 AF

PLYMPTON, A(LMIRA) G(EORGE). 1852-1939.
A Willing Transgressor, and other stories. Roberts, 1897 ss

POATE, ERNEST M. Ref: CC, MP. SC: Dr. Bentiron = B.
Behind Locked Doors. Chelsea, 1923 B [NYC]
Doctor Bentiron: Detective. Chelsea, 1930 B (3 novelets.) [NYC]
Murder on the Brain. Chelsea, 1930 [N.Y.]
Pledged to the Dead. Chelsea, 1925
The Trouble at Pinelands. Chelsea, 1922 [N.C.]

POCOCK, ROGER (S.). 1865-1941.
The Cheerful Blackguard; see The Splendid Blackguard
The Dragon Slayer. Chapman, 1896. Also published as: Sword and Dragon. Hodder, 1909
The Splendid Blackguard. Murray, 1915. U.S. title: The Cheerful Blackguard. Bobbs, 1915
Sword and Dragon; see The Dragon Slayer

POE, EDGAR A(LLAN). 1809-1849. Ref: all except CA. See also: Robert Brome, 1917- ; and: Dorothy Rose Gribble; and: Walter Ben Hare, 1870-1950. SC: C. Auguste Dupin = D (see also: Michael Harrison, 1907-).
The Prose Romances of Edgar A. Poe. Graham, 1843 (Contains only "The Murders in the Rue Morgue", with D, in its first book appearance.)
Tales. Wiley and Putnam (NYC & London), 1845. (Contains, in addition to "Rue Morgue", first book appearances of the other two D stories, "The Mystery of Marie Roget" and "The Purloined Letter.")
The Works of the Late Edgar A. Poe. Volume II. Redfield, 1850. (Contains the first book appearance of "Thou Art the Man".)

POE, EDGAR ALLAN, JR. 1896- .
The House Party Murders. Lippincott, 1940 [Del.]

POHL, FREDERIK. 1919- . Ref: CA.
Edge of the City. Ballantine, 1957 (Novelization of the movie.)

POLK, DORA (BEALE). 1923- . Ref: CA.
The Gilt Feather. Doubleday, 1979
The House on the Black Moor. Beagle, 1972 [Eng.]
The Linnet Estate. McKay, 1973
Tower of the Crow. McKay, 1975 [Ire.]

POLK, JAMES K.
The Camelia Caper. Vantage, 1978

POLLAND, MADELEINE (ANGELA CAHILL). 1918- . Ref: CA.
The Little Spot of Bother. Hutchinson, 1967. U.S. title: Minutes of a Murder. Holt, 1967 [Ire.]
Minutes of a Murder; see The Little Spot of Bother
Package to Spain. Hutchinson, 1971; Walker, 1971 [Sp.]
-Random Army. Hutchinson, 1969
Thicker Than Water. Hutchinson, 1967; Holt, 1965 [Ire.]

POLLARD, CAPTAIN A(LFRED) O(LIVER). 1893- . Set: Eng.
A.R.P. Spy. Hutchinson, 1940
Air Reprisal. Hutchinson, 1938
Black Out. Hutchinson, 1938
Blood Hunt. Hutchinson, 1946
-The Cipher Five. Hutchinson, 1932
Counterfeit Spy. Hutchinson, 1952
Criminal Airman. Hutchinson, 1953
Dead Man's Secret. Hutchinson, 1949
A Deal in Death. Hutchinson, 1947 [Buen. A.]
The Death Curse. Hutchinson, 1948
The Death Flight. Hutchinson, 1932
The Death Game. Hutchinson, 1936 [S. Am.]
Death Intervened. Hutchinson, 1951
The Death Parade. Hutchinson, 1951
The Death Squadron. Hutchinson, 1943
Double-Cross. Hutchinson, 1946
The Fifth Freedom. Hutchinson, 1945 [Balkans]
Flanders Spy. Hutchinson, 1938
Forged Evidence. Long, 1962
Gestapo Fugitive. Hutchinson, 1944

The Havenhurst Affair. Hutchinson, 1933
Hidden Cipher. Hutchinson, 1937
Homicidal Spy. Hutchinson, 1954
Invitation to Death. Hutchinson, 1944
The Iron Curtain. Hutchinson, 1947
The Murder Germ. Hutchinson, 1937
Murder Hide-and-Seek. Hutchinson, 1931
Murder in the Air. Hutchinson, 1935
Murder of a Diplomat. Hutchinson, 1935
The Phantom 'Plane. Hutchinson, 1934
-Pirdale Island. Hutchinson, 1930
Red Hazard. Hutchinson, 1950
The Riddle of Loch Lemman. Hutchinson, 1933
Rum Alley. Hutchinson, 1931
The Secret Formula. Hutchinson, 1939
The Secret of Castle Voxzel. Hutchinson, 1935
The Secret Pact. Hutchinson, 1940
The Secret Vendetta. Hutchinson, 1949
The Secret Weapon. Hutchinson, 1941
Sinister Secret. Hutchinson, 1956 [Austria]
Smuggler's Buoy. Hutchinson, 1958
Unofficial Spy. Hutchinson, 1936
Wanted by the Gestapo. Hutchinson, 1942
Wrong Verdict. Long, 1960

POLLARD, PERCIVAL. 1869-1911. Ref: EM.
Lingo Dan. Neale, 1903 ss

POLLINI, FRANCIS
-Glover. Putnam, 1965; Spearman, 1965
Pretty Maids All in a Row. Delacorte, 1968; Spearman, 1969

POLLITZ, EDWARD A., JR. 1937-   . Pseudonym: Nick Christian, q.v. Born in NYC; securities analyst and consultant in corporate finance.
The Forty-First Thief. Delacorte, 1975; Hart-Davis, 1976 [Fr.]
-The 200% Rule. Bobbs, 1974; New English Library, 1975

POLLOCK, CHANNING. 1880-1946.
Synthetic Gentleman. Farrar, 1934

POLLOCK, COURTENAY (EDWARD MAXWELL). 1877-1943.
The Mystery of Rapallo. Methuen, 1919 [It.]

POLLOCK, GUY C(AMERON) and ANNE (WETZELL) ARMSTRONG
To See Ourselves. Hutchinson, 1936

POLLOCK, ROBERT. 1930-   . Ref: CA.
Loophole, or "How to Rob a Bank." Hodder, 1972; Dutton, 1973

POLLOCK, TED [THEODORE MARVIN POLLOCK]. 1929-   . Ref: CA.
The Rainbow Man. McGraw, 1979 [Utah]

POLLOCK, WALTER HERRIES. 1850-1926.
A Nine Men's Morrice. Longmans, 1889 ss, some criminous

POLONSKY, ABRAHAM LINCOLN. 1910-   . Ref: CA. Joint pseudonym with Mitchell A. Wilson, 1913-1973, q.v.: Emmett Hogarth, q.v.

POLSKY, THOMAS. 1908-   . SC: L. F. "Scoop" Griddle = SG.
The Cudgel. Dutton, 1950; Boardman, 1952 [N.C.]
Curtains for the Copper. Dutton, 1941 SG
Curtains for the Editor. Dutton, 1939 SG
Curtains for the Judge. Dutton, 1939 SG

POND, E. J.
The Ince Murder Case. Heritage, 1934

POND, RUTH POWER
The Oaks of Bashan. Dorrance, 1969

PONDER, PATRICIA
Haven of Fear. Manor, 1977
Murder for Charity. Manor, 1977

PONDER, ZITA INEZ
The Bandaged Face. Selwyn, 1927; Macaulay, 1929

PONS, MAURICE. 1927-   . Ref: CA.
Mademoiselle B. St. Martin's, 1974 (Translation of "Mademoiselle B." Paris, 1973.) [Fr.]

PONSONBY, DORIS ALMON. 1907-   . Pseudonym: Sara Tempest, q.v.

PONTHIER, FRANCOIS. Novelist and TV critic in Paris.
Assignment Basra. Cassell, 1969; McKay, 1969 (Translation of "Le Rendevous de Bassora." Paris, 1966.) [Mid.

East, 1940s]
The Harpoon. Cassell, 1969; McKay, 1970 (Translation of "Le Harpon." Paris, 1966.)

POOLE, HELEN LEE
The House of Clouds. Lancer, 1966

POOLE, MICHAEL. Pseudonym of Reginald Heber Poole, 1885-   , q.v. See also: F(rederick) H(aydn) Dimmock, 1895-   . SC: Freddie Browne and Jim Fanshaw = B&F. Set: Eng.
-Browne Fights the Fifth Column. Oxford, 1942 B&F
-Browne Follows the Clue. Oxford, 1936 B&F
-Browne of the Secret Service. Oxford, 1940 B&F
-Browne's £50,000 Mystery. Oxford, 1937 B&F
-Browne's First Case. Oxford, 1935 B&F
Death Follows the Trail. Melrose, 1935
Gang's Orders. Amalgamated Press, 1930 (Sexton Blake)
-The Gwythyn Clay Mystery. Oxford, 1940 B&F
Let Justice Be Done! Mellifont, 1946
-The Missing Bank Manager. Oxford, 1938 B&F
-Mystery at Merrilees. Oxford, 1939 B&F
The Roll Film Mystery. Crowther, 1941
-The Vanished Stamps Mystery. Oxford, 1941
-The Wagoner's Halt Mystery. Blackie, 1940

POOLE, REGINALD HEBER. 1885-   . Pseudonym: Michael Poole, q.v. See also: F(rederick) H(aydn) Dimmock, 1895-   . SC (with many other authors): Sexton Blake, in those titles without publisher below, which were issued by Amalgamated Press. Set: Eng.
The Case of the Russian Crown Jewels. 1921
The Davenham Heritage. Long, 1928
The Great Trunk Mystery. 1927. Reprinted in 1939 as by H. Gregory.
John Quinton's Secret. Aldine, 1926
The King's Secret. 1920
The Prison Breakers. 1920
The Trail Under the Sea. 1920
Unjustly Branded. 1919

POPE, EDITH
-Colcorton. Scribner, 1944; Collins, 1945 [Fla.]

POPE, LEO
Malachi Breen Times Two. Caravelle, 1967

POPESCU, PETRU
Before and After Edith. Quartet, 1978

POPKIN, ZELDA. 1898-1983. SC: Mary Carner (Whittaker) = MC. Ref: CA, TC.
Dead Man's Gift. Lippincott, 1941; Hutchinson, 1948 MC [Pa.]
A Death of Innocence. Lippincott, 1971; Allen, 1972 [NYC]
Death Wears a White Gardenia. Lippincott, 1938; Hutchinson, 1939 MC [NYC]
Murder in the Mist. Lippincott, 1940; Hutchinson, 1941 MC [Mass.]
No Crime for a Lady. Lippincott, 1942 MC [NYC]
So Much Blood. Lippincott, 1944; Hutchinson, 1946 [L.I.]
Time Off for Murder. Lippincott, 1940; Hutchinson, 1940 MC [NYC]

POPPLEWELL, JACK. 1911-   . Ref: CA.
Busybody. French (London), 1965 (3-act play.)
Dead Easy. French (London), 1975 (Play)
Dead on Nine. French (London), 1956 (3-act play.)
The Last Word. French (London), 1960 (3-act play.)
Policy for Murder. French (London), 1963 (3-act play.)

POPPLEWELL, O(LIVE) M.
Mrs. Snagg—Detective. Deane, 1934; Baker, 1934 (1-act play.)

PORCELAIN, SIDNEY E. SC: Stephen Clay, in both titles.
The Crimson Cat Murders. Phoenix, 1946 [New Eng.]
The Purple Pony Murders. Phoenix, 1944; Partridge, 1946 [NYC]

PORLOCK, MARTIN. Pseudonym of Philip MacDonald, 1899-1981. Other pseudonym: Anthony Lawless. Joint pseudonym with Ronald MacDonald, 1860-1933: Oliver Fleming, q.v. Set: Eng.

Escape; see Mystery in Kensington Gore
Mystery at Friar's Pardon. Collins, 1931; Doubleday, 1932, as by Philip MacDonald
Mystery in Kensington Gore. Collins, 1932. U.S. title: Escape, as by Philip MacDonald. Doubleday, 1932
The Mystery of Mr. X; see X v. Rex
Mystery of the Dead Police; see X v. Rex
X v. Rex. Collins, 1933. U.S. title: Mystery of the Dead Police, as by Philip MacDonald. Doubleday, 1933. Also published as: The Mystery of Mr. X. Literary Press, 1934

PORTER, ADMIRAL (DAVID DIXON). 1813-1891.
Allan Dare and Robert le Diable. Appleton, 1884

PORTER, EDWARD SEFTON
At the Foot of the Stairs. (Boston), 1922 (3-act play.)
Five Floors Down. Baker, 1968 (3-act play.)

PORTER, HAROLD EVERETT. 1887-1936. Pseudonym: Holworthy Hall, q.v.

PORTER, JOYCE. 1924-   . Ref: CA, CC, EM, MC, TC. SC: Insp. Wilfred Dover = WD; Edmund Brown = EB; Constance Morrison-Burke = CM. Set: Eng.
The Cart Before the Crime. Weidenfeld, 1979 CM
The Chinks in the Curtain. Cape, 1967; Scribner, 1968 EB [Paris]
Dead Easy for Dover. Weidenfeld, 1978; St. Martin's, 1979 WD
Dover and the Claret Tappers. Weidenfeld, 1976 WD
Dover and the Unkindest Cut of All. Cape, 1967; Scribner, 1967 WD
Dover Beats the Band. Weidenfeld, 1980 WD
Dover Goes to Pott. Cape, 1968; Scribner, 1968 WD
Dover One. Cape, 1964; Scribner, 1964 WD
Dover Strikes Again. Weidenfeld, 1970; McKay, 1973 WD
Dover Three. Cape, 1965; Scribner, 1966 WD
Dover Two. Cape, 1965; Scribner, 1965 WD
It's Murder with Dover. Weidenfeld, 1973; McKay, 1973 WD
A Meddler and Her Murder. Weidenfeld, 1972; McKay, 1973 CM
Neither a Candle Nor a Pitchfork. Weidenfeld, 1969; McCall, 1970 EB [Russ.]
Only with a Bargepole. Weidenfeld, 1971; McKay, 1974 EB
The Package Included Murder. Weidenfeld, 1975; Bobbs, 1976 CM [Russ.]
Rather a Common Sort of Crime. Weidenfeld, 1970; McCall, 1970 CM
Sour Cream with Everything. Cape, 1966; Scribner, 1966 EB [Russ.]
Who the Heck Is Sylvia? Weidenfeld, 1977 CM

PORTER, LINN BOYD. 1851-1916. Pseudonym: Albert Ross, q.v.

PORTER, MONICA E.
The Mercy of the Court. Norton, 1955 [Mich.]

PORTER, REBECCA N(EWMAN). 1883-   .
The Rest Hollow Mystery. Century, 1922; Long, 1924 [Calif.]

PORTER, WILLIAM SYDNEY. 1862-1910. Pseudonym: O. Henry, q.v.

PORTNOY, HOWARD N. 1946-   . Ref: CA.
Hot Rain. Putnam, 1977; Sphere, 1979 [Neb.]

PORTWAY, CHRISTOPHER (JOHN). 1923-   . Ref: CA.
All Exits Barred. Hale, 1971; Pinnacle, 1974
Lost Vengeance. Hale, 1973
The Tirana Assignment. Hale, 1974; Pinnacle, 1975

PORTWINE, E(LIZABETH) T.
The Limping Wolf. Featherstone, 1946

POSNER, JACOB D. 1883-   . Pseudonym: Gregory Dean, q.v.

POSNER, RICHARD. 1944-   . Pseudonyms: Iris Foster, Beatrice Murray, Paul Todd, q.v. Ref: CA.
The Mafia Man. GM, 1973; Gold Lion, 1973 [NYC]
The Seven-Ups. GM, 1973; Futura, 1974 (Novelization of the movie.) [NYC]

The Trigger Man. GM, 1974

POSNICK, PAUL. See: Leonard Leokum.

POSSENDORF, HANS. Pseudonym of Hans Mahner-Mons.
The 77th Day. Hutchinson, 1937 (Translation of "Gerbergasse 7." Munich, 1933.)

POST, MELVILLE DAVISSON. 1871-1930. Ref: CC, DD, EM, MC, MP, TC. SC: Uncle Abner = A; Sir Henry Marquis = HM; Randolph Mason = RM.
The Bradmoor Murder. Sears, 1929. British title (with contents rearranged): The Garden in Asia. Brentano's (London), 1929 HM ss [Eng.]
The Corrector of Destinies. Clode, 1908. Also published as: Randolph Mason, Corrector of Destinies. Putnam, 1923 RM ss [NYC]
The Garden in Asia; see The Bradmoor Murder
The Man of Last Resort; or, The Clients of Randolph Mason. Putnam, 1897. Also published as: Randolph Mason: The Clients. Putnam, 1923 RM ss
The Methods of Uncle Abner. Aspen, 1974 A ss [Va., ca.1850]
Monsieur Jonquelle, Prefect of Police. Appleton, 1923 ss [Fr.]
The Mystery at the Blue Villa. Appleton, 1919 ss
The Nameless Thing. Appleton, 1912 ss
Randolph Mason: The Clients; see The Man of Last Resort
Randolph Mason, Corrector of Destinies; see The Corrector of Destinies
Randolph Mason: The Strange Schemes; see The Strange Schemes of Randolph Mason
The Silent Witness. Farrar, 1930 ss [Va., ca.1850]
The Sleuth of St. James's Square. Appleton, 1920 HM ss [Eng.]
The Strange Schemes of Randolph Mason. Putnam, 1896. Also published as: Randolph Mason: The Strange Schemes. Putnam, 1922 RM ss
Uncle Abner, Master of Mysteries. Appleton, 1918; Stacey, 1972 A ss [Va., ca.1850]
Walker of the Secret Service. Appleton, 1924 ss

POST, MORTIMER. Pseudonym of Walter Blair, 1900- . Born in Wash.; received Ph.D. from U. of Chicago, where he was in English department nearly 40 years; biographer, critic.
Candidate for Murder. Doubleday, 1936 [acad., Midwest]

POSTGATE, JOHN W(ILLIAM). 1851-1921.
The Mystery of Paul Chadwick. Laird, 1896
Private Detective No. 39; or, The Mysterious Client. Ogilvie, 1892 [Chi.]
The Stolen Laces. Laird, 1889 (Byline given as John T. Postgate.)
The Strange Case of Henry Toplass and Capt. Shiers. Homewood, 1893
Two Women in Black. Belford, 1886. Also published as by James Mooney: Donohue, 1894
A Woman's Devotion; or, The Mixed Marriage. Rand, 1887

POSTGATE, RAYMOND (WILLIAM). 1896-1971. Ref: all except MM. SC: Insp. Holly = H. Set: Eng.
The Ledger Is Kept. Joseph, 1953 H
Somebody at the Door. Joseph, 1943; Knopf, 1943 H
Verdict of Twelve. Collins, 1940; Doubleday, 1940

POTTER, DAN. 1932- . Born in Okla., educated at U. of Okla. and Yale; author of novels, ss, and plays.
The Way of an Eagle. Stein, 1970; Secker, 1970 [Midwest]

POTTER, GEORGE WILLIAM, JR. 1930- . Pseudonym: E. L. Withers, q.v.

POTTER, J. L. SC: Jeff Tyler, in all titles.
Kill, Sweet Charity—Kill. Chicago Paperback House, 1962 [New Or.]
—Or Murder for Free. Chicago Paperback House, 1962
Room at the Bottom. Chicago Paperback House, 1962

POTTER, JEREMY. 1922- . Ref: CA, CC. SC: Sgt./Insp. Hiscock, in at least those marked H. Set: Eng.
The Dance of Death. Constable, 1968; Walker, 1969 H
Death in Office. Constable, 1965 H
Death in the Forest. Constable, 1977 [past]
Disgrace and Favour. Constable, 1975
Foul Play. Constable, 1967
Going West. Constable, 1972
Hazard Chase. Constable, 1964
A Trail of Blood. Constable, 1970; McCall, 1971 [Eng., 1536]

POTTER, JERRY ALLEN
A Talent for Dying. Popular Library, 1980 [Calif.]

POTTS, JEAN. 1910- . Ref: CA, CC, EM, TC.
An Affair of the Heart. Scribner, 1970; Gollancz, 1970 [NYC]
Blood Will Tell; see Lightning Strikes Twice
Death of a Stray Cat. Scribner, 1955; Gollancz, 1955 [L.I.]
The Diehard. Scribner, 1956; Gollancz, 1956
The Evil Wish. Scribner, 1962; Gollancz, 1962 [NYC]
The Footsteps on the Stairs. Scribner, 1966; Gollancz, 1967 [NYC]
Go, Lovely Rose. Scribner, 1954; Gollancz, 1955 [Ill.]
Home Is the Prisoner. Scribner, 1960; Gollancz, 1960
Lightning Strikes Twice. Scribner, 1958. British title: Blood Will Tell. Gollancz, 1959 [Midwest]
The Little Lie. Scribner, 1968; Gollancz, 1969 [New Eng.]
The Man with the Cane. Scribner, 1957; Gollancz, 1958 [NYC]
My Brother's Killer. Scribner, 1975; Gollancz, 1976 [NYC]
The Only Good Secretary. Scribner, 1965; Gollancz, 1966 [NYC]
The Trash Stealer. Scribner, 1967; Gollancz, 1968
The Troublemaker. Scribner, 1972; Gollancz, 1973 [Maine]

POTTS, RUTH
The Lost Kachina. Manor, 1979
Nugget. Manor, 1979

POU, GENEVIEVE LONG. 1919- . Pseudonym: Genevieve Holden, q.v.

POURNELLE, JERRY EUGENE. 1933- . Pseudonym: Wade Curtis, q.v.

POWELL, FRANCES. Pseudonym of Frances Powell Case.
-The By-Ways of Braiths. Scribner, 1904; Harper (London), 1904
The House on the Hudson. Scribner, 1903; Harper (London), 1903 [N.Y.]
An Old Maid's Vengeance. Scribner, 1911
Old Mr. Davenant's Money. Scribner, 1908
The Prisoner of Ornith Farm. Scribner, 1906

POWELL, ISABELLA BAYNE. See: Isabella Bayne-Powell.

POWELL, JOHN D.
Silent Knife. Hale, 1979

POWELL, LARRY. Pseudonym: R. L. Brent, q.v.

POWELL, LESTER (EDWIN). 1912- . SC: Philip Odell, in at least those marked PO.
The Big M. Hale, 1973
The Black Casket. Collins, 1953 PO [Paris]
A Count of Six. Collins, 1948 PO
Shadow Play. Collins, 1949 PO
Spot the Lady. Collins, 1950 PO
Still of Night. Collins, 1952 PO

POWELL, MICHAEL. 1905- . British film maker.
A Waiting Game. Joseph, 1975; St. Martin's, 1976 [Ire.]

POWELL, P(ERCIVAL) H(ENRY). Ref: CC. SC: Supt. Gaden, in at least those marked G. Set: Eng.
Death of an Expert Witness. Hale, 1957
Fatal Mistake. Hale, 1956
Murder Premeditated. Jenkins, 1951; Roy, 1958
-No Moonlight. Nimmo, 1948
Now Lying Dead. Jenkins, 1953 G
Only Three Died. Low, 1951
The Police Murders. Hale, 1955
Why Kill a Butler? Jenkins, 1952; Roy, 1957 G

POWELL, RICHARD (PITTS). 1908- . Ref: CA, CC. SC: Arab & Andy Blake = B.
All Over But the Shooting. Simon, 1944; Hodder, 1949. Abridged version: Death Talks Out of Turn. U.S. Government Printing Office, 1944 B [Wash. D.C.]
And Hope to Die. Simon, 1947; Hodder, 1950 B [Fla.]
The Case of the Curious Chair; see Don't Catch Me
Death Talks Out of Turn; see All Over But the Shooting
Don't Catch Me. Simon, 1943; Hodder, 1949. Also published as: The Case of the Curious Chair. Handi-Books, 1944 B [Pa.]
False Colors. Simon, 1955; Hodder, 1956. Also published as: Masterpiece in Murder. Dell, 1956 [Phil.]
Lay That Pistol Down. Simon, 1945; Hodder, 1950 B [Wash. D.C.]
Leave Murder to Me; see A Shot in the Dark
Masterpiece in Murder; see False Colors
On the Hook; see Shark River
Say It with Bullets. Simon, 1953; Hodder, 1955 [West]
Shark River. Simon, 1950; Hodder, 1951. Also published as: On the Hook. Ace, 1954 [Fla.]
Shell Game. Simon, 1950; Hodder, 1952 [Fla.]
Shoot If You Must. Simon, 1946; Hodder, 1949 B [Wash. D.C.]
A Shot in the Dark. Simon, 1952. British title: Leave Murder to Me. Hodder, 1952 [Fla.]

POWELL, ROSAMUND BAYNE. 1879- . See: Rosamund Bayne-Powell.

POWELL, TALMAGE. 1920- . Pseudonym: Jack McCready, q.v. See also: Ellery Queen. Ref: CA. SC: Ed Rivers = ER.
Corpus Delectable. PB, 1965 ER [Tampa]
The Girl Who Killed Things. Zenith, 1960
The Girl's Number Doesn't Answer. PB, 1960 ER [Tampa]
The Killer Is Mine. PB, 1959 ER [Tampa]
Man-Killer. Ace, 1960
The Smasher. Macmillan, 1959
Start Screaming Murder. Permabooks, 1962 ER [Tampa]
With a Madman Behind Me. Permabooks, 1962 ER [Tampa]

POWER, PATRICIA. Lives in Montreal.
The Face of the Foe. Doubleday, 1973; Hale, 1974 [Montr.]
This Deadly Grief. Doubleday, 1972; Hale, 1973 [Montr.]

POWERS, J.
Big Slam. World Distributors, 1953
Front Page Murder. World Distributors, 1954

POWERS, JAMES
-Estate of Grace. Harper, 1979

POWLETT, NIGEL AMYAS ORDE. 1900- . See: Nigel (Amyas) Orde-Powlett.

POWLEY, JEAN. Pseudonym: Ann Cardwell, q.v.

POWNALL, DAVID. 1938- .
Music to Murder By. Faber, 1978 (Play.)

POYER, JOE [JOSEPH JOHN POYER, JR.]. 1939- . Ref: CA. SC: Cole Brogan = CB.
The Balkan Assignment. Doubleday, 1971; Gollancz, 1972 [Balkans]
The Chinese Agenda. Doubleday, 1972; Gollancz, 1973
The Contract. Atheneum, 1978; Gollancz, 1978 CB
Hell Shot; see The Shooting of the Green
North Cape. Doubleday, 1969; Gollancz, 1970
Operation Malacca. Doubleday, 1968; Sphere, 1976 [Ind. O.]
The Shooting of the Green. Doubleday, 1973; Barker, 1974. Also published as: Hell Shot. Sphere, 1978 CB [Ire.]
Tunnel War. Atheneum, 1979; Joseph, 1980 [Eng., 1911]

POYNTER, BEULAH
The Disappearance of Mary Amber. Greenberg, 1934 [Venice, Paris]
-Lost Rapture. Greenberg, 1934
Murder on 47th Street. Doubleday, 1931 [NYC]

The Murillo Mystery. Altemus, 1927 [NYC]

PRAED, MRS. CAMPBELL [ROSA CAROLINE MURRAY-PRIOR PRAED]. 1851-1925.
Outlaw and Lawmaker. Chatto, 1893; Appleton, 1894

PRAGER, J. SIMON
The Newman Factor. Dell, 1973

PRATHER, RICHARD S(COTT). 1921-   .
Pseudonyms: David Knight, Douglas Ring, qq.v. Ref: CA, CC, TC. SC: Shell Scott = SS (see also David Knight entry).
Always Leave 'Em Dying. GM, 1954; Fawcett (London), 1957 SS [L.A.]
Bodies in Bedlam. GM, 1951; Fawcett (London), 1957 SS [L.A.]
Case of the Vanishing Beauty. GM, 1950; Fawcett (London), 1957 SS [L.A.]
The Cheim Manuscript. PB, 1969 SS [L.A.]
The Cockeyed Corpse. GM, 1964 SS [Ariz.]
Dagger of Flesh. Falcon, 1952; Panther, 1961 [L.A.]
Dance with the Dead. GM, 1960; Muller pb, 1962 SS [Haw.]
Darling, It's Death. GM, 1952; Fawcett (London), 1957 SS [Mex.]
Dead-Bang. PB, 1971 SS [L.A.]
Dead Heat. PB, 1963 SS [L.A.]
Dead Man's Walk. PB, 1965; Four Square, 1968 SS [Carib.]
Dig That Crazy Grave. GM, 1961; Muller pb, 1962 SS [L.A.]
Double in Trouble, with Stephen Marlowe, q.v. GM, 1959 SS, plus Marlowe's series character Chester Drum
Everybody Had a Gun. GM, 1951; Muller, 1953 SS [L.A.]
Find This Woman. GM, 1951; Fawcett (London), 1959 SS [Las Veg.]
Gat Heat. Trident, 1967; Four Square, 1968 SS [L.A.]
Have Gat—Will Travel. GM, 1957; Fawcett (London), 1958 SS ss [L.A.]
Joker in the Deck. GM, 1964; Muller pb, 1965 SS [L.A.]
Kill Him Twice. PB, 1965 SS [L.A.]
Kill Me Tomorrow. PB, 1969 SS [L.A.]
Kill the Clown. GM, 1962; Muller pb, 1963 SS [L.A.]
The Kubla Khan Caper. Trident, 1966 SS [Calif.]
Lie Down, Killer. Lion, 1952; Fawcett (London), 1958 [L.A.]
The Meandering Corpse. Trident, 1965; Four Square, 1967 SS [L.A.]
Over Her Dead Body. GM, 1959; Panther, 1960 SS [L.A.]
Pattern for Panic. Abelard, 1954. Revised version, with SS: GM, 1961; Muller pb, 1962 [Mex. City]
Ride a High Horse. GM, 1953. Also published as: Too Many Crooks. GM, 1956; Fawcett (London), 1957 SS [L.A.]
The Shell Scott Sampler. PB, 1969 ss SS [L.A.]
Shell Scott's Seven Slaughters. GM, 1961; Muller pb, 1962 SS ss [L.A.]
Slab Happy. GM, 1958 SS [Calif.]
Strip for Murder. GM, 1956; Fawcett (London), 1957 SS [L.A.]
The Sure Thing. PB, 1975 SS [L.A.]
The Sweet Ride. PB, 1972 SS [Calif.]
Take a Murder, Darling. GM, 1958; Muller pb, 1961 SS [L.A.]
Three's a Shroud. GM, 1957; Gold Lion, 1973 (3 novelets.) SS [L.A.]
Too Many Crooks; see Ride a High Horse
The Trojan Hearse. PB, 1964; Four Square, 1967 SS [L.A.]
The Wailing Frail. GM, 1956; Fawcett (London), 1957 SS [L.A.]
Way of a Wanton. GM, 1952; Fawcett (London), 1958 SS [L.A.]

PRATT, AMBROSE. 1874-1944.
The Counterstroke. Ward, 1906; Fenno, 1907
The Great "Push" Experiment. Richards, 1902 [Australia]
-Her Assigned Husband. Simpkin, 1914
King of the Rocks. Hutchinson, 1900
The Leather Mask. Ward, 1907
The Living Mummy. Ward, 1910; Stokes, 1910
-Vigorous Daunt, Billionaire. Ward, 1905; Fenno, 1908

PRATT, CORNELIA ATWOOD.   -1929. See: Richard Slee.

PRATT, ELEANOR BLAKE ATKINSON COX. 1899-   . Pseudonym: Eleanor Blake, q.v.

PRATT, (MURRAY) FLETCHER. 1897-1956.
The Cunning Mulatto and Other Cases of Ellis Parker, American Detective. Smith & Haas, 1935. British title: Detective No. 1. Methuen, 1936 ss [N.J.]
Detective No. 1; see The Cunning Mulatto
Double Jeopardy. Doubleday, 1952 (2 stories.) [future]

PRATT, GRACE TYLER
The Bainbridge Mystery. Sherman, 1911

PRATT, THEODORE. 1901-1969. Pseudonym: Timothy Brace, q.v.

PRAVIEL, ARMAND. 1875-   .
The Murder of Monsieur Fualdes. Collins, 1923; Seltzer, 1924 (Translation of "L'Assassinat de Monsieur Fualdes." Paris, 1922.) [Fr., 1817]

PRAY, PAUL. Pseudonym of Richard Hill Wilkinson, 1904-   , q.v. Other pseudonyms: Julian Brocke, Eugene Hayford, E. Harrison Ott, qq.v.
The Ghost in the Belfrey. Drama Guild, 1941 (3-act play.)

PREBBLE, MARJORIE MARY CURTIS. 1912-   . Pseudonym: Marjorie Curtis, q.v.

PREEDY, GEORGE R. Pseudonym of Gabrielle Margaret Vere Campbell Long, 1886-1952. Other pseudonyms: Marjorie Bowen, Joseph Shearing, qq.v., Margaret Campbell.
-Beneath the Passion Flower. McBride, 1932 (British title?)
-Black Man—White Maiden. Hodder, 1941
The Devil Snard. Benn, 1932
-Dove in the Mulberry Tree. Jenkins, 1939
-Dr. Chaos and the Devil Snard. Cassell, 1933
The Fair Young Widow. Jenkins, 1939
-Findernes' Flowers. Hodder, 1941
-The Fourth Chamber. Hodder, 1944
-General Crack. Lane, 1928
-Julia Ballantyne. Hodder, 1952
-Lady in a Veil. Hodder, 1953
-Laurell'd Captains. Hutchinson, 1935
-Lyndley Waters. Hodder, 1942
My Tattered Loving. Jenkins, 1937
-Nightcap and Plume. Hodder, 1945
-No Way Home. Hodder, 1947
Painted Angel. Jenkins, 1938 [Ger., 1809-11]
-The Pavilion of Honour. Lane, 1932
The Prisoners. Hutchinson, 1936
-Primula. Hodder, 1940
The Prince's Darling; see The Rocklitz
-The Rocklitz. Lane, 1930. U.S. title: The Prince's Darling. Dodd, 1930
-The Sacked City. Hodder, 1949
-Tumult in the North. Lane, 1931; Dodd, 1931
-Violante. Cassell, 1946

PREISS, BYRON and RALPH REESE
Son of Sherlock Holmes: The Woman in Red. Pyramid, 1976

PRENTIS, JOHN H(ARCOURT). 1878-   .
The Case of Doctor Horace. Baker, 1907 [Mich.]

PRESCOT, JULIAN. Pseudonym of John Budd. SC: Julian Prescot, in all titles. Set: Eng.
Both Sides of the Case. Barker, 1958
The Case Continued. Barker, 1959
Case for Court. Barker, 1964
Case for Hearing. Barker, 1963
Case for the Accused. Barker, 1961
Case for Trial. Barker, 1962
Case Proceeding. Barker, 1960
The Case Re-Opened. Barker, 1965
The Krakatao Cult. Barker, 1966

PRESCOTT, H(ILDA) F(RANCES) M(ARGARET). 1896-   .
Dead and Not Buried. Constable, 1938; Dodd, 1938

PRESCOTT, S. C.
The Amber Gods. Ticknor, 1863 ss
The Bauer Murder; or, The Last of His Race. Elliott, 1863

PRESNELL, FRANK G. 1906-   . SC: John and Anne Webb = W.
No Mourners Present. Morrow, 1940; Nicholson, 1943 W [Ohio]
Send Another Coffin. Morrow, 1939; Heinemann, 1939 W [Ohio]
Too Hot to Handle. Mill, 1951 [L.A.]

PRESS, SYLVIA
-The Care of Devils. Beacon, 1958; Constable, 1958

PREST, THOMAS PECKET. 1810-1879. Many of the following were published anonymously and without dates. The publisher in most instances was Edward Lloyd. Set: Eng.
Adventures by Night. 1846
Agnes the Unknown; or, The Beggar's Secret. 1849
Almira's Curse; or, The Black Tower of Bransdorf. 1842
Angelina; or, The Mystery of St. Mark's Abbey. 1841
The Apparition. 1846
The Black Mantle; or, The Murder at the Old Ferry. 1851
The Black Monk; or, The Secret of the Grey Turret. 1844
Blanche Heriot; or, The Chertsey Curfew. 1851
Blanche; or, The Mystery of the Doomed House. 1847
The Blighted Heart; or, The Murder in the Old Priory Ruins. 1851
The Brigand; or, The Mountain Chief. 1851
The Child of Two Fathers; or, The Mysteries of the Days of Old. 1848
The Convict. 1846
Crime; or, The Gamester's Daughter. 1843?
The Death Grasp; or, A Father's Curse. 1842
The Death Ship; or, The Pirate's Bride and the Maniac of the Deep. 1846
The Divorce; or, The Mystery of the Wreck. 1847
Don Caesar de Bazan. 1845
Ela the Outcast; or, The Gipsy of Rosemary Dell. 1841
Emily Fitzormond. 1841
Emily Percy. 1842
Ernestine de Lacy; or, The Robber's Founding. 1842
Ethelinda; or, The Fatal Vow. 1848
Evelina, the Pauper's Child; or, Poverty, Crime and Sorrow. 1851
Fatherless Fanny; or, The Mysterious Orphan. 1841
The First False Step; or, The Path of Crime. 1846
Gallant Tom. 1841
Geraldine; or, The Secret Assassins of the Old Stone Cross. 1844
Gertrude of the Rock. 1842
The Gipsy Boy. 1847
Grace Walter. 1853
The Hebrew Maiden; or, The Lost Diamond. 1841
The Harvest Home. 1852
Jack Junk; or, The Tar for All Weathers. 1851
Jane Shore; or, London in the Reign of Edward the Fourth. 1846
Jonathan Bradford; or, The Murder at the Roadside Inn. 1846
Kathleen; or, The Secret Marriage. 1842
The Lone Cottage; or, Who's the Stranger? 1845
The Love Child. 1847
The Maniac Father; or, The Victim of Seduction.
Manuscripts from the Diary of a Physician. Two Series. 1844
Mariette; or, The Forger's Wife and the Child of Destiny. 1845
Martha Willis; or, The Maid, the Profligate, and the Felon. 1844
Mary Clifford; or, The Foundling Apprentice Girl. 1841
May Grayson; or, Love and Treachery. 1842
Mazeppa; or, The Wild Horse of the Ukraine. 1850
The Miller and His Men; or, The Secret Robbers of Bohemia. 1852
The Miller's Maid. 1849
The Miser of Shoreditch; or, The Curse of Avarice. 1847
My Poll and My Partner Joe. 1849
Newgate. 1847
The Old House of West Street; or, London in the Last Century. 1846
Paul Clifford. 1844
Pedlar's Acre; or, The Murderess of Seven Husbands. 1848
Phoebe, the Miller's Daughter. 1842
Ranger of the Tomb; or, The Gipsy's Prophecy. 1847
Retribution; or, The Murder at the Old Dyke. 1849
Richard Parker; or, The Mutiny at the Nore. 1851
The Rivals; or, The Spectre at the Hall. 1847
Rosalie; or, The Vagrant's Daughter. 1848
The Royal Twins; or, The Sisters of Mystery. 1848

Sawney Bean, the Man Eater of Midlothian. 1851
Schamyl, the Sultan, Warrior and Prophet of the Caucasus. 1854
The Skeleton's Clutch; or, The Goblet of Gore. 1842
The String of Pearls; or, The Sailor's Gift. 1849
Theresa; or, The Orphan of Geneva. 1844
Varney the Vampire; or, The Feast of Blood. 1847; Dover, 1972
Vice and Its Victim; or, Phoebe, the Peasant's Daughter. 1854
Widow Mortimer; or, The Marriage in the Dark. 1850
The Wife's Dream; or, A Profligate's Lesson. 1843?

PRESTON, ELLIOTT
- An American Venus. Drane, 1900

PRESTON, JACK. Pseudonym of John Preston Buschlen, 1888-
  Heil! Hollywood. Reilly, 1939 [L.A.]

PRESTON, JAMES. 1913-   . Ref: CA. SC: Det. Sgt. Bob Christie, in at least those marked BC.
  Axes of Hate. Long, 1963 BC [Australia]
  Breakdown. Long, 1965
  Bushfire. Long, 1969
  Crashout. Long, 1968
  Death Takes Revenge. Long, 1970
  The Empty Years. Cresset, 1962
  Gaol in Conflict. Long, 1966
  The Killer Came Riding. Long, 1963
  Murder at Sundown. Long, 1968
  Power Failure. Long, 1971
  Prison Fund. Long, 1962
  Racing Axes. Long, 1966 [Melb.]
  Shattered Steel. Long, 1964 BC [Australia]
  Valley of No Escape. Long, 1961

PRESTON, T. See: Jack Gratus, 1935-   .

PRICE, ANTHONY. 1928-   . Ref: CA, TC. SC: Dr. David Audley, in all titles.
  The Alamut Ambush. Gollancz, 1971; Doubleday, 1972
  Colonel Butler's Wolf. Gollancz, 1972; Doubleday, 1973
  The '44 Vintage. Gollancz, 1978; Doubleday, 1978 [Fr., 1944]
  The Labyrinth Makers. Gollancz, 1970; Doubleday, 1971
  October Men. Gollancz, 1973; Doubleday, 1974 [It.]
  Other Paths to Glory. Gollancz, 1974; Doubleday, 1975 [Fr.]
  Our Man in Camelot. Gollancz, 1975; Doubleday, 1976
  Tomorrow's Ghost. Gollancz, 1979; Doubleday, 1979
  War Game. Gollancz, 1976; Doubleday, 1977

PRICE, EVADNE. Pseudonym of Helen Zenna Smith, 1896-
  Diary of a Red-Haired Girl. Long, 1932
  The Haunted Light. Long, 1933
  Once a Crook, with Kenneth Attiwell. French, 1943 (3-act play.)
  The Phantom Light. French, 1949 (Play.)
  - Probationer! Hurst, 1934
  Red for Danger! Long, 1936

PRICE, FRANK J(OHN), JR. 1890-   . Born in St. Louis; newspaperman, then in public relations and advertising; ss writer, with over 100 published.
  Mind Wreckers, Limited, and Other Adventures of Barrow—Ace Insurance Detective. Spectator, 1933 ss

PRICE, J. L. See: Arthur W(illiam) Upfield, 1888-1964.

PRICE, LELAND. Pseudonym of Charles George, 1893-   , q.v. Other pseudonyms: Henry Rowland, Dorothy Sterling, qq.v.
  Bessie, the Bandit's Beautiful Baby. Northwestern, 1946 (1-act play.)
  The City Slicker and Our Nell. Northwestern, 1945 (Play.)
  Desperate Diamond's Dastardly Deed. Northwestern, 1946 (1-act play.)
  For His Brother's Crime. Northwestern, 1947 (1-act play.)
  Parted on Her Wedding Morn. Dramatists, 1942 (1-act play.)

PRICE, RICHARD. 1949-   . Ref: CA.
  Bloodbrothers. Houghton, 1976; Macdonald, 1977

PRICE, WESLEY
  Death Is a Stowaway. Godwin, 1933; Wright, 1935 [ship]

PRICHARD, (VERNON) HESKETH. 1876-1922. See also: K(atherine O'Brien) Prichard. Ref: DD, EM, MP.
  November Joe, the Detective of the Woods. Hodder, 1913; Houghton, 1913 ss [Can.]

PRICHARD, K(ATHERINE O'BRIEN) and (VERNON) HESKETH PRICHARD, 1876-1922, q.v. SC: Don Q = Q.
  The Cahusac Mystery. Heinemann, 1912; Sturgis, 1912
  The Chronicles of Don Q. Chapman, 1904; Lippincott, 1904 ss Q [Sp.]
  Don Q in the Sierra; see The New Chronicles of Don Q
  Don Q's Love Story. Greening, 1909; Grosset, 1925 Q [Sp.]
  Ghost Stories; see Ghosts
  Ghosts. Pearson, 1899 ss, of which the first 6 were published later as: Ghost Stories. Pearson, 1916, as by E. & H. Heron
  - Karadac, Count of Gerzy. Constable, 1901; Stokes, 1901
  - A Modern Mercenary. Smith Elder, 1899; Doubleday, 1899
  The New Chronicles of Don Q. Unwin, 1906. U.S. title: Don Q in the Sierra. Lippincott, 1906 ss Q [Sp.]
  - Roving Hearts. Smith Elder, 1903 ss

PRICKETT, (ALEXANDER THOMAS) STEPHEN. 1939-   . Ref: CA.
  Do It Yourself Doom. Gollancz, 1962

PRIDHAM, SYLVIA SANDYS
  Case of the Poisoned Pup. Arcadia, 1961 [Ohio]

PRIESTLEY, BRIAN
  The Island Emperor. Macmillan (London), 1978
  Makariri Gold. Macmillan (London), 1977

PRIESTLEY, CLIVE RYLAND. 1892-   . Pseudonym: Clive Ryland, q.v.

PRIESTLEY, J(OHN) B(OYNTON). 1894-   . See also: Ruth Holland. Ref: CA, CC, EM, TC. Set: Eng.
  Benighted. Heinemann, 1927. U.S. title: The Old Dark House. Harper, 1928
  Black-Out in Gretley. Heinemann, 1942; Harper, 1942
  Bright Shadow. French (London), 1950 (3-act play.)
  Dangerous Corner. Heinemann, 1932 (3-act play.)
  The Doomsday Men. Heinemann, 1938; Harper, 1938 [Calif.]
  I'll Tell You Everything, with Gerald (William) Bullett, 1893-1958, q.v. Heinemann, 1933; Macmillan, 1932
  An Inspector Calls. Heinemann, 1947; Dramatists Play Service, 1948 (3-act play.)
  Laburnum Grove. Heinemann, 1934; French (NYC), 1935 (3-act play.)
  Mystery at Greenfingers. French (London), 1937; French (NYC), 1938 (Play.)
  The Old Dark House; see Benighted
  Salt Is Leaving. Pan, 1966; Harper, 1975
  Saturn over the Water. Heinemann, 1961; Doubleday, 1961
  The Shapes of Sleep. Heinemann, 1962; Doubleday, 1962

PRIESTLEY, LEE (SHORE). 1904-   . Ref: CA.
  Murder Takes the Baths. Arcadia, 1952

PRINCE, DANIEL C. Pseudonym: Nick Carter, q.v.

PRINCE, PETER. 1942-   .
  Dogcatcher. Gollancz, 1974

PRIOR, ALLAN. 1922-   . Ref: CA, TC.
  - The Contract. Cassell, 1970; Simon, 1971
  - A Flame in the Air. Joseph, 1951
  The Interrogators. Cassell, 1965; Simon, 1965
  - The Joy Ride. Joseph, 1952
  - The Loving Cup. Cassell, 1968; Simon, 1969
  One Away. Eyre, 1961
  The Operators. Cassell, 1966; Simon, 1967
  Paradiso. Cassell, 1972; Simon, 1973
  Z Cars Again. Trust Books, 1963 (Novelization of the TV series.)

PRIOR, WILLIAM W.
  Not Our House. Vantage, 1979

PRITCHARD, JOHN LAURENCE. 1885-   . Pseudonym: John Laurence, q.v.

PRITCHARD, JOHN WALLACE. 1912-   . Pseudonym: Ian Wallace, q.v.

PRITCHETT, ARIADNE
  Ghosts of Kings. GM, 1972
  Karamour. GM, 1968 [Eng., past]
  Legacy of Evil. GM, 1973 [Eng., 1800s]
  The Malpas Legacy. GM, 1974 [Eng., 1800s]
  Mill Reef Hall. GM, 1968 [past, Eng.]

PRIWIN, H(ANS) W(OLFGANG)
  Inspector Hornleigh Investigates. Hodder, 1939

PROBY, WILLIAM C.
  The Mysterious Seal. Westley, 1799
  The Spirit of the Castle. Crosby, 1800

PROCTER, ARTHUR (WYMAN). 1889-1961.
  Murder in Manhattan. Morrow, 1930 [NYC]

PROCTER, MAURICE. 1906-1973. Ref: CA, CC, EM, TC. SC: Insp. Martineau, in at least those marked M; Supt. Philip Hunter, in at least those marked PH. Set: Eng.
  A Body to Spare. Hutchinson, 1962; Harper, 1962 M
  The Chief Inspector's Statement. Hutchinson, 1951. U.S. title: The Pennycross Murders. Harper, 1953 PH
  Death Has a Shadow. Hutchinson, 1965. U.S. title: Homicide Blonde. Harper, 1965 M
  Devil in Moonlight. Hutchinson, 1962
  The Devil Was Handsome. Hutchinson, 1961; Harper, 1961 M
  Devil's Due. Hutchinson, 1960; Harper, 1960 M
  The Dog Man. Hutchinson, 1969
  Each Man's Destiny. Longmans, 1947
  The End of the Street. Longmans, 1949
  Exercise Hoodwink. Hutchinson, 1967; Harper, 1967 M
  The Graveyard Rolls; see Moonlight Flitting
  Hell Is a City. Hutchinson, 1954. U.S. title: Somewhere in This City. Harper, 1954. Also published as: Murder, Somewhere in This City. Avon, 1956 M
  Hideaway. Hutchinson, 1968; Harper, 1968 M
  His Weight in Gold. Hutchinson, 1966; Harper, 1966 M
  Homicide Blonde; see Death Has a Shadow
  Hurry the Darkness. Hutchinson, 1952; Harper, 1951
  I Will Speak Daggers. Hutchinson, 1956. U.S. title: The Ripper. Harper, 1956. Also published as: The Ripper Murders. Avon, 1957 PH
  Killer at Large. Hutchinson, 1959; Harper, 1959 M
  Man in Ambush. Hutchinson, 1958; Harper, 1959 M
  The Midnight Plumber. Hutchinson, 1957; Harper, 1958 M
  Moonlight Flitting. Hutchinson, 1963. U.S. title: The Graveyard Rolls. Harper, 1964 M
  Murder, Somewhere in This City; see Hell Is a City
  No Proud Chivalry. Longmans, 1947
  The Pennycross Murders; see The Chief Inspector's Statement
  The Pub Crawler. Hutchinson, 1956; Harper, 1957
  Rich Is the Treasure. Hutchinson, 1952
  The Ripper; see I Will Speak Daggers
  The Ripper Murders; see I Will Speak Daggers
  Rogue Running. Hutchinson, 1967; Harper, 1966 M
  Somewhere in This City; see Hell Is a City
  The Spearhead Death. Hutchinson, 1960
  Three at the Angel. Hutchinson, 1958; Harper, 1958
  Two Men in Twenty. Hutchinson, 1964; Harper, 1964 M

PROCTOR, FRED J.
  Timothy Twill's Secret. Tarstow, 1891

PROKOSCH, FREDERIC. 1908-   . Ref: CA.
  The Conspirators. Harper, 1943; Chatto, 1943 [Lisbon]
  A Tale for Midnight. Little, 1955; Secker, 1956 [It., 1500s]

PRONZINI, BILL. 1943-   . Pseudonyms: Jack Foxx, Alex Saxon, qq.v. Ref: CA, TC. SC: unnamed private eye = PE.
  Acts of Mercy, with Barry (Norman) Malzberg, 1939-   , q.v. Putnam, 1977 [Wash. D.C.]
  Blowback. Random, 1977; Hale, 1978 PE [Calif.]
  Games. Putnam, 1976; Hamlyn, 1978 [Maine]

A Killing in Xanadu. Waves Press, 1980
  (20 pp pb.) PE
Labyrinth. St. Martin's, 1980; Hale,
  1981 PE [S.F.]
Night Screams, with Barry (Norman)
  Malzberg, 1939- , q.v. Playboy,
  1979 [Vt.]
Panic! Random, 1972; Hale, 1976 [S.W.]
The Running of Beasts, with Barry (Nor-
  man) Malzberg, 1939- , q.v. Put-
  nam, 1976 [N.Y.]
The Snatch. Random, 1971; Hale, 1974
  PE [Calif.]
Snowbound. Putnam, 1974; Weidenfeld,
  1975 [Calif.]
The Stalker. Random, 1971; Hale, 1974
  [Calif.]
Twospot, with Collin Wilcox, 1924- ,
  q.v. Putnam, 1978 PE, and Wilcox's
  series character Lt. Frank Hastings
  [S.F.]
Undercurrent. Random, 1973; Hale, 1975
  PE [Calif.]
The Vanished. Random, 1973; Hale, 1974
  PE [S.F.]

PROPPER, MILTON (MORRIS). 1906-1962. Ref:
  CC, EM, MP, TC. SC: Tommy Rankin, in
  all titles.
And Then Silence; see The Boudoir Mur-
  der
The Blood Transfusion Murders. Harper,
  1943. British title: Murders in Se-
  quence. Jenkins, 1947 [Phil.]
The Boudoir Murder. Harper, 1931. British title: And Then Silence. Faber,
  1931 [Phil.]
The Case of the Cheating Bride. Harper,
  1938; Harrap, 1939 [Phil.]
The Divorce Court Murder. Harper, 1934;
  Faber, 1934 [Phil.]
The Election Booth Murder. Harper,
  1935. British title: Murder at the
  Polls. Harrap, 1936 [Phil.]
The Family Burial Murders. Harper,
  1934; Harrap, 1935 [Phil.]
The Great Insurance Murders. Harper,
  1937; Harrap, 1938 [Phil.]
The Handwriting on the Wall. Harper,
  1941. British title: You Can't Gag
  the Dead. Jenkins, 1949 [Phil.]
Hide the Body! Harper, 1939; Harrap,
  1940 [Phil.]
Murder at the Polls; see The Election
  Booth Murder
Murder of an Initiate; see The Student
  Fraternity Murder
Murders in Sequence; see The Blood
  Transfusion Murders
One Murdered, Two Dead. Harper, 1936;
  Harrap, 1937 [Phil.]
The Station Wagon Murder. Harper, 1940
  [Pa.]
The Strange Disappearance of Mary
  Young. Harper, 1929; Harrap, 1929
  [Phil.]
The Student Fraternity Murder. Bobbs,
  1932. British title: Murder of an
  Initiate. Faber, 1933 [Phil., acad.]
The Ticker-Tape Murder. Harper, 1930;
  Faber, 1930 [N.J.]
You Can't Gag the Dead; see The Hand-
  writing on the Wall

PROSPER, JOHN. Joint pseudonym of John
  Chipman Farrar, 1896-1974, and Pros-
  per Buranelli, 1890-1960, q.v.
Gold-Killer. Doran, 1922 [NYC]

PROUD, FRANKLIN M. 1920- . Born and
  educated in Van.; correspondent,
  journalist and writer living in the
  Far East. SC: Joe Sanford, in both
  titles.
The Golden Triangle. St. Martin's,
  1978; Sphere, 1976 [Far East]
The Walking Wind. St. Martin's, 1979

PROUDFIT, DAVID LAW. See: Anonymous.

PROUDFOOT, WALTER. Pseudonym of John
  (George) Hazlette Vahey, 1881- ,
  q.v. Other pseudonyms: Henrietta
  Clandon, John Haslette, Anthony Lang,
  Vernon Loder, John Mowbray, qq.v.
  SC: Insp. Bill Vallance = BV.
  Set: Eng.
Arrest. Hutchinson, 1933 BV
Conspiracy. Hutchinson, 1933 BV
Crime in the Arcade. Hutchinson, 1931
  BV
The Trail of the Ruby. Hutchinson, 1932

PROUT, GEOFFREY. 1894-
The Mystery of the Marshes. Lloyd's,
  1923

PRUITT, ALAN. Pseudonym of Alvin Emanuel
  Rose. SC: Don Carson, in both titles,
  both set in Chi.
The Restless Corpse. Ziff-Davis, 1947
Typed for a Corpse. Handi-Books, 1951

PRYCE, LARRY. SC: Dick Barton = DB (see
  also: Mike Dorrell).
Black Gunn. Tandem, 1974
The Gold Bullion Swindle. Star, 1979
  DB

PRYCE, RICHARD. 1864-1942.
-The Quiet Mrs. Fleming. Methuen, 1891

PRYCE-JONES, DAVID. 1936- . Ref: CA.
The England Commune. Quartet, 1975

PRYDE, ANTHONY and R(OSE) K(IRKPATRICK)
  WEEKES, 1874- , q.v. Anthony Pryde
  is the pseudonym of A(gnes) R(ussell)
  Weekes, q.v.
The Purple Pearl. Allen, 1923; Dodd,
  1922

PRYOR, LARRY [LAWRENCE ALLDERDICE PRYOR].
  1938- . Ref: CA.
The Viper. Harper, 1978; Gollancz, 1979
  [L.A.]

PUCCETTI, ROLAND (PETER). 1924- .
The Death of the Fuhrer. Hutchinson,
  1972; St. Martin's, 1973
The Trial of John and Henry Norton.
  Hutchinson, 1973

PUDNEY, JOHN (SLEIGH). 1909-1977. Ref:
  CA.
-The Accomplice. Bodley, 1950
Hero of a Summer's Day. Lane, 1951
The Net. Joseph, 1952
-A Ring for Luck. Joseph, 1953
Thin Air. Joseph, 1961
-Trespass in the Sun. Joseph, 1957

PUGH, EDWIN (WILLIAM), 1874-1930, and
  CHARLES GLEIG, 1862- , q.v.
The Rogues' Paradise. Bowden, 1898

PUGH, MARSHALL. Born in Scot.; free-
  lance writer, columnist, film critic.
A Dream of Treason. Deutsch, 1974;
  Coward, 1974
Last Place Left. Deutsch, 1969; Harper,
  1969 [Hebrides]
A Murmur of Mutiny. Deutsch, 1962;
  Harper, 1972 [Mid. East]

PUIG, MANUEL. 1932- . Ref: CA.
The Buenos Aires Affair. Dutton, 1976
  (Translation of "The Buenos Aires
  Affair." Buenos Aires, 1973.)
  [Buen. A.]

PUISSESSEAU, RENE
Someone Will Die Tonight in the Carib-
  bean. Knopf, 1958; Allen, 1959
  (Translation of "Quelqu'un Mourra ce
  Soir aux Caraibes." Paris, 1957.)
  [Carib.]

PULLEIN-THOMPSON, JOANNA MAXWELL CANNAN.
  1898- . Pseudonym: Joanna Cannan,
  q.v.

PULLEIN-THOMPSON, JOSEPHINE (MARY WEDDER-
  BURN). Pseudonym: Josephine Mann,
  q.v. Ref: CA. SC: Insp. James Fleck-
  er, in all titles. Set: Eng.
Gin and Murder. Hammond, 1959
Murder Strikes Pink. Hammond, 1963
They Died in the Spring. Hammond, 1960

PULMAN, JACK. 1928?-1979. Ref: CA.
Fixation. H. Hamilton, 1978. U.S.
  title: Collision. Atheneum, 1979
  [U.S.]

PULSFORD, NORMAN GEORGE. 1902- . Pseudonym: A. C. Trevor, q.v.

PUNNETT, IVOR MACAULAY. Joint pseudonym
  with Margaret Punnett, 1932- :
  Roger Simons, q.v.

PUNNETT, MARGARET. 1932- . Joint pseudonym with Ivor Macaulay Punnett:
  Roger Simons, q.v.

PUNSHON, E(RNEST) R(OBERTSON). 1872-1956.
  Ref: CC, EM, MP. SC: Carter & Bell =
  C&B; Bobby Owen = BO. Set: Eng.
Arrows of Chance. Ward, 1917
The Attending Truth. Gollancz, 1952 BO
The Bath Mysteries. Gollancz, 1936;
  Hillman-Curl, 1938. Also published
  as: The Bathtub Murder Case. Detec-
  tive Novel Classics, 194? BO
The Bathtub Murder Case; see The Bath
  Mysteries
The Bittermeads Mystery. Knopf, 1922
The Blue John Diamond. Cherry Tree
  (abridged), 1946; Clode, 1929
Brought to Light. Gollancz, 1954 BO
Comes a Stranger. Gollancz, 1938 BO
The Conqueror Inn. Gollancz, 1943; Mac-
  millan, 1944 BO
The Cottage Murder. Benn, 1931; Hough-
  ton, 1932 C&B
The Crossword Murder; see Crossword
  Mystery
Crossword Mystery. Gollancz, 1934. U.S.
  title: The Crossword Murder. Knopf,
  1934 BO
The Dark Garden. Gollancz, 1941 BO
Dark Is the Clue. Gollancz, 1955 BO
Death Among the Sunbathers. Benn, 1934
  BO
Death Comes to Cambers. Gollancz, 1935
  BO
Death in the Chalkpit. Mystery Novel of
  the Month, 194? (British title?)
Death of a Beauty Queen. Gollancz,
  1935 BO
Death of a Tyrant; see Dictator's Way
Diabolic Candelabra. Gollancz, 1942 BO
Dictator's Way. Gollancz, 1938. U.S.
  title: Death of a Tyrant. Hillman-
  Curl, 1938 BO
Dunslow. Ward, 1922
The Dusky Hour. Gollancz, 1937; Hill-
  man-Curl, 1938 BO
Earth's Great Lord. Ward, 1901
  [Australia]
Everybody Always Tells. Gollancz, 1950
  BO
Four Strange Women. Gollancz, 1940 BO
Genius in Murder. Benn, 1932; Houghton,
  1933 C&B
The Glittering Desire. Ward, 1910
The Golden Dagger. Gollancz, 1951 BO
Helen Passes By. Gollancz, 1947 BO
Hidden Lives. Ward, 1913
The House of Godwinsson. Gollancz, 1948
  BO
Information Received. Benn, 1933;
  Houghton, 1934 BO
It Might Lead Anywhere. Gollancz, 1946;
  Macmillan, 1947 BO
Murder Abroad. Gollancz, 1939 BO
Music Tells All. Gollancz, 1948 BO
The Mystery of Lady Isobel. Hurst, 1907
Mystery of Mr. Jessop. Gollancz, 1937;
  Hillman-Curl, 1937 BO
Mystery Villa. Gollancz, 1934 BO
Night's Cloak. Gollancz, 1944; Macmil-
  lan, 1944 BO
Proof, Counter Proof. Benn, 1931 C&B
The Secret Search. Gollancz, 1951 BO
Secrets Can't Be Kept. Gollancz, 1944;
  Macmillan, 1946 BO
Six Were Present. Gollancz, 1956 BO
So Many Doors. Gollancz, 1949; Macmil-
  lan, 1950 BO
The Solitary House. Ward, 1919; Knopf,
  1918
The Spin of the Coin. Hurst, 1908
Strange Ending. Gollancz, 1953 BO
Suspects—Nine. Gollancz, 1939 BO
Ten Star Clues. Gollancz, 1941 BO
There's a Reason for Everything. Gol-
  lancz, 1945; Macmillan, 1946 BO
Triple Quest. Gollancz, 1955 BO
Truth Came Out. Benn, 1932; Houghton,
  1934 C&B
The Unexpected Legacy. Benn, 1929 C&B
The Woman's Footprint. Hodder, 1919

PURCELL, MARY. 1906- . Ref: CA.
The Pilgrim Came Late. Clanmore, 1947

PURDY, ANNE
Dark Boundary. Vantage, 1954

PURDY, CLAIRE LEE. 1906- . See:
  Benson Wheeler, 1905- .

PURDY, JENNIE BOUTON. Pseudonym: Shubael,
  q.v.

PURLEY, JOHN. Pseudonym of Reginald
  George Thomas, 1899- . SC (with
  many other authors): Sexton Blake =
  SB.
The Mansion on the Moor. Amalgamated,
  1943 SB

PURSER, PHILIP (JOHN). 1925- . Ref:
  CA. SC: Colin Pauton, in at least
  those marked CP.
Four Days to the Fireworks. Hodder,
  1964; Walker, 1965
Holy Father's Navy. Hodder, 1971
Night of Glass. Hodder, 1968
Peregrination 22. Cape, 1962 CP [Nor.]
The Twentymen. Hodder, 1967; Walker,
  1967 CP

PURTELL, JOSEPH. Senior editor for "Time"
  magazine, then newspaper publisher.
The Tiffany Caper. Coward, 1974; Cassell, 1975 [NYC]
To a Blindfold Lady. Reynal, 1942

PURVIS, JAMES L.
Weekend of Terror. Powell, 1970

PUTNAM, FRANK
The Raid on the Mint. Street, ca.1900

PUTNAM, GEORGE PALMER, 1887-1950, and NELL SHIPMAN [HELEN BARHAM SHIPMAN], 1892- .
   Hot Oil. Greenberg, 1935   [Tex.]

PUTNAM, SEAN
   Bomba, Bomba! Panther, 1979

PUTNAM, XENO
   Crystal Tower. Shores, 1917

PUZEY, F. G.
   Cupid Among the Clues. Hartley, 1931

PUZO, MARIO. 1920- . Pseudonym: Mario Cleri, q.v. Ref: CA.
   The Godfather. Putnam, 1969; Heinemann, 1969 [L.I.]

PYKE, RIVINGTON
   The Fellow Passengers. Greening, 1898
   The Man Who Disappeared. Bentley, 1896

"Q". Pseudonym of Sir Arthur T(homas) Quiller-Couch, 1863-1944, q.v.
   Dead Man's Rock. Cassell (London & NYC), 1887
   I Saw Three Ships, and other winter's tales. Cassell (London & NYC), 1892 ss

Q, JOHN. Pseudonym of John Edward Quirk, 1920- . At least some of the titles below were reprinted as by John Quirk. Ref: CA. SC: Peter Trees, in all titles.
   The Bunnies. Avon, 1965   [Det.]
   The Survivor. Avon, 1965   [S. Am.]
   The Tournament. Signet, 1966   [Bahamas]

QUARRY, NICK. Pseudonym of Marvin H(ubert) Albert, 1924- , q.v. Other pseudonyms: Mike Barone, Al Conroy, Albert Conroy, Ian MacAlister, Anthony Rome, qq.v. SC: Jake Barrow = JB.
   The Don Is Dead. GM, 1972; Coronet, 1972
   The Girl with No Place to Hide. GM, 1959; Muller pb, 1961 JB [NYC]
   The Hoods Come Calling. GM, 1958; Fawcett (London), 1959 JB [NYC]
   No Chance in Hell. GM, 1960; Muller pb, 1962 JB [NYC]
   Some Die Hard. GM, 1961; Muller pb, 1963 JB [NYC]
   Till It Hurts. GM, 1960; Muller pb, 1962 JB [NYC]
   Trail of a Tramp. GM, 1958; Muller pb, 1960 JB [NYC]
   The Vendetta. GM, 1973

QUARTERMAIN, H. J.
   Death Before Launching. H. Hamilton, 1964

QUARTERMAIN, JAMES. Pseudonym of James Broome Lynne, 1920- , q.v. SC: Carbo, in all titles.
   The Diamond Hook. Constable, 1970; Doubleday, 1970
   The Diamond Hostage. Constable, 1975
   The Man Who Walked on Diamonds. Constable, 1971; Doubleday, 1972
   Rock of Diamond. Constable, 1972; Doubleday, 1972 [U.S.]

QUEEN, ELLERY. Joint pseudonym of Frederic Dannay, 1905-1982, and Manfred Bennington Lee, 1905-1971. Other joint pseudonym: Barnaby Ross, q.v. Ref: all eight. SC: Ellery (and Insp. Richard) Queen = Q (see also: next entry).
   The Adventures of Ellery Queen. Stokes, 1934; Gollancz, 1935 ss Q
   The American Gun Mystery. Stokes, 1933; Gollancz, 1933. Also published as: Death at the Rodeo. Mercury, 1951 Q [NYC]
   And on the Eighth Day. Random, 1964; Gollancz, 1964 (Actually written by Avram Davidson, 1923- , q.v., from detailed story outline by Dannay.) Q [1943, Nev.]
   Calamity Town. Little, 1942; Gollancz, 1942 Q [New Eng.]
   Calendar of Crime. Little, 1952; Gollancz, 1952 ss Q
   The Case Book of Ellery Queen. Bestseller, 1945 (A pb collection of ss reprinted from The Adventures, and The New Adventures, qq.v., along with 3 Q radio plays uncollected elsewhere.) ss Q
   The Case of the Seven Murders; see Double, Double
   Cat of Many Tails. Little, 1949; Gollancz, 1949 Q [NYC]
   The Chinese Orange Mystery. Stokes, 1934; Gollancz, 1934 Q [NYC]
   Cop Out. World, 1969; Gollancz, 1969
   Death at the Rodeo; see The American Gun Mystery
   The Devil to Pay. Stokes, 1938; Gollancz, 1938 Q [L.A.]
   The Door Between. Stokes, 1937; Gollancz, 1937 Q [NYC]
   Double, Double. Little, 1950; Gollancz, 1950. Also published as: The Case of the Seven Murders. PB, 1958 Q [New Eng.]
   The Dragon's Teeth. Stokes, 1939; Gollancz, 1939. Also published as: The Virgin Heiresses. PB, 1954 Q [NYC]
   The Dutch Shoe Mystery. Stokes, 1931; Gollancz, 1931 Q [NYC]
   The Egyptian Cross Mystery. Stokes, 1932; Gollancz, 1932 Q [L.I.]
   Face to Face. New American Library, 1967; Gollancz, 1967 Q [NYC]
   A Fine and Private Place. World, 1971; Gollancz, 1971 Q [NYC]
   The Finishing Stroke. Simon, 1958; Gollancz, 1958 Q [N.Y.]
   The Four of Hearts. Stokes, 1938; Gollancz, 1939 Q [L.A.]
   The Fourth Side of the Triangle. Random, 1965; Gollancz, 1965 (Actually written by Avram Davidson, 1923- , q.v., from detailed story outline by Dannay.) Q [NYC]
   The French Powder Mystery. Stokes, 1930; Gollancz, 1930 Q [NYC]
   The Glass Village. Little, 1954; Gollancz, 1954 [New Eng.]
   The Greek Coffin Mystery. Stokes, 1932; Gollancz, 1932 Q [NYC]
   Halfway House. Stokes, 1936; Gollancz, 1936 Q [N.J.]
   The House of Brass. New American Library, 1968; Gollancz, 1968 (Actually written by Avram Davidson, 1923- , q.v., from detailed story outline by Dannay.) Q [N.Y.]
   Inspector Queen's Own Case. Simon, 1956; Gollancz, 1956 Q [Conn.]
   The King Is Dead. Little, 1952; Gollancz, 1952 Q
   The Lamp of God. Dell 10¢ pb, 1951 (A novelet originally appearing in The New Adventures of Ellery Queen, q.v.)
   The Last Woman in His Life. World, 1970; Gollancz, 1970 Q [New Eng.]
   More Adventures of Ellery Queen. Bestseller, 1940 (A pb collection of ss reprinted from The Adventures, and The New Adventures, qq.v.) ss Q
   The Murderer Is a Fox. Little, 1945; Gollancz, 1945 Q [New Eng.]
   The New Adventures of Ellery Queen. Stokes, 1940; Gollancz, 1940 ss Q
   The Origin of Evil. Little, 1951; Gollancz, 1951 Q [L.A.]
   The Player on the Other Side. Random, 1963; Gollancz, 1963 (Actually written by Theodore Sturgeon, 1918- , q.v., from detailed story outline by Dannay.) Q [NYC]
   QBI: Queen's Bureau of Investigation. Little, 1954; Gollancz, 1955 ss Q
   QED: Queen's Experiments in Detection. New American Library, 1968; Gollancz, 1969 ss Q
   Queens Full. Random, 1965; Gollancz, 1966 ss Q
   The Quick and the Dead; see There Was an Old Woman
   The Roman Hat Mystery. Stokes, 1929; Gollancz, 1929 Q [NYC]
   The Scarlet Letters. Little, 1953; Gollancz, 1953 Q [NYC]
   Sherlock Holmes vs. Jack the Ripper; see A Study in Terror
   The Siamese Twin Mystery. Stokes, 1933; Gollancz, 1934 Q
   The Spanish Cape Mystery. Stokes, 1935; Gollancz, 1935 Q
   A Study in Terror. Lancer, 1966. British title: Sherlock Holmes vs. Jack the Ripper. Gollancz, 1967 (Novelization of the movie, with Ellery added as a character in the "framing story"; Q sequences written by Dannay & Lee; Sherlock Holmes sequences primarily by Paul W. Fairman, 1916-1977, q.v., with Dannay-Lee input.) Q, Sherlock Holmes [Eng., 1888]
   Ten Days' Wonder. Little, 1948; Gollancz, 1948 Q [New Eng.]
   There Was an Old Woman. Little, 1943; Gollancz, 1944. Also published as: The Quick and the Dead. PB, 1956 Q [NYC]
   The Virgin Heiresses; see The Dragon's Teeth

QUEEN, ELLERY. House name. Actual authors of some titles have been identified: by Richard Deming, 1915- , q.v. = by RD; by Edward D(entinger) Hoch, 1930- , q.v. = by EH; by Stephen Marlowe, 1928- , q.v. = by SM; by Talmage Powell, 1920- , q.v. = by TP; by John Holbrook Vance, 1917- , q.v. = by JV. Note: all titles were edited and supervised by Lee except "The Blue Movie Murders," which was edited and supervised by Dannay after Lee's death. SC: Tim Corrigan = TC; Mike McCall = MM; Ellery Queen = EQ (see also: previous entry). See also: William Rand.
   Beware the Young Stranger. PB, 1965 (by TP.)
   The Black Hearts Murder. Lancer, 1970 MM (by RD.)
   Blow Hot, Blow Cold. PB, 1964
   The Blue Movie Murders. Lancer, 1972; Gollancz, 1973 MM (by EH.)
   The Campus Murders. Lancer, 1969 MM [acad.]
   The Copper Frame. PB, 1965; Four Square, 1966 [N.Y.] (by RD.)
   Dead Man's Tale. PB, 1961; Four Square, 1967 (by SM.)
   Death Spins the Platter. PB, 1962; Gollancz, 1975 (by RD.) [L.A.]
   The Devil's Cook. PB, 1966 [acad.]
   Ellery Queen, Master Detective. Grosset, 1941. Also published as: The Vanishing Corpse. Pyramid, 1968 (Novelization of the movie.) EQ [NYC]
   The Four Johns. PB, 1964. British title: Four Men Called John. Gollancz, 1976 (by JV.) [S.F.]
   Four Men Called John; see The Four Johns
   The Golden Goose. PB, 1964; Four Square, 1967
   Guess Who's Coming to Kill You? Lancer, 1968 [Jap.]
   How Goes the Murder? Popular Library, 1967 TC (by RD.) [NYC]
   Kill As Directed. PB, 1963 [NYC]
   The Killer Touch. PB, 1965 [Carib.]
   Kiss and Kill. Dell, 1969 [Mex.]
   The Last Man Club. Whitman, 1940 ("Novelettization" of the radio play.) EQ [NYC]
   The Last Man Club. Pyramid, 1968 (Reprint edition combining the earlier "novelettizations" The Last Man Club and The Murdered Millionaire, qq.v.)
   The Last Score. PB, 1964 [Mex.]
   Losers, Weepers. Dell, 1966 (by RD.) [L.A.]
   The Madman Theory. PB, 1966 (by JV.) [Calif.]
   Murder with a Past. PB, 1963 (by TP.)
   The Murdered Millionaire. Whitman, 1942 ("Novelettization" of the radio play.) EQ [NYC]
   The Penthouse Mystery. Grosset, 1941 (Novelization of the movie.) EQ [NYC]
   The Perfect Crime. Grosset, 1942 (Novelization of the movie.) EQ [NYC]
   A Room to Die In. PB, 1965 (by JV.) [Calif.]
   Shoot the Scene. Dell, 1966 (by RD.) [L.A.]
   The Vanishing Corpse; see Ellery Queen, Master Detective
   What's in the Dark? Popular Library, 1968. British title: When Fell the Night. Gollancz, 1970 TC (by RD.) [NYC]
   When Fell the Night; see What's in the Dark?
   Where Is Bianca? Popular Library, 1966; Four Square, 1966 TC (by TP.) [NYC]
   Which Way to Die? Popular Library, 1967 TC (by RD.) [NYC]
   Who Spies, Who Kills? Popular Library, 1966; Four Square, 1967 TC (by TP.) [NYC]
   Why So Dead? Popular Library, 1966; Four Square, 1966 TC (by RD.)
   Wife or Death. PB, 1963; Four Square, 1963 (by RD.)

QUENEAU, RAYMOND. 1903-1976. Ref: CA.
   -We Always Treat Women Too Well. Calder, 1980; New Directions, 1981 (Translation of "On est Toujours Trop Bon Avec les Femmes," originally published as by Sally Mara.) [Dublin]

QUENTIN, DOROTHY
   -The Cottage in the Woods. Ward, 1964
   -Dangerous Affair. Ward, 1962
   -The Dark Castle. Ward, 1963
   -Duel Across the Water. Ward, 1966
   -House of Illusion. Ward, 1966
   -Perilous Voyage. Ward, 1964 [ship]
   The Prisoner in the Square. Ward, 1961; Pyramid, 1968
   -What News of Kitty? Ward, 1967

QUENTIN, PATRICK. Joint pseudonym of Hugh Callingham Wheeler, 1912- , q.v., and Richard Wilson Webb, 1901- . Other joint pseudonyms: Q. Patrick, Jonathan Stagge, qq.v. SC: Peter Duluth = PD; Lt. Timothy Trant = TT (see also Q. Patrick entry).
Black Widow. Simon, 1952. British title: Fatal Woman. Gollancz, 1953 PD,TT [NYC]
Family Skeletons. Random, 1965; Gollancz, 1965 TT [NYC]
Fatal Woman; see Black Widow
The Fate of the Immodest Blonde; see Puzzle for Pilgrims
The Follower. Simon, 1950; Gollancz, 1950 [Mex.]
The Green-Eyed Monster. Random, 1960; Gollancz, 1960 [NYC]
Love Is a Deadly Weapon; see Puzzle for Fiends
The Man in the Net. Simon, 1956; Gollancz, 1956 [N.Y.]
The Man with Two Wives. Simon, 1955; Gollancz, 1955 TT [NYC]
My Son, the Murderer. Simon, 1954. British title: The Wife of Ronald Sheldon. Gollancz, 1954 TT [NYC]
The Ordeal of Mrs. Snow. Random, 1962; Gollancz, 1961 ss
Puzzle for Fiends. Simon, 1946; Gollancz, 1947. Also published as: Love Is a Deadly Weapon. PB, 1949 PD [Calif.]
A Puzzle for Fools. Simon, 1936; Gollancz, 1936 PD
Puzzle for Pilgrims. Simon, 1947; Gollancz, 1948. Also published as: The Fate of the Immodest Blonde. PB, 1950 PD [Mex. City]
Puzzle for Players. Simon, 1938; Gollancz, 1939 PD [NYC]
Puzzle for Puppets. Simon, 1944; Gollancz, 1944 PD [S.F.]
Puzzle for Wantons. Simon, 1945; Gollancz, 1946. Also published as: Slay the Loose Ladies. PB, 1948 PD [Reno]
Run to Death. Simon, 1948; Gollancz, 1948 PD [Mex.]
Shadow of Guilt. Random, 1959; Gollancz, 1959 TT [NYC]
Slay the Loose Ladies; see Puzzle for Wantons
Suspicious Circumstances. Simon, 1957; Gollancz, 1957 [L.A.]
The Wife of Ronald Sheldon; see My Son, the Murderer

QUEST, ERICA. Joint pseudonym of John Sawyer, 1919- , and Nancy Buckingham Sawyer, 1924- . Other joint pseudonym: Nancy Buckingham, q.v.
The October Cabaret. Doubleday, 1979
The Silver Castle. Doubleday, 1978 [Switz.]

QUEST, RODNEY. 1897- . Ref: CA. SC: Peter Quentin = PQ.
The Cerebus Murders. Harrap, 1969; McCall, 1970 PQ
Countdown to Doomsday. Harrap, 1966
Death of a Sinner. Harrap, 1971 PQ
The Fenton Affair. Harrap, 1967
Murder with a Vengeance. Harrap, 1971 PQ

QUICK, DOROTHY. 1900-1962. Writer of ss, poetry, book reviews; syndicated columnist; lived in NYC and L.I. SC: Lt. Peter Donnegan, in at least those marked PD.
The Cry in the Night. Arcadia, 1957; Cherry Tree, 1950
The Doctor Looks at Murder. Arcadia, 1959 PD [Mass.]
The Fifth Dagger. Scribner, 1947 PD [Boston]
Peril at Dune's Edge. Cherry Tree, 1945
Something Evil. Arcadia, 1958 [L.I.]
Too Strange a Hand. Arcadia, 1950

QUIGLEY, AILEEN. 1930- . Pseudonym: Erica Lindley, q.v.

QUIGLEY, JOHN. 1927- . Ref: CA.
The Last Checkpoint. Collins, 1971; McCall, 1971
The Secret Soldier. Hutchinson, 1966; New American Library, 1966 [Formosa]

QUILLER-COUCH, SIR ARTHUR T(HOMAS). 1863-1944. Pseudonym: "Q", q.v. Ref: CC.
Castle Dor, with Daphne du Maurier, 1907- , q.v. Dent, 1962; Doubleday, 1962
Foe-Farrell. Collins, 1918; Macmillan, 1918
Old Fires and Profitable Ghosts. Cassell, 1900; Scribner, 1900 ss
Poison Island. Smith, Elder, 1907; Scribner, 1906
Q's Mystery Stories. Dent, 1937 ss

QUILTY, RAFE
The Tenth Session. Cape, 1972

QUIN, ANN (MARIE). 1936-1973. Ref: CA.
-Berg. Calder, 1964; Scribner, 1965

QUIN, B(ASIL) G(ODFREY). SC: James Clarkson-Parry, in at least those marked JC. Set: Eng.
The Death Box. Hutchinson, 1929; Greenberg, 1932 JC
Mistigris. Hutchinson, 1932 JC
The Murder Rehearsal. Hutchinson, 1931; Greenberg, 1932 JC
The Mystery of the Black Gate. Hutchinson, 1930
The Phantom Murderer. Hutchinson, 1932 JC

QUINCE, JAMES
Casual Slaughters. Nicholson, 1935
Notice to Quit. Hodder, 1932
The Tin Tree. Hodder, 1930

QUINN, DERRY. Movie story editor; scriptwriter for films and TV.
The Fear of God. Barrie, 1978; St. Martin's, 1979
The Limbo Connection. Harrap, 1976; St. Martin's, 1977
The Solstice Man. Harrap, 1977; St. Martin's, 1977

QUINN, E(LEANOR) BAKER. SC: James Strange, in at least those marked JS. Set: Eng.
The Dead Harm No One. Heinemann, 1938
Death Is a Restless Sleeper. Heinemann, 1940; Mystery House, 1941 JS
One Man's Muddle. Heinemann, 1936; Macmillan, 1937 JS

QUINN, JAKE. SC: Patrick Shannon, in all titles.
The Mindbenders. Leisure, 1975 [NYC]
Shallow Grave. Leisure, 1974 [NYC]
The Undertaker. Leisure, 1974 [NYC]

QUINN, OLGA
Spies Go Running. Hale, 1971
Spies on the Roof. Hale, 1969

QUINN, PATRICK. SC: Pete Riley, in at least those marked PR.
The Barbed-Wire Hurdlers. Hale, 1969
The Big Game. Hale, 1970 PR
The Fatal Complaint. Hale, 1970 PR
Once Upon a Private Eye. Hale, 1968 PR
Thrice Upon a Killing Spree. Hale, 1970 PR
Twice Upon a Crime. Hale, 1969 PR

QUINN, SEABURY (GRANDIN). 1889-1969. Ref: CA. SC: Jules de Grandin, in all titles.
The Adventures of Jules de Grandin. Popular Library, 1976 ss
The Casebook of Jules de Grandin. Popular Library, 1976 ss
The Devil's Bride. Popular Library, 1976 [N.J.]
The Hellfire Files of Jules de Grandin. Popular Library, 1976 ss
The Horror Chambers of Jules de Grandin. Popular Library, 1977 ss
The Phantom-Fighter. Mycroft, 1966 ss
The Skeleton Closet of Jules de Grandin. Popular Library, 1976 ss

QUINN, SIMON. Pseudonym of Martin Cruz Smith, 1942- , q.v. Other pseudonym: Nick Carter, q.v. SC: The Inquisitor (Francis Xavier Killy) = I.
The Devil in Kansas. Dell, 1974 I
His Eminence, Death. Dell, 1974 I
The Human Factor. Dell, 1975; Futura, 1975 (Novelization of the movie.) [It.]
Last Rites for the Vulture. Dell, 1975 I
The Last Time I Saw Hell. Dell, 1974 I
The Midas Coffin. Dell, 1975 I
Nuplex Red. Dell, 1974 I

QUINN, TERRY. 1945- . Ref: CA.
The Great Bridge Conspiracy. St. Martin's, 1979; Allen, 1980 [S.F.]

QUINNELL, A. J. Pseudonym.
Man on Fire. Macmillan (London), 1981; Morrow, 1980 [It.]

QUINTANO, DOROTHY G. Author of 1949 book, "No Winds of Healing," as Dorothy Hines; lives in N.Y.
Weekend at the Villa. Doubleday, 1974 [N.Y.]

QUIRK, JOHN (EDWARD). 1920- . Pseudonym: John Q, q.v.

QUIRK, LESLIE (W.). 1882- . See: Horatio (Gates) Winslow, 1882- .

QUIROULE, PIERRE. Pseudonym of W(alter) W(illiam) Sayer, 1892- , q.v. Those titles listed below without publisher feature Sexton Blake and were published by Amalgamated Press. Note: Many Sexton Blake titles originally published as by W. W. Sayer were reprinted with new titles as by Pierre Quiroule; see the W. W. Sayer entry. See also: R. C. Armour.
The Circle of Death. Mellifont, 1936
The Golf Links Mystery. Mellifont, 1935
The Hated Eight. 1938
The Hour of Recognition. Mellifont, 1932
The Man with Two Souls. Amalgamated, 1935
The Mystery of the Missing Envoy. 1939
The Mystery of No. 7 Bitton Court. 1938
The Mystery of No. 13 Cavendish Square. 1936
The Painted Death. Nelson, 1935
The Riddle of the Evil Eye. 1939
The Riddle of the Ugly Face. 1939
The Secret of the Armaments King. 1935
Secret of the Circle. Mellifont, 1934
The Secret of the Woods. 1934
The Silhouette Symbol. Mellifont, 1935
The Slaver's Secret. 1934
The Three Lepers' Heads. 1937

RABE, PETER. Ref: CC. SC: Daniel Port = DP; Manny DeWitt = MD.
Agreement to Kill. GM, 1957; Fawcett (London), 1958
Anatomy of a Killer. Abelard (NYC & London), 1960
Benny Muscles In. GM, 1955; Fawcett (London), 1958
Black Mafia. GM, 1974
Blood on the Desert. GM, 1958; Muller pb, 1960
The Box. GM, 1962; Muller pb, 1963 [Afr., N.]
Bring Me Another Corpse. GM, 1959; Muller pb, 1960 DP [Cleve.]
Code Name Gadget. GM, 1967 MD
The Cut of the Whip. Ace, 1958
Dig My Grave Deep. GM, 1956; Fawcett (London), 1957 DP
Girl in a Big Brass Bed. GM, 1965 MD
A House in Naples. GM, 1956; Fawcett (London), 1958 [Naples]
It's My Funeral. GM, 1957; Fawcett (London), 1959 DP [L.A.]
Journey into Terror. GM, 1957; Fawcett (London), 1959
Kill the Boss Good-By. GM, 1956; Fawcett (London), 1957
Mission for Vengeance. GM, 1958
Murder Me for Nickels. GM, 1960; Muller pb, 1961
My Lovely Executioner. GM, 1960; Jenkins, 1967
The Out Is Death. GM, 1957; Fawcett (London), 1959 DP
A Shroud for Jesso. GM, 1955; Fawcett (London), 1956 [Ger.]
The Spy Who Was Three Feet Tall. GM, 1966 MD [Afr.]
Stop This Man! GM, 1955; Fawcett (London), 1957 [L.A.]
Time Enough to Die. GM, 1959; Muller pb, 1961 DP [Mex.]
War of the Dons. GM, 1972; Coronet, 1973 [L.A.]

RABINOWITZ, MAX
Cop Killers. Zebra, 1979

RABON, WALTER
Spider on the Belly. Vantage, 1967

RABOU, CHARLES (FELIX HENRI). 1803-1870.
The Widow's Walk; or, The Mystery of Crime. Appleyard, 18?? (Translation of "L'Alee des Veuves.")

RACE, PHILIP
Johnny Come Deadly. Hillman, 1960
Killer Take All. GM, 1959; Muller pb, 1961 [Calif.]
Self-Made Widow. GM, 1958; Fawcett (London), 1960 [L.A.]

RACINA, THOM. 1946- . Ref: CA.
Quincy, M.E. Ace, 1977 (Novelization of the TV series.)
Quincy, M.E. #2. Ace, 1977 (Novelization of the TV series.)
Sweet Revenge. Berkley, 1977 (Novelization of the "Baretta" TV series.) [L.A.]

RADANO, GENE. NYC policeman for 20 years; playwright.
  Stories Cops Only Tell Each Other. Stein, 1974 ss

RADCLIFFE, ANN (WARD). 1764-1823. Ref: CC, DD, EM.
  The Castles of Athlin and Dunbayne. Hookham, 1789; Bradford, 1796, as by Anne Rattcliffe [Scot., Middle Ages]
  The Confessional of the Black Penitents; see The Italian
  Gaston de Blondeville; or, The Court of Henry III. Colburn, 1826; Collins, 1826
  The Italian; or, The Confessional of the Black Penitents. Cadell, 1797; Magill, 1797. Also published as: The Confessional of the Black Penitents. Folio Society, 1956 [It.]
  The Mysteries of Udolpho. Robinson, 1794; White, 1795 [It., 1600s]
  The Romance of the Forest. Hookham, 1791; Etheridge, 1795
  A Sicilian Romance. Hookham, 1790; Rice, 1795 [Sic., 1580]

RADCLIFFE, (HENRY) GARNETT. 1899- . Set: Eng.
  The Flower Gang. Butterworth, 1929; Houghton, 1930
  Forgotten of Allah. Butterworth, 1936
  The Great Orme Terror. Butterworth, 1934
  In the Grip of the Brute. Butterworth, 1937 [ship]
  The Prisoners in the Wall. Butterworth, 1933
  -The Return of the Ceteosaurus, and other tales. Drane's, 1926 ss
  The Sky Wolves. Butterworth, 1938
  The Straight Road. Butterworth, 1935
  The 13th Mummy. Butterworth, 1936
  Top Floor Back. Macdonald, 1943

RADCLIFFE, JANETTE. Pseudonym of Janet Louise Roberts, 1925- , q.v. Other pseudonyms: Louisa Bronte, Rebecca Danton, qq.v.
  -The Blue-Eyed Gypsy. Dell, 1974
  -The Gentleman Pirate. Dell, 1975
  -The Moonlight Gondola. Dell, 1975

RADCLIFFE, JOCELYN. Pseudonym of Charles N. Beardsley.
  Blackwood. Curtis, 1974 [Calif.]

RADCLIFFE, MARY ANNE
  Manfrone; or, The One-Handed Monk. Hughes, 1809; Arno, 1972 [It.]

RADFORD, E(DWIN ISAAC), 1891- , and M(ONA) A(UGUSTA MANGAN). Ref: CA, TC. SC: Doctor Manson, in at least those marked M. Set: Eng.
  A Cosy Little Murder. Hale, 1963 M
  Crime Pays No Dividends. Melrose, 1945 M
  Dead Water. Hale, 1971 M
  Death and the Professor. Hale, 1961
  Death at the Chateau Noir. Hale, 1960 M [Fr.]
  Death Has Two Faces. Hale, 1972 M
  Death of an Ancient Saxon. Hale, 1969 M
  Death of a Frightened Editor. Hale, 1959 M
  Death of a "Gentleman". Hale, 1966 M
  Death of a Peculiar Rabbit. Hale, 1969 M
  Death on the Broads. Long, 1957 M
  Death Takes the Wheel. Hale, 1962 M
  Death's Inheritance. Hale, 1961 M
  From Information Received. Hale, 1962 M
  The Greedy Killers. Hale, 1971 M
  The Heel of Achilles. Melrose, 1950 M
  The Hungry Killer. Hale, 1964 M
  Inspector Manson's Success. Melrose, 1944 M
  It's Murder to Live. Melrose, 1947 M
  John Kyleing Died. Melrose, 1949 M
  Jones's Little Murders. Hale, 1967 M
  Look in at Murder. Long, 1956 M
  Married to Murder. Hale, 1959
  Mask of Murder. Hale, 1965 M
  The Middlefold Murders. Hale, 1967 M
  Murder Is Ruby Red. Hale, 1970 M
  Murder Isn't Cricket. Melrose, 1946 M
  Murder Jigsaw. Melrose, 1944 M
  Murder Magnified. Hale, 1965 M
  Murder of Three Ghosts. Hale, 1963 M
  Murder on My Conscience. Hale, 1960 M
  Murder Speaks. Hale, 1970 M
  No Reason for Murder. Hale, 1967 M
  The Safety First Murders. Hale, 1968 M
  The Six Men. Hale, 1958
  Trunk Call to Murder. Hale, 1968 M
  Two Ways to Murder. Hale, 1969 M
  Who Killed Dick Whittington? Melrose, 1947 M

RADFORD, JOHN P. SC: Joe Maguire (The Illusionist), in all titles.
  All of Our Aircraft Are Missing! Canyon, 1974 [Fr.]
  The Game Show Girls. Canyon, 1975
  The Most Happy Con Man. Canyon, 1974
  The Parisian Pigeon Drop. Canyon, 1974

RADFORD, M(ONA) A(UGUSTA MANGAN). See: E(dwin Isaac) Radford, 1891- .

RADFORD, RUBY L(ORRAINE). 1891-1971. Ref: CA.
  Crime and Judy. Avalon, 1960

RADLEY, EDWARD. See: Uri Dan.

RADLEY, SHEILA. Pseudonym. Other pseudonym: Hester Rowan, q.v. SC: Insp. Douglas Quantrill, in both titles. Set: Eng.
  The Chief Inspector's Statement. Constable, 1981; Scribner, 1980
  Death and the Maiden. H. Hamilton, 1978. U.S. title: Death in the Morning. Scribner, 1979

RADNOR, ALAN. SC: Dick Barton = DB (see also: Mike Dorrell; and: Larry Pryce).
  The Case of the Vanishing House. Star, 1978 DB
  The Force. Hamlyn, 1979
  Red Light Red. Sphere, 1980
  Whodunit? Arrow, 1978 (Novelization of the TV series.)

RAE, HUGH C(RAUFORD). 1935- . Pseudonyms: Robert Crawford, R. B. Houston, Stuart Stern, qq.v. Ref: CA, TC. SC: Insp./Supt. McCaig, in at least those marked M.
  A Few Small Bones. Blond, 1968. U.S. title: The House at Balnesmoor. Coward, 1969 M [Scot.]
  -The Haunting at Waverley Falls. Constable, 1980
  The House at Balnesmoor; see A Few Small Bones
  The Interview. Blond, 1969; Coward, 1969
  The Marksman. Constable, 1971; Coward, 1971 [Glasgow]
  Night Pillow. Blond, 1967; Viking, 1967
  The Rock Harvest. Constable, 1973
  The Rookery. Constable, 1974; St. Martin's, 1975 [Eng., ca.1850]
  The Saturday Epic. Blond, 1970; Coward, 1970 [Scot.]
  The Shooting Gallery. Constable, 1972; Coward, 1972 M [Scot.]
  Skinner. Blond, 1965; Viking, 1965 [Scot.]
  Sullivan. Constable, 1978; Playboy, 1978

RAE-BROWN, CAMPBELL
  The Avenging Kiss. Digby, 1912
  The Devil's Shilling. Drane, 1897
  The Great Newmarket Mystery. Long, 1909
  -The Resurrection of His Grace. Greening, 1899
  Very Long Odds and a Strange Finish. Routledge, 1893 ss

RAEF, LAURA (GLADYS) C(AUBLE). Ref: CA.
  Trade Winds over Kokio. Manor, 1979

RAFFALOVICH, GEORGE. 1880- .
  The Deuce and All. Equinox, 1910 ss, at least one criminous
  Planetary Journeys and Earthly Sketches. Fairbairns, 1908 ss, at least one criminous

RAFFERTY, S. S. Pseudonym of John Jerome Hurley, 1930- . Ref: CA, TC.
  Fatal Flourishes. Avon, 1979 ss [U.S., ca.1750]

RAGG, THOMAS MURRAY. 1897- . Pseudonym: Murray Thomas, q.v.

RAGOSTA, MILLIE J(ANE). 1931- . Ref: CA.
  House of Evil Winds. Avalon, 1973
  The House on Curtin Street. Doubleday, 1979
  King John's Treasure. Doubleday, 1976 [Eng.]
  The Lighthouse. Avalon, 1971
  Lorena Veiled. Ballantine, 1974 [Pa., ca.1905]
  Taverna in Terrazzo. Ballantine, 1975 [It.]
  Witness to Treason. Doubleday, 1977

RAGSDALE, LULAH
  The Crime of Philip Guthrie. Morrill, 1892
  -A Shadow's Shadow. Lippincott, 1893

RAINE, RICHARD. Pseudonym of Raymond H(arold) Sawkins, 1923- , q.v. Other pseudonyms: Jay Bernard, Colin Forbes, qq.v. SC: David Martini, in all titles.
  Bombshell. Dent, 1970; Harcourt, 1970
  The Corder Index; see A Wreath for America
  Night of the Hawk. Heinemann, 1968; Harcourt, 1968
  A Wreath for America. Heinemann, 1967. U.S. title: The Corder Index. Harcourt, 1967

RAINE, WILLIAM MacLEOD. 1871-1954.
  Cry Murder. Phoenix, 1947. British title: Cry Murder in the Market Place. Hodder, 1941
  Cry Murder in the Market Place; see Cry Murder
  Tangled Trails. Houghton, 1921; Hodder, 1921

RAINHAM, THOMAS. Pseudonym of Charles MacKinnon Barren, 1913- . Ref: CA.
  Too Late to Mend. Hurst, 1957

RAINIER, PAUL J.
  Scared Stiff. Merit, 1954 [Calif.]

RAINONE, CHRISTOPHER. Pseudonym: Violet Hawthorne, q.v.

RAINSFORD, W. H.
  BB of Ardlegay. Lane, 1923

RAISON, MILTON M(ICHAEL). 1903-1982. Born in NYC; newspaper feature writer and book reviewer, theatrical publicist, screenwriter. SC: Tony Woolrich = TW.
  The Gay Mortician. Murray, 1946; Archer, 1947 TW [S.F.]
  Murder in a Lighter Vein. Murray, 1947 TW [L.A.]
  No Weeds for the Widow. Murray, 1946; Kelly, 1951 TW [L.I.]
  Nobody Loves a Dead Man. Murray, 1945; Archer, 1946 TW [L.A.]
  The Phantom of Forty-Second Street, with Jack Harvey. Macaulay, 1936 TW [NYC]
  Tunnel 13. Murray, 1948

RALEIGH, ALAN. Pseudonym of Elijah Brown, 1867- .
  The Man in the Car. Long, 1913

RALEIGH, CECIL. Pseudonym of Cecil Rowlands, 1856-1914. See also: Richard Parker.
  The Sins of Society. Paul, 1909; Dillingham, 1910 (Novelization of the play by Cecil Raleigh and Henry Hamilton, 1853?-1918.)

RALEIGH, H(ILARY) M(ASON). 1893- .
  -The Chronicles of Slyme Court. Bles, 1935
  Excess Baggage. Methuen, 1932; Dutton, 1932
  The Machinations of Dr. Grue. Bles, 1938
  -The Merry Mug. Bles, 1936
  -Royal Exchange. Methuen, 1932
  -Sheikh Stuff. Bles, 1937

RALLI, CONSTANTINE (SCARAMANGA)
  The Strange Story of Falconer Thring. Hurst, 1907

RALPH, JULIAN. 1853-1903.
  The Millionairess. Lothrop, 1902; Methuen, 1902

RALSTON, GILBERT A(LEXANDER). 1912- . Ref: CA. SC: Dakota = D.
  Ben. Bantam, 1972 (Novelization of the movie.)
  Chain Reaction. Pinnacle, 1975 D [Nev.]
  Cat Trap. Pinnacle, 1974 D
  Dakota Warpath. Pinnacle, 1973 D
  The Deadly, Deadly Art. Pinnacle, 1974 [NYC]
  The Frightful Sin of Cisco Newman, with Richard (L.) Newhafer, 1922- . Prentice-Hall, 1972
  Murder's Money. Pinnacle, 1975 D [Nev.]
  Red Revenge. Pinnacle, 1974 D

RAMAGE, JENNIFER. Pseudonym: Howard Mason, q.v.

RAME, DAVID. Pseudonym of A(rthur) D(urham) Divine, 1904- , q.v. Other pseudonym: David Divine, q.v.

RAMIREZ, ALICE. Pseudonym: Candice Arkham, q.v.

RAMPAL, S. N. 1928-   .
   Unknown Skyjacker. Blue Band (New Delhi), 1972

RAMPO, EDOGAWA. Pseudonym of Taro Hirai, 1894-   . Ref: CC.
   Japanese Tales of Mystery and Imagination. Tuttle, 1956   ss [Jap.]

RAMRUS, AL, 1930-   , and JOHN SHANER. Ref for Ramrus: CA.
   -The Ludendorff Pirates. Doubleday, 1978; Arrow, 1979

RAMSAY, DIANA. Pseudonym of Rhoda Brandes. SC: Lt. Meredith, in at least those marked M
   The Dark Descends; see Descent into the Dark
   Deadly Discretion. Collins, 1973   M
   Descent into the Dark. Collins, 1975. U.S. title: The Dark Descends. Harper, 1975   [NYC]
   A Little Murder Music. Collins, 1972   M [NYC]
   No Cause to Kill. Collins, 1974   M
   You Can't Call It Murder. Collins, 1977

RAMSAY, JACK
   Deathgame. Sphere, 1978
   The Golden Lady. New English Library pb, 1977
   -The Rage. Sphere, 1977

RAMSAY, R(INA)
   The Step in the House. Hurst, 1926

RAMSDALE, FRED
   The Brand of the Crook. Mellifont, 1942
   Poison on the Menu. Grafton, 1945

RAMSEY, ERIC
   The Kummersdorf Connection. Playboy, 1978; Futura, 1978   [Ger.]

RAMSEY, GUY (HAYLETT WALKER)
   Stop Press Murder. Dakers, 1953

RANBERN, JAMES
   Unnatural Selection. New Horizon, 1978

RANCE, JOSEPH and AREI KATO
   Bullet Train. Souvenir, 1980; Morrow, 1981   [Jap.]

RAND, AYN. 1905-1982. Ref: CA.
   The Night of January 16. Longmans, 1936 (3-act play.)

RAND, JOHN. Pseudonym of James Reach, 1909?-1970, q.v. Other pseudonyms: Hilda Manning, Pete Williams, qq.v. Joint pseudonym with Tom (Barnard) Taggart, q.v.: Ross MacRoss, q.v.
   Cruise of Death. French (NYC), 1947 (3-act play.)
   Murder at the DeSoto. French (NYC), 1938 (1-act play.)

RAND, LOU
   The Gay Detective. Paperback Library, 1965. Also published as: Rough Trade. Paperback Library, 1965

RAND, REX
   Desperation. Modern Fiction, 1956
   -Playing for Time. Modern Fiction, 1956
   -She Wanted a Guy. Modern Fiction, 1955
   -Surrendered. Modern Fiction, 1955

RAND, STEVE. Pseudonym of Jay Bennett, 1912-   , q.v.
   All Her Vices. Monarch, 1961
   So Sweet, So Wicked. Monarch, 1961

RAND, WILLIAM. Pseudonym of William Roos, 1911-   . See also: Audrey (Kelley) Roos, 1912-1982. Joint pseudonym with Audrey (Kelley) Roos, 1912-1982: Kelley Roos, q.v.
   Ellery Queen's The Four of Hearts Mystery. Dramatic Publishing Co., 1949 (Dramatization of the novel by and about Ellery Queen, q.v.)

RANDALL, ANTHONY A(SHETON). 1923-   .
   SC: Roger Patten, in at least those marked RP.
   Flashpoint. Hale, 1966   RP
   Ride a Tiger. Hale, 1965   RP
   Suicide Passage. Hale, 1967
   To Catch a Spy. Hale, 1965

RANDALL, BOB
   The Fan. Random, 1977; Secker, 1977 [NYC]

RANDALL, FLORENCE ENGEL. 1917-   . Ref: CA.
   Haldane Station. Harcourt, 1973; Millington, 1975   [Mass.]
   Hedgerow. Harcourt, 1967   [N.Y.]
   The Place of Sapphires. Harcourt, 1969; Millington, 1974   [New Eng.]

RANDALL, JOHN
   Reserve Two for Murder. French, 19?? (Play.)

RANDALL, ROGER
   The Scarlet Death. Modern, 193?

RANDALL, RONA. Pseudonym of Rona (Green) Shambrook, q.v. These titles are at least mostly published in England as romances and in the U.S. as gothics.
   The Arrogant Duke. Collins, 1966; Ace, 1972
   Bright Morning. Collins, 1952
   Broken Tapestry. Hurst, 1969; Ace, 1973
   The Cedar Tree. Collins, 1957
   Dancing Cinderella. Collins, 1959
   Delayed Harvest. Collins, 1950
   Desert Flower. Collins, 1955
   The Doctor Falls in Love. Collins, 1958
   Dragonmede. Collins, 1974; Simon, 1974
   The Eagle at the Gate. H. Hamilton, 1978; Coward, 1978
   Enchanted Eden. Collins, 1960
   Faith, Hope and Charity. Collins, 1954
   The Fleeting Hour. Collins, 1947
   A Girl Called Ann. Collins, 1956; Ace, 1973
   Girl in Love. Collins, 1961
   Girls in White. Collins, 1952
   Glenrannoch. Collins, 1973. U.S. title: The Midnight Walker. Ace, 1973
   Hotel de Luxe. Collins, 1961; Ace, 1967
   House Surgeon at Luke's. Collins, 1962
   The Howards of Saxondale. Collins, 1946
   I Married a Doctor. Collins, 1947
   The Island Doctor. Collins, 1951
   Journey to Love. Collins, 1953; Ace, 1972
   Knight's Keep. Collins, 1967; Ace, 1967
   The Late Mrs. Lane. Collins, 1945
   Leap in the Dark. Collins, 1956; Ace, 1967
   Love and Dr. Maynard. Collins, 1959
   Lyonhurst; see Walk into My Parlour
   The Merry Andrew. Collins, 1954
   The Midnight Walker; see Glenrannoch
   The Moon Returns. Collins, 1942
   Moutain of Fear; see Silent Thunder
   Murmuring Willow; see The Willow Herb
   Nurse Stacey Comes Aboard. Collins, 1958
   Rebel Wife. Collins, 1944
   Runaway from Love. Collins, 1956
   Seven Days from Midnight. Collins, 1965; Ace, 1967
   Shadows on the Sand. Collins, 1949; Ace, 1973
   Silent Thunder. Hurst, 1971. U.S. title (?): Mountain of Fear. Ace, 1972
   Sister at Sea. Collins, 1960
   The Street of the Singing Fountain. Collins, 1948
   Time Remembered, Time Lost. Ace, 1973 (British title?)
   Walk into My Parlour. Collins, 1962; Ace, 1967. Revised edition: Lyonhurst. Fontana, 1977; Ballantine, 1977
   The Watchman's Stone. Collins, 1975; Simon, 1975   [Scot.]
   The Willow Herb. Collins, 1965. U.S. title: Murmuring Willow. Ace, 1967
   The Witching Hour. Hurst, 1970; Ace, 1970

RANDALL, WILLIAM. Pseudonym of William R. Gwinn.
   Deadly the Daring. Mystery House, 1958 [Mass.]

RANDALL, WILLIAM R.
   The Crystal Eye. Regent, 1935   [NYC]
   The Syndicate Murders. Greenberg, 1935

RANDAU, CARL (ALBERT), 1893-1969, and LEANE ZUGSMITH, 1903-1969. See also: Kenneth White, 1905-1953.
   The Visitor. Random, 1944; Gollancz, 1945

RANDELL, CHRISTINE. Several title correlations lacking below.
   Black Candle. Paperback Library, 1968 [Ire.]
   Curse of Deepwater. Paperback Library, 1974   [Eng.]
   Flower of the Judas. Jenkins, 1962
   House of Shadows. Jenkins, 1961. U.S. title: Whisper of Fear. Paperback Library, 1966
   Love Hath an Island. Jenkins, 1960
   Mallory Grange. Paperback Library, 1971 [Eng.]
   The Secret of Tarn-End House. Paperback Library, 1969
   Silent, My Love. Jenkins, 1959
   Valley of Silence. Hurst, 1969
   The Weeping Tower. Paperback Library, 1967   [Scot.]
   Whisper of Fear; see House of Shadows
   A Woman Possessed. Paperback Library, 1966

RANDISI, ROBERT J. See also: Warren B. Murphy, 1933-   .
   The Disappearance of Penny. Charter, 1980

RANDOLPH, ELLEN. Pseudonym of W(illiam) E(dward) D(aniel) Ross, 1912-   , q.v. Other pseudonyms: Laura Frances Brooks, Rose Dana, Jan Daniels, Clarissa Ross, Dan Ross, Dana Ross, Marilyn Ross, qq.v.
   The Castle on the Hill. Bouregy, 1964
   Paris in September. Bouregy, 1965 [Paris]
   Rendezvous in Amsterdam. Bouregy, 1965 [Amst.]
   The Secret of Graytowers. Bouregy, 1968
   -Threads of Love. Avalon, 1969

RANDOLPH, MARION. Pseudonym of Marie Fried Rodell, 1912-1975. Ref: CA, CC, TC.
   Breathe No More. Holt, 1940; Heinemann, 1940   [Conn.]
   Grim Grow the Lilacs. Holt, 1941; Museum, 1943   [N.Y.]
   This'll Kill You. Holt, 1940; Museum, 1944

RANDOLPH, VANCE, 1892-   , and NANCY CLEMENS, pseudonym. Ref for Randolph: CA.
   The Camp-Meeting Murders. Vanguard, 1936; Cassell, 1937   [Mo.]

RANDOLPHE, ARABELLA
   The Vampire Tapes. Berkley, 1977

RANK, MARY O. 1922-   .
   A Dream of Falling. Houghton, 1959. British title: Dream of Death. Hale, 1960

RANSOME, STEPHEN. Pseudonym of Frederick C(lyde) Davis, 1902-1977, q.v. Other pseudonyms: Murdo Coombs, Curtis Steele, qq.v. SC: Steve Ransome = SR; Det. Lt. Lee Barcello = LB.
   Alias His Wife. Dodd, 1965; Gollancz, 1965   LB   [Fla.]
   Death Checks In. Doubleday, 1939. British title: Whose Corpse? Davies, 1939   [NYC]
   False Bounty. Doubleday, 1948; Gollancz, 1949. Also published as: I, the Executioner. Ace, 1953   [Pa.]
   The Frazer Acquittal. Doubleday, 1955; Gollancz, 1955   [Pa.]
   Hear No Evil. Doubleday, 1953; Gollancz, 1954   SR   [Pa.]
   Hearses Don't Hurry. Doubleday, 1941
   The Hidden Hour. Dodd, 1966; Gollancz, 1966   LB   [Fla.]
   I, the Executioner; see False Bounty
   I'll Die for You. Doubleday, 1959; Gollancz, 1959   [Fla.]
   Meet in Darkness. Dodd, 1964; Gollancz, 1964   [Fla.]
   The Men in Her Death. Dodd, 1956; Gollancz, 1957   [Fla.]
   The Night, the Woman. Dodd, 1963; Gollancz, 1963   LB   [Fla.]
   One-Man Jury. Dodd, 1964; Gollancz, 1965   LB   [Fla.]
   A Shroud for Shylock. Doubleday, 1939 [N.Y.]
   The Shroud Off Her Back. Doubleday, 1953; Gollancz, 1953   SR   [Pa.]
   The Sin File. Dodd, 1965; Gollancz, 1966   LB   [Fla.]
   So Deadly My Love. Doubleday, 1957; Gollancz, 1958   [Fla.]
   Some Must Watch. Doubleday, 1961; Gollancz, 1961   [Pa.]
   Trap #6. Doubleday, 1971; Gollancz, 1972   LB   [Fla.]
   The Unspeakable. Doubleday, 1960; Gollancz, 1960   [Pa.]
   Warning Bell. Doubleday, 1960; Gollancz, 1960   [Pa.]
   Whose Corpse?; see Death Checks In
   Without a Trace. Doubleday, 1962; Gollancz, 1962   [Fla.]

RANVINS, AL. See: John Shaner.

RAPHAEL, CHAIM. 1908-   . Pseudonym: Jocelyn Davey, q.v.

RAPHAEL, FREDERIC (MICHAEL). 1931- .
Ref: CA.
Who Were You with Last Night? Cape, 1971

RAPHAEL, JOHN N(ATHANIEL). 1868-1917.
The Mystery of the Rue de Babylone. Grafton, 1916 [Paris]

RAPHAEL, MRS. L.
-The Double Mystery. Drane, 1924

RAPHAEL, RICK. 1919- . Ref: CA.
The Defector. Doubleday, 1980

RAPIER, JOHN
The Secret Mission of Colonel Death. Alliance, 1946

RASKIN, EUGENE. 1909- . Ref: CA.
Stranger in My Arms. Dell, 1971

RASKIN, JONAH. 1942- . Ref: CA.
Underground. Bobbs, 1978

RATCLIFFE, SUSAN
The Castle Captive. Avon, 1968 [Eng.]

RATH, E. J. Joint pseudonym of J. Chauncey Corey Brainerd and Edith Rathbone Jacobs Brainerd.
The Stolen Car. Nelson, 1929
Too Many Crooks. Watt, 1918

RATH, VIRGINIA (ANNE). 1905- . Educated at U. of Calif.; active in S.F. literary circles. SC: Rocky Allan = RA; Michael Dundas = MD.
The Anger of the Bells. Doubleday, 1937 RA [Calif.]
The Dark Cavalier. Doubleday, 1938 MD [S.F.]
Death at Dayton's Folly. Doubleday, 1935 RA [Calif.]
Death Breaks the Ring. Doubleday, 1941 MD [Calif.]
Death of a Lucky Lady. Doubleday, 1940 MD [S.F.]
A Dirge for Her. Ziff-Davis, 1947 MD [S.F.]
Epitaph for Lydia. Doubleday, 1942 MD [S.F.]
An Excellent Night for a Murder. Doubleday, 1937 RA [Calif.]
Ferryman, Take Him Across! Doubleday, 1936 RA [Calif., acad.]
Murder on the Day of Judgment. Doubleday, 1936 RA [Calif.]
Murder with a Theme Song. Doubleday, 1939 RA,MD [Calif.]
Posted for Murder. Doubleday, 1942 MD [S.F.]
A Shroud for Rowena. Ziff-Davis, 1947 MD [S.F.]

RATHBONE, CORNELIA KANE
Darkened Windows. Appleton, 1924 [NYC]
Jeremy Takes a Hand. Appleton, 1927 [NYC]

RATHBONE, EDWARD
-The Brass Knocker. Cape, 1934; Appleton, 1934

RATHBONE, JULIAN. 1935- . Ref: CA, TC. SC: Nur Bey, in at least those marked NB.
Bloody Marvelous. Joseph, 1975; St. Martin's, 1976 [Sp.]
Carnival! Joseph, 1976; St. Martin's, 1976 [Sp.]
Diamonds Bid. Joseph, 1967; Walker, 1967 NB [Turk.]
The Euro-Killers. Joseph, 1979; Pantheon, 1980
Hand Out. Joseph, 1968; Walker, 1968 NB [Turk.]
Kill Cure. Joseph, 1975; St. Martin's, 1975 [Turk.]
-King Fisher Lives. Joseph, 1976; St. Martin's, 1976
A Raving Monarchist. Joseph, 1977; St. Martin's, 1978 [Sp.]
Trip Trap. Joseph, 1972; St. Martin's, 1972 NB [Turk.]
With My Knives I Know I'm Good. Joseph, 1969; Putnam, 1970 [Mid. East]

RATHBONE, RICHARD A(DAMS). Born in W. Va.; prof. in Yale Art School; author of text on Composition, of poetry.
Death in the Drawing Room. Comet, 1954

RATHBORNE, ST. GEORGE (HENRY). 1854-1938. Pseudonyms: Nicholas Carter, Marline Manly, Doctor Mark Merrick, qq.v.
A Bar Sinister. Hobart, 1897. British title: A Cruel Case; or, The Bar Sinister. Aldine, 1897
Baron Sam. American News, 1893; Aldine, 1894
The Carteret Affair. Laird, 1891; Aldine, 1894. Also published as: Witch or Wife. Laird, 1895
A Cruel Case; see A Bar Sinister
The Detective and the Poisoner. Laird, 1892; Aldine, 1894
Masked in Mystery. Hobart, 1897; Henderson, 1897. Also published as: Under Egyptian Skies; or, Masked in Mystery. Street, 1900 [Egypt]
Miss Pauline of New York. American News, 1893; Aldine, 1894 [NYC]
-The Spider's Web. Street, 1898
Under Egyptian Skies; see Masked in Mystery
Witch or Wife; see The Carteret Affair

RATHBUN, F. P.
Suspected: A Story of Mystery. Henderson, 1894

RATHBURNE, FAY P.
Cruel Suspicion. Street (Magnet)
A Woman in the Case; or, Debtor to the Devil. Ogilvie, 1891

RATTCLIFFE, ANNE. See: Ann (Ward) Radcliffe, 1764-1823.

RATTRAY, SIMON. Pseudonym of Elleston Trevor, 1920- , q.v. Name originally: Trevor Dudley Smith, q.v. Other pseudonyms: Mansell Black, Adam Hall, Howard North, Warwick Scott, Caesar Smith, qq.v. SC: Hugo Bishop, in all titles. Set: Eng.
Bishop in Check. Boardman, 1953; Mill, 1961. Reprinted as by Adam Hall: Remploy, 1972; Pyramid, 1971
Dead Circuit. Boardman, 1955. U.S. title: Rook's Gambit, as by Adam Hall. Pyramid, 1972. Reprinted under the U.S. title as by Adam Hall: Remploy, 1972
Dead Sequence. Boardman, 1957
Dead Silence. Boardman, 1954. U.S. title: Pawn in Jeopardy, as by Adam Hall. Pyramid, 1971. Reprinted in Britain under the U.S. title: Remploy, 1972, as by Adam Hall
Knight Sinister. Boardman, 1951; Pyramid, 1971, as by Adam Hall. Reprinted in Britain as by Adam Hall: Remploy, 1972
Pawn in Jeopardy; see Dead Silence
Queen in Danger. Boardman, 1952; Pyramid, 1971, as by Adam Hall. Reprinted in Britain as by Adam Hall: Remploy, 1972
Rook's Gambit; see Dead Circuit

RAUCH, CONSTANCE. 1937- . Ref: CA.
The Landlady. Putnam, 1975 [N.Y.]
The Spy on Riverside Drive. Popular Library, 1977 [NYC, 1943]

RAVEN, CHARLES. Pseudonym.
Underworld Nights. Hulton, 1956 ss

RAVEN, JAMES
Pinnacle of Ice. Hale, 1978 [Green.]
The Triad Consignment. Hale, 1978
When Strangers Came. Hale, 1979

RAVEN, SIMON (ARTHUR NOEL). 1927- . Ref: CA, CC.
Brother Cain. Blond, 1959; Simon, 1960 [It.]
-Close of Play. Blond, 1962
Doctors Wear Scarlet. Blond, 1960; Simon, 1961
The Sabre Squadron. Blond, 1966; Harper, 1967 [Ger.]

RAVENSWOOD, FRITZEN
The Witching. Zebra, 1980

RAWLENCE, (E.) GUY. 1888- .
The Highwayman. Watt, 1911. British title (?): The Romantic Road. Unwin, 1910

RAWLINGS, FRANK
The Lisping Man. Gateway, 1942 [NYC]

RAWLS, PHILIP. SC: Richard Bronson, in all titles, which are novelizations of the TV series.
Blind Rage. Manor, 1975
Streets of Blood. Manor, 1975 (by Leonard Levinson, 1935- , q.v.) [NYC]
Switchblade. Manor, 1975

RAWSON, CLAYTON. 1906-1971. Pseudonym: Stuart Towne, q.v. Ref: CA, CC, DD, EM, MP, TC. SC: The Great Merlini, in all titles.
Death from a Top Hat. Putnam, 1938; Collins, 1938 [NYC]
The Footprints on the Ceiling. Putnam, 1939; Collins, 1939 [NYC]
The Great Merlini. Gregg, 1979 ss [NYC]
The Headless Lady. Putnam, 1940; Collins, 1942 [N.Y.]
No Coffin for the Corpse. Little, 1942; Stacey, 1972 [N.Y.]

RAWSON, TABOR. Pseudonym of Irving Shulman, 1913- , q.v.
I Want to Live! Signet, 1958 (Novelization of the movie.) [L.A.]

RAY, DAVID
All in a Day's Work. Panther, 1966 (Novelization of the "Rat Catchers" TV series.)

RAY, JEAN. Pseudonym of Jean Raymond de Kremer, 1887-1964.
Ghouls in My Grave. Berkley, 1965

RAY, RENE
-A Man Named Seraphin. Eyre, 1952
Wraxton Marne. Green, 1946

RAY, ROBERT (J.). Living in San Diego.
Cage of Mirrors. Lippincott, 1980

RAYMOND, CLIFFORD S(AMUEL). 1875- .
Four Corners. Doran, 1921
The Men on the Dead Man's Chest. Bobbs, 1930 [Chi.]
The Mystery of Hartley House. Doran, 1917
One of Three. Doran, 1919
-Our Very Best People. Bobbs, 1931

RAYMOND, DIANA (JOAN). 1916- . Ref: CA.
-The Five Days. Cassell, 1959
Incident on a Summer's Day. Cassell, 1974

RAYMOND, ERNEST. 1888-1974. Ref: CA.
-A Chorus Ending. Cassell, 1951
For Them That Trespass. Cassell, 1944
-The Marsh. Cassell, 1937
-The Tree of Heaven. Cassell, 1965
We, the Accused. Cassell, 1935; Stokes, 1935

RAYMOND, PATRICK (ERNEST). 1924- . Ref: CA.
A Matter of Assassination. Cassell, 1977 [Afr.]

RAYMOND, R. ALWYN
-The Cleft Chin Murder. Morris, 1945

RAYMOND, RENE BRABAZON. 1906- . Pseudonyms: James Hadley Chase, James L. Docherty, Ambrose Grant, Raymond Marshall, qq.v.

RAYNE, GODFREY
Earmarked for Murder. Hale, 1968
Headline—Murder! Hale, 1967

RAYNER, AUGUSTUS ALFRED. 1894- . Pseudonym: Whyte Hall, q.v.

RAYNER, CLAIRE (BERENICE). 1931- . Ref: CA.
The Baby Factory; see The Meddlers
Death on the Table. Corgi, 1969
The House on the Fen. Corgi, 1967; Bantam, 1967
-Lady Mislaid. Corgi, 1968
-The Meddlers. Cassell, 1970; Simon, 1970. Also published as: The Baby Factory. Lancer, 197?

RAYNER, RICHARD. Pseudonym of David MacIlwain, 1921- . Other pseudonym: Charles Eric Maine, q.v.
Darling Daughter. Hale, 1961
Dig Deep for Julie. Hale, 1963
Stand-In for Danger. Hale, 1963
The Trouble with Ruth. Hale, 1960

RAYNER, WILLIAM. 1929- . Ref: CA.
Eating the Big Fish. Collins, 1977. U.S. title: The Interface Assignment. Atheneum, 1977

RAYNES, JEAN
The Blood Carnelian. Doubleday, 1979
Legacy of the Wolf. Doubleday, 1977 [Scot., 1857]

RAYTER, JOE. Pseudonym of Mary F. McChesney. SC: Johnny Powers = JP.
Asking for Trouble. Mill, 1955; Ward, 1957 JP [Calif.]
Stab in the Dark. Mill, 1955; Ward, 1958 [Mex.]
The Victim Was Important. Scribner, 1954; Reinhardt, 1954 JP [S.F.]

RAZDAN, C. K. 1935- .
Stories of Crime and Murder. Hind Pocket Books (Delhi), 1972 ss

RAZIO, RICK. SC: Rick Razio, in both titles.
  Blondie Beg Your Bullet. M.C. Publications, 19?? [Chi.]
  Blondie Kiss Your Doom. M.C. Publications, 19??

REA, M(ARGARET LUCILE) P(AINE). SC: Lt. Powledge = P.
  Blackout at Rehearsal. Doubleday, 1943 [Fla.]
  Compare These Dead! Doubleday, 1941 P [Chi.]
  A Curtain for Crime. Doubleday, 1941 P [Chi.]
  Death of an Angel. Doubleday, 1943 P [Chi.]
  Death Walks the Dry Tortugas. Doubleday, 1942 [Fla.]

REACH, ANGUS BETHUNE. 1821-1856. Ref: EM.
  Clement Lorimer; or, The Book with the Iron Clasp. Bogue, 1849

REACH, JAMES. 1909?-1970. Joint pseudonym with Tom (Barnard) Taggart, q.v.: Ross MacRoss, q.v. Pseudonyms for plays: John Rand, Hilda Manning, Pete Williams, qq.v. The first four titles below are novels; the remainder are plays, published by Samuel French (NYC) unless otherwise indicated. The number of acts is given in parenthesis.
  Blind Gambit. Coward, 1954; Foulsham, 1956
  The Innocent One. Coward, 1953; Foulsham, 1956. Play version (3 acts): French, 1965
  Late Last Night. Morrow, 1949; Heinemann, 1950 [NYC]
  Sunset Strip. Popular Library, 1957 [L.A.]
  Afraid of the Dark. 1953 (3)
  Bear Witness. 1970 (2)
  The Black Hawk. 1952 (3)
  The Blackout Mystery. 1942 (1)
  The Case of the Laughing Dwarf. 1938 (3)
  The Case of the Squealing Cat. 1937 (3)
  The Clock Struck Twelve. 1949 (3)
  Danger—Girls Working! 1938 (?) [NYC]
  Dark Doings. 1951 (3)
  Dead of the Night. 1952 (3)
  Dragnet. 1956 (3) (Dramatization of the TV series.)
  For the Defense. 1967 (3)
  Fright. 1937 (1)
  The Girl in the Rain. 1953 (3)
  The Green Ghost. 1935 (3)
  House of Horrors. 1949 (3)
  The House on the Lake. 1949 (3)
  It Happened at Midnight. 1941 (3)
  It Walks at Midnight. Baker, 1956 (3)
  Lunatics at Large. 1936 (3)
  The Missing Witness. 1936 (3)
  Mr. Snoop Is Murdered. 1941 (3)
  Murder for the Bride. Bakers, 1955 (3)
  Murder Is My Business. 1958 (3) (Dramatization of the novel by Brett Halliday, q.v.)
  Murder, She Says! 1952 (3)
  Murder Takes the Stage. 1957 (3)
  The Night Was Dark. 1940 (3)
  The Old Man's Money. 1950 (3)
  Once upon a Midnight. 1948 (3)
  One Mad Night. 1935 (3)
  Shadows in the Night. 1942 (3)
  Storm over Hollywood. 1946 (3) [L.A.]
  Stranger in Town. 1955 (3)
  The Tennis Club Mystery. 1941 (1)
  Terror at Black Oaks. Dramatic, 1953 (3)
  Welcome, Danger! 1937 (3)
  We're All Guilty. 1952 (?)
  The Window. 1936 (1)
  Women in White. 1953 (3)
  You, the Jury. 1958 (3)

READ, HARLAN EUGENE. 1880-   .
  -Thurman Lucas. Macmillan, 1929

READ, OPIE (PERCIVAL). 1852-1939.
  The Mystery of Margaret. Wessels, 1907

READ, PIERS PAUL. 1941-   . Ref: CA.
  A Married Man. Secker, 1979; Lippincott, 1980
  The Upstart. Alison, 1973; Lippincott, 1973

READE, BILL. Pseudonym.
  A Bomb for Atuna. Barker, 1975
  I Wonder What Happened to Tom? Corgi, 1968
  The Ibiza Syndicate. Barker, 1975; St. Martin's, 1976 [Sp.]
  What Have They Done to You, Ben? Corgi, 1967; Bantam, 1968

READE, CHARLES. 1814-1884.
  Foul Play, with Dion(ysius Lardner) Boucicault, 1820-1890. Ticknor, 1868
  The Jilt. Chatto, 1884 ss, at least one criminous

READE, HAMISH. Pseudonym of Simon (James Holliday) Gray, 1936-   , q.v.
  A Comeback for Stark. Faber, 1968; Putnam, 1968

READUS, JAMES-HOWARD
  The Big Hit. Holloway, 1975
  The Black Assassin. Holloway, 1975
  Black Renegades. Holloway, 1976
  The Death Merchants. Holloway, 1974

READY, STUART
  Murder Deferred. French, 1976 (Play.)

REAGAN, THOMAS (JAMES) B(UTLER). 1916-   . Pseudonym: Jim Thomas, q.v. Ref: CA.
  Bank Job. Torquil/Dodd Mead, 1964; Hale, 1966 [Okla.]
  The Big Fall. Hammond, 1967
  Blood Money. Putnam, 1970; Long, 1971 [N.Y.]
  The Caper. Putnam, 1969; Long, 1970 [New Eng.]
  The Inside-Out Heist. Putnam, 1970; Hale, 1972 [N.J.]
  An Unkindness of Ravens. Hammond, 1967

REAKES, PAUL
  Act of Murder. New Playwright's Network, 1979 (Play.)
  Catspaw. New Playwright's Network, 1976 (1-act play.)

REARDON, DAN. Pseudonym: Nick Carter, q.v.

REASONER, JAMES M.
  Texas Wind. Manor, 1980 [Tex.]

REDD, REBECCA VERGUS
  The Brierfield Tragedy. Lovell, 1884

REDDER, GEORGE. Pseudonym of Jack Drummond, 1923?-1978.
  The Flight Instructor Murders. Exposition, 1977

REDDOCH, JENNIFER. Pseudonym of George McNeill.
  A Chair for Death. Popular Library, 1973
  The Legacy of Mendoubia. Popular Library, 1973
  Night of the Hellebore. Popular Library, 1974 [La.]

REDFERN, JOHN
  The Victim Needs a Nurse. Jarrolds, 1940

REDFIELD, MALISSA
  Games of Chance with Strangers. Doubleday, 1971

REDGATE, JOHN. Pseudonym of Adam Kennedy, q.v.
  The Killing Season. Trident, 1967; Cape, 1968
  The Last Decathlon. Delacorte, 1979 [Moscow]

REDGRAVE, MICHAEL (SCUDAMORE). 1908-
  The Aspern Papers. Heinemann, 1959 (Play based on the story by Henry James, 1843-1916, q.v.)

REDMAN, BEN RAY. 1896-1961. Pseudonym: Jeremy Lord, q.v.

REDMOND, A(NTON) E(DWARD)
  Cancelled Out. Hale, 1972
  Dead Is Forever. Hale, 1973
  No Exit. Hale, 1973

REDMOND, LIAM. Born in Dublin; actor, and writer for radio, stage and screen.
  Death Is So Kind. Devin-Adair, 1959 [Dub.]

REDMOND-HOWARD, L(OUIS) G. 1884-   .
  The Dilemma of Death. Modern, 1935
  Murder Was Never Bolder. Grafton, 1946
  The Mystery of Beacon Hill. Modern, 193?
  Radio Blackmail. Mellifont, 1936
  The Siege of Scotland Yard. Brentano's (London), 1929
  The Sin of Sacrifice. Modern, 193?

REDNOUR, HAROLD P.
  The Oblong Circle. French (NYC), 1954 (3-act play.)

REDWING, MORRIS. Pseudonym of James Milford Merrill, 1847-1936.
  Detective Against Detective; or, A Great Conspiracy. Laird, 1888
  Forced Apart; or, Exiled by Fate. Laird, 1886
  The Great Trunk Tragedy; or, Shadowed to Australia. Laird, 1888
  Tracked to Death; or, Eagle Gray, the Western Detective. Laird, 1886

REDWOOD, ALEC. Pseudonym of George Alexis Milkomanovich Milkomane, 1903-   . Other pseudonyms: George Braddon, Peter Conway, George Sava, qq.v.
  Deadline Moscow. New Horizon, 1978 [Moscow]
  The Lady Is Not Fooling. Hale, 1974
  Wine with Veronica. New Horizon, 1979

REED, BLAIR. Pseudonym: Adam Ring, q.v.
  Pass Key to Murder. Phoenix, 1948

REED, DAVID V. Pseudonym of David Vern, 1924-   .
  I Thought I'd Die. Green Dragon, 1946. Also published as: The Thing That Made Love. Unibook, 1951 [N.Y.]
  Murder in Space. Galaxy, 1954
  The Thing That Made Love; see I Thought I'd Die

REED, EDWARD CHARLES. 1891-   .
  Boothroyd's Mill. Long, 1929
  -Clowning Through. Long, 1928
  The Dream Murder. Long, 1929
  -The Free Heart. Long, 1927
  -History of Edward Brown. Long, 1932
  The Mirror. Long, 1925
  The Padgate Mystery. Long, 1930
  -Passionate Youth. Long, 1926
  The Strangler. Long, 1929
  -The Tents of Shame. Long, 1927
  -Venus Besieged. Long, 1927
  -A Wise Fool. Long, 1924

REED, EDWARD J(AMES). 1830-1906. Ref: CC.
  Fort Minster, M.P. Arrowsmith, 1885

REED, ELIOT. Joint pseudonym of Eric Ambler, 1909-   , q.v., and (Percival) Charles Rodda, 1891-   , q.v. Other Rodda pseudonyms: Gardner Low, Gavin Holt, qq.v. Note: Ambler was not involved with those marked * and only slightly with that marked #.
  Charter to Danger. Collins, 1954 *
  The Maras Affair. Collins, 1953; Doubleday, 1953 [Balkans] #
  Passport to Panic. Collins, 1958 [S. Am.] *
  Skytip. Hodder, 1951; Doubleday, 1950
  Tender to Danger; see Tender to Moonlight
  Tender to Moonlight. Hodder, 1952. U.S. title: Tender to Danger. Doubleday, 1951

REED, HARLAN. SC: Dan Jordan, in both titles.
  The Case of the Crawling Cockroach. Dutton, 1937 [ship]
  The Swing Music Murder. Dutton, 1938 [Seattle]

REED, HARRY
  A Piece of Something Big. Lancer, 1972 [Calif.]

REED, ISCHMAEL. 1938-   . Ref: CA, TC. SC: Papa LaBas, in both titles.
  The Last Days of Louisiana Red. Random, 1974 [S.F.]
  Mumbo Jumbo. Doubleday, 1972

REED, J(AMES) D(ONALD). 1940-   . Ref: CA.
  Free Fall. Delacorte, 1980; Futura, 1979 [West]

REED, LANGFORD. 1889-1954. See also: Frances Evelyn.
  -The Mantle of Methuselah, with Hetty Spiers. Rich, 1939

REED, MARK
  Lay Down and Die. Falcon, ca.1952
  Vice Cop. Rainbow, 1952

REED, WALLACE. SC: Sheriff Bill Lloyd = BL.
  Marked for Murder. Phoenix, 1941 BL [N.Y.]
  Motive for Murder. Arcadia, 1957 [NYC]
  No Sign of Murder. Phoenix, 1950 BL [N.Y.]
  Time to Kill. Phoenix, 1940 BL [NYC]

R

REES, ARTHUR J(OHN). 1872-1942. See also: John R(eay) Watson, 1872- . Ref: CC, MP. SC: David Colwyn = DC; Colwin Grey = CG; Insp. Luckraft = L. Set: Eng.
- Aldringham's Last Chance. Lane, 1933; Dodd, 1933 L
- The Brink. Lane, 1931. U.S. title: The Swaying Rock. Dodd, 1931 [Wales]
- The Corpse That Traveled. Dodd, 1938 L (British title?)
- Cup of Silence. Lane, 1924; Dodd, 1925
- -The Flying Argosy. Jarrolds, 1934
- Greymarsh. Jarrolds, 1927; Dodd, 1927 CG
- The Hand in the Dark. Lane (London & NYC), 1920 DC
- Investigations of Colwin Grey. Jarrolds, 1932 CG ss
- Island of Destiny. Lane, 1923; Dodd, 1923 L
- The Moon Rock. Lane, 1922; Dodd, 1922
- Mystery at Peak House; see Peak House
- The Pavilion by the Lake. Lane, 1930; Dodd, 1930 L
- Peak House. Jarrolds, 1933. U.S. title: Mystery at Peak House. Dodd, 1933
- The River Mystery. Jarrolds, 1932; Dodd, 1932 L
- The Shrieking Pit. Lane (London & NYC), 1919 DC
- Simon of Hangletree. Hutchinson, 1926. U.S. title: The Unquenchable Flame. Dodd, 1926 CG, with L in a walk-on role
- The Swaying Rock; see The Brink
- The Threshold of Fear. Hutchinson, 1925; Dodd, 1926 CG
- Tragedy at Twelvetrees. Lane, 1931; Dodd, 1931 L
- The Unquenchable Flame; see Simon of Hangletree

REES, DILWYN. Pseudonym of Glyn (Edmund) Daniel, 1914- , q.v. SC: Sir Richard Cherrington, in title below and that under the Glyn Daniel byline.
- The Cambridge Murders. Gollancz, 1945 [acad.]

REES, GEORGE. Titles below were published by Amalgamated Press and feature Sexton Blake.
- The Secret of the Jungle. 1953
- The Secret of the Suez Canal. 1954 [Egypt]

REES, JOAN. 1927- . Ref: CA.
- The Bride in Blue. Popular Library, 1977

REES, OLWEN
- Death of Virginia. Gifford, 1945
- There's No One in the Village. Gifford, 1949

REESE, JOHN (HENRY). SC: Jefferson Hewitt = JH.
- The Looters. Random, 1968; Hale, 1969 [Calif.]
- Omar, Fats and Trixie. GM, 1976 [Las Veg.]
- Pity Us All. Random, 1969; Hale, 1970 [L.A.]
- The Sharpshooter. Doubleday, 1974; Hale, 1978 JH [West, past]
- Texas Gold. Doubleday, 1975; Hale, 1978 JH [West, past]
- Weapon Heavy. Doubleday, 1973; Milton House, 1975 JH [Kan., 1800s]
- Wes Hardin's Gun. Doubleday, 1975; Hale, 1979 JH [West, past]

REESE, RALPH. See: Byron Preiss.

REESE, SAMMY [SAMUEL PHARR REESE]. 1930- . Ref: CA.
- I'm Waiting. Doubleday, 1974

REESE, TERENCE, 1913- , and JEREMY FLINT
- Trick Thirteen. Weidenfeld, 1979

REEVE, ARTHUR B(ENJAMIN). 1880-1936. Ref: CC, DD, EM, MM, MP, TC. SC: Craig Kennedy = CK.
- The Adventuress. Harper, 1917; Collins, 1918 CK [L.I.]
- Atavar, the Dream Dancer. Harper, 1924 CK [NYC]
- The Black Hand; see The Silent Bullet
- The Boy Scout's Craig Kennedy. Harper, 1925 CK ss
- The Clutching Hand. Reilly, 1934 CK [NYC]
- Constance Dunlap, Woman Detective. Hearst's, 1916; Hodder, 1916 ss [NYC]
- Craig Kennedy, Detective; see The War Terror
- Craig Kennedy Listens In. Harper, 1923; Hodder, 1924 CK ss [NYC]
- Craig Kennedy on the Farm. Harper, 1925 CK ss
- The Diamond Queen; see The Social Gangster
- The Dream Doctor. Hearst's, 1914; Hodder, 1916 CK ss
- The Ear in the Wall. Hearst's, 1916; Hodder, 1917 CK [NYC]
- Enter Craig Kennedy. Macaulay, 1935 (4 connected novelets.) CK
- The Exploits of Elaine. Hearst's, 1915; Hodder, 1915 CK ss [NYC]
- The Film Mystery. Harper, 1921; Hodder, 1922 CK [N.Y.]
- The Fourteen Points. Harper, 1925 CK ss
- Gold of the Gods. Hearst's, 1915; Hodder, 1916 CK ss [NYC]
- Guy Garrick. Hearst's, 1914; Hodder, 1916 [NYC]
- The Kidnap Club. Macaulay, 1932 CK [NYC]
- The Master Mystery. Grosset, 1919 (Novelization of the movie.)
- The Mystery Mind. Grosset, 1921 (Novelization of the movie.) [N.Y.]
- The Panama Plot. Harper, 1918; Collins, 1920 CK ss [S. Am.]
- Pandora. Harper, 1926 CK [NYC]
- The Poisoned Pen. Harper, 1911; Hodder, 1916 CK ss [NYC]
- The Radio Detective. Grosset, 1926 CK (Novelization of the movie.)
- The Romance of Elaine. Hearst's, 1916; Hodder, 1916 CK ss (The U.S. edition combines the text of the British edition with part of The Triumph of Elaine, q.v.) [NYC]
- The Silent Bullet. Dodd, 1912. British title: The Black Hand. Nash, 1912 CK ss [NYC]
- The Social Gangster. Hearst's, 1916. British title: The Diamond Queen. Hodder, 1917 CK ss [NYC]
- The Soul Scar. Harper, 1919 CK [NYC]
- The Stars Scream Murder. Appleton, 1936 CK [L.I.]
- The Treasure Train. Harper, 1917; Collins, 1920 CK ss [NYC]
- The Triumph of Elaine. Hodder, 1916 CK ss (Part of this is included in the U.S. edition of The Romance of Elaine, q.v.)
- The War Terror. Hearst's, 1915. British title: Craig Kennedy, Detective. Simpkin, 1916 CK ss [NYC]

REEVE, CHRISTOPHER. Set: Eng.
- The Emerald Kiss. Jarrolds, 1932; Morrow, 1931
- The Ginger Cat. Collins, 1929; Morrow, 1929
- The House That Waited. Ward, 1944
- Hunter's Way. Jarrolds, 1934
- Lady, Be Careful. Ward, 1948; Mill, 1950
- Murder Steps Out. Ward, 1942; Mill, 1951
- The Toasted Blonde. Collins, 1930; Morrow, 1930

REEVE, CLARA. 1729-1807.
- The Champion of Virtue. Keymer, 1777. Also published as: The Old English Baron. Dilly, 1778; Stewart, 1797
- The Old English Baron; see The Champion of Virtue
- The Progress of Romance, Through Times, Countries, and Manners. Keymer, 1785; Facsimile, 1930

REEVES, JOHN. 1926- . Born in Can., raised in Eng.; for many years a producer with Canadian Broadcasting Corporation.
- Murder by Microphone. Doubleday, 1978 [Toronto]

REEVES, ROBERT. ca.1912- . Born in NYC, graduate of New York U.; active in NYC theatre, magazine writer. SC: Cellini Smith, in all titles.
- Cellini Smith, Detective. Houghton, 1943 [Calif.]
- Come Out Killing; see No Love Lost
- Dead and Done For. Knopf, 1939; Cassell, 1940 [NYC]
- No Love Lost. Holt, 1941. Also published as: Come Out Killing. Mercury, 1953, abridged [L.A.]

REEVES, RUTH (ELIZABETH TRAUGHBER). 1902-
- Lament for a Lonesome Corpse. Phoenix, 1951 [Tex.]

REGAN, MARK
- Crash Landing. Hamlyn, 1979

REGESTER, SEELEY. Pseudonym of Mrs. M(eta) V(ictoria Fuller) Victor, 1831-1886, q.v. Ref: EM.
- The Dead Letter. Beadle, 1867
- The Figure Eight; or, The Mystery of Meredith Place. Beadle, 1869

REGIS, JULIUS. Pseudonym of Julius Pettersson, 1889-1925. SC: Maurice Wallion, in both titles.
- The Copper House. Holt, 1923; Hodder, 1923 (Translation of "Kopparhuset." Stockholm, 1918.) [Stock.]
- No. 13 Toroni. Holt, 1922; Hodder, 1922 (Translation of "Nr. 13 Toroni." Stockholm, 1919.) [Swed.]

REICH, RICHARD
- House Without Windows. Dramatists, 1952 (2-act play.)

REID, C. LESTOCK
- -The Greatest Game. Long, 1930
- -Masque of Mutiny. Temple, 1947
- -Peter's Profession. Long, 1927
- Revenge with a Vengeance. Robertson, 1952

REID, DESMOND. House name. Used by Wilfred (Glassford) McNeilly, 1921- , q.v. Other McNeilly pseudonyms: W. Howard Baker, W. A. Ballinger, William Glassford, Errol Lecale, Peter Saxon, qq.v. Also used by Michael (John) Moorcock, 1939- , q.v. Other Moorcock pseudonym: Bill Barclay, q.v. Also used by John Newton Chance, 1911- , q.v. Other Chance pseudonyms: J. Drummond, John Lymington, qq.v. Also used by Ross Richards, q.v. Other Richards pseudonym: Matt Mead, q.v. SC (with many other authors): Sexton Blake, in at least those marked SB.
- The Abductors. Mayflower, 1968 SB
- Anger at World's End. Amalgamated, 1963 (By John Newton Chance; revised by W. Howard Baker and Arthur MacLean.) SB
- The Babcock Boys. Mayflower, 1966
- Beat on an Orange Drum. Mayflower, 1965 [Ire.]
- Bullets Are Trumps. Amalgamated, 1961 SB
- Caribbean Crisis. Amalgamated, 1962 SB (By Michael Moorcock and James Cawthorn; revised by Philip Chambers.) [Carib.]
- The Case of the Renegade Agent. Mayflower, 1968 SB
- Conflict Within. Amalgamated, 1960 SB
- Contract for a Killer. Amalgamated, 1960 SB
- The Corpse Came Too. Amalgamated, 1961 SB
- Cult of Darkness. Amalgamated, 1963 SB
- Dead on Cue. Amalgamated, 1962 SB
- Dead Respectable. Mayflower, 1967 SB
- The Deadlier of the Species. Mayflower, 1966 SB
- Deadly Persuasion. Amalgamated, 1961 SB
- Death in Dockland. Amalgamated, 1962 SB
- Death on a High Note. Amalgamated, 1962 SB
- Death on the Spike. Mayflower, 1966 SB
- Death Waits in Tucson. Mayflower, 1966 [Tucson]
- Flashpoint for Treason. Amalgamated, 1957 SB
- Frenzy in the Flesh. Mayflower, 1966; Macfadden, 1968 SB
- The Girl Who Saw Too Much. Amalgamated, 1963 SB
- High Heels and Homicide. Amalgamated, 1958 SB
- Homicide Blues. Amalgamated, 1957 SB
- Hunt the Lady! Amalgamated, 1961 SB
- Let My People Be. Mayflower, 1965 SB
- The Man from Pecos. Mayflower, 1966
- Murder by Moonlight. Amalgamated, 1961 SB
- Murder Comes Calling! Amalgamated, 1960 SB
- Murder Made Easy. Amalgamated, 1960 SB
- Murder's Rock. Amalgamated, 1961 SB
- Roadhouse Girl. Amalgamated, 1957 SB
- Showdown in Sydney. Amalgamated, 1959 SB [Syd.]
- The Slave Brain. Mayflower, 1967 SB
- The Slaver. Mayflower, 1969
- The Snowman Cometh. Mayflower, 1966 SB
- Something to Kill About. Amalgamated, 1961 SB
- Stand-In for Murder. Amalgamated, 1957 SB
- State of Fear. Amalgamated, 1961 SB
- Victim Unknown. Amalgamated, 1957 SB
- Witch-Hunt! Amalgamated, 1960 SB
- The World-Shakers. Amalgamated, 1960 SB

REID, JAMES (W.). Born in Eng.; has been a teacher, in advertising, an art dealer, a magazine editor.
  The Offering. Putnam, 1978 [Boston]

REID, JOHN
  The Magician Kills and The Coffin Mystery. Stockwell, 1942 (2 stories.)

REID, PHILIP. Joint pseudonym of Richard Reid Ingrams, 1937- , and Andrew Osmond, 1938- , q.v. See also: Douglas (Richard) Hurd, 1930- .
  Harris in Wonderland. Cape, 1973. U.S. title: The Fun House. Houghton, 1974

REID, WALTER
  Off Lands End. Griffin, 1866 ss, two criminous

REIFFEL, LEONARD. 1927- .
  The Contaminant. Harper, 1978; Collins, 1978

REILLY, HELEN. 1891-1962. Pseudonym: Kieran Abbey, q.v. Ref: CC, EM, MP, TC. SC: Insp. Christopher McKee = CM.
  All Concerned Notified. Doubleday, 1939; Heinemann, 1939 CM [NYC]
  The Canvas Dagger. Random, 1956; Hale, 1957 CM [NYC]
  Certain Sleep. Random, 1961; Hale, 1962 CM [Conn.]
  Compartment K. Random, 1955. British title: Murder Rides the Express. Hale, 1956 CM [Can.]
  The Day She Died. Random, 1962; Hale, 1963 CM [N. Mex.]
  The Dead Can Tell. Random, 1940 CM [NYC]
  Dead for a Ducat. Doubleday, 1939; Heinemann, 1939 CM [Conn.]
  Dead Man Control. Doubleday, 1936; Heinemann, 1937 CM [NYC]
  Death Demands an Audience. Doubleday, 1940 CM [N.Y.]
  The Diamond Feather. Doubleday, 1930 CM [N.Y.]
  Ding Dong Bell. Random, 1958; Hale, 1959 CM [NYC]
  The Doll's Trunk Murder. Farrar, 1932; Hutchinson, 1933 [Pa.]
  The Double Man. Random, 1952; Museum, 1954 CM [Cape Cod]
  The Farmhouse. Random, 1947; Hammond, 1950 CM [N.Y.]
  File on Rufus Ray. Morrow, 1937; Jarrolds, 1937 [NYC]
  Follow Me. Random, 1960; Hale, 1961 CM [Sante Fe]
  Lament for the Bride. Random, 1951; Museum, 1954 CM [Fla.]
  The Line-Up. Doubleday, 1934; Cassell, 1935 CM [NYC]
  McKee of Centre Street. Doubleday, 1934 CM [NYC]
  Man with the Painted Head. Farrar, 1931 [Conn.]
  Mr. Smith's Hat. Doubleday, 1936; Cassell, 1936 CM [NYC]
  Mourned on Sunday. Random, 1941 CM [N.Y.]
  Murder at Arroways. Random, 1950; Museum, 1952 CM [Conn.]
  Murder in Shinbone Alley. Doubleday, 1940 CM [NYC]
  Murder in the Mews. Doubleday, 1931 CM [NYC]
  Murder on Angler's Island. Random, 1945; Hammond, 1948 CM [New Eng.]
  Murder Rides the Express; see Compartment K
  Name Your Poison. Random, 1942 CM [Conn.]
  Not Me, Inspector. Random, 1959; Hale, 1960 CM [NYC]
  The Opening Door. Random, 1944 CM [NYC]
  The Silver Leopard. Random, 1946; Hammond, 1959 CM [NYC]
  Staircase 4. Random, 1949; Hammond, 1950 CM [NYC]
  Tell Her It's Murder. Random, 1954; Museum, 1955 CM [N.Y.]
  The Thirty-First Bullfinch. Doubleday, 1930 [New Eng.]
  Three Women in Black. Random, 1941 CM
  The Velvet Hand. Random, 1953; Museum, 1955 CM [Conn.]

REINSMITH, RICHARD. Pseudonym of Richard Rein Smith, 1930- . Other pseudonym: Diana Tower, q.v. Ref: CA. SC: Ray Martin (The Bodyguard), in all titles.
  The Blonde Target. Tower, 1980
  Bodyguard. Tower, 1980
  Bury the Past. Tower, 1980
  An Extra Body. Tower, 1980
  The Five and Dime Murders. Tower, 1980

REISMAN, JOHN
  P.S. Your Shrink Is Dead. Leisure, 1979

REISNER, MARY
  Black Hazard. Belmont, 1966
  Bride of Death. Belmont, 1968
  Death Hall. Belmont, 1968
  The Four Witnesses. Dodd, 1947; Hammond, 1948. Also published as: Web of Fear. Belmont, 1967 [New Eng.]
  The House of Cobwebs. Dodd, 1944; Methuen, 1948 [Pa.]
  The Hunted. Belmont, 1967 [New Eng.]
  Katherine and the Dark Angel. Dodd, 1948; Hammond, 1949
  Mirror of Delusion. Dodd, 1946; Hammond, 1947
  Shadows on the Wall. Dodd, 1943. British title: Twelve Steps at Miramar. Methuen, 1946
  Twelve Steps at Miramar; see Shadows on the Wall
  Web of Fear; see The Four Witnesses

REISS, BOB [ROBERT]. 1951- . Born in NYC; reporter and magazine writer.
  Summer Fires. Simon, 1980; Secker, 1980 [NYC]

REITCI, JOHN GEORGE. 1922-1983. Pseudonym: Jack Ritchie, q.v.

REITCI, RITA KROHNE. 1930- . Pseudonym: Rita Ritchie, q.v.

REITER, B. P. 1945- .
  The Saturday Night Knife and Gun Club. Lippincott, 1977

REIZENSTEIN, ELMER L. 1892-1967. See: Elmer L. Rice; D. Torbett.
  On Trial. French, 1919 (Play.)

REMENHAM, JOHN. Pseudonym of John Alexander Vlasto, 1877-1958. Other pseudonym: John Alexander, q.v. SC: Insp. Bliss, in at least those marked B. Set: Eng.
  Arsenic. Skeffington, 1930 B
  The Canal Mystery. Skeffington, 1928 B
  The Crooked Bough. Macdonald, 1948
  The Dump. Skeffington, 1931 B
  Fog. Skeffington, 1929
  The Loom. Skeffington, 1933
  The Lurking Shadow. Macdonald, 1946
  -The Peacemaker. Macdonald, 1947
  Righteous Abel. Macdonald, 1943 [Wales]
  Sea Gold. Skeffington, 1931
  Seed of Envy. Macdonald, 1944
  -Tregear's Treasure. Skeffington, 1932

REMNANT, RICHARD
  At the Back o' Beyond. Chambers, 1930 ss, a few criminous

REMY, JACQUES. 1911- .
  Race for Life. Lane, 1957 (Translation of "Si Tous les Gars du Monde." Paris, 1956.)

REMY, PIERRE-JEAN. Pseudonym of Jean-Pierre Angremy, 1937- . French diplomat, then director in Ministry of Culture in Paris.
  Compartment East. Morrow, 1980. British title: Orient Express. Collins, 1981 (Translation of "Orient-Express." Paris, 1979.)

RENARD, MAURICE. 1875-1939.
  Blind Circle, with (Marie Joseph) Albert Jean, 1892- . Dutton, 1928; Gollancz, 1929 [Fr.]
  The Hands of Orlac. Dutton, 1929; Souvenir, 1981 (Translation of "Les Mains d'Orlac." Paris, 192?) [Fr.]
  New Bodies for Old. Macaulay, 1923 [Fr.]
  The Snake of Luvercy. Dutton, 1930 (Translation of "Lui?" Paris, 1927.) [Fr.]

RENAUD, JEAN-JOSEPH. 1874- .
  Doctor Mephisto. Hutchinson, 1930
  The Phantom Violin. Metropolitan, 1948 (Translation of "Le Violan Fantome.") [Fr.]

RENAUD, RON
  Fade to Black. Pinnacle, 1980 (Novelization of the movie.)

RENDELL, VERNON (HORACE). 1869- . Ref: CC.
  The London Nights of Belsize. Lane (London & NYC), 1917 ss

RENDELL, RUTH. 1930- . Ref: CC, TC. SC: Chief Insp. Wexford = W. Set: Eng.
  The Best Man to Die. Long, 1969; Doubleday, 1970 W
  A Demon in My View. Hutchinson, 1976; Doubleday, 1977
  The Face of Trespass. Hutchinson, 1974; Doubleday, 1974
  The Fallen Curtain, and other stories. Hutchinson, 1976; Doubleday, 1976 ss
  From Doon with Death. Long, 1964; Doubleday, 1965 W
  A Guilty Thing Surprised. Hutchinson, 1970; Doubleday, 1970 W
  In Sickness and in Health; see Vanity Dies Hard
  A Judgement in Stone. Hutchinson, 1977; Doubleday, 1978
  The Lake of Darkness. Hutchinson, 1980; Doubleday, 1980
  Make Death Love Me. Hutchinson, 1979; Doubleday, 1979
  Means of Evil. Hutchinson, 1979; Doubleday, 1979 W ss
  Murder Being Once Done. Hutchinson, 1972; Doubleday, 1972 W
  A New Lease of Death. Long, 1967; Doubleday, 1967. Also published as: Sins of the Fathers. Ballantine, 1970 W
  No More Dying Then. Hutchinson, 1971; Doubleday, 1972 W
  One Across, Two Down. Hutchinson, 1971; Doubleday, 1971
  The Secret House of Death. Long, 1968; Doubleday, 1969
  Shake Hands for Ever. Hutchinson, 1975; Doubleday, 1975 W
  Sins of the Fathers; see A New Lease of Death
  A Sleeping Life. Hutchinson, 1978; Doubleday, 1978 W
  Some Lie and Some Die. Hutchinson, 1973; Doubleday, 1973 W
  To Fear a Painted Devil. Long, 1965; Doubleday, 1965
  Vanity Dies Hard. Long, 1966. U.S. title: In Sickness and in Health. Doubleday, 1966. Reprinted under British title: Beagle, 1970
  Wolf to the Slaughter. Long, 1967; Doubleday, 1968 W

RENEK, MORRIS
  Heck. Harper's Magazine Press, 1971
  Las Vegas Strip. Knopf, 1975; Secker, 1975 [Las Veg.]

RENFROE, MARTHA KAY. 1938- . Pseudonym: M. K. Wren, q.v.

RENN, CHRIS. Pseudonym of a Pasadena, Calif. architect.
  The Violent Air. St. Martin's, 1980 [Calif.]

RENNERT, MAGGIE. 1922- . Ref: CA. SC: Guy Silvestri, in all titles.
  Circle of Death. Prentice-Hall, 1974 [Mass., acad.]
  Operation Alcestis. Prentice-Hall, 1975 [Mass., acad.]
  Operation Calpurnia. Prentice-Hall, 1976 [Mass.]

RENNIE, J(AMES) ALAN. 1899-1969. Ref: CA.
  -Aces Run Wild. Quality, 1950
  The Riddle of Rainbow Mountain. Muller, 1938

RENNIE, NEVILLE
  Strange Instrument. Aldor, 1948

RENO, MARIE R(OTH). Ref: CA.
  Final Proof. Harper, 1976 [NYC]

RENWICK, PETER. SC: Leatherface Lonergan, in at least those marked LL.
  Black Hogan Strikes Again. Low, 1937 LL [Australia]
  Leatherface Lonergan Stakes a Claim. Low, 1936 LL [Australia]
  Red Saunders Bites the Dust. Low, 1937

RESSICH, JOHN SELLAR MATHISON. 1877- . Joint pseudonym with Eric de Banzie, 1894- : Gregory Baxter, q.v.

RESTON, JAMES (B.), JR. 1941- .
  The Knock at Midnight. Norton, 1975 [Cin.]

RETCLIFF, JOHN. Pseudonym (?): Charles Felix, q.v.

REVELL, LOUISA. Ref: CC. SC: Julia Tyler, in all titles.
  The Bus Station Murders. Macmillan, 1947; Boardman, 1949 [Md.]
  The Kindest Use a Knife. Macmillan, 1952; Boardman, 1953 [Va.]
  The Men with Three Eyes. Macmillan, 1955 [Wash. D.C.]
  No Pockets in Shrouds. Macmillan, 1948; Boardman, 1959 [Louisville]
  A Party for the Shooting. Macmillan, 1960 [Va.]
  See Rome and Die. Macmillan, 1957; Gollancz, 1958 [Rome]

A Silver Spade. Macmillan, 1950; Boardman, 1950 [Maine]

REVELLI, GEORGE. SC: Amanda Nightingale, in all titles.
-Amanda in Berlin. Mayflower, 1978 [Berlin]
-Amanda in Spain. Mayflower, 1976 [Sp.]
Amanda's Castle. Bantam, 1972; Mayflower, 1973
Commander Amanda Nightingale. Grove, 1968; New English Library, 1969 [Fr.]
Resort to War. Grove, 1971; New English Library, 1971

REY, PIERRE
Out. Granada, 1980; Bantam, 1980 (Translation of "Out." Paris, 1977.) [Switz.]

REYBOLD, MALCOLM. Former advertising executive; lives in NYC.
The Inspector's Opinion. Saturday Review Press, 1975 [Mass.]

REYBURN, WALLACE (MacDONALD). 1913- . Ref: CA.
Follow a Shadow. Cassell, 1956
Good and Evil. Cassell, 1962
Port of Call. Cassell, 1957
The Street That Died. Cassell, 1960
Three Women. Cassell, 1960

REYMOND, HENRY
Deadlier Than the Male. Hodder pb, 1966; Signet, 1967 (Novelization of the Bulldog Drummond movie.) (Bulldog Drummond also appears in books by H. C. McNeile, 1888-1937, his creator, and by Gerard Fairlie, 1899- , qq.v.)

REYNAUD-FOURTON, ALAIN
The Reluctant Assassin. Collins, 1964; Coward, 1962 (Translation of (?): "Les Mystifies." Paris, 1962.) [Fr.]

REYNOLDS, ADRIAN. Pseudonym of Amelia Reynolds Long, 1904-1978, q.v. Other pseudonyms: Patrick Laing, Peter Reynolds, qq.v. Joint pseudonym with Edna McHugh: Kathleen Buddington Coxe, q.v. SC: Prof. Dennis Barrie, in all titles.
Formula for Murder. Phoenix, 1947
The Leprechaun Murders. Phoenix, 1950
The Round Table Murders. Phoenix, 1952

REYNOLDS, ANN. Pseudonym of Anne (Louise) Coulter Martens, 1906- , q.v. Other pseudonyms: Rilla Carlisle, Jane Kendall, qq.v.
Home Sweet Homicide. Dramatic, 1947 (Play based on the novel by Craig Rice, q.v.)

REYNOLDS, MRS. BAILLIE [GERTRUDE M. ROBINS REYNOLDS]. Set: Eng.
Accessory After the Fact. Hodder, 1928. U.S. title: The Innocent Accomplice. Doubleday, 1928 [Switz.]
The Affair at the Chateau. Hodder, 1929; Doubleday, 1929 [Switz.]
-Beware of the Dog. Mills, 1910; Brentano's, 1911
Black Light. Hodder, 1937; Doubleday, 1938
-Brother Wolf. Wright, 1931
A Castle to Let. Cassell, 1917; Doran, 1917
-Confession Corner, and other stories. Hurst, 1922 ss
-The Court Favourite. Mills, 1915
-The Flight of the Duchess, and other stories. Wright, 1935 ss
-The Gift of the Gauntlet. Hodder, 1927; Doran, 1927
The Innocent Accomplice; see Accessory After the Fact
The Intrusive Tourist. Hodder, 1935; Doubleday, 1935
It Is Not Safe to Know. Hodder, 1939; Doubleday, 1939
-The Kingdom and the Wall, and other tales. Mills, 1916 ss
-The Lonely Stronghold. Cassell, 1918; Doran, 1918
-The Lost Discovery. Hodder, 1923; Doran, 1923
-The Missing Two. Hodder, 1932; Doubleday, 1932
The Nameless Stranger and What Happened at Flaunce. Wright, 1933
The Notorious Miss Lisle. Hodder, 1911; Doran, 1911
-"Open, Sesame!". Skeffington, 1919; Doran, 1918
-Out of the Night. Hodder, 1910; Doran, 1910
The Prisoner of the Garret. Partridge, 1915
-The Queen's Hand. Mills, 1911 ss

-The Sheikh Touch, and other stories. Hurst, 1931 ss
-The Spell of Sarnia. Hodder, 1925; Doran, 1925
The Stranglehold. Doubleday, 1930 (British title?)
-The Swashbuckler, and other tales. Mills, 1913 ss
-The Terrible Baron, and other stories. Wright, 1933 ss
Trouble at Glaye. Hodder, 1936; Doubleday, 1936
Very Private Secretary. Hodder, 1933; Doubleday, 1933
-A Wayward Girl. Partridge, 1913
Whereabouts Unknown. Hutchinson, 1931; Doubleday, 1931 [Fr.]

REYNOLDS, BARBARA LEONARD
Alias for Death. Coward, 1950; Muller, 1953

REYNOLDS, BONNIE JONES
The Confetti Man. Stein, 1975
-The Truth About Unicorns. Stein, 1972; Garnstone, 1974

REYNOLDS, CATHERINE
Black Is the Colour of My True Love's Heart. New English Library, 1979

REYNOLDS, DALLAS McCORD. 1917- . Pseudonyms: Mack Reynolds, Maxine Reynolds, qq.v.

REYNOLDS, FREDERIC MANSELL. -1850.
Misserrimus. Davison, 1832, Harper, 1833

REYNOLDS, GEORGE
Victor Maury, the French Detective. Ogilvie, 1882 [Paris, 1807]

REYNOLDS, GEORGE WILLIAM MacARTHUR. 1814-1879. Ref: MC.
Grace Darling; or, The Heroine of the Fern Islands. 1839
The Loves of the Harem. 1855
The Mysteries of London (8 volumes). 1845-1850
The Mysteries of the Court of London. (8 volumes). 1848-1856
The Youthful Imposter. 1835

REYNOLDS, LOUISE (CLARISSA)
The Walton Mystery. Ward, 1872

REYNOLDS, MACK. Pseudonym of Dallas McCord Reynolds, 1917- . Other pseudonym: Maxine Reynolds, q.v.
The Case of the Little Green Men. Phoenix, 1951
Police Patrol: 2000 A.D. Ace, 1977 [2000]

REYNOLDS, MAXINE. Pseudonym of Dallas McCord Reynolds, 1917- . Other pseudonym: Mack Reynolds, q.v.
The Home of the Inquisitor. Beagle, 1972
The House in the Kasbah. Beagle, 1972

REYNOLDS, MINNIE JOSEPHINE. 1865- .
The Crayon Clue. Kennerley, 1915

REYNOLDS, PETER. Pseudonym of Amelia Reynolds Long, 1904-1978, q.v. Other pseudonyms: Patrick Laing, Adrian Reynolds, qq.v. Joint pseudonym with Edna McHugh: Kathleen Buddington Coxe, q.v.
Behind the Evidence. Visionary Pub. Co., 1936

REYNOLDS, QUENTIN (JAMES). 1902-1965. Ref: CA.
The Man Who Wouldn't Talk. Random, 1953 [Fr.]

REYNOLDS, W(ARWICK). -1946. An illustrator.
The Mawpeth Millions. Amalgamated, 1946 (Sexton Blake.)

REYWALL, JOHN. Pseudonym of NYC lawyer.
The Trial of Alvin Boaker. Random, 1948

RHEA, NICHOLAS. Pseudonym of Peter N(orman) Walker, 1936- , q.v. Other pseudonyms: Christopher Coram, Tom Ferris, qq.v.
Constable on the Hill. Hale, 1979

RHOADES, KNIGHT
She Died on the Stairway. Arcadia, 1947

RHODE, JOHN. Pseudonym of Cecil John Charles Street, 1884-1964. Other pseudonym: Miles Burton, q.v. Ref: all except CA. SC: Dr. Lancelot Priestley = LP. Set: Eng.
A.S.F.: The Story of a Great Conspiracy. Bles, 1924. U.S. title: The White Menace. McBride, 1926
The Affair of the Substitute Doctor; see Dr. Goodwood's Locum
The Alarm. Bles, 1925
An Artist Dies. Bles, 1956. U.S. title: Death of an Artist. Dodd, 1956 LP
Blackthorn House. Bles, 1949; Dodd, 1949 LP
The Bloody Tower. Collins, 1938. U.S. title: The Tower of Evil. Dodd, 1938 LP
Body Unidentified; see Proceed with Caution
The Bricklayer's Arms. Collins, 1945. U.S. title: Shadow of a Crime. Dodd, 1945 LP
By Registered Post. Bles, 1953. U.S. title: The Mysterious Suspect. Dodd, 1953 LP
The Case of the Forty Thieves; see Death at the Inn
The Claverton Affair; see The Claverton Mystery
The Claverton Mystery. Collins, 1933. U.S. title: The Claverton Affair. Dodd, 1933 LP
The Corpse in the Car. Collins, 1935; Dodd, 1935 LP
The Davidson Case. Bles, 1929. U.S. title: Murder at Bratton Grange. Dodd, 1929 LP
Dead Men at the Folly. Collins, 1932; Dodd, 1932 LP
Dead of the Night; see Night Exercise
Dead on the Track. Collins, 1943; Dodd, 1943 LP
Death at Breakfast. Collins, 1936; Dodd, 1936 LP
Death at the Dance. Bles, 1952; Dodd, 1952 LP
Death at the Helm. Collins, 1941; Dodd, 1941 LP
Death at the Inn. Bles, 1953. U.S. title: The Case of the Forty Thieves. Dodd, 1954 LP
Death in Harley Street. Bles, 1946; Dodd, 1946 LP
Death in the Hop Fields. Collins, 1937. U.S. title: The Harvest Murder. Dodd, 1937 LP
Death in Wellington Road. Bles, 1952; Dodd, 1952 LP
Death Invades the Meeting. Collins, 1944; Dodd, 1944 LP
Death of a Bridegroom. Bles, 1957; Dodd, 1958 LP
Death of a Godmother. Bles, 1955. U.S. title: Delayed Payment. Dodd, 1956 LP
Death of an Artist; see An Artist Dies
Death of an Author. Bles, 1947; Dodd, 1948 LP
Death on Sunday. Collins, 1939. U.S. title: The Elm Tree Murder. Dodd, 1939 LP
Death on the Board. Collins, 1937. U.S. title: Death Sits on the Board. Dodd, 1937 LP
Death on the Boat Train. Collins, 1940; Dodd, 1940 LP
Death on the Lawn. Bles, 1954; Dodd, 1955 LP
Death Pays a Dividend. Collins, 1939; Dodd, 1939 LP
Death Sits on the Board; see Death on the Board
Death Takes a Partner. Bles, 1958; Dodd, 1958 LP
Delayed Payment; see Death of a Godmother
Dr. Goodwood's Locum. Bles, 1951. U.S. title: The Affair of the Substitute Doctor. Dodd, 1951 LP
Dr. Priestley Investigates; see Pinehurst
Dr. Priestley Lays a Trap; see The Motor Rally Mystery
Dr. Priestley's Quest. Bles, 1926 LP
The Domestic Agency. Bles, 1955. U.S. title: Grave Matters. Dodd, 1955 LP
The Double Florin. Bles, 1924
Double Identities; see The Two Graphs
The Dovebury Murders. Bles, 1954; Dodd, 1954 LP
Drop to His Death, with Carter Dickson, q.v. (pseudonym of John Dickson Carr, 1905-1977, q.v.). Heinemann, 1939. U.S. title: Fatal Descent. Dodd, 1939
The Ellerby Case. Bles, 1927; Dodd, 1927 LP
The Elm Tree Murder; see Death on Sunday
Experiment in Crime; see Nothing But the Truth
Family Affairs. Bles, 1950. U.S. title: The Last Suspect. Dodd, 1951 LP
Fatal Descent; see Drop to His Death
The Fatal Garden; see Up the Garden Path
The Fatal Pool. Bles, 1960; Dodd, 1961 LP
The Fire at Greycombe Farm; see Mystery at Greycombe Farm

The Fourth Bomb. Collins, 1942; Dodd, 1942 LP
Grave Matters; see The Domestic Agency
The Hanging Woman. Collins, 1931; Dodd, 1931 LP
The Harvest Murder; see Death in the Hop Fields
Hendon's First Case. Collins, 1935; Dodd, 1935 LP
The House on Tollard Ridge. Bles, 1929; Dodd, 1929 LP
In Face of the Verdict. Collins, 1936. U.S. title: In the Face of the Verdict. Dodd, 1940 LP
In the Face of the Verdict; see In Face of the Verdict
Invisible Weapons. Collins, 1938; Dodd, 1938 LP
The Lake House. Bles, 1946. U.S. title: Secret of the Lake House. Dodd, 1946 LP
The Last Suspect; see Family Affairs
Licensed for Murder. Bles, 1958; Dodd, 1958 LP
The Links in the Chain; see The Paper Bag
-Mademoiselle from Armentieres. Bles, 1927
Men Die at Cyprus Lodge. Collins, 1943; Dodd, 1944 LP
The Motor Rally Mystery. Collins, 1933. U.S. title: Dr. Priestley Lays a Trap. Dodd, 1933 LP
Murder at Bratton Grange; see The Davidson Case
Murder at Derivale. Bles, 1958; Dodd, 1958 LP
Murder at Lilac Cottage. Collins, 1940; Dodd, 1940 LP
Murder at the Motor Show; see Mystery at Olympia
The Murders in Praed Street. Bles, 1928; Dodd, 1928 LP
The Mysterious Suspect; see By Registered Post
Mystery at Greycombe Farm. Collins, 1932. U.S. title: The Fire at Greycombe Farm. Dodd, 1932 LP
Mystery at Olympia. Collins, 1935. U.S. title: Murder at the Motor Show. Dodd, 1936 LP
Night Exercise. Collins, 1942. U.S. title: Dead of the Night. Dodd, 1942
Nothing But the Truth. Bles, 1947. U.S. title: Experiment in Crime. Dodd, 1947 LP
Open Verdict. Bles, 1956; Dodd, 1957 LP
The Paddington Mystery. Bles, 1925 LP
The Paper Bag. Bles, 1948. U.S. title: The Links in the Chain. Dodd, 1948 LP
Peril at Cranbury Hall. Bles, 1930; Dodd, 1930 LP
Pinehurst. Bles, 1930. U.S. title: Dr. Priestley Investigates. Dodd, 1930 LP
Poison for One. Collins, 1934; Dodd, 1934 LP
Proceed with Caution. Collins, 1937. U.S. title: Body Unidentified. Dodd, 1938 LP
Robbery with Violence. Bles, 1957; Dodd, 1957 LP
The Robthorne Mystery. Collins, 1934; Dodd, 1934 LP
The Secret Meeting. Bles, 1951; Dodd, 1951 LP
Secret of the Lake House; see The Lake House
Shadow of a Crime; see The Bricklayer's Arms
Shadow of an Alibi; see The Telephone Call
Shot at Dawn. Collins, 1934; Dodd, 1935 LP
Signal for Death; see They Watched by Night
The Telephone Call. Bles, 1948. U.S. title: Shadow of an Alibi. Dodd, 1948 LP
They Watched by Night. Collins, 1941. U.S. title: Signal for Death. Dodd, 1941 LP
Three Cousins Die. Bles, 1959; Dodd, 1960 LP
Too Many Suspects; see Vegetable Duck
The Tower of Evil; see The Bloody Tower
Tragedy at the Unicorn. Bles, 1928; Dodd, 1928 LP
Tragedy on the Line. Collins, 1931; Dodd, 1931 LP
Twice Dead. Bles, 1960; Dodd, 1960 LP
The Two Graphs. Bles, 1950. U.S. title: Double Identities. Dodd, 1950 LP
Up the Garden Path. Bles, 1949. U.S. title: The Fatal Garden. Dodd, 1949 LP
The Vanishing Diary. Bles, 1961; Dodd, 1961 LP
Vegetable Duck. Collins, 1944. U.S. title: Too Many Suspects. Dodd, 1945 LP
The Venner Crime. Odhams, 1933; Dodd, 1934 LP

The White Menace; see A.S.F.: The Story of a Great Conspiracy

RHODES, DENYS (GRAVENOR). 1919-
Flyaway Peter. Richards, 1952

RHODES, EVAN H. 1929- .
-The Carrion Eaters. Stein, 1974; Allen, 1975. Also published as: Safari. Charter, 1979

RHODES, KATHLYN
Crime on a Cruise. Hutchinson, 1935 [ship]
-In Search of Stephanie. Hutchinson, 1941
-It Happened in Cairo. Hutchinson, 1944 [Cairo]
The Lady Was Warned. Hutchinson, 1936
-Strange Quartet. Hutchinson, 1938

RHODES, RICHARD. 1937- . Born in Kan. City, graduate of Yale; contributing editor to "Playboy" magazine.
-The Last Safari. Doubleday, 1980; Deutsch, 1980 [Tanz.]

RHODES, RUSSELL (LAWRENCE). Graduate of Yale and Harvard Business School; advertising agency executive in NYC.
The Herod Conspiracy. Dodd, 1980 [Sp.]
The Styx Complex. Dodd, 1977; Bantam (London), 1978

RHYS, JEAN. 1894- . Ref: CA.
-Wide Sargasso Sea. Deutsch, 1966; Norton, 1966 [Carib., 1830s]

RHYS-WILLIAMS, JULIET (EVANGELINE GLYN). 1898- .
Forty-Nine Chances. Rich, 1947 (Novelization of the play "They Had His Number," by R. J. Minney, 1895- , and Juliet Rhys-Williams.)

RICE, CRAIG. Pseudonym of Georgiana Ann Randolph Craig, 1908-1957. Pseudonyms: Daphne Sanders, Michael Venning, qq.v. See also: Gypsy Rose Lee; and: Ann Reynolds; and: Stuart Palmer, 1905-1968. Ref: CC, DD, EM, MC, MP, TC. SC: John J. Malone and the Justuses = M&J (see also: Larry M. Harris); Ringo Riggs and Handsome Kusak = R&K.
The April Robin Murders, with Ed McBain, q.v. Random, 1958; Hammond, 1959 R&K [L.A.]
The Big Midget Murders. Simon, 1942 M&J [Chi.]
But the Doctor Died. Lancer, 1967 M&J [Chi.]
The Corpse Steps Out. Simon, 1940; Eyre, 1940 M&J [Chi.]
Death at Three; see Eight Faces at Three
The Double Frame; see Knocked for a Loop
Eight Faces at Three. Simon, 1939; Eyre, 1939. Also published as: Death at Three. Cherry Tree, 1941 M&J [Ill.]
The Fourth Postman. Simon, 1948; Hammond, 1951 M&J [Chi.]
Having Wonderful Crime. Simon, 1943; Nicholson, 1944 M&J [NYC]
Home Sweet Homicide. Simon, 1944
Innocent Bystander. Simon, 1949; Hammond, 1958
Knocked for a Loop. Simon, 1957. British title: The Double Frame. Hammond, 1958 M&J [Chi.]
The Lucky Stiff. Simon, 1945 M&J [Chi.]
My Kingdom for a Hearse. Simon, 1957; Hammond, 1959 M&J [Chi.]
The Name Is Malone. Pyramid, 1958; Hammond, 1960 M ss [Chi.]
The Right Murder. Simon, 1941; Eyre, 1948 M&J [Chi.]
The Sunday Pigeon Murders. Simon, 1942; Nicholson, 1948 R&K [NYC]
Telefair. Bobbs, 1942. Also published as: Yesterday's Murder. Popular Library, 1950 [Md.]
The Thursday Turkey Murders. Simon, 1943; Nicholson, 1946 R&K [Ia.]
Trial by Fury. Simon, 1941; Hammond, 1950 M&J [Wis.]
The Wrong Murder. Simon, 1940; Eyre, 1942 M&J [Chi.]
Yesterday's Murder; see Telefair

RICE, DESMOND CHARLES. 1924- . Pseudonym: Desmond Meiring, q.v.

RICE, ELMER L. 1892-1967. Name originally: Elmer L. Reizenstein, q.v. See also: D. Torbett.
Cock Robin, with Philip Barry, 1896- . French, 1929 (Play.)

RICE, JAMES. 1843-1882. See: Walter Besant, 1836-1901.

RICE, JEFF. 1944- . Born in R.I., living in Las Veg. since 1955; journalist, screenwriter. SC: Carl Kolchak, in both titles.
The Night Stalker. PB, 1973 (Novelization of the TV movie.) [Las Veg.]
The Night Strangler. PB, 1974 (Novelization of the TV movie.) [Seattle]

RICE, LAVERNE
Well-Dressed for Murder. Doubleday, 1938 [N.Y.]

RICE, LOUISE (GUEST). 1880- .
By Whose Hand? Macaulay, 1930 [Eng.]

RICH. Pseudonym: Nicholas Carter, q.v.

RICH, ARTHUR T.
The Curate Finds the Corpse. Bear, 1945

RICH, KATHLEEN
The Deadly Rose; see Jacqueminot
Jacqueminot. Tower, 1967. Also published as: The Deadly Rose. Belmont, 1972
The Lucifer Mask. Tower, 1967 [Lisbon]

RICH, NICHOLAS. SC: Adam Hood, in at least those marked AH.
The Blane Document. Hale, 1972 AH
The Seajet Spies. Hale, 1973
Spy Now, Pay Later. Hale, 1972 AH

RICH, WILLARD. Pseudonym.
Brain-Waves and Death. Scribner, 1940 [Boston]

RICHARD, JAMES L.
Never Kill for Sport. Hale, 1978

RICHARD, SUSAN. Pseudonym of Julie (M.) Ellis, q.v. Other pseudonyms: Susan Marino, Susan Marvin, qq.v.
Ashley Hall. Paperback Library, 1967 [Conn.]
Chateau Saxony. Paperback Library, 1970
Intruder at Maison Benedict. Paperback Library, 1967 [Vt.]
The Secret of Chateau Kendall. Paperback Library, 1967
Secret of the Chateau Leval. Avon, 1975
Terror at Nelson Woods. Paperback Library, 1973 [Can.]

RICHARDS, ALLEN. Pseudonym of Richard A. Rosenthal, 1925- . Ref: CA.
To Market, to Market. Macmillan, 1961. British title: The Merchandise Murders. Hammond, 1964. Also published as: The Luxury Merchants. Pyramid, 1975, as by Richard Rosenthal

RICHARDS, CLAY. Pseudonym of Kendell Foster Crossen, 1910-1981, q.v. Other pseudonyms: Bennett Barlay, M. E. Chaber, Richard Foster, Christopher Monig, qq.v. SC: Grant Kirby = GK; Kim Locke = KL (begun under the Kendell Foster Crossen byline).
Death of an Angel. Bobbs, 1963 GK [NYC, 1890s]
The Gentle Assassin. Bobbs, 1964; Boardman, 1965 KL [Cuba]
The Marble Jungle. Obolensky, 1961; Cassell, 1963 GK [New Or., 1890s]
Who Steals My Name. Bobbs, 1964; Boardman, 1965

RICHARDS, CURTIS
Halloween. Bantam, 1979; Corgi, 1980 (Novelization of the movie.)

RICHARDS, DAVID. Pseudonym of Richard (Leslie) Townshend Bickers, 1917- , q.v.
Double Game. Digit, 1958 [Berlin, 1939]

RICHARDS, FRANCIS. See: Frances (Louise Davis) Lockridge, 1896-1963; and Richard (Orson) Lockridge, 1898-1982.

RICHARDS, (FRANKLIN THOMAS) GRANT. 1872-1948.
Who Killed Aunt Caroline? French (NYC), 1942 (3-act play.)

RICHARDS, GUY
Red Kill. Dent, 1980. U.S. title: The Salekov Kill. GM, 1981

RICHARDS, HEDLEY
The Beautiful Suspect. Fiction House, 1937
The Deputy Avenger. Aldine, 1920
The Meshes of Fear; or, The Curse of the Blue Diamonds. Henderson
The Ossington Mystery. Henderson

RICHARDS, JAMES BRINSLEY. 1846-1892.
   The Alderman's Children. Bentley, 1891

RICHARDS, JONATHAN. Pseudonym: Canella Lewis, q.v.

RICHARDS, LESLIE
   Love's Deadly Silhouette. Zebra, 1979
   Pale Ghost at Graves End. Zebra, 1977
   Pursue the Wind. Manor, 1975

RICHARDS, MARK
   Vengeance Is Mine. Columbine, 1940

RICHARDS, MARSDEN
   -A Brace for the Law. Digby, 1892

RICHARDS, NAT. Pseudonym of James Nathaniel Richardson, 1942-   .
   Otis Dunn: Manhunter. Ashley, 1974

RICHARDS, PAUL. House name. SC: Grant Fowler, in all titles.
   Moscow at High Noon Is the Target. Award, 1973 (By Dan Streib and Chet Cunningham, qq.v.)
   Our Spacecraft Is Missing! Award, 1970 (By Jon Messmann and George Snyder, qq.v.) [Australia]
   The President Has Been Kidnapped! Award, 1971 (By George Snyder and Dan Streib, qq.v.) [Carib.]

RICHARDS, ROBIN
   Cold Blood. Hutchinson, 1920

RICHARDS, RONALD CHARLES WILLIAM. 1923-   . Pseudonym: K. Allen Sadler, q.v.

RICHARDS, ROSS. Pseudonym: Matt Mead, q.v.
   The Death Seekers. Hale, 1964
   Murder on the Monte. Mayflower, 1966 (Sexton Blake.)

RICHARDS, TAD
   The Killing Place. Dell, 1976

RICHARDS, WILLIAM
   Dead Man's Tide. Graphic, 1953 [Fla.]

RICHARDSON, ANTHONY (THOMAS STEWART CURRIE). 1899-   .
   The Rose of Kantara. Odhams, 1951 [Fr.]

RICHARDSON, CARL. 1938-   .
   Effigy of a Spy. Hale, 1971
   Jump the High Wall. Hale, 1969
   The Name of the Game Is Death. Hale, 1971

RICHARDSON, FRANK (COLLINS). 1870-1917. SC: Vincent Skrene = VS.
   Bunkum. Nash, 1907 ss, some criminous
   The King's Counsel. Chatto, 1902 VS
   The Mayfair Mystery; see 2835 Mayfair
   -The Secret Kingdom. Duckworth, 1905
   Semi-Society. Chatto, 1903 VS
   2835 Mayfair. Laurie, 1907; Kennerley, 1907. Also published as: The Mayfair Mystery. Collins, 1929
   Whiskers and Soda. Nash, 1910 ss, two criminous
   The Worst Man in the World. Nash, 1908

RICHARDSON, H(ENRY) M(ARRIOTT). 1876-   .
   The Rock of Justice. Hutchinson, 1928
   The Temple Murder. Hutchinson, 1926

RICHARDSON, JAMES NATHANIEL. 1942-   .
   Pseudonym: Nat Richards, q.v.

RICHARDSON, LEANDER P(EASE). 1856-1918.
   The Prairie Detective. Street, 1889

RICHARDSON, MOZELLE (GRONER). 1914-   .
   Ref: CA.
   A Candle in the Wind. Morrow, 1973 [Ire.]
   The Curse of Kalispoint. Paperback Library, 1971
   Daughter of the Sacred Mountain. Morrow, 1977 [Afr.]
   The Masks of Thespis. Warner, 1973
   Portrait of Fear. Paperback Library, 1971
   The Song of India. Morrow, 1973 [India]

RICHARDSON, SUSANNE
   The Green Cape. Lenox, 1973 [Wales]

RICHART, MARY. Born in Ga., living in Calif. in 1940s; magazine fiction writer.
   Murder in the Town. Farrar, 1947

RICHBERG, DONALD (RANDALL). 1881-1960.
   -In the Dark. Forbes, 1912
   The Shadow Men. Forbes, 1911 [Chi.]

RICHMOND, D.
   The Film Star Vanishes. Bear, 1945

RICHMOND, DONALD
   -The Dunkirk Directive. Stein, 1980 [Eng., WWII]

RICHMOND, MARY
   -All That Glitters. Wright, 1954
   -Barbed Wire. Hale, 1941
   -Be My Love. Wright, 1967
   -Beloved Enemy. Wright, 1965
   -Brides of Doom. Wright, 1946
   -Cabin Nineteen. Wright, 1953
   -The Clock Strikes Ten. Wright, 1944
   Concealed Identity. Wright, 1938
   Danger Ahead. Wright, 1937
   -The Dark Countess. Wright, 1958
   Dark Horizon. Wright, 1937
   -The Devil Laughed. Wright, 1950
   Disciples of Satan. Wright, 1936
   -Enchanted Wooing. Wright, 1946
   -Evening in Paris. Wright, 1949 [Paris]
   -Feast of Lanterns. Wright, 1968
   -Fettered Love. Wright, 1955
   -Flight from a Throne. Wright, 1951
   -Flower in the Desert. Wright, 1943
   Footprints in the Sand. Wright, 1939
   -For Ever Beloved. Wright, 1968
   -For Those in Peril. Wright, 1957
   -Garden of Memories. Wright, 1947
   -Good-Time Girl. Wright, 1956
   -The Grim Tomorrow. Wright, 1953
   -Hearts in Turmoil. Wright, 1946
   -Hell Hath No Fury. Wright, 1956
   The Hidden Horror. Wright, 1937
   Hounded! Wright, 1936
   -Hour of Destiny. Wright, 1954
   -I'll Always Remember. Wright, 1964
   In Deep Water. Wright, 1934
   In Fear of the Hangman. Wright, 1938
   In the Grip of the Dragon. Wright, 1939
   -Incredible Adventure. Wright, 1969
   -Indian Love Lyrics. Wright, 1958
   -Indian Lullaby. Wright, 1964
   Insurgent Love. Wright, 1940
   -I've Found My Love. Wright, 1955
   Jewels of Death. Wright, 1938
   -Journey to Happiness. Wright, 1963
   Judgment of Death. Wright, 1942
   -Justice for Julia. Wright, 1955
   -Kashmiri Love Song. Wright, 1967
   Lady in Distress. Wright, 1936
   -Lady of the Night. Wright, 1950
   -A Leap in the Dark. Wright, 1949
   -Look to the Dawn. Wright, 1946
   -Love Without Honour. Wright, 1956
   -Love's the Only Guide. Wright, 1964
   -Magnet for Danger. Wright, 1943
   -Maid of Athens. Wright, 1948
   -The Mandarin's Bride. Wright, 1945
   The Mark of the Dragon. Wright, 1935
   -Market of Venus. Hale, 1941
   -Marry in May. Wright, 1963
   The Masked Terror. Wright, 1934; Godwin, 1935 [Cape Town]
   -The Memory of You. Wright, 1950
   Murder by a Maniac. Wright, 1937
   -No Escape. Wright, 1952
   -Oasis of Tears. Wright, 1952
   -One Enchanted Evening. Wright, 1965
   -One Fine Day. Wright, 1966
   -One Glorious Spring. Wright, 1968
   -Only a Love Song. Wright, 1965
   -Paradise for Two. Wright, 1954
   -The Passionate Atonement. Wright, 1960
   Passport to Danger. Wright, 1938 [Sp.]
   -Perilous Adventure. Wright, 1962
   Pirate Love. Wright, 1937
   The Pointing Finger. Wright, 1940
   Poison Weed. Wright, 1940
   -Prisoner of Love. Wright, 1962
   -Put Back the Clock. Wright, 1952
   -Queen of My Heart. Wright, 1951
   Red Claws. Wright, 1940 [Russ.]
   Red Dawning. Wright, 1946
   -The Reluctant Duchess. Wright, 1957
   -Reluctant Rebel. Wright, 1967
   -Risk All for Love. Wright, 1959
   -The Secret Hour. Wright, 1949
   The Secret of the Marshes. Wright, 1940
   The Secret of the Priory. Wright, 1935
   The Seven Bloodhounds. Wright, 1937
   Shadow of the Gallows. Wright, 1940
   -Shadow of the Past. Wright, 1960
   -A Star Is Falling. Wright, 1960
   -The Steadfast Heart. Wright, 1961
   Stealthy Death. Wright, 1935
   Strange Cargo. Wright, 1933
   Suspicious Company. Wright, 1938
   -Tempest at Dawn. Wright, 1944
   Terror by Night. Wright, 1939
   Terror Stalks Abroad. Wright, 1935
   -That Fatal Night. Wright, 1949
   -Thin Ice. Wright, 1950
   -This Man Belongs to Me. Wright, 1951
   -This Road Is Dangerous. Wright, 1950
   To Have and to Hold. Wright, 1961
   To Make You Mine. Wright, 1963
   Tomorrow's Harvest. Wright, 1947
   -Tragedy at Blue Aloes. Wright, 1958
   Traitor's Harvest. Wright, 1942 [Scot.]
   -Troubled Heritage. Wright, 1942
   -Unnatural Death. Wright, 1952
   -Unwelcome Rapture. Wright, 1961
   -Unwilling to Wed. Wright, 1959
   -The Valley of Doom. Wright, 1947
   -The Valley of the Shadow. Wright, 1947
   -Waltz of My Heart. Wright, 1968
   -Web of Enchantment. Wright, 1962
   -Wild Reckoning. Wright, 1953
   The Woman Cain. Wright, 1936

RICKARD, JESSIE LOUISA (MOORE). 1879-   . Byline sometimes: Mrs. Victor Rickard. Set: Eng.
   -Ascendancy House. Jarrolds, 1944
   The Baccarat Club; see The Mystery of Vincent Dane
   -A Bird of Strange Plumage. Hodder, 1927
   -Blindfold. Cape, 1922
   -Cathy Rossiter. Hodder, 1919; Doran, 1920
   -The Dark Stranger. Hodder, 1930
   -Dregs. Rivers, 1914
   The Empty Villa. Hodder, 1929; Liveright, 1929
   -The Frantic Boast. Duckworth, 1917
   -The Guests of Chance. Hodder, 1928
   The Light Above the Crossroads. Duckworth, 1916; Dodd, 1918
   The Light That Lies. Hodder, 1927
   Murder by Night. Jarrolds, 1936
   The Mystery of Tara Heston. Jarrolds, 1938
   The Mystery of Vincent Dane. Hodder, 1930. U.S. title: The Baccarat Club. Liveright, 1929
   Not Sufficient Evidence. Constable, 1926
   -Old Sins Have Long Shadows. Constable, 1924; Houghton, 1924
   -The Passionate City. Hodder, 1928
   -A Perilous Elopement. Hodder, 1928
   -Sensation at Blue Harbour. Jarrolds, 1934
   -Shandon Hall. Jarrolds, 1950
   Upstairs. Constable, 1925; Doubleday, 1926
   -White Satin. Jarrolds, 1945
   -Without Justification. Cape, 1923
   -Yesterday's Love. Hodder, 1931
   -The Young Man in Question. Jarrolds, 1933
   -Young Mr. Gibbs. Nash, 1911
   -Young Mrs. Henniker. Jarrolds, 1931

RICKARD, MRS. VICTOR. 1879-   . Byline usually: Jessie Louisa (Moore) Rickard, q.v.

RICKETT, FRANCES. Born in Ind., later living in NYC; free-lance writer.
   The Prowler. Simon, 1963; Hale, 1964 [Ind.]
   Tread Softly. Simon, 1964; Hale, 1964 [Ind.]

RICO, DON. 1917-   . Ref: CA. SC: Burgess (Buzz) Cardigan, in at least those marked BC; Casey Grant, in at least those marked CG.
   The Daisy Dilemma. Lancer, 1967 BC [Calif.]
   Lorelei. Belmont, 1966
   The Man from Pansy. Lancer, 1967 BC
   Nightmare of Eyes. Lancer, 1967 [Calif.]
   The Passion Flower Puzzle. Lancer, 1969
   The Ring-a-Ding Girl. Paperback Library, 1969 CG
   So Sweet, So Deadly. Paperback Library, 1970 CG
   The Swinging Virgin. Paperback Library, 1969 CG

RIDDELL, FLORENCE
   The Valley of Suspicion. Bles, 1930. U.S. title: Suspicion. Lippincott, 1931

RIDDELL, GILBERT
   Murder with Music. Alliance, 1935 [NYC]

RIDDELL, MRS. J. H. [CHARLOTTE ELIZA LAWSON COWAN RIDDELL]. 1832-1906.
   Alaric Spenceley; or, A High Ideal. Skeet, 1881
   Handsome Phil, and other stories. White, 1899 ss, some criminous
   A Life's Assize. Tinsley, 1871; Harper, 1871

RIDDELL, JOHN. Pseudonym of Corey Ford, 1902-1969. Ref: CA, CC.
   The John Riddell Murder Case: A Philo Vance Parody. Scribner (NYC & London), 1930 [NYC] (Philo Vance.)

RIDEAL, CHARLES F. See: Maurice Moser.

RIDEAUX, CHARLES DE BALZAC. 1900-1971. Pseudonym: John Chancellor, q.v.

RIDEING, WILLIAM H(ENRY). 1853-1918.
How Tyson Came Home. Lane (London & NYC), 1904

RIDEOUT, HENRY MILNER. 1877-1927. Ref: MP.
-Admiral's Light. Houghton, 1907
Dulcarnon. Duffield, 1925; Hurst, 1926
Fern Seed. Duffield, 1921; Hurst, 1922
-Man Eater. Duffield, 1924; Hurst, 1927
No Man's Money; see Tin Cowrie Dass
The Siamese Cat. McClure, 1907; Jarrolds, 1922
-Tin Cowrie Dass. Duffield, 1918. British title: No Man's Money. Jarrolds, 1919
The Twisted Foot. Houghton, 1910; Constable, 1910

RIDER, ANNE. 1924- .
The Bad Samaritan. Bodley, 1965
A Safe Place. Bobbs, 1974 [Eng.]

RIDER, SARAH
The Misplaced Corpse. Houghton, 1940 [L.A.]

RIDER, WARRICK W.
Dyed for Death. Belmont, 1980 [Iran]

RIDGE, W(ILLIAM) PETT. -1930.
A Breaker of Laws. Harper (London), 1900; Macmillan, 1900
By Order of the Magistrate; see Mord Em'ly
An Important Man and others. Ward, 1896 ss, some criminous
Mord Em'ly. Pearson, 1898. U.S. title: By Order of the Magistrate. Harper, 1898. Also published as: "Mordemly"; or, By Order of the Magistrate. Harper, 1898

RIDGEWAY, PHILIP and COLIN FRASER
The Switch. Compact, 1964 (Novelization of the movie.)

RIDGWAY, JASON. Pseudonym of Stephen Marlowe, 1928- , q.v. Name originally: Milton Lesser. Other pseudonyms: Andrew Frazer, C. H. Thames, qq.v. See also: Richard S(cott) Prather, 1921- ; and: Ellery Queen. SC: Brian Guy = BG.
Adam's Fall. Permabooks, 1960 BG [NYC]
Hardly a Man Is Now Alive. Permabooks, 1962 BG [L.I.]
People in Glass Houses. Permabooks, 1961 BG [N.Y.]
The Treasure of the Cosa Nostra. PB, 1966 BG [It.]
West Side Jungle. Signet, 1958

RIDLEY, ARNOLD. 1896- . See also: Ruth Alexander.
The Ghost Train. French (London), 1930; French (NYC), 1931 (3-act play.)
Murder Happens. French (London), 1951 (3-act play)
Peril at End House. French (London), 1945 (3-act play based on the novel by Agatha Christie, 1890-1976, q.v.)
Recipe for Murder. Deane, 1936; Baker, 1936 (Play.)
The Wrecker, with Bernard Merivale, 1882-1939. French (London), 1930 (3-act play.)

RIDLEY, NAT, JR. House name. SC: Nat Ridley, in all titles.
The Crime on the Limited; or, Nat Ridley in the Follies. Garden City, 1926
A Daring Abduction; or, Nat Ridley's Biggest Fight. Garden City, 1926
The Double Dagger; or, Nat Ridley's Mexican Trail. Garden City, 1926
The Great Circus Mystery; or, Nat Ridley on a Crooked Trail. Garden City, 1926
Guilty or Not Guilty? or, Nat Ridley's Great Race Track Case. Garden City, 1926
In the Grip of the Kidnappers. Garden City, 1926
In the Nick of Time; or, Nat Ridley Saving a Life. Garden City, 1926
The Mountain Inn Mystery; or, Nat Ridley with the Forest Rangers. Garden City, 1927
The Race Track Crooks; or, Nat Ridley's Queerest Puzzle. Garden City, 1926
A Scream in the Dark; or, Nat Ridley's Crimson Clue. Garden City, 1926
A Secret of the Stage; or, Nat Ridley and the Bouquet of Death. Garden City, 1926
The Stolen Liberty Bonds. Garden City, 1926
The Stolen Nugget of Gold; or, Nat Ridley on the Yukon. Garden City, 1926 [Can.]
Tracked to the West; or, Nat Ridley at the Magnet Mine. Garden City, 1926
The Western Express Robbery; or, Nat Ridley and the Mail Thieves. Garden City, 1927

RIDYARD, RICHARD D.
The Final Destiny. Hale, 1980

RIEFE, ALAN. 1925- . Pseudonym: Barbara Reife, q.v. Ref: CA. SC: Huntington Cage = HC; Tyger (Tygrus Gerald) Decker = TD.
The Black Widower. Popular Library, 1975 HC
The Bullet-Proof Man. Popular Library, 1975 HC
The Conspirators. Popular Library, 1975; New English Library pb, 1977 HC [NYC]
The Killer with a Golden Touch. Popular Library, 1975 HC
The Lady Killers. Popular Library, 1975; New English Library pb, 1976 HC [NYC]
The Silver Puma. Popular Library, 1975 HC
Tyger at Bay. Popular Library, 1976 TD [Vir. Is.]
Tyger by the Tail. Popular Library, 1976 TD [Antwerp]

RIEFE, BARBARA. Pseudonym of Alan Riefe, 1925- , q.v.
Auldearn House. Popular Library, 1977 [Scot., 1930s]
The Barringher House. Popular Library, 1976
Rowleston. Popular Library, 1976

RIEMAN, (MILDRED) TERRY
Vamp Till Ready. Harper, 1954; Gollancz, 1955 [NYC]

RIENITS, REX. 1909-1971. Ref: CA.
Assassin for Hire. Muller, 1952

RIESENBERG, FELIX. 1879-1939. Seaman, explorer, engineer.
The Left-Handed Passenger. Doubleday, 1935; Nicholson, 1935 [ship]

RIESS, CURT. 1902- . Born in Ger.; newspaper correspondent.
High Stakes. Putnam, 1942 [NYC]

RIEWERTS, J. P. See: Bernard J. McOwen.

RIFE, ELLOUISE A.
Broken Promise. Major, 1976
The House at Windridge. Zebra, 1980

RIFKIN, SHEPARD. 1918- . Ref: CA. SC: Damian McQuaid = DM.
Ladyfingers. GM, 1969; Coronet, 1969 [NYC]
McQuaid. Putnam, 1974; Hale, 1975 DM [L.A.]
McQuaid in August. Doubleday, 1979; Hale, 1980 DM [NYC]
The Murderer Vine. Dodd, 1970; Hale, 1973 [South]
The Snow Rattlers. Putnam, 1977; Hale, 1978 DM [N. Mex.]

RIGG, JENNIFER. 1939- . Born in Eng., living in Toronto in the 1970s.
Pencarnan. Bobbs, 1977; Hale, 1980 [Wales, 1920]
The Slipperdown Chant. McKay, 1977; Hale, 1979 [Eng., ca.1910]

RIGONI, ORLANDO JOSEPH. 1897- .
Pseudonym: Leslie Ames, q.v.

RIGSBY, HOWARD. 1909- . Pseudonym: Vechel Howard, q.v. Ref: CA.
As a Man Falls. GM, 1954; Muller 1960 [Calif.]
The Avenger. Crowell, 1957. Also published as: Naked to My Pride. Popular Library, 1958
Calliope Reef. Doubleday, 1967 [Calif.]
Clash of Shadows. Lippincott, 1959; Hale, 1961 [NYC]
Kill and Tell. Morrow, 1951; Muller, 1954 [Calif.]
Lucinda. GM, 1954; Fawcett (London), 1955
Murder for the Holidays. Morrow, 1951; Muller, 1952 [S.F.]
Naked to My Pride; see The Avenger
-A Time for Passion. Dell, 1960
The Tulip Tree. Doubleday, 1963 [N.Y.]

RIIS, DAVID ALLEN
The Jerusalem Conspiracy. Dell, 1979

RILEY, DICK. 1946- . Ref: CA.
Rite of Expiation. Putnam, 1976 [N.J.]

RILEY, FRANK
Jesus II. Sherbourne, 1972
The Kocska Formula. Sherbourne, 1971

RILEY, JOE
Long Firm. New Horizon, 1979

RILLA, WOLF (PETER). 1925- . Ref: CA.
The Chinese Consortium. Futura, 1980; Signet, 1980
The Dispensable Man. Allen, 1973; Day, 1974 [Mex.]

RIMEL, DUANE W(ELDON). 1915- . Ref: CA.
The Curse of Cain. McKay, 1945 [Midwest]
The Jury Is Out. Cherry Tree, 1947
Motive for Murder. Cherry Tree, 1945
The River Is Cold. Vega, 1962

RIMMER, ROBERT H. 1917- . Ref: CA.
The Zolotov Affair. Sherbourne, 1967; New English Library pb, 1969

RINEHART, MARY ROBERTS. 1876-1958. Ref: CC, DD, EM, MC, MP, TC. SC: Hilda Adams = HA.
The After House. Houghton, 1914; Simpkin, 1915 [ship]
The Album. Farrar, 1933; Cassell, 1933
Alibi for Isabel. Farrar, 1944; Cassell, 1946. Title story published separately: Dell 10¢ pb, 1951 ss
The Amazing Adventures of Letitia Carberry. Bobbs, 1911; Hodder, 1919 ss
The Bat, with Avery Hopwood, 1884-1928. French (NYC & London), 1932 (A play based on Rinehart's novel The Circular Staircase, q.v.) [N.Y.]
The Bat, with Avery Hopwood, 1884-1928. Doran, 1926; Cassell, 1926 (Novelization of the play.) [N.Y.]
The Buckled Bag; see Mary Roberts Rinehart's Crime Book
The Case of Elinor Norton; see The State vs. Elinor Norton
The Case of Jennie Brice. Bobbs, 1913; Hodder, 1919 [Pitt.]
The Circular Staircase. Bobbs, 1908; Cassell, 1909
The Curve of the Catenary. Royce, 1945 (Originally published in the anthology "The Mystery Book." Farrar, 1939.)
Dangerous Days. Doran, 1919; Hodder, 1919
The Door. Farrar, 1930; Hodder, 1930
The Double Alibi; see Miss Pinkerton
Episode of the Wandering Knife. Rinehart, 1950. British title: The Wandering Knife. Cassell, 1951 (Three novelets.)
The Frightened Wife. Rinehart, 1953; Cassell, 1954 ss
The Great Mistake. Farrar, 1940; Cassell, 1941
Haunted Lady. Farrar, 1942; Cassell, 1942 HA
Locked Doors; see Mary Roberts Rinehart's Crime Book
The Man in Lower Ten. Bobbs, 1909; Cassell, 1909 [Wash. D.C.]
Mary Roberts Rinehart's Crime Book. Farrar, 1933 (Includes two otherwise uncollected HA novelets, The Buckled Bag and Locked Doors, of which the latter was later published separately: Dell 10¢ pb, 1951.)
Miss Pinkerton. Farrar, 1932. British title: The Double Alibi. Cassell, 1932 HA
The Mystery Lamp; see The Red Lamp
The Pool; see The Swimming Pool
The Red Lamp. Doran, 1925. British title: The Mystery Lamp. Hodder, 1925
Sight Unseen, and The Confession. Doran, 1921; Hodder, 1921 (Two novelets.)
The State vs. Elinor Norton. Farrar, 1934. British title: The Case of Elinor Norton. Cassell, 1934 [Mont.]
The Swimming Pool. Rinehart, 1952. British title: The Pool. Cassell, 1952 [N.Y.]
Two Flights Up. Doubleday, 1928; Hodder, 1928
The Wall. Farrar, 1938; Cassell, 1938 [New Eng.]
The Wandering Knife; see Episode of the Wandering Knife
Where There's a Will. Bobbs, 1912
The Window at the White Cat. Bobbs, 1910; Nash, 1911
The Yellow Room. Farrar, 1945; Cassell, 1949 [Maine]

RING, ADAM. Pseudonym of Blair Reed, q.v.
Killers Play Rough. Crown, 1946

RING, BASIL. Pseudonym of Wilbur Braun, 1896-   , q.v. Other pseudonyms: Walter Blake, Bruce Brandon, Fred Caldwell, Raymond Dumkey, Nan Fleming, Marsha Grable, Edwin F. Hornung, Jed Parish, Orville Snap, Mortimer Sprague, Bert Stoner, qq.v.
   The Leavenworth Case. French, 1936 (3-act play based on the novel by Anna Katharine Green, 1846-1935, q.v.)

RING, DOUGLAS. Pseudonym of Richard S(cott) Prather, 1921-   , q.v. Other pseudonym: David Knight, q.v.
   The Peddler. Lion, 1952. Reprinted as by Prather: GM, 1963; Muller pb, 1963 [S.F.]

RIOTI, R.
   Scarlet Widow. Milestone, 1953

RIPLEY, (HAROLD) AUSTIN. 1896-   .
   How Good a Detective Are You? Stokes, 1934; Foulsham, 1939 ss in quiz form
   Minute Mysteries. Houghton, 1932 ss in quiz form
   Minute Mysteries. PB, 1949 ss in quiz form (A pb original, not a reprint of the above volume.)
   Mystery Puzzles. Stokes, 1937 ss in quiz form

RIPLEY, CLEMENTS. 1892-1954.
   Murder Walks Alone. Messner, 1935; Eldon, 1935 [S.W.]

RIPLEY, JACK. Pseudonym of John (William) Wainwright, 1921-   , q.v. SC: John George Davis, in all titles. Set: Eng.
   Davis Doesn't Live Here Any More. H. Hamilton, 1971; Doubleday, 1971
   My God How the Money Rolls In. H. Hamilton, 1972
   My Word You Should Have Seen Us. H. Hamilton, 1972
   The Pig That Got Up and Slowly Walked Away. H. Hamilton, 1971

RIPPON, MARION (EDITH). 1921-   . Ref: CA. SC: Insp. Maurice Ygrec, in all titles, all set in Fr.
   Behold, the Druid Weeps. Doubleday, 1970; Hale, 1972
   The Hand of Solange. Doubleday, 1969
   Lucien's Tomb. Doubleday, 1979; Hale, 1979
   The Ninth Tentacle. Doubleday, 1974

RISCO, M.
   Corpse at College. Scion, 1952
   Over My Dead Body. Milestone, 1953
   Ramona. Milestone, 1953
   Visa for Violence. Milestone, 1954

RISING, LAWRENCE. 1891-   .
   She Who Was Helena Cass. Doran, 1920; Hodder, 1920 [Sp.]

RISKU, CILLAY
   White Midnight. Playboy, 1977 [Fin.]

RITA. Pseudonym of Eliza Margaret J. Gollan Humphreys, 1860-1938.
   -The Doctor's Secret. White, 1890; Lovell, 1890
   -Grim Justice. Newnes, 1907
   The Mystery of a Turkish Bath. White, 1888; Lovell, 1888
   -An Old Rogue's Tragedy. Hutchinson, 1899
   The Philanthropic Burglar. Odhams, 1919 ss
   -The Pointing Finger. Nash, 1907

RITCHIE, HETTY
   Death Runs on Skis. Methuen, 1935

RITCHIE, JACK. Pseudonym of John George Reitci, 1922-1983. Ref: TC.
   A New Leaf, and other stories. Dell, 1971 ss

RITCHIE, PAUL. 1923-   . Ref: CA.
   Pitfall. Milton House, 1973

RITCHIE, RITA. Pseudonym of Rita Krohne Reitci, 1930-   . Ref: CA.
   Grip of Fear. Major, 1976
   Shadow of the Pyramid. Carousel, 1980

RITCHIE, ROBERT WELLES. 1879-1942. See also: Earl Derr Biggers, 1844-1933.
   Deep Furrows. Crowell, 1927; Bles, 1927 [Calif.]

RITNER, PETER (VAUGHN). 1927-1976. Ref: CA.
   Red Carpet for the Shah. Morrow, 1975; Weidenfeld, 1976 [future]

RITSON, JOHN. Pseudonym of Douglas Gordon Baber, 1918-   .
   Beneath the Precipice. Boardman, 1962
   The Deadly Blunder. Boardman, 1964
   Death of a Mind. Boardman, 1962
   The Desperate Venture. Boardman, 1963

RITTENBERG, MAX. 1880-   .
   -Every Man His Price. Methuen, 1914; Dillingham, 1914
   -Gold and Thorns. Ward, 1915
   -The Mind Reader. Appleton (London & NYC), 1913
   -Swirling Waters. Methuen, 1913; Dillingham, 1913

RITTER, MARGARET
   The Burning Woman. Putnam, 1979; Hale, 1981
   Caroline, Caroline. Scribner, 1976 [Mass.]
   The Lady in the Tower. Avon, 1972

RIVERA, WILLIAM L.
   Panic Walks Alone. Major, 1976 [S.F.]

RIVERS, ANNE. Editor, ss writer, in London.
   Payment for Silence. Hurst, 1974; Walker, 1975

RIVERS, GAYLE, pseudonym, and JAMES HUDSON, 1937-   .
   -The Five Fingers. Doubleday, 1978; Corgi, 1979 [Viet Nam]

RIVERS, RONALD
   "The Coniackers"; or, The Driggs-Guyon Gang of Notorious Counterfeiters. Laird, 1889

RIVES, ANNE. Executive of French publishing house.
   The Incident. Dutton, 1962. British title: Over the Tunnel. Harvill, 1962 (Translation of "L'Incident." Paris, 1961.) [Fr.]

RIVES, HALLIE ERMINIE. 1876-1956.
   The Magic Man. Dodd, 1927; Hutchinson, 1928

RIVETT, EDITH CAROLINE. 1894-1958. Pseudonyms: Carol Carnac, E. C. R. Lorac, qq.v.

ROADARMEL, PAUL. 1942-   . Ref: CA.
   The Kaligarh Fault. Harper, 1979 [India]

ROAN, TOM
   The Dragon Strikes Back. Messner, 1936; Melrose, 1936 [S.F.]
   Greedy Fingers. Mellifont, 1953

ROBB, JOHN. Pseudonym of Norman Robson.
   -Advance South. Hamilton Stafford, 1955
   -American Legionnaire. Hamilton Stafford, 1952
   -Broken Ramparts. Hamilton Stafford, 1951
   Four Corpses in a Million. Big Ben, 1942
   I Shall Avenge. Hamilton Stafford, 1954
   -The Last Deserter. Hamilton Stafford, 1952
   -The Lost Garrison. Hamilton Stafford, 1952
   -March of the Legion. Hamilton Stafford, 1951
   Mission of Mercy. Hamilton Stafford, 1954
   -Patrol to Zaruse. Hamilton Stafford, 1952
   Punitive Action. Hamilton Stafford, 1954
   -Revolt in the Desert. Hamilton Stafford, 1952
   -Space Beam. Hamilton Stafford, 1951
   -State of Emergency. Hamilton Stafford, 1955
   Storm Evil. Hamilton Stafford, 1954
   We, the Condemned. Hamilton Stafford, 1954
   Zone Zero. Hamilton Stafford, 1954

ROBBE-GRILLET, ALAIN. 1922-   . Ref: CA, TC.
   The Erasers. Calder, 1963; Grove, 1964 (Translation of "Les Gommes." Paris, 1962.)
   -In the Labyrinth. Grove, 1960 (Translation of "Dans le Labyrinthe." Paris, 1959.)
   -Jealousy. Calder, 1960; Grove, 1959 (Translation of "La Jalousie." Paris, 1957.)
   Topology of a Phantom City. Grove, 1977 (Translation of "Topologie d'une Cite Fantome." Paris, 1976.)
   The Voyeur. Calder, 1959; Grove, 1958 (Translation of "Le Voyeur." Paris, 1959.)

ROBBINS, CLARENCE AARON. 1888-1949. Pseudonym: Tod Robbins, q.v.

ROBBINS, CLIFTON. 1890-   . Ref: CC. SC: Clay Harrison = CH; Staveley = S. Set: Eng.
   Death Forms Threes. Rich, 1940 S
   Death on the Highway. Benn, 1933 CH
   Dusty Death. Benn, 1931; Appleton, 1932 CH
   The Man Without a Face. Benn, 1932. U.S. title: The Mystery of Mr. Cross. Appleton, 1933 CH
   Methylated Murder. Butterworth, 1935 CH
   Murder by Twenty-Five. Butterworth, 1936
   The Mystery of Mr. Cross; see The Man Without a Face
   Six Sign-Post Murder. Rich, 1939 S
   Smash and Grab. Benn, 1934; Appleton, 1934 CH

ROBBINS, NORMAN
   A Tomb with a View. French (London), 1978 (Play.)

ROBBINS, TOD. Pseudonym of Clarence Aaron Robbins, 1888-1949.
   The Master of Murder; see Mysterious Martin
   Mysterious Martin. Ogilvie, 1912. British title: The Master of Murder. Allan, 1933 [NYC]
   The Three Freaks; see The Unholy Three
   The Unholy Three. Lane, 1917. British title: The Three Freaks. Allan, 1934

ROBENS, HOWARD and JACK WASSERMANN
   Hambro's Itch. Doubleday, 1979 [future]

ROBERTS, ANTHONY. Pseudonym of John B(asil) Watney, 1915-   , q.v.
   Scheme for One. Gifford, 1945

ROBERTS, ARTHUR GUY. 1903-   . Pseudonym: Guy Clifford, q.v.

ROBERTS, BEN. See: Ivan Goff.

ROBERTS, CARL ERIC BECHHOFER. 1894-1949. Pseudonym: Ephesian, q.v. See also: George Goodchild, 1888-   , and (Carl Eric) Bechhofer Roberts. Born in London; stationed in Russ. during WWI; newspaper correspondent, author of books on Russ., biographies, and novels.

ROBERTS, DAVID. 1924-   . With USIA since 1956, stationed in Mid. East, and more recently in Greece.
   Journey from Baghdad. Doubleday, 1969 [Mid. East]

ROBERTS, DOROTHY JAMES. 1903-   . Pseudonym (?): Peter Mortimer, q.v.

ROBERTS, DORRIS
   Beginning of a Crime. Dorrance, 1958 [Ill.]

ROBERTS, IRENE. 1926-   . Pseudonym: Irene Shaw, q.v.

ROBERTS, JAMES HALL. Pseudonym of Robert L(ipscomb) Duncan, 1927-   , q.v.
   -The Burning Sky. Morrow, 1966
   The February Plan. Morrow, 1967; Deutsch, 1967. Also published as by Robert L. Duncan: Sphere, 1981 [Jap.]
   The Q Document. Morrow, 1964; Cape, 1965

ROBERTS, JAN. Pseudonym of "a famous American author, raised and educated on the East Coast."
   The Judas Sheep. Souvenir, 1974; Saturday Review Press, 1975 [Athens]

ROBERTS, JANE. 1929-   .
   The Education of Oversoul Seven. Prentice-Hall, 1973

ROBERTS, JANET LOUISE. 1925-   . Ref: CA. Pseudonyms: Louisa Bronte, Rebecca Danton, Janette Radcliffe, qq.v. Some of the titles below are more straight romance than gothic.
   Black Pearls. Ballantine, 1979; Sphere, 1980
   The Cardross Luck. Dell, 1974
   Castlereagh. PB, 1975 [Eng., 1819]
   The Curse of Kenton. Avon, 1972
   The Dancing Doll. Dell, 1973
   Dark Rose. Lancer, 1971
   The Devil's Own. Avon, 1972
   The Dornstein Ikon. Avon, 1973 [Austria]

The First Waltz. Dell, 1974
Golden Lotus. Warner, 1979
The Golden Thistle. Dell, 1973
Her Demon Lover. PB, 1978
Island of Desire. Ballantine, 1977;
  Sphere, 1977
Isle of the Dolphins. Avon, 1973
Jade Vendetta. PB, 1976 [Eng., 1890s]
The Jewels of Terror. Lancer, 1970
La Casa Dorada. Dell, 1973
Love Song. Pinnacle, 1971
A Marriage of Inconvenience. Dell, 1972
My Lady Mischief. Dell, 1973
Ravenswood. Avon, 1971 [Eng., 1800s]
Rivertown. Avon, 1972
The Weeping Lady. Lancer, 1971
Wilderness Inn. PB, 1976 [West, 1795]

ROBERTS, KATHERINE. 1895-   .
  Center of the Web. Doubleday, 1942
    [Antwerp]
  Private Report. Doubleday, 1943

ROBERTS, LEE. Pseudonym of Robert (Lee)
  Martin, 1908-1976, q.v. SC: Dr.
  Clinton Shannon, in at least those
  marked CS.
  The Case of the Missing Lovers. Dodd,
    1957; Foulsham, 1957 [Midwest]
  Death of a Ladies' Man. GM, 1960;
    Muller pb, 1960. Reprinted in Britain
    as by Robert Martin: Hale, 1969 CS
    [N.Y.]
  If the Shoe Fits. Dodd, 1959; Hale,
    1960 CS [Ohio]
  Judas Journey. Dodd, 1956. British
    title: Mahogany Murder. Foulsham,
    1957 [Tex.]
  Little Murder. GM, 1952
  Mahogany Murder; see Judas Journey
  Once a Widow. Dodd, 1957; Hale, 1961
    CS [Ohio]
  The Pale Door. Dodd, 1955; Foulsham,
    1956 [Midwest]
  Suspicion. Curtis, 1971; Hale, 1964 CS
    [N.Y.]

ROBERTS, LILLIAN
  Rafferty and the Gold Dust Twins.
    Paperback Library, 1975 (Novelization
    of the movie.)

ROBERTS, MARION. SC: Anne and David Lay-
  ton, in at least those marked L.
  A Mask for Crime. Eldon, 1935 L
    [Burma]
  Red Greed. Eldon, 1934 L
  The Yellow Robed Wago. Eldon, 1936

ROBERTS, MARK K. See: Lionel Derrick.

ROBERTS, MARY CARTER. Ref: CC.
  Little Brother Fate. Farrar, 1957; Gol-
    lancz, 1958

ROBERTS, MORLEY. 1857-1942.
  -The Adventure of the Broad Arrow.
    Hutchinson, 1897
  -The Degradation of Geoffrey Alwith.
    Downey, 1895; Sergel, 1895
  -The Descent of the Duchess. Sands, 1900
  -The Fugitives; see Taken by Assault;
    or, The Fugitives
  -The Grinder's Wheel. Nelson, 1907
  -Midsummer Madness. Nash, 1909 ss, one
    criminous
  -The Plunderers. Methuen, 1900
  -The Prey of the Strongest. Hurst, 1906
  -The Scent of Death. Nash, 1931
  -Taken by Assault; or, The Fugitives.
    Sands, 1901. U.S. title: The Fugi-
    tives. McClure, 1900

ROBERTS, R(ICHARD) ELLIS. 1879-1953.
  -The Other End. Palmer, 1923 ss

ROBERTS, RINALDA. Pseudonym of Edythe
  Lachlan.
  The Four Marys. Popular Library, 1976

ROBERTS, ROY. Pseudonym of Alexander
  Brinchmann, 1888-1978.
  The Crayfish Club. Hodder, 1931
    (Translation of "Krebseklubben."
    Oslo, 1929.) [Oslo]

ROBERTS, SUZANNE
  House of Cain. Dell, 1975
  Terror at Tansey Hill. Dell, 1975
  To Kill a House. Lancer, 1973

ROBERTS, THOMAS A. 1947-   . Born in
  Boston, graduate of Harvard.
  The Heart of the Dog. Random, 1972
    [Mid. East]

ROBERTS, W(ALTER) ADOLPHE. 1886-1962.
  Pseudonym: Stephen Endicott, q.v.
  The Haunting Hand. Macaulay, 1926;
    Hutchinson, 1972 [L.I.]
  The Mind Reader. Macaulay, 1929 [NYC]

The Top-Floor Killer. Nicholson, 1935
  [NYC]

ROBERTS, WILLO DAVIS. 1928-   . Ref: CA.
  Act of Fear. Doubleday, 1977; Hale,
    1978
  Becca's Child. Lancer, 1972
  The Cade Curse. Popular Library, 1978
  Cape of Black Sands. Popular Library,
    1977
  Dangerous Legacy. Lancer, 1972
  Dark Dowry. Popular Library, 1978
  Devil Boy. Signet, 1970
  The Devil's Double. Popular Library,
    1979
  Didn't Anybody Know My Wife? Putnam,
    1974; Hale, 1978
  The Evil Children. Lancer, 1973
  Expendable. Doubleday, 1976; Hale, 1979
    [Calif.]
  The Face of Danger. Lancer, 1972
  The Gates of Montrain. Lancer, 1971
  The Ghosts of Harrel. Lancer, 1971
  The Girl Who Wasn't There. Arcadia,
    1957
  The Gods in Green. Lancer, 1973
  The Gresham Ghost. Popular Library,
    1980
  The Hellfire Heritage. Popular Library,
    1979
  The House at Fern Canyon. Lancer, 1970
  House of Imposters. Popular Library,
    1977
  Inherit the Darkness. Lancer, 1972
  Invitation to Evil. Lancer, 1970
    [Maine]
  The Jaubert Ring. Doubleday, 1976
    [S.F.]
  Key Witness. Putnam, 1975 [New Eng.]
  King's Pawn. Lancer, 1971
  The Macomber Menace. Popular Library,
    1979
  Murder at Grand Bay. Arcadia, 1955
    [Mich.]
  Murder Is So Easy. Vega, 1961
  The Radkin Revenge. Popular Library,
    1979
  Return to Darkness. Lancer, 1969
  The Search for Willie. Popular Library,
    1980 [Nev., ca.1900]
  Shadow of a Past Love. Lancer, 1970
    [Calif.]
  Shroud of Fog. Ace, 1970
  Sing a Dark Song. Lancer, 1972
  Sinister Gardens. Lancer, 1972
  The Stuart Stain. Popular Library, 1978
    [Calif., 1850]
  The Suspected Four. Vega, 1962
  The Tarot Spell. Lancer, 1970
  The Terror Trap. Lancer, 1971
  The Waiting Darkness. Lancer, 1970
  The Watchers. Lancer, 1971
  White Jade. Doubleday, 1975 [Calif.,
    1885]

ROBERTSHAW, JAMES
  -Merivale; or, Phases of Southern Life.
    Dillingham, 1898

ROBERTSON, ALEXANDER
  -Irish Monte Cristo Abroad; or, The
    Secrets of the Catacombs. Street,
    1889
  -Irish Monte Cristo's Search; or, The
    Bonanza King in New York. Street,
    1889 [NYC]
  -Irish Monte Cristo's Trail; or, Hunted
    from the Pyramids to Berlin. Street,
    1890
  -Joe Leslie's Wife; or, A Skeleton in
    the Closet. Smith, 1892
  Old Specie, the Treasury Detective; or,
    The Harbor Lights of New York.
    Street, 1890 [NYC]
  The Vestibule Limited Mystery. Street,
    1891

ROBERTSON, ANDREW
  The Kidnapped Squatter and other Aus-
    tralian tales. Longmans, 1891 ss
    [Australia]

ROBERTSON, BRIAN. 1951-   . Ref: CA.
  The Siege of Hampton Mall. Manor, 1979

ROBERTSON, CHARLES
  The Elijah Conspiracy. Bantam, 1980
    [Ger.]

ROBERTSON, COLIN. 1906-1980. Ref: CA. SC:
  Peter Grayleigh = PG; Supt. Bradley
  = B; Insp. John Martin, in at least
  those marked JM; Vicky McBain = VM;
  Edward North = EN; Insp. Robert
  Strong, in at least those marked RS;
  Alan Steel = AS. Set: Eng.
  Alibi in Black. Ward, 1944 PG
  The Amazing Corpse. Ward, 1942 PG
  The Black Onyx Ring. Mellifont, 1936
  Calling Peter Grayleigh. Ward, 1948 PG
  Clash of Steel. Hale, 1965 AS [Venice]
  Conflict of Shadows. Hale, 1963 B

The Dark Knight. Ward, 1946 PG
Dark Money. Hale, 1962
Dead on Time. Hale, 1964 B
Death Wears Red Shoes. Ward, 1949 PG
Demon's Moon. Ward, 1951
Devil or Saint? Ward, 1936
The Devil's Cloak. Hale, 1969 B
The Devil's Lady. Ward, 1947 PG
Double Take. Hale, 1967 B
Dusky Limelight. Ward, 1950 EN
The Eastlake Affair. Long, 1957 VM
Explosion! Ward, 1945 PG
The Fake. Ward, 1937 JM
The Frightened Widow. Hale, 1963 B
Ghost Fingers. Ward, 1941
The Golden Triangle. Hale, 1959 VM
The Green Diamonds. Hale, 1970 B
House of Intrigue. Ward, 1937
The Judas Spies. Hale, 1966 AS
Killer's Mask. Hale, 1966 B
Knaves' Castle. Ward, 1948 PG
Lady, Take Care. Allen, 1952 EN
A Lonely Place to Die. Hale, 1969 PG
The Marble Tomb Mystery. Ward, 1936 RS
Murder in the Morning. Long, 1957 VM
Murder Sits Pretty. Hale, 1961 VM
Night Shadows. Ward, 1935 JM
Night Trap. Hale, 1960
No Trial—No Error. Allen, 1953 EN
North for Danger. Allen, 1952 EN
Painted Faces. Ward, 1935 RS
Peter Grayleigh Flies High. Ward, 1951
  PG
Project X. Hale, 1968 AS
Sinister Moonlight. Hale, 1965 B
Smugglers' Moon. Ward, 1954 PG
Soho Spy. Ward, 1940 RS
The Stalking Stranger. Ward, 1939 JM
Sweet Justice. Ward, 1949
The Temple of Dawn. Ward, 1939 JM
The Threatening Shadows. Hale, 1959 VM
The Tiger's Claws. Ward, 1951 VM
Time to Kill. Hale, 1961 B
Twice Dead. Hale, 1968 B
Two Must Die. Ward, 1946 PG
Venetian Mask. Ward, 1956 VM
White Menace. Ward, 1938 RS
Who Rides a Tiger? Long, 1958 VM
Without Motive. Pendulum, 1946 ss
The Yellow Strangler. Ward, 1934;
  Hillman-Curl, 1938
You Can Keep the Corpse. Ward, 1955 VM
Zero Hour. Ward, 1942 PG

ROBERTSON, CONSTANCE PIERREPONT NOYES.
  1897-   . Pseudonym: Dana Scott,
  q.v.

ROBERTSON, HELEN. Pseudonym of Helen
  (Jean Mary) Edmiston, 1913-   , q.v.
  SC: Insp. Lathom Dynes, in at least
  those marked LD. Set: Eng.
  The Chinese Goose. Macdonald, 1960.
    U.S. title: Swan Song. Doubleday,
    1960 LD
  The Crystal-Gazers. Macdonald, 1957;
    Doubleday, 1958 LD
  Swan Song; see The Chinese Goose
  Venice of the Black Sea. Macdonald,
    1956 LD
  The Winged Witnesses. Macdonald, 1955

ROBERTSON, JOHN
  Death Goes to Sea. Foster, 1947

ROBERTSON, KEITH CARLTON. 1914-   .
  Pseudonym: Carlton Keith, q.v.

ROBERTSON, L(ILIAN) M.
  -Due to the Lion Tamer. Joseph, 1964
  Frederika and the Convict; see Mr.
    Cooper's Frederika
  Mr. Cooper's Frederika. Hodder, 1965.
    U.S. title: Frederika and the Con-
    vict. Doubleday, 1965

ROBERTSON, LILIAN MAY. Pseudonym: Glen
  Steuart, q.v.

ROBERTSON, MANNING K. SC: Steve Carra-
  dine, in at least those marked SC.
  Blueprint for Destruction. Badger, 196?
    SC
  Night Passage to Kano. Badger, 196?
    SC
  -Rosaria. Badger, 1961
  The Secret Enemy. Badger, 196?
  Seek and Destroy. Badger, 1965 SC
  Twelve Hours to Destiny. Badger, 19??
    SC

ROBERTSON, MARJORIE
  To Ripen or to Kill. Harrap, 1953
    [Australia]

ROBERTSON, MUIRHEAD. Pseudonym of Henry
  Johnson.
  A Lombard Street Mystery. Bartholomew,
    1888

ROBERTSON, NETTA
  A Long Day's Nightmare. Hale, 1980

ROBERTSON, WILFRID. 1892-   . Ref: CA.
-The House on the Broads. Quality, 1954

ROBERTSON, WILLIAM
  Morris Hume, Detective. Hodge, 1905 ss

ROBESON, KENNETH. House name. The first
  series listed below is all Doc Savage
  stories, reprinted from the pulps;
  the second series is all Avenger stories, reprinted from the pulps
  through #24, thereafter new stories
  by Ron(ald Joseph) Goulart, 1933-   ,
  q.v., under the Kenneth Robeson byline. The Doc Savage stories were all
  written by Lester Dent, 1905-1969
  (= LD), q.v., except where indicated
  otherwise. Authorship of The Avenger
  series is indicated by Paul Ernst
  (1886-   , q.v.) = PE (#1-24) and
  Ron Goulart = RG (#25-36). The series
  number is given in parenthesis for
  both series. Except where indicated
  otherwise, Doc Savage titles were
  first published in book form by Bantam; all Avenger titles were published by Warner Paperback Library.
  The Angry Ghost. 1977; Bantam (London),
    1977 (86) (by LD and William Bogart,
    1907-1977, q.v.)
  The Annihilist. 1968; Bantam (London),
    1969 (31) [NYC]
  The Awful Egg. 1978 (92)
  The Black Spot. 1974 (76) (by Laurence
    Donovan.) [NYC]
  The Boss of Terror. 1976 (85) [NYC]
  Brand of the Werewolf. 1965; Bantam
    (London), 1965 (5) [Can.]
  Cargo Unknown. 1980 (98)
  Cold Death. 1968; Bantam (London), 1968
    (21) (By Laurence Donovan.)
  The Crimson Serpent. 1974 (78) (By
    LD and Harold A. Davis.) [Ark.]
  The Czar of Fear. 1968; Bantam (Lon-
    don), 1968 (22)
  The Dagger in the Sky. 1969 (40)
    [Carib.]
  The Deadly Dwarf. 1968; Bantam (Lon-
    don), 1968 (28) [S. Pac.]
  Death in Silver. 1968; Bantam (London),
    1968 (26)
  The Derrick Devil. 1973 (74) [Okla.]
  The Devil Genghis. 1974 (79) [Arctic]
  Devil on the Moon. 1970 (50) [Va.]
  The Devil's Playground. 1968; Bantam
    (London), 1968 (25) (By Alan Hath-
    way.) [Mich.]
  Dust of Death. 1969; Bantam (London),
    1969 (35) (By LD and Harold A.
    Davis.) [S. Am.]
  The Evil Gnome. 1978 (82) [Mo.]
  The Fantastic Island. 1966; Bantam
    (London), 1967 (14) (By LD and
    Ryerson Johnson, 1901-   , q.v.)
    [S. Pac.]
  Fear Cay. 1966; Bantam (London), 1966
    (11)
  The Feathered Octopus. 1970 (48) [NYC]
  The Flaming Falcons. 1968; Bantam (Lon-
    don), 1969 (30) [Far East]
  The Flying Goblin. 1977; Bantam (Lon-
    don), 1977 (90) (By LD and William
    Bogart, 1907-1977, q.v.) [N.Y.]
  Fortress of Solitude. 1968; Bantam
    (London), 1968 (23) [Russ.]
  The Freckled Shark. 1972 (67) [S. Am.]
  The Giggling Ghosts. 1971 (56) [N.J.]
  The Gold Ogre. 1969 (42)
  The Golden Peril. 1970 (55) (By LD
    and Harold A. Davis.) [Cent. Am.]
  The Green Death. 1971 (65) (By LD and
    Harold A. Davis.) [Brazil]
  The Green Eagle. 1968; Bantam (London),
    1968 (24) [Wyo.]
  The Hate Genius. 1979 (94) [Lisbon]
  Haunted Ocean. 1970 (51) (By Laurence
    Donovan.) [Nor.]
  He Could Stop the World. 1970 (54)
    [Calif.]
  Hell Below. 1980 (99) [Mex.]
  Hex. 1969; Bantam (London), 1968 (37)
    (By LD and William Bogart, 1907-1977,
    q.v.) [Mass.]
  The King Maker. 1975 (80) (By LD and
    Harold A. Davis.) [Balkans]
  Land of Always-Night. 1966 (13) (By
    LD and Ryerson Johnson, 1901-   ,
    q.v.) [Can.]
  The Land of Fear. 1973 (75) [NYC]
  Land of Long Juju. 1970 (47) (By Lau-
    rence Donovan.) [Afr.]
  The Land of Terror. Street, 1935; Tan-
    dem, 1965 (8) [NYC]
  The Living Fire Menace. 1971 (61) (By
    LD and Harold A. Davis.) [Calif.]
  The Lost Giant. 1980 (100) [Arctic]
  The Lost Oasis. 1965; Bantam (London),
    1965 (6)
  Mad Eyes. 1969; Bantam (London), 1969
    (33) [NYC]
  Mad Mesa. 1972 (66) [Utah]
  The Magic Mountain. 1977; Bantam (Lon-
    don), 1977 (89)
  The Majii. 1971 (60) [NYC]
  The Man of Bronze. Street, 1935; Ban-
    tam (London), 1964 (1) [Cent. Am.]
  The Man Who Shook the Earth. 1969 (43)
    [Chile]
  The Men Who Smiled No More. 1970 (45)
    (By Laurence Donovan.) [NYC]
  The Mental Wizard. 1970 (53) (By LD
    and Harold A. Davis.) [NYC]
  Merchants of Disaster. 1969 (41) (By
    LD and Harold A. Davis.) [Wash. D.C.]
  The Metal Monster. 1973 (72)
  Meteor Menace. 1964; Bantam (London),
    1964 (3) [Tib.]
  The Midas Man. 1970 (46) [N.J.]
  The Monsters. 1965; Bantam (London),
    1965 (7) [Mich.]
  The Motion Menace. 1971 (64) (By LD
    and Ryerson Johnson, 1901-   , q.v.)
  The Mountain Monster. 1976 (84) (By
    LD and Harold A. Davis.) [Alaska]
  The Munitions Master. 1971 (58) (By
    LD and Harold A. Davis.) [Afr.]
  Murder Melody. 1967 (15) (By Laurence
    Donovan.) [Can.]
  Murder Mirage. 1972 (71) (By Laurence
    Donovan.)
  Mystery on Happy Bones. 1979 (96)
    [Carib.]
  The Mystery on the Snow. 1972 (69)
    [Can.]
  Mystery Under the Sea. 1968; Bantam
    (London), 1969 (27) [ship]
  The Mystic Mullah. 1965; Bantam (Lon-
    don), 1966 (9) (By LD and Richard
    Sale, 1911-   , q.v.) [NYC]
  The Other World. 1968; Bantam (London),
    1969 (29) [Can.]
  The Phantom City. 1966; Bantam (Lon-
    don), 1966 (10)
  The Pharaoh's Ghost. 1980 (101)
    [Cairo]
  Pirate of the Pacific. 1967; Bantam
    (London), 1967 (19)
  The Pirate's Ghost. 1971 (62) [Calif.]
  Poison Island. 1971 (57)
  The Polar Treasure. 1965; Bantam (Lon-
    don), 1965 (4) [Arctic]
  The Purple Dragon. 1978 (91) (By LD
    and Harold A. Davis.) [NYC]
  Quest of Qui. 1966; Bantam (London),
    1965 (12) [Can.]
  Quest of the Spider. Street, 1935 (68)
    [La.]
  The Red Skull. 1967; Bantam (London),
    1967 (17) [Ariz.]
  Red Snow. 1969 (38) [Miami]
  The Red Spiders. 1979 (95) [Moscow]
  The Red Terrors. 1976 (83) (By LD and
    Harold A. Davis.) [ship]
  Resurrection Day. 1969; Bantam (Lon-
    don), 1969 (36) [NYC]
  The Roar Devil. 1977; Bantam (London),
    1977 (88) [N.Y.]
  The Sargasso Ogre. 1967; Bantam (Lon-
    don), 1967 (18)
  Satan Black. 1980 (97)
  The Sea Angel. 1970 (49)
  The Sea Magician. 1970 (44) [Eng.]
  The Secret in the Sky. 1967; Bantam
    (London), 1968 (20)
  The Seven Agate Devils. 1973 (73) (By
    LD and Harold A. Davis.) [L.A.]
  The South Pole Terror. 1974 (77) (By
    LD and Harold A. Davis.) [Antarctica]
  Spook Hole. 1972 (70) [S. Am.]
  The Spook Legion. 1967; Bantam (Lon-
    don), 1967 (16) [NYC]
  The Spotted Men. 1977 (87) (By LD and
    William Bogart, 1907-1977, q.v.)
    [N.Y.]
  The Squeaking Goblin. 1969; Bantam
    (London), 1969 (32) [Maine]
  The Stone Man. 1976 (81) [Ariz.]
  The Submarine Mystery. 1971 (63)
  The Terror in the Navy. 1969; Bantam
    (London), 1969 (34)
  The Thousand-Headed Man. 1964; Bantam
    (London), 1964 (2) [Far East]
  The Time Terror. 1980 (102) [Can.]
  Tunnel Terror. 1979 (93) (By LD and
    William Bogart, 1907-1977, q.v.)
    [West]
  The Vanisher. 1970 (52)
  World's Fair Goblin. 1969 (39) (By LD
    and William Bogart, 1907-1977, q.v.)
    [NYC]
  The Yellow Cloud. 1971 (59) [NYC]

  The Black Chariots. 1974 (30) (RG)
    [Calif.]
  The Black Death. 1974 (22) (PE) [NYC]
  The Blood Countess. 1975 (33) (RG)
    [S. Am.]
  The Blood Ring. 1972 (6) (PE) (Wash.
    D.C.]
  The Cartoon Crimes. 1974 (31) (RG)
    [L.I.]
  Death in Slow Motion. 1973 (18) (PE)
    [NYC]
  The Death Machine. 1975 (32) (RG)
    [S.F.]
  Demon Island. 1975 (36) (RG) [Calif.]
  The Devil's Horns. 1972 (4) (PE)
  Dr. Time. 1974 (28) (RG) [L.I.]
  The Flame Breathers. 1973 (12) (PE)
    [NYC]
  The Frosted Death. 1972 (5) (PE)
    [NYC]
  The Glass Man. 1975 (34) (RG)
    [N. Mex.]
  The Glass Mountain. 1973 (8) (PE)
    [Ida.]
  The Green Killer. 1974 (20) (PE)
  The Happy Killers. 1974 (21) (PE)
    [NYC]
  The Hate Master. 1973 (16) (PE)
  House of Death. 1973 (15) (PE) [NYC]
  The Iron Skull. 1975 (35) (RG) [NYC]
  Justice, Inc. 1972 (1) (PE) [N.Y.]
  The Man from Atlantis. 1974 (25) (RG)
    [N.Y.]
  Midnight Murder. 1974 (24) (PE) [NYC]
  Murder on Wheels. 1973 (13) (PE)
    [NYC]
  Nevlo. 1973 (17) (PE) [Ohio]
  The Nightwitch Devil. 1974 (29) (RG)
    [Mass.]
  Pictures of Death. 1973 (19) (PE)
    [NYC]
  The Purple Zombie. 1974 (27) (RG)
    [L.A.]
  Red Moon. 1974 (26) (RG) [Conn.]
  River of Ice. 1973 (11) (PE) [NYC]
  The Sky Walker. 1972 (3) (PE) [Chi.]
  The Smiling Dogs. 1973 (10) (PE)
    [Wash. D.C.]
  Stockholders in Death. 1972 (7) (PE)
    [NYC]
  Three Gold Crowns. 1973 (14) (PE)
    [NYC]
  Tuned for Murder. 1973 (9) (PE)
    [N.Y.]
  The Wilder Curse. 1974 (23) (PE)
    [NYC]
  The Yellow Hoard. 1972 (2) (PE) [NYC]

ROBEY, GEORGE. 1869-1954.
  Bits and Pieces. Jarrolds, 1928 ss,
    some criminous

ROBIN, LILIANE
  Cruise of the Sphinx. Mystique, 1978
    (Translation of "Pour Oublier Jusqu'a
    Tou Nom." Paris, 1968.)
  Fury on the Pampas. Mystique, 1980
    (Translation of "Samantha." Paris,
    1978.)
  Gamble with Death. Mystique, 1980
    (Translation of "Les Aveux." Paris,
    1969.)
  Letter from a Stranger. Mystique, 1979
    (Translation of "Le Chant des Si-
    renes." Paris, 1966.)
  Night of the Scorpion. Mystique, 1980
    (Translation of "La Nuit des Scor-
    pions." Paris, 1975.)
  No Turning Back. Mystique, 1979
    (Translation of "Francesca." Paris,
    1961.)
  Sisters at War. Mystique, 1977 (Trans-
    lation of "Soeurs Ennemies." Paris,
    1962.)
  The Snare. Mystique, 1980 (Translation
    of "La Piege." Paris, 1969.)
  Spell of the Antilles. Mystique, 1979
    (Translation of "Le Sortilege des
    Antilles." Paris, 1963.)
  Stalked by Fear. Mystique, 1979
    (Translation of "Le Soir des Adieux."
    Paris, 1977.)
  Summer of Deceit. Mystique, 1979
    (Translation of "Une Fille Sous
    L'Orage." Paris, 1977.)

ROBINETT, STEPHEN (ALLEN). 1941-   .
  The Man Responsible. Ace, 1978
  Stargate. St. Martin's, 1976; Hale,
    1978 [future]

ROBINS, DENISE (NAOMI). 1897-   . Pseu-
  donym: Harriet Gray, q.v. Ref: CA.
-This One Night. Hutchinson, 1942;
  Avon, 1975

ROBINS, ELIZABETH. 1862-1952.
  The Messenger. Century, 1919; Hodder,
    1919
  The Secret That Was Kept. Harper, 1926;
    Hutchinson, 1926 [NYC]

ROBINS, PATRICIA DENISE [PATRICIA DENISE
  ROBINS CLARK]. 1921-   . Pseudonym:
  Claire Lorrimer, q.v.

ROBINS, RAYMOND. 1900-   . Born in
  Mich.; graduate of West Point, with
  degree in engineering from Mass.
  Institute of Technology.
  Murder at Bayside. Crowell, 1933;
    Hutchinson, 1934 [Md.]

ROBINSON, B(ERTRAM) FLETCHER
　The Chronicles of Addington Peace. Harper (London), 1905　ss
　The Trail of the Dead, with J. Malcolm Fraser. Ward, 1904; Langton (Toronto), 1904　[Ger.]

ROBINSON, DAVID. 1915-　. Ref: CA.
　The Confession of Andrew Clare. McKay, 1968　[Calif.]
　The Confessions of Alma Quartier. Signet, 1962

ROBINSON, DEREK. 1932-　. Ref: CA.
　The Eldorado Network. H. Hamilton, 1979; Norton, 1980　[Eng., 1941]
　Kramer's War. H. Hamilton, 1977; Viking, 1977　[Chan. Is.]
　Rotten with Honour. Barrie, 1973; Viking, 1973

ROBINSON, E(THELBERT) M(cKENNON)
　Death Designs a Dress. Hammond, 1958
　The Secret of the Swinging Room. Hammond, 1957　[Paris]

ROBINSON, EDWARD L(OUIS). 1921-　. Ref: CA.
　Sloth and Heathen Folly. Macmillan, 1972

ROBINSON, ELIOT H(ARLOW). 1884-1942.
　"Dee Dee." Small, 1925; Hutchinson, 1926
　The Scarred Hand. Page, 1931　[NYC]

ROBINSON, ERNEST H(ERBERT). 1880-1947.
　The Disappearance of "Straight Left" Smith. Lloyd's, 1921
　Dr. Quick, the Masked Detective. Aldine
　Gold for the Bank of England. Lloyd's, 1921
　The Will on the Watch. Lloyd's, 1922
　The Yellow Claws of Wong. Lloyd's, 1922

ROBINSON, F(REDERICK) W(ILLIAM). 1830-1901.
　-The Hands of Justice. Chatto, 1883; Harper, 1883
　The Keeper of the Keys. Hurst, 1890; Lovell, 1890
　Lazarus in London. Hurst, 1885; Harper, 1885
　Memoirs of Jane Cameron, Female Convict. Hurst, 1864
　99, Dark Street. Maxwell, 1887; Harper, 1887
　-The Woman in the Dark. Chatto, 1895
　-A Woman's Ransom. Hurst, 1863; Burnham, 1864
　-The Wrong That Was Done. Hurst, 1892; Lovell, 1891

ROBINSON, FRANK M(ALCOLM). 1926-　. See also: Thomas N(icholas) Scortia, 1926-　. Ref: CA.
　The Power. Lippincott, 1956; Eyre, 1957

ROBINSON, (DR.) J(OHN) H(OVEY). 1825-1867.
　-The Boston Conspiracy; or, The Royal Police. Dow, 1847　[Boston]
　-Cepherine; or, The Secret Cabal. Brady, 1862
　The House of Silence. Street, 1890
　-Nightshade; or, The Masked Robber of Hounslow Heath. Brady, 1861
　-Sibylla; or, The Mystery of the Brownstone House. Brady, 1864
　-The Uncle's Crime; or, The Doctor's Beautiful Ward. Starr, 1870

ROBINSON, JIM
　Together Brothers. Award, 1974; Tandem, 1974 (Novelization of the movie.)

ROBINSON, L(EONARD) W(ALLACE). 1918-　.
　Ref: CA.
　The Assassin. World, 1968; Macdonald, 1969. Also published as: With Time Running Out. Signet, 1973　[Wash. D.C.]

ROBINSON, LEWIS (GEORGE). 1886-　.
　Pseudonym: George Limnelius, q.v.
　Ref: CC.
　The General Goes Too Far. Nicholson, 1935; Putnam, 1936　[Afr., W.]
　-The Inward Glance. Chapman, 1940
　The Manuscript Murder. Barker, 1933; Doubleday, 1934, as by George Limnelius
　No More Ancestors. Nicholson, 1938

ROBINSON, MARY (DARBY). 1758-1800.
　Vancenza; or, The Dangers of Credulity. Bell, 1792

ROBINSON, PATRICIA COLBERT. 1923-　.
　Joint pseudonym with Ferdinan Stevenson: Daria Macomber, q.v. Ref: CA.

ROBINSON, PHILIP (BEDFORD). 1926-　.
　Ref: CA.
　-Masque of a Savage Mandarin. Macdonald, 1969
　The Pakistani Agent. Hart-Davis, 1965

ROBINSON, RICHARD
　High-Ballin'. Ballantine, 1978 (Novelization of the movie.)

ROBINSON, RICHARD BLUNDELL. 1905-　.
　Pseudonym: George Leaderman, q.v.

ROBINSON, ROBERT (HENRY). 1929-　.
　Ref: CA, CC.
　-The Conspiracy. Hodder, 1968
　Landscape with Dead Dons. Gollancz, 1956; Rinehart, 1956　[acad.]

ROBINSON, SONDRA TILL. 1931-　. See also: Susan Lee. Ref: CA.
　The Dark and Brilliant Places. Pyramid, 1977

ROBINSON, TIMOTHY (MICHAEL). 1934-　.
　Ref: CC.
　When Scholars Fall. Hutchinson, 1961　[acad.]

ROBISON, HAROLD R.
　Rat Alley. Monarch, 1965　[Carib.]

ROBSON, JAMES
　The Last Prisoner. Hamlyn, 1980

ROBSON, NORMAN. Pseudonym: John Robb, q.v.

ROBY, ADELAIDE Q.
　Sea Urchin. Milton House, 1974

ROBY, MARY LINN. 1930-　. Pseudonyms: Elizabeth Welles, Mary Wilson, qq.v. Ref: CA.
　Afraid of the Dark. Dodd, 1965
　All Your Lovely Words Are Spoken. Ace, 1970
　And Die Remembering. Signet, 1972
　Before I Die. Hale, 1966
　The Broken Key. Hawthorn, 1973; Milton House, 1974　[Eng.]
　Cat and Mouse. Hale, 1967
　Christobel. Berkley, 1976
　The Cry of the Peacock; see The White Peacock
　Dig a Narrow Grave. Signet, 1971
　-A Heritage of Strangers. Berkley, 1978
　The Hidden Book. Berkley, 1977　[Hung.]
　The House at Kilgallen. Signet, 1973　[Ire.]
　If She Should Die. Signet, 1970
　In the Dead of the Night. Signet, 1969
　Lie Quiet in Your Grave. Signet, 1970
　Marsh House. Hawthorn, 1974; Milton House, 1975　[Eng.]
　Pennies on Her Eyes. Signet, 1969　[Eng.]
　Reap the Whirlwind. Signet, 1972
　Shadow over Grove House. Signet, 1973
　The Silent Walls. Signet, 1974
　Some Die in Their Beds. Signet, 1970
　Speak No Evil of the Dead. Signet, 1973
　Still as the Grave. Dodd, 1964; Collins, 1965　[Eng.]
　That Fatal Touch. Signet, 1970
　This Land Turns Evil Slowly. Signet, 1971
　The Tower Room. Hawthorn, 1974; Milton House, 1975
　Trapped. Dell, 1977
　The Treasure Chest. Berkley, 1976
　When the Witch Is Dead. Signet, 1972
　The White Peacock. Hawthorn, 1972. British title: The Cry of the Peacock. Milton House, 1974

ROCCO, A.
　Build Me a Blonde. Milestone, 1953

ROCHE, ARTHUR SOMERS. 1883-1935. Ref: MP.
　Among Those Present. Sears, 1930　[NYC]
　Callingham's Girl, with Ethel P(ettit) Roche. Dodd, 1937　[NYC]
　The Case Against Mrs. Ames. Dodd, 1934; Archer, 1935　[NYC]
　Conspiracy. Sears, 1934
　Death Was a Wedding Guest. Cherry Tree, 1942 (U.S. title?)
　-Devil-May-Care. Century, 1926
　The Eyes of the Blind. Doran, 1919
　Find the Woman. Cosmopolitan, 1921; Hodder, 1921　[NYC]
　The Great Abduction. Sears, 1933　[NYC]
　Hard to Get. Dodd, 1937; Cherry Tree, 1940　[NYC]
　Honest Crook. Cherry Tree, 1941 (U.S. title?)
　In the Money. Dodd, 1936　[Fla.]
　A Lady of Resource. Dodd, 1938
　Loot. Bobbs, 1916　[NYC]
　-Marriage for Two. Sears, 1929
　No Stockings. Boston American, 1928
　Penthouse. Dodd, 1935　[NYC]
　The Pleasure Buyers. Macmillan, 1925　[Fla.]
　Plunder. Bobbs, 1917　[NYC]
　Ransom! Doran, 1918　[NYC]
　Shadow of Doubt. Dodd, 1935　[NYC]
　Slander. Sears, 1933　[NYC]
　The Sport of Kings. Bobbs, 1917
　The Star of Midnight. Dodd, 1936; Cherry Tree, 1940
　Uneasy Street. Cosmopolitan, 1920　[NYC]
　-The Wrong Wife. Sears, 1932

ROCHE, ETHEL P(ETTIT). See: Arthur Somers Roche, 1883-1935.

ROCHE, KAY
　-The Game and the Candle. Hurst, 1951
　The Shuttered House. Hurst, 1950

ROCHE, PETER
　Dean of Clonbury. Wright, 1957

ROCHE, REGINA MARIA (DALTON). 1764?-1845.
　The Children of the Abbey. Lane, 1796; Davis, 1798
　Clermont. Lane, 1798; Conrad, 1802　[Fr.]

ROCHESTER, DEVEREAUX
　Forever Timeless. Vantage, 1969

ROCHESTER, GEO(RGE) E(RNEST). Pseudonym: Jeffrey Gaunt, q.v. SC: Grey Shadow = GS. Set: Eng.
　Adventures at Greystones. Popular Library (London), 1936
　The Air Ranger. Hamilton, 1936
　The Air Trail. Popular Library (London), 1936
　The Black Bat Rides the Sky. Daniels, 1948
　The Black Chateau. Amalgamated, 1935
　The Black Hawk. Hamilton, 1936
　The Black Mole. Popular Library (London), 1936
　-The Black Octopus. Warne, 1954
　The Bulldog Breed. Hamilton, 1936
　Buzzard's Roost. Hutchinson, 1955
　The Crimson Threat. Amalgamated, 1934
　Dead Man's Gold. Amalgamated, 1935　[Scot.]
　-Drums of War. Warne, 1957
　The Flying Beetle. Hamilton, 1935
　The Flying Cowboys. Hamilton, 1936
　The Freak of St. Freda's! Popular Library (London), 1936
　Grey Shadow. Hamilton, 1936　GS
　Lair of the Vampire. Daniels, 1948
　The Mystery of Flying V Ranch. Hamilton, 1936
　North Sea Patrol. Hamilton, 1938
　Porson's Flying Service. Popular Library (London), 1936
　The Return of Grey Shadow. Eldon, 1949　GS　[Ger.]
　The Scarlet Squadron. Ace (London), 1938
　Secret Pilot. Epworth, 1954
　The Secret Squadron in Germany. Hamilton, 1938　[Ger.]
　The Shadow of the Guillotine. Popular Library (London), 1936
　The Sky Bandits. Ace (London), 1938
　Sons of the Legion. Daniels, 1948
　The Squadron Without a Number. Hamilton, 1937
　Traitor's Rock. Eldon, 1933
　The Vultures of Desolate Island. Ace (London), 1938
　Wings of Doom. Hamilton, 1936
　The Worst Squadron in France. Eldon, 1949　[Fr.]

ROCK, GILBERT
　The Crime of Golden Gully. Street (Magnet)

ROCK, PHILIP. 1927-　. Ref: CA.
　-The Dead in Guanajuato. Meredith, 1968
　Dirty Harry. Bantam (NYC & London), 1971 (Novelization of the movie.)　[S.F.]
　-The Extraordinary Seaman. Meredith, 1967; Souvenir, 1967
　Hickey and Boggs. Popular Library, 1972 (Novelization of the movie.)　[L.A.]
　Tick...Tick...Tick. Popular Library, 1970 (Novelization of the movie.)　[South]

ROCKEY, HOWARD. 1886-1934. Pseudonym: Oliver Panbourne, q.v.

ROCKLIN, ROSS LOUIS. 1913-　. Pseudonym: Ross Rocklynne, q.v.

ROCKWOOD, HARRY. Pseudonym of Ernest A. Young, q.v.
   Abner Ferret, the Lawyer Detective. Ogilvie, 1883
   Allan Keene, the War Detective. Ogilvie, 1884
   Clarice Dyke, the Female Detective. Ogilvie, 1883 [Boston]
   The Dexter Bank Robbery. Street (Magnet)
   Donald Dyke, the Down-East Detective. Ogilvie, 1882 [Boston]
   Dyke and Burr, the Rival Detectives. Ogilvie, 1883. Also published as: The Rival Detectives. Ogilvie, 1883
   Fred Danford, the Skillful Detective; or, The Watertown Mystery. Ogilvie, 1885. Also published as: The Watertown Mystery. Street (Magnet)
   The Handkerchief Clue. Street (Magnet)
   Harry Pinkurten, the King of Detectives. Ogilvie, 1882 [Boston]
   Harry Sharpe, the New York Detective. Ogilvie, 1893 [NYC]
   Luke Leighton, the Government Detective. Ogilvie, 1884
   The Man and the Crime. Street (Magnet)
   Mrs. Donald Dyke, Detective. Street, 1900
   Nat Foster, the Boston Detective. Ogilvie, 1883 [Boston]
   Neil Nelson, the Veteran Detective; or, Tracking Mail Robbers. Ogilvie, 1885 [NYC]
   The Railway Detective. Street (Magnet), 1900
   The Rival Detectives; see Dyke and Burr, Rival Detectives
   The Secret of the Missing Checks. Street (Magnet)
   Tales of Romance and Mystery. General Publishing, 1891 ss
   Walt Wheeler, the Scout Detective. Ogilvie, 1884 [Va., 1862]
   The Watertown Mystery; see Fred Danford, the Skillfull Detective

RODD, RALPH. Pseudonym of William North, 1869- . Set: Eng.
   Blind Man's Bluff. Collins, 1929
   The Claverton Case. Mellifont, 1940
   -From the House of Bondage. Collins, '1924
   -Madame Knits. Cassell, 1936
   -A Man Beguiled. Collins, 1929
   -Maureen Versus Fate. Collins, 1925
   Midnight Murder. Collins, 1931
   The Secret of the Flames. Collins, 1924; Dial, 1929
   Sleuth o' the World. Collins, 1933
   -The Story of Joan Courage. Cassell, 1932
   -The Whipping Girl. Collins, 1923
   Without Judge or Jury. Collins, 1928; Dial, 1929

RODDA, (PERCIVAL) CHARLES. 1891- . Pseudonyms: Gardner Low, Gavin Holt, qq.v. Ref: CA, CC. Joint pseudonym with Eric Ambler, 1909- , q.v.: Eliot Reed, q.v.
   -Golden Corn. Hodder, 1945
   -The House Upstairs. Barrie, 1949
   -Pilgrim Come Home. Hodder, 1945
   -Providence Hall. Hodder, 1943
   The Scarlet Mask. Nelson, 1926
   -South Sea Gold. Nelson, 1926
   -Tango. Benn, 1928

RODELL, MARIE FRIED. 1912-1975. Pseudonym: Marion Randolph, q.v.

RODELL, VIC
   Free-Lance Murder. Mystery House, 1957 [Colo.]

RODEN, H(ENRY) W(ISDOM). 1895-1963. Executive of corporations in food industry. SC: Sid Ames, in all titles.
   One Angel Less. Morrow, 1945; Hammond, 1949
   Too Busy to Die. Morrow, 1944; Hammond, 1947
   Wake for a Lady. Morrow, 1946; Hammond, 1950
   You Only Hang Once. Morrow, 1944; Hammond, 1946

RODNEY, BRYAN. Pseudonym of Cyril Edgeley. SC: Francis Villiers, in all titles.
   The Owl Flies Home. Wright, 1952 [Ire.]
   The Owl Hoots. Wright, 1945
   The Owl Meets the Devil. Wright, 1949

ROE, EDWARD PAYSON. 1838-1888.
   A Knight of the Nineteenth-Century. Dodd, 1877; Ward, 1877

ROE, IVAN. 1917- . Pseudonym: Richard Savage, q.v.

ROE, KIM
   The Gang Buster. Hale, 1961

ROE, WILLIAM JAMES. 1843- . Pseudonym: G. I. Cervius, q.v.

ROEBURT, JOHN. 1908?-1972. Ref: CA. SC: Johnny Devereaux = JD; Jigger Moran = JM.
   Al Capone. Pyramid, 1959 (Novelization of the movie.) [Chi., 1919-1929]
   Case of the Hypnotized Virgin; see Corpse on the Town
   Case of the Tearless Widow; see Jigger Moran
   The Climate of Hell. Abelard (NYC & London), 1958. Also published as: The Long Nightmare. Crest, 1958; Digit, 1959 [NYC]
   Corpse on the Town. Graphic, 1950. Revised edition: Case of the Hypnotized Virgin. Avon, 1956 JM [NYC]
   Did You Kill Mona Leeds?; see The Lunatic Time
   The Hollow Man. Simon, 1954; Jarrolds, 1955 JD [NYC]
   Jigger Moran. Greenberg, 1944; Wells Gardner, 1948. Also published as: Case of the Tearless Widow. Handi-Books, 1946. And as: Wine, Women and Murder. Avon, 1958 JM [NYC]
   The Lady and the Prowler; see The Unholy Wife
   The Long Nightmare; see The Climate of Hell
   The Lunatic Time. Simon, 1956. Also published as: Did You Kill Mona Leeds? Crest, 1958 [NYC]
   Manhattan Underworld; see There Are Dead Men in Manhattan
   The Mobster. Pyramid, 1960 [Chi., 1929]
   Murder in Manhattan; see There Are Dead Men in Manhattan
   Ruby Maclaine. Hillman, 196?
   Seneca, U.S.A. Curl, 1947
   Sing Out, Sweet Homicide. Dell, 1961 (Novelization of the "Roaring Twenties" TV series.)
   There Are Dead Men in Manhattan. Mystery House, 1946. Also published as (?): Manhattan Underworld. Harlequin, 1951. And as: Murder in Manhattan. Avon, 1957. And as: Triple Cross. Belmont, 1962 JM [NYC]
   They Who Sin. Avon, 1959
   Tough Cop. Simon, 1949 JD [NYC]
   Triple Cross; see There Are Dead Men in Manhattan
   The Unholy Wife. Avon, 1957. British title: The Lady and the Prowler (Novelization of the movie.)
   Wine, Women and Murder; see Jigger Moran

ROFFEY, JACK
   Hostile Witness. Evans, 1965; French (NYC), 1965 (2-act play.) Novel version: Evans, 1966; Arrow, 1968
   Night of the Fourth, with Gordon Harbord. French (London), 1957 (3-act play adapted from the play "Sprechstunde" by H. Bratt.)

ROFFMAN, JAN. Pseudonym of Margaret Summerton, q.v. SC: Sgt. Ratlin, in at least those marked R. Set: Eng.
   Ashes in an Urn. Doubleday, 1966 (British title?)
   A Bad Conscience. Doubleday, 1972 (British title?)
   A Daze of Fears. Doubleday, 1968 (British title?)
   Death of a Fox; see Winter of the Fox
   A Dying in the Night. Macdonald, 1975; Doubleday, 1974
   Grave of Green Water. Long, 1968; Doubleday, 1968
   The Hanging Woman. Bles, 1965 R
   Likely to Die. Bles, 1964
   Mask of Words; see A Penny for the Guy
   One Wreath with Love. Hale, 1979; Doubleday, 1978
   A Penny for the Guy. Bles, 1965; Doubleday, 1965. Also published as: Mask of Words. Ace, 1973 R
   Reflection of Evil; see Winter of the Fox
   Seeds of Suspicion. Long, 1968
   A Walk in the Dark. Long, 1969; Doubleday, 1970
   Why Someone Had to Die. Macdonald, 1976; Doubleday, 1976
   Winter of the Fox. Bles, 1964. U.S. title: Death of a Fox. Doubleday, 1964. Also published as: Reflection of Evil. Ace, 1967
   With Murder in Mind. Doubleday, 1963 (British title?)

ROGERS, BARBARA. 1935- . Born in St. Louis, raised in NYC; college teacher in N.J.
   The Doomsday Scroll. Dodd, 1979 [Isr.]
   Project WEB. Dodd, 1980

ROGERS, BEN. Set: Eng.
   The Murder at the Coffee Stall. Modern, 193?
   Murder Pays a Call. Modern, 1938
   The Vengeance of the Tong. Modern, 193?

ROGERS, DAVID
   The In-Laws. GM, 1979; Magnum, 1979

ROGERS, GARET. Ref: CA.
   Scandal in Eden. Dial, 1963; Putnam (London), 1964

ROGERS, J. TRUMBELL. See: Marian J. Herrick.

ROGERS, JAMES CASS
   Foul Play. Jove, 1978 (Novelization of the movie.) [S.F.]
   Silver Streak. Ballantine, 1976 (Novelization of the movie.)

ROGERS, JOEL TOWNSLEY. 1896- . Ref: EM, TC.
   Lady with the Dice. Handi-Books, 1946
   Never Leave My Bed; see The Stopped Clock
   Once in a Red Moon. Brentano's (NYC and London), 1923 [NYC]
   The Red Right Hand. Simon, 1945 [Conn.]
   The Stopped Clock. Simon, 1958. Also published as: Never Leave My Bed. Beacon, 1960 [Wash. D.C.]

ROGERS, KERK. Pseudonym of Edward Rogers Knowlton, 1909- , q.v.
   -Beach Patrol. Mill, 1943
   -Too Many Yesterdays. Mill, 1942
   Vantage Point. Mystery House, 1959 [New Eng.]
   With Intent to Destroy. Mill, 1944; Hammond, 1946

ROGERS, MILTON. 1924- .
   Born Reckless. Avon, 1959 (Novelization of the movie.)

ROGERS, RAY MOUNT
   The Negotiator. McKay, 1975 [Wash. D.C.]

ROGERS, RUTH. 1890- . Pseudonym: Ruth Alexander, q.v.

ROGERS, SAMUEL (GREENE ARNOLD). 1894- . Ref: CC. SC: Professor Paul Hatfield, in all titles.
   Don't Look Behind You! Harper, 1944
   Murder Is Grim; see You'll Be Sorry!
   You Leave Me Cold! Harper, 1946 H [Midwest]
   You'll Be Sorry! Harper, 1945. British title: Murder Is Grim. Hammond, 1955 H [Midwest]

ROGGER, L(OUIS) L(UCIEN)
   The Faceless Corpse Murders. Longmans, 1937

ROHAN, DONALD
   The Browning Touch. Dial, 1979 [Viet Nam]

ROHDE, ROBERT H.
   Hunted Down. Chelsea, 1928 [NYC]
   Sucker Money. Chelsea, 1927

ROHDE, WILLIAM L(AURENCE). Ref: CC. Living in Fla. in 1950s. Pseudonym: Nick Carter, q.v.
   -Give Me a Little Something. Pyramid, 1956
   The Heel. Pyramid, 1953 [NYC]
   Help Wanted—for Murder. GM, 1950; Fawcett (London), 1953
   High Red for Dead. GM, 1951; Fawcett (London), 1953. Also published as: Murder on the Line. GM, 1957 [Vt.]
   Murder on the Line; see High Red for Dead
   Uneasy Lies the Head. Ace, 1957 [Fla.]
   -V.I.P. Pyramid, 1957

ROHMER, ELIZABETH SAX. Pseudonym of Rose Elizabeth Knox Ward, 1886-1979.
   Bianca in Black. Mystery House, 1958

ROHMER, RICHARD (HEATH). 1924- . Ref: CA.
   Periscope Red. Beaufort, 1980
   Ultimatum. Clarke (Toronto), 1973; PB, 1974 [Ottawa]

ROHMER, SAX. Pseudonym of Arthur Henry
    Sarsfield Ward, 1883-1959. Other
    pseudonym: Michael Furey, q.v. Ref:
    CC, EM, MC, MM, TC. SC: Fu Manchu
    (and Nayland Smith) = FM; Nayland
    Smith alone = NS; Paul Harley = PH;
    Daniel "Red" Kerry = DK; Gaston Max
    = GM; Sumuru = S.
  The Bat Flies Low. Cassell, 1935;
    Doubleday, 1935 [Egypt]
  Bat-Wing. Cassell, 1921; Doubleday,
    1921 PH
  Bimbashi Baruk of Egypt; see Egyptian
    Nights
  The Bride of Fu Manchu. Cassell, 1933.
    U.S. title: Fu Manchu's Bride.
    Doubleday, 1933. Reprinted under the
    British title: Pyramid, 1962 FM
  Brood of the Witch-Queen. Pearson,
    1918; Doubleday, 1924
  Daughter of Fu Manchu. Cassell, 1931;
    Doubleday, 1931 FM [Egypt]
  The Day the World Ended. Cassell, 1930;
    Doubleday, 1930 GM [Ger.]
  The Devil Doctor. Methuen, 1916. U.S.
    title: The Return of Fu-Manchu.
    McBride, 1916 FM
  Dope. Cassell, 1919; McBride, 1919 DK
  The Dream-Detective. Jarrolds, 1920;
    Doubleday, 1925 ss
  The Drums of Fu Manchu. Cassell, 1939;
    Doubleday, 1939 FM
  Egyptian Nights. Hale, 1944. U.S.
    title: Bimbashi Baruk of Egypt.
    McBride, 1944 (British edition pre-
    sented as a novel, U.S. edition as a
    collection of ss.) [Mid. East]
  Emperor Fu Manchu. Jenkins, 1959; GM,
    1959 FM [China]
  The Emperor of America. Cassell, 1929;
    Doubleday, 1929 [NYC]
  The Exploits of Captain O'Hagan. Jar-
    rolds, 1916; Bookfinger, 1968 ss
  The Fire Goddess; see Virgin in Flames
  Fire-Tongue. Cassell, 1921; Doubleday,
    1922 PH
  Fu Manchu's Bride; see The Bride of
    Fu Manchu
  The Golden Scorpion. Methuen, 1919;
    McBride, 1920 GM,FM
  The Green Eyes of Bast. Cassell, 1920;
    McBride, 1920
  Grey Face. Cassell, 1924; Doubleday,
    1924
  The Hand of Fu-Manchu; see The Si-Fan
    Mysteries
  Hangover House. Jenkins, 1950; Random,
    1949
  The Haunting of Low Fennel. Pearson,
    1920 ss, including one about NS
    (All but one story appear in the U.S.
    edition of Tales of East and West,
    q.v.)
  The Insidious Dr. Fu-Manchu; see The
    Mystery of Dr. Fu-Manchu
  The Island of Fu Manchu. Cassell, 1941;
    Doubleday, 1941 FM
  The Mask of Fu Manchu. Cassell, 1933;
    Doubleday, 1932 FM [Mid. East]
  The Moon Is Red. Jenkins, 1954 [Fla.]
  Moon of Madness. Cassell, 1927; Double-
    day, 1927
  The Mystery of Dr. Fu-Manchu. Methuen,
    1913. U.S. title: The Insidious Dr.
    Fu-Manchu. McBride, 1913 FM
  Nude in Mink; see Sins of Sumuru
  -The Orchard of Tears. Methuen, 1918;
    Bookfinger, 1970
  President Fu Manchu. Cassell, 1936;
    Doubleday, 1936 FM [NYC]
  The Quest of the Sacred Slipper. Pear-
    son, 1919; Doubleday, 1919
  Re-Enter Dr. Fu Manchu. Jenkins, 1957.
    U.S. title: Re-Enter Fu Manchu. GM,
    1957 FM [NYC]
  Re-Enter Fu Manchu; see Re-Enter Dr. Fu
    Manchu
  The Return of Dr. Fu-Manchu; see The
    Devil Doctor
  Return of Sumuru; see Sand and Satin
  Salute to Bazarada and other stories.
    Cassell, 1939; Bookfinger, 1971
    ss, including three about PH
  Sand and Satin. Jenkins, 1955. U.S.
    title: Return of Sumuru. GM, 1954 S
    [Egypt]
  The Secret of Holm Peel and other
    strange stories. Ace, 1970 ss, in-
    cluding one about NS
  Seven Sins. Cassell, 1944; McBride,
    1943 GM
  Shadow of Fu Manchu. Jenkins, 1949;
    Doubleday, 1948 FM [NYC]
  She Who Sleeps. Cassell, 1929; Double-
    day, 1928 [Egypt]
  The Si-Fan Mysteries. Methuen, 1917.
    U.S. title: The Hand of Fu-Manchu.
    McBride, 1917 FM
  Sinister Madonna. Jenkins, 1956; GM,
    1956 S
  The Sins of Severac Bablon. Cassell,
    1914; Bookfinger, 1967
  Sins of Sumuru. Jenkins, 1950. U.S.
    title: Nude in Mink. GM, 1950 S
  Slaves of Sumuru. Jenkins, 1952. U.S.
    title: Sumuru. GM, 1951 S [NYC]
  Sumuru; see Slaves of Sumuru
  Tales of Chinatown. Cassell, 1922;
    Doubleday, 1922 ss, including PH,DK
  Tales of East and West. Cassell, 1932;
    Doubleday, 1933 (The British edition
    contains 10 ss, including PH, NS; the
    U.S. edition includes 6 of the 7 ss
    from The Haunting of Low Fennel,
    q.v., and 5 of the 10 ss from the
    British edition of Tales of East and
    West.)
  Tales of Secret Egypt. Methuen, 1918;
    McBride, 1919 ss [Egypt]
  The Trail of Fu Manchu. Cassell, 1934;
    Doubleday, 1934 FM
  Virgin in Flames. Jenkins, 1953. U.S.
    title: The Fire Goddess. GM, 1952 S
    [Jam.]
  White Velvet. Cassell, 1936; Doubleday,
    1936 [Egypt]
  The Wrath of Fu Manchu and other sto-
    ries. Stacey, 1973; Daw, 1976 ss,
    including 4 about FM
  The Yellow Claw. Methuen, 1915;
    McBride, 1915 GM
  Yellow Shadows. Cassell, 1925; Double-
    day, 1926 DK
  Yu'an Hee See Laughs. Cassell, 1932;
    Doubleday, 1932

ROHRBACH, PETER THOMAS. 1926- . Pseu-
    donym: James P. Cody, q.v.

ROLAND, BETTY. 1903- . Ref: CA.
  Beyond Capricorn. Collins, 1976

ROLEINE, ROBERTA. French byline: Roberte
    Roleine.
  Deadly Triangle. Mystique, 1979 (Trans-
    lation of "Le Baldu Chevalier."
    Paris, 1970.)
  Fated to Love. Mystique, 1979 (Trans-
    lation of "Le Jugement du Feu."
    Paris, 1971.)
  Flight into Peril. Mystique, 1979
    (Translation of "Les Fruits du Re-
    gret." Paris, 1976.)
  Kiss of Vengeance. Mystique, 1979
    (Translation of "La Prisonniere du
    Fjord." Paris, 1973.)
  The Sealed Fountain. Mystique, 1979
    (Translation of "La Fontaine Scel-
    lee." Paris, 1967.)
  Secret at Jester Moor. Mystique, 1979
    (Translation of "Irresistable Daf-
    fodil." Paris, 1965.)
  Storm over Ibiza. Mystique, 1980
    (Translation of "Tempete sur Ibiza."
    Paris, 1963.)
  Terror at Golden Sands. Mystique, 1977
    (Translation of "Noces aux Sables-
    D'Or." Paris, 1969.)
  Time of Illusion. Mystique, 1979
    (Translation of "Le Temps d'Une Illu-
    sion." Paris, 1967.)

ROLFE, EDWIN, 1909-1954, and LESTER
    FULLER, 1908- . Rolfe: reporter,
    editor, foreign and war correspond-
    ent; poet; publicist for shows.
  The Glass Room. Rinehart, 1946; Low,
    1948 [L.A.]

ROLFE, MARO O(RLANDO). 1852-1925.
  The Band of Mystery. Street (Magnet)
  The Branded Hand. Street (Magnet)
  -Clyde, the Trailer; or, The Brothers of
    Death. Beadle, 1872
  The Cross of the Dust. Street (Magnet)
  An Eye for an Eye. Street (Magnet)
  The Man Who Knew. Street (Magnet)
  -The Man-Hunter; or, The Counterfeiters
    of the Border. Beadle, 1873
  On the Stroke of Midnight. Street (Mag-
    net)
  A Queen of Blackmailers. Street (Mag-
    net)
  A Rascal's Nerve. Street (Magnet)
  A Secret Suspicion. Street (Magnet)
  A Transatlantic Puzzle. Street (Magnet)
  The Two Conspirators. Street (Magnet)

ROLLINS, ALICE (MARLAND) WELLINGTON.
    1847-1897.
  The Finding of the Gentian. (Author,
    NYC), 1895 5 ss, 2 criminous

ROLLINS DRESSER, KATHLEEN. Joint pseudo-
    nym with Davis Dresser, 1904-1977,
    q.v.: Hal Debrett, q.v.

ROLLINS, WILLIAM, JR. 1897- . Pseudo-
    nym: O'Connor Stacy, q.v. Born in
    Mass., served in French Army in WWI,
    later living in NYC; magazine writer.
  Midnight Treasure. Coward, 1929 [Ariz.]
  The Ring and the Lamp. Simon, 1947
    [Paris]

  The Shadow Before. McBride, 1934
  -The Wall of Men. Modern Age, 1938

ROLLS, ANTHONY. Pseudonym of C(olwyn)
    E(dward) Vulliamy, 1886-1971, q.v.
    Set: Eng.
  Clerical Error; see The Vicar's Experi-
    ments
  Family Matters. Bles, 1933
  Lobelia Grove. Bles, 1932
  Scarweather. Bles, 1934
  The Vicar's Experiments. Bles, 1932.
    U.S. title: Clerical Error. Little,
    1932

ROLT, JON
  The Syndrome Equation. Vantage, 1976

ROMAIN, NEVILLE H. See: Robin Moore.

ROMAINE, DALLAS
  The Malicious Madonna. Berkley, 1975
  Shadow of Evil. Berkley, 1976 [Eng.]

ROMAN, ERIC. 1926- . Ref: CA.
  After the Trial. Citadel, 1968
  A Year As a Lion. Stein, 1978

ROMAN, HOWARD
  Pitfall in August. Harper, 1960; Allen,
    1961
  When Victims Meet. Muller, 1980

ROMANES, NORMAN HUGH
  Young Lord Folliot. Jenkins, 1931. Also
    published as: The Case of Young Lord
    Folliot. Athenaeum, 1943

ROMANO, DEANE (LOUIS). 1927- . Ref:
    CA.
  Banacek. Bantam, 1973 (Novelization of
    the TV series.) [Boston]

ROMANO, DON. House name. All titles in a
    Mafia series. Those written by Paul
    Eiden = *; those written by Robert
    (Harry) Turner, 1915-1980, q.v., and
    Allan Nixon, 1918- , q.v. = #.
  Operation Cocaine. Pyramid, 1974 #
  Operation Hijack. Pyramid, 1974 *
  Operation Hit Man. Pyramid, 1974 #
  Operation Loan Shark. Pyramid, 1974 *
  Operation Porno. Pyramid, 1973 *

ROMANOFF, ALEXANDER NICHOLAYEVITCH. 1881-
    1945. Pseudonym: Achmed Abdullah,
    q.v.

ROME, ANTHONY. Pseudonym of Marvin H(u-
    bert) Albert, 1924- , q.v. Other
    pseudonyms: Mike Barone, Al Conroy,
    Albert Conroy, Ian MacAlister, Nick
    Quarry, qq.v. SC: Tony Rome, in all
    titles.
  The Lady in Cement. PB, 1961; Hale,
    1962 [Miami]
  Miami Mayhem. PB, 1960; Hale, 1961.
    Also published as: Tony Rome. Dell,
    1967, as by Marvin H. Albert [Miami]
  My Kind of Game. Dell, 1962 [Fla.]
  Tony Rome; see Miami Mayhem

ROME, TONY
  God's Gift to All Women. New English
    Library pb, 1971

ROMER, ISABELLA F(RANCES). -1852.
  -Sturmer. Lea, 1842; Bentley, 1841

ROMSEY, PETER
  The Lidless Eye. Jenkins, 1950; Roy,
    1957 [Buen. A.]

RONAL, PETER. Pseudonym: Maybeth Morgan,
    q.v.

RONALD, E. B. Pseudonym of Ronald (Er-
    nest) Barker, 1920-1976, q.v. SC:
    Rupert "Brad" Bradley, in all titles.
  The Cat and Fiddle Murders. Gollancz,
    1954; Rinehart, 1954
  Death by Proxy. Boardman, 1956
  A Sort of Madness. Boardman, 1958;
    Abelard, 1959 [Paris]

RONALD, JAMES. 1905- . Pseudonym: Kirk
    Wales. SC: Julian Medoza, in at least
    those marked JM. Set: Eng.
  Counsel for the Defense. Gramol, 1932
  Cross Marks the Spot. Hodder, 1933 JM
  The Dark Angel. Modern, 193?
  Death Croons the Blues. Hodder, 1934;
    Phoenix, 1940 JM
  Diamonds of Death. Gramol, 1934
  The Green Ghost Murder. Gramol, 1936
  Hanging's Too Good. Rich, 1938
  -Lord Peter Goes A-Wooing. Gramol, 1933
  The Man Who Made Monsters. Gramol, 1935
  The Monocled Man. Gramol, 1933
  Murder for Cash. Rich, 1938 [Chi.]
  The Murder in Gay Ladies; see Murder in
    the Family

Murder in the Family. Lane, 1936; Lippincott, 1940. Also published as: The Murder in Gay Ladies. Mercury, 1952
She Got What She Asked For. Lippincott, 1941 (British title?) [NYC]
Six Were to Die. Hodder, 1932; Mystery House, 1941, as by Kirk Wales
-Star Dust. Gramol, 1932
The Sundial Drug Mystery. Gramol, 1934
They Can't Hang Me! Rich, 1938; Doubleday, 1938
This Way Out. Rich, 1940; Lippincott, 1939
The Unholy Trio. Gramol, 1933

RONNS, EDWARD. Pseudonym of Edward S(idney) Aarons, 1916-1975, q.v. Other pseudonym: Paul Ayres, q.v. SC: Jerry Benedict = JB.
The Art Studio Murders. Handi-Books, 1950. Reprinted as by Aarons: Macfadden, 1965 [NYC]
The Big Bedroom. Pyramid, 1959
The Black Orchid. Pyramid, 1959 (Novelization of the movie.)
But Not for Me. Pyramid, 1959; World Distributors, 1960 (Novelization of the movie.)
Catspaw Ordeal. GM, 1950; Gaywood, 1953. Reprinted as by Aarons: GM, 1966 [Conn.]
The Corpse Hangs High. Phoenix, 1939 [N.J.]
The Cowl of Doom; see Death in a Lighthouse
Dark Destiny. Graphic, 1953. Reprinted as by Aarons: Macfadden, 1968 [Fla.]
Dark Memory. Handi-Books, 1950
Death in a Lighthouse. Phoenix, 1938. Also published as: The Cowl of Doom. Hangman's House, 1946 [NYC]
Death Is My Shadow. Mystery House, 1957. Reprinted as by Aarons: Macfadden, 1965 [La.]
The Decoy. GM, 1951. Reprinted as by Aarons: GM, 1966 [N.J.]
Don't Cry, Beloved. GM, 1952. Reprinted as by Aarons: GM, 1966 [N. Mex.]
Gang Rumble. Avon, 1958 [Phil.]
Gift of Death. McKay, 1948. Reprinted as by Aarons: Macfadden, 1964 JB [Conn.]
The Glass Cage. Pyramid, 1962
I Can't Stop Running. GM, 1951. Reprinted as by Aarons: GM, 196? [Fla.]
The Lady Takes a Flyer. Avon, 1958 (Novelization of the movie.)
Lady, the Guy Is Dead; see No Place to Live
Million Dollar Murder. GM, 1950; Fawcett (London), 1952. Reprinted as by Aarons: GM, 196? [Maine]
Murder Money. Phoenix, 1938. Also published as: $1,000,000 in Corpses. Best Detective Selections, 1943 [Maine]
The Net. Graphic, 1953. Reprinted as by Aarons: Macfadden, 1969 [New Eng.]
No Place to Live. McKay, 1947; Boardman, 1950. Also published as: Lady, the Guy Is Dead. Avon, 1950, abridged. Reprinted under original title as by Aarons: Macfadden, 1964 JB
$1,000,000 in Corpses; see Murder Money
Passage to Terror. GM, 1952. Reprinted as by Aarons: GM, 1966 [Cent. Am.]
Pickup Alley. Avon, 1957 (Novelization of the movie.)
Point of Peril. Mystery House, 1956. Reprinted as by Aarons: Macfadden, 1965 [Md.]
Say It with Murder. Graphic, 1954; Red Seal, 1960. Reprinted as by Aarons: Macfadden, 196? [L.I.]
State Department Murders. GM, 1950; Fawcett (London), 1957. Reprinted as by Aarons: GM, 196?; Coronet, 1974 [Va.]
Terror in the Town. McKay, 1947. Reprinted as by Aarons: Macfadden, 1964 [Mass.]
They All Ran Away. Graphic, 1955. Reprinted as by Aarons: Macfadden, 1970 [N.Y.]

RONSON, MARK
-Bloodthirst. Hamlyn, 1979
-Ghoul. Hamlyn, 1980
-Ogre. Hamlyn, 1980

RONZONE, BENJAMIN ANTHONY. 1848- . Pseudonym: Baron, q.v.

ROOF, KATHERINE METCALF. Ref: CC.
Murder on the Salem Road. Houghton, 1931 [Mass., ca.1840]

ROOK, CLARENCE. -1915.
The Hooligan Nights. Richards, 1899; Holt, 1899

ROOK, TONY. 1932- . Ref: CA.
Strange Mansion. Milton House, 1974

ROOKE, REBECCA
Murder in Store. Hale, 1978

ROOME, DOUGLAS
Faith, Hope and Cyanide. Dramatic, 1973 (1-act play.)

ROOS, AUDREY (KELLEY), 1912-1982, and WILLIAM ROOS, 1911- . Joint pseudonym: Kelley Roos, q.v. Pseudonym of William Roos: William Rand, q.v.
A Few Days in Madrid. Scribner, 1965; Deutsch, 1966 [Madrid]
Speaking of Murder. Random, 1957; French (London), 1959 (Play.)

ROOS, KELLEY. Joint pseudonym of Audrey (Kelley) Roos, 1912-1982, q.v., and William Roos, 1911- . Pseudonym of William Roos: William Rand, q.v. Ref: TC. SC: Jeff and Haila Troy = T.
Bad Trip. Dodd, 1971
Beauty Marks the Spot; see Triple Threat
The Blonde Died Dancing. Dodd, 1956. British title: She Died Dancing. Eyre, 1947 [NYC]
Cry in the Night. Dodd, 1966 [N.Y.]
Dangerous Blondes; see If the Shroud Fits
The Frightened Stiff. Dodd, 1942; Hale, 1951 T [NYC]
Ghost of a Chance. Wyn, 1947 T [NYC]
Grave Danger. Dodd, 1965; Eyre, 1966 [Conn.]
If the Shroud Fits. Dodd, 1941. Also published as: Dangerous Blondes. Jonathan, 1951 T [NYC]
Made Up for Murder; see Made Up to Kill
Made Up to Kill. Dodd, 1940. British title: Made Up for Murder. Jarrolds, 1941 T [NYC, theatre]
Murder in Any Language. Wyn, 1948 T [NYC]
Murder Noon and Night; see Requiem for a Blonde
Necessary Evil. Dodd, 1965; Eyre, 1965 [NYC]
One False Move. Dodd, 1966 T [Tex.]
Requiem for a Blonde. Dodd, 1958. British title (?): Murder Noon and Night. Eyre, 1959 [New Eng.]
Sailor, Take Warning! Dodd, 1944; Hale, 1952 T [NYC]
Scent of Mystery. Dell, 1959 (Novelization of the movie, which was based on Ghost of a Chance, q.v.) [Sp.]
She Died Dancing; see The Blonde Died Dancing
Suddenly One Night. Dodd, 1970 [Sp.]
There Was a Crooked Man. Dodd, 1945; Hale, 1953 T [NYC]
To Save His Life. Dodd, 1968; Cassell, 1969 [NYC]
Triple Threat. Wyn, 1949 (Three novelets, of which one was published separately as: Beauty Marks the Spot. Dell 10¢ pb, 1951.) T [NYC]
What Did Hattie See? Dodd, 1970; Cassell, 1970 [NYC]
Who Saw Maggie Brown? Dodd, 1967 [NYC]

ROOS, WILLIAM. 1911- . Pseudonym: William Rand, q.v. Joint pseudonym with Audrey (Kelley) Roos, 1912-1982, q.v.: Kelley Roos, q.v.

ROOSEVELT, FRANKLIN D(ELANO). 1882-1945.
The President's Mystery Story. Farrar, 1935; Lane, 1936. Revised edition. Prentice-Hall, 1967 (A mystery novel suggest by Roosevelt and written, a chapter each, by 7 mystery writers.)

ROOSEVELT, JAMES, 1907- , and SAM TOPEROFF, 1933- . Ref (both authors): CA.
-A Family Matter. Simon, 1980; Severn, 1981 [U.S., 1943]

ROOT, GROSVENOR T., M.D. Born in Detroit, trained at U. of Mich. and Mayo Clinic; surgeon in Calif.
Bird in the Hand. Carlton, 1972 [Eng.]

ROOT, PAT
The Devil on the Stairs. Simon, 1956 [NYC]
Evil Became Them. Simon, 1952; Redman, 1953 [W.I.]

ROOTE, MIKE. Pseudonym of Leonore Fleischer. Other pseudonyms: Alexander Edwards, Philip Fenty, qq.v.
Badge 373. Award, 1973 (Novelization of the movie.) [NYC]
Born to Win. Award, 1971 (Novelization of the movie.)
CC and Company. Award, 1970 (Novelization of the movie.)
Enter the Dragon. Award, 1973; Tandem, 1974 (Novelization of the movie.)
From Director, CIA: Burn Scorpio. Award, 1975
Prime Cut. Award, 1973 (Novelization of the movie.)
Scorpio. Award, 1973; Tandem, 1973 (Novelization of the movie.)

ROOTH, ANNE REED and JAMES P(ATRICK) WHITE, 1940- . Ref on White: CA.
The Ninth Car. Putnam, 1978 [Zurich]

ROPER, GAYLE G.
Death on an Island. Chime, 1980 [Can.]

ROPER, L. V. SC: Jerry "Renegade" Roe = JR.
Death—As in Matador. Popular Library, 1975 [Ariz.]
The Emerald Chicks Caper. Popular Library, 1976 JR
Hookers Don't Go to Heaven. Popular Library, 1976
Rage. Curtis, 1973 (Novelization of the movie.)
The Red Horse Caper. Popular Library, 1975 JR

ROPER, SUSAN BRONTHRON. 1948- . Pseudonym: Susan Brand, q.v.

ROSA, DENNIS
Sherlock Holmes and the Curse of the Sign of Four; or, "The Mark of Timber Toe." Dramatists, 1975 (Play based on The Sign of the Four by A. Conan Doyle, 1859-1930, q.v.) (Sherlock Holmes.)

ROSAIRE, FORREST. 1902- . Born in Chi.; for some years an oil explorer, then ss writer in Calif.
White Night. Lippincott, 1956; Cape, 1954 [L.A.]

ROSCOE, JOHN. 1921- . Joint pseudonym with Michael Ruso: Mike Roscoe, q.v.

ROSCOE, MIKE. Joint pseudonym of John Roscoe, 1921- , and Michael Ruso. SC: Johnny April, in all titles.
Death Is a Round Black Ball. Crown, 1952; Foulsham, 1954 [Kan. City]
The Midnight Eye. Ace, 1958
One Tear for My Grave. Crown, 1955; Foulsham, 1956 [Kan. City]
Riddle Me This. Crown, 1952; Foulsham, 1955 [Kan. City]
Slice of Hell. Crown, 1954; Foulsham, 1955 [S.F.]

ROSCOE, THEODORE. Born in Roch., N.Y.; specialist in naval affairs, served on presidential commissions in 1950s; TV writer.
A Grave Must Be Deep. Popular (London), 1947 (U.S. title?)
I'll Grind Their Bones. Dodge, 1936; Harrap, 1937
Murder on the Way! Dodge, 1935 [Haiti]
Only in New England. Scribner, 1959 [New Eng.]
Seven Men. Handi-Books, 1942
To Live and Die in Dixie. Scribner, 1961 [Va., 1902]

ROSE, ALVIN EMANUEL. Pseudonym: Alan Pruitt, q.v.

ROSE, EDWARD E(VERETT). 1862-1939.
"The Gold Flame." Northwestern, 1933 (4-act play.)
The Rear Car. French (NYC), 1926 (3-act play.)

ROSE, ELIZABETH. 1915- . Ref: CA.
Grand Jury. Avon, 1974

ROSE, F(REDERICK) HORACE (VINCENT). 1876-
-Bride of the Kalahari. Duckworth, 1940
-The Four Kings in the Street of Gold. Duckworth, 1942
-The Harp of Life. Duckworth, 1946
-Hell's Acre. Duckworth, 1941
-Kruger's Wagon. Duckworth, 1943
-The Maniac's Dream. Duckworth, 1946
-The Night of the World. Duckworth, 1944
-Palace and Prison. Duckworth, 1946
-Pharoah's Crown. Duckworth, 1943
-The Prodigal Soldier. Duckworth, 1942
-Rock of Ages. Duckworth, 1944

ROSE, GEOFFREY. 1932- .
The Bright Adventure. Macmillan (London), 1975; St. Martin's, 1976 [S. Am., 1900s]

A Clear Road to Archangel. Macmillan
 (London), 1973; St. Martin's, 1976
 [Russ., 1917]
Nobody on the Road. Macmillan (London),
 1972; St. Martin's, 1976

ROSE, GEORGE. 1817-1882. Pseudonym:
 Arthur Sketchley, q.v.

ROSE, LA ROMA. All titles are plays, with
 number of acts given in parenthesis.
Ghost at Punkin Holler. Art Craft, 1952
 (1)
The Haunted Bookshop. Art Craft, 1951
 (1)
The House Next Door. Heuer, 1949 (1)
The Laughing Ghost. Heuer, 1950 (1)
Mystery of the Locked Room. Art Craft,
 1950 (1)
Spooks Alive. Art Craft, 1953 (3)
Uninvited Guest. Heuer, 1949 (1)

ROSE, PATRICIA
Satan's Seal. Manor, 1978

ROSEN, NORMA STAHL. 1925-   . Ref: CA.
Touching Evil. Harcourt, 1969

ROSEN, VICTOR
Dark Plunder. Lion, 1955
A Gun in His Hand. GM, 1951; Red Seal,
 1958 [NYC, 1931]

ROSENBACH, A(BRAHAM) S(IMON) W(OLF).
 1876-1952. Ref: MP.
The Unpublishable Memoirs. Kennerley,
 1917; Castle, 1924 ss

ROSENBAUM, RON. Magazine contributor and
 staff writer.
Murder at Elaine's. Stonehill, 1978
 [NYC]

ROSENBERG, ELIZABETH. See: John Rosenberg, 1931-   .

ROSENBERG, JOHN. 1931-   .
-A Company of Strangers. Hogarth, 1959
-The Desperate Art. Longmans, 1955
Fanfare for a Murderer, with Elizabeth
 Rosenberg. Hogarth, 1960
-Mirror and Knife. Hogarth, 1961
Out Brief Candle, with Elizabeth Rosen-
 berg. Hogarth, 1959

ROSENBERG, PHILIP. 1942-   . Ref: CA.
Contract on Cherry Street. Crowell,
 1975; Secker, 1976 [NYC]
Point Blank, with Sonny Grosso. Grosset, 1978 [NYC]

ROSENBERG, STUART
When the Bough Breaks. Crowell, 1976
 [Miss.]

ROSENBERGER, JOSEPH. Pseudonyms: Nick
 Carter, Lee Chang, qq.v. SC: Richard
 Camellion (The Death Merchant) = RC;
 Murder Master (Louis Luther King) =
 MM.
Alaska Conspiracy. Pinnacle, 1979 RC
 [Alaska]
The Albanian Connection. Pinnacle,
 1973; Corgi, 1982 RC [Alb.]
Armageddon, USA! Pinnacle, 1976 RC
 [Mo.]
The Bermuda Triangle Action. Pinnacle,
 1980 RC
The Billionaire Mission. Pinnacle, 1974
 RC
Blueprint Invisibility. Pinnacle, 1980
 RC
The Budapest Action. Pinnacle, 1977 RC
 [Buda.]
The Burning Blue Death. Pinnacle, 1980
 RC
The Caribbean Caper. Manor, 1974 MM
 [Carib.]
The Castro File. Pinnacle, 1974 RC
 [Cuba]
The Chinese Conspiracy. Pinnacle, 1973;
 Corgi, 1981 RC
The Cosmic Reality Kill. Pinnacle, 1979
 RC
Deadly Manhunt. Pinnacle, 1979 RC
The Death Merchant. Pinnacle, 1972;
 Corgi, 1981 RC [Chi.]
Death Trap. Manor, 1973 MM [Ill.]
The Enigma Project. Pinnacle, 1977 RC
Fatal Formula. Pinnacle, 1978 RC
 [Russ.]
The Fourth Reich. Pinnacle, 1980 RC
Hell in Hindu Land. Pinnacle, 1977 RC
 [India]
High Command Murder. Pinnacle, 1980 RC
The Hooker-Smash Operation. Manor, 1974
 MM
Invasion of the Clones. Pinnacle, 1976
 RC [S. Afr.]
The Iron Swastika Plot. Pinnacle, 1976
 RC [ship]
The KGB Frame. Pinnacle, 1975 RC

The Kondrashev Chase. Pinnacle, 1977 RC
The Kronos Plot. Pinnacle, 1977 RC
 [Pan.]
The Laser War. Pinnacle, 1974 RC
The Mainline Plot. Pinnacle, 1974 RC
Manhattan Wipeout. Pinnacle, 1975 RC
 [NYC]
Massacre in Rome. Pinnacle, 1979 RC
 [Rome]
The Mato Grosso Horror. Pinnacle, 1975
 RC [Brazil]
The Mexican Hit. Pinnacle, 1978 RC
 [Mex.]
Nightmare in Algeria. Pinnacle, 1976 RC
 [Algeria]
Nipponese Nightmare. Pinnacle, 1978 RC
 [Jap.]
Operation Mind-Murder. Pinnacle, 1979
 RC [Arctic]
Operation Overkill. Pinnacle, 1972;
 Corgi, 1981 RC [NYC]
Operation Thunderbolt. Pinnacle, 1978
 RC [Kor.]
The Pole Star Secret. Pinnacle, 1977 RC
 [Arctic]
The Psychotron Plot. Pinnacle, 1972;
 Corgi, 1981 RC [Mid. East]
Satan Strike. Pinnacle, 1972; Corgi,
 1981 RC [Carib.]
The Shambhala Strike. Pinnacle, 1978 RC
The Shamrock Smash. Pinnacle, 1980 RC
 [Ire.]
The Surinam Affair. Pinnacle, 1978 RC
 [Suri.]
Vengeance of the Golden Hawk. Pinnacle,
 1976 RC [Mid. East]
The Zembya Expedition. Pinnacle, 1976
 RC

ROSENBLUM, ROBERT (J.). 1938-   .
Cover Stories. Delacorte, 1979. British
 title: Cover Story. Granada, 1980
 [Greece]
Cover Story; see Cover Stories
The Good Thief. Doubleday, 1974; Hart-
 Davis, 1975 [It.]
The Mushroom Cave. Doubleday, 1973;
 Gollancz, 1974 [Russ.]
The Sweetheart Deal. Putnam, 1976;
 Hart-Davis, 1978 [N.Y.]

ROSENHAYN, PAUL. 1877-1929. SC: Joe Jenkins, in both titles.
Joe Jenkins' Case Book. Heinemann, 1930
 ss [Den.]
Joe Jenkins: Detective. Heinemann,
 1929; Doubleday, 1930 ss

ROSENKRANTZ, BARON PALLE (ADAM VILHELM).
 1867-1941.
The Magistrate's Own Case. Methuen,
 1908; McClure, 1908 [Ger.]
The Man in the Basement. Empire, 1907
 [Den.]

ROSENTHAL, NORMAN C.
Silenced Witnesses. Ace, 1955 [Calif.]

ROSENTHAL, RICHARD A. 1925-   . Pseudonym: Allen Richards, q.v.

ROSENWALD, FRANCIS
A Big Man in Saludas. Ballantine, 1962

ROSER, VAL
Murder in the Wind. Long, 1947

ROSMANITH, OLGA L.
-Don't Say No. Popular Library, 1956
-The Long Thrill. Lion, 1954
-Passenger List. Murray, 1940
Signature to a Crime. Cassell, 1938
 [L.A.]
-Storm Cloud over Vienna. Murray, 1940
 [Vienna]
-Unholy Flame. GM, 1952

ROSMER, JEAN. Pseudonym of Jeanne Ichord
 Alcanter de Brahm, 1890-   .
In Secret Service. Lippincott, 1937
 (Translation of "Napoleone." Paris,
 1929.)

ROSNER, JOSEPH. 1914-   . Ref: CA.
The Habits of Command. Harcourt, 1975

ROSS, ALBERT. Pseudonym of Linn Boyd
 Porter, 1851-1916.
His Foster Sister. Dillingham, 1896

ROSS, ALBERT. Pseudonym of Arthur D(avid)
 Goldstein, 1937-   , q.v.
If I Knew What I Was Doing. Random,
 1974 [NYC]

ROSS, ANGUS. Pseudonym of Kenneth Giggal,
 1927-   . Ref: CA, TC. SC: Marcus
 Aurelius Farrow, in all titles.
The Aberdeen Conundrum. Long, 1977
The Ampurias Exchange. Long, 1976;
 Walker, 1977 [Sp.]

The Amsterdam Diversion. Long, 1974
 [Amst.]
The Bradford Business. Long, 1974
The Burgos Contract. Long, 1978; Walk-
 er, 1979 [Sp.]
The Congleton Lark. Long, 1979
The Dumfermline Affair. Long, 1973
The Edinburgh Exercise. Long, 1975
 [Edin.]
The Hamburg Switch. Long, 1980; Walker,
 1980 [Hamb.]
The Huddersfield Job. Long, 1971
The Manchester Thing. Long, 1970
The Leeds Fiasco. Long, 1975
The London Assignment. Long, 1972

ROSS, ANN B.
The Murder Cure. Avon, 1978 [Charles-
 ton, hosp.]

ROSS, BARNABY. Joint pseudonym of Fred-
 eric Dannay, 1905-1982, and Manfred
 Bennington Lee, 1905-1971. Other
 joint pseudonym: Ellery Queen, q.v.
 SC: Drury Lane, in all titles.
Drury Lane's Last Case. Viking, 1933;
 Cassell, 1933. Reprinted as by Ellery
 Queen: Little, 1946 [NYC]
The Tragedy of X. Viking, 1932; Cas-
 sell, 1932. Reprinted as by Ellery
 Queen: Stokes, 1940 [NYC]
The Tragedy of Y. Viking, 1932; Cas-
 sell, 1932. Reprinted as by Ellery
 Queen: Stokes, 1941 [NYC]
The Tragedy of Z. Viking, 1933; Cas-
 sell, 1933. Reprinted as by Ellery
 Queen: Little, 1942 [N.Y.]

ROSS, CAMERON
Case for Compensation. Hale, 1980

ROSS, CARLTON. Pseudonym of Edwy Searles
 Brooks, 1889-1965, q.v. Other pseudo-
 nyms: Berkeley Gray, Victor Gunn,
 qq.v.
The Black Skull Murders. Swan, 1942
Racketeers of the Turf. Swan, 1947

ROSS, MAJOR-GENERAL CHARLES
The Castle Fenham Case. Murray, 1927
-Every Man's Hand. Murray, 1923
The Fly-by-Nights. Murray, 1921
The Haunted Seventh. Murray, 1922
When the Devil Was Sick. Murray, 1924

ROSS, CHARLES H(ENRY). 1842-1897.
Hot and Cold. Routledge, 1872
A Private Enquiry. Tinsley, 1870

ROSS, CLARISSA. Pseudonym of W(illiam)
 E(dward) D(aniel) Ross, 1912-   ,
 q.v. Other pseudonyms: Laura Frances
 Brooks, Rose Dana, Jan Daniels, Ellen
 Randolph, Dan Ross, Dana Ross, Mar-
 ilyn Ross, qq.v.
Beware the Kindly Stranger. Lancer,
 1970
-Casablanca Intrigue. Warner, 1979; Ham-
 lyn, 1979 [Casa.]
China Shadow. Avon, 1974; Magnum, 1978
The Corridors of Fear. Avon, 1971
 [Maine]
Dark Harbor Hunting. Avon, 1975 [Mass.]
Drifthaven. Avon, 1974 [L.I.]
Durrell Towers. Pyramid, 1965 [Maine]
Evil of Dark Harbor. Avon, 1975 [Mass.]
Face in the Pond. Avon, 1968 [Scot.,
 1870]
Fogbound. Arcadia, 1967 [ship]
Gemini in Darkness. Lancer, 1970
 [Boston]
Ghost of Dark Harbor. Avon, 1974
 [Mass.]
The Ghosts of Grantmeer. Avon, 1972
 [Va.]
The Glimpse into Terror. Lancer, 1971
 [Conn.]
The Haunting of Villa Gabriel. Paper-
 back Library, 1971
A Hearse of Dark Harbor. Avon, 1974
 [Mass.]
Istanbul Nights. Jove, 1978 [Istan.,
 1861]
It Comes by Night. Lancer, 1972
The Jade Princess. Pyramid, 1977
 [H. Kong]
Jennifer by Moonlight. Bantam, 1973
-Kashmiri Passions. Warner, 1978; New
 English Library pb, 1978 [India,
 1856]
A Love to Cherish. Bantam, 1973
Mistress of Ravenswood. Arcadia, 1966
Mists of Dark Harbor. Avon, 1974
 [Mass.]
Moscow Mists. Avon, 1977; Magnum, 1978
 [Moscow, past]
Out of the Fog. Lancer, 1970 [Maine]
Phantom of Dark Harbor. Avon, 1972
 [Mass.]
Phantom of Glencourt. Lancer, 1972
A Scandalous Affair. Belmont, 1977
Secret of Mallet Castle. Arcadia, 1966

Secret of the Pale Lover. Lancer, 1970
Shadow on Capricorn. Bantam, 1972
Shadow over the Garden. Belmont, 1975
The Spectral Mist. Hale, 1968 [Calif.]
Terror at Dark Harbor. Avon, 1975 [Mass.]
Voice from the Grave. Lancer, 1971
Whisper of Danger. Bantam, 1974
Whispers in the Night. Bantam, 1971

ROSS, DAN. Pseudonym of W(illiam) E(dward) D(aniel) Ross, 1912-   , q.v. Other pseudonyms: Laura Frances Brooks, Rose Dana, Jan Daniels, Ellen Randolph, Clarissa Ross, Dana Ross, Marilyn Ross, qq.v. Several titles published as by W. E. D. Ross were reprinted in pb as by Dan Ross.
The Castle on the Cliff. Avalon, 1967 [Scot.]
Cliffhaven. Avalon, 1966 [Mass.]
Murder at City Hall. Avalon, 1965
The Mystery of Fury Castle. Avalon, 1965
Out of the Night. Avalon, 1963

ROSS, DANA. Pseudonym of W(illiam) E(dward) D(aniel) Ross, 1912-   , q.v. Other pseudonyms: Laura Frances Brooks, Rose Dana, Jan Daniels, Ellen Randolph, Clarissa Ross, Dan Ross, Marilyn Ross, qq.v.
Demon of the Darkness. PB, 1975 [Eng., 1889]
The Figure in the Shadows. Popular Library, 1971 [Maine, 1894]
The Haunting of Clifton Court. Popular Library, 1972
Lodge Sinister. PB, 1975 [Maine]
Night of the Dead. Popular Library, 1973
The Raven and the Phantom. PB, 1976 [Phil., 1800s]
This Shrouded Night. PB, 1975 [Eng.]

ROSS, DONALD
Dead Men Do Tell Tales. Methuen, 1938
The Devil Was Kind. Whitman, 1938 (British title?)
Five Keys to Mystery. Methuen, 1938
House of Horror. Methuen, 1939
M.D.—Doctor of Murder. Methuen, 1938
Murder C.O.D. Methuen, 1938 [NYC]

ROSS, FRANK. Joint pseudonym of Colin Northway and Michael Ewings. Pseudonym of Ewings alone: Blair Stuart, q.v.
Dead Runner. Macmillan (London), 1977; Atheneum, 1977
The Sixty-Fifth Tape. Macmillan (London), 1979; Atheneum, 1979 (Probably by Northway alone.)
Sleeping Dogs. Macmillan (London), 1978; Atheneum, 1978 (Probably by Ewings alone.) [New Eng.]

ROSS, GENE. SC: Shaun O'Malley, in at least those marked SO.
Corpse in the Boudoir. Harborough, 1953
"Lady, Throw Me a Curve." Archer, 1950 SO [Calif.]
Step Up, Sucker. Harborough, 1953
This Way for Hell. Archer, 1950
Two Smart Dames. Archer, 1949 SO [Calif.]
You're Dead, My Lovely. Archer, 1950

ROSS, GEORGE. See also: John (Frederick) Burke, 1922-   . And: Joseph (Arnold) Hayes, 1918-   .
Any Other Business, with Campbell Singer, 1909-   , q.v. French (London), 1959 (3-act play.)
Guilty Party, with Campbell Singer, 1909-   , q.v. French (London), 1962 (3-act play.)

ROSS, HAL. 1941-   . Ref: CA.
The Fleur de Lys Affair. Doubleday, 1975; New English Library, 1976 [Toronto]

ROSS, HELEN HALYBURTON
-Dark Gethryn. Jenkins, 1932
-The House of the Talisman. Butterworth, 1927
-The Lost Oasis. Hutchinson, 1933
-A Man with His Back to the East. Butterworth, 1926
The Mystery of the Lotus Queen. Jenkins, 1931 [ship]
-Peel Rocke—Black Sheep. Jenkins, 1932
The Scarab Clue. Hutchinson, 1935
-The Sea of Death. Jenkins, 1931
-The Shadow of Egypt. Butterworth, 1928
-The Silence of Jeremy Langton. Hutchinson, 1934
-Sin and Sand. Butterworth, 1929

ROSS, IAN. Pseudonym of John F(rancis) Rossmann, 1942-   , q.v. SC: Mind Masters, in both titles (see also Rossmann entry).
Amazons. Signet, 1976
Recycled Souls. Signet, 1976

ROSS, IVAN T. Pseudonym of Robert Rossner, 1932-   , q.v. SC: Ben Gordon = BG.
The Man Who Would Do Anything. Doubleday, 1963; Heinemann, 1964 [NYC]
Murder out of School. Simon, 1960; Heinemann, 1960 BG [NYC, acad.]
Old Students Never Die. Doubleday, 1962; Heinemann, 1963 BG [N.Y.]
Requiem for a Schoolgirl. Simon, 1961; Heinemann, 1962 BG [NYC, acad.]
Teacher's Blood. Doubleday, 1964; Hale, 1966 BG [NYC, acad.]

ROSS, JAMES. 1911-   . Born in N.C.; newspaperman.
They Don't Dance Much. Houghton, 1940; Jarrolds, 1940 [N.C.]

ROSS, JEROME. See: Dorothy Salisbury Davis, 1916-   .

ROSS, JOHN. SC: The Major (Major Hutton Seary), in at least those marked M. Set: Eng.
The Black Spot. Hodder, 1936
Bless the Wasp. Hodder, 1938
The Drone-Man. Hodder, 1937
Federal Agent. Collins, 1941
The Major. Hodder, 1938 M
The Major Steps Out. Hodder, 1939 M
The Man from the Chamber of Horrors. Hodder, 1939
The Moccasin Men. Hodder, 1936 M
The Tall Man. Collins, 1940

ROSS, JOHN. ca.1936-   .
Devil's Gate Road. Anderberg-Lund, 1980 [Reno]

ROSS, JONATHAN. Pseudonym of John Rossiter, 1916-   , q.v. SC: Insp. George Rogers, in all titles. Set: Eng.
The Blood Running Cold. Cassell, 1968
The Burning of Billy Toober. Constable, 1974; Walker, 1976
Dead at First Hand. Cassell, 1969
The Deadest Thing You Ever Saw. Cassell, 1969; McCall, 1970
Diminished by Death. Cassell, 1968
Here Lies Nancy Frail. Constable, 1972; Saturday Review Press, 1972
"I Know What It's Like to Die." Constable, 1976
A Rattling of Old Bones. Constable, 1979

ROSS, KATHLEEN
The Wounded Heart. Belmont, 1976

ROSS, LEONARD Q. Pseudonym of Leo (Calvin) Rosten, 1908-   , q.v.
-Adventure in Washington. Harcourt, 1940 [Wash. D.C.]
Balkan Express; see Dateline: Europe
The Dark Corner. Century, 1945; Edwards, 1946, as by L. C. Rosten
-Dateline: Europe. Harcourt, 1939. British title: Balkan Express. Heinemann, 1939
-Sleep My Love. Century, 1947

ROSS, MANDER
The Sorting Van Murder. Melrose, 1935

ROSS, MARILYN. Pseudonym of W(illiam) E(dward) D(aniel) Ross, 1912-   , q.v. Other pseudonyms: Laura Frances Brooks, Rose Dana, Jan Daniels, Ellen Randolph, Clarissa Ross, Dan Ross, Dana Ross, qq.v. Novelizations of the "Dark Shadows" TV series = DS (published by Paperback Library and set in Maine).
The Amethyst Tears. Beagle, 1975
The Aquarius Curse. Paperback Library, 1970
Assignment: Danger. Paperback Library, 1967
Awake to Terror. Popular Library, 1978
Barnabas Collins. 1968 DS
Barnabas Collins and Quentin's Demon. 1970 DS
Barnabas Collins and the Gypsy Witch. 1970 DS
Barnabas Collins and the Mysterious Ghost. 1970 DS
Barnabas Collins vs. the Warlock. 1969 DS
Barnabas, Quentin and Dr. Jekyll's Son. 1971 DS
Barnabas, Quentin and the Avenging Ghost. 1970 DS
Barnabas, Quentin and the Body Snatchers. 1971 DS
Barnabas, Quentin and the Crystal Coffin. 1970 DS
Barnabas, Quentin and the Frightened Bride. 1970 DS
Barnabas, Quentin and the Grave Robbers. 1971 DS
Barnabas, Quentin and the Haunted Cave. 1970 DS
Barnabas, Quentin and the Hidden Tomb. 1971 DS
Barnabas, Quentin and the Mad Magician. 1971 DS
Barnabas, Quentin and the Magic Potion. 1971 DS
Barnabas, Quentin and the Mummy's Curse. 1970 DS
Barnabas, Quentin and the Nightmare Assassin. 1970 DS
Barnabas, Quentin and the Scorpio Curse. 1970 DS
Barnabas, Quentin and the Sea Ghost. 1971 DS
Barnabas, Quentin and the Serpent. 1970 DS
Barnabas, Quentin and the Vampire Beauty. 1972 DS
Barnabas, Quentin and the Witch's Curse. 1970 DS
Behind the Purple Veil. Paperback Library, 1973 [L.A.]
Beware, My Love. Paperback Library, 1965 [Maine]
The Brides of Saturn. Berkley, 1975
Cameron Castle. Paperback Library, 1967
Cauldron of Evil. Popular Library, 1977 [Scot.]
Cellars of the Dead. Popular Library, 1976 [Scot.]
The Curse of Black Charlie. Popular Library, 1976 [Edin., 1774]
The Curse of Collinwood. 1968 DS
Dark Legend. Paperback Library, 1966 [Maine]
Dark Shadows. 1966 DS
Dark Stars over Seacrest. Paperback Library, 1972 [Cape Cod]
Dark Towers of Fog Island. Popular Library, 1975 [Can., 1877]
Dead of Winter! Popular Library, 1978
Death's Dark Music. Popular Library, 1977 [Scot., 1919]
-Delta Flame. Popular Library, 1978
The Demon of Barnabas Collins. 1969 DS
Desperate Heiress. Paperback Library, 1966
The Devil's Daughter. Paperback Library, 1973
Don't Look Behind You. Paperback Library, 1973 [Mass.]
Face in the Fog. Curtis, 1973
Face in the Shadows. Paperback Library, 1973 [N.Y.]
The Foe of Barnabas Collins. 1969 DS
Fog Island. Paperback Library, 1965 [Can.]
Fog Island Horror. Popular Library, 1978 [Can.]
Fog Island Secret. Popular Library, 1975 [Can.]
A Garden of Ghosts. Popular Library, 1974
A Gathering of Evil. Paperback Library, 1966
The Ghost and the Garnet. Beagle, 1975 [Eng., 1837]
Ghost Comes Knocking. Paperback Library, 1971
Ghost Ship of Fog Island. Popular Library, 1975 [Can., ca.1900]
The Haiti Circle. Popular Library, 1976 [Haiti]
Haunting of Fog Island. Curtis, 1973 [Can.]
House of Dark Shadows. Paperback Library, 1970 (Novelization of the movie.)
House of Ghosts. Paperback Library, 1973
The Light in the Tower. Paperback Library, 1965
Loch Sinister. Popular Library, 1974 [Hebrides]
The Locked Corridor. Paperback Library, 1965
The Long Night of Fear. Paperback Library, 1972 [Ga.]
Marta. Paperback Library, 1973 [Austria]
Mask of Evil. Popular Library, 1977 [Va., 1853]
Memory of Evil. Paperback Library, 1966
Message from a Ghost. Paperback Library, 1972
Mistress of Moorwood Manor. Paperback Library, 1972 [Eng., 1879]
Mistress of Ravenswood. Paperback Library, 1967
The Mystery of Collinwood. 1967 DS

The Mystery of Fury Castle. Paperback Library, 1967 [Maine]
Night of the Phantom. Paperback Library, 1972 [Greece]
The Peril of Barnabas Collins. 1969 DS
The Phantom and Barnabas Collins. 1969 DS
Phantom Manor. Paperback Library, 1966 [Eng., 1881]
The Phantom of Belle Acres. Curtis, 1973
Phantom of Fog Island. Paperback Library, 1971 [Can., 1870]
Phantom of the Snow. Popular Library, 1977 [Glasgow, 1854]
Phantom of the Swamp. Paperback Library, 1972
Phantom of the Thirteenth Floor. Popular Library, 1975
Phantom Wedding. Popular Library, 1976
-Pleasure's Daughter. Popular Library, 1978 [Eng., ca.1670]
Ravenhurst. Popular Library, 1975
Rothby. Popular Library, 1978
Satan's Island. Warner, 1975
Satan's Rock. Paperback Library, 1966 [Can., 1900]
The Secret of Barnabas Collins. 1969 DS
Secrets of Sedbury Manor. Curtis, 1973
Shadow over Emerald Castle. Beagle, 1975
Shadows over Denby. Popular Library, 1976
Shorecliff. Paperback Library, 1968
The Sinister Garden. Paperback Library, 1972 [Fr.]
Step into Terror. Paperback Library, 1973
Strangers at Collins House. 1967 DS
Temple of Darkness. Ballantine, 1976; Futura, 1977 [Eng., 1665]
This Evil Village. Popular Library, 1977
This Frightened Lady. Popular Library, 1977
Tread Softly, Nurse Scott. Paperback Library, 1966
The Twice Dead. Popular Library, 1978
The Vampire Contessa. Pinnacle, 1974 [Eng., 1800s]
Victoria Winters. 1967 DS
Waiting in the Shadows. Popular Library, 1976 [Scot.]
The Widows of Westwood. Popular Library, 1976
The Witch of Bralhaven. Paperback Library, 1972
Witches' Coven. Paperback Library, 1971

ROSS, MARK
Ace High. Warren, 1951
Alibi. Warren, 1951
Blackmail. Warren, 1951
Crisis for Two. Warren, 1952
Last Card. Warren, 1952
Manhunt. Warren, 1951
Night Ride. Warren, 1952
Noon Jury. Warren, 1952
Operator X. Warren, 1951
Quiet City. Warren, 1952
Strange Money. Warren, 1951
This Woman Is Dangerous. Warren, 1952

ROSS, PAUL. House name. SC: Terry Bunker (Chopper Cop) = TB.
The Assassin. Manor, 1974 (By William Crawford, 1929-   , q.v.)
Dynamite Monster Boogie Concert. Popular Library, 1975 TB (By Bill Amidon and Nathaniel Freedland.) [Calif.]
The Hitchhike Killer. Popular Library, 1972 TB (By Dan Streib, q.v.) [Calif.]
Valley of Death. Popular Library, 1972 TB (By Dan Streib, q.v.) [Calif.]

ROSS, PAUL B.
Freebie and the Bean. Warner, 1974; Futura, 1975 (Novelization of the movie.) [L.A.]

ROSS, PHYLLIS (FREEDMAN). 1926-1970. Ref: CA.
Miranda Clair. PB, 1965

ROSS, REGINA. Pseudonym of May MacKintosh, q.v.
The Devil Dances for Gold. Macdonald, 1976; Ballantine, 1977
Falls the Shadow. Barker, 1974; Delacorte, 1974 [Rum.]

ROSS, ROBERT
A French Finish. Putnam, 1977

ROSS, SAM. 1912-   . Ref: CA.
Hang-Up. Coward, 1968; Hale, 1969 [L.A.]
The Hustlers. Popular Library, 1956
He Ran All the Way. Farrar, 1947 [Chi.]
The Keepers; see Ready for the Tiger
Ready for the Tiger. Farrar, 1964; Barrie, 1965. Also published as: The Keepers. New English Library pb, 1969
The Tight Corner. Farrar, 1956; Boardman, 1957 [La.]
-You Belong to Me. Popular Library, 1955

ROSS, SHEILA (MURIEL). 1925-   .
-Five Days Till Noon. Collins, 1973
The Foam on the River. Collins, 1975
-A Log Across the Road. Collins, 1971. Reprinted in two volumes: A State of Emergency. Fontana, 1973; and: Wars Within Wars. Fontana, 1973
-The Perfect Carrier. Collins, 1972
A State of Emergency; see A Log Across the Road
-The Tower of Monte Rado. Collins, 1974
Wars Within Wars; see A Log Across the Road

ROSS, VICTOR. 1919-   .
A Stranger in My Midst. Hodder, 1949

ROSS, W(ILLIAM) E(DWARD) D(ANIEL). 1912-   . Pseudonyms: Laura Frances Brooks, Rose Dana, Jan Daniels, Ellen Randolph, Clarissa Ross, Dan Ross, Dana Ross, Marilyn Ross, qq.v. Ref: CA. At least some of the titles below are gothics.
An Act of Love. Avalon, 1970
Behind Locked Shutters. Arcadia, 1968
Castle on the Hill. Hale, 1968
Christopher's Mansion. Bouregy, 1969
Dark Is My Shadow. Arcadia, 1969 [Va.]
Dark Mansion. Avalon, 1970
Dark of the Moon. Arcadia, 1968
Dark Villa of Capri. Arcadia, 1968 [It.]
Destination Terror. Paperback Library, 1968
The Enchanted Voyage. Hale, 1968
The Forbidden Island. Lenox, 1972. British title: Rendezvous in Austria. Hale, 1967 [Paris, Austria]
The Ghost of Oaklands. Arcadia, 1967
The Haunted Garden. Paperback Library, 1970
The House on Mount Vernon Street. Lenox, 1972
Magic Valley. Hale, 1970
Mansion on the Moors. Avalon, 1971
The Music Room. Dell, 1971
Nightmare Abbey. Berkley, 1975
One Louisberg Square. Lenox, 1974; Remploy, 1975 [Boston]
Our Share of Love. Hale, 1969
Rendezvous in Austria; see The Forbidden Castle
Reunion in Renfrew. Avalon, 1972; Hale, 1974
The Room Without a Key. Lenox, 1971
Rothhaven. Avalon, 1972
Sable in the Rain. Lenox, 1970
The Third Spectre. Arcadia, 1967
This Man I Love. Hale, 1970
The Twilight Web. Arcadia, 1968. Reprinted as by Dan Ross: Macfadden, 1970 [Maine, 1892]
The Web of Love. Hale, 1970
The Whispering Gallery. Lenox, 1970 [Va., 1884]
Whispers in the Night. Lenox, 1970 [Va.]
Wind over the Citadel. Lenox, 1971
Witch of Goblin's Acres. Lenox, 1974; Remploy, 1974
The Yesteryear Phantom. Lenox, 1971

ROSS, WILLIAM. Born in Cin.; writer of dialogue for English-language movies in Japan; film company executive.
Bamboo Terror. Tuttle, 1969 [Viet Nam]

ROSS, Z(OLA) H(ELEN GIRDEY). 1912-   . Pseudonyms: Helen Arre, Bert Iles, qq.v. Ref: CA. SC: Beau Smith and Pogy Rogers = S&R
One Corpse Missing. Bobbs, 1948 S&R [Reno]
Overdue for Death. Bobbs, 1947 [Seattle]
Three Down Vulnerable. Bobbs, 1946 S&R [Nev.]

ROSSER, AUSTIN
Sweeney Todd. French (London), 1971 (2-act play.)

ROSSI, BRUNO. House name. Those by John Stevenson = *; those by Leonard Levinson, q.v. = #. SC: Johnny Rock (The Sharpshooter), in all titles.
Blood Bath. Leisure, 1974
Blood Oath. Leisure, 1974 [N.Y.]
A Dirty Way to Die. Leisure, 1975
Head Crusher. Leisure, 1974 # [NYC]
Hit Man. Leisure, 1974 *
The Killing Machine. Leisure, 1973 [Vt.]
Las Vegas Vengeance. Leisure, 1975 * [Las Veg.]
Mafia Death Watch. Leisure, 1975 [Det.]
Muzzle Blast. Leisure, 1974 [Cape Cod]
Night of the Assassins. Leisure, 1974 #
No Quarter Given. Leisure, 1974 [Va.]
Savage Slaughter. Leisure, 1975
Scarfaced Killer. Leisure, 1975 [Okla.]
Stiletto. Leisure, 1974
Triggerman. Leisure, 1975 [NYC]
The Worst Way to Die. Leisure, 1974 #

ROSSI, JEAN BAPTISTE. 1931-   . Pseudonym: Sebastien Japrisot, q.v.

ROSSITER, JOHN. 1916-   . Pseudonym: Jonathan Ross, q.v. Ref: CA, TC. SC: Roger Tallis, in at least those marked RT.
The Deadly Gold; see The Golden Virgin
The Deadly Green. Cassell, 1970; Walker, 1971 RT [S. Am.]
The Golden Virgin. Constable, 1975. U.S. title: The Deadly Gold. Walker, 1975 RT [Sp.]
The Man Who Came Back. H. Hamilton, 1978; Houghton, 1979
The Manipulators. Cassell, 1973; Simon, 1974
The Murder Makers. Cassell, 1970; Walker, 1977 RT [Ariz.]
A Rope for General Dietz. Constable, 1972; Walker, 1972 RT [Sp.]
The Victims. Cassell, 1971
The Villains. Cassell, 1974; Walker, 1976

ROSSMANN, JOHN F. 1942-   . Pseudonym: Ian Ross, q.v. SC: Britt St. Vincent (The Mind Masters), in all titles (see also Ian Ross entry). Ref: CA.
The Door. Signet, 1975
The Mind-Masters. Signet, 1974 [Sic.]
Shamballah. Signet, 1975

ROSSNER, ROBERT. 1932-   . Pseudonym: Ivan T. Ross, q.v. Ref: CA.
The End of Someone Else's Rainbow. Saturday Review Press, 1974

ROSTAND, ROBERT. Pseudonym of Robert (S.) Hopkins, q.v. SC: Mike Locken, in at least those marked ML.
The D'Artagnan Signature. Putnam, 1976; Hutchinson, 1976 [Fr.]
The Killer Elite. Delacorte, 1973; Hodder, 1974 ML
A Killing in Rome. Delacorte, 1977; Hutchinson, 1977 ML [Rome]
The Vengeance Run. Berkley, 1972; Arrow, 1976
Viper's Game. Delacorte, 1974; Hodder, 1975 ML [S. Pac.]

ROSTEN, LEO (CALVIN). 1908-   . Pseudonym: Leonard Ross, q.v. SC: Silky Pincus = SP. Ref: CA, CC.
King Silky! Harper, 1980 SP [N.J.]
A Most Private Intrigue. Atheneum, 1967; Gollancz, 1967
Silky! Harper, 1979 SP [NYC]

ROSTOV, MARA. Born in Switz.; graduate of U. of Calif.
Eroica. Putnam, 1977; Corgi, 1978 [Ger.]
Night Hunt. Putnam, 1979; Hale, 1980 [Ger., 1962]

ROTH, ARTHUR JOSEPH. 1925-   . Pseudonym: Slater McGurk, q.v.

ROTH, HOLLY. 1916-1964. Pseudonyms: K. G. Ballard, P. J. Merrill, qq.v. Ref: CA, CC, EM, TC. SC: Lt. Kelly = K; Insp. Medford = M.
Button, Button. Harcourt, 1966; H. Hamilton, 1967 K [NYC]
The Content Assignment. Simon, 1954; H. Hamilton, 1954. Also published as: The Shocking Secret. Dell, 1955 K [NYC]
The Crimson in the Purple. Simon, 1956; H. Hamilton, 1956 [NYC]
The Mask of Glass. Vanguard, 1954; H. Hamilton, 1955 [NYC]
Operation Doctors; see Too Many Doctors
Shadow of a Lady. Simon, 1957; H. Hamilton, 1957 M [Eng.]
The Shocking Secret; see The Content Assignment
The Sleeper. Simon, 1955; H. Hamilton, 1955 [NYC]

Too Many Doctors. Random, 1962. British title: Operation Doctors. H. Hamilton, 1962 M [ship]
The Van Dreisen Affair. Random, 1960; H. Hamilton, 1960

ROTHBERG, ABRAHAM. 1922- . Ref: CA.
The Great Waltz. Putnam, 1978 [Vienna]
The Heirs of Cain. Putnam, 1966
The Stalking Horse. Saturday Review Press, 1972 [N.J.]
The Thousand Doors. Holt, 1965; Heinemann, 1965 [Yugos.]

ROTHMAN, JUDITH
With Murder in Mind. Hale, 1975

ROTHROCK, KEN
The Deadly Welcome. Major, 1976

ROTHSTEIN, RAPHAEL
The Hand of Fatima. Manor, 1979 [Rome]

ROTHWEILER, PAUL R(OGER). 1931- . Ref: CA.
Blood Sports. Jove, 1980 [Austria]

ROTHWELL, H(ENRY) T(ALBOT). 1921- . SC: Mike Brooks, in all titles.
Dive Deep for Danger. Hale, 1966; Roy, 1966
Duet for Three Spies. Hale, 1967; Roy, 1967
Exit a Spy. Hale, 1966
No Honour Amongst Spies. Hale, 1969; Roy, 1969 [Rhod.]
No Kisses from the Kremlin. Hale, 1969

ROTHWELL, UNA
Death on the Run. Hale, 1965 [Australia]
Murder Is Lonely. Hale, 1964

ROTSSTEIN, AARON NATHAN. Born in Israel, raised in Can., living in U.S. since 1969; physicist and lawyer turned full-time writer.
Judgment in St. Peter's. Putnam, 1980; Pan, 1981 [Rome]

ROUDYBUSH, ALEXANDRA (BROWN). 1911- . Ref: CA.
Before the Ball Was Over. Doubleday, 1965. British title: A Season for Death. Hale, 1966 [Wash. D.C.]
A Capital Crime. Doubleday, 1969 [Wash. D.C.]
Death of a Moral Person. Doubleday, 1967; Hale, 1968 [Paris]
Female of the Species. Doubleday, 1978 [Paris]
A Gastronomic Murder. Doubleday, 1973; New English Library, 1974 [Fr.]
The House of the Cat. Doubleday, 1970; New English Library, 1975 [Paris]
A Season for Death; see Before the Ball Was Over
Suddenly in Paris. Doubleday, 1975 [Paris]
A Sybaritic Death. Doubleday, 1972; New English Library, 1972 [Wash. D.C., Turk.]

ROUECHE, BERTON. 1911- Ref: CA, CC.
Black Weather. Reynal, 1945. Also published as: Rooming House. Lion, 1953 [Midwest]
The Cats; see Feral
Fago. Harper, 1977; Gollancz, 1978 [L.I.]
Feral. Harper, 1974. British title: The Cats. Gollancz, 1975 [L.I.]
The Last Enemy. Dell, 1956; Gollancz, 1956 [Mo.]
Rooming House; see Black Weather

ROUGVIE, CAMERON. SC: Robert Belcourt, in all titles.
The Gredos Reckoning. Barker, 1966
Medal from Pamplona. Barker, 1964; Ballantine, 1964
Tangier Assignment. Barker, 1965; Ballantine, 1965 [Tangier]
When Johnny Died. Barker, 1967

ROURKE, JAMES FRANCIS ANTHONY. 1922- . Joint pseudonym with Hollis Spurgeon Summers, 1915- : Jim Hollis, q.v.

ROURKE, THOMAS. Pseudonym of Daniel Joseph Clinton, 1900- .
The Scarlet Flower. Farrar, 1933; Nicholson, 1934

ROUVEROL, JEAN
Storm Wind Rising. GM, 1974

ROVIN, JEFF. 1951- . Ref: CA. SC: Roger Garrison, in both titles.
Hollywood Detective: Garrison. Manor, 1975 [L.A., 1927]
Hollywood Detective: The Wolf. Manor, 1975 [L.A., 1920s]

ROWAN, DEIRDRE. Pseudonym of Jeanne Williams, 1930- . Other pseudonym: Jeanne Crecy, q.v. Ref: CA.
Dragon's Mount. GM, 1973; Coronet, 1975
Shadow of the Volcano. GM, 1975 [Mex.]
Silver Wood. GM, 1974; Coronet, 1975 [Eng.]

ROWAN, HESTER. Pseudonym of a "well-known author of romantic suspense." Other pseudonym: Sheila Radley, q.v.
Alpine Encounter; see Snowfall
-The Linden Tree. Collins, 1977
-Overture in Venice. Collins, 1976 [Venice]
Snowfall. Collins, 1978. U.S. title: Alpine Encounter. Scribner, 1979 [Austria]

ROWDEN, DICK
Bright Like Blood. Pyramid, 1969

ROWE, ANNE (VON MEIBOM). SC: Insp. Barry = B; Insp. Pettengill = P.
Cobra Venom; see Too Much Poison
Curiosity Killed a Cat. Morrow, 1941; Gifford, 1945
Deadly Intent. Mill, 1946 B
Fatal Purchase. Mill, 1945; Gifford, 1946 [Maine]
The Little Dog Barked. Morrow, 1942; Gifford, 1944 P [Maine]
-Men Are Strange Lovers. King, 1935
The Painted Monster. Gifford, 1945 P
Too Much Poison. Mill, 1944. British title: Cobra Venom. Gifford, 1946 B [NYC]
The Turn of a Wheel. Macaulay, 1930
Up to the Hilt. Mill, 1945; Nimmo, 1947 B [Conn.]

ROWE, JAMES N(ICHOLAS). 1938- . Ref: CA.
The Judas Squad. Little, 1977 [Pa.]

ROWE, JOHN G(ABRIEL). 1874- .
The Cartsley Mystery. Modern, 193?
The Death Flash; or, The Horror of Monkstone Wood. Modern, 193?
The Fighting Lieutenant. Modern, 1935
Gentleman George. Modern, 1935
The Man with the Seared Hand; see The Seared Hand
The Mystery of the Derelict. Modern, 1935; Cupples, 1927
The Seared Hand. Step, 1925. Also published as (?): The Man with the Seared Hand. Modern, 193?
The Secret of the Old Lighthouse. Crowther, 1945
Spies of the Secret Police. Modern, 193?
Struck Down. Modern, 193?

ROWE, JOHN
The Aswan Solution. Doubleday, 1979 [Mid. East]

ROWELL, GEORGE (RIGNALL). 1923- . Ref: CA.
The Lyons Mail. Heinemann, 1969 (Play)

ROWLAND, HENRY. Pseudonym of Charles George, 1893- , q.v. Other pseudonyms: Leland Price, Dorothy Sterling, qq.v.
Hearts and Flowers. Baker, 1937 (1-act play.)

ROWLAND, HENRY C(OTTRELL). 1874-1933. SC: Frank Clamart = FC.
-The Apple of Discord. Dodd, 1913
The Closing Net. Dodd, 1912; Hurst, 1913 FC [Paris]
Duds. Harper, 1920
Mile High. Harper, 1921
-The Mountains of Fears. Barnes, 1905 ss
-Pearl Island. Watt, 1919; Collins, 1921
The Peddler. Harper, 1920 [New Eng.]
The Return of Frank Clamart. Harper, 1923 FC [NYC]
-Sea Scamps. McClure, 1903 ss
The Sultana. Dodd, 1914 [Fr.]
-To Windward. Barnes, 1904; Nutt, 1905

ROWLAND, JOHN (HERBERT SHELLEY). 1907- . SC: Insp. Shelley, in at least those marked S. Set: Eng.
Bloodshed in Bayswater. Jenkins, 1935 S
Calamity in Kent. Jenkins, 1950 S
The Cornish Riviera Mystery. Jenkins, 1939 S
The Crooked House. Jenkins, 1940 S
Dangerous Company. Jenkins, 1937 S
Death Beneath the River. Jenkins, 1943 S
The Death of Nevill Norway. Jenkins, 1942
Death on Dartmoor. Jenkins, 1936 S
The Devil Comes to Devon. Jenkins, 1938 S
Grim Souvenir. Jenkins, 1944 S
Gunpowder Alley. Jenkins, 1941 S
Murder—By Persons Unknown. Mellifont, 1941
Murder in the Museum. Jenkins, 1938 S
The Orange-Tree Mystery. Jenkins, 1949 S
The Professor Dies. Jenkins, 1936 S
Puzzle in Pyrotechnics. Jenkins, 1947 S
Sinister Creek. Fiction House, 1946
Slow Poison. Jenkins, 1939
The Spy with the Scar. Jenkins, 1940 S
Suicide Alibi. Jenkins, 1937 S
Time for Killing. Jenkins, 1950 S

ROWLANDS, CECIL. 1856-1914. Pseudonym: Cecil Raleigh, q.v. See also: Richard Parker.

ROWLEY, J. DE LA MARE
The Passage in Park Lane. Butterworth, 1928

ROWSELL, E. P.
Recollections of a Relieving Officer. Ward, 1861. Also published as by Francis W. Rowsell: Maxwell, 1886

ROWSELL, FRANCIS W. See: E. P. Rowsell.

ROY, ARCHIE [ARCHIBALD EDMISTON ROY]. 1924- . Has Ph.D. in astrophysics from Glasgow U., where he teaches and does research in celestial mechanics; author of articles and books on these subjects.
All Evil Shed Away. Long, 1970; World, 1972 [Hebrides]
The Curtained Sleep. Long, 1969; World, 1971 [Scot.]
The Dark Host. Long, 1976
Deadlight. Long, 1968
Devil in the Darkness. Long, 1978 [Scot.]
Sable Night. Long, 1973

ROY, IAN
Lord Lynmore's Life. Nisbet, 1917

ROYCE, KENNETH. Pseudonym of Kenneth Royce Gandley, 1920- . Other pseudonym: Oliver Jacks, q.v. Ref: CA, TC. SC: Spider Scott = SS. Set: Eng.
The Angry Island. Cassell, 1963
Bones in the Sand. Cassell, 1967
Bustillo. Hodder, 1976; Coward, 1976 [Jap.]
The Concrete Boot. Hodder, 1971; McKay, 1971 SS
The Day the Wind Dropped. Cassell, 1964
The Long Corridor. Cassell, 1960
The Masterpiece Affair; see Spider Underground
The Miniatures Frame. Hodder, 1972; Simon, 1972 SS
My Turn to Die. Barker, 1958
The Night Seekers. Cassell, 1962
No Paradise. Cassell, 1961
A Peck of Salt. Cassell, 1968
The Satan Touch. Hodder, 1978
A Single to Hong Kong. Hodder, 1969
The Soft-Footed Moor. Barker, 1959
Spider Underground. Hodder, 1973. U.S. title: The Masterpiece Affair. Simon, 1973 SS
The Third Arm. Hodder, 1980; McGraw, 1980
Trap Spider. Hodder, 1974 SS
The Woodcutter Operation. Hodder, 1975; Simon, 1975 [hosp.]
The XYY Man. Hodder, 1970; McKay, 1970 SS

ROYDE-SMITH, NAOMI (GWLADYS). 1875?-1964. Set: Eng.
All Star Cast. Macmillan (London & NYC), 1936
The Altar-Piece. Macmillan (London & NYC), 1939
John Fanning's Legacy. Constable, 1927
Madam Julia's Tale and other queer stories. Gollancz, 1932 ss
-The Tortoiseshell Cat. Constable, 1925; Boni, 1925
-The Younger Venus. Macmillan (London), 1938; Macmillan (NYC), 1939

ROYER, LOUIS-CHARLES. 1885- .
-African Mistress. Pyramid, 1953
-French Doctor. Pyramid, 1951
-The Harem. Pyramid, 1951 (Translation of "Le Serai.")
-Love Camp. Pyramid, 1953
-The Man from Paris. Pyramid, 1956
The Redhead from Chicago. Pyramid, 1954

-Savage Triangle. Pyramid, 1954
-Unrepentent Sinners. Pyramid, 1957

ROYS, WILLIS E.
Flame Eternal and The Maharajah's Son. Osberg, 1936 (2 stories, the second criminous.)

RUARK, ERIC B.
The Campus Killings. Carlyle, 1980 [acad.]

RUBEL, JAMES L(YON). 1894- .
No Business for a Lady. GM, 1950; Fawcett (London), 1952 [L.A.]

RUBEN, WILLIAM S.
Murder: Love Story. Manor, 1977 [Eng.]

RUBENS, BERNICE. 1923- . Ref: CA.
Sunday Best. Summit, 1980 [Eng.]

RUBENS, ROBERT
The Cosway Miniature. Bachman, 1980

RUBENSTEIN, SAMUEL LEONARD. 1922-
Joint pseudonym with Robert G. Weaver: Rubin Weber, q.v.

RUBENSTEIN, STANLEY (JACK)
Merry Murder. Jarrolds, 1949

RUBIN, DANIEL N. 1892- .
Riddle Me This! French (NYC), 1933 (3-act play.)

RUBIN, RON(ALD)
The Annulment. Jove, 1978 [L.A.]

RUBINGTON, NORMAN. Pseudonym: Leslie Paige, q.v.

RUBINSTEIN, PAUL (ARTHUR). 1935- .
Ref: CA. See: Peter (Joseph) Tanous, 1938- .

RUCK, BERTA [AMY ROBERTA RUCK OLIVER]. 1878- . Ref: CA.
The Pearl Thief. Dodd, 1926; Hodder, 1926

RUD, ANTHONY M(ELVILLE). 1893-1942. SC: J. C. K. ("Jiggers") Masters = JM.
The Devil's Heirloom. Garden City, 1924
House of the Damned. Macaulay, 1934 JM
The Rose Bath Riddle. Macaulay, 1934 JM [L.I.]
-The Sentence of the Six-Gun. Garden City, 1926
The Stuffed Men. Macaulay, 1935; Newnes, 1936 JM [L.I.]

RUDD, COLIN
The Red Flowers of Death. Hale, 1970
The Violent Dawn. Hale, 1971

RUDORFF, RAYMOND. 1933- .
The Dracula Archives. Bruce & Watson, 1971; PB, 1972
The Venice Plot. Secker, 1977; Putnam, 1976 [Venice]

RUEGG, JUDGE (ALFRED HENRY). 1854-1941.
Ref: CC. SC: Rosie Bright = RB. Set: Eng.
David Betterton. Daniel, 1931 RB
Flash. Daniel, 1928
John Clutterbuck. Daniel, 1923 RB
A Staffordshire Knot; or, The Two Houses. Daniel, 1926

RUELL, PATRICK. Pseudonym of Reginald (Charles) Hill, 1936- , q.v.
The Castle of the Demon. Long, 1971; Hawthorn, 1973 [Scot.]
Death Takes the Low Road. Hutchinson, 1974
Red Christmas. Long, 1972; Hawthorn, 1972
Urn Burial. Hutchinson, 1975

RUNDLE, ANNE. Pseudonyms: Alexandra Manners, Joanne Marshall, qq.v. Ref: CA.
Amberwood. Hale, 1973; Bantam, 1974
-Forest of Fear. Hurst, 1969
Grey Ghyll. Hale, 1978; St. Martin's, 1979
Heronbrook. Hale, 1975; Bantam, 1975
-Lost Lotus. Hale, 1972
-The Moon Marriage. Hurst, 1967
-Rakehell. Hurst, 1970
-Swordlight. Hurst, 1968

RUNYON, CHARLES (W.). 1928- . Ref: CA.
The Anatomy of Violence. Ace, 1963
The Black Moth. GM, 1967 [Ill.]
Bloody Jungle. Ace, 1966
Color Him Dead. GM, 1963; Muller pb, 1964 [Carib.]
The Death Cycle. GM, 1963; New English Library, 1969

Kiss the Girls and Make Them Die. Pyramid, 1977
No Place to Hide. GM, 1970
Power Kill. GM, 1972
The Prettiest Girl I Ever Killed. GM, 1965
Something Wicked. Lancer, 1973
To Kill a Dead Man. Major, 1976 [Carib.]

RUNYON, DAMON, 1880-1946, and HOWARD LINDSAY, 1889- , q.v. Ref for Runyon: CC, EM.
A Slight Case of Murder. Dramatists, 1940 (2-act play.)

RUNYON, POKE
Commando X. Pyramid, 1967
Night Jump—Cuba. Pyramid, 1967 [Cuba]

RUSE, GARY ALAN. 1946- . Ref: CA.
A Game of Titans. Prentice-Hall (NYC & London), 1976
Houndstooth. Prentice-Hall, 1975; Sphere, 1979 [Russ.]

RUSE, PAUL
The Alumni Murders. Tower, 1980 [Kan.]

RUSHTON, CHARLES. Pseudonym of Charles Rushton Shortt, 1904- . SC: Insp. Cadman, in at least those marked C; James O'Hannay and Floyd East, in at least those marked O&E. Set: Eng.
Another Crime. Jenkins, 1934
Black Destiny. Jenkins, 1929
Bloody with Spurring. Jenkins, 1939 [Czech.]
Crime Looks Up. Jenkins, 1947
Danger in the Deed. Jenkins, 1933
Dark Amid the Blaze. Jenkins, 1950
The Dead Man. Jenkins, 1935
Death in the Wood. Jenkins, 1936
Devil's Power. Jenkins, 1952; Roy, 1956 C
The Doctor from Devil's Island. Jenkins, 1935
Furnace for a Foe. Jenkins, 1951; Roy, 1957 C
Madman's Manor. Jenkins, 1932
The Master of Fear. Jenkins, 1930 O&E
Murder in Bavaria. Jenkins, 1937 [Ger.]
The Murder Market. Jenkins, 1934
Murder on Trust. Jenkins, 1943 C
Murder out of Tune. Jenkins, 1939 C
Night of Murder. Jenkins, 1937
No Beast So Fierce. Jenkins, 1950; Roy, 1958 C [Calcutta]
No Second Stroke. Jenkins, 1938 [Ger.]
Terror Tower. Jenkins, 1933
The Trail of Blood. Jenkins, 1929 O&E

RUSO, MICHAEL. Joint pseudonym with John Roscoe, 1921- : Mike Roscoe, q.v.

RUSSELL. Pseudonym: Nicholas Carter, q.v.

RUSSELL, A(NDREW) J(OSEPH). Born in NYC; TV writer.
The Devalino Caper. Random, 1975; Collins, 1977 [Ind.]
Pour the Hemlock. Random, 1977; Gollancz, 1979 [Wash. D.C.]

RUSSELL, AGNES
A Flame in the Heather. Hale, 1974
Hill of the Wild Cat. Hale, 1975
Larksong at Dawn. Hale, 1977; Zebra, 1978 [Scot., past]
-A Red Rose for Annabel. Hale, 1973
Target Capricorn. Hale, 1976

RUSSELL, ARTHUR
The Croaker. Mellifont, 1936
The Mystery of the Luminous Ray. Mellifont, 1935
Tragedy at Cumberland Park. Fenland, 1933

RUSSELL, MAJOR C(HARLES) E(DMUND). 1878- .
Adventures of the D.C.I. Doubleday, 1924; Curtis Brown, 1924 ss [Fr.]
True Adventures of the Secret Service. Doubleday, 1923; Hurst, 1924 ss

RUSSELL, CHARLOTTE. Pseudonym of Carl Henry Rathjen, 1909- . Ref: CA.
Dark Music. Lancer, 1972

RUSSELL, CHARLOTTE MURRAY. Ref: MP. SC: Jane Amanda Edwards = JE; Homer Fitzgerald = HF.
The Bad Neighbor Murder. Doubleday, 1946 JE [Midwest]
Between Us and Evil. Doubleday, 1950 HF [Midwest]
The Careless Mrs. Christian. Doubleday, 1949 HF [Midwest]

The Case of the Topaz Flower. Doubleday, 1939 [Chi.]
The Clue of the Naked Eye. Doubleday, 1939 JE
Cook Up a Crime. Doubleday, 1951 JE [Midwest]
Death of an Eloquent Man. Doubleday, 1936 JE
Dreadful Reckoning. Doubleday, 1941 [Chi.]
Hand Me a Crime. Doubleday, 1949; Cherry Tree, 1950 JE
I Heard the Death Bell. Doubleday, 1940 JE [Wis.]
Ill Met in Mexico. Doubleday, 1948 JE [Mex.]
June, Moon, and Murder. Doubleday, 1952 HF [Midwest]
Lament for William. Doubleday, 1947 HF [Midwest]
Market for Murder. Doubleday, 1953 [Midwest]
The Message of the Mute Dog. Doubleday, 1942 JE [Midwest]
Murder at the Old Stone House. Doubleday, 1935 JE
Murder Steps In. Doubleday, 1942 [Miami]
Night on the Devil's Pathway; see Night on the Pathway
Night on the Pathway. Doubleday, 1938. British title: Night on the Devil's Pathway. World's Work, 1938 JE [Midwest]
No Time for Crime. Doubleday, 1945 JE [Midwest]
The Tiny Diamond. Doubleday, 1937; World's Work, 1937 JE

RUSSELL, DONN
A Difference in Death. Faber, 1957

RUSSELL, DORA
-Betrayed. White, 1885
The Broken Seal. Hurst, 1887; Lovell, 1886
The Drift of Fate. Chatto, 1895
-An Evil Reputation. Griffith, 1892
-A Fatal Past. Simpkin, 1896; Lovell, 1891
-Footprints in the Snow. Tinsley, 1877
-A Hidden Chain. Digby, 1894; Rand, 1896
-The Last Signal. White, 1893; Taylor, 1892
-The Secret of the River. Hurst, 1891
-The Silent Watchers. Low, 1889; Lovell, 1888
-A Torn-Out Page. Digby, 1899; Rand, 1897

RUSSELL, E(NID) S. Ref: CC. SC: Ben Louis = BL.
The Fortunate Island. Doubleday, 1973 [New Eng.]
Nice Enough to Murder. Doubleday, 1971 BL [Mass.]
She Should Have Cried on Monday. Doubleday, 1968; Hale, 1969 BL [Mass.]

RUSSELL, EARL LOUIS
Grandma's Best Years. Art Craft, 1949 (3-act play.)

RUSSELL, ERIC FRANK. 1905-1978.
Dreadful Sanctuary. Fantasy Press, 1951; Museum, 1953
The Mindwarpers; see With a Strange Device
With a Strange Device. Dobson, 1964. U.S. title: The Mindwarpers. Lancer, 1965

RUSSELL, FOX
The Escapades of Mr. Alfred Dimmock. Everett, 1906 ss, some criminous
-In the Wrong Box. Everett, 1904
The Phantom Spy. Nelson, 1904

RUSSELL, HERBERT
My Atlantic Bride. Digby, 1906

RUSSELL, JACK GOLDEN. See: George Clayton Johnson.

RUSSELL, JOHN. 1885-1956. Ref: EM.
Cops 'n Robbers. Norton, 1930; Butterworth, 1930 ss
-Far Wandering Men. Norton, 1929; Butterworth, 1929 ss
-In Dark Places. Knopf, 1923; Butterworth, 1923 ss
The Red Mark, and other stories. Knopf, 1919. British title: Where the Pavement Ends. Butterworth, 1921. Reprinted in the U.S. under the British title: Knopf, 1921 ss
Where the Pavement Ends; see The Red Mark

RUSSELL, MARTIN (JAMES). 1934-   . Pseudonym: Mark Lester, q.v. Ref: CA, TC. SC: Jim Larkin = JL. Set: Eng.
Advisory Service. Collins, 1971
Catspaw. Collins, 1980
The Client. Collins, 1975
Concrete Evidence. Collins, 1972 JL
Crime Wave. Collins, 1974 JL
Danger Money. Collins, 1968
A Dangerous Place to Dwell. Collins, 1978
Daylight Robbery. Collins, 1978
Deadline. Collins, 1971 JL
Death Fuse. Collins, 1980; St. Martin's, 1981
Dial Death. Collins, 1977
Double Deal. Collins, 1976
Double Hit. Collins, 1973
Hunt to Kill. Collins, 1969
The Man Without a Name; see Mr. T
Mr. T. Collins, 1977. U.S. title: The Man Without a Name. Coward, 1977
Murder by the Mile. Collins, 1975
No Return Ticket. Collins, 1966
No Through Road. Collins, 1965; Coward, 1966
Phantom Holiday. Collins, 1974 JL
Touchdown. Collins, 1979

RUSSELL, RAY. 1924-   . Ref: CA, TC.
The Case Against Satan. Obolensky, 1962; Souvenir, 1963

RUSSELL, RICHARD. SC: Angel Graham, in all titles.
Paperback. Belmont, 1979
Point of Reference. Belmont, 1979
Reunion. Belmont, 1979

RUSSELL, VICTOR
People of the Night. Harlequin, 1955

RUSSELL, W(ILLIAM) CLARK. 1844-1911. Ref: CC, EM.
Alone on a Wide, Wide Sea. Chatto, 1892; Taylor, 1892
-The Convict Ship. Chatto, 1895; Cassell (NYC), 1893
The Copsford Mystery; see Is He the Man?
-The Hunchback's Charge. Low, 1867
-In the Middle Watch. Chatto, 1885; Harper, 1885
Is He the Man? Tinsley, 1876. U.S. title: The Copsford Mystery; or, Is He the Man? New Amsterdam, 1896
-An Ocean Tragedy. Chatto, 1890; Harper, 1889
-The Phantom Death, and other stories. Chatto, 1895; Stokes, 1895 ss
The Tragedy of Ida Noble. Hutchinson, 1893; Appleton, 1891 [ship, 1838]

RUSSELL, WILLIAM. Pseudonyms: Inspector F, Waters, qq.v.

RUSSO, JOHN
The Majorettes. PB, 1979
-The Night of the Living Dead. Paperback Library, 1974 (Novelization of the movie.)
-Return of the Living Dead. Dale, 1978

RUTHERFORD, (SAMUEL) ANWORTH. 1877-   .
-The Bottle of Dust. Caxton, 1940
-Hidden Island. Little, 1927
-Sandlappers. Caxton, 1935
-Squaberry Canyon. Caxton, 1932

RUTHERFORD, CECILE
Desperate Encounter. Hale, 1971

RUTHERFORD, CONSTANCE. Ref: MP.
-The Blazing Star. Macdonald, 1914
The Door Without a Key. Hale, 1948
Double Entry. Heinemann, 1939
The Forgotten Terror. Heinemann, 1939
-The Lily Field. Hodder, 1913
-The Straight Furrow. Melrose, 1920

RUTHERFORD, DOUGLAS. Pseudonym of James Douglas Rutherford McConnell, 1915-   . Joint pseudonym with Francis Durbridge, 1912-   , q.v.: Paul Temple, q.v. Ref: CA, CC, TC.
The Black Leather Murders. Collins, 1966; Walker, 1966 [Fr.]
Clear the Fast Lane. Collins, 1971; Holt, 1972
Collision Course. Macmillan (London), 1978
Comes the Blind Fury. Faber, 1950 [Paris]
The Creeping Flesh. Collins, 1963; Walker, 1965 [Paris]
Flight into Peril; see Telling of Murder
The Gilt-Edged Cockpit. Collins, 1969; Doubleday, 1971
Grand Prix Murders. Collins, 1955 [It.]
-The Gunshot Grand Prix. Collins, 1972
Kick Start. Collins, 1973; Walker, 1974
-Killer on the Track. Collins, 1973
The Long Echo. Collins, 1957; Abelard, 1958 [It.]
Meet a Body. Faber, 1951
Murder Is Incidental. Collins, 1961
Mystery Tour. Collins, 1975; Walker, 1976 [It.]
On the Track of Death; see A Shriek of Tyres
The Perilous Sky. Collins, 1956
-Race Against the Sun. Collins, 1975
-Rally to the Death. Collins, 1974
Return Load. Collins, 1977; Walker, 1977 [It.]
A Shriek of Tyres. Collins, 1958. U.S. title: On the Track of Death. Abelard, 1959
Skin for Skin. Collins, 1968; Walker, 1968
Telling of Murder. Faber, 1952. U.S. title: Flight into Peril. Dodd, 1952 [It.]
Turbo. Macmillan (London), 1980; St. Martin's, 1980

RUTHERFORD, WARD
The Gallows Set. Bles, 1969
Great Big Laughing Hannah. Bles, 1970

RUTLAND, HARRIET. Ref: MP. SC: Mr. Winkley = W.
Bleeding Hooks. Skeffington, 1940. U.S. title: The Poison Fly Murder. Harrison-Hilton, 1940 W [Wales]
Blue Murder. Skeffington, 1950; Smith & Durrell, 1942
Knock, Murderer, Knock! Skeffington, 1938; Harrison-Hilton, 1939 W
The Poison Fly Murder; see Bleeding Hooks

RUTLAND, LYNN
The Death Ray Mystery. Northwestern, 1940 (3-act play.)
The Jeweled Cat. Northwestern, 1940 (3-act play.)

RUTLEDGE, (ARTHUR
Object of Jealousy. Barker, 1961; Tower, 1965

RUTLEDGE, BRETT. Pseudonym of Elliot (Harold) Paul, 1891-1958, q.v.
The Death of Lord Haw Haw. Random, 1940; Laurie, 1941

RUTLEDGE, MARYSE. Pseudonym of Mrs. Marice Rutledge Gibson Hale, 1884-   .
-The Sad Adventurers. Stokes, 1924; Constable, 1924
The Silver Peril. Fiction League, 1931

RUTLEDGE, NANCY. Pseudonym: Leigh Bryson, q.v. Born in Chi.; has degrees in chemistry and English literature.
Beware the Hoot Owl. Farrar, 1944; Boardman, 1946 [Midwest]
Blood on the Cat. Farrar, 1945; Boardman, 1946
Cry Murder. Dutton, 1954; Muller, 1955 [NYC]
Easy to Murder. Doubleday, 1951; Boardman, 1952 [New Eng.]
Emily Will Know. Doubleday, 1949. British title: Murder for Millions. Harrap, 1950. Reprinted in the U.S. under the British title: Bestseller, 1951 [NYC]
Escape into Danger. Hale, 1960
The Frightened Murderer. Random, 1957; Hale, 1959
Murder for Millions; see Emily Will Know
Murder on the Mountain. Muller, 1957
The Preying Mantis. Doubleday, 1947; Boardman, 1949 [Midwest]
Wanted for Murder. Random, 1956; Muller, 1956 [Midwest]

RUTTER, AMANDA
Murder at Eastover. Arcadia, 1958
Murder Is Where You Find It. Arcadia, 1959

RUTTER, OWEN. 1889-1944.
The Monster of Mu. Benn, 1932

RUUTH, MARIANNE. 1933-   . Ref: CA.
Game of Shadows. Ace, 1974
-Outbreak. Manor, 1977
Journey into Fear. Belmont, 1977
Tapestry of Terror. Ace, 1975

RUYLE, JOHN. SC: Turlock Loams, in all titles.
The Adventure of the Dancing Hen. Pequod, 1978
The Adventure of the Freckled Hand. Pequod, 1975
The Adventure of the Giant Bat of Sonoma. Pequod, 1976
The Adventure of the Jogging Man. Pequod, 1979
The Adventure of the Logophagous Client. Pequod, 1976
The Adventure of the Missing Third Quarter. Pequod, 1977
The Adventure of the Retired Weatherman. Pequod, 1976
His Last Vow. Pequod, 1977
Silver Haze. Pequod, 1978

RYAN, DONALD. Pseudonym.
The Dynamite Freaks. Manor, 1972

RYAN, FLOYD CURTISS
Murder on the Ranch. Nicholson, 1935; Empire, 1935 [N. Mex.]

RYAN, J. M.
Mother's Day. GM, 1969; Allen, 1970

RYAN, JESSICA (CADWALADER). 1914?-1972. Ref: CA. SC: Gregory (Grischa) Pavlov and O'Shaunnessey, in both titles.
Clue of the Frightening Coin; see The Man Who Asked Why
Exit Harlequin. Doubleday, 1947 [S.F.]
The Man Who Asked Why. Doubleday, 1945. Also published as: Clue of the Frightening Coin. Novel Selections, 194? [S.F.]

RYAN, JIM
The Bludgeon. Hale, 1973
The Vengeance Business. Hale, 1973

RYAN, LOFTUS A.
The Blue Waistcoat, and other stories. Drane, 1904 ss, some criminous

RYAN, DETECTIVE PATRICK. Pseudonym of A. Frank Pinkerton, q.v.
A Daring Horse Thief. Laird, 1890

RYAN, PAUL WILLIAM. 1906-1947. Pseudonym: Robert Finnegan, q.v.

RYAN, R(ACHEL) R.
Death of a Sadist. Jenkins, 1937
Echo of a Curse. Jenkins, 1939
Freak Museum. Jenkins, 1938
No Escape. Jenkins, 1940
The Right to Kill. Jenkins, 1936
The Subjugated Beast. Jenkins, 1938

RYAN, STELLA
Death Never Weeps. Coward, 1946 [N.J.]

RYAN, THOMAS J(OSEPH). 1942-   . A computer troubleshooter, in Calif.
The Adolescence of P-1. Macmillan, 1977

RYCK, FRANCIS
Account Rendered. Collins, 1975. U.S. title: The Sern Charter. Coward, 1976 (Translation of "Le Prix des Choses." Paris, 1973.)
Green Light, Red Catch. Collins, 1972; Stein, 1973 (Translation of "Feu Vert pour Poissons Rouge." Paris, 1967.) [Russ.]
Loaded Gun. Collins, 1971; Stein, 1971 (Translation of "Drole de Pistolet." Paris, 1969.) [Eng.]
Sacrificial Pawn. Collins, 1973; Stein, 1974 (Translation of "L'Incroyant." Paris, 1970.) [Fr.]
The Sern Charter; see Account Rendered
Undesirable Company. Collins, 1974; Stein, 1974 (Translation of "Le Compagnon Indesirable." Paris, 1972.) [Fr.]
Woman Hunt. Collins, 1972; Stein, 1972 (Translation of "Le Peau de Torpedo." Paris, 1968.) [Fr.]

RYDELL, FORBES. Joint pseudonym of (De Loris Florine) Stanton Forbes, 1923-   , q.v., and Helen B. Rydell. Other Forbes pseudonym: Tobias Wells, q.v.
Annalisa. Dodd, 1959; Gollancz, 1960 [La.]
If She Should Die. Doubleday, 1961; Gollancz, 1961 [Mass.]
No Questions Asked. Doubleday, 1963; Gollancz, 1963 [Mass.]
They're Not Home Yet. Doubleday, 1962; Gollancz, 1962 [New Eng.]

RYDELL, HELEN B. Joint pseudonym with (DeLoris Florine) Stanton Forbes, 1923-   , q.v.: Forbes Rydell, q.v.

RYDER, JONATHAN. Pseudonym of Robert Ludlum, 1927-   , q.v. Other pseudonym: Michael Shepherd, q.v.
The Cry of the Halidon. Delacorte, 1974; Weidenfeld, 1974 [Jam.]
Trevayne. Delacorte, 1973; Weidenfeld, 1974

RYDER, SABIN
Three on the Road. Avalon, 1963 [Calif.]

RYERSON, FLORENCE [FLORENCE RYERSON CLEMENTS], 1894- , and COLIN (CAMPBELL) CLEMENTS, 1894- . SC: Jimmy Lane = JL.
Blind Man's Buff. Long & Smith, 1933. British title: Sleep No More. Grayson, 1933 JL
The Borgia Blade. Appleton, 1937 [L.I.]
Fear of Fear. Appleton, 1931; Skeffington, 1931 JL [S.F.]
Seven Suspects. Appleton, 1930; Skeffington, 1930 JL [Calif.]
Shadows. Appleton, 1934 JL [L.A.]
Sky High (by Florence Ryerson and Alice Deur Miller, 1874-1942, q.v.). French (NYC), 1950 (3-act play.)
Sleep No More; see Blind Man's Buff
Stick 'Em Up! Penn, 1929 (1-act play.)
Through the Night. French, 1940 (Play)

RYERSON, MARTIN. Born in NYC; writer for numerous radio and TV network shows; pulp adventure writer.
Doctor vs. Murder. Vega, 1964
Press Agent for Murder. Vega, ca.1963

RYLAND, CLIVE. Pseudonym of Clive Ryland Priestley, 1892- . SC: Chief Insp. George Bassett, in at least those marked GB; Insp. Beck, in at least those marked B; Supt. Shannon, in at least those marked S. Set: Eng.
The Blind Beggar Murder. Hutchinson, 1935 B
The Case Against Alder. Hutchinson, 1941 B
The Case of the Back Seat Girl. Hutchinson, 1952 GB
The Case of the Brown-Eyed Housemaid. Hutchinson, 1951
The Dark Lady Murders. Hutchinson, 1940
Death at Screaming Pool. Hutchinson, 1937
Death Serves a Fault. Hutchinson, 1936
In Walks Murder. Hutchinson, 1951 GB
The Lone Crook Murders. Hutchinson, 1938
Monday Never Came. Hutchinson, 1947 GB
Murder in Queer Street. Hutchinson, 1941 GB
Murder of Margaret. Hutchinson, 1949
Murder on Bag Hill. Hutchinson, 1945 B
Murder on the Cliff. Grayson, 1934 S
Murder on the Common. Hutchinson, 1939 S
The Murders at the Manor. Grayson, 1933 S
The Notting Hill Murder. Grayson, 1932 S
The Selminster Murders. Hutchinson, 1952
So Death Came. Hutchinson, 1938
Three Died for Morson. Hutchinson, 1950
The Twelfth Night Murders. Hutchinson, 1939
Visitors for Venning. Hutchinson, 1948

RYLAND, JOHN KNOX. SC: Insp. Rodway, in all titles. Set: Eng.
Death Meets the Coroner. Paul, 1936
The Easter Guests Mystery. Paul, 1935
The Tragedy Near Tring. Paul, 1934

RYLEY, ELIZABETH
Homicide with Charm. Swan, 1946

RYMER, MALCOLM J. See: Anonymous.

S., I. Pseudonym of Isidor Schneider, 1896- .
-Doctor Transit. Boni, 1925

S., R., Esq. Pseudonym (?) of Richard Sickelmore.
The New Monk. Lane, 1798

SABATINI, RAFAEL. 1875-1950.
Turbulent Tales. Hutchinson, 1946 ss

SABER, ROBERT O. Pseudonym of Milton K. Ozaki, 1913- , q.v. SC: Carl Good, in at least those marked CG; Max Keene, in at least those marked MK.
The Affair of the Frigid Blonde. Handi-Books, 1950
The Black Dark Murders. Handi-Books, 1949. Canadian title (?): Out of the Dark. Harlequin, 1954 [Chi., acad.]
Chicago Woman; see The Dove
City of Sin. Original Novels, 1952
A Dame Called Murder. Graphic, 1955 MK [Chi.]
The Deadly Lover. Phantom, 1951 CG [Ind.]
The Dove. Handi-Books, 1951. Also published as: Chicago Woman. Pyramid, 1953 CG [Chi.]
Murder Doll. Phantom, 1952 CG [Chi.]
No Way Out. Phantom, 1952; Comyns, 1952
Out of the Night; see The Black Dark Murders
The Scented Flesh. Handi-Books, 1951 CG [Chi.]
Sucker Bait. Graphic, 1955 CG [Chi.]
A Time for Murder. Graphic, 1956 MK [Chi.]
Too Young to Die. Graphic, 1954 CG [Chi.]

SABER, W. J.
The Devious Defector. Banner, 1967

SABERHAGEN, FRED (THOMAS). 1930- . Ref: CA.
The Holmes-Dracula File. Ace, 1978 (Sherlock Holmes.) [Eng., 1897]

SABRE, DIRK. Pseudonym of John (Alfred Charles) Laffin, 1922- , q.v. Other pseudonyms: Carl Dekker, Mark Napier, qq.v.
Murder by Bamboo. Hammond, 1958

SACHAR, HOWARD M(ORLEY). 1928- . Ref: CA.
-The Man on the Camel. Times, 1980 [Isr., ca.1972]

SACHS, EMANIE (LOUISE) N(AHM)
The Octangle. Cape & Smith, 1930; Eyre, 1932 [NYC]

SACKVILLE, ORME
The Curse of Amen-Tah. Modern, 193? [Egypt]
The Island of Ghosts. Modern, 1935 [S. Pac.]
The Jungle Goddess. Modern, 193?
McLoon of the South Seas. Modern, 1935 [S. Pac.]
The Valley of Skulls. Modern, 1935

SACKVILLE-WEST, V(ICTORIA MARY). 1892-1962.
Devil at Westease. Doubleday, 1947

SADDLER, K. ALLEN. Pseudonym of Ronald Charles William Richards, 1923- . Ref: CA. SC: Dave Stevens, in all titles.
Gilt Edge. Elek, 1966
The Great Brain Robbery. Elek, 1966
Talking Turkey. Joseph, 1968

SADE, MARK. See: Roger Blake.

SADLER, MARK. Pseudonym of Dennis Lynds, 1924- , q.v. Other pseudonyms: William Arden, Nick Carter, Michael Collins, John Crowe, Carl Dekker, Maxwell Grant, Paul Shaw, qq.v. SC: Paul Shaw, in all titles.
Circle of Fire. Random, 1973 [Calif.]
The Falling Man. Random, 1970 [N.Y.]
Here to Die. Random, 1971 [L.A.]
Mirror Image. Random, 1972 [N.J.]

SADLIER, ANNA T(HERESA). 1854-1932.
Phileas Fox, Attorney. Ave Maria, 1909 [NYC]

SAFFRON, ROBERT. Has M.A. in playwriting from Yale School of Drama; TV writer, newspaper copy editor and feature writer in NYC, playwright.
The Demon Device. Putnam, 1979 [Ger., 1917]

SAFONOV, MADELEINE. See: Alice M. Dodge.

SAGE, DANA. Pseudonym of Glendon Allvine, 1893?-1977. Ref: CA. SC: Donald O'Keefe Adams, in both titles.
The Moon Was Red. Simon, 1944 [Bolivia]
The 22 Brothers. Simon, 1950 [Buen. A.]

SAGER, GORDON
The Formula. Lippincott, 1952. British title: The Rape of Europe. Chapman, 1952

SAGOLA, MARIO J. Pseudonym of a "well-known novelist."
The Manacle. Macmillan, 1978 [NYC]
The Naked Bishop. Coward, 1980 [NYC]

SAINT-ALBAN, DOMINIQUE. Novelist and screenwriter living in Paris.
Deja-Vu. St. Martin's, 1978 (Translation of "Les Etangs de Hollande." Paris, 1976.)

ST. AUBYN, ALAN. Pseudonym of Mrs. Francis Bridges Marshall.
-A Fair Imposter. White, 1898
A Fellow of Trinity, with Walt Wheeler. Chatto, 1890; Rand, 1890
-Mrs. Dunbar's Secret. Chatto, 1899
-The Red Van. Digby, 1906
-The Scarlet Lady. White, 1902
The Tremlett Diamonds. Chatto, 1895

ST. CLAIR, DEXTER. Pseudonym of Prentice Winchell, 1895- . Other pseudonyms: Spencer Dean, Jay de Bekker, Stewart Sterling, Dexter St. Clare, qq.v.
The Lady's Not for Living. GM, 1963; Muller pb, 1964 [Md.]

ST. CLAIR, EILEEN ADAMS
Murder Unplanned. Quality, 1949 [S.W.]
Murdered Man's Derby. Gramol, 1935

ST. CLAIR, ELIZABETH. Pseudonym of Susan Handler Cohen, 1938- . Ref: CA. SC: Marilyn Ambers = MA.
DeWitt Manor. Signet, 1977
The Jeweled Secret. Signet, 1978
Mansion in Miniature. Signet, 1977
Murder in the Act. Zebra, 1978 MA
Provenance House. Signet, 1976 [Pa.]
The Sandcastle Murders. Zebra, 1979 MA [Mass.]
Secret of the Locket. Signet, 1975
The Singing Harp. Signet, 1975 [Pa.]
Stonehaven. Signet, 1974
Trek or Treat. Zebra, 1980 MA

ST. CLAIR, IAN
Bled White. Stockwell, 1938

ST. CLAIR, JEANANNE
The House on Vickers' Island. Lenox, 1974; Remploy, 1975

ST. CLAIR, KATHERINE. Pseudonym of T(om) E. Huff, ca.1938- , q.v. Other pseudonyms: Edwina Marlow, Beatrice Parker, qq.v.
Room Beneath the Stairs. Bobbs, 1975 [Eng.]

ST. CLAIR, LEONARD. 1916- . Ref: CA.
The Emerald Trap. Putnam, 1974; Constable, 1975 [Paris]
A Fortune in Death. GM, 1972; Constable, 1976 [Mid. East]
Obsessions. Simon, 1980; Macmillan (London), 1980 [U.S., 1918-1958]

ST. CLAIR, MIKE
Daddy's Gone a'Hunting. Bantam, 1969 (Novelization of the movie.)

ST. CLAIR, ROBERT (R.). 1898- . All titles are plays, in 3 acts except where otherwise indicated.
Black Cat. Hardin, 1935
Caught in a Web. Eldridge, 1955
The Curse of Siva. Banner, 1940
The Curse of the Crystal Ball. Eldridge, 1938
The Death Bird. Northwestern, 1938
"The Fire-Bug." Northwestern, 1938
The Fury Within. Northwestern, 1951
The Ghost City. Penn, 1933
The Ghost House. (Cedar Rapids), 1946
"The Ghost in the Glass." Northwestern, 1934
The Ghost in the Wall. Bugbee, 1941
"Ghost of the Air." Northwestern, 1932
Ghostly Quarantine. Heuer, 1941
The Green Light. Northwestern, 1938
The High School Mystery. Northwestern, 1939 [acad.]
"The House of Greed." Northwestern, 1938
The House of Vengeance. Denison, 1949
Hurricane House. Penn, 1932
Kigi Sets a Trap. Denison, 1952
Margie and the Wolf Man. Eldridge, 1950
Mark Twain's A Double Barrelled Detective Story. Peterson, 1954 (Based on the novel by Mark Twain, q.v.)
The Mountain House Mystery. Heuer, 1942
Murder with Magic. Wetmore, 1941
The Mysterious Cane of Dr. Chang. Penn, 1934
Mystery in Hawaii. Denison, 1954 [Haw.]
Perilous Voyage. Northwestern, 1954 (Two acts.)
The Phantom Bells. Bugbee, 1935
The Phantom Bus. Dramatic, 1932
"The Phantom Dirigible." Northwestern, 1932
The Phantom Miner. Bugbee, 1940
"The Phantom Tiger." Northwestern, 1933
Queen from Mars. Northwestern, 1952
The Secret Door. Northwestern, 1939
The Singing Ghost. Northwestern, 1942
Sinister Station. Bugbee, 1936
"The Sixth Key." Northwestern, 1932
Susie and the F.B.I. Baker, 1958

The Television Mystery. Denison, 1949
Tiger House. Northwestern, 1930
The Tiger's Necklace. Northwestern, 1937
The Tower Room Mystery. Northwestern, 1932
The Trailer Mystery. Northwestern, 1954
The Vampire Bat. Peterson, 1940
Who Killed Ann Gage? Eldridge, 1943
The Woman in Red. Penn, 1941
The Zombie. Northwestern, 1941

ST. CLARE, DEXTER. Pseudonym of Prentice Winchell, 1895- . Other pseudonyms: Spencer Dean, Jay de Bekker, Stewart Sterling, Dexter St. Clair, qq.v.
Saratoga Mantrap. GM, 1951 [N.Y.]

ST. CLOUD, RUPERT. See: J(ohn Freeman) Fairfax-Blakeborough, 1883- .

ST. DAVID, JOHN. Pseudonym of David John Walsh, 1859-
The Vanishing of Ira Bouck. (Author), 1936

ST. DENNIS, MADELON. SC: Sydney Treherne, in both titles, both set in NYC.
The Death Kiss. Fiction League, 1932
The Perfumed Lure. Clode, 1932

ST. GEORGE, GEOFFREY
The Proteus Pact. Little, 1975; Gollancz, 1976 [Ger., WWII]

ST. GEORGE, JOSEPH
The Dangerous Impersonation. Hamilton, 1938

ST. GERMAIN, MARIE
Tales of the Weird and West Countree. Brendon, 1924 ss, some criminous

ST. JAMES, BERNARD. Pseudonym of Bernard William Treister, 1932- . Ref: CA.
April Thirtieth. Harper, 1978 [Paris, ca.1800]
-The Witch. Harper, 1979

ST. JAMES, IAN
The Money Stones. Collins, 1980; Atheneum, 1980

ST. JOHN, BARNETT. See: Phillip Andrews.

ST. JOHN, CHERYL. Pseudonym of Joseph Nathenson, q.v.
The Library of Alex Brandt. Manor, 1979

ST. JOHN, DARBY. Born in Wis., studied at U. of Wis. and U. of Chi.; living in L.A. in 1940s.
The Westgate Mystery. Random, 1941. Also published as: The Bride Brings Death. Mystery Novel Classic, 1943 [Wash.]

ST. JOHN, DAVID. Pseudonym of (Everette) Howard Hunt, 1918- , q.v. Other pseudonyms: Gordon Davis, Robert Dietrich, qq.v. SC: Peter Ward, in all titles.
The Coven. Weybright, 1971
Diabolus. Weybright, 1971 [Fr.]
Festival for Spies. Signet, 1966. Reprinted as by E. Howard Hunt: Signet, 1973 [Camb.]
Hazardous Duty; see On Hazardous Duty
The Mongol Mask. Weybright, 1968; Hale, 1969 [China]
On Hazardous Duty. Signet, 1965. British title: Hazardous Duty. Muller, 1966. Reprinted as by E. Howard Hunt: Signet, 1972 [Fr.]
One of Our Agents Is Missing. Signet, 1967. Reprinted as by E. Howard Hunt: Signet, 1973 [Tokyo]
Return from Vorkuta. Signet, 1965; Muller, 1967. Reprinted as by E. Howard Hunt: Signet, 1974 [Sp.]
The Sorcerers. Weybright, 1969
The Towers of Silence. Signet, 1966. Reprinted as by E. Howard Hunt: Signet, 1974 [India]
The Venus Probe. Signet, 1966. Reprinted as by E. Howard Hunt: Signet, 1974

ST. JOHN, GAIL. Pseudonym of Anita Grace. Dunsan House. Dell, 1969

ST. JOHN, GENEVIEVE
The Dark Watch. Belmont, 1966 [N.Y.]
Daughter of Evil. Belmont, 1967
Death in the Desert. Belmont, 1966 [Ariz.]
The Ghost of Channing House. Lancer, 1969
The Invisible Trap. Lancer, 1967 [Calif.]
Night of Evil. Belmont, 1967 [Md.]
The Secret of Dresden Farm. Belmont, 1971 [N.Y.]
The Secret of Kensington Manor. Belmont, 1965 [Conn.]
The Shadow on Spanish Swamp. Belmont, 1966 [La.]
The Sinister Voice. Belmont, 1967 [N.Y.]
Strangers in the Night. Paperback Library, 1967

ST. JOHN, NICOLE. Pseudonym of Norma Johnston.
Guinevere's Gift. Random, 1978; Heinemann, 1979 [Eng., ca.1905]
The Medici Ring. Random, 1975; Collins, 1976 [Boston, 1874]
Wychwood. Random, 1977; Heinemann 1978 [Eng., 1800s]

ST. JOHN, PERCY B(OLINGBROKE). 1821-1899.
The Blue Dwarf. Hogarth, ca.1870

SAINT-LAMBERT, PATRICK
Wheel of Fate. Mystique, 1980 (Translation of "La Fille Sans Nom." Paris, 1978.)

SAINT-LAURENT, CECIL. Pseudonym of Jacques Laurent-Cely, 1919- .
The Cautious Maiden. Crown, 1955 (Translation of "Une Sacree Salade." Paris, 1954.) [Paris]

ST. LEGER, WARHAM. 1850- . See: Henry Pottinger Stephens.

ST. MARS, F. 1883- .
Off the Beaten Track. Chambers, 1920 ss, some criminous

ST. MARTIN, THOMAS. Pseudonym of Peter Lincoln.
Jill. Dell, 1979 [S.F.]

ST. MICHAELS, DONELLA
The Prisoner. Lancer, 1966

ST. MOORE, A.
Angel Face Tatters the Kimono. International, 1969 (Translation from the French.) [Tokyo]

ST. THOMAS, HAROLD
Night of the Long Shadows. Harrap, 1967 [Australia]

SAKI. Pseudonym of Hector Hugh Munro, 1870-1916. See: James Fuller.

SAKOL, JEANNIE. 1928- . Ref: CA.
Hot 30. Delacorte, 1980

SAKS, ELMER ELIOT. Pseudonym of F(rank) Dubrez Fawcett, 1891-1968, q.v. Other pseudonyms: Spike Gordon (?), Griff, Ben Sarto, qq.v.
The Case of the Indiana Torturer. Bear, 1945
-Innocents on Broadway. Bear, 1944 [NYC]

SALA, GEORGE AUGUSTUS (HENRY). 1828-1896.
-Margaret Forster. Unwin, 1897
The Seven Sons of Mammon. Tinsley, 1862; Burnham, 1862

SALAS, FLOYD. 1931- . Born in Colo., educated in and living in Calif.
What Now My Love. Grove, 1969 [Calif., Mex.]

SALAWAY, RALPH. Pseudonym: Al Fray, q.v.

SALCIDO, CRAIG
Malago's Visit. Belmont, 1980

SALCROFT, ARTHUR
John Traile: Smuggler. Hutchinson, 1929
The Mystery of the Walled Garden. Hutchinson, 1928
The Twisted Grin. Hutchinson, 1929

SALE, RICHARD (BERNARD). 1911- . See also: Kenneth Robeson. Ref: CA, EM, TC. SC: Danile Webster = DW.
Benefit Performance. Simon, 1946 [L.A.]
Cardinal Rock. Cassell, 1940
Death at Sea. Popular Library, 1948. British title: Destination Unknown. World's Work, 1943 [ship]
Death Looks In; see Lazarus #7
Destination Unknown; see Death at Sea
For the President's Eyes Only. Simon, 1971. British title: The Man Who Raised Hell. Cassell, 1971
Home Is the Hangman. Popular Library, 1949 (Two novelets, one published separately in England as: Sailor, Take Warning. Big Ben, 1942.)
Lazarus Murder Seven; see Lazarus #7
Lazarus #7. Simon, 1942. British title: Death Looks In. Cassell, 1943. Also published as: Lazarus Murder Seven. Handi-Books, 1943 DW [L.A.]
The Man Who Raised Hell; see For the President's Eyes Only
Murder at Midnight. Popular Library, 1950 (2 novelets)
Not Too Narrow—Not Too Deep. Simon, 1936; Cassell, 1936 [Carib.]
Passing Strange. Simon, 1942 DW [L.A.]
Sailor, Take Warning; see Home Is the Hangman

SALINGER, PIERRE (EMILE GEORGE). 1925- . Ref: CA.
On the Instructions of My Government. Doubleday, 1971. British title: For the Eyes of the President Only. Collins, 1971 [Wash. D.C.]

SALISBURY, CAROLA (ISOBEL JULIEN). 1943- . Ref: CA.
Dark Inheritance. Collins, 1976; Doubleday, 1975 [Eng., ca.1850]
The Dolphin Summer. Collins, 1977; Doubleday, 1977 [ship]
Mallion's Pride. Collins, 1975. U.S. title: The Pride of the Trevallions. Doubleday, 1975
The Pride of the Trevallions; see Mallion's Pride
-The Shadowed Spring. Collins, 1980; Doubleday, 1980
The Winter Bride. Collins, 1978; Doubleday, 1978

SALISBURY, JOHN
The Baby Sitters. Secker, 1978; Atheneum, 1978. Also published as: The Hour Before Midnight. Dell, 1980
The Hour Before Midnight; see The Baby Sitters
Moscow Gold. Futura, 1980 [Moscow]

SALKELD, MICHAEL
Missing from the Shelf. Bles, 1936 [S. Am.]

SALMON, GERALDINE GORDON. 1897- . Pseudonym: J. G. Sarasin, q.v.

SALT, JONATHAN
Avenger at Large. Hale, 1977
Strange Fortune. Hale, 1976

SALT, SARAH. Pseudonym of Coralie von Werner Hobson, 1891- .
Murder for Love. Davies, 1937 (Two stories.)

SALTER, ELIZABETH (FULTON). 1925-1980. Ref: CA. SC: Insp. Michael Hornsley, in all titles.
Death in a Mist. Bles, 1957; Ace, 1968 [N.Z.]
Once Upon a Tombstone. Hutchinson, 1965; Ace, 1967 [Austria]
There Was a Witness. Bles, 1960; Ace, 1963 [Australia]
The Voice of the Peacock. Bles, 1962
Will to Survive. Bles, 1958; Ace, 1968 [Australia]

SALTER, MARION ARMOUR
The Cat's-Paw. Rinehart, 1952 [NYC]

SALTMARSH, MAX. SC: Archie Lumsden = AL.
The Clouded Moon. Joseph, 1937; Knopf, 1938 AL [Fr.]
Highly Inflammable. Joseph, 1936; Little, 1936 AL [Turk.]
Highly Unsafe. Joseph, 1936
Indigo Death. Joseph, 1938 AL [Ger.]

SALTUS, EDGAR (EVERTSON). 1855-1921. Ref: CA, CC.
The Ghost Girl. Boni, 1922
Mr. Incoul's Misadventure. Benjamin, 1887; Greening, 1903
-The Monster. Pulitzer, 1912
The Pace That Kills. Belford, 1889
The Paliser Case. Boni, 1919
A Transient Guest, and Other Episodes. Belford, 1889 ss, some criminous

SALVATO, SHARON ANNE. 1938- . Ref: CA.
Briarcliff Manor. Stein, 1974
The Meredith Legacy. Stein, 1975
Scarborough House. Stein, 1975; Collins, 1976

SALWEY, REGINALD E(RNEST)
-The Greater Call. Heath, 1916
-The Hand in the Web. Heath, 1925
-The Kestrel. Digby, 1911
My Masters. Heath, 1920 ss, some criminous
-A Peerage in Peril. Rivers, 1928
The Secret of Providence Lodge. Western Gazette, 1923 ss, some criminous
Wildwater Terrace. Digby, 1890

SAMACHSON, JOSEPH. 1906-1980. Pseudonym: John Miller, q.v.

SAMARAKIS, ANTONIS. 1919-   . Ref: CA.
　The Flaw. Weybright, 1969; Heinemann, 1969

SAMPSON, GEORGE (RICHARD). 1916-   . SC: Paola and George, in both titles.
　A Drug on the Market. Hale, 1967
　Playing with Fire. Hale, 1968

SAMPSON, RICHARD HENRY. 1896-1973. Pseudonym: Richard Hull, q.v.

SAMPSON, VICTOR. 1855-1940. SC: Insp. Downes and Sgt. Hopkins, in both titles.
　The Komani Mystery. Jenkins, 1930
　The Murder of Paul Rougier. Jenkins, 1928 [S. Afr.]

SAMSON, JOAN. 1937-1976. Ref: CA.
　The Auctioneer. Simon, 1975; Hodder, 1976 [N.H.]

SAMUEL, JOSEPH
　The Murdered Cliche. Quality, 1947

SAN ANTONIO. Pseudonym of F(rederic) Dard, q.v. Journalist who turned to novels and wrote some 65 about this character. SC: San Antonio, in all titles.
　Alien Archipelago. Joseph, 1971 (Translation of "L'Archipel des Malotrus." Paris, 1969.)
　Crooks' Hill. Sphere, 1969; Paperback Library, 1969 (Translation of "Le Gala des Emplumes." Paris, 1963.) Title on inside of British edition reads: Puck of Crooks' Hill.) [Fr.]
　From A to Z. Duckworth, 1968; Paperback Library, 1970 (Translation of "De l'A Jusqu'a Z." Paris, 1961.) [Paris]
　The Hatchet Man. Paperback Library, 1970 (Translation of "Vas-y Beru." Paris, 1960.) [Fr.]
　Knights of Arabia. Duckworth, 1969; Paperback Library, 1970 (Translation of "Berurier au Serail." Paris, 1964.) [Saud. Arab.]
　Puck of Crooks' Hill; see Crook's Hill
　Stone Dead. Sphere, 1969; Paperback Library, 1970 (Translation of "C'Est Mort et ca ne Sait Pas." Paris, 1954.) [Paris]
　The Strangler. Duckworth, 1968; Paperback Library, 1970 (Translation of "La Fin des Haricots." Paris, 1961.) [Paris]
　The Sub Killers. Joseph, 1971 (Translation of "La Rate au Court Bouillon." Paris, 1958.) [Paris]
　Thugs and Bottles. Sphere, 1969; Paperback Library, 1970 (Translation of "Du Brut Pour les Brutes." Paris, 1960.) [Paris]
　Tough Justice. Duckworth, 1967; Norton, 1969 (Translation of "Messieurs les Hommes." Paris, 1955.) [Fr.]

SANBORN, B. X. Pseudonym of Bill S(anborn) Ballinger, 1912-1980, q.v. Other pseudonym: Frederic Freyer, q.v.
　The Doom-Maker. Dutton, 1959; Boardman, 1959. Also published as: The Blonde on Borrowed Time. Zenith, 1960 [NYC]

SANBORN, RUTH BURR. 1894-1942. SC: Angeline Tredennick, in both titles.
　Murder by Jury. Little, 1932; Jarrolds, 1933
　Murder on the Aphrodite. Macmillan, 1935; Jarrolds, 1936 [Maine]

SANCHEZ, THOMAS. 1944-   . Ref: CA.
　Zoot-Suit Murders. Dutton, 1978; Secker, 1980 [L.A., 1943]

SAND, MARGARET. 1932-   . Ref: CA.
　-The Chanting of Children. Coward, 1978; Hale, 1979

SANDBERG, BERENT. Joint pseudonym of Mark Berent and Peter Lars Sandberg, 1934-   , q.v.
　Brass Diamonds. NAL, 1980 [Camb.]

SANDBERG, H. W.
　The Crazy Quilt Murders. Phoenix, 1938

SANDBERG, PETER LARS. 1934-   . Joint pseudonym with Mark Berent: Berent Sandberg, q.v. Ref: CA.
　King's Point. Playboy, 1978 [Carib.]
　Stubb's Run. Houghton, 1979; Hale, 1981
　Wolf Mountain. Playboy, 1975 [Colo.]

SANDERS, BRUCE. Ref: CC. SC: Howard Digburn, in at least those marked HD. Set: Eng.
　Blonde Blackmail. Jenkins, 1945
　Code of Dishonour. Jenkins, 1964 HD
　Deadly Jade. Jenkins, 1947
　Feminine for Spy. Jenkins, 1967 HD
　Kiss for a Killer. Jenkins, 1953; Roy, 1956
　Madame Bluebeard. Jenkins, 1951; Roy, 1957
　Midnight Hazard. Jenkins, 1955
　Pink Silk Alibi. Jenkins, 1946
　The Scarlet Widow. Jenkins, 1943
　Secret Dragnet. Jenkins, 1956; Roy, 1957 HD
　Tawny Menace. Jenkins, 1948
　To Catch a Spy. Jenkins, 1958; Roy, 1958 HD [Fr.]

SANDERS, CHARLES WESLEY
　The Memory Man. Lloyd's, 1921
　Murder to the North-West. Collins, 1931
　Murder Trail. Collins, 1929 [West]
　Poison Lockspur. Collins, 1930

SANDERS, DAPHNE. Pseudonym of Georgiana Ann Randolph Craig, 1908-1957. Other pseudonyms: Craig Rice, Michael Venning, qq.v. See also: Gypsy Rose Lee; and: George Sanders, 1906-1972.
　To Catch a Thief. Dial, 1943 [NYC]

SANDERS, DAVID. 1915-
　The Queen Sends for Mrs. Chadwick. Centaur, 1979; St. Martin's, 1980

SANDERS, DOROTHY (LUCIE). 1917-   . Ref: CA.
　Monday in Summer. Hodder, 1961

SANDERS, GEORGE. 1906-1972. Actor.
　Crime on My Hands. Simon, 1944; Edwards, 1948 (Ghost-written by Craig Rice, 1908-1957, q.v., and Cleve Cartmill, 1908-1964.) [Calif.]
　Stranger at Home. Simon, 1946; Pilot, 1947 (Ghost-written by Leigh Brackett, 1915-1978, q.v.) [L.A.]

SANDERS, JAMES (EDWARD). 1911-   .
　Frontiers of Fear. Hale, 1980

SANDERS, JOHN (EDWARD). 1930-   . SC: Nicholas Pym, in all titles.
　-Cromwell's Cavalier. Hale, 1968 [Eng., 1650s]
　A Firework for Oliver. Heinemann, 1964; Walker, 1965 [Fr., 1654]
　The Hat of Authority. Heinemann, 1965 [Carib., 1656]
　Roundhead Retreat. Hale, 1971 [1600s]
　Without Trumpet or Drum. Heinemann, 1966 [1600s]

SANDERS, LAWRENCE. 1920-   . Pseudonym: Lesley Andress, q.v. Ref: CA, TC. SC: Edward X. Delaney = ED; Peter Tangent = PT.
　The Anderson Tapes. Putnam, 1970; Allen, 1970 [NYC]
　The First Deadly Sin. Putnam, 1973; Allen, 1974 ED [NYC]
　The Second Deadly Sin. Putnam, 1977; Hart-Davis, 1978 ED [NYC]
　The Sixth Commandment. Putnam, 1979; Granada, 1979 [N.Y.]
　The Tangent Factor. Putnam, 1978; Hart-Davis, 1978 PT [Afr.]
　The Tangent Objective. Putnam, 1976; Hart-Davis, 1977 PT [Afr.]
　The Tenth Commandment. Putnam, 1980; Granada, 1981 [NYC]
　-The Tomorrow File. Putnam, 1975; Corgi, 1977

SANDERS, LEONARD. 1929-   . Ref: CA. SC: Clay Loomis, in both titles.
　The Hamlet Ultimatum. Scribner, 1979
　The Hamlet Warning. Scribner, 1976; Allen, 1977

SANDERS, MARION K., 1905-1977, and MORTIMER S. EDELSTEIN. Ref for Sanders: CA.
　The Bride Laughed Once. Farrar, 1943 [N.Y.]

SANDERS, W. FRANKLIN
　The Whip Hand. GM, 1961 [Dallas]

SANDERSON, AVERIL D.
　Long Shadows. Constable, 1935

SANDERSON, (RONALD) DOUGLAS. 1922-   . Born in Eng., Canadian citizen; author of radio plays and documentaries. Pseudonyms: Martin Brett, Malcolm Douglas, qq.v.
　Black Reprieve. Hale, 1965
　Catch a Fallen Starlet. Avon, 1960

Cry Wolfram. Secker, 1959. U.S. title: Mark It for Murder. Avon, 1959 [Sp.]
　Dark Passions Subdue. Avon, 1953
　A Dead Bullfighter. Hale, 1975
　The Final Run. Secker, 1956
　Lam to Slaughter. Hale, 1964
　Mark It for Murder; see Cry Wolfram
　Night of the Horns. Secker, 1958
　No Charge for Framing. Hale, 1969 [Cuba]

SANDFORD, KEN(NETH LESLIE). 1915-   . SC: Max Lamb, in both titles.
　Dead Reckoning. Hutchinson, 1955 [N.Z.]
　Dead Secret. Long, 1957

SANDROFF, RONNI. 1943-   . Ref: CA.
　Fighting Back. Knopf, 1978 [NYC]

SANDS, CHRISTOPHER NICHOLSON JOHNSTON. 1857-1934. Pseudonym: Christopher N(icholson) Johnston, q.v.

SANDS, LESLIE. 1921-   . TV actor and playwright in Eng.
　Intent to Murder. English Theatre, 1953 (Play.)
　Something to Hide. English Theatre, 1953 (3-act play.) Novel based on this play: Muller, 1965

SANDS, MARTIN. Pseudonym of John (Frederick) Burke, 1922-   , q.v. Other pseudonyms: Jonathan Burke, Robert Miall, qq.v. Joint pseudonym with his wife: Harriet Esmond, q.v. Joint pseudonym with George Theiner, 1927-   : Jonathan George, q.v.
　The Jokers. Pan, 1967 (Novelization of the movie.)
　Maroc 7. Pan, 1967 (Novelization of the movie.) [Mor.]

SANDULESCU, JACQUES and ANNIE GOTTLIEB. Sandulescu is the author of autobiographical works; NYC actor. Gottlieb is a book reviewer, article writer, and magazine publisher in NYC.
　The Carpathian Caper. Putnam, 1975 [Rum.]

SANDYS, JAMES. SC: James Charlesworth, in at least those marked JC; Insp. Millwall, in at least those marked M; Mr. Springfield, in at least those marked S. Set: Eng.
　And So We Die. Paul, 1941
　Darkest Under the Lamp. Paul, 1949 S
　The Death Echo. Paul, 1948
　Death Finds the Gloves. Paul, 1939
　Death Is Merciful. Paul, 1948 JC
　From Laughter to Death. Paul, 1945
　Green Eye of Death. Paul, 1943 M,JC
　The Hand Without Mercy. Paul, 1940 JC
　Harlequin of Doom. Paul, 1939
　The Lodestar of Death. Paul, 1946 S
　The Lone Commando. Paul, 1944
　The Man Who Wasn't There. Paul, 1953 S
　The Silken Shroud. Paul, 1947
　A Stripe for a Stripe. Paul, 1938 JC [Mid. East]
　Thicker Than Water. Paul, 1941 S
　This Is Death Calling. Paul, 1943
　The Vengeance Due. Paul, 1938 M
　Voices of the Storm. Paul, 1940

SANDYS, MILES
　Michael Carmichael. Laird, 1902

SANDYS, OLIVER. Pseudonym of Marguerite Helene Jervis Evans, 1894-   .
　Chicane. Long, 1912

SANFORD, HARRY. See: Max Lamb.

SANFORD, JOHN
　Make My Bed in Hell. Avon, 1954

SANFORD, URSULA
　The Poisoned Anemones. PB, 1974 [Wales]

SANG, BOB and DUSTY SANG
　Deadly Companions. Belmont, 1978
　The Terror Chronicle. Sang, 1979

SANG, DUSTY. See: Bob Sang.

SANGER, JOAN
　The Case of the Missing Corpse. Green Circle, 1936 [Havana]

SANGSTER, JIMMY. 1927-   . Ref: CA. SC: Katy Touchfeather = KT; John Smith = JS.
　Foreign Exchange. Triton, 1968; Norton, 1968 JS [Russ.]
　The Man Who Could Cheat Death, with Barre Lyndon, q.v. Avon, 1959
　Private I. Triton, 1967; Norton, 1967 JS
　The Terror of the Tongs. Digit, 1962 (Novelization of the movie.)

354 / Sann, Paul

Touchfeather. Triton, 1968; Norton, 1968   KT
Touchfeather, Too. Triton, 1970; Norton, 1970   KT   [Afr.]
Your Friendly Neighborhood Death Pedlar. Triton, 1971; Dodd, 1972 [S. Am.]

SANN, PAUL. 1914-   . Ref: CA.
Dead Heat. Dial, 1974 [NYC]

SANTIAGO, V. J. House name. SC: Joseph Madden (The Vigilante), in all titles.
Dead End Delivery. Pinnacle, 1976 [Det.]
Detour to a Funeral. Pinnacle, 1975 [L.A.]
An Eye for an Eye. Pinnacle, 1975 [NYC]
Kill or Be Killed. Pinnacle, 1976 [S.F.]
Knock, Knock, You're Dead. Pinnacle, 1976
This Gun for Justice. Pinnacle, 1978 [Wash. D.C.]

SAPIR, RICHARD. 1936-   . Ref: CA. See also: next entry.
Bressio. Random, 1975 [NYC]

SAPIR, RICHARD, 1936-   , and WARREN (B.) MURPHY, 1933-   , q.v. See also: previous entry. SC: Remo Williams (The Destroyer), in all titles (see also Warren Murphy).
Acid Rock. Pinnacle, 1973; Corgi, 1975
Assassin's Play-Off. Pinnacle, 1975; Corgi, 1978 [China]
Bottom Line. Pinnacle, 1979; Corgi, 1981 (By Murphy alone.)
Brain Drain. Pinnacle, 1976; Corgi, 1978 [L.A.]
Chained Reaction. Pinnacle, 1978; Corgi, 1980 [South]
Child's Play. Pinnacle, 1976; Corgi, 1978
Chinese Puzzle. Pinnacle, 1972; Corgi, 1973 [China]
Created: The Destroyer. Pinnacle, 1971; Corgi, 1973 [N.J.]
Deadly Seeds. Pinnacle, 1975; Corgi, 1978
Death Check. Pinnacle, 1971; Corgi, 1973 [Va.]
Death Therapy. Pinnacle, 1972; Corgi, 1974
Dr. Quake. Pinnacle, 1972; Corgi, 1974 [Calif.]
The Final Death. Pinnacle, 1977; Corgi, 1979 (By Murphy and Richard S. Meyers.) [Tex.]
Funny Money. Pinnacle, 1975; Corgi, 1977
The Head Men. Pinnacle, 1977; Corgi, 1979 [Wash. D.C.]
Holy Terror. Pinnacle, 1975; Corgi, 1978 [S.F.]
In Enemy Hands. Pinnacle, 1977; Corgi, 1978
Judgment Day. Pinnacle, 1974; Corgi, 1976
Kill or Cure. Pinnacle, 1973; Corgi, 1975 [Miami]
Killer Chromosomes. Pinnacle, 1978; Corgi, 1979
Last Call. Pinnacle, 1978; Corgi, 1981 (By Murphy alone.)
The Last Temple. Pinnacle, 1977; Corgi, 1978 (By Murphy and Richard S. Meyers.) [Isr.]
Last War Dance. Pinnacle, 1974; Corgi, 1977 [Mont.]
Mafia Fix. Pinnacle, 1972; Corgi, 1974 [N.J.]
Mugger Blood. Pinnacle, 1977; Corgi, 1979 [NYC]
Murder Ward. Pinnacle, 1974; Corgi, 1976 [Md., hosp.]
Murder's Shield. Pinnacle, 1973; Corgi, 1975 [N.Y.]
Oil Slick. Pinnacle, 1974; Corgi, 1977
Power Play. Pinnacle, 1979; Corgi, 1981 (By Murphy alone.) [Ind.]
Ship of Death. Pinnacle, 1977; Corgi, 1979 [ship]
Slave Safari. Pinnacle, 1973; Corgi, 1976 [Afr.]
Summit Chase. Pinnacle, 1973; Corgi, 1975 (By Murphy alone.) [Afr.]
Sweet Dreams. Pinnacle, 1976; Corgi, 1978 (By Murphy and Richard S. Meyers.) [St. Louis]
Terror Squad. Pinnacle, 1973; Corgi, 1975
Union Bust. Pinnacle, 1973; Corgi, 1974 (By Murphy alone.) [Chi.]
Voodoo Die. Pinnacle, 1978; Corgi, 1980 [Carib.]

SAPPER. Pseudonym of H(erman) C(yril) McNeile, 1888-1937, q.v. This author's works have variously appeared under his own name and/or his pseudonym, and are all collectively listed under his real name herein.

SARASIN, J. G. Pseudonym of Geraldine Gordon Salmon, 1897-   .
-Across the Border. Hutchinson, 1933
-The Ambush. Hutchinson, 1940
 The Black Glove. Hutchinson, 1925; Doran, 1926
-The Cargo of Gold. Hutchinson, 1933
-The Caspian Song. Hutchinson, 1935
-Chronicles of a Cavalier. Hutchinson, 1924
-City of Refuge. Hutchinson, 1928
-The Corsair. Hutchinson, 1951
-The Court of Dusty Feet. Hutchinson, 1942
-The Dark Turnpike. Hutchinson, 1943
-The Drums of War. Hutchinson, 1956
-The Eighth Wonder. Hutchinson, 1952
 Fleur de Lys. Hutchinson, 1929; Doubleday, 1929 [Fr., 1600s]
 Flittermouse. Hutchinson, 1931
-The Flying Palatine, and other stories. Hutchinson, 1935   ss
-The House of the Winds. Hutchinson, 1941
-Invasion Coast. Hutchinson, 1948
-The Iron Mask. Hutchinson, 1928
-The Island of Unrest. Hutchinson, 1955
-Lady and Leader. Hutchinson, 1931
-The Lost Duchess. Hutchinson, 1927
-The Lost Kingdom. Hutchinson, 1954
-The Lovers of Astrea. Hutchinson, 1930
-The Magpie on the Gallows. Hutchinson, 1953
-The Man from Troy. Hutchinson, 1937
 The Mystery of Martin Guerre. Hutchinson, 1934 [Fr., 1500s]
-No Land Without Liberty. Hutchinson, 1962
-A Phoenix in Castile. Hutchinson, 1950
-The Pirate's Pack. Hutchinson, 1934
-Quest of Youth. Hutchinson, 1923
-Remember! Hutchinson, 1946
-Six Ropes for Glory. Hutchinson, 1937
-Southern Fires. Hutchinson, 1929
-Star Above Paris. Hutchinson, 1938
-The State Torch. Hutchinson, 1944
-Storm-Bound. Hutchinson, 1930
-Thunderbolt. Hutchinson, 1958
-Tiger-Heart. Hutchinson, 1936
-Wings Without Freedom. Hutchinson, 1951

SARDOU, VICTORIEN. 1831-1908.
The Black Pearl. Brentano's, 1888. 3-act play version: French (NYC), 1915

SARGEANT, ADELINE. Variant spelling sometimes encountered on the U.S. editions of works by (Emily Frances) Adeline Sergeant, 1851-1904, q.v.

SARGENT, PATRICIA
Mortal Encounter. Avon, 1979; Piatkus, 1979

SARIOLA, MAURI. Born in Helsinki, studied law; newspaper editor.
The Helsinki Affair. Cassell, 1970; Walker, 1971 (Translation of "Lavaentien Laki." Finland, 1970.) [Fin.]
The Torvick Affair. Walker, 1972 [Helsinki]

SARL, ARTHUR J.
The Mystery of Flat 60. Aldine, 1921
Racing Ramp. Hutchinson, 1939

SARMIENTO, DOROTHY
Roles and Relations. Chapman, 1956

SARNE, MICHAEL. Pseudonym of T(homas) Arthur Plummer, q.v.
-The Scarlet Saint. Paul, 1932

SAROYAN, WILLIAM. 1908-1981. Ref: CA. See: Henry Cecil.

SARSFIELD, MAUREEN. SC: Insp. Lane Parry, in both titles. Set: Eng.
Dinner for None. Nicholson, 1948. U.S. title: A Party for Lawty. Coward, 1948
Green December Fills the Graveyard. Pilot, 1945; Coward, 1946
A Party for Lawty; see Dinner for None

SARTO, BEN. House name. Many of these were written by F(rank) Dubrez Fawcett, 1891-1968, q.v. Other Fawcett pseudonyms: Spike Gordon (?), Griff, Elmer Eliot Saks, qq.v. SC: Miss Otis, in at least those marked O.
Baby Moll. Modern Fiction, 1957
Beech of the Boulevard. Modern Fiction, 1952
Blonde Horror. Modern Fiction, 1956
Blood and Blondes. Modern Fiction, 1954
Bodies Fetch Good Prices. Beacon, 1954
Bowery Birdie. Modern Fiction, 1947 [NYC]
Call Me Shameless. Beacon, 1954
Chain-Gang Queenie. Beacon, 1955
Chicago Dames. Modern Fiction, 1949 [Chi.]
City of Sin. Modern Fiction, 1952
Claws for a Cutie. Modern Fiction, 1955
Corpse in the Cabin. Modern Fiction, 1954
Corrupted Women. Modern Fiction, 1952
Crooked Lady. Modern Fiction, 1956
Dames for Hire. Beacon, 1953
Dangerous Blonde. Modern Fiction, 1957
The Dead Don't Cry. Modern Fiction, 1956
Dead Reckoning. Modern Fiction, 1955
Death by the Seine. Modern Fiction, 1956 [Fr.]
Death for a Dumb-Bell. Modern Fiction, 1957
Death Rides the Train. Modern Fiction, 1954
Decoy Babes. Beacon, 1956
Diamonds for a Blonde. Modern Fiction, 1958
Disillusioned. Modern Fiction, 1955
Down-River Dolls. Modern Fiction, 1957
Dread. Modern Fiction, 1955
Duchess of Dope. Modern Fiction, 1948
Dynamite. Modern Fiction, 1956
Dynamite Doll. Beacon, 1954
Eastside Exposure. Modern Fiction, 1955
Elsa the Terrible. Modern Fiction, 1954
Espionage. Modern Fiction, 1957
Fear. Modern Fiction, 1955
Floozie Takes Lawman. Modern Fiction, 1952
Gangster Lady. Modern Fiction, 1953
Gorilla Moll. Modern Fiction, 1953
Grand Graft Hotel. Modern Fiction, 1947
Hi-Jacker's Lady. Modern Fiction, 1949
Hire Me a Rope. Modern Fiction, 1958
Hot Dames Die Cold. Modern Fiction, 1958
House of Sin. Modern Fiction, 1956
I Kill 'Em Inch by Inch. Modern Fiction, 1949
I'll Get By. Modern Fiction, 1948
"Jews" Pellegrini. Modern Fiction, 1947
Killer in Love. Modern Fiction, 1948
Kiss Me, Kill Me. Modern Fiction, 1953
Lady Bites. Milestone, 1953
Lidy Takes Plenty. Modern Fiction, 1952
Manhattan Terrors. Modern Fiction, 1952 [NYC]
Miami for Murder. Modern Fiction, 1954 [Miami]
Micky's Hide. Modern Fiction, 1956
Million Dollar Murder. Modern Fiction, 1957
Miss Otis Blows Town. Milestone, 1953 O
Miss Otis Comes to Piccadilly. Modern Fiction, 1949 O
Miss Otis Desires. Milestone, 1954 O
Miss Otis Gets Fresh. Milestone, 1954 O
Miss Otis Goes French. Milestone, 1953 O
Miss Otis Goes Up. Modern Fiction, 1949 O
Miss Otis Has a Daughter. Modern Fiction, 1948 O
Miss Otis Hits Back. Milestone, 1953 O
Miss Otis Makes a Date. Milestone, 1953 O
Miss Otis Makes Hay. Modern Fiction, 1954 O
Miss Otis Moves In. Milestone, 1953 O
Miss Otis Plays Ball. Milestone, 1954 O
Miss Otis Plays Eve. Milestone, 1954 O
Miss Otis Relents. Milestone, 1954   O
Miss Otis Says Yes. Milestone, 1953 O
Miss Otis Takes the Rap. Modern Fiction, 1953 O
Miss Otis Throws a Come-Back. Modern Fiction, 1947 O
The Oldest Profession. Modern Fiction, 1952
The Pace Grows Hotter. Modern Fiction, 1956
Pinday and the "White Slaver". Modern Fiction, 1947
Pleasure Girl. Modern Fiction, 1957
Queen of Crook's Harem. Modern Fiction, 1949
Rebecca of the Snatch Racket. Modern Fiction, 194?
Riviera Nights. Modern Fiction, 1958 [Fr.]
Rope for a Lady. Modern Fiction, 1954
Satan Is Blonde. Modern Fiction, 1953
She Ruled with a Rod. Modern Fiction, 1947
Sidewalk Floozie. Modern Fiction, 194?
Sinister Wooing. Modern Fiction, 1954
Snake Hips. Modern Fiction, 1954
Soho Spiv. Modern Fiction, 1948
Stay Out of Menchis. Modern Fiction, 1958

SUSIE Comes to Soho. Beacon, 1953
Swamp Fever. Modern Fiction, 1957
Take Over, Angel. Modern Fiction, 1955
Take What's Coming. Modern Fiction, 1952
There's Always a Dame. Modern Fiction, 1949
They Burn for Me. Modern Fiction, 1954
Tigress of Brazil. Modern Fiction, 1952 [Brazil]
Tombstones Are Free to Quitters. Modern Fiction, 1947
Vice City. Modern Fiction, 1957
Vice Volcano. Modern Fiction, 1956
The Vicious Breed. Modern Fiction, 1957
Viper's Brood. Modern Fiction, 1954
Where You Throw Blood. Modern Fiction, 1957
The Wolf Shows His Teeth. Modern Fiction, 1952
You Die in Valpaso. Modern Fiction, 1957

SATCHELL, WILLIAM
The Greenstone Door. Sidgwick, 1914

SATHIANADHAN, KAMALA
Detective Janaki. Thacker (Bombay), 1944

SATTERTHWAIT, WALTER
Cocaine Blues. Dell, 1980

SAUL, JOHN RALSTON
The Birds of Prey. McGraw, 1978; Macmillan (London), 1977 [Fr.]
-Comes the Blind Fury. Dell, 1980 [Mass.]
Cry for the Strangers. Dell, 1979; Coronet, 1980 [N.W.]
-Punish the Sinners. Dell, 1978; Coronet, 1979
-Suffer the Children. Dell, 1977; Coronet, 1978

SAUL, OSCAR. Pseudonym of Oscar Saul Halpern, 1932-   . Ref: CA.
The Dark Side of Love. Harper, 1974; Cassell, 1975 [L.A.]

SAUNDERS, ALLEN. 1899-   . Ref: CA.
The Big Cough. French, 1939 (1-act play.)
Three Taps at Twelve. French, 1933 (3-act play.)

SAUNDERS, CLARE CASTLER. See also: Babs Lee.
Design for Treachery. Scribner, 1947 [NYC]

SAUNDERS, DAVID. Pseudonym of Daniel Sontup, 1922-   . Ref: CA.
M-Squad. Belmont, 1962 (Novelization of the TV series.)

SAUNDERS, HILARY (AIDEN) ST. GEORGE. 1898-1951. Joint pseudonym with John (Leslie) Palmer, 1885-1944, q.v.: Francis Beeding, q.v. Joint pseudonym with Geoffrey Dennis: Barum Browne, q.v. Joint pseudonym with John deVere Loder: Cornelius Cofyn, q.v.
The Sleeping Bacchus. Joseph, 1951

SAUNDERS, LAWRENCE. Joint pseudonym of Burton Davis, 1893-   , and Clare Ogden Davis, 1892-   . SC: Wylie King and Nels Lundberg, in at least those marked K&L.
The Columnist Murder. Farrar, 1931 K&L [NYC]
The Devil's Den. Covici, 1933 K&L [Conn.]
-Six Weeks. Covici, 1932
Smoke Screen. Sears, 1933 [Houston]

SAUNDERS, MONTAGU
-The Mystery in the Drood Family. Cambridge University Press, 1914

SAUNDERS, THEODORE. Joint pseudonym with Mary Means: Denis Scott, q.v.

SAUNDERS, THOMAS J.
The Riddle of the Red Devil Costume. Vantage, 1975

SAVA, GEORGE. Pseudonym of George Alexis Milkomanovich Milkomane, 1903-   . Other pseudonyms: George Braddon, Peter Conway, Alec Redwood, qq.v.
Cocaine for Breakfast. Hale, 1973

SAVAGE, DAVID. Pseudonym of Harry Hossent, 1916-   , q.v.
The Spy Who Got Off at Las Vegas. Jenkins, 1969

SAVAGE, GEORGE M(ILTON), 1904-   , and EDOUARD H. PELTRET
Watch Your Step. Longmans, 1931 (3-act play.)

SAVAGE, JENNY. ca.1946-   .
The Nemesis Club. Macmillan (London), 1977; St. Martin's, 1978

SAVAGE, JOHN
A Shady Place to Die. Dell, 1957 [Ariz.]

SAVAGE, MARY
The Coach Draws Near. Dodd, 1964 [Calif.]

SAVAGE, RICHARD. Pseudonym of Ivan Roe, 1913-   . SC: Dr. Ferenc, in at least those marked F. Set: Eng.
The Horrible Hat. Jarrolds, 1948 F
The Innocents. Museum, 1958; Washburn, 1959
The Lightning's Eye. Museum, 1957
Murder for Fun. Jarrolds, 1947 F
Murder Goes to School. Jarrolds, 1946 [acad.]
The Poison and the Root. Jarrolds, 1950 F
Stranger's Meeting. Museum, 1957
When the Moon Died. Ward, 1955

SAVAGE, RICHARD HENRY. 1846-1903.
-After Many Years. Neely, 1895
-The Anarchist. Neely, 1894; Routledge, 1894. Also published as: Storm Signals. Rand, 1897
Brought to Bay. Home, 1900; White, 1900
Captain Landon. Rand, 1899; White, 1899
-A Captive Princess. Home, 1898; Routledge, 1898
Checked Through, Missing Trunk No. 17580. Rand, 1896; Routledge, 1896 [NYC]
Commander Leigh; see Special Orders for Commander Leigh
A Daughter of Judas. Neely, 1894; Routledge, 1894
-Delilah of Harlem. American News, 1893; Routledge, 1894
-An Egyptian Tragedy, and other stories. Digby, 1902 (U.S. title?) ss
-An Exile from London. Home, 1896; Routledge, 1897
-A Fascinating Traitor. Home, 1897; Routledge, 1897
-For a Young Queen's Bright Eyes. Home, 1902; White, 1902
-For Her Life. Rand, 1897; Routledge, 1897
-For Life and Love. Neely, 1893; Routledge, 1894
-The Golden Rapids of High Life. Home, 1902; French, 1903
-The Hacienda on the Hill. Home, 1899; Routledge, 1899
-Her Foreign Conquest. Home, 1896; Routledge, 1897
-His Cuban Sweetheart. Home, 1895; Routledge, 1896, with Mrs. Archibald Clavering Gunter
-In the Emperor's Villa. Ward, 1906 (U.S. title?)
-In the Esbekieyeh Gardens, and other stories. Routledge, 1901 ss (U.S. title?)
-In the Old Chateau. Neely, 1895; Routledge, 1895
-In the Shadow of the Pyramids. Rand, 1898; Routledge, 1898
-in the Swim. Rand, 1898; Routledge, 1898
The King's Secret. Home, 1900; White, 1901
The Last Traitor of Long Island. Home, 1903; French, 1903
The Little Lady of Lagunitas. American News, 1892; Routledge, 1892
Lost Countess Falka. Rand, 1896; Routledge, 1897
The Masked Venus. American News, 1893; Routledge, 1893
-The Midnight Passenger. Home, 1900; White, 1901
-Miss Devereux of the Mariquita. Routledge, 1895 (U.S. title?)
A Modern Corsair. Rand, 1897; Routledge, 1897
-A Monte Cristo in Khaki. Home, 1903; French, 1903
My Official Wife. Home, 1891; Routledge, 1891
The Mystery of a Shipyard. Home, 1901; White, 1902
Our Mysterious Passenger, and other stories. Street, 1899; Henderson, 1899 ss
-The Passing Show. Neely, 1893; Routledge, 1894. Also published as: The Spider of Truxillo. Neely, 1895
-Prince Schamyl's Wooing. Routledge, 1892 (U.S. title?)

-The Princess of Alaska. Nelly, 1894; Routledge, 1894
-The Shield of His Honor. Home, 1900; White, 1900
-Special Orders for Commander Leigh. Home, 1902. British title: Commander Leigh. White, 1903
The Spider of Truxillo; see The Passing Show
Storm Signals; see The Anarchist
-Tales of Adventure. Home, 1900 ss
-The White Lady of Khaminavatka. Home, 1898; Routledge, 1899

SAVAGE, THOMAS. 1915-   .
Midnight Line. Little, 1976

SAVAGE, WALLACE
A Bait of Perjury. Dorke House, 1970

SAVI, GERALD B(ARTON)
-Alive or Dead. Hodder, 1938
The Last Lap. Wright, 1935 [Burma]
-The Misfit. Wright, 1936
-The Mosquito Net. Wright, 1933
Raw Material. Wright, 1934

SAVIDGE, EUGENE COLEMAN. 1863-1924.
Wallingford. Lippincott, 1887 [Phil.]

SAVILE, FRANK (MACKENZIE)
The Pursuit. Arnold, 1910; Little, 1910

SAVILLE, MALCOLM. ca.1901-1982.
Dark Summer. Heinemann, 1965

SAWKINS, RAYMOND H(AROLD). 1923-   .
Pseudonyms: Jay Bernard, Colin Forbes, Richard Raine, qq.v. Ref: CA. SC: Supt. John Snow, in all titles.
Snow Along the Border. Heinemann, 1968; Harcourt, 1968
Snow in Paradise. Heinemann, 1967; Harcourt, 1967 [It.]
Snow on High Ground. Heinemann, 1966; Harcourt, 1967

SAWN, DAVID
Victims of the Devil's Triangle. Pioneer, 1975 (Play.)

SAWYER, EUGENE T. 1846-1924. Pseudonym: Nicholas Carter, q.v.
The Coleraine Tragedy. Street (Magnet), 1901
The Los Huecos Mystery. Street, 1900
The Maltese Cross; or, The Detective's Quest. Street, 1888
Old Quartz, the Nevada Detective. Street (Magnet), 1900; Henderson, 1890
The Prince of Fraud. Rose (Toronto), 1891
A Strike of Millions. Street (Magnet), 1907
The Tiger's Head Mystery. Street (Magnet), 1901

SAWYER, JOHN. 1919-   . Joint pseudonyms with Nancy Buckingham Sawyer, 1924-   : Nancy Buckingham, Erica Quest, qq.v.

SAWYER, NANCY BUCKINGHAM. 1924-   .
Joint pseudonyms with John Sawyer, 1919-   : Nancy Buckingham, Erica Quest, qq.v.

SAX, ANDRE. Joint pseudonym of Stephen Soitos and Jamie Kinney.
A Death in the Colony. Charter, 1980 [Mass.]
Salt Cat Bank. Charter, 1980 [Fla.]

SAXBY, CHARLES
Death Cuts the Film. Dutton, 1939 [ship]
Death in the Sun. Dutton, 1940; Hale, 1941 [Colo.]
Death Joins the Woman's Club. Dutton, 1940 [Calif.]
Death over Hollywood, with Louis Molnar. Dutton, 1937 [L.A.]
Death Wore Roses. Dutton, 1942 [Calif.]
Even Bishops Die. Dutton, 1942 [Carib.]
Murder at the Mike. Dutton, 1938 [L.A.]
Out of It All. Dutton, 1941 [Calif.]

SAXE, R. B. SC: John Dobbs (The Ghost), in at least those marked JD.
The Ghost Does a Richard III. Long, 1943 JD [Paris]
The Ghost Knows His Greengages. Constable, 1940 JD
The Ghost Pulls the Jackpot. Long, 1945 JD
What Can You Lose? Long, 1947

SAXON, ALEX. Pseudonym of Bill Pronzini, 1943-   , q.v. Other pseudonym: Jack Foxx, q.v.
A Run in Diamonds. PB, 1973 [Sp.]

SAXON, JOHN A. 1886-1947. SC: Sam Welpton, in both titles.
  Half-Past Mortem. Mill, 1947; Foulsham, 1951 (Ghost-written by Robert Leslie Bellem, q.v.) [Calif.]
  Liability Limited. Mill, 1947. British title: This Was No Accident. Foulsham, 1949 [L.A.]
  This Was No Accident; see Liability Limited

SAXON, PETER. House name. Used by W(illiam Arthur) Howard Baker, 1925- , q.v. Other Baker pseudonyms: W. A. Ballinger, William Arthur, Julie Wellsley, Richard Williams, qq.v. Also used by Wilfred (Glassford) McNeilly, 1921- , q.v. Other McNeilly pseudonyms: W(illiam Arthur) Howard Baker, William A. Ballinger, William Glassford, Errole Lecale, Desmond Reid, qq.v. Also used by Thomas Hector Martin, 1913- . Other Martin pseudonym: Martin Thomas, q.v. SC: Sexton Blake (with many other authors) = SB; The Guardians = G.
  Act of Violence. Amalgamated, 1957 SB
  Black Honey. Mayflower, 1968 SB
  Corruption. Sphere, 1968
  A Cry in the Night. Amalgamated, 1957 SB
  The Curse of Rathlaw. Baker, 1969; Lancer, 1968 G
  Danger Ahead. Amalgamated, 1956 SB
  Dark Ways to Death. Baker, 1968; Berkley, 1969 G
  The Darkest Night. Mayflower, 1966; Paperback Library, 1967
  Decoy for Murder. Amalgamated, 1956 SB
  The Disoriented Man. Mayflower, 1966. U.S. title: Scream and Scream Again. Paperback Library, 1967
  -The Enemy Sky. Corgi, 1969
  Flight into Fear. Amalgamated, 1956 SB
  Front Page Woman. Amalgamated, 1956 SB
  The Haunting of Alan Mais. Mayflower, 1970; Berkley, 1969 G
  The Killing Bone. Baker, 1970; Berkley, 1969 G
  The Last Days of Berlin. Amalgamated, 1957 SB [Berlin]
  Lovely—But Lethal! Amalgamated, 1961 SB
  The Naked Blade. Amalgamated, 1958 SB
  Satan's Child. Mayflower, 1967; Lancer, 1968 [Scot.]
  Scream and Scream Again; see The Disoriented Man
  The Sea Tigers. Amalgamated, 1958 SB
  This Spy Must Die. Mayflower, 1967 SB [Russ.]
  Through the Dark Curtain. Baker, 1968; Lancer, 1968 G
  -The Torturer. Mayflower, 1967; Paperback Library, 1967
  -The Unfeeling Sky. Corgi, 1968
  Vampire's Moon. Belmont, 1970 (British title?) [Rum.]
  The Vampires of Finistere. Baker, 1970; Berkley, 1970 G
  Vengeance Is Ours! Mayflower, 1965 SB
  The Violent Hours. Amalgamated, 1957.SB
  The Violent Ones. Amalgamated, 1959 SB
  The Voodoo Drum. Amalgamated, 1948 SB
  -The Warring Sky. Corgi, 1970
  White Mercenary. Amalgamated, 1962 SB
  Woman of Saigon. Amalgamated, 1968 SB [Saigon]

SAXON, VAN. Joint pseudonym of Marilyn Granbeck, 1927- , q.v., and Arthur Moore, q.v. Other joint pseudonym: Adam Hamilton, q.v. Pseudonyms of Marilyn Granbeck: Ben Grant, Clayton Moore, qq.v. For Arthur Moore, see also: Don Hoyt.
  Hollywood Hit Man. Zebra, 1975 [L.A.]

SAXTON, MARK. 1914- . Ref: CA.
  The Broken Circle. Farrar, 1941
  Danger Road. Farrar, 1939; Heinemann, 1940 [Mass.]
  -Paper Chase. Bobbs, 1964
  The Year of August. Farrar, 1943

SAYER, W(ALTER) W(ILLIAM). 1892- . Pseudonym: Pierre Quiroule, q.v. All titles without publisher below feature Sexton Blake and were issued by Amalgamated Press. Many of the books were reprinted (and retitled) and published as by a Sayer pseudonym, P. Quiro(u)le, as indicated. SC: Barnaby Grayle = BG.
  The Adventure of the Albanian Avenger. 1925. Reprinted as: The Mystery of the Albanian Avenger. 1936
  The Black Limousine. 1926. Reprinted as: The £100,000 Insurance Swindle. 1936
  The Case of the Cabaret Girl. 1923
  The Case of the Five Dummy Books. 1923. Reprinted: 1934
  The Case of the King's Spy. 1920. Reprinted as: The Missing Spy. 1934
  The Case of the Strange Wireless Message. 1920
  The Crimson Domino. 1922. Reprinted as: The Red Domino. 1934
  The Ethiopian's Secret. 1926. Reprinted 1936.
  The Forest of Fortune. 1924. Reprinted: 1935
  The Havana Mystery; see The Mystery of the Lost Battle-Ship
  The Living Shadow; see The Mystery of the Living Shadow
  The Lost Expedition. 1923. Reprinted: 1936
  The Man with the Black Wallet; see The Secret of the Black Wallet
  Mine Sinister Host. Wright, 1948 BG
  The Missing Spy; see The Case of the King's Spy
  The Mystery Box. 1920. Reprinted: 1934
  The Mystery of the Albanian Avenger; see The Adventure of the Albanian Avenger
  The Mystery of the Living Shadow. 1920. Reprinted as: The Living Shadow. 1934
  The Mystery of the Lost Battle-Ship. 1924. Reprinted as: The Havana Mystery. 1935
  The Mystery of the Missing Aviator; see The Secret of the Six Black Dots
  The Mystery of the Platinum Nugget! 1925. Reprinted as: The Soho Cafe Crime. 1935
  The Mystery of the Turkish Agreement. 1920
  The Nemesis Club. Wright, 1946 BG
  The £100,000 Insurance Swindle; see The Black Limousine
  The Outlaws of Yugo-Slavia. 1923. Reprinted: 1934 [Yugos.]
  The Phantom of the Pacific. 1922. Reprinted: 1934
  The Red Domino; see The Crimson Domino
  The Red Mountain; see The Secret of the Red Mountain
  The Riders of the Sands. 1922. Reprinted: 1934
  The Sacred City. 1921. Reprinted: 1934
  The Secret of the Black Wallet. 1924. Reprinted as: The Man with the Black Wallet. 1935
  The Secret of the Frozen North. 1921
  The Secret of the Oblong Chest. 1922
  The Secret of the Red Mountain. 1921. Reprinted as: The Red Mountain. 1934
  The Secret of the Six Black Dots. 1921. Reprinted as: The Mystery of the Missing Aviator. 1937
  The Secret of Thirty Years! 1925
  Sellers of Death. Wright, 1940 BG
  The Soho Cafe Crime; see The Mystery of the Platinum Nugget!
  The Vanished Million. 1924. Reprinted: 1935

SAYERS, DOROTHY L(EIGH). 1893-1957. Ref: all eight. SC: Lord Peter Wimsey = PW; Montague Egg = ME. Set: Eng.
  Busman's Honeymoon. Gollancz, 1937; Harcourt, 1937. 3-act play version, with M. St. Clare Byrne, 1895- : Gollancz, 1937 PW
  Clouds of Witness. Unwin, 1926; Dial, 1927 PW
  The Dawson Pedigree; see Unnatural Death
  The Documents in the Case, with Robert Eustace (pseudonym of Robert Eustace Barton, 1868-1943). Benn, 1930; Brewer, 1930
  The Five Red Herrings. Gollancz, 1931. U.S. title: Suspicious Characters. Brewer, 1931 PW [Scot.]
  Gaudy Night. Gollancz, 1935; Harcourt, 1936 PW
  Hangman's Holiday. Gollancz, 1933; Harcourt, 1933 (12 ss: 4 about PW, 6 about ME, 2 non-series.)
  Have His Carcase. Gollancz, 1932; Brewer, 1932 PW
  The Image in the Mirror. Todd, 1943 (16 pp booklet containing a ss from Hangman's Holiday, q.v.)
  In the Teeth of the Evidence. Gollancz, 1939; Harcourt, 1940 (17 ss: 2 about PW, 5 about ME, 10 non-series.)
  The Incredible Elopement of Lord Peter Wimsey. Todd, 1943 (16 pp booklet containing a ss from Hangman's Holiday, q.v.)
  Lord Peter. Harper, 1972 (All 21 PW ss, complete under one cover in the second edition, including the 3 ss uncollected in Sayers' lifetime.)
  Lord Peter Views the Body. Gollancz, 1928; Brewer, 1929 (12 ss about PW.)
  The Man with No Face. Todd, 1943 (16 pp booklet containing a ss from Lord Peter Views the Body, q.v.)
  Murder Must Advertise. Gollancz, 1933; Harcourt, 1933 PW
  The Nine Tailors. Gollancz, 1934; Harcourt, 1934 PW
  Striding Folly. New English Library, 1972 (The 3 PW ss uncollected in Sayers' lifetime.)
  Strong Poison. Gollancz, 1930; Brewer, 1930 PW
  Suspicious Characters; see The Five Red Herrings
  Unnatural Death. Benn, 1927. U.S. title: The Dawson Pedigree. Dial, 1928 PW
  The Unpleasantness at the Bellona Club. Benn, 1928; Payson, 1928 PW
  Whose Body? Unwin, 1923; Boni, 1923 PW

SCADUTO, ANTHONY. Ref: CA.
  A Terrible Time to Die. Putnam, 1978 [NYC]

SCANLON, D.
  Big Shot. World Distributors, 1953
  School for Murder. World Distributors, 1953
  Snatch. World Distributors, 1952

SCANLON, NOEL. SC: Quinn, in both titles.
  Quinn. Murray, 1973
  Quinn and the Desert Oil. Murray, 1975

SCANNELL, VERNON. 1922- . Ref: CA.
  The Big Chance. Long, 1960
  -The Big Time. Longmans, 1965
  -The Dividing Night. Putnam (London), 1962
  -The Face of the Enemy. Putnam (London), 1961
  -The Fight. Nevill, 1953
  The Shadowed Place. Long, 1961
  -The Wound and the Scar. Nevill, 1953

SCARBOROUGH, CHUCK. 1943- . TV news correspondent.
  Stryker. Macmillan, 1978; Piatkus, 1980 [NYC]

SCARBOROUGH, GEORGE. See also: Page Philips.
  The Lure. Dillingham, 1914

SCARLETT, ROGER. Pseudonym of Dorothy Blair, 1903- , and Evelyn Page, 1902- . Ref for Page: CA. SC: Insp. Kane, in all titles.
  The Back Bay Murders. Doubleday, 1930; Selwyn, 1931 [Boston]
  The Beacon Hill Murders. Doubleday, 1930; Heinemann, 1930 [Boston]
  Cat's Paw. Doubleday, 1931 [Boston]
  In the First Degree. Doubleday, 1933 [Boston]
  Murder Among the Angells. Doubleday, 1932 [Boston]

SCARLETT, SUSAN
  -The Man in the Dark. Hodder, 1940
  Murder While You Work. Hodder, 1944

SCARPETTA, FRANK. Pseudonym (?) of Aaron Fletcher. SC: Philip Magellan (The Marksman), in all titles (see also: Peter McCurtin).
  Bloody Sunday. Belmont, 1976. Reprinted as by Aaron Fletcher: Leisure, 1981
  Body Count. Belmont, 1974 [Fr.]
  Counterattack. Belmont, 1974
  Death to the Mafia. Belmont, 1973 [L.A.]
  Die, Killer, Die. Belmont, 1975 [Fr.]
  Headhunter. Belmont, 1973
  Icepick; see Icepick in the Spine
  Icepick in the Spine. Belmont, 1975. Also published as: Icepick, as by Aaron Fletcher: Leisure, 1982 [Mex.]
  Kill! Belmont, 1974 [N.J.]
  Kill Them All. Belmont, 1973 [Vir. Is.]
  Killer on the Prowl. Belmont, 1975
  Kiss of Death. Belmont, 1974
  Mafia Massacre. Belmont, 1974 [Miami]
  Mafia Wipe-Out. Belmont, 1973 [Chi.]
  The Murder Machine. Belmont, 1975
  Open Contract. Belmont, 1974
  Slaughterhouse. Belmont, 1973 [St. Louis]
  Stone Killer. Belmont, 1974 [Fr.]
  This Animal Must Die. Belmont, 1975
  The Times Square Connection. Belmont, 1976 [NYC]
  The Torture Contract. Belmont, 1975 [Calif.]

SCERBANENCO, GIORGIO. 1911-1969. Ref: CC.
  Duca and the Milan Murders. Cassell, 1970; Walker, 1970 (Translation of "Traditori di Tutti." Milan, 1966.) [Milan]

SCHAAP, DICK. 1934-   . See: Jimmy Breslin, 1930-

SCHABELITZ, R(UDOLPH) F(REDERICK). 1884-1959. See: Willetta Ann Barber, 1911-   .

SCHAEFER, FRANK. 1936-   . See: Kerry Newcomb, 1946-   .

SCHERE, MONROE. 1913-   . Pseudonym: Abigail Winter, q.v.

SCHERF, MARGARET (LOUISE). 1908-1979. Ref: CA, CC, EM, TC. SC: Emily & Henry Bryce = B; Rev. Martin Buell = MB; Lt. Ryan = R; Grace Severance = GS.
  Always Murder a Friend. Doubleday, 1948; Low, 1949 MB
  The Banker's Bones. Doubleday, 1968; Hale, 1969 GS [Ariz.]
  The Beaded Banana. Doubleday, 1978; Hale, 1979 GS [Mont.]
  The Beautiful Birthday Cake. Doubleday, 1971 GS [Mont.]
  The Case of the Hated Senator; see Dead: Senate Office Building
  The Case of the Kippered Corpse. Putnam, 1941
  The Cautious Overshoes. Doubleday, 1956 MB
  The Corpse Grows a Beard. Putnam, 1940; Partridge, 1941 [N.J.]
  The Corpse in the Flannel Nightgown. Doubleday, 1965; Hale, 1966 MB [Mont.]
  The Corpse with One Shoe; see The Green Plaid Pants
  The Curious Custard Pie. Doubleday, 1950. Also published as: Divine and Deadly. Bestseller, 1953 MB [Mont.]
  Dead: Senate Office Building. Doubleday, 1953. Also published as: The Case of the Hated Senator. Ace, 1954 [Wash. D.C.]
  Death and the Diplomat; see The Diplomat and the Gold Piano
  The Diplomat and the Gold Piano. Doubleday, 1963. British title: Death and the Diplomat. Hale, 1964 B [NYC]
  Divine and Deadly; see The Curious Custard Pie
  Don't Wake Me Up While I'm Driving. Doubleday, 1977; Hale, 1978 [N. Dak., 1920s]
  The Elk and the Evidence. Doubleday, 1952 MB [Mont.]
  For the Love of Murder; see Gilbert's Last Toothache
  Gilbert's Last Toothache. Doubleday, 1949. Also published as: For the Love of Murder. Bestseller, 1950 MB [Mont.]
  Glass on the Stairs. Doubleday, 1954; Barker, 1955 B [NYC]
  The Green Plaid Pants. Doubleday, 1951. Also published as: The Corpse with One Shoe. Detective Book Club, 1951 B [N.Y.]
  The Gun in Daniel Webster's Bust. Doubleday, 1949 B [NYC]
  If You Want a Murder Well Done. Doubleday, 1974 [Las Veg.]
  Judicial Body. Doubleday, 1957 [NYC]
  Murder Makes Me Nervous. Doubleday, 1948; Low, 1952 R
  Never Turn Your Back. Doubleday, 1959 MB [Mont.]
  The Owl in the Cellar. Doubleday, 1945; Nimmo, 1947 R [NYC]
  They Came to Kill. Putnam, 1942 [Mont.]
  To Cache a Millionaire. Doubleday, 1972 GS [Las Veg.]

SCHERMERHORN, DUANE R. Pseudonym: James Marcott, q.v.

SCHIER, NORMA. SC: Kay Barth = KB.
  The Anagram Detectives. Mysterious Press, 1979 ss
  Death Goes Skiing. Zebra, 1979 KB [Colo.]
  Death on the Slopes. Zebra, 1978 KB [Colo.]
  Demon of the Opera. Zebra, 1980 KB [Sante Fe, theatre]
  Murder by the Book. Zebra, 1979 KB [Colo.]

SCHIFF, BARRY (J.) and HAL FISHMAN
  The Vatican Target. St. Martin's, 1979; Severn, 1980 [Mid. East]

SCHIMMEL, ROBERT C(ARL). 1895-   .
  The Green Light. Baker, 1930. With J(oseph) C(arl) McMullen, 1882-   , q.v.; Fitzgerald, 1937 (3-act play.)
  Whispering Pines. Baker, 1929 (Play.)

SCHINKE, NORMA S.
  The Devil Wolf. Small, 1924; Unwin, 1924

SCHISGALL, OSCAR. 1901-   . Ref: CA.
  Baron Ixell, Crime Breaker. Longmans (NYC & London), 1929 (4 novelets.)
  The Devil's Daughter. Fiction League, 1932 [NYC]

SCHLEIFER, GERRY
  Five Million Francs. Joseph, 1973

SCHLEY, STURGES MASON. Born in NYC; magazine writer. SC: Dr. Quentin Toby = QT.
  Deepening Blue. Doubleday, 1935
  Dr. Toby Finds Murder. Random, 1941 QT [Miami]
  Dream Sinister. Morrow, 1950. British title: The Starry-Eyed Chipmonk. Gollancz, 1951 QT [L.I.]
  The Starry-Eyed Chipmonk; see Dream Sinister
  Vengeance Pulls the Trigger; see Who'd Shoot a Genius?
  Who'd Shoot a Genius? Random, 1940. Also published as: Vengeance Pulls the Trigger. Death House, 1944 QT [NYC]

SCHMIDT, JAMES H(ENRY). 1911-   . Ref: CA. SC: Telzey Amberdon and Trigger Argee = A&A. Set, all titles: future.
  Agent of Vega. Gnome, 1960 (4 novelets.)
  Legacy; see A Tale of Two Clocks
  The Lion Game. DAW, 1973 A&A
  A Tale of Two Clocks. Dodd, 1962. Also published as: Legacy. Ace, 1979 A&A
  The Telzey Toy. DAW, 1973 A&A ss
  The Universe Against Her. Ace, 1964 A&A

SCHMIDT, JAMES NORMAN. 1912-   . Pseudonym: James Norman, q.v.

SCHMITT, LEO F(RANCIS). 1891-   .
  The Shyster Lawyer. Schmitt, 1929 ss [Ia.]

SCHNURR, WILLIAM
  Johnny Death. PB, 1974 [1933-34]

SCHOENFELD, HOWARD
  Let Them Eat Bullets. GM, 1954; Fawcett (London), 1955 [NYC]

SCHOFIELD, SYLVIA ANNE MATHESON. 1918-   . Pseudonym: Max Mundy, q.v.

SCHOFIELD, WILLIAM G(REENOUGH). 1909-   . Ref: CA.
  The Cat in the Convoy. Macrae, 1946
  Payoff in Black. Macrae, 1947; Cherry Tree, 1948 [Boston]

SCHOLEFIELD, ALAN. 1931-   . Ref: CA.
  -The Alpha Raid. Heinemann, 1976; Morrow, 1977 [WWI]
  Berlin Blind. Heinemann, 1980; Morrow, 1981 [Berlin]
  Point of Honour. Heinemann, 1979; Morrow, 1979 [Fr.]
  Venom. Heinemann, 1977; Morrow, 1978

SCHOLEY, ERIC
  Answer in the Negative. Ward, 1952

SCHOLEY, JEAN. Ref: CC.
  The Dead Past. Heinemann, 1961; Macmillan, 1962 [Tang.]

SCHRADER, LEONARD
  The Yakuza. Futura, 1975 (Novelization of the movie.)

SCHUBERT, JOHN D. Pseudonym: Catherine Morland, q.v. Has degrees from Harvard and Stanford; high school and college teacher; scholarship fund director in Cleveland in 1970s.
  Castle Black. Lenox, 1971. Also published as: The Devil at Castelnero. Magnum, 197? And as by Catherine Morland: Beagle, 1972
  The Devil at Castelnero; see Castle Black
  The Keep. Lenox, 1972 [N.Y., 1880s]

SCHUETZ, DENNIS. Joint pseudonym with Michael McDowell, 1950-   , q.v.: Nathan Aldyne, q.v.

SCHULER, FRANK and ROBIN MOORE, q.v.
  The Pearl Harbor Cover-Up. Pinnacle, 1977 [Haw., 1941]

SCHURMACHER, EMILE C. 1903-1976. Ref: CA.
  Assignment X: Top Secret. Paperback Library, 1965

SCHURR, CATHLEEN. Ref: CA.
  Dark Encounter. Rinehart, 1955. British title: Dark Death. Foulsham, 1957

SCHWARTZ, ALAN. College English prof. in NYC.
  No Country for Old Men. NAL, 1980 [Chile]

SCHWARTZ, ALVIN. 1916-   .
  The Blowtop. Dial, 1948

SCHWARTZ, JOOST MARIUS WILLIAM VAN DER POORTEN. 1858-1915. Pseudonym: Maarten Maartens, q.v. See also: Anonymous ("The Black Box Murder").

SCHWARTZ, PAULA. 1925-   . Pseudonym: Elizabeth Mansfield, q.v.

SCHWARZ, BRUNO
  Crimson Clay. Hamilton, 1955
  Cry Vengeance. Hamilton, 1954
  Dames Are Dynamite. Hamilton, ca.1950
  The Dead and the Damned. Hamilton, 1954
  How Cold the Night. Hamilton, 1955
  The Long Revenge. Hamilton, 1955

SCHWEITZER, GERTRUDE. 1909-   . Ref: CA.
  The Ledge. Delacorte, 1972; Macdonald, 1973

SCIASCIA, LEONARDO. 1921-   . Ref: CA.
  Equal Danger. Harper, 1973; Cape, 1974 (Translation of "Il Contesto." Turin, 1971.) [Sic.]
  Mafia Vendetta. Knopf, 1964; Cape, 1973 (Translation of "Il Giorno della Avetta." Turin, 1961.)
  A Man's Blessing. Harper, 1968; Cape, 1969 (Translation of "A Ciascuno il Suo." Turin, 1966.) [Sic.]
  One Way or Another. Harper, 1977 (Translation of "Todo Modo." Italy, 1974.) [It.]

SCOBIE, ALASTAIR. 1918-   .
  The Cape Town Affair. Cassell, 1952 [Cape Town]
  Kangaroo Shoots Man. Cassell, 1949
  Murder a la Mozambique. Cassell, 1950 [Mozam.]

SCOFIELD, CHARLES J(OSIAH). 1853-   .
  A Subtle Adversary. Scofield, 1891

SCOPPETTONE, SANDRA. 1936-   . Ref: CA.
  Some Unknown Person. Putnam, 1977; H. Hamilton, 1978 [N.J., 1906-1977]
  Such Nice People. Putnam, 1978

SCORTIA, THOMAS N(ICHOLAS), 1926-   , and FRANK M(ALCOLM) ROBINSON, 1926-   , q.v. Ref for Scortia: CA.
  The Gold Crew. Warner hb, 1980
  The Nightmare Factor. Doubleday, 1978; Hodder, 1978 [S.F.]

SCOTLAND, JAY. Pseudonym of John (William) Jakes, 1932-   , q.v. Other pseudonyms: Alan Payne, Rachel Ann Payne, qq.v. See also: William (Thomas) Ard, 1922-1960.
  The Seventh Man. Mystery House, 1958 [Chi.]

SCOTT, LADY A(IMEE BYNG HALL)
  -Another Man's Wife. Nash, 1925
  The Blue Vase. Holden, 1922
  -The Open Prison. Eldon, 1934
  -The Painted Window. Eldon, 1934
  The Sealed Envelope. Hutchinson, 1927
  -The Unknown Path. Hutchinson, 1926

SCOTT, A. W.
  Life Experiences of a Detective. Detective's Museum Pub. Co., 1878 ss

SCOTT, ANNJEANETTE. Pseudonym of Scott Wright.
  Castle for the Left Hand. Popular Library, 1976 [Scot.]
  The Count of Van Rheeden Castle. Popular Library, 1976 [Holl.]

SCOTT, ANTONIA
  Falcon's Island. PB, 1973 [Maine]

SCOTT, BARBARA MONTAGU
  -And, Which, the Knave? Hutchinson, 1946
  -The Devil Within. Hutchinson, 1956
  -The Road Back. Hutchinson, 1952
  The Wolf Troubleth Not. Hurst, 1943

SCOTT, BRUCE
  A Hell of a Spot. Hale, 1971

SCOTT, CHRIS. 1945-   . Born in Eng.; living in Toronto since 1969.
  To Catch a Spy. Viking, 1978

SCOTT, DANA. Pseudonym of Constance Pierrepont Noyes Robertson, 1897- . Ref: CA.
 Five Fatal Letters. Farrar, 1937 [N.Y.]

SCOTT, DEBORAH
 Deathbed of Roses. Ace, 1976

SCOTT, DENIS. Joint pseudonym of Mary Means and Theodore Saunders. SC: Mike James, in both titles.
 The Beckoning Shadow. Bobbs, 1946; Hammond, 1956 [Ill.]
 Murder Makes a Villain. Bobbs, 1944; Hammond, 1955 [L.I.]

SCOTT, DOUGLAS. 1926- .
 Operation Artemis. Bobbs, 1979. British title: The Gift of Artemis. Secker, 1979 [WWII]

SCOTT, EVELYN. 1893- . Pseudonym: Ernest Souza, q.v.

SCOTT, G. FIRTH
 -At Friendly Point. Bowden, 1898 ss
 Possessed. Rider, 1912
 The Rider of Waroona. Long, 1912
 -The Track of Midnight. Low, 1897
 The Twillford Mystery. Everett, 1904

SCOTT, GAVIN. 1950- . Born in Eng., raised in N.Z.; BBC radio and TV reporter.
 A Flight of Lies. Deutsch, 1980; St. Martin's, 1981
 Hot Pursuit. Collins, 1977; St. Martin's, 1978 [N.Z.]

SCOTT, GENEVIEVE
 The Water Horse. Gollancz, 1974

SCOTT, SIR (JAMES) GEORGE. 1851-1935.
 Why Not? Arnold, 1929

SCOTT, HEDLEY. Pseudonym of Hedley Percival Angelo O'Mant, 1899-1955. SC (with many other authors): Sexton Blake, in both titles.
 The Mystery of the Missing Refugee. Amalgamated, 1939
 The Suspected Six. Amalgamated, 1938

SCOTT, HUGH STOWELL. 1862-1903. Pseudonym: Henry Seton Merriman, q.v.

SCOTT, J(AMES) M(AURICE). 1906- . Ref: CA.
 The Bright Eyes of Danger. Hodder, 1950
 -Cap Across the River. Hodder, 1949
 -I Keep My Word. Heinemann, 1957
 -Michael Anonymous. Chilton, 1971 (British title?)
 -The Other Half of the Orange. Heinemann, 1955; Dutton, 1955 [Switz.]
 Snowstone. Hodder, 1936 [Green.]
 -The Touch of the Nettle. Hodder, 1951
 Unknown River. Hodder, 1939 [Can.]
 -Where the River Bends. Heinemann, 1962

SCOTT, JACK DENTON. 1915- . See also: Anne Damer.
 Spargo. World, 1972

SCOTT, JACK S. Pseudonym of Jonathan Escott, 1922- . Ref: CA. SC: Alf Rosher, in at least those marked AR. Set: Eng.
 The Bastard's Name Was Bristow; see A Better Class of Business
 A Better Class of Business. Hale, 1976. U.S. title: The Bastard's Name Was Bristow. Harper, 1977
 A Clutch of Vipers. Collins, 1979; Harper, 1979 AR
 The Gospel Lamb. Collins, 1980; Harper, 1980 AR
 The Poor Old Lady's Dead. Hale, 1976; Harper, 1976 AR
 The Shallow Grave. Hale, 1977; Harper, 1978 AR
 A Walk in Dead Man's Wood. Allen, 1978

SCOTT, JEFFRY. Pseudonym of Shaun Usher, 1937- . Son of Gray Usher, 1903- , q.v. Ref: CA.
 Trust Them and Die. Hale, 1969

SCOTT, JEREMY. 1915- . Born in Cairo, educated in Eng.; TV writer and director, then partner in film production company in Eng.
 Angels in Your Beer. Allen, 1979. U.S. title: The Two Faces of Robert Just. Morrow, 1980. Also published as: Escape. Star, 1981 [Fr.]
 Escape; see Angels in Your Beer
 Hunted. Allen, 1980; Wyndham, 1981

SCOTT, JODY. 1923- . Joint pseudonym with George Thurston Leite, 1920- : Thurston Scott, q.v.

SCOTT, JOHN DICK. Pseudonym: Malcolm Gair, q.v.

SCOTT, JOHN REED. 1869- .
 The Cab of the Sleeping Horse. Putnam (NYC & London), 1916 [Wash. D.C.]
 -In Her Own Right. Lippincott (NYC & London), 1911
 The Man in Evening Clothes. Putnam (NYC & London), 1917 [Wash. D.C.]
 -The Red Emerald. Lippincott (NYC & London), 1914 [Wash. D.C.]
 The Woman in Question. Lippincott (NYC & London), 1909 [Va.]

SCOTT, JUNE (MEINDL)
 Bitter Honeycomb. Dorrance, 1972

SCOTT, JUSTIN (BLAZER). Pseudonym: J. S. Blazer, q.v. Ref: CA.
 Many Happy Returns. McKay, 1973
 The Shipkiller. Dial, 1978; Hart-Davis, 1979 [ship]
 Treasure for Treasure. McKay, 1974; Barker, 1974 [NYC]
 The Turning. Dell, 1978; Panther, 1980

SCOTT, LEROY. 1875-1929. SC: Bob Clifford, in at least those marked BC.
 Children of the Whirlwind. Houghton, 1921 [NYC]
 Cordelia the Magnificent. Holt, 1923
 Counsel for the Defense. Doubleday, 1912; Newnes, 1914
 -A Daughter of Two Worlds. Houghton, 1919
 Folly's Gold. Houghton, 1926 BC [NYC]
 The Living Dead Man. Washburn, 1929; Nash, 1929 [L.I.]
 Mary Regan. Houghton, 1918 BC [NYC]
 No. 13 Washington Square. Houghton, 1914 [NYC]
 Partners of the Night. Century, 1916; Nash, 1917 ss BC [NYC]
 -The Shears of Destiny. Doubleday, 1910; Hodder, 1910

SCOTT, LILY K.
 A House of Women. Pyramid, 1966

SCOTT, MANSFIELD. SC: Insp. Malcome Steele = MS.
 Behind Red Curtains. Small, 1919; Nash, 1920 MS [Boston]
 The Black Circle. Clode, 1928; Lane, 1929 MS [NYC]
 The Phantom Passenger. Clode, 1927; Lane, 1928 [ship]
 The Spider's Web. Clode, 1929 MS
 The Sportsman-Detective. Clode, 1930

SCOTT, MARGARET. Joint pseudonym with Will(iam Charles) Oursler, 1913- , q.v.: Gale Gallagher, q.v.

SCOTT, MARGERIE
 Mrs. Tenterden. Milton House, 1975

SCOTT, MARIAN GALLAGHER. 1892- . Pseudonyms: Gail Oliver, Katherine Wolffe, qq.v.

SCOTT, MARIANNE de JAY
 The Van Dyne Collection. Lancer, 1973

SCOTT, MARION. Actress and court reporter.
 Dead Hands Reaching. Macmillan, 1932

SCOTT, MARY (EDITH CLARKE), 1888- , and JOYCE (TARLTON) WEST
 The Mangrove Murder. Angus, 1964
 No Red Herrings. Angus, 1964
 -Such Nice People. Angus, 1962
 -Who Put It There? Angus, 1965

SCOTT, MARY SEMPLE
 Crime Hound. Scribner, 1940 [Midwest]

SCOTT, MAURICE
 -In the Thraldom of Fear. Stevens, 1936
 The Mark of the Broad Arrow. Henderson
 -A Modern Circe. Stevens, 1937

SCOTT, MILTON
 Dear, Dead Harry. Phoenix, 1949 [N.Y.]

SCOTT, R. McNAIR. See: T(erence) H(anbury) White, 1906-1964.

SCOTT, R(EGINALD) T(HOMAS) M(AITLAND). 1882- . Ref: CC, TC. SC: Aurelius Smith = AS; Richard Wentworth (The Spider); stories reprinted from pulp magazines; see also: Grant Stockbridge) = RW.
 The Agony Column Murders. Dutton, 1946 AS [NYC]
 Ann's Crime. Dutton, 1926; Heinemann, 1927. Also published as: Smith of the Secret Service (with no author given). Amalgamated, 1929 AS [NYC]
 Aurelius Smith—Detective. Dutton, 1927; Heinemann, 1928 AS ss [NYC]
 The Black Magician. Dutton, 1925; Heinemann, 1926 AS [NYC]
 The Mad Monk. Kendall, 1931; Rich, 1933 [Russ.]
 Murder Stalks the Mayor. Dutton, 1936; Rich, 1935 AS [NYC]
 The Nameless Ones. Dutton, 1947 AS [NYC]
 Secret Service Smith. Dutton, 1923; Hodder, 1924 AS ss
 Smith of the Secret Service; see Ann's Crime
 The Spider Strikes! Berkley, 1969 RW [NYC]
 The Wheel of Death. Berkley, 1969 RW [NYC]

SCOTT, RALPH. Pseudonym of George Scott Atkinson, 1899- .
 The Unknown Quest. Hurst, 1930 [Fr.]

SCOTT, RONEY. Pseudonym of William Campbell Gault, 1910- , q.v. Other pseudonym: Will Duke, q.v. SC: Joe Puma = JP (see also Gault entry).
 Shakedown. Ace, 1953 JP [L.A.]

SCOTT, STEVE. Pseudonym of William (Elbert) Crawford, 1929- , q.v. Other pseudonyms: Roger Brandt, Jim Peterson, Paul Ross, qq.v.
 The Cop-Killers. Manor, 1972

SCOTT, SUTHERLAND. Ref: CC. SC: Dr. Septimus Dodds, in at least those marked SD. Set: Eng.
 The A.R.P. Murder. Paul, 1939 SD
 Capital Punishment. Paul, 1949
 Crazy Murder Show. Paul, 1937; Hillman-Curl, 1937. Also published as: Murder on Stage. Mystery Novel of the Month, 1941 SD
 Diagnosis—Murder. Paul, 1954 SD
 Doctor Dodds' Experiment. Paul, 1956 SD
 Escape to Murder. Paul, 1946 SD
 The Influenza Mystery. Paul, 1938 SD
 The Mass Radiography Murders. Paul, 1947 SD
 Murder in the Mobile Unit. Paul, 1940 SD [hosp.]
 Murder Is Infectious. Paul, 1936 SD
 Murder on Stage; see Crazy Murder Show
 Murder Without Mourners. Paul, 1936 SD
 The Night Air Is Dangerous. Paul, 1943
 Operation Urgent. Paul, 1947
 Tincture of Murder. Paul, 1951 SD

SCOTT, TARN
 Don't Let Her Die. GM, 1957

SCOTT, THURSTON. Joint pseudonym of George Thurston Leite, 1920- , and Jody Scott, 1923- .
 Cure It with Honey. Harper, 1951. Also published as (?): I'll Get Mine. Popular Library, 1952 [Calif.]

SCOTT, VINCENT E. Pseudonym: Nicholas Carter, q.v.

SCOTT, VIRGIL (JOSEPH). 1914- . Ref: CA.
 The Dead Tree Gives No Shelter. Swallow, 1947; Archer, 1950
 The Kreutzman Formula, with Dominic Koski. Simon, 1974 [Jam.]
 -The Savage Affair. Harcourt, 1958; Methuen, 1958
 Walk-In, with Dominic Koski. Simon, 1976; Hodder, 1977

SCOTT, WARWICK. Pseudonym of Elleston Trevor, 1920- , q.v. Name originally: Trevor Dudley Smith, q.v. Other pseudonyms: Mansell Black, Adam Hall, Howard North, Simon Rattray, Caesar Smith, qq.v.
 Cockpit; see Image in the Dust
 Doomsday; see The Domesday Story
 The Domesday Story. Davies, 1952. U.S. title: Doomsday. Lion, 1953. Reprinted as by Elleston Trevor: Mayflower, 1966
 Image in the Dust. Davies, 1951. U.S. title: Cockpit. Lion, 1953. Reprinted as by Elleston Trevor: Mayflower, 1967
 Naked Canvas. Davies, 1954; Popular Library, 1955. Reprinted as by Elleston Trevor: Mayflower, 1965

SCOTT, WILL. 1894?-1964. Ref: MP. SC: Disher = D.
 The Black Stamp; see Disher-Detective
 Disher-Detective. Cassell, 1925. U.S. title: The Black Stamp. Macrae-Smith, 1926 D
 Giglamps. Cassell, 1924 ss
 The Man. Paul, 1930. U.S. title: The Mask. Macrae-Smith, 1929 D

The Mask; see The Man
Shadows. Cassell, 1928; Macrae-Smith,
1928 D
SCOTT, WILLIAM
Getting the Boy. Elek, 1966
SCOTT, WILLIAM RALPH. 1918-   . Pseudonym: Weldon Hill, q.v.
SCOTT-HERON, GIL. 1949-   . Ref: CA.
The Vulture. World, 1970 [NYC]
SCOTT-MONCRIEFF, DAVID (WILLIAM HARDY). 1907-
The Vaivaisukko's Bride. Scots Digest, 1949
SCOTTER, JOHN
The Golestan Episode. Hale, 1979
Operation Hercules. Hale, 1978
SCOWCROFT, RICHARD (PINGREE). 1916-   .
Ref: CA.
Back to Fire Mountain. Little, 1973
SCRIBNER, FRANK K(IMBALL). 1866-1935.
The Secret of Frontellac. Small, 1912; Gay, 1912 [Fr.]
SCRIBNER, HARVEY. 1850-1913.
My Mysterious Clients. Clarke, 1900 ss, some criminous [Mass.]
SCROPE, MASON. Pseudonym of Arthur Charles Mason, 1879-   .
The Man with the Big Head. Wells Gardner, 1929
SCUDDER, ANTOINETTE (QUINBY). 1898-1958.
-The Grey Studio. Ruth Hill, 1934
SEABROOKE, JOHN PAUL. House name.
The Eyewitness. Chelsea, 1925; Jarrolds, 1926 [N.Y.]
Four Knocks on the Door. Chelsea, 1925 Jarrolds, 1927 [Conn.]
The Green Bag. Chelsea, 1926 [L.I.]
Shadow Hall. Chelsea, 1926; Jarrolds, 1927 [Conn.]
The Woman in 919. Chelsea, 1926 [NYC]
SEAFARER. Pseudonym of C(larence) Hedley Barker, q.v. Other pseudonym: Frank Hedley, q.v. SC: Captain Firebrace, in at least those marked F.
Bold Buccaneer. Ward, 1953
Captain Firebrace. Ward, 1958 F
Captain Firebrace and the Java Queen. Ward, 1958 F
Crook's Cruise. Ward, 1960
Firebrace and Father Kelly. Ward, 1959 F
The Haunted Ship. Ward, 1956
Make Way for a Sailor. Ward, 1947
The Sailor and the Widow. Ward, 1957
Santa Maria. Ward, 1955
Smuggler's Pay for Firebrace. Ward, 1959 F
Voyage into Peril. Ward, 1954
SEAFORTH. Pseudonym of George C(ecil) Foster, 1893-   , q.v.
Misprision of Felony. Jenkins, 1941
SEA-LION. Pseudonym of Geoffrey Martin Bennett, 1909-   . Ref: CA. SC: Desmond Drake, in at least those marked DD; John Prentice, in at least those marked JP. Set: Eng.
Cargo for Crooks. Collins, 1948 JP
Damn Desmond Drake. Hutchinson, 1953 DD
Death in Russian Habit. Long, 1958
Death in the Dog Watches. Long, 1962
Desmond Drake Goes West. Hutchinson, 1956 DD
The Diamond Rock. Hutchinson, 1952
Down Among the Dead Men. Long, 1961
The Invisible Ships. Hutchinson, 1950
Meet Desmond Drake. Hutchinson, 1952 DD
Operation Fireball. Long, 1959
Phantom Fleet. Collins, 1946 JP
-The Quest of John Clare. Hutchinson, 1951
Sea of Troubles. Collins, 1947 JP
Sink Me the Ship. Collins, 1946 JP
The Stolen Cipher. Hutchinson, 1955
This Creeping Evil. Hutchinson, 1950
When Danger Threatens. Collins, 1949 JP
SEALE, C. S. ST. BRELADE. See: Hugh Beresford.
SEALIS, HATHERLY. Pseudonym of Charles Freeman Foster, 1830-   .
The Veiled Lady. Broadway, 1905
SEAMAN, DONALD (PETER). 1922-   . Reporter and foreign correspondent for London newspaper. SC: Sydenham = S.
The Bomb That Could Lip-Read. H. Hamilton, 1974; Stein, 1974 [Ire.]

The Chameleon Course; see The Defector
Chase Royal. H. Hamilton, 1980 [Eng., 1800s]
The Committee. H. Hamilton, 1977; Atheneum, 1978
The Defector. H. Hamilton, 1975. U.S. title: The Chameleon Course. Coward, 1976 S
The Duel. H. Hamilton, 1979; Doubleday, 1979
Island of Death. Muller, 1956
The Terror Syndicate. H. Hamilton, 1976; Coward, 1976 S
SEAMARK. Pseudonym of Austin J. Small, -1929, q.v. Set: Eng.
The Avenging Ray. Hodder, 1930; Doubleday, 1930, as by Austin J. Small
Down River. Hodder, 1929. U.S. title: The Needle's Kiss. Doubleday, 1929, as by Austin J. Small
The Master Mystery. Hodder, 1928; Doubleday, 1928, as by Austin J. Small
The Mystery Maker. Hodder, 1929; Doubleday, 1930, as by Austin J. Small
The Needle's Kiss; see Down River
Out of the Dark. Hodder, 1931 ss
Pawns and Kings. Hodder, 1931 ss
The Silent Six. Hodder, 1926
The Vantine Diamonds. Hodder, 1930; Doubleday, 1930, as by Austin J. Small
The Web of Destiny. Hodder, 1929. U.S. title: The Web of Murder. Doubleday, 1929, as by Austin J. Small
The Web of Murder; see The Web of Destiny
SEARLE, WESTON
The Honeyfall. Regency, 1972
SEARLS, HANK [HENRY HUNT SEARLS]. 1922-   . Ref: CA.
Never Kill a Cop. PB, 1977
Pentagon. Geis, 1971
SEARS, RUTH McCARTHY
The Gift of the Sea. Lenox, 1973; Remploy, 1973
The Golden Sentinals. Lenox, 1974; Remploy, 1974 [Calif.]
The Grangerfjord Monks. Lenox, 1974; Remploy, 1975. Also published as: Wind in the Cypress. Leisure, 1975 [Calif.]
Heir of Grangerfjord Castle. Lenox, 1974; Remploy, 1975 [Calif.]
In the Shadow of the Tower. Lenox, 1972; Remploy, 1973
A Lonely Place; see The Phantom Empire
The Phantom Empire. Lenox, 1974. Also published as: A Lonely Place. Leisure, 1976
Port of No Return. Lenox, 1973; Remploy, 1974 [ship]
St. George Manor. Lenox, 1973; Remploy, 1973
The Spirit of Cove Island. Leisure, 1975 [Wash.]
-Three Silver Birches. Dell, 1975
SEATON, STUART. SC: Insp. Martin Laidman, in at least those marked ML.
Cage of Fear. Long, 1960
Don't Take It to Heart. Boardman, 1955 ML
Dust in Your Eyes. Boardman, 1957 ML
SEA-WRACK. Pseudonym of Edward Horace Crebbin.
McInnes of the N.I.D. Rich, 1941 ss
SEBASTIAN, MARGARET. Pseudonym of Arthur M. Gladstone, 1921-   . Ref: CA.
Bow Street Brangle. Popular Library, 1977 [Eng., ca.1820]
Bow Street Gentleman. Popular Library, 1977 [Eng., ca.1820]
SEBASTIAN, PAUL
The Black Shadow. Fiction House, 1937
The Red Boulders Mystery. Fiction House, 1937
Secret Service. Fiction House, 1937
The Spy Gang. Fiction House, 1941
SEBENTHAL, ROBERTA ELIZABETH. 1917-   .
Pseudonyms: Harry Davis, Paul Kruger, qq.v.
SECRIST, KELLIHER. Joint pseudonym of Dan T. Kelliher and W. G. Secrist. Both Kan. City reporters in 1940s. SC: Sham Payne, in both titles.
Murder Makes By-Lines. Mystery House, 1941
Murder Melody. Phoenix, 1939. Also published as: She Screamed Blue Murder. Green Dragon, 1946

She Screamed Blue Murder; see Murder Melody
SECRIST, W. G. Joint pseudonym with Dan T. Kelliher: Kelliher Secrist, q.v.
SEDERBERG, ARELO (CHARLES). 1930-   .
Ref: CA.
60 Hours of Darkness. Sherbourne, 1974 [Las Veg.]
SEE, INGRAM
No Scars to See. Bouregy, 1965
SEELEY, CLINTON. 1921-   . Born in N.Y.; newspaperman in N.Y. and New Or.
Storm Fear. Holt, 1954; Ward, 1957 [N.Y.]
SEELEY, MABEL (HODNESFIELD). 1903-   .
Ref: CC, DD, EM, MP, TC.
The Beckoning Door. Doubleday, 1950; Collins, 1950 [Minn.]
The Blonde with the Deadly Past; see The Whistling Shadow
The Chuckling Fingers. Doubleday, 1941; Collins, 1942 [Minn.]
The Crying Sisters. Doubleday, 1939; Collins, 1940 [Minn.]
Eleven Came Back. Doubleday, 1943; Collins, 1943 [Wyo.]
The Listening House. Doubleday, 1938; Collins, 1939 [Minn.]
The Whispering Cup. Doubleday, 1940; Collins, 1941 [Minn.]
The Whistling Shadow. Doubleday, 1954; Jenkins, 1954. Also published as: The Blonde with the Deadly Past. Mercury, 1955 [Mpls.]
SEGAL, ALAN and DON SEGAL
The Croesus Affair. Carlyle, 1979
SEGAL, DON. See: Alan Segal.
SEGALL, DON. Pseudonym: Leo August, q.v.
SEIBERT, ELIZABETH G.
-The Abrus Necklace. Macrae-Smith, 1956
Death Follows the Flower Show. Arcadia, 1958
SEIDMAN, ROBERT J(EROME). 1941-   . Ref: CA.
-Bucks County Idyll. Simon, 1980 [Pa.]
SEIFERT, ADELE. See also: Shirley (Louise) Seifert, 1889-1971. SC: Gregory Trent, in all titles.
Deeds Ill Done. Mill, 1939. British title (?): Kill Your Own Snakes. Boardman, 1947 [Mo.]
Kill Your Own Snakes; see Deeds Ill Done
Shadows Tonight. Mill, 1939; Boardman, 1943 [Midwest]
3 Blind Mice. Mill, 1942; Boardman, 1945 [Mo.]
SEIFERT, SHIRLEY (LOUISE), 1889-1971, and ADELE SEIFERT, q.v.
Death Stops at the Old Stone Inn. Hillman-Curl, 1938; Big Ben, 1943 [Tenn.]
SEIGNOLLE, CLAUDE. 1917-   . Ref: CA.
-The Accursed. Coward, 1967; Allen, 1967 (Translation of "Les Maledictions." Paris, 1963.) (2 stories.)
SEILAZ, AILEEN
The Veil of Silence. Ace, 1965
SELA, OWEN. Partner in firm of chartered accountants in London. SC: Nicholas Maasten = NM.
The Bearer Plot. Hodder, 1972; Pantheon, 1973 NM
The Bengali Inheritance. Hodder, 1975; Pantheon, 1975 [H. Kong]
An Exchange of Eagles. Hodder, 1977; Atheneum, 1977 [Ger., 1940]
The Kiriov Tapes. Hodder, 1973; Pantheon, 1974 NM
The Petrograd Consignment. Joseph, 1979; Dial, 1979 [Russ., 1919]
The Portuguese Fragment. Hodder, 1974; Pantheon, 1973 NM [Cey.]
SELBORNE, JOHN
-The House of the Siren. Everett, 1911
The Thousand Secrets. Everett, 1911; Kennerley, 1915
SELBY, HUBERT, JR. 1928-   . Ref: CA.
Requiem for a Dream. Playboy, 1978; Boyars, 1979
SELDEN, CATHARINE
Villa Nova; or, The Ruined Castle. Lane, 1805
SELDES, GILBERT VIVIAN. 1893-1970. Pseudonym: Foster Johns, q.v.

SELIG, ELAINE BOOTH. 1935-   . Ref: CA.
    Mariner's End. PB, 1977 [New Eng.]
    Scorpion Summer. PB, 1977

SELIGSON, TOM. 1946-   . Ref: CA.
    Stalking. Everest, 1979

SELLAR, MAURICE
    The Allies. Cassell, 1979

SELLARS, ELEANORE KELLY. Ref: CC.
    Murder a la Mode. Dodd, 1941; Muller, 1943 [NYC]

SELLERS, CON(NIE LESLIE, JR.). 1922-   .
    Pseudonym: Robert Crane, q.v.
    The Algerian Incident. Powell, 1970 [Algeria]

SELLERS, MARY
    The Cry of the Cat. Warner, 1975 [Miss.]
    The House on Black Bayou. Warner, 1975 [La., 1700s]
    Night Shadows. Berkley, 1977 [N.W.]
    Raise the Dark Gambler. Berkley, 1977 [La.]

SELLERS, MICHAEL
    Leonardo and Others. Macmillan (London), 1980

SELLICKS, LESLIE EDWARD. 1902-   . Pseudonym: Edward Leslie, q.v.

SELLINGS, ARTHUR. Pseudonym of Arthur Gordon Ley, 1911-1968, q.v.

SELMAN, ROBERT. Actor.
    Once Upon a Crime. Morrow, 1947; Foulsham, 1949 [NYC]

SELMARK, GEORGE. Pseudonym of (Leslie) Seldon Truss, 1892-   , q.v. SC: Insp. Bass = B (see also Truss entry.)
    Murder in Silence. Cassell, 1939; Doubleday, 1940

SELTZER, CHARLES ALDEN. 1875-1942.
    Parade of the Empty Boots. Doubleday, 1937; Hodder, 1938

SELVER, (PERCY) PAUL. 1888-1970. Ref: CA.
    Private Life. Jarrolds, 1929; Harper, 1930

SELWYN. Pseudonym of Selwyn Victor Watson.
    Operation Ballerina. Hodder, 1953

SELWYN, FRANCIS. 1935-   . Ref: TC. SC: Sgt. William Verity, in all titles.
    Cracksman on Velvet. Deutsch, 1974; Stein, 1974. Also published as: Sergeant Verity and the Cracksman. Futura, 1975 [Eng., ca.1860]
    Sergeant Verity and the Blood Royal. Duetsch, 1979; Stein, 1979 [Phil., 1860]
    Sergeant Verity and the Cracksman; see Cracksman on Velvet
    Sergeant Verity and the Imperial Diamond. Deutsch, 1975; Stein, 1976 [India, ca.1860]
    Sergeant Verity and the Swell Mob. Deutsch, 1980; Stein, 1980 [Eng., ca.1860]
    Sergeant Verity Presents His Compliments. Deutsch, 1977; Stein, 1977 [Eng., 1860]

SEMENOV, JULIAN (SEMENOVICH). 1931-   .
    Ref: CA, CC.
    The Himmler Ploy. Popular Library, 1978; Arrow, 1979. Original title: The Seventeen Moments of Spring. Progress (Moscow), 1973 (Translation of "Semnadtsat Mgnovenii Visny." Moscow, 1970.) [Ger., WWII]
    Petrovka 38. MacGibbon, 1965; Stein, 1965 (Translation of "Petrovka 38." Moscow, 1964.) [Moscow]
    The Seventeen Moments of Spring; see The Himmler Ploy

SEMPRUN, JORGE. 1920?-   .
    The Second Death of Ramon Mercader. Weidenfeld, 1973; Grove, 1973 (Translation of "La Deuxieme Mort de Ramon Mercader." Paris, 1969.)

SENECAL, JEAN-MICHEL. Joint pseudonym with Yves Jacquemard: Jacquemard-Senecal, q.v.

SENNOCKE, T. J. R. SC: Sgt. Mallory, in at least those marked M.
    Inquest on a Lady. Rudkin, 1941 M
    Inquest on a Mistress. Rudkin, 1943 M
    Inquest Betraying. Rudkin, 1943 M
    Inquests by Jury. Rudkin, 1944
    Inquests on the Deceased. Rudkin, 1944
    What Is Your Verdict? Eyre, 1936 (Problems in detection, with solutions.)

SERAFIN, DAVID. British novelist who has lived many years in Sp.
    Saturday of Glory. Collins, 1979

SERAO, MATILDE. 1856-1927.
    The Severed Hand. Paul, 1925 (Translated from the Italian.)

SERENY, GITTA
    The Medallion. Gollancz, 1957

SERGE, VICTOR. 1890-1947.
    The Case of Comrade Tulayev. Doubleday, 1950; H. Hamilton, 1951 (Translation of L'Affaire Toulaev." Paris, 1949.)

SERGEANT, (EMILY FRANCES) ADELINE. 1851-1904. U.S. byline sometimes: Adeline Sargeant.
    -Accused and Accuser. Methuen, 1904
    -Beneath the Veil. Long, 1903
    -A Broken Idol. Hurst, 1893
    -A Deadly Foe. Hutchinson, 1895
    -Deveril's Diamond. Hurst, 1889
    -Dr. Endicott's Experiment. Chatto, 1894; Cassell (NYC), 1895
    An East London Mystery. Hurst, 1892
    The Great Mill Street Mystery. Lovell, 1890. Also published as: The Mill Street Mystery. Westbrook, ca.1920 (British title?)
    -The House in the Crescent. Long, 1907
    -A Life Sentence. Hurst, 1891; Lovell, 1889
    -The Master of Beechwood. Methuen, 1902; Burt, 1902
    The Mill Street Mystery; see The Great Mill Street Mystery
    -Miss Betty's Mistake. Hurst, 1898
    -The Missing Elizabeth. Chatto, 1905
    Mrs. Lygon's Husband. Methuen, 1905
    My Lady's Diamonds. Ward, 1901; Buckles, 1901
    The Mystery of the Moat. Methuen, 1905
    -An Open Foe. Bentley, 1884
    The Progress of Rachel. Methuen, 1904
    The Quest of Geoffrey Darrell. Methuen, 1907
    -The Sin of Laban Routh. Digby, 1905
    Sir Anthony. Hurst, 1892. U.S. title: Sir Anthony's Secret; or, A False Position. Taylor, 1891
    Sir Anthony's Secret; see Sir Anthony
    -This Body of Death. Hurst, 1891
    -The Treasure of Captain Scarlett. Hutchinson, 1901
    -Under False Pretences. Ward, 1892; Lovell, 1889
    Under Suspicion. Methuen, 1904
    The Yellow Diamond. Methuen, 1904

SERGEL, RUTH (FULLER). 1897-   .
    The Red House Mystery. Dramatic, 1956 (3-act play based on the novel by A. A. Milne, 1882-1956, q.v.)

SERLING, ROBERT J(EROME). 1918-   .
    Ref: CA.
    McDermott's Sky. Stein, 1977
    The President's Plane Is Missing. Doubleday, 1967; Cassell, 1968 [Wash. D.C.]

SERNER, MARTIN GUNNAR. 1886-1947. Pseudonym: Frank Heller, q.v.

SERRESTER, LEONARD
    The Frog Murders. Dorrance, 1955 [New Eng.]

SERVICE, ROBERT W(ILLIAM). 1876-1958. Ref: MM.
    The House of Fear. Dodd, 1927; Unwin, 1927 [Fr.]
    -The Master of the Microbe. Barse, 1926; Unwin, 1927 [Paris]
    The Poisoned Paradise. Dodd, 1922

SETH, RONALD (SYDNEY). 1911-   .
    -The Patriot. Owen, 1954
    Spy in the Nude. Hale, 1962

SETON, GRAHAM. Pseudonym of Graham Seton Hutchison, 1890-1946. SC: Col. Duncan Grant = DG.
    According to Plan. Rich, 1938 DG
    Blood Money. Hutchinson, 1934
    Colonel Grant's Tomorrow. Butterworth, 1931; Farrar, 1932 DG [Mor.]
    Eye for an Eye. Hutchinson, 1932; Farrar, 1933 [Russ.]
    The Governor of Kattowitz. Butterworth, 1930. U.S. title: The Sign of Arnim. Cosmopolitan, 1931
    The K Code Plan. Rich, 1938 DG [Paris, India]
    Minos Magnificent. Hutchinson, 1935
    The Red Colonel. Hutchinson, 1947 DG [Ger.]
    Scar 77. Rich, 1936 DG
    The Sign of Arnim; see The Governor of Kattowitz
    Tiger's Cub. Rich, 1940
    The V Plan. Eyre, 1941; Smith & Durrell, 1941 DG [Fr.]
    The Viper of Luxor. Hutchinson, 1933
    The W Plan. Butterworth, 1929; Cosmopolitan, 1930 DG [Fr., Ger.]

SETTLE, MARY LEE. 1918-   . Ref: CA.
    Blood Tie. Houghton, 1977 [Turk.]

SEUFFERT, MUIR. SC: Mike Hubbard, in all titles.
    Devil at the Door. Hale, 1972
    Hand of a Killer. Hale, 1967
    Trespassers Will Die. Hale, 1968

SEVERN, RICHARD. SC: Jeff Cass, in at least those marked JC.
    An Array of Eagles. Hale, 1971
    Blood and Gold. Hale, 1964
    The Desperate Rendezvous. Hale, 1966
    The Forest and the Damned. Hale, 1965
    A Game for Hawks. Hale, 1968   JC
    The Killing Match. Hale, 1970   JC
    The Long Echo. Hale, 1976
    Quest to Kill. Hale, 1974
    Stalk a Long Shadow. Hale, 1967   JC

SEVERNE, FLORENCE
    In the Meshes. Osgood, 1894

SEVERY, MARTIN (LINWOOD). 1863-   .
    SC: George Maitland, in all titles.
    The Darrow Enigma. Dodd, 1904; Richards, 1904 [Boston]
    Maitland's Master Mystery. Ball, 1912
    The Mystery of June 13. Dodd, 1905; Stevens, 1905

SEVILLE, MARJORIE
    The Quest of the Emerald. Hutchinson, 1927

SEWARD, JACK [JOHN NEIL SEWARD]. 1924-   . Ref: CA. SC: Curt Stone, in all titles.
    Assignment: Find Cherry. Tower, 1969 [Jap.]
    The Cave of the Chinese Skeletons. Tuttle, 1964 [Jap.]
    The Chinese Pleasure Girl. Tower, 1969
    The Frogman Assassination. Tower, 1969
    The Eurasian Virgins. Tower, 1969 [Jap.]

SEWARD, WILLIAM WARD. 1913-   . Ref: CA.
    Skirts of the Dead Night. Bookman, 1950

SEWART, ALAN
    Curiosity Killed the Cop. Hale, 1980
    Kyriakos and the Toad. Hale, 1979
    Loop Current. Hale, 1980
    A Ribbon for My Repute. Hale, 1979
    The Salome Syndrome. Hale, 1979
    Tough Tontine. Hale, 1978
    The Turn-Up. Hale, 1978
    A Very Ordinary Murder. Hale, 1979
    The Women of Morning. Hale, 1980

SEYMOUR, ARTHUR
    The Fall of the Mighty. Odhams, 1919

SEYMOUR, CYRIL
    The Magic of To-Morrow. Chatto, 1903

SEYMOUR, (WILLIAM HERSCHEL KEAN) GERALD. 1941-   . British TV news reporter.
    The Contract. Collins, 1980; Holt, 1981 [Ger.]
    The Glory Boys. Collins, 1976; Random, 1976
    The Harrison Affair; see Red Fox
    Harry's Game. Collins, 1975; Random, 1975 [Belfast]
    Kingfisher. Collins, 1977; Summit, 1978
    Red Fox. Collins, 1979. U.S. title: The Harrison Affair. Summit, 1980 [It.]

SEYMOUR, H(ENRY). Pseudonym of Helmut Henry Hartmann, 1931-   . Ref: CA.
    Appointment with Murder. Gifford, 1962
    The Big Steal. Hale, 1972
    The Bristol Affair. Gifford, 1960
    Cold Wind of Death. Hale, 1972
    Hot Ice. Gifford, 1966
    In the Still of the Night. Gifford, 1966 [Rio de J.]
    Infernal Idol. Gifford, 1967
    Intrigue in Tangier. Gifford, 1958 [Tangier]
    The Paperchase Murder. Gifford, 1961
    Run for Your Enemy. Gifford, 1959

SHABTAI, SABI H.
    Five Minutes to Midnight. Delacorte, 1980; Dent, 1980

SHAFER, ROBERT (JONES). 1920- . Ref: CA.
-The Conquered Place. Putnam (NYC), 1954; Putnam (London), 1955. Also published as: The Naked and the Damned. Popular Library, 1955, abridged

SHAFFER, ANTHONY (JOSHUA). 1926- . Joint pseudonym with Peter (Levin) Shaffer, 1926- , q.v.: Peter Antony, q.v. See also: Robin Hardy. Ref: CC, EM, MC, TC.
Absolution. Corgi, 1979
Murderer. Boyars (NYC & London), 1979 (2-act play.)
Sleuth. Calder, 1971; Dodd, 1970 (Play.)
Withered Murder, with P(eter Levin) Shaffer. Gollancz, 1955; Macmillan, 1956

SHAFFER, ERVIN ADAM
Major Washington. Hobson, 1947 [Va., 1754]

SHAFFER, JACK C. 1928- . Born in Ia.; employed in missile industry, later head of publishing firm.
Sweet Revenge. Vantage, 1965

SHAFFER, PETER (LEVIN). 1926- . Joint pseudonym with Anthony (Joshua) Shaffer, 1926- , q.v.: Peter Antony, q.v. Ref: CA, EM, MC, TC.

SHAFTEL, GEORG ARMIN. See: Robert Clark.

SHAGAN, STEVE. 1927- . Ref: CA.
City of Angels. Putnam, 1975; Joseph, 1975. Also published as: Hustle. Signet, 1975; Star, 1976 [L.A.]
The Formula. Morrow, 1979; Joseph, 1980
Hustle; see City of Angels

SHAH, DIANE K(IVER). 1945- . Ref: CA.
The Mackin Cover. Dodd, 1977

SHAIRP, (ALEXANDER) MORDAUNT. 1887-1939.
The Crime at Blossoms. Allen, 1932; Baker, 1933 (3-act play.)

SHAKESPEARE, BRIAN. See: John De St. Jorre, 1936- .

SHALLIT, JOSEPH. SC: Dan Morrison, in all titles.
The Billion Dollar Body. Lippincott, 1947; Hammond, 1952. Also published as: The Case of the Billion Dollar Body. Avon, 1954 [Phil.]
The Case of the Billion Dollar Body; see The Billion Dollar Body
Juvenile Hoods; see Kiss the Killer
Kiss the Killer. Lippincott, 1952; Hammond, 1954. Also published as: Juvenile Hoods. Avon, 1957 [Phil.]
Lady, Don't Die on My Doorstep. Lippincott, 1951; Hammond, 1952 [Phil.]
Yell Bloody Murder. Lippincott, 1951. British title: Yell Ruddy Murder. Hammond, 1953 [Pa.]
Yell Ruddy Murder; see Yell Bloody Murder

SHAMBROOK, RONA (GREEN). Pseudonym: Rona Randall, q.v.
The Silver Cord. Collins, 1963; Ace, 1968, as by Rona Randall

SHAND, WILLIAM. SC: Bill Tempest, in all titles.
A Man Called Tempest. Jenkins, 1957
Tempest in a Tea-Cup. Jenkins, 1958; Roy, 1959
Tempest Weaves a Shroud. Jenkins, 1957

SHANE, MARK. Pseudonym of Victor (George Charles) Norwood, 1920- , q.v. Other pseudonyms: Johnny Dark, Mark Hampton, Hank Janson, Nat Karta, qq.v.
Borrowed Time. Comyns, 1952
Death at Her Fingers. Comyns, 1953
Honey Ain't So Sweet. Comyns, 1953
Jail and Farewell. Comyns, 1953
The Lady Bites the Dust. Comyns, 1952
Obsession to Kill. Comyns, 1953

SHANE, SUSANNAH. Pseudonym of H(arriette Cora) Ashbrook, 1898-1946, q.v. SC: Christopher Saxe, in at least those marked CS.
The Baby in the Ash Can. Dodd, 1944; Nicholson, 1947 CS [N.J.]
Diamonds in the Dumplings. Doubleday, 1946 CS [Conn.]
Lady in a Million. Dodd, 1943; Nicholson, 1948 CS [NYC]
Lady in a Wedding Dress. Dodd, 1943
Lady in Danger. Dodd, 1942; Nicholson, 1948 CS [L.I.]
Lady in Lilac. Dodd, 1941 [NYC]

SHANER, JOHN. See: Al Ramrus.

SHANKS, EDWARD (BUXTON). 1892-1953.
The Dark Green Circle; see Old King Cole
Old King Cole. Macmillan (London), 1936. U.S. title: The Dark Green Circle. Bobbs, 1936
The Richest Man. Collins, 1923; Knopf, 1924

SHANN, B. V. See: Marten Cumberland, 1892-1972.

SHANNON, ALASTAIR
The Black Scorpion. Bles, 1926 [India]

SHANNON, BRAD. SC: Lefty O'Connor, in at least those marked LO.
The Big Snatch. Scion, 1950
Blues for My Baby. Scion, 1950
The Body Was Lonely. Scion, 1952
Bury the Guy! Scion, 1951 LO
Cons on the Run. Scion, 1951
The Countless Steps. Scion, 1952
The Dead Don't Cry. Scion, 1951
Death Pulls No Punches. Scion, 1951
Don't Mention It. Scion, 1951
Fall Guy. Scion, 1950
Heads You Lose. Scion, 1952
I Wake Screaming. Scion, 1953
The Lady's for Killing. Scion, 1950
Lefty Cuts Loose. Scion, 1951 LO
Lefty Hands It Out. Scion, 1951 LO
Lefty O'Connor Moves In. Scion, 1950 LO
Lefty Takes Over. Scion, 1952 LO
Murder!—So What? Scion, 1951
Rubberneck. Scion, 1952
Sadie Swings the Blues. Scion, 1953
Some Get It. Scion, 1953
"Stir" Crazy. Scion, 1950
They Say I'm Bad. Scion, 1953
You Talk Too Much. Scion, 1951

SHANNON, CARL. Pseudonym of Wilbur Owings Hogue, 1910?-1952.
Fatal Footsteps. Phoenix, 1948; Boardman, 1951 [Afr.]
Lady, That's My Skull. Phoenix, 1947; Boardman, 1948
Murder Me Never. Boardman, 1951

SHANNON, DELL. Pseudonym of (Barbara) Elizabeth Linington, 1921- , q.v. Other pseudonyms: Anne Blaisdell, Lesley Egan, qq.v. SC: Lt. Luis Mendoza, in all titles, all set in L.A.
The Ace of Spades. Morrow, 1961; Oldbourne, 1963, as by Barbara Elizabeth Linington
Appearances of Death. Morrow, 1977; Gollancz, 1978
Case Pending. Harper, 1960; Gollancz, 1960
Chance to Kill. Morrow, 1967; Gollancz, 1968
Coffin Corner. Morrow, 1966; Gollancz, 1967
Cold Trail. Morrow, 1978; Gollancz, 1978
Crime File. Morrow, 1974; Gollancz, 1975
Crime on Their Hands. Morrow, 1969; Gollancz, 1970
Death by Inches. Morrow, 1965; Gollancz, 1967
The Death-Bringers. Morrow, 1965; Gollancz, 1966
Death of a Busybody. Morrow, 1963; Oldbourne, 1963, as by Barbara Elizabeth Linington. Reprinted as by Dell Shannon: Gollancz, 1978
Deuces Wild. Morrow, 1975; Gollancz, 1975
Double Bluff. Morrow, 1963; Oldbourne, 1964, as by Barbara Elizabeth Linington. Reprinted as by Dell Shannon: Gollancz, 1978
Extra Kill. Morrow, 1962; Oldbourne, 1962, as by Barbara Elizabeth Linington
Felony at Random. Morrow, 1979; Gollancz, 1979
Felony File. Morrow, 1980; Gollancz, 1980
Kill with Kindness. Morrow, 1968; Gollancz, 1969
Knave of Hearts. Morrow, 1962; Oldbourne, 1963, as by Barbara Elizabeth Linington
Mark of Murder. Morrow, 1964; Gollancz, 1965
Murder with Love. Morrow, 1972; Gollancz, 1972
No Holiday for Crime. Morrow, 1973; Gollancz, 1974
Rain with Violence. Morrow, 1967; Gollancz, 1969
The Ringer. Morrow, 1971; Gollancz, 1972
Root of All Evil. Morrow, 1964; Gollancz, 1966
Schooled to Kill. Morrow, 1969; Gollancz, 1970
Spring of Violence. Morrow, 1973; Gollancz, 1974
Streets of Death. Morrow, 1976; Gollancz, 1977
Unexpected Death. Morrow, 1970; Gollancz, 1971
Whim to Kill. Morrow, 1971; Gollancz, 1971
With a Vengeance. Morrow, 1966; Gollancz, 1968
With Intent to Kill. Morrow, 1972; Gollancz, 1973

SHANNON, DORIS. 1924- . Ref: CA.
Hawthorn Hill. St. Martin's, 1976
The Lodestar Legacy. Popular Library, 1976 [Can.]
The Whispering Runes. Lenox, 1972

SHANNON, JOHN C.
Who Shall Condemn? and other stories. Robinson, 1894 ss, some criminous
Zylgrahof and other stories. Simpkin, 1901 ss, some criminous

SHANNON, JIMMY
The Devil's Passkey. Appleton, 1952 [NYC]

SHAPIRO, LIONEL (SEBASTIAN BERK). 1908- . Foreign correspondent for U.S. newspapers and broadcasts.
The Sealed Verdict. Doubleday, 1947; Jarrolds, 1950 [Ger.]
Torch for a Dark Journey. Doubleday, 1950; Jarrolds, 1951

SHAPIRO, MILTON J.
The Hawk. Ace, 1975

SHAPLEIGH, MARY YALE
-Johnny Counterfeit. Hopkins, 1938

SHARD, JOHN
I Am Maud Latimer. Laurie, 1941

SHARKEY, MRS. EMMA AUGUSTA BROWN. 1858- . Pseudonym: Mrs. E. Burke Collins, q.v.

SHARKEY, JACK [JOHN MICHAEL SHARKEY]. 1931- . Ref: CA. SC: George Herbert Henry = GH.
Death for Auld Lang Syne. Holt, 1962; Joseph, 1963 GH [NYC]
Murder, Maestro, Please. Abelard (NYC & London), 1960 GH [NYC]
The Murder Room. French (NYC), 1977 (3-act play.)
-Who's on First? French (NYC), 1975 (Play.)

SHARLAND, MICHAEL
Nervestorm. Ellis, 1975

SHARMAN, MIRIAM. Pseudonym of Maisie Sharman Bolton, 1915- . Other pseudonym: Stratford Davis, q.v. Ref: CA.
Death Pays All Debts. Gollancz, 1965
The Face of Danger. Gollancz, 1967
Law of Probability. Macdonald, 1971
Seeds of Violence. Gollancz, 1966

SHARMAN, NICK
The Cats. New English Library pb, 1977

SHARP, ALAN. 1934- . Ref: CA.
Night Moves. Paperback Library, 1975; Corgi, 1975 (Novelization of the movie.)

SHARP, DAVID. Ref: CC. SC: Prof. Henry Arthur Fielding, in at least those marked HF. Set: Eng.
The Code-Letter Mystery; see None of My Business
Disputed Quarry. Jenkins, 1938 HF
Elderly Gentleman Shot. Jenkins, 1939 HF
Everybody Suspect. Jenkins, 1939 HF
Exit Second Murderer. Jenkins, 1940
The Frightened Sailor. Jenkins, 1939 HF
I, the Criminal. Benn, 1932; Houghton, 1933 HF
The Inconvenient Corpse. Benn, 1933 HF
Marriage and Murder. Benn, 1934 HF
My Particular Murder. Benn, 1931; Houghton, 1931 HF
None of My Business. Benn, 1931. U.S. title: The Code-Letter Mystery. Houghton, 1932 HF
When No Man Pursueth. Benn, 1930 HF

SHARP, GUSTAVUS
The Confessions of an Attorney. Cornish, 1852 ss

SHARP, JACK
 The Telltale Tattoo. Street (Magnet)
 The Wall Street Swindlers. Street (Magnet)

SHARP, LUKE. Pseudonym of Robert Barr, 1850-1912, q.v.

SHARP, MARILYN. Wife of a U.S. congressman.
 Sunflower. Marek, 1979; Macmillan (London), 1979

SHARP, ROBERT (GEORGE). Pseudonym: Jon J. Deegan, q.v.
 The Blonde Gangster. Fiction House, 1935
 The Cry from the Ether. Fiction House, 1935
 Death Comes to Rehearsal. Hutchinson, 1951
 Death in the Headlines. Hutchinson, 1950
 Death Rides the Rail. Fiction House, 1947
 Horror Castle. Gray, 1936
 In the Hands of the Enemy. Fiction House, 1935
 -Love Is King. Fiction House, 1938
 The Racketeers. Fiction House, 1948

SHARP, WILLOUGHBY
 Murder in Bermuda. Kendall, 1933; Eyre, 1935 [Bermuda]
 Murder of the Honest Broker. Kendall, 1934 [NYC]

SHATTE, PHYLLIS
 Ninety Days to Nine-O. Stockwell, 1976

SHATTUCK, DORA (RICHARDS). Pseudonym: Richard Shattuck, q.v.
 The Wailing Woman. Paperback Library, 1973

SHATTUCK, RICHARD. Pseudonym of Dora (Richards) Shattuck, q.v.
 The Body in the Bridal Bed; see The Wedding Guest Sat on a Stone
 The Half-Haunted Saloon. Simon, 1945 [Calif.]
 Said the Spider to the Fly. Simon, 1944 [Utah]
 The Snark Was a Boojum. Morrow, 1941; Hale, 1941. Also published as: With Blood and Kisses. Mercury, 1954 [Mass.]
 The Wedding Guest Sat on a Stone. Morrow, 1940; Hale, 1941. Also published as: The Body in the Bridal Bed. Mercury, 1953 [Calif.]
 With Blood and Kisses; see The Snark Was a Boojum

SHAVELSON, MELVILLE. 1917-   . Ref: CA.
 The Eleventh Commandment. Reader's Digest, 1977; Allen, 1978

SHAW, BYNUM (GILLETTE). 1923-   . Ref: CA.
 The Nazi Hunter. Norton, 1968 [Ger.]

SHAW, CHARLES. 1900-   . Pseudonym: Bant Singer, q.v.

SHAW, D. B.
 Ten True Secret Service Stories. Ogilvie, ss

SHAW, DAVID. 1943-   . Ref: CA.
 -The Levy Caper. Macmillan, 1974

SHAW, FELICITY. 1918-   . Pseudonym: Anne Morice, q.v.

SHAW, FRANK H(UBERT). 1878-   .
 Atlantic Murder. Mathews, 1932; McBride, 1933 [ship]

SHAW, HERBERT. See also: Anthony Armstrong.
 The Man Who Lived Twice. Columbine, 1939

SHAW, (COLIN) HOWARD. 1934-   . Pseudonym: Colin Howard, q.v.

SHAW, IRENE. Pseudonym of Irene Roberts, 1926-   . Ref: CA.
 Murderer's Mansion. Wright, 1968; Doubleday, 1976

SHAW, IRWIN. 1913-   . Ref: CA.
 The Assassin. Random, 1946 (3-act play).
 The Gentle People. Random, 1939. 3-act play version: Dramatists, 1939
 -Nightwork. Delacorte, 1975; Weidenfeld, 1975

SHAW, JOSEPH T(HOMPSON). 1874-1952.
 Blood on the Curb. Dodge, 1936 [NYC]
 Danger Ahead. Mohawk, 1932
 Derelict. Knopf, 1930 [ship]
 It Happened at the Lake. Dodd, 1937 [N.Y.]

SHAW, ROBIN. 1936-   .
 Running. Putnam, 1973; Gollancz, 1974 [Ida.]

SHAW, STANLEY GORDON. 1884-1938? Brother of Frank H(ubert) Shaw, 1878-   , q.v.
 The Secret of the Monastery. Amalgamated, 1928 (Sexton Blake.)

SHAW, STOCKER
 "Eblis." Hornsey Journal, 1933

SHAW, W. J.
 Old Anthony's Secret. (Author), 1888
 Solomon's Story. Thomson, 1880

SHAW, WILENE
 -The Fear and the Guilt. Ace, 1954
 -Heat Lightning. Ace, 1954
 -The Mating Call. Ace, 1954
 -Out for Kicks. Ace, 1959

SHAY, FRANK. 1888-1954. SC: Dan (DeeDee) Doner, in both titles.
 The Charming Murder. Macaulay, 1930 [NYC]
 Murder on Cape Cod. Macaulay, 1931 [Cape Cod]

SHAYNE, GORDON. Pseudonym of Bevis Winter, 1918-   , q.v. Other pseudonyms: Al Bocca, Peter Cagney, qq.v.
 And So to Death. Jasmit, 1952
 Ticket to Eternity. Jasmit, 1954

SHEA, JOHN D.
 A Private Detective: The Marvelous Career of a Notorious Criminal. Laird, 1889

SHEA, ROBERT and ROBERT ANTON WILSON, 1932-   . Ref for Wilson: CA.
 -The Eye in the Pyramid. Dell, 1975
 -The Golden Apple. Dell, 1975
 -Leviathan. Dell, 1975

SHEAHAN, K. M. Set: Eng.
 -An Artist in Crime. Jenkins, 1936
 Dangerous Men. Jenkins, 1935
 The Stormberg Jewel Case. Jenkins, 1931

SHEARING, JOSEPH. Pseudonym of Gabrielle Margaret Vere Campbell Long, 1886-1952. Other pseudonyms: Marjorie Bowen, George R. Preedy, qq.v., Margaret Campbell. Ref: CC, MP, TC.
 The Abode of Love. Hutchinson, 1945
 Airing in a Closed Carriage. Hutchinson, 1943; Harper, 1943 [Eng., 1889]
 Album Leaf. Heinemann, 1933. U.S. title: The Spider in the Cup. Smith, 1934. Reprinted in the U.S. as by Margaret Campbell: Signet, 1975
 Aunt Beardie. Hutchinson, 1940; Harrison-Hilton, 1940 [Eng., 1794]
 Blanche Fury; or, Fury's Ape. Heinemann, 1939; Harrison-Hilton, 1939 [Eng., 1848-50]
 The Crime of Laura Sarelle; see Laura Sarelle
 The Fetch. Hutchinson, 1942. U.S. title: The Spectral Bride. Smith, 1942. Reprinted in the U.S. under the British title as by Margaret Campbell: Signet, 1975 [Eng., 1870]
 For Her to See. Hutchinson, 1947. U.S. title: So Evil My Love. Harper, 1947 [Eng., 1800s]
 Forget-Me-Not. Heinemann, 1932. U.S. title: Lucile Clery. Harper, 1932. Reprinted as: The Strange Case of Lucile Clery. World, 1944 [Fr., 1800s]
 The Golden Violet. Heinemann, 1936; Smith, 1941. Also published as: Night's Dark Secret. Signet, 1975, as by Margaret Campbell [Jam., 1860]
 The Heiress of Frascati; see Within the Bubble
 The Lady and the Arsenic. Heinemann, 1937; Smith, 1944 [Fr., 1869]
 Laura Sarelle. Hutchinson, 1940. U.S. title: The Crime of Laura Sarelle. Smith, 1941 [Eng., 1700s]
 Lucile Clery; see Forget-Me-Not
 Mignonette. Heinemann, 1949; Harper, 1948 [past]
 Moss Rose. Heinemann, 1934; Smith & Haas, 1935 [Eng., 1800s]
 Night's Dark Secret; see The Golden Violet
 Orange Blossoms. Heinemann, 1938
 So Evil My Love; see For Her to See
 The Spectral Bride; see The Fetch
 The Spider in the Cup; see Album Leaf
 The Strange Case of Lucile Clery; see Forget-Me-Not
 To Bed at Noon. Heinemann, 1951
 Within the Bubble. Heinemann, 1950. U.S. title: The Heiress of Frascati. Berkley, 1966

SHECKLEY, ROBERT. 1928-   . Ref: CA. SC: Stephen Dain = SD.
 Calibre .50. Bantam, 1961 SD [Carib.]
 Dead Run. Bantam, 1961 SD
 The Game of X. Delacorte, 1965; Cape, 1966 [Venice]
 Live Gold. Bantam, 1962 SD
 The Man in the Water. Regency, 1962
 The Tenth Victim. Ballantine, 1965; Mayflower, 1966 (Novelization of the movie.)
 Time Limit. Bantam, 1967; New English Library pb, 1967 SD [Mid. East]
 White Death. Bantam, 1963 SD [Iran]

SHEDD, GEORGE C(LIFFORD). 1877-1937.
 Gangster War on Bar "G". Swan, 1949
 -In the Shadow of the Hills. Macaulay, 1919
 The Invisible Enemy. Macaulay, 1918
 The Isle of Strife. Small, 1912
 The Lady of Mystery House. Macaulay, 1917; Gardner, 1920 [Fla.]
 -The Passport Invisible. Doran, 1918
 -Those Who Walk in Darkness. Doran, 1917

SHEDD, MARGARET (COCHRAN). 1900-   .
 Run. Doubleday, 1956; Gollancz, 1956

SHEDLEY, ETHAN I. Pseudonym of Boris Beizer, 1934-   . Ref: CA.
 The Medusa Conspiracy. Viking, 1980

SHEEHAN, PERLEY POORE. 1875-1943.
 The House with a Bad Name. Boni, 1920; Brentano's (London), 1923 [NYC]
 Three Sevens. Chelsea, 1927
 The Whispering Chorus. Watt, 1927; Benn, 1928

SHEEN, GEORGE
 Assignment Greece. Digit, 1958 [Greece]
 -Extermination Camp. Digit, 1958
 -Malayan Story. Digit, 1958 [Mal.]
 The Traitor. Digit, 1958

SHEERS, JAMES C.
 The Counterfeit Courier. Dell, 1961

SHEFLER, HARRY F.
 Devil Take the Hindmost. Exposition, 1955

SHELBY, BRIT. 1949-   . Ref: CA.
 The Great Pebble Affair. Putnam, 1976

SHELDON, MRS. GEORGIE. Pseudonym of Sarah Elizabeth Forbush Downs, 1843-   .
 Max. Street, 1892
 The Shadow of a Crime; see Trixy
 Trixy; or, The Shadow of a Crime. Burt, 1888. British title: The Shadow of a Crime. Aldine, 1897
 The Welfleet Mystery. Red Lion, 1901 (U.S. title?)

SHELDON, GILBERT. 1870-   . Pseudonym: James Colwall, q.v.

SHELDON, LOUISE VESCELIUS
 An I.D.B. in South Africa. Lovell, 1888; Trubner, 1889 [S. Afr.]

SHELDON, RICHARD
 Harsh Evidence. Hutchinson, 1950 [Eng., 1874]
 Poor Prisoner's Defense. Hutchinson, 1949; Simon, 1949

SHELDON, SIDNEY. 1917-   . Ref: CA.
 Bloodline. Morrow, 1978; Collins, 1978
 The Naked Face. Morrow, 1970; Hodder, 1971 [NYC]
 The Other Side of Midnight. Morrow, 1974; Hodder, 1974
 Rage of Angels. Morrow, 1980; Collins, 1980

SHELDON, WALTER J. 1917-   . Pseudonym: Shel Walker, q.v. Ref: CA.
 The Blue Kimono Kill. GM, 1965 [Tokyo]
 Devil's Box. Lancer, 1968
 Gold Bait. GM, 1973 [Kor.]
 The House of Happy Mayhem. Banner, 1967 [H. Kong]
 The Man Who Paid His Way. Lippincott, 1955; Corgi, 1957 [Calif.]
 The Red Flower Kill. GM, 1971 [Thai.]
 The Yellow Music Kill. GM, 1974 [China]

SHELLABARGER, SAMUEL. 1888-1954. Pseudonyms: John Esteven, Peter Loring, qq.v.

SHELLEY, M(ARY) W(OLLSTONECRAFT GODWIN).
  1797-1851. See also: Tim J. Kelly,
  1937-   . Ref: EM.
  Frankenstein. Lackington, 1818; Daggers, 1845
  Tales and Stories. Paterson, 1891 ss

SHELLEY, PERCY BYSSHE. 1792-1822.
  Zastrozzi. Wilkie, 1810; Arno, 1977

SHELLEY, SIDNEY (JOSEPH). 1921-   .
  -The Bay of Deception. Gibbs, 1964
  Bowmanville Break. Delacorte, 1968.
    Also published as: The Mackenzie
    Break. Dell, 1971; Sphere, 1971
    [Can., 1943]
  Francine. Belmont, 1963 [Sp., 1944]
  The Mackenzie Break; see Bowmanville
    Break

SHELYNN, JACK
  The Affair at Cralla Voe. Hale, 1978
  The Cuoto Snatch. Hale, 1978
  Epilogue for Selena. Hale, 1980
  A Fall of Snow. Hale, 1980
  For a Girl Called Isaiah. Hale, 1979
  The Judas Factor. Hale, 1980
  The Night Marchers. Hale, 1979
  A Place Called Purgatory. Hale, 1978

SHENKIN, ELIZABETH (SHOEMAKER).   -1975.
  Ref: CA. Raised in NYC.
  Brownstone Gothic. Holt, 1961. Also
    published as: The Secret Heart. Paperback Library, 1964 [NYC, 1871]
  Midsummer's Nightmare. Rinehart, 1960;
    Ward, 1961 [U.S., 1923]
  The Secret Heart; see Brownstone Gothic

SHENTON, ALAN. 1939-   .
  The Friendless Spy. Hale, 1980
  A Savage Way to Die. Hale, 1979

SHEPARD, SAM. 1943-   .
  Suicide in B-Flat. French (NYC), ca.
    1979 (Play.)

SHEPHERD, DONALD LEE. 1932-   . Pseudonym: Barbara Kevern, q.v.

SHEPHERD, ERIC. 1892-   . Ref: CC, MP.
  SC: Supt. Andrew Pearson, in both
    titles, both set in Eng.
  More Murder in a Nunnery. Sheed, 1954
  Murder in a Nunnery. Sheed, 1940
    [acad.]

SHEPHERD, FLORENCE. Joint pseudonym with
  John Marsh, 1907-   , q.v.: Harrington Hastings, q.v.

SHEPHERD, JOAN. Pseudonym of Betty Joan
  Buchanan. Worked variously in Hollywood studios; article writer, living
  in NYC in 1950s. SC: Insp. Jolivet,
  in both titles.
  The Girl on the Left Bank. Washburn,
    1953 [Paris]
  Tender Is the Knife. Washburn, 1956
    [Paris]

SHEPHERD, JOHN. Pseudonym of W(illis)
  T(odhunter) Ballard, 1903-1980, q.v.
  Other pseudonyms: P. D. Ballard, Neil
  MacNeil, qq.v. Joint pseudonym with
  Norbert Davis, q.v.: Harrison Hunt,
  q.v. SC (continued from the W. T.
  Ballard byline): Bill Lennox = BL.
  Lights, Camera, Murder. Belmont, 1960
    BL [Mex.]

SHEPHERD, L(OUIS) P. Ref: CA.
  Cape House. Dell, 1974

SHEPHERD, MICHAEL. Pseudonym of Robert
  Ludlum, 1927-   , q.v. Other pseudonym: Jonathan Ryder, q.v.
  The Road to Gandolfo. Dial, 1975; Hart-Davis, 1976. Reprinted as by Robert
    Ludlum. Bantam, 1982

SHEPHERD, NEAL. Pseudonym of Nigel Morland, 1905-   , q.v. Other pseudonyms: Mary Dane, John Donavan, Norman Forrest, Roger Garnett, Vincent
  McCall, qq.v. SC: Chief Insp. Michael
  "Napper" Tandy, in all titles. Set:
  Eng.
  Death Flies Low. Constable, 1938
  Death Rides Swiftly. Constable, 1939
  Death Walks Softly. Constable, 1938
  Exit to Music. Constable, 1940

SHEPPARD, MARY. Ref: CA.
  Devil Dunes. Arcadia, 1969
  The Humming Precipice. Lenox, 1970
  Strangers in the Sun. Lenox, 1972
    [P. Rico]

SHEPPARD, STEPHEN. 1945-   . Ref: CA.
  The Four Hundred. Summit, 1979; Secker,
    1979 [Eng., 1872]

SHER, JACK. 1913-   . Born in Mpls.;
  columnist, author of fiction and articles in magazines.
  The Cold Companion. Rinehart, 1948
    [NYC]

SHERARD, R(OBERT) H(ARBOROUGH). 1861-   .
  -After the Fault. Sisley's, 1906
  Agatha's Quest. Trischler, 1890; Minerva, 1890
  -The American Marquis. Simpkin, 1888
  -A Bartered Honour. Remington, 1883
  By Right Not Law. Cassell (London &
    NYC), 1891
  -The Ghost's Revenge, and other stories
    of modern Paris. Digby, 1902 ss
    [Paris]
  -The Iron Cross. Pearson, 1897
  -Jacob Niemand. Ward, 1895
  -Rogues. Chatto, 1889
  -The Typewritten Letter. Trischler, 1891
  An Underground Mystery. Digby, 1903

SHERATON, NEIL. Pseudonym of Norman Edward Mace Smith, 1914-   . Other
  pseudonym: Norman Shore, q.v.
  -African Terror. Hale, 1957 [Afr.]
  Cairo Ring. Hale, 1958 [Cairo]
  -Clear Sky Above. Hale, 1959
  -The Princess and the Pilot. Hale, 1961
  -They Found a Way Back. Hale, 1960

SHERBURNE, JAMES (ROBERT). 1925-   .
  Ref: CA.
  Death's Pale Horse. Houghton, 1980
    [N.Y., 1880s]

SHERIDAN, ANNE-MARIE. 1948-   . Ref: CA.
  Summoned to Darkness. Simon, 1978
    [Venice, 1891]

SHERIDAN, H. B. Pseudonym: Gordon Sherry,
  q.v.

SHERIDAN, JUANITA. See also: (Helen)
  Dorothy Dudley, 1895-   . SC: Lily
  Wu and Janice Cameron, in all titles.
  The Chinese Chop. Doubleday, 1949; Barker, 1951 [NYC]
  The Kahuna Killer. Doubleday, 1951;
    Heinemann, 1955 [Haw.]
  The Mamo Murders. Doubleday, 1952. British title: While the Coffin Waited.
    Heinemann, 1953 [Haw.]
  The Waikiki Widow. Doubleday, 1953
    [Haw.]
  While the Coffin Waited; see The Mamo
    Murders

SHERIDAN, LEE. Joint pseudonym of Elsie
  Lee, 1902-   , q.v., and Michael
  Sheridan. Other Lee pseudonym: Elsie
  Cromwell, q.v.
  The Pit and the Pendulum. Lancer, 1961
    (Novelization of the movie.)

SHERIDAN, MICHAEL. Joint pseudonym with
  Elsie Lee, 1902-   , q.v.: Lee
  Sheridan, q.v.

SHERIDAN, SOL(OMON) N(EIL). 1859-   .
  The Typhoon's Secret. Doubleday, 1920

SHERIDAN, WILFRED. SC: Tommy Weston, in
  both titles.
  The Five Brains. Jarrolds, 1924
  Tommy Weston, Adventuress. Jarrolds,
    1925

SHERIE, FENN. See: Ingram D'Abbes.

SHERLOCK, A. B.
  -Galleon Treasure. Sheldon, 1929
  Red Darkness. Hurst, 1940
  -The Sea Raiders. Sheldon, 1927
  The Yellow Beetle. Sheldon, 1931
    [Syd.]

SHERLOCK, JOHN. 1932-   . Ref: CA.
  The Ordeal of Major Grigsby. Morrow,
    1964; Hutchinson, 1964 [Mal.]

SHERMAN, CHARLOTTE A. Pseudonym of Jory
  (Tecumseh) Sherman, 1932-   , q.v.
  The Shuttered Room. Major, 1975

SHERMAN, DAN(IEL MICHAEL). 1950-   .
  Ref: CA. Joint pseudonym with Robin
  Williamson: Sherman Williamson, q.v.
  Dynasty of Spies. Arbor, 1980; Gollancz, 1982
  King Jaguar. Arbor, 1979 [Brazil]
  The Mole. Arbor, 1977; Hamlyn, 1979
  Riddle. Arbor, 1977; Hamlyn, 1979
  Swann. Arbor, 1978; Hamlyn, 1980

SHERMAN, JORY (TECUMSEH). 1932-   .
  Pseudonym: Charlotte A. Sherman,
  q.v. Ref: CA. SC: Dr. Russell V.
  Childers (Chill) = RC.
  The Bamboo Demons. Pinnacle, 1979; New
    English Library pb, 1981 RC

Chill. Pinnacle, 1978; New English Library pb, 1979 RC
  House of Scorpions. Pinnacle, 1980 RC
  The Phoenix Man. Pinnacle, 1980 RC
  The Reincarnation of Jenny James. Carlyle, 1979
  Satan's Seed. Pinnacle, 1978; New English Library pb, 1979 RC
  Shadows. Pinnacle, 1980 RC
  Vampire; see Vegas Vampire
  Vegas Vampire. Pinnacle, 1980. British
    title: Vampire. New English Library
    pb, 1981 RC

SHERMAN, PATRICIA J.
  Sleep off the Highway. Manor, 1979
    [Calif.]

SHERMAN, ROBERT J.
  Spooks. French, 1932 (3-act play.)

SHERMAN, ROBIN
  Jigsaw. Pinnacle, 1973 [Eng.]

SHERMAN, ROGER
  Beware of the Cat. Apollo, 1971

SHERMAN, WILLIAM
  Stacey. Playboy, 1977

SHERRIDANE, DAVID. Pseudonym.
  The Heart of a Gangster. Vantage, 1964
    [S.F.]

SHERRIFF, R(OBERT) C(EDRIC). 1896-1975.
  Ref: CA.
  Home at Seven. Gollancz, 1951 (3-act
    play.)
  Miss Mabel. Gollancz, 1949 (3-act
    play.)
  A Shred of Evidence. French (London),
    1961 (3-act play.)

SHERRING, A(LBERT) W(ILLIAM HENRY).
  1922-   .
  The Big Haul. Hale, 1962
  Double Exposure. Hale, 1965
  Night of Vengeance. Hale, 1960
  The Pay Off. Hale, 1961
  The Tip Off. Hale, 1959

SHERRY, EDNA.   -1967. See also: Milton
  Herbert Gropper, 1897-1955.
  Backfire. Dodd, 1956; Hodder, 1957.
    Also published as: Murder at Nightfall. Dell, 1957 [NYC]
  Call the Witness. Dodd, 1961; Hodder,
    1962
  The Defense Does Not Rest. Dodd, 1959;
    Hodder, 1960
  Girl Missing. Dodd, 1962; Hodder, 1963
    [NYC]
  Murder at Nightfall; see Backfire
  No Questions Asked. Dodd, 1949; Hodder,
    1950 [NYC]
  She Asked for Murder; see Tears for
    Jessie Hewitt
  Strictly a Loser. Dodd, 1965; Hodder,
    1966 [NYC]
  Sudden Fear. Dodd, 1948; Hodder, 1949
  The Survival of the Fittest. Dodd,
    1960; Hodder, 1961
  Tears for Jessie Hewitt. Dodd, 1958;
    Hodder, 1959. Also published as: She
    Asked for Murder. Dell, 1959 [N.Y.]

SHERRY, GORDON. Pseudonym of H. B. Sheridan.
  Black Limelight. French (NYC), 1937;
    Nelson, 1940 (3-act play.)
  -Whispers Can Kill. French (London),
    1947 (1-act play.)

SHERRY, JOHN
  The Loring Affair. PB, 1964 [Mor.]

SHERRY, OLIVER. Pseudonym of George Edmund Lobo.
  Mandrake. Jarrolds, 1929

SHERWOOD, EVELYN
  A Candidate for Danger. Melrose, 1910

SHERWOOD, JOHN (HERMAN MULSO). 1913-   .
  Ref: CA, CC. SC: Charles Blessington,
  in at least those marked CB.
  Ambush for Anatol. Hodder, 1952;
    Doubleday, 1952. Also published as:
    Murder of a Mistress. Mercury, 1954,
    abridged CB
  Disappearance of Dr. Bruderstein. Hodder, 1949. U.S. title: Dr. Bruderstein Vanishes. Doubleday, 1949 CB
    [Ger.]
  Dr. Bruderstein Vanishes; see Disappearance of Dr. Bruderstein
  The Half Hunter. Gollancz, 1961. U.S.
    title: The Sleuth and the Liar.
    Doubleday, 1961
  Honesty Will Get You Nowhere. Gollancz,
    1977

The Hour of the Hyenas. Macmillan (London), 1979
The Limericks of Lachasse. Macmillan (London), 1978 [Switz.]
Mr. Blessington's Imperialist Plot; see Mr. Blessington's Plot
Mr. Blessington's Plot. Hodder, 1951. U.S. title: Mr. Blessington's Imperialist Plot. Doubleday, 1951 CB [Balkans]
Murder of a Mistress; see Ambush for Anatol
The Sleuth and the Liar; see The Half Hunter
Two Died in Singapore. Hodder, 1954 CB [Sing.]
Undiplomatic Exit. Hodder, 1958; Doubleday, 1958 [Mid. East]
Vote Against Poison. Hodder, 1956 CB

SHERWOOD, PETE
Plugged Nickel. Carlyle, 1979

SHEW, E(DWARD) SPENCER. 1908-1977? Ref: CA.
Hands of the Ripper. Sphere, 1971

SHIEL, M(ATTHEW) P(HIPPS). 1865-1947. Sometime joint pseudonym with Louis Tracy, 1863-1928, q.v.: Gordon Holmes, q.v. Ref: CC, DD, EM, MC, MM, MP. Set: Eng.
The Best Short Stories of M. P. Shiel. Gollancz, 1948 ss
The Black Box. Richards, 1931; Vanguard, 1930
Dr. Krasinski's Secret. Jarrolds, 1930; Vanguard, 1929
-The Evil That Men Do. Ward, 1904
-Here Comes the Lady. Richards, 1928 ss
How the Old Woman Got Home. Richards, 1927; Vanguard, 1928
-The Lost Viol. Ward, 1908; Clode, 1905
-The Pale Ape. Laurie, 1911 ss
Prince Zaleski. Lane, 1895; Roberts, 1895 ss
The Rajah's Sapphire. Ward, 1896
Say Au R'Voir But Not Goodbye. Benn, 1933
Unto the Third Generation. Chatto, 1903
The Weird o'It. Richards, 1902
-Xelucha and Others. Arkham, 1975 ss
-The Yellow Danger. Richards, 1898; Fenno, 1899

SHIFFRIN, ABRAHAM B. 1902- .
Angel in the Pawnshop. Dramatists, 1951 (2-act play.)
Twilight Walk. Dramatists, 1952 (3-act play.)

SHILL, J.
Murder in Paradise. Blackfriars, 1946

SHIMER, R(UTH) H.
The Correspondent. Popular Library, 1974
The Cricket Cage. Harper, 1975; Prior, 1977 [Seattle, 1886]
Squaw Point. Harper, 1972 [Alaska]

SHINGLER, WILLIAM G., JR.
The Crooked Computer. Manor, 1979

SHIPMAN, NELL. 1892- . See: George Palmer Putnam, 1887-1950.

SHIPPEY, (HENRY) LEE. 1884-1969.
The Girl Who Wanted Experience. Houghton, 1937 [Calif.]
Where Nothing Ever Happens. Houghton, 1935 ss, some criminous [Calif.]

SHIPWAY, GEORGE. 1908- . Ref: CA.
The Chilean Club. Davies, 1971. U.S. title: The Yellow Room. Doubleday, 1971

SHIVELEY, THORNTON. Pseudonym: Thorne Lee, q.v.

SHIVELLEY, ANGELA
Dread of Night. Paperback Library, 1966

SHOEBRIDGE, MARJORIE
Ranleigh Court. Doubleday, 1980 [Eng., 1800s]
A Wreath of Orchids. Doubleday, 1978

SHOESMITH, KATHLEEN A(NNE). 1938- . Ref: CA.
Belltower. Hale, 1973; Ace, 1975
-Brackenthorpe. Hale, 1980
Cloud over Calderdown. Hale, 1969; Ace, 1973
-Elusive Legacy. Hale, 1976
-Guardian at the Gate. Hale, 1979
-The Highwayman's Daughter. Hale, 1973; Ace, 1977
Jack O'Lantern. Hale, 1969; Ace, 1973
Mallory's Luck. Hale, 1971; Ace, 1974
-The Miser's Ward. Hale, 1977

Reluctant Puritan. Hale, 1972; Ace, 1973
-Return of the Royalist. Hale, 1971
-Smuggler's Haunt. Hale, 1978
The Tides of Tremannion. Hale, 1970; Ace, 1973

SHOLL, ANNA McCLURE
The Mystery of Lostland Academy. Federation, 1925 [acad.]
This Way Out. Hearst's, 1915 ss
The Unclaimed Letter. Dorrance, 1921

SHORE, JULIAN
Rattle His Bones. Morrow, 1941

SHORE, NORMAN. Pseudonym of Norman Edward Mace Smith, 1914- . Other pseudonym: Neil Sheraton, q.v.
Hong Kong Nightstop. Hale, 1973
-The Lonely Russian. Hale, 1972
-Russian Hi-Jack. Hale, 1975

SHORE, P. R. Set: Eng.
The Bolt. Methuen, 1929; Dutton, 1929
The Death Film. Methuen, 1932

SHORE, VALERY
Final Payment. Major, 1979

SHORE, VIOLA BROTHERS. 1895- . SC: Colin Keats and Gwynn Leith, in both titles.
The Beauty-Mask Murder. Smith, 1930. British title: The Beauty-Mask Mystery. Hamilton, 1932
The Beauty-Mask Mystery; see The Beauty-Mask Murder
Murder on the Glass Floor. Smith, 1932; Harrap, 1933 [ship]

SHOREY, MRS. L. H.
The Mystery of Renille Castle. Thrilling Life Stories, 1898

SHORT, (CHARLES) CHRISTOPHER (DUDLEY). See also: Leslie Charteris, 1907- . Ref: CA.
The Big Cat. Chapman, 1962; Dodd, 1965 [NYC]
The Black Room. Cape, 1964; Dodd, 1966 [Ger., 1892]
The Blue-Eyed Boy. Stacey, 1972; Dodd, 1966 [South]
Dark Lantern. Chapman, 1962; Scribner, 1961. Also published as: The Swastika Rises. New English Library pb, 1968 [Ger.]
The Naked Skier. Stacey, 1972
The Swastika Rises; see Dark Lantern

SHORT, ERNEST (HENRY), 1875-1959, and ARTHUR COMPTON-RICKETT, 1869-1937, q.v. For Compton-Rickett, see also: Patrick Leyton.
The Hope Strange Mystery. Jenkins, 1927

SHORT, LUKE. Pseudonym of Frederick Dilley Glidden, 1908-1975. Ref: CA.
Barren Land Murders. GM, 1951; Muller, 1954. Also published as: Barren Land Showdown. GM, 1957

SHORT, MARION. See also: Pauline Phelps. All titles are plays, with number of acts given in parenthesis.
Aunt Sally and the Crime Wave. French (NYC), 1936 (3)
The Hidden Guest, with Pauline Phelps. French (NYC), 1926 (3)
The Jade Necklace. French (NYC), 1929 (3)
The Nervous Miss Miles. French (NYC), 1931 (3)
Nobody's Home. French (NYC), 1931 (3)
The Return of Mr. Benjamin. French (NYC), 1933 (1)

SHORTELL, L(ESLIE) T.
French for Trouble. Rich, 1947
The Hounds Are Restless Tonight. Rich, 1949
-People Apart. Rich, 1944

SHORTT, CHARLES RUSHTON. 1904- . Pseudonym: Charles Rushton, q.v.

SHORTT, VERE (DAWSON), 1872-1915, and FRANCES (H. SHORTT) MATHEWS
-The Rod of the Snake. Lane (London & NYC), 1917

SHOUBRIDGE, DONALD
-The Stories of Donald Shoubridge. Pendulum, 1945 ss
Yard Lengths. Pendulum, 1946 ss

SHREVE, SUSAN RICHARDS. 1939- . Ref: CA.
Children of Power. Macmillan, 1979 [Wash. D.C., 1954]

SHRIBER, IONE SANDBERG. 1911- . SC: Lt. Bill Grady = BG.
As Long As I Live. Rinehart, 1947 [Ohio]
A Body for Bill. Farrar, 1942; Nicholson, 1946 BG [Ohio]
The Dark Arbor. Farrar, 1940; Nicholson, 1945 BG [N.Y.]
Family Affair. Farrar, 1941 BG [N.Y.]
Head over Heels in Murder. Farrar, 1940 BG [N.Y.]
Invitation to Murder. Farrar, 1943; Nicholson, 1946 BG [Cleve.]
The Last Straw. Rinehart, 1946 BG [Calif.]
Murder Well Done. Farrar, 1941 BG [Mich.]
Never Say Die. Rinehart, 1950
Pattern for Murder. Farrar, 1944 BG [Cleve.]
Ready or Not. Rinehart, 1953; Boardman, 1954

SHROYER, FREDERICK (BENJAMIN). 1916- . Ref: CA.
It Happened in Wayland; see Wayland 13
There None Embrace. Ward, 1966; Nash, 1974
Tower of Hate; see Wayland 13
Wayland 13. Quadriga, 1962. U.S. title: It Happened in Wayland. Reynal, 1963. Also published as: Tower of Hate. Corgi, 1963. Revised edition: Welcome Back to Wayland. Major, 1978
Welcome Back to Wayland; see Wayland 13

SHRYACK, DENNIS. See: Michael Butler, 1941- .

SHUB, JOYCE L. Wife of a foreign correspondent stationed 2 years in Moscow.
Moscow by Nightmare. Coward, 1973; Collins, 1973 [Moscow]

SHUBAEL. Pseudonym of Jennie Bouton Purdy.
The Dark Stain. Abbey, 1903

SHUBIN, SEYMOUR. 1921- . Ref: CA.
-Anyone's My Name. Simon, 1953. British title: A Stranger to Myself. Benn, 1954

SHULMAN, IRVING. 1913- . Pseudonym: Tabor Rawson, q.v. Ref: CA.
The Amboy Dukes. Doubleday, 1947
The Big Brokers. Dial, 1951
-Calibre. Popular Library, 1957
Children of the Dark. Holt, 1956
Cry Tough. Dial, 1949
The Notorious Landlady. GM, 1962 (Novelization of the movie.)
Platinum High School. Bantam, 1960 (Novelization of the movie.)
-The Roots of Fury, with Peggy Bristol. Doubleday, 1961; Mayflower, 1967
-The Short End of the Stick, and other stories. Doubleday, 1959 ss

SHULMAN, MILTON. 1913- . Ref: CA.
Kill 3. Collins, 1967; Random, 1967

SHULMAN, SANDRA (DAWN). 1944- . Ref: CA.
The Bride of Devil's Leap. Paperback Library, 1968 [Eng., 1800s]
Castlecliff. Paperback Library, 1967 [Eng.]
The Daughters of Astaroth. Paperback Library, 1968. British title: The Daughters of Satan. New English Library pb, 1969
The Daughters of Satan; see The Daughters of Astaroth
The Lady of Arlac. Paperback Library, 1969 [Fr., 1892]
The Menacing Darkness. Paperback Library, 1966
The Prisoner of Garve. Paperback Library, 1970 [Scot.]
The Temptress. Paperback Library, 1972

SHUMATE, HAROLD. See: Robin Moore.

SHUMSKY, ZENA FELDMAN. 1926- . Pseudonym: Jane Collier, q.v.

SHURA, MARY FRANCIS (CRAIG). 1923- . Pseudonym: Mary Craig, q.v. Ref: CA.
The Shop on Threnody Street. Grosset, 1972 [Chi.]

SHURMAN, IDA
Death Beats the Band. Phoenix, 1943

SHUTE, NEVIL. Pseudonym of Nevil Shute Norway, 1899-1960. Ref: CA, TC.
So Disdained. Cassell, 1928. U.S. title: The Mysterious Aviator. Houghton, 1928

Author Index

SHUTE, WALTER. -ca.1940. Pseudonym: Walter Edwards, q.v. All titles were published by Amalgamated Press and feature Sexton Blake. Set: Eng.
The Affair of the Rival Cinema Kings. 1928
The Case of the Discharged P.C. 1929
The Fatal Number. 1929
The Mystery of Merlyn Mansions. 1929
The Mystery of the Uninvited Guest. 1929
The "Talkie" Murder Mystery. 1930

SIBLEY, CELESTINE. 1917-   . Ref: CA.
The Malignant Heart. Doubleday, 1958; Gollancz, 1958 [Atlanta]

SIBLEY, PATRICIA (HAYLES). 1928-   . Ref: CA.
-High Walk to Wandlemere. Hodder, 1973; Dell, 1974

SIBLY, JOHN. 1920-   .
Girl on the Run. Cape, 1958

SICKELMORE, RICHARD. Pseudonym (?): R. S., q.v.
Edgar; or, The Phantom of the Castle. Minerva, 1798
Osrick; or, Modern Horrors. Minerva, 1809 [S. Am.]

SIDDALL, R(OGER) B(EARD). 1896-   .
Travers, A Mystery Story. Beard, 1952 [NYC]

SIDDLE, CHARLES. 1892-   . Joint pseudonym with Frederick Peel, 1888-   : Rufus Slingsby, q.v.

SIDDONS, ANNE RIVERS
The House Next Door. Simon, 1978; Collins, 1979

SIDEMAN, ABNER
Murder on Both Sides. Charlton, 1945 [NYC]

SIEGEL, BENJAMIN. 1914-   . Ref: CA.
The Adventures of Richard O'Boy. Lippincott, 1980 [Eng., 1850s]
The Jurors. Delacorte, 1973; Hale, 1973

SIEGEL, DORIS. Pseudonym: Susan Wells, q.v. Ref: CC.
How Still, My Love. Mill, 1957; Gollancz, 1958 [Ga.]

SIEGEL, JACK [JACOB]. 1913-   . Ref: CA.
Dawn at Kahlenberg. Pyramid, 1966
The Ruby. Pyramid, 1972 [NYC]

SIEGRIST, ROBERT R.
Rotunda. Condor, 1977

SIEVEKING, LANCE (LOT DE GIBERNE). 1896-1972.
Stampede. Cayme, 1924; Brentano's, 1928
A Tomb with a View. Faber, 1950 [Fr.]
The Ultimate Island. Routledge, 1925

SIEVIER, R(OBERT) S(TANDISH)
Warned Off. Winning Post, 1910

SIGEL, EFREM. Harvard graduate; editor.
The Kermanshah Transfer. Macmillan, 1973 [Mid. East]

SILBERRAD, UNA L(UCY). 1872-1955.
-The Escape of Andrew Cole. Hutchinson, 1941
-The Lynwood Affair. Hutchinson, 1918
The Mystery of Barnard Hanson. Hutchinson, 1915
-The Strange Story in the Falconer Papers. Hutchinson, 1934

SILBERSKY, LEIF, 1938-   , and OLOV SVEDELID, 1932-   .
The Last Witness. Hale, 1979 (Translation of "Sista Vittnet." Stockholm, 1977.)

SILBERSTANG, EDWIN. 1930-   . Ref: CA.
Losers, Weepers. Doubleday, 1975 [NYC]
Rapt in Glory. PB, 1964

SILLER, VAN. Pseudonym of Hilda van Siller. Ref: CC, TC. SC: Richard Massey, in at least those marked RM; Pete Rector, in at least those marked PR; Allan Stewart, in at least those marked AS.
Bermuda Murder. Hammond, 1956 [Bermuda]
The Biltmore Call. Ward, 1967 AS
A Complete Stranger. Doubleday, 1965; Ward, 1966 AS [Conn.]
The Curtain Between. Doubleday, 1947; Jarrolds, 1949. Also published as: Fatal Bride. Mercury, 1948 RM [N.Y.]
Deception of Death; see The Old Friend

Echo of a Bomb. Doubleday, 1943; Jarrolds, 1944 RM [Va.]
Fatal Bride; see The Curtain Between
Fatal Lover; see The Last Resort
Good Night, Ladies. Doubleday, 1943; Jarrolds, 1945 PR [Wash. D.C.]
The Hell with Elaine. Doubleday, 1974; Hale, 1975 [Conn.]
It Had to Be You. Doubleday, 1970. British title (?): Whisper of Death. Hale, 1971 [NYC]
The Last Resort. Lippincott, 1951; Hammond, 1954. Also published as: Fatal Lover. Bestseller, 1953 [Bermuda]
The Lonely Breeze. Doubleday, 1965. British title: The Murders at Hibiscus Key. Hammond, 1965 [Fla.]
The Mood of Murder. Doubleday, 1966; Ward, 1967 AS [Fla.]
Murder Is My Business. Hammond, 1957
The Murders at Hibiscus Key; see The Lonely Breeze
The Old Friend. Doubleday, 1973. British title (?): Deception of Death. Hale, 1974 [N.Y.]
One Alone. Doubleday, 1946; Jarrolds, 1948 [Wash. D.C.]
Paul's Apartment. Doubleday, 1948; Hammond, 1953 [NYC]
The Red Geranium. Hammond, 1966
The Road. Hammond, 1960 [Dom. Rep.]
Somber Memory. Doubleday, 1945; Jarrolds, 1946 [Mont.]
Sudden Storm. Jenkins, 1968
Under a Cloud. Doubleday, 1944; Jarrolds, 1946 PR [Mont.]
The Watchers. Doubleday, 1969; Hale, 1969 [NYC]
Whisper of Death; see It Had to Be You
The Widower. Doubleday, 1958; Hammond, 1959 [N.Y.]

SILLIMAN, VERA
Haunted Wood Hollow. Commercial, 1928

SILLIPHANT, STIRLING (DALE). 1918-   .
Ref: CA. See also: Charles Einstein.
The Slender Thread. Signet, 1966 (Novelization of the movie.) [Seattle]

SILVER, ALFRED
Good Time Charlie's Back in Town Again. Avon, 1978 [Winnipeg]

SILVER, HY
Bogus Lover. Newstand, 1960 [S.F.]

SILVER, R. NORMAN
A Daughter of Mystery. Jarrolds, 1901; Page, 1901
A Double Mask. Jarrolds, 1918
The Golden Dwarf. Jarrolds, 1903; Page, 1903
Hate, the Destroyer. Ward, 1900
-Held Apart. Ward, 1905

SILVERMAN, MARGUERITE R(UTH). SC: Insp. Christopher Adrian, in all titles. Set: Eng.
9 Had No Vet. Nicholson, 1951
The Vet It Was That Died. Nicholson, 1945
Who Should Have Died? Nicholson, 1948

SILVERMAN, ROBERT S.
-The Colombian Connection. Manor, 1977
The Cumberland Decision. Manor, 1977
The Kingston Papers. Manor, 1978

SILVERWOOD, ROGER. 1932-   . SC: Supt. Cawthorne, in all titles. Set: Eng.
Deadly Daffodils. Hale, 1970
Dying for a Drink. Hale, 1971
The Illegitimate Spy. Hale, 1972

SIMART, HELENA
Cruel Masquerade. Mystique, 1979 (Translation of "Defense D'Aimer." Paris, 1975.)
Dangerous Pretense. Mystique, 1979 (Translation of "Pour une Inconnue." Paris, 1972.)
Dark Shadow of Love. Mystique, 1979 (Translation of "La Proie Pour L'Ombre." Paris, 1974.)

SIMENON, GEORGES. 1903-   . Pseudonym: Victor Kosta. Ref: all except MM. This entry is in two parts: the first, the Jules Maigret series; the second, the non-series novels, many if not all of which are criminous. Set: mostly Paris, or elsewhere in France.
At the Gai-Moulin. (Included in the twosome Maigret Abroad, q.v.) Routledge, 1940; Harcourt, 1940 (Translation of "La Danseuse du Gai-Moulin." Paris, 1931.)

Simenon, Georges / 365

A Battle of Nerves. (Included in the twosome The Patience of Maigret, q.v.) Routledge, 1939; Harcourt, 1940 (Translation of "Le Tete d'un Homme." Paris, 1931.)
The Crime at Lock 14. (Included in Britain in the twosome Triumph of Inspector Maigret, q.v. In the U.S., published in a twosome with The Shadow in the Courtyard, q.v.) Hurst, 1934; Covici, 1934. Also published as: Maigret Meets a Milord. Penguin, 1963 (Translation of "Le Charretier de la 'Providence'." Paris, 1931.)
A Crime in Holland. (Included in the twosome Maigret Abroad, q.v.) Routledge, 1940; Harcourt, 1940 (Translation of "Un Crime en Hollande." Paris, 1931.) [Holl.]
The Crime of Inspector Maigret. (Included in Britain in the twosome Introducing Inspector Maigret, q.v.; published as a separate volume in the U.S.) Hurst, 1933; Covici, 1932. Also published as: Maigret and the Hundred Gibbets. Penguin, 1963 (Translation of "Le Pende de St.-Pholien." Paris, 1931.)
The Crossroad Murders. (Included in Britain in the twosome Inspector Maigret Investigates, q.v.; published as a separate volume in the U.S.) Hurst, 1933; Covici, 1933. Also published as: Maigret at the Crossroads. Penguin, 1963 (Translation of "La Nuit du Carrefour." Paris, 1931.)
Death of a Harbourmaster. (Included in the twosome Maigret and Monsieur Labbe, q.v.) Routledge, 1941; Harcourt, 1942 (Translation of "Le Port des Brumes." Paris, 1932.)
The Death of Monsieur Gallet. (Included in Britain in the twosome Introducing Inspector Maigret, q.v.; published as a separate volume in the U.S.) Hurst, 1933; Covici, 1932. Also published as: Maigret Stonewalled. Penguin, 1963 (Translation of "M. Gallet Decede." Paris, 1931.)
A Face for a Clue. (Included in the twosome The Patience of Maigret, q.v.) Routledge, 1939; Harcourt, 1940 (Translation of "Le Chien Jaune." Paris, 1931.)
Five Times Maigret; see A Maigret Omnibus
The Flemish Shop. (Included in the twosome Maigret to the Rescue, q.v.) Routledge, 1940; Harcourt, 1941 (Translation of "Chez les Flamands." Paris, 1932.)
The Guinguette by the Seine. (Included in the twosome Maigret to the Rescue, q.v.) Routledge, 1940; Harcourt, 1941 (Translation of "La Guinguette a Deux Sous." Paris, 1932.)
Inspector Maigret and the Burglar's Wife; see Maigret and the Burglar's Wife
Inspector Maigret and the Dead Girl; see Maigret and the Dead Girl
Inspector Maigret and the Killers; see Maigret and the Gangsters
Inspector Maigret and the Strangled Stripper; see Maigret in Montmartre
Inspector Maigret in New York's Underworld; see Maigret in New York
Inspector Maigret Investigates. Hurst, 1933 (A twosome consisting of The Crossroad Murder and The Strange Case of Peter the Lett, qq.v.)
Introducing Inspector Maigret. Hurst, 1933 (A twosome consisting of The Death of Monsieur Gallet and The Crime of Inspector Maigret, qq.v.)
Liberty Bar. (Included in the twosome Maigret Travels South, q.v.) Routledge, 1940; Harcourt, 1940 (Translation of "Liberty Bar." Paris, 1932.)
The Lock at Charenton. (Included in the twosome Maigret Sits It Out, q.v.) Routledge, 1941; Harcourt, 1941 (Translation of "L'Ecluse No. 1." Paris, 1933.)
Madame Maigret's Friend. H. Hamilton, 1960. U.S. title: Madame Maigret's Own Case. Doubleday, 1959 (Translation of "L'Amie de Mme. Maigret." Paris, 1950.)
Madame Maigret's Own Case; see Madame Maigret's Friend
The Madman of Bergerac. (Included in the twosome Maigret Travels South, q.v.) Routledge, 1940; Harcourt, 1940 (Translation of "Le Four de Bergerac." Paris, 1932.)
Maigret Abroad. Routledge, 1940; Harcourt, 1940 (A twosome consisting of A Crime in Holland and At the Gai-Moulin, qq.v.; the first of these reprinted separately as: Maigret in Holland. Severn, 1980.)

Maigret Afraid. H. Hamilton, 1961; Harcourt, 1983 (Translation of "Maigret a Peur." Paris, 1953.)
Maigret and Monsieur Charles. H. Hamilton, 1973 (Translation of "Maigret et Monsieur Charles." Paris, 1972.)
Maigret and Monsieur Labbe. Routledge, 1941; Harcourt, 1942 (A twosome consisting of Death of a Harbourmaster, q.v., and The Man from Everywhere, a non-Maigret story listed in Part II hereof.)
Maigret and the Apparition; see Maigret and the Ghost
Maigret and the Black Sheep. H. Hamilton, 1976; Harcourt, 1976 (Translation of "Maigret et les Braves Gens." Paris, 1962.)
Maigret and the Bum; see Maigret and the Dosser
Maigret and the Burglar's Wife. H. Hamilton, 1955. U.S. title: Inspector Maigret and the Burglar's Wife. Doubleday, 1956 (Translation of "Maigret et la Grande Perche." Paris, 1951.)
Maigret and the Calame Report; see Maigret and the Minister
Maigret and the Concarneau Murders. Severn, 1980
Maigret and the Coroner. H. Hamilton, 1980. U.S. title: Maigret at the Coroner's. Harcourt, 1980 (Translation of "Maigret Chez la Coroner." Paris, 1949.) [Ariz.]
Maigret and the Dead Girl. H. Hamilton, 1955. U.S. title: Inspector Maigret and the Dead Girl. Doubleday, 1955. Also published as: Maigret and the Young Girl, in: The Second Maigret Omnibus. H. Hamilton, 1964; Harcourt, 1965, as Maigret Cinq (Translation of "Maigret et la Jeune Morte." Paris, 1954.)
Maigret and the Dosser. H. Hamilton, 1973. U.S. title: Maigret and the Bum. Harcourt, 1974 (Translation of "Maigret et le Clochard." Paris, 1963.)
Maigret and the Enigmatic Lett; see The Strange Case of Peter the Lett
Maigret and the Flea. H. Hamilton, 1972. U.S. title: Maigret and the Informer. Harcourt, 1973 (Translation of "Maigret et l'Indicateur." Paris, 1971.)
Maigret and the Gangsters. H. Hamilton, 1974. U.S. title: Inspector Maigret and the Killers. Doubleday, 1954 (Translation of "Maigret, Lognon et les Gangsters." Paris, 1952.)
Maigret and the Ghost. H. Hamilton, 1976. U.S. title: Maigret and the Apparition. Harcourt, 1976 (Translation of "Maigret et le Fantome." Paris, 1964.)
Maigret and the Headless Corpse. H. Hamilton, 1967; Harcourt, 1968 (Translation of "Maigret et le Corps sans Tete." Paris, 1955.)
Maigret and the Hotel Majestic. H. Hamilton, 1977; Harcourt, 1978 (Translation of "Maigret et les Caves du Majestic." Paris, 1942.)
Maigret and the Hundred Gibbets; see The Crime of Inspector Maigret
Maigret and the Informer; see Maigret and the Flea
Maigret and the Killer. H. Hamilton, 1971; Harcourt, 1971 (Translation of "Maigret et le Tueur." Paris, 1969.)
Maigret and the Lazy Burglar. (Published as a separate volume in Britain; included in the U.S. in the collection A Maigret Trio, q.v.) H. Hamilton, 1963; Harcourt, 1973 (Translation of "Maigret et le Voleur Paresseux." Paris, 1961.)
Maigret and the Loner. H. Hamilton, 1975; Harcourt, 1975 (Translation of "Maigret et l'Homme Tout Seul." Paris, 1971.)
Maigret and the Madwoman. H. Hamilton, 1972; Harcourt, 1972 (Translation of "La Folle de Maigret." Paris, 1970.)
Maigret and the Man on the Bench; see Maigret and the Man on the Boulevard
Maigret and the Man on the Boulevard. H. Hamilton, 1975. U.S. title: Maigret and the Man on the Bench. Harcourt, 1975 (Translation of "Maigret et l'Homme du Banc." Paris, 1953.)
Maigret and the Millionaires. H. Hamilton, 1974; Harcourt, 1974 (Translation of "Maigret Voyage." Paris, 1958.)
Maigret and the Minister. H. Hamilton, 1969. U.S. title: Maigret and the Calame Report. Harcourt, 1969 (Translation of "Maigret Chez le Ministre." Paris, 1955.)

Maigret and the Nahour Case. H. Hamilton, 1967; Harcourt, 1983 (Translation of "Maigret et l'Affaire Nahour." Paris, 1967.)
Maigret and the Old Lady. (Published as a separate volume in Britain; included in the U.S. in the collection Maigret Cinq, q.v.) H. Hamilton, 1958; Harcourt, 1965 (Translation of "Maigret et la Vieille Dame." Paris, 1950.)
Maigret and the Reluctant Witnesses. (Published as a separate volume in Britain; included in the U.S. in the twosome Versus Inspector Maigret, q.v.) H. Hamilton, 1959; Doubleday, 1960 (Translation of "Maigret et la Temoins Recalcitrants." Paris, 1959.)
Maigret and the Saturday Caller. H. Hamilton, 1964; White Lion, 1975 (Translation of "Maigret et le Client du Samedi." Paris, 1962.)
Maigret and the Spinster. H. Hamilton, 1977; Harcourt, 1977 (Translation of "Cecile est Morte." Paris, 1942.)
Maigret and the Toy Village. H. Hamilton, 1978; Harcourt, 1979 (Translation of "Felicie est La." Paris, 1944.)
Maigret and the Wine Merchant. H. Hamilton, 1971; Harcourt, 1971 (Translation of "Maigret et le Marchand de Vin." Paris, 1970.)
Maigret and the Young Girl; see Maigret and the Dead Girl
Maigret at the Coroner's; see Maigret and the Coroner
Maigret at the Crossroads; see The Crossroads Murders
Maigret Cinq; see The Second Maigret Omnibus
Maigret Goes Home; see The Saint-Fiacre Affair
Maigret Goes to School. (Published as a separate volume in Britain; included in the U.S. in the collection Five Times Maigret, q.v.) H. Hamilton, 1957; Harcourt, 1964 (Translation of "Maigret a l'Ecole." Paris, 1954.)
Maigret Has Doubts. H. Hamilton, 1968 (Translation of "Une Confidence de Maigret." Paris, 1959.)
Maigret Has Scruples. (Published as a separate volume in Britain; included in the U.S. in the twosome Versus Inspector Maigret, q.v.) H. Hamilton, 1959; Doubleday, 1960 (Translation of "Les Scrupules de Maigret." Paris, 1958.)
Maigret Hesitates. H. Hamilton, 1970; Harcourt, 1970 (Translation of "Maigret Hesite." Paris, 1968.)
Maigret in Court. H. Hamilton, 1961 (Translation of "Maigret aux Assises." Paris, 1960.)
Maigret in Exile. H. Hamilton, 1978; Harcourt, 1979 (Translation of "La Maison du Juge." Paris, 1942.)
Maigret in Holland; see Maigret Abroad
Maigret in Montmartre. (Included in Britain in the twosome Maigret Right and Wrong, q.v.) H. Hamilton, 1954. U.S. title: Inspector Maigret and the Strangled Stripper. Doubleday, 1954 (Translation of "Maigret au 'Picratt's'." Paris, 1951.)
Maigret in New York. H. Hamilton, 1979. U.S. title: Maigret in New York's Underworld. Doubleday, 1955. Also published as: Inspector Maigret in New York's Underworld. Signet, 1956 (Translation of "Maigret a New York." Paris, 1947.) [NYC]
Maigret in New York's Underworld; see Maigret in New York
Maigret in Retirement. PB, 1978 (Translation of "Maigret se Fache." Paris, 1949.)
Maigret in Society. (Published as a separate volume in Britain; included in the U.S. in the collection A Maigret Trio, q.v.) H. Hamilton, 1962; Harcourt, 1973 (Translation of "Maigret et les Vieillards." Paris, 1960.)
Maigret in Vichy; see Maigret Takes the Waters
Maigret Keeps a Rendezvous. Routledge, 1940; Harcourt, 1941 (A twosome consisting of The Sailors' Rendezvous and The Saint-Fiacre Affair, qq.v.)
Maigret Loses His Temper. H. Hamilton, 1965; Harcourt, 1974 (Translation of "La Colere de Maigret." Paris, 1963.)
Maigret Meets a Milord; see The Crime at Lock 14
Maigret Mystified; see The Shadow in the Courtyard
A Maigret Omnibus. H. Hamilton, 1962. U.S. title: Five Times Maigret. Harcourt, 1964 (A collection of five Maigret novels, of which the under-

lined titles were first U.S. appearances: Maigret in Montmartre; Maigret's Mistake; Maigret Has Scruples; Maigret and the Reluctant Witnesses; Maigret Goes to School.)
Maigret on Holiday. Routledge, 1950 (A twosome consisting of A Summer Holiday and To Any Lengths, qq.v.)
Maigret on the Defensive. H. Hamilton, 1966; Harcourt, 1981 (Translation of "Maigret se Defend." Paris, 1964.)
A Maigret Quartet. H. Hamilton, 1972. U.S. title: A Maigret Trio. Harcourt, 1973 (A collection of four Maigret novels, of which the last-named was omitted from the U.S. edition: Maigret's Failure; Maigret in Society; Maigret and the Lazy Burglar; Maigret's Special Murder. All three included in the U.S. edition are first U.S. appearances.)
Maigret Rents a Room; see Maigret Takes a Room
Maigret Returns. (Included in the twosome Maigret Sits It Out.) Routledge, 1941; Harcourt, 1941 (Translation of "Maigret." Paris, 1934.)
Maigret Right and Wrong. H. Hamilton, 1954 (A twosome consisting of Maigret in Montmartre and Maigret's Mistake, qq.v.)
Maigret Sets a Trap. H. Hamilton, 1965; Harcourt, 1972 (Translation of "Maigret Tend un Piege." Paris, 1955.)
Maigret Sits It Out. Routledge, 1941; Harcourt, 1941 (A twosome consisting of The Lock at Charenton and Maigret Returns, qq.v.)
Maigret Stonewalled; see The Death of Monsieur Gallet
Maigret Takes a Room. H. Hamilton, 1960. U.S. title: Maigret Rents a Room. Doubleday, 1961 (Translation of "Maigret en Meuble." Paris, 1951.)
Maigret Takes the Waters. H. Hamilton, 1969. U.S. title: Maigret in Vichy. Harcourt, 1969 (Translation of "Maigret a Vichy." Paris, 1968.)
Maigret to the Rescue. Routledge, 1940; Harcourt, 1941 (A twosome consisting of The Flemish Shop and The Guinguette by the Seine, qq.v.)
Maigret Travels South. Routledge, 1940; Harcourt, 1940 (A twosome consisting of Liberty Bar and The Madman of Bergerac, qq.v.)
A Maigret Trio; see A Maigret Quartet
Maigret's Boyhood Friend. H. Hamilton, 1970; Harcourt, 1970 (Translation of "L'Ami d'Enfance de Maigret." Paris, 1968.)
Maigret's Christmas. H. Hamilton, 1976; Harcourt, 1977 ss
Maigret's Dead Man; see Maigret's Special Murder
Maigret's Failure. (Published as a separate volume in Britain; included in the U.S. in the collection A Maigret Trio, q.v.) H. Hamilton, 1962; Harcourt, 1973 (Translation of "Un Echec de Maigret." Paris, 1956.)
Maigret's First Case. (Published as a separate volume in Britain; included in the U.S. in the collection Maigret Cinq, q.v.) H. Hamilton, 1958; Harcourt, 1965 (Translation of "La Premier Enquete de Maigret." Paris, 1949.)
Maigret's Little Joke. H. Hamilton, 1957. U.S. title: None of Maigret's Business. Doubleday, 1958 (Translation of "Maigret s'Amuse." Paris, 1957.)
Maigret's Memoirs. H. Hamilton, 1963; White Lion, 1974 (Translation of "Les Memoires de Maigret." Paris, 1951.)
Maigret's Mistake. (Included in Britain in the twosome Maigret Right and Wrong, q.v., and in the U.S. in the collection Five Times Maigret, q.v.) H. Hamilton, 1954; Harcourt, 1964 (Translation of "Maigret Se Trompe." Paris, 1953.)
Maigret's Pickpocket. H. Hamilton, 1968; Harcourt, 1968 (Translation of "Le Voleur de Maigret." Paris, 1967.)
Maigret's Pipe. H. Hamilton, 1977; Harcourt, 1977 ss (Translation of "La Pipe de Maigret." Paris, 19??.)
Maigret's Revolver. H. Hamilton, 1956 (Translation of "Le Revolver de Maigret." Paris, 1952.) [Eng.]
Maigret's Rival. H. Hamilton, 1979; Harcourt, 1979 (Translation of "L'Inspecteur Cadavre." Paris, 1944.)
Maigret's Special Murder. H. Hamilton, 1964. U.S. title: Maigret's Dead Man. Doubleday, 1964 (Translation of "Maigret et son Mort." Paris, 1948.)
The Methods of Maigret; see My Friend Maigret

My Friend Maigret. H. Hamilton, 1966. U.S. title: The Methods of Maigret. Doubleday, 1957 (Translation of "Mon Ami Maigret." Paris, 1949.)
No Vacation for Maigret; see A Summer Holiday
None of Maigret's Business; see Maigret's Little Joke
The Patience of Maigret. Routledge, 1939; Harcourt, 1940 (A twosome consisting of A Battle of Nerves and A Face for a Clue, qq.v.)
The Patience of Maigret. H. Hamilton, 1966 (Translation of "La Patience de Maigret." Paris, 1965.)
The Sailor's Rendezvous. (Included in the twosome Maigret Keeps a Rendezvous, q.v.) Routledge, 1940; Harcourt, 1941 (Translation of "Au Rendez-Vous des Terre-Neuvas." Paris, 1931.)
The Saint-Fiacre Affair. (Included in the twosome Maigret Keeps a Rendezvous, q.v.) Routledge, 1940; Harcourt, 1941. Also published as: Maigret Goes Home. Penguin, 1967 (Translation of "L'Affair Saint-Fiacre." Paris, 1932.)
The Second Maigret Omnibus. H. Hamilton, 1964. U.S. title: Maigret Cinq. Harcourt, 1965 (A collection of five Maigret novels, of which the underlined titles were first U.S. appearances: Maigret and the Young Girl; Maigret's Little Joke; Maigret and the Old Lady; Maigret's First Case; Maigret Takes a Room.)
The Shadow in the Courtyard. (Included in Britain in the twosome Triumph of Inspector Maigret, q.v. In the U.S., published in a twosome with The Crime at Lock 14, q.v.) Hurst, 1934; Covici, 1934. Also published as: Maigret Mystified. Penguin, 1964 (Translation of "L'Ombre Chinoise." Paris, 1932.)
The Short Cases of Inspector Maigret. Doubleday, 1959 (Five stories taken from various collections of Maigret short cases published in France.) ss
The Strange Case of Peter the Lett. (Included in Britain in the twosome Inspector Maigret Investigates, q.v. Published in the U.S. as a separate volume.) Hurst, 1933; Covici, 1933. Also published as: Maigret and the Enigmatic Lett. Penguin, 1963 (Translation of "Pietr-le-Letton." Paris, 1931.)
A Summer Holiday. (Included in Britain in the twosome Maigret on Holiday, q.v.) Routledge, 1950. U.S. title: No Vacation for Maigret. Doubleday, 1953 (Translation of "Les Vacances de Maigret." Paris, 1948.)
To Any Lengths. (Included in Britain in the twosome Maigret on Holiday, q.v.) Routledge, 1950 (Translation of "Signe Picpus." Paris, 1944.)
Triumph of Inspector Maigret. Hurst, 1934 (A twosome consisting of The Shadow in the Courtyard and The Crime at Lock 14, q.v.)
Versus Inspector Maigret. Doubleday, 1960 (A twosome consisting of Maigret and the Reluctant Witnesses and Maigret Has Scruples, q.v.)

II.

Aboard the Aquitaine. (Included in the collection African Trio, q.v.) H. Hamilton, 1979; Harcourt, 1979 (Translation of "45° a L'Ombre." Paris, 1936.)
The Accomplices. H. Hamilton, 1966; Harcourt, 1964 (U.S. edition is a twosome with The Blue Room, q.v.) (Translation of "Les Complices." Paris, 1955.)
Account Unsettled. H. Hamilton, 1962. U.S. title: The Fugitive. Doubleday, 1955 (Translation of "Crime Impuni." Paris, 1954.)
Across the Street. Routledge, 1954 (Translation of "La Fenetre des Rouet." Paris, 1945.)
Act of Passion. Routledge, 1953; Prentice-Hall, 1952 (Translation of "Lettre a Mon Juge." Paris, 1947.)
Affairs of Destiny. Routledge, 1952; Harcourt, 1945 (A twosome consisting of Newhaven-Dieppe and The Woman of the Grey House, qq.v.)
African Trio. H. Hamilton, 1979; Harcourt, 1979 (A collection containing Aboard the Aquitaine, and 2 others.)
Aunt Jeanne. Routledge, 1953; Harcourt, 1983 (Translation of "Tante Jeanne." Paris, 1951.)

Banana Tourist. (Included in the twosome Lost Moorings, q.v.) Routledge, 1946 (Translation of "Touriste de Bananes." Paris, 1938.)
Belle. (Included in Britain in the twosome Violent Ends, q.v., and in the U.S. in the collection Tidal Wave, q.v.) H. Hamilton, 1954; Doubleday, 1954 (Translation of "Le Mort de Belle." Paris, 1952.)
The Bells of Bicetre; see The Patient
Betty. H. Hamilton, 1975; Harcourt, 1975 (Translation of "Betty." Paris, 1961.)
Big Bob. H. Hamilton, 1969; Harcourt, 1981 (Translation of "Le Grand Bob." Paris, 1954.)
Black Rain. (Included in Britain in the twosome Black Rain, q.v.; published in the U.S. as a separate volume.) Routledge, 1949; Reynal, 1947 (Translation of "Il Pleut, Bergere." Paris, 1941.)
Black Rain. Routledge, 1949 (A twosome consisting of The Survivors and Black Rain, qq.v.)
Blind Alley; see Blind Path
Blind Path. (Included in Britain in the twosome Lost Moorings, q.v.; published in the U.S. as a separate volume.) Routledge, 1946. U.S. title: Blind Alley. Reynal, 1946 (Translation of "Chemin sans Issue." Paris, 1938.)
The Blue Room. H. Hamilton, 1965; Harcourt, 1964 (U.S. edition is a twosome with The Accomplices, q.v.) (Translation of "Le Chambre Bleue." Paris, 1964.)
The Bottom of the Bottle. (Included in the U.S. in the collection Tidal Wave, q.v.; published as a separate volume in Britain.) H. Hamilton, 1977; Doubleday, 1954 (Translation of "La Fond de la Bouteille." Paris, 1949.)
The Breton Sisters. (Included in the twosome Havoc by Accident, q.v.) Routledge, 1943; Harcourt, 1943 (Translation of "Les Demoiselles de Concarneau." Paris, 1936.)
The Brothers Rico. (Included in Britain in the twosome Violent Ends, q.v., and in the U.S. in the collection Tidal Wave, q.v.) H. Hamilton, 1954; Doubleday, 1954 (Translation of "Les Freres Rico." Paris, 1952.)
The Burgomaster of Furnes. Routledge, 1952 (Translation of "Le Bourgmestre de Furnes." Paris, 1939.)
The Buriel of M. Bouvet; see Inquest on Bouvet
The Cat. H. Hamilton, 1972; Harcourt, 1967 (Translation of "Le Chat." Paris, 1967.)
Chez Krull. (Included in Britain in the twosome A Sense of Guilt, q.v.; published in the U.S. as a separate volume.) H. Hamilton, 1955; White Lion, 1974 (Translation of "Chez Krull." Paris, 1939.)
Chit of a Girl. (Included in the twosome Chit of a Girl, q.v.) Routledge, 1949. Also published as: Girl in Waiting, in the twosome Girl in Waiting. Pan, 1957 (Translation of "La Marie du Port." Paris, 1938.)
Chit of a Girl. Routledge, 1949. Also published as: Girl in Waiting. Pan, 1957 (A twosome consisting of Chit of a Girl and Justice, q.v.)
The Clockmaker; see The Watchmaker of Everton
The Confessional. H. Hamilton, 1967; Harcourt, 1968 (Translation of "Le Confessional." Paris, 1966.)
The Country Doctor. (Included in Britain in the collection The White Horse Inn.) H. Hamilton, 1980. U.S. title: The Delivery. Harcourt, 1981 (Translation of "Bergelon." Paris, 1941.)
Danger Ahead. H. Hamilton, 1955 (A twosome consisting of Red Lights and The Watchmaker of Everton, qq.v.)
Danger Ashore; see The Window over the Way
Danger at Sea; see The Mystery of the 'Polarlys'
The Delivery; see The Country Doctor
Destinations. Doubleday, 1955 (A twosome consisting of The Hitchhiker and The Buriel of M. Bouvet, qq.v.)
The Disappearance of Odile. H. Hamilton, 1972; Harcourt, 1972 (Translation of "La Disparition d'Odile." Paris, 1971.)
The Disintegration of J.P.G. Routledge, 1937 (Translation of "L'evade." Paris, 1936.)
The Door. H. Hamilton, 1964 (Translation of "La Porte." Paris, 1962.)

Escape in Vain. Routledge, 1943; Harcourt, 1944 (A twosome consisting of The Lodger and One Way Out, q.v.)
The Family Lie. H. Hamilton, 1978; Harcourt, 1978 (Translation of "Malemprin." Paris, 1940.)
The Fate of the Malous. H. Hamilton, 1962 (Translation of "La Destin des Malou." Paris, 1947.)
The First-Born; see Magnet of Doom
Four Days in a Lifetime. (Included in the U.S. in the twosome Satan's Children, q.v.; published as a separate volume in Britain.) H. Hamilton, 1977; Prentice-Hall, 1953 (Translation of "Les Quatre Jours du Pauvre Homme." Paris, 1949.)
The Fugitive; see Account Unsettled
The Gendarme's Report. (Included in a twosome with The Window over the Way, q.v.) Routledge, 1951 (Translation of "La Rapport du Gendarme." Paris, 1944.)
The Girl in His Past. H. Hamilton, 1976; Prentice-Hall, 1953 (Translation of "Le Temps d'Anais." Paris, 1951.)
Girl in Waiting; see Chit of a Girl
The Girl with a Squint. H. Hamilton, 1978; Harcourt, 1978 (Translation of "Marie Qui Louche." Paris, 1951.)
The Glass Cage. H. Hamilton, 1973; Harcourt, 1973 (Translation of "La Cage de Verre." Paris, 1971.)
The Grandmother. (Included in Britain in the collection The White Horse Inn, q.v.) H. Hamilton, 1980; Harcourt, 1980 (Translation of "La Vieille." Paris, 1939.)
The Green Thermos. (Included in the twosome On the Danger Line, q.v.) Routledge, 1944; Harcourt, 1944 (Translation of "Le Suspect." Paris, 1938.)
The Hatter's Ghosts. (Included in the twosome The Judge and the Hatter, q.v.) H. Hamilton, 1956. U.S. title: The Hatter's Phantoms. Harcourt, 1976 (Translation of "Les Fantomes du Chapelier." Paris, 1949.)
The Hatter's Phantoms; see The Hatter's Ghosts
Havoc by Accident. Routledge, 1943; Harcourt, 1943 (A twosome consisting of Talatala and The Breton Sisters, qq.v.)
The Heart of a Man. (Included in Britain in the twosome A Sense of Guilt, q.v.; published in the U.S. as a separate volume.) H. Hamilton, 1955; Prentice-Hall, 1951 (Translation of "Les Volets Verts." Paris, 1950.)
The Hitchhiker; see Red Lights
Home Town. (Included in the twosome On the Danger Line, q.v.) Routledge, 1944; Harcourt, 1944 (Translation of "Faubourg." Paris, 1937.)
The House by the Canal. (Included in the twosome With The Ostenders, q.v.) Routledge, 1952 (Translation of "La Maison du Canal." Paris, 1933.)
The House on Quai Notre Dame; see The Others
I Take This Woman; see The Trial of Bebe Donge
In Case of Emergency. H. Hamilton, 1960; Doubleday, 1958 (Translation of "En Cas de Malheur." Paris, 1956.)
In Two Latitudes. Routledge, 1942 (A twosome consisting of The Mystery of the 'Polarlys' and Tropic Moon, qq.v.)
The Innocents. H. Hamilton, 1973; Harcourt, 1974 (Translation of "Les Innocents." Paris, 1972.)
Inquest on Bouvet. H. Hamilton, 1958. U.S. title: The Burial of M. Bouvet (Included in the twosome Destinations, q.v.) Doubleday, 1955 (Translation of "L'Enterrement de M. Bouvet." Paris, 1950.)
The Iron Staircase. H. Hamilton, 1963; Harcourt, 1977 (Translation of L'Escalier de Fer." Paris, 1953.)
The Judge and the Hatter. H. Hamilton, 1956 (A twosome consisting of The Witnesses and The Hatter's Ghosts, qq.v.)
Justice. (Included in the twosome Chit of a Girl, q.v.) Routledge, 1949 (Translation of "Cour d'Assises." Paris, 1941.)
The Little Doctor. H. Hamilton, 1978; Harcourt, 1981 ss (Translation of "Le Petit Docteur." Paris, 1943.)
The Little Man from Archangel. (Published as a separate volume in Britain; published in the U.S. in a twosome with Sunday, q.v.) H. Hamilton, 1957; Harcourt, 1966 (Translation of "Le Petit Homme d'Archangelsk." Paris, 1956.)

The Little Saint. H. Hamilton, 1966; Harcourt, 1965 (Translation of "Le Petit Saint." Paris, 1965.)
The Lodger. (Included in the twosome Escape in Vain, q.v.) Routledge, 1943; Harcourt, 1944 (Translation of "Le Locataire." Paris, 1934.)
Lost Moorings. Routledge, 1946 (A twosome consisting of Blind Path and Banana Tourist, qq.v.)
The Magician. (Published as a separate volume in Britain; included in the U.S. in the twosome The Magician and the Widow, q.v.) H. Hamilton, 1974; Doubleday, 1955 (Translation of "Antoine et Julie." Paris, 1953.)
The Magician and the Widow. Doubleday, 1955 (A twosome consisting of The Magician and The Widow, qq.v.)
Magnet of Doom. Routledge, 1948. U.S. title: The First-Born. Reynal, 1947 (Translation of "L'Aine des Ferchaux." Paris, 1945.)
Maigret and Monsieur Labbe. Routledge, 1941; Harcourt, 1942 (A twosome consisting of Death of a Harbourmaster, a Maigret novel listed in Part I hereof, and The Man from Everywhere, q.v.)
The Man from Everywhere. (Included in the twosome Maigret and Monsieur Labbe.) Routledge, 1941; Harcourt, 1942 (Translation of "Le Relais d'Alsace." Paris, 1931.)
The Man on the Bench in the Barn. H. Hamilton, 1970; Harcourt, 1969 (Translation of "La Main." Paris, 1968.) [Conn.]
The Man Who Watched the Trains Go By. Routledge, 1942; Reynal, 1946 (Translation of "L'Homme Qui Regardait Passer les Trains." Paris, 1938.)
The Man with the Little Dog. H. Hamilton, 1965 (Translation of "L'Homme au Petit Chien." Paris, 1964.)
Monsieur la Souris. (Included in the twosome Poisoned Relations, q.v.) Routledge, 1950 (Translation of "Monsieur la Souris." Paris, 1938.)
Monsieur Monde Vanishes. H. Hamilton, 1967; Harcourt, 1977 (Translation of "La Fuite de M. Monde." Paris, 1945.)
The Move; see The Neighbors
Mr. Hire's Engagement. (Included in the twosome Sacrifice, q.v.) H. Hamilton, 1956 (Translation of "Les Fiancailles de M. Hire." Paris, 1933.)
The Murderer. (Included in a twosome with A Wife at Sea, q.v.) Routledge, 1949 (Translation of "L'Assassin." Paris, 1937.)
The Mystery of the 'Polarlys'. (Included in Britain in the twosome In Two Latitudes, q.v., and in the U.S. in the twosome On Land and Sea, under the byline Victor Kosta.) Routledge, 1942; Hanover House, 1954 (Translation of "Le Passager du 'Polarlys'." Paris, 1932.)
The Negro. H. Hamilton, 1959 (Translation of "Le Negre." Paris, 1957.)
The Neighbors. H. Hamilton, 1968. U.S. title: The Move. Harcourt, 1968 (Translation of "Le Demenagement." Paris, 1967.)
A New Lease of Life. H. Hamilton, 1963. U.S. title: A New Lease on Life. Doubleday, 1963 (Translation of "Une Vie Comme Neuve." Paris, 1951.)
A New Lease on Life; see A New Lease of Life
Newhaven-Dieppe. (Included in the twosome Affairs of Destiny, q.v.) Routledge, 1942; Harcourt, 1945 (Translation of "L'Homme de Londres." Paris, 1934.)
The Night Club. H. Hamilton, 1979; Harcourt, 1979 (Translation of "L'Ane Rouge." Paris, 1933.)
November. H. Hamilton, 1970; Harcourt, 1970 (Translation of "Novembre." Paris, 1946.)
The Old Man Dies. H. Hamilton, 1968; Harcourt, 1967 (Translation of "La Mort d'Auguste." Paris, 1966.)
On Land and Sea (as by Victor Kosta). Hanover House, 1954 (A twosome consisting of Danger Ashore and Danger at Sea, qq.v., each of which was separately published: Berkley, 1955.)
On the Danger Line. Routledge, 1944; Harcourt, 1944 (A twosome consisting of Home Town and The Green Thermos, qq.v.)
One Way Out. (Included in the twosome Escape in Vain, q.v.) Routledge, 1943; Harcourt, 1944 (Translation of "Les Suicides." Paris, 1934.)
The Ostenders. (Included in a twosome with The House by the Canal, q.v.) Routledge, 1952 (Translation of "Le Clan des Ostendais." Paris, 1947.)
The Others. H. Hamilton, 1975. U.S. title: The House on Quai Notre Dame. Harcourt, 1975 (Translation of "Les Autres." Paris, 1962.)
The Patient. H. Hamilton, 1963. U.S. title: The Bells of Bicetre. Harcourt, 1964 (Translation of "Les Anneaux de Bicetre." Paris, 1963.)
Pedigree. H. Hamilton, 1962; London House, 1963 (Translation of "Pedigree." Paris, 1948.)
Poisoned Relations. (Included in the twosome Poisoned Relations, q.v.) Routledge, 1950 (Translation of "Les Soeurs Lacroix." Paris, 1938.)
Poisoned Relations. Routledge, 1950 (A twosome consisting of Monsieur la Souris and Poisoned Relations, qq.v.)
The Premier. (Published as a separate volume in Britain; included in the U.S. in a twosome with The Train, q.v.) H. Hamilton, 1961; Harcourt, 1966 (Translation of "Le President." Paris, 1958.)
The Prison. H. Hamilton, 1969; Harcourt, 1969 (Translation of "La Prison." Paris, 1968.)
Red Lights. (Included in Britain in the twosome Danger Ahead, q.v., and in the U.S. in the twosome Destinations, q.v.) H. Hamilton, 1955. U.S. title: The Hitchhiker. Doubleday, 1955 (Translation of "Feux Rouges." Paris, 1953.)
The Rich Man. H. Hamilton, 1971; Harcourt, 1971 (Translation of "Le Riche Homme." Paris, 1970.)
Sacrifice. H. Hamilton, 1956 (A twosome consisting of Mr. Hire's Engagement and Young Cardinaud, qq.v.)
Satan's Children. Prentice-Hall, 1953 (A twosome consisting of I Take This Woman and Four Days in a Lifetime, qq.v.)
A Sense of Guilt. H. Hamilton, 1955 (A twosome consisting of Chez Krull and The Heart of a Man, qq.v.)
The Shadow Falls. Routledge, 1945; Harcourt, 1945 (Translation of "Le Testament Donadieu." Paris, 1937.)
The Snow Was Black; see The Stain on the Snow
The Son. H. Hamilton, 1958 (Translation of "Le Fils." Paris, 1957.)
The Stain on the Snow. Routledge, 1953. U.S. title: The Snow Was Black. Prentice-Hall, 1950 (Translation of "La Neige Etait Sale." Paris, 1948.)
The Stowaway. H. Hamilton, 1957 (Translation of "Le Passager Clandestin." Paris, 1947.)
Strange Inheritance. Routledge, 1950 (Translation of "Le Voyageur de la Toussaint." Paris, 1941.)
Strangers in the House. Routledge, 1951; Doubleday, 1954 (Translation of "Les Inconnus dans la Maison." Paris, 1940.)
Striptease. H. Hamilton, 1959 (Translation of "Strip-Tease." Paris, 1958.)
Sunday. (Published as a separate volume in Britain; included in the U.S. in a twosome with The Little Man from Archangel, q.v.) H. Hamilton, 1960; Harcourt, 1956 (Translation of "Dimanche." Paris, 1958.)
The Survivors. (Included in the twosome Black Rain, q.v.) Routledge, 1949 (Translation of "Les Rescapes du Telemaque." Paris, 1938.)
Talatala. (Included in the twosome Havoc by Accident, q.v.) Routledge, 1943; Harcourt, 1943 (Translation of "Le Blanc a Lunettes." Paris, 1937.)
Teddy Bear. H. Hamilton, 1971; Harcourt, 1972 (Translation of "L'Ours en Peluche." Paris, 1960.)
Three Beds in Manhattan. H. Hamilton, 1976; Doubleday, 1964 (Translation of "Trois Chambres a Manhattan." Paris, 1946.)
Ticket of Leave. Routledge, 1954. U.S. title: The Widow. (Included in the twosome The Magician and the Widow, q.v.) Doubleday, 1955 (Translation of "La Veuve Couderc." Paris, 1942.)
Tidal Wave. Doubleday, 1954 (A collection consisting of Belle, The Bottom of the Bottle, and The Brothers Rico, qq.v.)
The Train. (Published as a separate volume in Britain; included in the U.S. in a twosome with The Premier, q.v.) H. Hamilton, 1964; Harcourt, 1966 (Translation of "Le Train." Paris, 1961.)
The Trial of Bebe Donge. (Published as a separate volume in Britain; included in the U.S. in the twosome Satan's Children, q.v.) Routledge, 1952. U.S. title: I Take This Woman. Prentice-Hall, 1953 (Translation of "La Verite sur Bebe Donge." Paris, 1942.)
Tropic Moon. (Included in Britain in the twosome Two Latitudes, q.v.; published in the U.S. as a separate volume.) Routledge, 1942; Harcourt, 1943 (Translation of "Le Coup de Lune." Paris, 1933.) [Afr.]
The Venice Train. H. Hamilton, 1974; Harcourt, 1974 (Translation of "Le Train de Venise." Paris, 1965.)
Violent Ends. H. Hamilton, 1954 (A twosome consisting of Belle and The Brothers Rico, qq.v.)
The Watchmaker; see The Watchmaker of Everton
The Watchmaker of Everton. (Included in Britain in the twosome Danger Ahead, q.v., and in the U.S. in the twosome The Witnesses and the Watchmaker, q.v.) H. Hamilton, 1955. U.S. title: The Watchmaker. Doubleday, 1956. Also published as: The Clockmaker. Jove, 1977 (Translation of "L'Horloger d'Everton." Paris, 1954.)
The White Horse Inn. (Included in the collection of the same title.) H. Hamilton, 1980; Harcourt, 1980.) (Translation of "Le Cheval Blanc." Paris, 1938.)
The White Horse Inn. H. Hamilton, 1980; Harcourt, 1980 (A collection consisting of the title story, The Grandmother, and The Country Doctor, qq.v.)
The Widow; see Ticket of Leave
The Widower. H. Hamilton, 1961; Harcourt, 1982 (Translation of "Le Veuf." Paris, 1959.)
A Wife at Sea. (Included in a twosome with The Murderer, q.v.) Routledge, 1949 (Translation of "Les Pitard." Paris, 1935.)
The Window over the Way. (Included in Britain in a twosome with The Gendarme's Report, q.v., and in the U.S. in the twosome On Land and Sea, q.v.) Routledge, 1951. U.S. title: Danger Ashore. Hanover House, 1954 (Translation of "Les Gens d'en Face." Paris, 1933.)
The Witnesses. (Included in Britain in the twosome The Judge and the Hatter, q.v., and in the U.S. in the twosome The Witnesses and the Watchmaker, q.v.) H. Hamilton, 1956; Doubleday, 1956 (Translation of "Les Temoins." Paris, 1954.)
The Witnesses and the Watchmaker. Doubleday, 1956 (A twosome consisting of The Witnesses, and The Watchmaker, qq.v.)
The Woman of the Grey House. (Included in the twosome Affairs of Destiny, q.v.) Routledge, 1942; Harcourt, 1945 (Translation of "Le Haut Mal." Paris, 1933.)
Young Cardinaud. (Included in the twosome Sacrifice, q.v.) H. Hamilton, 1956 (Translation of "Le Fils Cardinaud." Paris, 1942.)

SIMMAT, RUDOLPH
Murder on Mitcham Common. Newnes, 1936

SIMMEL, JOHANNES MARIO. 1924-   . Ref: CA.
The Affair of Nina B. Popular Library, 1978; Hamlyn, 1979 (Translation of "Affare Nina B." Hamburg, 1958.)
The Berlin Connection; see To the Bitter End
The Caesar Code. Popular Library, 1976; Futura, 1977 (Translation of "Und Jimmy Ging zum Regenbogen." Munich, 1970.) [Vienna]
The Cain Conspiracy; see Cain '67
Cain '67. McGraw, 1971. Also published as: The Cain Conspiracy. Popular Library, 1976; Hamlyn, 1979 (Translation of "Alle Menschen Werden Bruder." Munich, 1967.) [Ger.]
Dear Fatherland. Random, 1969; Deutsch, 1969. Also published as: Double Agent—Triple Cross. Popular Library, 1977; Hamlyn, 1980 (Translation of "Lieb Vaterland, Magst Ruhig Sein." Munich, 1965.) [Ger.]
Double Agent—Triple Cross; see Dear Fatherland
I Confess. Popular Library, 1977 (Translation of "Ich Gestehe Alles." Munich, 1958.)

It Can't Always Be Caviar. Doubleday, 1965; Blond, 1965. Also published as: The Monte Cristo Cover-Up. Popular Library, 1977 (Translation of "Es Muss Nicht Immer Kaviar Sein." Munich, 1960.)
Love Is Just a Word. McGraw, 1969 (Translation of "Liebe Ist Nur ein Wort." Munich, 1962.) [Ger.]
The Monte-Cristo Cover-Up; see It Can't Always Be Caviar
The Sybil Cipher. Popular Library, 1979; Hamlyn, 1982 (Translation of "Gott Schuetzt die Liebenden." Hamburg, 1957.) [Berlin, 1950s]
To the Bitter End. McGraw, 1970. Also published as: The Berlin Connection. Popular Library, 1977; Hamlyn, 1980 (Translation of "Bis zur Bitteren Neige." Munich, 1962.)
The Traitor Blitz. Popular Library, 1980 (Translation of "Der Stoff, aus dem die Traeume Sind." Munich, 1971.)
The Wind and the Rain. Popular Library, 1978 (Translation of "Die Antwort Kennt nur der Wind." Munich, 1973.) [Fr.]

SIMMONS, ADDISON. 1902- . Born in Boston; graduate of Harvard and Harvard Law School.
Dead Weight. Phoenix, 1946
Death on the Campus. Crowell, 1935 [acad.]

SIMMONS, ALBERT
-Saint and Cynic. Digby, 1895

SIMMONS, DENIS
The Stolen Laces. Laird, 1889

SIMMONS, DIANE. 1948- . Raised in Oreg.; newspaper reporter.
Let the Bastards Freeze in the Dark. Wyndham, 1980 [Alaska]

SIMMONS, GEOFFREY S. 1943- . Ref: CA.
The Z-Papers. Arbor, 1976

SIMMONS, MARY KAY. 1933- . Ref: CA.
Cameron Hill. Dell, 1972 [Calif.]
The Captain's House. Dell, 1970 [Cape Cod]
The Clock Face. Dell, 1976
-Crown of Stars. PB, 1977
Dark Holiday. Dell, 1976
The Diamonds of Alcazar. Dell, 1972 [Calif.]
Domino. PB, 1978
A Fire in the Blood. PB, 1977
Flight from Riversedge. Dell, 1975
The Girl with the Key. Dell, 1974
The Gypsy Grove. Dell, 1974 [N.J.]
Haggard's Cove. Dell, 1975
The Hermitage. Dell, 1970
The Kill Cross. Dell, 1976
Megan. Dell, 1971
The Saracen Gardens. Dell, 1973
Smuggler's Gate. Dell, 1976
The Willow Pond. Dell, 1972 [N.Y.]
The Year of the Rooster. Delacorte, 1971

SIMMONS, STEVE. Pseudonym: Nick Carter, q.v.

SIMMS, WILLIAM GILMORE. 1806-1870. Ref: CC.
Life in America; or, The Wigwam and the Cabin; see The Wigwam and Cabin
Martin Faber, The Story of a Criminal, and other tales. Harper, 1833 (Novel and ss.)
The Wigwam and Cabin. Wiley, 1845. Also published as: Life in America; or, The Wigwam and the Cabin. Clark, 1848 ss, at least one criminous

SIMON. Joint pseudonym of Roger d'Este Burford, 1904- , and Oswell Blakeston, 1907- , q.v. Pseudonym of Burford alone: Roger East, q.v.
The Cat with the Mustache. Wishart, 1935. Also published as: The Mystery of the Hypnotic Room. Curtis Warren, 1950
Death on the Swim. Wishart, 1934
Murder Among Friends. Wishart, 1933
The Mystery of the Hypnotic Room; see The Cat with the Mustache

SIMON, ANGELA
Seven Sons. Berkley, 1977

SIMON, C. E.
-The Second Tablet. Fiction House, 1947
Sleeping Draught. Houghton (London), 1934

SIMON, LEONARD. 1937- . Psychologist and psychoanalyst in NYC.
The Irving Solution. Arbor, 1977 [NYC]
-Reborn. Arbor, 1979

SIMON, ROBERT A(LFRED). 1897-1981.
The Weekend Mystery. Watt, 1926; Collins, 1927 [NYC]

SIMON, ROGER L(ICHTENBERG). 1943- .
Ref: TC. SC: Moses Wine, in all titles.
The Big Fix. Straight Arrow, 1973; Deutsch, 1973 [L.A.]
Peking Duck. Simon, 1979; Deutsch, 1979 [China]
Wild Turkey. Straight Arrow, 1975; Deutsch, 1976 [L.A.]

SIMON, RUTH (CORABEL SHIMER). 1918- .
-A Castle for Tess. Follett, 1967

SIMON, S. J. Pseudonym of Simon Jasha Skidelsky. See: Caryl Brahms (pseudonym of Doris Caroline Abrahams, 1901-1982).

SIMONDS, PETER. 1906- . Pseudonym: Richard Greaves, q.v.

SIMONS, ROGER. Joint pseudonym of Margaret Punnett, 1932- , and Ivor Macaulay Punnett. Ref: CC. SC: Insp. Fadiman Wace, in all titles. Set: Eng.
Arrangement for Murder. Bles, 1961; Roy, 1963
Bullet for a Beast. Bles, 1964; Roy, 1965
Dead Reckoning. Bles, 1965
Death on Display. Bles, 1968; Roy, 1969
A Frame for Murder. Bles, 1960
Gamble with Death. Bles, 1961; Roy, 1963
The Houseboat Killings. Bles, 1959
The Killing Chase. Bles, 1962
Murder by Design. Hale, 1973
Murder First Class. Bles, 1969; Roy, 1970 [ship]
Murder Joins the Chorus. Bles, 1960
Picture of Death. Hale, 1973
Reel of Death. Bles, 1970
Silver and Death. Bles, 1963
Taxed to Death. Bles, 1967
The Veil of Death. Bles, 1966; Roy, 1967

SIMPSON, ALAN (FRANCIS). 1929- . See: Ray(mond Percy) Galton, 1930- .

SIMPSON, ALBERTA. Pseudonym of Alfred Bercovici.
The Falmont Heiress. Curtis, 1973

SIMPSON, CHARLES H.
Life in the Far West; or, A Detective's Adventures Among the Indians and Outlaws of Montana. Rhodes, 1896 [Mont.]
Life in the Mines; or, Crime Avenged. Rhodes, 1896. (Note: The spines of at least some printings read Wild Life in the Far West.) [Calif.]

SIMPSON, DOROTHY. 1933- .
Harbingers of Fear. Macdonald, 1977

SIMPSON, GEORGE E(DWARD), 1944- , and NEAL R. BURGER
Fair Warning. Delacorte, 1980; New English Library, 1980 [WWII]
Thin Air. Dell, 1978; New English Library, 1978

SIMPSON, HAROLD. See: A. A. Willis.

SIMPSON, HELEN (DE GUERRY). 1897-1940. See also: Clemence Dane. Ref: CC, EM, TC.
Vantage Striker. Heinemann, 1931. U.S. title: The Prime Minister Is Dead. Doubleday, 1931

SIMPSON, HOWARD R(USSELL). 1925- .
Ref: CA.
Assignment for a Mercenary. Harper, 1965 [Afr.]
Rendezvous Off Newport. Curtis, 1973; Hale, 1974 [Conn.]
The Three Day Alliance. Doubleday, 1971; Hale, 1973 [Fr.]

SIMPSON, M. E.
And One for the Pot. Hale, 1973

SIMPSON, MARGARET. 1913- .
The Chrome Connection. Deutsch, 1975
Sorry Wrong Number. Deutsch, 1973

SIMPSON, ROBERT
The Gray Charteris. Hodder, 1922; McCann, 1922

Welcome Danger. London Book Co., 1930 (Novelization of the movie.) [S.F.]

SIMPSON, RONALD. Pseudonym of magazine writer and novelist, born and educated in Eng.
End of a Diplomat. Monarch, 1964 [Warsaw]
Make Every Kiss Count. Monarch, 1961
The Return of Colonel Pho. Monarch, 1965

SIMPSON, SPENCER. Set: Eng.
Crooks in Cabaret. Nicholson, 1935
The Four Dead Men. Methuen, 1936; Macaulay, 1937

SIMPSON, WARWICK. Pseudonym of William Pettridge.
Eighteen of Them—Singular Stories. Leadenhall, 1894 ss, some criminous

SIMS, DOROTHY RICE. See: (George) Valentine Williams, 1883-1946.

SIMS, GEORGE (FREDERICK ROBERT). 1923- .
Ref: CA, TC. Set: Eng.
Deadhand. Gollancz, 1971
The End of the Web. Gollancz, 1976; Walker, 1976
Hunters Point. Gollancz, 1973; Penguin, 1977 [S.F.]
The Last Best Friend. Gollancz, 1967; Stein, 1968
Rex Mundi. Gollancz, 1978
The Sand Dollar. Gollancz, 1969
Sleep No More. Gollancz, 1966; Harcourt, 1966
The Terrible Door. Bodley Head, 1964; Horizon, 1964

SIMS, GEORGE. 1902-1966. Pseudonym: Paul Cain, q.v.

SIMS, GEORGE R(OBERT). 1847-1922. Ref: EM, MC, MP. SC: Dorcas Dene = DD.
Anna of the Underworld. Chatto, 1916
As It Was in the Beginning. White, 1896 ss, some criminous
Behind the Veil. Greening, 1913 ss
Biographs of Babylon. Chatto, 1902 ss, at least one criminous
The Black Stain. Jarrolds, 1907
A Blind Marriage, and other stories. Chatto, 1901 ss
-A Cabinet Minister's Wife and other tales. Paul, 1910 ss
The Case of George Candlemas. Chatto, 1890
The Coachman's Club; or, Tales Told out of School. White, 1897 ss
The Death Gamble. Paul, 1909 ss
Detective Inspector Chance. Ferret Fantasy, 1974 ss
Dorcas Dene, Detective. White, 1897 ss DD
Dorcas Dene, Detective. Second Series. White, 1898 ss DD
Dramas of Life. Chatto, 1890; U.S. Book Co., 1890 ss
For Life and After. Chatto, 1906
His Wife's Revenge. Chatto, 1907
In London's Heart. Chatto, 1900
Buckles, 1900
-Joyce Pleasantry and other stories. Chatto, 1908 ss
-Li Ting of London and other stories. Chatto, 1905 ss
-The Life We Live. Chatto, 1904 ss
Mary Jane Married. Chatto, 1888 ss
Memoirs of a Landlady. Chatto, 1894 ss, some criminous
A Missing Husband and other tales. Chatto, 1890 ss
-My Two Wives and other stories. Chatto, 1894 ss
The Mysteries of Modern London. Pearson, 1906
The Mystery of Mary Anne and other stories. Chatto, 1907 ss
-Off the Track in London. Jarrolds, 1911
Once Upon a Christmas Time. Chatto, 1898 ss, some criminous
-The Ring o' Bells. Chatto, 1886 ss
Rogues and Vagabonds. Chatto, 1885; Munro, 1886
Scenes from the Show. Chatto, 1895 ss
The Small-Part Lady, and other stories. Chatto, 1900 ss
The Social Kaleidoscope. First Series. Francis, 1879 ss, some criminous
The Social Kaleidoscope. Second Series. Francis, 1881 ss, some criminous
-Stories in Black and White. Fuller, 1885 ss
Tales of Today. Chatto, 1889; Munro, 1887 ss
The Ten Commandments. Chatto, 1896 ss, some criminous

The Theatre of Life. Fuller, 1881 ss,
  some criminous
Three Brass Balls. Fuller, 1882 ss,
  some criminous
Tinkletop's Crime and other tales.
  Chatto, 1891; Webster, 1891 ss
-Watches of the Night. Greening, 1907 ss
-Young Mrs. Caudle. Chatto, 1904
Zeph and other stories. Fuller, 1882
  ss, some criminous

SIMSON, CICELY DEVENISH FRASER. See:
  Cicely (Devenish) Fraser-Simpson.

SIMSON, ERIC ANDREW. 1895-   . Pseudonym: Laurence Kirk, q.v.

SINCLAIR, ANDREW (ANNANDALE). 1935-   .
  Ref: CA.
  Cat; see The Surrey Cat
  The Facts in the Case of E. A. Poe.
    Weidenfeld, 1979; Holt, 1980
    (Edgar A. Poe.) [U.S., 1811 to pre-
    sent]
  A Patriot for Hire. Joseph, 1978. Also
    published as: Sea of the Dead.
    Sphere, 1981
  Sea of the Dead; see A Patriot for Hire
  The Surrey Cat. Joseph, 1976. Also pub-
    lished as: Cat. Sphere, 1977

SINCLAIR, CLAUDE EDWARD ROBERT
-The House at Ballyslane. Witherby, 1949
-Problem Island. Witherby, 1950

SINCLAIR, DENNIS. Pseudonym of "a best-
  selling suspense novelist."
  The Temple Dogs Guard My Fate. Signet,
    1969 [China]

SINCLAIR, DENNIS. SC: Greg Ballard, in
  all titles.
  The Blood Brothers. Corgi, 1977
  The Friends of Lucifer. Corgi, 1977
  The Third Force. Corgi, 1976

SINCLAIR, FIONA. Ref: CC. Actress, poet.
  SC: Insp. Paul Grainger, in all
  titles. Set: Eng.
  But the Patient Died; see Dead of a
    Physician
  Dead of a Physician. Bles, 1961. U.S.
    title: But the Patient Died. Double-
    day, 1962 [hosp.]
  Meddle with the Mafia. Bles, 1963
    [Sic.]
  Most Unnatural Murder. Bles, 1965
    (PG in very brief appearance.)
  Scandalize My Name. Bles, 1960
  Three Slips to a Noose. Bles, 1964

SINCLAIR, FREDRIC
  Drop One, Carry Four. Doubleday, 1947
    [Calcutta, Egypt]

SINCLAIR, MAY. 1865?-1946. Ref: CC.
  Uncanny Stories. Hutchinson, 1923;
    Macmillan, 1923 ss

SINCLAIR, MICHAEL
  How to Steal a Million. Signet, 1966;
    New English Library pb, 1966 (Novel-
    ization of the movie.) [Paris]

SINCLAIR, MICHAEL. Pseudonym of a "young
  international bureaucrat", born and
  educated (Ph.D.) in Scot.
  The Dollar Covenant. Gollancz, 1973;
    Norton, 1973 [Scot.]
  Folio Forty-One; see Norslag
  A Long Time Sleeping. Gollancz, 1975;
    Norton, 1976
  The Masterplayers. Gollancz, 1978; Nor-
    ton, 1978
  Norslag. Gollancz, 1972. U.S. title:
    Folio Forty-One. Putnam, 1972
  Sonntag. Gollancz, 1971; Putnam, 1971
    [Ger.]

SINCLAIR, MURRAY
  Tough Luck L.A. Pinnacle, 1980 [L.A.]

SINCLAIR, OLGA (ELLEN WATERS). 1923-   .
  Ref: CA.
  Bitter Sweet Summer. Hale, 1970; PB,
    1972
-Hearts by the Tower. Hale, 1968. U.S.
    title: Night of the Black Tower.
    Lancer, 1968
-The Man at the Manor. Gresham, 1967;
    Dell, 1972
-Man of the River. Hale, 1968
  Night of the Black Tower; see Hearts by
    the Tower
-Wild Dreams. Hale, 1973

SINCLAIR, ROBERT B(RUCE). 1905-   .
  Stage and film director.
  The Eleventh Hour. Mill, 1951; Cassell,
    1951
  It Couldn't Be Murder. Mill, 1954;
    Boardman, 1955 [N.Y.]

SINCLAIR, SALLY
  Muted Murder. Arcadia, 1953 [South]

SINGER, BANT. Pseudonym of Charles Shaw,
  1900-   . SC: Denis Delaney, in all
  titles.
  Blind Alley; see You're Wrong, Delaney
  Don't Slip, Delaney. Collins, 1954
    [Syd.]
  Have Patience, Delaney! Collins, 1954
  Your Move, Delaney! Collins, 1956
  You're Wrong, Delaney. Collins, 1953;
    Crown, 1953. Also published as: Blind
    Alley. Pyramid, 1954. And as by
    Charles Shaw under original title:
    Pyramid, 1957

SINGER, CAMPBELL. 1909-   . See: John
  (Frederick) Burke, 1927-   ; and:
  Joseph (Arnold) Hayes, 1918-   ;
  and: George Ross.

SINGER, LOREN. Born in N.Y.
-Boca Grande. Doubleday, 1974; New Eng-
    lish Library, 1976
  The Parallax View. Doubleday, 1970;
    New English Library, 1970
  That's the House, There. Doubleday,
    1973; New English Library, 1974
    [N.Y.]

SINGER, NORMAN. 1925-   . Ref: CA. SC:
  Robbie Jardino, in both titles.
  Diamond Stud. Manor, 1976 [Fla.,
    1930s]
  The Shakedown Kid. Manor, 1975 [1930s]

SINGER, SALLY M.
  For Dying You Always Have Time. Putnam,
    1971 [Isr.]

SINGLETON, FRANK. 1909-   .
-A Change of Sky. Chatto, 1953
  Independent Means. Chatto, 1948; Mac-
    millan, 1948

SINGLETON, JAMES R.
  Edisto Sanctuary. Carlyle, 1980

SINSTADT, GERALD. SC: Geoffrey Landon, in
  both titles.
  The Fidelio Score. Long, 1965; Lancer,
    1967 [Ger.]
  Ship of Spies; see Whisper in a Lonely
    Place
  Whisper in a Lonely Place. Long, 1966.
    U.S. title: Ship of Spies. Lancer,
    1967

SIODMAK, CURT. 1902-   . Born in Ger.,
  trained in engineering, resident of
  the U.S. since 1937; science fiction
  writer, movie director. SC: Dr. Patrick Cory = PC.
  Donovan's Brain. Knopf, 1943; Chapman,
    1944 PC [Ariz.]
  Hauser's Memory. Putnam, 1968; Jenkins,
    1969 PC
  The Third Ear. Putnam, 1971 [Ger.]

SIRENGO, CHARLES A.
  A Cowboy Detective. Ogilvie, 189?
  Further Adventures of a Cowboy Detec-
    tive. Ogilvie, 189?

SITWELL, S(YDNEY) M(ARY)
-A Great Revenge. Christian Knowledge
  Society, 1885

SJOWALL, MAJ, 1935-   , and PER WAHLOO,
  1926-1975, q.v. Ref: CA, CC, EM, MC,
  TC. SC: Martin Beck, in all titles.
  The Abominable Man. Pantheon, 1972;
    Gollancz, 1973 (Translation of "Den
    Vedervardige Mannen fran Saffle."
    Stockholm, 1971.) [Stock.]
  Cop Killer. Pantheon, 1975; Gollancz,
    1975 (Translation of "Polismord-
    aren." Stockholm, 1974.) [Swed.]
  The Fire Engine That Disappeared. Pan-
    theon, 1971; Gollancz, 1972 (Trans-
    lation of "Brandbilen som Forsvann."
    Stockholm, 1969.) [Stock.]
  The Laughing Policeman. Pantheon, 1970;
    Gollancz, 1971 (Translation of "Den
    Skrattande Polisen." Stockholm,
    1968.) [Stock.]
  The Locked Room. Pantheon, 1973; Gol-
    lancz, 1974 (Translation of "Det
    Slutna Rummet." Stockholm, 1972.)
    [Stock.]
  The Man on the Balcony. Pantheon, 1968;
    Gollancz, 1969 (Translation of "Man-
    nen pa Balkongen." Stockholm, 1967.)
    [Stock.]
  The Man Who Went Up in Smoke. Pantheon,
    1969; Gollancz, 1970 (Translation of
    "Mannen som Gick Upp in Rok." Stock-
    holm, 1966.) [Buda.]

Murder at the Savoy. Pantheon, 1971;
    Gollancz, 1972 (Translation of
    "Polis, Polis, Potatismos!" Stock-
    holm, 1970.) [Swed.]
  Roseanna. Pantheon, 1967; Gollancz,
    1968 (Translation of "Roseanna."
    Stockholm, 1965.) [Swed.]
  The Terrorists. Pantheon, 1976; Gol-
    lancz, 1977 (Translation of "Terror-
    isterna." Stockholm, 1975.) [Stock.]

SKALLAND, HARLEY L.
  The Wrong Slant of Red. Dorrance, 1967

SKEHAN, EVERETT M. Reporter in Mass.
  A Bullet for Georgie. Houghton, 1979
    [Boston]

SKENE, ANTHONY. Pseudonym of George Nor-
  man Philips, 1888?-   . SC (with
  many other authors): Sexton Blake, in
  those titles listed without publisher
  (which was Amalgamated Press).
  The Affair of the Bronzed Basilisk.
    1943
  The Circus Crime. 1933
  The Crook's Accomplice. 1930
  Crook Town. 1932
  The Death Gang. 1931; Red Mask, 194?
  The Death of Four. 1931
  The Death Trap. 1930
  Derelict House. 1933
  The Fatal Mascot. 1932
  Five Dead Men. Paul, 1932
  Gallows Alley. Paul, 1934
  Green Mask. 1932
  The Haunted Hotel Mystery. 1941
  The Legacy of Fear. 1931
  The Man Who Lost His Memory. 1947
  The Masks. Paul, 1933
  Missing Men. 1934
  Monsieur Zenith. Paul, 1936
  The Mystery of the Bombed Hotel. 1942
  The Nameless Five. 1931
  The Night-Club Crime. 1931
  The Night Raiders. 1930
  The £1,000,000 Plot. 1933
  The Red Stilleto. 1932
  The Ripper Returns. Pemberton, 1948
  The Riverside Club Murder. 1934
  The Road House Murder. 1933
  The Rush Hour Crime. 1935
  The Silent Menace. 1933
  The Silver Circle. Amalgamated, 1934
  The Terror of the Tenements. 1937
  The Vault of Doom. 1931

SKETCHLEY, ARTHUR. Pseudonym of George
  Rose, 1817-1882.
  Mrs. Brown on the Tichborne Case. Rout-
    ledge, 1872

SKIDELSKY, SIMON JASHA. Pseudonym: S. J.
  Simon. See: Caryl Brahms.

SKINNER, AINSLIE
  Mind's Eye. Secker, 1980. U.S. title:
  The Harrowing. Rawson, 1981

SKINNER, CONRAD ARTHUR. 1889-   . Pseudonym: Michael Maurice, q.v.

SKINNER, JOHN
  Murder in the Village. Methuen, 1930

SKINNER, JUNE O'GRADY. 1922-   . Pseudonym: Rohan O'Grady, q.v.

SKINNER, MICHAEL
  Among Those Hunted. Hale, 1978
  Somewhere in Hamburg. Hale, 1980
    [Hamb.]

SKIRROW, DESMOND.   -ca.1973. Born in
  Wales; painter, designer, jurnalist,
  creative director for advertising a-
  gency. SC: John Brock, in at least
  those marked JB. Set: Eng.
  I Was Following This Girl. Bodley,
    1967; Doubleday, 1968 JB
  I'm Trying to Give It Up. Bodley,
    1968; Doubleday, 1969 JB
  It Won't Get You Anywhere. Bodley,
    1966; Lippincott, 1966 JB
-Poor Quail. Bodley, 1969

SKLAR, GEORGE. See: Vera Caspary,
  1899-

SKOGGARD, BRUNO. 1921-1978.
  China Hand. Dodd, 1979; Hale, 1980
    [China]

SKOTTOWE, B(RITIFFE) C(ONSTABLE).
  1857-
  Sudden Death; or, My Lady the Wolf.
    Sonnenschein, 1886

Author Index

SKVORECKY, JOSEF (VOLCAV). 1924-   .
    Ref: CA.
    Miss Silver's Past. Grove, 1975; Bodley, 1976   (Translation of "Lvice." Prague, 1969.)   [Prague]
    The Mournful Demeanour of Lieutenant Boruvka. Gollancz, 1973 ss (Translation of "Smutek Porucika Boruvky." Prague, 1966.)   [Czech.]

SLABBER, I. G.
    The Carrion Experience. Hale, 1980

SLADE, H(ERBERT). See: W(alter) B(urton) Baldry, 1888-   .

SLADEK, JOHN (THOMAS). 1937-   . Joint pseudonyms with Thomas M(ichael) Disch, 1940-   , q.v.: Thom Demijohn, Cassandra Knye, qq.v. SC: Thackeray Phin, in both titles, both set in Eng.
    Black Aura. Cape, 1974; Walker, 1979
    Invisible Green. Gollancz, 1977; Walker, 1979

SLANEY, GEORGE WILSON. 1884-   . Pseudonym: George Woden, q.v.

SLAPPEY, STERLING G(REENE). 1917-   .
    Ref: CA.
    Exodus of the Damned. Signet, 1968

SLATE, JOHN. Pseudonym of John Russell Fearn, 1908-1960, q.v. Other pseudonyms: Hugo Blayn, Spike Gordon, Volsted Gribban, Griff, Nat Karta, qq.v. SC: Black Maria = BM. Set: Eng.
    Black Maria, M.A. Rich, 1944 BM
    Death in Silhouette. Rich, 1950 BM
    Framed in Guilt. Rich, 1948
    Maria Marches On. Rich, 1945 BM
    One Remained Seated. Rich, 1946 BM
    Thy Arm Alone. Rich, 1947 BM

SLATER, HUMPHREY. 1906-   .
    Calypso. Longmans, 1933
    The Conspirator. Lehmann, 1948; Harcourt, 1948
    -Three Among Mountains. Wingate, 1959

SLATER, IAN (DAVID). 1941-   . Ref: CA.
    -Fireshell. Bantam, 1977; Corgi, 1977
    Sea Gold. Bantam, 1979   [ship]

SLATER, MONTAGUE. 1902-   . Pseudonym: Richard Johns, q.v.

SLATER, WILL. 1944-   . Ref: CA.
    Falcon. Collins, 1979; Atheneum, 1979   [It.]

SLATER, WILL
    The Adventures of D'Arcy Dewpond, Detective. Drane, 1927 ss
    -The Bells of Palmdale, and other stories. Drane, 1925 ss
    "Land of the Free." Drane, 1928

SLAVITT, DAVID R(YTMAN). 1935-   . Ref: CA.
    -ABCD. Doubleday, 1972; H. Hamilton, 1974
    Cold Comfort. Methuen (NYC), 1980
    -Killing of the King. Doubleday, 1974; Allen, 1974

SLEAR, GENEVIEVE
    The Golden Bauble. Doubleday, 1977

SLEATH, MRS. ELEANOR
    The Orphan of the Rhine. Lane, 1798
    Who's the Murderer? or, The Mystery of the Forest. Lane, 1802

SLEATH, FREDERICK
    -A Breaker of Ships. Hutchinson, 1922
    -The Gold of the Sunset. Hutchinson, 1924
    Green Swallows. Hutchinson, 1930
    -The Hill of the Crows. Jenkins, 1921
    The Red Vulture. Hutchinson, 1923; Houghton, 1923
    -The Seventh Vial. Jenkins, 1920
    -Sniper Jackson. Jenkins, 1919

SLEE, RICHARD and CORNELIA ATWOOD PRATT, -1929.
    -Dr. Berkeley's Discovery. Putnam, 1899

SLESAR, HENRY. 1927-   . See also: Anne Coulter Martens. Ref: CA, TC.
    A Bouquet of Clean Crimes and Neat Murders. Avon, 1960 ss
    The Bridge of Lions. Macmillan, 1963; Gollancz, 1964
    A Crime for Mothers and Others. Avon, 1962 ss
    Enter Murderers. Random, 1960; Gollancz, 1961   [NYC]
    The Grey Flannel Shroud. Random, 1959; Deutsch, 1960   [NYC]
    The Seventh Mask. Ace, 1969 (Novelization of the "Edge of Night" TV series.)
    The Thing at the Door. Random, 1974; H. Hamilton, 1975   [NYC]

SLIGH, NIGEL
    -The Beast with Two Backs. Laurie, 1951
    -The Fugitives. Laurie, 1947
    -The Loved and the Loving. Laurie, 1953
    -The Overlords. Laurie, 1955
    -The Time and the Torture. Laurie, 1950
    -Tomorrow and Yesterday. Laurie, 1954
    Traitor's Bridge. Laurie, 1952

SLIMAN, DAVID
    Manhunting. Maclaren   ss

SLINGSBY, JONATHAN FREKE. Pseudonym of John Francis Waller.
    The Dead Bridal. Ward, 1856

SLINGSBY, RUFUS. Joint pseudonym of Charles Siddle, 1892-   , and Frederick Peel, 1888-   .
    The Murders at Highbridge. Long, 1929

SLOAN, SARAH
    Image of Stephanie. Lenox, 1972; Remploy, 1973
    Raventree. Lenox, 1972; Remploy, 1974

SLOANE, WILLIAM (MILLIGAN). 1906-1974.
    Ref: CA, MP.
    The Edge of Running Water. Farrar, 1939; Methuen, 1940. Also published as: The Unquiet Corpse. Dell, 1956   [Maine]
    To Walk the Night. Farrar, 1937; Barker, 1938   [L.I.]
    The Unquiet Corpse; see The Edge of Running Water

SMALL, AUSTIN J.   -1929. Pseudonym: Seamark, q.v. Set: Eng.
    The Death Maker; see Master Vorst
    Frozen Gold. Heinemann, 1924. U.S. title: The Frozen Trail. Houghton, 1924. Reprinted as by Seamark: Hodder, 1935
    Love's Enemy. Hodder, 1929
    The Man They Couldn't Arrest. Hodder, 1927; Doran, 1927
    Master Vorst. Hodder, 1926. U.S. title: The Death Maker. Doran, 1926
    Pearls of Desire. Heinemann, 1924; Houghton, 1925

SMALLEY, DAVE E.
    Stumbling. Barse, 1929   [Chi.]

SMART, HAWLEY. 1833-1893.
    At Fault. Chapman, 1883; Munro, 1883
    -Bad to Beat. White, 1886; Rand, 1886
    -Beatrice and Benedick. White, 1891; Taylor, 1891
    -Belles and Ringers. Chapman, 1880; Munro, 1881
    Bit and Bridal; see Bitter Is the Rind
    -Bitter Is the Rind. Bentley, 1870. Also published as: Bit and Bridal. Everett, 1909
    -A Black Business. White, 1890
    -Bound to Win. Chapman, 1877
    -Broken Bonds. Hurst, 1874
    -Cecile; or, Modern Idolators. Bentley, 1871
    -Cleverly Won. White, 1887
    False Cards. Hurst, 1873
    -A Family Failing. U.S. Book Co., 1891 (British title?)
    -From Post to Finish. Chapman, 1884; Harper, 1884
    The Great Tontine. Chapman, 1881; Munro, 1884
    -Hard Lines. Chapman, 1883
    -The Last Coup. White, 1889
    -Lightly Lost. White, 1885
    -Long Odds. White, 1889; Lovell, 1889
    -The Master of Rathkelly. White, 1885
    -A Member of Tattersall's. White, 1892; Lovell, 1892
    -The Outsider. White, 1886; Munro, 1887
    -Play or Pay. Chapman, 1878
    -Plucked. Diprose, 1886
    "The Plunger." White, 1891; Lippincott, 1891
    -The Pride of the Paddock. White, 1888; Lovell, 1888
    -A Race for a Wife. Bentley, 1870; Munro, 1882
    -A Racing Rubber. White, 1895
    -Saddle and Sabre. Chapman, 1888
    -Salvage. Ward, 1884 ss
    -Social Sinners. Chapman, 1880
    Struck Down. Warne, 1885; Munro, 1885
    -Sunshine and Snow. Chapman, 1878
    -Thrice Past the Post. White, 1891
    Tie and Trick. Chapman, 1885; Harper, 1885

Smith, David MacLeod / 371

    -Two Kisses. Bentley, 1875; Loring, 1877
    -Vanity's Daughter. White, 1893; Taylor, 1892
    Without Love or Licence. Chatto, 1890

SMILEY, VIRGINIA (KESTER). 1923-   .
    Ref: CA.
    The Cove of Fear. Avalon, 1974   [Can.]
    Guest at Gladehaven. Dell, 1972
    Mansion of Mystery. Dell, 1973

SMITH, A(NTHONY) C(HARLES) H.
    The Jericho Gun. Weidenfeld, 1977

SMITH, ADAM. Joint pseudonym of George (Jerome Waldo) Goodman, 1930-   , q.v., and Winthrop Knowlton.

SMITH, ANN T.
    Death in the Cards. Phoenix, 1946   [Boston]

SMITH, ANNIE L. [MRS. LYDIA ANNIE JOCELYN SMITH]. 1836-   .
    The Black Mask; or, Bonnie Orielle's Lovers. Neely, 1898

SMITH, ANTHONY HECKSTALL. 1904-   . See: Anthony Heckstall-Smith

SMITH, ARTHUR. 1896-   .
    -Against All Odds. Stockwell, 1973
    Cloggy Dick. Stockwell, 1974

SMITH, BEVAN. See: John (Dudley) Ball (Jr.), 1911-   .

SMITH, C.I.D. 1894-   . SC: Insp. Barlowe, in both titles, both set in Eng.
    No Epitaph for Mr. Zarke. Jenkins, 1941
    Thy Guilt Is Great. Jenkins, 1939

SMITH, CAESAR. Pseudonym of Elleston Trevor, 1920-   , q.v. Name originally: Trevor Dudley Smith, q.v. Other pseudonyms: Mansell Black, Adam Hall, Howard North, Simon Rattray, Warwick Scott, qq.v.
    Heatwave. Wingate, 1957; Ballantine, 1958. Reprinted as by Elleston Trevor: White Lion, 1972

SMITH, CARMICHAEL. Pseudonym of Paul Myron Anthony Linebarger, 1913-1966.
    Ref: CA.
    Atomsk. Duell, 1949   [Russ.]

SMITH, CATHERINE
    Barozzi; or, The Venetian Sorcerers. Newman, 1815; Arno, 1977   [Venice, 1500s]

SMITH, CHARLES MERRILL. A pastor (Methodist) for over 30 years, creative writing teacher; living in Kan.; father of Terrence Lore Smith, q.v. SC: Reverend C. P. "Con" Randollph, in all titles.
    Reverend Randollph and the Avenging Angel. Putnam, 1977; Hale, 1979   [Chi.]
    Reverend Randollph and the Fall from Grace, Inc. Putnam, 1978; Hale, 1979   [Chi.]
    Reverend Randollph and the Holy Terror. Putnam, 1980   [Chi.]
    Reverend Randollph and the Wages of Sin. Putnam, 1974; Barker, 1975   [Chi.]

SMITH, CHARLOTTE (TURNER). 1749-1806.
    The Old Manor House. Bell, 1793

SMITH, CHESTER ALFRED. 1920-   .
    The Web of Deceit. Comet, 1957

SMITH, (ALEXANDER) CLARK. 1919-   .
    Born in Glasgow; chartered accountant, then director of electronics company; author of auditing textbook. SC: Nicky Mahoun, in all titles. Ref: CC.
    The Case of Torches. Hammond, 1957
    The Deadly Reaper. Hammond, 1956
    The Speaking Eye. Hammond, 1955 [Scot.]

SMITH, COLIN
    The Cut-Out. Deutsch, 1980; Viking, 1981

SMITH, DAVE and GRAHAM MURDOCH
    Mystery of Achnaghoulash. Aberdeen People's, 1979

SMITH, DAVID. 1936-   . Born in N.Y.; graduate of and dean at Harvard Law School.
    The Leo Conversion. Dodd, 1980   [Afr.]

SMITH, DAVID MacLEOD. 1920-   . Pseudonym: David Mariner, q.v.

SMITH, DENNIS. 1940-   . Ref: CA.
　　Glitter and Ash. Dutton, 1980 [NYC]

SMITH, DEREK
　　Whistle Up the Devil. Gifford, 1953

SMITH, DODIE. Pseudonym of Dorothy Gladys
　　Smith, 1896-   . Ref: CA.
　　The Girl from the Candle-Lit Bath.
　　　Allen, 1978

SMITH, DON(ALD TAYLOR). 1909-   . Ref:
　　CA. SC: Tim Parnell = TP; Phil
　　Sherman = PS.
　　The Bavarian Connection. Charter, 1978
　　　PS
　　China Coaster. Holt, 1953 [Shanghai]
　　Corsican Takeover. GM, 1974; Coronet,
　　　1974 TP
　　The Dalmatian Tapes. Award, 1976 PS
　　　[Yugos.]
　　Death Stalk in Spain. Award, 1972 PS
　　　[Sp.]
　　Haitian Vendetta. Award, 1973 PS
　　　[Haiti]
　　The Libyan Contract. Award, 1974 PS
　　　[Libya]
　　The Man Who Played Thief. GM, 1969;
　　　Hale, 1971 TP [Fr.]
　　The Marseilles Enforcer. Award, 1972
　　　PS [Mars.]
　　Night of the Assassin. Award, 1972 PS
　　The Padrone. GM, 1971; Coronet, 1971 TP
　　　[It.]
　　The Payoff. GM, 1973; Coronet, 1974 TP
　　　[Fr.]
　　The Peking Connection. Award, 1975 PS
　　　[Peking]
　　Perilous Holiday. Holt, 1951 [Yugos.]
　　Secret Mission: Angola. Award, 1970 PS
　　　[Angola]
　　Secret Mission: Athens. Award, 1971 PS
　　　[Athens]
　　Secret Mission: Cairo. Award, 1970 PS
　　　[Cairo]
　　Secret Mission: Corsica. Award, 1968;
　　　Tandem, 1968 PS [Cors.]
　　Secret Mission: Istanbul. Award, 1969;
　　　Tandem, 1971 PS [Istan.]
　　Secret Mission: Morocco. Award, 1968;
　　　Tandem, 1968 PS [Mor.]
　　Secret Mission: Munich. Award, 1970 PS
　　　[Munich]
　　Secret Mission: North Korea. Award,
　　　1970 PS [Kor.]
　　Secret Mission: Peking. Award, 1968;
　　　Tandem, 1971 PS [Peking]
　　Secret Mission: Prague. Award, 1968;
　　　Tandem, 1971 PS [Prague]
　　Secret Mission: The Kremlin Plot.
　　　Award, 1971 PS [Moscow]
　　Secret Mission: Tibet. Award, 1969;
　　　Tandem, 1971 PS [Tib.]
　　The Strausser Transfer. Charter, 1978
　　　PS

SMITH, DOROTHY GLADYS. 1896-   . Pseudonym: Dodie Smith, q.v.

SMITH, EDGAR (HERBERT). 1934-   . Ref:
　　CA.
　　A Reasonable Doubt. Coward, 1970 [N.Y.]

SMITH, EDWARD PERCY. 1891-1968. Pseudonym: Edward Percy, q.v.

SMITH, ERNEST BRAMAH. 1868-1942. Pseudonym: Ernest Bramah, q.v.

SMITH, ESSEX. Pseudonym of Frances Essex
　　Theodora Hope.
　　The Wye Valley Mystery. Hutchinson,
　　　1929

SMITH, EVELYN E. 1927-   . Pseudonym:
　　Delphine Lyons, q.v.

SMITH, FRANK A(LLEN). 1927-   . Born in
　　Can. and educated in Eng.; employed
　　by government telephone company in
　　Can. SC: Supt. Pepper, in at least
　　those marked P.
　　Corpse in Handcuffs. Macmillan (Toronto), 1969; Hale, 1969 P
　　Defectors Are Dead Men. Macmillan (Toronto), 1971; Hale, 1971 P
　　Dragon's Breath. Beaufort, 1980; Hale,
　　　1981 [Can.]
　　The Traitor Mask. Hale, 1974

SMITH, FRANK E. 1919-   . Pseudonym:
　　Jonathan Craig, q.v.

SMITH, FRANK ELLIS. 1918-   . Pseudonym:
　　Jennifer Hale, q.v.

SMITH, (DAVID) FRED(ERICK). 1888-1976.
　　Ref: CA.
　　The Broadcast Murders. Day, 1931 [NYC]

SMITH, FREDERICK E(SCREET). 1922-   .
　　Pseudonym: David Farrell, q.v. Ref:
　　CA.
　　The Devil Behind Me. Hodder, 1962
　　The Grotto of Tiberius. Hodder, 1961
　　A Killing for the Hawks. Harrap, 1966;
　　　McKay, 1967
　　Laws Be Their Enemy. Hutchinson, 1955
　　Lydia Trendennis. Hutchinson, 1957;
　　　Paperback Library, 1964
　　Of Masks and Minds. Hutchinson, 1954
　　The Persuaders Again!; see The Persuaders #2
　　The Persuaders at Large; see The Persuaders #3
　　The Persuaders #1. Pan, 1972; Ballantine, 1972 (Two novelettizations of
　　　the TV series.)
　　The Persuaders #2. Pan, 1972; Ballantine, 1972. Also published as: The
　　　Persuaders Again! Ian Henry, 1976;
　　　State Mutual, 1977 (Two novelettizations of the TV series.)
　　The Persuaders #3. Pan, 1973. U.S.
　　　title: The Persuaders at Large.
　　　State Mutual, 1977 (Three novelettizations of the TV series.)
　　-Saffron's War. Futura, 1975
　　The Sin and the Sinners. Jarrolds, 1958
　　633 Squadron. Hutchinson, 1956; Signet,
　　　1964
　　633 Squadron, Operation Rhine Maiden.
　　　Cassell, 1975
　　-The Storm Knight. Harrap, 1966
　　-The Tormented. Cassell, 1974
　　-Waterloo. Baker, 1970; Award, 1971
　　　(Novelization of the movie.)
　　-The Wider Sea of Love. Harrap, 1969

SMITH, FREDERICK M(ILLER). 1870-   .
　　The Stolen Signet. Duffield, 1909

SMITH, FREDRIKA SHUMWAY. Biographer and
　　author of children's books; wife of
　　a Chicago banker.
　　The House and the Tower. Christopher,
　　　1951 [New Eng.]

SMITH, GARRET.   -1954.
　　I Did It! Chelsea, 1928 [N.Y.]

SMITH, GEORGE MALCOLM. 1901-   . See:
　　George Malcolm-Smith.

SMITH, GEORGE O(LIVER). 1911-1981. Ref:
　　CA.
　　Hellflower. Abelard, 1953; Bodley, 1955

SMITH, GODFREY. 1926-   . Ref: CA, CC.
　　-The Business of Loving. Gollancz, 1961;
　　　Stein, 1968
　　Caviare. Hodder, 1976; Coward, 1976
　　The Flaw in the Crystal. Gollancz,
　　　1954; Putnam, 1954
　　-The Friends. Gollancz, 1957; Stein,
　　　1968
　　-The Network. Hodder, 1965

SMITH, GUY N(EWMAN). 1939-   .
　　-Bamboo Guerillas. New English Library
　　　pb, 1977
　　-Bats Out of Hell. New English Library
　　　pb, 1978
　　-The Black Knights. New English Library
　　　pb, 1977
　　-Caracol. New English Library pb, 1980
　　-Deathbell. Hamlyn, 1980
　　-The Ghoul. Sphere, 1976
　　-Hi-Jack! New English Library pb, 1977
　　-Killer Crabs. New English Library pb,
　　　1978
　　-Locusts. Hamlyn, 1979
　　-Night of the Crabs. New English Library pb, 1976
　　-The Origin of the Crabs. New English
　　　Library pb, 1979
　　-Satan's Snowdrop. Hamlyn, 1980
　　-The Slime Beast. New English Library
　　　pb, 1975
　　-The Son of the Werewolf. New English
　　　Library pb, 1978
　　-The Sucking Pit. New English Library
　　　pb, 1975
　　-Thirst. New English Library pb, 1980
　　-Werewolf by Moonlight. New English Library, 1974

SMITH, H(ERBERT) MAYNARD. 1869-1949.
　　Ref: CC. SC: Insp. Frost, in all
　　titles. Set: Eng.
　　Inspector Frost and Lady Brassingham.
　　　Benn, 1930
　　Inspector Frost and the Waverdale Fire.
　　　Benn, 1931
　　Inspector Frost and the Whitbourne Murder. Benn, 1939
　　Inspector Frost in Crevenna Cove. Benn,
　　　1933; Minton, 1933
　　Inspector Frost in the Background.
　　　Faber, 1941
　　Inspector Frost in the City. Benn,
　　　1930; Doubleday, 1930
　　Inspector Frost's Jigsaw. Benn, 1929;
　　　Doubleday, 1929

SMITH, HELEN ZENNA. 1896-   . Pseudonym:
　　Evadne Price, q.v.

SMITH, HORACE (HERBERT). 1868-1936.
　　Crooks of the Waldorf. Macaulay, 1929;
　　　Long, 1930 (Fictionalized true
　　　crime.)

SMITH, J. C. S. Pseudonym of a "noted
　　writer of nonfiction."
　　Jacoby's First Case. Atheneum, 1980;
　　　Hale, 1981 [NYC]

SMITH, J(OHN) F(REDERICK)
　　Woman and Her Master. Bradley, 1897

SMITH, JACK NICKLE
　　-The Black Troopers. Hale, 1972
　　-Is He Dead, Miss Ffinch? Tallis, 1969

SMITH, JASPER
　　The Specialist. Hamlyn, 1979

SMITH, JOHN TALBOT. 1855-1923.
　　The Art of Disappearing. Young, 1902.
　　　Also published as: The Man Who Vanished. Benziger, 1922

SMITH, JOHNSTON
　　Murder in the Square. Archer, 1933

SMITH, JUNIUS B. See: J(ohn) U(lrich)
　　Giesy, 1877-1947.

SMITH, KAY NOLTE. 1932-   . Ref: CA.
　　The Watcher. Coward, 1980; Gollancz,
　　　1981 [NYC]

SMITH, L. NEIL
　　The Probability Broach. Ballantine,
　　　1980 [1987, U.S.]

SMITH, LAURA
　　-Cuckoo in the Nest. Hale, 1970
　　Friarsmead. Hale, 1969
　　From This Day Forth. Hale, 1970
　　-The Maitland Inheritance. Hale, 1969

SMITH, LAURENCE DWIGHT. SC: Dick Whelan
　　= DW.
　　The Case of the Rented Coffin; see
　　　Follow This Fair Corpse
　　The Corpse with the Listening Ear. Mystery House, 1940 DW [L.I.]
　　Death Is Thy Neighbor. Lippincott, 1938
　　　[L.I.]
　　Follow This Fair Corpse. Mystery House,
　　　1941. Also published as: The Case of
　　　the Rented Coffin. Mystery Novel of
　　　the Month, 1941 DW [L.I.]
　　Girl Hunt. Lippincott, 1937 [NYC]

SMITH, LOU. 1918-   . Ref: CA. SC: John
　　Spencer, in at least those marked JS.
　　Fear and the Dead Man. Collins, 1968
　　The Fourth Man; see Primrose: The
　　　Fourth Man
　　Master Plot. Hale, 1976; St. Martin's,
　　　1977 JS
　　Primrose: The Fourth Man. Hale, 1976;
　　　St. Martin's, 1976. Also published
　　　as: The Fourth Man. Signet, 1978 JS
　　Psycho in Focus. Macmillan (London),
　　　1969
　　The Secret of MI6. Hale, 1975; St. Martin's, 1978 JS

SMITH, MARK (RICHARD). 1935-   . Ref:
　　CA.
　　The Death of the Detective. Knopf,
　　　1974; Secker, 1975 [Chi.]
　　Toyland. Little, 1965 [Mich.]

SMITH, MARTIN CRUZ. 1942-   . Pseudonyms: Nick Carter, Simon Quinn, qq.v.
　　Ref: CA. SC: Roman Grey = RG.
　　The Analog Bullet. Belmont, 1972; Star,
　　　1982 [Wash. D.C.]
　　Canto for a Gypsy. Putnam, 1972; Barker, 1975 RG [NYC]
　　Gypsy in Amber. Putnam, 1971; Barker,
　　　1975 RG
　　-Nightwing. Norton, 1977; Deutsch, 1977
　　　[Ariz.]

SMITH, MICHAEL A(NTHONY). 1942-   .
　　Ref: CA.
　　Legacy of the Lake. Avon, 1980 [Mo.]

SMITH, NANCY CAROLYN
　　To Dwell in Shadows. Belmont, 1978

SMITH, NANCY TAYLOR
　　The Golden Fig. Ace, 1974

SMITH, NAOMI GLADISH
　　Buried Remembrance. Ace, 1976

SMITH, NAOMI GWLADYS ROYDE. 1875?-1964.
See: Naomi (Gwladys) Royde-Smith.

SMITH, NEVILLE
Gumshoe. Fontana, 1971; Ballantine, 1972 (Novelization of the movie.)

SMITH, NORMAN EDWARD MACE. 1914-   .
Pseudonyms: Neil Sheraton, Norman Shore, qq.v.

SMITH, PAULINE C(OGGESHALL). 1908-   .
Ref: CA.
Nothing But Blood. Chicago Paperback House, 1962 [L.A.]

SMITH, RICHARD N. 1937-   . Ref: CA.
Death Be Nimble. Signet, 1967 [Mass.]

SMITH, RICHARD REIN. 1930-   . Pseudonyms: Richard Reinsmith, Diana Tower, qq.v.

SMITH, ROBERT ARTHUR. 1944-   . Ref: CA.
The Fox Trap. GM, 1978 [Ger.]
The Kramer Project. Doubleday, 1976; Hale, 1977

SMITH, ROBERT CHARLES. 1938-   . Pseudonyms: Robert Charles, Charles Leader, qq.v.

SMITH, ROBERT KIMMEL. 1930-   . Ref: CA.
Ransom. McKay, 1971; Constable, 1972
Sadie Shapiro in Miami. Simon, 1977; Prior, 1978 [Miami]

SMITH, SHELLEY. Pseudonym of Nancy Hermione Bodington, 1912-   . Ref: CA, CC, MC, TC. Set: Eng. SC: Jacob Chaos, in at least those marked JC.
An Afternoon to Kill. Collins, 1953; Harper, 1954 [Eng., ca.1910]
Background for Murder. Swan, 1942 JC
The Ballad of the Running Man. H. Hamilton, 1961; Harper, 1962
The Cellar at No. 5; see The Party at No. 5
Come and Be Killed! Collins, 1946; Harper, 1947
The Crooked Man; see Man Alone
Death Stalks at Lady. Swan, 1945
A Game of Consequences. Macmillan (London), 1978
A Grave Affair. H. Hamilton, 1971; Doubleday, 1973
He Died of Murder! Collins, 1947; Harper, 1948 JC
The Lord Have Mercy. H. Hamilton, 1956; Harper, 1956. Also published as: The Shrew Is Dead. Dell, 1959
Man Alone. Collins, 1952. U.S. title: The Crooked Man. Harper, 1952
Man with a Calico Face. Collins, 1951; Harper, 1950
The Party at No. 5. Collins, 1954. U.S. title: The Cellar at No. 5. Harper, 1954
Rachel Weeping. H. Hamilton, 1957; Harper, 1957 (Three novelets.)
The Shrew Is Dead; see The Lord Have Mercy
This Is the House. Collins, 1945 [W.I.]
The Woman in the Sea. Collins, 1948; Harper, 1948

SMITH, SPENCER. Born in Eng.; journalist and feature writer in N.Z., then in Australia.
The Dead Don't Matter. Long, 1960 [Australia]

SMITH, STEVE. Pseudonym: Jane Fleming, q.v.

SMITH, SURREY. Pseudonym of William Dinner, q.v.
The Astonished Guardsman. Boardman, 1965
A Gun for Delilah. Hale, 1979
No Tears for Teddy. Boardman, 1964

SMITH, SYDNEY. 1912-   .
The Survivor. Eyre, 1979; St. Martin's, 1979

SMITH, TERRENCE LORE. Pseudonym: Phillips Lore, q.v. Son of Charles Merrill Smith, q.v.; Illinois resident. SC: Webster Daniels, in at least those marked WD.
The Devil and Webster Daniels. Doubleday, 1975 WD [N.Y.]
The Money War. Atheneum, 1978; H. Hamilton, 1979 [St. Louis]
The Thief Who Came to Dinner. Doubleday, 1971 WD [Chi.]

SMITH, (JAMES) THORNE. 1893-1934. Ref: CC.
Did She Fall? Cosmopolitan, 1930; Barker, 1936

SMITH, TREVOR DUDLEY. Original name of Elleston Trevor, 1920-   , q.v. Pseudonyms: Mansell Black, Trevor Burgess, Adam Hall, Howard North, Simon Rattray, Warwick Scott, Caesar Smith, qq.v.
Double Who Double Crossed. Swan, 1944
Escape to Fear. Swan, 1948
Now Try the Morgue. Swan, 1948 [U.S.]
Over the Wall. Swan, 1943

SMITH, VERN E.
The Jones Men. Regnery, 1974; Weidenfeld, 1975 [Det.]

SMITH, WALLACE. 1888-1937.
-The Happy Alienist. Smith & Haas, 1936; Heinemann, 1936

SMITH, WILBUR (ADDISON). 1933-   . Ref: CA.
The Dark of the Sun; see The Train from Katanga
The Delta Decision; see Wild Justice
The Diamond Hunters. Heinemann, 1971; Doubleday, 1972
The Eye of the Tiger. Heinemann, 1975; Doubleday, 1976 [ship]
-The Train from Katanga. Heinemann, 1965. U.S. title: The Dark of the Sun. Dell, 1977
Wild Justice. Heinemann, 1979. U.S. title: The Delta Decision. Doubleday, 1981

SMITH, WILLARD K. Ref: CC, MM. SC: Insp. Dan Carr, in both titles.
Bowery Murder. Doubleday, 1929; Collins, 1930 [NYC]
The Sultan's Skull. Archer, 1933 [L.I.]

SMITH, WILLIAM DALE. 1929-   . Pseudonym: David Anthony, q.v.

SMITH, WILLIAM J. Pseudonym: Stephanie Hall, q.v.

SMITH, WILLIAM R.
Court by Proceedings, and other stories. Stockwell, 1937 ss

SMITH, YORK
The Banana Murders. Macdonald, 1958 [NYC]
Night of Wrath. Macdonald, 1959

SMITH, Z. Z. Pseudonym of David Westheimer, 1917-   , q.v.
A Very Private Island. Signet, 1963

SMITHIES, MURIEL. Pseudonym: Muriel Howe, q.v.

SMITHIES, RICHARD H(UGO) R(IPMAN). 1936-   . Ref: CA, CC. SC: Insp. William McAlpin, in at least those marked WM.
An Academic Question. Horizon, 1965. Also published as: Death Gets an A. Signet, 1968 WM [NYC, acad.]
Death Gets an A; see An Academic Question
Death Takes a Gamble; see Disposing Mind
Disposing Mind. Horizon, 1966. Also published as: Death Takes a Gamble. Signet, 1968 WM [N.Y.]
Fern Dead. Barrie, 1971 (U.S. title?)
The Shoplifter. Horizon, 1968; Jenkins, 1969 [Conn.]
The Tease. Signet, 1975

SMOCK, JAMES. Joint pseudonym with Clyde Laurents: Harriet Fredericks, q.v.

SMYLES, L. E.
A Millionaire's Folly; or, The Beautiful Unknown. Signet (Magnet), 1900

SMYTHE, ALAN LYLE. 1914-   . Pseudonym: Alan Caillou, q.v.

SMYTHE, FRANK S. [FRANCIS SIDNEY SMYTHE]. 1900-   .
Secret Mission. Hodder, 1942

SMYTHIES, MRS. G. [HARRIET MARIA GORDON SMYTHIES]
Guilty or Not Guilty. Ward, 1864

SNAITH, J(OHN) C(OLLIS). 1876-1936.
-Broke of Covenden. Constable, 1904; Turner, 1905
The Council of Seven. Collins, 1921; Appleton, 1921
The Crime of Constable Kelly. Nelson, 1924
Curiouser and Curiouser. Hutchinson, 1935. U.S. title: Lord Cobleigh Disappears. Appleton, 1936

Henry Northcote. Constable, 1906; Turner, 1906
Lord Cobleigh Disappears; see Curiouser and Curiouser
-Mistress Dorothy Marvin. Ward, 1900
-One of the Ones. Hutchinson, 1937
Thus Far. Hodder, 1925; Appleton, 1925
The Unforeseen. Hodder, 1930; Appleton, 1930
-William Jordan Junior. Long, 1925

SNAPP, ORVILLE. Pseudonym of Wilbur Braun, 1896-   , q.v. Other pseudonyms: Walter Blake, Bruce Brandon, Fred Caldwell, Raymond Dumkey, Nan Fleming, Marsha Grable, Edwin F. Hornung, Jed Parrish, Basil Ring, Mortimer Sprague, Bert Stoner, qq.v.
Murder Mansion. French (NYC), 1942 (3-act play.)

SNEDDON, ROBERT W(ILLIAM). 1880-1944.
-The Galleon's Gold. Methuen, 1925
Monsieur X. Methuen, 1926; Dial, 1928 [Paris]

SNELL, DAVID. 1942-   . NYC actor.
Lights, Camera...Murder. St. Martin's, 1979 [NYC]

SNELL, EDMUND. 1889-   . SC: Reggie Faulkner, in at least those marked RF; Peter Pennington, in at least those marked PP. Set: Eng.
And Then...One Dark Night. Skeffington, 1933
Anti-Crime Ltd. Mellifont, 1939
Back from the Dead. Mellifont, 1940
Blue Murder. Unwin, 1927; Lippincott, 1933 [It.]
Calling All Cars. Mellifont, 1938
-Corrigan's Way. Unwin, 1924
The Crimson Butterfly. Unwin, 1924 [Borneo]
The Crimson Swastika. Mellifont, 1938
Crooks Limited. Skeffington, 1934
The Dope Dealer. Mellifont, 1941
Emerald of Death. Everybody's, 1944
The Finger of Destiny and other stories. Quality, 1938 ss
Grid Murder. Mellifont, 1937
-Kontrol. Benn, 1928; Lippincott, 1928
Murder at the Miramar. Skeffington, 1936
Murder in Switzerland. Hale, 1938; Hillman-Curl, 1938 RF [Switz.]
-The Purple Shadow. Unwin, 1927
The Red Spinner. Hale, 1937; Hillman-Curl, 1938 RF [Afr.]
The Sign of the Scorpion. Skeffington, 1935
-The Sound Machine. Skeffington, 1932
Suicide House. Mellifont, 1941
The White Owl. Hodder, 1930; Lippincott, 1930
Yellow Jacket. Skeffington, 1936 PP
The Yellow Seven. Unwin, 1923; Century, 1923 PP [Far East]
-The Yu-Chi Stone. Unwin, 1925; Macaulay, 1926 [Borneo]
The "Z" Ray. Skeffington, 1932; Lippincott, 1932 RF

SNELLING, LAURENCE. 1933-   .
The Heresy. H. Hamilton, 1973; Norton, 1973 [It.]

SNIDER, MYRTLE IRENE
The Man Behind the Badge. Exposition, 1959

SNODGRESS, G. M.
The Crestwood Traps. Papillon, 1974. Also published as: Device for Murder. Decade, 1980 [New Eng.]

SNOW, C(HARLES) P(ERCY). 1905-1980. Ref: CA, CC, EM, MC.
A Coat of Varnish. Macmillan (London), 1979; Scribner, 1979
Death Under Sail. Heinemann, 1932; Doubleday, 1932 [ship]
The Sleep of Reason. Macmillan (London), 1968; Scribner, 1969

SNOW, CHARLES H(ORACE). 1877-   . Pseudonym: Charles Bellew, q.v. SC: Tommy Thorne, in at least those marked TT.
The Bonanza Murder Case. Wright, 1934 TT [West]
The Brush Creek Murders. Wright, 1937
The Buckhorn Murder Case. Wright, 1952
The Desert Castle Mystery. Wright, 1936
The Highgrade Murder. Wright, 1949 [West]
Hollow Stump Mystery. Wright, 1934
The Lakeside Murder. Wright, 1933 TT [West]
The Mountain Murder Case. Wright, 1951
Murder on the Cattle Ranch. Wright, 1935

The Mysterious Missile. Wright, 1950
The Mystery of Devil's Canyon. Wright, 1941
The Sign of the Death Circle. Wright, 1935 TT [West]
The Silent Shot. Wright, 1932
Twice Murdered. Wright, 1954

SNOW, KATHLEEN. 1944-   . Ref: CA.
Night Waking. Simon, 1978; Arrow, 1980 [NYC]

SNOW, LYNDON. Pseudonym of Dorothy Phoebe Ansle. Other pseudonyms: Laura Conway, Hebe Elsna, qq.v. Titles under this byline were apparently published in Britain as romances; those also published in the U.S. as gothics are listed below.
Francesca. Collins, 1970; Saturday Review Press, 1973, as by Laura Conway
Moment of Truth. Collins, 1968; Saturday Review Press, 1975, as by Laura Conway

SNOW, WALTER. 1907-1973. Born in Conn.; NYC newspaperman, ss writer.
The Golden Nightmare. Austin-Phelps, 1952 [NYC]

SNOWDEN, (JAMES) KEIGHLEY. 1860-   .
-Hate of Evil. Hutchinson, 1907
-Jack the Outlaw. Simpkin, 1926
The Plunder Pit. Methuen, 1898

SNYDER, CHARLES M(cCOY). 1859-   .
The Flaw in the Sapphire. Metropolitan, 1909 [India]

SNYDER, GENE
Mind War. Playboy, 1980
The Ogden Enigma. Playboy, 1980 [Utah]

SNYDER, GEORGE. Pseudonyms: Nick Carter, Patrick Morgan, Paul Richards, qq.v.

SNYDER, ZILPHA KEATLEY. 1927-   .
Heirs of Darkness. Atheneum, 1978; Magnum, 1980 [Calif.]

SOBEL, IRWIN PHILIP. 1901-   . Ref: CA.
-Dr. Monte Cristo. Doubleday, 1978 [hosp.]

SODARO, CRAIG. 1948-   . Ref: CA.
Be Our Guest. Performance Pub., 1979 (Play)
Mummy Sea, Mummy Do. Art Craft, 1977 (3-act play)
Search Me. Performance Pub., 1977 (Play)
Tea and Arsenic. Art Craft, 1977 (3-act play)

SODERBERG, DALE L.
Pawns. Manor, 1979

SOHL, JERRY [GERALD ALLAN SOHL]. 1913-   . Ref: CA. Pseudonym: Sean Mei Sullivan, q.v.
The Altered Ego. Rinehart, 1954 [2000s]
The Odious Ones. Rinehart, 1959; Consul, 1961 [L.A.]
Prelude to Peril. Rinehart, 1957 [Midwest]
The Time Dissolver. Avon, 1957; Sphere, 1967

SOITOS, STEPHEN. Joint pseudonym with Jamie Kinney: Andre Sax, q.v.

SOLOMON, (NEAL) BRAD(LEY). 1945-   . Ref: CA.
The Gone Man. Random, 1977; New English Library, 1978 [L.A.]
Jake and Katie. Dial, 1979
The Open Shadow. Summit, 1978 [L.A.]

SOMERS, CHRISTOPHER. See: J(ohn Freeman) Fairfax-Blakeborough, 1883-   .

SOMERS, JOHN
The Brethren of the Axe. Murray, 1926; Dutton, 1927

SOMERS, MARK
Merely Mischief. Hutchinson, 1922. U.S. title: The Haunted House of Marley. Moffat, 1923

SOMERS, PAUL. Pseudonym of Paul Winterton, 1908-   . Other pseudonyms: Roger Bax, Andrew Garve, qq.v. SC: Hugh Curtis = HC. Set: Eng.
Beginner's Luck. Collins, 1958; Harper, 1958 HC
The Broken Jigsaw. Collins, 1961; Harper, 1961
Operation Piracy. Collins, 1958; Harper, 1959 HC
The Shivering Mountain. Collins, 1959; Harper, 1959 HC

SOMERS, SUZANNE. Pseudonym of Dorothy Daniels, 1915-   , q.v. Other pseudonyms: Danielle Dorsett, Angela Gray, Cynthia Kavanaugh, Geraldine Thayer, Helen Gray Weston, qq.v.
House of Eve. Avalon, 1962
The House on Thunder Hill. Curtis, 1973
Image of Truth. Avalon, 1963
The Mists of Morning. Tower, 1966
The Romany Curse. Belmont, 1971 [Fla.]
Until Death. Curtis, 1973

SOMERVILLE, CHARLES (CECIL LEE D'MONTRAL). 1876?-1931. NYC reporter.
An Artist in Crime. Curtiss, 1928; Paul, 1929 [NYC]
The Master Rogue. Lippincott, 1935

SOMERVILLE, HENRY. Set: Eng.
Black Triangle. Modern, 1938
The Leland Case. Modern, 193?

SOMERVILLE, IVAN
Scattered Death. Alexandrian, 1931 [NYC]

SOMERVILLE-LARGE, PETER. 1928-   . Ref: CA.
Couch of Earth. Gollancz, 1975 [Iran]
Eagles Near His Carcase. Gollancz, 1977

SOMMERSCALES, ROWLAND. 1912-   . Pseudonym: Robert Gaines, q.v.

SONIN, RAY. 1907-   . Set: Eng.
The Dance Band Mystery. Quality, 1940
The Death Pack. Fenland, 1933
Murder in Print. Jenkins, 1953; Roy, 1956
The Mystery of the Tailor's Dummy. Harrap, 1935
Twice Times Murder. Jenkins, 1954

SONTAG, SUSAN. 1933-   . Ref: CA.
Death Kit. Farrar, 1967; Secker, 1967

SONTUP, DANIEL. 1922-   . Pseudonym: David Saunders, q.v.

SORRENTINO, GILBERT. 1929-   . Ref: CA.
-Mulligan Stew. Grove, 1979; Boyars, 1980

SOUBERGE, LEALE
Mystery at Wadham Close. Bride's, 1942

SOULIE, FREDERICK. 1800-1847.
Pastourel; or, The Sorcerer of the Mountain. Williams, 1847; M'Glashan, 1849 (Translation from the French.)

SOUTAR, ANDREW. 1879-1941. SC: Phineas Spinnet, in at least those marked PS; Kharduni, in at least those marked K. Set: Eng.
Back from the Dead. Hodder, 1920
-Back to Eden. Hutchinson, 1927
-Battling Barker. Hutchinson, 1933
-A Beggar in Purple. Hodder, 1918
The Black Spot Mystery. Hutchinson, 1938 PS
-Broken Ladders. Cassell, 1912
-Butterflies in the Rain. Hutchinson, 1926
Chain Murder. Hutchinson, 1939 PS
The Chosen of the Gods. Harper (London), 1910 [India]
Consider Your Verdict. Hutchinson, 1928
-Corinthian Days. Hutchinson, 1923
-Cowards' Castle. Hutchinson, 1934
-Dear Fools. Hutchinson, 1927
-Delilah of Mayfair. Hutchinson, 1926
-The Devil's Triangle. Hutchinson, 1931
Eight Three Five. Hutchinson, 1935 PS
-Equality Island. Hodder, 1919
Facing East. Hutchinson, 1936 PS
The Great Conspiracy. Hutchinson, 1934 K
-The Green Orchard. Cassell, 1916
-Hagar, Called Hannah. Hutchinson, 1933
The Hanging Sword! Hutchinson, 1933 PS
Hornet's Nest. Murray, 1922
-The Imperfect Lover. Hodder, 1919
-In the Blood. Jarrolds, 1928
-The Island of Test. Harper (London), 1910
Justice Is Done. Hutchinson, 1936 K
Kharduni. Hutchinson, 1933; Macaulay, 1934 K
The Leopard's Spots. Hutchinson, 1928
-Magpie House. Cassell, 1913
-The Marquis. Hodder, 1919
The Master Key. Federation, 1926
The Money Spinners and other stories. Hutchinson, 1934 ss
Motive for the Crime. Hutchinson, 1941 PS
-Mr. Nobody of England. Hutchinson, 1942
The Museum Mystery. Hutchinson, 1936 PS
Neither Do I Condemn Thee. Hutchinson, 1924
Night of Horror. Hutchinson, 1934 PS

"Not Mentioned..." Hutchinson, 1930
One Page Missing. Hutchinson, 1938 PS
Opportunity. Hutchinson, 1932
-Ostrich Man. Hutchinson, 1937
-Other Men's Shoes. Hodder, 1918
-Pagans. Hutchinson, 1928
-The Perverted Village. Hutchinson, 1936
The Phantom in the House. Hutchinson, 1928
-The Prodigal, and other stories. Hodder, 1919 ss
Public Ghost Number One. Hutchinson, 1941
Pursuit. Hutchinson, 1927
-Rainbow Nights, and other stories. Hodder, 1919 ss
-The Road to Romance. Murray, 1921
Secret Ways. Hutchinson, 1932; Kendall, 1934
Silence! Hutchinson, 1930
Silent Accuser. Hutchinson, 1938 PS
Sinister River. Hutchinson, 1936
-Snow in the Desert. Hodder, 1919
"The Stars I'd Give—". Hutchinson, 1937
The Strange Case of Sir Merton Quest. Hutchinson, 1940 PS
A Stranger Came to Dinner. Hutchinson, 1939 PS
Study in Suspense. Hutchinson, 1941 PS
Thirty Pieces of Silver. Hutchinson, 1931
The White Lie Company, and The Woman with the Green Eyes. Hodder, 1927
The Wolves and the Lamb. Hutchinson, 1940 PS
-Worldly Goods. Hutchinson, 1928

SOUTH, MARSHALL
The Curse of the Sightless Fish. World's Work, 1948 [New Guinea]

SOUTH, ROBERT
Rogues' Nest. South, 1925

SOUTHCOTT, AUDLEY. With advertising agencies, TV scriptwriter, film producer in Eng.
The Black General. Macdonald, 1969; Morrow, 1969
Cross That Palm When I Come to It. Sphere, 1974 (Episodic novelization of the "Public Eye" TV series.)

SOUTHNEY, LYN
Deadly Fresco. Moray, 1939

SOUTHON, ARTHUR E(USTACE). 1887-   .
The Laughing Ghosts. Sheldon, 1928 ss [Afr.]

SOUTHWICK, ALBERT P(LYMPTON). 1855-1929.
The Catherwood Mystery. Taylor, 1929

SOUTHWOLD, STEPHEN. 1887-1964. Pseudonyms: Neil Bell, Paul Martens, qq.v.

SOUTHWORTH, MRS. E(MMA) D(OROTHY) E(LIZA) N(EVITTE). 1819-1899. At least some of these titles contain significant crime/gothic elements. Considerable bibliographic confusion surrounds this author, most of which has resisted removal, as will be evident below.
Allworth Abbey. Peterson, 1865
The Artist's Love. Peterson, 1872
Astrea; or, The Bridal Day. (London), 1862 (U.S. title?)
Beatrice; The Forsaken Daughter. 1872
Brandon Coyle's Wife. Bonner's, 1893
The Bridal Eve. Peterson, 1864; Milner, 1878
The Bride of an Evening; see The Gipsy's Prophecy
The Bride of Llewellyn. Peterson, 1866
The Bride's Fate. Milner, 1878 (U.S. title?)
The Broken Engagement; or, Speaking the Truth for a Day. Peterson, 1862
Broken Pledges. Peterson, 1891
Captain Rock's Pet. 1863
The Changed Brides. Peterson, 1869; Milner, 1878
The Christmas Guest. Peterson, 1870
The Coral Lady; or, The Bronzed Beauty of Paris. Alexander, 1867
Cruel As the Grave. Peterson, 1871
The Curse of Clifton; or, The Widowed Bride. Hart, 1853; Clarke, 1853
David Lindsay. Bonner's, 1893
The Deserted Wife. Appleton, 1851; Clarke, 1856
The Discarded Daughter; or, The Children of the Isle. Peterson, 1875
"Em." Bonner's, 1892
Em's Husband. Bonner's, 1892
An Exile's Bride. 1887
Fair Play; or, The Test of the Lone Island. 1868
Fallen Pride; or, The Mountain Girl's Love. Peterson, 1868

The Family Doom; or, The Sin of a
  Countess. Peterson, 1888
The Fatal Marriage. Peterson, 1863;
  Milner, 1878
The Fatal Secret. Peterson, 1877
For Woman's Love. Bonner's, 1890
The Fortune Seeker. Peterson, 1866;
  Milner, 1878
Gertrude Haddon. Bonner's, 1894
The Gipsy's Prophecy; or, The Bride of
  an Evening. Peterson, 1861. British
  title: The Bride of an Evening; or,
  The Gipsy's Prophecy. Milner, 18??
Gloria. Bonner's, 1891
Hagar; or, The Deserted Wife. Milner,
  18?? (U.S. title?)
The Haunted Homestead. Peterson, 1860
  ss
Hester Strong's Life Work. (Boston),
  1869
Hickory Hall; or, The Outcast. Peterson, 1861
The Hidden Hand. (U.S.), 18??; Ward,
  1859
How He Won Her. Peterson, 1869; (London), 1969
India. Peterson, 1856
Ishmael; or, In the Depths. (U.S.),
  1884
The Island Princess; or, The Double
  Marriage. Bryce, 1857
The Lady of the Isle. Peterson, 1859
A Leap in the Dark. Bonner's, 1890
Lilith. Bonner's, 1891
Little Ned's Engagement. Street, 1908
The Lost Bride. Lea, 1858 (U.S.
  title?)
The Lost Heir of Linlithgow. Peterson,
  1872
The Lost Heiress. (Phil.), 1855; Ward,
  1855
Love's Labor Won. Peterson, 1862
The Maiden Widow. Peterson, 1870
Mark Sutherland; or, Power and Principle. Cassell, 1853 (U.S. title?)
The Missing Bride; or, Miriam the
  Avenger. 1872
The Mother-in-Law; or, The Isle of
  Rays. Clarke, 1853 (U.S. title?)
Mother's Secret. (London), 1883 (U.S.
  title?)
The Mysterious Marriage. Street, 1908
The Mystery of Dark Hollow. Peterson,
  1875
Nearest and Dearest. Bonner's, 1889
A Noble Lord. Peterson, 1872
Only a Girl's Heart. Bonner's, 1893;
  Modern, 1935
The Phantom Wedding; or, The Fall of
  the House of Flint. Peterson, 1878
The Prince of Darkness. Peterson, 1869
The Red Hill Tragedy. Peterson, 1877
The Rejected Bride. Bonner's, 1894
Retribution. (NYC), 1849; Lea, 1858
Self-Made. 1861
Self-Raised; or, From the Depths.
  Peterson, 1876; Milner, 18??
Shannondale. (NYC), 1851. British
  title: Winny Darling; or, Three Beauties of Shannondale. Clarke, 1856
A Skeleton in the Closet. Bonner's,
  1893
The Spectre Lover. Peterson, 1875
Sybil Brotherton. Peterson, 1879
The Test of Love; see The Trail of the
  Serpent
A Tortured Heart; see The Trail of the
  Serpent
The Trail of the Serpent. (U.S.), 1879.
  Also published as: The Test of Love,
  plus: A Tortured Heart. Street, 1907
Tried for Her Life. (Phil.), 1871
The Two Sisters; or, Virginia and Magdalene; see Virginia and Magdalene
The Unknown. 1874
Unknown; or, the Mystery of Raven
  Rocks. Bonner's, 1889
The Unloved Wife. Bonner's, 1891
Virginia and Magdalene; or, The Foster
  Sisters. Peterson, 1852. Also published as: The Two Sisters; or, Virginia and Magdalene. Peterson, 1875.
  British title: The Two Sisters, Lea,
  1859
Vivia; or, The Secret of Power. Peterson, 1875
The Widow's Son. Peterson, 1867
The Wife's Victory. Peterson, 1854 ss
Winny Darling; see Shannondale
Woman's Fate. Modern, 1935 (U.S.
  title?)

SOUTHWORTH, LOUIS. Pseudonym of Thomas
  Louis Grealey, 1916- . Ref: CA.
  SC: Insp. Tom Anderson, in both
  titles. Set: Eng.
  Corpse on London Bridge. Hale, 1969
  Felon in Disguise. Hale, 1966

SOUVESTRE, PIERRE, 1874-1914, and MARCEL
  ALLAIN, 1885-1970. SC: Fantomas, in
  all titles; series continued by
  Allain, q.v.
  The Exploits of Juve. Paul, 1916; Brentano's, 1917 [Paris]
  Fantomas. Paul, 1915; Brentano's, 1915
  [Fr.]
  A Limb of Satan. Paul, 1924. U.S.
    title: The Long Arm of Fantomas.
    Macaulay, 1924 [Paris]
  The Long Arm of Fantomas; see A Limb of
    Satan
  Messengers of Evil. Paul, 1917; Brentano's, 1917 [Paris]
  A Nest of Spies. Paul, 1917; Brentano's, 1917 [Fr.]
  A Royal Prisoner. Paul, 1919; Brentano's, 1918 [Paris]
  Slippery As Sin. Paul, 1920; Moffat,
    1923 [Eng.]

SOUZA, ERNEST. Pseudonym of Evelyn Scott,
  1893- . Ref: CA.
  Blue Rum. Cape & Smith, 1930; Cape,
    1930 [Port.]

SOWMAN, GORDON
  Expendable Agent. Church, 1968

SPADE, DANNY. Pseudonym of Dail Ambler,
  q.v.
  The Dame Plays Rough. Scion, 1950
  'Frisco Rock. Scion, 1951
  A Gun for Sale. Scion, 1952
  Kiss Me As You Go. Milestone, 1953
  Lady Likes to Sin. Milestone, 1953
  Nothing to Hide. Milestone, 1953
  Silk and Cordite. Scion, 1951
  Story of a Killer. Milestone, 1953
  That's All I Need. Milestone, 1954
  Twice As Dead. Scion, 1952
  You Slay Me. Scion, 1950
  You'll Play This My Way. Scion, 1951

SPAIN, JOHN. Pseudonym of Cleve F(ranklin) Adams, 1895-1949, q.v. Joint
  pseudonym with Robert Leslie Bellem, q.v.: Franklin Charles, q.v.
  SC: Bill Rye = BR.
  Death Is Like That. Dutton, 1943 BR
    [L.A.]
  Dig Me a Grave. Dutton, 1942 BR [L.A.]
  The Evil Star. Dutton, 1944 [L.A.]

SPAIN, NANCY. 1917-1964. SC: Miriam
  Birdseye = MB; Johnny DuVivien = JD.
  Set: Eng.
  Cinderella Goes to the Morgue. Hutchinson, 1950 MB
  Death Before Wicket. Hutchinson, 1946
    JD [acad.]
  Death Goes on Skis. Hutchinson, 1949
    MB,JD
  The Kat Strikes. Hutchinson, 1955
  Murder, Bless It! Hutchinson, 1948 JD
  Not Wanted on Voyage. Hutchinson, 1951
    MB
  Out, Damned Tot! Hutchinson, 1952 MB
  Poison for Teacher. Hutchinson, 1949
    MB, JD [acad.]
  Poison in Play. Hutchinson, 1946 JD
  R in the Month. Hutchinson, 1950 MB

SPAIN, PETER. Pseudonym of "a young Irish
  writer."
  Blood Scenario. Coward, 1980 [Ire.]

SPAIN, RICHARD
  The Strange Citadel. Jenkins, 1931

SPAIN, TERRY. Pseudonym of Ted Stratton,
  1902- , q.v.
  Time to Kill. Popular Library, 1953
    [N.J.]

SPALDING, SAMUEL C. Pseudonym: Nicholas
  Carter, q.v.

SPANN, WELDON (OMA). 1924- . Ref: CA.
  Discharge to Danger. Hale, 1969
  Hunter for Hire. Hale, 1970
  Plunge into Peril. Hale, 1970
  Return to Violence. Hale, 1969
  The Stink of Murder. Hale, 1969
  Wall of Jeopardy. Hale, 1970

SPARK, MURIEL (SARAH). 1918- . Ref:
  CA.
  The Comforters. Macmillan (London),
    1957; Lippincott, 1957
  Robinson. Macmillan (London), 1958;
    Lippincott, 1958
  Territorial Rights. Macmillan (London), 1979; Coward, 1979 [Venice]

SPARKES, BOYDEN. 1890-1954. See: Claire
  Carvalho.

SPARKIA, ROY (BERNARD). 1924- . Ref:
  CA.
  Boss Man. Lion, 1954
  Build My Gallows High. GM, 1956; Fawcett (London), 1957
  Paradise County. Dell, 1974
  The Vanishing Vixen. Crest, 1959; Muller, 1960

SPARKS, CHRISTINE
  The Enigma Files. BBC, 1980 (Novelization of the TV series.)

SPARRE, CHRISTIAN. 1859-1936. Pseudonym:
  Fredrik Viller, q.v.

SPARROY, MASSICKS. Pseudonym.
  The Leper's Bell. Collins, 1921; Putnam, 1921 [Fr.]
  The Listening Woman. Faber, 1932; Little, 1932

SPATZ, H. DONALD. 1913-
  Death on the Nose. Phoenix, 1942 [NYC]
  Murder with Long Hair. Phoenix, 1940.
    Also published as (?): 3 Girls and a
    Killer. Crime Novel Selections, 1942
    [Pa.]
  3 Girls and a Killer; see Murder with
    Long Hair

SPEAR, ANNE B. Joint pseudonym with Bessie C. Morris: Forfex et Hesta, q.v.

SPEARMAN, FRANK H(AMILTON). 1859-1937.
  The Nerve of Foley, and other railroad
    stories. Harper, 1900, some criminous

SPEARS, RAYMOND S(MILEY). 1876-1950.
  Diamond Tolls. Doubleday, 1920

SPECTOR, ROBERT DONALD. 1922- . Ref:
  CA.
  The Candle and the Tower. Warner, 1974

SPEICHER, HELEN ROSS. 1915- . Joint
  pseudonym with Kathryn Kilby Borland,
  1916- : Alice Abbott, q.v.

SPEIGHT, T(HOMAS) W(ILKINSON). 1830-1915.
  As It Was Written. Chatto, 1902
  -Back to Life. Taylor, 1891 (British
    title?)
  -A Barren Life. Chatto, 1886; Harper,
    1885
  A Bootless Crime. Digby, 1909
  -Brought to Light. Wood, 1867; Hilton,
    1867
  -Burgo's Romance. Chatto, 1890
  -By Fate's Caprice. Digby, 1904
  -By Fortune's Whim. Digby, 1903
  The Celestial Ruby. Digby, 1904
  The Chains of Circumstance. Digby, 1900
  The Crime in the Wood. Long, 1899
  The Doom of Siva. Chatto, 1899
  The Fate of the Hara Diamond. Greening,
    1907
  Foiled. Digby, 1911
  -Foolish Margaret. Wood, 1867
  -For Himself Alone. Munro, 1884 (British title?)
  The Grey Monk. Chatto, 1895
  The Heart of a Mystery. Jarrolds, 1896;
    Fenno, 1896
  -Her Ladyship. Chatto, 1903
  In the Dead of Night. Bentley, 1874
  -Juggling Fortune. Long, 1900
  -A Late Repentence. Digby, 1901
  The Loudwater Tragedy. Chatto, 1892
  The Master of Trenance. Chatto, 1896
  A Minion of the Moon. Chatto, 1897; New
    Amsterdam, 1896
  -Mr. Spenyard's Two Experiments. Digby,
    1908
  The Mysteries of Heron Dyke. Bentley,
    1880; Harper, 1881
  -On the Fringe. Digby, 1912
  The Plotters. Digby, 1905
  The Price of a Secret. Digby, 1908
  Quittance in Full. Chatto, 18??
  The Sandycroft Mystery. Chatto, 1890
  -Second Love. Digby, 1900
  A Secret of the Sea. Bentley, 1876
  The Secret of Wyvern Towers. Chatto,
    1898
  The Sport of Chance. Digby, 1903
  -Stepping Blindfold. Chatto, 1903
  -The Strange Experience of Mr. Verschoyle. Chatto, 1901
  -Tangled Lives. Jarrolds, 1910
  -Time Bargains. Digby, 1907
  -Under a Cloud. Digby, 1906
  Under Lock and Key. Tinsley, 1869;
    Turner, 1869
  Ursula Lenorme: Lady Companion. Digby,
    1909 ss
  The Web of Fate. Chatto, 1900
  -Wife or No Wife?, and A Close Shave.
    Chatto, 1887 (Two stories.)

SPENCE, EDWARD F(ORDHAM). 1860- .
  The Crime of Sybil Cresswell. Benn, 1929
  -A Freak of Fate. White, 1886

SPENCE, (JAMES) LEWIS (THOMAS CHALMERS). 1874-1955.
  The Archer in the Arras, and other tales of mystery. Grant, 1932 ss

SPENCE, RALPH
  The Gorilla. French, 1950 (3-act play.)

SPENCE, WALL. All titles below are plays, with the number of acts given in parenthesis.
  The Case of the Weird Sisters. Baker's, 1944 (1)
  "Catch That Thief!" Northwestern, 1933 (3)
  The Dark House. Dramatists, 1939 (3)
  Four Frightened Sisters. Baker's, 1956 (1)
  The Full Moon. French (NYC), 1935 (1)
  "Ghostly Fingers." Northwestern, 1932 (3)
  "The Green Phantom." Northwestern, 1935 (3)
  "The House of Fear." Northwestern, 1937 (3)
  How Betty Butted In. Baker's, 1954 (3)
  The Locked Room. Baker's, 1956 (1)
  A Message from John. Baker's, 1953 (3)
  Mystery in Blue. Northwestern, 1942 (3)
  The Scarlet Shadow. Northwestern, 1947 (3)
  The Sign of the Four. Northwestern, 1940 (3) (Suggested by the story by A. Conan Doyle, 1859-1930, q.v.)
  Whispering Walls. French (NYC), 1935 (3)
  Wits' End. French (NYC), 1934 (1)
  The Woman in Black. Northwestern, 1938 (3)

SPENCER, MRS. BELLA Z(ILFA). 1840-1867.
  Right and Wrong; or, She Told the Truth at Last, with other stories. Holland, 1870 ss, title story criminous

SPENCER, CLAIRE. 1899- .
  -Gallows Orchard. Cape & Smith, 1930; Cape, 1930

SPENCER, ERLE
  The Death of the Captain Shand. Hodder, 1930 [Port.]
  The Four Lost Ships. Hodder, 1931
  The King of Spain's Daughter. Hodder, 1934
  Or Give Me Death! Harrap, 1936
  The Piccadilly Ghost. Hodder, 1929; Macmillan, 1930
  Stop, Press! Hodder, 1932

SPENCER, GEOFFREY. Pseudonym of Alexander (Douglas Chesney) Wilson, 1893- , q.v.
  -Confessions of a Scoundrel. Laurie, 1933

SPENCER, HANK
  Bad-Luck Cutie. Modern Fiction, 1953
  Dumb Babes Don't Die. Modern Fiction, 1954
  The Flesh Game. Modern Fiction, 1954
  The Gallows Are High. Modern Fiction, 1953
  Gentleman's Relish. Modern Fiction, 1954
  Neck of Sinners. Modern Fiction, 1954
  No Face for a Killer. Modern Fiction, 1953
  Vice Squad. Modern Fiction, 1954

SPENCER, JOHN. Pseudonym of Roy Vickers, 1888-1965, q.v. Other pseudonyms: David Durham, Sefton Kyle, qq.v.
  Swell Garrick. Hodder, 1933. Reprinted as by Vickers: Newnes, 1935
  The Whispering Death. Hodder, 1932. Reprinted as by Vickers: Newnes, 1935. U.S. edition, as by Vickers: Jefferson House, 1947

SPENCER, LEE
  The Furtive Men. Jarrolds, 1951

SPENCER, PHILIP (HERBERT). 1924- .
  Full Term. Faber, 1961 [acad.]

SPENCER, ROSS H(ARRISON). 1921- .
  Ref: CA. SC: Chance Purdue, in all titles.
  The Abu Wahab Caper. Avon, 1980 [Ill.]
  The DADA Caper. Avon, 1978
  The Regis Arms Caper. Avon, 1979 [Chi.]
  The Stranger City Caper. Avon, 1979 [Ill.]

SPENDER, J(EAN) M(AUDE)
  The Charge Is Murder! Eyre, 1934
  Death Comes in the Night. Eyre, 1938
  Death Renders Account. Hale, 1960
  Full Moon for Murder. Evans, 1948
  Murder on the Prowl. Hale, 1960
  Seven Days for Hanging. Hale, 1958

SPENDER, MRS. JOHN KENT [LILIAN HEADLAND SPENDER]. 1835-1895.
  The Recollections of a Country Doctor. Hurst, 1885 ss, at least one criminous

SPENSER, JOHN. Pseudonym of Francis Harold Guest, 1901- .
  -The Awkward Marine. Longmans, 1948
  Crime Against Society. Longmans, 1938
  The Five Mutineers. Longmans, 1935
  -Limey. Longmans, 1933
  -Limey Breaks In. Longmans, 1934
  -The Wheels. Longmans, 1938

SPERDUTI, DOMINICK ROCKE
  For You, I Commit Murder. Christopher, 1956
  That Night at Nine. Williams-Frederick, 1958

SPEWACK, BELLA COHEN, 1899- , and SAMUEL SPEWACK, 1899-1971, q.v.
  The Solitaire Man. French (NYC), 1934 (3-act play.)

SPEWACK, SAMUEL. 1899-1971. See also: Bella Cohen Spewack, 1899- . Ref: CA.
  Murder in the Gilded Cage. Simon, 1929 [Havana]
  The Skyscraper Murder. Macaulay, 1928 [NYC]

SPICER, BART. 1918- . Joint pseudonym with Betty Coe Spicer: Jay Barbette, q.v. Ref: CA, CC, TC. SC: Col. Peregrine White = PW; Benson Kellogg = BK; Carney Wilde = CW.
  Act of Anger. Atheneum, 1962; Barker, 1963 BK [N. Mex.]
  The Adversary. Putnam, 1974; Hart-Davis, 1974
  Black Sheep, Run. Dodd, 1951; Collins, 1952 CW [Phil.]
  Blues for the Prince. Dodd, 1950; Collins, 1951 CW [Phil.]
  The Burned Man. Atheneum, 1966; Hale, 1967 PW [Sp.]
  The Dark Light. Dodd, 1949; Collins, 1950 CW [Phil.]
  The Day of the Dead. Dodd, 1955; Hodder, 1956 PW [Sp.]
  Exit, Running. Dodd, 1959; Hodder, 1960 CW [Phil.]
  The Golden Door. Dodd, 1951; Collins, 1951 CW [Phil.]
  Kellogg Junction. Atheneum, 1969; Hodder, 1970 BK [N. Mex.]
  The Long Green. Dodd, 1952. British title: Shadow of Fear. Collins, 1953 CW [Ariz.]
  Shadow of Fear; see The Long Green
  The Taming of Carney Wilde. Dodd, 1954; Hodder, 1955 CW [ship]

SPICER, BETTY COE. Joint pseudonym with Bart Spicer, 1918- , q.v.: Jay Barbette, q.v.

SPICER, DOROTHY (GLADYS). Ref: CA.
  The Crystal Ball. Beagle, 1975
  Desert Adventure. Bouregy, 1968; Gold Lion, 1973
  Eye of the Cat. Lancer, 1973
  The Humming Top. Phillips, 1968
  The Tower Room. Avon, 1973; Remploy, 1973
  The Witch's Web. Ballantine, 1975

SPICER, HENRY. -1891.
  A White Hand and a Black Thumb. Chapman, 1864

SPIESS, CHRISTIAN H(EINRICH). 1755-1799.
  The Dwarf of Westerbourg. Morgan, 1827 (Translation of "Der Petermanchen." Prague, 1793.)

SPIESS, JAN
  The Amber Bead. Cassell, 1961

SPIKE, PAUL. 1947- . Ref: CA.
  The Night Letter. Putnam, 1979; Granada, 1979 [Mich., 1940]

SPILKEN, ARON, 1939- , and ED O'LEARY
  Burning Moon. Playboy, 1978 [West]

SPILLANE, MICKEY [FRANK MORRISON SPILLANE]. 1918- . Ref: CA, CC, EM, MC, TC. SC: Mike Hammer = MH; Tiger Mann = TM.
  The Big Kill. Dutton, 1951; Barker, 1952 MH [NYC]
  Bloody Sunrise. Dutton, 1965; Barker, 1965 TM [NYC]
  The Body Lovers. Dutton, 1967; Barker, 1967 MH
  The By-Pass Control. Dutton, 1966; Barker, 1967 TM [NYC, Fla.]
  Day of the Guns. Dutton, 1964; Barker, 1965 TM [NYC]
  The Death Dealers. Dutton, 1965; Barker, 1966 TM [NYC]
  The Deep. Dutton, 1961; Barker, 1961 [NYC]
  The Delta Factor. Dutton, 1967; Corgi, 1969
  The Erection Set. Dutton, 1972; Allen, 1972 [NYC]
  The Flier. Corgi, 1964 (2 novelets.)
  The Girl Hunters. Dutton, 1962; Barker, 1962 MH [NYC]
  I, the Jury. Dutton, 1947; Barker, 1952 MH [NYC]
  Killer Mine. Signet, 1968; Corgi, 1965 (2 novelets.)
  Kiss Me, Deadly. Dutton, 1952; Barker, 1953 MH [NYC]
  The Last Cop Out. Dutton, 1973; Allen, 1973 [NYC]
  The Long Wait. Dutton, 1951; Barker, 1953 [Midwest]
  Me, Hood! Corgi, 1963 (3 novelets.)
  Me, Hood! Signet, 1969 (2 novelets, only one from the British collection of the same name.) [NYC]
  My Gun Is Quick. Dutton, 1950; Barker, 1951 MH [NYC]
  One Lonely Night. Dutton, 1951; Barker, 1952 MH [NYC]
  Return of the Hood. Corgi, 1964 (2 novelets.)
  The Snake. Dutton, 1964; Barker, 1964 MH [NYC]
  Survival Zero. Dutton, 1970; Corgi, 1970 MH [NYC]
  The Tough Guys. Signet, 1969 (3 novelets from various British collections of Spillane's novelets.)
  The Twisted Thing. Dutton, 1966; Barker, 1966 MH [N.Y.]
  Vengeance Is Mine! Dutton, 1950; Barker, 1951 MH [NYC]

SPILLER, ANDREW. SC: Det. Insp. "Duck" Mallard, in at least those marked M. Set: Eng.
  Alias Mr. Orson. Paul, 1951 M
  And Thereby Hangs—. Paul, 1948 M
  As They Shall Sow. Paul, 1952 M
  Birds of a Feather. Paul, 1950
  Black Cap for Murder. Paul, 1956 M
  Brains Trust for Murder. Paul, 1956 M
  Brief Candle. Paul, 1949 M
  Crooked Highway. Archer, 1947
  Curtain Call for Murder. Long, 1957 M
  The Evil That Men Do. Paul, 1953 M
  If Murder Interferes with Business. Archer, 1945
  It's in the Bag. Paul, 1955 M
  Kiss the Book. Paul, 1952
  The Man Who Caught the 4:15. Paul, 1950
  The Man Who Dressed to Kill. Long, 1960
  Murder Has Three Dimensions. Archer, 1948 M
  Murder Is a Shady Business. Paul, 1954
  Murder on a Shoestring. Long, 1958 M
  Murder Without Malice. Paul, 1954 M
  Phantom Circus. Paul, 1950 M
  Queue Up to Listen. Archer, 1946 M
  Ring Twice for Murder. Paul, 1955 M
  Rope for Breakfast. Archer, 1945
  Sing a Song of Murder. Long, 1959
  They Tell No Tales. Paul, 1953
  What's in a Name? Archer, 1947 M
  When Crook Meets Crook. Archer, 1947
  Who Plays with Sin. Paul, 1951
  Whom Nobody Owns. Archer, 1945
  You Can't Get Away with Murder! Archer, 1948 M

SPINELLI, MARCOS. 1904-1970. Ref: CA.
  Assignment Without Glory. Lippincott, 1945; Davies, 1945 [Braz.]

SPLINT. Pseudonym: Nicholas Carter.

SPOFFORD, HARRIET (ELIZABETH PRESCOTT). 1835-1921.
  The Amber Gods and other stories. Ticknor, 1863 ss, at least one criminous
  -A Lost Jewel. Lee, 1891

SPOONER, JOHN D. 1937- . Ref: CA.
  The King of Terrors. Little, 1975; Arrow, 1976

SPORE, KEITH
  The Breaking Point. Major, 1977
  Death of a Scavenger. Belmont, 1980 [Wash. D.C.]
  The Hell Masters. Major, 1977

SPOUSE, MARY
   The Hammerword Technique. Tower, 1980 [Mid. East]

SPRAGUE, JOYCE CLAYPOOL
   Dynasty of Fear. Lenox, 1973; Remploy, 1974

SPRAGUE, MORTIMER. Pseudonym of Wilbur Braun, 1896-   , q.v. Other pseudonyms: Walter Blake, Bruce Brandon, Fred Caldwell, Raymond Dumkey, Nan Fleming, Marsha Grable, Edwin F. Hornung, Jed Parish, Basil Ring, Orville Snap, Bert Stoner, qq.v.
   Murder Comes in Threes. French (NYC), 1957 (3-act play.)

SPRIGG, C(HRISTOPHER) ST. JOHN. 1907-1937. Ref: EM, MC, TC. SC: Insp. Bernard Bray = BB; Charles Venables = CV. Set: Eng.
   The Corpse with the Sunburnt Face. Nelson, 1935; Doubleday, 1935
   Crime in Kensington. Eldon, 1933. U.S. title: Pass the Body. Dial, 1933 BB,CV
   Death of an Airman. Hutchinson, 1934; Doubleday, 1935 BB
   Death of a Queen. Nelson, 1935 CV
   Fatality in Fleet Street. Eldon, 1933 CV
   Pass the Body; see Crime in Kensington
   The Perfect Alibi. Eldon, 1934; Doubleday, 1934 CV,BB
   The Six Queer Things. Jenkins, 1937; Doubleday, 1937

SPRIGGE, S(AMUEL) SQUIRE. 1860-1937.
   An Industrious Chevalier. Chatto, 1902 ss
   Odd Issues. Smithers, 1899 ss, some criminous

SPRING, GERALD MAX. 1897-   . Pseudonym: Richard Bodwell, q.v.

SPRINGER, BOB. See: Charlotte Springer.

SPRINGER, CHARLOTTE and BOB SPRINGER
   Smugglers' Moon. Exposition, 1954 [Fla.]

SPRINGER, NORMAN
   -The Blood Ship. Watt, 1922; Unwin, 1923

SPRINGFIELD, LINCOLN. Joint pseudonym with Edward Card Mitchell: Captain Coe, q.v.

SPRISSLER, ALFRED
   The Avenging Note. Gernsback, 1932

SPROTT, HELEN
   The Fake. (Author), 1936

SPROUL, KATHLEEN. SC: Dick Wilson = DW.
   The Birthday Murder. Dutton, 1932 DW [NYC]
   Death Among the Professors; see Death and the Professors
   Death and the Professors. Dutton, 1933. British title: Death Among the Professors. Eyre, 1934 DW [New Eng., acad.]
   Death Listened In. Phoenix, 1946
   Murder Off Key. Dutton, 1934 DW
   The Mystery of the Closed Car. Dutton, 1935 DW [Fla.]

SPROULE, WESLEY (R.)
   Freeway to Murder. Hale, 1967
   Hell in the Afternoon. Hale, 1967
   Killer Waiting. Hale, 1967
   Violent Death. Hale, 1967
   Walk Softly. Hale, 1968

SPRUILL, JOOK
   Murder by Proxy. Vega, 1963

SPRUILL, STEVEN G(REGORY). 1946-   . Ref: CA.
   The Psychopath Plague. Doubleday, 1978; Hale, 1978 [future]

SPRY, THEODORE JAMES. 1898-   . Pseudonym: Palmer White, q.v.

SPURGEON, DOUGLAS W.
   The Ippletree Manor Mystery. Ward, 1925
   The Missing Witness. Ward, 1927
   The Wheel of Circumstance. Ward, 1926

SQUERENT, WILL. Pseudonym of Will [Wilbur] Bradbury, q.v.
   Your Golden Jugular. Macmillan, 1970; Hale, 1971 [NYC]

SQUIRE, ROBIN. 1937-   . Ref: CA.
   A Portrait of Barbara. Bachman, 1978; St. Martin's, 1978 [Eng., 1891]

STABLES, (WILLIAM) GORDON. 1840-1910.
   The Mystery of a Millionaire's Grave. Remington, 1890
   The Rose of Allandale. Digby, 1896

STACEY, BARNARD. 1889-   .
   Satan's Secret. Ward, 1956

STACKELBERG, GENE
   Double Agent. Popular Library, 1959 [Boston]

STACPOOLE, H(ENRY) DeVERE. 1863-1951. Pseudonym: Tyler De Saix, q.v. See also: Margaret (Robson) Stacpoole.
   The Cottage on the Fells. Laurie, 1908. Also published as: Murder on the Fell. Cherry Tree, 1937
   -Golden Ballast. Hutchinson, 1924; Dodd, 1924
   Green Coral. Hutchinson, 1935 ss, half of them criminous
   The House of Crimson Shadows. Hutchinson, 1925; Small, 1926 [Far East]
   Men, Women and Beasts. Hutchinson, 1922 ss, some criminous
   Murder on the Fell; see The Cottage on the Fells
   The Mystery of Uncle Ballard. Cassell, 1927; Doubleday, 1928 [S.F.]
   Stories of East and West. Hutchinson, 1926 ss, some criminous
   The Tales of Mynheer Amayat. Newnes, 1930 ss [Indon.]
   The Vengeance of Mynheer Van Lok and other stories. Hutchinson, 1934 ss

STACPOOLE, MARGARET (ROBSON)
   -London, 1913. Hutchinson, 1914; Duffield, 1914
   The Man Who Found Himself; see Uncle Simon
   Uncle Simon, with H(enry) DeVere Stacpoole, 1863-1951, q.v. Hutchinson, 1920. U.S. title: The Man Who Found Himself. Lane, 1920

STACTON, DAVID DEREK. 1925-1968. Pseudonyms: Bud Clifton, David West, qq.v.

STACY, O'CONNOR. Pseudonym of William Rollins, Jr., 1897-   , q.v.
   Murder at Cypress Hall. Macaulay, 1933 [South]

STADE, GEORGE. 1933-   . Ref: CA.
   Confessions of a Lady Killer. Norton, 1979; Muller, 1980 [NYC]

STADLEY, PAT. Born in Tex., raised in and living in Calif.; has been reporter and co-owner of trucking business.
   Autumn of a Hunter. Random, 1970; Collins, 1971. Also published as: The Murder Hunt. Major, 1977 [Calif.]
   The Black Leather Barbarians. Bobbs, 1960 [L.A.]
   -Daddy-O. Signet, 1960
   The Murder Hunt; see Autumn of a Hunter

STAFFORD, CAROLINE. Pseudonym of Carolyn L. T. Watjen. Ref: CA.
   The Honour of Ravensholme. Simon, 1979 [Eng., 1800s]
   The House by Exmoor. Simon, 1975; Millington, 1976 [Eng.]
   Moira. Simon, 1976 [Scot., past]
   The Teville Obsession. Simon, 1978 [Wales]

STAFFORD, EARL FRANKLIN
   A Kiss for a Killer. Jarrolds, 1941

STAFFORD, JOHN K.
   Back from the Grave. Street (Magnet)
   The Broken Pen. Street (Magnet)
   Cheating Justice. Street (Magnet)
   The Convent Mystery. Street (Magnet)
   The Crime of Bohemia. Street (New Magnet)
   A Daring Express Messenger. Street (Magnet)
   The Death Demon. Street (Magnet)
   The Divided Trail. Street (New Magnet)
   Forging the Links. Street (New Magnet)
   In After Years. Street (New Magnet)
   In the Clutch of the Law. Street (New Magnet)
   Into His Own Trap. Street (New Magnet)
   King Among Crooks. Street (Magnet)
   Millionaire's Crime. Street (Magnet)
   Morgan the Dauntless. Street (New Magnet)
   The Nameless Dread. Street (New Magnet)
   An Oath of Vengeance. Street (Magnet)
   On a Blind Trail. Street (New Magnet)
   Only a Bullet. Street (Magnet)
   Piece by Piece. Street (New Magnet)
   Shadowed Round the World. Street (Magnet)
   Shot from Above. Street (Magnet)
   A Skein Well Trangled. Street (New Magnet)
   Smugglers at Odds. Street (Magnet)
   The Spurious Note Maker. Street (Magnet)
   Tracked to His Doom. Street (New Magnet)
   The Trail to the End. Street (New Magnet)
   The Triple Cross. Street (New Magnet)
   Under the Surface. Street (Magnet)
   An Unknown Foe. Street (New Magnet)
   When Thieves Fall Out. Street (Magnet)
   When Threads Get Tangled. Street (New Magnet)
   When Trails Cross. Street (New Magnet)
   With Bullet and Steel. Street (New Magnet)

STAFFORD, MARJORIE
   Death Plays the Gramophone. Macmillan, 1953

STAFFORD, MURIEL [MURIEL STAFFORD SAUER]. 1903-   .
   X Marks the Dot. Duell, 1943

STAFFORD, PETER. Pseudonym (?) of Paul Tabori, 1908-1974, q.v.
   The Man Who Loved to Blow Up Trains. New English Library pb, 1974

STAGG, CLINTON H(OLLAND). 1890-1916. Ref: MP. SC: Thornley Colton, in at least those marked TC.
   High Speed. Watt, 1916; Richards, 1920
   Silver Sandals. Watt, 1916. British title (?): Thornley Colton, Blind Reader of Hearts. Simpkin, 1915 TC [NYC]
   Thornley Colton, Blind Detective. Watt, 1923 ss TC [NYC]
   Thornley Colton, Blind Reader of Hearts; see Silver Sandals

STAGG, JAMES. Pseudonym of Gilbert Johns, q.v. All titles below feature Sexton Blake and were published by Amalgamated Press.
   Assignment in Beirut. 1956 [Beirut]
   Crime of Violence. 1958
   Desert Intrigue. 1960
   Murder Down Below. 1958
   Nightmare in Naples. 1957 [Naples]
   Panic in the Night. 1957
   Passport to Danger. 1957
   Time for Murder. 1959

STAGGE, JONATHAN. Joint pseudonym of Richard Wilson Webb and Hugh Callingham Wheeler, 1912-   . Other joint pseudonyms: Q. Patrick, Patrick Quentin, qq.v. SC: Dr. Hugh Westlake, in all titles.
   Call a Hearse; see The Yellow Taxi
   Death and the Dear Girls; see Death, My Darling Daughters
   Death, My Darling Daughters. Doubleday, 1945. British title: Death and the Dear Girls. Joseph, 1946 [Mass.]
   Death's Old Sweet Song. Doubleday, 1946; Joseph, 1947 [Mass.]
   The Dogs Do Bark. Doubleday, 1937. British title: Murder Gone to Earth. Joseph, 1938 [Mass.]
   Funeral for Five; see Turn of the Table
   Light from a Lantern; see The Scarlet Circle
   Murder by Prescription. Doubleday, 1938. British title: Murder or Mercy. Joseph, 1937 [Mass.]
   Murder Gone to Earth; see The Dogs Do Bark
   Murder in the Stars; see The Stars Spell Death
   Murder or Mercy; see Murder by Prescription
   The Scarlet Circle. Doubleday, 1943. British title: Light from a Lantern. Joseph, 1943 [New Eng.]
   The Stars Spell Death. Doubleday, 1939. British title: Murder in the Stars. Joseph, 1940 [Mass.]
   The Three Fears. Doubleday, 1949; Joseph, 1949 [Mass.]
   Turn of the Table. Doubleday, 1940. British title: Funeral for Five. Joseph, 1940 [Mass.]
   The Yellow Taxi. Doubleday, 1942. British title: Call a Hearse. Joseph, 1942 [Mass.]

STAHL, NORMAN. 1931-   . Ref: CA.
   The Assault on "Mavis A". Random, 1978; Granada, 1979

STAHL, RAY
   Death Stalks "The Wild Goose". Hamilton Stafford, 1952 [ship]
   No Answer from a Corpse. Hamilton Stafford, 1953

STALL, MIKE
    The Dark Valley. Hale, 1979
    The Deadly Charade. Hale, 1980
    The Rossi Killings. Hale, 1979
    The Sprengler Cache. Hale, 1980

STALLWORTH, LYN. Graduate of Vassar; has been decorator, in public relations, translator; in late 1960s with Time-Life Books.
    Pot Shot. Walker, 1968 [Greece]

STAM, PAUL JUSTIN
    30° North 165° East. Avon, 1978

STAMPER, JOSEPH. 1886-   .
    The Shipyard Menace. Amalgamated, 1943 (Sexton Blake.)

STAND, MARGUERITE. SC: Bill Rice, in at least those marked BR; Police Constable Robins, in at least those marked R. Set: Eng.
    Death Came in Lucerne. Hale, 1966 BR [Switz.]
    Death Came in the Studio. Hale, 1969 BR
    Death Came to "Lighthouse Steps". Hale, 1968 BR
    Death Came Too Soon. Hale, 1970 BR
    Death Came with Darkness. Hale, 1965 BR
    Death Came with Diamonds. Hale, 1966 BR
    Death Came with Flowers. Hale, 1966 BR
    Diana Is Dead. Hale, 1967 R
    Escape from Murder. Hale, 1964 BR
    L for Murder. Hale, 1968
    Murder at Cloud Hospital. Hale, 1969 R
    Murder in the Camp. Hale, 1964 R

STANDER, SIEGFRIED. 1935-   . Ref: CA.
    Flight from the Hunter. Gollancz, 1977; St. Martin's, 1977 [S.W. Afr.]

STANDISH, BURT L. Pseudonym of Gilbert Patten, 1866-1945.
    Dick Merriwell's Detective Work. Street, 1911
    Dick Merriwell's Mystery; or, Working for Right. Street, 1903
    The Motor Wizard's Mystery. Street, 1914

STANDISH, ROBERT. Pseudonym of Digby George Gerahty.
    Green Fire. Davies, 1976
    Private Enterprise, and other stories. Davies, 1954   ss, some criminous
    The Window Hack. Davies, 1966

STANFORD, ALFRED (BOLLER) 1900-   . Ref: CA.
    The Mission in Sparrow Brush Lane. Morrow, 1965 [Eng., 1943]

STANFORD, DON(ALD KENT). 1918-   . Ref: CA. SC: Dallas Webster = DW.
    Bargain in Blood. GM, 1951; Muller, 1958 DW [Fla.]
    Mulligan's Pirates. Simon, 1966; Deutsch, 1967
    The Slaughtered Lovelies. GM, 1950; Red Seal, 1957 DW [N.Y.]

STANG, JO ANN. Magazine article writer; living in Conn.
    Shadows on the Sceptered Isle. Crown, 1980 [Eng.]

STANHOPE, LOUISA SIDNEY
    The Confessional of Valombre. Newman, 1812
    Treachery; or, The Grave of Antoinette. Newman, 1815

STANLEY, ARTHUR. Pseudonym of Arthur Stanley Megaw, 1872-   .
    The Monkhurst Case. Macdonald, 1946

STANLEY, BENNETT. Pseudonym of S(tanley) B(ennett) Hough, 1917-   , q.v.
    The Alscott Experiment. Hodder, 1954 [ship]
    Government Contract. Hodder, 1956

STANLEY, FAY GRISSOM (SHULMAN). 1924-
    Pseudonym: Fay Grissom, q.v.
    Murder Leaves a Ring. Rinehart, 1950 [NYC]

STANLEY, GEORGE. SC: Black Pilgrim, in at least those marked BP.
    The Adventure of the Black Pilgrim. Modern Fiction, 1945 BP ss
    The Blue Light. Blackie, 1935
    The Brotherhood of Death. Mitre, 1946
    Case of the Seven Keys. Modern Fiction, 1945
    Further Adventures of the Black Pilgrim. Modern Fiction, 1945 BP
    Gangsters All. Mitre, 1945
    Gangsters Parade. Mitre, 1945
    The League of Twelve. Mellifont, 1940
    Men of the Mist. Martin & Reid, 1947
    The Missing Million. Gifford, 1938
    Rubberface. Modern Fiction, 1945
    The Secret of the Seven Spiders. Fenland, 1932
    The Seven Saints. Swan, 1945
    The Seven Shadows. Blackie, 1935
    The Sign of Seven. Coker, 1950
    Silver Slave. Regency, 1945
    Sinister Valley. Bear, 1946

STANLEY, JACKSON
    The Florentine Ring. Doubleday, 1962

STANLEY, JOHN. 1940-   . Ref: CA. See also: Kenn Davis.
    Bogart 48, with Kenn Davis. Dell, 1980 [L.A., 1948]
    The Dark Side, with Kenn Davis. Avon, 1976 [S.F.]

STANLEY, MARTHA M. See: Adelaide Matthews

STANLEY, MICHAEL
    The Boomerang Conspiracy. Avon, 1977
    The Swiss Conspiracy. Avon, 1976; Futura, 1976 [Switz.]

STANLEY, OLIN. Pseudonym of agricultural pilot in Tex.
    Legal Fire. Vantage, 1959 [NYC]

STANLEY, RAY
    The Hippy Cult Murders. Macfadden, 1970 [L.A.]

STANLEY, SANDRA
    Rogue's Castle. PB, 1974 [Minn., past]

STANLEY, WILLIAM. Born in Eng.; an engineer.
    Mr. Holroyd Takes a Holiday. Abelard (London & NYC), 1966

STANNARD, HENRIETTA ELIZA VAUGHAN PALMER. 1856-1911. Pseudonym: John Strange Winter, q.v.

STANNERS, H(AROLD) H. 1894-   . Ref: CC. SC: Prof. Harding, in all titles. Set: Eng.
    At the Tenth Clue. Eyre, 1937
    The Crowning Murder. Eyre, 1938
    Murder at Markenden Court. Eyre, 1936

STANSFIELD, ANTHONY. Joint pseudonym with Peter Lilley: Bruce Buckingham, q.v.

STANTON, CORALIE. Pseudonym of Alice Cecil Seymour Hosken. Set: Eng.
    The Adventuress; see Miriam Lemaire, Money Lender
    The Amateur Adventuress. Thomson, 1930
    Called to Judgment, with (Ernest Charles) Heath Hosken, 1875-   . Paul, 1913
    The Dog Star, with (Ernest Charles) Heath Hosken, 1875-   . Cassell, 1913
    -Her Fugitive. Thomson, 1929
    Ironmouth. Paul, 1916
    The Love That Kills, with (Ernest Charles) Heath Hosken, 1875-   . Milne, 1909
    The Man Made Law, with (Ernest Charles) Heath Hosken, 1875-   . Everett, 1908
    Miriam Lemaire, Money Lender, with (Ernest Charles) Heath Hosken, 1875-   . Cassell, 1906. U.S. title: The Adventuress. McBride, 1907 ss
    The Muzzled Ox, with (Ernest Charles) Heath Hosken, 1875-   . Paul, 1911
    The Second Best, with (Ernest Charles) Heath Hosken, 1875-   . Long, 1907
    The Sinners' Syndicate, with (Ernest Charles) Heath Hosken, 1875-   . Hurst, 1907
    -The Way of Escape. Leng, 1932
    The White Horsemen, with (Ernest Charles) Heath Hosken, 1875-   . Nash, 1924

STANTON, KEN. Pseudonym of Manning Lee Stokes, q.v. Other pseudonyms. Paul Edwards, Nick Carter, qq.v. SC: William Martin (Tiger Shark), in all titles.
    Cold Blue Death. Macfadden, 1970 [Carib.]
    Evil Cargo. Manor, 1973
    Operation Deep Six. Manor, 1972
    Operation Mermaid. Manor, 1974
    Operation Sea Monster. Manor, 1974 [ship]
    Operation Steelfish. Manor, 1972
    Sargasso Secret. Macfadden, 1971
    Seek, Strike and Destroy. Macfadden, 1971 [Calif.]
    Stalkers of the Sea. Macfadden, 1972
    Ten Seconds to Zero. Macfadden, 1970
    Whirlwind Beneath the Sea. Manor, 1972

STANTON, MARTIN
    Apocalypse. Oxford, 1975 (Play.)

STANTON, PAUL. Pseudonym of (Arthur) David Beaty, 1919-   , q.v.
    -Call Me Captain. Joseph, 1959; Mill, 1960
    -The Gun Garden. Joseph, 1965; Mill, 1965
    -Village of Stars. Joseph, 1960; Mill, 1960

STANTON-HOPE, WILLIAM E(DWARD). 1889-1961. See also: (William Edward) Stanton Hope.
    Dead Man's Sands. Amalgamated, 1929 (Sexton Blake.)

STANWOOD, BROOKS. Joint pseudonym of Howard Kaminsky, 1940-   , and Susan Stanwood.
    -The Glow. McGraw, 1979; Macdonald, 1980

STANWOOD, DONALD (A.). ca.1950-   .
    The Memory of Eva Ryker. Coward, 1978; H. Hamilton, 1978

STANWOOD, SUSAN. Joint pseudonym with Howard Kaminsky, 1940-   : Brooks Stanwood, q.v.

STAPLES, REGINALD THOMAS. 1911-   .
    Pseudonym: R. T. Stevens, q.v.

STAPLETON, A.
    The Limping Death. Gnome, 1945

STAPLETON, D. (and D.). Joint pseudonym of Douglas Stapleton, 1904-   , q.v., and Dorothy Stapleton.
    Corpse and Robbers. Arcadia, 1954 [Va.]
    The Crime, the Place, and the Girl. Arcadia, 1953
    Late for the Funeral. Arcadia, 1953

STAPLETON, DOROTHY. Joint pseudonym with Douglas Stapleton, 1904-   , q.v.: D. (and D.) Stapleton, q.v.

STAPLETON, DOUGLAS. 1904-   . Joint pseudonym with Dorothy Stapleton: D. (and D.) Stapleton, q.v.
    The Corpse Is Indignant, with Helen A. Carey. Five Star, 1946

STAPP, ROBERT
    A More Perfect Union. Harper's Magazine Press, 1970 [U.S., 1981]

STARK, INSPECTOR
    At Death's Call. Street (New Magnet)
    The Call of the Deep. Street (New Magnet)
    The Cost of a Clue. Street (New Magnet)
    The Crimson Clue. Street (New Magnet)
    A Deed of Darkness. Street (Magnet)
    A Demand for Justice. Street (New Magnet)
    Eye of Gold. Street (Magnet)
    The Great Green Diamond. Street (New Magnet)
    The Hand in Red. Street (Magnet)
    Hunted and Haunted. Street (New Magnet)
    In League with Satan. Street (New Magnet)
    Kentucky Moonshiner. Street (Magnet)
    A Life at Stake. Street (New Magnet)
    A Long Baffled Capture. Street (New Magnet)
    The Mafia's Victim. Street (Magnet)
    The Missing Bracelet. Street (Magnet)
    A Modern Sorceress. Street (Magnet)
    The Nitroglycerine League. Street (Magnet)
    Out of the Underworld. Street (New Magnet)
    Revealed by Lightning. Street (Magnet)
    Ring of Iron. Street (Magnet)
    The Root of All Evil. Street (Magnet)
    The Secret of the Dead. Street (New Magnet)
    Shadow of an Assassin. Street (Magnet)
    The Shadow of the Rope. Street (New Magnet)
    A Telegraph Clue. Street (Magnet)
    Tricked and Trapped. Street (New Magnet)
    The Unseen Hand. Street (New Magnet)
    A Victim of the Occult. Street (New Magnet)
    The Victor's Spoils. Street (New Magnet)
    The Water Trail. Street (Magnet)
    The Western Ferret. Street (Magnet)
    When the Quarry Turns. Street (New Magnet)
    Where the Clue Leads. Street (New Magnet)
    With Chains of Brass. Street (New Magnet)

STARK, DELBERT RAYMOND. 1919- . Pseudonym: John Norwood, q.v.

STARK, ERNEST
Ed. Somers, the Pinkerton Detective; or, the Murdered Man. Ogilvie, 1886

STARK, JAMES. Pseudonym of Robert C(onroy) Goldston, 1927- , q.v.
The Greek Virgin. Avon, 1962 [Sp.]

STARK, MICHAEL. Pseudonym of Lawrence Lariar, 1908-1981, q.v. Other pseudonyms: Adam Knight, Michael Lawrence, qq.v.
Run for Your Life! Crown, 1946; Boardman, 1948. Also published as: Kill-Box. Ace, 1954 [NYC]

STARK, RICHARD. Pseudonym of Donald E(dwin) Westlake, 1933- , q.v. Other pseudonyms: Curt Clark, Tucker Coe, Timothy J. Culver, qq.v. SC: Parker = P; Alan Grofield = AG.
The Black Ice Score. GM, 1968; Coronet, 1969 P [NYC]
The Blackbird. Macmillan, 1969; Hodder, 1970 AG [Can.]
Butcher's Moon. Random, 1974; Coronet, 1977 P,AG [Midwest]
The Dame. Macmillan, 1969; Hodder, 1969 AG [P. Rico]
The Damsel. Macmillan, 1967; Hodder, 1968 AG [Mex.]
Deadly Edge. Random, 1971; Coronet, 1972 P [N.J.]
The Green Eagle Score. GM, 1967; Coronet, 1968 P [N.Y.]
The Handle. PB, 1966. British title: Run Lethal. Coronet, 1972 P,AG
The Hunter. PB, 1962. British title: Point Blank. Coronet, 1967 P [NYC]
The Jugger. PB, 1965; Coronet, 1971 P [Neb.]
Killtown; see The Score
Lemons Never Lie. World, 1971 AG
The Man with the Getaway Face. PB, 1963. British title: The Steel Hit. Coronet, 1971 P [N.J.]
The Mourner. PB, 1963; Coronet, 1971 P
The Outfit. PB, 1963; Coronet, 1971 P
Plunder Squad. Random, 1972; Coronet, 1974 P
Point Blank; see The Hunter
The Rare Coin Score. GM, 1967; Coronet, 1968 P [Indianapolis]
Run Lethal; see The Handle
The Score. PB, 1964. British title: Killtown. Coronet, 1971 P,AG [N. Dak.]
The Seventh. PB, 1966. British title: The Split. Coronet, 1969 P [N.Y.]
Slayground. Random, 1971; Coronet, 1973 P [Midwest]
The Sour Lemon Score. GM, 1969; Coronet, 1969 P
The Split; see The Seventh
The Steel Hit; see The Man with the Getaway Face

STARK, SHELDON. 1919- .
Too Many Sinners. Ace, 1954 [NYC]

STARKO, RICHARD
War of Nerves. PaperJacks, 1977

STARNES, RICHARD. 1922- . Born in Wash. D.C., newspaper editor there. SC: Barney Forge & Dr. St. George Peachy = F&P; Maxwell Speed = MS.
And When She Was Bad She Was Murdered. Lippincott, 1950; Muller, 1953 F&P [Wash. D.C.]
Another Mug for the Bier. Lippincott, 1950; Muller, 1952 F&P [Wash. D.C.]
The Flypaper War. Trident, 1969; Hutchinson, 1970 MS [Mid. East]
The Other Body in Grant's Tomb. Lippincott, 1951; Muller, 1954 F&P [Wash. D.C.]
Requiem in Utopia. Trident, 1967 MS [Swed.]

STARR, JIMMY. 1904- . Born in Tex.; Hollywood publicity agent, movie columnist. SC: Joe Medford, in all titles.
The Corpse Came C.O.D. Murray, 1944; Coker, 1951 [L.A.]
Heads You Lose. Fell, 1950 [L.A.]
Three Short Biers. Murray, 1945 [L.A.]

STARR, JONATHAN
Crook. Cape & Smith, 1930
Grapevine. Liveright, 1930 [N.Y.]

STARR, JULIAN
The Disagreeable Woman. Dillingham, 1895

STARR, RICHARD (HENRY). 1878- . Pseudonym: Richard Essex, q.v.
-Gangster's Girl. Jenkins, 1935
-Married to a Spy. Hurst, 1915
-Mary Elizabeth—Adventuress. Low, 1932

STARRETT, (CHARLES) VINCENT (EMERSON). 1886-1974. Ref: CA, CC, EM, MP, TC. SC: Riley Blackwood = RB; Walter Ghost = WG; Jimmie Lavender = JL
The Blue Door. Doubleday, 1930 ss, JL in two
The Case Book of Jimmie Lavender. Gold Label, 1944 JL ss [Chi.]
Coffins for Two. Covici, 1924 ss
Dead Man Inside. Doubleday, 1931; World's Work, 1935 WG [Chi.]
The End of Mr. Garment. Doubleday, 1932 WG [Chi.]
The Great Hotel Murder. Doubleday, 1935; Nicholson, 1935 RB [Chi.]
The Laughing Buddha. Magna, 1937 (A digest-size paperback, whose publisher scattered his own additions to the text throughout the book. Restored to its original condition, it was published as: Murder in Peking. Lantern, 1946; Edwards, 1947.) [China]
Midnight and Percy Jones. Covici, 1938; Nicholson, 1938 RB [Chi.]
Murder in Peking; see The Laughing Buddha
Murder on "B" Deck. Doubleday, 1929; World's Work, 1936 WG [ship]
-The Quick and the Dead. Arkham, 1965 ss
The Unique Hamlet. (Chicago), 1920 (Sherlock Holmes.)

STAUFFER, FRANK H. [FRANCIS HENRY STAUFFER]. 1832-1895.
Darke Darrell, the Boy Detective. Street, 1888

STAYTON, FRANK. 1874- .
-The Passionate Adventure. Nash, 1924; Century, 1924

STEAD, C(HRISTIAN) K(ARLSON). 1932- . Ref: CA.
Smith's Dream. Longman Paul (Auckland), 1971; Longmans, 1932

STEAD, PHILIP JOHN. 1916-
-The Charlatan. Macdonald, 1948
-Fausta. Macdonald, 1950
In the Street of the Angel. Art & Educ. Publishers, 1947 [Algiers]

STEAD, ROBERT J(OHN) C(AMPBELL). 1880-1959.
The Bail Jumper. Unwin, 1914 [Can.]
The Copper Disc. Doubleday, 1931 [Can.]

STEARN, JESS. Reporter for large city newspaper.
The Reporter. Doubleday, 1970

STEARNS, EDGAR FRANKLIN. 1879- . Pseudonym: Edgar Franklin, q.v.

STEBEL, S(IDNEY) L(EO). 1924- . Pseudonym: Leo Bergson, q.v. Ref: CA.
The Vorovich Affair. Viking, 1975. British: Constable, 1976. Reprinted in Britain under the U.S. title: Penguin, 1977

STED, RICHARD. ca.1902- . Newspaperman, freelance writer.
They All Bleed Red. Simon, 1954; Boardman, 1955 [NYC]

STEEGMULLER, FRANCIS. 1906- . Pseudonym: David Keith, q.v. Ref: CA.
Silence at Salerno. Holt, 1978 [It.]

STEEL, DAVID
Beauty Is Found in a Grave. Comyns, 1952
Death Is a Dame. Comyns, 1953
Lovely But Lethal. Comyns, 1952
Too Tough for Death. Comyns, 1953
You'll Have to Talk. Comyns, 1953

STEEL, KURT. Pseudonym of Rudolf Hornaday Kagey, 1904-1946. Ref: MP. SC: Hank Hyer = HH.
Ambush House. Harcourt, 1943 HH [N.Y.]
Crooked Shadow. Little, 1939; Swan, 1945 HH [L.I.]
Dead of Night. Little, 1940; Swan, 1944 HH [NYC]
The Imposter. Harcourt, 1942; Gifford, 1945 [Conn.]
Judas, Incorporated. Little, 1939 HH [Conn.]
Madman's Buff. Little, 1941; Swan, 1945 HH [NYC]
Murder for What? Bobbs, 1936 HH [NYC]
Murder Goes to College. Bobbs, 1936 HH [NYC, acad.]

Murder in G-Sharp. Bobbs, 1937. Also published as: Strangler's Holiday. Select, 1942, abridged HH [N.Y.]
Murder of a Dead Man. Bobbs, 1935. Also published as: The Traveling Corpses. Crime Novel Selection, 1942, abridged HH [NYC]
Strangler's Holiday; see Murder in G-Sharp
The Traveling Corpse; see Murder of a Dead Man

STEELE, CHESTER K. Pseudonym of Edward (L.) Stratemeyer, 1862-1930, q.v. Other pseudonym: Nicholas Carter, q.v. SC: Colonel Robert Lee Ashley = RA.
The Crime at Red Towers. Clode, 1927
The Diamond Cross Mystery. Sully, 1918; Jenkins, 1920 RA
The Golf Course Mystery. Sully, 1919 RA
The Great Radio Mystery. Chelsea, 1928
The House of Disappearances. Chelsea, 1927
The Mansion of Mystery. Cupples, 1911

STEELE, CURTIS. House name. All titles published by Corinth below are by Frederick C(lyde) Davis, 1902-1977, q.v. Other Davis pseudonyms: Murdo Coombs, Stephen Ransome, qq.v. SC: James Christopher (Operator 5), in all titles, which are pulp reprints.
The Army of the Dead. Corinth, 1966 [Pa.]
Blood Reign of the Dictator. Corinth, 1966 [Wash. D.C.]
Cavern of the Damned. Pulp Press, 1980
Hosts of the Flaming Death. Corinth, 1966
Invasion of the Yellow Warlords. Corinth, 1966
The Invisible Empire. Corinth, 1966 [NYC]
Legions of the Death Master. Corinth, 1966 [Wash. D.C.]
March of the Flame Marauders. Corinth, 1966 [NYC]
The Masked Invasion. Freeway, 1974 [NYC]
Master of Broken Men. Corinth, 1966
The Yellow Scourge. Freeway, 1974 [Calif.]

STEELE, DeFOREST C.
Glitter-Gold Mountain. Christopher, 1951

STEELE, DERWENT. SC: John Blackmore = JB. Set: Eng.
The Avenger. Modern, 1935 JB
The Black Gangster. Modern, 193?
The Phantom Slayer. Modern, 1935
The Poison Gang. Modern, 193? JB
The Purple Plague. Modern, 1935

STEELE, FRANCESCA MARIA. Pseudonym: Darley Dale, q.v.

STEELE, HARWOOD (ELMES ROBERT). 1897- .
The Ninth Circle. Doran, 1928; Hodder, 1927 [Can.]
Spirit-of-Iron-Mountain. Doran, 1923; Hodder, 1924 [Can.]
To Effect an Arrest. Ryerson, 1947; Jarrolds, 1946 ss [Can.]

STEELE, JACK
The House of Iron Men. FitzGerald, 1911 [NYC]

STEELE, JACLEN
The Forbidden Room. GM, 1952

STEELE, TEDD
Artists, Models and Murder. Crown (Canada), 1946

STEELE, TOM
Cunning Against Force. Street (Magnet)

STEELE, V. M. SC: Chief-Insp. Saunders, in at least those marked S. Set: Eng.
Beloved of Ishmael. Paul, 1937
Hunters of Humans. Paul, 1936 S
The Scarred Wrists. Paul, 1935 S

STEELE, WILBUR DANIEL. 1886-1970. Ref: CA.
Full Cargo. Doubleday, 1952 ss, some criminous
Land's End, and other stories. Harper, 1918 ss, some criminous
The Man Who Saw Through Heaven. Harper, 1927 ss, some criminous
The Post Road, with Norma Mitchell. French (NYC), 1935 (2-act play.)

The Shame Dance, and other stories. Harper, 1923; Unwin, 1924 ss, some criminous
-The Sound of Rowlocks. Harper, 1938
-The Way to Gold. Doubleday, 1955

STEELEY, ROBERT DEREK. Pseudonym: Nick Carter, q.v.
The Herzog Affair. Carlyle, 1980
Hot Ice. Carlyle, 1978

STEELNIB, JOCUNDUS. Pseudonym.
Freaks of Imagination. Kent, 1852 ss, some criminous

STEEMAN, (STANISLAUS) ANDRE. 1908- SC: Wenceslas Vorobeitchik, in both titles.
The Night of the 12th-13th. Lippincott, 1933 (Translation of "La Nuit du 12 au 13." Paris, 1931.) [Fr.]
Six Dead Men. Farrar, 1932; Hurst, 1933 (Translation of "Six Hommes Morts." Paris, 1931.) [Paris]

STEERS, HELEN. Pseudonym of Helen Steers Burgess.
Death Will Find Me. Dodd, 1947 [Boston]

STEEVES, HARRISON R(OSS). 1881-1981. Ref: CA, CC, EM, MP.
Good Night, Sheriff. Random, 1941; Rich, 1942 [New Eng.]

STEFAN, ILLY
Guilty, My Lord. Opium Books, 1968

STEFFENS, ARTHUR JOSEPH. 1873- . Pseudonym: A(rthur) S(teffens) Hardy, q.v.

STEIN, AARON MARC. 1906- . Pseudonyms: George Bagby, Hampton Stone, qq.v. Ref: CA, CC, EM, MP, TC. SC: Tim Mulligan & Elsie Mae Hunt = M&H; Matt Erridge = ME.
Alp Murder. Doubleday, 1970; Hale, 1971 ME [Switz.]
...and High Water. Doubleday, 1946 M&H
Blood on the Stars. Doubleday, 1964; Hale, 1967 ME [Tex., Mex.]
Body Search. Doubleday, 1977; Hale, 1978 ME [Athens]
The Case of the Absent-Minded Professor. Doubleday, 1943 M&H [acad., Midwest]
The Cheating Butler. Doubleday, 1980; Hale, 1981 ME [Venice]
Chill Factor. Doubleday, 1978; Hale, 1979 ME [New Eng.]
Coffin Country. Doubleday, 1976; Hale, 1976 ME [Maine]
The Cradle and the Grave. Doubleday, 1948 M&H [N.Y.]
Days of Misfortune. Doubleday, 1949 M&H [Mex.]
The Dead Thing in the Pool. Doubleday, 1952 M&H [Mex.]
Deadly Delight. Doubleday, 1967; Hale, 1969 ME [Istan.]
Death Meets 400 Rabbits. Doubleday, 1953 M&H [Mex.]
Death Takes a Paying Guest. Doubleday, 1947 M&H [Wash. D.C.]
Executioner's Rest; see I Fear the Greeks
Faces of Death; see Snare Andalucian
The Finger. Doubleday, 1973; Hale, 1974 ME [Czech.]
Frightened Amazon. Doubleday, 1950 M&H [Mex.]
Home and Murder. Doubleday, 1962 ME [Vir. Is.]
I Fear the Greeks. Doubleday, 1966. British title: Executioner's Rest. Hale, 1967 ME [Athens]
Kill Is a Four-Letter Word. Doubleday, 1968; Hale, 1969 ME [ship]
Lend Me Your Ears. Doubleday, 1976 ME [It.]
Lock and Key. Doubleday, 1973 [NYC]
Mask for Murder. Doubleday, 1952 M&H [Mex.]
Moonmilk and Murder. Doubleday, 1955; Macdonald, 1956 M&H [Fr.]
Never Need an Enemy. Doubleday, 1959; Boardman, 1960 ME [Yugos.]
A Nose for It. Doubleday, 1980; Hale, 1981 ME [Maine]
Nowhere? Doubleday, 1978; Hale, 1978 ME [Pa.]
One Dip Dead. Doubleday, 1979; Hale, 1980 ME [Florence]
Only the Guilty. Doubleday, 1942 M&H [Colombia]
Pistols for Two. Doubleday, 1951 M&H [NYC]
The Rolling Heads. Doubleday, 1979; Hale, 1979 ME [Fr.]
The Second Burial. Doubleday, 1949 M&H [Mex.]
Shoot Me Dacent. Doubleday, 1951; Macdonald, 1957 M&H [Dublin]
Sitting Up Dead. Doubleday, 1958; Macdonald, 1959 ME [Rome]
Snare Andalucian. Doubleday, 1968. British title: Faces of Death. Hale, 1968 ME [Fr., Sp.]
The Sun Is a Witness. Doubleday, 1940 M&H [S.W.]
Three—with Blood. Doubleday, 1950 M&H [Mex.]
Up to No Good. Doubleday, 1941 M&H [Peru]
We Saw Him Die. Doubleday, 1947 M&H [Calif.]

STEIN, BENJAMIN. 1944- .
The Croesus Conspiracy. Simon, 1978; Hamlyn, 1979 [1982-4]

STEIN, GERTRUDE. 1874-1946. Ref: CA.
Blood on the Dining Room Floor. Banyan, 1948

STEIN, PETER, 1932- , and RICHARD LIPEZ, 1938- .
Grand Scam. Dial, 1979 [Tex.]

STEIN, SOL. 1926- . Ref: CA.
The Resort. Morrow, 1980; Collins, 1980 [Calif.]

STEIRMAN, HY. 1921- . Ref: CA. SC: Zachary Jones, in both titles.
Cry of the Hawk. Paperback Library, 1970
Strike Terror. Paperback Library, 1968

STELLIER, KILSYTH. Pseudonym of A. Welbourne Summers.
Taken by Force. Gale, 1893

STEPHAN, LESLIE (BATES). 1933- . Ref: CA.
Murder in the Family. Hale, 1979
Murder R.F.D. Scribner, 1978; Curley, 1979 [Mass.]

STEPHENS, CASEY
The Porterfield Legacy. Zebra, 1980
The Shadows of Fieldcrest Manor. Zebra, 1980

STEPHENS, DAVE
The Elusive Clue. Vega, 1961

STEPHENS, DeVERE ASHMORE
Echoes from Castor Hills. Comet, 1959

STEPHENS, EDWARD (CARL). 1924- . Ref: CA.
The Submariner. Doubleday, 1973

STEPHENS, HENRIETTA HENKLE. 1909-1983. Pseudonym: Henrietta Buckmaster, q.v.

STEPHENS, HENRY POTTINGER and WARHAM ST. LEGER, 1850- .
The Basilisk. Sonnenschein, 1886. U.S. title: From Darkness to Light; or, The Basilisk's Love. Donnelley, 1886

STEPHENS, JENNIFER. Pseudonym of Kathleen Jenks.
Vengeance of the Cat Goddess. Avon, 1973

STEPHENS, REED
The Man Who Killed His Brother. Ballantine, 1980; Fontana, 1982

STEPHENS, RICCARDO
The Cruciform Mark. Chatto, 1896 [Edin.]
-The Eddy. Blackwood, 1907
-Mr. Peters. Bliss, 1897; Harper, 1897
The Mummy. Nash, 1912
-The Prince and the Undertaker, and What They Undertook. Sands, 1898 ss
-The Wooing of Grey Eyes, and other stories. Murray, 1901 ss

STEPHENS, ROBERT NEILSON. 1867-1906.
The Mystery of Murray Davenport. Page, 1903; Nash, 1903 [NYC]

STEPHENSON, H(UMPHREY) M(EIGH). 1882- . Ref: CC.
Death on the Deep; see Yo-Ho, and a Bottle of Rum!
A Killer and His Star. Hutchinson, 1935
The Missing Partner. Hutchinson, 1932
On the Highest Hill. Long, 1927
Yo-Ho, and a Bottle of Rum! Hutchinson, 1930. U.S. title (?): Death on the Deep. Doubleday, 1931 [ship]

STEPHENSON, MAUREEN. 1927- . Ref: CA.
The House on Wath Moor. Zebra, 1979 [Eng., 1800s]
Ride the Dark Moors. Zebra, 1977

STEPHENSON, (WILLIAM) RALPH (EWING). 1910- . Ref: CA.
Body in My Arms. Gifford, 1963 [N.Z.]
Darkest Death. Gifford, 1964
Down Among the Dead Men. Gifford, 1966
Festival Death. Gifford, 1966 [Fr.]
Spies in Concert. Gifford, 1965

STERLING, DOROTHY. Pseudonym of Charles George, 1893- , q.v. Other pseudonyms: Leland Price, Henry Rowland, qq.v.
Murder Will Out. Baker, 1941 (1-act play.)

STERLING, STEWART. Pseudonym of Prentice Winchell, 1895- . Other pseudonyms: Jay de Bekker, Spencer Dean, Dexter St. Clair, Dexter St. Clare, qq.v. Born in Ill., living in Fla. in 1960s; newspaperman, editor of trade publications, journalism lecturer; wrote and produced over 500 radio mystery shows, wrote for films and TV; published some 400 magazine detective stories, including 40 about Fire Marshal Ben Pedley, besides those below. SC: Ben Pedley = BP; Gil Vine = GV. Ref: CC.
Alarm in the Night. Dutton, 1949 BP [NYC]
Alibi Baby. Ives Washburn, 1955; Boardman, 1955 GV [NYC]
The Big Ear. Dutton, 1953; Boardman, 1955 [Md.]
The Blonde in Suite 14; see Dead to the World
The Body in the Bed. Lippincott, 1959; Boardman, 1960 GV [NYC]
Candle for a Corpse. Lippincott, 1957; Boardman, 1958. Also published as: Too Hot to Kill. Avon, 1958 BP [NYC]
Dead Certain. Ace, 1960 (2 novelets.) GV [NYC]
Dead of Night. Dutton, 1950 GV [NYC]
Dead Right. Lippincott, 1956; Boardman, 1957. Also published as: The Hotel Murders. Avon, 1957 GV [Fla.]
Dead Sure. Dutton, 1949; Hennel Locke, 1951 GV [NYC]
Dead to the World. Lippincott, 1958; Boardman, 1959. Also published as: The Blonde in Suite 14. Avon, 1959 GV [NYC]
Dead Wrong. Lippincott, 1947 GV [NYC]
Down Among the Dead Men. Putnam, 1943; Wells Gardner, 1949 [NYC]
Dying Room Only. Ace, 1960 BP [NYC]
Fire on Fear Street. Lippincott, 1958; Boardman, 1959 BP [NYC]
Five Alarm Funeral. Putnam, 1942 BP [NYC]
The Hinges of Hell. Ives Washburn, 1955; Boardman, 1956 BP [NYC]
The Hotel Murders; see Dead Right
Nightmare at Noon. Dutton, 1951 BP [NYC]
Too Hot to Handle. Random, 1961; Boardman, 1962 BP [NYC]
Too Hot to Kill; see Candle for a Corpse
Where There's Smoke. Lippincott, 1946 BP [NYC]

STERLING, THOMAS (L.). 1921- . Ref: CC. Born in Neb., lived mostly in NYC. SC: Capt. Rizzi = R.
The Evil of the Day. Simon, 1955; Gollancz, 1955. Also published as: Murder in Venice. Dell, 1959 R [Venice]
The House Without a Door. Simon, 1950; Boardman, 1951 [NYC]
Murder in Venice; see The Evil of the Day
The Silent Siren. Simon, 1958; Gollancz, 1958 R [Venice]
Strangers and Afraid. Simon, 1952; Boardman, 1952

STERN, DANIEL. 1928- . Ref: CA.
The Suicide Academy. McGraw, 1968; Allen, 1969

STERN, DAVID. 1909- . Pseudonym: Peter Stirling, q.v.

STERN, G(LADYS) B(RONWYN). 1890-1973. Ref: CA.
The Shortest Night. Heinemann, 1931; Knopf, 1931

STERN, PHILIP VAN DOREN. 1900- . Pseudonym: Peter Storme, q.v. Ref: CA, MP.
Love Is the One with Wings. Farrar, 1951. British title (?): It's Always Too Late to Mend. Jarrolds, 1952

STERN, RICHARD G(USTAV). 1928- . Ref: CA.
In Any Case. McGraw, 1962; MacGibbon, 1963

STERN, RICHARD MARTIN. 1915-   . Ref: CA, TC. SC: Johnny Ortiz = JO.
The Bright Road to Fear. Ballantine, 1958; Secker, 1959 [It.]
Cry Havoc. Scribner, 1963; Cassell, 1964 [N.Y.]
Death in the Snow. Scribner, 1973; Hale, 1974 JO [N. Mex.]
High Hazard. Scribner, 1962
I Hide, We Seek. Scribner, 1965; Deutsch, 1966 [Scot.]
The Kessler Legacy. Scribner, 1967; Cassell, 1968 [Austria]
Manuscript for Murder. Scribner, 1970; Hale, 1973 [Scot.]
Merry Go Round. Scribner, 1969; Cassell, 1970 [Austria]
Murder in the Walls. Scribner, 1971; Hale, 1973 JO [N. Mex.]
Power. McKay, 1975; Secker, 1975
Quidnunc County; see These Unlucky Deeds
Right Hand Opposite. Scribner, 1964
The Search for Tabitha Carr. Scribner, 1960; Secker, 1960
Suspense. Ballantine, 1959 (Four novelets.)
These Unlucky Deeds. Scribner, 1960. British title: Quidnunc County. Eyre, 1961 [N.Y.]
-The Tower. McKay, 1973; Secker, 1973
-The Will. Doubleday, 1976; Secker, 1976
You Don't Need an Enemy. Scribner, 1972; Hale, 1973 JO [N. Mex.]

STERN, STUART. Pseudonym of Hugh C(rauford) Rae, 1935-   , q.v. Other pseudonyms: R. B. Houston, Robert Crawford, qq.v.
The Minotaur Factor. Futura, 1977; Playboy, 1978
The Poison Tree. Futura, 1978; Playboy, 1978

STERNBERG, CECILIA. 1908-   .
-Masquerade. Rawson, 1979; Collins, 1979

STERNE, JULIAN. Pseudonym of Nosta H. Webster.
The Secret of the Zodiac. Boswell, 1933

STERREY, CHARLES E(RNEST)
-In the Grip of Destiny. Allen, 1913
The Voice from the Night. Allen, 1912

STEUART, GLEN. Pseudonym of Lilian May Robertson.
The Evil That Men Do. Long, 1937
The Glass Fish. Long, 1935

STEVEN, E. E.
Kat and Copy-Cat. Patten, 1929 [Haw.]

STEVENS, CURTIS
The Gravy Train Hit. Joseph, 1975

STEVENS, DAVID. 1933-   .
-White for Danger. Collins, 1979; Stein, 1979

STEVENS, DIANE (BARRETT). 1944-   . Ref: CA.
Labyrinth. Doubleday, 1976 [Colo.]
The Valley of the Shadows. Popular Library, 1976 [West]

STEVENS, FRANCES MOYER ROSS. 1895-1948. Pseudonym: Christopher Hale, q.v.

STEVENS, FRANK (EDMUND). 1909-   .
She Left a Silver Slipper. Mill, 1954; Foulsham, 1955 [Conn.]

STEVENS, FRANK. See: Warren B. Murphy, 1933-   .

STEVENS, FRANKLIN. 1933-   . Pseudonym: Steve Franklin, q.v.

STEVENS, JAMES. 1936-   .
In Shadows of Desire. Exposition, 1964

STEVENS, JON
Deadly Matrimony. Hale, 1972
The Nightmare Kick. Hale, 1971

STEVENS, K. M.
Panic in the Solomons. Bles, 1971 [Sol. Is.]

STEVENS, LUCILE VERNON. 1899-   . Ref: CA.
-Crepe Myrtle Tree. Avalon, 1970
Death Wore Gold Shoes. Avalon, 1966
-Dowry of Diamonds. Avalon, 1968
-Green Shadows. Avalon, 1973
-Home to Cypresswood. Avalon, 1972
-Love in a Mist. Avalon, 1967
-The Red Tower. Avalon, 1968
-The Redbird Affair. Avalon, 1974
Search Through the Mist. Avalon, 1971
-Threads of Gold. Avalon, 1968

STEVENS, R. T. Pseudonym of Reginald Thomas Staples, 1911-   .
Flight from Bucharest. Souvenir, 1977; Doubleday, 1978. Also published as: In My Enemy's Arms. Warner, 1980 [1918, Europe]

STEVENS, SHANE. 1941-   . Ref: CA.
By Reason of Insanity. Simon, 1979; Weidenfeld, 1979
Dead City. Holt, 1973; Barrie, 1974 [N.J.]
Go Down Dead. Morrow, 1967 [NYC]
Rat Pack. Seabury, 1974 [NYC]

STEVENSON, ANNE [ANNE KATHARINE STEVENSON ELVIN]. 1933-   . Born in Wales, educated at Oxford; employed in publishing research and journalism.
Coil of Serpents. Collins, 1977; Putnam, 1977 [It.]
-Flash of Splendour. Collins, 1968
The French Inheritance. Collins, 1974; Putnam, 1974 [Fr.]
A Game of Statues. Collins, 1972; Putnam, 1972
Mask of Treason. Piatkus, 1981; Putnam, 1979 [Scot.]
A Relative Stranger. Collins, 1970; Putnam, 1970

STEVENSON, BURTON E(GBERT). 1872-1962. Ref: CA, CC, MP. SC: Jim Godfrey = JG.
Affairs of State. Holt, 1906; Chatto, 1907
The Clue of the Red Carnation; see The Red Carnation
Death Wears a Carnation; see The Red Carnation
The Destroyer. Dodd, 1913; Nash, 1913 [Fr.]
The Girl from Alsace; see Little Comrade
The Gloved Hand. Dodd, 1912; Nash, 1920 JG [NYC]
The Holladay Case. Holt, 1903; Heinemann, 1903 JG [NYC]
The House Next Door. Dodd, 1932; Hutchinson, 1932 JG [NYC]
The Kingmakers. Dodd, 1922; Hutchinson, 1922 [Fr.]
Little Comrade. Holt, 1915; Hutchinson, 1915. Also published as: The Girl from Alsace. Grosset, 1919
The Marathon Mystery. Holt, 1904 JG [NYC]
The Mystery of the Boule Cabinet. Dodd, 1912; Nash, 1915 JG [NYC]
The Mystery of Villa Aurelia; see Villa Aurelia
The Red Carnation. Dodd, 1939. British title: Death Wears a Carnation. Cassell, 1940. Also published as: The Clue of the Red Carnation. Mystery Novel of the Month, 1942 [NYC]
The Storm Center. Dodd, 1924; Hutchinson, 1924
That Affair at Elizabeth. Holt, 1907 JG [N.J.]
Villa Aurelia. Dodd, 1932. British title: The Mystery of Villa Aurelia. Rich, 1933 [Fr.]

STEVENSON, D(OROTHY) E(MILY). 1892-1973. Ref: CA.
Crooked Adam. Farrar, 1942; Collins, 1969 [Scot.]

STEVENSON, FERDINAN. Joint pseudonym with Patricia Colbert Robinson, 1923-   : Daria Macomber, q.v.

STEVENSON, FLORENCE. SC: Kitty Telefair = KT.
Altar of Evil. Award, 1973 KT
Bianca, with Patricia Hagan Murray. Signet, 1975 [L.I.]
The Curse of the Concullens. World, 1970 [Ire., 1865]
Dark Encounter. Signet, 1977 [Mass.]
Dark Odyssey. Signet, 1974 [Calif., ca.1845]
A Darkness on the Stairs. Signet, 1976
Feast of Eggshells. Signet, 1970
The Horror from the Tombs. Award, 1977
The House at Luxor. Signet, 1976 [Egypt]
The Ides of November. Signet, 1975 [Calif., 1950s]
Kilmeny in the Dark Wood. Signet, 1973 [Eng., 1800s]
Mistress of Devil's Manor. Award, 1973 KT
Ophelia. Signet, 1969
A Shadow on the House. Signet, 1975 [Calif., 1905]
The Silent Watcher. Award, 1975 KT
The Sorcerer of the Castle. Award, 1974 KT [L.A.]
Where Satan Dwells. Award, 1971 KT
The Witching Hour. Award, 1971 KT
Witch's Crossing. Signet, 1975 [Mass., 1875]

STEVENSON, JOHN. Pseudonyms: Nick Carter, Mark Denning, Bruno Rossi, qq.v.
The Merchant of Menace. Belmont, 1980

STEVENSON, LOUIS LACY. 1879-1953.
Big Game. Brentano's, 1924 [Ohio]

STEVENSON, PHILIP EDWARD. Pseudonym: Lars Lawrence, q.v.

STEVENSON, ROBERT LOUIS. 1850-1894. See also: Robert Brome, 1917-   . Ref: CC, DD, EM, MC, MP.
The Body Snatcher. Merriam, 1895
The Dynamiter. Longmans, 1885; Munro, 1886
The Merry Men and other tales. Chatto, 1887; Harper, 1887 ss
New Arabian Nights. Chatto, 1882; Holt, 1882 (ss, a selection of which was published separately as: The Pavilion on the Links. Chatto, 1913.)
The Pavilion on the Links; see New Arabian Nights
The Strange Case of Dr. Jekyll and Mr. Hyde, with other tales. Longmans, 1896; Munro, 1886 ss
The Suicide Club. Munro, 1894
The Wrecker. Cassell, 1892; Scribner, 1892
The Wrong Box, with Lloyd Osbourne, 1868-1947, q.v. Longmans, 1889; Scribner, 1889

STEVENSON, TRAILL
The Diamond in the Hoof. Cassell, 1926
The Island Murder. Jenkins, 1936
Murder at the Bar. Jenkins, 1936 [Scot.]
The Nudist Murder. Jenkins, 1937
The Silver Arrow Murder. Jenkins, 1939

STEVERMER, C. J.
Death of a Borgia. Charter, 1980 [Rome, ca.1400]

STEWARD, BARBARA and DWIGHT STEWARD, q.v. Both born in Chi., both professors of English at Delaware State College. SC: Edgar Allan Poe, in both titles.
Evermore. Morrow, 1978 [Paris, 1889]
The Lincoln Diddle. Morrow, 1979 [U.S., 1860s]

STEWARD, DWIGHT. See also: Barbara Steward.
The Acupuncture Murders. Harper, 1973; Barker, 1973 [Conn.]

STEWARD, PAULL. SC: Donald Everhard, in all titles.
Dangerous Men. Harrap, 1926
Gaboreau. Harrap, 1927
Gaboreau the Terrible. Harrap, 1927 [U.S.]

STEWART, ALFRED WALTER. 1880-1947. Pseudonym: J. J. Connington, q.v.

STEWART, ANDREW. Pseudonym of Andrew Herbert Dakers, 1887-   .
Circumstantial Evidence. Bodley, 1928
-"Once I Was Blind." Cassell, 1926

STEWART, ANITA (MARIE). 1901-   .
The Devil's Toy. Dutton, 1935 [S.F., theatre]

STEWART, DICK
The Belrox Mystery. Street (Magnet)
The Brotherhood of Freedom. Street (Magnet)
Casting the Net. Street (New Magnet)
Checkmating a Countess. Street (Magnet)
A Clique of Knaves. Street (New Magnet)
Closing the Circle. Street (New Magnet)
Confederate Rogues. Street (Magnet)
A Crime Without a Name. Street (Magnet)
The Downward Path. Street (Magnet)
An Expert in Craft. Street (New Magnet)
A Game of Draw. Street (Magnet)
The Green Goods Speculator. Street (Magnet)
The Human Cat. Street (Magnet)
The Human Question Mark. Street (New Magnet)
In the Name of the Law. Street (New Magnet)
The King of Scamps. Street (Magnet)
The "L" Mystery. Street (Magnet)
The Lure of Mammon. Street (New Magnet)
The Man Who Hid. Street (Magnet)
On Death's Trail. Street (New Magnet)
Only a Headless Nail. Street (Magnet)
A Political Plotter. Street (Magnet)
A Queen of Chance. Street (New Magnet)
A Race with Death. Street (Magnet)
The Scamp Hunter. Street (New Magnet)
The Scarlet Spot. Street (New Magnet)

Search for a Motive. Street (Magnet)
The Sign of the Crescent. Street (New Magnet)
The Skeleton Clew. Street (Magnet)
The Strength of the Weak. Street (New Magnet)
The Unbidden Guests. Street (New Magnet)
An Unheeded Warning. Street (Magnet)
Villain's Work. Street (Magnet)
Welding the Chain. Street (New Magnet)
When the Clews Point Wrong. Street (New Magnet)
Without a Name. Street (New Magnet)

STEWART, DOROTHY MARY. 1917-1965. Pseudonym: Mary Elgin, q.v.

STEWART, DOUGLAS
Told by Twilight. Douglas, 1862 ss, some criminous

STEWART, EDWARD. 1938- . Graduate of Harvard, studied acting in Paris; has taught English, worked for a NYC publisher, been a staff film writer.
Heads. Macmillan, 1969; Deutsch, 1970 [NYC]
Launch! Doubleday, 1976; Collins, 1977
Rock Rude. Simon, 1970; Joseph, 1972 [N.H.]
They've Shot the President's Daughter. Doubleday, 1973; Allen Lane, 1973 [Wash. D.C.]

STEWART, FLORA. SC: Insp. Newsom, in both titles.
Blood Relations. Jenkins, 1967
Deadly Nightcap. Jenkins, 1966

STEWART, FRED MUSTARD. 1936- . Ref: CA.
The Mephisto Waltz. Coward, 1969; Joseph, 1969 [NYC]
-The Methuselah Enzyme. Arbor, 1970; Joseph, 1971

STEWART, FRED S.
The Crippled Hand. Street (Magnet)

STEWART, IAN. 1928- .
The Peking Payoff. Macmillan, 1975 [H. Kong]
The Seizing of Singapore. Hamlyn, 1980 [Sing.]

STEWART, JOHN INNES MACKINTOSH. 1906- . Pseudonym: Michael Innes, q.v.

STEWART, JAMES
Danger from Grassen. Black, 1946
Escape to Crime. Black, 1946
Spies over France. Nelson, 1941

STEWART, JAMES E.
The Mail Robber; or, The Clever Capture of a Dishonest Postal Clerk. Laird, 1889

STEWART, JAY. Pseudonym of (Charles) Stuart Palmer, 1905-1968, q.v.
Before It's Too Late. Mill, 1950. Reprinted as by Stuart Palmer: Dell, 1952 [Wash.]

STEWART, KENNETH LIVINGSTON. 1894- .
Pseudonym: Kenneth Livingston, q.v.

STEWART, KERRY. Pseudonym of Linda Stewart, q.v. Other pseudonyms: Nick Carter, Sam Stewart, qq.v.
The Concorde—Airport 1979. Jove, 1979 (Novelization of the movie.)
Ruby. Berkley, 1978

STEWART, LINDA. Pseudonyms: Nick Carter, Kerry Stewart, Sam Stewart, qq.v. Ref: CA.
Panic on Page One. Delacorte, 1979 [L.A.]

STEWART, MARY (FLORENCE ELINOR). 1916- . See also: Guy (Reginald) Bolton, 1884-1979. Ref: CA, CC, EM, TC.
Airs Above the Ground. Hodder, 1965; Mill, 1965 [Austria]
The Gabriel Hounds. Hodder, 1967; Mill, 1967 [Leb.]
The Ivy Tree. Hodder, 1961; Mill, 1961
Madam, Will You Talk? Hodder, 1955; Mill, 1956 [Fr.]
The Moon-Spinners. Hodder, 1962; Mill, 1963 [Crete]
My Brother Michael. Hodder, 1960; Mill, 1960 [Greece]
Nine Coaches Waiting. Hodder, 1958; Mill, 1959 [Fr.]
This Rough Magic. Hodder, 1964; Mill, 1964 [Greece]
Thunder on the Right. Hodder, 1957; Mill, 1958 [Fr.]
Touch Not the Cat. Hodder, 1976; Morrow, 1976
Wildfire at Midnight. Hodder, 1956; Appleton, 1956

STEWART, MICHAEL
Belle. Macmillan, 1977

STEWART, NEIL. Joint pseudonym with Pamela Hansford Johnson, 1912-1981: Nap Lombard, q.v.

STEWART, RAMONA. 1922- . Ref: CA.
The Apparition. Little, 1973; Deutsch, 1974 [NYC]
The Nightmare Candidate. Delacorte, 1980
The Possession of Joel Delany. Little, 1970; Deutsch, 1971 [NYC]
Sixth Sense. Delacorte, 1979; Magnum, 1980 [NYC, N.H.]

STEWART, SAM. Pseudonym of Linda Stewart, q.v. Other pseudonyms: Nick Carter, Kerry Stewart, qq.v.
The Big Rip-Off. Dell, 1976; Star, 1976 (Novelization of the TV movie.) [L.A.]
Fun with Dick and Jane. Dell, 1977; Sphere, 1977

STICKNEY, F. L.
The Rubber Mask. Chelsea, 1937

STIEPER, DONALD R.
It Seemed Like a Good Idea at the Time. Art Craft, 1975 (3-act play.)

STILES, W(ILLIAM) C(URTIS). 1851-1911.
Double Jeopardy. Home, 1898

STILGEBAUER, EDWARD. 1868- .
The Star of Hollywood. Paul, 1927; World, 1929 (Translation from the German.) [L.A.]

STILSON, CHARLES B(ILLINGS)
The Seven Blue Diamonds. Watt, 1927; Hutchinson, 1927 [Pa.]

STIMSON, FREDERICK JESUP. See: Anonymous.

STIMSON, MARY (DRAKE STURDIVANT). 1897- .
Marijuana Murder. Dorrance, 1940

STIMSON, ROBERT G. and JAMES BELLAH
The Avenger Tapes. Pinnacle, 1971

STINE, GEORGE HARRY. 1928- . Pseudonym: Lee Correy, q.v.

STINE, HANK [HENRY EUGENE STINE]. 1945- .
The Prisoner #3: A Day in the Life. Ace, 1970 (Novelization of "The Prisoner" TV series.)

STINSON, HUNTER
Fingerprints. Holt, 1925 [NYC]

STIRLING, PETER. Pseudonym of David Stern, 1909- .
Stop Press—Murder! Phoenix, 1947

STITT, DAVID E.
The Stars of Evil. Pageant, 1967

STITT, MILAN
The Runner Stumbles. Dramatists, 1976 (2-act play.)

STIVENS, DAL(LAS GEORGE). 1911- . Ref: CA.
The Wide Arch. Angus (Sydney), 1958

STOCK, RALPH. 1882- .
The Recipe for Rubber. Lynwood, 1912 [Fiji]

STOCKBRIDGE, GRANT. Pseudonym of Norvell W. Page, 1904-1961. SC: Richard Wentworth (The Spider), in all titles, which are reprinted from 1930's pulp magazines (see also: R. T. M. Scott, 1882-).
Builder of the Black Empire. Dimeda, 1980
The City Destroyer. PB, 1975; New English Library pb, 1976 [NYC]
City of Flaming Shadows. Berkley, 1970 [NYC]
Death and the Spider. PB, 1975; New English Library pb, 1976 [NYC]
Death Reign of the Vampire King. PB, 1975; New English Library pb, 1976
Hordes of the Red Butcher. PB, 1975; New English Library pb, 1976
Master of the Death Madness. Dimeda, 1980
Overlord of the Damned. Dimeda, 1980
Wings of the Black Death. Berkley, 1969 [NYC]

STOCKTON, FRANK R(ICHARD). 1834-1902. Ref: EM.
The Lady, or the Tiger, and other stories. Scribner, 1884; Douglas, 1884 ss
The Stories of Three Burglars. Dodd, 1889; Low, 1890

STOCKWELL, GAIL. SC: Kingsley Toplitt = KL
The Candy Killings. Greystone, 1940 [NYC]
Death by Invitation. Macmillan, 1937 KT
The Embarrassed Murderer. Macmillan, 1938; Lane, 1938 KT [NYC]

STODDARD, CHARLES. Pseudonym of Charles Stanley Strong, 1906-1962. SC: Mallory, in at least those marked M.
The Caribou Patrol. Foulsham, 1957 M (U.S. title?)
Death Rides the Rails. Foulsham, 1955 M (U.S. title?)
-Devil's Portage. Gateway, 1942; Cassell, 1940
The Golden Arrow. Foulsham, 1956 M (U.S. title?)
The Killer at Fort Norman. Arcadia, 1944 M
The Killer of Sheep River. Arcadia, 1946 M
Mallory of the Royal Mounted. Arcadia, 1944; Wells Gardner, 1946 M
-North of the Stars. Dodge, 1937; Cassell, 1938
-Northwest Trouble. Phoenix, 1948
-Prairie Peril. Arcadia, 1946; Wright, 1949
Timber Beasts. Arcadia, 1945 M
The Trapper of Rat River. Arcadia, 1941; Wells Gardner, 1943 M
Trooper MacLean. Caslon, 1936; Cassell, 1938 [Can.]
Tundra Trail. Arcadia, 1947; Wells Gardner, 1948 M
The Wilderness Patrol. Dodge, 1938; Cassell, 1938

STOHLMAN, RICHARD
An Overflowing Rain. Avon, 1979 [Russ.]

STOKER, ALAN. 1930- . Pseudonym: Alan Evans, q.v.

STOKER, BRAM [ABRAHAM STOKER]. 1847-1912. See also: Hamilton Deane, Crane Johnson, Ted Tiller. Ref: CA, CC, EM, TC.
Dracula. Constable, 1897; Doubleday, 1899 [Rum.]
Dracula's Guest. Routledge, 1914; Hillman-Curl, 1937 ss
The Garden of Evil; see The Lair of the White Worm
The Jewel of Seven Stars. Heinemann, 1903; Harper, 1904
The Lady of the Shroud. Heinemann, 1909; Paperback Library, 1966
The Lair of the White Worm. Rider, 1911. U.S. title: The Garden of Evil. Paperback Library, 1966, abridged
The Man. Heinemann, 1905
The Mystery of the Sea. Heinemann, 1902; Doubleday, 1902
The Snake's Pass. Low, 1891; Harper, 1890
Under the Sunset. Low, 1882

STOKES, ARTHUR M.
Checkmate! Goldscheider, 1980 (Sherlock Holmes.)

STOKES, CEDRIC. Pseudonym of George Beardmore, 1908- , q.v. Other pseudonym: George Wolfenden, q.v.
The Staffordshire Assassins. Macdonald, 1945

STOKES, DONALD (HUBERT). 1913- .
Appointment with Fear. Coward, 1950
Captive in the Night. Coward, 1951 [Algiers]

STOKES, FRANCIS WILLIAM. 1883- . Pseudonym: Francis Everton, q.v.

STOKES, MANNING LEE. Pseudonyms: Nick Carter, Paul Edwards, Ken Stanton, qq.v. SC: Christopher Fenn, in at least those marked CF; Barnabas Jones, in at least those marked BJ.
The Case of the Judas Spoon. Arcadia, 1957 CF [Eng.]
The Case of the Presidents' Heads. Arcadia, 1956 CF [NYC]
The Case of the Winking Buddha. St. John, 1950

The Crooked Circle. Graphic, 1951. Also
  published as: Too Many Murderers.
  Graphic, 1955
The Dying Room. Phoenix, 1947 [L.I.]
The Grave's in the Meadow. Arcadia,
  1959
Green for a Grave. Phoenix, 1946 BJ
Hang the Hangman. Arcadia, 1956
The Iron Tiger. Arcadia, 1958 [Ohio]
The Lady Lost Her Head. Phoenix, 1950
  [NYC]
Murder Can't Wait. Graphic, 1955
Too Many Murderers; see The Crooked
  Circle
Under Cover of Night. Dell, 1958 [Kor.]
The Wolf Howls "Murder". Phoenix, 1945
  BJ [Ill.]

STOKES, ROBERT S.
  Walking Wounded. Dell, 1980

STOKESBERRY, BOB. Pseudonym: Nick Carter,
  q.v.

STONE, A.
  American Pep. Shores, 1918 [Pa.]
  Fighting Byng. Britton, 1919

STONE, ANDREW L.
  Cry Terror. Signet, 1958 (Novelization
    of the movie.)
  The Decks Ran Red. Signet, 1958 (No-
    velization of the movie.) [ship]
  Julie. Signet, 1956; Panther, 1957
    (Novelization of the movie.) [Calif.]

STONE, AUSTIN. Set: Eng.
  Blood Stays Red. Gifford, 1949
  Deadly Night-Blade. Gifford, 1950
  Death Throws a Party. Gifford, 1949
  The Headsman. Eldon, 1936
  Murders in the Mortuary. Eldon, 1935;
    Putnam, 1936

STONE, CLARA
  Death in Cranford. Hutchinson, 1959

STONE, DAVID (ANTHONY). 1929-   . Ref:
  CA.
  The Tired Spy. Putnam, 1961; Davies,
    1961 [It.]

STONE, EDDIE
  Black Fugitive. Holloway, 1977
  Black Hunter. Holloway, 1976
  Street Games. Holloway, 1977
  Twenty Miles to Terror. Holloway, 1978
  A Victim of Rape. Holloway, 1976

STONE, EDMUND
  Dawn for Danger. Consul, 1965

STONE, ELINORE COWAN. 1884-   . Born in
  Mich., raised in Pitt. and Boston;
  newspaperwoman, teacher, magazine ss
  writer; living in Pitt. in 1930s.
  Fear Rides the Fog. Appleton, 1937
    [Pitt.]

STONE, ELIZABET M. SC: Maggie Slone, in
  both titles, both set in New Or.
  Murder at the Mardi Gras. Sheridan,
    1947
  Poison, Poker and Pistols. Sheridan,
    1946

STONE, ELNA (BURCHFIELD). Ref: CA.
  Dark Masquerade. Lancer, 1973 [Fla.]
  Ghost at the Wedding. Belmont, 1971
  Secret of the Willows. Belmont, 1971
    [South]
  The Visions of Esmaree. St. Martin's,
    1976 [South, 1930s]
  Whisper of Fear. Beagle, 1973

STONE, GEORGE
  Blizzard. Grosset, 1977; Hale, 1979

STONE, GRACE ZARING. 1891-   . Pseudonym: Ethel Vance, q.v. Ref: CA, CC.
  Dear Deadly Cara. Random, 1968
    [New Eng.]

STONE, HAMPTON. Pseudonym of Aaron Marc
  Stein, 1906-   , q.v. Other pseudo-
  nym: George Bagby, q.v. SC: Jeremiah
  X. (Gibby) Gibson, in all titles.
  The Babe with the Twistable Arm. Simon,
    1962; Hale, 1964 [NYC]
  The Corpse in the Corner Saloon. Simon,
    1948 [NYC]
  The Corpse That Refused to Stay Dead.
    Simon, 1952; Dobson, 1954 [NYC]
  The Corpse Was No Bargain at All.
    Simon, 1968; Hale, 1969 [NYC]
  The Corpse Who Had Too Many Friends.
    Simon, 1953; Foulsham, 1954 [NYC]
  The Funniest Killer in Town. Simon,
    1967 [NYC]
  The Girl Who Kept Knocking Them Dead.
    Simon, 1957; Foulsham, 1957 [NYC]

The Girl with the Hole in Her Head.
  Simon, 1949; Boardman, 1958 [NYC]
The Kid Was Last Seen Hanging Ten.
  Simon, 1966 [NYC]
The Kid Who Came Home with a Corpse.
  Simon, 1972 [NYC]
The Man Who Had Too Much to Lose.
  Simon, 1955; Foulsham, 1955 [NYC]
The Man Who Looked Death in the Eye.
  Simon, 1961 [NYC]
The Man Who Was Three Jumps Ahead.
  Simon, 1959; Boardman, 1960 [NYC]
The Murder That Wouldn't Stay Solved.
  Simon, 1951 [NYC]
The Needle That Wouldn't Hold Still.
  Simon, 1950; Boardman, 1958 [NYC]
The Real Serendipitous Kill. Simon,
  1964 [NYC]
The Strangler; see The Strangler Who
  Couldn't Let Go
The Strangler Who Couldn't Let Go.
  Simon, 1956. British title: The
  Strangler. Foulsham, 1957 [L.I.]
The Swinger Who Swung by the Neck.
  Simon, 1970 [NYC]

STONE, HARRIET
  Heiress of Bayou Vache. Lancer, 1965

STONE, JAMES F(LOYD). 1898-   .
  Calling All Ghosts. Dramatists, 1941
    (3-act play.)
  "The Haunted Chair." Northwestern, 1937
    (3-act play.)
  Spooky Junction. Northwestern, 1946
    (3-act play.)

STONE, MERRITT
  The Moonstone. French (NYC), 1944
    (3-act play based on the novel by
    Wilkie Collins, 1824-1889, q.v.)

STONE, PETER H(ESS). 1930-   . Ref: CA.
  Charade. GM, 1965; Fontana, 1964
    (Novelization of the movie.)

STONE, SCOTT C(LINTON) S(TUART).
  1932-   . Ref: CA.
  The Dragon's Eye. GM, 1969 [Far East]
  Spies. St. Martin's, 1980 [Far East]

STONE, SIMON. Pseudonym of Howard Bar-
  rington, 1906-   . Born in Eng.;
  has been bookseller, advertising
  executive, furniture designer, and
  civil servant. SC: Sir Brian Dinsmore
  Conway, in at least those marked BC.
  Bookmaker's Body. Hutchinson, 1947 BC
  Conway, K.C. Hutchinson, 1945 BC
  Demi-Paradise Regained. Hutchinson,
    1945
  I, Spy. Hutchinson, 1941
  Knight Missing. Hutchinson, 1944; Mac-
    millan, 1945 BC
  Murder Gone Mad. Hutchinson, 1951 BC
  The Price of Admiralty. Hutchinson,
    1942

STONE, THOMAS H. Pseudonym of Terry Hark-
  nett, 1936-   , q.v. Other pseudo-
  nyms: Joseph Hedges, William Pine,
  William Terry, qq.v. SC: Chester For-
  tune, in at least those marked CF.
  Black Death. New English Library pb,
    1973
  Dead Set. New English Library pb, 1972
    CF
  One Horse Race. New English Library pb,
    1972 CF
  Squeeze Play. New English Library pb,
    1973
  Stopover for Murder. New English Li-
    brary pb, 1973

STONE, ZACHARY
  The Modigliani Scandal. Collins, 1976
  Paper Money. Collins, 1977

STONEBRAKER, FLORENCE. 1896-   . Pseudonym: Florenz Branch, q.v.

STONEHAM, C(HARLES) THURLEY. 1895-   .
  Pseudonym: Norgrove Thurley, q.v.
  -Adventure for Wealth. Long, 1957
  Kenya Mystery. Museum, 1954 [Kenya]
  The Man in the Pig Mask. Hutchinson,
    1929
  The Prowling Terror. Long, 1957
  Rogues in the Forest. Long, 1958

STONER, BERT. Pseudonym of Wilbur Braun,
  1896-   , q.v. Other pseudonyms:
  Walter Blake, Bruce Brandon, Fred
  Caldwell, Raymond Dumkey, Nan Flem-
  ing, Marsha Grable, Edwin F. Hornung,
  Jed Parish, Basil Ring, Orville Snap,
  Mortimer Sprague, qq.v.
  Was This Murder? French (NYC), 1951
    (3-act play.)

STOOKEY, RICHARD
  A Still and Woven Blue. Popular Li-
    brary, 1975

STOPPARD, TOM. Pseudonym of Tom Straussler, 1937-   . Ref: CA.
  The Real Inspector Hound. Faber, 1968;
    Grove, 1969 (Play.)

STORER, MARIA LONGWORTH (NICHOLS). 1849-
  1932.
  The Borodino Mystery. Herder, 1916
  -Probation. Herder, 1916
  -Sir Christopher Leighton; or, The Mar-
    quis de Vaudreuil's Story. Herder,
    1915
  -The Villa Rossignol; or, The Advance of
    Islam. Herder, 1918

STOREY, ANTHONY. 1928-   . Ref: CA.
  -Brothers Keepers. Boyars, 1975
  -The Centre Holds. Calder, 1973
  Platinum Ass. Allen, 1975
  Platinum Jag. Calder, 1972

STOREY, MICHAEL. 1941-   .
  Soft in the Middle. Knopf, 1972; Cape,
    1972

STORM, JOAN. SC: Sarah Vanessa, in all
  titles.
  Bitter Rubies. Hammond, 1952 [Vienna]
  Dark Emerald. Hammond, 1951 [Ger.]
  Deadly Diamond. Hammond, 1953

STORM, LESLEY. Pseudonym of Mabel Margar-
  et Cowie Clark, 1903-1975.
  The Day's Mischief. French (London),
    1952 (2-act play.)
  Gallows-Bird. Hutchinson, 1937

STORM, MICHAEL. SC: Nick Cranley, in at
  least those marked NC.
  Baby Don't Love Hoodlums. Harborough,
    1953
  Baby Don't Say Goodbye. Harborough,
    1953
  Carmen Was a Virgin. Leisure, 1952 NC
  Chicago Terror. Harborough, 1952 [Chi.]
  A Corpse Spells Danger. Leisure, 1953
  Curtains for Carla. Leisure, 1952 NC
  The Devil Has a Racket. Harborough,
    1954
  Dragons Come Expensive. Harborough,
    1953
  Elvira Digs a Grave. Harborough, 1952
  The Grey Messengers. Blackie, 1940
  Hot Dames on Cold Slabs. Archer, 1950;
    Leisure, 195?
  Kiss the Corpse Goodbye. Harborough,
    1952
  Lovelies Are Never Lonely. Harborough,
    1952
  Make Mine a Corpse. Archer, 1950
  Make Mine a Harlot. Archer, 1949
  Make Mine a Redhead. Harborough, 1952
  Make Mine a Shroud. Leisure, 195?
  Make Mine a Virgin. Archer, 1949
  Make Mine Beautiful. Archer, 1949
  Make Mine Dangerous. Archer, 1949
  Me and My Ghoul. Harborough, 1953
  Satan Buys a Wreath. Archer, 1951
  Stella Buys a Shroud. Harborough, 1952
  "Sucker for a Red-Head." Archer, 1950
  Sweetheart with a Wreath. Harborough,
    1953
  This Woman Is Death. Leisure, 1953 NC
  Tiptoe Thro' a Graveyard. Harborough,
    1953
  A Woman's Friend. Curtis Warren, 1950
  You'll Be Better Off Dead. Harborough,
    1953

STORM, MICHAEL
  China Cane. Mystery House, 1959
  Cry, Tiger! Mystery House, 1958
    [Boston]
  Edge of Danger. Mystery House, 1957
    [New Eng.]

STORME, PETER. Pseudonym of Philip Van
  Doren Stern, 1900-   , q.v.
  The Thing in the Brook. Simon, 1937;
    Hale, 1937

STORRS, LEWIS AUSTIN. 1866-1945.
  Koheleth. Dillingham, 1897

STORY, JACK TREVOR. 1917-   . Ref: CA.
  SC: Sexton Blake (with many other
  authors) = SB; Albert Argyle, in at
  least those marked AA; Horace Spur-
  geon Fenton, in at least those marked
  HF.
  Assault and Pepper. Fleetway, 1961 SB
  The Big Steal! Fleetway, 1960 SB
  The Blonde and the Boodle. Amalgamated,
    1957 SB
  Collapse of Stout Party. Amalgamated,
    1958 SB
  Company of Bandits. Mayflower, 1965 SB
  Courier for Crime. Amalgamated, 1959 SB

-Crying Makes Your Nose Run. Bruce, 1974
Danger on the Flip Side. Amalgamated, 1960 SB
Danger's Child. Fleetway, 1961 SB
-Dishonourable Member. Secker, 1969
The Frightened People. Amalgamated, 1958 SB
-Green to Pagan Street. Harrap, 1952
-Hitler Needs You. Allison, 1971 HF
Home Sweet Homicide. Amalgamated, 1959 SB
Invitation to a Murder! Amalgamated, 1959 SB
-I Sit in Hanger Lane. Secker, 1968
-Little Dog's Day. Allison, 1971
-Live Now, Pay Later. Secker, 1963 AA
Mix Me a Person. Allen, 1959; Macmillan, 1960
-The Money Goes Round and Round. Redman, 1958
Murder in the Sun. Amalgamated, 1958 SB
Murder—with Love. Amalgamated, 1956 SB
Nine O'Clock Shadow. Amalgamated, 1958 SB
-One Last Mad Embrace. Allison, 1970 HF
Protection for a Lady. Laurie, 1950
Rogue's Harbour. Fleetway, 1961 SB
The Season of the Skylark. Amalgamated, 1957 SB
She Ain't Got No Body. Amalgamated, 1958 SB
-Something for Nothing. Secker, 1963 AA
Suddenly It's Murder. Fleetway, 1961 SB
The Trouble with Harry. Boardman, 1949; Macmillan, 1950
-Up River. Duckworth, 1979
-The Urban District Lover. Secker, 1964 AA
Vacation with Fear. Amalgamated, 1957 SB
Violence in Quiet Places. Amalgamated, 1960 SB
The Wind in the Snottygobble Tree. Allison, 1971

STOUT, REX. 1886-1975. Ref: all except MM. SC: Nero Wolfe & Archie Goodwin = W&G; Insp. Cramer (also in the W&G stories) = C; Tecumseh Fox = TF; Dol Bonner (also in some of the W&G series) = DB. See also: Anonymous ("The President Vanishes").
Alphabet Hicks. Farrar, 1941; Collins, 1942. Also published as: The Sound of Murder. Pyramid, 1965 [NYC]
And Be a Villain. Viking, 1948. British title: More Deaths Than One. Collins, 1949 W&G [NYC]
And Four to Go. Viking, 1958. British title: Crime and Again. Collins, 1959 (4 W&G novelets.) [NYC]
Bad for Business. Farrar, 1940 (in the omnibus "The Second Mystery Book"); Collins, 1945 TF
Before Midnight. Viking, 1955; Collins, 1956 W&G [NYC]
The Black Mountain. Viking, 1954; Collins, 1955 W&G [Yugos.]
Black Orchids. Farrar, 1942; Collins, 1943. Also published as: The Case of the Black Orchids. Avon, 1950 (Two W&G novelets. Some paperback editions contain only the first of these, the title story. The second novelet has been reprinted separately as: Cordially Invited to Meet Death. Jonathan, 1945. And as: Invitation to Murder. Avon, 1956.) [NYC]
The Broken Vase. Farrar, 1941; Collins, 1942 TF [NYC]
The Case of the Black Orchids; see Black Orchids
Case of the Red Box; see The Red Box
Champagne for One. Viking, 1958; Collins, 1959 W&G [NYC]
Cordially Invited to Meet Death; see Black Orchids
Corsage. Rock, 1977 (Contains a 1940 W&G novelet in its first book publication, plus nonfiction by and about Rex Stout.)
Crime and Again; see And Four to Go
Crime on Her Hands; see The Hand in the Glove
Curtains for Three. Viking, 1951; Collins, 1951 (3 W&G novelets.) [NYC]
Death of a Doxy. Viking, 1966; Collins, 1967 W&G [NYC]
Death of a Dude. Viking, 1969; Collins, 1970 W&G [Mont.]
Door to Death; see Three Doors to Death
The Doorbell Rang. Viking, 1965; Collins, 1966 W&G [NYC]
Double for Death. Farrar, 1939; Collins, 1940 TF [N.Y.]
Even in the Best Families; see In the Best Families
A Family Affair. Viking, 1975; Collins, 1976 W&G [NYC]
The Father Hunt. Viking, 1968; Collins, 1969 W&G [NYC]
Fer-de-Lance. Farrar, 1934; Cassell, 1935. Also published as: Meet Nero Wolfe. Mercury, 194? W&G [NYC]
The Final Deduction. Viking, 1961; Collins, 1962 W&G [NYC]
Gambit. Viking, 1962; Collins 1963 W&G [NYC]
The Golden Spiders. Viking, 1953; Collins, 1954 W&G [NYC]
The Hand in the Glove. Farrar, 1937. British title: Crime on Her Hands. Collins, 1939 DB [N.Y.]
Homicide Trinity. Viking, 1962; Collins, 1963 (3 W&G novelets.) [NYC]
If Death Ever Slept. Viking, 1957; Collins, 1958 W&G [NYC]
In the Best Families. Viking, 1950. British title: Even in the Best Families. Collins, 1951 W&G [NYC]
Invitation to Murder; see Black Orchids
Justice Ends at Home, and other stories. Viking, 1977 ss
The League of Frightened Men. Farrar, 1935; Cassell, 1935 W&G [NYC]
Meet Nero Wolfe; see Fer-de-Lance
Might As Well Be Dead. Viking, 1956; Collins, 1957 W&G [NYC]
More Deaths Than One; see And Be a Villain
The Mother Hunt. Viking, 1963; Collins, 1964 W&G [NYC]
Mountain Cat. Farrar, 1939; Collins, 1940. Also published as: The Mountain Cat Murders. Dell, 1943 [Wyo.]
The Mountain Cat Murders; see Mountain Cat
Murder by the Book. Viking, 1951; Collins, 1952 W&G [NYC]
Murder in Style; see Plot It Yourself
Not Quite Dead Enough. Farrar, 1944 (2 W&G novelets.) [NYC]
Out Goes She; see Prisoner's Base
Over My Dead Body. Farrar, 1940; Collins, 1940 W&G [NYC]
Please Pass the Guilt. Viking, 1973; Collins, 1974 W&G [NYC]
Plot It Yourself. Viking, 1959. British title: Murder in Style. Collins, 1960 W&G [NYC]
Prisoner's Base. Viking, 1952. British title: Out Goes She. Collins, 1953 W&G [NYC]
The Red Box. Farrar, 1937; Cassell, 1937. Also published as: Case of the Red Box. Avon, 1945 W&G [NYC]
The Red Bull; see Some Buried Caesar
Red Threads. Farrar, 1939 (in the omnibus "The Mystery Book"); Collins, 1941 C [NYC]
A Right to Die. Viking, 1964; Collins, 1965 W&G [NYC]
The Rubber Band. Farrar, 1936; Cassell, 1936. Also published as: To Kill Again. Hillman, 1960 W&G [NYC]
The Second Confession. Viking, 1949; Collins, 1950 W&G [NYC]
The Silent Speaker. Viking, 1946; Collins, 1947 W&G [NYC]
Some Buried Caesar. Farrar, 1939; Collins, 1939. Also published as: The Red Bull. Dell, 1945 W&G [N.Y.]
The Sound of Murder; see Alphabet Hicks
Three at Wolfe's Door. Viking, 1960; Collins, 1961 (3 W&G novelets.) [NYC]
Three Doors to Death. Viking, 1950; Collins, 1950 (3 W&G novelets, of which one was reprinted separately as: Door to Death. Dell 10¢ pb, 1951.) [NYC]
Three for the Chair. Viking, 1957; Collins, 1958 (3 W&G novelets.) [NYC]
Three Men Out. Viking, 1954; Collins, 1955 (3 W&G novelets.) [NYC]
Three Witnesses. Viking, 1956; Collins, 1956 (3 W&G novelets.) [NYC]
To Kill Again; see The Rubber Band
Too Many Clients. Viking, 1960; Collins, 1961 W&G [NYC]
Too Many Crooks. Farrar, 1938; Collins, 1938 W&G [W. Va.]
Too Many Women. Viking, 1947; Collins, 1948 W&G [NYC]
Trio for Blunt Instruments. Viking, 1964; Collins, 1965 (3 W&G novelets) [NYC]
Triple Jeopardy. Viking, 1951; Collins, 1952 (3 W&G novelets.) [NYC]
Trouble in Triplicate. Viking, 1949; Collins, 1949 (3 W&G novelets.) [NYC]
Where There's a Will. Farrar, 1940; Collins, 1941 W&G [NYC]

STOVALL, WALTER
The Minus Pool. Wyndham, 1980 [NYC]
Presidential Emergency. Dutton, 1978; Hodder, 1978

STOWE, JAMES L(EWIS). 1950-   . Ref: CA.
Winter Stalk. Simon, 1979; Hamlyn, 1980 [N. Mex.]

STOWELL, WILLIAM AVERILL. 1882-1950.
The Marston Murder Case. Appleton, 1930 [NYC]
The Mystery of the Singing Walls. Appleton, 1925 [NYC]
The Wake of the Setting Sun. Appleton, 1923 [San Diego]

STRACHAN, T(ONY) S(IMPSON). 1920-   .
Ref: CA.
Fire Escape. Laurie, 1950
Key Major. Heinemann, 1954
No Law in Illyria. Heinemann, 1957
No One to Worry Us. Laurie, 1949
The Short Weekend. Hammond, 1953 [Madrid]

STRAHAN, KAY CLEAVER. 1888-1941. SC: Lynn MacDonald, in all titles. Ref: CC, MP. Born, educated and died in Oreg.
Death Traps. Doubleday, 1930; Gollancz, 1930 [S.F.]
The Desert Lake Mystery. Bobbs, 1936; Methuen, 1937 [Nev.]
The Desert Moon Mystery. Doubleday, 1928; Gollancz, 1928 [Nev.]
Footprints. Doubleday, 1929; Gollancz, 1929 [Oreg.]
The Hobgoblin Murder. Bobbs, 1934; Methuen, 1935 [Calif.]
The Meriweather Mystery. Doubleday, 1932 [Oreg.]
October House. Doubleday, 1932; Gollancz, 1931 [Oreg.]

STRAKER, J(OHN) F(OSTER). 1904-   .
Ref: CA, TC. SC: Johnny Inch, in at least those marked JI; Insp. Pitt, in at least those marked P; David Wright, in at least those marked DW. Set: Eng.
Arthurs' Night. Hale, 1976
A Coil of Rope. Harrap, 1962 DW
Countersnatch. Hale, 1980
Death of a Good Woman. Harrap, 1961 P
Death on a Sunday Morning. Hale, 1978
Final Witness. Harrap, 1963 DW
The Ginger Horse. Harrap, 1956 P
The Goat. Harrap, 1972 JI
Goodbye, Aunt Charlotte! Harrap, 1958 P
A Gun to Play With. Harrap, 1956 P
Hell Is Empty. Harrap, 1958
A Letter for Obi. Harrap, 1971 JI
A Man Who Cannot Kill. Harrap, 1969
Miscarriage of Murder. Harrap, 1967
Murder for Missemily. Harrap, 1961 P
Pick Up the Pieces. Harrap, 1955 P
A Pity It Wasn't George. Hale, 1979
Postman's Knock. Harrap, 1954 P
Ricochet. Harrap, 1965
The Shape of Murder. Harrap, 1964
Sin and Johnny Inch. Harrap, 1968 JI
Swallow Them Up. Hale, 1977
Tight Circle. Harrap, 1970 JI

STRANGE, CARLTON
The Beechcourt Mystery. Newnes, 1894

STRANGE, DOROTHY. See: Arthur W(illiam) Upfield, 1888-1964.

STRANGE, JEREMY
Tragedy on a Trooper. Stockwell, 1944

STRANGE, JOHN STEPHEN. Pseudonym of Dorothy Stockbridge Tillett, 1896-   .
Ref: CC, MP, TC. SC: Barney Gantt = BG; Lt./Capt. George Honegger = GH; Van Dusen Ormsberry = VO.
All Men Are Liars. Doubleday, 1948. British title: Come to Judgment. Collins, 1949 GH [NYC]
The Ballot Box Murders; see Rope Enough
The Bell in the Fog. Doubleday, 1936; Collins, 1937 BG
Black Hawthorn. Doubleday, 1933. British title: The Chinese Jar Mystery. Collins, 1934 [Conn.]
Catch the Gold Ring. Doubleday, 1955. British title: A Handful of Silver. Collins, 1955 [Paris]
The Chinese Jar Mystery; see Black Hawthorn
The Clue of the Second Murder. Doubleday, 1929; Collins, 1929 VO [Conn.]
Come to Judgment; see All Men Are Liars
The Corpse and the Lady; see Silent Witnesses
Dead End; see Let the Dead Past—
Deadly Beloved. Doubleday, 1952; Collins, 1952 BG [NYC]
Eye Witness. Doubleday, 1961; Collins, 1962 GH [NYC]
The Fair and the Dead; see Reasonable Doubt
For the Hangman. Doubleday, 1934; Collins, 1935 [Balt.]
A Handful of Silver; see Catch the Gold Ring
The House on 9th Street. Doubleday, 1976 BG [NYC]

Let the Dead Past—. Doubleday, 1953. British title: Dead End. Collins, 1953 [NYC]
Look Your Last. Doubleday, 1943; Collins, 1944 BG [NYC]
Make My Bed Soon. Doubleday, 1948; Collins, 1948 BG [Pa.]
The Man Who Killed Fortescue. Doubleday, 1928; Collins, 1929. Also published as by Dorothy Stockbridge Tillett. Perennial, 1981 VO [NYC]
Murder at World's End; see The Strangler Fig
Murder Game; see Murder on the Ten-Yard Line
Murder Gives a Lovely Light. Doubleday, 1941; Collins, 1942 GH [NYC]
Murder on the Ten-Yard Line. Doubleday, 1931. British title: Murder Game. Collins, 1931 VO [N.Y.]
Night of Reckoning. Doubleday, 1958; Collins, 1959 [Conn.]
A Picture of the Victim. Doubleday, 1940; Collins, 1940 BG [L.I.]
Reasonable Doubt. Doubleday, 1951; Collins, 1951. Also published as: The Fair and the Dead. Bestseller, 1953 [Vt.]
Rope Enough. Doubleday, 1938; Collins, 1939. Also published as: The Ballot Box Murders. Mystery Novel Classic, 1943 BG [NYC]
Silent Witnesses. Doubleday, 1938. British title: The Corpse and the Lady. Collins, 1938 BG [NYC]
The Strangler Fig. Doubleday, 1930; Collins, 1931. Also published as: Murder at World's End. Mystery Novel Classic, 1943 [Fla.]
Uneasy Is the Grave; see Unquiet Grave
Unquiet Grave. Doubleday, 1949. British title: Uneasy Is the Grave. Collins, 1950 [Mass.]

STRANGE, MARK. Pseudonym.
Midnight. Faber, 1927 [acad.]

STRANGER, L. D.
The Great Snake Murder. Richmond, 1915
-The Odd One Out. Nelson, 1936

STRATEMEYER, EDWARD (L.). 1862-1930. Pseudonyms: Nicholas Carter, Chester K. Steele, qq.v. Ref: CA.
Reuben Stone's Discovery; or, The Young Miller of Torrent Bend. Merriam, 1895

STRATENUS, LOUISE
Suspected. Chapman, 1892 (Translation of "Gewroken." Arnheim, 1890.)

STRATFORD, MICHAEL. Pseudonym of Bruce (Bingham) Cassiday, 1920-   , q.v. Other pseudonyms: Carson Bingham, Nick Carter, Mary Anne Drew, Annie Laurie McAllister, Annie Laurie McMurdie, qq.v.
The Sniper. Award, 1974; Tandem, 1974 (Novelization of the "Adam 12" TV series.) [L.A.]

STRATTON, CHRIS. Pseudonym of Richard Hubbard,   -ca.1974, q.v. Other pseudonyms: Nick Carter, Marie Eyre, Regina Hubbard, qq.v.
Change of Mind. Pyramid, 1969 (Novelization of the movie.)
Dead on Arrival. Award, 1972 (Novelization of the "Adam 12" TV series.) [L.A.]
A Fine Pair. Popular Library, 1969 (Novelization of the movie.)
The Hostage. Award, 1974; Tandem, 1974 (Novelization of the "Adam 12" TV series.) [L.A.]
Rock! Pyramid, 1970 (Novelization of the "Then Came Bronson" TV series.) [Ariz.]
The Runaway. Award, 1974 (Novelization of the "Adam 12" TV series.) [L.A.]
The Ticket. Pyramid, 1970; New English Library pb, 1970 (Novelization of the "Then Came Bronson" TV series.)
Underground. Popular Library, 1970 (Novelization of the movie.)

STRATTON, HENRY. Pseudonym of Michael Harrington Nelson, 1921-   . Ref: CA.
Blanket. Macdonald, 1959

STRATTON, ROY (OLIN). 1909?-   . Ref: CA. SC: Scott Gregory and Justin Bassett, in both titles.
The Decorated Corpse. Mill, 1962; Boardman, 1963 [Cape Cod]
One Among None. Mill, 1965; Boardman, 1965 [Mass.]

STRATTON, TED [JOHN THEODORE STRATTON]. 1902-   . Pseudonym: Terry Spain, q.v. Ref: CA.
Tourist Trap. Putnam, 1975; Hale, 1977 [N.J.]

STRATTON, THOMAS. Joint pseudonym of (Thomas Eu)Gene DeWeese, 1934-   , q.v., and Robert Stratton Coulson, 1918-   . Other DeWeese pseudonym: Jean DeWeese, q.v.
The Invisibility Affair. Ace, 1967 (Novelization of the "Man from UNCLE" TV series.) [Wis.]
The Mind-Twisters Affair. Ace, 1967 (Novelization of the "Man from UNCLE" TV series.) [Ind.]

STRAUB, PETER (FRANCIS). 1943-   . Ref: CA.
Julia. Coward, 1975; Cape, 1976 [Eng.]

STRAUS, RALPH. 1882-1950. Pseudonym: Robert Erstone Forbes, q.v.
Five Men Go to Prison. Chapman, 1935
Pengard Awake. Methuen, 1920; Appleton, 1920 [Chi.]

STRAUSS, THEODORE. 1912-   .
Black Caesar; see Night at Hogwallow
Dark Hunger; see Moonrise
The Haters; see Night at Hogwallow
Moonrise. Viking, 1946; H. Hamilton, 1947. Also published as: Dark Hunger. Bantam, 1951
Night at Hogwallow. Little, 1937. British title: Black Caesar. Heinemann, 1937. Also published as: The Haters. Bantam, 1951

STRAUSSLER, TOM. 1937-   . Pseudonym: Tom Stoppard, q.v.

STRECKFUSS, ADOLF. 1823-1895.
The Lonely House. Lippincott, 1907 (Translation from the German.)

STREET, A(RTHUR) G(EORGE). 1892-1966. Ref: CA.
A Crook in the Furrow. Faber, 1940

STREET, BRADFORD
For Pete's Sake. Avon, 1974 (Novelization of the movie.)
The Glass Bottom Boat. Dell, 1966 (Novelization of the movie.)
In Like Flint. Dell, 1967 (Novelization of the movie.)
Primus. Bantam, 1971 (Novelization of the movie.)

STREET, CECIL JOHN CHARLES. 1884-1961. Pseudonyms: Miles Burton, John Rhode, qq.v.

STREET, JAMES. SC: Eugene Mulcahy = EM. Set: Eng.
Carbon Monoxide. Low, 1937
Death in an Armchair. Jenkins, 1936 EM
A Wastrel Goes West. Low, 1937 EM

STREET, PENNY
The Chinese Bottle. Pocket Editions, 1945
Murder in a Barge. Pocket Editions, 1946
The Sign of Blood. Pictorial Art, 1946

STREIB, DAN(IEL T.). Pseudonyms: Nick Carter, Paul Richards, qq.v. SC: Michael Hawk = MH.
The Deadly Crusader. Jove, 1980; Sphere, 1982 MH [Greece]
The Mind Twisters. Jove, 1980; Sphere, 1982 MH
Operation: Count Down, with R(obert) P(age) Jones, q.v. Powell, 1970
The Power Barons. Jove, 1980; Sphere, 1982 MH
The Predators. Jove, 1980; Sphere, 1982 MH [ship]

STREVENS, ROBERT
Murder in Manuscript. Rich, 1948

STRIBLING, T(HOMAS) S(IGISMUND). 1881-1965. Ref: CC, EM, MC, MP, TC. SC: Prof. Henry Poggioli, in both titles.
Best Dr. Poggioli Detective Stories. Dover (NYC), 1975; Dover (London), 1976 ss
Clues of the Caribbees. Doubleday, 1929; Heinemann, 1930 ss [Carib.]

STRIEBER, WHITLEY. 1945-   . Ref: CA.
-The Wolfen. Morrow, 1978; Hodder, 1978 [NYC]

STRINGER, ARTHUR (JOHN ARBUTHNOTT). 1874-1950. Ref: EM. SC: James Durkin, in at least those marked JD.
The City of Peril. Knopf, 1923 [NYC]
The Diamond Thieves. Bobbs, 1923; Hodder, 1925 ss [NYC]
The Door of Dread. Bobbs, 1916; Amalgamated, 1925 [NYC]
-Empty Hands. Bobbs, 1924; Hodder, 1924
The Ghost Plane. Bobbs, 1940
The Gun-Runner. Dodge, 1909
The Hand of Peril. Macmillan, 1915
The House of Intrigue. Bobbs, 1918 [NYC]
In Bad with Sinbad. Bobbs, 1926
The Man Who Couldn't Sleep. Bobbs, 1919 ss [NYC]
-Manhandled, with Russell Holmen. Grossett, 1924 (Novelization of the movie.)
-Marriage by Capture. Bobbs, 1933; Methuen, 1934
Never-Fail Blake; see The Shadow
Night Hawk. McClure, 1908 [NYC]
Phantom Wires. Little, 1907; Daily Mail, 1909 JD
The Shadow. Century, 1913. Also published as: Never-Fail Blake. Burt, 1924
-Shadowed Victory. Bobbs, 1943; Hodder, 1944
-The Silver Poppy. Appleton, 1903; Methuen, 1904
-Star in a Mist. Bobbs, 1943
-The Story Without a Name, with Russell Holman. Grosset, 1924 (Novelization of the movie.)
-Twin Tales. Bobbs, 1921 (2 novelets.)
The Under Groove. McClure, 1908 ss
The Wire Tappers. Little, 1906 JD [NYC]
-The Wolf Woman. Bobbs, 1928; Paul, 1929

STROBEL, MARION. 1895-   . SC: A. Lincoln Lacy, in both titles.
Ice Before Killing. Scribner, 1943 [Chi.]
Kiss and Kill. Scribner, 1946 [N.Y.]

STRONG, BEN. Joint pseudonym of Emeric Hulme-Beaman, q.v., and William Senior Ellis. SC: Prof. Adrian Criddle = AC.
The Secret of Gnome Head. Hodder, 1928 AC
The Shadow on the Course. Hamilton, 1926
The Studdingly Stables Mystery. Hodder, 1926
The Track of the Slayer. Hodder, 1925 AC

STRONG, CHARLES STANLEY. 1906-1962. Pseudonyms: Kelvin McKay, Charles Stoddard, qq.v.

STRONG, EDMUND C.
Manacle and Bracelet; or, The Dead Man's Secret. Laird, 1888

STRONG, HARRINGTON. Pseudonym of Johnston McCulley, q.v.
The Brand of Silence. Chelsea, 1924 [NYC]
The Hooded Stranger. Hutchinson, 1926
Legal Settlement. Lloyd, 1922
The Scarlet Scourge. Hutchinson, 1927
The Spider's Den. Hutchinson, 1926
Who Killed William Drew? Chelsea, 1925; Skeffington, 1926

STRONG, HERO. Pseudonym of Clara Augusta Jones. Other pseudonym: Clara Augusta, q.v.
A Beautiful Woman's Sin; or, The Scarred Arm. Street, 1890
-Born to Command; or, The Mistress of Hillmere. Street, 1890
Found Dead; or, The Charles Street Mystery. Street, 1892

STRONG, L(EONARD) A(LFRED) G(EORGE). 1896-1958. Ref: CC. SC: Insp. Ellis McKay = EM. Set: Eng.
All Fall Down. Collins, 1944; Doubleday, 1944 EM
Murder Plays an Ugly Scene; see Othello's Occupation
Odd Man In. Pitman, 1938 ss
Othello's Occupation. Collins, 1945. U.S. title: Murder Plays an Ugly Scene. Doubleday, 1945 EM
Slocombe Dies. Collins, 1942
Treason in the Egg. Collins, 1958 EM
Which I Never. Collins, 1950; Macmillan, 1952 EM

STRONG, MICHAEL. 1929-   . Was with the Colonial Service in Afr.; studied law, was with a financial organization, then returned to Afr.

Danger Feeds My Fear. Hutchinson, 1980; Walker, 1980 [Fr.]
The Wolves Came Down from the Mountain. Long, 1979; Walker, 1979

STROTHER, ELSIE (FRANCES) W(ARMOTH WEITZEL). 1912- .
Island of Terror. Avalon, 1976
-Rendezvous at Live Oaks. Avalon, 1975

STROUP, WILLIAM
The Mark of Pak San Ri. Book Company of America, 1965 [Kor.]

STRUTTON, BILL [WILLIAM HAROLD STRUTTON]. 1918- . Ref: CA.
The Carpaccio Caper; see A Glut of Virgins
A Glut of Virgins. Macdonald, 1974. U.S. title: The Carpaccio Caper. Coward, 1973 [Venice]
A Jury of Angels. Hodder, 1957

STUART, AIMEE (McHARDY), 1890- , and PHILIP STUART, 1887- .
Nine Till Six. French (NYC), 1931 (3-act play.)

STUART, ALAN
The Unwilling Angel. Ward, 1955

STUART, ANNE [ANNE KRISTINE STUART OHLRAGGE]
Cameron's Landing. Doubleday, 1977
The Demon Count. Dell, 1980
The Demon Count's Daughter. Dell, 1980
Demonwood. Dell, 1979

STUART, ANTHONY. Pseudonym of Julian Anthony Stuart Hale, 1940- . SC: Vladimir Gull, in all titles.
Force Play. Macdonald, 1980; Arbor, 1979 [NYC]
Midwinter Madness. Arbor, 1979
Snap Judgment. Macdonald, 1977. U.S. title: That Man Gull. Arbor, 1979 [Rum.]
That Man Gull; see Snap Judgment
Vicious Circles. Macdonald, 1978; Arbor, 1979 [Rome]

STUART, BLAIR. Pseudonym of Michael Ewings. Joint pseudonym with Colin Northway: Frank Ross, q.v.
Bloodwealth. Macmillan (London), 1980

STUART, BRIAN. Pseudonym of Brian Arthur Worthington-Stuart. Other pseudonym: Peter Meredith, q.v. SC: Knock-Out Kavanagh, in at least those marked KK.
The Affair at Sidi Brahim. Ward, 1948 KK
Beth Takes Charge. Ward, 1954
The Case Is Altered. Ward, 1955
Diamond Cut Diamond. Ward, 1955
Knock-Out Kavanagh. Ward, 1948 KK
Mysterious Monsieur Moray. Ward, 1950
The Serpent's Fang. Ward, 1951
The Silver Phantom Murder. Ward, 1950 KK

STUART, DEE. Pseudonym: Nick Carter, q.v.
Christina. Pyramid, 1977

STUART, DONALD. 1897-1980. Pseudonym: Gerald Verner, q.v. Those titles listed below without publisher were issued by Amalgamated Press and feature Sexton Blake. Other SC: Lionel Crane, in at least those marked LC.
The Bells of Doom. 1936
The Burmese Daggar. 1939
The Case of the Missing Estate Agent. 1932
The Cottage of Terror. 1935
Danger at Westway's. 1938
Dead Man's Secret. 1932
The Death Road. 1930
The Embankment Crime. 1932
The Empty House Murder. 1933
The Fence's Victim. 1930
The Garden City Crime. 1931
Guilty, But Insane. 1933
The Hidden Menace. 1933
The Hodded Raider. 1931
The Man in the Dark. Wright, 1935
The Man Outside. Wright, 1934
Midnight Murder. Wright, 1935 LC
The Motor Bus Murder. 1934
The Next Victim. 1931
The £1,000,000 Film Murder. 1933
The Riddle of the Sunken Garden. 1937
The Secret of the Moor House. 1938
The Secret of Seven. 1932
The Secret of the Hulk. 1940
The Secret of the Sealed Room. 1935
The Shadow. Wright, 1934
The Squealer's Secret. 1932
The Terror of Lonely Tor. 1931
The Third Victim. 1939
The Three Who Paid. 1938
The Time of the Crime. 1938
The Truth About Lord Tench. 1935
Twenty Years of Hate. 1940
The Unknown Menace. 1937
The Valley of Terror. Wright, 1935
The Village of Fear. 1934
The White Friar. Wright, 1934; Godwin, 1935 LC

STUART, ELIZABETH [ELIZABETH STUART PRATT]
The Shaking Shadow. Signet, 1967 [Maine]

STUART, ESME. Pseudonym of Amelie Claire Leroy, 1851- .
Arrested. White, 1896; Appleton, 1897

STUART, IAN. Pseudonym of Alistair (Stuart) MacLean, 1922- , q.v. Both titles reissued as by Alistair MacLean.
The Black Shrike; see The Dark Crusader
The Dark Crusader. Collins, 1961. U.S. title: The Black Shrike. Scribner, 1961 [Fiji]
The Satan Bug. Collins, 1962; Scribner, 1962

STUART, IAN. 1927- . Ref: CA.
Death from Disclosure. Hale, 1976
Fatal Switch. Hale, 1978
Flood Tide. Hale, 1977
Pictures in the Dark. Hale, 1979
The Renshaw Strike. Hale, 1980
Sand Trap. Hale, 1977
The Snow on the Ben. Ward, 1961
A Weekend to Kill. Hale, 1978

STUART, ILIAN
The Man in the Rolls-Royce. Heinemann, 1958

STUART, JANE. 1942- . Ref: CA.
Passerman's Hollow. McGraw, 1974

STUART, JOHN
Ashes to Ashes. International Publishers, 1969 [Fr.]

STUART, MIRANDA. Pseudonym of Muriel Lillah Stuart Thompson, 1902- .
Dead Men Sing No Songs. Hodder, 1939

STUART, ROBERT
Duncan Ross—Detective-Sergeant. Blackie, 1935

STUART, SIDNEY. Pseudonym of Michael (Angelo) Avallone (Jr.), 1924- , q.v. Other pseudonyms: Nick Carter, Mark Dane, Jean-Anne de Pre, Priscilla Dalton, Dora Highland, Stuart Jason, Steve Michaels, Dorothea Nile, Edwina Noone, Max Walker, qq.v.
The Beast with the Red Hands. Popular Library, 1973
The Night Walker. Award, 1964 (Novelization of the movie.)
Young Dillinger. Belmont, 1965 (Novelization of the movie.)

STUART, VIVIAN. Pseudonym of Charles Stuart-Vernon.
The Darkness of Love. Pyramid, 1977
Darnley's Bride. Pyramid, 1976 [Scot.]
The New Mrs. Aldrich. Pyramid, 1976

STUART, WARREN
The Sword and the Net. Morrow, 1941; Joseph, 1942

STUART, WILLIAM L(ISLE). 1915- .
Dead Ahead; see The Dead Lie Still
The Dead Lie Still. Farrar, 1945. Also published as: Dead Ahead. Ace, 1953 [NYC]
Night Cry. Dial, 1948; Boardman, 1951

STUART-VERNON, CHARLES. Pseudonym: Vivian Stuart, q.v.

STUBBS, HARRY CLEMENT. 1922- . Pseudonym: Hal Clement, q.v.

STUBBS, JEAN. 1926- . Ref: CA, TC. SC: Insp. John Lintott = JL.
The Case of Kitty Ogilvie. Macmillan (London), 1970; Walker, 1971 [Scot., 1700s]
Dear Laura. Macmillan (London), 1973; Stein, 1973 JL [Eng., 1800s]
The Golden Crucible. Macmillan (London), 1976; Stein, 1976 JL [S.F., 1906]
My Grand Enemy. Macmillan (London), 1967; Stein, 1968 [Eng., 1750s]
The Painted Face. Macmillan (London), 1974; Stein, 1974 [Paris, 1902] JL

STUDER, PAUL
In the Shadow of Gold. Greenberg, 1935

STURGEON, THEODORE (HAMILTON). 1918- . Name originally: Edward Hamilton Waldo. See also: Ellery Queen. Ref: CA.
Some of Your Blood. Ballantine, 1961; Sphere, 1967
Sturgeon's West, with Don(ald G.) Ward, 1911- , q.v. Doubleday, 1973 ss

STURROCK, JEREMY. U.S. byline: J. G. Jeffreys. Pseudonym of Ben(jamin James) Healey, 1908- , q.v. SC: Jeremy Sturrock, in all titles, set in Eng., ca.1800.
A Conspiracy of Poisons. Hale, 1977; Walker, 1977
The Thief Taker; see The Village of Rogues
The Village of Rogues. Macmillan (London), 1972. U.S. title: The Thief Taker. Walker, 1972
A Wicked Way to Die. Macmillan (London), 1973; Walker, 1973
The Wilful Lady. Macmillan (London), 1975; Walker, 1975

STURT, E. M. LEADER
A Detective's Memoirs and other stories. Drane, 1921 ss

STUTLEY, S. J. and A. E. COPP
The Melbourne Mystery. Bodley, 1929 [Melb.]
The Poisoned Glass. Bodley, 1930 [Australia]

STUYVESANT, ALICE. Pseudonym of Alice M(uriel Livingston) Williamson, 1869-1933, q.v. Other pseudonym: Dona Teresa de Savallo, q.v. See also: C(harles) N(orris) Williamson, 1859-1920.

STYLES, (FRANK) SHOWELL. 1908- . Pseudonym: Glyn Carr, q.v. Ref: CA, CC, MP, TC. SC: Abercrombie Lewker, in at least those marked AL (see also the Glyn Carr entry).
Dark Hazard. Selwyn, 1948
Hammer Island. Selwyn, 1947 AL
Kidnap Castle. Selwyn, 1947 AL
-Land from the Sea. Faber, 1952
-Path to Glory. Faber, 1951
The Rising of the Lark. Selwyn, 1948
-Shadow Buttress. Faber, 1959
-Sir Devil. Selwyn, 1949
Traitor's Mountain. Selwyn, 1945; Macmillan, 1946 AL

SUBOND, VALERIE. Pseudonym of V(alerie) Merle (Spanner) Grayland, q.v. Other pseudonym: Lee Belvedere, q.v.
The Heights of Havenrest. Beagle, 1972
The House over Hell Valley. Beagle, 1974 [N.Z.]

SUDAK, EUNICE
The Icepick in Ollie Birk. Lancer, 1966 [NYC]
The Raven. Lancer, 1963 (Novelization of the movie.)
Tales of Terror. Lancer, 1962 (Novelization of the movie.)
-X. Lancer, 1963 (Novelization of the movie.)

SUE, (MARIE JOSEPH) EUGENE. 1804-1857. Ref: CC, DD, EM, MC, MP.
The Female Bluebeard; or, The Adventurer. (London), 1845; Winchester, 1844
The Mysteries of Paris. Wiley, 1843; Winchester, 1844 (Translation of "Les Mysteres de Paris." Paris, 1843-4.)

SUGAR, ANDREW. SC: Alex Jason (The Enforcer) = AJ; Israeli Commandos = IC.
The Alps Assignment. Manor, 1975 IC
The Aswan Assignment. Manor, 1974 IC [Egypt]
Bio Blitz. Manor, 1975 AJ
Calling Dr. Kill. Lancer, 1973 AJ
Caribbean Kill; see The Enforcer
The Cult Breaker. Manor, 1979
The Enforcer. Lancer, 1973. Also published as: Caribbean Kill. Manor, 1975 AJ [Carib.]
The Fireball Assignment. Manor, 1974 IC
The Kamikaze Assignment. Manor, 1975 IC
Kill City. Lancer, 1973 AJ [NYC]
Kill Deadline. Lancer, 1973 AJ
Steel Trap. Manor, 1975 AJ
-Yank. Manor, 1975

SULLIVAN, (EDWARD) ALAN. 1868-1947. Pseudonym: Sinclair Murray, q.v.
The Jade God. Bles, 1924; Century, 1925

SULLIVAN, LEWIS W.
The Scarlet Cord. Major, 1977

SULLIVAN, SEAN MEI. Pseudonym of Jerry Sohl, 1913-   , q.v.
 Super Man Chu. Ballantine, 1974 (Novelization of the movie.) [China]

SULLIVAN, TIM (D.)
 Glitter Street. Rawson, 1979

SULLIVAN, VERNON. Pseudonym of Boris Vian, 1920-1959.
 I Spit on Your Grave. Audubon, 1971 (Translation of "J'Irai Cracher Sur Vos Tombes." 1947.)

SULLIVAN, VIRGINIA
 Permanent Wave. Macrae Smith, 1929

SULLY, KATHLEEN (M.). 1910-   . Ref: CA.
 -Merrily to the Grave. Davies, 1958
 -Through the Wall. Davies, 1957

SULZBERGER, C(YRUS) L(EO). 1912-   .
 Ref: CA.
 The Tooth Merchant. Quadrangle, 1973; Collins, 1973

SUMMERS, A. WELBOURNE. Pseudonym: Kilsyth Stellier, q.v.

SUMMERS, DENNIS
 -A Madness from Mars. Hale, 1976

SUMMERS, HOLLIS SPURGEON. 1915-   .
 Ref: CA. Joint pseudonym with James Francis Anthony Rourke, 1922-   : Jim Hollis, q.v.

SUMMERS, KEITH
 Design for Death. Boardman, 1957 [Tangier]

SUMMERSCALES, ROWLAND. 1912-   . Pseudonym: Robert Gaines, q.v.
 The Ballot. Hale, 1979; St. Martin's, 1979

SUMMERTON, MARGARET. Pseudonym: Jan Roffman, q.v. Ref: TC.
 A Dark and Secret Place. Collins, 1977; Doubleday, 1977 [It.]
 The Ghost Flowers. Collins, 1973; Doubleday, 1973 [Cyprus]
 A Memory of Darkness. Hodder, 1967; Dutton, 1967
 Nightingale at Noon. Hodder, 1963; Dutton, 1963 [Fr.]
 Quin's Hide. Hodder, 1964; Dutton, 1965
 The Red Pavilion. Hodder, 1968
 Ring of Mischief. Hodder, 1965; Dutton, 1965 [Switz.]
 The Saffron Summer. Collins, 1975; Doubleday, 1975
 The Sand Rose. Collins, 1969; Doubleday, 1969 [Tun.]
 The Sea House. Hodder, 1961; Holt, 1961
 A Small Wilderness. Hodder, 1959
 The Sunset Hour. Hodder, 1957
 Sweetcrab. Collins, 1971; Doubleday, 1971
 Theft in Kind. Hodder, 1962

SUMNER, CID RICKETTS. 1890-1970. Ref: CA.
 Withdraw Thy Foot. Coward, 1964; Hale, 1966 [Mass.]

SUMNER, E. E. Pseudonym.
 Chance Encounter. Hale, 1967
 The Juryman. Hale, 1968
 Second-Hand Death. Hale, 1966

SUNAGEL, LOIS A(NN) 1926-   . Ref: CA.
 The Amethyst Quest. Avalon, 1975
 Deception on Peregrine Island. Manor, 1979
 The Last Member of the Family. Manor, 1980
 -A Promise to Keep. Manor, 1980
 The Shadow of the Needle. Avalon, 1976
 The Tangled Web. Major, 1979

SUNDERLAND, KAYE
 Late Harvest. Paul, 1933
 The Third Seat Back. Benn, 1930

SUNDMAN, PER OLOF. 1922-   . Born in Swed., educated in Stockholm; owner of farm and tourist hotel; elected to Swedish Parliament in 1968.
 Two Days, Two Nights. Pantheon, 1969 (Translation of "Tva Dagar, Tva Natter." Stockholm, 1965.) [Swed.]

SUNMAN, WILLIAM R.
 The Mystery of Wolverston Grange. Crombie, 1889

SUSSMAN, BARTH JULES
 Shanghai. Signet, 1980 [Shanghai, 1945]

SUTCLIFFE, HALLIWELL. 1870-1932.
 Persons Unknown. Long, 1928

SUTHERLAND, DAN
 Mystery at Blackwater. French (London), 1955 (3-act play based on "The Woman in White" by Wilkie Collins, 1824-1889, q.v.)

SUTHERLAND, MORRIS. Pseudonym of Gwendolen Sutherland Morris.
 -The Hunting Ground. Rich, 1934
 -Mountain Fires. Rich, 1937
 The Perilous Errand. Rich, 1935
 -Second Storm. Butterworth, 1930
 -Send Danger. Rich, 1934

SUTHERLAND, NEIL PULSFORD
 The Pawn. Heinemann, 1952

SUTHERLAND, WILLIAM. Pseudonym of John Murray Cooper, 1908-   . SC: Insp. Haskell = H.
 Behind the Head-Lines. Arrowsmith, 1933 H
 Death Rides the Air Line. Arrowsmith, 1934; Kendall, 1934 [U.S.]
 The Proverbial Murder Case. Arrowsmith, 1935 H

SUTPHEN, (WILLIAM GILBERT) VAN TASSEL. 1861-1945.
 The Cardinal's Rose. Harper (NYC), 1900; Harper (London), 1901
 The Gates of Chance. Harper, 1904; Ward, 1908 ss
 In Jeopardy. Harper, 1922 [Md.]

SUTTON, ELIZABETH
 Dead Fingers. Fly, 1918 [N.Y.]

SUTTON, GRAHAM. Pseudonym: Antony Marsden, q.v.

SUTTON, HENRY. Ref: CA.
 The Sacrifice. Grosset, 1978; Sphere, 1980 [acad., Conn.]

SUTTON, JEFFERSON (H.). 1913-   . Ref: CA.
 Cassady. St. Martin's, 1979; Hale, 1981 [L.A.]

SVEDELID, OLOF. 1932-   . See: Leif Silbersky, 1938-   .

SWAIM, LAWRENCE. 1942-   . Ref: CA.
 The Killing. Holt, 1980 [S.F.]

SWAIN, DWIGHT VREELAND. 1915-   . Pseudonym: Nick Carter, q.v. Ref: CA.

SWAIN, VIRGINIA. 1899-   .
 -The Hollow Skin. Farrar, 1938

SWAN, ANNIE S. [MRS. ANNIE S. SWAN BURDETT-SMITH]. 1859-1943.
 -The Curse of Cowden. Hutchinson, 1897
 -The Dark House. Leng, 1941
 -A Mask of Gold. Hodder, 1906
 The Maclure Mystery. Leng, 1932 [Glasgow]
 -The Secret of Skye. Leng, 1940
 -The Secret Panel. Oliphant, 1888

SWAN, PHYLLIS. SC: Anna J (Anna Jagedinski), in all titles.
 The Death Inheritance. Leisure, 1980
 Find Sherri! Leisure, 1979
 Trigger Lady. Leisure, 1979

SWANN, FRANCIS. 1913-   . Ref: CA.
 Angelica. Lancer, 1973
 The Brass Key. Simon, 1964; Gollancz, 1965 [Maine]
 Hacienda Triste. Lancer, 1968
 Hellgate Plantation. Lancer, 1973
 House of Terror. Lancer, 1968
 Royal Street. Lancer, 1966
 You'll Hang, My Love!, with Lucille Emerick. Lancer, 1967

SWANN, INGO. 1933-   . Ref: CA.
 Star Fire. Souvenir, 1978; Dell, 1978

SWANTON, SCOTT
 Sweetheart. Bantam, 1980 [Calif.]

SWARTHOUT, GLENDON (FRED). 1918-   . Ref: CA.
 Skeletons. Doubleday, 1979; Secker, 1979 [N. Mex.]

SWARTWOUT, R(OBERT) E(GERTON)
 The Boat Race Murder. Grayson, 1933

SWATRIDGE, CHARLES JOHN. Pseudonym: Leslie Lance. Joint pseudonym with Irene Maude Mossop Swatridge: Theresa Charles, q.v. Pseudonym of Irene Maude Mossop Swatridge alone: Jan Tempest, q.v. Ref: CA.

SWATRIDGE, IRENE MAUDE MOSSOP. Pseudonym: Jan Tempest, q.v. Joint pseudonym with Charles John Swatridge: Theresa Charles, q.v. Pseudonym of Charles John Swatridge alone: Leslie Lance, q.v. Ref: CA.

SWAZEE, RUTH
 A Time of Night. Manor, 1979

SWEENEY, R. L. See also: R. A. Anderson.
 The Hangman's Loose. Eldridge, 1963 (1-act play.)

SWEENEY, W. A.
 Murder by Legacy. Modern Fiction, 1945

SWEM, CHARLES LEE. For many year secretary to President Woodrow Wilson.
 Werewolf. Doubleday, 1928; Hutchinson, 1929 [N.J.]

SWERDLOW, JOEL. Newspaper columnist; author of magazine articles.
 Code Z. Putnam, 1979; Secker, 1979 [Wash. D.C.]

SWIFT, ANTHONY. Pseudonym of J(oseph) Jefferson Farjeon, 1883-1955, q.v.
 Interrupted Honeymoon. Hale, 1945
 Murder at a Police Station. Hale, 1943; Bobbs, 1943, as by J. Jefferson Farjeon
 November 9th at Kersea. Hale, 1944

SWIFT, BENJAMIN. Pseudonym of William Romaine Paterson, 1871-   .
 The Death Man. Chapman, 1908
 -The Destroyer. Unwin, 1898; Stokes, 1898
 Lady of the Night. Nash, 1913
 -Ludus Amoris. Wellby, 1902
 -The Tormenter. Unwin, 1897; Scribner, 1897
 -What Lies Beneath. Chapman, 1917

SWIFT, IKE
 Sketches of Gotham. Fox, 1906 ss, some criminous

SWIGGETT, HOWARD. 1891-1957. Graduate of Yale; businessman and author. SC: Garrett Maynard = GM.
 The Corpse in the Derby Hat. Little, 1937. British title: The Stairs Lead Nowhere. Heinemann, 1937 GM [N.Y.]
 The Hidden and the Hunted. Morrow, 1950; Heinemann, 1951
 Most Secret...Most Immediate. Houghton, 1944 GM
 The Stairs Lead Nowhere; see The Corpse in the Derby Hat
 The Strongbox. Houghton, 1955; Hodder, 1956 [Eng.]

SWINGLER, J. H.
 Circumstantial Evidence. Digby Long, 1897

SWINNERTON, FRANK (ARTHUR). 1884-1982. Ref: CC.
 On the Shady Side. Hutchinson, 1970; Doubleday, 1971

SWINSON, ARTHUR. 1915-1970. Ref: CA. SC: Sergeant Cork, in both titles, taken from the British TV series.
 Sergeant Cork's Casebook. Arrow, 1965 ss [Eng., 1890]
 Sergeant Cork's Second Casebook. Arrow, 1966 ss [Eng., 1890]

SWITZER, ROBERT
 I Was Going Anyway. Macmillan, 1961 [Can.]

SWORD, JOHN, SENIOR. 1877-   .
 The Bullitzer Baby Case. Jarrolds, 1925

SYDNEY, GEORGE. House name.
 Countdown for Murder. Amalgamated, 1962 (Sexton Blake.)

SYKES, CHRISTOPHER (HUGH). 1907-   . Ref: CA.
 High-Minded Murder. Home, 1944

SYKES, CLAUDE W(ALTER). 1883-   .
 The Nine Pointed Star. Hamilton, 1926
 The Strange Adventures of Handel Archimedes. Hamilton, 1929

SYKES, W(ILLIAM) STANLEY. 1894-1961. Ref: CC. SC: Insp. Dennis Drury, in at least those marked DD. Set: Eng.
 The Harness of Death. Lane, 1932; Dodd, 1932 DD
 The Man Who Was Dead; see The Missing Money-Lender
 The Missing Money-Lender. Lane, 1931. U.S. title: The Man Who Was Dead. Dodd, 1931 DD

The Ray of Doom. Hodder, 1935

SYLVAINE, VERNON. 1897-   .
   A Spot of Bother. French (London), 1938 (3-act play.)
-Warn That Man! French (London), 1943 (3-act play.)

SYLVESTER, JOHN. Pseudonym of Hector Hawton, 1901-   , q.v.
   The Phantom. Lunn, 1946
   The Terror of Tregarwith. Amalgamated, 1943 (Sexton Blake.)

SYLVESTER, ROBERT (McPHIERSON). 1907-1975. Ref: CA.
   The Big Boodle. Random, 1954; Hammond, 1957. Also published as: Night in Havana. Corgi, 1958 [Havana]

SYMONDS, F(RANCIS) ADDINGTON. 1893-   .
   Those titles listed below without publisher feature Sexton Blake and were issued by Amalgamated Press. Other SC: Insp./Supt. Maxwell Quayne, in at least those marked MQ. Set: Eng.
   By Order of the Soviet. 1925
   The Case of the Golden Stool. 1925
   The Case of the Hold-Up King. 1927
   The Case of the Twisted Trail. 1922
   Death Goes Window Shopping. Ward, 1961 MQ
   The Golden Casket. 1921
   The Iron Claw. 1921
   The Man from Australia. 1928
   Murder of Me. Wells Gardner, 1946
   Out of the Fog. 1926
   Portrait of the Accused. Boardman, 1952
   The Red Dwarf. 1922
   Smile and Murder. Boardman, 1954
   Spotlight on Murder. Ward, 1962 MQ
   Stone Dead. Ward, 1961 MQ
   The Valley of Fear. 1921

SYMONS, BERYL (MARY ELIZABETH TAUBMAN).
   SC: Jane Carberry, in at least those marked JC; Insp. Henry Doight, in at least those marked HD. Set: Eng.
   Blind Justice. Jenkins, 1933
   By Whose Hand? Jenkins, 1936
   The Devine Court Mystery. Jenkins, 1928 HD
   Haunted Hollow. Jenkins, 1934
   Jane Carberry and the Laughing Fountain. Jenkins, 1943 JC
   Jane Carberry: Detective. Jenkins, 1940 JC [Brus.]
   Jane Carberry Investigates. Jenkins, 1940 JC
   Jane Carberry's Week-End. Jenkins, 1947 JC
   The Leering House. Jenkins, 1929 HD
   Magnet for Murder. Jenkins, 1941 JC
   The Opal Murder Case. Jenkins, 1932 HD
   Strange Witness. Jenkins, 1934
   Through a Glass Darkly. Jenkins, 1938

SYMONS, JULIAN (GUSTAVE). 1912-   . SC: CA, CC, DD, EM, MC, TC. SC: Insp. Bland = B; Francis Quarles = FQ. Set: Eng.
   The Belting Inheritance. Collins, 1965; Harper, 1965
   The Blackheath Poisonings. Collins, 1978; Harper, 1978 [Eng., 1890s]
   Bland Beginning. Gollancz, 1949; Harper, 1949 B [Eng.,1924]
   Bogue's Fortune; see The Paper Chase
   The Broken Penny. Gollancz, 1953; Harper, 1953
   The Colour of Murder. Collins, 1957; Harper, 1958
   The End of Solomon Grundy. Collins, 1964; Harper, 1964
   Francis Quarles Investigates. Panther, 1965 ss FQ
   The Gigantic Shadow. Collins, 1958. U.S. title: The Pipe Dream. Harper, 1959
   The Immaterial Murder Case. Gollancz, 1945; Macmillan, 1957 B
   The Killing of Francie Lake. Collins, 1962. U.S. title: The Plain Man. Harper, 1962
   A Man Called Jones. Gollancz, 1947 B
   The Man Who Killed Himself. Collins, 1967; Harper, 1967
   The Man Who Lost His Wife. Collins, 1970; Harper, 1971 [Yugos.]
   The Man Whose Dreams Came True. Collins, 1968; Harper, 1969
   Murder! Murder! Fontana, 1961 ss FQ
   The Narrowing Circle. Gollancz, 1954; Harper, 1955
   The Paper Chase. Collins, 1956. U.S. title: Bogue's Fortune. Harper, 1957 [acad.]
   The Pipe Dream; see The Gigantic Shadow
   The Plain Man; see The Killing of Francie Lake
   The Players and the Game. Collins, 1972; Harper, 1972
   The Plot Against Roger Rider. Collins, 1973; Harper, 1973 [Sp.]
   The Progress of a Crime. Collins, 1960; Harper, 1960
   Sweet Adelaide. Collins, 1980; Harper, 1980 [Eng., 1880s]
   The Thirty-First of February. Gollancz, 1950; Harper, 1951
   A Three-Pipe Problem. Collins, 1975; Harper, 1975

SYMONS, MAURICE (ALBERT). 1904-   .
   SC: George Roberts, in all titles. Set: Eng.
   The Girl in Ocean View. Boardman, 1961
   Lot 41—Dead Auctioneer. Boardman, 1964
   Pattern of Murder. Boardman, 1962

TABOR, MARGARET
   Unity Penfold. Heinemann, 1980. U.S. title (?): Nightmare Street. PB, 1982

TABORI, GEORGE. 1914-   . Ref: CA.
   The Good One. Permabooks, 1960 [Afr., W.]

TABORI, PAUL. 1908-1974. Ref: CA. SC: The Hunters = H.
-Bricks Upon Dust. Hodder, 1945
   Diana Meets Murder. Progressive Press, 1949
   The Doomsday Brain. Tandem, 1968; Pyramid, 1967 H
-The Frontier. Low, 1950
   Hazard Island. New English Library, 1973
   He Never Came Back; see The Leaf of a Lime Tree
-Heritage of Mercy. Low, 1949
   The Invisible Eye. Tandem, 1969; Pyramid, 1967 H
-Japanese Jeopardy. Hodder, 1943
   The Leaf of a Lime Tree. Hodder, 1945. U.S. title: He Never Came Back. Dutton, 1947
-Lily Dale. New English Library, 1972; Belmont, 1972
   Murder in Majorca. Consul, 1961 [Maj.]
   Perdita's End. Cassell, 1952 [Paris]
-The Pleasure House. New English Library, 1974
-Salvatore. Cassell, 1951
   Sneeze on a Monday. Hodder, 1941
-Song of the Scorpions. New English Library, 1971
   They Came to London. Hodder, 1943; Macmillan, 1943
   The Torture Machine. Pyramid, 1969 H

TACK, ALFRED. 1906-   . Ref: CA, CC. SC: John Harley, in at least those marked JH. Set: Eng.
   The Big Kidnap. Long, 1969
   Death Kicks a Pebble. Jenkins, 1951
   Death Takes a Dive. Jenkins, 1950; Roy, 1957 JH
   Forecast—Murder. Long, 1967
   The Great Hijack. Long, 1970; Doubleday, 1970
   Interviewing's Killing. Jenkins, 1947 JH
   Killing Business. Jenkins, 1949
   A Murder Is Staged. Jenkins, 1949
   Murder Takes Over. Long, 1966
   P.A. to Murder. Long, 1966
   The Prospect's Dead. Jenkins, 1948 JH
   Return of the Assassin. Barker, 1975; Putnam, 1974
   Selling's Murder! Jenkins, 1946 JH
   The Spy Who Wasn't Exchanged. Long, 1968; Doubleday, 1969 [Moscow]
   The Test Match Murder. Jenkins, 1948
   The Top Steal. Long, 1968; Doubleday, 1968

TAFFRAIL. Pseudonym of Henry Taprell Dorling, 1883-1968, under which byline some of these titles may have appeared.
-Arctic Convoy. Hodder, 1956
-Chenies. Hodder, 1943
   Cypher K. Hodder, 1932
   Dover-Ostend. Hodder, 1933
-Euridice. Hodder, 1936
-Fred Travis, A.B. Hodder, 1939
-H.M.S. Anonymous. Jenkins, 1920
-The Jade Lizard. Hodder, 1951
-Kerrell. Hodder, 1931
   The Lonely Bungalow. Hodder, 1930
   The Man from Scapa Flow. Hodder, 1933
-Michael Bray. Hodder, 1925
-Mid-Atlantic. Hodder, 1936
-Minor Operation. Pearson, 1917 ss
   Mystery of Milford Haven. Hodder, 1936
   Mystery Cruise. Hodder, 1937
-The Navy in Action. Hodder, 1940
-The New Moon. Hodder, 1952
-Off Shore. Pearson, 1917 ss
-"Oh, Joshua!" Hodder, 1920
   Operation 'M.O.'. Hodder, 1938
-Pincher Martin, O.D. Chambers, 1916
-Pirates. Hodder, 1929
-Sea, Spray and Spindrift. Pearson, 1917 ss
   Second Officer. Hodder, 1935
   Seventy North—70°N. Hodder, 1934
   The Shetland Plan. Hodder, 1939 [Scot.]
-Stand By! Pearson, 1916 ss
-The Sub. Hodder, 1917
-Toby Shad. Hodder, 1949
-The Watch Below. Pearson, 1918 ss

TAFT, WILLIAM NELSON. 1889-   .
   On Secret Service. Harper, 1921 ss

TAGGART, DONALD
   Dial M for Money. GM, 1972

TAGGART, TOM (BARNARD). Joint pseudonym with James Reach, 1909?-1970, q.v.: Ross MacRoss, q.v. All titles are plays; number of acts in parenthesis.
   Deadwood Dick. French (NYC), 1953 (3)
   Dear Phoebe, with James Reach. French (NYC), 1956
   Do—or Die! French (NYC), 1955 (3)
   Gentle Hearts and Murder. French (NYC), 1952 (3)
   Lay Down, You're Dead! French (NYC), 1943 (3)
   Lily, the Felon's Daughter. French (NYC), 1949 (3)
   Nick of the Woods. French (NYC), 1940 (3)
   Short and Sweet. French (NYC), 1957 (Plays, some criminous.)
   Sinister House. French (NYC), 1938 (3)
   Spider Island. French (NYC), 1942 (3)
   Three Dots and a Dash. French (NYC), 1942 (3)

TAILLET, EDMOND and RACHEL DESMOND
   The Real Connection. Zebra, 1977

TAIN, ISABEL
   The Cherrycake Death. Long, 1967 [Scot.]

TAIT, EUPHEMIA MARGARET. Pseudonym: John Ironside, q.v.

TAIT, JAMES SELWIN. 1846-1917.
   My Friend Pasquale and other stories. Tait, 1892 ss, some criminous
-Who Is the Man? Tait, 1892; Chapman, 1890

TAIT, WILLIAM
   Tip and Run. Hutchinson, 1940

TAKAGI, AKIMITSU. 1920-   .
   Honeymoon to Nowhere. Anthos (Australia), 1972. U.S. title: No Patent on Murder. Playboy, 1977 (Translation from the Japanese.) [Jap.]
   The Informer. Anthos (Australia), 1971 (Translation from the Japanese.) [Jap.]
   No Patent on Murder; see Honeymoon to Nowhere

TALBOT, CARL. Pseudonym of Charles Hammond Hipkins, 1893-   .
   The Cameron Mystery. Eldon, 1935
   Love in Danger. Eldon, 1934
   The White Badger. Eldon, 1935

TALBOT, HAKE. Pseudonym of Henning Nelms, 1900-   . SC: Rogan Kincaid, in both titles.
   The Hangman's Handyman. Simon, 1942 [N.C.]
   Rim of the Pit. Simon, 1944 [New Eng.]

TALBOT, HENRY
   Catch Me a Traitor. Hale, 1966
   Cold Line to Moscow. Hale, 1968
   A Spy in the Hand. Hale, 1966

TALMY, SHEL
   "Whadda We Do Now, Butch?" Pan, 1978

TANENBAUM, BARRY. 1944-   . See: Linda J. LaRosa, 1951-   .

TANJONG
   The Scarlet Bee. Hutchinson, 1919

TANNER, MARTIN
   Cut and Run. Cherry Tree, 1949

TANNOCK, MALCOLM
   The Humming Cliff. Ward, 1950
   Uneasy Money. Ward, 1951

TANOUS, PETER (JOSEPH). 1938-   . Ref: CA.
-The Earhart Mission. Simon, 1979; Deutsch, 1980
   The Petrodollar Takeover, with Paul (Arthur) Rubinstein, 1935-   . Putnam, 1975; Deutsch, 1976

The Wheat Killing, with Paul (Arthur)
  Rubinstein, 1935-   . Doubleday,
  1979; Deutsch, 1980
TARG, WILLIAM, 1907-   , and LOUIS HER-
  MAN, 1905-   . Ref for Targ: CA.
  The Case of Mr. Cassidy. Phoenix, 1939
    [Chi.]
TARMEY, MARTIN. 1932-   .
  Murphy's Game; see Outrage
  Outrage. Barrie, 1970. U.S. title: Mur-
    phy's Game. Harcourt, 1971 [Sp.]
  Skinman. Barrie, 1970; Harcourt, 1970
TARNE, ROSINA
  You Murdered Me. Crowther, 1946
TARPEY, J(ESSE TOLER) KINGSLEY
  The Bulldog Murder. Butterworth, 1930
TARRANT, C. A. Pseudonym.
  The Cat Climbs. Secker, 1936; Lippin-
    cott, 1937
TARRANT, JOHN. Pseudonym of Clive (Fred-
  erick) Egleton, 1927-   , q.v.
  The Clauberg Trigger. Macdonald, 1978;
    Atheneum, 1979 [Ger., 1945]
  The Rommel Plot. Macdonald, 1977; Lip-
    pincott, 1977 [Fr., WWII]
TARRANT, NOELINE
  Dead on Noon. Hale, 1965 [N.Z.]
TASCHDJIAN, CLAIRE (LOUISE). 1914-   .
  Ref: CA.
  Classified Death. Raven, 1980 [Vt.]
  The Peking Man Is Missing. Harper,
    1977; New English Library, 1978
    [Peking, 1940s]
TASHKENT, RENN
  The Ambiguous Man. Tallis, 1969
  Wreath for a Spy. Tallis, 1967
TATE, PETER. Science fiction writer and
  newspaper editor, living in Wales.
  -Country Love and Poison Rain. Double-
    day, 1973
TATE, RICHARD. Pseudonym of Anthony Mas-
  ters, 1940-   , q.v.
  Birds of a Bloodied Feather. Constable,
    1974
  The Dead Travel Fast. Constable, 1971
  The Donor. Constable, 1970
  The Emperor on Ice. Constable, 1973
    [U.S.]
TATE, SYLVIA. 1919-   . Ref: CC.
  Never by Chance. Harper, 1947
TATE, VELMA. 1913-   . Pseudonym: Fran-
  cine Davenport, q.v.
TATTERSALL, IVAN. Pseudonym of Ivan Tat-
  tersall Hodgkinson, 1891-   .
  The Society of Nobles. Chapman, 1928.
    U.S. title: The Avenging Brotherhood.
    McBride, 1929 [Fr.]
TATTERSALL, (HONOR) JILL (BLUNT).
  1931-   . Ref: CA. Set: Eng.
  Chanter's Chase. Hodder, 1978; Morrow,
    1978 [Eng., ca.1800]
  Damnation Reef. Hodder, 1980; Morrow,
    1979 [Carib., ca.1890]
  Dark at Noon. Hodder, 1979; Morrow,
    1979 [Wales, past]
  Enchanter's Castle. Collins, 1966
  Lady Ingram's Secret. Collins, 1970.
    U.S. title: Lady Ingram's Room. Mor-
    row, 1971 [Eng., 1808]
  Lady Ingram's Room; see Lady Ingram's
    Retreat
  Lyonesse Abbey. Collins, 1968; Morrow,
    1968
  The Midnight Oak. Collins, 1967
  Midsummer Masque. Collins, 1972; Mor-
    row, 1972 [Eng., ca.1810]
  The Shadows of Castle Fosse. Hodder,
    1976; Morrow, 1976
  A Summer's Cloud. Collins, 1965
  A Time at Tarragon. Collins, 1969
  The Wild Hunt. Hodder, 1974; Morrow,
    1974 [Eng., 1809]
  The Witches of All Saints. Hodder,
    1975; Morrow, 1975 [Eng., 1811]
TAUB, HAROLD J.
  The Takers. Pyramid, 1968
TAUB, LESTER S. 1920-   . Ref: CA.
  The Cossack Cowboy. Allen, 1971
  The Diamond Boomerang; see The Grabbers
  The Grabbers. Allen, 1969. U.S. title:
    The Diamond Boomerang. PB, 1970
    [S. Afr.]
  Myer for Hire. Allen, 1970
  Peter Krimsov. Allen, 1969

TAUBES, FRANK
  Run...Run...Run. Crowell, 1955; Muller,
    1955
TAUBMAN-GOLDIE, VALENTINE FRANCIS
  The Case of Sir Edward Talbot. Heine-
    mann, 1922; Dutton, 1922
TAUNTON, H(AROLD) R(OBY). 1880-   .
  Death in Diamonds. Hurst, 1936
  It Prowls at Dark. Hurst, 1937
  The Red Club. Hurst, 1926
  The Second Wager. Hurst, 1927
  Six Foot of Rope. Hurst, 1938
TAVIS, ALEC. Pseudonym of Alastair
  (MacTavish) Dunnett, 1908-   , q.v.
  The Duke's Day. H. Hamilton, 1970;
    Houghton, 1970 [Scot.]
TAYLOR, A. FRANK. Advertising copywriter,
  juvenile writer, detective in L.A.
  Sheriff's Office, article writer.
  How I Made a Million Dollars. Pageant,
    1960 [L.A.]
TAYLOR, BEATRICE
  Journey into Danger. Beagle, 1974
TAYLOR, BERNARD. 1937-   . Ref: CA.
  The Godsend. Souvenir, 1976; St. Mar-
    tin's, 1976
  -The Reaping. Souvenir, 1980; St. Mar-
    tin's, 1980
  Sweetheart, Sweetheart. Souvenir, 1977;
    St. Martin's, 1978
TAYLOR, BERT L(ESTON), 1866-1921, and
  ALVIN V. THOITS
  Under Three Flags. Rand, 1896
TAYLOR, C(ONSTANCE) LINDSAY. 1907-   .
  Pseudonym: Guy Cullingford, q.v.
  Ref: CC, TC.
  Murder with Relish. Skeffington, 1948
TAYLOR, CHARLES D(OONAN). 1938-   .
  Ref: CA.
  Show of Force. St. Martin's, 1980;
    Macdonald, 1981
TAYLOR, EDITH. 1913-   . Ref: CA.
  The Serpent Under It. Norton, 1973;
    Barker, 1973 [N.Y., acad.]
TAYLOR, ELSPETH
  Second Thursday. Bles, 1967
TAYLOR, FRANK
  House of the Hunter. Chicago Paperback
    House, 1962 [L.A.]
TAYLOR, GEORGIA ELIZABETH
  The Death of Jason Darby. World, 1970
    [Eng., 1778]
TAYLOR, GORDON. 1943-   .
  Place of the Dawn. Holt, 1975; Hamlyn,
    1979
TAYLOR, (FRANK HERBERT) GRIFFIN. 1917-   .
  Ref: CA.
  Mortlake. Houghton, 1960; H. Hamilton,
    1961
TAYLOR, H. BALDWIN. Pseudonym of Hillary
  (Baldwin) Waugh, 1920-   , q.v.
  Other pseudonyms: Elissa Grandower,
  Harry Walker, qq.v. SC: David Halli-
  day = DH.
  The Duplicate. Doubleday, 1964; Heine-
    mann, 1965 DH [Conn.]
  The Missing Tycoon; see The Trouble
    with Tycoons
  The Triumverate. Doubleday, 1966;
    Heinemann, 1966 DH [Conn.]
  The Trouble with Tycoons. Doubleday,
    1967. British title: The Missing Ty-
    coon. Hale, 1967 [N.Y.]
TAYLOR, HENDERSON
  Counterpoise of Death. Modern, 193?
  Phantom Killer. Modern, 1938
TAYLOR, IRIS
  Pussy Cat, Pussy Cat. Stockwell, 1978
TAYLOR, JACK. Pseudonym: Jonathan Gray,
  q.v.
TAYLOR, JUDSON R. Pseudonym of Harlan
  Page Halsey, 1837-1898, q.v. Other
  pseudonyms: Old Sleuth, Tony Pastor,
  qq.v.
  Abner Ferret, the Lawyer Detective.
    Published in an omnibus by Ogilvie
    under the Judson R. Taylor byline,
    but originally published as by Harry
    Rockwood, q.v.
  Gipsy Blair, the Western Detective.
    Ogilvie, 1882 [West]

Macon Moore, the Southern Detective.
  Ogilvie, 1882 [South]
The Man from the South. Street (Magnet)
Old Stonewall, the Colorado Detective.
  Street, 1888 [Colo.]
Phil Scott, the Indian Detective. Ogil-
  vie, 1882
TAYLOR, KATHARINE HAVILAND. 1888-1941.
  The Secret of the Little Gods. Hodder,
    1927
TAYLOR, MARY
  Murder on Tuesday. Hale, 1972
TAYLOR, MARY ANN. 1912-   . Ref: CA. SC:
  Emil Martin = EM.
  Appointment in Verona. Popular Library,
    1975 [It.]
  Portrait of a Dead Lady. Popular Li-
    brary, 1975
  Red Is for Shrouds. Raven, 1980 EM
    [Nev.]
  Return to Murder. Raven, 1980 EM
    [Nev.]
  The Serpent Heart. Pyramid, 1971
TAYLOR, MARY IMLEY. 1878-1938.
  The Man Who Awoke. Chelsea, 1927; Nel-
    son, 1929 [Boston]
TAYLOR, MATT
  The Famous McGarry Stories. Detective
    Book Club, 1958 ss [NYC]
TAYLOR, CAPTAIN (PHILIP) MEADOWS. 1808-
  1876.
  Confessions of a Thug. Bentley, 1839
TAYLOR, P(HILIP NEVILLE) WALKER. 1903-   .
  Byline also: Walker Taylor, q.v.
  SC: Commander Wraithlea, in all
  titles.
  Murder in the Flagship. Butterworth,
    1936; Mill, 1937 [S. Afr., ship]
  Murder in the Game Reserve. Butter-
    worth, 1937; Mill, 1938 [S. Afr.]
  Murder in the Suez Canal. Butterworth,
    1937 [Egypt]
  Murder in the Taj Mahal. Butterworth,
    1938 [India]
TAYLOR, PHOEBE ATWOOD. 1909-1976. Pseudo-
  nyms: Freeman Dana, Alice Tilton,
  qq.v. Ref: CA, CC, DD, EM, MP, TC.
  SC: Asey Mayo, in all titles.
  The Annulet of Guilt. Norton, 1938;
    Collins, 1939 [Cape Cod]
  The Asey Mayo Trio. Messner, 1946; Col-
    lins, 1946 (3 novelets.) [Cape Cod]
  Banbury Bog. Norton, 1938; Collins,
    1939 [Cape Cod]
  The Cape Cod Mystery. Bobbs, 1931
    [Cape Cod]
  The Criminal C.O.D. Norton, 1940; Col-
    lins, 1940 [Cape Cod]
  The Crimson Patch. Norton, 1936; Gol-
    lancz, 1936 [Cape Cod]
  The Deadly Sunshade. Norton, 1940; Col-
    lins, 1941 [Cape Cod]
  Death Lights a Candle. Bobbs, 1932
    [Cape Cod]
  Deathblow Hill. Norton, 1935; Gollancz,
    1936 [Cape Cod]
  Diplomatic Corpse. Little, 1951; Col-
    lins, 1951 [Cape Cod]
  Figure Away. Norton, 1937; Collins,
    1938 [Cape Cod]
  Going, Going, Gone. Norton, 1943; Col-
    lins, 1944 [Cape Cod]
  The Mystery of the Cape Cod Players.
    Norton, 1933; Eyre, 1934 [Cape Cod]
  The Mystery of the Cape Cod Tavern.
    Norton, 1934; Eyre, 1935 [Cape Cod]
  Octagon House. Norton, 1937; Collins,
    1938 [Cape Cod]
  Out of Order. Norton, 1936; Gollancz,
    1937
  The Perennial Boarder. Norton, 1941;
    Collins, 1942 [Cape Cod]
  Proof of the Pudding. Norton, 1945;
    Collins, 1945 [Cape Cod]
  Punch with Care. Farrar, 1946; Collins,
    1947 [Cape Cod]
  Sandbar Sinister. Norton, 1934; Gol-
    lancz, 1936 [Cape Cod]
  The Six Iron Spiders. Norton, 1942;
    Collins, 1943 [Cape Cod]
  Spring Harrowing. Norton, 1939; Gol-
    lancz, 1939 [Cape Cod]
  Three Plots for Asey Mayo. Norton,
    1942 (3 novelets.) [Cape Cod]
  The Tinkling Symbol. Norton, 1935; Gol-
    lancz, 1935 [Cape Cod]
TAYLOR, R. M.
  Detective Bob Bridger; or, The Man from
    Scotland Yard. Street, 1890

TAYLOR, R. W. "Author of dozens of books, fiction and nonfiction, under several names," living in Fla. in 1960s.
   Whiplash. Gold Star, 1964

TAYLOR, RAY WARD. 1908- . Ref: CA.
   Doomsday Square. Dutton, 1966; Gollancz, 1967 [S.W.]

TAYLOR, ROGER
   Snatch! Melbourne, 1980; Bantam, 1981

TAYLOR, SAM S. Radio and film scriptwriter, ss writer, living in Calif. in 1950s. SC: Neal Cotten, in all titles.
   No Head for Her Pillow. Dutton, 1952; Foulsham, 1954 [L.A.]
   Sleep No More. Dutton, 1949; Boardman, 1951 [L.A.]
   So Cold, My Bed. Dutton, 1953; Foulsham, 1955 [L.A.]

TAYLOR, SAMUEL W(OOLLEY). 1907- . Ref: CA.
   The Grinning Gismo. Wyn, 1951; Hodder, 1952 [S.F.]
   The Man with My Face. Wyn, 1948; Hodder, 1949 [Calif.]

TAYLOR, SELMAN
   The Marshmead Murders. Hale, 1967
   Murder Grows Roots. Hale, 1970

TAYLOR, THEODORE. 1921- . Ref: CA.
   The Body Trade. GM, 1968 [China]

TAYLOR, TOM. 1817-1880. See also: H. C. Williams. Ref: DD.
   The Ticket-of-Leave Man. Lacy's, 1863; French, 186? (4-act play.)

TAYLOR, WALKER. 1903- . Byline also: P(hillip Neville) Walker Taylor, q.v.
   The Admiral's a Spy. Hodder, 1941 [Wash. D.C.]
   Spylight. Eyre, 1943
   Spyrocket. Eyre, 1944

TAYLOR, WILLIAM C. 1924- .
   The Yellow Paint War. Vantage, 1977

TEAGLE, MIKE
   Death over San Silvestro. Hillman-Curl, 1936 [NYC]
   Murders in Silk. Hillman-Curl, 1938; Long, 1939 [NYC]

TEAGUE, JOHN JESSOP. 1856-1929. Pseudonym: Morice Gerard, q.v.

TEAGUE, RUTH (TOWNSEND MILLS), 1896- , and WALTER (DORWIN) TEAGUE, 1883-1960. Pseudonym of Ruth Teague: Ruth Mills, q.v.
   You Can't Ignore Murder. Putnam, 1942 [N.J.]

TEAGUE, WALTER (DORWIN). 1883-1960. See: Ruth (Townsend Mills) Teague, 1896- .

TEARLE, CHRISTIAN. Pseudonym of Edward Tyrrell Jaques.
   A Legal Practitioner. Routledge, 1907 ss, some criminous

TEBBETTS-TAYLOR, ELIZABETH. Ref: CA.
   Now I Lay Me Down to Die. Arcadia, 1955 [L.A.]

TEDESCHI, FRANK L. See: Barbara Ninde Byfield, 1930- .

TEED, G(EORGE) H(AMILTON). 1878-1939. Byline sometimes: Hamilton Teed. Those titles below listed without publisher were issued by Amalgamated Press and feature Sexton Blake. Other SC: Grant Rushton, in at least those marked GR.
   The Adventure of the Bogus Sheik. 1928
   The Adventure of the Voodoo Queen. 1928
   The Bailiff's Secret. 1938
   The Black Eagle. 1925
   The Black Emperor. 1926
   Bottom of Suez. Columbine, 1939 GR [Egypt]
   The Cabaret Crime. 1929
   The Case of the Bogus Monk. 1928
   The Case of the Chinese Puzzle. 1925
   The Case of the Clairvoyant's Ruse. 1924
   The Case of the Courtlandt Jewels. 1922
   The Case of the Disguised Apache. 1927
   The Case of the Jade-Handled Knife. 1924
   The Case of the Mummified Hand. 1926
   The Case of the Portuguese Giantess. 1928
   The Case of the Ten Diamonds. 1925
   Cassidy the Con Man. 1930
   The China Town Mystery. 1932
   The Clue of the Four Wigs. 1925
   The Crime of the Catacombs. 1931
   The Crime on Gallows Hill. 1931
   The Crimson Belt. 1923
   The Crook of Canada. 1930
   The Crook of Costa Blanca. 1931
   The Crook of Marsden Manor. 1930
   The Crook of Monte Carlo. 1932
   The Crook of Paris. 1930
   The Crook of Shanghai. 1932
   The Crook's Decoy. 1933
   Crooks in Clover. 1928
   Crooks' Vendetta. Columbine, 1939 GR
   The Cross-Channel Crime. 1931
   The Diamond Dragon. 1922
   The Diamond Sunburst. 1917
   The Dictator's Secret. 1936
   The Eight-Pointed Star. 1923
   The Eighth Millionaire. 1928
   The Fatal Amulet. 1934
   Five in Fear. Smith, 1936 GR [Manila]
   Gang War. 1931
   The Great Canal Plot. 1925
   The Great Ivory Swindle. 1924
   The Gunners. 1929
   The Hand of Vengeance. Mellifont, 1935
   The House of Cellars. 1932
   The House of Curtains. 1931
   The House of Silence. 1930
   The Island of the Guilty. 1926
   The Isle of Horror. 1933
   The Ivory Screen. 1922
   Killer Aboard. Amalgamated, 1934 [ship]
   The Martello Tower Mystery. 1935
   The Masked Killer. 1930
   Missing at Lloyds. Mellifont, 1935
   The Mitcham Murder Mystery. Mellifont, 1935
   Murder in Manchuria. 1934 [China]
   Murder Ship. Smith, 1935 GR [ship]
   The Mystery of Cell 13. 1934
   The Mystery of the Cashiered Officer. 1935
   The Mystery of the Film City. 1927
   The Mystery of the Man from Rio. 1929
   The Mystery of the Old Age Pensioner. 1933
   The Mystery of the Seine. 1925 [Fr.]
   Mystery on the Broads. Mellifont, 1935
   The Night-Club Mystery. 1927
   The Orloff Diamond. 1923
   The Pearls of Doom. 1929
   The Phantom of the Creek. 1932
   Prisoner of the Chateau. 1929
   The Riddle of the Russian Gold. 1926
   Rogues of Ransom. 1933
   The Rogues' Republic. 1927
   The Rubber Smugglers. 1928
   The Secret Emerald Mines. 1923
   The Secret of the Coconut Groves. 1925
   The Secret of the President's Daughter. 1929
   The Secret of the Strong Room. 1930
   The Secret of the Thieves' Kitchen. 1930
   The Shadow Crook. Smith, 1936
   Spies Ltd. Wright, 1938
   The Spirit Smuggler. 1922
   The Terror of Gold-Digger Creek. 1928
   The Terror of Tangier. 1927 [Tangier]
   The Tiger of Canton. 1927 [China]
   The Two Mysteries. 1916
   Under the Eagle's Wing. 1925
   The Victim of Black Magic. 1928
   The Victim of the Gang. 1930
   Voodoo Island. Columbine, 1939 GR [Haiti]
   The Yellow Skull. 1931
   The Yellow Tiger. 1915

TEED, HAMILTON. See: G(eorge) H(amilton) Teed, 1878-1939.

TEILHET, DARWIN L. 1904-1964. Pseudonym: William H. Fielding, q.v. See also: Hildegarde Tolman Teilhet, 1906- . Ref: MC, MP. SC: Jean Henri St. Amand = JS; Baron von Kaz = K.
   The Big Runaround. Coward, 1964; Gollancz, 1964. Also published as: Dangerous Encounter. Paperback Library, 1965 [Calif.]
   The Broken Face Murders, with Hildegarde Tolman Teilhet. Doubleday, 1940; Gollancz, 1940 K [Calif.]
   The Crimson Hair Murders, with Hildegarde Tolman Teilhet. Doubleday, 1936; Gollancz, 1937 K [S.F.]
   Dangerous Encounter; see The Big Runaround
   Death Flies High. Morrow, 1931; Long, 1932 JS [air.]
   The Fear Makers. Appleton, 1945; Gollancz, 1946 [Wash. D.C.]
   The Feather Cloak Murders, with Hildegarde Tolman Teilhet. Doubleday, 1936; Gollancz, 1937 K [Haw.]
   Murder in the Air. Morrow, 1931 JS [Paris]
   Odd Man Pays. Little, 1944 [Eng.]
   The Talking Sparrow Murders. Morrow, 1934; Gollancz, 1934 [Ger.]
   The Ticking Terror Murders. Doubleday, 1935; Methuen, 1936 K [S.F.]

TEILHET, HILDEGARDE TOLMAN 1906- . Pseudonym: Hildegarde Tolman, q.v. See also: Darwin L. Teilhet, 1904-1964. SC: Sam Hook = SH (see also Tolman entry).
   The Assassins. Doubleday, 1946; Gollancz, 1947 SH [China]
   The Double Agent. Doubleday, 1945; Gollancz, 1946, as by Darwin L. and Hildegarde Tolman Teilhet SH [Fr.]
   A Private Undertaking. Coward, 1952; Macdonald, 1953. Also published as: The Screaming Bride. Mercury, 1954 [Fr.]
   The Rim of Terror. Coward, 1950; Gollancz, 1950, as by Darwin L. and Hildegarde Tolman Teilhet [West]
   The Screaming Bride; see A Private Undertaking
   The Terrified Society. Doubleday, 1947

TELENGA, SUZETTE. 1915- . Pseudonym: Susan York, q.v.

TELFAIR, RICHARD. Pseudonym of Richard Jessup, 1925-1982. SC: Monty Nash = MN.
   The Bloody Medallion. GM, 1959; Muller pb, 1960 MN
   The Corpse That Talked. GM, 1959; Muller pb, 1960 MN [NYC]
   Good Luck, Sucker. GM, 1961; Muller pb, 1962 MN [P. Rico]
   Scream Bloody Murder. GM, 1960; Muller pb, 1961 MN
   The Slavers. GM, 1961; Muller pb, 1962 MN [Afr.]
   Target for Tonight. Dell, 1962 (Novelization of the "Danger Man" TV series.) [Lisbon]

TELFER, DARIEL. 1905- . Ref: CA.
   The Corrupters. Simon, 1964; Muller, 1964
   The Guilty Ones. Simon, 1961; Muller, 1961 [Calif.]
   Love Is for Hating. Muller, 1963

TELFORD, DON
   Party. Telfreight, 1978

TELLET, ROY. Pseudonym of Albert Eubule Evans, 1839-1896.
   A Draught of Lethe. Smith Elder, 1891; Lippincott, 1891

TEMMEY, BOB
   Blueprint for Terror. Major, 1976

TEMPERLEY, ROSEMARY
   Nameless One. Firecrest, 1979

TEMPEST, BURTON
   Murder by Dart. Mitre, 1946

TEMPEST, JAN. Pseudonym of Irene Maude Mossop Swatridge. Joint pseudonym with Charles John Swatridge, q.v.: Theresa Charles, q.v.
   House of the Pines. Mills, 1946; Ace, 1968

TEMPEST, SARAH. Pseudonym of Doris Almon Ponsonby, 1907- . Ref: CA.
   A Winter of Fear. Hurst, 1967; Pyramid, 1968 [Eng., 1872]

TEMPLE, PAUL. Joint pseudonym of Francis (Henry) Durbridge, 1912- , q.v., and James Douglas Rutherford McConnell, 1915- . Other McConnell pseudonym: Douglas Rutherford, q.v. SC: Paul Temple (see also Francis Durbridge entry), in both pseudonyms.
   East of Algiers. Hodder, 1959. Reprinted as by Francis Durbridge: Hodder pb, 1962 [Afr., N.]
   The Tyler Mystery. Hodder, 1957. Reprinted as by Francis Durbridge: Hodder pb, 1960

TEMPLE, RICHARD. SC: Simon Leigh, in both titles.
   The Schulsinger Affair. Hale, 1971
   Spy Is a Dirty Word. Hale, 1970

TEMPLE, ROBIN. Pseudonym of (Samuel) Andrew Wood, 1890- , q.v.
   -Cuckoo Fair. Ward, 1932
   -The Dark Man. Jenkins, 1939
   -Escape If You Can. Ward, 1934
   -The Golden Stranger. Mellifont, 1953
   -Hoodwink. Ward, 1933
   -It Always Happens. Ward, 1934
   -Little White Hen. Jenkins, 1938
   -London Lights Were Shining. Jenkins, 1941

-Maureen of the Island. Jenkins, 1938
-Spaniard's House. Macdonald, 1946
-Street Paved with Water. Jenkins, 1939. Reprinted as by Samuel Andrew Wood: Cherry Tree, 1946
-The Sweet Enemy. Jenkins, 1940
-Tide Rip. Ward, 1933. Reprinted as by Samuel Andrew Wood: Mellifont, 1951
-Till Doomsday. Ward, 1932

TEMPLE, WILLIAM F(REDERICK). 1914- . British science fiction writer and early member of British Interplantary Society.
The Dangerous Edge. Long, 1951
Shoot at the Moon. Whiting, 1966; Simon, 1966

TEMPLE-ELLIS, N. A. Pseudonym of Neville Aldridge Holdaway, 1894- . Ref: CC. SC: Montrose Arbuthnot, in at least those marked MA; Insp. Wren, in at least those marked W. Set: Eng.
The Case in Hand. Hodder, 1933
The Cauldron Bubbles. Methuen, 1930
Dead in No Time. Hodder, 1935. U.S. title: Murder in the Ruins. Dial, 1936 MA,W
Death of a Decent Fellow. Hodder, 1941 W
The Hollow Land. Hodder, 1934
The Inconsistent Villains. Methuen, 1929; Dutton, 1929 MA
The Man Who Was There. Methuen, 1930; Dutton, 1930 MA
Murder in the Ruins; see Dead in No Time
Quest. Methuen, 1931 MA
Six Lines. Hodder, 1932
Three Went In. Hodder, 1934 W

TEMPLETON, CHARLES (B.). 1915- . Ref: CA.
-An Act of God. Joseph, 1978; Little, 1978
The Kidnapping of the President. McClelland (Toronto), 1974; Simon, 1975; Quartet, 1976 [NYC]

TEMPLETON, GEORGE
The Silent Barrier. Curtiss, 1933 [Can.]
-The Silver Trail. Curtiss, 1932 [Can.]

TEMPLETON, JESSE. Pseudonym of George Goodchild, 1888-1969, q.v. Other pseudonym: Alan Dare, q.v.
-Between the Tides. Ward, 1929. Reprinted as by George Goodchild: Ward, 1936
-The Bitter Test. Ward, 1930
The Call of the North (as by George Goodchild); see Jake Canuke
-Clay-Face. Ward, 1930
Dead or Alive. Ward, 1929. Reprinted as by George Goodchild: Ward, 1937 [Can.]
-The Eternal Conflict. Hurst, 1925. Reprinted as by George Goodchild: Archer, 1950
-The Feud. Hurst, 1925. Reprinted as by George Goodchild: Hodder, 1935
Inch of the C.I.D. Ward, 1932. Reprinted as by George Goodchild: Ward, 1936
-Jake Canuck. Hurst, 1924. Reprinted as by George Goodchild: Hodder, 1932. Also published as: The Call of the North, as by George Goodchild. Newnes, 1938
-Love's Challenge. Mellifont, 1932
-Ten Fathoms Deep. Ward, 1931. Reprinted as by George Goodchild: Ward, 1938
-The Timber Wolf. Hurst, 1927
-Virginia's Quest. Mellifont, 1934
-Winning Through. Ward, 1932. Reprinted as by George Goodchild: Ward, 1935
The Woman Accused. Mellifont, 1934
The Yellow Hibiscus. Ward, 1931 [Bangkok]

TENNANT, EMMA. 1937- . Ref: CA.
-The Bad Sister. Gollancz, 1978; Coward, 1978
The Last of the Country House Murders. Cape, 1974

TEPPERMAN, EMILE C. Pseudonym: Brant House, q.v.

TERAMOND, EDMOND GAUTIER. 1869-1957. Pseudonym: Guy de Teramond, q.v.

TERESA, VINCENT (CHARLES). 1928- . Mafia member turned government informer.
Wiseguys. Dutton, 1978; Panther, 1978

TERHUNE, ALBERT PAYSON. 1872-1942.
The Amateur Inn. Doran, 1923; Hodder, 1924 [N.Y.]
Black Caesar's Clan. Doran, 1922; Hodder, 1924 [Miami]
Black Gold. Doran, 1922; Hodder, 1922 [Calif.]
Blundell's Last Guest. Chelsea, 1927 [N.J.]
Grudge Mountain. Harper, 1939. British title: The Mystery of Grudge Mountain. Chapman, 1939 [Calif.]
Letters of Marque. Harper, 1934 [N.J.]
Loot! Harper, 1940 [N.J.]
The Man in the Dark. Dutton, 1921
The Mystery of Grudge Mountain; see Grudge Mountain
The Pest. Dutton, 1923
The Runaway Bag. Doran, 1925
The Secret of Sea-Dream House. Harper, 1929; Butterworth, 1929 [Fla.]
The Tiger's Claw. Doran, 1924; Hodder, 1925
Unseen! Harper, 1937 [N.J.]

TERMAN, DOUGLAS. 1933- . Jet pilot, missile site commander; has been in military intelligence.
First Strike; see The 3 Megaton Gamble
Free Flight. Scribner, 1980; Macdonald, 1981 [Can.]
The 3 Megaton Gamble. Vermont Crossroads, 1978. Revised edition: First Strike. Scribner, 1979; Joseph, 1980

TERRALL, ROBERT. 1914- . Pseudonyms: John Gonzales, Robert Kyle, qq.v. See also: Brett Halliday. Ref: CA.
A Killer Is Loose Among Us. Duell, 1948 [South]
Madam Is Dead. Duell, 1947 [Fr.]
Sand Dollars. St. Martin's, 1978; New English Library, 1978 [Jam.]
They Deal in Death. Simon, 1943 [NYC]

TERRELL, THOMAS. 1853-1928.
The City of the Just. Trischler, 1892

TERRIS, E. WILMOT. Set: Eng.
The Hidden Death. Modern, 1938
Mystery of the Purple Cloak. Modern, 193?

TERROT, CHARLES (HUGH). 1917- .
The Chelsea Rainbow. Collins, 1955. U.S. title: The Neon Rainbow. Dutton, 1956

TERRY, J. E. HAROLD. See: Beamish Tinker.

TERRY, MAY. Pseudonym: Terry Kendrick, q.v.

TERRY, WILLIAM. Pseudonym of Terry Harknett, 1936- , q.v. Other pseudonyms: Joseph Hedges, William Pine, Thomas H. Stone, qq.v.
Once a Copper. Hammond, 1965

TESSIER, ERNEST MAURICE. 1885-1973. Pseudonym: Maurice Dekobra, q.v.

TESSIER, THOMAS. Born in Conn., moved to Eng. ca.1975; poet and playwright.
The Nightwalker. Macmillan (London), 1979; Atheneum, 1980

TETA, JON (ANTHONY). 1933- . Ref: CA.
The Clock at Ravenswood. Pyramid, 1969 [L.I.]

TEY, JOSEPHINE. Pseudonym of Elizabeth MacKintosh, 1896-1952. Other pseudonym: Gordon Daviot, q.v. Ref: CC, EM, MC, TC. SC: Insp. Alan Grant (see also Gordon Daviot entry) = AG. Set: Eng.
Brat Farrar. Davies, 1949; Macmillan, 1950. Also published as: Come and Kill Me. PB, 1951
Come and Kill Me; see Brat Farrar
The Daughter of Time. Davies, 1951; Macmillan, 1952 AG
The Franchise Affair. Davies, 1948; Macmillan, 1948 AG
Miss Pym Disposes. Davies, 1946; Macmillan, 1948 [acad.]
A Shilling for Candles. Methuen, 1936; Macmillan, 1954 AG
The Singing Sands. Davies, 1952; Macmillan, 1953 AG
To Love and Be Wise. Davies, 1950; Macmillan, 1951 AG

THACKERAY, ALEC
One Way Ticket. Hutchinson, 1975; Pyramid, 1976

THACKERAY, KIT. ca.1946- . British cameraman and director.
Counterflood. Davies, 1979; Morrow, 1979 [Brazil]

THAMES, C. H. Pseudonym of Stephen Marlowe, 1928- . Name originally: Milton Lesser. Other pseudonyms: Andrew Frazer, Jason Ridgway, qq.v. See also: Richard (Scott) Prather, 1921- ; and: Ellery Queen.
Blood of My Brother. Permabooks, 1963
Violence Is Golden. Boureguy, 1956 [Fla.]

THANET, OCTAVE. Pseudonym of Alice French, 1850-1934.
The Lion's Share. Bobbs, 1907

THATCHER, JULIA. Pseudonym of Donald R. Bensen, 1927- , q.v.
Home to the Night. Ballantine, 1976; Futura, 1977
Inherit the Mirage. Ballantine, 1976
Mask of Love. Popular Library, 1980
Nightgleams. Ballantine, 1976 [NYC, ca.1900]
Tempest at Summer's End. Ballantine, 1976
Tower in the Sea. Popular Library, 1979

THAYER, CHARLES W(HEELER). 1910-1969. Ref: CA.
Checkpoint. Harper, 1964 [Berlin]
Moscow Interlude. Harper, 1962. British title: Natasha. Joseph, 1962 [Moscow]
Natasha; see Moscow Interlude

THAYER, GERALDINE. Pseudonym of Dorothy Daniels, 1915- , q.v. Other pseudonyms: Danielle Dorset, Angela Gray, Cynthia Kavanaugh, Suzanne Somers, Helen Gray Weston, qq.v.
The Dark Rider. Avalon, 1961 [Ky.]

THAYER, JAMES STEWART. 1949- . Ref: CA.
The Earhart Betrayal. Putnam, 1980; Hamlyn, 1982 [Far East, 1946]
The Hess Cross. Putnam, 1977; Arrow, 1979 [Chi., 1942]
The Stettin Secret. Putnam, 1979 [Poland, 1947]

THAYER, (EMMA REDINGTON) LEE. 1874-1973. Ref: CA, CC, EM, MP, TC. SC: Peter Clancy, in all titles except "Doctor S.O.S."
Accessory After the Fact. Dodd, 1943; Hurst, 1944 [Calif.]
Accident, Manslaughter or Murder? Dodd, 1945; Hurst, 1946 [Maine]
Alias Dr. Ely. Doubleday, 1927; Hurst, 1927 [L.I.]
And One Cried Murder. Dodd, 1961; Long, 1962 [S.F.]
Blood on the Knight. Dodd, 1952; Hurst, 1953 [Calif.]
Clancy's Secret Mission; see Do Not Disturb
A Clue for Clancy; see Pig in a Poke
Counterfeit. Sears, 1933. British title: The Counterfeit Bill. Hurst, 1934 [NYC]
The Counterfeit Bill; see Counterfeit
Dark of the Moon. Dodd, 1936. British title: Death in the Gorge. Hurst, 1937 [Conn.]
The Darkest Spot. Sears, 1928; Hurst, 1928 [NYC]
Dead End Street. Dodd, 1936. British title: Murder in the Mirror. Hurst, 1936 [NYC]
Dead Men's Shoes. Sears, 1929; Hurst, 1929 [N.J.]
Dead on Arrival. Dodd, 1960; Long, 1962 [S.F.]
Dead Reckoning. Dodd, 1954. British title: Murder on the Pacific. Hurst, 1955 [ship]
Dead Storage. Dodd, 1935. British title: The Death Weed. Hurst, 1935 [NYC]
Death in the Gorge; see Dark of the Moon
Death Walks in Shadow; see Dusty Death
The Death Weed; see Dead Storage
Death Within the Vault; see Within the Vault
Do Not Disturb. Dodd, 1951. British title: Clancy's Secret Mission. Hurst, 1952 [Calif.]
Doctor S.O.S. Doubleday, 1925; Hurst, 1925
Dusty Death. Dodd, 1966. British title: Death Walks in Shadow. Long, 1966 [Calif.]
Evil Root. Dodd, 1949; Hurst, 1951 [N.Y.]
Fatal Alibi; see Who Benefits?
Five Bullets. Dodd, 1944; Hurst, 1947 [Fla.]
The Glass Knife. Sears, 1932; Hurst, 1932 [N.J.]
Guilt Edged. Dodd, 1951. British title: Guilt-Edged Murder. Hurst, 1953 [New Or.]

Guilt-Edged Murder; see Guilt Edged
Guilt Is Where You Find It. Dodd, 1957;
    Long, 1958 [Calif.]
Guilty! Dodd, 1940; Hurst, 1941 [L.A.]
A Hair's Breadth. Dodd, 1946; Hurst,
    1947 [S.F.]
Hallowe'en Homicide. Dodd, 1941; Hurst,
    1942 [NYC]
Hanging's Too Good. Dodd, 1943; Hurst,
    1945 [Conn.]
Hell-Gate Tides. Sears, 1933; Hurst,
    1933 [NYC]
The Jaws of Death. Dodd, 1946; Hurst,
    1948 [Fla.]
The Key. Doubleday, 1924; Hurst, 1924
    [N.Y.]
The Last Shot. Sears, 1931; Hurst, 1931
    [N.J.]
Last Trump. Dodd, 1937; Hurst, 1937
    [ship]
Lightning Strikes Twice. Dodd, 1939;
    Hurst, 1939 [ship]
A Man's Enemies. Dodd, 1937. British
    title: This Man's Doom. Hurst, 1938
    [L.I.]
Murder in the Mirror; see Dead End
    Street
Murder Is Out. Dodd, 1942; Hurst, 1943
    [NYC]
Murder on Location. Dodd, 1942; Hurst,
    1944 [Calif.]
Murder on the Pacific; see Dead Reckon-
    ing
Murder Stalks the Circle. Dodd, 1947;
    Hurst, 1949 [Conn.]
The Mystery of the 13th Floor. Century,
    1919 [NYC]
No Holiday for Death. Dodd, 1954;
    Hurst, 1955 [S.F.]
Out, Brief Candle! Dodd, 1948; Hurst,
    1950 [S.F.]
Persons Unknown. Dodd, 1941; Hurst,
    1942 [L.I.]
Pig in a Poke. Dodd, 1948. British
    title: A Clue for Clancy. Hurst, 1950
    [Calif.]
A Plain Case of Murder. Dodd, 1944;
    Hurst, 1945 [N.J.]
Poison. Doubleday, 1926; Heinemann,
    1926 [N.J.]
The Prisoner Pleads "Not Guilty". Dodd,
    1953; Hurst, 1954 [Bermuda]
The Puzzle; see Q.E.D.
Q.E.D. Doubleday, 1922. British title:
    The Puzzle. Hurst, 1923 [N.J.]
Ransom Racket. Dodd, 1938; Hurst, 1938
    [N.Y.]
Red-Handed; see Sudden Death
The Scrimshaw Millions. Sears, 1932;
    Hurst, 1933 [NYC]
The Second Bullet. Sears, 1934. British
    title: The Second Shot. Hurst, 1935
    [N.J.]
The Second Shot; see The Second Bullet
Set a Thief. Sears, 1931. British
    title: To Catch a Thief. Hurst, 1932
    [N.Y.]
The Sinister Mark. Doubleday, 1923;
    Hurst, 1923 [NYC]
Stark Murder. Dodd, 1939; Hurst, 1940
    [N.Y.]
Still No Answer. Dodd, 1958. British
    title: Web of Hate. Long, 1959 [Can.]
The Strange Sylvester Affair; see That
    Sylvester Affair
Sudden Death. Dodd, 1935. British
    title: Red-Handed. Hurst, 1936 [NYC]
That Affair at the Cedars. Doubleday,
    1921; Hurst, 1924 [L.I.]
That Strange Sylvester Affair. Dodd,
    1938. British title: The Strange Syl-
    vester Affair. Hurst, 1939 [Conn.]
They Tell No Tales. Sears, 1930; Hurst,
    1930 [NYC]
This Man's Doom; see A Man's Enemies
To Catch a Thief; see Set a Thief
Too Long Endured. Dodd, 1950; Hurst,
    1952 [Conn.]
Two Ways to Die. Dodd, 1959; Long, 1961
    [Jap.]
The Unlatched Door. Century, 1920 [NYC]
Web of Hate; see Still No Answer
Who Benefits? Dodd, 1955. British
    title: Fatal Alibi. Hurst, 1956
    [Calif.]
Within the Vault. Dodd, 1950. British
    title: Death Within the Vault. Hurst,
    1951 [N.J.]
X Marks the Spot. Dodd, 1940; Hurst,
    1941 [Calif.]

THAYER, TIFFANY (ELLSWORTH). 1902-1959.
    Pseudonym: John Doe, q.v.
    The Illustrious Corpse. Fiction League,
        1930 [NYC]
    Thirteen Men. Kendall, 1930; Long, 1938

THEINER, GEORGE. 1927-   . Joint pseudo-
    nym with John (Frederick) Burke,
    1922-   , q.v.: Jonathan George,
    q.v. Ref: CA.

THELWELL, MICHAEL
    -The Harder They Come. Grove, 1980;
        Pluto, 1980

THEMERSON, STEFAN. 1910-   . Ref: CA.
    Tom Harris. Gaberbocchus, 1967; Knopf,
        1968

THEROUX, PAUL. 1941-   . Ref: CA.
    The Family Arsenal. Houghton, 1976;
        H. Hamilton, 1976 [Eng.]
    Murder in Mount Holly. Ross, 1969

THIELEN, BERNARD
    A Charm of Finches. Mystery House, 1959
        [Vt.]
    Open Season. Mystery House, 1958 [New
        Eng.]

THIENES, THOMAS L. Pseudonym: Tom T.
    Ness, q.v.

THIERRY, JAMES FRANCIS
    The Adventure of the Eleven Cuff-But-
        tons. Neale, 1918 [Eng.]

THIESSEN, VAL
    My Brother, Cain. Monarch, 1964 [Okla.
        City]

THIMBLETHORPE, JUNE SYLVIA. Pseudonym:
    Sylvia Thorpe, q.v.

THOITS, ALVIN T. See: Bert L(eston) Tay-
    lor, 1866-1921.

THOM, ROBERT. 1929-1979. Ref: CA.
    Bloody Mama. Paperback Library, 1970;
        New English Library pb, 1970 (Novel-
        ization of the movie.)

THOMAS, A(LBERT) E(LLSWORTH). 1872-1947.
    The Double Cross. Dodd, 1924; Methuen,
        1925 [NYC]

THOMAS, ALAN (ERNEST WENTWORTH).
    1896-   . Ref: CC. SC: Insp. Wid-
    geon, in at least those marked W.
    Set: Eng.
    -The Calverton Story. Gollancz, 1970
    Daggers Drawn. Benn, 1930; Brewer,
        1930
    The Death of Laurence Vining. Benn,
        1928; Lippincott, 1929 W
    Death of the Home Secretary. Benn, 1933
        W
    -The Director. Gollancz, 1958
    The Fugitives. Gollancz, 1953
    -The Governor. Gollancz, 1961
    -The Judge. Gollancz, 1966
    -The Lonely Years. Benn, 1930
    The Mask and the Man. Gollancz, 1951
    -The Professor. Gollancz, 1969
    The Stolen Cellini. Benn, 1931; Holt,
        1932
    Summer Adventure. Benn, 1933
    -The Surgeon. Gollancz, 1964
    -That We Might Live. Harrap, 1935
    The Tremayne Case. Benn, 1929; Lippin-
        cott, 1930

THOMAS, ANNIE [ANNIE HALL THOMAS CUDLIP].
    1838-1918.
    A Dangerous Secret. Low, 1864
    -False Colours. Tinsley, 1869; Harper,
        1869
    -False Pretenses. Digby, 1895
    Four Women in the Case. White, 1896
    A Mystery and other stories. Munro,
        1892 ss (British title?)
    -A Narrow Escape. Chapman, 1875; Gill,
        1876
    -The Sloan Square Scandal and other sto-
        ries. Swan, 1890; U.S. Book Co.,
        1890 ss

THOMAS, AUGUSTUS. 1857-1934.
    Arizona. Russell, 1899 (4-act play.)
        [Ariz.]
    The Witching Hour. Harper, 1908. Play
        version: French (NYC), 1916 (4-acts)

THOMAS, CAROLYN. Pseudonym of Actea Caro-
    lyn Duncan, 1913-   .
    The Cactus Shroud. Lippincott, 1957;
        Boardman, 1957 [Las Veg.]
    The Hearse Horse Snickered. Lippincott,
        1954; Boardman, 1955 [N. Mex.]
    Narrow Gauge to Murder. Lippincott,
        1953; Boardman, 1956 [Colo.]
    Prominent Among the Mourners. Lippin-
        cott, 1946; Cherry Tree, 1949
        [Midwest, acad.]

THOMAS, CRAIG. 1942-   . Pseudonym:
    Donald Grant, q.v.
    Firefox. Joseph, 1977; Holt, 1977
    Rat Trap. Joseph, 1976
    Snow Falcon. Joseph, 1979; Holt, 1980
        [Russ.]
    Wolfsbane. Joseph, 1978; Holt, 1978
        [Fr., 1963]

THOMAS, CURTIS. Pseudonym: Thomas Kinney,
    q.v.

THOMAS, D.
    Gulf Coast Run. Leisure, 1980 [Fla.]

THOMAS, DYLAN (MARLAIS). 1914-1953. Ref:
    CA.
    The Death of the King's Canary, with
        John Davenport, 1908-1966. Hutchin-
        son, 1976; Viking, 1977
    The Doctor and the Devils. Dent, 1953;
        New Directions, 1953

THOMAS, EUGENE. 1894-   . SC: Mrs. Cay-
    wood Weston = CW; Chu-Sheng = C.
    The Dancing Dead. Sears, 1933 CW [Va.]
    Death Rides the Dragon. Sears, 1932 CW
        [NYC]
    The Intimate Stranger. Sears, 1932;
        Smith, 1936
    Shadow of Chu-Sheng. Sears, 1933 C
        [Panama]
    Yellow Magic. Sears, 1934 C [NYC]

THOMAS, FRANK. SC: Sherlock Holmes, in
    both titles.
    Sherlock Holmes and the Golden Bird.
        Pinnacle, 1979; L.S.P. Books, 1980
        [Eng., 1890s]
    Sherlock Holmes and the Sacred Sword.
        Pinnacle, 1980 [Eng., 1890s]

THOMAS, H(ENRY) W(ILTON). 1867-   .
    The Long Shadow. Methuen, 1927
        [Florence]

THOMAS, JACK W(ILLIAM). 1931-   . Ref:
    CA.
    Burnout. Bantam, 1979
    The Fear Dealers. Bantam, 1975

THOMAS, JACQUES
    Machine Gun Murder. Fiction House, 1935

THOMAS, JIM. Pseudonym of Thomas (James)
    B(utler) Reagan, 1916-   , q.v.
    Cross Purposes. McCall, 1971 [NYC]

THOMAS, JOHN ORAM. Pseudonym: John Oram,
    q.v.

THOMAS, KATE. Pseudonym of Katharine
    Thomas Jarboe Bull.
    "Aila." Doxey, 1896

THOMAS, LESLIE (JOHN). 1931-   . Ref:
    CA.
    Dangerous Davies: The Last Detective.
        Eyre, 1976; Dell, 1982
    Orange Wednesday. Constable, 1967;
        Delacorte, 1968 [Ger.]
    Ormerod's Landing. Eyre, 1978; St. Mar-
        tin's, 1979 [Fr., 1940]
    That Old Gang of Mine. Eyre, 1979;
        Elliott, 1980

THOMAS, LOUIS (C.). 1921-   . Prize-
    winning French novelist.
    Good Children Don't Kill. Frewin, 1967;
        Dodd, 1968 (Translation of "Les Mau-
        vaises Frequentations." Paris, 1964.)
        [Mars.]

THOMAS, MARTIN. Pseudonym of Thomas Hec-
    tor Martin, 1913-   . All titles
    without publisher below feature Sex-
    ton Blake (= SB) and were issued by
    Amalgamated Press, Fleetway, or
    Mayflower.
    Assignment Doomsday. 1961
    Brainwashed. 1968
    Bred to Kill. 1960
    Catch a Tiger. 1959
    A Cold Night for Murder. 1959
    The Copy-Cat Killings. 1957
    Date with Danger! 1960
    Dead Man's Destiny. 1960
    Death and a Dark Horse. Mayflower, 1967
    Death in Small Doses. 1963
    Design for Vengeance. 1960
    An Event Called Murder. 1967
    The Evil Eye. 1958
    Fear Is My Shadow. 1959
    The Hand of Cain. Mayflower, 1966;
        Lancer, 1967
    Lady in Distress. 1958
    Laird of Evil. 1965 [Scot.]
    The Mind Killers. 1965
    The Mini-Skirt Murders. Baker, 1969 SB
    Shadow of a Gun. 1959
    Sorcerers of Set. 1966
    The Sound of Murder. 1963
    Spotlight on Murder. 1962
    Such Men Are Dangerous. 1965

THOMAS, MAUDE M(AY)
    Wait Long, Wait Still. Arcadia, 1954

THOMAS, MICHAEL M.
    Green Monday. Wyndham, 1980; Hutchin-
        son, 1980

THOMAS, MURRAY. Pseudonym of Thomas Murray Ragg, 1897-   . SC: Insp. Wilkins, in all titles.
Buzzards Pick the Bones. Longmans, 1932 [Wales]
Inspector Wilkins Reads the Proofs. Jenkins, 1935
Inspector Wilkins Sees Red. Jenkins, 1934

THOMAS, OWEN
Rope Fodder. Rivers, 1932

THOMAS, PAUL
Cargo—Trouble. Avon, 1960
Code Name: Rubble. Tower, 1967 [Ger.]
The Defector; see The Spy
The Spy. Midwood, 1963. Also published as: The Defector. Tower, 1966 [Ger.]

THOMAS, REGINALD GEORGE. 1899-   .
Pseudonym: John Purley, q.v.

THOMAS, RICHARD H. 1854-1904.
-Penelve; or, Among the Quakers. Headley, 1898; Winston, 1898

THOMAS, ROBERT
Dead Ringer. GM, 1964 (Novelization of the movie.)

THOMAS, ROBERT
Trap for a Lonely Man. English Theatre, 1964 (Translation of "Piege Pour un Homme Seul." Paris, 1960.) (3-act play.)

THOMAS, RONALD WILLS. 1910-   . Pseudonyms: Jeff Bogar, Ronald Wills, qq.v.

THOMAS, ROSS. 1926-   . Pseudonym: Oliver Bleeck, q.v. Ref: CA, TC. SC: McCorkle & Padillo = M&P.
The Backup Men. Morrow, 1971; Hodder, 1971 M&P [Wash. D.C.]
Cast a Yellow Shadow. Morrow, 1967; Hodder, 1968 M&P [Wash. D.C.]
Chinaman's Chance. Simon, 1978; H. Hamilton, 1978 [Calif.]
The Cold War Swap. Morrow, 1966. British title: Spy in the Vodka. Hodder, 1967 M&P [Ger.]
The Eighth Dwarf. Simon, 1979; H. Hamilton, 1979 [Ger., 1946]
The Fools in Town Are on Our Side. Morrow, 1971; Hodder, 1970 [South]
If You Can't Be Good. Morrow, 1973; H. Hamilton, 1974
The Money Harvest. Morrow, 1975; H. Hamilton, 1975 [Wash. D.C.]
The Porkchoppers. Morrow, 1972; H. Hamilton, 1974 [Chi.]
The Seersucker Whipsaw. Morrow, 1967; Hodder, 1968
The Singapore Wink. Morrow, 1969; Hodder, 1969 [Sing.]
Spy in the Vodka; see The Cold War Swap
Yellow-Dog Contract. Morrow, 1977; H. Hamilton, 1977

THOMAS, TAMMY
Wild Is My Heart. Exposition, 1965

THOMAS, VERNON
The Meteren Road. Ward, 1930

THOMAS, W(ILLIAM) MOY. 1828-1910.
Pictures in a Mirror. Groombridge, 1861 ss, one criminous

THOMAS-STANFORD, CHARLES. 1858-1932.
The Ace of Hearts. Methuen, 1912

THOMES, WILLIAM H(ENRY). 1824-1895.
-The Belle of Australia; or, Who Am I? DeWolfe, 1883; Henderson, 1890 [Australia]
The Bushrangers. Lee, 1865 [Australia]
-The Gold-Hunters' Adventures; or, Life in Australia. Loyd, 1883. British title (?): A Gold-Hunter's Adventures Between Melbourne and Ballarat. Ward, 1885 [Australia]
A Gold-Hunter's Adventures Between Melbourne and Ballarat; see The Gold-Hunters' Adventures
-The Gold-Hunters in Europe; or, The Dead Alive. Lee, 1869
Running the Blockade; or, U.S. Secret Service Adventures. Lee, 1875

THOMEY, TEDD. 1920-   . Ref: CA.
And Dream of Evil. Abelard, 1954 [L.A.]
Flight to Takla-Ma. Monarch, 1962 [China]
I Want Out. Ace, 1959
Killer in White. GM, 1956; Fawcett (London), 1958 [L.A.]

THOMPSON, ANN LORRAINE
-A Cry for Love. Avon, 1974
-Hands of Fate. Avon, 1975
House of Strange Music. Avon, 1973
Love, the Sorcerer. Avon, 1978 [Calif.]

THOMPSON, ANNE ARMSTRONG. 1939-   . Ref: CA.
Message from Absalom. Simon, 1975; Hodder, 1976 [Bulg.]
The Romanov Ransom. Simon, 1978; Hodder, 1978
The Swiss Legacy. Simon, 1974; Hodder, 1979

THOMPSON, ARTHUR
The Starved. Belmont, 1965

THOMPSON, ARTHUR LEONARD BELL. 1917-1975.
Pseudonym: Francis Clifford, q.v.

THOMPSON, CHARLES MINER. 1864-1941.
The Calico Cat. Houghton, 1908
The Nimble Dollar, with other stories. Houghton, 1895 ss

THOMPSON, CHINA. Pseudonym of Mary Christianna Milne Lewis, 1907-   . Other pseudonyms: Mary Ann Ashe, Christianna Brand, qq.v.
-Starrbelow. Hutchinson, 1958; Scribner, 1958

THOMPSON, D(ANIEL) P(IERCE). 1795-1868.
Centeola; and other tales. Carleton, 1864 5 ss, 3 criminous

THOMPSON, DONALD
The Corpse Wore No Shoes. Eerie Series, 1945

THOMPSON, EDWARD ANTHONY. 1928-   .
Pseudonym: Anthony Lejeune, q.v.

THOMPSON, ESTELLE. Born in and living in Australia.
The Edge of Nowhere. Hodder, 1965
Find a Crooked Sixpence. Hodder, 1970; Walker, 1977 [Australia]
The Glass Houses. Hodder, 1967
Hunter in the Dark. Hale, 1978; Walker, 1979 [Australia]
The Lawyer and the Carpenter. Hodder, 1963; Washburn, 1964
The Meadows of Tallon. Hale, 1974; Ace, 1974
-A Mischief Past. Hale, 1971
Three Women in the House. Hale, 1973; Avon, 1973
-To Catch a Rainbow. Hale, 1979; Walker, 1980 [Australia, 1868]
A Twig Is Bent. Abelard (London & NYC), 1961 [Australia]
The Wrong Saturday. Hodder, 1968

THOMPSON, FRANK
The Transgressor. Badger, 1920 [Ky.]

THOMPSON, (EU)GENE (ALLEN). 1924-   .
Ref: CA.
-Lupe. Random, 1977; Macdonald, 1978
Murder Mystery. Random, 1980; Gollancz, 1981 [L.A.]

THOMPSON, GRACE E. Pseudonym: Camilla Hope, q.v.

THOMPSON, HARRISON R.
Seventh Sense. Manor, 1979

THOMPSON, J. LEE
Murder Without Crime. French (London), 1943; French (NYC), 1944 (3-act play.)

THOMPSON, JIM [JAMES MYERS THOMPSON]. 1906-1977. Born on Indian reservation in Okla., graduate of U. of Neb.; newspaperman.
After Dark, My Sweet. Popular Library, 1955
The Alcoholics. Lion, 1953
Bad Boy. Lion, 1953
Child of Rage. Lancer, 1972 [NYC]
The Criminal. Lion, 1953
Cropper's Cabin. Lion, 1952
The Getaway. Signet, 1959; Allen, 1972
The Golden Gizmo. Lion, 1954
The Grifters. Regency, 1963
Heed the Thunder. Greenberg, 1946
A Hell of a Woman. Lion, 1954
Ironside. Popular Library, 1967 (Novelization of the TV series.) [S.F.]
The Kill-Off. Lion, 1957 [New Eng.]
The Killer Inside Me. Lion, 1952; Sphere, 1973 [Tex.]
King Blood. Sphere, 1973 (Published in U.S. in 1954—title?)
Nothing But a Man. Popular Library, 1970 (Novelization of the movie.)
The Nothing Man. Dell, 1954 [Calif.]
Nothing More Than Murder. Harper, 1949
-Now and on Earth. Modern Age, 1942
Pop. 1280. GM, 1964
Recoil. Lion, 1953
Roughneck. Lion, 1954
Savage Night. Lion, 1953
South of Heaven. GM, 1967
A Swell-Looking Babe. Lion, 1954
Texas by the Tail. GM, 1965 [Tex.]
The Transgressors. Signet, 1961
The Undefeated. Popular Library, 1969 (Novelization of the movie.)
Wild Town. Signet, 1957

THOMPSON, KENNETH (PUGH). 1909-   .
Member's Lobby. Joseph, 1966; London House, 1967
Pattern of Conquest. Joseph, 1967

THOMPSON, LLOYD S. Drama critic in S.F., movie publicist. SC: Lt. Claude Greenway, in both titles.
Death Stops the Show. Crown, 1946 [S.F.]
Hear Not My Steps. Abelard, 1953

THOMPSON, MURIEL LILLAH STUART. 1902-   .
Pseudonym: Miranda Stuart, q.v.

THOMPSON, RAYMOND, 1949-   , and TREVE DALY, pseudonym. Thompson is actor, musician, singer and songwriter turned screenwriter.
The Number to Call Is... St. Martin's, 1979; Souvenir, 1979 [Ala.]

THOMPSON, STEPHEN L.
Recovery. Warner hc, 1980; New English Library pb, 1981 [Ger.]

THOMPSON, VANCE. 1863-1925. SC: Mr. Guelpa = G.
Diplomatic Mysteries. Lippincott, 1905 ss
The Green Ray. Bobbs, 1924; Hutchinson, 1925 [NYC]
Mr. Guelpa. Bobbs, 1925; Hutchinson, 1926 G [N.Y.]
The Pointed Tower. Bobbs, 1922; Hutchinson, 1923 G [Paris]
The Scarlet Iris. Bobbs, 1924. British title: The Tarnished Woman. Hutchinson, 1924 [It.]
Spinners of Life. Lippincott, 1903; Methuen, 1904
The Tarnished Woman; see The Scarlet Iris

THOMPSON, W. CRAWFORD
A Suitcase Full of Money. Curtis, 1973 [Fla.]

THOMSEN, FRIEDA
The Second Lady Cameron. Belmont, 1977 [Scot., 1800s]

THOMSON, A(RTHUR) A(LEXANDER MALCOLM). 1894-1969. Ref: CA.
But Once a Year, with (Thomas) F(alkland) L(itton) Cary, q.v. Jenkins, 1951
The Late Lamented. French, 1949 (Play.)
Murder at the Ministry, with (Thomas) F(alkland) L(itton) Cary, q.v. Jenkins, 1947

THOMSON, BASIL (HOME). 1861-1939. Ref: CC, MC, MP, TC. SC: Peter Graham = PG; P. C. (Supt.) Richardson = R. Set: Eng.
Carfax Abbey. Methuen, 1928
The Case of Naomi Clynes; see Inspector Richardson C.I.D.
The Case of the Dead Diplomat; see Richardson Goes Abroad
-A Court Intrigue. Heinemann, 1896
The Dartmoor Enigma; see Richardson Solves a Dartmoor Mystery
Death in the Bathroom. Eldon, 1936. U.S. title: Who Killed Stella Pomeroy? Doubleday, 1936 R
Inspector Richardson C.I.D. Eldon, 1934. U.S. title: The Case of Naomi Clynes. Doubleday, 1934 R
The Kidnapper. Eldon, 1933 PG
The Metal Flask. Methuen, 1929 PG
Milliner's Hat Mystery. Eldon, 1937. U.S. title: The Mystery of the French Milliner. Doubleday, 1937 R
Mr. Pepper, Investigator. Castle, 1925 ss
A Murder Arranged. Eldon, 1937. U.S. title: When Thieves Fall Out. Doubleday, 1937 R
The Mystery of the French Milliner; see Milliner's Hat Mystery
P. C. Richardson's First Case. Eldon, 1933; Doubleday, 1933 R
Richardson Goes Abroad. Eldon, 1935. U.S. title: The Case of the Dead Diplomat. Doubleday, 1935 R [Paris]

Richardson Scores Again. Eldon, 1934.
U.S. title: Richardson's Second Case.
Doubleday, 1934 R
Richardson Solves a Dartmoor Mystery.
Eldon, 1935. U.S. title: The Dartmoor
Enigma. Doubleday, 1936 R
Richardson's Second Case; see Richardson Scores Again
When Thieves Fall Out; see A Murder Arranged
Who Killed Stella Pomeroy?; see Death in the Bathroom

THOMSON, DAVID LANDSBOROUGH. 1901-1964.
Pseudonym: T. L. Davidson, q.v.

THOMSON, EDWARD. 1810-1870.
The Adventures of Burnaby Lee; or, The Struggle of a Son and Heir. Tegg, 1852

THOMSON, JUNE. 1930- . Ref: CA, TC.
SC: Insp. Finch, in all titles (but called Insp. Rudd in the U.S. Doubleday editions). Set: Eng.
Alibi in Time. Constable, 1980; Doubleday, 1980
Case Closed. Constable, 1977; Doubleday, 1977
Deadly Relations. Constable, 1979. U.S. title: The Habit of Loving. Doubleday, 1979
Death Cap. Constable, 1973; Doubleday, 1977
The Habit of Loving; see Deadly Relations
The Long Revenge. Constable, 1974; Doubleday, 1975
Not One of Us. Constable, 1972; Harper, 1971
A Question of Identity. Constable, 1978; Doubleday, 1977

THORBURN, C. H.
The Mysterious Stranger. Derby, 1890

THOREAU, DAVID
City at Bay. Arbor, 1979 [S.F.]

THORMANBY. Pseudonym of W(illmott) Willmott Dixon, 1843- , q.v.
The Black Bean. Heath, 1913
-Romances of the Road. Everett, 1901

THORN, RONALD SCOTT. Pseudonym of Ronald Wilkinson, 1920- . Ref: CA.
The Dark Shadow; see Second Opinion
-Experiment with Eros. Hale, 1967
-The Full Treatment. Heinemann, 1959
Second Opinion. Heinemann, 1961; Macmillan, 1961. Also published as: The Dark Shadow. Macfadden, 1964
The Twin Serpents. Heinemann, 1965; Macmillan, 1965
-Upstairs and Downstairs. Spearman, 1957; Greenberg, 1958

THORNBURG, NEWTON (KENDALL). 1930- .
Ref: CA.
Cutter and Bone. Little, 1976; Heinemann, 1977 [Calif.]
Knockover. GM, 1968; Coronet, 1968 [Milw.]
To Die in California. Little, 1973 [Calif.]

THORNBURY, ETHEL (M.). 1894-
We've Been Waiting for You. Bobbs, 1947 [Wash. D.C.]

THORNDYKE, (ARTHUR) RUSSELL. 1885-1972.
Ref: CA. SC: Mr. Macauley, in at least those marked M; Dr. Syn = S (books set in Eng., ca.1780).
The Amazing Quest of Doctor Syn. Rich, 1938 S
The Courageous Exploits of Doctor Syn. Rich, 1939 S
The Devil in the Belfry; see Herod's Peal
Doctor Syn. Nelson, 1915; Doubleday, 1915 S
Doctor Syn on the High Seas. Rich, 1936 S [ship]
Doctor Syn Returns. Rich, 1935. U.S. title: The Scarecrow Rides. Dial, 1935 S
-The First Englishman. Rich, 1949
The Forbidden Room. Dial, 1933 (British title?)
The Further Adventures of Doctor Syn. Rich, 1936 S
Herod's Peal. Butterworth, 1931. U.S. title: The Devil in the Belfry. Dial, 1932 M
-The House of Jeffreys. Rich, 1943
-Jet and Ivory. Rich, 1934
The Scarecrow Rides; see Doctor Syn Returns
The Shadow of Doctor Syn. Rich, 1944 S
-Show House—Sold. Rich, 1941

The Slype. Holden, 1927; Dial, 1928 M
The Vandekkers. Butterworth, 1929; Appleton, 1930
-The Watch Witch. Butterworth, 1932

THORNE, (ERIC) ANTHONY. 1904- .
So Long at the Fair. Heinemann, 1947; Random, 1947

THORNE, E(RNEST) P(OLLETT). SC: Major "Brains" Cunningham, in at least those marked C; Quentin Eady, in at least those marked QE; Geoff Fennell, in at least those marked GF.
The Angel Steps In. Wright, 1960
Assignment Haiti. Wright, 1963 GF [Haiti]
The Bengal Spider Plan. Wright, 1961 C [India]
The Black Sadhu. Wright, 1935
Black Sunset. Wright, 1963 [Far East]
The Caribbean Affair. Wright, 1966 C [Haiti]
Chinese Poker. Wright, 1964 C [Cairo]
Code Word "Proton." Wright, 1968
Date with the Departed. Wright, 1955 C
The Death Rust. Wright, 1965 [India]
The Devil's Chapel. Wright, 1957 QE
Die Wearing a Rose. Wright, 1959 QE
Evil in the Cup. Wright, 1958 QE
Expect No Mercy. Wright, 1962 QE
The Face of Inspector Britt. Wright, 1947 C
Gallows Inn. Wright, 1958 QE
Ganges Mud. Wright, 1936 [India]
The House of the Fragrant Lotus. Wright, 1962 C [Far East]
The Jungle Hut. Wright, 1966 [Mal.]
Justice Is Mine. Wright, 1950 C
Lady with a Gun. Wright, 1955 C
The Moon Dance. Wright, 1953 C
The Moscow File. Wright, 1967
Operation Dragnet. Wright, 1966 C
Red Bamboo. Wright, 1954 C
Seven Red Herrings. Wright, 1956 QE
The Shadow of Dr. Ferrari. Wright, 1950 C
Sinister Sanctuary. Wright, 1949 C
The Smile of Cheng Su. Wright, 1946 C [China]
They Never Came Back. Wright, 1961 GF [Mid. East]
Three Silent Men. Wright, 1939
White Arab. Wright, 1936
Yoga Mist. Wright, 1937
Zero Minus Nine. Wright, 1964 C

THORNE, EMILY
Aaron's Serpent. Avalon, 1962
The House on Sixteenth Street. Avalon, 1966
The Mystery of Knickbocker Towers. Avalon, 1960
Nothing to Pretend. Avalon, 1963

THORNE, GUY. Pseudonym of C(yril Arthur Edward) Ranger Gull, 1876-1923, q.v.
-Back to Lilac Land. Dillingham, 1920 (British title?)
-A Butterfly on the Wheel. Readers Library, 1928
-Chance in Chains. Laurie, 1913; Sturgis, 1914
-The Charioteer. Ward, 1907
-The Cruiser on Wheels. Jack, 1915
-Divorce. Greening, 1911
Doris Moore. Ward, 1919
-The Drunkard. Greening, 1912; Sturgis, 1912
-The Eyes of Pharaoh. Ward, 1924
-False Gods. Ward, 1923
The Fanshawe Murder. In "An Omnibus Thriller of Murder and Mystery" (four novels by different authors). Laurie, 1931
First It Was Ordained. Ward, 1906
-Fishport. Ward, 1922
The Gentleman from Nowhere. Modern, 193?
-The Hammers of Hate. Skeffington, 1919
-Harder Than Steel. Laurie, 1919
-The Lapse of the Bishop. Ward, 1920
Lucky Mr. Loder. Ward, 1918
-Muriel Wins Through. Long, 1923
The Mystery of St. Michael's. Jenkins, 1924
-An Officer and a Gentleman? and other stories. White, 1909 ss
The Oven. Greening, 1902
-The Polluted City. Ward, 1917
Rescuing Rupert. Long, 1917
The Secret Sea-Plane. Hodder, 1915
The Secret Service Submarine. Jack 1915; Scully, 1915
-Sweetheart Submarine. Greening, 1911
-The Tears of Hate. Ward, 1921
-The Voiceless Victims. Laurie, 1922
-When It Was Dark. Greening, 1903; Putnam, 1904
-When the Wicked Man. Allen, 1916
-A Year and a Day. Ward, 1922

THORNE, JIM
The White Hand of Athene. Pinnacle, 1974

THORNE, MABEL. See: Paul Thorne.

THORNE, PAUL
Murder in the Fog. Penn, 1929 [Chi.]
The Secret Toll, with Mabel Thorne. Dodd, 1922
The Sheridan Road Mystery, with Mabel Thorne. Dodd, 1921 [Chi.]
Spiderweb Clues. Penn, 1928 [Chi.]
That Evening in Shanghai. Penn, 1931 [Shanghai]

THORNER, WILLIAM E. Practicing homoeopath and osteopath.
The Cat of Bast and other stories of mystery. Regency, 1958 ss

THORNETT, ERNEST BASIL CHARLES. Pseudonym: Rupert Penny, q.v.

THORNTON, CHARLES
The Story of the Fast Mail. Continental, 1891. Also published as: The Fast Mail. Donohue, 189?

THORNTON, FRANCIS JOHN. 1938- . Ref: CA.
The Snake Harvest. Coward, 1978 [Phil., 1898]

THORP, RODERICK (MAYNE, JR.). 1936- .
Ref: CA, CC. SC: Joseph Leland, in both titles.
The Detective. Dial, 1966; Barker, 1967
Nothing Lasts Forever. Norton, 1979; Corgi, 1981 [L.A.]

THORPE, EDWARD. 1926- .
The Night I Caught the Sante Fe Chief. Joseph, 1972; St. Martin's, 1973 [S.W.]

THORPE, SYLVIA. Pseudonym of June Sylvia Thimblethorpe, 1926- .
Smuggler's Moon. Rich, 1955. U.S. title: Strangers on the Moor. Pyramid, 1974

THORSON, DELOS RUSSELL. 1906- . Joint pseudonym with Sara Winfree Thorson, 1906- : Kit Christian, q.v.

THORSON, SARA WINFREE. 1906- . Joint pseudonym with Delos Russell Thorson, 1906- : Kit Christian, q.v.

THRELFALL, T. R.
The Strange Adventures of a Magistrate. Everett, 1903

THUM, MARCELLA. Ref: CA.
Abbey Court. Doubleday, 1976 [Ire., 1800s]
Fernwood. Doubleday, 1973. British title: The Haunting Cavalier. Milton House, 1974 [Va., 1860s]
The Haunting Cavalier; see Fernwood

THURLEY, NORGROVE. Pseudonym of C(harles) Thurley Stoneham, 1895- , q.v.
Bamboo Elephants. Paul, 1956
Death for Dollars. Paul, 1951
The Devil's Steps. Paul, 1947
Giants of Darkness. Paul, 1957
Grow Grey with Fear. Paul, 1952
Lonely Water. Paul, 1948
Murder Strikes North. Paul, 1951 [Can.]
The Trail of the Ghosts. Paul, 1955
The Treacherous Border. Long, 1958
The Woman in the Case. Long, 1959

THURLOW, DAVID
Double Double-Cross. Hale, 1978
Hate for Eight, with Ross Peers. Hale, 1978
Incubus, with Ross Peers. Hale, 1977
Ransom for the First Lady. Hale, 1979
Schade, with Ross Peers. Hale, 1977
-The Sleepers. Hale, 1980
Takeover. Hale, 1978

THURMAN, CARYL. 1938- . See: Irene King, 1943- .

THURMAN, STEVE. Pseudonym of Frank Castle, q.v.
"Mad Dog" Coll. Monarch, 1961 (Novelization of the movie.) [NYC, 1932]
Night After Night. Monarch, 1959

THURSTON, KATHERINE CECIL. 1875-1911.
-The Masquerader. Harper, 1904
-The Mystics. Blackwood, 1970; Harper, 1907

THURSTON, (ERNEST) TEMPLE. 1879-1933.
The Diamond Pendant. Doubleday, 1932 (British title?)

John Boddy: Leaves from a Constable's Notebook. Ward, 1931 ss
Man in a Black Hat. Cassell, 1930; Doubleday, 1931
Portrait of a Spy. Putnam (London), 1928; Doubleday, 1929 [Fr.]

THURSTON, WESLEY S.   -1966.
The Trumpets of November. Geis, 1966

THWAITES, FREDERICK J(OSEPH)
-The Dark Abyss. Harcourt (London), 1955
The Mad Doctor. Quality, 1938
The Mad Doctor in Harley Street. Quality, 1939

THYNNE, ALEXANDER
The Carry-Cot. Allen, 1972. Also published as: Blue Blood. Star, 1974

THYNNE, MOLLY. SC: Dr. Constantine = C.
The Case of Sir Adam Braid. Nelson, 1930
The Crime at the "Noah's Ark". Nelson, 1931 C
The Draycott Murder Mystery; see The Red Dwarf
He Dies and Makes No Sign. Hutchinson, 1933 C
Murder in the Dentist Chair. Hutchinson, 1932; Covici, 1932 C
The Murder on the "Enriqueta". Nelson, 1929. U.S. title: The Strangler. Minton, 1929
The Red Dwarf. Nelson, 1928. U.S. title: The Draycott Murder Mystery. Stokes, 1928
The Strangler; see The Murder on the "Enriqueta"

THYNNE, ROBERT
Boffin's Find. Long, 1899 [Australia, 1850s]

TIBBITTS, GEORGE F(RANKLIN). 1864-   .
The Mystery of Kun-Ja-Muck Cave. Brieger, 1924 [N.Y.]

TIBBLE, ANN (NORTHGRAVE). 1912-   . Ref: CA.
The God Spigo. Duckworth, 1976

TICKELL, JERRARD. 1905-1966. Born in Ire.
Appointment with Venus. Hodder, 1951. U.S. title: Island Rescue. Doubleday, 1952
-At Dusk All Cats Are Grey. Chapman, 1940
-Dark Adventure. Mellifont, 1953
High Water at Four. Hodder, 1965; Doubleday, 1966
The Hunt for Richard Thorpe; see Whither Do You Wander?
Island Rescue; see Appointment with Venus
Jill Fell Down. Heinemann, 1938; Morrow, 1939
-Silk Purse. Heinemann, 1937
-Soldier from the Wars Returning. Chapman, 1942
Villa Mimosa. Hodder, 1960; Doubleday, 1961
Whither Do You Wander? Hodder, 1959. U.S. title: The Hunt for Richard Thorpe. Doubleday, 1960
Yolan; see Yolan of the Plains
Yolan of the Plains. Richards, 1928. U.S. title: Yolan. Putnam, 1929 [Buda.]

TICKNER, F. C. All titles are 16-32 page booklets.
The Dance of Death. Danceland, 1946
Death at the Towers. Danceland, 1946
Line-Up for Murder. Beverley, 1944
Murder Makes a Call. Danceland, 1946
Murderers Three. Danceland, 1946
Three Were to Die. Danceland, 1946

TIDYMAN, ERNEST. 1928-   . Ref: CA, TC. SC: John Shaft = JS.
Goodbye, Mr. Shaft. Dial, 1973; Weidenfeld, 1974 JS [Eng.]
The Last Shaft. Weidenfeld, 1975 JS
Line of Duty. Little, 1974; Allen, 1974 [Cleve.]
Shaft. Macmillan, 1970; Joseph, 1971 JS [NYC]
Shaft Among the Jews. Dial, 1972; Weidenfeld, 1973 JS [NYC]
Shaft Has a Ball. Bantam, 1973; Corgi, 1973 JS
Shaft's Big Score. Bantam, 1972; Corgi, 1972 JS
Shaft's Carnival of Killers. Bantam, 1974; Bantam (London), 1974 JS [Jam.]
Starstruck. Allen, 1975

TIGER, JOHN. Pseudonym of Walter (Herman) Wager, 1924-   , q.v. Other pseudonym: Walter Hermann, q.v. S: novelizations of the "I Spy" TV series = IS; novelizations of the "Mission Impossible" TV series = MI.
Code Name: Little Ivan. Popular Library, 1969 MI [Ger.]
Countertrap. Popular Library, 1967 IS [Moscow]
Death Hits the Jackpot. Avon, 1954 [Chi.]
Death-Twist. Popular Library, 1968 IS
Doomdate. Popular Library, 1967 IS [Mid. East]
I Spy. Popular Library, 1965 IS
Masterstroke. Popular Library, 1966 IS
Mission Impossible. Popular Library, 1967 MI [S. Am.]
Superkill. Popular Library, 1967 IS [Berlin]
Wipeout. Popular Library, 1967 IS [Carib.]

TIGHE, HARRY. 1877-   .
The Man in the Fog. Heath, 1916

TILBURN, E. O. Pseudonyms: Nevada Ned, Dr. N. T. Oliver, qq.v.

TILDEN, FREEMAN. 1883-   .
The Spanish Prisoner. Doubleday, 1928 [Sp.]

TILLER, TED
Count Dracula. French (NYC), 1972 (3-act play based on the novel by Bram Stoker, 1847-1912, q.v.)

TILLETT, DOROTHY STOCKBRIDGE. 1896-   . Pseudonym: John Stephen Strange, q.v.

TILTON, ALICE. Pseudonym of Phoebe Atwood Taylor, 1909-1976, q.v. Other pseudonym: Freeman Dana, q.v. SC: Leonidas Witherall, in all titles.
Beginning with a Bash. Norton, 1972; Collins, 1937 [Boston]
Cold Steal. Norton, 1939; Collins, 1940 [Mass.]
The Cut Direct. Norton, 1938; Collins, 1938 [Mass.]
Dead Ernest. Norton, 1944; Collins, 1945 [Mass.]
File for Record. Norton, 1943; Collins, 1944 [Mass.]
The Hollow Chest. Norton, 1941; Collins, 1942 [Mass.]
The Iron Clew. Farrar, 1947. British title: The Iron Hand. Collins, 1947 [Mass.]
The Iron Hand; see The Iron Clew
The Left Leg. Norton, 1940; Collins, 1941 [Mass.]

TIMINS, DOUGLAS
A Double Quest. Methuen, 1930
The Extra Passenger. Hutchinson, 1928 [Arg.]
The Phantom Train. Hutchinson, 1926

TIMLETT, PETER VALENTINE
The Seedbreakers. Quartet, 1974; Bantam, 1976

TIMPERLEY, ROSEMARY (KENYON). 1920-   . Ref: CA.
The House of Mad Children. Hale, 1980
Suspicion. Hale, 1978

TINAYRE, (MARGUERITE SUZANNE) MARCELLE (CHASTEAU). 1872-1948.
Death at the Chateau. Jarrolds, 1934 (Translation of "Chateau en Limousin." Paris, 1934.)

TINDALL, GILLIAN. 1938-   . Ref: CA.
The Intruder. Hodder, 1979

TINE, ROBERT. ca.1955-   .
State of Grace. Viking,   1980 [Rome]

TINKER, BEAMISH. Pseudonym of F(ryniwyd) Tennyson Jesse, 1889?-1958, q.v.
The Man Who Stayed at Home. Mills, 1915 (Novelization of the play by Lechmere Worrall and J. E. Harold Terry.)

TIPPETTE, GILES. 1936-   . Ref: CA. SC: Wilson Young = WY.
The Bank Robber. Macmillan, 1970 WY [West, 1800s]
The Mercenaries. Delacorte, 1976; Sphere, 1977 [Afr.]
-The Sunshine Killers. Dell, 1980
Wilson's Gold. Dell, 1980 WY [West, 1800s]
Wilson's Luck. Dell, 1980 WY [West, 1800s]

TIRBUTT, HONORIA. Pseudonym: Emma Page, q.v.

TITHERADGE, DION. 1889-   .
The Crooked Billet. French (London), 1930 (3-act play.)

TITTERTON, J.
Death Ray Dictator. Organ, 1946

TOBIAS, JAY. 1896-   . All titles are plays; number of acts in parenthesis.
The Black Widow. Denison, 1939 (1)
Gangway for Ghosts. Denison, 1940 (3)
Ghost-Farm. Drama Guild, 1943 (1)
House for Sale Haunted! Drama Guild, 1947 (3)
Lucifer's Lodge. Denison, 1935
The Scarecrow Creeps. Denison, 1934 (3)
Spooks and Spasms. Baker's, 1942 (3)
Spooky Tavern. Denison, 1932 (3)
Tune in on Terror. Eldridge, 1959 (3)
The Valley of Ghosts. Dramatic, 1931 (3)
You'll Die Laughing! Drama Guild, 1944 (3)

TOBIAS, KATHERINE. Pseudonym of Theodore Mark Gottfried, 1928-   . Other pseudonym: Harry Gregory, q.v. Ref: CA.
The Lady in the Lightning. Lancer, 1966 [Ger.]

TODD, IAN (MENZIES). 1923-   . Ref: CA.
Ghost of the Assassins. Seemann, 1976

TODD, PAUL. Pseudonym of Richard Posner, 1944-   , q.v. Other pseudonyms: Iris Foster, Beatrice Murray, qq.v.
Blood All Over. Warner, 1975 [L.I.]

TODD, PETER. Pseudonym of Charles Harold St. John Hamilton, 1876-1961. Incredibly prolific British author of juvenile fiction: some 5000 stories, about 100 million words.
The Adventures of Herlock Sholmes. Mysterious Press, 1976 ss

TODD, ROBERT HENRY
The Solver of Mysteries and other stories. Charters, 1930 ss

TODD, RUTHVEN. 1914-   . Pseudonym: R. T. Campbell, q.v.

TOEPFER, RAY GRANT. 1923-   . Ref: CA.
Endplay. GM, 1975; Coronet, 1976 [NYC]
The Witness. Muller, 1966

TOFTE, ARTHUR. 1902-1980. Ref: CA.
The Ghost Hunters. Major, 1978

TOKSON, ELLIOT. SC: Alec Cavender = AC.
Appointment in Calcutta. GM, 1979; Magnum, 1981 AC [Calcutta]
Cavender's Balkan Quest. GM, 1977; Magnum, 1981 AC [Balkans, ca.1914]
Desert Captive. GM, 1977; Magnum, 1980 AC [Afr.]
The Quintana Inheritance. GM, 1980

TOLER, BUCK. Pseudonym of Harold Ernest Kelly, 1899-   . Other pseudonyms: Eugene Ascher, Darcy Glinto, Gordon Holt, qq.v.
The Bronsville Massacre. Mitre, 1943
It's Only Saps That Die. Everybody's, 1944
Killer on the Run. Everybody's, 1946
Tough on the Wops. Robin Hood, 1947

TOLER, SIDNEY
Somebody's Crooked. French (NYC), 1929 (3-act play.)

TOLLEMACHE, E(DWARD) D(EVEREUX) H(AMILTON). See: P. P. Muir.

TOLLER, ERNEST. 1893-1939.
The Blind Goddess. Lane, 1934 (Translation of "Die Blinde Gottin." Berlin, 1933.) (5-act play.) Adapted by Denis Johnston as: Blind Man's Bluff. Cape, 1938

TOLMAN, HILDEGARDE. Pseudonym of Hildegarde Tolman Teilhet, 1906-   , q.v. See also: Darwin L. Teilhet, 1904-1964. SC: Sam Hook = SH (see also Hildegarde Tolman Teilhet entry).
Hero by Proxy. Little, 1942; Gollancz, 1943 as by Darwin L. Teilhet SH [Cent. Am.]

TOMA, DAVID and JACK PEARL, q.v.
The Airport Affair. Dell, 1975 [Newark]

TOMERLIN, JOHN (E.). 1930- . Joint pseudonym with Charles Nutt, 1929-1967: Keith Grantland, q.v.
  Comeback. Paperback Library, 1969 [Fr.]
  Return to Vikki. GM, 1959; Consul, 1961 [N.Y.]

TOM-GALLON, NELLIE and CALDER WILSON
  He Who Walked in Scarlet. Unwin, 1924
  Monsieur Zero. Unwin, 1923 ss [Fr.]

TOMLINSON, GERALD. 1933- . Ref: CA.
  On a Field of Black. Nellin, 1980 [Pa., 1875]

TOMS, BERNARD. 1931- . Ref: CA, CC.
  The Strange Affair. Constable, 1966

TONKIN, PETER (FRANCIS). 1950- . Ref: CA.
  -Killer. Hodder, 1979; Coward, 1979

TOOLE, WYC(LIFFE D., JR.). A rear admiral in the U.S. Navy; author of mystery ss and articles on military affairs.
  Death in Deep Shadows. Stickley, 1977 [Fla.]

TOOMBS, JANE JENKE
  The Fog Maiden. Ballantine, 1976
  Point of Lost Souls. Avon, 1975 [Mich.]
  A Topaz for My Lady Fair. Ballantine, 1975
  Tule Witch. Avon, 1973

TOOMBS, JOHN. Pseudonym: Fortune Kent, q.v.

TOPEROFF, SAM. 1933- . See: James Roosevelt, 1907- .

TOPOL, ALLAN. 1941- . Ref: CA.
  -The Fourth of July War. Morrow, 1978 [Iran, 1983]
  A Woman of Valor. Morrow, 1980 [Mid. East]

TOPOR, ROLAND. 1938- .
  The Tenant. Allen, 1966; Doubleday, 1966 (Translation of "Le Locataire Chemerique." Paris, 1964.)

TOPOR, TOM. 1938- . Ref: CA.
  Bloodstar. Norton, 1978 [NYC]
  Tightrope Minor. Doubleday, 1971

TORBETT, D.
  Kick-In. Clode, 1915 (Novelization of the play by Willard Mack, 1878-1934, q.v.) [NYC]
  On Trial. Dodd, 1951 (Novelization of the play by Elmer L. Reizenstein, 1892-1967, q.v.) [NYC]
  -Sinners. Clode, 1915 (Novelization of the play by Owen Davis, 1874-1956, q.v.)

TORDAY, URSULA. 1888- . Pseudonyms: Paula Allardyce, Charity Blackstock, Charlotte Keppel, qq.v., Lee Blackstock.

TORGERSON, EDWIN DIAL. SC: Pierre Montigny, in both titles.
  The Cold Finger Curse. Falcon, 1933 [NYC]
  The Murderer Returns. Lane, 1931; Smith, 1930 [Montr.]

TORQUEMADA. Pseudonym of Edward Powys Mathers, 1892-1939.
  The Torquemada Puzzle Book. Gollancz, 1934 (Includes one criminous puzzle story.)

TORR, DOMINIC. Pseudonym of John Branfrost Simpson Pedler. Ref: CC. Diplomat educated in Boston; has been war correspondent and lecturer on foreign affairs.
  Diplomatic Cover. Barker, 1965; Harcourt, 1966 [Paris]
  A Mission of Mercy. Hodder, 1969; Stein, 1969
  The Treason Line. Cape, 1968; Stein, 1968 [Geneva]

TORRES, EDWIN. Grew up in NYC's Spanish Harlem, was first Puerto Rican Assistant D.A. in NYC. SC: Carlito = C.
  After Hours. Dial, 1979; Futura, 1979 C
  Carlito's Way. Saturday Review Press, 1975; Star, 1977 C [NYC]
  Q & A. Dial, 1977; Futura, 1978 [NYC]

TORREY, ROGER
  42 Days for Murder. Hillman-Curl, 1938 [Reno]

TORREY (BUDLONG), WARE. 1905-1967. Pseudonyms: Lee Crosby, Meg Padget, Judith Ware, Joan Winslow, qq.v.

TORRIE, MALCOLM. Pseudonym of Gladys (Maude Winifred) Mitchell, 1901- q.v. SC: Timothy Herring, in all titles. Set: Eng.
  Bismarck Herrings. Joseph, 1971
  Churchyard Salad. Joseph, 1969
  Heavy As Lead. Joseph, 1966
  Late and Cold. Joseph, 1967
  Shade of Darkness. Joseph, 1970
  Your Secret Friend. Joseph, 1968

TORRIO, VINCENTE. SC: Jim Sheridan, in all titles, set in Chi. in 1920s.
  Bootlegger. New English Library pb, 1975
  Dealer. New English Library pb, 1976
  The Executioner. New English Library, 1975
  Politician. New English Library pb, 1976

TOURGEE, ALBION (WINEGAR). 1838-1905.
  With Gauge and Swallow, Attorneys. Lippincott, 1889 ss

TOURNEY, LEONARD (D.). Prof. of Eng. at U. of Tulsa, Okla.
  The Players' Boy Is Dead. Harper, 1980; Hale, 1982 [Eng., 1601]

TOUSSAINT-SAMAT, JEAN. 1865- . SC: M. Levert = L.
  The Dead Man at the Window. Lippincott, 1934 (Translation of "Le Mort a la Fenetre." Paris, 1933.) L [Fr.]
  Ships Aflame! Lippincott, 1935 [ship]
  Shoes That Had Walked Twice. Lippincott, 1933 (Translation of "L'Horrible Mort de Miss Gildchrist." Paris, 1932.) L [Fr.]

TOWER, DIANA. Pseudonym of Richard Rein Smith, 1930- . Other pseudonym: Richard Reinsmith, q.v.
  Dark Diamond. Beagle, 1975
  A Gleam of Sapphire. Ballantine, 1975
  Prisoner of Evil. Major, 1976
  Red Lion. Ballantine, 1974

TOWER, STELLA (MARY HODGSON). 1891- . Pseudonym: Faith Wolseley, q.v.
  Dumb Vengeance. Hutchinson, 1933
  Yesterday's Bones. Hutchinson, 1934

TOWNE, STUART. Pseudonym of Clayton Rawson, 1906-1971, q.v. SC: Don Diavolo, in both titles.
  Death from Nowhere. Yogi, 194? (Two DD novelets disguised as a novel.)
  Death out of Thin Air. Coward, 1941; Cassell, 1947 (Two DD novelets.) [NYC]

TOWNEND, PAUL. 1925- .
  Died o' Wednesday. Collins, 1959; Walker, 1962 [Switz.]
  The Man on the End of the Rope. Collins, 1960; Dutton, 1960 [Switz.]
  The Road to El Saida. Collins, 1961 [Afr.]

TOWNEND, PETER (ROBERT GASCOIGNE). 1935- . Graduate of Cambridge; magazine publisher, photographer, correspondent for travel magazine. Pseudonym: Peter Gascoigne, q.v. SC: Philip Quest, in at least those marked PQ.
  Fisheye. Pinnacle, 1976
  Out of Focus. Heinemann, 1971; St. Martin's, 1972 PQ [Sp.]
  Triple Exposure. Pinnacle, 1977 PQ
  Zoom! Heinemann, 1972; St. Martin's, 1972 PQ [Sard.]

TOWNER, (JAMES) AUSBURN. 1836-1909.
  -The House Terrible. Collier, 1893
  -Seven Days in a Pullman Car. Ogilvie, 1883 ss

TOWNLEY, HOUGHTON
  -The Bishop's Emeralds. Greening, 1907; Watt, 1908
  The Case of the Human Mole. Amalgamated Press, 1927 (Sexton Blake.)
  -Dazzled. Trischler, 1891
  -The Gay Lord Waring. Greening, 1910; Watt, 1910
  His Own Accuser. Ward, 1894
  -The Scarlet Feather. Watt, 1909 (British title?)
  The Secret of the Raft. Greening, 1909
  The Sin of the Duchess. Greening, 1909
  -The Splendid Coward. Greening, 1908

TOWNSEND, CHARLES. 1857-1914.
  The Mahoney Million. New Amsterdam, 1903

TOWNSEND, EDWARD W(ATERMAN). 1855-1942.
  -Lees and Leaven. McClure, 1903

TOWSON, HAZEL
  The Black and the White. Stockwell, 1977

TOY, BARBARA. See: Moie Charles.

TOYE, NINA
  The Twice Murdered Man. Eyre, 1935 [It.]

TOYE, STANLEY (PERCIVAL). SC: Anthony Read, in at least those marked AR.
  Cyanide! Nelson, 1940 AR
  The Laughing Cat. Melrose, 1950
  The Line Between. Melrose, 1948
  Murder in the Lady Chapel. Melrose, 1944
  Prelude to Peril. Melrose, 1946 AR
  Sinners in Clover. Melrose, 1945 AR

TOZER, ALFRED B. Pseudonym: Nicholas Carter, q.v.

TOZER, BASIL (JOHN JOSEPH). 1872- .
  A Daughter of Belial. Redman, 1908
  A Dealer in Antiques. Ward, 1923
  The Elusive Lord Bagtor. Laurie, 1939
  The Riddle of the Forest. Laurie, 1931 [Eng., 1890s]
  Secret Traffic. Laurie, 1935
  Vengeance. Ward, 1916

TRACEY, GRANT
  Call It Murder. Hale, 1972
  The Paradise Conspiracy. Hale, 1972
  The Take-Away Girl. Hale, 1973

TRACY, DON(ALD FISKE). 1905-1976. Pseudonym: Roger Fuller, q.v. Ref: CA. SC: Giff Speer = GB.
  The Big Blackout. Detective Book Club, 1959
  The Big Brass Ring. Trident, 1963
  The Big X. PB, 1976 GS [Md.]
  The Black Amulet. PB, 1968
  A Corpse Can Sure Louse Up a Weekend! PB, 1973 [Fla.]
  The Cheat; see Criss-Cross
  Criss-Cross. Vanguard, 1934; Constable, 1935. Also published as: The Cheat. Lion, 1951
  Deadly to Bed. PB, 1960 GS
  Death Calling—Collect. PB, 1976 GS [Conn.]
  The Editor. PB, 1973 [U.S., 1932]
  Flats Fixed—Among Other Things. PB, 1974 GS [Fla.]
  Fun and Deadly Games. PB, 1968 GS [Fla.]
  The Hated One. Simon, 1963; Cassell, 1963 [Fla.]
  High, Wide and Ransom. PB, 1976 GS
  How Sleeps the Beast. Mill, 1938; Constable, 1937 [Md.]
  Last Year's Snow. Mill, 1937; Constable, 1937. Also published as: White Hell. Berkley, 1955
  Look Down on Her Dying. PB, 1968 GS [La.]
  Naked She Died. PB, 1962 GS [La.]
  -No Trespassing. Lippincott, 1961
  Pot of Trouble. PB, 1971 GS [Ariz.]
  Round Trip. Vanguard, 1934; Constable, 1935 [Md.]
  White Hell; see Last Year's Snow

TRACY, HUGH
  Career with Death. Hale, 1970
  Death in Disguise. Hale, 1969
  Death in Reserve. Gollancz, 1976

TRACY, LOUIS. 1863-1928. Pseudonym, jointly in part with M(atthew) P(hipps) Shiel, 1865-1947, q.v.: Gordon Holmes, q.v. Ref: CC, EM, MM, MP. SC: Insp. Furneau, in at least those marked F (see also Gordon Holmes entry); Reginald Brett, in at least those marked RB. Set: Eng.
  The Albert Gate Affair. Ward, 1904. U.S. title: The Albert Gate Mystery. Fenno, 1904 RB
  The Albert Gate Mystery; see The Albert Gate Affair
  -At the Court of the Maharaja. American News, 1906 (British title?)
  The Bartlett Mystery. Clode, 1919 (British title?) [NYC]
  The Black Cat. Hodder, 1925; Clode, 1925 F
  -The Captain of the Kansas. Jarrolds, 1931; Clode, 1907
  The Case of Mortimer Fenley. Cassell, 1915. U.S. title: The Strange Case of Mortimer Fenley. Clode, 1919 F

-Cynthia's Chauffeur. Clode, 1910 (= Sylvia's Chauffeur?)
-A Dangerous Situation. Clode, 1932 (British title?)
-The Darkest Hour. Digby, 1903; Westbrook, 1920?
-The Day of Wrath. Chambers, 1916; Clode, 1916
Diana of the Moorland; see Diana of the Moors
Diana of the Moors. Cassell, 1914. U.S. title: Diana of the Moorland. Clode, 1918
A Fatal Legacy. Ward, 1903
Fennell's Tower. Ward, 1908
-Flower of the Gorse. Cassell, 1916; Clode, 1915
The Gleave Mystery. Hodder, 1926; Clode, 1926 F
-The Great Mogul. Clode, 1905 (British title?)
-Heart's Delight. Ward, 1906
-His Unknown Wife. Cassell, 1915; Clode, 1916
The House of Peril. Clode, 1922 (British title?) F [NYC]
The House of Silence; see The Silent House
A Japanese Revenge. Westbrook, ca.1920 (British title?)
-The King's Messenger. White, 1905
The Lastingham Murder; see The Third Miracle
The Law of the Talon. Hodder, 1926; Clode, 1926 F
The Manning-Burke Murder; see The One Girl in a Million
The Message. Ward, 1909; Clode, 1908
-Minkie. Ward, 1910; Clode, 1907
-Mirabil's Island. Ward, 1912; Clode, 1912
-A Morganatic Wife. White, 1904
A Mysterious Disappearance. Hodder, 1928; Clode, 1905, as by Gordon Holmes
No Other Way. Ward, 1913; Clode, 1912, as by Gordon Holmes [U.S.]
Number Seventeen. Cassell, 1916; Clode, 1915 F
The One Girl in a Million. Hodder, 1928. U.S. title: The Manning-Burke Murder. Clode, 1930 F
-One Wonderful Night. Ward, 1913; Clode, 1913
The Park Lane Mystery. Hodder, 1924
The Passing of Charles Lanson. Hodder, 1925; Clode, 1924 F
The Pelham Affair. Clode, 1923 (British title?)
The Pillar of Light. Ward, 1905; Clode, 1904. Also published as: The Wreck of the Chinook. Clode, 1930
The Postmaster's Daughter. Cassell, 1917; Clode, 1916 F
-Princess Kate. White, 1903
-Rainbow Island. Ward, 1903
The Revellers. White, 1904; Clode, 1917
The Sandling Case; see What Would You Have Done?
-The Second Baronet. Hodder, 1923
The Silent Barrier. Ward, 1909; Clode, 1911
The Silent House. Nash, 1911. U.S. title: The House of Silence. Clode, 1911, as by Gordon Holmes
-A Son of the Immortals. Ward, 1912; Clode, 1909
-Souls on Fire. Clode, 1904 (British title?)
-The Stowaway. Ward, 1910; Clode, 1909. Also published as: The Stowaway Girl. Clode, 1912
The Stowaway Girl; see The Stowaway
The Stowmarket Mystery. Ward, 1904; Fenno, 1904 RB
The Strange Case of Mortimer Fenley; see The Case of Mortimer Fenley
The Strange Disappearance of Lady Delia. Pearson, 1901
Sylvia's Chauffeur. Ward, 1911 (= Cynthia's Chauffeur?)
-The Terms of Surrender. Cassell, 1914; Clode, 1913 [S. Am.]
The Third Miracle. Hodder, 1927. U.S. title: The Lastingham Murder. Clode, 1929 F
The Token. Hodder, 1924; Clode, 1924 F
-Waifs of Circumstance. Hodder, 1906
What Would You Have Done? Hodder, 1928. U.S. title: The Sandling Case. Clode, 1931 F
The Wheel o' Fortune. Ward, 1908; Clode, 1907
-The Winning of Winifred. White, 1906
The Women in the Case. Hodder, 1927; Clode, 1928 F
-The Wooing of Esther Gray. Pearson, 1902
The Wreck of the Chinook; see The Pillar of Light

TRACY, VIRGINIA
The Moment After. Doubleday, 1930; Mathews, 1931 [NYC]
Personal Appearance of a Lioness. Lippincott, 1937 [NYC]
"Persons Unknown." Century, 1914

TRAFTON, EDWIN H.
"Cell 13." Ogilvie, 1888

TRAIL, ARMITAGE. Pseudonym of Maurice Coons.
Scarface. Clode, 1930; Long, 1931
The Thirteenth Guest. Whitman, 1929

TRAILL, PETER. Pseudonym of Guy (Mainwaring) Morton, 1896-   , q.v.
-The Angel. Grayson, 1934
-Carry Me Home. Grayson, 1934
The Deceiving Mirror. Jenkins, 1947
-The Divine Spark. Faber, 1926
-Golden Oriole. Methuen, 1940
-Great Dust. Grayson, 1932
-Half Mast. Grayson, 1936
-The Life Fashionable. Brentano's (London), 1929
-Mutation Mink. Jenkins, 1950
Not Proven. Barker, 1938
The Portly Peregrine. Jenkins, 1948
-Red, Green and Amber. Grayson, 1935 ss
-The Rope of Sand. Jenkins, 1951
-Six of One. Barker, 1938 ss
The Sleeve of Night. Grayson, 1937
-So Sits the Turtle. Jenkins, 1948
-Under the Cherry Tree. Faber, 1926
-The White Hen. Faber, 1927
-Wings of Tomorrow. Jenkins, 1950

TRAIN, ARTHUR. 1875-1945. Ref: CC, EM, MP, TC. SC: Ephraim Tutt = ET.
The Adventures of Ephraim Tutt. Scribner, 1930 ET
The Blind Goddess. Scribner, 1926 [NYC]
By Advice of Counsel. Scribner, 1921 ET ss [NYC]
The Confessions of Artemas Quibble. Scribner, 1911 [NYC]
"C.Q."; or, In the Wireless House. Century, 1912
The Hermit of Turkey Hollow. Scribner, 1921 ET
McAllister and His Double. Scribner, 1905; Newnes, 1905 ss [NYC]
Manhattan Murder. Scribner, 1936 [NYC]
Mortmain. Appleton, 1907 ss
Mr. Tutt Comes Home. Scribner, 1941 ET ss
Mr. Tutt Finds a Way. Scribner, 1945 ET ss
Mr. Tutt Takes the Stand. Scribner, 1936 ET ss [NYC]
Mr. Tutt's Case Book. Scribner, 1936 ET
Murderer's Medicine. Constable, 1937 (U.S. title?)
Old Man Tutt. Scribner, 1938 ET ss
Page Mr. Tutt. Scribner, 1926 ET ss [NYC]
Tut, Tut! Mr. Tutt. Scribner, 1923; Nash, 1924 ET [NYC]
Tutt and Mr. Tutt. Scribner, 1920 ET ss [NYC]
Tutt for Tutt. Scribner, 1934 ET ss
When Tutt Meets Tutt. Scribner, 1927 ET ss [NYC]
Yankee Lawyer—The Autobiography of Ephraim Tutt. Scribner, 1943 ET

TRALINS, (STANLEY) ROBERT. 1926-   . Ref: CA. SC: Lee Crosley = LC.
The Chic Chic Spy. Belmont, 1966 LC
Dragnet '67. Popular Library, 1967 (Novelization of the TV series.) [L.A.]
The Miss from S.I.S. Belmont, 1966 LC
The Ring-a-Ding UFOs. Belmont, 1967 LC [Fla.]

TRANTER, NIGEL (GODWIN). Pseudonym of Nye Tredgold, 1909-   . Ref: CA.
-Balefire. Hodder, 1958
-Bridal Path. Ward, 1952
Cable from Kabul. Hodder, 1968
-Cheviot Chase. Ward, 1952
-The Chosen Course. Ward, 1949
-Colours Flying. Ward, 1948
-Delayed Action. Ward, 1944
-Drug on the Market. Hodder, 1962
-Ducks and Drakes. Ward, 1953
-Eagle's Feathers. Ward, 1941
-The Enduring Flame. Hodder, 1957
-Fair Game. Ward, 1950
-Fast and Loose. Ward, 1951
-Flight of Dutchmen. Hodder, 1947
-The Flockmasters. Hodder, 1960
-The Freebooters. Ward, 1950
-The Gilded Fleece. Ward, 1942
-Gold for Prince Charlie. Hodder, 1962
-Harsh Heritage. Ward, 1939
-High Spirits. Collins, 1950
-Island Twilight. Ward, 1947
-Kettle of Fish. Hodder, 1961

-The Long Coffin. Ward, 1956
-Mammon's Daughter. Ward, 1939
The Man Behind the Curtain. Hodder, 1959
-Man's Estate. Ward, 1946
-The Night Riders. Ward, 1954
-The Queen's Grace. Ward, 1953
-Rio d'Oro. Ward, 1955
-Root and Branch. Ward, 1948
-Rum Week. Ward, 1954
-Spanish Galleon. Hodder, 1960
The Stone. Hodder, 1958; Putnam, 1959
-There Are Worse Jungles. Ward, 1955
-Tidewrack. Ward, 1951
-Tinker's Pride. Ward, 1945
-Trespass. Moray, 1937
-Watershed. Ward, 1941

TRASK, KEITH. Born in NYC, educated at Columbia U.; mechanical engineer, magazine writer; living in Calif. in 1930s.
Captain King Investigates; see Murder Incidental
Dead Men Do Tell. Farrar, 1931 [Calif.]
Murder Incidental. Farrar, 1931. British title: Captain King Investigates. Butterworth, 1932 [ship]

TRASK, MERRILL. Pseudonym of Hal Braham, q.v. Other pseudonym: Mel Colton, q.v.
Murder in Brief. Mystery House, 1956 [L.A.]

TRAUBEL, HELEN
The Metropolitan Opera Murders. Simon, 1951 (Ghost-written by Harold Q. Masur, 1909-   , q.v.) [NYC, theatre]

TRAUGOT, LEANORE
The Curious Locket. Major, 1976

TRAVER, ROBERT. Pseudonym of John Donaldson Voelker, 1903-   . See also: Elihu Winner. Ref: CA, CC.
Anatomy of a Murder. St. Martin's, 1958; Faber, 1958 [Mich.]
-Laughing Whitefish. McGraw, 1965; Allen, 1967
Small-Town D.A. Dutton, 1954; Faber, 1959 (Dramatized autobiographical episodes.) [Mich.]

TRAVERS, HUGH. Pseudonym of Hugh (Travers) Mills, q.v. SC: Madame Aubry, in both titles.
Madame Aubry and the Police. Elek, 1966; Harper, 1967 [Paris]
Madame Aubry Dines with Death. Elek, 1967; Harper, 1967 [Fr.]

TRAVERS, ROBERT (JOHN). 1911?-1974. Ref: CA.
The Apartment on K Street. Little, 1972

TRAVIS, GERRY. Pseudonym of Louis (Preston) Trimble, 1917-   , q.v. Other pseudonym: Stuart Brock, q.v.
The Big Bite. Mystery House, 1957 [Mex.]
A Lovely Mask for Murder. Mystery House, 1956
-Tarnished Love. Phoenix, 1942

TRAVIS, GRETCHEN A. Ref: CA.
The Cottage. Putnam, 1973; Franklin, 1974 [N.Y.]
Holiday of Fear. Signet, 1968 [Yugos.]
She Fell Among Thieves. Doubleday, 1963; Hale, 1964 [NYC]
Too Old to Die. Putnam, 1968; Hale, 1969 [Neb.]
2 Spruce Lane. Putnam, 1975

TREAT, LAWRENCE. 1903-   . Name originally: Lawrence Arthur Goldstone, q.v. Ref: CA, CC, TC. SC: Bill Decker = BD; Jub Freeman = JF; Mitch Taylor = MT; Carl Wayward = CW.
B as in Banshee. Duell, 1940. Also published as: Wail for the Corpses. Best Detective Selection, 1943 CW [N.Y.]
Big Shot. Harper, 1951; Boardman, 1952 MT,BD,JF [N.Y.]
D As in Dead. Duell, 1941 CW [New Or.]
F As in Flight. Morrow, 1948; Boardman, 1949 JF,BD [N.Y.]
H As in Hangman. Duell, 1942 CW [N.Y.]
H As in Hunted. Duell, 1946; Boardman, 1950 JF [NYC]
Lady, Drop Dead. Abelard (NYC & London), 1960 MT,JF [N.Y.]
The Leather Man. Duell, 1944; Rich, 1947
O As in Omen. Duell, 1943 CW [N.Y.]
Over the Edge. Morrow, 1948; Boardman, 1958 JF,BD [N.Y.]
P As in Police. Davis, 1970 MT,JF ss

Q As in Quicksand. Duell, 1947. British title: Step into Darkness. Boardman, 1959 MT,JF
Step into Quicksand; see Q As in Quicksand
T As in Trapped. Morrow, 1947 MT,JF [NYC]
Trial and Terror. Morrow, 1949; Boardman, 1958 [N.Y.]
V As in Victim. Duell, 1945; Rich, 1950 MT,JF [NYC]
Venus Unarmed. Doubleday, 1961 [Paris]
Wail for the Corpses; see B As in Banshee
Weep for a Wanton. Ace, 1956; Boardman, 1957 MT,JF

TREBOR, SNIVIG C. Pseudonym of Robert Cartwright Givens, 1845-1915.
The Millionaire Tramp. Cook County Review, 1886. Also published as by Robert C. Givins: Around the World Publishing Co., 1913

TREDGOLD, NYE. 1909- . Pseudonym: Nigel (Godwin) Trantor, q.v.

TREE, GREGORY. Pseudonym of John Franklin Bardin, 1916-1981, q.v. Other pseudonym: Douglas Ashe, q.v. SC: Bill Bradley and Noel Mayberry = B&M.
The Case Against Butterfly. Scribner, 1951 B&M [NYC]
The Case Against Myself. Scribner, 1950; Gollancz, 1951 B&M [NYC]
So Young to Die. Scribner, 1953; Gollancz, 1953

TREE, HERBERT BEERBOHM. 1853-1917.
Nothing Matters, and other stories. Cassell, 1917; Houghton, 1917 ss, at least one criminous

TREECE, HENRY. 1911-1966. Ref: CA.
Ask for King Billy. Faber, 1955
Bang, You're Dead! Faber, 1966
Desperate Journey. Faber, 1954
Don't Expect Any Mercy. Faber, 1958
Hunter Hunted. Faber, 1957
Killer in Dark Glasses. Faber, 1965

TREETON, ERNEST A.
The Crooked Finger. Lloyd's, 1921
The Entombed Convict. Lloyd's, 1921
The Instigator. Chatto, 1903
A New Jack Sheppard. Routledge, 1907
The Saving of Christian Sergison. Hodder, 1903

TREGARRON, YATE
-Murderer's Island. Methuen, 1925

TREGASKIS, RICHARD (WILLIAM). 1916-1973. Ref: CA.
China Bomb. Washburn, 1967

TREHEARNE, ELIZABETH
Storm at Midnight. Ace, 1973 [South]

TREIBICH, S(TEPHEN) J(OHN). 1936-1972.
Burwyck's Wander. Lancer, 1967
Haelstrom Manor. Lancer, 1967

TREISTER, BERNARD WILLIAM. 1932- .
Pseudonym: Bernard St. James, q.v.

TREMAYNE, RAYMOND
Some Rogues and Daphne. Low, 1924

TREMBATH, HAROLD
Double Dealing. Cole, 1942
Murder in Berlin. Cole, 1942 [Berlin]

TREMBATH, HEDLEY
The Fighting Cartoonist Detective. Swan, 1946

TREMONTE, JULIA
The Devil's House. Pinnacle, 1974

TRENCH, JOHN. 1920- . Ref: TC. SC: Martin Cotterell = MC. Set: Eng.
Beyond the Atlas. Macdonald, 1963; Macmillan, 1963 [Ethio.]
Dishonoured Bones. Macdonald, 1953; Macmillan, 1955 MC
Docken Dead. Macdonald, 1953; Macmillan, 1954 MC
What Rough Beast. Macdonald, 1957; Macmillan, 1957 MC

TRENT, ILONA
Too Many Crooks. Vantage, 1968

TRENT, LEE
A Bird in the Hand. Hale, 1972

TRENT, PAUL. Pseudonym of Edward Platt. SC: Peter Quayle, in at least those marked PQ. Set: Eng.
-Adair and Son. Ward, 1940
-Adam. Ward, 1917
 The Air Bandits. Ward, 1935
-Andrew Reforms. Ward, 1946
-At the World's Mercy. Ward, 1924
-A Battle of Giants. Ward, 1931
-Baxter's Son. Ward, 1929
-Bentley's Conscience. Ward, 1916
-The Best of Three. Ward, 1942
 The Blackguard. Hayes, 1923
 The Blackmailer. Ward, 1914
-"Blue Peter." Odhams, 1919
-The Broken Way. Ward, 1933
-Brotherhood. Odhams, 1922
-Brotherly Love. Ward, 1930
-The Bush King. Ward, 1926
-Celia. Hayes, 1921
-Celia's Career. Ward, 1928
 Churstons. Ward, 1920
-Clubs and Hearts. Ward, 1933
-The Counterbalance. Ward, 1918
 The Craven Mystery. Ward, 1929
 The Crooked Samaritan. Ward, 1933
-Delilah. Hayes, 1920
-The Devil in Her. Ward, 1944
 Ethel Norman's Secret. Ward, 1915
-Eve. Hayes, 1919
-Falkland's Choice. Ward, 1930
-Family Property. Ward, 1940
-Fettered. Ward, 1924
-A Final Chance. Ward, 1932
-The First-Born. Ward, 1943
-Flying Peter. Wright, 1938
-The Foundling. Ward, 1913
-From Father to Son. Ward, 1939
-Gentleman of the Sea. Ward, 1915
-Gold Poison. Ward, 1942
-The Golden Rat. Ward, 1932
-The Great Autumn Double. Wright, 1934
-The Heart Specialist. Odhams, 1921
-Her Month of Freedom. Ward, 1932
-Her Wild Oats. Ward, 1930
-The Honour of the Family. Ward, 1941
-In the Toils. Long, 1925
-The Ironmaster's Daughter. Ward, 1939
 The Island Murder. Ward, 1934
-It Might Have Been. Ward, 1933
-Ivor's Chance. Ward, 1936
-Jane Ventures. Ward, 1944
-John and Son. Ward, 1946
-The Judgment of Ann. Ward, 1931
-The Lady of Longbourne. Ward, 1915
-A Legacy of Vengeance. Ward, 1923
-A Long Lane. Ward, 1943
-The Lost Generation. Ward, 1938
-Love Cruisers. Ward, 1935
-The Maid of Mansfield. Ward, 1915
-The Man Who Made Good. Odhams, 1920
-The Man Who Stood Alone. Ward, 1920
-Mark Ryder's Vow. Ward, 1922
 The Master of the Skies. Odhams, 1920
-Max Logan. Ward, 1914
-Maxine. Ward, 1937
-Michael Durrant. Ward, 1925
-The Million Heiress. Ward, 1941
 A Modern Portia. Ward, 1938
-The Money Sense. Ward, 1928
-Mortgaged Lives. Wright, 1935
 Mr. Justice Philbank. Ward, 1934
-Natalie Limited. Ward, 1936
-A Naval Adventuress. Ward, 1919
 Nesbit's Compact. Ward, 1915
-Nurse to Dives. Ward, 1937
-The Pathway to Fame. Ward, 1931
-The Peacemaker. Ward, 1927
-Peter Hyde, M.P. Ward, 1920
-The Price of a Soul. Mills, 1916
-Private and Confidential. Ward, 1940
 Quayle of the Yard. Ward, 1935 PQ
 Quayle's First Case. Ward, 1936 PQ
-Red Mirage. Wright, 1937
-The Red Streak. Ward, 1930
-The Ruling Vice. Ward, 1917
 The Sacrifice. Ward, 1928
-The Second Chance. Ward, 1913
 Shattered. Ward, 1934
-A Soviet Marriage. Laurie, 1930
-Stephen Vale. Ward, 1918
-The Strange Inheritance. Ward, 1921
-The Strong Right Arm. Odhams, 1922
-The Supplanter. Ward, 1914
-Tainted Gold. Ward, 1918
-The Unexpected Daughter. Ward, 1930
-The Vow. Hodder, 1911; Stokes, 1911
-Wheat and Tares. Ward, 1914
-When Greek Meets Greek. Ward, 1916
-A Wife by Purchase. Milne, 1909
-Wilton's Silence. Ward, 1921
-Wings Behind Bars. Wright, 1940
-Wings of Love. Wright, 1935
-A Woman of Action. Ward, 1919
-Workers All. Ward, 1923
-The Years Between. Ward, 1939

TRENT, TIMOTHY. Pseudonym of Carl Malmberg, 1904- . Ref: CA.
-All Dames Are Dynamite. Godwin, 1935
 Fall Guy. Godwin, 1936
-Night Boat. Godwin, 1934

TREVANIAN. Pseudonym of Rodney W. Whitaker, 1925- . Ref: TC. SC: Jonathan Hemlock = JH.
The Eiger Sanction. Crown, 1972; Heinemann, 1973 [Switz.] JH
The Loo Sanction. Crown, 1973; Heinemann, 1974 JH
The Main. Harcourt, 1976; Granada, 1977 [Montr.]
Shibumi. Crown, 1979; Granada, 1979

TREVELYAN, JULIA
Blackmoor. Signet, 1976
Greythorne. Signet, 1974 [Eng., 1800s]
The Landsend Terror. Signet, 1979 [Mass.]
The Tower Room. Signet, 1979

TREVELYAN, ROBERT. Pseudonym of Robert Forrest-Webb, 1929- . Other pseudonym: Forrest Webb, q.v. Joint pseudonym with David Eliades: David Forrest, q.v.
The Montenegran Plot. Hodder, 1977; St. Martin's, 1978

TREVOR, A. C. Pseudonym of Norman George Pulsford, 1902- .
Death Haunts the Lounge. Harrap, 1936

TREVOR, ELLESTON. 1920- . Name originally: Trevor Dudley Smith, q.v. Pseudonyms: Mansell Black, Trevor Burgess, Adam Hall, Howard North, Simon Rattray, Warwick Scott, Caesar Smith, qq.v. Ref: CA, EM, TC.
-The Billboard Madonna. Heinemann, 1960; Morrow, 1961
 A Blaze of Roses. Heinemann, 1952; Harper, 1952. Also published as: The Fire Raiser. New English Library pb, 1970
-The Burning Shore. Heinemann, 1961. U.S. title: The Pasang Run. Harper, 1962
-Bury Him Among Kings. Heinemann, 1970; Doubleday, 1970
-Chorus of Echoes. Boardman, 1950
-Dream of Death. Digit, 1958
 The Fire-Raiser; see A Blaze of Roses
-The Flight of the Phoenix. Heinemann, 1964; Harper, 1964
-The Mind of Max Duvine. Swan, 1960; Wehman, 1960
 Night Stop; see The Paragon
 The Paragon. New English Library, 1975. U.S. title: Night Stop. Doubleday, 1975 [Nev.]
 The Pasang Run; see The Burning Shore
-The Passion and the Pity. Heinemann, 1953
 A Place for the Wicked. Heinemann, 1968; Doubleday, 1968
-Redfern's Miracle. Boardman, 1951
-The Second Chance. Digit, 1965
-Secret Arena. Jenkins, 1951
-The Shoot. Heinemann, 1966; Doubleday, 1966
-The Sibling. New English Library, 1980; Playboy, 1979, as by Adam Hall
-Silhouette. Swan, 1959
 The Theta Syndrome. New English Library, 1977; Doubleday, 1977 [hosp.]
-Tiger Street. Boardman, 1951; Lion, 1954
-Touch of Purple. French (London & NYC), 1973 (Play.)
 The V.I.P. Heinemann, 1959; Morrow, 1960
-Weave a Rope of Sand. Consul, 1965

TREVOR, G. S. and M. E. TREVOR
The Bloodhound of the Law. Sea-Side Times Print, 1908

TREVOR, GLEN. Pseudonym of James Hilton, 1900-1954. Ref: CC, EM, TC.
Murder at School. Benn, 1931. U.S. title: Was It Murder? Harper, 1933. Reprinted as by James Hilton.

TREVOR, JAMES. SC: John Savage, in both titles.
The Savage Game. Award, 1967; Gibbs, 1967 [S. Am.]
The Savage Height. Award, 1969; Tandem, 1970

TREVOR, LESLIE. SC: Sgt. Pepper Anderson, in all titles, which are novelizations of the "Policewoman" TV series. Set: L.A., in all titles
Code 1013: Assassin. Award, 1975
Death of a Call Girl. Award, 1975
The Rape. Award, 1975; Tandem, 1975

TREVOR, M. E. See: G. S. Trevor.

TREVOR, RALPH. Pseudonym of J(ames) R(eginald) Wilmot, 1897- , q.v. SC: Insp./Supt. Curtis Burke, in at least those marked CB. Set: Eng.

The Ace of Clubs Murder. Wright, 1939
Behind the Green Mask. Wright, 1940
The Corpse in the Caravan. Wright, 1939
Death Burns the Candle. Wright, 1938 CB
Death Comes Too Late. Wright, 1938
Death in the Surgery. Wright, 1937
The Deputy Avenger. Wright, 1938
Easy for the Crook. Wright, 1939
The Eyes Through the Mask. Wright, 1935
Front Page Murder. Wright, 1942 CB
The Ghost Counts Ten. Wright, 1938
The Girl in the Crimson Cloak. Wright, 1940
High Spy. Wright, 1942
The House of Silence. Wright, 1935
Invitation to Murder. Wright, 1936
Meet Doctor Death. Wright, 1940
The Monday Night Murder. Wright, 1935
The Moorcroft Manor Mystery. Wright, 1935
Murder for Two Pins. Wright, 1939 CB
A Murder Has Been Arranged. Wright, 1942
Murder in Silk. Wright, 1937
Murder in the Fifth Column. Wright, 1940
Murder Without Regrets. Wright, 1937
On the Night of the Ninth. Wright, 1935
The Phantom Raider. Wright, 1941
Red Stands for Danger. Wright, 1941
Sky-High Terror. Wright, 1940 CB
Some Persons Unknown. Wright, 1935
Under Suspicion. Wright, 1936
Viper's Vengeance. Wright, 1938
Who Killed the Crooner? Wright, 1941

TREW, ANTONY (FRANCIS). 1906-   . Ref: CA.
The Antonov Project. Collins, 1979; St. Martin's, 1979 [ship]
Death of a Supertanker. Collins, 1978; St. Martin's, 1978
-Sea Fever. Collins, 1980; St. Martin's, 1980
The Soukour Deadline; see Ultimatum
Ultimatum. Collins, 1976; St. Martin's, 1976. Also published as: The Soukour Deadline. Fontana, 1977
The Zhukov Briefing. Collins, 1975; St. Martin's, 1976

TREYNOR, ALBERT M.
The Long Patrol. Dodd, 1926; Hutchinson, 1927
-Rogues of the North. Chelsea, 1922; Hutchinson, 1924
Snow Blind. Dodd, 1929; Hamilton, 1930 [Can.]
The Trail from Devil's Country. Dodd, 1926; Hutchinson, 1926

TREYNOR, BLAIR
If You Should Ever Need Me; see She Ate Her Cake
She Ate Her Cake. Morrow, 1946. British title: If You Should Ever Need Me. Nimmo, 1948 [L.A.]
Silver Doll. Holt, 1952 [L.A.]
Widow's Pique. Mill, 1956; Ward, 1958 [L.A.]

TRICE, BOROUGH. Pseudonym of Arthur Bruce Allen, 1903-1975. Ref: CA.
'Orrible Murder. Big Ben, 1942

TRIEM, PAUL ELLSWORTH. 1882-   .
Alias John Doe. Chelsea, 1930; Hamilton, 1931

TRIESCHMAN, CHARLES
Two. Dell, 1974 (Novelization of the movie.)

TRILL
Removals Limited. Everyday, ca.1930s
The Sickle Murders. Williams, 1935

TRIMBLE, JACQUELYN WHITNEY. 1927-   . Pseudonym: J. L. H. Whitney, q.v.

TRIMBLE, LOUIS (PRESTON). 1917-   . Pseudonyms: Stuart Brock, Gerry Travis, qq.v. Ref: CA. SC: Anthropol Detective Agency = AA; Martin Zane = MZ.
Anthropol. Ace, 1968 AA
Blondes Are Skin Deep. Lion, 1951 [Portland]
Cargo for the Styx. Ace, 1959 MZ [Calif.]
The Case of the Blank Cartridge. Phoenix, 1942 [Calif.]
The Corpse Without a Country. Ace, 1959 [Wash.]
Date for Murder. Phoenix, 1942 [Calif.]
The Dead and the Deadly. Ace, 1963 MZ [Mex. City]
Design for Dying. Phoenix, 1945 [S.F.]
The Duchess of Skid Row. Ace, 1960 [Wash.]
Fit to Kill. Phoenix, 1941 [Ariz.]

Girl on a Slay Ride. Avon, 1960 [Wash.]
Give Up the Body. Superior, 1946 [Oreg.]
Love Me and Die. Ace, 1960 [Ariz.]
Murder Trouble. Phoenix, 1945; Wells Gardner, 1949 [Wash.]
The Noblest Experiment in the Galaxy. Ace, 1970 AA
Nothing to Lose But My Life. Ace, 1957 [Calif.]
Obit Deferred. Ace, 1959
The Smell of Trouble. Ace, 1958 [Wash.]
Stab in the Dark. Ace, 1956
The Surfside Caper. Ace, 1961   [Calif.]
The Tide Can't Wait. Mystery House, 1957; Wright, 1959
Till Death Do Us Part. Ace, 1959 [Mex. City.]
Tragedy in Turquoise. Phoenix, 1942 [N. Mex.]
You Can't Kill a Corpse. Phoenix, 1946

TRINIAN, JOHN
Any Number Can Win. Pyramid, 1963
A Game of Flesh. Lancer, 1963
House of Evil. Pyramid, 1962 [L.A.]
North Beach Girl. GM, 1960; Muller pb, 1961. Also published as: Strange Lovers. Macfadden, 1967 [S.F.]
The Savage Breast. GM, 1961; Muller pb, 1962
Scandal on the Sand. GM, 1964 [Calif.]
Scratch a Thief. Ace, 1961 [S.F.]
Strange Lovers; see North Beach Girl

TRIPP, C. E. Pseudonym of Charles (Smith) Morris, 1833-1922, q.v.
Ace High, the 'Frisco Detective. Book Club of America, 1948

TRIPP, MILES (BARTON). 1923-   . Pseudonyms: John Michael Brett, Michael Brett, qq.v. SC: John Samson, in at least those marked JS. Ref: CA, MC, TC.
The Chicken. Macmillan (London), 1966. Also included in: The Chicken and Zella. Pan, 1968
The Chicken and Zella; see The Chicken
The Claws of God. Macmillan (London), 1972
Cruel Victim. Macmillan (London), 1979 JS
-The Eighth Passenger. Heinemann, 1969
-The Fifth Point of the Compass. Macmillan (London), 1967
Five Minutes with a Stranger. Macmillan (London), 1971
A Glass of Red Wine. Macdonald, 1960
High Heels. Macmillan (London), 1980
The Image of Man. Finlayson, 1955
Kilo Forty. Macmillan (London), 1963; Holt, 1964 [Mid. East]
Malice and the Maternal Instinct. Macmillan (London), 1969
A Man Without Friends. Macmillan (London), 1970
Obsession. Macmillan (London), 1973 JS
The Once a Year Man. Macmillan (London), 1977 JS
A Quarter of Three. Macmillan (London), 1965
One Is One. Macmillan (London), 1968
-The Skin Dealer. Macmillan (London), 1964; Holt, 1965
The Wife-Smuggler. Macmillan (London), 1978 JS [Warsaw]
Woman at Risk. Macmillan (London), 1974
A Woman in Bed. Macmillan (London), 1976

TROKE, MOLLY. Pseudonym: Hester Bourne, q.v.

TROLLOPE, ANTHONY. 1815-1882. Ref: CC, MC.
The Eustace Diamonds. Chapman, 1873; Harper, 1872

TROLLOPE, T(HOMAS) ADOLPHUS. 1810-1892.
A Siren. Smith & Elder, 1870; Arno, 1976

TRONSON, ROBERT
Afternoon of a Counterspy. Hutchinson, 1969

TROTT, NICHOLAS
Monkey Boat. Macmillan, 1932 [ship]

TROTT, SUSAN. 1937-   . Ref: CA.
The Housewife and the Assassin. St. Martin's, 1979; Gollancz, 1979 [Calif.]

TROTTA, GERI [GERALDINE TROTTA]
Dead As Diamonds. Boardman, 1956
Veronica Died Monday. Dodd, 1952; Boardman, 1953 [NYC]

TROUBETZKOY, PRINCESS PAUL
-The Clock Strikes. Rich, 1943
Gallows Seed. Grayson, 1934; Kendall, 1935
-Spider Spinning. Hale, 1936
-Storm Tarn. Grayson, 1933

TROWN, ROBERT C(OOPER)
Battle Without Glory. Hutchinson, 1947

TROY, JONATHAN
The Haunted Honeymoon. Dramatists, 1970 (3-act play.)
No Drums at Midnight, with Robert Birchall. Dramatic, 1962   (2-act play.)
Web of Murder. Dramatists, 1964   (Play)

TROY, KATHERINE. Pseudonym of Anne Buxton. Other pseudonym: Anne Maybury, q.v. Set: Eng.
Enchanter's Nightshade. Collins, 1963. U.S. title: The Winds of Night. Ace, 1967, as by Anne Maybury
Falcon's Shadow. Collins, 1964; Ace, 1967, as by Anne Maybury
Farramonde. McKay, 1968 (British title/byline?)
The House of Fand. Collins, 1966; Ace, 1966, as by Anne Maybury
The Night of the Enchantress. Hodder, 1967
Roseheath; see Storm over Roseheath
Someone Waiting. Collins, 1961; Ace, 1966, as by Anne Maybury
Storm over Roseheath. Hodder, 1969. U.S. title: Roseheath. McKay, 1969
Whisper in the Dark. Collins, 1961; Ace, 1966, as by Anne Maybury

TROY, SIMON. Pseudonym of Thurman Warriner, q.v. Other pseudonym: John Kersey, q.v. SC: Insp. Smith, in at least those marked S. Set: Eng.
Blind Man's Garden. Gollancz, 1970 S
Cease upon the Midnight. Gollancz, 1964; Macmillan, 1965 S
Don't Play with the Rough Boys. Gollancz, 1963; Macmillan, 1964 S
Drunkard's End. Gollancz, 1960; Walker, 1961
Half-Way to Murder. Gollancz, 1955 S
No More A-Roving. Gollancz, 1965 S
Road to Rhuine. Collins, 1952; Dodd, 1952 S
Second Cousin Removed. Gollancz, 1961; Macmillan, 1962 S
Sup with the Devil. Gollancz, 1967 S
Swift to Its Close. Gollancz, 1969; Stein, 1969 S [Wales]
Tonight and Tomorrow. Gollancz, 1967 S
Waiting for Oliver. Gollancz, 1963; Macmillan, 1963 [Chan. Is.]

TRUAX, RHODA. 1891-   .
The Accident Ward Mystery. Little, 1937 [hosp.]

TRUESDELL, JUNE
Be Still, My Love. Dodd, 1947; Boardman, 1948 [L.A.]
Burden of Proof. Boardman, 1951
The Morgue the Merrier. Dodd, 1945; Boardman, 1947

TRUMAN, MAJOR BEN(JAMIN) C(UMMINGS). 1835-1916.
Occidental Sketches. San Francisco News, 1881 ss, at least one criminous

TRUMAN, MARCUS GEORGE. 1890-   . Pseudonym: Mark Beckett, q.v.

TRUMAN, (MARY) MARGARET. 1924-   . Ref: CA.
Murder in the White House. Arbor, 1980; Severn, 1981 [Wash. D.C.]

TRUSCOTT, LUCIAN K(ING) IV. 1947-   . Ref: CA.
Dress Gray. Doubleday, 1979; Collins, 1979 [Md.]

TRUSS, (LESLIE) SELDON. 1892-   . Pseudonym: George Selmark, q.v. Ref: CA, CC. SC: Chief Insp. Gidleigh = G; Det. Insp. Shane = S; Insp. Bass = B (see also the Selmark entry). Set: Eng.
Always Ask a Policeman. Hodder, 1953; Doubleday, 1952 G
The Barberton Intrigue. Hodder, 1956. U.S. title: A Store of Wrath. Doubleday, 1956 G
The Bride That Got Away. Hale, 1967; Doubleday, 1967, as by George Selmark
The Coroner Presides; see Mr. Coroner Presides
The Corpse That Got Away. Hale, 1969
The Crooks' Shepherd; see Draw the Blinds

The Daughters of Belial. Jarrolds, 1934
Deadline for a Diplomat; see Rooksmiths
Death Was No Lady. Hodder, 1952; Doubleday, 1952 G
The Disappearance of Julie Hintz. Hodder, 1940 G
The Doctor Was a Dame; see Put Out the Light
Draw the Blinds. Hodder, 1936. U.S. title: The Crooks' Shepherd. Lothrop, 1936
Escort to Danger. Hodder, 1935 S
Eyes at the Window. Hodder, 1966; Doubleday, 1966, as by George Selmark
False Face; see The Long Night
Footsteps Behind Them. Hodder, 1937 G
Foreign Bodies. Hodder, 1938 B
Gallows Bait. Butterworth, 1928. U.S. title: The Living Alibi. Coward, 1929 S
The Hands of the Shadow. Hale, 1968
The Hidden Men. Hodder, 1959. U.S. title: A Man to Match the Hour. Doubleday, 1959 G
The High Wall. Hodder, 1954. U.S. title: The Other Side of the Wall. Doubleday, 1955 G
The Hunterstone Outrage. Butterworth, 1931; Mystery League, 1931
In Secret Places. Hodder, 1958; Doubleday, 1958 G
Ladies Always Talk. Hodder, 1950. U.S. title: Why Slug a Postman. Doubleday, 1950 G
The Living Alibi; see Gallows Bait
The Long Night. Hodder, 1956. U.S. title: False Face. Doubleday, 1955 G
A Man to Match the Hour; see The Hidden Men
The Man Who Played Patience. Hodder, 1937 G
The Man Without Pity. Butterworth, 1930. U.S. title: Number Nought. Dodd, 1930 S
Mr. Coroner Presides. Harrap, 1932. U.S. title: The Coroner Presides. Minton, 1932 S
Murder Paves the Way. Hodder, 1936 S
Never Fight a Lady. Hodder, 1951; Doubleday, 1950 G
Number Nought; see The Man Without Pity
One Man's Death. Hale, 1960. U.S. title: One Man's Enemies. Doubleday, 1960 G
One Man's Enemies; see One Man's Death
The Other Side of the Wall; see The High Wall
Put Out the Light. Hodder, 1954. U.S. title: The Doctor Was a Dame. Doubleday, 1953 G
Rooksmiths. Hodder, 1936 B (Also published as: Deadline for a Diplomat. Merit, 1954, with SC changed from Bass to Gidleigh.)
Seven Years Dead. Hale, 1961; Doubleday, 1961 G
She Could Take Care. Hodder pb, 1937
The Stolen Millionaire. Butterworth, 1929; Coward, 1929
A Store of Wrath; see The Barberton Intrigue
Sweeter for His Going. Hodder, 1950 G
Technique for Treachery. Hale, 1963; Doubleday, 1963 G
They Came by Night. Jarrolds, 1933
A Time to Hate. Hale, 1962; Doubleday, 1962 G
The Town That Went Sick. Hale, 1965 G
The Truth About Claire Veryan. Hodder, 1957; Doubleday, 1957 G
Turmoil at Brede. Harrap, 1932; Mystery League, 1931 S
Walk a Crooked Mile. Hale, 1964 G
Where's Mr. Chumley? Hodder, 1949; Doubleday, 1948 G
Why Slug a Postman?; see Ladies Always Talk

TRYON, THOMAS. 1926-   . Ref: CA.
The Other. Knopf, 1971; Cape, 1971 [Conn., 1930s]

TUBB, EDWIN CHARLES. 1919-   . Pseudonym: Mike Lantry, q.v. See also: Arthur (George) McLean.

TUCKER, (ALLAN) JAMES. 1929-   . Pseudonym: David Craig, q.v. Ref: CA.
Blaze of Riot. Hutchinson, 1979 [Berlin, 1933]

TUCKER, TERRY
What's Become of Anna? Hale, 1972

TUCKER, (ARTHUR) WILSON. 1914-   . Ref: CA. SC: Charles Horne = CH.
The Chinese Doll. Rinehart, 1946; Cassell, 1948 CH [Ill.]
The Dove. Rinehart, 1948; Cassell, 1950 CH [Ill., Calif.]
The Hired Target. Ace, 1957
Last Stop. Doubleday, 1963; Hale, 1965

The Man in My Grave. Rinehart, 1956; Macdonald, 1958 [Midwest]
A Procession of the Damned. Doubleday, 1965; Hale, 1967 [Las Veg.]
Red Herring. Rinehart, 1951; Cassell, 1953 CH [Midwest]
The Stalking Man. Rinehart, 1949; Cassell, 1950 CH
This Witch. Doubleday, 1971; Gollancz, 1972 [Isr.]
Time Bomb. Rinehart, 1955. Also published as: Tomorrow Plus X. Avon, 1957
To Keep or Kill. Rinehart, 1947; Cassell, 1950 CH [Ill.]
To the Tombaugh Station. Ace, 1960
Tomorrow Plus X; see Time Bomb
The Warlock. Doubleday, 1967; Hale, 1968 [Russ.]

TUDOR, ANTHONY
The Case of Paul Breen. Page, 1911

TUITE, HUGH (GEORGE SPENCER)
-Mr. Dovecourt's Decoy. Collins, 1926
The Secret of the Blue Vase. Jenkins, 1924

TULLETT, TOM
Murder Squad. Panther, 1980

TULLY, ANDREW (FREDERICK, JR.). 1914-   . Ref: CA.
The Brahmin Arrangement. Coward, 1974 [Wash. D.C.]

TUPPER, EDITH SESSIONS.   -1927.
By a Hair's Breadth. Street (Magnet), 1900
By Whose Hand? Fracher, 1889

TUPPER, MARTIN FARQUAR. 1810-1889.
The Crock of Gold. Bentley, 1844

TUREK, IONE FRANCES. Pseudonym of Otto O(scar) Binder, 1911-1974, q.v.
Terror in the Bay. Curtis, 1971

TURLAND, EILEEN
Evil Genius. Hale, 1976

TURNBULL, AGNES SLIGH. 1888-1982. Ref: CA.
The Flowering. Houghton, 1972; Collins, 1972
The Richlands. Houghton, 1974; Collins, 1975
The Wedding Bargain. Houghton, 1966; Collins, 1967 [N.Y., 1935]

TURNBULL, DORA AMY DILLON. 1878-1961. Pseudonym: Patricia Wentworth, q.v.

TURNBULL, MARGARET.   -1942. SC: Juliet Jackson, in at least those marked JJ.
The Bride's Mirror; see In the Bride's Mirror
-The Close Up. Harper, 1918
The Coast Road Murder. Lippincott, 1934 JJ [N.J.]
-In the Bride's Mirror. Lippincott, 1934. British title: The Bride's Mirror. Ward, 1934
Madame Judas. Lippincott, 1926; Jenkins, 1926 JJ [Pa.]
The Return of Jenny Weaver. Lippincott, 1932; Ward, 1932 JJ [Maine]
Rogues' March. Lippincott, 1928 JJ [NYC]

TURNBULL, PATRICK (EDWARD XENOPHON). 1908-   . Ref: CA.
Dead for a Dead Thing. New English Library, 1976
-Death Is Our Playmate. Pan, 1971

TURNER, BESSIE (A.)
Circumstantial Evidence. Munro, 1884
A Woman in the Case. Carleton, 1875

TURNER, BILL. 1927-   . U.S. byline is sometimes the author's full name: William Price Turner. Ref: CA, CC. SC: Sgt. Louis Solden, in at least those marked LS. Set: Eng.
Another Little Death. Constable, 1970; Walker, 1971
Bound to Die. Constable, 1967; Walker, 1967
Circle of Squares. Constable, 1969; Walker, 1969 LS
Hot-Foot. Constable, 1973
Sex Trap. Constable, 1968 LS
Solden's Women. Constable, 1972 LS

TURNER, CHARLES (CYRIL). 1870-1952. London news correspondent.
Unlawful. Paul, 1927

TURNER, EDGAR
-The Armada Gold, with (William) Reginald Hodder, q.v. Richards, 1908
-The Lady and the Burglar. Ward, 1904
The Purloined Prince, with (William) Reginald Hodder, q.v. Caxton, 1905
-The Submarine Girl. Paul, 1909

TURNER, ELAINE
-Garlic, Grapes, and a Pinch of Heroin. Manor, 1978
Your Secret Is in a Well. Manor, 1977 [Saud. Arab.]

TURNER, J(OHN) V(ICTOR). 1900-1945. Pseudonyms: Nicholas Brady, David Hume, qq.v. Crime reporter in Eng. SC: Amos Petrie, in all titles. Set: Eng.
Amos Petrie's Puzzle. Bles, 1933
Below the Clock. Collins, 1936; Appleton, 1936
Death Joins the Party. Bles, 1935
Death Must Have Laughed. Putnam (London), 1932. U.S. title: First Round Murder. Holt, 1932
First Round Murder; see Death Must Have Laughed
Homicide Haven. Collins, 1935; Appleton, 1936
Murder—Nine and Out. Bles, 1934
Who Spoke Last? Putnam (London), 1932; Holt, 1933

TURNER, JAMES (ERNEST). 1909-   . SC: Rampion Savage, in all titles. Set: Eng.
The Blue Mirror. Cassell, 1965
The Crystal Wave. Cassell, 1957
The Dark Index. Cassell, 1959
A Death by the Sea. Cassell, 1955
The Frontiers of Death. Cassell, 1957; British Book Centre, 1959
The Glass Interval. Cassell, 1961
Murder at Landred Hall. Cassell, 1954
The Nettle Shade. Cassell, 1963
Requiem for Two Sisters. Cassell, 1968
The Slate Landscape. Cassell, 1964
The Stone Dormitory. Cassell, 1971
The Strange Little Snakes. Cassell, 1956

TURNER, JOHN HASTINGS. 1892-1956. See: Roland Pertwee, 1885-1963.

TURNER, MARY. Pseudonym of Isobel (Mary) Lambot, 1926-   , q.v.
The Justice Hunt. Hale, 1975
Perilous Love. Gresham, 1966
-So Bright a Lady. Hale, 1977

TURNER, PEARL. 1913-   .
Comrades in Death. Hale, 1980

TURNER, PHILIP WILLIAM. 1925-   . Pseudonym: Stephen Chance, q.v.

TURNER, RAY
Arson by Proxy. Hale, 1971

TURNER, ROBERT (HARRY). 1915-1980. Pseudonyms: Mercer B. Cook, Don Romano, qq.v. Ref: CA.
The Girl in the Cop's Pocket. Ace, 1956
The Night Is for Screaming. Pyramid, 1960
Shroud 9. Powell, 1970 ss
The Tobacco Auction Murders. Ace, 1954

TURNER, RUSSELL
The Short Night. Hillman-Curl, 1957

TURNER, WILLIAM PRICE. 1927-   . See: Bill Turner.

TURNEY, CATHERINE. 1906-   . Ref: CA.
The Other One. Holt, 1952. Also published as: Possessed. Paperback Library, 1968 [Calif.]

TURNGREN, ANNETTE. 1902-1980. Pseudonym: A. T. Hopkins, q.v.

TURNI, MARIE
Cousin Jess. Vega, ca.1962
The Opposite Six. Vega, 1961

TURPIN, ALLAN
The Little Medicine Bottle. H. Hamilton, 1977 [1930s]

TURTLE, JEREMY
Black Mastery. Hodder, 1939

TUTE, WARREN (STANLEY). 1914-   . Ref: CA. SC: George Mado, in all titles.
The Cairo Sleeper. Constable, 1977 [Cairo]
A Matter of Diplomacy. Dent, 1969; Coward, 1970 [Athens]

Next Saturday in Milan. Constable, 1975 [Milan]
The Powder Train. Dent, 1970; Ballantine, 1975
The Resident. Constable, 1973; Ballantine, 1975
The Tarnham Connection. Dent, 1971; Ballantine, 1974

TUTT, MERVYN C.
Odd Man In. Hale, 1980

TUTTIETT, MARY GLEED.   -1923. Pseudonym: Maxwell Grey, q.v.

TUTTLE, GENE
Slade, Range Detective. Avalon, 1973; Hale, 1975

TUTTLE, W(ILBUR) C(OLEMAN). 1883- .
Ref: CA. An American author of mostly westerns, many of which have strong detective elements. Note that some uncorrelated title changes likely persist in the following list, and that many of Tuttle's books were apparently published only in Britain. SC: Hashknife Hartley, in at least those marked HH. Set: mostly West.
Arizona Drifters. Collins, 1964
Bluffer's Luck. Houghton, 1937; Collins, 1932
Buckshot Range. Collins, 1966
Danger Trail. Collins, 1958
The Dead-Line. Collins, 1927 HH
The Deputy. Avalon, 1959
The Devil's Payday. World's Work, 1929
Diamond Hitch. Collins, 1962
Double-Crossers of Ghost Tree. Collins, 1965 HH
Double Trouble. Collins, 1964
Dynamite Days. Collins, 1960
The Flood of Fate. Collins, 1926
Galloping Gold. Collins, 1961
Ghost Guns. Collins, 1957
Ghost Trails. Houghton, 1940; Collins, 1926
Gold at K-BAR-T. Collins, 1961
Gun Feud. Popular Library, 1951
Hashknife of Stormy River. Houghton, 1935; Collins, 1931 HH
Hashknife of the Canyon Trail. Collins, 1928 HH
Hashknife of the Double Bar 8. Houghton, 1936; Collins, 1927 HH
Henry the Sheriff. Houghton, 1936
Hidden Blood. Houghton, 1943; Collins, 1929 HH
Horse-Shoe Luck. Collins, 1934
The House of the Hawk. Collins, 1963
The Keeper of Red Horse Pass. Houghton, 1937; Collins, 1930
The King of Dancing Valley. Collins, 1958
The Lone Wolf. Collins, 1967
Loot of the Lazy F. Collins, 1933
Lucky Partners. Collins, 1967
Me and Rudolph. Avalon, 1958
Medicine Maker. Collins, 1967 HH
The Medicine-Man. Houghton, 1939; Collins, 1925 HH
Mission River Justice. Avalon, 1955; Collins, 1956
Montana Man. Avalon, 1966
The Morgan Trail. Houghton, 1928 HH
Mystery at the JHC Ranch. Houghton, 1932
The Mystery of the Red Triangle. Houghton, 1942; Collins, 1929 HH
Outlaw Empire. Avalon, 1960
Passengers for Painted Rock. Collins, 1962
The Payroll of Fate. Collins, 1966 HH
Piperock Tales. Avalon, 1963
Reddy Brant, His Adventures. Century, 1920
The Redhead from Sun Dog. Houghton, 1930; Collins, 1929
Renegade Sheriff. Avalon, 1953; Collins, 1954
Rifled Gold. Houghton, 1934; Collins, 1934 HH
The Rim Rider. Collins, 1959
Road to the Moon. Collins, 1965
Rocky Rhodes. Collins, 1936
Rustlers' Roost. Collins, 1927
Sad Sontag Plays His Hunch. Garden City, 1926. British title (?): Sontag of Sundown. World's Work, 1929
Salt for the Tiger. Avalon, 1952; Collins, 1954
The Santa Dolores Stage. Houghton, 1934; Collins, 1935 HH
The Shadow Shooter. Collins, 1955
The Shame of Arizona. Collins, 1957
Shotgun Gold. Houghton, 1940; Collins, 1941 HH
The Silver Bar Mystery. Houghton, 1933; Collins, 1932
Silver Buckshot. Collins, 1959
The Singing Kid. World's Work, 1953
Singing River. Houghton, 1939; Collins, 1931
Sontag of Sundown; see Sad Sontag Plays His Hunch
Spawn of the Desert. World's Work, 1929
Spooky Riders. Collins, 1930
Stockade. Collins, 1965
Straight Shooting. Garden City, 1926
Straws in the Wind. Houghton, 1948; Collins, 1948
Sun Dog Loot. Collins, 1926
Thicker Than Water. Houghton, 1927 HH
Thunderbird Range. Avalon, 1954; Collins, 1955
The Tin God of Twisted River. Houghton, 1941; Collins, 1942
The Trail of Deceit. Houghton, 1951
The Trail to Kingdom Come. Collins, 1960
Trouble at the JHC. Hillman, 1950
The Trouble Trailer. Houghton, 1946; Collins, 1946 HH
Tumbling River Range. Houghton, 1935; Collins, 1929 HH
The Turquoise Trail. Collins, 1935
Twisted Trails. Popular Library, 1950
Valley of Suspicion. Collins, 1964 HH
The Valley of Twisted Trails. Houghton, 1931; Collins, 1932 HH
The Valley of Vanishing Herds. Houghton, 1942 HH
Wandering Dogies. Houghton, 1938; Collins, 1939
West of Aztec Pass. Collins, 1963
Wild Horse Valley. Houghton, 1938; Collins, 1939
Wolf Creek Valley; see The Wolf Pack of Lobo Butte
The Wolf Pack of Lobo Butte. Houghton, 1945. British title: Wolf Creek Valley. Collins, 1946

TUTTON, BARBARA (IVY CURTIS). 1914- .
Black Widow. Hale, 1963
Plague Spot. Hale, 1965
Rich to Die. Hale, 1962
Take Me Alive. Hale, 1961

TWAIN, MARK. Pseudonym of Samuel Langhorne Clemens, 1835-1910. See also: Robert (R.) St. Clair, 1898- . Ref: CA, CC, EM, MC, MP.
A Double-Barrelled Detective Story. Harper, 1902; Chatto, 1902
A Murder, a Mystery, and a Marriage. Manuscript House, 1945
Simon Wheeler, Detective. New York Public Library, 1963
The Stolen White Elephant. Osgood, 1882; Chatto, 1882
Tom Sawyer, Detective, and other stories. Harper, 1896; Chatto, 1897 ss

TWEDT, JERRY L.
Murder on Center Stage. Dramatic, 1976 (3-act play.)

TWEEDALE, VIOLET (CHAMBERS).   -1936.
The Beautiful Mrs. Davenant. Jenkins, 1920; Stokes, 1920
Unsolved Mysteries. Digby, 1895 ss

TWIST, PETER. Pseudonym of C. P. Hewitt.
The Gilded Hideaway. Ace, 1955 [Mex.]

TYLER, ANNE. 1941- . Ref: CA.
-Celestial Navigation. Knopf, 1974; Chatto, 1975

TYLER, CHARLES W(ALLER). 1841-1920. SC: Blue Jean Billy Race, in both titles.
Blue Jean Billy. Chelsea, 1926; Lloyd's, 1921 [New Eng.]
Quality Bill's Girl. Chelsea, 1925; Hutchinson, 1926 [New Eng.]

TYLER, ESTHER
Murder on the Bluff. Simon, 1936. British title: The Family Skeleton. Bell, 1937 [Conn.]

TYLER, FROOM. 1904- .
Gallows Parade. Dickson, 1933 ss

TYLER, ROBERT LEE
Lawyer Bell from Boston. Street, 1893

TYLER, W. T. Pseudonym of an American diplomat, recently assigned to the Arab world.
The Man Who Lost the War. Dial, 1980; Collins, 1981 [Europe, 1945-47]

TYNAN, KATHARINE [KATHARINE TYNAN HINKSON]. 1861-1931. Ref: CA.
The Rattlesnake. Ward, 1917

TYNAN, KATHLEEN. Ref: CA.
Agatha. Weidenfeld, 1978; Ballantine hc, 1978 [Eng., 1926]

TYNDALL, JOHN. SC: Roger Turnbull, in both titles.
Death in Lebanon. Bles, 1971 [Leb.]
Death in the Jordan. Bles, 1970 [Mid. East]

TYNER, PAUL. 1939- . Has degrees in mathematics from U. of Ill.
Shoot It. Little, 1968; Heinemann, 1969

TYRE, NEDRA. 1921- . Ref: CA, CC, EM, TC.
Death Is a Lover; see Mouse in Eternity
Death of an Intruder. Knopf, 1953; Collins, 1954
Everyone Suspect. Macmillan, 1964; Gollancz, 1965
Hall of Death. Simon, 1960. Also published as: Reformatory Girls. Ace, 1962
Journey to Nowhere. Knopf, 1954; Collins, 1954
Mouse in Eternity. Knopf, 1952; Macdonald, 1953. Also published as: Death Is a Lover. Mercury, 1953
Reformatory Girls; see Hall of Death
Twice So Fair. Random, 1971

TYRELL, PATRICK
The Robber King. Laird, 1889

TYRER, WALTER. 1900- . Prolific author of juvenile fiction in Eng., perhaps 20 million words of output. Ref: CC. Those titles below listed without publisher feature Sexton Blake and were issued by Amalgamated Press.
The Affair of Danny the "Dip". 1950
The Affair of the Hollywood Contract. 1949
The Case Against Dr. Ripon. 1948
The Case of the Bogus Baron. 1952
The Case of the Conscript Miner. 1944
The Case of the Cottage Crime. 1950
The Case of the Council Swindle. 1954
The Case of the Forbidden Island. 1955
The Case of the Missing Nazi. 1953
The Case of the Naval Defaulter. 1950
The Case of the Naval Stores Bucket. 1953
The Case of the Returning Soldier. 1955
The Case of the Swindled Guarantor. 1954
The Case of the Two Crooked Baronets. 1951
The Clue of the Pin-Up Girl. 1956
The Crime in Room 27. 1954
The Crime on the Moors. 1946
The Crimes at Fenton Towers. 1951
The Curse of the Carrington's. 1943
Daughter of the Scaffold. Amalgamated, 1935
The Dilemma of Dr. Hiley. 1952
Ellen Morgan. Columbine, 1939
The Evil Spell. 1950
The Hangman's Daughter. Amalgamated, 1936
The Hire-Purchase Fraud. 1952
The Holiday Camp Mystery. 1947
Jane the Ripper. Columbine, 1939
The Motor Coach Mystery. 1948
The Mystery of Squadron X. 1943
The Mystery of the Mad Millionaires. 1955
The Mystery of the Missing Angler. 1949
The Mystery of the Rio Star. 1950
The Mystery of the Swindler's Stooge. 1953
The Mystery of the Three Demobbed Men. 1956
The Mystery of the Woman Overboard. 1948
One of the Eleven. 1949
The Riddle of the French Alibi. 1954
The Scrap-Metal Mystery. 1952
The Secret of the Sands. 1945
The Secret of the Snows. 1953
She Sent Her Mother to the Scaffold. Amalgamated, 1936
The Strange Affair of the Shot Gun Sniper. 1955
Such Friends Are Dangerous. Staples, 1954
Trunk Crime Number Three. Columbine, 1939

TYRRELL, MABEL L(OUISE)
-The Forgotten Hills. Hodder, 1936
-Mysterious Journey. Hodder, 1940
-The Noble Error. Hodder, 1930
-Patchwork Palace. Hodder, 1933
-Pull the House Down. Hodder, 1938
-The Street of Fortune. Hodder, 1939
-That's Mark Avery. Hodder, 1942
-The Thief. Hodder, 1953
-Thirteen Moons. Hodder, 1937
-The Toledo Sword. Hodder, 1957

TYRRELL, ROSS
 The Pathway of Adventure. Knopf, 1920

TYSON. Pseudonym: Nicholas Carter, q.v.

TYSON, J(OHN) AUBREY. 1870-   .
 The Barge of Haunted Lives. Macmillan, 1923; Mills, 1924
 The Rhododendron Man. Dutton, 1930; Mills, 1930 [L.I.]
 The Scarlet Tanager. Macmillan, 1922; Mills, 1922 [Wash. D.C., 1930]
 -The Stirrup Cup. Appleton, 1903

TYTLER, SARAH. Pseudonym of Henrietta Keddie, 1827-1914.
 The Blackhall Ghosts. Chatto, 1888; Rand, 1888

UDOFF, YALE M(AURICE). 1935-   . Ref: CA.
 A Gun Play. French (NYC), 1972 (Play.)

UHNAK, DOROTHY. 1933-   . Ref: CA, EM, TC. SC: Christie Opara = CO.
 The Bait. Simon, 1968; Hodder, 1968 CO [NYC]
 The Investigation. Simon, 1977; Hodder, 1977 [NYC]
 Law and Order. Simon, 1973; Hodder, 1973 [NYC]
 The Ledger. Simon, 1970; Hodder, 1971 CO [NYC]
 The Witness. Simon, 1969; Hodder, 1970 CO [NYC]

ULLMAN, ALBERT E(DWARD)
 The Kidnappers. Amour, 1932. Canadian title (?): Hoodlum Alley. Harlequin, 1955

ULLMAN, ALLAN. 1909(?)-1982.
 The Naked Spur, with Rolfe Bloom. Random, 1953; Corgi, 1955 (Novelization of the movie.) [Tex.]
 Night Man, with Lucille Fletcher, 1912-   , q.v. Random, 1951; Gollancz, 1951 (Novelization of the screenplay by Lucille Fletcher.)
 Sorry, Wrong Number, with Lucille Fletcher, 1912-   , q.v. Random, 1948; Gollancz, 1948 (Novelization of the radio play by Lucille Fletcher.) [NYC]

ULLMAN, BETTY E. Artist and photographer in Wash. D.C.
 The Voluptuaries. Putnam, 1978 [Wash. D.C.]

ULLMAN, JAMES MICHAEL. Newspaperman in Chicago.
 Full Coverage; see Good Night, Irene
 Good Night, Irene. Simon, 1965. British title: Full Coverage. Cassell, 1966 [Chi.]
 House of Cards; see The Venus Trap
 Lady on Fire. Simon, 1968; Cassell, 1969 [Chi.]
 The Neon Haystack. Simon, 1963; Cassell, 1964
 The Venus Trap. Simon, 1966. British title: House of Cards. Cassell, 1967 [Chi.]

ULLMANN, RICHARD (EDWIN)
 A Taste of Poison. Laurie, 1954

ULRICH, MAX
 Bank Robbery. Constable, 1967 (Translation of "Raub in der Munchner Lombard-Bank." Munich, 1965.) [Munich]

ULSH, WAYNE C.
 Rip-Off. Pyramid, 1975

UMBSTAETTER, H(ERMAN) D(ANIEL). 1851-1913.
 The Red Hot Dollar and other stories from "The Black Cat". Page, 1911 ss

UNDERHILL, G(EORGE) F(REDERICK)
 -The Hand of Vengeance. Trischler, 1890
 -In at the Death. Swan, 1888
 -A Nasty Cropper. Trischler, 1889
 -The Rogues of Society, and The Doctor of Duddlestone. Diprose, 1899

UNDERWOOD, MICHAEL. Pseudonym of John Michael Evelyn, 1916-   .   Ref: CA, CC, TC. SC: Martin Ainsworth, in at least those marked MA; Sgt. Nick Atwell, in at least those marked NA; Insp./Supt. Simon Manton, in at least those marked SM; Richard Monk, in at least those marked RM. Set: Eng.
 Adam's Case. Hammond, 1961; Doubleday, 1961 SM
 The Anxious Conspirator. Macdonald, 1965; Doubleday, 1965 SM
 Anything But the Truth. Macmillan (London), 1978; St. Martin's, 1978
 Arm of the Law. Hammond, 1959 SM [Trin.]
 The Case Against Philip Quest. Macdonald, 1962 SM
 Cause of Death. Hammond, 1960 SM
 A Clear Case of Suicide. Macmillan (London), 1980; St. Martin's, 1980
 A Crime Apart. Macdonald, 1966
 The Crime of Colin Wise. Macdonald, 1964; Doubleday, 1964 SM
 Crime upon Crime. Macmillan (London), 1980; St. Martin's, 1981
 Crooked Wood. Macmillan (London), 1978; St. Martin's, 1978 NA
 Death by Misadventure. Hammond, 1960 SM
 Death on Remand. Hammond, 1956 SM
 False Witness. Hammond, 1957; Walker, 1961 SM
 The Fatal Trip. Macmillan (London), 1977; St. Martin's, 1977 NA
 Girl Found Dead. Macdonald, 1963   SM
 The Juror. Macmillan (London), 1975; St. Martin's, 1975 NA
 Lawful Pursuit. Hammond, 1958; Doubleday, 1958 SM
 The Man Who Died on Friday. Macdonald, 1967 RM
 The Man Who Killed Too Soon. Macdonald, 1968 RM
 Menaces, Menaces. Macmillan (London), 1976; St. Martin's, 1976
 Murder Made Absolute. Hammond, 1955; Washburn, 1957 SM
 Murder on Trial. Hammond, 1954; Washburn, 1958 SM
 Murder with Malice. Macmillan (London), 1977; St. Martin's, 1977 NA
 A Pinch of Snuff. Macmillan (London), 1974; St. Martin's, 1974
 Reward for a Defector. Macmillan (London), 1973; St. Martin's, 1973
 The Shadow Game. Macdonald, 1969 MA
 Shem's Demise. Macmillan (London), 1970
 The Silent Liars. Macmillan (London), 1970; Doubleday, 1970
 Smooth Justice. Macmillan (London), 1979; St. Martin's, 1979
 A Trout in the Milk. Macmillan (London), 1971; Walker, 1972
 The Unprofessional Spy. Macdonald, 1964; Doubleday, 1964 MA [Berlin]
 Victim of Circumstances. Macmillan (London), 1979; St. Martin's, 1980

UNDERWOOD, REGINALD
 Secret Fear. Fortune, 1943

UNEKIS, RICHARD
 The Chase. Walker, 1962; Gollancz, 1963. Also published as: Pursuit. Signet, 1964 [Ill.]

UNSWORTH, BARRY (FORSTER). 1930-   . Ref: CA.
 The Big Day. Joseph, 1976; Mason/Charter, 1977
 The Idol Hunter; see Pascali's Island
 Pascali's Island. Joseph, 1980. U.S. title: The Idol Hunter. Simon, 1980 [Turk., 1908]

UNSWORTH, MAIR
 Wild Winds. Hurst, 1968; Ace, 1972 [Scot., 1800s]

UNTERMEYER, WALTER, JR. 1915-   .
 Dark the Summer Dies. Lion, 1953
 Evil Roots. Lion, 1954

UPCHURCH, BOYD. 1919-   . Ref: CA.
 Scarborough Hall. Berkley, 1976 [Ga.]

UPFIELD, ARTHUR W(ILLIAM). 1888-1964. Ref: CC, EM, MC, TC. SC: Insp. Napoleon Bonaparte = NB. Set: Australia, in all titles.
 An Author Bites the Dust. Angus, 1948; Doubleday, 1948 NB
 The Bachelors of Broken Hill. Heinemann, 1958; Doubleday, 1950 NB
 The Barrakee Mystery. Hutchinson, 1929. U.S. title: The Lure of the Bush. Doubleday, 1965 NB
 The Battling Prophet. Heinemann, 1956 NB
 The Beach of Atonement. Hutchinson, 1930
 The Body at Madman's Bend; see Madman's Bend
 The Bone Is Pointed. Angus, 1938; Doubleday, 1947 NB
 Bony and the Black Virgin. Heinemann, 1959; Collier pb, 1965 NB
 Bony and the Kelly Gang. Heinemann, 1960. U.S. title: Valley of Smugglers. Doubleday, 1960 NB
 Bony and the Mouse. Heinemann, 1959. U.S. title: Journey to the Hangman. Doubleday, 1959 NB
 Bony and the White Savage. Heinemann, 1961. U.S. title: The White Savage. Doubleday, 1961 NB
 Bony Buys a Woman. Heinemann, 1957. U.S. title: The Bushman Who Came Back. Doubleday, 1957 NB
 The Bushman Who Came Back; see Bony Buys a Woman
 Bushranger of the Skies. Angus, 1940. U.S. title: No Footprints in the Bush. Doubleday, 1944 NB
 Cake in the Hat Box. Heinemann, 1955. U.S. title: Sinister Stones. Doubleday, 1954 NB
 The Clue of the New Shoe; see The New Shoe
 Death of a Lake. Heinemann, 1954; Doubleday, 1954 NB
 Death of a Swagman. Aldor, 1946; Doubleday, 1945 NB
 The Devil's Steps. Aldor, 1948; Doubleday, 1946 NB
 Gripped by Drought. Hutchinson, 1932
 The House of Cain. Hutchinson, 1928; Dorrance, 1929
 Journey to the Hangman; see Bony and the Mouse
 The Lake Frome Monster. Heinemann, 1966 (Completed by J. L. Price and Dorothy Strange.) NB
 The Lure of the Bush; see The Barrakee Mystery
 Madman's Bend. Heinemann, 1963. U.S. title: The Body at Madman's Bend. Doubleday, 1964 NB
 The Man of Two Tribes. Heinemann, 1956; Doubleday, 1956 NB
 Mr. Jelly's Business. Angus, 1937. U.S. title: Murder Down Under. Doubleday, 1943 NB
 The Mountains Have a Secret. Heinemann, 1952; Doubleday, 1948 NB
 Murder Down Under; see Mr. Jelly's Business
 Murder Must Wait. Heinemann, 1953; Doubleday, 1953 NB
 The Mystery of Swordfish Reef. Angus, 1939; Doubleday, 1943 NB
 The New Shoe. Heinemann, 1952; Doubleday, 1951. Also published as: The Clue of the New Shoe. Thorpe, 1974 NB
 No Footprints in the Bush; see Bushranger of the Skies
 A Royal Abduction. Hutchinson, 1932
 The Sands of Windee. Hutchinson, 1931; British Book Centre, 1959 NB
 Sinister Stones; see Cake in the Hat Box
 Valley of Smugglers; see Bony and the Kelly Gang
 Venom House. Heinemann, 1953; Doubleday, 1952 NB
 The White Savage; see Bony and the White Savage
 The Widows of Broome. Heinemann, 1951; Doubleday, 1950 NB
 The Will of the Tribe. Heinemann, 1962; Doubleday, 1962 NB
 Winds of Evil. Angus, 1937; Doubleday, 1944 NB
 Winged Mystery; see Wings Above the Diamantina
 Wings Above the Claypan; see Wings Above the Diamantina
 Wings Above the Diamantina. Angus, 1936. U.S. title: Wings Above the Claypan. Doubleday, 1943. Also published as: Winged Mystery. Hamilton, 1937 NB

UPHILL, THOMAS
 Strange Heritage. Hutchinson, 1926

UPSHAW, HELEN
 The Return of Jennifer. Dodd, 1964; Redman, 1965

UPTON, PETER
 The Eve of April Twenty. Arlington, 1978

UPTON, ROBERT. Ref: CA.
 A Golden Fleecing. St. Martin's, 1979 [Geneva]
 Who'd Want to Kill Old George? Putnam, 1977 [S.F.]

UPWARD, ALLEN. 1863-1926. SC: Monsieur V, in at least those marked V; Dr. Frank Tarleton, in at least those marked FT. Set: Eng.
 The Accused Princess. Pearson, 1900
 The Ambassador's Adventure. Cassell, 1901
 -Athelstane Ford. Pearson, 1899
 A Bride's Madness. Arrowsmith, 1897

The Club of Masks; see The Domino Club
A Crown of Straw. Chatto, 1896; Dodd, 1896
A Day's Tragedy: A Novel in Rhyme. Chapman, 1897
The Domino Club. Faber, 1926. U.S. title: The Club of Masks. Lippincott, 1926 FT
-God Save the Queen! Chatto, 1897
High Treason. Primrose, 1903
The House of Sin. Faber, 1926; Lippincott, 1927 FT
The International Spy; see The Phantom Torpedo-Boats
-Lord Alistair's Rebellion. Rivers, 1909
On Her Majesty's Service. Primrose, 1904
-One of God's Dilemmas. Heinemann, 1896; Arnold, 1896
-The Ordeal by Fire. Digby, 1904
The Phantom Torpedo-Boats. Chatto, 1905. U.S. title: The International Spy. Dillingham, 1905 V
The Prince of Balkistan. Chatto, 1895; Lippincott, 1895
The Queen Against Owen. Chatto, 1894
Romance of Politics. Tyndale, 1904
Secret History of Today. Chapman, 1904 ss V
Secrets of the Courts of Europe. Arrowsmith, 1897 ss
The Venetian Key. Faber, 1927; Lippincott, 1927 FT
The Wonderful Career of Ebenezer Lobb. Hurst, 1900 ss
The Wrongdoer. Arrowsmith, 1900
The Yellow Hand. Digby, 1904

URELL, WILLIAM FRANCIS. Pseudonym: William Francis, q.v.

URIS, LEON (MARCUS). 1924- . Ref: CA.
Topaz. McGraw, 1967; Kimber, 1968

URNER, NATHAN D(ANE). 1839-1893. Pseudonym: Burke Brentford, q.v.
The Detective's Secret. Laird, 1888
Link by Link; or, The Chain of Evidence. Laird, 1888

URQUHART, MACGREGOR. Ref: CC. SC: Chief Insp. Joshua Smarles, in at least those marked JS.
-Alamein. Digit, 1958
The Bitter Lemon Mob. Boardman, 1966 JS [Sic.]
The Bluebottle. Boardman, 1964 JS
-Breakthrough. Digit, 1958
Contact Lens. Boardman, 1964 JS
Dig the Missing. Boardman, 1963 JS
-First Stop to Hell. Digit, 1962
-Foxhole. Digit, 1958
Frail on North Circular. Boardman, 1962 JS
Girl on the Waterfront. Boardman, 1962 JS
The Grey Man. Boardman, 1965 JS [Scot.]
-Hungary Fights. Digit, 1957
Investigation, with Cecil Madden. Evans, 1958 (3-act play.)
The Open Mouth. Boardman, 1967 JS
-Partisan. Digit, 1958
-Private Death. Digit, 1958
-Speedo! Digit, 1958
-Through the Bamboo Curtain. Digit, 1960

URQUHART, PAUL. Pseudonym of Ladbroke (Lionel Day) Black, 1877-1940, q.v. See also: T. C. St. C. Morton. Those titles below without publisher feature Sexton Blake and were issued by Amalgamated Press.
The Boro Council Ramp. 1937
The Brooklands Mystery. 1932
The Building Estate Murder. 1934
The Bungalow Crime. 1932
The Crime at the Crossroads. 1934
The Crime of Count Dureen. 1935
The Double Cross. 1933
The Exploits of a Dead Man. Amalgamated, 1934
Found in Possession. Amalgamated, 1935
Gun Rule. 1931
The Man on the Dole. 1938
Mr. Kilmer Sees Red. 1933
Murder by Mistake. 1934
The Mystery of the Lorry Driver. 1939
The Mystery of the Rajah's Jewels. 1932
The Mystery of the Thirteenth Chest. 1931
Presumed Dead. 1932
The Secret of the Dead Man. 1938
The Secret of the Evacuee. 1940
-The Shadow. Ward, 1908
The Victim of Devil's Alley. 1933
-The Web. Ward, 1907
Yellow Vengeance. 1933

USHER, FRANK (HUGH). 1909-1976. Pseudonyms: Charles Franklin, Frank Lester, qq.v. Ref: CA. SC: Amanda Curzon and Oscar Sallis, in at least those marked C&S; Daye Smith, in at least those marked DS. Set: Eng.
Body in Velvet. Hale, 1963
The Boston Crab. Hale, 1970 C&S
Deadly Legacy. Hale, 1971
Death in Error. Hale, 1959 DS
Death Is Waiting. Long, 1958 DS
Die, My Darling. Hale, 1960 DS
The Faceless Stranger. Hale, 1961 DS
Fall into My Grave. Hale, 1962 DS
First to Kill. Long, 1959 DS
Ghost of a Chance. Long, 1956 DS
The Lonely Cage. Long, 1965 DS
The Man from Moscow. Hale, 1965 C&S
No Flowers in Brazlov. Hale, 1968 C&S
Portrait of Fear. Long, 1957 DS
The Price of Death. Long, 1957 DS
Shot in the Dark. Hale, 1961 DS
Stairway to Murder. Hale, 1964 DS [Fr.]
Who Killed Rosa Gray? Hale, 1962 DS

USHER, GRAY. 1903- . SC: Supt. Michael Drexel, in at least those marked MD. Set: Eng.
A Dame to Discover. Scion, 1952
Death Goes Caving. Long, 1959
Death in the Bag. Long, 1958 MD
Death in the Straw. Long, 1955 MD
Death Sped the Plough. Long, 1956 MD
Death Takes a Teacher. Long, 1957 MD
Don't Crowd Me. Scion, 1952
Double Snatch. Scion, 1951
Flames Burn High. Baker, 1954
For Pete's Sake! Scion, 1951
I Was a Spy in Britain. Baker, 1952
Intrigue. Scion, 1951
Sleep If You Dare. Milestone, 1953
Triggerman! Scion, 1951

USHER, JACK. Ref: CC. Born in L.A.
Brothers and Sisters Have I None. Mill, 1958; Heinemann, 1959. Also published as: Reason for Murder. PB, 1960 [Calif.]
The Fix. Mill, 1959. British title: The Girl in the White Mercedes. Heinemann, 1960 [Calif.]
The Girl in the White Mercedes; see The Fix
Reason for Murder; see Brothers and Sisters Have I None

USHER, SHAUN. 1937- . Pseudonym: Jeffrey Scott, q.v.

USHER, WILFRID
Creeping Shadows. Paul, 1929
The Great Hold-Up Mystery. Paul, 1928; International Fiction Library, 1929
The Mystery of the Seven. Paul, 1930

UTECHIN, NICHOLAS. See also: Austin Mitchelson.
Sherlock Holmes at Oxford. Dugdale, 1977 (Sherlock Holmes.)

VACHA, ROBERT
The Black Orchestra. Star, 1979
-Moscow 1980. Star, 1979 [Moscow]
O.P.E.C. Project. Star, 1979
Phantoms over Potsdam. Everest, 1975
Requiem for a Crown. Star, 1978
Spy for Churchill. Everest, 1974

VACHELL, HORACE ANNESLEY. 1861-1955. Ref: EM. SC: Joe Quinney = JQ. Set: Eng.
The Disappearance of Martha Penny. Hodder, 1934
The Enchanted Garden and other stories. Cassell, 1929 ss
Experiences of a Bond Street Jeweler. Cassell, 1932 ss
An Impending Sword. Murray, 1909
Loot from the Temple of Fortune. Murray, 1913; Doran, 1914 ss, some criminous
The Mote House Mystery; see Mr. Allen
Mr. Allen, with Archibald Marshall, q.v. (pseudonym of Arthur Hammond Marshall, 1866-1934). Hodder, 1926. U.S. title: The Mote House Mystery, as by Archibald Marshall and H. A. Vachell. Dodd, 1926
-Quinneys'. Murray, 1914; Doran, 1914 JQ
Quinney's Adventures. Murray, 1924; Doran, 1924 ss JQ

VACHETTE, EUGENE. 1827-1902. Pseudonym: Eugene Chavette, q.v.

VACULIK, LUDVIK. 1926- . Ref: CA.
The Guinea Pigs. Third Press, 1973; London Magazine Editions, 1974 (Translation of "Morcata.")

VACZEK, LOUIS CHARLES. 1913- . Pseudonym: Peter Hardin, q.v.

VAHEY, JOHN (GEORGE) HASLETTE. 1881- . Pseudonyms: Henrietta Clandon, John Haslette, Anthony Lang, Vernon Loder, John Mowbray, Walter Proudfoot, qq.v. Set: Eng.
Death by the Gaff. Skeffington, 1932
-Down River. Ward, 1925
Fiddlestrings. Ward, 1925
Mr. Nemesis. Ward, 1930 [S. Afr.]
-The Money Barons. Ward, 1928
Mystery at the Inn. Ward, 1931
-Payment Down. Ward, 1927
Secrets for Sale. Eyre, 1935
-Solitude Limited. Ward, 1928
Spies in Ambush. Eyre, 1934
The Storm Lady. Ward, 1926 [Wales]
Tragic Lesson. Hutchinson, 1933
-Up North. Ward, 1926
Witness in Support. Skeffington, 1932

VAIL, LAURENCE. 1891- .
Murder! Murder! Davies, 1931 [Paris]

VAIL, THOMAS
Blackmail and Old Lace. NSL, 1961
Weekend to Danger. Vega, 1963

VAILE, WILLIAM N(EWELL). 1876-1927.
The Mystery of the Golconda. Doubleday, 1925; Heinemann, 1925 [Colo.]

VAIZEY, GEORGE (DE HORNE). 1900- . Was executive with Lloyds of London.
-The Chairman. Harrap, 1941
-The Failure. Harrap, 1947
-Give Me Yesterday. Harrap, 1964
Guile Wears a Coronet. Harrap, 1939
-Inherit the Wind. Harrap, 1952
Into Thin Air. Harrap, 1939
-The Mirror Lies. Harrap, 1943
-Or By Default. Harrap, 1957
-The Road Home. Harrap, 1954
-Sister Theatre. Harrap, 1950
Tangled Web. Faith, 1974
-Through Another Gate. Harrap, 1945

VAIZEY, JOHN (ERNEST). 1929- . Ref: CA.
The Sleepless Lunch. Weidenfeld, 1968

VALBECK, MICHAEL
Headlong from Heaven. Unie-Volkspers (Cape Town), 1947; Mill, 1947

VALDES, IVY. 1921- . Ref: CA.
Chase a Dark Shadow. Hurst, 1971; Signet, 1972
-The Drury Affair. Hurst, 1974; Pyramid, 1975
Gift from a Stranger. Hurst, 1965; Signet, 1972
Over My Shoulder. Hurst, 1968; Signet, 1972

VALDEZ, PAUL. Pseudonym. All titles published in Australia.
Ghosts Don't Kill.
Hypnotic Death. Transport, ca.1941
Satan's Sabbath.

VALE, G. B.
The Mystery of the Papyrus. Methuen, 1929

VALE, MARTIN. Pseudonym of Marguerite Veiller.
The Two Mrs. Carrolls. Allen, 1936; French (NYC), 1951 (3-act play.)

VALE, RENA M. 1898- .
The House on Rainbow Leap. PB, 1973 [Ill., 1865]

VALENTINE. Pseudonym of Archibald Thomas Pechey, 1876-1961. Other pseudonym: Mark Cross, q.v. SC: Daphne Wrayne and the Four Adjusters = DW (see also the Mark Cross entry).
The Adjusters. Anglo-Eastern, 1930 DW (3 novelets.)
A Flight to a Finish. Ward, 1929
Strange Experiment. Ward, 1937
The Unseen Hand. Jarrolds, 1924

VALENTINE, DOUGLAS. Pseudonym of (George) Valentine Williams, 1893-1946, q.v. SC: Dr. Adolph Grundt (Clubfoot) = AG (see also Valentine Williams entry); Desmond Okewood = DO. Set: Eng.
The Man with the Clubfoot. Jenkins, 1918; McBride, 1918, as by Valentine Williams AG,DO
Okewood of the Secret Service; see The Secret Hand

The Secret Hand. Jenkins, 1919. U.S. title: Okewood of the Secret Service, as by Valentine Williams. McBride, 1919 DO

VALENTINE, JO. Pseudonym of Charlotte Armstrong, 1905-1969, q.v.
The Trouble in Thor. Coward, 1953; Davies, 1953. Also published as: And Sometimes Death. PB, 1955 [Mich.]

VALIN, JONATHAN (LOUIS). 1948- . Ref: CA. SC: Harry Stoner, in both titles.
Final Notice. Dodd, 1980; Collins, 1981 [Cin.]
The Lime Pit. Dodd, 1980; Collins, 1981 [Cin.]

VALLANCE, DOUGLAS
The Amateur Agent. Hale, 1976
The Kildallon Affair. Hale, 1969
Man in the Lubianka. Hale, 1971
The Milngavie Collection. Hale, 1977
A Prize of Traitors. Hale, 1970
A Safe Job. Hale, 1969

VALLEY, MEL
Magnum Force. Paperback Library, 1974; Star, 1977 (Novelization of the movie.) [S.F.]

VALLINGS, GABRIELLE (FRANCESCA LILLIAN MAY)
Jury of Four. Hutchinson, 1938

VALLS-RUSSELL, JOSEPH LAWRENCE. Pseudonym: Ray Alan, q.v.

VANARDY, VARICK. Pseudonym of Frederic Merrill Van Rensselaer Dey, 1861-1922. Other pseudonyms: Nicholas Carter, Marmaduke Dey, Frederic Ormond, qq.v. Ref: TC. SC: Bingham Harvard = BH; Crewe (Birge Moreau) = C.
Alias the Night Wind. Dillingham, 1913 BH [NYC]
The Girl by the Roadside. Macaulay, 1917; Jarrolds, 1923
The Lady of the Night Wind. Macaulay, 1919; Skeffington, 1926 BH [L.I.]
The Night Wind's Promise. Dillingham, 1914 BH [NYC]
The Return of the Night Wind. Dillingham, 1914 BH [NYC]
Something Doing. Macaulay, 1919 C (3 novelets.) [NYC]
The Two-Faced Man. Macaulay, 1918; Jarrolds, 1920 C [NYC]
Up Against It. Macaulay, 1920 [Can.]

VAN ARSDALE, WIRT. Pseudonym of Martha Wirt Davis.
The Professor Knits a Shroud. Doubleday, 1951 [N.Y.]

VAN ATTA, WINFRED (LOWELL). 1910- . Ref: CA.
The Adam Sleep. Doubleday, 1980; Hale, 1981 [NYC]
A Good Place to Work and Die. Doubleday, 1970; Hale, 1971 [Ill.]
Hatchet Man. Doubleday, 1962; Boardman, 1964 [Ill.]
Shock Treatment. Doubleday, 1961; Boardman, 1964 [Ill.]

VAN BEEVER, ROBERT F. Joint pseudonym with Fred(erick) G(ordon) Jarvis (Jr.), 1930- , q.v.: Fritz Gordon, q.v.

VANCE, ETHEL. Pseudonym of Grace Zaring Stone, 1891- , q.v.
Escape. Little, 1939; Collins, 1939 [Ger.]
Reprisal. Little, 1942; Collins, 1943 [Fr.]
The Secret Thread. Harper, 1948; Collins, 1948

VANCE, JACK. 1917- . Byline also: John Holbrook Vance, q.v. Pseudonyms: Peter Held, Alan Wade, qq.v. See also: Ellery Queen. SC: Keith Gersen = KG.
The Face. DAW, 1979 KG [future]
Galactic Effectuator. Underwood, 1980 (2 stories.) [future]
The House on Lily Street. Underwood, 1979
The Killing Machine. Berkley, 1964; Dobson, 1967 KG [future]
-The Many Worlds of Magnus Ridolph. Ace, 1966 ss
Marune: Alastor 933. Ballantine, 1975; Coronet, 1975
The Palace of Love. Berkley, 1967; Dobson, 1968 KG [future]
The Star King. Berkley, 1964; Dobson, 1966 KG [future]
To Live Forever. Ballantine, 1956; Sphere, 1976
The View from Chickweed's Window. Underwood, 1979 [S.F.]

VANCE, JOHN HOLBROOK. 1917- . Byline also: Jack Vance, q.v. Pseudonyms: Peter Held, Alan Wade, qq.v. See also: Ellery Queen. Ref: CA, CC, EM, TC. SC: Sheriff Joe Bain = JB.
Bad Ronald. Ballantine, 1973
The Deadly Isles. Bobbs, 1969; Hale, 1970 [Tahiti]
The Fox Valley Murders. Bobbs, 1966; Hale, 1967 JB [Calif.]
The Man in the Cage. Random, 1960; Boardman, 1960 [Algeria]
The Pleasant Grove Murders. Bobbs, 1967; Hale, 1968 JB [Calif.]

VANCE, LOUIS JOSEPH. 1879-1933. Ref: EM, MP, TC. SC: Michael Lanyard (The Lone Wolf) = ML; Terence O'Rourke = TO.
Alias the Lone Wolf. Doubleday, 1921; Hodder, 1921 ML [Fr.]
The Bandbox. Little, 1912; Richards, 1912 [N.Y., Eng.]
Baroque. Dutton, 1923; Hodder, 1923 [NYC]
-Beau Revel. Nash, 1920 (U.S. title?)
The Black Bag. Bobbs, 1908; Richards, 1908 [Eng.]
The Brass Bowl. Bobbs, 1907; Richards, 1907 [NYC]
The Bronze Bell. Dodd, 1909; Richards, 1909 [India]
Cynthia-of-the-Minute. Dodd, 1911; Richards, 1911
-The Dark Mirror. Doubleday, 1920; Hurst, 1921 [NYC]
The Dark Power. Bles, 1925 (U.S. title?)
The Dead Ride Hard. Lippincott, 1926; Bles, 1927 [Vienna]
The Destroying Angel. Little, 1912; Richards, 1913 [NYC]
Detective. Lippincott, 1932; Jarrolds, 1933 [NYC]
Encore the Lone Wolf. Lippincott, 1933; Jarrolds, 1934 ML [NYC]
The False Faces. Doubleday, 1918; Skeffington, 1920 ML [NYC]
-Lip-Service. Bles, 1928 (U.S. title?)
The Lone Wolf. Little, 1914; Nash, 1915 ML [Paris]
The Lone Wolf Returns. Dutton, 1923; Hodder, 1924 ML [NYC]
The Lone Wolf's Last Prowl. Lippincott, 1934; Jarrolds, 1935 ML [ship]
The Lone Wolf's Son. Lippincott, 1931; Jarrolds, 1932 ML [ship]
No Man's Land. Dodd, 1910; Stevens, 1910 [Conn.]
Nobody. Doran, 1915; Hodder, 1916
The Pool of Flame. Dodd, 1909; Richards, 1910 TO
Red Masquerade. Doubleday, 1921; Hodder, 1921 ML [Eng.]
Sheep's Clothing. Little, 1915 [NYC, ship]
The Street of Strange Faces. Lippincott, 1934; Jarrolds, 1934 [NYC]
-Terence O'Rourke, Gentleman Adventurer. Wessels, 1905; Richards, 1906 TO
The Trembling Flame. Lippincott, 1931; Jarrolds, 1932 [NYC]
The Woman in the Shadow. Lippincott, 1930; Jarrolds, 1931 [Hung.]

VANCE, WILLIAM E. 1911- . Ref: CA.
Homicide Lost. Graphic, 1956 [Miss.]

VANDAM, ALBERT D(RESDEN). 1843-1903. Ref: CC.
A Court Tragedy. Chatto, 1892
Masterpieces of Crime. Remington, 1892 ss
The Mystery of the Patrician Club. Chapman, 1894; Lippincott, 1894

VANDEBURG, MILLIE BIRD
The Clean Hand. Cassell, 1928
The Door to the Moor. Cassell, 1927; Dorrance, 1925

VANDENPANHUISE, GASTON. Joint pseudonym with Jean Libert: Paul Kenny, q.v.

VANDERCOOK, JOHN W(OMACK). 1902-1963. Ref: CC, EM. SC: Bertram Lynch and Robert Deane, in all titles.
Murder in Fiji. Doubleday, 1936; Heinemann, 1936 [Fiji]
Murder in Haiti. Macmillan, 1956; Eyre, 1956. Also published as: Out for a Killing. Avon, 1958 [Haiti]
Murder in New Guinea. Macmillan, 1959; Allen, 1960 [New Guinea]
Murder in Trinidad. Doubleday, 1933; Heinemann, 1934 [Trin.]
Out for a Killing; see Murder in Haiti

VAN DER ELST, VIOLET. 1882-1966. Composer, artist, traveller and psychic.
The Brain Master. Modern Fiction, 1946 ss
Death of the Vampire Baroness. Modern Fiction, 1946 ss
The Mummy Comes to Life. Modern Fiction, 1945 ss
The Satanic Power. Van Der Elst Press, 1945 ss
The Secret Power. Van Der Elst Press, 1945 ss
The Strange Doctor and other mystic stories. Van Der Elst Press, 1945 ss
The Torture Chamber and other stories. Doge, 1937 ss

VANDERGRIFF, (LOLA) AOLA. 1920- . Ref: CA.
The Bell Tower of Wyndspelle. Warner, 1975; New English Library pb, 1978 [Mass., ca.1770]
House of the Dancing Dead. Warner, 1974
Sisters of Sorrow. Warner, 1974
Wyndspelle. Warner, 1975; New English Library pb, 1978 [Mass., ca.1770]
Wyndspelle's Child. Warner, 1976 [Mass., 1815]

VANDERPUIJE, NII AKRAMPHAHENE. 1925- .
The Counterfeit Corpse. Comet, 1956

VANDERVEER, STEWART
Death for the Lady. Phoenix, 1939 [New Or.]

VAN DER ZEE, JOHN. 1936- . Ref: CA.
Blood Brotherhood. Harcourt, 1970 [S.F.]
Stateline. Harcourt, 1976 [Nev.]

VAN DEUSEN, DELIA
The Garden Club Murders. Bobbs, 1941; Selwyn, 1943 [N.Y.]
Many a Murder; see Murder Bicarb
Murder Bicarb. Bobbs, 1940; Selwyn, 1943. Also published as: Many a Murder. Croydon, 1944, abridged [South]

VAN DEVENTER, EMMA MURDOCH. Pseudonym: Lawrence L. Lynch, q.v.

VAN DE WATER, FREDERIC F(RANKLYN). 1890-1968. SC: John Tarleton = JT.
Alibi. Doubleday, 1930 [New Eng.]
The Eye of Lucifer. Appleton, 1927 [N.Y.]
Havoc. Doubleday, 1931; Skeffington, 1931 [Can.]
Hidden Ways. Bobbs, 1935; Jenkins, 1937 [NYC]
Horsemen of the Law. Appleton, 1926 ss
Hurrying Feet. Appleton, 1928
Plunder. Doubleday, 1933 JT [NYC]
Still Waters. Doubleday, 1929; Skeffington, 1932 JT [N.Y.]

VAN DE WETERING, JANWILLEM. 1931- . Ref: CA, TC. SC: Detectives Grijpstra and De Gier, in all titles.
The Blond Baboon. Houghton, 1978; Heinemann, 1978 [Amst.]
The Corpse on the Dike. Houghton, 1976; Heinemann, 1976 [Amst.]
Death of a Hawker. Houghton, 1977; Heinemann, 1977 [Amst.]
The Japanese Corpse. Houghton, 1977; Heinemann, 1977 [Amst.]
The Maine Massacre. Houghton, 1979; Heinemann, 1979 [Maine]
Outsider in Amsterdam. Houghton, 1975; Heinemann, 1976 [Amst.]
Tumbleweed. Houghton, 1976; Heinemann, 1976 [Amst.]

VAN DINE, S. S. Pseudonym of Willard Huntington Wright, 1888-1939. Ref: all except CA. SC: Philo Vance, in all titles.
The Benson Murder Case. Scribner, 1926; Benn, 1926 [NYC]
The Bishop Murder Case. Scribner, 1929; Cassell, 1929 [NYC]
The Canary Murder Case. Scribner, 1927; Benn, 1927 [NYC]
The Casino Murder Case. Scribner, 1934; Cassell, 1934 [NYC]
The Dragon Murder Case. Scribner, 1933; Cassell, 1934 [NYC]
The Garden Murder Case. Scribner, 1935; Cassell, 1935 [NYC]
The Gracie Allen Murder Case. Scribner, 1938; Cassell, 1938. Also published as: The Smell of Murder. Bantam, 1950 [NYC]
The Greene Murder Case. Scribner, 1928; Benn, 1928 [NYC]
The Kennel Murder Case. Scribner, 1933; Cassell, 1933 [NYC]
The Kidnap Murder Case. Scribner, 1936; Cassell, 1936 [NYC]

The Scarab Murder Case. Scribner, 1930; Cassell, 1930 [NYC]
The Smell of Murder; see The Gracie Allen Murder Case
The Winter Murder Case. Scribner, 1939; Cassell, 1939 [N.Y.]

VAN DOREN, RONALD. See: Robin Moore.

VAN DRUTEN, JOHN (WILLIAM). 1901-1957.
Somebody Knows. Gollancz, 1932; French (NYC), 1935 (3-act play.)

VAN DYCKE, TOM and BEN KERNER
Not with My Neck. Messner, 1947 [S.F.]

VAN DYKE, HENRY. 1928-   . Ref: CA.
-Blood of Strawberries. Farrar, 1969
Dead Piano. Farrar, 1971

VAN DYKE, JULIUS. Pseudonym of Frederick Anthony Edwards, 1896-   . Other pseudonym: Charman Edwards, q.v.
The Black Market Murders. Fore, 1945

VANE, DEREK. Pseudonym of Mrs. B. Eaton-Back. Set: Eng.
Dancer's End. Eldon, 1934
The Ferrybridge Mystery. Moffat, 1920 (British title?)
£500 Reward. Eldon, 1933
Intrigue and Matrimony. Hurst, 1928
-Lady Varley. Paul, 1914
The Mystery of the Moat House. Cosmopolitan (London), 1901
-The Paradise of Fools. Everett, 1913
The Scar. Bles, 1924; Clode, 1925
The Secret Door. Everett, 1907
The Sign of the Snake. Hurst, 1927; Macrae-Smith, 1928
-The Sin and the Woman. Remington, 1893
-The Soul of a Man. Holden, 1913
-The Three Daughters of Night. Hutchinson, 1897
The Trump Card. Hurst, 1925
-The Unguarded Hour. Thomson, 1929
-What Fools Women Are! Nash, 1928
The White Panthers. Nash, 1930; Macmillan, 1930
Who Goes There? Eldon, 1933

VANE, NIGEL. SC: Li-Sin = L; Philip Quest, in at least those marked PQ. Set: Eng.
The Devil's Dozen. Modern, 1935
The Menace of Li-Sin. Modern, 193? L
The Midnight Men. Smith, 1936
The Vanishing Death. Modern, 193? PQ
The Veils of Death. Modern, 1935 PQ
The Vengeance of Li-Sin. Modern, 1935 L

VANE, NORMAN T.
The Exorcism of Angela Gray. Belmont, 1974

VANE, PHILIPPA. Pseudonym of Phyllis Mac-Vean, 1892-   . Other pseudonym: Phyllis Hambledon, q.v.
Here Is the Evidence. Hammond, 1950 [Chan. Is.]
Priority for Death. Hammond, 1948

VANGE, NORMAN
A Spy in Damascus. Low, 1940 [Damascus]

VAN GELDER, LAWRENCE. Pseudonym: Nick Carter, q.v.

VAN GREENAWAY, PETER. 1929-   . Born in London; lawyer turned full-time writer.
The Destiny Man. Gollancz, 1977
The Dissident. Gollancz, 1980
Doppelganger. Gollancz, 1975
Judas! Gollancz, 1972. U.S. title: Judas Gospel. Atheneum, 1972
The Judas Gospel; see Judas!
A Man Called Scavener. Gollancz, 1978
The Man Who Held the Queen to Ransom and Sent Parliament Packing. Weidenfeld, 1968; Atheneum, 1969
The Medusa Touch. Gollancz, 1973; Stein, 1973
-Suffer! Little Children. Gollancz, 1976
-Take the War to Washington. Gollancz, 1974; St. Martin's, 1975

VAN GULIK, ROBERT (HANS). 1910-1967.
Ref: CA, CC, EM, MC, TC. SC: Judge Dee, in all titles, set in 7th century China.
Celebrated Cases of Judge Dee; see Dee Goong An
The Chinese Bell Murders. Joseph, 1958; Harper, 1959
The Chinese Gold Murders. Joseph, 1959; Harper, 1961
The Chinese Lake Murders. Joseph, 1960; Harper, 1960
The Chinese Maze Murders. Joseph, 1962

The Chinese Nail Murders. Joseph, 1961; Harper, 1962
Dee Goong An (translated by Robert Van Gulik). (Author), 1949; Arno, 1976. Also published as: Celebrated Cases of Judge Dee. Dover, 1976
The Emperor's Pearl. Heinemann, 1963; Scribner, 1964
The Fox-Magic Murders; see Poets and Murder
The Haunted Monastery. Heinemann, 1963; Scribner, 1969
Judge Dee at Work. Heinemann, 1967; Scribner, 1973 ss
The Lacquer Screen. Heinemann, 1964; Scribner, 1970
The Monkey and the Tiger. Heinemann, 1965; Scribner, 1966
Murder in Canton. Heinemann, 1966; Scribner, 1967
Necklace and Calabash. Heinemann, 1967; Scribner, 1971
New Year's Eve in Lan-Fang. (Beirut), 1958 (32 pp.)
The Phantom of the Temple. Heinemann, 1966; Scribner, 1966
Poets and Murder. Heinemann, 1968; Scribner, 1972. Also published as: The Fox-Magic Murders. Panther, 1973
The Red Pavilion. Heinemann, 1964; Scribner, 1968
The Willow Pattern. Heinemann, 1965; Scribner, 1965

VAN HAZINGA, CYNTHIA
Balance of Terror. Berkley, 1976
Ghost River Inn. Popular Library, 1973
The House on Gannet's Point. Popular Library, 1974 [Mass.]

VAN HEARN, J.
Don't Betray Me. Belmont, 1962 [Carib.]

VAN HORN, CHARLES
The Quest of Krang. Hutchinson, 1938

VAN ITALLIE, JEAN-CLAUDE. 1935-   .
Mystery Play. Dramatists, 1973 (Play.)

VAN LHIN, ERIK. Pseudonym of Lester del Rey, 1915-   . Ref: CA.
Police Your Planet. Avalon, 1956. Revised edition: Ballantine, 1975, as by Erik van Lhin and Lester del Rey

VAN LOON, MRS. ELIZABETH
The Mystery of Allanwold. Peterson, 1880
The Shadow of Hampton Road. Peterson, 1878
-Under the Willows; or, The Three Countesses. Peterson, 1879

VAN LUSTBADER, ERIC. 1946-   . Ref: CA.
The Ninja. Evans, 1980; Granada, 1980 [NYC]

VAN ORSDELL, JOHN
Ragland. World, 1972 [Wash. D.C.]

VAN RAALTE, JOSEPH
The Vice Squad. Vanguard, 1931
The Walls Are High. Vanguard, 1931 [N.Y.]

VAN RENSBURG, HELEN and LOUWRENS VAN RENSBURG
Death in a Dark Pool. Joseph, 1954
The Man with Two Ties. Joseph, 1955 [S. Afr.]

VAN RENSBURG, LOUWRENS. See: Helen Van Rensburg.

VAN RJNDT, PHILIPPE. Pseudonym. 1950-   .
Ref: CA.
Blueprint. Putnam, 1977; Macdonald, 1978 [Russ.]
The Tetramachus Collection. Putnam, 1976; Macdonald, 1977 [It.]
-The Trial of Adolph Hitler. Summit, 1978; Macdonald, 1979

VAN SCOFIELD, HENRY
The Frigorific Ghost. Vantage, 1976

VAN SICKLE, V. A. Pseudonym of Arthur Hawthorne Carhart, 1892-   . Ref: CA.
The Wrong Body. Knopf, 1937 [Chi.]

VAN SILLER, HILDA. Pseudonym: Van Siller, q.v.

VAN SLYKE, HELEN.   -1979. Pseudonym: Sharon Ashton, q.v.

VAN URK, VIRGINIA (NELLIS). SC: Tom Craig, in both titles, both set in NYC.
Grounds for Murder. Arcadia, 1958
Speaking of Murder. Phoenix, 1951

VAN VOGT, A(LFRED) E(LTON). 1912-   .
Ref: CA.
The House That Stood Still. Greenberg, 1950. Revised edition: The Mating Cry. Beacon, 1960

VAN WEDDINGTON, MARTHE. 1924-   . Pseudonym: Claire Dumas, q.v.

VAN WIJK, J(ACQUELINE) LOUW
Iselane. Houghton, 1961; Allen, 1961 [S. Afr.]

VAN ZANDT, EDMUND. ca.1919-   . Pseudonym: Tom Pendleton, q.v.

VAN ZILE, EDWARD S(IMS). 1863-1931.
-Kings in Adversity. Neely, 1897
The Last of the Van Slacks. Neely, 1894

VAN ZYL, P. R. Lawyer in S. Afr.
The Prosecutor. Putnam, 1974 [S. Afr.]

VARDEMAN, ROBERT E. Pseudonym: Nick Carter, q.v.

VARDRE, LESLIE. Pseudonym of L(eslie) P(urnell) Davies, 1914-   , q.v.
A Grave Matter (as by L. P. Davies); see The Nameless Ones
The Nameless Ones. Long, 1967. U.S. title: A Grave Matter, as by L. P. Davies. Doubleday, 1968
The Reluctant Medium (as by L. P. Davies); see Tell It to the Dead
Tell It to the Dead. Long, 1966. U.S. title: The Reluctant Medium, as by L. P. Davies. Doubleday, 1967

VARLEY, HENRY
The R.O.F. Murders. Mitre, 1945

VARLEY, JOHN. 1947-   . Ref: CA.
The Barbie Murders and other stories. Berkley, 1980 ss, at least one criminous

VARNADO, DONALD (ROBERT)
Washington Woman. Vantage, 1956

VARNAM, JOHN. SC: Insp. Semlake, in all titles, set in Eng.
Beware of the Dog. Hodder, 1954
Death Rehearses. Hodder, 1950
Travelling Deadman. Hodder, 1951 [acad.]

VARNEY, GEORGE
The Bungalow of Dead Birds. Nelson, 1929 [China]
The Missing Link. Jarrolds, 1927

VASE, GILLAN. Pseudonym of Elizabeth Newton.
A Great Mystery Solved. Remington, 1878; McBride, 1914

VASQUEZ, RICHARD
The Giant Killer. Manor, 1978 [L.A.]

VAUGHAN, GARY
The Belgrade Drop. Hale, 1978
East Zone Snatch. Hale, 1977
Radar Target. Hale, 1979

VAUGHAN, JULIAN
Jamo and the Bent Playboy. Hale, 1973

VAUGHAN, MATTHEW
The Discretion of Dominick Ayres. Secker, 1976; Little, 1976 [Eng., 1896]

VAUGHAN, ROBERT (RICHARD). 1937-   .
Ref: CA.
The Sin. Zebra, 1979
The Valkyrie Mandate. Simon, 1974; New English Library, 1975 [Saigon, 1963]

VAUGHN, JASON
Trailor Park. Vantage, 1975

VEDDER, JOHN K. Pseudonym of Frank Gruber, 1904-1969, q.v. Other pseudonyms: Stephen Acre, Charles K. Boston, qq.v.
The Last Doorbell. Holt, 1941. Also published as: Kiss the Boss Goodbye, as by Frank Gruber. Mercury, 1954 [Chi.]

VEIGA, JOSE J(ACINTO DA). 1915-   .
Ref: CA.
The Three Trials of Manirema. Knopf, 1970 (Translation of "A Hora dos Ruminentes." Rio de Janeiro, 1968.)

VEILLER, BAYARD. 1869-1943. See also: Marvin Dana, 1867-   ; and: William Almon Wolff, 1885-1933. Playwright.
Bait for a Tiger. Reynal, 1941 [NYC]

The Thirteenth Chair. French (NYC), 1922 (3-act play.)
The Trial of Mary Dugan. French (NYC), 1928 (3-act play.) [NYC]
Within the Law. Fly, 1913. Also as a 4-act play: French (NYC), 1917

VEILLER, MARGUERITE. Pseudonym: Martin Vale, q.v. See also: William Almon Wolff, 1885-1933.

VEITCH, JAMES
Crime and the Curator. Fiction House, 1946
Wait for Death. Blackfriars, 1944

VELEY, CHARLES. 1943-   .
-Children of the Dark. Doubleday, 1979; Granada, 1979
Night Whispers. Doubleday, 1980; Mayflower, 1981 [NYC]

VENABLES, TERRY. See: Gordon M(acLean) Williams, 1934-   . Joint pseudonym with Williams: P. B. Yuill, q.v.

VENNING, MICHAEL. Pseudonym of Georgiana Ann Randolph Craig, 1908-1957. Other pseudonyms: Daphne Sanders, Craig Rice, qq.v. See also: Gypsy Rose Lee; and: Ann Reynolds; and: Stuart Palmer, 1905-1968. SC: Melville Fairr, in all titles.
Jethro Hammer. Coward, 1944; Nicholson, 1947 [NYC]
The Man Who Slept All Day. Coward, 1942 [N.Y.]
Murder Through the Looking Glass. Coward, 1943; Nicholson, 1947 [NYC]

VENTERS, ARCHIE
Highland Vengeance. Hale, 1978
Kennedy's Killing. Hale, 1980
Macaterick's Revenge. Hale, 1979

VERALDI, ATTILIO. 1925-   . Born in Naples; translator of more than 100 mystery novels from English.
The Payoff. H. Hamilton, 1978; Harper, 1978 (Translation of "La Mazzetta." Milan, 1976.) [Naples]

VERALDI, GABRIEL. 1926-   . Born in France; publishing executive.
Spies of Good Intent. Atheneum, 1969; Deutsch, 1969 (Translation of "Les Espions de Bonne Volonte." Paris, 1969.)

VERCORS. Pseudonym of Jean Marcel Bruller, 1902-   . Ref: CA.
You Shall Know Them. Little, 1953. British title: Borderline. Macmillan (London), 1954. Also published as: The Murder of the Missing Link. PB, 1958 (Translation of "Les Animaux Denatures." Paris, 1952.)

VERMANDEL, JANET GREGORY. Born in N.Y.; advertising copywriter in Montr.; later living in Fla.
The Claverse Affair. Dodd, 1974; Milton House, 1975 [Montr.]
Dine with the Devil. Dodd, 1970; Hale, 1972 [Montr.]
Last Seen in Samarra. Dodd, 1972; Milton House, 1975 [Montr.]
Murder Most Fair; see So Long at the Fair
Of Midnight Honor. Dodd, 1972 [Montr.]
Scratch a Lover. Dodd, 1969; Hale, 1970 [Can.]
So Long at the Fair. Dodd, 1968. British title: Murder Most Fair. Jenkins, 1968 [Montr.]

VERN, DAVID. 1924-   . Pseudonym: David V. Reed, q.v.

VERNEDE, R(OBERT) E(RNEST). 1875-1917.
The Flight of Faviel; see The Pursuit of Mr. Faviel
The Port Allington Stories and others. Heinemann, 1921. U.S. title: Port Allington Stories. Doran, 1920 ss
The Pursuit of Mr. Faviel. Rivers, 1905. U.S. title (somewhat revised): The Flight of Faviel. Holt, 1912

VERNER, GERALD. Pseudonym of Donald Stuart, 1897-1980, q.v. SC: Sexton Blake (with many other authors), in those titles given without publisher (which was Amalgamated Press); Supt. Robert Budd, in at least those marked RB; Trevor Lowe, in at least those marked TL; Simon Gale, in at least those marked SG; Peter Chard, in at least those marked PC; Felix Heron, in at least those marked FH; Michael Dene, in at least those marked MD. Set: Eng.

Alias the Ghost. Wright, 1933
The Angel. Wright, 1939
The Black Hunchback. Wright, 1933
Black Skull. Wright, 1933
The Black Skull. 1929
The Box of Doom. 1928
The Case of Mr. Budd; see The Cleverness of Mr. Budd
The Cleverness of Mr. Budd. Wright, 1935. U.S. title: The Case of Mr. Budd. Macaulay, 1938 RB (3 novelets.)
The Clue of the Green Candle. Wright, 1938 TL
The Clue of the Second Tooth. 1927
The Con Man. Wright, 1934 [L.A.]
The Coupon Crimes. Mellifont, 1946
The Crime of Four. 1930
The Crimson Ramblers. Wright, 1960 (Novelization of the TV play.)
The Crooked Circle. Wright, 1935; Macaulay, 1937 RB
Dead Secret. Wright, 1967 FH
The Death Play. Wright, 1933
Death Set in Diamonds. Wright, 1965 TL
Dene of the Secret Service. Wright, 1941 DN,TL [Wales]
The Embankment Murder. Wright, 1933
The Faceless Ones. Wright, 1964 [Tangier]
The Fatal Manuscript. 1929
The Football Pool Murders. Wright, 1939 RB
The Frightened Man. Wright, 1937
Ghost House. Wright, 1961
The Ghost Man. Wright, 1936; Macaulay, 1936
The Ghost Squad. Wright, 1963
The Glass Arrow. Wright, 1937 TL
Green Mask. Wright, 1934 RB
Grim Death. Wright, 1960
The Grim Joker. Wright, 1936 RB
The Hand of Fear. Wright, 1936
The Hangman. Wright, 1934; Godwin, 1935 TL
The Heel of Achilles. Wright, 1945 MD
The Huntsman. Wright, 1940
I Am Death. Wright, 1963
The Jockey. Wright, 1937 RB
The Lady of Doom. Wright, 1934 TL
The Last Warning. Wright, 1962 RB
Meet Mr. Callaghan. French (London), 1953 (Play based on "The Urgent Hangman" by Peter Cheyney, 1896-1951, q.v.)
Mister Big. Wright, 1966 RB
Mr. Budd Again. Wright, 1939 RB
Mr. Budd Investigates. Wright, 1940 RB (3 novelets.)
Mr. Midnight. Wright, 1933 RB
Mr. Whipple Explains. Wright, 1936 (3 novelets.)
The Moor House Murders. Wright, 1964
Murder in Manuscript. Wright, 1963 RB
The Mystery of Sherwood Towers. 1928 Reprinted in 1940 as by Donald Stuart
The Mystery of the Phantom Blackmailer. 1928
The Next to Die. Wright, 1934 TL
Noose for a Lady. Wright, 1952 (Novelization of the radio play.) SG
The Nursery Rhyme Murders. Wright, 1960 RB
Phantom Hollow. Wright, 1933 TL
The Poisoner. Wright, 1940
The "Q" Squad. Wright, 1935; Macaulay, 1938
Queer Face. Wright, 1935
The Red Tape Murders. Wright, 1962 RB
The Return of Mr. Budd. Wright, 1938 RB
The Riddle of the Phantom Plague. 1928
The River House Mystery. Wright, 1938 TL
The River Men. Wright, 1936
The Royal Flush Murders. Wright, 1948 RB
The Secret of the Vault. 1930
The Seven Clues. Wright, 1936 MD
The Seven Lamps. Wright, 1947 RB
The Shadow Men. Wright, 1961 TL
The Show Must Go On. Wright, 1950 (Novelization of the radio play.) [theatre]
The Silent Slayer. 1929
The Silver Horseshoe. Wright, 1935 RB
Sinister House. Wright, 1934 RB (3 novelets.)
Six Men Died. Wright, 1964 RB
Sorcerer's House. Hutchinson, 1956 SG
The Squealer. Wright, 1934
Terror Tower. Wright, 1935 TL
They Walk in Darkness. Wright, 1947 PC
The Third Key. Wright, 1961
Thirsty Evil. Westhouse, 1945 PC
The Three Gnomes. Wright, 1937 TL
The Tipster. Wright, 1949 (Novelization of the radio play.) RB
The Token. Wright, 1937 TL
Towards Zero. French (London), 1957; Dramatists, 1957 (Play based on the novel by Agatha Christie, 1890-1976, q.v.)

The Tudor Gardens Mystery. Wright, 1966 FH
The Twelve Apostles. Wright, 1946 RB
The Vampire Man. Wright, 1941
The Watcher. Wright, 1936 TL
The Whispering Woman. Wright, 1949 RB
White Wig. Wright, 1935
The Witches' Moon. Wright, 1938 RB

VERNEY, F(RANK) E(DWIN)
The Man with the Black Patch. Hutchinson, 1931

VERNIER, PATRICIA
The California Factor. Dell, 1980 [Calif.]

VERNON, GEORGE SHIRRA GIBB. 1885-   . Pseudonym: Vernon George, q.v.

VERNON, HARRY M. 1878-   . See: Louise Jordan Miln, 1864-1933.

VERNON, KAY R.
The Ardreys. Zebra, 1979. Also published as: The Dark Seas of Maltern Manor. Zebra, 1981
The Dark Seas of Maltern Manor; see The Ardreys
The Phantom of Fonthill Park. Doubleday, 1976; Hale, 1977

VERNON, MARJORIE
-Flamenco and Orange Blossoms. Hale, 1976

VERNON-HARCOURT, F. C. 1845-   . See: F(rederick) C. Vernon Harcourt.

VERRON, ROBERT. Set: Eng.
The Country Club Murder. Wright, 1948
The Curse at Craig's End. Wright, 1953
The Day of the Dust. Wright, 1964 [future, Eng.]
Death Waits Outside. Wright, 1953
The Fifth Must Die! Wright, 1949
Freak Island Murders. Wright, 1947
Moon Killer. Wright, 1962
Murder Calls the Tune. Wright, 1958
Murder Indicted. Wright, 1957
Murder Lands the Odds. Wright, 1963
Murder Lifts the Veil. Wright, 1955
Murder Most Black. Wright, 1954
Murder Most Monstrous. Wright, 1958
Murder of No Consequence. Wright, 1960
Murder on Demand. Wright, 1961
Murder Points East. Wright, 1956
Murder with Impatience. Wright, 1944
Party to Murder. Wright, 1960
Return a Gain for Murder. Wright, 1961
Right Turn for Murder. Wright, 1952

VESCELIUS-SHELDON, LOUISE. See: Louise Vescelius Sheldon.

VESEY, ARTHUR H(ENRY). 1869-   . Byline also: Arthur Henry Veysey, q.v.
The Castle of Lies. Appleton, 1906
The Clock and the Key. Appleton, 1905; Sidney Appleton, 1905 [Venice]

VESTAL, STANLEY. Pseudonym of Walter Stanley Campbell, 1887-1957.
The Wine Room Murder. Little, 1935 [Fr.]

VEXIN, NOEL
Murder in Montmartre. Dell, 1960 [Paris]

VEYSEY, ARTHUR HENRY. 1869-   . Byline also: Arthur H(enry) Vesey, q.v.
A Cheque for Three Thousand. Dillingham, 1897; Arrowsmith, 1905, as by Arthur Henry Vesey
-Hats Off! Dillingham, 1899
-A Pedigree in Pawn. Dillingham, 1898
The Stateroom Opposite. Dillingham, 1900
-The Two White Elephants. Dillingham, 1899

VIAN, BORIS. 1920-1959. Pseudonym: Vernon Sullivan, q.v.

VICAR, EDWARD C.
Illegal Tender. Selwyn, 1936

VICARY, JEAN
Castle at Glencarris. Avon, 1972 [Scot.]
The Ice Maiden. Avon, 1972 [Fin.]
Saverstall. Ace, 1967

VICAS, VICTOR and VICTOR HAIM
The Impromptu Impostor. Abelard, 1971 (Translation of "L'Inconnu de la Mer Mort." Paris, 1969.)

VICKERS, RALPH
  The Confrontation. Hale, 1970
  Enticement to Danger. Hale, 1969

VICKERS, ROY. 1888-1965. Pseudonyms: David Durham, Sefton Kyle, John Spencer, qq.v. Ref: CC, DD, EM, MC, TC. SC: Insp. J. Rason = JR; Insp. George Rason = GR; Insp. Kyle = K; Hugh Stanton = HS; Insp. Peter Curwen = PC; James Segrove = JS. SC named Rason also found in pseudonymous titles. Set: Eng.
  Bardelow's Heir. Jenkins, 1933 JR
  Best Detective Stories of Roy Vickers. Faber, 1965 ss, GR in 1
  Brenda Gets Married. Jenkins, 1941
  A Date with Danger. Jenkins, 1942; Vanguard, 1944
  The Department of Dead Ends. Bestseller, 1947 ss GR
  The Department of Dead Ends. Faber, 1949; Detective Book Club, 1949 ss GR
  The Department of Dead Ends. Dover, 1978 ss GR
  The Deputy for Cain. Jenkins, 1931
  Double Image and other stories. Jenkins, 1955; Detective Book Club, 1955 ss, PC in 1, K in 2
  Eight Murders in the Suburbs. Jenkins, 1954. U.S. title: Six Murders in the Suburbs. Detective Book Club, 1958 (Two stories omitted from the U.S. edition.) ss, PC in 1, GR in 5
  The Enemy Within. Jenkins, 1938
  Find the Innocent. Jenkins, 1959 PC
  Four Past Four. Jenkins, 1925; Jefferson House, 1945 JS
  The Girl in the News. Jenkins, 1937 JR
  Gold and Wine. Jenkins, 1949; Walker, 1961 HS,PC
  The Gold Game. Jenkins, 1930
  Hide Those Diamonds! Newnes, 1935
  I'll Never Tell. Jenkins, 1937
  Ishmael's Wife. Jenkins, 1924 JS
  Kidnap Island. Newnes, 1935 JR
  -The Life Between. Jenkins, 1938 JR
  Maid to Murder; see Murdering Mr. Velfrage
  The Man in the Red Mask. Newnes, 1935 JR
  -The Marriage for the Defence. Jenkins, 1932
  Money Buys Everything. Jenkins, 1934 JR
  A Murder for a Million. Jenkins, 1924
  Murder in Two Flats. Jenkins, 1951; Mill, 1952 HS,PC
  Murder of a Snob. Jenkins, 1949; British Book Centre, 1958
  Murder Will Out. Faber, 1950; Detective Book Club, 1954 ss GR
  Murdering Mr. Velfrage. Faber, 1950. U.S. title: Maid to Murder. Mill, 1950 K
  The Mystery of the Scented Death. Jenkins, 1922 JR
  Playgirl Wanted. Jenkins, 1940
  The Radingham Mystery. Jenkins, 1928
  Seven Chose Murder. Jenkins, 1959; Detective Book Club, 1959 ss, GR in 2, PC in 2, K in 1
  She Walked in Fear. Jenkins, 1940 JR
  Six Came to Dinner. Jenkins, 1948 HS,PC
  Six Murders in the Suburbs; see Eight Murders in the Suburbs
  The Sole Survivor and The Kynsard Affair. Gollancz, 1952; Detective Book Club, 1951 (2 novelets.)
  Terror of Tongues. Jenkins, 1937 JR
  They Can't Hang Caroline. Jenkins, 1950 HS,PC
  The Unforbidden Sin. Jenkins, 1926
  The Vengeance of Henry Jarroman. Jenkins, 1923 JS

VICKERY, WILLIAM P(AUL)
  The Racketeer's Will. Amalgamated, 1932 (Sexton Blake.)

VICTOR, H(AROLD) L(AUDER). 1897-   .
  A Doctor in Eng.
  Deceptions. Paul, 1935
  Fate and Four Sinners. Paul, 1934
  Murder in Duplicate. Low, 1935

VICTOR, MRS. M(ETTA) V(ICTORIA FULLER). 1831-1886. Pseudonym: Seeley Regester, q.v.
  -Born to Betray; or, A Game Well Played. Street, 1890; Aldine, 1895
  -The Brown Princess. Street, 1888
  Dora Elmyr's Worst Enemy; or, Guilty or Not Guilty. Street, 1878. Also published as: Guilty or Not Guilty; or, Dora Elmyr's Worst Enemy. Street, 1890
  -The Gay Captain. Street, 1891; Aldine, 1896
  Guilty or Not Guilty; see Dora Elmyr's Worst Enemy

  -The Phantom Wife. Street, 1888
  -Who Owned the Jewels? or, The Heiress of the Sandalwood Chest. Street, 1891
  -Who Was He? Beadle, 1866

VIDAL, EUGENE GORE. 1925-   . Pseudonym: Edgar Box, q.v.

VIDOCQ, (EUGENE FRANCOIS). 1775-1857. Ref: DD, EM, MC, MP.
  Memoirs of Vidocq. Carey & Hart, 18??; Hunt and Clarke, 18?? Also published as: Vidocq, the Police Spy. Routledge, 1866 (Translation of "Memoires de Vidocq." Paris, 1828-9.) ss [Paris]

VIELE, HERMAN KNICKERBOCKER. 1856-1908.
  On the Lightship. Duffield, 1909 ss, some criminous

VIGILANT. Pseudonym. Series character: Barry Link (Lynx), in at least those marked BL.
  Fighting the Red Shadow. Hamilton, 1932
  Lynx, Counter Spy. Hamilton, 1937 BL
  Lynx, Spyflyer. Hamilton, 1936 BL
  Lynx, V.C. Hamilton, 1936 BL
  Lynx, V.C., Flies Again. Crowther, 1944 BL

VIGNANT, JEAN FRANCOIS. Pseudonym of Jean Beliard, wartime intelligence officer, later diplomat and government minister in Paris.
  The Alpine Affair. Chelsea, 1970 (Translation of "Meurtre a l'Alpe d'Heuz." Paris, 1968.) [Fr.]

VILLER, FREDRIK. Pseudonym of Christian Sparre, 1859-1936.
  The Black Tortoise. Doubleday, 1901; Heinemann, 1901 (Translation of "Gamle Friks Diamant." Oslo, 1898.) [Nor.]

VILLIERS, DAVID HUGH. Pseudonym: David Buckingham, q.v.

VILLIERS, MARGOT
  The Serpent of Lilith. PB, 1976 [Eng., ca.1860.]

VILLIERS-STUART, GERALD
  The Flight of Lord Rhincrew. Everett, 1909
  -The Soul of Croesus. Laurie, 1908

VINCE, HENRY SCOTT
  Two Pardons. Ward, 1889

VINCENT, CLAIRE. Pseudonym of Miriam Lynch, q.v. Other pseudonym: Mary Wallace, q.v.
  Garden of Satan. Lancer, 1970. Also published as by Miriam Lynch: Pinnacle, 1978
  -The Pink Castle. Arcadia, 1959
  Spellbound. Tower, 1966. Also published as: Unholy Spell. Belmont, 1972. Also published under original title as by Miriam Lynch: Pinnacle, 1979
  Unholy Spell; see Spellbound

VINCENT, DWIGHT. See: Day Keene.

VINCENT, LADY KITTY (EDITH BLANCHE). 1887-   . SC: Gyp Kidnadze, in at least those marked GK. Set: Eng.
  "No. 3." Jenkins, 1924 GK
  The Ruby Cup. Jenkins, 1928 GK
  These Within. Jenkins, 1943
  An Untold Tale. Jenkins, 1934 GK

VINCENT, (A.) LOUIS. 1876-   .
  Youth at Bay. Hutchinson, 1934

VINCENT, RICHARD
  Portrait in Black. Bantam, 1960 (Novelization of the movie.)

VINES, T. H.
  S. Botolph; or, The Missing Key. Church Press, 1868

VINEY, ALBERT
  -The Ballet of Moments Unborn. Melrose, 1947

VINING, KEITH
  Too Hot for Hell. Ace, 1952

VINN, WALGER. Head of Chi. construction firm.
  Suddenly He Knew. Greenwich, 1957

VINTER, MICHAEL. 1927-   .
  All This Shall Perish. Hale, 1970
  Colour of Dried Blood. Hale, 1967
  Die Here a Stranger. Hale, 1968
  A Place of Execution. Hale, 1969

  Rat in a Trap. Hale, 1971
  A Vintage So Evil. Hale, 1968
  The Wounds of Treason. Hale, 1972

VINTON, ALDIN. Pseudonym of Adelin Sumner Briggs Linton, 1899-   .
  Mystery in Green. Phoenix, 1937. Also published as: The Corpse in the Cab. Hangman's House, 1942 [Chi.]

VINTON, ARTHUR DUDLEY. 1852-1906.
  The Pomfret Mystery. Ogilvie, 1886
  The Unpardonable Sin. Ogilvie, 1889

VIOLETT, ELLEN
  Double Take. Doubleday, 1977 [NYC]

VIPOND, DON (HARRY). 1932-   . Ref: CA.
  Night of the Shooting Star. Bobbs, 1975 [Can.]

VIRDEN, KATHARINE
  The Crooked Eye. Doubleday, 1930; Chapman, 1930
  The Thing in the Night. Doubleday, 1930

VIRMONNE, CLAUDE. Pseudonym. See: Claudette Virmonne.

VIRMONNE, CLAUDETTE. Pseudonym. French byline: Claude Virmonne.
  Bound by Honor. Mystique, 1980 (Translation of "La Mariee du Chateau Noir." Paris, 1977.)
  Circle of Deception. Mystique, 1980 (Translation of "Un Etranger sur la Colline." Paris, 1970.)
  Falcon's Heir. Mystique, 1980 (Translation of "Lune de Miel en Irlande." Paris, 1969.)
  Haven of Deceit. Mystique, 1980 (Translation of "La Nuit du Rossignol." Paris, 1976.)
  Valley of No Return. Mystique, 1979 (Translation of "Le Cavalier du Soir." Paris, 1976.)
  The Venetian Portrait. Mystique, 1980 (Translation of "Le Portrait Venitian." Paris, 1968.)
  Voices of Terror. Mystique, 1980 (Translation of "Comme un Oiseau Blesse." Paris, 1968.)

VIVIAN, E(VELYN) CHARLES (H.). 1882-1947. Pseudonyms: Charles Cannell, Jack Mann, qq.v. SC: Insp. Byrne, in at least those marked B; Insp. Head, in at least those marked H. Set: Eng.
  Accessory After. Ward, 1934 H
  And Then There Was None. Ward, 1941
  Arrested. Hale, 1949
  The Barking Dog Murder Case; see Tramp's Evidence
  The Capsule Mystery. Ward, 1935
  Cigar for Inspector Head. Ward, 1935 H
  Curses Come Home. Hale, 1942
  Dangerous Guide. Hale, 1943
  Delicate Fiend. Ward, 1930
  Double or Quit. Ward, 1930
  Evidence in Blue. Ward, 1938. U.S. title: The Man in Gray. Hillman-Curl, 1938 H
  False Truth. Ward, 1932
  Following Feet. Melrose, 1911
  The Forbidden Door. Ward, 1927
  Girl in the Dark. Ward, 1933 H
  House for Sale. Amalgamated, 1934
  The Impossible Crime. Ward, 1940
  Infamous Fame. Ward, 1932
  Innocent Guilt. Ward, 1931
  Jewels Go Back. Ward, 1934
  The Keys of the Flat. Ward, 1933
  Ladies in the Case. Ward, 1933
  -Lone Isle. Ward, 1932
  Man Alone. Ward, 1928
  The Man in Gray; see Evidence in Blue
  The Man with a Scar. Ward, 1940 B
  Nine Days. Ward, 1928
  One Tropic Night. Ward, 1930
  Other Gods. Hale, 1945
  Problem by Rail. Ward, 1939 H
  The Rainbow Puzzle. Ward, 1938 H
  Samson. Hale, 1944
  Seventeen Cards. Ward, 1935 H
  Shadow on the House. Ward, 1934 H
  She Who Will Not—. Hale, 1945
  The Tale of Fleur. Ward, 1929
  .38 Automatic. Ward, 1937 H
  Touch and Go. Ward, 1939 H
  Tramp's Evidence. Ward, 1937. U.S. title: The Barking Dog Murder Case. Hillman-Curl, 1937 H
  Unwashed Gods. Ward, 1931
  Vain Escape. Hale, 1952 B
  Who Killed Gatton? Ward, 1936 H
  With Intent to Kill. Ward, 1936 H

VIVIAN, FRANCIS. Pseudonym of Arthur Ernest Ashley, 1906-   . Ref: CA, CC. SC: Supt. Gordon Knollis, in at least those marked GK; Insp. John

Burnell = JB; Sgt. Ronnie Drew, in at least those marked RD. Set: Eng.
　The Arrow of Death. Jenkins, 1938　RD
　Black Alibi. Jenkins, 1938　JB
　Dark Moon. Jenkins, 1939　RD
　Darkling Death. Jenkins, 1956; Roy, 1957　GK
　Dead Opposite the Church. Jenkins, 1959
　Death at the Salutation. Jenkins, 1937　JB
　The Death of Mr. Lomas. Jenkins, 1941　GK
　The Elusive Bowman. Hodder, 1951　GK
　The Frog Was Yellow. Jenkins, 1940　RD
　The Ladies of Locksley. Jenkins, 1953; Roy, 1957　GK
　The Laughing Dog. Hodder, 1949　GK
　Murder in Angel Yard. Fiction House, 1949
　The Ninth Enemy. Hodder, 1948　GK
　Sable Messenger. Jenkins, 1947　GK
　The Singing Masons. Hodder, 1950　GK
　The Sleeping Island. Hodder, 1951　GK
　The Three Short Men. Jenkins, 1939　GK
　The Threefold Cord. Jenkins, 1947　GK

VIZETELLY, ERNEST A(LFRED). 1853-1922.
　The Scorpion. Chatto, 1894　[Sp.]

VLASTO, JOHN ALEXANDER. 1877-1958. Pseudonyms: John Alexander, John Remenham, qq.v.

VOELKER, JOHN DONALDSON. 1903- . Pseudonym: Robert Traver, q.v.

VOGAN, ARTHUR JAMES
　The Black Police. Hutchinson, 1891

VOGEL, HARRY B(ENJAMIN). 1868- .
　-Gentleman Garnet. Smith, 1902
　-The Tragedy of a Flirtation. Greening, 1909
　Two Million. Unwin, 1925

VOLDENG, KARL E.
　The X-Ray Solution. Carlyle, 1979

VOLK, GEORGE. Pseudonym: Janet Kidde, q.v.

VOLK, GORDON. 1885- . See also: Raymond Knotts.
　-Bamboo Bay. Skeffington, 1934
　The Cliff Mill Mystery. Skeffington, 19??
　Cliffs of Sark. Skeffington, 1936
　-Cornish Cruise. Paul, 1947
　-The Devil's Whirlpool. Skeffington, 1928
　-Fifty-Fifty. Skeffington, 1935
　-Galleon Rock. Hale, 1939
　-Gold out of China. Paul, 1946
　-The Green Ship. Skeffington, 1931
　-In Brighton Waters. Skeffington, 1936
　-Island Schooner. Paul, 1950
　-The Isle of Men. Skeffington, 1932
　The Lighthouse Mystery. Skeffington, 1930
　-The Lobster Pot. Paul, 1949
　-The Lonely Shore. Skeffington, 1937
　-The "Maid of Sussex". Paul, 1948
　-The Sea Case. Skeffington, 1929
　-South of the Line. Skeffington, 1934
　-Thunder Island. Skeffington, 1933
　-The Tideless Sea. Skeffington, 1932
　-The Zoo Ship. Skeffington, 1938

VOLTAIRE, (FRANCOIS MARIE AROUET DE). 1694-1778. Ref: CC, DD, MC, MP.
　Zadig; or, The Book of Fate. Brindley (London), 1749

VON BLOCK, BELA (WILLIAM). 1927- . Pseudonyms: Jonathan Black, Mercedes Endfield, E. L. McGinnis, qq.v.
　The World Rapers. Hart-Davis, 1974

VON CONTA, MANFRED. 1931- .
　The Deathbringer. Calder, 1971 (Translation of "Der Totmacher." Zurich, 1969.)

VON DODERER, HEIMITO. 1896-1966. Born in Austria; doctorate in history from U. of Vienna; poet and novelist.
　Every Man a Murderer. Knopf, 1964 (Translation of "Ein Mord den Jeder Begeht." Munich, 1938.)　[Austria]

VON ELSNER, DON (BYRON). 1909- . Ref: CA. SC: David Danning = DD; Jake Winkman = JW.
　The Ace of Spies. Award, 1966; Tandem, 1968　JW　[Wash. D.C.]
　A Bullet for Your Dreams. Lancer, 1968　DD
　Countdown for a Spy. Signet, 1966　DD　[Haw.]
　Don't Just Stand There, Do Someone. Signet, 1962　DD　[L.A.]
　How to Succeed at Murder Without Really Trying. Signet, 1963. Also published as: The Jake of Diamonds. Award, 1967; Tandem, 1967　JW　[Haw.]
　The Jack of Hearts. Award, 1968　JW
　The Jake of Diamonds; see How to Succeed at Murder Without Really Trying
　Just Not Making Mayhem Like They Used To. Signet, 1961　DD
　Pour a Swindle Through a Loophole. Belmont, 1964　DD　[Calif.]
　Those Who Prey Together Slay Together. Signet, 1961; New English Library pb, 1962　DD　[Haw.]
　Who Says a Corpse Has to Be Dull. Signet, 1963　DD　[Calif.]
　You Can't Do Business with Murder. Signet, 1962　DD　[Wis.]

VON HARBOU, THEA. 1888- .
　The Spy. Readers Library, 1928. U.S. title: Spies. Putnam, 1928 (Translation of "Spione." Berlin, 1928.)　[Eng.]

VON HINDENBURG, AGNES BLANCHE MARIE. 1873- . Pseudonym: Marie Hay, q.v.

VON HUTTEN, BARONESS [BETTINA RIDDLE FREIFRAU VON HUTTEN ZUM STOLZENBERG]. 1874-1957.
　Cowardly Custard. Hutchinson, 1936. U.S. title: Gentleman's Agreement. Dutton, 1936
　Die She Must. Hutchinson, 1934; Dutton, 1936
　-The Elgin Marble. Hutchinson, 1937. U.S. title: Youth Without Glory. Dutton, 1938
　Flies. Mills, 1927　ss, some criminous
　Gentleman's Agreement; see Cowardly Custard
　Monkey-Puzzle. Long, 1932
　What Happened Is This. Hutchinson, 1938; Dutton, 1939
　Youth Without Glory; see The Elgin Marble

VON LINSINGEN, F(REDERICK) W(ILLIAM) B(ERRY). 1901- .
　The Pressure-Gauge Murder. Methuen, 1929; Dutton, 1930　[S. Afr.]

VONNEGUT, KURT, JR. 1922- . Ref: CA.
　Mother Night. GM, 1961; Cape, 1968

VON RABE, BARONESS ANN CRAWFORD. 1846- . Pseudonym: Von Degan, q.v.

VON RIMANOCZY, CHARLES ADOLPH. 1906- . Pseudonym: Charles Eland, q.v.

VOS, DAVID. See: James McDonald.

VOSPER, FRANK. 1899- .
　Love from a Stranger. Collins, 1936 (3-act play based on the ss "Philomel Cottage" by Agatha Christie, 1890-1976, q.v.)
　Murder on the Second Floor. Putnam, 1929 (Play.) Novelization of the play: Readers Library, 1929
　People Like Us. Putnam (London & NYC), 1929 (3-act play.)

VOSPER, G. VENNING
　The Squire of Landrewn. Paul, 1946　[Eng., 1838]
　Who Killed the Chauffeur? Paul, 1941

VOSS BARK, CONRAD. See: Bark, Conrad Voss

VOUTE, EMILE
　The Passport. Kennerley, 1915

VOWELL, DAVID
　The Assassinator. Bantam (NYC & London), 1975　[L.A.]
　Dragnet 1968. Popular Library, 1967 (Novelization of the TV series.)　[L.A.]

VREELAND, (WILLIAM CANTWELL) FRANK (THORPE). 1891- .
　Dishonored. Grosset, 1931 (Novelization of the movie.)　[Vienna]
　June 13. Longmans, 1930 (3-act play, from the movie "The Night of June 13", based on a story by Vera Caspary, 1899- , q.v.)

VROOMAN, H(ENRY) WELLINGTON
　Half a Million Insurance; or, Dr. Lauterback's Strange Patient. American News, 1888

VULLIAMY, C(OLWYN) E(DWARD). 1886-1971. Pseudonym: Anthony Rolls, q.v. Ref: CC, DD, EM, MC, MP, TC. Set: Eng.
　Body in the Boudoir. Joseph, 1956
　Cakes for Your Birthday. Joseph, 1959; British Book Centre, 1959
　Don Among the Dead Men. Joseph, 1952　[acad.]
　Floral Tribute. Joseph, 1963
　Justice for Judy. Joseph, 1960
　Tea at the Abbey. Joseph, 1961

VULPIUS, C(HRISTIAN) A(UGUST). 1762-1827.
　Rinaldo Rinaldini, Captain of Banditti. Maiden, 1801

W., W. Pseudonym of Mrs. Fortune.
　The Detective's Album: Tales of the Australian Police. Clarson (Melbourne), 1871　ss　[Australia]

WADDELL, C. C.
　You're My Man! Queensway, 1936

WADDELL, C(HARLES) C(AREY). 1868-1930. Pseudonym: Charles Carey, q.v.
　The Girl of the Guard Line. Moffat, 1915
　Juror No. 17. Long, 1931　[NYC]
　Midnight to High Noon. Whitman, 1929　[NYC]

WADDELL, E(LEANOR) LEE
　Murder at Drake's Anchorage. Dutton, 1949　[Calif.]

WADDELL, MARTIN. 1941- . Born in Ireland. SC: Gerald Otley = GO.
　-Come Back When I'm Sober. Hodder, 1969
　Otley. Hodder, 1966; Stein, 1966　GO
　Otley Forever. Hodder, 1968; Stein, 1968　GO
　Otley Pursued. Hodder, 1967; Stein, 1967　GO
　Otley Victorious. Hodder, 1969; Stein, 1969　GO

WADE, ALAN. Pseudonym of John Holbrook Vance, 1917- , q.v. Byline also: Jack Vance, q.v. Other pseudonym: Peter Held, q.v. See also: Ellery Queen.
　Isle of Peril. Mystery House, 1957　[Calif.]

WADE, BOB [ROBERT WADE], 1920- , and BILL MILLER, 1920-1961. Joint pseudonyms: Will Daemer, Whit Masterson, Wade Miller, Dale Wilmer, qq.v. See also: Robert Wade.
　Pop Goes the Queen. Farrar, 1947. Also published as: Murder—Queen High. Graphic, 1949; Allen, 1958, as by Wade Miller　[Calif.]

WADE, GARRISON. Pseudonym.
　Alias John Smith. Vantage, 1966

WADE, HARRISON
　So Lovely to Kill. Graphic, 1956　[N.Y.]

WADE, HENRY. Pseudonym of Henry Lancelot Aubrey-Fletcher, 1887-1969. Ref: CC, EM, MP, TC. SC: Constable John Bragg = JB; Major Faide = F; Chief Insp. Poole = P. Set: Eng.
　Be Kind to the Killer. Constable, 1952
　Bury Him Darkly. Constable, 1936　P
　Constable, Guard Thyself! Constable, 1934; Houghton, 1935　P
　Diplomat's Folly. Constable, 1951; Macmillan, 1952
　The Duke of York's Steps. Constable, 1929; Payson, 1929　P
　The Dying Alderman. Constable, 1930; Brewer, 1930
　A Dying Fall. Constable, 1955; Macmillan, 1955
　Gold Was Our Grave. Constable, 1954; Macmillan, 1954　P
　The Hanging Captain. Constable, 1932; Harcourt, 1933
　Heir Presumptive. Constable, 1935; Macmillan, 1953
　Here Comes the Copper. Constable, 1938　JB　ss
　The High Sheriff. Constable, 1937　F
　The Litmore Snatch. Constable, 1957; Macmillan, 1957
　Lonely Magdalen. Constable, 1940. Revised edition: Constable, 1946　P
　The Missing Partners. Constable, 1928; Payson, 1928
　Mist on the Saltings. Constable, 1933
　New Graves at Great Norne. Constable, 1947
　No Friendly Drop. Constable, 1931; Brewer, 1932　P,F
　Policeman's Lot. Constable, 1933　P　ss
　Released for Death. Constable, 1938　JB
　Too Soon to Die. Constable, 1953; Macmillan, 1954　P
　The Verdict of You All. Constable, 1926; Payson, 1927

WADE, JENNIFER. Pseudonym of Joy DeWeese Wehen, 1926- . Ref: CA.
  The Singing Wind. Coward, 1977

WADE, JONATHAN. 1926-
  Back to Life. Collins, 1961; Pantheon, 1962
  The Boy with the Sling. Collins, 1965
  Running Sand. Collins, 1962; Random, 1963

WADE, KATHLEEN (NESTA KNIGHT). 1903- .
  Act of Violence. Hutchinson, 1954
  A Cloak for Malice. Hutchinson, 1949
  Crime at Gargoyles. Hutchinson, 1947
  The Dark Moment. Hutchinson, 1951
  Death at Aranshore. Gifford, 1942
  Death on "Calamity". Gifford, 1945

WADE, ROBERT. 1920- . Joint pseudonyms with Bill Miller, 1920-1961: Will Daemer, Whit Masterson, Wade Miller, Dale Wilmer, qq.v. See also: Bob Wade.
  Knave of Eagles. Random, 1969; Hale, 1970 [Havana]
  The Stroke of Seven. Morrow, 1965; Heinemann, 1966

WADELTON, MAGGIE-OWEN [MAGGIE JEANNE MELODY WADELTON]. 1895- .
  Sarah Mandrake. Bobbs, 1946

WADHAM, RUTH
  Weekend in Baghdad. Gollancz, 1958; Macmillan, 1959 [Baghdad]

WAER, JACK. Born in Poland; gambling casino manager.
  Murder in Las Vegas. Avon, 1955 [Las Veg.]
  -Sweet and Low-Down. Popular Library, 1955
  17 and Black. Viking, 1954 [Mex. City]

WAGER, WALTER (HERMAN). 1924- . Pseudonyms: Walter Hermann, John Tiger, qq.v. Ref: CA. SC: Alison Gordon = AG.
  Blue Leader. Arbor, 1979; Futura, 1980 AG
  Blue Moon. Arbor, 1980; Futura, 1981 AG [Las Veg.]
  Sledgehammer. Macmillan, 1970; Hodder, 1971
  Swap. Macmillan, 1972; Futura, 1977
  Telefon. Macmillan, 1975; Barker, 1975
  Time of Reckoning. Playboy, 1977; Futura, 1978 [Ger.]
  Viper Three. Macmillan, 1971

WAGNER, CONSTANCE. 1903-
  The Major Has Seven Guests. Stokes, 1940; Hale, 1941

WAGNER, ELAINE. 1939- . Ref: CA.
  A Case of Bottled Murder. Doubleday, 1973 [Mass.]

WAGNER, GEOFFREY (ATHELING). 1927- . Ref: CA.
  -Born of the Sun. Falcon, 1949; Popular Library, 1954
  -The Dispossessed. Ward, 1957; Devin-Adair, 1956
  -The Lake Lovers. Quadriga, 1962; Macmillan, 1963
  The Passionate Land. Ward, 1956; Simon, 1953
  The Passionate Strangers. Popular Library, 1964 (British title?)
  Season of Assassins. Quadriga, 1961; GM, 1961 [1940s]
  -A Summer Stranger. Redman, 1959
  Venables. Murray, 1952; Simon, 1952

WAGNER, KARL EDWARD
  -Bloodstone. Warner, 1975; Coronet, 1977
  Death Angel's Shadow. Warner, 1973; Hodder pb, 1980

WAGNER, SHARON (BLYTHE). 1936- . Ref: CA.
  Bride of the Dullahan. Doubleday, 1976
  Circle of Evil. Lancer, 1971
  Colors of Death. Beagle, 1974
  Country of the Wolf. Lancer, 1970
  The Cove in Darkness, with Bernard L. Casey. Lancer, 1973 [Eng.]
  Cry of the Cat. Belmont, 1973
  Curse of Still Valley. Lancer, 1969
  Dark Side of Paradise. Beagle, 1974
  Dark Waters of Death. Beagle, 1975
  Echoes of an Ancient Love. Ballantine, 1976
  -Embraces. Zebra, 1980
  Haitian Legacy, with Bernard L. Casey. Avon, 1974
  The Haunted Honeymoon. Popular Library, 1980
  Havenhurst. Beagle, 1975
  House of Doom, House of Desire. Zebra, 1980
  Legacy of Loneliness. Avon, 1974
  Maridu. Lancer, 1970
  Moonwind. Lancer, 1971
  Satan's Acres. Ace, 1974
  -Secrets. Zebra, 1980
  Shades of Evil. Beagle, 1974
  Shadow on the Sun, with Bernard L. Casey. Lancer, 1972
  The Turquoise Talisman. Ballantine, 1975

WAGONER, DAVID (RUSSELL). 1926- . Ref: CA.
  The Man in the Middle. Harcourt, 1954; Gollancz, 1955 [Chi.]

WAHL, ALBERTA (ELIZABETH) HUGHES. 1904- . Born in N.J.; magazine fiction writer.
  Handsome, But Dead. Howell, 1942; Boardman, 1946 [N.J.]

WAHLOO, PER [PETER]. 1926-1975. See also: Maj Sjowall, 1935- . SC: Chief Insp. Peter Jensen = PJ.
  The Assignment. Joseph, 1965; Knopf, 1966 (Translation of "Uppdraget." Stockholm, 1963.) [S. Am.]
  The Generals. Joseph, 1974; Pantheon, 1974 (Translation of "Generalerna." Stockholm, 1965.)
  The Lorry. Joseph, 1968. U.S. title: A Necessary Action. Pantheon, 1969 (Translation of "Lastbilen." Stockholm, 1962.) [Sp.]
  Murder on the Thirty-First Floor. Joseph, 1966. U.S. title: The Thirty-First Floor. Knopf, 1967 (Translation of "Mord pa 31: a Vaningen." Stockholm, 1966.) PJ
  A Necessary Action; see The Lorry
  The Steel Spring. Joseph, 1970; Delacorte, 1970 (Translation of "Stalspranget." Stockholm, 1968.) PJ
  The Thirty-First Floor; see Murder on the Thirty-First Floor

WAINWRIGHT, JOHN (WILLIAM). 1921- . Pseudonym: Jack Ripley, q.v. Ref: CC, TC. SC: Chief Insp./Supt. Lennox, in at least those marked L; Supt. Gilliant, in at least those marked G; Supt. Charles Ripley, in at least those marked CR; Insp. Lyle, in at least those marked IL. Set: Eng.
  Acquittal. Macmillan (London), 1976; St. Martin's, 1976
  The Bastard. Macmillan (London), 1976; St. Martin's, 1977
  The Big Tickle. Macmillan (London), 1969
  Brainwash. Macmillan (London), 1979; St. Martin's, 1979 IL
  Cause for a Killing. Macmillan (London), 1974
  Coppers Don't Cry. Macmillan (London), 1975
  The Crystallised Carbon Pig. Collins, 1966; Walker, 1967 G
  The Darkening Glass. Collins, 1968
  The Day of the Peppercorn Kill. Macmillan (London), 1977; St. Martin's, 1981
  Death Certificate. Macmillan (London), 1978
  Death in a Sleeping City. Collins, 1965
  Death of a Big Man. Macmillan (London), 1975; St. Martin's, 1975 CR
  The Devil You Don't. Macmillan (London), 1973
  Dig the Grave and Let Him Die. Macmillan (London), 1971
  Do Nothin' Till You Hear from Me. Macmillan (London), 1977; St. Martin's, 1978
  Dominoes. Macmillan (London), 1980; St. Martin's, 1980 L
  Duty Elsewhere. Macmillan (London), 1979; St. Martin's, 1979 IL
  Edge of Extinction. Collins, 1968
  The Evidence I Shall Give. Macmillan (London), 1974 L
  Evil Intent. Collins, 1966 CR
  The Eye of the Beholder. Macmillan (London), 1980; St. Martin's, 1980
  Freeze Thy Blood Less Coldly. Macmillan (London), 1970 CR
  The Hard Hit. Macmillan (London), 1974; St. Martin's, 1975 CR
  High-Class Kill. Macmillan (London), 1973
  Home Is the Hunter, and The Big Kayo. Macmillan (London), 1979 (2 stories)
  The Jury People. Macmillan (London), 1978; St. Martin's, 1978
  A Kill of Small Consequences. Macmillan (London), 1980
  Kill the Girls and Make Them Cry. Macmillan (London), 1974
  Landscape with Violence. Macmillan (London), 1975; St. Martin's, 1976 L
  The Last Buccaneer. Macmillan (London), 1971
  Man of Law. Macmillan (London), 1980; St. Martin's, 1980
  A Nest of Rats. Macmillan (London), 1977; St. Martin's, 1977
  Night Is a Time to Die. Macmillan (London), 1972
  Pool of Tears. Macmillan (London), 1977; St. Martin's, 1977 L
  A Pride of Pigs. Macmillan (London), 1973
  Prynter's Devil. Macmillan (London), 1970
  The Reluctant Sleeper. Macmillan (London), 1979
  Requiem for a Loser. Macmillan (London), 1972 G
  A Ripple of Murders. Macmillan (London), 1978; St. Martin's, 1979 G
  Square Dance. Macmillan (London), 1975; St. Martin's, 1975 L
  Take Murder... Macmillan (London), 1979; St. Martin's, 1981 L
  The Take-Over Man. Collins, 1969
  Talent for Murder. Collins, 1967; Walker, 1967
  Ten Steps to the Gallows. Collins, 1967
  Tension. Macmillan (London), 1979
  Thief of Time. Macmillan (London), 1978; St. Martin's, 1978
  A Touch of Malice. Macmillan (London), 1973 CR
  The Venus Fly-Trap. Macmillan (London), 1980; St. Martin's, 1980
  Walther P.38. Macmillan (London), 1976
  Web of Silence. Collins, 1968
  Who Goes Next? Macmillan (London), 1976; St. Martin's, 1977
  The Worms Must Wait. Collins, 1967 CR

WAINWRIGHT, RICHARD A.
  Hunted Down. Street (Magnet)
  A Kidnapped Millionaire. Street (Magnet)

WAITT, ISABEL (WOODMAN)
  Death a la King. Phoenix, 1943. British title: It's Murder, Miss King. Morris, 1946 [Boston]
  It's Murder, Miss King; see Death a la King
  Murder at Pirate's Head. Edwards, 1946

WAKE, EDITH
  Death and Mrs. Lovely. Wells Gardner, 1947

WAKEFIELD, H(ERBERT) RUSSELL. 1888-1965. Ref: CC. Set: Eng.
  Belt of Suspicion. Collins, 1936
  Hearken to the Evidence. Bles, 1933; Doubleday, 1934
  Hostess to Death. Collins, 1938
  Imagine a Man in a Box. Allan, 1931; Appleton, 1931 ss, at least one criminous

WAKEFIELD, JOHN. 1921- . Ref: CC.
  Death the Sure Physician. Constable, 1965; Dodd, 1966 [hosp.]

WAKEFIELD, MAUREEN E.
  Secret at Midwinter End. Lenox, 1974 [Eng.]

WAKEFIELD, R. I. Pseudonym of Gertrude Mason White, 1915- . Ref: CA.
  You Will Die Today! Dodd, 1953 [acad.]

WAKEVAINEN, CLARA A. Pseudonym: Carol West, q.v.

WALCOTT, EARLE ASHLEY. 1859- .
  Blindfolded. Bobbs, 1906 [S.F.]
  The Open Door. Dodd, 1910 [S.F.]

WALD, MALVIN (DANIEL), 1927- , and ALBERT MALTZ, 1908- . Ref (both authors): CA.
  The Naked City. Southern Illinois U. Press, 1979 (Screenplay.)

WALDMAN, FRANK. SC: Insp. Clouseau, in both titles, which are movie novelizations.
  The Pink Panther Strikes Again. Ballantine, 1976; Futura, 1976
  The Return of the Pink Panther. Ballantine, 1977; Futura, 1977

WALDRON, SIMON. SC: Steve Essex, in at least those marked SE.
  Caught in the Middle. Hale, 1972
  The Grayson Affair. Hale, 1975
  Hot Ice. Hale, 1969 SE
  Leap Before You Look. Hale, 1968 SE
  Time to Run. Hale, 1968

WALES, HUBERT. Pseudonym of William Charter Piggott, 1870-1943.
-Blue Flames. Long, 1918
The Brocklebank Riddle. Century, 1914. British title: The Thirty Days. Cassell, 1915
The Thirty Days; see The Brocklebank Riddle

WALES, KIRK. Pseudonym of James Ronald, 1905- , q.v.

WALK, CHARLES EDMONDS. 1875- .
The Crimson Cross. McClurg, 1913; Cazenove, 1913
The Green Seal. McClurg, 1914
The Paternoster Ruby. McClurg, 1910 [U.S., 1892]
The Silver Blade. McClurg, 1908 [South]
The Time Lock. McClurg, 1912 [NYC]
The Yellow Circle. McClurg, 1909 [Va.]

WALKER, CHARLES M(AURICE)
Death of a Jazz King. Paul, 1936

WALKER, DAVID (ESDAILE). 1907- .
Diamonds for Danger; see Diamonds for Moscow
Diamonds for Moscow. Chapman, 1953. U.S. title: Diamonds for Danger. Harper, 1954 [Port.]
-The Rigoville Match. Chapman, 1955

WALKER, DAVID (HARRY). 1911- . Ref: CA.
Ash. Collins, 1976; Houghton, 1976 [Scot.]
Black Dougal. Collins, 1973; Houghton, 1974 [Can.]
CAB-Intersec; see Devil's Plunge
Devil's Plunge. Collins, 1968. U.S. title: CAB-Intersec. Houghton, 1968 [Switz.]
Mallabec. Collins, 1965; Houghton, 1965 [Can.]
The Storm and the Silence. Cape, 1950; Houghton, 1949
Winter of Madness. Collins, 1964; Houghton, 1964 [Scot.]

WALKER, G. LEITCH. See: R(ichard) Andre.

WALKER, GEORGE. 1772-1847.
The House of Tynian. Lane, 1795

WALKER, GERALD. 1928- . Ref: CA.
Cruising. Stein, 1970; Allen, 1971 [NYC]

WALKER, GERTRUDE
Diamonds Don't Burn. Jenkins, 1955
So Deadly Fair. Putnam, 1948 [Minn.]
The Suspect. Major, 1978

WALKER, HARRY. Pseudonym of Hillary (Baldwin) Waugh, 1920- , q.v. Other pseudonyms: Elissa Grandower, H. Baldwin Taylor, qq.v.
The Case of the Missing Gardener. Arcadia, 1954 [Conn.]

WALKER, IRA. Pseudonym of Irma (Ruth Roden) Walker, 1921- , q.v. Other pseudonym: Andrea Harris, q.v. SC: Steve Rhoden, in both titles (see also Irma Walker entry).
The Man in the Driver's Seat. Abelard (NYC & London), 1964
Someone's Stolen Nellie Grey. Abelard (NYC & London), 1963 [Ky.]

WALKER, IRMA (RUTH RODEN). 1921- .
Pseudonyms: Andrea Harris, Ira Walker, qq.v. Ref: CA. SC: Steve Rhoden = SR (see also Ira Walker entry).
The Lucifer Wine. Bobbs, 1977 [Calif.]
The Maumaloa Curse. Bobbs, 1978 [Haw.]
Murder in 25 Words or Less. Raven, 1980 SR [Colo.]

WALKER, JERRY. SC: Lawrence Marley, in at least those marked LM.
The Crimson Trail. Cosmos, 1949
A Date with Destiny. Cosmos, 1949 LM
Mission Accomplished. Cosmos, 1947; Mitre, 1948 LM

WALKER, KEITH. 1927- .
The Escape. Vantage, 1970

WALKER, MARK. Born and educated in Maine; author of articles and manuals on technical subjects, playwright.
Cassis...Resort to Violence. Walker, 1979 [Fr.]

WALKER, MARTIN. 1947- . Ref: CA. SC: Maddox, in both titles.
The Infiltrator. Hart-Davis, 1978; Dial, 1978 [Port.]
A Mercenary Calling. Granada, 1980. U.S. title: The Money Soldiers. Doubleday, 1980 [Angola]
The Money Soldiers; see A Mercenary Calling

WALKER, MAURICE
The Roof. Evans, 1970 (1-act play.)

WALKER, MAX
Code Name: Judas. Popular Library, 1968 (Novelization of the "Mission Impossible" TV series.) [Geneva]
Code Name: Rapier. Popular Library, 1968 (Novelization of the "Mission Impossible" TV series.) [Carib.]
The Last Escape. Popular Library, 1970 (Novelization of the movie. Although signed by Walker, this book was in fact written by Michael Avallone, 1924- , q.v.)

WALKER, PAUL
Who Killed Utopia? Carlyle, 1980

WALKER, PETER
Mirth and Mayhem. Performance, 1974 (Play.)

WALKER, PETER N(ORMAN). 1936- . Pseudonyms: Christopher Coram, Tom Ferris, Nicholas Rhea, qq.v. SC: Carnaby, in at least those titles containing his name. Set: Eng.
The Carlton Plot. Hale, 1980
Carnaby and the Assassins. Hale, 1968
Carnaby and the Conspirators. Hale, 1969
Carnaby and the Counterfeiters. Hale, 1980
Carnaby and the Demonstrators. Hale, 1972
Carnaby and the Eliminators. Hale, 1971
Carnaby and the Gaolbreakers. Hale, 1968
Carnaby and the Hijackers. Hale, 1967
Carnaby and the Infiltrators. Hale, 1974
Carnaby and the Kidnappers. Hale, 1976
Carnaby and the Saboteurs. Hale, 1970
The Dovingsby Death. Hale, 1975
Fatal Accident. Hale, 1970
Identification Parade. Hale, 1972
The MacIntyre Plot. Hale, 1977
Major Incident. Hale, 1974
Missing from Home. Hale, 1977
Panda One Investigates. Hale, 1973
Panda One on Duty. Hale, 1971
Special Duty. Hale, 1971
Target Criminal. Hale, 1978
Witchcraft for Panda One. Hale, 1978

WALKER, ROBERT W(AYNE). 1948- . Ref: CA.
Sub-Zero! Belmont, 1979

WALKER, ROWLAND. 1876- . SC: Deville McKeene, in at least those marked DM. Set: Eng.
Captain McBlaid of the Air Police. Partridge, 1932
Covenant with Death. Blackie, 1939
Death Flies High. Low, 1936
Deville McKeene, the British Ace. Partridge, 1919 DM
The Exploits of Capt. McKeene. Aldine, 1926 DM
-The Fifth Form Detective. Partridge, 1924
-The Phantom Airman. Partridge, 1920
-Phantom Island. Ward, 1925
When Spy Meets Spy. Blackie, 1935
The Woman in Whitehall. Low, 1937 [Eng., 1917]

WALKER, SHEL. Pseudonym of Walter J. Sheldon, 1917- , q.v.
-The Man I Killed. Lion, 1952
Tokyo Escapade. Phoenix pb, 1955 [Tokyo]

WALKER, T. MIKE. 1937- .
Voices from the Bottom of the World. Grove, 1970

WALKER, THOMAS
Felonry of New South Wales. Dymock (Sydney), 1891 ss [Australia]

WALKER, THOMAS P. Pseudonym of Thomas Page, 1942- , q.v.
Recall. Seaview, 1979 [L.A.]

WALL, JOHN
Guardian Angel in the Underworld. Vantage, 1958

WALL, WILLIAM
Devils in Candy Houses. Papillon, 1974. Reprinted as: Murder with Grace. Decade, 1980
Murder with Grace; see Devils in Candy Houses
Quiet Terror; see Wake Up Dead
Wake Up Dead. Papillon, 1974. Reprinted as: Quiet Terror. Decade, 1980

WALLACE, ARTHUR
Passion Pulls the Trigger. Valhalla, 1936 [NYC]

WALLACE, BRYAN EDGAR. 1904- . Son of (Richard Horatio) Edgar Wallace, 1875-1932, q.v. Educated at Cambridge; screenwriter, Diplomatic Secretary at British embassy in Madrid. SC: Bill Tern = BT.
Death Packs a Suitcase. Hodder, 1961 BT
The Device. Hodder, 1962 BT
The Man Who Would Not Swim. Hodder, 1963 [Sp.]
Murder in Touraine. Hodder, 1966 [Fr.]
Murder Is Not Enough. Hodder, 1964
Murder on the Night Ferry. Hodder, 1965

WALLACE, C. H. Pseudonym of Rosaylmer Burger. Joint pseudonym with Julia Perceval, q.v.: Jessyca Paul, q.v. SC: Steve Ramsay, in all titles.
Crashlanding in the Congo. Belmont, 1965 [Bel. Congo]
E.T.A. for Death. Belmont, 1967
Highflight to Hell. Belmont, 1966 [Eng.]
Tailwind to Danger. Belmont, 1966 [Ecua.]

WALLACE, C. S. Living in Calif. in 1940s.
Westbound Murder. Farrar, 1941 [West]

WALLACE, CARLTON. British journalist and criminologist. SC: Supt. Edmund Bendilow, in at least those marked EB.
Death at No. 47. Mellifont, 1937
Death in the Kettle. Long, 1938 EB
Death of a Libertine. Long, 1936 EB
Death of a Wife. Long, 1936 EB
The Devil Breathes But Once. Long, 1937 EB
Mr. Death; see Mr. Death Walks Abroad
Mr. Death Walks Abroad. Long, 1933. U.S. title: Mr. Death. Doubleday, 1934 EB
Sinister Alibi. Long, 1934; Doubleday, 1934 EB

WALLACE, (RICHARD HORATIO) EDGAR. 1875-1932. See also: Robert (G.) Curtis, -ca.1936. Ref: all except CA. SC: J. G. Reeder = JR; Four Just Men = JM; Educated Evans = EE; Det. Sgt./Insp. Elk = E; The Ringer = R; Sanders = S (continued in books by Francis Gerard, 1905- , q.v.); Supt. Minter = M; T. B. Smith = TS. Set: Eng.
The Admirable Carfew. Ward, 1914 ss, some criminous TS
The Adventures of Heine. Ward, 1919 ss
The African Millionaire. Davis-Poynter, 1972 (Play.)
Again Sanders. Hodder, 1928; Doubleday, 1929 ss S [Afr., W.]
Again the Ringer. Hodder, 1929. U.S. title: The Ringer Returns. Doubleday, 1931 R
Again the Three; see Again the Three Just Men
Again the Three Just Men. Hodder, 1928. U.S. title: The Law of the Three Just Men. Doubleday, 1931. Also published as: Again the Three. Pan, 1968 ss JM
Again the Three Just Men (U.S. edition); see The Law of the Four Just Men
Angel Esquire. Arrowsmith, 1908; Holt, 1908
The Angel of Terror. Hodder, 1922; Small, 1922. Also published as: The Destroying Angel. Pan, 1959
The Arranways Mystery; see The Coat of Arms
The Avenger. Long, 1926. U.S. title: The Hairy Arm. Small, 1925
Barbara on Her Own. Newnes, 1926
Big Foot. Long, 1927 M
The Big Four. Readers Library, 1929 ss
The Black. Readers Library, 1929 ss (Not to be confused with the title below.)
The Black; see The Man from Morocco
The Black Abbot. Hodder, 1926; Doubleday, 1927
Blue Hand. Ward, 1925; Small, 1926
Bones. Ward, 1915 ss S [Afr., W.]
Bones in London. Ward, 1921 ss, S in some of them
Bones of the River. Newnes, 1923 ss S [Afr., W.]

The Book of All Power. Ward, 1923 [Russ.]
Bosambo of the River. Ward, 1914 ss S [Afr., W.]
The Brigand. Hodder, 1927 ss
The Calendar. Collins, 1930; Doubleday, 1931
Captains of Souls. Long, 1923; Small, 1922
Captain Tatham of Tatham Island. Gale & Polden, 1909. Revised edition: The Island of Galloping Gold. Newnes, 1916. Also published as: Eve's Island. Newnes, 1926
The Case of the Frightened Lady. French (London), 1932. U.S. title: Criminal at Large. French (NYC), 1934 (Play, based on The Frightened Lady, q.v.)
The Cat Burglar; see Forty-Eight Short Stories
Chick. Ward, 1923
Circumstantial Evidence; see Forty-Eight Short Stories
The Clever One; see The Forger
The Clue of the New Pin. Hodder, 1923; Small, 1923
The Clue of the Silver Key. Hodder, 1930. U.S. title: The Silver Key. Doubleday, 1930
The Clue of the Twisted Candle. Newnes, 1917; Small, 1916
The Coat of Arms. Hutchinson, 1931. U.S. title: The Arranways Mystery. Doubleday, 1932
The Colossus; see The Joker
The Council of Justice. Ward, 1908 (See also the U.S. edition of The Four Just Men.) JM
Criminal at Large; see The Case of the Frightened Lady
The Crimson Circle. Hodder, 1922; Doubleday, 1929
The Daffodil Murder; see The Daffodil Mystery
The Daffodil Mystery. Ward, 1920. U.S. title: The Daffodil Murder. Small, 1921
The Dark Eyes of London. Ward, 1924; Doubleday, 1929
The Daughters of the Night. Newnes, 1925
The Day of Uniting. Hodder, 1926; Mystery League, 1930
A Debt Discharged. Ward, 1916
The Destroying Angel; see The Angel of Terror
The Devil Man. Collins, 1931; Doubleday, 1931 [Eng., 1875]
Diana of Kara-Kara; see Double Dan
The Door with Seven Locks. Hodder, 1926; Doubleday, 1926
The Double. Hodder, 1928; Doubleday, 1928
Double Dan. Hodder, 1924. U.S. title: Diana of Kara-Kara. Small, 1924
Down Under Donovan. Ward, 1918
The Duke in the Suburbs. Ward, 1909
The Edgar Wallace Reader. World, 1943 (ss, reassembled from earlier collections.)
Educated Evans. Webster, 1924 ss EE
The Educated Man; see Good Evans!
Elegant Edward. Readers Library, 1928 ss
Eve's Island; see Captain Tatham of Tatham Island
The Face in the Night. Long, 1924; Doubleday, 1929
The Feathered Serpent. Hodder, 1927; Doubleday, 1928
The Fellowship of the Frog. Ward, 1925; Doubleday, 1928 E
Fighting Snub Reilly; see Forty-Eight Short Stories
Flat 2. Long, 1927; Garden City, 1924
The Flying Fifty-Five. Hutchinson, 1922
The Flying Squad. Hodder, 1928; Doubleday, 1929
The Forger. Hodder, 1927. U.S. title: The Clever One. Doubleday, 1928
For Information Received. Newnes, 1929 ss
Forty-Eight Short Stories. Newnes, 1929 ss This collection precedes by one month six separate collections assembled from this title, as follows: The Cat Burglar. Newnes, 1929 (8 ss). Circumstantial Evidence. Newnes, 1929; World, 1934 (8 ss). Fighting Snub Reilly. Newnes, 1929; World, 1934 (8 ss in British edition; U.S. edition has 11 ss from Forty-Eight Short Stories and For Information Received, q.v.). The Governor of Chi-Foo. Newnes, 1929; World, 1933 (8 ss in British edition; U.S. edition contains 13 ss). The Little Green Man. Newnes, 1929 (8 ss). The Prison Breakers. Newnes, 1929 (8 ss)

The Four Just Men. Tallis, 1905; Tallis, 1906 (with solution to mystery); Newnes, 1911 (with complete final chapter); Small, 1920 (The U.S. edition includes The Council of Justice, abridged, q.v.)
Four Square Jane. Readers Library, 1929; World Wide, 19?? ss
The Fourth Plague. Ward, 1913; Doubleday, 1930
The Frightened Lady. Hodder, 1933. U.S. title: The Mystery of the Frightened Lady. Doubleday, 1933 (For play version, see: The Case of the Frightened Lady.)
The Gaol Breaker; see We Shall See
The Gaunt Stranger. Hodder, 1925. U.S. title: The Ringer. Doubleday, 1926 (See also: the play and the British novel titled The Ringer.)
The Ghost of Down Hill. Readers Library, 1929; World Wide, 19?? (2 novelets.)
The Girl from Scotland Yard; see The Square Emerald
The Golden Hades. Collins, 1929
Good Evans! Webster, 1926. Also published as: The Educated Man. Readers Library, 1929 ss EE
The Governor of Chi-Foo; see Forty-Eight Short Stories
The Green Archer. Hodder, 1923; Small, 1924
The Green Pack. French (London), 1933 (Play).
The Green Ribbon. Hutchinson, 1929; Doubleday, 1930
Green Rust. Ward, 1919; Small, 1920
Grey Timothy. Ward, 1913. Also published as: Pallard the Punter. Ward, 1914
Gunman's Bluff; see The Gunner
The Gunner. Long, 1928. U.S. title: Gunman's Bluff. Doubleday, 1929
The Guv'nor; see The Guv'nor and other stories
The Guv'nor and other stories. Collins, 1932. U.S. title: Mr. Reeder Returns. Doubleday, 1932 (4 novelets, also published in two volumes: The Guv'nor. Collins, 1933; and: Mr. J. G. Reeder Returns. Collins, 1934.) JR
The Hairy Arm; see The Avenger
The Hand of Power. Long, 1926; Mystery League, 1930
The India-Rubber Men. Hodder, 1929; Doubleday, 1930
The Iron Grip. Readers Library, 1930 ss
The Island of Galloping Gold; see Captain Tatham of Tatham Island
Jack o' Judgment. Ward, 1920; Small, 1921
The Joker. Hodder, 1926. U.S. title: The Colossus. Doubleday, 1932 E
The Just Men of Cordova. Ward, 1917; Doubleday, 1930, in "Mammoth Mystery Book" JM
Kate Plus Ten. Ward, 1919; Small, 1917 TS
The Keepers of the King's Peace. Ward, 1917 ss S [Afr., W.]
Killer Kay. Newnes, 1930 ss
A King by Night. Long, 1925; Doubleday, 1926
The Lady Called Nita. Newnes, 1930 ss
The Lady of Ascot. Hutchinson, 1930
The Lady of Little Hell. Newnes, 1929 ss
The Last Adventure. Hutchinson, 1934 ss
The Law of the Four Just Men. Hodder, 1921. U.S. title: Again the Three Just Men. Doubleday, 1933 ss JM
The Law of the Three Just Men; see Again the Three Just Men
Lieutenant Bones. Ward, 1918 ss S [Afr., W.]
The Little Green Man; see Forty-Eight Short Stories
The Lone House Mystery. Collins, 1929 (1 novelet and 3 ss.) SM
The Man at the Carlton. Hodder, 1931; Doubleday, 1932
The Man from Morocco. Long, 1925. U.S. title: The Black. Doubleday, 1930 [Tangier]
The Man Who Bought London. Ward, 1915
The Man Who Changed His Name. Hodder, 1929 (Play.)
The Man Who Knew. Newnes, 1919; Small, 1918
-The Man Who Married His Cook and other stories. White Lion, 1976 ss
The Man Who Was Nobody. Ward, 1927
The Melody of Death. Arrowsmith, 1915; Dial, 1927
The Million Dollar Story. Newnes, 1926
The Mind of Mr. J. G. Reeder. Hodder, 1925. U.S. title: The Murder Book of Mr. J. G. Reeder. Doubleday, 1929 ss JR

The Missing Million. Long, 1923. U.S. title: The Missing Millions. Small, 1925
Mr. Commissioner Sanders; see Sanders
Mr. J. G. Reeder Returns; see The Guv'nor and other stories
Mr. Justice Maxell. Ward, 1922
Mr. Reeder Returns; see The Guv'nor and other stories
The Mixer. Long, 1927 ss
More Educated Evans. Webster, 1927 ss EE
The Murder Book of Mr. J. G. Reeder; see The Mind of Mr. J. G. Reeder
The Mystery of the Frightened Lady; see The Frightened Lady
Nig-Nog. World, 1934 ss
The Nine Bears. Ward, 1910. U.S. title: The Other Man. Dodd, 1911. Revised editions: The Secret House, and Silinski, Master Criminal, qq.v. TS
The Northing Tramp. Hodder, 1926; Doubleday, 1929. Also published as: The Tramp. Pan, 1965
Number Six. Newnes, 1922
On the Spot. Long, 1931; Doubleday, 1931 [Chi.]
The Orator. Hutchinson, 1928 ss
The Other Man; see The Nine Bears
Pallard the Punter; see Grey Timothy
Penelope of the Polyantha. Hodder, 1926
The People of the River. Ward, 1912 ss S [Afr., W.]
Planetoid 127 and The Sweizer Pump. Readers Library, 1929 (2 novelets.)
The Prison Breakers; see Forty-Eight Short Stories
Red Aces. Hodder, 1929; Doubleday, 1930 (3 novelets about JR.)
The Reporter. Readers Library, 1929 ss
The Ringer. Hodder, 1929; French, 1929 (Play based on The Gaunt Stranger, q.v.) Novelization of the play: The Ringer. Hodder, 1927; Doubleday, 1926 R
The Ringer Returns; see Again the Ringer
The River of Stars. Ward, 1913 S, in brief appearance [Afr., W.]
Room 13. Long, 1924 JR
Sanders. Hodder, 1926. U.S. title: Mr. Commissioner Sanders. Doubleday, 1930 S ss [Afr., W.]
Sanders of the River. Ward, 1911; Doubleday, 1930 S ss [Afr., W.]
Sandi, the King Maker. Ward, 1922 S ss [Afr., W.]
The Secret House. Ward, 1917; Small, 1919 (Revised edition of The Nine Bears, q.v.) TS
Sergeant Sir Peter. Chapman, 1932; Doubleday, 1933 ss
Silinski, Master Criminal. World, 1930 (Revision of The Nine Bears, q.v.)
The Silver Key; see The Clue of the Silver Key
The Sinister Man. Hodder, 1924; Small, 1925
The Square Emerald. Hodder, 1926. U.S. title: The Girl from Scotland Yard. Doubleday, 1927
The Squeaker. Hodder, 1927. U.S. title: The Squealer. Doubleday, 1928
The Squealer; see The Squeaker
The Steward. Collins, 1932 ss
The Strange Countess. Hodder, 1925; Small, 1926
The Stretelli Case and other mystery stories. World, 1930 ss, from earlier collections
The Terrible People. Hodder, 1926; Doubleday, 1926
The Terror. Hodder, 1929 (Play.) Novelization: Collins, 1929 E
Terror Keep. Hodder, 1927; Doubleday, 1927 JR
The Thief in the Night. Readers Library, 1929; World Wide, 19??
The Three Just Men. Hodder, 1926; Doubleday, 1930 JM
The Three Oak Mystery. Ward, 1924
The Tomb of T'sin. Ward, 1916. Abridged edition: Hutchinson, 1973 [China]
The Traitor's Gate. Hodder, 1927; Doubleday, 1927
The Tramp; see The Northing Tramp
The Twister. Long, 1928; Doubleday, 1929 E
The Undisclosed Client. Digit, 1963 ss, some from earlier collections
The Valley of Ghosts. Odhams, 1922; Small, 1923
We Shall See. Hodder, 1926. U.S. title: The Gaol Breaker. Doubleday, 1930, in "Mammoth Mystery Book"
When the Gangs Came to London. Long, 1932; Doubleday, 1932
White Face. Hodder, 1930; Doubleday, 1931 E
The Woman from the East. Hutchinson, 1934 ss

The Yellow Snake. Hodder, 1926
WALLACE, F(LOYD) L.
   Three Times a Victim. Ace, 1957 [L.A.]
   Wired for Scandal. Ace, 1959 [L.A.]
WALLACE, FRANCIS. 1894-1977. Graduate of Notre Dame; magazine sportswriter in NYC.
   Front Man. Rinehart, 1952 [Midwest, acad.]
   Little Hercules. Mill, 1939; Cherry Tree, 1941 [L.A.]
WALLACE, IAN. Pseudonym of John Wallace Pritchard, 1912- . Ref: CA. SC: Claudine St. Cyr = CS; Croyd = C. Set: future (all titles).
   Croyd. Putnam, 1967 C
   Deathstar Voyage. Putnam, 1969; Dobson, 1972 CS
   Door to Enigma. DAW, 1979 C
   Heller's Leap. DAW, 1979
   The Purloined Prince. McCall, 1971 CS
   The Sign of the Mute Medusa. Popular Library, 1977 CS
   Z-Sting. DAW, 1978 C
WALLACE, IRVING. 1916- . Ref: CA.
   -The Pigeon Project. Simon, 1979; Cassell, 1979 [Venice]
   The Plot. Simon, 1967; Cassell, 1967 [Paris]
   The R Document. Simon, 1976; Cassell, 1976 [Wash. D.C.]
   The Second Lady. NAL, 1980; Hutchinson, 1980
WALLACE, JOHN
   Invasion. Popular Publications, 193? [Australia]
   Millionaire Gangster. Long, 1937 [Australia]
   The Sedan Murder Mystery. Windsor, 1938
   Vengeance of ?. Popular Publications, 193?
WALLACE, MARY. Pseudonyms: Miriam Lynch, Claire Vincent, qq.v.
   From This Death Forward. Arcadia, 1959
WALLACE, PAT. 1929- . Ref: CA.
   House of Scorpio. Avon, 1975
WALLACE, ROBERT
   The Body on the Beach. Watt, 1932
   The Jig-Saw Murder Case. Gabriel, 1933
   Seven Men Are Murdered. Fiction League, 1930
WALLACE, ROBERT. House name. Used by W(illis) T(odhunter) Ballard, 1903-1980, q.v.; Robert Sidney Bowen, 1900-1977, q.v.; Ed Burkholder; Norman Daniels, q.v. (title marked +); Jack D'Arcy; Laurence Donovan (titles marked #); Anatole France Feldman; Charles Green (titles marked *); (Walter) Ryerson Johnson, 1901- , q.v.; C(arleton) S(tevens) Montayne, 1892-1948, q.v.; and others. SC: Richard Curtis Van Loan (The Phantom Detective), in all titles, which are reprints from pulp magazines.
   The Beast-King Murders. Regency, 1965 [NYC]
   The Broadway Murders. Regency, 1965 # [NYC]
   The Corpse Parade. Regency, 1966 [NYC]
   The Curio Murders. Regency, 1966 # [NYC]
   The Daggers of Kali. Regency, 1965 [NYC]
   The Dancing Doll Murders. Regency, 1965 [NYC]
   Death Glow. Regency, 1966 [NYC]
   Death Under Contract. Regency, 1966 * [L.A.]
   Fangs of Murder. Regency, 1966 [NYC]
   The Forty Thieves. Regency, 1966
   The Green Glare Murders. Regency, 1966 [Wash. D.C.]
   The Melody Murders. Regency, 1966 * [NYC]
   Murder Money. Regency, 1966
   Murder Stalks a Billion. Regency, 1966 # [N.Y.]
   Murder Trail. Regency, 1966
   Murder Under the Big Top. Regency, 1965 +
   Stones of Satan. Regency, 1966 [NYC]
   The Trail to Death. Regency, 1965 [NYC]
   Tycoon of Crime. Regency, 1965
   The Uniformed Killers. Regency, 1966 [Tex.]
   The Vampire Murders. Regency, 1965
   Yellow Shadows of Death. Regency, 1965 * [S.F.]

WALLACE, TREVOR. SC: John Tracy, in at least those marked JT.
   The Air Cavalier. Wright, 1937
   Bandits Aloft. Wright, 1936
   The Battling Skyman. Wright, 1938
   Cargo for Death. Wright, 1938 JT
   The Curse of the Silver Wings. Wright, 1938
   The Flying Headhunter. Wright, 1939
   Galahad of the Air. Wright, 1937 JT
   The Mystery of DS 24. Wright, 1937 JT [New Guinea]
   Raiders of the Southern Seas. Wright, 1936
   The Skyriders. Wright, 1937 JT [New Guinea]
   Tail Spin Morgan. Wright, 1938
   Two Gun Hedgehopper. Wright, 1938
WALLACE, WILLIAM. 1843-1921.
   After the Revolution and Other Holiday Fantasies. Hodge, 1893 ss, some criminous
WALLACE, WILLIAM
   Tales of Mystery and Crime. Edmund Ward, 1948 ss
WALLENSTEIN, MARCEL (H.)
   Merlin's Forest. Constable, 1965
WALLER, BRUCE
   The Crime Squadron. Columbine, 1939
WALLER, JOHN FRANCIS. Pseudonym: Jonathan Freke Slingsby, q.v.
WALLER, LESLIE. 1923- . Pseudonyms: C. S. Cody, Patrick Mann, qq.v. Ref: CA.
   The Coast of Fear. Doubleday, 1974; Allen, 1975 [It., WWII]
   "K". GM, 1963. British title: The "K" Assignment. Mayflower, 1976 [Chi.]
   The "K" Assignment; see "K"
   The Swiss Account. Doubleday, 1976; Hart-Davis, 1976 [Switz.]
   Trocadero. Delacorte, 1978; Hart-Davis, 1978 [Paris]
WALLING, R(OBERT) A(LFRED) J(OHN). 1869-1949. Refs: CC, EM, MC, MP, TC. SC: Garstang = G; Philip Tolefree = PT. Set: Eng.
   The Bachelor Flat Mystery; see VIII to IX
   Behind the Yellow Blind. Hodder, 1932. U.S. title: Murder at Midnight. Morrow, 1932 G
   Bury Him Deeper. Hodder, 1937. U.S. title: Marooned with Murder. Morrow, 1937 PT
   By Hook or by Crook. Hodder, 1941. U.S. title: By Hook or Crook. Morrow, 1941 PT
   By Hook or Crook; see By Hook or by Crook
   Castle-Dinas. Hodder, 1942. U.S. title: The Corpse with the Eerie Eye. Morrow, 1942 PT
   The Cat and the Corpse. Hodder, 1935. U.S. title: The Corpse in the Green Pajamas. Morrow, 1935 PT
   The Coroner Doubts. Hodder, 1938. U.S. title: The Corpse with the Blue Cravat. Morrow, 1938 PT
   A Corpse by Any Other Name; see The Doodled Asterisk
   The Corpse in the Coppice; see Mr. Tolefree's Reluctant Witnesses
   The Corpse in the Crimson Slippers. Hodder, 1936; Morrow, 1936 PT
   The Corpse in the Green Pajamas; see The Cat and the Corpse
   The Corpse with the Blistered Hand; see Dust in the Vault
   The Corpse with the Blue Cravat; see The Coroner Doubts
   The Corpse with the Dirty Face. Hodder, 1936; Morrow, 1936. Also published as: The Crime in Cumberland Court. Hodder, 1938 PT
   The Corpse with the Eerie Eye; see Castle-Dinas
   The Corpse with the Floating Foot; see The Mystery of Mr. Mock
   The Corpse with the Grimy Glove; see More Than One Serpent
   The Corpse with the Missing Watch. Morrow, 1949 PT
   The Corpse with the Red-Headed Friend; see They Liked Entwhistle
   The Corpse Without a Clue. Hodder, 1944; Morrow, 1944 PT
   The Crime in Cumberland Court; see The Corpse with the Dirty Face
   The Dinner-Party at Bardolph's. Jarrolds, 1927. U.S. title: That Dinner at Bardolph's. Morrow, 1928
   The Doodled Asterisk. Hodder, 1943. U.S. title: A Corpse by Any Other Name. Morrow, 1943 PT

   Dust in the Vault. Hodder, 1939. U.S. title: The Corpse with the Blistered Hand. Morrow, 1939 PT
   VIII to IX. Hodder, 1934. U.S. title: The Bachelor Flat Mystery. Morrow, 1934 PT
   The Fatal Five Minutes. Hodder, 1932; Morrow, 1932 PT
   The Five Suspects. Hodder, 1935. U.S. title: Legacy of Death. Morrow, 1934 PT
   Follow the Blue Car. Hodder, 1933. U.S. title: In Time for Murder. Morrow, 1933 PT
   In Time for Murder; see Follow the Blue Car
   The Late Unlamented. Hodder, 1948; Morrow, 1948 PT
   Legacy of Death; see The Five Suspects
   The Man with the Squeaky Voice. Methuen, 1930; Morrow, 1930
   Marooned with Murder; see Bury Him Deeper
   More Than One Serpent. Hodder, 1938. U.S. title: The Corpse with the Grimy Glove. Morrow, 1938 PT
   Mr. Tolefree's Reluctant Witnesses. Hodder, 1936. U.S. title: The Corpse in the Coppice. Morrow, 1936 PT
   Murder at Midnight; see Behind the Yellow Blind
   Murder at the Keyhole. Methuen, 1929; Morrow, 1929
   The Mystery of Mr. Mock. Hodder, 1937. U.S. title: The Corpse with the Floating Foot. Morrow, 1936 PT
   Prove It, Mr. Tolefree; see The Tolliver Case
   The Spider and the Fly; see Why Did Trethewy Die?
   Stroke of One. Methuen, 1931; Morrow, 1931 G
   The Strong Room. Jarrolds, 1927
   That Dinner at Bardolph's; see The Dinner-Party at Bardolph's
   They Liked Entwhistle. Hodder, 1939. U.S. title: The Corpse with the Red-Headed Friend. Morrow, 1939 PT
   The Tolliver Case. Hodder, 1934. U.S. title: Prove It, Mr. Tolefree. Morrow, 1933 PT
   Why Did Trethewy Die? Hodder, 1940. U.S. title: The Spider and the Fly. Morrow, 1940 PT
WALLIS, A(RTHUR) J(AMES) and CHARLES F. BLAIR, JR.
   Thunder Above. Holt, 1956; Jarrolds, 1959
WALLIS, HENRY MARRIAGE. Pseudonym: Ashton Hilliers, q.v.
WALLIS, J(AMES) H(AROLD). 1885-1958. Ref: EM. Born in Ia., educated at Yale; newspaperman in Ia. turned full-time writer in N.Y. SC: Insp. Wilton Jacks = WJ.
   The Capital City Mystery. Dutton, 1932; Jarrolds, 1933 WJ [Wash. D.C.]
   Cries in the Night. Dutton, 1933; Jarrolds, 1935 WJ [NYC]
   House of Murder; see Murder Mansion
   Murder by Formula. Dutton, 1931; Jarrolds, 1932 WJ [NYC]
   Murder Mansion. Dutton, 1934. British title: House of Murder. Jarrolds, 1934 WJ [NYC]
   The Mystery of Vaucluse. Dutton, 1933; Jarrolds, 1934 WJ [Conn., acad.]
   The Niece of Abraham Pein. Dutton, 1943; Jarrolds, 1944 [N.H.]
   Once Off Guard. Dutton, 1942; Jarrolds, 1943. Also published as: The Woman in the Window. World, 1944 [NYC]
   The Servant of Death. Dutton, 1932; Jarrolds, 1933 WJ [NYC]
   The Synthetic Philanthropist. Dutton, 1943; Jarrolds, 1945
   The Woman He Chose. Dutton, 1934 [Ill.]
   The Woman in the Window; see Once Off Guard
WALLIS, RUTH (OTIS) SAWTELL. 1895-1978. Ref: CA, CC. SC: Eric Lund = EL.
   Blood from a Stone. Dodd, 1945; Hammond, 1955 [Fr.]
   Cold Bed in the Clay. Dodd 1947 EL [Midwest]
   Forget My Fate. Dodd, 1950 EL [Minn.]
   No Bones About It. Dodd, 1944; Hammond, 1950 EL [Mass.]
   Too Many Bones. Dodd, 1943; Hammond, 1947 [Midwest]
WALLMANN, JEFFREY M(INER). 1941- . Ref: CA.
   Clean Sweep. Avon, 1978; Barrie, 1976
   Judas Cross. Random, 1974; Barrie, 1974 [N.J.]
   The Spiral Web. Signet, 1969 [N.J.]

WALMSLEY, LEO. 1892-1966. Ref: CA.
 The Lure of Thunder Island. Jenkins, 1923

WALPOLE, HORACE. 1717-1797. Ref: CC, DD.
 The Castle of Otranto. Lownds, 1765; Longworth, 1801

WALPOLE, HUGH (SEYMOUR). 1884-1941. See also: Edward Chodorov, 1904-   . Ref: CA, MC.
 Above the Dark Circus. Macmillan (London), 1931. U.S. title: Above the Dark Tumult. Doubleday, 1931
 Above the Dark Tumult; see Above the Dark Circus
 -All Souls' Night. Macmillan (London), 1933; Doubleday, 1933 ss
 The Killer and the Slain. Macmillan (London), 1942; Doubleday, 1942
 Portrait of a Man with Red Hair. Macmillan (London), 1925; Doran, 1925

WALSH, DAVID JOHN. 1859-   . Pseudonym: John St. David, q.v.

WALSH, GEO(RGE) E(THELBERT). 1865-1941.
 The Mysterious Burglar. Buckles, 1901; Ward, 1903

WALSH, GOODWIN
 The Voice of the Murderer. Putnam, 1926

WALSH, J(AMES) M(ORGAN). 1897-1952. Pseudonyms: H. Haverstock Hill, Stephen Maddock, George M. White, qq.v. Born in Australia, came to Eng. in 1925; full-time writer after 1923. SC: Bromley Kay, in at least those marked BK; Oliver Keene, in at least those marked OK; Colonel Ormiston, in at least those marked O; Mike Harman, in at least those marked MH; Insp. Quaile, in at least those marked Q; Insp. Storm, in at least those marked S. Set: Eng.
 The Bandits of the Night. Hamilton, 1932
 The Black Cross. Hamilton, 1928
 Black Dragon. Collins, 1938 OK
 The Black Ghost. Hamilton, 1930; Brewer, 1931
 The Brethren of the Compass, with E. J. Blythe. Jarrolds, 1925
 Bullets for Breakfast. Collins, 1939 OK
 Chalk-Face. Hodder, 1937
 The Company of Shadows. Hamilton, 1926; Brewer, 1931
 The Crimes of Cleopatra's Needle. Hamilton, 1928
 Danger Zone. Collins, 1942 OK [Can. Is.]
 Death at His Elbow. Collins, 1941 OK [Istan.]
 Dial 999. Collins, 1938 OK
 Exit Simeon Hex. Hamilton, 1930; Brewer, 1931
 Express Delivery. Collins, 1946 MH
 Face Value. Collins, 1944 OK [Far East]
 A Girl of the Islands. Hamilton, 1932 [S. Pac.]
 The Hairpin Mystery. Hamilton, 1926
 The Half Ace. Collins, 1936 O
 The Hand of Doom. Hamilton, 1927 Q
 The Images of Han. Hamilton, 1927
 Island Alert. Collins, 1943 OK [Far East]
 Island of Spies. Collins, 1937 OK
 King of Tiger Bay. Collins, 1952
 King's Enemies. Collins, 1939 OK
 King's Messenger. Collins, 1933 O [Egypt]
 Lady Incognito. Collins, 1932 Q
 The League of Missing Men. Hamilton, 1932 BK
 The Man Behind the Curtain. Hamilton, 1931 BK
 The Man from Whitehall. Collins, 1934 O
 The Man Who Grew Bulbs. Vallancey, 1945
 Mutton Dressed As Lamb, and Live Bait. Polybooks, 1944 (2 stories.)
 Mystery House. Hamilton, 1931
 The Mystery Man. Hamilton, 1931
 The Mystery of the Green Caterpillars. Hamilton, 1929
 Next, Please. Collins, 1951
 Once in Tiger Bay. Collins, 1947
 The Purple Stain. Hamilton, 1928
 Return to Tiger Bay. Collins, 1950
 The Secret Service Girl. Collins, 1933 O
 Secret Weapons. Collins, 1940 OK
 The Silent Man. Collins, 1935 O
 The Silver Greyhound. Hamilton, 1928 S
 Spies Are Abroad. Collins, 1933 O
 Spies from the Skies. Collins, 1941 OK
 Spies in Pursuit. Collins, 1934 O
 Spies in Spain. Collins, 1937 O [Sp.]
 Spies Never Return. Collins, 1935 O
 Spies' Vendetta. Collins, 1936 O
 The Tempania Mystery. Hamilton, 1929 Q
 Tiger in the Night. Collins, 1935 O
 Time to Kill. Collins, 1949 MH
 Walking Shadow. Collins, 1948 MH
 The Week-End Crime Book, with Audrey Baldwin. Hamilton, 1929 quiz ss
 The Whisperer. Hamilton, 1931 S
 Whispers in the Dark. Collins, 1945 OK
 The White Mask. Hamilton, 1925; Doran, 1927 BK

WALSH, MAURICE. 1879-1964.
 Danger Under the Moon. Chambers, 1956; Lippincott, 1957
 The Man in Brown. Chambers, 1945. U.S. title: Nine Strings to Your Bow. Lippincott, 1945 [Scot.]
 Nine Strings to Your Bow; see The Man in Brown

WALSH, PAUL E.
 KKK. Avon, 1956 [Ga.]
 Murder in Baracoa. Avon, 1958 [Cuba]
 The Murder Room. Avon, 1957 [NYC]

WALSH, PERCY
 Chin-Chin-Chinaman. French, 1929 (1-act play.)
 The Clueless Trail. Eldon, 1933

WALSH, R. F. Pseudonym: Nicholas Carter, q.v.

WALSH, ROBERT
 Violent Hours. Signet, 1958 [S.W.]

WALSH, THOMAS (FRANCIS MORGAN). 1908-   . Ref: TC.
 The Action of the Tiger. Simon, 1968; Hale, 1969 [N.Y.]
 Dangerous Passenger. Little, 1959 [NYC]
 The Dark Window. Little, 1956; H. Hamilton, 1956 [NYC]
 The Eye of the Needle. Simon, 1961; Cassell, 1962 [NYC]
 The Face of the Enemy. Simon, 1966; Cassell, 1968 [N.Y.]
 The Night Watch. Little, 1952; H. Hamilton, 1952 [NYC]
 Nightmare in Manhattan. Little, 1950; H. Hamilton, 1951 [NYC]
 The Resurrection Man. Simon, 1966; Cassell, 1967 [NYC]
 The Tenth Point. Simon, 1965; Cassell, 1965 [N.Y.]
 A Thief in the Night. Simon, 1962; Cassell, 1963 [NYC]
 To Hide a Rogue. Simon, 1964; Cassell, 1965 [NYC]

WALSH, WILLIAM THOMAS. 1891-1949.
 Out of the Whirlwind. McBride, 1935. British title: A Murder Makes a Man. Longmans, 1935 [New Eng.]

WALSHE, DOUGLAS. 1880-   .
 -Close-Up. Wright, 1934
 -Dancing Cheat. Gramol, 1935
 -Duty Be Damned! Hutchinson, 1932
 Fairly Caught. Leng, 1937
 Find the Lady! Hutchinson, 1929
 Guilty! Gramol, 1935
 -Hartington's Luck. Mowl, 1935
 -Her Lips Betrayed. Gramol, 1935
 -His First Affair. Leng, 1931
 The Man Behind the Curtain. Hutchinson, 1929
 -Siren in Satin. Gramol, 1935
 The Smoke-Screen. Hutchinson, 1928
 -Spider Girls. Hutchinson, 1930
 -Their Wife. Wright, 1934
 -Two for a Pair. Wright, 1936

WALTER, A(LEXIA) E. and H(UBERT) C(ONRAD) WALTER. SC: Sir Edgar Ewart, in both titles.
 Betrayal. Methuen, 1929; Dutton, 1930
 The Patriot. Methuen, 1928; Dutton, 1928

WALTER, DOROTHY BLAKE. 1908-   . Pseudonym: Katherine Blake, q.v.

WALTER, ELIZABETH
 Dead Woman and Other Haunting Experiences. Harvill, 1975; St. Martin's, 1977 ss
 Snowfall and Other Chilling Events. Harvill, 1965; Stein, 1966 ss

WALTER, H(UBERT) C(ONRAD). See: A(lexia) E. Walter.

WALTER, HUGH. Born in Scot.; rubber planter in Mal.
 A Bullet for Charles. Macdonald, 1955 [Swed.]

WALTERMIRE, BEECHER W(ESLEY). 1858-1932.
 -The Adventures of a Skeleton. Ogilvie, 1890

WALTERS, SHELLY. Pseudonym.
 The Dunes. McKay, 1974

WALTHEW, NICHOLAS
 Murder at the "Black Swan". Hutchinson, 1939

WALTMORE, IAIN
 No Doubts After Friday. Cassell, 1961

WALTON, EVANGELINE
 Witch House. Arkham, 1945; Skeffington, 1950 [New Eng.]

WALTON, FRANCIS. Pseudonym of Alfred Hodder, 1866-1907. See: Josiah Flynt.

WALTON, GEORGE LINCOLN. 1854-1941.
 Oscar Montague—Paranoiac. Lippincott, 1919 [Conn.]

WALTON, MARION. 1928-   . SC: Insp. James Cardinal, in both titles.
 Cardinal Error. Hale, 1973
 The Paduan Conspiracy. Hale, 1973

WALTON, THOMAS
 -Married or Trapped. Stockwell, 1936
 The Sins of the Fathers; or, The Wye Valley Mystery. Stock, 1908

WALTON, THOMAS
 The Haunted Wing. Stockwell, 1935

WALWORTH, JEANNETTE (RITCHIE) H(ADERMANN). 1837-1918.
 The Silent Witness. Cassell, 1888

WALWORTH, MANSFIELD TRACY. 1830-1873.
 -Beverly; or, The White Mask. Carleton, 1872
 -Delaplaine; or, The Sacrifice of Irene. Carleton, 1871
 -Hotspur. Carleton, 1864
 Lulu. Carleton, 1863
 -Married in Mask. Burt, 1888
 The Mission of Death. Sadlier, 186?
 -Stormcliff. Carleton, 1866
 -Warwick. Carleton, 1869
 -Zahara; or, A Leap for Empire. Dillingham, 1888

WALZ, AUDREY BOYERS. 1906-1983. Pseudonym: Francis Bonnamy, q.v.

WAMBAUGH, JOSEPH. 1937-   . Ref: CA, TC.
 The Black Marble. Delacorte, 1978; Weidenfeld, 1978 [L.A.]
 The Blue Knight. Little, 1972; Joseph, 1973
 The Choirboys. Delacorte, 1975; Weidenfeld, 1976 [S.F.]
 The New Centurions. Little, 1970; Joseph, 1971 [L.A.]
 The Onion Field. Delacorte, 1973; Weidenfeld, 1974

WANDERER. Pseudonym of Elim Henry d'Avigdor, 1841-1895.
 Whims. Gilbert, 1889 ss, at least one criminous

WARBURTON, D. See: Hank Janson.

WARBY, MARJORIE
 More Than All. Collins, 1975

WARD, ARTHUR HENRY SARSFIELD. 1883-1959. Pseudonyms: Michael Furey, Sax Rohmer, qq.v.

WARD, B. E. M.
 Black Cat Murders. Regency, 1945
 Hellmouth Horrors. Regency, 1945
 Murder at the Playhouse. Mitre, 1945
 -A Night of Love. Regency, 1946
 -School on Lone Island. Regency, 1945
 She Was No Angel. Regency, 1945
 Viper's Vengeance. Regency, 1945

WARD, CANDICE. 1948-   . Pseudonym: Lee O'Brien, q.v.

WARD, CHRISTOPHER (LONGSTRETH). 1868-1943.
 Twisted Tales. Holt, 1924 ss, including 2 detective/mystery parodies

WARD, COLIN. Ref: CC.
 House Party Murder. Collins, 1933; Morrow, 1934

WARD, (DOROTHY) DEWEY (COMSTOCK)
 The Curse of Seabrea; see The Unsheltered
 The House in Paris. Dell, 1971 [Paris]
 Reception at High Tower. Dell, 1969
 The Unsheltered. Random, 1963. British title: The Curse of Seabrea. Muller, 1964

WARD, DON(ALD G.). 1911-   . See: Alfred (Joseph) Hitchcock, 1899-1980; and: Theodore (Hamilton) Sturgeon, 1918-   . Ref: CA.

WARD, EDMUND. 1928-   . Playwright, TV writer.
The Hanged Man. Weidenfeld, 1976 (Novelization of the TV series.)
The Main Chance. Weidenfeld, 1977; Coward, 1977 (Novelization of the TV series.)

WARD, ELIZABETH CAMPBELL. 1936-   . Pseudonym: E. C. Allen, q.v.

WARD, ERNEST
Five for Bridge. Crowell, 1940 [NYC]

WARD, GERALD
Time to Kill. Jarrolds, 1957

WARD, HAROLD. Pseudonym: Zorro, q.v. SC: The Vulture = V.
The Blood of Buddha. Melrose, 1937 [U.S.]
Murder of a Painted Lady. Melrose, 1937
The Vulture. Pearson, 1936 V [U.S.]
"The Vulture" Strikes. Pearson, 1936 V [NYC]

WARD, HENRY (L.). 1913-   .
The Green Suns. Sidgwick, 1961 (Translation of "Les Soleils Verts." Paris, 1956.)
Hell's Above Us. Sidgwick, 1960 (Translation of "L'Enfer est dans le Ciel." Paris, 1960.)

WARD, HERBERT D(ICKINSON). 1861-1932.
The Burglar Who Moved Paradise. Houghton, 1897
The White Crown and other stories. Houghton, 1894 ss, some criminous

WARD, MRS. HUMPHREY [MARY AUGUSTA ARNOLD WARD]. 1851-1920.
The Case of Richard Meynell. Smith Elder, 1911; Doubleday, 1911

WARD, I(RENE) E(LLEN)
Death Came Too Soon. Hale, 1975

WARD, JULIAN. 1908-   . Born in Rhodesia, living in Eng.; ss writer, movie and TV writer. Set: Eng.
The Compass Points to Fear. Hodder, 1949
Death Sleeps in Kensington. Hodder, 1951
Death Without a Funeral. Hutchinson, 1957
No Medal If I Die. Hutchinson, 1956
We Died in Bond Street. Hodder, 1952

WARD, ROBERT. 1943-   . Ref: CA.
The Sandman. Rawson, 1978 [NYC, hosp.]

WARD, ROSE ELIZABETH KNOX. 1886-1979. Pseudonym: Elizabeth Sax Rohmer, q.v.

WARD, STEVE
Odds Against Linda. Ace, 1960 [S.F.]

WARD, WILLIAM. House name. See also: H(arry) F(reeman) Wood; and: Anonymous ("The Black Box Murder"). SC: Jeff Clayton, in all titles bearing his name.
Jeff Clayton and the Outlaws. Westbrook, 1911
Jeff Clayton in the Heart of Trouble. Westbrook, 1910
Jeff Clayton's Blind Trail. Westbrook, 1910
Jeff Clayton's Brigand Foe. Westbrook, 1911
Jeff Clayton's Dancing Bubble. Westbrook, 1911
Jeff Clayton's Daring Leap. Westbrook, 1911
Jeff Clayton's Deal with Death. Westbrook, 1911
Jeff Clayton's Decoy. Westbrook, 1911
Jeff Clayton's Demon Pursuer. Westbrook, 1911
Jeff Clayton's Discovery. Westbrook, 1911
Jeff Clayton's Fatal Shot. Westbrook, 1911
Jeff Clayton's Golden Ladder. Westbrook, 1911
Jeff Clayton's Last Bullet. Westbrook, 1911
Jeff Clayton's Last Ship. Westbrook, 1911
Jeff Clayton's Long Chase. Westbrook, 1911
Jeff Clayton's Lost Clue. Westbrook, 1910
Jeff Clayton's Man-Trap. Westbrook, 1910
Jeff Clayton's Master Stroke. Westbrook, 1910
Jeff Clayton's Mexican Plot. Westbrook, 1912
Jeff Clayton's Pursuit. Westbrook, 1911
Jeff Clayton's Puzzle. Westbrook, 1911
Jeff Clayton's Red Mystery. Westbrook, 1911
Jeff Clayton's Riddle. Westbrook, 1910
Jeff Clayton's Strange Quest. Westbrook, 1910
Jeff Clayton's Surprise. Westbrook, 1910
Jeff Clayton's Thunder Bolt. Westbrook, 1910
Jeff Clayton's Triumph. Westbrook, 1910
Jeff Clayton's White Mission. Westbrook, 1910
Jeff Clayton's Winged Flight. Westbrook, 1911
The Murderer of New Orleans. Buckeye, 1907 [New Or.]

WARD-THOMAS, EVELYN BRIDGET PATRICIA STEPHENS. 1928-   . Pseudonym: Evelyn Anthony, q.v.

WARDEN, FLORENCE. Pseudonym of Florence Alice Price James, 1857-1929. Set: Eng.
Abbot's Moat. White, 1913
-Adela's Ordeal. Stevens, 1894; International News, 1893
The Adventures of a Pretty Woman. Paul, 1909
-At the World's Mercy. Stevens, 1884; Munro, 1884
The Bad Lord Lockington. Long, 1912
-The Baronet's Wife. Unwin, 1908
Beatrice Foyle's Crime. Pearson, 1903
-The Beauty Doctor. Greening, 1911
The Beauty of the Family. White, 1910
-Blindman's Marriage. Laurie, 1907
-The Bohemian Girls. White, 1899
The Case for the Lady. Greening, 1910
The Case of Sir Geoffrey. Long, 1908
-City and Suburban. White, 1890; Lovell, 1890
Cliff's End Farm and other stories. White, 1905 ss, some criminous
The Colonel's Past. Ward, 1910
Cross-Fires. Cassell, 1915
The Dazzling Miss Davison. Unwin, 1908; Fly, 1910
Deldee; or, The Iron Hand; see A Dog with a Bad Name
Deldee, the Ward of Warington; see A Dog with a Bad Name
A Desperate Game. Burt, 1902 (British title?)
A Devil's Bargain. Long, 1908
The Disappearance of Nigel Blair. Ward, 1911
-Doctor Darch's Wife. White, 1896; Collier, 1896
A Dog with a Bad Name. Bentley, 1885. U.S. title: The Iron Hand; or, Deldee, the Ward of Warington. Munro, 1884. Also published as: Deldee, the Ward of Warington. Appleton, 1885. And as: Deldee; or, The Iron Hand. Lovell, 1887
-Dolly the Romp. White, 1897
-Doris's Fortune. Stevens, 1886; Appleton, 1886
The Empress of the Andes. Laurie, 1909
The Face in the Flashlight. Long, 1905
-The Farm in the Hills. Sands, 1899
-The Fight for a Soul. Digby, 1912
A Fight to a Finish. Chatto, 1901
-The Financier's Wife. Laurie, 1906
-The Fog Princes. Ward, 1889; Lovell, 1889
-Forge and Furnace. New Amsterdam, 1896 (British title?)
-A Girl with Money. Ward, 1917
The Girl with the Haunting Eyes. Ward, 1920
-The Girls at the Grange. White, 1897
-Girls Will Be Girls. White, 1898
-The Good Ship "Dove". Ward, 1919
-Grave Lady Jane. White, 1893; Taylor, 1892
-The Grey Moth. Ward, 1920
-The Half-Smart Set. Milne, 1908
The Harlingham Case. Ward, 1918
-The Heart of a Girl. Chatto, 1903
-Heiress of Densley Wold. Cassell, 1907
-"Highest References." Railway and General Automatic Library, 1892; Lovell, 1891
-A Hole and Corner Marriage. Pearson, 1902
-The House by the River. Unwin, 1905; Ogilvie, 1905
A House in the Hills. Fenno, 1899 (British title?)
The House on the Marsh. Stevens, 1877; Munro, 1883
-A House with a History. White, 1901
-An Impossible Husband. Long, 1904

The Inn by the Shore. Jarrolds, 1897. U.S. title: The Mystery of the Inn by the Shore. Bonner's, 1895
The Iron Hand; or, Deldee, the Ward of Waringham; see A Dog with a Bad Name
-Joan, the Curate. Chatto, 1898; Buckles, 1899
-Kitty's Engagement. White, 1895; Appleton, 1895
-Lady Anne's Trustee, and other stories. White, 1908 ss
A Lady in Black. White, 1896
-The Lady in Furs. Ward, 1922
-Lady Joan's Companion. Digby, 1902
-Lady Lee. Laurie, 1908
-Lady Rodway's Ordeal. Ward, 1909
Lady Ursula's Husband. Ward, 1914
-Laidlaw's Wife. Long, 1911
Law Not Justice. Hurst, 1906
A Life's Arrears. Cassell, 1908
-The Light in the Upper Storey. Ward, 1917
-Lilith. Ward, 1923
-The Little Grey Mouse. White, 1915
Little Miss Prim. White, 1898
-Lord Penworth's Daughter. Ward, 1913
-Lord Quare's Visiter. Long, 1915
-Love and Lordship. Chatto, 1906
-The Love That Lasts. Ward, 1900; Street, 1899
Love's Sentinel. Long, 1913
-The Lovely Mrs. Pemberton. Long, 1901; Buckles, 1901
-A Lowly Lover. White, 1900
-Mad Sir Geoffrey. Everett, 1907
-The Major. White, 1913
The Man with the Amber Eyes. Long, 1907
-The Marriage Broker. Laurie, 1907
-Married by Stealth. Ward, 1918
-The Master-Key. Pearson, 1898
-The Matheson Money. Long, 1906
The Mill House Mystery. Jarrolds, 1911
-The Millionaire's Son. Ward, 1908
The Mis-Rule of Three. Unwin, 1903; Wycil, 1903
Miss Ferriby's Clients. Laurie, 1910
Missing—A Young Girl. U.S. Book Co., 1890 (British title?)
-Mollie the Handful. White, 1912
-Morals and Millions. White, 1901
My Child and I. White, 1894; Lippincott, 1894
-My Lady of Whims. Chatto, 1907
The Mystery of Dudley Horne. White, 1897
The Mystery of Fourways. Fenno, 1900 (British title?)
The Mystery of the Inn by the Shore; see The Inn by the Shore
A Mystery of the Thames. Ward, 1913
A Night Surprise. Ward, 1919
-No. 3 the Square. Long, 1903
-Nurse Revel's Mistake. Simpkin, 1889; Lovell, 1899
The Old House at the Corner. Chatto, 1906
Once Too Often. Long, 1901
-Our Widow. White, 1896; International News, 1895. Also published as: Three Wayward Girls. International News, 1895
-An Outsider's Year. Long, 1903
A Passage Through Bohemia. Ward, 1893; Hovendon, 1893
-A Patched-Up Affair. Pearson, 1901
-A Perfect Fool. White, 1894; International News, 1894
-The Plain Miss Cray. White, 1900; Buckles, 1900
Playing the Knave. Laurie, 1905
The Precipice. Ward, 1923
-Pretty Miss Smith. Heinemann, 1891; U.S. Book Co., 1891
-The Price of Silence. Ward, 1916
A Prince of Darkness. Ward, 1886; Appleton, 1885
-Ralph Ryder of Brent. Bentley, 1892; National Book Co., 1892. Also published as: A Young Wife's Trial; or, Ralph Ryder of Brent. White, 1893
-The Real Mrs. Daybrook. Long, 1906
Rogues Fall Out. Ward, 1908
Room Nineteen. Ward, 1915
St. Cuthbert's Tower. Cassell, 1889; Lovell, 1889
-A Scarborough Romance. Ward, 1894
-Scherherazade. Ward, 1887; Appleton, 1887
Seamew Abbey. Heinemann, 1892; Lovell, 1891
The Secret of Lynndale. White, 1899
A Sensational Case. Ward, 1898; International News, 1894
Serle's Secret. Everett, 1909
-A Shock to Society. White, 1892; Lovell, 1892
Sir Julian's Crime. Ward, 1921
Sir Penywern's Wife. Ward, 1915
-The Socialism of Lady Jim. Digby, 1908
A Society Scare. Hurst, 1909
Something in the City. Long, 1902; Buckles, 1902

-A Spoilt Girl. White, 1895; Lippincott, 1895
-A Sporting Offer. Ward, 1918
-A Terrible Family. Stevens, 1893; International News, 1893
-The Things That Women Do. White, 1912
-Those Westerton Girls. Bentley, 1891; Lovell, 1891
Three Wayward Girls; see Our Widow
-Tom Dawson. Chatto, 1904
-Town Lady and Country Lass. White, 1900
-Two Lads and a Lass, and other stories. White, 1896 ss
-A Vagrant Wife. Stevens, 1885; Appleton, 1885
The Veiled Lady. Long, 1909
-A Very Rough Diamond. Nisbet, 1899
-Wedded But Not a Wife. White, 1911
-What She Ought to Be. Chatto, 1904
-When the Devil Drives. Ward, 1910
The White Countess. Long, 1907
The White Witch. Bentley, 1884
Who Was Lady Thurne? Long, 1905
-Why She Left Him. Long, 1914
-A Wild Wooing. White, 1893
-The Wiles of Wilhelmina. White, 1913
-A Wilful Ward. White, 1891
-A Witch of the Hills. Bentley, 1888; Lovell, 1888
-The Wolf at the Door. Digby, 1909; Roberts, 1877
The Woman with the Diamonds. White, 1895
A Woman's Face; or, A Lakeland Mystery. Ward, 1888; Appleton, 1888
-Woman's Story. Everett, 1903
-The Wraith of Overstone. Ward, 1916
-The Youngest Miss Brown. Chatto, 1905
A Young Wife's Trial; see Ralph Ryder of Brent

WARDEN, GERTRUDE
-An Actress's Husband. White, 1909
An Angel of Evil. Stevens, 1897
As a Bird to the Snare. Arrowsmith, 1888
-Beauty in Distress. Digby, 1903
Beyond the Law. Ward, 1902
The Crime in the Alps. White, 1908
-The Dancing Leaves. Ward, 1908
-The Dark Arches. Dicks, 189?
-Diana of Dartmoor. Digby, 1913
-Five Old Maids. Stevens, 1895
-The Game of Love. Digby, 1904
-The Grey Wolf's Daughter. International News, 1894 (British title?)
Haunted. Ward, 1911
-The Haunted House at Kew. Stevens, 1893
-A Heart of Stone. Digby, 1905
-Her Fairy Prince. Stevens, 1896; Lippincott, 1895
-Her Faithful Knight. Street, 1899 (British title?)
-Merely Man. White, 1909
-The Millionaire and the Lady. Long, 1907
The Moth and the Footlights. Digby, 1906
Nobody's Widow. Digby, 1903
The Nut-Browne Mayd: A Riviera Mystery. White, 1907 [Fr.]
-The Path of Virtue. White, 1912
Robert the Devil. Digby, 1906
-Scoundrel or Saint? Digby, 1902
A Secret Foe. International News, 1896 (British title?)
The Secret of a Letter. International News, 1894 (British title?)
-The Sentimental Sex. Lane, 1896; Appleton, 1896
Set to Partners. Digby, 1902
-The Severn Affair. Long, 1909
Stand and Deliver. White, 1910
The Stolen Pearl, with Robert Eustace, q.v. Ward, 1903
A Syndicate of Sinners. Digby, 1901
-Two Girls and a Saint. White, 1915
Whose Was the Crime? Street, 1899 (British title?)
-A Wise and Foolish Virgin. White, 1904
-The Woman Who Tempted. Ward, 1912
-The Wooing of a Fairy. Hurst, 1897

WARDEN, LEWIS (CHRISTOPHER). 1913- . Ref: CA.
Murder on Wheels. Avalon, 1964 [South]

WARDEN, MIKE
Dead Ringer. Carousel, 1980 [Seattle]

WARE, JUDITH. Pseudonym of Ware Torrey (Budlong), 1905-1967. Other pseudonyms: Lee Crosby, Meg Padget, Joan Winslow, qq.v.
Detour to Denmark. Paperback Library, 1967
The Faxon Secret. Paperback Library, 1966
The Fear Place. Paperback Library, 1967
Quarry House. Paperback Library, 1965
Thorne House. Paperback Library, 1965
A Touch of Fear. Signet, 1969

WARE, WALLACE. Pseudonym of David Karp, 1922- , q.v.
The Charka Memorial. Doubleday, 1954

WARING, D. GAINSBOROUGH
-Against My Fire. Long, 1941
-And If I Laugh... Long, 1940
Deep Malice. Long, 1939
Fortune Must Follow. Long, 1937
Hated Therewith. Long, 1942
-Not Quite So Black. Hale, 1948
-Nothing Irredeemable. Long, 1936
The Oldest Road. Long, 1938
Out of Evil. Long, 1937
This Day's Madness. Long, 1939
-This New Corn. Long, 1940

WARING, J(AMES) H(ENRY)
Murder on the Camp. Stockwell, 1973
Was It Murder? Stockwell, 1969 ss

WARING, MAIN. Pseudonym of William Thomas Mainwaring Hughes, 1893- .
Clinging Shadows. Melrose, 1936

WARMAN, CY. 1855-1914.
The Express Messenger and other tales of the rail. Scribner, 1897; Chatto, 1897 ss, some criminous

WARMAN, (WILLIAM) ERIK. 1904- . Ref: CA, CC. SC: Insp. John Isidore Bloom, in at least those marked JB. Set: Eng.
Incident. Grasshopper Press, 1943
No Place for the Young. Fortune, 1934
Pattern for Murder. Harrap, 1943 JB
Relative to Murder. Harrap, 1940 JB
Soft at the Centre. Dakers, 1953

WARNEFORD, LIEUTENANT (ROBERT)
Tales of the Coast Guard. Brown, 1856 ss

WARNER, DOUGLAS. Joint pseudonym of John Desmond Currie and Elizabeth Warner. Set: Eng.
Death of a Bogey. Cassell, 1962
Death of a Dreamer. Cassell, 1964; Walker, 1965
Death of a Nude. Cassell, 1964
Death of a Snout. Cassell, 1961; Walker, 1962
Death of a Tom. Cassell, 1963; Macmillan, 1964
Death on a Warm Wind. Rapp, 1968; Doubleday, 1968

WARNER, ELIZABETH. Joint pseudonym with John Desmond Currie: Douglas Warner, q.v.

WARNER, KENNETH LEWIS. 1918- . Pseudonym: Dighton Morel, q.v.

WARNER, MIGNON. Born in Australia; living in Eng. SC: Mrs. Charles, in at least those marked C. Set: Eng.
Grave Error. Hale, 1977
A Medium for Murder; see A Nice Way to Die
A Nice Way to Die. Hale, 1976. U.S. title: A Medium for Murder. McKay, 1977 C
Old Ghosts Never Die. Hale, 1976
The Tarot Murders. Hale, 1978; McKay, 1978 C
Who Saw Her Die? Hale, 1976

WARNER, OLIVER (MARTIN WILSON). 1903-1976. Ref: CA.
A Secret of the Marsh. Chatto, 1927; Dutton, 1927

WARNER, PETER. 1942- .
Loose Ends. McGraw, 1972

WARNER, WARREN. Pseudonym of Samuel Warren, 1807-1877, q.v.
The Experiences of a Barrister. Brown (anonymously), 1856; Cornish Lamport (with an excerpt from Charles Dickens' "Household Words"), 1852. Also published in (with 11 ss added): The Experiences of a Barrister and Confessions of an Attorney (as by Samuel Warren). Estes, 1884. And as: The Lawyer-Detective; or, Twenty-Two Celebrated Criminal Cases Unraveled. Loyd, 1887 ss

WARREN, C. DELVES
Some Cases of Sherwood Lang, Detective. Drane's, 1923 ss

WARREN, CHARLES MARQUIS. 1912- .
Deadhead. Coward, 1949; Boardman, 1950 [Balt.]

WARREN, DOUG(LAS). 1935- . Ref: CA.
A Case of Rape. Pyramid, 1975 (Novelization of the TV movie.) [L.A.]
Scarlet Starlet. Ace, 1959 [L.A.]
Walking Tall. Pinnacle, 1973 (Novelization of the movie.)

WARREN, GEORGE. Pseudonym: Nick Carter, q.v.
-The Bike Bastards. Brandon, 1975
Body for the Widow. Brandon, 1973
The Laughing Widow. Brandon, 1974 [Mex.]
Run for Blood. Playboy, 1980

WARREN, J(OHN) RUSSELL. 1886- . Pseudonym: Gilbert Coverack, q.v. Ref: MP. London journalist and ss writer. SC: Insp. M'Guire, in at least those marked M (see also Coverack entry). Set: Eng.
A Bride for Bombay. Ward, 1931
Castle Enigma. Ward, 1930
Gas-Mask Murder. Heinemann, 1939. U.S. title: Murder in the Blackout. Sheridan, 1940 M
Half a Clue. Ward, 1930
Missing from His Home. Melrose, 1950
Murder from Three Angles. Heinemann, 1939; Furman, 1939 M
Murder in the Blackout; see Gas-Mask Murder
"Princess Proxy." Ward, 1932
Snow upon the Desert. Ward, 1932
This Inward Horror; see This Mortal Coil
This Mortal Coil. Melrose, 1947. U.S. title: This Inward Horror. Dutton, 1948

WARREN, JAMES. SC: James Warren, in at least those marked W; James Weston, in at least those marked JW. Set: Eng.
Brush of Death. Collins, 1958 JW
Cold Steel. Collins, 1957 JW
The Disappearing Corpse; see The Runaway Corpse
The Gold Pistol. Collins, 1956
The Lady Was Disturbed. Collins, 1956 W
No Sleep at All. Collins, 1941; Alliance, 1941 JW
Prowl No More, Lady. Collins, 1942
The Runaway Corpse. Collins, 1957. U.S. title: The Disappearing Corpse. Washburn, 1958 W
She Fell Among Actors. Collins, 1944; Doubleday, 1946 JW

WARREN, JOSEPH
-Revenge. Grosset, 1928 (Novelization of the movie.)

WARREN, MARY DOUGLAS. Pseudonym of Maysie Greig, 1902-1971, q.v. Other pseudonym: Jennifer Ames, q.v.

WARREN, PAULETTE. Pseudonym of Paul W. Fairman, 1916-1977, q.v. Other pseudonym: Ivar Jorgensen, q.v. See also: Ellery Queen. Caliban series = C.
Apprentice in Terror. Berkley, 1976 C [New Eng.]
Brooding Mansion; see The Nurse at Brooding Mansion
Caliban's Castle. Berkley, 1976 C
Castle of Dreams. Berkley, 1977 C [U.S., ca.1860]
Dark Shadow at Bitterhill. Lancer, 1970
Ghost at Ravenkill Manor. Lancer, 1969 [Maine]
-Golden Girl. Manor, 1976
Hazard House. Popular Library, 1972
Horror House. Lancer, 1973
I Take This Stranger. Berkley, 1977 C
Lady Sinister. Berkley, 1976 C
Night Falls at Bitterhill. Lancer, 1969
The Nurse at Brooding Mansion. Lancer, 1969. Also published as: Brooding Mansion. Lancer, 1973
Ravenkill. Lancer, 1965 [Maine]
Search in the Shadows. Berkley, 1976 C
The Shadowed Staircase. Lancer, 1971
Some Beckoning Wraith. Lancer, 1965
Storm over Bitterhill. Lancer, 1969

WARREN, ROBERT PENN. 1905- . Ref: CA.
Meet Me in the Green Glen. Random, 1971; Secker, 1972 [Tenn.]

WARREN, SAMUEL. 1807-1877. Pseudonym: Warren Warner, q.v.
Passages from the Diary of a Late Physician. (London), 1832-8 (3 volumes); Harper, 1831 ss

WARREN, VERNON. Pseudonym of George Warren Vernon Chapman, 1925- . Ref: CA, CC. SC: Mark Brandon = MB.
Appointment in Hell. Gifford, 1956
Backlash. Gifford, 1960
The Blue Mauritius. Gifford, 1954 MB

Brandon in New York. Gifford, 1953 MB [NYC]
Brandon Returns. Gifford, 1954 MB [Ill.]
Brandon Takes Over. Gifford, 1953 MB
Bullets for Brandon. Gifford, 1955 MB
By Fair Means or Foul. Gifford, 1956 [NYC]
Farewell by Death. Gifford, 1961 [U.S.]
Invitation to Kill. Gifford, 1963 [Seattle]
Mister Violence. Gifford, 1961
No Bouquets for Brandon. Gifford, 1955 MB
Runaround. Gifford, 1958 MB [Chi.]
Stop-Over Danger. Gifford, 1959
Three Steps to Hell. Gifford, 1957

WARRICK, MILLIGAN. SC: William Harkness, in at least those marked WH.
The Bandit Trust. Moray, 1934 WH [Scot.]
Granite Shadows. Moray, 1937
The Yawning Lion. Grant, 1932 WH [Scot.]

WARRINER, CORNELIA. Joint pseudonym with James A. MacPhail: James Crockett, q.v.

WARRINER, THURMAN. Pseudonyms: John Kersey, Simon Troy, qq.v. Ref: CC, TC. SC: Mr. Scotter = S. Set: Eng.
Death's Bright Angel. Hodder, 1956 S
Death's Dateless Night. Hodder, 1952 S [Fr.]
The Doors of Sleep. Hodder, 1955 S
Ducats in Her Coffin. Hodder, 1951 S
The Golden Lantern. Hodder, 1958
Heavenly Bodies. Hodder, 1960 S
Method in His Murder. Hodder, 1950; Macmillan, 1951 S
She Died, Of Course. Hodder, 1958 S

WARTHEN, RON
No More Witnesses. Pinnacle, 1975

WARWICK, CHESTER
My Pal, the Killer. Ace, 1961 [N.Y.]

WARWICK, FREDERICK
The Shadow Behind. Modern, 1938

WARWICK, JAMES
Blind Alley. French (NYC), 1936 (3-act play.)

WARWICK, JOHN
Telekiller. New English Library pb, 1978
The Violator. New English Library pb, 1979

WARWICK, PAULINE. Pseudonym of Betty Evelyn Davies.
Death of a Sinner. Cassell, 1944

WARWICK, SIDNEY. 1870-1953. Set: Eng.
-Cat's Eyes. Newnes, 1911
-Conscience Money. Greening, 1914
-Dreams to Sell. Hodder, 1923
-A Girl's Temptation. Thomson, 1928
-The Great Temptation. Thomson, 1923
A Guilty Silence, with John Mulvy Ouseley. Gay, 1907
Harvest of Guilt. Newnes, 1911
-A House of Lies. Cassell, 1909
In a Bad Man's Grip. Thomson, 1921
-An Irregular Marriage. Greening, 1911
Justice Astray. Hodder, 1924
-The Lone Hand. Hodder, 1922
The Night of Secrets. Newnes, 1919
Night of the Thirteenth. Mellifont, 1937
The River Road Mystery. Newnes, 1910
-The Road Back. Cassell, 1910
The Silver Basilisk. Hodder, 1924
-A Slip of a Girl. Hodder, 1923
-That American Woman. Leng, 1934
-The Woman Pays. Newnes, 1915

WASHBURN, MARK. 1948- . Ref: CA.
The Armageddon Game. Putnam, 1977; Davies, 1978
The Omega Threat. Dell, 1980

WASHBURN, ROBERT COLLYER
The Jury of Death. Doubleday, 1930; Paul, 1931

WASSERMAN, JACK. See: Howard Robens.

WASSERMAN, (CARL) JACOB. 1873-1934.
The Maurizius Case. Liveright, 1929; Allen, 1930 (Translation of "Der Fall Maurizius." Berlin, 1928.)

WATEN, JUDAH L(EON). 1911- .
Shares in Murder. Australasian Book Society, 1957

WATERBURY, JENNIE BULLARD
-A New Race Diplomatist. Lippincott, 1900

WATERMAN, WILLIAM. See: Monique Van Cleef.

WATERS. Pseudonym of William Russell. Other pseudonym: Inspector F, q.v. Ref: DD, EM, TC.
Autobiography of a London Detective; see Autobiography of an English Detective
Autobiography of an English Detective. Maxwell, 1863. U.S. title: Autobiography of a London Detective. Dick, 1864 ss
The Detective Officer; see The Recollections of a Policeman
Diary of a Detective Police Officer; see The Recollections of a Policeman
The Experiences of a French Detective Officer. Clarke, 1861; Arno, 1976 ss [Fr.]
The Game of Life. Ward, 1857. Also published as: Leonard Harlowe; or, The Game of Life. Ward, 1862
The Heir-at-Law, and other tales. Lea, 1861 ss
-Kirke Webbe, the Privateer Captain. Knight, 1858. Also published as: The Privateer Captain. Clarke, 1861
Leaves from the Diary of a Law Clerk. Brown, 1857 ss
Leaves from the Journal of a Custom-House Officer. (London), 1868 ss
Leonard Harlowe; see The Game of Life
The Privateer Captain; see Kirke Webbe, the Privateer Captain
Recollections of a Detective; see Recollections of a Detective Police Officer
Recollections of a Detective Police Officer. Brown, 1856. U.S. title: The Recollections of a Policeman. Cornish Lamport, 1852. Also published as: Diary of a Detective Police Officer. Dick, 1864. And as: The Detective Officer and other tales (with 3 ss added). Chambers, 1878. And as: The Recollections of a Detective. Loyd, 1887 ss
Recollections of a Detective Police Officer. Second Series. Kent, 1859 ss (A volume of this main title, containing both first and second series: Ward, 1875.)
The Recollections of a Policeman; see Recollections of a Detective Police Officer
Recollections of a Sheriff's Officer. Aldine Chambers, 1860 ss
-The Romance of a Common Life. Clarke, 1861
A Skeleton in Every House. Clarke, 1860; Dick, 18?? ss
Strange Stories of a Detective; or, Curiosities of Crime. Dick, 1863 ss (British title?)
-Traditions of London. Kent, 1859 ss
Undiscovered Crimes. Ward, 1862 ss
The Valazy Family and other narratives. Ward, 1869 ss

WATERS, THOMAS A. 1938- . Born in Ohio; a magician living in Calif.
Blackwood Cult. Lancer, 1969 [N.Y.]
Bow Street Terror. Lancer, 1970
-Centerforce. Dell, 1974
In the Halls of Evil. Lancer, 1967 [Mass.]
The Lost Victim. Random, 1973 [Calif.]
Love That Spy. Lancer, 1968
The Psychedelic Spy. Lancer, 1967

WATJEN, CAROLINE L. T. Pseudonym: Caroline Stafford, q.v.

WATKINS, ALAN
Till the Dying Day. Horwitz, 1965 [Australia]

WATKINS, ALEX. Pseudonym: Joseph Lane Linklater, q.v.

WATKINS, ARTHUR THOMAS LEVI. 1907-1965. Pseudonym: Arthur Watkyn, q.v.

WATKINS, IVOR
The Bloodsnarl. Futura, 1980

WATKINS, LESLIE. British journalist.
The Killing of Idi Amin. Everest, 1976; Avon, 1977 [Uganda]
The Unexploded Man. H. Hamilton, 1978; Morrow, 1978

WATKINS, LUCY
Frederick and Sophie; or, The Fortunate Discovery. Dean, n.d.

WATKINS, MAURINE
Chicago. Knopf, 1927 (3-act play.) [Chi.]

WATKINS, RICHARD HOWELLS
The Air Murders. Doubleday, 1929; Selwyn, 1929 [L.I.]
Half a Clew. Clode, 1927 [L.I.]
The Master of Revels. Doubleday, 1928 [Eng.]

WATKINS, RON
Death Draws the Curtain. Hale, 1973
Make Haste to Die. Hale, 1976
No Useless Coffin. Hale, 1976
A Paper Chase. Hale, 1972
Sinner Takes All. Hale, 1979

WATKINSON, VALERIE [VALERIE MAE WATKINSON ELLISTON]. 1929- .
The Sped Arrow. Scribner, 1964

WATKYN, ARTHUR. Pseudonym of Arthur Thomas Levi Watkins, 1907-1965. Ref: CA.
Amber for Anna. French (London), 1965 (3-act play.)
Not in the Book. French (London), 1958 (3-act play.)
Out of Bounds. French (London), 1963 (2-act play.)

WATNEY, JOHN B(ASIL). 1915- . Pseudonym: Anthony Roberts, q.v. Ref: CA.
-Common Love. Putnam, 1954
-The Glass Facade. Cape, 1963
Leopard with a Thin Skin. Cape, 1959
The Quarrelling Room. Cape, 1960
The Unexpected Angel. Collins, 1949

WATSON, CLARISSA. Ref: CA. SC: Persis Willum, in both titles.
The Bishop in the Back Seat. Atheneum, 1980; Hale, 1981 [L.I.]
The Fourth Stage of Gainsborough Brown. McKay, 1977; Joseph, 1978 [NYC]

WATSON, COLIN. 1920- . Ref: CA, CC, EM, MC, TC. SC: Insp. Purbright, in at least those marked P. Set: Eng.
Blue Murder. Eyre, 1979 P
Broomsticks over Flaxborough. Eyre, 1972. U.S. title: Kissing Covens. Putnam, 1972 P
Bump in the Night. Eyre, 1960; Walker, 1961
Charity Ends at Home. Eyre, 1968; Putnam, 1968 P
Coffin, Scarcely Used. Eyre, 1958; Putnam, 1967 P
The Flaxborough Crab. Eyre, 1969. U.S. title: Just What the Doctor Ordered. Putnam, 1969 P
Hopjoy Was Here. Eyre, 1962; Walker, 1963
It Shouldn't Happen to a Dog; see One Man's Meat
Just What the Doctor Ordered; see The Flaxborough Crab
Kissing Covens; see Broomsticks over Flaxborough
Lonelyheart 4122. Eyre, 1967; Putnam, 1967 P
The Naked Nuns. Eyre, 1975. U.S. title: Six Nuns and a Shotgun. Putnam, 1975 P
One Man's Meat. Eyre, 1977. U.S. title: It Shouldn't Happen to a Dog. Putnam, 1977 P
Plaster Sinners. Eyre, 1980; Doubleday, 1981 P
The Puritan. Eyre, 1966
Six Nuns and a Shotgun; see The Naked Nuns

WATSON, E(LLIOT) L(OVEGOOD) GRANT. 1885-1970. Ref: CA.
It's Up to You. Douglas, 1933

WATSON, GEOFFREY. 1942- . Born in Eng. and later living in It.; newspaper reporter.
Black Jack. Davies, 1979. U.S. title: The Nooriabad File. Scribner, 1979 [It.]

WATSON, H(ENRY) B(RERETON) MARRIOTT. 1863-1921. SC: Dick Ryder = DR. Set: Eng.
The Adventurers. Harper (London), 1898; Harper (NYC), 1899
Aftermath. Chapman, 1919 ss, some criminous
Alise of Astra. Methuen, 1910; Little, 1911 [Ger.]
As It Chanced. Methuen, 1916 DR
At a Venture. Methuen, 1911 ss, some criminous
The Castle by the Sea. Methuen, 1909; Little, 1909
Chapman's Wares. Mills, 1915 ss, some criminous
Diogenes of London and other fantasies and sketches. Methuen, 1893 ss, some criminous
The Excelsior. Methuen, 1918

Galloping Dick. Lane, 1896; Stone, 1896 DR
The Golden Precipice. Cassell, 1908
The High Toby. Methuen, 1906 DR
Hurricane Island. Isbister, 1904; Doubleday, 1905
The King's Highway. Mills, 1910 DR
The Pester Finger. Skeffington, 1919
The Privateers. Methuen, 1907; Doubleday, 1907
Romances at Random. Hutchinson, 1909
The Web of the Spider. Hutchinson, 1891

WATSON, JACK
Conspire to Kill. Penn Medos (Salisbury), 1976; New English Library pb, 1979

WATSON, JAMES L.
The Accidental Spy. Apollo, 1971
The Agent Orange Affair. Apollo, 1971

WATSON, JOHN. 1921- .
The File of the Golden Goose. Sphere, 1969 (Novelization of the movie.)

WATSON, JOHN R(EAY), 1872- , and ARTHUR J(OHN) REES, 1872-1942, q.v. Ref: MM. SC: Crewe, in both titles. Set: Eng.
The Hampstead Mystery. Lane (London & NYC), 1916
The Mystery of the Downs. Lane (London & NYC), 1918

WATSON, LAWRENCE
In a Dark Time. Scribner, 1980 [Minn., 1973]

WATSON, LEWIS H. Pseudonym: Lewis Harrison, q.v.

WATSON, MARJORIE
Heir to Polventon. Collins, 1973; Saturday Review Press, 1974

WATSON, MAURICE (THORPE). 1916- .
Reclining Nude. Cassell, 1960

WATSON, PATRICK. 1929- . TV journalist and interviewer in Can.
Alter Ego. Viking, 1979 [Toronto]

WATSON, ROBERT (PATRICK)
Louisa Reignier: The Communion of Crime and Criminals. Smith, 1895

WATSON, SELWYN VICTOR. Pseudonym: Selwyn, q.v.

WATSON, STERLING. 1947- .
Weep No More My Brother. Morrow, 1978 [Fla.]

WATT, LAUCHLIN MacLEAN. 1867- .
The Advocate's Wig. Jenkins, 1932

WATTERS, (EUGENE) RUTHERFORD. 1919- .
Murder in Three Moves. Figgis (Dublin), 1960

WATTS, EDGAR JOHN PALMER. 1904- .
Pseudonym: John Palmer, q.v.

WATTS, JOHN
Head of State. New English Library, 1979

WAUGH, ALEC [ALEXANDER RABAN WAUGH]. 1898-1981. Ref: CA.
Married to a Spy. Allen, 1976
A Spy in the Family. Allen, 1970; Farrar, 1970

WAUGH, HILLARY (BALDWIN). 1920- .
Pseudonyms: Elissa Grandower, H. Baldwin Taylor, Harry Walker, qq.v. Ref: CA, CC, EM, MC, TC. SC: Chief Fred Fellows = FF; Frank Sessions = FS; Sheridan Wesley = SW.
Born Victim. Doubleday, 1962; Gollancz, 1963 FF [Conn.]
A Bride for Hampton House. Doubleday, 1975; Gollancz, 1976
Case of the Brunette Bombshell; see Rich Man, Dead Man
The Con Game. Doubleday, 1968; Gollancz, 1968 FF [Conn.]
Death and Circumstance. Doubleday, 1963; Gollancz, 1963 FF [Conn.]
Doctor on Trial; see Parrish for the Defense
The Eighth Mrs. Bluebeard. Doubleday, 1958; Foulsham, 1959
End of a Party. Doubleday, 1965; Gollancz, 1965 FF [Conn.]
Finish Me Off. Doubleday, 1970; Gollancz, 1971 FS [NYC]
Girl on the Run. Doubleday, 1965; Gollancz, 1966

The Girl Who Cried Wolf. Doubleday, 1958; Foulsham, 1960 [NYC]
The Glenna Powers Case. Raven, 1980; Gollancz, 1981
Hope to Die. Coward, 1948; Boardman, 1949 SW [NYC]
If I Live to Dine; see Madam Will Not Dine Tonight
Jigsaw; see Sleep Long, My Love
Last Seen Wearing—. Doubleday, 1952; Gollancz, 1953 [Mass., acad.]
The Late Mrs. D. Doubleday, 1962; Gollancz, 1962 FF [Conn.]
Madam Will Not Dine Tonight. Coward, 1947; Boardman, 1949. Also published as: If I Live to Dine. Graphic, 1949 SW [N.Y.]
Madman at My Door. Doubleday, 1978; Gollancz, 1979 [Conn.]
The Missing Man. Doubleday, 1964; Gollancz, 1964 FF [Conn.]
Murder on the Terrace. Foulsham, 1961
The Odds Run Out. Coward, 1949; Boardman, 1950 SW
Parrish for the Defense. Doubleday, 1974; Gollancz, 1975. Also published as: Doctor on Trial. Dell, 1977 [Conn.]
Prisoner's Plea. Doubleday, 1963; Gollancz, 1964 FF [Conn.]
Pure Poison. Doubleday, 1966; Gollancz, 1967 FF [Conn.]
A Rag and a Bone. Doubleday, 1954; Foulsham, 1955 [Conn.]
Rich Man, Dead Man. Doubleday, 1956. British title: Rich Man, Murder. Foulsham, 1956. Also published as: Case of the Brunette Bombshell. Crest, 1957 [NYC]
Rich Man, Murder; see Rich Man, Dead Man
Road Block. Doubleday, 1960; Gollancz, 1961 FF [Conn.]
Run When I Say Go. Doubleday, 1969; Gollancz, 1969
The Shadow Guest. Doubleday, 1971; Gollancz, 1971 [Eng.]
Sleep Long, My Love. Doubleday, 1959; Gollancz, 1960. Also published as: Jigsaw. Pan, 1962 FF [Conn.]
That Night It Rained. Doubleday, 1961; Gollancz, 1961 FF [Conn.]
"30" Manhattan East. Doubleday, 1968; Gollancz, 1969 FS [NYC]
The Young Prey. Doubleday, 1969; Gollancz, 1970 FS [NYC]

WAY, ISABEL STEWART. 1904- .
Bell, Book and Candleflame. Beagle, 1971
Fleur Macabre. Tower, 1967
The House on Sky High Road. Belmont, 1970 [Calif.]

WAY, PETER. Poet, scientist, military historian, former "Reader's Digest" editor; living in London and Fr.
Dirty Tricks; see Super-Celeste
Icarus. Gollancz, 1980; Coward, 1980
Sunrise. Gollancz, 1979
Super-Celeste. Gollancz, 1977. U.S. title: Dirty Tricks. St. Martin's, 1977 [1982, Fr.]

WAYDE, BERNARD. All titles published by Street, ca.1900.
An Anarchist's Oath.
The Belt of Diamonds.
The Coiner's League.
A Compact of Crime.
The Crooked Inspector.
A Custom House Fraud.
A False Claim.
A Golden Clue.
A Government Trust.
The Hand on the Window Sill.
In the Secret Vault.
The King of Anarchists.
The Man from Texas.
The Man Who Made Money.
The Money Jugglers.
A Privateer's Defiance.
A Question of Policy.
The Smuggler's Ally.
The Tracker Tracked.
The Treasury's Millions.
The Untaxed Whiskey.

WAYE, CECIL. Ref: CC. SC: Christopher Perrin, in all titles, set in Eng.
The End of the Chase. Hodder, 1932
The Figure of Eight. Hodder, 1931; Kinsey, 1933
Murder at Monk's Barn. Hodder, 1931
The Prime Minister's Pencil. Hodder, 1933; Kinsey, 1933

WAYLAND, PATRICK. Pseudonym of Richard O'Connor, 1915-1975. Other pseudonym: Frank Archer, q.v. Ref: CA, TC. SC: Lloyd Nicolson, in all titles.
Counterstroke. Doubleday, 1964; Hale, 1965 [Calif.]
Double Defector. Doubleday, 1964; Hale, 1966 [Wash. D.C., Montr.]
The Waiting Game. Doubleday, 1965; Hale, 1967 [Vt.]

WAYNAR, CHRIS
Fire on the Cliffs. Ace, 1975

WAYNE, CHARLES STOKES. 1858- . Pseudonym: Horace Hazeltine, q.v.

WAYNE, HILARY
Tickletoby. Jenkins, 1949

WEARE-GIFFARD, J.
-Lure of Contraband. Jarrolds, 1920
The Riddle of the River. Jarrolds, 1923

WEATHERBY, W(ILLIAM) J(OHN). Pseudonym: Will Perry, q.v.

WEATHERHEAD, JOHN. SC: David Connell, in at least those marked DC.
A Force of Innocence. Harrap, 1966 DC
-The Sacred Shaft. Harrap, 1967 DC
-Transplant. Harrap, 1969

WEATHERLY, (JOHN) MAX. 1921- . Ref: CA.
The Mantis and the Moth. Houghton, 1964; Gollancz, 1965

WEATHERS, PHILIP. 1908- . See also: A(rthur) A(lexander Malcolm) Thomson, 1894-1969; and: (Thomas) Falkland L(itton) Cary.
Murder Isn't Cricket. French (London), 1961 (3-act play.)
Tell-Tale Murder. French (London), 1956 (Play.)

WEATHERS, WINSTON. 1926- . Ref: CA.
Mysteries for Radio. Eldridge, 1946 (10 radio plays.)

WEAVER, GRAHAM. See: Leslie Charteris, 1907- .

WEAVER, NICKY. SC: Nicky Weaver, in both titles.
Love, Blood and Tears. Kozy, 1963
Love or Kill Them All. Kozy, 1963

WEAVER, ROBERT G. Joint pseudonym with Samuel Leonard Rubenstein, 1922- : Rubin Weber, q.v.

WEBB, ANTHONY. Pseudonym of Norman Scarlyn Wilson, 1901- . SC: Mr. Pendlebury, in at least those marked P. Set: Eng.
Bill Blunders Through. Jenkins, 1944
Mr. Pendlebury and the Suicide Club. Harrap, 1941 P
Mr. Pendlebury Makes a Catch. Harrap, 1939 P
Mr. Pendlebury's Hat Trick. Harrap, 1938 P
Mr. Pendlebury's Second Case. Harrap, 1938 P
Murder in Reverse. Harrap, 1945 P
One Man Saw Them Die. Harrap, 1940 P
Pass Along, Madam! Harrap, 1940
A Queer Bag of Bodies. Harrap, 1947 P
Thank You, Mr. Pendlebury. Harrap, 1939 P
Verdict Without Jury. Harrap, 1937 P

WEBB, DOROTHY ANNA. Pseudonym: Jermyn March, q.v.

WEBB, E. KANE
Temple, K.C. Hodder, 1928

WEBB, FORREST. Pseudonym of Richard Forrest-Webb, 1929- . Other pseudonym: Robert Trevelyan, q.v. Joint pseudonym with David Eliades: David Forrest, q.v. Ref: CA.
-Brannington's Leopard. Hodder, 1973; Doubleday, 1974
The Cavair Cruise. Hodder, 1975; Doubleday, 1977 [ship]
Go for Out. Allen, 1977
-The Snowboys. Hodder, 1973; Doubleday, 1973

WEBB, JACK. 1920- . Pseudonym: John Farr, q.v. Ref: TC. SC: Father Shanley and Sammy Golden = S&G.
The Bad Blonde. Rinehart, 1956; Boardman, 1957 S&G [L.A.]
The Big Sin. Rinehart, 1952; Boardman, 1953 S&G [L.A.]
The Brass Halo. Rinehart, 1957; Boardman, 1958 S&G [L.A.]

The Broken Doll. Rinehart, 1955; Boardman, 1956 S&G [L.A.]
The Damned Lovely. Rinehart, 1954; Boardman, 1955 S&G [Calif.]
The Deadly Sex. Rinehart, 1959; Boardman, 1960 S&G [L.A.]
The Delicate Darling. Rinehart, 1959; Boardman, 1960 S&G [L.A.]
The Gilded Witch. Regency, 1963; Boardman, 1963 S&G [L.A.]
Make My Bed Soon. Holt, 1963; Boardman, 1964 [Ariz.]
The Naked Angel. Rinehart, 1953. British title: Such Women Are Dangerous. Boardman, 1954 S&G [L.A.]
One for My Dame. Holt, 1961; Boardman, 1962 [L.A.]
Such Women Are Dangerous; see The Naked Angel

WEBB, JEAN FRANCIS. 1910-   . Pseudonym: Roberta Morrison, q.v. Ref: CA.
The Bride of Cairngorn. McKay, 1974
Carnavaron's Castle. Meredith, 1969 [Maine]
The Craigshaw Curse. Meredith, 1968 [Fla.]
Is This Coffin Taken? Zebra, 1978 [Haw.]
No Match for Murder. Macmillan, 1942 [N.Y.]
Roses from a Haunted Garden. McKay, 1971
Somewhere Within This House. McKay, 1973 [Haw., 1887]

WEBB, L. J. Pseudonym of "one of the best-known women in America."
Walking the Dusk. Coward, 1932 [L.I.]

WEBB, MARTHA T(OOKE)
The Will and the Willful. Dorrance, 1969

WEBB, MICHAEL
Club—Mink Lined Murder. New Horizon, 1978

WEBB, RICHARD WILSON. 1901- . Joint pseudonym with Mary Louise Aswell; with Martha Mott Kelley; and with Hugh Callingham Wheeler, 1912- , q.v.; as well as solo pseudonym: Q. Patrick, q.v. Joint pseudonyms with Wheeler: Patrick Quentin, Jonathan Stagge, qq.v.

WEBB, SIDNEY HASTINGS
The Painted Honeymoon. Low, 1925

WEBBER, F. SIDNEY
A Baltic Mystery. Nelson, 1926

WEBER, RUBIN. Joint pseudonym of Robert G. Weaver and Samuel Leonard Rubinstein, 1922- . Ref: CC.
The Grave-Maker's House. Harper, 1964 [Pa.]

WEBLING, PEGGY
Strange Enchantment. Hutchinson, 1929

WEBSTER, ERNEST
The Friulan Plot. Hale, 1980

WEBSTER, F(REDERICK) A(NNESLEY) M(ICHAEL). 1886- . Ref: CC. SC: Ebbie Entwhistle = EE.
-The Adventures of Husky Hillier. Mellifont, 1937
All Is Not Gold. Thames,   ss
Beneath the Mask. Skeffington, 1948
-Beyond All Fear. Wright, 1934
-Beyond the Frontier. Shaw, 1931 ss
-The Black Shadow. Nisbet, 1922; Moffat, 1923 [Afr.]
-By Peak and Pass. Shaw, 1931
The Crime Scientist. Warne, 1930 EE ss
Dark Trails Go East. Wright, 1932
East of Kashgar. Skeffington, 1940
Echoing Footsteps. Thames,   ss
Gathering Storm. Wright, 1933
-The Hill of Riches. Hutchinson, 1923
The Islands of the Condemned. Wright, 1933
Killing No Murder. Thames,   ss
The Man in the Portrait. Thames, ss
The Man Who Knew. Selwyn, 1927
-M'Sango, the Witch Doctor. Shaw, 1927
Old Ebbie: Detective Up-to-Date. Chapman, 1923 EE ss
Old Ebbie Returns. Chapman, 1925 EE ss
On Government Service. Thames,   ss
-Stirring Adventures. Shaw, 1931
To Meet the Law. Thames,   ss
-The White Nigger. Mellifont, 1937

WEBSTER, H. M. SC: Shamus Burke, in all titles. Set: Eng.
The Ballycronin Mystery. Hurst, 1947
The Secret of Baron's Folly. Hurst, 1949
The Tontine Treasure. Hurst, 1951

WEBSTER, HENRY KITCHELL. 1875-1932. Ref: CC, EM. SC: Arthur Jeffrey = AJ.
The Alleged Great-Aunt, with Janet Ayer Fairbank, 1878?-1951, and Margaret Ayer Barnes, 1886-1967. Bobbs, 1935; Paul, 1935 [N.Y.]
The Butterfly. Appleton, 1914 [Midwest]
The Clock Strikes Two. Bobbs, 1928; Hamilton, 1928
The Corbin Necklace. Bobbs, 1926. British title: The Mystery of the Corbin Necklace. Hamilton, 1929
The Ghost Girl. Appleton, 1913 AJ [NYC]
The Man with the Scarred Hand. Bobbs, 1930
The Mystery of the Corbin Necklace; see The Corbin Necklace
Philopena. Bobbs, 1927; Nash, 1927
The Quartz Eye. Bobbs, 1928; Hodder, 1929
The Sealed Trunk. Bobbs, 1929; Paul, 1929 [Chi.]
The Whispering Man. Appleton, 1908; Nash, 1908 AJ [NYC]
Who Is the Next? Bobbs, 1931; Garland (London), 1976 [Ill.]

WEBSTER, (ALICE) JEAN (CHANDLER). 1876-1916.
The Four-Pools Mystery. Century, 1908; Hodder, 1916 [Va.]

WEBSTER, NOAH. Pseudonym of Bill Knox, 1928- , q.v. Other pseudonyms: Robert McLeod (under which byline the Noah Webster titles are published in Britain), q.v.; Michael Kirk.

WEBSTER, NOSTA H. Pseudonym: Julian Sterne, q.v.

WEDLAKE, GEORGE E. C.
Looted Gold. Jenkins, 1934
The Wrecking Ray. Jenkins, 1935

WEEKES, A(GNES) R(USSELL). See also: next entry. Pseudonym: Anthony Pryde, q.v.
The Rowforest Plot. Constable, 1927. U.S. title: Rowforest. Dodd, 1927, as by Anthony Pryde
The Story of Leland Gay. Constable, 1932; Dodd, 1932, as by Anthony Pryde

WEEKES, A(GNES) R(USSELL) and R(OSE) K(IRKPATRICK) WEEKES, 1894- , q.v. Pseudonym of Agnes Russell Weekes: Anthony Pryde, q.v. See also: preceding entry.
Affair at the "Vere Arms." Ward, 1935
Alda Abducted. Ward, 1942
-The Duke of Cameron Avenue. Macmillan, 1904 (British title?)
The Emerald Necklace. Ward, 1931; Dodd, 1931, as by Anthony Pryde and R. K. Weekes
The Figure on the Terrace. Ward, 1933
The Girl in the Other Seat. Appleton, 1911 (British title?)
-The Green Cross. Ward, 1937
Ninety in the Shade. Ward, 1937
-Real Life. Bobbs, 1921 (British title?)
-Traitor and Loyalist. Macmillan, 1904 (British title?)

WEEKES, R(OSE) K(IRKPATRICK). 1894- . See also: previous entry.
B14. Allen, 1920. U.S. title: Convict B14. Brentano's, 1920

WEEKS, HERBERT
The Mystery of Cedar Bluff. Colonial, 1928

WEEKS, JACK
The Grey Affair. Dell, 1961. British title (?): A Time to Kill. Cassell, 1961
The Limbo Touch. GM, 1968 [Carib.]
A Time to Kill; see The Grey Affair

WEEKS, WILLIAM E. Boston attorney.
All in the Racket. Boni, 1930

WEEKS, WILLIAM RAWLE. 1920- . Born in Denver, educated at Stanford U.
Knock and Wait a While. Houghton, 1957 Muller, 1957

WEES, FRANCES SHELLEY. 1902- . Ref: CA, CC. SC: Michael Forrester = MF.
The Country of the Strangers. Doubleday, 1960. British title: Dangerous Deadline. Ward, 1961 [Russ.]
Dangerous Deadline; see The Country of the Strangers
Detectives, Ltd.; see The Maestro Murders
Faceless Enemy. Doubleday, 1966; Cassell, 1967 [Toronto]
The Keys of My Prison. Doubleday, 1956; Jenkins, 1956
The Last Concubine. Abelard, 1970 [China]
Lost House. Macrae Smith, 1938; Hurst, 1939
The Maestro Murders. Mystery League, 1931. British title: Detectives, Ltd. Eyre, 1933 MF
M'Lord, I Am Not Guilty. Doubleday, 1954; Jenkins, 1954 [Can.]
The Mystery of the Creeping Man. Macrae Smith, 1931; Eyre, 1934 MF [acad.]
This Unnecessary Murder. Jenkins, 1957
Under the Quiet Water. Macrae Smith, 1949; Hurst, 1951
Where Is Jenny Now? Doubleday, 1958; Jenkins, 1958 [Toronto]

WEHEN, JOY DeWEESE. Pseudonym: Jennifer Wade, q.v.

WEIDMAN, JEROME. 1913- . Ref: CA.
A Family Fortune. Simon, 1978; Bodley, 1978
"I, and I Alone." Pockettes, 1972

WEIGALL, ARTHUR (EDWARD PEARSE BROME). 1880-1934.
The King Who Preferred Moonlight. Hutchinson, 1928 [Egypt]

WEIL, BARRY
Dossier IX. H. Hamilton, 1969; Bobbs, 1969 [Fr.]

WEIL, JERRY. 1928- . Ref: CA.
Daughter of Evil. Signet, 1961
A Real Cool Cat. Signet, 1960 [NYC]
The Spy Who Came Home to Die. Five Star, 1967 [Sp.]

WEILL, GUS. 1933- . Ref: CA.
The Bonnet Man. Macmillan, 1978 [Miss.]
The Fuhrer Seed. Morrow, 1979; New English Library, 1980 [Ger.]
A Woman's Eyes. Dial, 1975; Constable, 1976 [NYC]

WEIN, JACQUELINE. 1938- . Ref: CA.
Roommate. Crown, 1979 [NYC]

WEIN, LEN and MARV WOLFMAN
Mayhem in Manhattan. PB, 1978 [NYC]

WEINER, HENRI. Pseudonym of Stephen Longstreet, 1907- . Other pseudonym: Paul Haggard, q.v.
Crime on the Cuff. Morrow, 1936. Also published as: The Case of the Severed Skull. Mystery Novel of the Month, 1940 [NYC]

WEINER, JACK B. 1929- .
The Morning After. Delacorte, 1973; Hart-Davis, 1974

WEINER, MORRIS COLBY
The Price of Silence. Vantage, 1967

WEINSTEIN, SOL. 1928- . Ref: CA. SC: Israel Bond, in all titles.
Loxfinger. PB, 1965
Matzohball. PB, 1966
On the Secret Service of His Majesty, the Queen. PB, 1966
You Only Live Until You Die. Trident, 1968

WEINSTOCK, JACK and WILLIE GILBERT
Catch Me If You Can. French (NYC), 1965 (Play.)

WEINTRAUB, SIDNEY. 1922- . Ref: CA.
Mexican Slay Ride. Hale, 1962; Abelard, 1962 [Mex. City]
The Siamese Coup Affair. Boardman, 1963

WEIR, DONALD
-Balkan Saga. Oliver, 1937 [Balkans]
-Black Lobster. Wright, 1951
-The Death Stone. Wright, 1939
-The Hot Seat. Wright, 1940
-Red Flows the Barada. Wright, 1948

WEIR, HUGH C(OSGRO). 1884-1934.
Miss Madelyn Mack, Detective. Page, 1914 ss [NYC]

WEIR, MARIPOSA
  A Chase Round the World; or, A Detective by Chance. Street, 1890

WEISMAN, JOHN. 1942-   . Ref: CA. SC: The Headhunters = H.
  Evidence. Viking, 1980 [Det.]
  Heroin Triple Cross, with Brian (D.) Boyer, 1939-   . Pinnacle, 1974 H [Det.]
  Quadraphone Homicide, with Brian (D.) Boyer, 1939-   . Pinnacle, 1975 H [L.A.]
  The Starlight Motel Incident, with Brian (D.) Boyer, 1939-   . Pinnacle, 1974 H [Det.]
  Three Faces of Death, with Brian (D.) Boyer, 1939-   . Pinnacle, 1974 H [Chi.]

WEISMILLER, EDWARD (RONALD). 1915-   . Ref: CA.
  The Serpent Sleeping. Putnam, 1962

WEISS, DAVID. 1909-   . Ref: CA.
  The Assassination of Mozart. Hodder, 1970; Morrow, 1971

WEISS, MARTIN L.
  Death Hitches a Ride. Ace, 1954 [S.W.]
  Hate Alley. Ace, 1957

WEISS, MELFORD S(TEPHEN). 1937-   . Ref: CA.
  The Korean Conspiracy. Manor, 1978

WEISSL, AUGUST
  The Mystery of the Green Car. Nelson, 1913 (Translation of "Der Grune Auto." Stuttgart, 1911.) [Vienna]

WEISSMAN, JERRY
  The Zodiac Killer. Pinnacle, 1979 [S.F., 1960s]

WELCH, TIMOTHY L. 1935-   . Ref: CA. Pseudonym: Patrick Cake, q.v. SC: Dion Quince, in title below and that by Patrick Cake.
  The Tennis Murders. Popular Library, 1976

WELCOME, JOHN. Pseudonym of John Needham Huggard Brennan, 1914-   . Ref: CA, CC, TC. SC: Richard Graham = RG; Simon Harald = SH.
  Beware of Midnight. Faber, 1961; Knopf, 1961
  Go for Broke. Faber, 1972; Walker, 1972 RG
  -Grand National. H. Hamilton, 1976; Simon, 1977
  Hard to Handle. Faber, 1964 RG
  Hell Is Where You Find It. Faber, 1968 RG [Fr.]
  -Mr. Merston's Money. Constable, 1951
  On the Stretch. Faber, 1969 RG
  -Red Coats Galloping. Constable, 1949
  Run for Cover. Faber, 1958; Knopf, 1959 RG [Fr.]
  Stop at Nothing. Faber, 1959; Knopf, 1960 SH
  Wanted for Killing. Faber, 1965; Holt, 1967 SH [Cors.]

WELDEN, ELLIS
  Sudden Death of the M.F.H. Heath Cranston, 1938

WELDON, DAVID
  The Chaos Contract. New English Library pb, 1977
  The Million Pound Bus Fare. New English Library pb, 1976

WELFORD, MAURICE. Set: Eng.
  Queen of Crookdom. Modern, 193?
  The Secret Guest Mystery. Modern, 1938
  Thameside Gold. Modern, 1938

WELLARD, JAMES (HOWARD). 1909-   . Ref: CA. SC: Lucius Hunt = LH.
  Action of the Tiger. St. Martin's, 1955; Macmillan (London), 1955 [Alb.]
  A Moment in Time. Dodd, 1947. British title: Spotlight on Murder. Foulsham, 1949 LH [NYC]
  The Snake in the Grass. Dodd, 1946; United Authors, 1946 LH [Ga.]
  Spotlight on Murder; see A Moment in Time

WELLEN, EDWARD (PAUL). 1919-   . Ref: CA.
  Hijack. Beagle, 1971

WELLER, MARY ELIZABETH PHYLLIS. Joint pseudonym with Agnes Rosemary Cooper: Ramsay Bell, q.v.

WELLES, ELIZABETH. House name. SC: Jannine West, in all titles
  Captain's Walk. PB, 1976 [Cape Cod]
  Fahnworth Manor. PB, 1976 [Ire.]
  Seagull Crag. PB, 1977 (By Mary Linn Roby, 1930-   , q.v.)
  Spaniard's Gift. PB, 1977 [Fla.]
  Waterview Manor. PB, 1976 [Md.]

WELLES, (GEORGE) ORSON. 1915-   . Ref: CA.
  Mr. Arkadin. Crowell, 1956; Allen, 1956

WELLES, PATRICIA
  Angels in the Snow. PB, 1980 [Mich.]

WELLMAN, MANLY WADE. 1905-   . Ref: CA, EM.
  A Double Life. Century, 1947 (Novelization of the movie.)
  Find My Killer. Farrar, 1947; Low, 1948
  Sherlock Holmes's War of the Worlds, with Wade Wellman, 1939-   . Warner, 1975 [Eng., 1902] (Sherlock Holmes)

WELLMAN, WADE. 1939-   . See: Manly Wade Wellman, 1905-   .

WELLS, A(RTHUR) W(ALTER). 1894-   .
  All This Is Ended. Melrose, 1936 ss, two criminous

WELLS, ANNA MARY. 1906-   . Ref: CA. SC: Dr. Hillis Owen = HO.
  Fear of Death. Wingate, 1951
  Murderer's Choice. Knopf, 1943; Hammond, 1950 [NYC]
  The Night of May Third. Doubleday, 1956; Foulsham, 1957
  Sin of Angels. Simon, 1948; Hammond, 1951 HO [NYC]
  A Talent for Murder. Knopf, 1942; Hammond, 1948 HO [NYC]

WELLS, CAROLYN. 1870-1942. Pseudonym: Rowland Wright, q.v. Ref: CC, DD, EM, MC, MP, TC. SC: Kenneth Carlisle = KC; Alan Ford = AF; Lorimer Lane = LL; Fleming Stone = FS; Pennington Wise = PW.
  The Affair at Flower Acres. Doran, 1923 PW [NYC]
  All at Sea. Lippincott (Phil. and London), 1927 FS [N.J.]
  Anybody But Anne. Lippincott (Phil. and London), 1914 FS [New Eng.]
  Anything But the Truth. Lippincott (Phil. and London), 1925 FS
  The Beautiful Derelict. Lippincott (Phil. and London), 1935 FS [Mass.]
  The Black Night Murders. Lippincott, 1941 FS [Conn.]
  The Bride of a Moment. Doran, 1916; Hodder, 1920 AF [N.Y.]
  The Broken O. Lippincott (Phil. and London), 1933 FS [L.I.]
  The Bronze Hand. Lippincott (Phil. and London), 1926 FS [ship]
  Calling All Suspects. Lippincott, 1939 FS [NYC]
  A Chain of Evidence. Lippincott, 1912 FS [NYC]
  The Clue. Lippincott, 1909; Hodder, 1920 FS [N.J.]
  The Clue of the Eyelash. Lippincott (Phil. and London), 1933 FS [L.I.]
  The Come-Back. Doran, 1921; Hodder, 1921 PW [NYC]
  Crime Incarnate. Lippincott, 1940 FS [N.Y.]
  The Crime in the Crypt. Lippincott (Phil. and London), 1928 FS [N.Y.]
  Crime Tears On. Lippincott, 1939 FS [L.I.]
  The Curved Blades. Lippincott (Phil. and London), 1916 FS [L.I.]
  The Daughter of the House. Lippincott (Phil. and London), 1925 FS [N.Y.]
  Deep-Lake Mystery. Doubleday, 1928 [Wis.]
  Devil's Work. Lippincott, 1940 FS [L.I.]
  The Diamond Pin. Lippincott (Phil. and London), 1919 FS [N.Y.]
  The Doomed Five. Lippincott (Phil. and London), 1930 FS [NYC]
  The Doorstep Murders. Doubleday, 1930 KC [Conn.]
  The Elusive Vicky Van; see Vicky Van
  Eyes in the Wall. Lippincott (Phil. and London), 1934 FS [NYC]
  Face Cards. Putnam (NYC and London), 1925 [Conn.]
  Faulkner's Folly. Doran, 1917 AF [L.I.]
  Feathers Left Around. Lippincott (Phil. and London), 1923 FS [N.Y.]
  For Goodness' Sake. Lippincott (Phil. and London), 1935 FS [L.I.]
  The Fourteenth Key. Putnam (NYC and London), 1924 LL [N.Y.]
  Fuller's Earth. Lippincott (Phil. and London), 1932 FS [Mass.]
  The Furthest Fury. Lippincott (Phil. and London), 1924 FS
  The Ghosts' High Noon. Lippincott (Phil. and London), 1930 FS [N.Y.]
  Gilt-Edged Guilt. Lippincott, 1938 FS [N.Y.]
  The Gold Bag. Lippincott (Phil. and London), 1911 FS [N.Y.]
  Horror House. Lippincott (Phil. and London), 1931 FS [Conn.]
  The Huddle. Lippincott (Phil. and London), 1936 FS [NYC]
  The Importance of Being Murdered. Lippincott, 1939 FS [Mass.]
  In the Onyx Lobby. Doran, 1920; Hodder, 1920 PW [NYC]
  In the Tiger's Cage. Lippincott (Phil. and London), 1936 FS [Mass.]
  The Killer. Lippincott, 1938 FS [Vt.]
  The Luminous Face. Doran, 1921 PW [NYC]
  The Man Who Fell Through the Earth. Doran, 1919; Harrap, 1924 PW [NYC]
  The Mark of Cain. Lippincott (Phil. and London), 1917 FS [NYC]
  The Master Murderer. Lippincott (Phil. and London), 1933 FS [NYC]
  The Maxwell Mystery. Lippincott (Phil. and London), 1913 FS [N.J.]
  The Missing Link. Lippincott, 1938 FS [N.Y.]
  Money Musk. Lippincott (Phil. and London), 1936 FS [NYC]
  More Lives Than One. Boni, 1923; Hutchinson, 1924 LL [NYC]
  The Moss Mystery. Garden City, 1924 [N.Y.]
  Murder at the Casino. Lippincott, 1941 FS [N.Y.]
  Murder in the Bookshop. Lippincott (Phil. and London), 1936 FS [NYC]
  Murder on Parade. Lippincott, 1940 FS [Maine]
  Murder Plus. Lippincott, 1940 FS [Conn.]
  Murder Will In. Lippincott, 1942 FS [NYC]
  The Mystery Girl. Lippincott (Phil. and London), 1922 FS [New Eng., acad.]
  The Mystery of the Sycamore. Lippincott (Phil. and London), 1921 FS [Mass.]
  The Mystery of the Tarn. Lippincott (Phil. and London), 1937 FS [Mass.]
  Prilligirl. Lippincott (Phil. and London), 1924 FS [NYC]
  The Radio Studio Murder. Lippincott (Phil. and London), 1937 FS [NYC]
  Raspberry Jam. Lippincott (Phil. and London), 1920 FS [NYC]
  The Red-Haired Girl. Lippincott (Phil. and London), 1926 FS [NYC]
  The Roll-Top Desk Mystery. Lippincott (Phil. and London), 1932 FS [Mass.]
  The Room with the Tassels. Doran, 1918 PW [Vt.]
  The Sixth Commandment. Doran, 1927 [L.I.]
  The Skeleton at the Feast. Doubleday, 1931 KC [NYC]
  Sleeping Dogs. Doubleday, 1929 KC [L.I.]
  Spooky Hollow. Lippincott (Phil. and London), 1923 FS [Vt.]
  The Tannahill Tangle. Lippincott (Phil. and London), 1928 FS [New Eng.]
  The Tapestry Room Murder. Lippincott (Phil. and London), 1929 FS [N.Y.]
  Triple Murder. Lippincott (Phil. and London), 1929 FS [N.Y.]
  The Umbrella Murder. Lippincott (Phil. and London), 1931 FS [N.J.]
  The Vanishing of Betty Varian. Doran, 1922; Collins, 1924 PW [Maine]
  The Vanity Case. Putnam (NYC and London), 1926 [L.I.]
  Vicky Van. Lippincott (Phil. and London), 1918. Also published as: The Elusive Vicky Van. Mellifont, 1934 FS [NYC]
  The Visiting Villain. Lippincott (Phil. and London), 1934 FS [NYC]
  Wheels Within Wheels. Doran, 1923 PW [Conn.]
  Where's Emily. Lippincott (Phil. and London), 1927 FS [New Eng.]
  The White Alley. Lippincott (Phil. and London), 1915 FS [N.Y.]
  Who Killed Caldwell? Lippincott, 1942 FS [NYC]
  The Wooden Indian. Lippincott (Phil. and London), 1935 FS [Conn.]

WELLS, CHARLIE [CHARLES HARDING WELLS]. Born in Miss.
  The Last Kill. Signet, 1955 [Memphis]
  Let the Night Cry. Abelard (NYC), 1953; Abelard (London), 1959 [New Or.]

WELLS, ELAINE F.
  The Legend of Lostwithiel. Zebra, 1979
  The Lords of Castle Weirwyck. Zebra, 1980

WELLS, GEORGE
    The Weird Idol of Penang Towers. Macdonald, 1928

WELLS, H(ERBERT) G(EORGE). 1866-1946. Ref: EM.
    The Stolen Bacillus, and other incidents. Methuen, 1895 ss, at least one criminous

WELLS, MICHAEL
    The Doublecrossers. Hale, 1961

WELLS, ROBERT M.
    The Finger of Smoke. Street (New Magnet)
    A Fortune in Peril. Street (New Magnet)
    On Fortune's Wheel. Street (New Magnet)
    Out of Chaos. Street (New Magnet)
    A Woman of Nerve. Street (New Magnet)

WELLS, SUSAN. Pseudonym of Doris Siegel, q.v. SC: Anthony Ware, in all titles.
    Death Is My Name. Scribner, 1942; Cherry Tree, 1943 [San Diego]
    Footsteps in the Air. Simon, 1940; Cassell, 1941 [Calif.]
    Murder Is Not Enough. Simon, 1939; Cassell, 1939 [ship, Calif.]
    The Witches' Pond. Doubleday, 1947 [Calif.]

WELLS, TOBIAS. Pseudonym of DeLoris Florine Stanton Forbes, 1923-   .
    Other pseudonym: Stanton Forbes, q.v. Joint pseudonym with Helen B. Rydell: Forbes Rydell, q.v. SC: Knute Severson, in all titles.
    Brenda's Murder. Doubleday, 1973; Hale, 1974
    A Creature Was Stirring. Doubleday, 1977; Hale, 1978 [Mass.]
    Dead by the Light of the Moon. Doubleday, 1967; Gollancz, 1968 [Boston]
    A Die in the Country. Doubleday, 1972; Hale, 1974
    Die Quickly, Dear Mother. Doubleday, 1969; Hale, 1969 [Boston]
    Dinky Died. Doubleday, 1970; Hale, 1970 [Boston]
    The Foo Dog. Doubleday, 1971. British title: The Lotus Affair. Hale, 1973
    Hark, Hark, the Watchdogs Bark. Doubleday, 1975; Hale, 1976 [Carib.]
    Have Mercy Upon Us. Doubleday, 1974; Hale, 1975 [Mass.]
    How to Kill a Man. Doubleday, 1972; Hale, 1973 [Conn.]
    The Lotus Affair; see The Foo Dog
    A Matter of Love and Death. Doubleday, 1966; Gollancz, 1966 [Boston]
    Murder Most Fouled Up. Doubleday, 1968; Hale, 1969 [Boston]
    What Should You Know of Dying? Doubleday, 1967; Gollancz, 1967 [Boston]
    What to Do Until the Undertaker Comes. Doubleday, 1971; Hale, 1973 [Boston]
    The Young Can Die Protesting. Doubleday, 1969; Hale, 1970 [Boston]

WELLSLEY, JULIE. Pseudonym of W(illiam) Howard Baker, 1925-   , q.v. Other pseudonyms: William Arthur, W. A. Ballinger, Peter Saxon, Richard Williams, qq.v. Uncorrelated title changes are likely in the list below.
    The Castle on the Mountain. Baker, 1973; Dell, 1972 [Wales]
    Chateau of Secrets. Mayflower, 1970
    Climb the Dark Mountain. Lancer, 1970
    Companion of Dishonour. Baker, 1969
    The Fateful Tide. Baker, 1969
    House Malign. Mayflower, 1967; Lancer, 1967
    House of Secrets. Baker, 1969
    Stranger in a Dark Land. Lancer, 1969
    Tall, Dark Stranger. Mayflower, 1968
    Two Faces of Fear. Lancer, 1971
    The Wine of Vengeance. Lancer, 1969 [Fr.]

WELTON, ARTHUR D(ORMAN). 1867-1940.
    The 27th Ride. Sears, 1932 [Chi.]

WEMPE, IRENE
    Come to My Funeral. Ballantine, 1967

WENLOCK, ARTHUR
    The Countermine. Rivers, 1904

WENTWORTH, PATRICIA. Pseudonym of Dora Amy Dillon Turnbull, 1878-1961. Ref: CC, EM, MP, TC. SC: Maud Silver = MS; Insp. Ernest Lamb, in many MS books, and alone in those marked EL. Set: Eng.
    Account Rendered; see Who Pays the Piper?
    The Alington Inheritance. Hodder, 1960; Lippincott, 1958 MS

    The Amazing Chance. Hodder, 1926; Lippincott, 1927
    Anna, Where Are You? Hodder, 1953; Lippincott, 1951. Also published as: Death at Deep End. Pyramid, 1963 MS
    The Annam Jewel. Melrose, 1924; Small, 1925
    Anne Belinda. Hodder, 1927; Lippincott, 1928
    The Astonishing Adventure of Jane Smith. Melrose, 1923; Small, 1923
    Beggar's Choice. Hodder, 1930; Lippincott, 1931
    The Benevent Treasure. Hodder, 1956; Lippincott, 1954 MS
    The Black Cabinet. Hodder, 1925; Small, 1926
    The Blind Side. Hodder, 1939; Lippincott, 1939 EL
    Blindfold. Hodder, 1935; Lippincott, 1935
    The Brading Collection. Hodder, 1952; Lippincott, 1950 MS
    The Case Is Closed. Hodder, 1937; Lippincott, 1937 MS
    The Case of William Smith. Hodder, 1950; Lippincott, 1948 MS
    The Catherine Wheel. Hodder, 1951; Lippincott, 1949 MS
    The Chinese Shawl. Hodder, 1943; Lippincott, 1943 MS
    The Clock Strikes Twelve. Hodder, 1945; Lippincott, 1944 MS
    The Coldstone. Hodder, 1930; Lippincott, 1930
    Danger Calling. Hodder, 1931; Lippincott, 1931
    Danger Point. Hodder, 1942. U.S. title: In the Balance. Lippincott, 1941 MS
    Dark Threat; see Pilgrim's Rest
    Dead or Alive. Hodder, 1936; Lippincott, 1936
    Death at Deep End; see Anna, Where Are You?
    Devil-in-the-Dark. Hodder, 1934. U.S. title: Touch and Go. Lippincott, 1934
    The Dower House Mystery. Hodder, 1925; Small, 1925
    Down Under. Hodder, 1937; Lippincott, 1937
    Eternity Ring. Hodder, 1950; Lippincott, 1948 MS
    Fear by Night. Hodder, 1934; Lippincott, 1934
    The Fingerprint. Hodder, 1959; Lippincott, 1956 MS
    Fool Errant. Hodder, 1929; Lippincott, 1929
    The Gazebo. Hodder, 1958; Lippincott, 1956. Also published as: The Summerhouse. Pyramid, 1967 MS
    The Girl in the Cellar. Hodder, 1961 MS
    Grey Mask. Hodder, 1928; Lippincott, 1929 MS
    Hole and Corner. Hodder, 1936; Lippincott, 1936
    Hue and Cry. Hodder, 1927; Lippincott, 1927
    In the Balance; see Danger Point
    The Ivory Dagger. Hodder, 1953; Lippincott, 1951 MS
    The Key. Hodder, 1946; Lippincott, 1944 MS
    Kingdom Lost. Hodder, 1931; Lippincott, 1930
    Ladies' Bane. Hodder, 1954; Lippincott, 1952 MS
    Latter End. Hodder, 1949; Lippincott, 1947 MS
    The Listening Eye. Hodder, 1957; Lippincott, 1955 MS
    Lonesome Road. Hodder, 1939; Lippincott, 1939 MS
    Miss Silver Comes to Stay. Hodder, 1951; Lippincott, 1949 MS
    Miss Silver Deals with Death; see Miss Silver Intervenes
    Miss Silver Intervenes. Hodder, 1944. U.S. title: Miss Silver Deals with Death. Lippincott, 1943 MS
    Mr. Zero. Hodder, 1938; Lippincott, 1938
    Nothing Venture. Cassell, 1932; Lippincott, 1932
    Out of the Past. Hodder, 1955; Lippincott, 1953 MS
    Outrageous Fortune; see Seven Green Stones
    Pilgrim's Rest. Hodder, 1948; Lippincott, 1946. Also published as: Dark Threat. Popular Library, 1951 MS
    Poison in the Pen. Hodder, 1957; Lippincott, 1955 MS
    Pursuit of a Parcel. Hodder, 1942; Lippincott, 1942 EL
    Red Danger. Cassell, 1932. U.S. title: Red Shadow. Lippincott, 1932
    The Red Lacquer Case. Melrose, 1924; Small, 1925
    Red Shadow; see Red Danger
    Red Stefan. Hodder, 1935; Lippincott, 1935 [Russ.]

    Rolling Stone. Hodder, 1940; Lippincott, 1940
    Run! Hodder, 1938; Lippincott, 1938
    Seven Green Stones. Cassell, 1933. U.S. title: Outrageous Fortune. Lippincott, 1933
    She Came Back; see The Traveller Returns
    Silence in Court. Hodder, 1947; Lippincott, 1945
    The Silent Pool. Hodder, 1956; Lippincott, 1954 MS
    Spotlight. Hodder, 1949. U.S. title: Wicked Uncle. Lippincott, 1947 MS
    The Summerhouse; see The Gazebo
    Through the Wall. Hodder, 1952; Lippincott, 1950 MS
    Touch and Go; see Devil-in-the-Dark
    The Traveller Returns. Hodder, 1948. U.S. title: She Came Back. Lippincott, 1945 MS
    Unlawful Occasions. Hodder, 1941. U.S. title: Weekend with Death. Lippincott, 1941
    Vanishing Point. Hodder, 1955; Lippincott, 1953 MS
    Walk with Care. Cassell, 1933; Lippincott, 1933
    The Watersplash. Hodder, 1953; Lippincott, 1951 MS
    Weekend with Death; see Unlawful Occasions
    Who Pays the Piper? Hodder, 1940. U.S. title: Account Rendered. Lippincott, 1940 EL
    Wicked Uncle; see Spotlight
    Will-o'-the-Wisp. Hodder, 1928; Lippincott, 1928

WENZELL, ISABEL D'ESTE
    The Dragon's Lair. Lancer, 1967

WERLIN, MARVIN. 1929-   .
    Shadow Play. Morrow, 1976 [Calif.]

WERNER, GEORGE. Reporter, magazine staff writer, in NYC.
    One Helluva Blow. Gold Star, 1964 [Calif.]

WERNICK, SAUL. 1921-   . Pseudonym: Nick Carter, q.v. Ref: CA.
    Blood Tide. Dell, 1979 [Mass.]

WERRY, RICHARD R. 1916-   . Ref: CA.
    Hammer Me Home. Dodd, 1955 [Tex.]

WESLEY, MARY. 1912-   . Ref: CA.
    The Sixth Seal. Macdonald, 1969; Stein, 1971 [future, Eng.]

WESLEY, ROBERT
    The Rogue with a Past. Street (Magnet)

WEST, ALROY
    The Baying Hound. Wright, 1934
    The Beach of Skulls. Wright, 1937
    The Black Matador. Wright, 1937
    The Crouching Men. Wright, 1933
    Hate Island. Wright, 1934; Godwin, 1935
    The Knife Terror. Wright, 1934
    The Man Who Didn't Exist. Wright, 1935
    The Messengers of Death. Wright, 1935

WEST, CAROL. Pseudonym of Clara A. Wakevainen.
    Laughing Malefactor. Vantage, 1965

WEST, CHARLES
    The Destruction Man. Hale, 1976

WEST, DAVID. Pseudonym of David Derek Stacton, 1925-1968. Other pseudonym: Bud Clifford, q.v.
    Wish Me Dead. Eyre, 1960 [S.W.]

WEST, EDWARD (CHARLES) SACKVILLE
    The Ruin. Heinemann, 1926

WEST, ELLIOT. 1924-   . Ref: CA.
    The Killing Kind. Houghton, 1974
    Man Running. Little, 1959; Weidenfeld, 1959 [Sp., Fr.]
    The Night Is a Time for Listening. Random, 1966; Gollancz, 1966 [Eng.]
    These Lonely Victories. Putnam, 1972; Gollancz, 1973 [Berlin]

WEST, GEOFFREY PHILIP
    How Did Elmer Die? Longmans, 1938

WEST, GORDON. 1896-   . Ref: CA.
    Murder for Charity. Cherry Tree, 1943
    Murder in Mayfair. Cherry Tree, 1943

WEST, JOHN B.   -ca.1960. Born in Wash. D.C., educated at Howard and Harvard Universities; physician, specialist in tropical diseases, with practice in Liberia. SC: Rocky Steele, in all titles.

Bullets Are My Business. Signet, 1960 [NYC]
Cobra Venom. Signet, 1959 [Wash. D.C.]
Death on the Rocks. Signet, 1961
An Eye for an Eye. Signet, 1959 [NYC]
Never Kill a Cop. Signet, 1961 [NYC]
A Taste for Blood. Signet, 1960 [NYC]

WEST, JOYCE (TARLTON). See: Mary (Edith Clarke) Scott, 1888- .

WEST, KEITH. Pseudonym of Kenneth Westmacott Lane, 1893- .
-Bamboo. Jarrolds, 1931
Hanging Waters. Lovat Dickson, 1933; Putnam, 1933
-The Hollow Hub. Hale, 1951
The House That Chak Built. Jenkins, 1935
-The Widows of the Magistrate. Hale, 1949

WEST, LYN
Corpse Without a Jacket. Everybody's, 1946
The Lost House Mystery. Mitre, 1944

WEST, MORRIS L(ANGLO). 1916- . Pseudonym: Michael East, q.v. SC: George Harlequin = GH. Ref: CA.
The Ambassador. Heinemann, 1965; Morrow, 1965
Backlash; see The Second Victory
The Big Story. Heinemann, 1957. U.S. title: The Crooked Road. Morrow, 1957 GH [It.]
The Crooked Road; see The Big Story
Daughter of Silence. Heinemann, 1961; Morrow, 1961. 3-act play based on this novel: Morrow, 1962
Harlequin. Collins, 1974; Morrow, 1974 GH
-The Heretic. Heinemann, 1970; Morrow, 1969 (Play.)
-Kundu. Angus, 1957; Dell, 1956
Proteus. Collins, 1979; Morrow, 1979
The Salamander. Heinemann, 1973; Morrow, 1973 [It.]
The Second Victory. Heinemann, 1958. U.S. title: Backlash. Morrow, 1958
Summer of the Red Wolf. Heinemann, 1971; Morrow, 1971 [Scot.]
The Tower of Babel. Heinemann, 1968; Morrow, 1968 [Mid. East]

WEST, NICHOLSON
-Gold Island. Cassell, 1904
The Mysterious Millionaire. Greening, 1906

WEST, PAUL. See: William (Andrew) Johnston, 1871-1929.

WESTALL, SHEILA
The Galmart Affair. Hale, 1975

WESTALL, WILLIAM (BURY). 1835-1903.
-As a Man Sows. Ward, 1894
-As Luck Would Have It. Chatto, 1900
-Back to Africa. Ward, 1891
-Ben Clough and other stories. Ward, 1892; Lovell, 1891 ss
-Birch Dene. Ward, 1889; Harper, 1889
Dr. Wynne's Revenge. Chatto, 1904
-Don or Devil? Pearson, 1901
-A Fair Crusader. Hurst, 1888; Harper, 1887
-For Honour and Life. Osgood, 1894; Harper, 1894
Her Ladyship's Secret. Chatto, 1901
-Her Two Millions. Ward, 1887; Harper, 1887
John Brown & Larry Lohengrin; see Larry Lohengrin
-Larry Lohengrin. Tinsley, 1881. Also published as: John Brown & Larry Lohengrin. Ward, 1889
Mr. Fortescue; see Nigel Fortescue
-Nigel Fortescue. Ward, 1888. U.S. title: Mr. Fortescue. Lovell, 1888
The Old Bank. Chatto, 1902
-The Old Factory. Tinsley, 1881
-The Princess of Peele. Lovell, 1892 (British title?)
-A Queer Race. Cassell (London & NYC), 1887
-Ralph Norbreck's Trust. Tinsley, 1883
-A Red Bridal. Chatto, 1899
-Red Rivington. Hurst, 1882
-Roy of Roy's Court. Ward, 1892
The Sacred Crescents. Chatto, 1902 [Turk.]
-Sons of Belial. Chatto, 1895; Cassell, 1895
Strange Crimes. Ward, 1890; Lovell, 1890 ss
-Trust Money. Chatto, 1892
-Two Pinches of Snuff. Ward, 1886; Harper, 1886
A Very Queer Business, and other stories. Chatto, 1904 ss
-A Woman Tempted Him. Chatto, 1898

WESTBIE, CONSTANCE LOVEALL. 1910- .
Ref: CA.
The Birdcage Murders. Bouregy, 1964

WESTBROOK, PERRY D(ICKIE). 1916- .
Ref: CA, CC. SC: Dr. Samuel Cutting = SC.
Happy Deathday. Phoenix, 1947 SC
Infra Blood. Phoenix, 1950 SC [Maine]
It Boils Down to Murder. Arcadia, 1953 [Vt.]
The Red Herring Murder. Phoenix, 1949 SC [Maine]
The Sting of Death. Arcadia, 1955 [Vt.]

WESTCOTT, KATHLEEN. Pseudonym of Christine Elizabeth Abrahamson, 1916- .
Bride of Kilkerran. PB, 1974

WESTERBY, ROBERT
Wide Boys Never Work. Barker, 1937

WESTERHAM, JULIA. Pseudonym of Ella Griffiths Ormhaug, 1926- .
Web of Murder. (Oslo), 1970

WESTERHAM, S. C. Pseudonym of Cyril A(rgentine) Alington, 1872-1955, q.v.
Mixed Bags. Christopher, 1929; McBride, 1929

WESTGATE, TED
Death Writes a Message. Banner, 1949 (1-act play.)
The Mystery of Mouldy Manor. Row, 1950 (Play.)

WESTHEIMER, DAVID. 1917- . Pseudonym: Z. Z. Smith, q.v. Ref: CA.
The Avila Gold. Putnam, 1974; Joseph, 1975 [L.A.]
Going Public. Mason, 1973; Joseph, 1973 [Calif.]
The Olmec Head. Little, 1974; Joseph, 1974 [Mex.]
Over the Edge. Little, 1972; Joseph, 1974

WESTLAKE, DONALD E(DWIN). 1933- .
Pseudonyms: Curt Clark, Tucker Coe, Timothy J. Culver, Richard Stark, qq.v. Ref: CA, EM, TC. SC: John Dortmunder = JD.
Bank Shot. Simon, 1972; Hodder, 1972 JD [L.I.]
-Brothers Keepers. Evans, 1975; Hodder, 1977 [NYC]
The Busy Body. Random, 1966; Boardman, 1966 [NYC]
Castle in the Air. Evans, 1980; Hodder, 1981 [Paris]
Cops and Robbers. Evans, 1972; Hodder, 1973 [NYC]
The Curious Facts Preceding My Execution. Random, 1968 ss
Dancing Aztecs. Evans, 1976. British title: A New York Dance. Hodder, 1979 [NYC]
Enough! Evans, 1977; Hodder, 1980 (2 novelets.) [NYC]
The Fugitive Pigeon. Random, 1965; Boardman, 1966 [NYC]
Gangway!, with Brian (Francis Wynne) Garfield, 1939- , q.v. Evans, 1973; Barker, 1974 [S.F., 1874]
God Save the Mark. Random, 1967; Joseph, 1968 [NYC]
Help I Am Being Held Prisoner. Evans, 1974; Hodder, 1975
The Hot Rock. Simon, 1970; Hodder, 1971 JD [NYC]
I Gave at the Office. Simon, 1971; Hodder, 1972 [Carib.]
Jimmy the Kid. Evans, 1974; Hodder, 1975 JD [N.J.]
Killing Time. Random, 1961; Boardman, 1962. Also published as: The Operator. Dell, 1964
Killy. Random, 1963; Boardman, 1964 [N.Y.]
The Mercenaries. Random, 1960; Boardman, 1961. Also published as: The Smashers. Dell, 1962; Four Square, 1963
A New York Dance; see Dancing Aztecs
Nobody's Perfect. Evans, 1977; Hodder, 1978 JD
The Operator; see Killing Time
Pity Him Afterwards. Random, 1964; Boardman, 1965
The Smashers; see The Mercenaries
Somebody Owes Me Money. Random, 1969; Hodder, 1970 [NYC]
The Spy in the Ointment. Random, 1966; Boardman, 1967 [NYC]
361. Random, 1962; Boardman, 1962
Two Much! Evans, 1975; Hodder, 1976 [NYC]
Who Stole Sassi Manoon? Random, 1969; Hodder, 1971 [Carib.]

WESTLAW, STEVEN
The Mystery of Lombardy Chambers. Hodder, 1926 [Melb.]
-The White Peril. Hodder, 1926

WESTMINSTER, AYNN
Moon in Shadow. Dell, 1974 [N.Y.]

WESTON, ALLEN. Joint pseudonym of Alice Mary Norton, 1912?- , and Grace Allen Hogarth, 1905- . Other Norton pseudonym: Andre Norton, q.v.
Murders for Sale. Hammond, 1954

WESTON, CAROLYN. 1921- . Ref: TC. SC: Casey Kellog and Al Krug = K&K.
Danju Gig. Random, 1969. British title: Spy in Black. Hale, 1972 [Afr., W.]
Poor, Poor Ophelia. Random, 1972; Gollancz, 1973 K&K [L.A.]
Rouse the Demon. Random, 1976; Gollancz, 1977 K&K [L.A.]
Spy in Black; see Danju Gig
Susannah Screaming. Random, 1975; Gollancz, 1976 K&K [L.A.]
Tormented. Berkley, 1958

WESTON, GARNETT (JAMES). SC: Highway = H.
Citizens—to Arms!; see The Man with the Monocle
Dead Men Are Dangerous. Stokes, 1937; Hutchinson, 1937 H [Calif.]
Death Never Forgets; see Murder in Haste
The Hidden Portal. Doubleday, 1946 [Afr., N.]
Legacy of Fear. Mill, 1950 [Can.]
The Man with the Monocle. Doubleday, 1943. British title (?): Citizens—to Arms! Cassell, 1943
Murder in Haste. Stokes, 1935. British title: Death Never Forgets. Hutchinson, 1935 H [Calif.]
Murder on Shadow Island. Farrar, 1933; Hutchinson, 1933 [Can.]
Poldrate Street. Messner, 1944
The Undertaker Dies. Hutchinson, 1940 H [L.A.]

WESTON, GEORGE. 1880-1965.
Queen of the World. Dodd, 1923
Wings of Destiny. Dodd, 1929 [Paris]
The Wondering Moon. Dodd, 1926 [Conn.]

WESTON, HELEN GRAY. Pseudonym of Dorothy Daniels, 1915- , q.v. Other pseudonyms: Danielle Dorsett, Angela Gray, Cynthia Kavanaugh, Suzanne Somers, Geraldine Thayer, qq.v.
House of False Faces. Paperback Library, 1967 [La., 1860s]
Mystic Manor. Paperback Library, 1966 [N.Y., 1890]

WESTON, JOHN (HARRISON). 1932- . Ref: CA.
The Walled Parrot. McGraw, 1975

WEST-WATSON, KEITH CAMPBELL. Pseudonym: Keith Campbell, q.v.

WESTWOOD, A(NNE) M(cDOUGALL). 1887- .
The Flying Firs. Hurst, 1930

WETHERELL, JUNE (PAT). 1909- .
The Cottage at Avalanche. Popular Library, 1972 [Wash.]
Her Stepfather's House. Lancer, 1972 [N.Y.]
House by the Bay. Dell, 1971
The House of Cabra. Belmont, 1966
Legacy of the Lost. Lancer, 1970
The Mahogany House. Manor, 1976
Maiden of Glory Island. Berkley, 1976 [Carib.]
Night of Secrets. Dell, 1977
Opal Street. Lancer, 1967
13 Winston Street. Popular Library, 1971
A Touch of the Witch. Lancer, 1969
When the Century Blooms. Avon, 1973
Willoughby Manor. Ballantine, 1974

WEVERKA, ROBERT. 1926- . Pseudonym: Robert McMahon; see Leo Bergson. Ref: CA.
Griff. Bantam, 1973 (Novelization of the TV movie.) [L.A.]
Moonrock. Bantam (NYC), 1973; Bantam (London), 1975 (Novelization of the "Search" TV series.)
Murder by Decree. Ballantine, 1979; Corgi, 1979 (Novelization of the movie.) (Sherlock Holmes.)
One Minute to Eternity. Morrow, 1969 [Mex.]
Search. Bantam, 1973 (Novelization of the TV series.)
Spectre. Bantam, 1979 (Novelization of the movie.)
The Sting. Bantam, 1973; Corgi, 1973 (Novelization of the movie.) [Chi.]

WEXLER, WARREN. See: John Paul Hudson.

WEXLEY, JOHN. 1907-
    The Last Mile. French (NYC), 1930 (3-act play.)

WEYMAN, STANLEY J(OHN). 1855-1928.
    The Man in Black. Cassell (London & NYC), 1894 [Fr., 1637]

WEYMOUTH, ANTHONY. Pseudonym of Ivo Geikie Cobb, 1887-   . Ref: CC. A doctor. SC: Insp. Treadgold = T. Set: Eng.
    Cornish Crime. Hodder pb, 1943 T
    The Doctors Are Doubtful. Barker, 1935 T
    Frozen Death. Barker, 1934 T
    Hard Liver. Barker, 1936 T
    Inspector Treadgold Investigates. Rich, 1941 ss T
    No, Sir Jeremy. Barker, 1935 T
    Surgical Emergency: Tales Told by a Doctor. Littlebury, 1951 ss, some criminous
    Tempt Me Not. Rich, 1937 T

WHALEY, BARTON. Pseudonym: S. W. Barton. See: Michael (J.) Kurland, 1938-   .

WHALEY, CHARLES N(ORMAN), 1940-   , and TERRY W(AYMAN) LYNCH, 1940-   .
    The Erring Way. Carlton, 1960

WHALEY, F(RANCIS) J(OHN). 1897-1977. Ref: CC. Set: Eng.
    Challenge to Murder. Skeffington, 1937
    Death at Datchets. Hale, 1941
    Enter a Spy. Hale, 1941
    The Mystery of Number Five. Hale, 1940
    Reduction of Staff. Skeffington, 1936 [acad.]
    Southern Electric Murder. Skeffington, 1938
    Swift Solution. Hale, 1939
    This Path Is Dangerous. Hale, 1938
    Trouble in College. Skeffington, 1936 [acad.]

WHARTON, ALTHEA
    The White Ghost of Fenwick Hall. PB, 1974 [N.Y.]

WHARTON, ANTHONY. Pseudonym of Alister McAlister, 1877-1943. Other pseudonym: Lynn Brock, q.v.
    The Two of Diamonds. Collins, 1926 [Fr.]

WHEATLEY, CHRIS
    Baby, Don't Get Rough. Gray, 1953
    Dames, Diamonds and Death! Grayling, 1951
    Date for a Dame. Gray, 1951
    Dizzy Dames Die Fast. Gray, 1951
    Hot Dames—Cold Lead. Grayling, 1951
    Murder at the Blue Garter. Gray, 1951
    Never Trust a Dame. Gray, 1956
    This Dame Spells Death. Grayling, 1950

WHEATLEY, DENNIS (YATES). 1897-1977. Ref: CA, CC, EM, MC, TC. SC: Roger Brook, in at least those marked RB; Julian Day, in at least those marked JD; Duke de Richleau, in at least those marked DR; Gregory Sallust, in at least those marked GS.
    Bill for the Use of a Body. Hutchinson, 1964 JD [H. Kong, Jap.]
    Black August. Hutchinson, 1934; Dutton, 1934 GS [Eng., future]
    The Black Baroness. Hutchinson, 1940; Macmillan, 1942 GS
    Code Word—Golden Fleece. Hutchinson, 1946 DR [Pol., 1939]
    Come into My Parlour. Hutchinson, 1946 GS [Russ., 1941]
    Contraband. Hutchinson, 1936 GS [Fr.]
    Curtain of Fear. Hutchinson, 1953 [Prague]
    Dangerous Inheritance. Hutchinson, 1965 DR [Cey., Greece]
    The Dark Secret of Josephine. Hutchinson, 1955 RB [W.I., 1793-4]
    Desperate Measures. Hutchinson, 1974 RB [Belg., Paris, 1814-5]
    The Devil Rides Out. Hutchinson, 1935; Hutchinson (U.S.), 1978 DR
    The Eunich of Stamboul. Hutchinson, 1935; Little, 1935 [Istan.]
    Evil in a Mask. Hutchinson, 1969 RB [Russ., Port., 1806-09]
    The Fabulous Valley. Hutchinson, 1934 [S. Am.]
    Faked Passports. Hutchinson, 1940; Macmillan, 1943 GS [Ger.]
    File on Bolitho Blane; see Murder Off Miami
    File on Robert Prentice; see Who Killed Robert Prentice?
    The Forbidden Territory. Hutchinson, 1933; Dutton, 1933 DR [Russ.]
    Gateway to Hell. Hutchinson, 1970; Ballantine, 1973 DR [Arg., 1953]
    The Golden Spaniard. Hutchinson, 1938 DR [Sp.]
    Gunmen, Gallants, and Ghosts. Hutchinson, 1943 ss
    The Haunting of Toby Jugg. Hutchinson, 1948; Hutchinson (U.S.), 1978
    Herewith the Clues! Hutchinson, 1939
    The Irish Witch. Hutchinson, 1973 RB [U.S., Ire., 1812-14]
    The Island Where Time Stands Still. Hutchinson, 1954 GS [China]
    The Ka of Gifford Hillary. Hutchinson, 1956; Hutchinson (U.S.), 1978
    The Launching of Roger Brook. Hutchinson, 1947 RB [Fr., Eng., 1783-87]
    The Malinsay Massacre. Hutchinson, 1938 [Scot.]
    The Man Who Killed the King. Hutchinson, 1951; Putnam, 1965 RB [Fr., 1793-4]
    The Man Who Missed the War. Hutchinson, 1945 [Antarctic]
    Mayhem in Greece. Hutchinson, 1962 [Greece]
    Mediterranean Nights. Hutchinson, 1942 ss
    Murder Off Miami. Hutchinson, 1936. U.S. title: File on Bolitho Blane. Morrow, 1936 [ship]
    The Prisoner in the Mask. Hutchinson, 1957 DR [Paris, 1890s]
    The Quest of Julian Day. Hutchinson, 1939 JD [Egypt]
    The Rape of Venice. Hutchinson, 1959 RB [India, Venice, 1796-98]
    The Ravishing of Lady Mary Ware. Hutchinson, 1971 RB [Port., Russ., 1809-12]
    The Rising Storm. Hutchinson, 1949 RB [Naples, Fr., 1789-92]
    The Satanist. Hutchinson, 1960; Ballantine, 1974
    The Scarlet Imposter. Hutchinson, 1940; Macmillan, 1942 GS [Ger.]
    The Second Seal. Hutchinson, 1950 DR [Vienna, Ger., 1914]
    The Secret War. Hutchinson, 1937 [Afr., N.]
    The Shadow of Tyburn Tree. Hutchinson, 1948; Ballantine, 1973 RB [Scand., Russ., 1787-9]
    Sixty Days to Live. Hutchinson, 1939
    Star of Ill-Omen. Hutchinson, 1952 [S. Am.]
    Strange Conflict. Hutchinson, 1941; Hutchinson (U.S.), 1978 DR [Haiti]
    The Strange Story of Linda Lee. Hutchinson, 1972 [Can., U.S.]
    Such Power Is Dangerous. Hutchinson, 1933; Hutchinson (U.S.), 1979 [L.A.]
    The Sultan's Daughter. Hutchinson, 1963 RB [Egypt, Fr., 1798-9]
    The Sword of Fate. Hutchinson, 1941; Macmillan, 1944 JD [Afr., N.]
    They Found Atlantis. Hutchinson, 1936; Lippincott, 1936 [Azores]
    They Used Dark Forces. Hutchinson, 1964; Hutchinson (U.S.), 1978 GS [Ger., 1943]
    Three Inquisitive People. Hutchinson, 1940 DR
    To the Devil—a Daughter. Hutchinson, 1953; Hutchinson (U.S.), 1978 [Fr.]
    Traitor's Gate. Hutchinson, 1958 GS [Hung., 1942]
    Uncharted Seas. Hutchinson, 1938 [ship]
    Unholy Crusade. Hutchinson, 1967 [Mex.]
    "V" for Vengeance. Hutchinson, 1942; Macmillan, 1942 GS [Paris]
    Vendetta in Spain. Hutchinson, 1961 DR [Sp.]
    The Wanton Princess. Hutchinson, 1966; Hutchinson (U.S.), 1979 RB [1800-05]
    The White Witch of the South Seas. Hutchinson, 1968 GS [S. Pac.]
    Who Killed Robert Prentice? Hutchinson, 1937. U.S. title: File on Robert Prentice. Greenberg, 1937

WHEELER, BENSON, 1905-   , and CLAIRE LEE PURDY, 1906-   .
    The Riddle of the Eighth Guest. Speller, 1936

WHEELER, EDW(ARD) L(YTTON). 1854?-1885. Ref: EM.
    Deadwood Dick's Last Shot. Ogilvie, 1902
    Fritz, the Bound Boy Detective. Westbrook, ca.1920
    Fritz to the Front. Westbrook, ca.1920
    The Frontier Detective. Westbrook, ca.1920
    The Heart of Oak Detective. Westbrook, ca.1920

WHEELER, FRANCIS
    Sylvanian Adventure. Hurst, 1939

WHEELER, GORDON. Raised in Tex., educated at Harvard and Boston College; child psychologist.
    Easy Come. Random, 1974 [Mass.]

WHEELER, H. E. SC: Kendal Graydon, in at least those marked KG; Stephen Rant, in at least those marked SR. Set: Eng.
    Dead Men Turn Green. Jenkins, 1939 KG
    Death Calls the Jester. Jenkins, 1936 KG
    Death Takes a Ride. Jenkins, 1942 SR
    No Crime Is Perfect. Jenkins, 1935
    The Syndicate of Death. Jenkins, 1937
    The Third Attempt. Jenkins, 1946 SR

WHEELER, HUGH CALLINGHAM. 1913-   . Joint pseudonyms with Richard Wilson Webb, 1901-   : Q. Patrick, Patrick Quentin, Jonathan Stagge, qq.v.
    Sweeney Todd, the Demon Barber of Fleet Street. Dodd, 1979 (Play.)
    We Have Always Lived in the Castle. Dramatists, 1967 (3-act play based on the novel by Shirley Jackson, 1920-1965, q.v.)

WHEELER, KEITH. 1911-   . Ref: CA.
    Epitaph for Mister Wynn. Putnam, 1971; Hodder, 1972
    The Last Mayday. Doubleday, 1968; Hodder, 1969

WHEELER, PAUL. 1934-   . Ref: CA.
    And the Bullets Were Made of Lead. Hutchinson, 1968; Doubleday, 1969 [Paris]
    Ransom. Fontana, 1975; Ballantine, 1974. Also published as: The Terrorists. Tempo, 1975 (Novelization of the movie.)

WHEELER, SAMUEL WATSON
    Count de Mornay; or, Back from the Dead. (Author), 1894

WHEELER-NICHOLSON, MALCOLM. 1890-   .
    Death over London. Gateway, 1940

WHEELOCK, DOROTHY
    Dead Giveaway. Phoenix, 1942 [NYC]
    Murder at Montauk. Phoenix, 1940 [L.I.]

WHELTON, PAUL. Born in Boston, and living near Boston in late 1940s; a rewrite man on large city newspapers. SC: Garry Dean, in all titles.
    Angels Are Painted Fair. Lippincott, 1947; Foulsham, 1951. Also published as (?): Lures of Death. Graphic, 1950
    Call the Lady Indiscreet. Lippincott, 1946; Aldor, 1946
    Death and the Devil. Lippincott, 1944. Also published as: Flash—Hold for Murder. Graphic, 1949
    Flash—Hold for Murder; see Death and the Devil
    In Comes Death. Lippincott, 1951; Gifford, 1952
    Lures of Death; see Angels Are Painted Fair
    Pardon My Blood. Lippincott, 1950; Gifford, 1951
    Uninvited Corpse; see Women Are Skin Deep
    Women Are Skin Deep. Lippincott, 1948; Foulsham, 1951. Also published as (?): Uninvited Corpse. Graphic, 1950

WHELTON, CLARK
    CB Baby. Avon, 1976

WHIPPLE, KENNETH. 1894-   .
    The Fires at Fitch's Folly. Crowell, 1935 [New Eng.]
    The Killings in Carter Cave. King, 1934 [Va.]
    The Murders at Loon Lake. King, 1933 [New Eng.]

WHISHAW, FRED(ERICK J.)
    -The Adventures of a Stowaway. Griffith, 1897
    -The Brothers of the People. Pearson, 1898
    -Called Back to Tsarland. Jarrolds, 1899
    -The Caxborough Scandal. White, 1910
    -Clutterbuck's Treasure. Griffith, 1898
    -Countess Ida. Long, 1904
    -The Degenerate. Everett, 1909
    -The Diamond of Evil. Long, 1902 [S. Afr.]
    -A Fool with Women. Long, 1904
    -The Great Green God. White, 1906
    -The Heart of Noel. Everett, 1910
    -Her Highness. Long, 1906

The Informer. Long, 1905
-Lost Sir Brian. Wells Gardner, 1903
-Lovers at Fault. White, 1904
-The Madness of Gloria. Digby, 1907
-Mazeppa. Chatto, 1902
-My Terrible Twin. Arrowsmith, 1896
-Mystery Island. Shaw, 1904
-The Patriots. Digby, 1906
-The Persecuted. Laurie, 1907
-A Race for Life. Griffith, 1898
-The Revolt of Beatrix. Long, 1908
-The Romance of the Woods. Longmans, 1895
-A Royal Hoax. Everett, 1908
-A Russian Coward. Laurie, 1906
-A Russian Judas. White, 1911
-A Secret of Berry Pomeroy. Griffith, 1902
-The Secret Syndicate. Long, 1907
-A Splendid Imposter. Chatto, 1903
-A Village Temptress. Everett, 1909
-The Vortex. Paul, 1909
-The White Witch of the Matabele. Griffith, 1897
The Yellow Satchel. Routledge, 1903; Dutton, 1903

WHITAKER, BERYL (SALISBURY). 1916- .
SC: John Abbot, in all titles.
The Chained Crocodile. Hale, 1967
The Man Who Wasn't There. Hale, 1968
A Matter of Blood. Hale, 1967
Of Mice and Murder. Hale, 1967

WHITAKER, C(UTHBERT) W(ILFRID)
The Gift of Hermes. Blackwood, 1924
-The House of Lyes. Blackwood, 1923

WHITAKER, H(ERMAN). 1867-1919.
The Mystery of the Barranca. Harper (NYC & London), 1913 [Mex.]
-Over the Border. Harper (NYC & London), 1909

WHITAKER, LEO
Return to Hawkeston Hall. Major, 1975 [Vt.]

WHITAKER, RODNEY W. 1925- . Pseudonym: Trevanian, q.v.

WHITE, ALAN. 1924- . Pseudonyms: James Fraser, Alec Whitney, qq.v. Ref: CA, CC. SC: Det. Insp. Armstrong, in at least those marked A.
Armstrong. Barrie, 1973; Doubleday, 1977, as by Alec Whitney A
Cassidy's Yard. Granada, 1980
Climate of Revolt. Barrie, 1971
Death Finds the Day; see The Long Day's Dying
Death in Darkness. Barrie, 1975; Doubleday, 1977, as by Alec Whitney A
Death in Duplicate. Barrie, 1974 A
-Kibbutz. Barrie, 1970. U.S. title: Possess the Land. Harcourt, 1970
The Long Day's Dying. Hodder, 1965. U.S. title: Death Finds the Day. Harcourt, 1965
The Long Drop. Jenkins, 1969; Harcourt, 1970 [Belg., WWII]
The Long Fuse. Barrie, 1973; Harcourt, 1974
-The Long Hand of Death. Barrie, 1977 [WWII]
The Long Midnight. Barrie, 1972; Harcourt, 1974
The Long Night's Work. Hodder, 1968; Harcourt, 1969 [Ger., WWII]
-The Long Silence. Barrie, 1976; Mason/Charter, 1977
The Long Summer. Barrie, 1974; Harcourt, 1975
The Long Watch. Barrie, 1971; Harcourt, 1971
Possess the Land; see Kibbutz
-The Wheel. Hodder, 1966; Harcourt, 1967

WHITE, ALICEN. Ref: CA.
Dirge for a Lady. Lancer, 1968
Evil That Walks Invisible. Dell, 1973 [Eng.]
Nor Spell Nor Charm. Lancer, 1971
The Traitor Within. Dell, 1974
The Watching Eye. Dell, 1977 [Madeira]

WHITE, ARED. SC: Captain Fox Elton = FE.
Agent B-7. Houghton, 1934; Eyre, 1935 FE
Seven Tickets to Singapore. Houghton, 1939; Rich, 1941
The Spy Net. Houghton, 1931; Eyre, 1931 FE [Switz.]

WHITE, EDWARD LUCAS. 1866-1934.
-Lukundoo, and other stories. Doran, 1927; Benn, 1927 ss

WHITE, ETHEL LINA. 1887-1944. See also: F(rederic) Andrew Leslie, 1927- .
Ref: CC, EM, MC, MP, TC. Set: Eng.
The Elephant Never Forgets. Collins, 1937; Harper, 1938
Fear Stalks the Village. Ward, 1932; Harper, 1942
The First Time He Died. Collins, 1935
Her Heart in Her Throat; see Midnight House
The Lady Vanishes; see The Wheel Spins
The Man Who Loved Lions. Collins, 1943. U.S. title: The Man Who Was Not There. Harper, 1943
The Man Who Was Not There; see The Man Who Loved Lions
Midnight House. Collins, 1942. U.S. title: Her Heart in Her Throat. Harper, 1942. Also published as: The Unseen. Paperback Library, 1966
Put Out the Light. Ward, 1931; Harper, 1933. Also published as: Sinister Light. Paperback Library, 1966
She Faded into Air. Collins, 1941; Harper, 1941
Sinister Light; see Put Out the Light
Some Must Watch. Ward, 1933; Harper, 1941. Also published as: The Spiral Staircase. World, 1946
The Spiral Staircase; see Some Must Watch
Step in the Dark. Collins, 1938; Harper, 1939 [Swed.]
They See in Darkness. Collins, 1944
The Third Eye. Collins, 1937; Harper, 1937
The Unseen; see Midnight House
Wax. Collins, 1935; Doubleday, 1935
The Wheel Spins. Collins, 1936; Harper, 1936. Also published as: The Lady Vanishes. Paperback Library, 1966
While She Sleeps. Collins, 1940; Harper, 1940

WHITE, FRED(ERICK) M(ERRICK). 1859- .
Set: Eng.
Ambition's Slave. Ward, 1916
The Argus Eye. Ward, 1919
Blackmail! Ward, 1918
The Brand of Silence. Ward, 1911
A Broken Memory. Long, 1930
The Cardinal Moth. Ward, 1905; Street, 19??
The Case for the Crown. Ward, 1919
Claxton's Mill. Ward, 1912
A Clue in Wax. Ward, 1930
The Corner House. Ward, 1906; Fenno, 1906
The Councillors of Falconhoe. Ward, 1924
Craven Fortune. Ward, 1908
A Crime on Canvas. Ward, 1909; Fenno, 1909
The Crimson Blind. Ward, 1905; Fenno, 1905. Also published as: The Mystery of the Crimson Blind. Westbrook, ca. 1911
A Deal in Letters. Long, 1923
The Devil's Advocate. Long, 1930
Dropped from the Fast Express; or, A Daughter's Sacrifice. Laird, 1911 (British title?)
The Edge of the Sword. Ward, 1908
The Ends of Justice. Ward, 1916
A Fatal Dose. Ward, 1907
The Fight for the Child. Long, 1925
The Five Knots. Ward, 1910; Little, 1908
The Four Fingers. Ward, 1911. U.S. title: The Mystery of the Four Fingers. Watt, 1908
A Front of Brass. Ward, 1912
The Garden o' Dreams. Ward, 1909
The Golden Bat. Shoe Lane, 19??
The Golden Rose. Ward, 1913
The Green Bungalow. Long, 1930
The Grey Woman. Ward, 1928
The Happy Exile. Skeffington, 1920
A Harbour of Refuge. Ward, 1918
Hard Pressed. Ward, 1913; Fenno, 1910
The Honour of His House. Ward, 1921
The House of Mammon. Ward, 1914
A House of Sorrows. Ward, 1911
Jim Crowshaw's Mary. Ward, 1913
The King Diamond. Ward, 1927
Lady Clara. Ward, 1913
The Lady in Blue. Ward, 1918
The Law of the Land. Ward, 1908
The Leopard's Spots. Ward, 1920
The Lord of the Manor. Ward, 1908
Love, the Foe. Ward, 1911
The Man Called Gillray. Ward, 1912
The Man Who Was Two. Ward, 1922
The Man with the Vandyk Beard. Long, 1925
A Matter of Millions. Ward, 1909
The Midnight Guest. Cassell, 1907; McBride, 1907
My Lady Bountiful. Ward, 1915
The Mystery of the Crimson Blind; see The Crimson Blind

The Mystery of the Four Fingers; see The Four Fingers
The Mystery of the Ravenspurs. Ward, 1912; Ogilvie, 1911
The Nether Millstone. Little, 1907 (British title?)
Netta. Ward, 1909
Number 13. Ward, 1914
On the Night Express. Long, 1930
The Open Door. Ward, 1912
Paul Quentin. Ward, 1915
Paul, the Sage. Ward, 1910
The Phantom Car. Ward, 1929
Powers of Darkness. Ward, 1915
The Psalm Stone. Ward, 1923
A Queen of the Stage. Ward, 1911
The Riddle of the Rail. Ward, 1926
The Robe of Lucifer. Innes, 1896 ss
A Royal Wrong. Ward, 1913
The Salt of the Earth. Ward, 1916
The Scales of Justice. Ward, 1909; Kearney, 1909
The Secret of the Sands. Ward, 1912
The Seed of Empire. Ward, 1916
The Sentence of the Court. Ward, 1917
A Shadowed Love. Ward, 1914
The Slave of Silence. Ward, 1907; Little, 1906
A Society Jezebel. Ward, 1917
The Sundial. Ward, 1910; Dodge, 1908
Tregarthen's Wife. Newnes, 1901
The Turn of the Tide. Ward, 1923
The Weight of the Crown. Ward, 1906; Fenno, 1906
The White Bride. Ward, 1910
The White Glove. Ward, 1919
The Wings of Victory. Ward, 1921
The Yellow Face. White, 1906; Fenno, 1907

WHITE, GEORGE M. Pseudonym of J(ames) M(organ) Walsh, 1897-1952, q.v. Other pseudonyms: H. Haverstock Hill, Stephen Maddock, qq.v.
The Mystery of the Crystal Skull. Hamilton, 1926. Reprinted as by J. M. Walsh: Hamilton, 1929

WHITE, GERTRUDE MASON. 1915- . Pseudonym: R. I. Wakefield, q.v.

WHITE, GRACE MILLER.   -1965.
-The Confessions of a Wife. Ogilvie, 1905
Convict 999. Ogilvie, 1907
-Dangers of Working Girls. Ogilvie, 1904
-Fast Life in New York. Ogilvie, 1905 [NYC]
-From the Valley of the Missing. Watt, 1911; Hutchinson, 1912
-The Ghost of Glen George. Macaulay, 1925; Hodder, 1926
The Great Express Robbery. Ogilvie, 1907
The House of Mystery. Ogilvie, 1905
Kidnapped for Revenge. Ogilvie
The King of the Opium Ring. Ogilvie, 1901
The Life That Kills. Ogilvie
Lured from Home. Ogilvie, 1906
-A Marked Woman. Ogilvie, 1907
-New York by Night. Ogilvie, 1904 [NYC]
-Prisoner of War. Ogilvie, 1904
The Queen of the White Slaves. Ogilvie, 1904
-Ruled Off the Turf. Ogilvie, 1906
Secrets of the Police. Ogilvie, 1906 (Play.)
-The Secret of the Storm Country. Fly, 1917; Hodder, 1924
The Square Mark, with H(ilda) L. Deakin, q.v. Dutton, 1930; Methuen, 1929
-The Warning Bell. Ogilvie, 1905 (Play.)
-When Tragedy Grins. Watt, 1912; Palmer, 1916

WHITE, HERBERT OLIVER. 1885- . Pseudonym: Oliver Martyn, q.v.

WHITE, JAMES DILLON. Pseudonym of Stanley White, 1913- . Other pseudonym: Felix Krull, q.v. Ref: CA. SC: Sebastian Kettle, in at least those marked SK.
The Brandenburg Affair. Hutchinson (London & U.S.), 1979 SK
-The Edge of the Forest. Heinemann, 1952
Fair Wind to Malabar. Hutchinson (London & U.S.), 1978
-Flamingo Lake. Heinemann, 1954
-The Hound of Heaven. Hutchinson, 1966
The Leipzig Affair. Hutchinson, 1974
-Lords of Human Kind. Hutchinson, 1971
Night on the Bare Mountain. Heinemann, 1957
-The Princess of Persia. Hutchinson, 1961
-The Quiet River. Heinemann, 1953
-The Running Lions. Hutchinson, 1972
The Salzberg Affair. Hutchinson (London & U.S.), 1977 SK

-The Spoletta Story. Heinemann, 1952
-A Spread of Sail. Hutchinson, 1975
-A Stranger in Town. Heinemann, 1953
Sweet Evil. Hutchinson, 1968

WHITE, JAMES P(ATRICK). 1940-   . See: Anne Reed Rooth.

WHITE, JOHN B(LAKE). 1781-1859.
The Mysteries of the Castle; or, The Victim of Revenge. (Author), 1807 (5-act play.)

WHITE, JON (EWBANK) MANCHIP. 1924-   .
Ref: CA, TC. SC: Colonel Rickman = R.
The Game of Troy. Chatto, 1971; McKay, 1971 R [Tex.]
The Garden Game. Chatto, 1973; Bobbs, 1974 R
The Mercenaries. Long, 1958; Major, 1979
The Moscow Papers. Major, 1979 (British title?)
Nightclimber. Chatto, 1968; Morrow, 1968 R
-The Robinson Factor. Panther, 1976
Send for Mr. Robinson. Panther, 1974; Pinnacle, 1975

WHITE, KENNETH. 1905-1953.
The Visitor. Dramatic, 1945 (Play based on the novel by Carl Randau, 1893-1969, q.v., and Leane Zugsmith, 1903-1969.)

WHITE, LESLIE T(URNER). 1903-   . Ref: CA. SC: Capt. Barnaby = B.
5,000 Trojan Horses. World's Work, 1943
Harness Bull. Harcourt, 1937; Hamilton, 1938. Also published as: Vice Squad. Bestseller, 1954 B
Homicide. Harcourt, 1937; Hamilton, 1938 B
Me, Detective. Harcourt, 1936 [L.A.]
River of Fear; see The River of No Return
The River of No Return. Macrae Smith, 1941; World's Work, 1947. Also published as: River of Fear. Adventure Novel Classic, 194?
Six Weeks South of Texas. World's Work, 1948
Vice Squad; see Harness Bull

WHITE, LIONEL. 1905-   . Pseudonym: Nick Carter, q.v. Ref: CC, TC.
Before I Die; see To Find a Killer
The Big Caper. GM, 1955; Fawcett (London), 1956
Clean Break. Dutton, 1955; Boardman, 1955. Also published as: The Killing. Signet, 1956 [L.I.]
Coffin for a Hood. GM, 1958; Fawcett (London), 1959
The Crimshaw Memorandum. Dutton, 1967; Macdonald, 1968 [Md.]
A Death at Sea. Dutton, 1961; Boardman, 1962 [Fla.]
Death of a City. Bobbs, 1970; Hale, 1972 [South]
Death Takes the Bus. GM, 1957; Fawcett (London), 1958 [Calif.]
Flight into Terror. Dutton, 1955; Boardman, 1957 [Fla., NYC]
A Grave Undertaking. Dutton, 1961; Boardman, 1962 [NYC]
Hijack. Macfadden, 1969; Hale, 1970
Hostage for a Hood. GM, 1957; Fawcett (London), 1958
The House Next Door. Dutton, 1956; Boardman, 1958 [N.Y.]
The House on K Street. Dutton, 1965; Boardman, 1966 [Wash. D.C.]
Invitation to Violence. Dutton, 1958; Boardman, 1958 [L.I.]
Jailbreak. Hale, 1976
The Killing; see Clean Break
Lament for a Virgin. GM, 1960; Muller, 1960 [Fla.]
Love Trap. Signet, 1955
Marilyn K. Monarch, 1960 [Md.]
The Merriweather File. Dutton, 1959; Boardman, 1960 [L.I.]
The Mexico Run. GM, 1974 [Mex.]
The Money Trap. Dutton, 1963; Boardman, 1964 [NYC]
The Night of the Rape. Dutton, 1967; Hale, 1969 [Del.]
Obsession. Dutton, 1962; Boardman, 1963
Operation—Murder. GM, 1956; Fawcett (London), 1958 [Colo.]
A Party to Murder. GM, 1966; Jenkins, 1968 [NYC]
Rafferty. Dutton, 1959; Boardman, 1960
The Ransomed Madonna. Dutton, 1964; Boardman, 1965
A Rich and Dangerous Game. McKay, 1974 [ship]
Right for Murder. Boardman, 1957 (U.S. title?)
Run, Killer, Run. Avon, 1959

The Snatchers. GM, 1953; Red Seal, 1958 [L.I.]
Steal Big. GM, 1960; Muller, 1961 [NYC]
The Time of Terror. Dutton, 1960; Boardman, 1961 [L.I.]
To Find a Killer. Dutton, 1954; Boardman, 1956. Also published as: Before I Die. Tower, 1964 [NYC]
Too Young to Die. GM, 1958; Fawcett (London), 1959 [NYC]

WHITE, MARION. 1901-   .
Out of the Night. Mill, 1938 [NYC]

WHITE, OSMAR (EGMONT DORKIN). 1909-   . Ref: CA.
A Silent Reach. Macmillan (London), 1978; Scribner, 1980 [Australia]

WHITE, PALMER. Pseudonym of Theodore James Spry, 1898-   .
-The Circle of Confusion. Chapman, 1930
-Mystery Island. Chapman, 1930

WHITE, PERCY. 1852-   .
-Corruption. Heinemann, 1895; Appleton, 1895
-The Grip of the Bookmaker. Hutchinson, 1901
-The Heart of the Dancer. Hutchinson, 1900
-The House of Intrigue. Hurst, 1909

WHITE, R.
Corollary to Murder. Stockwell, 1942

WHITE, R(EGINALD) J(AMES). 1905-1971.
Ref: CA. SC: Insp. David Brock = DB.
A Second-Hand Tomb. Macmillan (London), 1971; Harper, 1971
The Smartest Grave. Collins, 1961; Harper, 1961 DB [Eng., 1901)
The Women of Peasenhall. Macmillan (London), 1969; Harper, 1969 DB [Eng., 1902]

WHITE, SAMUEL ALEXANDER. 1885-   .
Morgan of the Mounted. Phoenix, 1939; Coker, 1949 [Can.]
Nighthawk of the Northwest. Phoenix, 1938; Foulsham, 1944 [Can.]
North of the Law. Doubleday, 1920
Northwest Law. Phoenix, 1942. British title: Northwest Patrol. Coker, 1949 [Can.]
Northwest Patrol; see Northwest Law
-Secret Harbour. Doubleday, 1926; Hodder, 1926

WHITE, STANLEY. 1913-   . Pseudonyms: Felix Krull, James Dillon White, qq.v.

WHITE, STEWART EDWARD. 1873-1946. SC: Percy Darrow, in both titles.
-The Mystery, with Samuel Hopkins Adams, 1871-1958, q.v. McClure, 1907; Hodder, 1907
-The Sign at Six. Bobbs, 1912; Hodder, 1912 [NYC]

WHITE, T(HOMAS) H(ENRY)
Bellgrove Castle; or, The Horrid Spectre! Minerva, 1803

WHITE, T(ERENCE) H(ANBURY). 1906-1964.
Ref: CA. Set: Eng.
Darkness at Pemberly. Gollancz, 1932; Century, 1933
Dead Mr. Nixon, with R. McNair Scott. Cassell, 1931
-Gone to Ground. Collins, 1935

WHITE, TERENCE DeVERE. 1912-   . Ref: CA.
My Name Is Norval. Gollancz, 1978; Harper, 1979 [Ire.]

WHITE, TRENTWELL MASON. 1901-   .
The Thing in the Road. Marshall Jones, 1930

WHITE, VALERIE. SC: John Case = JC.
Case. Barker, 1954
Case for Treachery. Barker, 1955
Lost Person. Heinemann, 1957

WHITE, W(ILLIAM) J(OHN). 1920-   .
The Devil You Know. Cape, 1962
The Hard Man. Cape, 1958
One for the Road. Cape, 1956 [Dublin]

WHITE, W(ILLIAM EDWARD BRADDON) HOLT. 1878-   . See: W(illiam Edward Braddon) Holt-White, 1878-   .

WHITE, WILLIAM ANTHONY PARKER. 1911-1968. Pseudonyms: Anthony Boucher, H. H. Holmes, qq.v. See also: Theo Durrant.

WHITE, WILLIAM PATTERSON. 1884-   .
Cloudy in the West. Little, 1928; Hodder, 1928

WHITECHURCH, VICTOR L(ORENZO). 1868-1933.
Ref: CC, EM, MM, MP, TC. Set: Eng.
The Adventures of Captain Ivan Koravitch. Blackwood, 1925 ss
The Canon in Residence. Unwin, 1904; Baker, 1911
The Crime at Diana's Pool. Unwin, 1927; Duffield, 1927
Murder at Exbridge; see Murder at the College
Murder at the College. Collins, 1932. U.S. title: Murder at Exbridge. Dodd, 1932 [acad.]
Murder at the Pageant. Collins, 1930; Duffield, 1931
The Robbery at Rudwick House. Duffield 1929
Shot on the Downs. Unwin, 1927; Duffield, 1928
Stories of the Railway; see Thrilling Stories of the Railway
The Templeton Case. Long, 1924; Clode, 1924
Thrilling Stories of the Railway. Pearson, 1912. Also published as: Stories of the Railway. Routledge, 1977 ss

WHITED, CHARLES
The Brandon Affair. Signet, 1977

WHITEHEAD, JANE
The House on the Hill. Lancer, 1967 [Ill.]

WHITEHOUSE, ARCHIBALD. Pseudonym of Arthur George Joseph Whitehouse, 1895-1979. Ref: CA.
Crime on a Convoy Carrier. World's Work, 1943
-Wings of Adventure. Hamilton, 1936

WHITEHOUSE, ARTHUR GEORGE JOSEPH. 1895-1979. Pseudonym: Archibald Whitehouse, q.v.

WHITEHOUSE, WESLEY L(EONARD). ca.1915-   .
In insurance business, a County Magistrate, in Eng.
Confidential Mission. Robertson, 1951
The Man from Australia. Robertson, 1953

WHITEHURST, BEN and FAITH WILEY
Death on Capitol Hill. Vantage, 1970 [Wash. D.C.]

WHITELAW, DAVID. Set: Eng.
The Big Picture. Bles, 1936
Black Out. Hutchinson, 1928
Black-Out Murder. Bles, 1943
Blackmail de Luxe. Bles, 1939
A Castle in Bohemia. Hodder, 1914
The Face. Bles, 1937
The Feud. Bles, 1937
A Flutter in Kings. Hodder, 1916
For Conduct Unbefitting. Holden, 1925
Frame-Up. Bles, 1939
The Gang. Greening, 1908
Garments of Repentence. Macdonald, 1948
Girl Friday. Bles, 1940
The Girl from the East. Greening, 1912
A Hair of the Dog. Holden, 1925
Horace Steps Out. Bles, 1941
Horror on the Loch. Bles, 1938 [Scot.]
Hotel Sinister. Bles, 1935
The House in Cavendish Square. Macdonald, 1950
I Could a Tale Unfold. Jenkins, 1957; Roy, 1959
The Imposter. Hodder, 1915
-The Island of Romance. Holden, 1926
The Jackal. Bles, 1940
The League of St. Louis. Hodder, 1913 [Fr.]
Legacy in Green. Macdonald, 1954
The Lexicon Murders. Macdonald, 1945
-The Little Hour of Peter Wells. Hodder, 1913
-Little Lady of Arrock. Chapman, 1921
Lovers in Waiting. Macdonald, 1947
-MacStodger's Affinity. Greening, 1906
Madcap Betty. Hutchinson, 1927
The Madgwick Affair. Ward, 1918
The Man from Mexico City. Hutchinson, 1927
The Man on the Dover Road. Hodder, 1919
The Man with the Red Beard. Greening, 1911
The Master of Merlains. Ward, 1918
-Moon of Valleys. Greening, 1909
The Moor. Macdonald, 1949
Murder Besieged. Macdonald, 1953
Murder Calling. Bles, 1934; Kendall, 1934
Murder in Motley. Bles, 1935 [U.S.]
Mystery at Furze Acres. Nash, 1929
The Mystery of Enid Belairs. Hodder, 1915. Also published as: The Odean Theatre Mystery. Shoe Lane, 19??

Number Fifteen. Nash, 1931
The Odean Theatre Mystery; see The Mystery of Enid Belairs
-Pirates' Gold. Hodder, 1920
Presumed Dead. Macdonald, 1952
The Princess Galva. Greening, 1910
The Roof. Bles, 1933
The Ryecroft Verdict. Macdonald, 1946
The Secret of Chauville. Greening, 1911
Spanish Heels. Grayson, 1932
-The Stones of Khor. Hutchinson, 1924
-The Valley of Bells. Jarrolds, 1918
The Villa Petroff. Hutchinson, 1926
Wolf's Crag. Bles, 1936
The Yellow Door. Macdonald, 1951

WHITELOCK, LOUISE CLARKSON. 1865-1928.
Pseudonym: L. Clarkson, q.v.

WHITFIELD, RAOUL. 1898-1945. Pseudonym: Temple Field, q.v.
Death in a Bowl. Knopf, 1931 [L.A.]
Green Ice. Knopf, 1930. Also published as: The Green Ice Murders. Avon, 1947 [Pitt.]
The Green Ice Murders; see Green Ice
The Virgin Kills. Knopf, 1932 [ship]

WHITING, CHARLES. 1926- . Spymaster series = S; Destroyer series = D.
The Big Breakout. Sphere, 1976
Double Cross. Futura, 1977 S
Highway Through Hell. Sphere, 1976
Kill Patton. Ballantine, 1974 (British title?)
The Last Mission. Sphere, 1976
Massacre at Metz. Sphere, 1976
Operation Afrika. Sphere, 1974; Pinnacle, 1975 D
Operation Caucasian Fox. Sphere, 1974 D
Operation Fox Hunt. Pinnacle, 1977 (British title?)
Operation Il Duce. Sphere, 1974 D
Operation Kill Ike. Sphere, 1975 D
Operation Stalag. Sphere, 1974; Pinnacle, 1976 D
Operation Werewolf. Sphere, 1975 D
Orders to Kill. Corgi, 1974
Wolf Hunt. Futura, 1976 S

WHITLACH, JOHN
Gannon's Line. PB, 1976 [Mex.]

WHITMAN, CHARLES. 1916- . SC: Insp. Lindon, in all titles.
Death Out of Focus. Cassell, 1970 [Australia]
Death Suspended. Cassell, 1971
Doctor Death. Cassell, 1970

WHITMAN, H(ENRY) E(SMOND) O(RAM). 1900- .
The Pirate of Pittsburgh. Houghton, 1925. British title: The High Jacker. Hodder, 1925 [ship]

WHITNEY, ALEC. Pseudonym of Alan White, 1924- , q.v. Other pseudonym: James Fraser, q.v.
Every Man Has His Price. Allen, 1968
-The Triple Zero. Allen, 1971

WHITNEY, E. G.
The Sleeping Cupid. Daily Mirror, 1967 (Novelization of "Man in a Suitcase" TV series.)

WHITNEY, J. L. H. Pseudonym of Jacquelyn Whitney Trimble, 1927- . Ref: CA.
The Whisper of Shadows. Ace, 1965 [Can.]

WHITNEY, PHYLLIS A(YAME). 1903- .
Ref: CA, EM, TC.
Black Amber. Appleton, 1964; Hale, 1965 [Istan.]
Blue Fire. Appleton, 1961; Hodder, 1962 [S. Afr.]
Columbella. Doubleday, 1966; Hale, 1967 [Vir. Is.]
Domino. Doubleday, 1979; Heinemann, 1980 [Colo.]
The Glass Flame. Doubleday, 1978; Heinemann, 1979 [Tenn.]
The Golden Unicorn. Doubleday, 1976; Heinemann, 1977 [L.I.]
Hunter's Green. Doubleday, 1968; Heinemann, 1969 [Eng.]
Listen for the Whisperer. Doubleday, 1972; Heinemann, 1972 [Nor.]
Lost Island. Doubleday, 1970; Heinemann, 1971 [Ga.]
The Mask and the Moonflower; see The Moonflower
The Moonflower. Appleton, 1958. British title: The Mask and the Moonflower. Hurst, 1960 [Jap.]
Poinciana. Doubleday, 1980; Heinemann, 1981 [Fla.]
The Quicksilver Pool. Appleton, 1955; Coronet, 1973 [NYC, ca.1860]
Red Carnelian; see Red Is for Murder

Red Is for Murder. Ziff-Davis, 1943. Also published as: Red Carnelian. Paperback Library, 1968; Coronet, 1976 [Chi.]
Sea Jade. Appleton, 1964; Hale, 1966 [New Eng., 1870s]
Seven Tears for Apollo. Appleton, 1963; Coronet, 1969 [Greece]
Silverhill. Doubleday, 1967; Heinemann, 1968 [N.H.]
Skye Cameron. Appleton, 1957; Hurst, 1959
Snowfire. Doubleday, 1973; Heinemann, 1973 [Pa.]
Spindrift. Doubleday, 1975; Heinemann, 1975 [Conn.]
The Stone Bull. Doubleday, 1977; Heinemann, 1977 [N.Y.]
Thunder Heights. Appleton, 1960; Coronet, 1973 [N.Y.]
The Trembling Hills. Appleton, 1956; Coronet, 1974 [S.F., 1906]
The Turquoise Mask. Doubleday, 1974; Heinemann, 1975 [Sante Fe]
Window on the Square. Appleton, 1962; Coronet, 1969 [NYC, 1870s]
The Winter People. Doubleday, 1969; Heinemann, 1970 [N.J.]

WHITNEY, STEVEN. 1946- . Ref: CA.
Singled Out. Morrow, 1978; New English Library, 1979 [NYC]

WHITSON, JOHN H(ARVEY). 1854-1936.
-The Castle of Doubt. Little, 1907

WHITTAKER, CAPT. FREDERICK. 1838-1889.
The Red Rajah. Westbrook, ca.1920
-Transgressing the Law. Bonner's, 1893

WHITTEN, LESLIE H(UNTER). 1928- . Ref: CA.
Death of a Nurse; see Moon of the Wolf
Moon of the Wolf. Doubleday, 1967. British title: Death of a Nurse. Hale, 1969 [Miss.]
Progeny of the Adder. Doubleday, 1965; Hodder, 1966 [Wash. D.C.]

WHITTINGTON, HARRY (BENJAMIN). 1915- .
Pseudonym: Whit Harrison, q.v. Ref: CA, TC.
-Across That River. Ace, 1957
Backwoods Tramp. GM, 1959; Muller pb, 1961
The Brass Monkey. Handi-Books, 1951 [Haw.]
Brute in Brass. GM, 1956; Red Seal, 1958
Burden's Mission. Avon, 1968 [Viet Nam]
Call Me Killer. Graphic, 1951
Connolly's Woman. GM, 1960; Muller pb, 1962
Cross the Red Creek. Avon, 1964
Desire in the Dust. GM, 1956; Fawcett (London), 1957
The Devil Wears Wings. Abelard (NYC and London), 1960
Die, Lover; see Vengeful Sinner
Don't Speak to Strange Girls. GM, 1963; Muller pb, 1963 [L.A.]
The Doomsday Affair. Ace, 1965; Four Square, 1965 (Novelization of "The Man from UNCLE" TV series.) [Calif.]
-Doomsday Mission. Banner, 1967
Drawn to Evil. Ace, 1952
Fires That Destroy. GM, 1951
God's Back Was Turned. GM, 1961; Muller pb, 1962
Guerrilla Girls. Pyramid, 1960; New English Library pb, 1970 [Algeria]
Halfway to Hell. Avon, 1959
A Haven for the Damned. GM, 1962; Muller pb, 1963
Heat of Night. GM, 1960; Muller pb, 1961 [Fla.]
Hell Can Wait. GM, 1960; Muller pb, 1962
Hot As Fire, Cold As Ice. Belmont, 1962
The Humming Box. Ace, 1956 [Tampa]
Journey into Violence. Pyramid, 1961
The Lady Was a Tramp. Handi-Books, 1951
Man in the Shadow. Avon, 1957 (Novelization of the movie.)
Married to Murder. Phantom, 1951 [Fla.]
Mourn the Hangman. Graphic, 1952 [Fla.]
Murder Is My Mistress. Graphic, 1951
The Naked Jungle. Ace, 1955
A Night for Screaming. Ace, 1960 [Kan.]
Nita's Place. Pyramid, 1960
One Deadly Dawn. Ace, 1957 [Calif.]
One Got Away. Ace, 1955
Play for Keeps. Abelard (NYC & London), 1957
Rebel Woman. Avon, 1960 [Cuba]
Satan's Widow. Phantom, 1952
Saturday Night Town. Crest, 1956; Fawcett (London), 1958
69 Babylon Park. Avon, 1962
Slay Ride for a Lady. Handi-Books, 1950
So Dead My Love! Ace, 1953 [Fla.]
Strange Bargain. Avon, 1959

Strangers on Friday. Abelard (NYC & London), 1959 [Fla.]
Teen-Age Jungle. Avon, 1958
Temptations of Valerie. Avon, 1957 (Novelization of the movie.)
A Ticket to Hell. GM, 1959; Muller pb, 1960 [N. Mex.]
-Trouble Rides Tall. Abelard (NYC & London), 1958
Vengeful Sinner. Croydon, 1953. Also published as: Die, Lover. Avon, 1960, abridged
Web of Murder. GM, 1958; Fawcett (London), 1959
Wild Lonesome. Ballantine, 1965
A Woman on the Place. Ace, 1956; Red Seal, 1960
You'll Die Next! Ace, 1954; Red Seal, 1959

WHITTLESEY, ELSIE LEIGH
The Hemlock Swamp, and A Season at the White Sulfur Springs. Claxton, 1873

WHITTON, CHARLES
The Judas Way. Long, 1923
The Purple Trident. Long, 1924

WHORF, RICHARD B.
At the Sign of the Eel. Baker, 1930 (3-act play.)
Creaking Floors. Baker, 1930 (3-act play.)
The ? Crime. Fitzgerald, 1932   (Play.)

WIBBERLEY, LEONARD PATRICK O'CONNOR. 1915- . Pseudonym: Leonard Holton, q.v.
Black Jack Rides Again. Dramatic, 1971 (2-act play.)

WICK, CARTER. Pseudonym of Collin Wilcox, 1924- , q.v.
The Faceless Man. Saturday Review Press, 1975; H. Hamilton, 1976 [S.F.]

WICK, STUART MARY. Pseudonym of Kathleen Freeman, 1897-1959, q.v. Other pseudonym: Mary Fitt, q.v.
And Where's Mr. Bellamy? Hutchinson, 1948
-The Statue and the Lady. Hodder, 1950

WICKER, TOM [THOMAS GREY WICKER]. 1926- . Ref: CA. Pseudonym: Paul Connolly, q.v.
The Devil Must. Harper, 1957
-The Judgment. Sloane, 1961; Cassell, 1962

WICKES, MARTHA
The Mystery of Sun Dial Court. Penn, 1926

WICKHAM, HARVEY. 1872-1930. SC: Ferris McClue, in at least those marked FM.
The Boncoeur Affair. Clode, 1923; Skeffington, 1925 FM [Paris]
The Clue of the Primrose Petal. Clode, 1921; Brentano's (London), 1923 FM [Conn.]
Jungle Terror. Doubleday, 1920
The Scarlet X. Clode, 1922; Brentano's (London), 1923 FM [S. Pac.]
The Trail of the Squid. Clode, 1924 FM [Paris]

WICKING, G(EORGE) W(ALTER).
Bales of Trouble. Wright, 1937 [Australia]
Boom-Time Gold. Angus, 1936
The Glory Box Mystery. Angus, 1937 [Australia]
The Mysterious Valley. Angus, 1938

WICKS, FREDERICK. 1840-1910.
Golden Lives. Blackwood, 1891. Also published as: A Woman's Courage. Remington, 1892
The Infant. Remington, 1895
My Undiscovered Crimes. Blackwood, 1909 ss
The Stories of the Broadmoor Patient, and the Poor Clerk. Remington, 1893
The Veiled Hand. Remington, 1892; Harper, 1893
A Woman's Courage; see Golden Lives

WICKWARE, FRANCIS SILL. 1911- . Ref: CC.
Dangerous Ground. Doubleday, 1946 [Mass.]

WIDDEMER, MARGARET. 1894-1978. Ref: CA.
The Red Castle Women. Doubleday, 1968; Jenkins, 1969 [N.Y.]

WIEGAND, WILLIAM (GEORGE). 1928-   .
  Ref: CA, CC, DD, TC.
  At Last, Mr. Tolliver. Rinehart, 1950;
    Hodder, 1951

WIENER, WILLARD. 1900-   . Born in St.
  Louis; newspaperman in Calif.
  Four Boys and a Gun. Dial, 1944. Also
    published as: Four Boys, a Girl and
    a Gun. Avon, 1951

WIESELBERG, HELEN
  The Lords of Dair. Putnam, 1978

WIGHT, NATALIE
  Death in the Inner Office. Phoenix,
    1938 [Chi.]

WIGNALL, TREVOR C. 1883-1958. Both
  titles below were published by Amal-
  gamated Press and feature Sexton
  Blake.
  The Case of the Japanese Detective.
    1920
  The House with the Red Blinds. 1920

WILCOX, COLLIN. 1924-   . Pseudonym:
  Carter Wick, q.v. Ref: CA, CC, TC.
  See also: Bill Pronzini, 1943-   .
  SC: Lt. Frank Hastings = FH (see
  the Pronzini entry); Stephen Drake =
  SD; McCloud (novelizations of the
  TV series) = M.
  Aftershock. Random, 1975; Hale, 1976
    FH [S.F.]
  The Black Door. Dodd, 1967; Cassell,
    1968 SD [S.F.]
  Dead Aim. Random, 1971; Hale, 1973 FH
    [S.F.]
  The Disappearance. Random, 1970; Hale,
    1971 FH [S.F.]
  Doctor, Lawyer... Random, 1976; Hale,
    1978 FH [S.F.]
  Hiding Place. Random, 1973; Hale, 1974
    FH [S.F.]
  The Lonely Hunter. Random, 1969; Hale,
    1971 FH [S.F.]
  Long Way Down. Random, 1974; Hale, 1975
    FH [S.F.]
  McCloud. Award, 1974 M [NYC]
  Mankiller. Random, 1980; Hale, 1981 FH
    [S.F.]
  The New Mexico Connection. Award, 1974;
    Tandem, 1974 M
  Power Plays. Random, 1979; Hale, 1982
    FH [S.F.]
  The Third Figure. Dodd, 1968; Hale,
    1969 SD [Calif.]
  The Third Victim. Dell, 1976; Hale,
    1977 FH [S.F.]
  The Watcher. Random, 1978; Hale, 1979
    [Calif.]

WILCOX, HARRY. Pseudonym: Mark Derby,
  q.v.

WILCOX, HENRY S. 1855-   .
  A Strange Flaw. Thompson, 1908

WILCOX, JESS. Pseudonym of Morris Hersh-
  man, 1920-   , q.v. Other pseudonym:
  Evelyn Bond, q.v.
  Kill Me, Sweet. Monarch, 1960

WILCOX, RONALD
  -The Rig. Leisure, 1978

WILDE, OSCAR (FINGAL O'FLAHERTIE WILLS).
  1854-1900. See also: Constance Cox,
  1915-   . Ref: CA.
  Lord Arthur Savile's Crime, and other
    stories. Osgood, 1891; Dodd, 1891
    ss, one criminous

WILDE, PERCIVAL. 1887-1953. Ref: CC, EM,
  MP.
  Design for Murder. Random, 1941; Gol-
    lancz, 1942 [Conn.]
  Inquest. Random, 1940; Gollancz, 1939
    [Conn.]
  Mystery Week-End. Harcourt, 1938; Gol-
    lancz, 1938 [Conn.]
  P. Moran, Operative. Random, 1947; Gol-
    lancz, 1947 ss [Conn.]
  Rogues in Clover. Appleton, 1929 ss
  Tinsley's Bones. Random, 1942; Gol-
    lancz, 1943 [Conn.]

WILDEN, THEODORE. 1936-   . Czech citizen, born in Greece, living in London.
  To Die Elsewhere. Heinemann, 1976; Har-
    court, 1976 (Translation of "Umrit
    Nekde Jinde.") [Fr.]

WILDER, ROBERT (INGERSOLL). 1901-1974.
  Ref: CA.
  An Affair of Honor. Putnam, 1969;
    Allen, 1970
  Fruit of the Poppy. Putnam, 1965;
    Allen, 1965

Walk with Evil. Crest, 1957; Allen,
  1958

WILDER, THORNTON (NIVEN). 1897-1975.
  Ref: CA.
  The Eighth Day. Harper, 1967; Long-
    mans, 1967 [Ill., ca.1900]

WILES, DOMINI. 1942-   . Ref: CA.
  The Betrayer. Collins, 1979
  Death Flight. Collins, 1977; Coward,
    1977 (The U.S. edition is revised
    and expanded.) [L.A.]

WILES, FRANK(LIN)
  Hell of Make Believe. Research Publish-
    ing Co., 1978

WILEY, FAITH. See: Ben Whitehurst.

WILEY, HUGH. 1884-   . Ref: EM.
  The Copper Mask, and other stories.
    Knopf, 1932 ss [S.F.]
  Jade, and other stories. Knopf, 1921;
    Heinemann, 1922 ss [S.F.]
  Manchu Blood. Knopf, 1927 ss [S.F.]
  Murder by the Dozen. Popular Library,
    1951 ss [S.F.]

WILHELM, KATE [KATE WILHELM KNIGHT].
  1928-   . Ref: CA.
  City of Cain. Little, 1974; Gollancz,
    1975 [Wash. D.C.]
  More Bitter Than Death. Simon, 1963;
    Hale, 1965
  -The Nevermore Affair. Doubleday, 1966

WILK, MAX. 1920-   . Ref: CA.
  Eliminate the Middle Man. Norton, 1974
    [Greece]
  The Kissinger Noodles; or, Westward,
    Mr. Ho. Norton, 1976
  The Moving Picture Boys. Norton, 1978
    [L.A.]

WILKES, ALLENE TUPPER
  The Creaking Chair. French (NYC & Lon-
    don), 1926 (Play.)

WILKES-HUNTER, R(ICHARD). 1906-   .
  Pseudonyms: Marc Brody, Tod Conrad,
  Alex Crane, qq.v. Ref: CA. All data
  below refer to Australian editions,
  the relative criminous content of
  which has not been ascertained.
  Badge for a Gunfighter. Leisure, 1954
  Bank Robbery Hostage. Leisure, 1956
  Borneo Patrol. Webster, 1958 [Borneo]
  Commando. Webster, 1958
  Commandos Are Expendable. Cleveland
    Publishing, 1954
  Crusade into Crime. Australian Pub-
    lishing, 1948
  The Day I Stopped Running. Leisure,
    1953
  Death Date. Leisure, 1957
  Deserters Don't Come Back. Leisure,
    1955
  Fast with a Gun. Cleveland Publishing,
    1955
  Fighter Pilot. Leisure, 1955
  Five Came to Kill. Leisure, 1954
  Five Days to Kill. Horwitz, 1956
  Fool from Down Under. Cleveland Pub-
    lishing, 1954
  Gunsmoke Haze. Cleveland Publishing,
    1955
  Heritage of the Horned Steer. Leisure,
    1954
  Hostage. Cleveland Publishing, 1955
  Kid with a Gun. Cleveland Publishing,
    1955
  Kokoda Trail. Webster, 1958
  Partisans Die Alone. Leisure, 1954
  Patient Is the Hunter. Leisure, 1953
  Range Justice. Cleveland Publishing,
    1955
  Ride West of the Law. Leisure, 1953
  Run with the Weasel. Leisure, 1953
  Six Gun Empire. Cleveland Publishing,
    1954
  Take This Gun. Cleveland Publishing,
    1954
  Task Demolition. Leisure, 1954
  A Tomb for Mr. Lee. Leisure, 1954
  Trail of the Hunted. Leisure, 1954
  Train a Fast Gun. Leisure, 1955
  Violent Holiday. Leisure, 1954
  White Trails over London. Leisure, 1953

WILKINS, W. A.
  The Cleverdale Mystery; or, The Machine
    and Its Wheels. Fords Howard, 1882
    [N.Y.]

WILKINSON, (JOHN) BURKE. 1913-   . Ref:
  CA. SC: Geoffrey Mildmay = GM.
  Black Judas; see Run, Mongoose.
  Last Clear Chance. Little, 1954; Hod-
    der, 1954 GM [Wash. D.C.]
  Night of the Short Knives. Scribner,
    1964; Hodder, 1965 [Paris]

Proceed at Will. Little, 1948; Hodder,
  1949 GM [Fr.]
Run, Mongoose. Little, 1950; Hodder,
  1951. Also published as: Black Judas.
  Permabooks, 1951 GM [Dublin]

WILKINSON, ELLEN (CICELY). 1891-   .
  Ref: CC.
  -Clash. Harrap, 1929
  The Division Bell Mystery. Harrap, 1932

WILKINSON, G(EOFFREY) K(EDINGTON).
  1907-   . Ref: CA.
  Nick the Click. Cassell, 1968; Putnam,
    1968

WILKINSON, LAURENCE
  Appointment in Tangier. Collins, 1955
    [Tangier]
  The Salamander Sword. Collins, 1953
  A Touch of Judas. Ward, 1952

WILKINSON, RICHARD HILL. 1904-   . Pseu-
  donyms: Julian Brocke, Eugene Hay-
  ford, E. Harrison Ott, Paul Pray,
  qq.v.
  The Ghost of Grand Canyon. Baker, 1936
    (3-act play)
  Mad Murder. Meador, 1931 [New Eng.]
  Murder on the High Seas. Drama Guild,
    1938 (3-act play.) [ship]
  Night of Terror. Baker, 1936 (3-act
    play.)
  The Pennington Case. Drama Guild, 1937
    (3-act play.)
  Tea at Four. Drama Guild, 1934 (1-act
    play.)
  The Terror. Denison, 1952 (3-act
    play.)

WILKINSON, (WILLIAM) RODERICK. 1917-   .
  Ref: CA.
  The Big Still. Long, 1958; British Book
    Centre, 1959 [Scot.]
  Everything Goes Dead. Hale, 1967
  Murder Belongs to Me! Museum, 1956
  The Network. Hale, 1969
  The Pressure Man. Hale, 1967

WILKINSON, RONALD. 1920-   . Pseudonym:
  Ronald Scott Thorn, q.v.

WILKINSON, SARAH (SCUDGELL)
  The Eve of St. Mark; or, The Mysterious
    Spectre. Bailey, 1805
  The Mysterious Novice; or, Convent of
    the Grey Penitents. Arliss, 1809
  Priory of St. Clair; or, The Spectre of
    the Murdered Nun. Harrild, 1811
  The Spectre of Lanmere Abbey; or, The
    Mystery of the Blue and Silver Bag.
    Mason, 1820
  Zittaw the Cruel; or, The Woodsman's
    Daughter. Mace, n.d. [Pol.]

WILLARD. Pseudonym: Nicholas Carter, q.v.

WILLARD, JOHN. 1885-1942. Ref: EM.
  The Cat and the Canary. Readers Li-
    brary, 1927. U.S. title: The Cat
    Creeps. Jacobson, 1930. The play:
    French (NYC & London), 1927

WILLARD, JOSHUA
  The Thorne Theatre Mystery. Phoenix,
    1937 [N.Y.]

WILLARD, JOSIAH FLYNT. 1869-1907. Pseudonym: Josiah Flynt, q.v.

WILLARDS, E(RNST) S(EYMOUR)
  My Mother Was Hanged. Heinemann, 1958
    (Translation of "Mijn Moeder Werd Op-
    gehangen." Amsterdam, 1956.)

WILLEFORD, CHARLES RAY III. 1919-   .
  Pseudonym: Will Charles, q.v.

WILLETS, GILSON. 1869-   .
  Anita, the Cuban Spy. Neely, 1898
    [Cuba]
  The Double Cross. Dillingham, 1910;
    Unwin, 1910
  The First Law. Dillingham, 1911; Unwin,
    1911 [Eng.]

WILLETT, E(RNEST) NODALL
  The Sitting Emperor. Gardner, 1920

WILLETT, HILDA. 1878-   . Set: Eng.
  Accident in Piccadilly. Paul, 1935
  -April, May and June. Paul, 1931
  Bucket in a Well. Paul, 1932
  Diamonds of Death. Longmans, 1930
  Found Shot. Paul, 1934
  It's Quiet in the Country. Gifford,
    1946
  Murder at the Party. Paul, 1931
  Mystery on the Centre Court. Paul, 1933
  Peril in Darkness. Paul, 1935
  -So It Goes On. Paul, 1930
  Tragedy in Pewsey Chart. Longmans, 1929

WILLIAM, PETER
  The Affair at Abu Mina. Macrae Smith, 1944. Also published as: Death at Abu Mina. Thriller Novel Classic, 194?, abridged [Afr., N.]

WILLIAMS, ALAN. 1890-   .
  Room Service. Godwin, 1936 [NYC]

WILLIAMS, ALAN (EMLYN). 1935-   . Son of actor-playwright (George) Emlyn Williams, 1905-1974, q.v.; a newspaper correspondent. SC: Rupert Quinn = RQ.
  Barbourze. Blond, 1964. U.S. title: The False Beards. Harper, 1965 RQ [Afr., N.]
  The Beria Papers. Blond, 1973; Simon, 1973
  The Brotherhood. Blond, 1968. U.S. title: The Purity League. Putnam, 1969
  A Bullet for the Shah; see Shah-Mak
  Dead Secret. Granada, 1980
  The False Beards; see Barbouze
  Gentleman Traitor. Blond, 1974; Harcourt, 1975 [Russ.]
  Holy of Holies. Granada, 1981; Rawson, 1980
  Long Run South. Blond, 1962; Little, 1962 RQ [Algeria]
  The Purity League; see The Brotherhood
  Shah-Mak. Blond, 1976; Coward, 1976. Also published as: A Bullet for the Shah. GM, 1978 [Switz.]
  Snake Water. Blond, 1965; Harper, 1965
  The Tale of the Lazy Dog. Blond, 1970; Simon, 1970 [Viet Nam]
  -The Widow's War. Hart-Davis, 1978; Rawson, 1980

WILLIAMS, ALEXANDER (HAZARD). 1894-1952. Pseudonym: Forrester Hazard, q.v. SC: Det. Sgt. Pietro Tonelli, in all titles.
  Death over Newark. Payson, 1933 [NYC]
  The Jinx Theatre Murder. Payson, 1933
  Murder in the WPA. McBride, 1937 [NYC]

WILLIAMS, BEN AMES. 1889-1953. Ref: CC, MP. SC: Insp. Tope, in at least those marked T.
  Audacity. Dutton, 1924
  The Bellmer Mystery; see Death on Scurvy Street
  Crucible. Dutton, 1937
  Death on Scurvy Street. Dutton, 1929. British title: The Bellmer Mystery. Paul, 1930 T
  The Dreadful Night. Dutton, 1928; Paul, 1929 [Maine]
  An End to Mirth. Dutton, 1931 [L.A.]
  Hostile Valley. Dutton, 1934. Also published as: Valley Vixen. Avon, 1948
  A Killer Among Us; see Silver Forest
  Lady in Peril; see Money Musk
  -Leave Her to Heaven. Houghton, 1944; Hale, 1946
  Mischief. Dutton, 1933 [Maine]
  Money Musk. Dutton, 1932. Also published as: Lady in Peril. Popular Library, 1948 T
  Pascal's Mill. Dutton, 1943 [Maine]
  Pirate's Purchase. Dutton, 1931 [Ga.]
  The Silver Forest. Dutton, 1926; Mills, 1927 [Maine]
  Valley Vixen; see Hostile Valley

WILLIAMS, BRAD. 1918-   . Ref: CA, CC. SC: Sam Benedict = SB (who also appears in books by Elsie Lee, 1912-   , and Howard L. Oleck, 1911-   , qq.v.).
  A Borderline Case. Mill, 1960. British title: Death Lies in Waiting. Jenkins, 1961 [Calif.]
  A Conflict of Interest, with J(acob) W(ilburn) Ehrlich, 1900-1971. Holt, 1971 SB [S.F.]
  Death Lies in Waiting; see A Borderline Case
  Make a Killing. Mill, 1961; Jenkins, 1962 [L.A.]
  A Matter of Confidence, with J(acob) W(ilburn) Ehrlich, 1900-1971. Holt, 1973 SB [S.F.]
  A Stranger to Herself. Doubleday, 1964; Gollancz, 1965 [L.A., Las Veg.]
  Tumulto. Avon, 1974 [Mex.]
  The Well-Dressed Skeleton. Mill, 1962; Jenkins, 1963 [L.A., Mex.]

WILLIAMS, CHARLES
  A Master of Crime. Odhams, 1919

WILLIAMS, CHARLES. 1909-1975. Ref: CC, TC. SC: John Ingram = JI.
  Aground. Viking, 1960; Cassell, 1961 JI [ship]
  All the Way. Dell, 1958. British title: The Concrete Flamingo. Cassell, 1960 [Fla.]
  And the Deep Blue Sea. Signet, 1971; Cassell, 1972
  The Big Bite. Dell, 1956; Cassell 1957 [Okla.]
  Big City Girl. GM, 1951; Fawcett (London), 1953 [South]
  The Catfish Tangle; see River Girl
  The Concrete Flamingo; see All the Way
  Dead Calm. Viking, 1963; Cassell, 1964 JI [ship]
  The Diamond Bikini. GM, 1956; Consul, 1962
  Don't Just Stand There; see The Wrong Venus
  Girl Out Back. Dell, 1958. British title: Operator. Cassell, 1958
  Go Home, Stranger. GM, 1954; Red Seal, 1957 [Fla.]
  Gulf Coast Girl; see Scorpion Reef
  Hell Hath No Fury. GM, 1953; Red Seal, 1958. Also published as: The Hot Spot. Cassell, 1965
  Hill Girl. GM, 1951; Red Seal, 1958
  The Hot Spot; see Hell Hath No Fury
  The Long Saturday Night. GM, 1962; Cassell, 1964 [Ala.]
  Man in Motion; see Man on the Run
  Man on a Leash. Putnam, 1973; Cassell, 1974
  Man on the Run. GM, 1958. British title: Man in Motion. Cassell, 1959 [Fla.]
  Mix Yourself a Redhead; see A Touch of Death
  Nothing in Her Way. GM, 1953; Fawcett (London), 1954 [S.F.]
  Nude on Thin Ice. Avon, 1961
  Operator; see Girl Out Back
  River Girl. GM, 1951
  The Sailcloth Shroud. Viking, 1960; Cassell, 1960
  Scorpion Reef. Macmillan, 1955; Cassell, 1956. Also published as: Gulf Coast Girl. Dell, 1956
  Stain of Suspicion; see Talk of the Town
  Talk of the Town. Dell, 1958. British title: Stain of Suspicion. Cassell, 1959. Reprinted in the U.S. under the British title: PB, 1973 [Fla.]
  A Touch of Death. GM, 1954; Fawcett (London), 1955. Also published as: Mix Yourself a Redhead. Cassell, 1965
  Uncle Sagamore and His Girls. GM, 1959
  The Wrong Venus. New American Library, 1966. British title: Don't Just Stand There. Cassell, 1967 [Fr.]

WILLIAMS, DAVID (FFRANCON). 1909-   .
  Agent from the West. Cape, 1956 [Balkans]

WILLIAMS, DAVID. 1926-   . Born in Wales; founder and executive of London advertising agency. SC: Mark Treasure, in all titles. Set: Eng.
  Murder for Treasure. Collins, 1980; St. Martin's, 1980
  Treasure by Degrees. Collins, 1977; St. Martin's, 1977 [acad.]
  Treasure Up in Smoke. Collins, 1978; St. Martin's, 1978 T
  Unholy Writ. Collins, 1976; St. Martin's, 1977

WILLIAMS, DAVID. 1939-   . Ref: CA.
  The Brandenburg Concerto. Cassell, 1980
  Second Sight. Simon, 1977; H. Hamilton, 1978 [N.Y.]

WILLIAMS, EDWIN ALFRED. Pseudonym: Edwin De Caire, q.v.

WILLIAMS, ELIOT CRAWSHAY. 1879-   .
  -No Apparent Motive. Long, 1948
  -Stay of Execution. Jarrolds, 1933
  -The Stroud Case. Long, 1953

WILLIAMS, ELMA M(ARY). 1913-   .
  Escape to Death. Ward, 1961
  Strange Legacy. Ward, 1961
  Tomorrow a Stranger. Ward, 1962

WILLIAMS, (GEORGE) EMLYN. 1905-1974. Ref: EM.
  A Murder Has Been Arranged. Collins, 1930; French (NYC), 1931 (3-act play.)
  Night Must Fall. Gollancz, 1935; Random, 1936 (3-act play.)
  Someone Waiting. Dramatists, 1956 (3-act play.)

WILLIAMS, ERIC (ERNEST). 1911-   . Ref: CA. SC: Roger and Kate Starte, in both titles.
  The Borders of Barbarism. Heinemann, 1961; Coward, 1962
  Dragoman Pass. Collins, 1959; Coward, 1959

WILLIAMS, F(RANK) CHENHALLS. 1880-   .
  -The Inner Number. Longmans, 1927

WILLIAMS, G. MOUNTFORD
  Silk Rope. Duckworth, 1947 [acad.]

WILLIAMS, GILBERT M. 1917-   . Pseudonym: Michael Wolfe, q.v.

WILLIAMS, GORDON M(acLEAN). 1934-   . Born in Scot. Joint pseudonym with Terry Venables: P. B. Yuill, q.v.
  Big Morning Blues. Hodder, 1974
  -The Camp. Secker, 1966; Stein, 1966
  -From Scenes Like These. Secker, 1968; Morrow, 1969
  The Last Day of Lincoln Charles. Secker, 1965; Stein, 1965
  The Siege of Trencher's Farm. Secker, 1969; Morrow, 1969
  -They Used to Play on Grass, with Terry Venables. Hodder, 1971

WILLIAMS, H. C.
  The Ticket-of-Leave Man. (London), 1875 (Novelization of the play by Tom Taylor, 1817-1880, q.v.)

WILLIAMS, H(UGH) NOEL. 1870-1925.
  Tainted Gold. Paul, 1915

WILLIAMS, HAROLD. 1853-1926. Pseudonym: George Afterem, q.v.

WILLIAMS, HARPER
  The Thing in the Woods. McBride, 1924

WILLIAMS, HENRY. Pseudonym of W(illiam) H(enry) Manville, 1930-   , q.v.
  How to Murder Your Wife. Dell, 1965 (Novelization of the movie.) [NYC]

WILLIAMS, HENRY LLEWELLYN. 1842-   . Pseudonym: Matt Mizzen, q.v.

WILLIAMS, HENRY SMITH. 1863-1943.
  The Witness of the Sun. Doubleday, 1920 [NYC]

WILLIAMS, J. ARTHUR
  The Clue of the Cone. Hutchinson, 1946

WILLIAMS, J(OHN) ELLIS
  Murder at the Eisteddfod. Gomer, 1973

WILLIAMS, JAY. 1914-1978. Pseudonym: Michael Delving, q.v.

WILLIAMS, JEANNE. 1930-   . Pseudonyms: Jeanne Crecy, Deirdre Rowan, qq.v.

WILLIAMS, JOHN. 1908-   . Ref: CA.
  Suddenly at the Priory. Heinemann, 1957; British Book Service, 1958

WILLIAMS, JOHN (STANLEY). 1925-   . Ref: CA.
  -Death Is a Lizard. Hutchinson, 1963
  -The God-Seeker. Hutchinson, 1966
  -On the Way Out. New Authors, 1962
  The Spinsters. Hutchinson, 1967

WILLIAMS, JOHN B., M.D.
  The Baronet's Crime. Westbrook, 1912
  Dead Yet Living; or, The Baltimore Bank Robbery. Westbrook, 1912 [Balt.]
  Leaves from the Note-Book of a New York Detective. Dick, 1865 ss [NYC]
  The Secret Compact; or, The Lone House by the River. Westbrook, 1912
  Under a Mask. Westbrook, 1912
  The Vial with the White Powder; or, Deadly Foes to the Grave. Westbrook, 1912

WILLIAMS, KIRBY. Pseudonym. SC: Dr. Thackeray Place, in both titles.
  The C.V.C. Murders. Doubleday, 1929; Hutchinson, 1929 [Chi.]
  The Opera Murders. Scribner, 1933 [Chi.]

WILLIAMS, LAWRENCE. 1915-   .
  -The Fiery Furnace. Simon, 1960; Muller, 1960
  -The Smoke-Filled Boudoir. Simon, 1965

WILLIAMS, LAWRENCE
  A Copper Snare. Hale, 1980

WILLIAMS, LYNN. Pseudonym of Arlene Hale, 1924-   .
  Lake of the Wind. Dell, 1971
  Medley of Mystery. Dell, 1974
  Once Upon a Nightmare. Dell, 1971
  Picture Her Missing. Dell, 1973
  Rendezvous with Danger. Dell, 1973
  The Secret of Hedges Hall. Dell, 1973
  Shadows over Seascape. Dell, 1972
  Threads of Intrigue. Dell, 1973
  Where Is Jane? Dell, 1972

WILLIAMS, MARGARET WETHERBY. Pseudonym: Margaret Erskine, q.v.

WILLIAMS, MARY
Carnecrane. Kimber, 1979

WILLIAMS, MONA (GOODWYN). 1906- .
The Messenger. Rawson, 1977
This House Is Burning. Rawson, 1978 [Calif.]

WILLIAMS, MOSES
Shadows of a City Care Forgotten. Vantage, 1980

WILLIAMS, MOUNTFORD
Hound Island. Nelson, 1940

WILLIAMS, NATHAN WINSLOW. 1860-1924. Pseudonym: Richard Dallas, q.v.

WILLIAMS, NEIL
Also Ran. New English Library pb, 1974
-Scorch. New English Library pb, 1975

WILLIAMS, NEIL WYNN
-The Electric Theft. Greening, 1906; Small, 1906

WILLIAMS, OSCAR
The Dance of Death and other stories. Morris, 1946 ss
The Dawn Must Come. Morris, 1948
Death Stalks the River. Pan, 1945
Devil's Luck. Mellifont, 1934
Harringay's Last Gamble. Morris, 1946 ss
Justice Never Sleeps. Morris, 1945
Reparation. Mellifont, 1934
The Sign of the Tiger. Morris, 1945
The Vengeance of Sheevra. Morris, 1945

WILLIAMS, P(HILIP) C(LAXTON). SC: Mr. Hoyland, in at least those marked H.
Hoyland Intervenes. Atlas, 1944 H
Hoyland Steps Out. Pictorial Art, 1946 H
Mr. Hoyland Looks Round. Hale, 1941 H ss
Murder Will Out. Pictorial Art, 194? H
Time for Crime. Pocket Editions, 1945

WILLIAMS, PETE. Pseudonym of James Reach, 1909?-1970. Joint pseudonym with Tom (Barnard) Taggart, q.v.: Ross MacRoss, q.v. Other pseudonyms: John Rand, Hilda Manning, qq.v.
Over My Dead Body. French (NYC), 1950 (3-act play.)

WILLIAMS, RAYMOND
The Volunteers. Eyre, 1978 [Wales]

WILLIAMS, RICHARD. House name, used by W(illiam Arthur) Howard Baker, 1925- , q.v., and others. Other Baker pseudonyms: William Arthur, W. A. Ballinger, Julie Wellsley, qq.v. SC: Sexton Blake (with many other authors), in all titles.
Hurricane Warning! Amalgamated, 1960
Large Type Killer. Amalgamated, 1960
The Man with the Iron Chest. Mayflower, 1965
Murder by Proxy. Amalgamated, 1963
The Slaying of Julian Summers. Amalgamated, 1963
The Sniper. Mayflower, 1965
Somebody Wants Me Dead. Amalgamated, 1962
Speak Ill of the Dead. Amalgamated, 1963
Torment Was a Redhead. Amalgamated, 1962
Vendetta! Amalgamated, 1961

WILLIAMS, RUTH
Cry Rape. Award, 1974 (Novelization of the TV movie.)

WILLIAMS, SIDNEY (CLARK). 1878-1949. Born in Maine. Reporter, literary editor, drama critic, on newspapers in Maine, Boston and Philadelphia. SC: Jabez Twombley = JT.
The Aconite Murders. Dodd, 1956 JT [Phil.]
The Body in the Blue Room. Penn, 1922; Hurst, 1924
The Drury Club Case. Penn, 1927
In the Tenth Moon. Penn, 1923; Hurst, 1924 [NYC]
The Murder of Miss Betty Sloan. Appleton, 1935 JT [Phil.]
Mystery in Red. Penn, 1925; Hurst, 1925 [Mass.]

WILLIAMS, STEPHEN DANIEL
The Adventures of Shylar Homes. Carlton, 1966 ss

WILLIAMS, T. JEFF
Sonny. Bantam, 1978; New English Library pb, 1978
Strangler. Bantam, 1979

WILLIAMS, THOMAS. 1926- . Novelist, teacher at U. of N.H.
The Followed Man. Marek, 1978; Sidgwick, 1980 [N.H.]

WILLIAMS, (GEORGE) VALENTINE. 1883-1946. Pseudonym: Douglas Valentine, q.v. Ref: CC, EM, MM, MP, TC. SC: Sgt. Trevor Dene = TD; Dr. Adolph Grundt (Clubfoot) = AG (see also Douglas Valentine entry); Insp. Manderton = M; Mr. Treadgold = T.
The Clock Ticks On. Hodder, 1933; Houghton, 1933 TD [L.I.]
Clubfoot the Avenger. Jenkins, 1924; Houghton, 1924 AG
The Clue of the Rising Moon. Hodder, 1935; Houghton, 1935 TD [New Eng.]
Courier to Marrakesh. Hodder, 1944; Houghton, 1946 AG [It.]
The Crouching Beast. Hodder, 1928; Houghton, 1928 AG [Ger.]
The Curiosity of Mr. Treadgold; see Mr. Treadgold Cuts In
Dead Man Manor. Hodder, 1936; Houghton, 1936 T [Can.]
Death Answers the Bell. Hodder, 1931; Houghton, 1932 TD,M
The Eye in Attendance. Hodder, 1927; Houghton, 1927 TD,M
Fog, with Dorothy Rice Sims. Hodder, 1933; Houghton, 1933 [ship]
The Fox Prowls. Hodder, 1939; Houghton, 1939 [Buch.]
The Gold Comfit Box. Hodder, 1932. U.S. title: The Mystery of the Gold Box. Houghton, 1932 AG
Island Gold; see The Return of Clubfoot
The Key Man; see The Pigeon House
The Knife Behind the Curtain. Hodder, 1930; Houghton, 1930 ss
Mannequin. Hodder, 1930. U.S. title: The Mysterious Miss Morrisot. Houghton, 1930 [Fr.]
Masks Off at Midnight. Hodder, 1934; Houghton, 1934 TD [L.I.]
Mr. Ramosi. Hodder, 1926; Houghton, 1926
Mr. Treadgold Cuts In. Hodder, 1937. U.S. title: The Curiosity of Mr. Treadgold. Houghton, 1937 T ss
The Mysterious Miss Morrisot; see Mannequin
The Mystery of the Gold Box; see The Gold Comfit Box
The Orange Divan. Jenkins, 1923; Houghton, 1923 M
The Pigeon House. Hodder, 1926. U.S. title: The Key Man. Houghton, 1926 [Fr.]
The Portcullis Room. Hodder, 1934; Houghton, 1934 [Scot.]
The Red Mass. Hodder, 1925; Houghton, 1925 [Fr.]
The Return of Clubfoot. Jenkins, 1923. U.S. title: Island Gold. Houghton, 1923 AG [S. Pac.]
Skeleton Out of the Cupboard. Hodder, 1946 T
The Spider's Touch. Hodder, 1936; Houghton, 1936 AG
The Three of Clubs. Hodder, 1924; Houghton, 1924 [Hung.]
The Yellow Streak. Jenkins, 1922; Houghton, 1922 M

WILLIAMS, WILLIAM FREDERICK
The Witcheries of Craig Isuff. Newman, 1804

WILLIAMS, WYNN. Pseudonym of Canadian born author living in Portland since about 1955.
Take the Money and Die. Raven, 1980 [Portland]

WILLIAMSON, ALICE M(URIEL LIVINGSTON) [MRS. C. N. WILLIAMSON]. 1869-1933. See also: C(harles) N(orris) Williamson, 1859-1920. Pseudonym: Dona Teresa de Savallo, q.v.
-The Barn Stormers. Hutchinson, 1897; Stokes, 1897, as by Mrs. Harcourt Williamson
-Bewitched. Wright, 1934
-A Bid for a Coronet. Routledge, 1901
Black Incense; see Told at Monte Carlo
Black Sleeves. Chapman, 1928 [L.A.]
-The Castle of Shadows. Methuen, 1905; Hudson, 1909

-Children of the Zodiac. Chapman, 1929
-The Flower Forbidden. Hodder, 1911
-Fortune's Sport. Pearson, 1898
-Frozen Slippers. Chapman, 1930
-The Girl in the Secret. Wright, 1934
-The Girl in the Passion Play. Hodder, 1911
The Girl Who Had Nothing. Ward, 1905
-The Golden Carpet. Chapman, 1931
-Hollywood Love. Chapman, 1928
-Honeymoon Hate. Chapman, 1931
The House by the Lock. Bowden, 1899; Dodge, 1906
-The Indian Princess. Mills, 1924 ss
-Keep This Door Shut. Benn, 1933
Lady Mary of the Dark House. Bowden, 1898
-Last Year's Wife. Benn, 1932
-The Lightning Conductor Comes Back. Chapman, 1933
-The Little White Nun. White, 1903
-The Man Himself. Philpot, 1925
-My Lady Cinderella. Routledge, 1900; Dodge, 1906
-Name the Woman. Methuen, 1924
-The Newspaper Girl. Pearson, 1899
-Ordered South. Routledge, 1900
-Papa. Methuen, 1902
-Princess Mary's Locked Book. Cassell (London), 1912; Cassell (NYC), 1913
-Publicity for Anne. Mills, 1926
-Queen Sweetheart. White, 1901
-The Sea Could Tell. Methuen, 1904
Secret Gold. Methuen, 1925; Doubleday, 1925 [N. Mex.]
-Sheikh Bill. Mills, 1927
-The Silent Battle. Hurst, 1902
Told at Monte Carlo. Mills, 1926. U.S. title: Black Incense. Doran, 1926 ss
The Turnstile of Night. Hurst, 1904
-'Twixt Devil and Deep Sea. Pearson, 1901
-The Underground Syndicate. Hodder, 1910
The Vanity Box. Hodder, 1913; Doubleday, 1911, as by Alice Stuyvesant
A Woman in Grey. Routledge, 1898; Burt, (date?)
The Woman Who Cared. Methuen, 1903

WILLIAMSON, AUDREY. 1913- . SC: Supt. Richard York, in both titles.
Death of a Theatre Filly. Elek, 1980 [theatre]
Funeral March for Siegfried. Elek, 1979 [theatre]

WILLIAMSON, B(EATRICE) G(LYNN)
Death Stalks the Ward. Hutchinson, 1942 [hosp.]

WILLIAMSON, C(HARLES) N(ORRIS), 1859-1920, and A(LICE) M(URIEL LIVINGSTON) WILLIAMSON, 1869-1933, q.v. Pseudonym of A(lice) M(uriel Livingston) Williamson: Dona Teresa de Savallo, q.v.
Alias Richard Power. Hodder, 1921
-Berry Goes to Monte Carlo. Mills, 1921 ss [Fr.]
-Briar Rose. Odhams, 1919
-Champion. Cassell, 1913
-The Cowboy Countess. Methuen, 1917
-The Demon. Methuen, 1912
-The Fortune Hunters and others. Mills, 1923 ss
The Great Pearl Secret. Methuen, 1921; Doubleday, 1921
The House of Silence. Hodder, 1921
-The Lady from the Air. Hodder, 1922; Doubleday, 1923
The Lion's Mouse. Methuen, 1919; Doubleday, 1919
-Lord John in New York. Methuen, 1918 [NYC]
Love and the Spy. Leng, 1908
-The Marquis of Loveland. McClure, 1908 (British title?)
-The Minx Goes to the Front. Mills, 1919 ss
The Night of the Wedding. Hodder, 1921; Doran, 1923
-The Powers and Maxine. Empire, 1907 (British title?)
-Scarlet Runner. Methuen, 1908 ss
The Second Latchkey. Doubleday, 1920 (British title?)
-The Shop-Girl. Methuen, 1916; Grosset, 1916
-A Soldier of the Legion. Nelson, 1915
-This Woman to This Man. Methuen, 1917
-Tiger Lily. Mills, 1917
-The Wedding Day. Methuen, 1914

WILLIAMSON, MRS. HARCOURT. Pseudonym of A(lice) M(uriel Livingston) Williamson, 1869-1933, q.v. Other pseudonym: Dona Teresa de Savallo, q.v.

WILLIAMSON, HUGH ROSS. 1901-1978.
A Wicked Pack of Cards. Joseph, 1961; Guild, 1965

WILLIAMSON, MARGARET
    The White Feather Mystery. Regency, 1945

WILLIAMSON, ROBIN. Joint pseudonym with Dan(iel Michael) Sherman, 1950-   , q.v.: Sherman Williamson, q.v.

WILLIAMSON, S(AMUEL) C(HARLES)
    The Compost Heap Corpses. Regency, 1966

WILLIAMSON, SHERMAN. Joint pseudonym of Robin Williamson and Dan(iel Michael) Sherman, 1950-   , q.v.
    The Glory Trap. New English Library, 1977; Walker, 1977   [Mor.]

WILLIAMSON, TONY [ANTHONY GEORGE WILLIAMSON]. 1932-   . Television reporter, writer for films and TV. SC: Lee Corey = LC.
    The Connector. Collins, 1976; Stein, 1976 LC [It.]
    Doomsday Contract. Collins, 1977; Stein, 1978 LC [Mid. East]
    The Samson Strike. Collins, 1979; Atheneum, 1980
    Technicians of Death. Collins, 1978; Atheneum, 1978 LC [Bangkok]

WILLIE, ENNIS
    Vice Town. Vega, 1962

WILLIS, G(RANVILLE) P(RATT)
    Escape at Dawn, with Michael P(atrick) O'Connor. Hale, 1961
    It Began in Singapore, with Michael P(atrick) O'Connor. Hale, 1958
    Somebody Killed Milner. Hale, 1968

WILLIS, GEORGE ANTHONY ARMSTRONG. 1897-1976. Pseudonym: Anthony Armstrong, q.v.

WILLIS, M(ABEL) AUDREY
    Flowers of Vengeance. Jarrolds, 1925

WILLIS, MAUD. Pseudonym of Eileen (Shubb) Lottman, 1927-   , q.v.
    The Devil's Rain. Dell, 1975 (Novelization of the movie.)

WILLIS, TED [EDWARD HENRY WILLIS]. 1918-   . See also: Henry Cecil. Ref: CA, TC. SC: George Dixon, in at least those marked GD. Set: Eng.
    The Blue Lamp. Convoy, 1950 GD
    The Buckingham Palace Connection. Macmillan (London), 1978; Morrow, 1978
    The Churchill Commando. Macmillan (London), 1977; Morrow, 1977
    Death May Surprise Us. Macmillan (London), 1974. U.S. title: Westminster One. Putnam, 1975
    The Devil's Churchyard. Parrish, 1957   GD
    Dixon of Dock Green, with Charles Hatton. Kimber, 1960 GD
    Dixon of Dock Green, with Paul Graham. Mayflower, 1961 GD
    The Left-Handed Sleeper. Macmillan (London), 1975; Putnam, 1976
    The Lions of Judah. Macmillan (London), 1979; Holt, 1980 [Ger., 1939]
    -The Naked Sun. Macmillan (London), 1980
    Seven Gates to Nowhere. Parrish, 1958   GD
    Westminster One; see Death May Surprise Us

WILLOCK, COLIN (DENNISTOUN). 1918-   . Ref: CA, CC. SC: Nathaniel Goss, in all titles. Set: Eng.
    Death at Flight. Heinemann, 1956
    Death at the Strike. Heinemann, 1957
    Death in Covert. Heinemann, 1961

WILLOCK, RUTH. 1904-   . Ref: CA.
    I, Victoria Strange. Hawthorn, 1975; Collins, 1975 [Scot.]
    The Moonlit Trap. Hawthorn, 1973; Collins, 1974
    The Night of the Visitor. Ace, 1965; Hodder, 1966 [Eng.]
    The Street of the Small Steps. Hawthorn, 1972; Collins, 1972 [Zurich]
    The Twisted Key. Collins, 1977

WILLOUGHBY, JOHN
    Crimsoned Millions. Clode, 1927 [L.I.]

WILLS, C(HARLES) J(AMES). 1842-1912.
    The Pit Town Coronet. Ward, 1888

WILLS, (MAITLAND) CECIL M(ELVILLE). 1891-   . Ref: TC. SC: Roger Ellerdine = RE; Geoffrey Boscobell = GB; Sylvester Horatio Pinkney = SP. Set: Eng.
    Author in Distress. Heritage, 1934. Also published as: Number 19. Bodley, 1934 GB

    A Body in the Dawn. Hodder, 1938 GB
    The Case of the Calabar Bean. Hodder, 1939 GB
    The Case of the Empty Beehive. Hale, 1959 SP
    The Case of the R. E. Pipe. Hodder, 1940 GB,RE
    The Chamois Murder. Heritage, 1935 GB
    The Clue of the Golden Ear-Ring. Hodder, 1950 RE,GB [Cyprus]
    The Clue of the Lost Hour. Hodder, 1949 GB,RE
    The Colonel's Foxhound. Hale, 1960 SP [Fr.]
    The Dead Voice. Hodder, 1952 RE
    Death at the Pelican. Heritage, 1934 GB
    Death in the Dark. Hutchinson, 1955 RE
    Death of a Best Seller. Hale, 1959 SP
    Death on the Line. Hutchinson, 1954
    "Death Treads—". Heritage, 1935 GB
    Defeat of a Detective. Hodder, 1936 GB
    Fatal Accident. Hodder, 1936 GB
    It Pays to Die. Hodder, 1953 RE
    Justice in Jeopardy. Hale, 1961 RE
    Mere Murder. Hale, 1958 RE
    Midsummer Murder. Hutchinson, 1956
    Number 18; see Author in Distress
    On the Night in Question. Hodder, 1937 GB
    Then Came the Police. Heritage, 1935 GB
    The Tiger Strikes Again. Hutchinson, 1957 RE
    What Say the Jury? Hodder, 1952 RE
    Who Killed Brother Treasurer? Hodder, 1951 RE

WILLS, GARRY. 1934-   . Ref: CA.
    At Button's. Andrews, 1979 [New Or.]

WILLS, HELEN (NEWINGTON), 1906-   , and ROBERT W(ILLIAM) MURPHY, 1902-1971, q.v.
    Death Serves an Ace. Scribner, 1939; Hutchinson, 1939 [Eng.]

WILLS, RONALD. Pseudonym of Ronald Wills Thomas, 1910-   . Other pseudonym: Jeff Bogar, q.v.
    The Big Fish. Wingate, 1951; Roy, 1954
    The Black Weaver. Wingate, 1952; Roy, 1955
    Food for Fishes. Dakers, 1954
    Live Bait. Wingate, 1950

WILLS, THOMAS. Pseudonym of William (Thomas) Ard, 1922-1960, q.v. Other pseudonyms: Ben Kerr, Mike Moran, qq.v.
    Mine to Avenge. GM, 1955; Fawcett (London), 1956
    You'll Get Yours. Lion, 1952. Also published as by William Ard: Berkley, 1960 [NYC]

WILLS, W. G. and MRS. GREEN
    Whose Hand?; or, The Mystery of No Man's Heath. Rand, 1890

WILLSDON, ANDREW
    Murder Breeds Murder. Hale, 1971
    The One-Off Job. Hale, 1970

WILMER, DALE. Joint pseudonym of Robert Wade, 1920-   , q.v., and Bill Miller, 1920-1961. Other joint pseudonyms: Will Daemer, Wade Miller, Whit Masterson, qq.v. See also: Bob Wade.
    Dead Fall. Bouregy, 1954 [Calif.]
    Jungle Heat. Pyramid, 1954; Panther, 1962
    Memo for Murder. Graphic, 1951 [L.A.]

WILMOT, EILEEN
    Dangerous Search. Wright, 1958
    Holiday with Danger. Wright, 1959
    Homicide at Saxondale. Progressive, 1949
    The Lurking Terror. Mellifont, 1956
    Murder Insoluble. Progressive, 1950
    Murder Will. Coker, 1951
    Not a Nice Murder! Brown Watson, 1949
    Poison for One. Fiction House, 1947
    Voodoo Drums. Fiction House, 1947

WILMOT, J(AMES) R(EGINALD). 1897-   . Pseudonym: Ralph Trevor, q.v.
    Death in the Stalls. Nicholson, 1934. U.S. title: Death in the Theatre. Kendall, 1934 [theatre]
    Death in the Theatre; see Death in the Stalls
    Night Tide. Nicholson, 1936
    -A Young Girl's Bondage. Newnes, 1935

WILMOT, ROBERT PATRICK. Born in Mont.; reporter and newspaper editor, radio and song lyric writer; living in NYC in 1950s. SC: Steve Considine, in all titles.
    Blood in Your Eye. Lippincott, 1952; Boardman, 1954 [NYC]

    Death Rides a Painted Horse. Lippincott, 1954; Boardman, 1955 [NYC]
    Murder on Monday. Lippincott, 1953; Boardman, 1954 [NYC]

WILSON, A. G. Pseudonym of W. G. A. Harrison.
    Come Away Death. Hurst, 1936
    Spider Ballet. Hurst, 1938

WILSON, ALEXANDER (DOUGLAS CHESNEY). 1893-   . Pseudonym: Geoffrey Spencer, q.v. SC: Sir Leonard Wallace, in at least those marked LW. Set: Eng.
    Chronicles of the Secret Service. Jenkins, 1940 ss LW
    The Crimson Dacoit. Jenkins, 1933 [India]
    The Death of Dr. Whitelaw. Longmans (London & NYC), 1930
    The Devil's Cocktail. Longmans (London & NYC), 1928 LW [India]
    Double Events. Jenkins, 1937
    Double Masquerade. Jenkins, 1940
    Get Wallace! Jenkins, 1934 LW
    His Excellency, Governor Wallace. Jenkins, 1936 LW
    The Magnificent Hobo. Jenkins, 1935
    Microbes of Power. Jenkins, 1937 LW
    Mr. Justice. Jenkins, 1937
    Murder Mansion. Longmans (London & NYC), 1929
    The Mystery of Tunnel 51. Longmans (London & NYC), 1928 LW [India]
    Scapegoats for Murder. Jenkins, 1939
    The Sentimental Crook. Jenkins, 1934
    Wallace at Bay. Jenkins, 1938 LW
    Wallace Intervenes. Jenkins, 1939 LW [Ger.]
    Wallace of the Secret Service. Jenkins, 1933 ss LW

WILSON, ALEXANDER. 1893-   . See: Ruth Wilson.

WILSON, CALDER. See: Nellie Tom-Gallon.

WILSON, CAROLYN (SCHISLER). 1938-   . Ref: CA.
    The Scent of Lilacs. Ace, 1966

WILSON, CHRISTOPHER
    For a Woman's Honour. Paul, 1911
    -The Heart of Delilah. Blackwood, 1912
    The Missing Millionaire. Blackwood, 1911
    -The Wings of Destiny. Daily Mail, 1909

WILSON, COLIN (HENRY). 1931-   . Ref: CA, CC, TC. Set: Eng.
    The Black Room. Weidenfeld, 1971
    The Glass Cage. Barker, 1966; Random, 1967
    -The God of the Labyrinth. Hart-Davis, 1970. U.S. title: The Hedonists. Signet, 1971
    The Hedonists; see The God of the Labyrinth
    The Killer. New English Library, 1970. U.S. title: Lingard. Crown, 1970
    Lingard; see The Killer
    Necessary Doubt. Barker, 1964; Trident, 1964
    -The Philosopher's Stone. Barker, 1969; Crown, 1971
    Ritual in the Dark. Gollancz, 1960; Houghton, 1960
    The Schoolgirl Murder Case. Hart-Davis, 1974; Crown, 1974
    The Violent World of Hugh Greene; see The World of Violence
    The World of Violence. Gollancz, 1963. U.S. title: The Violent World of Hugh Greene. Houghton, 1963

WILSON, DANA
    Make with the Brains, Pierre. Messner, 1946. British title: Scenario for Murder. Foulsham, 1949. Also published as: Uneasy Virtue. Avon, 1948 [L.A.]

WILSON, DAVID. Pseudonym of D(avid) Wilson MacArthur, 1903-   , q.v.
    Murder in Mozambique. Jenkins, 1963 [Mozam.]
    The Search for Geoffrey Goring. Jenkins, 1962

WILSON, DAVID. SC: McCloud, in all titles, which are novelizations of the TV series.
    The Corpse Maker. Award, 1974; Tandem, 1974 [NYC]
    A Dangerous Place to Die. Award, 1975; Tandem, 1975
    The Killing. Award, 1974; Tandem, 1974 [NYC]
    Park Avenue Executioner. Award, 1975; Tandem, 1975 [Mex. City]

WILSON, E. LEA
The Vanishing Hand. (Author), 1893 (3 stories.)

WILSON, G(ERTRUDE) M(ARY BRYANT). 1899- . SC: Insp. Lovick, in at least those marked L. Set: Eng.
Bury That Poker. Hale, 1957 L
The Bus Ran Late. Hale, 1971 L
Cake for Caroline. Hale, 1967 L
A Deal of Death Caps. Hale, 1970 L
Death Is Buttercups. Hale, 1969 L
Death on a Broomstick. Hale, 1977
The Devil's Skull. Hale, 1965 L
Do Not Sleep. Hale, 1968 L [Fr.]
Gipsies Don't Have Them. Hale, 1974
The Headless Man. Hale, 1967 L
I Was Murdered. Hale, 1957; Walker, 1961 L
It Rained That Friday. Hale, 1960
Murder on Monday. Hale, 1963 L
Nightmare Cottage. Hale, 1963
Roberta Died. Hale, 1962 L
Shadows on the Landing. Hale, 1959 L
She Kept on Dying. Hale, 1972 L
She Sees Things. Hale, 1975
Shot at Dawn. Hale, 1964 L
Thirteen Stannergate. Hale, 1958
Three Fingered Death. Hale, 1961
Witchwater. Hale, 1961 L

WILSON, GREGORY. Set: Eng.
The Boxing Mystery. Modern, 1938
The Factory Mystery. Modern, 1938

WILSON, GROVE. 1883-1954.
The Monster of Snowdon Hall. Washburn, 1932; Skeffington, 1933 [N.Y.]
The Mysterious Wife. Frank-Maurice, 1927
Sport of the Gods. Frank-Maurice, 1926

WILSON, IVOR (ARTHUR). 1924- . SC: Greg Flamm, in all titles. Ref: CA.
But Not for Love. Collins, 1962
Empty Tigers. Collins, 1965 [Greece]
Lilies That Fester. Collins, 1964
That Feeds on Men. Collins, 1963

WILSON, JACK [JOHN AITKEN WILSON]. 1937- . Ref: CA.
-Adam Grey. Muller, 1964. Also published as: The Night Comer. Corgi, 1966
The Night Comer; see Adam Grey
-The Tomorrow Country. Muller, 1967
-The Wild Summer. Muller, 1963

WILSON, JACQUELINE. 1945- . Ref: CA.
Hide and Seek. Macmillan (London), 1972; Doubleday, 1973
Let's Pretend. Macmillan (London), 1976
Making Hate. Macmillan (London), 1977; St. Martin's, 1978
Snap. Macmillan (London), 1974
Truth or Dare. Macmillan (London), 1973; Doubleday, 1974

WILSON, JEANNE (PATRICIA PAULINE). 1920- . Ref: CA.
Model for Murder. Ward, 1968
No Medicine for Murder. Ward, 1967

WILSON, JOHN ANTHONY BURGESS. 1917- . Pseudonym: Anthony Burgess, q.v.

WILSON, JOS(EPH) N(ATHANIEL PUBLICOVER). 1894- .
-Hell's Harvest. Meador, 1940

WILSON, JOYCE
Shadow Hill. Popular Library, 1977

WILSON, LANFORD. 1938- .
The Rimers of Eldritch. Dramatists, 1967 (2-act play.)

WILSON, LEE. Pseudonym of Laura Elizabeth Lemmon, 1917- .
This Deadly Drop. Dodd, 1946 [S.F.]

WILSON, MARIE BEATRICE. 1922- . Pseudonym: Jeanne Marie, q.v.

WILSON, MARY. Pseudonym of Mary Linn Roby, 1930- , q.v. Other pseudonym: Elizabeth Welles, q.v.
The Changeling. Dell, 1975
The Wind of Death. Dell, 1976 [Eng.]

WILSON, MITCHELL A. 1913-1973. Joint pseudonym with Abraham Lincoln Polonsky, 1910- : Emmett Hogarth, q.v. Ref: CA.
Footsteps Behind Her. Simon, 1941 [NYC]
The Huntress. Doubleday, 1966; Secker, 1966
None So Blind. Simon, 1945; Allen, 1947
The Panic-Stricken. Simon, 1946 [ship]
Stalk the Hunter. Simon, 1943 [NYC]

WILSON, NORMAN SCARLYN. 1901- . Pseudonym: Anthony Webb, q.v.

WILSON, P(HILIP) W(HITWELL). 1875-1956. Ref: CC. SC: Sir Julian Morthoe, in all titles, all set in Eng.
Black Tarn. Farrar, 1945; Boardman, 1948 [1909]
Bride's Castle. Farrar, 1944; Boardman, 1946 [1893]
The Old Mill. Rinehart, 1946; Boardman, 1948 [1912]

WILSON, ROBERT ANTON. 1932- . See: Robert Shea.

WILSON, ROBERT McNAIR. 1882-1963. Pseudonym: Anthony Wynne, q.v.

WILSON, RUTH and ALEXANDER WILSON, 1893- .
The Town Is Full of Rumors. Simon, 1941. Also published as: Death Watch. Ace, 1955

WILSON, SLOAN. 1920- . Ref: CA.
The Greatest Crime. Arbor, 1980 [ship]

WILSON, STANLEY KIDDER. 1879-1944.
The Scream of the Doll. Duffield, 1931

WILSON, STEVE. 1943- .
Dealer's Move. Macmillan (London), 1978
Dealer's War. Macmillan (London), 1980

WILSON, T(REVOR) E(DWARD)
Fugitive from Fear. Hale, 1972
Knock Softly on Death's Door. Hale, 1971
-The Parasites. Hale, 1973

WILSON, WILLIAM. 1935- .
Detour. Putnam, 1974

WILSON-BARRETT, ALFRED. 1871- . See: Alfred Wilson Barrett, 1871- .

WILSTACH, JOHN
-The Fate of Fay Delray. Macaulay, 1933
Under Cover Man. Morrow, 1931

WIMBERLY, ROBERT L.
Willy Velvet, Homicide Detective. Dramatic, 1956 (1-act play.)

WIMHURST, CECIL GORDON EUGENE. 1905- . Pseudonym: Nigel Brent, q.v.

WINCH, EDGAR
The Hunting of Hillary. Skeffington, 1929
-The Mountain of Gold. Hurst, 1928
-When the Tide Runs Out. Hurst, 1930

WINCHELL, PRENTICE. 1895- . Pseudonyms: Spencer Dean, Jay de Bekker, Dexter St. Clair, Dexter St. Clare, Stewart Sterling, qq.v.

WINCHESTER, CLARENCE (ARTHUR CHARLES). 1892- .
City of Lies. Collins, 1942
-The Devil Rides High. Collins, 1933
Three Men in a Plane. Collins, 1941

WINCHESTER, JACK. Pseudonym of "a veteran British writer of espionage fiction."
The Solitary Man. H. Hamilton, 1980; Coward, 1980 [NYC]

WINCHESTER, STANLEY
Ten Per Cent of Your Life. Allen, 1973

WINCOR, RICHARD
The St. Ives Murders. Oceana, 1958
Sherlock Holmes in Tibet. Weybright, 1968 (Sherlock Holmes.) [Tib.]

WINDSOR, GEORGE
Nelson Lord—One of Our Agents. Stockwell, 1974

WINDSOR, HUGH. Set: Eng.
Dead Man's Shoes. Gifford, 1964
Lead Him to Death. Gifford, 1963
The Source of Death. Gifford, 1964

WINDSOR-RICHARDS, A(RTHUR BEDLINGTON). 1904- . Ref: CA.
Of Hidden Depths. Gifford, 1966

WINDUST, CHARLES
Some Crime Stories. Weekly Dispatch, 1899 ss

WINER, ELIHU
Anatomy of a Murder. French (NYC), 1966 (3-act play based on the novel by Robert Traver, q.v.)

WING, WILLIS KINGSLEY. Pseudonym: Michael Bryan, q.v.

WINGARD, ALAN
The Graffiti Gambit. Paperback Library, 1974

WINGATE, JOHN. 1920- . Ref: CA.
Avalanche. Weidenfeld, 1977; St. Martin's, 1977 [Austria]
Oil Strike. Weidenfeld, 1976; St. Martin's, 1976
Seawaymen. Weidenfeld, 1979
-Target Risk. Weidenfeld, 1978

WINGATE, WILLIAM. Pseudonym of Ronald Ivan Grbich, 1939- .
Bloodbath. Hutchinson, 1978; St. Martin's, 1980 [Afr.]
Fireplay. Hutchinson, 1977; Coward, 1977
Shotgun. St. Martin's, 1980 [Tenn.]

WINN, PATRICK. 1906- . Born in Eng. but living in Australia after 1927; author of ss and plays. SC: Insp. Lyon, in at least those marked L.
Colour of Murder. Hale, 1965
Dead Innocent. Hale, 1966 L [Australia]
Dusty Sunset. Hale, 1962
Fact X. Hale, 1966 L [Australia]
Invisible Evidence. Hale, 1963
Postscript to Murder. Hale, 1964 L [Australia]

WINNER, PERCY. 1899-1974. Ref: CA.
Scene in the Ice-Blue Eyes. Harcourt, 1947

WINNINGTON, ALAN
Berlin Epitaph; see Berlin Halt
Berlin Halt. Hale, 1973. U.S. title: Berlin Epitaph. Pinnacle, 1974 [Berlin]
Catseyes. Cassell, 1967
The Fairfax Millions. Hale, 1974

WINSLOW, DORIAN. Pseudonym of Daoma Winston, 1922- , q.v.
The Sorcerers. Avon, 1973

WINSLOW, HORATIO (GATES), 1882- , and LESLIE (W.) QUIRK, 1882- . Ref: CC.
Into Thin Air. Doubleday, 1929; Gollancz, 1928

WINSLOW, JOAN. Pseudonym of Ware Torrey (Budlong), 1905-1967. Other pseudonyms: Lee Crosby, Meg Padget, Judith Ware, qq.v.
Griffin Towers. Ace, 1966

WINSLOW, PAULINE GLEN. Ref: CA. SC: Supt. Merlin Capricorn = MC. Set: Eng.
The Brandenburg Hotel. Macmillan (London), 1976; St. Martin's, 1976 MC
Copper Gold; see Coppergold
Coppergold. Collins, 1978. U.S. title: Copper Gold. St. Martin's, 1978 MC
The Counsellor Heart. Collins, 1980; St. Martin's, 1980 MC
Death of an Angel. Macmillan (London), 1975; St. Martin's, 1975 MC
Gallows Child; see The Strawberry Marten
The Strawberry Marten. Macmillan (London), 1973. U.S. title: Gallows Child. St. Martin's, 1978
The Witch Hill Murder. Collins, 1977; St. Martin's, 1977 MC

WINSOR, DIANA. 1946- . Born in Belfast; worked on newspapers, edited a company magazine; ss writer and painter.
The Death Convention. Macmillan (London), 1974; Stein, 1978 [Amst.]
Red on Wight. Macmillan (London), 1972; Stein, 1978

WINSOR, G(EORGE) McLEOD
The Mysterious Disappearances. Faber, 1926. U.S. title: Vanishing Men. Morrow, 1927
-Once Bitten, and What Ensued. Jenkins, 1930
-Station X. Jenkins, 1919
Vanishing Men; see The Mysterious Disappearances

WINSOR, ROY. 1912- . Ref: CA. SC: Ira Cobb, in all titles.
Always Lock Your Bedroom Door. GM, 1976 [Mass.]
The Corpse That Walked. GM, 1974 [Mass.]
Three Motives for Murder. GM, 1976 [N.Y.]

WINSTANLEY, L(ILIAN). 1875- .
  The Double Disappearance. Hutchinson, 1925
  The Face on the Stair. Hutchinson, 1927

WINSTEAD, REBECCA NOYES
  Tunnel of Darkness. Canyon, 1974. Also published as: The Forbidden Mansion. Carousel, 1981, as by Angel Davidson

WINSTON, DAOMA. 1922- . Ref: CA.
  The Adventuress. Simon, 1978; Macdonald, 1979 [Md., ca.1900]
  Carnaby Curse. Belmont, 1967
  Castle of Closing Doors. Belmont, 1967 [Mex.]
  The Death Watch. Ace, 1975 [Calif.]
  Dennison Hill. Paperback Library, 1970
  The Devil's Daughter. Lancer, 1971
  The Devil's Princess. Lancer, 1971; Piatkus, 1980
  The Dream Killers. Ace, 1976
  Emerald Station. Avon, 1974; Futura, 1977 [New Eng.]
  Flight of a Fallen Angel. Lancer, 1971; Piatkus, 1982
  -Gallows Way. Simon, 1976; Macdonald, 1978 [N.C., 1858]
  The Golden Valley. Simon, 1975
  The Haversham Legacy. Simon, 1974; Futura, 1977 [Wash. D.C., 1860s]
  House of Mirror Images. Lancer, 1970; Piatkus, 1981
  The Inheritance. Avon, 1972
  Kingdom's Castle. Berkley, 1972; Piatkus, 1981
  The Long and Living Shadow. Belmont, 1968
  The Lotteries. Morrow, 1980; Macdonald, 1980 [Vt.]
  The Love of Lucifer. Lancer, 1971 [Md.]
  The Mansion of Smiling Masks. Signet, 1967
  -Mills of the Gods. Simon, 1979; Macdonald, 1979
  Moorhaven. Avon, 1974; Futura, 1980
  Pity My Love. Belmont, 1967
  The Return. Avon, 1972
  The Secrets of Cromwell Crossing. Lancer, 1965 [N. Mex.]
  Seminar in Evil. Lancer, 1972
  Shaow of an Unknown Woman. Lancer, 1967; Piatkus, 1979
  Shadow on Mercer Mountain. Lancer, 1967
  Sinister Stone. Paperback Library, 1966
  Skeleton Key. Piatkus, 1980 (U.S. title?)
  The Trap. Popular Library, 1973
  The Trificante Treasure. Lancer, 1968 [Fla.]
  The Unforgotten. Berkley, 1973
  The Vampire Curse. Paperback Library, 1971
  The Victim. Popular Library, 1972
  The Wakefield Witches. Award, 1966
  Walk Around the Square. Ace, 1975

WINSTON, PETER. SC: Peter Winston, in all titles (novelizations of "The Adjusters" TV series).
  The ABC Affair. Award, 1967; Tandem, 1967
  Assignment to Bahrein. Award, 1967; Tandem, 1967 [Mid. East]
  Doomsday Vendetta. Award, 1968 [Mor.]
  The Glass Cipher. Award, 1968; Tandem, 1968

WINSTON, ROBERT ALEXANDER. 1907-1974.
  Pseudonym: Col. Victor J. Fox, q.v.

WINTER, ABIGAIL. Pseudonym of Monroe Schere.
  Olivia's Story. Dell, 1976
  Whispering Caverns. Simon, 1974 [New Eng.]

WINTER, BEVIS. 1918- . Pseudonyms: Al Bocca, Peter Cagney, Gordon Shayne, qq.v. See also: Eric Maschwitz, 1901-1969. Ref: CA. SC: Steve Craig, in at least those marked SC.
  Blondes End Up Dead. Jenkins, 1959 SC
  The Dark and Deadly. Jenkins, 1961 SC
  Darker Grows the Street. Jenkins, 1955 SC
  The Dead Sleep for Keeps. Jenkins, 1955 SC
  Let the Lady Die. Jenkins, 1957 SC
  Make Murder. Warren, 1949
  Next Stop—the Morgue. Jenkins, 1956 SC
  The Night Was Made for Murder. Jenkins, 1957 SC [Calif.]
  A Noose of Emeralds. Mystery House, 1956 (British title?) SC
  Redheads Are Poison. Hamilton & Co., 1948
  Redheads Cool Fast. Jenkins, 1954 SC
  Sleep Long, My Lovely. Jenkins, 1958 SC

WINTER, JOHN STRANGE. Pseudonym of Henrietta Eliza Vaughan Palmer Stannard, 1856-1911.
  A Mystery of Mayfair. White, 1908

WINTERBOTHAM, RUSSELL ROBERT. 1904-1971. Pseudonym: J. Harvey Bond, q.v.

WINTERS, JON. Pseudonym of Gilbert B. Cross. Ref: CA.
  The Drakov Memoranda. Avon, 1979

WINTERTON, PAUL. 1908- . Pseudonyms: Roger Bax, Andrew Garve, Paul Somers, qq.v.

WINTHROP, WILMA
  Hostage of Evil. Lancer, 1966
  Island of the Accursed. Lancer, 1965 [Carib.]
  Tryst with Terror. Lancer, 1965

WINTLE, ALFRED DANIEL. Pseudonym: Michael Cobb, q.v.

WINTLE, GILBERT
  -The Gentleman Tramp. Ward, 1907
  -Gold of Cathay. Ward, 1908
  -Meshes of Mischance. Ward, 1906
  Strange Partners. Ward, 1905

WINTLE, HAROLD
  -The Great Betrayal. Ouseley, 1911

WINTLE, W(ILLIAM) J(AMES)
  Nights with an Old Lag. Ouseley, 1911 ss

WINWARD, (RICHARD) WALTER. 1938- . Ref: CA.
  -The Conscripts. Cassell, 1968
  Fives Wild. Weidenfeld, 1975; Atheneum, 1976
  Hammerstrike. H. Hamilton, 1978; Simon, 1979 [Eng., 1942]
  -Rough Deal. Weidenfeld, 1977
  Seven Minutes Past Midnight. H. Hamilton, 1979; Simon, 1980 [Berlin, 1945]

WIRE, H(AROLD) C(HANNING). 1899- . Born in Calif., and has lived there most of his life; author of some 300 magazine stories.
  Marked Man. Appleton, 1934; World's Work, 1950 [Nev.]
  Mountain Man. Crowell, 1929; Skeffington, 1930
  -The Witness Tree. Crowell, 1930

WISE, ARDATH
  Dark Waters. Lenox, 1974; Remploy, 1974
  The Gold Door. Lenox, 1972
  Tiger Hill. Lenox, 1975

WISE, ARTHUR. 1923- . Ref: CA, CC.
  The Death's-Head. Cassell, 1962
  Leatherjacket. Weidenfeld, 1970
  The Little Fishes. Gollancz, 1961
  The Naughty Girls. Allen, 1971
  Who Killed Enoch Powell? Weidenfeld, 1970; Harper, 1971

WISE, WILLIAM
  The Amazon Factor. Raven, 1980 [N.J.]

WISEMAN, RICHARD
  Duncan Is in His Grave. Hale, 1978
  First Person Plural. Macmillan (London), 1975

WISEMAN, THOMAS. 1931- . Ref: CA.
  The Day Before Sunrise. Cape, 1976; Holt, 1976 [Berlin, 1945]
  A Game of Secrets. Cape, 1979; Delacorte, 1979 [Wash. D.C., 1947]

WISER, WILLIAM. Ref: CA.
  Disappearances. Atheneum 1980

WISHART, GERTRUDE
  Madame Lies Murdered. Long, 1940

WISHART, NAN
  Fatal Entrance. New Horizon, 1979

WISHMAN, SEYMOUR
  Nothing Personal. Delacorte, 1978 [NYC]

WISSMAN, RUTH (LESLIE). 1914- . Ref: CA.
  Celebration for Murder. Doubleday, 1979; Hale, 1980
  The Claws of the Crow. Paperback Library, 1974
  Desert of Darkness. Paperback Library, 1972 [Calif.]
  Dreamer Beware. Doubleday, 1977; Hale, 1978
  Fear Waits on Cypress Road. Doubleday, 1975; Hale, 1976
  The Shadow of Sheila Ann. Paperback Library, 1974
  To Hang a Witch. Paperback Library, 1974
  -Whispers in the Wind. Doubleday, 1980

WITHERS, E. L. Pseudonym of George William Potter, Jr., 1930- . Ref: CA, CC.
  The Birthday. Doubleday, 1962
  Diminishing Returns. Rinehart, 1960; Harrap, 1961
  Heir Apparent. Doubleday, 1961; Harrap, 1962 [It., 1941]
  The House on the Beach. Rinehart, 1957; Harrap, 1958
  The Salazar Grant. Rinehart, 1959; Harrap, 1960 [N. Mex.]

WITHERS, JULIA
  Caprice. Dell, 1967 (Novelization of the movie.)
  Echo in a Dark Wind. Signet, 1966 [Eng.]
  The Shuttered Room. Dell, 1966; Mayflower, 1967 (Novelization of the movie.)

WITLEY, A. F. Pseudonym of Sandor Forbat, 1890- .
  Dangerously Blonde. Pallas, 1938 (Translation of "Je Suis Innocent." Paris, 19??.)

WITNEY, FREDERIC C.
  Grand Guignol. Constable, 1947 (1-act play.)

WITTING, CLIFFORD. 1907- . Ref: CA, CC, TC. SC: Insp. Charlton = C; Sgt./Insp. Peter Bradfield = PB. Set: Eng.
  A Bullet for Rhino. Hodder, 1950 C
  The Case of the Busy Bees. Hodder, 1952 C,PB
  The Case of the Michaelmas Goose. Hodder, 1938 C,PB
  Catt out of the Bag. Hodder, 1939 C
  Crime in Whispers. Hodder, 1964 PB
  Dead on Time. Hodder, 1948 C,PB
  Driven to Kill. Hodder, 1961 PB
  Let X Be the Murderer. Hodder, 1947 C,PB
  Measure for Murder. Hodder, 1941 C
  Midsummer Murder. Hodder, 1937 C
  Mischief in the Offing. Hodder, 1958 C
  Murder in Blue. Hodder, 1937; Scribner, 1937 C
  Silence After Dinner. Hodder, 1953 PB,C
  Subject—Murder. Hodder, 1945 C,PB
  There Was a Crooked Man. Hodder, 1960; British Book Centre, 1962 PB
  Villainous Saltpeter. Hodder, 1962

WITTMAN, GEORGE
  A Matter of Intelligence. Macmillan, 1975

WLASCHIN, KEN(NETH). See also: Troy Kennedy Martin.
  To Kill the Pope. New English Library pb, 1971 [Rome]

WODEHOUSE, P(ELHAM) G(RENVILLE). 1881-1975. Ref: CA.
  -Do Butlers Burgle Banks? Jenkins, 1968; Simon, 1968
  He Rather Enjoyed It; see Ukridge
  -Hot Water. Jenkins, 1932; Doubleday, 1933
  -Ice in the Bedroom. Jenkins, 1961; Simon, 1961
  -The Little Nugget. Methuen, 1913; Watt, 1914
  -The Old Reliable. Jenkins, 1951; Doubleday, 1951
  -Piccadilly Jim. Jenkins, 1918; Dodd, 1917
  -Pigs Have Wings. Jenkins, 1952; Doubleday, 1952
  -Ukridge. Jenkins, 1924. U.S. title: He Rather Enjoyed It. Doran, 1925 ss
  The Uncollected Wodehouse. Seabury, 1976 ss, one criminous

WODEN, GEORGE. Pseudonym of George Wilson Slaney, 1884- . Ref: CA.
  The Cathkin Mystery. Hutchinson, 1937
  -Mungo. Hutchinson, 1932
  The Mystery of the Amorous Music Master. Hutchinson, 1951
  The Puzzled Policeman. Hutchinson, 1949
  -The Queer Folk Next Door. Hutchinson, 1942
  The Wrenfield Mystery. Parsons, 1923

WOGAN, CHARLES. SC: Sebastian Stole, in all titles. Set: Eng.
  Cyanide for the Chorister. Long, 1950
  The Hangman's Hands. Long, 1947
  The Horror at Wardens Hall. Long, 1948

WOHL, BURTON
China Syndrome. Bantam, 1979; Corgi, 1979 (Novelization of the movie.)
-High Encounter. Bantam (NYC & London), 1975
Rollercoaster. Dell, 1977; Mayflower, 1977
The Ten Tola Bars. Delacorte, 1975; Hamlyn, 1978

WOHL, JAMES P(AUL). 1937- . Pseudonym: James Coltrane, q.v. Ref: CA. SC: Sam Gross, in both titles.
The Blind Trust Kills. Bobbs, 1978; Hale, 1980 [Phoenix]
The Nirvana Contracts. Bobbs, 1977 [NYC]

WOHLFROM, CLARENCE J.
Bite of the Tigress. Vantage, 1976

WOLF, JACK (CLIFFORD). 1922- . Ref: CA. SC: Timothy Rourke = TR.
Death Rides a Camel. Hammond, 1960 [Afr., N.]
Payoff on Fever Street. Hammond, 1962 TR
Two Shadows for Death. Hammond, 1961 TR [Calif.]

WOLF, MARI. 1927- .
The Golden Frame. Permabooks, 1961

WOLFE, JOHN. Lives in Houston. SC: Johnny McCoy, in both titles.
Drilling for Death. Raven, 1980 [Houston]
The Wrong Target. Major, 1978

WOLFE, JONATHAN
Killer See, Killer Do. Leisure, 1977

WOLFE, LINDA
Private Practices. Simon, 1980; Allen, 1980

WOLFE, MICHAEL. Pseudonym of Gilbert M. Williams, 1917- . SC: Michael Keefe, in all titles.
The Chinese Fire Drill. Harper, 1976 [Viet Nam]
Man on a String. Harper, 1973 [Viet Nam]
The Panama Paradox. Harper, 1977 [Pan.]
The Two-Star Pigeon. Harper, 1975 [Viet Nam]

WOLFE, WINIFRED (HARRIET). 1929- .
Ref: CA.
Never Step on a Rainbow. Harper, 1965; Gollancz, 1966

WOLFENDEN, GEORGE. Pseudonym of George Beardmore, 1908- , q.v. Other pseudonym: Cedric Stokes, q.v.
The House in Spitalfields. Hurst, 1937
-The Little Doves of Destruction. Hurst, 1942
The Spy Who Died in Bed. Hurst, 1941

WOLFERT, IRA
Tucker's People. Fischer, 1943. Also published as: The Underworld. Bantam, 1950

WOLFF, RUTH
I, Keturah. Day, 1963; Dent, 1964. Also published as: Hawthorne. Paperback Library, 1965

WOLFF, WILLIAM ALMON. 1885-1933. SC: Sgt./Lt. Charley Mitchell = CM.
Manhattan Night. Minton, 1930 CM [NYC]
Murder at Endor. Minton, 1933; Putnam (London), 1933 CM [N.J.]
The Trial of Mary Dugan. Doubleday, 1928; Heinemann, 1928 [NYC]

WOLFFE, KATHERINE. Pseudonym of Marian Gallagher Scott, 1892- . Other pseudonym: Gail Oliver, q.v. SC: Capt. Courtney Brade = CB.
The Attic Room. Morrow, 1942 CB
Bride of Death; see Tall Man Walking
Death's Long Shadow. Five Star, 1946 CB [Minn.]
Tall Man Walking. Doubleday, 1936. British title: Bride of Death. Bell, 1937

WOLFSON, P(INCUS) J(ACOB). 1903- .
Ref: CA.
Bodies Are Dust. Vanguard, 1931 [NYC]

WOLFSON, VI
Nothing Happens to Children in Beverly Hills. Putnam, 1975; Hale, 1976 [L.A.]

WOLFSON, VICTOR. 1910- . Pseudonym: Langdon Dodge, q.v. Ref: CA.
The Lonely Steeple. Simon, 1945

WOLK, GEORGE. Born in NYC; graduate of Cornell U.
400 Brattle Street. Wyden, 1978; Sphere, 1980 [Boston]
-Jeremiah Painter. Dell, 1973; New English Library, 1976
The Leopold Contract. Random, 1969 [Rome]
The Man Who Dealt in Blood. Warner, 1974 [NYC]

WOLSELEY, FAITH. Pseudonym of Stella (Mary Hodgson) Tower, 1891- , q.v.
-Old Mrs. Warren. Crisp, 1945
Screened. Murray, 1937
Which Way Came Death? Murray, 1936 [acad.]

WOOD, (SAMUEL) ANDREW. 1890- . Byline sometimes: S. Andrew Wood, but all works are listed here. Pseudonym: Robin Temple, q.v. SC: Magnus Keeble, in at least those marked MK; Sasha, in at least those marked S; Koregorvsky, in at least those marked K. Set: Eng.
Big Ben Struck Twelve. Hurst, 1948 MK
Blind Man's Buff. Jenkins, 1943
Bright Angel. Ward, 1933; Dutton, 1933 K
Castle Dangerous. Cherry Tree, 1941
-Cinderella All Alone. Jenkins, 1926
Deep Flows the River. Mellifont, 1950
Eros Is No Hangman. Hurst, 1949 MK
-The Flower of Desire. Dutton, 1927 (British title?)
The Four Pitiful People. Hurst, 1947
Hangman's Child. Hodder, 1936
Hell for Leather. Jarrolds, 1930
-Her Second Self. Thomson, 1933
-I'll Blackmail the World. Hodder, 1935
-The Isle of Enchantment. Jenkins, 1925
It's Easy to Kill. Hodder, 1938
Judgement Castle. Dragon, 1955
King Vagabond. Hodder, 1936 S
The Little Widow Murder. Fiction House, 1949
The Man Who Came Back. Cherry Tree, 1942
The Midnight Road. Mellifont, 1943
-The Misleading Lady. Cassell, 1926
Murder at the Wishing Well. Mellifont, 1944
Murder by the Minute. Dragon, 1955 MK
Not Proven Castle. Hodder, 1936
Odds Against Her. Leng, 1929
-Phantom Railway. Muller, 1954
Port of Little Ships. Hurst, 1947
The Prom Concert Murders. Hurst, 1948 MK
Red-Handed They Came. Mellifont, 1945
Red Square. Ward, 1934; Dutton, 1934 K,S [Moscow]
Release the Prisoner. Hodder, 1937
The River Will Hide Me. Cherry Tree, 1949
Serenade for Murder. Cherry Tree, 1944
Sinister Island. Cherry Tree, 1945
Sinners' Castle. Jenkins, 1941; Swift, 1941
Stick at Nothing. Jenkins, 1939
Street Paved with Water. Cherry Tree, 1946
Ten Peacocks. Ward, 1934
There Is No Ogpu. Jenkins, 1940
-Volcano Island. Venturebooks, 1950
-Wed for Wealth. Thomson, 1931
White Sin. Ward, 1933

WOOD, BARBARA. 1947- .
Curse This House. Dell, 1978; Magnum, 1979 [Eng., 1800s]
Hounds and Jackals. Doubleday, 1978; Eyre, 1979 [Egypt]
The Magdalene Scrolls. Doubleday, 1978; Eyre, 1978
Night Trains, with Gareth Wootton. Morrow, 1979; Eyre, 1979 [Poland, WWII]
-Yesterday's Child. Doubleday, 1979

WOOD, BARI. 1936- . Ref: CA.
The Killing Gift. Putnam, 1975; Heinemann, 1976 [NYC]
Twins. Putnam, 1977; Heinemann, 1977

WOOD, CHRISTOPHER (HOVELLE). 1935- . Ref: CA. SC: James Bond = JB (following Ian Fleming, 1908-1964, q.v.)
Dead Center. Joseph, 1980 [Australia]
James Bond and Moonraker. Panther, 1979; Jove, 1979 (Novelization of the movie.) JB
James Bond, The Spy Who Loved Me. Cape, 1977; Warner, 1977 (Novelization of the movie.) JB
North to Rabaul. Arbor, 1979

WOOD, CLEMENT. 1888-1950. Born in Ala.; lawyer, educator, poet and novelist. SC: Skelton Keyne = SK; Lal Reed = LR; Capt./Insp. Colin = C.
The Corpse in the Guest Room. Arcadia, 1945 SK
Death in Ankara. Mystery House, 1944 LR [Turk.]
Death on the Pampas. Mystery House, 1944 LR [Arg.]
Double Jeopardy. Arcadia, 1947 SK
The Shadow from the Bogue. Dutton, 1928 C [La.]
The Tabloid Murders. Macaulay, 1930 C [N.Y.]

WOOD, DEBORAH
The Mistress of Soundcliff Manor. Zebra, 1980

WOOD, ELLEN PRICE. 1814-1887. See: Mrs. Henry Wood.

WOOD, ERIC. SC: Arnold Keene and Bernard Young = K&Y. Set: Eng.
Death in the Mews. Hamilton, 1937 K&Y
Death of an Oddfellow. Hamilton, 1938 K&Y
Hands of Death. Hamilton, 1937 K&Y
Murder from the Grave. Hamilton, 1938
The Mystery of Maybury Manor. Cassell, 1920

WOOD, ERNEST
Feloniously and Wilfully. Long, 1947

WOOD, H(ARRY) F(REEMAN)
-Avenged on Society. Heinemann, 1893; Lovell, 1892
The Englishman of the Rue Cain. Chatto, 1889; Rand, 1889 [Paris]
The Night Mail; see The Passenger from Scotland Yard
The Night of the 3rd Ult. Lovell, 1890
The Passenger from Scotland Yard. Chatto, 1888; Munro, 1888. Also published as: The Night Mail; or, The Passenger from Scotland Yard. Munro, 1894. Also published as by William Ward: Economy Book League, 1933
-Under Masks. Sisley's, 1908

WOOD, MRS. HENRY [ELLEN PRICE WOOD]. 1814-1887. Ref: DD, MM, MP, TC. Here listed is the book fiction attributed to this British author. No attempt has been made to distinguish among her works on the basis of criminous content. Note that a number of U.S. titles remain uncorrelated with their British originals.
About Ourselves. Nisbet, 1883
Adam Grainger. Bentley, 1876. U.S. title: Adam Grainger and other stories. Macmillan, 18?? ss
Anne Hereford. Tinsley, 1868. U.S. title: The Mystery; or, Anne Hereford. Peterson, 1862
Ashley, and other stories. Bentley, 1897 ss
Barren Honor. Dick, 1968 (British title?)
Bessy Rane. Bentley, 1870; Peterson, 1870
Bessy Wells. Daldy, 1875
Castle Wafer; or, The Plain Gold Ring. Dick, 1868 (British title?)
Castle's Heir; see Lady Adelaide's Oath
The Channings. Bentley, 1862; Peterson, 1862
Clara Lake's Dream. Peterson, ca.1873 (British title?)
Count Netherleigh. Bentley, 1881; Munro, 1881
Cyrilla Maude's First Love. Peterson, ca.1873 (British title?)
Danesbury House. Scottish Temperance League, 1860; Harper, 18??
Dene Hollow. Bentley, 1871; Peterson, 1871
The Diamond Bracelet; see The Lost Will
Doctor's Daughter. Ogilvie, 1881 (British title?)
East Lynne. Bentley, 1861; Dick, 1861
Edina. Bentley, 1876; Peterson, 1876
Elster's Folly. Tinsley, 1866; Peterson, 1866
Featherstone's Story. Bentley, 1889
Final Ending of It. Ogilvie, 1881 (British title?)
Five Thousand a Year. Peterson, ca.1873 (British title?)
The Foggy Night at Offord. Nisbet, 1863; Peterson, 1863
Frances Hildyard. Peterson, ca.1873 (British title?)
George Canterbury's Will. Tinsley, 1870; Peterson, 1870
Gervase Castonel; or, The Six Grey Powders. Dick, 1863 (British title?)
Great Feast. Ogilvie, 1881 (British title?)

The Haunted Tower. Peterson, 1864 (British title?)
The Heir to Ashly. Dick, 1863 (British title?)
Helen Whitney's Edding, and other stories. Munro, 1885 ss (British title?)
The House of Halliwell. Bentley, 1890; U.S. Book Co., 1890
Johnny Ludlow. Bentley, 1874; Munro, 1881 ss, some reprinted as: Under the Rose. Carleton, 1878
Johnny Ludlow. Second Series. Bentley, 1880 ss
Johnny Ludlow. Third Series. Bentley, 1885; Macmillan, 18?? ss
Johnny Ludlow. Fourth Series. Bentley, 1890 ss
Johnny Ludlow. Fifth Series. Bentley, 1890; Macmillan, 189? ss
Johnny Ludlow. Sixth Series. Bentley, 1899; Macmillan, 1901 ss
Lady Adelaide's Oath. Bentley, 1867. U.S. title: Castle's Heir; or, Lady Adelaide's Oath. Peterson, ca.1871
Lady Grace and other stories. Bentley, 1887; Lovell, 1887 ss
A Life's Secret. Wood, 1867; Peterson, ca.1873
Light and a Dark Christmas. Peterson, 1866 (British title?)
Lord Oakburn's Daughters. Bradbury, 1864; Peterson, 1865
The Lost Bank Note. Peterson, 1863 (British title?)
Lost in the Post, and other tales. Munro, 1881 ss (British title?)
The Lost Will. Peterson, 1865. Also published as: The Diamond Bracelet. Peterson, ca.1873 (British title?)
Marrying Beneath Your Station. Peterson, ca.1873 (British title?)
Martyn Ware's Temptation. Peterson, ca.1873 (British title?)
The Master of Graylands. Bentley, 1873; Peterson, 1873
Mildred Arkell. Peterson, 1856 (British title?)
Mrs. Halliburton's Troubles. Bentley, 1862; Dick, 1863
Missing Letter. Ogilvie, 1882 (British title?)
My Cousin Caroline's Wedding. Peterson, ca.1873 (British title?)
My Husband's First Love. Peterson, ca.1873 (British title?)
The Mystery; see Anne Hereford
The Mystery of Jessie Page, and other stories. Munro, 1885 ss (British title?)
The Nobleman's Wife. Peterson, ca.1873 (British title?)
Orville College. Tinsley, 1867; Peterson, ca.1873
Oswald Gray. Black, 1864; Peterson, 1864
Out of the Deep; or, Cast Up by the Sea. Gill, 1875 (British title?)
Parkwater. Bentley, 1876; Peterson, ca.1873
Pomeroy Abbey. Bentley, 1878; Munro, 1878
The Red Court Farm. Tinsley, 1868; Peterson, 1865
Robert Ashton's Wedding Day, and other stories. Munro, 1881 ss (British title?)
Roland Yorke. Bentley, 1869; Peterson, 1869
Rose Lodge. Munro, 1881 ss (British title?)
The Runaway Match. Peterson, 1863 (British title?)
Rupert Hall. Peterson, 1876 (British title?)
St. Martin's Eve. Tinsley, 1866; Peterson, 1866
Self-Convicted. Peterson, ca.1873 (British title?)
The Shadow of Ashlydyat. Bentley, 1863; Peterson, 1863
Smuggler's Ghost. Peterson, ca.1873 (British title?)
Squire Trevlyn's Heir; see Trevlyn Hold
The Story of Charles Strange. Bentley, 1888; Laird, 1889
The Story of Dorothy Grape, and other tales. Munro, 1885 ss (British title?)
A Tale of Sin, and other tales. Munro, 1881 ss (British title?)
Told in the Twilight. Bentley, 1875
Trevlyn Hold; or, Squire Trevlyn's Heir. Tinsley, 1864. U.S. title: Squire Trevlyn's Heir; or, Trevlyn Hold. Peterson, 1863
Under the Rose; see Johnny Ludlow
The Unholy Wish, and other stories. Bentley, 1890; Munro, 1885 ss
Verner's Pride. Bradbury, 1863; Peterson, 1863

Was He Severe? Ogilvie, 1881 (British title?)
Will He Betray Her? Ogilvie, 1882 (British title?)
William Allair; or, Running Away to Sea. Griffith, 1864; Peterson, 1864
Within the Maze. Bentley, 1872; Peterson, 1872

WOOD, JAMES (ALEXANDER FRASER). 1918-   . Ref: CA. SC: James Fraser, in at least those marked JF.
Bay of Seals. Hutchinson, 1964 JF
Be Thou My Judge. Hutchinson, 1966. U.S. title: Voyage into Nowhere. Vanguard, 1967
A Black Horse Running. Hutchinson, 1972; Vanguard, 1977
Cry of the Kestrel. Hutchinson, 1962
Fire Rock. Hutchinson, 1965; Vanguard, 1966 JF
The Friday Run. Hutchinson, 1967; Vanguard, 1971 JF [ship]
Highland Gathering. Hutchinson, 1970
The Lisa Bastian. Hutchinson, 1960; Vanguard, 1961 JF [ship]
North Beat. Hutchinson, 1973
North Kill. Hutchinson, 1975
Northern Mission. Duckworth, 1954
The Rain Islands. Duckworth, 1957
Road to Canossa. Hutchinson, 1971
The Sealer. Hutchinson, 1959; Vanguard, 1960
The Seine Fishers. Duckworth, 1965
The Shop in Loch Street. Hutchinson, 1958
Star Witness. Hutchinson, 1972
Three Blind Mice. Hutchinson, 1969; Vanguard, 1973
The Uist Project. Hutchinson, 1973
Voyage into Nowhere; see Be Thou My Judge

WOOD, LESLIE
Hardship Our Garment. Hutchinson, 1947

WOOD, S(AMUEL) ANDREW. 1890-   . See: (Samuel) Andrew Wood.

WOOD, SALLY (CALKINS). 1897-   . Ref: CC.
Death in Lord Byron's Room. Morrow, 1948 [Switz.]
Murder of a Novelist. Simon, 1941; Swan, 1946 [Conn.]

WOOD, WALTER. 1866-1961.
-The Lord of the Dyke. Cassell, 1907
-Margaret the Peacemaker. Cassell, 1910
The Revenge of Gilbert Strange. Cassell, 1908
The Secret Paper. Cassell, 1909 [NYC]

WOODBRIDGE, H. HORATIO
Dig: Two Heads Wanted. Price, 1876 [Eng., 1847]

WOODBURY, DAVID O(AKES). 1896-   . SC: George Riam, in both titles.
Five Days to Oblivion. Devin-Adair, 1963 [New Eng., acad.]
Mr. Faraday's Formula. Devin-Adair, 1965 [New Eng., acad.]

WOODFIN, HENRY. Born in Buffalo, N.Y.; a music (jazz) critic there.
Virginia's Thing. Harper, 1968 [acad.]

WOODFORD, JACK. Pseudonym of Josiah Pitt Woolfolk, 1894-1971. Ref: CA.
Find the Motive. Long & Smith, 1932; Paul, 1933. Also published as: The Motive Key. Dawn Press, 1956
Five Fatal Days. Carlyle, 1933
The Motive Key; see Find the Motive

WOODGATE, M(ILDRED) V(IOLET). 1904-   . Ref: CA.
The Mystery of Pauline's Lady; see Pauline's Lady
Pauline's Lady. Hurst, 1931. Also published as (abridged): The Mystery of Pauline's Lady. Mellifont, 1945
The Secret of the Sapphire Ring. Hurst, 1930
The Silver Mirror. Bles, 1935
The Two Houses on the Cliff. Hurst, 1931

WOODHALL, EDWIN THOMAS. 1886-   .
The Atlantic Murders. Mellifont, 1939
Eleven Men Died. Mellifont, 1937
The Greyhound Stadium Plot. Mellifont, 1940
The Kidnap Murders. Mellifont, 1939
-The Mystery Flier. Mellifont, 1940
-Nazi Speedway Plot. Mellifont, 1940

WOOD-HILL, H.
The Reluctant Spy. Gifford, 1946

WOODHOUSE, MARTIN (CHARLTON). 1932-   .
Ref: CA. Pseudonym: John Charlton, q.v. SC: Giles Yoeman = GY.
Blue Bone. Heinemann, 1973; Coward, 1973 GY
Bush Baby; see Rock Baby
Mama Doll. Heinemann, 1972; Coward, 1972 GY
Moon Hill. Macmillan (London), 1976; Coward, 1976 GY [S. Am.]
Phil and Me. Heinemann, 1970; Coward, 1970 [Carib.]
Rock Baby. Heinemann, 1968. U.S. title: Bush Baby. Coward, 1968 GY [Yugos.]
Traders. Macdonald, 1980
Tree Frog. Heinemann, 1966; Coward, 1966 GY

WOODIWISS, JOHN C(ECIL). SC: Insp. Hopton, in at least those marked H. Set: Eng.
Death's Visiting Card. Melrose, 1936 H
The Ebony Torso. Gifford, 1939 H
Mouseback. Melrose, 1937

WOODLEY, RICHARD
Deadly Encounter. Jove, 1980 (Novelization of the movie.) [Eng.]
It's Alive. Ballantine, 1977 (Novelization of the movie.)

WOODMAN, MICHAEL. 1948-   . SC: Paul Gane, in both titles.
Bullion. Sphere, 1971
The Medusa Kiss. Sphere, 1970; Beagle, 1971 [Far East]

WOODROW, MRS. WILSON [NANCY MANN WADDEL WOODROW]. 1870-1935.
Burned Evidence. Putnam (NYC), 1925; Putnam (London), 1926 [NYC]
-Come Alone. Macaulay, 1929
The Hornet's Nest. Little, 1917
The Moonhill Mystery. Macaulay, 1930
Pawns of Murder. Smith, 1932; Paul, 1933 [NYC]
-The Second Chance. Watt, 1925; Collins, 1925
The Silver Butterfly. Bobbs, 1908
-Swallowed Up. Brentano's (NYC), 1922; Brentano's (London), 1923

WOODRUFF, PHILIP. Pseudonym of Philip Mason, 1906-   . Ref: CA.
Call the Next Witness. Cape, 1945; Harcourt, 1946 [India]
Whatever Dies. Cape, 1948 ss

WOODS, KATHERINE (IRVIN). 1886-1968. Ref: CC.
Murder in a Walled Town. Houghton, 1934; Eyre, 1936 [Fr.]

WOODS, SARA. Pseudonym of Sara Hutton Bowen-Judd, 1922-   . Other pseudonyms: Anne Burton, Mary Challis, Margaret Leek, qq.v. Ref: CA, CC, EM, TC. SC: Antony Maitland, in all titles, all set in Eng.
And Shame the Devil. Collins, 1967; Holt, 1972
Bloody Instructions. Collins, 1962; Harper, 1962
The Case Is Altered. Collins, 1967; Harper, 1967
Done to Death. Macmillan (London), 1974; Holt, 1975
Enter Certain Murderers. Collins, 1966; Harper, 1966
Enter the Corpse. Macmillan (London), 1973; Holt, 1974
Error of the Moon. Collins, 1963
Exit Murderer. Macmillan (London), 1978; St. Martin's, 1978
An Improbable Fiction. Collins, 1970; Holt, 1971
The Knavish Crows. Collins, 1971; Raven, 1980
Knives Have Edges. Collins, 1968; Holt, 1970
The Law's Delay. Macmillan (London), 1977; St. Martin's, 1977
Let's Choose Executors. Collins, 1966; Harper, 1967
Malice Domestic. Collins, 1962
My Life Is Done. Macmillan (London), 1976; St. Martin's, 1976
Past Praying For. Collins, 1968; Harper, 1968
Proceed to Judgement. Macmillan (London), 1979; St. Martin's, 1980
Serpent's Tooth. Collins, 1971; Holt, 1973
A Show of Violence. Macmillan (London), 1975; McKay, 1975
Tarry and Be Hanged. Collins, 1969; Holt, 1971
The Taste of Fears. Collins, 1963. U.S. title: The Third Encounter. Harper, 1963
They Love Not Poison. Macmillan (London), 1972; Holt, 1972

They Stay for Death. Macmillan (London), 1980; St. Martin's, 1980
A Thief or Two. Macmillan (London), 1977; St. Martin's, 1977
The Third Encounter; see The Taste of Fears
This Fatal Writ. Macmillan (London), 1979; St. Martin's, 1979
This Little Measure. Collins, 1964
Though I Know She Lies. Collins, 1965; Holt, 1972
Trusted Like the Fox. Collins, 1964; Harper, 1965
Weep for Her. Macmillan (London), 1980; St. Martin's, 1981
The Windy Side of the Law. Collins, 1965; Harper, 1965
Yet She Must Die. Macmillan (London), 1973; Holt, 1974

WOODS, STOCKTON. Pseudonym of Richard Forrest, 1932-   , q.v.
The Laughing Man. GM, 1980 [Conn.]

WOODS, VIRNA. 1864-1903.
An Elusive Lover. Houghton, 1898; Constable, 1898

WOODS, WILLIAM B.
Lancaster Triple Thousand. Exposition, 1956

WOODTHORPE, R(ALPH) C(ARTER). 1886-   .
Ref: CC, MP. SC: Matilda Perks = MP; Nicholas Slade = NS. Set: Eng.
A Dagger in Fleet Street. Nicholson, 1934
Death in a Little Town. Nicholson, 1935; Doubleday, 1935 MP
Death Wears a Purple Shirt; see Silence of a Purple Shirt
The Necessary Corpse. Nicholson, 1939; Doubleday, 1939 NS
The Public School Murder. Nicholson, 1932 [acad.]
Put Out That Light. Hale, 1941
Rope for a Convict. Nicholson, 1939; Doubleday, 1940
The Shadow on the Downs. Nicholson, 1935; Doubleday, 1935 MP
Silence of a Purple Shirt. Nicholson, 1934. U.S. title: Death Wears a Purple Shirt. Doubleday, 1934 NS

WOODWARD, EDWARD (EMBERLIN)
Bill Marshall, Turf Sleuth. Mellifont, 1942
Black Sheep. Unwin, 1926
-Blizzard. Hutchinson, 1932
Dead Man's Plaything. Kemsley, 1950
-Dear Delusion. Long, 1947
Death Amidst Satin. Long, 1940
-Dr. Greenfingers. Long, 1933
Each Night We Die. Hutchinson, 1936
-False Colours. Mellifont, 1941
-Fingers Before Forks. Selwyn, 1931
-The Gamblers. Unwin, 1925
-Gentlemen at Large. Long, 1948
-A Hive of Glass. Long, 1950
The House of Terror. Selwyn, 1929; Mystery League, 1930
-A Lady Fell in Love. Long, 1945
Love Is a Fiend. Long, 1945
-Noughts and Crosses. Mellifont, 1943
-Panther Face. Mellifont, 1942
-The Pigeon Wins. Unwin, 1924
-Promise for Tomorrow. Long, 1949
-Race Gang. Cherry Tree, 1940
-Shake Hands for Ever. Long, 1947
-The Sky's the Limit. Cherry Tree, 1940
-So This Is Love! Long, 1943
-Tiger Tooth. Cherry Tree, 1944
-Troubled Harvest. Long, 1951
The Turf Bandits. Mellifont, 1941
Winter Wheat. Hutchinson, 1932
-Women Are Like That. Long, 1942

WOODWARD, HELEN (ROSEN). 1882-   . Ref: CA.
The Bowling Green Murders, with Frances Amherst. Random, 1940; Hale, 1942 [NYC]
Money to Burn. McKay, 1945 [NYC]

WOODWARD, R(OBERT) PITCHER
Trains That Met in the Blizzard. Salmagundi, 1896. Also published as: Frozen Humor. Dillingham, 1896 ss, some criminous

WOODWARD, S(HERMAN) M(ELVILLE). 1871-1953
Shot in the Pulpit. Quality, 1939

WOODY, WILLIAM
Mistress of Horror House. Ace, 1959 [Tex.]

WOOLF, PHILIP, M.D. 1848-1903.
Who Is Guilty? Cassell, 1886; Maxwell, 1886

WOOLFOLK, JOSIAH PITT. 1894-1971. Pseudonym: Jack Woodford, q.v.

WOOLFOLK, WILLIAM. Born on L.I., educated at New York U.; writer for comic strips, radio, magazines and books; magazine publisher.
Blacker Than Murder; see The Naked Hunter
-My Name Is Morgan. Doubleday, 1963; Allen, 1963
The Naked Hunter. Popular Library, 1954. British title (?): Blacker Than Murder. Hale, 1958 [NYC]
The Overlords. Doubleday, 1973; Allen, 1973
The President's Doctor. Playboy, 1975; Allen, 1976 [Wash. D.C.]
Run While You Can. Popular Library, 1956; Hale, 1958 [NYC]
Way of the Wicked. Monarch, 1959

WOOLL, EDWARD. 1878-   .
Libel. Heinemann, 1934 (Play.) Novel based on this play: Blackie, 1935; Macrae-Smith, 1936
-The Lodestar. Heinemann, 1935
-The Nettle. Macdonald, 1947
-There Is a Tide—. Blackie, 1934

WOOLLCOTT, ALEXANDER (HUMPHREYS). 1887-1943, and GEORGE S(IMON) KAUFMAN, 1889-1961.
The Dark Tower. Random, 1934 (3-act play.)

WOOLRICH, CORNELL (GEORGE HOPLEY). 1903-1968. Pseudonyms: George Hopley, William Irish, qq.v. Ref: CA, CC, EM, MC, MP, TC.
Angels of Darkness. Mysterious Press, 1978 ss
Beware the Lady; see The Bride Wore Black
Beyond the Night. Avon, 1959 ss
Black Alibi. Simon, 1942; Hale, 1951 [S. Am.]
The Black Angel. Doubleday, 1943; Hale, 1949 [NYC]
The Black Curtain. Simon, 1941 [NYC]
The Black Path of Fear. Doubleday, 1944 [Havana]
The Bride Wore Black. Simon, 1940; Hale, 1942. Also published as: Beware the Lady. Pyramid, 1953 [NYC]
The Dark Side of Love. Walker, 1965 ss
Death Is My Dancing Partner. Pyramid, 1959
-The Doom Stone. Avon, 1960 [1757-1941]
Hotel Room. Random, 1958 ss, some with criminous elements [NYC]
Manhattan Love Song. Godwin, 1932 [NYC]
Nightmare. Dodd, 1956 ss
Nightwebs. Harper, 1971; Gollancz, 1973 (Four ss and the complete Woolrich bibliography omitted from the British edition.)
Rendezvous in Black. Rinehart, 1948; Hale, 1950
Savage Bride. GM, 1950 [Mex.]
The Ten Faces of Cornell Woolrich. Simon, 1965; Boardman, 1966 ss
Violence. Dodd, 1958 ss

WOOLRYTH, HUMPHREY WILLIAM. See: Anonymous.

WOOTTON, GARETH. See: Barbara Wood, 1947-   .

WORBOYS, ANNE (ETTE ISOBEL). Pseudonym: Vicky Maxwell, q.v. Ref: CA.
The Barrancourt Destiny. Hodder, 1977; Scribner, 1977
The Bhunda Jewels. Mayflower, 1980; Ace, 1981
Every Man a King. Hodder, 1975; Scribner, 1976. Also published as: Rendezvous with Fear. Ace, 1977 [Sp.]
The Lion of Delos. Hodder, 1975; Delacorte, 1974 [Greece]
Rendezvous with Fear; see Every Man a King

WORDEN, ALONZO T. See: W(illiam) J. Arkell.

WORKMAN, GARNET
The Gardens at Moontower. Vantage, 1976

WORKMAN, JAMES
-The Apologetic Tiger. Hodder, 1958
Contrabandits. Horwitz, 1968 [Australia]
-Face of Fortune. Hodder, 1961
-Lucifer at Ponsfordville. Hodder, 1959

WORLEY, WILLIAM
My Dead Wife. Simon, 1948   [S.F.]

WORMSER, RICHARD (EDWARD). 1908-1977.
Pseudonym: Ed Friend, q.v. SC: Sgt. Joe Dixon = JD; Lt. Andy Bastian = AB.
The Body Looks Familiar. Dell, 1958
The Communist's Corpse. Smith & Haas, 1935; Gollancz, 1935 JD [NYC]
Drive East on 66. GM, 1961; Muller, 1962 AB [S.W.]
The Hanging Heiress. Mill, 1949. Also published as: The Widow Wore Red. Crest, 1958 [L.A.]
The Invader. GM, 1972 [Calif.]
The Late Mrs. Five. GM, 1960 [Midwest]
The Man with the Wax Face. Smith & Haas, 1934 JD [NYC]
A Nice Girl Like You. GM, 1963; Muller, 1963 AB [Calif.]
Perfect Pigeon. GM, 1962
The Takeover. GM, 1971; Coronet, 1972
Torn Curtain. Dell, 1966; Mayflower, 1966 (Novelization of the movie.) [Ger.]
The Widow Wore Red; see The Hanging Heiress

WORRALL, LECHMERE. See: Beamish Tinker.

WORSLEY, T(HOMAS) C(UTHBERT). 1907-   .
Five Minutes, Sir Matthew. Ross, 1969

WORSLEY-GOUGH, BARBARA (KATHLEEN). 1903-   . SC: Aloysius Kelly, in both titles. Ref: CC. Set: Eng.
Alibi Innings. Joseph, 1954
Lantern Hill. Joseph, 1957

WORTH, CEDRIC. 1900-   . Ref: MP. SC: Insp. Sevrel, in both titles.
The Corpse That Knew Everybody. Dutton, 1941 [NYC]
The Trail of the Serpent. Dutton, 1940 [Calif.]

WORTH, MARGARET. Pseudonym of Helen Arvonen, q.v.
Red Wine of Rapture. Avon, 1973

WORTH, MAURICE. Joint pseudonym of Maurice H. B. Mash and Willan George Bosworth, 1904-   . Other pseudonym of Willan George Bosworth: Willan G. Borth, q.v. SC: Derek Harding, in all titles. Set: Eng.
The Golden Pheasant Mystery. Hutchinson, 1927
The Pagoda Mystery. Hutchinson, 1928
The Plaza Mystery. Hutchinson, 1928

WORTH, NIGEL. Pseudonym of Noel Wright, 1890-1975.
-The Arms of Phaedra. Mills, 1924
The Man in the Box. Mills, 1923
Roger Sinclair's Treasure. Hutchinson, 1927
The Wise Man of Welby. Mills, 1924

WORTH, RICHARD
The Amateur Boxer. Modern, 1938
The Coup That Failed. Lloyd's, 1921
The Murder in the Fog. Aldine, 1927

WORTHINGTON-STUART, BRIAN ARTHUR. Pseudonyms: Peter Meredith, Brian Stuart, qq.v.

WORTS, GEORGE F(RANK). 1892-   . Pseudonym: Loring Brent, q.v.
The Blue Lacquer Box. Kinsey, 1939; Hurst, 1940. Also published as: The Case of the Blue Lacquered Box. Mystery Novel Classic, 1942 [L.I.]
The Case of the Blue Lacquered Box; see The Blue Lacquer Box
Dangerous Young Man. Kinsey, 1940; Hurst, 1940 [NYC]
Five Who Vanished. McBride, 1945
The Greenfield Mystery. Whitman, 1929
The House of Creeping Horror. King, 1934
Laughing Girl. Kinsey, 1941. Also published as: Murder and the Secret Weapon. Thriller Novel Classic, 194? [West]
The Monster of the Lagoon. Popular Publications (London), 1947
Murder and the Secret Weapon; see Laughing Girl
Overboard. Kinsey, 1943
Peter the Brazen. Lippincott (Phil. and London), 1919
The Phantom President. Cape & Ballou, 1932
Red Darkness. Harper Allen, 1928 [Fla.]
The Silver Fang. McClurg, 1930 [ship]
Where Some Men Are Men. Wright, 1937 (U.S. title?)

WOUK, HERMAN. 1915- . Ref: CA.
 The Traitor. French (NYC), 1949
 (2-act play.)

WRAY, G. W.
 Death on the Roads. Hale, 1938

WRAY, I. Pseudonym. SC: Insp. Digby, in
 both titles. Set: Eng.
 Murder—and Ariadne. Methuen, 1931
 The Vye Murder. Methuen, 1930

WRAY, J(AMES) JACKSON
 -Jonas Haggerley. Shaw, 1887
 -The Secret of the Mere; or, Under the
 Surface. Nisbet, 1885

WRAY, NICHOLAS
 Dale of the Secret Service. Mellifont,
 1940
 Death Deals a Diamond. Mellifont, 1942
 The Fortune Cheats. Mellifont, 1943
 The Lightship Murders. Mellifont, 1940
 Who Was the Killer? Mellifont, 1942

WRAY, ROGER. Pseudonym of James William
 Marriott, 1884-1953.
 The Rayner Case. Jarrolds, 1925

WREN, LASSITER and RANDLE McKAY, q.v.
 The Baffle Book. Doubleday, 1928;
 Heinemann, 1930 puzzle ss
 The Mystery Puzzle Book. Crowell, 1933;
 Hurst, 1934 puzzle ss
 The Second Baffle Book. Doubleday, 1929
 puzzle ss
 The Third Baffle Book. Doubleday, 1930
 puzzle ss

WREN, M. K. Pseudonym of Martha Kay Ren-
 froe, 1938- . Ref: CA. SC: Conan
 Flagg, in all titles.
 Curiosity Didn't Kill the Cat. Double-
 day, 1973; Hale, 1975 [Oreg.]
 A Multitude of Sins. Doubleday, 1975;
 Hale, 1976 [Oreg.]
 Nothing's Certain But Death. Doubleday,
 1978; Hale, 1978 [Oreg.]
 Oh, Bury Me Not. Doubleday, 1976; Hale,
 1978 [Oreg.]

WREN, P(ERCIVAL) C(HRISTOPHER). 1885-
 1941.
 Bubble Reputation. Murray, 1936. U.S.
 title: The Cortenay Treasure. Hough-
 ton, 1936
 Cardboard Castle. Murray, 1938; Hough-
 ton, 1938
 The Cortenay Treasure; see Bubble Repu-
 tation
 Mammon; see The Mammon of Righteousness
 The Mammon of Righteousness. Murray,
 1930. U.S. title: Mammon. Stokes,
 1930
 The Man the Devil Didn't Want; see
 Paper Prison
 Mysterious Waye. Murray, 1930; Stokes,
 1930
 -Odd—But Even So. Murray, 1941; Macrae
 Smith, 1942 ss
 Paper Prison. Murray, 1939. U.S. title:
 The Man the Devil Didn't Want. Macrae
 Smith, 1940
 Two Feet from Heaven. Murray, 1940

WRENN, HAROLD A(LBERT). 1909- . SC:
 William Mitchell, in at least those
 marked WM.
 The Clue of the Stone. French, 1964
 (1-act play.)
 Due to Expire. Hale, 1958 WM
 Infamous Conduct. Hale, 1961. As a 1-
 act play: French, 1963
 The Lady Prefers Murder. Hammond, 1954
 WM
 Tangle. Hammond, 1953 WM
 The Toby Jug Murders. Hammond, 1955 WM
 Unguarded Moment. Hale, 1959 WM

WRIGHT, ARTHUR
 -A Colt from the Country. Newnes, 1922
 A Crooked Game. Newnes, 1928
 -Fettered by Fate. Newnes, 1921
 -Gambler's Gold. Newnes, 1923
 -Gaming for Gold. Newnes, 1929
 -A Good Recovery. Newnes, 1928
 -Keane of Kalgoorlie. Newnes, 1907
 A Rogue's Luck. Newnes, 1923
 [Australia]
 -A Rough Passage. Newnes, 1920
 Rung In. Newnes, 1924 [Australia]

WRIGHT, ELSIE N. 1907- .
 Strange Murders at Greystones. International Fiction Library, 1931

WRIGHT, GLOVER
 The Torch. Hutchinson, 1981; Putnam,
 1980

WRIGHT, JOHN. Pseudonym: Wade Wright,
 q.v.

WRIGHT, JOSEPH E.
 Memorandum of a Murder. Manor, 1977

WRIGHT, JUNE
 The Devil's Caress. Hutchinson, 1952
 [Australia]
 Faculty of Murder. Long, 1961
 Make-Up for Murder. Long, 1966
 Murder in the Telephone Exchange.
 Hutchinson, 1948 [Australia]
 Reservation for Murder. Long, 1958
 So Bad a Death. Hutchinson, 1949
 [Australia]

WRIGHT, LAURIE ROBESON
 The Perfect Corpse. Major, 1977

WRIGHT, MARY PATRICIA. 1932- . Pseudonym: Mary Napier, q.v.

WRIGHT, MASON
 The Army Post Murders. Farrar, 1931
 [Okla.]
 Murder on Polopel, with William R(eno)
 Kane, 1885- . Doubleday, 1929
 [N.Y.]

WRIGHT, NOEL. 1890-1975. Pseudonym: Nigel
 Worth, q.v.

WRIGHT, OLIVER
 The Riverport Mail. Nash, 1912

WRIGHT, RICHARD
 Savage Holiday. Avon, 1954

WRIGHT, RICHARD B(RUCE). 1937- .
 Final Things. Dutton, 1980 [Toronto]

WRIGHT, ROWLAND. Pseudonym of Carolyn
 Wells, 1870-1942, q.v.
 The Disappearance of Kimball Webb.
 Dodd, 1926 [NYC]

WRIGHT, S(YDNEY) FOWLER. 1874-1965. Pseudonym: Sydney Fowler, q.v.

WRIGHT, SCOTT. Pseudonym: Annjeanette
 Scott, q.v.

WRIGHT, SEAN M. See: Michael P. Hodel.

WRIGHT, THOMAS. 1859-1936.
 The Mystery of St. Dunstans. Low, 1882

WRIGHT, WADE. Pseudonym of John Wright.
 SC: Bart Condor, in at least those
 marked BC; Paul Cameron, in at least
 those marked PC.
 Blonde Target. Hale, 1966 BC [NYC]
 Blood in the Ashes. Hale, 1964 BC
 Don't Come Back! Hale, 1973
 The Hades Hello. Hale, 1973
 A Hearse Waiting. Hale, 1965 BC
 No Haloes in Hell. Hale, 1969
 Shadows Don't Bleed. Hale, 1967 PC
 The Sharp Edge. Hale, 1968 PC
 Suddenly You're Dead. Hale, 1964 BC
 Two Faces of Death. Hale, 1970 BC
 Until She Dies. Hale, 1965 BC

WRIGHT, WILLARD HUNTINGTON. 1888-1939.
 Pseudonym: S. S. Van Dine, q.v.

WRIXON, FRED
 Moonstalker. Exposition, 1977

WUORIO, EVA-LIS. 1918- . Ref: CA.
 Explosion; see Midsummer Lokki
 Midsummer Lokki. Dobson, 1967; Holt,
 1967. Also published as: Explosion.
 Lancer, 1968 [Fin.]
 The Terror Factor; see Z for Zaborra
 The Woman with the Portuguese Basket.
 Dobson, 1963; Holt, 1964 [Vienna]
 Z for Zaborra. Dobson, 1965; Holt,
 1966. Also published as: The Terror
 Factor. Lancer, 1970

WURR, H. J. SC: Insp. Grierson = G.
 The Giant Hunchback. Rich, 1939 G
 [Scot.]
 Hunt in the Highlands. Bell, 1937
 [Scot.]
 Who Dies Next? Rich, 1939 G [Scot.]

WYKES, ALAN. 1914- . Ref: CA.
 The Pen-Friend. Duckworth, 1950
 Pursuit Till Morning. Duckworth, 1948;
 Random, 1947

WYLIE, I(DA) A(LEXA) R(OSS). 1885-1959.
 Rogues and Company. Lane, 1921; Mills,
 1921

WYLIE, NOEL
 Dumb Witness. Hammond, 1958 [Ire.]
 Saddle a Killer. Hammond, 1960 [Ire.]

WYLIE, PHILIP (GORDON). 1902-1971. See
 also: Edwin Balmer, 1883-1959; and:
 Anonymous ("The Smiling Corpse").
 Ref: CA, CC, EM.
 Corpses at Indian Stones. Farrar, 1943
 [N.Y.]
 Danger Mansion. Bantam (Los Angeles),
 1940
 Experiment in Crime; see Three to Be
 Read
 The Murderer Invisible. Farrar, 1931
 [N.J.]
 The Savage Gentleman. Farrar, 1932
 [NYC]
 The Smuggled Atom Bomb; see Three to Be
 Read
 The Spy Who Spoke Porpoise. Doubleday,
 1969 [Haw.]
 Three to Be Read. Rinehart, 1951 (Con-
 tains: Experiment in Crime, The Smug-
 gled Atom Bomb, and Sporting Blood,
 of which the first two were each pub-
 lished separately by Avon in 1956.)

WYLLIE, JOHN (VECTIS CAREW). 1914- .
 Ref: CA. SC: Dr. Quarshie = Q, all
 set in Afr., W.
 The Butterfly Flood. Doubleday, 1975;
 Barrie, 1977 Q
 Death Is a Drum...Beating Forever.
 Doubleday, 1977; Hale, 1979 Q
 Johnny Purple. Zenith, 1958
 The Killer Breath. Doubleday, 1979;
 Hale, 1980 Q
 A Pocket Full of Dead. Doubleday, 1978;
 Hale, 1979 Q
 Skull Still Bone. Doubleday, 1975; Bar-
 rie, 1975 Q
 A Tiger in Red Weather. Doubleday,
 1980; Hale, 1981 Q
 To Catch a Viper. Doubleday, 1977;
 Hale, 1979 Q

WYMAN, EDWARD. Pseudonym (?): Franz, q.v.

WYMARK, EDWARD. 1933- .
 As Good As Gold. Coward, 1967; Longmans, 1967

WYND, OSWALD (MORRIS). 1913- . Pseudo-
 nym: Gavin Black, q.v. Ref: CA, TC.
 Death the Red Flower. Cassell, 1965;
 Harcourt, 1965 [ship]
 -The Forty Days. Collins, 1972; Har-
 court, 1973
 -The Hawser Pirates. Cassell, 1970; Har-
 court, 1970
 -Stars in the Heather. Blackwood, 1956
 Sumatra Seven Zero. Cassell, 1968; Har-
 court, 1968 [Burma]
 Walk Softly, Men Praying. Cassell,
 1967; Harcourt, 1967 [Jap.]
 -A Wall in the Long Dark Night. Cassell,
 1962
 -When Ape Is King. Home & Van Thal, 1949

WYNNE, ANTHONY. Pseudonym of Robert
 McNair Wilson, 1882-1963. Ref: CC,
 MP. SC: Dr. Eustace Hailey, in all
 titles. Set: Eng.
 The Blue Vesuvius. Hutchinson, 1930;
 Lippincott, 1931
 The Case of the Gold Coins. Hutchinson,
 1933; Lippincott, 1934
 The Case of the Green Knife. Hutchin-
 son, 1932. U.S. title: The Green
 Knife. Lippincott, 1932
 The Case of the Red-Haired Girl. Hutch-
 inson, 1932. U.S. title: The Cotswold
 Case. Lippincott, 1933
 The Cotswold Case; see The Case of the
 Red-Haired Girl
 The Dagger. Hutchinson, 1928; Lippin-
 cott, 1929
 Death of a Banker. Hutchinson, 1934;
 Lippincott, 1934
 Death of a Golfer. Hutchinson, 1937;
 Lippincott, 1937. Also published as:
 Murder in the Morning. Detective
 Novel Classic, 194?
 Death of a King. Hutchinson, 1938. U.S.
 title: Murder Calls Dr. Hailey. Lip-
 pincott, 1938
 Death of a Shadow. Hutchinson, 1950
 Death Out of the Night; see The Loving
 Cup
 Door Nails Never Die. Hutchinson, 1939;
 Lippincott, 1939
 The Double Thirteen; see The Double-
 Thirteen Mystery
 The Double-Thirteen Mystery. Hutchin-
 son, 1926. U.S. title: The Double
 Thirteen. Lippincott, 1926
 Emergency Exit. Hutchinson, 1941; Mess-
 ner, 1944
 The Fourth Finger. Hutchinson, 1929;
 Lippincott, 1929
 The Green Knife; see The Case of the
 Green Knife
 The Holbein Mystery. Hutchinson, 1935.
 U.S. title: The Red Lady. Lippincott,
 1935

The Horseman of Death. Hutchinson,
    1927; Lippincott, 1928
The House on the Hard. Hutchinson, 1940
The Loving Cup. Hutchinson, 1933. U.S.
    title: Death Out of the Night. Lip-
    pincott, 1933 [Scot.]
Murder Calls Dr. Hailey; see Death of a
    King
Murder in a Church. Hutchinson, 1942
Murder in the Morning; see Death of a
    Golfer
Murder in Thin Air. Hutchinson, 1936;
    Lippincott, 1936 [Scot.]
Murder of a Lady. Hutchinson, 1931.
    U.S. title: The Silver Scale Mystery.
    Lippincott, 1931 [Scot.]
The Mystery of the Ashes. Hutchinson,
    1927; Lippincott, 1927
The Mystery of the Evil Eye. Hutchin-
    son, 1925. U.S. title: The Sign of
    Evil. Lippincott, 1925
The Red Lady; see The Holbein Mystery
Red Scar. Hutchinson, 1928; Lippincott,
    1928
The Room with the Iron Shutters. Hutch-
    inson, 1929; Lippincott, 1929
The Sign of Evil; see The Mystery of
    the Evil Eye
The Silver Arrow. Hutchinson, 1931.
    U.S. title: The White Arrow. Lippin-
    cott, 1932
The Silver Scale Mystery; see Murder of
    a Lady
Sinners Go Secretly. Hutchinson, 1927;
    Lippincott, 1927 ss
The Toll-House Murder. Hutchinson,
    1935; Lippincott, 1935
The White Arrow; see The Silver Arrow
The Yellow Crystal. Hutchinson, 1930;
    Lippincott, 1930

WYNNE, BARRY. 1929-   .
-The Day Gibraltar Fell. Macdonald, 1969
-The Sniper. Macdonald, 1968
The Spies Within. Jenkins, 1964

WYNNE, F. C.
A Wild Goose Chase. Stockwell, 1978

WYNNE, FRED(ERICK) E(DWARD). 1870-   .
-Digby's Miracle. Jenkins, 1924
-Faith Unfaithful. Brown, 1908
-Fortune's Fool. Brown, 1907
A Mediterranean Mystery. Jenkins, 1923;
    Duffield, 1923 [Egypt]

WYNNE-JONES, TIM. 1948-   . Ref: CA.
Odd's End. Little, 1980; Deutsch, 1981
    [Can.]

WYNNTON, PATRICK. 1899-   .
The Agent Outside. Longmans, 1931
The Black Turret. Hodder, 1925; Bobbs,
    1925
The Honourable Pursuit. Hodder, 1930.
    U.S. title: Strange Pursuit. Lippin-
    cott, 1930
The Lady Zia; see Zia
The Lost Mark. Hodder, 1929; Lippin-
    cott, 1929
Spider's Parlour. Longmans, 1933
Strange Pursuit; see The Honourable
    Pursuit
The Ten Jewels. Hodder, 1931; Lippin-
    cott, 1931
The Third Messenger. Hodder, 1926;
    Doran, 1927
Zia. Hodder, 1928. U.S. title: The Lady
    Zia. Doubleday, 1928

XV 8
Narcissus Murders. Libra, 1945

XANTIPPE. Pseudonym of (?) Edith Meiser,
    writer and producer of radio pro-
    grams, including the Sherlock Holmes
    hour. Ref: CC.
Death Catches Up with Mr. Kluck.
    Doubleday, 1935 [NYC]

YABLONSKY, YABO
Jaguar Lives. Futura, 1980

YAFFE, JAMES. 1927-   . Ref: CA, EM.
The Deadly Game. Dramatists, 1960 (2-
    act play adapted from the novel "A
    Dangerous Game" by Friedrich Duerren-
    matt, 1921-   , q.v.)
Nothing But the Night. Little, 1957;
    Cape, 1958 [NYC]

YARBOROUGH, CHARLOTTE
The Condor Conspiracy. Leisure, 1980
    [Panama]
Murder on the Long Straight. Leisure,
    1979

YARBRO, CHELSEA QUINN. 1942-   . Ref:
CA. SC: Charlie Spotted Moon, in both
titles.
Music When Sweet Voices Die. Putnam,
    1979 [S.F., theatre]
Ogilvie, Tallant & Moon. Putnam, 1976

YARDLEY, HERBERT O(SBORN). 1889-1958.
SC: Mr. Greenleaf = G.
The Blonde Countess. Longmans, 1934;
    Faber, 1934 G [Wash. D.C.]
Crows Are Black Everywhere, with Carl
    Grabo. Putnam, 1945 [China]
Red Sun of Nippon. Longmans, 1934 G
    [Wash. D.C.]

YARDLEY, JAMES. SC: Kiss Darling, in both
titles.
A Kiss a Day Keeps the Corpses Away.
    Joseph, 1971; Signet, 1971
Kiss the Boys and Make Them Die.
    Joseph, 1970; Signet, 1970

YARDLEY, MAUDE H.
-Sinless. Sisley's, 1906; Fenno, 1907

YARNELL, DUANE
Mantrap. Crest, 1957 [Fla.]
Murder Bait. Crest, 1958

YARROW, ARNOLD. 1920-   .
-Death Is a Z. Hale, 1978
Softly, Softly Casebook. Pan, 1973
    (Novelets adapted from scripts for
    the British TV series "Softly,
    Softly".)

YATES, A. L.
-Nick Westerman, Detective. Reed, n.d.
    ss

YATES, ALAN GEOFFREY. 1923-   . Pseudonyms: Carter Brown, Caroline Farr,
qq.v. Ref: CA.
The Cold Dark Hours. Horwitz, 1958

YATES, BROCK (WENDEL). 1933-   . Ref:
CA.
Dead in the Water. Farrar, 1975 [Can.]

YATES, DORNFORD. Pseudonym of Cecil Wil-
liam Mercer, 1885-1960. Ref: CC, EM.
SC: Chandos = C; Jonah Mansel = JM;
Bertram Pleydell = BP; Supt. Falcon
= F. (Note: Characters overlap series
in Yates' work, and most books about
BP are not criminous.)
Adele & Co. Hodder, 1932; Minton, 1931
    BP,JM
Berry and Co. Ward, 1921; Minton, 1928
    ss, three criminous   BP,JM
Blind Corner. Hodder, 1927; Minton,
    1927 C,JM
Blood Royal. Hodder, 1929; Minton, 1930
    C [Austria]
By Royal Command; see Fire Below
Cost Price. Ward, 1949. U.S. title: The
    Laughing Bacchante. Putnam, 1949
    C,JM [Austria]
An Eye for a Tooth. Ward, 1943; Putnam,
    1944 C,JM [Austria]
Fire Below. Hodder, 1930. U.S. title:
    By Royal Command. Minton, 1931 C
    [Austria]
Gale Warning. Ward, 1939; Putnam, 1940
    C,JM [Fr.]
The House That Berry Built. Ward, 1945;
    Putnam, 1945 BP,JM,F
The Laughing Bacchante; see Cost Price
Ne'er-Do-Well. Ward, 1954 C,JM,F
Period Stuff. Ward, 1942 ss, some cri-
    minous F
Perishable Goods. Hodder, 1928; Minton,
    1928 C,JM,BP
Red in the Morning. Ward, 1946. U.S.
    title: Were Death Denied. Putnam,
    1946 C,JM [Fr.]
Safe Custody. Hodder, 1932; Minton,
    1932
She Fell Among Thieves. Hodder, 1935;
    Minton, 1935 C,JM [Fr.]
She Painted Her Face. Ward, 1937; Put-
    nam, 1937 [Austria]
Shoal Water. Ward, 1940; Putnam, 1941
    JM [Fr.]
Storm Music. Hodder, 1934; Minton, 1934
    [Austria]
Were Death Denied; see Red in the Morn-
    ing

YATES, EDMUND (HODGSON). 1831-1894.
-After Office-Hours. Ward, 1861
-Black Sheep. Tinsley, 1867; Harper,
    1867
-Broken to Harness. Bentley, 1864; Lor-
    ing, 1866

-Cast Away. Chapman, 1872
A Dangerous Game; see The Impending
    Sword
-Dr. Wainwright's Patient. Chapman, 1871
-The Forlorn Hope. Tinsley, 1867; Lor-
    ing, 1867
Going to the Bad. Gill, 1876 (British
    title?)
The Impending Sword. Tinsley, 1874.
    U.S. title: A Dangerous Game. Gill,
    1874
-Kissing the Rod. Tinsley, 1866; Harper,
    1866
-Land at Last. Chapman, 1866; Harper,
    1866
-Nobody's Fortune. Chapman, 1872; Estes,
    187?
-A Righted Wrong. Tinsley, 1870
-The Rock Ahead. Tinsley, 1868
-Running the Gauntlet. Chapman, 1865;
    Loring, 1866
A Silent Witness. Tinsley, 1875; Gill,
    1875
-Two by Tricks. Routledge, 1874
-Wages of Sin. Gill, 1875 (British
    title?)
-A Waiting Place. Tinsley, 1872; Apple-
    ton, 187?
-Wrecked in Port. Chapman, 1869; Harper,
    1869
-The Yellow Flag. Tinsley, 1872; Estes,
    187?

YATES, GEORGE WORTHING. Joint pseudonym
with Charles Hunt Marshall: Peter
Hunt, q.v. Ref: MP. Born in NYC; ci-
trus farmer in Calif. SC: Hazlitt
Woar = H.
The Body That Came by Post. Morrow,
    1937; Dickson & Davies, 1937 HW
    [Sp.]
The Body That Wasn't Uncle. Morrow,
    1939; Davies, 1939 HW [N.J.]
If a Body. Morrow, 1941 HW
There Was a Crooked Man. Morrow, 1936;
    Dickson & Davies, 1936 [NYC]

YATES, J. MICHAEL. 1938-   . Ref: CA.
Night Freight. Playwrights, 1972
    (1-act play.)

YATES, LIONEL (PEEL) and HONOR (MAHON)
    GOODHART
The Eclipse of James Trent. D. I.
    Murray, 1924

YATES, MARGARET (POLK), 1915-   , and
    PAULA BRAMLETTE. 1917-   .
Death Casts a Vote. Dutton, 1948 [NYC]
The Widow's Walk. Dutton, 1945
    [Cape Cod]

YATES, MARGARET (EVELYN) TAYLER. 1887-
1952. Born in Calif.; newspaper cor-
respondent. SC: Anne ("Davvie")
Davenport McLean, in all titles.
Death Sends a Cable. Macmillan, 1938;
    Davies, 1939 [Cuba]
The Hush-Hush Murders. Macmillan, 1937;
    Dickson, 1938 [ship]
Midway to Murder. Macmillan, 1941
    [Midway Is.]
Murder by the Yard. Macmillan, 1942
    [Haw.]

YATES, PETER. Pseudonym of William Long,
    1922-   . Other pseudonym: Will
    Creed, q.v. SC: Sandy Blunt = SB;
    the Thatcher family = T.
Curtain Call for Murder. Five Star,
    1945 T [Pa.]
Death Comes to Dinner. Five Star, 1945
    T [NYC]
Death in the Hands of Talent. Five
    Star, 1945 SB [NYC]
The Dress Circle Murders. Five Star,
    1945 SB [NYC]

YELDHAM, PETER
But She Won't Lie Down. French (NYC &
    London), 1978 (2-act play.)

YELOUSHAN, JAMES N.
Revenge Shall Be Mine. Vantage, 1979

YERBY, FRANK G(ARVIN). 1916-   .
A Rose for Ana Maria. Dial, 1976;
    Heinemann, 1976

YORCK, RUTH L(ANDSHOFF). 1909-1966. Ref:
CA.
So Cold the Night. Harper, 1948 [NYC]

YORK, ANDREW. Pseudonym of Christopher
    Robin Nicole, 1930-   . Other pseu-
    donym: Robin Cade, q.v. Ref: CA, CC,
    TC. SC: Col. Munro Tallant = MT;
    Jonas Wilde = JW.
The Captivator. Hutchinson, 1973;
    Doubleday, 1974 JW [ship]
The Co-Ordinator. Hutchinson, 1967;
    Lippincott, 1967 JW [Scand.]

Dark Passage. Hutchinson, 1976; Doubleday, 1977
The Deviator. Hutchinson, 1969; Lippincott, 1969 JW
The Dominator. Hutchinson, 1969 JW
The Eliminator. Hutchinson, 1966; Lippincott, 1967 JW
The Expurgator. Hutchinson, 1972; Doubleday, 1973 JW
The Fascinator. Hutchinson, 1975; Doubleday, 1975 JW [ship]
The Infiltrator. Hutchinson, 1971; Doubleday, 1971 JW
The Predator. Hutchinson, 1968; Lippincott, 1968 JW
Tallant for Disaster. Hutchinson, 1978; Doubleday, 1978 MT [W.I.]
Tallant for Trouble. Hutchinson, 1977; Doubleday, 1977 MT [W.I.]

YORK, (MARGARET) ELIZABETH. 1927- . Ref: CA.
The Medea Legend. PB, 1975 [Eng., past]

YORK, HELEN. 1918- . Ref: CA.
Malverne Manor. Doubleday, 1974 [Eng., 1800s]
Pennhaven. Dale, 1978
Tremorra Towers. Doubleday, 1976 [Eng., 1870]
A Venetian Charade. Doubleday, 1978 [Vienna, 1881]

YORK, JEREMY. Pseudonym of John Creasey, 1908-1973, q.v. Other pseudonyms: Gordon Ashe, M. E. Cooke, Norman Deane, Robert Caine Frazer, Michael Halliday, Patrick Gill, Charles Hogarth, Brian Hope, Colin Hughes, Kyle Hunt, Abel Mann, Peter Manton, J. J. Marric, Richard Martin, Rodney Mattheson, Anthony Morton, qq.v. SC (in revised editions of books that originally lacked such a character): Supt. Folly = F. Some titles published in the U.S. as by Jeremy York were originally issued in England as by Michael Halliday, and are listed in that entry herein. Set: Eng.
By Persons Unknown. Bles, 1941
Close the Door on Murder. Melrose, 1948; McKay, 1973,F
Death to My Killer. Melrose, 1950; Macmillan, 1966
Find the Body. Melrose, 1945; Macmillan, 1967,F
The Gallows Are Waiting. Melrose, 1949; McKay, 1973,F
Hide and Kill. Long, 1959; Scribner, 1960
Let's Kill Uncle Lionel. Melrose, 1947; McKay, 1976,F
Murder Came Late. Melrose, 1946; Macmillan, 1969,F
Murder in the Family. Melrose, 1944; McKay, 1976, as by John Creasey
Murder Unseen. Bles, 1942
My Brother's Killer. Long, 1958; Scribner, 1959
No Alibi. Melrose, 1943
Run Away to Murder. Melrose, 1947; Macmillan, 1970,F
Safari with Fear. Melrose, 1953 [S. Afr.]
Seeds of Murder. Paul, 1956; Scribner, 1958
Sentence of Death. Melrose, 1950; Macmillan, 1964
Sight of Death. Paul, 1956; Scribner, 1958
So Soon to Die. Paul, 1955; Scribner, 1957
To Kill or Die; see To Kill or to Die
To Kill or to Die. Long, 1960. U.S. title: To Kill or Die. Macmillan, 1965
Voyage with Murder. Melrose, 1952 [ship]
Wilful Murder. McNaughton, 1956 (British title? Byline?)
Yesterday's Murder. Melrose, 1945

YORKE, CLIFTON
The Swift Hand of Vengeance. Modern, 1938
The Voice from the Grave. Modern, 193?

YORKE, CURTIS. Pseudonym of Susan Richmond Lee.
The Brown Portmanteau and other stories. Jarrolds, 1889
The Mystery of Belgrave Square. White, 1889

YORKE, MARGARET. Pseudonym of Margaret Beda Larminie Nicholson, 1924- . Ref: CA, TC. SC: Patrick Grant = PG. Set: Eng.
Cast for Death. Hutchinson, 1976; Walker, 1976 PG [acad.]
The Come-On; see The Point of Murder

The Cost of Silence. Hutchinson, 1977; Walker, 1977
Dead in the Morning. Bles, 1970 PG
Death on Account. Hutchinson, 1979
Grave Matters. Bles, 1973; Bantam, 1983 PG [Greece]
Mortal Remains. Bles, 1974 PG [Crete]
No Medals for the Major. Bles, 1974 PG
The Point of Murder. Hutchinson, 1978. U.S. title: The Come-On. Harper, 1979
The Scent of Fear. Hutchinson, 1980; St. Martin's, 1981
Silent Witness. Bles, 1972; Walker, 1975 PG [Austria]
The Small Hours of the Morning. Bles, 1975; Walker, 1975

YORKE, PRESTON
The Case of the Strangled Seven. Everybody's, 1943
The Case of the Swinging Spider. Everybody's, 1944
Death on Priority! Mitre, 1945
The Gamma Ray Murders. Everybody's, 1943

YORKE, SUSAN. Pseudonym of Suzette Telenga, 1915- .
Agency House, Malaya. Farrar, 1962. Also published as: The Girl in the Cheongsam. Macfadden, 1963 [Mal.]

YORKE, VICTORIA
-Five of Hearts. Long, 1927
-Sealed Lips. Long, 1928
-Suppressed Evidence. Long, 1931

YOUD, (CHRISTOPHER) SAMUEL. 1922- . Pseudonyms: John Christopher, Hilary Ford, Peter Graaf, Peter Nichols, qq.v. Ref: CA.
Holly Ash. Cassell, 1955. U.S. title: The Opportunist. Harper, 1957

YOUNG, AL. 1939- . Ref: CA.
Ask Me Now. McGraw, 1980; Sidgwick, 1980

YOUNG, COLLIER. 1908-1980. Producer-director of movies and TV series.
The Todd Dossier. Delacorte, 1969; Macmillan (London), 1969 (Ghost-written by Robert Bloch, 1917- , q.v.)

YOUNG, DAVID. 1946- .
Agent Provocateur. Coach House, 1976

YOUNG, DONALD JORDAN
Demented. Gold Star, 1964

YOUNG, EDWARD (PRESTON). 1913- . Ref: CC.
The Fifth Passenger. Cassell, 1963; Harper, 1963

YOUNG, ERIC BRETT. Ref: CC.
The Dancing Beggars. Hutchinson, 1929; Lippincott, 1929
The Murder at Fleet. Hutchinson, 1927; Lippincott, 1928

YOUNG, ERNEST A. Pseudonym: Harry Rockwood, q.v.
-Barbara's Rival; or, Only a Woman's Heart. Lovell, 1885
A Criminal Queen; or, The Fatal Shot. Laird, 1888
Defending a Home. Ogilvie, 1891
File No. 114. Ogilvie, 1886 (A sequel to File No. 113 by Emile Gaboriau, 1833-1873, and possibly published as by Gaboriau.)
-Fugitives of Pearl Hill. Ogilvie, 1891
Luke Darby, the "World" Detective; or, Romance of the Dexter, Maine, Bank Robbery and Murder. Ogilvie, 1887 [Maine]
-A Wife's Honor. Ogilvie, 1885. Also published as: A Woman's Honor. Lovell, 1886
A Woman's Honor; see A Wife's Honor

YOUNG, FRANCIS BRETT. 1884-1954.
The Case Bird and other stories. Heinemann, 1933; Harper, 1933 ss, at least one criminous

YOUNG, G. H. R.
The Talking Skull and other selected short stories grave and gay. Wells Gardner, 1947 ss

YOUNG, GEORGE. 1919- .
Code-Name Caruso. Hutchinson, 1961 [It.]
The Man Called Lenz. Hutchinson, 1954; Coward, 1955

YOUNG, GORDON (RAY). 1886-1948.
Crooked Shadows. Garden City, 1924
The Devil's Passport. Century, 1933; Cassell, 1934 [Paris]
Hurricane Williams' Vengeance; see The Vengeance of Hurricane Williams
The Vengeance of Hurricane Williams. Doran, 1925. British title: Hurricane Williams' Vengeance. Unwin, 1925 [S. Pac.]

YOUNG, HOWARD IRVING. 1893- . Ref: CA.
Not Herbert. French (NYC), 1926 (4-act play.)

YOUNG, KENDAL. Pseudonym of Phyllis Brett Young, q.v.
The Ravine. Allen, 1961

YOUNG, MARSHA
A Chateau in Brittany. Popular Library, 1979 [Fr.]

YOUNG, MARY JULIA
Donalda; or, The Witches of Glenshiel. Hughes, 1805

YOUNG, PHYLLIS BRETT. Pseudonym: Kendal Young, q.v. Born in Toronto; lived in Geneva before returning to Toronto.
A Question of Judgment. Allen, 1970; Putnam, 1969
Undine. Longmans, 1964; Putnam, 1964

YOUNG, R(OSE) E(MMET). 1869-1941. Editor, staff writer and feature writer for magazines; active in suffrage movement; ss writer and novelist.
Murder at Manson's. Day, 1927 [NYC]

YOUNG, RICHARD. -1972. Pseudonym: Richard Macnaughtan, q.v.

YOUNGER, ELIZABETH HELY. 1913- . Pseudonym: Elizabeth Hely, q.v.

YOUNGER, JACK
-Claw. Manor, 1976
-The Curse of Anubis. Manor, 1976
The Curse of the Pharoahs. Manor, 1976
-Devlin. Manor, 1976

YOUNGER, WILLIAM ANTONY. 1917-1962. Pseudonym: William Mole, q.v.

YUDKOFF, ALVIN. Born and living in NYC in 1950s; radio and TV writer.
Circumstances Beyond Control. Rinehart, 1955. Also published as: Network of Fear. Bestseller, 1956, abridged

YUILL, P. B. Pseudonym of Gordon M(acLean) Williams, 1934- , q.v., and Terry Venables. Ref: TC. SC: James Hazell = JH. Set: Eng.
The Bornless Keeper. Macmillan (London), 1974; Walker, 1975
Hazell and the Menacing Jester. Macmillan (London), 1976 JH
Hazell and the Three Card Trick. Macmillan (London), 1975; Walker, 1976 JH
Hazell Plays Solomon. Macmillan (London), 1974; Walker, 1975 JH

Z., Z. Pseudonym of Louis Zangwill, 1869- .
A Nineteenth Century Miracle. Chatto, 1897

ZACHARY, HUGH. 1928- . Ref: CA.
To Guard the Right. Raven, 1980 [N.C.]

ZACKEL, FRED. Living in S.F. SC: Michael Brennan, in both titles.
Cinderella After Midnight. Coward, 1980 [S.F.]
Cocaine and Blue Eyes. Coward, 1978 [S.F.]

ZAKE, S. JOSHUA L. Former Ugandan Minister of Education and Attorney General, then Ambassador to U.S.
Truckful of Gold. Regnery, 1980 [Uganda]

ZANE, LEHI
Brenda. GM, 1952; Red Seal, 1957 [Calif.]

ZANGWILL, ISRAEL. 1864-1926. Ref: CC, DD, EM, MC, MP, TC.
The Big Bow Mystery. Henry, 1892; Rand, 1895

ZANGWILL, LOUIS. 1869- . Pseudonym: Z. Z., q.v.

ZAREMBA, EVE
　A Reason to Kill. PaperJacks, 1978

ZAROULIS, N(ANCY) L.
　The Poe Papers. Putnam, 1977; Allen, 1978 [Mass., 1890s]

ZARUBICA, MLADIN
　Scutari, Farrar, 1967
　-The Year of the Rat. Harcourt, 1964; Collins, 1965

ZAWADSKY, PATIENCE. 1927-　. Pseudonym: Patience Day.
　The Demon of Raven's Cliff. Belmont, 1971. Reprinted as by Patience Day: Belmont, 1973 [N.J.]

ZEC, DONALD
　The Face. New English Library, 1980

ZEIGER, (HENRY) ANTHONY. Pseudonym of a playwright and author "whose books have sold close to a million copies."
　Serenade for a Shylock. Putnam, 1976 [NYC]

ZELAZNY, ROGER. 1937-　. Ref: CA.
　My Name Is Legion. Ballantine, 1976; Faber, 1979 (3 novelets.)

ZENO. Pseudonym.
　Grab. Macmillan (London), 1970; Stein, 1970 [Afr.]

ZHDANOV, ALEKSANDR IVANOVICH. Pseudonym.
　Shadow of Peril. Doubleday, 1963

ZIEMANN, HANS HEINRICH. 1944-　.
　The Explosion. New English Library, 1978. U.S. title: The Accident. St. Martin's, 1979 (Translation of "Die Explosion." Hamburg, 1978; the translation is revised in the U.S. edition.)

ZIMMER, EGON MARIA. 1910-　. Pseudonym: C. C. Bergius, q.v.

ZINBERG, LEONARD S. 1911-1968. Pseudonym: Ed Lacy, q.v.

ZIRAN, GOLAND
　The Don. Pyramid, 1972

ZOCHERT, DONALD (PAUL, JR.). 1938-　. Ref: CA.
　Another Weeping Woman. Holt, 1980 [Mont.]
　Murder in the Hellfire Club. Holt, 1978 [Eng., 1775]

ZOLAR. Pseudonym of Bruce King,　-1976. Ref: CA.
　Zolar's Astrological Murder Mysteries. Zolar, 1971　ss

ZORE, H.
　Alibi Off Broadway. Scion, 1954 [NYC]
　Black Orchid. Scion, 1953
　Blue Orchid. Scion, 1953
　Carnival of Death. Scion, 1953
　Cover That Corpse. Scion, 1953
　Flame. Scion, 1953
　It's a Sin. Scion, 1953
　The Lady Is a Tramp. Scion, 1953
　Savage Siren. Scion, 1953
　Shadow of a Sin. Scion, 1953
　This Was a Woman. Scion, 1953
　What's Ya Problem? Scion, 1953

ZORRO. Pseudonym of Harold Ward, q.v. SC: Dr. Death (Dr. Rance Mandarin), in all titles.
　The Gray Creatures. Corinth, 1966 [Egypt]
　The Shriveling Murders. Corinth, 1966
　12 Must Die. Corinth, 1966

ZUCKERMAN, ALBERT
　The Head of the House. Dell, 1978
　Tiger Kittens. Doubleday, 1973

ZUCKMAYER, CARL. 1896-1977. Ref: CA.
　Carnival Confession. Methuen, 1961 (Translation of "Die Fastnachtsbeichte." Frankfurt, 1959.)

ZUGSMITH, LEANE. 1903-1969. See: Carl (Albert) Randau, 1893-1969; and: Kenneth White, 1905-1953.

ZUKAS, EDGAR V.
　A Handful of Stars. Vantage, 1964

ZUMWALT, EVA. 1936-　. Ref: CA.
　Briarlea. Ace, 1976
　The Deathday Song. Major, 1977
　Masquerade of Evil. Ace, 1975 [Miss.]

Title Index

Title Index

ABC Affair. P. Winston
ABCD. D. R. Slavitt
A.B.C. Investigates. Ephesian
ABC Murders. A. Christie
A.B.C. Solves Five. Ephesian
A.B.C.'s Test Case. Ephesian
A. J. Alan's Second Book. A. J. Alan
A-100. Bruce Harrison
A.R.P. Murder. Sutherland Scott
A.R.P. Mystery. B. Perowne
A.R.P. Spy. A. O. Pollard
A.S.F. J. Rhode
ATS Mystery. G. Coverack
Aamon Always. D. E. L. Patch
Aardvark Affair. G. Brandner
Aaron Rodd, Diviner. E. P. Oppenheim
Aaron's Serpent. E. Thorne
Abaft 'Midships. E. L. Long
Abandon Hope. I. Garland
Abandoned Car Crime. Gwyn Evans
Abandoned Claim. F. H. Loughead
Abandoned Doll. L. Meynell
Abandoned Power. J. Fores
Abandoned Room. Wadsworth Camp
Abbey Court. M. Thum
Abbey Court Murder. A. Haynes
Abbey Murder. J. Hatton
Abbey Mystery. R. M. Gilchrist
Abbey of St. Asaph. I. Kelly
Abbeygate. C. Crowe
Abbot of Montserrat. W. C. Green
Abbot's Cup. C. A. Alington
Abbot's House. L. Conway
Abbot's Moat. F. Warden
Abduction. T. Burke
Abduction. S. Cohen
Abduction. G. F. Newman
Abduction of Princess Chriemhild. L. F. Griffin
Abduction of Virginia Lee. F. O'Rourke
Abductor. D. Hitchens
Abductors. D. Reid
Abel Coincidence. J. N. Chance
Aberdeen Conundrum. Angus Ross
Abimelech Pott, the Don Quixote of the Bar. H. W. Jessup
Abner Crane's Vengeance. A. G. Hales
Abner Ferret, the Lawyer Detective. H. Rockwood
Abner Ferret, the Lawyer Detective. J. R. Taylor
Aboard the American Duchess. H. Hill
Aboard "The American Duchess." G. L. Myers
Aboard the Aquitaine. G. Simenon
Abode of Love. J. Shearing
Abolition of Death. James Anderson
Abominable Man. M. Sjowall
Abominable Twilight. Reginald Campbell
Abomination. H. Janson
About Doctor Ferrel. D. Keene
About Face. F. Kane
About Ourselves. H. Wood
About the Murder of a Man Afraid of Women. A. Abbot
About the Murder of a Startled Lady. A. Abbot
About the Murder of Geraldine Foster. A. Abbot
About the Murder of the Circus Queen. A. Abbot
About the Murder of the Clergyman's Mistress. A. Abbot
About the Murder of the Night Club Lady. A. Abbot
About Two A.M. C. F. Coe
Above and Below. J. Palmer
Above Suspicion. R. O. Chipperfield
Above Suspicion. Helen MacInnes
Above the Dark Circus. H. Walpole
Above the Dark Tumult. H. Walpole
Above the Law. J. Goodwin
Abra-Cadaver. C. Monig
Abracadabra. W. Mankowitz
Abracadaver. P. Lovesey
Abrams and Jones, Homicide. M. Dines
Abrus Necklace. E. G. Seibert
Absense. M. Eyre
Absent Friends. C. J. C. Hyne
Absolutely Murder. G. Le Pelley
Absolutely True. I. Montagu
Absolution. A. Shaffer
Abu Wahab Caper. R. H. Spencer
Abyssinian Mystery. G. Chester
Academic Factor. C. A. Haddad
Academic Murder. D. Fiske
Academic Question. R. H. R. Smithies
Acapulco Rampage. D. Pendleton
Accent on Murder. R. Lockridge
Accessory. M. Lockwood
Accessory After. E. C. Vivian
Accessory After the Fact. W. A. Hobday
Accessory After the Fact. B. Reynolds
Accessory After the Fact. L. Thayer
Accessory for Murder. J. M. Howe
Accessory to Murder. P. Barrington
Accident. A. A. Josey
Accident by Design. E. C. R. Lorac
Accident for Inspector West. J. Creasey
Accident in Piccadilly. H. Willett
Accident, Manslaughter or Murder? L. Thayer

Accident or Murder? Nicholas Carter
Accident to Adeline. E. Burgess
Accident Ward Mystery. R. Truax
Accidental Accomplice. W. A. Johnston
Accidental Adventurer. S. M. Parkman
Accidental Clue. B. Graeme
Accidental Don Juan. E. Jepson
Accidental Murder. C. F. Gregg
Accidental Password. Nicholas Carter
Accidental Spy. James Watson
Accidents Do Happen. M. Burton
Accidents Will Happen. V. Bridges
Accomplice. J. Bland
Accomplice. M. Head
Accomplice. F. T. Hill
Accomplice. J. Pudney
Accomplices. Leonard Cooper
Accomplices. David Fletcher
Accomplices. G. Simenon
According to Gibson. D. MacKail
According to Orders. F. B. Austin
According to Plan. L. Jackson
According to Plan. G. Seton
According to the Evidence. H. Cecil
According to the Evidence. F. Douglas
Account Closed. S. M. Parkman
Account Paid. C. Brooks
Account Rendered. P. Barrington
Account Rendered. P. Cheyney
Account Rendered. F. Ryck
Account Rendered. P. Wentworth
Account to Render. S. Coulter
Account Unsettled. G. Simenon
Accounting. B. Marshall
Accounting for Murder. E. Lathen
Accursed. C. Seignolle
Accuse the Toff. J. Creasey
Accused. H. R. Daniels
Accused and Accuser. A. Sergeant
Accused Princess. A. Upward
Accusing Finger. M. Doran
Accusing Spirit. Mrs. Pilkington
Ace High. G. Goodchild
Ace High. Mark Ross
Ace High, the 'Frisco Detective. C. E. Tripp
Ace in the Hole. F. Martin
Ace-in-the-Hole Haggarty. R. M. Hankins
Ace of Clubs Murder. R. Trevor
Ace of Danger. L. Grex
Ace of Danger. Augustus Muir
Ace of Death. J. Callahan
Ace of Death. T. A. Plummer
Ace of Diamonds. A. Hurry
Ace of Hearts. F. Du Boisgobey
Ace of Hearts. C. Thomas-Stanford
Ace of Jades. S. Palmer
Ace of Knaves. L. Charteris
Ace of Spades. R. Andre
Ace of Spades. H. Holt
Ace of Spades. A. Nasielski
Ace of Spades. Dell Shannon
Ace of Spades Murder. H. S. Keeler
Ace of Spies. D. Von Elsner
Ace Up My Sleeve. J. H. Chase
Aces & Eights. P. Garlington
Aces, Eights, and Murder. M. V. Heberden
Aces High. William Hughes
Aces of the White Death. R. J. Hogan
Aces Run Wild. J. A. Rennie
Achievements of John Carruthers. E. C. Cox
Achievements of Luther Trant. E. Balmer
Achilles Affair. B. Mather
Achilles' Isle. R. Batchelor
Achilles Mandate. M. Fogarty
Acid. H. Imbert-Terry
Acid Drop. S. George
Acid Rock. R. Sapir
Ackroyd. J. Feiffer
Aconite Murders. S. Williams
Acquainted with Murder. F. Hurt
Acquittal. G. Lorimer
Acquittal. W. Wainwright
Acquitted! M. Frazer
Acrefield Mystery. F. Grierson
Across 110th. W. Ferris
Across That River. H. Whittington
Across the Border. J. G. Sarasin
Across the Common. E. Berridge
Across the Divide. A. Murray
Across the Footlights. F. Hume
Across the Frontiers. H. Edmonds
Across the Narrow Seas. J. Pattinson
Across the Pacific. C. E. Blaney
Across the Street. G. Simenon
Across the Water. S. Binnie
Across the World for a Wife. G. Boothby
Act of Anger. B. Spicer
Act of Darkness. P. Hastings
Act of Fear. Michael Collins
Act of Fear. W. D. Roberts
Act of God. C. Templeton
Act of Impulse. H. Bayliss
Act of Love. W. E. D. Ross
Act of Mercy. F. Clifford
Act of Murder. P. Reakes
Act of Passion. Wenzell Brown
Act of Passion. G. Simenon
Act of Providence. H. C. McNeile
Act of Silence. Anthony Graham
Act of Terror. P. A. Foxall

Act of Violence. E. Fadiman
Act of Violence. B. Heatter
Act of Violence. P. Saxon
Act of Violence. K. Wade
Act of War. B. Callison
Acting Second Mate. S. M. Parkman
Action Along the Humboldt. K. Kramer
Action at Arcanum. W. C. MacDonald
Action at World's End. W. Chambers
Action for the Picaroon. J. Cassells
Action in Diamonds. C. R. Cooper
Action Man. J. Flynn
Action of the Tiger. A. Kent
Action of the Tiger. T. Walsh
Action of the Tiger. J. Wellard
Actor Manager. A. Askew
Actor's Blood. B. Hecht
Actor's Knife. Howel Evans
Actor's Secret. H. E. Hill
Actress. A. Applin
Actress Detective. Anonymous
Actress's Daughter. M. A. Fleming
Actress's Husband. G. Warden
Acts of Black Night. K. M. Knight
Acts of Mercy. B. Pronzini
Acts of Theft. A. A. Cohen
Acupuncture Murders. D. Steward
Ada Vernham, Actress. R. Marsh
Adair and Son. P. Trent
Adam. P. Trent
Adam and Evelina. P. Allardyce
Adam Grainger. H. Wood
Adam Grey. Jack Wilson
Adam Sleep. W. Van Atta
Adam's Case. M. Underwood
Adam's Child. R. Breen
Adam's Fall. J. Ridgway
Adam's Rib. P. Allardyce
Adam's Tale. G. Honeycombe
Adapted to Stress. C. D. Peel
Add a Pinch of Cyanide. E. Page
Adders Abounding. J. Lukens
Adder's Brood. Nicholas Carter
Adders on the Heath. G. Mitchell
Addicted to Murder. T. S. Drachman
Addle. D. Durrant
Address Unknown. E. Phillpotts
Adela's Ordeal. F. Warden
Adele & Co. D. Yates
Adelgitha. Matthew Gregory Lewis
Adeline Saint Julian. A. Ker
Adjuster. P. Malloch
Adjusters. Valentine
Adjustments. I. R. G. Hart
Admirable Carfew. E. Wallace
Admirable Lady Biddy Fane. F. Barrett
Admiral Teach. C. J. C. Hyne
Admiral's a Spy. W. Taylor
Admiral's Light. H. M. Rideout
Admiral's Million. A. D. Divine
Admiral's Secret. A. Murray
Admiralty Murders. M. Adam
Admiralty Regrets—. Reginald Campbell
Admiralty's Secret. C. Dawe
Adolescence of P-1. T. J. Ryan
Adopted. A. L. Halstead
Adopted Face. A. S. Carter
Adopters. W. Hegner
Adrian and Jonathan. Richard Martin
Adriana. G. Dyer
Adriatic Formula. M. Lederer
Adrienne de Portalis. A. C. Gunter
Adrift with a Vengeance. K. Cornwallis
Advance Agent. J. August
Advance South. J. Robb
Advancement of Learning. R. Hill
Advancement of Mr. Simpkin. J. Last
Adventure. B. Deal
Adventure. C. Moberly
Adventure at Eighty. J. J. Farjeon
Adventure Calling! S. Horler
Adventure for Nine. J. J. Farjeon
Adventure for Two. A. Applin
Adventure for Wealth. C. T. Stoneham
Adventure in the Night. W. Dawson
Adventure in Washington. L. Ross
Adventure Isle. G. A. England
Adventure Mysterious. F. Marlowe
Adventure of Red Head of the Red Sea. W. J. Makin
Adventure of the Albanian Avenger. W. W. Sayer
Adventure of the Annamese Prince. W. M. Graydon
Adventure of the Blue Room. S. Fowler
Adventure of the Bogus Sheik. G. H. Teed
Adventure of the Broad Arrow. Morley Roberts
Adventure of the Christmas Pudding. A. Christie
Adventure of the Dancing Hen. J. Ruyle
Adventure of the Egyptian Student. R. C. Armour
Adventure of the Freckled Hand. J. Ruyle
Adventure of the Eleven Cuff-Buttons. J. F. Thierry
Adventure of the Giant Bat of Sonoma. J. Ruyle
Adventure of the Jogging Man. J. Ruyle
Adventure of the Logophagous Client. J. Ruyle

Adventure of the Lost Manuscript. E. Pearson
Adventure of the Man "On Bail". W. J. Mayfield
Adventure of the Marked Man and One Other. S. Palmer
Adventure of the Missing Third Quarter. J. Ruyle
Adventure of the Mysterious Lodger. G. Gravatt
Adventure of the Oil Pirates. R. C. Armour
Adventure of the Orient Express. A. Derleth
Adventure of the Peerless Peer. P. J. Farmer
Adventure of the Red-Headed Man. W. J. Bayfield
Adventure of the Retired Weatherman. J. Ruyle
Adventure of the Rogue's Apprentice. W. M. Graydon
Adventure of the Silk Smugglers. R. C. Armour
Adventure of the Speed Mad Camden. A. Murray
Adventure of the Stalwart Companions. H. P. Jeffers
Adventure of the Unique Dickensians. A. Derleth
Adventure of the Voodoo Queen. G. H. Teed
Adventure Trail. D. B. Hobart
Adventure with a Goat. R. T. Campbell
Adventure with Crime. Josephine Bell
Adventurer. R. Miall
Adventurer from the West. M. J. Pemberton
Adventurer of the Bay. O. Binns
Adventurers. J. A. Hodge
Adventurers. H. B. M. Watson
Adventurers of the Night. G. A. Birmingham
Adventures at Greystones. G. E. Rochester
Adventures by Night. T. P. Prest
Adventure's End. J. Harris
Adventures of a Bashful Bachelor. C. Augusta
Adventures of a Chemist. F. A. Fawcett
Adventures of a Chemist. F. A. Hawkes
Adventures of a Coquette. G. Leroux
Adventures of a Journalist. H. Cadett
Adventures of a Lady Detective. Mrs. G. Corbett
Adventures of a Lady Pearl Broker. B. Heron-Maxwell
Adventures of a Nice Young Man. Aix
Adventures of a Pretty Woman. F. Warden
Adventures of a Skeleton. B. W. Waltermire
Adventures of a Social Detective. C. Bramley
Adventures of a Solicitor. W. Chesney
Adventures of a Stowaway. F. Whishaw
Adventures of a Turf Detective. F. D. A. C. De L'Isle
Adventures of Ah Foo, the Chinese Sherlock Holmes. C. Bishop
Adventures of Alonzo MacTavish. P. Cheyney
Adventures of an Attorney in Search of Practice. Anonymous
Adventures of an Engineer. W. Chesney
Adventures of an Equerry. M. Gerard
Adventures of an Ugly Girl. Mrs. G. Corbett
Adventures of Antoine. H. Collinson Owen
Adventures of Archer Dawe, Sleuth-Hound. J. S. Fletcher
Adventures of Blackshirt. B. Graeme
Adventures of Burnaby Lee. E. Thomson
Adventures of Caleb Williams. W. Godwin
Adventures of Captain Ivan Koravitch. V. L. Whitechurch
Adventures of Captain Jack. M. Pemberton
Adventures of Captain Kettle. C. J. C. Kyne
Adventures of Captain Mounsell. W. W. Dixon
Adventures of Creighton Holmes. N. Hubell
Adventures of D'Arcy Dewpond, Detective. W. Slater
Adventures of Detective Barney. H. J. O'Higgins
Adventures of Dick Boss. Maz
Adventures of Dr. Burton. A. C. Gunter
Adventures of Dr. Thorndyke. R. A. Freeman
Adventures of Ellery Queen. E. Queen
Adventures of Ephraim Tutt. A. Train
Adventures of Felix Boyd. S. Campbell
Adventures of Francois. S. W. Mitchell
Adventures of Harrison Keith, Detective. Nicholas Carter
Adventures of Heine. E. Wallace
Adventures of Herlock Sholmes. Peter Todd
Adventures of Hiram Holliday. P. Gallico
Adventures of Husky Hillier. F. A. M. Webster
Adventures of Jimmie Dale. F. Packard

Adventures of Jimmy Strange. E. Dudley
Adventures of John Johns. F. Carrell
Adventures of Johnnie Pascoe. G. Norway
Adventures of Judith Lee. R. Marsh
Adventures of Jules de Grandin. Seabury Quinn
Adventures of Julia. P. Cheyney
Adventures of Julia and Two Other Spy Stories. P. Cheyney
Adventures of Kathlyn. H. MacGrath
Adventures of Kerlock Shomes and Dr. Warsaw. T. Gross
Adventures of Latimer Field, Curate. S. Hocking
Adventures of Louis Dural. Marguerite Bryant
Adventures of Marmaduke Clegg. M. Gerard
Adventures of Martin Hewitt. Arthur Morrison
Adventures of Miranda. L. T. Meade
Adventures of Miss Gregory. P. Gibbon
Adventures of Mr. Topham, Comedian. C. R. Gull
Adventures of Mr. Joseph P. Cray. E. P. Oppenheim
Adventures of M. D'Haricot. J. S. Clouston
Adventures of Napoleon Prince. M. Edginton
Adventures of Picklock Holes. R. C. Lehman
Adventures of Police Constable Vane, M.A. A. Askew
Adventures of Private Faust. H. H. Kirst
Adventures of Richard O'Boy. B. Siegel
Adventures of Romney Pringle. C. Ashdown
Adventures of Sam Spade and other stories. D. Hammett
Adventures of Scout Grey. R. L. Bellamy
Adventures of Sherlaw Kombs. R. Barr
Adventures of Sherlock Holmes. A. C. Doyle
Adventures of Sherlock Holmes' Smarter Brother. G. Pearlman
Adventures of Shylar Homes. S. D. Williams
Adventures of Solar Pons. A. Derleth
Adventures of the Black Pilgrim. G. Stanley
Adventures of the D.C.I. C. E. Russell
Adventures of the Five Puce Map Tacks. P. Nizza
Adventures of the Infallible Godahl. F. I. Anderson
Adventures of Tyler Tatlock, Private Detective. D. Donovan
Adventuress. A. B. Reeve
Adventuress. C. Stanton
Adventuress. D. Winston
Adventuress of France. E. Gaboriau
Adventurous Annie. E. Everett-Green
Adventurous Exploits of the Younger Brothers. H. Dale
Adversaries. E. Linn
Adversary. B. Spicer
Advice Limited. E. P. Oppenheim
Advisory Service. M. Russell
Advocate's Wig. L. M. Watt
Aelian Fragment. G. Bartram
Aerial Burglars. J. Blyth
Aerie. J. S. McClean
Aero Clubs Mystery. E. J. Millward
Aeroplane Mystery. D. T. Hughes
Affacombe Affair. E. Lemarchand
Affair at Abu Mina. P. William
Affair at Aliquid. G. D. H. Cole
Affair at Alkali. V. Coffman
Affair at Cralla Voe. J. Shelynn
Affair at Dead End. J. N. Chance
Affair at Falconers. M. Howe
Affair at Flower Acres. C. Wells
Affair at Helen's Court. C. Carnac
Affair at Little Todsham. G. Greenaway
Affair at Little Wokeham. F. W. Crofts
Affair at Lover's Leap. R. G. Dean
Affair at Palm Springs. C. Knight
Affair at Pine Court. N. R. Gilbert
Affair at Quala. T. Helmore
Affair at Ritos Bay. Muriel Bradley
Affair at Royalties. G. Baxt
Affair at Sidi Brahim. Brian Stuart
Affair at the Boat Landing. A. B. Cunningham
Affair at the Chateau. B. Reynolds
Affair at the Grotto. E. H. Fonseca
Affair at the Semiramis Hotel. A. E. W. Mason
Affair at the "Vere Arms." A. R. Weekes
Affair at Tideways. E. A. Heath
Affair at Timber Lake. A. Anderson
Affair for the Baron. Anthony Morton
Affair in Araby. T. Mundy
Affair in Death Valley. C. Knight
Affair in Duplex 9B. W. A. Johnston
Affair in Hong Kong. D. Daniels
Affair in Marakesh. D. Daniels
Affair in Tokyo. J. McPartland
Affair of Chief Strongheart. P. O'Malley
Affair of Danny the "Dip". W. Tyrer
Affair of Hearts. D. Noel
Affair of Honor. R. Wilder
Affair of John Donne. P. O'Malley

Affair of Jolie Madame. P. O'Malley
Affair of Nina B. J. M. Simmel
Affair of Sorcerers. G. Chesbro
Affair of State. P. Frank
Affair of Strangers. J. Crosby
Affair of Swan Lake. P. O'Malley
Affair of the Atlantic Mail Robbery. R. C. Armour
Affair of the Black Sombrero. C. Knight
Affair of the Blackfriars Financier. L. H. Brooks
Affair of the Bloodstained Egg-Cosy. James Anderson
Affair of the Blue Pig. P. O'Malley
Affair of the Bronzed Basilisk. A. Skene
Affair of the Bumbling Briton. P. O'Malley
Affair of the Circus Queen. C. Knight
Affair of the Corpse Escort. C. Knight
Affair of the Country Club. H. H. C. Gibbons
Affair of the Crimson Gull. C. Knight
Affair of the Crook Explorer. R. C. Armour
Affair of the Cross-Roads. H. H. C. Gibbons
Affair of the Dead Stranger. C. Knight
Affair of the Demobilized Soldier. W. J. Bayfield
Affair of the Diamond Star. H. H. C. Gibbons
Affair of the Exotic Dancer. B. Benson
Affair of the Fainting Butler. C. Knight
Affair of the Family Diamonds. W. J. Bayfield
Affair of the Fraternizing Soldier. P. Meriton
Affair of the Frigid Blonde. R. O. Saber
Affair of the Gallows Tree. S. Chalmers
Affair of the Ginger Lei. C. Knight
Affair of the Golden Buzzard. C. Knight
Affair of the Heart. J. Potts
Affair of the Heavenly Voice. C. Knight
Affair of the Hollywood Contract. W. Tyrer
Affair of the Jade Monkey. C. Knight
Affair of the Kidnapped Crook. H. H. C. Gibbons
Affair of the Limping Sailor. C. Knight
Affair of the Malacca Stick. C. Andrews
Affair of the Missing Parachutist. A. Parsons
Affair of the Missing Witness. W. M. Graydon
Affair of the Oriental Doctor. Jack Lewis
Affair of the Phantom Car. E. J. Murray
Affair of the Red Mosaic. P. O'Malley
Affair of the Rival Cinema Kings. W. Shute
Affair of the Scarlet Crab. C. Knight
Affair of the Seven Mummy Cases. W. J. Bayfield
Affair of the Seven Warnings. G. N. Philips
Affair of the Sixth Button. C. Knight
Affair of the Skiing Clown. C. Knight
Affair of the Smuggled Millions. M. B. Dix
Affair of the Spiv's Secret. J. Hunter
Affair of the Splintered Heart. C. Knight
Affair of the Substitute Doctor. J. Rhode
Affair of the Syrian Dagger. C. Andrews
Affair of the Three Gunmen. W. M. Graydon
Affair of the Trade Rivals. R. C. Armour
Affair of the World's Champion. Jack Lewis
Affair on the Bridge. J. M. DeGroot
Affair on the Painted Desert. C. Knight
Affair on Thor's Head. E. C. R. Lorac
Affair Ravel. J. Courage
Affair with a Rich Girl. J. N. Chance
Affairs of Death. N. Fitzgerald
Affairs of Destiny. G. Simenon
Affairs of O'Malley. W. MacHarg
Affairs of Paula. H. Janson
Affairs of State. B. E. Stevenson
Affairs of the Generals. H. H. Kirst
Affairs of the Heart. M. Muggeridge
Afghan Assault. A. Caillou
Afraid in the Dark. M. Derby
Afraid in the Dark. J. Reach
Afraid of the Dark. M. L. Roby
African Contract. S. Jason
African Gold. W. M. Graydon
African Millionaire. G. Allen
African Millionaire. E. Wallace
African Mistress. L. Royer
African Poison Murders. E. Huxley
African Terror. N. Sheraton
African Trio. G. Simenon
Afrit Affair. K. Laumer
After Baxtow's Death. M. Farrow
After Dark. W. Collins
After-Dark. Ron Fraser
After Dark, My Sweet. J. Thompson
After Darvray Died. P. Meriton
After-Dinner Story. W. Irish
After Doomsday. P. Anderson

Title Index

After Hours. E. Torres
After House. M. R. Rinehart
After Innocence. I. Gordon
After Many Days. C. Dawe
After Many Years. R. H. Savage
After Midnight. M. Albrand
After Midnight. W. F. Fauley
After Midnight. H. Nielsen
After Office-Hours. E. Yates
After Rome, Africa. B. Glanville
After Sundown. W. W. Penn
After the Act. Winston Graham
After the Ball. E. Dewhurst
After the Battle. D. Learmonth
After the Bribe Takers. Lieut. Carlton
After the Deacon Was Murdered. C. Penfield
After the Deed. J. S. Clouston
After the Execution. T. Hyde
After the Fact. A. Brock
After the Fault. R. H. Sherard
After the Fine Weather. M. Gilbert
After the First Death. Lawrence Block
After the First Death. R. Cormier
After the Funeral. A. Christie
After the Island. H. Bourne
After the Kill. S. Cunningham
After the Lady. P. Allardyce
After the Last Race. D. Koontz
After the Night Has Passed. A. L. Halstead
After the Revolution. W. Wallace
After the Trial. E. Roman
After the Verdict. Nicholas Carter
After the Verdict. Anthony Gilbert
After the Verdict. R. Hichens
After the Verdict. P. Johnson
After the Verdict. E. Jordan
After the Wedding. K. Lindsay
After the Widow Changed Her Mind. C. Penfield
After Things Fell Apart. R. Goulart
After You with the Pistol. K. Bonfiglioli
Aftermath. O. T. Jackson
Aftermath. H. B. M. Watson
Aftermath of Murder. M. Fitt
Aftermath of Murder. R. Harrison
Aftermath of Murder. T. Newman
Afternoon at the Seaside. A. Christie
Afternoon for Lizards. D. Eden
Afternoon of a Counterspy. R. Tronson
Afternoon of a Loser. T. Pace
Afternoon of Violence. C. Barling
Afternoon to Kill. Shelley Smith
Afternoon Walk. D. Eden
Aftershock. L. O'Donnell
Aftershock. C. Wilcox
Afterwards. M. B. Lowndes
Again Inspector Flagg. J. Cassells
Again McLean. G. Goodchild
Again, Mr. Sandyman. Neill Graham
Again Sanders. E. Wallace
Again the Dreamer. W. M. Duncan
Again the Remover. Roland Daniel
Again the Ringer. E. Wallace
Again the Three. E. Wallace
Again the Three Just Men. E. Wallace
Against All Odds. Arthur Smith
Against Desperate Odds. Nicholas Carter
Against My Fire. D. G. Waring
Against Odds. L. L. Lynch
Against the Evidence. L. Egan
Against the F.B.I. R. Carni
Against the Flame. Evelyn Harris
Against the Law. D. Durham
Against the Public Interest. R. Gaines
Against the Stream. J. Hatton
Agatha. K. Tynan
Agatha Webb. A. K. Green
Agatha's Quest. R. H. Sherard
Age of Death. W. Marshall
Age of the Junkman. P. D. Ballard
Agency. P. Gottlieb
Agency House, Malaya. S. Yorke
Agent. T. Hinde
Agent B-7. Ared White
Agent Counter Agent. Nick Carter
Agent Extraordinary. S. Bayne
Agent from the West. D. Williams
Agent in Place. Helen MacInnes
Agent Intervenes. M. Annesley
Agent No. 5. J. Corbett
Agent of Death. N. De Mille
Agent of the Devil. H. Habe
Agent of the Id. B. Byers
Agent of Vega. J. H. Schmitz
Agent on the Other Side. G. O'Toole
Agent Orange Affair. James Watson
Agent Outside. P. Wynnton
Agent Provocateur. D. Young
Agents of Influence. P. Harcourt
Agents of the League. C. Davy
Aggravating Joe, the Prince of Mischief. Old Sleuth
Agnes the Unknown. T. P. Prest
Agony Column. E. D. Biggers
Agony Column Murders. R. T. M. Scott
Agony Terrace. A. Griffiths
Agreement to Kill. P. Rabe
Aground. C. Williams
Ah King. W. S. Maugham

Ahead of the Game. Nicholas Carter
Aila. K. Thomas
Aim to Kill. R. Gatenby
Ainceworth Mystery. G. Baxter
Air Apparent. J. Gardner
Air Bandits. D. T. Lindsay
Air Bandits. P. Trent
Air Bridge. H. Innes
Air Cavalier. T. Wallace
Air Devil. B. Beverley
Air Disaster. H. Innes
Air for Murder. F. L. Cary
Air Force One. E. Corley
Air Gold. Colin Hope
Air Killer. J. Corbett
Air Ministry, Room 28. G. Frankau
Air Murders. R. H. Watkins
Air of Glory. S. Neilan
Air Peril. Colin Hope
Air Pilot. R. Parrish
Air Pirate. C. R. Gull
Air Ranger. G. E. Rochester
Air Reprisal. A. O. Pollard
Air-Ship. J. S. Fletcher
Air Sleuth. J. Bolton
Air Smugglers. J. Bolton
Air That Kills. Francis King
Air That Kills. M. Millar
Air Trail. G. E. Rochester
Airing in a Closed Carriage. J. Shearing
Airline Pirates. J. Gardner
Airport Affair. D. Toma
Airport Cop. C. Miron
Airs Above the Ground. Mary Stewart
Airtight Alibi. C. F. Gregg
Akin to Murder. K. M. Knight
Al Capone. J. Roeburt
Aladdin in London. F. Hume
Aladdin in London. M. Pemberton
Alain of Halfdene. A. Burr
Alamein. M. Urquhart
Alamut Ambush. A. Price
Alan Fitz Osborne. Miss Fuller
Alan Thorne. M. L. Moodey
Alaric Spenceley. J. H. Riddell
Alarm. J. Rhode
Alarm at Black Brake. J. N. Chance
Alarm in the Night. S. Sterling
Alarm of the Black Cat. D. B. Olsen
Alarming Clock. M. Avallone
Alarum. G. Marton
Alarum and Excursion. V. Perdue
Alas for Her That Met Me! M. A. Ashe
Alas, Poor Father. Joan Fleming
Alaska Conspiracy. J. Rosenberger
Alaskan. G. Goodchild
Albanian Connection. J. Rosenberger
Albatross. C. Armstrong
Albatross Murders. I. Jones
Albert Gate Affair. L. Tracy
Albert Gate Mystery. L. Tracy
Albino's Double. G. N. Philips
Albion Case. D. Craig
Album. M. R. Rinehart
Album Leaf. J. Shearing
Alcatraz Incident. R. O'Neil
Alchemy Deception. H. W. Holzer
Alchemy Murder. P. Oldfeld
Alcoholics. J. Thompson
Alda Abducted. A. R. Weekes
Aldeburg Cezanne. J. A. Graham
Alden Case. R. Bridges
Alderman's Double. J. B. Richards
Aldringham's Last Chance. A. J. Rees
Aleph Solution. S. Frankel
Aleta's Terrible Secret. L. J. Libbey
Aletta. B. Mitford
Aleutian Blue Mink. J. M. Fox
Alexandrovitch Is Missing! Anne Edwards
Alexena. Anonymous
Algarve Affair. R. Derwent
Algerian Incident. C. Sellers
Algonquin Project. F. Nolan
Alias. F. Andreas
Alias Basil Willing. H. McCloy
Alias Ben Alibi. T. S. Cobb
Alias Blackshirt. B. Graeme
Alias Blue Mask. Anthony Morton
Alias Dr. Ely. L. Thayer
Alias for Death. B. L. Reynolds
Alias His Wife. S. Ransome
Alias John Doe. P. E. Triem
Alias John Smith. G. Wade
Alias Man. D. Craig
Alias Mr. Death. G. W. Jones
Alias Mr. Orson. A. Spiller
Alias Norman Conquest. B. Gray
Alias Red Ryan. C. N. Buck
Alias Richard Power. W. Allison
Alias Richard Power. C. N. Williamson
Alias the Baron. Anthony Morton
Alias—The Crimson Snake. T. A. Plummer
Alias the Dead. G. H. Coxe
Alias the Eagle. M. Harvey
Alias the Ghost. G. Verner
Alias the Hangman. V. Gunn
Alias the Lone Wolf. L. J. Vance
Alias the Night Wind. V. Vanardy
Alias the Saint. L. Charteris
Alias the Thunderbolt. J. McCulley
Alias the Victim. L. Gribble
Alias Uncle Hugo. M. Coles

Alibeg, the Tempter. W. C. Child
Alibi. H. Carmichael
Alibi. J. Creasey
Alibi. G. A. England
Alibi. Mark Ross
Alibi. F. F. Van De Water
Alibi and Dr. Morelle. E. Dudley
Alibi at Dusk. B. Benson
Alibi Baby. S. Sterling
Alibi for a Corpse. E. Lemarchand
Alibi for a Judge. H. Cecil
Alibi for a Witch. E. Ferrars
Alibi for Isabel. M. R. Rinehart
Alibi for Murder. C. Armstrong
Alibi in Black. Colin Robertson
Alibi in the Rough. S. Box
Alibi in Time. J. Thomson
Alibi Innings. B. Worsley-Gough
Alibi of Guilt. Philip Daniels
Alibi Off Broadway. H. Zore
Alibi Too Much. H. Kaner
Alice. E. Bulwer-Lytton
Alice. E. V. Cunningham
Alice. F. W. Pangborn
Alice and Me. W. Judson
Alice Devine. E. Jepson
Alice Dies Twice. B. Grant
Alice, Where Art Thou? E. Cadell
Alicia's Trump. J. Mathewson
Alien. Josephine Bell
Alien Archipelago. San Antonio
Alien Minds. E. E. Evans
Alien Souls. A. Abdullah
Alien Virus. A. Caillou
Alington Inheritance. P. Wentworth
Alinsky's Diamond. T. McHale
Alise of Astra. H. B. M. Watson
Alive and Dead. E. Ferrars
Alive or Dead. G. B. Savi
Alixe Derring. E. Nisot
All Along the River. M. E. Braddon
All at Sea. C. Wells
All Brides Are Beautiful. M. Corrigan
All Cats Are Grey. C. G. Givens
All Change for Murder. V. Gunn
All Change, Humanity! C. Houghton
All Concerned Notified. H. Reilly
All Dames Are Dynamite. T. Trent
All Done by Kindness. Doris Langley Moore
All England at Home. John Gloag
All Evil Shed Away. A. Roy
All Exits Barred. C. Portway
All Exits Blocked. B. Perowne
All Fall Down. A. Kennington
All Fall Down. L. A. G. Strong
All for a Woman. J. J. Dratler
All for Him. Anonymous
All for One and One for Death. S. Forbes
All for the Apple. J. MacKenzie
All for the Love of a Lady. L. Ford
All God's Children. A. Lyons
All Grass Isn't Green. A. A. Fair
All Heads Turn When the Hunt Goes By. J. Farris
All Her Vices. S. Rand
All Honorable Men. D. Karp
All I Can Get. W. Ard
All in a Day. L. Barbee
All in a Day's Work. D. Ray
All in Good Crime. M. Hervey
All in the Dark. J. S. Le Fanu
All in the Night's Work. E. W. Mumford
All in the Racket. W. E. Weeks
All Is Discovered. J. Cannan
All Is Not Gold. F. A. M. Webster
All Is Vanity. Josephine Bell
All Killers Aren't Ugly. T. K. Makagon
All Leads Negative. P. Alding
All Men Are Liars. J. S. Strange
All Men Are Lonely Now. F. Clifford
All Men Are Murderers. C. Blackstock
All My Dead Men. B. Byers
All My Enemies. S. Baron
All My Enemies. Rosemary Harris
All My Pretty Chickens. A. Hocking
All Night at Mr. Stanyhurst's. H. Edwards
All Night Long. F. Metcalfe
All of Our Aircraft Are Missing. J. P. Radford
All on a Summer's Day. J. Garden
All or Nothing. A. Bocca
All or Nothing. M. Catto
All or Nothing. R. Marlowe
All Other Perils. Robert MacLeod
All over But the Shooting. R. Powell
All-Purpose Bodies. P. McCutchan
All Roads Lead to Friday. H. Innes
All Roads Lead to Sospel. G. Bellairs
All Set for Murder. B. Carter
All Shot Up. C. Himes
All Souls' Night. H. Walpole
All Square with Fate. T. C. St. C. Morton
All Star Cast. N. Royde-Smith
All Stations to Malta. G. Hackforth-Jones
All Suspect. K. Methold
All Suspected. W. J. Bayfield
All That Glitters. M. Coles
All That Glitters. N. B. Gerson
All That Glitters. M. Richmond

All the Better to Kill You. F. Carmichael
All the Colors of Darkness. L. Biggle
All the King's Men. J. L. Johnson
All the Nice Girls. E. Kyle
All the Queen's Men. G. DeMontfort
All the Silent Voices. Roger Fuller
All the Skeletons in All the Closets. K. Fowler
All the Way. C. Williams
All the Way Down. M. E. Chaber
All the Way Home and All the Night Through. T. Lewis
All the World to Nothing. W. Martyn
All These Condemned. J. D. MacDonald
All This Is Ended. A. W. Wells
All This Shall Perish. M. Vinter
All Through the Night. W. Masterson
All Thugs Are Dangerous. Roland Daniel
All Very Irregular. V. Bridges
All Your Lovely Words Are Spoken. M. L. Roby
"Allah's Eye." A. Parsons
Allan Dare and Robert le Diable. A. Porter
Allan Keene, the War Detective. H. Rockwood
Alleged Great Aunt. H. K. Webster
Allegra's Child. J. Letton
Alley Girl. Jonathan Craig
Alley Kids. B. Appel
Allie Baird, the Settler's Son. Old Sleuth
Allies. M. Sellar
Alligator. I*n Fl*m*ng
Allingham Case-Book. M. Allingham
Allingham Minibus. M. Allingham
All's Fair on Lake Garda. A. J. Evans
Allworth Abbey. E. Southworth
Almack, the Detective. E. H. Cragg
Almagro and Claude. Anonymous
Almeda. N. T. Oliver
Almira's Curse. T. P. Prest
Almon Mitchell's Double. Old Sleuth
Almost Dead. W. Herber
Almost Midnight. M. Caidin
Almost Perfect Murder. H. Footner
Almost Without Murder. B. Graeme
Aloha. Robin Moore
Aloha Means Goodbye. N. A. Hintze
Alone at Night. V. Packer
Alone in the Grass. C. Phillips
Alone on a Wide, Wide Sea. W. C. Russell
Along a Dark Path. V. Johnston
Along Came a Spider. E. Davis
Along Came a Spider. Maude Parker
Along for the Ride. T. Newman
Along the Road. M. Hodges
Alonzo MacTavish Again. P. Cheyney
Alp Murder. A. M. Stein
Alperfol Affair. A. Kullar
Alpha and Omega. N. Bell
Alpha-I Conspiracy. R. Jontas
Alpha List. T. Allbeury
Alpha List. James Anderson
Alpha-Omega. W. Glassford
Alpha Raid. A. Scholefield
Alpha Trip. G. Billing
Alphabet Hicks. R. Stout
Alphabet Murders. A. Christie
Alphonsine. A. Belot
Alpine Affair. J. F. Vignant
Alpine Coach. V. Coffman
Alpine Crack-Up. J. W. Hornby
Alpine Encounter. H. Rowan
Alps Assignment. A. Sugar
Alscott Experiment. B. Stanley
Also Ran. N. Williams
Alster Case. J. R. Gillies
Altar of Evil. F. Stevenson
Altar-Piece. N. Royde-Smith
Altars of the Heart. R. Lebherz
Alter Ego. P. Watson
Altered Ego. J. Sohl
Alternate Case. J. F. Dinneen
Althea. M. McDonell
Althea's Falcon. D. M. Carlisle
Altheimer Inheritance. J. Herbrand
Aluminum Turtle. B. Kendrick
Alumni Murders. P. Ruse
Alvarez Journal. R. Burns
Always Ask a Policeman. S. Truss
Always Expect the Unexpected. B. Graeme
Always Fight Back. A. MacKenzie
Always in August. A. Head
Always Kill a Stranger. R. L. Fish
Always Leave 'Em Dying. R. S. Prather
Always Lock Your Bedroom Door. R. Winsor
Always Murder a Friend. M. Scherf
Always Say Die. E. Ferrars
Always Say Goodbye. M. Heath-Miller
Always Take the Big Ones. Peter Chambers
Always Tell the Truth. Kevin O'Hara
Always the Wolf. N. Easton
Amanda in Berlin. K. Steel
Amanda in Spain. G. Revelli
Amanda's Castle. G. Revelli
Amaranth Club. J. S. Fletcher
Amateur Adventuress. C. Stanton
Amateur Agent. Christopher Adams
Amateur Agent. D. Vallance
Amateur Boxer. R. Worth

Amateur Corpse. Simon Brett
Amateur Cracksman. E. W. Hornung
Amateur Crime. A. B. Cox
Amateur Criminal. G. S. Lavard
Amateur Crook. H. Clevely
Amateur Detective. S. Janney
Amateur Detectives. C. B. Booth
Amateur Emigrants. T. Cobb
Amateur Gentleman. J. Farnol
Amateur Governess. M. A. Gibbs
Amateur Hour. R. Hardin
Amateur in Crime. W. M. Graydon
Amateur in Violence. M. Gilbert
Amateur Inn. A. P. Terhune
Amateur Murderer. C. J. Daly
Amateurs. W. Cook
Amazing Adventures of Carolus Herbert. G. Leroux
Amazing Adventures of Lester Leith. E. S. Gardner
Amazing Adventures of Letitia Carberry. M. R. Rinehart
Amazing Adventures of Mr. Henry Button. L. Despard
Amazing Adventures of Sophie Lyons. S. Lyons
Amazing Affair of the Renegade Prince. G. N. Philips
Amazing Affair of the Shipyard Sabotage. S. Hope
Amazing Chance. P. Wentworth
Amazing Corpse. Colin Robertson
Amazing Count. W. LeQueux
Amazing Dr. Clitterhouse. B. Lyndon
Amazing Dr. Khan. H. Metcalfe
Amazing Duke. W. Magnay
Amazing Judgment. E. P. Oppenheim
Amazing Mr. Blackshirt. R. Graeme
Amazing Mr. Bunn. B. Atkey
Amazing Mr. Lutterworth. D. Leslie
Amazing Mr. Sandyman. Neill Graham
Amazing Mrs. Pollifax. D. Gilman
Amazing Partnership. E. P. Oppenheim
Amazing Quest of Doctor Syn. R. Thorndike
Amazing Quest of Mr. Ernest Bliss. E. P. Oppenheim
Amazing Scoundrel. Nicholas Carter
Amazing Test Match Crime. A. Alington
Amazing Verdict. M. Leighton
Amazing Web. H. S. Keeler
Amazing Wizard. Old Sleuth
Amazon. Nick Carter
Amazon Factor. W. Wise
Amazons. I. Ross
Ambart Trial. K. Ingram
Ambassador. S. Longstreet
Ambassador. M. L. West
Ambassador of Death. J. F. Fishter
Ambassador's Adventure. A. Upward
Ambassador's Glove. R. Machray
Ambassador's Kiss. W. J. Lomax
Ambassador's Plot. S. D. Frances
Ambassador's Trunk. G. Barton
Ambassador's Wife. P. Gibbs
Amber and Jade. A. Griffin
Amber Cat. Elizabeth Ford
Amber Bead. J. Spiess
Amber Eyes. F. Crane
Amber Eyes. Roland Daniel
Amber Eyes of the Lion. S. Dembo
Amber for Anna. A. Watkyn
Amber Girl. C. Mayne
Amber Gods. S. C. Prescott
Amber Gods and Other Stories. H. Spofford
Amber Junk. M. E. Hanshew
Amber Nine. J. Gardner
Amber Palace. J. Freytag
Amber to Red. V. Hill
Amber Twilight. M. Lynch
Ambergris! A. Murray
Amberleigh. M. E. Edward
Amberley Diamonds. A. W. Madden
Amberstone. P. Bennetts
Amberwood. A. Rundle
Ambiguous Man. R. Tashkent
Ambition's Slave. F. M. White
Ambitious Lady. J. S. Fletcher
Amblers. B. L. Farjeon
Amboy Dukes. I. Shulman
Ambrose in London. P. Levene
Ambrose in Paris. P. Levene
Ambrose Lavendale, Diplomat. E. P. Oppenheim
Ambrosio. M. G. Lewis
Ambrotox and Limping Dick. O. Fleming
Ambulance. H. Miller
Ambush. W. Edwards
Ambush. B. G. High
Ambush. J. G. Sarasin
Ambush at Derati Wells. P. McCurtin
Ambush for Anatol. J. Sherwood
Ambush for the Hunter. F. L. Green
Ambush House. K. Steel
Ambushers. D. Hamilton
American Baron. J. De Mille
American Cavalier. W. C. Hudson
American Counterfeits. G. P. Burnham
American Detective in Russia. Old Sleuth
American Gothic. R. Bloch
American Gun Mystery. E. Queen

American Legionnaire. J. Robb
American Marquis. Nicholas Carter
American Marquis. R. H. Sherard
American Monte Cristo. J. Hawthorne
American Monte Cristo. Old Sleuth
American Penman. J. Hawthorne
American Pep. A. Stone
American Prisoner. E. Phillpotts
American Surrender. Michael Brady
American Thug. Old Sleuth
American Tragedy. T. Dreiser
American Venus. E. Preston
Amethyst Box. A. K. Green
Amethyst Button. B. Baskerville
Amethyst Cross. F. Hume
Amethyst Quest. L. A. Sunagel
Amethyst Spectacles. F. Crane
Amethyst Tears. Marilyn Ross
Amiable Charlatan. E. P. Oppenheim
Amiable Crimes of Dirk Memling. Rupert Hughes
Amigo, Amigo. F. Clifford
Ammie, Come Home. B. Michaels
Amnesia Trap. R. Ormerod
Among Arabian Sands. J. Mitchell
Among the Brigands. J. De Mille
Among the Counterfeiters. Nicholas Carter
Among the Nihilists. Nicholas Carter
Among the Ruins and Other Stories. M. C. Hay
Among Thieves. G. Cuomo
Among Those Absent. M. Coles
Among Those Hunted. M. Skinner
Among Those Present. P. Barrington
Among Those Present. A. Feist
Among Those Present. A. S. Roche
Amongst Those Missing. P. Capon
Amoret. C. Gibbon
Amorous Captive. H. Janson
Amorous Rogue. R. Foxall
Amos Petrie's Puzzle. J. V. Turner
Ampersand Papers. M. Innes
Amphetamines and Pearls. J. Harvey
Amphitheatre Plot. Nicholas Carter
Amphorae Pirates. L. Cameron
Ampurias Exchange. Angus Ross
Amsterdam. Nick Carter
Amsterdam Connection. L. Grimsey
Amsterdam Diversion. Angus Ross
Amusement Only. R. Marsh
Amy. K. W. Eyre
Amyas Egerton, Cavalier. M. H. Hervey
Amzi, the Detective. Old Sleuth
Anagram Detectives. N. Schier
Analog Bullet. Martin Smith
Anarchaos. Curt Clark
Anarchist. R. H. Savage
Anarchist's Moon. J. Griffin
Anarchist's Oath. B. Wayde
Anathema Stone. J. B. Hilton
Anatomy Lesson. M. Goldberg
Anatomy of a Crime. J. F. Dinneen
Anatomy of a Killer. P. Rabe
Anatomy of a Murder. R. Traver
Anatomy of a Murder. E. Winer
Anatomy of an Arsonist. G. Mahoney
Anatomy of Violence. C. Runyon
Ancestor. R. Carol
Anchor Island. P. Malloch
Anchor's Aweigh. E. L. Long
Ancient Evil. C. Arkham
Ancient Pond. Courtney Browne
Ancient Rage. J. La Tourrette
Ancient Records. T. J. H. Curties
Ancora Scipio. T. Gates
And a Bottle of Rum. B. Graeme
And All That Beauty—. R. Bridges
And Be a Villain. J. Cannan
And Be a Villain. L. Meynell
And Be a Villain. R. Stout
And Be My Love. Ledru Baker
And Being Dead. M. Erskine
And Billy Disappeared. W. B. Hare
And Call It Accident. M. B. Lowndes
And Cauldron Bubble. B. Flynn
And Dangerous to Know. E. Daly
And Death Came Too. Anthony Gilbert
And Death Came Too. R. Hull
And Death Came Too. H. Mace
And Death Drove On. Robert Fleming
And Die Remembering. M. L. Roby
And Die She Did. J. Oellrichs
And Died So? V. Gielgud
And Dream of Evil. T. Thomey
And Four to Go. R. Stout
...And Hang Him. K. P. Arbuthnot
And Here Is the Noose! Kevin O'Hara
...And High Water. A. M. Stein
And Home Came Ted. W. B. Hare
And Hope to Die. L. Charbonneau
And Hope to Die. R. Powell
And If I Laugh. D. G. Waring
...And Incidentally, Murder! B. E. Lovell
And Justice for All. R. Grossbach
And Kill Once More. A. Fray
And Left for Dead. F. Lockridge
And Let the Coffin Pass. K. Abbey
And Love Survived. R. Chetwynd-Hayes
And Loving It! W. Johnston
And Murder Came Too. G. Compton
And Murder Won. H. C. Davis

Title Index

And Next the King. Nick Carter
And No One Wept. A. Hocking
And Not for Love. P. Mechem
And Now the Screaming Starts. D. Case
And on the Eighth Day. E. Queen
And One Cried Murder. L. Thayer
And One for the Dead. P. Audemars
And One for the Pot. M. E. Simpson
And One Must Die. P. Henneker
And Only Man. A. Dick
...And Presumed Dead. L. Fletcher
"And Shall Trelawney Die?" J. Hocking
And Shame the Devil. Sara Woods
And She Had a Little Knife. J. L. Linklater
And So He Had to Die. D. C. Cameron
And So to Bed. W. Ard
And So to Death. W. Irish
And So to Death. G. Shayne
And So to Eternity. Whitney Brown
And So to Murder. Carter Dickson
And So We Die. J. Sandys
And Sometimes Death. J. Valentine
And Still I Cheat the Gallows. E. P. Oppenheim
And Sudden Death. C. F. Adams
And Sudden Death. J. S. Fletcher
And the Body Came Too. L. Boden
And the Bullets Were Made of Lead. P. Wheeler
And the Deep Blue Sea. R. Knotts
And the Deep Blue Sea. C. Williams
And the Devil. C. Cannell
And the Girl Screamed. G. Brewer
And the Moon Was Full. H. McCutcheon
And the Shouting Dies. Robert Mason
And the Undead Sing. Carter Brown
And the Winds Blew. H. J. Heinecke
And Then Came Fear. M. Cumberland
And Then Look Down. M. Garratt
And Then Murder. J. Fast
And Then...One Dark Night. E. Snell
And Then Put Out the Light. E. C. R. Lorac
And Then Silence. M. Propper
And Then the Screaming Started. O. Blakeston
And Then There Was Georgia. J. Blackmore
And Then There Was None. E. C. Vivian
And Then There Were Nine. W. H. L. Crauford
And Then There Were None. A. Christie
And Thereby Hangs—. A. Spiller
And They Say You Can't Buy Happiness. M. Lovell
And to My Beloved Husband—. P. Loraine
And Turned to Clay. L. G. Offord
And Two Shall Meet. Raymond Mason
And When She Was Bad She Was Murdered. R. Starnes
And Where She Stops. T. B. Dewey
And Where's Mr. Bellamy? S. M. Wick
And, Which, the Knave? B. M. Scott
And Why Not? V. G. Malo
And Worms Have Eaten Them. M. Cumberland
"And Worms Have Eaten Them... W. J. Elliott
Andean Murders. L. Hazard
Anderson Crow, Detective. G. B. McCutcheon
Anderson Tapes. L. Sanders
Andra Fiasco. W. Garner
Andre Cornelis. P. Bourget
Andrew and His Wife. T. Cobb
Andrew Reforms. P. Trent
Andrewlina. J. S. Fletcher
Andrew's Wife. K. Booton
Andromache. H. Monteilhet
Andromeda Assignment. David Lewis
Angel. G. Brewer
Angel! Carter Brown
Angel. P. Traill
Angel. G. Verner
Angel Abroad. G. Montrose
Angel Among Witches. A. Gale
Angel and the Cuckoo. G. Kersh
Angel and the Nero. G. Montrose
Angel and the Red Admiral. G. Montrose
Angel, Angel, Down We Go. W. Johnston
Angel Astray. H. Janson
Angel at Arms. G. Montrose
Angel Came Down. M. Pereira
Angel Dance. M. F. Beal
Angel Death. P. Moyes
Angel Esquire. E. Wallace
Angel Eyes. R. Dietrich
Angel Face. F. Nichols
Angel Face Tatters the Kimono. A. St. Moore
Angel for Paradise. J. Canon
Angel Hold Fire. K. T. McCall
Angel in Paradise. G. Montrose
Angel in the Case. E. Elder
Angel in the Pawnshop. A. B. Shiffrin
Angel Loves Nobody. R. Miles
Angel of Death. James Anderson
Angel of Death. P. D. Ballard
Angel of Death. Nicholas Carter
Angel of Death. P. Loraine
Angel of Death. G. Montrose
Angel of Destruction. J. Hedges
Angel of Evil. G. Warden

Angel of Light. H. McCutcheon
Angel of No Mercy. G. Montrose
Angel of Terror. E. Wallace
Angel of the Bells. F. Du Boisgobey
Angel of the Chimes. F. Du Boisgobey
Angel of the Covenant. J. M. Cobban
Angel of Vengeance. G. De Villiers
Angel of Vengeance. G. Montrose
Angel Possessed. C. Conaway
Angel, Shoot to Kill. H. Janson
Angel Steps In. E. P. Thorne
Angel Street. P. Hamilton
Angel Take Care. R. Lakin
Angel with Dirty Wings. J. E. Hasty
Angelic Avengers. P. Andrezel
Angelica. J. A. Bartlett
Angelica. F. Swann
Angelina. T. P. Prest
Angell, Pearl and Little God. Winston Graham
Angels Are Cowards. D. Garth
Angels Are Painted Fair. P. Whelton
Angels Fell. B. Fischer
Angel's Flight. L. Cameron
Angels in Aldgate. W. J. Passingham
Angels in Chains. M. Franklin
Angels in the Gutter. J. Hilton
Angels in the Snow. Derek Lambert
Angels in the Snow. P. Welles
Angels in Your Beer. Jeremy Scott
Angels of Darkness. C. Woolrich
Angels of Doom. L. Charteris
Angels of Double Faces. R. O. Abio
Angels on a String. M. Franklin
Angels on Ice. M. Franklin
Angel's Ransom. D. Dodge
Angel's Tear. J. Blackmore
Angels Weep! D. Leslie
Angeltread. K. Mendenhall
Anger at World's End. D. Reid
Anger of Fear. J. Ashford
Anger of Olivia. T. Cobb
Anger of the Bells. V. Rath
Angle of Attack. R. Burns
Angry Amazons. Carter Brown
Angry Battalion. Herbert Harris
Angry Darkness. C. Leader
Angry Dream. G. Brewer
Angry Dust. C. R. Hoopes
Angry Ghost. K. Robeson
Angry Heart. L. Edgley
Angry Island. J. Pattinson
Angry Island. K. Royce
Angry Millionaire. S. Jepson
Angry Mountain. H. Innes
Angry Night. W. H. Baker
Angry Ocean. R. Johnston
Angry Silence. John Burke
Angry Wind. L. Ames
Animal Game. L. Derrick
Animal-Lover's Book of Beastly Murder. P. Highsmith
Animated Skeleton. Anonymous
Anita, the Cuban Spy. G. Willets
Ann, the Gentle. K. Kimbrough
Ann Turns Detective. Roland Daniel
Anna of the Plains. A. Askew
Anna of the Underworld. G. R. Sims
Anna, the Adventuress. E. P. Oppenheim
Anna, Where Are You? P. Wentworth
Annalisa. F. Rydell
Annals of the Age. Anonymous
Annam Jewel. P. Wentworth
Anna's. C. N. Boyle
Anne Belinda. P. Wentworth
Anne Hereford. H. Wood
Anne of Destiny House. Wilma Forrest
Anne of the Flying Cap. H. H. Hill
Annette of the Argonne. W. LeQueux
Annexation Society. J. S. Fletcher
Annie Deane. R. H. Adelman
Annie Wallace. H. P. Halsey
Annihilation. I. Ostrander
Annihilist. K. Robeson
Anniversary Murder. E. Phillpotts
Announcer. D. H. Landels
Ann's Crime. R. T. M. Scott
Annulet of Guilt. P. A. Taylor
Annulment. R. Rubin
Anonymous Assassin. J. F. Drexler
Anonymous Footsteps. J. M. O'Connor
Another Case for Inspector Jackson. D. T. Lindsay
Another Chorus. John Burke
Another Crime. C. Rushton
Another Day. J. Farnol
Another Day—Another Death. G. Bagby
Another Day, Another Stiff. Michael Brett
Another Day Toward Tying. M. Marlette
Another Death in Venice. R. Hill
Another Little Death. Bill Turner
Another Little Drink. P. Cheyney
Another Little Murder. L. N. Morgan
Another Man's Life. M. Head
Another Man's Murder. M. G. Eberhart
Another Man's Poison. H. Holman
Another Man's Shadow. J. Bude
Another Man's Shoes. V. Bridges
Another Man's Wife. J. Chancellor
Another Man's Wife. M. B. Lowndes
Another Man's Wife. Lady A. Scott

Another Morgue Heard From. F. C. Davis
Another Mug for the Bier. R. Starnes
Another Mystery in Suva. F. Arthur
Another Night, Another Day. D. F. Gardiner
Another Spring. H. S. Maxfield
Another Time, Another Woman. W. Kaylin
Another Way of Dying. F. Clifford
Another Way to Die. J. Crowe
Another Weeping Woman. D. Zochert
Another Woman's House. M. G. Eberhart
Another Woman's Love. K. Lindsay
Another Woman's Man. Norma Lee
Another Woman's Poison. W. H. L. Crauford
Another Woman's Shoes. F. Durbridge
Another's Burden. J. Payn
Another's Crime. J. Hawthorne
Answer from a Dead Man. G. P. Cronin
Answer in the Negative. H. Hamilton
Answer in the Negative. E. Scholey
Answer That Bell! M. Baillie-Saunders
Answer to Heaven. P. Gallagher
Answered. F. Hume
Ant Heap. A. Mills
Antagonists. O. Cameron
Antagonists. W. Haggard
Antarctic Convergence. J. Griffin
Antenna Syndrome. A. Marks
Anthill. D. Gilles
Anthony Ravenhill, Crime Merchant. R. Francis Foster
Anthony Trent: Avenger. W. Martyn
Anthropol. L. Trimble
Anti-Crime Ltd. E. Snell
Anti-Death League. K. Amis
Antidote. S. Murray
Antidote to Venom. F. W. Crofts
Antiphonary. H. Aquin
Antoinette. G. Ohnet
Antonov Project. A. Trew
Antrobus Trust. R. Haig
Anxious Conspirator. M. Underwood
Anxious Lady. J. Pendower
Any Body for Tennis? J. Last
Any Kind of Danger. E. G. Cousins
Any Man's Girl. B. Heatter
Any Minute Now. A. Bocca
Any Number Can Die. F. Carmichael
Any Number Can Play. D. Bloodworth
Any Number Can Play. E. H. Heth
Any Number Can Win. J. Trinian
Any Old Port in a Storm. Henry Clement
Any Shape or Form. E. Daly
Any War Will Do. E. Pace
Anybody But Anne. C. Wells
Anybody's Pearls. H. Footner
Anyone's Grief. K. Drayton
Anyone's My Name. S. Shubin
Anything But Saintly. R. Deming
Anything But the Truth. M. Underwood
Anything But the Truth. C. Wells
Anything Can Happen. G. F. Gibbs
Anything for a Quiet Life. A. A. Avery
Anything for Kicks. Morton Cooper
Anything Might Happen. H. Balfour
Anything Once. Douglas Grant
Anything to Declare? F. W. Crofts
Anytime, Anywhere. M. Caidin
Anywhere Else. H. J. Kaplan
Apache. A. Askew
Apache Girl. A. Mills
Apaches of New York. Alfred H. Lewis
Apartment Next Door. W. A. Johnston
Apartment on K Street. R. Travers
Apartment 13. J. C. McMullen
Ape, a Dog, and a Serpent. G. Kersh
Ape and the Diamond. Richard Marsh
Ape in Velvet. R. Foley
Ape Man. H. T. Johnson
Ape of London. F. Crisp
Ape, the Idiot and Other People. W. C. Morrow
Aphrodite. D. Chandler
Aphrodite Inheritance. M. J. Bird
Aphrodite Means Death. J. Appleby
Apocalypse. M. Stanton
Apollo Fountain. D. Daniels
Apollo Legacy. A. Barker
Apollo Wore a Wig. R. T. Campbell
Apologetic Tiger. J. Workman
Apostles of Violence. M. G. Braun
Apostles of Violence. D. Perring
Apparition. G. Bishop
Apparition. T. P. Prest
Apparition. R. Stewart
Appearance of Evil. James Anderson
Appearances of Death. Dell Shannon
Apperson's Folly. A. Mallory
Apple a Day. H. Brinton
Apple of Discord. H. C. Rowland
Apple Tree. D. Du Maurier
Appleby at Allington. M. Innes
Appleby File. M. Innes
Appleby on Ararat. M. Innes
Appleby Plays Chicken. M. Innes
Appleby Talking. M. Innes
Appleby Talks Again. M. Innes
Appleby's Answer. M. Innes

Appleby's End. M. Innes
Appleby's Other Story. M. Innes
Applegreen Cat. F. Crane
Apples of Sin. C. Kernahan
Appleshaw. C. Damien
Applewood Mystery. F. Burleigh
Appointed Date. J. J. Farjeon
Appointment at Eight. H. Desmond
Appointment at Nine. D. M. Disney
Appointment in Andalusia. M. MacKintosh
Appointment in Cairo. G. Brewer
Appointment in Calcutta. E. Tokson
Appointment in Hell. G. Brewer
Appointment in Hell. V. Warren
Appointment in Iran. S. Jason
Appointment in Manila. Elinor Chamberlain
Appointment in New Orleans. T. Claymore
Appointment in Peking. F. Drake
Appointment in Tangier. L. Wilkinson
Appointment in Tenerife. R. Harding
Appointment in Tibet. W. H. Murray
Appointment in Verona. M. A. Taylor
Appointment in Vienna. S. Gainham
Appointment in Zahrein. Michael Barrett
Appointment with Danger. W. H. Baker
Appointment with Danger. D. Garth
Appointment with Death. C. Barling
Appointment with Death. A. Christie
Appointment with Death. P. Frankau
Appointment with Death. M. Hervey
Appointment with Desire. H. Luger
Appointment with Dishonor. W. H. Gage
Appointment with Fear. D. Stokes
Appointment with Murder. H. Seymour
Appointment with My Lady. F. Griffin
Appointment with the Hangman. T. C. H. Jacobs
Appointment with Venus. J. Tickell
Appointment with Yesterday. C. Fremlin
Apprehensive Dog. H. C. Bailey
Apprentice in Terror. P. Warren
Apprentice to Fear. H. Brinton
April Evil. J. D. MacDonald
April, May and June. H. Willett
April Robin Murders. C. Rice
April Shroud. R. Hill
April Thirtieth. B. St. James
April's Grave. S. Howatch
Apron-Strings. R. Marsh
Aquanauts. D. Bard
Aquarius Angel. L. Bullock
Aquarius Curse. Marilyn Ross
Aquarius Mission. M. Caidin
Aquarius, My Evil. J. De Pre
Arab Agent. Robert Mason
Arab Plague. Nick Carter
Arabesque. G. Household
Arabian Nights Murder. J. D. Carr
Araby's Husband. A. Askew
Arafat Is Here! Lionel Black
Araminta and the River. Alan Graham
Araway Oath. H. Adams
Arch-Criminal. Roland Daniel
Archdeacons Afloat. C. A. Alington
Archdeacons Ashore. C. A. Alington
Architect's Secret. W. J. Bayfield
Archer in the Arras, and other tales of mystery. L. Spence
Archer Plus Twenty. H. Clevely
Archie the Tumbler. Old Sleuth
Arctic Assignment. R. Charles
Arctic Convoy. Taffrail
Arctic Submarine. A. Mars
Arctic Trail. W. M. Graydon
Arden Mystery. M. Harvey
Ardreys. K. R. Vernon
Are You Mr. Butterworth? F. Metcalfe
Are You My Wife? M. Marcin
Area of Suspicion. J. D. MacDonald
Arena. W. Haggard
Argus Eye. F. M. White
Argus Pheasant. J. C. Beecham
Argyle Case. A. Hornblow
Argyll Killings. Daniel Benson
Ariel. Lawrence Block
Aries Rising. A. Herzog
Arigato. R. Condon
Arising from an Accident. P. Dewdney
Aristocratic Detective. R. Marsh
Aristocrats. Gwen Davis
Aristotle Detective. M. Doody
Arizona. Augustus Thomas
Arizona Ambush. D. Pendleton
Arizona Drifters. W. C. Tuttle
Arkansas Ranger. M. M. Murray
Arkie, the Runaway. Old Sleuth
Arlie Bright. Old Sleuth
Arm of Mrs. Egan and other strange stories. W. F. Harvey
Arm of the Law. Lieut. Carlton
Arm of the Law. M. Underwood
Armada Gold. Edgar Turner
Armadale. W. Collins
Armageddon Game. M. Washburn
Armageddon, USA! J. Rosenberger
Armchair in Hell. H. Kane
Armed...Dangerous... B. Halliday
Armed with a New Terror. T. Du Bois
Armitage Case. Michael Kent
Armitage Secret. H. Howard
Armorer of Tyre. S. Cobb

Arms and the Spy. M. McKenna
Arms for Adonis. C. Jay
Arms for Oblivion. J. Hedges
Arms for the Love of Allah. Anthony Harding
Arms'-Length. J. Metcalfe
Arms of Phaedra. N. Worth
Arms of the Law. J. L. Latham
Arms of the Mantis. R. Charles
Arms of Venus. J. Appleby
Armstrong. Alan White
Army Defaulter's Secret. L. C. Douthwaite
Army Doctor's Romance. G. Allen
Army of the Dead. C. Steele
Army of the Undead. Rafe Bernard
Army Post Murders. M. Wright
Arncliffe Puzzle. Gordon Holmes
Arnholt Makes His Bow. G. Latta
Around Dark Corners. H. Pentecost
Arrangement for Murder. R. Simons
Arranways Mystery. E. Wallace
Array of Eagles. R. Severn
Arrest. W. Proudfoot
Arrest and Trial. N. Daniels
Arrest of Arsene Lupin. M. Leblanc
Arrest the Bishop? W. Peck
Arrest the Saint. L. Charteris
Arrest These Men! B. Perowne
Arrested. Eame Stuart
Arrested. E. C. Vivian
Arrested for Murder. Roland Daniel
Arresting Delia. S. Fowler
Arrival in Suspicion. S. Harvester
Arriverderci, Baby! James Peterson
Arrogant Alibi. C. D. King
Arrogant Duke. Rona Randall
Arrow of Death. Roland Daniel
Arrow of Death. F. Vivian
Arrow of God. R. Cassilis
Arrow of Terror. J. Marie
Arrow Pointing Nowhere. E. Daly
Arrow Points to Murder. F. De Laguna
Arrows of Chance. E. R. Punshon
Arsenal Stadium Mystery. L. Gribble
Arsene Lepine—Herlock Soames Affair. S. B. Chester
Arsene Lupin. E. Jepson
Arsene Lupin, Gentleman Burglar. M. Leblanc
Arsene Lupin Intervenes. M. Leblanc
Arsene Lupin, Super Sleuth. M. Leblanc
Arsene Lupin Versus Herlock Sholmes. M. Leblanc
Arsene Lupin Versus Holmlock Shears. M. Leblanc
Arsenic. J. Remenham
Arsenic and Gold. B. Atkey
Arsenic and Old Lace. J. Kesselring
Arsenic for the Teacher. O. Keystone
Arsenic in Richmond. D. Frome
Arsenic on the Menu. B. H. Homersham
Arson and Old Lace. S. Angus
Arson by Proxy. Ray Turner
Arson Job. J. Moss
Art for Keeps. C. B. Block
Art of Disappearing. J. T. Smith
Art School Murders. M. Dalton
Art Studio Murders. E. Ronns
Art Thou the Man? G. Berton
Art Treasure Murders. J. L. Benton
Arterial Road Murder. A. Blair
Artful Schemer. Nicholas Carter
Arthur. J. A. Graham
Arthur Mervyn. C. B. Brown
Arthur's Night. J. F. Straker
Article 92: Murder-Rape. W. Beech
Artifex Intervenes. R. Keverne
Artificial Fate. C. Boutelle
Artificial Girl. R. W. Cole
Artificial Man. L. P. Davies
Artist and a Magician. H. Fleetwood
Artist and Model. R. de Pont-Jest
Artist Detective. Anonymous
Artist Dies. J. Rhode
Artist in Crime. R. Ottolengui
Artist in Crime. K. M. Sheahan
Artist in Crime. C. Somerville
Artist's Daughter. L. O'Grady
Artists in Crime. N. Mash
Artist's Love. E. Southworth
Artist's Mother. Mrs. C. Kernahan
Artists, Models and Murder. Tedd Steele
Artist's Murder. F. L. Cary
Artless Heiress. C. B. Kelland
Arundel Motto. M. C. Hay
Aryan Onslaught. L. Derrick
As a Bird to the Snare. G. Warden
As a Crook Sows. Nicholas Carter
As a Man Falls. H. Rigsby
As a Man Lives. E. P. Oppenheim
As a Man Sows. W. Westall
As a Thief in the Night. R. A. Freeman
As Bad As I Am. W. Ard
As Darker Grows the Night. E. Giles
As Deadly Does. J. Corby
As Empty As Hate. M. Halliday
As for the Woman. F. Iles
As Good As a Mile. E. Albert
As Good As Dead. T. B. Dewey
As Good As Gold. E. Wymark
As Good As Murdered. J. D. O'Hanlon

As I Was Going to St. Ives. A. Hocking
As It Chanced. H. B. M. Watson
As If She Were Mine. Alex Hamilton
As It Was in the Beginning. G. R. Sims
As It Was Written. S. Luska
As It Was Written. T. W. Speight
As Lonely As the Damned. M. Halliday
As Long As I Live. I. S. Shriber
As Luck Would Have It. W. Westall
As Merry As Hell. M. Halliday
As Old As Cain. M. E. Chaber
As Strange a Maze. F. Leighton
As the Devil Burned. H. Kemp
As the Sparks Fly. M. Eastvale
As the Stars Fade. B. Hector
As They Rise. E. L. Long
As They Shall Sow. A. Spiller
As We Forgave Them. W. LeQueux
As We Sow. John O'Neill
Asbestos Mask. J. Nicholas
Ascendancy House. J. L. Rickard
Ascent of D-13. A. Garve
Aseptic Murders. Carter Brown
Asey Mayo Trio. P. A. Taylor
Ash. C. Cannel
Ash. D. Walker
Ashenden. W. S. Maugham
Ashes. C. F. Coe
Ashes. H. Nisbet
Ashes and Diamonds. J. Andrzeyevski
Ashes for the Living. N. Cromarty
Ashes in an Urn. J. Roffman
Ashes in the Cellar. T. C. H. Jacobs
Ashes of Evidence. E. Levison
Ashes of Falconwyck. Angela Gray
Ashes of Loda. A. Garve
Ashes of Murder. G. Morton
Ashes to Ashes. E. Lathen
Ashes to Ashes. I. Ostrander
Ashes to Ashes. John Stuart
Ashiel Mystery. C. Bryce
Ashley, and other stories. H. Wood
Ashley Hall. S. Richard
Ashton-Kirk: Criminologist. J. T. MacIntyre
Ashton Kirk: Investigator. J. T. MacIntyre
Ashton-Kirk: Secret Agent. J. T. MacIntyre
Ashton-Kirk: Special Detective. J. T. MacIntyre
Asian Mantrap. Nick Carter
Asimov's Mysteries. I. Asimov
Ask a Policeman. Detection Club
Ask a Policeman. E. C. R. Lorac
Ask Agamemnon. Jenni Hall
Ask an Angel. G. Montrose
Ask for King Billy. H. Treece
Ask for Linda. F. Nichols
Ask for Lois. J. Matcha
Ask for Me Tomorrow. M. Millar
Ask for Ronald Standish. H. C. McNeile
Ask for Trouble. M. Cronin
Ask Me No Questions. L. Edwards
Ask Me Now. A. Young
Ask Miss Mott. E. P. Oppenheim
Ask No Mercy. B. Perowne
Ask No Question. M. Hocking
Ask No Questions. L. Dean
Ask No Questions. B. Duff
Ask the Rattlesnake. P. Loraine
Ask the Right Question. M. Z. Lewin
Asking for It. J. Mayo
Asking for Trouble. L. Meynell
Asking for Trouble. J. Rayter
Asking Price. H. Cecil
Aspen Incident. T. Murphy
Aspern Papers. M. Redgrave
Asphalt Jungle. W. R. Burnett
Asphalt Jungle. B. Maddow
Asphodel. M. E. Braddon
Assassin. James Anderson
Assassin. Evelyn Anthony
Assassin. M. Edwards
Assassin. E. M. Harper
Assassin. E. Jepson
Assassin. U. Levi
Assassin. Liam O'Flaherty
Assassin. L. W. Robinson
Assassin. Paul Ross
Assassin. Irwin Shaw
Assassin—Code Name Vulture. Nick Carter
Assassin for Hire. R. Rienits
Assassin of Saint Glenroy. A. F. Holstein
Assassin Trail. Dan Morgan
Assassin Who Gave Up His Gun. E. V. Cunningham
Assassination. B. Abro
Assassination Affair. J. H. Hunter
Assassination Brigade. Nick Carter
Assassination Bureau, Ltd. J. London
Assassination Day. O. Jacks
Assassination File. G. Gardner
Assassination Is Set for July 4. L. Parker
Assassination of Mozart. D. Weiss
Assassination Run. J. Gerson
Assassinator. D. Vowell
Assassinators. P. Boast
Assassins. J. A. Brown
Assassins. L. Falk

Title Index

Avengers / 447

Assassins. N. Mosley
Assassins. F. Mullally
Assassins. H. T. Teilhet
Assassins and Victims. C. Black
Assassins Don't Die in Bed. M. Avallone
Assassins for Peace. R. Charles
Assassins for Tomorrow. P. Heath
Assassins Have Starry Eyes. D. Hamilton
Assassins in White. Robert Callahan
Assassin's Playoff. R. Sapir
Assassins Road. S. Harvester
Assault and Matrimony. James Anderson
Assault and Pepper. J. T. Story
Assault on a Queen. J. Finney
Assault on Agathon. A. Caillou
Assault on Aimata. A. Caillou
Assault on England. Nick Carter
Assault on Fellawi. A. Caillou
Assault on Kolchak. A. Caillou
Assault on Loveless. A. Caillou
Assault on Mavis A. N. Stahl
Assault on Ming. A. Caillou
Assault on Soho. D. Pendleton
Assessor. H. Henry
Assignment. P. Wahloo
Assignment Abacus. L. P. Davies
Assignment—Amazon Queen. E. S. Aarons
Assignment Andalusia. R. C. Galway
Assignment—Angelina. E. S. Aarons
Assignment—Ankara. E. S. Aarons
Assignment Argentina. R. C. Galway
Assignment: Assassination. J. Milton
Assignment—Bangkok. E. S. Aarons
Assignment Basra. F. Ponthier
Assignment—Black Gold. E. S. Aarons
Assignment—Black Viking. E. S. Aarons
Assignment—Budapest. E. S. Aarons
Assignment—Burma Girl. E. S. Aarons
Assignment—Carlotta Cortez. E. S. Aarons
Assignment—Ceylon. E. S. Aarons
Assignment—Cong Hai Kill. E. S. Aarons
Assignment: Danger. Marilyn Ross
Assignment Death Squad. R. C. Galway
Assignment Doomsday. Martin Thomas
Assignment Fenland. R. C. Galway
Assignment: Find Cherry. J. Seward
Assignment for a Mercenary. Howard R. Simpson
Assignment for Trouble. M. Carrel
Assignment Gaolbreak. R. C. Galway
Assignment—Golden Girl. E. S. Aarons
Assignment Greece. G. Sheen
Assignment Haiti. E. P. Thorne
Assignment—Helene. E. S. Aarons
Assignment Hong Kong. James Dark
Assignment in Algeria. John Lee
Assignment in Andorra. M. MacKintosh
Assignment in Beirut. J. Stagg
Assignment in Brittany. Helen MacInnes
Assignment in Guiana. G. H. Coxe
Assignment in Iraq. J. MacKinnon
Assignment in the Islands. J. Blair
Assignment in Tokyo. J. T. Elton
Assignment: Intercept. Nick Carter
Assignment: Israel. Nick Carter
Assignment K. H. Howard
Assignment—Karachi. E. S. Aarons
Assignment—Lili Lemaris. E. S. Aarons
Assignment London. R. C. Galway
Assignment—Lowlands. E. S. Aarons
Assignment—Madeleine. E. S. Aarons
Assignment Malta. R. C. Galway
Assignment—Maltese Maiden. E. S. Aarons
Assignment—Manchurian Doll. E. S. Aarons
Assignment—Mara Tirana. E. S. Aarons
Assignment Mermaid. W. B. Aarons
Assignment—Moon Girl. E. S. Aarons
Assignment, Murder. Neill Graham
Assignment: Murder. D. Hamilton
Assignment New York. R. C. Galway
Assignment New York. M. Lantry
Assignment—Nuclear Nude. E. S. Aarons
Assignment—Palermo. E. S. Aarons
Assignment—Peking. E. S. Aarons
Assignment—Quayle Question. E. S. Aarons
Assignment—School for Spies. E. S. Aarons
Assignment Sea Bed. R. C. Galway
Assignment Sheba. W. B. Aarons
Assignment—Silver Scorpion. E. S. Aarons
Assignment—Sorrento Siren. E. S. Aarons
Assignment—Star Stealers. E. S. Aarons
Assignment—Stella Marni. E. S. Aarons
Assignment—Suicide. E. S. Aarons
Assignment—Sulu Sea. E. S. Aarons
Assignment Sydney. R. C. Galway
Assignment Tahiti. A. Gardner
Assignment—The Cairo Dancers. E. S. Aarons
Assignment—The Girl in the Gondola. E. S. Aarons
Assignment 13th Princess. W. B. Aarons
Assignment Tiger Devil. W. B. Aarons
Assignment to Bahrein. P. Winston
Assignment to Death. C. L. Leonard
Assignment to Disaster. E. S. Aarons
Assignment to Sante Fe. Dan Morgan

Assignment to Vengeance. B. Cleeve
Assignment—Tokyo. E. S. Aarons
Assignment Tokyo. James Dark
Assignment—Treason. E. S. Aarons
Assignment Tyrant's Bride. W. B. Aarons
Assignment—White Rajah. E. S. Aarons
Assignment Without Glory. M. Spinelli
Assignment X. E. C. Schurmacher
Assignment—Zoraya. E. S. Aarons
Assisted by Lessinger. R. Essex
Assisted by Sadie. W. B. Hare
Assize of the Dying. E. Pargeter
Assurance Double Sure. J. Esteven
Asterisk Destiny. C. Black
Astonished Guardsman. Surrey Smith
Astonishing Adventure of Jane Smith. P. Wentworth
Astounding Crime on Torrington Road. W. Gillette
Astounding Dr. Yell. L. A. Knight
Astrakhan Coat. P. Macaulay
Astrea. E. Southworth
Astrid Factor. D. Orgill
Astronaut. J. Baumgarten
Aswan Assignment. A. Sugar
Aswan Solution. J. Rowe
Asylum. W. Johnston
Asylum. O. Knox
Asylum. Isaac Mitchell
At a Farthing's Rate. H. Gibbs
At a Venture. H. B. M. Watson
At Bay. Mrs. Alexander
At Bay. G. Greenfield
At Bay. P. Philips
At Bertram's Hotel. A. Christie
At Button's. G. Wills
At Dark of the Moon. A. C. Ley
At Dawn I Die. J. Corbett
At Dead of Night. N. Perrelli
At Death's Call. I. Stark
At Death's Door. L. Bruce
At Dusk All Cats Are Grey. J. Tickell
At Face Value. Nicholas Carter
At Fault. H. Smart
At Friendly Point. G. F. Scott
At Her Mercy. J. Payn
At High Risk. P. Harcourt
At Large. E. W. Hornung
At Last, Mr. Tolliver. W. Wiegand
At Market Value. G. Allen
At Midnight and Other Stories. A. Cambridge
At Midnight's Chime. W. J. Newton
At Mystery's Threshold. Nicholas Carter
At Night to Die. H. Hamilton
At Nine Bells. S. Emery
At 9:45. Owen Davis
At Odds with Scotland Yard. Nicholas Carter
At One Fell Swoop. O. Mills
At One Fell Swoop. S. Palmer
At One-Thirty. I. Ostrander
At Sixty Miles Per Hour. J. Drummond
At Some Forgotten Door. D. M. Disney
At Ten Paces. C. G. Booth
At the Altar Steps. J. Middlemass
At the Back o' Beyond. R. Remnant
At the Back of the World. L. T. Meade
At the Bar. C. A. Collins
At the Blue Gates. R. Keverne
At the Call of Honour. A. W. Marchmont
At "The Cedars". A. Hocking
At the Change of the Moon. B. C. Blake
At the Court of the Maharaja. L. Tracy
At the End of a Road. C. Houghton
At the Foot of the Rainbow. J. B. Hendryx
At the Foot of the Stairs. E. S. Porter
At the Gai-Moulin. G. Simenon
At the Green Dragon. J. J. Farjeon
At the House of Dree. G. Gardiner
At the House of the Priest. J. Adye
At the Knife's Point. Nicholas Carter
At the Point of a .38. B. Halliday
At the Shrine of the Buddha. W. M. Graydon
At the Sign of the Clove and Hoof. Z. Johnson
At the Sign of the Eel. R. B. Whorf
At the Sign of the Golden Horn. J. K. Leys
At the Sign of the Sword. W. LeQueux
At the Silver Butterfly. Roland Daniel
At the Tenth Clue. H. H. Stanners
At the Time Appointed. A. M. Barbour
At the Villa Rose. A. E. W. Mason
At the World's Mercy. P. Trent
At the World's Mercy. F. Warden
At Thompson's Ranch. Nicholas Carter
At War with Society. J. M'Levy
At War with the Unknown. C. Frisbie
At What Cost, and Other Stories. H. Conway
Atavar, the Dream Dancer. A. B. Reeve
Athabasca. Alistair MacLean
Athelstane Ford. A. Upward
Athens Affair. H. Greene
Atherwood Terminal. H. Henn
Atlanta Deathwatch. R. Dennis
Atlantic City. W. B. Murphy
Atlantic City Murder Mystery. N. Goldsmith

Atlantic City Proof. C. C. Gilmore
Atlantic Fury. H. Innes
Atlantic Incident. Jack Davies
Atlantic Murder. F. H. Shaw
Atlantic Murders! E. T. Woodhall
Atlantis Fire. G. Goshgarian
Atom at Spithead. D. Divine
Atom-Busters. P. Graham
Atom of Doubt. B. George
Atomic Death. H. Karlson
Atomic Murder. L. Gribble
Atomic Submarine. A. Mars
Atoms and Evil. R. Bloch
Atomsk. Carmichael Smith
Atone with Evil. J. Fiedler
Attack. C. Ehrlich
Attack Alarm. H. Innes
Attack on Vienna. Alan Nixon
Attack the Baron. Anthony Morton
Attack the Lusitania. R. Hitchcock
Attar's Revenge. Robert Graham
Attending Physician. R. B. Dominic
Attending Truth. E. R. Punshon
Attention! Saturnin Dax. M. Cumberland
Attic Child. G. Corren
Attic Murder. S. Fowler
Attic Room. K. Wolffe
Attic Rope. D. Daniels
Attorney. Anonymous
Attorney. H. Q. Masur
Auber File. M. Home
Auction. R. Cox
Auction. T. Murphy
Auctioned. H. Janson
Auctioneer. J. Samson
Audacious Picaroon. J. Cassells
Audacity. B. A. Williams
Audit in Death. E. Norwood
Auditorium Affair. Hugh C. McDonald
Audrey Rose. F. De Felitta
August Incident. A. Dean
Augusta, the First. K. Kimbrough
Augusta, the Second. K. Kimbrough
Auldearn House. B. Riefe
Aunt Beardie. J. Shearing
Aunt Cathie's Cat. F. Metcalfe
Aunt Isabel's Lover. M. Fox
Aunt Ivy Diddit. E. G. Gless
Aunt Jeanne. G. Simenon
Aunt Miranda's Murder. J. N. Chase
Aunt Phipps. T. Gallon
Aunt Sally and the Crime Wave. M. Short
Aunt Sunday Sees It Through. J. J. Farjeon
Aunt Sunday Takes Command. J. J. Farjeon
Aunt Susie Shoots the Works! F. Caldwell
Aunt What's-Her-Name! W. B. Hare
Aupres de ma Blonde. N. Freeling
Aurelius Smith—Detective. R. T. M. Scott
Aurora Floyd. M. E. Braddon
Aussie Lawman. Glenn Holt
Austenbury Castle. Anonymous
Australian Bush Track. D. Hennessey
Australian Life. F. Adams
Authentic Death of Hendry Jones. C. Neider
Author Bites the Dust. A. W. Upfield
Author in Distress. C. M. Wills
Author Unknown. C. Dane
Authorized Murder. I. Asimov
Author's Choice. M. Kantor
Autobiography of a Blackguard. R. Paton
Autobiography of a Bottle of Bourbon. Old Sleuth
Autobiography of a French Detective. M. Canler
Autobiography of a London Detective. Waters
Autobiography of a Quack, and The Case of George Dedlow. S. W. Mitchell
Autobiography of an English Detective. Waters
Autobiography of an Italian Police-Officer. Anonymous
Autopsy. J. R. Feegel
Autumn Accelerator. P. Leslie
Autumn Heroes. O. Jacks
Autumn Lace. Eileen Jackson
Autumn of a Hunter. P. Stadley
Autumn Rose. Margery Lawrence
Ava Mining Syndicate. C. C. Lewis
Avalanche. G. Atherton
Avalanche. K. Boyle
Avalanche. J. Wingate
Avalanche Express. C. Forbes
Avenged on Society. H. F. Wood
Avenger. Anonymous
Avenger. M. Blood
Avenger. R. Gar
Avenger. J. Goodwin
Avenger. Samuel Gordon
Avenger. H. Kane
Avenger. E. P. Oppenheim
Avenger. H. Rigsby
Avenger. D. Steele
Avenger. E. Wallace
Avenger at Bay. J. Salt
Avenger of Blood. J. M. Cobban
Avenger Strikes. W. S. Masterman
Avenger Tapes. R. G. Stimson
Avengers. D. Enefer

448 / Avengers — Title Index

Avengers. H. Hill
Avenging Brotherhood. I. Tattersall
Avenging Eagle. T. P. Hurley
Avenging Ikon. C. Barry
Avenging Kiss. C. Rae-Brown
Agenging Maid. J. S. May
Avenging Note. A. Sprissler
Avenging Nymph. H. Janson
Avenging of Ruthanna. Mrs. C. Kernahan
Avenging Parrot. Anne Austin
Avenging Picaroon. J. Cassells
Avenging Ray. Seamark
Avenging Saint. L. Charteris
Avenging Seven. L. H. Brooks
Avenging Twins. J. McCulley
Avenging Twins Collect. J. McCulley
Average Jones. S. H. Adams
Average Man. A. C. Fox-Davies
Averno. B. Mitford
Avery's Fortune. W. M. Green
Avila Gold. D. Westheimer
Avima Affair. N. Calmer
Awake and Die. R. Ames
Awake Deborah! E. Phillpotts
Awake to Terror. Marilyn Ross
Awakening. R. C. Meredith
Awakening Dream. K. Cameron
Awakening of Theodore Wrenn. M. Crombie
Award of Justice. A. M. Barbour
Away Went the Little Fish. M. Bennett
Away with Murder. J. Pattinson
Awful Egg. K. Robeson
Awkward Lie. M. Innes
Awkward Marine. J. Spenser
Ax. E. McBain
Ax of Atlantis. L. Grimes
Axe for the Rani. R. Bond
Axe Is Laid. J. Mackworth
Axe to Grind. A. A. Fair
Axes of Hate. James Preston
Axis. Clive Irving
Axmann Agenda. M. Pettit
Axwater. Jennie Melville
Aynsley's Case. G. M. Fenn
Azanian Assignment. I. Finlay
Azor! J. Henaghan
Aztec Avenger. Nick Carter
Azure Rose. R. W. Kauffman

A

B As in Banshee. L. Treat
BB of Ardlegay. W. H. Rainsford
B14. R. K. Weekes
Babbington Case. Nicholas Carter
Babcock Boys. D. Reid
Babe in the Woods. W. Ard
Babe Jardine. Stuart Martin
Babe with the Twistable Arm. Hampton Stone
Babes in the Woods. L. O'Donnell
Babes Up in Arms. K. T. McCall
Babiole, the Pretty Milliner. F. Du Boisgobey
Baboon's Paw. R. C. Armour
Baby Doll Murders. J. O. Causey
Baby, Don't Dare Squeal. H. Janson
Baby, Don't Get Rough. C. Wheatley
Baby Don't Love Hoodlums. M. Storm
Baby Don't Say Goodbye. M. Storm
Baby Face. M. Corrigan
Baby Face. Dulcie Gray
Baby Factory. C. Rayner
Baby Grand and other stories. S. Aumonier
Baby in the Ash Can. S. Shane
Baby Merchants. L. O'Donnell
Baby Moll. S. Brackeen
Baby Moll. B. Sarto
Baby Sitter. R. Boyle
Baby Sitters. J. Salisbury
Baby-Snatcher. C. Kendall
Baby, the Rain Must Fall. H. Foote
"Baby" Wilkinson's V. C. and other stories. N. Newham-Davis
Baby, Your Type's Murder. M. Brody
Baby, You're Guilt-Edged. Carter Brown
Babylon. G. Allen
Babysitter. A. Coburn
Babysitter. John Fraser
Baccarat. H. Malot
Baccarat Club. J. L. Rickard
Bach Festival Murders. B. Bloch
Bachelor Flat Mystery. R. A. J. Walling
Bachelor Party. H. Hickman
Bachelors Get Lonely. A. A. Fair
Bachelors of Broken Hill. A. W. Upfield
Bachelor's Widow. O. Dekobra
Back-Alley Blond. Griff
Back Bay Murders. R. Scarlett
Back Country. W. Fuller
Back Door to Death. R. Foley
Back from the Dead. E. Snell
Back from the Dead. A. Soutar
Back from the Grave. W. S. Masterman
Back from the Grave. J. K. Stafford
Back Home. I. S. Cobb
Back in Daylight. E. H. Clements
Back Number. E. Everett-Green

Back Room Girl. F. Durbridge
Back-Seat Murder. Herman Landon
Back to Africa. W. Westall
Back to Eden. A. Soutar
Back to Fire Mountain. R. Scowcroft
Back to Life. W. Speight
Back to Life. Jonathan Wade
Back to Lilac Land. G. Thorne
Back to the Old Country. M. C. Hay
Back to the Wall. R. P. Hansen
Back to Victoria. J. J. Farjeon
Backfire. C. Egleton
Backfire. D. J. Marlowe
Backfire. E. Sherry
Backfire Is Hostile. J. Barnett
Background for Murder. Shelley Smith
Background to Danger. E. Ambler
Background to Death. J. W. Lee
Background to Murder, and other stories. T. S. Denham
Backing Winds. Josephine Bell
Backlash. P. Durst
Backlash. J. B. O'Sullivan
Backlash. J. Philips
Backlash. V. Warren
Backlash. M. L. West
Backlash of Infamy. H. Janson
Backslider. G. Allen
Backstage Mystery. O. R. Cohen
Backup Men. Ross Thomas
Backwash. P. Malloch
Backwaters. M. S. Boyd
Backwoods Princess. H. Footner
Backwoods Teaser. G. Brewer
Backwoods Tramp. H. Whittington
Backyard. J. Femling
Bad Blonde. J. Webb
Bad Blood. B. Petty
Bad Boy. S. D. Frances
Bad Boy. J. Thompson
Bad Communist. M. Crawford
Bad Companions. D. Lee
Bad Conscience. J. Roffman
Bad Day at Black Rock. M. Niall
Bad Day for a Black Brother. B. B. Johnson
Bad Die Young. Peter Chambers
Bad Dream. M. Gair
Bad Dream of Death. J. N. Chance
Bad End Valley. W. B. Bannerman
Bad for Business. R. Stout
Bad for the Baron. Anthony Morton
Bad Girl. H. Janson
Bad Girls. B. Clifton
Bad Guy. N. Brady
Bad Investment. L. Cassels
Bad Lord Lockington. F. Warden
Bad-Luck Cutie. H. Spencer
Bad Man of Cairo. A. Parsons
Bad Men Make Good Wives. M. Hayes
Bad Moon Rising. J. Kirsch
Bad Name. J. J. Ellis
Bad Neighbor Murder. C. M. Russell
Bad Night's Work. O. J. Currington
Bad Ronald. J. H. Vance
Bad Samaritan. W. C. Gault
Bad Samaritan. A. Rider
Bad Seed. Maxwell Anderson
Bad Seed. W. March
Bad Sister. E. Tennant
Bad Step. M. Derby
Bad Summer. J. Appleby
Bad to Beat. H. Smart
Bad Track. M. Booth
Bad Trip. K. Roos
Baddington Horror. W. S. Masterman
Badge. B. Bolt
Badge for a Gunfighter. R. Wilkes-Hunter
Badge of Evil. W. Masterson
Badge of Honor. D. Barnes
Badge of Honor. D. Brennan
Badge of Infamy. P. Durst
Badge 373. M. Roote
Badger in the Dusk. N. Brent
Badger's Daughter. P. Crawford
Badmen on Halfaday Creek. J. B. Hendryx
Baffle Book. L. Wren
Baffled, But Not Beaten. Nicholas Carter
Baffled Conspirators. W. E. Norris
Baffled Imposter. S. W. Hopkins
Baffled Oath. Nicholas Carter
Baffling Quest. R. Dowling
Bag and Baggage. B. Capes
Bag Man. F. McAuliffe
Bag of Diamonds. G. M. Fenn
Bagful of Bones. A. Kennington
Baghdad Blues. S. Greenlee
Baghdad Defections. B. Keller
Bagman in Jewels. M. Pemberton
Bags of Blackmail. C. Litchfield
Bagshot Mystery. O. Gray
Bahama Crisis. D. Bagley
Bahamas Murder Case. L. Ford
Bail Jumper. R. J. C. Stead
"Bail Up!" H. Nisbet
Bailiff's Secret. G. H. Teed
Bainbridge Holme. Charles Henry
Bainbridge Murder. C. Fitzsimmons
Bainbridge Mystery. G. T. Pratt
Bait. Lionel Black
Bait. M. Carroll
Bait. L. Martin

Bait. D. Uhnak
Bait for a Killer. G. Bagby
Bait for a Tiger. B. Veiller
Bait for Murder. K. M. Knight
Bait Money. Max Collins
Bait of Perjury. W. Savage
Baited Blonde. R. MacLean
Baiting the Trap. J. Middlemass
Baja Bandidos. L. Derrick
Baker Street. J. Coopersmith
Balance. W. D. Orcutt
Balance of Fear. H. Matheson
Balance of Fear. G. Osborne
Balance of Terror. C. Van Hazinga
Balaoo. G. Leroux
Balcony. F. Cowen
Balcony. D. C. Disney
Balcony. J. Genet
Baldragon. J. B. Harris-Burland
Balefire. N. Tranter
Bales of Trouble. G. W. Wicking
Bali Ballet Murder. C. Conyn
Balkan Assignment. J. Poyer
Balkan Express. L. Ross
Balkan Saga. D. Weir
Balkan Spy. D. Betteridge
Ball of Fortune. C. E. Pearce
Ballad of Loving Jenny. Carter Brown
Ballad of the Running Man. Shelley Smith
Ballarat. Eric Lambert
Ballet! T. Murphy
Ballet of Death. Elizabeth Anthony
Ballet of Fear. Elizabeth Anthony
Ballet of Moments Unborn. A. Viney
Balloon Girl. M. MacKintosh
Balloon Man. C. Armstrong
Ballot. R. Summerscales
Ballot Box Murders. J. S. Strange
Ballot Box Mystery. H. H. C. Gibbons
Ballots for Violence. S. Dave
Ballycronin Mystery. H. M. Webster
Ballyho Bey. A. C. Gunter
Baltic Mystery. F. S. Webber
Baltimore Madame. H. Knowland
Bamboo. K. West
Bamboo Bay. G. Volk
Bamboo Blonde. D. B. Hughes
Bamboo Bloodbath. P. Anthony
Bamboo Bomb. James Dark
Bamboo Demons. J. Sherman
Bamboo Elephants. N. Thurley
Bamboo Girl. F. Lester
Bamboo Guerillas. G. N. Smith
Bamboo Prison. H. Gibbs
Bamboo Screen. S. Harvester
Bamboo Terror. W. Ross
Bamboo Whistle. C. V. Frost
Banacek. Deane Romano
Banana Men. M. Catto
Banana Murders. Y. Smith
Banana Tourist. G. Simenon
Banbury Bog. P. A. Taylor
Bancaster Mystery. A. N. Hodges
Bancock Murder Case. A. B. Cunningham
Band of Mystery. M. O. Rolfe
Band Played Murder. E. Howie
Bandaged Face. Z. I. Ponder
Bandaged Nude. R. Finnegan
Bandar-Log Murder. C. Comstock
Bandbox. L. J. Vance
Bandersnatch. D. Lowden
Bandicoot. R. Condon
Bandit. L. Charteris
Bandit of Syracuse. S. Cobb
Bandit Trust. M. Warrick
Bandits Aloft. T. Wallace
Bandit's Moon. N. MacKenzie
Bandits of the Air. Nicholas Carter
Bandits of the Night. J. M. Walsh
Bang! Bang! G. Ade
Bang Bang Birds. A. Diment
Bang! Bang! You're Dead! June Drummond
Bang, You're Dead! H. Treece
Bangkok Murders. Reginald Campbell
Banishment of Jessop Blythe. J. Hatton
Banjo. J. Curtis
Bank Draft Puzzle. Nicholas Carter
Bank Job. R. L. Pike
Bank Job. T. B. Reagan
Bank Manager. E. P. Oppenheim
Bank Note Plates. Lieut. Carlton
Bank Robber. G. Tippette
Bank Robbers. A. Griffiths
Bank Robbers. Old Sleuth
Bank-Robbers and the Detectives. A. Pinkerton
Bank Robbery. M. Ulrich
Bank Robbery Hostage. R. Wilkes-Hunter
Bank Shot. D. E. Westlake
Bank Tragedy. M. R. Hatch
Bank Vault Mystery. L. F. Booth
Bank with the Bamboo Door. D. Hitchens
Banker's Bones. M. Scherf
Banker's Millions. Warren Miller
Banker's Trust. J. W. Bobin
Banker's Victim. O. Bradbury
Banking on Death. E. Lathen
Banksters. Robin Moore
Bannantyne Sapphires. F. Hird
Banner for Pegasus. J. Bonett
Bannerman. J. Flynn
Bannerman Case. J. Lord

Title Index

Banners of Blood. J. H. Hunter
Banners Yellow. J. E. Gordon
Bannon. A. Evans
Banquet Ceases. M. Pitt
Banyon. W. Johnston
Bar Sinister. K. G. Ballard
Bar Sinister. C. A. Collins
Bar Sinister. J. M. DeGroot
Bar Sinister. P. MacTyre
Bar Sinister. S. Rathbone
Barbara. M. E. Braddon
Barbara Heathcote's Trial. R. N. Carey
Barbara on Her Own. E. Wallace
Barbara, the Valiant. K. Kimbrough
Barbara's Rival. E. A. Young
Barbarous Coast. R. Macdonald
Barbary Freight. R. Burke
Barbary Hoard. J. Appleby
Barbary Kate. F. Hay
Barbed Wire. E. Everett-Green
Barbed Wire. M. Richmond
Barbed-Wire Hurdlers. P. Quinn
Barber of Littlewick. M. Drewe
Barber's Shop Crime. W. Edwards
Barber's Wife. C. Phillips
Barberton Intrigue. S. Truss
Barbie Murders. J. Varley
Barbouse. Alan Williams
Barboza Credentials. P. Driscoll
Barca. L. Cameron
Barclay Place. R. Foley
Bardelow's Heir. Roy Vickers
Bardel's Murder. E. McGirr
Bare Bodkin. F. Gerard
Bare Trap. F. Kane
Barefoot Witch. M. Clare
Barely Seen. F. Kane
Bargain. M. Gilbert
Bargain for Death. Robert Martin
Bargain in Blood. Arthur MacLean
Bargain in Blood. D. Stanford
Bargain in Crime. Nicholas Carter
Bargain in Souls. E. D. Pierson
Bargain with Death. H. Pentecost
Barge Girl. C. Clements
Barge of Haunted Lives. J. A. Tyson
Barker Case. G. Barrett
Barker's Drift. M. Cannell
Barking Clock. H. S. Keeler
Barking Dog Murder Case. E. C. Vivian
Barlow Casebook. Elwyn Jones
Barlow Comes to Judgment. Elwyn Jones
Barlow Down Under. Elwyn Jones
Barlow Exposed. Elwyn Jones
Barlow in Charge. Elwyn Jones
Barn Stormers. A. M. Williamson
Barnabas Collins. Marilyn Ross
Barnabas Collins and Quentin's Doom.
  Marilyn Ross
Barnabas Collins and the Gypsy Witch.
  Marilyn Ross
Barnabas Collins and the Mysterious
  Ghost. Marilyn Ross
Barnabas Collins vs. the Warlock.
  Marilyn Ross
Barnabas, Quentin and Dr. Jekyll's Son.
  Marilyn Ross
Barnabas, Quentin and the Avenging Ghost.
  Marilyn Ross
Barnabas, Quentin and the Body Snatchers.
  Marilyn Ross
Barnabas, Quentin and the Crystal Coffin.
  Marilyn Ross
Barnabas, Quentin and the Frightened
  Bride. Marilyn Ross
Barnabas, Quentin and the Grave Robbers.
  Marilyn Ross
Barnabas, Quentin and the Haunted Cave.
  Marilyn Ross
Barnabas, Quentin and the Hidden Tomb.
  Marilyn Ross
Barnabas, Quentin and the Mad Magician.
  Marilyn Ross
Barnabas, Quentin and the Magic Potion.
  Marilyn Ross
Barnabas, Quentin and the Mummy's Curse.
  Marilyn Ross
Barnabas, Quentin and the Nightmare
  Assassin. Marilyn Ross
Barnabas, Quentin and the Scorpio Curse.
  Marilyn Ross
Barnabas, Quentin and the Sea Ghost.
  Marilyn Ross
Barnabas, Quentin and the Serpent.
  Marilyn Ross
Barnabas, Quentin and the Vampire Beauty.
  Marilyn Ross
Barnabas, Quentin and the Witch's Curse.
  Marilyn Ross
Barney. W. Johnston
Baron Again. Anthony Morton
Baron and the Arrogant Alibi. Anthony
  Morton
Baron and the Beggar. Anthony Morton
Baron and the Chinese Puzzle. Anthony
  Morton
Baron and the Missing Old Masters.
  Anthony Morton
Baron and the Mogul Swords. Anthony Mor-
  ton
Baron and the Stolen Legacy. Anthony
  Morton

Baron and the Unfinished Portrait.
  Anthony Morton
Baron at Bay. Anthony Morton
Baron at Large. Anthony Morton
Baron Branches Out. Anthony Morton
Baron Comes Back. Anthony Morton
Baron Goes A-Buying. Anthony Morton
Baron Goes East. Anthony Morton
Baron Goes Fast. Anthony Morton
Baron in France. Anthony Morton
Baron Ixell, Crime Breaker. O. Schisgall
Baron—King Maker. Anthony Morton
Baron Montez of Panama and Paris.
  A. C. Gunter
Baron of Hong Kong. N. Daniels
Baron on Board. Anthony Morton
Baron Returns. Anthony Morton
Baron Sam. St. George Rathborne
Baron Sinister. J. Milton
Baron Trigault's Vengeance. E. Gaboriau
Baroness of Bow Street. G. Clark
Baronet Rag-Picker. C. S. Coom
Baronet's Bride. M. A. Fleming
Baronet's Crime. J. B. Williams
Baronet's Wife. F. Warden
Baroni. Alfred Harris
Baron's Daughter. I. Kelly
Baron's Mission to Peking. N. Daniels
Baroque. L. J. Vance
Barotique Mystery. G. H. Coxe
Barozzi. Catherine Smith
Barracuda. I. A. Greenfield
Barracuda. R. Magowan
Barradine Detects. E. Jepson
Barrakee Mystery. A. W. Upfield
Barrancourt Destiny. A. Worboys
Barred from the West End. J. Hunter
Barrel Mystery. Nicholas Carter
Barrel Mystery. W. J. Flynn
Barren Harvest. C. M. Nelson
Barren Heritage. L. R. Davis
Barren Honor. H. Wood
Barren Land Murders. L. Short
Barren Land Showdown. L. Short
Barren Title. T. W. Speight
Barrier. S. L. Bell
Barrier. R. Maugham
Barrier Reef. M. Grant
Barrier Reef Mystery. A. Murray
Barringher House. B. Riefe
Barrington Mystery. L. Brock
Barronwell Mystery. H. Leyford
Barrow Sinister. Elsie Lee
Bars of Gold. G. Ellinger
Bars of Steel. L. Noel
Bartenstein Case. J. S. Fletcher
Bartenstein Mystery. J. S. Fletcher
Bartered Honour. R. H. Sherard
Bartlett Mystery. L. Tracy
Barton Manor Mystery. Gwyn Evans
Barton Mystery. G. Goodchild
Barton Mystery. W. Hackett
Barush Mystery. T. A. Plummer
Basement Room and other stories. G.
  Greene
Basil. W. Collins
Basil and Annette. B. L. Farjeon
Basilisk. H. P. Stephens
Basket of Summer Fruit. R. McCullough
Basle Express. M. Coles
Bass Derby Murder. K. M. Knight
Bassington Murder. C. Hough
Bastard. J. Wainwright
Bastard Brigade. P. Leslie
Bastard Verdict. Winifred Duke
Bastard's Name Was Bristow. J. S. Scott
Bastion of the Damned. J. Cassells
Bat. M. R. Rinehart
Bat Flies Low. S. Rohmer
Bat of the Belfrey. Anonymous
Bat Out of Hell. F. Durbridge
Bat Staffel. R. J. Hogan
Bat That Flits. N. Collins
Bat-Wing. S. Rohmer
Bat Woman. C. Gibbons
Bateman Household. J. Payn
Bath Mysteries. E. R. Punshon
Bath of Acid. C. Franklin
Bathchair Mystery. A. Murray
Bathing Pool Mystery. A. Blair
Bathtub Murder. D. Lyon
Bathtub Murder Case. E. R. Punshon
Bathurst Complex. W. Martyn
Batman. B. Kane
Batman vs. the Fearsome Foursome.
  W. Lyon
Batman vs. Three Villains of Doom.
  W. Lyon
Bats Fly at Dusk. A. A. Fair
Bats Fly Up for Inspector Ghote.
  H. R. F. Keating
Bats in the Belfry. E. C. R. Lorac
Bats out of Hell. G. N. Smith
Bats with Baby Faces. W. S. Moss
Battered Caravanserai. P. Capon
Battle for Inspector West. J. Creasey
Battle for the Cup. P. Gill
Battle for the Right. Nicholas Carter
Battle Mask. D. Pendleton
Battle of Basinghall Street. E. P.
  Oppenheim
Battle of Giants. P. Trent

Battle of Hate. N. Buntline
Battle of Nerves. G. Simenon
Battle of the April Storm. L. Forrester
Battle of the Singing Men. G. Kersh
Battle of Wits. S. Campbell
Battle Pay. P. McCurtin
Battle Road. S. Harvester
Battle Song. W. H. Baker
Battle Without Glory. R. C. Trown
Battling Barker. A. Soutar
Battling Prophet. A. W. Upfield
Battling Skyman. T. Wallace
Bauer Murder. S. C. Prescott
Bavarian Connection. Don Smith
Bawlerout. F. Halsey
Baxter Family. A. Askew
Baxter Letters. D. Hitchens
Baxter's Second Death. I. Greig
Baxter's Son. P. Trent
Bay City Blast. W. B. Murphy
Bay of Deception. S. Shelley
Bay of Seals. J. Wood
Bay of the Damned. W. Carrier
Bay Prowler. M. Barry
Baying Hound. A. West
Bayou Road. M. G. Eberhart
Bazi Bazoum. C. Matthew
Be a Good Boy. Joan Fleming
Be Absolute for Death. R. Chance
Be All and End All. E. Berckman
Be Careful How You Live. E. Lacy
Be Home by Eleven. A. Dean
Be Kind to the Killer. Henry Wade
Be My Ghost. R. Chapman
Be My Love. M. Richmond
Be My Victim. R. Dietrich
Be Our Guest. C. Sodaro
Be Shot for Sixpence. M. Gilbert
Be Silent, Love. F. Nichols
Be Still, My Love. J. Truesdell
Be Thou My Judge. J. Wood
Beach Girls. J. D. MacDonald
Beach House. V. Coffman
Beach of Atonement. A. W. Upfield
Beach of Skulls. A. West
Beach of Terror, and other stories.
  B. Grimshaw
Beach Patrol. R. Rogers
Beach Queen Blowout. P. Morgan
Beachcomber. A. Murray
Beachy Head Murder. A. Gask
Beacon Fires. M. Gerard
Beacon Hill Murders. R. Scarlett
Beacon in the Night. B. S. Ballinger
Beacons of Death. M. B. Dix
Beaded Banana. M. Scherf
Beads of Silence. L. Bamburg
Beagle Scented Murder. F. Gruber
Beak of Death. L. Bennet-Thompson
Beam of Black Light. O. John
Beam of Malice. Alex Hamilton
Bear Island. Alistair MacLean
Bear Raid. K. Follett
Bear Squeeze. M. M. Bodkin
Bear Witness. J. Reach
Beard the Lion. W. Manchester
Bearer Plot. O. Sela
Bearers of the Burden. W. P. Drury
Beast. L. Allan
Beast. H. Fleetwood
Beast. E. C. Litsey
Beast in View. M. Millar
Beast-King Murders. R. Wallace
Beast Must Die. N. Blake
Beast of the City. J. Lait
Beast with Five Fingers. W. F. Harvey
Beast with the Red Hands. S. Stuart
Beast with Two Backs. N. Sligh
Beastmark the Spy. J. B. Clouston
Beasts of Brahm. M. Hansom
Beat Back the Tide. D. Hitchens
Beat Not the Bones. C. Jay
Beat on an Orange Drum. D. Reid
Beat the Devil. J. Helvick
Beaten at the Post. B. Delannoy
Beating the Nobblers. J. Fairfax-
  Blakeborough
Beatrice. E. Southworth
Beatrice and Benedick. H. Smart
Beatrice Foyle's Crime. F. Warden
Beatrice Mystery. D. Johns
Beatrix Randolph. J. Hawthorne
Beau Blackstone. R. Falkirk
Beau Revel. L. J. Vance
Beaufort Dossier. D. Mariner
Beaumaroy Home from the Wars. Anthony
  Hope
Beamont Tradition. D. Daniels
Beaurand Mystery. H. Greville
Beautiful Alien. S. Hocking
Beautiful and Dead. R. MacRoss
Beautiful Birthday Cake. M. Scherf
Beautiful Blackmailer. Old Sleuth
Beautiful But Bad. R. Colby
Beautiful But Dangerous. T. W. Hanshew
Beautiful Crook. M. O'Nair
Beautiful Dead. H. Pentecost
Beautiful Derelict. C. Wells
Beautiful Devil. Detective Dunn
Beautiful Frame. W. Pearson
Beautiful Friend. R. Collier
Beautiful Fugitive. Old Sleuth

B

Beautiful Golden Frame. Peter Chambers
Beautiful Gunner. Norma Lee
Beautiful Jack, the Double-Edged Detective. Anonymous
Beautiful Mrs. Davenant. V. Tweedale
Beautiful Murder. J. Ingersol
Beautiful Savage. Mrs. C. Kernahan
Beautiful Schemer. D. T. Hughes
Beautiful Scourge. E. Gaboriau
Beautiful Stranger. Bernice Carey
Beautiful Suspect. H. Richards
Beautiful Trap. B. S. Ballinger
Beautiful White Devil. G. Boothby
Beautiful Woman's Sin. Hero Strong
Beauty—A Snare. Glint Green
Beauty and the Beat. H. Janson
Beauty and the Policeman and other stories. S. Horler
Beauty Can Kill. M. McCretton
Beauty Doctor. F. Warden
Beauty for Inspector West. J. Creasey
Beauty in Distress. G. Warden
Beauty Is a Beast. K. M. Knight
Beauty Is Found in a Grave. D. Steel
Beauty Kill. R. Hawkes
Beauty-Killer. B. Fleming
Beauty Marks the Spot. K. Roos
Beauty-Mask Murder. V. B. Shore
Beauty-Mask Mystery. V. B. Shore
Beauty of the Family. F. Warden
Beauty Parlor Murder. G. Chester
Beauty Queen Killer. J. Creasey
Beauty Sleep. R. Darby
Beauty Sleep. H. Dolson
Beauty Spot. H. Mee
Beauty That Must Die. Barbara James
Beauty Vanishes. D. Brande
Beauty's Queen. M. Leighton
Because of Misella. A. W. Marchmont
Because of the Cats. N. Freeling
Because of the Woman. C. H. Bullivant
Because Their Hearts Were Pure. M. Cary
Becca's Child. W. D. Roberts
Beckoning. V. Coffman
Beckoning Door. M. Seeley
Beckoning Dream. E. Berckman
Beckoning Finger. H. Harding
Beckoning Hand and other stories. G. Allen
Beckoning Lady. M. Allingham
Beckoning Shadow. Denis Scott
Becky. H. Janson
Bed Disturbed. Elbur Ford
Bed of Ashes. D. Daniels
Bedelia. V. Caspary
Bedeviled. Libbie Block
Bedford Row Mystery. J. S. Fletcher
Bedroom Agent. F. Branch
Bedroom Bang Bang. D. Davis
Bedroom Bolero. M. Avallone
Bedrooms Have Windows. A. A. Fair
Bedside Corpse. M. Friedman
Bee Sting Deal. G. Beare
Beech of the Boulevard. B. Sarto
Beechcourt Mystery. C. Strange
Beehive. M. O'Donnell
Beelfontaine. S. O'Brien
Beelzebub Business. G. Brandner
Beer for Psyche. D. Gardiner
Beetle. R. Marsh
Before and After Edith. P. Popescu
Before I Die. G. Joseph
Before I Die. H. McCloy
Before I Die. M. L. Roby
Before I Die. L. White
Before I Wake. H. Debrett
Before I Wake. M. Echard
Before It's Too Late. L. Cameron
Before It's Too Late. Jay Stewart
Before Midnight. R. Stout
Before the Ball Was Over. A. Roudybush
Before the British Raj. A. Griffiths
Before the Cock Crowed. W. E. Hayes
Before the Crossing. S. Jameson
Before the Fact. F. Iles
Before the Party. R. Ackland
Before the Storm. M. B. Lowndes
Before the Wind. E. F. Charles
Before the Wind. J. Laing
Beg Pardon, Sir! R. W. Kauffman
Beggar, and other stories. D. Newton
Beggar in Purple. A. Soutar
Beggar on Horseback. J. Payn
Beggars All. K. N. Burt
Beggar's Choice. H. C. Branson
Beggar's Choice. P. Wentworth
Beggar's Manor. R. M. Gilchrist
Begin, Murderer! D. Cory
Begin with a Gun. M. Cronin
Beginner's Luck. P. Somers
Beginning of a Crime. Dorris Roberts
Beginning the Adventure. Augustus Muir
Beginning with a Bash. A. Tilton
Beginnings of Mr. P. J. Davenant. F. S. Hamilton
Begins with Murder. W. Collison
Begonia Walk. Gavin Holt
Begotten Murder. M. Carroll
Beguiling Shore. D. F. Gardiner
Begumbagh. Anonymous
Behind a Mask. L. M. Alcott
Behind a Mask. Nicholas Carter

Behind a Mask. T. Douglas
Behind a Mask. J. Hatton
Behind a Throne. Nicholas Carter
Behind Closed Doors. Nicholas Carter
Behind Closed Doors. A. K. Green
Behind Locked Doors. E. M. Poate
Behind Locked Shutters. W. E. D. Ross
Behind Red Curtains. Mansfield Scott
Behind Shuttered Windows. A. Askew
Behind That Curtain. E. D. Biggers
Behind That Door. G. Goodchild
Behind That Mask. H. S. Keeler
Behind the Arras. Anthony Graham
Behind the Black Mask. Nicholas Carter
Behind the Bolted Door? A. E. McFarlane
Behind the Bronze Door. W. LeQueux
Behind the Crimson Blind. Carter Dickson
Behind the Curtain. H. R. Addison
Behind the Curtain. M. Pemberton
Behind the Devil Screen. M. Keck
Behind the Door. E. J. Anders
Behind the Enemy. G. Marlowe
Behind the Evidence. L. Blackledge
Behind the Evidence. P. Reynolds
Behind the First Wall. P. Graham
Behind the Fog. H. H. Bashford
Behind the German Lines. W. LeQueux
Behind the Granite Gateway. W. S. King
Behind the Green Mask. R. Trevor
Behind the Head-Lines. W. Sutherland
Behind the Headlines. R. Chapman
Behind the Monocle. J. S. Fletcher
Behind the Panel. J. S. Fletcher
Behind the Picture. M. M. Bodkin
Behind the Purple Mask. J. H. Chase
Behind the Purple Veil. Marilyn Ross
Behind the Ranges. O. Binns
Behind the Scarlet Door. L. Cameron
Behind the Screen. D. Doubtfire
Behind the Throne. W. LeQueux
Behind the Veil. D. E. L. Patch
Behind the Veil. George R. Sims
Behind the Veils. W. M. Graydon
Behind the Wire Fence. L. Allan
Behind the Yellow Bind. R. A. J. Walling
Behold a Fair Woman. F. Duncan
Behold, Here's Poison! G. Heyer
Behold the Body! O. Cecil
Behold the City. R. W. Howe
Behold, the Druid Weeps. M. Rippon
Behold! The Executioner! E. Harding
Behold the Fire. M. Blankfort
Behold the Judge. J. Brophy
Behold This Woman. D. Goodis
Beholder. P. Freund
Beirut Incident. Nick Carter
Beirut Pipeline. R. Alan
Belfast Connection. G. DeVilliers
Belfriere. K. Gooding
Belfry Murder. M. Dalton
Belgrade Case. S. Bradley
Belgrade Drop. G. Vaughan
Belgrave Manor Crime. M. Dalton
Belgravia. D. Linzee
Believe This...You'll Believe Anything. J. H. Chase
Believed Violent. J. H. Chase
Belinda's Beaux. A. Kenealy
Bell. D. Daniels
Bell, Book and Candleflame. I. S. Way
Bell in the Fog. J. S. Strange
Bell Is Answered. R. East
Bell of Death. Anthony Gilbert
Bell on Lonely. M. P. Hood
Bell Street Murders. S. Fowler
Bell Tower of Wyndspelle. A. Vandergriff
Bella. D. Eden
Bella Donna Was Poisoned. Carter Brown
Bella on the Roof. H. Ford
Belladonna. E. Lindley
Bellamy Case. J. Hay
Bellamy Trial. F. N. Hart
Belle. G. Simenon
Belle. Michael Stewart
Belle Claudine. P. Muse
Belle of Australia. W. H. Thomas
Belle of the Ballet. A. Applin
Belle of Toorak. E. W. Hornung
Belle Starr, the Bandit Queen. Anonymous
Belles and Ringers. H. Smart
Bellgrove Castle. T. H. White
Bellini Look. C. Brink
Bellman and True. D. Lowden
Bellmer Mystery. B. A. Williams
Bellringer. L. Kamarck
Bells at Old Bailey. D. Bowers
Bells for the Dead. K. M. Knight
Bells of Bicetre. G. Simenon
Bells of Doom. A. S. Falkner
Bells of Doom. Donald Stuart
Bells of Old Bailey. D. Bowers
Bells of Palmdale, and other stories. W. Slater
Bells of Penraven. B. L. Farjeon
Bells of St. Martin. Karen Campbell
Bells of Widows Bay. M. Lynch
Belltower. K. A. Shoesmith
Bellwood. E. Ogilvie
Beloved Diana. A. C. Ley
Beloved Enemy. P. Allardyce
Beloved Enemy. M. K. Douglas

Beloved Enemy. A. Maybury
Beloved Enemy. M. Richmond
Beloved Lady. B. Jefferis
Beloved of Ishmael. V. M. Steele
Beloved Stranger. J. Blackmore
Beloved Traitor. E. Bond
Beloved Traitor. H. Janson
Beloved Victim. J. Arliss
Below Bridge. R. Dowling
Below Suspicion. J. D. Carr
Below the Belt. David Hume
Below the Clock. J. V. Turner
Below the Dead-Line. S. Campbell
Below the Surface. E. K. Chatterton
Belrox Mystery. Dick Stewart
Belt of Diamonds. B. Wayde
Belt of Suspicion. H. R. Wakefield
Beltane the Smith. J. Farnol
Belting Inheritance. J. Symons
Belvedere. Elizabeth Ford
Belvedere. R. Pearsall
Ben. G. A. Ralston
Ben Bradley's Puzzle. W. G. Forbes
Ben Bradley's Weirdest Case. W. G. Forbes
Ben Clough and other stories. W. Westall
Ben Gates Is Hot. R. Kyle
Ben Hassan's Secret. W. V. Cook
Ben on the Job. J. J. Farjeon
Ben Sees It Through. J. J. Farjeon
Beneath the Mask. F. A. M. Webster
Beneath the Passion Flower. G. R. Preedy
Beneath the Precipice. J. Ritson
Beneath the Sea. G. M. Fenn
Beneath the Veil. A. Sergeant
Beneath the Wheels. F. E. M. Notley
Beneath Your Very Boots. C. J. C. Hyne
Benedict Arnold Connection. J. DiMona
Benefactors' Club. A. Abdullah
Benefit. N. Mayo
Benefit Performance. R. Sale
Benefits of Death. R. Jeffries
Benevent Treasure. P. Wentworth
Benevolent Blackmail. W. R. M. Churcher
Benevolent Blackmailer. T. Harknett
Benevolent Picaroon. J. Cassells
Bengal Fire. L. G. Blochman
Bengal Spider Plan. E. P. Thorne
Bengali Inheritance. O. Sela
Benighted. J. B. Priestley
Benjamin Butts Junr. Anonymous
Benjamin Seven. M. Kerr
Bennett. D. Cory
Benny Muscles In. P. Rabe
Benny Went First. V. Kathrens
Benson Murder Case. S. S. Van Dine
Bent Copper. J. Ashford
Bent for Blackmail. G. Monro
Bent Man. A. Maling
Bent, Not Broken. G. M. Fenn
Bentinck's Tutor. J. Payn
Bentley's Conscience. P. Trent
Benton of the Royal Mounted. R. S. Kendall
Benwell Mystery. Hawkshaw
Bequeath Them No Tumbled House. Y. MacManus
Berenice. E. P. Oppenheim
Berg. A. Quin
Berg Case. John Bentley
Bergen Worth. W. Lloyd
Bergman's Blitz. T. Barling
Beria Papers. Alan Williams
Berkeley Street Mystery. M. R. Hatch
Berkshire Mystery. G. D. H. Cole
Berlin. Nick Carter
Berlin at Midnight. R. Joseph
Berlin Blind. A. Scholefield
Berlin Couriers. J. McGovern
Berlin Ending. Howard Hunt
Berlin Epitaph. A. Winnington
Berlin Halt. A. Winnington
Berlin Indictment. E. Fischer
Berlin Memorandum. Adam Hall
Berlin Spy Trap. Geoffrey Davison
Berlin Tunnel 21. D. Lindquist
Bermuda Burial. C. D. King
Bermuda Calling. D. Garth
Bermuda Murder. V. Siller
Bermuda Triangle Action. J. Rosenberger
Bernan Affair. J. Kessel
Bernard Treve's Boots. L. Clarke
Berry And Co. D. Yates
Berry Goes to Monte Carlo. C. N. Williamson
Berry Green. E. H. Clements
Berryhill. B. C. Bennett
Bertha, the Bartender's Beautiful Baby. C. George
Bertha, the Beautiful Typewriter Girl. C. George
Bertha's Secret. F. Du Boisgobey
Bertie Bland, the Detective. Old Sleuth
Bertram. C. R. Maturin
Beryl of the Biplane. W. LeQueux
Besides the Wench Is Dead. M. Erskine
Besieged. L. Cullinan
Bess of Bentley's. A. Askew
Bessie, the Bandit's Beautiful Baby. L. Price
Bessy Rane. H. Wood
Bessy Wells. H. Wood

Title Index

Best Detective Stories of Cyril Hare. Cyril Hare
Best Detective Stories of Roy Vickers. Roy Vickers
Best Dr. Poggioli Detective Stories. T. S. Stribling
Best Go First. F. O'Malley
Best Laid Plans. F. Carmichael
Best Laid Plans. A. Hocking
Best-Laid Schemes. Mark Cross
Bessie Kitson. G. Norway
Best Man. H. MacGrath
Best Man to Die. R. Rendell
Best of Her Sex. F. Hume
Best of Husbands. J. Payn
Best of Mr. Fortune. H. C. Bailey
Best of Three. P. Trent
Best Short Stories of M. P. Shiel. M P. Shiel
Best Stories of Peter Cheyney. P. Cheyney
Best Story Ever. J. S. Clouston
Best That Ever Did It. E. Lacy
Best Thinking Machine Detective Stories. J. Futrelle
Best Will Always Do. E. Clarke
Betencourt Five. S. F. Griffin
Beth Takes Charge. Brian Stuart
Betray Me—If You Dare. P. Carlon
Betrayal. E. P. Oppenheim
Betrayal. A. E. Walter
Betrayal and other stories. H. Acton
Betrayal at Blackcrest. Beatrice Parker
Betrayal in Eden. P. Chase
Betrayal into Darkness. R. S. S. Hall
Betrayal of John Fordham. B. L. Farjeon
Betrayed. D. Essex
Betrayed!! C. M. Lindsay
Betrayed. J. Pendower
Betrayed. Dora Russell
Betrayer. D. Wiles
Betrayers. D. Hamilton
Betrayers. P. Leslie
Better Angels. C. McCarry
Better Class of Business. J. S. Scott
Better Corpses. C. J. Daly
Better Dead. G. Bagby
Better Dead. J. M. Barrie
Better Dead. J. Bonett
Better Luck Next Crime. M. Hervey
Better Off Dead. R. M. Laurenson
Better Off Dead. H. McCloy
Better Part of Valour. B. Heatter
Better Than a Kick in the Pants. J. MacLaren-Ross
Better Than Dying. R. Faherty
Better Than Weapons. L. Christie
Better to Eat You. C. Armstrong
Better Wed Than Dead. H. Kane
Betty. G. Simenon
Between Darkness and Day. G. Merrick
Between Life and Death. F. Barrett
Between Midnight and Dawn. I. L. Cassilis
Between Murders. Sherwood King
Between the Dark and the Daylight. R. Marsh
Between the Lines. B. Delannoy
Between the Tides. J. Templeton
Between Twelve and One. V. Loder
Between Us and Evil. C. M. Russell
Beverly. M. T. Walworth
Beware, My Love. Marilyn Ross
Beware of Johnny Washington. F. Durbridge
Beware of Midnight. J. Welcome
Beware of the Bouquet. Joan Aiken
Beware of the Cat. Roger Sherman
Beware of the Dawn. K. Lindsay
Beware of the Dog! Charles North
Beware of the Dog. B. Reynolds
Beware of the Dog. J. Varnam
Beware of the Trains. E. Crispin
Beware, Sweet Maggie. D. Olson
Beware the Bog. M. Kingsbury
Beware the Crimson Cord. B. Edmunds
Beware the Curves. A. A. Fair
Beware the Hoot Owl. N. Rutledge
Beware the Kindly Stranger. Clarissa Ross
Beware the Lady. C. Woolrich
Beware the Lurking Scorpion. S. Milne
Beware the Night. J. Blackmore
Beware the Pale Horse. B. Benson
Beware! The Picaroon. J. Cassells
Beware the Hunter. H. Jones
Beware the Shadows. J. Carrick
Beware the Young Stranger. E. Queen
Beware Young Lovers. H. Pentecost
Beware Your Neighbor. M. Burton
Bewitched. R. Gilmour
Bewitched. A. M. Williamson
Bewitching Grace. Patricia Maxwell
Beyond a Reasonable Doubt. C. W. Grafton
Beyond All Fear. F. A. M. Webster
Beyond Baker Street. M. Jaffee
Beyond Capricorn. B. Roland
Beyond Compare. C. Gibbon
Beyond Control. G. Leonard
Beyond Desire. R. Himmel
Beyond Dover. V. Gielgud
Beyond Mombassa. J. Hilton

Beyond Pursuit. Nicholas Carter
Beyond Reasonable Doubt. R. Hull
Beyond Recall. Dorothy Fletcher
Beyond the Atlas. J. Trench
Beyond the Danube. R. Meade
Beyond the Dark. K. Abbey
Beyond the Dark. Jennifer Hale
Beyond the End. C. Boutelle
Beyond the Fourth Door. J. J. Deegan
Beyond the Frontier. F. A. M. Webster
Beyond the Frontiers. L. Cargill
Beyond the Law. E. Dalton
Beyond the Law. A. Murray
Beyond the Law. A. Patrick
Beyond the Law. G. Warden
Beyond the Locked Door. L. Allan
Beyond the Night. C. Woolrich
Beyond the Outposts. J. B. Hendryx
Beyond the Prize. M. Denning
Beyond the Skyline. R. Aitken
Beyond the Skyline. R. Hardinge
Beyond These Voices. M. E. Braddon
Beyond This Place. A. J. Cronin
Beyond This Point Are Monsters. M. Millar
Beyond Tolerance. Hank Hobson
Bhunda Jewels. A. Worboys
Bianca. F. Stevenson
Bianca in Black. E. S. Rohmer
Bicycle Detective. Old Sleuth
Bicycle Highwayman. F. M. Bicknell
Bicycle Jim. Old Sleuth
Bid for a Coronet. A. M. Williamson
Bid for Beauty. H. Janson
Bid for Empire. A. Griffiths
Bid for Fortune. G. Boothby
Bid for Freedom. G. Boothby
Bid for Life. S. Campbell
Bid Me Discourse. M. C. Hay
Bid the Babe Bye-Bye. Carter Brown
Bidders. John Baxter
Bidding. John Baxter
Bier for a Chaser. R. Foster
Bier for a Hussy. A. Holt
Big Apple. S. Myles
Big Bedroom. E. Ronns
Big Ben Alibi. Neil Gordon
Big Ben Looks On! J. Guildford
Big Ben Strikes Eleven. D. Magarshack
Big Ben Struck Twelve. A. Wood
Big Bet. E. H. Heth
Big Bite. Gerry Travis
Big Bite. C. Williams
Big Black. S. Myles
Big Blackmail. Frank King
Big Blackout. D. Tracy
Big Blue Death. J. Milton
Big Bob. G. Simenon
Big Boodle. R. Sylvester
Big Boss. R. Gar
Big Bounce. E. Leonard
Big Bow Mystery. I. Zangwill
Big Boys. D. Leach
Big Boys Don't Cry. M. Corrigan
Big Brain. B. Gray
Big Brass Ring. D. Tracy
Big Breakout. C. Whiting
Big Brokers. I. Shulman
Big Bruiser. A. Eichler
Big Business Murder. G. D. H. Cole
Big Bust. E. Lacy
Big C. C. M. Cronin
Big Call. G. Ashe
Big Caper. L. White
Big Cat. C. Short
Big Chance. V. Scannell
Big Chill. B. Copper
Big Chip. E. Cannon
Big Circus Mystery. H. King
Big City. J. G. Brandon
Big City Girl. C. Williams
Big Clock. K. Fearing
Big Cough. A. Saunders
Big Dano. R. Arana
Big Day. B. Unsworth
Big Deal. E. Ellison
Big Deal. A. Evans
Big Deal. P. Malloch
Big Deal in Veraqua. P. Morales
Big Dig. S. McGurk
Big Dive. K. F. Crossen
Big Dream. S. Fisher
Big Ear. S. Sterling
Big Easy. J. Conaway
Big Enough Wreath. W. Garner
Big Fall. Ralph Hayes
Big Fall. T. B. Reagan
Big Fear. T. Durrant
Big Feeling. D. Karp
Big Fish. F. Beeding
Big Fish. R. Charles
Big Fish. R. Wills
Big Fix. A. Barker
Big Fix. M. Colton
Big Fix. Spike Gordon
Big Fix. E. Hunter
Big Fix. E. Jarvis
Big Fix. E. Lacy
Big Fix. R. L. Simon
Big Foot. E. Wallace
Big Four. A. Christie
Big Four. E. Wallace

Big Frame. J. K. Baxter
Big Frame. The Gordons
Big Frame. Sam Merwin
Big Gamble. G. H. Coxe
Big Game. M. Brand
Big Game. P. Quinn
Big Game. L. L. Stevenson
Big Gold Dream. C. Himes
Big Goodbye. Peter Chambers
Big Greed. K. Giles
Big Guy. Wade Miller
Big H. H. Janson
Big H. Bryan Peters
Big Hand for the Corpse. G. Bagby
Big Haul. A. W. Sherring
Big Heart. J. G. Brandon
Big Heat. W. P. McGivern
Big Heist. H. C. Davis
Big Hit. J. Readus
Big House. J. Lait
Big Ivy. J. McCague
Big Job. D. Boland
Big Kidnap. A. Tack
Big Kill. M. Spillane
Big Killing. P. Malloch
Big Killing. N. Morland
Big Kiss-Off. D. Keene
Big Kiss-Off of 1944. A. Bergman
Big Knockover. D. Hammett
Big Loser. E. Kennedy
Big M. L. Powell
Big Make. G. Paul
Big Man. Edward Brown
Big Man. R. Marston
Big Man, a Fast Man. B. Appel
Big Man in Saludas. F. Rosenwald
Big Midget Murders. M. Rice
Big Mike. C. G. Givens
Big Money. H. Atkinson
Big Money. H. Q. Masur
Big Money-Box. A. La Bern
Big Morning Blues. Gordon M. Williams
Big Needle. S. Myles
Big Nick. P. Buranelli
Big Night. I. Andersen
Big Night. S. Ellin
Big Night at Mrs. Maria's. B. Parrish
Big Noise. G. Courtis
Big Paddle. Robin Moore
Big Payoff. J. Law
Big Payoff. R. Novak
Big Phil's Kid. M. M. Parker
Big Picture. D. Whitelaw
Big Racket. Roland Daniel
Big Radium Mystery. M. E. Cooke
Big Red Sun. D. Larany
Big Red's Daughter. J. McPartland
Big Rip-Off. B. Copper
Big Rip-Off. S. Stewart
Big Rumble. Wenzell Brown
Big Runaround. D. L. Teilhet
Big Score. Clayton Matthews
Big Secret Suzuki. J. P. Conty
Big Shot. Roland Daniel
Big Shot. F. Packard
Big Shot. D. Scanlon
Big Shot. L. Treat
Big Sin. J. Webb
Big Slam. J. Powers
Big Sleep. R. Chandler
Big Smear. W. H. Baker
Big Snatch. Anthony Ferguson
Big Snatch. H. Howard
Big Snatch. B. Shannon
Big Squeal. Roland Daniel
Big Squeeze. B. Arthur
Big Squeeze. M. Corrigan
Big Stake. R. Jocelyn
Big Stan. J. Monahan
Big Stash. R. Peters
Big Steal. W. H. Baker
Big Steal. E. Basinsky
Big Steal. P. Malloch
Big Steal. H. Seymour
Big Steal! J. T. Story
Big Stick-Up at Brinks! N. Behn
Big Stiffs. M. Avallone
Big Still. Roderic Wilkinson
Big Story. M. L. West
Big, Strong Man! C. Edwards
Big Success. I. Gordon
Big Take. W. B. M. Ferguson
Big Tickle. M. Cronin
Big Tickle. J. Wainwright
Big Time. V. Scannell
Big Time Girl. R. Marlowe
Big-Time Racketeer. D. Linton
Big Timer. W. M. Duncan
Big-Timer. P. A. Foxall
Big Tomorrow. D. Bateson
Big Top Dame. N. Karta
Big Trail. C. Houghton
Big Twist. Hank Hobson
Big Water. M. Derby
Big Wind for Summer. G. Black
Big Woman. M. Colton
Big X. D. Tracy
Bigamist. J. J. Chichester
Bigamy Kiss. S. Harragan
Bigger They Are. J. Ditton
Bigger They Are. H. Luger
Bigger They Come. A. A. Fair

Biggest Holdup. J. F. Dinneen
Biggle's Wharf. Brothers Owen
Bijoux. F. Des Ligneris
Bike Bastards. G. Warren
Bikini Bombshell. B. McKnight
Bill Blunders Through. A. Webb
Bill for Damages. N. Easton
Bill for the Use of a Body. D. Wheatley
Bill Marshall, Turf Sleuth. E. Woodward
Billboard Madonna. E. Trevor
Billiard-Room Mystery. B. Flynn
Billie Finds the Answer. H. C. McNeile
Billikin Courier. T. C. Lewellen
Billion Dollar Body. J. Shallit
Billion Dollar Brain. L. Deighton
Billion Dollar Death. J. Nazel
Billion-Dollar Hold-Up. M. Calland
Billion Dollar Killing. P. E. Erdman
Billion Dollar Sure Thing. P. E. Erdman
Billionaire Mission. J. Rosenberger
Billions. I. K. Martin
Billy Binks, Hero, and other stories. G. Boothby
Billy Hamilton. A. C. Gunter
Billy Mischief, a Regular Trained Detective. Old Sleuth
Billy Preston. Old Sleuth
Billy Rags. T. Lewis
Billy, the Tramp. Old Sleuth
Billy's Bargain. E. Everett-Green
Biltmore Call. V. Siller
Bimbashi Baruk of Egypt. S. Rohmer
Bimini Run. Howard Hunt
Binary. J. Lange
Bind. S. Ellin
Binnacle Jack. Anonymous
Binnacle Jack. M. Mizzen
Bio Blitz. A. Sugar
Biographs of Babylon. G. R. Sims
Birch Dene. W. Westall
Birchwood. J. Banville
Bird. T. Hinde
Bird Cage. E. O'Duffy
Bird-Cage. Kenneth O'Hara
Bird in a Guilt-Edged Cage. Carter Brown
Bird in Last Year's Nest. S. Herron
Bird in the Chimney. D. Eden
Bird in the Hand. G. T. Root
Bird in the Hand. Lee Trench
Bird of Paradise. E. P. Oppenheim
Bird of Prey. V. Canning
Bird of Prey. M. Cumberland
Bird of Strange Plumage. J. L. Rickard
Bird Walking Weather. G. Bagby
Bird Watcher. J. A. Morris
Birdcage. J. Cannan
Birdcage Murders. G. L. Westbie
Birds and other stories. D. Du Maurier
Birds in the Belfry. L. Payne
Bird's Nest. S. Jackson
Birds of a Bloodied Feather. R. Tate
Birds of a Feather. A. Spiller
Birds of a Feather Affair. M. Avallone
Birds of Ill Omen. K. M. Knight
Birds of Prey. M. E. Braddon
Birds of Prey. G. Bronson-Howard
Birds of Prey. A. C. Brown
Birds of Prey. Nicholas Carter
Birds of Prey. G. Fairlie
Birds of Prey. J. R. Saul
Birds of the Night. Austin Moore
Birdwatcher. E. Gordon
Birdwatcher's Quarry. M. Coles
Birth of a Dark Soul. B. Cleeve
Birthday. E. L. Withers
Birthday, Deathday. M. Pentecost
Birthday Gift. U. Curtiss
Birthday Gifts and other stories. G. D. H. Cole
Birthday Murder. Lange Lewis
Birthday Murder. K. Sproul
Birthmark. C. Houghton
Birthmark of Fear. Marsha Alexander
Bishop As Pawn. R. McInerny
Bishop in Check. S. Rattray
Bishop in the Back Seat. Clarissa Watson
Bishop Misbehaves. Frederick Jackson
Bishop Murder Case. S. S. Van Dine
Bishop Must Move. K. Bird
Bishop of Hell. M. Bowen
Bishop Pendle. F. Hume
Bishop's Amazement. D. C. Murray
Bishop's Bible. D. C. Murray
Bishop's Cap. J. L. Linklater
"Bishop's Cap" Murder. J. L. Linklater
Bishop's Crime. H. C. Bailey
Bishop's Emeralds. H. Townley
Bishop's Gambit. T. Cobb
Bishop's Move. L. Hiscott
Bishop's Palace. Jan Alexander
Bishop's Park Mystery. D. Dike
Bishop's Pawn. Ritchie Perry
Bishop's Purse. C. Moffett
Bishop's Scapegoat. T. B. Clegg
Bishop's Secret. F. Hume
Bishop's Sword. N. Berrow
Bismarck Herrings. M. Torrie
Bit and Bridal. H. Smart
Bit of a Shunt Up the River. D. Cory
Bit of Human Nature. D. C. Murray
Bit of Red May. O. Dale
Bitch. G. Brewer

Bite. E. Corder
Bite. C. E. Dibb
Bite of an Apple, and other stories. Nicholas Carter
Bite of the Leech. W. A. MacKenzie
Bite of the Tigress. C. J. Wohlfrom
Bite the Hand. R. Fenisong
Biter. Jack Lang
Biting Fortune. W. Mills
Bits and Pieces. J. C. Masterman
Bits and Pieces. G. Robey
Bits of Broken China. W. E. S. Fales
Bitten by the Tarantula. J. MacLaren-Ross
Bitter Autumn. C. D. Peel
Bitter Conquest. C. Blackstock
Bitter Enders. P. Leslie
Bitter Ending. A. Irving
Bitter Fortune. J. Boland
Bitter Harvest. W. Haggard
Bitter Honey. J. Blackmore
Bitter Honey. D. Noel
Bitter Honeycomb. June Scott
Bitter Is the Fruit. C. J. Collins
Bitter Is the Harvest. T. Craig
Bitter Is the Rind. H. Smart
Bitter Justice. S. Cowan
Bitter Lemon Mob. M. Urquhart
Bitter Love. J. Blackmore
Bitter Love. E. Woodward
Bitter Orange. Desmond Hamill
Bitter Reason. F. Cowen
Bitter Reckoning. J. Payn
Bitter Rubies. J. Storm
Bitter Springs. Clifford King
Bitter Sweet Summer. O. Sinclair
Bitter Tea. G. Black
Bitter Test. J. Templeton
Bittermeads Mystery. E. R. Punshon
Bittern Point. V. MacFadyen
Bitters Wood. U. Nightingale
Black. E. Wallace
Black Abbot. E. Wallace
Black Abolitionist. J. F. Bradley
Black Account. D. Jordan
Black Ace. G. Dilnot
Black Ace. K. Gordon
Black Agent. B. Flynn
Black Alibi. F. Vivian
Black Alibi. C. Woolrich
Black Alice. T. Demijohn
Black Amber. P. A. Whitney
Black Amulet. D. Tracy
Black and Deadly. C. A. Harris
Black and the Red. Elliot Paul
Black and the White. H. Towson
Black Angel. B. Kingsley
Black Angel. C. Woolrich
Black Arab. J. Halstead
Black Arab. Operator 1384
Black Arrows. F. Beeding
Black As He's Painted. N. Marsh
Black Asp. J. L. Hamilton
Black Assassin. J. Readus
Black Attendant. H. McCutcheon
Black August. D. Wheatley
Black Aura. J. Sladek
Black Automatic. W. B. Mowery
Black Autumn. F. Evans
Black Bag. E. Jones-Evans
Black Bag. L. J. Vance
Black Ball. E. D. Pierson
Black Band. Anonymous
Black Band. M. E. Braddon
Black Bar. G. M. Fenn
Black Baroness. D. Wheatley
Black Bartlemy's Treasure. J. Farnol
Black Bat. A. Murray
Black Bat Rides the Sky. G. E. Rochester
Black Beadle. E. C. R. Lorac
Black Bean. Thormanby
Black Beret. P. Fry
Black Bird. Alexander Edwards
Black, Black Hearse. F. Freyer
Black Blood. G. M. Fenn
Black Blood. A. L. Martin
Black Book. G. Bronson-Howard
Black Bottle. R. S. L. Harding
Black Box. T. C. H. Jacobs
Black Box. E. P. Oppenheim
Black Box. M. P. Shiel
Black Box Murder. Anonymous
Black Bread. W. B. M. Ferguson
Black Buck. L. C. Hopkins
Black Bullets. Gavin Holt
Black Burying. H. Carstairs
Black Business. H. Smart
Black Butterfly. W. A. MacKenzie
Black Cabinet. A. Feist
Black Cabinet. P. Wentworth
Black Caesar. T. Strauss
Black Caesar's Clan. A. P. Terhune
Black Camel. E. D. Biggers
Black Camelot. D. Kyle
Black Camels. R. Johnston
Black Camels of Qashran. R. Johnston
Black Candle. C. Randell
Black Cap. Gwyn Evans
Black Cap for Murder. A. Spiller
Black Cap Murder. V. Gunn
Black Card. P. Brebner
Black Card. C. Lys

Black Cargo. W. M. Graydon
Black Carnation. F. Hume
Black Casket. L. Powell
Black Castle. Anonymous
Black Castle. J. J. Farjeon
Black Cat. R. Brome
Black Cat. R. St. Clair
Black Cat. L. Tracy
Black Cats Are Lucky. A. Fielding
Black Chalice. C. Goodall
Black Champagne. G. B. Mair
Black Charade. John Burke
Black Chariots. K. Robeson
Black Chateau. G. E. Rochester
Black Christmas. L. Hays
Black Chronicle. W. E. Hayes
Black Chrysanthemum. A. Murray
Black Circle. C. Baines
Black Circle. Mansfield Scott
Black Cloak Murders. C. Buchanan
Black Coat. Constance Little
Black Coffee. A. Christie
Black Company. W. B. M. Ferguson
Black Connection. Randolph Harris
Black Cop. D. Gober
Black Corridors. Constance Little
Black Cotton Gloves. P. Fry
Black Cripple. R. Keverne
Black Cross. J. M. Walsh
Black Curl. Constance Little
Black Curtain. F. H. Loughead
Black Curtain. C. Woolrich
Black Cypress. F. Crane
Black Dagger. E. S. Brooks
Black Dark Murders. R. O. Saber
Black Death. H. Adams
Black Death. Nick Carter
Black Death. M. Dalton
Black Death. Anthony Gilbert
Black Death. M. McCracken
Black Death. K. Robeson
Black Death. T. H. Stone
Black Destiny. C. Rushton
Black Devil. T. C. H. Jacobs
Black Doctor and other tales of terror and mystery. A. C. Doyle
Black Dog. G. Goff
Black Doll. W. E. Hayes
Black Door. C. F. Adams
Black Door. V. Markham
Black Door. C. Wilcox
Black Dougal. D. Walker
Black Dragon. J. M. Walsh
Black Dream. Constance Little
Black Drop. H. Nisbet
Black Dudley Murder. M. Allingham
Black Eagle. Roland Daniel
Black Eagle. G. H. Teed
Black Eagle Mystery. G. Bonner
Black Eagles Are Flying. F. V. Morse
Black Edged. B. Flynn
Black Emperor. F. Gerard
Black Emperor. G. H. Teed
Black Envelope. D. Frome
Black Exorcist. J. Nazel
Black Express. Constance Little
Black Eye. Constance Little
Black Eye Snapshot. B. Lebhar
Black-Eyed Stranger. C. Armstrong
Black Fame. J. C. Ellis
Black Fan. M. B. O'Reilly
Black Fear. J. Halstead
Black Feather. B. Atlee
Black Fedora. H. Luger
Black Fetish. D. T. Lindsay
Black Finger. P. Newton
Black Fire. L. Goldman
Black Flame. J. Halstead
Black Flamingo. V. Canning
Black Flamingo. K. Norris
Black Fog. C. J. Dutton
Black Folder. D. Brett
Black for a Bride. J. Marie
Black for the Baron. Anthony Morton
Black Fox. H. F. Heard
Black Friday. D. Goodis
Black Fugitive. Eddie Stone
Black Fury. J. Nazel
Black Gambit. Eric Clark
Black Gang. H. C. McNeile
Black Gangster. D. Goines
Black Gangster. D. Steele
Black Garden. C. Arnothy
Black Gardenia. Elliot Paul
Black General. A. Southcott
Black Gestapo. J. Nazel
Black Ghost. R. Carlisle
Black Ghost. J. M. Walsh
Black Ghost of the Highway. G. Linnell
Black Girl Lost. D. Goines
Black-Girl, White-Lady. A. Hyder
Black Glass City. J. Philips
Black Glove. J. G. Sarasin
Black Gloves. Constance Little
Black Goatee. Constance Little
Black Gold. G. Morton
Black Gold. A. P. Terhune
Black Gold Murders. J. B. Ethan
Black Gold of Malverde. R. L. Graves
Black Grandee. J. McCulley
Black Gull Rock. M. Gerard
Black Gunn. L. Pryce

Black Hammer. M. McCracken
Black Hand. W. C. Blakeman
Black Hand. A. B. Reeve
Black Hate. J. Halstead
Black Hawk. J. Reach
Black Hawk. G. E. Rochester
Black Hawthorn. J. S. Strange
Black Hazard. M. Reisner
Black-Headed Pins. Constance Little
Black Heart. M. E. Cooke
Black Heart. S. Horler
Black Hearts Murder. E. Queen
Black Heather. V. Coffman
Black Highway. J. N. Chance
Black-Hill Murder Case. R. Hardinge
Black Hogan Strikes Again. P. Renwick
Black Honey. C. R. Gull
Black Honey. P. Saxon
Black Honeymoon. Constance Little
Black Horse Running. J. Wood
Black Horse Tavern. R. Danton
Black House. R. Bridges
Black House. Constance Little
Black House in Harley Street. J. S. Fletcher
Black Hunchback. G. Verner
Black Hunter. Eddie Stone
Black Ice Score. R. Stark
Black Image. F. Hume
Black Incense. A. M. Williamson
Black Inheritance. J. MacEnery
Black Ink Mystery. Gareth H. Browning
Black Inquisitor. Rex Madison
Black Iris. Constance Little
Black Is Beautiful. B. B. Johnson
Black Is Black. J. Nazel
Black Is the Color. J. Brunner
Black is the Colour of My True Love's Heart. Ellis Peters
Black Is the Colour of My True Love's Heart. C. Reynolds
Black Is the Fashion for Dying. Jonathan Latimer
Black Italian. S. Jepson
Black Jack. G. Watson
Black Jack Rides Again. L. Wibberley
Black Jess, the Outlaw. Old Sleuth
Black John of Halfaday Creek. J. B. Hendryx
Black Joker. I. Ostrander
Black Joss. J. G. Brandon
Black Judas. B. Wilkinson
Black Key. M. S. Michel
Black Knights. G. N. Smith
Black Lace Blackmail. K. T. McCall
Black Lace Hangover. Carter Brown
Black Lady. Constance Little
Black Lake. W. Magnay
Black Land, White Land. H. C. Bailey
Black Leather Barbarians. P. Stadley
Black Leather Case. M. Cronin
Black Leather Murders. D. Rutherford
Black Light. T. Howard
Black Light. G. Kinnell
Black Light. T. Mundy
Black Light. B. Reynolds
Black Limelight. G. Sherry
Black Limousine. W. W. Sayer
Black Lobster. D. Weir
Black Look. M. Butterworth
Black Mafia. P. Rabe
Black Magic. "Capstan"
Black Magic. T. S. King
Black Magician. R. T. M. Scott
Black Mail. D. M. Disney
Black Mamba. A. Broome
Black Man—White Maiden. G. R. Preedy
Black Man, White Man, Dead Man. M. J. Kingsley
Black Mantle. T. P. Prest
Black Marble. J. Wambaugh
Black Maria, M.A. J. Slate
"Black Maria" Mystery. W. J. Bayfield
Black Market. Roland Daniel
Black Market. B. Newman
Black Market Murders. H. Keyworth
Black Market Murders. J. Van Dyke
Black Mask. J. Cournos
Black Mask. E. W. Hornung
Black Mask. A. L. Smith
Black Mass. F. Breton
Black Massacre. L. Derrick
Black Master. M. Grant
Black Mastery. J. Turtle
Black Matador. A. West
Black Midnight. A. Lowing
Black Mirror. B. Benson
Black Mirror. Winifred Duke
Black Mitre. W. M. Duncan
Black Mole. G. E. Rochester
Black Money. R. Macdonald
Black Monk. Anonymous
Black Monk. T. P. Prest
Black Morning. A. Bocca
Black Moth. C. Runyon
Black Motor-Cat. J. B. Harris-Burland
Black Mountain. R. Stout
Black Nail. A. Applin
Black Nat. J. Halstead
Black Night Murders. C. Wells
Black Octopus. G. E. Rochester
Black Onyx Ring. Colin Robertson

Black Opal. A. De Bremont
Black Opal. L. Allan
Black Opal. J. L. Linklater
Black Opal Mine. A. Murray
Black Orchestra. R. Vacha
Black Orchid. G. Goodchild
Black Orchid. N. Meyer
Black Orchid. E. Ronns
Black Orchid. H. Zore
Black Orchids. R. Stout
Black Out. A. O. Pollard
Black Out. D. Whitelaw
Black-Out Crime. G. Chester
Black-Out in Gretley. J. B. Priestley
Black-Out Murder. D. Whitelaw
Black-Out Murders. L. Grex
Black Owl. W. LeQueux
Black Panther. D. Barton
Black Parrot. H. Hervey
Black Parrot. O. Lethbridge
Black Patch. F. Hume
Black Path of Fear. C. Woolrich
Black Pavilion. Augustus Muir
Black Paw. Constance Little
Black Pawn. Bruce Norman
Black Pearl. V. Sardou
Black Pearl and the Vikings. P. O'Donnell
Black Pearl Murders. M. S. Buchanan
Black Pearl of Passion. D. Fay
Black Pearls. J. L. Roberts
Black Piano. Constance Little
Black Pigeon. Anne Austin
Black Plume. D. Madsen
Black Plumes. M. Allingham
Black Police. A. J. Vogan
Black Prophet. F. Hume
Black Rain. G. Simenon
Black Rat. T. A. Plummer
Black Raven. Roland Daniel
Black Renegades. J. Readus
Black Reprieve. D. Sanderson
Black Ribbon Murders. T. A. Plummer
Black Robber. E. Ball
Black Robe. W. Collins
Black Robe. G. Morton
Black Room. C. Short
Black Room. Colin Wilson
Black Rose. G. Croudace
Black Rose Murder. P. McGuire
Black Royalty. A. Mills
Black Bustle. Constance Little
Black Sabbat. J. B. Herman
Black Sadhu. E. P. Thorne
Black Sambo Affair. V. Gielgud
Black Samurai. M. Olden
Black Satchel. H. S. Keeler
Black Scorpion. A. Shannon
Black Sea Caper. Robin Moore
Black Sea Connection. Robin Moore
Black Seven. C. Kendall
Black Shadow. P. Sebastian
Black Shadow. F. A. M. Webster
Black Shadows. A. M. Fenn
Black Sheep. S. P. Hyatt
Black Sheep. B. Spicer
Black Sheep. E. Woodward
Black Sheep. E. Yates
Black Sheep, White Lamb. D. S. Davis
Black Ship. P. Mandel
Black Shrike. I. Stuart
Black Shrouds. Constance Little
Black Shrouds the Bride. P. G. Larbalester
Black Silence. M. Leighton
Black Sister. D. Edgvist
Black Skull. G. Verner
Black Skull Murders. Carlton Ross
Black Sleeves. A. M. Williamson
Black Smith. Constance Little
Black Sombrero Mystery. H. Pink
Black Spear. J. DeVries
Black Spectacles. J. D. Carr
Black Spider. Mark Cross
Black Spider. C. Dawe
Black Spider. S. P. B. Mais
Black Spiders. J. Creasey
Black Spot. K. Robeson
Black Spot. John Ross
Black Spot Mystery. A. Soutar
Black Stage. Anthony Gilbert
Black Stain. G. R. Sims
Black Stamp. Will Scott
Black Star. J. McCulley
Black Star Again. J. McCulley
Black Star's Campaign. J. McCulley
Black Star's Return. J. McCulley
Black Star's Revenge. J. McCulley
Black Stocking. Constance Little
Black Stone. G. F. Gibbs
Black Streak. W. M. Graydon
Black Sunday. Thomas Harris
Black Sunday. A. Kent
Black Sunset. E. P. Thorne
Black Sunshine. Dorothea Martin
Black Swan. Nancy Graham
Black Swan. R. C. Payes
Black Swan. W. Penmare
Black Swastika. J. G. Brandon
Black Tarn. P. W. Wilson
Black Templar. J. Halstead
Black Terrace. K. Kendall

Black Terror. C. Bishop
Black Terror. F. W. Irwin
Black Terror. J. K. Leys
Black Thumb. Constance Little
Black Tide Rising. L. P. Greene
Black Tortoise. F. Viller
Black Tower. P. D. James
Black Trail. E. M. Hall
Black Triangle. H. Somerville
Black Trinity. T. C. H. Jacobs
Black Troopers. J. N. Smith
Black Troopers and other stories. Anonymous
Black Tulip. S. Bate
Black Turret. P. Wynnton
Black Unicorn. June Drummond
Black Uprising. J. Nazel
Black Valley Murders. A. Mallory
Black Vanguard. E. Atiyah
Black Velvet. C. B. Dignan
Black Vendetta. M. Gattzden
Black Venus Contract. P. Atlee
Black Vintage. M. Gerard
Black Vulture. G. Ashcroft
Black Watcher. A. Partridge
Black Weather. B. Roueche
Black Weever. R. Wills
Black Welcome. N. Fitzgerald
Black, White, and Brindled. E. Phillpotts
Black Widow. R. Harrison
Black Widow. P. Quentin
Black Widow. B. Tutton
Black Widow. J. Tobias
Black Widow Weeps. Carter Brown
Black Widower. P. Moyes
Black Widower. A. Riefe
Black Wind. M. Asher
Black Windmill. C. Egleton
Black Wings. M. Dalton
Black Wings Has My Angel. E. Chaze
Black Wolf Mystery. R. J. Diven
Black Work. M. Frederics
Blackadder. G. Croudace
Blackbird. R. Stark
Blackbird Sings of Murder. W. M. Duncan
Blackbirder. D. B. Hughes
Blackboard Jungle. E. Hunter
Blackbourne Hall. E. Grandower
Blackdrop Hall. H. Carstairs
Blacker Than Murder. W. Woolfolk
Blackfingers. J. Cassells
Blackgable Inn. M. Eyre
Blackguard. P. Trent
Blackhall Ghosts. S. Tytler
Blackheath Poisonings. J. Symons
Blackjack Hijack. C. Einstein
Blackladies. E. Everett-Green
Blacklash. J. Brunner
Blacklight. B. Knox
Blackmail. Ruth Alexander
Blackmail. C. Bennett
Blackmail. W. T. Call
Blackmail. V. Chute
Blackmail. J. Goodwin
Blackmail. H. I. Hancock
Blackmail. J. Ironside
Blackmail. R. Mounteney-Jephson
Blackmail. Mark Ross
Blackmail! F. M. White
Blackmail and Old Lace. T. Vail
Blackmail de Luxe. D. Whitelaw
Blackmail Gang. C. Bishop
Blackmail in Blankshire. C. A. Alington
Blackmail in Red. F. Grierson
Blackmail, Inc. R. Kyle
Blackmail Is Murder. Craig Cooper
Blackmail North. P. McCutchan
Blackmailed. A. Applin
Blackmailed. W. LeQueux
Blackmailed Baronet. H. E. Hill
Blackmailed Refugee. A. Parsons
Blackmailer. G. Axelrod
Blackmailer. Roland Daniel
Blackmailer. R. C. Elliott
Blackmailer. R. Fenisong
Blackmailer. E. Klein
Blackmailer. J. Miles
Blackmailer. J. Oakley
Blackmailer. P. Trent
Blackmailer and the Blonde. Leslie Carroll
Blackmailers. H. Cecil
Blackmailers. E. Gaboriau
Blackmailers & Co. J. C. Ellis
Blackmailer's Bluff. Nicholas Carter
Blackman's Wood. E. P. Oppenheim
Blackmarket Brains. K. Hoffman
Blackmoor. J. Trevelyan
Blackout. Mark Andrews
Blackout. H. Aquin
Blackout. Constance Little
Blackout at Rehearsal. M. P. Rea
Blackout Mystery. J. Reach
Blackpool Vanishes. R. H. Francis
Blackshirt. B. Graeme
Blackshirt Again. B. Graeme
Blackshirt at Large. R. Graeme
Blackshirt, Counter-Spy. B. Graeme
Blachshirt Finds Trouble. R. Graeme
Blackshirt Helps Himself. R. Graeme
Blackshirt in Peril. R. Graeme

Blackshirt Interferes. B. Graeme
Blackshirt Meets the Lady. R. Graeme
Blackshirt Mystery. W. M. Graydon
Blackshirt on the Spot. R. Graeme
Blackshirt Passes By. R. Graeme
Blackshirt Saves the Day. R. Graeme
Blackshirt Sees It Through. R. Graeme
Blackshirt Sets the Pace. R. Graeme
Blackshirt Stirs Things Up. R. Graeme
Blackshirt Strikes Back. B. Graeme
Blackshirt Takes a Hand. B. Graeme
Blackshirt Takes the Trail. R. Graeme
Blackshirt the Adventurer. B. Graeme
Blackshirt the Audacious. B. Graeme
Blackshirt Wins the Trick. R. Graeme
Blackstock Affair. F. Bandy
Blackstone. R. Falkirk
Blackstone and the Scourge of Europe. R. Falkirk
Blackstone on Broadway. R. Falkirk
Blackstone Underground. R. Falkirk
Blackstone's Fancy. R. Falkirk
Blackthorn. D. Daniels
Blackthorn. A. J. Fitzgerald
Blackthorn House. J. Rhode
Blacktower. M. Lynch
Blackwater Bayou. Marilyn Austin
Blackwell's Ghost. Angela Gray
Blackwood. J. Radcliffe
Blackwood Cult. T. A. Waters
Blade Is Bright. S. Horler
Blade of Castlemayne. A. Esler
Blade-o'-Grass. B. L. Farjeon
Blade of Light. D. Carpenter
Blag. J. Balham
"Blairmount?" Blinkhoolie
Blair's Attic. J. C. Lincoln
Blame the Baron. Anthony Morton
Blame the Dead. G. Lyall
Blanche. T. P. Prest
Blanche Coningham's Surrender. J. Middlemass
Blanche de Maletroit. A. E. W. Mason
Blanche Fury. J. Shearing
Blanche Heriot. T. P. Prest
Blanco Case. S. Horler
Bland Beginning. J. Symons
Blane Document. N. Rich
Blank Cheque. Richard Brown
Blank Cheque for Murder. O. Beeby
Blank Page. K. C. Constantine
Blank Wall. E. S. Holding
Blanket. A. A. Murray
Blanket. H. Stratton
Blanket of the Dark. B. Healey
Blast of Trumpets. G. Ashe
Blasted Acre. G. Ellinger
Blatchington Tangle. G. D. H. Cole
Blaze at Noon. M. Clare
Blaze of Riot. J. Tucker
Blaze of Roses. E. Trevor
Blazing Affair. M. Avallone
Blazing Garage Crime. A. Blair
Blazing Launch Murder. R. Hardinge
Blazing Star. Constance Rutherford
Bleak House. C. Dickens
Bleak November. R. O'Grady
Bleak Strand. G. K. Hohn
Bled White. I. St. Clair
Bledding Sorrow. Marilyn Harris
Bleeding Hooks. H. Rutland
Bleeding House. Hilda Lawrence
Bleeding Scissors. B. Fischer
Bleke, the Butler. W. LeQueux
Bless the Wasp. John Ross
Blessed Among Women. A. MacLeod
Blessed Plot. E. Berckman
Blessing Way. T. Hillerman
Blessington Method, and other strange tales. S. Ellin
Bleston Mystery. R. M. Kennedy
Blight. J. Creasey
Blighted Heart. T. P. Prest
Blind Alley. G. Simenon
Blind Alley. B. Singer
Blind Alley. James Warwick
Blind Allies. B. Kendrick
Blind Barber. J. D. Carr
Blind Bargain. T. B. Morris
Blind Beak. E. Dudley
Blind Beggar Murder. C. Ryland
Blind Beggar of Bethnal Green and Bessy. Anonymous
Blind Cartridges. W. C. MacDonald
Blind Cave. L. Katcher
Blind Chance. J. James
Blind Chance. B. Kingsley
Blind Chance. Mary Napier
Blind Circle. M. Renard
Blind Corner. D. Yates
Blind Date. Leigh Howard
Blind Date. J. Pattinson
Blind Date for a Private Eye. B. Graeme
Blind Drifts. C. B. Clason
Blind Eyes. M. Peterson
Blind Frog. F. Grierson
Blind Fury. S. Gluck
Blind Gambit. J. Reach
Blind Geese. Winifred Duke
Blind Girl's Buff. E. Berckman
Blind Goddess. E. Toller
Blind Goddess. A. Train

Blind Hypnotist. M. Lovell
Blind Justice. I. L. Cassilis
Blind Justice. H. B. Mathers
Blind Justice. B. Symons
Blind Lead. L. L. Lynch
Blind Love. W. Collins
Blind Man. R. W. Kauffman
Blind Man with a Pistol. C. Himes
Blind Man's Bluff. B. Kendrick
Blind Man's Bluff. R. Rodd
Blind Man's Bluff. E. Toller
Blind Man's Buff. J. Futrelle
Blind Man's Buff. F. Lynde
Blind Man's Buff. A. M. Meadows
Blind Man's Buff. F. Ryerson
Blind Man's Buff. A. Wood
Blind Man's Daughter. Nicholas Carter
Blind Man's Eyes. W. MacHarg
Blind Man's Garden. S. Troy
Blind Man's Mark. B. Palmer
Blind Man's Night. J. Esteven
Blind Man's Secret. C. Brisbane
Blind Marriage, and other stories. G. R. Sims
Blind Miller. C. A. Cookson
Blind Murder. P. Perelli
Blind Obsession. D. Noel
Blind Path. G. Simenon
Blind Pig. J. A. Jackson
Blind Plot. A. Clancy
Blind Policy. G. M. Fenn
Blind Quest. W. Dainton
Blind Rage. P. Rawls
Blind Reckoning. W. Mills
Blind Run. Ken Blake
Blind Saw Murder. H. C. Huston
Blind Search. L. Egan
Blind Side. F. Clifford
Blind Side. N. Cromarty
Blind Side. D. Klein
Blind Side. P. Wentworth
Blind Spot. J. Creasey
Blind Spot. Joseph Harrington
Blind Terror. W. Hughes
Blind Trust Kills. J. P. Wohl
Blind Villain. E. Berckman
Blindfold. L. Fletcher
Blindfold. F. Marryat
Blindfold. A. Melville-Ross
Blindfold. J. L. Rickard
Blindfold. P. Wentworth
Blindfold Mystery. Nicholas Carter
Blindfolded. E. A. Walcott
Blinding Light. C. Collins
Blindman. E. C. Mayne
Blindman's Bluff. M. Carr
Blindman's Marriage. F. Warden
Blindness of Flynn. E. L. Long
Blindpits. Anonymous
Blinkey Morgan, the Detective's Foe. Hawkshaw
Blitzlicht Passage. D. Mason
Blizzard. G. Stone
Blizzard. W. Woodward
Block Busters. L. Cameron
Blockbuster. S. Barlay
Blockade Runners. W. M. Graydon
Blocked Trail. J. McCulley
Blond Baboon. J. Van de Wetering
Blond Spider. V. Brun
Blonde. Carter Brown
Blonde and Beautiful. R. Foster
Blonde and Johnny Malloy. B. Kerr
Blonde and the Boodle. J. T. Story
Blonde at Bay. M. Brody
Blonde, Bad and Beautiful. Carter Brown
Blonde Baggage. M. Holland
Blonde Bait. E. Lacy
Blonde Bait. S. Marlowe
Blonde, Beautiful and—BLAM! Carter Brown
Blonde Betrayer. J. Godey
Blonde Blackmail. B. Sanders
Blonde Body. Michael Morgan
Blonde Bombshell. D. Foster
Blonde Countess. H. O. Yardley
Blonde Cried Murder. J. Creighton
Blonde Cried Murder. B. Halliday
Blonde Died Dancing. K. Roos
Blonde Died First. D. Chambers
Blonde Dynamite. A. Bocca
Blonde for Danger. B. Gray
Blonde for Danger. L. Lambert
Blonde for Danger. M. Perelli
Blonde for Murder. W. B. Gibson
Blonde Gangster. R. Sharp
Blonde Genius. J. T. Edson
Blonde Horror. B. Sarto
Blonde in Black. B. Benson
Blonde in Suite 14. S. Sterling
Blonde Is Dead. J. Dow
Blonde Lady. M. Leblanc
Blonde Madonna. H. D. Dearden
Blonde Menace. Don Martin
Blonde Murder Case. Roland Daniel
Blonde on a Broomstick. Carter Brown
Blonde on Borrowed Time. B. X. Sanborn
Blonde on the Rocks. Carter Brown
Blonde on the Spot. H. Janson
Blonde on the Street Corner. D. Goodis
Blonde Target. R. Reinsmith
Blonde Target. W. Wright

Blonde, the Gangster and the Private Eye. Dale Clark
Blonde Verdict. Carter Brown
Blonde with the Deadly Past. M. Seeley
Blonde Without Escort. B. Perowne
Blonde Wore Black. Peter Chambers
Blondel Parva. J. Payn
Blondes Are My Trouble. Martin Brett
Blondes Are Skin Deep. L. Trimble
Blondes Die Young. Bill Peters
Blondes Don't Cry. M. Mace
Blondes End Up Dead. B. Winter
Blondes' Requiem. Raymond Marshall
Blondie Beg Your Bullet. R. Razio
Blondie Iscariot. E. Lustgarten
Blondie Kiss Your Doom. R. Razio
Blood. Allan Morgan
Blood All Over. Paul Todd
Blood and Blondes. B. Sarto
Blood and Caviare. M. Dekobra
Blood and Gold. R. Severn
Blood and Honey. G. G. Fickling
Blood and Judgment. M. Gilbert
Blood and Sun-Tan. T. C. H. Jacobs
Blood and Thirsty. F. Bonnamy
Blood and Thunder. H. Clevely
Blood and Water. P. De Polnay
Blood Bargain. Michael Bradley
Blood Bath. H. Janson
Blood Bath. B. Rossi
Blood Beast. D. Ballenger
Blood Bond. E. Cave
Blood Bond. H. Curties
Blood Brother, Blood Brother. N. N. Peebles
Blood Brotherhood. R. Barnard
Blood-Brotherhood. A. Murray
Blood Brotherhood. J. Van Der Zee
Blood Brothers. D. Sinclair
Blood Carnelian. J. Raynes
Blood Countess. K. Robeson
Blood Cries for Vengeance. H. Desmond
Blood Debt. S. Jason
Blood Eagle, and other mystery tales. P. H. Emerson
Blood Emerald. V. Blake
Blood Fix. D. Ballenger
Blood Flies Upwards. E. Ferrars
Blood for Breakfast. D. Ballenger
Blood from a Stone. R. S. Wallis
Blood Group O. D. Brierley
Blood Hunt. A. O. Pollard
Blood in the Ashes. W. Wright
Blood in the Bank. N. Brent
Blood in Your Eye. R. P. Wilmot
Blood Innocents. T. H. Cook
Blood Is a Beggar. T. Kyd
Blood Is a Personal Thing. J. Moffat
Blood Kin. B. A. Pauley
Blood, M'Lud. H. Carstairs
Blood Money. C. H. Bullivant
Blood Money. Max Collins
Blood Money. A. Drummond
Blood Money. J. Goodwin
Blood Money. D. Hammett
Blood Money. Jack Lewis
Blood Money. Roy Lewis
Blood Money. F. J. Lowe
Blood Money. P. Malloch
Blood-Money. W. C. Morrow
Blood Money. T. B. Reagan
Blood Money. G. Seton
Blood Money, and other stories. C. Gibbon
Blood Moon. Jan Alexander
Blood Oath. B. Rossi
Blood of an Englishman. J. McClure
Blood of Angels. A. Barker
Blood of Buddha. Harold Ward
Blood of My Brother. C. H. Thames
Blood of October. D. Lippincott
Blood of Strawberries. H. Van Dyke
Blood of the Dragon. E. Ellison
Blood of the North. J. B. Hendryx
Blood of the Vampire. F. Marryat
Blood of Vintage. T. Kyd
Blood on a Harvest Moon. D. Anthony
Blood on a Window's Cross. James Fraser
Blood on Baker Street. A. Boucher
Blood on Biscayne Bay. B. Halliday
Blood on Blue Denim. R. Cooper
Blood on Frisco Bay. J. Flynn
Blood on Her Shoe. Medora Field
Blood on His Hands! M. Afford
Blood on Lake Louisa. B. Kendrick
Blood on My Rug. E. L. Cushing
Blood on My Shadow. A. J. Merak
Blood on My Shoes. Jean Leslie
Blood on My Sleeve. I. Baker
Blood on Nassau's Moon. W. McCully
Blood on Pale Fingers. P. Malloch
Blood on the Beach. H. Holley
Blood on the Black Market. B. Halliday
Blood on the Blonde. G. Jackson
Blood on the Blotter. L. Marshall
Blood on the Boards. W. C. Gault
Blood on the Bosom Devine. T. Kyd
Blood on the Cat. N. Rutledge
Blood on the Common. A. Fuller
Blood on the Curb. J. T. Shaw
Blood on the Desert. P. Rabe
Blood on the Dining Room Floor. G. Stein

Title Index

Blood on the Floor. W. S. Masterman
Blood on the Heather. S. Chalmers
Blood on the Ivy. H. Ellson
Blood on the Knight. L. Thayer
Blood on the Lake. R. Hobart
Blood on the Pavement. Neill Graham
Blood on the River. W. L. Heath
Blood on the Sand. F. Martin
Blood on the Shrine. J. G. Brenter
Blood on the Snow. E. Litvinoff
Blood on the Snow. N. MacKenzie
Blood on the Stars. B. Halliday
Blood on the Stars. N. Morland
Blood on the Stars. A. M. Stein
Blood on the Strip. L. Derrick
Blood on the Yukon Trail. J. B. Hendryx
Blood Pearls of Sulu. D. Del Mar
Blood Pit. M. Carrel
Blood Red. Anthony Morton
Blood-Red Badge. Nicholas Carter
Blood Red Death. M. Bardon
Blood-Red Dream. Michael Collins
Blood Red Gold. G. Blumberg
Blood Red Leaf. W. M. Duncan
Blood Red Oscar. Elsie Lee
Blood Reign of the Dictator. C. Steele
Blood Relations. F. Stewart
Blood Relatives. E. McBain
Blood Ring. K. Robeson
Blood Risk. B. Coffey
Blood Royal. G. Allen
Blood Royal. D. Yates
Blood Ruby. Jan Alexander
Blood Run. Al Conroy
Blood Run East. P. McCutchan
Blood Running Cold. Jonathan Ross
Blood Runs Cold. R. Bloch
Blood Runs Cold. A. B. Cunningham
Blood Runs Cold. L. Eby
Blood Scenario. P. Spain
Blood Secrets. C. Jones
Blood Ship. N. Springer
Blood Sport. D. K. Cohler
Blood Sport. V. Cross
Blood Sport. D. Francis
Blood Sports. P. R. Rothweiler
Blood Stays Red. Austin Stone
Blood Tells. T. Armour
Blood Tide. S. Wernick
Blood Tie. M. L. Settle
Blood Trail. W. H. Baker
Blood Transfusion Murders. M. Propper
Blood Upon the Snow. Hilda Lawrence
Blood Velvet. A. Kennington
Blood Vengeance. M. Carroll
Blood Vengeance. S. Jason
Blood White Rose. B. L. Farjeon
Blood Will Out. M. Carr
Blood Will Tell. G. Bagby
Blood Will Tell. Nicholas Carter
Blood Will Tell. A. Christie
Blood Will Tell. Maude Parker
Blood Will Tell. J. Potts
Blood Wrath. C. Krone
Bloodbath. W. Wingate
Bloodbrothers. R. Price
Bloodhound of the Law. G. S. Trevor
Bloodhounds Bay. W. S. Masterman
Bloodhound's Revenge. W. M. Graydon
Bloodhouse. K. Cook
Bloodline. S. Sheldon
Bloodline to Murder. E. McDowell
Bloodroots Manor. Claudette Nicole
Bloodshed in Bayswater. J. Rowland
Bloodsnarl. I. Watkins
Bloodspoor. J. McVean
Bloodstain. David Alexander
Bloodstained Bokhara. W. C. Gault
Bloodstained Toy. Alice Campbell
Bloodstar. T. Topor
Bloodstone. K. J. Bjorgum
Bloodstone. L. Benedict
Bloodstone. K. E. Wagner
Bloodstone Terror. Nicholas Carter
Bloodthirst. M. Ronson
Bloodwater. J. Crowe
Bloodwealth. Blair Stuart
Bloody Benders. R. H. Adleman
Bloody Bokhara. W. C. Gault
Bloody Boston. L. Derrick
Bloody Chamber. Angela Carter
Bloody Chasm. J. W. De Forrest
Bloody Hand. Anonymous
Bloody Hand. M. Braun
Bloody Instructions. Sara Woods
Bloody Jungle. C. Runyon
Bloody Mama. R. Thom
Bloody Marvelous. J. Rathbone
Bloody Medallion. R. Telfair
Bloody Monday Conspiracy. Ralph Hayes
Bloody Moonlight. F. Brown
'Bloody Murder.' S. C. Mason
Bloody Passage. J. Graham
Bloody Precinct. B. Douglas
Bloody September. C. A. Haddad
Bloody Spur. C. Einstein
Bloody Sun at Noon. G. Beare
Bloody Sunday. F. Scarpetta
Bloody Sunrise. M. Spillane
Bloody Tower. J. Rhode
Bloody Vengeance. J. Ehrlich

Bloody Wednesday. Joel Harrison
Bloody Wig Murders. G. Bagby
Bloody with Spurring. C. Rushton
Bloody Wood. M. Innes
Bloomsbury Treasure. S. Kyle
Bloomsbury Wonder. T. Burke
Blotting Book. E. F. Benson
Blow-Down. L. G. Blochman
Blow for Vengeance. Nicholas Carter
Blow Hot, Blow Cold. Gerald Butler
Blow Hot, Blow Cold. E. Queen
Blow of a Hammer and other stories. Nicholas Carter
Blow out My Torch. J. A. Howard
Blow over the Heart. R. Machray
Blow the Four Winds. H. Arvay
Blow the House Down. J. Blackburn
Blowback. B. Pronzini
Blowdown. C. MacHardy
Blown Away. Hal Kantor
Blowtop. A. Schwartz
Bludgeon. Jim Ryan
Blue Red. Glyn Jones
Blue Blood. A. Thynne
Blue Blood Flows East. D. Glinto
Blue Blood Runs Red. W. E. Johns
Blue Blood Will Out. T. Heald
Blue Bone. M. Woodhouse
Blue Bonnet. Augustus Muir
Blue Bucket Mystery. F. Grierson
Blue Bucket. W. H. Osborne
Blue Bungalow. W. LeQueux
Blue Car Mystery. N. S. Lincoln
Blue Circle. E. Jordan
Blue City. K. Millar
Blue Dahlia. R. Chandler
Blue Days and Fair. H. Gibbs
Blue Death. Michael Collins
Blue Devil Suite. D. Daniels
Blue Diamond. A. Askew
Blue Diamond. P. Costello
Blue Diamond. A. Haynes
Blue Diamond. W. K. Keene
Blue Diamond. Mrs. C. Kernahan
Blue Diamond. L. T. Meade
Blue Door. V. Starrett
Blue Dwarf. P. B. St. John
Blue Envelope. S. Kerr
Blue-Eyed Boy. C. Short
Blue-Eyed Gypsy. Janette Radcliff
Blue-Eyed Manchu. A. Abdullah
Blue Eyes. J. Charyn
Blue Fire. P. A. Whitney
Blue Flames. H. Wales
Blue Flower Mystery. N. Cassera
Blue Geranium. D. Birkley
Blue Germ. M. Swayne
Blue Ghost. B. J. McOwen
Blue Guitar. N. Hasluck
Blue Hammer. R. Macdonald
Blue Hand. M. E. Braddon
Blue Hand. E. Wallace
Blue Harpsichord. D. Keith
Blue Horse of Taxco. K. M. Knight
Blue Hour. J. Godey
Blue Ice. H. Innes
Blue Invective. J. C. Manning
Blue Jean Billy. C. W. Tyler
Blue John Diamond. E. R. Punshon
Blue Key. K. Krause
Blue Kimono Kill. W. J. Sheldon
Blue Knight. J. Wambaugh
Blue Lacquer Box. G. F. Worts
Blue Lamp. W. D. Pelley
Blue Lamp. T. Willis
Blue Leader. W. Wager
Blue Lenses and other stories. D. Du Maurier
Blue Light. G. Stanley
Blue Lightning. G. Baxter
Blue Lights. A. Fredericks
Blue Line Murder. J. Moffatt
Blue Macaw. C. Edwards
Blue Man. T. Atkins
Blue Mandarin. D. Lenton
Blue Marsh. T. R. Bernard
Blue Mascara Tears. J. McKimmey
Blue Mask. J. Cassells
Blue Mask at Bay. Anthony Morton
Blue Mask Strikes Again. Anthony Morton
Blue Mask Victorious. Anthony Morton
Blue Mauritius. V. Warren
Blue Mirror. J. Turner
Blue Mist and Mystery. E. Everett-Green
Blue Moon. W. Wager
Blue Mountains Murderer. F. P. Clune
Blue Movie Murders. E. Queen
Blue Murder. R. L. Bellem
Blue Murder. E. Hale
Blue Murder. B. Halliday
Blue Murder. H. Rutland
Blue Murder. E. Snell
Blue Murder. Colin Watson
Blue Octavo. J. Blackburn
Blue Orchid. H. Zore
Blue Parakeet Murders. R. P. Koehler
Blue Paroquet. E. Y. Miller
Blue Parrot. M. Dekobra
Blue Pavilion. W. Buchan
Blue Pete. L. Allan
Blue Pete and the Kid. L. Allan
Blue Pete and the Pinto. L. Allan

Blue Pete at Bay. L. Allan
Blue Pete Breaks the Rules. L. Allan
Blue Pete: Detective. L. Allan
Blue Pete: Half-Breed. L. Allan
Blue Pete in the Badlands. L. Allan
Blue Pete: Indian Scout. L. Allan
Blue Pete: Outlaw. L. Allan
Blue Pete Pays a Debt. L. Allan
Blue Pete: Rebel. L. Allan
Blue Pete Rides the Foothills. L. Allan
Blue Pete to the Rescue. L. Allan
Blue Pete, Unofficially. L. Allan
Blue Pete Works Alone. L. Allan
Blue Pete's Dilemma. L. Allan
Blue Pete's Vendetta. L. Allan
"Blue Peter." P. Trent
Blue Pheasant. J. Boswell
Blue Poppy. C. Baines
Blue Print for Execution. L. Parker
Blue Print Murders. J. G. Brandon
Blue Rajah Murder. H. MacGrath
Blue Ribbon. W. Irish
Blue Ridge Crime. W. Martyn
Blue Ridge Mystery. Caroline Martin
Blue Room. G. Simenon
Blue Rum. E. Souza
Blue Russell. W. Bryant
Blue Santo Murder Mystery. M. Armstrong
Blue Sash. O. Binns
Blue Scarab. D. G. Adee
Blue Scarab. R. A. Freeman
Blue Sea & Yellow Sun. R. Batchelor
Blue Shadow Mystery. J. H. Chase
Blue Silver. V. Bridges
Blue Spectacles. H. S. Keeler
Blue Spider. A. Mills
Blue Sunshine. K. Johnson
Blue Talisman. F. Hume
Blue Taper. Gimone Hall
Blue Taxi. A. W. Barrett
Blue Vase. Lady A. Scott
Blue Veil. F. Du Boisgobey
Blue Vesuvius. A. Wynne
Blue Waistcoat. L. A. Ryan
Blue Wall. R. W. Child
Blue Water. C. H. Barker
Blue Water Murder. P. Atkey
Blue Wolf. W. L. Amy
Blueback. B. Knox
Bluebeard's Daughter. M. Z. Bradley
Bluebeard's Keys. Gwyn Evans
Bluebeard's Seventh Wife. W. Irish
Bluebeard's Wife. H. Desmond
Bluebolt One. P. McCutchan
Bluebottle. M. Urquhart
Bluefeather. L. Meynell
Blueprint. P. Van Rjndt
Blueprint for Destruction. M. K. Robertson
Blueprint for Larceny. P. Chester
Blueprint for Murder. R. Bax
Blueprint for Terror. B. Temmey
Blueprint to Kill. K. Evans
Blueprints for a Blonde. M. Brody
Blues for a Black Sister. B. B. Johnson
Blues for My Baby. B. Shannon
Blues for the Prince. B. Spicer
Bluethorne. F. Y. McHugh
Bluff. H. Adams
Bluff! H. M. Paull
Bluffer's Luck. W. C. Tuttle
Bluffing of Gaston Leroux. W. Dinner
Blundell's Last Guest. A. P. Terhune
Blunderer. P. Highsmith
Blunt Instrument. G. Heyer
Blunted Sword. D. Divine
Blushing Monkey. R. McDougald
Blye, Private Eye. N. Pileggi
Board Stiff. Robert James
Boarding-House Mystery. E. S. Brooks
Boarding House Mystery. M. Osborne
Boast. M. Donald
Boat-House Riddle. J. J. Connington
Boat Race Murder. R. E. Swartwout
Boat Train Mystery. C. Barry
Bob Bridger, Detective. Anonymous
Bob Covington. A. C. Gunter
Bob Ford, the Slayer of Jesse James. W. B. Lawson
Bob Hits the Headlines. J. J. Farjeon
Bob Martin's Little Girl. D. C. Murray
Bob Younger's Fate. Anonymous
Bob Younger's Fate. E. S. Deane
Boca Grande. L. Singer
Boden's Boy. T. Gallen
Bodies Are Dust. P. J. Wolfson
Bodies Are Where You Find Them. B. Halliday
Bodies Fetch Good Prices. B. Sarto
Bodies in a Bookshop. R. T. Campbell
Bodies in a Cupboard. H. Desmond
Bodies in Bedlam. R. S. Prather
Body. Carter Brown
Body and Passion. Whit Harrison
Body and Soul. A. Dare
Body at Busman's Hollow. F. Hurt
Body at Madman's Bend. A. W. Upfield
Body Beautiful. B. S. Ballinger
Body Beautiful Murder. K. Platt
Body Behind the Bar. C. F. Gregg
Body Behind the Curtain. E. G. Cousins
Body Below. Howard Mason

Body Beneath a Mandarin Tree. F. Crane
Body Blow. K. Hopkins
Body Came Back. B. Halliday
Body Count. P. McCurtin
Body Count. F. Scarpetta
Body Drank Coffee. N. Hill
Body Fell on Berlin. R. Lakin
Body for a Blonde. K. McLeod
Body for Bill. I. S. Shriber
Body for McHugh. J. Flynn
Body for Sale. R. Deming
Body for the Bride. G. Bagby
Body for the Widow. G. Warren
Body Found Stabbed. J. Cameron
Body Goes Round and Round. T. Du Bois
Body in Bedford Square. D. Frome
Body in My Arms. R. Stephenson
Body in the Barrage Balloon. Colin Curzon
Body in the Basket. G. Bagby
Body in the Beck. J. Cannan
Body in the Bed. B. S. Ballinger
Body in the Bed. S. Sterling
Body in the Blue Room. S. Williams
Body in the Boathouse. J. Mack
Body in the Bonfire. C. Bush
Body in the Boot. V. Gunn
Body in the Boudoir. C. E. Vulliamy
Body in the Bridal Bed. R. Shattuck
Body in the Bungalow. J. Corbett
Body in the Bunker. H. Adams
Body in the Car. A. Hodges
Body in the Dawn. C. M. Wills
Body in the Drum Mystery. M. Harvey
Body in the Dumb River. G. Bellairs
Body in the Library. A. Christie
Body in the Pound. O. Martyn
Body in the Road. M. Dalton
Body in the Safe. C. F. Gregg
Body in the Safe. S. Kyle
Body in the Shaft. R. Francis Foster
Body in the Silo. R. A. Knox
Body in the Trawl. A. Glanville
Body in the Turl. D. Frome
Body in Velvet. F. Usher
Body Lies. E. J. Millward
Body Looks Familiar. R. Wormser
Body Lovers. M. Spillane
Body Made Alive. John Marsh
Body Missed the Boat. J. Iams
Body Next Door. E. K. Goldthwaite
Body of a Girl. M. Gilbert
Body of the Crime. L. Heller
Body on Mount Royal. D. Montrose
Body on Page One. D. Ames
Body on the Beach. S. Brackeen
Body on the Beach. J. Decrest
Body on the Beach. R. Hardinge
Body on the Beach. R. Wallace
Body on the Beam. Anthony Gilbert
Body on the Bench. D. B. Hughes
Body on the Bus. L. Hollingsworth
Body on the Floor. N. B. Mavity
Body on the Line. Mary Archer
Body on the Pavement. G. Meyrick
Body on the Sidewalk. Bernice Carey
Body Ran Home. M. Perelli
Body Rolled Downstairs. I. H. Irwin
Body Rub. Mark Andrews
Body Search. A. M. Stein
Body Snatcher. R. L. Stevenson
Body Snatchers. C. Brooks
Body That Came by Post. G. W. Yates
Body That Wasn't Uncle. G. W. Yates
Body to Spare. M. Procter
Body Trade. Theodore Taylor
Body Unidentified. J. Rhode
Body Unknown. B. Graeme
Body Vanishes. V. Gunn
Body Vanishes. Jacquemard-Senecal
Body Was Lonely. B. Shannon
Body Was of No Account. J. C. Cooper
Body Was Quite Cold. R. G. Dean
Bodyguard. R. Reinsmith
Bodyguard Man. Philip Evans
Body's Name Was Jones. P. Jaye
Bodysnatch. J. Hallums
Boffin's Find. R. Thynne
Bogart 48. John Stanley
Bogey Men. R. Bloch
Bogmail. P. McGinley
Bogue's Fortune. J. Symons
Bogus Clew. Nicholas Carter
Bogus Lover. H. Silver
Bogus Tourist-Agency. W. M. Graydon
Boheme Combination. R. Close
Bohemian Girls. F. Warden
Boiled Alive. B. Buckingham
Boka Lives! H. Calvin
Bold Vuccaneer. Seafarer
Bold House Murders. Eugene Franklin
Boldt. T. Lewis
Bolero. M. Pflaum
Bolero Murders. M. Avallone
Bolo the Super-Spy. W. LeQueux
Bolt. J. F. Howard
Bolt. P. R. Shore
Bolt from the Blue. Scott Graham
Bolthole. D. Craig
Bolts and Bars. F. C. V. Harcourt
Bolts from Blue Skies. Nicholas Carter
Bomb. A. Badger

Bomb for Atuna. B. Reade
Bomb Job. H. Kane
Bomb-Makers. W. LeQueux
Bomb Makers. V. Mayhew
Bomb-Shell. M. Leblanc
Bomb Squad. Mark Andrews
Bomb That Could Lip Read. D. Seaman
Bomba, Bomba! S. Putnam
Bombay Mail. L. G. Blochman
Bombay Murder. S. K. Chettur
Bombers. P. Leslie
Bombs Burst Once. G. Church
Bombs from the Murder Wolves. R. J. Hogan
Bombshell. Carter Brown
Bombshell. G. G. Fickling
Bombshell. R. Raine
Bombship. B. Knox
Bonanza Murder Case. C. H. Snow
Bonaparte Kiss. S. Cardiff
Bonaventure. C. Hastings
Boncoeur Affair. H. Wickham
Bond. M. Ehrlich
Bond Grayson Murdered! N. S. Bortner
Bond of Black. W. LeQueux
Bond of Evil. M. Cordell
Bond of Hate. J. Carrick
Bond Street Murder. J. G. Brandon
Bond Street Raiders. J. G. Brandon
Bondage of Brandon. B. Hemyng
Bonded Dead. M. E. Chaber
Bonded Villain. Nicholas Carter
Bone. I. Blair
Bone and a Hank of Hair. L. Bruce
Bone House. W. Butler
Bone Is Pointed. A. W. Upfield
Bone of the Dinosaur. G. D. H. Cole
Bonecrack. D. Francis
Bonegrinder. J. Lutz
Bones. E. Wallace
Bones Don't Lie. C. T. Gardner
Bones in London. E. Wallace
Bones in the Marrow. Josephine Bell
Bones in the Brickfield. M. Burton
Bones in the Sand. K. Royce
Bones in the Wilderness. G. Bellairs
Bones of Contention. E. Candy
Bones of Contention. R. Foley
Bones of Contention. N. Gage
Bones of Frankenstein. D. F. Glut
Bones of Napoleon. J. W. Bellah
Bones of the River. E. Wallace
Bonesetter's Brawl. C. Calderwood
Bonfire Murder. T. A. Plummer
Bonnet Man. G. Weill
Bonnie. H. Barron
Bonnie and Clyde. B. Hirschfeld
Bonus for Murder. J. G. Brandon
Bony and the Black Virgin. A. W. Upfield
Bony and the Kelly Gang. A. W. Upfield
Bony and the Mouse. A. W. Upfield
Bony and the White Savage. A. W. Upfield
Bony Buys a Woman. A. W. Upfield
Boodle. L. Charteris
Boogie Was a Gent. P. Lauben
Book for Banning. N. Easton
Book Her for Murder. M. Brody
Book of All Power. E. Wallace
Book of Bargains. V. O'Sullivan
Book of Changes. R. H. W. Dillard
Book of Master Crimes. M. Hervey
Book of Murder. F. I. Anderson
Book of Murder. R. Cowen
Book of Strange Sins. C. Kernahan
Book of the Crime. E. Daly
Book of the Dead. E. Daly
Book of the Lion. E. Daly
Book with Orange Leaves. H. S. Keeler
Booked for Death. M. Cumberland
Bookmaker's Body. S. Stone
Bookmaker's Crime. A. Steffens Hardy
Books and Crooks. N. Mitzman
Books for the Baron. Anthony Morton
Bookshop Mystery. J. S. Childers
Boom-Time Gold. G. W. Wicking
Boomerang. A. Garve
Boomerang. B. Graeme
Boomerang. W. H. Osborne
Boomerang Clue. A. Christie
Boomerang Conspiracy. M. Stanley
Boomerang Murder. F. Grierson
Boon Companions. June Drummond
Boondocks. D. Lowden
Boothroyd's Mill. E. C. Reed
Bootlaces for Bastion. R. Harrison
Bootleg Angel. E. Mazzaro
Bootlegger. V. Torrio
Bootlegger's Victim. R. C. Armour
Bootless Crime. T. W. Speight
Booty. Douglas Grant
Booty for a Babe. Carter Brown
Border Incident. Jay Flynn
Border Line. W. S. Masterman
Border of Darkness. John Latimer
Border Scourge. B. Mulford
Border Town Girl. J. D. MacDonald
Border Trail. H. Bindloss
Borderlanders. J. Laing
Borderline. J. Keener
Borderline. Vercors
Borderline Case. H. McLeave

Borderline Case. B. Williams
Borderline Cases. C. F. Adams
Borderline Murder. A. Amos
Borderlines. A. Madsen
Borders of Barbarism. Eric Williams
Bored to Death. M. Delving
Borgia Blade. F. Ryerson
Borgia Cabinet. J. S. Fletcher
Borgia Head Mystery. V. Gunn
Borgia Testament. N. Balchin
Boris Story. V. Leigh
Bormann Brief. C. Egleton
Bormann Receipt. M. Duke
Born Bad. Anonymous
Born Beautiful. Keith Campbell
Born Innocent. B. J. Hurwood
Born Loser. Carter Brown
Born Loser. M. Cronin
Born of the Son. G. Wagner
Born Reckless. M. Rogers
Born Survivor. J. K. Lucas
Born to Be Hanged. M. E. Chaber
Born to Be Hanged. P. McGuire
Born to Be Murdered. Dennis Allan
Born to Betray. M. V. Victor
Born to Command. Hero Strong
Born to Die. K. David
Born to Evil. B. Lippincott
Born to Sin. H. L. Gates
Born to Win. M. Roote
Born Victim. H. Waugh
Borneo Patrol. R. Wilkes-Hunter
Bornless Keeper. P. B. Yuill
Boro Council Ramp. P. Urquhart
Borodino Mystery. M. L. Storer
Borough Council Murders. J. Austwick
Borough Treasurer. J. S. Fletcher
Borrow the Night. H. Nielsen
Borrowdale Tragedy. W. J. Dawson
Borrowed Alibi. L. Egan
Borrowed Alibi. M. Murphy
Borrowed Cottage. Alice Campbell
Borrowed Crime. W. Irish
Borrowed Liner. L. Clarke
Borrowed Shield. R. E. Enright
Borrowed Time. M. Shane
Borrower of the Night. Elizabeth Peters
Bosambo of the River. E. Wallace
Boss. J. W. McConaughy
Boss, and How He Came to Rule New York. Alfred Henry Lewis
Boss Man. R. B. Sparkia
Boss of Taroomba. E. W. Hornung
Boss of Terror. K. Robeson
Boss of the Skeletons. W. B. M. Ferguson
Boston Avenger. M. Barry
Boston Belle Meets Murder. J. C. Lenehan
Boston Blackie. J. Boyle
Boston Blitz. D. Pendleton
Boston Bust Out. P. McCurtin
Boston Conspiracy. J. H. Robinson
Boston Crab. F. Usher
Botany Bay. John Lang
Both Sides of the Case. J. Prescot
Both Sides of the Veil. R. Marsh
Botticelli Madonna. R. Cox
Bottle. Anonymous
Bottle of Dust. A. Rutherford
Bottle Organ. R. Masson
Bottle with the Black Label. Nicholas Carter
Bottle with the Green Wax Seal. H. S. Keeler
Bottles of Scented Sweets. M. J. Pemberton
Bottletop Affair. G. Cotler
Bottom Deal. J. Philips
Bottom Line. F. Knebel
Bottom Line. R. Sapir
Bottom of Suez. G. H. Teed
Bottom of the Bottle. G. Simenon
Bottom of the Matter. A. Burr
Bottom of the Well. F. U. Adams
Boudapesti 3. D. Lowden
Boudoir Murder. M. Propper
Boulevard. L. H. Brennan
Boulevard Mutes. Nicholas Carter
Boulevard Nights. D. Gram
Bound by a Spell. H. Conway
Bound by Honor. C. Virmonne
Bound to Die. Bill Turner
Bound to John Company. M. E. Braddon
Bound to Kill. J. Blackburn
Bound to Win. H. Smart
Bound Together. H. Conway
Bounty Hunter. M. Franklin
Bouquet of Clean Crimes and Neat Murders. H. Slesar
Bourbon Street. G. H. Otis
Bourne Identity. R. Ludlum
Bournewick Murders. L. Blow
Bout with the Mildew Gang. S. Fowler
Bow Street Brangle. M. Sebastian
Bow Street Gentleman. M. Sebastian
Bow Street Terror. T. A. Waters
Bowerings' Breakwater. P. McCutchan
Bowery Birdie. B. Sarto
Bowery Murder. W. K. Smith
Bowling Green Murders. H. Woodward
Bowman at a Venture. H. Howard
Bowman on Broadway. H. Howard
Bowman Strikes Again. H. Howard

Title Index

Bowman Test. A. J. Elias
Bowman Touch. H. Howard
Bowmanville Break. S. Shelley
Bowsham Puzzle. J. Habberton
Bowstring Murders. Carr Dickson
Box. P. Rabe
Box for a Long Journey. E. E. Cameron
Box from Japan. H. S. Keeler
Box Hill Murder. J. S. Fletcher
Box of Doom. G. Verner
Box of Secrets. M. Crossley
Box Office Murders. F. W. Crofts
Box 100. F. Leonard
Box with Broken Seals. E. P. Oppenheim
Boxing Mystery. Gregory Wilson
Boxwood Maze. B. Plagemann
Boy at the Bank. A. Philips
Boy Behind the Gun. C. E. Blaney
Boy Detective. Anonymous
Boy Detective. C. E. Blaney
Boy Detective. Old Sleuth
Boy Fugitive. Old Sleuth
Boy in the Pool. C. R. Bittle
Boy on a Chain. R. Parker
Boy on a Dolphin. D. Divine
Boy Scout's Craig Kennedy. A. B. Reeve
Boy Who Followed Ripley. P. Highsmith
Boy Who Invented the Bubble Gun. P. Gallico
Boy with a Sling. Jonathan Wade
Boy Without a Memory. J. W. Bobin
Boys from Brazil. I. Levin
Boys of Red House. E. Everett-Green
Brace for the Law. Marsden Richards
Brace of Rogues. N. Islay
Brackenridge Enigma. L. Geoghegan
Brackenroyd Inheritance. E. Lindley
Brackenthorpe. K. A. Shoesmith
Bracknell's Law. W. Hildick
Brad Dolan's Blonde Cargo. W. Fuller
Brad Dolan's Miami Manhunt. W. Fuller
Braddigan Murder. I. Ostrander
Bradfield Case. J. Graystone
Bradford Business. Angus Ross
Brading Collection. P. Wentworth
Bradmoor Murder. M. D. Post
Braes of Yarrow. C. Gibbon
Braganza Pursuit. S. Neilan
Brahmin Arrangement. A. Tully
Brain and Ten Fingers. G. Kersh
Brain Drain. R. Sapir
Brain Drain Docket. S. Dave
Brain Guy. B. Appel
Brain Master. V. Van Der Elst
Brain of Paul Menoloff. John Marsh
Brain Robbers. H. Munro
Brain Scavengers. P. Edwards
Brain Trust Murder. Diplomat
Brain Twister. Mark Phillips
Brain-Waves and Death. W. Rich
Brainfire. C. Black
Brains Trust for Murder. A. Spiller
Brainstorm. Reginald Campbell
Brainwash. J. Wainwright
Brainwashed. Martin Thomas
Brainwrack. K. Pedler
Bramble Bush. D. Duncan
Branch Bearers. G. Petrie
Branch for the Baron. Anthony Morton
Branches of Evil. M. J. Kinglsey
Brand for the Burning. H. McCutcheon
Brand Image. H. Janson
Brand Inheritance. Dorothy Fletcher
Brand of Cain. G. Norway
Brand of Fear. B. Lang
Brand of Silence. Harrington Strong
Brand of Silence. F. M. White
Brand of the Beast. Michael Lewis
Brand of the Broad Arrow. A. Griffiths
Brand of the Crook. F. Ramsdale
Brand of the Metal Maiden. B. House
Brand of the Werewolf. K. Robeson
Brand X. C. Brand
Branded. G. Biss
Branded Hand. M. O. Rolfe
Branded Prince. W. Chesney
Branded Spy. O. Merland
Branded Spy Murders. W. W. Mason
Branded Woman. Wade Miller
Brandenburg Affair. J. D. White
Brandenburg Concerto. D. Williams
Brandenburg Hotel. P. G. Winslow
Brandon Affair. C. Whited
Brandon Case. J. J. Connington
Brandon Coyle's Wife. E. Southworth
Brandon in New York. V. Warren
Brandon Is Missing. Dennis Allan
Brandon Returns. V. Warren
Brandon Takes Over. V. Warren
Brandy for a Hero. W. O'Farrell
Brandy for the Parson. R. Foxall
Brandy on the Rocks. Maryl James
Brandy Pole. J. N. Chance
Brangwyn Mystery. D. C. Murray
Brannington's Leopard. F. Webb
Brant Adams, the Emperor of Detectives. Anonymous
Brass Bed. F. Flora
Brass Bound Book. J. Letton
Brass Bowl. L. J. Vance
Brass Chills. H. Pentecost
Brass Cupcake. J. D. MacDonald

Brass Diamonds. B. Sandberg
Brass Go-Between. O. Bleeck
Brass Gong Tree. J. W. Bellah
Brass Halo. J. Webb
Brass Key. F. Swann
Brass Knocker. E. Rathbone
Brass Knuckle. L. Grex
Brass Knuckles. F. Gruber
Brass Monkey. H. Whittington
Brass Rainbow. Michael Collins
Brass Ring. L. Padgett
Brass Shroud. B. Cassiday
Brass Target. F. Nolan
Brassbound. M. D. Bickel
Brat. G. Brewer
Brat Farrar. J. Tey
Brave, Bad Girls. T. B. Dewey
Brave Cannot Yield. I. MacKintosh
Brave Heart of Youth. K. Lindsay
Brave Interlude. G. Goodchild
Brave Little Woman. M. A. Denison
Bravo Charlie. C. M. Filgate
Bravo 9. W. B. Day
Bravo of London. E. Bramah
Braydon Mystery. E. Healey
Brazen. Carter Brown
Brazen Bull. G. Kersh
Brazen Confession. C. F. Gregg
Brazen Head. L. A. Knight
Brazen Seductress. H. Janson
Brazen Tongue. G. Mitchell
Brazilian Sleigh Ride. R. L. Fish
Brazilian Stardust. M. McEvoy
Breach of Fate. J. P. Evans
Breach of Reason. E. H. John
Breach of Security. M. Penoyre
Breach of Trust. W. M. Graydon
Bread. E. McBain
Bread and a Stone. A. Bessie
Bread and Olives. P. Arundale
Bread for the Dead. B. Carson
Bread of Deceit. M. B. Lowndes
Breadfruit Lotteries. R. Elman
Break. J. Giovanni
Break. B. Mather
Break a Leg. L. DuBreuil
Break for a Lovely. H. Janson
Break for Summer. L. Meynell
Break in the Circle. P. Loraine
Break in the Line. B. Mather
Break of Day. B. King
Break-Out. O. J. Currington
Break Out. W. McNeilly
Break the Toff. J. Creasey
Break-Through. P. Malloch
Breakaway. Lionel Black
Breakaway. E. Cannon
Breakdown. J. Boland
Breakdown. P. Marsh
Breakdown. James Preston
Breaker of Laws. W. P. Ridge
Breaker of Ships. F. Sleath
Breakers Ahead. A. M. Barbour
Breakfast for Three. Marguerite Bryant
Breakfast with a Corpse. Max Murray
Breakheart Pass. Alistair MacLean
Breaking Point. B. Copper
Breaking Point. D. Du Maurier
Breaking Point. A. A. Flint
Breaking Point. W. Hewlett
Breaking Point. L. Meynell
Breaking Point. K. Spore
Breaking Strain. J. Masters
Breaking the Shackles. F. Barrett
Breaking the Shell. Joseph Norwood
Breakthrough. M. Urquhart
Breastplate for Aaron. S. Harvester
Breath of Brimstone. Anthea Fraser
Breath of Murder. W. M. Duncan
Breath of Scandal. E. Balmer
Breath of Suspicion. H. Desmond
Breath of Suspicion. E. Ferrars
Breath of Suspicion. W. LeQueux
Breathe No More. C. Franklin
Breathe No More. M. Randolph
Breathe No More, My Lady. H. Bailey
Breathe No More, My Lady. E. Lacy
Brecon Castle. C. Farr
Bred in the Bone. J. Payn
Bred in the Bone. E. Phillpotts
Bred to Kill. Martin Thomas
Breed of the Beverleys. S. Horler
Breezy Frank. Old Sleuth
Bren Hardy Again. W. J. Elliott
Bren Hardy, Tough Dame. W. J. Elliott
Brenda. L. Zane
Brenda Gets Married. Roy Vickers
Brenda Yorke, and other tales. M. C. Hay
Brenda's Murder. T. Wells
"Brent"—of Bleak House. T. A. Plummer
Bressant. J. Hawthorne
Bressio. R. Sapir
Bretherton. W. F. Morris
Brethren of the Axe. J. Somers
Brethren of the Compass. J. M. Walsh
Breton Sisters. G. Simenon
Brezhnev Memo. M. Marcus
Briar Patch. C. Blackstock
Briar Rose. C. N. Williamson
Briarcliff Manor. S. A. Salvato
Briarlea. E. Zumwalt
Briarwood. K. Ashby

Bribe Was Beautiful. Carter Brown
Bric-a-Brac Man. R. H. Greenan
Brickbats for Bastian. R. Harrison
Bricklayer's Arms. J. Rhode
Bricks upon Dust. P. Tabori
Bridal Bed Murders. A. E. Martin
Bridal Eve. E. Southworth
Bridal Path. N. Tranter
Bride Brings Death. Darby St. John
Bride by Candlelight. D. Eden
Bride Dined Alone. V. Kelsey
Bride for Arundel. Jan Daniels
Bride for Bedivere. Hilary Ford
Bride for Bombay. J. R. Warren
Bride for Hampton House. H. Waugh
Bride from the Bush. E. W. Hornung
Bride from the Desert. G. Allen
Bride from the Sea. G. Boothby
Bride in Black. A. Askew
Bride in Blue. J. Rees
Bride Laughed Once. M. K. Sanders
Bride of a Day. F. Du Boisgobey
Bride of a Moment. C. Wells
Bride of a Stranger. Patricia Maxwell
Bride of Alderman. M. Neilson
Bride of an Evening. E. Southworth
Bride of Cairngore. J. F. Webb
Bride of Chance. V. Blake
Bride of Darkness. Margery Lawrence
Bride of Death. N. Marsh
Bride of Death. M. Reisner
Bride of Death. K. Wolffe
Bride of Devil's Leap. S. Shulman
Bride of Donnybrook. L. Ames
Bride of Doom. Harriet Gray
Bride of Dutton Market. M. Leighton
Bride of Emersham. L. Lance
Bride of Fu Manchu. S. Rohmer
Bride of Fury. R. C. Payes
Bride of Gaylord Hall. S. O'Brien
Bride of Infelice. A. L. Halstead
Bride of Invercoe. C. Massey
Bride of Kilkerran. K. Westcott
Bride of Lenore. C. Kavanaugh
Bride of Llewellyn. E. Southworth
Bride of Lowther Fell. M. Forster
Bride of Menace. A. Barron
Bride of Misfortune. V. Blake
Bride of Moat House. P. Curtis
Bride of Newgate. J. D. Carr
Bride of Pendorric. V. Holt
Bride of Raven Island. E. Orford
Bride of Tancred. D. Pearson
Bride of Terror. E. Bond
Bride of the Dark Castle. Dorine Moore
Bride of the Dullahan. S. Wagner
Bride of the Kalahari. F. H. Rose
Bride of the Shadows. L. M. Jansen
Bride of the Sun. G. Leroux
Bride of the Tomb. A. M. Miller
Bride of the Unliving. L. Churchill
Bride of the Wolf. W. E. Groves
Bride Regrets. M. Carleton
Bride That Got Away. S. Truss
Bride Wears Black. W. H. L. Crauford
Bride Wore Black. C. Woolrich
Bride Wore Weeks. H. Janson
Bridegroom. C. V. McFadden
Bride's Bouquet. K. Gordon
Bride's Castle. P. W. Wilson
Bride's Fate. E. Southworth
Bride's Madness. A. Upward
Bride's Mirror. M. Turnbull
Brides of Bellenmore. A. Maybury
Brides of Doom. M. Richmond
Brides of Friedberg. Gwendoline Butler
Brides of Lucifer. M. Lynch
Brides of Mertonbridge Hall. H. C. McNeile
Brides of Saturn. Marilyn Ross
Brides of Solomon and other stories. G. Household
Brides Ransom. S. Clausse
Bridge House. L. Crosby
Bridge of Asses. J. Gautier
Bridge of Fear. D. Eden
Bridge of Lions. H. Slesar
Bridge of Magpies. G. Jenkins
Bridge of Sand. F. Gruber
Bridge of Strange Music. J. Blackmore
Bridge of Wonder. Margery Lawrence
Bridge Players. C. R. Gull
Bridge That Went Nowhere. R. L. Fish
Bridge to Nowhere. L. R. Humes
Bridge to the Moon. A. Maybury
Bridge to Vengeance. Winston Graham
Bridgeport Dagger. J. Milbrook
Brief Candle. A. Spiller
Brief Candles. F. Gaite
Brief Case of Murder. P. Laing
Brief for O'Leary, and two other episodes in his career. B. Graeme
Brief Return. M. G. Eberhart
Brief Suspicion. Patricia Gordon
Brief Tales from the Bench. H. Cecil
Brierfield Tragedy. R. F. Redd
Brig Jane May. F. Marlowe
Brigand. T. P. Prest
Brigand. E. Wallace
Brigand's Secret. W. M. Graydon
Briggs Investigates. D. MacDonald
Bright Adventure. G. Rose

Bright Angel. A. Wood
Bright As a Diamond. A. Allyson
Bright Blue Death. Nick Carter
Bright Cantonese. A. Cordell
Bright Corner. J. B. Priestley
Bright Danger. H. M. Kahler
Bright Day. M. Hocking
Bright Deadly Summer. Barbara James
Bright Eyes of Danger. J. M. Scott
Bright Face of Danger. J. Fast
Bright Face of Danger. L. Meynell
Bright Face of Danger. R. Ormerod
Bright Green Waistcoat. P. Fry
Bright Lights. R. O. Chipperfield
Bright Lights, Dark Rooms. D. Nemec
Bright Like Blood. D. Rowden
Bright Morning. Rona Randall
Bright Nemesis. J. Gunther
Bright Orange for the Shroud. J. D. MacDonald
Bright Promise. J. Lukens
Bright Red Business Men. P. McCutchan
Bright Road to Fear. R. M. Stern
Bright Serpent. J. M. Fox
Bright Star of Danger. W. Chambers
Brighter Buccaneer. L. Charteris
Brightlight. T. Bernard
Brighton Alibi. A. Mills
Brighton Beach Mystery. C. Kingston
Brighton Belle. A. La Bern
Brighton Belle and other stories. Francis King
Brighton Monster and others. G. Kersh
Brighton Murder Trial. B. Hamilton
Brighton Mystery. B. Hemyng
Brighton Rock. G. Greene
Brighton Tragedy. G. Boothby
Brimstone. R. L. Duncan
Brimstone Red. D. Keene
Bring Back Her Body. S. Brock
Bring 'Em Back Dead! David Hume
Bring Him Back Dead. D. Keene
Bring Me Another Corpse. P. Rabe
Bring Me Another Murder. W. Chambers
Bring Me My Bow. M. Moiseiwitsch
Bring the Bride a Shroud. D. B. Olsen
Brink. A. J. Rees
Brink of Disaster. G. Cullingford
Brink of Murder. H. Nielsen
Brink of Silence. G. M. Jay
Brink's. N. Behn
Bristol Affair. H. Seymour
British Museum Mystery. W. Jardine
Brittany Stones. Lynna Cooper
Brittle Thread. D. Hall
Britz of Headquarters. M. Barber
Brixham Manor Mystery. E. S. Brooks
Broad Highway. J. Farnol
Broadcast. J. Mackworth
Broadcast Murder. "Capstan"
Broadcast Murders. F. Smith
Broadcast Mystery. W. LeQueux
Broads Don't Scare Easy. H. Janson
Broadway Bab. J. McCulley
Broadway Bob, the Bounder Detective. Anonymous
Broadway Butterfly Murders. T. Bliss
Broadway Cross. Nicholas Carter
Broadway Jungle. Norma Lee
Broadway Murders. E. J. Doherty
Broadway Murders. R. Wallace
Broadway Racket. W. R. Hutton
Broadway Virgin. L. Bull
Brock. G. Kersh
Brocken Spectre. Karen Campbell
Brocklebank Riddle. H. Wales
Broderick. W. Heffernan
Broke of Covenden. J. C. Snaith
Broken Alibi. T. C. H. Jacobs
Broken Angel. F. Mahannah
Broken Bars. Nicholas Carter
Broken Blossoms. T. Burke
Broken Body. F. Mahannah
Broken Bond. Nicholas Carter
Broken Bonds. H. Smart
Broken Boy. J. Blackburn
Broken Branch. Keith Campbell
Broken Circle. R. Goyne
Broken Circle. M. Saxton
Broken Doll. A. Kent
Broken Doll. J. Webb
Broken Engagement. E. Southworth
Broken Face Murders. D. L. Teilhet
Broken Faith. I. D. Hardy
Broken Fang. U. Key
Broken Fetter. J. K. Leys
Broken Glass. E. Kyle
Broken Heart. Mary Bennett
Broken Honeymoon. C. H. Bullivant
Broken Idol. A. Sergeant
Broken Jigsaw. P. Somers
Broken Key. M. L. Roby
Broken Knife. T. C. H. Jacobs
Broken Ladders. A. Soutar
Broken Law. J. B. Harris-Burland
Broken Marriage. S. Murray
Broken Memory. F. M. White
Broken Men. V. Gielgud
Broken Necks and other stories. B. Hecht
Broken Net. H. Bindloss
Broken O. C. Wells
Broken on Crime's Wheel. Nicholas Carter

Broken Pen. J. K. Stafford
Broken Penny. J. Symons
Broken Pledges. E. Southworth
Broken Promise. E. A. Rife
Broken Ramparts. J. Robb
Broken River. J. Hawkins
Broken Rosary. G. Johnson
Broken Seal. H. Hill
Broken Seal. Dora Russell
Broken Shield. B. Benson
Broken Sphinx. K. Kimbrough
Broken Stirrup-Leather. C. Granville
Broken Sword. M. Gerard
Broken Sword. A. Mills
Broken Tapestry. Rona Randall
Broken Thread. W. LeQueux
Broken Three. K. Detzer
Broken to Harness. E. Yates
Broken Toy. Arthur MacLean
Broken Trail. H. Bindloss
Broken Trail. Nicholas Carter
Broken Trail. A. Murray
Broken Trust. T. A. Plummer
Broken Vase. R. Stout
Broken Vase Mystery. M. Plum
Broken Waters. F. Packard
Broken Way. P. Trent
Broken Window. E. Booth
Broker. Max Collins
Broker's End. L. F. Booth
Broker's Wife. Max Collins
Bronkhurst Case. T. C. H. Jacobs
Bronsville Massacre. B. Toler
Bronze Bell. L. J. Vance
Bronze Buddha. C. L. Daniels
Bronze Claws. P. Kruger
Bronze Door. Augustus Muir
Bronze Face. W. LeQueux
Bronze Hand. C. Wells
Bronze Heist. M. F. Callan
Bronze Mermaid. P. Ernst
Bronze Perseus. S. B. Hough
Brood of Folly. M. Erskine
Brood of the Witch-Queen. S. Rohmer
Brooding House. Alice Brennan
Brooding Lake. D. Eden
Brooding Mansion. P. Warren
Brooding Mist. Rose Dana
Brooding Wild. R. Cullum
Brookham Mystery. E. De Wil
Brooklands Mystery. W. B. Baldry
Brooklands Mystery. P. Urquhart
Brooklyn Angel. M. Hervey
Brooklyn Moll Shoots Bedmate. Griff
Brooklyn Murders. G. D. H. Cole
Broomstick. I. Karlova
Broomstick in the Hall. J. Blackmore
Broomsticks over Flaxborough. Colin Watson
Brother and Sister. M. Nickolay
Brother Berserk. J. W. Hanson
Brother Cain. P. Capon
Brother Cain. S. Raven
Brother Death. J. Lodwick
Brother for Hugh. M. Coles
Brother Orchid. L. Brady
Brother Rat. N. Karta
Brother Rogue and Brother Saint. T. Gallon
Brother Sinister. C. Bramwell
Brother Spy. T. C. H. Jacobs
Brother Wolf. B. Reynolds
Brotherhood. L. J. Carlino
Brotherhood. P. Trent
Brotherhood. Alan Williams
Brotherhood of Death. Nicholas Carter
Brotherhood of Death. G. Stanley
Brotherhood of Freedom. Dick Stewart
Brotherhood of Satan. L. Q. Jones
Brotherhood of the Seven Kings. L. T. Meade
Brotherhood of Velvet. D. Karp
Brotherly Love. P. Trent
Brothers and Sisters Have I None. J. Usher
Brothers Brannigan. H. E. Helseth
Brothers in Arms. H. H. Kirst
Brothers in Blood. P. D. Ballard
Brothers in Law. H. Cecil
Brothers Karamazov. J. Copeau
Brothers Karamazov. F. Dostoevskii
Brothers Keepers. A. Storey
Brothers Keepers. D. E. Westlake
Brothers of Benevolence. J. Cassells
Brothers of Judgment. W. M. Duncan
Brothers of Silence. F. Gruber
Brothers of the Chain. George Griffith
Brothers of the People. F. Whishaw
Brothers of the Thin Wire. F. Pitt
Brothers Rico. G. Simenon
Brothers Sackville. G. D. H. Cole
Brought in Dead. Harry Patterson
Brought to Bay. Nicholas Carter
Brought to Bay. J. M'Govan
Brought to Bay. M. Pereira
Brought to Bay. R. H. Savage
Brought to Light. E. Punshon
Brought to Light. T. W. Speight
Brought to the Mark. Nicholas Carter
Brown Book. J. B. Harris-Burland
Brown Mask. P. Brebner
Brown Murder Case. Roland Daniel

Brown Paper Twice. C. Davy
Brown Portmanteau and other stories. Curtis Yorke
Brown Princess. M. V. Victor
Brown Suede Jacket. P. Fry
Browne Fights the Fifth Column. M. Poole
Browne Follows the Clue. M. Poole
Browne of the Secret Service. M. Poole
Browne's £50,000 Mystery. M. Poole
Browne's First Case. M. Poole
Brownie's Plot. T. Cobb
Browning Touch. D. Rohan
Browns of the Yard. A. Brock
Brownstone Gothic. E. Shenkin
Brownstone House. R. Foley
Brownsville Murders. B. S. Keirstead
Bruce Angelo. Anonymous
Bruce Angelo, the City Detective. Old Sleuth
Bruce Douglas, A Man of the People. R. A. Gunn
Bruce Lee Lives? M. Caulfield
Brumblingham Hall. J. Blyth
Brunettes Are Dangerous. Roland Daniel
Brunettes Are No Better. S. Coburn
Brush Creek Murders. C. H. Snow
Brush of Death. James Warren
Brush with a Baby. M. McLoughlin
Brush with Death. S. Pim
Brush with Fate. C. Dawe
Brussels Dossier. W. H. Baker
Brutal Kook. M. Avallone
Brutal Question. O. W. Bayer
Brutal Years. G. Ledig
Brute. G. Des Cars
Brute. F. A. Kummer
Brute. D. Newton
Brute in Brass. H. Whittington
Bubble Moon. R. Bridges
Bubble Reputation. P. C. Wren
Bubbles. M. Foster
Bubbles We Buy. A. Jones
Buccaneer in Spats. A. Abdullah
Buccaneer's Parrot. J. Courage
Buccaneer's Pride. B. Bolt
Buchanan of "The Press." S. Bent
Bucharest Ballerina Murders. V. M. Mason
Bucholz and the Detectives. A. Pinkerton
Bucket in a Well. H. Willett
Buckhorn Murder Case. C. H. Snow
Buckingham Palace Connection. T. Willis
Buckled Bag. M. R. Rinehart
Bucks. P. Chandler
Bucks County Idyll. R. J. Seidman
Buckshot Range. W. C. Tuttle
Budapest Action. J. Rosenberger
Budapest Parade Murders. V. M. Mason
Budapest Tradeoff. R. Carroll
Buddha of Fleet Street. F. Grierson
Buddha's Secret. Roland Daniel
Buenos Aires Affair. M. Puig
Buffalo Box. F. Gruber
Buffalo Hook. Richard Butler
Bugged for Murder. E. Lacy
Bugles Blowing. N. Freeling
Build Me a Blonde. A. Rocco
Build My Gallows High. G. Homes
Build My Gallows High. R. B. Sparkia
Builders of Ships. M. Leighton
Builders of the Black Empire. G. Stockbridge
Building Estate Murder. P. Urquhart
Built for Trouble. A. Fray
Bulgarian Exchange. A. Grey
Bull Moose. R. Cullum
Bulldog and Rats. M. Allain
Bulldog Breed. G. E. Rochester
Bulldog Drummond. H. C. McNeile
Bulldog Drummond and the Female of the Species. H. C. McNeile
Bulldog Drummond at Bay. H. C. McNeile
Bulldog Drummond Attacks. G. Fairlie
Bulldog Drummond Meets a Murderess. H. C. McNeile
Bulldog Drummond on Dartmoor. G. Fairlie
Bulldog Drummond Returns. H. C. McNeile
Bulldog Drummond Stands Fast. G. Fairlie
Bulldog Drummond Strikes Back. H. C. McNeile
Bulldog Drummond's Third Round. H. C. McNeile
Bulldog Has the Key. F. W. Bronson
Bulldog Murder. J. K. Tarpey
Bullet for a Beast. R. Simons
Bullet for a Blonde. P. Kruger
Bullet for a Star. S. Kaminsky
Bullet for Charles. H. Walter
Bullet for Cinderella. J. D. MacDonald
Bullet for Fidel. Nick Carter
Bullet for Georgie. E. M. Skehan
Bullet for Midas. N. Morland
Bullet for My Baby. Carter Brown
Bullet for My Lady. M. Mara
Bullet for My Love. O. R. Cohen
Bullet for Pretty Boy. M. Avallone
Bullet for Rhino. C. Witting
Bullet for the Bride. J. Messmann
Bullet for the Countess. S. Horler
Bullet for the Shah. Alan Williams
Bullet for Your Dreams. D. Von Elsner
Bullet in His Cap. Robert Fleming

Title Index

Bullet in the Ballet. C. Brahms
Bullet in the Cornice. M. Beckett
Bullet Proof. R. Angel
Bullet Proof. A. Dean
Bullet Proof. F. Kane
Bullet-Proof Man. A. Riefe
Bullet-Proof Martyr. J. A. Howard
Bullet Train. P. Rance
Bullets and Brown Eyes. M. Corrigan
Bullets Are Final. E. Kennedy
Bullets Are My Business. J. B. West
Bullets Are Trumps. D. Reid
Bullets Bite Deep. David Hume
Bullets for a Blonde. W. Oursler
Bullets for Brandon. V. Warren
Bullets for Breakfast. J. M. Walsh
Bullets for Macbeth. Marvin Kaye
Bullets for Snoopers. Griff
Bullets for the Bridegroom. D. Dodge
Bullets in the Bush. E. Norwood
Bullets Make Holes. John Bentley
Bullets Speak Louder. R. Marlowe
Bullets to Baghdad. Philip Chambers
Bullion. M. Woodman
Bullion Mystery. Nicholas Carter
Bullitt. R. L. Pike
Bullitzer Baby Case. J. Sword
Bull's Eye. M. Kennedy
Bulls Like Death. M. Fitt
Bulls of Ronda. E. P. Benson
Bullshot Crummond. R. House
Bulton's Revenge. H. C. McNeile
Bump and Grind Murders. Carter Brown
Bump in the Night. Colin Watson
Bunce. M. Delarrabeiti
Bunch of Crooks. Roland Daniel
Bundle for the Toff. J. Creasey
Bundle of Clews. Nicholas Carter
Bundle of Lies. L. Castletown
Bundle of Nerves. Joan Aiken
Bungalow Crime. P. Urquhart
Bungalow Mystery. A. Haynes
Bungalow of Dead Birds. G. Varney
Bungalow on the Roof. A. Abdullah
Bungalow Tragedy. W. J. Bayfield
Bungalow Under the Lake. C. E. Pearce
Bungay Castle. E. Bonhote
Bunker at the 5th. M. Dods
Bunkum. F. Richardson
Bunnies. J. Quirk
Bunny Lake Is Missing. E. Piper
Buns from the Gutter. N. Melides
Buoyed Cables. E. L. Long
Burden of Guilt. Carter Brown
Burden of Guilt. I. Gordon
Burden of Isabel. J. M. Cobban
Burden of Proof. J. Ashford
Burden of Proof. J. Barlow
Burden of Proof. V. Canning
Burden of Proof. Nicholas Carter
Burden of Proof. M. Challis
Burden of Proof. J. Truesdell
Burden's End. B. Lowry
Burden's Mission. H. Whittington
Burdock. A. L. Elsworthy
Burglar. D. Goodis
Burglar and the Lady. O. Harper
Burglar in Baulk. F. Martyn
Burglar in the Closet. Lawrence Block
Burglar of White Birches. W. M. Graydon
Burglar Who Liked to Quote Kipling. Lawrence Block
Burglar Who Moved Paradise. H. D. Ward
Burglar's Accomplice. Beechwood
Burglar's Can't Be Choosers. Lawrence Block
Burglars' Club. H. A. Hering
Burglar's Fate and the Detectives. A. Pinkerton
Burglars in Bucks. G. D. H. Cole
Burglars Must Dine. E. P. Oppenheim
Burglary. E. A. Dillwyn
Burgle the Baron. Anthony Morton
Burgled Heart. G. Leroux
Burglings of Tutt. R. Andom
Burgomaster of Furnes. G. Simenon
Burgos Contract. Angus Ross
Burgo's Romance. T. W. Speight
Burial in Portugal. Robert MacLeod
Burial of M. Bouvet. G. Simenon
Burial of the Fruit. D. Dortort
Burial Service. P. McGuire
Buried for Pleasure. E. Crispin
Buried in So Sweet a Place. S. Forbes
Buried in the Past. E. Lemarchand
Buried Motive. B. Cassiday
Buried Once. M. Dalman
Buried Remembrance. N. G. Smith
Buried Rubies. E. Jepson
Buried Secret. Nicholas Carter
Burke's Law. Roger Fuller
Burleigh Murders. G. Morton
Burma Battle. G. Marlowe
Burma Ruby. J. S. Fletcher
Burmese Dagger. Donald Stuart
Burn. N. Gant
Burn Forever. L. Ford
Burn, Killer, Burn. P. Crump
Burn This. H. McCloy
Burn, Witch, Burn! A. Merritt
Burned Evidence. W. Woodrow
Burned Man. C. Monig
Burned Man. B. Spicer
Burning. R. Charles
Burning Beacon. T. Charles
Burning Blue Death. J. Rosenberger
Burning Conscience. C. Kingston
Burning Court. J. D. Carr
Burning Eye. V. Canning
Burning Fuse. B. Benson
Burning Fuse. Jay Bernard
Burning Gold. F. L. Cary
Burning Hill. E. Kyle
Burning Is a Substitute for Loving. Jennie Melville
Burning Man. T. J. Kelly
Burning Moon. A. Spilken
Burning of Billy Toober. Jonathan Ross
Burning of Troy. M. Gair
Burning Question. C. Carnac
Burning Sappho. G. Baxt
Burning Secret. G. McDonell
Burning Shore. E. Trevor
Burning Sky. R. Faust
Burning Sky. J. H. Roberts
Burning Woman. M. Ritter
Burnout. J. W. Thomas
Burnt Bones Mystery. M. Dalman
Burnt Caravan. B. Bolt
Burnt Earth. W. F. Fauley
Burnt Million. J. Payn
Burnt Offering. R. Lockridge
Burnt Offerings. R. Marasco
Burnt-Out Case. G. Greene
Burnt Powder. A. P. Morris
Burqa. H. Campbell
Burwyck's Wander. S. J. Treibich
Bury by Night. L. Foley
Bury Her Deep. D. Macomber
Bury Him Among Kings. E. Trevor
Bury Him Darkly. J. Blackburn
Bury Him Darkly. Henry Wade
Bury Him Deeper. R. A. J. Walling
Bury in Haste. A. Eichler
Bury Me Deep. H. L. Ingham
Bury Me Deep. D. Linton
Bury Me Deep. H. Q. Masur
Bury Me in Gold Lame. S. Forbes
Bury Me in Lead. I. Goodwin
Bury Me Not. W. Francis
Bury Me Not at Sea. M. Eyre
Bury That Poker. G. M. Wilson
Bury the Guy! B. Shannon
Bury the Hatchet. Manning Long
Bury the Past. R. Reinsmith
Bury Their Dead. Alex Fraser
Bus Ran Late. G. M. Wilson
Bus Station Murders. L. Revell
Bus That Vanished. L. Groc
Bush Baby. M. Woodhouse
Bush King. P. Trent
Bush Mystery. J. Mackie
Bush Track. D. Hennessey
Bushfire. James Preston
Bushido. B. Osborne
Bushigrams. G. Boothby
Bushman. A. Crane
Bushman Who Came Back. A. W. Upfield
Bushmaster. B. Bolt
Bushranger of the Skies. A. W. Upfield
Bushrangers. W. H. Thomes
Business at Blanche Capel. B. Morgan
Business of Bodies. S. Forbes
Business of Loving. Godfrey Smith
Busman's Holiday. J. Pattinson
Busman's Honeymoon. D. L. Sayers
Busted Wheeler. Carter Brown
Bustillo. K. Royce
Busy Body. E. Ferrars
Busy Body. D. E. Westlake
Busy Whisper. T. Cobb
Busybody. J. Popplewell
But a Short Time to Live. Raymond Marshall
But Death Runs Faster. W. P. McGivern
But Don't Go Alone. K. Court
But I Wouldn't Want to Die There. S. Forbes
But Ill He Lived. Bradshaw Jones
But Nellie Was So Nice. M. McMullen
But Not for Love. I. Wilson
But Not for Me. E. Ronns
But Not Forgotten. R. Fenisong
But Not Yet Slain. B. Appel
But Once a Year. A. A. Thomson
But She Won't Lie Down. P. Yeldham
But Soft—We Are Observed. H. Belloc
But the Doctor Died. C. Rice
But the Patient Died. J. G. Edwards
But the Patient Died. Fiona Sinclair
But We Are Exiles. E. Kyle
But We Didn't Get the Fox. R. Llewellyn
Butcher of Belgrade. Nick Carter
Butcher of Bruton Street. A. Applin
Butcherknife Killings. S. Harkins
Butcher's Moon. R. Stark
Butcher's Wife. O. Cameron
Butler Did It. T. J. Kelly
Butler Died in Brooklyn. R. Fenisong
Butler in a Box. C. H. Abrahall
Butter Market House. Elizabeth Ford
Buttercup Case. F. Crane
Buttercup Spell. H. Cecil
Butterflies in the Rain. A. Soutar
Butterfly. J. M. Cain
Butterfly. H. K. Webster
Butterfly Flood. J. Wyllie
Butterfly Murder. C. Andrews
Butterfly of Paris. L. H. Brennan
Butterfly on the Wheel. G. Thorne
Butterfly Picnic. Joan Aiken
Butterfly Plague. T. Findley
Butterfly Revolution. W. Butler
Butterfly Wings. M. Peterson
Butterscotch Prince. Richard Hall
Button, Button. M. Bramhall
Button, Button. W. L. Doty
Button, Button. H. Roth
Button in the Plate. V. Loder
Buy Back Blues. R. Dennis
Buy Back the Dawn. H. Garland
Buy My Silence! Herman Landon
Buyer Beware. J. Lutz
Buzzards Pick the Bones. Murray Thomas
Buzzard's Roost. G. E. Rochester
By a Hair's Breadth. H. Hill
By a Hair's Breadth. E. S. Tupper
By a Vanished Hand. A. Feeny
By Advice of Counsel. A. Train
By an Unseen Hand. Nicholas Carter
By Birth a Lady. G. M. Fenn
By Bitter Experience. Scott Graham
By Blood Alone. F. Corey
By Breathless Ways. B. Bolt
By Candle-Light. G. Knevels
By Dawn's Early Light. Henry Clement
By Demons Possessed. E. Grayson
By Executive Arrangement. T. McMordie
By Fair Means. J. Middlemass
By Fair Means or Foul. T. W. Speight
By Fate's Caprice. T. W. Speight
By Flower and Dean Street, and The Love Apple. P. Chaplin
By Force of Circumstances. Gordon Holmes
By Fortune's Whim. T. W. Speight
By Foul Means. H. Leyford
By Hand Unseen. A. W. Marchmont
By Her Own Hand. F. Bonham
By His Own Hand. M. Cronin
By Hook or by Crook. Anthony Gilbert
By Hook or by Crook. E. Lathen
By Hook or by Crook. R. A. J. Walling
By Hook or Crook. R. A. J. Walling
By Horror Haunted. C. Fremlin
By-Line for Murder. A. Garve
By Love Forgotten. C. Gayet
By Mead and Stream. C. Gibbon
By Misadventure. F. Barrett
By Misadventure. A. Brock
By Misadventure. R. J. Fletcher
By Night. R. Clay
By Night at Dinsmore. J. Esteven
By Order of the Brotherhood. Le Voleur
By Order of the Czar. J. Hatton
By Order of the Dead. W. V. Cook
By Order of the Five. H. Adams
By Order of the King. A. Askew
By Order of the King! W. M. Graydon
By Order of the Magistrate. W. P. Ridge
By Order of the Soviet. F. A. Symonds
By Order of the Tong. J. G. Brandon
By Papuan Waters. O. Binns
By-Pass Control. M. Spillane
By-Pass Murder. D. Frome
By Peak and Pass. F. A. M. Webster
By Persons Unknown. J. York
By Proxy. J. Payn
By Reason of Insanity. S. Stevens
By Registered Post. J. Rhode
By Right Not Law. R. H. Sherard
By Right of Sword. A. W. Marchmont
By Royal Command. D. Yates
By Saturday. S. Fowler
By Snare of Love. A. W. Marchmont
By Some Person Unknown. P. Barrington
By Telegraph. J. M. Cobban
By That Sin. B. Malim
By the Gate of the Sea. D. C. Murray
By the Night Express. K. Fleming
By the North Door. M. E. Atkins
By the Pricking of My Thumbs. A. Christie
By the Skin of His Teeth. R. C. Armour
By the Terms of the Will. W. M. Graydon
By the Watchman's Clock. L. Ford
By the Waters of Babylon. N. DeMille
By the World Condemned. John Marsh
By Their Deeds. A. Peters
By Third Degree. H. S. Keeler
By Way of Confession. R. Gore-Brown
By-Ways of Braithe. F. Powell
By Whose Hand? B. Baskerville
By Whose Hand. F. Crisp
By Whose Hand? R. Hardinge
By Whose Hand? H. H. Lewis
By Whose Hand? Louise Rice
By Whose Hand? B. Symons
By Whose Hand? E. S. Tupper
By Wit of Woman. A. W. Marchmont
Bye, Baby Bunting. D. Keene
Bye, Bye, Baby! J. H. Bond
Bye-Bye, Blackbeard! N. Mapple
Byzantine Encounter. Andrea Harris

B

460 / CAB-Intersec — Title Index

CAB-Intersec. D. Walker
CB Baby. C. Whelton
CC and Company. M. Roote
C.I.D. T. Mundy
C.I.D. of Dexter Drake. E. Barker
C.I.D. Room. P. Alding
C.I.G. J. H. Jones
C.L.A.W. R. Graves
C.O.D. N. S. Lincoln
"C.Q." A. Train
C.V.C. Murders. K. Williams
Cab Driver's Secret. Nicholas Carter
Cab No. 44. Richard F. Foster
Cab of the Sleeping Horse. J. R. Scott
Cabal. N. Garbo
Cabana Murders. J. Y. Dane
Cabaret. L. H. Brennan
Cabaret Crime. F. Grierson
Cabaret Crime. G. H. Teed
Cabbages and Crime. A. Nash
Cabbages and Kings. O. Henry
Cabin Nineteen. M. Richmond
Cabin of Fear. D. Hitchens
Cabinda Affair. M. Head
Cabine de Luxe. E. L. Long
Cabinet Minister Resigns. A. Duncan
Cabinet Minister's Wife and other stories. G. R. Sims
Cabinet Secret. G. Boothby
Cable-Car. June Drummond
Cable from Kabul. N. Tranter
Cable-Man. W. Chesney
Cache. L. Damore
Cache-Cache. A. Marsland
Cactus. C. Chadwick
Cactus Shroud. Carolyn Thomas
Cad Metti, the Female Detective. Old Sleuth
Cadaver of Gideon Wyck. A. Laing
Cade. J. H. Chase
Cade Curse. W. E. D. Ross
Cade's County. A. Lawrence
Caesar Code. J. M. Simmel
Caesar Dies. T. Mundy
Cafe in Montparnasse. A. Mills
Cage. R. Gadney
Cage. S. Horler
Cage Five Is Going to Break. E. R. Johnson
Cage for the Nightingale. P. Paul
Cage of Corruption. Griff
Cage of Darkness. R. Masson
Cage of Fear. S. Seaton
Cage of Ice. D. Kyle
Cage of Mirrors. R. Ray
Cage of Shadows. Archie Hill
Cage of Violence. R. Magowan
Cage Until Tame. L. Henderson
Cage Without Bars. P. Barrington
Caged. T. Brykczynski
Caged. C. R. Cooper
Caged! H. Hill
Caged. F. Nichols
Cahusac Mystery. K. Prichard
Cain '67. J. M. Simmel
Cain's Girl Friend. W. Grote
Cain's Hundred. E. L. Heyman
Cain's Woman. O. G. Benson
Cairo Cabal. A. Caillou
Cairo Communique. Robert Mason
Cairo Counterplot. L. J. Burke
Cairo Crisis. W. Martyn
Cairo Garter Murders. V. W. Mason
Cairo Intrigue. W. Manchester
Cairo Mafia. Nick Carter
Cairo Ring. N. Sheraton
Cairo Sleeper. W. Tute
Cake for Caroline. G. M. Wilson
Cakes for Your Birthday. C. E. Vulliamy
Cakes to Kill. H. C. Beck
Calabrian Summer. M. McEvoy
Calamity at Harwood. G. Bellairs
Calamity Comes of Age. G. Baxter
Calamity Comes to Flenton. C. Ashton
Calamity Conquest. B. Gray
Calamity Fair. Wade Miller
Calamity House. M. Billett
Calamity in Kent. J. Rowland
Calamity Town. E. Queen
Calcroft Case. E. J. Murray
Calculated Risk. R. Foley
Calculated Risk. J. Hayes
Calderwood. M. Heath
Caldwell Shadow. D. Daniels
Caleb, Who Is Hotter Than a $2 Pistol. S. Ashley
Caleb Williams. W. Godwin
Calendar. E. Wallace
Calendar of Crime. E. Queen
Caliban's Castle. P. Warren
Calibre. I. Shulman
Calibre .50. R. Sheckley
Calico Cat. C. M. Thompson
California Detective. Anonymous
California Factor. P. Vernier
California Hit. D. Pendleton
Caligari Complex. B. Copper
Calina. L. Gardner
Caliph Intrigue. L. James
Call a Hearse. J. Stagge
Call After Midnight. M. G. Eberhart
Call Back to Crime. P. Alding

Call Back Yesterday. G. Ferrand
Call-Box Murder. G. Barnett
Call-Box Mystery. J. Ironside
Call Conquest for Danger. B. Gray
Call Down the Sky. H. Lillie
Call for Blackshirt. R. Graeme
Call for Michael Shayne. B. Halliday
Call for Simon Shard. P. McCutchan
Call for Superintendent Flagg. J. Cassells
Call for the Baron. Anthony Morton
Call for the Dead. J. Le Carre
Call for the Saint. L. Charteris
Call from Austria. M. Albrand
Call from the Past, and other stories. L. Merrick
Call Girl Murders. J. G. Brandon
Call Girls for Murder. J. B. Ethan
Call Her Savage. J. Grecco
Call Him Early for the Murder. N. Morland
Call in Miss Hogg. A. Lee
Call in the Feds. "G-Man"
Call in the Night. Nicholas Carter
Call in the Night. S. Howatch
"Call in the Yard." M. A. Clune
Call in the Yard. David Hume
Call It Accident. R. Foley
Call It Coincidence. F. Lockridge
Call It Murder. G. Tracey
Call It Rhodesia. W. A. Ballinger
Call It Treason. G. Howe
Call McLean. G. Goodchild
Call Me Al. D. Linton
Call Me Captain. P. Stanton
Call Me Deadly. H. Braham
Call Me Duke. H. Grey
Call Me Killer. H. Whittington
Call Me Pandora. A. Dean
Call Me Shameless. B. Sarto
Call Me Sometime. R. Angel
Call Mr. Fortune. H. C. Bailey
Call of Death. T. S. King
Call of Glengarron. N. Buckingham
Call of the Blood. K. Kellow
Call of the Deep. I. Stark
Call of the Flesh. V. Coffman
Call of the North. J. Templeton
Call of the People. L. Clarke
Call of the World. C. H. Bullivant
Call Off the Corpse. John Bentley
Call on Kuprin. M. Edelman
Call on the Phone. Nicholas Carter
Call Out the Flying Squad! H. Holt
Call the Lady Indiscreet. P. Whelton
Call the Next Witness. P. Woodruff
Call the Toff. J. Creasey
Call the Witness. E. Sherry
Call the Yard! H. Clevely
Call the Yard. J. Mowbray
Call to Danger. C. Coram
Call to Die. C. Coram
Callaghan. P. Cheyney
Callaghan Meets His Fate. M. Chesney
Callaghan of Intelligence. M. Chesney
Callan. J. Mitchell
Callander Square. A. Perry
Callao Clue. R. Howes
Called Back. H. Conway
Called to Account. Nicholas Carter
Called to Judgment. C. Stanton
Called to the Bar. B. Hemyng
Caller. M. R. Hayes
Callers for Dr. Morelle. E. Dudley
Calling Alan Fraser. H. Desmond
Calling All Cars. H. Holt
Calling All Cars. E. Snell
Calling All Ghosts. J. F. Stone
Calling All Suspects. C. Wells
Calling Bulldog Drummond. G. Fairlie
Calling Dr. Kill. A. Sugar
Calling Dr. Patchwork. R. Goulart
Calling Lord Blackshirt. B. Graeme
Calling Mr. Callaghan. P. Cheyney
Calling Peter Grayleigh. Colin Robertson
Calling Scotland Yard. H. Holt
Calling Whitehall 1212. H. Clevely
Calling Whitehall 1212. A. Parsons
Callingham's Girl. A. S. Roche
Calliope Reef. H. Rigsby
Calloused Eye. E. H. Loban
Calverston Story. Alan Thomas
Caly. S. M. Combes
Calypso. E. McBain
Calypso. H. Slater
Calypso Murders. P. H. Mulholland
Cambodia. Nick Carter
Cambodian Quest. R. J. Casey
Cambri Plot. J. Moffatt
Cambridge Murders. A. Broome
Cambridge Murders. D. Rees
Camden Ruby Murder. A. Bliss
Came the Dawn. R. Bax
Camel. L. Berners
Camelia Caper. J. K. Polk
Camelion's Dish. R. Pertwee
Camelot Caper. Elizabeth Peters
Camelot Club. B. Killick
Camelot Conundrum. J. Griffin
Cameos. O. R. Cohen
Camera Clue. G. H. Coxe
Camera Fiend. E. W. Hornung

Cameron Castle. Marilyn Ross
Cameron Hill. M. Flavin
Cameron Hill. M. K. Simmons
Cameron Mystery. C. Talbot
Cameron's Landing. Anne Scott
Camerton Slope. R. F. Bishop
Camilla. P. Paul
Camouflage! E. W. Alais
Camouflage. L. Meynell
Camouflage Revolution. H. McKay
Camp. Gordon M. Williams
Camp-Meeting Murders. V. Randolph
Camp of Fear. L. H. Gordon
Camp 7 Last Stop. H. H. Kirst
Camp, the Battlefield, and the Hospital. L. P. Brockett
Campaign Train. The Gordons
Campanile Murders. W. Chambers
Campbell's Kingdom. H. Innes
Campden Hill Mystery. Elliot Bailey
Campus Corpse. K. Hopkins
Campus Killings. E. B. Ruark
Campus Murders. E. Queen
Can a Mermaid Kill? T. B. Dewey
Can Death Be Sleep? H. Brinton
Can Ellen Be Saved? M. Z. Bradley
Can Ladies Kill? P. Cheyney
Can of Worms. J. H. Chase
Cana Diversion. W. C. Gault
Canadian Bomber Contract. P. Atlee
Canadian Crisis. D. Pendleton
Canadian Kill. J. Nazel
Canal Mystery. J. Remenham
Canaries Also Sing. E. Allen
Canaries Sometimes Croak. J. Cooper
Canaris Legacy. R. Hitchcock
Canary Murder Case. W. Butterfield
Canary Murder Case. S. S. Van Dine
Canary That Died. James Lewis
Canary Yellow. E. Cadell
Canceled Czech. Lawrence Block
Cancelled Accounts. H. Greene
Cancelled in Red. H. Pentecost
Cancelled Out. A. E. Redmond
Cancelled Score Mystery. Gret Lane
Cancelled Will. E. A. Dupuy
Candace. Alice Brennan
Candid Escort. T. B. Marle
Candid Imposter. G. H. Coxe
Candid Killer. J. Giltene
Candidate. R. Alonso
Candidate for a Coffin. J. G. Brandon
Candidate for a Coffin. Neill Graham
Candidate for Danger. E. Sherwood
Candidate for Hell. D. P. Neeley
Candidate for Lilies. R. East
Candidate for Murder. M. Post
Candidate's Blood. L. Derrick
Candidates for Glory. J. Fores
Candidates for Murder. A. Hocking
Candidates for Murder. Frank King
Candidate's Wife. V. Coffman
Candied Peel. F. L. Cary
Candle. L. C. Hopkins
Candle and the Tower. R. D. Spector
Candle at Midnight. F. Lynch
Candle for a Corpse. S. Sterling
Candle for the Dead. H. Marlowe
Candle for the Dragon. M. Craig
Candle-Holders. V. Gielgud
Candle in the Sun. D. Daniels
Candle in the Wind. M. Richardson
Candle of the Night. M. Clare
Candle of the Wicked. E. Balmer
Candle of the Wicked. Elizabeth Brown
Candlelight in Avalon. Augustus Muir
Candles Are All Out. N. Fitzgerald
Candles for the Dead. H. Carmichael
Candles in the Night. A. Carr
Candles in the Wood. A. Manners
Candleshoe. M. Innes
Candlestick with Seven Branches. M. Leblanc
Candy Kid. D. B. Hughes
Candy Killings. G. Stockwell
Candy Man. R. Cullum
Candyleg. O. Demaris
Candywine Development. John Morris
Cane-Patch Mystery. A. B. Cunningham
Canfield Decision. S. T. Agnew
Canisbay Conspiracy. A. MacVicar
Cankerworm. G. M. Fenn
Cannibal. N. De Mille
Cannibal Heart. M. Millar
Cannibal Who Overate. H. Pentecost
Cannibals and Missionaries. M. McCarthy
Cannon Law. T. C. Paynter
Cannon, the Falling Blonde. P. Denver
Cannonball. J. Chamier
Canon in Residence. V. L. Whitechurch
Canon Lucifer. J. D. Delille
Canon's Ward. J. Payn
Canterbury Kilgrims. J. N. Chance
Canterbury Mystery. J. S. Fletcher
Canter's Chase. Margaret Archer
Canto for a Gypsy. Martin Smith
Canvas Coffin. W. C. Gault
Canvas Dagger. H. Reilly
Canvas Jungle. Arthur MacLean
Cap Across the River. J. M. Scott
Cap and Gown for a Shroud. E. N. Gilla

Title Index

Cap Colt, the Quaker Detective. C. Morris
Capablanca Opening. D. T. Chantler
Capac Legacy. S. Gianetta
Cape. M. Caidin
Cape Cod Caper. M. Arnold
Cape Cod Caper. Carey Phillips
Cape Cod Mystery. P. A. Taylor
Cape Fear. J. D. MacDonald
Cape House. L. P. Shepherd
Cape Jasmine Murder. M. M. Mott
Cape of Black Sands. W. D. Roberts
Cape of Shadows. H. Gibbs
Cape Town Affair. A. Scobie
Caper. L. Andress
Caper. T. B. Reagan
Caper of the Golden Bulls. W. P. McGivern
Caper Sauce. S. P. B. Mais
Capful o' Nails. D. C. Murray
Capillary Crime and other stories. F. D. Millett
Capital City Mystery. J. H. Wallis
Capital Crime. L. Ford
Capital Crime. A. Roudybush
Capital Murder. J. Z. Alner
Capital Punishment. Stuart Martin
Capital Punishment. Sutherland Scott
Capitol Crime. Lawrence Meyer
Capitol Hell. L. Derrick
Capitol Hill Affair. L. James
Capitol Offense. J. Davey
Caprice. S. Hylton
Caprice. J. Withers
Capricorn One. R. Goulart
Capricorn Run. D. J. Cleary
Capricorn Stone. M. Brent
Caprifoil. W. P. McGivern
Caprimulgus. W. F. Harvey
Capsule. D. Hagberg
Capsule Mystery. E. C. Vivian
Captain Black. M. Pemberton
Captain Blood. M. Blodgett
Captain Bowker. S. M. Parkmam
Captain Bulldog Drummond. G. Fairlie
Captain Castle. C. Dawe
Captain Christine. Basil Carey
Captain Clew, the Flying Detective. Anonymous
Captain Crash. G. Goodchild
Captain Cut-Throat. J. D. Carr
Captain Dack. P. Meriton
Captain Firebrace. Seafarer
Captain Firebrace and the Java Queen. Seafarer
Captain Flynn. E. L. Long
Captain Flynn Ret'd. E. L. Long
Captain Flynn, Sheriff. E. L. Long
Captain Gardiner of the International Police. R. Allen
Captain Gault. W. H. Hodgson
Captain Incognito. G. Gibson
Captain Jack. H. Outerbridge
Captain Kettle, Ambassador. C. J. C. Hyne
Captain Kettle, K.C.B. C. J. C. Hyne
Captain Kettle on the War-Path. C. J. C. Hyne
Captain Kettle's Bit. C. J. C. Hyne
Captain King Investigates. K. Trask
Captain Landon. R. H. Savage
Captain Lucifer. B. Bolt
Cap'n Luke, Filibuster. "Capstan"
Captain Marraday's Marriage. T. Cobb
Captain McBlaid of the Air Police. R. Walker
Captain Millett's Island. K. N. Burt
Captain Must Die. R. Colby
Captain Nash and the Honour of England. Ragan Butler
Captain Nash and the Wroth Inheritance. Ragan Butler
Captain Nice. W. Johnston
Captain of the Guard. C. Houghton
Captain of the Kansas. L. Tracy
Captain of the Polestar, and other stories. A. C. Doyle
Captain of the Vulture. M. E. Braddon
Captain Overboard. F. Andreas
Captain Rock's Pet. E. Southworth
Captain Samson, A.B. Gavin Douglas
Captain Sentimental and other stories. E. Jepson
Captain Shannon. C. Kernahan
Captain Sinister. G. Goodchild
Captain Sparkle, Pirate. Nicholas Carter
Cap'n Sue. H. Footner
Captain Tatham of Tatham Island. E. Wallace
Captain Wardlaw's Kitbags. H. MacGrath
Captain's Cabin. Edward Jenkins
Captain's Curio. E. Phillpotts
Captain's House. M. K. Simmons
Captain's Lady. Rachelle Edwards
Captains of Souls. E. Wallace
Captains of the "Calabar". F. Knight
Captain's Pawn. A. Lowing
Captain's Walk. E. Welles
Captivator. A. York
Captive. N. Daniels
Captive. The Gordons
Captive. B. Kingsley
Captive Audience. Jessica Mann
Captive City. J. Appleby
Captive City. D. DaCruz
Captive in Paradise. Magali
Captive in the Land. J. Aldridge
Captive in the Night. D. Stokes
Captive Princess. R. H. Savage
Captive Years. D. Lee
Captives of Mora Island. V. Canning
Captors. J. Farris
Capture. W. Martyn
Capture of Paul Beck. M. M. Bodkin
Capture of the Paddy Ryan Gang of Burglars. L. A. Newcome
Captured by Cannibals. J. Hatton
Captured Cruiser. C. J. C. Hyne
Car Park Mystery. A. Parsons
Caracal. G. N. Smith
Caracol Reef. Michael Andrews
Carambola. D. Dodge
Caravan Adventure. J. J. Farjeon
Caravan Crime. G. Chester
Caravan Mystery. F. Hume
Caravan of Crime. E. O'Donnell
Caravan of Night. M. Erskine
Caravan to Vaccares. Alistair MacLean
Caravanners. J. Dering
Caravans by Night. H. Hervey
Carbon Copy. Anthony Brennan
Carbon Monoxide. J. Street
Carbuncle Clue. F. Hume
Carcellini Emerald, with other tales. Mrs. B. Harrison
Card Games. A. Fletcher
Card 13. M. L. Luther
Cardboard Castle. Margery Lawrence
Cardboard Castle. P. C. Wren
Cardboard Hero. L. Noel
Cardinal Error. M. Walton
Cardinal Moth. F. M. White
Cardinal Rock. E. Sale
Cardinal Sin. H. Conway
Cardinalli Contract. E. R. Johnson
Cardinal's Rose. V. Sutphen
Cardross Luck. J. L. Roberts
Cards of the Gambler. B. Kiely
Cards on the Table. A. Christie
Cardyce for the Defence. B. Graeme
Care of Devils. S. Press
Care of the Commander. R. L. Dearden
Careen. V. Coffman
Career for the Baron. Anthony Morton
Career in C Major and other stories. J. M. Cain
Career with Death. H. Tracy
Careful, He Might Hear You. S. L. Elliott
Careful Man. R. Deming
Careless Corpse. B. Halliday
Careless Corpse. C. D. King
Careless Hangman. N. Morland
Careless Lives. P. Leslie
Careless Mrs. Christian. C. M. Russell
Caress Before Killing. Carter Brown
Caress of Conquest. S. D. Frances
Caretaker. F. Hume
Carfax Abbey. B. Thomson
Carfax Baines. W. M. Graydon
Cargo for Crooks. Sea Lion
Cargo for Death. T. Wallace
Cargo for the Styx. L. Trimble
Cargo of Death. H. McCutcheon
Cargo of Eagles. M. Allingham
Cargo of Fear. J. L. Currier
Cargo of Gold. J. G. Sarasin
Cargo of Spent Evil. J. M. Brett
Cargo Risk. Robert MacLeod
Cargo to Saigon. C. Leader
Cargo-Trouble. P. Thomas
Cargo Unknown. K. Robeson
Caribbean Affair. E. P. Thorne
Caribbean Caper. Robin Moore
Caribbean Caper. J. Rosenberger
Caribbean Conspiracy. B. Conrad
Caribbean Crisis. D. E. Bingley
Caribbean Crisis. D. Reid
Caribbean Cutie. Griff
Caribbean Kidnap. M. Cronin
Caribbean Kill. D. Pendleton
Caribbean Kill. A. Sugar
Caribbean Mystery. A. Christie
Caribbean Strip. I. S. Black
Caribou Patrol. C. Stoddard
Carlent Manor Crime. L. Grex
Carleton Case. E. H. Clark
Carlito's Way. E. Torres
Carlos Contract. D. A. Phillips
Carlos Must Die. U. Dan
Carlton Plot. P. N. Walker
Carlyon's Year. J. Payn
Carmen Was a Virgin. M. Storm
Carmen's Messenger. H. Bindloss
Carnaby and the Assassins. P. N. Walker
Carnaby and the Conspirators. P. N. Walker
Carnaby and the Counterfeiters. P. N. Walker
Carnaby and the Demonstrators. P. N. Walker
Carnaby and the Eliminators. P. N. Walker
Carnaby and the Gaolbreakers. P. N. Walker
Carnaby and the Hijackers. P. N. Walker
Carnaby and the Infiltrators. P. N. Walker
Carnaby and the Kidnappers. P. N. Walker
Carnaby and the Saboteurs. P. N. Walker
Carnaby Curse. D. Winston
Carnaby Rex. R. MacLeish
Carnacki, the Ghost Finder. W. H. Hodgson
Carnacki, the Ghost Finder, and a Poem. W. H. Hodgson
Carnage of the Realm. C. A. Goodrum
Carnavaron's Castle. J. F. Webb
Carnecrane. Mary Williams
Carnelian Cat. J. Deweese
Carnellian Circle. H. John
Carney's Burlesque. S. Harragan
Carnival! J. Rathbone
Carnival Confession. C. Zuckmayer
Carnival for Killing. Nick Carter
Carnival Girl. R. Glendinning
Carnival Murder. N. Brady
Carnival of Crime. Nicholas Carter
Carnival of Death. A. Eadie
Carnival of Death. D. Keene
Carnival of Death. D. Kirby
Carnival of Death. J. C. Lenehan
Carnival of Death. H. Zore
Carny Kill. R. E. Alter
Caro. B. J. Packer
Carol, the Pursued. K. Kimbrough
Carolina House. E. Kyle
Caroline Affair. C. H. Gibbs-Smith
Caroline, Caroline. M. Ritter
Caroline Ormesby's Crime. H. Adams
Carp Country. E. Kyle
Carpaccio Caper. B. Strutton
Carpathian Caper. J. Sandulescu
Carpenter, Detective. H. T. Caine
Carpet Courtship. T. Cobb
Carpet from Bagdad. H. MacGrath
Carpet of Death. R. McNear
Carpet-Slipper Murder. A. C. MacLean
Carquake. M. Avallone
Carr of Dimscaur. T. Douglas
Carriage 7 Seat 15. C. Aveline
Carried Away. E. L. Long
Carriers of Death. J. Creasey
Carrington Assignment. R. Child
Carrington's Cases. J. S. Clouston
Carrion Crows. Dorothy Bennett
Carrion Eaters. W. A. Ballinger
Carrion Eaters. E. H. Rhodes
Carrion Experience. I. G. Slobber
Carrismore Ruby. J. S. Fletcher
Carriston's Gift and other stories. F. J. Fargus
Carroll Moore. Old Sleuth
Carry-Cot. A. Thynne
Carry Me Home. P. Traill
Carry My Coffin Slowly. L. Herrington
Carson Inheritance. D. Daniels
Carson Loan Mystery. A. De Brune
Cart Before the Crime. J. Porter
Cart Before the Hearse. R. Ormerod
Cartel. E. J. Epstein
Carter Kidnapping Case. A. R. Long
Carteret Affair. S. Rathbone
Carteret Hotel Mystery. J. Corbett
Carteret's Cure. R. Keverne
Carter's Triumph. H. Bindloss
Carthusian Friar. Sarah Green
Cartoon Crimes. K. Robeson
Cartsley Mystery. J. G. Rowe
Cartwright Gardens Murder. J. S. Fletcher
Cartwright Is Dead, Sir! H. Baker
Caruthers Affair. W. N. Harben
Carved Emerald. V. France
Carven Ball. J. Haslette
Carver. P. Barker
Carver of the Swamp. "Capstan"
Casa Madrone. M. G. Eberhart
Casablack. C. Leopold
Casablanca Intrigue. Clarissa Ross
Casanova Embrace. W. Adler
Casbah Killers. Nick Carter
Case. V. White
Case Against Aldor. C. Ryland
Case Against Andrew Fane. Anthony Gilbert
Case Against Butterfly. G. Tree
Case Against Dr. Ripon. W. Tyrer
Case Against Love. D. Decoin
Case Against Mrs. Ames. A. S. Roche
Case Against Myself. G. Tree
Case Against Paul Raeburn. J. Creasey
Case Against Philip Quest. M. Underwood
Case Against Satan. Ray Russell
Case and Exceptions. F. T. Hill
Case and the Girl. R. Parrish
Case Bird and other stories. F. B. Young
Case-Book of Anthony Slade. L. Gribble
Case Book of Ellery Queen. E. Queen
Case Book of Jimmie Lavender. V. Starrett
Case Book of Mr. Campion. M. Allingham
Case-Book of Sherlock Holmes. A. C. Doyle

C

Case Books of X 37. A. J. Dawson
Case Closed. J. Thomson
Case Continued. J. Prescott
Case Dead and Buried. C. Barry
Case File: FBI. The Gordons
Case for Appeal. L. Egan
Case for Compensation. Cameron Ross
Case for Court. J. Prescot
Case for Equity. K. Hill
Case for Hearing. J. Prescot
Case for Inspector Flagg. J. Cassells
Case for Inspector West. J. Creasey
Case for Mason. W. McCleery
Case for M.I.5. W. Jardine
Case for Mr. Crook. Anthony Gilbert
Case for Mr. Fortune. H. C. Bailey
Case for Mr. Paul Savoy. Jackson Gregory
Case for Mrs. Heydon. R. Bridges
Case for Punishment. H. Hunter
Case for Sergeant Beef. L. Bruce
Case for Solomon. B. Graeme
Case for the Accused. J. Prescot
Case for the Baron. Anthony Morton
Case for the C.I.D. P. C. De Crespigny
Case for the Courts. Mrs. C. Kernahan
Case for the Crown. F. M. White
Case for the Defence. M. Fitt
Case for the Defendent. H. Aufricht-Ruda
Case for the Dreamer. W. M. Duncan
Case for the Lady. F. Warden
Case for the Prosecution. W. M. Graydon
Case for Three Detectives. L. Bruce
Case for Treachery. V. White
Case for Tressider. C. Barry
Case for Trial. J. Prescot
Case in Camera. O. Onions
Case in Hand. N. A. Temple-Ellis
Case in Madrid. E. Naughton
Case in Nullity. E. Berckman
Case in the Clinic. E. C. R. Lorac
Case Is Altered. H. L. Jones
Case Is Altered. W. Plomer
Case Is Altered. Brian Stuart
Case Is Altered. Sara Woods
Case Is Closed. P. Wentworth
Case Load—Maximum. E. R. Johnson
Case No. 561. D. Knight
Case of Alisa Gray. G. M. Fenn
Case of Alan Copeland. M. Dalton
Case of Anne Bickerton. S. Fowler
Case of Blackmail. E. W. Alais
Case of Blackmail. C. K. Moore
Case of Books. B. Graeme
Case of Bottled Murder. E. Wagner
Case of Caroline Animus. D. Chambers
Case of Casper Gault. W. Morton
Case of Colonel Marchand. E. C. R. Lorac
Case of Comrade Tulayev. V. Serge
Case of Constable Shields. R. Greaves
Case of Dan Morris. C. Jude
Case of Doctor Horace. J. H. Prentis
Case of Dr. Morel. K. Bramson
Case of Doctor Plemen. R. De Pont-Jest
Case of Doctor Tracey. R. A. Here
Case of Elinor Norton. M. R. Rinehart
Case of Elymas the Sorcerer. B. Flynn
Case of George Candlemas. G. R. Sims
Case of Identity. L. Brain
Case of Identity. R. Marsh
Case of Indelicate Champagne. F. Halliday
Case of Jennie Brice. M. R. Rinehart
Case of John Muir of Merchant Navy. L. Jackson
Case of Joshua Locke. R. G. Dean
Case of Kitty Ogilvie. J. Stubbs
Case of L. A. C. Dickson. J. Drummond
Case of Lady Broadstone. A. W. Marchmont
Case of Larachi the Lascar. O. Merland
Case of Libel. J. Bingham
Case of Lord Greyburn's Son. D. Long
Case of Many Clues. Nicholas Carter
Case of Marie Corwin. G. Dean
Case of Mary Fielding. M. Erskine
Case of Mary Sherman. J. E. Brady
Case of Matthew Crake. A. G. MacLeod
Case of Miss Dunstable. J. Hocking
Case of Miss Elliott. B. Orczy
Case of Mr. Budd. G. Verner
Case of Mr. Cassidy. W. Targ
Case of Mrs. Wingate. O. Micheaux
Case of Mortimer Fenley. L. Tracy
Case of Naomi Clynes. B. Thomson
Case of Need. J. Hudson
Case of Oscar Brodsky. R. A. Freeman
Case of Paul Breen. A. Tudor
Case of Rape. D. Warren
Case of Reuben Malachi. H. Sutherland Edwards
Case of Richard Eden. Mark Allerton
Case of Richard Meynell. Mrs. H. Ward
Case of Robert Quarry. A. Garve
Case of Robert Robertson. S. Elvestad
Case of Sir Adam Braid. M. Thynne
Case of Sir Edward Talbot. V. F. Taubman-Goldie
Case of Sir Geoffrey. F. Warden
Case of Sonia Wayward. M. Innes
Case of Spirits. P. Lovesey
Case of the Abominable Snowman. N. Blake
Case of the Absent Corpse. K. Hill

Case of the Absent-Minded Professor. A. M. Stein
Case of the Ace Accomplice. W. J. Passingham
Case of the Acid Throwers. J. Creasey
Case of the Adopted Daughter. W. M. Graydon
Case of the Advertised Murder. M. Bardon
Case of the African Emigrant. R. Hardinge
Case of the African Hoodoo. R. Hardinge
Case of the African Trader. R. Hardinge
Case of the Amateur Actor. C. Bush
Case of the Amber Crown. A. Murray
Case of the American Tourists. J. Hunter
Case of the Amorous Aunt. E. S. Gardner
Case of the Angels' Trumpets. Michael Burt
Case of the Angry Mourner. E. S. Gardner
Case of the April Fools. C. Bush
Case of the Back Seat Girl. C. Ryland
Case of the Backward Mule. E. S. Gardner
Case of the Baited Hook. E. S. Gardner
Case of the Baker Street Irregulars. A. Boucher
Case of the Banned Film. A. Parsons
Case of the Barking Clock. H. S. Keeler
Case of the Baronet's Memoirs. Richard Grant
Case of the Beautiful Beggar. E. S. Gardner
Case of the Beautiful Body. Jonathan Craig
Case of the Beckoning Dead. J. Donavan
Case of the Bendigo Heirlooms. Jack Lewis
Case of the Benevolent Bookie. C. Bush
Case of the Berlin Spy. D. Betteridge
Case of the Bigamous Spouse. E. S. Gardner
Case of the Billion Dollar Body. J. Shallit
Case of the Biscay Pirate. L. Jackson
Case of the Bismarck Memoirs. P. Quiroule
Case of the Black-Eyed Blonde. E. S. Gardner
Case of the Black Magician. R. Hardinge
Case of the Black Orchids. R. Stout
Case of the Black Sheep. S. Finley
Case of the Black Twenty-Two. B. Flynn
Case of the Blackmailed Banker. A. Blair
Case of the Blackmailed King. Roland Daniel
Case of the Blackmailed Prince. A. Parsons
Case of the Blank Cartridge. L. Trimble
Case of the Blind Mouse. M. J. Freeman
Case of the Blonde Bonanza. E. S. Gardner
Case of the Blood-Stained Dime. M. Bardon
Case of the Bludgeoned Teacher. J. Hollis
Case of the Blue Lacquered Box. G. F. Worts
Case of the Blue Orchid. H. Desmond
Case of the Bogus Baron. W. Tyrer
Case of the Bogus Bride! H. H. C. Gibbons
Case of the Bogus Ingots. W. J. Bayfield
Case of the Bogus Laird. J. W. Bobin
Case of the Bogus Monk. G. H. Teed
Case of the Bogus Prince. G. Chester
Case of the Bogus Treasure Hunt. W. M. Graydon
Case of the Bonfire Body. C. Bush
Case of the Bookmaker Baronet. J. W. Bobin
Case of the Borrowed Brunette. E. S. Gardner
Case of the Bouncing Betty. M. Avallone
Case of the Brass-Bound Chest. G. Chester
Case of the Brazen Beauty. Jonathan Craig
Case of the Bronze Statue. J. Hunter
Case of the Brooklyn Mobsters. L. Dexter
Case of the Brown-Eyed Housemaid. C. Ryland
Case of the Brunette Bombshell. H. Waugh
Case of the Buried Clock. E. S. Gardner
Case of the Burmese Dagger. A. Murray
Case of the Burnt Bohemian. C. Bush
Case of the Busy Bees. C. Witting
Case of the Cabaret Girl. W. W. Sayer
Case of the Calabar Bean. C. M. Wills
Case of the Calendar Girl. E. S. Gardner
Case of the Cancelled Redhead. H. Daly
Case of the Canny Killer. H. S. Keeler
Case of the Careless Cupid. E. S. Gardner
Case of the Careless Kitten. E. S. Gardner
Case of the Careless Thief. C. Bush
Case of the Caretaker's Cat. E. S. Gardner
Case of the Cashiered Officer. W. M. Graydon
Case of the Cautious Coquette. E. S. Gardner

Case of the Chased and the Unchaste. T. B. Dewey
Case of the Cheating Bride. M. Propper
Case of the Chinese Courier. R. Hardinge
Case of the Chinese Gong. C. Bush
Case of the Chinese Pearls. G. H. Teed
Case of the Cinema Star. A. Murray
Case of the Clairvoyant's Ruse. G. H. Teed
Case of the Climbing Corpse. Gwyn Evans
Case of the Climbing Rat. C. Bush
Case of the Cold Coquette. Jonathan Craig
Case of the Cold Murderer. E. Godfrey
Case of the Coloured Wind. J. Donavan
Case of the Conscript Miner. W. Tyrer
Case of the Constant God. R. King
Case of the Constant Suicides. J. D. Carr
Case of the Copper Cat. L. W. Douglas
Case of the Cop's Wife. M. K. Ozaki
Case of the Copy-Hook Killing. R. Howes
Case of the Corner Cottage. C. Bush
Case of the Corporal's Leave. C. Bush
Case of the Cottage Crime. W. Tyrer
Case of the Cotton Beetle. A. Murray
Case of the Council Swindle. W. Tyrer
Case of the Counterfeit Colonel. C. Bush
Case of the Counterfeit Eye. E. S. Gardner
Case of the Courtlandt Jewels. G. H. Teed
Case of the Crawling Cockroach. Harlan Reed
Case of the Crazy Atom. H. Hawton
Case of the Crazy Pilot. P. Conde
Case of the Crime Reporter. R. Hardinge
Case of the Criminal's Daughter. H. Clevely
Case of the Crimson Conjuror. Gwyn Evans
Case of the Crimson Kiss. E. S. Gardner
Case of the Crimson Wizard. E. J. Murray
Case of the Crook Banker. Ladbroke Black
Case of the Crook Councilor. A. Blair
Case of the Crook Iron Master. M. Osborne
Case of the Crook M.P. G. N. Philips
Case of the Crook Rajah. A. Parsons
Case of the Crooked Candle. E. S. Gardner
Case of the Crooked Skipper. J. Hunter
Case of the Crumpled Knave. A. Boucher
Case of the Crying Swallow. E. S. Gardner
Case of the Cultured Pearls. J. W. Bobin
Case of the Curious Bride. E. S. Gardner
Case of the Curious Chair. R. Powell
Case of the Curious Client. C. Bush
Case of the Curious Heel. K. F. Crossen
Case of the Dancing Sandwiches. F. Brown
Case of the Dangerous Dowager. E. S. Gardner
Case of the Dangra Millions. A. Parsons
Case of the Daring Decoy. E. S. Gardner
Case of the Daring Divorcee. E. S. Gardner
Case of the Dark Hero. P. Cheyney
Case of the Dark Stranger. M. Dalton
Case of the Dark Wanton. P. Cheyney
Case of the Dead Cadet. R. P. Koehler
Case of the Dead Diplomat. B. Thomson
Case of the Dead Divorcee. W. Holder
Case of the Dead Doctor. V. Loder
Case of the Dead Grandmother. M. Bardon
Case of the Dead Man Gone. C. Bush
Case of the Dead Shepherd. C. Bush
Case of the "Dead" Spy. J. Drummond
Case of the Deadly Diamonds. C. Bush
Case of the Deadly Diary. William Du Bois
Case of the Deadly Drops. G. Benedict
Case of the Deadly Kiss. M. K. Ozaki
Case of the Deadly Toy. E. S. Gardner
Case of the Deadly Triangle. R. Ayers
Case of the Death Computer. J. N. Chance
Case of the Defaulting Sailor. J. Hunter
Case of the Demented Spiv. G. Bellairs
Case of the Demure Defendant. E. S. Gardner
Case of the Deported Aliens. W. J. Bayfield
Case of the Deportee. G. Chester
Case of the Deserted War Bride. J. Hunter
Case of the Deserted Wife. W. J. Bayfield
Case of the Dictator's Double. A. Blair
Case of the Discharged P.C. W. Shute
Case of the Discharged Policeman. L. Jackson
Case of the Disguised Apache. G. H. Teed
Case of the Dope Dealers. M. Frazer
Case of the Doped Favourite. J. Hunter
Case of the Doped Heavyweight. L. Jackson
Case of the Double Event. J. Hunter
Case of the Double Tangle. W. J. Bayfield
Case of the Dowager's Etchings. R. King
Case of the Drowning Duck. E. S. Gardner

Title Index

Case of the Drowsy Mosquito. E. S. Gardner
Case of the Dubious Bridegroom. E. S. Gardner
Case of the Duplicate Daughter. E. S. Gardner
Case of the Ebony Queen. C. Adkins
Case of the Eccentric Will. R. C. Armour
Case of the Eight Brothers. M. V. Heberden
Case of the Eighteenth Ostrich. Colin Curzon
Case of the Empty Beehive. C. M. Wills
Case of the Empty Tin. E. S. Gardner
Case of the Extra Grave. C. Bush
Case of the Extra Man. C. Bush
Case of the Fabulous Fake. E. S. Gardner
Case of the Faithful Heart. B. Flynn
Case of the Famished Parson. G. Bellairs
Case of the Fan-Dancer's Horse. E. S. Gardner
Case of the Fast Young Lady. Michael Burt
Case of the Fatal Film. J. Hunter
Case of the Fatal Souvenir. L. Jackson
Case of the Fatal Taxi Cab. W. M. Graydon
Case of the Fear Makers. J. N. Chance
Case of the Fenced-In Woman. E. S. Gardner
Case of the Fiery Fingers. E. S. Gardner
Case of the Fifth Key. G. Dean
Case of the Fighting Padre. L. Jackson
Case of the Fighting Soldier. C. Bush
Case of the First-Class Carriage. C. Carnac
Case of the Five Dummy Books. W. W. Sayer
Case of the Five Fugitives. L. Jackson
Case of the Five Merchants. W. M. Graydon
Case of the Five Red Herrings. L. Jackson
Case of the Flowery Corpse. C. Bush
Case of the Flying Ass. C. Bush
Case of the Flying Fifteen. O. Mills
Case of the Foot-Loose Doll. E. S. Gardner
Case of the Forbidden Island. W. Tyrer
Case of the Forty Thieves. J. Rhode
Case of the Foster Father. V. Perdue
Case of the Four Barons. W. M. Graydon
Case of the Four Friends. J. C. Masterman
Case of the Four Pages. John Norman
Case of the Fourth Detective. C. Bush
Case of the Frantic Ladies. L. Floyd
Case of the French Raiders. J. Hunter
Case of the Frightened Brother. Frank King
Case of the Frightened Fish. William Du Bois
Case of the Frightened Girl. R. Hardinge
Case of the Frightened Lady. E. Wallace
Case of the Frightened Man. A. Parsons
Case of the Frightened Mannequin. C. Bush
Case of the Frozen Scream. T. B. Haughey
Case of the Fugitive Nurse. E. S. Gardner
Case of the Gambler's Corpse. R. Clarke
Case of the Gangster's Moll. J. G. Brandon
Case of the Giant Killer. H. C. Branson
Case of the Gilded Fly. E. Crispin
Case of the Gilded Lily. E. S. Gardner
Case of the Girl on Remand. J. Hunter
Case of the Girl Reporter. J. W. Bobin
Case of the Glamorous Ghost. E. S. Gardner
Case of the Glass Slipper. N. MacKenzie
Case of the Gloating Landlord. R. Fenisong
Case of the Gold Coins. A. Wynne
Case of the Gold-Digger's Purse. E. S. Gardner
Case of the Golden Stool. F. A. Symonds
Case of the Good Employer. C. Bush
Case of the Grand Alliance. C. Bush
Case of the Greedy Rainmaker. George Douglas
Case of the Green Caravan. R. Hardinge
Case of the Green-Eyed Sister. E. S. Gardner
Case of the Green Felt Hat. C. Bush
Case of the Green Knife. A. Wynne
Case of the Grieving Monkey. V. Perdue
Case of the Grinning Gorilla. E. S. Gardner
Case of the Half-Wakened Wife. E. S. Gardner
Case of the Hanging Lady. N. Jones
Case of the Hanging Rope. C. Bush
Case of the Happy Medium. C. Bush
Case of the Happy Warrior. C. Bush
Case of the Hated Senator. M. Scherf
Case of the Haunted Brides. William Du Bois
Case of the Haunted Husband. E. S. Gardner
Case of the Haven Hotel. C. Bush
Case of the Head Dispenser. J. W. Bobin
Case of the Headless Corpse. Dennis Allan
Case of the Headless Jesuit. G. Bellairs
Case of the Heavenly Twin. C. Bush
Case of the Hesitant Hostess. E. S. Gardner
Case of the Hold-Up King. F. A. Symonds
Case of the Hollow Man. M. Carrel
Case of the Horrified Heirs. E. S. Gardner
Case of the Housekeeper's Hair. C. Bush
Case of the Howling Dog. E. S. Gardner
Case of the Hula Clock. D. Gardner
Case of the Human Ape. W. M. Graydon
Case of the Human Mole. H. Townley
Case of the Hypnotized Virgin. J. Roeburt
Case of the Ice-Cold Hands. E. S. Gardner
Case of the Income-Tax Frauds. W. J. Bayfield
Case of the Indian Dancer. A. Parsons
Case of the Indian Millionaire. A. Parsons
Case of the Indian Watcher. A. Parsons
Case of the Indiana Torturer. E. E. Saks
Case of the Innocent Victims. J. Creasey
Case of the Innocent Wife. N. Morland
Case of the Innocent Witness. M. Carrel
Case of the International Adventurer. J. W. Bobin
Case of the Invisible Thief. T. B. Haughey
Case of the Irate Witness. E. S. Gardner
Case of the Island Princess. R. C. Armour
Case of the Island Trader. J. W. Bobin
Case of the Ivory Arrow. H. S. Keeler
Case of the Jack of Clubs. Gwyn Evans
Case of the Jade-Handled Knife. G. H. Teed
Case of the Japanese Contract. A. Parsons
Case of the Japanese Detective. T. C. Wignall
Case of the Jeweled Ragpicker. H. S. Keeler
Case of the Journeying Boy. M. Innes
Case of the Judas Spoon. M. L. Stokes
Case of the Jumbo Sandwich. C. Bush
Case of the Kidnapped Colonel. C. Bush
Case of the Kidnapped Legatee. R. C. Armour
Case of the Kidnapped Prisoner. A. Blair
Case of the Kidnapped Shadow. T. B. Haughey
Case of the Kidnapped Specialist. R. Hardinge
Case of the King of Montavia. Roland Daniel
Case of the King's Spy. W. W. Sayer
Case of the Kippered Corpse. M. Scherf
Case of the Lame Canary. E. S. Gardner
Case of the Late Pig. M. Allingham
Case of the Laughing Dwarf. J. Reach
Case of the Laughing Jesuit. Michael Burt
Case of the Laughing Virgin. Jonathan Craig
Case of the Lavender Gripsack. H. S. Keeler
Case of the Lazy Lover. E. S. Gardner
Case of the Leaning Man. C. Bush
Case of the Legion Deserter. H. Clevely
Case of the Little Doctor. Hilda Lewis
Case of the Little Green Man. M. Reynolds
Case of the Lone Plantation. E. J. Murray
Case of the Lonely Heiress. E. S. Gardner
Case of the Lonely Lovers. W. Daemer
Case of the Long-Firm Frauds. J. W. Bobin
Case of the Long-Legged Models. E. S. Gardner
Case of the Lucky Legs. E. S. Gardner
Case of the Lucky Loser. E. S. Gardner
Case of the Mad Inventor. J. Creasey
Case of the Magic Mirror. C. Bush
Case of the Malevolent Twin. L. Eby
Case of the Maltese Treasure. T. B. Haughey
Case of the Malverne Diamonds. L. Gribble
Case of the Man in Black. O. Merland
Case of the Man on Leave. G. Chester
Case of the Man Who Never Slept. Gwyn Evans
Case of the Man with No Name. J. Drummond
Case of the Marsden Rubies. L. Gribble
Case of the Master Organizer. A. Murray
Case of the Mexican Knife. G. Homes
Case of the Michaelmas Goose. C. Witting
Case of the Mill Owner's Son. W. M. Graydon
Case of the Millionaire Newspaper Owner. R. C. Armour
Case of the Millionaire's Blackmail. W. J. Bayfield
Case of the Mischievous Doll. E. S. Gardner
Case of the Missing Airmen. G. Elliott
Case of the Missing Bridegroom. G. Dilnot
Case of the Missing Bullion. Peter Gordon
Case of the Missing Co-Ed. W. Hardy
Case of the Missing Corpse. E. Lanham
Case of the Missing Corpse. J. Sanger
Case of the Missing D.F.C. A. Parsons
Case of the Missing Diary. A. Fielding
Case of the Missing Estate Agent. Donald Stuart
Case of the Missing G.I. Bride. A. Parsons
Case of the Missing Gardener. H. Walker
Case of the Missing Hand. M. Hervey
Case of the Missing Lovers. Lee Roberts
Case of the Missing Major. A. Parsons
Case of the Missing Men. C. Bush
Case of the Missing Minutes. C. Bush
Case of the Missing Musician. R. Hardinge
Case of the Missing Nazi. W. Tyrer
Case of the Missing Sandals. N. B. Mavity
Case of the Missing Scientist. A. Parsons
Case of the Missing Ships. S. Hope
Case of the Missing Stoker. L. Jackson
Case of the Missing Surgeon. A. Parsons
Case of the Monday Murders. C. Bush
Case of the Monta Grandee Diamonds. S. Hope
Case of the Moth-Eaten Mink. E. S. Gardner
Case of the Moving Finger. A. Christie
Case of the Muckrakers. W. McNeilly
Case of the Mummified Hand. G. H. Teed
Case of the Murdered Caretaker. C. Gates
Case of the Murdered Commissionaire. J. G. Brandon
Case of the Murdered Financier. J. Creasey
Case of the Murdered Madame. H. Kane
Case of the Murdered Mahout. W. M. Graydon
Case of the Murdered Major. C. Bush
Case of the Murdered Model. T. B. Dewey
Case of the Murdered Pawn Broker. W. Edwards
Case of the Murdered Postman. R. Hardinge
Case of the Murdered Redhead. F. Lockridge
Case of the Murdered Taxi Driver. A. Blair
Case of the Murdered Wedding Guest. W. Jardine
Case of the Murderer's Bride. E. S. Gardner
Case of the Musical Cow. E. S. Gardner
Case of the Mysterious Germs. R. C. Armour
Case of the Mysterious Jockey. W. M. Graydon
Case of the Mysterious Moll. H. S. Keeler
Case of the Mystery Champion. A. Steffens Hardy
Case of the Mystery Millionaire. A. Murray
Case of the Mythical Monkeys. E. S. Gardner
Case of the Nabob's Son. W. M. Graydon
Case of the Nameless Corpse. C. B. Kelland
Case of the Nameless Man. O. Merland
Case of the Nameless Millionaire. A. Parsons
Case of the Naval Defaulter. W. Tyrer
Case of the Naval Stores Bucket. W. Tyrer
Case of the Negligent Nymph. E. S. Gardner
Case of the Nervous Accomplice. E. S. Gardner
Case of the Nervous Nude. Jonathan Craig
Case of the Night Club Queen. J. G. Brandon
Case of the Night Lorry Driver. L. Jackson
Case of the Old Oak Chest. H. H. C. Gibbons
Case of the One-Eyed Witness. E. S. Gardner
Case of the 100% Alibis. C. Bush
Case of the One-Penny Orange. E. V. Cunningham
Case of the Open Drawer. L. Allan
Case of the Painted Girl. Frank King
Case of the Painted Ladies. B. Flynn
Case of the Paralyzed Man. A. Murray
Case of the Perfect Alibi. M. Carrel
Case of the Perfumed Mouse. T. Du Bois
Case of the Perjured Parrot. E. S. Gardner
Case of the Petticoat Murder. Jonathan Craig
Case of the Phantom Fingerprints. K. F. Crossen

C

Case of the Phantom Fortune. E. S. Gardner
Case of the Philosper's Ring. R. Collins
Case of the Plastic Man. J. Donavan
Case of the Plastic Mask. J. Donavan
Case of the Platinum Blonde. C. Bush
Case of the Poisoned Cat. K. P. Bahadur
Case of the Poisoned Cocktails. O. Boyd
Case of the Poisoned Eclairs. E. V. Cunningham
Case of the Poisoned Pen. Gwyn Evans
Case of the Poisoned Pup. S. S. Pridham
Case of the Pornographic Photos. Lawrence Block
Case of the Portuguese Giantess. G. H. Teed
Case of the Postponed Murder. E. S. Gardner
Case of the Preying Evangelist. D. W. F. Hardie
Case of the President's Heads. M. L. Stokes
Case of the Press Photographer. W. J. Bayfield
Case of the Prince's Diary. A. Parsons
Case of the Prince's Prisoners. A. Parsons
Case of the Prodigal Daughter. C. Bush
Case of the Purloined Picture. C. Bush
Case of the Purple Calf. B. Flynn
Case of the Queenly Contestant. E. S. Gardner
Case of the R. E. Pipe. C. M. Wills
Case of the Radioactive Redhead. G. G. Fickling
Case of the Rajah's Son. H. E. Hill
Case of the Red Box. R. Stout
Case of the Red Brunette. C. Bush
Case of the Red Crimona's. H. H. C. Gibbons
Case of the Red-Haired Girl. A. Wynne
Case of the Redoubled Cross. R. King
Case of the Rejuvenated Millionaire. G. N. Philips
Case of the Reluctant Model. E. S. Gardner
Case of the Renegade Agent. D. Reid
Case of the Renegade Naval Officer. A. Parsons
Case of the Rented Coffin. L. D. Smith
Case of the Repatriated Prisoner. G. Chester
Case of the Restless Redhead. E. S. Gardner
Case of the Returning Soldier. W. Tyrer
Case of the Rival Race Gangs. H. C. Miln
Case of the River Smugglers. D. T. Hughes
Case of the Rolling Bones. E. S. Gardner
Case of the Runaway Corpse. E. S. Gardner
Case of the Running Man. C. Bush
Case of the Running Mouse. C. Bush
Case of the Russian Cross. C. Bush
Case of the Russian Crown Jewels. R. H. Poole
Case of the Russian Diplomat. E. V. Cunningham
Case of the Rusted Room. J. Donavan
Case of the Sapphire Brooch. C. Bush
Case of the Scared Rabbits. G. Bellairs
Case of the Screaming Woman. E. S. Gardner
Case of the Seaside Crooks. A. Murray
Case of the Second Chance. C. Bush
Case of the Second Crime. A. Parsons
Case of the Secret Agent. R. Hardinge
Case of the Secret Plans. C. H. Barker
Case of the Secret Road. A. Parsons
Case of the Seven Bells. C. Bush
Case of the Seven Keys. G. Stanley
Case of the Seven Murders. E. Queen
Case of the Seven of Calvary. A. Boucher
Case of the Seven Sneezes. A. Boucher
Case of the Seven Whistlers. G. Bellairs
Case of the Severed Skull. H. Weiner
Case of the Shapely Shadow. E. S. Gardner
Case of the Shaven Blonde. R. Hobart
Case of the Shivering Chorus Girls. J. A. Phillips
Case of the Shoplifter's Shoe. E. S. Gardner
Case of the Shot Looter. M. Frazer
Case of the Silent Partner. E. S. Gardner
Case of the Silent Safe-Cutters. H. H. C. Gibbons
Case of the Silent Stranger. Jonathan Craig
Case of the Silken Petticoat. C. Bush
Case of the Singing Skirt. E. S. Gardner
Case of the Sinister Farm. A. Parsons
Case of the Six Bullets. R. M. Laurenson
Case of the Six Mistresses. B. Maxwell
Case of the Six O'Clock Scream. A. Parsons
Case of the 16 Beans. H. S. Keeler
Case of the Sleeping Partner. E. S. Brooks
Case of the Sleepwalker's Niece. E. S. Gardner
Case of the Smoking Chimney. E. S. Gardner
Case of the Smuggled Currency. H. Clevely
Case of the Society Blackmailer. W. M. Graydon
Case of the Solid Key. A. Boucher
Case of the Spanish Legatee. A. Parsons
Case of the Spiv's Secret. A. Parsons
Case of the Spurious Spinster. E. S. Gardner
Case of the Squealing Cat. J. Reach
Case of the Stag at Bay. W. McNeilly
Case of the Stepdaughter's Secret. E. S. Gardner
Case of the Stolen Bridegroom. H. Adams
Case of the Stolen Evidence. A. Parsons
Case of the Stolen Mine. R. Hardinge
Case of the Stolen Police Dossier. A. Blair
Case of the Stolen Ransom. J. Hunter
Case of the Stranded Touring Company. L. Carlton
Case of the Strange Beauties. Frank King
Case of the Strange Wireless Message. W. W. Sayer
Case of the Strangled Seven. P. Yorke
Case of the Strangled Starlet. J. H. Chase
Case of the Straw Man. D. M. Disney
Case of the Stuttering Bishop. E. S. Gardner
Case of the Subtitute Face. E. S. Gardner
Case of the Sulky Girl. R. F. Fernand
Case of the Sulky Girl. E. S. Gardner
Case of the Sun Bather's Diary. E. S. Gardner
Case of the Suppressed Will. W. M. Graydon
Case of the "Suspect" Watchmaker. L. Jackson
Case of the Swindled Guarantor. W. Tyrer
Case of the Swindler's "Stooge". A. Parsons
Case of the Swinging Spider. P. Yorke
Case of the Tainted Token. K. M. Knight
Case of the Talking Bug. The Gordons
Case of the Talking Dust. J. Donavan
Case of the Tea-Cosy's Aunt. Anthony Gilbert
Case of the Tearless Widow. J. Roeburt
Case of the Ten Diamonds. G. H. Teed
Case of the Terrified Typist. E. S. Gardner
Case of the Theatrical Profiteer. W. M. Graydon
Case of the 13th Coach. E. G. Bartlett
Case of the Three Absconding Swindlers. C. Brisbane
Case of the Three Broken Necks. A. McClintock
Case of the Three Lost Letters. C. Bush
Case of the Three-Ring Puzzle. C. Bush
Case of the Three Strange Faces. C. Bush
Case of the Three Survivors. H. Clevely
Case of the Topaz Flower. C. M. Russell
Case of the Trade Secret. J. W. Bobin
Case of the Transatlantic Flyers. Jack Lewis
Case of the Transposed Legs. H. S. Keeler
Case of the Treble Twist. C. Bush
Case of the Triple Twist. C. Bush
Case of the Troubled Trustee. E. S. Gardner
Case of the Tudor Queen. C. Bush
Case of the Turning Tide. E. S. Gardner
Case of the Twin Detectives. C. Brooks
Case of the Twisted Scarf. F. Durbridge
Case of the Twisted Trail. F. A. Symonds
Case of the Two Bankers. J. W. Bobin
Case of the Two Brothers. A. Murray
Case of the Two Crooked Baronets. W. Tyrer
Case of the Two Doctors. Nicholas Carter
Case of the Two-Faced Swindler. J. Drummond
Case of the Two Guardians. W. M. Graydon
Case of the Two Pearl Necklaces. A. Fielding
Case of the Two Scapegraces. W. M. Graydon
Case of the Two Strange Ladies. H. S. Keeler
Case of the Unconquered Sisters. T. Downing
Case of the Uncut Gems. A. Murray
Case of the Undischarged Bankrupt. A. Murray
Case of the Unfortunate Village. C. Bush
Case of the Unhappy Angels. G. Homes
Case of the Unknown Heir. A. Parsons
Case of the Un-Named Film. A. Murray
Case of the Vagabond Virgin. E. S. Gardner
Case of the Vanished Husband. W. J. Bayfield
Case of the Vanishing Artist. Frank King
Case of the Vanishing Beauty. R. S. Prather
Case of the Vanishing Woman. R. Archer
Case of the Velvet Claws. E. S. Gardner
Case of the Village Tramp. Jonathan Craig
Case of the Violent Virgin. M. Avallone
Case of the Violet Smoke. J. Donavan
Case of the Walking Corpse. A. Livingston
Case of the Walking Corpse. B. Halliday
Case of the Waylaid Wolf. E. S. Gardner
Case of the Weird Sisters. C. Armstrong
Case of the Weird Sisters. W. Spence
Case of the Wicked Three. A. Parsons
Case of the Wicked Twin. L. Eby
Case of the Winking Buddha. M. L. Stokes
Case of the Withered Hand. J. G. Brandon
Case of the Woman in Black. A. Murray
Case of the Worried Waitress. E. S. Gardner
Case of the Would-Be Widow. J. G. Brandon
Case of the Wounded Mastiff. N. Harman
Case of Torches. Clark Smith
Case of William Smith. P. Wentworth
Case of Young Lord Folliot. N. H. Romanes
Case on Cloud Nine. L. Freeman
Case Pending. Dell Shannon
Case Proceeding. J. Prescott
Case Re-Opened. J. Prescot
Case to Answer. E. Lustgarten
Case 29. J. Cassells
Case with Four Clowns. L. Bruce
Case with Nine Solutions. J. J. Connington
Case with No Conclusion. L. Bruce
Case with Ropes and Rings. L. Bruce
Case with Three Husbands. M. Erskine
Case with Three Threads. Anthony Lang
Case Without a Clue. Nicholas Carter
Case Without a Clue. N. Morland
Case Without a Corpse. L. Bruce
Casebook of a Victorian Detective. J. M'Levy
Casebook of Crime. A. Brock
Casebook of Jules de Grandin. Seabury Quinn
Casebook of Lucius Leffing. J. P. Brennan
Casebook of Solar Pons. A. Derleth
Casebook of the Black Widowers. I. Asimov
Cases of Susan Dare. M. G. Eberhart
Cash and Carry. C. Megahy
Cash on Delivery. F. Du Boisgobey
Cash on Destruction. S. Howatch
Cashelmara. S. Howatch
Cashier's Secret. Nicholas Carter
Casino. G. Norsworthy
Casino for Sale. C. Brahms
Casino Greystone. L. Bronte
Casino Murder Case. S. S. Van Dine
Casino Mystery. M. E. Cooke
Casino Mystery. Elaine Hamilton
Casino Royale. I. Fleming
Casinopoly. H. Janson
Cask. F. W. Crofts
Cask of Amontillado. D. R. Gribble
Casket of Death. J. B. O'Sullivan
Caspian Song. J. G. Sarasin
Cassady. J. Sutton
Cassandra Crossing. R. Katz
Cassandra, Goodbye. A. W. Berg
Cassia. M. Conte
Cassidy the Con Man. G. H. Teed
Cassidy's Girl. D. Goodis
Cassidy's Yard. Alan White
Cassiodore Case. A. R. Martin
Cassis...Resort to Vengeance. Mark Walker
Cast a Green Shadow. M. V. Hunt
Cast a Long Shadow. H. Elsna
Cast a Yellow Shadow. Ross Thomas
Cast Away. E. Yates
Cast for Death. M. Yorke
Cast, in Order of Disappearance. Simon Brett
Cast Iron Alibi. D. Betteridge
Cast of Death. N. Orde-Powlette
Cast Out. M. Gerard
Castang's City. N. Freeling
Castilian Caper. V. A. Paradis
Casting of the Shadows. J. Dory
Casting the Net. Dick Stewart
Castle and the Key. C. Knye
Castle at Glencarris. J. Vicary
Castle at Witch's Coven. V. Coffman
Castle Barebane. Joan Aiken
Castle Barra. V. Coffman
Castle Black. J. Schubert
Castle by the Sea. B. M. Watson
Castle Captive. S. Ratcliffe
Castle Clodha. Alanna Knight
Castle Cloud. Joan Grant
Castle Cloud. Elizabeth Norman
Castle Conquest. B. Gray
Castle Craggs. V. Maas
Castle Craneycross. G. B. McCutcheon
Castle Danger. W. O'Meara

Title Index / Centurion's Story / 465

Castle Dangerous. V. Gunn
Castle Dangerous. A. Wood
Castle-Dinas. R. A. J. Walling
Castle Doom. M. McEvoy
Castle Dor. A. T. Quiller-Couch
Castle Enigma. J. R. Warren
Castle Fell. D. Duff
Castle Fenham Case. Charles Ross
Castle Foam. H. W. French
Castle for Sale. M. Messer
Castle for Tess. R. Simon
Castle for the Left Hand. Annjeanette Scott
Castle Garac. N. Monsarrat
Castle Gay. J. Buchan
Castle Heritage. E. Barr
Castle Hohenfels. Dorinne Moore
Castle in Bohemia. D. Whitelaw
Castle in Canada. C. Farr
Castle in Spain. J. De Mille
Castle in Spain. C. Farr
Castle in the Air. D. E. Westlake
Castle Island Case. V. W. Mason
Castle Malindone. H. Ford
Castle Mandragora. M. Durham
Castle Midnight. E. McKenna
Castle Minerva. V. Canning
Castle Mirage. Alice Brennan
Castle Morvant. D. Daniels
Castle of Berry Pomeroy. E. Montague
Castle of Caithness. F. H. P.
Castle of Closing Doors. D. Winston
Castle of Dark Evil. Melissa Napier
Castle of Doubt. J. H. Whitson
Castle of Dreams. P. Warren
Castle of Eagles. C. Heaven
Castle of Ehrenstein. G. P. R. James
Castle of Evil. S. Abbott
Castle of Fear. S. Abbott
Castle of Fear. J. J. Farjeon
Castle of Fear. R. S. L. Harding
Castle of Lies. A. H. Vesey
Castle of Lindenburg. M. G. Lewis
Castle of Lugas. A. Fernandez
Castle of Mowbray. N. Harley
Castle of Otranto. H. Walpole
Castle of St. Vallery. Anonymous
Castle of Shadows. A. M. Williamson
Castle of Sin. J. Cassells
Castle of Terror. C. Farr
Castle of the Demon. P. Ruell
Castle of Vengeance. M. Hastings
Castle of Villeroy. F. M. Mills
Castle of Vivaldi. C. Harwood
Castle of Wolfenbach. Mrs. Parsons
Castle on the Cliff. Dan Ross
Castle on the Hill. E. Randolph
Castle on the Hill. W. E. D. Ross
Castle on the Island. L. Ames
Castle on the Loch. C. Farr
Castle on the Mountain. J. Wellsley
Castle on the Rhine. C. Farr
Castle Perilous. V. Johnston
Castle Raven. Laura Black
Castle Rock Mystery. G. F. Gibbs
Castle Sinister. Gwyn Evans
Castle Skull. J. D. Carr
Castle Spectre. M. G. Lewis
Castle Terror. M. Z. Bradley
Castle That Whispered. M. Farnsworth
Castle to Let. B. Reynolds
Castle Ugly. Marianne Barrett
Castle Wafer. H. Wood
Castle Walk. M. Le Bas
Castlecliff. S. Shulman
Castlecourt Diamond Case. G. Bonner
Castledoom. E. Lecale
Castleford Conundrum. J. J. Connington
Castlereagh. M. Heath
Castlereagh. J. L. Roberts
Castles Burning. A. Lyons
Castle's Heir. H. Wood
Castles in the Air. Augustus Muir
Castles in the Air. B. Orczy
Castles of Athlin and Dunbayne. A. Radcliffe
Castro File. J. Rosenberger
Casual Murderer. H. Footner
Casual Slaughters. V. Hanson
Casual Slaughters. J. Quince
Cat. V. Gielgud
Cat. G. Simenon
Cat. A. Sinclair
Cat Among the Pigeons. A. Christie
Cat and Capricorn. D. B. Olsen
Cat and Feather. D. Basil
Cat and Fiddle Murders. E. B. Ronald
Cat and Mouse. C. Brand
Cat and Mouse. E. K. Goldthwaite
Cat and Mouse. M. Halliday
Cat and Mouse. H. Pentecost
Cat and Mouse. M. L. Roby
Cat and Mouse Murder. E. K. Goldthwaite
Cat and the Canary. G. Kingsley
Cat and the Canary. John Willard
Cat and the Cherub. C. B. Fernald
Cat and the Clock. C. G. Booth
Cat and the Corpse. R. A. J. Walling
Cat and the Fiddle. P. Costello
Cat Burglar. E. Wallace
Cat Cay Warrant. Allen Morgen
Cat Climbs. C. A. Tarrant

Cat Creeps. John Willard
Cat Dies First. W. H. L. Crauford
Cat-Eye. Lucille Palmer
Cat Got Your Tongue? C. Carpenter
Cat Got Your Tongue? A. Pearson
Cat in Gloves. D. Delaney
Cat in the Convoy. W. G. Schofield
Cat in the Hat Box. A. W. Upfield
Cat Jumps. M. Burton
Cat of Bast and other stories of mystery. W. E. Thorner
Cat of Many Tails. E. Queen
Cat o' Nine Tails. P. J. Gillette
Cat of Nine Tales. V. Leigh
Cat Saw Murder. D. B. Olsen
Cat Screams. T. Downing
Cat Trap. G. A. Ralston
Cat Trapper. P. Bryers
Cat Walk. D. B. Olsen
Cat Watchers. J. N. Chance
Cat Wears a Mask. D. B. Olsen
Cat Wears a Noose. D. B. Olsen
Cat Who Ate Danish Modern. L. J. Braun
Cat Who Could Read Backwards. L. J. Braun
Cat Who Turned On and Off. L. J. Braun
Cat Will Mew. Frederick Jackson
Cat with the Mustache. Simon
Catacombs. Jay Bennett
Catacombs of Death. Operator 1384
Catafalque. R. C. Goldston
Catalyst. Josephine Bell
Catalyst. K. Lowe
Catalyst Club. G. Dyer
Catastrophe. E. Gaboriau
Catastrophe at Cliff Haven. T. K. Cook
Catastrophe Club. Frank King
Catastrophe in Bohemia and other stories. H. S. Brooks
Catch. J. Boland
Catch a Fallen Starlet. D. Sanderson
Catch a Falling Spy. N. Benchley
Catch a Falling Spy. L. Deighton
Catch a Killer. U. Curtiss
Catch a Killer. Robert Martin
Catch a Tiger. O. Cameron
Catch a Tiger. Martin Thomas
Catch and Kill. N. Blake
Catch and Squeeze. Craig Cooper
Catch-as-Catch-Can. C. Armstrong
Catch as Catch Can. F. Lockridge
Catch-'Em-Alice-O! Michael Burt
Catch Me a Phoenix. Carter Brown
Catch Me a Renegade. H. Janson
Catch Me a Spy. G. Marton
Catch Me a Traitor. Henry Talbot
Catch Me—If You Can. B. Cobb
Catch Me If You Can. P. McGerr
Catch Me If You Can. J. Weinstock
Catch Me, Kill Me. W. H. Hallahan
Catch That Thief! W. Spence
Catch the Brass Ring. S. Marlowe
Catch the Gold Ring. J. S. Strange
Catch the Saint. L. Charteris
Catching a Tartar. G. W. Appleton
Cater Street Hangman. A. Perry
Caterpillar Cop. J. McClure
Catfish Tangle. C. Williams
Cathedral Option. R. Montana
Catherine Wheel. P. Wentworth
Catherwood Mystery. A. P. Southwick
Cathkin Mystery. G. Woden
Cathra Mystery. A. G. MacLeod
Cathy Rossiter. J. L. Rickard
Catmur's Caves. R. Dowling
Catnapped. The Gordons
Cats. B. Roueche
Cats. N. Sharman
Cat's Claw. D. B. Olsen
Cat's Cradle. P. Flower
Cat's Cradle. S. Harvester
Cat's Cradle Murder. Jerome Barry
Cat's Don't Need Coffins. D. B. Olsen
Cats Don't Smile. D. B. Olsen
Cat's Eye. C. Aveline
Cat's Eye. R. A. Freeman
Cat's-Eye Ring. F. Du Boisgobey
Cat's Eyes. S. Warwick
Cats Have Tall Shadows. D. B. Olsen
Cats in Crime...and others. A. L. Germeshausen
Cat's Paw. J. Heron
Cat's Paw. H. Hocking
Cat's Paw. C. B. Kelland
Cat's Paw. N. S. Lincoln
Cat's-Paw. M. Salter
Cat's Paw. R. Scarlett
Cat's Prey. D. Eden
Cats Prowl at Night. A. A. Fair
Cat's Whisker. H. C. Bailey
Catseyes. A. Winnington
Catspaw. W. LeQueux
Catspaw. A. Murray
Catspaw. W. H. Osborne
Catspaw. P. Reakes
Catspaw. M. Russell
Catspaw for Murder. D. B. Olsen
Catspaw Ordeal. E. Ronns
Catspaws. C. Brooks
Catt Among the Pigeons. C. Connell
Catt Out of the Bag. C. Witting
Caught and Bowled. Anonymous

Caught at Last! D. Donovan
Caught by Fate. Mageli
Caught Dead. B. Halliday
Caught in a Trap. J. C. Hutcheson
Caught in a Web. R. St. Clair
Caught in a Whirlpool. Nicholas Carter
Caught in Mid-Ocean. Anonymous
Caught in Mid-Ocean. O. Harper
Caught in Terror. M. Bardsley
Caught in the Act. John Lee
Caught in the Machine. C. Campbell
Caught in the Middle. S. Waldron
Caught in the Net. E. Gaboriau
Caught in the Toils. Nicholas Carter
Caught Wet. R. Crothers
Cauldron Bubble. G. Goodchild
Cauldron Bubbles. N. A. Temple-Ellis
Cauldron of Evil. Marilyn Ross
Cause for a Killing. J. Wainwright
Cause for Alarm. E. Ambler
Cause for Alarm. J. Pendower
Cause for Malice. F. Hurt
Cause for Suspicion. T. C. H. Jacobs
Cause of Death. M. Underwood
Cause of the Crime. L. Frank
Cause of the Screaming. D. Elias
Cause Unknown. J. J. Farjeon
Causeway. P. M. Hubbard
Causeway to the Past. W. O'Farrell
Cautious Assassin. D. Orgill
Cautious Maiden. C. Saint-Laurent
Cautious Overshoes. M. Scherf
Cautley Conundrum. A. Fielding
Cautley Mystery. A. Fielding
Cavalier Conquest. B. Gray
Cavalier of Chance. S. Horler
Cavalier of Crime. F. Hedley
Cavalier of the Night. R. Armstrong
Cavalier's Corpse. T. Du Bois
Cavalier's Cup. Carter Dickson
Cavaliers of Death. R. Forbes
Cavanaugh Keep. M. Leslie
Cavanaugh Quest. T. Gifford
Cave and the Beast. I. Garrick
Cave of Bats. Robert MacLeod
Cave of the Chinese Skeletons. J. Seward
Cave of the Moaning Wind. J. Deweese
Cave of the Moon. N. McGill
Cave with Two Exits. H. H. Cooper
Cavender's Balkan Quest. E. Tokson
Cavern. A. MacVicar
Cavern of Horrors. Anonymous
Cavern of the Damned. C. Steele
Caverns of Falkenhorst. Dorinne Moore
Caves of Alienation. Stuart Evans
Caves of Blackscar. Haydon Dean
Caves of Claro. J. Palmer
Caves of Death. V. Norwood
Caves of Fear. P. Morton
Caves of Guernica. Samuel Edwards
Caves of Night. J. Christopher
Caves of Shend. D. Hennessey
Caves of Steel. I. Asimov
Caves of Terror. T. Mundy
Caviar Cruise. F. Webb
Caviar to Kill. K. T. McCall
Caviare. Godfrey Smith
Cawthorn Journals. S. Marlowe
Caxborough Scandal. F. Whishaw
Cease upon the Midnight. S. Troy
Cecile. H. Smart
Cecile's Fortune. F. Du Boisgobey
Cecile's Tryst. J. Payn
Cecily. I. Holland
Cedar Haven. P. Campbell
Cedar Tree. Rona Randall
Celebate's Wife. H. Flowerdew
Celebrated Cases of Dick Tracy, 1931-1951. C. Gould
Celebrated Cases of Judge Dee. R. Van Gulik
Celebrated Detective. Anonymous
Celebration for Murder. R. Wissman
Celestial City. B. Orczy
Celestial Navigation. A. Tyler
Celestial Ruby. T. W. Speight
Celia. P. Trent
Celia's Career. P. Trent
Cell. D. Case
Cell Car 54. J. M. Fox
Cell Murder Mystery. D. B. Hobart
"Cell 13". E. H. Trafton
Cellar. R. Laymon
Cellar at No. 5. Shelley Smith
Cellar Boys. W. H. Baker
Cellars of the Dead. Marilyn Ross
Cellini Plaque. H. MacGrath
Cellini Smith, Detective. Robert Reeves
Celluloid Caper. C. Miron
Cemetery First Stop! David Hume
Cemetery in Munich. C. Hilton
Censor. J. Gardner
Centeola; and other tales. D. P. Thompson
Center of the Web. K. Roberts
Centerforce. T. A. Waters
Centipede. B. Boothby
Central Park Murder. B. Duff
Central Park Mystery. Old Sleuth
Centre Court Murder. B. Newman
Centre Holds. A. Storey
Centurion's Story. P. C. MacFarlane

C

466 / Cepherine   **Title Index**

Cepherine. J. H. Robinson
Cerebus Murders. R. Quest
Ceremony in the Lincoln Tunnel. R. Cunningham
Certain Blindness. Roy Lewis
Certain Dr. Mellor. P. P. Maguire
Certain Dr. Thorndyke. R. A. Freeman
Certain Evil. D. Kraslow
Certain Liveliness. H. F. Moulton
Certain Sleep. H. Reilly
Certified Check. Nicholas Carter
Certified Insane. R. C. Armour
Chaff Before the Wind. S. Christiansen
Chain-Gang Queenie. B. Sarto
Chain Invisible. C. R. Gull
Chain Murder. A. Soutar
Chain of Chance. S. Lem
Chain of Clues. Nicholas Carter
Chain of Command. I. R. Blacker
Chain of Command. D. Buttenshaw
Chain of Darkness. K. Cook
Chain of Death. N. McLarty
Chain of Death. S. Noel
Chain of Evidence. Nicholas Carter
Chain of Evidence. C. Wells
Chain of Infamy. G. Beare
Chain Reaction. C. Hodder-Williams
Chain Reaction. G. Pape
Chain Reaction. G. A. Ralston
Chained. F. Hird
Chained Reaction. R. Sapir
Chained Crocodile. B. Whitaker
Chains. B. Moss
Chains of Circumstance. T. W. Speight
Chair for Death. J. Reddoch
Chair for Martin Rome. H. E. Helseth
Chair-Lift. E. H. Clements
Chairman. J. K. Kennedy
Chairman. G. Vaizey
Chalet Bougy-Villars. S. Marvin
Chalet Diabolique. V. Coffman
Chalice Caper. D. MacKenzie
Chalk Face. W. Frank
Chalk-Face. J. M. Walsh
Chalk Garden. E. Bagnold
Chalk Stream Killing. R. Pertwee
Challenge. H. C. McNeile
Challenge at Le Mans. L. Kenyon
Challenge Blue Mask! Anthony Morton
Challenge for the Dreamer. W. M. Duncan
Challenge for the Picaroon. J. Cassells
Challenge for Three. D. Garth
Challenge of Evil. A. Metcalfe
Challenge of the Bush. C. R. Cooper
Challenge to Murder. F. J. Whaley
Challenge to the Four. Mark Cross
Challoners of Bristol. L. Hayes
Chamber of Horrors. R. Bloch
Chambered Tomb. Charlotte Hunt
Chameleon. H. S. Keeler
Chameleon. W. LeQueux
Chameleon Course. D. Seaman
Chameleon File. L. James
Chameleon Variant. C. K. Mack
Chamois Murder. C. M. Wills
Champagne Blues. N. Lyons
Champagne for One. R. Stout
Champagne Killer. H. Pentecost
Champagne Marxist. R. Gadney
Champagne Mystery. G. Garston
Champdoce Mystery. E. Gaboriau
Champington Mystery. Le Voleur
Champion. C. N. Williamson
Champion and Crook. T. Lloyd
Champion Clue-Finder. Anonymous
Champion from Far Away. B. Hecht
Champion of Virtue. Clara Reeve
Championship Crime. J. G. Brandon
Chance Awakening. G. Markstein
Chance Child. Mrs. C. Kernahan
Chance Discovery. Nicholas Carter
Chance Elson. W. T. Ballard
Chance Encounter. E. E. Sumner
Chance in Chains. G. Thorne
Chance Marriage. E. Gaboriau
Chance Meeting. Leigh Howard
Chance to Die. Lionel Black
Chance to Die. F. Drake
Chance to Kill. R. Lait
Chance to Kill. Dell Shannon
Chance to Poison. G. Bromley
Chancellor Manuscript. R. Ludlum
Chancer. J. Brown
Chandler. W. Denbow
Chandler Policy. D. M. Disney
Chandu Men. F. Crisp
Change for Heaven. A. Hillgarth
Change for the Worse. E. Lemarchand
Change Here for Babylon. N. Bawden
Change of Heart. M. McCloy
Change of Heir. M. Innes
Change of Mind. C. Stratton
Change of Pace. T. Cobb
Change of Sky. F. Singleton
Changed Brides. E. Southworth
Changed Face. T. Craig
Changeling. M. Higgins
Changeling. A. Murray
Changeling. E. Phillpotts
Changeling. M. Wilson
Changeling Conspiracy. H. McCloy
Changing Heart. P. Barrington

Changing Pulse of Madame Touraine. A. C. Gunter
Changing Road. H. MacGrath
Channay Syndicate. E. P. Oppenheim
Channel Million. G. Collins
Channel Mystery. L. H. Brennan
Channel Mystery. W. F. Morris
Channel Tunnel Mystery. S. G. Hedges
Channing Affair. R. Dark
Channings. H. Wood
Chant of Jimmie Blacksmith. T. Keneally
Chanter's Chase. J. Tattersall
Chantic Bird. D. Ireland
Chanticleer's Muffled Crow. A. Dean
Chanting of Children. M. Sand
Chaos Contract. D. Weldon
Chaperone. E. Gordon
Chaplain's Craze. G. M. Fenn
Chapman's Wares. H. B. M. Watson
Charabanc Mystery. M. Burton
Charade. P. Stone
Charg, Monster. M. Grant
Charge from the Grave. S. Gibney
Charge Is Murder. M. Cumberland
Charge Is Murder! J. M. Spender
Charge Is Rape. J. MacGowan
Charge Is Treason. W. H. Baker
Charing Cross Mystery. J. S. Fletcher
Chariot of Desire. D. Nabarro
Chariot of the Sun. M. Clare
Charioteer. G. Thorne
Charitable End. Jessica Mann
Charity. S. Nichols
Charity Ends at Home. Colin Watson
Charity Fund Mystery. G. Chester
Charity Ghost. T. Gallon
Charity Murders. P. Manton
Charka Memorial. W. Ware
Charlatan. S. Horler
Charlatan. P. J. Stead
Charles and Elizabeth. W. J. Burley
Charles Fort Never Mentioned Wombats. G. DeWeese
Charleston Knife's in Town. Ralph Dennis
Charley Hunter. Anonymous
Charlie Boy. P. Feibleman
Charlie Chan Carries On. E. D. Biggers
Charlie Chan Returns. D. Lynds
Charlie Finds a Corpse. R. Denton
Charlie M. B. Freemantle
Charlie Muffin. B. Freemantle
Charlie Muffin U.S.A. B. Freemantle
Charlie Muffin's Uncle Sam. B. Freemantle
Charlie Sent Me! Carter Brown
Charlie's Angels. M. Franklin
Charlie's Back in Town. Jacqueline Park
Charlotte. N. Lofts
Charlotte Wade. A. McElfresh
Charlotte's Inheritance. M. E. Braddon
Charm of Finches. B. Thielen
Charmer Chased. Carter Brown
Charmian, Lady Vibard. J. Farnol
Charming Couple. Elizabeth Ford
Charming Murder. F. Shay
Charred Witness. G. H. Coxe
Charter Lane Mystery. G. C. Keech
Charter to Danger. E. Reed
Charteris Mystery. A. Fielding
Chase. N. Daniels
Chase. K. R. Dwyer
Chase. H. Foote
Chase. R. M. Gilchrist
Chase. R. G. Hubler
Chase. J. Lermina
Chase. R. Unekis
Chase a Dark Shadow. I. Valdes
Chase Around the World. Anonymous
Chase for Millions. Nicholas Carter
Chase in the Dark. Nicholas Carter
Chase of the Golden Plate. J. Futrelle
Chase of the Linda Belle. H. Footner
Chase of the Ruby. R. Marsh
Chase Round the World. R. Overton
Chase Round the World. M. Weir
Chase Royal. D. Seaman
Chase the Snowman. M. C. McDougall
Chased by Fire. N. Gould
Chasm. V. Canning
Chasm. R. W. Kauffman
Chastity House. John Burke
Chateau Chaumond. A. Delmonico
Chateau d'Or. M. J. Holmes
Chateau in Brittany. M. Young
Chateau in the Shadows. S. Marvin
Chateau of Mystery. L. T. Meade
Chateau of Secrets. J. Wellsley
Chateau of Shadows. M. Heath
Chateau of Wolves. C. Farr
Chateau Rocca. E. H. England
Chateau Saxony. S. Richard
Chateau Sinister. I. Moore
Chatham Rats. D. Mariner
Chattering Gods. R. Crawley
Chatterton Mystery. E. Everett-Green
Chauffeur-Driven Pyre. J. Hedges
Chautauqua. D. Keene
Cheap Detective. R. Grossbach
Cheat. R. Dietrich
Cheat. D. Tracy
Cheat the Hangman. E. Ferrars

Cheaters. Ledru Baker
Cheating Butler. A. M. Stein
Cheating Cheaters. M. Marcin
Cheating Justice. J. K. Stafford
Check No. 77. Nicholas Carter
Check to the King. M. Gerard
Checked Through, Missing Trunk No. 17580. R. H. Savage
Checkerboard Caper. John Morris
Checkmate. S. Horler
Checkmate. J. S. Le Fanu
Checkmate. N. Lofts
Checkmate. P. Meredith
Checkmate. A. M. Stokes
Checkmate and Deathmate. M. Ashley
Checkmate and Stalemate. D. Learmonth
Checkmate by the Colonel. G. Griswold
Checkmate for China. G. Osborne
Checkmate in Rio. Nick Carter
Checkmate to Murder. E. C. R. Lorac
Checkmated Scoundrel. Nicholas Carter
Checkmating a Countess. Dick Stewart
Checkpoint. C. W. Thayer
Checkpoint Charlie. G. De Villiers
Cheer for the Dead. E. Colter
Cheerful Blackguard. R. Pocock
Cheerful Knave. Keble Howard
Cheese from a Mousetrap. J. M. Fox
Cheim Manuscript. R. S. Prather
Chekhov Proposal. Constance Carey
Chelsea Murders. L. Davidson
Chelsea Mystery. Elaine Hamilton
Chelsea Rainbow. C. Terrot
Cheltenham Square Murder. J. Bude
Chemes. Taffrail
Cheng Ling Mystery. Elliot Bailey
Chengtu Strain. M. Goldberg
Cheque for Three Thousand. A. H. Veysey
Cherbourg Mystery. J. Maske
Cherchez la Femme. B. Graeme
Cheri-Bibi and Cecily. G. Leroux
Cheri-Bibi, Mystery Man. G. Leroux
Cherished Ones. H. Elsna
Cherry-Fair. Winifred Duke
Cherry Harvest. E. H. Clements
Cherry in the Wine Glass. J. B. O'Sullivan
Cherrycake Death. I. Tain
Cherry's Choice. L. Cargill
Chess Murders. Means Davis
Chessboard Spies. Geoffrey Davison
Chest of Opium. Mr. M—
Chestermarke Instinct. J. S. Fletcher
Cheung, Detective. H. S. Keeler
Chevalier Casse-Cou. F. Du Boisgobey
Cheviot Chase. N. Tranter
Cheyne Mystery. F. W. Crofts
Cheyney's Law. P. Cosgrove
Chez Krull. G. Simenon
Chez Torpe. F. Billetdoux
Chianti Flask. M. B. Lowndes
Chic Chick Spy. R. Tralins
Chicago. C. Carroll
Chicago. M. Watkins
Chicago Chick. H. Janson
Chicago Dames. B. Sarto
Chicago Deadline. E. Mazzaro
Chicago 11. D. Keene
Chicago Girl. T. Kenrick
Chicago Hustle. O. Hawkins
Chicago Payoff. A. Capelli
Chicago Princess. R. Barr
Chicago Rod. L. Martin
Chicago-7. W. P. McGivern
Chicago Slaughter. M. Barry
Chicago Terror. M. Storm
Chicago Winter's Tale. A. B. Crunden
Chicago Wipeout. D. Pendleton
Chicago Woman. R. O. Saber
Chicane. O. Sandys
Chichester Intrigue. T. Cobb
Chick. E. Wallace
Chicken. M. Tripp
Chicken and Zella. M. Tripp
Chickens in the Airshaft. S. Franklin
Chief. C. Dawe
Chief Constable. Vincent Brown
Chief Constable. C. F. Gregg
Chief Counsel. A. L. Furman
Chief in Embryo. E. L. Long
Chief Inspector McLean. G. Goodchild
Chief Inspector's Daughter. S. Radley
Chief Inspector's Statement. M. Procter
Chief Legatee. A. K. Green
Chief of the Counterfeiters. Old Sleuth
Chief Witness. H. Adams
Chiffon Scarf. M. G. Eberhart
Child and the Serpent. S. Cook
Child at the Window. W. Hewlett
Child Divided. H. Cecil
Child Is Missing. C. Paul
Child Killer. E. T. Hamill
Child of Darkness. D. Daniels
Child of Evil. O. R. Cohen
Child of Mystery. H. M. Jones
Child of Night. Anne Edwards
Child of Rage. J. Thompson
Child of Satan. Melissa Napier
Child of the North. R. Cullum
Child of the Regiment. C. E. Blaney
Child of Two Fathers. T. P. Prest
Child of Value. P. Morton

Title Index

Child Slaves of New York. C. E. Blaney
Child Witness. H. C. Davis
Child Witness. H. N. Halsey
Childerbridge Mystery. G. Boothby
Children Are Gone. A. Cavanaugh
Children Are Watching. P. L. Dixon
Children of Chance. A. Carlyle
Children of Chance. H. Lloyd
Children of Despair. J. Creasey
Children of Earth. S. Paternoster
Children of Hate. J. Creasey
Children of Hermes. H. Hisbet
Children of Houndstooth. K. Kimbrough
Children of Light. Robert (G.) Curtis
Children of Light. H. L. Lawrence
Children of Mammon. J. K. Leys
Children of Power. S. R. Shreve
Children of the Abbey. R. M. Roche
Children of the Cloven Hoof. A. Dorrington
Children of the Dark. I. Shulman
Children of the Dark. C. Veley
Children of the Griffin. E. Giles
Children of the Gutter. A. Applin
Children of the Mist. B. Knox
Children of the Night. J. Blackburn
Children of the Reich. James Gregory
Children of the Storm. D. Dwyer
Children of the Whirlwind. L. Scott
Children of the Zodiac. A. M. Williamson
Children's Overture. H. Gibbs
Children's Party. Arthur H. Lewis
Child's Garden of Death. R. Forrest
Child's Play. Alice Campbell
Child's Play. K. Christie
Child's Play. U. Curtiss
Child's Play. R. Marasco
Child's Play. R. Sapir
Chilean Club. G. Shipway
Chill. E. C. Bentley
Chill. R. Macdonald
Chill. J. Sherman
Chill and the Kill. Joan Fleming
Chill Factor. J. Falkirk
Chill Factor. A. M. Stein
Chill of a Corpse. G. Peters
Chill Wind of Freedom. J. Midgley
Chillers and Thrillers. Anonymous
Chillery Court Mystery. R. Francis Foster
Chimney Murder. E. M. Channon
Chin-Chin-Chinaman. P. Walsh
Chin Chin, the Chinese Detective. A. W. Aiken
China Alley. H. Henn
China Bomb. R. Tregaskis
China Cane. M. Storm
China Card. D. Freed
China Coaster. Don Smith
China Doll. Nick Carter
China Expert. M. Delving
China Governess. M. Allingham
China Hand. B. Skoggard
China Kill. S. Hamill
China Rose. L. Crichton
China Roundabout. Josephine Bell
China Sea Murders. V. W. Mason
China Shadow. Clarissa Ross
China Servant. C. S. Archer
China Shepherdess. F. Y. McHugh
China Syndrome. B. Wohl
China Town Mystery. G. H. Teed
Chinaman's Chance. Ross Thomas
Chinatown Connection. D. Park
Chinatown Stories. C. B. Fernald
Chinatown Trunk Mystery. O. Harper
Chinese Agenda. J. Poyer
Chinese Agent. M. Moorcock
Chinese Assassin. A. Grey
Chinese Bed Mysteries. A. E. Martin
Chinese Bell Murders. R. Van Gulik
Chinese Blake. James Bennett
Chinese Bottle. P. Street
Chinese Box. K. W. Eyre
Chinese Box. M. McEvoy
Chinese Brown of Scotland Yard. C. Bishop
Chinese Cabinet. A. Applin
Chinese Cabinet. "Capstan"
Chinese Chanty. V. Clemov
Chinese Chop. J. Sheridan
Chinese Coats. F. Heller
Chinese Coffin. J. Hedges
Chinese Connection. William Crawford
Chinese Consortium. W. Rilla
Chinese Conspiracy. J. Rosenberger
Chinese Conundrum. W. Manson
Chinese Crimson. A. S. Fleischman
Chinese Doll. W. Tucker
Chinese Doll Affair. A. Nuttall
Chinese Donovan. Carter Brown
Chinese Door. V. Coffman
Chinese Executioner. P. Boulle
Chinese Fire Drill. M. Wolfe
Chinese Fish. J. Bommart
Chinese Godfather. P. Gillette
Chinese Gold Murders. R. Van Gulik
Chinese Goose. H. Robertson
Chinese Hammer. S. Harvester
Chinese Jade Affair. D. Miller
Chinese Jar. F. Hume
Chinese Jar Mystery. J. S. Strange

Chinese Keyhole. R. Himmel
Chinese Kiss. J. J. Montague
Chinese Label. J. F. Davis
Chinese Lake Murders. R. Van Gulik
Chinese Letter. Claudette Nicole
Chinese Mask. B. S. Ballinger
Chinese Maze Murders. R. Van Gulik
Chinese Nail Murders. R. Van Gulik
Chinese Nightmare. H. Pentecost
Chinese Orange Mystery. E. Queen
Chinese Parrot. E. D. Biggers
Chinese Paymaster. Nick Carter
Chinese Pleasure Girl. J. Seward
Chinese Poison. G. Hackforth-Jones
Chinese Poker. E. P. Thorne
Chinese Puzzle. M. Bower
Chinese Puzzle. M. Burton
Chinese Puzzle. M. Dekobra
Chinese Puzzle. R. Sapir
Chinese Red. R. Burke
Chinese Red. G. Collins
Chinese Shawl. P. Wentworth
Chinese Straight. J. J. Lamb
Chinese Ultimatum. Robin Moore
Chinese Visitor. J. Eastwood
Chinese White. H. B. Drake
Chinese Widow. J. Leasor
Ching Ching on the Trail. E. H. Burrage
Chink in the Armour. Jack Lewis
Chink in the Armour. M. B. Lowndes
Chinks in the Curtain. J. Porter
Chink's Victim. J. G. Brandon
Chip on My Shoulder. Eric North
Chipstead of the Lone Hand. S. Horler
Chiselers. Albert Conroy
Chiseller. Duff Johnson
Chislehurst Mystery. E. L. Mann
Chit of a Girl. G. Simenon
Chivalry and the Gibbet. G. Curtis
Chocolate Charlie. T. Fitzgerald
Chocolate Cobweb. C. Armstrong
Chocolate Mousse Murders. F. Halliday
Chocolate Spy. D. M. Alexander
Chog. Q. Crisp
Choice. M. Brandel
Choice. P. MacDonald
Choice Cuts. P. Boileau
Choice of Angels. H. Arvonen
Choice of Assassins. W. P. McGivern
Choice of Crimes. L. Egan
Choice of Enemies. T. Allbeury
Choice of Evils. Mrs. Alexander
Choice of Theodora. T. Cobb
Choice of Two Women. Gerald Butler
Choice of Violence. H. Pentecost
Choirboys. J. Wambaugh
Choke Chain. J. B. O'Sullivan
Choose Your Weapon. V. Loder
Chopin Express. H. Kaplan
Chord in Crimson. G. Gallagher
Chorine Makes a Killing. Carter Brown
Chorus Ending. E. Raymond
Chorus of Echoes. E. Trevor
Chosen Child. V. Maxwell
Chosen Course. N. Tranter
Chosen Girl. J. Buell
Chosen Instrument. H. Calvin
Chosen Man. Anonymous
Chosen Man. H. P. Halsey
Chosen of the Gods. A. Soutar
Chosen Sparrow. V. Caspary
Chowra's Revenge. F. E. Penny
Chris: A Love Story. J. Ironside
Christ Commission. O. Mandino
Christabel's Room. A. Clement
Christie in Love. H. Brenton
Christina. Dee Stuart
Christine Diamond. M. B. Lowndes
Christmas at Candleshoe. M. Innes
Christmas at Poverty Castle. T. Gallon
Christmas Bomber. T. Chastain
Christmas Card Murders. D. W. Meredith
Christmas Day and How It Was Spent. C. Le Ros
Christmas Egg. M. Kelly
Christmas Guest. E. Southworth
Christmas Hirelings. M. E. Braddon
Christmas Murder. C. Hare
Christmas Spy. J. Howlett
Christmas Tree Murders. J. Y. Dane
Christmas Without Roddy. W. Fennerton
Christobel. M. L. Roby
Christopher Bond, Adventurer. W. Martyn
Christopher Henrick. J. Hatton
Christopher Quarles, College Professor and Master Detective. P. Brebner
Christopher's Mansion. W. E. D. Ross
Chrome Connection. M. Simpson
Chromium Cat. W. Martyn
Chronicles of a Cavalier. J. G. Sarasin
Chronicles of Addington Peace. B. F. Robinson
Chronicles of Cardew Manor. L. Farmer
Chronicles of Dennis Chetwynd. H. J. Fidler
Chronicles of Don. K. J. Prichard
Chronicles of Golden Friars. J. S. Le Fanu
Chronicles of Lucius Leffing. J. P. Brennan
Chronicles of Martin Hewitt. Arthur Morrison

Chronicles of Melhampton. E. P. Oppenheim
Chronicles of Michael Danevitch of the Russian Secret Service. D. Donovan
Chronicles of Quincy Adams Sawyer, Detective. C. F. Pidgin
Chronicles of Slyme Court. H. M. Raleigh
Chronicles of Solar Pons. A. Derleth
Chronicles of the Bow Street Police-Office. Percy Fitzgerald
Chronicles of the Imp. J. Farnol
Chronicles of the Secret Service. A. Wilson
Chrysanthanum Chain. James Melville
Chuckling Fingers. M. Seeley
Church of Humanity. D. C. Murray
Churchill Commando. T. Willis
Churchill Mission. K. Netzen
Churchill's Gold. J. Follett
Churchyard Salad. M. Torrie
Churstons. P. Trent
Cider Row. W. K. McIntire
Cigar for Inspector Head. E. C. Vivian
Cigarette Clew. Nicholas Carter
Cinderella After Midnight. F. Zackel
Cinderella All Alone. A. Wood
Cinderella Goes to the Morgue. N. Spain
Cinderell's Dead. M. F. Callan
"Cinders" of Harley Street. W. LeQueux
Cinema City. C. R. Gull
Cinema Crime. R. Goyne
Cinema Crimes. J. Creasey
Cinema Murder. E. P. Oppenheim
Cinnabar Shroud. K. Ashley
Cinnamon Murder. F. Crane
Cintra Story. M. Clare
Cipher. Alex Gordon
Cipher Detective. A. P. Morris
Cipher Five. A. O. Pollard
Cipher of Death. F. L. Gregory
Cipher Six. W. LeQueux
Cipher Stories Puzzle Book. K. S. Cooper
Ciphered. S. Keech
Circe Complex. D. Cory
Circle. L. E. McCormick
Circle in the Water. J. McKimmey
Circle of Confusion. Palmer White
Circle of Danger. P. Alding
Circle of Darkness. J. Griffin
Circle of Death. H. Arvonen
Circle of Death. C. J. Dutton
Circle of Death. Richard Grant
Circle of Death. P. Quiroule
Circle of Death. M. Rennert
Circle of Deception. C. Virmonne
Circle of Dust. J. Cassells
Circle of Evil. V. Johnston
Circle of Evil. S. Wagner
Circle of Fear. P. Carlon
Circle of Fire. M. Sadler
Circle of Freedom. Mark Cross
Circle of Guilt. D. Daniels
Circle of Guilt. C. Kingston
Circle of Justice. P. Manton
Circle of Secrets. Claudette Nicole
Circle of Shadows. D. Holt
Circle of Squares. Bill Turner
Circle of Vengeance. N. Jorgenson
Circle of Von Boden. R. Harrison
Circle of Women. D. L. Pifer
Circle Round a Corpse. Hilary Landon
Circular Staircase. M. R. Rinehart
Circular Study. A. K. Green
Circumstances Beyond Control. A. Yudkoff
Circumstantial Evidence. A. I. Abbott
Circumstantial Evidence. Nicholas Carter
Circumstantial Evidence. F. W. Crofts
Circumstantial Evidence. F. J. Fargus
Circumstantial Evidence. E. Fitzmaurice
Circumstantial Evidence. Andrew Stewart
Circumstantial Evidence. J. H. Swingler
Circumstantial Evidence. Bessie Turner
Circumstantial Evidence. E. Wallace
Circus. Alistair MacLean
Circus Crime. A. Skene
Circus Couronne. R. W. Campbell
Circus Detective. Anonymous
Cire Perdue. W. Butler
Citadel of the Bats. M. Hastings
Citizens—to Arms! Garnett Weston
City and Suburban. F. Warden
City at Bay. D. Thoreau
City Beyond. L. Emerick
City Destroyer. G. Stockbridge
City for Sale. J. Messmann
City in Heat. W. B. Murphy
City Limit Blonde. A. Bocca
City Limits. N. Marino
City of Angels. S. Shagan
City of Anger. W. Manchester
City of Apes. A. Murray
City of Brass, and other Simon Ark stories. E. D. Hoch
City of Cain. K. Wilhelm
City of Crooks. S. Blake
City of Fear. P. Lady
City of Fear. John Marsh
City of Flaming Shadows. G. Stockbridge
City of Forever. B. Blackburn
City of Gold and Shadows. Ellis Peters
City of Horrors. W. J. Bayfield
City of Kites. T. Callas

City of Lies. C. Winchester
City of Lost Women. Griff
City of Masks. E. J. Murray
City of Mystery. A. C. Gunter
City of Peril. A. Stringer
City of Purple Dreams. Anonymous
City of Refuge. J. G. Sarasin
City of Shadows. P. Meredith
City of Silent Men. J. A. Moroso
City of Sin. R. O. Saber
City of Sin. B. Sarto
City of the Dead. H. Lieberman
City of the Golden Gate. E. Everett-Green
City of the Just. T. Terrell
City of the Living Dead. B. House
City of the Soul. M. Home
City Primeval. E. Leonard
City Slicker and Our Nell. L. Price
City of Whispering Stone. G. Chesbro
Claim of the Fleshless Corpse. G. Bruce
Claimant. W. Chesney
Claire. D. Malm
Clairvoyant Countess. D. Gilman
Clairvoyante. B. L. Farjeon
Clancumara's Keep. M. Heath
Clancy. F. Mullally
Clancy of the Mounted Police. O. Binns
Clancy's Secret Mission. L. Thayer
Clang on the Anvil. H. C. Danby
Clangor in the Bell Tower. M. Graff
Clap Hands, Here Comes Charlie. B. Freemantle
Clap Hands If You Believe in Fairies. John Fraser
Clara Lake's Dream. H. Wood
Clara Reeve. L. Hargrave
Clara Vaughan. R. D. Blackmore
Clare of Claresmede. C. Gibbon
Claret, Sandwiches and Sin. M. Donne
Clarice Dyke, the Female Detective. H. Rockwood
Clash. E. Wilkinson
Clash by Night. C. Clarke
Clash by Night. R. Croft-Cooke
Clash of Distant Thunder. A. C. Marin
Clash of Hawks. R. Charles
Clash of Shadows. H. Rigsby
Clash of Steel. Colin Robertson
Classified Death. C. Taschjian
Clauberg Trigger. J. Tarrant
Claud the Charmer. E. Everett-Green
Claude Beauclerc. Ambofilius
Claude Duval of Ninety-Five. F. Hume
Claude Melnotte as a Detective, and other stories. A. Pinkerton
Claudia Pole. C. Dawe
Clause in the Will. W. M. Graydon
Claustrophobia. R. Child
Claverse Affair. J. G. Vermandel
Claverton Affair. J. Rhode
Claverton Case. R. Rodd
Claverton Mystery. J. Rhode
Claw. J. Younger
Claw of a Cat. G. Peters
Claws for a Cutie. B. Sarto
Claws of Fate. D. Dayle
Claws of God. M. Tripp
Claws of Mercy. J. Harris
Claws of the Cougar. N. Berrow
Claws of the Crow. P. Wissmann
Claws of the Night. V. Hansen
Claws of the Red Dragon. C. Bishop
Claws of the Scorpion. G. Johnston
Claws of the Tiger. Nicholas Carter
Claxton's Mill. F. M. White
Clay. H. Imbert-Terry
Clay Assassin. J. Godey
Clay-Face. J. Templeton
Clay Hand. D. S. Davis
Clean Break. L. White
Clean, Bright, and Slightly Oiled. G. Kersh
Clean Hand. M. B. Vandeburg
Clean Kill. M. Gilbert
Clean Sweep. J. M. Wallmann
Clean Up. Joe Barry
Clean-Up. L. C. Douthwaite
Clear and Present Danger. B. Kendrick
Clear Case of Murder. H. Desmond
Clear Case of Suicide. M. Underwood
Clear Road to Archangel. G. Rose
Clear Round. E. L. Long
Clear Sky Above. N. Sheraton
Clear the Fast Lane. D. Rutherford
Clearer Vision. E. C. Mayne
Clearing in the Fog. D. Macomber
Cleek of Scotland Yard. T. W. Hanshew
Cleek, the Man of the Forty Faces. T. W. Hanshew
Cleek, the Master Detective. T. W. Hanshew
Cleek's Government Cases. T. W. Hanshew
Cleek's Greatest Riddles. T. W. Hanshew
Cleft Chin Murder. R. A. Raymond
Cleft of Stars. G. Jenkins
Clement Lorimer. A. B. Reach
Clemmie. J. D. MacDonald
Cleopatra Jones. R. Goulart
Cleopatra Jones and the Casino of Gold. R. Goulart
Cleopatra Needle Mystery. J. N. Pentelow

Cleopatra's Nose. T. B. Marle
Cleopatra's Tears. H. S. Keeler
Clerical Cracksman. A. F. King
Clerical Error. A. Rolls
Clerk of Portwick. G. M. Fenn
Clermont. R. M. Roche
Clerycastle. M. Heath
Clevedon Case. N. Oakley
Cleveland Pipeline. D. Pendleton
Clever Celestial. Nicholas Carter
Clever Criminals. John Lang
Clever Detective. Old Sleuth
Clever One. E. Wallace
Clever Ones. R. R. King
Clever Ones. J. E. Middleton
Cleverdale Mystery. W. A. Wilkins
Cleverest Woman in England. L. T. Meade
Cleverly Won. H. Smart
Cleverness of Mr. Budd. G. Verner
Clew Against Clew. Nicholas Carter
Clew by Clew. Nicholas Carter
Clew by Clew. Old Sleuth
Clew in the Glass. W. B. M. Ferguson
Clew of the Forgotten Murder. C. Kendrake
Click of the Gate. Alice Campbell
Client. M. Russell
Client Is Cancelled. R. Lockridge
Clients of Omega. D. Bloodworth
Cliff Face. D. Buckingham
Cliff Mill Mystery. G. Volk
Cliff Mystery. H. Aide
Cliff-Path Mystery. H. Hill
Cliffhaven. Dan Ross
Clifford Affair. A. Fielding
Clifford Mystery. A. Fielding
Cliff's End Farm and other stories. F. Warden
Cliff's Head. D. Kamm
Cliffs of Death. Claude Nicole
Cliffs of Dread. V. Coffman
Cliffs of Night. Beatrice Brandon
Cliffs of Sark. G. Volk
Cliffside Castle. D. Daniels
Climate for Conspiracy. P. Harcourt
Climate of Courage. J. Cleary
Climate of Hell. H. Lieberman
Climate of Hell. J. Roebuck
Climate of Revolt. Alan White
Climax. G. C. Jenks
Climax. N. Karta
Climax. F. J. Lewis
Climax at the Falls. G. Baxter
Climb a Dark Cliff. K. Ashby
Climb the Dark Mountain. J. Wellsley
Climb the Wall. M. Cronin
Climbing Corpse. A. Brede
Cling of the Clay. M. Hayes
Clinging Shadows. M. Waring
Clinic of Dr. Aicadre. Muriel Harris
Clinton Is Assigned. M. McConnell
Clip-Joint. E. Olmstead
Clipped Hedges. F. Hird
Clique of Gold. E. Gaboriau
Clique of Knaves. Dick Stewart
Clive Lorimer's Marriage. E. Everett-Green
Cloak and Dagger Lover. M. Greig
Cloak for Malice. K. Wade
Cloak of Darkness. W. Magnay
Cloak of Guilt. Nicholas Carter
Cloakroom Murder. W. Jardine
Clock. R. Goyne
Clock. A. E. W. Mason
Clock and Bell. S. Claudia
Clock and the Key. A. H. Vesey
Clock at Ravenswood. J. Teta
Clock Face. M. J. Simmons
Clock in the Hatbox. Anthony Gilbert
Clock Strikes. P. Troubetzkoy
Clock Strikes Ten. M. Richmond
Clock Strikes Thirteen. H. Brean
Clock Strikes Twelve. P. Wentworth
Clock Strikes Two. H. K. Webster
Clock Struck One. F. Hume
Clock Struck Seven. G. Goodchild
Clock Struck Twelve. J. Reach
Clock That Wouldn't Stop. E. Ferrars
Clock Ticks. C. Houghton
Clock Ticks On. V. Williams
Clock Without Hands. G. Kersh
Clockmaker. G. Simenon
Clockmaker of Heidelberg. H. Edmonds
Clocks. A. Christie
Clocktower. G. McDonell
Clockwork Orange. A. Burgess
Cloggy Dick. Arthur Smith
Cloisonne Vase. E. Noone
Clone People. M. Johnson
Close All Roads to Sospel. G. Bellairs
Close Call. J. L. Berry
Close Call. E. Phillpotts
Close Doesn't Count. John Craig
Close Her Pale Blue Eyes. H. Hull
Close His Eyes. O. Dwight
Close of Play. S. Raven
Close Quarters. M. Gilbert
Close Shave. S. Maddock
Close the Door on Murder. J. York
Close the Frontier. L. A. Knight
Close to Death. J. Crowe
Close to the Wind. J. Harris

Close-Up. M. Turnbull
Close-Up. D. Walshe
Close-Up of a Killing. R. M. Douglas
Close-Up of a Killing. Richard Hubbard
Closed Book. W. LeQueux
Closed Circuit. W. Haggard
Closed Door. R. M. Douglas
Closed Door. F. Du Boisgobey
Closed Door. S. Horler
Closely Confined. E. Burgess
Closeout. D. Conger
Closet Bones. T. Bunn
Closing Ceremonies. Harold King
Closing Circle. L. Cameron
Closing Door. J. E. Blackmore
Closing Net. H. C. Rowland
Closing the Circle. Dick Stewart
Cloud. R. Bridges
Cloud over Calderwood. K. A. Shoesmith
Cloud over Malverton. N. Buckingham
Cloud the Smiter. A. Gask
Clouded in Mystery. M. A. A. B.
Clouded Mirror. E. Bond
Clouded Moon. S. Nichols
Clouded Moon. M. Saltmarsh
Clouds in the Wind. F. L. Green
Clouds of Fear. R. Bryant
Clouds of War. Ralph Hayes
Clouds of Witness. D. L. Sayers
Clouds over Vellanti. Elsie Lee
Cloudy in the West. W. P. White
Cloudy Ladder. V. Barlow
Clough Plays Murder. L. Parsons
Clove Crest. I. A. Greenfield
Cloven Foot. M. E. Braddon
Cloven Foot. O. C. Kerr
Cloven-Footed Angel. M. Dekobra
Cloverdale Skeleton. C. L. Hooper
Clown. Carter Brown
Clowning Through. E. C. Reed
Cloze Papers. K. Livingston
Club Car Mystery. G. I. Colbron
Club—Mink Lined Murder. M. Webb
Club of Masks. A. Upward
Club of Queer Trades. G. K. Chesterton
Club of Skulls. Wilfred Barclay
Club 17. B. Kerr
Clubbable Woman. R. Hill
Clubfoot the Avenger. V. Williams
Clubs and Hearts. P. Trent
Clue. A. V. Arnold
Clue. C. Wells
Clue for Clancy. L. Thayer
Clue for Clutha. H. Munro
Clue for Mr. Fortune. H. C. Bailey
Clue for Murder. R. Barker
Clue from the Past. E. Langdon
Clue from the Stars. E. Phillpotts
Clue from the Unknown. Nicholas Carter
Clue in the Air. I. Ostrander
Clue in the Clay. D. B. Olsen
Clue in the Glass. W. B. M. Ferguson
Clue in the Mirror. N. Morland
Clue in Two Flats. R. L. F. McCombs
Clue in Wax. F. M. White
Clue of the Artificial Eye. J. S. Fletcher
Clue of the Bricklayer's Aunt. N. Morland
Clue of the Careless Hangman. N. Morland
Clue of the Charred Diary. W. J. Bayfield
Clue of the Cloakroom Ticket. R. C. Armour
Clue of the Clock. M. Harvey
Clue of the Clot. C. Barry
Clue of the Cone. J. Arthur Williams
Clue of the Curious Cat. R. Brode
Clue of the Dead Goldfish. V. MacClure
Clue of the Eyelash. C. Wells
Clue of the Forgotten Murder. C. Kendrake
Clue of the Four Wigs. G. H. Teed
Clue of the Fourteen Keys. M. Burton
Clue of the Frightening Coin. Jessica Ryan
Clue of the Golden Ear-Ring. C. M. Wills
Clue of the Golden Tooth. J. Brooks
Clue of the Green Candle. G. Verner
Clue of the Cross-Eyed Girl. N. Burnaby
Clue of the Hungry Corpse. I. Jones
Clue of the Ivory Claw. F. H. Dimmock
Clue of the Judas Tree. L. Ford
Clue of the Leather Noose. D. B. Hobart
Clue of the Lost Hour. C. M. Wills
Clue of the Missing Link. Gwyn Evans
Clue of the Naked Eye. C. M. Russell
Clue of the New Pin. E. Wallace
Clue of the New Shoe. A. W. Upfield
Clue of the Pin-Up Girl. W. Tyrer
Clue of the Poor Man's Shilling. K. M. Knight
Clue of the Postage Stamp. A. Bray
Clue of the Primrose Petal. H. Wickham
Clue of the Purple Asters. J. Cassells
Clue of the Rising Moon. V. Williams
Clue of the Second Murder. J. S. Strange
Clue of the Second Tooth. G. Verner
Clue of the Silver Brush. M. Burton
Clue of the Silver Cellar. M. Burton
Clue of the Silver Key. E. Wallace

Title Index

Clue of the Six Kissing Girls. C. Herbert
Clue of the Stolen Rupees. A. Parsons
Clue of the Stone. H. A. Wrenn
Clue of the Tattooed Man. J. G. Brandon
Clue of the Twisted Candle. E. Wallace
Clue of the Twisted Face. F. A. Kummer
Clue Sinister. C. Carnac
Clue to Danger. A. Furness
Clue to the Labyrinth. C. B. Clason
Clueless Trail. P. Walsh
Clues. W. Henderson
Clues for Dr. Coffee. L. G. Blochman
Clues from a Detective's Camera. H. Hill
Clues of the Caribbees. T. S. Stribling
Clues to Burn. L. G. Offord
Clues to Christabel. M. Fitt
Clunk's Claimant. H. C. Bailey
Cluny Problem. A. Fielding
Cluster of Gems. R. Carr
Cluster of Separate Sparks. Joan Aiken
Clutch of Circumstance. J. Barnes
Clutch of Circumstance. M. B. Cooke
Clutch of Constables. N. Marsh
Clutch of Coppers. G. Ashe
Clutch of Dread. Nicholas Carter
Clutch of Vipers. J. S. Scott
Clutching Claw. R. Kettering
Clutching Hand. C. J. Dutton
Clutching Hand. A. B. Reeve
Clutha and the Lady. H. Munro
Clutha Plays a Hunch. H. Munro
Clutterbuck's Treasure. F. Whishaw
Clyde, the Resolute Detective. Old Sleuth
Clyde, the Trailer. M. O. Rolfe
Clyffards of Clyffe. J. Payn
Clytie. J. Hatton
Coach Draws Near. M. Savage
Coach North. P. McCutchan
Coachman's Club. George R. Sims
Coachman's Daughter. D. Creekmore
Coal Tom. Old Sleuth
Coals of Fire and other stories. D. C. Murray
Coast of Adventure. H. Bindloss
Coast of Chance. Esther Chamberlain
Coast of Fear. K. G. Ballard
Coast of Fear. J. D'Astor
Coast of Fear. L. Waller
Coast of Intrigue. W. Chambers
Coast of No Return. M. Hastings
Coast Road Murder. M. Turnbull
Coat of Arms. E. Wallace
Coat of Blackmail. J. T. McIntosh
Coat of Varnish. C. P. Snow
Coatine Case. A. J. Colton
Cobalt 60. R. L. Graves
Cobra Candlestick. E. Barker
Cobra Diamond. A. Lillie
Cobra Kill. Nick Carter
Cobra Strike. R. Charles
Cobra Team. E. E. Mayer
Cobra Venom. A. Rowe
Cobra Venom. J. B. West
Cobweb. P. Flower
Cobweb Across the Moon. C. Darby
Cobweb Castle. J. S. Fletcher
Cobweb House. E. H. Holloway
Cobwebs. Mabel Collins
Cobwebs and Clues. E. Malan
Cocaine. D. Forde
Cocaine. M. Olden
Cocaine and Blue Eyes. F. Zackel
Cocaine Blues. W. Satterthwait
Cocaine Caper. V. A. Paradis
Cocaine Connection. R. L. Brent
Cocaine for Breakfast. G. Sava
Cocaine Kill. A. Destefano
Cock Crow. A. Carlyle
Cock o' the North. T. Mundy
Cock-Pit of Roses. James Fraser
Cock Robin. E. L. Rice
Cockatoo Crime. B. Knox
Cockeyed Corpse. R. S. Prather
Cockleburr. R. Crawford
Cockney Cavalcade. G. Ingram
Cockpit. J. Kosinski
Cockpit. Warwick Scott
Cockroach Sings. Alice Campbell
Cock's Tail Murder. H. Austin
Cocksure Dame. J. Cairo
Cocktail for Cupid and other stories. P. Cheyney
Cocktail Party and other stories. P. Cheyney
Cocktails and the Killer. P. Cheyney
Cocktails with a Stranger. C. Franklin
Coconut Killings. P. Moyes
Coconut Wireless. F. Kauffman
Code. Nick Carter
Code-Letter Mystery. D. Sharp
Code-Name Caruso. George Sims
Code Name Gadget. P. Rabe
Code Name Hangman. P. Geddes
Code Name "Icy". L. Agniel
Code Name: Judas. M. Walker
Code Name: Little Ivan. J. Tiger
Code Name: Mamba. M. Marler
Code Name Nimrod. J. Leasor
Code Name: Rapier. M. Walker
Code Name: Rubble. P. Thomas
Code Name Sebastian. J. L. Johnson
Code Name: Werewolf. Nick Carter
Code of Conduct. Elliott Arnold
Code of Dishonour. B. Sanders
Code 1013: Assassin. L. Trevor
Code Seven. L. Cameron
Code Three. J. M. Fox
Code Word Christmas Tree. J. J. Parnell
Code Word—Golden Fleece. D. Wheatley
Code Word "Proton". E. P. Thorne
Code Z. J. Swerdlow
Codename—Bastille. B. Musto
Codename, Starlight. Hartshorne
Codeword Cromwell. P. Kelly
Codfish Watch. E. R. Knowlton
Coffee for None. A. B. Caldwell
Coffee for One. E. Hale
Coffee for One. J. Last
Coffee in the Morning. G. Greenaway
Coffin Bird. Carter Brown
Coffin Corner. G. Bagby
Coffin Corner. Dell Shannon
Coffin Country. A. M. Stein
Coffin Fits. A. Bocca
Coffin Following. Gwendoline Butler
Coffin for a Cutie. S. Morelli
Coffin for a Hood. L. White
Coffin for a Murderer. Reginald Campbell
Coffin for Baby. Gwendoline Butler
Coffin for Christopher. D. Ames
Coffin for Dimitrios. E. Ambler
Coffin for One. F. Beeding
Coffin for Pandora. Gwendoline Butler
Coffin for the Body. N. Morland
Coffin for the Canary. Gwendoline Butler
Coffin for Two. Robert Martin
Coffin from Hong Kong. J. H. Chase
Coffin from the Past. Gwendoline Butler
Coffin in Malta. Gwendoline Butler
Coffin in Oxford. Gwendoline Butler
Coffin Island. M. Leblanc
Coffin, Scarcely Used. Colin Watson
Coffin Things. M. Avallone
Coffin Waiting. Gwendoline Butler
Coffin's Dark Number. Gwendoline Butler
Coffins for Three. F. C. Davis
Coffins for Two. Gwyn Evans
Coffins for Two. V. Starrett
Coffy. P. W. Fairman
Cogan's Trade. G. V. Higgins
Co-Heiresses. E. Everett-Green
Coil of Mystery. B. Bolt
Coil of Rope. J. F. Straker
Coil of Serpents. A. Stevenson
Coin of Edward VII. F. Hume
Coiner's Cave. J. Herbrand
Coiner's League. B. Wayde
Colchicine Factor. R. Bryce
Colcorton. E. Pope
Cold and Unhonoured. F. Hurt
Cold Bed in the Clay. R. S. Wallis
Cold Blood. L. Bruce
Cold Blood. Robin Richards
Cold-Blooded Murder. F. W. Crofts
Cold Blue Death. K. Stanton
Cold Chill of Coptos. K. Ashley
Cold Chills. R. Bloch
Cold Chisel. J. B. O'Sullivan
Cold Comfort. D. R. Slavitt
Cold Coming. M. Kelly
Cold Companion. J. Sher
Cold Cream. A. Applin
Cold Dark Hours. A. G. Yates
Cold Dark Night. S. Gainham
Cold Dead Coed. H. Janson
Cold Death. K. Robeson
Cold Evil. B. Flynn
Cold Eyes. J. F. Dwyer
Cold Finger Curse. E. D. Torgerson
Cold Front. B. Everitt
Cold Hand in Mine. R. Aickman
Cold Is the Sea. E. L. Beach
Cold Jungle. G. Black
Cold Line to Moscow. Henry Talbot
Cold Moon over Babylon. M. McDowell
Cold Night for Murder. Martin Thomas
Cold Night's Death. Barbara Harrison
Cold Ones. P. Kruger
Cold Poison. S. Palmer
Cold Room. J. Caine
Cold Route to Freedom. C. D. Peel
Cold Spell. J. Bruce
Cold Steal. A. Tilton
Cold Steel. James Warren
Cold Terror. R. Chetwynd-Hayes
Cold Trail. Dell Shannon
Cold Turkey. T. Childs
Cold War. D. Brierley
Cold War in a Country Garden. L. Gutteridge
Cold War Swap. Ross Thomas
Cold Waters. P. M. Hubbard
Cold Waters. L. Moore
Cold Wind of Death. H. Seymour
Coldharbour. M. Cobb
Coldstone. P. Wentworth
Cole of Spyglass Mountain. A. P. Hankins
Coleraine Tragedy. E. T. Sawyer
Coleville Skeleton. R. C. Finney
Colfax Book-Plate. Agnes Miller
Coliseum. B. Cohen
Collapse of Stout Party. J. T. Story
Collar for the Killer. H. Brean
Collected Stories of Ben Hecht. B. Hecht
Collection. P. Montana
Collection of Strangers. D. Hitchens
Collector. J. Fowles
Collector's Choice. Peter Marks
Collector's Item. A. Dean
Collegians. G. Griffin
Collision. J. Pulman
Collision Ahead. R. Johnston
Collision Course. D. Rutherford
Collusion. T. Cobb
Collusion. T. D. Irwin
Colombian Connection. R. S. Silverman
Colonel and the Corpse. Tod Conrad
Colonel Blessington. P. Frankau
Colonel Bogus. J. Blackburn
Colonel Butler's Wolf. A. Price
Colonel Dam. J. S. Clouston
Colonel Gore's Second Case. L. Brock
Colonel Gore's Third Case. L. Brock
Colonel Grant's Tomorrow. G. Seton
Colonel Paternoster. R. Inchbald
Col. Ross of Piedmont. J. E. Cooke
Colonel Sun. R. Markham
Colonel Thorndyke's Secret. G. A. Henty
Colonel's Foxhound. C. M. Wills
Colonel's Past. F. Warden
Colonial King. H. Nisbet
Color Him Dead. C. Runyon
Color of Hate. J. L. Hensley
Colorado Jim. G. Goodchild
Colorado Kill-Zone. D. Pendleton
Colors of Death. S. Wagner
Colossus. E. Wallace
Colossus of Arcadia. E. P. Oppenheim
Colour Blind. C. A. Cookson
Colour Blind. S. P. B. Mais
Colour of Darkness. A. Dipper
Colour of Dried Blood. M. Vinter
Colour of Fear. R. Ormerod
Colour of Murder. J. Symons
Colour of Murder. P. Winn
Colour of Violence. J. Ashford
Colour Scheme. N. Marsh
Coloured Glass. I. R. G. Hart
Colours Flying. N. Tranter
Colt from the Country. A. Wright
Columbella. P. A. Whitney
Columbia. Anonymous
Columbine Cabin Murders. P. Mechem
Columbo. A. Lawrence
Columnist Murder. L. Saunders
Colwyn Dane—the Outlawed Detective. M. Grimshaw
Coma. R. Cook
Comanche Scalp. W. C. MacDonald
Combat Pay. Robin Moore
Combat Zone—Miami. T. Conners
Combination-Lock Mystery. Anonymous
Come Alone. W. Woodrow
Come Along with Me. S. Jackson
Come and Be Killed. Dorothy Bennett
Come and Be Killed! Shelley Smith
Come and Get Me. Griff
Come and Go. F. Gaite
Come and Kill Me. S. Gluck
Come and Kill Me. J. Tey
Come Away, Death. J. Kirkpatrick
Come Away, Death. G. Mitchell
Come Away Death. A. G. Wilson
Come Back. Duff Johnson
Come-Back. C. Wells
Come Back and Die. I. Lambot
Come Back, Charleston Blue. C. Himes
Come Back for More. A. Fray
Come Back for the Body. David Hume
Come Back, My Love. E. S. Aarons
Come Back to Murder. S. H. Courtier
Come Back When I'm Sober. M. Waddell
Come Blonde, Came Murder. P. George
Come Dark, Come Evil. W. McNeilly
Come Destroy Me. V. Packer
Come Die for Me. D. P. Lyday
Come Die with Me. James Dark
Come Die with Me. J. Eastwood
Come Die with Me. W. C. Gault
Come Dwell with Death. M. W. Glidden
Come Feed on Me. Morton Cooper
Come Hell and High Water. R. Petrie
Come Here and Die. M. Halliday
Come Home and Be Killed. Jennie Melville
Come Home to Crime. N. Deane
Come Home to Death. G. Ashe
Come In. E. C. Mayne
Come In Number One, Your Time Is Up. D. Jewell
Come into My Parlour. D. Wheatley
Come Kill with Me. H. Kane
Come Kill with Me. F. Kassak
Come Like a Storm. E. G. Cousins
Come Love, Come Death. S. P. B. Mais
Come Murder Me. J. Kieran
Come Night, Come Evil. Jonathan Craig
Come-On. W. Chambers
Come-On. M. Yorke
Come Out, Come Out. G. Malcolm-Smith
Come Out, Come Out, Whoever You Are. T. McCann
Come Out Fighting. Duff Johnson
Come Out Killing. Robert Reeves
Come Out with Your Hands Up. H. Luger

Come Over, Red Rover. S. Marlowe
Come Quickly, Honey. H. Janson
Come See Me Die. M. Neville
Come See Them Die. H. Hadley
Come Sweet Death. M. S. Curry
Come, Sweet Death. S. Mitchell
Come, Thick Night. M. Neville
Come to Castlemoor. Beatrice Parker
Come to Dust. F. Drake
Come to Dust. E. Lathen
Come to Grief. H. Foley
Come to Judgment. J. S. Strange
Come to My Funeral. I. Wempe
Come-Uppance of Arthur Hearne. Angus Hall
Come Watch Him Die. S. Jason
Comeback. J. Tomerlin
Comeback for Stark. H. Reade
Comedian. K. Hewitt
Comedian Dies. Simon Brett
Comedians. G. Greene
Comedy of Terrors. A. Carr
Comedy of Terrors. J. De Mille
Comedy of Terrors. M. Innes
Comedy of Terrors. Elsie Lee
Comedy of the Unexpected. G. W. Appleton
Comes a Stranger. E. R. Punshon
Comes the Blind Fury. H. McCutcheon
Comes the Blind Fury. D. Rutherford
Comes the Blind Fury. J. R. Saul
Comes the Dark Stranger. Harry Patterson
Comethup. T. Gallon
Comets Have Long Tails. M. Johnston
Comforters. M. Spark
Comic Strip. G. Panetta
Comic Tragedy. G. R. Kuhn
Coming Back of Laurence Averil. M. Drake
Coming Home to Roost. G. M. Fenn
Coming of Age. R. Marsh
Coming of Aurora. P. C. De Crespigny
Coming of Carew. B. Graeme
Coming of Cosgrove. L. Y. Erskine
Coming of Jonathan Smith. H. Ludlam
Coming of the Monster. O. F. Dudley
Coming-Out Party. R. Frede
Coming Out Party. G. Petrie
Comlyn Alibi. H. Hill
Command Strike. D. Pendleton
Commander Amanda Nightingale. G. Revelli
Commander Leigh. R. H. Savage
Commander-1. P. George
Commandments Six and Eight. A. Griffin
Commando. R. Wilkes-Hunter
Commando Escape. Stagg Green
Commando X. P. Runyon
Commandos Are Expendable. R. Wilkes-Hunter
Commemorations. H. Herlin
Commencement Day Murders. L. M. Floyd
Commerce Patrol. I. F. Anderson
Commission for Disaster. J. N. Chance
Commissioner. R. Dougherty
Commitment. C. Illing
Committal Chamber. R. Braddon
Committee. H. Braxton
Committee. D. Seaman
Commodore Junk. G. M. Fenn
Common Love. J. B. Watney
Common or Garden Crime. S. Pim
Common Sense Is All You Need. J. J. Connington
Commons Killing. J. Fairfax
Communicating Door. S. Allan
Communicating Door. Wadsworth Camp
Communist's Corpse. R. Wormser
Compact. R. Cullum
Compact of Crime. B. Wayde
Companion of Dishonour. J. Wellsley
Companion to Evil. M. Farnsworth
Companion to Sirius. G. Goodchild
Company. J. Ehrlichman
Company Man. J. Maggio
Company of Bandits. J. T. Story
Company of Friends. J. Crosby
Company of St. George. Kenneth O'Hara
Company of Shadows. J. M. Walsh
Company of Sinners. W. M. Duncan
Company of Strangers. J. Rosenberg
Compare These Dead! M. P. Rea
Compartment East. P. Remy
Compartment K. H. Reilly
Compass Points to Fear. J. Ward
Compassionate Crook. P. Goulden
Compassionate Rogue. G. Goodchild
Compleat Werewolf and other tales of fantasy and science fiction. A. Boucher
Complete Change. A. J. Philip
Complete State of Death. J. Gardner
Complete Steel. C. Aird
Complete Stranger. V. Siller
Compliments of a Fiend. F. Brown
Composite Lady. T. Cobb
Composition for Four Hands. Hilda Lawrence
Compost Heap Corpses. S. C. Williamson
Compound for Death. D. M. Disney
Compromising Positions. S. Isaacs
Sompton Effect. L. Horvitz
Compulsion. M. Levin
Computer Connection. A. Bester
Computer Kill. R. E. Banks

Computer Kill. L. Derrick
Comrade Jill. H. Adams
Comrade Souvarin. M. Moiseiwitsch
Comrade Spy. L. S. Ovalov
Comrades in Death. P. Turner
Comrades of Peril. R. Parrish
Comrades of the Black Cross. H. Nisbet
Comrades of the Right Hand. Nicholas Carter
Con Game. M. Cronin
Con Game. H. Waugh
Con Man. C. A. Harris
Con Man. E. McBain
Con Man. G. Verner
Conant. W. R. Burnett
Conceal and Disguise. H. Kane
Concealed Identity. M. Richmond
Concept for Murder. Margo Lewis
Concerning a Woman of Sin and other stories. B. Hecht
Concerning Blackshirt. R. Graeme
Concerning Miss Duncan. Mary Archer
Concerning Peter Jackson and others. G. Frankau
Concerning the Saint. L. Charteris
Concerning This Woman. W. LeQueux
Concert Party Murders. John Norman
Concerto. P. Austin
Concerto for Fear. N. W. Firth
Concerto in the Key of Death. B. Fried
Concerto of Death. G. J. Barrett
Concorde—Airport 1979. K. Stewart
Concrete Boot. K. Royce
Concrete Cage. R. Novak
Concrete Castle. F. Gerard
Concrete Castle Murders. F. Gerard
Concrete Crime. M. Coles
Concrete Curtain. J. Bogar
Concrete Evidence. M. Russell
Concrete Flamingo. C. Williams
Concrete Kimono. J. P. Carstairs
Concrete Maze. N. Morland
Concrete Nymph. N. Karta
Concubine. M. East
Condamine Case. M. Dalton
Condemned. H. Carmichael
Condemned. H. Desmond
Condemned. J. Pagano
Condemned as a Nihilist. G. A. Henty
Condemned Door. F. Du Boisgobey
Condemned to Death. J. R. Eyre
Condemned to Live. T. A. Plummer
Condition Green. N. Goble
Conditional Sentence. H. Fleetwood
Condor Conspiracy. C. Yarborough
Conduct of a Member. V. Gielgud
Cone of Silence. D. Beaty
Coney Island Quickstep. G. Gipe
Confederate. J. Fielding
Confederate Rogues. Dick Stewart
Confederate Spy. T. N. Conrad
Confess Fletch. G. McDonald
Confess to Dr. Morelle. E. Dudley
Confession. H. Carmichael
Confession. R. Francis Foster
Confession Corner, and other stories. B. Reynolds
Confession of a Thug. Warren Miller
Confession of Andrew Clare. David Robinson
Confession of Hercule. P. Audemars
Confession of Lorraine Herschel. N. T. Oliver
Confession of Murder. C. Barling
Confession of Murder. M. Neville
Confession of Murder. F. Arthur
Confessional. G. Simenon
Confessional of the Black Penitents. A. Radcliffe
Confessional of Valombre. L. S. Stanhope
Confessions of a Chinatown Doll. J. Bogar
Confessions of a Con Man. Will Irwin
Confessions of a Convict. P. A. Foxall
Confessions of a Court Milner. L. T. Meade
Confessions of a Currency Girl. C. Dawe
Confessions of a Detective. Alfred H. Lewis
Confessions of a Detective Policeman. Anonymous
Confessions of a Ladies' Man. W. LeQueux
Confessions of a Lady Killer. G. Stade
Confessions of a Private Dick. T. Lea
Confessions of a Scoundrel. G. Spencer
Confessions of a Thug. Meadows Taylor
Confessions of a Ticket-of-Leave Man. Anonymous
Confessions of a Vagabond. C. Massie
Confessions of a Wife. Grace M. White
Confessions of Alma Quartier. David Robinson
Confessions of Alphonse. B. Pain
Confessions of an Attorney. G. Sharp
Confessions of an Imp. Old Sleuth
Confessions of an Old Burglar. Charles Morley
Confessions of Arsene Lupin. M. Leblanc
Confessions of Artemas Quibble. A. Train
Confessions of Cleodora. C. Dawe
Confessions of Stephen Whopshare. E. Brooke

Confessor. J. Donohue
Confetti Can Be Red. M. Cumberland
Confetti for a Killing. C. Edwards
Confetti Man. B. J. Reynolds
Confidence King. Nicholas Carter
Confidence Man. L. V. Erskine
Confident Morning. V. Gielgud
Confidential. D. H. Clarke
Confidential Agent. G. Greene
Confidential Agent. J. Payn
Confidential Mission. W. L. Whitehouse
Conflict. M. E. Braddon
Conflict. H. Janson
Conflict. C. B. Kelland
Conflict of Evidence. R. Ottolengui
Conflict of Interest. B. Williams
Conflict of Shadows. Colin Robertson
Conflict of Women. E. Darby
Conflict Within. D. Reid
Confounding of Sergeant Cluff. G. North
Confrontation. N. Garbo
Confrontation. Ralph Vickers
Confucius in a Tail-Coat. M. Dekobra
Confusion at Campden Trig. V. B. Harris
Cong Kiss. J. J. Montague
Congleton Lark. Angus Ross
Congo. W. A. Ballinger
Congo Venus. M. Head
Congo War Cry. A. Caillou
"Coniackers." R. Rivers
Conjure Man Dies. Rudolph Fisher
Conjurer of Phantoms. J. W. Harding
Conjurer's Coffin. G. Cullingford
Conjurers. Marilyn Harris
Connecting Link. Nicholas Carter
Connecting Rooms. W. Hughes
Connector. T. Williamson
Connie Burt. G. Boothby
Connie Morgan Hits the Trail. J. B. Hendryx
Connie Morgan in Alaska. J. B. Hendryx
Connie Morgan in Barren Lands. J. B. Hendryx
Connie Morgan in the Arctic. J. B. Hendryx
Connie Morgan in the Cattle Country. J. B. Hendryx
Connie Morgan in the Fur Country. J. B. Hendryx
Connie Morgan in the Lumber Camps. J. B. Hendryx
Connie Morgan, Prospector. J. B. Hendryx
Connie Morgan with the Forest Rangers. J. B. Hendryx
Connie Morgan with the Mounted. J. B. Hendryx
Connoisseur's Case. M. Innes
Connolly's Woman. H. Whittington
Conor Sands. E. Kyle
Conover's Folly. D. Daniels
Conquered Place. R. Shafer
Conqueror Inn. E. R. Punshon
Conqueror's Road. L. A. Knight
Conquest After Midnight. B. Gray
Conquest Before Autumn. M. Eden
Conquest Calls the Tune. B. Gray
Conquest Goes Home. B. Gray
Conquest Goes West. B. Gray
Conquest in California. B. Gray
Conquest in Command. B. Gray
Conquest in Ireland. B. Gray
Conquest in Scotland. B. Gray
Conquest in the Underworld. B. Gray
Conquest Likes It Hot. B. Gray
Conquest Marches On. B. Gray
Conquest of Fortune. George Griffith
Conquest on the Run. B. Gray
Conquest Overboard. B. Gray
Conquest Takes All. B. Gray
Conquest Touch. B. Gray
Cons on the Run. B. Shannon
Conscience. A. Griffin
Conscience Makes Heroes. G. Abrahams
Conscience Money. S. Warwick
Conscience of a Killer. M. Arrighi
Conscience of a King. A. C. Gunter
Conscience of Dr. Holt. A. Clare
Conscripts. W. Winward
Consequence of Crime. E. Linington
Consequence of Fear. T. Allbeury
Consequences of a Duel. F. Du Boisgobey
Conservatory. P. Hastings
Consider the Evidence. J. Ashford
Consider the Lilies. H. Ainsworth
Consider the Verdict. A. Bodelsen
Consider Your Verdict. R. Hardinge
Consider Your Verdict. N. MacKenzie
Consider Your Verdict. T. Mason
Consider Your Verdict. A. Soutar
Consider Yourself Dead. J. H. Chase
Consider Yourself Dead. G. Fredrics
Conspiracy. R. Baker
Conspiracy. P. Meriton
Conspiracy. W. Proudfoot
Conspiracy. Robert Robinson
Conspiracy. A. S. Roche
Conspiracy at Angel. B. Flynn
Conspiracy Island. Peter Craig
Conspiracy of Love. L. Hoffman
Conspiracy of Poisons. J. Sturrock
Conspiracy of Rumors. Nicholas Carter
Conspiracy of Silence. M. Blizard

Title Index

Conspiracy of Silence. E. Butler
Conspiracy of Vipers. P. Ordway
Conspiracy to Kill. C. Jauniere
Conspirator. H. Slater
Conspirator of Cordova. S. Cobb
Conspirators. W. Haggard
Conspirators. F. Kane
Conspirators. E. P. Oppenheim
Conspirators. F. Prokosch
Conspirators. A. Riefe
Conspirators at Large. S. Maddock
Conspirators in Capri. S. Maddock
Conspirators Three. S. Maddock
Conspire to Kill. Jack Watson
Constable and the Lady. J. Bude
Constable 42Z. E. A. D. B.
Constable, Guard Thyself! Henry Wade
Constable on the Hill. N. Rhea
Constables Don't Count. Alex Fraser
Constance, and Calbot's Rival. J. Hawthorne
Constance Dunlap, Woman Detective. A. B. Reeve
Constantine Cay. C. Dillon
Consultant. J. McNeil
Consulting Room Crime. M. Osborne
Consulting Room Mystery. M. Osborne
Consummate Rose. L. Meynell
Consummate Scoundrel. G. Boothby
Contact and other stories. F. N. Hart
Contact Lens. J. Urquhart
Contact Lost. D. Craig
Contact Man. D. Betteridge
Contact Mercury. L. H. Nason
Contact Mr. Delgado. J. Pattinson
Container. M. Kaufman
Contaminant. L. Reiffel
Contango Day. B. Jefferis
Content Assignment. H. Roth
Contents of the Coffin. J. S. Fletcher
Contents Unknown. L. Barbee
Contessa Came Too. J. Bryan
Contesting the County, and other tales. B. Hemyng
Continental Conspiracy. F. W. Irwin
Continental Contract. D. Pendleton
Continental Drift. J. D. Houston
Continental Op. D. Hammett
Contraband. C. F. Adams
Contraband. H. Janson
Contraband. C. B. Kelland
Contraband. L. A. Knight
"Contraband." R. Parrish
Contraband. D. Wheatley
Contraband Coast. W. Chambers
Contraband Cruises. Will Allen
Contrabandits. J. Workman
Contrabando. K. Detzer
Contract. H. Carlisle
Contract. O. Demaris
Contract. J. Poyer
Contract. A. Prior
Contract. G. Seymour
Contract for a Homicide. Dan Morgan
Contract for a Killer. D. Reid
Contract for a Killing. R. L. Brent
Contract for Death. D. Ingham
Contract on Cherry Tree. P. Rosenberg
Contract on Stone. D. R. Addleman
Contract on the President. J. Crosby
Contract with a Killer. H. Jobson
Controller. O. John
Convent Mystery. J. K. Stafford
Convent on Styx. G. Mitchell
Convention. F. Knebel
Conversation with a Corpse. R. C. Dennis
Convertible Hearse. W. C. Gault
Convict. N. Buntline
Convict. T. P. Prest
Convict B 14. R. K. Weekes
Convict by Proxy. A. Murray
Convict Captain. D. W. MacArthur
Convict Colonel. F. Du Boisgobey
Convict 413L. M. Leighton
Convict Has Escaped. J. Budd
Convict International. W. D. Maydwell
Convict 999. Grace M. White
Convict 99. M. Leighton
Convict 100. M. Leighton
Convict 1066. B. Gray
Convict 72. N. Ned
Convict Ship. W. C. Russell
Convict's Hoard. M. G. Hugi
Convict's Marriage. A. Bouvier
Convict's Sweetheart. Anonymous
Convict's Sweetheart. O. Harper
Conway, K. C. S. Stone
Cook General. J. Cashman
Cook Up a Crime. C. M. Russell
Cool Cottontail. J. Ball
Cool Day for Killing. W. Haggard
Cool Jade. B. Girard
Cool Man. W. R. Burnett
Cool Murder. P. George
Cool Sleeps Balaban. D. MacKenzie
Cool Sugar. H. Janson
Cooler. G. Markstein
Coolie Tramp. E. L. Long
Coombsberrow Mystery. J. Colwall
Co-Ordinator. A. York
Cop. J. Karney
Cop Hater. E. McBain

Cop in a Tight Frame. Neill Graham
Cop-Kill. William Crawford
Cop Killer. G. Bagby
Cop Killer. M. Sjowall
Cop Killers. M. Rabinowitz
Cop Killers. Steve Scott
Cop-Lover. P. Malloch
Cop on the Corner. J. Kirkpatrick
Cop Out. E. Queen
Cop Story. P. Andrews
Copacabana Stud. John Allen
Copenhagen Affair. S. McGurk
Copenhagen Affair. J. Oram
Copley's Hunch. J. Ditton
Copper at Sea. G. Fairlie
Copper Beeches. Arthur H. Lewis
Copper Bottle. E. J. Millward
Copper Box. J. S. Fletcher
Copper Butterfly. S. Harvester
Copper Disc. R. J. C. Stead
Copper Frame. E. Queen
Copper House. J. Regis
Copper Lady. H. L. Nelson
Copper Mask, and other stories. H. Wiley
Copper Snare. Lawrence Williams
Coppergold. P. G. Winslow
Copperhead. J. Henderson
Coppers and Gold. H. Brinton
Coppers Don't Cry. J. Wainwright
Coppersmith. R. J. Griffin
Coppersmith's Dolls. R. J. Griffin
Cops. J. Pearl
Cops and Robbers. O. Henry
Cops and Robbers. D. E. Westlake
Cops 'n Robbers. J. Russell
Copsford Mystery. W. C. Russell
Copy-Cat Killings. Martin Thomas
Copy for Crime. C. Carnac
Coral Kill. B. Chandler
Coral Lady. E. Southworth
Coral Pin. F. Du Boisgobey
Coral Princess Murders. F. Crane
Corbin Necklace. H. K. Webster
Cord and Cheese. J. De Mille
Cord for a Killer. W. M. Duncan
Cordelia the Magnificent. L. Scott
Corder Index. R. Raine
Cordially Invited to Meet Death. R. Stout
Cordley's Castle. J. Pattinson
Cords of Vanity. D. Hennessey
Co-Respondent. G. W. Appleton
Corfu Affair. J. T. Phillifent
Corinthian Days. A. Soutar
Corinthian Jack. C. E. Pearce
Corioli Affair. M. Deasy
Cork and the Serpent. Macdonald Hastings
Cork in Bottle. Macdonald Hastings
Cork in the Doghouse. Macdonald Hastings
Cork on Location. Macdonald Hastings
Cork on the Telly. Macdonald Hastings
Cork on the Water. Macdonald Hastings
Cork Street Crime. J. G. Brandon
Cormac Legend. D. Daniels
Cormorant Crag. G. M. Fenn
Cormorant's Isle. A. MacKinnon
Corner House. F. M. White
Corner in Coffee. C. T. Brady
Corner in Corpses. A. Bocca
Corner in Crime. Norman Lucas
Corner in Diamonds. M. Gerard
Corner Men. J. Gardner
Corner of Paradise. L. Holton
Corner of the Playground. S. Harvester
Corner Shop. E. Cadell
Cornered. L. King
Cornered! J. McKimmey
Cornered. T. A. Plummer
Cornered at Last. Nicholas Carter
Cornered at Last. A. F. Pinkerton
Cornered at Six. T. P. McMahon
Cornish Coast Conspiracy. D. Ames
Cornish Coast Murder. J. Bude
Cornish Crime. A. Weymouth
Cornish Cruise. G. Volk
Cornish Fox. C. H. B. Kitchin
Cornish Interlude. S. Murray
Cornish Mystery. M. Durham
Cornish Penny. C. T. Cade
Cornish Pixie Affair. P. Leslie
Cornish Riviera Mystery. J. Rowland
Corollary to Murder. R. White
Coronation Mysteries and other stories. H. Hill
Coronation Mystery. G. Chester
Coroner Doubts. R. A. J. Walling
Coroner Presides. S. Truss
Coroner's Pidgin. M. Allingham
Coroner's Understudy. Captain Coe
Coroner's Verdict. R. Keverne
Corporal Cameron. R. Connor
Corporal Cameron of the North West Mounted Police. R. Connor
Corporal Died in Bed. B. Graeme
Corporal Downey Takes the Trail. J. B. Hendryx
Corporate Caper. S. Jason
Corpse. Carter Brown
Corpse. P. McCutchan
Corpse and Robbers. D. Stapleton
Corpse and the Lady. J. S. Strange

Corpse and the Three Ex-Husbands. P. MacTyre
Corpse at Camp Two. G. Carr
Corpse at Casablanca. B. Cobb
Corpse at College. M. Risco
Corpse at Least. S. H. Courtier
Corpse at the Carnival. G. Bellairs
Corpse at the Quill Club. A. R. Long
Corpse Awaits. O. F. Jerome
Corpse-Bird Cries. O. Norton
Corpse by Any Other Name. R. A. J. Walling
Corpse by the River. H. Arre
Corpse Came Back. A. R. Long
Corpse Came C.O.D. Jimmy Starr
Corpse Came Calling. G. C. Bestor
Corpse Came Calling. B. Halliday
Corpse Came Too. D. Reid
Corpse Can Sure Louse Up a Weekend! D. Tracy
Corpse Candle. G. Bagby
Corpse Can't Walk. H. Long
Corpse Comes Ashore. J. Mersereau
Corpse de Ballet. L. Cores
Corpse Died Twice. B. Frost
Corpse Diplomatique. D. Ames
Corpse Errant. M. Durham
Corpse for a Candidate. M. Geller
Corpse for a Client. H. W. Gabriel
Corpse for Breakfast. Max Murray
Corpse for Charlie. J. Courage
Corpse for Charybdis. S. Gilruth
Corpse for Christmas. W. A. Ballinger
Corpse for Christmas. Carter Brown
Corpse for Christmas. H. Kane
Corpse for Kofi Katt. G. North
Corpse from "The City". J. G. Brandon
Corpse from the Sky. J. M. Crouch
Corpse Grows a Beard. M. Scherf
Corpse Guards Parade. M. Kennedy
Corpse Had Red Hair. Alice Campbell
Corpse Hangs High. E. Ronns
Corpse in Camera. D. Launay
Corpse in Canonicals. G. D. H. Cole
Corpse in Cold Storage. M. Kennedy
Corpse in Community. D. Fisher
Corpse in Company K. Avery
Corpse in Diplomacy. M. Borgenicht
Corpse in Handcuffs. F. A. Smith
Corpse in My Bed. David Alexander
Corpse in the Boudoir. Gene Ross
Corpse in the Cab. Aldin Vinton
Corpse in the Cabin. B. Sarto
Corpse in the Car. J. Rhode
Corpse in the Caravan. R. Trevor
Corpse in the Cargo. B. Cobb
Corpse in the Castle. E. Friend
Corpse in the Church. T. F. W. Hickey
Corpse in the Circus. N. Morland
Corpse in the Circus and other stories. N. Morland
Corpse in the Clouds. P. Conde
Corpse in the Constable's Garden. G. D. H. Cole
Corpse in the Coppice. R. A. J. Walling
Corpse in the Corner Saloon. Hampton Stone
Corpse in the Coupe. W. Paddon
Corpse in the Cove. E. Mack
Corpse in the Crevasse. G. Carr
Corpse in the Crimson Slippers. R. A. J. Walling
Corpse in the Derby Hat. H. Swiggett
Corpse in the Elevator. M. Mannon
Corpse in the Flannel Nightgown. M. Scherf
Corpse in the Green Pajamas. R. A. J. Walling
Corpse in the Guest Room. Clement Wood
Corpse in the Picture Window. B. Cassiday
Corpse in the Snowman. N. Blake
Corpse in the Waxworks. J. D. Carr
Corpse in the Wind. R. P. Koehler
Corpse Incognito. B. Cobb
Corpse Is Indignant. Douglas Stapleton
Corpse Maker. David Wilson
Corpse Moved Upstairs. F. Gruber
Corpse Next Door. J. Farris
Corpse of the Old School. J. Iams
Corpse on Ice. J. Hedges
Corpse on London Bridge. L. Southworth
Corpse on the Bridge. C. Barry
Corpse on the Dike. J. Van de Wetering
Corpse on the Flying Trapeze. N. Morland
Corpse on the Hearth. Harry Lang
Corpse on the Mat. M. Kennedy
Corpse on the Town. J. Roebuck
Corpse on the White House Lawn. Diplomat
Corpse Parade. M. Hervey
Corpse Parade. R. Wallace
Corpse Road. G. Moffat
Corpse Rode On. J. G. Brandon
Corpse Said No. B. Frost
Corpse Spells Danger. M. Storm
Corpse Steps Out. C. Rice
Corpse That Came Back. P. Piper
Corpse That Got Away. S. Truss
Corpse That Knew Everybody. C. Worth
Corpse That Never Was. B. Halliday
Corpse That Refused to Stay Dead. Hampton Stone

Corpse That Spoke. R. H. Leitfred
Corpse That Talked. R. Telfair
Corpse That Traveled. A. J. Rees
Corpse That Walked. O. R. Cohen
Corpse That Walked. R. Winsor
Corpse to Bury. J. B. Fearnley
Corpse to Cairo. M. O'Brine
Corpse to Copenhagen. Jonathan Burke
Corpse to Cuba. A. Kent
Corpse Too Many. J. Callendar
Corpse Was No Bargain at All. Hampton Stone
Corpse Was No Lady. N. Morland
Corpse Who Had Too Many Friends. Hampton Stone
Corpse Who Wouldn't Die. E. J. Doherty
Corpse with Camera. Jean Fraser
Corpse with Knee Action. B. J. Maylon
Corpse with One Shoe. M. Scherf
Corpse with the Blistered Hand. R. A. J. Walling
Corpse with the Blue Cravat. R. A. J. Walling
Corpse with the Dirty Face. R. A. J. Walling
Corpse with the Eerie Eye. R. A. J. Walling
Corpse with the Floating Foot. R. A. J. Walling
Corpse with the Grimy Glove. R. A. J. Walling
Corpse with the Listening Ear. L. D. Smith
Corpse with the Missing Watch. R. A. J. Walling
Corpse with the Purple Thighs. G. Bagby
Corpse with the Red-Headed Friend. R. A. J. Walling
Corpse with the Sticky Fingers. G. Bagby
Corpse with the Sunburnt Face. C. S. Sprigg
Corpse Without a Clue. R. A. J. Walling
Corpse Without a Country. L. Trimble
Corpse Without a Jacket. L. West
Corpse Without Boots. L. Hill
Corpse Without Flesh. G. Bruce
Corpse Won't Sing. S. H. Courtier
Corpse Wore a Wig. G. Bagby
Corpse Wore Nylon. L. Paradise
Corpse Wore No Shoes. D. Thompson
Corpse Wore Rubies. F. Lester
Corpses at Enderby. G. Bellairs
Corpses at Indian Stones. P. Wylie
Corpses Can't Walk. Robert (G.) Curtis
Corpses Don't Care. E. Ellison
Corpses Galore. J. Bruce
Corpses Never Argue. David Hume
Corpus Delectable. T. Powell
Corrector of Destinies. M. D. Post
Correspondent. R. H. Shimer
Corridor of Death. Lieut. Carlton
Corridor of Mirrors. Archie Hill
Corridor of Mirrors. C. Massie
Corridor of Venus. N. Bell
Corridor of Whispers. E. Noone
Corridors of Fear. S. Horler
Corridors of Fear. J. D. Perry
Corridors of Fear. Clarissa Ross
Corrie Who? M. Foster
Corrigan's Way. E. Snell
Corrupt and Ensnare. F. M. Nevins
Corrupt City. E. Ellison
Corrupt Ones. J. C. Barton
Corrupted Women. B. Sarto
Corrupter. H. Barron
Corrupters. Clayton Moore
Corrupters. D. Telfer
Corruption. R. Curle
Corruption. P. Saxon
Corruption. Percy White
Corruption City. H. McCoy
Corruption in Cantock. J. Notley
Corruption's Tutor. J. Cello
Corruptors. W. Francis
Corruptors. G. G. Griffin
Corsage. R. Stout
Corsair. J. G. Sarasin
Corsican. B. S. Ballinger
Corsican. J. Bazal
Corsican Contract. E. Clark
Corsican Cross. Michael Bradley
Corsican Death. R. Hawkes
Corsican Takeover. Don Smith
Cortenay Treasure. P. C. Wren
Cosa Nostra. P. McCurtin
Cosa Nostra Circus. G. Corbin
Cosgrove: Detective. M. M. Innes
Cosgrove Report. G. O'Toole
Cosmic Reality Kill. J. Rosenberger
Cossack Cowboy. L. S. Taube
Cossack Mystery. H. Pink
Cost of a Clue. I. Stark
Cost of Living. R. D. MacDougall
Cost of Silence. M. Yorke
Cost Price. D. Yates
Costello—Psychic Investigator. J. Nicholson
Cosway Miniature. R. Rubens
Cosy Little Murder. E. Radford
Cotfold Conundrums. D. G. Browne
Cotswold Case. A. Wynne
Cottage. Gretchen Travis

Cottage at Avalanche. J. Wetherell
Cottage at Chapelyard. F. Keinzley
Cottage at Drimble. Elizabeth Ford
Cottage in the Chine. H. Hill
Cottage in the Woods. D. Quentin
Cottage Murder. E. R. Punshon
Cottage of Terror. Donald Stuart
Cottage on Catherine Cay. J. Aeby
Cottage on the Fells. H. D. Stacpoole
Cottage Sinister. Q. Patrick
Cotton Comes to Harlem. C. Himes
Couch. R. Bloch
Couch of Earth. P. Somerville-Large
Couch Trip. K. Kolb
Could It Be Murder? N. MacKenzie
Coulson Alone. Jack Mann
Coulson Goes South. Jack Mann
Council of Comforters. W. M. Duncan
Council of Crooks. W. J. Bayfield
Council of Death. Nicholas Carter
Council of Justice. E. Wallace
Council of Seven. J. C. Snaith
Council of Ten. S. Cobb
Council of the Rat. J. B. Cassells
Councillors of Falconhoe. F. M. White
Counsel for the Defense. J. Ashford
Counsel for the Defense. J. Ronald
Counsel for the Defense. I. Scott
Counsel for the Killer. M. Carrel
Counsellor. J. J. Connington
Counsellor Heart. P. G. Winslow
Counsels of the Night. L. Cleeve
Count Backwards to Zero. B. Halliday
Count Bruga. B. Hecht
Count Bunker. J. S. Clouston
Count de Mornay. S. W. Wheeler
Count-Down. H. Howard
Count-Down. C. E. Maine
Count Down for Conquest. B. Gray
Count Dracula. T. Tiller
Count in Kensington. C. A. Alington
Count Me In. F. Nichols
Count Netherleigh. H. Wood
Count Not the Cost. I. MacKintosh
Count of Nine. A. A. Fair
Count of Six. L. Powell
Count of Van Rheeden Castle. Annjeanette Scott
Count on the Saint. L. Charteris
Count Philip. P. Benoit
Count Remeny. J. Middlemass
Count Roderic's Castle. Anonymous
Count the Cost. E. Ferrars
Count the Hours. C. Fraser-Simson
Count the Ways. D. M. Disney
Count Zarka. W. Magnay
Countdown at Monaco. L. Kenyon
Countdown for a Spy. D. Von Elsner
Countdown for Murder. G. Sydney
Countdown 1000. D. Mariner
Countdown to Crisis. M. Eden
Countdown to Doomsday. R. Quest
Countdown to Murder. H. D. Kastle
Countdown to Terror. L. Derrick
Counter Currents. E. Janis
Counter-Feat. H. Janson
Counter Paradise. N. Fleming
Counter Plot. E. Z. Frank
Counter-Spy. G. Dilnot
Counterattack. F. Scarpetta
Counterbalance. P. Trent
Countercrime. O. Chase
Counterfeit. H. Howard
Counterfeit. L. Thayer
Counterfeit Agent. Nick Carter
Counterfeit Bill. L. Thayer
Counterfeit Bridegroom. L. M. Borden
Counterfeit Corpse. F. Findley
Counterfeit Corpse. N. A. Vanderpuije
Counterfeit Courier. J. C. Sheers
Counterfeit Gentleman. C. B. Kelland
Counterfeit Heiress. Andrea Hill
Counterfeit Kill. Gordon Davis
Counterfeit Murder. W. Bannister
Counterfeit Murders. V. MacClure
Counterfeit Spy. A. O. Pollard
Counterfeit Wife. B. Halliday
Counterfeiter's Roguery. E. C. Derby
Counterfeiter's Wake. Lieut. Carlton
Counterflood. K. Thackeray
Countermine. A. Wenlock
Counterpoint. I. Holland
Counterpoint Murder. G. D. H. Cole
Counterpoise of Death. H. Taylor
Counterpol. J. Boland
Counterpol in Paris. J. Boland
Countersnatch. J. F. Straker
Counterspy. B. Cleeve
Counterspy Express. A. S. Fleischman
Counterspy Murders. P. Cheyney
Counterstroke. A. Garve
Counterstroke. A. Pratt
Counterstroke. P. Wayland
Countertrap. J. Tiger
Counterweight. D. Brown
Countess and the Spy. G. De Villiers
Countess Ida. F. Whishaw
Countess Londa. G. Boothby
Countess Muta. C. H. Montague
Countess of Lowndes Square. E. F. Benson
Countess of Zelle. M. Gerard
Countess Vera. A. M. Miller

Countless Steps. B. Shannon
Country and Fatal. G. Bagby
Country Club Murder. R. Verron
Country Coffins. Dale Clark
Country Family. J. S. Clouston
Country Holiday. Elizabeth Ford
Country-House Burglar. M. Gilbert
Country Killing. M. F. Harris
Country Kind of Death. M. McMullen
Country Love and Poison Rain. P. Tate
Country of Again. P. M. Hubbard
Country of the Kind. S. Jennifer
Country of the Strangers. F. S. Wees
Country of the Wolf. S. Wagner
Country Squire. G. M. Fenn
Country Tragedy. F. C. Hall
Count's Chauffeur. W. LeQueux
Count's Millions. F. Du Boisgobey
Count's Millions. E. Gaboriau
Count's Secret. E. Gaboriau
County Affairs. R. Armfelt
County Family. J. Payn
County Kill. W. C. Gault
County Library Murders. J. Austwick
Coup That Failed. R. Worth
Coupon Crimes. G. Verner
Coupons for Death. N. Brady
Courage for Sale. Robert Mason
Courage of the North. J. B. Hendryx
Courageous Exploits of Doctor Syn. R. Thorndike
Courier for Crime. J. T. Story
Courier Job. J. Pattinson
Courier of Fortune. A. W. Marchmont
Courier to Marrakesh. V. Williams
Courier to Peking. J. Goodfield
Course in Murder. L. Chaytor
Course of Villainy. J. Moffatt
Court by Proceedings. W. R. Smith
Court Favorite. B. Reynolds
Court Intrigue. B. Thomson
Court Martial. J. Ehrlich
Court-Martial. Robin Moore
Court of Crows. R. A. Knowlton
Court of Dusty Feet. J. G. Sarasin
Court of Honor. W. LeQueux
Court of Last Resort. L. H. Hart
Court of St. Simon. E. P. Oppenheim
Court of Shadows. G. Jackson
Court of Silver Shadows. Beatrice Brandon
Court of the Thorn Tree. Patricia Maxwell
Court Short. J. Balfour
Court Tragedy. A. D. Vandam
Courtesy Dame. R. M. Gilchrist
Courtesy of Death. G. Household
Courthouse. J. N. Iannuzzi
Courtier to Death. Anthony Gilbert
Courtland's Crime. A. M. Burrage
Courtney Entry. J. Harris
Courts of Morning. J. Buchan
Courtway Case. R. Goyne
Courtyard. J. Moffatt
Cousin Jess. M. Turni
Cousin to Terror. C. Bramwell
Cove in Darkness. S. Wagner
Cove of Fear. V. Smiley
Coven. Carter Brown
Coven. J. Hampton
Coven. David St. John
Coven Gibbet. J. N. Chance
Covenant with Death. S. Becker
Covenant with Death. F. Grierson
Covenant with Death. J. Harris
Covenant with Death. R. Walker
Covent Garden Murder. W. J. Makin
Covent Garden Mystery. W. J. Bayfield
Coventry Option. Anthony Burton
Cover Girls. P. W. Fairman
Cover Her Face. P. D. James
Cover Her Face. H. McCutcheon
Cover Her with Roses. R. Anderson
Cover His Face. T. Kyd
Cover of Darkness. L. A. Olmsted
Cover Stories. R. Rosenblum
Cover Story. R. Rosenblum
Cover That Corpse. H. Zore
Cover-Up Story. M. Babson
Cove's End. S. Hufford
Coward. A. Meredith
Coward Behind the Curtain. R. Marsh
Cowardly Custard. B. Von Hutten
Cowards' Castle. A. Soutar
Coward's Club. F. Grierson
Cowboy Countess. C. N. Williamson
Cowboy Detective. Old Sleuth
Cowboy Detective. C. A. Sirengo
Cowl of Doom. E. Ronns
Cowled Menace. W. E. Hawkins
Crabtree Affair. M. Innes
Crabtree House. Howel Evans
Crack in the Bell. P. C. MacFarlane
Crack in the Mirror. M. Haedrich
Crack in the Sidewalk. B. Copper
Crack in the Teacup. M. Gilbert
Crack of Dawn. L. Ford
Crack of Doom. L. Bruce
Crack of Doom. R. Cromie
Crack of Doom. G. Hackforth-Jones
Crack-Up. H. Atkinson
Crackerjack. W. B. M. Ferguson

Title Index

Cracking of Spines. Roy Lewis
Crackshot Detective. Anonymous
Cracksman on Velvet. F. Selwyn
Cracksmen All. G. C. Foster
Crackswoman. Roland Daniel
Crackswoman. C. Dawe
Cradle and the Grave. A. M. Stein
Cradle Snatch. P. Conway
Cradle Will Fall. M. H. Clark
Cradled in Fear. A. Boutell
Cradled in Murder. Rudd Fleming
Cradle's Revenge. Eric Bailey
Craft and Cunning. W. M. Graydon
Crafty Foe. H. Nisbet
Crag Island. W. M. Graydon
Craghold Creatures. E. Noone
Craghold Crypt. E. Noone
Craghold Curse. E. Noone
Craghold Legacy. E. Noone
Cragsmoor. J. Letton
Craig and the Jaguar. K. Benton
Craig and the Midas Touch. K. Benton
Craig and the Tunisian Tangle. K. Benton
Craig Kennedy, Detective. A. B. Reeve
Craig Kennedy Listens In. A. B. Reeve
Craig Kennedy on the Farm. A. B. Reeve
Craig Poisoning Mystery. A. Fielding
Craigallen Castle. Mrs. Gore
Craig's Spur. E. S. Madden
Craigshaw Curse. J. F. Webb
Craine's First Case. E. P. Healey
Crambo. M. O'Brine
Cranes of Ibycus. M. Craig
Crank in the Corner. C. Bush
Cranmer. S. Knickmeyer
Cranshaw Inheritance. C. Etheridge
Crash! A. Applin
Crash. H. Franklin
Crash and Carry. S. Christie
Crash Course. S. Barlay
Crash into Murder. T. B. Morris
Crash Landing. M. Regan
Crash Programme. J. R. Daniels
Crashlanding in the Congo. C. H. Wallace
Crashout. James Preston
Crater. R. Gore-Brown
Crater's Gold. P. E. Curtiss
Crave Pity from the Wind. B. Freestone
Craven Castle. L. Churchill
Craven Fortune. F. M. White
Craven Mystery. P. Trent
Crawlspace. H. Lieberman
Crawshay Jewel Mystery. Roland Daniel
Crayfish Club. Roy Roberts
Crayfish Dinner. C. Keith
Crayon Clue. M. J. Reynolds
Craze of Christian Englehart. H. F. Darnell
Crazy Joe. M. Barone
Crazy Kill. C. Hamblett
Crazy Kill. C. Himes
Crazy Mixed-Up Corpse. M. Avallone
Crazy Mixed-Up Nude. G. G. Fickling
Crazy Murder Show. Sutherland Scott
Crazy-Quilt. F. Hume
Crazy Quilt Murders. H. W. Sandberg
Crazy to Kill. A. Cardwell
Crazy to Kill. D. Linton
Crazy Woman Blues. J. F. Burke
Creaking Chair. L. Meynell
Creaking Chair. A. T. Wilkes
Creaking Floors. R. B. Whorf
Creaking Gallows. T. A. Plummer
Creaking Gate. V. Bridges
Creaking Tree Mystery. L. A. Knight
Cream and Cider. H. Gibbs
Created: The Destroyer. R. Sapir
Creative Murders. Carter Brown
Creator. M. T. Hinkemeyer
Creature of the Night. F. Hume
Creature Was Stirring. T. Wells
Creatures. R. Masson
Creatures of Satan. John Muir
Creatures of the Night. V. Hanson
Creco the Swordsman. Old Sleuth
Credit for a Murder. S. Dean
Creedy Case. F. Crankshaw
Creep, Shadow! A. Merritt
Creep, Shadow, Creep! A. Merritt
Creepers. J. Creasey
Creeping Death. M. Grant
Creeping Death. L. A. Knight
Creeping Flesh. D. Rutherford
Creeping Hours. H. Pentecost
Creeping Jenny Mystery. B. Flynn
Creeping Shadow. Sam Merwin
Creeping Shadows. W. Usher
Creeping Siamese. D. Hammett
Creeping Venom. S. Pim
Creeping Vicar. I. Hamilton
Creeps. A. Abbot
Creeps by Night. T. J. Kelly
Creeps Medley. M. Hervey
Creggan Peerage. C. R. Gull
Creighton's Castle. M. Lynch
Crenland Castle. M. Gerard
Creole. S. J. Arnold
Creole Slave's Revenge. O. Harper
Creole's Crime. M. Pinkerton
Crepe Myrtle Tree. L. V. Stevens
Crescent Brotherhood. Nicholas Carter
Crescent Moon. L. Noel

Cresselly Inheritance. J. Blackmore
Cressida. M. B. Lowndes
Crested Key. K. Orbison
Creston, the Detective. Old Sleuth
Crestwood Traps. G. M. Snodgrass
Cretan. E. Ayrton
Cretan Cipher. J. Palmer
Cretan Counterfeit. K. Farrer
Crevice. W. J. Burns
Crew of L.C. 454. E. L. Long
Cricket Cage. R. H. Shimer
Cries in the Night. J. H. Wallis
Crilly Court Mystery. H. S. Keeler
Crime. G. Bernanos
Crime. Anthony Lang
Crime. S. Longstreet
Crime. T. P. Prest
Crime a la Carte. M. Hervey
Crime Across the Way. F. Millington
Crime Against Judy Bishop. C. Barling
Crime Against Marcella. G. Milner
Crime Against Society. J. Spenser
Crime and a Clock. Whyte Hall
Crime and Again. R. Stout
Crime and Co. S. Fowler
Crime and Judy. R. L. Radford
Crime and Punishment. R. Ackland
Crime and Punishment. M. Dubois
Crime and Punishment. F. M. Dostoevski
Crime and the Casket. J. Ironside
Crime and the Confessor. H. G. Hutchinson
Crime and the Criminal. R. Marsh
Crime and the Curator. J. Veitch
Crime and the Motive. Nicholas Carter
Crime and the Underworld. C. Bishop
Crime Apart. M. Underwood
Crime at Black Dudley. M. Allingham
Crime at Blossoms. M. Sharp
Crime at Cape Folly. S. Browning
Crime at Christmas. C. H. B. Kitchin
Crime at Cloysters. R. Bayne-Powell
Crime at Cobb's House. H. Corey
Crime at Crooked Gables. T. A. Plummer
Crime at Crown Inn. M. Frazer
Crime at Diana's Pool. V. L. Whitechurch
Crime at Gargoyles. K. Wade
Crime at Grandison Hall. H. Leyford
Crime at Guildford. F. W. Crofts
Crime at Halfpenny Bridge. G. Bellairs
Crime at Honotassa. M. G. Eberhart
Crime at Keeper's. T. Cobb
Crime at Lock 14. G. Simenon
Crime at Nornes. F. W. Crofts
Crime at Orcival. E. Gaboriau
Crime at Porches Hill. R. Bayne-Powell
Crime at Red Towers. C. K. Steele
Crime at Tattenham Corner. A. Haynes
Crime at the Conquistador. S. Callaway
Crime at the Crossroads. P. Urquhart
Crime at the Crossways. B. Flynn
Crime at the Fair. H. King
Crime at the "Noah's Ark." M. Thynne
Crime at the Quay. A. Blair
Crime at the Quay Inn. E. Aldhouse
Crime at the Seaside Hotel. A. Blair
Crime at the Villa Gloria. G. Norsworthy
Crime at 3 A.M. H. Clevely
Crime Beat Crisis. H. Janson
Crime by Chance. E. Linington
Crime Cargo. M. Knight
Crime Club. Anonymous
Crime Club. F. Froest
Crime Club. W. Holt-White
Crime Coast. E. Gill
Crime Code. W. LeQueux
Crime Combine. David Hume
Crime Commandoes. P. Cave
Crime Conductor. P. MacDonald
Crime Confessions. J. W. Firth
Crime Cop. L. Holden
Crime Counter Crime. E. C. R. Lorac
Crime Cruise. E. L. Long
Crime Cult. M. Grant
Crime de Luxe. E. Gill
Crime Doctor. E. W. Hornung
Crime File. Dell Shannon
Crime for Christmas. M. Lynch
Crime for Mothers and others. H. Slesar
Crime Gang. M. E. Cooke
Crime, Gentleman, Please. D. Ames
Crime Haters. A. Ashe
Crime Hound. M. S. Scott
Crime in a Big Way. C. Bishop
Crime in Cabin 66. A. Christie
Crime in Car 13. S. Chalmers
Crime in Carson's Shack. R. Hardinge
Crime in Concrete. M. Coles
Crime in Corn-Weather. M. M. Atwater
Crime in Crystal. H. R. Campbell
Crime in Cumberland Court. R. A. J. Walling
Crime in Holland. G. Simenon
Crime in Ink. C. Carvalho
Crime in Kensington. C. S. Sprigg
Crime in Lepers' Hollow. G. Bellairs
Crime in Paradise. Nicholas Carter
Crime in Park Lane. W. Jardine
Crime in Quarantine. Rosa Lambert
Crime in Reverse. J. D. Kennedy
Crime in Room 27. W. Tyrer
Crime in the Alps. G. Warden

Crime in the Arcade. W. Proudfoot
Crime in the Boulevard Raspail. R. Massey
Crime in the Close. A. Dick
Crime in the Crypt. F. W. Gumley
Crime in the Crypt. C. Wells
Crime in the Crystal. R. Hare
Crime in the Dutch Garden. H. Adams
Crime in the Kiosk. J. G. Brandon
Crime in the Wood. W. M. Graydon
Crime in the Wood. T. W. Speight
Crime in Threadneedle Street. George Davis
Crime in Time. M. Burton
Crime in Washington Mews. H. Crooken
Crime in Whispers. C. Witting
Crime Inc. J. S. Endicott
Crime Incarnate. C. Wells
Crime Insoluble. M. Durham
Crime Is Murder. H. Nielsen
Crime Is My Business. W. H. Baker
Crime Is of the Essence. J. Csida
Crime Legitimate. P. Luck
Crime Limited. L. C. Douthwaite
Crime Looks Up. C. Rushton
Crime Maker. B. Fleming
Crime Master. W. M. Duncan
Crime Medley. M. Hervey
Crime Most Foul. George Douglas
Crime of a Century. Nicholas Carter
Crime of a Christmas Toy. H. Herman
Crime of a Countess. Nicholas Carter
Crime of Bohemia. J. K. Stafford
Crime of Colin Wise. M. Underwood
Crime of Constable Kelly. J. C. Snaith
Crime of Convict 13. W. M. Graydon
Crime of Corporal Sherwood. G. Chester
Crime of Count Dureen. P. Urquhart
Crime of Four. G. Verner
Crime of Golden Gully. G. Rock
Crime of Gunga Dass. C. Brisbane
Crime of Hallowe'en. L. J. Libbey
Crime of Henry Vane. Anonymous
Crime of Herbert Wratislaus. Michael Lewis
Crime of His Life. C. Conrad
Crime of Honor. G. Arpino
Crime of Inspector Maigret. G. Simenon
Crime of Jane Dacre. S. C. Lethbridge
Crime of Julian Masters. E. Atiyah
Crime of Keziah Keene. V. Campbell
Crime of Laura Sarelle. J. Shearing
Crime of Maunsell Grange. F. Breton
Crime of Mildred Bentham. T. B. Morris
Crime of Monte Carlo. Anonymous
Crime of One's Own. E. Grierson
Crime of Peter Ropner. H. Heslop
Crime of Philip Garrison. F. Marlowe
Crime of Philip Guthrie. L. Ragsdale
Crime of Silence. P. Carlon
Crime of Sybil Cresswell. F. E. Spence
Crime of the Boulevard. J. Claretie
Crime of the Camera. Nicholas Carter
Crime of the Cashiered Major. A. Parsons
Crime of the Catacombs. G. H. Teed
Crime of the Century. A. Abbot
Crime of the Century. D. Donovan
Crime of the Century. R. Ottolengui
Crime of the Chromium Bowl. E. B. Black
Crime of the Crossword. J. Garland
Crime of the Crystal. F. Hume
Crime of the French Cafe and other stories. Nicholas Carter
Crime of the 'Liza Jane. F. Hume
Crime of the Midnight Express. A. F. Pinkerton
Crime of the Opera House. F. Du Boisgobey
Crime of the Reckaviles. W. S. Masterman
Crime of the Under-Seas. G. Boothby
Crime of Their Life. F. Kane
Crime of Vera Seymour. B. Heygate
Crime of Violence. R. King
Crime of Violence. J. Stagg
Crime of Wilfred Hanson. Alfred James Alderson
Crime on a Convoy Carrier. A. Whitehouse
Crime on a Cruise. K. Rhodes
Crime on Canvas. F. M. White
Crime on Cote des Neiges. D. Montrose
Crime on Gallows Hill. G. H. Teed
Crime on Her Hands. L. Gribble
Crime on Her Hands. R. Stout
Crime on My Hands. R. Chapman
Crime on My Hands. R. Drayton
Crime on My Hands. C. G. Hodges
Crime on My Hands. H. Janson
Crime on My Hands. J. Laffin
Crime on My Hands. G. Sanders
Crime on the Cliff. L. Jackson
Crime on the Clyde. G. Chester
Crime on the Cuff. H. Weiner
Crime on the French Frontier. J. Hunter
Crime on the Heath. C. V. Frost
Crime on the Kennet. C. A. Alington
Crime on the Limited. N. Ridley
Crime on the Moor. T. C. Bridges
Crime on the Moors. W. Tyrer
Crime on the Promenade. J. Hunter
Crime on the Solent. F. W. Crofts
Crime on Their Hands. Dell Shannon
Crime or Folly? B. M. Clay

Crime Oracle. M. Grant
Crime Out of Mind. D. Ames
Crime over Casco. W. B. Gibson
Crime Partners. A. C. Clark
Crime Pays No Dividends. E. Radford
Crime Philosopher. R. Goyne
Crime Photographers. S. Bristol
Crime Reporter's Secret. G. Dilnot
Crime School. M. Cumberland
Crime Scientist. F. A. M. Webster
Crime Specialist. D. Newton
Crime Squadron. B. Waller
Crime Syndicate. P. Manton
Crime Takes the Count. Elliott Dane
Crime Takes Wings. J. S. Dawe
Crime Tears On. C. Wells
Crime, the Place, and the Girl. D. Stapleton
Crime to Fit the Punishment. C. Joyce
Crime to Music. P. Drax
Crime Unlimited. David Hume
Crime Upon Crime. A. Gask
Crime Upon Crime. M. Underwood
Crime Wave. M. Russell
Crime Wave at Little Cornford. H. Adams
Crime Wind. M. Holbrook
Crime with Many Voices. M. Halliday
Crime with Ten Solutions. H. Leyford
Crime Within Crime. F. Drax
Crime Without a Clue. T. Cobb
Crime Without a Flaw. L. Despard
Crime Without a Name. Dick Stewart
Crime Without Reason. George Douglas
Crimes at Fenton Towers. W. Tyrer
Crimes at Rillington Place. J. N. Chance
Crimes Club. W. LeQueux
Crime's Masquerader. A. MacVicar
Crimes of Cleopatra's Needle. J. M. Walsh
Crimes of Passion. J. Orton
Crimes Past. M. Challis
Criminal. J. Thompson
Criminal Airman. A. O. Pollard
Criminal at Large. E. Wallace
Criminal C.O.D. P. A. Taylor
Criminal Conversation. N. Freeling
Criminal Court. W. Lyon
Criminal Croesus. George Griffith
Criminal Link. Nicholas Carter
Criminal Mischief. P. Chevigny
Criminal Queen. E. A. Young
Criminal Reminiscences and Detective Sketches. A. Pinkerton
Criminal Square. H. Hastings
Criminal Tendencies. J. Goodman
Criminal Yarns. T. C. Bridges
Criminals All. W. Martyn
Criminals Caught. J. M'Govan
Criminals I Have Known. A. Griffiths
Criminals Run Down. Old Sleuth
Crimshaw Memorandum. L. White
Crimson Alibi. O. R. Cohen
Crimson Belt. G. H. Teed
Crimson Blade. M. S. Buchanan
Crimson Blind. F. M. White
Crimson Blotter. I. Ostrander
Crimson Box. H. S. Keeler
Crimson Butterfly. E. Snell
Crimson Candle. E. Bond
Crimson Car. F. Grierson
Crimson Cat Murders. S. E. Porcelain
Crimson Chair, and other stories. R. Dowling
Crimson Circle. E. Wallace
Crimson Claw. W. Hewlett
Crimson Clay. B. Schwarz
Crimson Clown. J. McCulley
Crimson Clown Again. J. McCulley
Crimson Clue. G. H. Coxe
Crimson Clue. I. Stark
Crimson Crescent. Augustus Muir
Crimson Crime. G. M. Fenn
Crimson Cross. C. E. Walk
Crimson Cryptogram. F. Hume
Crimson Dacoit. A. Wilson
Crimson Dice. G. N. McCain
Crimson Domino. G. Goodchild
Crimson Domino. W. W. Sayer
Crimson Feather. M. Crossley
Crimson Feather. S. E. Mason
Crimson Flash. Nicholas Carter
Crimson Frame. A. L. Martin
Crimson Friday. D. C. Disney
Crimson Glove. Warren Miller
Crimson Goddess. E. S. Carrington
Crimson Hair Murders. D. L. Teilhet
Crimson Hairs. Whidden Graham
Crimson Hand. R. C. Finney
Crimson Honeymoon. H. Hill
Crimson Ice. C. Fitzsimmons
Crimson in the Purple. H. Roth
Crimson Jade. G. B. Mair
Crimson Madness of Little Doom. M. McShane
Crimson Mascot. C. E. Pearce
Crimson Mask. W. H. L. Crauford
Crimson Mask. A. Steffens Hardy
Crimson Moon. I. Foster
Crimson Pall. W. Dawson
Crimson Patch. P. A. Taylor
Crimson Paw. M. G. Eberhart
Crimson Poppies. M. Benson
Crimson Query. A. Eadie
Crimson Quest. D. Barr
Crimson Ramblers. G. Verner
Crimson Rope. H. Asbury
Crimson Serpent. K. Robeson
Crimson Shadow. Roland Daniel
Crimson Stain. A. Bradshaw
Crimson Swastika. E. Snell
Crimson Thread. L. Lauferty
Crimson Threat. G. E. Rochester
Crimson Trail. J. Walker
Crimsoned Millions. J. Willoughby
Crinkled Crown. W. LeQueux
Crippled Canary. V. Gunn
Crippled Hand. F. S. Stewart
Crises. M. Level
Crisis. J. Cello
Crisis. D. E. Fisher
Crisis Comes to Mister Smith. Richard Fisher
Crisis for Two. Mark Ross
Criss-Cross. D. Tracy
Crisscross. P. Flower
Crisscross. H. Henkin
Criton Hunt Mystery. R. Jocelyn
Croaked the Raven. B. Fischer
Croaker. G. Ashe
Croaker. R. Garnett
Croaker. Arthur Russell
Croaking Raven. G. Mitchell
Croation. T. B. Marle
Crock of Gold. M. F. Tupper
Crockett on the Loose. B. Lang
Crockett's Woman. E. Hatch
Crocodile Club. A. Broome
Crocodile Down the River. G. C. Foster
Crocodile Man. P. Meredith
Crocodile on the Sandbank. Elizabeth Peters
Croesus Affair. A. Segal
Croesus Conspiracy. B. Stein
Cromwell's Cavalier. John Sanders
Cromwell's Spy. Eva McDonald
Cronin Mystery. John Arthur Fraser
Crook. Jonathan Starr
Crook Bait. L. C. Douthwaite
Crook Cargo. J. Hunter
Crook from Chicago. S. Hood
Crook in the Furrow. A. G. Street
Crook of Canada. G. H. Teed
Crook of Chinatown. W. M. Graydon
Crook of Costa Blanca. G. H. Teed
Crook of Crauford Court. L. Essex
Crook of Fleet Street. Gwyn Evans
Crook o' Lune. E. C. R. Lorac
Crook of Marsden Manor. G. H. Teed
Crook of Mayfair. H. H. C. Gibbons
Crook of Monte Carlo. G. H. Teed
Crook of Newmarket. A. Steffens Hardy
Crook of Paris. G. H. Teed
Crook of Shanghai. G. H. Teed
Crook Ship. M. Frazer
Crook Stuff. R. Keverne
Crook Town. A. Skene
Crooked. M. Foster
Crooked Adam. D. E. Stevenson
Crooked Alley. Irene Alexander
Crooked Billet. D. Titheradge
Crooked Bough. J. Remenham
Crooked Business. F. Marlowe
Crooked Circle. M. L. Stokes
Crooked Circle. G. Verner
Crooked City. R. Kyle
Crooked Coffins. Griff
Crooked Company. F. Marlowe
Crooked Computer. W. G. Shingler
Crooked Cop. Bob Parker
Crooked Coronet. M. Arlen
Crooked Cross. C. J. Dutton
Crooked Eye. K. Virden
Crooked Finger. A. MacVicar
Crooked Finger. E. A. Treeton
Crooked Five! J. G. Brandon
Crooked Frame. W. P. McGivern
Crooked Furrow. J. Farnol
Crooked Gambler. R. Hardinge
Crooked Game. A. Wright
Crooked Highway. A. Spiller
Crooked Hinge. J. D. Carr
Crooked House. A. Christie
Crooked House. B. Fleming
Crooked House. J. Rowland
Crooked Inn. E. Dudley
Crooked Inspector. B. Wayde
Crooked Jacket. D. Dayle
Crooked Killer. P. Manton
Crooked Lady. B. Sarto
Crooked Lane. F. N. Hart
Crooked Lanes. R. S. Holland
Crooked Letter. L. DuBreuil
Crooked Lip. H. Adams
Crooked Man. Shelley Smith
Crooked Men Came. R. F. Lambert
Crooked Mile. N. Fagan
Crooked Money. J. E. Day
Crooked Paths. F. Allingham
Crooked Paths. D. Lee
Crooked Phoenix. Bradshaw Jones
Crooked Road. M. L. West
Crooked Samaritan. P. Trent
Crooked Shadow. K. Steel
Crooked Shadows. J. Crowe
Crooked Shadows. Gordon Young
Crooked Shamrock. C. B. Gilford
Crooked Sign. B. Bolt
Crooked Sixpence. L. Grex
Crooked Staircase. V. Gunn
Crooked Straight. E. Dudley
Crooked Tree. T. B. Morris
Crooked Way. W. LeQueux
Crooked Wood. M. Underwood
Crooked Wreath. C. Brand
Crookedshaws. Winifred Duke
Crookery Inn. M. Crossley
Crooking Finger. C. F. Adams
Crook's Accomplice. A. Skene
Crooks and Vagabonds. R. Keverne
Crook's Blind. Nicholas Carter
Crooks' Caravan. Frank King
Crook's Cargo. J. G. Brandon
Crooks' Castle. B. Atkey
Crook's Castle. G. Dilnot
Crooks Convoy. A. Blair
Crooks' Cross. Frank King
Crook's Crossing. V. Lester
Crook's Cruise. Seafarer
Crook's Decoy. G. H. Teed
Crook's Deputy. A. Parsons
Crook's Double. W. J. Bayfield
Crook's Double. Nicholas Carter
Crook's Double. A. Murray
Crooks' Game. G. Dilnot
Crooks' Hill. San Antonio
Crooks in Cabaret. S. Simpson
Crooks in Clover. G. H. Teed
Crooks in the Sunshine. E. P. Oppenheim
Crooks Ltd. L. Bidston
Crooks Limited. E. Snell
Crook's Loot. W. Jardine
Crooks of Paris. D. Lenton
Crooks of the Waldorf. Horace Smith
Crooks of Tunis. A. Parsons
Crook's Shadow. J. J. Farjeon
Crooks' Shepherd. S. Truss
Crook's Turning. John Muir
Crooks' Vendetta. G. H. Teed
Crookshaven Murder. Alexander Morrison
Crooner's Swan Song. L. Grex
Cropper's Cabin. J. Thompson
Cross-Channel Crime. G. H. Teed
Cross-Country. H. D. Kastle
Cross Current. C. T. Cline
Cross Cut. C. R. Cooper
Cross-Eyed Bear. D. B. Hughes
Cross-Eyed Bear Murders. D. B. Hughes
Cross-Fires. F. Warden
Cross for Tomorrow. M. Farnsworth
Cross Marks the Spot. J. Ronald
Cross of Gold Affair. F. Davies
Cross of Lazzaro. J. Harris
Cross of Murder. Carter Dickson
Cross of the Dust. M. O. Rolfe
Cross Over Nine. W. C. Butler
Cross Purposes. A. Dick
Cross Purposes. Jim Thomas
Cross That Palm When I Come to It. A. Southcott
Cross the Red Creek. H. Whittington
Crossbow Murder. Carter Dickson
Crossed Needles. Nicholas Carter
Crossed Path. W. Collins
Crossed Skis. C. Carnac
Crossed Wires. Nicholas Carter
Crossfire. D. Lynds
Crossing. C. Keane
Crossing of Clues. E. C. Derby
Crossover. W. Greatorex
Crossroad Murders. G. Simenon
Crossroads. J. D. MacDonald
Crosstalk. D. Bloodworth
Crossword Murder. E. R. Punshon
Crossword Mystery. R. Gillespie
Crossword Mystery. E. R. Punshon
Crotchet Castle. T. L. Peacock
Crouching Beast. V. Williams
Crouching Men. A. West
Crouching Spy. A. MacVicar
Crow and the Cat. P. De Polnay
Crow Hollow. D. Eden
Crowded and Dangerous. A. Lejeune
Crowing Hen. R. Davis
Crown: Bamboo Shoot-Out. T. Harknett
Crown Colony. N. Harman
Crown Court. J. Follett
Crown Diamond. Nicholas Carter
Crown Estate. E. Berckman
Crown Kidnap. A. Crofts
Crown: Macao Mayhem. T. Harknett
Crown of India. S. Fuller
Crown of Night. P. Audemars
Crown of Stars. M. K. Simmons
Crown of Straw. A. Upward
Crown Swindle. M. L. Eades
Crown: The Sweet and Sour Kill. T. Harknett
Crown Valley. K. Ashby
Crowned Skull. F. Hume
Crowner's Quest. A. Broome
Crowning Murder. H. H. Stanners
Crowning of Esther. M. Gerard
Crows Can Kill. H. Janson
Crows Are Black Everywhere. H. O. Yardley
Crows Can't Count. A. A. Fair

Crow's Inn Tragedy. A. Haynes
Croyd. Ian Wallace
Crozart Story. K. Fearing
Crucible. S. Murray
Crucible. B. A. Williams
Crucible of Circumstance. P. Brebner
Crucible of Evil. Lydia Belknap Long
Cruciform Mark. Riccardo Stephens
Cruel As a Cat. M. Halliday
Cruel As the Grave. I. Bayne
Cruel As the Grave. H. McCloy
Cruel As the Grave. E. Southworth
Cruel Case. S. Rathbone
Cruel Dart. H. Carstairs
Cruel Deadline. R. Gaines
Cruel Fire. E. Atiyah
Cruel Heart. J. La Tourrette
Cruel Is the Night. Howard Hunt
Cruel Lady. M. Corrigan
Cruel Legacy. L. H. Hudson
Cruel London. J. Hatton
Cruel Masquerade. H. Simart
Cruel Secret. Anonymous
Cruel Suspicion. F. P. Rathburne
Cruel Victim. M. Tripp
Cruise into Chaos. L. Derrick
Cruise of Death. J. Rand
Cruise of Terror. S. Hope
Cruise of the Albatross. G. Allen
Cruise of the Carefree. John Marsh
Cruise of the Jasper B. Appleton. D. Marquis
Cruise of the Motor-Boat Conqueror. S. Paternoster
Cruise of the Sphinx. L. Robin
Cruise with Death. F. Draco
Cruiser in Action. Reginald Campbell
Cruiser on Wheels. G. Thorne
Cruising. Gerald Walker
Crumblerock Crime! W. J. Bayfield
Crumpled Cup. H. Kane
Crumpled Leaf. Mrs. Alexander
Crumpled Lilies. C. Dawe
Crusade into Crime. R. Wilkes-Hunter
Crusader's Cross. J. Pattinson
Crusoe Harry. Old Sleuth
Crusoe Test. Mark Nelson
Cry Aloud for Murder. P. McGuire
Cry at Dusk. L. Dent
Cry, Baby, Cry! J. Ehrlich
Cry Baby Killer. J. Hilton
Cry Blood. H. V. Dixon
Cry, Brother, Cry. J. Karney
Cry Flesh. D. Karp
Cry Flood! E. J. Fredericks
Cry for Help. Nicholas Carter
Cry for Help. D. M. Disney
Cry for Kit. V. Heley
Cry for Love. A. L. Thompson
Cry for My Lovely. S. D. Frances
Cry for the Baron. Anthony Morton
Cry for the Lost. G. Dessart
Cry for the Strangers. J. R. Saul
Cry from the Dark. W. H. Baker
Cry from the Ether. R. Sharp
Cry Hallelujah! K. Orvis
Cry Hard, Cry Fast. J. D. MacDonald
Cry Havoc. R. M. Stern
Cry Hold! P. Harris
Cry in Absence. Madison Jones
Cry in the Jungle. K. M. Knight
Cry in the Night. K. Brosnan
Cry in the Night. A. Golsworthy
Cry in the Night. W. Masterson
Cry in the Night. D. Quick
Cry in the Night. K. Roos
Cry in the Night. P. Saxon
Cry in the Valley. G. K. Cowan
Cry Kill. Wenzell Brown
Cry Killer! K. Fearing
Cry Me a Killer. Garrity
Cry Murder. E. Howie
Cry Murder. W. M. Raine
Cry Murder. N. Rutledge
Cry Murder in the Market Place. W. M. Raine
Cry of Blood. F. Du Boisgobey
Cry of Neptune. A. Bretonne
Cry of the Beast. V. Norwood
Cry of the Cat. M. Sellers
Cry of the Cat. S. Wagner
Cry of the Dingo. C. Phillips
Cry of the Flesh. R. Himmel
Cry of the Halidon. A. Dick
Cry of the Hawk. H. Steirman
Cry of the Hunter. Harry Patterson
Cry of the Kestrel. J. Wood
Cry of the Nighthawk. N. Dorer
Cry of the Owl. P. Highsmith
Cry of the Owl. M. Mayhew
Cry of the Peacock. M. L. Roby
Cry of the Wind. S. MacIvers
Cry of Whiteness. T. J. Fleming
Cry on My Shoulder. H. Howard
Cry on the Wind. W. H. Boore
Cry Passion. R. Jessup
Cry Plague! T. S. Drachman
Cry Rape. R. Boyle
Cry Rape. Ruth Williams
Cry Revenge! A. C. Clark
Cry Scandal. W. Ard
Cry Shadow. M. Grant

Cry the Soft Rain. A. Dwyer-Joyce
Cry Terror. A. L. Stone
Cry, Tiger! M. Storm
Cry Tough. I. Shulman
Cry Treason Thrice. Eva McDonald
Cry Uncle! Michael Brett
Cry Vengeance. L. Peters
Cry Vengeance. B. Schwarz
Cry Witch. N. A. Hintze
Cry Wolf. M. Carleton
Cry Wolfram. D. Sanderson
Crying Child. B. Michaels
Crying Makes Your Nose Run. J. T. Story
"Crying Pig" Murder. V. MacClure
Crying Sisters. M. Seeley
Cryogenic Nightmare. L. Derrick
Cryptogram. J. De Mille
Cryptogram. W. M. Graydon
Crystal Ball. D. Spicer
Crystal Beads Murder. A. Haynes
Crystal Cell. Gwyn Evans
Crystal Claw. W. LeQueux
Crystal Clear. E. Cadell
Crystal Clear Case. L. Head
Crystal Crow. Joan Aiken
Crystal Eye. W. R. Randall
Crystal-Gazers. H. Robertson
Crystal Mouse. B. H. Deal
Crystal Mystery. Nicholas Carter
Crystal Palace. Max Barrett
Crystal Pawns. B. T. Haaf
Crystal Skull. Warren Hill
Crystal Skull. J. McLaren
Crystal Stopper. W. Leblanc
Crystal Tower. X. Putnam
Crystal Wave. J. Turner
Crystal Window. P. Brisco
Crystallized Carbon Pig. J. Wainwright
Cub. C. L. Pancoast
Cuban Connection. P. Pembroke
Cuban Expedition. G. Null
Cuban Heel. B. Carson
Cuban Heel. S. Harragan
Cuban Heel. P. Jefferson
Cuban Legacy. S. M. Parkman
Cuban Treasure Island. W. P. Kelly
Cubano Caper. S. Jason
Cubwood. W. R. S. Lewis
Cuckoo Clock. M. K. Ozaki
Cuckoo Fair. Robin Temple
Cuckoo in Harley Street. S. Fairway
Cuckoo in the Nest. Laura Smith
Cuckoo Line Affair. A. Garve
Cuckoo Run. I. Pitt
Cuckoo Woman. H. Parker
Cuckoos on the Hearth. P. Fennelly
Cudgel. T. Polsky
Cue for Murder. Matt Bryant
Cue for Murder. H. McCloy
Cue for Passion. E. Chodorov
Cuernavaca Question. Lydia Kirk
Cuirass of Diamonds. E. Jepson
Cul-de-Sac. S. Dewes
Cult Breaker. A. Sugar
Cult of Darkness. D. Reid
Cult of Killers. D. MacIvers
Cult of the Queer People. W. M. Duncan
Cumberland Decision. R. S. Silverman
Cummings Report. J. Brogan
Cumsha Cruise. E. L. Long
Cunning. R. Bloch
Cunning Against Force. Tom Steele
Cunning and the Haunted. R. Jessup
Cunning As a Fox. M. Halliday
Cunning Enemy. V. Hill
Cunning Mulatto and Other Cases of Ellis Parker, American Detective. F. Pratt
Cuoto Snatch. J. Shelynn
Cup and the Lip. E. Ferrars
Cup Final Crime. L. Bidston
Cup Final Murder. B. Newman
Cup Final Mystery. A. Edgar
Cup of Cold Poison. Joan Fleming
Cup of Silence. A. J. Rees
Cup of Thanatos. Charlotte Hunt
Cup That Kills. G. J. Barrett
Cup, the Blade or the Gun. M. Eberhart
Cup-Tie Mystery. F. W. Irwin
Cupid Among the Clues. F. G. Puzey
Cupid and the Creeds. W. J. Newton
Cupid's Executioners. H. Monteilhet
CUPPI. Sandy Johnson
Curate Finds the Corpse. A. T. Rich
Curate's Crime. A. Dick
Cure for Cancer. M. Moorcock
Cure It with Honey. Thurston Scott
Cure of Souls. J. M. Cobban
Curio Murders. R. Wallace
Curios. R. Marsh
Curiosities of Crime in Edinburgh. J. M'Levy
Curiosities of Detection. Robert Curtis
Curiosity Didn't Kill the Cat. M. K. Wren
Curiosity Killed a Cat. A. Rowe
Curiosity Killed Kitty. R. C. Payes
Curiosity Killed the Cat. J. Cockin
Curiosity of Etienne MacGregor. P. Cheyney
Curiosity of Mr. Treadgold. V. Williams
Curious Affair of the Third Dog. P. Moyes

Curious Case of Gen. Delaney Smythe. W. H. Gardner
Curious Case of Marie Dupont. A. Luehrmann
Curious Case of the Crook's Memoirs. W. M. Graydon
Curious Crime. A. E. Martin
Curious Crime of Miss Julia Blossom. L. Meynell
Curious Crimes. B. Hemyng
Curious Custard Pie. M. Scherf
Curious Facts Preceding My Execution. D. E. Westlake
Curious Happenings to the Rooke Legatees. E. P. Oppenheim
Curious Locket. L. Traugot
Curious Mr. Tarrant. C. D. King
Curious Quest. E. P. Oppenheim
Curious Were Killed. Dorothy Bennett
Curiouser and Curiouser. J. C. Snaith
Curiously Planned. Camilla Hope
Curl Up and Die Day. F. Dickens
Curlew Coombe Mystery. Gret Lane
Currie, Curtis & Co., Crammers. C. J. C. Hyne
Curs in Clover. I. Mercer
Curse! N. Buntline
Curse. F. Hume
Curse at Craig's End. R. Verron
Curse in the Colophon. E. Goodspeed
Curse of Amen-Tah. O. Sackville
Curse of Anubis. J. Younger
Curse of Black Charlie. Marilyn Ross
Curse of Cain. D. W. Rimel
Curse of Cantire. W. S. Masterman
Curse of Carlyon. E. Everett-Green
Curse of Carne's Hold. G. A. Henty
Curse of Carranca. Elsie Lee
Curse of Clement Waynflete. B. Mitford
Curse of Clifton. E. Southworth
Curse of Cloud. J. B. Harris-Burland
Curse of Collinwood. Marilyn Ross
Curse of Cowden. A. S. Swan
Curse of Deepwater. C. Randell
Curse of Doone. S. Horler
Curse of Halewood. B. Paul
Curse of Kali. A. Greening
Curse of Kali. H. E. Hill
Curse of Kalispoint. M. Richardson
Curse of Kama. W. F. Lovatt
Curse of Kenton. J. L. Roberts
Curse of Khatra. T. C. H. Jacobs
Curse of Leo. R. Lory
Curse of Mallory Hall. D. Daniels
Curse of Nightwind. Regina Hubbard
Curse of Pengrail Park. S. Farrant
Curse of Rathlaw. P. Saxon
Curse of Ravenswood. S. MacIvers
Curse of Red Shiva. V. Meik
Curse of Scotland. Gordon Bligh
Curse of Seabrea. Dewey Ward
Curse of Siva. R. St. Clair
Curse of Still Valley. S. Wagner
Curse of the Bronze Lamp. Carter Dickson
Curse of the Carrington's. W. Tyrer
Curse of the Casa Del Monte. E. E. Cameron
Curse of the Clodaghs. F. Cowen
Curse of the Concullens. F. Stevenson
Curse of the Crystal Ball. R. St. Clair
Curse of the Fleers. B. Copper
Curse of the Fultons. W. E. Grogan
Curse of the Golden Skull. J. Kains
Curse of the Island Pool. V. Coffman
Curse of the Kings. V. Holt
Curse of the Mandarin's Fan. B. House
Curse of the Moors. F. Hurd
Curse of the Pharoahs. J. Younger
Curse of the Reckaviles. W. S. Masterman
Curse of the Santyres. Gwyn Evans
Curse of the Sightless Fish. M. South
Curse of the Silver Wings. T. Wallace
Curse of the Snake. G. Boothby
Curse of the Track. J. Hunter
Curse of the Two-Headed Bull. L. Falk
Curse of the Wolfskin. J. Crecy
Curse of Whispering Hills. K. Cameron
Curse This House. Barbara Wood
Curse You, Jack Dalton! W. Braun
Cursed Be the Treasure. H. B. Drake
Cursed by a Fortune. G. M. Fenn
Curses Come Home. E. C. Vivian
Cursing Stones Murder. G. Bellairs
Curtailed Voyage. E. L. Long
Curtain. A. Christie
Curtain at Eight. O. R. Cohen
Curtain Between. V. Siller
Curtain Call. M. Cronin
Curtain Call. R. Foley
Curtain Call for a Corpse. Josephine Bell
Curtain Call for Murder. A. Spiller
Curtain Call for Murder. P. Yates
Curtain Fall. E. Dewhurst
Curtain for a Jester. F. Lockridge
Curtain for Crime. M. P. Rea
Curtain Has Lace Fringes. G. Joseph
Curtain of Fear. D. Wheatley
Curtain of Glass. D. Ambler
Curtain of Hate. J. Moffatt
Curtain of Storm. J. Gollomb
Curtain of the Dark. H. McElroy

Curtained Sleep. A. Roy
Curtains for a Chorine. Carter Brown
Curtains for a Lover. R. Dietrich
Curtains for Carla. M. Storm
Curtains for Carrie. D. Glinto
Curtains for Conquest? B. Gray
Curtains for Komespi. Ernest Paul
Curtains for the Copper. T. Polsky
Curtains for the Editor. T. Polsky
Curtains for the Judge. T. Polsky
Curtains for Three. R. Stout
Curtis Wives. Marsha Alexander
Curve of the Catenary. M. R. Rinehart
Curved Blades. C. Wells
Curves Can Cast Shadows. Griff
Curves for a Coroner. Carter Brown
Curves for Danger. A. Bocca
Curzon. F. Durbridge
Custom House. Francis King
Custom House Fraud. B. Wayde
Custom of the Country. P. M. Hubbard
Customer's Always Wrong. Kevin O'Hara
Cut and Run. B. McGhee
Cut and Run. M. Tanner
Cut by Society. A. M. Meadows
Cut by the County. M. E. Braddon
Cut Direct. A. Tilton
Cut for Partners. E. K. Goldthwaite
Cut Me In. H. Collins
Cut Me In. J. Karney
Cut of the Whip. P. Rabe
Cut-Out. Colin Smith
Cut Price Murder. M. Hervey
Cut the Cards, Lady. D. Lee
Cut Thin to Win. A. A. Fair
Cut Throat. C. Bush
Cute and Deadly Surf Twins. P. Morgan
Cute Boy Detective. Old Sleuth
Cuthbert Grahame's Will. R. Marsh
Cutie Cashed His Chips. Carter Brown
Cutie on Call. H. Janson
Cutie Takes the Count. Carter Brown
Cutie Wins a Corpse. Carter Brown
Cutter and Bone. N. Thornberg
Cutting Edge. K. Jackson
Cyanide! S. Toye
Cyanide for the Chorister. C. Wogan
Cyanide with Compliments. E. Lemarchand
Cyborg. M. Caidin
Cyborg IV. M. Caidin
Cyclops Goblet. J. Blackburn
Cynic Fortune. D. C. Murray
Cynic's Desperate Mission. H. Kaner
Cynthia. M. Brenner
Cynthia. E. V. Cunningham
Cynthia-of-the-Minute. L. J. Vance
Cynthia Wakeham's Money. A. K. Green
Cynthia's Chauffeur. L. Tracy
Cypher 8. I. F. Anderson
Cypher K. Taffrail
Cypress Chest. G. Cumberland
Cypress Man. Jane Beynon
Cypress Road. M. Home
Cyrilla Maude's First Love. H. Wood
Czar of Fear. K. Robeson
Czar of Halfaday Creek. J. B. Hendryx
Czar's Spy. W. LeQueux
Czech Mate. W. Fennerton
Czech Point. N. Fleming
Czechmate. L. Johns

D.A. Breaks a Seal. E. S. Gardner
D.A. Breaks an Egg. E. S. Gardner
D.A. Calls a Turn. E. S. Gardner
D.A. Calls It Murder. E. S. Gardner
D.A. Cooks a Goose. E. S. Gardner
D.A. Draws a Circle. E. S. Gardner
D.A. Goes to Trial. E. S. Gardner
D.A. Holds a Candle. E. S. Gardner
D.A. Takes a Chance. E. S. Gardner
D.A.'s Daughter. H. Peterson
D As in Dead. L. Treat
D.E.Q. L. Gorell
D for Delinquent. B. Clifton
D.I. J. Ashford
D Is for Danger. C. Emery
D.N.A. Business. H. Calvin
"D" Notice. B. Graeme
Da Vinci Rose. A. O'Neill
Dachau Treasure. A. Destefano
Dacobra. J. B. Harris-Burland
DADA Caper. R. H. Spencer
Daddy Cool. D. Goines
Daddy Goriot. H. Balzac
Daddy-O. P. Stadley
Daddy's Gone a'Hunting. M. St. Clair
Daffodil Affair. M. Innes
Daffodil Blonde. F. Crane
Daffodil Murder. E. Wallace
Daffodil Mystery. E. Wallace
Dagger. A. Wynne
Dagger Affair. D. McDaniel
Dagger and Cord. A. De Brune
Dagger and the Cross. J. Hatton
Dagger Before Me. M. O'Brine
Dagger Drawn. L. Hill
Dagger in Fleet Street. R. C. Woodthorpe
Dagger in the Dark. W. F. Eberhardt

Dagger in the Sky. K. Robeson
Dagger in the Sleeve. K. Maclaren
Dagger of Fate. R. Marsh
Dagger of Flesh. R. S. Prather
Dagger of the Mind. K. Fearing
Daggerman. R. H. Francis
Daggers Drawn. M. Carr
Daggers Drawn. Alan Thomas
Daggers of Kali. R. Wallace
Dago. J. March
Dagwort Coombe Murder. L. Brock
Dahlia. B. Goldie
Dain Curse. D. Hammett
Dainty Was a Jane. D. Glinto
Daisy Canfield. B. Haas
Daisy-Chain for Satan. Joan Fleming
Daisy Dilemma. D. Rico
Dakota Project. J. Beeching
Dakota Warpath. G. A. Ralston
Dale of the Secret Service. N. Wray
Dalehouse Murder. F. Everton
Dally with a Deadly Doll. J. Miles
Dalmation Tapes. Don Smith
Dalmayne Mystery. H. Leyford
Dalton Boys and the M. K. and T. Robbery. W. B. Lawson
Dalton Boys in California. W. B. Lawson
Damascus Countdown. H. Arvay
Dame. Carter Brown
Dame. R. Stark
Dame Ain't Safe. A. Bocca
Dame Between Two. D. Glinto
Dame Called Murder. R. O. Saber
Dame Came Late. R. Angel
Dame Dies Greedy. N. Perrelli
Dame Doles Death. M. Perelli
Dame in Danger. T. B. Dewey
Dame in Distress. Craig Cooper
Dame Is Snatched. R. Commorde
Dame on a Death Round. M. Brody
Dame on the Lam. Johnny Dark
Dame on the Make. K. T. McCall
Dame Plays Rough. D. Spade
Dame to Discover. G. Usher
Dame Trouble There. R. Angel
Dames Are Dynamite. B. Schwarz
"Dames Are Out." D. Glinto
Dames Can Be Deadly. Peter Chambers
Dames, Diamonds and Death! C. Wheatley
Dames Die Too. D. Linton
Dames Don't Care. P. Cheyney
Dames Don't Dictate. R. Angel
Dames Don't Forget. Griff
Dames-Errant. G. Norsworthy
Dames for Danger. J. Cairo
Dames for Hire. B. Sarto
Dames Play Rough. N. W. Firth
Dames Spell Trouble. M. Hervey
Dame's the Game. A. Fray
Damn Desmond Drake. Sea Lion
Damnation of Adam Blessing. V. Packer
Damnation Reef. J. Tattersall
Damned. J. D. MacDonald
Damned and Destroyed. K. Orvis
Damned and the Destroyed. K. Orvis
Damned If He Does. B. Kerr
Damned Innocents. R. Neely
Damned Lovely. J. Webb
Damned One. G. Des Cars
Damned Spot. H. Adams
Damned to Success. H. H. Kirst
Damning Trifles. M. C. Johnson
Damocles Factor. R. Chester
Damosel Croft. R. M. Gilchrist
Damsel. R. Stark
Dan Gunn, the Man from Mauston. L. Armstrong
Dan, the Detective. H. Alger
Dance Band Mystery. R. Sonin
Dance for a Dead Uncle. C. Ashton
Dance for Diplomats. P. Harcourt
Dance Hall of the Dead. T. Hillerman
Dance in Darkness. D. Daniels
Dance of Death. Carter Brown
Dance of Death. H. McCloy
Dance of Death. L. Potter
Dance of Death. F. C. Ticknor
Dance of Death and other stories. O. Williams
Dance of Love. D. B. Dodson
Dance of the Dwarfs. G. Household
Dance on a Hornet's Nest. J. Blackmore
Dance to Your Daddy. G. Mitchell
Dance with a Ghost. K. Ostrander
Dance with Me Deadly. K. T. McCall
Dance with the Dead. R. S. Prather
Dance with the Devil. D. Dwyer
Dance Without Music. P. Cheyney
Dancer and the King. C. E. Blaney
Dancer in Yellow. E. Ogilvie
Dancer of San Jose. J. Laffin
Dancer's Daughter. J. Edgar
Dancer's End. D. Vane
Dancers in Mourning. M. Allingham
Dancers in the Reeds. L. Meynell
Dancing Aztecs. D. E. Westlake
Dancing Bear. P. Conway
Dancing Beggars. E. B. Young
Dancing Cheat. D. Walshe
Dancing Cinderella. Rona Randall
Dancing Dead. E. Thomas
Dancing Death. C. Bush

Dancing Detective. W. Irish
Dancing Dodo. J. Gardner
Dancing Doll. F. Condon
Dancing Doll. J. L. Roberts
Dancing Doll Murders. W. Wallace
Dancing Druids. G. Mitchell
Dancing Floor. J. Buchan
Dancing Floor. M. M. McNamara
Dancing Ghost. L. Greth
Dancing Girl. G. Leroux
Dancing Horse. A. MacVicar
Dancing Leaves. G. Warden
Dancing Men. P. M. Hubbard
Dancing of the Fox. Winifred Duke
Dancing Silhouette. N. S. Lincoln
Dancing Spy. C. H. Bullivant
Dancing Star. Captain Ingram
Dancing Stones. L. A. Knight
Dancing Water. Y. Pickering
Dancing with a Tiger. S. Morrow
Dancing with Death. J. Coggin
Dancing with Death. J. Corbett
Dandy. L. Meynell
Dandy. J. Middlemass
Dandy in Aspic. D. Marlowe
Danes Abbey. M. Gerard
Danesbury House. H. Wood
Danger Aft. N. Ashe
Danger After Dark. S. Maddock
Danger Ahead. M. Richmond
Danger Ahead. P. Saxon
Danger Ahead. J. T. Shaw
Danger Ahead. G. Simenon
Danger! and other stories. A. C. Doyle
Danger Ashore. G. Simenon
Danger at Bravo Key. Ronald Johnston
Danger at Cliff House. C. F. Gregg
Danger at Dahlkari. E. Marlow
Danger at Hand. Anne-Marie Cox
Danger at Midnight. F. Griffin
Danger at My Heels. G. Meyrick
Danger at Olduvai. J. Blair
Danger at Ringside. H. R. Cleaver
Danger at Sea. G. Simenon
Danger at Westway's. Donald Stuart
Danger Below. G. Goodchild
Danger Below. G. Hackforth-Jones
Danger by My Side. A. MacKinnon
Danger Calling. P. Wentworth
Danger—Dame at Work. P. Muller
Danger—Death at Work. R. Garnett
Danger Feeds My Fear. M. Strong
Danger Follows. C. Fraser-Simson
Danger for Blackshirt. R. Graeme
Danger for Breakfast. J. McPartland
Danger for Love. R. Lacroix
Danger for the Baron. Anthony Morton
Danger from Grassen. James Stewart
Danger Game. E. Hunt
Danger Game. A. Mills
Danger—Girls Working! J. Reach
Danger: Hospital Zone. U. Curtiss
Danger in Diamonds. G. J. Barrett
Danger in Eden. J. Ames
Danger in My Blood. S. Brackeen
Danger in Numbers. Noel Lee
Danger in Paradise. O. R. Cohen
Danger in Paradise. A. S. Fleischman
Danger in Suburbia. R. Goyne
Danger in the Cards. M. MacDougall
Danger in the Dark. P. Carlon
Danger in the Dark. A. M. Chase
Danger in the Dark. M. G. Eberhart
Danger in the Dark. C. F. Gregg
Danger in the Deed. R. Rushton
Danger Inside. F. L. Cary
Danger Is My Line. S. Marlowe
Danger Key. Nick Carter
Danger Line. G. Goodchild
Danger Line. L. L. Lynch
Danger Mansion. D. Daniels
Danger Mansion. P. Wylie
Danger Merchant. I. Lambot
Danger Money. M. G. Eberhart
Danger Money. T. C. H. Jacobs
Danger Money. M. Russell
Danger Next Door. Q. Patrick
Danger of Folly. Nicholas Carter
Danger on Cue. Rebecca Holland
Danger on the Flip Side. J. T. Story
Danger on the Map. A. Aldous
Danger Point. P. Wentworth
Danger Preferred. S. Horler
Danger Road. M. Saxton
Danger Round the Corner. L. Meynell
Danger Signal. P. Bottome
Danger Signal and other tales. B. Hemyng
Danger Trail. W. C. Tuttle
Danger Under the Moon. M. Walsh
Danger Wakes My Heart. J. Ames
Danger Within. M. Gilbert
Danger Woman. Abel Mann
Danger: Woman at Work! Kevin O'Hara
Danger Zone. J. M. Flynn
Danger Zone. K. Lindsay
Danger Zone. J. M. Walsh
Dangerfield Talisman. J. J. Connington
Dangerous Affair. D. Quentin
Dangerous Age. A. J. Baker
Dangerous American. A. E. Hotchner
Dangerous Angel. C. B. Kelland
Dangerous Assignment. J. Blair

Dangerous Beauty. J. J. Farjeon
Dangerous Blonde. B. Sarto
Dangerous Blondes. K. Roos
Dangerous Brute. R. Jocelyn
Dangerous Business. E. Balmer
Dangerous by Nature. M. Coles
Dangerous Cargo. H. Footner
Dangerous Cargoes. R. Hobart
Dangerous Catspaw. D. C. Murray
Dangerous Child. F. Cowen
Dangerous Company. J. Rowland
Dangerous Connection. C. Gibbon
Dangerous Conspirator. G. Norway
Dangerous Corner. Ruth Holland
Dangerous Course. M. K. Douglas
Dangerous Cross-Roads. Laurence Kirk
Dangerous Curves. P. Cheyney
Dangerous Davies: The Last Detective. Leslie Thomas
Dangerous Days. R. Overton
Dangerous Days. M. R. Rinehart
Dangerous Dead. W. Brandon
Dangerous Deadline. F. S. Wees
Dangerous Design. L. Goldman
Dangerous Dilemmas. J. Peddie
Dangerous Diversion! E. Nepean
Dangerous Domicile. E. C. R. Lorac
Dangerous Dream. V. Nielsen
Dangerous Edge. E. L. Hewitt
Dangerous Edge. W. F. Temple
Dangerous Enchantment. M. Garratt
Dangerous Encounter. D. L. Teilhet
Dangerous Escapade. J. A. Park
Dangerous Exchange. M. Eden
Dangerous Fortune. T. C. H. Jacobs
Dangerous Funeral. M. McMullen
Dangerous Game. A. Applin
Dangerous Game. F. Duerrenmatt
Dangerous Game. W. LeQueux
Dangerous Game. E. Yates
Dangerous Games. W. B. Murphy
Dangerous Ground. L. L. Lynch
Dangerous Ground. F. S. Wickware
Dangerous Guest. L. Leete-Hodge
Dangerous Guide. E. C. Vivian
Dangerous Harbour. W. E. Huntsberry
Dangerous Haven. G. Bettany
Dangerous Holiday. Elizabeth Ford
Dangerous Homecoming. V. F. Freethy
Dangerous Honeymoon. A. Kielland
Dangerous House. J. Herbrand
Dangerous Impersonation. J. St. George
Dangerous Inheritance. V. Black
Dangerous Inheritance. G. Ferrand
Dangerous Inheritance. I. L. Forrester
Dangerous Inheritance. D. Wheatley
Dangerous Islands. A. Bridge
Dangerous Isles. Basil Carey
Dangerous Journey. N. Deane
Dangerous Knowledge. K. Bennett
Dangerous Knowledge. L. A. Knight
Dangerous Ladies. H. Manning
Dangerous Lady. O. R. Cohen
Dangerous Lady. M. Cronin
Dangerous Lady. M. O'Nair
Dangerous Landing. P. McGerr
Dangerous Legacy. G. H. Coxe
Dangerous Legacy. J. Holden
Dangerous Legacy. M. Murphy
Dangerous Legacy. W. D. Roberts
Dangerous Limelight. R. Armstrong
Dangerous Love. J. Blackmore
Dangerous Love. D. Dayle
Dangerous Lovers. A. Applin
Dangerous Madonna. K. Lindsay
Dangerous Magic. F. Lynch
Dangerous Maze. Brian Jones
Dangerous Memory. L. A. Olmsted
Dangerous Men. K. M. Sheahan
Dangerous Men. P. Steward
Dangerous Mission. Roland Daniel
Dangerous Mission. B. Marchant
Dangerous Mr. Dell. David Hume
Dangerous Mr. X. F. Duncan
Dangerous Moment. Roland Daniel
Dangerous Money. R. Hardinge
Dangerous Nan McGrew. G. Batson
Dangerous Oasis. M. Hastings
Dangerous One. R. Ames
Dangerous Ones. C. Franklin
Dangerous Passenger. T. Walsh
Dangerous Paths. H. S. Cooper
Dangerous Pawn. Winston Graham
Dangerous Place to Die. David Wilson
Dangerous Place to Dwell. M. Russell
Dangerous Playmate. Philip Chambers
Dangerous Pretense. H. Simart
Dangerous Promise. R. Bell
Dangerous Quest. J. Creasey
Dangerous Quest. E. D. Pierson
Dangerous Refuge. Joyce Bentley
Dangerous Refuge. I. Lambot
Dangerous Sanctuary. Andrea Hill
Dangerous Search. E. Wilmot
Dangerous Secret. Annie Thomas
Dangerous Shadow. J. B. Priestley
Dangerous Silence. D. MacKenzie
Dangerous Situation. L. Tracy
Dangerous Stable. N. Gould
Dangerous Sunlight. J. Bude
Dangerous to Know. M. Babson
Dangerous to Know. J. P. Duff
Dangerous to Know. K. Lindsay
Dangerous to Lean Out. K. Fitzgerald
Dangerous to Me. R. Foley
Dangerous Trade. G. Hackforth-Jones
Dangerous Twin. H. C. Davis
Dangerous Twins. E. Jepson
Dangerous Visit. F. Hurt
Dangerous Water. W. Chambers
Dangerous Waters. John Bentley
Dangerous Waters. M. Frazer
Dangerous Woman. M. Blount
Dangerous Woman. G. A. Pierce
Dangerous Young Man. G. F. Worts
Dangerously Blonde. A. F. Witley
Danger's Bright Eyes. S. Horler
Danger's Child. J. T. Story
Danger's Green Eyes. M. Corrigan
Dangers of Working Girls. Grace M. White
Dangerville Inheritance. A. C. Fox-Davies
Dangling Carrot. D. Keene
Dangling Man. H. Kane
Daniel P. Wack, "Dumb-Bell." H. M. Kohler
Danju Gig. C. Weston
Danny Spade Sees Red. D. Ambler
Danny Spade Spells Danger. D. Ambler
Danish Gambit. W. Butler
Danse Macabre. K. Kellow
Danton, the "Shadow-Sharp." Anonymous
Danube Covenant. J. M. Elliot
Danube Flows Red. A. Melville
Danube Runs Red. R. Meade
Danvers Jewels. M. Cholmondeley
Danziger Transcript. C. Fick
D'Arblay Mystery. R. A. Freeman
Darby Trial. D. Pearce
Darcourt. I. Holland
Dardanelles Derelict. V. W. Mason
Dare-Devil Conquest. B. Gray
Dare Lorimer's Heritage. E. Everett-Green
Dare the Devil. M. Carr
Dared by a Dame. Griff
Daredevil. L. Charteris
Daring Abduction. N. Ridley
Daring Anna Alcott. A. Applin
Daring Conspiracy. Old Sleuth
Daring Diana. Anthony Lang
Daring Experiment and other stories. L. D. Blake
Daring Express Messenger. J. K. Stafford
Daring Horse Thief. P. Ryan
Daring Maddie. Old Sleuth
Daringfords. Mrs. Lodge
Dark. M. Derby
Dark. M. Franklin
Dark. J. Herbert
Dark Abyss. C. Knight
Dark Abyss. F. J. Thwaites
Dark Adventure. Augustus Muir
Dark Adventure. J. Tickell
Dark Amid the Blaze. C. Rushton
Dark and Brilliant Places. S. T. Robinson
Dark and Deadly. B. Winter
Dark and Deadly Love. E. Evans
Dark and Light Stories. M. Hope
Dark and Secret Place. M. Summerton
Dark Angel. L. Della
Dark Angel. J. Ronald
Dark Arbor. I. S. Shriber
Dark Arches. G. Warden
Dark at Noon. J. Tattersall
Dark Avenue. F. Hume
Dark Avenue. J. Pendower
Dark Backward. Eric Lambert
Dark Bahama. P. Cheyney
Dark Before Dawn. T. Dick
Dark Beginnings. K. Blickle
Dark Below. M. T. Hinkemeyer
Dark Beneath the Pines. A. Eliot
Dark Between the Stars. J. Blackmore
Dark Beyond Moura. V. Coffman
Dark Blood, Dark Terror. B. Cleeve
Dark Boundary. A. Purdy
Dark Brings Death. D. Linton
Dark Brown. P. Johnson
Dark Bureau. E. Dudley
Dark Calypso. Dulcie Gray
Dark Carnival. J. Ames
Dark Castle. D. Quentin
Dark Cavalier. V. Rath
Dark Chamber. L. Cline
Dark Chase. D. Goodis
Dark Circle. G. Ashe
Dark Citadel. C. Farr
Dark Cliffs. D. Farrell
Dark Conflict. A. J. Merak
Dark Corner. M. Blizard
Dark Corner. C. Dale
Dark Corner. L. Ross
Dark Corners. F. E. Penny
Dark Corners of the Night. L. Olay
Dark Corsican. J. Appleby
Dark Countess. M. Richmond
Dark Crusade. J. M. Fox
Dark Crusader. I. Stuart
Dark Curtain. J. Packer
Dark Cypress. E. Noone
Dark Dame. W. Collison
Dark Danger. S. Horler
Dark Danger. M. Saville
Dark Days. F. J. Fargus
Dark Dealing. A. C. Brown
Dark Death. Anthony Gilbert
Dark Death. C. Schurr
Dark Deception. Jane McCarthy
Dark Deeds. H. Desmond
Dark Deeds. D. Donovan
Dark Descends. D. Ramsay
Dark Design. F. Hurt
Dark Desires. P. J. Cooper
Dark Destiny. K. Lindsay
Dark Destiny. E. Ronns
Dark Device. H. Lees
Dark Diamond. D. Tower
Dark Disguise. John Bentley
Dark Doings. J. Reach
Dark Don't Catch Me. V. Packer
Dark Door. M. Collis
Dark Dowry. W. D. Roberts
Dark Dream. H. Elsna
Dark Dream. Robert Martin
Dark Duet. P. Cheyney
Dark Echo. H. L. Nelson
Dark Eden. B. Kevern
Dark Edge of Violence. M. Carrel
Dark Emerald. J. Storm
Dark Enchantment. D. Macardle
Dark Encounter. Howard Hunt
Dark Encounter. W. Mills
Dark Encounter. C. Schurr
Dark Encounter. F. Stevenson
Dark Eyes and Danger. H. Clevely
Dark Eyes of London. E. Wallace
Dark Fantastic. M. Echard
Dark Fantastic. W. Masterson
Dark Forest. R. Foxall
Dark Frontier. E. Ambler
Dark Frontier. Arthur MacLean
Dark Garden. M. G. Eberhart
Dark Garden. E. R. Punshon
Dark Geraldine. J. Ferguson
Dark Gethryn. H. H. Ross
Dark God. J. Chancellor
Dark Goddess. M. H. Albert
Dark Gondola. V. Coffman
Dark Green Circle. E. Shanks
Dark Guardian. V. Blake
Dark Harbor Hunting. Clarissa Ross
Dark Harvest. J. Creasey
Dark Harvest. C. Kenyon
Dark Hazard. W. R. Burnett
Dark Hazard. S. Styles
Dark Heritage. D. Daniels
Dark Heritage. John Foster
Dark Heritage. M. McEvoy
Dark Hero. P. Cheyney
Dark Highway. A. Gask
Dark Hill. R. Foley
Dark Holiday. M. K. Simmons
Dark Hollow. A. K. Green
Dark Horizon. M. Richmond
Dark Horse. N. Gould
Dark Horse. F. Knebel
Dark Horseman. J. Budd
Dark Host. A. Roy
Dark Hostess. S. Horler
Dark House. M. Cumberland
Dark House. M. K. Douglas
Dark House. G. M. Fenn
Dark House. W. Spence
Dark House. A. S. Swan
Dark House in Florissant. R. W. Kauffman
Dark Hunger. Don James
Dark Hunger. T. Strauss
Dark Index. J. Turner
Dark Inheritance. M. C. Hay
Dark Inheritance. C. Salisbury
Dark Intent. R. Foley
Dark Interlude. P. Cheyney
Dark Interval. John Aiken
Dark Intruder. R. Dowling
Dark Intruder. V. Packer
Dark Is My Destiny. H. S. Hurst
Dark Is My Shadow. W. E. D. Ross
Dark Is the Clue. E. R. Punshon
Dark Is the Tunnel. M. Burton
Dark Island. R. Barr
Dark Island. D. Daniels
Dark Journey. F. W. Crofts
Dark Journey. Julien Green
Dark Journey. S. Horler
Dark Kiss. D. Enefer
Dark Knight. Colin Robertson
Dark Labyrinth. L. Barth
Dark Labyrinth. S. Leigh
Dark Lady. D. M. Disney
Dark Lady. J. J. Farjeon
Dark Lady. Gavin Holt
Dark Lady Murders. C. Ryland
Dark Lantern. C. Short
Dark Legacy. M. Alan
Dark Legacy. T. Charles
Dark Legend. L. Hayes
Dark Legend. Marilyn Ross
Dark Light. B. Spicer
Dark Love, Dark Magic. O. T. Jackson
Dark Lucy. P. King
Dark Mambo. W. H. Baker
Dark Man. R. Chetwynd-Hayes
Dark Man. Robin Temple
Dark Mansion. C. Farr

Dark Mansion. H. R. Kaye
Dark Mansion. W. E. D. Ross
Dark Masquerade. Anonymous
Dark Masquerade. Patricia Maxwell
Dark Masquerade. Elna Stone
Dark Memories. J. Morella
Dark Memory. E. Ronns
Dark Menace. C. Birkin
Dark Messenger. C. L. Cooper
Dark Mill. Claudette Nicole
Dark Mill Stream. A. Gask
Dark Mind. R. Goyne
Dark Mirror. B. Copper
Dark Mirror. P. Mason
Dark Mirror. L. J. Vance
Dark Moment. K. Wade
Dark Money. Colin Robertson
Dark Moon. A. D. Divine
Dark Moon. F. Vivian
Dark Moon, Lost Lady. Elsie Lee
Dark Moonshine. J. M. English
Dark Mosaic. C. Brooker
Dark Music. C. Russell
Dark Mystery. G. Ashe
Dark Nantucket Noon. J. Langton
Dark Night. R. Francis Foster
Dark Night. S. Horler
Dark Night. N. MacKenzie
Dark Night of Love. C. Clements
Dark Nights. T. Burke
Dark Number. E. Boyd
Dark Odyssey. F. Stevenson
Dark of Memory. P. Minton
Dark of Summer. D. Dwyer
Dark of the Moon. J. D. Carr
Dark of the Moon. W. E. D. Ross
Dark of the Moon. L. Thayer
Dark of the Sun. Wilbur Smith
Dark on Monday. M. Avallone
Dark on the Other Side. B. Michaels
Dark Page. N. Bell
Dark Page. S. Fuller
Dark Palazzo. V. Coffman
Dark Paradise. M. MacKintosh
Dark Passage. D. Goodis
Dark Passage. A. York
Dark Passions Subdue. D. Sanderson
Dark Path. M. Neilson
Dark Pathway. D. Newton
Dark Peril. J. Creasey
Dark Peril. M. Leighton
Dark Place. Mildred Davis
Dark Places. C. Allen
Dark Places. Alex Fraser
Dark Places. P. Gibbon
Dark Plot. S. Cobb
Dark Plunder. V. Rosen
Dark Power. W. Arden
Dark Power. E. S. Holding
Dark Power. L. J. Vance
Dark Prophecy. M. Alan
Dark Purpose. Doris Hume
Dark Rainbow. Gerald Butler
Dark Refuge. N. McFather
Dark Returners. J. P. Brennan
Dark Rider. G. Thayer
Dark River. P. Clark
Dark Road. J. Cross
Dark Road. D. M. Disney
Dark Road. C. Knight
Dark Road. G. Leroux
Dark Road. N. MacKenzie
Dark Road of Danger. C. H. Barker
Dark Roots of Fear. B. Gaston
Dark Rose. J. L. Roberts
Dark Rose the Phoenix. W. H. Murray
Dark Satanic. M. Z. Bradley
Dark Saviour. R. Harling
Dark Sea. P. C. De Crespigny
Dark Seas of Maltern Mansion. K. Vernon
Dark Secret. E. C. Clapp
Dark Secret. M. A. Fleming
Dark Secret of Josephine. D. Wheatley
Dark Secrets. W. M. Graydon
Dark Seed, Dark Flower. V. Leigh
Dark Shadow. H. Desmond
Dark Shadow. R. Mattheson
Dark Shadow. R. S. Thorn
Dark Shadow at Bitterhill. P. Warren
Dark Shadow of Love. H. Simart
Dark Shadows. K. Lynn
Dark Shadows. Marilyn Ross
Dark Ships. P. Footner
Dark Shore. S. Howatch
Dark Side. John Stanley
Dark Side Also. P. Conway
Dark Side of Love. O. Saul
Dark Side of Love. C. Woolrich
Dark Side of Magic. R. Aspinall
Dark Side of Paradise. J. A. Creighton
Dark Side of Paradise. S. Wagner
Dark Side of the Island. M. Hebden
Dark Side of the Island. Harry Patterson
Dark Side of the Moon. W. Corlett
Dark Side of the Street. M. Fallon
Dark Sonata. E. Bond
Dark Sonata. B. Murray
Dark Spot. L. Allan
Dark Square. J. Meynell
Dark Stage. D. Daniels
Dark Stain. B. Appel
Dark Stain. Shubael

Dark Star. R. W. Chambers
Dark Star. A. Maybury
Dark Star Rising. D. Lee
Dark Stars over Seacrest. Marilyn Ross
Dark Stone. Mildred Nelson
Dark Stranger. L. Lance
Dark Street. P. Cheyney
Dark Street. Gavin Holt
Dark Street Murders. P. Cheyney
Dark Summer. N. Buckingham
Dark Sun, Pale Shadows. N. Grey
Dark Suspicion. C. Gayet
Dark Symmetry. L. Conway
Dark Talisman. A. Bretonne
Dark the Summer Dies. W. Untermeyer
Dark Threat. P. Wentworth
Dark Threshold. G. Corren
Dark Tide. G. Croudace
Dark Tower. J. Edgar
Dark Tower. A. Woollcott
Dark Towers of Fog Island. Marilyn Ross
Dark Trade. A. Lejeune
Dark Trails Go East. F. A. M. Webster
Dark Tunnel. K. Millar
Dark Turnpike. J. G. Sarasin
Dark Understudy. E. Greenwood
Dark Valley. M. Stall
Dark Vendetta. R. Charles
Dark Vengeance. A. Barron
Dark Villa. T. Daniels
Dark Villa of Capri. W. E. D. Ross
Dark Voyage. H. Addis
Dark Wanton. P. Cheyney
Dark Watch. Genevieve St. John
Dark Waterfront. M. Hervey
Dark Waters. F. Cockrell
Dark Waters. W. Corcoran
Dark Waters. Ardath Wise
Dark Waters of Death. S. Wagner
Dark Ways of Death. P. Saxon
Dark Wheel. P. MacDonald
Dark Whispers. Claudette Nicole
Dark Window. T. Walsh
Dark Woman. Anonymous
Dark Wood. M. Farnsworth
Darke Darrell, the Boy Detective. F. H. Stauffer
Darken the Moon. F. B. Clark
Darkened Room. A. Clarke
Darkened Room. R. Goyne
Darkened Room. M. Harrison
Darkened Windows. C. K. Rathbone
Darkening Door. B. S. Ballinger
Darkening Glass. J. Wainwright
Darkening Night. Jane Elliott
Darkening Willows. P. Dalton
Darker Grows the Street. B. Winter
Darker Grows the Valley. Q. Patrick
Darker Heritage. G. A. Cerra
Darker Than Amber. J. D. MacDonald
Darker the Night. H. Brean
Darker Traffic. Martin Brett
Darkest Death. R. Stephenson
Darkest Hour. W. P. McGivern
Darkest Hour. H. Nielsen
Darkest Hour. L. Tracy
Darkest Night. P. Saxon
Darkest Room. G. Corren
Darkest Spot. L. Thayer
Darkest Under the Lamp. J. Sandys
Darkhaven. D. Daniels
Darkling Death. F. Vivian
Darkness As a Bride. M. Cumberland
Darkness at Bromley Hall. Maybeth Morgan
Darkness at Indian Key. K. Hess
Darkness at Mantia. I. Barry
Darkness at Noon. S. Kingsley
Darkness at Noon. A. Koestler
Darkness at Pemberley. W. H. White
Darkness at Sunrise. Rae Brown
Darkness Falling. B. Kevern
Darkness Falls from the Air. N. Balchin
Darkness I Leave You. N. W. Hooke
Darkness of Love. V. Stuart
Darkness of Slumber. R. Kutak
Darkness on the Stairs. F. Stevenson
Darkness Outside. G. H. Johnston
Darkness over Hycroft. F. A. Chittenden
Darkness Visible. N. Lewis
Darkroom. C. Banks
Darkwater. Jan Alexander
Darkwater. D. Eden
Darkwater Hall Mystery. K. Amis
Darling Clementine. D. Eden
Darling Daughter. R. Rayner
Darling Delinquent. H. Janson
Darling, Don't. Keith Campbell
Darling, Don't Be Dumb. P. G. Larbalestier
Darling, I Hate You. T. S. Matthews
Darling, It's Death. R. S. Prather
Darling Lili. H. Clement
Darling Murderess. C. Franklin
Darling Sin. Jean Leslie
Darling, This Is Death. D. Chambers
Darling You're Doomed. Carter Brown
Darnley's Bride. V. Stuart
Darrell Markham. M. E. Braddon
Darrow Enigma. M. Severy
Darsham's Folly. H. Esmond
Darsham's Tower. H. Esmond
Dart Board Mystery. W. D. Maydwell

D'Artagnan Signature. R. Rostand
Dartmoor. M. H. Hervey
Dartmoor Enigma. B. Thomson
Dartmoor Mystery. M. B. Dix
Dartmouth Murders. C. Orr
Darwich Castle. B. Kingsley
Dash for a Throne. A. W. Marchmont
Dashiell Hammett Omnibus. D. Hammett
Dashiell Hammett Story Omnibus. D. Hammett
Dashing Dick's Daughter. E. Everett-Green
Dashing Female Detective. Anonymous
Dashing Fugitive. Old Sleuth
Dastard "Dr." Anonymous
Datchet Diamonds. R. Marsh
Datchley Inheritance. S. McKenna
Date After Dark and other stories. P. Cheyney
Date for a Dame. C. Wheatley
Date for Homicide. R. Carni
Date for Murder. L. Trimble
Date with a Dead Man. B. Halliday
Date with a Spy. S. Maddock
Date with Danger. J. Ames
Date with Danger. G. Chester
Date with Danger! Martin Thomas
Date with Danger. Roy Vickers
Date with Darkness. D. Hamilton
Date with Death. W. H. L. Crauford
Date with Death. L. Ford
Date with Death. E. K. Goldthwaite
Date with Death. E. Linington
Date with Destiny. J. Walker
Date with Doom. Ray Owen
Date with Fear. J. Pendower
Date with Murder. L. Marshall
Date with the Departed. E. P. Thorne
Dateless Bargain. C. L. Pirkis
Dateline Darlene. H. Janson
Dateline Debbie. H. Janson
Dateline Diane. H. Janson
Dateline: Europe. L. Ross
Daughter Fair. P. Graaf
Daughter of Allah. C. H. Bullivant
Daughter of Anderson Crow. G. B. McCutcheon
Daughter of Astrea. E. P. Oppenheim
Daughter of Belial. B. Tozer
Daughter of Bonnie & Clyde. L. W. Brent
Daughter of Darkness. R. Goyne
Daughter of Darkness. E. Gresham
Daughter of Darkness. J. R. Lowell
Daughter of Darkness. P. McGerr
Daughter of Darkness. E. Noone
Daughter of Despair. Richard Hubbard
Daughter of Evil. P. Norton
Daughter of Evil. Genevieve St. John
Daughter of Evil. J. Weil
Daughter of France. J. Hatton
Daughter of Fu Manchu. S. Rohmer
Daughter of Illusion. J. Budd
Daughter of Judas. R. H. Savage
Daughter of Kings. G. W. Gough
Daughter of Mars. B. Kingsley
Daughter of Mystery. R. N. Silver
Daughter of Satan. Harry Mills
Daughter of Shame. H. Janson
Daughter of Silence. M. L. West
Daughter of the House. C. Wells
Daughter of the Marionis. E. P. Oppenheim
Daughter of the Pangaran. D. Divine
Daughter of the Sacred Mountain. M. Richardson
Daughter of the Scaffold. W. Tyrer
Daughter of the Sidewalk. D. Linton
Daughter of the Stars and other tales. H. Conway
Daughter of the States. M. Pemberton
Daughter of the Veldt. B. Marnan
Daughter of Time. J. Tey
Daughter of Two Worlds. L. Scott
Daughters in Law. H. Cecil
Daughters of Ardmore Hall. D. Eden
Daughters of Astaroth. S. Shulman
Daughters of Belial. S. Truss
Daughters of Cain. M. Lynch
Daughters of Lizzie. S. Lawrence
Daughters of Satan. S. Shulman
Daughters of the Night. E. Wallace
Dave Sulkin Cares. F. Knebel
Davenham Heritage. R. H. Poole
David Betterton. J. Ruegg
David Dimsdale, M.D. M. H. Hervey
David Lindsay. E. Southworth
David Poindexter's Disappearance, and other tales. J. Hawthorne
Davidian Report. D. B. Hughes
Davidson Case. J. Rhode
Davis Doesn't Live Here Any More. J. Ripley
Davy Jones. A. Hillgarth
Dawn at Kahlenberg. J. Siegal
Dawn Comes Soon. U. Nightingale
Dawn for Danger. Edmund Stone
Dawn Must Come. O. Williams
Dawn of Darkness. J. Creasey
Dawson Pedigree. D. L. Sayers
Day and Night Stories. A. Blackwood
Day Before Sunrise. T. Wiseman
Day Before Tomorrow. D. Helwig

Title Index

Day for Angels. E. Lindall
Day for Murder. K. McComb
Day Gibraltar Fell. B. Wynne
Day He Died. L. Padgett
Day I Died. L. Lariar
Day I Stopped Running. R. Wilkes-Hunter
Day in Monte Carlo. M. Albrand
Day It Rained Diamonds. M. E. Chaber
Day Khrushchev Panicked. G. B. Mair
Day Miss Bessie Lewis Disappeared. D. M. Disney
Day New York Trembled. I. Lewis
Day of Dark Memory. J. Phillips
Day of Disaster. J. Creasey
Day of Dwarfs. P. Everett
Day of Fear. G. Ashe
Day of Judgement. J. Higgins
Day of Judgment. E. Lipsky
Day of Judgment. N. MacKenzie
Day of Murder. B. Bearshaw
Day of Reckoning. Nicholas Carter
Day of Reckoning. F. Du Boisgobey
Day of Reckoning. J. Garden
Day of Temptation. W. LeQueux
Day of Terror. M. E. Cooke
Day of the Adder. N. Fitzgerald
Day of the Arrow. P. Loraine
Day of the Big Dollar. Peter Chambers
Day of the Coastwatch. P. McCutchan
Day of the Dead. C. Murray
Day of the Dead. B. Spicer
Day of the Dingo. Nick Carter
Day of the Dolphin. R. Merle
Day of the Donkey Derby. Joan Fleming
Day of the Dust. R. Verron
Day of the Fox. N. Lewis
Day of the Guns. M. Spillane
Day of the Jackal. F. Forsyth
Day of the Peppercorn Kill. J. Wainwright
Day of the Ram. W. C. Gault
Day of the Storm. Elizabeth Ford
Day of Uniting. E. Wallace
Day of Vengeance. D. Dayle
Day of Wrath. W. Coughlin
Day of Wrath. L. Tracy
Day One. J. Maccabee
Day She Died. H. Reilly
Day That I Die. P. F. Kluge
Day the Bookies Took a Bath. A. P. Hagan
Day the Call Came. T. Hinde
Day the Children Vanished. H. Pentecost
Day the Fish Came Out. K. Cicellis
Day the Sun Fell. R. L. Duncan
Day the Wind Dropped. K. Royce
Day the World Ended. S. Rohmer
Day They Hijacked Death. James Lake
Day They Invaded New York. I. Lewis
Day They Kidnapped Queen Victoria. H. K. Fleming
Day They Robbed the Bank of England. J. Brophy
Day Will Come. M. E. Braddon
Daybreak at Deest. R. Gaines
Daylight Fear. F. Cowen
Daylight Murder. P. McGuire
Daylight Robbery. J. W. Bobin
Daylight Robbery. M. Russell
Days Among the Dead. I. Baker
Days and Nights of Peril. Old Sleuth
Days Are Long. R. Barker
Day's Mischief. L. Storm
Days of Danger. J. Creasey
Days of Darkness. D. Orgill
Days of Doubt. A. M. Meadows
Days of Misfortune. A. M. Stein
Days of Thunder. M. Hartmann
Days of Vengeance. D. Enefer
Days of Vengeance. C. H. Guenter
Day's Tragedy. A. Upward
Daze of Fears. J. Roffman
Daze, the Magician. A. Baerlein
Dazzled. H. Townley
Dazzling Miss Davison. F. Warden
De Bercy Affair. Gordon Holmes
De Marigny Affair. M. C. Pain
Deacon and Actress. A. C. Gunter
Deacon Brodie. D. Donovan
Deacon's Daughter. R. Marsh
Deacon's Second Wind. A. C. Gunter
Dead Accomplice. Nicholas Carter
Dead Account. G. Burnett
Dead Against My Principles. K. Hopkins
Dead Against the Lawyers. R. Jefferies
Dead Ahead. W. L. Stuart
Dead Aim. C. Wilcox
Dead and Alive. H. Innes
Dead and Done For. Robert Reeves
Dead, and Done With. M. Cronin
Dead and Dumb. E. Crispin
Dead and Gone. B. Bird
Dead—and Kicking. F. Castle
Dead and Not Buried. H. F. M. Prescott
Dead and Paid For. M. Olden
Dead and the Damned. W. H. Baker
Dead and the Damned. B. Schwarz
Dead and the Deadly. L. Trimble
Dead Angel. J. Dolph
Dead Are Blind. M. Afford
Dead Are Dangerous. L. Marshall
Dead Are Discreet. A. Lyons
Dead Are Prowling. V. Markham
Dead Are Silent. L. Marshall
Dead As a Dinosaur. F. Lockridge
Dead As a Dodo. M. O'Brine
Dead As a Dummy. G. Homes
Dead As Diamonds. G. Trotta
Dead As They Come. K. Platt
Dead at First Hand. Jonathan Ross
Dead at the Take-Off. L. Dent
Dead Babes in the Wood. D. B. Olsen
Dead-Bang. R. S. Prather
Dead Beat. R. Bloch
Dead Before Midnight. R. Charles
Dead Bones Tell Tales. Griff
Dead Branch. G. Norham
Dead Bridal. J. F. Slingsby
Dead Bullfighter. D. Sanderson
Dead Butler Caper. F. Norman
Dead by Now. M. Erskine
Dead by the Light of the Moon. T. Wells
Dead Calm. C. Williams
Dead Can Tell. H. Reilly
Dead Canary. J. M. Fox
Dead Can't Love. J. Philips
Dead Center. Mary Collins
Dead Center. L. Langley
Dead Center. Christopher Wood
Dead Cert. D. Francis
Dead Certain. S. Sterling
Dead Certainty. N. Gould
Dead Certainty. H. Janson
Dead Circuit. S. Rattray
Dead City. S. Stevens
Dead City Round Up. E. Z. Frank
Dead Copy. H. Monteilhet
Dead Corse. M. Kelly
Dead Darling. Jonathan Craig
Dead Do Talk. John Bentley
Dead Dogs Bite. E. M. Curtiss
Dead Dolls Don't Talk. D. Keene
Dead Don't Bite. D. G. Browne
Dead Don't Care. Jonathan Latimer
Dead Don't Cry. B. Sarto
Dead Don't Cry. B. Shannon
Dead Don't Matter. Spencer Smith
Dead Don't Rise. Duff Johnson
Dead Don't Scare. P. Marlowe
Dead Don't Speak. M. Erskine
Dead Drop in Havana. C. H. Guenter
Dead Drunk. G. Bagby
Dead Drunk. H. Howard
Dead Duck. P. MacNee
Dead Easy. R. Angel
Dead Easy. J. Popplewell
Dead Easy for Dover. J. Porter
Dead End. M. Cruz
Dead End. C. Hilton
Dead End. S. Kingsley
Dead End. E. Lacy
Dead End. Ritchie Perry
Dead End. J. S. Strange
Dead End Delivery. T. J. Santiago
Dead-End Option. R. Obstfeld
Dead End Street. W. B. Murphy
Dead End Street. L. Thayer
Dead Ending. J. Philips
Dead Ernest. A. Tilton
Dead Fall. D. Wilmer
Dead Fellah. M. Palmer
Dead File. B. Copper
Dead Fingers. E. Sutton
Dead for a Ducat. L. Bruce
Dead for a Ducat. H. Reilly
Dead for a Dead Thing. P. Turnbull
Dead for a Penny. C. A. Goodrum
Dead for Danger. J. Foley
Dead Game. M. Avallone
Dead Game. G. Hammond
Dead Girl's Shoes. B. Cobb
Dead Give Away. Dulcie Gray
Dead Giveaway. S. Allan
Dead Giveaway. D. Blunt
Dead Giveaway. H. L. Nelson
Dead Giveaway. D. Wheelock
Dead Hand. I. R. G. Hart
Dead Hands Reaching. Marion Scott
Dead Harm No One. E. B. Quinn
Dead Have No Friends. J. Donavan
Dead Have No Mouths. C. Barry
Dead Heart. C. Gibbon
Dead Heat. P. Ayres
Dead Heat. B. Hemyng
Dead Heat. R. S. Prather
Dead Heat. P. Saxon
Dead Heat on a Merry-Go-Round. E. L. Heyman
Dead Hero. W. C. Gault
Dead If I Remember. S. H. Courtier
Dead in a Ditch. V. Gunn
Dead in a Row. Gwendoline Butler
Dead in Aqaba. C. H. Guenter
Dead in Bed. H. Kane
Dead in Bed. D. Keene
Dead in Guanajuato. P. Rock
Dead in No Time. N. A. Temple-Ellis
Dead in the Eye of the Law. G. Parker
Dead in the Morning. M. Yorke
Dead in the Water. B. Yates
Dead in Transit. M. Cronin
Dead Indeed. M. R. Hodgkin
Dead Ingleby. T. Gallon
Dead Innocent. P. Winn
Dead Is Forever. A. E. Redmond

Dead Men Are Dangerous / 479

Dead Is the Door-Nail. P. Haggard
Dead Letter. M. Ehrlich
Dead Letter. S. Regester
Dead Letters. J. George
Dead Level. Russell Gordon
Dead Liberty. D. Craig
Dead Lie Still. W. L. Stuart
Dead Line. P. McCutchan
Dead-Line. W. C. Tuttle
Dead Lion. J. Bonett
Dead Little Rich Girl. N. Davis
Dead Little Rich Girl. T. Harknett
Dead Look Down. S. Esmond
Dead Loss. M. Cronin
Dead Loss. R. Petrie
Dead Love Has Chains. M. E. Braddon
Dead Low Tide. J. D. MacDonald
Dead Man at the Window. J. Toussaint-Samat
Dead Man Blues. W. Irish
Dead Man Calling. G. Black
Dead Man Control. H. Reilly
Dead, Man, Dead. David Alexander
Dead Man Falling. D. Cory
Dead Man Friday. J. F. Hutton
Dead Man Inside. V. Starrett
Dead Man Laughs. V. Gunn
Dead Man Manor. V. Williams
Dead Man Murder. B. Newman
Dead Man Out. C. B. Gilford
Dead Man Running. J. Blackburn
Dead Man Running. S. Picard
Dead Man Sings. Roland Daniel
Dead Man Talks Too Much. W. Dickinson
Dead Man Twice. C. Bush
Dead Man's Alibi. L. Hollingsworth
Dead Man's Bay. C. Arley
Dead Man's Bay. M. Osborne
Dead Man's Bluff. B. Dunne
Dead Man's Bluff. R. Jeffries
Dead Man's Booty. O. Bradshaw
Dead Man's Chest. P. Capon
Dead Man's Chest. Jack Mann
Dead Man's Cocktail. B. Crowther
Dead Man's Corner. Roland Daniel
Dead Man's Court. M. H. Hervey
Dead Man's Cross. H. C. Davis
Dead Man's Destiny. Martin Thomas
Dead Man's Diary. B. Halliday
Dead Man's Diary. C. Kernahan
Dead Man's Dower. S. Kyle
Dead Man's Effects. H. C. Bailey
Dead Man's Evidence. J. G. Brandon
Dead Man's Face. F. J. Fargus
Dead Man's Float. A. Dean
Dead Man's Folly. A. Christie
Dead Man's Gang. F. Delmere
Dead Man's Gate. J. Hunter
Dead Man's Gift. Z. Popkin
Dead Man's Gold. R. Bridges
Dead Man's Gold. J. A. Dunn
Dead Man's Gold. G. E. Rochester
Dead Man's Grip. Nicholas Carter
Dead Man's Handle. J. Blackburn
Dead Man's Hat. H. Footner
Dead Man's Heath. J. J. Farjeon
Dead Man's Hoard. T. J. O'Connell
Dead Man's Island. J. Hunter
Dead Man's Knock. J. D. Carr
Dead Man's Knock. J. N. Chance
Dead Man's Love. T. Gallon
Dead Man's Mirror. A. Christie
Dead Man's Money. J. S. Fletcher
Dead Man's Music. C. Bush
Dead Man's Peak. C. Brisbane
Dead Man's Plaything. E. Woodward
Dead Man's Quarry. I. Jerrold
Dead Man's Riddle. M. Kelly
Dead Man's Rock. Q
Dead Man's Rooms. B. Delannoy
Dead Man's Sands. W. E. Stanton-Hope
Dead Man's Secret. J. Paeon
Dead Man's Secret. M. Plum
Dead Man's Secret. A. O. Pollard
Dead Man's Secret. Donald Stuart
Dead Man's Shadow. Basil Carey
Dead Man's Shoes. R. C. Armour
Dead Man's Shoes. H. C. Bailey
Dead Man's Shoes. L. Bruce
Dead Man's Shoes. E. Cameron
Dead Man's Shoes. J. N. Chance
Dead Man's Shoes. M. Innes
Dead Man's Shoes. H. Windsor
Dead Man's Step. L. L. Lynch
Dead Man's Story, and other tales. H. Herman
Dead Man's Tale. H. Pentecost
Dead Man's Tale. E. Queen
Dead Man's Tide. W. Richards
Dead Man's Treasure. M. Brand
Dead Man's Treasure. J. Goodwin
Dead Man's Vengeance. Roland Daniel
Dead Man's Walk. R. S. Prather
Dead Man's Warning. V. Gunn
Dead Man's Watch. G. D. H. Cole
Dead March for Penelope. G. Bellairs
Dead March for Penelope Blow. G. Bellairs
Dead March in Three Keys. P. Curtis
Dead Men. C. Rushton
Dead Men Alive. D. Cory
Dead Men Are Dangerous. Garnett Weston

D

Dead Men at the Folly. J. Rhode
Dead Men Do Tell. K. Trask
Dead Men Do Tell Tales. Donald Ross
Dead Men Don't Answer. T. Claymore
Dead Men Don't Ski. P. Moyes
Dead Men Grin. B. Fischer
Dead Men Leave No Fingerprints. W. Chambers
Dead Men of Eden. V. M. Grayland
Dead Men of Sestos. P. Loraine
Dead Men Rise Up Never. C. Landon
Dead Men Sing No Songs. M. Stuart
Dead Men Tell... R. Dark
Dead Men Tell No Tales. E. W. Hornung
Dead Men Turn Green. H. E. Wheeler
Dead Men's Bells. V. Gunn
Dead Men's Dollars. M. Crommelin
Dead Men's Fingers. P. Helm
Dead Men's Morris. G. Mitchell
Dead Men's Plans. M. G. Eberhart
Dead Men's Shoes. M. E. Braddon
Dead Men's Shoes. L. Thayer
Dead Men's Tales. F. H. Kitchin
Dead Mr. Nixon. T. H. White
Dead Mrs. Stratton. A. Berkeley
Dead Mouse. Austen Allen
Dead Needle. Alex Hamilton
Dead-Nettle. J. B. Hilton
Dead Nigger. Anthony Gray
Dead of a Counterplot. S. Nash
Dead of a Physician. Fiona Sinclair
Dead of Night. J. C. McMullen
Dead of Night. K. Steel
Dead of Night. S. Sterling
Dead of Summer. Josephine Gill
Dead of Summer. M. Kelly
Dead of Summer. D. Moseley
Dead of the Night. H. Carmichael
Dead of the Night. J. Reach
Dead of the Night. J. Rhode
Dead of Winter. D. Cooper
Dead of Winter. C. Cornish
Dead of Winter. C. Hale
Dead of Winter. W. H. Hallahan
Dead of Winter. Marilyn Ross
Dead on Arrival. G. Bagby
Dead on Arrival. H. Gordon
Dead on Arrival. S. Marlowe
Dead on Arrival. S. Mitchell
Dead on Arrival. S. Stratton
Dead on Arrival. L. Thayer
Dead on Course. M. Black
Dead on Cue. G. Compton
Dead on Cue. D. Reid
Dead on Delivery. A. Bocca
Dead on Delivery. George Douglas
Dead on Departure. A. MacKinnon
Dead on Nine. J. Popplewell
Dead on Noon. T. Tarrant
Dead on Prediction. O. Norton
Dead on the Dot. George Douglas
Dead on the Level. H. Nielsen
Dead on the Stone. R. Amberley
Dead on the Track. J. Rhode
Dead on Time. A. Bocca
Dead on Time. P. Denver
Dead on Time. C. F. Gregg
Dead on Time. Stephen Grey
Dead on Time. O. John
Dead on Time. N. Perrelli
Dead on Time. Colin Robertson
Dead on Time. C. Witting
Dead One in Berlin. U. Miehe
Dead Ones Don't Talk. R. Gar
Dead Opposite the Church. F. Vivian
Dead or Alive. Anonymous
Dead or Alive. J. Creasey
Dead or Alive. J. Templeton
Dead or Alive. P. Wentworth
Dead Orchid. D. Lawrence
Dead Parrot. M. Keyes
Dead Past. J. Scholey
Dead Piano. H. Van Dyke
Dead Pigeon. J. M. Fox
Dead Pigeon. R. P. Hansen
Dead Pigeon on Beethoven Street. S. Fuller
Dead Pigs at Hungry Farm. B. Graeme
Dead Prior. C. D. Lampen
Dead Reckoning. Ken Blake
Dead Reckoning. J. E. Bloundelle-Burton
Dead Reckoning. F. Bonnamy
Dead Reckoning. E. Cannon
Dead Reckoning. P. Conde
Dead Reckoning. George Douglas
Dead Reckoning. B. Hamilton
Dead Reckoning. G. Mitcham
Dead Reckoning. K. Sandford
Dead Reckoning. B. Sarto
Dead Reckoning. R. Simons
Dead Reckoning. L. Thayer
Dead Regimental. B. Bavin
Dead Respectable. D. Reid
Dead Return. W. Carter
Dead Ride Hard. L. J. Vance
Dead Riders. E. O'Donnell
Dead Right. Jennette Lee
Dead Right. S. Sterling
Dead Ringer. F. Brown
Dead-Ringer. E. Cannon
Dead Ringer. J. H. Chase
Dead Ringer. F. Findley

Dead Ringer. A. Lyons
Dead Ringer. Robert Thomas
Dead Ringer. M. Warden
Dead Rite. F. Kane
Dead Run. J. Foxx
Dead Run. H. Holley
Dead Run. R. Lockridge
Dead Run. R. Sheckley
Dead Runner. F. Ross
Dead Say No. Max Gordon
Dead Sea Cipher. Elizabeth Peters
Dead Sea Fruit. M. E. Braddon
Dead Sea Submarine. A. Caillou
Dead Secret. R. Ackland
Dead Secret. W. Collins
Dead Secret. K. Sandford
Dead Secret. G. Verner
Dead Secret. Alan Williams
Dead: Senate Office Building. M. Scherf
Dead Sequence. S. Rattray
Dead Set. T. H. Stone
Dead Shall Be Raised. G. Bellairs
Dead, She Was Beautiful. W. Masterson
Dead Shot. J. M. Fox
Dead Side. K. Davis
Dead Side of the Mike. Simon Brett
Dead Silence. J. Bruce
Dead Silence. S. Rattray
Dead Skip. J. Gores
Dead Sleep for Keeps. B. Winter
Dead Sleep Late. E. Kennedy
Dead Snakes' Venom. H. Kemp
Dead So Soon. Richard Grayson
Dead Stay Dumb. J. H. Chase
Dead Stop. M. Burton
Dead Stop. D. M. Disney
Dead Storage. G. Bagby
Dead Storage. L. Thayer
Dead Straight. D. MacKenzie
Dead Straight. Old Sleuth
Dead Stranger. Nicholas Carter
Dead Sure. H. Brean
Dead Sure. S. Sterling
Dead Take No Bows. R. Burke
Dead Tale-Tellers. J. N. Chance
Dead Thing in the Pool. A. M. Stein
Dead to Rights. Dennis Allan
Dead to Rites. S. Angus
Dead to the World. N. Baker
Dead to the World. F. Durbridge
Dead to the World. D. X. Manners
Dead to the World. S. Sterling
Dead Travel Fast. R. Tate
Dead Tree Gives No Shelter. V. Scott
Dead Trouble. M. Carroll
Dead Trouble. D. Devine
Dead, Upstairs in the Tub. Michael Brett
Dead Voice. C. M. Wills
Dead Walk. G. Collins
Dead Water. N. Marsh
Dead Water. E. Radford
Dead Weight. R. Fenisong
Dead Weight. F. Kane
Dead Weight. B. Lecomber
Dead Weight. A. Simmons
Dead Were Strangers. M. Clinten
Dead with Sorrow. P. Audemars
Dead Witness. Old Spicer
Dead Woman. E. Walter
Dead Woman of the Year. H. Pentecost
Dead Woman's Ditch. S. Nash
Dead Wood. B. Parvin
Dead Wrong. G. Bagby
Dead Wrong. M. Cruz
Dead Wrong. W. S. Doxey
Dead Wrong. R. S. Hastings
Dead Wrong. L. Holden
Dead Wrong. S. Sterling
Dead Yellow Women. D. Hammett
Dead Yesterday. R. Fenisong
Dead Yet Living. J. B. Williams
Dead Zone. Stephen King
Deader They Fall. Peter Chambers
Deadest Thing You Ever Saw. Jonathan Ross
Deadfall. D. Cory
Deadfall. K. Laumer
Deadfall. J. MacLean
Deadhand. G. Sims
Deadhead. C. Carpenter
Deadhead. C. M. Warren
Deadlier of the Species. D. Reid
Deadlier Sex. B. S. Ballinger
Deadlier Sex. G. Manceron
Deadlier Than the Male. J. C. Conaway
Deadlier Than the Male. James Gunn
Deadlier Than the Male. G. Holden
Deadlier Than the Male. H. Reymond
Deadliest Game. M. Jahn
Deadliest Game. P. McCurtin
Deadlight. A. Roy
Deadline. P. Brickhill
Deadline. T. B. Dewey
Deadline. J. Eastwood
Deadline. H. Howard
Deadline. T. Heald
Deadline. A. Irving
Deadline. D. Linton
Deadline. P. MacNee
Deadline. M. Russell
Deadline at Dawn. W. Irish
Deadline Dolly. D. Enefer

Deadline for a Diplomat. S. Truss
Deadline for a Dream. B. Knox
Deadline for Danger. Arthur MacLean
Deadline for Destruction. C. L. Leonard
Deadline for Loren. M. Clare
Deadline for Lovers. F. Nichols
Deadline for Macall. G. Fairlie
Deadline for Murder. H. Gould
Deadline Moscow. A. Redwood
Deadline 2 A.M. R. L. Pike
Deadlock. R. Busby
Deadlock. R. Fenisong
Deadlocked! L. P. Kelley
Deadly Advice. L. Ericson
Deadly Affair. E. Lacy
Deadly Affair. J. Le Carre
Deadly Alliance. William Crawford
Deadly Bedfellows. F. C. Davis
Deadly Beloved. W. Ard
Deadly Beloved. J. S. Strange
Deadly Blunder. J. Ritson
Deadly Boodle. J. M. Flynn
Deadly But Delectable. K. T. McCall
Deadly Charade. M. Stall
Deadly Chase. Carter Cullen
Deadly Chase. J. M. Eshleman
Deadly Climate. U. Curtiss
Deadly Combo. J. Farr
Deadly Companions. B. Sang
Deadly Company. G. Kent
Deadly Contact. A. Dean
Deadly Cotton Heart. R. Dennis
Deadly Crusade. P. Chase
Deadly Crusader. D. Streib
Deadly Cyborgs. P. Edwards
Deadly Daffodils. R. Silverwood
Deadly Dames. Malcolm Douglas
Deadly Date. A. F. Daniels
Deadly, Deadly Art. G. A. Ralston
Deadly Deal. S. Jason
Deadly Deceit. E. Burgess
Deadly Decree. J. C. Lenehan
Deadly Deep. J. Messmann
Deadly Delight. A. M. Stein
Deadly Desire. R. Colby
Deadly Diamond. J. Storm
Deadly Diary. William Du Bois
Deadly Discretion. D. Ramsay
Deadly Ditto. C. Hale
Deadly Doctor. S. Jason
Deadly Document. M. Bar-Zohar
Deadly Doll. J. Barbette
Deadly Doll. H. Kane
Deadly Doubles. Nick Carter
Deadly Dove. R. King
Deadly Dowager. E. Greenwood
Deadly Downbeat. Jonathan Burke
Deadly Duo. M. Allingham
Deadly Duo. R. Jessup
Deadly Dwarf. K. Robeson
Deadly Dyke. B. Parvin
Deadly Edge. R. Stark
Deadly Election. M. Castle
Deadly Encounter. R. Woodley
Deadly Ernest. A. Bocca
Deadly Ernest. J. Cockin
Deadly Errand. M. Hillary
Deadly Eurasian. A. Cordell
Deadly Feast. Jane Collier
Deadly Finger. H. Kane
Deadly Foe. A. Sergeant
Deadly Fresco. L. Southney
Deadly Friend. H. Pentecost
Deadly Friendship. C. Arkham
Deadly Frost. T. Moan
Deadly Game. N. Daniels
Deadly Game. Graham Hastings
Deadly Game. J. MacKenzie
Deadly Game. W. Manson
Deadly Game. J. Yaffe
Deadly Gold. J. Rossiter
Deadly Green. J. Rossiter
Deadly Group Down Under. P. Morgan
Deadly Hall. J. D. Carr
Deadly Harvest. P. Mallory
Deadly Homecoming. T. George
Deadly Honeymoon. Lawrence Block
Deadly Honeymoon. A. C. MacLean
Deadly Image. G. H. Coxe
Deadly Inheritance. A. Andre
Deadly Intent. A. Rowe
Deadly Interlude. M. O'Brine
Deadly Is the Diamond. M. G. Eberhart
Deadly Is the Evil Tongue. A. Hocking
Deadly Isles. J. H. Vance
Deadly Jade. B. Sanders
Deadly Jest. V. Markham
Deadly Jigsaw. R. Bay
Deadly Joke. H. Pentecost
Deadly Joker. N. Blake
Deadly Kind of Lonely. S. Forbes
Deadly Kitten. Carter Brown
Deadly Knighthood. J. O. Mayo
Deadly Lady. J. Dial
Deadly Lampshade. Dulcie Gray
Deadly Legacy. W. Arden
Deadly Legacy. F. Usher
Deadly Lover. R. O. Saber
Deadly Lovers. Anthony Graham
Deadly Lure. W. Chambers
Deadly Manhunt. J. Rosenberger
Deadly Marriage. R. Jeffries

Title Index

Deadly Matrimony. Jon Stevens
Deadly Meeting. R. Bernard
Deadly Memorial. P. Perry
Deadly Mermaid. J. A. Phillips
Deadly Messiah. Andrea Hill
Deadly Miss. Carter Brown
Deadly Miss Ashley. F. C. Davis
Deadly Mission. Roland Daniel
Deadly Mission. H. Janson
Deadly Night-Blade. Austin Stone
Deadly Night Call. W. Irish
Deadly Night-Cap. H. Carmichael
Deadly Nightcap. H. Hawton
Deadly Nightcap. F. Stewart
Deadly Nightshade. K. Cameron
Deadly Nightshade. E. Daly
Deadly Nightshade. James Fraser
Deadly Nightshade. Jean Fraser
Deadly Noose. R. Foley
Deadly One. H. McCutcheon
Deadly Orbit Mission. V. M. Mason
Deadly Party. L. DuBreuil
Deadly Pattern. Douglas Clark
Deadly Pavilion. Hilda Lawrence
Deadly Pawn. Magali
Deadly Pay-Off. W. H. Duhart
Deadly Payoff. M. Clerc
Deadly Payoff. F. Mullally
Deadly Pearl. M. Olden
Deadly Percheron. J. F. Bardin
Deadly Persuasion. S. Mitchell
Deadly Persuasion. D. Reid
Deadly Pickup. M. K. Ozaki
Deadly Picnic. J. Bingham
Deadly Piece. P. Hamill
Deadly Poison. M. Pertwee
Deadly Prey. Ralph Hayes
Deadly Purpose. R. P. Hanson
Deadly Putter. T. Dexter
Deadly Quiet. D. Enefer
Deadly Race. T. C. H. Jacobs
Deadly Reaper. Clark Smith
Deadly Record. N. W. Hooke
Deadly Relations. R. Gatenby
Deadly Relations. J. Thomson
Deadly Return. I. Lambot
Deadly Reunion. W. L. Harter
Deadly Revenge. A. Askew
Deadly Rose. M. Lynch
Deadly Rose. K. Rich
Deadly Scarab. Nicholas Carter
Deadly Sea, Deadly Sand. I. Foster
Deadly Secret. A. Abbot
Deadly Seeds. R. Sapir
Deadly September. K. Kramer
Deadly Sex. J. Webb
Deadly Shade of Gold. J. D. MacDonald
Deadly Shore. J. Pattinson
Deadly Silence. L. Derrick
Deadly Streets. H. Ellison
Deadly Summer. G. M. Barnes
Deadly Sunshade. P. A. Taylor
Deadly the Daring. W. Randall
Deadly to Bed. D. Tracy
Deadly Trade. Bradshaw Jones
Deadly Trap. H. Pentecost
Deadly Travelers. D. Eden
Deadly Triangle. R. Roleine
Deadly Truth. H. McCloy
Deadly Weapon. Wade Miller
Deadly Welcome. J. D. MacDonald
Deadly Welcome. K. Rothrock
Deadman's Bay. L. A. Knight
Deadman's Rest. N. Dorer
Deadwood Dick. T. Taggart
Deadwood Dick's Last Shot. E. L. Wheeler
Deaf, Dumb and Blonde. Anthony Morton
Deaf-Mute Murders. V. Loder
Deal in Death. A. O. Pollard
Deal in Diamonds. Nicholas Carter
Deal in Letters. F. M. White
Deal in Violence. W. Arden
Deal Me Out. J. S. Blazer
Deal Me Out. S. Morelli
Deal of Death Caps. G. M. Wilson
Deal of the Century. I. K. Martin
Dealer. Max Collins
Dealer. V. Torrie
Dealer in Antiques. B. Tozer
Dealer in Death and other stories. Arthur Morris
Dealer of Death. F. MacIsaac
Dealer's Move. Steve Wilson
Dealer's War. Steve Wilson
Dealing Out Death. W. T. Ballard
Deals. B. Pain
Dean Dunham. H. Alger
Dean of Clonbury. P. Roche
Dean's Daughters. H. Adams
Dean's Death. A. Lawrence
Dear Brother, Here Departed. Stella Phillips
Dear Conspirator. G. Goodchild
Dear Daughter Dead. S. B. Hough
Dear, Dead Days. J. Barbette
Dear, Dead Girls. N. Morland
Dear, Dead Harry. Milton Scott
Dear Dead Mother-in-Law. K. Hill
Dear Dead Professor. K. A. LaRoche
Dear Dead Woman. Anthony Gilbert
Dear, Dead Woman. D. Chambers
Dear, Deadly Beloved. J. Flagg

Dear Deadly Cara. G. Z. Stone
Dear Delusion. E. Woodward
Dear Departed. Anne Burton
Dear Fatherland. J. M. Simmel
Dear Fools. A. Soutar
Dear Hungarian Friend. G. Napier
Dear John. Susan Lee
Dear Judgment. J. Crosby
Dear Laura. J. Stubbs
Dear Liar. D. M. Low
Dear Life. H. E. Bates
Dear Lost Love. A. Maybury
Dear Old Gentleman. G. Goodchild
Dear Phoebe. T. Taggart
Dear Traitor. J. March
Dearly Beloved Wives. W. H. L. Crauford
Death. Woody Allen
Death a la King. I. Waitt
Death About Face. F. Kane
Death Across the Tamagash. M. Hastings
Death After Breakfast. H. Pentecost
Death After Dark. F. Griffin
Death After Evensong. Douglas Clark
Death After Lunch. R. D. Abrahams
Death After School. A. Holden
Death Against the Clock. Anthony Gilbert
Death Against Venus. D. Chambers
Death Ain't Commercial. G. Bagby
Death Amidst Satin. E. Woodward
Death Among Doctors. J. G. Edwards
Death Among Friends. H. Ainsworth
Death Among Friends. Lange Lewis
Death Among the Orchids. T. B. Morris
Death Among the Professors. K. Sproul
Death Among the Sands. E. Mack
Death Among the Stars. K. Giles
Death Among the Stars. Jean Marsh
Death Among the Sunbathers. E. R. Punshon
Death Among the Tulips. A. Hocking
Death Among the Writers. E. De Caire
Death and a Dark Horse. Martin Thomas
Death and Benedict. I. Bayne
Death and Bitters. K. Christian
Death and Bright Water. J. Mitchell
Death and Chicanery. P. MacDonald
Death and Circumstance. H. Waugh
Death and Daisy Bland. N. Blake
Death and Festivals. Richard Blum
Death and His Brother. M. Bidwell
Death and His Sweetheart. Winifred Duke
Death and Letters. E. Daly
Death and Lilacs. F. Bayard
Death and Little Brother. C. Knight
Death and Little Girl Blue. V. J. Hanson
Death and Mary Dazill. M. Fitt
Death and Mr. Gilly. W. M. Duncan
Death and Mr. Potter. R. Foley
Death and Mr. Prettyman. K. Giles
Death and Mrs. Lovely. E. Wake
Death and Still Life. D. Launay
Death and Taxes. T. B. Dewey
Death and Taxes. T. B. Dodge
Death and the Archdeacon. N. Harman
Death and the Bridegroom. L. Hurt
Death and the Bright Day. M. Fitt
Death and the Dancing Footman. N. Marsh
Death and the Dark Daughter. F. Hurt
Death and the Dear Girls. J. Stagge
Death and the Devil. P. Whelton
Death and the Diplomat. M. Scherf
Death and the Durlings. V. Fletcher
Death and the Dutch Uncle. P. Moyes
Death and the Dutiful Daughter. A. Morice
Death and the Gentle Bull. R. Lockridge
Death and the Gilded Man. Carter Dickson
Death and the Golden Boy. N. Morland
Death and the Golden Image. Whyte Hall
Death and the I Ching. E. Michaels
Death and the Joyful Woman. Ellis Peters
Death and the Leaping Ladies. C. Drummond
Death and the Maiden. E. Lindall
Death and the Maiden. J. K. MacDougall
Death and the Maiden. G. Mitchell
Death and the Maiden. Q. Patrick
Death and the Maiden. S. Radley
Death and the Naked Lady. J. Flagg
Death and the Night Watches. V. Bell
Death and the Pleasant Voices. M. Fitt
Death and the Pregnant Virgin. S. T. Haymon
Death and the Professor. E. Radford
Death and the Professors. K. Sproul
Death and the Shortest Day. M. Fitt
Death and the Sky Above. A. Garve
Death and the South Wind. F. Lester
Death and the Spider. G. Stockbridge
Death and the Visiting Fireman. H. R. F. Keating
Death and the Women. A. Golsworthy
Death and Variations. I. Baker
Death Angel. C. B. Clason
Death Angel's Shadow. K. E. Wagner
Death Answers the Bell. V. Williams
Death—As in Matador. L. V. Roper
Death at a Masquerade. M. E. Corne
Death at Abu Mina. P. William
Death at Aranshore. K. Wade
Death at Ash House. M. Burton
Death at Breakfast. J. Rhode
Death at Broadcasting House. V. Gielgud

Death at Chestnut Hill. C. Nicolai
Death at Court Lady. S. Horler
Death at Crane's Court. E. Dillon
Death at Dakar. K. O'Neil
Death at Dale's End. J. Brooke
Death at Dancing Stones. M. Fitt
Death at Datchets. F. J. Whaley
Death at Dayton's Folly. V. Rath
Death at Deep End. P. Wentworth
Death at Devil-Fish Point. D. Boyle
Death at Dusk. P. Ketchum
Death at Dyke's Corner. E. C. R. Lorac
Death at Eight Bells. F. A. Kummer
Death at Flight. C. Willock
Death at Flood Tide. L. A. Brennan
Death at Four Corners. Anthony Gilbert
Death at Half-Term. Josephine Bell
Death at Hallows End. L. Bruce
Death at Heel. F. Andreas
Death at Her Elbow. D. C. Cameron
Death at Her Fingers. M. Shane
Death at His Elbow. J. M. Walsh
Death at Lord's. B. Newman
Death at Lover's Leap. R. G. Dean
Death at Low Tide. M. Burton
Death at My Elbow. H. Desmond
Death at My Heels. D. Kirby
Death at My Heels, and other stories. M. Hervey
Death at No. 47. C. Wallace
Death at One Below. H. Hamilton
Death at Peak Hour. Jean Marsh
Death at Pyford Hall. D. Fisher
Death at Roman Farm. John Lloyd
Death at St. Asprey's School. L. Bruce
Death at Salterton Court. R. Marr
Death at Screaming Pool. C. Ryland
Death at Sea. R. Sale
Death at Sea. L. White
Death at 7:10. H. F. S. Moore
Death at Shinglestrand. P. Capon
Death at Slack Water. D. W. MacArthur
Death at Springtime. D. C. Andrews
Death at Swaythling Court. J. J. Connington
Death at the Bank. B. Francis
Death at the Bar. C. Drummond
Death at the Bar. N. Marsh
Death at "The Bottoms". A. B. Cunningham
Death at the Cascades. J. B. Farmer
Death at the Chase. M. Innes
Death at the Chateau. M. Tinayre
Death at the Chateau Noir. E. Radford
Death at the Club. M. Burton
Death at the Crossroads. M. Burton
Death at the Dam. C. F. Adams
Death at the Dance. J. Rhode
Death at the Depot. D. G. Hastings
Death at the Dog. J. Cannan
Death at the Dolphin. N. Marsh
Death at the Door. Anthony Gilbert
Death at the Dowager. B. Rhode
Death at the Drome. W. R. Hutton
Death at the Easel. M. Baker
Death at the Feast. Nicholas Carter
Death at the Furlong Post. C. Drummond
Death at the Games. J. MacGowan
Death at the Golden Cockerel. W. R. Hutton
Death at the Golden Crown. A. Dick
Death at the Helm. B. Rhode
Death at the Horse Show. V. Loder
Death at the Inn. R. A. Freeman
Death at the Inn. J. Rhode
Death at the Isthmus. G. H. Coxe
Death at the Manor. M. E. Corne
Death at the Medical Board. Josephine Bell
Death at the Mike. A. Eichler
Death at the Opera. G. Mitchell
Death at the Pelican. C. M. Wills
Death at the President's Lodging. M. Innes
Death at the Rodeo. E. Queen
Death at the Salutation. F. Vivian
Death at the Strike. C. Willock
Death at the Towers. F. C. Tickner
Death at the Villa. M. Dalton
Death at the Wedding. M. Duke
Death at the Wedding. A. Hocking
Death at the Wheel. V. Loder
Death at Three. C. Rice
Death at Traitor's Gate. V. Gunn
Death at Windward Hill. H. J. Hultman
Death Awaits Thee. M. Lang
Death Be Nimble. R. N. Smith
Death Beats the Band. I. Shurman
Death Beckons Quietly. W. M. Duncan
Death Bed. S. Greenleaf
Death Before Bedtime. E. Box
Death Before Breakfast. C. F. Adams
Death Before Breakfast. G. Bellairs
Death Before Breakfast. D. Fearon
Death Before Day. M. Dalman
Death Before Dinner. E. C. R. Lorac
Death Before Honour. David Hume
Death Before Launching. H. J. Quartermain
Death Before Wicket. N. Spain
Death Begs the Question. L. Eby
Death Behind the Door. F. W. Gumley
Death Behind the Door. V. MacClure

D

Death Bell. Edison Marshall
Death Below the Dam. E. H. Fonseca
Death Below Zero. H. S. Head
Death Below Zero. T. Muir
Death Beneath Jerusalem. R. Bax
Death Beneath the River. J. Rowland
Death Beyond the Go-Thru. B. Kendrick
Death Bids for Corners. A. Dickson
Death Bird. R. St. Clair
Death Bird Contract. P. Atlee
Death Blanks the Screen. L. O'Donnell
Death Blew Out the Match. K. M. Knight
Death Boards the Lazy Lady. R. Darby
Death Box. E. Lecale
Death Box. L. N. Morgan
Death Box. B. G. Quin
Death Breaks the Ring. V. Rath
Death Bringers. D. Orgill
Death-Bringers. Dell Shannon
Death Brings a Storke. A. Boutell
Death Brings in the New Year. G. Bellairs
Death Brokers. P. D. Ballard
Death Burns the Candle. R. Trevor
Death Business. Anthony Graham
Death by Apparition. Reginald Campbell
Death by Appointment. F. Bonnamy
Death—by Appointment. J. Corbett
Death by Appointment. C. Goodall
Death by Arrangement. J. Kershaw
Death by Arrangement. L. Meynell
Death by Association. R. Lockridge
Death by Ballot. John Laffin
Death by Bequest. F. Hurt
Death by Bequest. M. McMullen
Death by Chalk Face. J. Gale
Death by Clue. H. C. Beck
Death by Computer. D. M. Disney
Death by Demonstration. P. Carlon
Death by Design. A. Derleth
Death by Design. A. Nash
Death by Desire. R. Goyne
Death by Drowning. Robin Daniel
Death by Dynamite. J. L. Bonney
Death by Hoax. Lionel Black
Death by Inches. Dell Shannon
Death by Invitation. G. Stockwell
Death by Marriage. E. G. Cousins
Death by Misadventure. B. Malim
Death by Misadventure. M. Underwood
Death by Moonlight. M. Innes
Death by Night. J. Creasey
Death by Order. W. Byford-Jones
Death by Proxy. J. Crosby
Death by Proxy. E. B. Ronald
Death by Remote Control. E. Hogarth
Death by Request. P. John
Death by the Day. Lawrence Fisher
Death by the Gaff. J. H. Vahey
Death by the Lake. L. Bruce
Death by the Lake. Roland Daniel
Death by the Lake. W. Martyn
Death by the Mistletoe. A. MacVicar
Death by the Nile. A. Parsons
Death by the Radio. J. W. Lee
Death by the Sea. J. Turner
Death by the Seine. B. Sarto
Death by the Zodiac. M. Farnsworth
Death by Treble Chance. E. G. Cousins
Death by Two Hands. P. Drax
Death by Water. M. Innes
Death Called China. R. Carni
Death Called Twice. C. B. Molyneaux
Death Calling—Collect. D. Tracy
Death Calls at Scotland Yard. J. E. Nyson
Death Calls on the Witches. J. Martenson
Death Calls the Jester. H. E. Wheeler
Death Calls the Shots. B. Knox
Death Calls the Tune. F. W. Gumley
Death Calls Three Times. G. Barnett
Death Came Back. E. Hale
Death Came Back. C. Kingston
Death Came by Night. G. Bligh
Death Came Dancing. K. M. Knight
Death Came in Lucerne. M. Stand
Death Came in Straw. P. Piper
Death Came in the Studio. M. Stand
Death Came Late. J. B. O'Sullivan
Death Came Smiling. E. Dewhurst
Death Came Softly. E. C. R. Lorac
Death Came to Lighthouse Steps. M. Stand
Death Came Too Soon. M. Stand
Death Came Too Soon. I. E. Ward
Death Came Uninvited. E. Backhouse
Death Came with Darkness. M. Stand
Death Came with Diamonds. M. Stand
Death Came with Flowers. M. Stand
Death Can Wait. G. W. Cooke
Death Cancels the Evidence. R. H. Leitfred
Death Cap. S. Brydon
Death Cap. R. T. Campbell
Death Cap. J. Thomson
Death Car Surfside. P. Morgan
Death Card. J. B. O'Sullivan
Death Carries a Cane. Sherwood King
Death Casts a Long Shadow. Anthony Gilbert
Death Casts a Lure. M. Johnston
Death Casts a Shadow. L. Marshall
Death Casts a Vote. M. Yates

Death Casts No Shadow. P. G. Larbalestier
Death Catches Up with Mr. Kluck. Xantippe
Death Certificate. J. Wainwright
Death Changes His Mind. Frank King
Death Charge. A. Caillou
Death Charter. E. L. Adams
Death Check. R. Sapir
Death Checks In. S. Ransome
Death Chime. L. Gribble
Death Circle. Nicholas Carter
Death Claims. J. Hansen
Death Climbs a Hill. E. Backhouse
Death Coins. W. S. Masterman
Death Collection. M. Arrighi
Death Comes As the End. A. Christie
Death Comes Ashore. E. F. Charles
Death Comes at Night. K. Ingram
Death Comes by Air. N. Leslie
Death Comes by Post. J. Carr
Death Comes Courting. I. Garland
Death Comes Early. W. R. Cox
Death Comes Easy. B. Feltner
Death Comes Grinning. W. Creed
Death Comes in the Night. J. M. Spender
Death Comes Laughing. V. Gunn
Death Comes Like a Thief. V. Ellis
Death Comes on Derby Day. Alan Muir
Death Comes on Friday. L. Day
Death Comes Swiftly. J. G. Brandon
Death Comes to a Party. A. McAllister
Death Comes to Cambers. E. R. Punshon
Death Comes to Casanova. H. G. Coulter
Death Comes to Dinner. A. Colin
Death Comes to Dinner. S. Gluck
Death Comes to Dinner. P. Yates
Death Comes to Fanshawe. J. Corbett
Death Comes to Kenya. N. Leslie
Death Comes to Lady's Steps. W. M. Duncan
Death Comes to Perigord. J. Ferguson
Death Comes to Rehearsal. R. Sharp
Death Comes to Tea. T. Du Bois
Death Comes to the Hermit. J. Harrell
Death Comes Too Late. R. Trevor
Death Comes Wholesale. R. Drayton
Death Commits Bigamy. J. M. Fox
Death Conducts a Tour. R. Darby
Death Connection. R. Brandt
Death Convention. D. Winsor
Death Counts Five. H. L. Gates
Death Counts Three. H. Carmichael
Death Cracks a Bottle. K. Giles
Death Crag. B. Gaston
Death Cries in the Street. S. A. Krasney
Death Cries Ole. M. Mundy
Death Croons the Blues. J. Ronald
Death Crosses the Line. E. F. Charles
Death Cruises South. R. Denbie
Death Cry. D. Hauck
Death Cues the Pageant. E. Ainsworth
Death Curse. A. O. Pollard
Death Cuts a Caper. D. Magarshack
Death Cuts a Silhouette. D. B. Olsen
Death Cuts the Deck. R. L. Fish
Death Cuts the Film. C. Saxby
Death Cycle. C. Runyon
Death Dams the Tide. J. Guildford
Death Dances Thrice. J. C. Lenehan
Death Darkens Council. V. Bell
Death Date. R. Wilkes-Hunter
Death Dates a Dame. J. Death
Death Deal. Anonymous
Death Deal. B. E. Miller
Death Dealers. I. Asimov
Death Dealers. B. Gaston
Death Dealers. F. Meadows
Death Dealers. M. Spillane
Death Deals a Diamond. N. Wray
Death Deals a Double. J. Bude
Death Deals in Diamonds. Bradshaw Jones
Death Dealt the Cards. E. Hale
Death Deep Down. D. J. Marlowe
Death Defies the Doctor. B. Cobb
Death Defies the Doctor. Denis Muir
Death Defies the Doctor. D. Munro
Death Delivers a Postcard. J. Philips
Death Demands an Audience. H. Reilly
Death Demon. J. K. Stafford
Death Department. B. Knox
Death Descending. Karen Campbell
Death Designs a Dress. E. M. Robinson
Death Devils. P. Edwards
Death Dines Out. T. Du Bois
Death Disciple. Robin Moore
Death Disposes. M. Dalman
Death Disturbs Mr. Jefferson. A. Hocking
Death Dives Deep. M. Avallone
Death Do Us Part. S. Noel
Death Do Us Part. Maude Parker
Death-Doctor. W. LeQueux
Death Doubles Death. G. Braddon
Death Down East. E. Blake
Death Down East. H. Norwood
Death Draws the Curtain. R. Watkins
Death Draws the Line. J. Iams
Death Dreams. W. Katz
Death Drive. M. E. Cooke
Death Drives the Lead Car. P. Moore
Death Drop. B. M. Gill
Death Drops Delilah. Q. Mario

Death Drops the Pilot. G. Bellairs
Death Drum. M. Peterson
Death Duel. A. Hocking
Death Dupes a Lady. R. Howes
Death Duty Swindle. W. J. Bayfield
Death Echo. J. Sandys
Death Elects a Mayor. J. G. Edwards
Death Enters the Lists. O. Mills
Death Enters the Ward. I. Bayne-Powell
Death Express. A. Eadie
Death Fear. W. Martyn
Death Files for Congress. T. O. Henle
Death Filled the Glass. C. Armstrong
Death Film. P. R. Shore
Death Finds a Foothold. G. Carr
Death Finds a Target. M. Fitt
Death Finds the Day. Alan White
Death Finds the Gloves. J. Sandys
Death Fire. L. Bennet-Thompson
Death Fires. R. Faust
Death Flash. J. G. Rowe
Death Flies High. J. R. Holden
Death Flies High. D. L. Teilhet
Death Flies Low. H. Park
Death Flies Low. N. Shepherd
Death Flies West. J. F. Bonnell
Death Flight. C. Miron
Death Flight. A. O. Pollard
Death Flight. D. Wiles
Death Follows a Formula. N. Gayle
Death Follows the Flower Show. E. G. Seibert
Death Follows the Trail. M. Poole
Death for a Doll. S. Morelli
Death for a Dropout. P. Bloxham
Death for a Dumb-Bell. B. Sarto
Death for a Holiday. D. P. Le Huray
Death for a Hussy. A. Holt
Death for a Hussy. A. L. Martin
Death for a Playmate. J. Ball
Death for a Theatre Filly. A. Williamson
Death for a Traitor. N. MacKenzie
Death for Auld Lang Syne. J. Sharkey
Death for Dear Clara. Q. Patrick
Death for Deborah. V. Heley
Death for Dollars. N. Thurley
Death for Hire. J. Nazel
Death for Love. A. F. Garner
Death for Madame. R. T. Campbell
Death for Mr. Big. J. Gonzales
Death for My Beloved. D. M. Disney
Death for My Neighbor. Muriel Bradley
Death for Safe Custody. B. Francis
Death for Safety. E. Dennis
Death for Sale. H. Kane
Death for Sale. N. Morland
Death for Short. J. Gale
Death for the Lady. S. Vanderveer
Death for the Surgeon. G. Eldredge
Death for Two. C. Ashton
Death Forms Threes. C. Robbins
Death Framed in Silver. Alice Campbell
Death Freak. J. Luckless
Death from a Top Hat. C. Rawson
Death from Below. G. Ashe
Death from Disclosure. Ian Stuart
Death from Nowhere. S. Towne
Death from the Air. P. Conde
Death Fugue. P. McGuire
Death Fungus. W. Allen
Death Fuse. M. Russell
Death Gamble. J. A. Dunn
Death Gamble. G. R. Sims
Death Game. A. O. Pollard
Death Gang. D. Dell
Death Gang. A. Skene
Death Gets a Head. A. R. McKenzie
Death Gets a Place. J. Brown
Death Gets an A. R. H. R. Smithies
Death Giver. M. Grant
Death Glides In. A. L. Elsworthy
Death Glow. R. Wallace
Death Goes Ashore. A. Glanville
Death Goes by Bus. L. Cargill
Death Goes Caving. G. Usher
Death Goes Fishing. Edward Lee
Death Goes Hunting. C. Massie
Death Goes Native. Max Long
Death Goes on Skis. N. Spain
Death Goes Skiing. N. Schier
Death Goes to a Party. M. Jaffe
Death Goes to a Reunion. K. M. Knight
Death Goes to Brussels. Rosa Lambert
Death Goes to School. Q. Patrick
Death Goes to Sea. J. Robertson
Death Goes to the Fair. J. Courage
Death Goes Touring. F. W. Gumley
Death Goes Window Shopping. F. A. Symonds
Death Gong. S. Jepson
Death Grasp. T. P. Prest
Death Greets a Guest. C. Ashton
Death Grip. Al Conroy
Death Hall. M. Reisner
Death Has a Double. Frank King
Death Has a Past. A. Boutell
Death Has a Shadow. M. Procter
Death Has a Small Voice. F. Lockridge
Death Has a Thousand Doors. W. Cooper
Death Has a Thousand Doors. M. Marlette
Death Has a Thousand Entrances. P. Helm
Death Has a Will. A. R. Long

Title Index

Death Has Deep Roots. M. Gilbert
Death Has Four Hands. Hilda Lawrence
Death Has Green Eyes! Nicholas Carter
Death Has Green Fingers. Lionel Black
Death Has Many Doors. F. Brown
Death Has Many Doors. S. MacKenzie
Death Has My Number. J. Laffin
Death Has No Tongue. J. Cowdroy
Death Has No Weight. B. Luigi
Death Has Scarlet Candles. D. Lockwood
Death Has Seven Faces. H. Austin
Death Has Ten Thousand Doors. B. Chetwynd
Death Has Three Lives. B. Halliday
Death Has Two Doors. V. Bell
Death Has Two Faces. N. Herries
Death Has Two Faces. E. Radford
Death Has Two Hands. J. Lawrence
Death Haunts the Charnel Estate. Jackson Evans
Death Haunts the Dark Lane. A. B. Cunningham
Death Haunts the Lounge. A. C. Trevor
Death Haunts the Repertory. T. A. Plummer
Death Heads North. J. B. Hendryx
Death Her Destination. W. Jardine
Death Hides a Mask. M. E. Corne
Death Hitches a Ride. M. L. Weiss
Death Hits the Jackpot. L. J. Tiger
Death Holds His Court. N. MacKenzie
Death House. C. Brisbane
Death House. Roland Daniel
Death House Doll. D. Keene
Death Hunch. R. Humphreys
Death Hunt. P. McCurtin
Death in a Bowl. R. Whitfield
Death in a Chilly Corner. I. Oellrichs
Death in a Cold Climate. R. Barnard
Death in a Dark Pool. H. Van Rensburg
Death in a Deck-Chair. M. Kennedy
Death in a Domino. R. Pertwee
Death in a Downpour. K. McComb
Death in a Duffle Coat. M. Burton
Death in a Hurry. G. Ashe
Death in a Lighthouse. E. Ronns
Death in a Little Town. R. C. Woodthorpe
Death in a Million Living Rooms. P. McGerr
Death in a Mist. E. Salter
Death in a Pheasant's Eye. James Fraser
Death in a Quiet Place. E. G. Cousins
Death in a Salubrious Place. W. J. Burley
Death in a Sleeping City. J. Wainwright
Death in a Small World. L. Colburn
Death in a Sunny Place. R. Lockridge
Death in a Tokyo Family. D. Kenrick
Death in a Tranquil Place. Clare Dawson
Death in a White Tie. N. Marsh
Death in Aberration. J. C. Cooper
Death in Act IV. B. Francis
Death in Albert Park. L. Bruce
Death in Ambush. J. Bude
Death in Ambush. S. Gilruth
Death in Amsterdam. N. Freeling
Death in an Armchair. J. Street
Death in Ankara. Clement Wood
Death in April. A. Greeley
Death in Arcady. Stella Phillips
Death in Arms. R. Philmore
Death in B-Minor. J. Lilly
Death in Bermuda. Q. Patrick
Death in Botanist's Bay. E. Ferrars
Death in Budapest. V. Gielgud
Death in Captivity. M. Gilbert
Death in Clairvoyance. Josephine Bell
Death in Cold Print. J. Creasey
Death in Cold Storage. E. Healey
Death in Connecticut. D. Linzee
Death in Costume. A. McRoyd
Death in Covert. C. Willock
Death in Cranford. C. Stone
Death in "D" Division. J. G. Brandon
Death in Dark Glasses. G. Bellairs
Death in Darkness. C. Barry
Death in Darkness. George Douglas
Death in Darkness. Alan White
Death in Deakins Wood. R. Petrie
Death in Deep Green. M. Hastings
Death in Deep Shadows. W. Toole
Death in Desolation. G. Bellairs
Death in Despair. G. Bellairs
Death in Diamonds. G. Ashe
Death in Diamonds. K. Giles
Death in Diamonds. H. R. Taunton
Death in Disguise. M. Tracy
Death in Dockland. D. Reid
Death in Don Mills. H. Garner
Death in Downing Street. J. G. Brandon
Death in Dream Time. S. H. Courtier
Death in Duplicate. J. G. Brandon
Death in Duplicate. George Douglas
Death in Duplicate. Alan White
Death in Dwelly Lane. F. V. Morley
Death in Ecstasy. N. Marsh
Death in Error. F. Usher
Death in Fancy Dress. J. J. Farjeon
Death in Fancy Dress. Anthony Gilbert
Death in Five Boxes. Carter Dickson
Death in Flames. G. Ashe
Death in Four Colors. B. Bird

Death in Four Letters. F. Beeding
Death in Gelly Wood. H. Keyworth
Death in Gentle Grove. F. K. Allan
Death in Goblin Waters. M. Peterson
Death in Grease Paint. S. Palmer
Death in Harbour. R. Goyne
Death in Harley Street. J. Rhode
Death in High Heels. C. Brand
Death in High Places. G. Ashe
Death in High Provence. G. Bellairs
Death in Jermyn Street. J. G. Brandon
Death in Lebanon. J. Tyndall
Death in Life. Nicholas Carter
Death in Lilac Time. F. Crane
Death in Lord Byron's Room. S. Wood
Death in Melting. Richard Grayson
Death in Mermaid Lane. Gret Lane
Death in Midwinter. J. B. Hilton
Death in Office. N. Longmate
Death in Office. J. Potter
Death in 1-2-3. R. D. Abrahams
Death in Our Wake. A. Glanville
Death in Passing. E. Lacy
Death in Perpetuity. D. G. Browne
Death in Piccadilly. Elliot Bailey
Death in Piccadilly. R. Garnett
Death in Ptarmigan Forest. C. Coram
Death in Pursuit. G. Leaderman
Death in Quiet Places. Elliot Bailey
Death in Real Life. R. Latimer
Death in Regatta Week. Charles Mason
Death in Reserve. T. Muir
Death in Reserve. H. Tracy
Death in Retirement. Josephine Bell
Death in Retreat. George Douglas
Death in Room Five. G. Bellairs
Death in Russian Habit. Sea Lion
Death in Sanctuary. I. Baker
Death in Santiago. G. DeVilliers
Death in Seven Hours. Stratford Davis
Death in Seven Volumes. D. G. Browne
Death in Shallow Water. M. Burton
Death in Sheep's Clothing. Stella Phillips
Death in Silhouette. J. Slate
Death in Silver. K. Robeson
Death in Slow Motion. K. Robeson
Death in Small Doses. Martin Thomas
Death in Soundings. T. Muir
Death in Stanley Street. W. J. Burley
Death in Still Water. A. Handley
Death in Sunlight. F. Lester
Death in Ten Point Bold. E. Bruton
Death in the A.R.P. G. Davison
Death in the Air. A. Christie
Death in the Back Seat. D. C. Disney
Death in the Bag. G. Usher
Death in the Bathroom. B. Thomson
Death in the Blackout. Anthony Gilbert
Death in the Blue Hour. F. Crane
Death in the Blue Lake. B. Borge
Death-in-the-Box. M. Magill
Death in the Canongate. P. Piper
Death in the Cards. A. T. Smith
Death in the Caribbean. J. R. L. Anderson
Death in the Castle. P. S. Buck
Death in the Cemetery. A. L. Matthison
Death in the Chalkpit. E. L. Punshon
Death in the Channel. J. R. L. Anderson
Death in the Church. K. Giles
Death in the City. J. R. L. Anderson
Death in the Clouds. A. Christie
Death in the Colony. A. Sax
Death in the Copse. A. G. E. Cromwell
Death in the Coverts. R. Jeffries
Death in the Crease. Richard Curtis
Death in the Cup. M. Dalton
Death in the Dark. Stacey Bishop
Death in the Dark. M. Dalton
Death in the Dark. C. M. Wills
Death in the Deep South. Ward Greene
Death in the Desert. J. R. L. Anderson
Death in the Desert. Genevieve St. John
Death in the Dimness. I. B. Colley
Death in the Ditch. J. G. Brandon
Death in the Diving Pool. C. Carnac
Death in the Dog Watches. Sea Lion
Death in the Doll's House. H. Lees
Death in the Dormitory. M. Brucker
Death in the Dovecote. Q. Patrick
Death in the Drawing Room. R. A. Rathbone
Death in the Dunes. P. H. Dobbins
Death in the Dusk. V. Markham
Death in the East. C. Franklin
Death in the Fearful Night. G. Bellairs
Death in the Fens. Colin Hope
Death in the Fifth Position. E. Box
Death in the Fog. M. G. Eberhart
Death in the Forest. N. Brand
Death in the Forest. M. Dalton
Death in the Forest. J. Potter
Death in the Glass. N. Gayle
Death in the Gorge. L. Thayer
Death in the Grand Manor. A. Morice
Death in the Greenhouse. J. R. L. Anderson
Death in the Hands of Talent. P. Yates
Death in the Headlines. R. Sharp
Death in the Hop Fields. J. Rhode
Death in the House. A. Berkeley

Death in the Inkwell. J. J. Farjeon
Death in the Inner Office. N. Wight
Death in the Jordan. J. Tyndall
Death in the Jungle. Gwyn Evans
Death in the Kettle. C. Wallace
Death in the Library. J. Greenfield
Death in the Library. P. Ketchum
Death in the Life. D. S. Davis
Death in the Life Department. C. P. Cleary
Death in the Limelight. A. Applin
Death in the Limelight. A. E. Martin
Death in the Loch. T. Muir
Death in the Mews. T. C. H. Jacobs
Death in the Mews. Eric Wood
Death in the Middle Watch. L. Bruce
Death in the Mind. R. Lockridge
Death in the Mist. R. C. Finney
Death in the Mist. F. Hurt
Death in the Morning. S. Radley
Death in the Night. P. Ketchum
Death in the Night Watches. G. Bellairs
Death in the North Sea. J. R. L. Anderson
Death in the Past. R. A. Moore
Death in the Past. B. Parvin
Death in the Picture. G. Braddon
Death in the Quadrangle. E. Dillon
Death in the Quarry. J. G. Brandon
Death in the Quarry. G. D. H. Cole
Death in the Ring. R. Gilmour
Death in the Rising Sun. J. Creasey
Death in the Round. A. Morice
Death in the Scillies. H. C. Davis
Death in the Senate. Diplomat
Death in the Shingle. H. Desmond
Death in the Signal Box. H. Keyworth
Death in the Silver Ring. J. Brown
Death in the Smog. N. MacKenzie
Death in the Snow. R. M. Stern
Death in the Spanish Sun. N. Deane
Death in the Spring. M. J. Law
Death in the Stalls. J. R. Wilmot
Death in the State House. T. Knox
Death in the Stocks. G. Heyer
Death in the Straw. G. Usher
Death in the Sun. G. D. H. Cole
Death in the Sun. S. Coulter
Death in the Sun. C. Saxby
Death in the Sunday Supplement. Sam Merwin
Death in the Surgery. R. Trevor
Death in the Tankard. G. D. H. Cole
Death in the Thames. J. R. L. Anderson
Death in the Theatre. D. Dayle
Death in the Theatre. J. R. Wilmot
Death in the Thicket. W. Loder
Death in the 13th Dose. V. Loder
Death in the Top Twenty. W. McNeilly
Death in the Tote Box. W. D. Maydwell
Death in the Trees. G. Ashe
Death in the Tunnel. M. Burton
Death in the Village. J. Garden
Death in the Virgins. R. H. Barbour
Death in the Wasteland. G. Bellairs
Death in the Wet. G. Mitchell
Death in the Wheelbarrow. W. Gore
Death in the Willows. R. Forrest
Death in the Wind. J. A. Jordan
Death in the Wind. E. Lanham
Death in the Wind. R. Massey
Death in the Wood. C. Rushton
Death in the Wrong Bed. S. Farrar
Death in the Wrong Room. Anthony Gilbert
Death in the Yew Alley. M. Ervin
Death in Three Masks. B. Healey
Death in Tiger Valley. Reginald Campbell
Death in Triplicate. E. C. R. Lorac
Death in View. T. Macrae
Death in Waiting. J. Bland
Death in Wellington Road. J. Rhode
Death in White Pajamas. J. Bude
Death in Willow Pattern. W. J. Burley
Death in Zanzibar. M. M. Kaye
Death Inheritance. P. Swan
Death Intervened. A. O. Pollard
Death Invades the Meeting. J. Rhode
Death Is a Black Camel. H. B. Kaye
Death Is a Cold, Keen Edge. E. Basinsky
Death Is a Dame. D. Steel
Death Is a Dark Man. D. Highland
Death Is a Dirty Trick. J. Philips
Death Is a Drag. D. Hoyt
Death Is a Drum...Beating Forever. J. Wyllie
Death Is a Friend. D. MacKenzie
Death Is a Gold Coin. R. Fenisong
Death Is a Habit. O. Kensch
Death Is a Liar. Marc Miller
Death Is a Lizard. John Williams
Death Is a Lovely Dame. M. Blood
Death Is a Lovely Lady. R. Fenisong
Death Is a Lover. N. Tyre
Death Is a Red Rose. D. Eden
Death Is a Restless Sleeper. E. B. Quinn
Death Is a Round Black Ball. M. Roscoe
Death Is a Silent Room. Jay Bennett
Death Is a Stowaway. W. Price
Death Is a Swinger. Jason Morgan
Death Is a Tiger. M. Mundy
Death Is a Tory. K. Patrick
Death Is a Z. A. Yarrow

Death Is Academic. A. MacKay
Death Is an Artist. S. Gardiner
Death Is an Early Riser. J. M. Bigelow
Death Is Buttercups. G. M. Wilson
Death Is Confidential. L. Lariar
Death Is for Ever. L. Marshall
Death Is for Losers. W. F. Nolan
Death Is Forever. M. O'Callaghan
Death Is in the Garden. M. Marlette
Death Is Late to Lunch. T. Du Bois
Death Is Like That. J. Spain
Death Is Merciful. J. Sandys
Death Is My Bridegroom. D. M. Devine
Death Is My Comrade. S. Marlowe
Death Is My Dancing Partner. C. Woolrich
Death Is My Lover. S. Brock
Death Is My Name. S. Wells
Death Is My Shadow. J. Corbett
Death Is My Shadow. E. Ronns
Death Is No Lady. M. E. Corne
Death Is No Sportsman. C. Hare
Death Is Not a Passing Grade. V. B. Miller
Death Is Our Playmate. P. Turnbull
Death Is Skin Deep. C. Percy
Death Is So Final. Alex Fraser
Death Is So Kind. L. Redmond
Death Is So Lonely. L. Amino
Death Is the End. G. W. Cooke
Death Is the Host. L. Lariar
Death Is the Last Lover. H. Kane
Death Is the Pay-Off. Simon Burke
Death Is Thy Neighbor. L. D. Smith
Death Is Too Good for You. M. Alexander
Death Is Waiting. F. Usher
Death Is Where You Meet It. Max James
Death Joins the Party. R. Boyd
Death Joins the Party. J. V. Turner
Death Joins the Woman's Club. C. Saxby
Death Keeps a Secret. C. B. Kelland
Death Kicks a Pebble. A. Tack
Death Kiss. M. St. Dennis
Death Kit. S. Sontag
Death Knell. C. T. Cline
Death Knell. B. Kendrick
Death Knocks Three Times. Anthony Gilbert
Death Knows No Calendar. J. Bude
Death Laughs Aloft. P. Conde
Death Leaves a Diary. H. Carmichael
Death Leaves No Card. M. Burton
Death Leaves Us Naked. L. Hollingsworth
Death Let Loose. H. Desmond
Death Letter. T. A. Plummer
Death Lies Deep. W. Guinn
Death Lies in Waiting. B. Williams
Death Lifts the Latch. Anthony Gilbert
Death Light. Richard Grant
Death Lights a Candle. P. A. Taylor
Death Like Thunder. H. Holman
Death Likes It Hot. E. Box
Death List. R. Casler
Death List. A. C. Clark
Death List. R. Hawkes
Death List. R. McKew
Death Listened In. K. Sproul
Death Lives in the Mansion. D. Locke
Death Lives Next Door. Gwendoline Butler
Death Looks Down. A. R. Long
Death Looks In. R. Sale
Death Looks On. P. Manton
Death Loop. P. Conde
Death Lottery. E. Hyams
Death Loves a Shining Mark. A. Hocking
Death Machine. K. Robeson
Death Maker. A. J. Small
Death Makers. J. Milton
Death Makers Conspiracy. Ralph Hayes
Death Makes a Claim. Hank Hobson
Death Makes a Date. J. Corbett
Death Makes a Date. F. W. Irwin
Death Makes a Deal. Maude Parker
Death Makes a Prophet. J. Bude
Death Makes the Scene. Stella Phillips
Death Man. D. Kirby
Death Man. B. Swift
Death Mask. A. Applin
Death-Mask. R. Parkes
Death Mask. H. Pentecost
Death Mask. Ellis Peters
Death-Mask of War. G. Marlowe
Death-Masque. K. Hayles
Death Master. B. Appel
Death May Surprise Us. T. Willis
Death Mechanic. A. D. Hutter
Death Meets 400 Rabbits. A. M. Stein
Death Meets the Coroner. J. K. Ryland
Death Meets the Deadline. D. R. George
Death Meets the King's Messenger. G. Collins
Death Merchant. J. Rosenberger
Death Merchants. J. Readus
Death Message: Oil 74-2. Nick Carter
Death Miser. J. Creasey
Death Mission: Havana. Nick Carter
Death Must Have Laughed. J. V. Turner
Death Must Wait. D. Kingery
Death, My Darling Daughters. J. Stagge
Death, My Lover. P. Allardyce
Death-Mystery. N. Buntline
Death Near the River. Monte Cooper
Death Needs No Alibi. L. Gribble

Death Never Forgets. Robin Moore
Death Never Forgets. Garnett Weston
Death Never Weeps. S. Ryan
Death Notes. R. Rendell
Death Occurred. N. Hoult
Death of a Banker. A. Wynne
Death of a Barrow Boy. Charles Harris
Death of a Beauty Queen. E. R. Punshon
Death of a Best Seller. C. M. Wills
Death of a Big Man. J. Wainwright
Death of a Big Shot. George Douglas
Death of a Big Shot. C. Knight
Death of a Blue-Eyed Soul Brother. B. B. Johnson
Death of a Bogey. D. Warner
Death of a Bookseller. B. J. Farmer
Death of a Borgia. C. J. Stevermer
Death of a Bovver Boy. L. Bruce
Death of a Bride. G. D. H. Cole
Death of a Bridegroom. J. Rhode
Death of a Bridge Expert. C. C. Nicolet
Death of a Bullionaire. A. B. Cunningham
Death of a Busybody. G. Bellairs
Death of a Busybody. Dell Shannon
Death of a Cad. J. Bude
Death of a Call Girl. L. Trevor
Death of a Canary. Neill Graham
Death of a Celebrity. H. Footner
Death of a Cheat. J. M. Eshleman
Death of a Citizen. D. Hamilton
Death of a City. L. White
Death of a Cloven Hoof. Frank King
Death of a Clown. E. Backhouse
Death of a Commuter. L. Bruce
Death of a Con Man. Josephine Bell
Death of a Convict. T. Herd
Death of a Corinthian. E. Lanham
Death of a Courier. R. Hawkes
Death of a Curate. K. H. Ashley
Death of a Dandie Dinmont. M. Duke
Death of a Dastard. H. Kane
Death of a Decent Fellow. N. A. Temple-Ellis
Death of a Delegate. G. P. Cronin
Death of a Delft Blue. G. Mitchell
Death of a Designer. N. Brand
Death of a Detective. L. W. Brent
Death of a Diplomat. P. Oldfeld
Death of a Dissenter. L. Lamb
Death of a Doctor. J. Armour
Death of a Dog. L. Eyles
Death of a Doll. Carter Brown
Death of a Doll. Hilda Lawrence
Death of a Doxy. R. Stout
Death of a Dreamer. D. Warner
Death of a Dude. R. Stout
Death of a Dwarf. H. Kemp
Death of a Fashion Writer. M. Charlton
Death of a Fat God. H. R. F. Keating
Death of a Favorite Girl. M. Gilbert
Death of a Fellow Traveller. D. Ames
Death of a Fire-Raiser. George Davis
Death of a First Mate. C. Barry
Death of a Flack. H. Kane
Death of a Flower Child. R. Clarke
Death of a Fool. N. Marsh
Death of a Fox. J. Pohlman
Death of a Friend. M. Masterman
Death of a Frightened Editor. E. Radford
Death of a Frightened Traveller. F. Lester
Death of a Gay Dog. A. Morice
Death of a Gentleman. J. Courage
Death of a "Gentleman." E. Radford
Death of a Ghost. M. Allingham
Death of a Goblin. G. Hythe
Death of a Godmother. J. Rhode
Death of a Golden Goose. H. Mace
Death of a Golfer. A. Wynne
Death of a Good Woman. J. F. Straker
Death of a Governor. A. Parsons
Death of a Greek. J. G. Brandon
Death of a Halo. Frank King
Death of a Harbourmaster. G. Simenon
Death of a Harlot. B. Newman
Death of a Hawker. J. Van De Wetering
Death of a Heavenly Twin. A. Morice
Death of a Hippie. Michael Brett
Death of a Hittite. S. Angus
Death of a Holy Murderer. M. Duke
Death of a Hooker. H. Kane
Death of a Jazz King. C. M. Walker
Death of a King. A. Wynne
Death of a Ladies' Man. Lee Roberts
Death of a Lady Killer. C. Carnac
Death of a Lake. A. W. Upfield
Death of a Lawyer. E. Jones-Evans
Death of a Libertine. C. Wallace
Death of a Literary Widow. R. Barnard
Death of a Love. R. Hobart
Death of a Low-Handicap Man. B. Ball
Death of a Lucky Man. Yu. Rath
Death of a Marine. C. Leader
Death of a Merchant of Death. N. S. Bortner
Death of a Mermaid. G. Brandon
Death of a Millionaire. G. D. H. Cole
Death of a Millionaire. R. Dana
Death of a Mind. J. Ritson
Death of a Moral Person. A. Roudybush
Death of a Mystery Writer. R. Barnard
Death of a Nude. D. Warner

Death of a Nurse. R. Masten
Death of a Nurse. L. H. Whitten
Death of a Nymph. E. Piper
Death of a Painted Lady. B. Cleeve
Death of a Pale Man. F. Lester
Death of a Patriot. R. E. Harrington
Death of a Peculiar Rabbit. E. Radford
Death of a Peeping Tom. B. Cobb
Death of a Peer. N. Marsh
Death of a Philanderer. L. Meynell
Death of a Player. L. O'Donnell
Death of a Poison-Tongue. Josephine Bell
Death of a Politician. R. Condon
Death of a Pornographer. A. Lejeune
Death of a Portrait. E. Mack
Death of a Postman. J. Creasey
Death of a Prima Donna. L. Colburn
Death of a Punk. J. Browner
Death of a Puppet. G. Hythe
Death of a Puppeteer. W. G. Beyer
Death of a Pusher. R. Deming
Death of a Queen. C. S. Sprigg
Death of a Racehorse. J. Creasey
Death of a Revolutionist. J. Dall
Death of a Saboteur. H. Footner
Death of a Sadist. R. R. Ryan
Death of a Sardine. Joan Fleming
Death of a Scapegoat. G. Hythe
Death of a Scavenger. K. Spore
Death of a Scoundrel. T. C. H. Jacobs
Death of a Shadow. G. Bellairs
Death of a Shadow. A. Wynne
Death of a Shrew. C. Barling
Death of a Shrew. A. Kennington
Death of a Sinner. R. Arnold
Death of a Sinner. R. Quest
Death of a Sinner. P. Warwick
Death of a Skin-Diver. S. Jay
Death of a Snout. D. Warner
Death of a Socialite. J. G. Brandon
Death of a Source. R. A. Moore
Death of a Spinster. M. Dalton
Death of a Spinster. F. Duncombe
Death of a Spinster. Dorothy Johnson
Death of a Spy. S. Horler
Death of a Star. G. D. H. Cole
Death of a Stranger. M. Halliday
Death of a Stranger. D. Noel
Death of a Stray Cat. J. Potts
Death of a Supertanker. A. Trew
Death of a Swagman. A. W. Upfield
Death of a Tall Man. F. Lockridge
Death of a Tax Inspector. S. Chance
Death of a Thin-Skinned Animal. P. Alexander
Death of a Tin God. G. Bellairs
Death of a Tom. D. Warner
Death of a Train. F. W. Crofts
Death of a Tyrant. E. R. Punshon
Death of a Viewer. H. Adams
Death of a Village. J. Courage
Death of a Wedding Guest. A. Morice
Death of a Weirdy. G. Carr
Death of a White Witch. I. Oellrichs
Death of a Wicked Servant. B. Cleeve
Death of a Wide-Boy. W. R. Hutton
Death of a Wife. C. Wallace
Death of a Wild Bird. J. N. Chance
Death of a Witch. H. Hawton
Death of a World. J. J. Farjeon
Death of a Worldy Woman. A. B. Cunningham
Death of an Ad Man. A. Eichler
Death of an Admiral. G. Hackforth-Jones
Death of an Airman. C. S. Sprigg
Death of an Alderman. J. B. Hilton
Death of an Ambassador. M. Coles
Death of an Ancient Saxon. E. Radford
Death of an Angel. F. Lockridge
Death of an Angel. M. P. Rea
Death of an Angel. C. Richards
Death of an Angel. P. G. Winslow
Death of an Artist. A. Eichler
Death of an Artist. J. Rhode
Death of an Aryan. E. Huxley
Death of an Assassin. J. Creasey
Death of an Aunt. T. Harknett
Death of an Author. E. C. R. Lorac
Death of an Author. J. Rhode
Death of an Editor. V. Loder
Death of an Eloquent Man. C. M. Russell
Death of an Expert Witness. P. D. James
Death of an Expert Witness. P. H. Powell
Death of an Extra. V. Gielgud
Death of an Idol. W. A. Harbinson
Death of an Informer. W. Perry
Death of an Innocent. J. N. Chance
Death of an Intruder. N. Tyre
Death of an Oddfellow. Eric Wood
Death of an Old Girl. E. Lemarchand
Death of an Old Goat. R. Barnard
Death of an Old Sinner. D. S. Davis
Death of an Uncle. P. Hambledon
Death of an Undertaker. D. Lynn
Death of Anton. A. Melville
Death of Captain Shand. E. Spencer
Death of Cecelia. H. Hartley
Death of Cold. L. Bruce
Death of Cosmo Revere. C. Bush
Death of Daddy-O. David Alexander
Death of Dr. Whitelaw. A. Wilson
Death of Duboyne. W. J. Bayfield

Title Index

Death of Four. A. Skene
Death of Gold. Mervyn Lewis
Death of Henrietta. L. M. Armistead
Death of His Uncle. C. H. B. Kitchin
Death of Humpty-Dumpty. David Alexander
Death of Innocence. Z. Popkin
Death of Jason Darby. G. E. Taylor
Death of Jezebel. C. Brand
Death of John Tait. A. Fielding
Death of Kings. J. L. Johnson
Death of Kyralessa. C. V. Gheorghiu
Death of Laura. H. C. Davis
Death of Laurence Vining. Alan Thomas
Death of Lord Haw Haw. B. Rutledge
Death of Maurice. B. Pain
Death of Me Yet. W. Masterson
Death of Miss Cunningham. J. Cousseau
Death of Miss X. M. McMullen
Death of Mr. Balishberger. B. Hrabel
Death of Mr. Dodsley. J. Ferguson
Death of Mr. Gantley. M. Burton
Death of Mr. Lomas. F. Vivian
Death of Mrs. Preedy. L. Jackson
Death of Monsieur Gallet. G. Simenon
Death of My Aunt. C. H. B. Kitchin
Death of Nevill Norway. J. Rowland
Death of Our Dear One. M. Erskine
Death of the Claimant. A. R. Martin
Death of the Deputy. F. Didelot
Death of the Detective. Mark Smith
Death of the Doctor's Wife. Whyte Hall
Death of the Dragon. F. Drake
Death of the Falcon. Nick Carter
Death of the Fuhrer. R. Puccetti
Death of the Good Samaritan. O. D. Johnston
Death of the Home Secretary. Alan Thomas
Death of the King's Canary. Dylan Thomas
Death of the Party. R. Fenisong
Death of the Red King. P. Bennetts
Death of the Vampire Baroness. V. Van Der Elst
Death of Two Brothers. M. Burton
Death of Virginia. O. Rees
Death off the Fairway. H. Adams
Death on a Back Bench. F. Hobson
Death on a Broomstick. G. M. Wilson
Death on a Downbeat. Carter Brown
Death on a Dude Ranch. F. Bonnamy
Death on a Ferris Wheel. A. L. Martin
Death on a High Note. D. Reid
Death on a Pale Horse. Bradshaw Jones
Death on a Quiet Beach. S. Challis
Death on a Quiet Day. M. Innes
Death on a Smokeboat. Ross Graham
Death on a Summer Day. E. Booth
Death on a Sunday Morning. J. F. Straker
Death on a Warm Wind. D. Warner
Death on a Wet Sunday. P. Capon
Death on Account. M. Yorke
Death on All Hallows. A. C. MacLean
Death on Allhallowe'en. L. Bruce
Death on an Island. G. G. Roper
Death on Bodmin Moor. V. Gunn
Death on "Calamity". K. Wade
Death on Capitol Hill. B. Whitehurst
Death on Danger Hill. T. A. Plummer
Death on Dartmoor. J. Rowland
Death on Delivery. E. Allen
Death on Delivery. J. G. Brandon
Death on Delivery. R. Gore-Browne
Death on Delivery. F. W. Gumley
Death on Demand. G. Ashe
Death on Deposit. F. Grierson
Death on Display. R. Simons
Death on Doomsday. E. Lemarchand
Death on Herons' Mere. M. Fitt
Death on Ice. J. B. O'Sullivan
Death on Jerusalem Road. D. Angus
Death on Location. W. R. Cox
Death on May Morning. M. Dalman
Death on Milestone Buttress. G. Carr
Death on My Left. P. MacDonald
Death on My Shoulder. C. Franklin
Death on Paper. J. Bude
Death on Priority! P. Yorke
Death on Raven's Scar. Albert Harding
Death on Remand. M. Underwood
Death on Romney Marsh. L. Bruce
Death on Scurvy Street. B. A. Williams
Death on Shivering Sand. V. Gunn
Death on Sunday. J. Rhode
Death on the Agenda. M. Bidwell
Death on the Agenda. P. Moyes
Death on the Agenda. T. Muir
Death on the Air. Herman Landon
Death on the Aisle. F. Lockridge
Death on the Atoll. B. Francis
Death on the Barrier Reef. E. Antill
Death on the Beach. P. Broad
Death on the Black Sands. L. Bruce
Death on the Board. J. Rhode
Death on the Boat Train. J. Rhode
Death on the Border. R. P. Holden
Death on the Borough Council. Josephine Bell
Death on the Bridge. R. Howes
Death on the Broads. E. Radford
Death on the Campus. A. Simmons
Death on the Centre Court. G. Goodchild
Death on the Champs-Elysees. F. Didelot
Death on the Cherwell. M. D. Hay

Death on the Circuit. J. Ellery
Death on the Cliff. T. Cobb
Death on the Clock. G. Knevels
Death on the Cuff. M. G. MacKnutt
Death on the Deep. H. M. Stephenson
Death on the Diamond. C. Fitzsimmons
Death on the Door Mat. M. V. Heberden
Death on the Doorstep. George Douglas
Death on the Dordogne. Jean Fraser
Death on the Double. H. Kane
Death on the Down Beat. S. Farr
Death on the Downbeat. Carter Brown
Death on the Downs. A. Marsden
Death on the Files. M. Penrose
Death on the First Tee. H. Adams
Death on the Grass. L. O'Donnell
Death on the High C's. R. Barnard
Death on the Highway. C. Robbins
Death on the Hit Parade. B. Gray
Death on the Hour. R. Lockridge
Death on the Last Train. G. Bellairs
Death on the Late Show. J. Michaels
Death on the Lawn. J. Rhode
Death on the Limited. R. Denbie
Death on the Line. C. M. Wills
Death on the Machar. A. MacVicar
Death on the Mall. A. Parsons
Death on the Moor. J. Pendower
Death on the Motorway. C. Coram
Death on the Mountain. D. Ogburn
Death on the Move. G. Ashe
Death on the Nile. A. Christie
Death on the Nose. H. D. Spatz
Death on the Outer Shoal. A. Fuller
Death on the Oxford Road. E. C. R. Lorac
Death on the Pack Road. H. Andover
Death on the Pampas. Clement Wood
Death on the Piazza. Jean Fraser
Death on the Reserve. Josephine Bell
Death on the River Kwai. G. De Villiers
Death on the Riviera. J. Bude
Death on the Roads. G. W. Wray
Death on the Rocks. J. R. L. Anderson
Death on the Rocks. J. B. West
Death on the Roof. B. Francis
Death on the Run. J. M. Hickman
Death on the Run. U. Rothwell
Death on the Set. V. MacClure
Death on the Sixth Day. H. Farrell
Death on the Slopes. N. Schier
Death on the Spike. D. Reid
Death on the Swim. Simon
Death on the Table. C. Rayner
Death on the Trooper. T. Muir
Death on the Waterfront. R. Archer
Death on the Way. F. W. Crofts
Death on Tiptoe. R. C. Ashby
Death on Tour. J. Courage
Death Opens the Ball. J. R. Benson
Death Out of Darkness. M. Halliday
Death Out of Focus. W. C. Gault
Death Out of Focus. C. Whitman
Death Out of Season. E. Litvinoff
Death Out of the Night. A. Wynne
Death Out of Thin Air. S. Towne
Death over Deep Water. S. Nash
Death over Her Shoulder. D. C. Meade
Death over Hollywood. C. Saxby
Death over London. M. Wheeler-Nicholson
Death over Newark. Alexander Williams
Death over San Silvestro. M. Teagle
Death over Sunday. J. F. Bonnell
Death Overseas. C. Barry
Death Pack. R. Sonin
Death Packs a Suitcase. B. E. Wallace
Death Paints a Picture. M. Burton
Death Paints a Portrait. W. Herber
Death Paints the Picture. L. Lariar
Death Parade. H. Desmond
Death Parade. A. O. Pollard
Death Pays a Dividend. J. Rhode
Death Pays All Debts. M. Sharman
Death Pays Dividends. J. W. Hornby
Death Pays the Piper. L. Gribble
Death Pays the Wages. E. McGirr
Death Penalty. A. Draper
Death Play. G. Verner
Death Plays a Duet. A. L. Davies
Death Plays Solitaire. R. L. Goldman
Death Plays the Gramophone. Marjorie Stafford
Death Plays the Last Card. H. H. Kirst
Death Plot. L. H. Brenning
Death Points a Finger. W. Levinrew
Death Pool. J. Corbett
Death Pool. V. Loder
Death Prowls the Cove. Gret Lane
Death Pulls a Doublecross. Lawrence Block
Death Pulls No Punches. B. Shannon
Death Race. S. Jason
Death Raid. Jon Hart
Death Rattle. A. B. Caldwell
Death Ray Dictator. J. Titterton
Death Ray Mystery. L. Rutland
Death Ray Terror. L. Derrick
Death Reel. Hamish MacInnes
Death Registers at the Eagle Arms. K. Frost
Death Rehearses. J. Varnam
Death Reign of the Vampire King. G. Stockbridge

Death Renders Account. J. M. Spender
Death Ride. M. Franklin
Death Ride. N. MacNeil
Death-Riders. C. Cofyn
Death Rides a Black Steed. L. Churchill
Death Rides a Camel. J. Wolf
Death Rides a Hobby. R. Howes
Death Rides a Painted Horse. R. P. Wilmot
Death Rides a Sorrel Horse. A. B. Cunningham
Death Rides Swiftly. N. Shepherd
Death Rides Tandem. W. McCully
Death Rides the Air Line. W. Sutherland
Death Rides the Deep. F. MacIsaac
Death Rides the Desert. D. Adair
Death Rides the Dragon. E. Thomas
Death Rides the Forest. Rupert Grayson
Death Rides the Rail. R. Sharp
Death Rides the Rails. J. Hopwood
Death Rides the Rails. C. Stoddard
Death Rides the Range. B. Netton
Death Rides the Speedway. D. Forde
Death Rides the Storm. K. Kendall
Death Rides the Train. B. Sarto
Death Ring. E. S. Drewry
Death Rings a Bell. C. Fitzsimmons
Death Rings No Bell. G. Braddon
Death Road. Donald Stuart
Death Rocks the Cradle. P. Martens
Death Rope Island. P. Goulden
Death Round the Corner. J. Creasey
Death Runs on Skis. H. Ritchie
Death Rust. E. P. Thorne
Death Sails in a High Wind. T. Du Bois
Death Sails the Bay. J. Feegel
Death Sails the Nile. F. B. McKinley
Death Says Good-Morning. J. O. Mayo
Death-Scented Flower. P. Hastings
Death Schuss. L. O'Donnell
Death Seance. F. W. Gumley
Death Seat. J. B. O'Sullivan
Death Seekers. Ross Richards
Death Sends a Cable. M. T. Yates
Death Sends for the Doctor. G. Bellairs
Death Sentence. B. Garfield
Death Sentence. A. D. Miller
Death Serves a Fault. C. Ryland
Death Serves an Ace. H. Wills
Death Set in Diamonds. G. Verner
Death Set to Music. M. Hebden
Death Sets the Pace. L. Cargill
Death Shall Overcome. E. Lathen
Death Ship. A. Blair
Death Ship. M. Edmonds
Death Ship. S. Hope
Death Ship. T. P. Prest
Death Sign. Gwyn Evans
Death Singer. J. A. Jordan
Death Sits In. C. Glick
Death Sits In. H. A. Keller
Death Sits on the Board. J. Rhode
Death Slams the Door. P. Cade
Death Sleeps in Kensington. J. Ward
Death Sleeps Lightly. R. C. Payes
Death Smiles. R. R. Phillips
Death Song. R. Hawkes
Death Speaking. Gwyn Evans
Death Specialists. G. Paulsen
Death Sped the Plough. G. Usher
Death Spins the Platter. E. Queen
Death Spins the Wheel. G. Bellairs
Death Spoke Sweetly. R. Garnett
Death Springs the Trap. E. K. Goldthwaite
Death Squad. B. Copper
Death Squad. H. Kastle
Death Squad. D. Pendleton
Death Squadron. A. O. Pollard
Death Stalk. T. Chastain
Death Stalk. B. Langley
Death Stalk in Spain. Don Smith
Death Stalked the Fells. A. G. MacLeod
Death Stalks a Lady. Shelley Smith
Death Stalks a Marriage. R. W. Larson
Death Stalks in Kenya. A. Peverett
Death Stalks in Soho. J. G. Brandon
Death Stalks the Bride. Jean Marsh
Death Stalks the Cobbled Square. J. N. Chance
Death Stalks the Dykes. A. Lloyd
Death Stalks the Fleet. H. Cope
Death Stalks the Punjab. M. A. Casberg
Death Stalks the River. O. Williams
Death Stalks the Stadium. J. B. O'Sullivan
Death Stalks the Wakely Family. A. Derleth
Death Stalks the Ward. B. G. Williamson
Death Stalks the Waterway. S. Dewes
Death Stalks "The Wild Goose." R. Stahl
Death Stands By. J. Creasey
Death Stands Near. L. A. Knight
Death Stands Round the Corner. W. M. Duncan
Death Starts a Rumour. M. Fitt
Death Steals the Show. J. Bude
Death Stills the Brush. F. W. Gumley
Death Stone. D. Weir
Death Stops at the Old Stone Inn. S. Seifert
Death Stops the Bells. R. M. Baker

Death Stops the Frolic. G. Bellairs
Death Stops the Manuscript. R. M. Baker
Death Stops the Rehearsal. R. M. Baker
Death Stops the Show. L. S. Thompson
Death Strain. Nick Carter
Death Strikes at Dawn. H. Desmond
Death Strikes at Heron House. K. O'Neil
Death Strikes at Six Bells. G. Baxter
Death Strikes from the Rear. A. Marsden
Death Strikes Home. M. W. Glidden
Death Strikes in Darkness. L. Marshall
Death Strikes Out. G. Finley
Death Suspended. C. Whitman
Death Switch. H. Henn
Death Symbol. T. A. Plummer
Death Syndicate. J. Philips
Death Takes a Bow. F. Lockridge
Death Takes a Detour. M. Burton
Death Takes a Dive. G. W. Cooke
Death Takes a Dive. E. Heath
Death Takes a Dive. A. Tack
Death Takes a Flat. M. Burton
Death Takes a Gamble. H. R. Smithies
Death Takes a Hand. F. Griffin
Death Takes a Hand. T. A. Plummer
Death Takes a Holiday. N. MacKenzie
Death Takes a Partner. J. Rhode
Death Takes a Paying Guest. A. M. Stein
Death Takes a Redhead. Anthony Gilbert
Death Takes a Ride. R. C. Finney
Death Takes a Ride. H. E. Wheeler
Death Takes a Sabbatical. R. Bernard
Death Takes a Star. N. Morland
Death Takes a Teacher. G. Usher
Death Takes a Wife. Anthony Gilbert
Death Takes an Editor. N. Morland
Death Takes an Option. N. MacNeil
Death Takes Over. J. McFerran
Death Takes Revenge. James Preston
Death Takes Small Bites. G. H. Johnston
Death Takes the Bus. L. White
Death Takes the Joystick. P. Conde
Death Takes the Last Train. R. Bernard
Death Takes the Living. M. Burton
Death Takes the Low Road. P. Ruell
Death Takes the Stage. Gavin Holt
Death Takes the Stump. E. H. Duthoit
Death Takes the Wheel. E. Radford
Death Talks Out of Turn. H. Powell
Death Talks Shop. P. Haggard
Death Tears a Comic Strip. T. Du Bois
Death That Lurks Unseen. J. S. Fletcher
Death the Red Flower. O. Wynd
Death the Showman. John Fraser
Death the Sure Physician. J. Wakefield
Death Therapy. R. Sagar
Death Through the Looking Glass. R. Forrest
Death Through the Mill. L. Colburn
Death Throws a Party. Austin Stone
Death Throws No Shadow. L. Grex
Death Thumbs a Ride. J. Lilly
Death to a Left-Handed Woman. C. Joyce
Death to Comrade X. John Morgan
Death to Drumbeat. J. Lane
Death to My Beloved. R. Neely
Death to My Killer. J. York
Death to Slow Music. B. Nichols
Death to the Dancing Masters. R. Harper
Death to the Fifth Column. R. Newman
Death to the Killer. C. F. Caunter
Death to the Ladies. N. Morland
Death to the Landlords! Ellis Peters
Death to the Mafia. F. Scarpetta
Death to the Rescue. M. Kennedy
Death to the Spy. D. Dayle
Death to the Spy. R. Newman
Death to Windward. H. Brinton
Death Toll. W. E. Chambers
Death Tolls the Bell. M. Hervey
Death Tolls the Bell. P. McGuire
Death Tolls the Gong. J. G. Brandon
Death Took a Greek God. N. Forrest
Death Took a Publisher. N. Forrest
Death-Torch Terror. B. House
Death Tour. D. J. Michael
Death Tower. M. Grant
Death Trap. H. Carmichael
Death Trap. R. W. Cole
Death Trap. P. H. Dobbins
Death Trap. E. P. Green
Death Trap. J. D. MacDonald
Death Trap. J. Rosenberger
Death Trap. A. Skene
Death Traps. K. C. Strahan
Death Traps the Killer. Mary Dane
"Death Treads—." C. M. Wills
Death Treads Softly. G. Bellairs
Death Trick. J. F. Burke
Death Trust. Anonymous
Death Trust. A. L. Halstead
Death Turns Right. T. B. Dewey
Death Turns the Tables. J. D. Carr
Death Turns Traitor. W. S. Masterman
Death-Twist. J. Tiger
Death Under Contract. R. Wallace
Death Under Desolate. J. N. Chance
Death Under Gibraltar. B. Newman
Death Under Sail. C. P. Snow
Death Under Snowdon. G. Carr
Death Under the Moonflower. T. Downing
Death Under the Stars. V. Bell

Death Under the Table. P. Godfrey
Death Under Virgo. T. Muir
Death Unheralded. George Douglas
Death Valley. K. Netzen
Death Visits Downspring. M. Burton
Death Visits the Apple Hole. A. B. Cunningham
Death Visits the Cinema. F. W. Irwin
Death Visits the Circus. Jean Marsh
Death Visits the Parish. F. W. Gumley
Death Visits the Summer-House. Gret Lane
Death Waits in Tucson. D. Reid
Death Waits Outside. R. Verron
Death Walked In. B. Manktelow
Death Walked In. L. A. Olmsted
Death Walked in Berlin. M. M. Kaye
Death Walked in Cyprus. M. M. Kaye
Death Walked in Kashmir. M. M. Kaye
Death Walkers. G. Brandner
Death Walks by the River. V. Bell
Death Walks In. G. Chester
Death Walks in Eastrepps. F. Beeding
Death Walks in Marble Halls. L. G. Blochman
Death Walks in Scarlet. L. Cargill
Death Walks in Shadow. L. Thayer
Death Walks on Cat Feet. P. Haggard
Death Walks on Cat Feet. D. B. Olsen
Death Walks Softly. Hazel C. MacDonald
Death Walks Softly. N. Shepherd
Death Walks the Dry Tortugas. M. P. Rea
Death Walks the Post. V. Hanson
Death Walks the Woods. C. Hare
Death Warmed Over. Mary Collins
Death Was a Wedding Guest. A. S. Roche
Death Was Her Escort. E. Pawley
Death Was No Lady. S. Truss
Death Was the Echo. R. Dana
Death-Watch. J. D. Carr
Death Watch. D. Creed
Death Watch. J. Hawkins
Death Watch. D. Winston
Death Watch. R. Wilson
Death Watch Ladies. J. N. Chance
Death Wears a Carnation. B. E. Stevenson
Death Wears a Copper Necktie and other stories. H. Pentecost
Death Wears a Green Hat. W. Creed
Death Wears a Mask. Therese Benson
Death Wears a Mask. D. G. Browne
Death Wears a Mask. Anthony Gilbert
Death Wears a Purple Shirt. R. C. Woodthorpe
Death Wears a Red Hat. W. X. Kienzle
Death Wears a Scarab. A. R. Long
Death Wears a Silk Stocking. W. M. Duncan
Death Wears a Veil. K. M. Knight
Death Wears a White Shirt. T. Du Bois
Death Wears a White Gardenia. Z. Popkin
Death Wears Cat's Eyes. D. B. Olsen
Death Wears Pink Shoes. Robert James
Death Wears Red Shoes. Colin Robertson
Death Weed. L. Thayer
Death Went Hunting. George Douglas
Death When She Wakes. N. Morland
Death When You Want It. Desmond Martin
Death Whispers. J. B. Carr
Death Whispers Softly. P. Malloch
Death Whistle. R. Marsh
Death Will Find Me. H. Steers
Death Wish. R. Beck
Death Wish. V. Caspary
Death Wish. B. Garfield
Death Wish. E. S. Holding
Death-Wish Green. F. Crane
Death with a Difference. B. Cobb
Death with Blue Ribbon. L. Bruce
Death Within the Vault. L. Thayer
Death Without a Funeral. J. Ward
Death Without Question. T. Muir
Death Woman. J. N. Chance
Death Won a Prize. I. Montgomery
Death Won't Wait. Anthony Gilbert
Death Won't Wash. N. Longmate
Death Wore a Petticoat. H. Janson
Death Wore Fins. Dale Clark
Death Wore Gold Shoes. L. V. Stevens
Death Wore Roses. C. Saxby
Death Works to Rule. J. Bowyer
Death Writes a Message. T. Westgate
Death Writes an Ad. M. Holbrook
Deathbed of Roses. Deborah Scott
Deathbell. G. N. Smith
Deathbird Stories. H. Ellison
Deathblow Hill. P. A. Taylor
Deathbringer. M. Von Conta
Deathday Song. E. Zumwalt
Deathgame. J. Ramsay
Deathless and the Dead. A. Clarke
Deathmaster. W. M. Duncan
Death's Bright Angel. T. Warriner
Death's Bright Dart. V. C. Clinton-Baddeley
Death's Busy Crossroads. S. Mitchell
Death's Counterfeit. H. Clevely
Death's Dark Deceit. S. Clausse
Death's Dark Music. Marilyn Ross
Death's Dateless Night. T. Warriner
Death's Doorway. V. Gunn
Death's Duet. H. Carstairs
Death's Eye. L. Meynell

Death's Foot Forward. G. B. Mair
Death's Head. C. Black
Death's Head. Arthur Wise
Death's Head Conspiracy. Nick Carter
Death's Inheritance. E. Radford
Death's Juggler. C. J. Daly
Death's Long Shadow. J. Barbette
Death's Long Shadow. K. Wolffe
Death's Lovely Mask. J. Flagg
Death's Mannikens. M. Afford
Death's No Antidote. G. Osborne
Deaths of Lora Karen. R. McDougald
Death's Old Sweet Song. J. Stagge
Death's Pale Horse. J. Sherburne
Death's Second Self. J. F. Drabble
Death's Sweet Music. N. Morland
Death's Sweet Song. Clifton Adams
Death's Treasure Hunt. W. C. Harvey
Death's Visiting Card. J. C. Woodiwiss
Deathsport. William Hughes
Deathstar Voyage. Ian Wallace
Deathstone. E. L. Arch
Deathtrap. I. Levin
Deathwishers. T. Journet
Deathwork. J. McLendon
Deaves Affair. H. Footner
Debriefing. R. Littell
Debt. O. Hogstrand
Debt Discharged. E. Wallace
Debt of Hatred. G. Ohnet
Debt of Vengeance. Mrs. E. B. Collins
Debt to Dishonour. A. Furness
Decayed Gentlewoman. E. Ferrars
Deceit and Deadly Lies. F. Bandy
Deceivers. R. Goldhurst
Deceivers. J. D. MacDonald
Deceiver's Door. C. B. Booth
Deceiving Mirror. P. Traill
Deception. C. Dale
Deception. C. Kavanaugh
Deception of Death. V. Siller
Deception of Ursula. T. Cobb
Deception on Peregrine Island. L. A. Sunagel
Deceptions. H. L. Victor
Decimate Decision. A. Heal
Decision. E. Chodorov
Decision. W. A. Hackett
Decision. H. Kane
Decision at Dawn. A. Calin
Decision at Delphi. Helen MacInnes
Decision Before Dawn. G. Howe
Deck with Flowers. E. Cadell
Decker. W. Graeme-Holder
Decks Ran Red. A. L. Stone
Decoding of Edwin Drood. C. Forsyte
Decorated Corpse. R. Stratton
Decoration. K. Hewitt
Decoy. C. F. Adams
Decoy. J. D. Beresford
Decoy. Francis Dana
Decoy. A. Maling
Decoy. Michael Morgan
Decoy. E. Ronns
Decoy Babes. B. Sarto
Decoy Detective. Anonymous
Decoy for Murder. P. Saxon
Decoy in Diamonds. N. Gates
Decoy Murders. A. Douglas
Decoyed Across the Seas. R. Overton
Decoys. R. Hoyt
Deductions of Colonel Gore. L. Brock
Dee Dee. E. H. Robinson
Dee Goong An. R. Van Gulik
Deed Is Drawn. W. A. Barber
Deed of a Night. Warren Miller
Deed of Darkness. I. Stark
Deed of Innocence. J. Blackmore
Deed Without a Name. D. Bowers
Deed Without a Name. E. Phillpotts
Deeds Ill Done. A. Seifert
Deeds of Darkness. G. T. Morley
Deeds of Dr. Deadcert. Joan Fleming
Deep. M. Spillane
Deep Among the Dead Men. J. Blackburn
Deep and Crisp and Even. L. Payne
Deep As the Grave. O. Keystone
Deep Blue Cradle. Peter Chambers
Deep Blue Good-By. J. D. MacDonald
Deep Channels. E. L. Long
Deep Cold Green. Carter Brown
Deep Cover. B. Garfield
Deep Currents. A. Fielding
Deep, Dark and Dead. D. MacKenzie
Deep, Deep Freeze. W. Garner
Deep End. F. Brown
Deep End. O. Dudley
Deep End. J. Hayes
Deep Fall. B. Knox
Deep Flows the River. A. Wood
Deep Freeze. J. Bruce
Deep Furrows. R. W. Ritchie
Deep Green Death. B. Gaston
Deep in Dark Country. P. Drew
Deep Is My Desire. I. Gordon
Deep Is My Grave. J. Death
Deep Is the Blue. M. Ehrlich
Deep Is the Lake. M. Clare
Deep Is the Pit. H. V. Dixon
Deep Kill. D. Da Cruz
Deep-Lake Mystery. C. Wells
Deep Lay the Dead. F. C. Davis

Title Index

Deep Malice. D. G. Waring
Deep Moat Grange. S. R. Crockett
Deep Pocket. M. Kenyon
Deep Pool. J. Blackmore
Deep Sand. B. Munslow
Deep-Sea Tow. C. McManus
Deep Secret. R. Chapman
Deep Six. J. Cartwright
Deep Six. J. M. Flynn
Deep Valley. W. Anthony
Deep Water. P. Highsmith
Deep Waters. M. Leighton
Deepening Blue. S. M. Schley
Deeper Game. Nicholas Carter
Deeper Scar. S. Gluck
Deeper Stain. F. Hird
Deepsea Shootout. L. Derrick
Defame and Destroy. P. Chase
Defeat of a Detective. C. M. Wills
Defection of A. J. Lewinter. R. Littell
Defector. Evelyn Anthony
Defector. Nick Carter
Defector. C. Collingwood
Defector. R. Raphael
Defector. D. Seaman
Defector. P. Thomas
Defectors Are Dead Men. F. A. Smith
"Defend the Rock." P. Groom
Defenders. E. S. Aarons
Defending a Home. E. A. Young
Defense Does Not Rest. E. Sherry
Defense Rests. E. Pierson
Deferred Payment. J. Owen
Definite Object. J. Farnol
Defrauded Yeggman. H. S. Keeler
Defy the Tempest. S. Dannett
Degenerate. F. Whishaw
Degradation of Geoffrey Alwith. Morley Roberts
Deirdre. J. Nicholas
Deja-Vu. D. Saint-Alban
Delacott Mystery. C. Kingston
Delafield Affair. F. F. Kelly
Delaplaine. M. T. Walworth
Delaware Dick. M. Mizzen
Delay in Danger. S. Harvester
Delay of Doom. P. Capon
Delayed Action. R. W. Hatch
Delayed Action. N. Tranter
Delayed Harvest. Rona Randall
Delayed Payment. J. Rhode
Deldee. F. Warden
Deldee, the Ward of Warington. F. Warden
Delfina. S. Brackeen
Delgado Killings. R. Hawkes
Delia's Dilemma. A. Griffin
Delicate Ape. D. B. Hughes
Delicate Case of Murder. S. Gluck
Delicate Darling. J. Webb
Delicate Deceit. S. Hufford
Delicate Dust of Death. P. Audemars
Delicate Fiend. E. C. Vivian
Delicious Danger. H. Janson
Delilah. P. Trent
Delilah of Harlem. R. H. Savage
Delilah of Mayfair. A. Soutar
Delilah Was Deadly. Carter Brown
Delinquent! Morton Cooper
Delinquents. A. Bloomfield
Delinquents. P. Malloch
Deliver Us from Evil. H. Desmond
Deliver Us from Wolves. L. Holton
Deliver Us to Evil. J. L. Hensley
Delivery. G. Simenon
Delivery of Furies. V. Canning
Delorme in Deep Water. S. Lister
Delphi Calculus. M. Green
Delta Decision. Wilbur Smith
Delta Deputies. Carl Martin
Delta Factor. M. Spillane
Delta Flame. Marilyn Ross
Delta Knife. Kenneth O'Hara
Delta November. C. M. Filgate
Demagogue. C. Dawe
Demand for Justice. I. Stark
Demarest Inheritance. M. Carleton
DeMaury Papers. I. Holland
Demented. D. J. Young
Demented Empire. L. Derrick
Demi-Paradise Regained. S. Stone
Demise of a Louse. W. T. Ballard
Democrat Dies. P. Frankau
Demolished Man. A. Bester
Demon. J. McCulley
Demon. C. N. Williamson
Demon Again. E. M. Keate
Demon Barber of Broadway. Griff
Demon Cat. L. B. Clark
Demon Child. D. Dwyer
Demon Count. Anne Stuart
Demon Count's Daughter. Anne Stuart
Demon Detective. Anonymous
Demon Device. R. Saffron
Demon in My View. R. Rendell
Demon in the Blood. P. Marlowe
Demon Island. K. Robeson
Demon Jockey. B. Hemyng
Demon of Barnabas Collins. Marilyn Ross
Demon of Desire. W. J. Elliott
Demon of Hong Kong. R. S. L. Harding
Demon of Raven's Cliff. P. Zawadsky
Demon of Sicily. E. Montague

Demon of the Air. E. M. Keate
Demon of the Darkness. Dana Ross
Demon of the Opera. N. Schier
Demon Stirs. O. Cameron
Demon Tower. V. Coffman
Demon Within. Brook Hastings
Demoniacs. J. D. Carr
Demon's Eye. Nicholas Carter
Demon's Moon. Colin Robertson
Demons of Highpoint House. C. Cunningham
Demons of the Night. Nicholas Carter
Demonwood. Anne Stewart
Dempsey Diamonds. A. Arnot
Den of Savage Men. Bradshaw Jones
Denbigh Affair. A. Lowing
Dene Hollow. H. Wood
Dene of the Secret Service. J. S. Barlow
Dene of the Secret Service. G. Verner
Denis Dent. E. W. Hornung
Denmark Bus. S. McGurk
Denmede Mystery. W. Martyn
Dennisdale Tragedy. H. Andover
Dennison Hill. D. Winston
Denton's Army. R. D. Cross
Denver Lil. F. Foden
Denver's Double. George Griffith
Denzil Emeralds. P. Meredith
Denzil's Device. B. Delannoy
Depart This Life. E. Ferrars
Department K. H. Howard
Department of Dead Ends. Roy Vickers
Department of Death. J. Creasey
Department of Queer Complaints. Carter Dickson
Departure Deferred. W. H. Baker
Departure Delayed. W. Oursler
Departure of Mr. Gaudette. D. M. Disney
Deposit Vault Puzzle. Nicholas Carter
Depository Mystery. G. Chester
Depths. J. Creasey
Depths of Yesterday. D. Lyons
Deputy. W. C. Tuttle
Deputy Avenger. H. Richards
Deputy Avenger. R. Trevor
Deputy for Cain. Roy Vickers
Derelict. C. J. C. Hyne
Derelict. J. T. Shaw
Derelict House. A. Skene
Derelicts. W. M. Graydon
Derfflinger. B. Garland
Derision. C. Edwards
Derrick Devil. K. Robeson
Derring-Do. H. Craigie
Derry Down Death. A. Curry
Deruga Trial. R. Huch
Desborough Mystery. A. M. Diehl
Descent into the Dark. D. Ramsay
Desert Adventure. D. Spicer
Desert Bride. H. Nisbet
Desert Captive. E. Tokson
Desert Castle Mystery. C. H. Snow
Desert Convoy. M. Hastings
Desert Crime. Roland Daniel
Desert Desire. J. Chancellor
Desert Episode. G. Greenfield
Desert Flower. Rona Randall
Desert Flyer. J. Bolton
Desert Fury. H. Janson
Desert Intrigue. E. Ellison
Desert Intrigue. J. Stagg
Desert Lake Mystery. K. C. Strahan
Desert Moon Mystery. K. C. Strahan
Desert Night. W. E. Johns
Desert of Darkness. P. Wissmann
Desert of Doom. W. M. Graydon
Desert of Salt. K. R. Butler
Desert Shadows. B. Netton
Desert Squadron. J. R. Holden
Desert Stalker. M. Barry
Desert Trail. R. C. Armour
Desert Trail. D. Lenton
Desert Wooing. C. H. Bullivant
Deserted by the Devil. T. Irving-Jones
Deserted Night. T. B. Morris
Deserted Wife. E. Southworth
Deserter of the Foreign Legion. W. M. Graydon
Deserters. G. C. Jenks
Deserters Don't Come Back. R. Wilkes-Hunter
Design for an Accident. D. Egerton
Design for Blackmail. J. L. Morrissey
Design for Danger. E. Ellison
Design for Death. J. Day
Design for Death. K. Summers
Design for Destruction. Deryck Phillips
Design for Dupes. H. Janson
Design for Dying. A. Jeffers
Design for Dying. S. A. Krasney
Design for Dying. H. McCloy
Design for Dying. L. Trimble
Design for Murder. G. Batson
Design for Murder. F. Durbridge
Design for Murder. F. A. Kummer
Design for Murder. P. Wilde
Design for Murder, and five other stories. L. H. Fox
Design for November. R. E. Mitchell
Design for Treachery. C. C. Saunders
Design for Treason. G. Dickson
Design for Vengeance. Martin Thomas
Design in Diamonds. K. M. Knight

Design in Evil. R. King
Designs on Life. E. Ferrars
Desirable Alien. A. Kennington
Desirable Dictator. J. Fores
Desirable Woman. C. Dawe
Desire in the Dust. H. Whittington
Desire of the Eyes and other stories. G. Allen
Desire to Kill. Alice Campbell
Desired. Carter Brown
Desmond Dare. Old Sleuth
Desmond Drake Goes West. Sea Lion
Desmond Rourke, Irishman. J. Haslette
Desouza in Stardust. F. Olbrich
Desouza Pays the Price. F. Olbrich
Despair. V. Nabokoff-Sirin
Despair and Delight. R. Arnold
Despair's Last Journey. D. C. Murray
Despatch of a Dove. R. Petrie
Desperado. J. Hunter
Desperate Adversaries. J. Hoffenberg
Desperate Art. J. Rosenberg
Desperate Chance. Nicholas Carter
Desperate Chance. O. Harper
Desperate Chance. J. D. J. Kelley
Desperate Chance. Old Sleuth
Desperate Conspiracy. G. Boothby
Desperate Criminals. R. Longrigg
Desperate Cure. R. Fenisong
Desperate Deed. N. T. Oliver
Desperate Desmond's Dastardly Deed. L. Price
Desperate Dilemma. M. Danvers
Desperate Encounter. Cecile Rutherford
Desperate Expedient. C. N. Boyle
Desperate Gamble. H. Desmond
Desperate Game. J. K. Leys
Desperate Game. Old Spicer
Desperate Game. F. Warden
Desperate Games. P. Boulle
Desperate Heiress. Marilyn Ross
Desperate Holiday. F. Cowen
Desperate Hours. J. Hayes
Desperate Journey. H. Treece
Desperate Justice. Dan Morgan
Desperate Love. C. Dawe
Desperate Measures. D. Wheatley
Desperate Moment. M. Albrand
Desperate People. H. C. Davis
Desperate People. F. Durbridge
Desperate Remedy. B. Bolt
Desperate Rendezvous. R. Severn
Desperate Search. C. Eland
Desperate Search. A. Mayse
Desperate Steps. Mark Cross
Desperate Venture. J. Ritson
Desperate Voyage. E. F. Knight
Desperate Witch. Anthony Graham
Desperation. R. Rand
Despite the Evidence. P. Alding
Despoilers. E. Mitchell
Destination Dames. H. Janson
Destination Danger. W. C. MacDonald
Destination: Death. G. Bishop
Destination—Death. H. Desmond
Destination Dieppe. W. H. Baker
Destination: Terror. J. Paull
Destination Terror. W. E. D. Ross
Destination Unknown. A. Christie
Destination Unknown. R. Goyne
Destination Unknown. J. Hunter
Destination Unknown. R. Sale
Destinations. G. Simenon
Destiny. A. Askew
Destiny Is My Name. David Hume
Destiny Man. P. Van Greenaway
Destiny on Demand. M. Butcher
Destiny's Child. P. Morton
Destiny's Daughter. C. H. Bullivant
Destroy the U.S.A. W. F. Jenkins
Destroyer. C. Goodall
Destroyer. J. Lodwick
Destroyer. B. E. Stevenson
Destroyer. B. Swift
Destroyer and the Red-Haired Death. S. Horler
Destroying Angel. J. Creighton
Destroying Angel. N. Klein
Destroying Angel. L. J. Vance
Destroying Angel. E. Wallace
Destruction Committee. W. J. Coughlin
Destruction Man. Charles West
Destruction of Eva. K. Hurst
Destructive Vice. B. Bavin
Destructors. M. Franklin
Detail. W. McCarthy
Detail for the Dreamer. W. M. Duncan
Details of Jeremy Stratton. A. E. Lindop
Detection in a Topper. J. Oliver
Detection Unlimited. G. Heyer
Detections of Dr. Sam: Johnson. L. De La Torre
Detective. P. Ferris
Detective. R. Thorp
Detective. L. J. Vance
Detective Against Detective. D. J. MacKenzie
Detective Against Detective. M. Redwing
Detective and the Poisoner. S. Rathbone
Detective and the Somnambulist. A. Pinkerton
Detective Archie. Old Sleuth
Detective Ben. J. J. Farjeon

Detective Bob Bridger. R. M. Taylor
Detective Burr's Seven Clues. Anonymous
Detective Coulson. Jack Mann
Detective Crime Stories. L. Dexter
Detective Dale. Old Sleuth
Detective Duff Unravels It. H. J. O'Higgins
Detective Fleet of London. Anonymous
Detective for Vengeance. Anonymous
Detective Gay. Old Sleuth
Detective Gordon's Grip. Anonymous
Detective Hanley. Old Sleuth
Detective in Distress. B. Cobb
Detective in Italy. H. Forbes
Detective in Spite of Himself. H. Manning
Detective Inspector Chance. G. R. Sims
Detective Janaki. K. Sathianadhan
Detective Johnson of New Orleans. H. I. Hancock
Detective Kennedy. Old Sleuth
Detective Murdock, the Silent. Old Sleuth
Detective No. 1. F. Pratt
Detective Officer. Waters
Detective on the Prowl. L. W. Brent
Detective Payne. Old Sleuth
Detective Payne's Shadow. Old Sleuth
Detective Reynold's Hardest Case. G. Macias
Detective Sketches. Anonymous
Detective Stories. Anonymous
Detective Stories. W. Henderson
Detective Stories. Alexander Morton
Detective Story. S. Kingsley
Detective Sylvia Shale. S. Groom
Detective Thrash. Old Sleuth
Detective Trio. Old Sleuth
Detective Unawares. G. F. P. Lea
Detective Wore Silk Drawers. P. Lovesey
Detectives. N. Daniels
Detective's Album. W. W.
Detective's Clew. Old Hutch
Detective's Crime. F. Du Boisgobey
Detective's Crime. C. Morris
Detective's Daughter. L. L. Lynch
Detective's Daughter. Old Sleuth
Detective's Dilemma. F. Du Boisgobey
Detective's Dilemma. H. L. Phillips
Detective's Due. L. Egan
Detective's Enigma. Old Sleuth
Detective's Eye. F. Du Boisgobey
Detective's Holiday. C. Barry
Detective's Honeymoon. M. Danvers
Detectives in Gum Boots. R. East
Detectives, Ltd. F. S. Wees
Detective's Memoirs and other stories. E. M. L. Sturt
Detective's Note-Book. C. Martel
Detective's Notebook. Anonymous
Detectives of Europe and America. G. S. McWatters
Detective's Pretty Neighbor and other stories. Nicholas Carter
Detective's Secret. N. D. Urner
Detective's Tale. G. F. Newman
Detective's Theory. Nicholas Carter
Detective's Triumph. F. Du Boisgobey
Detective's Triumphs. D. Donovan
Detective's Victory. Anonymous
Dethroned Heiress. E. A. Dupuy
Detour. M. M. Goldsmith
Detour. H. Nielsen
Detour. W. Wilson
Detour at Night. G. Endore
Detour Through Devon. G. Endore
Detour to a Funeral. V. J. Santiago
Detour to Death. H. Nielsen
Detour to Denmark. J. Ware
Detour to Oblivion. F. C. Davis
Detours. O. R. Cohen
Detroit Deathwatch. D. Pendleton
Detroit Massacre. M. Barry
Deuce and All. G. Raffalovich
Deuces Wild. H. MacGrath
Deuces Wild. Dell Shannon
Devalino Caper. A. J. Russell
Devastation. Mrs. C. Kernahan
Devastators. D. Hamilton
Devereux Court Mystery. M. Burton
Deveril's Diamond. A. Sergeant
Deveron Hall. V. Johnston
Deviant Death. G. Moffat
Deviations of Diana. H. Mitchell
Deviator. A. York
Device. B. E. Wallace
Device for Murder. G. M. Snodgress
Devices of Darkness. J. M. English
Devil and Ben Franklin. T. Mathieson
Devil and Destiny. T. Du Bois
Devil and Mary Ann. C. Cookson
Devil and Miss Thrace, and other stories. M. Hervey
Devil and Mrs. Devine. Josephine Leslie
Devil and the C.I.D. E. C. R. Lorac
Devil and the Crusader. A. Askew
Devil and the Deep. S. Horler
Devil and the Deep. H. Janson
Devil and the Deep Blue Sea. E. Jordan
Devil and Webster Daniels. T. L. Smith
Devil and X.Y.Z. B. Browne
Devil at Castelnero. J. Schubert

Devil at Saxon Wall. G. Mitchell
Devil at the Door. M. Seuffert
Devil at Westease. V. Sackville-West
Devil at Your Elbow. D. M. Devine
Devil Behind Me. F. E. Smith
Devil Boy. W. D. Roberts
Devil Breathes But Once. C. Wallace
Devil Builds a Chapel. M. Marlette
Devil by the Sea. N. Bawden
Devil Child. P. J. Cooper
Devil Comes to Bolobyn. S. Horler
Devil Comes to Devon. J. Rowland
Devil Daddy. J. Blackburn
Devil Dances for Gold. Regina Ross
Devil, Devil. M. Avallone
Devil Doctor. S. Rohmer
Devil Drives. R. Ames
Devil Drives. J. N. Chance
Devil Drives. V. Markham
Devil Dunes. M. Sheppard
Devil Finds Work. M. Delving
Devil Fish. P. Groom
Devil for the Witch. E. Lacy
Devil Genghis. K. Robeson
Devil Has a Racket. M. Storm
Devil Has Four Faces. J. Jakes
Devil Has the Best Tunes. H. L. V. Fletcher
Devil Has Wings. P. Conde
Devil Held the Aces. P. Doncaster
Devil His Due. W. O'Farrell
Devil in a Domino. C. L'Epine
Devil in Broad Daylight. J. Bramlett
Devil in Crystal. E. Lindley
Devil in Davos. G. Brewer
Devil in Downing Street. R. Ladline
Devil in Dungarees. Albert Conroy
Devil in Greenlands. J. N. Chance
Devil in Harbour. C. Gavin
Devil in Her. H. Duval
Devil in Her. P. Trent
Devil in Kansas. Simon Quinn
Devil in Moonlight. M. Procter
Devil in Tartan. E. Ogilvie
Devil in the Belfry. R. Thorndike
Devil in the Bush. M. Head
Devil-in-the-Dark. P. Wentworth
Devil in the Darkness. A. Roy
Devil in the Maze. V. Gunn
Devil in the Pines. L. Cameron
Devil in the Pulpit. E. O'Donnell
Devil in the Sky. Muriel Bradley
Devil in the Wind. G. Greenaway
Devil in Velvet. J. D. Carr
Devil Kinsmere. R. Fairbairn
Devil Laughed. M. Richmond
Devil Loves Me. M. Millar
Devil Man. E. Wallace
Devil Mask Mystery. J. Kains
Devil May Care. Wade Miller
Devil-May-Care. Elizabeth Peters
Devil-May-Care. A. S. Roche
Devil Must. T. Wicker
Devil of Aske. Pamela Hill
Devil of Danehurst. J. Hunter
Devil of Pei-Ling. H. Asbury
Devil of the Depths. J. McLaren
Devil on Board. G. T. Ockley
Devil on His Trail. J. Hawkins
Devil on Horseback. V. Holt
Devil on Lammas Night. S. Howatch
Devil on the Moon. K. Robeson
Devil on the Stairs. P. Root
Devil on Two Sticks. Wade Miller
Devil or Saint? Colin Robertson
Devil Rides Out. D. Wheatley
Devil Snard. G. R. Preedy
Devil Spider. Glint Green
Devil-Stick. F. Hume
Devil Take All. Alice Brennan
Devil Take All. M. Caidin
Devil Take Her. F. Nichols
Devil Take Him. R. DeToledano
Devil Take the Blue-Tail Fly. J. F. Bardin
Devil Take the Foremost. T. Kinney
Devil Take the Hindmost. H. F. Shefler
Devil Takes a Hill Town. C. G. Givens
Devil That Slumbers. W. Allen
Devil Threw Dice. A. Dean
Devil Thumbs a Ride. R. C. Du Soe
Devil to Pay. P. Conway
Devil to Pay. R. Dolphin
Devil to Pay. George Douglas
Devil to Pay. F. N. Greene
Devil to Pay. H. Kane
Devil to Pay. E. Queen
Devil to Play. L. Holton
Devil Was a Woman. B. Graeme
Devil Was Handsome. M. Procter
Devil Was Kind. Donald Ross
Devil Was Sick. M. Durham
Devil Wears Wings. H. Whittington
Devil Within. B. M. Scott
Devil Within Us. D. Basinger
Devil Wolf. N. S. Schinke
Devil Woman. Roland Daniel
Devil Wore Scarlet. Dulcie Gray
Devil You Don't. R. Moody
Devil You Don't. J. Wainwright
Devil You Know. W. J. White
Devilday. Angus Hall

Deville McKeene, the British Ace. R. Walker
Devil's Ace. F. Hume
Devil's Admiral. F. F. Moore
Devil's Advocate. H. T. Johnson
Devil's Advocate. F. M. White
Devil's Agent. H. Habe
Devil's Alternative. F. Forsyth
Devil's Apprentice. G. Davison
Devil's Bargain. F. Warden
Devil's Behind You. H. E. Helseth
Devil's Bell. E. M. McMillan
Devil's Birthday. J. Lie
Devil's Box. W. J. Sheldon
Devil's Bread. D. Mariner
Devil's Brew. M. W. Kaye
Devil's Bride. Rachelle Edwards
Devil's Bride. Seabury Quinn
Devil's Bridge. M. Deasy
Devil's Brood. C. H. Barker
Devils Burn Too. Clay Henry
Devil's Cameo. W. H. Dye
Devil's Can-Can. W. H. Baker
Devil's Caress. J. Wright
Devil's Carnival. W. LeQueux
Devil's Cavern. C. Morgan
Devil's Chapel. E. P. Thorne
Devil's Chaplain. G. Bronson-Howard
Devil's Church. F. Draco
Devil's Churchyard. T. Willis
Devil's Cloak. Colin Robertson
Devil's Cockpit. Nick Carter
Devil's Cocktail. A. Wilson
Devil's Coffin. H. Gordon
Devil's Cook. E. Queen
Devil's Court. R. C. Payes
Devil's Current. K. Bennett
Devil's Dagger. M. G. Kiddy
Devil's Dance. Jan Alexander
Devil's Daughter. Griff
Devil's Daughter. E. Lipsky
Devil's Daughter. Marilyn Ross
Devil's Daughter. O. Schisgall
Devil's Daughter. D. Winston
Devil's Den. L. Saunders
Devil's Derelicts. F. C. V. Harcourt
Devil's Diamond. R. Marsh
Devil's Diamonds. G. Davison
Devil's Dice. W. LeQueux
Devil's Die. G. Allen
Devil's Diplomats. Operator 1384
Devil's Dominion. K. Lindsay
Devil's Door. L. Halliday
Devil's Door. R. Neill
Devil's Doorstep. D. Kamm
Devil's Double. C. H. Bullivant
Devil's Double. W. D. Roberts
Devil's Doubloons. J. McCulley
Devil's Dozen. Nick Carter
Devil's Dozen. N. Vane
Devil's Dreamer. Alice Brennan
Devil's Dress. M. M. Fletcher
Devil's Drive. A. W. Allan
Devil's Drum. L. Gorell
Devil's Drum. W. C. MacDonald
Devils' Drum. V. Meik
Devil's Due. Lanora Miller
Devil's Due. M. Procter
Devil's Edge. J. N. Chance
Devil's Elbow. G. Mitchell
Devil's Emissary. J. Laffin
Devil's End. P. Dalton
Devil's Eye. J. A. Jordan
Devil's Fire, Love's Revenge. B. Paul
Devil's Footprints. E. Bond
Devil's Footsteps. John Burke
Devil's Gate. A. J. Fitzgerald
Devil's Gate Road. John Ross
Devil's Goad. J. Laffin
Devil's Gold. J. B. Hendryx
Devil's Guard. T. Mundy
Devil's Heirloom. A. M. Rud
Devil's Henchmen. J. Oldrey
Devil's Highway. H. Janson
Devil's Hole. P. Ainsworth
Devil's Horns. K. Robeson
Devil's Horseman. J. Davison
Devil's Host. C. Glick
Devil's House. J. Tremonte
Devils in Candy Houses. W. Wall
Devil's Innocents. J. Edgar
Devil's Instrument. M. M. Fletcher
Devil's Keg. R. Cullum
Devils' Kloof. L. P. Greene
Devil's Lady. H. L. Gates
Devil's Lady. Linden Howard
Devil's Lady. Colin Robertson
Devil's Laughter. L. H. Grenning
Devil's Lieutenant. M. Fagyas
Devil's Lighter. J. Ballem
Devil's Luck. O. Williams
Devil's Mansion. R. Jardin
Devil's Mantle. F. Packard
Devil's Mirror. M. Lynch
Devil's Mistress. J. W. Brodie-Innes
Devil's Mistress. V. Coffman
Devil's Nest. H. H. Harper
Devil's Own. G. Bowman
Devil's Own. P. Curtis
Devil's Own. J. L. Roberts
Devil's Paradise. E. Cannon
Devil's Passkey. J. Shannon

Title Index

Devil's Passport. Gordon Young
Devil's Paw. E. P. Oppenheim
Devil's Pawn. E. Bruton
Devil's Payday. W. C. Tuttle
Devil's Playground. K. Robeson
Devil's Plunge. D. Walker
Devil's Portage. C. Stoddard
Devil's Post Office. John Muir
Devil's Power. C. Rushton
Devil's Princess. D. Winston
Devil's Punchbowl. D. Decker
Devil's Quill. D. Horner
Devil's Rain. M. Willis
Devil's Reckoning. M. Burton
Devil's Ring. L. Kenyon
Devil's Shilling. C. Rae-Brown
Devil's Signpost. A. Drummond
Devil's Skull. G. M. Wilson
Devil's Smile. R. Foxall
Devil's Snare. M. Cumberland
Devil's Son. Nicholas Carter
Devil's Sonata. S. Hufford
Devil's Spawn. C. Birkin
Devil's Spawn. R. Foxall
Devil's Steps. N. Thurley
Devil's Steps. A. W. Upfield
Devil's Stronghold. L. Ford
Devil's Tea-Party. T. A. Plummer
Devils' Tears. E. Hale
Devil's Torch. G. Dickson
Devil's Toy. Anita Stewart
Devil's Triangle. A. Soutar
Devil's Vicar. V. Coffman
Devil's Vineyard. B. Kevern
Devil's Virgin. V. Coffman
Devil's Walk. G. Hall
Devil's Whirlpool. G. Volk
Devil's Whisper. R. Barnett
Devil's Whisper. L. Borden
Devil's Work. C. Wells
Deviltower. U. Nightingale
Devilweek. B. Knox
Devine Court Mystery. B. Symons
Devious Defector. W. J. Saber
Devious Design. D. B. Olsen
Devious Murder. G. Bellairs
Devious Ones. F. Lockridge
Devious Ways. P. Freund
Devlin. J. Younger
Devlin the Barber. B. J. Farjeon
Devlin's Triangle. B. Heatter
Devon Maze. J. D. Fitz
Devouring Fire. L. Gorell
Dew in the Morning. Marjorie Curtis
Dewey Death. C. Blackstock
Dewey Decimated. C. A. Goodrum
DeWitt Manor. E. St. Clair
Dexter Bank Robbery. H. Rockwood
Diablo Manor. D. Daniels
Diabolic Candelabra. E. R. Punshon
Diabolist. M. A. Drew
Diabolist. P. W. Fairman
Diabolus. David St. John
Diagnosis: Homicide. L. G. Blochman
Diagnosis: Murder. J. Kahn
Diagnosis: Murder. R. King
Diagnosis—Murder. Sutherland Scott
Dial Death. M. Russell
Dial 577 R-A-P-E. L. O'Donnell
Dial M for Money. D. Taggart
Dail "M" for Murder. F. Knott
Dial 999. J. M. Walsh
Diamond. E. Byrd
Diamond and the Lady. J. Blyth
Diamond Beach. L. Forrester
Diamond Bikini. C. Williams
Diamond Boomerang. L. S. Taube
Diamond Bracelet. H. Wood
Diamond Bubble. R. L. Fish
Diamond-Buckled Shoe. B. Bolt
Diamond Button. B. North
Diamond Coterie. L. L. Lynch
Diamond Crime Detective. Benett Hill
Diamond Cross Mystery. C. K. Steele
Diamond Cut Diamond. J. Bunker
Diamond Cut Diamond. Nicholas Carter
Diamond Cut Diamond. Brian Stuart
Diamond Dragon. G. H. Teed
Diamond Dress. O. John
Diamond Duel. S. G. Hedges
Diamond Feather. H. Reilly
Diamond Fingers. J. Ingersol
Diamond Fix. A. Barker
Diamond Flood. R. C. Armour
Diamond from the Sky. R. L. McCardell
Diamond Hair Slide. H. C. McNeile
Diamond Hitch. W. C. Tuttle
Diamond Hook. J. Quartermain
Diamond Hostage. J. Quartermain
Diamond Hunters. Wilbur Smith
Diamond in the Hoof. T. Stevenson
Diamond Kill. Michael Brett
Diamond Master. J. Futrelle
Diamond Mercenaries. J. Carter
Diamond Mine Case. Nicholas Carter
Diamond Mountain. T. Keeping
Diamond Murders. J. S. Fletcher
Diamond Necklace. Frederick Jackson
Diamond of Evil. F. Whishaw
Diamond of Ti Lingo. J. G. Brandon
Diamond Pendant. T. Thurston
Diamond Pin. C. Wells

Diamond Queen. M. Dekobra
Diamond Queen. A. B. Reeve
Diamond Racket. N. Anthony
Diamond Ransom Murders. N. Child
Diamond Rock. Sea Lion
Diamond Rose Mystery. G. Knevels
Diamond Seeker of Brazil. Leon Lewis
Diamond Ship. M. Pemberton
Diamond Spitfire. Robin Moore
Diamond Stud. N. Singer
Diamond-Studded Typewriter. C. Keith
Diamond Sunburst. G. H. Teed
Diamond Thieves. A. Stringer
Diamond Tolls. R. S. Spears
Diamond Trail. O. Binns
Diamond Trail. Nicholas Carter
Diamond Trail. T. Gallon
Diamond Trip. Jenni Hall
Diamonds. J. S. Fletcher
Diamonds. A. Michaels
Diamonds and Blood. Robin Moore
Diamonds and Hearts. J. C. Goodwin
Diamonds Are Deadly. J. Eastwood
Diamonds Are Forever. I. Fleming
Diamonds Are Trumps. H. Adams
Diamonds Bid. J. Rathbone
Diamonds Can Be Dangerous. B. O'Keefe
Diamonds Can Be Trouble. E. Harrison
Diamonds Don't Burn. Gertrude Walker
Diamonds for a Blonde. B. Sarto
Diamonds for Danger. J. Pendower
Diamonds for Danger. D. Walker
Diamonds for Moscow. D. Walker
Diamonds Going and Coming. H. G. Dyar
Diamonds in the Dumplings. S. Shane
Diamonds of Alcazar. M. K. Simmons
Diamonds of Death. B. Chase
Diamonds of Death. W. Jackson
Diamonds of Death. J. Ronald
Diamonds of Death. H. Willett
Diamonds of Loreta. I. Drummond
Diamonds See in the Dark. T. Mundy
Diamonds Spell Death. L. Edgley
Diamonds to Amsterdam. M. Coles
Diamonds Wild. A. Caillou
Diamonds Worth a Death or Two. P. Campion
Diana Defiant. A. Applin
Diana Is Dead. M. Stand
Diana K.C. R. Lichfield
Diana Meets Murder. P. Tabori
Diana of Dartmoor. G. Warden
Diana of Kara Kara. E. Wallace
Diana of the Moorland. L. Tracy
Diana of the Moors. L. Tracy
Diana of the Woods. L. C. Douthwaite
Diana's Luck. A. Applin
Diane and Her Friends. A. Sherburne Hardy
Diane Game. S. Cohen
Diane of the Islands. B. Bolt
Diary. W. Ard
Diary of a Detective Police Officer. Waters
Diary of a Drop-Out. S. Box
Diary of a Great French Detective. Anonymous
Diary of a Judge. H. R. Addison
Diary of a Police Surgeon. G. Graham
Diary of a Red-Haired Girl. E. Price
Diary of a Scoundrel. M. Pemberton
Diary of an Ex-Detective. C. Martel
Diary of Death. W. Collison
Diary of Death. F. W. Gumley
Diary of Evil. V. Hawthorne
Diavolo. M. E. Braddon
Dibchick. Richard Dark
Dice Are Dark. B. Flynn
Dice Spelled Murder. A. Fray
Dice Were Loaded. M. Cumberland
Dick. B. J. Friedman
Dick Barton, Special Agent. Elwyn Jones
Dick Merriwell's Detective Work. B. L. Standish
Dick Merriwell's Mystery. B. L. Standish
Dick, the Boy Detective. Old Sleuth
Dick Tracy. W. Johnston
Dick Tracy and the Woo Woo Sisters. C. Gould
Dick Tracy: The Thirties. C. Gould
Dicker in Souls, and other stories. W. S. Gidley
Dictator. Justin McCarthy
Dictator of Death. Frank King
Dictator's Daughter. E. Jepson
Dictator's Destiny. D. Betteridge
Dictators Die Hard. R. A. Levey
Dictator's Secret. G. H. Teed
Dictator's Way. E. R. Punshon
Dictatorship of the Dove. F. Gerard
Did She Fall? T. Smith
Did She Fall or Was She Pushed? D. M. Disney
Did You Kill Mona Leeds? J. Roeburt
Didn't Anybody Know My Wife? W. D. Roberts
Die a Little Every Day. Lawrence Fisher
Die After Dark. H. Pentecost
Die All, Die Merrily. L. Bruce
Die Anytime, After Tuesday! Carter Brown
Die—As in Murder. L. Grex
Die by Night. M. S. Marble

Diplomatic Adventures / 489

Die by the Book. L. Meynell
Die, Damn You! P. Durst
Die, Darling, Die. E. Bruton
Die Fast, Die Happy. M. Denning
Die for Big Betsy. B. Knox
Die for Love. J. Oxford
Die Here a Stranger. M. Vinter
Die in the Country. T. Wells
Die in the Dark. Anthony Gilbert
Die, Jessica, Die. J. De Pre
Die, Killer, Die. F. Scarpetta
Die Laughing. R. Lockridge
Die Laughing. P. McGerr
Die Like a Dog. F. Gruber
Die Like a Dog. B. Halliday
Die Like a Man. M. Delving
Die, Little Goose. David Alexander
Die, Lover. H. Whittington
Die, My Beloved. P. Malloch
Die, My Darling. F. Usher
Die Now, Live Later. B. Copper
Die of a Rose. W. Maner
Die on Easy Street. J. A. Howard
Die Quickly, Brother. J. W. Hornby
Die Quickly, Dear Mother. T. Wells
Die Rich Die Happy. J. Munro
Die Screaming. J. Pagano
Die She Must. B. Von Hutten
Die to a Distant Drum. W. Arden
Die Wearing a Rose. E. P. Thorne
Die with Me, Lady. R. Cocking
Diecast. Michael Brett
Died in the Grass. C. Franklin
Died in the Red. Dulcie Gray
Died in the Wool. N. Marsh
Died o'Wednesday. S. Carver
Died o'Wednesday. Paul Townend
Died on a Rainy Sunday. Joan Aiken
Diehard. J. A. Jackson
Diehard. J. Potts
Difference in Death. Donn Russell
Difference to Me. J. Bryan
Different Kind of Rain. D. S. Copp
Different Kind of Summer. Jennie Melville
Different Night. O. Hesky
Difficult Problem and other stories. A. K. Green
Dig a Dead Doll. G. G. Fickling
Dig a Little Deeper. U. Curtiss
Dig a Narrow Grave. M. L. Roby
Dig Another Grave. D. C. Cameron
Dig Deep for Julie. R. Rayner
Dig for a Corpse. M. Mundy
Dig Her a Grave. P. Kruger
Dig Me a Grave. J. Spain
Dig Me Later. M. Hagen
Dig My Grave Deep. P. Rabe
Dig That Crazy Grave. R. S. Prather
Dig the Grave and Let Him Die. J. Wainright
Dig the Grave Deep. N. Brent
Dig the Missing. M. Urquhart
Dig Those Heels. H. Janson
Dig: Two Heads Wanted. H. H. Woodbridge
Digby's Miracle. F. E. Wynne
Digger of the Pit. M. Hastings
Diggers Die Hard. Eric Lambert
Digger's Game. G. V. Higgins
Dignity and Purity. I. Jefferies
Dil Dies Hard. K. P. Gast
Dilemma. J. Brampton
Dilemma. N. Edwards
Dilemma. H. C. McNeile
Dilemma. E. Phillpotts
Dilemma for Dax. M. Cumberland
Dilemma of Commander Brett. W. Chesney
Dilemma of Death. L. G. Redmond-Howard
Dilemma of Dr. Riley. W. Tyrer
Dilemma of the Dead Lady. W. Irish
Dilemmas. A. E. W. Mason
Dillinger. Henry Clement
Dimbleby's. L. C. Douthwaite
Diminished by Death. Jonathan Ross
Diminishing Returns. E. L. Withers
Dinah Faire. V. Coffman
Dinah for Danger. J. Bogar
Dinard Mystery. J. Maske
Dine and Be Dead. Gwendoline Butler
Dine with Murder. M. Halliday
Dine with the Devil. J. G. Vermandel
Ding Dong Bell. H. Reilly
Dingdong. A. Maling
Dinky Died. T. Wells
Dinner After Death. T. Irving-James
Dinner at Antoine's. F. P. Keyes
Dinner at Dupre's. B. Halliday
Dinner Club. H. C. McNeile
Dinner for None. M. Sarsfield
Dinner in New York. S. Fowler
Dinner-Party at Bardolph's. R. A. J. Walling
Dinner with the Dead. M. McLaren
Dinosaur. L. Kamarck
Diogenes of London and other fantasies and sketches. H. B. M. Watson
Dion O'Dare. C. E. Blaney
Dip into Murder. R. Ormerod
Diplomat. J. Aldridge
Diplomat and the Gold Piano. M. Scherf
Diplomat Dies. L. Gribble
Diplomatic Adventures. S. W. Mitchell

D

Diplomatic Corpse. P. A. Taylor
Diplomatic Cover. D. Torr
Diplomatic Death. C. Forsyte
Diplomatic Incident. Judith Kelly
Diplomatic Lover. Elsie Lee
Diplomatic Mysteries. V. Thompson
Diplomatic Traffic. D. Miller
Diplomatic Woman. H. Mee
Diplomat's Diary. Julien Gordon
Diplomat's Folly. Henry Wade
Dire Departed. J. Matheson
Director. O. Fraley
Director. Alan Thomas
Directors' Corridor. Caroline Francis
Dirge for a Dead Witch. Winifred Duke
Dirge for a Dog. Jennifer Jones
Dirge for a Lady. Alicen White
Dirge for Her. V. Rath
Dirty Area. N. Luard
Dirty Business. L. Edgley
Dirty Butter for Servants. Joan Fleming
Dirty Game. W. H. Baker
Dirty Gertie. H. Kane
Dirty Hands. R. Neely
Dirty Harry. P. Rock
Dirty Laundry. P. Hamill
Dirty Linen. Elliott Lewis
Dirty Money Can't Wash Both Hands at Once. J. M. Glazner
Dirty Pool. G. Bagby
Dirty Scenario. J. Ballem
Dirty Story. E. Ambler
Dirty Tricks. C. Pincher
Dirty Tricks. P. Way
Dirty Way to Die. G. Bagby
Dirty Way to Die. B. Rossi
Dirty Work. R. Pertwee
Dirty Work at the Crossroads. B. Johnson
Disagreeable Woman. Julian Starr
Disappearance. R. Carroll
Disappearance. J. Cowdroy
Disappearance. Derek Marlowe
Disappearance. C. Wilcox
Disappearance of a Niece. K. Field
Disappearance of Archibald Forsyth. Ian Alexander
Disappearance of Cropton. J. Fairfax-Blakeborough
Disappearance of Dr. Bruderstein. J. Sherwood
Disappearance of George Driffell. J. Payn
Disappearance of Julie Hintz. S. Truss
Disappearance of Kimball Webb. R. Wright
Disappearance of Lady Diana. R. Machray
Disappearance of Martha Penny. H. A. Vachell
Disappearance of Mary Amber. B. Poynter
Disappearance of Mr. Derwent. T. Cobb
Disappearance of Nicholson. C. Ainsworth
Disappearance of Nigel Blair. F. Warden
Disappearance of Norman Langdale. P. Lancaster
Disappearance of Odile. G. Simenon
Disappearance of Penny. R. J. Randisi
Disappearance of Roger Tremayne. B. Graeme
Disappearance of "Straight Left" Smith. Ernest H. Robinson
Disappearance of the Duke. Mrs. C. Kernahan
Disappearance of Uncle David. J. J. Farjeon
Disappearances. W. Wiser
Disappearing Bridegroom. M. Erskine
Disappearing Bullets. G. J. Brenn
Disappearing Corpse. James Warren
Disappearing Eye. F. Hume
Disappearing Island. G. Jenkins
Disappearing Parson. M. Burton
Disappearing Princess. Nicholas Carter
Disaster at Dungeness. R. Johnston
Disc. J. B. Harris-Burland
Discarded Daughter. E. Southworth
Discharge to Danger. W. Spann
Disciple of Satan. Nicholas Carter
Disciples of Nemesis. B. Osborne
Disciples of Satan. M. Richmond
Discipline of Christine. B. Goldie
Disclosures of a Press Agent. D. Miall
Disco Deathbeat. M. Geller
Discord in Harmony. P. K. McAfee
Discord in the Air. L. H. Clements
Discords of the Deep. L. A. Cunningham
Discourse with Shadows. J. Malcolm
Discovery. J. Parry
Discretion. D. Linzee
Discretion of Dominick Ayres. M. Vaughan
Disentanglers. Andrew Lang
Disgrace and Favour. J. Potter
Disgrace to the College. G. D. H. Cole
Disguise for a Dead Gentleman. G. Compton
Disher-Detective. Will Scott
Dishonest Murderer. F. Lockridge
Dishonest Way to Die. P. A. Foxall
Dishonor Among Thieves. S. Dean
Dishonored. F. Vreeland
Dishonour Among Thieves. David Hume
Dishonour Among Thieves. E. C. R. Lorac
Dis-Honourable. D. Hennessey
Dishonourable Member. J. T. Story
Dishonoured Bones. J. Trench

Disillusioned. B. Sarto
Disinformer. O. John
Disinherited. K. Orvis
Disintegration of J.P.G. G. Simenon
Disintegrator. Arthur Morgan
Disordered Death. J. B. O'Sullivan
Disoriented Man. P. Saxon
Dispatch and Secrecy. G. Grison
Dispensable Man. W. Rilla
Disposal Unit. J. Roland
Disposing Mind. R. H. R. Smithies
Disposing of Henry. R. Bax
Dispossessed. G. Wagner
Disputed Barricade. H. Gibbs
Disputed Quarry. D. Sharp
Disqualified. F. Johnston
Dissector. H. Miller
Dissemblers. T. Cobb
Dissemblers. J. Creasey
Dissident. P. Van Greenaway
Distant Banner. Roy Lewis
Distant Clue. R. Lockridge
Distant Landscape. H. Elsna
Distinguished Gathering. James Parish
Distracting Guest. R. Jocelyn
Distributors. A. Partridge
District Bungalow. C. C. Lewis
Disturbance on Berry Hill. Elizabeth Fenwick
Disturbing Affair of Noel Blake. N. Bell
Ditto, Brother Rat! W. Garner
Diva's Emeralds. V. MacClure
Dive Deep for Danger. H. T. Rothwell
Dive Deep for Death. E. Messenger
Dive into Danger. C. Forsyte
Dive into Darkness. L. O'Donnell
Dive into Death. Clayton Matthews
Diver Went Down. J. McLaren
Divers. H. Nisbet
Divers Diamonds. A. Dekker
Diversions of Dawson. B. Copplestone
Dives and Son. E. Davies
Divide by Seven. R. Chambers
Divide the Night. D. Honig
Divided Trail. J. K. Stafford
Divided We Fall. E. Burgess
Dividend of Death. G. Malcolm-Smith
Dividend on Death. B. Halliday
Dividend Was Death. W. J. Coughlin
Dividing Line. R. Maugham
Dividing Night. V. Scannell
Divinations of Kala Persad and other stories. H. Hill
Divine and Deadly. M. Scherf
Divine Death. L. Derrick
Divine Gift. C. McLaren
Divine Spark. P. Traill
Diving Dames Affair. P. Leslie
Diving Death. C. Forsyte
Divining Rod for Murder. M. Neville
Divinitas. J. Knowler
Division Bell Mystery. E. Wilkinson
Divorce. T. P. Prest
Divorce. G. Thorne
Divorce Court Murder. M. Propper
Divorced Princess. R. de Pont-Jest
Dixie Convoy. D. Pendleton
Dixie Death Squad. L. Derrick
Dixon Hawke, Secret Agent. J. Creasey
Dixon Hawke's Case Book. Anonymous
Dixon of Dock Green. Rex Edwards
Dixon of Dock Green. T. Willis
Dizzy Dames Die Fast. C. Wheatley
Do Butlers Burgle Banks? P. G. Wodehouse
Do Evil in Return. M. Millar
Do It Yourself Doom. S. Prickett
Do Me a Favor, Drop Dead. J. H. Chase
Do No Evil. F. Noro
Do Not Disturb. H. McCloy
Do Not Disturb. L. Thayer
Do Not Fold, Spindle or Mutilate. D. M. Disney
Do Not Murder Before Christmas. J. Iams
Do Not Sleep. G. M. Wilson
Do Nothin' Till You Hear from Me. J. Wainwright
Do—or Die! T. Taggart
Do Unto Others. D. M. Disney
Do You Deal in Murder? A. Allyson
Do You Know This Voice? E. Berckman
Do You Like Tahiti? E. Clerk
Do You Remember England? Derek Marlowe
Doc Churston. O. Binns
Doc Grip, the Sporting Detective. Anonymous
Dock Brief. D. Barr
"Dock Rats" of New York. Old Sleuth
Dock Walloper. B. Appel
Docken Dead. J. Trench
Dockyard Mystery. S. Hope
Doctor and the Corpse. Max Murray
Doctor and the Devil. C. W. Gardner
Doctor and the Devils. D. Thomas
Doctor Artz. R. Hichens
Doctor Baxter's Invention. W. P. Kelly
Doctor Bentiron: Detective. E. M. Poate
Dr. Berkeley's Discovery. R. Slee
Doctor Bernard St. Vincent. H. Nisbet
Dr. Bruderstein Vanishes. J. Sherwood
Doctor Burton. A. C. Gunter
Doctor Burton's Success. A. C. Gunter
Doctor Claude. H. Malot

Doctor Caro. B. J. Packer
Dr. Chaos and the Devil Snard. G. R. Preedy
Doctor Cobb's Game. R. V. Cassill
Doctor Cockaigne. N. E. Davies
Dr. Cook's Garden. I. Levin
Dr. Cunliffe—Investigator. H. Frankish
Doctor Dale's Dilemma. G. W. Appleton
Doctor Darch's Wife. F. Warden
Doctor Deals with Murder. W. M. Duncan
Dr. Death. Nick Carter
Doctor Death. J. Hartenfels
Doctor Death. C. Whitman
Doctor Detective. P. Graham
Doctor Didn't Prescribe Murder. H. B. May
Doctor Died at Dusk. G. Homes
Doctor Disappears. M. Dalman
Doctor Dodds' Experiment. Sutherland Scott
Dr. Duvene's Crime. G. Chester
Dr. Endicott's Experiment. A. Sergeant
Dr. Falke of Harley Street. S. Fairway
Doctor Falls in Love. Rona Randall
Dr. Feel Good. J. Nazel
Dr. Fell, Detective, and other stories. J. D. Carr
Dr. Ferraro's Frame-Up. C. Brisbane
Doctor Fischer of Geneva. G. Greene
Doctor Fix. H. Janson
Doctor for the Dead. M. Higgins
Doctor Fram. S. Mackenzie
Doctor Frigo. E. Ambler
Doctor from Devil's Island. C. Rushton
Doctor Garrett's Girl. M. Lynch
Dr. Gatskill's Blue Shoes. P. Conant
Dr. Glazebrook's Revenge. A. C. Brown
Doctor Glennie's Daughter. B. L. Farjeon
Dr. Goodwood's Locum. J. Rhode
Dr. Greenfingers. E. Woodward
Dr. Grimshawe's Secret. N. Hawthorne
Dr. Gully. Elizabeth Jenkins
Dr. Gully's Story. Elizabeth Jenkins
Doctor Havelock's Wife. Rona Randall
Doctor, His Wife, and the Clock. A. K. Green
Doctor Is Sick. A. Burgess
Doctor Izard. A. K. Green
Dr. Jekyll and Mr. Holmes. L. D. Estleman
Dr. Krasinski's Secret. M. P. Shiel
Doctor Krook. A. Mallory
Doctor, Lawyer... C. Wilcox
Doctor Looks at Murder. D. Quick
Dr. Mabuse, Master of Mystery. N. Jacques
Dr. Manton. M. Gerard
Doctor Mephisto. J. Joseph-Renaud
Dr. Monte Cristo. I. P. Sobel
Doctor Moon. C. Meadows
Dr. Morel. K. Bramson
Doctor Morelle. E. Dudley
Dr. Morelle and Destiny. E. Dudley
Dr. Morelle and the Doll. E. Dudley
Dr. Morelle and the Drummer Girl. E. Dudley
Dr. Morelle at Midnight. E. Dudley
Dr. Morelle Meets Murder and other new adventures. E. Dudley
Dr. Morelle Takes a Box. E. Dudley
Dr. Nicholas Stone. E. S. De Puy
Doctor Nikola. G. Boothby
Dr. Nikola's Experiment. G. Boothby
Doctor No. I. Fleming
Doctor of Pimlico. W. LeQueux
Doctor of Souls. W. K. Knight
Dr. Orient. F. Lauria
Dr. Palliser's Patient. G. Allen
Doctor Paradise. J. J. Dratler
Dr. Phibes. W. Goldstein
Dr. Phibes Rises Again. W. Goldstein
Dr. Priestley Investigates. J. Rhode
Dr. Priestley Lays a Trap. J. Rhode
Dr. Priestley's Quest. J. Rhode
Dr. Quake. R. Sapir
Doctor Quartz, Magician. Nicholas Carter
Doctor Quartz's Quick Move. Nicholas Carter
Dr. Quick, the Masked Detective. Ernest H. Robinson
Dr. Ricardo. W. Garrett
Dr. Rumsey's Patient. L. T. Meade
Doctor S.O.S. L. Thayer
Dr. Sam: Johnson, Detector. L. De La Torre
Doctor Samovar, Crook. Spike Gordon
Dr. Scarlett. A. Laing
Doctor Severin's Secret. S. Fairway
Doctor Sinister. G. Chester
Dr. Sinister. Gwyn Evans
Dr. Somerville's Crime. M. H. Hervey
Dr. Strangelove. P. George
Doctor Syn. R. Thorndike
Doctor Syn on the High Seas. R. Thorndike
Doctor Syn Returns. R. Thorndike
Dr. Tancred Begins. G. D. H. Cole
Doctor—There's Danger. F. L. Cary
Dr. Thorndyke Intervenes. R. A. Freeman
Dr. Thorndyke Investigates. R. A. Freeman
Dr. Thorndyke Omnibus. R. A. Freeman

Title Index

Dr. Thorndyke's Case-Book. R. A. Freeman
Dr. Thorndyke's Cases. R. A. Freeman
Dr. Thorndyke's Dilemma. J. H. Dirckx
Dr. Thorndyke's Discovery. R. A. Freeman
Dr. Time. K. Robeson
Doctor to the Stars. M. Leinster
Dr. Toby Finds Murder. S. M. Schley
Doctor Transit. I. S.
Doctor Vandyke. J. E. Cooke
Doctor vs. Murder. M. Ryerson
Doctor Villagos. F. Du Boisgobey
Dr. Wainwright's Patient. E. Yates
Doctor Was a Dame. S. Truss
Doctor Who Held Hands. H. Footner
Doctor Who Wouldn't Tell. W. M. Graydon
Dr. Wilbur's Note Book. N. T. Oliver
Dr. Wynne's Revenge. W. Westall
Doctor Xavier. M. Pemberton
Dr. Zollinoff's Revenge. E. R. Owen
Doctors Also Die. D. M. Devine
Doctors Are Doubtful. A. Weymouth
Doctors Beware! W. McCully
Doctor's Crime. M. Danvers
Doctor's Daughter. P. Allardyce
Doctor's Daughter. H. Wood
Doctor's Defence. S. Fairway
Doctor's Double. E. W. Alais
Doctor's Double. N. Gould
Doctor's First Murder. R. Hare
Doctor's Idol. C. Lys
Doctor's Mistake. C. H. Montague
Doctor's Murder Case. R. P. Koehler
Doctor's Office. Elsie Lee
Doctor's Secret. W. J. Bayfield
Doctor's Secret. Rita
Doctor's Strategem. Nicholas Carter
Doctors Wear Scarlet. S. Raven
Doctor's Wife. M. E. Braddon
Document of the Last Nazi. M. Eden
Documentary Evidence. R. Halket
Documents in the Case. D. L. Sayers
Documents Marked "Secret." John Gloag
Documents of Death. J. Creasey
Documents of Murder. T. C. H. Jacobs
Dodd Cases. K. Livingston
Dodge City Bombers. L. Derrick
Dodging the Law. Nicholas Carter
Dodos Don't Duck. M. O'Brine
Doesn't Everyone. I. A. Greenfield
Dog and Duck Mystery. H. Bogue
Dog Day Afternoon. P. Mann
Dog Detective. Anonymous
Dog Detective and His Young Master. M. M. Murray
Dog Eat Dog. W. Chambers
Dog Eat Dog. Mary Collins
Dog-Face. J. Easton
Dog Fight with Death. G. Davison
Dog Fox. W. B. M. Ferguson
Dog It Was. R. Harrison
Dog It Was That Died. G. Braddon
Dog It Was That Died. H. R. F. Keating
Dog It Was That Died. E. C. R. Lorac
Dog Man. M. Procter
Dog Star. C. Stanton
Dog Track Murder. M. Osborne
Dog with a Bad Name. F. Warden
Dogcatcher. P. Prince
Dogs. R. Calder
Dog's Death. P. Motte
Dogs Do Bark. J. Stagge
Dogs of War. W. H. Baker
Dogs of War. F. Forsyth
Dog's Ransom. P. Highsmith
Dogwatch. C. Coffin
Doings of Raffles Haw. A. C. Doyle
Doll. E. McBain
Doll Baby. H. Barron
Doll Castle. M. Monigle
Doll for the Big House. Carter Brown
Doll for the Toff. J. Creasey
Doll Who Ate His Mother. Ramsey Campbell
Doll with Opal Eyes. J. DeWeese
Dollar Covenant. Michael Sinclair
Dolls and Dollars. J. Dekker
Dolls Are Deadly. B. Halliday
Dolls Are Murder. H. Q. Masur
Doll's Bad News. J. H. Chase
Doll's Done Dancing. B. Flynn
Doll's Trunk Murder. H. Reilly
Dolls with Sad Faces. C. Phillips
Dolly and the Cookie Bird. D. Halliday
Dolly and the Doctor Bird. D. Halliday
Dolly and the Nanny Bird. D. Halliday
Dolly and the Singing Bird. D. Halliday
Dolly and the Starry Bird. D. Halliday
Dolly Dolly Spy. A. Diment
Dolly the Romp. F. Warden
Dolly's Walk. C. Edwards
Dolomite Cavern. W. P. Kelly
Dolores. G. Kelton
Dolores and Some Others. M. Pemberton
Dolores Divine, Guilty or Innocent? K. M. Ellis
Dolorosa Deal. B. Littell
Dolphin. Eric Lambert
Dolphin Mystery. J. P. Hutton
Dolphin Summer. C. Salisbury
Dombey and Daughter. R. Nicholson
Domes of Silence. O. J. Friend
Domesday Story. Warwick Scott
Domestic Agency. J. Rhode

Domestic Animal. Francis King
Dominant Third. E. Hely
Dominator. A. York
Dominici Affair. J. Laborde
Domino. M. K. Simmons
Domino. P. A. Whitney
Domino Club. A. Upward
Domino Plan. E. Granville
Domino Principle. A. Kennedy
Dominoes. J. Wainwright
Don. F. V. Perrin
Don. G. Ziran
Don Algonah. Anonymous
Don Among the Dead Men. C. E. Vulliamy
Don Belasco of Key West. A. C. Gunter
Don Caesar de Bazan. T. P. Prest
Don Is Dead. N. Quarry
Don or Devil? W. Westall
Don Q in the Sierra. K. Prichard
Don Q's Love Story. K. Prichard
Donald Dyke, the Down-East Detective. H. Rockwood
Donalda. M. J. Young
Donavan. Carter Brown
Donavan's Day. Carter Brown
Donavan's Delight. Carter Brown
Done in the Dark. Nicholas Carter
Done to Death. F. Carmichael
Done to Death. Sara Woods
Donkey from the Mountains. E. Atiyah
Donna. R. T. Larkin
Donna Died Laughing. Carter Brown
Donor. R. Tate
Donovan. J. Midgley
Donovan Affair. Owen Davis
Donovan Case. J. Monmouth
Donovan of Whitehall. W. LeQueux
Donovan's Brain. C. Siodmak
Don't Argue with Death. L. Gribble
Don't Ask Questions. J. P. Marquand
Don't Be Afraid of the Dark. P. Henneker
Don't Be No Hero. Leonard Harris
Don't Bet on Living, Alice. K. Carr
Don't Betray Me. J. Berry
Don't Betray Me. J. Van Hearn
Don't Bleed on Me. B. Copper
Don't Bother to Knock. Peter Chambers
Don't Bother to Knock. C. Dekker
Don't Break the Seal. A. M. Burrage
Don't Call Back. R. O'Neil
Don't Call Me Madame. H. Kane
Don't Call Tonight. W. C. Gault
Don't Catch Me. R. Powell
Don't Come Back! W. Wright
Don't Come Crying to Me. W. Ard
Don't Count the Corpses. C. Monig
Don't Crowd Me. E. Hunter
Don't Crowd Me. G. Usher
Don't Cry, Beloved. E. Ronns
Don't Cry for Long. T. B. Dewey
Don't Cry for Me. W. C. Gault
Don't Cry, Little Girl. N. Parker
Don't Cry Little Sister. J. Letton
Don't Dare Me, Sugar. H. Janson
Don't Dig Deeper. W. Francis
Don't Drop Dead Tomorrow. H. Pentecost
Don't Embarrass the Bureau. B. F. Connors
Don't Ever Love Me. O. R. Cohen
Don't Expect Any Mercy. H. Treece
Don't Feed the Animals. J. Farr
Don't Get Caught. M. E. Chaber
Don't Get Caught. Carter Cullen
Don't Get Me Wrong. P. Cheyney
Don't Go Away Dead. H. Kane
Don't Go Away Mad. J. Hayes
Don't Go in Alone. G. Holden
Don't Go into the Woods Today. D. M. Disney
Don't Go Out After Dark. N. Berrow
Don't Go to Ceuta. H. Franklin
Don't Go to Sleep in the Dark. C. Fremlin
Don't Hang Me Too High. J. B. O'Sullivan
Don't Jump, Mr. Boland! N. Berrow
Don't Just Stand There. C. Williams
Don't Just Stand There, Do Someone. D. Von Elsner
Don't Kill, My Love. R. Foley
Don't Let Her Die. Tarn Scott
Don't Let Him Burn! F. MacIsaac
Don't Let Him Kill. G. Ashe
Don't Lie to Me. T. Coe
Don't Lie to the Police. B. Cobb
Don't Look Back. M. Borgenicht
Don't Look Behind You. M. Erskine
Don't Look Behind You! S. Rogers
Don't Look Behind You. Marilyn Ross
Don't Look Down. V. Katcha
Don't Look Now. D. Du Maurier
Don't Make Me Kill. M. Clinten
Don't Mention It. B. Shannon
Don't Mention My Name. E. K. Goldthwaite
Don't Mess with Murder. A. Allyson
Don't Monkey with Murder. E. Ferrars
Don't Mourn for Me. E. Ellison
Don't Mourn Me, Toots. H. Janson
Don't Neglect the Body. Kevin O'Hara
Don't Open the Door. U. Curtiss
Don't Open the Door! Anthony Gilbert
Don't Play with the Rough Boys. S. Troy

Don't Point That Thing at Me. K. Bonfiglioli
Don't Push Me Around. E. Gilbert
Don't Push Your Luck. P. Muller
Don't Rely on Gemini. V. Packer
Don't Say No. O. L. Rosmanith
Don't Scare Easy. H. Janson
Don't Scare Me, Sister. D. Foster
Don't Shoot, Darling. H. Holt
Don't Shoot the Pianist. James Grant
Don't Shut Me Out. H. Elsna
Don't Slip, Delaney. B. Singer
Don't Speak to Strange Girls. H. Whittington
Don't Stop for Hooky Heffernan. L. Meynell
Don't Take It to Heart. S. Seaton
Don't Talk to Strangers. Beverly Hastings
Don't Tell the Police. Kevin O'Hara
Don't Tempt Me. S. Coburn
Don't Tempt the Hangman. Spike Gordon
Don't Tie Me Down. V. Lloyd
Don't Touch Me. Spike Gordon
Don't Touch the Body. A. Mills
Don't Try Anything Funny. J. M. Fox
Don't Wear Your Wedding Ring. L. O'Donnell
Don't Whistle "MacBeth". David Fletcher
Doodled Asterisk. R. A. J. Walling
Doom. H. Imbert-Terry
Doom! Justin Huntly McCarthy
Doom Campaign. M. McMullen
Doom Candle. Richard Grant
Doom Dealer. D. Fox
Doom in the Midnight Sun. E. M. Boyd
Doom-Maker. B. X. Sanborn
Doom of Glendour. K. Ostrander
Doom of Siva. T. W. Speight
Doom of the Demon Band. Old Sleuth
Doom of the Reds. Nicholas Carter
Doom Service. D. J. Marlowe
Doom Stone. C. Woolrich
Doom Window. M. Drake
Doomdate. J. Tiger
Doomed Five. C. Wells
Doomed Flight. J. R. Holden
Doomed Men. W. Jardine
Doomed Oasis. H. Innes
Doomed Sinner. D. Brennan
Doomed to Failure. Nicholas Carter
Doomed to Hate. J. Bowman
Doomington Wanderer. L. Golding
Doom's Caravan. G. Household
Doomsday. Warwick Scott
Doomsday Affair. H. Whittington
Doomsday Bag. M. Avallone
Doomsday Bells. M. Lynch
Doomsday Book. J. MacLaren-Ross
Doomsday Brain. P. Tabori
Doomsday Carrier. V. Canning
Doomsday Committee. R. Gallagher
Doomsday Conspiracy. Ralph Hayes
Doomsday Contract. T. Williamson
Doomsday Deposit. Stanley Johnson
Doomsday England. M. Cooney
Doomsday Formula. Nick Carter
Doomsday List. K. Orvis
Doomsday Men. J. B. Priestley
Doomsday Mission. H. Whittington
Doomsday Morning. C. L. Moore
Doomsday Scroll. Barbara Rogers
Doomsday Spore. Nick Carter
Doomsday Squad. D. Gober
Doomsday Squad. Clark Howard
Doomsday Square. R. W. Taylor
Doomsday Ultimatum. J. Follett
Doomsday Vendetta. P. Winston
Doomsters. R. Macdonald
Doomway. E. Bond
Door. M. R. Rinehart
Door. J. F. Rossmann
Door. G. Simenon
Door Between. E. Queen
Door Closed Softly. Alice Campbell
Door Fell Shut. M. Albrand
Door in the Wall. L. Meynell
Door into Terror. J. Coulson
Door Nails Never Die. A. Wynne
Door of Death. J. Esteven
Door of Doubt. Nicholas Carter
Door of Dread. A. Stringer
Door of the Unreal. G. Biss
Door to Death. R. Stout
Door to Doom. J. D. Carr
Door to Enigma. Ian Wallace
Door to the Moor. M. B. Vandeburg
Door to the Tower. S. Dannett
Door Was Violence. G. Leaderman
Door with Seven Locks. E. Wallace
Door Without a Key. Constance Rutherford
Doorbell Rang. R. Stout
Doors. E. Hannon
Doors of Sleep. T. Warriner
Doors of the Night. F. Packard
Doors Open. M. Gilbert
Doors to Death. L. Crosby
Doorstep Murders. C. Wells
Doorway to Danger. S. Maddock
Doorway to Death. H. Arvonen
Doorway to Death. J. Creasey
Doorway to Death. H. Desmond

D

Doorway to Death. D. J. Marlowe
Doorways to Death. Mark Napier
Doowinkle, D.A. H. Klingsberg
Dope. S. Rohmer
Dope-Darling. Leda Burke
Dope Dealer. E. Snell
Dope Dealers. L. Cross
Dope Devils. W. J. Elliott
Dope Doll. S. Harragan
Dope Is for Dopes. Griff
Dope Ring. J. Hill
Dope Runners. G. Grantham
Dope Ship. E. L. Long
Dope Specialist. F. Johnston
Doped and the Damned. Griff
Dopefiend. D. Goines
Doppelganger. H. Innes
Doppelganger. P. Van Greenaway
Doppelganger Gambit. L. Killough
Doppelgangers. H. F. Heard
Dora Elmyr's Worst Enemy. M. V. Victor
Dora Myrl, the Lady Detective. M. M. Bodkin
Dora's Device. G. P. Cather
Dorcas Dene, Detective. G. R. Sims
Doris. Dorothy Johnson
Doris Moore. G. Thorne
Doris's Fortune. F. Warden
Dormant. E. Nesbit
Dormitory Women. R. V. Cassill
Dormouse Has Nine Lives. Frank King
Dormouse—Peacemaker. Frank King
Dormouse—Undertaker. Frank King
Dornstein Ikon. J. L. Roberts
Dorothy Marlow. A. W. Marchmont
Dorothy the Rope Dancer. M. Leblanc
Dorothy, the Terrified. K. Kimbrough
Dorothy's Double. G. A. Henty
Dorothy's Venture. M. C. Hay
Dorrien of Cranston. B. Mitford
Dorrington Deed-Box. Arthur Morrison
Dossier Closed. C. Eland
Dossier 51. G. Perrault
Dossier IX. B. Weil
Dossier No. 113. E. Gaboriau
Dossier of Solar Pons. B. Copper
Dossier on a Mantis. W. R. Bennett
Dotmakers. J. F. Beaman
Double. E. Wallace
Double Acrostic. G. Goodchild
Double Agent. J. Bingham
Double Agent. G. Stackelberg
Double Agent. H. T. Teilhet
Double Alibi. M. R. Rinehart
Double Banked. E. L. Long
Double Barrel. N. Freeling
Double-Barrelled Detective Story. M. Twain
Double Blackmail. G. D. H. Cole
Double Bluff. S. Mitchell
Double Bluff. Dell Shannon
Double Chance. J. S. Fletcher
Double Crime. J. J. Farjeon
Double Crime. Old Sleuth
Double Cross. A. Capelli
Double Cross. George Douglas
Double Cross. M. Moran
Double-Cross. A. O. Pollard
Double Cross. A. E. Thomas
Double Cross. P. Urquhart
Double Cross. G. Willets
Double-Cross Circuit. M. Dorland
Double Cross Inn. J. Laurence
Double-Cross Murder. R. Gilmour
Double Cross Purposes. R. A. Knox
Double Cross Purposes. Kenneth O'Hara
Double Crossed. D. Newton
Double-Crosser. J. Cassells
Double-Crossers of Ghost Tree. W. C. Tuttle
Double-Crossing Traitor. Roland Daniel
Double Cunning. G. M. Fenn
Double Dagger. N. Ridley
Double Dan. E. Wallace
Double Darkness. E. Fenton
Double Deal. H. Miller
Double Deal. M. Russell
Double Dealers. M. MacKintosh
Double Dealing. F. P. Jordan
Double Dealing. Harold Trembath
Double Death. J. N. Chance
Double Death. F. W. Crofts
Double Death. Detection Club
Double Death. C. Forsyte
Double Death Mystery. L. Geoghegan
Double Death of Frederic Belot. C. Aveline
Double Deception. Jan Allen
Double Defector. P. Wayland
Double Detection. B. Cobb
Double Diamond. B. Pendower
Double Disappearance. L. Winstanley
Double Doom. Josephine Bell
Double, Double. E. Queen
Double Double-Cross. D. Thurlow
Double, Double, Oil and Trouble. E. Lathen
Double Duel. S. Cobb
Double Entry. Constance Rutherford
Double Events. A. Wilson
Double Exposure. D. MacKenzie
Double Exposure. H. McLeave

Double Exposure. A. W. Sherring
Double Fault. L. Meynell
Double Feature. A. Fowles
Double Finesse. H. Howard
Double Florin. J. Rhode
Double for Blackshirt. R. Graeme
Double for Death. G. Ashe
Double for Death. R. Stout
Double for Murder. N. Deane
Double for the Toff. J. Creasey
Double Fortune. B. L. Hoskins
Double Four. E. P. Oppenheim
Double Frame. Anthony Morton
Double Frame. C. Rice
Double Game. D. Richards
Double-Handed Game. Nicholas Carter
Double Hit. M. Russell
Double House. E. Dejeans
Double Identities. J. Rhode
Double Identity. Nick Carter
Double Identity. G. H. Coxe
Double Identity. F. Drake
Double Image. I. R. G. Hart
Double Image. Helen MacInnes
Double Image and other stories. Roy Vickers
Double in Diamonds. F. Carmichael
Double in Trouble. R. S. Prather
Double Indemnity. J. M. Cain
Double Jeopardy. M. M. Goldsmith
Double Jeopardy. E. Lanham
Double Jeopardy. F. Pratt
Double Jeopardy. W. C. Stiles
Double Jeopardy. Clement Wood
Double Kill. D. Bogard
Double Kill. D. Da Cruz
Double Knot. G. M. Fenn
Double Life. O. F. Jerome
Double Life. G. Leroux
Double Life. M. W. Wellman
Double Life and the Detectives. A. Pinkerton
Double Life of Mr. Alfred Burton. E. P. Oppenheim
Double Lives. S. Murray
Double M Man. C. Leader
Double Man. H. Reilly
Double Mask. R. N. Silver
Double Masquerade. A. Wilson
Double Menace. B. Newman
Double Motive. J. Creasey
Double Mystery. Nicholas Carter
Double Mystery. L. Raphael
Double Mystery. A. Wynne
Double Negative. P. Carkeet
Double Negative. J. B. O'Sullivan
Double Nought. W. LeQueux
Double or Quit. E. C. Vivian
Double or Quits. M. Dekobra
Double or Quits. A. A. Fair
Double or Quits. H. Luger
Double Plot. Nicholas Carter
Double Problem. J. L. Morrissey
Double Quest. D. Timins
Double Revenge. L. T. Meade
Double Run. J. Ashford
Double Scoop. B. Cable
Double Shadow. W. LeQueux
Double Shadow Murders. A. McRoyd
Double Shuffle. J. H. Chase
Double Shuffle. D. B. Hobart
Double Shuffle Club. Nicholas Carter
Double Sin and other stories. A. Christie
Double Smile. M. Leblanc
Double Snare. Rosemary Harris
Double Snatch. G. Usher
Double Solution. C. F. Gregg
Double Spy. M. McKenna
Double Standard. L. DuBreuil
Double Take. D. Bloch
Double Take. J. Bruce
Double Take. M. Colton
Double Take. D. Craig
Double Take. R. Huggins
Double Take. H. Janson
Double Take. Roy Lewis
Double Take. R. Ormerod
Double Take. L. Peters
Double Take. Colin Robertson
Double Take. E. Violett
Double the Bluff. G. Fairlie
Double Thirteen. P. Marlowe
Double-Thirteen Mystery. A. Wynne
Double Thumb. F. Grierson
Double Tragedy. Anonymous
Double Tragedy. F. W. Crofts
Double Traitor. E. P. Oppenheim
Double Treasure. C. B. Kelland
Double Trouble. A. Bocca
Double Trouble. B. Graeme
Double Trouble. E. Lacy
Double Trouble. R. Mallory
Double Trouble. W. C. Tuttle
Double Turn. C. Carnac
Double Who Double Crossed. T. D. Smith
Double Z. M. Grant
Doublecross. A. Livingston
Doublecross of Death. J. Creasey
Doublecross. Roland Daniel
Doublecrossers. M. Wells
Doubled in Diamonds. V. Canning

Doubles in Death. W. Grew
Doubling of Joseph Brereton. R. Hodder
Doubloons. E. Phillpotts
Doubly Dead. R. Cobb
Doubly Dead. E. Ferrars
Doubly Dead. J. M. Patterson
Doubtful Diciple. W. Haggard
Douce. E. Kyle
Dough for the Dormouse. Frank King
Douglas Affair. A. Mair
Douglas Castle. C. F. Barrett
Dove. R. O. Saber
Dove. W. Tucker
Dove in the Mulberry Tree. G. R. Preedy
Dove of War. Ian Mitchell
Dovebury Murders. J. Rhode
Dover and the Claret Tappers. J. Porter
Dover and the Unkindest Cut of All. J. Porter
Dover Beats the Band. J. Porter
Dover Goes to Pott. J. Porter
Dover One. J. Porter
Dover-Ostend. Taffrail
Dover Strikes Again. J. Porter
Dover Three. J. Porter
Dover Train Mystery. Anthony Gilbert
Dover Two. J. Porter
Doverfields' Diamonds. L. L. Lynch
Dovingsby Death. P. N. Walker
Dower Chest. A. Dean
Dower Court Manor. E. D. Bennett
Dower House Mystery. M. Beckett
Dower House Mystery. P. Wentworth
Dowker-Detective. F. Hume
Down. W. Grove
Down a Dark Alley. G. Holden
Down Among the Ad Men. W. A. Ballinger
Down Among the Dead Men. Evelyn Harris
Down Among the Dead Men. James Lake
Down Among the Dead Men. P. Moyes
Down Among the Dead Men. Sea Lion
Down Among the Dead Men. R. Stephenson
Down Among the Dead Men. S. Sterling
Down Among the Jocks. R. Dennis
Down and Dirty. Frank King
Down and Dirty. W. B. Murphy
Down and Out. W. J. Bayfield
Down and Out. Nicholas Carter
Down-Beat Kill. Peter Chambers
Down East. W. M. Graydon
Down East! L. Jackson
Down Express. G. W. Appleton
Down I Go. B. Kerr
Down Payment on Death. J. Eldridge
Down "Plug Street" Way, and other stories. G. Goodchild
Down River. Seamark
Down River. J. H. Vahey
Down-River Dolls. B. Sarto
Down the Dark Street. J. Fenton
Down the Green Stairs and other stories. J. J. Farjeon
Down the Last Slide. H. T. Hopkinson
Down the Water. E. Kyle
Down There. D. Goodis
Down Through the Night. J. Fast
Down to Death. Stella Phillips
Down Under. P. Wentworth
Down Under Donovan. E. Wallace
Down Yonder with Judge Priest. I. S. Cobb
Downbeat for a Dirge. B. Bird
Downbeat on a Debutante. J. J. McCall
Downe Reserve. M. Blount
Downey of the Mounted. J. B. Hendryx
Downhill Ride of Leeman Popple. G. Bellairs
Downing Street Discovery. J. G. Brandon
Downriver. P. Collier
Downtown Doll. H. Janson
Downward Path. R. Chapman
Downward Path. E. Gaboriau
Downward Path. Dick Stewart
Downwind. B. McKnight
Dowry. M. Gould
Dowry of Diamonds. L. V. Stevens
Dracula. H. Deane
Dracula. C. Johnson
Dracula. B. Stoker
Dracula Archives. R. Rudorff
Dracula's Guest. B. Stoker
Draftsman. F. Cockain
Drag the Dark. F. C. Davis
Dragnet. J. G. Brandon
Dragnet. J. Reach
Dragnet: Case No. 561. D. Knight
Dragnet 1968. D. Vowell
Dragnet '67. R. Tralins
Dragnet: The Case of the Courteous Killer. R. Deming
Dragnet: The Case of the Crime King. R. Deming
Dragoman Pass. Eric Williams
Dragon. Jack Bennett
Dragon. Alfred Coppel
Dragon Flame. Nick Carter
Dragon for Christmas. G. Black
Dragon Hunt. Garrity
Dragon in Harness. S. Gluck
Dragon in Spring. A. Barker
Dragon Island. M. Hastings
Dragon Keepers. Rodney Hughes

Dragon Murder Case. S. S. Van Dine
Dragon of Lung Wang. M. Harvey
Dragon Road. S. Harvester
Dragon Roars. C. Leader
Dragon Shadows. James Bennett
Dragon Slayer. R. Pocock
Dragon Spoor. J. H. Crisp
Dragon Strikes Back. T. Roan
Dragon Tree. V. Canning
Dragon Tree Island. N. Lewis
Dragon Under Ground. R. Bell
Dragon Under the Hill. G. Honeycombe
Dragonfly. K. R. Dwyer
Dragonhead Deal. R. J. Harper
Dragonmede. Rona Randall
Dragons at the Gate. R. L. Duncan
Dragon's Breath. F. A. Smith
Dragon's Cave. C. B. Clason
Dragon's Claw. Roland Daniel
Dragon's Claw. J. A. Dunn
Dragon's Claw. P. O'Donnell
Dragons Came Expensive. M. Storm
Dragons Drive You. E. Balmer
Dragon's Eye. Jennie Melville
Dragon's Eye. S. C. S. Stone
Dragon's Gap. G. Harding
Dragon's Jaws. F. Packard
Dragon's Lair. I. D. Wenzell
Dragon's Mount. D. Rowan
Dragon's Silk. P. Herring
Dragon's Spine. L. Cameron
Dragon's Teeth. E. Queen
Dragons to Slay. Bok
Dragonseeds. B. Banks
Dragonship. Robert MacLeod
Drakmere Must Die. W. H. L. Crauford
Drakov Memorandum. J. Winters
Dram of Poison. C. Armstrong
Dram of Poison. M. Jackson
Drama of Mr. Dilly. C. Edwards
Drama of Mount Street. H. Flatau
Drama of the Rue de la Paix. A. Belot
Drama of the Telephone and other tales. R. Marsh
Dramas of Life. G. R. Sims
Dramatic Murder. Elizabeth Anthony
Draught of Lethe. R. Tellet
Draughts in the Sun. R. Parker
Draw Batons! B. Knox
Draw the Blinds. S. Truss
Draw the Curtain Close. T. B. Dewey
Draw the Dragon's Teeth. B. Newman
Draw the Teeth of a Dragon. M. Ashton
Drawback to Murder. W. A. Barber
Drawn Blanc. R. Gadney
Drawn Blank. R. Jocelyn
Drawn Conclusion. W. A. Barber
Drawn to Evil. H. Whittington
Drawstring. D. Locke
Draycott Murder Mystery. M. Thynne
Dread. B. Sarto
Dread and Water. Douglas Clark
Dread Cave. J. Courage
Dread Journey. D. B. Hughes
Dread of Night. A. Shivelley
Dread the Sunset. M. Carleton
Dreadful Hollow. N. Blake
Dreadful Hollow. I. Karlova
Dreadful Lemon Sky. J. D. MacDonald
Dreadful Night. B. A. Williams
Dreadful Reckoning. C. M. Russell
Dreadful Sanctuary. E. F. Russell
Dreadful Summit. S. Ellin
Dream. L. Freeman
Dream and a Forgetting. J. Hawthorne
Dream and the Dead. P. Audemars
Dream—and the Woman. T. Gallon
Dream Apart. L. Egan
Dream Before Dying. M. Alexander
Dream Buyers. M. Land
Dream Daughter. A. Askew
Dream-Detective. S. Rohmer
Dream Doctor. A. B. Reeve
Dream Girl Caper. J. D. Lawrence
Dream Hunter. M. Fredericks
Dream Is Deadly. Carter Brown
Dream Killers. D. Winston
Dream Merchant. Carter Brown
Dream Murder. A. Broome
Dream Murder. E. C. Reed
Dream of a Woman. J. J. Dratler
Dream of Death. M. O. Bank
Dream of Death. E. Trevor
Dream of Fair Serpents. C. Darby
Dream of Fair Women. C. Armstrong
Dream of Falling. M. O. Rank
Dream of Freedom. H. Nisbet
Dream of Raven. Anonymous
Dream of Romy Jackson. A. J. Benchley
Dream of Terror. R. Abbey
Dream of Treason. M. Edelman
Dream of Treason. M. Pugh
Dream of Unicorns. M. Naismith
Dream Sinister. S. M. Schley
Dream Walker. C. Armstrong
Dreamer at Large. W. M. Duncan
Dreamer Beware. R. Wissman
Dreamer Deals with Murder. W. M. Duncan
Dreamer Intervenes. W. M. Duncan
Dreamer, Lost in Terror. Alison King
Dreamers. R. Manvell
Dreamers: A Club. J. K. Bangs

Dreamers in a Haunted House. M. Lovell
Dreaming God. Basil Carey
Dreaming of Babylon. R. Brautigan
Dreaming Summer. E. Ogilvie
Dreaming Witness. J. Davison
Dreamland. G. V. Higgins
Dreams Die Hard. M. Hayman
Dream's Fulfillment. H. C. Bentley
Dreams to Sell. S. Warwick
Dreamwalker. J. Fitzpatrick
Drearloch. D. Kamm
Dregs. J. L. Rickard
Dresden Green. N. Freeling
Dress Circle Murders. P. Yates
Dress Gray. L. Truscott
Dress Her in Indigo. J. D. MacDonald
Dress to Die In. Marion Cooper
Dress Up and Die. D. Elias
Dressed to Kill. C. Black
Dressed to Kill. A. Bocca
Dressed to Kill. B. Channing
Dressed to Kill. P. Cheyney
Dressed to Kill. E. L. Fetta
Dressed to Kill. K. Gordon
Dressed to Kill. D. H. Hyde
Dressed to Kill. N. Morland
Dressed to Kill. M. K. Ozaki
Dressed Up to Kill. E. G. Cousins
Dressing of Diamond. N. Freeling
Dressing-Room Murder. J. S. Fletcher
Drexel Dream. W. A. MacKenzie
Drift of Fate. Dora Russell
Drifthaven. Clarissa Ross
Drifting Death. H. Carstairs
Drifting Death. B. Gaston
Drifting Diamond. L. Colcord
Drifting Sands. Elsie Lee
Driftwood and Other Tales. J. C. Haywood
Drill Is Death. F. Lockridge
Drilling for Death. John Wolfe
Drink Alone and Die. B. Cobb
Drink for Mr. Cherry. D. Gardiner
Drink No Deeper. C. Edwards
Drink the Green Water. H. Austin
Drink This. E. Dewhurst
Drink to Yesterday. M. Coles
Drink with the Dead. J. M. Flynn
Drinks on the Victim. M. V. Heberden
Drip Dry Man. Eric Lambert
Dripping Tamarinds. C. C. Lowis
Driscoll's Diamonds. I. MacAlister
Drive East on 66. R. Wormser
Driven. R. Gehman
Driven Death. N. Orde-Powlett
Driven Flesh. L. Easton
Driven from Cover. Nicholas Carter
Driven from Home. Anonymous
Driven to Bay. F. Marryat
Driven to Death. J. C. Lenehan
Driven to Desperation. Nicholas Carter
Driven to Kill. D. M. Disney
Driven to Kill. R. Dolphin
Driven to Kill. C. Witting
Driven to Murder. O. Chase
Driven to the Wall. S. Campbell
Driver. C. B. Phillips
Drone-Man. John Ross
Droonin' Watter. J. S. Fletcher
Drop Dead. G. Ashe
Drop Dead. G. Bagby
Drop Dead. W. Braun
Drop Dead. June Drummond
Drop Dead. B. McKnight
Drop Dead. M. Neville
Drop Detective. Anonymous
Drop of a Hat. R. Fenisong
Drop of Hot Gold. J. N. Chance
Drop One, Carry Four. Frederic Sinclair
Drop Out. H. Miller
Drop That Gun. R. Angel
Drop to His Death. J. Rhode
Dropped from the Fast Express. F. M. White
Dropped Living Room. F. Y. McHugh
Drought. J. Creasey
Drove Road. Winifred Duke
Drown Her Remembrance. S. Gilruth
Drown Him Deep. Barbara Cooper
Drown the Wind. M. P. Hood
Drowned Queen. K. Laumer
Drowned Rat. E. Ferrars
Drowner. J. D. MacDonald
Drowning. J. Ehrlich
Drowning Day. A. Dipper
Drowning Pool. J. R. MacDonald
Drowning Stone. H. Fosburgh
Drowning Wire. M. Claire
Drug Called Power. I. MacKintosh
Drug in the Market. C. Baines
Drug of Choice. J. Lange
Drug on the Market. H. Brinton
Drug on the Market. D. Dodge
Drug on the Market. G. Sampson
Drug on the Market. N. Tranter
Drug Run. William Crawford
Drug-Run. P. Pettit
Drum Beat—Berlin. S. Marlowe
Drum Beat—Dominique. S. Marlowe
Drum Beat—Erica. S. Marlowe
Drum Beat—Madrid. S. Marlowe
Drum Beat—Marianne. S. Marlowe

Drum Madness. The Edingtons
Drum of Power. Robert MacLeod
Drum of Ungara. Robert MacLeod
Drummer in the Dark. F. Clifford
Drums Beat at Dusk. S. Maddock
Drums Beat at Night. Gavin Holt
Drums Beat Red. D. Graeme
Drums Call the Major. L. P. Greene
Drums Never Beat. M. McKenna
Drums of Darkness. M. Z. Bradley
Drums of Death. J. Addiscombe
Drums of Doom. O. Binns
Drums of Fu Manchu. S. Rohmer
Drums of Jeopardy. H. MacGrath
Drums of Kufu. J. Delft
Drums of Sacrifice. W. R. Foran
Drums of the Dark Gods. W. A. Ballinger
Drums of War. G. E. Rochester
Drums of War. J. G. Sarasin
Drums of Youth. Margery Lawrence
Drunkard. G. Thorne
Drunkard's End. S. Troy
Drury Affair. I. Valdes
Drury Lane's Last Case. B. Ross
Drury Club Case. S. Williams
Dry Spell. J. Creasey
Dry Taste of Fear. Dorothea Bennett
Dry Tortugas. W. Chambers
Dual Identity. C. G. Mitford
Duane and the Art Murders. J. L. Benton
Duane of the FBI. J. L. Benton
Duane of the G-Men. J. L. Benton
Dubai. Robin Moore
Dublin Nightmare. P. Loraine
Dublin Pawn. J. Keckhut
Duca and the Milan Murders. G. Scerbanenco
Ducats in Her Coffin. T. Warriner
Duchess. J. Edgar
Duchess de Langeais. H. Balzac
Duchess Grace. M. Leighton
Duchess in Difficulties. A. Griffiths
Duchess of Dope. B. Sarto
Duchess of Pontifex Square. G. W. Appleton
Duchess of Powysland. G. Allen
Duchess of Skid Row. L. Trimble
Duchess of Videl. D. Lindsey
Ducking of Herbert Polton, and Coincidence. H. C. McNeile
Ducks and Drakes. M. Leighton
Ducks and Drakes. N. Tranter
Ducks in Thunder. J. J. Dratler
Duckworth's Diamonds. E. Everett-Green
Ducrow Folly. J. N. Chance
Dude Ranch Murders. M. F. Ford
Dudie Dunne. Old Sleuth
Dudley Carleon. M. E. Braddon
Duds. H. C. Rowland
Due or Die. F. Kane
Due to a Death. M. Kelly
Due to Expire. H. A. Wrenn
Due to the Lion Tamer. L. M. Robertson
Duel. R. Marsh
Duel. D. Seaman
Duel Across the Water. D. Quentin
Duel for a Dark Lady. M. Marais
Duel in Glenfinnan. A. MacVicar
Duel in the Shadows. A. Lejeune
Duel in the Snow. H. Meissner
Duel Murder. B. Gray
Duel of Brains. Nicholas Carter
Duel of Shadows. L. R. Brown
Duel Reserrection. B. Mitford
Dueling Oaks. D. Dorsett
Duenna to a Murder. R. King
Duet. D. Daniels
Duet for Death. M. Cronin
Duet for Three Spies. H. T. Rothwell
Duet for Two Guns. D. Ambler
Duet for Two Hands. M. H. Bell
Duet in Death. Hilda Lawrence
Duet of Death. Hilda Lawrence
Duet to Corruption. J. Cello
Duff. I. Blair
Duffy. H. J. Brown
Duffy. D. Kavanagh
Dugdale Millions. W. C. Hudson
Duke. J. S. Clouston
Duke. H. Ellson
Duke. W. Manson
Duke Decides. H. Hill
Duke in the Suburbs. E. Wallace
Duke of Arcanum. F. C. Long
Duke of Cameron Avenue. A. R. Weekes
Duke of Clarence. E. M. F.
Duke of Omaha. Old Sleuth
Duke of York's Steps. Henry Wade
Dukedom of Portsea. A. M. Meadows
Duke's Daughters, and The Fugitives. M. Oliphant
Duke's Day. A. Tavis
Duke's Dilemma. W. Magnay
Duke's Last Trick. C. F. Gregg
Duke's Sweetheart. R. Dowling
Dulcarnon. H. M. Rideout
Dulcie Bligh. G. Clark
Dull Dead. Gwendoline Butler
Dull Thud. Manning Long
Dull Tree. H. Canelstein
Dum-Dum for the President. Martin Brett
Dumaresq's Daughter. G. Allen

Dumb Alibi. N. Morland
Dumb As They Come. M. Corrigan
Dumb Babes Don't Die. H. Spencer
Dumb Detective. Anonymous
Dumb Gods Speak. E. P. Oppenheim
Dumb Vengeance. S. Tower
Dumb Witness. A. Christie
Dumb Witness. M. Hervey
Dumb Witness. T. A. Plummer
Dumb Witness. N. Wylie
Dumb Witness and other stories. Nicholas Carter
Dumbo Dossier. E. Cannon
Dumdum Murder. Carter Brown
Dummy. H. J. O'Higgins
Dummy Murder Case. M. K. Ozaki
Dummy Robberies. M. E. Cooke
Dump. J. Remenham
Dumpling. C. Kernahan
Duncan Dynasty. D. Daniels
Duncan Is in His Grave. R. Wiseman
Duncan Ross—Detective-Sergeant. R. Stuart
Duncraig. M. Heath
Dunes. S. Walters
Dunfermline Affair. Angus Ross
Dungeon. M. L. Falcon
Dungeons of Crowley Hall. C. Alcott
Dunkirk Directive. D. Richmond
Dunleary. M. Heath
Dunleath Abbey. H. P. Diltz
Dunsan House. Gail St. John
Dunslow. E. R. Punshon
Dunthorpes of Westleigh. C. Lys
Duo. C. Armstrong
Dupe. G. Biss
Dupe. L. Cody
Dupe Negative. A. Fowles
Dupes. E. W. Mumford
Duplicate. H. B. Taylor
Duplicate Death. A. C. Fox-Davies
Duplicate Death. G. Heyer
Duplicate Duke. H. Hill
Duplicate Stiff. A. O'Neill
Dupre Blues. D. Curran
Durable Fire. Sheila Bishop
Durand Case. S. Kyle
During Her Majesty's Pleasure. M. E. Braddon
During His Majesty's Pleasure. S. Kyle
Durrell Towers. Clarissa Ross
Dusk at Penarder. Gavin Holt
Dusk to Dawn. C. Graves
Dusky Cactus. M. McEvoy
Dusky Death. R. Garnett
Dusky Hour. E. R. Punshon
Dusky Limelight. Colin Robertson
Dusky Night. V. Bridges
Dusseldorf. A. M. Mackenzie
Dust. J. Hawthorne
Dust and the Curious Boy. P. Graaf
Dust and the Heat. M. Gilbert
Dust in My Throat. J. Farrimond
Dust in the Sun. J. Cleary
Dust in the Vault. R. A. J. Walling
Dust in Your Eyes. S. Seaton
Dust of Death. K. Robeson
Dust to Dust. I. Ostrander
Dusty Coinage. W. Mills
Dusty Death. M. Burning
Dusty Death. O. Mills
Dusty Death. C. Robbins
Dusty Death. L. Thayer
Dusty Sunset. P. Winn
Dutch Courage. Ritchie Perry
Dutch Detective. W. B. Hare
Dutch Shoe Mystery. E. Queen
Dutch the Diver. G. M. Fenn
Dutch Treat. T. Jones
Dutch Uncle. S. Gray
Duty Be Damned! D. Walshe
Duty Elsewhere. J. Wainwright
Duty Free. F. Gaite
Dureen Letter. E. Leather
Dwarf of Westerbourg. C. H. Spiess
Dwarf's Chamber and other stories. F. Hume
Dwelly Lane. F. V. Morley
Dyed for Death. W. W. Rider
Dying Alderman. Henry Wade
Dying Business. E. Dewar
Dying Echo. K. M. Knight
Dying Fall. H. Dolson
Dying Fall. G. Milner
Dying Fall. Henry Wade
Dying for a Drink. R. Silverwood
Dying High. A. Curry
Dying in the Night. J. Roffman
Dying Room. M. L. Stokes
Dying Room Only. S. Sterling
Dying to Live and other stories. S. Horler
Dying Ukrainian. P. Howarth
Dying Witnesses. M. Halliday
Dyke and Burr, the Rival Detectives. H. Rockwood
Dyke Darrel, the Railroad Detective. A. F. Pinkerton
Dynamite! R. P. Connolly
Dynamite. B. Sarto
Dynamite Days. W. C. Tuttle
Dynamite Doll. B. Sarto

Dynamite Drury. L. P. Greene
Dynamite Drury Again. L. P. Greene
Dynamite Drury Patrols. L. P. Greene
Dynamite Freaks. D. Ryan
Dynamite Monster Boogie Concert. Paul Ross
Dynamite on Wheels. Duff Johnson
Dynamite Trap. Nicholas Carter
Dynamiter. R. L. Stevenson
Dynasty of Doom. P. A. Foxall
Dynasty of Fear. J. C. Sprague
Dynasty of Spies. D. Sherman

E Pluribus Bang! D. Lippincott
E.T.A. for Death. C. H. Wallace
Each Dawn I Die. J. Odlum
Each Life to Live. R. Gehman
Each Man's Destiny. M. Procter
Each Night We Die. E. Woodward
Eagle and the Wren. R. Pertwee
Eagle at the Gate. R. Randall
Eagle Flies from England. E. Atiyah
Eagle Has Landed. J. Higgins
Eagle Six. P. Long
Eagle's Eye. W. J. Flynn
Eagle's Feathers. N. Tranter
Eagles Fly. S. Flannery
Eagles Near His Carcase. P. Somerville-Large
Eagle's Nest. J. Carter
Eagle's Nest. D. Daniels
Eaglescliffe. M. McEvoy
Eagrave Square Mystery. A. W. Marchmont
Eames-Erskine Case. A. Fielding
Ear for Murder. Michael Brett
Ear in the Wall. A. B. Reeve
Ear to the Ground. J. H. Chase
Earhart Betrayal. J. S. Thayer
Earhart Mission. P. Tanous
Earl Derr Biggers Tells Ten Stories. E. D. Biggers
Earl Without an Earldom. Scott Graham
Earl's End. L. Gorell
Earl's Return. W. M. Graydon
Earl's Ward. S. Cobb
Early Boyd. Carter Brown
Early Days of August. J. B. Kovalsky
Early Doors. Hugh Mills
Early Frost. D. F. Parkhirst
Early Morning Murder. M. Burton
Early Morning Poison. B. Cobb
Early Warning. C. Fitzsimons
Earmarked for Murder. G. Rayne
Ears of the Jungle. P. Boulle
Earth-Bound. D. Macardle
Earth to Ashes. A. Brock
Earthly Pargatory. L. Dougall
Earthquake Machine. A. Mitchelson
Earth's Great Lord. E. R. Punshon
East All the Way. J. G. Lockhart
East and West. T. Mundy
East Coast Mystery. H. Edmonds
East Hampton. Richard Hubbard
East India and Company. P. Morand
East London Mystery. A. Sergeant
East Lynne. H. Wood
East of Algiers. P. Temple
East of Broadway. O. R. Cohen
East of Desolation. J. Higgins
East of Kashgar. F. A. M. Webster
East of Mansion House. T. Burke
East of Piccadilly. S. Maddock
East of Singapore. G. Goodchild
East of Singapore. M. McGrath
East of Singapore. S. M. Parkman
East Side Assignment. R. Kirby
East Side Detective. Anonymous
East Wind Coming. A. B. Cover
East Wind, Rain. N. R. Nash
East Zone Snatch. G. Vaughan
Easter Dinner. D. Downes
Easter Guests Mystery. J. K. Ryland
Eastern Men—Chicago Women. Griff
Eastern Vendetta. Old Sleuth
Eastlake Affair. Colin Robertson
Eastside Exposure. B. Sarto
Eastward in Eden. D. Garth
Eastwind/Westwind. J. Nordhoff
Easy Come. G. Wheeler
Easy Come, Easy Go. A. Bocca
Easy for the Crook. R. Trevor
Easy Go. J. Lange
Easy Money. B. Atkey
Easy Money. F. Johnston
Easy Money. A. Mather
Easy Prey. Josephine Bell
Easy to Kill. A. Christie
Easy to Kill. H. Footner
Easy to Murder. N. Rutledge
Easy Victim. L. Farago
Easy Way to Go. G. H. Coxe
Eat Me If You Must. N. Karta
Eating the Big Fish. W. Rayner
Eavesdropper. J. Payn
Eavesdropping on Death. C. C. Estes
Ebenezer Investigates. N. Brady
"Eblis." S. Shaw
Ebony Bed Murder. J. R. Gillies
Ebony Box. J. S. Fletcher

Ebony Cross. Nick Carter
Ebony Mirror. F. A. Gallimore
Ebony Stag. B. Flynn
Ebony Torso. J. C. Woodiwiss
Echo Answers Murder. N. Fitzgerald
Echo from Silence. M. Pereira
Echo in a Dark Wind. J. Withers
Echo in the Cave. L. Meynell
Echo My Tears. Jan Foster
Echo of a Bomb. M. Derby
Echo of a Bomb. V. Siller
Echo of a Curse. R. R. Ryan
Echo of Barbara. Jonathan Burke
Echo of Guilt. P. Paul
Echo of Margaret. V. Black
Echo of Treason. Jonathan Burke
Echo of Weeping. M. Lynch
Echo on the Stairs. M. Jenson
Echoes from Castor Hills. D. A. Stephens
Echoes from the Macabre. D. Du Maurier
Echoes of an Ancient Love. S. Wagner
Echoes of Celandine. D. Marlowe
Echoes of Evil. K. Cameron
Echoes of Evil. I. Comfort
Echoes of the Past. M. McEvoy
Echoing Footsteps. F. A. M. Webster
Echoing Shore. Robert Martin
Echoing Strangers. G. Mitchell
Echoing Wave. D. Giberson
Eclipse of James Trent, D.I. L. Yates
Ecstasy. H. Janson
Ecstasy Business. R. Condon
Ecstasy's Captive. N. McFather
Ecstatic Thief. G. K. Chesterton
Ed Noon in London. M. Avallone
Ed. Somers, the Pinkerton Detective. E. Stark
Eddie and the Cruisers. P. F. Kluge
Eddie Macon's Run. J. McLendon
Eddy. Riccardo Stephens
Eden. J. Ellis
Eden Eden. H. K. Fleming
Edgar. R. Sickelmore
Edgar Huntly. C. B. Brown
Edgar Wallace Reader. E. Wallace
Edge of Beauty. B. Ferm
Edge of Beyond. J. B. Hendryx
Edge of Danger. M. Storm
Edge of Darkness. B. Clemens
Edge of Despair. M. L. Hinkel
Edge of Doom. L. Brady
Edge of Doom. M. Dalton
Edge of Extinction. J. Wainwright
Edge of Glass. C. Gaskin
Edge of Hate. E. Cannon
Edge of Hazard. G. Horton
Edge of Honesty. C. Gleig
Edge of Horror. H. Desmond
Edge of Nowhere. E. Thompson
Edge of Panic. H. Kane
Edge of Running Water. W. Sloan
Edge of Terror. F. Cowen
Edge of Terror. B. Flynn
Edge of Terror. M. Halliday
Edge of the City. F. Pohl
Edge of the Forest. R. Barr
Edge of the Forest. J. D. White
Edge of the Law. R. Deming
Edge of the Pond. Robin Moore
Edge of the Sword. F. M. White
Edge of the Tightrope. J. H. Drew
Edge of Violence. J. Clausse
Edge of Violence. A. English
Edina. H. Wood
Edinburgh Caper. S. McKelway
Edinburgh Exercise. Angus Ross
Edisto Sanctuary. J. R. Singleton
Edith Heron. Anonymous
Edith's Diary. P. Highsmith
Editor. D. Tracy
Edric Forester. A. Ker
Educated Evans. E. Wallace
Educated Man. E. Wallace
Education of Don Juan. Robin Hardy
Education of Mr. P. J. Davenant. F. S. Hamilton
Education of Oversoul Seven. Jane Roberts
Education of Patrick Silver. J. Charyn
Edwin of the Iron Shoes. M. Muller
Edwina Black. W. Dinner
Eel Pie Murders. D. Frome
Eel Pie Mystery. D. Frome
Eenie, Meenie, Minie—Murder! W. G. Beyer
Eeny Meeny Miny Mole. M. D'Agneau
Efficiency Expert. E. R. Burroughs
Effigy of a Spy. C. Richardson
Efford Tangle. G. Goodchild
Egad, the Woman in White. T. J. Kelly
Egg-Shaped Thing. C. Hodder-Williams
Egremont Mystery. L. Elmont
Egyptian Cross Mystery. E. Queen
Egyptian Nights. Jack Mann
Egyptian Nights. S. Rohmer
Egyptian Tragedy and other stories. R. H. Savage
Egypt's Choice. D. Broun
Eichmann Syndrome. U. Dan
Eiger Sanction. Trevanian
Eight Candles Glowing. P. Muse
Eight Card Stud. Nick Carter

Title Index

Eight Crooked Trenches. F. Beeding
Eight Faces at Three. C. Rice
Eight Murders in the Suburbs. Roy Vickers
Eight O'Clock Alibi. C. Bush
Eight of Diamonds. H. G. Hutchinson
Eight of Swords. J. D. Carr
Eight Penny Spy. A. Mallary
Eight-Pointed Star. G. H. Teed
Eight Strokes of the Clock. M. Leblanc
813. M. Leblanc
Eight Three Five. A. Soutar
VIII to IX. R. A. J. Walling
Eight Went Cruising. C. H. Barker
Eight Women—and a Ghost. J. Kirkpatrick
Eighteen of Them—Singular Stories. W. Simpson
Eighteenth Summer. L. Holland
Eighth Circle. S. Ellin
Eighth Day. T. Wilder
Eighth Deadly Sin. Jessica Mann
Eighth Dwarf. Ross Thomas
Eighth Millionaire. G. H. Teed
Eighth Mrs. Bluebeard. H. Waugh
Eighth Passenger. M. Tripp
Eighth Sacrament. T. Cullinan
Eighth Seal. A. MacLeod
Eighth Square. H. Lieberman
Eighth Veil. J. Moffatt
Eighth Wonder. J. G. Sarasin
Eighty Dollars to Stamford. L. Fletcher
81st Site. T. Kenrick
Eighty Million Eyes. E. McBain
Eileen the Spy. Anonymous
El Dorado. R. Cromie
El Greco Puzzle. J. Murphy
El Rancho Rio. M. G. Eberhart
Ela the Outcast. T. P. Prest
Elderly Gentleman Shot. D. Sharp
Eldorado Network. Derek Robinson
Eldorado Red. D. Goines
Eldrida, the Red Rover's Daughter. N. Buntline
Eleanor's Victory. M. E. Braddon
Election Booth Murder. M. Propper
Election by Murder. A. Eichler
Electric Theft. N. W. Williams
Electric Train. D. Beaty
Electro Pete, the Man of Fire. A. P. Morris
Elegant Edward. E. Wallace
Elegy for a Revolutionary. C. J. Driver
Element of Chance. Emma Page
Element of Doubt. A. Booth
Element of Risk. E. Cannon
Element of Risk. M. Derby
Elemental. R. Chetwynd-Hayes
Elementary, My Dear. P. King
Elementary, My Dear Freddie. W. H. L. Craufurd
Elena. E. Francis
Elephant. G. Goodchild
Elephant God. G. Casserly
Elephant Murders. E. S. Brown
Elephant Never Forgets. Ethel L. White
Elephant Valley. F. Farr
Elephants Can Remember. A. Christie
Elephant's Work. E. C. Bentley
Elevated Railroad Mystery and other stories. Nicholas Carter
Eleven. P. Highsmith
Eleven Bullets for Mohammed. H. Arvay
Eleven Came Back. M. Seeley
11 for Danger. A. MacVicar
11 Harrowhouse. G. A. Browne
Eleven Men Died. E. T. Woodhall
Eleven of Diamonds. B. Kendrick
Eleven-Thirty Till Twelve. R. Greene
Eleven Thrilling Mysteries. V. McCall
11.20 Glasgow Central. P. Malloch
Eleven Were Brave. F. Beeding
Eleventh Commandment. M. Shavelson
Eleventh Hour. A. Armstrong
Eleventh Hour. J. S. Fletcher
Eleventh Hour. Donald Forbes
Eleventh Hour. H. C. McNeile
Eleventh Hour. R. B. Sinclair
Eleventh Little Indian. Jacquemard-Senecal
Eleventh Little Nigger. Jacquemard-Senecal
Eleventh Plague. N. Berrow
Eleventh Plague. L. T. Peters
Elfa. A. W. Marchmont
Elgin Marble. B. Von Hutten
Eligible Connection. Elsie Lee
Elijah Conspiracy. Charles Robertson
Eliminate the Middle Man. M. Wilk
Elimination Process. C. Joyce
Elimination Syndicate. J. A. Dunn
Eliminator. A. York
Eliza. J. A. Bartlett
Eliza Grimwood. Anonymous
Elizabeth. J. Hamilton
Elizabeth Finds the Body. F. Kilpatrick
Elizabeth Is Missing. L. De La Torre
Elizabeth R.I.P. D. Lee
Elizabeth the Sleuth. F. Kilpatrick
Elizabeth X. V. Caspary
Elk and the Evidence. M. Scherf
Ellen Morgan. W. Tyrer
Ellena. C. Connell

Ellerby Case. J. Rhode
Ellery Queen, Master Detective. E. Queen
Ellery Queen's The Four of Hearts Mystery. W. Rand
Elm Tree Murder. J. Rhode
Elope to Death. G. Ashe
Elsa the Terrible. B. Sarto
Elspeth. S. Nichols
Elster's Folly. H. Wood
Elusive Bachelor. F. E. Penny
Elusive Bowman. F. Vivian
Elusive Clue. D. Stephens
Elusive Corpse. N. Karta
Elusive Criminal. R. Broemel
Elusive Epicure. C. Keith
Elusive Four. W. LeQueux
Elusive Isabel. J. Futrelle
Elusive Killer. T. A. Plummer
Elusive Knave. Nicholas Carter
Elusive Lady. M. Cronin
Elusive Legacy. K. A. Shoesmith
Elusive Lord Bagtor. B. Tozer
Elusive Lover. V. Woods
Elusive Mr. Drago. T. C. H. Jacobs
Elusive Mrs. Pollifax. D. Gilman
Elusive Nephew. M. Dalman
Elusive Picaroon. J. Cassells
Elusive Picaroon. H. Landon
Elusive Quest. F. Cowen
Elusive Vicky Van. C. Wells
Elusive Witness. D. E. Bingley
Elvin Court Mystery. A. I. Etheridge
Elvira Digs a Grave. M. Storm
"Em." E. Southworth
Emancipation of Ambrose. M. Cobb
Embankment Crime. Donald Stuart
Embankment Murder. G. Verner
Embarrassed Ladies Affair. H. Catalan
Embarrassed Murderer. G. Stockwell
Embarrassing Death. R. Jeffries
Embarrassment of Riches. M. Fischer
Embassy. V. Brome
Embassy. S. Coulter
Embassy Ball. V. R. Coxe
Embassy Case. H. Hill
Embassy Detective. W. M. Graydon
Embassy Madonna. Lydia Kirk
Embassy Murder. A. Hodges
Embers of Hate. Bradshaw Jones
Embezzler. J. M. Cain
Embrace of Death. C. C. Estes
Embraces. S. Wagner
Embroidered Sunset. Joan Aiken
Emerald Buddha. J. B. Ames
Emerald Buddha. E. Morse
Emerald Chicks Caper. L. V. Roper
Emerald Clasp. F. Beeding
Emerald Decision. David Grant
Emerald Elephant Gambit. L. Maddock
Emerald Embassy. F. Gerard
Emerald Heart. M. Carrel
Emerald Hill. D. Daniels
Emerald Kiss. C. Reeve
Emerald Mountain. F. Y. McHugh
Emerald Murder Case. Dennis Dean
Emerald Murder Trap. Jackson Gregory
Emerald Necklace. E. Fraser
Emerald Necklace. A. R. Weekes
Emerald of Catherine the Great. H. Belloc
Emerald of Death. E. Snell
Emerald Oil Caper. J. D. Lawrence
Emerald Spider. Gavin Holt
Emerald Station. D. Winston
Emerald Tiger. E. Jepson
Emerald Trap. L. St. Clair
Emergency Exit. H. Carmichael
Emergency Exit. M. Cronin
Emergency Exit. A. Wynne
Emergency in the Pyrenees. A. Bridge
Emergency Procedure. M. Frederics
Emergency Room. J. Kerr
Emigrants de Luxe. M. Dekobra
Emily. C. F. Barrington
Emily Coulton Dies. M. B. Dix
Emily Fitzormond. T. P. Prest
Emily Moreland. H. M. Jones
Emily Percy. T. P. Prest
Emily Will Know. N. Rutledge
Emissary. Michael Mainwaring
Emma of Alkistan. Margery Lawrence
"Emma Slasky." J. Grecco
Emperor Fu Manchu. S. Rohmer
Emperor of America. S. Rohmer
Emperor of Detectives. Anonymous
Emperor of Evil. C. J. Daly
Emperor of Hallelujah Island. G. Goodchild
Emperor of Ice. R. Tate
Emperor's Old Clothes. F. Heller
Emperor's Pearl. R. Van Gulik
Emperor's Snuff-Box. J. D. Carr
Empire of Crime. Nicholas Carter
Empire of Evil. S. Noel
Empire of the World. C. J. C. Hyne
Empire on Arumac. M. Hale
Empress Eugenie. M. B. Lowndes
Empress of the Andes. F. Warden
Empty Bed. H. Adams
Empty Copper Sea. J. D. MacDonald
Empty Cot. C. Phillips
Empty Flat. Frank King

Enduring Flame / 495

Empty Glass. D. Learmonth
Empty Hands. A. Stringer
Empty Heart. Elizabeth Ford
Empty Hills. A. Holden
Empty Hotel. A. C. Gunter
Empty Hours. E. McBain
Empty House. M. Gilbert
Empty House. F. Grierson
Empty House. I. Karlova
Empty House Murder. Donald Stuart
Empty House Mystery. B. Bolt
Empty Mail Bags. E. C. Derby
Empty Man. M. Heimer
Empty Palace. Ben Barclay
Empty Quarter. L. Cameron
Empty Saddle. L. Meynell
Empty Tiger. M. Catto
Empty Tigers. I. Wilson
Empty Trap. J. D. MacDonald
Empty Villa. J. L. Rickard
Empty Years. James Preston
Em's Husband. E. Southworth
Emu's Head. C. Dawe
Enchanted Circle. A. Grace
Enchanted Eden. Rona Randall
Enchanted Garden and other stories. H. A. Vachell
Enchanted Grotto. V. Black
Enchanted Hat. H. MacGrath
Enchanted Isle. M. McEvoy
Enchanted Stone. C. L. Hind
Enchanted Type-Writer. J. K. Bangs
Enchanted Voyage. W. E. D. Ross
Enchanted Wooing. M. Richmond
Enchanter. R. Newman
Enchanter's Castle. J. Tattersall
Enchanter's Nightshade. K. Troy
Enchantment. H. MacGrath
Enchantress. G. Bolton
Enchantress. C. H. Bullivant
Enchantress of the Nile. K. Lindsay
Encore Allain! B. Graeme
Encore the Lone Wolf. L. J. Vance
Encore to Murder. H. P. Martin
Encounter Darkness. S. Forbes
Encounter in Athens. G. Ferrand
Encounter Three. M. Caidin
Encounter with Evil. A. Dean
End Game in Paris. I. Adams
End in Sight. Clifford King
End Is Known. G. H. Hall
End of a Big Wheel. C. Fox
End of a Call Girl. W. C. Gault
End of a Cigarette. E. Gellibrand
End of a Diplomat. Ronald Simpson
End of a Good Woman. M. Hinxman
End of a JD. J. Gonzales
End of a Life. E. Phillpotts
End of a Millionaire. P. D. Ballard
End of a Party. H. Waugh
End of a Shadow. A. Clarke
End of a Stripper. R. Dietrich
End of an Ancient Mariner. G. D. H. Cole
End of an Author. J. J. Farjeon
End of an Iron Man. J. N. Chance
End of Andrew Harrison. F. W. Crofts
End of Chapter. N. Blake
End of Count Rollo. E. Phillpotts
End of Count Rollo and other stories. E. Phillpotts
End of Her Honeymoon. M. B. Lowndes
End of It All. J. Danvers
End of Mr. Garment. V. Starrett
End of Reckoning. Clayton Moore
End of Solomon Grundy. J. Symons
End of Someone Else's Rainbow. R. Rossner
End of Steel. C. R. Cooper
End of the Affair. G. Greene
End of the Chase. C. Waye
End of the Game. J. Cortazar
End of the Game. F. Duerrenmatt
End of the Kill. V. J. Hanson
End of the Line. S. Baron
End of the Line. George Douglas
End of the Line. Graham Fisher
End of the Line. B. Hitchens
End of the Long Hot Summer. L. Meynell
End of the Mildew Gang. S. Fowler
End of the Night. J. D. MacDonald
End of the Road. A. Armstrong
End of the Road. Ray Owen
End of the Rug. R. Llewellyn
End of the Running. A. Evans
End of the Street. M. Procter
End of the Tiger and other stories. J. D. MacDonald
End of the Track. A. Garve
End of the Trail. L. Allan
End of the Web. G. Sims
End of Violence. B. Benson
End Play. R. Braddon
End to Mirth. B. A. Williams
Endangered. Barnaby Conrad
Endgame. H. Ardman
Endless Chain. N. Bell
Endless Colonnade. R. Harling
Endless Night. A. Christie
Endplay. R. G. Toepfer
Ends of Justice. F. M. White
Endure No Longer. M. Albrand
Enduring Flame. N. Tranter

E

Enduring Old Charms. D. M. Disney
Enemies. Richard Harris
Enemies of England. C. R. Gull
Enemies of the Bride. O. Mills
Enemies Within. M. Z. Lewin
Enemy. D. Bagley
Enemy Agent. S. MacKinlay
Enemy and Brother. D. S. Davis
Enemy in the House. M. G. Eberhart
Enemy of Love. V. Coffman
Enemy of Women. B. Perowne
Enemy Sky. P. Saxon
Enemy to Society. G. Bronson-Howard
Enemy Unseen. F. W. Crofts
Enemy Within. J. Creasey
Enemy Within. N. Herbert
Enemy Within. Roy Vickers
Enemy Within the Gates. S. Horler
Enforcer. W. Morgan
Enforcer. B. Appel
Enforcer. J. Cassells
Enforcer. O. Demaris
Enforcer. W. Morgan
Enforcer. A. Sugar
Engaged in Murder. N. Forde
Engaged to Murder. M. V. Heberden
Engagement with Death. G. Ashe
Engaging Picaroon. J. Cassells
England Commune. D. Pryce-Jones
England Made Me. G. Greene
England's Peril. W. LeQueux
English Assassin. M. Moorcock
English Murder. C. Hare
English Rose. Elizabeth Ford
English Wife. C. Blackstock
Englishman of the Rue Cain. H. F. Wood
Englishwoman. A. Askew
Engraved in Evil. P. Minton
Enigma. M. Barak
Enigma Files. C. Sparkes
Enigma of Conrad Stone. C. Houghton
Enigma Project. J. Rosenberger
Enigma Sacrifice. M. Barak
Enjoy Such Liberty. M. Latham
Enoch Strone. E. P. Oppenheim
Enormous Hour Glass. R. Goulart
Enormous Shadow. R. Harling
Enough. D. E. Westlake
Enough Blue Sky. Elizabeth North
Enough Rope. D. Linton
Enough to Kill a Horse. E. Ferrars
Enquiries Are Continuing. J. Ashford
Enquiries of Dr. Eszterhazy. A. Davidson
Enquiry. D. Francis
Enquiry into the Existence of Vampires. M. Lovell
Enrollment Concelled. D. B. Olsen
Ensign Knightley and other stories. A. E. W. Mason
Enter a Murderer. N. Marsh
Enter a Spy. F. J. Whaley
Enter Bridget. T. Cobb
Enter Certain Murderers. Sara Woods
Enter Craig Kennedy. A. B. Reeve
Enter Dr. Nikola. G. Boothby
Enter Murderers. H. Slesar
Enter Sir John. C. Dane
Enter Sleeping. D. Karp
Enter Superintendent Flagg. J. Cassells
Enter the Ace. S. Horler
Enter the Corpse. Sara Woods
Enter the Dormouse. Frank King
Enter the Dragon. M. Roote
Enter the Lion. M. P. Hodel
Enter the Picaroon. J. Cassells
Enter the Saint. L. Charteris
Enter Three Witches. P. McGuire
Enter Two Murderers. Hurst Marshall
Enter Without Desire. E. Lacy
Enterprising Burglar. H. Balfour
Enterprising Picaroon. J. Cassells
Entertaining Murder. F. Grierson
Enthusiast. Peter Hill
Enticement to Danger. Ralph Vickers
Entombed Convict. E. A. Treeton
Entrapped. F. G. Bissager
Entrapped. A. M. Diehl
Entry from San Sebastian. B. Adkins
Entry of Death. E. McGirr
Entwining. R. Condon
Envious Casca. G. Heyer
Envoy Extraordinary. E. P. Oppenheim
Envoy of the Emperor. F. Gerard
Envoy on Excursion. C. Brahms
Epidemic 9. M. Gunther
Epilogue. B. Graeme
Epilogue for Selena. J. Shelynn
Episode at Toledo. A. Bridge
Episode in Rome. T. Lester
Episode of the Stolen Voice. R. C. Armour
Episode of the Wandering Knife. M. R. Rinehart
Epitaph for a Blonde. I. Mercer
Epitaph for a Dead Actor. Dulcie Gray
Epitaph for a Dead Beat. D. Markson
Epitaph for a Lady. M. Cronin
Epitaph for a Lobbyist. R. B. Dominic
Epitaph for a Nurse. A. Hocking
Epitaph for a Spy. E. Ambler
Epitaph for a Teddy Bear. L. Barth
Epitaph for a Tramp. D. Markson

Epitaph for Emily. D. W. Christner
Epitaph for Joanna. H. Howard
Epitaph for Lemmings. S. Harvester
Epitaph for Love. H. Clewes
Epitaph for Lydia. V. Rath
Epitaph for Meredith. N. Cromarty
Epitaph for Mister Wynn. K. Wheeler
Epitaph to a Bad Cop. J. Fredman
Epitaph to Treason. W. A. Ballinger
Eppworth Case. I. Patterson
Epsom Mystery. H. Hill
Equal Antagonism. M. Pereira
Equal Danger. L. Sciascia
Equal Partners. H. Fielding
Equality Island. A. Soutar
Erase My Name. J. Donahue
Erasers. A. Robbe-Grillet
Erection Set. M. Spillane
Eric Allen's Broadcast Stories. Eric Allen
Eric Hearle, Detective. A. Joscelyn
Eric the Archer. M. H. Hervey
Ermine. M. A. Fleming
Ernest Maltravers. E. Bulwer-Lytton
Ernestine de Lacy. T. P. Prest
Eroica. M. Rostov
Eros Affair. P. McCutchan
Eros Is No Hangman. A. Wood
Errant Knights. M. Hebden
Erring Under-Secretary. F. Beeding
Erring Way. C. N. Whaley
Error in Judgment. A. Corliss
Error of Her Ways. F. Barrett
Error of Judgment. G. H. Coxe
Error of Judgment. H. Denker
Error of Judgment. Roy Lewis
Error of the Moon. Sara Woods
Escalation. H. Janson
Escalator. A. Gardner
Escapade. A. Mills
Escapades of Mr. Alfred Dimmock. F. Russell
Escape. M. Aldanov
Escape. Royal Brown
Escape. H. Desmond
Escape. C. Franklin
Escape. H. Janson
Escape. M. Porlock
Escape. Jeremy Scott
Escape. E. Vance
Escape. K. Walker
Escape a Killer. J. Philips
Escape Agents. C. J. C. Hyne
Escape and Be Secret. C. H. Gibbs-Smith
Escape and Return. M. McLaren
Escape at Dawn. G. P. Willis
Escape at Sunrise. M. Cronin
Escape for Sandra. P. Cheyney
Escape from Dartmoor. M. Beckett
Escape from Devil's Island. P. McCurtin
Escape from Julia. C. Massie
Escape from Liberty. L. P. Greene
Escape from Murder. M. Stand
Escape from Prague. R. Cleeve
Escape from Spain. A. D. Divine
Escape from Zahrein. Michael Barrett
Escape If You Can. Robin Temple
Escape in Vain. G. Simenon
Escape into Danger. M. S. Gaffney
Escape into Danger. M. Rutledge
Escape into Murder. M. Jackson
Escape of Andrew Cole. U. L. Silberrad
Escape of General Gerard. D. Betteridge
Escape of Mr. Trimm. I. S. Cobb
Escape of the Notorious Sir William Heans, and The Mystery of Mr. Daunt. W. Hay
Escape Route M6. J. H. Date
Escape the Night. M. G. Eberhart
Escape to Athena. P. Blake
Escape to Crime. James Stewart
Escape to Danger. P. Conway
Escape to Death. C. Franklin
Escape to Death. E. M. Williams
Escape to Eternity. W. B. M. Ferguson
Escape to Fear. S. Bate
Escape to Fear. T. D. Smith
Escape to Love. E. S. Aarons
Escape to Murder. Sutherland Scott
Escape to Nowhere. P. Covert
Escape to Nowhere. D. Karp
Escape to Quebec. M. Kennedy
Escape While I Can. M. Marlette
Escape with Gun Cotton. Rupert Grayson
Escaped from Sing Sing. Hawkshaw
Escapemanship. J. Ditton
Escaping Club. A. J. Evans
Escort Job. H. Kane
Escort to Adventure. A. MacVicar
Escort to Danger. S. Truss
Espionage. W. S. Doxey
Espionage! G. Marlowe
Espionage. B. Sarto
Espionage for a Lady. T. Ferris
Espionage Infection. D. Haysom
Espionage Killings. J. G. Brandon
Esprit de Corpse. F. Kane
Essence of Murder. M. Klinger
Essential Man. Al Morgan
Essex Murders. V. Loder
Essex Road Crime. J. Drummond
Establishment. Robin Moore

Establishment of Innocence. H. Aronson
Estate of Grace. J. Powers
Estate of the Beckoning Lady. M. Allingham
Esther Lawes. E. Jepson
Esther, Ruth and Jennifer. Jack Davies
Etched in Murder. K. Jones
Etched in Violence. M. Cumberland
Eternal Conflict. J. Templeton
Eternal Instinct. A. Applin
Eternal Moment. B. H. Logan
Eternity, Here I Come! David Hume
Eternity Ring. P. Wentworth
Ethel Norman's Secret. P. Trent
Ethel Opens the Door. D. Fox
Ethelinde. T. P. Prest
Ethical Solution. J. V. Gordon
Ethiopian's Secret. W. W. Sayer
Etonian. A. Askew
Etruscan Bull. F. Gruber
Etruscan Net. M. Gilbert
Etruscan Smile. V. Johnston
Eugene Aram. E. Bulwer-Lytton
Eugene Vidocq: Soldier, Thief, Spy, Detective. D. Donovan
Eugenia. Anonymous
Eugenia. A. Hurlba
Eulalie. M. A. Earl
Eulalie. W. S. Hayward
Eunuch of Stamboul. D. Wheatley
Eurasian Virgins. J. Seward
Euridice. Taffrail
Euro-Killers. J. Rathbone
Europe That Was. G. Household
Euryale in London. C. Dane
Eustace Diamonds. A. Trollope
Euston Road Mystery. A. Parsons
Euthanasia. Anonymous
Eve. J. H. Chase
Eve. P. Trent
Eve—and the Law. A. Askew
Eve Finds the Killer. R. Garnett
Eve—It's Extortion. Carter Brown
Eve of April Twenty. P. Upton
Eve of His Dying. Carter Brown
Eve of Judgment. Roger Fuller
Eve of the Wedding. Lionel Black
Eve Was No Lady. R. Drayton
Evelina, the Pauper's Child. T. P. Prest
Evelyn. A. Askew
Evelyn, the Ambitious. K. Kimbrough
Even Bishops Die. C. Saxby
Even Doctors Die. L. Anson
Even from the Law. M. Latham
Even If You Run. D. Cory
Even in Death. S. Devine
Even in the Best Families. R. Stout
Even Jericho. Warner Hall
Even Keel. R. Kruger
Even the Rainbow's Bent. C. Noone
Even the Rich Girl. H. L. Gates
Even the Wicked. R. Marsten
Evening in Paris. M. Richmond
Event Called Murder. Martin Thomas
Eventide. B. Ferm
Events of That Week. N. Bentley
Ever-Loving Blues. Carter Brown
Ever Mohun. F. T. Jane
Ever Singing Die Oh! Die. O. Blakeston
Evergreen Death. James Fraser
Evermore. B. Steward
Every Bet's a Sure Thing. T. B. Dewey
Every Cloud. M. Peterson
Every Inch a Lady. Joan Fleming
Every Little Crook and Nanny. E. Hunter
Every Man a King. A. Worboys
Every Man a Murderer. H. Von Doderer
Every Man an Enemy. W. H. Baker
Every Man for Himself. H. Moorhouse
Every Man Has His Price. M. Leighton
Every Man Has His Price. A. Whitney
Every Man His Price. M. Rittenberg
Every Man's Brother. P. Lewis
Every Man's Hand. Charles Ross
Every Night About Half Past Eight, and other stories. L. J. Beeston
Every Third Thought. D. Malm
Everybody Adored Cara. A. Head
Everybody Always Tells. E. R. Punshon
Everybody Does It. J. M. Cain
Everybody Had a Gun. R. S. Prather
Everybody Loves Opal. J. Patrick
Everybody Makes Mistakes. M. S. Marble
Everybody Suspect. D. Sharp
Everybody's Ready to Die. J. Frederics
Everyone Suspect. N. Tyre
Everything Goes Dead. Roderic Wilkinson
Everything Happens to Hector. D. Batchelor
Everything Happens to Joe. D. O'Flanagan
Everything Has Its Price. H. H. Kirst
Everything He Touched. M. Cumberland
Everything Is Thunder. J. L. Hardy
Eve's Island. E. Wallace
Evidence. Anthony Lang
Evidence. J. Weisman
Evidence Before Gabriel. Conrad Forst
Evidence by Telephone. Nicholas Carter
Evidence I Shall Give. J. Wainwright
Evidence in Blue. E. C. Vivian
Evidence Most Blind. D. Keene

Title Index

Evidence of the Accused. R. Jeffries
Evidence of Things Seen. E. Daly
Evidence Unseen. L. R. Davis
Evidence You Will Hear. H. Jobson
Evidently Murdered. Jay Hall
Evil Among Us. J. Crecy
Evil Angel. J. Middlemass
Evil at Bayou Laforche. E. Hayworth
Evil at Hillcrest. J. Ellis
Evil at Nunnery Manor. R. Abbey
Evil at Queen's Priory. V. Coffman
Evil at Roger's Cross. C. Cookson
Evil at Whispering Hills. K. Cameron
Evil Became Them. P. Root
Evil Cargo. K. Stanton
Evil Chateau. S. Horler
Evil Children. W. D. Roberts
Evil Come, Evil Go. W. Masterson
Evil Cross. S. Esmond
Evil Damp. K. R. Butler
Evil Days. B. Fischer
Evil Ever After. B. Myers
Evil, Evil. L. DuBreuil
Evil Eye. P. Boileau
Evil Eye. Martin Thomas
Evil Eyes. Roland Daniel
Evil Formula. Nicholas Carter
Evil Friendship. V. Packer
Evil Genius. G. Bagby
Evil Genius. W. Collins
Evil Genius. E. Turland
Evil Gnome. K. Robeson
Evil Guest. J. S. Le Fanu
Evil Harvest. Margery Lawrence
Evil Hour. L. Meynell
Evil in a Mask. D. Wheatley
Evil in High Places. P. Lunn
Evil in the Cup. E. P. Thorne
Evil in the Family. C. Corren
Evil in the House. E. Bond
Evil in the House. Elbur Ford
Evil Innocence. H. Munro
Evil Intent. J. Wainwright
Evil Is As Evil Does. R. Gatenby
Evil Is the Night. J. Chadwick
Evil Is the Night. J. Creighton
Evil Island. J. Blair
Evil Lives Here. H. S. Nuelle
Evil Men Do. C. Fitzsimmons
Evil Men Do. D. Nile
Evil Messenger. S. Horler
Evil Money. T. Harknett
Evil of Dark Harbor. Clarissa Ross
Evil of the Day. T. Sterling
Evil of Time. E. Berckman
Evil Ones. G. J. Barrett
Evil Phoenix. B. Newman
Evil Reputation. Dora Russell
Evil Root. L. Thayer
Evil Roots. W. Untermeyer
Evil Shadows. Roland Daniel
Evil Shepherd. E. P. Oppenheim
Evil Side of Eden. Sara North
Evil Sleep. E. Hunter
Evil Spell. W. Tyrer
Evil Star. J. Spain
Evil That Men Do. S. A. Curtis
Evil That Men Do. E. Fawcett
Evil That Men Do. R. L. Hill
Evil That Men Do. A. Hocking
Evil That Men Do. H. Pentecost
Evil That Men Do. M. P. Shiel
Evil That Men Do. A. Spiller
Evil That Men Do. G. Steuart
Evil That Waited. M. Farnsworth
Evil That Walks Invisible. Alicen White
Evil Under the Sun. A. Christie
Evil Vanguard. M. Hay
Evil Wish. J. Potts
Evvie. V. Caspary
Ewe Lamb. M. Erskine
Ex-Con. S. Friedman
Ex-Detective. E. P. Oppenheim
Ex-Duke. E. P. Oppenheim
Ex-Gangster. C. F. Caunter
Ex Officio. T. J. Culver
Ex-Pugilist Detective. Old Sleuth
Ex-Serviceman's Secret. H. Hardinge
Ex-Soldier Employment Swindle. A. Murray
Excalibur Disaster. J. Bickham
Excavator's Secret. H. H. C. Gibbons
Excellency. D. Beaty
Excellent Intentions. R. Hull
Excellent Knave. J. F. Molloy
Excellent Mystery. C. D. Jones
Excellent Night for a Murder. V. Rath
Excelsior. H. B. M. Watson
Except for One Thing. H. Blayn
Excess Baggage. H. M. Raleigh
Exchange. R. L. Brent
Exchange of Eagles. O. Sela
Exchanged Identity. F. Du Boisgobey
Exclusive. H. Janson
Excuse My Gun. R. Angel
Execution. M. Blais
Execution. O. Crawford
Execution. R. Mayer
Execution Exchange. J. Gluckman
Execution of Diamond Deutsch. C. F. Gregg
Executioner. P. Boulle
Executioner. V. Torrio
Executioners. Nick Carter
Executioners. J. Creasey
Executioners. J. D. MacDonald
Executioners. B. Moore
Executioner's Axe. P. Lancaster
Executioner's Rest. A. M. Stein
Executioner's Song. N. Mailer
Executive Privilege. G. Perrett
Executive Wife. R. Colby
Exercise for Madmen. B. Paul
Exercise Hoodwink. M. Procter
Exhibit No. Thirteen. R. Jeffries
Exhumed! A. Blair
Exile from London. R. H. Savage
Exiled to Siberia. W. M. Graydon
Exile's Bride. E. Southworth
Exit a Dictator. E. P. Oppenheim
Exit a Spy. H. T. Rothwell
Exit a Star. K. M. Knight
Exit Actors, Dying. M. Arnold
Exit an Admiral. A. W. Allen
Exit and Curtain. Kevin O'Hara
Exit Arnholt. G. Latta
Exit Charlie. A. Atkinson
Exit Dying. H. Olesker
Exit for a Dame. R. Ellington
Exit from Prague. B. Cleeve
Exit Harlequin. C. F. Gregg
Exit Harlequin. Jessica Ryan
Exit in Green. Martin Brett
Exit John Horton. J. J. Farjeon
Exit Laughing. S. Palmer
Exit Mr. Brent. G. Davison
Exit Mr. Marlowe. V. Bridges
Exit Mr. Shane. J. Cassells
Exit Murderer. Sara Woods
Exit Only. S. Maddock
Exit Pretty Poll. E. Burgess
Exit, Running. B. Spicer
Exit Screaming. H. Dalmas
Exit Screaming. C. Hale
Exit Second Murderer. D. Sharp
Exit Sherlock Holmes. R. L. Hall
Exit Silas Danvers. H. Leyford
Exit Simeon Hex. J. M. Walsh
Exit Sir John. B. Flynn
Exit Sir Toby Belch. Hilary Landon
Exit the Body. P. Carmichael
Exit the Disguiser. S. Horler
Exit—the Killer. J. Dyan
Exit the Skeleton. H. Adams
Exit This Way. M. V. Heberden
Exit to Music. N. Shepherd
Exit to Music and other stories. N. Morland
Exit to Violence. H. Jobson
Exit with Emeralds. I. Andrews
Exit with Intent. P. Loraine
Exit Without Permit. C. Franklin
Exodus: 20. O. B. Davis
Exodus of the Damned. S. Slappey
Exorcism. C. Blackstock
Exorcism of Angela Gray. N. T. Vane
Exorcism of Jenny Slade. D. Daniels
Exotic. Carter Brown
Exotic Seductress. H. Janson
Expect No Mercy. E. P. Thorne
Expectant Nymph. H. Janson
Expected Death. M. Fitt
Expendable. W. D. Roberts
Expendable Agent. G. Sowman
Expendable Man. D. B. Hughes
Expendable Spy. J. D. Hunter
Expensive Place to Die. L. Deighton
Experience with Evil. J. R. MacDonald
Experiences of a Barrister. W. Warner
Experiences of a Bond Street Jeweler. H. A. Vachell
Experiences of a French Detective Officer. Waters
Experiences of a Lady Detective. Anonymous
Experiences of a Real Detective. Inspector F
Experiences of an American Detective. Anonymous
Experiences of Loveday Brooke, Lady Detective. C. L. Pirkis
Experiment. W. Butler
Experiment at Proto. P. Oakes
Experiment in Crime. J. Rhode
Experiment in Crime. P. Wylie
Experiment in Springtime. M. Millar
Experiment in Terror. The Gordons
Experiment of Doctor Nevill. E. Hulme-Beaman
Experiment Perilous. M. Carpenter
Experiment with Eros. R. S. Thorn
Experiments in Crime. G. Frankau
Expert. B. Picton
Expert Evidence. C. F. Gregg
Expert Evidence. R. Pertwee
Expert in Craft. Dick Stewart
Expert in Murder. C. L. Leonard
Expert Witness. P. Conway
Expiation. E. P. Oppenheim
Expiation of Lady Anne. L. S. Oliver
Expiation of Wynne Palliser. B. Mitford
Exploited Woman. J. Keating
Exploiters. Samuel Edwards
Exploits of a Dead Man. P. Urquhart
Exploits of a Physician Detective. George Butler
Exploits of a Private Detective. S. Campbell
Exploits of a Race-Course Detective. N. Gould
Exploits of Arsene Lupin. M. Leblanc
Exploits of Asaf Khan. Afghan
Exploits of Black Thumb. W. Bouchier
Exploits of Capt. McKeene. R. Walker
Exploits of Captain O'Hagan. S. Rohmer
Exploits of Danby Croker. R. A. Freeman
Exploits of Dick Tracy, Detective. C. Gould
Exploits of Elaine. A. B. Reeve
Exploits of Fidelity Dove. D. Durham
Exploits of Jo Salis, a British Spy. W. O. Greener
Exploits of Jonathan Jow. W. J. Makin
Exploits of Juve. P. Souvestre
Exploits of Kesho Naik, Dacoit. E. C. Cox
Exploits of Pudgy Pete & Co. E. P. Oppenheim
Exploits of Sherlock Holmes. Adrian C. Doyle
Exploits of the Chevalier Dupin. M. Harrison
Explosion. D. C. Disney
Explosion! Colin Robertson
Explosion. E. Wuorio
Explosion. H. H. Ziemann
Explosive Situation. G. Hackforth-Jones
Expo 80. John Burke
Exporters. G. Norham
Express Delivery. J. M. Walsh
Express Messenger and other tales of the rail. C. Warman
Express Train Murder. John Norman
Expressman and the Detective. A. Pinkerton
Expresso Jungle. W. H. Baker
Expressway. H. North
Expropriators. J. Blythe
Expurgator. A. York
Exquisite Corpse. Alfred Chester
Exquisite Lady. G. Fairlie
Extenuating Circumstances. E. Nisot
Exterior to the Evidence. J. S. Fletcher
Extermination Camp. G. Sheen
Exterminator. P. McCurtin
Extinction Bomber. S. B. Hough
Extortion. H. Howard
Extortion Incorporated. J. Cooper
Extortioners. J. Creasey
Extortioners. O. Demaris
Extortionists. B. Bavin
Extra Body. R. Reinsmith
Extra Kill. Dell Shannon
Extra Passenger. D. Timins
Extraordinary Adventures of Arsene Lupin, Gentleman Burglar. M. Leblanc
Extraordinary Case of Mr. Bell. W. Jackson
Extraordinary Experience. L. Bryce
Extraordinary Seaman. P. Rock
Extreme License. Jerome Barry
Extreme Penalty. A. M. Meadows
Extreme Remedies. M. Borgenicht
Extremes Meet. C. MacKenzie
Extremists. P. Leslie
Extricating Obadiah. J. C. Lincoln
Extro. A. Bester
Eye at the Keyhole. S. Maddock
Eye for a Tooth. D. Yates
Eye for an Eye. O. W. Bayer
Eye for an Eye. L. Brackett
Eye for an Eye. F. Hickok
Eye for an Eye. M. Leighton
Eye for an Eye. W. LeQueux
Eye for an Eye. M. O. Rolfe
Eye for an Eye. V. J. Santiago
Eye for an Eye. G. Seton
Eye for an Eye. J. B. West
Eye in Attendance. J. N. Chance
Eye in Attendance. V. Williams
Eye in the Museum. J. J. Connington
Eye in the Pyramid. R. Shea
Eye of a God. W. A. Fraser
Eye of a Serpent. G. Peters
Eye of Fate. A. M. Meadows
Eye of Gold. I. Stark
Eye of Isis. M. Peterson
Eye of Jinas and other stories. T. A. Fraser
Eye of Kali. E. R. Brayshaw
Eye of Lucifer. F. F. Van De Water
Eye of Nemesis. P. C. De Crespigny
Eye of One. G. Merrick
Eye of Osiris. R. A. Freeman
Eye of Shiva. L. Grimes
Eye of the Beholder. M. Behm
Eye of the Beholder. J. Wainwright
Eye of the Cat. D. Spicer
Eye of the Devil. P. Loraine
Eye of the Eagle. D. O'Connor
Eye of the Gods. J. Neil
Eye of the Gods. Richard Owen
Eye of the Hurricane. H. Howard
Eye of the Needle. K. Follett
Eye of the Needle. Ronald Johnston
Eye of the Needle. T. Walsh

498 / Eye of the Peacock — Title Index

Eye of the Peacock. A. M. Dodge
Eye of the Peacock. O. Goff
Eye of the Sun. E. S. Ellis
Eye of the Tiger. Wilbur Smith
Eye of the Tornado. C. Pincher
Eye of Zeitoon. T. Mundy
Eye Spy. M. Finch
Eye Stones. H. Esmond
Eye with Mascara. M. Finch
Eye-Witness. G. H. Coxe
Eye-Witness! J. Doe
Eye Witness. E. Levison
Eye Witness. J. S. Strange
Eyes Around Me. G. Black
Eyes at the Window. O. S. Cornelius
Eyes at the Window. S. Truss
Eyes in the Night. Gavin Holt
Eyes in the Night. C. M. Howarth
Eyes in the Night. B. Kendrick
Eyes in the Wall. C. Wells
Eyes of Alicia. C. E. Pearce
Eyes of Buddha. J. Ball
Eyes of Death. John Bentley
Eyes of Desire. C. H. Bullivant
Eyes of Green. N. Bawden
Eyes of Laura. H. B. Gilmour
Eyes of Max Carrados. E. Bramah
Eyes of Men. D. Newton
Eyes of Omar. L. C. Douthwaite
Eyes of Pharaoh. G. Thorne
Eyes of St. Emlyn. A. Feist
Eyes of the Blind. A. S. Roche
Eyes of the Shadow. M. Grant
Eyes of the Tiger. Nick Carter
Eyes of Tlaloc. A. E. Peterson
Eyes That Watch You. W. Irish
Eyes Through the Mask. R. Trevor
Eyes Through the Tree. M. C. Keator
Eyewitness. M. Hebden
Eyewitness. J. P. Seabrooke
Eyre's Acquittal. H. B. Mathers
Eyrie of an Eagle. A. Delmonico
Eyrie of the Fox. M. Eyre

F As in Flight. L. Treat
F.B.I. Showdown. "G-Man"
F.B.I. Special Agent. "G-Man"
FBI Story. The Gordons
"F" Cipher. J. G. Bethune
F Corridor. J. G. Edwards
F.E.U.D. H. Janson
F.O.B. Murder. B. Hitchens
FSO-1. H. Greene
Fabulists. B. Capes
Fabulous. Carter Brown
Fabulous Clipjoint. F. Brown
Fabulous Finn. D. Cushman
Fabulous Valley. D. Wheatley
Fabulous Wink. K. Bennett
Face. J. Vance
Face. D. Whitelaw
Face. D. Zec
Face and the Mask. R. Barr
Face Cards. C. Wells
Face for a Clue. G. Simenon
Face in the Film. O. Merland
Face in the Flashlight. F. Warden
Face in the Fog. Marilyn Ross
Face in the Mirror. G. F. Bradby
Face in the Mirror. M. Chittenden
Face in the Mirror. A. Furness
Face in the Night. E. Wallace
Face in the Pond. Clarissa Ross
Face in the Shadow. Nicholas Carter
Face in the Shadows. V. Johnston
Face in the Shadows. P. Ordway
Face in the Shadows. Marilyn Ross
Face Me When You Walk Away. B. Freemantle
Face of a Hero. P. Boulle
Face of Air. G. L. Knapp
Face of an Angel. M. Paradise
Face of Chalk. Melissa Davies
Face of Danger. Graham Fisher
Face of Danger. W. D. Roberts
Face of Danger. M. Sharman
Face of Death. M. Gault
Face of Evil. J. McPartland
Face of Fear. B. Coffey
Face of Fear. L. Crump
Face of Fortune. J. Workman
Face of Hate. T. Du Bois
Face of Him. I. A. Greenfield
Face of Innocence. E. Ogilvie
Face of Inspector Britt. E. P. Thorne
Face of Jalanath. Ronald Hardy
Face of Night. B. Brunner
Face of Rosenfel. C. H. Montagne
Face of Stone. S. Horler
Face of Terror. U. Dan
Face of Terror. E. Litvinoff
Face of the Crime. L. O'Donnell
Face of the Enemy. V. Scannell
Face of the Enemy. T. Walsh
Face of the Foe. J. Millson
Face of the Foe. P. Power
Face of the Lion. J. Blackburn

Face of the Man from Saturn. H. S. Keeler
Face of the Tiger. U. Curtiss
Face of Trespass. R. Rendell
Face on the Cutting Room Floor. C. McCabe
Face on the Stair. L. Winstanley
Face Out Front. R. R. Irvine
Face the Music. C. Franklin
Face to Face. J. Lynch
Face to Face. D. J. MacKenzie
Face to Face. E. Queen
Face to Face with Death. A. W. Marchmont
Face Value. L. P. Greene
Face Value. J. M. Walsh
Faceless Adversary. F. Lockridge
Faceless Corpse Murders. L. L. Rogger
Faceless Enemy. F. S. Wees
Faceless Fugitive. R. Charles
Faceless Man. C. Wick
Faceless Men. O. Beeby
Faceless Ones. L. Hardy
Faceless Ones. G. Verner
Faceless Stranger. P. Usher
Faces in the Dark. P. Boileau
Faces of a Bad Girl. J. N. Chance
Faces of Danger. R. King
Faces of Death. A. M. Stein
Faces of Murder. J. T. MacCargo
Facets. I. R. G. Hart
Facing Death. J. J. Farjeon
Facing East. A. Soutar
Fact X. P. Winn
Factor's Wife. C. Blackstock
Factory Girl. C. E. Blaney
Factory Girl. M. E. Braddon
Factory Mystery. Gregory Wilson
Factory on the Cliff. Neil Gordon
Factotum and other stories. W. LeQueux
Facts About Floyd. S. M. Parkman
Facts in the Case of E. A. Poe. A. Sinclair
Faculty of Murder. J. Wright
Fade into Murder. S. Holmes
Fade out the Stars. M. Cumberland
Fade to Black. R. Renaud
Fadeout. J. Hansen
Fago. B. Roueche
Failure. G. Vaizey
Fainting Lady. M. Frazer
Faintley Speaking. G. Mitchell
Fair Affair. P. Champagne
Fair and the Dead. J. S. Strange
Fair Brigand. G. Horton
Fair Colonist. E. Glanville
Fair Criminal. Nicholas Carter
Fair Crusader. W. Westall
Fair Devil. E. Greenwood
Fair Exchange. E. Colles
Fair Exchange. Anne-Marie Cox
Fair Exchange. K. Gordon
Fair Exchange. P. Harcourt
Fair Freebooter. B. Marnan
Fair Freelance. G. Campbell
Fair Game. G. Bartram
Fair Game. P. Harcourt
Fair Game. K. Kramer
Fair Game. N. Tranter
Fair-Haired Lady. M. Leblanc
Fair Imposter. A. St. Aubyn
Fair in the Fearless Old Fashion. C. Farmlet
Fair Insurgent. E. Horton
Fair Intruder. K. Lindsay
Fair-Isle Jumper Mystery. Hallam James
Fair Kilmeny. V. Black
Fair Maids Missing. P. Audemars
Fair Murder. N. Brady
Fair Mystery. Anonymous
Fair Mystery. B. M. Clay
Fair Play. E. Southworth
Fair Prey. Will Duke
Fair Prisoner. M. Gerard
Fair Quakeress. O. Bradbury
Fair Refuge. M. Gerard
Fair Sinner. Mrs. C. Kernahan
Fair Trial. J. Laborde
Fair Warning. M. G. Eberhart
Fair Warning. G. E. Simpson
Fair Wind to Malabar. J. D. White
Fair Winds of Love. R. Laker
Fair Young Widow. G. R. Preedy
Fairbairn Case. John Bentley
Fairer Than She. T. Charles
Fairfax Millions. A. Winnington
Fairfax Mystery. J. Keating
Fairly Caught. D. Walshe
Fairly Dangerous Thing. R. Hill
Fairly Innocent Little Man. L. Meynell
Fairway Island. H. G. Hutchinson
Fairways and Foul. J. Carrick
Fairy of the Film. H. T. Johnson
Faith Has No Country. R. V. Beste
Faith-Healer. A. W. Marchmont
Faith, Hope and Charity. I. S. Cobb
Faith, Hope and Charity. Rona Randall
Faith, Hope and Cyanide. B. Roome
Faith, Hope and Death. D. Craig
Faith That Kills. E. Hulme-Beaman
Faith Unfaithful. F. E. Wynne
Faithful Achates. A. Gould

Faithless. Clayton Matthews
Fake. P. Lunn-Rockliffe
Fake. Colin Robertson
Fake. H. Sprott
Faked Passports. D. Wheatley
Fakers. P. Leslie
Faking It. Gerald Green
Fakir's Curse. K. Bruce
Falcon. N. Slater
Falcon and the Dove. J. Laborde
Falcon and the Moon. C. Darby
Falcon Cuts In. D. Drake
Falcon for a Witch. C. Darby
Falcon Meets a Lady. D. Drake
Falcon Mystery. S. Guise
Falcon of the Foreign Office. D. Newton
Falcon Rising. C. Darby
Falcon Road. C. Massie
Falcon Royal. C. Darby
Falcon Sunset. C. Darby
Falcon to the Lure. C. Darby
Falcon Tree. C. Darby
Falconer's Hall. J. Aeby
Falconlough. M. Heath
Falconridge. E. Marlow
Falcon's Claw. C. Darby
Falcon's Heir. C. Virmonne
Falcon's Island. Antonia Scott
Falcon's Nest. A. Lloyd
Falcon's Prey. D. Drake
Falcon's Shadow. K. Troy
Falkland's Choice. P. Trent
Falkner's of Greenhurst. J. Middlemass
Fall, Darkness, Fall. J. Corby
Fall from Grace. V. Canning
Fall Girl. Ken Blake
Fall Girl. R. Deming
Fall Guy. Jerome Barry
Fall Guy. Joe Barry
Fall Guy. H. Howard
Fall Guy. J. Mack
Fall Guy. Ray Owen
Fall Guy. Ritchie Perry
Fall Guy. B. Shannon
Fall Guy. T. Trent
Fall Guy for a Killer. S. Acre
Fall Guy for Murder. L. Goldman
Fall into My Grave. F. Usher
Fall of a Dictator. A. Gask
Fall of a Sparrow. V. Gielgud
Fall of a Star. W. Magnay
Fall of an Eagle. J. Cleary
Fall of Marty Moon. A. Frazer
Fall of Midas. J. Astley
Fall of Rock. K. R. Butler
Fall of Snow. J. Shelynn
Fall of Terror. L. Peters
Fall of the Curtain. P. Motte
Fall of the House of Usher. R. Brome
Fall of the Mighty. A. Seymour
Fall of the Sparrow. N. Balchin
Fall-Out of Thieves. J. N. Chance
Fall Over Cliff. Josephine Bell
Fallen Among Thieves. A. W. A'Beckett
Fallen Among Thieves. A. Applin
Fallen Among Thieves. S. P. Hyatt
Fallen Angel. M. Avallone
Fallen Angel. W. Ericson
Fallen Angel. M. Holland
Fallen Curtain. R. Rendell
Fallen Eagles. Geoffrey Davison
Fallen Fortunes. J. Payn
Fallen from Favour. J. Middlemass
Fallen into the Pit. E. Pargeter
Fallen Leaves. W. Collins
Fallen Pride. E. Southworth
Fallen Sparrow. D. B. Hughes
Fallen Staircase. K. Hess
Fallen Star. Jack Lewis
Falling Angel. W. Hjortsberg
Falling Blonde. P. Denver
Falling Man. W. Forma
Falling Man. M. Sadler
Falling Star. P. Moyes
Falling Star. L. O'Donnell
Falling Star. E. P. Oppenheim
Fallout for a Spy. R. L. Hershatter
Falls the Shadow. Regina Ross
Falmont Claiments. A. Bercovici
Falmont Heiress. A. Simpson
False. G. Fleming
False Alarm. Manning Long
False Alibi. J. G. Brandon
False Alibi. Jack Lewis
False Beards. Alan Williams
False Bounty. S. Ransome
False Cards. H. Smart
False Claim. B. Wayde
False Claimant. Nicholas Carter
False Colors. R. Powell
False Colours. Annie Thomas
False Colours. E. Woodward
False Combination. Nicholas Carter
False Evidence. H. Carmichael
False Evidence. E. P. Oppenheim
False Face. V. Caspary
False Face. L. Edgley
False-Face. S. Horler
False Face. J. Lilly
False-Face. F. MacIsaac
False Face. S. Truss
False Face of Death. Anita Allen

Title Index

False Faces. L. J. Vance
False Finger Tip. S. Kearney
False Flags. N. Hynd
False Freedom. L. Emsley
False Front. Lawrence Meyer
False Gods. G. H. Lorimer
False Gods. G. Thorne
False Idols. B. Ferm
False Intruder. G. Goodchild
False Joanna. J. Fredman
False Pretences. T. Cobb
False Pretences. W. J. Elliott
False Pretences. Annie Thomas
False Purple. S. Horler
False Scent. Mrs. Alexander
False Scent. J. S. Fletcher
False Scent. I. Greig
False Scent. N. Marsh
False Scents. W. J. Bayfield
False to Any Man. L. Ford
False Truth. E. C. Vivian
False Witness. Mark Allerton
False Witness. Mary Cross
False Witness. S. Milne
False Witness. H. Nielsen
False Witness. E. Nisot
False Witness. M. Underwood
Falsely Accused. G. Norway
Familiar Stranger. F. E. Penny
Familiar Strangers. B. Forbes
Families Repaired. J. S. Fletcher
Family Affair. L. Benedict
Family Affair. H. Conway
Family Affair. M. Innes
Family Affair. I. S. Shriber
Family Affair. R. Stout
Family Affairs. J. Ellery
Family Affairs. J. Rhode
Family and Friends. Emma Page
Family Arsenal. P. Theroux
Family at Tammerton. M. Erskine
Family Burial Murders. M. Propper
Family Doom. E. Southworth
Family Failing. H. Smart
Family Fortune. M. G. Eberhart
Family Fortune. J. Weidman
Family Lie. G. Simenon
Family Likeness. Anna Gilbert
Family Man. Robin Moore
Family Matter. F. Gaite
Family Matter. J. Roosevelt
Family Matters. A. Rolls
Family on Vendetta Street. L. Longo
Family Plot. V. Canning
Family Property. P. Trent
Family Scapegrace. J. Payn
Family Skeleton. D. M. Disney
Family Skeleton. J. Hawk
Family Skeleton. E. Tyler
Family Skeletons. P. Quentin
Family Tomb. M. Gilbert
Family Trouble. J. Masiello
Family Vault. C. MacLeod
Famine. J. Creasey
Famine Plot. L. Freivalds
Famous Boy. Old Sleuth
Famous Burdick Case. Anonymous
Famous Cases of Dr. Thorndyke. R. A. Freeman
Famous McGarry Stories. Matt Taylor
Fan. B. Randall
Fan Fare. H. Janson
Fanatic of Fez. C. L. Leonard
Fanatics. Peter Hill
Fanatics of Al Asad. Nick Carter
Fancies and Goodnights. John Collier
Fancy Dress Ball. J. J. Farjeon
Fancy Free. E. Phillpotts
Fancy Free and other stories. C. Gibbon
Fancy's Knell. B. H. Deal
Fanfare for a Murderer. J. Rosenberg
Fanfare for Angel. L. Montrose
Fanfare for Murder. H. Desmond
Fangs of Murder. R. Wallace
Fangs of the Serpent. G. R. Fox
Fangs of the Sky Leopard. R. J. Hogan
Fannin. D. Markson
Fanny. H. Janson
Fanny McBride. C. Cookson
Fanny White and Her Friend Jack Rawlings. Anonymous
Fanshaw Case. G. K. Cowan
Fanshawe Court Mystery. J. Laurence
Fanshawe Murder. G. Thorne
Fantastic Island. K. Roberts
Fantastic Summer. D. Macardle
Fantasy and Fugue. Roy Fuller
Fantine Avenel. L. Maddock
Fantoccini. F. Barrett
Fantomas. P. Souvestre
Fantomas Captured. M. Allain
Far and Away. A. Boucher
Far Better Dead! M. Cumberland
Far Cry. F. Brown
Far Forests. Joan Aiken
Far Place. B. Fuller
Far Pursuit. O. Binns
Far Sands. A. Garve
Far Side of the Dollar. R. Macdonald
Far to Go. M. Aswell
Far Traveller. F. Gaite
Far Wandering Men. J. Russell

Far West Detective. Anonymous
Fare Prey. Laine Fisher
Farewell by Death. V. Warren
Farewell Crown and Goodbye King. M. Bennett
Farewell, La Jolla. Demouzon
Farewell, Little Sister. D. Enefer
Farewell, My Lovely. R. Chandler
Farewell Nikola. G. Boothby
Farewell Party. F. Bandy
Farewell Party. June Drummond
Farewell, Pretty Ladies. C. Massie
Farewell to Passion. D. Keene
Farewell to the Admiral. P. Cheyney
Farewell to the Castle. J. Corby
Farewell to Vienna. Dorothy Fletcher
Farm at Paranao. Laurence Kirk
Farm at Sante Fe. Laurence Kirk
Farm in the Hills. F. Warden
Farm Villains. J. N. Chance
Farmhouse. H. Reilly
Farnsworth Score. R. Burns
Farrowshot Park Affair. W. J. Bayfield
Farther Off from England. L. Chancellor
Fascinating Traitor. R. H. Savage
Fascinator. A. York
Fashion in Shrouds. M. Allingham
Fashioned for Murder. G. H. Coxe
Fast and Loose. L. Della
Fast and Loose. A. Griffiths
Fast and Loose. N. Tranter
Fast Buck. J. H. Chase
Fast Buck. B. Fischer
Fast Buck. H. Janson
Fast Buck. R. Laurence
Fast Colors. M. Doran
Fast Company. Marco Page
Fast Exit. M. Cronin
Fast Life in New York. Grace M. White
Fast Mail. C. Thornton
Fast Man with a Dollar. R. Avery
Fast Money. E. A. Clancy
Fast Money Shoots from the Hip. J. M. Glazner
Fast One. P. Cain
Fast Shuffle. T. Herd
Fast Shuffle. Robin Moore
Fast with a Gun. R. Wilkes-Hunter
Fast Work. P. Cheyney
Fast Work and other stories. P. Cheyney
Faster She Runs. R. Colby
Faster We Live. B. Brennan
Fastest Boy in New York. Old Sleuth
Fat Boy Must Die. R. E. Pearson
Fat Chance. V. Laumer
Fat Death. M. Avallone
Fat Man's Agony. G. Carr
Fata Morgana. W. Kotzwinkle
Fatal Accident. P. N. Walker
Fatal Accident. C. M. Wills
Fatal Ace. A. Applin
Fatal Affinity. S. L. Cumberland
Fatal Alibi. G. Bellairs
Fatal Alibi. L. Bidston
Fatal Alibi. L. Thayer
Fatal Amateur. D. L. Mathews
Fatal Amulet. G. H. Teed
Fatal Bargain. Nicholas Carter
Fatal Beauty. D. H. Cole
Fatal Bonds. R. Dowling
Fatal Bride. V. Siller
Fatal Call. A. Dorrington
Fatal Car. R. Hardinge
Fatal Cast. C. T. Gardner
Fatal Chair. Hawkshaw
Fatal Choice. J. D'Astor
Fatal Choice. D. M. Disney
Fatal Complaint. P. Quinn
Fatal Cruise. Arthur MacLean
Fatal Curiosity. G. Lillo
Fatal Descent. J. Rhode
Fatal Diamonds. E. C. Donnelly
Fatal Dose. B. Cobb
Fatal Dose. F. M. White
Fatal Element. E. C. Clark
Fatal Entrance. R. Barratt
Fatal Entrance. N. Wishart
Fatal Error. J. Boland
Fatal Error. C. F. Gregg
Fatal Face. W. LeQueux
Fatal Falsehood. Nicholas Carter
Fatal Fascination. J. N. Chance
Fatal Fetish. P. Hochstein
Fatal Fifth. M. Penrose
Fatal Finale. P. H. Dobbins
Fatal Finger Mark, Rose Courtenay's First Case. M. Danvers
Fatal Fingers. W. LeQueux
Fatal Five Minutes. R. A. J. Walling
Fatal Flaw. L. Meynell
Fatal Flaw. B. Musto
Fatal Flirt. D. Hitchens
Fatal Flourishes. S. B. Rafferty
Fatal Flower. L. Benedict
Fatal Footsteps. C. Shannon
Fatal Forgery. J. G. Brandon
Fatal Formula. J. Rosenberger
Fatal Fortune. F. Hurt
Fatal Fortune. A. Murray
Fatal Foursome. F. Kane
Fatal Fragrance. D. M. Locke
Fatal Frails. D. J. Marlowe

Fatal Friday. F. Gerard
Fatal Friends. K. Netzen
Fatal Friendship. Gwyn Evans
Fatal Garden. J. Rhode
Fatal Glove. C. Augusta
Fatal Grace. G. M. Edwards
Fatal Harvest. A. Amos
Fatal Holiday. B. Cobb
Fatal Hour. Nicholas Carter
Fatal Hour. E. Harrison
Fatal Image. T. S. King
Fatal in Furs. J. M. Fox
Fatal in My Fashion. P. McGerr
Fatal Kiss Mystery. R. King
Fatal Lady. R. Foley
Fatal Legacy. L. Linares
Fatal Legacy. L. Tracy
Fatal Lover. V. Siller
Fatal Manuscript. G. Verner
Fatal Marriage. M. E. Braddon
Fatal Marriage. E. Southworth
Fatal Mascot. A. Skene
Fatal Memoirs. W. Edwards
Fatal Mistake. P. H. Powell
Fatal Move, and other stories. C. Conall
Fatal Nugget. E. H. Burrage
Fatal Number. W. Shute
Fatal Past. Dora Russell
Fatal Picnic. Bernice Carey
Fatal Pit. J. W. Bobin
Fatal Pool. J. Rhode
Fatal Power. C. H. Bullivant
Fatal Prescription. Nicholas Carter
Fatal Purchase. A. Rowe
Fatal Record. C. B. Booth
Fatal Relations. M. Erskine
Fatal Request. A. L. Harris
Fatal Resemblance. E. Ellerton
Fatal Resemblance. C. Faber
Fatal Revenge. Dennis J. Murphy
Fatal Ring. D. Donovan
Fatal Ring of Light. H. Eastwood
Fatal Ruby. C. Garvice
Fatal Second. H. C. McNeile
Fatal Secret. Anonymous
Fatal Secret. E. Southworth
Fatal Secrets. I. Crookenden
Fatal Shadows. S. George
Fatal Shadows. D. C. Meade
Fatal Shadows. M. Peterson
Fatal Silence. F. Marryat
Fatal Song. F. Hume
Fatal Step. C. F. Cushman
Fatal Step. Wade Miller
Fatal Switch. Ian Stuart
Fatal Talisman. C. Brisbane
Fatal Thirteen. W. LeQueux
Fatal Three. M. E. Braddon
Fatal Trip. M. Underwood
Fatal Undertaking. F. Kane
Fatal V Sign. M. Frazer
Fatal Venture. F. W. Crofts
Fatal Vow. F. Lathom
Fatal Wager. A. Blair
Fatal Woman. D. Donovan
Fatal Woman. P. Quentin
Fatality in Fleet Street. C. S. Sprigg
Fate—and Drusilla. A. Askew
Fate and Fernand. P. Audemars
Fate and Four Sinners. H. L. Victor
Fate and the Man. T. W. Hanshew
Fate and the Watcher. M. Peterson
Fate at the Fair. M. Burton
Fate Laughs. H. Adams
Fate of Austin Craige. S. Campbell
Fate of Fay Delray. J. Wilstach
Fate of Felix. Mrs. C. Kernahan
Fate of Felix Brand. F. F. Kelly
Fate of Herbert Wayne. E. J. Goodman
Fate of Jane McKenzie. N. B. Mavity
Fate of Luke Ormerod. R. Dowling
Fate of O'Loughlin. D. McCarthy
Fate of Osmund Brett. H. G. Hutchinson
Fate of the Hara Diamond. T. W. Speight
Fate of the Immodest Blonde. P. Quentin
Fate of the Lying Jade. J. N. Chance
Fate of the Malous. G. Simenon
Fate Strikes Twice. C. Ashton
Fated Five. G. Biss
Fated to Love. R. Roleine
Fateful Abduction. M. A. Fleming
Fateful Departure. D. M. Disney
Fateful Hand. N. T. Oliver
Fateful Star Murder. H. Kerkow
Fateful Tide. J. Wellsley
Fate's Pendulum. G. Comley
Father Brown Omnibus. G. K. Chesterton
Father Goriot. H. Balzac
Father Hayes. P. Leslie
Father Hunt. R. Stout
"Father Pig." B. Hirschfeld
Father Pink. A. W. Barrett
Fatherless Fanny. T. P. Prest
Fathers in Law. H. Cecil
Fathom. M. Hammond
Fauconberg. W. Magnay
Faulkner's Folly. C. Wells
Fault in the Structure. G. Mitchell
Faust of the F.B.I. J. Mack
Fausta. P. J. Stead
Favourite Scratched. B. Hemyng
Faxon Secret. J. Ware

Fayolle Formula. T. G. Courtenay
Fazackerley's Millions. F. Crisp
Fear! L. C. Douthwaite
Fear. T. Keneally
Fear. E. Nesbit
Fear. B. Sarto
Fear Among the Shadows. L. Hoffman
Fear and Miss Betony. D. Bowers
Fear and the Dead Man. L. Smith
Fear and the Guilt. W. Shaw
Fear and Trembling. B. Flynn
Fear Business. H. Hossent
Fear by Installments. Jonathan Burke
Fear by Night. P. Wentworth
Fear Came First. V. Kelsey
Fear Cay. K. Robeson
Fear Comes Calling. A. L. Martin
Fear Comes to Chalfont. F. W. Crofts
Fear Comes to Euston Road. R. Holmes
Fear Dealers. R. Cade
Fear Dealers. Jack Thomas
Fear Followed On. C. Kingston
Fear for Francis. V. Heley
Fear for Miss Betony. D. Bowers
Fear Fortune, Father. S. B. Hough
Fear Haunts the Fells. R. Goyne
Fear Haunts the Roses. C. Edwards
Fear Holds the Key. F. Duncan
Fear in a Desert Town. Roger Fuller
Fear in a Handful of Dust. J. Ives
Fear in Borzano. W. Jay
Fear in the Forest. Reginald Campbell
Fear in the Wind. S. Jepson
Fear Is a Weapon. F. Ford
Fear Is My Shadow. Martin Thomas
Fear Is the Key. Alistair MacLean
Fear Is the Same. Carter Dickson
Fear Kissed My Lips. J. Ames
Fear Makers. D. L. Teilhet
Fear No Evil. L. Brackett
Fear No Evil. Alice Brennan
Fear No More. L. Edgley
Fear of a Stranger. R. Foley
Fear of Death. C. Conte
Fear of Death. A. M. Wells
Fear of Fear. F. Ryerson
Fear of Felix Corder. J. Creasey
Fear of God. D. Quinn
Fear of Heights. V. Coffman
Fear of Life. G. Maxwell
Fear of Mr. Taltry. E. G. Cousins
Fear of the Night. J. S. Fletcher
Fear Place. J. Ware
Fear Rides the Fog. E. C. Stone
Fear Round About. G. Bellairs
Fear Runs Softly. C. Franklin
Fear Shadowed. M. Peterson
Fear Sign. M. Allingham
Fear Stalks the Bayou. J. Coulson
Fear Stalks the City. N. MacKenzie
Fear Stalks the Footlights. Don Boyd
Fear Stalks the Village. Ethel L. White
Fear the Light. E. Ferrars
Fear to Tread. M. Gilbert
Fear Today—Gone Tomorrow. R. Bloch
Fear Treads Soft Shod. M. Clare
Fear Waits on Cypress Road. P. Wissmann
Fear Walked Behind. S. Horler
Fear Walks the Island. H. Desmond
Fear Without End. Noel Lee
Fearful Paradise. J. Ames
Fearful Passage. H. C. Branson
Fearful Thing. V. Gielgud
Fearful Way to Die. J. C. Nolan
Fearless Investigator. F. U. Eaton
Fearless Lovers. A. Applin
Fearsome Riddle. M. Ehrmann
Feast for Spiders. K. Evans
Feast of Eggshells. F. Stevenson
Feast of Lanterns. M. Richmond
Feast of the Dead. G. M. Jay
Feast of the Scorpions. J. Pattinson
Feather Cloak Murders. D. L. Teilhet
Feather Your Nest. G. Greenaway
Feathered Octopus. K. Robeson
Feathered Serpent. E. Wallace
Feathers for the Toff. J. Creasey
Feathers in the Fire. C. Cookson
Feathers Left Around. C. Wells
Featherstone's Story. H. Wood
Featuring the Saint. L. Charteris
February Doll Murders. M. Avallone
February Plan. J. H. Roberts
Fed Up. G. A. Birmingham
Federal Agent. "G-Man"
Federal Agent. John Ross
Federal Bullets. G. F. Eliot
Fedora. A. Belot
Fedora of the Halls. A. Applin
Feedback. B. Copper
Feedback. H. Miller
Feeding the Wind. J. E. Gurdon
Feet of Death. B. Flynn
Feet of Death. M. Peterson
Feldisham Mystery. Gordon Holmes
Felicia. Mark Dane
Felicia. G. A. Effinger
Felix Boyd's Final Problems. S. Campbell
Felix Boyd's Revelations. S. Campbell
Felix Running. H. Ford
Felix Stone. A. Askew
Felix Walking. H. Ford

Fell Clutch. P. Motte
Fell Murder. E. C. R. Lorac
Fell of Dark. R. Hill
Fell of Dark. J. Judson
Fell Purpose. A. Derleth
Fellow of Trinity. A. St. Aubyn
Fellow Passenger. G. Household
Fellow Passengers. R. Pyke
Fellow-Traveler. D. Montross
Fellowship of Five. F. Johnston
Fellowship of the Feather. H. Pink
Fellowship of the Frog. E. Wallace
Fellowship of the Hand. E. D. Hoch
Felo De Se? R. A. Freeman
Felon Angel. Carter Brown
Felon in Disguise. L. Southworth
Feloniously and Wilfully. Ernest Wood
Felony of New South Wales. T. Walker
Felon's Bequest. F. Du Boisgobey
Felon's Daughter. J. Middlemass
Felony at Random. Dell Shannon
Felony File. Dell Shannon
Felony Squad. M. Avallone
Felony Tank. M. Braly
Felthams. Franz
Female Bluebeard. E. Sue
Female Depravity. Anonymous
Female Depravity. O. Bradbury
Female Detective. A. Forrester
Female Detective. Old Sleuth
Female of the Species. H. C. McNeile
Female of the Darkness. A. Roudybush
Female Spy. Emerson Bennett
Female Spy. Roland Daniel
Female Target. D. Onyeama
Female Ventriloquist. Old Sleuth
Feminine for Spy. B. Sanders
Fen Country. E. Crispin
Fen Tiger. C. Marchant
Fence. H. L. Nelson
Fence's Victim. Donald Stuart
Fengriffin. D. Case
Fenland Mystery. C. A. Brandreth
Fennell's Tower. L. Tracy
Fenner. G. H. Coxe
Fennister Affair. Josephine Bell
Fenokee Project. Roy Lewis
Fenton Affair. P. Quest
Fenton of the Foreign Office. M. Annesley
Fentons. R. Goyne
Fenton's Quest. M. E. Braddon
Fenwick Houses. C. A. Cookson
Fenwood Murders. G. E. Locke
Feo. M. Pemberton
Fer-de-Lance. R. Stout
Fer-de-Lance Contract. P. Atlee
Feral. B. Roueche
Feramontov. D. Cory
Ferguson. R. Kruger
Ferguson Affair. R. Macdonald
Fern Dead. R. H. R. Smithies
Fern Seed. H. M. Rideout
Fernanda. V. Miller
Fernande's Choice. F. Du Boisgobey
Fernwood. M. Thum
Ferret Detective. Anonymous
Ferrol Bond. J. Easton
Ferry Boat. F. Du Boisgobey
Ferrybridge Mystery. D. Vane
Ferryman, Take Him Across! V. Rath
Festival. J. R. L. Anderson
Festival! M. Butterworth
Festival Death. R. Stephenson
Festival for Spies. David St. John
Festival of Darkness. M. Garratt
Fetch. P. Everett
Fetch. J. Shearing
Fetch Me a Rope. R. Boyd
Fetish. K. Hewitt
Fetish Murders. A. Curry
Fettered. P. Trent
Fettered by Fate. G. W. Miller
Fettered by Fate. A. Wright
Fettered for Life. F. Barrett
Fettered Love. M. Richmond
Feud. "Capstan"
Feud. J. Templeton
Feud. D. Whitelaw
Feud of Fear. W. M. Graydon
Feudal Tyrants. M. G. Lewis
Fever Grass. John Morris
Fever of Live. F. Hume
Feversham. Diane Davidson
Few Days in Endel. Diana Gordon
Few Days in Madrid. A. Roos
Few Die Well. S. Noel
Few Drops of Murder. I. Capeto
Few Fiends to Tea. V. Coffman
Few Small Bones. H. C. Rae
Fiasco in Fulham. Josephine Bell
Ficciones. J. L. Borges
Fickle Heart. F. Du Boisgobey
Fictional Lives. H. Fleetwood
Fiddler's Place. R. Parker
Fiddlestrings. J. H. Vahey
Fiddling Cracksman. H. S. Keeler
Fidel Castro Assassinated. Lee Duncan
Fidelio Score. G. Sinstadt
Fidgets. G. A. Birmingham
Field of Fire. P. Alding

Field of the Forty Footsteps. P. Hastings
Fields of Eden. M. T. Hinkemeyer
Fiend. M. Millar
Fiend in Need. M. K. Ozaki
Fiend Incarnate. D. Malcolm
Fiends. P. Boileau
Fiends of the Family. P. Flower
Fiery Chariot. E. Everett-Green
Fiery Furnace. Lawrence Williams
Fiery Serpent. A. Mallory
Fiesta for Murder. P. O. McGuire
Fifteen Cells. Stuart Martin
Fifteen Keys. C. Dawe
Fifteen Streets. C. Cookson
Fifth Ace. Douglas Grant
Fifth Answer. M. Pereira
Fifth Caller. H. Nielsen
Fifth Cord. D. M. Devine
Fifth Dagger. D. Quick
Fifth Defector. P. Jones
Fifth Estate. Robin Moore
Fifth Finger. W. LeQueux
Fifth Form Detective. R. Walker
Fifth Freedom. A. O. Pollard
Fifth Grave. Jonathan Latimer
Fifth Horseman. N. M. Adams
Fifth Horseman. L. Collins
Fifth House. J. Godey
Fifth Key. G. H. Coxe
Fifth Latchkey. N. S. Lincoln
Fifth Man. M. Coles
Fifth Must Die! R. Verron
5th of November. M. Franklin
Fifth Passenger. E. Young
Fifth Point of the Compass. M. Tripp
Fifth Seal. M. Aldanov
Fifth Tumbler. C. B. Clason
Fifth Victim. D. Collins
Fifth Woman. M. Fagyas
Fifty Candles. E. D. Biggers
Fifty-Five. G. Volk
55 Guineas Reward. F. C. Milford
£50 Marriage Case. J. G. Brandon
Fifty Roads to Town. F. Nebel
Fifty Thousand Dollars Ransom. D. Malcolm
Fifty-Two Pickup. E. Leonard
Fig Leaves for a Lady. Johnny Dark
Fight. V. Scannell
Fight for a Fortune. F. Du Boisgobey
Fight for a Soul. F. Warden
Fight for a Throne. Nicholas Carter
Fight for Right. Nicholas Carter
Fight for the Child. F. M. White
Fight for the Luck. J. Blyth
Fight to a Finish. W. G. Forbes
Fight to a Finish. G. Hackforth-Jones
Fight to a Finish. E. Phillpotts
Fight to a Finish. F. Warden
Fight with a Fiend. Nicholas Carter
Fighter Pilot. R. Wilkes-Hunter
Fighting Against Millions. Nicholas Carter
Fighting an Unknown Power. W. G. Forbes
Fighting Back. C. Alverson
Fighting Back. R. Sandroff
Fighting Blood. J. Addiscombe
Fighting Byng. A. Stone
Fighting Cartoonist Detective. Hedley Trembath
Fighting Fool. G. Dilnot
Fighting Footballers. P. Gill
Fighting for a Fortune. Old Sleuth
Fighting Hearts. J. Dorrance
Fighting His Way. Old Sleuth
Fighting Lieutenant. J. G. Rowe
Fighting Men. J. Cartwright
Fighting Snub Reilly. E. Wallace
Fighting the Red Shadow. Vigilant
Fighting Through. A. Abdullah
Fighting Tramp. P. Gill
Fighting Troubadour. A. C. Gunter
"Fightingcocks." W. P. Drury
Figure Away. P. A. Taylor
Figure Eight. S. Regester
Figure in the Corner and other stories. M. E. Braddon
Figure in the Dusk. J. Creasey
Figure in the Shadows. Dana Ross
Figure It Out for Yourself. J. H. Chase
Figure of Eight. C. Waye
Figure on the Terrace. A. R. Weekes
Figurehead. B. Knox
File for Death. Janet Hart
File for Record. A. Tilton
File No. 115. H. Harper
File No. 114. E. A. Young
File No. 113. E. Gaboriau
File of the Golden Goose. John Watson
File on a Missing Redhead. L. Cameron
File on Bolitho Blane. D. Wheatley
File on Charlie. B. Copeland
File on Claudia Cragge. Q. Patrick
File on Death. K. Giles
File on Devlin. C. Gaskin
File on Fenton and Farr. Q. Patrick
File on Lester. A. Garve
File on Robert Prentice. D. Wheatley
File on Rufus Ray. H. Reilly
Filibusters. C. J. C. Hyne
Filibuster's Warning. G. Jerome

Title Index

Filigree Ball. A. K. Green
Fillets on the Menu. J. Hague
Filly. I. Herbert
Filly Wore Red. H. Janson
Film Mystery. A. B. Reeve
Film of Fear. A. Fredericks
Film Star Vanishes. D. Richmond
Film Studio Murder. C. Kenwood
Filmi, Filmi, Inspector Ghote. H. R. F. Keating
Filthy Five. Nick Carter
Final. J. Greaves
Final Act. J. H. Crisp
Final Act. C. Hudson
Final Agenda. E. Hyams
Final Appearance. J. C. Nolan
Final Appointment. M. Blair
Final Approach. P. Griffiths
Final Approach. C. Hodder-Williams
Final Chance. P. Trent
Final Copy. J. Barbette
Final Count. H. C. McNeile
Final Crossroads. Maude Parker
Final Curtain. W. H. L. Crauford
Final Curtain. F. Kane
Final Curtain. N. Marsh
Final Death. R. Sapir
Final Deduction. R. Stout
Final Destiny. R. D. Ridyard
Final Encore. M. Albrand
Final Ending of It. H. Wood
Final Exploits of Nick Carter. Nicholas Carter
Final Exposure. P. H. Mansfield
Final Fear. M. Blair
Final Fear. L. M. Janifer
Final Guest. M. Blair
Final Installment. M. Cronin
Final Judgement. P. Barrington
Final Judgment. M. Benjoya
Final Lie. M. Blair
Final Night. R. Gaines
Final Notice. J. Gores
Final Notice. J. Valin
Final Payment. A. Applin
Final Payment. T. C. H. Jacobs
Final Payment. V. Shore
Final Portrait. V. Caspary
Final Pose. M. Blair
Final Proof. D. MacVicar
Final Proof. R. Ottolengui
Final Proof. M. Reno
Final Reckoning. L. Edgley
Final Ring. M. Blair
Final Run. J. Pattinson
Final Run. D. Sanderson
Final Score. George Douglas
Final Score. G. Goodchild
Final Score. E. Grogan
Final Sentence. M. Maurice
Final Set. P. Harris
Final Steal. P. George
Final Target. M. Blair
Final Things. R. B. Wright
Final Triumph. Old Sleuth
Final Witness. J. F. Straker
Finale. M. Blair
Finalists. R. Braddon
Finances of Sir John Kynnersley. A. C. Fox-Davies
Financier. J. B. Harris-Burland
Financier's Wife. F. Warden
Finch Takes to Crime. F. Lester
Find a Crooked Sixpence. E. Thompson
Find a Victim. J. R. Macdonald
Find Actor Hart. H. S. Keeler
Find Eileen Hardin—Alive! A. Frazer
Find Inspector West. J. Creasey
Find Me a Killer! Arthur MacLean
Find My Killer. M. W. Wellman
Find Sherri! P. Swan
Find the Body. J. York
Find the Clock. H. S. Keeler
Find the Diamonds. J. Pattinson
Find the Don's Daughter. J. Jacks
Find the Innocent. Roy Vickers
Find the Lady. G. Barnett
Find the Lady. R. C. Finney
Find the Lady! G. Goodchild
Find the Lady! D. Walshe
Find the Motive. J. Woodford
Find the Professor. Mark Cross
Find the Tiger. P. Brooks
Find the Woman! W. Braun
Find the Woman. G. Burgess
Find the Woman. D. M. Disney
Find the Woman. J. S. Fletcher
Find the Woman. A. Hornblow
Find the Woman. H. J. Hultman
Find the Woman. A. S. Roche
Find This Woman. R. S. Prather
Find Tracy George. Ray Owen
Findernes' Flowers. G. R. Preedy
Finders Keepers. G. Homes
Finders, Losers—. P. Muller
Finding Maubee. A. H. Z. Carr
Finding of the Gentian. A. W. Rollins
Findings Is Keepings. J. B. Clarke
Findlay's Landing. M. Chittenden
Fine and Handsome Captain. F. Lynch
Fine and Private Place. M. Fitt
Fine and Private Place. E. Queen

Fine Day for Dying. J. T. MacCargo
Fine Day for Murder. J. Ingersol
Fine Feathers. Margery Lawrence
Fine Feathers. W. LeQueux
Fine Night for Dying. M. Fallon
Fine Pair. C. Stratton
Finger. H. Kane
Finger. A. M. Stein
Finger! Finger! H. S. Keeler
Finger in the Sky Affair. P. Leslie
Finger Man and other stories. R. Chandler
Finger of Death. H. Connolly
Finger of Destiny and other stories. E. Snell
Finger of Fate. H. C. McNeile
Finger of Fire. M. Braine
Finger of Saturn. V. Canning
Finger of Smoke. R. M. Wells
Finger of Suspicion. Nicholas Carter
Finger-Prints Never Lie! J. G. Brandon
Finger to Her Lips. E. Berckman
Fingered City. D. Hatch
Fingered Man. B. Fischer
Fingernail Beach. Richard Butler
Fingerprint. Anthony Gilbert
Fingerprint. P. Wentworth
Fingerprints. H. Stinson
Fingerprints of Fate! L. H. Brooks
Fingers Before Forks. E. Woodward
Fingers for Ransom. H. Berrow
Fingers of Death. M. Grant
Fingers of Fate. L. G. Moberly
Fingers of Fear. P. MacDonald
Fingers of Fear. J. U. Nicolson
Finish Line. P. Kruger
Finish Me Off. H. Waugh
Finish of a Rascal. Nicholas Carter
Finishing Stroke. E. Queen
Finishing Touch. A. Hocking
Finlay of the Sentinel. C. F. Gregg
Finnegan's Dilemma. C. Belmar
Finsbury Lot. G. Burnett
Finsbury Mob. E. Bruton
Fiona. C. Gaskin
Fire and the Clay. P. Audemars
Fire Ant. J. F. Drexler
Fire at Greycombe Farm. J. Rhode
Fire at Will. D. M. Disney
Fire Below. D. Yates
Fire Bomb. S. Jason
Fire-Bomb Jack. Old Sleuth
Fire Bug. E. Bruton
"Fire-Bug." R. St. Clair
Fire, Burn! J. D. Carr
Fire Circle. W. Marshall
Fire Cloud. K. McKenney
Fire Engine That Disappeared. M. Sjowall
Fire Escape. T. S. Strachan
Fire Flingers. W. J. Neidig
Fire Goddess. S. Rohmer
Fire in Anger. A. Mars
Fire in His Hand. M. Grieg
Fire in His Hand. L. Phillips
Fire in the Barley. F. Parrish
Fire in the Blood. M. K. Simmons
Fire in the Flesh. D. Goodis
Fire in the Ice. A. D. Divine
Fire in the Snow. H. Innes
Fire in the Streets. J. Messmann
Fire in the Thatch. E. C. R. Lorac
Fire Island. G. M. Fenn
Fire Kill. D. DaCruz
Fire Mountain. M. Hastings
Fire of Death. M. E. Cooke
Fire of the Witches. Lydia Belknap Long
Fire on Fear Street. S. Sterling
Fire on the Cliffs. C. Waynar
Fire on the Seven Peaks. R. Arnold
Fire on the Wind. D. Garth
Fire Opal. Robert Fraser
Fire Opal. P. Monnow
Fire Opals. R. Danton
Fire over Baghdad. G. Griffith
Fire over India. W. H. Baker
Fire Past the Future. C. E. Maine
Fire-Raiser. E. Trevor
Fire Rock. J. Wood
Fire Storm. R. L. Duncan
Fire-Tongue. S. Rohmer
Fire Trap. O. Cameron
Fire Trumpet. B. Mitford
Fire-Watcher's Night. H. Kaner
Fire Will Freeze. M. Millar
Fire Within. G. F. Gibbs
Fire Zone. J. Bogar
Fireball. H. Janson
Fireball Assignment. A. Sugar
Firebase. J. Crowther
Firebase Seattle. D. Pendleton
Firebird. W. Marchant
Firebrace and Father Kelly. Seafarer
Firebrand. S. R. Crockett
Firebug. R. Bloch
Firecrest. V. Canning
Fireflash 5. G. Masterton
Fireflood. P. Cave
Firefox. Craig Thomas
Firegold. J. R. Daniels
Firemen Hot. C. J. C. Hyne
Fireplay. W. Wingate
Fires at Fairlawn. Josephine Bell

Fires at Fitch's Folly. K. Whipple
Fires of Ballymorris. V. Connolly
Fires of Brimstone. P. Gallagher
Fires of Fate. W. F. Fauley
Fires of Glenlochy. C. Heaven
Fires of Hate. R. Bridges
Fires of Kiwai. E. Lindall
Fires of Love. M. Leighton
Fires That Destroy. H. Whittington
Fireside Omnibus. Anonymous
Firespill. I. Slater
Firestarter. Stephen King
Firework for Oliver. John Sanders
Firing Line. W. B. Murphy
Firm Hand. H. Bindloss
Firmly by the Tail. P. N. Gwynne
First a Murder. M. Halliday
First Blood. P. McCurtin
First Blood. D. Morrell
First Body. L. Payne
First Born. R. M. Gilchrist
First-Born. G. Simenon
First-Born. P. Trent
First Born of Egypt. Demouzon
First-Born Son. A. Murray
First Came a Murder. J. Creasey
First Case of Mr. Paul Savoy. Jackson Gregory
First Come, First Kill. F. Allan
First Come, First Kill. F. Lockridge
First Deadly Sin. L. Sanders
First Englishman. R. Thorndike
First False Step. T. P. Prest
First Flight. J. R. Daniels
First Gravedigger. B. Paul
First Immortals. E. L. Arch
First It Was Ordained. B. Thorne
First Lady. R. Nessen
First Law. G. Willets
First Mrs. Winston. R. Foley
First Night Murder. F. G. Parke
First of the English. A. C. Gunter
First Person Plural. R. Wiseman
First Person Singular. W. R. Benet
First Person Singular. D. C. Murray
First Round Murder. J. V. Turner
First Saint Omnibus. L. Charteris
First Steps Inside the Zoo. J. Lodwick
First Stone. M. S. Boyd
First Stone. M. Peterson
First Stop to Hell. M. Urquhart
First Strike. D. Terman
First Team. J. Ball
First Television Murder. V. Gielgud
First Time He Died. Ethel L. White
First to Kill. F. Usher
First Train to Babylon. M. Ehrlich
First Waltz. J. L. Roberts
Fish and Company. R. Arnold
Fish and Kill. Macdonald Hastings
Fish Are So Trusting. N. Morland
Fish for Murder. Edward Lee
Fish Lane. L. Corkill
Fish on a Hook. P. MacTyre
Fish or Cut Bait. A. A. Fair
Fish Out of Water. G. Hackforth-Jones
Fisherman's End. K. D. Guinness
Fisherman's Gat. E. Noble
Fisherman's Luck. T. Pace
Fishers of Men. C. Dawe
Fisheye. Peter Townend
Fishing Is Dangerous. F. N. Millar
Fishport. G. Thorne
Fist in the Sky. M. Jopson
Fist of Fatima. P. Edwards
Fistful of Death. H. Kane
Fit As a Filly. Howard Mason
Fit to Kill. B. Halliday
Fit to Kill. M. Cronin
Fit to Kill. F. Kane
Fit to Kill. H. C. Owen
Fit to Kill. L. Trimble
Fitch and His Fortunes. G. Dick
Fits and Starts. T. A. Fitzgerald
Five. T. Field
Five Aces. David Hume
Five Against the House. J. Finney
Five Alarm Funeral. S. Sterling
Five and Dime Murders. R. Reinsmith
Five Arrows. Allan Chase
Five Assassins. O. F. Jerome
Five Brains. W. Sheridan
Five Bullets. L. Thayer
Five Came to Kill. R. Wilkes-Hunter
Five-Day Nightmare. F. Brown
Five Days. D. Raymond
Five Days Till Noon. Sheila Ross
Five Days to Kill. R. Wilkes-Hunter
Five Days to Oblivion. D. O. Woodbury
Five Dead Men. A. Skene
Five Deceivers. F. Armitage
Five Devils of Kilmainham. E. M. McCullough
Five Diamonds. W. M. Graydon
5.18 Mystery. J. J. Farjeon
Five Faces of Murder. J. Flynn
Five Fatal Days. J. Woodford
Five Fatal Letters. Dana Scott
Five Fatal Words. E. Balmer
Five Fingers. G. Rivers
Five Flamboys. F. Beeding
Five Floors Down. E. S. Porter

Five for Bridge. Ernest Ward
Five for One. L. Allan
5:45 to Suburbia. V. Packer
Five Fowlers. E. Morris
Five Fragments. G. Dyer
Five Frontiers. W. H. Murray
Five Gates to Armageddon. J. Christian
Five Hours from Isfahan. W. Copeland
520%. B. North
$500. H. Alger
Five Hundred Keys. M. Carin
Five Hundred Pounds Reward. Anonymous
Five Hundred Pounds Reward. A. O. Cooke
£500 Reward. D. Vane
Five in Fear. G. H. Teed
Five Inns. R. Inchbald
Five Keys to Mystery. Donald Ross
Five Knots. F. M. White
Five-Leafed Clover. James Fraser
Five Little Pigs. A. Christian
Five Man War. C. Belanger
Five Matchboxes. H. Blayn
Five Men Go to Prison. R. Straus
Five Million Francs. G. Schleifer
Five Million in Case. O. B. King
Five-Minute Marriage. Joan Aiken
Five Minutes, Sir Matthew. T. C. Worsley
Five Minutes to Midnight. S. H. Shabtai
Five Minutes with a Stranger. M. Tripp
Five Murderers. R. Chandler
Five Mutineers. J. Spenser
Five Nights in Singapore. M. Derby
Five of Hearts. V. Yorke
Five of My Best. M. G. Eberhart
Five of Spades. P. C. De Crespigny
Five Old Maids. G. Warden
Five Passengers from Lisbon. M. G. Eberhart
Five Pieces of Jade. J. Ball
Five Plays. J. Mortimer
Five Red Fingers. B. Flynn
Five Red Herrings. D. L. Sayers
Five Red Stars. B. Bolt
Five Roads Inn. R. Goyne
Five Roads to Death. J. Philips
Five Roads to S'Agaro. K. G. Ballard
Five Roundabouts to Heaven. J. Bingham
Five Signs from Ruby. H. C. McDonald
Five Silver Buddahs. H. S. Keeler
Five Sinister Characters. R. Chandler
Five Star Fugitive. J. D. MacDonald
Five Survive. C. Graves
Five Suspects. R. A. J. Walling
Five Thousand a Year. H. Wood
$5000 Reward. G. Fleming
Five Thousand Dollars Reward. A. F. Pinkerton
5,000 Trojan Horses. L. T. White
Five Times Maigret. G. Simenon
Five to Five. D. E. Muir
Five to Kill. J. Halliday
Five Ways to Die. Richard Grant
Five Were Doomed. D. Dayle
Five Were Missing. Lois Duncan
Five Were Murdered! T. A. Plummer
Five Who Vanished. G. F. Worts
Five Years After. W. M. Graydon
Fives Wild. W. Winward
Fix. L. Clancy
Fix. D. Fliegel
Fix. J. Gannold
Fix. J. Usher
Fix Like This. K. C. Constantine
Fixation. J. Pulman
Fixed Alibi. Nicholas Carter
Fixer. M. B. Dix
Flag in the City. C. Landon
Flagdown. M. Muller
Flagellator. Carter Brown
Flags at Doney. H. Greene
Flail and the Fish. F. Gerard
Flame. L. P. Greene
Flame. H. Zore
Flame and the Wind. J. Blackburn
Flame Breathers. K. Robeson
Flame Dancer. F. A. Mathews
Flame Eternal and the Maharajah's Son. W. E. Roys
Flame in the Air. A. Prior
Flame in the Heather. Agnes Russell
Flame in the Mist. P. Audemars
Flame in the Snow. V. Black
Flame Lily. C. K. MacKinnon
Flame of Evil. D. M. Disney
Flame of Folly. L. Noel
Flame of Murder. M. Neville
Flame of the Forest. A. Broome
Flame of the Khan. M. B. Dix
Flame Too Hot. K. Kramer
Flamenco and Orange Blossoms. M. Vernon
Flameout. C. D. Peel
Flames Burn High. G. Usher
Flames of Velvet. M. Dekobra
Flames of Vengeance. M. S. Jones
Flames on the Bosphorus. J. Motta
Flames over the Castle. D. La Pointe
Flaming Belt. H. H. C. Gibbons
Flaming Crescent. O. Binns
Flaming Falcons. K. Robeson
Flaming Jewel. R. W. Chambers
Flaming Man. M. E. Chaber
Flaming Wilderness. R. Cullum

Flamingo Lake. J. D. White
Flamstock Mystery. J. S. Fletcher
Flanders Spy. A. O. Pollard
Flannelfoot, Phantom Crook. Jack Henry
Flash. J. Ruegg
Flash Casey, Detective. G. H. Coxe
Flash D 13. V. K. Kaledin
Flash—Hold for Murder. P. Whelton
Flash of Green. J. D. MacDonald
Flash of Light. C. Frisbie
Flash of Lightning. J. Adye
Flash of Splendour. A. Stevenson
Flash Point. J. Bruce
Flash Point. M. Gilbert
Flashback. H. Carmichael
Flashback. R. Dooley
Flashpoint. H. Blayn
Flashpoint. H. Janson
Flashpoint. G. La Fountaine
Flashpoint. D. J. Marlowe
Flashpoint. A. A. Randall
Flashpoint for Treason. D. Reid
Flask for the Journey. F. L. Green
Flat Aback. E. L. Long
Flat Beneath. B. Delannoy
Flat No. 4. W. J. Bayfield
Flat 2. E. Wallace
Flat Tyre in Fulham. Josephine Bell
Flats Fixed—Among Other Things. D. Tracy
Flaunting Moon. C. Darby
Flaw. J. Laflin
Flaw. A. Samarakis
Flaw in the Crystal. Godfrey Smith
Flaw in the Sapphire. C. M. Snyder
Flaxborough Crab. Colin Watson
Fledgling. D. Lee
Flee from Terror. Martin Brett
Flee from the Past. C. G. Hart
Flee the Night in Anger. D. Keller
Fleeced. Stuart Buchan
Fleet Hall Inheritance. R. Keverne
Fleeting Hour. Rona Randall
Fleetwood Mansions Mystery. M. B. Dix
Flemish Shop. G. Simenon
Flesh and Blood. J. Foss
Flesh and Blood. B. Palmer
Flesh and Fire. G. Arnaud
Flesh and Mr. Rawlie. Morton Cooper
Flesh and the Devil. Elbur Ford
Flesh Game. H. Spencer
Flesh of the Orchid. J. H. Chase
Flesh Peddlers. F. Boyd
Flesh Traders. Morton Cooper
Flesh Was Cold. B. Fischer
Fletch. G. Mcdonald
Fletch's Fortune. G. Mcdonald
Fleur. S. Nichols
Fleur de Lys. J. G. Sarasin
Fleur de Lys Affair. H. Ross
Fleur Macabre. I. S. Way
Flic Story. R. Borniche
Flick of a Fin. G. Peters
Flickering Death. Robert MacLeod
Flier. M. Spillane
Flies. B. Von Hutten
Flies in the Web. F. Hume
Flies on the Wall. Alex Hamilton
Flight. A. Omre
Flight by Night. D. Keene
Flight Errant. Laurence Kirk
Flight 409. S. Frazee
Flight from a Dark Equator. N. Lewis
Flight from a Firing Wall. B. Kendrick
Flight from a Throne. M. Richmond
Flight from Bucharest. R. T. Stevens
Flight from Eden Key. Dorinne Moore
Flight from Fear. H. Janson
Flight from Fear. Ray Owen
Flight from Montego Bay. A. Haig
Flight from Riversedge. M. K. Simmons
Flight from the Grave. R. J. Hogan
Flight from the Hunter. S. Stander
Flight in Darkness. S. Harvester
Flight Instructor Murders. G. Redder
Flight into Danger. J. Castle
Flight into Danger. J. England
Flight into Darkness. P. Clark
Flight into Fear. J. Ames
Flight into Fear. F. Gerard
Flight into Fear. D. Kyle
Flight into Fear. P. Saxon
Flight into Love. J. Blackmore
Flight into Peril. R. Roleine
Flight into Peril. D. Rutherford
Flight into Terror. L. White
Flight of a Fallen Angel. D. Winston
Flight of a Witch. Ellis Peters
Flight of an Angel. V. Chute
Flight of an Angel. J. F. W. Hannay
Flight of Chariots. J. Cleary
Flight of Dutchmen. N. Tranter
Flight of Faviel. R. E. Vernede
Flight of Hawks. M. Eden
Flight of Lies. Gavin Scott
Flight of Lord Rhincrew. G. Villiers-Stuart
Flight of the Bamboo Saucer. F. Gordon
Flight of the Bat. Donald Gordon
Flight of the Duchess, and other stories. B. Reynolds
Flight of the Falcon. D. Du Maurier

Flight of the Phoenix. E. Trevor
Flight of the Raven. R. Charles
Flight of the Shadows. N. Herbert
Flight of the Stiff. Michael Brett
Flight One. C. Carpentier
Flight 685 Is Overdue. Edward Moore
Flight to a Finish. Valentine
Flight to Afar. W. L. Andersch
Flight to Darkness. G. Brewer
Flight to Fear. P. Conway
Flight to Takla-Ma. T. Thomey
Flight to the Villa Mistra. V. Maxwell
Flight Without Wings. M. Latham
Flighty Phyllis. R. A. Freeman
Flip-Side. B. Copper
Flittermouse. J. G. Sarasin
Floater. B. Cassiday
Floating Admiral. Detection Club
Floating Cafe, and other stories. Margery Lawrence
Floating Dutchman. N. Bentley
Floating Game. J. Garforth
Floating Head. Old Sleuth
Floating Peril. E. P. Oppenheim
Floating Prison. G. Leroux
Flock of Ships. B. Callison
Flockmasters. N. Tranter
Flood. Lionel Black
Flood. J. Creasey
Flood Light. C. Massie
Flood of Fate. W. C. Tuttle
Flood Tide. Ian Stuart
Flood's First Case. M. O'Driscoll
Floods of Fear. J. Hawkins
Floodwater. P. Meredith
Floozie Takes Lawman. B. Sarto
Floral Tribute. C. E. Vulliamy
Florence. E. A. Dupuy
Florentine Dagger. B. Hecht
Florentine Finish. C. Hirschberg
Florentine Madonna. J. Griffin
Florentine Ring. Jackson Stanley
Florian Signet. H. Esmond
Florian Slappey. O. R. Cohen
Flotsam of the Line. O. Binns
Flow My Tears, the Policeman Said. P. K. Dick
Flower and Weed. M. E. Braddon
Flower-Bed Murder. C. P. Cleary
Flower-Covered Corpse. M. Avallone
Flower Forbidden. A. M. Williamson
Flower Gang. G. Radcliffe
Flower in the Desert. M. Richmond
Flower of Crime. A. Belot
Flower of Desire. H. Janson
Flower of Desire. A. Wood
Flower of Evil. D. Lyons
Flower of the Forest. O. Bradbury
Flower of the Forest. C. Gibbon
Flower of the Gods. E. Phillpotts
Flower of the Gorse. L. Tracy
Flower of the Judas. C. Randell
Flower o' the Orange, and other stories. A. Castle
Flower o' the Peach. W. A. MacKenzie
Flowered Box. T. J. Green
Flowering. A. S. Turnbull
Flowering Death. A. MacVicar
Flowers by Request. L. Holton
Flowers for a Dead Witch. M. Butterworth
Flowers for Lilian. Anna Clark
Flowers for Teacher. Margaret Archer
Flowers for the Judge. M. Allingham
Flowers in the Attic. V. C. Andrews
Flowers of Darkness. E. Barr
Flowers of the Forth. J. Hone
Flowers of Vengeance. M. A. Willis
Fluke. J. Herbert
Flush As May. P. M. Hubbard
Flutter in Kings. D. Whitelaw
Fluttered Dovecote. G. M. Fenn
Fly Away Death. P. Malloch
Fly by Night. M. Afford
Fly-by-Nights. Charles Ross
Fly Country. Anthony Lang
Fly Me a Killer. F. Lester
Fly on the Wall. T. Hillerman
Fly South to Danger. S. Clausse
Flyaway. D. Bagley
Flyaway Ned. Old Sleuth
Flyaway Peter. D. Rhodes
Flying Argosy. A. J. Rees
Flying Armada. D. T. Lindsay
Flying Arrow. M. Mizzen
Flying Beast. W. S. Masterman
Flying Beetle. G. E. Rochester
Flying Blind. Alice Campbell
Flying Blood. T. Burtis
Flying Chinaman. H. H. Fein
Flying Clues. C. J. Dutton
Flying Cowboys. G. E. Rochester
Flying Crusader. D. T. Lindsay
Flying Dagger Murder. J. Cowdroy
Flying Death. S. H. Adams
Flying Death. E. Balmer
Flying Dutchman. M. Arlen
Flying Dutchman. W. C. Russell
Flying Eye. B. McKnight
Flying Fifty-Five. E. Wallace
Flying Finish. D. Francis
Flying Firs. A. M. Westwood
Flying Girl. R. Marsh

Flying Goblin. K. Robeson
Flying Headhunter. T. Wallace
Flying Hooligans. Martin Kent
Flying Horse. S. Harvester
Flying Kidnappers. Martin Kent
Flying Palatine, and other stories. J. G. Sarasin
Flying Peter. P. Trent
Flying Porcupine. R. Haligon
Flying Red Horse. F. Crane
Flying Saucer. B. Newman
Flying Saucer Gambit. L. Maddock
Flying Squad. E. Wallace
"Flying Squad" Tragedy. W. J. Bayfield
Flying Visitor. A. Kennington
Flynn. G. Mcdonald
Flynn, A.B. E. L. Long
Flynn of the "Martagon". E. L. Long
Flynn's Sampler. E. L. Long
Flypaper War. R. Starnes
Foam on the River. Sheila Ross
Focus on Murder. Dale Clark
Focus on Murder. G. H. Coxe
Foe-Farrell. A. T. Quiller-Couch
Foe in the Family. N. Cay
Foe in the Shadow. C. E. Pearce
Foe of Barnabas Collins. Marilyn Ross
Foe to Sleep. E. Cannon
Foes of Justice. H. Hill
Fog. Elizabeth Ford
Fog. J. Herbert
Fog. J. Remenham
Fog. V. Williams
Fog Comes. Mary Collins
Fog for a Killer. B. Graeme
Fog Hides the Fury. P. Minton
Fog Is a Shroud. M. Malmer
Fog Island. D. Osborne
Fog Island. Marilyn Ross
Fog Island Horror. Marilyn Ross
Fog Island Secret. Marilyn Ross
Fog Maiden. J. Toombs
Fog of Doubt. C. Brand
Fog Off Weymouth. H. Clandon
Fog on the Mountain. F. De Laguna
Fog over Fundy. L. A. Cunningham
Fog Princess. F. Warden
Fog Sinister. M. Lovell
Fogarty and Co. J. Flaherty
Fogbound. Clarissa Ross
Foggerty's Fairy and other tales. W. S. Gilbert
Foggy, Foggy Death. R. Lockridge
Foggy, Foggy Dew. C. Blackstock
Foggy Foggy Dew. A. Dean
Foggy Night at Offord. H. Wood
Foghorn. A. Atherton
Foiled. Anonymous
Foiled. T. W. Speight
Foiled by an Innocent Mind. F. Carmichael
Foiling a Counterfeiter. E. C. Derby
Folded Paper Mystery. H. Footner
Folio Forty-One. Michael Sinclair
Folio on Florence White. W. Oursler
Follow a Shadow. G. Greenaway
Follow a Shadow. J. Marshall
Follow a Shadow. W. Reyburn
Follow, As the Night. P. McGerr
Follow McLean. G. Goodchild
Follow Me. H. Reilly
Follow Me Down. S. Foote
Follow My Leader. G. Greenaway
Follow That Hearse! J. Gonzales
Follow the Blue Car. R. A. J. Walling
Follow the Lady. B. Gray
Follow the Leader. L. DuBreuil
Follow the Leader. J. Logue
Follow the Little Pictures. Alan Graham
Follow the Saint. L. Charteris
Follow the Toff. J. Creasey
Follow This Fair Corpse. L. D. Smith
Follow Your Heart. A. Maybury
Followed Man. T. Williams
Follower. P. Quentin
Following a Chance Clew. Nicholas Carter
Following Ann. K. R. G. Browne
Following Feet. E. C. Vivian
Following Footsteps. J. J. Farjeon
Folly. D. Anne
Folly Hall. Lynna Cooper
Folly Morrison. F. Barrett
Folly of Fear. K. C. Groom
Folly of the Wise. S. Paternoster
Folly's Gold. J. Scott
Fontego's Folly. A. Garve
Fontenay, the Swordsman. F. Du Boisgobey
Foo Dog. T. Wells
Food for Felony. B. Cobb
Food for Fishes. R. Wills
Fool and His Money. E. Colles
Fool Beloved. J. Farnol
Fool Errant. P. Wentworth
Fool for a Client. Roy Lewis
Fool from Down Under. R. Wilkes-Hunter
Fool Killer. H. Eustis
Fool of Nature. J. Hawthorne
Fool of the "Yard." T. A. Plummer
Fool the Toff. J. Creasey
Fool with Women. F. Whishaw
Foolish Cargo. N. Carta
Foolish Margaret. T. W. Speight

Foolish Virgin. N. Karta
Foolish Virgin Returns. N. Karta
Foolish Virgin Says No! N. Karta
Foolproof Murder. Walter Blake
Fool's Apple. M. K. Douglas
Fool's Bet. C. Campbell
Fool's Fair. C. Campbell
Fool's Gamble. S. Gibbons
Fools' Gold. D. Hitchens
Fool's Gold. S. H. Page
Fools in Town Are on Our Side. Ross Thomas
Fools' Parade. D. Grubb
Fool's Proof. A. S. Carter
Fools Walk In. B. Fischer
Foot in the Grave. E. Ferrars
Football Pool Murders. G. Verner
Football Pools Mystery. W. D. Maydwell
Football Racket. W. D. Maydwell
Football Racketeers. F. W. Gumley
Footbridge to Death. K. M. Knight
Footfall in the Mist. V. Black
Foothills of Fear. J. Creasey
Footlight Glare. A. Askew
Footlights. A. Applin
Footlights. M. McGrath
Footlight's Call. G. Goodchild
Footpath. L. Meynell
Footpath Murder. M. Bringle
Footprints. K. C. Strahan
Footprints in the Sand. W. J. Elliott
Footprints in the Sand. W. Richmond
Footprints in the Snow. Dora Russell
Footprints of Death. N. MacKenzie
Footprints of Satan. N. Berrow
Footprints on the Ceiling. C. Rawson
Footsteps. T. Du Bois
Footsteps at the Lock. R. A. Knox
Footsteps Behind Her. M. A. Wilson
Footsteps Behind Me. Anthony Gilbert
Footsteps Behind Them. S. Truss
Footsteps in the Air. S. Wells
Footsteps in the Dark. G. Heyer
Footsteps in the Dark. L. Mearson
Footsteps in the Fog. P. Bennetts
Footsteps in the Night. C. Fraser-Simson
Footsteps in the Night. D. Hitchens
Footsteps in the Park. M. Joseph
Footsteps of Death. V. Gunn
Footsteps of the Cat. L. A. Olmsted
Footsteps on the Stairs. L. Ford
Footsteps on the Stairs. J. Potts
Footsteps That Follow. M. Farnsworth
Footsteps That Stopped. A. Fielding
For a Girl Called Isaiah. J. Shelynn
For a Madman's Millions. Nicholas Carter
For a Noble Cause. P. Boulle
For a Pawned Crown. Nicholas Carter
For a Woman's Honour. Christopher Wilson
For a Young Queen's Bright Eyes. R. H. Savage
For Cash Only. J. Payn
For Conduct Unbefitting. D. Whitelaw
For Crying Out Shroud. O. Blakeston
For Dying You Always Have Time. S. M. Singer
For England. M. Gerard
For Ever Beloved. M. Richmond
For Ever You'll Be Mine. K. Lindsay
For Fear of Little Men. J. Blackburn
For France. M. Gerard
For Gain Not Glory. J. W. McGaw
For Godmother and Country. R. T. Larkin
For Goodness' Sake. C. Wells
For Her Dear Sake. M. C. Hay
For Her Life. R. H. Savage
For Her Sister's Sake. M. E. Cooke
For Her to See. J. Shearing
For Himself Alone. T. W. Speight
For His Brother's Crime. C. E. Blaney
For His Brother's Crime. L. Price
For His Friend's Honor. S. Norris
For Honour and Life. W. Westall
For Honour or Death. D. Donovan
For Information Received. E. Wallace
For Jacques' Sake. J. Claretie
For Kicks. D. Francis
For Lack of Gold. C. Gibbon
For Liberty. H. Nisbet
For Life and After. G. R. Sims
For Life and Love. R. H. Savage
For Love and Honour. F. Barrett
For Love of a Bedouin Maid. Le Voleur
For Love of Her. G. Boothby
For Love of Imabelle. C. Himes
For Love or Crown. A. W. Marchmont
For Love or Money. M. Leighton
For Maimie's Sake. G. Allen
For Murder I Charge More. F. McAuliffe
For Murder Will Speak. J. J. Connington
For Old Crime's Sake. D. Ames
For One Season Only. R. Jocelyn
For Pete's Sake. B. Street
For Pete's Sake! G. Usher
For Reasons Unknown. G. Goodchild
For Richer, For Poorer, Til Death. P. McGerr
For Richer for Richer. Dulcie Gray
For Sale—Murder. W. Levinrew
"For So Little". Helen Davis
For the Asking. H. R. Daniels

For the Defence: Dr. Thorndyke. R. A. Freeman
For the Defense. B. L. Farjeon
For the Defense. F. Hume
For the Defense. J. Reach
For the Eyes of the President Only. P. Salinger
For the Hangman. J. S. Strange
For the Love of Murder. M. Scherf
For the President's Eyes Only. R. Sale
For the Queen. E. P. Oppenheim
For the Sake of Revenge. Nicholas Carter
For Them That Trespass. E. Raymond
For Those in Peril. M. Richmond
For Us the Living. H. Chevalier
For Valour. F. R. Adams
For Value Received. T. Cobb
For Very Life. Hamilton Marshall
For Woman's Love. E. Southworth
For You, I Commit Murder. D. R. Sperduti
For Your Eyes Only. I. Fleming
For Your Eyes Only: Read and Destroy. L. Honig
Forbidden. A. Maybury
Forbidden Area. P. Frank
Forbidden by Law. B. Cottingham
Forbidden by Law. A. Griffiths
Forbidden Cargo. S. Box
Forbidden Castle. W. E. D. Ross
Forbidden Cave. A. Furness
Forbidden Door. Herman Landon
Forbidden Door. E. C. Vivian
Forbidden Frontiers. L. Noel
Forbidden Frontiers. S. Maddock
Forbidden Garden. U. Curtiss
Forbidden Hour. M. Crossley
Forbidden Island. R. C. Payes
Forbidden Land. D. Cushman
Forbidden Mansion. R. N. Winstead
Forbidden Road. V. Canning
Forbidden Road. G. Morton
Forbidden Room. Jaclen Steele
Forbidden Room. R. Thorndike
Forbidden Shrine. C. Dawe
Forbidden Territory. "Capstan"
Forbidden Territory. D. Wheatley
Forbidden Tower. E. Cook
Forbidden Valley. L. P. Greene
Forbidden Wine. F. A. Kummer
Forbidden Word. W. LeQueux
Forbidden Years. Wadsworth Camp
Force. A. Radnor
Force of Innocence. J. Weatherhead
Force Play. Anthony Stuart
Force Red. M. R. Bass
Force 10 from Navarone. Alistair MacLean
Forced Apart. M. Redwing
Forced Landing. G. Goodchild
Fordham's Feud. B. Mitford
Ford's Folly, Ltd. A. Griffiths
Forecast—Murder. A. Tack
Foreign Affair. Graeme Douglas
Foreign Affairs. H. Fleetwood
Foreign Bodies. R. Petrie
Foreign Bodies. S. Truss
Foreign Body. Moira Field
Foreign Exchange. J. Sangster
Foreign Harry Complot. G. Hertz
Foreign Matter. C. Byron
Foreign Secretary Who Vanished. H. G. Hutchinson
Foreign Squad. G. Kent
Forest Affair. N. J. N. Chance
Forest and the Damned. R. Severn
Forest Exile. O. Binns
Forest Inn. H. L. V. Fletcher
Forest Mystery. N. Burnaby
Forest of Death. Jon Barton
Forest of Eyes. V. Canning
Forest of Fear. A. Rundle
Forest of Fortune. W. W. Sayer
Forest Officer. F. E. Penny
Forest Ranger. B. Bolt
Forests of the Night. Elliott Arnold
Forests of the Night. J. Cleary
Forests of the Night. I. R. G. Hart
Forever Is Today. Raymond Mason
Forever McLean. G. Goodchild
Forever Timeless. D. Rochester
Forever Wilt Thou Die. B. N. Byfield
Forfeit. R. Cullum
Forfeit. D. Francis
Forge and Furnace. F. Warden
Forged Evidence. A. O. Pollard
Forged Note. O. Micheau
Forged in Strong Fires. J. Ironside
Forged Will. Emerson Bennett
Forged Note. H. M. Jones
Forger. E. Wallace
Forgers and Confidence Men. G. S. McWatters
Forget-Me-Not. J. Shearing
Forget My Fate. R. S. Wallis
Forget What You Saw. J. Ashford
Forging the Blades. B. Mitford
Forging the Links. J. K. Stafford
Forgive Me, Lovely Lady. N. Easton
Forgive the Executioner. A. Lane
Forgotten Fleet Mystery. G. Coffin
Forgotten Hills. M. L. Tyrrell
Forgotten Honeymoon. D. Durham
Forgotten Love. Lynna Cooper

Forgotten of Allah. G. Radcliffe
Forgotten Place. J. Fores
Forgotten Road. S. Harvester
Forgotten Story. Winston Graham
Forgotten Terror. Constance Rutherford
Forked Lightning. M. Durham
Forked Tongue. R. L. De Havilland
Forlorn Hope. E. Yates
Form of Release. G. Petrie
Formula. S. Horler
Formula. G. Sager
Formula. S. Shagan
Formula for Crime. Richard Grant
Formula for Murder. B. S. Ballinger
Formula for Murder. Adrian Reynolds
Forsaken. T. Kingsley-Smith
Forsaken Inn. A. K. Green
Forsythia Finds Murder. R. C. Payes
Fort. J. Hale
Fort Minster, M.P. E. J. Reed
Fort Terror Murders. V. W. Mason
FORTEC Conspiracy. R. M. Garvin
Fortenberry Rites. M. Ogan
Fortescue Candle. B. Flynn
Fortieth Victim. C. Franklin
Fortnight by the Sea. Emma Page
Fortnight of Fear. S. Drew
Fortnightly Club. J. G. Hutchinson
Fortress. Gabrielle Lord
Fortress of Ashes. A. Pelham
Fortress of Solitude. K. Robeson
Fortress of the Maquis. Stagg Green
Fortress of Yadasara. C. Lys
Fortunate Island. E. S. Russell
Fortunate Miss East. L. Meynell
Fortunate Prisoner. M. Pemberton
Fortunate Wayfarer. E. P. Oppenheim
Fortune A-Begging. T. Gallon
Fortune Cheats. N. Wray
Fortune Favors Fools. R. Arnold
Fortune for a Falcon. C. Darby
Fortune for Four. D. H. Barber
Fortune for the Taking. C. Dixon
Fortune Hunters. Joan Aiken
Fortune Hunters and others. C. N. Williamson
Fortune in Death. L. St. Clair
Fortune in Peril. R. M. Wells
Fortune in the Sky. J. Pattinson
Fortune Is a Woman. Winston Graham
Fortune Must Follow. D. G. Waring
Fortune of Bridget Malone. M. B. Lowndes
Fortune Road. J. McCague
Fortune Seeker. E. Southworth
Fortune's Apprentice. L. Cargill
Fortune's Fool. J. Hawthorne
Fortune's Fool. F. E. Wynne
Fortunes of Conrad. S. Cobb
Fortunes of Flynn. E. L. Long
Fortune's Sport. A. M. Williamson
Fortune's Wheel. M. Gerard
Fortune's Wheel. George Long
Forty Days. O. Wynd
48 Hours. H. Janson
Forty-Eight Short Stories. E. Wallace
Forty-First Passenger. K. Hopkins
Forty-First Thief. E. A. Pollitz
.44. J. Breslin
'44 Vintage. A. Price
Forty-Nine Chances. J. Rhys-Williams
49 Days of Death. B. S. Ballinger
Forty Pieces of Alloy. P. Carlon
Forty Thieves. R. Wallace
Forty-Three Candles for Mr. Beamish. P. Barrington
42 Days for Murder. R. Torrey
Forty Whacks. G. Hume
Forty Years On. J. Owen
Forward from Youth. L. A. Pavey
Forza Trap. K. Davis
Foss River Ranch. R. Cullum
Foul Deeds Will Arise. Mark Cross
Foul Deeds Will Rise. R. Harrison
Foul Hawsers. E. L. Long
Foul Play. J. Potter
Foul Play. C. Reade
Foul Play. J. C. Rogers
Foul Play at Lentwood. H. Leyford
Foul Play Suspected. John Beynon
Foul Play Suspected. M. Halliday
Foul Weather. G. F. Gibbs
Found—Adventure. R. Hardinge
Found and Fettered. D. Donovan
Found Dead. C. Brooks
Found Dead. J. Payn
Found Dead. Hero Strong
Found Drowned. M. Burton
"Found Drowned." E. Phillpotts
Found Floating. F. W. Crofts
Found Guilty. F. Barrett
Found in Possession. P. Urquhart
Found in the Jungle. Nicholas Carter
Found on the Beach. Nicholas Carter
Found on the Road. Gret Lane
Found Out. H. B. Mathers
Found Shot. H. Willett
Founder Member. J. Gardner
Foundered Galleon. W. Chesney
Foundling. P. Trent
Fountain at Marlieux. C. Aveline
Fountain of Beauty. L. T. Meade
Fountain of Death. H. L. Nelson

Fountain of Green Fire. P. Brebner
Four Against the Mob. O. Fraley
Four-and-Twenty Blackbirds. H. V. O'Brien
Four and Twenty Virgins. J. McClure
Four Answers. J. Cobnor
Four Armourers. F. Beeding
Four at Bay. Mark Cross
Four Blind Mice. C. C. Lowis
Four Boys, a Girl and a Gun. W. Wiener
Four Brains. W. J. Makin
Four Callers in Razor Street. S. Fowler
Four Came Back. M. Caidin
Four Chambered Villian. G. Madderom
Four Cornered Story. F. A. Chittenden
Four Corners. C. S. Raymond
Four Corners of the World. A. E. W. Mason
Four Corpses in a Million. J. Robb
Four Days. J. Buell
Four Days. Harold King
Four Days in a Lifetime. G. Simenon
Four Days in June. Elizabeth Ford
Four Days to the Fireworks. P. Purser
Four Days' Wonder. A. A. Milne
Four Dead Men. S. Simpson
Four Dead Mice. T. B. Black
Four Defences. J. J. Connington
Four Doors to Death. J. Courage
Four Extra Daughters. J. Maconechy
Four Faces. W. LeQueux
Four Faces of Siva. R. J. Casey
Four False Weapons. J. D. Carr
Four Faultless Felons. G. K. Chesterton
Four Feet in the Grave. A. R. Long
4:50 from Paddington. A. Christie
Four Find Danger. M. Halliday
Four-Fingered Glove. Nicholas Carter
Four Fingers. F. M. White
Four for the Money. D. J. Marlowe
Four Frightened Sisters. W. Spence
Four Frightened Women. G. H. Coxe
Four Get Going. Mark Cross
Four Green Fish. E. Jepson
Four Guns to Carson City. Dan Morgan
Four Hoodoo Charms. Nicholas Carter
Four Horses. C. Pincher
Four Hours. M. Brenner
Four Hours to Fear. F. Lockridge
Four Hundred. S. Sheppard
400 Brattle Street. G. Wolk
Four in a Fairleand. E. L. Long
Four in Hand. J. Middlemass
Four Jealous Men. M. Frazer
Four Johns. E. Queen
Four Just Men. E. Wallace
Four Kings in the Street of Gold. F. H. Rose
Four Knocks on the Door. J. P. Seabrooke
Four Letter Crowd. P. Leslie
Four Liars. E. Murray
Four Lost Ladies. S. Palmer
Four Lost Ships. E. Spencer
Four Mad Monarchs. R. E. Cooke
Four Make Holiday. Mark Cross
Four Marys. Rinalda Roberts
Four Men and a Prayer. D. Garth
Four Men Called John. E. Queen
Four Million. O. Henry
Four Million a Year. J. Webster
Four More Sherlock Holmes Plays. Michael Hardwick
Four Motives for Murder. B. Hope
Four of a Kind. Dan Morgan
Four of Hearts. E. Queen
Four of Us Meet Again. L. Barbee
4 P.M. Express. F. Hume
Four Past Four. Roy Vickers
Four Philanthropists. E. Jepson
Four Pitiful People. A. Wood
Four Plus One. J. H. Hurst
Four-Ply Yarn. M. Burton
Four Pools Mystery. Anonymous
Four-Pools Mystery. J. Webster
Four Red Nightcaps. W. Chesney
Four Roads to Death. B. Appel
Four Sherlock Holmes Plays. Michael Hardwick
Four Square Jane. E. Wallace
Four Stars for Danger. Jonathan Burke
Four Stragglers. F. Packard
Four Strange Women. E. R. Punshon
Four Strike Home. Mark Cross
Four-Time Loser. D. Lynch
Four Times a Widower. A. Bliss
Four Tragedies of Memworth. Ernest Hamilton
Four Trails. W. M. Graydon
Four Unfaithful Servants. G. Bellairs
Four Way Proof. R. A. Henriquez
Four Winds. H. Adams
Four Winds. A. Atkinson
Four Winds. S. Gluck
Four Winds. R. Pertwee
"Four Winds" Mystery. Norman Lee
Four Witnesses. M. Reisner
Four Women in the Case. Annie Thomas
Four Women Went. O. Cecil
Fourfingers. L. Brock
Fourflush Island. L. C. Douthwaite
Foursome. Lionel Black
Foursquare Murder. David Hume

Fourteen Dilemma. H. Pentecost
Fourteen Points. A. B. Reeve
14 Seconds to Hell. Nick Carter
Fourteen Years After! J. Hunter
14th Agent. D. C. Cooke
Fourteenth Key. C. Wells
Fourteenth Trump. J. Philips
Fourth Agency. J. Fredman
Fourth at Junction. J. Barker
Fourth Bomb. J. Rhode
Fourth Challenge. R. H. Hutchinson
Fourth Chamber. G. R. Preedy
Fourth Dagger. L. Allan
Fourth Day of Fear. Berrie Davis
Fourth Degree. K. S. Daiger
Fourth Down to Death. B. Halliday
Fourth Finger. A. Wynne
Fourth Funeral. C. L. Leonard
Fourth Gambler. D. Castle
Fourth Grave. J. Boland
Fourth Horseman. G. Bocca
Fourth King. H. S. Keeler
Fourth Letter. F. Gruber
Fourth Man. W. McCarthy
Fourth Man. H. Mitchell
Fourth Man. Lou Smith
Fourth Man on the Rope. E. Berckman
Fourth Monkey. R. Parkes
Fourth Murder. D. M. Glew
Fourth of Forever. B. S. Ballinger
Fourth of July War. A. Topol
Fourth Plague. E. Wallace
Fourth Postman. C. Rice
Fourth Reich. M. Hale
Fourth Reich. J. Rosenberger
Fourth Reich Death Squad. A. Kilgore
Fourth Road. F. Hird
Fourth Seal. P. Groom
Fourth Shadow. R. Charles
Fourth Ship. C. E. Mayne
Fourth Side of the Triangle. E. Queen
Fourth Stage of Gainsborough Brown. Clarissa Watson
Fourth Star. R. Burke
Fourth Theory. W. J. Bayfield
Fourth Victim. P. Barrington
Fourth Wall. A. A. Milne
Fourth Wall. B. Paul
Fowl Murder. R. H. Lindsay
Fowl Play. T. Du Bois
Fowler Formula. H. Dalmas
Fox from His Lair. E. Cadell
Fox in the Sea. R. Magowan
Fox-Magic Murders. R. Van Gulik
Fox of Maulen. H. H. Kirst
Fox Potential. K. Hagenbach
Fox Prowls. V. Williams
Fox Trap. R. A. Smith
Fox Valley Murders. J. H. Vance
Foxbat. P. Cave
Foxbat Spiral. M. Karman
Foxfire Cove. K. Ostrander
Foxglove Country. Linden Howard
Foxglove Manor. R. Buchanan
Foxglove Summer. N. Grey
Foxhole. M. Urquhart
Fracas in the Foothills. Elliot Paul
Fractured Silence. F. Cowen
Fragment of Fear. J. Bingham
Fragment of Glass. F. L. Green
Fragrant Death. C. Blake
Frail Ghost. M. Maurice
Frail on North Circular. M. Urquhart
Frails Can Be So Tough. H. Janson
Frame. J. Harvey
Frame for Murder. K. Mechem
Frame for Murder. R. Simons
Frame Is Beautiful. Carter Brown
Frame the Baron. Anthony Morton
Frame-Up. J. G. Brandon
Frame-Up. C. Brooks
Frame-Up. A. Garve
Frame-Up. Neill Graham
Frame Up. Stephan Gregory
Frame-Up. D. Whitelaw
Framed. E. Ellison
Framed. H. Janson
Framed Evidence. J. Cowdroy
Framed for Hanging. G. Cullingford
Framed in Blood. B. Halliday
Framed in Guilt. D. Keene
Framed in Guilt. J. Slate
Framework of Fate. Nicholas Carter
Framing of Carol Woan. B. Cobb
Frampton—of "the Yard"! T. A. Plummer
Frampton Sees Red. T. A. Plummer
Frances. F. F. Kelly
Frances Hildyard. H. Wood
Francesca. S. Marlowe
Francesca. L. Snow
Franchise Affair. J. Tey
Francine. S. Shelley
Francis Quarles Investigates. J. Symons
Francois the Valet. G. W. Appleton
Frangipani. N. Easton
Frank James in St. Louis. W. B. Lawson
Frank Redland, Recruit. Mrs. C. Kernahan
Frankenstein. T. J. Kelly
Frankenstein. M. W. Shelley
Frankenstein Factory. E. D. Hoch
Frankenstein Lives Again. D. F. Glut
Frankenstein Meets Dracula. D. F. Glut

Title Index

Frankincense and Murder. B. Kendrick
Frantic. N. Calef
Frantic Boast. J. L. Rickard
Fraser Butts In. H. Clevely
Frass. J. Chancellor
Fratricide Is a Gas. L. Gutteridge
Fratricides. M. Edelman
Fraud, Mrs. C. Kernahan
Frauds. M. Hastings
Fraulein. J. McGovern
Fraulein Is Feline. Carter Brown
Fraulein Spy. Nick Carter
Frazer Acquittal. S. Ransome
Freak Island Murders. R. Verron
Freak Museum. R. R. Ryan
Freak of Fate. E. F. Spence
Freak of St. Freda's! G. E. Rochester
Freak-Out. M. Arrighi
Freak Racket. W. J. Elliott
Freak Show Murders. W. B. Gibson
Freaked Out Stranger. P. Morgan
Freaks of Imagination. J. Steelnib
Freckled Shark. K. Robeson
Fred Bennett, the Mormon Detective. F. E. Bennett
Fred Danford, the Skillful Detective. H. Rockwood
Fred in Situ. G. Hammond
Fred Travis, A.B. Taffrail
Frederick and Sophia. L. Watkins
Frederick Lonton. D. W. Croft
Frederika and the Convict. L. M. Robertson
Free Agent. P. Murray
Free Are the Dead. S. Friedman
Free As Air. E. Kyle
Free Fall. J. D. Reed
Free Flight. D. Terman
Free Heart. E. C. Reed
Free-Lance Murder. V. Rodell
Free-Lance Spy. P. Armstrong
Free Lovers. R. W. Kauffman
Free Ride. J. M. Fox
Freebie and the Bean. P. B. Ross
Freebody Heiress. E. Gordon
Freebooters. N. Tranter
Freebooty. J. Foxx
Freedman. J. Pattinson
Freedom. A. Askew
Freedom for Two. J. Carr
Freedom from Fear. I. Perrot
Freedom Trap. D. Bagley
Freedom Trail to Greystone. L. Bronte
Freeloaders. E. Lacy
Freer's Cove. E. Gordon
Freeway. D. Barkley
Freeway to Murder. W. Sproule
Freeze Frame. R. R. Irvine
Freeze Thy Blood Less Coldly. J. Wainwright
French Atlantic Affair. E. P. Lehman
French Connection II. Robin Moore
French Decision. D. Osborn
French Doctor. L. Royer
French Doll. V. McConnor
French Farce. E. Greenwood
French Finish. Robert Ross
French for Murder. B. Mara
French for Trouble. L. T. Shortell
French Girl. A. Mills
French Hazard. W. Mills
French Inheritance. A. Stevenson
French Key. F. Gruber
French Killing. J. P. Cody
French Kiss. P. Israel
French Kiss. J. J. Montague
French Master. A. W. Barrett
French Powder Mystery. E. Queen
French Strikes Oil. F. W. Crofts
Frenchman. V. Johnston
Frenchman Must Die. K. Boyle
Frenchwoman. B. Paul
Frenzied Fiction. S. Leacock
Frenzy. J. O. Causey
Frenzy. A. La Bern
Frenzy in the Flesh. D. Reid
Frenzy of Evil. H. Kane
Frenzy of Merchantmen. B. Callison
Frequent Hearses. E. Crispin
Fresh Air. G. Hughes
Fresh Waters and other stories. R. W. Child
Friarsmead. Laura Smith
Friday Before Bank Holiday. George Davis
Friday for Death. L. Lariar
Friday Market. C. Meadows
Friday Run. J. Wood
Friday the Rabbi Slept Late. H. Kemelman
Friday the 13th. J. J. Farjeon
Friday to Monday. W. Garrett
Friday's Feast. D. Pendleton
Friend in Deed. R. Jagoda
Friend in the Police. J. Givens
Friend of Mary Rose. Elizabeth Fenwick
Friend or Foe. R. Cawley
Friendless Millionaire. H. L. Phillips
Friendless Spy. A. Shenton
Friendly Fiends. P. Muller
Friendly Place to Die. M. P. Faur
Friends. H. Herlin
Friends. Godfrey Smith
Friends at Court. H. Cecil

Friends of Eddie Coyle. G. V. Higgins
Friends of Lucifer. D. Sinclair
Friend's Victim. A. Hurlba
Friendship of Veronica. T. Cobb
Friendships, Secrets and Lies. B. H. Deal
Fright. G. Hopley
Fright. J. Reach
Frightened Amazon. A. M. Stein
Frightened Angels. J. Cannan
Frightened Bowerbird. F. Y. McHugh
Frightened Brides. M. Cumberland
Frightened Chameleon. L. Gribble
Frightened Child. D. Lyon
Frightened Dove. P. Hardin
Frightened Eyes. Roland Daniel
Frightened Fiancee. G. H. Coxe
Frightened Fingers. S. Dean
Frightened Fisherman. J. N. Chance
Frightened Girl. M. Crombie
Frightened Heart. J. Ames
Frightened Ladies. B. Benson
Frightened Lady. W. H. Baker
Frightened Lady. E. Wallace
Frightened Man. D. Chambers
Frightened Man. L. Meynell
Frightened Man. G. Verner
Frightened Murderer. N. Rutledge
Frightened One. F. Gamble
Frightened Ones. M. Marlette
Frightened People. J. T. Story
Frightened Pigeon. R. Burke
Frightened Sailor. D. Sharp
Frightened Stiff. K. Roos
Frightened to Death. Hilary Gray
Frightened Village. N. Edwards
Frightened Widow. Bernice Carey
Frightened Widow. Colin Robertson
Frightened Wife. M. R. Rinehart
Frighteners. R. Busby
Frighteners. P. Leslie
Frightening Talent. L. Golding
Frightful Sin of Cisco Newman. G. A. Ralston
Frigorific Ghost. H. Van Scofield
Fringe of the Law. C. H. Bullivant
Frisco Detective. Anonymous
Frisco Hi-Jack. A. Capelli
'Frisco Rock. D. Spade
Fritz, the Bound Boy Detective. E. L. Wheeler
Fritz, the German Detective. T. Pastor
Fritz to the Front. E. L. Wheeler
Fritzi. A. Kennington
Friulan Plot. E. Webster
Frivolities. R. Marsh
Frog in the Moonflower. I. Drummond
Frog in the Throat. E. Ferrars
Frog Murders. L. Serrester
Frog Was Yellow. F. Vivian
Frogman Assassination. J. Seward
Frogs at the Bottom of the Well. K. Edgar
Froler Case. J. L. Jacolliot
From a Dark Place. L. Charbonneau
From a High Tower. T. Newman
From a Prison Cell. Nicholas Carter
From a Surgeon's Diary. C. Ashdown
From A to Z. San Antonio
From All Blindness. H. Gibbs
From Behind the Arras. P. C. De Crespigny
From Clue to Capture. D. Donovan
From Clue to Climax. W. N. Harben
From Clue to Clue. Nicholas Carter
From Dance Hall to Opium Den. Griff
From Death to Life. Old Sleuth
From Despair to Triumph. W. G. Forbes
From Director, CIA: Burn Scorpio. M. Roote
From Doon with Death. R. Rendell
From Dusk Till Dawn. W. Garrett
From Exile. J. Payn
From Father to Son. P. Trent
From Information Received. D. Donovan
From Information Received. C. F. Gregg
From Information Received. E. Radford
From Lake to Wilderness. W. M. Graydon
From Laughter to Death. J. Sandys
From London Far. M. Innes
From Midnight to Morning. M. Leblanc
From Natural Causes. Josephine Bell
From 9 O'Clock to Jamaica Bay. D. Broun
From Now On. P. Packard
From Out the Vasty Deep. M. B. Lowndes
From Outer Space. H. Clement
From Paris with Love. Lynna Cooper
From Peril to Peril. Nicholas Carter
From Post to Finish. H. Smart
From Russia, with Love. I. Fleming
From Satan, with Love. V. Coffman
From Scenes Like These. Gordon M. Williams
From Secret Places. M. Lynch
From Shadow to Light. G. Campbell
From Sing Sing to Liberty. H. C. Blaney
From Six to Six. W. B. Foster
From the Bosom of the Deep. J. E. Muddock
From the Cliffs of Croaghaun. R. Cromie
From the Hand of the Hunter. L. T. Meade
From the House of Bondage. R. Rodd

From the Scourge of the Tongue. B. Marchant
From the Valley of the Missing. Grace M. White
From Thief to Detective. F. Hume
From This Dark Stairway. M. G. Eberhart
From This Day Forth. Laura Smith
From This Death Forward. R. Bloomfield
Front Door Key. J. Brophy
Front for Murder. G. Emery
Front Man. F. Wallace
Front of Brass. F. M. White
Front Page Murder. John Bentley
Front Page Murder. J. Powers
Front Page Murder. R. Trevor
Front Page Mystery. G. M. Dean
Front Page Woman. P. Saxon
Frontier. M. Leblanc
Frontier. P. Tabori
Frontier Detective. E. L. Wheeler
Frontier Incident. S. B. Hough
Frontier Mystery. B. Mitford
Frontier Mystery. J. Mowbray
Frontier of Fear. I. R. G. Hart
Frontiers. B. Ledwidge
Frontiers of Death. J. Turner
Frontiers of Fear. J. Sanders
Frontiers of Violence. C. Leader
Frontiersman. H. Bindloss
Frontiersmen. H. Bindloss
Frost. Andrew Hall
Frost on the Moon. C. Darby
Frosted Death. K. Robeson
Frozen Death. Winifred Graham
Frozen Death. A. Weymouth
Frozen Deep. W. Collins
Frozen Fire. H. Hawton
Frozen Flame. M. E. Hanshew
Frozen Gold. A. J. Small
Frozen Ground. G. N. Hoult
Frozen Hearts. G. W. Appleton
Frozen Humor. R. P. Woodward
Frozen Inlet Post. J. B. Hendryx
Frozen Slippers. A. M. Williamson
Frozen Stiff. R. Chapman
Fruit of Folly. L. Bennet-Thompson
Fruit of Indiscretion. W. Magnay
Fruit of the Poppy. R. Wilder
Fruit of the Tree. G. S. Donisthorpe
Fruits of Deception. Marian Murray
Fu Manchu's Bride. S. Rohmer
Fuehrer Dies. H. Desmond
Fugitive. W. H. Baker
Fugitive. R. Bridges
Fugitive. R. L. Fish
Fugitive. G. Simenon
Fugitive Affair. R. Gatenby
Fugitive Eye. C. Jay
Fugitive from Fear. T. E. Wilson
Fugitive from Murder. M. V. Heberden
Fugitive Men. R. Goyne
Fugitive Millionaire. A. Carlyle
Fugitive Pigeon. D. E. Westlake
Fugitive Sleuth. H. Footner
Fugitives. W. Hackett
Fugitives. Morley Roberts
Fugitives. N. Sligh
Fugitives. Alan Thomas
Fugitives of Pearl Hill. E. A. Young
Fugitive's Road. A. MacVicar
Fugitive's Road. P. Malloch
Fuhrer Seed. G. Weill
Fulfilling of the Law. E. Gwynne
Fulfillment. Elsie Lee
Full Cargo. W. D. Steele
Full Circle. H. Cecil
Full Coverage. J. M. Ullman
Full Crash Dive. A. R. Bosworth
Full Fare for a Corpse. T. Davis
Full Fathom Five. H. S. Davies
Full Fathom Five. G. V. Galwey
Full Fury. R. Ormerod
Full House. Frederick Jackson
Full Moon. T. Mundy
Full Moon. W. Spence
Full Moon for Murder. J. M. Spender
Full Stop. G. Mitcham
Full Term. P. Spencer
Full Treatment. R. S. Thorn
Fuller's Earth. C. Wells
Fullerton Case. R. Doubleday
Fully Dressed and in His Right Mind. M. Fessier
Fully Ripe. P. H. Irving
Fun and Deadly Games. D. Tracy
Fun City. H. Barron
Fun Fair. H. H. Lee
Fun House. P. Reid
Fun with Dick and Jane. S. Stewart
Funeral for a Commissar. R. Magowan
Funeral for a Physicist. P. Bloxham
Funeral for Five. J. Stagge
Funeral in Berlin. L. Deighton
Funeral in Eden. P. McGuire
Funeral March for Siegfried. A. Williamson
Funeral March of a Marionette. Winifred Duke
Funeral of Figaro. Ellis Peters
Funeral Rites. J. Hedges
Funeral Urn. Jane Drummond
Funeral Was in Spain. E. McGirr

Funerals Are Fatal. A. Christie
Funhouse. B. Appel
Funniest Killer in Town. Hampton Stone
Funny Bob. Old Sleuth
Funny Bone. J. MacLaren-Ross
Funny, Jonas, You Don't Look Dead. M. McMullen
Funny Money. R. Sapir
Fur Bringers. H. Footner
Fur Raiders. H. H. C. Gibbons
Furious Old Women. L. Bruce
Furnace for a Foe. C. Rushton
Furnished for Murder. E. Ferrars
Further Adventures of a Cowboy Detective. C. A. Sirengo
Further Adventures of Captain Kettle. C. J. C. Hyne
Further Adventures of Doctor Syn. R. Thorndike
Further Adventures of Jimmie Dale. F. Packard
Further Adventures of Quincy Adams Sawyer. C. F. Pidgin
Further Adventures of Romney Pringle. C. Ashdown
Further Adventures of Solar Pons. B. Copper
Further Adventures of the Black Pilgrim. G. Stanley
Further Evidence. A. Brock
Further Exploits of Nick Carter, Detective. Nicholas Carter
Further Foolishness. S. Leacock
Further Outlook Unsettled. H. Clevely
Further Secrets of Potsdam. W. LeQueux
Further Side of Fear. H. McCloy
Furthest Fury. C. Wells
Furtive Flame. H. Janson
Furtive Men. L. Spencer
Fury. J. Farris
Fury of Rachel Monnet. P. Abrahams
Fury on Sunday. R. Matheson
Fury on the Pampas. L. Robin
Fury with Legs. G. Lawrence
Fury Within. R. St. Clair
Futile Alibi. F. W. Crofts
Future Mrs. Dering. T. Cobb
Fuzz. E. McBain

F

"G.B." W. F. Morris
G.B.H. T. Lewis
G Is for Ghoul. M. Hervey
G Man. C. F. Coe
G Man at the Yard. P. Cheyney
G-Men on Murder Island. L. Jamieson
G-String Murders. G. R. Lee
Gabbart Destiny. E. L. Long
Gables Mystery. C. E. Perry
Gaboreau. P. Steward
Gaboreau the Terrible. P. Steward
Gabriel Comes to 24. R. Braddon
Gabriel Hounds. Mary Stewart
Gabriel Praed's Castle. A. Jones
Gabriel Samara. E. P. Oppenheim
Gabriel Samara, Peacemaker. E. P. Oppenheim
Gabriel Sounds for Africa. C. Edwards
Gabriella. A. Maybury
Gabrielle. J. Maass
Gabrielle. K. Norris
Gabrielle de Vergy. Anonymous
Gad. S. Geller
Gadget. N. Freeling
Gage. D. Chako
'Gainst Chink and Gunman. T. Lloyd
Galactic Effectuator. J. Vance
Galactic Sue Blue. R. G. Brown
Galahad of the Air. T. Wallace
Galatea. J. M. Cain
Galaxy Lot. W. A. Ballinger
Gale Force. G. Black
Gale Gallyon Takes a Hand. Spike Gordon
Gale of the World. Laurence Kirk
Gale Warning. H. Innes
Gale Warning. D. Yates
Gallagher Plot. Nick Carter
Gallant. C. Blackstone
Gallant Adventuress. Therese Benson
Gallant Affair. Hank Hobson
Gallant Tom. T. P. Prest
Galleon Gold. M. Drake
Galleon Rock. G. Volk
Galleon Treasure. A. B. Sherlock
Galleon's Gold. R. W. Sneddon
Galleys of St. John. E. L. Long
Galloping Dick. H. B. M. Watson
Galloping Gold. D. Learmonth
Galloping Gold. W. C. Tuttle
Galloway Case. A. Garve
Gallows Alley. A. Skene
Gallows Are High. H. Spencer
Gallows Are Waiting. J. York
Gallows Bait. S. Truss
Gallows-Bird. L. Storm
Gallows Child. P. G. Winslow
Gallows' Foot. V. Gielgud
Gallows for a Fool. C. Franklin
Gallows for the Groom. D. B. Olsen
Gallows' Fruit. H. Desmond

Gallows Garden. M. E. Chaber
Gallows Orange. H. Holt
Gallows in My Garden. R. Deming
Gallows in My Garden. Joan Fleming
Gallows Inn. E. P. Thorne
Gallows March. G. Norham
Gallows of Chance. E. P. Oppenheim
Gallows Orchard. C. Spencer
Gallows Parade. F. Tyler
Gallows Seed. P. Troubetzkoy
Gallows Set. W. Rutherford
Gallows Stands in Salem. A. Bretonne
Gallows Wait. J. Corbett
Gallows Waits. J. Budd
Gallows Way. D. Winston
Gallowsbird's Song. T. Nielsen
Galmart Affair. S. Westall
Galton Case. R. Macdonald
Gambit. L. Kendall
Gambit. K. Lane
Gambit. R. Stout
Gambit for Mr. Groode. C. Griswold
Gamble My Last Game. R. W. Krepps
Gamble of Life. A. Applin
Gamble with Death. L. Robin
Gambler. C. Burdett
Gambler. O. Hogstrand
Gambler. W. Krasner
Gambler of the West. O. Harper
Gambler, the Minstrel, and the Dance Hall Queen. W. Downing
Gamblers. L. LeQueux
Gamblers. E. Woodward
Gambler's Choice. J. B. Hendryx
Gambler's Girl. J. Matcha
Gambler's Gold. A. Wright
Gambler's Last Throw. Anonymous
Gambler's Syndicate. Nicholas Carter
Gambler's Throw. E. L. Adams
Gambler's Wax Finger and other startling detective experiences. G. S. McWatters
Gambling Man. C. Cookson
Gambling with Fire. D. Montrose
Game. M. Hastings
Game and the Candle. E. M. Ingram
Game and the Candle. K. Roche
Game at Chess. J. Fogerty
Game Called Murder. J. Ingerson
Game for Eagles. O. M. Hall
Game for Hawks. R. Severn
Game for Heroes. J. Graham
Game for the Living. P. Highsmith
Game for Three Losers. E. Lustgarten
Game for Vultures. M. Hartmann
Game in Diamonds. E. Cadell
Game Keeper's Secret. W. M. Graydon
Game Men Play. V. Bourjaily
Game of Chance. Anthony Ferguson
Game of Consequences. Shelley Smith
Game of Craft. Nicholas Carter
Game of Danger. Lois Duncan
Game of Draw. Dick Stewart
Game of Falcons. C. Darby
Game of Flesh. J. Trinian
Game of Hazard. P. Allardyce
Game of Liberty. E. P. Oppenheim
Game of Life. Waters
Game of Life and Death. L. Colcord
Game of Love. G. Warden
Game of Murder. P. Barrington
Game of Murder. F. Durbridge
Game of Plots. Nicholas Carter
Game of Secrets. T. Wiseman
Game of Shadows. M. Ruuth
Game of Soldiers. S. Jackman
Game of Statues. A. Stevenson
Game of the Golden Ball. Elizabeth Johnson
Game of Terror. J. Messmann
Game of Titans. G. A. Ruse
Game of Troy. J. M. White
Game of X. R. Sheckley
Game Show Girls. J. P. Radford
Game Well Played. Nicholas Carter
Game Without Rules. M. Gilbert
Game Without Winners. Dorothy Bennett
Gamecock. M. Baldwin
Gamecock Murders. F. Gruber
Gamekeeper's Gallows. J. B. Hilton
Gamemaker. D. K. Cohler
Games. H. Ellson
Games. B. Pronzini
Game's Afoot. M. Hardwick
Games Murderers Play. C. Carpenter
Games of Chance. P. Delacorte
Games of Chance. T. Hinde
Games of Chance with Strangers. M. Redfield
Games of 80. W. H. Mefford
Gaming for Gold. A. Wright
Gamma Ray Murders. P. Yorke
Gammon and Espionage. N. Bentley
Gang. H. Kastle
Gang. D. Whitelaw
Gang Buster. K. Roe
Gang Girl. Wenzell Brown
Gang Girls. C. Bingham
Gang Law. H. Clevely
Gang Rumble. E. Ronns
Gang Smasher. H. Clevely
Gang Smasher Again. H. Clevely

Gang That Couldn't Shoot Straight. J. Breslin
Gang War. J. G. Brandon
Gang War. F. Colter
Gang War. G. H. Teed
Gangdom's Doom. M. Grant
Ganges Mud. E. P. Thorne
Gang's Deserter. C. Brisbane
Gang's Orders. M. Poole
Gang's Prisoners. L. Bidston
Gangster. Roland Daniel
Gangster and the Private Eye. Dale Clark
Gangster Girl. R. Campert
Gangster Girl. J. Lait
Gangster Lady. B. Sarto
Gangster Payoff. N. W. Firth
Gangster War on Bar "G". G. C. Shedd
Gangsers. D. Chandler
Gangsters. P. Martin
Gangsters #2. P. Martin
Gangsters All. G. Stanley
Gangster's Daughter. Roland Daniel
Gangster's Deputy. S. Drew
Gangster's Girl. J. Hunter
Gangster's Girl. R. Starr
Gangster's Glory. E. P. Oppenheim
Gangster's Isle. J. Brooke
Gangster's Last Shot. Roland Daniel
Gangsters of the Air. J. Noy
Gangsters Parade. G. Stanley
Gangster's Revenge. G. N. Philips
Gangway! D. E. Westlake
Gangway for Ghosts. J. Tobias
Gannon's Line. J. Whitlach
Gantry Episode. June Drummond
Gaol Breaker. E. Wallace
Gaol Gates Are Open. David Hume
Gaol in Conflict. James Preston
Gap in the Curtain. J. Buchan
Garage Boy. E. Forrest
Garde Save the World. J. La Plante
Garden at No. 19. E. Jepson
Garden City Crime. Donald Stuart
Garden Club Murders. D. Van Deusen
Garden Court Mystery. B. Delannoy
Garden Game. J. M. White
Garden in Asia. M. D. Post
Garden Murder Case. S. S. Van Dine
Garden o' Dreams. F. M. White
Garden of Evil. B. Stoker
Garden of Ghosts. Marilyn Ross
Garden of Grief. H. Arvonen
Garden of Memories. M. Richmond
Garden of Mystery. R. Marsh
Garden of Satan. C. Vincent
Garden of Shadows. V. Coffman
Garden of Silent Beasts. Gavin Holt
Garden of Swords. M. Pemberton
Garden of the Gods. E. M. Keate
Garden of Weapons. J. Gardner
Gardenias Bruise Easily. J. P. Carstairs
Gardens of Moontower. G. Workman
Gargantua Falls. P. Bair
Gargoni Girdle. Nicholas Carter
Gargoyle Conspiracy. M. Albert
Gargoyle of Polgelly. R. Hardinge
Gargrave Mystery. H. C. Davidson
Garlands of Sylvia. Gavin Holt
Garlic, Grapes and a Pinch of Heroin. Elaine Turner
Garment. C. Cookson
Garment of Immortality. A. Askew
Garments of Repentence. D. Whitelaw
Garmiscath. J. S. Clouston
Garnered. R. Marsh
Garnett Bell, Detective. C. H. Bullivant
Garonsky Missile. A. Caillou
Garrison Tales from Tonquin. James O'Neill
Garrity. Allan Nixon
Garston Murder Case. H. C. Bentley
Garstons. H. C. Bailey
Garth. J. Hawthorne
Garthoyle Gardens. E. Jepson
Garvey's Code. R. Busby
Garvock. C. Gibbon
Gas. B. Hirschfeld
Gas Light. P. Hamilton
Gas Mask Gang. H. Pink
Gas-Mask Murder. J. R. Warren
Gascoyne. S. Crawford
Gaslight. W. Drummond
Gaspar Trenchard. B. Hemyng
Gasparoni Detective. Aldine
Gaston de Blondeville. A. Radcliffe
Gastronomic Murder. A. Roudybush
Gat Heat. R. S. Prather
Gate Fever. J. B. O'Sullivan
Gate of Ivory, Gate of Horn. Philip Craig
Gate of Sinners. Mrs. C. Kernahan
Gate of Temptation. P. Brebner
Gates of Birth. R. Bridges
Gates of Brass. F. J. Kelly
Gates of Chance. V. Sutphen
Gates of Dawn. F. Hume
Gates of Death. J. Hedges
Gates of Flame. R. R. Hobbs
Gates of Montrain. W. D. Roberts
Gates of Sagittarius. R. Cutler
Gates of Sorrow. M. Leighton
Gates of Tien T'ze. L. H. Gordon

Title Index

Gateway to Escape. N. Deane
Gateway to Hell. D. Wheatley
Gateway to the Grave. M. Lynch
Gathering at Greystone. L. Bronte
Gathering of Eagles. E. Lindall
Gathering of Evil. Marilyn Ross
Gathering of Moondust. P. Morton
Gathering Storm. F. A. M. Webster
'Gator. G. Ford
Gaudy Night. D. L. Sayers
Gaudy Shadows. J. Brunner
Gauge of Deception. K. G. Ballard
Gauges Steady. E. L. Long
Gaunt Stranger. E. Wallace
Gaunt Woman. J. Blackburn
Gauntlet. M. Butler
Gauntlet of Alceste. H. Moorhouse
Gautran. B. L. Farjeon
Gay Adventure. A. Applin
Gay Adventures. W. Hackett
Gay Captain. M. V. Victor
Gay-Cat. P. Casey
Gay Conspirators. P. Curtiss
Gay Deceiver. P. Leslie
Gay Deceivers. Athur Moore
Gay Deception. R. Harding
Gay Desperado. B. Gray
Gay Detective. L. Rand
Gay Gallant. V. Blake
Gay Ghastly Holiday. S. Blayne
Gay Head Conspiracy. C. Baker
Gay Lord Waring. H. Townley
Gay Mortician. M. M. Raison
Gay of Heart. A. Maybury
"Gay Phoenix." M. Innes
Gay Pilgrimage. B. Bolt
Gay Triangle. W. LeQueux
Gay World. J. Hatton
Gaynor Women. V. Coffman
Gazebo. Alec Coppel
Gazebo. P. Wentworth
Gees' First Case. Jack Mann
Gelignite. W. Marshall
Gelignite Gang. J. Creasey
Gem of a Murder. C. Keith
Gemini Contenders. R. Ludlum
Gemini in Darkness. Clarissa Ross
Gemini Revenged. Charlotte Hunt
Gemini Run. M. Kerr
Gemini Smile, Gemini Kill. R. Lory
Gemini Trip. J. Law
Gendarme's Report. G. Simenon
General Besserley's Puzzle Box. E. P. Oppenheim
General Besserley's Second Puzzle Box. E. P. Oppenheim
General Crack. G. R. Preedy
General Died at Dawn. C. G. Booth
General Goes Too Far. L. Robinson
Generals. P. Wahloo
Generals Died Together. J. Bedford
General's Will. G. Allen
Generous Heart. K. Fearing
Genesis. W. A. Harbinson
Genesis 38. Brian Cooper
Genesta. A. Griffin
Geneva Mystery. F. Durbridge
Genghis Coppersmith. R. J. Griffin
Genial Stranger. D. MacKenzie
Genius in Murder. E. R. Punshon
Gentle Albatross. E. Foote-Smith
Gentle Assassin. C. Richards
Gentle Binns. E. Jepson
Gentle Giant. A. Eichler
Gentle Grafter. A. Henry
Gentle Hangman. J. M. Fox
Gentle Hearts and Murder. T. Taggart
Gentle Highwayman. P. Allardyce
Gentle Hook. F. Durbridge
Gentle Killer. P. Barrington
Gentle Kiss of Murder. A. Barron
Gentle Murderer. D. S. Davis
Gentle Obsession. F. Cowen
Gentle People. Irwin Shaw
Gentle Rain. Margaret Archer
Gentle Sex. Angus Hall
Gentle Thespians. R. M. Gilchrist
Gentleman Anonymous. M. B. Lowndes
Gentleman Called. D. S. Davis
Gentleman Crook. M. Crombie
Gentleman-Crook. Sheilah Graham
Gentleman for the Gallows. S. Horler
Gentleman from Chicago. J. Cashman
Gentleman from Nowhere. G. Thorne
Gentleman from Portland. C. R. Gull
Gentleman from Texas. H. Balfour
Gentleman Garnet. H. B. Vogel
Gentleman George. J. G. Rowe
Gentleman Hangs. J. Dolland
Gentleman in Pajamas. C. N. Buck
Gentleman-in-Waiting. S. Horler
Gentleman Junkie and other stories of the Hung-Up Generation. H. Ellison
Gentleman Juror. C. L. Marsh
Gentleman of London. M. Gerard
Gentleman of Rio. A. Mills
Gentleman of the Road. H. Bleackley
Gentleman of Virginia. P. Brebner
Gentleman Pirate. Janette Radcliffe
Gentleman Thorne. Old Sleuth
Gentleman Traitor. Alan Williams
Gentleman Tramp. G. Wintle

Gentleman Who Vanished. F. Hume
Gentleman's Agreement. B. Von Hutten
Gentleman's Daughters. M. Masterman
Gentleman's Gentleman. M. Pemberton
Gentleman's Relish. H. Spencer
Gentleman at Large. J. Boland
Gentleman at Large. E. Woodward
Gantlemen Go By. L. Meynell
Gentlemen in Hades. F. A. Kummer
Gentlemen March. R. Pertwee
Gentlemen of Crime. A. Gask
Gentlemen of the Jury. H. Leyford
Gentlemen of the Night. S. Maddock
Gentlemen of the Sea. P. Trent
Gentlemen Reform. J. Boland
Gently at a Gallop. A. Hunter
Gently by the Shore. A. Hunter
Gently Coloured. A. Hunter
Gently Continental. A. Hunter
Gently Does It. Janet Green
Gently Does It. A. Hunter
Gently Down the Stream. A. Hunter
Gently Dust the Corpse. S. H. Courtier
Gently Floating. A. Hunter
Gently French. A. Hunter
Gently Go Man. A. Hunter
Gently in the Highlands. A. Hunter
Gently in the Sun. A. Hunter
Gently in Trees. A. Hunter
Gently Instrumental. A. Hunter
Gently North-West. A. Hunter
Gently Sahib. A. Hunter
Gently Through the Mill. A. Hunter
Gently Through the Woods. A. Hunter
Gently to a Sleep. A. Hunter
Gently to the Summit. A. Hunter
Gently Where the Birds Are. A. Hunter
Gently Where the Roads Go. A. Hunter
Gently with Love. A. Hunter
Gently with the Innocents. A. Hunter
Gently with the Ladies. A. Hunter
Gently with the Painters. A. Hunter
Genuine Article. A. B. Guthrie
George and Georgina. E. Phillpotts
George Canterbury's Will. H. Wood
George Caulfield's Journey. M. E. Braddon
George Elvaston. Mrs. Lodge
Georgia Detective. Anonymous
Geraldine. T. P. Prest
Geraldine Walton—Woman! M. Leighton
Geranium Kiss. J. Harvey
Gerard. M. E. Braddon
German Helmet. P. McCutchan
German Spy. W. LeQueux
German Spy. B. Newman
German Spy System from Within. W. LeQueux
Germany Company. N. Lewis
Gerrard Street Mystery and other weird tales. J. C. Dent
Gertrude Haddon. E. Southworth
Gertrude of the Rock. T. P. Prest
Gervase Castonel. H. Wood
Gestapo Dormouse. Frank King
Gestapo File. D. Cory
Gestapo Fugitive. A. O. Pollard
Gestapo Gauntlet. L. Cargill
Gestapo Trial. J. Petersen
Get a Load o' Dis. R. Drayton
Get Carter. T. Lewis
Get Clutha. H. Munro
Get Down There and Die. J. Lash
Get Dumm! J. Brewer
Get Garrity. Allan Nixon
Get Me Headquarters. A. Capelli
Get Out and Stay Out. R. Angel
Get Out of Town. P. Connolly
Get Out of Town. H. V. Dixon
Get Out the Cuffs. David Hume
Get Ready to Die. B. Gray
Get-Rich-Quick Wallingford. G. R. Chester
Get Smart! W. Johnston
Get Smart Once Again! W. Johnston
Get That Man. R. Drayton
Get Wallace! A. Wilson
Get Your Man. E. Dorrance
Getaway. L. Charteris
Getaway. J. Harris
Getaway. O. John
Getaway. J. Thompson
Getaway Gang. D. J. Gammon
Geth Straker. B. Mather
Getting Away with Murder. Armine Campbell
Getting Even. B. Behr
Getting Rid of Anne. T. Cobb
Getting the Boy. William Scott
Ghost. A. Bennett
Ghost and the Garnet. Marilyn Ross
Ghost at Punkin Holler. L. Rose
Ghost at Ravenkill Manor. P. Warren
Ghost at Stagmere. Alice Brennan
Ghost at the Wedding. Elna Stone
Ghost Blonde. M. Derby
Ghost Breaker. R. Goulart
Ghost Car. B. Knox
Ghost City. R. St. Clair
Ghost City Killings. W. Martyn
Ghost Comes Knocking. Marilyn Ross
Ghost Counts Ten. R. Trevor

Ghosts of Grantmeer / 507

Ghost Dancers. Angela Gray
Ghost Does a Richard III. R. B. Saxe
Ghost-Farm. J. Tippette
Ghost Fingers. Colin Robertson
Ghost Flowers. M. Summerton
Ghost from Outer Space. L. Greth
Ghost from the Past. Colin Hope
Ghost from the Past. A. M. Meadows
Ghost Girl. E. E. Saltus
Ghost Girl. H. K. Webster
Ghost Guns. W. C. Tuttle
Ghost House. N. Berrow
Ghost House. F. Daingerfield
Ghost House. R. St. Clair
Ghost House. G. Verner
Ghost-Hunter and His Family. O'Hara Family
Ghost Hunters. R. Aiken
Ghost Hunters. C. Brooks
Ghost Hunters. G. Meyrick
Ghost Hunters. A. Tofte
Ghost in Green Velvet. Elizabeth Peters
Ghost in the Bank of England. Anonymous
Ghost in the Belfry. P. Pray
"Ghost in the Glass." R. St. Clair
Ghost in the Making. N. Fitzgerald
Ghost in the Wall. R. St. Clair
Ghost It Was. R. Hull
Ghost Knows His Greengages. R. B. Saxe
Ghost Lane. E. P. Hoyt
Ghost Makers. M. Grant
Ghost Man. G. Verner
Ghost Mesa. T. Craig
Ghose Murder. L. Allan
Ghost of a Cardinal. J. Maske
Ghost of a Chance. K. Roos
Ghost of a Chance. F. Usher
Ghost of a Clue. C. Barry
Ghost of a Clue. O. Mills
Ghost of Archie Gilroy. P. Allardyce
Ghost of Cemetery Ridge. L. Greth
Ghost of Channing House. Genevieve St. John
Ghost of Coquina Key. J. Bellamy
Ghost of Dark Harbor. C. Ross
Ghost of Downhill. E. Wallace
Ghost of Gaston Revere. M. Hansom
Ghost of Glen George. Grace M. White
Ghost of Grand Canyon. R. H. Wilkinson
Ghost of Graveyard Hill. P. W. Fairman
Ghost of Greystone Grange. A. W. A'Beckett
Ghost of Lost Lover's Lake. J. A. Blackwood
Ghost of Megan. M. Lovell
Ghost of Oaklands. W. E. D. Ross
Ghost of Roaring Pines. P. S. McCoy
Ghost of the Air. R. St. Clair
Ghost of the Assassins. I. Todd
Ghost of the Dunsany. E. L. Long
Ghost of Thomas Penry. Kenneth O'Hara
Ghost of Truth. J. N. Chance
Ghost of Windy Hill. E. B. Cook
Ghost on the Balcony. D. Marfield
Ghost Party. H. Clandon
Ghost Plane. P. Conde
Ghost Plane. J. Corbett
Ghost Plane. N. Fleming
Ghost Plane. A. Stringer
Ghost Pulls the Jackpot. R. B. Saxe
Ghost River. H. Hale
Ghost River Inn. C. Van Hazinga
Ghost Road. B. Johnson
Ghost Ship of Fog Island. Marilyn Ross
Ghost Song. D. Daniels
Ghost Squad. G. Verner
Ghost Stories. K. Prichard
Ghost Stories and Mysteries. J. S. Le Fanu
Ghost Town. C. Blackstock
Ghost Trail. L. C. Douthwaite
Ghost Trails. W. C. Tuttle
Ghost Train. Ruth Alexander
Ghost Train. A. Ridley
Ghost Voice. M. Hervey
Ghost Walks. C. Brogan
Ghost Walks. N. MacKenzie
Ghost Wanted. G. Le Pelley
Ghost Wanted. F. McDermid
Ghost Wore Black. F. Y. McHugh
Ghost Writer. D. Carter
Ghostflight. W. Katz
Ghosting. R. Goulart
"Ghostly Fingers." W. Spence
Ghostly Quarantine. R. St. Clair
Ghostly Strength. Winifred Graham
Ghosts. A. Crabb
Ghosts. E. McBain
Ghosts. K. Prichard
Ghosts Can't Kill. M. V. Heberden
Ghosts Don't Kill. P. Valdez
Ghosts, Ghouls and Gallows. G. F. Marson
Ghosts' Gloom. I. G. Holmes
Ghosts' High Noon. J. D. Carr
Ghosts' High Noon. C. Wells
Ghosts I Have Met and Some Others. J. K. Bangs
Ghosts Never Die. R. Heed
Ghosts of Ardnamore. A. Andre
Ghosts of Ballyduff. K. Ostrander
Ghosts of Chambord Affair. H. Catalan
Ghosts of Grantmeer. Clarissa Ross

Ghosts of Harrel. W. D. Roberts
Ghosts of Kings. A. Pritchett
Ghosts of Perranprah. H. Lea
Ghosts of Rhodes Manor. J. L. Latham
Ghosts of Sin-Chang. A. Gervais
Ghosts of Slave Driver's Bend. H. H. Kroll
Ghosts of Society. A. Partridge
Ghost's Revenge, and other stories of modern Paris. R. H. Sherard
Ghost's Touch and other stories. W. Collins
Ghostwater. E. Phillpotts
Ghostwind. R. A. Payne
Ghoul. Frank King
Ghoul. M. Ronson
Ghoul. G. N. Smith
Ghoul Friend. G. Donovan
Ghoul Goalie. F. W. Gumley
Ghouls in My Grave. J. Ray
Giant Athlete. Old Sleuth
Giant City Swindle. Anonymous
Giant City Swindle. G. N. Phillips
Giant Detective. Anonymous
Giant Detective Among the Cowboys. Old Sleuth
Giant Detective Among the Italian Brigands. Old Sleuth
Giant Detective in France. Old Sleuth
Giant Detective in Ireland. Anonymous
Giant Hunchback. H. J. Wurr
Giant Kill. K. Platt
Giant Killer. R. Vasquez
Giant Rat of Sumatra. R. L. Boyer
Giantkiller. C. Pincher
Giant's Chair. Winston Graham
Giant's Gate. M. Pemberton
Giants of Darkness. N. Thurley
Gibraltar Conspiracy. D. Betteridge
Gibraltar Prisoner. B. Perowne
Gibraltar Road. P. McCutchan
Gideon Drexel's Millions. Nicholas Carter
Gideon Drexel's Millions and other stories. Nicholas Carter
Gideon of Scotland Yard. J. J. Marric
Gideon's Art. J. J. Marric
Gideon's Badge. J. J. Marric
Gideon's Day. J. J. Marric
Gideon's Fear. J. Creasey
Gideon's Fire. J. J. Marric
Gideon's Fog. J. J. Marric
Gideon's Force. W. V. Butler
Gideon's Lot. J. J. Marric
Gideon's March. J. J. Marric
Gideon's Men. J. J. Marric
Gideon's Month. J. J. Marric
Gideon's Night. J. J. Marric
Gideon's Power. J. J. Marric
Gideon's Press. J. J. Marric
Gideon's Ride. J. J. Marric
Gideon's Risk. J. J. Marric
Gideon's River. J. J. Marric
Gideon's Sport. J. J. Marric
Gideon's Staff. J. J. Marric
Gideon's Vote. J. J. Marric
Gideon's Week. J. J. Marric
Gideon's Wrath. J. J. Marric
Gift from a Stranger. I. Valdes
Gift from Berlin. A. Barker
Gift Horse. M. R. Douglas
Gift in the Gauntlet. B. Reynolds
Gift of Artemis. Douglas Scott
Gift of Death. E. Ronns
Gift of Hermes. C. W. Whitaker
Gift of Murder. G. Batson
Gift of the Desert. R. Parrish
Gift of the Gods. Nicholas Carter
Gift of the Sea. R. M. Sears
Gift Shop. C. Armstrong
Gift Supreme. G. A. England
Gigantic Shadow. J. Symons
Giggling Ghosts. K. Robeson
Gigins Court. B. Graeme
Giglamps. Will Scott
Gilbert the Ghost. R. R. King
Gilbert's Last Toothache. M. Scherf
Gilchrist Case. J. Barclay
Gilded Cage. G. Ferrand
Gilded Fleece. N. Tranter
Gilded Fly. H. Payne
Gilded Hideaway. P. Twist
Gilded Kiss. D. Enefer
Gilded Lady. W. M. Clemens
Gilded London. A. Askew
Gilded Man. Carter Dickson
Gilded Needles. M. McDowell
Gilded Nightmare. H. Pentecost
Gilded Sarcophagus. Charlotte Hunt
Gilded Serpent. D. Donovan
Gilded Snatch Caper. J. D. Lawrence
Gilded of Spurs. G. Ingram
Gilded Witch. J. Webb
Gilead Balm, Knight Errant. B. Capes
Gillespie Suicide Mystery. L. Gribble
Gillingham Rubies. E. Jepson
Gilt Edge. K. A. Saddler
Gilt-Edge Mystery. E. M. Channon
Gilt-Edge Tom, Conductor. E. L. Coolidge
Gilt-Edged Cockpit. D. Rutherford
Gilt-Edged Guilt. C. Wells
Gilt-Edged Traitor. M. Eden

Gilt Feather. D. Polk
Gilt Kid. J. Curtis
Gimmel Flash. Douglas Clark
Gin and Ginger. J. F. W. Hannay
Gin and Murder. J. Pullein-Thompson
Ginger Cat. C. Reeve
Ginger Cat Mystery. R. Forsythe
Ginger Horse. J. F. Straker
Gingerbread House. M. Dobner
Gingerbread Man. R. Parker
Ginkgo Tree. C. Jarrett
Ginny. Morton Cooper
Ginzberg Circle. A. O'Neill
Gioconda Smile. A. Huxley
Gipsey Chief. H. M. Jones
Gipsey Girl. H. M. Jones
Gipsey Mother. H. M. Jones
Gipsies Don't Have Them. G. M. Wilson
Gipsy Blair, the Western Detective. J. R. Taylor
Gipsy Boy. T. P. Prest
Gipsy in Evening Dress. W. J. Makin
Gipsy of the North. O. Binns
Gipsy or Gentleman? W. M. Graydon
Gipsy Reno, the Detective. Old Sleuth
Gipsy Rose, the Female Detective. Old Sleuth
Gipsy's Prophecy. E. Southworth
Gipsy's Warning. E. A. Dupuy
Girl Alone. J. Blackmore
Girl Alone. Howel Evans
Girl and the Bill. B. Merwin
Girl and the Detective. C. E. Blaney
Girl and the Miracle. R. Marsh
Girl at Central. G. Bonner
Girl, a Man and a River. J. Hawkins
Girl at Pine Creek. G. Goodchild
Girl Behind the Keys. T. Gallon
Girl Between. B. Fischer
Girl by the Roadside. Roland Daniel
Girl by the Roadside. V. Vanardy
Girl Cage. J. Ehrlich
Girl Called Ann. Rona Randall
Girl Called Fathom. L. Forrester
Girl Champion. Old Sleuth
Girl Chase. D. Enefer
Girl Died Laughing. V. Paradise
Girl Died Singing. N. Morland
Girl Factory. R. F. Murphy
Girl for Danny. W. Ard
Girl Found Dead. M. Underwood
Girl Friday. D. Whitelaw
Girl from Alsace. B. E. Stevenson
Girl from Belfast. V. Bridges
Girl from Easy Street. R. Foster
Girl from Farris's. E. R. Burroughs
Girl from H.A.R.D. M. Moffat
Girl from Hateville. G. Brewer
Girl from Las Vegas. J. M. Flynn
Girl from Malta. F. Hume
Girl from Midnight. Wade Miller
Girl from Moscow. M. Corrigan
Girl from Nippon. C. Dawe
Girl from Nowhere. E. Bond
Girl from Nowhere. R. Foley
Girl from Nowhere. P. Minton
Girl from Outer Space. Carter Brown
Girl from Peking. G. B. Mair
Girl from Scotland Yard. M. McGrath
Girl from Scotland Yard. E. Wallace
Girl from Taiping. H. C. James
Girl from Texas. C. E. Blaney
Girl from the Candle-Lit Bath. Dodie Smith
Girl from the East. D. Whitelaw
Girl from the Mimosa Club. L. Ford
Girl from the Sea. R. Abbey
Girl from Toronto. H. Clevely
Girl He Left Behind Him. H. F. Moulton
Girl Hunt. L. D. Smith
Girl Hunters. M. Spillane
Girl in a Big Brass Bed. P. Rabe
Girl in a Hurry. T. A. Plummer
Girl in a Mask. H. K. Maxwell
Girl in a Million. D. Enefer
Girl in a Net. John Marsh
Girl in a Shroud. Carter Brown
Girl in a Thousand. J. Middlemass
Girl in Arms. D. Enefer
Girl in Asses' Milk. W. H. Baker
Girl in Black. V. Bridges
Girl in Black Velvet. L. De Jean
Girl in Blue Pants. R. Nettell
Girl in Cabin B54. L. Fletcher
Girl in Green. A. Carr
Girl in Hand. H. Janson
Girl in His House. H. McGrath
Girl in His Past. G. Simenon
Girl in Love. Rona Randall
Girl in My Grave. H. Davie-Martin
Girl in 906. D. Hall
Girl in Ocean View. M. Symons
Girl in Shadow. C. Franklin
Girl in the Blue Dress. R. Marsh
Girl in the Cage. B. Benson
Girl in the Cage. C. Fitzsimmons
Girl in the Case. R. Barr
Girl in the Case. Nicholas Carter
Girl in the Cellar. P. Wentworth
Girl in the Cheongsam. S. Yorke
Girl in the Cockpit. M. Avallone
Girl in the Cop's Pocket. Robert Turner

Girl in the Crime Belt. J. N. Chance
Girl in the Crimson Cloak. R. Trevor
Girl in the Dark. Roland Daniel
Girl in the Dark. E. C. Vivian
Girl in the Death Seat. F. Nichols
Girl in the Fog. J. Gollomb
Girl in the Frame. W. Fuller
Girl in the Green Beret. N. Penley
Girl in the Killer's Bed. A. Curry
Girl in the News. Roy Vickers
Girl in the Other Seat. A. R. Weekes
Girl in the Plain Brown Wrapper. J. D. MacDonald
Girl in the Punchbowl. T. B. Dewey
Girl in the Rain. J. Reach
Girl in the Red Jaguar. J. Manor
Girl in the River. V. B. Miller
Girl in the Secret. A. M. Williamson
Girl in the Spy Racket. W. J. Blackledge
Girl in the Telltale Bikini. P. Morgan
Girl in the Tiffany Dress. M. Eyre
Girl in the Tower. J. Corby
Girl in the Train. B. Bolt
Girl in the Trunk. B. Cassiday
Girl in the Wall. R. Hampton
Girl in the Web. Mark Allerton
Girl in the Wet-Look Bikini. S. Mitchell
Girl in the White Mercedes. J. Usher
Girl in 304. H. R. Daniels
Girl in Waiting. A. Eyre
Girl in Waiting. G. Simenon
Girl in White. J. Ellis
Girl Known As D 13. S. Kyle
Girl Meets Body. J. Iams
Girl Missing. E. Sherry
Girl Named Tamiko. R. Kirkbride
Girl Nobody Knows. M. McShane
Girl of Ghost Mountain. J. A. Dunn
Girl of Grit. A. Griffiths
Girl of Lost Island. W. H. Osborne
Girl of the Guard Line. C. C. Waddell
Girl of the Islands. J. M. Walsh
Girl of the Passion Play. A. M. Williamson
Girl of the Yellow Diamonds. M. Leighton
Girl on a High Wire. R. Foley
Girl on a Slay Ride. L. Trimble
Girl on Crown Street. D. Karp
Girl on the Beach. M. Cronin
Girl on the Beach. A. Holden
Girl on the Best Seller List. V. Packer
Girl on the Left Bank. Joan Shepherd
Girl on the Loose. G. G. Fickling
Girl on the M6. D. Enefer
Girl on the Prowl. G. G. Fickling
Girl on the Run. E. S. Aarons
Girl on the Run. E. Hunt
Girl on the Run. J. Sibly
Girl on the Run. H. Waugh
Girl on the Volkswagen Floor. W. A. Clark
Girl on the Waterfront. M. Urquhart
Girl on Zero. B. Perowne
Girl Out Back. C. Williams
Girl Out in Corsica. A. Philips
Girl Prisoner. Nicholas Carter
Girl Raffles. C. E. Blaney
Girl Running. Adam Knight
Girl, the City, and the Soldier. W. H. Baker
Girl, the Gold Watch & Everything. J. D. MacDonald
Girl Watcher's Funeral. H. Pentecost
Girl Who Cried Wolf. H. Waugh
Girl Who Dared. D. Durham
Girl Who Didn't Die. R. Jensen
Girl Who Died. K. Hopkins
Girl Who Failed Him. G. Goodchild
Girl Who Had Everything. R. Foley
Girl Who Had Nothing. A. M. Williamson
Girl Who Had to Die. E. S. Holding
Girl Who Kept Knocking Them Dead. Hampton Stone
Girl Who Killed Things. T. Powell
Girl Who Knew Too Much. J. G. Brandon
Girl Who Never Was. Jan Alexander
Girl Who Never Was. T. B. Dewey
Girl Who Passed for Normal. H. Fleetwood
Girl Who Saw Too Much. D. Reid
Girl Who Wanted Experience. L. Shippey
Girl Who Was Possessed. Carter Brown
Girl Who Wasn't There. T. B. Dewey
Girl Who Wasn't There. W. D. Roberts
Girl with a Golden Bar. Brenda Conrad
Girl with a Secret. C. Armstrong
Girl with a Squint. G. Simenon
Girl with Money. F. Warden
Girl with No Place to Hide. N. Quarry
Girl with Red Hair. Giles Gordon
Girl with Six Fingers. H. Pentecost
Girl with the Dynamite Bangs. L. Cameron
Girl with the Frightened Eyes. L. Lariar
Girl with the Golden Eyes. H. Balzac
Girl with the Green Eyes. M. Leblanc
Girl with the Haunting Eyes. F. Warden
Girl with the Hole in Her Head. Hampton Stone
Girl with the Key. M. K. Simmons
Girl with the Leopard-Skin Bag. M. Halliday
Girl with the Long Green Heart. Lawrence Block

Title Index

Girl with the Sweet Plump Knees. T. B. Dewey
Girl with the X-Ray Eyes. M. O'Nair
Girl with Two Faces. J. Kendall
Girls Are Missing. C. Crane
Girls at the Grange. F. Warden
Girl's Head. E. Jepson
Girls in 5J. R. S. Bernhard
Girls in White. Rona Randall
Girl's Number Doesn't Answer. T. Powell
Girl's Temptation. S. Warwick
Girls Who Came to Murder. K. Carr
Girls Will Be Girls. F. Warden
Giselle. Brian Cooper
Give a Corpse a Bad Name. E. Ferrars
Give a Man a Gun. J. Creasey
Give a Man a Rope. Gavin Holt
Give Daddy the Knife, Darling. J. Lymington
Give Death a Name. Anthony Gilbert
Give 'em the Ax. A. A. Fair
Give It to Me Straight. S. Morelli
Give Me a Gun. R. Angel
Give Me a Little Something. W. L. Rohde
Give Me a Ship! C. Edwards
Give Me Back Myself. L. P. Davies
Give Me Death. I. B. Myers
Give Me Murder. G. Ashe
Give Me That Man. E. G. Cousins
Give Me the Knife. L. Meynell
Give Me the Lowdown. D. Linton
Give Me This Woman. W. Ard
Give Me Yesterday. G. Vaizey
Give Thanks to Death. H. Bailey
Give the Boys a Great Big Hand. E. McBain
Give the Devil His Due. P. Graaf
Give the Girl a Gun. R. Deming
Give the Lady a Camel. W. J. Blackledge
Give the Little Corpse a Great Big Hand. G. Bagby
Give up the Body. L. Trimble
Give up the Ghost. M. Erskine
Give Us the World. F. L. Green
Given the Ammunition. H. Gilbert
Giver in Secret. T. Cobb
Glad Eye. C. R. Gull
Glad Summer. J. Farnol
Glamour Girl. K. Lindsay
Glare. C. Dawe
Glass Alibi. L. Gribble
Glass Arrow. G. Verner
Glass Bottom Boat. B. Street
Glass Cage. E. Ronns
Glass Cage. G. Simenon
Glass Cage. Colin Wilson
Glass Cell. P. Highsmith
Glass Centipede. T. Painter
Glass Cipher. P. Winston
Glass Dagger. J. G. Brandon
Glass Dagger. C. J. C. Hyne
Glass Facade. J. B. Watney
Glass Fish. G. Stuart
Glass Flame. P. A. Whitney
Glass Heart. M. Holland
Glass House. Jan Alexander
Glass Houses. E. Thompson
Glass Interval. J. Turner
Glass Key. D. Hammett
Glass Knife. L. Thayer
Glass Ladder. P. W. Fairman
Glass Lady. A. Bordages
Glass Man. K. Robeson
Glass Mask. L. G. Offord
Glass Mountain. K. Robeson
Glass of Red Wine. M. Tripp
Glass on the Stairs. M. Scherf
Glass Painting. Jan Alexander
Glass Play Pen. E. Fadiman
Glass Room. E. Rolfe
Glass-Sided Ants' Nest. P. Dickinson
Glass Slipper. M. G. Eberhart
Glass Spear. S. H. Courtier
Glass Too Many. Jack Mann
Glass Totem. D. Chandler
Glass Tower. D. Osborne
Glass Triangle. G. H. Coxe
Glass Village. E. Queen
Glass Virgin. C. Cookson
Gleam of Sapphire. D. Tower
Gleaming Blade. K. Kane
Gleaming Rails. G. M. Dean
Gleave Mystery. L. Tracy
Glenbeg Mystery. C. S. Lamont
Glencairly Castle. H. G. Hutchinson
Glendower Legacy. T. Gifford
Glendraco. Laura Black
Glenlitten Murder. E. P. Oppenheim
Glenmove Abbey. Mrs. Isaacs
Glenna Powers Case. H. Waugh
Glenrannoch. Rona Randall
Glenvirgin's Ghost. Winifred Graham
Glimpse into Terror. Clarissa Ross
Glimpse of Death. R. Ormerod
Glimpse of Evil. T. Irving-James
Glimpse of Forever. C. D. Peel
Glimpse of Paradise. A. Hale
Glimpse of Paradise. John Marsh
Glimpses of the Moon. E. Crispin
Glint of Spears. A. Lejeune
Glitter and Ash. Dennis Smith
Glitter-Dust. A. Dwyer-Joyce

Glitter-Gold Mountain. D. C. Steele
Glitter Street. T. Sullivan
Glitterburn. H. Gould
Glittering Desire. E. R. Punshon
Glittering Hour. A. Hodges
Glittering Isle. W. Collison
Glittering Prizes. B. Flynn
Glittering Road. W. A. MacKenzie
Global Globules Affair. S. Latter
Globe Hollow Mystery. H. Gartland
Gloria. E. Southworth
Glorious Masquerade. K. Lindsay
Glory Box Mystery. G. W. Wicking
Glory Boys. G. Seymour
Glory Hunter. J. Burmeister
Glory Thrown In. Eric Lambert
Glory Trap. S. Williamson
Gloved Hand. L. Bryson
Gloved Hand. Nicholas Carter
Gloved Hand. B. E. Stevenson
Gloved Saskia. W. C. MacDonald
Glover. F. Pollini
Glover Undercover. G. Blumberg
Glow. B. Stanwood
Glow Job. H. Kane
Glow-Worm Tales. J. Payn
Glowering Gables. L. Churchill
Gloyne Murder. C. Clausen
Glut of Red Herrings. J. Bude
Glut of Virgins. B. Strutton
Glyphs of Gold. P. Edwards
Gnat. L. H. Brooks
Gnome Mine Mystery. P. De Mar
Go Ahead with Murder. H. Halliday
Go Away Death. J. Creasey
Go Away to Murder. J. Creasey
Go Back for Murder. A. Christie
Go-Between. Mrs. C. Kernahan
Go-Between. A. Maling
Go Down Dead. S. Stevens
Go Down, Death. S. B. Hays
Go Find a Shadow. K. Hewitt
Go for Broke. J. Welcome
Go for Garrity. Allan Nixon
Go for Out. F. Webb
Go for the Body. E. Lacy
Go Home, Stranger. C. Williams
Go, Honeylou. T. B. Dewey
Go, Lovely Rose. J. Potts
Go, Man, Go. E. De Roo
Go South, Go Crazy. K. Howard
Go to Sleep, Jennie. T. B. Dewey
Go to Thy Death Bed. S. Forbes
Go with a Jerk. H. Janson
Goat. J. F. Straker
Goat Island. W. Fuller
Gobblecock Mystery. L. Austen-Leigh
Gobelin Grange. H. Drummond
Goblin Market. H. McCloy
God and All His Angels. Graham Lord
God Bless America. Stanley Johnson
God Cell. W. Bradbury
God for Tomorrow. M. Dibner
God Keepers. E. R. Johnson
God Machine. M. Caidin
God of the Forest. N. Dorer
God of the Labyrinth. Colin Wilson
God Player. E. Constantine
God Save the Child. R. B. Parker
God Save the Mark. D. E. Westlake
God Save the Queen! A. Upward
God-Seeker. John Williams
God Speed the Night. D. S. Davis
God Spigo. A. Tibble
God with Four Arms and other stories. H. T. W. Bousfield
Goddess. R. Marsh
Goddess Game. H. Barron
Goddess Gone Bad. Carter Brown
Goddess of Evil. J. Huslig
Goddess of Terror. A. Gale
Goddesses Never Die. G. B. Mair
Godfather. M. Puzo
Godfather Killer. D. Brennan
Godfather Must Live. T. Halstead
Godkillers. T. Journet
Godmother. H. Fleetwood
Godmother. R. T. Larkin
Godmother Caper. J. D. Lawrence
Godolphin. E. Bulwer-Lytton
God's Back Was Turned. H. Whittington
God's Clay. A. Askew
God's Defector. J. Bingham
God's Gift to All Women. T. Rome
Gods in Green. W. D. Roberts
Gods of the Lightning. Maxwell Anderson
God's Winepress. A. Jenkinson
Godsend. Bernard Taylor
Godwulf Manuscript. R. B. Parker
Goering Testament. G. Markstein
Goering Treasure. Gordon Davis
Goggle-Box Affair. V. Gielgud
Goggle-Eyed Pirates. L. Falk
Going Down. D. Markson
Going, Going, Gone. C. Hale
Going, Going, Gone. P. A. Taylor
Going It Alone. M. Innes
Going Public. E. Westheimer
Going Straight. D. Clement
Going to St. Ives. Colver Harris
Going to Jerusalem. R. Dixon
Going to the Bad. E. Yates

Going West. J. Potter
Golconda Necklace. H. St. J. Cooper
Gold. K. Perkins
Gold and Copper Delamonds. A. Autumn
Gold and Flesh. B. Appel
Gold and Gaiters. C. A. Alington
Gold and Guns on Halfaday Creek. J. B. Hendryx
Gold—and the Mounted. J. B. Hendryx
Gold and Thorns. M. Rittenberg
Gold and Wine. Roy Vickers
Gold at K-BAR-T. W. C. Tuttle
Gold Bag. C. Wells
Gold Bait. W. J. Sheldon
Gold Ballast. E. L. Long
Gold Bomb. K. Laumer
Gold Brick Island. J. J. Connington
Gold Bug. W. B. Hare
Gold Bullets. C. G. Booth
Gold Bullion Swindle. L. Pryce
Gold by Gemini. J. Gash
Gold Cat. A. Mills
Gold Coast Nocturne. H. Nielsen
Gold Comes in Bricks. A. A. Fair
Gold Comfit Box. V. Williams
Gold Connection. Robin Moore
Gold Crew. T. N. Scortia
Gold Cup Murder. F. Duke
Gold Digger, and fourteen other short stories. M. Hervey
Gold Door. Ardath Wise
Gold Drain. Stanley Johnson
Gold Dust Darrell. B. Brentford
Gold Express. J. Budd
Gold Flame. E. E. Rose
Gold Foil. R. Pennant-Rea
Gold for My Girl. J. Blackmore
Gold for Prince Charlie. N. Tranter
Gold for the Bank of England. Ernest H. Robinson
Gold from Gemini. J. Gash
Gold Game. Roy Vickers
Gold Gap. F. Gruber
Gold Girl. J. B. Hendryx
Gold, Gore and Gehenna. G. A. Birmingham
Gold Hijack. C. Eland
Gold-Hunters' Adventures. W. H. Thomes
Gold-Hunter's Adventures Between Melbourne and Ballarat. W. H. Thomes
Gold-Hunters in Europe. W. H. Thomes
Gold in Every Grave. H. L. Nelson
Gold Is King. O. Binns
Gold Is the Color of Blood. J. M. Patterson
Gold Is Where You Find It. J. B. Hendryx
Gold Is Where You Find It. H. C. James
Gold Island. N. West
Gold-Killer. J. Prosper
Gold Machine. Martin Davies
Gold Makers. N. P. McCoy
Gold Maker's Secret. E. C. Derby
Gold Marked Charm. B. Marchant
Gold of Cathay. G. Wintle
Gold of Gabria. S. C. Mason
Gold of Lubra Rock. Michael Barrett
Gold of Malabar. B. Mather
Gold of Ophir. E. J. Lysaght
Gold of St. Matthew. D. Hart-Davis
Gold of the Gods. A. B. Reeve
Gold of the Sunset. F. Sleath
Gold of Troy. R. L. Fish
Gold of Vale. G. V. Morris
Gold Ogre. K. Robeson
Gold out of China. G. Volk
Gold Pistol. James Warren
Gold Plated Hearse. J. Hedges
Gold-Plated Sewer. O. Demaris
Gold Poison. P. Trent
Gold Run. D. Bickerton
Gold Scoop. S. Gall
Gold Skull Murders. F. Packard
Gold Slippers. F. P. Keyes
Gold-Spinner. D. Donovan
Gold Star Detective from Kentucky. Anonymous
Gold Star Line. L. T. Meade
Gold Trap. A. Applin
Gold-Trackers. D. Hart-Davis
Gold Treasure Msytery. J. Laurence
Gold Was Our Grave. Henry Wade
Gold Without Glitter. B. O'Keefe
Gold Worshippers. J. B. Harris-Burland
Golden Alaskan. J. Dorrance
Golden Angel. N. Brent
Golden Angel. M. Corrigan
Golden Ape. H. Adams
Golden Apple. R. Shea
Golden Arrow. D. Clarke
Golden Arrow. C. Stoddard
Golden Ashes. F. W. Crofts
Golden Ball. L. Bennet-Thompson
Golden Ball and other stories. A. Christie
Golden Ballast. H. D. Stacpoole
Golden Barrier. A. M. Burrage
Golden Bat. F. M. White
Golden Bauble. G. Slear
Golden Beast. E. P. Oppenheim
Golden Belts. A. Murray
Golden Boats of Taradata Affair. S. Latter
Golden Bough. G. F. Gibbs
Golden Bowl. A. Joscelyn

Golden Box. F. Crane
Golden Bull. I. Brook
Golden Bullet. P. Denver
Golden Calf. M. E. Bradden
Golden Carpet. A. M. Williamson
Golden Casket. F. A. Symonds
Golden Cat. H. Long
Golden Cat. D. Newton
Golden Chalice. K. L. Meredith
Golden Child. Penelope Fitzgerald
Golden Circle. L. Falk
Golden Clue. B. Wayde
Golden Cockatrice. G. Black
Golden Corn. C. Rodda
Golden Crucible. J. Stubbs
Golden Crystal. F. Hird
Golden Dagger. E. R. Punshon
Golden Dart. S. Jepson
Golden Dawns the Sun. E. Messenger
Golden Death. N. Deane
Golden Deed. A. Garve
Golden Door. B. Spicer
Golden Dress. I. Montgomery
Golden Drum. B. Freestone
Golden Dwarf. R. N. Silver
Golden Earnest. A. Bright
Golden Enchantress. M. Clare
Golden-Eyed Venus. M. Dekobra
Golden-Eyes. S. Jepson
Golden Face. W. LeQueux
Golden Face. B. Mitford
Golden Fear. S. Harvester
Golden Fig. N. T. Smith
Golden Fleece. J. Boland
Golden Fleece. J. Hawthorne
Golden Fleece. N. Lofts
Golden Fleece. Ernest Paul
Golden Fleecing. R. Upton
Golden Fluid. M. B. Dix
Golden Fool. D. Divine
Golden Foundling. S. Murray
Golden Frame. J. Chadwick
Golden Frame. M. Wolf
Golden Gate. Alistair MacLean
Golden Girl. A. Askew
Golden Girl. I. Flanders
Golden Girl. P. Warren
Golden Girl and All. R. Dennis
Golden Girls. S. Box
Golden Gizmo. J. Thompson
Golden Glory. E. M. Channon
Golden Gloves. J. Ingersol
Golden God. Ralph Hayes
Golden Goddess. H. E. Hill
Golden Goddess Gambit. L. Maddock
Golden Goose. F. Mahannah
Golden Goose. B. Queen
Golden Goose Murders. A. McRoyd
Golden Grin. Colin Lewis
Golden Guilt. F. Gerard
Golden Hades. E. Wallace
Golden Harvest. H. H. Hill
Golden Helmet. H. Bogue
Golden Hoard. E. Balmer
Golden Hoard. Robert Morgan
Golden Hole. J. Blyth
Golden Hooligan. T. B. Dewey
Golden Hooves. Scarlet Grey
Golden Horn. B. Davidson
Golden Horse. A. Kennington
Golden Horseshoes. R. Aitken
Golden Imp. J. H. Chase
Golden Isle. H. H. Hill
Golden Keel. D. Bagley
Golden Key. W. O'Farrell
Golden Kill. M. Olden
Golden Knot. C. Gibbon
Golden Lady. B. Atkey
Golden Lady. J. Ramsay
Golden Land. B. L. Farjeon
Golden Lantern. T. Warriner
Golden Legacy. Old Sleuth
Golden Lives. F. Wicks
Golden Lode. A. Davidson
Golden Lotus. A. W. Barrett
Golden Lotus. G. E. Locke
Golden Lotus. J. L. Roberts
Golden Lure. J. Davison
Golden Lure. G. W. Leader
Golden Man. F. Lockridge
Golden Milestone. Scott Graham
Golden Milestone. K. Hewitt
Golden Monkey. V. Gunn
Golden Murder. F. Lester
Golden Nightmare. W. Snow
Golden Obsession. G. Cogswell
Golden Oriole. P. Traill
Golden Oyster. Donald Gordon
Golden Packet. Angela Gray
Golden Panther. S. Gluck
Golden Pebble. M. Bennett
Golden Peril. K. Robeson
Golden Pheasant Mystery. Maurice Worth
Golden Pig. F. Du Boisgobey
Golden Plough. P. Merritt
Golden Precipice. H. B. M. Watson
Golden Quest. A. Askew
Golden Rain. Douglas Clark
Golden Rapids of High Life. R. H. Savage
Golden Rat. P. Trent
Golden Reef. J. Pattinson

Golden Rendezvous. Alistair MacLean
Golden Rope. J. W. Brodie-Innes
Golden Rose. F. M. White
Golden Salamander. V. Canning
Golden Scarab. J. Adye
Golden Scarab. P. Goulden
Golden Scarab. H. Moorhouse
Golden Sceptre. G. H. Thornhill
Golden Scorpion. S. Rohmer
Golden Sentinels. R. M. Sears
Golden Serpent. Nick Carter
Golden Shadow. L. T. Meade
Golden Shaft. J. Nazel
Golden Shroud. H. Arre
Golden Sickle. M. Grubb
Golden Slipper and Other Problems for Violet Strange. A. K. Green
Golden Soak. H. Innes
Golden Spaniard. D. Wheatley
Golden Spiders. R. Stout
Golden Spike. H. Ellson
Golden Spur. J. S. Fletcher
Golden Stag. B. Heatter
Golden Statuette. J. Pendower
Golden Stone. D. A. G. Pearson
Golden Stranger. Robin Temple
Golden Swan Murder. D. C. Disney
Golden Teddybear. John Marsh
Golden Temptress. H. Hill
Golden Thistle. J. L. Roberts
Golden Thread. E. Carballido
Golden Thread. T. Gallon
Golden Three. W. LeQueux
Golden Tooth. J. M. Cobban
Golden Torrent. J. Davison
Golden Torrent. Alan Graham
Golden Trap. H. Pentecost
Golden Tress. F. Du Boisgobey
Golden Triangle. P. Bonnecarrere
Golden Triangle. M. Leblanc
Golden Triangle. F. M. Proud
Golden Triangle. Colin Robertson
Golden Unicorn. P. A. Whitney
Golden Urge. R. Kyle
Golden Valley. D. Winston
Golden Venus Affair. A. MacVicar
Golden Violet. J. Shearing
Golden Virgin. A. Dipper
Golden Virgin. J. Rossiter
Golden Wag-Ho. F. Hume
Golden Web. E. P. Oppenheim
Golden Widow. F. Mahannah
Golden Witch. Gavin Holt
Golden Woman. R. Cullum
Golden Woman. E. Hatch
Golden Years Caper. R. Carson
Goldfinger. I. Fleming
Goldfish Have No Hiding Place. J. H. Chase
Goldfish Murders. W. Mitchell
Goldhawk. B. Hayles
Goldilocks. E. McBain
Goldmine—London W.1. Philip Daniels
Goldsmith's Row. Sheila Bishop
Golem. B. Anson
Golem 100. A. Bestor
Golestan Episode. J. Scotter
Golf Club Murder. O. F. Jerome
Golf-Course Murder. O. F. Jerome
Golf Course Mystery. C. K. Steele
Golf House Murder. H. Adams
Golf Links Mystery. P. Quiroule
Golgotha. J. Gardner
Goliath Scheme. W. Arden
Gondez the Monk. W. H. Ireland
Gondreville Mystery. H. Balzac
Gone Man. B. Solomon
Gone, No Forwarding. J. Gores
Gone to Ground. T. H. White
Gone Tomorrow. F. C. Davis
Gonzaga's Woman. J. Jakes
Good and Evil. W. Reyburn
Good and the Bad. Joan Fleming
Good Books. R. Philmore
Good by Stealth. H. Clandon
Good-Bye and Amen. F. Clifford
Good-Bye to Life. David Hume
Good-Bye to Market. R. M. Gilchrist
Good-Bye Tomorrow. Griff
Good Children Don't Kill. L. Thomas
Good Citizens. J. Boland
Good Day to Die. T. Blackburn
Good Day to Die. Jim Harrison
Good Day to Die. J. A. Hoffman
Good Evans! E. Wallace
Good Girls Don't Get Murdered. P. S. Parker
Good Guys Were Black. M. Franklin
Good Knight, Sailor. T. C. H. Jacobs
Good Luck, Mr. Cain. B. Freeborn
Good Luck, Sucker. R. Telfair
Good Luck to the Corpse. Max Murray
Good Men and Bad. J. B. Hendryx
Good Men and True. S. Harvester
Good Men Do Nothing. J. Brunner
Good Morning, Mavis. Carter Brown
Good-Natured Lady. J. E. Buckrose
Good Neighbor Murder. E. Pierson
Good Night and Goodbye. Timothy Harris
Good Night for Murder. P. Ketchum
Good Night, Garrity. Allan Nixon
Good Night, Irene. J. M. Ullman

Good Night, Kathy. N. J. Krinkel
Good Night, Ladies. V. Siller
Good Night, Little Spy. E. Koch
Good Night, Sheriff. H. R. Steeves
Good Old Anna. M. B. Lowndes
Good Old Boys. W. L. Heath
Good Old Charlie. J. Bingham
Good Old Potts! C. N. Boyle
Good One. G. Tabori
Good Place for Murder. C. Mullen
Good Place to Die. B. Copper
Good Place to Die. R. Gaulden
Good Place to Work and Die. W. Van Atta
Good Recovery. A. Wright
Good Riddance. B. Abercrombie
Good Ship "Dove." F. Warden
Good Ship Rajah. E. L. Long
Good Thief. R. Rosenblum
Good Time Charlie's Back in Town Again. A. Silver
Good-Time Girl. M. Richmond
Good Year for Dwarfs? Carter Brown
Goodbye. W. H. Manville
Goodbye, Aunt Charlotte! J. F. Straker
Goodbye, Aunt Elva. Elizabeth Fenwick
Goodbye Blonde. D. Enefer
Goodbye California. Alistair MacLean
Goodbye Chairman Mao. C. New
Goodbye Charlie. M. H. Albert
Goodbye, Dear Elizabeth. G. Hoster
Goodbye, Dr. Thorndyke. N. Donaldson
Goodbye, Friend. S. Japrisot
Goodbye, Gemini. Jenni Hall
Goodbye, Gillian. Jonathan Burke
Goodbye Gorgeous. Keith Campbell
Goodbye Is Forever. M. Carroll
Goodbye Is Not Worthwhile. W. Mole
Goodbye, Julie Scott. A. Abbott
Goodbye Look. R. Macdonald
Goodbye, Miss Lizzie Borden. L. De La Torre
Goodbye, Mr. Shaft. E. Tidyman
Goodbye Piccadilly. T. Barling
Goodbye Piccadilly, Farewell Leicester Square. A. La Bern
Goodbye, Pussy. S. Kemp
Goodbye, Shirley. P. Muller
Goodbye, Stranger. D. Heyes
Goodbye, Sweet William. P. Flower
Goodbye to an Old Friend. B. Freemantle
Goodbye to Istanbul. J. Banning
Goodbye to Murder. D. Henderson
Goodey's Last Stand. C. Alverson
Goose Is Cooked. E. Hogarth
Gooseberry Fool. J. McClure
Gorgeous Ghoul. D. V. Babcock
Gorgeous Ghoul Murder Case. D. V. Babcock
Gorgon. J. L. Hamilton
Gorgon's Head. Ladbroke Black
Gorgon's Head. F. Hurd
Gorgonzola, Won't You Please Come Home? C. Ames
Gorilla. R. Spence
Gorilla Moll. B. Sarto
Goring's First Case. P. Kippax
Gory Details. D. Elias
Gory Dew. G. Mitchell
Gory Knight. M. R. Larminie
Gory Story. J. Kirkpatrick
Gospel Lamb. J. S. Scott
Gospel of Death. W. Harrington
Gospel of Death. M. Judd
Gossamer Thread. A. Lowing
Gossip. M. Olden
Gossip to the Grave. Jonathan Burke
Gossip Truth. Jonathan Burke
Gothic Story of Courville Castle. Anonymous
Gotland Deal. N. J. Crisp
Gouffe Case. J. Maass
Goulden Fleece. R. Obstfeld
Government Contract. B. Stanley
Government Special Detective. Anonymous
Government Spy. Lieut. Carlton
Government Trust. B. Wayde
Government's Man. E. C. Derby
Governess. E. Cromwell
Governor. Alan Thomas
Governor of Chi-Foo. E. Wallace
Governor of Kattowitz. G. Seton
Governors. E. P. Oppenheim
Gown and Shroud. K. Freeman
Gownsman's Gallows. K. Farrer
Grab. P. Aalben
Grab. J. P. Heggy
Grab. P. Malloch
Grab. Zeno
Grab Operators. J. N. Chance
Grabbers. L. S. Taube
Grace Darling. G. W. M. Reynolds
Grace O'Malley, Princess and Pirate. R. Machray
Grace Walter. T. P. Prest
Gracie Allen Murder Case. S. S. Van Dine
Gracious Lily Affair. V. W. Mason
Graffiti Gambit. A. Wingard
Grafin Rinsky. Hilarion
Graft Town. Neill Graham
Grafter. J. Cassells
Grafters. Nicholas Carter
Grafters. F. Lynde

Title Index

Grail Tree. J. Gash
Grammarian's Funeral. E. Acheson
Grand Babylon Hotel. A. Bennett
Grand Catch. G. Buhet
Grand Central Murder. P. MacTyre
Grand Central Murders. S. McGurk
Grand Duchess. A. Duffield
Grand Duke. C. Dawe
Grand Duke's Finances. F. Heller
Grand Graft Hotel. B. Sarto
Grand Guignol. F. C. Witney
Grand Guignol Stories. M. Level
Grand Jury. E. Rose
Grand Man. C. Cookson
Grand Modena Murder. L. Gribble
Grand National. J. Welcome
Grand National Mystery, and other tales. T. S. Denham
Grand National Night. D. Christie
Grand Ole Opry Murders. M. Kaye
Grand Opening. B. Glemser
Grand Prix Murders. D. Rutherford
Grand Scam. P. Stein
Grand Slam. Ritchie Perry
Grand Street Collector. J. Arleo
Grandma's Best Years. E. L. Russell
Grandmother. M. Masterman
Grandmother. G. Simenon
Grandmother Martin Is Murdered. J. Courtney
Grandmother's House. J. B. Herman
Granduca. M. Brand
Grangerfjord Monks. R. M. Sears
Granite Folly. C. Farr
Granite Shadows. M. Warrick
Grant McKenzie. Old Sleuth
Grantham Mystery. M. Danvers
Grant's Overture. F. N. Miller
Granville Crypt Murders. Melville Burt
Grape from a Thorn. J. Payn
Grape Vine. H. Janson
Grapevine. Jonathan Starr
Graphics. H. M. Lyon
Grasp at Straws. J. Y. Dane
Grasp of the Sultan. Anonymous
Grass Spinster. C. C. Lowis
Grass-Widow's Tale. Ellis Peters
Grasshopper Summer. J. L. Cooper
Grassleyes Mystery. E. P. Oppenheim
Grasville Abbey. G. Moore
Grave Affair. Shelley Smith
Grave Between Them. C. Boutelle
Grave Can Wait. H. B. Kaye
Grave Case of Murder. R. Bax
Grave Consequences. M. Cumberland
Grave Danger. F. Kane
Grave Danger. K. Roos
Grave Descend. J. Lange
Grave-Digger of Monks Arden. A. Gask
Grave-Digger's Apprentice. V. M. Grayland
Grave Doubt. I. Baker
Grave Error. S. Greenleaf
Grave Error. M. Warner
Grave for Coyotes. S. D. Frances
Grave for Madam. P. Cagney
Grave for Miss Carling. D. W. F. Hardie
Grave for Two. H. Carmichael
Grave Gives Up. P. MacCormack
Grave Is Waiting. A. MacKenzie
Grave Journey. M. Hebden
Grave Lady Jane. F. Warden
Grave-Maker's House. R. Weber
Grave Matter. L. Vardre
Grave Matters. J. Rhode
Grave Matters. M. Yorke
Grave Must Be Deep. T. Roscoe
Grave of Green Water. J. Roffman
Grave of Heroes. J. Cross
Grave of Sand. D. Graham
Grave of Truth. Evelyn Anthony
Grave Undertaking. Lionel White
Grave Without Grass. D. C. Cameron
Gravedigger's Funeral. A. Arent
Gravel Patch. R. Goyne
Gravelhanger. V. Gielgud
Graven Image. J. D. Fitz
Graven Image. Mrs. C. Kernahan
Grave's Company. S. Nichols
Graves Ghost. A. W. Clark
Graves, I Dig! Carter Brown
Grave's in the Meadow. M. L. Stokes
Graveswood. S. Lloyd
Gravetide. C. McKnight
Graveyard. P. M. Hubbard
Graveyard Never Closes. F. C. Davis
Graveyard Plot. M. Erskine
Graveyard Rolls. M. Procter
Graveyard Shift. Harry Patterson
Graveyard to Let. Carter Dickson
Graveyard Watch. A. D. Divine
Graveyard Watch. J. Esteven
Gravy Train. W. Masterson
Gravy Train Hit. C. Stevens
Gray Amber. Basil Carey
Gray Canaan. D. Garth
Gray Charteris. Robert Simpson
Gray Creatures. Zorro
Gray Dusk. O. R. Cohen
Gray Eyes. S. Friedman
Gray Fist. M. Gray
Gray Flannel Shroud. H. Slesar
Gray Gull. H. F. Granger
Gray Magic. Herman Landon
Gray Man Walks. H. Bellamann
Gray Mask. Wadsworth Camp
Gray Phantom. Herman Landon
Gray Phantom's Return. Herman Landon
Gray Stranger. F. Crane
Gray Terror. Herman Landon
Graymists. M. Lynch
Grayson Affair. S. Waldron
Great Abduction. A. S. Roche
Great Abduction Mystery. W. M. Graydon
Great Adams Express Robbery. A. F. Pinkerton
Great Adventure and Out of a Dark Sky. S. Horler
Great Aeroplane Mystery. J. Laurence
Great Affair. V. Canning
Great Air Swindle. J. Creasey
Great Airport Racket. J. Hunter
Great Airways Plot. J. Noy
Great Alone. G. Goodchild
Great Alternative. C. H. Bullivant
Great Amherst Mystery. W. Hubbell
Great Art-Gallery Crime. M. Osborne
Great Autumn Double. P. Trent
Great Awakening. E. P. Oppenheim
Great Bank Mystery. N. Ned
Great Bank Robbery. J. Hawthorne
Great Bank Robbery. Old Sleuth
Great Baruma Mystery. W. P. Brown
Great Bear. E. P. Oppenheim
Great Becklesthwaite Mystery. H. Herman
Great Berwyck Bank Burglary. J. G. Bethune
Great Betrayal. H. Wintle
Great Big Laughing Hannah. W. Rutherford
Great Billy. Old Sleuth
Great Black Kanba. Constance Little
Great Bluff. H. Hill
Great Boy. Old Sleuth
Great Brain Robbery. K. A. Saddler
Great Bridge Conspiracy. T. Quinn
Great Brighton Mystery. J. S. Fletcher
Great Buxton Mystery. Anonymous
Great Canal Plot. G. H. Teed
Great Capture. Old Sleuth
Great Cases of the Thinking Machine. J. Futrelle
Great Circus Mystery. E. J. Murray
Great Circus Mystery. N. Ridley
Great Conspiracy. Nicholas Carter
Great Conspiracy. A. Soutar
Great Court Scandal. W. LeQueux
Great Craneboro' Conspiracy. J. Oakley
Great Cronin Mystery. Anonymous
Great Currency Racket. G. Chester
Great Dandelion. J. L. Cooper
Great Day for Dying. J. Dillon
Great Deception. M. K. Douglas
Great Detective Puzzle Book. E. R. Emmet
Great "Detectives". T. Mathieson
Great Diamond Bluff. J. W. Bobin
Great Diamond Robbery. S. O'Donnell
Great Diamond Syndicate. Nicholas Carter
Great Dinosaur Robbery. D. Forrest
Great Dollar Fraud. A. Parsons
Great Dumping Mystery. W. Jardine
Great Dusk. P. Traill
Great Elk. E. G. Cousins
Great Enigma. Nicholas Carter
Great Explosion. A. Murray
Great Express Robbery. Grace M. White
Great Fear. R. Goyne
Great Feast. H. Wood
Great Flood. Louise Collis
Great Fog and other weird tales. H. F. Heard
Great Game. H. C. Bailey
Great Gay Road. T. Gallon
Great Gift. S. Paternoster
Great God Gold. W. LeQueux
Great Gorme. Colleen Cairus
Great Green Diamond. I. Stark
Great Green God. F. Whishaw
Great Hesper. F. Barrett
Great Hijack. A. Tack
Great Hold-Up Mystery. W. Usher
Great Hotel Murder. V. Starrett
Great House in the Park. A. Burr
Great Hush-Hush Mystery. M. B. Dix
Great Impersonation. E. P. Oppenheim
Great Indian Scout Detective. Old Sleuth
Great Insurance Murders. M. Propper
Great Ivory Swindle. G. H. Teed
Great Jekyll Diamond. J. L. Owen
Great Jewel Mystery. F. Du Boisgobey
Great Journey and other stories. M. E. Braddon
Great K & A Train Robbery. P. L. Ford
Great Ling Plot. W. Martyn
Great London Mystery. S. Gluck
Great London Mystery. C. Kingston
Great Magor Diamond, and The Creaking Door. H. C. McNeile
Great Mail Racket. G. Dilnot
Great Mail Robbery. C. B. Kelland
Great Marl-Pit. G. Ohnet
Great Merlini. C. Rawson
Great Mill Street Mystery. A. Sergeant
Great Mistake. M. R. Rinehart
Great Mogul. L. Tracy
Great Money-Mail Mystery. Margaret Douglas
Great Money Order Swindle. Nicholas Carter
Great Museum Mystery. H. E. Hill
Great Mystery Solved. G. Vase
Great Newmarket Mystery. C. Rae-Brown
Great Opium Case. Nicholas Carter
Great Orme Terror. G. Radcliffe
Great Pearl Secret. C. N. Williamson
Great Pebble Affair. B. Shelby
Great Pimlico Mystery. K. Kingston
Great Plot. W. LeQueux
Great Porter Square. B. L. Farjeon
Great Portrait Mystery. R. A. Freeman
Great Pretender. J. Deane
Great Prince Shan. E. P. Oppenheim
Great "Push" Experiment. A. Pratt
Great Radio Mystery. C. K. Steele
Great Revenge. S. M. Sitwell
Great Revue Mystery. H. H. C. Gibbons
Great River Mystery. Old Sleuth
Great Ruby. T. W. Hanshew
Great Salvage Swindle. H. H. C. Gibbons
Great Secret. Roland Daniel
Great Secret. E. P. Oppenheim
Great Shakes. B. Moodie
Great Shipyard Mystery. J. Ascott
Great Skene Mystery. W. Masterson
Great Snake Murder. L. D. Stranger
Great Southern Mystery. G. D. H. Cole
Great Spy Race. A. Diment
Great Stone Heart. M. Farnsworth
Great Stores Crime. W. Edwards
Great Stores Mystery. W. Edwards
Great Syndicate. George Griffiths
Great Taxi-Cab Mystery. J. H. Collins
Great Taxi-Cab Ramp. J. G. Brandon
Great Temptation. R. Marsh
Great Temptation. S. Warwick
Great Tontine. H. Smart
Great "Tote" Fraud. J. W. Bobin
Great Train Hijack. W. Masterson
Great Train Robbery. M. Crichton
Great Tavers Case. D. M. Merrick
Great Trunk Mystery. R. H. Poole
Great Trunk Tragedy. M. Redwing
Great Tunnel Mystery. A. Blair
Great Turf Fraud. D. J. Belgrave
Great Turf Fraud. A. Blair
Great Turf Fraud, and Other Notorious Crimes. D. Donovan
Great Turf Mystery. C. Frisbie
Great Van Suttart Mystery. G. A. Chamberlain
Great Victorian Mystery. P. Menegas
Great Waltz. A. Rothberg
Great Wash. G. Kersh
Great Waxworks Crime. Gwyn Evans
Great White Army. M. Pemberton
Great Yant Mystery. A. B. Cunningham
Great Year for Dying. B. Copper
Greater Call. R. E. Salwey
Greater Claim. R. Applin
Greater Crime. G. A. England
Greater Punishment. S. Chalmers
Greatest Crime. Sloan Wilson
Greatest Fool. G. Hackforth-Jones
Greatest Game. C. L. Reid
Greatest Gift. A. W. Marchmont
Grecian Bloodbath. S. Jason
Gredos Reckoning. C. Rougvie
Greed. M. Leighton
Greedy Fingers. T. Roan
Greedy Killers. E. Radford
Greedy Ones. V. Kelly
Greek Affair. F. Gruber
Greek Coffin Mystery. E. Queen
Greek Fire. Winston Graham
Greek God Affair. R. Deming
Greek Tragedy. G. D. H. Cole
Greek Virgin. J. Stark
Greek Wedding. J. A. Hodge
Green Ace. S. Palmer
Green Archer. Margery Lawrence
Green Archer. E. Wallace
Green Arrow. B. Bolt
Green Bag. A. Leaman
Green Bag. J. P. Seabrooke
Green Beetle. Elizabeth Ford
Green Blot. S. Gluck
Green Bondage. F. Ogilvie
Green Bough. Margery Lawrence
Green Bracken. D. Lee
Green Bungalow. F. M. White
Green Cape. S. Richardson
Green Cat. S. Guise
Green Circle. Mark Cross
Green Circle. C. Massie
Green Cloak. Y. Davis
Green Complex. H. MacGrath
Green Coral. H. D. Stacpoole
Green Cross. A. R. Weekes
Green Curtain. M. E. Braddon
Green Death. Elaine Hamilton
Green Death. K. Robeson
Green Death and other stories. B. Hutton
Green December Fills the Graveyard. M. Sarsfield
Green Diamond. Arthur Morrison
Green Diamond Mystery. F. Grierson

Green Diamonds. Colin Robertson
Green Domino. K. Lindsay
Green Dragon. J. J. Farjeon
Green Eagle. K. Robeson
Green Eagle Score. R. Stark
Green Evil. F. Grierson
Green Eye of Death. J. Sandys
Green Eye of Goona. Arthur Morrison
Green-Eyed Monster. G. Bronson-Howard
Green-Eyed Monster. P. Quentin
Green Eyes. E. S. Brooks
Green Eyes. M. Grant
Green Eyes Are Dangerous. E. L. MacKeag
Green Eyes of Bast. S. Rohmer
Green Fields of Eden. F. Clifford
Green Fire. G. Hughes
Green Fire. A. Maybury
Green Fire. R. Standish
Green Flag and other stories of war and sport. A. C. Doyle
Green Flames of Aries. R. Lory
Green Flash and other tales of horror, suspense and fantasy. Joan Aiken
Green for a Grave. M. L. Stokes
Green for a Season. P. H. Irving
Green for Danger. C. Brand
Green for Danger. Gavin Holt
Green for Danger. P. Johnson
Green Gene. P. Dickinson
Green Ghost. Stuart Martin
Green Ghost. J. Reach
Green Ghost Murder. J. Ronald
Green Glare Murders. R. Wallace
Green Glove. J. L. Linklater
Green God. F. A. Kummer
Green Goddess. P. Edwards
Green Gold. Frank King
Green Goods Speculator. Dick Stewart
Green Grass. M. Kenyon
Green Grassy Slopes. W. A. Ballinger
Green Grow the Graves. M. E. Chaber
Green Grow the Tresses-O. S. Hyland
Green Hazard. M. Coles
Green Hell Rampage. Dan Morgan
Green Hell Treasure. R. L. Fish
Green Ice. G. A. Browne
Green Ice. R. Whitfield
Green Ice Murders. R. Whitfield
Green Ink. J. S. Fletcher
Green Jacket. Jennette Lee
Green Jade Buddha. J. Gibbons
Green Jade God. Roland Daniel
Green Jade Hand. H. S. Keeler
Green Jade Necklace. J. H. Chase
Green Killer. C. Dawe
Green Killer. K. Robeson
Green Knife. A. Wynne
Green Knight. W. M. Duncan
Green Lama Mystery. J. Kains
Green Lane. Alec Brown
Green Lantern. B. Bolt
Green Lantern. Augustus Muir
Green Light. L. Landon
Green Light. R. St. Clair
Green Light. R. C. Schimmel
Green Light for Death. F. Kane
Green Light, Red Catch. F. Ryck
Green Lipstick. G. C. Foster
Green Mandarin Mystery. G. Galcom
Green Mask. A. Skene
Green Mask. G. Verner
Green Monday. M. M. Thomas
Green Moth. G. E. Mitton
Green Mountain Murders. C. Culley
Green Mummy. F. Hume
Green Murder. V. Barlow
Green Opal. H. C. James
Green Oranges. R. Masson
Green Orb. C. Massie
Green Orchard. A. Soutar
Green Overcoat. H. Belloc
Green Pack. Robert (G.) Curtis
Green Pack. E. Wallace
Green Parrot. B. Capes
Green Phantom. G. Meyrick
"Green Phantom." W. Spence
Green Plaid Pants. J. Scherf
Green Plush. J. E. Middleton
Green Ray. W. LeQueux
Green Ray. D. T. Lindsay
Green Ray. V. Thompson
Green Ribbon. E. Wallace
Green Ripper. J. D. MacDonald
Green River High. D. Kyle
Green Room Crime. G. Chester
Green Rope. J. S. Fletcher
Green Rust. E. Wallace
Green Sandals. C. C. Lewis
Green Scarab. G. Hughes
Green Scarf. P. Fry
Green Scorpion. W. Hawton
Green Seal. C. E. Walk
Green Shade. H. Hill
Green Shadow. J. E. Grant
Green Shadow. Herman Landon
Green Shadows. L. V. Stevens
Green Ship. G. Volk
Green Shiver. C. B. Clason
Green Shutters. E. Addyman
Green Silence. M. Hastings
Green Stone. S. Blanc
Green Stone. H. MacGrath
Green Stones of Evil. M. Peterson
Green Suns. Henry Ward
Green Swallows. F. Sleath
Green Tablets. B. Goldie
Green Tabloids. B. Goldie
Green Talons. Gavin Holt
Green Thermos. G. Simenon
Green to Pagan Street. J. T. Story
Green Toad. W. S. Masterman
Green Tree Mystery. R. Doubleday
Green Triangle. W. M. Duncan
Green Triangle Mystery. H. Pink
Green Tunnel. C. C. Lewis
Green Turban. W. M. Graydon
Green Turbans. J. M. Cobban
Green Willows. Jan Alexander
Green Windmill. I. Mercer
Green Wolf Connection. Nick Carter
Green Wood Burns Slow. M. Brice
Green Wound. P. Atlee
Green Wound Contract. P. Atlee
Green Wounds. P. P. Muir
Greene Murder Case. S. S. Van Dine
Greenface. Frank King
Greenfield Mystery. G. F. Worts
Greengage Summer. Ruth Perry
Greengirl. V. Black
Greenhouse. A. Lamb
Greenmantle. J. Buchan
Greenmask. J. J. Farjeon
Greenmask. E. Linington
Greensea Island. V. Bridges
Greenstone Door. W. Satchell
Greenwell Mystery. E. C. R. Lorac
Greenwell's Glory Case. H. G. Hutchinson
Greenwood. J. Phillips
Grell Mystery. F. Froest
Gremlin's Grampa. R. L. Pike
Grenelle. I. Holland
Grenencourt. I. Charles
Grenfell Legacy. M. McEvoy
Grenson Murder Case. T. C. H. Jacobs
Gresham Ghost. W. D. Roberts
Gretna Green. H. M. Jones
Grey Affair. J. Weeks
Grey Cat. J. B. Harris-Burland
Grey Doctor. F. Hume
Grey Domino. F. C. De Crespigny
Grey Face. J. Cassells
Grey Face. S. Rohmer
Grey Fair. M. Gerard
Grey Fish. W. V. Cook
Grey Gables. G. E. Locke
Grey Ghost. J. Cassells
Grey Ghyll. A. Rundle
Grey Man. M. Urquhart
Grey Mask. P. Wentworth
Grey Mask Gang. J. A. Jordan
Grey Mask Murders. Hugh C. McDonald
Grey Messengers. M. Storm
Grey Mist Murders. Constance Little
Grey Monk. T. W. Speight
Grey Moth. F. Warden
Grey Phantom's Triumph. Herman Landon
Grey Rat. O. Binns
Grey Room. E. Phillpotts
Grey Sentinels. B. Knox
Grey Shadow. G. E. Rochester
Grey Shapes. Jack Mann
Grey Shepherds. A. MacVicar
Grey Sisters. M. D. Anderson
Grey Sombrero. P. Fry
Grey Studio. A. Scudder
Grey Timothy. E. Wallace
Grey Wolf's Daughter. G. Warden
Grey Woman. F. M. White
Greybreek. A. MacVicar
Greygallows. B. Michaels
Greyhound Murder Mystery. W. D. Maydwell
Greyhound Stadium Plot. E. T. Woodhall
Greymarsh. A. J. Rees
Greyslaer. Anonymous
Greystone Heritage. L. Bronte
Greystone Tavern. L. Bronte
Greystones. A. Lamb
Greystones. H. Leigh
Greythorn Woman. J. Brennan
Greythorne. J. Trevelyan
Greyvale School Mystery. P. Manton
Grid Murder. E. Snell
Grief Before Night. P. Loring
Grierson Mystery. L. Osbourne
Grieve for the Past. S. Forbes
Grievous Bodily Harm. T. Lewis
Grif. B. L. Farjeon
Griff. R. Weverka
Griffin Towers. J. Winslow
Griffith Case. John Bentley
Grifters. J. Thompson
Grim Caretaker. E. Ascher
Grim Chancery. W. Mills
Grim Death. G. Verner
Grim Death and the Barrow Boys. Joan Fleming
Grim Game. S. Horler
Grim Grow the Lilacs. M. Randolph
Grim Inheritance. H. Leyford
Grim Joker. G. Verner
Grim Justice. Rita
Grim Maiden. B. Flynn
Grim Rehearsal. R. Fenisong
Grim Smile of the Five Towns. A. Bennett
Grim Souvenir. J. Rowland
Grim Tales. E. Nesbit
Grim Tomorrow. M. Richmond
Grim Vengeance. J. J. Connington
Grimm Death. D. F. Brown
Grin and Dare It. R. Drayton
Grinder's Wheel. Morley Roberts
Grindle Nightmare. Q. Patrick
Grinning Avenger. E. Jepson
Grinning Ghoul. L. Churchill
Grinning Gismo. S. W. Taylor
Grinning Pig. N. Lombard
Grip Finds the Lady. J. Dory
Grip of Fear. S. H. Burchell
Grip of Fear. V. Hansen
Grip of Fear. I. Lambot
Grip of Fear. Nick Carter
Grip of Fear. M. Level
Grip of Fear. R. Ritchie
Grip of Gold. R. Halifax
Grip of Sin. A. Askew
Grip of the Bookmaker. Percy White
Grip of the Four. Mark Cross
Grip of the Law. J. W. Bobin
Grip of the Strangler. J. C. Cooper
Grip of the Wolf. M. Gerard
Gripped. S. Hocking
Gripped by Drought. A. W. Upfield
Gristmill. G. S. Caldwell
Groaning Spinney. G. Mitchell
Groom Lay Dead. G. H. Coxe
Groote Park Murder. F. W. Crofts
Groovy Way to Die. R. Deming
Gross Carriage of Justice. R. L. Fish
Grossbeak Mansion. N. Buntline
Grosvenor Square Goodbye. F. Clifford
Grotto of Tiberius. F. E. Smith
Ground for Suspicion. M. Burton
Grounds for Indecency. M. H. Gropper
Grounds for Murder. J. Appleby
Grounds for Murder. T. D. Carroll
Grounds for Murder. V. Van Urk
Group Flashing Two. D. Howarth
Grouse Moor Murder. J. Ferguson
Grouse Moor Mystery. J. Ferguson
Grouser Investigates. E. S. Brooks
Grove of Doom. M. Grant
Grow Cold Along with Me. M. Lynch
Grow Grey with Fear. N. Thurley
Grow Young and Die. W. O'Farrell
Growing Evil. E. Messenger
Grubstake Gold. J. B. Hendryx
Grudge. P. Chevalier
Grudge. B. Hitchens
Grudge Mountain. A. P. Terhune
Grue of Ice. G. Jenkins
Gruesome Grange. Robert Marshall
"Grumpy." H. Hodges
Guaranteed to Fade. G. Bagby
Guard the Girl. R. Clifford
Guarded Room. J. S. Fletcher
Guarded Soul. A. Dare
Guarded Woman. C. Cannell
Guardian. C. Dilke
Guardian. J. Hough
Guardian Angel in the Underworld. J. Wall
Guardian at the Gate. K. A. Shoesmith
Guardian of the Cup. C. Cannell
Guardian of Willow House. D. Daniels
Guardian Spectre. M. Lovell
Guardians. W. H. Baker
Guardians. S. Brackeen
Guardians. R. Parkes
Guardian's Mystery. C. Faber
Guardians of the Treasure. H. C. McNeile
Guaymas Assignment. L. Lambert
Guerrilla Attack. Jon Hart
Guerrilla Girls. H. Whittington
Guess Who's Coming to Kill You? E. Queen
Guest at Gladehaven. V. Smiley
Guest in the House. P. MacDonald
Guest with the Scythe. Gret Lane
Guests at the Villa. A. Hesse
Guests of Chance. J. L. Rickard
Guile. H. Hill
Guile Wears a Coronet. G. Vaizey
Guilt. H. J. Forman
Guilt Edged. W. J. Burley
Guilt Edged. J. B. O'Sullivan
Guilt Edged. L. Thayer
Guilt-Edged Cage. Carter Brown
Guilt-Edged Frame. F. Kane
Guilt-Edged Murder. L. Thayer
Guilt for Innocence. C. Franklin
Guilt Is Plain. D. Frome
Guilt Is Where You Find It. L. Thayer
Guilt Merchants. R. Harwood
Guilt of Innocence. M. Halliday
Guilt Without Proof. P. Alding
Guilty? J. W. Arctander
Guilty! L. Thayer
Guilty! D. Walshe
Guilty Answer. A. Livingston
Guilty Are Afraid. J. H. Chase
Guilty As Charged. E. Hanley
Guilty As Hell. B. Halliday
Guilty Be Damned. G. J. Barrett
Guilty Bonds. W. LeQueux
Guilty, But—. S. Kyle
Guilty, But Insane. Donald Stuart
Guilty But Not Insane. J. C. Lenehan
Guilty Bystander. Mike Brett

Title Index

Guilty Bystander. Wade Miller
Guilty Gold. H. Hill
Guilty Governor. Nicholas Carter
Guilty Hands. J. A. Jordan
Guilty House. F. Hume
Guilty House. C. Kingston
Guilty Man. F. Coppee
Guilty, My Lord. M. Peterson
Guilty, My Lord. I. Stefan
Guilty of Love. M. Cambards
Guilty Ones. D. Telfer
Guilty or Innocent? M. Leighton
Guilty or Not Guilty? M. M. Bodkin
Guilty, or Not Guilty? W. G. Hamley
Guilty or Not Guilty? N. Ridley
Guilty or Not Guilty. G. Smythies
Guilty or Not Guilty. M. V. Victor
Guilty Party. John Burke
Guilty Party. R. Dolphin
Guilty Party. T. Herd
Guilty Party. George Ross
Guilty River. W. Collins
Guilty Secret. M. Pemberton
Guilty Silence. S. Warwick
Guilty Thing Surprised. R. Rendell
Guilty Until Proven Guilty. B. McNaughton
Guilty Witness. J. N. Chance
Guilty Witness. M. Hershman
Guilty You Must Be. C. Franklin
Guinea Pigs. L. Vaculik
Guinea Pigs Tail. F. Hope
Guinevere's Gift. N. St. John
Guinguette by the Seine. G. Simenon
Gulf Coast Girl. C. Williams
Gulf Coast Run. D. Thomas
Gull Cove Murders. E. Colter
Gull Yard. Margaret Archer
Gulls Fly Low. V. Bridges
Gull's Kiss. P. Graaf
Gumshoe. N. Smith
Gun. M. T. Kaufman
Gun and Mr. Smith. J. Godey
Gun Before Butter. N. Freeling
Gun-Brand. J. B. Hendryx
Gun Business. G. Dickson
Gun Business. V. B. Miller
Gun Cotton. Rupert Grayson
Gun Cotton—Ace High. Rupert Grayson
Gun Cotton—Adventure Nine. Rupert Grayson
Gun Cotton—Adventurer. Rupert Grayson
Gun Cotton at Blind Man's Hood. Rupert Grayson
Gun Cotton Goes to Russia. Rupert Grayson
Gun Cotton in Hollywood. Rupert Grayson
Gun Cotton in Mexico. Rupert Grayson
Gun Cotton—Murder at the Bank. Rupert Grayson
Gun Cotton—Outside the Law. Rupert Grayson
Gun Cotton, Secret Agent. Rupert Grayson
Gun Cotton—Secret Airman. Rupert Grayson
Gun Feud. W. C. Tuttle
Gun Fever. E. Ellison
Gun for a God. N. Morland
Gun for Company. A. Bocca
Gun for Delilah. Surrey Smith
Gun for Honey. G. G. Fickling
Gun for Inspector West. J. Creasey
Gun for Sale. G. Greene
Gun for Sale. D. Spade
Gun Fury. J. K. Baxter
Gun Garden. P. Stanton
Gun in Daniel Webster's Bust. M. Scherf
Gun in His Hand. V. Rosen
Gun in My Back. C. Edmunds
Gun Merchants. G. Harding
Gun Moll for Hire. H. Janson
Gun Play. Y. M. Udoff
Gun Rule. P. Urquhart
Gun-Runner. B. Mitford
Gun-Runner. A. Stringer
Gun Runners. J. Crosbie
Gun to Play With. J. F. Straker
Gunboat Mystery. J. G. Brandon
Gunboat Mystery. J. A. Jordan
Gungu Sahib. T. Mundy
Gunman. C. F. Coe
Gunman at Large. George Douglas
Gunman of Gozo. H. C. Davis
Gunman's Bluff. E. Wallace
Gunman's Holiday. M. Knight
Gunmen, Gallants, and Ghosts. D. Wheatley
Gunner. E. Wallace
Gunners. G. H. Teed
Gunner's Island. A. Glanville
Gunning in England. W. J. Elliott
Gunpowder Alley. J. Rowland
Gunpowder Treason and Plot. Moira Field
Gunrunners. J. Murphy
Guns. E. McBain
Guns and Saddles. E. Ellison
Guns Covered with Flowers. S. Jackman
Guns for Achin. M. Leinster
Guns in the Desert. B. Netton
Guns of Calliope. N. W. Firth
Guns of Darkness. F. Clifford
Guns of Mazatlan. L. Parker

Guns of Navarone. Alistair MacLean
Guns of Palembang. P. McCurtin
Guns of the Gods. T. Mundy
Guns over the Border. S. Brydon
Gunshot Grand Prix. D. Rutherford
Gunsmoke Haze. R. Wilkes-Hunter
Gunsmoke in Her Eyes. H. Janson
Gunston Cotton. Rupert Grayson
Gup Bahadur. T. Mundy
Guru Docket. S. Dave
Gusher. J. Boland
Gutenberg Murders. G. Bristow
Gutter Gang. Jay De Bekker
Gutter Tragedies. S. Paternoster
Guttersnipe. G. Kersh
Guvnor. G. F. Newman
Guv'nor. E. Wallace
Guv'nor and other stories. E. Wallace
Guy Deverell. J. S. Le Fanu
Guy Fawkes. Anonymous
Guy Fawkes Murder. E. C. Lester
Guy Garrick. A. B. Reeve
Guy Gets His. J. Cello
Guy Must Live. Johnny Dark
Gwendoline's Harvest. J. Payn
Gwenyth. R. Carol
Gwythyn Clay Mystery. M. Poole
Gyfford of Weare. J. Farnol
Gypsies and the Detectives. A. Pinkerton
Gypsum Flower. P. Bair
Gypsy Detective. Anonymous
Gypsy Detective. Old Sleuth
Gypsy, Go Home. W. O'Farrell
Gypsy Grove. M. K. Simmons
Gypsy in Amber. Martin Smith
Gypsy's Curse. R. Carol
Gypsy's Luck. J. Fairfax-Blakeborough
Gypsy's Warning. G. Kent
Gyrth Chalice Mystery. M. Allingham

H As in Hangman. L. Treat
H As in Hunted. L. Treat
H.M.S. Anonymous. Taffrail
Ha-Ha Case. J. J. Connington
Habeas Corpus and other stories. P. Green
Habit of Loving. J. Thomson
Habits of Command. J. Rosner
Hacienda on the Hill. R. H. Savage
Hacienda Triste. F. Swann
Had. R. Gehman
Had I But Groaned. Carter Brown
Hades and Hocus Pocus. L. Dent
"Hades Belle." C. McManus
Hades Hello. W. Wright
Hadfield Mystery. M. E. Cooke
Hadrian Ransom. A. Duane
Haelstrom Manor. S. J. Treibich
Hagar. E. Southworth
Hagar, Called Hannah. A. Soutar
Hagar of the Pawn-Shop. F. Hume
Hagar's Castle. Clayton Matthews
Haggard's Cove. M. K. Simmons
Haggard's Manor. E. Hayworth
Hag's Nook. J. D. Carr
Haigerloch Project. I. Melchior
Haight Is the Killer. W. J. Lucas
Hail, Hail, the Gang's All Here! E. McBain
Hail McLean! G. Goodchild
Hail to the Chief. E. McBain
Hail, Victor, Hail! Michael Kent
Hailey Street Murder. W. Jardine
Hair Divides. C. Houghton
Hair of the Dog. Jean Leslie
Hair of the Dog. D. Whitelaw
Hairpin Mystery. J. M. Walsh
Hair's Breadth. L. Thayer
Hairy Arm. E. Wallace
Haiti Circle. Marilyn Ross
Haitian Legacy. S. Wagner
Haitian Vendetta. Don Smith
Haldane Station. F. E. Randall
Half a Bag of Stringer. P. McCutchan
Half a Chance. F. S. Isham
Half a Clew. R. H. Watkins
Half a Clue. J. R. Warren
Half a Corpse. R. Millar
Half a Million Insurance. H. W. Vrooman
Half Ace. J. M. Walsh
Half Angel. B. Jefferis
Half Brothers. E. P. Frankland
Half-Caste. A. Murray
Half Devil, Half Tiger. R. J. Fletcher
Half-God. A. Dorrington
Half-Haunted Saloon. R. Shattuck
Half Hours of a Blind Man's Holiday. W. W. Fenn
Half Hunter. J. Sherwood
Half Interest in Murder. J. Creighton
Half Mast. P. Traill
Half-Mast for the Deemster. G. Bellairs
Half-Mast Murder. M. Kennedy
Half Moon Street. J. J. Lydecker
Half-Open Door. B. Gray
Half-Past Mortem. J. A. Saxon
Half-Sister's Secret. F. Du Boisgobey

Half-Smart Set. F. Warden
Half-Way to Murder. S. Troy
Halford's Adventure. H. Bindloss
Halfway House. E. Queen
Halfway to Hell. H. Whittington
Halfway to Horror. David Hume
Halfway to Paradise. Laurence Kirk
Hall of Death. N. Tyre
Hallam Moor Mystery. C. H. Barker
Hallelujah Corner. J. Harris
Halloween. B. Greer
Halloween. Curtis Richards
Hallowe'en Homicide. L. Thayer
Halloween Murder. D. M. Disney
Halloween Murders. J. N. Chance
Hallowe'en Party. A. Christie
Hallowmass Abbey. Winifred Graham
Halo for Nobody. H. Kane
Halo for Satan. John Evans
Halo Highway. Rafe Bernard
Halo in Blood. John Evans
Halo in Brass. John Evans
Halo Jump. Alistair Hamilton
Halo Solution. R. Neebel
Halves. J. Payn
Hambro's Itch. H. Robens
Hamburg Switch. Angus Ross
Hamish Munro's Experiment. V. George
Hamlet Problem. Bradshaw Jones
Hamlet, Revenge! M. Innes
Hamlet Ultimatum. Leonard Sanders
Hamlet Warning. Leonard Sanders
Hammer in His Hand. W. Masterson
Hammer Island. S. Styles
Hammer Me Home. R. R. Werry
Hammer of Doom. F. Everton
Hammer of God. C. H. Bullivant
Hammer of God. N. De Mille
Hammer of Justice. S. Milne
Hammer of Thor. Carter Brown
Hammer the Toff. J. Creasey
Hammerhead. D. Cory
Hammerhead. J. Mayo
Hammerhead Reef. K. Conway
Hammers of Fingal. A. MacVicar
Hammers of Hate. G. Thorne
Hammersleigh. R. Ellerbeck
Hammersmith Maggot. W. Mole
Hammersmith Murders. D. Frome
Hammerstrike. W. Winward
Hammerwood Technique. M. Spouse
Hammett. J. Gores
Hammett Homicides. D. Hammett
Hampstead Mystery. F. Marryat
Hampstead Mystery. J. R. Watson
Hampton Mystery. Mrs. H. Lewis
Hamydal, the Vagabond Philosopher. M. Dekobra
Hand. J. Farrington
Hand. T. F. W. Hickey
Hand and Land. George Long
Hand and Ring. A. K. Green
Hand in Glove. M. G. Eberhart
Hand in Glove. N. Marsh
Hand in Murder. C. Dixon
Hand in Red. I. Stark
Hand in the Dark. A. J. Rees
Hand in the Game. G. Hunting
Hand in the Glove. R. Stout
Hand Me a Crime. C. M. Russell
Hand of a Killer. M. Seuffert
Hand of a Thousand Rings. R. Bachmann
Hand of Allah. W. LeQueux
Hand of Cain. Martin Thomas
Hand of Doom. J. M. Walsh
Hand of Fatima. R. Rothstein
Hand of Fear. G. Verner
Hand of Fu-Manchu. S. Rohmer
Hand of Horror. O. F. Jerome
Hand of Justice. F. Duncan
Hand of Mary Constable. P. Gallico
Hand of Peril. A. Stringer
Hand of Power. E. Wallace
Hand of Seeta. J. G. Brandon
Hand of Solange. M. Rippon
Hand of the Chimpanzee. R. Hare
Hand of the Four. Mark Cross
Hand of the Imposter. P. Minton
Hand of the Mafia. J. Baynes
Hand of the Spoiler. S. Paternoster
Hand of the Unseen. M. Leighton
Hand of the Waverleys. B. Goldie
Hand of Vengeance. H. Desmond
Hand of Vengeance. G. H. Teed
Hand of Vengeance. G. F. Underhill
Hand on the Alibi. J. Bude
Hand on the Cobbler's Safe. S. Bailey
Hand on the Web. R. E. Salwey
Hand on the Window Sill. B. Wayde
Hand Out. J. Rathbone
Hand over Mind. M. Lovell
Hand-Picked for Murder. Robert Martin
Hand-Picked to Die. R. Deming
Hand-Print Mystery. S. Fowler
Hand That Hid in Darkness. W. M. Graydon
Hand That Won. Nicholas Carter
Hand to Burn. J. Cannan
Hand to Hand. Nicholas Carter
Hand Without Mercy. J. Sandys
Handcuff Wizard. Nicholas Carter
Handful of Dominoes. J. L. Johnson
Handful of Fire. N. R. Nash

H

Handful of Murder. F. Findley
Handful of Silver. V. Canning
Handful of Silver. J. S. Strange
Handful of Sinners. C. Franklin
Handful of Stars. E. V. Zukas
Handkerchief Clue. H. Rockwood
Handle. R. Stark
Handle of Sin. E. Metcalfe
Handle with Care. H. Luger
Handle with Fear. T. B. Dewey
Hands in the Dark. M. Grant
Hands in the Darkness. A. Golsworthy
Hands of Clay. E. R. Beach
Hands of Death. A. Colin
Hands of Death. Eric Wood
Hands of Fate. A. L. Thompson
Hands of Healing Murder. B. D'Amato
Hands of Innocence. J. Ashford
Hands of Justice. B. Flynn
Hands of Justice. F. W. Robinson
Hands of Orlac. M. Renard
Hands of Terror. J. Crecy
Hands of the Ripper. E. S. Shew
Hands of the Shadow. S. Truss
Hands Off Bulldog Drummond. G. Fairlie
Hands Unseen. Herman Landon
Hands Up! J. G. Bethune
Hands Without Healing. P. Conway
Handsome, But Dead. A. H. Wahl
Handsome Phil, and other stories. J. H. Riddell
Handwriting on the Wall. D. Fox
Handwriting on the Wall. M. Propper
Handy Death. R. L. Fish
Hang by Your Neck. H. Kane
Hang Dead Hawaiian Style. P. Morgan
Hang the Hangman. M. L. Stokes
Hang the Little Man. J. Creasey
Hang the Man High. G. Household
Hang-Up. Sam Ross
Hang-Up Kid. Carter Brown
Hanged by a Thread. D. Haddow
"Hanged by the Neck." F. G. Layton
Hanged for a Sheep. R. Gatenby
Hanged for a Sheep. F. Lockridge
Hanged I'll Be! R. Goyne
Hanged Man. Edmund Ward
Hanged Man's House. E. Ferrars
Hanged Men. D. Harper
Hanging. L. Halegua
Hanging Captain. Henry Wade
Hanging Heiress. R. Wormser
Hanging Judge. Gwyn Evans
Hanging Judge. B. Hamilton
Hanging Matter. M. H. Bradley
Hanging of Constance Hillier. S. Fowler
Hanging Rope. Martin Kent
Hanging Sword! A. Soutar
Hanging Waters. K. West
Hanging Woman. J. Rhode
Hanging Woman. J. Roffman
Hanging's Too Good. J. Ronald
Hanging's Too Good. L. Thayer
Hangman. P. Geddes
Hangman. G. Verner
Hangman for Paradise. J. Canon
Hangman Never Waits. M. Dekobra
Hangman Waits. Roland Daniel
Hangman Waits. H. Desmond
Hangman's Child. A. Wood
Hangman's Choice. C. Knight
Hangman's Crusade. J. Barwick
Hangman's Curfew. G. Mitchell
Hangman's Daughter. W. Tyrer
Hangman's Dozen. David Alexander
Hangman's Guests. Stuart Martin
Hangman's Hands. C. Wogan
Hangman's Handyman. Hake Talbot
Hangman's Harvest. M. E. Chaber
Hangman's Hat. P. Ernst
Hangman's Hill. F. Pell
Hangman's Holiday. D. L. Sayers
Hangman's Honeymoon. C. H. Barker
Hangman's Knot. A. Gask
Hangman's Loose. R. L. Sweeney
Hangman's Moon. L. Gribble
Hangman's Noose. G. Batson
Hangman's Noose. J. D. Green
Hangman's Tale. G. Griffith
Hangman's Tide. J. B. Hilton
Hangman's Tie. C. Hale
Hangman's Tree. D. C. Disney
Hangman's Whip. M. G. Eberhart
Hangover House. S. Rohmer
Hangover Murders. A. Hobhouse
Hangover Square. P. Hamilton
Hangsaman. S. Jackson
Hank of Hair. C. Jay
Hank Tries the Sidewalk. Griff
Hankow Return. C. S. Archer
Hannah Massey. C. Cookson
Hannah Says Foul Play. D. V. Babcock
Hanno's Doll. E. Piper
Hanoi. Nick Carter
Hans, Who Goes There? F. Helitzer
Happening. E. Curry
Happy Alienist. W. Smith
Happy Anniversary, Harrison High. J. Farris
Happy Deathday. P. D. Westbrook
Happy Exile. F. M. White
Happy Harvest. J. Farnol
Happy Highwayman. L. Charteris
Happy Holiday! T. O'Finn
Happy Hostage. V. Brome
Happy Hunting Ground. L. Greth
Happy Killers. K. Robeson
Happy Murderers. V. Bridges
Happy New Year, Herbie and other stories. E. Hunter
Happy Nightmare. P. Buranelli
Happy Now I Go. T. Charles
Happy Prodigal. E. Denny
Happy Returns. F. Gaite
Happy Thieves. R. Condon
Harassed Hero. E. Dudley
Harbingers of Fear. D. Simpson
Harbor of the Little Boats. W. E. Huntsberry
Harbour. P. MacDonald
Harbour of Refuge. F. M. White
Hard and Fast. U. S. Andersen
Hard Edge. A. Destefano
Hard Kill. L. Grex
Hard Knot. C. Gibbon
Hard Lines. H. Smart
Hard Liver. A. Weymouth
Hard Luck. A. W. A'Beckett
Hard Man. L. Katcher
Hard Man. W. J. White
Hard Man to Kill. Ritchie Perry
Hard Men. J. Burmeister
Hard Option. G. Moffat
Hard Pressed. F. M. White
Hard Rock Man. J. B. Hendryx
Hard Sell. W. Haggard
Hard to Get. A. S. Roche
Hard to Handle. J. Welcome
Hard to Kill. J. Marcott
Hard Trip. A. Dipper
Hardenbrass and Harverill. Anonymous
Harden's Escape. H. Bindloss
Harder Than Steel. G. Thorne
Harder They Come. M. Thelwell
Harder They Fall. A. Bocca
Harder Thing than Triumph. B. N. Byfield
Hardican's Hollow. J. S. Fletcher
Hardiman's Landing. P. Malloch
Harding Mystery. A. J. Alderson
Harding Scandal. F. Barrett
Hardliners. W. Haggard
Hardly a Man Is Now Alive. H. Brean
Hardly a Man Is Now Alive. J. Ridgway
Hardman. D. Karp
Hardship Our Garment. L. Wood
Hardway Diamonds Mystery. M. Burton
Hare in March. V. Packer
Hare Sitting Up. M. Innes
Harem. L. Royer
Harem Mystery. A. Parsons
Hark, Hark, the Watchdogs Bark. T. Wells
Harker File. M. Olden
Harlan Legacy. J. A. Creighton
Harlem Hit. R. Mallory
Harlem Is My Heaven. I. Gordon
Harlem Showdown. M. Barry
Harlem Underground. E. Lacy
Harlequin. M. L. West
Harlequin House. L. Hayes
Harlequin of Death. S. Horler
Harlequin of Doom. J. Sandys
Harlequin Opal. F. Hume
Harley Greenoak's Charge. B. Mitford
Harlingham Case. F. Warden
Harlot's Daughter. P. Hastings
Harlot's House. E. G. Cousins
Harm in Trying. M. Dedina
Harm Intended. R. Parker
Harmattan. T. Klop
Harmonetics Invesigtation. G. M. Heldman
Harmony in Autumn. K. Hewitt
Harne Grange Mystery. Colin Hope
Harness Bull. L. T. White
Harness of Death. W. S. Sykes
Harp of Life. F. H. Rose
Harper. John Macdonald
Harpinger's Hunch. H. Carstairs
Harpoon. F. Ponthier
Harpoon of Death. W. O'Farrell
Harriet. Elizabeth Jenkins
Harriet Farewell. M. Erskine
Harriet Said... B. Bainbridge
Harriet, the Haunted. K. Kimbrough
Harringa's Last Gamble. O. Williams
Harrington Street Mystery. W. P. Kelly
Harris in Wonderland. P. Reid
Harrison Affair. G. Seymour
Harrison Keith and the Phantom Heiress. Nicholas Carter
Harrison Keith at Bay. Nicholas Carter
Harrison Keith, Magician. Nicholas Carter
Harrison Keith, Sleuth. Nicholas Carter
Harrison Keith—Star Reporter. Nicholas Carter
Harrison Keith's Abduction Tangle. Nicholas Carter
Harrison Keith's Battle of Nerve. Nicholas Carter
Harrison Keith's Big Stakes. Nicholas Carter
Harrison Keith's Cameo Case. Nicholas Carter
Harrison Keith's Chance Clue. Nicholas Carter
Harrison Keith's Chance Shot. Nicholas Carter
Harrison Keith's Close Quarters. Nicholas Carter
Harrison Keith's Crooked Trail. Nicholas Carter
Harrison Keith's Cyclone Clue. Nicholas Carter
Harrison Keith's Danger. Nicholas Carter
Harrison Keith's Death Compact. Nicholas Carter
Harrison Keith's Death Watch. Nicholas Carter
Harrison Keith's Diamond Case. Nicholas Carter
Harrison Keith's Dilemma. Nicholas Carter
Harrison Keith's Double Cross. Nicholas Carter
Harrison Keith's Double Mystery. Nicholas Carter
Harrison Keith's Drag Net. Nicholas Carter
Harrison Keith's Dual Role. Nicholas Carter
Harrison Keith's Fight for Life. Nicholas Carter
Harrison Keith's Greatest Task. Nicholas Carter
Harrison Keith's Green Diamond. Nicholas Carter
Harrison Keith's Haunted Client. Nicholas Carter
Harrison Keith's Labyrinth. Nicholas Carter
Harrison Keith's Lucky Strike. Nicholas Carter
Harrison Keith's Mummy Mystery. Nicholas Carter
Harrison Keith's Mystic Letter. Nicholas Carter
Harrison Keith's Oath. Nicholas Carter
Harrison Keith's Padlock Mystery. Nicholas Carter
Harrison Keith's Perilous Contact. Nicholas Carter
Harrison Keith's Poison Problem. Nicholas Carter
Harrison Keith's Queer Clue. Nicholas Carter
Harrison Keith's River Front Ruse. Nicholas Carter
Harrison Keith's River Mystery. Nicholas Carter
Harrison Keith's Sparkling Trail. Nicholas Carter
Harrison Keith's Strange Summons. Nicholas Carter
Harrison Keith's Struggle. Nicholas Carter
Harrison Keith's Studio Crime. Nicholas Carter
Harrison Keith's Tact. Nicholas Carter
Harrison Keith's Time Lock Case. Nicholas Carter
Harrison Keith's Triple Tragedy. Nicholas Carter
Harrison Keith's Triumph. Nicholas Carter
Harrison Keith's Wager. Nicholas Carter
Harrison Keith's Warning. Nicholas Carter
Harrison Keith's Weird Partner. Nicholas Carter
Harrison Keith's Wireless Message. Nicholas Carter
Harrowing. A. Skinner
Harry Ambler. S. Marlow
Harry Ambler and How He Saved the Homestead. S. Marlow
Harry and the Bikini Bandits. B. Heatter
Harry Blount, the Detective. T. J. Flanagan
Harry Hogbin. D. W. MacArthur
Harry-O. L. Hays
Harry-O #2. L. Hays
Harry Pinkurten, the King of Detectives. H. Rockwood
Harry Roughton. L. J. F. Hexham
Harry Sharpe, the New York Detective. H. Rockwood
Harry Williams, the New York Detective. F. L. Broughton
Harry's Game. G. Seymour
Harsh Evidence. R. Sheldon
Harsh Heritage. N. Tranter
Hart Hit. J. Wainwright
Hartinger's Mouse. P. McCutchan
Hartington's Luck. D. Walshe
Hartland Case. John Bentley
Hartness Millions. G. Norsworthy
Hartwell Case. R. L. Goldman
Harvest for Harpies. H. Luger
Harvard Has a Homicide. T. Fuller
Harvest Home. T. P. Prest
Harvest Moon. J. S. Fletcher
Harvest Murder. J. Rhode
Harvest of Death. G. Hart
Harvest of Deceit. K. Lindsay
Harvest of Guilt. S. Warwick

Title Index

Harvest of Hate. R. Goyne
Harvest of Hate. H. Leyford
Harvest of Javelins. B. Atkey
Harvest of Love. C. R. Gull
Harvest of Sin. M. Leighton
Harvest of Tares. M. Dalton
Harvest of Terror. A. Gale
Harvest of Violence. S. Brydon
Harvey Garrard's Crime. E. P. Oppenheim
Has Anybody Here Seen Abby? C. Joyce
Has Anyone Seen Jean? W. B. Hare
Hash. N. Fleming
Hashish. T. King
Hashknife of Stormy River. W. C. Tuttle
Hashknife of the Canyon Trail. W. C. Tuttle
Hashknife of the Double Bar 8. W. C. Tuttle
Hasington. E. Fyhrlund
Hastings Conspiracy. Alfred Coppel
Hasty Heiress. P. Muller
Hasty Wedding. M. G. Eberhart
Hat of Authority. John Sanders
Hat-Pin Murder. G. Dilnot
Hatanee. A. Eggar
Hatchet Man. M. Arrighi
Hatchet Man. J. Cassells
Hatchet Man. W. Marshall
Hatchet Man. San Antonio
Hatchet Man. W. Van Atta
Hatchet Murders. N. Morland
Hatchetman. D. Dodge
Hatchett. L. McGraw
Hatchie, the Guardian Slave. W. J. Ashton
"Hate!" R. Gar
Hate. H. Janson
Hate Alley. M. L. Weiss
Hate Begins at Home. Joan Aiken
Hate Finds a Way. M. Cumberland
Hate for Eight. D. Thurlow
Hate for Sale. M. Cumberland
Hate Genius. K. Robeson
Hate Is for the Hunted. S. D. Frances
Hate Is My Livery. M. Durham
Hate Island. A. West
Hate Master. K. Robeson
Hate of Evil. K. Snowden
Hate of Man. H. Hill
Hate Ship. B. Graeme
Hate That Kills. Nicholas Carter
Hate, the Destroyer. R. N. Silver
Hate Thy Neighbor. M. Lynch
Hate Thy Neighbor. John Marsh
Hate to Kill. W. Halliday
Hate Will Find a Way. M. Cumberland
Hated by All! J. Drummond
Hated Eight. P. Quiroule
Hated One. D. Tracy
Hated Therewith. D. G. Waring
Hateful Voyage. M. Neville
Haters. T. Strauss
Hatfield-McCoy Feud. W. B. Lawson
Hatred's Web. P. Nottingham
Hats Off! A. H. Veysey
Hatter's Ghosts. G. Simenon
Hatter's Phantoms. G. Collins
Hatton Garden Mystery. F. Marlowe
Haughton Diamond Robbery. Roland Daniel
Haunt of the "Queen" Makers. Lieut. Carlton
Haunted. Janice Bennett
Haunted. C. G. Kurtz
Haunted. G. Warden
Haunted Abbey. H. Leyford
Haunted and Hunted. E. O'Donnell
Haunted Bells. M. S. Buchanan
Haunted Bookshop. C. Morley
Haunted Bookshop. L. Rose
Haunted Castle. O. Bradbury
Haunted Cavern. J. Palmer
Haunted Chair. G. Leroux
Haunted Chair. J. F. Stone
Haunted Chamber. Duchess
Haunted Farm. L. Austen-Leigh
Haunted Garden. W. E. D. Ross
Haunted Hammock. E. Lockwood
Haunted Harbor. D. Douglas
Haunted Heart. T. Brun
Haunted Heart. Claudette Nicole
Haunted Heirloom. M. Eatock
Haunted Hills. B. M. Bower
Haunted Hollow. B. Symons
Haunted Homestead. E. Southworth
Haunted Honeymoon. J. Troy
Haunted Honeymoon. S. Wagner
Haunted Hotel. W. Collins
Haunted Hotel Mystery. A. Skene
Haunted House. H. Belloc
Haunted House. A. Bernede
Haunted House. Owen Davis
Haunted House at Kew. G. Warden
Haunted House of Marley. M. Somers
Haunted Ice Rink. E. R. Home-Gall
Haunted Island. H. Bourne
Haunted Lady. M. R. Rinehart
Haunted Landscape. I. Bromige
Haunted Light. E. Price
Haunted Lives. J. S. Le Fanu
Haunted Looking Glass. G. Darrell
Haunted Man. J. Gaunt
Haunted Monastery. R. Van Gulik

Haunted Ocean. K. Robeson
Haunted Pajamas. F. P. Elliott
Haunted Place. V. Coffman
Haunted Portrait. A. Ashton
Haunted Priory. S. Cullen
Haunted Rectory. H. C. McNeile
Haunted Rock. R. C. Finney
Haunted Sea. J. Pattinson
Haunted Seventh. Charles Ross
Haunted Ship. Seafarer
Haunted Shore. M. Gerard
Haunted Station, and other stories. H. Nisbet
Haunted Strangler. J. C. Cooper
Haunted Suit. N. Mapple
Haunted Summer. Anne Edwards
Haunted Tower. B. Cane
Haunted Tower. H. Wood
Haunted Wing. T. Walton
Haunted Woman. Melissa Napier
Haunted Wood Hollow. V. Silliman
Haunting at Waverly Falls. H. C. Rae
Haunting Cavalier. M. Thum
Haunting Fingers. Herman Landon
Haunting Hand. W. A. Roberts
Haunting Image. S. Clausse
Haunting Lights. T. A. Plummer
Haunting Me. P. Allardyce
Haunting of Abbotsgarth. E. Lyons
Haunting of Alan Mais. P. Saxon
Haunting of Bally Moran. H. S. Nuelle
Haunting of Cliffside. J. Letton
Haunting of Clifton Court. Dana Ross
Haunting of Drumroe. Claudette Nicole
Haunting of Fog Island. Marilyn Ross
Haunting of Helen Farley. F. Cowen
Haunting of Helen Wren. Jan Alexander
Haunting of Hill House. S. Jackson
Haunting of Hill House. F. Andrew Leslie
Haunting of Kathleen Saunders. Reginald Campbell
Haunting of Low Fennel. S. Rohmer
Haunting of Sara Lessingham. P. Bennetts
Haunting of Toby Jugg. D. Wheatley
Haunting of Villa Gabriel. Clarissa Ross
Haunting Shadow. J. A. Jordan
Haunting Shadow. Old Sleuth
Hauser's Memory. C. Siodmak
Havana Hit. M. Barry
Havana Hotel Murders. F. Dudley
Havana Mystery. W. W. Sayer
Havana X. S. Gross
Have a Change of Scene. J. H. Chase
Have a Lovely Funeral. A. T. Hopkins
Have Gat—Will Travel. R. S. Prather
Have His Carcase. D. L. Sayers
Have Mercy Upon Us. T. Wells
Have Nude, Will Travel. C. Allison
Have Patience, Delaney! B. Singer
Have This One on Me. J. H. Chase
Have You Seen This Man? G. Hurley
Haven for the Damned. S. Mitchell
Haven for the Damned. H. Whittington
Haven of Deceit. C. Virmonne
Haven of Fear. P. Ponder
Haven of St. Garth. E. L. Long
Haven of Unrest. S. Wagner
Havenhurst. S. Wagner
Havenhurst Affair. A. O. Pollard
Havering Plot. R. Keverne
Haversham Legacy. D. Winston
Haviland's Chum. B. Mitford
Having No Hearts. G. Goodchild
Having Wonderful Crime. C. Rice
Havoc. E. P. Oppenheim
Havoc. F. F. Van De Water
Havoc by Accident. G. Simenon
Hawaii. Nick Carter
Hawaii Five-O. M. Avallone
Hawaii for Danger. N. A. Hintze
Hawaiian Cruise. J. Lester
Hawaiian Eye. F. Castle
Hawaiian Hellground. D. Pendleton
Hawaiian Trackdown. L. Derrick
Hawk. R. Hardwick
Hawk. S. Kyle
Hawk. M. J. Shapiro
Hawk of Rede. H. Harding
Hawk over Hollyhedge Manor. D. K. Dowdell
Hawk Shadow. M. Heath
Hawk Watch. B. Bird
Hawkeland Cache. E. Fitzmaurice
Hawkline Monster. R. Brautigan
Hawkmoor Mystery. W. H. L. Crauford
Hawkridge. J. Blackmore
Hawks. J. J. Amiel
Hawks of Glenaerie. Ruth MacLeod
Hawksbill Manor. A. Grace
Hawkshaw. R. Goulart
Hawkshaw the Detective. T. J. Kelly
Hawkshead. J. Flores
Hawser Pirates. O. Wynd
Hawthorn Hill. Doris Shannon
Hawthorn Wood. Jane Fleming
Hawthorne. R. Wolff
Hayes Hall Affair. W. Hunt
Hazard. G. A. Browne
Hazard. R. Chanslor
Hazard Chase. J. Potter
Hazard House. P. Warren
Hazard Island. P. Tabori

Hazard of the Snows. O. Binns
Hazardous Duty. David St. John
Hazardous Holiday. E. Nisot
Haze of Evil. K. Lowe
Hazel Verne. A. L. Halstead
Hazell and the Menacing Jester. P. B. Yuill
Hazell and the Three Card Trick. P. B. Yuill
Hazell Plays Solomon. P. B. Yuill
He Arrived at Dusk. C. R. Ashby
He Came by Night. Anthony Gilbert
He Could Not Have Slipped. F. Beeding
He Could Stop the World. K. Robeson
He Dared Not Look Behind. Cledwyn Hughes
He Didn't Mind Danger. M. Gilbert
He Didn't Mind Hanging. N. B. Mavity
He Died Laughing. R. P. Connolly
He Died Laughing. L. Larier
He Died of Murder! Shelley Smith
He Died Thrice. M. G. Hugi
He Died Twice. G. J. Barrett
He Died Twice. M. Hadley
He Dies and Makes No Sign. M. Thynne
He Fell Among Thieves. D. C. Murray
He Fell Down Dead. V. Perdue
He Found Himself Murdered. D. Ames
He Had It Coming to Him. F. Grierson
He Had to Die. A. Hocking
He Hanged His Mother on Monday. N. Morland
He Isn't Dead Yet. R. A. Anderson
He Laughed at Murder. R. Keverne
He Liked Them Murderous. L. Dundas
He Loved Freedom. S. Fairway
He Never Came Back. H. McCloy
He Never Came Back. P. Tabori
He Ought to Be Shot. Joan Fleming
He Ran All the Way. Sam Ross
He Rather Enjoyed It. P. G. Wodehouse
He Shot to Kill. P. Drax
He Should Have Been King. K. Lindsay
He Should Have Died Hereafter. C. Hare
He Travels Alone. P. Loring
He Walked in Her Sleep. P. Cheyney
He Walked in Her Sleep and other stories. P. Cheyney
He Walks by Night. F. Nichols
He Was Found in the Road. A. Armstrong
He Who Digs a Grave. D. Delman
"He Who Fights..." L. Gorell
He Who Hesitates. E. McBain
He Who Walked in Scarlet. N. Tom-Gallon
He Who Whispers. J. D. Carr
He Won't Need It Now. J. L. Docherty
He Would Provoke Death. C. G. Jarvis
He Wouldn't Kill Patience. Carter Dickson
He Wouldn't Stay Dead. F. C. Davis
He Wouldn't Talk. M. Adams
Head. D. Cory
Head Crusher. B. Rossi
Head for Death. N. Longmate
Head Held High. C. B. Bass
Head Hunter. A. P. Morris
Head Hunters. J. Luceno
Head Hunter's Secret. A. Murray
Head in the Soup. P. Levi
Head Men. R. Sapir
Head of a Girl. E. O'Duffy
Head of a Traveler. N. Blake
Head of Medusa. A. Grace
Head of Pasht. W. B. Allen
Head of State. J. Watts
Head of the Force. J. Barnett
Head of the House. A. Zuckerman
Head of the Household. T. Cobb
Head on the Sill. M. Neville
Head over Heels in Murder. I. S. Shriber
Headed for a Hearse. Jonathan Latimer
Headhunter. F. Scarpetta
Heading for a Wreath. David Hume
Headland House Affair. W. Martyn
Headless Beings. M. Malcolm
Headless Ghost. T. S. King
Headless Girl of the North River. Old Sleuth
Headless Hound, and other stories. R. H. Mottram
Headless Lady. C. Rawson
Headless Man. G. M. Wilson
Headless Mystery. Old Sleuth
Headless Victory. D. S. Lifson
Headline for Murder. E. Lanham
Headline—Murder! G. Rayne
Headlined for Murder. E. Lanham
Headlines Make Murder. O. Mills
Headlong for Murder. M. Mace
Headlong from Heaven. M. Valbeck
Headmaster. D. H. Landels
Headmaster's Secret. R. Hardinge
Headquarters Budapest. Robert Parker
Heads. E. Stewart
Heads for Death. L. Johnson
Heads I Win. Q. Downes
Heads Off at Midnight. F. Beeding
Heads or Tails. S. Jepson
Heads You Die. L. Gribble
Heads You Live. David Hume
Heads You Lose. C. Brand
Heads You Lose. L. Cargill

516 / Heads You Lose

Heads You Lose. B. Halliday
Heads You Lose. B. Shannon
Heads You Lose. Jimmy Starr
Headsman. Austin Stone
Headsman's Holiday. D. Hawkins
Healing Hands of Death. P. Audemars
Healthy Grave. M. Leek
Healthy Way to Die. Lionel Black
Heap of Trouble. E. Messenger
Hear No Evil. N. Bowen
Hear No Evil. M. Carroll
Hear No Evil. S. Ransome
Hear Not My Steps. L. S. Thompson
Hear the Stripper Scream. P. Cagney
Heard in the Dark. Nicholas Carter
Hearken to the Evidence. H. R. Wakefield
Hearse. Henry Clement
Hearse Class Male. F. Kane
Hearse for Cinderella. H. Howard
Hearse for McNally. G. J. Barrett
Hearse for the Boss. A. Eichler
Hearse Horse Snickered. Carolyn Thomas
Hearse in May-Day. G. Mitchell
Hearse of a Different Color. M. Constiner
Hearse of Another Color. M. E. Chaber
Hearse of Dark Harbor. Clarissa Ross
Hearse Waiting. W. Wright
Hearse with Horses. E. McGirr
Hearsed in Death. M. Cumberland
Hearses Don't Hurry. S. Ransome
Heart and Science. W. Collins
Heart Beat. E. Dong
Heart Cut Diamond. S. Horler
Heart in Exile. R. Garland
Heart in the Box. F. Grierson
Heart in the Highlands. N. Kennedy
Heart Merchants. L. Goldman
Heart of a Gangster. D. Sherridane
Heart of a Girl. F. Warden
Heart of a Hero. M. Gerard
Heart of a Man. G. Simenon
Heart of a Mystery. T. W. Speight
Heart of a Princess. W. LeQueux
Heart of Delilah. Christopher Wilson
Heart of Gold. R. H. Greenan
Heart of Ice. F. Hume
Heart of Marble. N. Buckingham
Heart of Noel. F. Whishaw
Heart of Oak Detective. E. S. Ellis
Heart of Oak Detective. E. L. Wheeler
Heart of Penelope. M. B. Lowndes
Heart of Stone. G. Warden
Heart of the Dancer. Percy White
Heart of the Dog. T. A. Roberts
Heart of the Harbor. K. Blickle
Heart of the Matter. G. Greene
Heart of the Underworld. Nicholas Carter
Heart of the West. O. Henry
Heart of Unaga. R. Cullum
Heart Specialist. P. Trent
Heart to Heart. P. Boileau
Heartache. H. Janson
Hearts. D. C. Murray
Hearts and Flowers. H. Rowland
Hearts by the Tower. O. Sinclair
Heart's Delight. C. Gibbon
Heart's Delight. L. Tracy
Hearts Ease in Death. James Fraser
Heart's Grown Brutal. D. Brewster
Hearts in the Highlands. Lynna Cooper
Hearts in Turmoil. M. Richmond
Hearts of Gold and Hearts of Steel. H. Herman
Hearts or Diamonds. I. D. Hardy
Heart's Problem. C. Gibbon
Heart's Ransom. C. Gayet
Heartstone. P. Margolin
Heat Lightning. R. F. Carroll
Heat Lightning. W. Shaw
Heat Not a Furnace. H. Kemp
Heat of Night. H. Whittington
Heat of the Day. E. Bowen
Heat of the Sun. M. Birmingham
Heat Wave. Timothy Harris
Heath Hover Mystery. B. Mitford
Heathcliff. J. Caine
Heather. M. Dobner
Heather-Bells. R. Gover
Heather Mixture. M. Gerard
Heather Mystery. M. Gerard
Heatherton Heritage. Pamela Hill
Heat's On. R. Drayton
Heat's On. C. Himes
Heatwave. Caesar Smith
Heaven-Kissed Hill. J. S. Fletcher
Heaven Ran Last. W. P. McGivern
Heaven-Sent Witness and other stories. J. S. Fletcher
Heaven Will Be Ours. E. Lindsay
Heavenly Bodies. T. Warriner
Heavenly Body. G. Morgan
Heaviest Pipe. A. M. Patterson
Heavy As Lead. M. Torrie
Heavy, Heavy Hangs. D. M. Disney
Heavy Stakes. M. K. Douglas
Heberden's Seat. Douglas Clark
Hebrew Maiden. T. P. Prest
Hec Ramsey. D. Owen
Hecatomb. B. Palmer
Heck. M. Renek
Heckler. E. McBain

Hector Duval. H. Collinson
Hector Tumbler Investigates. S. Crabtree
He'd Rather Be Dead. G. Bellairs
Hedgerow. F. E. Randall
Hedonists. Colin Wilson
Hedri. H. B. Mathers
Heed the Thunder. J. Thompson
Heel. W. L. Rohde
Heel of Achilles. L. H. Fox
Heel of Achilles. E. Radford
Heel of Achilles. G. Verner
Height of Day. D. Cory
Heights of Havenrest. V. Subond
Heights of Rimring. D. Hart-Davis
Heights of Zervos. C. Forbes
Heil Britannia. P. Long
Heil Harris! J. Garforth
Heil! Hollywood. Jack Preston
Heir. C. Keane
Heir Apparent. E. L. Withers
Heir-at-Law, and other tales. Waters
Heir Hunters. B. S. Ballinger
Heir of Ashly. H. Wood
Heir of Douglas. L. De La Torre
Heir of Frinton Park. F. M. Long
Heir of Grangerfjord Castle. R. M. Sears
Heir of Greymount. J. E. Cooke
Heir of Kings. Winifred Duke
Heir of Starvelings. E. Berckman
Heir of the Ages. J. Payn
Heir to Lucifer. M. Burton
Heir to Murder. M. Burton
Heir to Murder. M. Halliday
Heir to Polventon. Marjorie Watson
Heir to the Throne. A. W. Marchmont
Heiress Apparent. L. Conway
Heiress of Bayou Vache. Harriet Stone
Heiress of Bellefront. Emerson Bennett
Heiress of Densley Wold. F. Warden
Heiress of Fear. C. Farr
Heiress of Frascati. J. Shearing
Heiress of Glen Gower. M. A. Fleming
Heiress of the Season. W. Magnay
Heiress to Corsair Keep. C. Farr
Heiress to Evil. S. O'Brien
Heiress to Wolfskill. K. Kimbrough
Heirloom of Tragedy. E. Noone
Heirs of Cain. A. Rothberg
Heirs of Darkness. Z. K. Snyder
Heirs of Merlin. P. Atkey
Heirs to Kildrennan. A. Foxe
Heist Me Higher. B. S. Ballinger
Heisters. R. P. Jones
Held Apart. R. N. Silver
Held for Ransom. N. M. Murray
Held for Trial. Nicholas Carter
Held in Suspense. Nicholas Carter
Held in the Toils. J. K. Leys
Held in Thrall. B. Hemyng
Held in Trust! W. M. Graydon
Held Open for Death. E. Payne
Held to Ransom. R. Gover
Helen. E. V. Cunningham
Helen All Alone. W. Buchan
Helen Elwood, the Female Detective. B. and R.
Helen of London. J. Goodwin
Helen of the Moor. A. Askew
Helen Passes By. E. R. Punshon
Helen Vardon's Confession. R. A. Freeman
Helen Whitney's Edding, and other stories. H. Wood
Helena. H. S. Irwin
Helga's Web. J. Cleary
Helix File. W. D. Blankenship
Hell and High Water. R. Drayton
Hell and High Water. R. Garland
Hell Below. W. Robeson
Hell-Bent for Danger. W. Grove
Hell-Black Night. S. Fisher
Hell-Bomb Floozies. Griff
Hell Can Wait. H. Whittington
Hell Candidate. T. Luke
Hell for Heather. P. Flower
Hell for Leather. A. Wood
Hell for Tomorrow. P. Leslie
Hell Gate. James Dawson
Hell-Gate Tides. L. Thayer
Hell Has No Exit. J. L. Gilmer
Hell Hath No Fury. L. Eby
Hell Hath No Fury. M. Richmond
Hell Hath No Fury. C. Williams
Hell House. R. Matheson
Hell in Harness. J. Auslander
Hell in Hindu Land. J. Rosenberger
Hell in the Afternoon. W. Sproule
Hell Is a City. W. Ard
Hell Is a City. M. Procter
Hell Is Always Today. Harry Patterson
Hell Is Empty. J. F. Straker
Hell Is Forever. J. L. Gilmore
Hell Is My Destination. J. Conway
Hell Is Sold Out. M. Dekobra
Hell Is Too Crowded. Harry Patterson
Hell Is Where You Find It. J. Welcome
Hell Let Loose. F. Beeding
Hell Masters. K. Spore
Hell of a Murder. W. Carrier
Hell of a Spot. B. Scott
Hell of a Woman. J. Thompson
Hell of Make Believe. F. Wiles
Hell on Friday. W. Bogart

Hell on the Way. J. M. Fox
Hell! Said the Duchess. M. Arlen
Hell Seed. C. D. Peel
Hell Ship to Kuma. C. Clements
Hell Shot. J. Poyer
Hell Street. M. Franklin
Hell to Pay! H. Clevely
Hell to Pay. W. R. Cox
Hell with Elaine. V. Siller
Hellbirds. A. Mitchelson
Hellbomb Flight. L. Derrick
Hellbottom. E. Corder
Hellcat. Carter Brown
Helldorado. H. Janson
Heller's Leap. Ian Wallace
Hellfire Conspiracy. Ralph Hayes
Hellfire Files of Jules de Grandin. Seabury Quinn
Hellfire Heritage. W. D. Roberts
Hellflower. G. O. Smith
Hellgate Plantation. F. Swann
Hellinger's Law. J. Barr
Hellions. R. T. Bickers
Hello Cruel World, Goodbye. J. Goodman
Hello Summer, Goodbye. M. G. Coney
Hell's Above Us. Henry Ward
Hell's Acre. F. H. Rose
Hell's Angel. H. Janson
Hell's Angel Kidnapping. P. A. Foxall
Hell's Belle. Joan Fleming
Hell's Belles. R. Drayton
Hell's Belles. H. Janson
Hell's Brew. S. Horler
Hell's Full. William Harrison
Hell's Harbour. H. P. Lee
Hell's Harvest. H. S. Banner
Hell's Harvest. Jos. N. Wilson
Hell's Kitchen. B. Appel
Hell's Loose. R. Pertwee
Hell's Our Destination. G. Brewer
Hell's Wenches. V. Norwood
Hellspout. B. Knox
Help from the Baron. Anthony Morton
Help I Am Being Held Prisoner. D. E. Westlake
Help, Please. E. Bahr
Help Wanted—for Murder. W. L. Rohde
Help Yourself to Happiness. F. R. Adams
Helping Hand. C. Dale
Helping with Enquiries. C. Dale
Helsinki Affair. M. Sariola
Hemlock Avenue Mystery. R. Doubleday
Hemlock Galore. A. Kennington
Hemlock Swamp. E. L. Whittlesey
Hemlock Tree. E. Lottman
Henbane. C. Meadows
Hendon's First Case. J. Rhode
Hennessy. M. Franklin
Henrietta Who? C. Aird
Henry Broch, Old Sleuth's Assistant. Old Sleuth
Henry Cassland. H. Druce
Henry Dunbar. M. E. Braddon
Henry in a Silver Frame. J. Eastwood
Henry Massinger. R. Jocelyn
Henry Northcote. J. C. Snaith
Henry Prince in Action. C. F. Gregg
Henry the Sheriff. W. C. Tuttle
Hepsworth Millions. C. Lys
Her Assigned Husband. A. Pratt
Her Convict. M. E. Braddon
Her Convict Husband. Ladbroke Black
Her Convict Husband. M. Leighton
Her Crooked Lover. B. Delane
Her Dangerous Memory. N. Norman
Her Death of Cold. R. McInerny
Her Demon Lover. L. Bronte
Her Demon Lover. J. L. Roberts
Her Empty Trimph. A. Askew
Her Fairy Prince. G. Warden
Her Faithful Knight. G. Warden
Her Fatal Sin. M. E. Holmes
Her Fate and His. M. Leighton
Her Father's Daughter. A. Askew
Her Foreign Conquest. R. H. Savage
Her Fugitive. C. Stanton
Her Garden of Eden. J. Chancellor
Her Grace at Bay. H. Hill
Her Great Moment. E. Balmer
Her Great Surprise. H. P. Halsey
Her Happy Face. L. T. Meade
Her Heart in Her Throat. Ethel L. White
Her Heart's Awakening. M. Leighton
Her Heart's Desire. Lynna Cooper
Her Heart's Gift. O. Kent
Her Hidden Past. B. M. Clay
Her Highness. F. Whishaw
Her Highness's Secretary. C. Dawe
Her Honour. R. Machray
Her Ladyship. T. W. Speight
Her Ladyship's Jewels and What Became of Them. R. H. Gooch
Her Ladyship's Secret. W. Westall
Her Ladyship's Silence. M. Leighton
Her Lips Betrayed. D. Walshe
Her Lover's Peril. A. Eadie
Her Loving Slave. H. Nisbet
Her Majesty the Queen. J. E. Cooke
Her Majesty's Minister. W. LeQueux
Her Marriage Lines. M. Leighton
Her Month of Freedom. P. Trent
Her Mother's Child. A. Askew

Her Own Affair. T. A. Plummer
Her Private Murder. J. Corbett
Her Private Passions. M. Holland
Her Reputation. T. Mundy
Her Right Divine. O. Kent
Her Royal Highness. W. LeQueux
Her Royal Highness's Love Affair.
   J. M. Cobban
Her Sacrifice. A. Applin
Her Second Murder. J. Corbett
Her Second Self. A. Wood
Her Secret Life. R. Machray
Her Senator. A. C. Gunter
Her Sentinel. A. W. Marchmont
Her Soul's Desire. A. M. Meadows
Her Splendid Sin. H. Hill
Her Stepfather's House. J. Wetherell
Her Two Millions. W. Westall
Her Ways Are Death. J. Mann
Her Weapon Is Passion. H. Janson
Her Wedding Night. M. Pemberton
Her Wild Oats. P. Trent
Herald of Death. M. Dalman
Herald of Doom. G. Ashe
Herald Personal and other stories.
   Nicholas Carter
Herapath Property. J. S. Fletcher
Hercule and the Gods. P. Audemars
Hercule Poirot's Christmas. A. Christie
Hercule Poirot's Early Cases. A. Christie
Hercules and the Marionettes. R. M.
   Gilchrist
Hercules, Esq. Gwyn Evans
Hercules—Sportsman. B. Atkey
Here Come the Dead. R. P. Koehler
Here Comes a Candle. F. Brown
Here Comes a Candle. J. A. Hodge
Here Comes a Chopper. G. Mitchell
Here Comes a Hero. Lawrence Block
Here Comes Charlie M. B. Freemantle
Here Comes the Copper. Henry Wade
Here Comes the Corpse. G. Bagby
Here Comes the Corpse. G. Brandon
Here Comes the Lady. M. P. Shiel
Here Comes the Toff. J. Creasey
Here in Eden. K. Lindsay
Here Is an S.O.S. S. Horler
Here Is Danger. G. Ashe
Here Is the Evidence. P. Vane
Here Lies. D. M. Disney
Here Lies Blood. M. M. Mannon
Here Lies Georgeia Linz. P. Mason
Here Lies My Wife. E. McGirr
Here Lies Nancy Frail. Jonathan Ross
Here Lies the Body. R. Burke
Here Lies the Shadow. R. Foxall
Here There Be Dragons. R. Bentley
Here to Die. M. Sadler
Here Today—Dead Tomorrow. J. W. Hornby
Here's a Villain! J. Mitchell
Here's Blood in Your Eye. Manning Long
Here's Misery. E. V. Knox
Here's Murder Done. C. Ashton
Here's Why. F. Collins
Heresy. L. Snelling
Heretic. M. L. West
Herewith the Clues! D. Wheatley
Heritage in Trust. C. Davy
Heritage of Cain. I. Ostrander
Heritage of Danger. M. Lynch
Heritage of Evil. J. L. Finn
Heritage of Fear. E. Bond
Heritage of Folly. C. Marchant
Heritage of Kid McCleod. H. Pink
Heritage of Mercy. P. Tabori
Heritage of Peril. A. W. Marchmont
Heritage of Strangers. M. L. Roby
Heritage of the Horned Steer. R. Wilkes-Hunter
Heritage of Trouble. Nicholas Carter
Heritage Perilous. J. Farnol
Hermit of Turkey Hollow. A. Train
Hermitage. M. K. Simmons
Hermitage Bell. M. McEvoy
Hermitage Hill. D. Daniels
Hermit's Island. J. Phillips
Hero. P. Haining
Hero at Large. A. J. Carothers
Hero by Proxy. H. Tolman
Hero for Leanda. A. Garve
Hero Game. W. H. Baker
Hero in the Tower. H. H. Kirst
Hero of a Summer's Day. J. Pudney
Hero of Romance. R. Marsh
Hero Rat. W. Charleston
Herod Conspiracy. Russell Rhodes
Herod's Peal. R. Thorndike
Heroes of Yuca. Michael Barrett
Heroin Triple Cross. J. Weisman
Heroine. E. S. Barrett
Heroine of the Desert. A. Eadie
Heron Tree. E. Kyle
Heronbrook. A. Rundle
Heron's Nest. Elizabeth Ford
Heronstroke Mystery. E. Everett-Green
Hero's Lust. K. Jaediker
Herr Nightingale and the Satin Woman.
   W. Kotzwinkle
Hers Is a Hearse. M. Brody
Herzog Affair. R. D. Steeley
He's Dead All Right. J. Gainfort

He's Late This Morning. C. Hale
Heseltine Mystery. H. E. Chapman
Hess Cross. J. S. Thayer
Hester and I. P. C. De Crespigny
Hester Strong's Life Work. E. Southworth
Heston House Horror. V. Leigh
Hex. K. Robeson
Hex Marks the Spot. J. Dekker
Hex Murder. F. Hazard
Hi-Fi Fadeout. Carter Brown
Hi-Jack! G. N. Smith
Hi-Jack for a Jill. Carter Brown
Hi-Jack That Dame. Griff
Hi-Jacker's Lady. B. Sarto
Hi-Spy-Kick-the-Can. V. MacClure
Hibernation of Ginger Scrubb. A. Gardner
Hick Town Dame. F. Foden
Hickey and Boggs. P. Rock
Hickory Dickory Death. A. Christie
Hickory Dickory Dock. A. Christie
Hickory Hall. E. Southworth
Hidden and the Hunted. H. Swiggett
Hidden Answer. John Marsh
Hidden Blood. W. C. Tuttle
Hidden Book. M. L. Roby
Hidden Chain. Dora Russell
Hidden Chapel. L. Ames
Hidden Cipher. A. O. Pollard
Hidden Clue. E. D. Pierson
Hidden Clues. D. Deane
Hidden Death. C. Goodall
Hidden Death. M. Grant
Hidden Death. E. W. Terris
Hidden Door. A. Gask
Hidden Door. F. Packard
Hidden Enemy. V. Lloyd
Hidden Eyes. E. Levison
Hidden Face. V. Canning
Hidden Fear. J. Blyth
Hidden Flame. R. Dowling
Hidden Foe. G. A. Henty
Hidden Foes. Nicholas Carter
Hidden Gang. D. T. Hughes
Hidden Gold. W. Anthony
Hidden Gold. F. Barrett
Hidden Grave. P. Hardin
Hidden Guest. M. Short
Hidden Hand. C. J. Daly
Hidden Hand. S. Horler
Hidden Hand. E. Phillpotts
Hidden Hand. E. Southworth
Hidden Hands. M. Leighton
Hidden Hands. W. LeQueux
Hidden Hoard. J. Creasey
Hidden Horror. M. Richmond
Hidden Hour. J. B. Harris-Burland
Hidden Hour. S. Ransome
Hidden House. J. C. Dane
Hidden Island. A. Rutherford
Hidden Key. G. H. Coxe
Hidden Kingdom. F. Beeding
Hidden Light. M. Dalman
Hidden Lives. C. H. Merritt
Hidden Lives. E. R. Punshon
Hidden Man. C. Pidgin
Hidden Mask. C. G. Mitford
Hidden Men. S. Truss
Hidden Menace! J. W. Bobin
Hidden Menace. Donald Stuart
Hidden Message. A. Murray
Hidden Million. P. Merritt
Hidden, Not Lost. Anonymous
Hidden Out. H. Fielding
Hidden Paths. W. S. King
Hidden Perils. M. C. Hay
Hidden Portal. Garnett Weston
Hidden Record. E. W. Blaisdell
Hidden Sin. E. A. Dupuy
Hidden Submarine. C. Holland
Hidden Target. Helen MacInnes
Hidden Terror. Anonymous
Hidden Valley. D. C. Percy
Hidden Ways. F. F. Van De Water
Hidden Witness. H. C. McNeile
Hidden Woman. J. Hay
Hidden Wrath. Stella Phillips
Hide and Go Seek. A. Garve
Hide and Go Seek. Colver Harris
Hide and Kill. J. York
Hide and Seek. W. Collins
Hide and Seek. Jacqueline Wilson
Hide Away. N. Bond
Hide Her from Every Eye. H. Pentecost
Hide in Hell. F. Cannon
Hide in the Dark. F. N. Hart
Hide My Body. F. Lester
Hide My Eyes. M. Allingham
Hide-Out. L. Holden
Hide the Baron. Anthony Morton
Hide the Body! M. Propper
Hide the Children. V. Miller
Hide Those Diamonds. Roy Vickers
Hideaway. N. Content
Hideaway. J. Gardner
Hideaway. F. Nichols
Hideaway. M. Procter
Hiding Place. C. Keith
Hiding Place. C. Wilcox
Hiding to Nothing. Ken Blake
High Adventure. J. Farnol
High Adventure. P. Groom
High Anxiety. R. H. Pilpel

High Ballin'. Richard Robinson
High Bid for Murder. A. O'Neill
High-Bouncing Lover. Angus Hall
High Bright Sun. I. S. Black
High Citadel. D. Bagley
High-Class Kill. J. Wainwright
High Class Swindler. Old Spicer
High Command Murder. J. Rosenberger
High Commissioner. J. Cleary
High Corniche. D. Dodge
High Cost of Living. L. Hays
High Cost of Murder. H. Barron
High Crimes and Misdemeanors. J. Greenberg
High Crystal. M. Caidin
High Disaster. L. Derrick
High Dive. F. O'Rourke
High Doom. J. L. Morrissey
High Dudgeon. A. C. Frost
High Encounter. B. Wohl
High Explosive. N. Mapple
High Explosive. G. Phillips
High Fashion in Homicide. Carter Brown
High Game. P. Geddes
High Game. S. Horler
High Ground. C. Hastings
High Hand. J. Futrelle
High Hazard. S. Horler
High Hazard. R. M. Stern
High Heel Homicide. F. C. Davis
High Heels. M. Tripp
High Heels and Homicide. D. Reid
High Hostage. V. Maxwell
High Jacker. H. E. O. Whitman
High Jump. V. Gielgud
High Kill. P. Ordway
High-Minded Murder. C. Sykes
High Noon to High Noon. E. L. Long
High on a Hill. F. Y. McHugh
High Pastures. H. L. V. Fletcher
High Pavement. E. Bonett
High Place. G. Household
High Places. P. Ferris
High Red for Dead. W. L. Rohde
High Rendezvous. K. M. Knight
High Requiem. D. Cory
High Road to China. J. Cleary
High Road to Hell. H. L. Gates
High Roller. F. Du Boisgobey
High School Confidential. Morton Cooper
High School Mystery. R. St. Clair
High Seas Murder. P. Drax
High Season. E. Kyle
High Sheriff. Henry Wade
High Sierra. W. R. Burnett
High Slaughter. Jon Hart
High Speed. C. H. Stagg
High Spirits. N. Tranter
High Spy. R. Trevor
High Stakes. L. Dent
High Stakes. D. Francis
High Stakes. S. Horler
High Stakes. L. L. Lynch
High Stakes. C. Riess
High Street. C. Edwards
High Strung. J. Ellery
High Summer Homicide. A. Kirby
High Tension. E. H. Clements
High Tension. T. Du Bois
High Tension. Alex Fraser
High Terrace. V. Coffman
High Terror. I. A. Greenfield
High Tide. P. M. Hubbard
High Tide at Midnight. R. Cocking
High Tide for Hanging. G. Compton
High Tide Temptress. M. Brody
High Toby. H. B. M. Watson
High Treason. J. Bruce
High Treason. L. A. Knight
High Treason. A. Upward
High Valley. J. North
High Voltage. T. Chastain
High Walk to Wandlemere. P. Sibley
High Wall. B. Copper
High Wall. S. Truss
High Water at Four. J. Tickell
High Water Mark. R. Dowling
High Water Mark. F. Hume
High, Wide and Ransom. D. Tracy
High Wind in Brittany. C. Gayet
High Window. R. Chandler
High Wire. W. Haggard
High Wray. K. Hughes
High Yield in Death. Nick Carter
Highbinders. O. Bleeck
Higher Animals. H. E. F. Donohue
Higher They Fly. C. Hodder-Williams
"Highest References." F. Warden
Highflight to Hell. C. H. Wallace
Highgate Mystery. C. Kingston
Highgrade Murder. C. H. Snow
Highland Fire. A. Clements
Highland Fling. M. MacKintosh
Highland Gathering. J. Wood
Highland Homicide. J. Austwick
Highland Masquerade. M. Elgin
Highland Vengeance. A. Venters
Highly Inflammable. M. Saltmarsh
Highly Unsafe. M. Saltmarsh
Highway of Fear. Donald Moore
Highway Robber's Derby. F. Johnston
Highway Through Hell. C. Whiting

Highway to Hell. D. Forde
Highway to Murder. H. Howard
Highwayman. G. Rawlence
Highwayman's Daughter. K. A. Shoesmith
Highways of Death. H. Desmond
Hijack. E. Wellen
Hijack. L. White
Hijacked. D. Harper
Hijacker's Morgue. L. Mantz
Hijacking Manhattan. L. Derrick
Hiker's Secret. W. Edwards
Hilary. J. Jenkins
Hilary's Terms. H. Janson
Hilda, Take Heed. M. Halliday
Hilda Wade. G. Allen
Hildegarde Withers Makes the Scene. S. Palmer
Hill Fog. J. N. Chance
Hill Girl. C. Williams
Hill of Ashes. L. Ames
Hill of Riches. F. A. M. Webster
Hill of the Crows. F. Sleath
Hill of the Terrified Monk. G. Homes
Hill of the Wild Cat. Agnes Russell
Hillerway Letters. T. Cobb
Hilliare Henderson. N. Buntline
Hillman. E. P. Oppenheim
Hills of Fire. D. Daniels
Hills Sleep On. J. Cannan
Hills Were Higher Then. H. M. Kahler
Hilltop. J. Letton
Hilltop Murders. M. Baker
Hilma. W. T. Eldridge
Himalayan Assignment. V. W. Mason
Himalayan Concerto. J. Masters
Himmler Ploy. J. Semenov
Himself Again. R. E. Pickering
Hindoo Khan. M. J. Pemberton
Hinges of Hell. S. Sterling
Hint of Murder. N. Kent
Hippo's Coup. Sean Graham
Hippy Cult Murders. R. Stanley
Hire Me a Hearse. P. Marlowe
Hire Me a Rope. B. Sarto
Hire Purchase Crime. G. Chester
Hire-Purchase Fraud. W. Tyrer
Hired Girl. Mrs. C. Kernahan
Hired Girl's Millions. C. E. Blaney
Hired Target. W. Tucker
Hired Wife. Lynna Cooper
Hiroshima Reef. Eric Lambert
His Aunt Came Late. L. Meynell
His Beautiful Client. George Griffith
His Better Half. George Griffith
His Bones Are Coral. V. Canning
His Brother's Keeper. M. M. Bodkin
His Brother's Keeper. E. Phillpotts
His Burial Too. C. Aird
His Chinese Concubine. M. Dekobra
His Crooked Highness. K. Lindsay
His Cuban Sweetheart. R. H. Savage
His Dainty Whim. C. G. Mitford
His Darling Sin. M. E. Braddon
His Downward Path. Harry Mills
His Eminence, Death. Simon Quinn
His Evil Eye. H. I. Hancock
His Excellency, Governor Wallace. A. Wilson
His Excellency Regrets... H. Marchant
His Excellency's Secret. A. Murray
His Fabulous Fortune. Rupert Hughes
His Fatal Success. M. Bell
His Father's Crime. W. M. Graydon
His Father's Crime. E. P. Oppenheim
His Father's Ghost. Stratford Davis
His Father's Honour. D. C. Murray
His Father's Son. B. Matthews
His Father's Wife. D. Keene
His Final Choice. A. Applin
His First Affair. D. Walshe
His First Offense. J. S. Clouston
His Fortunate Foe. A. S. Arnold
His Foster Sister. Albert Ross
His Friend the Enemy. W. W. Cook
His Great Revenge. F. Du Boisgobey
His Greatest "Shadow." Old Sleuth
His Hand Betrays. P. Conway
His Helpmeet. F. Barrett
His Heritage. L. Gardiner
His Honor. C. E. Cleveland
His Kind of Woman. Michael Morgan
His Last Bow. A. C. Doyle
His Last Vow. J. Ruyle
His Lawful Wife. J. Middlemass
His Lordship the Crook. E. Louis
His Lordship the Judge. D. H. Landels
His Love or His Life. R. Marsh
"His Majesty." A. W. Marchmont
His Majesty—the Crook. Gwyn Evans
His Majesty's Peacock. W. A. MacKenzie
His Master's Voice. I. Litvinoff
His Mexican Wife. A. Applin
His Name Was Death. F. Brown
His Natural Life. M. Clarke
His Other Self. R. W. Cole
His Other Self. E. J. Goodman
His Own Accuser. S. Hocking
His Own Accuser. H. Townley
His Own Appointed Day. D. M. Devine
His Own Funeral. G. J. Barrett
His Own Ghost. D. C. Murray
His Own Law. F. Barrett

His Patients Died. C. Lillingston
His Prey Was Man. A. Gask
His Reverence the Rogue. H. Desmond
His Robe of Honor. E. Dorrance
His Royal Highness. George Hastings
His Secret. M. E. Braddon
His Silence. I. D. Hardy
His Son's Honour. J. W. Bobin
His Terrible Secret. C. E. Blaney
His Unknown Wife. L. Tracy
His Weight in Gold. M. Procter
His Wife's Revenge. G. R. Sims
His Wife's Soul. J. F. Molloy
Histoire des Treize. H. D. Balzac
Historic China. H. A. Giles
History of Edward Brown. E. C. Reed
Hit. R. Deming
Hit. B. Garfield
Hit and Run. J. Ashford
Hit and Run. J. Creasey
Hit and Run. R. Deming
Hit and Run. V. Kathrens
Hit and Run. Raymond Marshall
Hit and Run, Run, Run. A. Bodelsen
Hit It Rich. M. Bardsley
Hit Man. J. Fairburn
Hit Man. R. J. Flood
Hit Man. B. Rossi
Hit Me Hard. Neill Graham
Hit #29. Joey
Hit Squad. H. Kastle
Hit the Jackpot. Rick Madison
Hit Woman. G. Blumberg
Hitch in Time. C. Joyce
Hitchhike Killer. Paul Ross
Hitchhike to Hell. B. Grant
Hitchhiker. G. Simenon
Hitler Diamonds. D. Cory
Hitler Has Won. F. Mullally
Hitler Needs You. J. T. Story
Hive of Glass. E. Woodward
Hive of Glass. P. M. Hubbard
Hive of Suspects. S. Pim
Hoax. L. Lawrence
Hobgoblin Murder. K. C. Strahan
Hochmann Miniatures. R. L. Fish
Hodak. T. Pendleton
Hoffman Episode. J. Dell
Hoffman's Row. W. H. Carnahan
Hog Murders. W. L. DeAndrea
Hogdown Farm Mystery. M. Butcher
Hog's Back Mystery. F. W. Crofts
Holbein Mystery. A. Wynne
Holcroft Covenant. R. Ludlum
Hold Back the Night. D. Leslie
Hold Everything. D. Linton
Hold Out. E. Bruton
Hold That Tiger. D. Ambler
Hold-Up. Jack Davies
Hold-Up. W. F. Morris
Holden with the Cords. W. L. M. Jay
Hole and Corner. P. Wentworth
Hole and Corner Marriage. F. Warden
Hole in the Ground. Josephine Bell
Hole in the Ground. A. Garve
Hole in the Mountain. "Capstan"
Hole in the Vault. Nicholas Carter
Hole in the Wall. F. MacIsaac
Hole in the Wall. Arthur Morrison
Holes in the Wall. J. Bahr
Holiday Adventures of Mr. P. J. Davenant. F. S. Hamilton
Holiday Arrangement. Elizabeth Ford
Holiday at Half-Mast. J. J. Farjeon
Holiday Camp Murder. B. Francis
Holiday Camp Mystery. W. Tyrer
Holiday Express. J. J. Farjeon
Holiday for a Spy. B. Graeme
Holiday for Inspector West. J. Creasey
Holiday for Murder. A. Christie
Holiday Homicide. R. King
Holiday in a Manor House. E. Everett-Green
Holiday in Gaol. F. Martyn
Holiday of Fear. Gretchen Travis
Holiday with a Vengeance. Ritchie Perry
Holiday with Danger. E. Wilmot
Holiday with Murder. G. Carr
Holladay Case. B. E. Stevenson
Holland Suggestions. J. Dunning
Hollow. A. Christie
Hollow Ash Hall. M. Blount
Hollow Chest. A. Tilton
Hollow Crown Affair. D. McDaniel
Hollow House. U. Curtiss
Hollow Hub. K. West
Hollow Land. N. A. Temple-Ellis
Hollow Man. J. D. Carr
Hollow Man. J. Roeburt
Hollow Mountain. Alec Brown
Hollow Needle. G. H. Coxe
Hollow Needle. M. Leblanc
Hollow Sea. G. Jenkins
Hollow Shell. J. Farrimond
Hollow Skin. V. Swain
Hollow Stump Mystery. C. H. Snow
Hollow Sunday. R. Harling
Hollow Target. P. Bryers
Hollow Triumph. M. Forbes
Hollwood Mystery. Anonymous
Holly Ash. S. Youd
Hollywood and LeVine. A. Bergman

Hollywood Assassin. S. Jason
Hollywood Detective: Garrison. J. Rovin
Hollywood Detective: The Wolf. J. Rovin
Hollywood Gothic. T. Gifford
Hollywood Hit Man. V. Saxon
Hollywood Hoax. R. C. Frazer
Hollywood Love. A. M. Williamson
Hollywood Murder. P. B. Myers
Hollywood Murder Mystery. H. Crooken
Hollywood Mystery! B. Hecht
Holm Oaks. P. M. Hubbard
Holmes-Dracula File. F. Saberhagen
Holocaust. A. McCall
Holocaust Auction. P. Edwards
Holy Disorders. E. Crispin
Holy Father's Navy. P. Purser
Holy of Holies. Alan Williams
Holy Spirit. P. Leslie
Holy Terror. L. Charteris
Holy Terror. R. Sapir
Hombre from Sonora. W. Charles
Home and Murder. A. M. Stein
Home at Seven. R. C. Sherriff
Home for Stray Cats. J. Kirkpatrick
Home Guard Mystery. B. Cobb
Home in the Dark. W. Perry
Home Is the Hangman. R. Sale
Home Is the Heart. A. Meredith
Home Is the Hunter. J. Wainwright
Home Is the Prisoner. J. Potts
Home Is the Sailor. D. Keene
Home Is Where the Quick Is. William Johnston
Home of His Children. W. J. Bayfield
Home of Silence. L. T. Meade
Home of the Inquisitor. Maxine Reynolds
Home Secretary Affair. C. Franklin
Home Sweet Homicide. C. Rice
Home Sweet Homicide. Ann Reynolds
Home Sweet Homicide. J. T. Story
Home Through the Dark. Anthea Fraser
Home to Cypresswood. L. V. Stevens
Home to Our Valley. D. Lee
Home to Roost. A. Garve
Home to the Highlands. J. Eliot
Home to the Night. J. Thatcher
Home Town. G. Simenon
Homecoming. R. O'Neil
Homeward Tide. J. MacKenzie
Homeward Trail. G. Goodchild
Homicidal Colonel. R. Player
Homicidal Holiday. G. Brandon
Homicidal Horse. H. Pentecost
Homicidal Lady. D. Keene
Homicidal Spy. A. O. Pollard
Homicidal Virgin. B. Halliday
Homicide. M. Charlton
Homicide. L. T. White
Homicide at Saxondale. E. Wilmot
Homicide at Yuletide. H. Kane
Homicide Blonde. M. Procter
Homicide Blues. D. Reid
Homicide Call. S. A. Krasney
Homicide Club. Gwyn Evans
Homicide Dragnet. R. Marlowe
Homicide for Hannah. D. V. Babcock
Homicide Handicap. B. McKnight
Homicide Harem and Felon Angel. Carter Brown
Homicide Haven. J. V. Turner
Homicide Honeymoon. D. B. Hobart
Homicide Hotel. Joe Barry
Homicide House. D. Frome
Homicide Hoyden. Carter Brown
Homicide Hussy. A. McGuire
Homicide Is My Game. S. Marlowe
Homicide Johnny. S. Gould
Homicide Lost. W. Vance
Homicide Trinity. R. Stout
Homicide West. S. A. Krasney
Homicide with Charm. E. Ryley
Homicide Zone Four. N. Christian
Homing. J. Campbell
Honduras Double Cross. K. Edgar
Honest Crook. A. S. Roche
Honest Davie. F. Barrett
Honest Dealer. F. Gruber
Honest Lawyer. G. V. McFadden
Honest Reliable Corpse. G. Bagby
Honest Rogue. M. Park
Honesty Will Get You Nowhere. J. Sherwood
Honey Ain't So Sweet. M. Shane
Honey for Me. H. Janson
Honey for the Marshal. E. H. Clements
Honey Harlot. C. Brand
Honey, Here's Your Hearse! Carter Brown
Honey, Hold That Scream. T. Angelo
Honey in the Flesh. G. G. Fickling
Honey on Her Tail. G. G. Fickling
Honey Siege. G. Buhet
Honey Take My Gun. H. Janson
Honeybath's Haven. M. Innes
Honeycombers. J. Laing
Honeyfall. W. Searle
Honeymoon Caper. J. Pattinson
Honeymoon Hate. A. M. Williamson
Honeymoon in Shanghai. M. Dekobra
Honeymoon Killers. P. Buck
Honeymoon Murder. R. C. Finney
Honeymoon Mystery. J. Laurence
Honeymoon to Nowhere. A. Takagi

Title Index

Honeymoon with Death. H. Pentecost
Honeysuckle Rogue. R. M. Gilchrist
Honfleur Decision. A. Hunter
Hong Kong. Clayton Matthews
Hong Kong Aftermath. Wenzell Brown
Hong Kong Airbase Murders. V. W. Mason
Hong Kong Caper. Carter Brown
Hong Kong Incident. James Dark
Hong Kong Kill. Bryan Peters
Hong Kong Nightstop. N. Shore
Honky in the Woodpile. J. Brunner
Honolulu Murder Story. L. Ford
Honolulu Murders. L. Ford
Honolulu Snatch. M. Corrigan
Honolulu Story. L. Ford
Honor Legion. E. F. Droge
Honor of a Black Sheep. S. Campbell
Honor of the Name. E. Gaboriau
Honor Thy Godfather. T. P. Mulkeen
Honor Thy Godmother. R. T. Larkin
Honorable Gentleman and Others. A. Abdullah
Honorary Consul. G. Greene
Honour Among Thieves. H. C. Bailey
Honour Lost. E. V. De Fontmell
Honour of His House. F. M. White
Honour of Ravensholme. C. Stafford
Honour of the Family. P. Trent
Honour of Thieves. C. J. C. Hyne
Honourable Algernon Knox, Detective. E. P. Oppenheim
Honourable Assassins. Geoffrey Davison
Honourable Mister Death and other stories. S. Gluck
Honourable Mr. Tawnish. J. Farnol
Honourable Pursuit. P. Wynnton
Honourable Roger. C. A. Brandreth
Honourable Schoolboy. J. Le Carre
Hooch! C. F. Coe
Hood of Death. Nick Carter
Hooded Asp. J. A. McManis
Hooded Man. W. M. Duncan
Hooded Monster. W. S. Masterman
Hooded Raider. Donald Stuart
Hooded Riders. J. W. Bobin
Hooded Skull. P. Monnow
Hooded Snake. W. Phillips
Hooded Stranger. Harrington Strong
Hooded Vulture Murders. R. P. Koehler
Hoodlum. E. Lipsky
Hoodlum Alley. A. E. Ullman
Hoodlum Was a Honey. Carter Brown
Hoodlums. J. Eagle
Hoodmen's Bait. J. Bogar
Hoodoo Half-Back. F. W. Gumley
Hoods. H. Grey
Hoods Come Calling. N. Quarry
Hoods Incorporated. P. J. Andrews
Hoods Ride In. Wenzell Brown
Hoods Take Over. O. Demaris
Hoodwink. Robin Temple
Hook. D. J. Cleary
Hook, Line and Sinker. K. Nicholson
Hooker-Smash Operation. J. Rosenberger
Hookers Don't Go to Heaven. L. V. Roper
Hooky and the Crock of Gold. L. Meynell
Hooky and the Prancing Horse. L. Meynell
Hooky and the Villainous Chauffeur. L. Meynell
Hooky Gets the Wooden Spoon. L. Meynell
Hooky Goes to Blazes. L. Meynell
Hooligan. D. Dodge
Hooligan Nights. C. Rook
Hooligan's Rant. I. Blair
Hop Thief. O. Blakeston
Hope Strange Mystery. E. Short
Hope to Die. H. Waugh
Hopeless Case. E. Fawcett
Hopjoy Was Here. Colin Watson
Hopkinson and the Devil of Hate. P. McCutchan
Hopscotch. B. Garfield
Horace Steps Out. D. Whitelaw
Horatio and Camilla. Anonymous
Hordern Mystery. E. Finn
Hordes of the Red Butcher. G. Stockbridge
Horizon. Helen MacInnes
Horizontal Hold. R. R. Irvine
Horizontal Lieutenant. G. Cotler
Horizontal Man. H. Eustis
Horn. B. Flynn
Horn of Roland. Ellis Peters
Horned Cat. J. M. Cobban
Horned Owl. W. B. Cooke
Hornet's Nest. E. Bond
Hornet's Nest. B. Fischer
Hornet's Nest. J. R. Holden
Hornet's Nest. C. Landon
Hornets Nest. A. Soutar
Hornet's Nest. W. Woodrow
Horns for the Devil. L. Malley
Horns of Truth. T. B. Morris
Horrible Dummy and other stories. G. Kersh
Horrible Hat. R. Savage
Horrible Man. M. Avallone
Horrible Man in Heron's Wood. B. Cobb
Horrible Revenge. I. Crookenden
Horrid Mysteries. K. F. A. Grosse
Horror at Gull House. P. Brisco
Horror at the Hacienda. B. Y. Mosler

Horror at the Moated Mill. H. Desmond
Horror at Wardens Hall. C. Wogan
Horror Castle. R. Sharp
Horror Chambers of Jules de Grandin. Seabury Quinn
Horror Comes to Thripplands. G. Collins
Horror Expert. F. B. Long
Horror from the Tombs. F. Stevenson
Horror Hall. F. W. Irwin
Horror House. L. C. Douthwaite
Horror House. P. Warren
Horror House. C. Wells
Horror in the Dark. N. MacKenzie
Horror Medley. M. Hervey
Horror of the Juvenal Manse. K. Perkins
Horror on the Loch. D. Whitelaw
Horror on the Ruby X. F. Crane
Horror-7. R. Bloch
Horror Story. O. McNab
Horror's Head. S. Horler
Horrors of Oakendale Abbey. Mrs. Carver
Horrors of Smiling Manor. M. B. Gardner
Horse of Darius. J. Cartwright
Horse-Shoe Luck. W. C. Tuttle
Horse Under Water. L. Deighton
Horsehair Santa Claus and other stories. R. J. McLaughlin
Horsemen of Death. A. Wynne
Horsemen of the Law. F. F. Van De Water
Horses. J. Helvick
Horse's Head. E. Hunter
Horses of Winter. A. A. T. Davies
Horstmann Inheritance. B. Healey
Hospital Homicides. E. S. De Puy
Hospital Horror. O. O. Binder
Hospital Murders. Means Davis
Hospital Thief. T. A. Plummer
Hospitality for Murder. Gerard Fisher
Hospitality of Miss Tolliver and other stories. G. Kersh
Hospitality of the House. D. M. Disney
Host for Dying. P. Audemars
Host of Extras. J. Leasor
Hostage. P. Cave
Hostage. E. Garth
Hostage. Charles Henry
Hostage. S. Horler
Hostage. M. McShane
Hostage. Colin Mason
Hostage. R. Wilkes-Hunter
Hostage for a Hood. L. White
Hostage Heart. Gerald Green
Hostage in Illyria. C. Leonard
Hostage in Tokyo. G. DeVilliers
Hostage: London. G. Household
Hostage of Evil. W. Winthrop
Hostage of the Damned. P. A. Foxall
Hostage to Death. J. Ashford
Hostage to Death. H. Desmond
Hostage Tower. D. Denis
Hostages. George Fisher
Hostages. S. Heym
Hostages. C. Israel
Hostages. G. R. Lomas
Hostages. C. Stratton
Hostages of Hell. Ralph Hayes
Hostages to Fortune. M. E. Braddon
Hostages to Fortune. P. Conway
Hostess to Death. H. R. Wakefield
Hostess to Murder. E. S. Holding
Hostile Valley. B. A. Williams
Hostile Witness. J. Roffey
Hosts of Midian. P. Capon
Hosts of the Flaming Death. C. Steele
Hot. F. Lorenz
"Hot Air" Clew. Nicholas Carter
Hot and Cold. C. H. Ross
Hot As Fire, Cold As Ice. H. Whittington
Hot Blood—Cold Blood. J. W. Mason
Hot Body. M. Avallone
Hot Bullets for Love. G. Nyland
Hot Cargo. S. Coburn
Hot Cargo. G. H. Otis
Hot Chariot. J. M. Flynn
Hot Dam. N. MacNeil
Hot Dames—Cold Lead. C. Wheatley
Hot Dames Die Cold. B. Sarto
Hot Dames on Cold Slabs. M. Storm
Hot Day Hot Night. C. Himes
Hot Diary. H. J. Olmsted
Hot End of the Stick. A. Nuttall
Hot Fire. J. McKimmey
Hot-Foot. Bill Turner
Hot Freeze. Martin Brett
Hot Gold. F. MacIsaac
Hot Half-Million. R. Chapman
Hot House. H. Janson
Hot Ice. R. Angel
Hot Ice. R. J. Casey
Hot Ice. A. W. Clark
Hot Ice. H. Seymour
Hot Ice. R. D. Steeley
Hot Ice. S. Waldron
Hot-Line. J. Bruce
Hot Line. H. Janson
Hot Line—Capricorn. D. E. Mandeville
Hot Line for a Honey. M. Brody
Hot Mods. Garrity
Hot Oil. M. Carlton
Hot Oil. G. P. Putnam
Hot Pick-Up. J. T. Crawford
Hot Potato. R. Esser

Hot Prowl. H. D. Kastle
Hot Pursuit. L. Katcher
Hot Pursuit. Gavin Scott
Hot Rain. H. Portnoy
Hot Red Money. B. Kendrick
Hot Rock. D. E. Westlake
Hot Rod Gang Rumble. M. Dolinsky
Hot Season. G. Merrick
Hot Seat. D. Weir
Hot Seat for a Honey. Carter Brown
Hot Shot. D. Appell
Hot-Shot Rita. Griff
Hot Spot. M. Davidson
Hot Spot. C. Williams
Hot Stuff. S. Koperwas
Hot Summer Killing. J. Philips
Hot Swag. H. Kaner
Hot 30. J. Sakol
Hot Times. W. R. Cox
Hot Tip. J. Dolph
Hot Town. F. Malachy
Hot Type. M. Lipsyte
Hot Water. P. G. Wodehouse
Hot Wind from Hell. H. McCutcheon
Hotel Cremona Mystery. Gret Lane
Hotel de Luxe. Rona Randall
Hotel for Scandal. R. Lacroix
Hotel Geneva. J. Notley
Hotel Homicide. A. Parsons
Hotel Murders. S. Sterling
Hotel Richelieu Murders. A. Blackmon
Hotel Sinister. D. Whitelaw
Hotel X. W. LeQueux
Hotels with Empty Rooms. H. Gilbert
Hotshot. F. Flora
Hotspur. M. T. Walworth
Hotsy, You'll Be Chilled. H. Janson
Hound and the Fox and the Harper. S. Herron
Hound from the North. R. Cullum
Hound Island. Mountford Williams
Hound of Death. J. Corbett
Hound of Death and other stories. A. Christie
Hound of Heaven. J. D. White
Hound of Ireland. D. Byrne
Hound of the Baskervilles. A. C. Doyle
Hound of the Baskervilles. T. J. Kelly
Hound of the Baskervilles. F. A. Leslie
Hounded! M. Richmond
Hounded Down. D. Durham
Hounded Man. F. Carco
Hounded to Death. Nicholas Carter
Hounds. V. Coffman
Hounds and Jackals. Barbara Wood
Hounds Are Restless Tonight. L. T. Shortell
Hounds of Carvello. F. Cowen
Hounds of Justice. R. Forsythe
Hounds of Sparta. Barry Norman
Hounds of the Moon. E. O. Allen
Hounds of Vengeance. J. Creasey
Hound's Tooth. R. E. McDowell
Houndstooth. G. A. Ruse
Hour After Westerley. R. M. Coates
Hour Before Midnight. V. Johnston
Hour Before Midnight. J. Salisbury
Hour Before Moonrise. N. Buckingham
Hour Before Zero. S. Harvester
Hour-Glass. Winifred Duke
Hour-Glass Mystery. H. Hill
Hour-Glass to Eternity. M. Hastings
Hour Is Forever. E. H. Blackledge
Hour of Death. L. Morningstar
Hour of Destiny. M. Richmond
Hour of Evil. A. Grace
Hour of Maximum Danger. J. Barlow
Hour of Recognition. P. Quiroule
Hour of the Assassins. A. Kaplan
Hour of the Bishop. W. M. Duncan
Hour of the Blue Fox. H. C. McDonald
Hour of the Cat. J. De Weese
Hour of the Harp. Lynna Cooper
Hour of the Hyenas. J. Sherwood
Hour of the Oxrun Dead. C. L. Grant
Hour of the Wolf. Nick Carter
Hour of the Wolf. R. Charles
Hour of Truth. D. Egerton
Hour Struck. D. E. L. Patch
Hours After Midnight. J. Hayes
Hours Before Dawn. C. Fremlin
Hours to Kill. V. Curtiss
House Above Hollywood. V. Johnston
House Across the River. Josephine Bell
House Across the Park. Max Barrett
House Across the River. M. Bonham
House Across the Street. Nicholas Carter
House Across the Water. H. Bourne
House Across the Way. F. Daingerfield
House and the Tower. F. S. Smith
House at Ballyslane. C. E. R. Sinclair
House at Balnesmoor. H. C. Rae
House at Canterbury. F. Kent
House at Fern Canyon. W. D. Roberts
House at Gray Eagle. Elizabeth MacDonald
House at Hag's Curtain. P. Motte
House at Hawk's End. Claudette Nicole
House at Kilgallen. M. L. Roby
House at Landsdowne. C. Farr
House at Luxor. F. Stevenson
House at Norwood. W. P. Kelly
House at Parson's Landing. C. Connell

House at Pluck's Gutter. M. Coles
House at River's Bend. R. J. Jensen
House at Rose Point. Jan Alexander
House at Sandalwood. V. Coffman
House at Satan's Elbow. J. D. Carr
House at Serraville. R. Bagot
House at Swansea. A. Grace
House at the Corner. A. M. Meadows
House at the Crossroads. N. Bell
House at the Estuary. A. MacKenzie
House at Waterloo. E. S. Brooks
House at Windridge. E. A. Rife
House Behind the Mint. L. Huffman
House Between the Trees. J. Russell Lane
House-Boat Mystery. J. K. Leys
House by Exmoor. C. Stafford
House by the Way. J. Wetherell
House by the Bridge. M. G. Easton
House by the Bridge. Melissa Napier
House by the Canal. K. Hewitt
House by the Canal. G. Simenon
House by the Church-Yard. J. S. Le Fanu
House by the Common. T. Cobb
House by the Lake. Hugh Mills
House by the Lock. A. M. Williamson
House by the River. A. P. Herbert
House by the River. F. Warden
House by the Road. C. J. Dutton
House by the Sea. M. G. Eberhart
House by the Sea. H. B. Lowndes
House by the Tarn. R. Abbey
House Called Edenhythe. N. Buckingham
House Called Whispering Winds. M. M. Fletcher
House Cried Murder. F. Nash
House Dick. Gordon Davis
House for Sale. E. C. Vivian
House for Sale Haunted. J. Tobias
House in Belmont Square. M. Erskine
House in Brook Street. R. Cocking
House in Candle Square. P. Bennetts
House in Cavendish Square. D. Whitelaw
House in Charlton Crescent. A. Haynes
House in Gowderdale. T. Lang
House in Green Street. S. Horler
House in Harlem. M. S. Michel
House in Hook Street. M. Erskine
House in Lordship Lane. A. E. W. Mason
House in Marsh Road. L. Meynell
House in Munich. D. K. Dowdell
House in Naples. P. Rabe
House in Paris. D. Ward
House in Queen Anne Square. W. D. Lyell
House in Ralston Place. A. B. Moody
House in Sinister Lane. T. A. Plummer
House in Spitalfields. G. Wolfenden
House in Spite Street. W. M. Duncan
House in Spring Gardens. A. Griffiths
House in the Country. D. M. Low
House in the Crescent. A. Sergeant
House in the Fog. L. Geumlek
House in the Forest. M. Cumberland
House in the Hills. L. Meynell
House in the Hills. F. Warden
House in the Kasbah. Maxine Reynolds
House in the Mist. A. K. Green
House in the Shadows. C. McKnight
House in the Way. Colin Hope
House in the Wood. G. Chester
House in the Woods. J. Drummond
House in the Woods. L. Lance
House in Tuesday Market. J. S. Fletcher
House in White Mist. Melissa Napier
House Is Dark. Rebecca James
House Is Falling. N. Fitzgerald
House Is Just a House. J. Lindsay
House Malign. J. Wellsley
House Next Door. A. Askew
House Next Door. L. Rose
House Next Door. A. R. Siddons
House Next Door. B. E. Stevenson
House Next Door. L. White
House Nobody Lived In. R. Dumkey
House of a Thousand Candles. Meredith Nicholson
House of a Thousand Lanterns. V. Holt
House of Anna. A. J. Evans
House of Athena. Janice Bennett
House of Black Magic. L. T. Meade
House of Blight. Mrs. C. Kernahan
House of Brass. E. Queen
House of Broken Dolls. D. Daniels
House of Cain. S. Roberts
House of Cain. A. W. Upfield
House of Candles. P. Brisco
House of Cards. P. Cave
House of Cards. S. Ellin
House of Cards. H. Gartland
House of Cards. J. M. Ullman
House of Carson. A. Mallory
House of Cellars. G. H. Teed
House of Certain Death. B. Cossery
House of Clouds. H. L. Poole
House of Clystevill. B. Atkey
House of Cobwebs. M. Reisner
House of Counted Hatreds. S. Jennifer
House of Creeping Horror. G. F. Worts
House of Crimson Shadows. H. D. Stacpoole
House of Curtains. G. H. Teed
House of Dark Illusions. C. Farr
House of Dark Laughter. Melissa Napier

House of Dark Secrets. G. M. Allen
House of Dark Shadows. Marilyn Ross
House of Darkness. J. Hunter
House of Darkness. K. Laing
House of Darkness. A. MacKinnon
House of Darkness. J. Phillips
House of Deadly Calm. M. Farnsworth
House of Deadly Night. I. Barry
House of Dearth. V. MacClure
House of Death. E. J. Capocy
House of Death. C. Goodall
House of Death. L. Groc
House of Death. K. Robeson
House of Delusion. R. S. Holland
House of Destiny. C. Farr
House of Disappearance. J. J. Farjeon
House of Disappearance. C. K. Steele
House of Discord. M. E. Hanshew
House of Distant Voices. E. Bond
House of Dr. Edwardes. F. Beeding
House of Dogs. R. Elliott
House of Doom. Nicholas Carter
House of Doom. S. Wagner
House of Dread. R. Dorien
House of Echoes. John Marsh
House of Elnora Garland. W. Luttrell
House of En-Dor. A. Hocking
House of Eve. S. Somers
House of Evil. H. Clevely
House of Evil. W. LeQueux
House of Evil. C. Lipman
House of Evil. M. Lynch
House of Evil. J. Trinian
House of Evil Winds. M. J. Ragosta
House of Faith. M. G. Kiddy
House of False Faces. H. G. Weston
House of Fand. K. Troy
House of Fatal Mirrors. F. W. Gumley
House of Fear. Wadsworth Camp
House of Fear. M. Dalton
House of Fear. Jack Lewis
House of Fear. R. W. Service
"House of Fear." W. Spence
House of Fears. J. England
House of Fendon. R. Bridges
House of Flesh. B. Fischer
House of Fools. Jan Alexander
House of Fortune. M. Pemberton
House of Four Windows. D. Lyons
House of Fury. J. A. Creighton
House of Ghosts. L. H. Brooks
House of Ghosts. Marilyn Ross
House of Glass. G. Ferrand
House of Godwinsson. E. R. Punshon
House of Gold. Ann Anderson
"House of Greed." R. St. Clair
House of Green Turf. Ellis Peters
House of Haddon. L. Ames
House of Halliwell. H. Wood
House of Happy Mayhem. W. J. Sheldon
House of Hate. J. Bowman
House of Hate. J. E. Ferris
House of Hate. Dorothy Fletcher
House of Hate. H. Mace
House of Horror. M. Crombie
House of Horror. R. Halifax
House of Horror. T. C. H. Jacobs
House of Horror. N. MacKenzie
House of Horror. Donald Ross
House of Horrors. J. Reach
House of Illusion. N. Devon
House of Illusion. D. Quentin
House of Imposters. W. D. Roberts
House of Intrigue. L. Hoffman
House of Intrigue. Colin Robertson
House of Intrigue. A. Stringer
House of Intrigue. Percy White
House of Iron Men. Jack Steele
House of Jackals. S. Horler
House of Jeffreys. R. Thorndike
House of Lies. J. Audrenn
House of Lies. Austin Moore
House of Lies. S. Warwick
House of Living Death. T. Blore
House of Lyes. C. W. Whitaker
House of Mad Children. R. Timperley
House of Malory. H. McElroy
House of Mammon. F. M. White
House of Many Doors. D. Daniels
House of Many Mirrors. V. Hunt
House of Many Shadows. B. Michaels
House of Many Voices. B. Capes
House of Marney. J. Goodwin
House of Masks. Barbara Cooper
House of Masques. P. Kent
House of Men. C. Marchant
House of Menace. A. Furness
House of Merrilees. A. Marshall
House of Mirror Images. D. Winston
House of Moreys. P. Bentley
House of Murder. H. L. Gates
House of Murder. J. H. Wallis
House of Mystery. Will Irwin
House of Mystery. Hilary Lang
House of Mystery. R. Marsh
House of Mystery. W. J. Newton
House of Mystery. Grace M. White
House of Night. L. H. Gordon
House of Numbers. J. Finney
House of Ogilvie. Winifred Duke
House of Peril. M. B. Lowndes
House of Peril. L. Tracy

House of Rancour. S. Nichols
House of Ravensbourne. M. A. Gibbs
House of Retrogression. C. Patrick
House of Rhinestad. D. M. Parish
House of Rising Water. Melissa Napier
House of Rogues. C. B. Booth
House of Scorpio. P. Wallace
House of Scorpions. J. Sherman
House of Seclusion. M. Harvey
House of Secrets. E. Ames
House of Secrets. C. Farr
House of Secrets. S. Horler
House of Secrets. W. Martyn
House of Secrets. D. Noel
House of Secrets. S. Noel
House of Secrets. H. Peters
House of Secrets. H. L. Phillips
House of Secrets. J. Wellsley
House of Shade. M. Home
House of Shade. M. M. Kaye
House of Shadows. Marsha Alexander
House of Shadows. E. Bond
House of Shadows. J. J. Farjeon
House of Shadows. F. Hurd
House of Shadows. D. Martyn
House of Shadows. C. Randell
House of Shayle. John Alexander
House of Silence. C. Collins
House of Silence. D. Daniels
House of Silence. H. W. Jarvis
House of Silence. J. H. Robinson
House of Silence. G. H. Teed
House of Silence. L. Tracy
House of Silence. R. Trevor
House of Silence. C. N. Williamson
House of Sin. B. Sarto
House of Sin. H. Upward
House of Sinister Shadows. Cynthia Hyde
House of Sleep. Michael Burt
House of Sleep. Frank King
House of Soldiers. A. Garve
House of Sorcery. Carter Brown
House of Sorrows. F. M. White
House of Stolen Memories. D. Daniels
House of Storm. M. G. Eberhart
House of Storms. H. Bridges
House of Strange Guests. N. Brady
House of Strange Music. A. L. Thompson
House of Strange Victims. B. Atkey
House of Strangers. Jennifer Hale
House of Strangers. M. Padget
House of Sudden Sleep. J. Hawk
House of Tarot. R. C. Payes
House of Tears. E. Downey
House of Terror. E. Berckman
House of Terror. G. Biss
House of Terror. F. Swann
House of Terror. E. Woodward
House of the Apricots. H. Imber
House of the Arrow. A. E. W. Mason
House of the Bears. J. Creasey
House of the Black Ring. F. L. Pattee
House of the Cat. A. Roudybush
House of the Damned. A. M. Rud
House of the Dancing Dead. A. Vandergriff
House of the Darkest Death. A. Grace
House of the Dead Ones. J. N. Chance
House of the Deadly Nightshade. L. B. Long
House of the Enchantress. M. Erskine
House of the Fiery Cauldron. Alice Brennan
House of the Flashing Light. J. C. McMullen
House of the Four Winds. J. Buchan
House of the Fragrant Lotus. E. P. Thorne
House of the Hatchet and other tales of horror. R. Bloch
House of the Hawk. W. C. Tuttle
House of the Hunter. F. Taylor
House of the Lost. B. Gray
House of the Lost Court. M. D'Alpins
House of the Lost Court. D. T. De Savallo
House of the Lost Woman. Louise O'Flaherty
House of the Missing. S. Gluck
House of the Moving Room. J. J. Chichester
House of the Opal. Jackson Gregory
House of the Pines. J. Tempest
House of the Purple Stairs. J. Helm
House of the Secret. C. Farrere
House of the Seven Courts. D. Daniels
House of the Seven Flies. V. Canning
House of the Seven Keys. M. E. Hanshew
House of the Siren. J. Selborne
House of the Soul. J. B. Harris-Burland
House of the Spaniard. A. Behrend
House of the Strange Woman. M. Heath
House of the Sword. D. G. Browne
House of the Talisman. H. H. Ross
House of the Third Sense. L. Holt
House of the Three Ganders. I. A. Bacheller
House of the Twelve Caesars. P. Hastings
House of the Uneasy Dead. S. Horler
House of the Unicorn. L. Harper
House of the Vanishing Goblets. L. Edgley

Title Index

House of the Weeping Women. Coningsby Dawson
House of the Whispering Pines. A. K. Green
House of the Whispering Winds. E. McCrae
House of the White Shadows. B. L. Farjeon
House of the Wicked. W. LeQueux
House of the Winds. C. Hodge
House of the Winds. J. G. Sarasin
House of the Yellow Door. Nicholas Carter
House of Three Eagles. C. Miron
House of Tombs. C. Farr
House of Torment. C. R. Gull
House of Torture. L. C. Douthwaite
House of Tragedy. A. J. Fitzgerald
House of Treachery. C. Farr
House of Treason. D. Allan
House of Two Green Eyes. S. Chalmers
House of Two Wives. D. Locke
House of Tynian. George Walker
House of Valhalla. C. Farr
House of Vengeance. A. L. McAllister
House of Vengeance. R. St. Clair
House of Wailing Winds. W. M. Duncan
House of Whipplestaff. E. F. Boyd
House of Whispering Death. M. Farnsworth
House of Whispers. J. Baer
House of Whispers. Nicholas Carter
House of Whispers. W. A. Johnston
House of Whispers. W. LeQueux
House of Women. L. K. Scott
House of Wraith. E. J. Millward
House of Yesteryear. M. Lynch
House on Black Bayou. M. Sellars
House on Cabra. J. Wetherell
House on Charles Street. A. Burr
House on Cheyne Walk. P. Organ
House on Circus Hill. D. Daniels
House on Curtin Street. M. J. Ragosta
House on Doubloon Inlet. J. A. Dunn
House on Eagle Ledge. A. Mallet
House on Gannet's Point. C. Van Hazinga
House on Greenapple Road. H. R. Daniels
House on Hall Hill. D. Eden
House on K Street. L. White
House on Key Diablo. Jennifer Hale
House on Lily Street. J. Vance
House on Malador Street. P. Hastings
House on Mount Vernon Street. W. E. D. Ross
House on 9th Street. J. S. Strange
House on Q Street. R. Dietrich
House on Quai Notre Dame. G. Simenon
House on Rainbow Leap. R. M. Vale
House on Russian Hill. F. Hurd
House on Sixteenth Street. E. Thorne
House on Sky High Road. I. S. Way
House on Smith Square. A. Burr
House on Somber Lake. A. De Marquand
House on Telegraph Hill. D. Lyon
House on Washington Place. P. G. Demarest
House on the Bay. Arthur MacLean
House on the Beach. E. E. Cameron
House on the Beach. E. L. Withers
House on the Black Moor. D. Polk
House on the Broads. Wilfrid Robertson
House on the Cliff. G. Batson
House on the Cliff. L. Meynell
House on the Cliffs. G. Chester
House on the Cliffs. C. Farr
House on the Downs. G. E. Locke
House on the Drive. B. Kingsley
House on the Fen. C. Rayner
House on the Fens. C. Cookson
House on the Fens. A. Gask
House on the Hard. A. Wynne
House on the Hill. J. Drummond
House on the Hill. J. Whitehead
House on the Hudson. F. Powell
House on the Island. A. Gask
House on the Lake. J. Reach
House on the Left Bank. V. Johnston
House on the Mall. E. Jepson
House on the Marsh. J. J. Farjeon
House on the Marsh. H. R. Martin
House on the Marsh. F. Warden
House on the Moat. V. Coffman
House on the River. J. Drummond
House on the Rocks. T. Charles
House on the Roof. M. G. Eberhart
House on the Saltings. V. Bridges
House on the Strand. D. Du Maurier
House on the Thames. G. W. Appleton
House on Thunder Hill. S. Somers
House on Tollard Ridge. J. Rhode
House on Trevor Street. F. Hurd
House on Twyford Street. C. Gluyas
House on Vickers' Island. J. St. Clair
House on Wathmoor. M. Stephenson
House on Windswept Ridge. K. Kimbrough
House on Wolf Trail. Lanora Miller
House Opposite. J. J. Farjeon
House Opposite. E. Kent
House over Hell Valley. V. Subond
House over the Tunnel. J. J. Farjeon
House over the Way. A. W. Barrett
House Party Murder. Colin Ward
House Party Murders. E. A. Poe
House-Party Mystery. G. Norsworthy

House Possessed. C. Blackstock
House Possessed. L. Paige
House 'Round the Corner. Gorden Holmes
House-Surgeon. I. Jefferies
House Surgeon at Luke's. Rona Randall
House Terrible. A. Towner
House That Berry Built. D. Yates
House That Chak Built. K. West
House That Died. H. Bordeaux
House That Died. Josephine Gill
House That Fear Built. C. Knye
House That Hate Built. S. E. Mason
House That Hated People. V. Black
House That Samael Built. R. Jensen
House That Stood Still. A. E. Van Vogt
House That Waited. C. Reeve
House That Whispered. S. Emery
House Upstairs. C. Rodda
House with a Bad Name. P. P. Sheehan
House with a History. F. Warden
House with a Past. J. Courage
House with Black Blinds. H. Bridges
House with Blind Eyes. H. Jobson
House with Crooked Walls. B. Graeme
House with Green Shutters. A. R. Long
House with No Address. E. M. Channon
House with No Address. E. Nesbit
House with Steel Shutters. A. Parsons
House with Strange Secrets. A. E. Bayly
House with the Blue Door. H. Footner
House with the Double Moat. E. S. Brooks
House with the Green Shutters. George Douglas
House with the High Wall. A. Gask
House with the Light. S. Horler
House with the Myrtle Trees. Elizabeth Ford
House with the Red Blinds. T. C. Wignall
House with the Stained Glass Windows. Winston Graham
House with the Watching Eyes. N. A. Hintze
House with Two Faces. Sheila Bishop
House Without a Door. T. Sterling
House Without a Key. E. D. Biggers
House Without a Key. J. L. Latham
House Without the Door. E. Daly
House Without Windows. L. Constable
House Without Windows. R. Reich
Houseboat Enigma. R. R. Hillman
Houseboat Killings. R. Simons
Houseboat Mystery. J. Edwards
Household of Hertz. W. J. Newton
Household Skeleton. G. L. Aiken
Household Traitors. J. Blackburn
Householders. Margaret Henry
Housekeeper's Secret. H. Fielding
Houseparty. K. P. Britton
Houses of Glass. W. Lloyd
Housesitter. L. Karr
Housespy. M. Duffy
Housewife and the Assassin. S. Trott
Hovering Darkness. E. Berckman
How Are You, Johnnie? P. King
How Awful About Allan. H. Farrell
How Bad Can They Be? N. Leslie
How Betty Butted In. W. Spence
How Briggs Died. D. E. Harding
How Came He Dead? J. F. Molloy
How Cold the Night. B. Schwarz
How Could They? C. N. Boyle
How Dark Are the Dunes? C. Herbert
How Dead Can You Be? D. Linton
How Did Elmer Die? G. P. West
How Doth the Little Crocodile? P. Antony
How Evil the Word. H. G. Farrar
How Goes the Murder? E. Queen
How Good a Detective Are You? A. Ripley
How Hard to Kill. T. B. Dewey
How He Did It. E. A. Dupuy
How He Won Her. E. Southworth
How He Won Her, and A False Friend. G. Fleming
How I Became Eminent. J. Middlemass
How I Found a Five Pound Note and What Came of It. G. S. Jealous
How I Made a Million Dollars. A. F. Taylor
How Like an Angel. M. Millar
How Many Cards? I. Ostrander
How Many Coupons for a Shroud? N. Morland
How Many to Kill? M. Halliday
How Murder Speaks. R. S. Holland
How Now, McLean? G. Goodchild
How Sleeps the Beast. D. Tracy
How Slow the Snooth. C. Herbert
How Still My Love. D. Siegel
How Strange a Thing. Dorothy Bennett
How the Old Woman Got Home. M. P. Shiel
How to Kill a Man. T. Wells
How to Live Dangerously. Joan Fleming
How to Murder Your Wife. Henry Williams
How to Steal a Million. Michael Sinclair
How to Succeed at Business Spying by Trying. S. Mead
How to Succeed at Murder Without Really Trying. D. Von Elsner
How Tyson Came Home. W. H. Rideing
How Was It Done? Mark Cross
Howard Hughes Affair. S. M. Kaminsky
Howards of Saxondale. Rona Randall

Howling. G. Brandner
Howling II. G. Brandner
Howling Dog. R. Drayton
Howling in the Woods. V. Johnston
Hoxton Mystery. T. W. Hanshew
Hoyland Intervenes. P. C. Williams
Hoyland Steps Out. P. C. Williams
Hubberthwaite Horror. J. Austwick
Hubschmann Effect. T. P. McMahon
Huddersfield Job. Angus Ross
Huddle. C. Wells
Hue and Cry. T. B. Dewey
Hue and Cry. B. Hamilton
Hue and Cry. J. B. O'Sullivan
Hue and Cry. P. Wentworth
Hugger-Mugger in the Louvre. Elliot Paul
Human Bacillus. R. Eustace
Human Bloodhound. E. S. Brooks
Human Cat. Dick Stewart
Human Chase. E. P. Oppenheim
Human Element. J. Fores
Human Equation. C. E. Bowman
Human Factor. G. Greene
Human Factor. Simon Quinn
Human Fiend. Nicholas Carter
Human Mole. C. Collins
Human Nature. M. Leighton
Human Question Mark. Dick Stewart
Human Time Bomb. Nick Carter
Human Vampire. T. F. Elstow
Human Vultures. Roland Daniel
Humdrum House. M. Foster
Humming Box. H. Whittington
Humming Cliff. M. Tannock
Humming Precipice. M. Sheppard
Humming Top. D. Spicer
Humours and Oddities of the London Police Courts. Dogberry
Hump's First Case. R. Dennis
Hunch. R. Humphreys
Hunchback House. D. B. Hobart
Hunchback of Hatton Garden. G. Bowman
Hunchback of Hatton Garden! H. E. Hill
Hunchback of Soho. Roland Daniel
Hunchback of Westminster. W. LeQueux
Hundred Days. T. Mundy
Hundred-Dollar Girl. W. C. Gault
Hundred Per Cent. H. C. McNeile
Hundred Thousand Guineas. E. Jepson
Hundredth Acre. J. Campden
Hundredth Door. R. Foley
Hung by an Eyelash. L. Anson
Hung Until Dead. P. Johnson
Hung Up to Die. Martin Meyers
Hungarian Game. Roy Hayes
Hunger and other stories. C. Beaumont
Hunger and the Hate. H. V. Dixon
Hungering Shame. R. V. Cassill
Hungry Dog. F. Gruber
Hungry Goblin. J. D. Carr
Hungry Heart. H. B. Kaye
Hungry House. L. Lauferty
Hungry Killer. M. O'Brine
Hungry Killer. E. Radford
Hungry One. G. Brewer
Hungry Sea. L. Ames
Hungry Spider. S. Jepson
Hunslett's Yard. E. L. Long
Hunt. A. Alvarez
Hunt. W. Carrier
Hunt and Kill. R. T. Bickers
Hunt at Desolation. Michael Barrett
Hunt Ball Murder. F. W. Crofts
Hunt Ball Mystery. W. Magnay
Hunt Club. N. Daniels
Hunt for Danger. A. Curry
Hunt for Richard Thorpe. J. Tickell
Hunt in the Highlands. H. J. Wurr
Hunt Is Up. A. Hocking
Hunt the Body. P. Flower
Hunt the Evidence. R. Clifford
Hunt the Killer. D. Keene
Hunt the Lady! D. Reid
Hunt the Man. W. Pearson
Hunt the Man Down. W. Pearson
Hunt the Slipper. H. Cecil
Hunt the Spy. M. McKenna
Hunt the Toff. J. Creasey
Hunt the Tortoise. E. Ferrars
Hunt to Kill. M. Russell
Hunt with the Hounds. M. G. Eberhart
Hunted. G. F. Gibbs
Hunted. M. Hartmann
Hunted. E. Leonard
Hunted. M. Millard
Hunted! T. A. Plummer
Hunted. M. Reisner
Hunted. Jeremy Scott
Hunted and Haunted. I. Stark
Hunted Down. C. Dickens
Hunted Down. M. Hillary
Hunted Down. J. M'Govan
Hunted Down. R. H. Rohde
Hunted Down. R. A. Wainwright
Hunted Man. W. S. Masterman
Hunted to Death. W. S. Hayward
Hunted Woman. M. Albrand
Hunted Woman. J. Pendower
Hunter. R. Holland
Hunter. R. Stark
Hunter and the Trapped. Josephine Bell

Hunter at Large. T. B. Dewey
Hunter for Hire. W. Spann
Hunter Hunted. Ken Blake
Hunter Hunted. H. Treece
Hunter, Hunter, Get Your Gun. D. Macomber
Hunter in the Dark. E. Thompson
Hunter in the Shadows. Jennie Melville
Hunter Is the Hunted. A. B. Cunningham
Hunter-Killer. G. Jenkins
Hunter of Men. Nicholas Carter
Hunter of Men. C. H. Guenter
Hunter of the Blood. W. Masterson
Hunters. J. Ambler
Hunters. Peter Hill
Hunters. Clark Howard
Hunters and the Hunted. L. Egan
Hunter's Blood. J. Cunningham
Hunter's Green. P. A. Whitney
Hunter's Mate. J. Blackmore
Hunter's Moon. N. Benchley
Hunters of Humans. V. M. Steele
Hunters Point. G. Sims
Hunter's Walk. Ted Hart
Hunter's Way. C. Reeve
Hunterstone Outrage. S. Truss
Hunting for Gold. H. Nisbet
Hunting-Ground. F. Clifford
Hunting Ground. M. Sutherland
Hunting of Hillary. E. Winch
Hunting Party. G. Landers
Hunting Party. J. Millard
Hunting Shack. G. Landers
Huntingtower. J. Buchan
Huntress. H. Footner
Huntress. Williams Forrest
Huntress. C. C. Lowis
Huntress. M. A. Wilson
Huntress Is Dead. B. Benson
Huntress of Death. S. Horler
Huntsman. G. Verner
Hurricane. J. D. MacDonald
Hurricane Drift. J. N. Chance
Hurricane House. R. St. Clair
Hurricane Island. H. B. M. Watson
Hurricane Tex. G. Goodchild
Hurricane Wake. R. Ashe
Hurricane Warning! Richard Williams
Hurricane Williams' Vengeance. Gordon Young
Hurry the Darkness. M. Procter
Hurrying Feet. F. F. Van De Water
Hurt Me No More. I. Batista-Olivieri
Hurton Treasure Mystery. F. Hume
Husband. V. Caspary
Husband and Wife. M. Leighton
Husband of the Corpse. M. Judd
Husband's Secret. R. Dowling
Husband's Story. N. Collins
Hush-a-Bye Murder. David Alexander
Hush, Gabriel! V. P. Johns
Hush Hush Johnson. N. Gates
Hush-Hush Murder. A. Murphy
Hush-Hush Murders. M. T. Yates
Hush, It's a Game. P. Carlon
Hush Money. P. Israel
Hush Money. J. Middlemass
Hushed Up! W. LeQueux
Hushed Up at German Headquarters. W. LeQueux
Husky Voice. Roland Daniel
Hustle. S. Shagan
Hustle into Death. S. Arroyo
Hustler Paul. J. Cleveland
Hustlers. C. Megahy
Hustlers. Sam Ross
Hut. L. Meynell
Hyacinth Spell. F. Y. McHugh
Hyde Park Corner. W. Hackett
Hyde Place. V. Coffman
Hydra Conspiracy. P. Kirk
Hydra Head. C. Fuentes
Hydra-Head. S. Noel
Hydra Monster. L. Falk
Hydra with Six Heads. Josephine Bell
Hymn Tune Mystery. G. A. Birmingham
Hypnotic Death. P. Valdez
Hypnotic Demon. M. E. Cooke
Hypnotist Detective. Anonymous
Hypnotist of Hilary Mansion. Susan James
Hypnotized. M. Brandon
Hypocrite. C. R. Gull

I Accuse. C. Kingston
I Am a Smuggler. C. Evelyn
I Am Afraid. E. K. Lobaugh
I Am Being Poisoned. L. Phraile
I Am Death. R. Conner
I Am Death. G. Verner
I Am Gabriella! A. Maybury
I Am Jonathan Scrivener. C. Houghton
I Am Maud Latimer. J. Shard
I Am Saxon Ashe. S. Ashe
I Am the Captain. G. Hackforth-Jones
I Am the Cat. R. Kutak
I Am the Withered Man. N. Deane
"I, and I Alone." J. Weidman

I and My True Love. Helen MacInnes
I Came to a Castle. V. Johnston
I Came to Kill. Gordon Davis
I Came to the Highlands. V. Johnston
I Can Cope. M. Cronin
"I Can't Die Here." J. C. Nolan
I Can't Stop Running. E. Ronns
I Charge You Both. A. M. Meadows
I Come to Kill You. B. Halliday
I Confess. J. M. Simmel
I Could a Tale Unfold. D. Whitelaw
I Could Be Good to You. C. Keppel
I Could Have Died. G. Bagby
I Could Murder Her. E. C. R. Lorac
I Crown Thee King. M. Pemberton
I.D.B. E. W. T.
I.D.B. in South Africa. L. V. Sheldon
I Did It! Garret Smith
I Did Not Kill Osborne. V. Bridges
I Die Possessed. J. B. O'Sullivan
I Die Slowly. K. Millar
I Don't Die Easy. R. Drayton
I Don't Get It. Spike Gordon
I Don't Get It. Griff
I Don't Like Cats. L. Anson
I Don't Scare Easy. B. Dougall
I Don't Scare Easy. M. Hampton
I Escape. J. L. Hardy
I Fear the Greeks. A. M. Stein
I Fear You Not. B. Kerr
I Fell Among Thieves. B. Cobb
I for Intrigue. H. Janson
"I Forbid the Banns." F. Frankfort Moore
I Found Him Dead. G. Gallagher
I Gave at the Office. D. E. Westlake
I Get What I Want. Larry Heller
I Had to Kill Her. E. Connell
I Hardly Knew You. E. O'Brien
I Hate Actors! B. Hecht
I Hate Blondes. W. Kaufman
I Hate You to Death. K. Edgar
I Have Gloria Kirby. R. Himmel
I Have Killed a Man! C. F. Gregg
I Heard the Death Bell. C. M. Russell
I Hide, We Seek. R. M. Stern
I Hold the Four Aces. J. H. Chase
I Keep My Word. J. M. Scott
I, Keturah. R. Wolff
I Kill 'Em Inch by Inch. B. Sarto
I Killed Stalin. S. Noel
I Killed the Count. Alec Coppel
I Knew MacBean. M. Erskine
I Knew Mrs. Lang. G. Barnett
I Know a Secret. P. Hambledon
I Know My Love. F. Nichols
I Know What It's Like to Die. Jonathan Ross
I Know What You Did Last Summer. Lois Duncan
"I.L.F." D. Dallas
I Let Him Go. J. Brophy
I Like a Good Murder. M. Magill
I Like Danger. M. Corrigan
I Like 'Em Tough. C. Cannon
I Like It Cool. Michael Lawrence
I Like It Tough. J. A. Howard
I Love, I Kill. J. Bingham
I Love You Again. O. R. Cohen
I, Lucifer. P. O'Donnell
I Married a Dead Man. W. Irish
I Married a Doctor. Rona Randall
I Married Mr. Richardson. J. Ames
I Met a Man. M. Blankfort
I Met Murder. S. Jepson
I Met Murder on the Way. C. Blackstock
I Met Murder on the Way. M. Echard
I Never Killed. Max Gordon
I Never Miss Twice. B. Cobb
I.O.U. Murder. T. B. Dewey
I.O.U.—Murder. W. Francis
I Prefer Murder. B. Norton
I Said I Was Sorry. M. Dines
"I" Said the Demon. G. Baxt
I, Said the Fly. E. Ferrars
I, Said the Spy. D. Lambert
I, Savaran! D. Newton
I Saw Him Die. June Drummond
I Saw Murder. G. Cobden
I Saw Three Ships, and other winter's tales. Q
I Say "No". W. Collins
I See Red. S. Noel
I See You. C. Armstrong
I Shall Avenge. J. Robb
I, Sherlock Holmes. M. Harrison
I Should Have Sold Petunias. D. Honig
I Should Have Stayed Home. H. McCoy
I Sit in Hanger Lane. J. T. Story
I Smell the Devil. C. Magoon
I Spit on Your Grave. Griff
I Spit on Your Grave. Vernon Sullivan
I Spy. N. S. Lincoln
I, Spy. D. MacKenzie
I Spy. K. Medusa
I, Spy. S. Stone
I Spy. J. Tiger
I Start Counting. A. E. Lindop
I Stood in the Shadow of the Black Cap. J. Budd
I Take This Stranger. P. Warren
I Take This Woman. G. Simenon
I Thank a Fool. A. E. Lindop

I, the Criminal. D. Sharp
I, the Executioner. S. Ransome
I, the Hangman. W. A. Ballinger
I, the Jury. M. Spillane
I Thought I'd Die. D. V. Reed
I, Victoria Strange. R. Willock
I Wake Screaming. B. Shannon
I Wake Up Screaming. S. Fisher
I Want a Policeman! R. King
I Want Out. T. Thomey
I Want to Be a Lady. M. Foster
I Want to Go Home. R. Lockridge
I Want to Live. T. Rawson
I Wanted the Killer. A. Howe
I Wanted to Murder. C. F. Cushman
I Was a Spy in Britain. G. Usher
I Was Alone. K. David
I Was Following This Girl. D. Skirrow
I Was Going Anyway. R. Switzer
I Was Murdered. M. E. Longman
I Was Murdered. G. M. Wilson
I Was Walking Down Below. T. Gates
I Will Speak Daggers. M. Procter
I Wonder What Happened to Tom? B. Reade
I Would Rather Stay Poor. J. H. Chase
I Wouldn't Be in Your Shoes. W. Irish
Ibiza Syndicate. B. Reade
Icarus. P. Way
Ice. J. Follett
Ice-Axe Murders. G. Carr
Ice Before Killing. M. Strobel
Ice Bomb Zero. Nick Carter
Ice-Cold in Alex. C. Landon
Ice Cold in Ermine. Carter Brown
Ice-Cold Nude. Carter Brown
Ice Forest. V. Coffman
Ice Goddess. P. Edwards
Ice in the Bedroom. P. G. Wodehouse
Ice in the Sun. D. Enefer
Ice Maiden. J. Vicary
Ice Maidens. J. N. Chance
Ice Man. W. L. Morgan
Ice Pilot. H. Leverage
Ice Pond Mystery. J. Kipley
Ice Station Zebra. Alistair MacLean
Ice Trap. D. Haysom
Ice Trap Terror. Nick Carter
Iceberg. C. Cussler
Icepick. F. Scarpetta
Icepick in Ollie Birk. E. Sudak
Icepick in the Spine. F. Scarpetta
Iceworld. H. Clement
Icing of Balthazar. J. Goldsmith
I'd Crowns Resign. J. M. Cobban
Identical Strangers. V. Hawthorne
Identification Parade. P. N. Walker
Identity. Winifred Graham
Identity Crisis. L. Latham
Identity Trap. I. Lambot
Identity Unknown. T. C. H. Jacobs
Identity Unknown. Lorena
Identity Unknown. R. Marlowe
Identity Unwanted. Jean Marsh
Ides of March Conspiracy. Clyde Matthews
Ides of November. F. Stevenson
Idle Island. E. Hueston
Idol Hunter. B. Unsworth
Idol of Last Chance. Anonymous
Idol of the Blind. T. Gallon
Idol of the Town. W. LeQueux
Idols. R. DeNavery
Idol's Eye. H. E. Hill
If a Body. G. W. Yates
If a Body Kill a Body. P. Mortimer
If a Body Meet a Body. P. Clapp
If a Body Meet a Body. G. Malcolm-Smith
If Anything Happens to Hester. Anthony Morton
If Anything Should Happen. Kevin O'Hara
If Anything Should Happen to Me. A. Barker
If Death Ever Slept. R. Stout
If Dying Was All. R. Goulart
If Hate Could Kill. J. Bradley
If I Die Before I Wake. Sherwood King
If I Die—It's Murder. M. Ervin
If I Don't Tell. D. Olson
If I Kill Him. J. Hawkins
If I Knew What I Was Doing. Albert Ross
If I Live to Dine. H. Waugh
If I Should Die. P. Bannon
If I Should Die Before I Wake. W. Irish
If I Should Lose You. M. Richmond
If I Should Murder. P. Laing
If It Please You. Richard Marsh
If Laurel Shot Hardy the World Would End. S. Forbes
If Love Be Ours. K. Lindsay
If Murder Interferes with Business. A. Spiller
If She Should Die. M. L. Roby
If She Should Die. F. Rydell
If Sinners Entice Thee. W. LeQueux
If the Coffin Fits. D. Keene
If the Price Is Right. W. Newton
If the Reaper Ride. Elizabeth Norman
If the Shoe Fits. Lee Roberts
If the Shroud Fits. P. Kruger
If the Shroud Fits. K. Roos
If They Fall—. V. MacClure
If This Be Murder. R. Darby
If This Be Treason. M. Echard

Title Index

If Two of Them Are Dead. S. Forbes
If Two of Them Are Dead. M. Gregory
If Wishes Were Hearses. J. H. Bond
If Wishes Were Hearses. G. Cullingford
If You Can't Be Good. E. Cannon
If You Can't Be Good. Ross Thomas
If You Have Tears. John Evans
If You Should Ever Need Me. B. Treynor
If You Want a Murder Well Done. M. Scherf
If You Want to See Your Wife Again. John Craig
If Your Cover Is Blown. J. Browning
Ilene, the Superstitious. K. Kimbrough
Ilion Like a Mist. J. Mitchell
I'll Always Remember. M. Richmond
I'll Be Glad When You're Dead. D. Lyon
I'll Be Judge, I'll Be Jury. E. Hely
I'll Be Judge, I'll Be Jury. M. Kennedy
I'll Blackmail the World. A. Wood
I'll Bring Her Back. P. Cheyney
I'll Bury My Dead. J. H. Chase
I'll Come Quietly. T. McCoy
Ill Deeds Done. A. Hocking
I'll Die for You. S. Ransome
I'll Die Tonight. J. Laffin
I'll Die Too Soon. D. Boyce
I'll Do Anything. D. Bateson
I'll Eat You Last. H. C. Branson
I'll Find You. R. Himmel
I'll Fix You. H. Ellson
I'll Fry Yet. R. Angel
I'll Get By. B. Sarto
I'll Get Mine. Thurston Scott
I'll Get You for This. J. H. Chase
I'll Get You Yet. J. A. Howard
I'll Go Anywhere. D. Bateson
Ill Gotten Gains. A. Murray
I'll Grind Their Bones. T. Roscoe
I'll Hate Myself in the Morning, and Summer in December. Elliot Paul
I'll Kill You Last. H. C. Branson
I'll Kill You Next! Adam Knight
Ill Met by a Fish Shop on George Street. M. McShane
Ill Met by Moonlight. L. Ford
Ill Met in Mexico. C. M. Russell
I'll Never Leave You. E. Lustgarten
I'll Never Let You Go. F. Nichols
I'll Never Like Friday Again. S. Maddock
I'll Never Tell. Roy Vickers
I'll Say She Does! P. Cheyney
I'll See You In Hell. J. McPartland
I'll Sing at Your Funeral. H. Pentecost
I'll Sing You the Death of Bill Brown. B. Dexter
I'll Take What's Mine. N. Jones
I'll Tell You Everything. J. B. Priestley
Ill-Tempered Clavicord. S. J. Perelman
Ill Wind. H. Brinton
Ill Wind. R. Fenisong
Ill Wind. M. Fitt
Ill Wind. W. L. Heath
Ill Wind Contract. P. Atlee
Illegal Entry. R. Bernard
Illegal Tender. D. M. Devine
Illegal Tender. E. C. Vicar
Illegitimate Spy. R. Silverwood
Illicit Cargo. R. Lacroix
Illusion. F. Keinzley
Illusion at Haven's Edge. D. Daniels
Illusionist. S. D. Frances
Illustrious Corpse. T. Thayer
Illustrious Prince. E. P. Oppenheim
I'm Afraid I'll Live! K. S. Cole
I'm Cannon—for Hire. C. Cannon
I'm King of the Castle. Susan Hill
I'm No Hero. H. Howard
I'm No Murderer. B. Perowne
I'm Trying to Give It Up. D. Skirrow
I'm Waiting. S. Rsse
Image. C. Paul
Image in the Dust. Warwick Scott
Image in the Mirror. D. L. Sayers
Image Killer. W. Maner
Image Maker. P. Hastings
Image Makers. B. V. Dryer
Image of a Ghost. D. Daniels
Image of a Murder. P. Capon
Image of Evil. R. A. Crawford
Image of Hell. S. Fisher
Image of Man. M. Tripp
Image of Stephanie. S. Sloan
Image of the Beast. P. J. Farmer
Image of Truth. S. Somers
Image Seller. K. Ostrander
Images of Han. J. M. Walsh
Images of Rose. Anna Gilbert
Imagine a Man. N. Fitzgerald
Imagine a Man in a Box. H. R. Wakefield
Imbroglio. R. O. Collin
Imitation Thieves. M. Lovell
Immaculate Murders. K. Brooks
Immaterial Murder Case. J. Symons
Immediate Jewel. A. Applin
Immoralist. A. Gide
Immortal Dawn. R. Bridges
Immortals of the Mountain. C. V. Gheorghiu
Impact. B. Copper
Impact. H. Olesker

Impact of Evidence. C. Carnac
Impact-20. W. F. Nolan
Impartial Eye. P. Boulle
Impeached! B. Graeme
Impeccable People. Elizabeth Fenwick
Impending Sword. H. A. Vachell
Impending Sword. E. Yates
"Impenetrable Mystery" of Zora Burns. Anonymous
Imperfect Alibi. H. Hervey
Imperfect Crime. B. Graeme
Imperfect Lover. R. Gore-Brown
Imperfect Lover. A. Soutar
Imperial Blue. E. Bond
Imperial Marriage. A. W. Marchmont
Imperial 109. R. Doyle
Imperial Treasure. V. Gielgud
Impersonators. E. S. Brooks
Impetuous Mistress. G. H. Coxe
Implacable Hunter. G. Kersh
Implied Immunity. D. F. Holmes
Implosion. J. Montgomerie
Implosion Effect. G. Paulsen
Import of Evil. J. N. Chance
Importance of Being Murdered. C. Wells
Important Man and others. W. P. Ridge
Impossible Apollo. T. Cobb
Impossible Crime. E. C. Vivian
Impossible Dream. L. Hoffman
Impossible Guest. J. J. Farjeon
Impossible Husband. F. Warden
Impossible Lover. B. Bolt
Impossible Spy. K. Carr
Impossible Virgin. P. O'Donnell
Impossibles. Mark Phillips
Imposter. W. H. Baker
Imposter. M. Cumberland
Imposter. J. Jakes
Imposter. E. Keeley
Imposter. H. McCloy
Imposter. K. Steel
Imposter. D. Whitelaw
Imprint. Michael Bradley
Improbable Fiction. Sara Woods
Impromptu Imposter. V. Vicas
Impulse. I. Ostrander
In a Bad Man's Grip. S. Warwick
In a Dark Time. J. Watson
In a Deadly Vein. M. Culpan
In a Deadly Vein. B. Halliday
In a Fair Ground. L. G. Moberly
In a Glass Darkly. J. Caird
In a Glass Darkly. J. S. Le Fanu
In a House Unknown. D. Hitchens
In a Little House. T. Gallon
In a Lonely Place. D. B. Hughes
In a Silver Sea. B. L. Farjeon
In a Telephone Cabinet. G. D. H. Cole
In a Vain Shadow. Raymond Marshall
In a Vanishing Room. R. Colby
In a Wild Sanctuary. William Harrison
In Accordance with the Evidence. O. Onions
In After Years. J. K. Stafford
In All Shades. G. Allen
In All Simplicity. P. Capon
In an Alpine Valley. G. M. Fenn
In an Ancient Mirror. H. Flowerdew
In an Iron Grip. L. T. Meade
In and Out. Edgar Franklin
In Another Man's Shoes. M. L. Eades
In Any Case. R. G. Stern
In at the Death. F. Duncan
In at the Death. D. Frome
In at the Death. G. F. Underhill
In at the Kill. E. Ferrars
In at the Kill. B. Knox
In at the Kill. E. McDowell
In Bad with Sinbad. A. Stringer
In Barracks and Wigwam. W. M. Graydon
In-Between Spy. P. Fuller
In Black & Whitey. E. Lacy
In Brighton Waters. G. Volk
In Camera. John Gloag
In Camera. C. G. Mitford
In Case of Emergency. G. Simenon
In Chinatown. T. Burke
In Cold Blood. G. Bagby
In Cold Blood. T. Capote
In Cold Blood. A. Livingston
In Cold Pursuit. U. Curtiss
In Comes Death. P. Whelton
In Connection with Kilshaw. P. Driscoll
In Council Rooms Apart. John Craig
In Court. F. Andreas
In Crime's Disguise. F. C. Milford
In Cupid's Wars. C. Gibbon
In Dark Places. J. Russell
In Darkest Madras. H. E. Hill
In Deadly Peril. E. Gaboriau
In Deadly Peril. D. Lechmere
In Death's Grip. Nicholas Carter
In Deep. D. Kyle
In Deep Abyss. G. Ohnet
In Deep Water. M. Richmond
In Defense of Mrs. Maxon. G. A. Chamberlain
In Direst Peril. D. C. Murray
In Double Disguise. W. M. Graydon
In Enemy Hands. R. Sapir
In Extremis. Mrs. Greenough
In Face of the Verdict. J. Rhode

In False Attire. G. Norway
In Fear of a Woman. Winifred Graham
In Fear of the Hangman. M. Richmond
In Fear of the Night. H. Desmond
In Fort and Prison. W. M. Graydon
In Friendship's Guise. W. M. Graydon
In Full Commission. E. L. Long
In Full Cry. J. Goodwin
In Full Cry. R. Marsh
In Garde We Trust. J. La Plante
In God's Good Time. M. Leighton
In Great Danger. N. MacKenzie
In Great Waters. M. E. Braddon
In Her Own Right. J. R. Scott
In High Places. M. E. Braddon
In His Blood. H. R. Daniels
In His Grip. D. C. Murray
In Honour Bound. C. Gibbon
In Hot Blood. M. B. Cook
In Hot Pursuit. N. Cay
In Jeopardy. V. Sutphen
In Jeopardy, and other stories of peril. G. M. Fenn
In Lands of Terror. D. Lenton
In-Laws. D. Rogers
In League with Counterfeiters. E. C. Derby
In League with Satan. I. Stark
In Letters of Fire. Nicholas Carter
In Like Flint. B. Street
In London's Heart. G. R. Sims
In Love and War. C. Gibbon
In Lovers' Lane. A. Askew
In Loving Memory. Emma Page
In Male Attire. J. Hutton
In Market Overt. J. Payn
In Memory of Murder. D. Hawkins
In Memory of Sarah Bailey. Louise Cooper
In Mid-Atlantic. B. Delannoy
In Minden Town. M. A. Curtois
In Muffled Night. D. E. Muir
In My Enemy's Arms. R. T. Stevens
In My Father's Den. M. Gee
In Pastures Green and other stories. C. Gibbon
In Peril of His Life. G. D. H. Cole
In Peril of His Life. E. Gaboriau
In Pursuit of a Million. F. Marlowe
In Pursuit of Evil. Hugh Mills
In Queer Quarters. Nicholas Carter
In Queer Street. F. Hume
In re Sherlock Holmes. A. Derleth
In Record Time. Nicholas Carter
In Satan's Bonds. C. E. Perry
In Savage Hayti. R. C. Armour
In Savage Surrender. W. Chambers
In Scarlet and Plain Clothes. T. M. Longstreth
In Search of a Villain. R. Gore-Brown
In Search of Emily Crew. A. Furness
In Search of Himself. Nicholas Carter
In Search of Stephanie. K. Rhodes
In Search of Sybil. Magali
In Secret. R. W. Chambers
In Secret. W. LeQueux
In Secret Places. S. Truss
In Secret Service. J. Rosmer
In Shadows of Desire. James Stevens
In Sheep's Clothing. H. Nisbet
In Sickness and in Health. R. Rendell
In Sin or Folly? A. Nestorien
In Spite of Thunder. J. D. Carr
In Spite of the Czar. G. Boothby
In Storm and Strife. J. Middlemass
In Strange Company. G. Boothby
In Strange Shoes. A. Askew
In Such a Night... V. Gielgud
In Suspicion's Shadow. Nicholas Carter
In Terror's Grasp. Warren Miller
In the Absence of a Body. G. Bromley
In the Absence of Mrs. Peterson. N. Balchin
In the Balance. P. Wentworth
In the Beginning. P. O'Donnell
In the Best Families. R. Stout
In the Blood. L. Lamensdurf
In the Blood. A. Soutar
In the Bride's Mirror. M. Turnbull
In the Brooding Wild. R. Cullum
In the Cause of Freedom. A. W. Marchmont
In the Clutch of the Law. J. K. Stafford
In the Dark. S. Horler
In the Dark. D. Richberg
In the Dark Night. M. P. Hood
In the Days of Marlborough. George Long
In the Dead of Night. Mark Cross
In the Dead of Night. J. T. MacIntyre
In the Dead of Night. T. W. Speight
In the Dead of the Night. M. L. Roby
In the Death of a Man. L. Egan
In the Dentist's Chair. A. Armstrong
In the Depths of the First Degree. J. Doran
In the Distance. G. P. Lathrop
In the Emperor's Villa. R. H. Savage
In the Esbekieyeh Gardens, and other stories. R. H. Savage
In the Event of My Death. H. Bourne
In the Eye of the Law. L. Hagen
In the Eye of the Law. W. D. Lyell
In the Face of Evidence. Nicholas Carter

In the Face of Night. D. Donovan
In the Face of the Verdict. J. Rhode
In the First Degree. R. Scarlett
In the Flashlight. O. Binns
In the Fog. R. H. Davis
In the Force. Anonymous
In the Force. B. Hemyng
In the Frame. D. Francis
In the Gloom of Night. Nicholas Carter
In the Grip of a Lie. M. Leighton
In the Grip of Destiny. C. E. Sterrey
In the Grip of Fate. Nicholas Carter
In the Grip of the Brute. G. Radcliffe
In the Grip of the Dragon. M. Richmond
In the Grip of the Gestapo. S. Hope
In the Grip of the Kidnappers. N. Ridley
In the Grip of the Law. D. Donovan
In the Grip of the Tong. J. W. Bobin
In the Hag's Hands. C. C. Lowis
In the Halls of Evil. T. A. Waters
In the Hand of the Riffs. W. M. Graydon
In the Hands of Spies. J. G. Brandon
In the Hands of the Enemy. R. Sharp
In the Heat of the Night. J. Ball
In the Highest Tradition. E. F. Droge
In the Hour Before Midnight. J. Higgins
In the House of Another. B. Mantle
In the House of Dark Music. F. Lynch
In the House of the Eye. W. A. MacKenzie
In the Key of Black. P. Broadley
"In the King's Name—!" H. D. Dearden
In the Labyrinth. A. Robbe-Grillet
In the Lamb White Days. F. H. Hall
In the Lap of Danger. Nicholas Carter
In the Lap of Fortune. J. Hatton
In the Last Act. R. Goyne
In the Last Analysis. A. Cross
In the Lion's Den. J. Cotton
In the Mayor's Parlour. J. S. Fletcher
In the Meshes. F. Severne
In the Middle Watch. W. C. Russell
In the Midnight Express. A. Murray
In the Midst of Death. Lawrence Block
In the Midst of Death. H. Luce
In the Money. A. S. Roche
In the Name of a Woman. A. W. Marchmont
In the Name of Liberty. F. Marryat
In the Name of the Law. Dick Stewart
In the Name of the People. A. W. Marchmont
In the Name of the Tzar. J. B. Dayne
In the National Interest. M. Kalb
In the Nick of Time. Nicholas Carter
In the Nick of Time. N. Ridley
In the Night. L. Gorell
In the Night Watch. E. S. Brooks
In the Old Chateau. R. H. Savage
In the Onyx Lobby. C. Wells
In the Plotter's Web. M. Leighton
In the Potter's House. G. D. Eldridge
In the Province of Darkness. P. Morton
In the Queen's Service. D. Donovan
In the Red. Joan Fleming
In the Russian Secret Service. Old Sleuth
In the Secret State. R. McCrum
In the Secret Vault. B. Wayde
In the Serpent's Coils. F. Du Boisgobey
In the Service of Love. R. Marsh
In the Shadow. Old Spicer
In the Shadow of Fear. Nicholas Carter
In the Shadow of Gold. P. Studer
In the Shadow of Guilt. M. Leighton
In the Shadow of Night. E. W. Alais
In the Shadow of Pa-Menkh. D. Langlois
In the Shadow of the Bush. John Bell
In the Shadow of the Cheka. J. D. Kennedy
In the Shadow of the Dragon. P. A. Crisp
In the Shadow of the Guillotine. J. W. Bobin
In the Shadow of the Hills. G. C. Shedd
In the Shadow of the Pyramids. R. H. Savage
In the Shadow of the Tower. R. M. Sears
In the Shadow of Tyburn. Rachelle Edwards
In the Shadows. D. Daniels
In the Shadows. N. Harris
In the Still of the Night. H. Seymour
In the Street of the Angel. P. J. Stead
In the Swim. R. H. Savage
In the Teeth of the Evidence. D. L. Sayers
In the Tenth Moon. S. Williams
In the Thraldom of Fear. Maurice Scott
In the Tiger's Cage. C. Wells
In the Toils. J. T. MacIntyre
In the Toils. F. Trent
In the Toils of Fear. Nicholas Carter
In the Tsar's Dominions. Le Voleur
In the Wake of a Stranger. I. S. Black
In the Web. W. W. Cook
In the Whirl of the Rising. B. Mitford
In the Wrong Box. F. Russell
In Those Dark Woods. D. Ince
In Tight Places. A. Griffiths
In Time for Murder. R. A. J. Walling
In Times Square. D. L. Mitchell
In Triple Disguise. W. M. Graydon
In 25 Words—or Death. N. Mitzman
In Two Latitudes. G. Simenon

In Walks Murder. C. Ryland
In White Raiment. W. LeQueux
In Whose Dim Shadow. J. J. Connington
Inca Death Squad. Nick Carter
Ince Affair. J. Morella
Ince Murder Case. E. J. Pond
Incendiary. W. A. Leahy
Incendiary Blonde. K. Edgar
Incense of Death. N. Deane
Inch of the C.I.D. J. Templeton
Inch of Time. James Norman
Incident. M. Avallone
Incident. A. Rives
Incident. E. Warman
Incident at a Corner. C. Armstrong
Incident at Hendon. J. Letton
Incident at La Junta. O. Lange
Incident at Naha. M. J. Bosse
Incident at 125th Street. J. E. Brown
Incident at the Merry Hippo. E. Huxley
Incident at Villa Rahmana. A. Eliot
Incident Closed. H. J. Dellar
Incident in Ireland. Robert MacLeod
Incident on a Summer's Day. D. Raymond
Incidental Bishop. G. Allen
Incidental Murder. J. Champion
Incidental Murder. C. Joyce
Incitement to Murder. R. Amberley
Inclination to Murder. R. Ellerbeck
Inclination to Murder. H. Hunter
Inclining to Crime. A. Kent
Incognito. N. R. Nusbaum
Income Tax Conspiracy. A. Parsons
Incomparable Doll. K. Lindsay
Inconsistent Villains. N. A. Temple-Ellis
Inconvenient Bride. J. M. Fox
Inconvenient Corpse. E. P. Fenwick
Inconvenient Corpse. D. Sharp
Incorporated. W. Ash
Incredible Adventure. M. Richmond
Incredible Adventures of Rowland Hern. N. Olde
Incredible Crime. L. Austen-Leigh
Incredible Elopement of Lord Peter Wimsey. D. L. Sayers
Incredible Schlock Homes. R. L. Fish
Incredible Theft. A. Christie
Incredible Truth. C. Massie
Incredulity of Father Brown. G. K. Chesterton
Incubated Girl. F. T. Jane
Incubus. D. Thurlow
Incumbent. Pamela Hill
Indecent Exposure. E. Berckman
"Independent." T. Newman
Independent Detective. Anonymous
Independent Means. F. Singleton
Independent Witness. H. Cecil
India. E. Southworth
India-Rubber Men. E. Wallace
Indian Bangle. F. Hume
Indian Drum. W. MacHarg
Indian Idol Mystery. H. J. Andrews
Indian Love Lyrics. M. Richmond
Indian Lullaby. M. Richmond
Indian Mystery. G. Allen
Indian Point Conspiracy. R. Felber
Indian Police. Richard Fisher
Indian Princess. A. M. Williamson
Indian Wizard. A. Lillie
Indigo Death. M. Saltmarsh
Indigo Necklace. F. Crane
Indigo Necklace Murders. F. Crane
Indiscretions of a Lady's Maid. W. LeQueux
Induna's Wife. B. Mitford
Industrious Chevalier. S. S. Sprigge
Inevitable Crime. H. Leyford
Inevitable Fatality. Roy Lewis
Inevitable Hour. M. Boggan
Inevitable Law. F. E. Penny
Inevitable Millionaires. E. P. Oppenheim
Inexpendable. W. H. Baker
Infallible System. C. Kingston
Infallible Witness. P. Luck
Infamous Conduct. H. A. Wrenn
Infamous Fame. E. C. Vivian
Infamous Gentleman. G. Goodchild
Infant. F. Wicks
Infatuation of Marcella. A. M. Meadows
Infernal Device. M. Kurland
Infernal Idol. H. Seymour
Infernal Light. E. Friend
Inferno. J. Creasey
Inferno. R. Dundee
Infidel. M. E. Braddon
Infiltrator. Martin Walker
Infiltrator. A. York
Infinite Morning. D. Newton
Infinity of Mirrors. R. Condon
Influenza Mystery. Sutherland Scott
Informant. The Gordons
Informant. M. Olden
Information Man. C. Joyce
Information Received. E. R. Punshon
Information Received and other stories. P. Cheyney
Informed Sources. L. Kamarck
Informer. Ladbroke Black
Informer. Liam O'Flaherty
Informer. J. McGreevey

Informer. A. Takagi
Informer. F. Whishaw
Infra Blood. P. D. Westbrook
Ingenious Captain Cobbs. G. W. Appleton
Ingenious Mr. Stone. R. Player
Ingenious Stratagem. Nicholas Carter
Inherit the Darkness. W. D. Roberts
Inherit the Mirage. J. Thatcher
Inherit the Shadows. J. Lovesmith
Inherit the Stars. J. P. Hogan
Inherit the Wind. G. Vaizey
Inheritance. O. Brookes
Inheritance. P. J. Cooper
Inheritance. Stuart Martin
Inheritance. D. Winston
Inheritors. J. Messmann
Initials Only. A. K. Green
Injured. T. Grainger
Injured Lover. M. B. Lowndes
Ink Street Murder. F. Grierson
Inkosi-Carver Investigates. "Capstan"
Inland Passage. G. H. Coxe
Inn at the Red Oak. L. Griswold
Inn by the Shore. F. Warden
Inn Closes for Christmas. Cledwyn Hughes
Inn of Evil. J. A. Creighton
Inn of the Thirteen Swords. D. Graeme
Inn-Side Murder. C. C. Garner
Inn with the Wooden Door. N. MacSwan
Inner Circle. J. Fast
Inner Circle. M. Harvey
Inner Circle. E. C. Mayne
Inner City Hoodlum. D. Goines
Inner Number. F. C. Williams
Inner Room. P. H. Irving
Inner Steps. S. Cardiff
Innocence. C. H. Bullivant
Innocence at Play. J. Middlemass
Innocence of Father Brown. G. K. Chesterton
Innocence of Rosamond Prior. A. Dick
Innocent. E. Piper
Innocent Abroad. M. Carr
Innocent Accomplice. B. Reynolds
Innocent and Willing. Morton Cooper
Innocent Blood. P. D. James
Innocent Bottle. Anthony Gilbert
Innocent Bystander. G. Bagby
Innocent Bystander. B. Frost
Innocent Bystander. M. F. Page
Innocent Bystander. G. Rice
Innocent Bystanders. J. Munro
Innocent Criminal. J. D. Beresford
Innocent Flower. C. Armstrong
Innocent Guilt. E. C. Vivian
Innocent Gunman. J. P. Lacroix
Innocent House. F. Lockridge
Innocent Imposter and other stories. M. Grey
Innocent Mrs. Duff. E. S. Holding
Innocent Murder. L. D. Allen
Innocent Murderers. W. A. Johnston
Innocent One. J. Reach
Innocent Sinner. A. M. Meadows
Innocents. W. Archibald
Innocents. R. Savage
Innocents. G. Simenon
Innocents on Broadway. E. E. Saks
Innoculate! N. Bayne
Inquest. M. Barringer
Inquest. H. Clandon
Inquest. R. Newmann
Inquest. M. K. Ozaki
Inquest. P. Wilde
Inquest Betraying. T. J. R. Sennocke
Inquest—Eleven Thirty. S. Darrell
Inquest on a Lady. T. J. R. Sennocke
Inquest on a Mistress. T. J. R. Sennocke
Inquest on Bouvet. G. Simenon
Inquest on Miriam. M. Dalton
Inquests by Jury. T. J. R. Sennocke
Inquests on the Deceased. T. J. R. Sennocke
Inquiries by the Yard. A. Brock
Inquisition. M. Olden
Inquisitors. D. Lyle
Inquisitory. R. Pinget
Insanity Machine. Peter Maxwell
Inscrutable Charlie Muffin. B. Freemantle
Inscrutable Miss Stone. A. Askew
Inside Information. N. Bentley
Inside Job. S. Allan
Inside Job. N. Brady
Inside Job. J. Boland
Inside Lester. F. Carmichael
Inside Man. G. H. Coxe
Inside Man. E. R. Johnson
Inside Out. William Hughes
Inside Out. David Miles
Inside-Out Heist. T. B. Reagan
Inside Out Man. F. Cockain
Inside the Lines. E. D. Biggers
Inside Track. G. Dilnot
Insider. G. Joseph
Insiders. S. Morrow
Insiders. M. Pflaum
Insidious Dr. Fu-Manchu. S. Rohmer
Insoluble. F. Everton
Inspector Answers. N. P. Hart
Inspector Bedison and the Sunderland Case. T. Cobb

Title Index

Inspector Bedison Risks It. T. Cobb
Inspector Burmann's Black-Out. B. Cobb
Inspector Burmann's Busiest Day. B. Cobb
Inspector Calls. J. B. Priestley
Inspector Cole. R. Batchelor
Inspector Dickins Retires. E. P. Oppenheim
Inspector Derben and the Widow Maker. P. A. Foxall
Inspector Derben's War. P. A. Foxall
Inspector Flagg and the Scarlet Skeleton. J. Cassells
Inspector French and the Cheyne Mystery. F. W. Crofts
Inspector French and the Starvel Tragedy. F. W. Crofts
Inspector French's Greatest Case. F. W. Crofts
Inspector Frost and Lady Brassingham. H. M. Smith
Inspector Frost and the Waverdale Fire. H. M. Smith
Inspector Frost and the Whitbourne Murder. H. M. Smith
Inspector Frost in Crevenna Cove. H. M. Smith
Inspector Frost in the Background. H. M. Smith
Inspector Frost in the City. H. M. Smith
Inspector Frost's Jigsaw. H. M. Smith
Inspector Ghote Breaks an Egg. H. R. F. Keating
Inspector Ghote Caught in Meshes. H. R. F. Keating
Inspector Ghote Draws a Line. H. R. F. Keating
Inspector Ghote Goes by Train. H. R. F. Keating
Inspector Ghote Hunts the Peacock. H. R. F. Keating
Inspector Ghote Plays a Joker. H. R. F. Keating
Inspector Ghote Trusts the Heart. H. R. F. Keating
Inspector Ghote's Good Crusade. H. R. F. Keating
Inspector Henderson, the Central Office Detective. H. I. Hancock
Inspector Higgins Goes Fishing. C. F. Gregg
Inspector Higgins Hurries. C. F. Gregg
Inspector Higgins Sees It Through. C. F. Gregg
Inspector Hornleigh Investigates. H. W. Priwin
Inspector Jackson Goes North. D. T. Lindsay
Inspector Jackson Investigates. D. T. Lindsay
Inspector McLean's Casebook. G. Goodchild
Inspector McLean's Holiday. G. Goodchild
Inspector Maigret and the Burglar's Wife. G. Simenon
Inspector Maigret and the Dead Girl. G. Simenon
Inspector Maigret and the Killers. G. Simenon
Inspector Maigret and the Strangled Stripper. G. Simenon
Inspector Maigret in New York's Underworld. G. Simenon
Inspector Maigret Investigates. G. Simenon
Inspector Murphy Sails In. David J. Murphy
Inspector Manson's Success. E. Radford
Inspector Morgan's Dilemma. J. Bingham
Inspector Queen's Own Case. E. Queen
Inspector Richardson C.I.D. B. Thomson
Inspector Rusby's Finale. V. Markham
Inspector Treadgold Investigates. A. Weymouth
Inspector West Alone. J. Creasey
Inspector West at Bay. J. Creasey
Inspector West at Home. J. Creasey
Inspector West Cries Wolf. J. Creasey
Inspector West Kicks Off. J. Creasey
Inspector West Leaves Town. J. Creasey
Inspector West Makes Haste. J. Creasey
Inspector West Regrets. J. Creasey
Inspector West Takes Charge. J. Creasey
Inspector Wilkins Reads the Proofs. Murray Thomas
Inspector Wilkins Sees Red. Murray Thomas
Inspector's Holiday. R. Lockridge
Inspector's Opinion. M. Reybold
Inspector's Puzzle. C. Matthew
Instant Dead. S. Jason
Instant Enemy. R. Macdonald
Instar. R. Brady
Instead of Murder. J. Goodman
Instigator. E. A. Treeton
Instinct at Fault. Nicholas Carter
Instinctive Criminal. G. Coleridge
Institute. J. M. Cain
Instrument. P. Everett
Instrument of Destiny. J. D. Beresford
Instrument of Vengeance. H. McCutcheon
Instruments of Darkness. S. Horler
Instruments of Death. W. A. Harbinson

Insufficient Evidence. M. Hervey
Insulators. J. Creasey
Insurgent Love. M. Richmond
Insurrection! D. Brennan
Insurrection of Hippolytus Brandenberg. R. Friedman
Insurrectionist. A. McCoy
"Intelligence" Game of Secret Service Cases and Problems. R. McKay
Intelligence Quotient. G. C. Leppanen
Intensive Fear. N. Christian
Intent to Kill. M. Bryan
Intent to Kill. H. Desmond
Intent to Murder. N. Deane
Intent to Murder. L. Sands
Intercept. K. Bernstein
Intercom Conspiracy. E. Ambler
Interface. J. Gores
Interface Assignment. W. Rayner
Interference. R. Pertwee
Interloper. Gwendoline Butler
Interloper. E. P. Oppenheim
Interlopers. D. Hamilton
Interlude. S. P. B. Mais
Intermind. R. Luther
Intermission. M. Albrand
International Affair. B. Graeme
International Commando. J. Courage
International Crook League. Nicholas Carter
International Spy. A. Upward
Interrogators. A. Prior
Interrupted Honeymoon. A. Swift
Interrupted Kiss. R. Marsh
Interrupted Wedding. M. Gerard
Interview. H. C. Rae
Interviewing's Killing. A. Tack
Interworld. I. Haiblum
Intimate Journal of Warren Winslow. Jean Leslie
Intimate Relations. Fredrick Jackson
Intimate Stranger. E. Thomas
Intimate Victims. V. Packer
Intimidators. D. Hamilton
Into a Dark Mirror. K. Orvis
Into His Own Trap. J. K. Stafford
Into Nick Carter's Web. Nicholas Carter
Into the Fog. Winston Graham
Into the Jaws of Death. W. G. Forbes
Into the Night. F. N. Greene
Into the Shade, and other stories. M. C. Hay
Into Temptation. K. Lindsay
Into the Arena. E. Darby
Into the Void. F. Converse
Into Thin Air. H. Carmichael
Into Thin Air. J. Iams
Into Thin Air. G. Vaizey
Into Thin Air. H. Winslow
Into This Universe. Fredrick Jackson
Into Thy Hands. A. Applin
Intrigue. D. Cory
Intrigue. Clive Desmond
Intrigue. W. Hackett
Intrigue. A. J. Merak
Intrigue. J. Usher
Intrigue and Matrimony. D. Vane
Intrigue for Empire. K. M. Knight
Intrigue in Morocco. Coriola
Intrigue in Paris. S. Noel
Intrigue in Rome. E. Morley
Intrigue in Tangier. H. Seymour
Intrigue Island. A. Mills
Intrigue on Halfaday Creek. J. B. Hendryx
Intrigue on the Upper Level. T. T. Hoyne
Intriguer. Maude Parker
Intriguers. T. Cobb
Intriguers. D. Hamilton
Intriguers. W. LeQueux
Intrigues of a Prisoner. E. Gaboriau
Introducing C. B. Greenfield. L. Kallen
Introducing Inspector Maigret. G. Simenon
Introducing Mr. Brandon. Anthony Morton
Introducing Mr. Robinson. Rupert Grayson
Introducing the Super. R. Goyne
Introducing the Toff. J. Creasey
Introducing William Allison. W. Hewlett
Intruder. L. Charbonneau
Intruder. O. R. Cohen
Intruder. M. Cronin
Intruder. C. Farr
Intruder. H. Horn
Intruder. S. Laforest
Intruder. Hadley Lawrence
Intruder. D. M. Low
Intruder. R. Maugham
Intruder. A. Myrer
Intruder. G. Tindall
Intruder at Maison Benedict. S. Richard
Intruder from the Sea. G. McDonell
Intruder in the Dark. G. Bellairs
Intruder in the Dust. W. Faulkner
Intruders. P. Montandon
Intrusion. E. McCrae
Intrusive Tourist. B. Reynolds
Invader. R. Wormser
Invaders. E. P. Frankland
Invaders. W. Kempley
Invaders from the Dark. G. La Spina
Invasion. H. Janson

Invasion. J. Wallace
Invasion Coast. J. G. Sarasin
Invasion of Privacy. H. Kurnitz
Invasion of the Clones. J. Rosenberger
Invasion of the Yellow Warlords. C. Steele
Inverness Murder. C. A. Byers
Inverted Crime. L. Gribble
Investigation. S. Lem
Investigation. D. Uhnak
Investigation. M. Urquhart
Investigation at Holman Square. N. M. Hopkins
Investigations Are Proceeding. J. Ashford
Investigations of Colwin Grey. A. J. Rees
Investigations of John Pym. D. C. Murray
Investigators. J. S. Fletcher
Investment in Crime. J. C. Crowley
Invisibility Affair. Thomas Stratton
Invisible Border. Mildred Davis
Invisible Bridge. F. Allan
Invisible Companion and other stories. J. J. Farjeon
Invisible Cord. V. Castang
Invisible Cord. C. Cookson
Invisible Darkness. P. Paul
Invisible Death. B. Flynn
Invisible Empire. C. Steele
Invisible Enemy. G. C. Shedd
Invisible Evidence. P. Winn
Invisible Evil. R. Gaines
Invisible Eye. P. Tabori
Invisible Flamini. Carter Brown
Invisible Foe. L. J. Miln
Invisible Green. J. Sladek
Invisible Hand. R. Dark
Invisible Host. G. Bristow
Invisible Image. F. Chabrey
Invisible Man Murders. R. Foster
Invisible Pickpocket. J. M'Govan
Invisible Red. Maude Parker
Invisible Ships. Sea Lion
Invisible Trap. Genevieve St. John
Invisible Verdict. R. Goyne
Invisible Weapons. J. Rhode
Invisible Worm. M. Millar
Invisibles. E. E. Christopher
Invisibles. James Dark
Invitation. C. Cookson
Invitation to a Ball. P. Meredith
Invitation to a Dynamite Party. P. Lovesey
Invitation to a Funeral. T. Harknett
Invitation to a Murder. R. King
Invitation to a Murder. J. T. Story
Invitation to a Strangling. R. L. Brent
Invitation to Adventure. G. Ashe
Invitation to an Inquest. R. Hull
Invitation to Danger. F. Murray
Invitation to Death. A. R. Long
Invitation to Death. A. O. Pollard
Invitation to Die. F. French
Invitation to Evil. W. D. Roberts
Invitation to Kill. G. Low
Invitation to Kill. V. Warren
Invitation to Mather. B. Graeme
Invitation to Murder. Robert (G.) Curtis
Invitation to Murder. L. Ford
Invitation to Murder. Manning Long
Invitation to Murder. I. S. Shriber
Invitation to Murder. R. Stout
Invitation to Murder. R. Trevor
Invitation to Paradise. Lesley Howard
Invitation to Terror. P. Hambledon
Invitation to the Grave. David Hume
Invitation to Vengeance. K. M. Knight
Invitation to Violence. L. White
Invited. Z. Davis
Involved. Johnny Morgan
Involvement in Austria. J. N. Chance
Involvement of Arnold Wechsler. J. A. Graham
Inward Eye. P. Bacon
Inward Glance. L. Robinson
Ipcress File. L. Deighton
Ippletree Manor Mystery. D. W. Spurgeon
Iras. T. Douglas
Irena. J. Land
Irene. T. Alexander
Irina. Gavin Holt
Iris the Avenger. F. Marryat
Irish Affair. Andrea Harris
Irish Beauty Contract. P. Atlee
Irish Detective. Anonymous
Irish Detective. Old Sleuth
Irish Monte Cristo Abroad. A. Robertson
Irish Monte Cristo's Search. A. Robertson
Irish Monte Cristo's Trail. A. Robertson
Irish Police Officer. Robert Curtis
Irish Witch. D. Wheatley
Iron Apple. G. Bowman
Iron Box. C. R. Gull
Iron Burgess, the Government Detective. Anonymous
Iron Burgess, the Government Detective. Old Sleuth
Iron Butterflies. A. Norton
Iron Chalice. O. R. Cohen
Iron Claw. F. A. Symonds

Iron Clew. A. Tilton
Iron Cobweb. U. Curtiss
Iron Cross. S. Cobb
Iron Cross. R. H. Sherard
Iron Curtain. A. O. Pollard
Iron Door. O. Martin
Iron Egg. D. W. F. Hardie
Iron Facade. C. Marchant
Iron Gates. M. Millar
Iron Grip. E. Wallace
Iron Hand. J. M. Cobban
Iron Hand. Howard Dean
Iron Hand. A. Tilton
Iron Hand. F. Warden
Iron Horse. R. M. Ballantyne
Iron Maiden. Carter Brown
Iron Mask. F. Du Boisgobey
Iron Mask. Gwyn Evans
Iron Mask. J. G. Sarasin
Iron Orchid. John Bentley
Iron Pirate. M. Pemberton
Iron Ring. H. S. Keeler
Iron Sanctuary. Robert MacLeod
Iron Skull. K. Robeson
Iron Spiders. B. Kendrick
Iron Spiders Murder. B. Kendrick
Iron Staircase. G. Simenon
Iron Swastika Plot. J. Rosenberger
Iron Tiger. Harry Patterson
Iron Tiger. M. L. Stokes
Iron Virgin. J. M. Fox
Iron Will. C. N. Buck
Ironies. R. Connell
Ironmaster's Daughter. P. Trent
Ironmouth. C. Stanton
Ironside. J. Thompson
Ironsides Abroad. Anonymous
Ironsides' Lone Hand. V. Gunn
Ironsides of the Yard. V. Gunn
Ironsides on the Spot. V. Gunn
Ironsides Sees Red. V. Gunn
Ironsides Smashes Through. V. Gunn
Ironsides Smells Blood. V. Gunn
Ironwood. Jennie Melville
Irralie's Bushranger. E. W. Hornung
Irregular Marriage. S. Warwick
Irresistable Stranger. A. Applin
Irresponsibles. Elizabeth Ford
Irrespressible Peccadillo. F. Flora
Irving Solution. L. Simon
Is and Was. H. Hewlett
Is He Dead, Miss Ffinch? J. N. Smith
Is He the Man? W. C. Russell
Is No One Innocent? M. H. Gropper
Is She Dead Too? Anthony Gilbert
Is Skin Deep, Is Fatal. H. R. F. Keating
Is There a Traitor in the House? P. McGerr
Is This Coffin Taken? J. F. Webb
Is This Revenge? L. Gribble
Isa. A. W. Marchmont
Isabel Broderick—"Bubbles We Buy". A. Jones
Isabelle. A. Gide
Isabelle, the Frantic. K. Kimbrough
Iselane. J. L. Van Wijk
Ishmael. M. E. Braddon
Ishmael. E. Southworth
Ishmaelite. M. E. Braddon
Ishmael's Wife. Roy Vickers
Island. Mildred Nelson
Island Alert. J. M. Walsh
Island Doctor. Rona Randall
Island Emperor. B. Priestley
Island Feud. S. M. Parkman
Island Gold. V. Williams
Island Heirs. J. Judson
Island in Waiting. Anthea Fraser
Island Murder. T. Stevenson
Island Murder. P. Trent
Island Mystery. G. A. Birmingham
Island Mystery. J. W. Bobin
Island Mystery. J. Bolton
Island Mystery. T. Lester
Island of Atonement. H. Leyford
Island of Bitter Memories. D. Daniels
Island of Creeping Death. V. Norwood
Island of Dangerous Men. A. Drummond
Island of Death. A. Broome
Island of Death. D. Seaman
Island of Deceit. A. Andrew
Island of Deceit. E. Habersham
Island of Desire. J. L. Roberts
Island of Destiny. A. J. Rees
Island of Disaster. Michael Lewis
Island of Dogs. L. Falk
Island of Eden. B. Mitford
Island of Escape. H. L. Nelson
Island of Evil. D. Daniels
Island of Evil. C. Farr
Island of Fear. J. D. Conway
Island of Fear. R. Dent
Island of Fear. Domenica
Island of Fear. H. Footner
Island of Fog. M. Kingsbury
Island of Fu Manchu. S. Rohmer
Island of Galloping Gold. E. Wallace
Island of Ghosts. O. Sackville
Island of Gold. James Grant
Island of Intrigue. I. Ostrander
Island of Mystery. A. Hale
Island of Peril. J. Creasey

Island of Romance. D. Whitelaw
Island of Sheep. J. Buchan
Island of Silence. C. B. Norris
Island of Spies. J. M. Walsh
Island of Surprises. W. B. M. Ferguson
Island of Terror. H. C. McNeile
Island of Terror. E. W. Strother
Island of Test. A. Soutar
Island of the Accursed. W. Winthrop
Island of the Guilty. G. H. Teed
Island of the Pit. V. James
Island of the Seven Hills. Z. Cass
Island of Unrest. J. G. Sarasin
Island Princess. E. Southworth
Island Rescue. J. Tickell
Island Schooner. G. Volk
Island Secret. W. M. Graydon
Island Twilight. N. Trayton
Island Where Time Stands Still. D. Wheatley
Islands of the Condemned. F. A. M. Webster
Isle for a Stranger. D. W. Low
Isle of Confusion. Douglas Christie
Isle of Desire. Basil Carey
Isle of Desire. Douglas Christie
Isle of Dragons. Robert MacLeod
Isle of Enchantment. A. Wood
Isle of Hate. A. Dare
Isle of Horror. G. H. Teed
Isle of Illusion. G. Gibbs
Isle of Innocence. L. Noel
Isle of Men. G. Volk
Isle of Peril. A. Wade
Isle of Strife. G. C. Shedd
Isle of Surrey. R. Dowling
Isle of the Dolphins. J. L. Roberts
Isle of the Drums. J. A. Dunn
Isle of the Seventh Sentry. F. Kent
Isle of the Snakes. R. L. Fish
Isle of the Undead. V. Coffman
Isotope Man. C. E. Maine
Isoworg. H. Bentinck
Israel Rank. R. Horniman
Issac Docket. S. Dave
Issue. E. Noble
Issue of the Bishop's Blood. T. P. McMahon
Istanbul. Nick Carter
Istanbul Elopement. D. T. Hughes
Istanbul Nights. Clarissa Ross
It Adds Up to Trouble. A. Nuttall
It Ain't Hay. D. Dodge
It Always Happens. Robin Temple
It Always Rains on Sunday. A. La Bern
It Began in New York. M. Kennedy
It Began in Singapore. G. P. Willis
It Began in Vauxhall Gardens. K. Kellow
It Boils Down to Murder. P. D. Westbrook
It Came to Pass. S. Fairway
It Came to Pass. G. M. Fenn
It Can't Always Be Caviar. J. M. Simmel
It Comes by Night. Clarissa Ross
It Could Happen to You. A. Booth
It Could Happen to You. J. B. O'Sullivan
It Couldn't Be Caroline. D. Egerton
It Couldn't Be Murder. H. Austin
It Couldn't Be Murder. Mark Cross
It Couldn't Be Murder. R. B. Sinclair
It Couldn't Be Suicide. Caroline Francis
It Couldn't Happen to Me. J. Blackmore
It Couldn't Matter Less. P. Cheyney
It Doesn't Add Up. R. Drayton
It Had to Be You. V. Siller
It Happened at Midnight. J. Reach
It Happened at Night. Roland Daniel
It Happened at the Cape. K. Lindsay
It Happened at the Lake. J. T. Shaw
It Happened in Boston. R. H. Greenan
It Happened in Cairo. K. Rhodes
It Happened in Essex. V. Bridges
It Happened in Hamburg. W. H. Baker
It Happened in Melgrove Square. J. Hunter
It Happened in Vienna. T. B. Marle
It Happened in Wayland. F. Shroyer
It Happened on Halfaday Creek. J. B. Hendryx
It Happened to Susan. J. Blackmore
It Howls at Night. N. Berrow
"It Is Expedient..." K. Ingram
It Is No Wonder. J. F. Molloy
It Is Not Safe to Know. B. Reynolds
It Leaves Them Cold. Kevin O'Hara
It Makes You Think. A. E. Jones
It Means Mischief. R. Pertwee
It Might Have Been. P. Trent
It Might Have Meant Murder. L. Cargill
It Might Lead Anywhere. E. R. Punshon
It Never Rains—. V. Bridges
It Never Rains in Los Angeles. C. Flowers
It Only Hurts a Minute. D. M. Mankiewicz
It Pays to Die. C. M. Wills
It Prowls at Dark. H. R. Taunton
It Rained That Friday. G. M. Wilson
It Seemed Like a Good Idea at the Time. D. R. Stieper
It Shouldn't Happen to a Dog. E. Lanham
It Shouldn't Happen to a Dog. Colin Watson
It Takes a Thief. D. Billany

It Walks at Midnight. J. Reach
It Walks by Night. J. D. Carr
It Walks the Woods. Alan Grant
It Was Christmas Every Day. A. La Bern
It Was Locked. J. Hawk
It Was Murder, They Said. John Bentley
It Wasn't a Nightmare. L. F. Hay
It Wasn't Me! I. Jefferies
"It Will Be All Right!" T. Gallon
It Will Be Warmer When It Snows. A. La Bern
It Won't Get You Anywhere. D. Skirrow
Italian. A. Radcliffe
Italian Assets. Richard Butler
Italian Bandit. Old Sleuth
Italian Called Mario. P. H. Irving
Italian Connection. Robin Moore
Italian Gadget. H. Calvin
Italian Job. T. K. Martin
Italian Maze. E. Lascelles
Italian Mysteries. F. Lathom
Item 7. Alan Nixon
It's a Battlefield. G. Greene
It's a Crime. R. Ellington
It's a Free Country. L. Brain
It's a Sin. H. Zore
It's a Sin to Kill. D. Keene
It's a Wise Child. T. Curley
It's About Crime. M. Kantor
It's Alive. R. Woodley
It's All Yours. R. Angel
It's Always Eve That Weeps. H. Janson
It's Always Too Late to Mend. P. V. Stern
It's an Ill Wind. D. Mayor
It's Bedtime, Baby! H. Janson
It's Cold Next Door. P. De Polnay
It's Death, My Darling! A. R. Long
It's Different Abroad. H. Calvin
It's Different in July. K. Fitzgerald
It's Easier for Homicide. K. David
It's Easy to Kill. A. Wood
It's Her Own Funeral. C. Carnac
It's in the Bag. A. Spiller
It's Later Than You Think. M. M. Kaye
It's Loaded, Mr. Bauer. J. P. Marquand
It's Locked in with You. G. Mayo
It's Lonely on the Sidewalk. D. Bogard
It's Murder. R. Drayton
It's Murder! T. T. Flynn
It's Murder If You Say So! A. Aldous
It's Murder, McHugh. J. Flynn
It's Murder, Maguire. R. Himmel
It's Murder, Miss King. I. Waitt
It's Murder, Mr. Potter. R. Foley
It's Murder, Senorita. D. Bateson
It's Murder She Says. R. Angel
It's Murder to Live. E. Radford
It's Murder with Dover. J. Porter
It's My Funeral. P. Rabe
It's My Own Funeral. D. Lyon
It's Only Saps That Die. B. Toler
It's Quiet in the Country. H. Willett
It's Raining Violence. T. Du Bois
It's Safe in England. K. Fitzgerald
It's Up to You. E. L. G. Watson
It's Your Funeral. A. Bocca
It's Your Funeral. Kevin O'Hara
It's Your Turn to Die. Gerard Fisher
Ivan Greet's Masterpiece. G. Allen
Ivan the Serf. S. Cobb
I've Found My Love. M. Richmond
I've Got Viktor Schalkenburg. W. Mulvihill
Ivor's Chance. P. Trent
Ivorstone Manor. E. Cromwell
Ivory Ball. C. C. Hotchkiss
Ivory Dagger. P. Wentworth
Ivory Disc. P. Brebner
Ivory God. J. S. Fletcher
Ivory Goddess. W. H. L. Crauford
Ivory Grin. J. R. Macdonald
Ivory Ladies. Gavin Holt
Ivory Locket. M. Alan
Ivory Penguin. John Morgan
Ivory Queen. N. Hurst
Ivory Screen. G. H. Teed
Ivory Snuff Box. A. Fredericks
Ivory Tower. M. Eatock
Ivory Trail. T. Mundy
Ivory Tusk. R. Hardinge
Ivory Valley. C. J. C. Hyne
Ivy Halls. B. H. Hyatt
Ivy Tree. Mary Stewart
Izelle of the Dunes. C. G. Mitford

"J for Jennie" Murders. T. A. Plummer
J for Jupiter. T. Fuller
J. P. Dunbar. W. C. Hudson
Jacaranda Murders. H. Desmond
Jack Allyn's Friends. G. W. Appleton
Jack and Jill. Old Sleuth
Jack Breakaway. Old Sleuth
Jack Carter and the Law. T. Lewis
Jack Carter and the Mafia Pigeon. T. Lewis

Title Index

Jack Carter's Law. T. Lewis
Jack Chanty. H. Footner
Jack Curzon. A. C. Gunter
Jack Gordon, Night Errant, Gotham 1883. W. C. Hudson
Jack-in-the-Box. J. J. Connington
Jack Junk. T. P. Prest
Jack O'Judgment. E. Wallace
Jack O'Lantern. G. Goodchild
Jack O'Lantern. K. A. Shoesmith
Jack o' the Cudgel. Anonymous
Jack of Clubs. J. Ironside
Jack of Hearts. W. Von Elsner
Jack on the Gallows Tree. L. Bruce
Jack Ranworth. J. Blyth
Jack Sheppard, the Bandit King. Anonymous
Jack Sheppard. W. H. Ainsworth
Jack Sheppard, the Bandit King. O. Harper
Jack Spot. H. Janson
Jack the Juggler. Old Sleuth
Jack the Juggler's Ordeal. Old Sleuth
Jack the Juggler's Trial. Old Sleuth
Jack the Outlaw. K. Snowden
Jack the Rascal. G. M. Fenn
Jack the Ripper. Stuart James
Jack the Ripper. Richard Gordon
Jack the Ripper. R. Pember
Jack Vinton, the Boy Detective. Anonymous
Jack Warleigh. D. J. Belgrave
Jackal. D. Whitelaw
Jackals. C. Kernahan
Jackals and others. F. E. Penny
Jackal's Head. Elizabeth Peters
Jackals of the Secret Service. Operator 1384
Jackanapes Jacket. E. M. Keate
Jackdaw. C. Hill
Jackdaw Mystery. F. Grierson
Jack's Father, and other stories. W. E. Norris
Jack's Return Home. T. Lewis
Jacob Niemand. R. H. Sherard
Jacob Street Mystery. R. A. Freeman
Jacob's Ladder. E. P. Oppenheim
Jacob's Ladder, and other stories. W. B. Maxwell
Jacobs Park Killings. William Camp
Jacoby's First Case. J. C. S. Smith
Jacqueline of Olzeburg. Anonymous
Jacqueminot. K. Rich
Jade; and other stories. H. Wiley
Jade Box. N. Faulkner
Jade Cat. G. B. Mair
Jade Dragon. N. Buckingham
Jade Elephant. E. Fraser
Jade Elephants. T. Allen
Jade Eye. F. Hume
Jade Eye. J. Ingersol
Jade-Eyed Jinx. Carter Brown
Jade-Eyed Jungle. Carter Brown
Jade Figurine. J. Foxx
Jade Figurines. Jan Alexander
Jade for a Lady. M. E. Chaber
Jade God. W. E. Barry
Jade God. A. Sullivan
Jade Green. D. Daniels
Jade Green Cats. E. Blake
Jade-Green Garter. D. Newton
Jade Green Judy. D. Enefer
Jade Hatpin. M. G. Kiddy
Jade in Aries. T. Coe
Jade Lizard. Taffrail
Jade Necklace. M. Short
Jade of Death. R. Gar
Jade of Destiny. J. Farnol
Jade Pagoda. B. H. Hyatt
Jade Princess. Clarissa Ross
Jade Rabbit. A. Blood
Jade Unicorn. J. Halpern
Jade Vendetta. J. L. Roberts
Jade Venus. G. H. Coxe
Jade Wind. J. Harris
Jade's Progress. J. S. Clouston
Jadoo. N. Newham-Davis
Jaguar Lives. Y. Yablonsky
Jail and Farewell. M. Shane
Jail Bait! R. Angel
Jail Bait. S. Chayes
Jail Bait. J. W. Mason
Jail Break. D. Barton
Jail-Breakers. Roland Daniel
Jail-Breakers. B. Newman
Jail Gates Are Open. David Hume
Jailbait Jungle. Wenzell Brown
Jailbait Street. H. Ellson
Jailbreak. L. White
Jailer, My Jailer. M. Gavin
Jailer's Pretty Wife. F. Du Boisgobey
Jake and Sadie. B. Solomon
Jake Canuke. J. Templeton
Jake of Diamonds. D. Von Elsner
Jamaica Inn. D. Du Maurier
Jamaican Exchange. Nick Carter
James Ballingray, Murderer. J. Maconechy
James Bond and Moonraker. Christopher Wood
James Bond, the Spy Who Loved Me. Christopher Wood
James Cope. C. Barmby
James Joyce Murder. A. Cross

James Knowland: Deceased. H. Carmichael
James Tarrant, Adventurer. F. W. Crofts
James Whitaker's Dukedom. E. Jepson
Jamintha. Beatrice Parker
Jamo and the Bent Playboy. J. Vaughan
Jane Carberry and the Laughing Fountain. B. Symons
Jane Carberry: Detective. B. Symons
Jane Carberry Investigates. B. Symons
Jane Carberry's Week End. B. Symons
Jane Shore. T. P. Prest
Jane, the Courageous. K. Kimbrough
Jane the Ripper. W. Tyrer
Jane Ventures. P. Trent
Jane with Green Eyes. H. Janson
Janissary. A. L. Gelb
Janson, Go Home. H. Janson
Janus Imperative. Evelyn Anthony
Janus Murder. J. N. Datesh
Janus Pope. G. Marton
Japanese Corpse. J. Van De Wetering
Japanese Girl. Winston Graham
Japanese Jeopardy. P. Tabori
Japanese Mistress. R. Neely
Japanese Revenge. L. Tracy
Japanese Tales of Mystery and Imagination. E. Rampo
Japanese Umbrella and other stories. Francis King
Jarrah Tree. M. Kistler
Jarvis. R. W. Kauffman
Jarvis of Harvard. R. W. Kauffman
Jarwick the Prodigal. T. Gallon
Jasius Pursuit. D. Orgill
Jasmine for My Grave. Sara North
Jasmine Trail. H. J. Hagerty
Jason Affair. J. N. Chance
Jason and the Sleep Game. J. N. Chance
Jason Burr's First Case. D. Kent
Jason Goes West. J. N. Chance
Jason King. R. Miall
Jason Murders. J. N. Chance
Jasper Dane's Secret. M. E. Braddon
Jaubert Ring. W. D. Roberts
Java Jack. O. Binns
Javelin for Jonah. G. Mitchell
Jaws of Circumstance. C. Clausen
Jaws of Darkness. Mark Cross
Jaws of Death. G. Allen
Jaws of Death. L. Thayer
Jaws of Doom. B. Ludwig
Jaws of the Watchdog. I. Drummond
Jazz Jungle. H. Janson
Jealous in Honour. T. Heald
Jealous One. C. Fremlin
Jealous Woman. J. M. Cain
Jealousy. N. Karta
Jealousy. A. Robbe-Grillet
Jealousy Pulls the Trigger. M. E. Corne
Jean of the Lazy J Ranch. H. Pink
Jeanie with the Light Brown Corpse. J. Cello
Jeanne of the Marshes. E. P. Oppenheim
Jedcrow. Mark Elder
Jeff Clayton and the Outlaws. W. Ward
Jeff Clayton in the Heart of Trouble. W. Ward
Jeff Clayton's Blind Trail. W. Ward
Jeff Clayton's Brigand Foe. W. Ward
Jeff Clayton's Dancing Bubble. W. Ward
Jeff Clayton's Daring Leap. W. Ward
Jeff Clayton's Deal with Death. W. Ward
Jeff Clayton's Decoy. W. Ward
Jeff Clayton's Demon Pursuer. W. Ward
Jeff Clayton's Discovery. W. Ward
Jeff Clayton's Fatal Shot. W. Ward
Jeff Clayton's Golden Ladder. W. Ward
Jeff Clayton's Last Bullet. W. Ward
Jeff Clayton's Last Ship. W. Ward
Jeff Clayton's Long Chase. W. Ward
Jeff Clayton's Lost Clue. W. Ward
Jeff Clayton's Man-Trap. W. Ward
Jeff Clayton's Master Stroke. W. Ward
Jeff Clayton's Mexican Plot. W. Ward
Jeff Clayton's Pursuit. W. Ward
Jeff Clayton's Puzzle. W. Ward
Jeff Clayton's Red Mystery. W. Ward
Jeff Clayton's Riddle. W. Ward
Jeff Clayton's Strange Quest. W. Ward
Jeff Clayton's Surprise. W. Ward
Jeff Clayton's Thunder Bolt. W. Ward
Jeff Clayton's Triumph. W. Ward
Jeff Clayton's White Mission. W. Ward
Jeff Clayton's Winged Flight. W. Ward
Jeff Utter. C. C. Hamilton
Jefferson Boone, Handyman. J. Messmann
Jefferson Secret. H. Blaker
Jenkin's Green. R. Arnold
Jennerton & Co. E. P. Oppenheim
Jennie Barlowe, Adventures. E. O'Donnell
Jennie Baxter, Journalist. R. Barr
Jennifer. J. Goodwin
Jennifer by Moonlight. Clarissa Ross
Jennifer Disappears. M. O'Nair
Jennifer Pontefracte. A. Askew
Jenny and I. J. Letton
Jenny Be Good. W. F. Fauley
Jenny Kissed Me. R. Fenisong
Jenny Newstead. M. B. Lowndes
Jenny Nobody. M. Hutton
Jenny Wren. R. Kirkbridge
Jenny's Case. E. F. Pinsent

Jensen Scenario. W. Fennerton
Jeopardy. M. Conte
Jeopardy Is My Job. S. Marlowe
Jeremiah and the Princess. E. P. Oppenheim
Jeremiah Painter. G. Wolk
Jeremy Takes a Hand. C. K. Rathbone
Jericho Commandment. J. Patterson
Jericho Gun. A. C. H. Smith
Jericho Man. J. Lutz
Jerry the Lag. P. Baron
Jersey Guns. D. Pendleton
Jersey Plunder. J. Chancellor
Jerusalem Conspiracy. D. A. Riis
Jerusalem Diamond. Noah Gordon
Jerusalem File. Nick Carter
Jesmond Mystery. H. Hill
Jess. M. G. Lowe
Jessamy Court. A. Maybury
Jesse James, and His Band of Notorious Outlaws. W. Gordon
Jesse James at Coney Island. W. B. Lawson
Jesse James at Long Branch. W. B. Lawson
Jesse James' Double. W. B. Lawson
Jesse James in New York. W. B. Lawson
Jesse James' Oath. W. B. Lawson
Jessica. A. Maybury
Jessie Trim. B. L. Farjeon
Jessie Vandeleur. E. C. Mayne
Jessop Bequest. A. Burr
Jest of Darkness. V. M. Grayland
Jesus Factor. E. Corley
Jesus Man. R. Casey
Jesus II. F. Riley
Jet and Ivory. R. Thorndike
Jet Race. J. B. Lynne
Jet Stream. Austin Ferguson
Jethro Hammer. M. Venning
Jetsam. V. Bridges
Jew Detective. Anonymous
Jew of Prague. A. W. Barrett
Jewel in the Crypt. O. Baster
Jewel Island. Andrea Hill
Jewel Mysteries from a Dealer's Notebook. M. Pemberton
Jewel Mysteries I Have Known. M. Pemberton
Jewel of Death. E. Berckman
Jewel of Death. H. Mee
Jewel of Destiny. G. Davison
Jewel of Doom. Nick Carter
Jewel of Seven Stars. B. Stoker
Jewel of the Java Sea. D. Cushman
Jewel Thief. A. Mills
Jewel: Undercover Cop. G. Fogelson
Jeweled Cat. L. Rutland
Jeweled Dagger. J. Ellis
Jeweled Daughter. A. Maybury
Jeweled Hand. C. George
Jeweled Mummy. Nicholas Carter
Jeweled Secret. E. St. Clair
Jewels. R. Perrin
Jewels for a Shroud. W. De Steiguer
Jewels Go Back. E. C. Vivian
Jewels in Jeopardy. Ernest Paul
Jewels of Death. R. Halifax
Jewels of Death. M. Richmond
Jewels of Prince de Janville. Almhain
Jewels of Sin. B. Bolt
Jewels of Terror. J. L. Roberts
Jewels of Wu Ling. Jack Lewis
Jewels That Got Away. G. Madderom
Jew's House. F. Hume
"Jews" Pellegrini. B. Sarto
Jews Without Jehovah. G. Kersh
Jezebel's Daughter. W. Collins
Jig-Saw. E. Phillpotts
Jig-Saw Murder Case. R. Wallace
Jig-Saw Puzzle Murder. W. F. Eberhardt
Jig-Time Murders. C. G. Givens
Jigger Moran. J. Roeburt
Jigsaw. D. Hoddinott
Jigsaw. E. McBain
Jigsaw. Robin Sherman
Jigsaw. H. Waugh
Jigsaw John. A. Martinez
Jigsaw Man. Dorothea Bennett
Jill. T. St. Martin
Jill Fell Down. J. Tickell
Jilt. C. Reade
Jim. R. W. Kauffman
Jim Barnett Intervenes. M. Leblanc
Jim Brent. H. C. McNeile
Jim Crowshaw's Mary. F. M. White
Jim Cummings. F. Ferrars
Jim Cummings. A. F. Pinkerton
Jim Goes North. G. Goodchild
Jim Hanvey, Detective. O. R. Cohen
Jim Maitland. H. C. McNeile
Jim the Penman. C. H. Bullivant
Jim the Penman. D. Donovan
Jim the Penman. W. Gordon
Jim Trelawney. O. Binns
Jim Trent. R. W. Kauffman
Jimgrim. T. Mundy
Jimgrim and Allah's Peace. T. Mundy
Jimgrim Sahib. T. Mundy
Jimmie Dale and the Blue Envelope Murder. F. Packard
Jimmie Dale and the Missing Hour. F. Packard

J

Jimmie Dale and the Phantom Clue. F. Packard
Jimmie Rezaire. A. Armstrong
Jimmy the Kid. D. E. Westlake
Jink. T. P. McMahon
Jinx Theatre Murder. Alexander Williams
Joan in Jeopardy. R. R. King
Joan Mar, Detective. M. Leighton
Joan of the Hills. T. B. Clegg
Joan, the Curate. F. Warden
Joanna. J. Blackmore
Joanna Sets to Work. T. Cobb
Job Abroad. G. Bartram
Job Lot Sketches and Stories. J. P. Marsden
Job of Murder. F. Gruber
Jock MacKay, Crook. Scarlet Grey
Jockey. G. Verner
Jockey Club Stories. F. Barrett
Jockey Died First. A. Mills
Jockey's Revenge. N. Gould
Joe Jenkins' Case Book. P. Rosenhayn
Joe Jenkins: Detective. P. Rosenhayn
Joe Leslie's Wife. A. Robertson
Joe Muller, Detective. G. I. Colbron
Joe Phoenix, Private Detective. A. W. Aiken
Joe Phoenix Puzzled. Anonymous
Joe Phoenix, the Police Spy. A. W. Aiken
Joey Collects. Joey
Joey Kills. Joey
Jogger's Moon. J. Messmann
Johanna, the Unpredictable. K. Kimbrough
John Allard. E. M. Ingram
John Ames, Native Commissioner. B. Mitford
John and Son. P. Trent
John Armiger's Revenge. P. H. Hunter
John Boddy. T. Thurston
John Brand, Fugitive. J. Creasey
John Brand's Will. H. Adams
John Brown & Larry Lohengrin. W. Westall
John Brown's Body. E. C. R. Lorac
John Carruthers: Indian Policeman. E. C. Cox
John Carstairs, Space Detective. F. B. Long
John Clutterbuck. J. Ruegg
John Dene of Toronto. H. Jenkins
John Dighton, Mystery Millionaire. M. Pemberton
John Doe—Murderer. W. Dale
John Fanning's Legacy. N. Royde-Smith
John Ford. F. Barrett
John Hazel's Vengeance. W. S. Hayward
John Heriot's Wife. A. Askew
John Horsleydown. T. L. Holt
John Jasper's Gatehouse. Edwin Harris
John Jasper's Secret. Anonymous
John Jasper's Secret. E. Jones-Evans
John Jenkin, Public Enemy. B. Graeme
John Jeremy—Cracksman. Jeffrey Montague
John Kyleing Died. E. Radford
John Lillibud. F. G. Hurrell
John Lisbon, Agent. J. Budd
John Macnab. J. Buchan
John Marchmont's Legacy. M. E. Braddon
John Montcalm. M. Gerard
John Needham's Double. J. Hatton
John o' the Green. J. Farnol
John Parmelee's Curse. J. Hawthorne
John Quinton's Secret. R. H. Poole
John Riddell Murder Case. J. Riddell
John Rutland's Romance. J. P. Bessell
John Silence. A. Blackwood
John Smith Hears Death Walking. W. Blassingame
John Solomon, Incognito. A. Hawkwood
John Thorndyke's Cases. R. A. Freeman
John Topp, Pirate. W. Chesney
John Traile: Smuggler. A. Salcroft
John Vale's Guardian. D. C. Murray
John Webb's End. F. Adams
Johnnie. D. B. Hughes
Johnnie Madison. J. Haslette
Johnny Belinda. E. B. Harris
Johnny Blood. P. Malloch
Johnny Come Deadly. P. Race
Johnny Come Lately. F. Kane
Johnny Counterfeit. M. Y. Shapleigh
Johnny Danger. P. Allardyce
Johnny Death. W. Schnurr
Johnny Get Your Gun. J. Ball
Johnny Gets His! D. Ambler
Johnny Goes East. D. Cory
Johnny Goes North. D. Cory
Johnny Goes South. D. Cory
Johnny Goes West. D. Cory
Johnny Havoc. J. Jakes
Johnny Havoc and the Doll Who Had "It". J. Jakes
Johnny Havoc Meets Zelda. J. Jakes
Johnny, I Hardly Knew You. E. O'Brien
Johnny Liddell's Morgue. F. Kane
Johnny Lost. P. Jones
Johnny Ludlow. H. Wood
Johnny Ludlow. Fifth Series. H. Wood
Johnny Ludlow. Fourth Series. H. Wood
Johnny Ludlow. Second Series. H. Wood
Johnny Ludlow. Sixth Series. H. Wood
Johnny Ludlow. Third Series. H. Wood
Johnny on the Spot. A. Dell

Johnny Purple. J. Wyllie
Johnny Staccato. F. Boyd
Johnny Under Ground. P. Moyes
Johnstown Stage, and other stories. R. H. Fletcher
Joker. H. Osborne
Joker. E. Wallace
Joker Deals with Death. W. M. Duncan
Joker in the Deck. R. S. Prather
Joker in the Pack. J. H. Chase
Joker Takes Queen. B. Munslow
Jokers. M. Sands
Jolly Jess. Old Sleuth
Jolly Roger Mystery. P. Lancaster
Jonah Game. J. S. Abel
Jonah's Luck. F. Hume
Jonas Haggerley. J. J. Wray
Jonathan Bradford. T. P. Prest
Jonathan Guest. Margaret Archer
Jones, A., Finds the Body. H. McEvoy
Jones Men. V. E. Smith
Jones's Little Murders. E. Radford
Jordan Intercept. J. A. MacKenzie
Jordans Murder. S. Fowler
Joseph File. Alfred Harris
Joseph Prickett, the Scotland Yard Detective. I. Murray
Joseph Proctor's Money. W. H. L. Craufurd
Joseph Stone. J. La Tourrette
Joseph's Coat. D. C. Murray
Joshua Haggard's Daughter. M. E. Braddon
Joshua Humble. E. R. Reach
Joss. R. Marsh
Josselin Takes a Hand. A. C. Brown
Journey Downstairs. R. Philmore
Journey from Baghdad. David Roberts
Journey in the Dark. J. Ames
Journey into Danger. D. Faber
Journey into Danger. J. M. Fox
Journey into Danger. Beatrice Taylor
Journey into Darkness. I. Mercer
Journey into Death. Jack Jones
Journey into Fear. E. Ambler
Journey into Fear. V. Norwood
Journey into Fear. M. Ruuth
Journey into Stone. A. E. Lindop
Journey into Terror. D. Daniels
Journey into Terror. P. Rabe
Journey into Twilight. M. Lynch
Journey into Violence. D. Orgill
Journey into Violence. H. Whittington
Journey Past Repentance. G. Arnaud
Journey to a Safe Place. I. S. Black
Journey to Cuzco. M. R. Myers
Journey to Genoa. F. D. Fawcett
Journey to Happiness. M. Richmond
Journey to Love. Rona Randall
Journey to Murder. R. P. Koehler
Journey to Nowhere. N. Tyre
Journey to Orassia. A. Caillou
Journey to Romance. L. Ames
Journey to the Hangman. A. W. Upfield
Journey with a Stranger. The Gordons
Journeying Boy. M. Innes
Journey's End. E. Berckman
Journey's Eve. J. Cadell
Joy House. D. Keene
Joy Ride. J. G. Brandon
Joy Ride. A. Prior
Joy Wheel. P. W. Fairman
Joyce Harrington's Trust. B. Marchant
Joyce Pleasantry and other stories. G. R. Sims
Joyce, the Beloved. K. Kimbrough
Joyful Jays. J. C. Lenehan
Joyous Adventures of Aristide Pujol. W. J. Locke
Joyous Conspirator. G. F. Gibbs
Juanita Carrington. R. Jocelyn
Judah Lion Contract. P. Atlee
Judas. E. R. Johnson
Judas! P. Van Greenaway
Judas C.I.D. F. Grierson
Judas Cat. D. S. Davis
Judas Conspiracy. J. Ballem
Judas Country. G. Lyall
Judas Cross. J. M. Wallmann
Judas Diary. W. H. Baker
Judas Factor. J. Shelynn
Judas Flight. T. Beattie
Judas Freak. H. Pentecost
Judas Gene. J. Klainer
Judas Goat. B. Cleeve
Judas Goat. L. Edgley
Judas Goat. R. B. Parker
Judas Gospel. P. Van Greenaway
Judas Hour. Howard Hunt
Judas, Incorporated. K. Steel
Judas Journey. Lee Roberts
Judas Judge. S. Jason
Judas Kiss. H. Adams
Judas Kiss. J. J. Dratler
Judas Mandate. C. Egleton
Judas Pair. J. Gash
Judas Sheep. Jan Roberts
Judas Spies. Colin Robertson
Judas Spy. Nick Carter
Judas Squad. J. N. Rowe
Judas Way. C. Whitton
Judas Window. Carter Dickson
Judd for the Defense. L. Goldman

Judge. E. W. Peattie
Judge. Alan Thomas
Judge and His Hangman. F. Duerrenmatt
Judge and the Hatter. G. Simenon
Judge Dee at Work. R. Van Gulik
Judge Is Reversed. F. Lockridge
Judge Me Not. J. D. MacDonald
Judge Me Tomorrow. H. Jobson
Judge Not. C. H. Bullivant
Judge of Men. J. A. Ford
Judge Priest Turns Detective. I. S. Cobb
Judge Robinson Murdered! R. L. Goldman
Judge Speaks. R. Monroe
Judge Sums Up. J. J. Farjeon
Judge Will Call It Murder. S. M. Lott
Judge's Chair. E. Phillpotts
Judge's Daughters. G. E. Mitton
Judge's Dilemma. S. Kyle
Judges of Hades, and other Simon Ark stories. E. D. Hoch
Judgment. T. Wicker
Judgment Castle. A. Wood
Judgment Day. R. Sapir
Judgment Deferred. G. Braddon
Judgment in St. Peter's. A. N. Rotsstein
Judgement in Stone. R. Rendell
Judgment in Suspense. G. Bullett
Judgment Night. D. Honig
Judgment of Ann. P. Trent
Judgment of Death. A. Mills
Judgment of Death. M. Richmond
Judgment of Deke Hunter. G. V. Higgins
Judgment of Helen. T. Cobb
Judgment of Larose. A. Gask
Judgment on Deltchev. E. Ambler
Judgment Rock. L. A. Knight
Judicial Body. M. Scherf
Judson Murder Case. A. B. Leonard
Judy—and the Philosopher. T. Gallon
Judy Ashbane, Police Decoy. M. O'Nair
Judy of Bunter's Buildings. E. P. Oppenheim
Judy the Torch. A. P. Hankins
Jugger. R. Stark
Juggernaut. Alice Campbell
Juggernaut. A. Hine
Juggler and the Soul. H. B. Mathews
Juggler of Nankin. S. Cobb
Juggling Fortune. T. W. Speight
Juice. S. Becker
Juju. D. Onyeama
Juke Box King. F. Kane
Julia. P. Straub
Julia Ballantyne. G. R. Preedy
Julia Bicknell. O. Bradbury
Julie. A. L. Stone
Juliet Bravo. Mollie Hardwick
Juliet Dies Twice. Lange Lewis
Juliet Room. G. Hall
Julius Caesar Is Alive and Well. I. A. Greenfield
Julius Caesar Murder Case. Wallace Irwin
Julius Vernon. P. L. MacDermott
July at Fritham. M. Home
July 14 Assassination. B. Abro
Jump Cut. R. R. Irvine
Jump for Glory. G. McDonell
Jump into the Sun. P. Gregor
Jump the Gun. M. Cronin
Jump the High Wall. C. Richardson
Jumping Jenny. A. Berkeley
June, Moon, and Murder. C. M. Russell
June 13. F. Vreeland
Jungle Crime. L. Allan
Jungle Goddess. O. Sackville
Jungle Heat. D. Wilmer
Jungle Hut. E. P. Thorne
Jungle Jest. T. Mundy
Jungle Kids. E. Hunter
Jungle Manhunt. J. Laffin
Jungle Murder. A. Amos
Jungle of Stars. J. L. Chalker
Jungle She. D. Cushman
Jungle Terror. H. Wickham
Junior League Murders. C. Canyon
Juniper Hill. D. Daniels
Juniper Rock. P. Atkey
Junk Market. H. Janson
Junkyard Angel. J. Harvey
Jupiter Crisis. W. Harrington
Jupiter Missile Mystery. E. Beatty
Juror. M. Underwood
Juror in Waiting. H. Cecil
Juror No 17. C. C. Waddell
Jurors. B. Siegal
Jury. C. Bullett
Jury. E. Phillpotts
Jury Disagree. G. Goodchild
Jury Is Out. D. W. Rimel
Jury of Angels. B. Strutton
Jury of Death. R. C. Washburn
Jury of Four. G. Vallings
Jury of Her Peers. S. Glaspell
Jury of His Peers. J. Pearl
Jury of One. M. G. Eberhart
Jury People. J. Wainwright
Juryman. D. MacKenzie
Juryman. E. E. Sumner
Just a Corpse at Twilight. Robert Martin
Just a Matter of Time. J. H. Chase
Just a Song at Twilight. J. Lodwick

Title Index

Just an Ordinary Case. B. Graeme
Just and the Unjust. Nicholas Carter
Just and the Unjust. J. G. Cozzens
Just Another Murder. D. Furber
Just Another Sucker. J. H. Chase
Just Around the Corner. Elizabeth Ford
Just Around the Coroner. S. Brock
Just As I Am. M. E. Braddon
Just Desserts. T. Heald
Just Desserts. R. Jeffries
Just Fate. G. Long
Just for the Bread. R. Kelly
Just for the Bride. D. P. Clark
Just Killing Time. R. Ellington
Just Let Me Be. J. Cleary
Just Men of Cordova. E. Wallace
Just Murder, Darling. J. A. Brussel
Just Not Making Mayhem Like They Used To. D. Von Elsner
Just One Slip. Nicholas Carter
Just Sheaffer, or Storms in the Troubled Heir. I. Mowatt
Just the Way It Is. Raymond Marshall
Just Vengeance. L. P. Greene
Just What the Doctor Ordered. Colin Watson
Justice! C. F. Gregg
Justice. G. Simenon
Justice Astray. S. Warwick
Justice Be Damned. A. Hilliard
Justice By Accident. V. Lester
Justice by Midnight. J. Farnol
Justice by Proxy. G. H. Davies
Justice-Clerk. W. D. Lyell
Justice Ends at Home. R. Stout
Justice Enough. H. Carmichael
Justice for a Dead Spy. J. Moffatt
Justice for Judas. I. Baker
Justice for Judy. C. E. Vulliamy
Justice for Julia. M. Richmond
Justice Has No Sword. M. Franklin
Justice Hunt. M. Turner
Justice in Jeopardy. C. M. Wills
Justice, Inc. K. Robeson
Justice Is Done. A. Soutar
Justice Is Mine. E. P. Thorne
Justice Limited. F. Duncan
Justice Never Sleeps. O. Williams
Justice of Revenge. George Griffith
Justice of Sanders. F. Gerard
Justice on Halfaday Creek. J. B. Hendryx
Justice on the Rocks. B. Knox
Justice Peeps over the Handkerchief. C. Herbert
Justice Returns. F. Duncan
Justice—Suspended. R. Marsh
Justification of Andrew Lebrun. F. Barrett
Justified Sinner. J. F. Molloy
Justin Bayard. J. Cleary
Justine. W. Calvert
Justus Wise. A. W. Barrett
Juve in the Dock. M. Allain
Juvenile Delinquent. R. Deming
Juvenile Delinquents. L. Kaufman
Juvenile Hoods. J. Shallit
Juvenile Jungle. F. Counsel
Juvies. H. Ellison

"K." L. Waller
K Assignment. L. Waller
K Code Plan. G. Seton
KG 200. J. D. Gilman
KGB Frame. J. Rosenberger
KGB Is Here. C. Franklin
KKK. P. E. Walsh
K.O. for Keeps. R. Angel
K Section. T. Lilley
Ka of Gifford Hillary. D. Wheatley
Kabaka. C. Johnston
Kabbalah. D. S. Milton
Kabul Contract. Ian Mitchell
Kahuna Killer. J. Sheridan
Kaiser's Blonde Spy. G. Ladoux
Kak-Abdullah Conspiracy. M. Macao
Kalahari. H. Kolarz
Kalahari Kill. S. Dembo
Kalee's Shrine. G. Allen
Kaleidoscope. M. Avallone
Kaligarh Fault. P. Roadarmel
Kama Sutra Tango. J. F. Burke
Kamakaze Assignment. A. Sugar
Kanaga. K. R. Butler
Kane and Abel. J. Archer
Kane and Miss Able. Tod Conrad
Kanesbrake. J. Blair
Kang-He Vase. J. S. Fletcher
Kangaroo Shoots Man. A. Scobie
Kara. J. Ellis
Kara Yerta Tragedy. J. E. Harrison
Karadac, Count of Gerzy. K. Prichard
Karamanov Equations. M. Goldberg
Karamour. A. Pritchett
Karl, the Lion. S. Cobb
Karlyn. J. Jenkins
Kashmiri Love Song. M. Richmond
Kashmiri Passions. Clarissa Ross

Kastle Krags. A. Martin
Kat and Copy-Cat. E. E. Steven
Kat Strikes. N. Spain
Katana. M. Olden
Kate Hannigan. C. Cookson
Kate Meredith, Financier. C. J. C. Hyne
Kate, Plus Ten. E. Wallace
Kate Scott, the Decoy Detective. Anonymous
Kate, the Curious. K. Kimbrough
Kath. K. Henshaw
Katharine Beresford. H. M. Jones
Katherine and the Dark Angel. M. Reisner
Kathleen. T. P. Prest
Kathrine, the Returned. K. Kimbrough
Katie Mulholland. C. Cookson
Katmandu Affair. P. Davidson
Katmandu Contract. Nick Carter
Katrina. R. Kirkbridge
Kaufman Snatch. Robin Moore
Keane of Kalgoorlie. A. Wright
Kearny Died Twice. K. Howard
Keeban. E. Balmer
Keegan. B. Ball
Keegan: The No-Option Contract. B. Ball
Keegan: The One-Way Deal. B. Ball
Keep. J. Schubert
Keep Away from Water! Alice Campbell
Keep Back the Dark. A. McElfresh
Keep Cool, Mr. Jones. T. Fuller
Keep It a Secret. Philip Chambers
Keep It Crisp. S. J. Perelman
Keep It Quiet. R. Hull
Keep It Simple. L. Johnson
Keep Moving, Bud. D. Linton
Keep Murder Quiet. S. Jepson
Keep the Coffins Coming. J. Long
Keep This Door Shut. A. M. Williamson
Keep Your Fingers Crossed. S. Maddock
Keep Your Fingers Crossed. Kevin O'Hara
Keeper. H. Le Roy
Keeper of Black Hounds. Nicholas Carter
Keeper of Red Horse Pass. W. C. Tuttle
Keeper of the Children. W. H. Hallahan
Keeper of the Keys. E. D. Biggers
Keeper of the Keys. F. W. Robinson
Keepers. R. H. Greenan
Keepers. Sam Ross
Keepers of Death. S. Jason
Keepers of the King's Peace. E. Wallace
Keeping Time. D. Bear
Keeps Death His Court. M. Durham
Keerboskloof. N. Giles
Kefton, the Detective. Old Sleuth
Kek Huuygens, Smuggler. R. L. Fish
Keller's Bomb. L. Dunning
Kellogg Junction. B. Spicer
Kelly. Eric Lambert
Kelly Among the Nightingales. J. F. Burke
Kelpie's Burn. John Latimer
Kemmler. Hawkshaw
Kennedy for the Defense. G. V. Higgins
Kennedy's Killing. A. Venters
Kennel Murder Case. S. S. Van Dine
Kennels Crime. M. Osborne
Kentucky Detective. Anonymous
Kentucky Moonshiner. I. Stark
Kenya Mystery. C. T. Stoneham
Kenya Tragedy. Roland Daniel
Kenyatta's Escape. A. C. Clark
Kenyatta's Last Hit. A. C. Clark
Kept Women Can't Quit. A. A. Fair
Kermanshah Transfer. E. Sigel
Kerrell. Taffrail
Kessler Alliance. T. Horstman
Kessler Legacy. R. M. Stern
Kestrel. R. E. Salwey
Kestrel House Mystery. T. C. H. Jacobs
Kestrel Syndicate. Jack Lewis
Kestrel's Clue. Jack Lewis
Kestrel's Conspiracy. Jack Lewis
Kettel Mill Mystery. J. Oellrichs
Kettle of Fish. R. Duncan
Kettle of Fish. N. Tranter
Key. M. Aldanov
Key. B. Kevern
Key. M. B. Lowndes
Key. L. Thayer
Key. P. Wentworth
Key Diablo. D. Daniels
Key Major. T. S. Strachan
Key Man. C. B. Kelland
Key Man. V. Williams
Key Man. A. Feist
Key Ring Clew. Nicholas Carter
Key to Death. F. Lockridge
Key to Hawthorn Heath. A. P. Huff
Key to Midnight. I. Nichols
Key to Murder. Stewart Burke
Key to Murder. R. D. Cross
Key to Murder. L. Marshall
Key to Nicholas Street. S. Ellin
Key to Rebecca. K. Follett
Key to the Case. K. Orbison
Key to the Morgue. H. Howard
Key to the Morgue. Robert Martin
Key to the Suite. J. D. MacDonald
Key to Yesterday. C. N. Buck
Key West. B. Hirschfeld
Key Without a Lock. Jack Lloyd
Key Witness. M. Brett

Key Witness. F. Kane
Key Witness. W. D. Roberts
Keyhole Peeper. J. De Bekker
Keys for the Criminal. P. Hambledon
Keys of Chance. Winston Graham
Keys of Hell. M. Fallon
Keys of Hell. L. Osborne
Keys of My Prison. F. S. Wees
Keys of the Flat. E. C. Vivian
Keys to Crime. Richard Martin
Keys to Queenscourt. J. Hines
Keys to the House. R. Marion
Khaki Mafia. Robin Moore
Khan's Tale. J. B. Fraser
Kharduni. A. Soutar
Khufra Run. J. Graham
Kiai. P. Anthony
Kibbutz. Alan White
Kick-In. W. Mack
Kick-In. D. Torbett
Kick Start. D. Rutherford
Kickback. P. Malloch
Kicked to Death by a Camel. C. J.-L. Jackson
Kid. P. McCutchan
Kid Glove Charlie. J. Cashman
Kid Was a Killer. C. Chessman
Kid Was Last Seen Hanging Ten. Hampton Stone
Kid Who Came Home with a Corpse. Hampton Stone
Kid with a Gun. R. Wilkes-Hunter
Kiddy. T. Gallon
Kidnap. J. Boland
Kidnap. I. Morris
Kidnap Castle. S. Styles
Kidnap Club. A. B. Reeve
Kidnap Island. Roy Vickers
Kidnap Kid. T. Kenrick
Kidnap Murder Case. S. S. Van Dine
Kidnap Murders. E. T. Woodhall
Kidnapped. A. S. Manly
Kidnapped Again. J. Crozier
Kidnapped Child. G. Ashe
Kidnapped Child. J. Creasey
Kidnapped for a Million. D. Dayle
Kidnapped for Revenge. C. E. Blaney
Kidnapped for Revenge. Grace M. White
Kidnapped Heiress. Old Sleuth
Kidnapped King. R. Arnold
Kidnapped Millionaire. R. A. Wainwright
Kidnapped Millionaires. F. U. Adams
Kidnapped President. G. Boothby
Kidnapped Prince. T. S. King
Kidnapped Scientist. M. B. Dix
Kidnapped Squatter and other Australian tales. Andrew Robertson
Kidnapped Wife. Roland Daniel
Kidnapped Witness. A. Blair
Kidnapper. C. Bishop
Kidnapper. R. Bloch
Kidnapper, and Railway Line Murder. W. G. Mack
Kidnapper of Women. M. J. Pemberton
Kidnappers. W. Kiefer
Kidnappers. B. Thomson
Kidnappers. A. E. Ullman
Kidnapper's Victim. R. Goyne
Kidnapping of Lincoln and other war detective stories. J. C. Harris
Kidnapping of Madame Storey. H. Footner
Kidnapping of the President. C. Templeton
Kidnapping Syndicate. C. B. Booth
Kidneyed Caper. Alan Chase
Kigi Sets a Trap. R. St. Clair
Kiki. John Gill
Kilbourne Connection. G. P. Larsen
Kildallon Affair. D. Vallance
Kilgaren. I. Holland
Kill! F. Scarpetta
Kill a Wicked Man. K. Hunt
Kill All the Young Girls. B. Halliday
Kill and Be Damned. M. Carrel
Kill and Desire. D. Linton
Kill and Tell. H. Rigsby
Kill As Directed. E. Queen
Kill at Dusk. P. Ketchum
Kill-Box. M. Stark
Kill City. A. Sugar
Kill Claudio. P. M. Hubbard
Kill Cure. J. Rathbone
Kill Deadline. A. Sugar
Kill Dog. J. George
Kill 'Em All. A. G. Ball
Kill 'Em with Kindness. F. Dickenson
Kill for It. R. Hawkes
Kill for the Millions. H. Kane
Kill Gently, But Sure. S. Jason
Kill Her If You Can. H. Janson
Kill Her with Passion. H. Janson
Kill Her—You'll Like It! M. Avallone
Kill Him Gently, Nurse. K. Fitzgerald
Kill Him Quickly, It's Raining. Michael Brett
Kill Him Tonight. J. Lane
Kill Him Twice. R. S. Prather
Hill Hitler. Jon Barton
Kill Huggy Bear. M. Franklin
Kill in the Ring. V. Loder
Kill Is a Four-Letter Word. A. M. Stein

Kill Jason King. R. Miall
Kill Joy. E. S. Holding
Kill Kissinger. G. De Villiers
Kill Me a Fortune. R. Colby
Kill Me a Priest. J. Farrimond
Kill Me Again. John Bentley
Kill Me and Live. C. Franklin
Kill Me for Kicks. H. Janson
Kill Me in Atami. Earl Norman
Kill Me in Shimbashi. Earl Norman
Kill Me in Shinjuku. Earl Norman
Kill Me in Tokyo. Earl Norman
Kill Me in Yokohama. Earl Norman
Kill Me in Yoshiwara. Earl Norman
Kill Me on the Ginza. Earl Norman
Kill Me, Sweet. J. Wilcox
Kill Me Tomorrow. R. S. Prather
Kill Me with Kindness. J. H. Bond
Kill My Love. K. Hunt
Kill Now—Pay Later. L. Grex
Kill Now, Pay Later. R. Kyle
Kill of Small Consequences. J. Wainwright
Kill-Off. J. Thompson
Kill Once, Kill Twice. K. Hunt
Kill 1 Kill 2. W. W. Anderson
Kill One, Kill Two. R. Kelston
Kill or Be Killed. G. Ashe
Kill or Be Killed. V. J. Santiago
Kill or Cure. E. Ferrars
Kill or Cure. Joan Fleming
Kill or Cure. W. Francis
Kill or Cure. R. Sapir
Kill Patton. C. Whiting
Kill Petrosino! F. Nolan
Kill Quick or Die. S. Jason
Kill Squad. W. Bond
Kill Squad. M. Cruz
Kill, Sweet Charity, Kill. J. L. Potter
Kill the Boss Good-By. P. Rabe
Kill the Clown. R. S. Prather
Kill the Dragon. R. Hawkes
Kill the Girls and Make Them Cry. J. Wainwright
Kill the Hack! Michael Bradley
Kill the Reporter. M. Olden
Kill the Toff. J. Creasey
Kill Them All. F. Scarpetta
Kill Them Silently. S. Jason
Kill This Man. H. Janson
Kill 3. M. Shulman
Kill Time. S. Jason
Kill to Fit. B. Fischer
Kill Two Birds. P. Levene
Kill with Care. H. L. Nelson
Kill with Kindness. R. Bloomfield
Kill with Kindness. Dell Shannon
Kill with Style. H. Gulliver
Kill Your Own Snakes. A. Seifert
Killed by Scandal. S. Nash
Killed in the Ratings. W. L. DeAndrea
Killer. Roland Daniel
Killer. L. C. Douthwaite
Killer. E. Ionesco
Killer. Wade Miller
Killer. R. Parker
Killer. P. Tonkin
Killer. C. Wells
Killer. Colin Wilson
Killer Aboard. G. H. Teed
Killer Among Us. Robert Martin
Killer Among Us. Ben Ames Williams
Killer and His Star. H. M. Stephenson
Killer and the Slain. H. Walpole
Killer at His Back. J. Godey
Killer at Large. D. Bannon
Killer at Large. Ladbroke Black
Killer at Large. N. MacKenzie
Killer at Large. M. Procter
Killer at Scotland Yard. G. Davison
Killer Bait. D. Linton
Killer Be Killed. K. Chase
Killer Boy Was Here. G. Bagby
Killer Breath. J. Wyllie
Killer by Night. H. Keyworth
Killer by Proxy. S. Jepson
Killer Came Riding. James Preston
Killer Chromosomes. R. Sapir
Killer Conference. J. Carrick
Killer Conquest. B. Gray
Killer Cop. F. Findley
Killer Cop. D. Gober
Killer Corps. P. Leslie
Killer Crabs. G. N. Smith
Killer Dies Twice. L. R. Banks
Killer Dolphin. N. Marsh
Killer Elite. R. Rostand
Killer for a Song. J. Gardner
Killer for the Chairman. M. Hebden
Killer from the Grave. F. J. Lowe
Killer Genesis. A. Kilgore
Killer Grew Tired. George Davis
Killer in Canvas Jeans. M. McCracken
Killer in Dark Glasses. H. Treece
Killer in Love. B. Sarto
Killer in My Mind. G. Blumberg
Killer in Silk. H. V. Dixon
Killer in the Crowd. G. Daviot
Killer in the House. B. Deal
Killer in the Kitchen. F. James
Killer in the Rain. R. Chandler
Killer in the Shade. P. Marlowe

Killer in the Straw. R. Lockridge
Killer in the Street. H. Nielsen
Killer in White. T. Thomey
Killer Inside Me. J. Thompson
Killer Instinct. D. Boggis
Killer Is Kissable. Carter Brown
Killer Is Loose. G. Brewer
Killer Is Loose. C. Nicolai
Killer Is Loose Among Us. R. Terrall
Killer Is Mine. T. Powell
Killer Kay. E. Wallace
Killer Keep. W. M. Duncan
Killer Loose! G. Holden
Killer Mine. H. Innes
Killer Mine. M. Spillane
Killer Moon. G. Black
Killer Mountain. M. Hammond
Killer of Fort Norman. C. Stoddard
Killer of Sheep River. C. Stoddard
Killer on the Catwalk. J. Philips
Killer on the Heights. M. Jahn
Killer on the Keys. M. Avallone
Killer on the Line. A. Hyde
Killer on the Prowl. F. Scarpetta
Killer on the Run. B. Toler
Killer on the Track. D. Rutherford
Killer on the Turnpike. W. P. McGivern
Killer Pack. W. McNeilly
Killer Pine. L. Gutteridge
Killer Reaction. J. N. Chance
Killer Road. M. Hastings
Killer Satellites. P. Kirk
Killer See, Killer Do. Jonathan Wolfe
Killer Squad. J. Creasey
Killer Take All. J. O. Causey
Killer Take All. M. Hampton
Killer Take All. P. Race
Killer That's Dead! Carl L. Brown
Killer to Come. Sam Merwin
Killer Touch. E. Queen
Killer Waiting. W. Sproule
Killer Warrior. M. Olden
Killer Watches the Manhunt. A. B. Cunningham
Killer Wind. H. Hiscock
Killer with a Badge. W. Masterson
Killer with a Golden Touch. A. Riefe
Killer with a Key. D. J. Marlowe
Killers. W. H. Fear
Killers Are My Meat. S. Marlowe
Killers Are on Velvet. Neill Graham
Killers at Sea. A. Joseph
Killers at Sea. J. Messmann
Killer's Bargain. D. Owen
Killer's Blade. P. Malloch
Killers Cannot Live. A. Kinlay
Killer's Cargo. S. Jason
Killer's Carnival. T. Field
Killer's Category. J. Armour
Killer's Choice. S. Brock
Killer's Choice. E. McBain
Killer's Choice. Wade Miller
Killers Come Cheap. E. I. English
Killer's Conscience. J. Ingersol
Killer's Contract. T. C. Bridges
Killer's Cookbook. N. S. Gray
Killers End. H. Luger
Killers for Hire. F. Colter
Killers from the Keys. B. Halliday
Killer's Game. E. Hudiburg
Killer's Highway. M. Avallone
Killers in the Sun. J. E. Dixon
Killer's Kiss. H. Ellson
Killer's Kiss. H. Kane
Killer's Laughter. I. Lambot
Killer's Manual. John Morgan
Killer's Mask. Colin Robertson
Killer's Moon. H. McCutcheon
Killers Must Die. Roland Daniel
Killers Must Eat. M. O'Brine
Killers of Innocence. J. Creasey
Killers of Karawala. E. Lindall
Killers of Starfish. J. Gillis
Killer's Payoff. E. McBain
Killers Play Rough. A. Ring
Killer's Playground. E. Harrison
Killer's Progress. F. Griffin
Killer's Rope. J. Cassells
Killer's Town. L. Falk
Killer's Wedge. E. McBain
Killfactor Five. Peter Maxwell
Killigrew. A. Dare
Killing. L. Swaim
Killing. L. White
Killing. David Wilson
Killing Affair. P. Baker
Killing at the Big Tree. D. McCarthy
Killing Bone. P. Saxon
Killing Bottle Murder. L. A. Fenn
Killing Business. A. Tack
Killing Chase. R. Simons
Killing Comes Easy. P. Chester
Killing Cousins. F. Flora
Killing Edge. R. Forrest
Killing Experiment. J. N. Chance
Killing Floor. A. Lyons
Killing for Charity. Arthur Kaplan
Killing for the Hawks. F. E. Smith
Killing Frost. M. Catto
Killing Frost. E. Burgess
Killing Game. P. Cheyney
Killing Game. B. Knox

Killing Game. L. Peters
Killing Gift. Bari Wood
Killing Ground. D. Gober
Killing Ground. S. Linakis
Killing in Black and White. M. Hastings
Killing in Gold. J. L. Hensley
Killing in Hats. J. Davey
Killing in Malta. Robert MacLeod
Killing in Rome. R. Rostand
Killing in Swords. R. Bretnor
Killing in the Market. J. Ball
Killing in the Market. N. Daniels
Killing in the Market. G. Goodman
Killing in Xanadu. B. Pronzini
Killing Is Easy. M. Cronin
Killing Jar. E. M. Beekman
Killing Jazz. C. B. Booth
Killing Kin. A. Hocking
Killing Kind. M. Franklin
Killing Kind. E. West
Killing Kindness. R. Hill
Killing Machine. B. Rossi
Killing Machine. J. Vance
Killing Match. R. Severn
Killing No Murder. Colin Howard
Killing No Murder. M. G. Kiddy
Killing No Murder. F. A. M. Webster
Killing of Alquin Judd. P. Monnow
Killing of Ezra Burgoyne. P. Luck
Killing of Francie Lake. J. Symons
Killing of Idi Amin. Leslie Watkins
Killing of Judge MacFarlane. M. Plum
Killing of Katie Steelstock. M. Gilbert
Killing of Kings. R. W. Campbell
Killing of Paris Norton. R. Garnett
Killing of R. F. K. D. Freed
Killing of the Fallow Deer. T. H. Cook
Killing of the Golden Goose. R. J. Black
Killing of the King. D. R. Slavitt
Killing Place. T. Richards
Killing Run. M. Barry
Killing Season. J. Redgate
Killing Star. M. Avallone
Killing Strike. J. Creasey
Killing the Goose. F. Lockridge
Killing Time. T. Berger
Killing Time. D. E. Westlake
Killing Touch. W. Murray
Killing Wind. John Lee
Killing with Kindness. A. Morice
Killings. Clark Howard
Killings in Carter Cave. K. Whipple
Killing's No Murder. N. MacKenzie
Killings on Kersivay. A. MacVicar
Killraven. M. Bishop
Killshot. T. Alibrandi
Killtest. G. King
Killtown. R. Stark
Killy. D. E. Westlake
Kilman's Landing. W. Judson
Kilmeny in the Dark Wood. Florence Stevenson
Kilo Forty. M. Tripp
Kilroy Gambit. I. R. Blacker
Kim. R. Colby
Kim Ruff. R. Gover
Kind Lady. E. Chodorov
Kind Man. H. Nielsen
Kind of Anger. E. Ambler
Kind of Courage. J. Harris
Kind of Justice. R. Gaines
Kind of Justice. E. Lindall
Kind of Misfortune. R. Parker
Kind of Nightmare. E. Cannon
Kind of Prisoner. J. Creasey
Kind of Treason. R. S. Elegant
Kind Uncle Buckby. John Gloag
Kindest Use a Knife. L. Revell
Kindly Dig Your Grave, and other wicked stories. S. Ellin
Kinds of Love, Kinds of Death. T. Coe
King Against Anne Bickerton. S. Fowler
King Among Crooks. J. A. Stafford
King and Joker. P. Dickinson
King and the Corpse. Max Murray
King and Two Queens. M. MacKintosh
King Blood. J. Thompson
King by Night. E. Wallace
King Cobra. M. Channing
King Cobra. F. Dudley
King Comes Back. V. Bridges
King Coppersmith. R. J. Griffin
King Dan, the Factory Detective. G. W. Goode
King Diamond. E. Bruton
King Diamond. F. M. White
King Edward Intervenes. A. Keneally
King Edward Plot. R. L. Hall
King Fisher Lives. J. Rathbone
King Fritz's A.D.C. F. Hird
King in Bohemia. H. Herman
King in Check. T. Mundy
King in Jeopardy. Eva McDonald
King Is Dead. E. Queen
King Is Dead on Queen Street. F. Bonnamy
King Jaguar. D. Sherman
King John's Treasure. M. J. Ragosta
King Killers. T. B. Dewey
King Maker. K. Robeson
King Murder. C. R. Jones
King of Anarchists. B. Wayde
King of Bigamists. O. Harper

Title Index

King of Crooks. W. H. Ainsworth
King of Crooks. C. H. Bullivant
King of Dancing Valley. W. C. Tuttle
King of Detectives. Anonymous
King of Diamonds. J. J. Chichester
King of Fun. Old Sleuth
King of Gold. N. Ned
King—of Kearsarge. A. O. Friel
King of Scamps. Dick Stewart
King of Spain's Daughter. E. Spencer
King of Terrors. R. Bloch
King of Terrors. J. D. Spooner
King of the Castle. G. M. Fenn
King of the Castle. V. Holt
King of the Detectives. Old Sleuth
King of the Khyber Rifles. T. Mundy
King of the Opium Ring. C. E. Blaney
King of the Opium Ring. Grace M. White
King of the Peak. S. Cranbrook
King of the Rainy Country. N. Freeling
King of the Rocks. A. Pratt
King of the Sea. D. Bickerton
King of the Underworld. Nicholas Carter
King of the Underworld. Gwyn Evans
King of the World. G. Morton
King of Tiger Bay. J. M. Walsh
King of White Lady. R. L. Hill
King Pin. H. Miller
King Silky. L. Rosten
King-Sized Murder. W. Herber
King Spiv. L. Grex
King Vagabond. A. Wood
King Versus Wargrave. J. S. Fletcher
King Waits. M. Gerard
King Who Preferred Moonlight. A. Weigall
Kingdom and the Wall, and other tales. B. Reynolds
Kingdom Lost. P. Wentworth
Kingdom of Death. M. Allingham
Kingdom of Death. C. Leader
Kingdom of Death. H. Pentecost
Kingdom of Earth. A. Partridge
Kingdom of Hate. T. Gallon
Kingdom of Johnny Cool. J. McPartland
Kingdom of the Blind. E. P. Oppenheim
Kingdom's Castle. D. Winston
Kingdoms of the World. L. Osbourne
Kingfisher. G. Seymour
Kingfisher Scream. A. Fox
Kingmakers. B. E. Stevenson
King's Assegai. B. Mitford
King's Castle. L. Ames
King's Club Murder. I. Greig
King's Coil. C. B. Pallen
King's Counsel. F. Richardson
King's Crew. F. R. Adams
King's Curse. R. Sapir
King's Detective. Old Sleuth
Kings Die Hard. C. G. Booth
King's Elm Mystery. J. Goodwin
King's Enemies. Reginald Campbell
King's Enemies. J. M. Walsh
King's Falcon. C. Darby
King's Gambit. G. Chesbro
King's Highway. H. B. M. Watson
Kings in Adversity. E. S. Van Zile
King's Incognito. W. LeQueux
King's Justice. L. Galletley
King's Mate. R. F. Murphy
King's Messenger. J. M. Walsh
Kings of Crime. M. Grant
King's Pawn. W. D. Roberts
King's Point. P. L. Sandberg
King's Prisoner. Nicholas Carter
King's Ransom. Ralph Hayes
King's Ransom. E. McBain
King's Red-Haired Girl. S. Jepson
King's Secret. H. H. C. Gibbons
King's Secret. R. H. Poole
King's Secret. R. H. Savage
King's Signature. A. Askew
King's Signet. M. Gerard
King's Stockbroker. A. C. Gunter
King's Talisman. S. Cobb
Kingsclere Mystery. M. Dalton
Kingsford Mark. V. Canning
Kingsley the Detective. Old Sleuth
Kingston Black. R. East
Kingston Papers. R. S. Silverman
Kink. L. Brock
Kinks. A. Ambrose
Kinsman to Death. B. Cottingham
Kinsmen. W. Haggard
Kiriov Tapes. O. Sela
Kirkby's Changeling. M. Brent
Kirke Webbe, the Privateer Captain. Waters
Kirkland Revels. V. Holt
Kirkwood Fires. Deborah Lewis
Kirsty Affair. D. Hall
Kiss a Day Keeps the Corpses Away. J. Yardley
Kiss and Kill. Joe Barry
Kiss and Kill. Carter Brown
Kiss and Kill. R. Deming
Kiss and Kill. Adam Knight
Kiss and Kill. R. McCary
Kiss and Kill. Martin Meyers
Kiss and Kill. E. Queen
Kiss and Kill. M. Strobel
Kiss Before Dying. I. Levin
Kiss—But Never Tell. C. Linden

Kiss Daddy Goodbye. T. Altman
Kiss for a Killer. C. C. Fickling
Kiss for a Killer. D. B. Hughes
Kiss for a Killer. B. Sanders
Kiss for a Killer. E. F. Stafford
Kiss Her Goodbye. Wade Miller
Kiss Kiss. R. Dahl
Kiss! Kiss! Kill! Kill! H. Kane
Kiss Me Again, Stranger. D. Du Maurier
Kiss Me As You Go. D. Spade
Kiss Me Deadly. Carter Brown
Kiss Me, Deadly. M. Spillane
Kiss Me Hard. T. Brandt
Kiss Me, Kill Me. K. Cameron
Kiss Me, Kill Me. B. Sarto
Kiss Me Quick. K. Kramer
Kiss My Fist! J. H. Chase
Kiss of Death. L. P. Bachmann
Kiss of Death. C. Birkin
Kiss of Death. Malcom Knight
Kiss of Death. E. Lipsky
Kiss of Death. F. Scarpetta
Kiss of Hot Sun. N. Buckingham
Kiss of the Damned. S. Harragan
Kiss of the Enemy. H. Hill
Kiss of Vengeance. R. Roleine
Kiss-Off. D. Heyes
Kiss off the Dead. Garrity
Kiss That Failed. G. Leroux
Kiss the Babe Goodbye. B. McKnight
Kiss the Blonde Goodbye. F. McDermid
Kiss the Blood off My Hands. Gerald Butler
Kiss the Book. A. Spiller
Kiss the Boss Goodbye. R. Crawford
Kiss the Boys and Make Them Die. J. Yardley
Kiss the Corpse Goodbye. M. Storm
Kiss the Girls and Make Them Die. C. W. Runyon
Kiss the Killer. J. Shallit
Kiss the Tiger. F. M. Davis
Kiss the Toff. J. Creasey
Kiss Tomorrow Goodbye. Griff
Kiss Tomorrow Goodbye. H. McCoy
Kiss Your Elbow. A. Handley
Kissed Corpse. A. Baker
Kissed Corpse. W. J. Elliott
Kisses Can Kill. Donnell Carey
Kisses from Satan. G. B. Mair
Kisses Leave No Fingerprints. M. Fredman
Kisses of Death. H. Kane
Kissing Covens. Colin Watson
Kissing Gourami. K. Platt
Kissing the Rod. E. Yates
Kissinger Noodles. M. Wilk
Kit. J. Payn
Kit Wyndham. F. Barrett
Kitchen Cake Murder. C. Bush
Kitten with a Whip. Wade Miller
Kitten with Blue Eyes. J. Godden
Kitterman Legacy. A. McCaffrey
Kitty Atherton. M. Blount
Kitty Brown's Princess. E. Jepson
Kitty Shafton—Swindler. A. Askew
Kitty the Madcap. M. M. Bodkin
Kitty's Engagement. F. Warden
Kitty's Father. F. Barrett
Kiwi Club. N. Leslie
Kiwi Contract. P. Atlee
Kleinert Case. Jack Mann
Klondike Claim. Nicholas Carter
Klondyke Kit's Revenge. G. Goodchild
Klondyker. B. Knox
Klute. W. Johnston
Knave of Diamonds. J. Karney
Knave of Diamonds. Percy Marks
Knave of Eagles. R. Wade
Knave of Hearts. Dell Shannon
Knave Takes Queen. P. Cheyney
Knaves & Co. S. Horler
Knaves' Castle. Colin Robertson
Knaves in High Places. Nicholas Carter
Knaves of Diamonds. George Griffith
Knaves Rampant. W. Mills
Knavish Crows. Sara Woods
Knee-Deep in Death. B. Fischer
Knife. H. Adams
Knife. H. Ellson
Knife at My Back. Adam Knight
Knife Behind the Curtain. V. Williams
Knife Behind You. J. Benet
Knife Edge. W. Ellis
Knife Edge. D. MacKenzie
Knife-Edged Thing. S. Mitchell
Knife for Celeste. E. Burgess
Knife for Harry Dodd. G. Bellairs
Knife for the Juggler. M. Coles
Knife for the Killer. N. Morland
Knife for the Toff. J. Creasey
Knife for Your Heart. P. Marlowe
Knife in My Back. Sam Merwin
Knife in the Dark. G. D. H. Cole
Knife in the Night. W. M. Duncan
Knife Is Feminine. C. Jay
Knife Is Silent. D. Kent
Knife Terror. A. West
Knife Will Fall. M. Cumberland
Knifed in the Back. Chet Moore
Knifeman. D. Craig
Knight and the Castle. J. N. Chance
Knight at Arms. S. Horler

Knight Errant. E. Jepson
Knight in Red Armor. D. Daniels
Knight Missing. S. Stone
Knight of Evil. D. Donovan
Knight of the Nineteenth Century. E. P. Roe
Knight of the Silver Star. C. Lys
Knight Reluctant. C. Headlam
Knight Sinister. S. Rattray
Knight Takes Queen. G. Goodchild
Knight Templar. L. Charteris
Knight's Gambit. G. Dickson
Knight's Gambit. W. Faulkner
Knight's Keep. Rona Randall
Knight's Move. F. L. Cary
Knights of Arabia. San Antonio
Knightsbridge Affair. C. Dawe
Knives Have Edges. S. Woods
Knock and Come In. G. Goodchild
Knock and Wait a While. W. R. Weeks
Knock at Midnight. C. Blackstock
Knock at Midnight. J. Reston
Knock Down. D. Francis
Knock 'Em Dead. J. Karney
Knock, Knock! Who's There? J. H. Chase
Knock, Knock, Who's There? Anthony Gilbert
Knock, Knock, You're Dead. V. J. Santiago
Knock, Murderer, Knock! H. Rutland
Knock on Any Head. F. S. Miller
Knock on Wood. G. Hughes
Knock-Out. H. C. McNeile
Knock-Out Kavanagh. Brian Stuart
Knock Softly on Death's Door. T. E. Wilson
Knock Three-One-Two. F. Brown
Knocked for a Loop. C. Rice
Knocker on Death's Door. Ellis Peters
Knockout. C. F. Coe
Knockover. N. Thornburg
Knots in the Noose. Nicholas Carter
Knots Untied. G. S. McWatters
Knotted Silk. Monte Barrett
Know Then Thyself. H. Gibbs
Known as Z.1. G. Goodchild
Knuckles. C. B. Kelland
Knutsford Mystery. D. Donovan
Koberg Link. A. Maling
Kobra Manifesto. Adam Hall
Kocska Formula. F. Riley
Koheleth. L. A. Storrs
Kojak. Abby Mann
Kokoda Trail. R. Wilkes-Hunter
Kolchak's Gold. B. Garfield
Komani Mystery. V. Sampson
Komespi Affair. Ernest Paul
Kondrasher Chase. J. Rosenberger
Konigsmark. P. Benoit
Kono Diamond. N. Daniels
Kontrol. E. Snell
Korean Conspiracy. M. S. Weiss
Korean Tiger. Nick Carter
Kosygin Is Coming. T. Ardies
Kowloon Contract. P. Atlee
Krakatao Cult. J. Prescot
Kramer Project. R. A. Smith
Kramer's War. Derek Robinson
Krazny Connection. P. Lauben
Kregoff Necklace. Nicholas Carter
Kremlin Conspiracy. S. Flannery
Kremlin File. Nick Carter
Kremlin Letter. N. Behn
Kremlin Watcher. W. Perry
Kreutzman Formula. V. Scott
Kriegspiel. F. H. Groome
Kristiana Killers. H. Burland
Kronos Plot. J. Rosenberger
Kronstadt. M. Pemberton
Kruger's Wagon. F. H. Rose
Krush. H. Janson
Kubla Khan Caper. R. S. Prather
Kukri Killer. R. Gilmour
Kumbh Docket. S. Dave
Kummersdorf Connection. E. Ramsey
Kundu. M. L. West
Kung Fu Avengers. M. Minick
Kyd for Hire. Timothy Harris
Kyle Contract. D. MacKenzie
Kyriakos and the Toad. A. Sewart

L

L for Murder. M. Stand
"L" Mystery. Dick Stewart
LSD Dossier. Roger Harris
L.2002. E. Jepson
La Belle Laurine. B. Graeme
La Bora. P. Jones
La Casa Dorada. J. L. Roberts
La Masque. C. M. Carleton
Label It Murder. Neill Graham
Laboratory Murder and other stories. N. Morland
Labour of Hercules. M. B. Lowndes
Labours of Hercules. A. Christie
Laburnum Grove. J. B. Priestley
Labyrinth. R. M. Gilchrist
Labyrinth. E. MacKenzie-Lamb

Labyrinth. B. Pronzini
Labyrinth. Diane Stevens
Labyrinth Makers. A. Price
Labyrinthine Ways. G. Greene
Labyrinths. J. L. Borges
Lace in the Mews. R. Glover
LaChance Mine Mystery. S. Carleton
Lachlan's Woman. A. Dwyer-Joyce
Lackey and the Lady. T. Gallon
Lacquer Screen. R. Van Gulik
Lad of Mettle. N. Gould
Ladder of Cards. J. Chancellor
Ladder of Death. B. Flynn
Ladies Always Talk. S. Truss
Ladies and Gentlemen. B. Hecht
Ladies' Bane. P. Wentworth
Ladies' Bar. W. Dinner
Ladies Can Be Dangerous. L. Marshall
Ladies in Boxes. G. Burgess
Ladies in Danger. J. Carlton
Ladies in Ermine. Gavin Holt
Ladies in Ermine. F. A. Kummer
Ladies in Retirement. E. Percy
Ladies in Retreat. B. Perowne
Ladies in the Case. E. C. Vivian
Ladies in the Dark. M. Neville
Ladies in Waiting. C. Campion
Ladies' Juggernaut. A. C. Gunter
Ladies Leave the Castle. A. Athen
Ladies' Man. Rupert Hughes
Ladies of Holderness. D. Fowler
Ladies of Locksley. F. Vivian
Ladies Prefer Bruisers. A. Applin
Ladies Sleep Alone. L. Della
Ladies Won't Wait. P. Cheyney
Lady. C. Massie
Lady Adelaide's Oath. H. Wood
Lady Afraid. L. Dent
Lady All Alone. L. Noel
Lady and Her Doctor. E. Piper
Lady and Leader. J. G. Sarasin
Lady and the Arsenic. J. Shearing
Lady and the Burglar. Edgar Turner
Lady and the Cheetah. J. Flagg
Lady and the Giant. C. B. Kelland
Lady and the Pirate. P. Allardyce
Lady and the Prowler. J. Roeburt
Lady and the Snake. J. Farr
Lady and the Unicorn. P. H. Irving
Lady Anne's Trustee, and other stories. F. Warden
Lady at Bay. E. Maass
Lady Audley's Secret. M. E. Braddon
Lady Audley's Secret. C. Cox
Lady Bachelor. H. P. Halsey
Lady, Be Bad. B. Halliday
Lady, Be Careful. C. Reeve
Lady, Behave! P. Cheyney
Lady Beware. P. Cheyney
Lady Bites. B. Sarto
Lady Bites the Dust. M. Shane
Lady Borrodale's Ordeal. A. Askew
Lady Bug. F. Nordstrom
Lady Called Nita. E. Wallace
Lady Came by Night. B. Halliday
Lady Came to Kill. M. E. Chaber
Lady Can Do. S. Merwin
Lady Cat. N. Greenwald
Lady Christ. D. MacGregor
Lady Clara. F. M. White
Lady Death. G. Braddon
Lady Detective. Anonymous
Lady Detective. Rebecca Marsh
Lady Detective. Old Sleuth
Lady Doctor—Woman Spy. B. Newman
Lady, Don't Die on My Doorstep. J. Shallit
Lady, Don't Shroud Me! M. Brody
Lady—Don't Turn Over. D. Glinto
Lady Dorothy's Indiscretion. A. Applin
Lady Doth Protest. B. Graeme
Lady, Drop Dead. L. Treat
Lady Eleanor, Lawbreaker. R. Barr
Lady Elverton's Emeralds. D. Conyers
Lady Evelyn. L. Pemberton
Lady Fell in Love. E. Woodward
Lady Finger. G. Malcolm-Smith
Lady for Botany Bay. K. Lindsay
Lady for Sale. N. Daniels
Lady Forgot. M. S. Marble
Lady from Boston. T. McHale
Lady from Hamburg. V. Hill
Lady from Lisbon. V. Blake
Lady from Long Acre. V. Bridges
Lady from Nowhere. F. Hume
Lady from Shanghai. Sherwood King
Lady from the Air. C. N. Williamson
Lady from Tokyo. M. Corrigan
Lady, Get Your Gun. P. Ernst
Lady Gets Wise. Rick Madison
Lady Gift. J. Crecy
Lady Glenroy. G. McKeand
Lady Gone Astray. K. Hewitt
Lady Grace and other stories. H. Wood
Lady Grace's Mistake. C. Gibbon
Lady Gwendoline. T. Cobb
Lady Had a Gun. N. Morland
Lady Had a Tiger. B. Brodie
Lady Has a Scar. H. Janson
Lady Has Claws. H. Desmond
Lady Has No Convictions. Carter Brown
Lady Helena. G. Leroux

Lady, Here's Your Wreath. Raymond Marshall
Lady in a Cage. R. Durand
Lady in a Frame. J. N. Chance
Lady in a Million. S. Shane
Lady in a Veil. G. R. Preedy
Lady in a Wedding Dress. S. Shane
Lady in Armour. O. R. Cohen
Lady in Black. A. Clarke
Lady in Black. B. Graeme
Lady in Black. F. Warden
Lady in Blue. A. Groner
Lady in Blue. F. M. White
Lady in Cement. A. Rome
Lady in Danger. M. Afford
Lady in Danger. S. Shane
Lady in Darkness. E. Bond
Lady in Darkness. K. Booton
Lady in Distress. M. Richmond
Lady in Distress. Martin Thomas
Lady in Dread. R. Johnson
Lady in Furs. F. Warden
Lady in Green and other stories. P. Cheyney
Lady in Leicester Square. N. W. Firth
Lady in Lilac. S. Shane
Lady in Mink. V. Caspary
Lady in No. 4. R. Keverne
Lady in Peril. L. Dent
Lady in Peril. H. Desmond
Lady in Peril. B. A. Williams
Lady in Sables. G. W. Appleton
Lady in Scarlet. Roland Daniel
Lady in Shadows. A. Lamb
Lady in Tears and other stories. P. Cheyney
Lady in the Black Mask. T. Gallon
Lady in the Blue Veil. L. Clarke
Lady in the Car. W. LeQueux
Lady in the Car with Glasses and a Gun. S. Japrisot
Lady in the Case. J. Futrelle
Lady in the Lake. R. Chandler
Lady in the Lightning. K. Tobias
Lady in the Mist. T. Charles
Lady in the Morgue. Jonathan Latimer
Lady in the Tapestry. Deborah Lewis
Lady in the Tower. K. N. Burt
Lady in the Tower. M. Ritter
Lady in the Veil. A. Abdullah
Lady in the Wood. J. Dellbridge
Lady-in-Waiting. W. LeQueux
Lady Incognito. J. M. Walsh
Lady Ingram's Retreat. J. Tattersall
Lady Ingram's Room. J. Tattersall
Lady Is a Spitfire. B. Carson
Lady Is a Spy. Lionel Black
Lady Is a Tramp. H. Zore
Lady Is a Vamp. M. Dekobra
Lady Is Afraid. G. H. Coxe
Lady Is Available. Carter Brown
Lady Is Chased. Carter Brown
Lady Is Dead. P. Laing
Lady Is in Danger. R. A. Eames
Lady Is Lethal. P. Muller
Lady Is Not Available. Carter Brown
Lady Is Not Fooling. A. Redwood
Lady Is Poison. B. Gray
Lady Is Transparent. Carter Brown
Lady Is Waiting. J. Mitchell
Lady Jezebel. F. Hume
Lady Jim of Curzon Street. F. Hume
Lady Joan's Companion. F. Warden
Lady Judas. F. Barrett
Lady Kate, the Dashing Female Detective. Anonymous
Lady Killer. G. H. Coxe
Lady Killer. Anthony Gilbert
Lady Killer. W. Hardy
Lady Killer. E. S. Holding
Lady Killer. E. McBain
Lady Killer Affair. J. Arliss
Lady Killers. J. Kirkpatrick
Lady Killers. A. Riefe
Lady Kills. B. Fischer
Lady, Lady, I Did It! E. McBain
Lady Lee. F. Warden
Lady, Lie Low. H. Janson
Lady Likes to Sin. D. Spade
Lady Lisle. M. E. Braddon
Lady Living Alone. P. Curtiss
Lady Lost. D. Cory
Lady Lost Her Head. M. L. Stokes
Lady Loved Too Well. J. Donahue
Lady Make-Believe. K. Lindsay
Lady Makes News. V. Kathrens
Lady Marked for Murder. P. Bacon
Lady Mary of the Dark House. A. M. Williamson
Lady Mary's Experiences. R. Jocelyn
Lady Maude's Mania. G. M. Fenn
Lady, Mind that Corpse. H. Janson
Lady Mislaid. C. Rayner
Lady Molly of Scotland Yard. B. Orczy
Lady Muriel's Secret. J. Middlemass
Lady Noggs, Peeress. E. Jepson
Lady of a Thousand Sorrows. L. W. Mason
Lady of Arlac. S. Shulman
Lady of Ascot. E. Wallace
Lady of Balmerino. M. Leighton
Lady of Burlesque. Gypsy Rose Lee
Lady of Chantry Glades. S. Farrant

Lady of China Street. M. Corrigan
Lady of Despair. F. Grierson
Lady of Doom. G. Verner
Lady of Drawbridge Court. S. Farrant
Lady of Little Hell. E. Wallace
Lady of Longbourne. P. Trent
Lady of Lyon House. E. Marlow
Lady of Mallow. D. Eden
Lady of Mariner's Mead. S. Farrant
Lady of Monkswood Manor. S. Farrant
Lady of Mystery House. G. C. Shedd
Lady of Night. Jerome Barry
Lady of No Compassion. P. Malloch
Lady of Ravensedge. Jack Lewis
Lady of Resource. A. S. Roche
Lady of Regan's Tower. S. Farrant
Lady of Shadows. Nicholas Carter
Lady of Storm House. E. Bond
Lady of the Barge. W. W. Jacobs
Lady of the Blue Motor. S. Paternoster
Lady of the Cameo. T. Gallon
Lady of the Guns. Andrew Murray
Lady of the Hundred Dresses. S. R. Crockett
Lady of the Ice. J. De Mille
Lady of the Island. G. Boothby
Lady of the Isle. E. Southworth
Lady of the Lens. F. C. Long
Lady of the Leopard. C. L'Epine
Lady of the Lilacs. E. D. Pierson
Lady of the Miniature. O. Binns
Lady of the Night. S. Horler
Lady of the Night. B. Swift
Lady of the Night. V. Vanardy
Lady of the North Star. O. Binns
Lady of the Rifle. F. E. Penny
Lady of the Shadows. D. Daniels
Lady of the Shroud. B. Stoker
Lady of the Swamp. C. A. Brandreth
Lady of Wildersley. J. Edgar
Lady of Winston Park. S. Farrant
Lady on a Train. L. Charteris
Lady on Fire. J. M. Ullman
Lady on Loan. E. Ellison
Lady on Platform One. L. Meynell
Lady, or the Tiger, and other stories. F. R. Stockton
Lady Ottoline. Mrs. Lodge
Lady Pamela's Pearls. J. Ironside
Lady Passenger. A. W. Marchmont
Lady Pays. S. Coburn
Lady Prefers Murder. H. A. Wrenn
Lady Regrets. J. M. Fox
Lady Richly Left. M. B. Dix
Lady Rodway's Ordeal. F. Warden
Lady Said No. A. Allyson
Lady Sarah's Deed of Gift. A. Griffin
Lady Sativa. F. Lauria
Lady Saw Red. A. R. Long
Lady Says When. D. Ambler
Lady Screams. H. Kaner
Lady Shadower. Old Sleuth
Lady Sharlow's Secret. W. M. Graydon
Lady, Shed Your Head. D. Foster
Lady Sinister. P. Warren
Lady So Silent. L. Dent
Lady Sylvia's Imposter. T. Cobb
Lady, Take Care. Colin Robertson
Lady Takes a Flyer. E. Ronns
Lady Takes Care. G. Goodchild
Lady, That's My Skull. C. Shannon
Lady—This Is It! H. Lugar
Lady, This Is Murder. Peter Chambers
Lady, Throw Me a Curve. Gene Ross
Lady to Kill. L. Dent
Lady, Toll the Bell. H. Janson
Lady Turned Traitor. Roland Daniel
Lady Turpin. H. Herman
Lady Ursula's Husband. F. Warden
Lady Vanishes. Ethel L. White
Lady Varley. D. Vane
Lady Velvet. Nicholas Carter
Lady Was a Spy. Roland Daniel
Lady Was a Tramp. H. Whittington
Lady Was Disturbed. James Warren
Lady Was Elusive. L. Cargill
Lady Was Warned. K. Rhodes
Lady Wept Alone. C. B. Dawson
Lady, What's Your Game? T. C. H. Jacobs
Lady, Where Are You? H. Desmond
Lady with a Cool Eye. G. Moffat
Lady with a Gun. E. P. Thorne
Lady with a Rose. F. Hay
Lady with the Dice. J. T. Rogers
Lady with the Limp. S. Horler
Lady Without Mercy. R. McDougald
Lady, You're Killing Me. Peter Chambers
Lady Zia. P. Wynnton
Ladybirds Are In. H. Janson
Ladye Annabel. G. Lippard
Ladyfingers. Jackson Gregory
Ladyfingers. S. Rifkin
Ladygrove. John Burke
Ladykiller. T. Mallanson
Lady's a Decoy. K. T. McCall
Lady's Eyes Were Green. A. Aldous
Lady's for Killing. B. Shannon
Lady's in Danger. N. Berrow
Lady's Mile. M. E. Braddon
Lady's Not for Burning. C. Fry
Lady's Not for Living. D. St. Clair
Lagden's Luck. T. Gallon

Title Index

Lago. John Lee
Laguna Contracts. E. C. Allen
Laidlaw. W. McIlvanney
Laidlaw's Wife. F. Warden
Lair. L. Charbonneau
Lair. J. Herbert
Lair of the Vampire. G. E. Rochester
Lair of the White Worm. B. Stoker
Laird. Winifred Duke
Laird and the Lady. Joan Grant
Laird of Evil. Martin Thomas
Lairds of Turriff Hall. A. Jamison
Lake District Murder. J. Bude
Lake Frome Monster. A. W. Upfield
Lake House. J. Rhode
Lake Isle. N. Freeling
Lake Loot. H. Janson
Lake Lovers. G. Wagner
Lake Mystery. M. Dana
Lake of Darkness. F. Cowen
Lake of Darkness. R. Rendell
Lake of Fire. L. Houser
Lake of Fury. Robert MacLeod
Lake of Ghosts. R. Bell
Lake of the Dead. L. P. Greene
Lake of the Wind. Lynn Williams
Lake of Wine. B. Capes
Lakeland Tragedy. J. Courage
Lakeside Murder. C. H. Snow
Lakeside Zero. D. Enefer
Lalru Murders. E. N. Mangat Rai
Lam to Slaughter. D. Sanderson
Lam to the Slaughter. A. A. Fair
Lamaar Ransom—Private Eye. D. Galloway
Lama's Secret. W. M. Graydon
Lamb to the Slaughter. D. Eden
Lambert's Son. A. Maling
Lambs of Fire. P. Gascar
Lame Dog Murder. M. Halliday
Lament for a Lonesome Corpse. Ruth Reeves
Lament for a Lousy Lover. Carter Brown
Lament for a Lover. P. Highsmith
Lament for a Maker. M. Innes
Lament for a Virgin. L. White
Lament for Four Brides. E. Berckman
Lament for Julie. R. Colby
Lament for Leto. G. Mitchell
Lament for Lost Lovers. Alanna Knight
Lament for the Bride. H. Reilly
Lament for William. C. M. Russell
Lammas Grove. C. Dawe
Lamontane. S. Blackwood
Lamp Burns Blood. Leslie Carroll
Lamp of God. E. Queen
Lamp-Post 592. S. Maddock
Lampton Dreamers. L. P. Davies
Lanagan, Amateur Detective. E. H. Hurlbut
Lancaster Triple Thousand. W. B. Woods
Lance for the Devil. R. Charles
Lancer Spy. M. McKenna
Land at Last. E. Yates
Land from the Sea. S. Styles
Land God Gave to Cain. H. Innes
Land o' the Leal. H. B. Mathers
Land of Big Things. L. H. Gordon
Land of Eucalyptus. G. Ferrand
Land of Fear. K. Robeson
Land of Leys. L. P. Davies
Land of Long Juju. K. Robeson
Land of Eldorado. G. Goodchild
Land of No Escape. G. Horne
Land of Promises. S. P. Hyatt
Land of Shadows. F. C. Matranga
Land of Terror. K. Robeson
Land of the Free. W. McNeilly
"Land of the Free." W. Slater
Land Pirate. J. Bogar
Land Where Our Fathers Died. H. S. Nuelle
Land Without Shadow. M. Mewshaw
Landed at Last. H. Q. Gould
Landed Gently. A. Hunter
Landfall. D. W. MacArthur
Landfall Finesse. D. Da Cruz
Landlady. C. Rauch
Landlord of "The Sun". W. Gilbert
Landor Case. John Bentley
Landru. W. LeQueux
Landru. R. Masson
Land's End, and other stories. W. D. Steele
Landscape with Corpse. D. Ames
Landscape with Corpses. M. Barnes
Landscape with Dead Dons. Robert Robinson
Landscape with Violence. J. Wainwright
Landsend Terror. J. Trevelyan
Landslide. D. Bagley
Lane of Darkness. M. Clare
Langley Murder Case. Roland Daniel
Lanier Riddle. D. Daniels
Lansing Legacy. A. Hyman
Lantern for Diogenes. S. Harvester
Lantern Hill. B. Worsley-Gough
Lantern House Affair. Gret Lane
Lantern Network. T. Allbeury
Lantern of Luck. H. Douglas
Lapse of the Bishop. G. Thorne
Larceny in Her Heart. L. Grex
Large Type Killer. Richard Williams

Larksong at Dawn. Agnes Russell
Larkspur Conspiracy. J. Philips
Larrabee Heiress. D. Daniels
Larry Lohengrin. W. Westall
Las Vegas. Arthur Moore
Las Vegas Strip. M. Renek
Las Vegas Vengeance. B. Rossi
Laser War. J. Rosenberger
Lashed But Not Leashed. M. McShane
Lasko Tangent. R. N. Patterson
Last Act. J. A. Hodge
Last Act in Bermuda. D. Burnham
Last Adventure. E. Wallace
Last Alive. J. M. Cobban
Last Appointment. H. Howard
Last Assignment. N. Fisher
Last Best Friend. G. Sims
Last Believers. D. Karp
Last Breath. H. O. Masur
Last Bridge. B. Garfield
Last Bridge. D. Mariner
Last Buccaneer. J. Wainwright
Last Bus to Woodstock. C. Dexter
Last Cab on the Rank. H. Grisewood
Last Caesar. E. McGhee
Last Call. Nicholas Carter
Last Call. R. Dowling
Last Call. R. Sapir
Last Call for Lissa. D. Mayor
Last Call of Mourning. C. L. Grant
Last Card. H. H. Kirst
Last Card. Mark Ross
Last Checkpoint. J. Quigley
Last Chronicles of Ballyfungus. M. Manning
Last Clear Chance. B. Wilkinson
Last Clue. W. J. Bayfield
Last Clue. Eugene Jones
Last Command. C. Houghton
Last Commandment. G. H. Coxe
Last Concubine. F. S. Wees
Last Contract. Clark Howard
Last Cop Out. M. Spillane
Last Coup. H. Smart
Last Cruise of the "Majestic". G. Goodchild
Last Dance. J. Briley
Last Day in Limbo. P. O'Donnell
Last Day of Lincoln Charles. Gordon M. Williams
Last Days of Berlin. P. Saxon
Last Days of Louisiana Red. I. Reed
Last Days of Miss Jenkinson. N. Hoult
Last Days of New York. C. Mandeville
Last Decathalon. J. Redgate
Last Deception. H. Howard
Last Deserter. J. Robb
Last Ditch. G. Goodchild
Last Ditch. V. Hunt
Last Ditch. M. McGrath
Last Domino Contract. P. Atlee
Last Door. O. Binns
Last Door. D. Enefer
Last Doorbell. Joseph Harrington
Last Doorbell. J. K. Vedder
Last Drop. B. Cobb
Last Embrace. M. T. Bloom
Last Enemy. Keith Ayling
Last Enemy. V. M. Methley
Last Enemy. B. Roueche
Last Escape. E. C. R. Lorac
Last Escape. M. Walker
Last Express. B. Kendrick
Last Fathom. M. Caidin
Last First. R. Hull
Last Flight. M. Land
Last Flowers. Michael Barrett
Last Flying Tiger. D. E. Fisher
Last Frontier. Alistair MacLean
Last Galley. A. C. Doyle
Last Gamble. J. Fairfax-Blakeborough
Last Gamble. R. Foley
Last Gamble. H. Q. Masur
Last Good Kiss. J. Crumley
Last Great Death Stunt. Clark Howard
Last Hero. L. Charteris
Last Heroes. John Gill
Last Hope House. Wilma Forrest
Last Hour. C. Bennett
Last Hours Before Dawn. R. Gadney
Last House. G. Dessart
Last House. M. Maurice
Last Indictment. M. Cronin
Last Journey. Keith Campbell
Last Kill. Charlie Wells
Last King of Yewle. P. L. MacDermott
Last Known Address. Joseph Harrington
Last Lady. H. Janson
Last Lap. G. B. Savi
Last Laugh. C. Einstein
Last Laugh. Winifred Graham
Last Laugh and No Pictures for Cathy. P. Denver
Last Laugh for the Baron. Anthony Morton
Last Laugh, Mr. Moto. J. P. Marquand
Last Liberator. J. Clive
Last Link. M. Gerard
Last Lord Avanley. G. Maxwell
Last Magic. N. R. Nash
Last Man at Arlington. J. Di Mona
Last Man Club. E. Queen
Last Mandarin. S. Becker

Last Man's Head. Jessica Anderson
Last Mayday. K. Wheeler
Last Meeting. B. Matthews
Last Member of the Family. L. A. Sunagel
Last Mile. J. Wexley
Last Mission. C. Whiting
Last Move in the Game. Nicholas Carter
Last Movement. Joan Aiken
Last Mystery of Edgar Allan Poe. Manny Meyers
Last Nazi. M. Lamb
Last Night. J. McPartland
Last Night on Masada. Gavin Douglas
Last Note for a Lovely. Carter Brown
Last of Lysandra. Elizabeth Fenwick
Last of Mr. Moto. J. P. Marquand
Last of Mrs. Cheyney. D. G. Herriot
Last of Philip Banter. J. F. Bardin
Last of Sheila. Alexander Edwards
Last of the Armageddon Wars. R. Dennis
Last of the Country House Murders. E. Tennant
Last of the Crazy People. T. Findley
Last of the Cybernauts. P. Cave
Last of the Darrells. C. E. Pearce
Last of the Dog Team. W. W. Johnstone
Last of the Grenvilles. B. Copplestone
Last of the Mansions. D. Daniels
Last of the Pleasure Gardens. Francis King
Last of the Ruthvens. L. Barbee
Last of the Van Slacks. E. S. Van Zile
Last One Kills. W. Masterson
Last Page. J. H. Chase
Last Parable. Alex Coppel
Last Place God Made. J. Higgins
Last Place Left. M. Pugh
Last Plane from Uli. C. Keary
Last Post for a Partisan. C. Egleton
Last President. M. Kurland
Last Prisoner. J. Robson
Last Quarter Hour. J. Bruce
Last Redoubt. G. Goodchild
Last Refuge of a Scoundrel and other stories. W. Howard
Last Resort. V. Siller
Last Rights. H. H. Dooley
Last Rites for the Vulture. Simon Quinn
Last Run South. R. Hiscock
Last Safari. Richard Rhodes
Last Score. E. Queen
Last Scourge. W. Martyn
Last Secret. D. Chambers
Last Secret. G. Goodchild
Last Seen Alive. J. McCormick
Last Seen Alive. A. Mills
Last Seen Hitchhiking. B. Halliday
Last Seen in Samarra. J. G. Vermandel
Last Seen Wearing. C. Dexter
Last Seen Wearing—. H. Waugh
Last Sentence. J. Goodman
Last Set. J. Ellery
Last Seven Hours. J. N. Chance
Last Shaft. E. Tidyman
Last Sherlock Holmes Story. M. Dibdin
Last Shot. L. Thayer
Last Shot and other stories. R. Goyne
Last Signal. Dora Russell
Last Spin and other stories. E. Hunter
Last Stop. W. Tucker
Last Stop Camp 7. H. H. Kirst
Last Straw. D. M. Disney
Last Straw. F. Hume
Last Straw. I. S. Shriber
Last Stroke. L. L. Lynch
Last Stronghold. J. Pattinson
Last Survivor. E. Dale
Last Suspect. J. Rhode
Last Temple. R. Sapir
Last Tenant. B. L. Farjeon
Last Tiger. W. A. Ballinger
Last Time I Saw Hell. Simon Quinn
Last Time I Saw Mary. G. Corbin
Last Tomb. J. Lange
Last Train from Berlin. G. Blagowidow
Last Train Out. E. P. Oppenheim
Last Train to Limbo. J. N. Chance
Last Train to Rock Ferry. D. Enefer
Last Traitor of Long Island. R. H. Savage
Last Trap. S. Gluck
Last Trump. J. Gardner
Last Trump. L. Thayer
Last Trumpet. T. Downing
Last Twist of the Knife. M. Bonner
Last Two Weeks of Georges Rivac. G. Household
Last Vanity. H. Howard
Last Victim. A. Dramann
Last Voyage. A. Clarke
Last Voyage. R. Kytle
Last War Dance. R. Sapir
Last Warning. Wadsworth Camp
Last Warning. T. Fallon
Last Warning. G. Verner
Last Will and Testament. G. D. H. Cole
Last Will and Testament. E. Ferrars
Last Will and Testament of Constance Cobble. S. Forbes
Last Witness. W. Collison
Last Witness. L. Silbersky
Last Woman. R. Beeckman

Last Woman in His Life. E. Queen
Last Word. J. Popplewell
Last Year's Blood. H. C. Branson
Last Year's Snow. D. Tracy
Last Year's Wife. A. M. Williamson
Lastingham Murder. L. Tracy
Late and Cold. M. Torrie
Late Bill Smith. A. Garve
Late Boy Wonder. Angus Hall
Late Bride. T. Du Bois
Late Clara Beame. T. Caldwell
Late Contessa. Dorothy Fletcher
Late Demented. B. Carson
Late Edwina Black. W. Dinner
Late Final Blonde. M. Brody
Late for the Funeral. D. Stapleton
Late Harvest. K. Sunderland
Late into the Night. H. Bigden
Late Lamented. F. Brown
Late Lamented. A. A. Thomson
Late, Lamented Lady. M. Blizard
Late Last Night. J. Reach
Late, Late in the Evening. G. Mitchell
Late Miss Cordell. P. Johnson
Late Miss Trimming. C. Carnac
Late Mr. Beverly. T. Cobb
Late Mrs. D. H. Waugh
Late Mrs. Five. R. Wormser
Late Mrs. Fonsell. V. Johnston
Late Mrs. Lane. Rona Randall
Late Night Revel. H. Janson
"Late of London Wall..." Bruce Norman
Late Phoenix. C. Aird
Late Recovery. S. Fairway
Late Repentance. T. W. Speight
Late Tenant. Gordon Holmes
Late Uncle Max. M. Fitt
Late Unlamented. C. N. Boyle
Late Unlamented. H. Carmichael
Late Unlamented. D. L. Mathews
Late Unlamented. R. A. J. Walling
Lately Deceased. B. Picton
Later Than You Think. M. M. Kaye
Latigo. F. O'Rourke
Latter End. P. Wentworth
Lattimore Arch. Angela Gray
Laugh Was on Lazarus. J. Garforth
Laughing Bacchante. D. Yates
Laughing Buddha. C. Glick
Laughing Buddha. W. Starrett
Laughing Buddha Murders. R. Foster
Laughing Cat. S. Toye
Laughing Death. W. C. Brown
Laughing Death. P. Edwards
Laughing Dog. F. Vivian
Laughing Dragon Mystery. J. Kains
Laughing Fish. L. Bell
Laughing Fish. S. Jepson
Laughing Fox. F. Gruber
Laughing Gangster. D. Newton
Laughing Ghost. D. Eden
Laughing Ghost. L. Rose
Laughing Ghosts. A. E. Southon
Laughing Girl. R. W. Chambers
Laughing Girl. G. F. Worts
Laughing Grave. V. Gunn
Laughing Lightweight. P. Gill
Laughing Loon. J. E. Greene
Laughing Malefactor. Carol West
Laughing Man. Stockton Woods
Laughing Men. T. C. H. Jacobs
Laughing Mill and other stories. J. Hawthorne
Laughing Mountains. K. Lynn
Laughing Peril. H. L. Gates
Laughing Policeman. E. Bruton
Laughing Policeman. M. Sjowall
Laughing Rider. L. Y. Erskine
Laughing Whitefish. R. Traver
Laughing Widow. C. Warren
Laughter and Fear. D. Campton
Laughter Came Screaming. H. Kane
Laughter in the Alehouse. H. Kane
Laughter in the Night. F. Ford
Laughter in the Ranks. M. Hervey
Laughter Trap. J. Philips
Launch. E. Stewart
Launching of Roger Brook. D. Wheatley
Laura. V. Caspary
Laura Possessed. Anthea Fraser
Laura Sarelle. J. Shearing
Laurel and Hardy Murders. Marvin Kaye
Laurell'd Captains. G. R. Preedy
Laurels Are Poison. G. Mitchell
Laurels for McLean. G. Goodchild
Laurels for the Dreamer. W. M. Duncan
Laurine. B. Graeme
Lava Flow Murders. Max Long
Lavender Dagger. D. C. Calthrop
Lavender Gripsack. H. S. Keeler
Lavender's Inheritance. A. Askew
Lavenham Mystery. B. Bolt
Law. B. S. Ballinger
Law and Order. D. Uhnak
Law and Order on Halfaday Creek. J. B. Hendryx
Law and Order, Unlimited. W. C. MacDonald
Law and the Lady. W. Collins
Law Breakers. R. Cullum
Law-Breakers and other stories. Robert Grant
Law Courts Mystery. A. Blair
Law Not Justice. F. Warden
Law of Love. C. Jauniere
Law of Nemesis. A. Carlyle
Law of Probability. M. Sharman
Law of the Bolo. S. P. Hyatt
Law of the Four Just Men. E. Wallace
Law of the Gun. R. Cullum
Law of the Hills. O. Binns
Law of the Knife. C. Dawe
Law of the Land. F. M. White
Law of the River. F. Gerard
Law of the Streets. A. Le Breton
Law of the Talon. L. Tracy
Law of the Three Just Men. E. Wallace
Lawful Pursuit. M. Underwood
Lawless. C. Dawe
Lawless Hand. W. LeQueux
Lawless Justice. A. Edgar
Lawless Voyage. A. D. Divine
Lawrence Barclay File. B. Musto
Laws Be Their Enemy. F. E. Smith
Law's Delay. Sara Woods
Lawton Mystery. W. J. Burns
Lawyer and the Carpenter. E. Thompson
Lawyer Bell from Boston. R. L. Tyler
Lawyer-Detective. W. Warner
Lawyer Manton of Chicago. Le Jemlys
Lawyers Don't Hang. A. M. Barnes
Lawyer's Purpose. J. Leitch
Lawyer's Secret. M. E. Braddon
Lawyer's Secret. J. K. Leys
Lawyer's Secret. H. Lloyd
Lawyer's Story. J. A. Maitland
Laxham Haunting. J. Lymington
Lay Down and Die. M. Reed
Lay Down, You're Dead. T. Taggart
Lay Her Among the Lilies. J. H. Chase
Lay On, MacDuff! C. Armstrong
Lay-Over Town. D. Brennan
Lay That Pistol Down. R. Powell
Layers of Deceit. Bradshaw Jones
Laying on of Hands. A. Arent
Layoff. R. G. Dean
Layout for a Corpse. G. Goldsmith
Layout for Murder. J. Karney
Layton Court Mystery. A. Berkeley
Lazarus in London. F. W. Robinson
Lazarus Man. J. Lutz
Lazarus Inheritance. N. V. Carter
Lazarus Murder Seven. R. Sale
Lazarus #7. R. Sale
Lazy Detective. G. Dilnot
Lazy Lawrence Murders. T. Downing
Le Pere Goriot. H. D. Balzac
Lead Astray. Carter Brown
Lead Her Gently to the Grave. D. Bogard
Lead Him to Death. H. Windsor
Lead-Lined Coffin. E. McGirr
Lead Me into Temptation. F. Heller
Lead Me to the Gallows. F. Lester
Lead On, McLean! G. Goodchild
Lead with Your Left. E. Lacy
Leaden Bubble. R. W. Branson
Leading Lady. G. Bonner
Leading Lady. H. Herman
Leading Lady. R. Mills
Leaf of a Lime Tree. P. Tabori
League of Counterfeiters. Old Sleuth
League of Crime. F. Balfour
League of Dark Men. J. Creasey
League of Discontent. F. Beeding
League of 89. M. Hebden
League of Five. D. Lenton
League of Frightened Men. R. Stout
League of Gentlemen. J. Boland
League of Guilt. I. Murray
League of Justice. F. Duncan
League of Life. M. Gerard
League of Light. J. Creasey
League of Matthias. B. Flynn
League of Missing Men. J. M. Walsh
League of Nameless Men. J. Cassells
League of St. Louis. D. Whitelaw
League of the Lotus. A. Eadie
League of the Ring and Torn Apart. M. O'Brien
League of the Triangle. L. Lurgan
League of the White Hand. O. Crawford
League of Three. Old Sleuth
League of Twelve. G. Boothby
League of Twelve. G. Stanley
Lean Years. H. Bindloss
Leaning Man. C. Bush
Leap Before You Look. S. Waldron
Leap for the Sun. M. Hartmann
Leap in the Dark. Donald Gordon
Leap in the Dark. A. McCandless
Leap in the Dark. L. G. Moberly
Leap in the Dark. Rona Randall
Leap in the Dark. M. Richmond
Leap in the Dark. E. Southworth
Lease of Convict 308. E. W. Alais
Leases of Death. M. B. Gaunt
Least of All Evils. H. Arvonen
Leather Albatross. W. C. Odell
Leather Duke. F. Gruber
Leather Man. L. Treat
Leather Mask. A. Pratt
Leatherface. E. Dudley
Leatherface Lonergan Stakes a Claim. P. Renwick
Leatherjacket. Arthur Wise
Leathermouth. C. Dawe
Leathermouth's Luck. C. Dawe
Leave Everything to Me. O. F. Jerome
Leave Her to Heaven. Ben Ames Williams
Leave Her to Hell! F. Flora
Leave It to Amanda. H. K. Maxwell
Leave It to Conquest. B. Gray
Leave It to Me. M. Cronin
Leave It to Me. G. Joseph
Leave It to Me. H. Luger
Leave It to the Hangman. B. Knox
Leave It to the Toff. J. Creasey
Leave Murder to Me. R. Powell
Leave of Absence. Eric Bailey
Leave the Dead Behind Us. P. McCutchan
Leaven of Malice. Clare Curzon
Leavenworth Case. A. K. Green
Leavenworth Case. B. Ring
Leavenworth Irregulars. W. D. Blankenship
Leaves from the Diary of a Law Clerk. Waters
Leaves from the Journal of a Custom-House Officer. Waters
Leaves from the Note Book of a Chief of Police. A. Hughes
Leaves from the Note-Book of a New York Detective. J. B. Williams
Leaves from the Notebook of a New York Detective. Anonymous
Leavetaking. Anna Gilbert
Leavetaking. G. Milner
Leaving Mt. Venus. W. Hanley
Lebanon Paradise. E. Atiyah
Lecoq, the Detective's Daughter. W. Busnach
Led to the Light. M. A. Denison
Ledge. G. Schweitzer
Ledger. D. Uhnak
Ledger Is Kept. R. Postgate
Leech Club. G. W. Owen
Leeds Fiasco. Angus Ross
Leering House. B. Symons
Lees and Leaven. E. W. Townsend
Leffert's Disease. P. A. Lake
Left for Dead. Basil Carey
Left Hand Left. M. Massey
Left Hand of God. J. Lane
Left-Handed Death. R. Hull
Left-Handed Murder. A. Carruthers
Left-Handed Passenger. F. Riesenberg
Left-Handed Shell. James Grant
Left-Handed Sleeper. T. Willis
Left Leg. A. Tilton
Lefty Cuts Loose. B. Shannon
Lefty Hands It Out. B. Shannon
Lefty O'Connor Moves In. B. Shannon
Lefty Takes Over. B. Shannon
Legacy. A. Askew
Legacy. F. Hurd
Legacy. J. H. Schmitz
Legacy in Blood. M. Allingham
Legacy in Green. D. Whitelaw
Legacy Lenders. H. Q. Masur
Legacy of a Spy. H. S. Maxfield
Legacy of Cain. W. Collins
Legacy of Danger. A. Andre
Legacy of Danger. Richard Grant
Legacy of Danger. P. McGerr
Legacy of Death. M. Burton
Legacy of Death. R. A. J. Walling
Legacy of Doom. E. J. Murray
Legacy of Emeralds. Dorinne Moore
Legacy of Evil. A. Clarke
Legacy of Evil. Lydia Belknap Long
Legacy of Evil. A. Pritchett
Legacy of Fear. V. Coffman
Legacy of Fear. F. D. Hancock
Legacy of Fear. J. Lovesmith
Legacy of Fear. A. Skene
Legacy of Fear. Garnett Weston
Legacy of Hate. Nicholas Carter
Legacy of Hate. T. Douglas
Legacy of Hate. R. Hardinge
Legacy of Lanshore. F. Howe
Legacy of Loneliness. S. Wagner
Legacy of Mendoubia. J. Reddoch
Legacy of Redfern. J. Judson
Legacy of Shadows. R. Batchelor
Legacy of Shame. J. W. Bobin
Legacy of Terror. K. Cameron
Legacy of Terror. D. Dwyer
Legacy of the Golden Key. W. H. Brown
Legacy of the Granite Hills. B. Mitford
Legacy of the Lake. M. A. Smith
Legacy of the Lost. J. Wetherell
Legacy of the Wolf. J. Raynes
Legacy of Vengeance. J. W. Bobin
Legacy of Vengeance. P. Trent
Legacy of Winterwyck. C. Morland
Legal Fiction. E. Ferrars
Legal Fire. O. Stanley
Legal Practitioner. C. Tearle
Legal Settlement. Harrington Strong
Legal Wreck. W. Gillette
Legend. Evelyn Anthony
Legend in Blue Steel. S. Page
Legend in Green Velvet. Elizabeth Peters
Legend of Baverstock Manor. N. Buckingham
Legend of Blackhurst. M. Heath

Title Index

Legend of Crownpoint. M. Heath
Legend of Death. D. Daniels
Legend of Hatred. A. Andre
Legend of Holderly Hall. K. Cameron
Legend of Joseph Nokato. L. P. Bachmann
Legend of Lizzie. Reginald Lawrence
Legend of Lostwithiel. E. F. Wells
Legend of Molly Moor. L. Du Breuil
Legend of Monk's Court. Dorinne Moore
Legend of Piper's Hole. P. Farmer
Legend of the Grey Castle. R. Eldridge
Legend of the Loch. Alanna Knight
Legend of the Seventh Virgin. V. Holt
Legend of the Thirteenth Pilgrim. J. North
Legend of Witchwind. J. Hines
Legion. R. Bridges
Legion of the Living Dead. C. J. Daly
Legion of the Lost. J. Creasey
Legionnaire Spy. W. B. Bannerman
Legions of the Death Master. C. Steele
Legislative Body. J. L. Hensley
Legs. W. Kennedy
Leighton Grange. M. E. Braddon
Leila and Her Lover. M. Pemberton
Leipzig Affair. J. D. White
Leisure Dying. L. O'Donnell
Leland Case. H. Somerville
Leland Legacy. D. Daniels
Lemmings. C. Blackstock
Lemon in the Basket. C. Armstrong
Lemons Never Lie. R. Stark
Lemoyne Heritage. L. B. Long
Lena Hates Men. M. Neville
Lend a Hand. J. S. Blazer
Lend a Hand to Murder. M. Halliday
Lend Me a Rod. D. Linton
Lend Me Your Ears. A. M. Stein
Lenient Beast. F. Brown
Lenore. M. E. Edward
Leo Conversion. David Smith
Leo Wyoming Caper. J. Mandelkau
Leonard Harlowe. Waters
Leonardo and Others. Michael Sellers
Leonardo Touch. J. Eyerly
Leonardo's Law. W. B. Murphy
Leopard and the Cliff. W. Breem
Leopard Cat's Cradle. Jerome Barry
Leopard Died Too. N. Brent
Leopard Man. R. C. Armour
Leopard-Paw Orchid. K. Allsop
Leopard Valley. C. K. MacKinnon
Leopard with a Thin Skin. J. B. Watney
Leopard's Spots. A. Soutar
Leopard's Spots. F. M. White
Leopold Contract. G. Wolk
Leper's Bell. M. Sparroy
Lepke. J. Pearl
Leprechaun Murders. Adrian Reynolds
Lerouge Case. E. Gaboriau
Less Black Than We're Painted. J. Payn
Less Than the Dust. L. Crichton
Less Than the Dust. K. Lindsay
Lesser Antilles Case. R. King
Lesser Evil. R. Chambers
Lesser Evil. I. D. Hardy
Lessing Murder Case. S. Horler
Lessinger Comes Back. R. Essex
Lessinger Laughs Last. R. Essex
Lesson in Crime. G. D. H. Cole
Lesson in Crime and other stories. G. D. H. Cole
Lesson in Crime, and The Motive. G. D. H. Cole
Lesson in Murder. S. Claydon
Lesson Is Murder. J. Hoppe
Lester Affair. A. Garve
Lester Grayling, K.C. L. J. Lynwood
Lester's Secret. M. C. Hay
L'Estrange Case. John Bentley
Let Dead Enough Alone. R. Lockridge
Let Him Die. E. H. Clements
Let Him Go Hang. B. Clifton
Let Him Go, Let Him Tarry. M. Penoyre
Let Him Have Judgment. B. Hamilton
Let Him Stay Dead. T. C. H. Jacobs
Let It Lie. J. Goodwin
Let Justice Be Done. Mark Allerton
Let Justice Be Done! M. Poole
Let Me Kill You, Sweetheart. K. Carr
Let Me Kill You, Sweetheart. F. Flora
Let My People Be. D. Reid
Let Not Thy Left Hand. L. Gorell
Let or Hindrance. E. H. Clements
Let or Hindrance. E. Lemarchand
Let Sleeping Dogs Lie. T. Heald
Let Sleeping Girls Lie. J. Mayo
Let the Bastards Freeze in the Dark. D. Simmons
Let the Crags Comb Out Her Dainty Hair. J. Marten
Let the Dead Past—. J. S. Strange
Let the Lady Die. B. Winter
Let the Man Die. S. H. Courtier
Let the Night Cry. Charlie Wells
Let the Skeletons Rattle. F. C. Davis
Let the Tiger Die. M. Coles
Let the Witness Die. I. Lambot
Let Them Eat Bullets. H. Schoenfeld
Let Them Pray. S. Harvester
Let Tomorrow Come. A. J. Barr
Let Well Alone. E. C. R. Lorac
Let X Be the Murderer. C. Witting
Let X Equal Murder. E. Healey
Lethal in Love. Carter Brown
Lethal Lady. R. King
Lethal Playground. D. Franklin
Lethbridge of the Moor. M. Drake
Let's Ask Aunt. M. Godwyn
Let's Choose Executioners. Sara Woods
Let's Face It. A. Bocca
Let's Go Play at the Adams'. M. W. Johnson
Let's Hear It for the Deaf Man. E. McBain
Let's Kill George. L. Cores
Let's Kill Uncle. R. O'Grady
Let's Kill Uncle Lionel. J. York
Let's Not Get Smart. A. Bocca
Let's Pretend. Jacqueline Wilson
Let's Shoot This Out. R. Angel
Let's Talk of Graves, of Worms, and Epitaphs. R. Player
Letter E. W. LeQueux
Letter for Obi. J. F. Straker
Letter from a Stranger. L. Robin
Letter from Kiev. H. C. McDonald
Letter from Spain. F. P. Keyes
Letter from the Dead. A. Clarke
Letter of Intent. U. Curtiss
Letter to a Dead Girl. S. Jepson
Letter to a Ghost. A. Furness
Letters for a Spy. A. C. Ley
Letters of Discredit. P. Harris
Letters of Marque. A. P. Terhune
Letty Lynton. M. B. Lowndes
Levanter. E. Ambler
Levantine Trade. J. Pattinson
Lever's Folly. B. Care
Leviathan. R. Shea
Levity Hicks. T. Gallon
Levkas Man. H. Innes
Levy Caper. D. Shaw
Lew Archer, Private Investigator. R. Macdonald
Lewker in Norway. G. Carr
Lewker in Tirol. G. Carr
Lexicon Murders. D. Whitelaw
Lezaire Mystery. A. Griffiths
Li Kwang's Dagger. F. Johnston
Li Ting of London and other stories. G. R. Sims
Liability Limited. J. A. Saxon
Liar Dice. J. S. Mosher
Liars. Peter Hill
Liars and Tyrants and People Who Turn Blue. B. Paul
Libel. E. Wooll
Liberation. I. Ostrander
Liberators. J. Cleary
Liberators. J. Pattinson
Libertines. Douglas Clark
Libertines. H. Clewes
Liberty Bar. G. Simenon
Library of Alex Brandt. C. St. John
Library of Death. R. S. L. Harding
Library of Fiction. Anonymous
Libyan Kill. W. O'Neil
License to Kill. N. Daniels
License to Murder. E. Morgan
Licensed for Murder. J. Rhode
Lid Off. John Aiken
Lidless Eye. P. Romsey
Lidy Takes Plenty. B. Sarto
Lie a Little, Die a Little. Michael Brett
Lie Down, I Want to Talk to You. W. P. McGivern
Lie Down in Darkness. H. R. Hays
Lie Down, Killer. R. S. Prather
Lie Fallow My Acre. G. Joseph
Lie Like a Lady. C. S. Cody
Lie Quiet in Your Grave. M. L. Roby
Liers in Wait. Raymond Lawrence
Lies. R. Neely
Lieutenant and Others. H. C. McNeile
Lieutenant Barnabas. F. Barrett
Lieutenant Bones. E. Wallace
Lieutenant Flynn, R. N. E. L. Long
Lieutenant Must Be Mad. H. H. Kirst
Lieutenant of the King. M. Gerard
Lt. Pascal's Tastes in Homicide. H. Pentecost
Lieutenant What's-His-Name. M. Futrelle
Life, Adventure and Opinions of a Liverpool Policeman and His Contemporaries. Anonymous
Life—and a Fortnight. M. Peterson
Life and Anecdotes of the Black Dwarf. Anonymous
Life and Death of a Tough Guy. B. Appel
Life and Death of Peter Wade. Lionel Black
Life at Stake. P. Andreae
Life at Stake. I. Stark
Life Between. Roy Vickers
Life Cycle. H. Carmichael
Life Experiences of a Detective. A. W. Scott
Life Fashionable. P. Traill
Life for a Death. G. Ashe
Life for a Life. A. Bloomfield
Life for a Life. H. Fanger
Life for a Life. M. M. Murray
Life for Ruth. W. Drummond
Life for Sale. S. Horler
Life Has No Price. D. O'Neill
Life He Stole. S. Kyle
Life in America. W. G. Simms
Life in New York. Old Sleuth
Life in the Far West. C. H. Simpson
Life in the Mines. C. H. Simpson
Life Is No Bargain. P. Graham
Life Is Short. L. Della
Life Must Go On. M. Crombie
Life of a Nobody. Winifred Graham
Life of Anson Bunker, "The Bloody Hand." Anonymous
Life of Ease. P. De Polnay
Life of the Party. E. Jordan
Life on the Ocean Wave. G. Hackforth-Jones
Life Perilous. C. Dawe
Life Sentence. H. C. Bailey
Life Sentence. W. W. Burgess
Life Sentence. M. A. Hamilton
Life Sentence. O. Hesky
Life Sentence. A. Sergeant
Life Story of Madame Zelle, the World's Most Beautiful Spy. H. De Halsalle
Life That Kills. Grace M. White
Life to Lose. L. Hammond
Life We Live. G. R. Sims
Lifeline. P. Bottome
Lifer. J. Phelan
Life's Arrears. F. Warden
Life's Assize. J. H. Riddell
Life's Atonement. D. C. Murray
Life's Golden Web. J. B. Harris-Burland
Life's Reminiscences of Scotland Yard. A. Lansdowne
Life's Secret. H. Wood
Lift and the Drop. G. V. Galwey
Lift Murder. R. Francis Foster
Lift-Off at Satan. Richard Butler
Lift Shaft Crime. W. Jardine
Lift up the Lid. Anthony Gilbert
Lifted Latch. T. Frank
Lifting of the Shadow. O. Binns
Light Above the Crossroads. J. L. Rickard
Light and a Dark Christmas. H. Wood
Light and the Shadows. R. W. Howe
Light Beyond. E. P. Oppenheim
Light Cavalry Action. J. Harris
Light Fingered Ladies. A. Livingston
Light-Fingered Lady. L. Barbee
Light from a Lantern. J. Stagge
Light in Dends Wood, and other stories. T. Dagless
Light in the Swamp. V. Johnston
Light in the Tower. M. Lynch
Light in the Tower. Marilyn Ross
Light in the Upper Storey. F. Warden
Light in the Window. M. Lynn
Light of Day. E. Ambler
Light on Murder. E. Messenger
Light Side of the Law. G. A. MacDonald
Light That Lies. J. L. Rickard
Light That Lures. P. Brebner
Lightbody on Liberty. N. Balchin
Lighted Way. E. P. Oppenheim
Lighter of Candles. O. Cecil
Lighthearted Quest. A. Bridge
Lighthouse. M. J. Ragosta
Lighthouse Mystery. R. C. Armour
Lighthouse Mystery. G. Volk
Lighting Seven Candles. C. Lombardi
Lightly Lost. H. Smart
Lightning Conductor Comes Back. A. M. Williamson
Lightning May Strike Anywhere. M. Eldridge
Lightning over Mayfair. J. Monmouth
Lightning Strikes. Jon Barton
Lightning Strikes Twice. J. Potts
Lightning Strikes Twice. L. Thayer
Lightning Tree. Joan Aiken
Lightning Tree. J. Crecy
Lightning's Eye. R. Savage
Lights, Camera, Murder. John Shepherd
Lights, Camera...Murder. D. Snell
Lights of Skaro. D. Dodge
Lights Out. J. Cello
Lights Out. P. S. McCoy
Lights That Did Not Fail. M. Annesley
Lightship Murders. N. Wray
Ligny's Lake. S. H. Courtier
Like a Guilty Thing. B. Cobb
Like a Hole in the Head. J. H. Chase
Like a Man. J. Lane
Like a Rose. M. Peterson
Like an Evening Gone. J. Burrows
Like and Unlike. M. E. Braddon
Like Another Helen. G. Horton
Like Any Other Fugitive. J. Hayes
Like Crazy. H. Janson
Like Father, Like Son. J. Payn
Like Ice She Was. W. Ard
Like Lethal. H. Janson
Like Love. E. McBain
Like Poison. H. Janson
Like Shadows on the Wall. W. B. Maxwell
Like Water. I. R. G. Hart
Likely to Die. J. Roffman
Lil. J. Middlemass

Lil of the Slums. D. Donovan
Lila My Lovely. Dudley Dean
Lilac Bride Mystery. M. Crossley
Lilac Is for Sharing. J. Blackmore
Lilac Mansion. E. Hehl
Lilies for Madame. H. Austin
Lilies for My Lovely. H. Janson
Lilies in Her Garden Grew. F. C. Davis
Lilies That Fester. I. Wilson
Lilith. K. Kellow
Lilith. E. Southworth
Lilith. F. Warden
Lilla Hart. C. Burdett
Lilli Marlene. K. Lindsay
Lillian's Vow. Mrs. E. B. Collins
Lily and the Devil. A. Askew
Lily Dale. P. Tabori
Lily Field. Constance Rutherford
Lily in Her Coffin. B. Benson
Lily Pond. D. Daniels
Lily-Pond Mystery. G. Davison
Lily, the Felon's Daughter. T. Taggart
Limb of Satan. P. Souvestre
Limbo. J. Hammil
Limbo Affair. A. Firth
Limbo Connection. D. Quinn
Limbo Line. V. Canning
Limbo Lover. H. Janson
Limbo Touch. J. Weeks
Lime Pit. J. Valin
Limehouse Nights. T. Burke
Limelight for Jane. Elizabeth Ford
Limericks of Lachasse. J. Sherwood
Limey. J. Spenser
Limey Breaks In. J. Spenser
"Limited" Hold-Up. Nicholas Carter
Limited Liability. H. H. C. Gibbons
Limits of Pain. K. A. Blom
Limmerston Hall. H. W. Chapman
Limner. P. D. Boles
Limping Death. A. Stapleton
Limping Goose. F. Gruber
Limping Man. M. Erskine
Limping Man. F. Grierson
Limping Sailor. J. Brooke
Limping Wolf. E. T. Portwine
Lincoln Diddle. B. Steward
Lincoln McKeever. E. Lipsky
Lincoln's Inn Tragedy. W. J. Bayfield
Lincoln's Inn Tragedy. A. Blair
Linda Walked Alone. J. MacKenzie
Linden Affair. M. Albrand
Linden Tree. H. Rowan
Linden Walk Tragedy. F. Daingerfield
Line Between. S. Toye
Line of Duty. E. Tidyman
Line of Fire. D. Hamilton
Line of Fire. R. Parkes
Line of Succession. B. Garfield
Line on Ginger. R. Maugham
Line-Up. F. Kane
Line-Up. H. Luger
Line-Up. H. Reilly
Line Up for Murder. M. Babson
Line-Up for Murder. F. C. Ticknor
Lingala Code. W. Kiefer
Lingard. Colin Wilson
Lingo Dan. P. Pollard
Link. H. Carmichael
Link. P. MacDonald
Link. R. Maugham
Link by Link. J. W. Bobin
Link by Link. C. Courtenay
Link by Link. D. Donovan
Link by Link. N. D. Urner
Linked by Peril. B. Bolt
Linked to Crime. B. North
Linked with Fate. J. L. Berry
Linkram Jewels. J. Laurence
Links in the Chain. S. Campbell
Links in the Chain. H. Hill
Links in the Chain. J. Rhode
Linnet. G. Allen
Linnet Estate. D. Polk
Linnet Singing. D. Eden
Linnet's Folly. J. Aeby
Lint House Mystery. N. Oakley
Linton Memorial. L. Lloyd
Lion and the Lamb. E. P. Oppenheim
Lion and the Mouse. A. Hornblow
Lion by the Mane. Eva Dane
Lion Game. J. H. Schmitz
Lion in the Cellar. P. Branch
Lion in Wait. D. Gardiner
Lion Is Rampant. R. Laidlaw
Lion Men. J. Crosbie
Lion of Cooling Bay. P. Paul
Lion of Delos. A. Worboys
Lion of Petra. T. Mundy
Lion of the Law. S. Campbell
Lion? or Murder? D. Gardiner
Lion Triumphant. P. Carr
Lions at Night. R. Himmel
Lions at the Kill. S. Kent
Lion's Claws. F. Delmere
Lion's Gate. Jan Alexander
Lion's Mouse. C. N. Williamson
Lion's Mouth. J. Corbett
Lions of Judah. T. Willis
Lion's Ransom. P. Loraine
Lion's Share. O. Thanet
Lip-Service. L. J. Vance

Lipstick Clue. R. Goyne
Lipstick Larceny. Carter Brown
Liquid Death. Griff
Liquid Terror. E. Graves
Liquidated and The Seer. R. Lindau
Liquidator. R. L. Brent
Liquidator. Nick Carter
Liquidator. J. Gardner
Liquor Is Quicker. H. Janson
Lisa Bastian. J. Wood
Lisping Man. F. Rawlings
List. Nick Carter
List. G. F. Newman
List of Adrian Messenger. P. MacDonald
Listen for a Stranger. S. Devine
Listen for the Whisperer. P. A. Whitney
Listen, Lovely. Keith Campbell
Listen, Please Listen. N. A. Hintze
Listen to Danger. D. Eden
Listen to the Mocking Bird. S. H. Courtier
Listener. T. Du Bois
Listener. John Gill
Listening Boy. P. Hambledon
Listening Eye. P. Wentworth
Listening House. M. Seeley
Listening In. C. Moore
Listening Man. J. A. Moroso
Listening Silence. H. Lillie
Listening Walls. M. Millar
Listening Woman. T. Hillerman
Listening Woman. M. Sparroy
Lister Legacy. J. Drabek
Listerdale Mystery. A. Christie
Litany of Evil. Alice Brennan
Litmore Snatch. Henry Wade
Little Anarchist. A. W. Marchmont
Little Angie. E. Cave
Little Blue Goddess. W. LeQueux
Little Boy Laughed. J. Dow
Little Boy Lost. J. Ludwig
Little Brother Fate. M. C. Roberts
Little Brother of God. L. H. Gordon
Little Brothers. D. S. Davis
Little Caesar. W. R. Burnett
Little Caesars. E. De Roo
Little Captain. H. C. Bailey
Little Colonel. Old Sleuth
Little Comrade. B. E. Stevenson
Little Cowboy. Old Sleuth
Little Cowboy in New York. Old Sleuth
Little Crime. J. N. Chance
Little Dead-Sure. Old Sleuth
Little Doctor. G. Simenon
Little Dog Barked. A. Rowe
Little Dog's Day. J. T. Story
Little Doll. P. Garrod
Little Doves of Destruction. G. Wolfenden
Little Dragon from Peking. J. Eastwood
Little Drops of Blood. B. Knox
Little Ferret. R. Foxall
Little Fishes. Arthur Wise
Little Fortune. A. Fredericks
Little Game. F. Farrington
Little Gentleman from Okehampstead. E. P. Oppenheim
Little Giant. Old Sleuth
Little Girl Lost. C. Bolton
Little Girl Who Lives Down the Lane. L. Koenig
Little God Ben. J. J. Farjeon
Little Green Man. E. Wallace
Little Grey Man. W. Bouchier
Little Grey Mouse. F. Warden
Little Grey Shoe. P. Brebner
Little Hanging Men. P. Groom
Little Hangman. F. Cowen
Little Heiress. F. Cowen
Little Hercules. F. Gruber
Little Hercules. F. Wallace
Little Hour of Peter Wells. D. Whitelaw
Little Killer. G. Paul
Little Lady Linton. F. Barrett
Little Lady of Arrock. D. Whitelaw
Little Lady of Lagunitas. R. H. Savage
Little Lady of the Shot-Gun. L. H. Gordon
Little Less Than Kind. C. Armstrong
Little Lie. J. Potts
Little Lightning, the Shadow Detective. Police Captain James
Little Local Murder. R. Barnard
Little Lost Lady. W. Morton
Little Man from Archangel. G. Simenon
Little Man Murders. V. Loder
Little Man Who Wasn't There. Mildred Gordon
Little Matter of Arson. L. Meynell
Little Medicine Bottle. A. Turpin
Little Men, Big World. W. R. Burnett
Little Miss David—and Goliath. M. Croll
Little Miss Murder. M. Avallone
Little Miss Prim. F. Warden
Little Murder Music. D. Ramsay
Little Mysteries. K. Mikolowski
Little Ned's Engagement. E. Southworth
Little Novels. W. Collins
Little Nugget. P. G. Wodehouse
Little Old Lady. Roland Daniel

Little Old Man of the Batignolles. E. Gaboriau
Little People. J. Christopher
Little Pig-Alee. Y. Audouard
Little Red Captain. C. J. C. Hyne
Little Red Monkey. E. Maschwitz
Little Rosebud's Lovers. L. J. Libbey
Little Saint. G. Simenon
Little Sally Does It Again. R. Gillespie
Little Sin. W. Hardy
Little Sister. R. Chandler
Little Sister. Lee Roberts
Little Spot of Bother. M. Polland
Little Squaw Big Hurry. S. F. Griffin
Little Tales of Misogyny. P. Highsmith
Little Tales of Smethers, and other stories. Lord Dunsany
Little Terror. C. E. Blaney
Little Time to Stay. J. Garden
Little Tragedy at Tien-Tsin. F. A. Mathews
Little Tramp. G. Brewer
Little Treachery. P. Paul
Little Victim. T. P. McMahon
Little Victims Play. A. Hocking
Little Walls. Winston Graham
Little Wax Doll. P. Curtis
Little White God. E. Brock
Little White Hag. F. Beeding
Little White Hen. Robin Temple
Little White Nun. A. M. Williamson
Little Widow Murder. A. Wood
Little Woman in Black. M. E. Braddon
Littlejohn on Leave. G. Bellairs
Live Again, Love Again. D. Keene
Live and Let Die. I. Fleming
Live Bait. B. Knox
Live Bait. A. Mills
Live Bait. R. Wills
Live Bait for Murder. W. Herber
Live Cartridge. C. Dawe
Live Dangerously. A. Kielland
Live Gold. R. Sheckley
Live Like a Hero. Angus Hall
Live, Love, and Cry. G. B. Mair
Live Lumber. E. L. Long
Live Men's Shoes. R. Marsh
Live Now, Pay Later. J. T. Story
Live Till You Die. R. Angel
Live Wire. Austen Allen
Live Wire. J. Bruce
Live Wire Clue. Nicholas Carter
Lively Corpse. M. Millar
Lively Dead. P. Dickinson
Lively Form of Death. E. Lindall
Lively Game of Death. Marvin Kaye
Lively Luke. Old Sleuth
Lives and Times of Bernardo Brown. G. Household
Lives in a Box. Richard Grant
Lives to Give. S. De Gramont
Living Alibi. S. Truss
Living and the Dead. P. Boileau
Living Bomb. M. Avallone
Living Come First. J. Danvers
Living Dangerously. F. E. Penny
Living Dead Man. L. Scott
Living Death. Nick Carter
Living Demons. R. Bloch
Living End. F. Kane
Living Fire Menace. K. Robeson
Living Image. G. S. Gallant
Living in Fear. A. Parsons
Living Link. J. De Mille
Living Mask. Nicholas Carter
Living Mummy. A. Pratt
Living or Dead. H. Conway
Living Shadow. M. Grant
Living Shadow. W. W. Sayer
Living Skeleton. W. J. Fraser
Living Too Fast. W. T. Adams
Living's a Dying Game. R. Hamilton
Livingston Heirs. H. K. Maxwell
Liz. F. Kane
Lizard in the Cup. P. Dickinson
Lizard's Tail. M. Brandel
Lizzie. S. Jackson
Lizzie and Caroline. Ruth Moore
Lizzie Borden. M. B. Lowndes
Lizzie Borden of Fall River. T. J. Kelly
Llewellin. Anonymous
'Lo Sweeny Gang. Roland Daniel
Loaded Dice. E. H. Clark
Loaded Dice. M. Cumberland
Loaded Dice. E. Fawcett
Loaded Dice. P. Marlowe
Loaded Gun. F. Ryck
Loaded Orange. G. Jerome
Loadstone of Love. J. Middlemass
Loanshark. P. McCurtin
Loaves and Fishes. B. Capes
Lobelia Grove. A. Rolls
Lobster Guerrillas. W. Mole
Lobster Pick Murder. M. V. Heberden
Lobster Pot. G. Volk
Local Call. M. P. Berthold
Local Talent. W. Fuller
Local Talent. H. M. Kahler
Location Shots. J. F. Burke
Loch. J. Caird
Loch Sinister. Marilyn Ross
Loch Spy. D. Duff

Title Index

Lock and Key. A. M. Stein
Lock and the Key. F. Gruber
Lock at Charenton. G. Simenon
Lock the Door, Mademoiselle. T. C. H. Jacobs
Locked Book. F. Packard
Locked Corridor. Marilyn Ross
Locked Door. J. Hawk
Locked Doors. M. R. Rinehart
Locked Room. Herbert Ashton, Jr.
Locked Room. M. Sjowall
Locked Room. W. Spence
Locked Tower. C. Carfax
Locked Up. A. Griffiths
Loco-Motion, Commotion, Dr. Gorilla and Me. T. J. Kelly
Locust in the Wind. R. Collin
Locusts. G. N. Smith
Lodestar. M. Pemberton
Lodestar. E. Wooll
Lodestar Legacy. Doris Shannon
Lodestar of Death. J. Sandys
Lodge Sinister. Dana Ross
Lodger. M. B. Lowndes
Lodger. G. Simenon
Lodging-House Mystery. R. Hardinge
Lofoten Run. R. Middlemiss
Log Across the Road. Sheila Ross
Logan. A. Joseph
Logan. J. Neal
Lola Brought Her Wreath. H. Janson
Lola of the Isles. D. W. MacArthur
Lombard Street Mystery. A. Blair
Lombard Street Mystery. Muirhead Robertson
Lona. John Evans
London. G. Brandner
London Adventures of Mr. Collin. F. Heller
London After Midnight. M. Coolidge-Rask
London Assignment. Angus Ross
London, Bloody London. M. Avallone
London Bridge Mystery. J. Arnold
London by Night. Anonymous
London Calling. V. Gielgud
London Cobweb. P. Brebner
London Cobweb. C. Lys
London Connection. Robin Moore
London Deal. N. J. Crisp
London Detective's Thrilling Adventures. Anonymous
London Lamb. W. B. M. Ferguson
London Lights Were Shining. V. Rendell
London, 1913. M. Stacpoole
London Particular. C. Brand
London Plot. C. Dawe
London Pride. M. E. Braddon
London Spy Murders. P. Cheyney
London Switch. Robin Moore
London's Heart. B. L. Farjeon
Lone Commando. J. Sandys
Lone Cottage. T. P. Prest
Lone Crook Murders. C. Ryland
"Lone Cross Manor" Mystery. M. Danvers
Lone Hand. H. Bindloss
Lone Hand. S. Warwick
Lone House by the Sea. Old Sleuth
Lone House Mystery. E. Wallace
Lone Inn. F. Hume
Lone Isle. E. C. Vivian
Lone Kiwi. F. N. Millar
Lone Lodge Mystery. J. Hawk
Lone Trail. L. Allan
Lone Vendetta. Jean Fraser
Lone Wolf. W. C. Tuttle
Lone Wolf. L. J. Vance
Lone Wolf Returns. L. J. Vance
Lone Wolf's Last Prowl. L. J. Vance
Lone Wolf's Son. L. J. Vance
Loneliest Girl in the World. K. Fearing
Lonely Astronomer. V. Gridban
Lonely Beat. W. Keenan
Lonely Breeze. V. Siller
Lonely Bungalow. Taffrail
Lonely Cage. F. Usher
Lonely Church. F. Hume
Lonely God. C. Kernahan
Lonely Graves. C. Monig
Lonely Heritage. A. Furness
Lonely Hollow Mystery. T. A. Plummer
Lonely House. J. Blackmore
Lonely House. A. Gask
Lonely House. M. B. Lowndes
Lonely House. A. Streckfuss
Lonely Hunter. C. Wilcox
Lonely Inn Mystery. L. Grex
Lonely Is the Grave. G. J. Barrett
Lovely Island. H. L. V. Fletcher
Lovely, Lovely Lady. J. Monmouth
Lonely Magdalen. Henry Wade
Lonely Man. G. Frankau
Lonely Man. J. T. Phillifent
Lonely Pathway. John Marsh
Lonely Place. B. Copper
Lonely Place. D. Daniels
Lonely Place. R. M. Sears
Lonely Place to Die. W. Ebersohn
Lonely Place to Die. Colin Robertson
Lonely Road. J. Farnol
Lonely Russian. N. Shore
Lonely Shore. G. Volk
Lonely Shroud. S. Mitchell

Lonely Side of the River. D. MacKenzie
Lonely Skier. H. Innes
Lonely Steeple. Victor Wolfson
Lonely Stronghold. B. Reynolds
Lonely Subaltern. F. Hume
Lonely Target. M. Pentecost
Lonely Terror. S. Mayfield
Lonely Toys. M. Lynch
Lonely Voyage. J. Harris
Lonely Walk. M. E. Chaber
Lonely Water. N. Thurley
Lonely Way to Die. A. Bourgeau
Lonely Way to Die. H. Debrett
Lonely Years. Alan Thomas
Lonelyheart 4122. Colin Watson
Loner. O. Friedrich
Loner. F. Nichols
Lonesome Badger. F. Gruber
Lonesome Road. P. Wentworth
Lonesome Town. E. Dorrance
Long and Living Shadow. D. Winston
Long Arm. H. Cecil
Long Arm. S. M. Gardenhire
Long Arm. E. P. Oppenheim
Long Arm of Fantomas. P. Souvestre
Long Arm of Gil Hamilton. L. Niven
Long Arm of Mannister. E. P. Oppenheim
Long Arm of Murder. F. Gruber
Long Arm of the Mounted. J. Dorrance
Long Arm of the Mounted. W. B. Mowery
Long Arm of the Prince. E. Berckman
Long Baffled Capture. I. Stark
Long Body. H. McCloy
Long Branch Detective. Anonymous
Long Chance. D. Enefer
Long Chase. J. M. Eshleman
Long Chase. J. B. Hendryx
Long Coffin. N. Tranter
Long Cool Day in Hell. G. Kersh
Long Corridor. C. Cookson
Long Corridor. K. Ross
Long Count. R. Faust
Long Dark Night. J. Hayes
Long Dark Night of the Soul. J. Ellis
Long Day's Dying. Alan White
Long Day's Nightmare. N. Robertson
Long Deadly Summer. P. Barnaby
Long Death. G. Dyer
Long Distance. J. A. Dale
Long Distance—Wrong Number. N. Gifford
Long Divorce. E. Crispin
Long Drop. Alan White
Long Echo. K. Hughes
Long Echo. D. Rutherford
Long Echo. R. Severn
Long Escape. D. Dodge
Long Farewell. M. Innes
Long Fast Ride. A. F. Libby
Long Firm. J. Riley
Long Fuse. Alan White
Long Goodbye. R. Chandler
Long Goodnight. C. D. Burton
Long Green. B. Spicer
Long Green Gaze. V. Fuller
Long-Haired Bill. J. A. Dunn
Long Hand. W. Magnay
Long Hand of Death. Alan White
Long Hard Cure. D. Anthony
Long Hard Look. M. Gair
Long Hate. S. Forbes
Long Haul. F. Mills
Long Hot Night. D. Enefer
Long Island Murders. M. W. Glidden
Long Journey Home. M. F. Ford
Long Knife. E. S. De Puy
Long Lane. P. Trent
Long Lankin. J. Banville
Long Lavender Look. J. D. MacDonald
Long Leaf. R. Brock
Long Live the King. G. Boothby
Long Memory. H. Clewes
Long Memory. M. Cronin
Long Midnight. Alan White
Long Night. F. R. Adams
Long Night. O. Demaris
Long Night. P. B. Gallagher
Long Night. B. Graeme
Long Night. H. Howard
Long Night. A. Lyttle
Long Night. S. Truss
Long Night of Fear. Marilyn Ross
Long Night Through. H. McCutcheon
Long Nightmare. J. Roeburt
Long Night's Journey. I. MacKersey
Long Night's Walk. Alan White
Long Odds. M. Clarke
Long Odds. H. Smart
Long Overcoat. P. Fry
Long Patrol. H. A. Cody
Long Patrol. A. M. Treynor
Long Portage. H. Bindloss
Long Pursuit. J. Cleary
Long Reach. K. Hayles
Long Reconnaissance. J. Murphy
Long Revenge. B. Schwarz
Long Revenge. J. Thomson
Long Ride. J. McKimmey
Long Ride Out. W. James
Long Road. A. Furness
Long Run South. Alan Williams
Long Saturday Night. C. Williams
Long Search. G. Ashe

Long Search. S. L. Bell
Long Shadow. F. Bryan
Long Shadow. J. Cleary
Long Shadow. C. Fremlin
Long Shadow. Anthony Gilbert
Long Shadow. J. Pendower
Long Shadow. H. W. Thomas
Long Shadows. J. Cannan
Long Shadows. C. Carnac
Long Shadows. Camilla Hope
Long Shadows. A. D. Sanderson
Long Short Cut. A. Garve
Long Shot. Ken Blake
Long Shot. E. Hely
Long Silence. P. Costello
Long Silence. N. Freeling
Long Silence. Alan White
Long Skeleton. F. Lockridge
Long Sleep. A. Bocca
Long Spoon. J. Bryce
Long Spoon. J. B. O'Sullivan
Long Straight Road. G. Horton
Long Summer. Alan White
Long Thrill. O. L. Rosmanith
Long Time No Leola. Carter Brown
Long Time No See. E. McBain
Long Time Sleeping. Michael Sinclair
Long Tunnel. S. Fairway
Long Vendetta. J. Gant
Long Wait. M. Spillane
Long Walk to Wimbledon. H. R. F. Keating
Long Watch. Alan White
Long Way Down. Elizabeth Fenwick
Long Way Down. D. Hall
Long Way Down. C. Wilcox
Long Way from Shiloh. L. Davidson
Long Way Home. V. Norwood
Long Way Round. M. Maurice
Long Way to Fall. Angus Hall
Long Way to Pitt Street. D. Enefer
Long Week. P. Doncaster
Long White Con. R. Beck
Long White Night. Eric Lambert
Long Window. J. M. Eshleman
Longbow Murder. V. Luhrs
Longbridge Murders. M. Dalton
Longer Bodies. G. Mitchell
Longer the Thread. E. Lathen
Longest Second. B. S. Ballinger
Longstreet Legacy. D. Ashe
Loo Loo's Legacy. D. Dodge
Loo Sanction. Trevanian
Look Alive. M. Burton
Look at Murder. N. Deane
Look Back on Death. L. Egan
Look Back on Murder. D. M. Disney
Look Back to Love. V. Packer
Look Behind You. J. Barbette
Look Behind You, Lady. M. Erskine
Look Behind You, Lady. A. S. Fleischman
Look Down for Mercy. Max Gordon
Look Down on Her Dying. D. Tracy
Look for the Body. M. F. Christopher
Look in Any Doorway. N. Morland
Look in at Murder. E. Radford
Look of Innocence. Anna Gilbert
Look Out Behind You. K. Lewis
Look Out for Lucifer! E. Dudley
Look over Your Shoulder. A. McAllister
Look Three Ways at Murder. J. Creasey
Look to the Dawn. M. Richmond
Look to the Lady. M. Allingham
Look to the Lady! J. L. Bonney
Look Upon the Prisoner. H. Desmond
Look Who's Talking. R. Adam
Look Your Last. J. S. Strange
Looker-On. W. LeQueux
Looking for Ginger North. J. Dunning
Looking for Rachel Wallace. R. B. Parker
Looking-Glass. V. Coffman
Looking Glass Murder. Anthony Gilbert
Looking-Glass Murders. D. G. Browne
Looking Glass Murders. P. Lore
Looking Glass War. J. Le Carre
Looking Out for #1. M. Monsky
Lookout Cartridge. J. McElroy
Looks That Kill. W. B. Gibson
Loom. J. Remenham
Loom and the Web. C. Gibson-Jarvie
Loom of Tancred. D. Pearson
Loom of Terror. P. Minton
Loom of the Law. Anonymous
Loop. W. Hildick
Loop Current. A. Sewart
Loophole. A. Maling
Loophole. R. Pollock
Loose End. M. Cronin
Loose Ends. P. Warner
Loose Lady Death. L. Marshall
Loose Rib. Austen Allen
Loose Screw. G. Hammond
Loot! A. Murray
Loot. J. Orton
Loot. A. S. Roche
Loot! A. P. Terhune
Loot Curran, R. N. E. L. Long
Loot from the Temple of Fortune. H. A. Vachell
Loot of Cities. A. Bennett
Loot of France. A. Parsons
Loot of Nana Sahib. H. E. Hill
Loot of Pakistan. A. Parsons

L

L

Loot of the Lazy F. W. C. Tuttle
Looted Gold. G. E. C. Webster
Looters. Albert Conroy
Looters. J. Reese
Lopsided Man. B. S. Ballinger
Lord Alistair's Rebellion. A. Upward
Lord and Mary Ann. C. Cookson
Lord Arthur Savile's Crime. C. Cox
Lord Arthur Savile's Crime, and other stories. O. Wilde
Lord Blackshirt. B. Graeme
Lord Cobleigh Disappears. J. C. Snaith
Lord Edgware Dies. A. Christie
Lord Have Mercy. Shelley Smith
Lord Heathbury's Revenge. Rachelle Edwards
Lord, I Was Afraid. N. Balchin
Lord John in New York. C. N. Williamson
Lord Lynmore's Life. I. Roy
Lord Mayor of Death. M. Babson
Lord Mayor's Show Mystery. A. Blair
Lord Oakburn's Daughters. H. Wood
Lord of Irongray. J. B. Harris-Burland
Lord of Ravensley. C. Heaven
Lord of Terror. M. Allain
Lord of Terror. S. Horler
Lord of the Dyke. W. Wood
Lord of the Falcons. L. Harper
Lord of the Far Island. V. Holt
Lord of the Gallows. J. Neil
Lord of the Hollow Dark. R. Kirk
Lord of the Manor. J. Blackmore
Lord of the Manor. F. M. White
Lord of the Sorcerers. Carter Dickson
Lord Penworth's Daughter. F. Warden
Lord Peter. D. L. Sayers
Lord Peter Goes A-Wooing. J. Ronald
Lord Peter Views the Body. D. L. Sayers
Lord Quare's Visitor. F. Warden
Lord Satan. L. Bronte
Lords and Ladies. R. M. Gilchrist
Lords of Castle Weirwyck. E. F. Wells
Lords of Akchasaz. Y. Kemal
Lords of Dair. H. Wieselberg
Lords of Human Kind. J. D. White
Lordship, the Passen, and We. F. T. Jane
Lorelei. L. P. Bachmann
Lorelei. D. Rico
Lorena Veiled. M. J. Ragosta
Lorie. Old Sleuth
Loring Affair. J. Sherry
Loring Mystery. J. Farnol
Lorry. P. Wahloo
Los Angeles Holocaust. M. Barry
Los Huecos Mystery. E. T. Sawyer
Lose This Gun. H. Janson
Loser by a Head. H. Giddings
Loser Takes All. G. Greene
Loser Takes Nothing. M. Cronin
Losers. Clifford Irving
Loser's Blues. P. Harcourt
Losers Keepers. A. Mason
Losers Take All. J. J. Lamb
Losers, Weepers. E. Queen
Losers, Weepers. L. Silberstang
Losing Game. F. W. Crofts
Losing Game. H. Nisbet
Losing Game. W. Payne
Loss of a Head. J. Bude
Loss of Innocence. Magali
Loss of the Jane Vosper. F. W. Crofts
Lost! A Day. F. C. Milford
Lost Ambassador. E. P. Oppenheim
Lost American. A. C. Gunter
Lost and Found Man. N. Guild
Lost and the Damned. W. Carrier
Lost Bank Note. H. Wood
Lost Bride. C. Augusta
Lost Bride. E. Southworth
Lost Caesar. R. Fenisong
Lost Casket. F. Du Boisgobey
Lost Cause. Winifred Duke
Lost Cavern. H. F. Heard
Lost Chittendens. Nicholas Carter
Lost Countess Falka. H. Savage
Lost Despatch. N. S. Lincoln
Lost Diamond. D. G. Adee
Lost Diamonds. F. Marryat
Lost Diaries. M. Baring
Lost Diary. H. Bleackley
Lost Discovery. B. Reynolds
Lost Duchess. J. G. Sarasin
Lost Eden. M. E. Braddon
Lost Emeralds of Zarinthia. H. Beauchamp
Lost Endeavor. G. Boothby
Lost Expedition. W. W. Sayer
Lost for Love. M. E. Braddon
Lost Fraulein. R. Meade
Lost Friday. E. J. Fredericks
Lost Gallows. J. D. Carr
Lost Garrison. J. Robb
Lost Generation. P. Trent
Lost Giant. K. Robeson
Lost Girl. J. Boswell
Lost Golfer. H. G. Hutchinson
Lost Half Hour. L. Meynell
Lost Hat. E. Percy
Lost Heir. S. Cobb
Lost Heir. G. A. Henty
Lost Heir of Linlithgow. E. Southworth
Lost Heiress. E. Southworth
Lost Heritage. J. Herbrand

Lost Honeymoon. C. Jauniere
Lost House. F. S. Wees
Lost House Mystery. L. West
Lost Hyena. C. K. MacKinnon
Lost Identity. D. Hennessey
Lost Idol. A. Askew
Lost in Cambodia. W. M. Graydon
Lost in the Post, and other tales. H. Wood
Lost in the Slave Land. W. M. Graydon
Lost Inheritance. Scott Graham
Lost Island. P. A. Whitney
Lost Jewel. H. Spofford
Lost Judge. C. R. Gull
Lost Kachina. R. Potts
Lost Karim. E. Kyle
Lost Key. Forfex et Hesta
Lost Kingdom. J. G. Sarasin
Lost Lady. O. R. Cohen
Lost Lake. R. Kirk
Lost Lawyer. G. A. Birmingham
Lost Leader. E. P. Oppenheim
Lost Liner. R. Cromie
Lost Lotus. A. Rundle
Lost Man's Lane. A. K. Green
Lost Mark. P. Wynnton
Lost Million. W. Alden
Lost Million. W. LeQueux
Lost Mr. Linthwaite. J. S. Fletcher
Lost Moorings. G. Simenon
Lost Name. J. S. Le Fanu
Lost Naval Papers. B. Copplestone
Lost Oasis. K. Robeson
Lost Oasis. H. H. Ross
Lost One. F. Cowen
Lost One. A. Kennington
Lost One. D. Lyon
Lost Paradise. F. A. Kummer
Lost Parchment. F. Hume
Lost Pearl. F. Grierson
Lost Person. V. White
Lost Pibroch. N. Munro
Lost Rapture. B. Poynter
Lost Sir Brian. F. Whishaw
Lost Sir Massingberd. J. Payn
Lost Souls in Bohemia. W. J. Elliott
Lost Square. L. T. Meade
Lost Stradivarius. J. M. Falkner
Lost Tale. D. Estey
Lost Trooper. F. H. Dimmock
Lost Trooper. T. Mundy
Lost Vengeance. C. Portway
Lost Victim. T. A. Waters
Lost Victory. P. Bonnecarrere
Lost Viol. M. P. Shiel
Lost Will. H. Wood
Lost Without Trace. B. Cobb
Lost Witness. L. L. Lynch
Lost World. L. K. Vincent
Lot 41—Dead Auctioneer. M. Symons
Lotteries. D. Winston
Lottery. S. Jackson
Lottery Ticket. F. Du Boisgobey
Lottie, the Poor Saleslady. C. E. Blaney
Lotus Affair. T. Wells
Lotus for Miss Quon. J. H. Chase
Lotus Leaves and Larceny. Philip Chambers
Lotus Vellum. Charlotte Hunt
Loudwater Mystery. E. Jepson
Loudwater Tragedy. T. W. Speight
Louis Beretti. D. H. Clarke
Louisa. G. D. Hernon
Louisa Reignier. R. Watson
Louise. J. Dering
Louise Martin, the Village Maiden. O. Bradbury
Louise, the Restless. K. Kimbrough
Loup-Garou. E. Phillpotts
Louse for the Hangman. L. Bruce
Lovable Man. David Fletcher
Love After Five. Raymond Mason
Love Against the World. W. S. Hayward
Love-All. J. Leasor
Love and a Title. H. Flowerdew
Love and Bullets. J. Heddon
Love and Death in a Barn. Anonymous
Love and Dr. Hawkins. S. Gainsley
Love and Dr. Maynard. Rona Randall
Love and Hatred. M. B. Lowndes
Love—and Helen. S. Jepson
Love and I. M. Aiken
Love and Lordship. F. Warden
Love and the Land Beyond. J. Leasor
Love and the Law. H. Curties
Love and the Spy. C. N. Williamson
Love Bade Me Welcome. J. Lodwick
Love Besieged. C. E. Pearce
Love, Blood and Tears. N. Weaver
Love Calling. M. Dekobra
Love Camp. L. Royer
Love Can Be Dangerous. O. R. Cohen
Love Child. T. B. Clegg
Love Child. T. P. Prest
Love Clinic. M. Dekobra
Love Clouds. J. Latey
Love Comes Lethal. L. Della
Love Cruisers. P. Trent
Love-Death Thing. T. B. Dewey
Love for Sale. M. Corrigan
Love for the Baron. Anthony Morton
Love Forbidden. J. Blackmore

Love from a Stranger. F. Vosper
Love from Elizabeth. M. Fitt
Love Has No Alibi. O. R. Cohen
Love-Hate Relationship. J. N. Chance
Love Hath an Island. C. Randell
Love in a Mist. L. V. Stevens
Love in Amsterdam. N. Freeling
Love in Burma. R. Carr
Love in Danger. C. Talbot
Love in Fetters. R. Marsh
Love in Lilac-Land. C. G. Mitford
Love in Peril. S. Jepson
Love in Suburbia. J. Conway
Love in the Purple. M. Gerard
Love Insurance. E. D. Biggers
Love Is a Deadly Weapon. P. Quentin
Love is a Fiend. E. Woodward
Love Is a Flame. M. B. Lowndes
Love Is a Spirit. J. Hawthorne
Love Is Enough. M. Peterson
Love Is for Hating. D. Telfer
Love Is for the Living. E. Kyle
Love Is Just a Word. J. M. Simmel
Love Is King. R. Sharp
Love Is Murder. E. C. Barcelo
Love Is the One with Wings. P. V. Stern
Love Kills. Dan Greenberg
Love Letters. C. Massie
Love Lies Bleeding. E. Crispin
Love Like an Arrow. F. Y. McHugh
Love Like That. D. Garth
Love, Lust and Larceny. Sam Evans
Love Makers. H. Janson
Love Me and Die. D. Keene
Love Me and Die. L. Trimble
Love Me, Hurt Me. N. Karta
Love Me in Death. D. B. Olsen
Love Me Now. J. McPartland
Love Me Now. F. Nichols
Love Me to Death. F. Diamond
Love Me to Death. P. Kirk
Love, Mystery, and Misery! A. F. Holstein
Love Not Denied. K. Lindsay
Love of Lucifer. D. Winston
Love on the Set. A. Kennington
Love—or a Name. J. Hawthorne
Love or Kill Them All. N. Weaver
Love or Whatever It Is. W. Leslie
Love Remembered. E. Beresford
Love Rides the Rails. M. Cary
Love Secretaries. H. Janson
Love Song. A. Kennedy
Love Song. J. L. Roberts
Love Spell. Anonymous
Love Spy, Love. R. C. Kasper
Love Stone. A. Askew
Love Talker. Elizabeth Peters
Love Tap. L. Brady
Love Test. J. A. Jordan
Love That Believeth. O. Binns
Love That Kills. C. Stanton
Love That Lasts. F. Warden
Love That Spy. T. A. Waters
Love the Criminal. J. B. Harris-Burland
Love, the Foe. F. M. White
Love the Harvester. M. Pemberton
Love the Jester. A. Askew
Love, the Sorcerer. A. L. Thompson
Love the Sportsman. S. Horler
Love, the Thief. M. B. Mathers
Love Thieves. P. Packer
Love Thing. H. Barron
Love to Cherish. Clarissa Ross
Love Trap. L. White
Love Under Smoke. T. Craig
Love Was Married. S. Kyle
Love with a Gun and other stories. P. Cheyney
Love Without Honour. M. Richmond
Loved and the Loving. N. Sligh
Loved Enemy. S. Coulter
Lovehead. Jackie Collins
Lovel Castle. Anonymous
Loveless Isle. N. Penley
Lovelies Are Never Lonely. M. Storm
Lovels of Arden. M. E. Braddon
Lovely and Lethal. F. Castle
Lovely and the Damned. R. Collier
Lovely But Dangerous. Roland Daniel
Lovely—But Lethal! P. Saxon
Lovely But Lethal. D. Steel
Lovely Corpse. M. Cumberland
Lovely in Death. W. O'Farrell
Lovely Ladies. N. Freeling
Lovely Lady. M. Corrigan
Lovely Lady, Pity Me. R. Huggins
Lovely Mask for Murder. Gerry Travis
Lovely Mrs. Blake. R. Marsh
Lovely Mrs. Pemberton. F. Warden
Lover. Carter Brown
Lover. H. Janson
Lover Come Home. D. Lee
Lover, Don't Come Back! Carter Brown
Lover for Cindy. H. V. Dixon
Lover, Let Me Live. N. Daniels
Lover—Say It With Mink. Norma Lee
Lover Too Many. Roy Lewis
Lover Who Lost Himself. D. Newton
Lovers and Heretics. John Hale
Lovers Are Losers. Howard Hunt
Lovers at Fault. F. Whishaw

Title Index

Lover's Feud. R. C. Finney
Lovers in a Winter Circle. J. Kirsch
Lovers in the Dark. J. Ames
Lovers in Waiting. D. Whitelaw
Lovers of Astrea. J. G. Sarasin
Love's Atonement. K. Lindsay
Love's Burden. M. Peterson
Love's Challenge. J. Templeton
Love's Deadly Silhouette. L. Richards
Love's Enemy. A. J. Small
Love's Fiery Dagger. F. Hurd
Love's Great Surrender. C. H. Bullivant
Love's Harvest. B. L. Farjeon
Love's Labor Won. E. Southworth
Love's Legacy. R. Ashe King
Love's Lovely Counterfeit. J. M. Cain
Loves of the Harem. G. W. M. Reynolds
Loves Old and New. J. Middlemass
Love's Ordeal. D. Dayle
Love's Prisoner. R. C. Finney
Love's Rebel. D. Noel
Love's Revenge. M. B. Lowndes
Love's Sentinel. F. Warden
Love's Service. M. Peterson
Love's Testimony. M. Andrau
Love's the Only Guide. M. Richmond
Love's Triumph. F. Du Boisgobey
Love's Victory. B. L. Farjeon
Loving a Dream, and One of His Inventions. C. Gibbon
Loving and the Dead. Carter Brown
Loving Cup. A. Prior
Loving Cup. A. Wynne
Loving Sands, Deadly Sands. C. Keppel
Low Company. H. Atkinson
Low Road. H. Morrison
Lowdown. R. Chanslor
Lowdown. R. Jessup
Lowdown on G Men. K. Medusa
Lower Part of the Sky. L. Kaufman
Lower Underworld. A. R. L. Gardner
Lowly Lover. F. Warden
Loxfinger. S. Weinstein
Loyal Lady. K. Lindsay
Loyalty of Peter Drayton, and Mrs. Peter Skeffington's Revenge. H. C. McNeile
Lucienne. M. Pemberton
Lucien's Tombs. M. Rippon
Lucifer and Partner. Jack Henry
Lucifer at Ponsfordville. J. Workman
Lucifer at Sunset. S. Harvester
Lucifer Cell. W. Fennerton
Lucifer Cult. I. Benedict
Lucifer Mask. K. Rich
Lucifer Was Tall. E. Gresham
Lucifer Wine. Irma Walker
Lucifer's Dream. J. L. Curtis
Lucifer's Lodge. J. Tobias
Lucile Clery. J. Shearing
Lucile Dare, Detective. M. Leighton
Lucinda. H. Rigsby
Lucius Davoreen. M. E. Braddon
Luck and a Lady. J. A. Dunn
Luck of Bella Barton. G. W. Appleton
Luck of Gerard Ridgeley. B. Mitford
Luck of Jocelyn Pinner, R. N. Bruce Norman
Luck of Luce. D. Deane
Luck of Norman Dale. B. Pain
Luck of St. Boniface. L. C. Douthwaite
Luck of the Darrells. A. Murray
Luck of the Darrells. J. Payn
Luck of the Golden Star. H. J. Andrews
Luck of the Irish. H. MacGrath
Luck of the Kid. R. Cullum
Luck of the Mounted. R. S. Kendall
Luck of the Secret Service. W. LeQueux
Luck of the Vails. E. F. Benson
Luck of Udaipur. J. I. Emery
Luck Runs Out. C. MacLeod
Luck Was No Lady. Carter Brown
Luckless Lady. George Douglas
Lucky Devil. A. Maling
Lucky Ham. S. McCarthy
Lucky Jane. D. Ames
Lucky Mr. Loder. G. Thorne
Lucky Partners. W. C. Tuttle
Lucky Pierre. M. Endfield
Lucky Policeman. R. Penny
Lucky Shot. E. W. Elkington
Lucky Stiff. C. Rice
Lucky to Be Alive? A. Cromie
Lucretia. E. Bulwer-Lytton
Lucy and the Dark Gods. E. Jepson
Ludi Victor. J. Leigh
Ludus Amoris. B. Swift
Luger Lullaby. R. Angel
Lugger Audace. E. L. Long
Lugs O'Leary. A. Kimmins
Luigi of Catanzaro. L. Golding
Luke Darby, the "World" Detective. E. A. Young
Luke Leighton, the Government Detective. H. Rockwood
Luke's Summer. D. Lee
Lukundoo, and other stories. Edward L. White
Lullaby with Lugers. J. Crockett
Lulu. M. T. Walworth
Lumber Ship. E. L. Long
Luminous Face. C. Wells
Lumley Wood Mystery. G. W. L. Banbury

Lunatic at Large. J. S. Clouston
Lunatic at Large Again. J. S. Clouston
Lunatic Fringe. W. L. De Andrea
Lunatic in Charge. J. S. Clouston
Lunatic in Love. J. S. Clouston
Lunatic Still at Large. J. S. Clouston
Lunatic, the Lover. B. Cobb
Lunatic Time. J. Roeburt
Lunatic View. D. Campton
Lunatics at Large. J. Reach
Lunge Wire. J. B. O'Sullivan
Lupe. G. Thompson
Lure. C. Cavendish
Lure. F. Picano
Lure. J. Scarborough
Lure of Contraband. J. Wear-Gifford
Lure of Gold. Nicholas Carter
Lure of Love. W. LeQueux
Lure of Mammon. Dick Stewart
Lure of the Black Pool. Old Sleuth
Lure of the Bush. A. W. Upfield
Lure of Thunder Island. L. Walmsley
Lured by Greed. A. Andre
Lured from Home. Grace M. White
Lures of Death. P. Whelton
Lurking Death. F. W. Gumley
Lurking Man. Gerald Butler
Lurking Policeman. G. Kent
Lurking Shadow. A. Askew
Lurking Shadow. J. Remenham
Lurking Terror. A. Peverett
Lurking Terror. E. Wilmot
Lust for Innocence. D. Doubtfire
Lust for Murder. H. Klinger
Lust for Vengeance. R. Bloomfield
Lust for Vengeance. H. Janson
Lust Is No Lady. M. Avallone
Lust of Hate. G. Boothby
Lust of Power. H. Kane
Lust of Treasure. H. C. Marksman
Lust to Kill. Edward Lee
Lustful Ape. R. Gray
Lustful Summer. R. V. Cassill
Lusting Drive. O. Demaris
Lustre Jug. F. Hird
Lusty Men. W. R. Cox
Lute and the Glove. K. W. Eyre
Luther Wing. H. Maurice
Luxembourg Run. S. Ellin
Luxury Merchants. A. Richards
Luxury Tour. L. Handley
Lycanthia. F. Layland-Barratt
Lycanthrope, the Mystery of Sir William Wolf. E. Phillpotts
Lyddon House Mystery. G. Ellinger
Lydia. E. V. Cunningham
Lydia Trendennis. F. E. Smith
Lying at Death's Door. M. Cumberland
Lying Down Below. H. Carstairs
Lying Jade. L. Ford
Lying Ladies. R. Finnegan
Lying Lips. W. LeQueux
Lying Lips. T. A. Plummer
Lying Three. R. McInerny
Lying Voices. E. Ferrars
Lynch Town. W. B. Murphy
Lynching of Orin Newfield. G. J. Goldberg
Lynch's Law. J. Balnave
Lyndley Waters. G. R. Preedy
Lyndwood Affair. U. L. Silberrad
Lynmara Legacy. C. Gaskin
Lynne Court Spinney. J. S. Fletcher
Lynx, Counter Spy. Vigilant
Lynx, Spyflyer. Vigilant
Lynx, V. C. Vigilant
Lynx, V. C., Flies Again. Vigilant
Lyona Grimswood, Spinster. L. Higgin
Lyonesse Abbey. J. Tattersall
Lyonhurst. Rona Randall
Lyons Mail. G. Rowell
Lyttleton Case. R. A. V. Morris

MacAlastair Looks On. A. Dick
Macall Gets Curious. G. Fairlie
McAllister and His Double. A. Train
Macaterick's Revenge. A. Venters
McCabe. E. Naughton
McCabe and Mrs. Miller. E. Naughton
McCarthy, C.I.D. J. G. Brandon
McCarthy's List. M. Mackey
McCarty, Incog. I. Ostrander
McCloud. C. Wilcox
McCreary Moves In. M. East
McDermott's Sky. R. Serling
McGarr and the Politician's Wife. B. Gill
McGarr and the Sienese Conspiracy. B. Gill
McGarr at the Dublin Horse Show. B. Gill
McGarr on the Cliffs of Moher. B. Gill
MacGilleroy's Millions. I. D. Hardy
McGregor's Island. O. John
McHugh. J. Flynn
McInnes of the N.I.D. Sea-Wrack
MacIntyre Plot. P. M. Walker

McIver's Secret. L. Grimes
McKee of Centre Street. N. Reilly
Mackenzie Break. S. Shelley
Mackenzie's Glen. Janis Dawson
Mackintosh Man. D. Bagley
McLean at the Golden Owl. G. Goodchild
McLean Carries On. G. Goodchild
McLean Deduces. G. Goodchild
McLean Disposes. G. Goodchild
McLean Excels. G. Goodchild
McLean Finds a Way. G. Goodchild
McLean Incomparable. G. Goodchild
McLean Intervenes. G. Goodchild
McLean Investigates. G. Goodchild
McLean Invincible. G. Goodchild
McLean Keeps Going. G. Goodchild
McLean Knows Best. G. Goodchild
McLean Knows the Answers. G. Goodchild
McLean: Non-Stop. G. Goodchild
McLean of Scotland Yard. G. Goodchild
McLean Plays a Hand. G. Goodchild
McLean Predominant. G. Goodchild
McLean Prevails. G. Goodchild
McLean Remembers! G. Goodchild
McLean Scores Again. G. Goodchild
McLean Sees It Through. G. Goodchild
McLean Solves It. G. Goodchild
McLean Steps In. G. Goodchild
McLean Takes a Holiday. G. Goodchild
McLean Takes Charge. G. Goodchild
McLean Takes Over. G. Goodchild
McLean the Magnificent. G. Goodchild
McLean to the Dark Tower Came. G. Goodchild
McLoon of the South Seas. O. Sackville
Maclure Mystery. A. S. Swan
MacLurg Goes West. R. Petrie
McNeills Chase a Ghost. T. Du Bois
McQ. Alexander Edwards
McQuaid. S. Rifkin
McQuaid in August. S. Rifkin
MacStodger's Affinity. D. Whitelaw
MacTaggart's War. R. Dennis
MacTavish. P. Cheyney
McTodd. C. J. C. Hune

M. L. Falkner
M.D.—Doctor of Murder. Donald Ross
M.F.H.'s Daughter. R. Jocelyn
M for Murder. J. G. Brandon
M.R.C.S. B. Delannoy
M.S. Bradford, Special. A. C. Gunter
M-Squad. D. Saunders
MW-XX.3. R. Pertwee
Mabel Seymour. C. Matthew
Macabre Manor. E. Grayson
Macabre Mansion. L. Churchill
Macamba Project. M. Cronin
Macao. Nick Carter
Macedonian Mixup. John Bentley
Machinations of Dr. Grue. H. M. Raleigh
Machinations of the Myo-ok. C. C. Lowis
Machine Gun McCann. O. Demaris
Machine Gun Murder. Jacques Thomas
Machine to Kill. G. Leroux
Mackin Cover. D. K. Shah
Macomber Menace. W. D. Roberts
Macon Moore, the Southern Detective. J. R. Taylor
Macowen Murder. E. Y. Miller
Maculan's Daughter. S. Gainham
Mad. G. M. Fenn
Mad Baxter. Wade Miller
Mad Doctor. J. Thwaites
Mad Doctor in Harley Street. F. J. Thwaites
"Mad Dog" Coll. S. Thurman
Mad Eyes. K. Robeson
Mad Hatter Murder. F. Grierson
Mad Hatter Mystery. J. D. Carr
Mad Hatter's Holiday. P. Lovesey
Mad Hatter's Rock. V. Gunn
Mad Interlude. A. L. Martin
Mad Mesa. K. Robeson
Mad Mike. G. Goodchild
Mad Monk. R. T. M. Scott
Mad Murder. R. H. Wilkinson
Mad Scientist Affair. J. T. Phillifent
Mad Shepherdess. H. Brooke
Mad Sir Geoffrey. F. Warden
Mad with Much Heart. Gerald Butler
Madam. G. Cherrell
Madam Ambassador. N. Calmer
Madam and Eve. M. Corrigan
Madam Captain. E. L. Long
Madam Crowl's Ghost, and other tales of mystery. J. S. Le Fanu
Madam Is Dead. R. Terrall
Madam Julia's Tale and other queer stories. N. Royde-Smith
Madam Tic-Tac. F. L. Cary
Madam Will Not Dine Tonight. H. Waugh
Madam, Will You Talk? Mary Stewart
Madam, You Must Die. C. Keppel
Madam You're Mayhem. Carter Brown
Madame. E. P. Oppenheim
Madame and Her Twelve Virgins. E. P. Oppenheim

M

Madame Aubrey and the Police. H. Travers
Madame Aubrey Dines with Death. H. Travers
Madame Baltimore. H. Knowland
Madame Bluebeard. B. Sanders
Madame Flirt. C. E. Pearce
Madame Holle. Margery Lawrence
Madame Judas. M. Turnbull
Madame Knits. R. Rodd
Madame Lies Murdered. G. Wishart
Madame Lucien. A. Hodges
Madame Maigret's Friend. G. Simenon
Madame Maigret's Own Case. G. Simenon
Madame Merlin. G. Beardmore
Madame Midas. F. Hume
Madame "Q". Nicholas Carter
Madame Shadow. F. Grierson
Madame Sly. M. Corrigan
Madame Spy. B. Graeme
Madame Storey. H. Footner
Madame X. M. Avallone
Madball. F. Brown
Madcap Betty. D. Whitelaw
Maddening Scar. D. R. Clinton
Maddon's Rock. H. Innes
Made for Murder. Elizabeth Anthony
Made for Murder. F. McGrew
Made in America. P. Maas
Made to Murder. J. Courage
Made Up for Murder. K. Roos
Made Up to Kill. K. Roos
Madeleine. C. Campion
Madeleine Smith. Winifred Duke
Madeline. I. Kelly
Madeline Brown's Murderer. F. Adams
Madeline Payne, the Detective's Daughter. L. L. Lynch
Madeline Power. A. W. Marchmont
Mademoiselle B. M. Pons
Mademoiselle from Armentieres. J. Rhode
Mademoiselle of Monte Carlo. W. LeQueux
Madgwick Affair. D. Whitelaw
Madhouse. Angus Hall
Madhouse in Washington Square. David Alexander
Madigan. R. Dougherty
Madigan's Women. J. Conway
Madison Murder. L. Grex
Madman. M. Hansom
Madman at My Door. H. Waugh
Madman of Bergerac. G. Simenon
Madman of the Marshes. W. Jardine
Madman on a Drum. N. R. De Mexico
Madman Theory. E. Queen
Madman's Bend. A. W. Upfield
Madman's Buff. K. Steel
Madman's Manor. C. Rushton
Madman's Whisper. Richard Grayson
Madmen Die Alone. J. E. Greene
Madness at the Castle. S. Claudia
Madness from Mars. D. Summers
Madness of Charlie Pierce. H. C. James
Madness of Gloria. F. Whishaw
Madness of the Heart. R. Neely
Madonna Creek Witch. J. La Tourrette
Madonna in Hollywood. M. Dekobra
Madonna of Hell. K. Lindsay
Madonna of the Music Halls. W. LeQueux
Madonna of the Seven Moons. Margery Lawrence
Madonna of the Sleeping Cars. M. Dekobra
Madonna Red. J. P. Carroll
Madrigal. J. Gardner
Madrone Tree. D. Duncan
Maelstrom. F. Froest
Maelstrom. Howard Hunt
Maelstrom. W. H. Murray
Maestro Murders. F. S. Wees
Mafalda. J. Goodwin
Mafia. N. Clad
Mafia Death Watch. B. Rossi
Mafia Fix. R. Sapir
Mafia Kiss. P. Loraine
Mafia Man. R. Posner
Mafia Massacre. F. Scarpetta
Mafia Vendetta. L. Sciascia
Mafia Wipe-Out. F. Scarpetta
Mafia Women. J. Cenni
Mafia's Victim. I. Stark
Mafioso. P. McCurtin
Magdalene Scrolls. Barbara Wood
Maggie? F. Barrett
Maggie Rowan. C. Cookson
Magic Casket. R. A. Freeman
Magic Change Detective. Anonymous
Magic Dick, a Boy Detective. Old Sleuth
Magic Eardrums. H. S. Keeler
Magic for Murder. A. Livingston
Magic Grandfather. D. M. Disney
Magic Island. K. Robeson
Magic Lantern Murders. Carter Dickson
Magic Makes Murder. H. R. Campbell
Magic Man. H. E. Rives
Magic Necklace. Nicholas Carter
Magic of Chez Finnie. C. E. Elvy
Magic of To-Morrow. C. Seymour
Magic Ring. D. Daniels
Magic Valley. W. E. D. Ross
Magic Year. J. Maas
Magician. F. L. Green
Magician. G. Simenon
Magician and the Widow. G. Simenon

Magician Kills and The Coffin Mystery. John Reid
Magicians. James Gunn
Magician's Daughter. M. Granbeck
Magician's Wife. J. M. Cain
Maginot Line Murder. B. Newman
Magistrate's Own Case. B. P. Rosenkrantz
Magnate Detective. Anonymous
Magnet. A. O. Crozier
Magnet for Danger. M. Richmond
Magnet for Murder. M. E. Corne
Magnet for Murder. B. Symons
Magnet of Doom. G. Simenon
Magnetic Girl. R. Marsh
Magnetic Man. N. Daniels
Magnetism of Sin. Aesculapius
Magnificent Hoax. E. P. Oppenheim
Magnificent Hobo. A. Wilson
Magnificent Moll. J. Gonzales
Magnolia Curse. L. Murfi
Magnolia Murder. W. Bell
Magnolias. J. Ellis
Magnum for Schneider. J. Mitchell
Magnum Force. M. Valley
Magpie House. A. Soutar
Magpie Murder. G. Coverack
Magpie on the Gallows. J. G. Sarasin
Mahatma's Pupil. R. Marsh
Mahme Nousie. G. M. Fenn
Mahogany House. J. Wetherell
Mahogany Murder. Lee Roberts
Mahoney Million. C. Townsend
Maid for Murder. Carter Brown
Maid for Murder. C. Franklin
Maid for Murder. M. K. Ozaki
Maid from Norway. A. Munch
Maid in Paris. F. Kane
Maid Indomitable. L. T. Meade
Maid of Athens. M. Richmond
Maid of Honour. R. Aitken
Maid of Mansfield. P. Trent
Maid of Mystery. L. T. Meade
"Maid of Sussex." G. Volk
Maid of the Village. Mrs. Kentish
Maid to Murder. Roy Vickers
Maiden Armour. John Marsh
Maiden Fair and other stories. C. Gibbon
Maiden Flight That Never Was. M. D. Morrison
Maiden of Glory Island. J. Wetherell
Maiden Possessed. J. N. Chance
Maiden Widow. E. Southworth
Maiden's Prayer. Joan Fleming
Maigret Abroad. G. Simenon
Maigret Afraid. G. Simenon
Maigret and Monsieur Charles. G. Simenon
Maigret and Monsieur Labbe. G. Simenon
Maigret and the Apparition. G. Simenon
Maigret and the Black Sheep. G. Simenon
Maigret and the Bum. G. Simenon
Maigret and the Burglar's Wife. G. Simenon
Maigret and the Calame Report. G. Simenon
Maigret and the Concarneau Murders. G. Simenon
Maigret and the Coroner. G. Simenon
Maigret and the Dead Girl. G. Simenon
Maigret and the Dosser. G. Simenon
Maigret and the Enigmatic Lett. G. Simenon
Maigret and the Flea. G. Simenon
Maigret and the Gangsters. G. Simenon
Maigret and the Ghost. G. Simenon
Maigret and the Headless Corpse. G. Simenon
Maigret and the Hotel Majestic. G. Simenon
Maigret and the Hundred Gibbets. G. Simenon
Maigret and the Informer. G. Simenon
Maigret and the Killer. G. Simenon
Maigret and the Lazy Burglar. G. Simenon
Maigret and the Loner. G. Simenon
Maigret and the Madwoman. G. Simenon
Maigret and the Man on the Bench. G. Simenon
Maigret and the Man on the Boulevard. G. Simenon
Maigret and the Millionaires. G. Simenon
Maigret and the Minister. G. Simenon
Maigret and the Nahour Case. G. Simenon
Maigret and the Old Lady. G. Simenon
Maigret and the Reluctant Witnesses. G. Simenon
Maigret and the Saturday Caller. G. Simenon
Maigret and the Spinster. G. Simenon
Maigret and the Toy Village. G. Simenon
Maigret and the Wine Merchant. G. Simenon
Maigret and the Young Girl. G. Simenon
Maigret at the Coroner's. G. Simenon
Maigret at the Crossroads. G. Simenon
Maigret Cinq. G. Simenon
Maigret Goes Home. G. Simenon
Maigret Goes to School. G. Simenon
Maigret Has Doubts. G. Simenon
Maigret Has Scruples. G. Simenon
Maigret Hesitates. G. Simenon
Maigret in Court. G. Simenon
Maigret in Exile. G. Simenon

Maigret in Holland. G. Simenon
Maigret in Montmartre. G. Simenon
Maigret in New York's Underworld. G. Simenon
Maigret in Retirement. G. Simenon
Maigret in Society. G. Simenon
Maigret in Vichy. G. Simenon
Maigret Keeps a Rendezvous. G. Simenon
Maigret Loses His Temper. G. Simenon
Maigret Meets a Milord. G. Simenon
Maigret Mystified. G. Simenon
Maigret Omnibus. G. Simenon
Maigret on Holiday. G. Simenon
Maigret on the Defensive. G. Simenon
Maigret Quartet. G. Simenon
Maigret Rents a Room. G. Simenon
Maigret Returns. G. Simenon
Maigret Right and Wrong. G. Simenon
Maigret Sets a Trap. G. Simenon
Maigret Sits It Out. G. Simenon
Maigret Stonewalled. G. Simenon
Maigret Takes a Room. G. Simenon
Maigret Takes the Waters. G. Simenon
Maigret to the Rescue. G. Simenon
Maigret Travels South. G. Simenon
Maigret Trio. G. Simenon
Maigret's Boyhood Friend. G. Simenon
Maigret's Christmas. G. Simenon
Maigret's Dead Man. G. Simenon
Maigret's Failure. G. Simenon
Maigret's First Case. G. Simenon
Maigret's Little Joke. G. Simenon
Maigret's Memoirs. G. Simenon
Maigret's Mistake. G. Simenon
Maigret's Pickpocket. G. Simenon
Maigret's Pipe. G. Simenon
Maigret's Revolver. G. Simenon
Maigret's Rival. G. Simenon
Maigret's Special Murder. G. Simenon
Mail for McNair. S. Lock
Mail Robber. J. E. Stewart
Mail Robbers' Syndicate. E. C. Derby
Mail Train. K. A. Dobson
Mail Van Mystery. J. G. Brandon
Main. Trevanian
Main Attraction. S. Michaels
Main Chance. Edmund Ward
Main Experiment. C. Hodder-Williams
Main Line Kill. R. Busby
Main Street Morgue. Griff
Maine Massacre. J. Van De Wetering
Mainline Plot. J. Rosenberger
Maitland Inheritance. Laura Smith
Maitland Street Murder. Mark Allerton
Maitland's Master Mystery. M. Severy
"Majestic" Mystery. D. Mackail
Majesty of the Law. M. Danning
Majii. K. Robeson
Major. John Ross
Major. F. Warden
Major Adventures. L. P. Greene
Major Crime. O. Keystone
Major Developments. L. P. Greene
Major—Diamond Buyer. L. P. Greene
Major Enquiry. L. Henderson
Major Exploits. L. P. Greene
Major Has Seven Guests. C. Wagner
Major Hazards. L. P. Greene
Major Incident. P. N. Walker
Major—Knight Errant. L. P. Greene
Major Occasions. L. P. Greene
Major Owen, and other tales. C. N. Johnston
Major Steps Out. John Ross
Major Washington. E. A. Shaffer
Majorca. S. Dodson
Majorettes. J. Russo
Makariri Gold. B. Priestley
Makassar Strait Contract. P. Atlee
Make a Killing. H. Q. Masur
Make a Killing. B. Williams
Make Believe. P. DePolnay
Make-Believe Man. Elizabeth Fenwick
Make Death Love Me. R. Rendell
Make Do with Spring. E. Bonnet
Make Every Kiss Count. Ronald Simpson
Make Fame a Monster. E. H. Clements
Make Haste to Die. R. Watkins
Make Haste to Live. The Gordons
Make It Lethal. R. Drayton
Make It Look Like an Accident. J. R. Nolan
Make It Murder. J. Last
Make It Nylons. J. P. Heggy
Make Me a Murderer. Gwendoline Butler
Make Me a Widow. D. Ellis
Make Mine a Corpse. M. Storm
Make Mine a Harlot. M. Storm
Make Mine a Redhead. M. Storm
Make Mine a Shroud. M. Storm
Make Mine a Virgin. M. Storm
Make Mine Beautiful. M. Storm
Make Mine Dangerous. M. Storm
Make Mine Maclain. B. Kendrick
Make Mine Mavis. W. Ard
Make Mine Mayhem. P. Muller
Make Mine Mink. H. Janson
Make Mine Murder. R. S. Bowen
Make Mine Murder. Neill Graham
Make Mine Murder. M. Hervey
Make Mine Murder. B. Winter
Make Mine Vengeance. R. Colby

Title Index

Make My Bed in Hell. J. Sanford
Make My Bed Soon. J. S. Strange
Make My Bed Soon. J. Webb
Make My Coffin Big. J. B. O'Sullivan
Make My Coffin Strong. W. R. Cox
Make Out with Murder. C. Harrison
Make Sure I'm Dead. D. Bogard
Make the Corpse Walk. Raymond Marshall
Make-Up for Murder. J. Wright
Make-Up for the Toff. J. Creasey
Make Way for a Sailor. Seafarer
Make Way for Murder. A. A. Marcus
Make Way for the Mourners. David Hume
Make with the Brains, Pierre. Dana Wilson
Maker of Frocks. E. C. Davies
Maker of History. E. P. Oppenheim
Maker of Mischief. S. P. Hyatt
Maker of Nations. G. Boothby
Maker of Opportunities. G. F. Gibbs
Maker of Secrets. W. LeQueux
Maker of Shadows. Jack Mann
Maker of Ware. S. Edge
Making Crime Pay. P. Cheyney
Making Good Again. L. Davidson
Making Hate. Jacqueline Wilson
Making It Big. J. Jakes
Making Progress. A. Bailey
Makra Mystery. H. Campbell
Malabang Pearl. F. Archer
Malabar Magician. F. E. Penny
Malachi Breen Times Two. L. Pope
Malachite Jar. J. S. Fletcher
Malady in Madeira. A. Bridge
Malago's Visit. C. Salcido
Malaret Mystery. O. Hartley
Malaspiga Exit. Evelyn Anthony
Malay Manhunt. A. S. Fleischman
Malay Woman. A. S. Fleischman
Malayan Rose. M. Derby
Malayan Story. G. Sheen
Malcolm Sage, Detective. H. Jenkins
Malcolm the Wonder. Old Sleuth
Malcontents. S. Franklin
Male Order. C. E. Bowman
Malefactor. E. P. Oppenheim
Malefactors. C. Blair
Malice Aforethought. F. Iles
Malice and the Maternal Instinct. M. Tripp
Malice Domestic. E. Cameron
Malice Domestic. P. Capon
Malice Domestic. R. Foley
Malice Domestic. Sara Woods
Malice in Wonderland. N. Blake
Malice in Wonderland. R. King
Malice Matrimonial. Joan Fleming
Malice of Monday. E. Burgess
Malice with Murder. N. Blake
Malicious Madonna. D. Romaine
Malicious Mischief. L. Egan
Maliday Mystery. A. Mills
Malignant Heart. C. Sibley
Malignant Snowman. K. Laing
Malignant Stars. Jerome Barry
Malinsay Massacre. D. Wheatley
Mallabec. D. Walker
Mallen Girl. C. Cookson
Mallen Litter. C. Cookson
Mallen Lot. C. Cookson
Mallen Streak. C. Cookson
Mallion's Pride. C. Salisbury
Mallison Mystery. T. W. Hanshew
Mallory. Raymond Marshall
Mallory Case. L. Barbee
Mallory Grange. C. Randell
Mallory of the Royal Mounted. C. Stoddard
Mallory's Luck. K. A. Shoesmith
Malloy's Tryst. P. C. De Crespigny
Mally Lee. E. Kyle
Malpas Legacy. A. Pritchett
Malta Conspiracy. F. Mullally
Malta Mystery. S. G. Hedges
Maltese Cross. E. T. Sawyer
Maltese Falcon. D. Hammett
Maluti Murder. E. Haldane
Malverne Hall. R. C. Payes
Malverne Manor. H. York
Malvery Hold. J. S. Fletcher
Malvie Inheritance. Pamela Hill
Mama Doll. M. Woodhouse
Mambo to Murder. Dale Clark
Mamizelle Bon Voyage. G. Buhet
Mammon. P. C. Wren
Mammon of Righteousness. P. C. Wren
Mammon's Daughter. N. Tranter
Mammoth. S. P. Hyatt
Mammoth Mansions Mystery. H. Hill
Mamo Murders. J. Sheridan
M'amselle It's Murder. K. T. McCall
Man. M. Dinelli
Man. Will Scott
Man. B. Stoker
Man About a Dog. Alec Coppel
Man About Town. W. LeQueux
Man Above Suspicion. J. Mayo
Man Against Fear. Mike Brewer
Man Against Man. Nicholas Carter
Man Alive. M. Cronin
Man Alone. Shelley Smith
Man Alone. E. C. Vivian

Man and a Half. F. Gamble
Man and His Kingdom. E. P. Oppenheim
Man and His Money. F. S. Isham
Man and His Price. Nicholas Carter
Man and Master. L. L. Lynch
Man and the Crime. H. Rockwood
Man and Two Gods. Jean Morris
Man and Wife. W. Collins
Man at Large. M. Cronin
Man at Six. J. Celestin
Man at Six. J. De Leon
Man at the Carlton. E. Wallace
Man at the Manor. O. Sinclair
Man at the Window. Nicholas Carter
Man at Willow Ranch. H. Bindloss
Man Beguiled. R. Rodd
Man Behind. A. Dax
Man Behind. J. Hunter
Man Behind Me. J. N. Chance
Man Behind the Badge. M. I. Snider
Man Behind the Chair. Winifred Graham
Man Behind the Curtain. A. Murray
Man Behind the Curtain. N. Tranter
Man Behind the Curtain. J. M. Walsh
Man Behind the Curtain. D. Walshe
Man Behind the Door. A. C. Gunter
Man Behind the Face. J. March
Man Behind the Mask. G. M. Cooke
Man Behind the Tinted Glasses. Diana Forbes
Man Between. W. A. Frost
Man Called Black. W. Manson
Man Called Eighty-Eight. R. W. Hinds
Man Called Gillray. F. M. White
Man Called Harry Brent. F. Durbridge
Man Called Jones. J. Symons
Man Called Jordan. A. Aricha
Man Called Lenz. George Young
Man Called Scavener. P. Van Greenaway
Man Called Spade. D. Hammett
Man Called Tempest. W. Shand
Man Condemned. P. Alding
Man Could Get Killed That Way. Weldon Hill
Man Dead. S. Jepson
Man Died Here. G. Dessart
Man Died Talking. R. Garnett
Man Dormant. J. Lodwick
Man Drowning. H. Kuttner
Man Eater. H. M. Rideout
Man Everybody Was Afraid Of. J. Hansen
Man for Me. T. Charles
Man from Algiers. W. Jardine
Man from Arnheim. L. Jackson
Man from Atlantis. K. Robeson
Man from Australia. F. A. Symonds
Man from Australia. W. L. Whitehouse
Man from AVON. M. Avallone
Man from Bar Harbour. G. Mitcham
Man from Checkmate. W. R. Bennett
Man from Chicago. L. C. Douthwaite
Man from China. A. Parsons
Man from Chun King. R. Hardinge
Man from Dartmoor. Gwyn Evans
Man from Destiny. I. MacKintosh
Man from Dieppe. H. King
Man from Downing Street. W. LeQueux
Man from Dublin. A. Blair
Man from Egypt. H. Hill
Man from Everywhere. G. Simenon
Man from Fleet Street. J. Creasey
Man from Greek and Roman. J. Goldman
Man from Holland. R. Hardinge
Man from India. Nicholas Carter
Man from Italy. J. G. Brandon
Man from Kabul. G. De Villiers
Man from Kenya. A. Parsons
Man from Kura-Kura. A. Murray
Man from Limbo. G. Endore
Man from Lisbon. T. Gifford
Man from London. Nicholas Carter
Man from M.O.D. W. B. Day
Man from Madagascar. F. Grierson
Man from Madrid. P. Meriton
Man from Maloba. O. Binns
Man from Manchester. D. Donovan
Man from Manhattan. L. Grex
Man from Maybrick Road. A. Parsons
Man from Mexico City. D. Whitelaw
Man from Michigan. B. Graeme
Man from Mongolia. R. Hardinge
Man from Morocco. E. Wallace
Man from Moscow. G. Chester
Man from Moscow. P. McCutchan
Man from Moscow. F. Usher
Man from MOTHER. Harry Gregory
Man from Norway. G. Chester
Man from Nowhere. V. Bridges
Man from Nowhere. S. Ellin
Man from Nowhere. Joan Fleming
Man from Nowhere. E. Huxley
Man from Occupied France. A. Parsons
Man from Pansy. D. Rico
Man from Paris. Roland Daniel
Man from Paris. L. Royer
Man from Pecos. D. Reid
Man from Persia. L. Jackson
Man from Prison. Roland Daniel
Man from Scapa Flow. Taffrail
Man from Scotland Yard. D. Frome
Man from Scotland Yard. S. Horler
Man from Sing Sing. E. P. Oppenheim

Man from Singapore. J. G. Brandon
Man from Space. R. Hardinge
Man from Texas. B. Wayde
Man from the Bomb. R. Chetwynd-Hayes
Man from the Chamber of Horrors. John Ross
Man from the Clouds. J. S. Clouston
Man from the Diner's Club. S. Baol
Man from the Far East. J. Hunter
Man from the Gallows. E. L. McKeag
Man from the Jungle. R. Hardinge
Man from the Lias River. R. Cullum
Man from the Mist. M. Elgin
Man from the Norlands. J. Buchan
Man from the Past. S. P. Hyatt
Man from the Past. A. MacKenzie
Man from the Rhine. L. Cargill
Man from the River. G. D. H. Cole
Man from the Rock. D. Bateson
Man from the S.A.S. J. B. Coyle
Man from the Sea. M. Innes
Man from the South. J. R. Taylor
Man from the Turkish Slave. V. Canning
Man from the West. Anonymous
Man from the West. G. Goodchild
Man from the West, and other stories of adventure. G. Goodchild
Man from Tibet. C. G. Clason
Man from Tokyo. W. Jardine
Man from Troy. J. G. Sarasin
Man from Whitehall. J. M. Walsh
Man from Yesterday. D. Daniels
Man from Yesterday. G. Markstein
Man Gets into His Tomb. L. Mercer
Man Himself. A. M. Williamson
Man; His Mark. W. C. Morrow
Man Hunt. G. Bettany
Man Hunt. O. Cameron
Man Hunt! L. Como
Man Hunt. T. Gallon
Man Hunt. G. Household
Man Hunt. L. A. Knight
Man-Hunter. D. Donovan
Man-Hunter. M. O. Rolfe
Man I Didn't Kill. N. Deane
Man I Killed. M. Halliday
Man I Killed. S. Walker
Man in a Black Hat. T. Thurston
Man in a Mist. L. Lamb
Man in a Net. W. Butler
Man in a Net. P. Garrod
Man in Ambush. M. Procter
Man in Aspic. Andrew Hall
Man in Black. S. J. Weyman
Man in Blue. M. A. Denison
Man in Brown. W. Edwards
Man in Brown. M. Walsh
Man in Charge. R. Jessup
Man in Evening Clothes. J. R. Scott
Man in Gray. F. Crane
Man in Gray. B. Orczy
Man in Gray. E. C. Vivian
Man in Half Moon Street. B. Lyndon
Man in Lower Ten. M. R. Rinehart
Man in Mail. Lieut. Carlton
Man in Motion. C. Williams
Man in Motley. T. Gallon
Man in My Chair. H. B. Kaye
Man in My Grave. W. Tucker
Man in My Shoes. J. N. Chance
Man in No. 3. J. S. Fletcher
Man in Question. J. Godey
Man in Ratcatcher, and other stories. H. C. McNeile
Man in Room 3. A. Carr
Man in Stripes. Lieut. Carlton
Man in the Auto. Nicholas Carter
Man in the Basement. B. P. Rosenkrantz
Man in the Bird Cage. K. MacLean
Man in the Blue Mask. Anthony Morton
Man in the Bottle. B. Knox
Man in the Box. N. Worth
Man in the Brown Derby. W. S. Hastings
Man in the Brown Suit. A. Christie
Man in the Button Boots. Anthony Gilbert
Man in the Cage. J. H. Vance
Man in the Cape. H. C. Bailey
Man in the Car. A. Raleigh
Man in the Check Suit. T. W. H. Delf
Man in the Cloak. S. Horler
Man in the Corner. B. Orczy
Man in the Dark. W. Cook
Man in the Dark. J. Ferguson
Man in the Dark. D. Orgill
Man in the Dark. S. Scarlett
Man in the Dark. Donald Stuart
Man in the Dark. A. P. Terhune
Man in the Driver's Seat. Ira Walker
Man in the Fog. H. Tighe
Man in the Fur Coat. J. S. Fletcher
Man in the Garden. P. Mason
Man in the Green Hat. M. Coles
Man in the Grey Cowl. A. Murray
Man in the Hood. S. Horler
Man in the Jury Box. R. O. Chipperfield
Man in the Lubianka. D. Vallance
Man in the Mews. J. Packer
Man in the Middle. H. Atkinson
Man in the Middle. M. E. Chaber
Man in the Middle. F. Findley
Man in the Middle. A. Heal
Man in the Middle. D. Wagoner

Man in the Middle / 541

Man in the Mirror. F. Ayer
Man in the Mirror. H. Douglas
Man in the Mist. F. Bonnamy
Man in the Monkey Suit. A. Hathaway
Man in the Moonlight. R. S. Holland
Man in the Moonlight. H. McCloy
Man in the Net. P. Quentin
Man in the Night Mail Train. A. Philips
Man in the Pig Mask. C. T. Stoneham
Man in the Portrait. F. A. M. Webster
Man in the Purple Gown. C. Haddon
Man in the Queue. G. Daviot
Man in the Red Hat. R. Keverne
Man in the Red Mask. Roy Vickers
Man in the Rolls-Royce. Ilian Stuart
Man in the Sandhills. A. Marsden
Man in the Shadow. R. Foley
Man in the Shadow. S. Kyle
Man in the Shadow. H. Whittington
Man in the Shadows. C. Bidmead
Man in the Shadows. C. J. Daly
Man in the Shadows. S. Horler
Man in the Sopwith Camel. M. Butterworth
Man in the Spike. Michael Barrett
Man in the Tricorn Hat. D. Ames
Man in the Trilby Hat. R. Goyne
Man in the Turkish Bath. H. F. Moulton
Man in the Twilight. R. Cullum
Man in the Water. R. Sheckley
Man in the White Raincoat. R. Lebherz
Man in the White Slicker. L. H. Nason
Man in the Wood. M. S. Boyd
Man in White. S. Horler
Man in Yellow, and The Empty House. H. C. McNeile
Man Inside. M. E. Chaber
Man Inside. N. S. Lincoln
Man-Killer. T. Powell
Man Lay Dead. N. Marsh
Man, Let's Go On. P. McCutchan
Man Made Angry. H. Brooke
Man Made Law. C. Stanton
Man Made of Tin. Shane Martin
Man Made Woman. R. F. Murphy
Man Missing. M. G. Eberhart
Man Must Live. H. Holland
Man Named Seraphin. R. Ray
Man Named Thin. D. Hammett
Man Next Door. M. G. Eberhart
Man No One Knew. L. Meynell
Man Nobody Knew. D. T. Lindsay
Man Nobody Saw. P. Cheyney
Man of a Hundred Faces. G. Leroux
Man of a Hundred Masks. G. Leroux
Man of Affairs. S. Horler
Man of Affairs. J. D. MacDonald
Man of Bronze. R. Robeson
Man of Character. D. H. Landels
Man of Cold Rages. Jordan Park
Man of Dangerous Secrets. M. March
Man of Dartmoor. O. Binns
Man of Death. A. Gask
Man of Double Deed. L. Daventry
Man of Evil. S. Horler
Man of Forty. G. Bullett
Man of Iron. Nicholas Carter
Man of Last Resort. M. D. Post
Man of Law. J. Wainwright
Man of Little Evils. S. Dobyns
Man of Many Colours. D. Braza
Man of Many Faces. Nicholas Carter
Man of Many Minds. E. E. Evans
Man of Miracles. M. Leblanc
Man of Mystery. Nicholas Carter
Man of Mystery. Leon Lewis
Man of Mystery. Old Sleuth
Man of No Sorrows. C. Kernahan
Man of Power. J. Blackmore
Man of Riddles. Nicholas Carter
Man of Sentiment. T. Cobb
Man of Silver Mount. M. Pemberton
Man of Substance. A. Hodges
Man of Talent. E. Kyle
Man of the Avenue. F. Dard
Man of the Crag. G. Boothby
Man of the Forty Faces. T. W. Hanshew
Man of the Hour. W. Magnay
Man of the Moment. M. Gerard
Man of the North. J. B. Hendryx
Man of the River. O. Sinclair
Man of Two Tribes. A. W. Upfield
Man of Wrath. P. Allardyce
Man on a Horse. H. Clewes
Man on a Leash. C. Williams
Man on a Nylon String. W. Masterson
Man on a Rope. G. H. Coxe
Man on a Short Leash. O. Jacks
Man on a String. M. Wolfe
Man on All Fours. A. Derleth
Man on Fire. A. J. Quinnell
Man on His Shoulder. K. Methold
Man on Horseback. A. Abdullah
Man on the Balcony. M. Sjowall
Man on the Bench in the Barn. G. Simenon
Man on the Box. H. MacGrath
Man on the Bridge. I. S. Black
Man on the Camel. H. M. Sachar
Man on the Couch. E. C. Derby
Man on the Crater's Edge. J. Gerson
Man on the Dole. P. Urquhart
Man on the Dover Road. D. Whitelaw
Man on the End of the Rope. Paul Townend

Man on the Left. W. J. Gardiner
Man on the Marsh. D. Leach
Man on the Raffles Verandah. Lydia Kirk
Man on the Run. M. Cronin
Man on the Run. M. Halliday
Man on the Run! A. Kirby
Man on the Run. C. Williams
Man on the Spot. S. C. Mason
Man on the Stairs. Carnaby Brown
Man on the Right Rope. N. Paterson
Man on the Tower. C. Haubold
Man on the Twenty-Fourth Floor. L. Allan
Man on Watch. T. Filer
Man Out of Nowhere. L. P. Davies
Man Out of the Rain. P. MacDonald
Man Outside. S. Campbell
Man Outside. W. Martyn
Man Outside. Donald Stuart
Man Overboard! F. W. Crofts
Man Overboard. A. MacKinnon
Man Overboard! F. Metcalfe
Man Pays. A. Applin
Man Peter. G. Goodchild
Man Responsible. S. Robinett
Man Running. S. Jepson
Man Running. E. West
Man That I Love. D. Egerton
Man the Devil Didn't Want. P. C. Wren
Man They Could Not Convict. R. Hardinge
Man They Could Not Kill. C. H. Barker
Man They Could Not Kill. J. Corbett
Man They Couldn't Arrest. A. J. Small
Man They Couldn't Buy. Gilbert Chester
Man They Couldn't Escape. M. Fiaschetti
Man They Couldn't Hang. O. Martyn
Man They Couldn't Hang. R. L. Meyers
Man They Feared. T. A. Plummer
Man They Held Back. Nicholas Carter
Man They Put Away. T. A. Plummer
Man to be Feared. Nicholas Carter
Man to Match the Hour. S. Truss
Man Trap. Anonymous
Man Trap. J. A. Dunn
Man-Trap. J. D. MacDonald
Man-Trap. W. Magnay
Man-Trapper. Old Sleuth
Man Under the Window. G. T. Ockley
Man Underground. K. Cook
Man Upstairs. P. Hamilton
Man Who Asked Why. Jessica Ryan
Man Who Awoke. M. I. Taylor
Man Who Backed Out! A. Parsons
Man Who Bailed Out. G. Chester
Man Who Bombed the World. J. Milton
Man Who Bought London. E. Wallace
Man Who Butted In. V. Bridges
Man Who Called Himself Devlin. W. M. Green
Man Who Called Too Soon. A. M. Griffin
Man Who Came Back. J. Bryan
Man Who Came Back. W. M. Graydon
Man Who Came Back. M. Hastings
Man Who Came Back. E. Jepson
Man Who Came Back. H. W. Leggett
Man Who Came Back. J. Rossiter
Man Who Came Back. A. Wood
Man Who Came Back from the Dead. G. Leroux
Man Who Cannot Kill. J. F. Straker
Man Who Caught the 4:15. A. Spiller
Man Who Changed Faces. Nicholas Carter
Man Who Changed His Face. T. A. Plummer
Man Who Changed His Name. Robert (G.) Curtis
Man Who Changed His Name. E. Wallace
Man Who Changed His Plea. E. P. Oppenheim
Man Who Chose Death. E. Allen
Man Who Convicted Himself. D. Fox
Man Who Could Cheat Death. J. Sangster
Man Who Could Not Shudder. J. D. Carr
Man Who Could Read Cards. R. L. Broyles
Man Who Could Still Laugh. C. Houghton
Man Who Could Stop War. W. Penmare
Man Who Couldn't Sleep. A. Stringer
Man Who Covered Mirrors. M. Cumberland
Man Who Crawled Away. L. Butler
Man Who Cried All the Way Home. D. Hitchens
Man Who Dealt in Blood. G. Wolk
Man Who Did Not Die. T. Harknett
Man Who Did Not Hang. S. Horler
Man Who Didn't Answer. I. Oellrichs
Man Who Didn't Count. G. M. Glaskin
Man Who Didn't Exist. S. Homes
Man Who Didn't Exist. A. West
Man Who Didn't Fly. M. Bennett
Man Who Didn't Mind Hanging. N. B. Mavity
Man Who Died on Friday. M. Underwood
Man Who Died Too Soon. G. H. Coxe
Man Who Died Twice. G. H. Coxe
Man Who Died Twice. M. Dekobra
Man Who Died Twice. S. Horler
Man Who Died Twice. L. Paxton
Man Who Died Twice. S. A. Peeples
Man Who Disappeared. E. Bohle
Man Who Disappeared. R. Pyke
Man Who Dressed to Kill. A. Spiller
Man Who Drove On. W. M. Graydon
Man Who Drove the Car. M. Pemberton
Man Who Escaped. S. Bedford

Man Who Fainted. Nicholas Carter
Man Who Feared. P. Forsyth
Man Who Feared. W. F. Jenkins
Man Who Fell. M. Eden
Man Who Fell Through the Earth. C. Wells
Man Who Finally Died. John Burke
Man Who Followed Women. B. Hitchens
Man Who Forgot. R. C. Armour
Man Who Forgot. H. Holt
Man Who Forgot. J. Mackie
Man Who Found Himself. M. Stacpoole
Man Who Found His Way. F. O'Rourke
Man Who Got Away. S. L. Elliott
Man Who Got Away with It. Bernice Carey
Man Who Grew Bulbs. J. M. Walsh
Man Who Grew Tomatoes. G. Mitchell
Man Who Guided Missiles. P. Denman
Man Who Had to Quit. A. Parsons
Man Who Had Too Much to Lose. Hampton Stone
Man Who Haunted Himself. Ralph Martin
Man Who Held Five Aces. Jean Leslie
Man Who Held the Queen to Ransom and Sent Parliament Packing. P. Van Greenaway
Man Who Hid. Dick Stewart
Man Who Japed. P. K. Dick
Man Who Killed. C. Farrere
Man Who Killed Fortescue. J. S. Strange
Man Who Killed Himself. J. Symons
Man Who Killed His Brother. Reed Stephens
Man Who Killed Hitler. R. P. Jones
Man Who Killed Me. Arthur MacLean
Man Who Killed the King. D. Wheatley
Man Who Killed Too Soon. M. Underwood
Man Who Knew. H. Leyford
Man Who Knew. M. O. Rolfe
Man Who Knew. E. Wallace
Man Who Knew. F. A. M. Webster
Man Who Knew All. M. Leighton
Man Who Knew the Date. S. Kerr
Man Who Knew Too Much. Ruth Alexander
Man Who Knew Too Much. W. H. Baker
Man Who Knew Too Much and other stories. G. K. Chesterton
Man Who Laughed. G. Fairlie
Man Who Laughed at Murder. G. Ashe
Man Who Left Home. L. Jackson
Man Who Left Well Enough. M. McShane
Man Who Liked to Look at Himself. K. C. Constantine
Man Who Limped. V. Bridges
Man Who Lived Twice. H. Shaw
Man Who Looked Back. Joan Fleming
Man Who Looked Death in the Eye. Hampton Stone
Man Who Lost an Hour. F. Marlowe
Man Who Lost Everything. P. Kuttner
Man Who Lost His Memory. A. Skene
Man Who Lost His Shadow. B. Denham
Man Who Lost His Way. W. E. Johns
Man Who Lost His Wife. J. Symons
Man Who Lost the War. W. T. Tyler
Man Who Loved Chocolates. D. Batchelor
Man Who Loved His Wife. V. Caspary
Man Who Loved Lions. Ethel L. White
Man Who Loved Spiders. S. Horler
Man Who Loved to Blow Up Trains. P. Stafford
Man Who Loved Zoos. M. J. Bosse
Man Who Made a King. R. Ladline
Man Who Made Diamonds. Warren Miller
Man Who Made Good. P. Trent
Man Who Made Money. B. Wayde
Man Who Made Monsters. J. Ronald
Man Who Made Roubles. J. Ingersol
Man Who Mislaid the War. S. Horler
Man Who Missed the War. D. Wheatley
Man Who Murdered Goliath. G. Homes
Man Who Murdered Himself. G. Homes
Man Who Needed Action. M. Geller
Man Who Never Blundered. S. Gluck
Man Who Never Laughed. A. Hare
Man Who Never Slept! Gwyn Evans
Man Who Never Was. S. Picard
Man Who Paid. Nicholas Carter
Man Who Paid His Way. W. J. Sheldon
Man Who Played Patience. S. Truss
Man Who Played Thief. Don Smith
Man Who Plundered the City. S. Elvestad
Man Who Preferred Cocktails. S. Horler
Man Who Pulled the Strings. J. Haslette
Man Who Raised Hell. R. Sale
Man Who Ran Away. D. B. Dodson
Man Who Rang the Bell. M. Kennedy
Man Who Said No. W. Grove
Man Who Saw the Devil. J. Corbett
Man Who Saw Through Heaven. W. D. Steele
Man Who Seduced a Bank. T. E. B. Clarke
Man Who Shook the Earth. S. Horler
Man Who Shook the Earth. K. Robeson
Man Who Shook the World. J. Creasey
Man Who Shot Birds and other tales. M. Fitt
Man Who Slept All Day. M. Venning
Man Who Sold Death. Nick Carter
Man Who Sold Death. J. Munro
Man Who Sold Secrets. Roland Daniel
Man Who Sought Trouble. Roland Daniel
Man Who Squealed. G. N. Philips
Man Who Stayed Alive. G. Ashe
Man Who Stayed at Home. B. Tinker

Title Index

Man Who Stole Heaven. J. Ingersol
Man Who Stole Millions. Nicholas Carter
Man Who Stole Millions and other stories. Nicholas Carter
Man Who Stole the Crown Jewels. Augustus Muir
Man Who Stole the Earth. W. Holt-White
Man Who Stood Alone. P. Trent
Man Who Thought He Was a Pauper. E. P. Oppenheim
Man Who Turned King's Evidence. J. Hunter
Man Who Used Perfume. S. Horler
Man Who Vanished. V. Bridges
Man Who Vanished. Nicholas Carter
Man Who Vanished. F. Hume
Man Who Vanished. Old Sleuth
Man Who Vanished. J. T. Smith
Man Who Walked Away. C. Jay
Man Who Walked Like a Dancer. R. Brennan
Man Who Walked on Diamonds. J. Quartermain
Man Who Walked with Death. S. Horler
Man Who Wanted to Die. A. MacKenzie
Man Who Wanted Tomorrow. B. Freemantle
Man Who Was Bormann. Derek Boyd
Man Who Was Chief. G. Horne
Man Who Was Cursed. Nicholas Carter
Man Who Was Dead. A. W. Marchmont
Man Who Was Dead. W. S. Sykes
Man Who Was Guilty. F. H. Loughead
Man Who Was London. J. K. Keith
Man Who Was Murdered Twice. R. H. Leitfred
Man Who Was Nobody. E. Wallace
Man Who Was Not Himself. J. Graffy
Man Who Was Not Himself. M. Halliday
Man Who Was Not There. Ethel L. White
Man Who Was Ten Years Late for Breakfast. C. Herbert
Man Who Was There. D. G. Barron
Man Who Was There. N. A. Temple-Ellis
Man Who Was Three Jumps Ahead. Hampton Stone
Man Who Was Thursday. G. K. Chesterton
Man Who Was Too Clever. Anthony Gilbert
Man Who Was Too Much. A. Gardner
Man Who Was Two. F. M. White
Man Who Wasn't. G. Goodchild
Man Who Wasn't Himself. L. Cargill
Man Who Wasn't Murdered. H. C. Davis
Man Who Wasn't There. Anthony Gilbert
Man Who Wasn't There. R. MacLeish
Man Who Wasn't There. J. Sandys
Man Who Wasn't There. F. Whitaker
Man Who Watched the Trains Go By. G. Simenon
Man Who Went Away. K. David
Man Who Went Up in Smoke. M. Sjowall
Man Who Went Wrong. L. Jackson
Man Who Would Do Anything. I. T. Ross
Man Who Would Not Swim. B. E. Wallace
Man Who Wouldn't Quit. G. Chester
Man Who Wouldn't Talk. Q. Reynolds
Man Whose Dreams Came True. J. Symons
Man Will Be Kidnapped Tomorrow. J. Ashford
Man with a Background of Flames. R. Johns
Man with a Calico Face. Shelley Smith
Man with a Crutch. Nicholas Carter
Man with a Double. Nicholas Carter
Man with a Grievance. W. Jardine
Man with a Gun. Lieut. Carlton
Man with a Monocle. C. F. Gregg
Man with a Number. S. Blakesley
Man with a Paper Skull. D. Marfield
Man with a Past. J. M. Patterson
Man with a Scar. E. C. Vivian
Man with a Secret. F. Hume
Man with a Shadow. G. M. Fenn
Man with a Thumb. W. C. Hudson
Man with a Weak Heart. G. Gardiner
Man with Bated Breath. J. B. Carr
Man with Bogart's Face. A. J. Fenady
Man with Dry Hands. S. Horler
Man with Expensive Tastes. E. Percy
Man with Fifty Complains. M. McMullen
Man with Five Enemies. R. Hardinge
Man with Good Intentions. J. Barlow
Man with Half a Face. G. Davison
Man with His Back to the East. H. H. Ross
Man with Jitters. J. G. Brandon
Man with My Face. S. W. Taylor
Man with Nine Lives. J. Corbett
Man with Nine Lives. R. Marsh
Man with No Bones. P. Helm
Man with No Face. M. Armstrong
Man with No Face. J. N. Chance
Man with No Face. D. L. Sayers
Man with No Shadow. S. Marlowe
Man with Talent. G. Fairlie
Man with the Amber Eyes. E. Jepson
Man with the Amber Eyes. F. Warden
Man with the Big Head. M. Scrope
Man with the Black Cord. A. Groner
Man with the Black Feather. G. Leroux
Man with the Black Patch. F. E. Verney
Man with the Black Wallet. W. W. Sayer
Man with the Brooding Eyes. J. Goodwin

Man with the Brown Paper Face. I. Hamilton
Man with the Cane. J. Potts
Man with the Chocolate Egg. J. Noone
Man with the Clubfoot. D. Valentine
Man with the Crimson Box. H. S. Keeler
Man with the Crooked Arm. T. A. Plummer
Man with the Dark Beard. A. Haynes
Man with the Getaway Face. R. Stark
Man with the Glaring Eyes. A. Blair
Man with the Glass Eye. N. Leslie
Man with the Gloved Hand. J. McKimmey
Man with the Golden Gun. I. Fleming
Man with the Green Eyes. N. Goddard
Man with the Iron Chest. Richard Williams
Man with the Little Dog. G. Simenon
Man with the Lumpy Nose. L. Lariar
Man with the Magic Eardrums. H. S. Keeler
Man with the Magnetic Eyes. Roland Daniel
Man with the Million Pounds. R. M. Newman
Man with the Monocle. Garnett Weston
Man with the Opals. A. W. Barrett
Man with the Painted Head. H. Reilly
Man with the Parrots. A. E. Bayly
Man with the President's Mind. T. Allbeury
Man with the Rake. M. B. Lee
Man with the Red Beard. P. Cheyney
Man with the Red Beard. D. Whitelaw
Man with the Scar. J. Lomas
Man with the Scarlet Skull, and other tales. Gwyn Evans
Man with the Scarred Hand. H. K. Webster
Man with the Seared Hand. J. G. Rowe
Man with the Squeaky Voice. R. A. J. Walling
Man with the Tattooed Face. M. Burton
Man with the Tiny Head. I. Drummond
Man with the Twisted Face. G. Davison
Man with the Vandyk Beard. F. M. White
Man with the Wax Face. R. Wormser
Man with the White Face. M. Gerard
Man with the Wooden Spectacles. H. S. Keeler
Man with the Yellow Eyes. A. S. Burrage
Man with Three Chins. D. Ames
Man with Three Jaguars. D. Ames
Man with Three Names. H. MacGrath
Man with Three Passports. D. Ames
Man with Three Witches. J. N. Chance
Man with Tin Trumpet. F. Mullally
Man with Two Clocks. W. Masterson
Man with Two Faces. S. Horler
Man with Two Heads. J. N. Chance
Man with Two Shadows. R. Maugham
Man with Two Souls. P. Quiroule
Man with Two Ties. H. Van Rensburg
Man with Two Wives. P. Quentin
Man with Two Wives and other stories. P. Cheyney
Man with Yellow Eyes. B. Atkey
Man with Yellow Eyes. A. Heckstall-Smith
Man Within. G. Greene
Man Without a Conscience. Nicholas Carter
Man Without a Face. A. Boissiere
Man Without a Face. J. E. Hasty
Man Without a Face. C. Robbins
Man Without a Head. J. Bowen
Man Without a Head. T. De Saix
Man Without a Head. W. S. Masterman
Man Without a Memory. A. W. Marchmont
Man Without a Mouth. J. Charles
Man Without a Name. S. Kyle
Man Without a Name. M. Russell
Man Without a Passport. A. Parsons
Man Without a Will. Nicholas Carter
Man Without Friends. N. Echard
Man Without Friends. M. Tripp
Man Without Nerves. E. P. Oppenheim
Man Without Pity. T. Truss
Man, Woman and Sin. E. Jepson
Manacle. M. J. Sagola
Manacle and Bracelet. E. C. Strong
Manasco Road. V. Canning
Manchester Thing. Angus Ross
Manchu Blood. H. Wiley
Manchu Cloud. James Bennett
Manchu Jade. S. Jepson
Manchurian Candidate. R. Condon
Mandarin Cypher. Adam Hall
Mandarin's Bride. M. Richmond
Mandarin's Dagger. L. Crichton
Mandarin's Fan. F. Hume
Mandarin's Pearl. Jeffrey Montague
Mandarin's Sapphire. D. Marfield
Mandarin's Seal. A. Murray
Mandate for Murder. J. A. S. McCombie
Manderley Mystery. B. Ketterer
Mandragora. J. Palmer
Mandrake. D. Sherry
Mandrake the Magician. H. Ashman
Mandrakes in the Cupboard. T. B. Morris
Mandura Mystery. I. Barry
Manfred the Magic Trick Detective. Anonymous
Manfredi, Baron St. Osmund. S. Lansdell
Manfrone. M. Radcliffe

Mangrove Murder. Mary Scott
Manhandled. W. Chambers
Manhandled. A. Stringer
Manhattan Bombshell. N. W. Firth
Manhattan Cowboy. Carter Brown
Manhattan File. I. K. Martin
Manhattan Masquerade. F. A. Kummer
Manhattan Massacre. P. McCurtin
Manhattan Murder. A. Train
Manhattan Night. W. A. Wolff
Manhattan North. M. Albrand
Manhattan Terrors. B. Sarto
Manhattan Underworld. J. Roeburt
Manhattan Wipeout. J. Rosenberger
Manhood Ceremony. R. Berliner
Manhunt. D. MacKenzie
Manhunt. Mark Ross
Manhunt in Manhattan. J. Dekker
Manhunt in Murder. W. Martyn
Manhunt in Sicily. S. Brydon
Manhunt Is My Mission. S. Marlowe
Manhunting. D. Sliman
Mania for Blondes. S. A. Krasney
Maniac. A. MacVicar
Maniac Father. T. P. Prest
Maniac Rendezvous. M. Brandel
Maniac Responsible. R. Gover
Maniac's Dream. F. H. Rose
Manila Hemp. Elinor Chamberlain
Manila Masquerade. D. Garth
Manila Stranger. F. Crisp
Manipulator. L. Cook
Manipulators. H. Atkinson
Manipulators. G. V. Basile
Manipulators. W. Garner
Manipulators. J. Rossiter
Mankill Sport. L. Derrick
Mankiller. C. Wilcox
Mannequin. V. Williams
Mannequin Doll. D. Glinto
Manning-Burke Murder. L. Tracy
Mannix. M. Avallone
Manoeuvres of Celeste. M. E. G.
Manor House Menace. J. Drummond
Manor House Mystery. J. S. Fletcher
Manor Inn. G. H. R. Dabbs
Manordale Mystery. Old Sleuth
Man's Blessing. L. Sciascia
Man's Enemies. L. Thayer
Man's Estate. J. Cleary
Man's Estate. N. Tranter
Man's Shadow. W. H. L. Crauford
Mansel Disappearance Mystery. G. Comley
Mansfield Mystery. J. C. Lenehan
Mansion House Mystery. S. Drew
Mansion in Miniature. E. St. Clair
Mansion Malevolent. C. Farr
Mansion of Deadly Dreams. G. Corren
Mansion of Evil. C. Farr
Mansion of Evil. J. Millard
Mansion of Lost Memories. D. Daniels
Mansion of Menace. C. Farr
Mansion of Mystery. V. Smiley
Mansion of Mystery. C. K. Steele
Mansion of Peril. C. Farr
Mansion of Shadows. E. J. Murray
Mansion of Smiling Masks. D. Winston
Mansion of the Golden Windows. Elsie Lee
Mansion on the Moor. J. Purley
Mansion on the Moors. W. E. D. Ross
Manslaughter. A. D. Miller
Mantis. P. Fox
Mantis and the Moth. M. Weatherly
Mantle of Ishmael. J. S. Fletcher
Mantle of Methuselah. L. Reed
Mantouche Factor. Michael Bradley
Mantrackers. W. Mulvihill
Mantrap. J. N. Chance
Mantrap. A. Evans
Mantrap. D. Yarnell
Mantrapper. Anonymous
Manufacturer's Daughter. A. C. Gunter
Manuscript for Murder. R. M. Stern
Manuscript Murder. L. Robinson
Manuscripts from the Diary of a Physician. T. P. Prest
Manville Murders. C. Fitzsimmons
Manx Cat. F. Levon
Many a Monster. R. Finnegan
Many a Murder. D. Van Deusen
Many a Slip. F. W. Crofts
Many a Slip. O. Mills
Many Brave Hearts. D. M. Douglass
Many-Coloured Thread. L. Allan
Many Deadly Returns. P. Moyes
Many Engagements. J. S. Fletcher
Many Happy Returns. Justin Scott
Many-Headed Monster. G. Lett
Many Murders. I. H. Irwin
Many Parts. John Marsh
Many Thanks, Ben Hassett. H. De Hamel
Many Ways of Death. F. Didelot
Many Worlds of Magnus Ridolph. J. Vance
Maori Murder Case. A. L. Albert
Map of Mistrust. A. MacKinnon
Maple Hall Mystery. E. Parmer
Maplethorpe Tangle. Elliot Bailey
Maracaibo Mission. V. W. Mason
Marakano Formula. J. Pattinson
Maras Affair. E. Reed
Maraskar Bound. R. T. Bickers
Marathon Man. W. Goldman

M

Marathon Mystery. B. E. Stevenson
Marauders by Night. A. Gask
Marbeau Cousins. Harry S. Edwards
Marble Angel. D. Daniels
Marble Arch Mystery. W. J. Bayfield
Marble Forest. T. Durrant
Marble Forest. E. K. Goldthwaite
Marble Heart. H. Luger
Marble Hills. D. Daniels
Marble Jungle. C. Richards
Marble Leaf. D. Daniels
Marble Orchard. B. Copper
Marble Tomb Mystery. Colin Robertson
Marcadia. K. Ashby
Marceau Case. H. S. Keeler
Marcel Levignet. E. Barron
March Hare Murders. E. Ferrars
March of Fate. B. L. Farjeon
March of the Flame Marauders. C. Steele
March of the Legion. J. Robb
March to the Gallows. M. Kelly
Marchand Woman. J. Ives
Marches of Honour. Ganpat
Marchester Royal. J. S. Fletcher
Marching Home. D. Honig
Marchington Inheritance. I. Holland
Marcia, the Innocent. K. Kimbrough
Marco. S. Cobb
Marcus Device. I. Melchior
Marcus Hay. S. P. Hyatt
Marcus Holbeach's Daughter. A. Jones
Mardi. K. Hewitt
Mardi Gras Massacre. L. Derrick
Mardi Gras Murders. G. Bristow
Mardi-Gras Mystery. H. Bedford-Jones
Mare's Nest. C. Coffin
Margaret Benson's Vow. T. A. Plummer
Margaret Carmichael. C. Gibbon
Margaret Forster. G. A. Sala
Margaret Rutland. T. Cobb
Margaret, the Faithful. K. Kimbrough
Margaret, the Peacemaker. W. Wood
Margate Murder Mystery. B. Delannoy
Margie. E. V. Cunningham
Margie and the Wolf Man. R. St. Clair
Margin for Doubt. M. Borgenicht
Margin for Error. Clare Booth
Margin for Terror. F. Kane
Margin of Error. P. Henissart
Margin of Terror. P. Capon
Margin of Terror. W. P. McGivern
Margo. J. Jenkins
Margot—and Her Judges. R. Marsh
Margot Leck. P. Piper
Margravine. L. Hiscott
Maria. Brian Cooper
Maria Marches On. J. Slate
Marianna. N. Buckingham
Marianne. J. Dering
Marianne. F. Mullally
Marianne the Outcast. Anonymous
Marianne's Kingdom. P. J. Cooper
Maridu. S. Wagner
Marie Arnaud, Spy. F. Hope
Marie de Brinvilliers. E. Gaboriau
Marie Halkett. R. W. Chambers
Marie-Rose. F. Du Boisgobey
Marie, the Dancing Girl. Old Sleuth
Marie Vee. D. Newton
Mariella—Spy! C. Davy
Mariette. T. P. Prest
Marihuana. W. Irish
Marijuana Girl. N. R. De Mexico
Marijuana Mob. J. H. Chase
Marijuana Murder. M. Stimson
Marilyn K. L. White
Marilyn the Wild. J. Charyn
Marine Residence, and other stories. J. Payn
Mariner's End. E. B. Selig
Marinova of the Secret Service. R. Essex
Mario. J. Carrick
Marion. J. Bingham
Marionette. P. Bennetts
Marji and the Kidnap Plot. John Benton
Marjorie Daw and Other People. T. B. Aldrich
Marjorie Daw and other stories. T. B. Aldrich
Marjorie Daw and other tales. T. B. Aldrich
Mark. P. C. De Crespigny
Mark. C. E. Israel
Mark Castle—Cable Address: Roma. C. Marcus
Mark Danver's Sin, and The Madman of Coral Reef Lighthouse. H. C. McNeile
Mark Heffron. A. W. Bailey
Mark It for Murder. D. Sanderson
Mark Kilby and the Manhattan Murders. R. C. Frazer
Mark Kilby and the Miami Mob. R. C. Frazer
Mark Kilby and the Secret Syndicate. R. C. Frazer
Mark Kilby Solves a Murder. R. C. Frazer
Mark Kilby Stands Alone. R. C. Frazer
Mark Kilby Takes a Risk. R. C. Frazer
Mark Magic, the Detective. A. P. Morris
Mark of a Buoy. G. Peters
Mark of a Witch. H. Kemp
Mark of Cain. S. A. Key

Mark of Cain. Andrew Lang
Mark of Cain. C. Wells
Mark of Cosa Nostra. Nick Carter
Mark of Displeasure. E. Hely
Mark of Kane. C. Franklin
Mark of Lucifer. E. P. Green
Mark of Merlin. A. McCaffrey
Mark of Murder. Dell Shannon
Mark of Pak San Ri. W. Stroup
Mark of Satan. A. Loring
Mark of the Beast. R. W. Kauffman
Mark of the Broad Arrow. Maurice Scott
Mark of the Crescent. J. Creasey
Mark of the Dead. The Aresbys
Mark of the Dragon. M. Richmond
Mark of the Four. Mark Cross
Mark of the Hand. C. Armstrong
Mark of the Leech. J. Cassells
Mark of the Moccasin. K. Perkins
Mark of the Moon. F. Gerard
Mark of the Paw. Gavin Holt
Mark of the Rat. A. Fredericks
Mark of the Red Diamond. J. H. Chase
Mark of the Rope. M. Lynch
Mark of the Shadow. M. Grant
Mark of the Tong. J. G. Brandon
Mark of the Vulture. R. J. Hogan
Mark of the Vulture. M. Macao
Mark of Treachery. C. B. Kelland
Mark of Yekel. E. Y. Miller
Mark One: The Dummy. J. Ball
Mark Ryder's Vow. P. Trent
Mark Sutherland. E. Southworth
Mark the Sparrow. Clark Howard
Mark Three for Murder. R. P. Hansen
Mark Twain's A Double Barrelled Detective Story. R. St. Clair
Marked! B. Bristow
Marked "Cancelled." N. S. Lincoln
Marked Cards. J. Addiscombe
Marked Dangerous. E. Y. Miller
Marked Down for Murder. S. Dean
Marked for a Victim. S. C. Cumberland
Marked for Death. Nicholas Carter
Marked for Death. D. Plantz
Marked for Life. A. F. Pinkerton
Marked for Murder. Ronald Campbell
Marked for Murder. B. Halliday
Marked for Murder. C. R. Jones
Marked for Murder. J. R. Macdonald
Marked for Murder. V. B. Miller
Marked for Murder. W. Reed
Marked Hand. Nicholas Carter
Marked Man. C. Barling
Marked Man. H. Carmichael
Marked Man. W. LeQueux
Marked Man. H. C. Wire
Marked Men. C. N. Buck
Marked "Personal". A. K. Green
Marked Pistol. J. C. Lenehan
Marked to Die. M. Cronin
Marked with a Cross. G. Monro
Marked Woman. M. Leighton
Marked Woman. D. Newton
Marked Woman. Grace M. White
Markenmore Mystery. J. S. Fletcher
Market for Murder. F. Gruber
Market for Murder. C. M. Russell
Market of Venus. M. Richmond
Markham Affair. S. P. Hyatt
Marksman. M. Cronin
Marksman. H. C. Rae
Marl-Pit Mystery. G. Ohnet
Marley's Empire. P. McCutchan
Marloe Mansions Murder. A. G. MacLeod
Marlowe. R. Chandler
Marnie. Winston Graham
Maroc 7. M. Sands
Marooned. M. Maurice
Marooned! A. Murray
Marooned with Murder. R. A. J. Walling
Marozia. A. G. Hales
Marquis. A. Soutar
Marquis of Loveland. C. N. Williamson
Marquis of Murray Hill. Baron
Marquis of Putney. R. Marsh
Marquise de Brinvilliers. E. Gaboriau
Marrendon Mystery, and other stories of crime and detection. J. S. Fletcher
Marriage and Murder. D. Sharp
Marriage at a Venture. E. Gaboriau
Marriage Bed. H. V. Dixon
Marriage-Broker. M. B. Lowndes
Marriage Broker. F. Warden
Marriage Bureau Murders. J. Bingham
Marriage by Capture. A. Stringer
Marriage by Mistake. W. Carter
Marriage Cage. W. Johnston
Marriage Chest. D. Eden
Marriage for the Defence. Roy Vickers
Marriage for Two. A. S. Roche
Marriage Has Been Arranged. P. Allardyce
Marriage Lines. J. S. Fletcher
Marriage Mystery. F. Hume
Marriage of Adventure. E. Gaboriau
Marriage of Captain Kettle. C. J. C. Hyne
Marriage of Esther. G. Boothby
Marriage of Inconvenience. T. Cobb
Marriage of Inconvenience. J. L. Roberts
Marriage of Kettle. C. J. C. Hyne
Marriage of Margot. A. Applin

Marriage of Meldrum Strange. T. Mundy
Marriage of Yussuf Khan. F. Heller
Marriage Pact. L. Cheatham
Married Beneath Him. I. Payn
Married by Stealth. F. Warden
Married for Love. F. Du Boisgobey
Married in Haste. M. E. Braddon
Married in Mask. M. T. Walworth
Married into Murder. Reginald Campbell
Married Man. P. P. Read
Married or Trapped. T. Walton
Married to a Spy. R. Starr
Married to a Spy. A. Waugh
Married to Murder. E. Radford
Married to Murder. H. Whittington
Marriott Hall. D. Daniels
Marrowby Myth. W. Martyn
Marry in Haste. J. A. Hodge
Marry in May. M. Richmond
Marrying Beneath Your Station. H. Wood
Marsanne. V. Coffman
Marseilles. A. Caillou
Marseilles Enforcer. Don Smith
Marsh. E. Raymond
Marsh Blood. J. Marcus
Marsh Gang. H. N. Field
Marsh House. M. L. Roby
Marshmallow Pie. Graham Lord
Marshmead Murders. S. Taylor
Marshwood. M. Heath
Marston Murder Case. W. A. Stowell
Marta. Marilyn Ross
Martello Tower Mystery. G. H. Teed
Marten Mystery. J. Ironside
Martha Willis. T. P. Prest
Martha's Vineyard Affair. S. Hart
Marthe and the Madman. J. De Bosschere
Martin Faber, The Story of a Criminal. W. G. Simms
Martin Hewitt, Investigator. Arthur Morrison
Martin Speed Versus "The Snatcher". M. G. Hugi
Martineau Murders. R. Hull
Martini Murders. Roger Fuller
Martinis and Murder. H. Kane
Martyn Ware's Temptation. H. Wood
Martyr or Criminal? I. L. Cassilis
Martyred Fool. D. C. Murray
Marune: Alastor 933. J. Vance
Marvellous Coincidence. K. Cornwallis
Marvelous Escape. Old Sleuth
Marvels and Mysteries. R. Marsh
Marworth Mystery. W. A. Frost
Mary. M. E. Braddon
Mary Clifford. T. P. Prest
Mary Deare. H. Innes
Mary Elizabeth—Adventuress. R. Starr
Mary Jane Married. George R. Sims
Mary Regan. L. Scott
Mary Roberts Rinehart's Crime Book. M. R. Rinehart
Maryjane Tonight at Angels Twelve. M. Caidin
Marylebone Miser. E. Phillpotts
Masada Plan. Leonard Harris
Mascarada Pass. W. C. MacDonald
Masinglee Murders. M. B. Dix
Mask. J. Cowdroy
Mask. A. Hornblow
Mask. W. LeQueux
Mask. Will Scott
Mask and the Man. P. Andreae
Mask and the Man. Alan Thomas
Mask and the Moonflower. P. A. Whitney
Mask for Crime. Marion Roberts
Mask for Murder. M. Dalman
Mask for Murder. H. Kane
Mask for Murder. A. M. Stein
Mask for the Toff. J. Creasey
Mask of Alexander. M. Albrand
Mask of Danger. M. Clare
Mask of Death. A. Bachelin
Mask of Dimintrios. E. Ambler
Mask of Evil. C. Armstrong
Mask of Evil. J. A. Creighton
Mask of Evil. D. M. Disney
Mask of Evil. Marilyn Ross
Mask of Fear. Ross Alexander
Mask of Fu Manchu. S. Rohmer
Mask of Fury. Arthur MacLean
Mask of Glass. H. Roth
Mask of Gold. A. S. Swan
Mask of Love. J. Thatcher
Mask of Medusa. P. Minton
Mask of Memory. V. Canning
Mask of Mephisto. W. B. Gibson
Mask of Mephisto. M. Grant
Mask of Murder. E. Radford
Mask of Pursuit. J. N. Chance
Mask of Shadows. Ray Owen
Mask of Terror. H. Desmond
Mask of the Andes. J. Cleary
Mask of the Enchantress. V. Holt
Mask of Treason. A. Stevenson
Mask of Violence. M. Hebden
Mask of Words. J. Roffman
Masked Alibi. M. A. Clune
Masked Ball. A. Lowing
Masked Ball Murder. D. Fairfax
Masked Blackmailer. J. C. Lenehan
Masked Dancer. W. J. Bayfield

Title Index

Masked Dancer. B. Bolt
Masked Detective. Anonymous
Masked Detective. H. P. Halsey
Masked Dictator. W. M. Graydon
Masked Forgers. W. J. Bayfield
Masked Gunman. G. Ashe
Masked in Mystery. S. Rathbone
Masked Invasion. C. Steele
Masked Judgment. D. T. Lindsay
Masked Killer. G. H. Teed
Masked Lady. M. M. Murray
Masked Man. G. Leroux
Masked Man of the Desert. C. Brisbane
Masked Marauder. R. M. Graydon
Masked Motorist. Anonymous
Masked Murder. M. Alan
Masked Raiders. R. C. Armour
Masked Slayer. R. Hardinge
Masked Stranger. L. Allan
Masked Terror. H. Pink
Masked Terror. R. Richmond
Masked Venus. R. H. Savage
Masked Woman. J. McCulley
Masks. B. Fleming
Masks. A. Skene
Masks of Malevolence. L. Amino
Masks of Thespis. M. Richardson
Masks Off at Midnight. V. Williams
Masque. S. Holland
Masque by Gaslight. V. Coffman
Masque of a Savage Mandarin. P. Robinson
Masque of Mutiny. C. L. Reid
Masque of Satan. V. Coffman
Masque of the Red Death. Elsie Lee
Masque World. A. Panshin
Masquerade. W. Morton
Masquerade. M. Pereira
Masquerade. C. Sternberg
Masquerade at Monfalcone. Dorinne Moore
Masquerade in Blue. G. M. Barnes
Masquerade in Venice. V. Johnston
Masquerade into Madness. Samuel Merwin
Masquerade Mystery. F. Hume
Masquerade of Evil. E. Zumwalt
Masquerader. R. M. Graydon
Masquerader. K. C. Thurston
Mass for a Dead Witch. A. Grace
Mass Radiography Murders. Sutherland Scott
Massacre at Metz. C. Whiting
Massacre at Umtali. P. McCurtin
Massacre in Milan. Nick Carter
Massacre in Rome. J. Rosenberger
Massingham Affair. E. Grierson
Massingham Butterfly. J. S. Fletcher
Massy's Game. B. Olsen
Master. M. Braly
Master. Carter Brown
Master and Man. A. Askew
Master Criminal. Nicholas Carter
Master Criminal. J. J. Farjeon
Master Criminal. S. Paternoster
Master Detective. P. Brebner
Master Dudley. P. Johnson
Master Hand. R. Dallas
Master Hand. J. Futrelle
Master Key. A. Soutar
Master-Key. F. Warden
Master Manhunters. J. Gollomb
Master Mind. M. Dana
Master-Mind. F. Hume
Master Mind. H. Janson
Master Mind. C. Moffett
Master Mummer. E. P. Oppenheim
Master Murderer. C. Wells
Master Must Die. V. Gribban
Master Mystery. L. Dowsett
Master Mystery. A. B. Reeve
Master Mystery. Seamark
Master of Aysgarth. M. Mayhew
Master of Beechwood. A. Sergeant
Master of Blacktower. B. Michaels
Master of Blue Mire. V. Coffman
Master of Broken Men. C. Steele
Master of Charteris Towers. W. M. Graydon
Master of Crime. C. Williams
Master of Deception. R. Marsh
Master of Deviltry. Nicholas Carter
Master of Evil. H. Long
Master of Evrington. V. Blake
Master of Fear. C. Rushton
Master of Fortune. C. J. C. Hyne
Master of Foxhallow. S. Claudia
Master of Frinton Park. F. M. Long
Master of Graylands. H. Wood
Master of Greystone. G. Carrington
Master of High Beck. John Marsh
Master of Malcarew. V. Black
Master of Men. E. P. Oppenheim
Master of Merlains. D. Whitelaw
Master of Merripit. E. Phillpotts
Master of Millions. G. C. Lorimer
Master of Money. F. Lady
Master of Montrolfe Hall. R. O'Grady
Master of Murder. T. Robbins
Master of Mysteries. Anonymous
Master of Mysteries. L. T. Meade
Master of Palowar. Magali
Master of Penrose. J. A. Hodge
Master of Phoenix Hall. E. Marlow
Master of Rathkelly. H. Smart

Master of Revels. R. H. Watkins
Master of Roxton. E. Barr
Master of Shadows. Margery Lawrence
Master of Souls. M. Hansom
Master of the Ceremonies. G. M. Fenn
Master of the Dark. J. Cassells
Master of the Day of Judgment. L. Perutz
Master of the Death Madness. G. Stockbridge
Master of the Microbe. R. W. Service
Master of the Priory. A. Haynes
Master of the Skies. P. Trent
Master of Trenance. T. W. Speight
Master of Venom. S. Horler
Master Planner. N. Brady
Master Plot. Lou Smith
Master Rogue. D. G. Phillips
Master Rogue. C. Somerville
Master Schemer. V. Campbell
Master Sniper. S. Hunter
Master Spirit. W. Magnay
Master Spy. R. J. Buckley
Master Spy. A. Gask
Master Spy. J. Pendower
Master Stroke. E. C. Derby
Master Villain. Nicholas Carter
Master Vorst. A. J. Small
Masterful Voice. H. Buchanan
Masterly Trick. Nicholas Carter
Masterman's Mistake. T. Cobb
Masterpiece Affair. K. Royce
Masterpiece in Murder. R. Powell
Masterpiece of Crime. Nicholas Carter
Masterpiece of Nice Mr. Breen. H. Hunvald
Masterpieces of Crime. A. D. Vandam
Masterpieces of Mystery. A. K. Green
Masterplayers. Michael Sinclair
Masters Affair. B. Hirschfeld
Masters of Kaolina. E. L. Long
Masters of the Parachute Mail. J. Carr
Masterstroke. J. Tiger
Masterwork. J. Miglis
Matador Dies. J. Peyre
Matador's Fortune. J. W. Bobin
Matapan Affair. F. Du Boisgobey
Matapan Jewels. F. Du Boisgobey
Matarese Circle. R. Ludlum
Match for a Murderer. D. Halliday
Match Point for Murder. K. Platt
Matched with Mystery. J. A. Jordan
Matchless Detective. Anonymous
Material Witness. H. Messenger
Mathematician. W. Manson
Mathematics of Guilt. I. Ostrander
Mathematics of Murder. K. Bedford
Mather Graeme. B. Graeme
Mather Investigates. B. Graeme
Matheson Fever. J. Easton
Matheson Formula. J. S. Fletcher
Matheson Money. F. Warden
Matilda Hunter Murder. H. S. Keeler
Mating Call. W. Shaw
Mating Cry. A. E. Van Vogt
Mating in the Wilds. O. Binns
Mating of the Blades. A. Abdullah
Matlock Paper. R. Ludlum
Mato Grosso Horror. J. Rosenberger
Matorni's Vineyard. E. P. Oppenheim
Matrimonial Mixture. C. J. C. Hyne
Matrimony Most Dangerous. L. Cargill
Matsu Dossier. W. Dainton
Matt. R. Buchanan
Matter of Accent. D. Keith
Matter of Assassination. P. Raymond
Matter of Blood. B. Whitaker
Matter of Business and other stories. J. Farnol
Matter of Confidence. B. Williams
Matter of Conscience. E. P. Hoyt
Matter of Conviction. E. Hunter
Matter of Diplomacy. W. Tute
Matter of Fact. H. Brean
Matter of Intelligence. G. Wittman
Matter of Iodine. D. Keith
Matter of Love and Death. T. Wells
Matter of Luck and other stories. P. Cheyney
Matter of Mandrake. Barry Norman
Matter of Millions. W. J. Bayfield
Matter of Millions. A. K. Green
Matter of Millions. F. M. White
Matter of Motive. G. Montrose
Matter of Murder. Neill Graham
Matter of Nerves. R. Hull
Matter of Opportunity. C. Arley
Matter of Paradise. B. Meggs
Matter of Policy. Sam Merwin
Matter of Record. D. Morrison
Matter of Revenge. C. Demaine
Matter of Scents. T. Fitzgerald
Matter of Sixpence. J. La Tourrette
Matter of Size. H. Homewood
Matter of Skill. Nicholas Carter
Matter of Tar. H. C. McNeile
Matter of Taste. R. Lockridge
Matter of Thousands. Old Spicer
Matter of Witchcraft. Alice Brennan
Matthew's Hand. C. Larson
Matzohball. S. Weinstein
Maud Blackstone, the Millionaire's Daughter. R. R. Johnston

Maulever Hall. J. A. Hodge
Mauleverer Murders. A. C. Fox-Davies
Maumbury Rings. G. V. McFadden
Maunaloa Curse. Irma Walker
Maundy. Julian Gloag
Maureen of the Island. Robin Temple
Maureen Versus Fate. R. Rodd
Maurice Mystery. J. E. Cooke
Maurizius Case. J. Wasserman
Mausoleum Key. N. Daniels
Mauve Front Door. L. Meynell
Mavde Baxter. C. C. Hitchkiss
Mawpeth Millions. W. Reynolds
Max. Mrs. G. Sheldon
Max Carrados. E. Bramah
Max Carrados Mysteries. E. Bramah
Max Fargus. O. Johnson
Max Logan. P. Trent
Max Smart and the Ghastly Ghost Affair. W. Johnston
Max Smart and the Perilous Pellets. W. Johnston
Max Smart Loses Control. W. Johnston
Max Smart—The Spy Who Went Out to the Cold. W. Johnston
Maxims by a Man of the World. J. Payn
Maximum Credible Accident. J. Howlett
Maximum Game. E. Naughton
Maximus Zone. C. Keane
Maxine. P. Trent
Max's Marriage. E. Gaboriau
Maxwell Mystery. C. Wells
May Day Mystery. O. R. Cohen
May Grayson. T. P. Prest
May We Come Through? and other stories. R. Pertwee
May-Week Murders. D. G. Browne
May You Die in Ireland. M. Kenyon
Maya Temple. D. Daniels
Maybe a Trumpet. S. Harvester
Maybe He's Dead. S. Oakroyd
Maybe It's Murder. A. Barron
Mayday. C. Cussler
Mayday. T. P. McMahon
Mayday over Manhattan. S. Jason
Mayfair Lou. A. Hurry
Mayfair Magician. G. Griffith
Mayfair Murder. H. Holt
Mayfair Mystery. L. Clarke
Mayfair Mystery. H. Holt
Mayfair Mystery. F. Richardson
Mayfair Nights. H. Duval
Mayfair Slayride. H. Janson
Mayhem in B-Flat. Elliot Paul
Mayhem in Greece. D. Wheatley
Mayhem in Manhattan. L. Wein
Mayhem in Morton Episcopi. D. Lees
Mayhem Madchen. J. N. Chance
Mayhem on the Coney Beat. M. Geller
Maynard Hayes Affair. Dorothea Bennett
Maynard's Wives. H. Flowerdew
Mayor Harding of New York. S. Endicott
Mayor on Horseback. E. P. Oppenheim
Mayor's Wife. A. K. Green
Mazaroff Murder. J. S. Fletcher
Mazaroff Mystery. J. S. Fletcher
Maze. P. MacDonald
Maze. E. Orford
Maze of Crime. Anonymous
Maze of Death. P. K. Dick
Maze of Justice. T. El Hakim
Maze of Motives. Nicholas Carter
Maze of the Past. Magali
Mazeppa. T. P. Prest
Mazeppa. F. Whishaw
Me and My Ghoul. M. Storm
Me and Rudolph. W. C. Tuttle
Me, Detective. L. T. White
Me—Gangster. C. F. Coe
Me, Hood! M. Spillane
Me Tanner, You Jane. Lawrence Block
Meadows of Tallon. E. Thompson
Meadowsweet. Gwendoline Butler
Mean Streets. T. B. Dewey
Meandering Corpse. R. S. Prather
Means of Escape. S. Dunleavy
Means of Evil. R. Rendell
Meanwhile Back at the Morgue. M. Avallone
Measure for Murder. C. Witting
Measured for Murder. Babs Lee
Meat for Murder. Lange Lewis
Mecca for Murder. S. Marlowe
Mechanic. L. J. Carlino
Mechanic's Son. Old Sleuth
Medal from Pamplona. C. Rougvie
Medallion. L. Johnson
Medallion. G. Sereny
Medbury Fort Murder. G. Limnelius
Meddle with the Mafia. Fiona Sinclair
Meddler and Her Murder. J. Porter
Meddlers. C. Rayner
Medea Legend. E. York
Median Line. W. Haggard
Medical Examiner. W. H. A. Carr
Medical Witness. Richard Gordon
Medici Ring. N. St. John
Medicine Lady. L. T. Meade
Medicine Maker. W. C. Tuttle
Medicine-Man. W. C. Tuttle
Mediterranean Caper. G. Brewer
Mediterranean Caper. C. Cussler

Mediterranean Murder. A. Hocking
Mediterranean Murder. Rosa Lambert
Mediterranean Mystery. S. G. Hedges
Mediterranean Mystery. F. E. Wynne
Mediterranean Nights. D. Wheatley
Medium for Murder. G. Compton
Medium for Murder. Evelyn Harris
Medium for Murder. M. Warner
Medley of Mystery. Lynn Williams
Medusa. E. H. Visiak
Medusa Complex. M. H. Albert
Medusa Connection. F. Cowen
Medusa Conspiracy. E. I. Shedley
Medusa Emerald. G. F. Gibbs
Medusa Kiss. M. Woodman
Medusa Touch. P. Van Greenaway
Medusa's Head. J. D. Bacon
Meet a Body. J. Decrest
Meet a Body. D. Rutherford
Meet a Dark Stranger. L. Belvedere
Meet a Dark Stranger. T. E. Huff
Meet Desmond Drake. Sea Lion
Meet Doctor Death. R. Trevor
Meet Dr. Morelle. E. Dudley
Meet Dr. Morelle Again. E. Dudley
Meet in Darkness. S. Ransome
Meet Inspector Bourne. R. C. Finney
Meet Me at Philippi. C. Connell
Meet Me at the Morgue. J. R. Macdonald
Meet Me in Darkness. R. E. Banks
Meet Me in the Green Glen. R. P. Warren
Meet Me Tonight. M. Albrand
Meet Mike Desmond. J. V. Nolan
Meet Mr. Callaghan. G. Verner
Meet Mr. Fortune. H. C. Bailey
Meet Morocco Jones. J. Baynes
Meet Morocco Jones in the Case of the Syndicate Hoods. J. Baynes
Meet Murder, My Angel. Carter Brown
Meet Nero Wolfe. R. Stout
Meet the Baron. Anthony Morton
Meet the Don. B. Gray
Meet the Dragon. David Hume
Meet the Dreamer. W. M. Duncan
Meet the Falcon. D. J. Gannon
Meet the Picaroon. J. Cassells
Meet the Rev. G. Pedrick
Meet the Tiger. L. Charteris
Meet You in Munich. R. Jansson
Meeting by Moonlight. R. Knotts
Meeting Her Fate. M. E. Braddon
Meeting in Casa. J. Kershaw
Meeting in Madrid. Dorothy Fletcher
Meeting in Spring. Elizabeth Ford
Meeting Place and other stories. J. D. Beresford
Meeting with Murder. M. Lynch
Meg. D. Daniels
Meg the Lady. T. Gallon
Megacull. D. Hart-Davis
Megadeath. Peter Evans
Megan. M. K. Simmons
Megawind Cancellation. B. Boucher
Megeve Mystery. J. Mowbray
Megstone Plot. A. Garve
Meirovity Plan. H. Arvay
Melamare Mystery. M. Leblanc
Melander's Millions. C. F. Gregg
Melbourne Mystery. J. G. Brandon
Melbourne Mystery. S. J. Stutley
Mellbridge Mystery. A. O. Cooke
Mallona. K. Krause
Melmoth. C. R. Maturin
Melody Murders. R. Wallace
Melody of Death. T. A. Plummer
Melody of Death. E. Wallace
Melody of Malice. S. Hufford
Melody of Murder. Dina Allan
Melody of Terror. S. Forbes
Melon in the Cornfield. C. Blackstock
Melora. M. G. Eberhart
Meltdown. R. Kytle
Melting Man. V. Canning
Melwood Mystery. J. Hay
Melyonen. A. Lowing
Member of Tattersall's. H. Smart
Member of the Club. P. Niesewand
Member's Lobby. K. Thompson
Memo for Murder. D. Wilmer
Memo to a Firing Squad. F. H. Brennan
Memoirs to a Bow Street Runner. Henry Goddard
Memoirs of a Landlady. G. R. Sims
Memoirs of a Veteran Detective. M. Canler
Memoirs of an Aberdeen Detective. J. C. Philip
Memoirs of Arsene Lupin. M. Leblanc
Memoirs of Constantine Dix. B. Pain
Memoirs of J. (Paddy) MacDowell. M. J. Hobbs
Memoirs of Jane Cameron, Female Convict. F. W. Robinson
Memoirs of Monsieur Claude. M. Claude
Memoirs of Murder. R. C. Payes
Memoirs of Schlock Homes. R. L. Fish
Memoirs of Sherlock Holmes. A. C. Doyle
Memoirs of Solar Pons. A. Derleth
Memoirs of Vidocq. Vidocq
Memoirs of Villain. I. Crookenden
Memorandum of a Murder. J. E. Wright
Memorial Hall Murder. J. Langton

Memory Man. D. Lambert
Memory Man. C. W. Sanders
Memory of a Scream. D. X. Manners
Memory of Darkness. M. Summerton
Memory of Eva Ryker. D. Stanwood
Memory of Evil. Marilyn Ross
Memory of Megan. M. Lovell
Memory of Murder. H. Pentecost
Memory of Passion. G. Brewer
Memory of Treason. H. Hossent
Memory of You. M. Richmond
Memos from Purgatory. H. Ellison
Men and the Mirror. R. Rocklynne
Men Are Strange Lovers. A. Rowe
Men Are What Women Make Them. A. Belot
Men Die at Cyprus Lodge. J. Rhode
Men for Counters. G. Fairlie
Men for Pieces. B. Flynn
Men from the Boys. E. Lacy
Men in Blue Glasses. S. P. B. Mais
Men in Chains. M. Clarke
Men in Her Death. M. Blizard
Men in Her Death. P. Marlowe
Men in Her Death. S. Ransome
Men in Knots. Richard Grant
Men, Maids and Murder. J. Creasey
Men of Affairs. R. Pertwee
Men of Career. J. Lorraine
Men of Mystery. W. Anthony
Men of Silence. L. Forgione
Men of the Bureau. E. Gaboriau
Men of the Mist. G. Stanley
Men on Foot. F. R. Adams
Men on the Dead Man's Chest. C. S. Raymond
Men v. Devils. T. K. Clarke
Men Who Die Twice. P. Heath
Men Who Died Laughing. J. Creasey
Men Who Explained Miracles. J. D. Carr
Men Who Smiled No More. K. Robeson
Men Who Wrought. R. Cullum
Men with the Double Faces. V. Loder
Men with Three Eyes. L. Revell
Men Without Bones and other stories. G. Kersh
Men Without Faces. W. Martyn
Men, Women and Beasts. H. D. Stacpoole
Men, Women and Guns. H. C. McNeile
Menace. L. G. Blochman
Menace! J. Creasey
Menace. The Gordons
Menace. S. Horler
Menace. H. Janson
Menace. R. Keverne
Menace. P. MacDonald
Menace for Dr. Morelle. E. Dudley
Menace from the East. D. Holden
Menace in Siam. M. Corrigan
Menace of Death. E. Churchill
Menace of Li-Sin. N. Vane
Menace of Marble Hill. M. Farnsworth
Menace of the Silent Death. E. J. Murray
Menace of X. A. Kahn
Menace on the Downs. M. Burton
Menace to Mrs. Kershaw. Austen Allen
Menace Within. U. Curtiss
Menacers. D. Hamilton
Menaces, Menaces. M. Underwood
Menacing Darkness. S. Shulman
Menagerie. C. Cookson
Mendelov Conspiracy. M. Caidin
Mender of Images. N. Lorimer
Mendip Mystery. L. Brock
Mendocino Menace. Ruth MacLeod
Mendon Mystery. J. Mary
Mendoza File. Clayton Matthews
Mene Tekel. A. Groner
Menfreya. V. Holt
Menfreya in the Morning. V. Holt
Menorah Men. L. Davidson
Mental Marvel. F. MacIsaac
Mental Wizard. K. Robeson
Mentons. C. F. R. Hayward
Mephisto Waltz. F. M. Stewart
Mercenaries. J. Harris
Mercenaries. G. Tippette
Mercenaries. D. E. Westlake
Mercenary. H. Barron
Mercenary. J. Freytag
Mercenary. A. Marsden
Mercenary Calling. Martin Walker
Merchandise. R. Bridges
Merchandise Murders. A. Richards
Merchant of Menace. K. Bedford
Merchant of Menace. J. Stevenson
Merchant of Murder. S. Dean
Merchants of Death. P. Chase
Merchants of Disaster. K. Robeson
Merchant's Secret. J. W. Bobin
Merciless Ladies. Winston Graham
Mercy at the Manor Manor. H. J. Mundis
Mercy Flight. A. MacVicar
Mercy of the Court. M. E. Porter
Mere Murder. C. M. Wills
Meredith Legacy. S. A. Salvato
Meredith Mystery. N. S. Lincoln
Merely Man. G. Warden
Merely Michael. M. Somers
Merely Murder. G. Heyer
Merely Players. J. F. Molloy
Merindol. F. Du Boisgobey
Merivale. J. Robertshaw

Meriweather Mystery. K. C. Strahan
Merlewood Mystery. Mrs. J. O. Arnold
Merlin's Forest. M. Wallenstein
Merlin's Furlong. G. Mitchell
Merlin's Keep. M. Brent
Mermaid. O. Martin
Mermaid of Dark Mountain. Melissa Napier
Mermaid on the Rocks. B. Halliday
Merrily to the Grave. K. Sully
Merrivale Mystery. J. Corbett
Merriweather File. L. White
Merry Andrews. Rona Randall
Merry-Go-Round. J. Cowdrey
Merry Go Round. R. M. Stern
Merry-Go-Round of Murder. J. F. Dinneen
Merry Hippo. E. Huxley
Merry Men and other tales. R. L. Stevenson
Merry Mug. H. M. Raleigh
Merry Murder. S. Rubenstein
Merry Murders at Montmarie. T. J. Kelly
Merry Widower. Joan Fleming
Merrylees Mystery. R. Goyne
Meryl. W. T. Eldridge
Mesalliance. W. F. Fauley
Mesh. J. Haslette
Meshes of Fear. H. Richards
Meshes of Mischance. G. Wintle
Mesmerists. B. L. Farjeon
Message. H. C. McNeile
Message. L. Tracy
Message Ends. D. Craig
Message from a Corpse. Sam Merwin
Message from a Ghost. Marilyn Ross
Message from a Spy. D. Helwig
Message from Absalom. A. A. Thompson
Message from Hong Kong. M. G. Eberhart
Message from John. W. Spence
Message from Julie. Sara North
Message from Malaga. Helen MacInnes
Message from Marise. P. Kruger
Message from Sirius. C. Jenkins
Message of the Mute Dog. C. M. Russell
Messenger. E. Robins
Messenger. Mona Williams
Messenger from Munich. N. Pierce
Messenger from the Unknown. J. Hawthorne
Messengers of Death. A. West
Messengers of Evil. P. Souvestre
Metal Box. T. Cobb
Metal Flash. B. Thomson
Metal Monster. K. Robeson
Metamorphosis. R. Marsh
Metcalfe Mystery. Elliot Bailey
Meteor Men. A. LeBaron
Meteor Menace. K. Robeson
Meteren Road. V. Thomas
Methinks the Lady—. G. Endore
Method in His Murder. T. Warriner
Method in Madness. D. M. Disney
Method of Murder. Whyte Hall
Methods of Dr. Scarlett. A. Laing
Methods of Maigret. G. Simenon
Methods of Mr. Ames. F. Carrel
Methods of Sergeant Cluff. G. North
Methods of Uncle Abner. M. D. Post
Methuselah Enzyme. F. M. Stewart
Methylated Murder. C. Robbins
Metropolitan Opera Murders. H. Traubel
Mexican Adventure. L. Oliver
Mexican Affair. C. W. Burleson
Mexican Assassin. Hartshorne
Mexican Bill, the Cowboy Detective. N. Ned
Mexican Brown. L. Derrick
Mexican Connection. A. Mason
Mexican Deadline. J. Grecco
Mexican Hit. J. Rosenberger
Mexican Mourning. J. Hedges
Mexican Slayride. T. B. Dewey
Mexican Slay Ride. N. MacNeil
Mexican Slay Ride. S. Weintraub
Mexico Run. L. White
Mezzoni, the Brigand. M. M. Murray
Miami 59. D. Keene
Miami for Murder. B. Sarto
Miami Golden Boy. H. Kastle
Miami Marauder. M. Barry
Miami Massacre. D. Pendleton
Miami Mayhem. A. Rome
Miami Mob and Mark Kilby Stands Alone. R. C. Frazer
Miami Murder-Go-Round. M. La France
Miami Undercover. E. L. Heyman
Miasma. E. S. Holding
Micah Faraday, Adventurer. L. T. Meade
Mice Are Not Amused. K. Hewitt
Michael and All Angels. N. Lofts
Michael Anonymous. J. M. Scott
Michael Bray. Taffrail
Michael Carmichael. M. Sandys
Michael Cassidy, Sergeant. H. C. McNeile
Michael Dred, Detective. M. Leighton
Michael Durrant. P. Trent
Michael Intervenes. G. Clifford
Michael Shayne Investigates. B. Halliday
Michael Shayne Takes a Hand. B. Halliday
Michael Shayne's 50th Case. B. Halliday
Michael Shayne's Long Chance. B. Halliday

Title Index
Miracle Gold / 547

Michael Shayne's Triple Mystery. B. Halliday
Michaelmas Girls. J. B. Barry
Michael's Crag. G. Allen
Michael's Evil Deeds. E. P. Oppenheim
Michael's Wife. M. Millhiser
Mick Cardby Works Overtime. David Hume
Micky's Ride. B. Sarto
Microbe Murders. F. G. Eberhard
Microbe of Crime. Nicholas Carter
Microbe's Kiss. G. Braddon
Microbes of Power. A. Wilson
Microwave Factor. N. Brady
Mid-Atlantic. Taffrail
Mid-Ocean Tragedy. J. Hawk
Mid the Thick Arrows. M. Pemberton
Midas Coffin. Simon Quinn
Midas Man. K. Robeson
Midas Operation. J. Griffin
Midas Touch. J. Boland
Midday Moon. D. Daniels
Middle Class Murder. B. Hamilton
Middle Distance. O. Martin
Middle Kingdom. W. Marshall
Middle Link. Nicholas Carter
Middle of Midnight. W. G. Beymer
Middle of Nowhere. M. Brenner
Middle of the Negro's Head. C. Brisbane
Middle of Things. J. S. Fletcher
Middle Temple Murder. J. S. Fletcher
Middle Wall. Edward Marshall
Middlefold Murders. E. Radford
Midge. P. MacTyre
Midget Marvel. P. Manton
Midnight. O. R. Cohen
Midnight. G. Hughes
Midnight. M. Strange
Midnight Adventure and other stories. J. J. Farjeon
Midnight Alibi. E. Ellison
Midnight and Percy Jones. V. Starrett
Midnight at Mallyncourt. T. E. Huff
Midnight at Mallyncourt. E. Marlow
Midnight at Mears House. H. J. Holt
Midnight Bell. F. Latham
Midnight Cavalier. R. Armstrong
Midnight Cry. J. M. Parker
Midnight Dancers. A. Maybury
Midnight Eye. M. Roscoe
Midnight Guest. F. M. White
Midnight Hag. Joan Fleming
Midnight Hazard. B. Sanders
Midnight Horrors. Anonymous
Midnight Hostess. Griff
Midnight House. Ethel L. White
Midnight House and other tales. W. F. Harvey
Midnight King. G. Delamare
Midnight Lace. W. Drummond
Midnight Lady. G. Leroux
Midnight Lady. H. Parker
Midnight Lady and the Mourning Man. D. Anthony
Midnight Line. T. Savage
Midnight Lorry Crime. E. S. Brooks
Midnight Mail. H. Holt
Midnight Male. R. Drayton
Midnight Man. H. Kane
Midnight Men. A. E. Fisher
Midnight Men. N. Vane
Midnight Message. Nicholas Carter
Midnight Minute. C. Herbert
Midnight Murder. P. Herring
Midnight Murder. John Morgan
Midnight Murder. K. Robeson
Midnight Murder. R. Rodd
Midnight Murder. Donald Stuart
Midnight Mystery. Anonymous
Midnight Mystery. B. Atkey
Midnight Mystery. R. Hardinge
Midnight Mystery. F. Hume
Midnight Never Comes. M. Fallon
Midnight Oak. J. Tattersall
Midnight on the Place Pigalle. M. Dekobra
Midnight Passenger. R. H. Savage
Midnight Patient. E. Hostovsky
Midnight Plumber. M. Procter
Midnight Plus One. G. Lyall
Midnight Queen. Anonymous
Midnight Quest. Old Sleuth
Midnight Road. A. Wood
Midnight Sailing. L. G. Blochman
Midnight Sailing. S. Hufford
Midnight Sister. H. Luger
Midnight Sleep. Frank King
Midnight Special. B. Delannoy
Midnight Surrender. E. Nepean
Midnight Tales. W. F. Harvey
Midnight to High Noon. C. C. Waddell
Midnight Treasure. W. Rollins
Midnight Vigil. Warren Miller
Midnight Visitor. L. Dartey
Midnight Walker. Rona Randall
Midnight Walkers. K. Laing
Midnight Webs. G. M. Fenn
Midnight Wireless. C. A. Alington
Midst Balkan Perils. E. S. Brooks
Midsummer Loki. E. Wuorio
Midsummer Madness. Langdon Dodge
Midsummer Madness. Morley Roberts
Midsummer Malice. N. Fitzgerald

Midsummer Masque. J. Tattersall
Midsummer Mink. P. Coke
Midsummer Mischief. N. Mapple
Midsummer Murder. C. M. Wills
Midsummer Murder. C. Witting
Midsummer Mystery. G. H. Gerould
Midsummer Nightmare. C. Hale
Midsummer Night's Crime. G. Bromley
Midsummer Night's Murder. R. F. Baylus
Midsummer Night's Murder. L. Crosby
Midsummer Slay Ride. L. Gribble
Midsummer's Nightmare. E. Shenkin
Midtown North. Mike Curtis
Midway to Murder. M. T. Yates
Midwinter Madness. Anthony Stuart
Miernik Dossier. C. McCarry
Might As Well Be Dead. R. Stout
Mighty Arm. C. Dawe
Mighty Blockhead. F. Gruber
Mignon. J. M. Cain
Mignonette. G. Norway
Mignonette. J. Shearing
Mignon's Peril. J. Middlemass
Mikado Jewel. F. Hume
Mike Dime. B. Fantoni
Miklos Alexandrovitch Is Missing. Anne Edwards
Milady Charlotte. K. Kellow
Milady Took the Rap. H. Janson
Milan Grill Room. E. P. Oppenheim
Mild Case of Murder. G. Brandon
Mildred Arkell. H. Wood
Mildred Pierce. J. M. Cain
Mile-Away Murder. A. Armstrong
Mile Deep Grave. J. Hedges
Mile High. R. Condon
Mile High. H. C. Rowland
Military Crime. F. M. Peacock
Milk Churn Murder. M. Burton
Milk of Human Kindness. E. Ferrars
Milkmaid's Millions. H. Austin
Mill. Mark Allerton
Mill House Murder. J. S. Fletcher
Mill House Mystery. F. Warden
Mill-Lass of Idderleigh. H. E. Inman
Mill Mystery. A. K. Green
Mill of Fear. L. Bidston
Mill of Many Windows. J. S. Fletcher
Mill of Silence. B. Capes
Mill Pond Mystery. H. E. Hill
Mill Reef Hall. A. Pritchett
Mill Street Mystery. A. Sergeant
Millbank Case. G. D. Eldridge
Miller and His Men. T. P. Prest
Miller's Maid. T. P. Prest
Millie. E. V. Cunningham
Millie Lynn, Shop Investigator. C. H. Bullivant
Millijoy, the Determined. K. Kimbrough
Milliner's Hat Mystery. B. Thomson
Million a Minute. H. Douglas
Million Dollar Babe. Carter Brown
Million-Dollar Diamond. J. S. Fletcher
Million Dollar Gamble. F. Johnston
Million Dollar Handle. B. Halliday
Million Dollar Mayhem. K. T. McCall
Million Dollar Murder. T. B. Black
Million Dollar Murder. E. Ronns
Million Dollar Mystery. B. Sarto
Million Dollar Mystery. H. MacGrath
Million Dollar Snapshot. H. Howard
Million Dollar Story. E. Wallace
Million Dollar Snatch. J. Grecco
Million Dollar Suitcase. A. MacGowan
Million Dollar Tramp. W. C. Gault
Million Heiress. P. Trent
Million in Diamonds. Nicholas Carter
Million in Diamonds. Old Sleuth
Million in Jewels. Old Sleuth
Million of Money. A. M. Meadows
Million Pound Bus Fare. D. Weldon
Million Pound Cipher. R. Pertwee
Million Pound Deposit. E. P. Oppenheim
Million Pounds Reward. F. Lady
Million to Burn. M. S. Jones
Millionaire and the Lady. G. Warden
Millionaire and the Policeman's Wife. O. Harper
Millionaire Baby. A. K. Green
Millionaire Crook. Roland Daniel
Millionaire Detective. C. E. Blaney
Millionaire Gangster. J. Wallace
Millionaire Girl. A. W. Marchmont
Millionaire Mystery. F. Hume
Millionaire Mystery. A. W. Marchmont
Millionaire of Yesterday. E. P. Oppenheim
Millionaire Partner. Nicholas Carter
Millionaire Tramp. S. C. Trebor
Millionaires. H. D. Kastle
Millionaire's Crime. J. K. Stafford
Millionaire's Daughter. D. Eden
Millionaire's Fate. F. Du Boisgobey
Millionaire's Folly. Le Jemlys
Millionaire's Folly. L. E. Smyles
Millionaire's Island. M. Pemberton
Millionaire's Love Story. G. Boothby
Millionaire's Mania. Nicholas Carter
Millionaire's Nest Egg. A. Parsons
Millionaire's Revenge. O. Harper
Millionaire's Son. F. Warden
Millionairess. J. Ralph

Millions at Stake and other stories. Nicholas Carter
Millions for Murder. F. MacIsaac
Millions of Mischief. H. Hill
Millions of Money. L. Clarke
Mills. M. O'Brine
Mills Bomb. C. Egleton
Mills of the Gods. D. Winston
Mills of the Law. Nicholas Carter
Millstone Man. B. Healey
Milly Darrell and other tales. M. E. Braddon
Milly the Actress. A. Askew
Milngavie Collection. D. Vallance
Mimic a Murderer. S. H. Courtier
Mind Benders. J. Kennaway
Mind Breaker. A. Mather
Mind Brothers. Peter Heath
Mind Killers. Nick Carter
Mind Killers. Martin Thomas
Mind-Masters. J. F. Rossmann
Mind of a Killer. J. Kirkpatrick
Mind of Dr. Morelle. E. Dudley
Mind of John Meredith. F. Gerard
Mind of Max Duvine. E. Trevor
Mind of Mr. J. G. Reeder. E. Wallace
Mind over Murder. R. S. Hastings
Mind over Murder. C. Noone
Mind Poisoners. Nick Carter
Mind Reader. M. Rittenberg
Mind Reader. W. A. Roberts
Mind Readers. M. Allingham
Mind to Murder. A. Clarke
Mind to Murder. P. D. James
Mind Twisters. D. Streib
Mind-Twisters Affair. Thomas Stratton
Mind War. G. Snyder
Mind Wreckers, Limited, and Other Adventures of Barrow—Ace Insurance Detective. F. J. Price
Mind Your Own Murder. Y. Foldes
Mindanao Pearl. A. Caillou
Mindbenders. J. Quinn
Mind's Eye. A. Skinner
Mindwarpers. E. F. Russell
Mindy Lindy May Surprise. M. Erlanger
Mine. R. Jeffery
Mine Enemy My Friend. T. B. Morris
Mine in the Desert. D. Footman
Mine Is the Power. H. J. Lukens
Mine of Ill Omen. H. Lea
Mine Own Executioner. N. Balchin
Mine Sinister Host. W. W. Sayer
Mine to Avenge. T. Wills
Miner Detective. Anonymous
Minerva Stone. A. Maybury
Ming Vase Mystery. R. Dark
Ming Yellow. J. P. Marquand
Mingled with Venom. G. Mitchell
Mini-Murders. Carter Brown
Mini-Skirt Murders. Martin Thomas
Miniatures Frame. K. Royce
Minimum Man. A. Marvell
Minion of the Moon. T. W. Speight
Minister of Death. J. Bingham
Minister of Evil. W. LeQueux
Minister of Injustice. M. Culpan
Minister of Police. H. Mountjoy
Ministers of Vengeance. R. E. Conot
Ministers Too Are Mortal. F. Duncan
Ministry Murder. C. Dixon
Ministry of Fear. G. Greene
Mink and Murder. H. Holt
Mink-Lined Coffin. Jonathan Latimer
Mink Steel. M. Dedina
Minkie. L. Tracy
Minnesota Gothic. W. O'Meara
Minnesota Strip. P. McCurtin
Minnie Santangelo and the Evil Eye. A. Mancini
Minnie Santangelo's Mortal Sin. A. Mancini
Minor Murders. J. L. Hensley
Minor Operation. J. J. Connington
Minor Operation. Taffrail
Minority. F. T. Hill
Minos Magnificent. G. Seton
Minotaur Country. H. McCloy
Minotaur Factor. S. Stern
Minotaur Garden. L. Hosegood
Minot's Folly. R. S. Holland
Minstrel Code. W. Nelson
Minstrel's Leap. V. Black
Mint Mystery. W. J. Bayfield
Minus a Shamus. Anthony Graham
Minus Man. R. Maxwell
Minus One Corpse. J. Cleveland
Minus Pool. W. Stovall
Minus X. S. Gluck
Minute for Murder. N. Blake
Minute Mysteries. A. Ripley
Minute to Pray, a Second to Die. A. Destefano
Minuteman Murder. J. Langton
Minutes of a Murder. M. Polland
Minutes to Impact. Michael Gray
Minx Goes to the Front. C. N. Williamson
Minx Is Murder. Carter Brown
Mirabilis Diamond. J. Odlum
Mirabil's Island. L. Tracy
Miracle at St. Bruno's. P. Carr
Miracle Gold. R. Dowling

Miracle in the Drawing Room. E. Greenwood
Miracle Man. F. Packard
Mirador Collection. B. Flynn
Mirage. W. Ericson
Mirage. P. P. Muir
Miramar Seduction. K. Jordan
Miranda. J. Blackmore
Miranda. M. E. Braddon
Miranda. C. Larner
Miranda Clair. Phyllis Ross
Miranda Must Die. H. Calvin
Miranda Said Murder. M. Carroll
Miranda's Curse. Dorinne Moore
Miranda's Folly. Rachelle Edwards
Miriam Lemaire, Money Lender. C. Stanton
Miriam Rozella. B. L. Farjeon
Mirk Abbey. J. Payn
Miro. S. Herron
Miro Papers. S. Herron
Mirror. E. C. Reed
Mirror and Knife. J. Rosenberg
Mirror Crack'd. A. Christie
Mirror Crack'd from Side to Side. A. Christie
Mirror Dance. E. Kyle
Mirror Image. L. Du Breuil
Mirror Image. S. Harper
Mirror Image. M. Sadler
Mirror Lies. G. Vaizey
Mirror, Mirror on the Wall. S. Ellin
Mirror, Mirror on the Wall. H. B. Freeman
Mirror Murder. L. Z. Adams
Mirror of a Dead Lady. H. D. Irvine
Mirror of Delusion. M. Reisner
Mirror of Hell. L. Holton
Mirror of Shadows. D. Daniels
Mirror of Silver. R. Bridges
Mirror Room. C. Landon
Mirror Train. J. N. Chance
Mirrored Murder. A. W. Eyles
Mirrors of the Apocalypse. D. L. Moore
Mirth and Mayhem. Peter Walker
Mis-Rule of Three. F. Warden
Misadventures of Athelstan Digby. W. F. Harvey
Misadventures of Mr. Larkin. D. Lynn
Miscarriage of Justice. Nicholas Carter
Miscarriage of Justice. C. Kingston
Miscarriage of Murder. J. F. Straker
Miscast for Murder. R. Fenisong
Miscellanea. J. H. Ewing
Mischief. C. Armstrong
Mischief. B. A. Williams
Mischief at Frinton Park. F. M. Long
Mischief in the Air. M. Afford
Mischief in the Lane. A. Derleth
Mischief in the Stone. P. Loring
Mischief in the Offing. C. Witting
Mischief-Maker. E. P. Oppenheim
Mischief of a Glove. P. C. De Crespigny
Mischief Past. E. Thompson
Miser Farebrother. B. L. Farjeon
Miser Hoadley's Secret. A. W. Marchmont
Miser of Maida Vale. B. Orczy
Miser of Shoreditch. T. P. Prest
Misercordia Drop. F. Greenland
Miser's Money. E. Phillpotts
Miser's Ward. K. A. Shoesmith
Miser's Will. F. Hume
Misfire. Jonathan Evans
Misfit. G. B. Savi
Misfit. S. Kyle
Misfits. G. F. Forrest
Misfortunes of Mr. Teal. L. Charteris
Misguided Angel. R. Angel
Misguided Missile. O. Mills
Misleading Lady. A. Wood
Misplaced Corpse. S. Rider
Misprision of Felony. Seaforth
Miss Agatha. H. L. V. Fletcher
Miss Agatha Doubles for Death. H. L. V. Fletcher
Miss Arnott's Marriage. R. Marsh
Miss Bantling Is Missing. J. W. Meagher
Miss Betty's Mistake. A. Sergeant
Miss Blake's Husband. E. Jordan
Miss Bones. Joan Fleming
Miss Bracegirdle and others. S. Aumonier
Miss Brandt. Margery Lawrence
Miss Brown of X.Y.O. E. P. Oppenheim
Miss Cadogna. J. Hawthorne
Miss Callaghan Comes to Grief. J. H. Chase
Miss Called Murder. Carter Brown
Miss Cayley's Adventures. G. Allen
Miss Charley. C. Blackstock
Miss Devereux of the Mariquita. R. H. Savage
Miss Dividends. A. C. Gunter
Miss Doll, Go Home. D. Markson
Miss Dynamite. B. Gray
Miss Fenny. C. Blackstock
Miss Ferriby's Clients. F. Warden
Miss Francis Baird, Detective. R. W. Kauffman
Miss from S.I.S. R. Tralins
Miss Gloria Gets Wise. E. Ellison
Miss Hamblett's Ghost. A. Brock
Miss Hogg and the Bronte Murders. A. Lee
Miss Hogg and the Covent Garden Murders. A. Lee
Miss Hogg and the Dead Dean. A. Lee

Miss Hogg and the Missing Sisters. A. Lee
Miss Hogg and the Squash Club Murder. A. Lee
Miss Hogg Flies High. A. Lee
Miss Hogg's Last Case. A. Lee
Miss Hurd. A. K. Green
Miss Information. C. George
Miss Ivory White. R. Haggard
Miss Mabel. R. C. Sherriff
Miss Madelyn Mack, Detective. H. C. Weir
Miss Maitland, Private Secretary. G. Bonner
Miss Maitland's Spy. G. A. Birmingham
Miss Malevolent. C. R. Gull
Miss Marple and the Thirteen Problems. A. Christie
Miss Marple's Final Cases. A. Christie
Miss Martha Mary Crawford. C. Marchant
Miss Melbourn's Million. N. Penley
Miss Mephistopheles. F. Hume
Miss Merewether's Money. T. Cobb
Miss Milverton. A. Hocking
Miss Mitchell. H. Brooke
Miss Mystery. S. Horler
Miss Nobody of Nowhere. A. C. Gunter
Miss or Mrs? W. Collins
Miss Otis Blows Town. B. Sarto
Miss Otis Comes to Piccadilly. B. Sarto
Miss Otis Desires. B. Sarto
Miss Otis Gets Fresh. B. Sarto
Miss Otis Goes French. B. Sarto
Miss Otis Goes Up. B. Sarto
Miss Otis Has a Daughter. B. Sarto
Miss Otis Hits Back. B. Sarto
Miss Otis Makes a Date. B. Sarto
Miss Otis Makes Hay. B. Sarto
Miss Otis Moves In. B. Sarto
Miss Otis Plays Ball. B. Sarto
Miss Otis Plays Eve. B. Sarto
Miss Otis Relents. B. Sarto
Miss Otis Says Yes. B. Sarto
Miss Otis Takes the Rap. B. Sarto
Miss Otis Throws a Come-Back. B. Sarto
Miss Pauline of New York. St. George Rathborne
Miss Pegham. P. Conway
Miss Pell Is Missing. L. Gershe
Miss Pink at the Edge of the World. G. Moffat
Miss Pinkerton. M. R. Rinehart
Miss Pinnegar Disappears. Anthony Gilbert
Miss Private Eye. G. Batson
Miss Pym Disposes. J. Tey
Miss Rayburn's Diamonds. R. Jocelyn
Miss Rolling Stone. P. Loring
Miss Schuyler's Alias. G. Horton
Miss Seeton Bewitched. H. Carvic
Miss Seeton Draws the Line. H. Carvic
Miss Seeton Sings. H. Carvic
Miss Shumway Waves a Wand. J. H. Chase
Miss Silver Comes to Stay. P. Wentworth
Miss Silver Deals with Death. P. Wentworth
Miss Silver Intervenes. P. Wentworth
Miss Silver's Past. J. Skorvecky
Miss Turquoise. G. B. Mair
Miss White of Mayfair. G. W. Appleton
Miss Withers Regrets. S. Palmer
Miss X. S. Kyle
Missed It by That Much. W. Johnston
Misserrimus. M. P. Reynolds
Missile. A. MacKenzie
Missile Mob. H. Janson
Missing! M. Avallone
Missing. M. Halliday
Missing. E. Hostovsky
Missing! S. Kyle
Missing! F. E. Penny
Missing—A Lady. N. MacKenzie
Missing—A Young Girl. F. Warden
Missing Ace. W. H. L. Crauford
Missing Agent. M. Annesley
Missing! and other tales. M. C. Hay
Missing...and Presumed Dead. J. Hayes
Missing Archduke. G. Leroux
Missing at Lloyds. G. H. Teed
Missing Aunt. G. D. H. Cole
Missing Background. L. Cargill
Missing Bank Manager. M. Poole
Missing Banker. C. Brandon
Missing Baronet. G. D. H. Cole
Missing, Believed Dead. N. MacKenzie
Missing Body. Roland Daniel
Missing Book-Keeper. C. Keith
Missing Bracelet. I. Stark
Missing Bride. E. Southworth
Missing Bridegroom. J. K. Leys
Missing Bullet. Warren Miller
Missing Cashier. E. D. Pierson
Missing Chancellor. J. S. Fletcher
Missing Chauffeur. H. C. McNeile
Missing Clue. C. Dawe
Missing Cotton King. Nicholas Carter
Missing Cyclist and other stories. B. Delannoy
Missing Delora. E. P. Oppenheim
Missing Deputy Chief. Nicholas Carter
Missing Doctor. R. J. Fletcher
Missing Elizabeth. A. Sergeant
Missing Finger. A. Boissiere

Missing Formula. J. Decrest
Missing from Her Home. Anthony Gilbert
Missing from His Home. Mark Cross
Missing from His Home. C. Hosken
Missing from His Home. J. R. Warren
Missing from Home. S. Green
Missing from Home. M. Halliday
Missing from Home. P. Johnson
Missing from Home. P. N. Walker
Missing from Monte Carlo. B. Malim
Missing from the Shelf. M. Salkeld
Missing Gates. R. Francis Foster
Missing Grandfather. F. Y. McHugh
Missing Grave. M. Dalman
Missing Heiress. Bernice Carey
Missing Heiress. Roland Daniel
Missing Hoard. J. Creasey
Missing Hour. J. Blackmore
Missing Husband and other tales. G. R. Sims
Missing in Mexico. J. N. Pentelow
Missing Initial. N. S. Lincoln
Missing Lady. Roland Daniel
Missing Letter. H. Wood
Missing Link. K. Farrer
Missing Link. W. B. Murphy
Missing Link. G. Varney
Missing Link. C. Wells
Missing Man. B. Cane
Missing Man. Nicholas Carter
Missing Man. H. Sutherland Edwards
Missing Man. M. R. Hatch
Missing Man. K. MacLean
Missing Man. H. Waugh
Missing Masterpiece. H. Belloc
Missing Matisse. B. Levy
Missing Mayor. T. S. King
Missing Men. G. Leroux
Missing Men. A. Skene
Missing Million. A. Askew
Missing Million. E. H. Burrage
Missing Million. G. Stanley
Missing Million. E. Wallace
Missing Millionaire. Christopher Wilson
Missing Miniature. E. Kastner
Missing Minx. R. Goyne
Missing Miss Randolph. M. Leighton
Missing Money-Lender. W. S. Sykes
Missing Note. Mrs. G. Corbett
Missing or Dead. G. Ashe
Missing or Murdered. R. Forsythe
Missing Partner. J. M. Cobban
Missing Partner. H. M. Stephenson
Missing Partners. Henry Wade
Missing Person. P. Brooks
Missing Person. O. Millard
Missing Piece. P. C. De Crespigny
Missing, Presumed Dead. C. Keith
Missing, Presumed Dead. J. V. Gordon
Missing Rajah. R. Gilmour
Missing Rope. C. Carnac
Missing Rubies. F. Du Boisgobey
Missing Scapegoat. B. Cobb
Missing Ships. A. Murray
Missing Spy. W. W. Sayer
Missing Treaty. C. Dawe
Missing Two. B. Reynolds
Missing Tycoon. H. B. Taylor
Missing Widow. Anthony Gilbert
Missing Will. H. Conway
Missing Witness. F. Barrett
Missing Witness. M. E. Braddon
Missing Witness. I. Cabot
Missing Witness. N. Daniels
Missing Witness. J. M. Hickman
Missing Witness. J. Reach
Missing Witness. D. W. Spurgeon
Missing Woman. E. Page
Mission Accomplished. J. Walker
Mission for Betty Smith. Brian Cooper
Mission for Vengeance. P. Rabe
Mission House Murder. Hank Hobson
Mission Impossible. J. Tiger
Mission in Black. G. Cotler
Mission in Guemo. S. B. Hough
Mission in Sparrow Brush Lane. A. Stanford
Mission in Tunis. J. Pendower
Mission into Auschwitz. K. Netzen
Mission of Death. M. T. Walworth
Mission of Doom. Gwyn Evans
Mission of Fear. G. H. Coxe
Mission of Menace. R. Hardinge
Mission of Mercy. J. Robb
Mission of Mercy. D. Torr
Mission of Murder. R. Charles
Mission of Vengeance. R. Hardinge
Mission: Police Action. M. Kurland
Mission River Justice. W. C. Tuttle
Mission: Tank War. M. Kurland
Mission: Third Force. M. Kurland
Mission to Beirut. E. Mannin
Mission to Burundi. J. M. Bernier
Mission to Majorca. I. Mercer
Mission to Malaspiga. Evelyn Anthony
Mission to Mexico. Arthur MacLean
Mission to Murder. R. Glendinning
Mission to Siena. Raymond Marshall
Mission to Venice. Nick Carter
Mission to Venice. Raymond Marshall
Missioner. E. P. Oppenheim

Title Index

Mississippi Outlaws and the Detectives. A. Pinkerton
Mississippi Run. P. D. Boles
Missouri Legend. E. B. Ginty
Mist of Darkness. V. Coffman
Mist of Error. M. A. Dickens
Mist of Evil. P. Brisco
Mist on the Saltings. Henry Wade
Mist on the Waters. F. L. Green
Mist over Talla. A. E. Lindop
Mistake Me Not. N. Easton
Mistakenly in Mallorca. R. Jeffries
Mr. Ace. H. Christy
Mr. Allen. H. A. Vachell
Mr. & Mrs. North. Owen Davis
Mr. & Mrs. North and the Poisoned Playboy. F. Lockridge
Mr. & Mrs. North Meet Murder. F. Lockridge
Mr. Angel Comes Aboard. C. G. Booth
Mr. Arkadin. O. Welles
Mr. Babbacombe Dies. M. Burton
Mr. Balkram's Band. Frank King
Mr. Ball of Fire. B. Gray
Mr. Barnes, American. A. C. Gunter
Mr. Barnes of New York. A. C. Gunter
Mr. Bazalgette's Agent. L. Merrick
Mr. Benson's Business. Elliot Bailey
Mr. Big. M. Kenyon
Mister Big. G. Verner
Mr. Billingham, the Marquis and Madelon. E. P. Oppenheim
Mr. Birdsall Breezes Through. W. H. Mack
Mr. Blessington's Imperialist Plot. J. Sherwood
Mr. Blessington's Plot. J. Sherwood
Mr. Bobadil. F. Beeding
Mr. Bowling Buys a Newspaper. D. Henderson
Mr. Braddy's Safe and other humorous tales. R. Connell
Mister Brown's Bodies. J. Blackburn
Mr. Buckby Is Not at Home. John Gloag
Mr. Budd Again. G. Verner
Mr. Budd Investigates. G. Verner
Mr. Burnside's Responsibility. T. Cobb
Mr. Byculla. E. Linklater
Mr. Campion and others. M. Allingham
Mr. Campion: Criminologist. M. Allingham
Mr. Campion's Falcon. Y. Carter
Mr. Campion's Farthing. Y. Carter
Mr. Campion's Quarry. Y. Carter
Mr. Capon. Jenni Hall
Mr. Caution—Mr. Callaghan. P. Cheyney
Mr. Chang of Scotland Yard. A. E. Apple
Mr. Chang's Crime Ray. A. E. Apple
Mr. Christopoulos. C. Blackstock
Mr. Clackworthy. C. B. Booth
Mr. Clackworthy, Con Man. C. B. Booth
Mr. Clerihew: Wine Merchant. W. Allen
Mr. Clunk's Text. H. C. Bailey
Mr. Collin Is Ruined. F. Heller
Mr. Commissioner Sanders. E. Wallace
Mr. Cooper's Frederika. L. M. Robertson
Mr. Coroner Presides. S. Truss
Mr. Cromwell Is Dead. L. Ford
Mr. Cronk's Cases. W. A. Darlington
Mr. Crook Lifts the Mask. Anthony Gilbert
Mr. Daddy-Detective. C. Brooks
Mr. Dass. B. Atkey
Mr. Death. C. Wallace
Mr. Death Walks Abroad. C. Wallace
Mr. Denning Drives North. Alec Coppel
Mr. Diabolo. A. Lejeune
Mr. Digweed & Mr. Lumb. E. Phillpotts
Mr. Dorillon. J. Middlemass
Mr. Dovecourt's Decoy. H. Tuite
Mr. Dunton's Invention, and other stories. J. Hawthorne
Mr. Essington in Love. J. S. Clouston
Mr. Evans. C. A. Alington
Mr. Fairlie's Final Journey. A. Derleth
Mr. Faraday's Formula. D. O. Woodbury
Mr. Fortescue. W. Westall
Mr. Fortune Explains. H. C. Bailey
Mr. Fortune Finds a Pig. H. C. Bailey
Mr. Fortune Here. H. C. Bailey
Mr. Fortune Objects. H. C. Bailey
Mr. Fortune, Please. H. C. Bailey
Mr. Fortune Speaking. H. C. Bailey
Mr. Fortune Wonders. H. C. Bailey
Mr. Fortune's Practice. H. C. Bailey
Mr. Fortune's Trials. H. C. Bailey
Forty-Five. R. Angel
Mr. Grantley's Idea. J. E. Cooke
Mr. Grex of Monte Carlo. E. P. Oppenheim
Mr. Guelpa. V. Thompson
Mr. Hedley's Private Hell. P. Barrington
Mr. Hercules. Gwyn Evans
Mr. Hire's Engagement. G. Simenon
Mr. Holmes and the Fair Armenian. C. V. Bark
Mr. Holmes and the Love Bank. C. V. Bark
Mr. Holmes at Sea. C. V. Bark
Mr. Holmes Goes to Ground. C. V. Bark
Mr. Holroyd Takes a Holiday. W. Stanley
Mr. Horrocks, Purser. C. J. C. Hyne
Mr. Hoyland Looks Round. P. C. Williams
Mr. Incoul's Misadventure. E. E. Saltus
Mr. J. G. Reeder Returns. E. Wallace
Mr. Jackson. H. Green

Mr. Jelly's Business. A. W. Upfield
Mr. Justice. A. Wilson
Mr. Justice Maxell. E. Wallace
Mr. Justice Philbank. P. Trent
Mr. Justice Raffles. E. W. Hornung
Mr. Kettle, Third Mate. C. J. C. Hyne
Mr. Kilmer Sees Red. P. Urquhart
Mr. Laxworthy's Adventures. E. P. Oppenheim
Mr. Lessingham Goes Home. E. P. Oppenheim
Mr. Lucky. Albert Conroy
Mr. Lyndon at Liberty. V. Bridges
Mr. Majestyk. E. Leonard
Mr. Malcolm Presents. G. Fairlie
Mr. Marlow Chooses Wine. John Bentley
Mr. Marlow Stops for Brandy. John Bentley
Mr. Marlow Takes to Rye. John Bentley
Mr. Marx's Secret. E. P. Oppenheim
Mr. Mason. J. Last
Mr. Meeson's Will. H. R. Haggard
Mr. Merston's Money. J. Welcome
Mister Midas. M. Catto
Mr. Midnight. G. Verner
Mr. Mirakel. E. P. Oppenheim
Mr. Moon's Last Case. B. Patten
Mr. Mortimer Gets the Jitters. B. Gray
Mr. Moto Is No Sorry. J. P. Marquand
Mr. Moto Takes a Hand. J. P. Marquand
Mr. Munt Carries On. H. Clevely
Mr. Murray and the Boococks. W. F. Harvey
Mr. Nemesis. J. H. Vahey
Mr. Nobody of England. A. Soutar
Mr. Parker Pyne, Detective. A. Christie
Mr. Passingham. T. Cobb
Mr. Pendlebury and the Suicide Club. A. Webb
Mr. Pendlebury Makes a Catch. A. Webb
Mr. Pendlebury's Hat Trick. A. Webb
Mr. Pendlebury's Second Case. A. Webb
Mr. Pennington Barges In. J. G. Brandon
Mr. Pennington Comes Through. J. G. Brandon
Mr. Pennington Goes Nap. J. G. Brandon
Mr. Pennington Sees Red. J. G. Brandon
Mr. Penny. M. Moiseiwitsch
Mr. Penny at War. M. Moiseiwitsch
Mr. Penny Comes Down Heads. M. Moiseiwitsch
Mr. Pepper, Investigator. B. Thomson
Mr. Perkins of New Jersey. G. Parker
Mr. Peters. Riccardo Stephens
Mr. Pidgeon's Island. A. Berkeley
Mr. Pinkerton and the Old Angel. D. Frome
Mr. Pinkerton at the Old Angel. D. Frome
Mr. Pinkerton Finds a Body. D. Frome
Mr. Pinkerton Goes to Scotland Yard. D. Frome
Mr. Pinkerton Grows a Beard. D. Frome
Mr. Pinkerton Has the Clue. D. Frome
Mr. Pinkerton: Passage for One. D. Frome
Mr. Polton Explains. R. A. Freeman
Mr. Pond of Borneo. P. Blundell
Mr. Potter of Texas. A. C. Gunter
Mr. Pottermack's Oversight. R. A. Freeman
Mr. Preed Investigates. Ladbroke Black
Mr. Preed's Gangster. Ladbroke Black
Mr. Preston's Daughter. T. Cobb
Mr. Priestley's Problem. A. B. Cox
Mr. Punt of Chelsea. H. G. Hutchinson
Mister Q33. G. Goodchild
Mr. Quentin Investigates. Anthony Morton
Mr. Quixley of the Gate House. P. Brebner
Mr. Ramosi. V. Williams
Mr. Reeder Returns. E. Wallace
Mr. Right. C. Banks
Mr. Sandeman Loses His Life. E. P. Healey
Mister Scipio. T. Gates
Mr. Sefton, Murderer. F. W. Crofts
Mr. Simpson Finds a Body. D. Frome
Mr. Smith's Hat. H. Reilly
Mr. Snoop Is Murdered. J. Reach
Mr. South Burned His Mouth. G. Nyland
Mr. Spenyard's Two Experiments. T. W. Speight
Mr. Spirket Reforms. T. E. B. Clarke
Mr. Splitfoot. H. McCloy
Mr. Standfast. J. Buchan
Mr. Stimpson and Mr. Gorse. P. Hamilton
Mr. Strang. C. J. Daly
Mister Target. W. Harrington
Mr. Three. W. Butler
Mr. Tolefree's Reluctant Witnesses. R. A. J. Walling
Mr. Treadgold Cuts In. V. Williams
Mr. Trouble. W. Ard
Mr. Tutt Comes Home. A. Train
Mr. Tutt Finds a Way. A. Train
Mr. Tutt Takes the Stand. A. Train
Mr. Tutt's Case Book. A. Train
Mister Violence. V. Warren
Mr. Walker Wants to Know. E. Dudley
Mr. Watson Intervenes. D. Gardiner
Mr. Westerby Missing. M. Burton
Mr. Whimset Buys a Gun. B. Graeme
Mr. Whipple Explains. G. Verner

Mix Me a Person / 549

Mr. Wingrave, Millionaire. E. P. Oppenheim
Mr. Wray's Cash Box. W. Collins
Mr. Wu. L. J. Miln
Mr. X. C. Brooks
Mr. Zero. P. Wentworth
Mistigris. B. G. Quin
Mistress. Carter Brown
Mrs. Balfame. G. Atherton
Mrs. Barthelme's Madness. S. Claudia
Mrs. Belfort's Strategem. T. Cobb
Mrs. Blarney from Ireland. C. E. Blaney
Mrs. Brown on the Tichborne Case. A. Sketchley
Mrs. Brown's Pearls. A. Crabb
Mistress Devon. V. Coffman
Mrs. Dimmock's Worries. B. L. Farjeon
Mrs. Donald Dyke, Detective. H. Rockwood
Mistress Dorothy Marvin. J. C. Snaith
Mrs. Druse's Case, and Maggie Houghtaling. Anonymous
Mrs. Dunbar's Secret. A. St. Aubyn
Mrs. Erricker's Reputation. T. Cobb
Mrs. Fuller. Marguerite Bryant
Mrs. Gainsborough's Diamonds. J. Hawthorne
Mrs. Gaskell's Tales of Mystery and Horror. E. C. Gaskell
Mrs. Gray's Past. H. Flowerdew
Mrs. Greet's Story of the Golden Owl. Mrs. Greet
Mrs. Greystone—Murdered. Roland Daniel
Mrs. Grundy's Victim. G. Corbett
Mrs. Gunness Mystery. Anonymous
Mrs. Halliburton's Troubles. H. Wood
Mrs. Homicide. D. Keene
Mrs. Inspector Jones. James Parish
Mrs. Isaac. B. L. Farjeon
Mrs. John Foster. C. Granville
Mrs. Jonathan Abroad. George Hastings
Mrs. Knox's Profession. Jessica Mann
Mrs. Latham's Extravagance. T. Cobb
Mrs. Lygon's Husband. A. Sergeant
Mrs. McGinty's Dead. A. Christie
Mrs. McThing. M. Chase
Mrs. Maitland's Affair. M. Lynn
Mrs. Marden's Ordeal. J. Hay
Mrs. Meeker's Money. D. M. Disney
Mrs. Munck. E. Leffland
Mistress Murder. P. Cheyney
Mistress Murder. B. Picton
Mrs. Murdock Takes the Case. G. H. Coxe
Mrs. Murphy's Underpants. F. Brown
Mrs. Musgrave—and Her Husband. R. Marsh
Mistress of Bonaventure. H. Bindloss
Mistress of Corey's Landing. M. Harmon
Mistress of Death. P. Anthony
Mistress of Destiny. B. Kingsley
Mistress of Devil's Manor. F. Stevenson
Mistress of Falcon Hill. D. Daniels
Mistress of Farrondale. D. Nile
Mistress of Fear. H. Janson
Mistress of Ghosthaven. J. Bellamy
Mistress of Horror House. W. Woody
Mistress of Lost River. M. Craig
Mistress of Mellyn. V. Holt
Mistress of Mellyn. M. C. Kuner
Mistress of Moorwood Manor. Marilyn Ross
Mistress of Mount Fair. Jane Gordon
Mistress of Orion Hall. Claudette Nicole
Mistress of Ravenstone. M. Heath
Mistress of Ravenswood. Clarissa Ross
Mistress of Ravenswood. Marilyn Ross
Mistress of Shades. N. McFather
Mistress of Soundcliff Manor. D. Wood
Mistress of Tara. C. Laffeaty
Mistress of the Moor. A. Clements
Mistress of the Moor. E. Lockwood
Mistress on a Deathbed. N. Daniels
Mrs. Pollifax on Safari. D. Gilman
Mrs. Pillifax, Spy. D. Gilman
Mrs. Pomeroy's Reputation. T. Cobb
Mrs. Pym and other stories. N. Morland
Mrs. Pym of Scotland Yard. N. Morland
Mrs. Raffles. J. K. Bangs
Mrs. Snagg—Detective. O. M. Popplewell
Mrs. Sparks of Paris. A. C. Bond
Mrs. Starr Lives Alone. J. Godden
Mrs. Tenterden. Margerie Scott
Mistress to Murder. R. Dietrich
Mrs. Vanderstein's Jewels. C. Bryce
Mrs. Vannock. A. Griffin
Mrs. Waldegrave's Will and other tales. Inspector F
Mrs. Warrender's Profession. G. D. H. Cole
Mrs. Whiston's Party. T. Cobb
Mrs. Winterton's Rebellion. J. Dering
Mrs. W's Last Sandwich. E. Denby
Mrs. Wylde. L. Gardiner
Mists Came Down. E. Backhouse
Mists of Dark Harbor. C. Ross
Mists of Fear. J. Creasey
Mists of Memory. C. Cookson
Mists of Mourning. S. Somers
Mists of Treason. J. N. Chance
Misty Curtain. L. Cores
Misty Pathway. H. Desmond
Mitcham Murder Mystery. G. H. Teed
Mittenwald Syndicate. F. Nolan
Mix Me a Murder. L. Grex
Mix Me a Person. J. T. Story

Mix Yourself a Redhead. C. Williams
Mixed Bags. S. C. Westerham
Mixed-Up Mess. Nicholas Carter
Mixer. E. Wallace
Mixture of Plays. I. Gass
Mizmaze. M. Fitt
Moab Is My Washpot. E. G. Cousins
Moat Farm Mystery. M. E. Cooke
Moat House Mystery. B. M. Clay
Moat House Mystery. R. Francis Foster
Mob Says Murder. Albert Conroy
Mobile Library Murders. J. Austwick
Mobius Trip. W. Garner
Mobsmen on the Spot. M. Grant
Mobster. F. Arrigio
Mobster. J. Roeburt
Moccasin Men. John Ross
Moccasin Murders. K. Perkins
Mockery in Arms. J. Aldridge
Mocking Face of Murder. S. Horler
Moday Mystery. M. E. Hively
Model Corpse. M. B. Clark
Model Father. D. C. Murray
Model for Murder. Carter Brown
Model for Murder. P. Campion
Model for Murder. J. Fast
Model for Murder. R. Kyle
Model for Murder. S. Marlowe
Model for Murder. Jeanne Wilson
Model for the Toff. J. Creasey
Model in Mayhem. H. Janson
Model Is Murdered. Babs Lee
Model Murders. J. H. Demarest
Model of No Virtue. Carter Brown
Model Town and the Detectives. A. Pinkerton
Modeled in Murder. Manning Long
Moderate Murderer and The Honest Quack. G. K. Chesterton
Modern Cameos. A. Mills
Modern Circe. Maurice Scott
Modern Corsair. R. H. Savage
Modern Delilah. B. Bolt
Modern Dick Whittington. J. Payn
Modern Magician. J. F. Molloy
Modern Man-Hunt. P. H. Lockwood
Modern Mercenary. K. Prichard
Modern Portia. P. Trent
Modern Prometheus. E. P. Oppenheim
Modern Quixote. August Berkeley
Modern Robyn Hood. M. M. Bodkin
Modern Sorceress. I. Stark
Modern Ulysses. J. Hatton
Modern Wizard. R. Ottolengui
Modesty Blaise. P. O'Donnell
Modesty Blaise's The Black Pearl. P. O'Donnell
Modigliani Scandal. Z. Stone
Mogul Men. P. Leslie
Mohawks. M. E. Braddon
Mohune's Nine Lives. P. Groom
Moina. L. L. Lynch
Mole. D. Sherman
Molehill File. M. Kenyon
Moles of Death. J. Dellbridge
Mollie the Handful. F. Warden
Molls Mean Murder. Griff
Molly and the Confidence Man. S. Overholser
Molly Maguires. James O'Neill
Molly Maguires and the Detectives. A. Pinkerton
Molly on the Spot. Frank King
Molly's Aunt at Angmering. H. C. McNeile
Molly's Husband. R. Marsh
Molting Season. C. Ferguson
Moment. E. Davies
Moment After. R. Buchanan
Moment After. V. Tracy
Moment for Murder. A. Eichler
Moment for Murder. L. Marshall
Moment in Time. J. Wellard
Moment More. J. Laing
Moment of Danger. D. MacKenzie
Moment of Decision. S. B. Hough
Moment of Fiction. D. Estow
Moment of Madness. C. J. Bellamy
Moment of Need. M. Coombs
Moment of Silence. D. Estow
Moment of the Predator. G. Bernard
Moment of Truth. K. A. Blom
Moment of Truth. W. M. Goeney
Moment of Truth. Magali
Moment of Truth. L. Snow
Moment of Untruth. E. Lacy
Moment of Violence. G. H. Coxe
Moment on Ice. N. Easton
Moment to Moment. Alec Coppel
Momentary Stoppage. A. F. Grey
Moment's Error. A. W. Marchmont
Mona. Lawrence Block
Mona Intercept. D. Hamilton
Monastery Mystery. G. Chester
Moncasket Mystery and How Tom Hardy Solved It. S. Marlow
Moncrieff. I. Holland
Monday in Summer. Dorothy Sanders
Monday Never Came. C. Ryland
Monday Night. K. Boyle
Monday Night Murder. R. Trevor
Monday the Rabbi Took Off. H. Kemelman
Monday, Tuesday, Wednesday! R. Houston

Monday's Mob. D. Pendleton
Mondo. A. De Stefano
Moneta Papers. J. Messmann
"Money." M. Leighton
Money Barons. J. H. Vahey
Money Buys Everything. Roy Vickers
Money by Menaces. S. Adams
Money for Murder. H. Carmichael
Money for Murder. Neill Graham
Money for the Taking. D. M. Disney
Money from Holme. M. Innes
Money from Rome. R. Holt
Money Goes Round and Round. J. T. Story
Money Harvest. Ross Thomas
Money in the Air. M. Franklin
Money Jugglers. B. Wayde
Money Lender. B. Delannoy
Money-Lender in Gloves. F. Blane
Money Means Murder. L. Marshall
Money Men. W. Haggard
Money Moon. J. Farnol
Money Movers. D. Minchin
Money Murder. J. Ingersol
Money, Murder and the McNeills. T. Du Bois
Money Murders. Eugene Franklin
Money Musk. C. Wells
Money Musk. B. A. Williams
Money on Murder. H. Gardiner
Money on the Black. A. MacKinnon
Money Order Murder. Stafford Edwards
Money People. C. C. Katcher
Money Sense. P. Trent
Money Soldiers. Martin Walker
Money Spider. M. Leighton
Money-Spider. W. LeQueux
Money Spinners. S. Murray
Money Spinners and other stories. A. Soutar
Money Stones. I. St. James
Money That Money Can't Buy. J. Munro
Money to Burn. W. Douglas
Money to Burn. R. W. Kauffman
Money to Burn. H. Woodward
Money Trap. L. White
Money Walks. J. J. Farjeon
Money War. T. L. Smith
Money with Menaces and To the Public Danger. P. Hamilton
Money's Worth of Murder. C. Conrad
Mongol Mask. David St. John
Mongolian Interlude. L. Oliver
Mongolian Mystery. G. Collins
Mongo's Back in Town. E. R. Johnson
Monique. B. Blankfort
Monitor Affair. C. B. Kelland
Monk. M. G. Lewis
Monk of Cruta. E. P. Oppenheim
Monk of Hambleton. A. Livingston
Monk of Udolpho. T. J. H. Curties
Monkey and the Tiger. R. Van Gulik
Monkey Boat. N. Trott
Monkey Business. L. Isom
Monkey Game. G. Kent
Monkey Murder, and other Hildegarde Withers stories. S. Palmer
Monkey on a Chain. C. Blackstock
Monkey on a Chain. E. Lanham
Monkey-Puzzle. B. Von Hutten
Monkey Trick. J. E. Gurdon
Monkey Wrench. J. Griffith
Monkey Wrench Gang. E. Abbey
Monkhurst Case. A. Stanley
Monkhurst Murder. F. Grierson
Monk's Bridge Mystery. W. G. Borth
Monk's Court. K. W. Eyre
Monk's Croft Mystery. T. S. King
Monk's Hollow. John Marsh
Monk's Hood. Ellis Peters
Monk's Hood Murders. L. Edgley
Monk's Retreat. Susannah Curtis
Monk's Treasure. G. Horton
Monksglade Mystery. H. Hill
Monkshood. E. Phillpotts
Monocled Man. J. Ronald
Monocled Monster. H. S. Keeler
Monomark Mystery. L. Carlton
Monopoly Menace. J. Hunter
Monopoly to Murder. R. Magowan
Monsieur Blackshirt. D. Graeme
Monsieur Brunner. D. A. Grant
Monsieur Faux-Pas. Rosa Lambert
Monsieur Jonquelle, Prefect of Police. M. D. Post
Monsieur Judas. F. Hume
Monsieur la Souris. G. Simenon
Monsieur Lecoq. E. Gaboriau
Monsieur Monde Vanishes. G. Simenon
Monsieur X. R. W. Sneddon
Monsieur Zenith. A. Skene
Monsieur Zero. N. Tom-Gallon
Monsoon Murder. Brian Cooper
Monster. H. Hext
Monster. E. Saltus
Monster Club. R. Chetwynd-Hayes
Monster in the Pool. A. Livingston
Monster of Dagenham Hall. J. Corbett
Monster of Grammont. G. Goodchild
Monster of Lazy Hook. Thorne Lee
Monster of Mu. O. Rutter
Monster of Snowdon Hall. Grove Wilson
Monster of the Lagoon. G. F. Worts

Monster Unto Many. P. Giles
Monster Wheel Affair. D. McDaniel
Monsters. K. Robeson
Monstrous Enemy. C. R. Gull
Monstrous Regiment. J. N. Chance
Montana Man. W. C. Tuttle
Monte Carlo Mission. V. Connell
Monte Carlo Stories. J. M. Barrett
Monte Cristo Cover-Up. J. M. Simmel
Monte Cristo in Khaki. R. H. Savage
Montenegran Plot. R. Trevelyan
Montenegrin Gold. B. Ball
Monterant Affair. Richard Grayson
Montezuma's Revenge. H. Harrison
Month of the Evil Moon. R. Pitt
Month of the Falling Leaves. B. Marshall
Month of the Mangled Models. R. Player
Month of the Pearl. P. Jones
Monument of Terror. V. Jones
Mood for Murder. F. Gruber
Mood for Murder. V. Siller
Moods and Tenses. W. F. Harvey
Moon Cat. E. Neely
Moon Chapel. Lynna Cooper
Moon Dance. E. P. Thorne
Moon Dancers. S. Nichols
Moon Endureth. J. Buchan
Moon Express. N. Daniels
Moon Fire. L. Benedict
Moon for Killers. G. Black
Moon Garden. Jan Alexander
Moon Gate. C. C. Estes
Moon Hill. M. Woodhouse
Moon in Pisces. C. Darby
Moon in Shadows. A. Westminster
Moon in the Gutter. D. Goodis
Moon Is Red. S. Rohmer
Moon Killer. J. Corbett
Moon Killer. R. Verron
Moon Marriage. A. Rundle
Moon Murders. N. Morland
Moon of Darkness. M. Lynch
"Moon of Death!" R. Gar
Moon of Joy. Camilla Hope
Moon of Madness. S. Rohmer
Moon of the Wolf. L. H. Whitten
Moon of Valleys. D. Whitelaw
Moon of Violence. E. Douglas
Moon over Miami. J. Deane
Moon over the Danube. M. McEvoy
Moon over the Water. M. Greig
Moon over Willow Run. D. E. L. Patch
Moon Returns. Rona Randall
Moon Rock. A. J. Rees
Moon Saw Murder. G. Oliver
Moon Shadow. K. Allyson
Moon Shadows. A. Boyle
Moon-Spinners. Mary Stewart
Moon Was Made for Murder. N. Morland
Moon Was Red. D. Sage
Moonbathers. R. Miles
Moonbeams. R. V. Beste
Moonblood. P. J. Cooper
Mooney Moves Around. K. O'Neil
Moonflete. V. Black
Moonflower. B. Nichols
Moonflower. P. A. Whitney
Moonflower Murder. B. Nichols
Moonflowers. M. Peterson
Moonhaunt. U. Nightingale
Moonhill Mystery. W. Woodrow
Moonlake Manor. L. Churchill
Moonlight at Greystone. L. Bronte
Moonlight Can Betray. L. Harper
Moonlight Flitting. M. Procter
Moonlight Gondola. Janette Radcliffe
Moonlight Madness. E. Nepean
Moonlight Path. K. Lindsay
Moonlight Red. D. Morel
Moonlighter. H. Kane
Moonlighters. S. Morrow
Moonlit Door. A. Maybury
Moonlit Trap. R. Willock
Moonlit Way. R. W. Chambers
Moonlit Way. R. A. Dwyer-Joyce
Moonmilk and Murder. A. M. Stein
Moonraker. I. Fleming
Moonrakers and Mischief. G. J. Feakes
Moonraker's Bride. M. Brent
Moonrise. T. Strauss
Moonrock. R. Weverka
Moons in Gold. C. S. Montanye
Moonshadow Mansion. T. R. Bernard
Moonshine. R. Carr
Moonshine Momma. Carter Brown
Moonshine Mountain. C. Glore
Moonshine War. E. Leonard
Moonshiners. J. Carr
Moonshiner's Dupe. Lieut. Carlton
Moonstalker. F. Wrixon
Moonstone. W. Collins
Moonstone. M. Stone
Moonstone Jungle. S. Harvester
Moonstone Mystery. A. Marsden
Moonstone Spirit. J. Deweese
Moonwater. Claudia Nicole
Moonwind. S. Wagner
Moor. D. Whitelaw
Moor Barn Mystery. H. L. Phillips
Moor Fires Mystery. H. R. Campbell
Moor House Murders. G. Verner
Moorcroft Manor Mystery. R. Trevor

Title Index

Moorhaven. D. Winston
Moorland Mystery. A. S. Falkner
Moorland Terror. H. Broadbridge
Moorlands Murder. C. Jude
Moorsend Manor. F. Hurd
Moorwood Legacy. I. Foster
Morals and Millions. F. Warden
Morals and Mysteries. H. Aide
Morals Squad. J. S. A. Krasney
Moran Chambers Smiled. E. P. Oppenheim
Moran's Women. D. Keene
Morbid Taste for Bones. Ellis Peters
Mord Em'ly. W. P. Ridge
More About P.J., the Secret Service Boy. F. S. Hamilton
More Adventures of Captain Kettle. C. J. C. Hyne
More Adventures of Ellery Queen. E. Queen
More Beautiful Than Murder. O. R. Cohen
More Bitter Than Death. K. Wilhelm
More Crook Stuff. R. Keverne
More Dangerous Than the Moon. Richard Butler
More Dead Than Alive. R. Ormerod
More Deadly Than the Male. Ambrose Grant
More Deadly Than the Male. L. Meynell
More Deaths for Sergeant Cluff. G. North
More Deaths Than One. S. Engstrand
More Deaths Than One. B. Fischer
More Deaths Than One. R. Stout
More Educated Evans. E. Wallace
More Exploits of Sherlock Holmes. Adrian Conan Doyle
More Goon Show Scripts. S. Milligan
More Knaves Than One. F. Packard
More Limehouse Nights. T. Burke
More Lives Than One. C. Houghton
More Lives Than One. C. Wells
More Murder in a Nunnery. E. Shepherd
More Mysteries of a Great City. W. LeQueux
More News from Middle East. Robert Mason
More Nightmares. R. Bloch
More Perfect Union. R. Stapp
More Secrets of Potsdam. W. LeQueux
More Stories from Thriller. Ted Hart
More Tales of the Black Widowers. I. Asimov
More Tales of the Uneasy. V. Hunt
More Tales of the Unexpected. R. Dahl
More Than All. M. Warby
More Than Flesh. L. A. Brennan
More Than Kisses, Baby. S. Morelli
More Than Once Upon a Time. G. Kersh
More Than One Serpent. R. A. J. Walling
More to Be Pitied Than Scorned. C. E. Blaney
More Trouble for Archer. H. Clevely
More Work for the Undertaker. M. Allingham
Moreton Abbey. H. Chilcot
Moreton Mystery. E. Dejeans
Morgan of the Mounted. S. A. White
Morgan the Dauntless. J. K. Stafford
Morgan Trail. W. C. Tuttle
Morganatic Marriage. C. Dawe
Morganatic Marriage. M. Leighton
Morganatic Wife. L. Tracy
Morgan's Castle. J. Hilliard
Morgan's Horror. G. M. Fenn
Morgan's Mountain. A. Mayse
Morgan's Wife. V. James
Morgue Amour. Carter Brown
Morgue for Venus. Jonathan Craig
Morgue Is Always Open. J. Odlum
Morgue the Merrier. J. Truesdell
Moriarty. J. Gardner
Morituri. W. J. Luddecke
Morlo. L. A. Knight
Morning After. J. B. Weiner
Morning After Death. N. Blake
Morning of the Tiger. D. J. Fretland
Moroccan. C. A. Haddad
Morocco Episode. W. P. Brothers
Morocco Jones and the Case of the Golden Angel. J. Baynes
Moron. M. Brandel
Morosco. R. Pertwee
Morris Hume, Detective. William Robertson
Mort Castle. Anonymous
Mortal Affair. S. Allan
Mortal Coils. A. Huxley
Mortal Encounter. P. Sargent
Mortal Fire. H. Gibbs
Mortal Gods. J. Fast
Mortal Remains. M. Yorke
Mortal Stakes. R. B. Parker
Mortal Storm. P. Bottome
Mortdecai's Endgame. K. Bonfiglioli
Mortgage for Murder. P. Costello
Mortgaged Lives. P. Trent
Mortimer Story. P. Barrington
Mortissimo. P. E. H. Durston
Mortlake. Griffin Taylor
Mortmain. H. C. Asterley
Mortmain. A. Train
Morton Mystery. E. D'Arcy
Mortover Grange Affair. J. S. Fletcher
Mortover Grange Mystery. J. S. Fletcher
Morwenna. A. Goring

Mosaic Earring. C. Boyer
Mosaic of Death. W. Keenan
Moscow. Nick Carter
Moscow at High Noon Is the Target. P. Richards
Moscow by Nightmare. J. L. Shub
Moscow Coach. P. McCutchan
Moscow File. E. P. Thorne
Moscow 500. David Grant
Moscow Gold. J. Salisbury
Moscow Intercept. H. Arvay
Moscow Interlude. C. W. Thayer
Moscow Manhunt. Philip Chambers
Moscow Mists. Clarissa Ross
Moscow Murder. B. Newman
Moscow Mystery. I. Litvinoff
Moscow 1980. R. Vacha
Moscow Papers. J. M. White
Moscow Quadrille. T. Allbeury
Moscow Road. S. Harvester
Moscow Tape. J. N. Datesh
Moses Bottle. R. Mead
Mosque of the Mahdi. A. Murray
Mosquito Net. G. B. Savi
Mosquito Serenade. N. McGuire
Mosquitoes Don't Kill. R. Hamilton
Moss Mystery. C. Wells
Moss Rose. J. Shearing
Mossbank Murder. Harry Mills
Mosshaven. S. Hancock
Most Beautiful Lady. D. Brande
Most Contagious Game. C. Aird
Most Contagious Game. S. Grafton
Most Dangerous Game. G. Lyall
Most Deadly Game. E. Friend
Most Deadly Hate. H. Carmichael
Most Delicious Poison. C. Connell
Most Happy Con Man. J. P. Radford
Most Immoral Murder. H. Ashbrook
Most Likely to Love. F. Flora
Most Men Don't Kill. David Alexander
Most Private Intrigue. L. Rosten
Most Sacred of All. J. Farnol
Most Savage Animal. H. Atkinson
Most Secret. J. D. Carr
Most Secret...Most Immediate. H. Swiggett
Most Unnatural Murder. Fiona Sinclair
Mostly by Moonlight. D. Daniels
Mostly Murder. F. Brown
Mote House Mystery. H. A. Vachell
Moteley's Concession. C. N. Boyle
Moth. J. M. Cain
Moth and the Flame. A. M. Meadows
Moth and the Footlights. G. Warden
Moth in a Rag Shop. R. Chambers
"Moth" Murder. L. Blow
Moth-Watch Murder. M. Burton
Moth-Woman. F. Hume
Mother Finds a Body. G. R. Lee
Mother Goose Murders. W. B. Gibson
Mother Hunt. R. Stout
Mother-in-Law. E. Southworth
Mother Mandarin. F. Hume
Mother Night. K. Vonnegut
Mother of Jack the Ripper. J. Kirkpatrick
Mother of the Year. B. B. Johnson
Mother Russia. R. Littell
Mother's Day. J. M. Ryan
Mother's Sacrifice. C. Faber
Mother's Secret. E. Southworth
Moths. R. Ashe
Motion Menace. K. Robeson
Motive. H. Carmichael
Motive. M. B. Lowndes
Motive. E. Piper
Motive for a Kill. J. N. Chance
Motive for Murder. C. Barling
Motive for Murder. S. Bate
Motive for Murder. N. Brent
Motive for Murder. Neill Graham
Motive for Murder. A. Griffin
Motive for Murder. E. T. Hamill
Motive for Murder. H. Manningham
Motive for Murder. W. Reed
Motive for Murder. D. W. Rimel
Motive for Revenge. S. Clausse
Motive for Revenge. P. Conway
Motive for the Crime. A. Soutar
Motive in Shadow. L. Egan
Motive Key. J. Woodward
Motive Not the Deed. A. Arden
Motives for Murder. G. Croudace
Motives of Nicholas Holtz. T. Painter
Motley and Murder. H. Holt
Motley Menace. L. Cargill
Motor Bus Murder. Donald Stuart
Motor City Blue. L. D. Estleman
Motor Coach Murder. L. Bidston
Motor Coach Mystery. A. Murray
Motor Coach Mystery. W. Tyrer
Motor Cracksman. Charles Carey
Motor-Gun. H. C. McNeile
Motor Horn Mystery. T. S. King
Motor Pirate. S. Paternoster
Motor Rally Mystery. J. Rhode
Motor Show Mystery. H. H. C. Gibbons
Motor Show Mystery. R. Hardinge
Motor Wizard's Mystery. B. L. Standish
Mottled Death. J. Creasey
Motto for Murder. M. Mace

Mouche. Demouzon
Mouls House Mystery. C. Barry
Mound Hill Mystery. Max Burton
Mount Desolation. C. Dawe
Mount Despair, and other stories. D. C. Murray
Mount Royal. M. E. Braddon
Mountain Cabin Mystery. C. Bussell
Mountain Cat. R. Stout
Mountain Cat Murders. R. Stout
Mountain Fires. M. Sutherland
Mountain Gold. Basil Carey
Mountain Gold. G. Goodchild
Mountain House Mystery. R. St. Clair
Mountain Inn Mystery. N. Ridley
Mountain Justice. C. N. Buck
Mountain Limited. E. L. Coolidge
Mountain Madness. L. Ford
Mountain Man. H. C. Wire
Mountain Meadow. J. Buchan
Mountain Monster. K. Robeson
Mountain Murder. J. T. Adams
Mountain Murder Case. C. H. Snow
Mountain Mystery. J. J. Farjeon
Mountain Mystery. L. L. Lynch
Mountain of Fear. Rona Randall
Mountain of Terror. H. S. Banner
Mountain of the Blind. J. Creasey
Mountain Terror. M. E. Cooke
Mountaineer Detective. Anonymous
Mountaineer Detective. C. W. Cobb
Mountaineers. H. Bindloss
Mountainhead. D. Cory
Mountains Have a Secret. A. W. Upfield
Mountains Have No Shadow. O. Cameron
Mountains of Fears. H. C. Rowland
Mountains West of Town. W. Downing
Mounted Justice. K. Mayo
Mountford Show. Elizabeth Ford
Moura. V. Coffman
Mourn the Hangman. H. Whittington
Mourned on Sunday. H. Reilly
Mourner. R. Stark
Mourner's Voyage. Shane Martin
Mournful Demeanor of Lieutenant Boruvka. J. Skvorecky
Mourning After. T. B. Dewey
Mourning After. Z. Johnson
Mourning After. F. Kane
Mourning Brooch. H. Miller
Mourning of the Dove. I. Betz
Mourning Raga. Ellis Peters
Mourning Tree. V. Johnston
Mouse in Eternity. N. Tyre
Mouse in the Mountain. N. Davis
Mouse Trap. M. Messer
Mouse Who Wouldn't Play Ball. Anthony Gilbert
Mouse with Red Eyes. E. Eastman
Mouseback. J. C. Woodiwiss
Mousetrap. A. Christie
Mousetrap and Other Plays. A. Christie
Mouth of the Wolf. W. Murray
Mouthpiece. Robert (G.) Curtis
Move. G. Simenon
Move Along. F. Castle
Move in the Dark. Nicholas Carter
Move On, Miss Mayhem. M. Brody
Movement Toward Eden. Clark Howard
Movie Mystery. R. C. Armour
Moving Day. Charles Henry
Moving Eye. M. E. Cooke
Moving Finger. J. H. Barrington
Moving Finger. A. Christie
Moving Finger. C. Fitzsimmons
Moving Finger. N. S. Lincoln
Moving Finger. E. P. Oppenheim
Moving Graveyard. M. Avallone
Moving House of Foscaldo. C. Chadwick
Moving Picture Boys. M. Wilk
Moving Picture Mystery. Nicholas Carter
Moving Target. John Macdonald
Moving Toyshop. E. Crispin
Mowbray Mystery. B. Holt
Mox. M. Grant
Mozard Fiddle. K. Bird
"Mozart" Leaves at Nine. H. Greene
Mozart Score. E. Leather
M'Sango, the Witch Doctor. F. A. M. Webster
Much Ado About Murder. F. Levon
Much Ado About Something. B. Graeme
Much Darker Days. A. H. Longway
Much in Evidence. H. Cecil
Mud in His Eye. G. Hammond
Muddles of Solon Mudhen, the Blacksmith Detective. Anonymous
Muddy Leaf Mystery. T. B. Morris
Mudflats of the Dead. G. Mitchell
Muertalma. M. Dey
Muffled Man. G. Ingram
Mufti. H. C. McNeile
Mugger. E. McBain
Mugger Blood. R. Sapir
Mugger's Day. G. Bagby
Mugs, Molls and Dr. Harvey. G. Malcolm-Smith
Muir's Blood. C. Larson
Mullenthorpe Thing. C. Hood
Mulligan Stew. G. Sorrentino
Mulligan's Pirates. D. Stanford
Mulligan's Seed. H. Burkholz

M

Multi-Million-Dollar Murders. V. W. Mason
Multi-Millionaire. A. Hodges
Multiple Man. B. Bova
Multiple Murder. T. Macrae
Multitude of Shadows. A. Calin
Multitude of Sins. M. K. Wren
Mumbo Jumbo. I. Reed
Mummer Case Mystery. D. Morrah
Mummy. Riccardo Stephens
Mummy Case. D. Morrah
Mummy Comes to Life. V. Van Der Elst
Mummy Moves. M. Gaunt
Mummy Sea, Mummy Do. C. Sodaro
Mummy's Curse. T. S. King
Mummy's Hand. Mrs. C. Kernahan
Mum's the Word for Murder. A. Baker
Mumsy, Nanny, Sonny, and Girly. B. Comport
Mungo. G. Woden
Munich Involvement. F. Mullally
Munitions Master. K. Robeson
Mura, the Western Detective. Old Sleuth
Mura, the Western Lady Detective. Anonymous
Murder! John Arnold
Murder!! M. Crombie
Murder. H. Janson
Murder. Evelyn Johnson
Murder a Day! R. Avery
Murder a la Mode. P. Moyes
Murder a la Mode. E. K. Sellars
Murder a la Mozambique. A. Scobie
Murder a la Richelieu. A. Blackman
Murder a la Stroganoff. C. Brahms
Murder a Mile High. E. Dean
Murder, a Mystery, and a Marriage. M. Twin
Murder Abroad. W. C. Harvey
Murder Abroad. E. R. Punshon
Murder, Absolutely Murder. H. Cloutier
Murder Adrift. G. Bellairs
Murder After a Fashion. S. Dean
Murder After Christmas. R. Latimer
Murder After Dark. J. Gannett
Murder After Hours. A. Christie
Murder After the Blitz. P. Piper
Murder Against the Grain. E. Lathen
Murder Ahead. N. Deane
Murder al Fresco. Jennifer Jones
Murder All Over. C. F. Adams
Murder Amid Proofs. M. Bremner
Murder Among Children. T. Coe
Murder Among Friends. B. Barry
Murder Among Friends. I. E. Cox
Murder Among Friends. E. Ferrars
Murder Among Friends. Lange Lewis
Murder Among Friends. Simon
Murder Among Members. C. Carnac
Murder Among the Angells. R. Scarlett
Murder Among the Nudists. P. Hunt
Murder Among the Well-To-Do. E. Godfrey
Murder Among Thieves. P. Alding
Murder Among Those Present. H. Mace
Murder—and Ariadne. I. Wray
Murder and Blueberry Pie. F. Lockridge
Murder and Chips. L. Mantell
Murder & Co. B. Gray
Murder and Gardenias. M. Neville
Murder and Magic. R. Garrett
Murder and Marigold. G. Brandon
Murder and Miss Ming. P. Hambledon
Murder and Music. G. Lee
Murder and Mystery. Evelyn Johnson
Murder and Poor Jenny. M. Neville
Murder and the Married Virgin. B. Halliday
Murder and the Red-Haired Girl. H. Balfour
Murder and the Secret Weapon. G. F. Worts
Murder and the Shocking Miss Williams. H. J. Kennedy
Murder and the Wanton Bride. B. Halliday
Murder Anonymous. Anthony Gilbert
Murder Arranged. J. Philips
Murder Arranged. B. Thomson
Murder As a Fine Art. F. Bonnamy
Murder As a Fine Art. C. Carnac
Murder As an Ornament. M. Boniface
Murder As Arranged. Mark Cross
Murder As Usual. O. F. Jerome
Murder As Usual. H. Pentecost
Murder Assured. M. Halliday
Murder at a Cottage. Roland Daniel
Murder at a Dog Show. D. F. Gardiner
Murder at a Police Station. A. Swift
Murder at Arondale Farm. J. Hawk
Murder at Arroways. H. Reilly
Murder at Auction. E. Beatty
Murder at Avalon Arms. O. F. Jerome
Murder at Bador. S. C. Mason
Murder at Barclay House. K. McKay
Murder at Bayside. R. Robins
Murder at Belle Butte. T. M. Longstreth
Murder at Belle Camille. Monte Barrett
Murder at Benfleet. G. Bettany
Murder at Brambles. G. Collins
Murder at Bratton Grange. J. Rhode
Murder at Bridge. Anne Austin
Murder at Brownhill. T. A. Plummer
Murder at Buzzards Bay. A. Abbot

Murder at Calamity House. A. Cardwell
Murder at Cambridge. Q. Patrick
Murder at Castle Deeping. W. E. Johns
Murder at Charters. J. Fethaland
Murder at Chartres Towers. M. Beard
Murder at City Hall. Dan Ross
Murder at Cloud Hospital. M. Stand
Murder at Coney Island. J. D. O'Hanlon
Murder at Constantia. C. M. Lindsay
Murder at Cost Price. L. H. Hart
Murder at Covent Garden. W. J. Makin
Murder at Crawford Notch. M. L. Burns
Murder at Crome House. G. D. H. Cole
Murder at Cypress Hall. O. Stacey
Murder at Daybreak. G. A. Mayhew
Murder at Deem House. S. Bate
Murder at Deer Lick. A. B. Cunningham
Murder at Derivale. J. Rhode
Murder at Drake's Anchorage. E. L. Waddell
Murder at Eastover. A. Rutter
Murder at Eight. S. Bate
Murder at Eight Bells. E. L. McReay
Murder at Elaine's. R. Rosenbaum
Murder at Elstree. T. Burke
Murder at End House. M. Halliday
Murder at Endor. W. A. Wolff
Murder at Exbridge. V. L. Whitechurch
Murder at Fenwold. C. Bush
Murder at Fleet. E. B. Young
Murder at Four Dot Ranch. F. L. Gregory
Murder at Full Moon. W. J. Makin
Murder at Glen Athol. N. Lippincott
Murder at Government House. E. Huxley
Murder at Grand Bay. W. D. Roberts
Murder at Grassmere Abbey. M. B. Dix
Murder at H.Q. H. Hawton
Murder at Hazelmoor. A. Christie
Murder at Hermit's Cottage. R. Hardinge
Murder at Hide and Seek. E. O'Donnell
Murder at High Noon. P. McGuire
Murder at High Tide. C. G. Booth
Murder at Horsethief. J. D. O'Hanlon
Murder at King's Kitchen. M. Halliday
Murder at Le Touquet. R. Lacroix
Murder at Lancaster Gate. F. Grierson
Murder at Landred Hall. J. Turner
Murder at Lantern Corner. T. A. Plummer
Murder at Large. L. Frost
Murder at Leisure. J. G. Edwards
Murder at Leisure. H. Monteilhet
Murder at Liberty Hall. A. Clutton-Brock
Murder at Lilac Cottage. J. Rhode
Murder at Linpara. H. Horn
Murder at Lintercombe. I. Greig
Murder at Little Malling. Roland Daniel
Murder at Lover's Lake. M. Brucker
Murder at Maison Manche. H. Burleigh
Murder at Malibu. J. D. O'Hanlon
Murder at Maneuvers. R. Howes
Murder at Manor House. L. Gorell
Murder at Manson's. R. E. Young
Murder at Marble Arch. Gavin Holt
Murder at Markenden Court. H. H. Stanners
Murder at Marks Caris. W. M. Duncan
Murder at Marlington. T. A. Plummer
Murder at Marston Manor. R. Forsythe
Murder at Mavering. L. Gorell
Murder at Melton Peveril. C. Ashton
Murder at Mid-Day. A. Hocking
Murder at Midnight. L. Allan
Murder at Midnight. J. Blackburn
Murder at Midnight. M. Cumberland
Murder at Midnight. H. Desmond
Murder at Midnight. C. F. Gregg
Murder at Midnight. P. Hoar
Murder at Midnight. R. Sale
Murder at Midnight. R. A. J. Walling
Murder at Midyears. Marion Mainwaring
Murder at Mocking House. W. C. Brown
Murder at Monk's Barn. C. Waye
Murder at Montauk. D. Wheelock
Murder at Monte Carlo. E. P. Oppenheim
Murder at Moreby. A. Cartlidge
Murder at Morning Prayers. Hilary Landon
Murder at Mornington. C. Carnac
Murder at Mulberry Cottage. G. Norsworthy
Murder at Night. J. Corbett
Murder at Nightfall. E. Sherry
Murder at No. 3. L. G. Horsefield
Murder at Our House. C. J. Daly
Murder at Out-Patients. A. W. Eyles
Murder at Pirate's Head. I. Waitt
Murder at Plenders. F. Everton
Murder at Pringlehurst. J. Corbett
Murder at Prospect, Kentucky. A. W. Lyons
Murder at Puck's Cottage. M. Alan
Murder at Quay Cottage. S. Amberley
Murder at Radio City. N. Morland
Murder at Red Grange. J. Corbett
Murder at Red Pass. The Aresbys
Murder at St. Dennis. M. A. Hubbard
Murder at School. G. Trevor
Murder at Scotland Yard. G. Dilnot
Murder at Sea. R. Connell
Murder at Shirttail Flats. K. Franklin
Murder at Stone House. E. Howie
Murder at Sundown. James Preston
Murder at Sunset Gables. D. Heffernan

Murder at Sunset Rock. D. P. Neeley
Murder at Tall Tip. E. G. Gless
Murder at 10,000 Feet. P. Conde
Murder at the ABA. I. Asimov
Murder at the Admiralty. Eric Bennett
Murder at the Angel. H. McCutcheon
Murder at the Arab Stud. S. Miles
Murder at the Bar. T. Stevenson
Murder at the Black Crook. C. H. Matschat
Murder at the "Black Swan." N. Walthew
Murder at the Blue Garter. C. Wheatley
Murder at the Boarding House. A. S. Bradshaw
Murder at the Bookstall. H. Holt
Murder at the Bugginses. M. Constanduros
Murder at the Casino. C. Wells
Murder at the Class Reunion. C. Andrews
Murder at the Club. L. Allan
Murder at the Coffee Stall. Ben Rogers
Murder at the College. V. L. Whitechurch
Murder at the Cookout. G. De Fraga
Murder at the DeSoto. J. Rand
Murder at the Dome. G. Burgess
Murder at the Eclipse. John Alexander
Murder at the Eisteddfod. J. E. Williams
Murder at the Festival. V. Lucas
Murder at the Flea Club. M. Head
Murder at the Flood. M. E. Allan
Murder at the Flower Show. M. Beckett
Murder at the Frankfurt Book Fair. H. Monteilhet
Murder at the Gallop. A. Christie
Murder at the Hunting Club. M. Plum
Murder at the Inn. L. Brock
Murder at the Inn. R. Goyne
Murder at the Kentucky Derby. C. Parmer
Murder at the Keyhole. R. A. J. Walling
Murder at the Mardi Gras. E. M. Stone
Murder at the Margin. M. Jevons
Murder at the Met. F. G. Jarvis
Murder at the Microphone. D. Hogg
Murder at the "Mike". Margaret Douglas
Murder at the Mike. C. Saxby
Murder at the Ministry. A. A. Thomson
Murder at the Miramar. E. Snell
Murder at the Moorings. M. Burton
Murder at the Motel. V. Gunn
Murder at the Motor Show. J. Rhode
Murder at the Movies. M. Hervey
Murder at the Munition Works. G. D. H. Cole
Murder at the New York's World Fair. Freeman Dana
Murder at the Nook. A. Fielding
Murder at the Old Stone House. C. M. Russell
Murder at the Open. A. MacVicar
Murder at the Pageant. V. L. Whitechurch
Murder at the Palace. J. Corbett
Murder at the Party. H. Willett
Murder at the Piano. G. Bagby
Murder at the Play. J. Corrie
Murder at the Polls. M. Propper
Murder at the Red Cockatoo. A. Parsons
Murder at the Savoy. M. Sjowall
Murder at the Schoolhouse. A. B. Cunningham
Murder at the "Signal". M. Byrne
Murder at the Stadium. A. Parsons
Murder at the U.N. W. Perry
Murder at the Varsity. F. L. Cary
Murder at the Varsity. Q. Patrick
Murder at the Vicarage. M. Charles
Murder at the Vicarage. A. Christie
Murder at the Wedding. F. Grierson
Murder at the Wedding. David Martin
Murder at the White Tulip. D. Cole
Murder at the Wishing Well. A. Wood
Murder at the Women's City Club. Q. Patrick
Murder at the World's Fair. M. Plum
Murder at the Yard! J. G. Brandon
Murder at 300 to 1. J. D. O'Hanlon
Murder at 28:10. N. Gayle
Murder at Vista Point? N. Fenton
Murder at Willow Run. Michelle Collins
Murder at Wrides Park. J. S. Fletcher
Murder Backstairs. Anne Austin
Murder Bait. D. Yarnell
Murder Beacon. L. P. Greene
Murder Beat. R. Drennen
Murder Beat. A. Lenton
Murder Before Breakfast. L. G. Offord
Murder Before Dinner. C. Franklin
Murder Before Marriage. M. Neville
Murder Before Midnight. A. B. Cunningham
Murder Before Tuesday. Elaine Hamilton
Murder Began Yesterday. L. Johnson
Murder Begets Murder. J. Corbett
Murder Begets Murder. M. G. Hugi
Murder Begets Murder. R. Jeffries
Murder Begins at Home. D. Ames
Murder Behind Closed Doors. P. Lore
Murder Behind the Mask. Adrian Dale
Murder Behind the Mike. R. L. Goldman
Murder Being Once Done. R. Rendell
Murder Belongs to Me! Roderic Wilkinson
Murder Below Wall Street. R. Delancey
Murder Beneath the Trees. C. Coram
Murder Besieged. D. Whitelaw
Murder Between Dark and Dark. Max Long

Title Index

Murder Between Drinks. A. Gibbs
Murder Beyond the Pale. M. Neville
Murder Bicarb. D. Van Deusen
Murder, Bless It! N. Spain
Murder Blues. B. Edwards
Murder Bound. Poul Anderson
Murder Breaks Trail. E. M. Boyd
Murder Breeds Murder. A. Willsdon
Murder Brewing. A. W. Eyles
Murder Business. P. C. Herring
Murder But Gently. F. Duncan
Murder—But Natch. M. Hagen
Murder Buttoned Up. P. A. Holmes
Murder by a Maniac. M. Richmond
Murder by Accident. L. Mason
Murder by Air. W. E. Johns
Murder by an Aristocrat. M. G. Eberhart
Murder—by an Idiot. T. A. Plummer
Murder by Appointment. E. Browne
Murder by Appointment. J. Paul
Murder by Arrangement. W. G. Beyer
Murder by Bamboo. D. Sabre
Murder by Bequest. R. Foley
Murder by Burial. S. Casson
Murder by Chance. P. Drax
Murder by Contract. Griff
Murder by Dart. B. Tempest
Murder by Death. H. Keating
Murder by Decree. R. Weverka
Murder by Degrees. J. B. Fearnley
Murder by Degrees. A. Pearson
Murder by Design. R. Simons
Murder by Experiment. L. A. Knight
Murder by Experts. Anthony Gilbert
Murder by Formula. J. H. Wallis
Murder by Gemini. R. Gallagher
Murder by Inches. S. Hopkins
Murder by Inspiration. E. H. Bierstadt
Murder by Installment. M. Hervey
Murder by Invitation. R. Hull
Murder by Invitation. A. C. MacLean
Murder by Jury. R. B. Sanborn
Murder by Latitude. R. King
Murder by Legacy. W. A. Sweeney
Murder by Magic. J. Creasey
Murder by Magic. M. J. Freeman
Murder by Magic. W. B. Gibson
Murder by Magic. M. Grant
Murder by Magic. A. R. Long
Murder by Mail. F. McGrew
Murder by Marriage. R. G. Dean
Murder by Matchlight. E. C. R. Lorac
Murder by Mathematics. H. Hawton
Murder by Microphone. J. Reeves
Murder by Miss-Demeanour. Carter Brown
Murder by Mistake. P. Urquhart
Murder by Moonlight. M. Grant
Murder by Moonlight. D. Reid
Murder by Multiplication. M. Durham
Murder by Nail. J. Farnol
Murder by Neglect. Elizabeth Jenkins
Murder by Night. J. L. Rickard
Murder by Numbers. J. Phelan
Murder—by Persons Unknown. J. Rowland
Murder by Precedent. R. Petrie
Murder by Prescription. J. Stagge
Murder by Proxy. B. Boyer
Murder by Proxy. H. Carmichael
Murder by Proxy. P. Drax
Murder by Proxy. B. Halliday
Murder by Proxy. Colver Harris
Murder by Proxy. A. Morice
Murder by Proxy. H. Nielsen
Murder by Proxy. J. Spruill
Murder by Proxy. Richard Williams
Murder by Reflection. H. F. Heard
Murder by Request. B. Nichols
Murder by Schedule. J. Hinckley
Murder by Scripture. A. R. Long
Murder by Stealth. J. W. Booth
Murder by Suggestion. E. Acheson
Murder by Telecopter. D. T. Hughes
Murder by Telephone. B. Herbert
Murder by the Arch. H. W. Higginson
Murder by the Book. H. Arre
Murder by the Book. L. Hays
Murder by the Book. F. Lockridge
Murder by the Book. N. Schier
Murder by the Book. R. Stout
Murder by the Clock. R. King
Murder by the Day. V. P. Johns
Murder by the Dozen. H. Wiley
Murder by the Lake. C. Coram
Murder by the Law. P. McGuire
Murder by the Mile. M. Russell
Murder by the Minute. A. Wood
Murder by the Pack. C. G. Hodges
Murder by the Way. M. Halliday
Murder by the Yard. M. T. Yates
Murder by Treason. A. R. Long
Murder by Twenty-Five. C. Robbins
Murder by Warrant. E. T. Collis
Murder by Wash of Light. G. De Fraga
Murder C.O.D. Donald Ross
Murder Calling. D. Whitelaw
Murder Calling "50". G. Bagby
Murder Calls Dr. Hailey. A. Wynne
Murder Calls the Tune. W. M. Duncan
Murder Calls the Tune. R. Verron
Murder Came Late. J. York
Murder Came Tumbling. Martin Brett
Murder Can Be Fun. F. Brown

Murder Can Be Such Fun! L. Beresford
Murder Cancels All Debts. M. V. Heberden
Murder Can't Stop. W. T. Ballard
Murder Can't Wait. R. Lockridge
Murder Can't Wait. M. L. Stokes
Murder Caravan. T. T. Flynn
Murder Case Number 33. L. Cornell
Murder Cave. H. Hawton
Murder Challenges Valcour. R. King
Murder Charge. Wade Miller
Murder Chase. E. Elton
Murder Cheats the Bride. Anthony Gilbert
Murder Children. J. Ball
Murder, Chop Chop. James Norman
Murder City. O. M. Hall
Murder City. A. Lenton
Murder Clear, Track Fast. J. Philips
Murder Club. Howel Evans
Murder Column. C. Franklin
Murder Comes Home. M. Halliday
Murder Comes at Night. I. Oellrichs
Murder Comes Back. H. Ashbrook
Murder Comes Calling. Malcolm Douglas
Murder Comes Calling! D. Reid
Murder Comes First. F. Lockridge
Murder Comes High. H. L. Nelson
Murder Comes Home. M. Chappell
Murder Comes Home. N. Child
Murder Comes Home. Anthony Gilbert
Murder Comes in Threes. M. Sprague
Murder Comes Smiling. G. Brandon
Murder Comes to Dinner. Robert Fleming
Murder Comes to Eden. L. Ford
Murder Comes to Rothesay. J. Cassells
Murder Could Not Kill. G. Baxter
Murder, Country Style. M. F. Ford
Murder Cries Out. A. Hocking
Murder Cruise. M. Keyes
Murder Cum Laude. J. Y. Dane
Murder Curve. A. B. Ross
Murder Day by Day. I. S. Cobb
Murder Deferred. S. Ready
Murder Defies the Roman Emperor. C. E. Gray
Murder Delayed. D. Greenwood
Murder DeLuxe. R. King
Murder Disqualifies. Alan Graham
Murder Does Light Housekeeping. M. Bardon
Murder Doesn't Always Out. F. C. Davis
Murder Doll. M. K. Ozaki
Murder Doll. R. O. Saber
Murder, Double Murder. Neill Graham
Murder Down Below. J. Stagg
Murder Down South. L. Ford
Murder Down Under. A. W. Upfield
Murder Draws a Line. W. A. Barber
Murder Each Way. J. Brown
Murder En Route. B. Flynn
Murder Ends the Song. A. Meyers
Murder Enters the Picture. W. A. Barber
Murder Every Monday. P. Branch
Murder Expert. R. P. Koehler
Murder Fantastical. P. Moyes
Murder First Class. R. Ellis
Murder First Class. R. Simons
Murder—First Edition. T. Garrett
Murder Flies the Atlantic. S. H. Page
Murder Flight. K. Hemingway
Murder Follows Desmond Shannon. M. V. Heberden
Murder for a Hollow Shell. A. L. Albert
Murder for a Million. J. G. Brandon
Murder for a Million. C. B. Kelland
Murder for a Million. Roy Vickers
Murder for a Wanton. W. Chambers
Murder for Art's Sake. R. Lockridge
Murder for Breakfast. P. Hunt
Murder for Cash. J. Ronald
Murder for Charity. O. Dudley
Murder for Charity. P. Ponder
Murder for Charity. G. West
Murder for Christmas. A. Christie
Murder for Christmas. F. Duncan
Murder for Christmas. E. Howie
Murder for Empire. K. M. Knight
Murder for Fun. R. Savage
Murder for Hannah. D. V. Babcock
Murder for Her Birthday. G. Cobden
Murder for His Money. G. Cobden
Murder for Love. D. E. Boocock
Murder for Love. S. Salt
Murder for Madame. Adam Knight
Murder for Millions. N. Rutledge
Murder for Missemily. J. F. Straker
Murder for Money. Jay Bennett
Murder for Money. H. Liggett
Murder for Real. M. Bardon
Murder for Sale. M. Bardsley
Murder for Sale. N. W. Firth
Murder for Sale. S. Horler
Murder for Tea. E. Howie
Murder for the Asking. G. H. Coxe
Murder for the Bride. J. D. MacDonald
Murder for the Bride. J. Reach
Murder for the Holidays. H. Rigsby
Murder for the Million. R. Chapman
Murder for the Millions. H. Kane
Murder for Treasure. D. Williams
Murder for Two. G. H. Coxe
Murder for Two. N. MacKenzie
Murder for Two Pins. R. Trevor

Murder for What? K. Steel
Murder Forestalled. P. Chester
Murder, Four Miles High. R. A. Braun
Murder from Beyond. R. Francis Foster
Murder from Heaven. P. Palmer
Murder from the East. C. J. Daly
Murder from the Grave. W. Levinrew
Murder from the Grave. Eric Wood
Murder from the Mind. P. Laing
Murder from Three Angles. V. Loder
Murder from Three Angles. J. R. Warren
Murder Game. R. Batchelor
Murder Game. C. Cox
Murder Game. J. S. Strange
Murder Games. L. Davidson
Murder Gang. Roland Daniel
Murder Germ. A. O. Pollard
Murder Gets Around. R. S. Bowen
Murder Gives a Lovely Light. J. S. Strange
Murder-Go-Round. J. Christopher
Murder-Go-Round. C. P. Donnel
Murder Goes Astray. M. V. Heberden
Murder Goes Fishing. T. Brace
Murder Goes Free. Roland Daniel
Murder Goes in a Trailer. T. Brace
Murder Goes Nap. R. Dolphin
Murder Goes Rolling Along. H. F. S. Moore
Murder Goes South. A. R. Long
Murder Goes to Bank Night. W. C. Clark
Murder Goes to College. K. Steel
Murder Goes to Press. Cicely Cairns
Murder Goes to Press. N. Loomis
Murder Goes to School. H. Farrar
Murder Goes to School. R. Savage
Murder Goes to Sea. A. R. Bosworth
Murder Goes to the Dogs. T. Brace
Murder Goes to the World's Fair. T. Brace
Murder Goes West. L. C. Douthwaite
Murder Gone Mad. G. Bellairs
Murder Gone Mad. P. MacDonald
Murder Gone Mad. S. Stone
Murder Gone Minoan. C. B. Clason
Murder Gone to Earth. J. Stagge
Murder Greets Jean Holton. K. M. Knight
Murder Grows Roots. S. Taylor
Murder Half Baked. G. Bagby
Murder Happens. A. Ridley
Murder Has a Motive. F. Duncan
Murder Has an Echo. J. Notley
Murder Has Been Arranged. R. Trevor
Murder Has Been Arranged. Emlyn Williams
Murder Has Been Done. Neill Graham
Murder Has Its Points. F. Lockridge
Murder Has Many Faces. W. Grew
Murder Has No Friends. Bradshaw Jones
Murder Has No Tongue. Anthony Gilbert
Murder Has Three Dimensions. A. Spiller
Murder Has Your Number. H. Garner
Murder Hath Charms. M. Durham
Murder Helps. I. Oellrichs
Murder Hide-and-Seek. A. O. Pollard
Murder Hole Road. A. Douglas
Murder House. T. A. Plummer
Murder Humane. H. Kemp
Murder Hunt. P. Stadley
Murder in a Barge. P. Street
Murder in a Blue Room. M. Neville
Murder in a Church. A. Wynne
Murder in a Dark Room. Neill Graham
Murder in a Haystack. D. Aldis
Murder in a Hurry. F. Lockridge
Murder in a Library. C. J. Dutton
Murder in a Lighter Vein. M. M. Raison
Murder in a Madhouse. C. B. Molyneaux
Murder in a Maze. M. Alan
Murder in a Muffler. G. Davison
Murder in a Nunnery. E. Lavery
Murder in a Nunnery. E. Shepherd
Murder in a Road Gang. M. Cresswell
Murder in a Shell. M. Beam
Murder in a Walled Town. K. Woods
Murder in Absence. M. Burton
Murder in Amber. Colver Harris
Murder in Angel Yard. F. Vivian
Murder in Any Degree. O. Johnson
Murder in Any Language. K. Roos
Murder in Baracoa. P. E. Walsh
Murder in Bavaria. C. Rushton
Murder in Beacon Street. W. Martyn
Murder in Berkeley Square. R. Dark
Murder in Berlin. Harold Trembath
Murder in Bermuda. W. Sharp
Murder in Bethnel Square. S. Fowler
Murder in Black. Mark Cross
Murder in Black. F. Grierson
Murder in Black and White. David Alexander
Murder in Black and White. E. Elder
Murder in Black Letter. Poul Anderson
Murder in Blue. C. Witting
Murder in Blue Street. F. Crane
Murder in Bostall. P. McGuire
Murder in Brass. L. Padgett
Murder in Brief. M. Trask
Murder in Bright Red. F. Crane
Murder in Broad Daylight. G. D. H. Cole
Murder in Camera. W. A. Ballinger
Murder in Canton. R. Van Gulik
Murder in Cardigan Square. N. MacKenzie

Murder in Chelsea. E. C. R. Lorac
Murder in Church. Babette Hughes
Murder in College. J. Y. Dane
Murder in Company. P. King
Murder in Crown Passage. M. Burton
Murder in Dawson City. Roland Daniel
Murder in Devil's Hollow. L. N. Morgan
Murder in Disguise. C. Kingston
Murder in Duplicate. P. Conway
Murder in Duplicate. H. L. Victor
Murder in Earl's Court. Neil Gordon
Murder in False Face. G. Childerness
Murder in False-Face. R. Lockridge
Murder in Fancy Dress. I. H. Irwin
Murder in Fancy Dress. L. Mantell
Murder in Fiji. J. W. Vandercook
Murder in Five Columns. F. Diamond
Murder in Flat 14. A. G. E. Cromwell
Murder in Focus. D. Halliday
Murder in Four Degrees. J. S. Fletcher
Murder in Four Parts. G. D. H. Cole
Murder in Full Flight. M. Magill
Murder in Full View. J. D. Forbes
Murder in G-Sharp. K. Steel
Murder in Gay Ladies. J. Ronald
Murder in Haiti. J. W. Vandercook
Murder in Haste. E. P. Fenwick
Murder in Haste. H. Gardiner
Murder in Haste. B. Halliday
Murder in Haste. P. McGuire
Murder in Haste. Garnett Weston
Murder in Havana. G. H. Coxe
Murder in Hawthorn. J. Armour
Murder in Her Big Blue Eyes. J. Long
Murder in High Place. R. B. Dominic
Murder in Hollywood. W. Braun
Murder in Hollywood. C. Gibbons
Murder in Hospital. Josephine Bell
Murder in Hospital. A. W. Eyles
Murder in Jackson Hole. Maude Parker
Murder in Las Vegas. J. Waer
Murder in Lima. R. A. Levey
Murder in Majorca. M. Bryan
Murder in Majorca. P. Tabori
Murder in Make-Up. C. Ashton
Murder in Makeup. Lorenz Heller
Murder in Mallorca. W. Angus
Murder in Man. F. Duncan
Murder in Manchuria. G. H. Teed
Murder in Manhattan. A. Procter
Murder in Manhattan. J. Roeburt
Murder in Manuscript. R. Strevens
Murder in Manuscript. G. Verner
Murder in Marble. J. Philips
Murder in Marrakech. C. Leader
Murder in Married Life. A. Morice
Murder in Marseilles. C. Lefevre
Murder in Maryland. L. Ford
Murder in Mayfair. J. G. Brandon
Murder in Mayfair. F. Goldsmith
Murder in Mayfair. R. J. Lawrence
Murder in Mayfair. G. West
Murder in Maytime. G. Brandon
Murder in Medora Mansions. J. S. Fletcher
Murder in Melancholy. W. Keenan
Murder in Melbourne. Dulcie Gray
Murder in Mesopotamia. A. Christie
Murder in Mid-Air. D. Dayle
Murder in Mid-Atlantic. E. Antill
Murder in Midsummer. M. M. Atwater
Murder in Millenium VI. C. Gray
Murder in Mimicry. A. Morice
Murder in Mind. Dulcie Gray
Murder in Mind. J. A. Howard
Murder in Miniature. E. Mack
Murder in Miniatures. S. Merwin Jr.
Murder in Mink. R. G. Dean
Murder in Mink. B. Iles
Murder in Mocking Valley. W. Crowell
Murder in Monaco. J. Flagg
Murder in Montana. Muriel Bradley
Murder in Montmartre. N. Vexin
Murder in Montparnasse. J. Bude
Murder in Mortimer Square. F. Grierson
Murder in Moscow. A. Garve
Murder in Motley. I. D'Abbes
Murder in Motley. D. Whitelaw
Murder in Mount Holly. P. Theroux
Murder in Mozambique. David Wilson
Murder in New Guinea. J. W. Vandercook
Murder in Newport. G. B. Lambert
Murder in November. M. Alan
Murder in Ocean Drive. Roland Daniel
Murder in Odd Sizes. H. J. Hultman
Murder in Oil. J. Avrach
Murder in Oils. J. N. Chance
Murder in Okefenokee. C. H. Matschat
Murder in Outline. A. Morice
Murder in Paradise. R. Dana
Murder in Paradise. G. Joseph
Murder in Paradise. J. Laffin
Murder in Paradise. J. Shill
Murder in Paris. Alice Campbell
Murder in Pastiche. Marion Mainwaring
Murder in Peking. V. Starrett
Murder in Piccadilly. Roland Daniel
Murder in Piccadilly. C. Kingston
Murder in Pimlico. J. G. Brandon
Murder in Plain Sight. G. Brown
Murder in Port Afrique. B. V. Dryer
Murder in Print. R. Sonin

Murder in Public. J. Crozier
Murder in Queer Street. C. Ryland
Murder in Red. F. Castle
Murder in Retrospect. A. Christie
Murder in Reverse. A. Webb
Murder in Rockwater. M. Neville
Murder in Romney Marsh. E. Jepson
Murder in Room 700. M. H. Bradley
Murder in Room 13. Albert Conroy
Murder in Rosemary Lane. H. M. Keynes
Murder in St. John's Wood. E. C. R. Lorac
Murder in Season. O. R. Cohen
Murder in Shinbone Alley. H. Reilly
Murder in Silence. G. Selmark
Murder in Silk. R. Trevor
Murder in Soho. J. G. Brandon
Murder in Space. D. V. Reed
Murder in Stained Glass. M. Armstrong
Murder in Store. R. Rooke
Murder in Strange Houses. R. Peckham
Murder in Style. E. L. Fetta
Murder in Style. D. Hoddinott
Murder in Style. R. Stout
Murder in Suffolk. A. Fielding
Murder in Sussex. G. Norsworthy
Murder in Switzerland. E. Snell
Murder in Sydney. L. Mann
Murder in Texas. A. E. Lingo
Murder in the Act. E. St. Clair
Murder in the Air. C. Brisbane
Murder in the Air. Mark Cross
Murder in the Air. J. Hunter
Murder in the Air. A. O. Pollard
Murder in the Air. D. L. Teilhet
Murder in the Atlantic. Carter Dickson
Murder in the Ballroom. K. Hewitt
Murder in the Bank. R. Essex
Murder in the Basement. A. Berkeley
Murder in the Bath. F. Didelot
Murder in the Bazaar. D. Lynn
Murder in the Bedroom. G. Leroux
Murder in the Blackout. J. R. Warren
Murder in the Bookshop. C. Wells
Murder in the Borough Library. J. Austwick
Murder in the Brownstone House. W. Collison
Murder in the Bud. P. Bottome
Murder in the Calais Coach. A. Christie
Murder in the Camp. M. Stand
Murder in the Cellar. L. Eppley
Murder in the Clinic. Edmond Hamilton
Murder in the Coalhole. M. Burton
Murder in the Cockpit. P. Conde
Murder in the Consulting Room. M. S. Michel
Murder in the Dark. C. J. Dutton
Murder in the Delhi Mail. K. P. Bahadur
Murder in the Dentist Chair. M. Thynne
Murder in the Embassy. Diplomat
Murder in the Family. M. H. Bradley
Murder in the Family. D. Emerson
Murder in the Family. M. Leinster
Murder in the Family. J. Ronald
Murder in the Family. L. Stephan
Murder in the Family. J. York
Murder in the Family Way. Carter Brown
Murder in the Ferris-Wheel. G. George
Murder in the Fifth Column. R. Trevor
Murder in the Fine Arts. C. Nicolai
Murder in the First Person. S. Adams
Murder in the Flagship. P. W. Taylor
Murder in the Fog. H. L. Gates
Murder in the Fog. Elaine Hamilton
Murder in the Fog. P. Thorne
Murder in the Fog. R. Worth
Murder in the French Room. H. J. Hultman
Murder in the Game Reserve. P. W. Taylor
Murder in the Garden. F. Grierson
Murder in the Gilded Cage. S. Spewack
Murder in the Green Sedan. R. P. Koehler
Murder in the Gunroom. H. B. Piper
Murder in the Harem Club. Carter Brown
Murder in the Haunted Sentry-Box. N. Gayle
Murder in the Hellfire Club. D. Zochert
Murder in the Highlands. P. Manton
Murder in the Home Guard. R. Adam
Murder in the Hotel. H. P. Hanshew
Murder in the House of Commons. M. A. Hamilton
Murder in the House with the Blue Eyes. J. N. Darby
Murder in the Hurricane. E. L. Adams
Murder in the Key Club. Carter Brown
Murder in the King's Road. J. Boyd
Murder in the Kitchen. F. Halliday
Murder in the Laboratory. K. Brooks
Murder in the Laboratory. T. L. Davidson
Murder in the Lady Chapel. S. Toye
Murder in the Madhouse. Jonathan Latimer
Murder in the Making. H. Petersen
Murder in the Maze. J. J. Connington
Murder in the Melody. N. Berrow
Murder in the Mews. A. Christie
Murder in the Mews. H. Reilly
Murder in the Mill-Race. E. C. R. Lorac
Murder in the Mills. H. S. Keeler
Murder in the Mind. K. T. Knoblock
Murder in the Mirror. W. W. Masters
Murder in the Mirror. L. Thayer

Murder in the Mist. W. Chambers
Murder in the Mist. H. L. Gates
Murder in the Mist. Z. Popkin
Murder in the Mobile Unit. Sutherland Scott
Murder in the Moonlight. F. Brown
Murder in the Moor. T. Kindon
Murder in the Morning. G. Pahlow
Murder in the Morning. Colin Robertson
Murder in the Morning. A. Wynne
Murder in the Museum. F. W. Gumley
Murder in the Museum. E. Heath
Murder in the Museum. J. Rowland
Murder in the Navy. R. Marsten
Murder in the News Room. H. C. Beck
Murder in the Newspaper Guild. H. C. Beck
Murder in the Night. A. Gask
Murder in the North-West. C. W. Sanders
Murder in the O.P.M. L. Ford
Murder in the Old Jail. Michael Henry
Murder in the Opera House. Q. Mario
Murder in the Outlands. J. B. Hendryx
Murder in the Pallant. J. S. Fletcher
Murder in the Park. C. F. Gregg
Murder in the Pool. Mark Cross
Murder in the Procession. L. Cargill
Murder in the Radio Department. A. Eichler
Murder in the Rain. W. Collison
Murder in the Rain Forest. N. MacKenzie
Murder in the Raw. B. Fischer
Murder in the Raw. W. C. Gault
Murder in the Raw. B. Grant
Murder in the Rough. L. Allen
Murder in the Round. D. Halliday
Murder in the Rue Royale. M. Harrison
Murder in the Ruins. N. A. Temple-Ellis
Murder in the Sacristy. D. A. Lord
Murder in the Sanctuary. L. Grex
Murder in the Senate. G. Coffin
Murder in the Square. Johnston Smith
Murder in the Squire's Pew. J. S. Fletcher
Murder in the Stacks. M. Boyd
Murder in the Stars. M. Halliday
Murder in the Stars. J. Stagge
Murder in the State Department. Diplomat
Murder in the Stork Club. V. Caspary
Murder in the Stratosphere. G. Eldredge
Murder in the Stratosphere. J. Laurence
Murder in the Submarine Zone. Carter Dickson
Murder in the Suez Canal. P. W. Taylor
Murder in the Sun. H. Footner
Murder in the Sun. J. T. Story
Murder in the Surgery. J. G. Edwards
Murder in the Surgery. T. A. Plummer
Murder in the Taj Mahal. P. W. Taylor
Murder in the Telephone Exchange. J. Wright
Murder in the Temple. J. Brooke
Murder in the Theatre. E. M. McDuff
Murder in the Tomb. L. A. Osgood
Murder in the Top Drawer. E. G. Cousins
Murder in the Town. M. Richert
Murder in the Tropic Night. F. Arthur
Murder in the Vestry. M. Crossley
Murder in the Village. T. A. Plummer
Murder in the Village. J. Skinner
Murder in the WPA. Alexander Williams
Murder in the Walls. R. M. Stern
Murder in the White House. M. Truman
Murder in the Willett Family. R. King
Murder in the Wind. J. D. MacDonald
Murder in the Wind. G. Ogan
Murder in the Wind. V. Roser
Murder in the Zoo. E. Balneaves
Murder in the Zoo. Babette Hughes
Murder in Thin Air. A. Wynne
Murder in Three Acts. A. Christie
Murder in Three Moves. R. Watters
Murder in Time. L. Day
Murder in Time. E. Ferrars
Murder in Touraine. B. E. Wallace
Murder in Tow. C. Hale
Murder in Transit. W. R. Hutton
Murder in Trinidad. J. W. Vandercook
Murder in Triplicate. H. Austin
Murder in Triplicate. L. Marshall
Murder in 25 Words or Less. Irma Walker
Murder in Two Flats. Roy Vickers
Murder in Vegas. W. R. Cox
Murder in Venice. Anne-Mariel
Murder in Venice. T. Sterling
Murder in Vienna. E. C. R. Lorac
Murder in Vision. K. Bird
Murder in Waiting. M. G. Eberhart
Murder in Waiting. R. Murphy
Murder in Wardour Street. N. Morland
Murder in Wax. P. Baron
Murder in White Pit. J. H. Barrington
Murder in Whitehall. T. Hyde
Murder in Windy Coppice. T. A. Plummer
Murder in Wonderland. G. Bagby
Murder in Y Division. J. G. Brandon
Murder in Your Home. E. Cobb
Murder Incidental. M. Cronin
Murder Incidental. K. Trask
Murder Included. J. Cannan
Murder Incognito. M. Dare
Murder Inc. J. Eastwood

Title Index

Murder Indicated. R. Verron
Murder Inherited. G. Cobden
Murder Insoluble. E. Wilmot
Murder Intended. F. Beeding
Murder Is a Best Seller. M. Judd
Murder Is a Collector's Item. E. Dean
Murder Is a Furtive Thing. R. Boyd
Murder Is a Gamble. G. M. Barnes
Murder Is a Gentle Kiss. A. Barron
Murder Is a Habit. B. Halliday
Murder Is a House Guest. I. Cabot
Murder Is a Kill-Joy. E. S. Holding
Murder Is a Maiden's Handicap. M. Brody
Murder is a Package Deal. Carter Brown
Murder Is a Serious Business. E. Dean
Murder Is a Shady Business. A. Spiller
Murder Is a Witch. J. Bingham
Murder Is Absurd. P. McGerr
Murder Is an Art. A. B. Correll
Murder Is an Art. M. Innes
Murder Is an Evil Business. M. Bramhall
Murder Is Announced. A. Christie
Murder Is Announced. L. Darbon
Murder Is Catching. M. Ainsworth
Murder Is Cheap. Anthony Gilbert
Murder Is Contagious. M. Bramhall
Murder Is Dangerous. S. Levinson
Murder Is Easy. A. Christie
Murder Is Easy! A. Livingston
Murder Is for Keeps. Peter Chambers
Murder Is Forgetful. W. Bogart
Murder Is Grim. S. Rogers
Murder Is Incidental. D. Rutherford
Murder Is Infectuous. Sutherland Scott
Murder Is Insane. G. M. Barnes
Murder Is Justified. H. Desmond
Murder Is Lonely. U. Rothwell
Murder Is Mutuel. J. Dolph
Murder Is My Business. B. Halliday
Murder Is My Business. J. Reach
Murder Is My Business. V. Siller
Murder Is My Dish. S. Marlowe
Murder Is My Mistress. Carter Brown
Murder Is My Mistress. H. Whittington
Murder Is My Racket. R. H. Leitfred
Murder Is My Shadow. C. Nash
Murder Is My Weakness. Neill Graham
Murder Is No Accident. Jerome Barry
Murder Is Not Enough. B. E. Wallace
Murder Is Not Enough. S. Wells
Murder Is Not Mute. A. Newell
Murder Is Out. L. Thayer
Murder Is Ruby Red. E. Radford
Murder Is Served. F. Lockridge
Murder Is So Easy. W. D. Roberts
Murder Is So Nostalgic! Carter Brown
Murder Is So Simple. S. Horler
Murder Is Staged. A. Tack
Murder Is Suggested. F. Lockridge
Murder Is Suspected. P. Alding
Murder Is Swift. C. Fitzsimmons
Murder Is the Message. Carter Brown
Murder Is the Pay-Off. L. Ford
Murder Is the Reason. L. Marshall
Murder Is Where You Find It. R. P. Hansen
Murder Is Where You Find It. A. Rutter
Murder Island. L. Jamieson
Murder Island. W. Martyn
Murder Isn't Cricket. E. Radford
Murder Isn't Cricket. P. Weathers
Murder Isn't Easy. R. Hull
Murder Isn't Funny. J. H. Bond
Murder Isn't Private. J. Garden
Murder Jigsaw. E. Radford
Murder Joins the Chorus. R. Simons
Murder Kick. Wenzell Brown
Murder Knows No Master. S. Miles
Murder Lady. N. Chambers
Murder Lands the Odds. R. Verron
Murder Las Vegas Style. W. T. Ballard
Murder Laughs Last. J. Ford
Murder Lays a Golden Egg. E. T. Hull
Murder Lays the Odds. J. Letherby
Murder League. R. L. Fish
Murder Leaves a Ring. F. G. Stanley
Murder Lies in Waiting. Neill Graham
Murder Lifts the Veil. R. Verron
Murder Limited. C. R. Gull
Murder Limps By. T. A. Plummer
Murder Line. P. Alding
Murder Link. H. T. Johnson
Murder Listens In. E. Daly
Murder, London-Australia. J. Creasey
Murder, London-Miami. J. Creasey
Murder, London-New York. J. Creasey
Murder, London-South Africa. J. Creasey
Murder Looks Back. M. Alan
Murder: Love Story. W. S. Ruben
Murder Loves Company. J. Mersereau
Murder, M.A. A. Kennington
Murder M.D. M. Burton
Murder Machine. P. A. Foxall
Murder Machine. F. Scarpetta
Murder Made Absolute. M. Underwood
Murder Made Easy. R. Goyne
Murder Made Easy. Neill Graham
Murder Made Easy. D. Reid
Murder Madness. M. Leinster
Murder, Maestro, Please. D. Ames
Murder, Maestro, Please. J. Sharkey
Murder Magnified. E. Radford

Murder Makers. J. N. Chance
Murder Makers. J. Rossiter
Murder Makes a Call. F. C. Tickner
Murder Makes a Date. Neill Graham
Murder Makes a Deadline. S. Fuller
Murder Makes a Man. W. T. Walsh
Murder Makes a Marriage. S. Broocks
Murder Makes a Merry Widow. R. G. Dean
Murder Makes a Racket. M. V. Heberden
Murder Makes a Villain. Denis Scott
Murder Makes an Entrance. C. B. Kelland
Murder Makes By-Lines. K. Secrist
Murder Makes Haste. J. Creasey
Murder Makes It Certain. Neill Graham
Murder Makes Its Mark. M. Judd
Murder Makes Me Laugh. J. Jackson
Murder Makes Me Mad. F. Findley
Murder Makes Me Nervous. M. Scherf
Murder Makes Merry. F. W. Irwin
Murder Makes Mistakes. G. Bellairs
Murder Makes Murder. H. Ashbrook
Murder Makes Murder. H. Halliday
Murder Makes the Mare Go. J. Dolph
Murder Makes the News. Neill Graham
Murder Makes the Wheels Go Round. E. Lathen
Murder Makes Us Gay. I. Oellrichs
Murder Man. W. Bogart
Murder Man. W. M. Duncan
Murder Manana. S. Bandolier
Murder Maniac. R. S. L. Harding
Murder Manor. A. Eadie
Murder Manor. P. Manton
Murder Mansion. J. H. Barry
Murder Mansion. Herman Landon
Murder Mansion. O. Snapp
Murder Mansion. J. H. Wallis
Murder Mansion. A. Wilson
Murder Maritime. C. Cranston
Murder Market. T. C. H. Jacobs
Murder Market. C. Rushton
Murder Mars the Tour. M. Fitt
Murder Mask. G. Begbie
Murder Mask. S. Horler
Murder Mask. J. A. Jordan
Murder Masks Miami. R. King
Murder Masquerade. G. Bellairs
Murder Masquerade. G. Dilnot
Murder Masquerade. I. H. Irwin
Murder Matinee. B. Carson
Murder Matrix. E. J. Fredericks
Murder May Follow. S. Morrow
Murder May Pass Unpunished. F. Everton
Murder Maze. H. Liggett
Murder Me for Nickels. P. Rabe
Murder Me Never. C. Shannon
Murder Medley. H. Hervey
Murder Meets Mephisto. Q. Mario
Murder Melody. K. Robeson
Murder Melody. K. Secrist
Murder Memo to the Commissioner. W. Oursler
Murder: Men Only. B. Cobb
Murder Menagerie. J. Lane
Murder Minus Motive. J. Corbett
Murder Mirage. K. Robeson
Murder Mislaid. M. Cronin
Murder Mission! Al Conroy
Murder Mission. F. W. Irwin
Murder Mistaken. Janet Green
Murder Mistress. R. Colby
Murder Money. Jay Bennett
Murder Money. E. Ronns
Murder Money. R. Wallace
Murder Moon. P. H. Dobbins
Murder Moon. H. Leyford
Murder Most Artistic. W. Gore
Murder Most Black. R. Verron
Murder Most Fair. J. G. Vermandel
Murder Most Familiar. H. Bremner
Murder Most Foul. G. Ashe
Murder Most Foul. K. B. Coxe
Murder Most Foul. H. Hawton
Murder Most Fouled Up. T. Wells
Murder Most Ingenious. K. Chase
Murder Most Intimate. W. H. Baker
Murder Most Monstrous. R. Verron
Murder Most Opportune. R. G. Dean
Murder Moves In. E. Ferrars
Murder Moves On. J. Dall
Murder! Murder! J. Symons
Murder! Murder! L. Vail
Murder, Murder, Little Star. M. Babson
Murder Muscles In. M. Franklin
Murder Must Advertise. D. L. Sayers
Murder Must Wait. J. Creasey
Murder Must Wait. A. W. Upfield
Murder Mutuel. B. McKnight
Murder, My Love. E. Atiyah
Murder, My Sweet. H. Holt
Murder Mystery. G. Thompson
Murder Needs a Face. R. Fenisong
Murder Needs a Name. R. Fenisong
Murder Next Door. M. Alan
Murder Next Door. Jean Marsh
Murder Next Year. B. J. Farmer
Murder—Nine and Out. J. V. Turner
Murder '97. F. Gruber
Murder Noon and Night. K. Roos
Murder Now and Again. J. A. Knipe
Murder Now and Then. H. Brean
Murder Now, Pay Later. F. Bosworth

Murder of a Bad Man. H. Footner
Murder of a Banker. J. S. Fletcher
Murder of a Black Cat. Neill Graham
Murder of a Bookmaker. Roland Daniel
Murder of a Chemist. M. Burton
Murder of a Cop. W. M. Duncan
Murder of a Dead Man. W. H. L. Crauford
Murder of a Dead Man. K. Steel
Murder of a Diplomat. A. O. Pollard
Murder of a Film Star. H. Holt
Murder of a Headmistress. E. Pickering
Murder of a Lady. L. Marshall
Murder of a Lady. A. Wynne
Murder of a Magnate. M. Beckett
Murder of a Man Afraid of Women. A. Abbot
Murder of a Marriage. R. Armstrong
Murder of a Martinet. E. C. R. Lorac
Murder of a Matriarch. H. Austin
Murder of a Midget. M. J. Freeman
Murder of a Missing Man. A. M. Chase
Murder of a Mistress. H. Kuttner
Murder of a Mistress. J. Sherwood
Murder of a Mouse. M. Fitt
Murder of a Musician. "Capstan"
Murder of a Mystery Writer. J. Hawk
Murder of a Mystery Writer. E. Heath
Murder of a Novelist. S. Wood
Murder of a Nymph. M. Neville
Murder of a Painted Lady. Harold Ward
Murder of a Professor. J. Miller
Murder of a Quack. G. Bellairs
Murder of a Redhaired Man. M. Plum
Murder of a Snob. Roy Vickers
Murder of a Startled Lady. A. Abbot
Murder of a Student. P. Malloch
Murder of a Stuffed Shirt. M. V. Heberden
Murder of a Suicide. E. Ferrars
Murder of a Wanton. Dorothea Gray
Murder of a Wife. H. Kuttner
Murder of Alonzo. P. Cheyney
Murder of an Initiate. M. Propper
Murder of an M.P. R. Gore-Browne
Murder of an M.P. B. H. Homersham
Murder of an Old Man. D. Frome
Murder of an Owl. G. Carr
Murder of an Unpopular Man. D. R. Forbes
Murder of Ann Avery. H. Kuttner
Murder of Augustin Dench. E. Jepson
Murder of Bishop Conrad. L. Hebach
Murder of Busy Lizzie. G. Mitchell
Murder of Caroline Bundy. Alice Campbell
Murder of Cecily Thane. H. Ashbrook
Murder of Christine Wilmerding. W. Morton
Murder of Constable Cartwright. A. Blair
Murder of Convenience. R. G. Dean
Murder of Crows. P. Buchanan
Murder of Dave Brandon. T. Lund
Murder of Doctor Grey. T. A. Plummer
Murder of Edwin Drood. P. T. Carden
Murder of Eleanor Pope. H. Kuttner
Murder of Estelle Cantor. C. F. Gregg
Murder of Eve. M. Dalton
Murder of Geraldine Foster. A. Abbot
Murder of Guy Thorpe. Roland Daniel
Murder of Harvey Blake. R. L. Goldman
Murder of Jacob Canansey. P. Capon
Murder of Lalla Lee. H. Burnham
Murder of Lawrence of Arabia. M. Eden
Murder of London Lew. H. S. Keeler
Murder of Love. Dulcie Gray
Murder of Lydia. J. Cowdroy
Murder of Margaret. C. Ryland
Murder of Margot Midnight. P. Herring
Murder of Marion Mason. T. B. Dewey
Murder of Martin Fotherill. E. C. Lester
Murder of Mary Steers. Brian Cooper
Murder of Me. J. F. W. Hannay
Murder of Me. M. S. Michel
Murder of Me. F. A. Symonds
Murder of Miranda. M. Millar
Murder of Miss Betty Sloan. S. Williams
Murder of Mr. Mallabee. Winifred Duke
Murder of Mrs. Davenport. Anthony Gilbert
Murder of Monsieur Fualdes. A. Praviel
Murder of My Aunt. R. Hull
Murder of My Patient. M. G. Eberhart
Murder of My Wife. Reginald Campbell
Murder of No Consequence. R. Verron
Murder of Olympia. M. Neville
Murder of Paul Rougier. V. Sampson
Murder of Quality. J. Le Carre
Murder of Roger Ackroyd. A. Christie
Murder of Santa Klaus. T. La Cour
Murder of Sigurd Sharon. H. Ashbrook
Murder of Sir Edmund Godfrey. J. D. Carr
Murder of Some Importance. B. Graeme
Murder of Steven Kester. H. Ashbrook
Murder of Suzy Pommier. E. Bove
Murder of the Admiral. S. Gould
Murder of the Circus Queen. A. Abbot
Murder of the Clergyman's Mistress. A. Abbot
Murder of the Dainty-Footed Model. F. E. Hewens
Murder of the Fifth Columnist. L. Ford
Murder of the Honest Broker. W. Sharp
Murder of the Lawyer's Clerk. J. S. Fletcher

M

Murder of the Maharajah. H. R. F. Keating
Murder of the Man Next Door. P. Malloch
Murder of the Missing Link. Vercors
Murder of the Night Club Lady. A. Abbot
Murder of the Ninth Baronet. J. S. Fletcher
Murder of the Only Witness. J. S. Fletcher
Murder of the Park Avenue Playgirl. H. Kane
Murder of the Pigboat Skipper. S. Fisher
Murder of the Prime Minister. L. Clark
Murder of the Secret Agent. J. S. Fletcher
Murder of the U.S.A. W. F. Jenkins
Murder of the Well-Beloved. M. Neville
Murder of Three Ghosts. E. Radford
Murder of Whistler's Brother. David Alexander
Murder Off Broadway. L. Falkner
Murder Off Broadway. H. Klinger
Murder Off Key. K. Sproul
Murder Off Miami. D. Wheatley
Murder Off Stage. Monte Barrett
Murder Off Stage. A. Eichler
Murder Off the Record. J. Bingham
Murder on a Bad Trip. June Drummond
Murder on a Monument. E. C. R. Lorac
Murder on a Saturday. Dulcie Gray
Murder on a Shoestring. A. Spiller
Murder on a Tangent. D. M. Disney
Murder on Alternate Tuesdays. T. Davis
Murder on Angler's Island. H. Reilly
Murder on Arrival. G. Batson
Murder on "B" Deck. V. Starrett
Murder on Bag Hill. C. Ryland
Murder on Beacon Hill. G. Brown
Murder on Both Sides. A. Sideman
Murder on Broadway. H. Q. Masur
Murder on Cape Cod. F. Shay
Murder on Center Stage. J. L. Twedt
Murder on Coney Island. Dan Morgan
Murder on Delivery. S. Dean
Murder on Demand. Neill Graham
Murder on Demand. R. Verron
Murder on Display. C. Hale
Murder on Duty. M. Burton
Murder on Every Floor. A. Demarest
Murder on Fifth Avenue. C. Cranston
Murder on Fire. M. Bardsley
Murder on Flight 354. John Laffin
Murder on 47th Street. B. Poynter
Murder on French Leave. A. Morice
Murder on Friday. H. Ashbrook
Murder on Ghost Tree Island. K. S. Daiger
Murder on Halfaday Creek. J. B. Hendryx
Murder on Her Mind. R. Dietrich
Murder on Her Mind. Vechel Howard
Murder on High. Carter Brown
Murder on High Heels. R. Burke
Murder on His Mind. G. Goldsmith
Murder on Holiday. B. Malim
Murder on Honeymoon. Dulcie Gray
Murder-on-Hudson. Jennifer Jones
Murder on Ice. M. Bardsley
Murder on Ice. V. Gunn
Murder on Largo Island. C. Hogarth
Murder on Leave. G. V. Galwey
Murder on Location. L. Thayer
Murder on Manoeuvres. S. C. Mason
Murder on Margin. R. G. Dean
Murder on Mitcham Common. R. Simmat
Murder on Monday. G. Barnett
Murder on Monday. C. Barry
Murder on Monday. C. Bush
Murder on Monday. R. P. Wilmot
Murder on Monday. G. M. Wilson
Murder on Monk's Wood. H. G. Hutchinson
Murder on Mount Capita. L. W. Martin
Murder on My Conscience. E. Radford
Murder on My Hands. C. Franklin
Murder on My Hands. Neill Graham
Murder on My Street. E. Lanham
Murder on Parade. C. Wells
Murder on Paradise Island. R. Forsythe
Murder on Playboy Island. M. Franklin
Murder on Polopel. M. Wright
Murder on Queer Street. Gene Evans
Murder on Route 40. H. J. Hultman
Murder on Russian Hill. L. G. Offord
Murder on Safari. E. Huxley
Murder-on-Sea. R. Harrison
Murder on Shadow Island. Garnett Weston
Murder on Shark Island. J. De Witt
Murder on Show. M. Babson
Murder on Stage. Sutherland Scott
Murder on Stilts. G. Dean
Murder on Sundays. E. Gilzean
Murder-on-Thames. D. Fearon
Murder on the Aphrodite. R. B. Sanborn
Murder on the Beam. J. G. Brandon
Murder on the Blackboard. S. Palmer
Murder on the Bluff. E. Tyler
Murder on the Boat Express. R. Hardinge
Murder on the Brain. A. Heckstall-Smith
Murder on the Brain. E. M. Poate
Murder on the Brampton. G. Camacho
Murder on the Bridge. L. Brock
Murder on the Broads. G. Chester
Murder on the Burrows. E. C. R. Lorac

Murder on the Bus. C. F. Gregg
Murder on the Camp. J. H. Waring
Murder on the Cattle Ranch. C. H. Snow
Murder on the Cliff. C. Ryland
Murder on the Common. C. Ryland
Murder on the Costa Brava. J. Bonett
Murder on the Day of Judgment. V. Rath
Murder on the Downbeat. R. Avery
Murder on the "Duchess." Neill Graham
Murder on the Eighteenth Hole. C. Miron
Mirder on the "Enriqueta." M. Thynne
Murder on the Face of It. E. L. Fetta
Murder on the Fell. H. D. Stacpoole
Murder on the Fourth Floor. J. G. Brandon
Murder on the Frontier. E. Haycox
Murder on the Glass Floor. V. B. Shore
Murder on the High Seas. J. G. Brandon
Murder on the High Seas. R. H. Wilkinson
Murder on the Ice Rink. J. G. Brandon
Murder on the Left Bank. Elliot Paul
Murder on the Line. J. Creasey
Murder on the Line. W. L. Rohde
Murder on the Links. A. Christie
Murder on the List. Neill Graham
Murder on the Loire. T. B. Morris
Murder on the Long Straight. C. Yarborough
Murder on the Marsh. J. Ferguson
Murder on the Marshes. G. Chester
Murder on the Matterhorn. G. Carr
Murder on the Menu. M. Byrne
Murder on the Merry-Go-Round. Josephine Bell
Murder on the Mistral. V. G. Malo
Murder on the Monte. Ross Richards
Murder on the Moon. C. MacDaniel
Murder on the Moor. H. Desmond
Murder on the Moor. W. Edwards
Murder on the Moors. C. Campbell
Murder on the Mountain. C. N. Govan
Murder on the Mountain. A. H. Hill
Murder on the Mountain! F. W. Irwin
Murder on the Mountain. N. Rutledge
Murder on the Night Ferry. B. E. Wallace
Murder on the Nile. A. Christie
Murder on the Nose. G. Bagby
Murder on the Orient Express. A. Christie
Murder on the Pacific. D. K. Patton
Murder on the Pacific. L. Thayer
Murder on the Palisades. W. Levinrew
Murder on the Pier. G. Chester
Murder on the Pike. A. Nonweiler
Murder on the Program. M. M. Mannon
Murder on the Prowl. J. M. Spender
Murder on the Purple Water. F. Crane
Murder on the Ranch. F. C. Ryan
Murder on the River. R. Gar
Murder on the Rocks. R. Dietrich
Murder on the Roof. E. J. Doherty
Murder on the S-23. S. Fisher
Murder on the Salem Road. K. M. Roof
Murder on the Second Floor. C. Bishop
Murder on the Second Floor. F. Vosper
Murder on the Side. D. Keene
Murder on the Sixth Hole. D. Frome
Murder on the Square. D. Frome
Murder on the Stage. J. G. Brandon
Murder on the Stairs. Dulcie Gray
Murder on the Ten-Yard Line. J. S. Strange
Murder on the Terrace. H. Waugh
Murder on the Thirty-First Floor. P. Wahloo
Murder on the Tropic. T. Downing
Murder on the Underground. W. Boggs
Murder on the Veld. R. Hardinge
Murder on the Way! T. Roscoe
Murder on the Wild Side. J. Jacks
Murder on the Wing. A. Eadie
Murder on the Yacht. R. King
Murder on the Yellow Brick Road. S. M. Kaminsky
Murder on Their Minds. G. H. Coxe
Murder on Tour. T. Downing
Murder on Trial. M. Underwood
Murder on Trust. C. Rushton
Murder on Tuesday. Mary Taylor
Murder on Vacation. Ruth MacLeod
Murder on Wall Street. J. B. Ethan
Murder on Wheels. S. Palmer
Murder on Wheels. K. Robeson
Murder on Wheels. L. Warden
Murder on Whispering Sands. V. Gunn
Murder Once Removed. I. G. Neiman
Murder One! M. E. Cohane
Murder One. B. Copper
Murder One. F. Gruber
Murder One. H. Howard
Murder One. E. Lipsky
Murder: One, Two, Three. J. Creasey
Murder or Manslaughter. H. B. Mathers
Murder or Mercy. J. Stagge
Murder or Three. L. Mantell
Murder Out of Class. H. C. Davis
Murder Out of Commission. R. B. Dominic
Murder Out of Court. J. Cowdroy
Murder Out of Court. R. B. Dominic
Murder Out of Mind. K. F. Crossen
Murder Out of School. M. Burton
Murder Out of School. I. T. Ross

Murder Out of Season. L. Gribble
Murder Out of the Past. J. Creasey
Murder Out of Tune. F. L. Cary
Murder Out of Tune. M. Magill
Murder Out of Tune. C. Rushton
Murder Out of Turn. F. Lockridge
Murder over Broadway. F. Malina
Murder over Dorval. D. Montrose
Murder over Karmak. N. MacKenzie
Murder—Paris Fashion. Carter Brown
Murder Party. H. Bordeaux
Murder Party. F. L. Cary
Murder Paves the Way. S. Truss
Murder Pays a Call. Ben Rogers
Murder Pays No Dividends. C. Cookson
Murder Picks the Jury. Harrison Hunt
Murder, Plain and Fancy. Garland Lord
Murder Plan Six. J. Bingham
Murder Plays an Ugly Scene. L. A. G. Strong
Murder Pluperfect. K. Giles
Murder Plus. C. Wells
Murder Point. Coningsby Dawson
Murder Points a Finger. David Alexander
Murder Points East. R. Verron
Murder Pool. E. Heath
Murder Premeditated. P. H. Powell
Murder Proof. J. B. O'Sullivan
Murder—Queen High. B. Wade
Murder R.F.D. H. Petersen
Murder R.F.D. L. Stephan
Murder Recalls Van Kill. S. Bayne
Murder Red-Handed. Richard Grayson
Murder Reflected. J. Caird
Murder Rehearsal. R. East
Murder Rehearsal. B. G. Quin
Murder Remote. J. Caird
Murder Rents a Room. S. E. Mason
Murder, Repeat Murder. A. MacKinnon
Murder Rides a Rocket. F. Diamond
Murder Rides the Campaign Train. The Gordons
Murder Rides the Express. H. Reilly
Murder Rings the Bell. Neill Graham
Murder Rings Twice. H. J. Hultman
Murder Road. G. J. Barrett
Murder Room. J. Sharkey
Murder Room. P. E. Walsh
Murder Round the Corner. N. MacKenzie
Murder Roundabout. R. Lockridge
Murder Run Riot. J. Courage
Murder Run Wild. H. Desmond
Murder Runs a Fever. R. Fenisong
Murder Runs in the Family. H. Footner
Murder Runs Riot. S. Forbes
Murder Runs Wild. N. Morland
Murder Sails at Midnight. M. Babson
Murder Sails at Midnight. K. Gordon
Murder Scholastic. J. Caird
Murder Secretary. W. G. Beyer
Murder Seeks an Agent. Wenzell Brown
Murder Set to Music. H. R. Campbell
Murder Sets the Pace. E. W. Freeman
Murder, She Said. A. Christie
Murder She Says! Reginald Campbell
Murder, She Says! J. Reach
Murder Ship. G. H. Teed
Murder Sits Pretty. Colin Robertson
Murder So Real. A. Bird
Murder!—So What? B. Shannon
Murder Solves a Problem. M. Bramhall
Murder, Somewhere in This City. M. Procter
Murder Sonata. F. Fletcher
Murder Speaks. E. Radford
Murder Special. F. MacIsaac
Murder Specialist. B. Clifton
Murder Spins the Wheel. B. Halliday
Murder Spoils Everything. J. Lane
Murder Squad. E. Meade
Murder Squad. T. Tullett
Murder Stalks a Billion. R. Wallace
Murder Stalks the Bay. E. Messenger
Murder Stalks the Circle. L. Thayer
Murder Stalks the Mayor. R. T. M. Scott
Murder Stalks the Wakely Family. A. Derleth
Murder Starts from Fishguard. H. C. Davis
Murder Steals the Show. L. Hirsch
Murder Steps In. C. M. Russell
Murder Steps Out. C. Reeve
Murder Story. L. Kennedy
Murder Strikes an Atomic Unit. T. Du Bois
Murder Strikes at Dawn. H. Desmond
Murder Strikes North. N. Thurley
Murder Strikes Pink. J. Pullein-Thompson
Murder Strikes Three. D. MacDuff
Murder Strikes Thrice. C. G. Booth
Murder Strikes Twice. M. B. Dix
Murder Strikes Twice. J. V. Nolan
Murder, Sunny Side Up. R. B. Dominic
Murder Swings High. N. Brent
Murder Syndicate. J. Chancellor
Murder Takes a Honeymoon. E. Fleming
Murder Takes a Wife. J. A. Howard
Murder Takes No Holiday. B. Halliday
Murder Takes Over. A. Tack
Murder Takes the Baths. L. Priestley
Murder Takes the Stage. J. Reach
Murder Takes the Veil. M. A. Hubbard

Title Index

Murder That Had Everything. H. Footner
Murder That Wouldn't Stay Solved. Hampton Stone
Murder Through Room 45. T. A. Plummer
Murder Through the Looking Glass. R. G. Dean
Murder Through the Looking Glass. A. Garve
Murder Through the Looking Glass. M. Venning
Murder Through the Window. F. Everton
Murder Thy Neighbor. M. Hervey
Murder Times Five. R. Colby
Murder Times 4. C. Nuetzel
Murder Times Three. A. R. Long
Murder Tips the Scales. J. Creasey
Murder to Follow. K. Field
Murder to Go. E. Lathen
Murder to Hounds. E. Acheson
Murder to Make You Grow Up Little Girl. L. Oriol
Murder to Measure. Robert Mason
Murder to Music. G. Burne
Murder to Music. G. Chester
Murder to Music. P. Colson
Murder to Music. W. H. L. Crauford
Murder to Music. L. Edgley
Murder to Music. J. Kilgore
Murder to Music. M. Newman
Murder to Order. L. Marshall
Murder to Type. A. R. Long
Murder to Welcome Her. M. Neville
Murder Today, Money Tomorrow. J. Messmann
Murder Too Late. G. Ashe
Murder Town. L. Marshall
Murder Trail. M. Grant
Murder Trail. C. W. Sanders
Murder Trail. R. Wallace
Murder Train. Gavin Holt
Murder Trap. Howel Evans
Murder Trap. J. A. Jordan
Murder Trap. A. Livingston
Murder Trapp. Eugene Franklin
Murder Tree. L. McFarlane
Murder Trial. S. Box
Murder Trouble. L. Trimble
Murder Tunes In. C. Kingston
Murder Twice Removed. Muriel Bradley
Murder Twice Told. D. Hamilton
Murder Under Construction. P. MacTyre
Murder Under the Big Top. R. Wallace
Murder Under the Sun. L. O'Donnell
Murder Underground. W. Arden
Murder Underground. M. D. Hay
Murder Unleashed. Dorothy Bennett
Murder Unlimited. Nicholas Carter
Murder Unlimited. M. V. Heberden
Murder Unmourned. George Douglas
Murder Unplanned. E. A. St. Clair
Murder Unrecognized. M. Burton
Murder Unseen. J. York
Murder Unsolved. S. Adams
Murder Unsuspected. J. Cowdroy
Murder up My Sleeve. E. S. Gardner
Murder up the Glen. C. Campbell
Murder Upstairs. A. Bliss
Murder—Very Dry! S. S. Baker
Murder Walks Alone. J. V. Nolan
Murder Walks Alone. C. Ripley
Murder Walks on Tiptoe. Neill Graham
Murder Walks the Corridors. J. D. Perry
Murder Walks the Deck. W. Martyn
Murder Walks the Stairs. G. M. Barnes
Murder Ward. R. Sapir
Murder Was My Neighbor. G. Cobden
Murder Was Never Bolder. L. G. Redmond-Howard
Murder Was Their Medicine. G. Cobden
Murder Wears a Friendly Face. V. M. Perry
Murder Wears a Mantilla. Carter Brown
Murder Wears a Mummer's Mask. B. Halliday
Murder Wears Mukluks. E. M. Boyd
Murder Week-End. M. Halliday
Murder Well Begun. S. Adams
Murder Well Done. I. S. Shriber
Murder When Necessary. P. Levene
Murder While You Wait. J. Corbett
Murder While You Work. S. Scarlett
Murder Will. E. Wilmot
Murder Will Be Committed. G. Goodchild
Murder Will In. C. Wells
Murder Will Out. E. M. Bowen
Murder Will Out. M. Leinster
Murder Will Out. H. Leyford
Murder Will Out. G. E. Minot
Murder Will Out. Jeannette Covert Nolan
Murder Will Out. D. Sterling
Murder Will Out. R. Vickers
Murder Will Out. P. C. Williams
Murder Will Speak. G. Bellairs
Murder Will Speak. J. J. Connington
Murder Will Speak. Mark Cross
Murder with a Kiss. V. Gunn
Murder with a Past. E. Queen
Murder with a Theme Song. V. Rath
Murder with a Vengeance. R. Quest
Murder with Gloves. B. Huber
Murder with Grace. W. Wall
Murder with Impatience. R. Verron

Murder with Long Hair. H. D. Spatz
Murder with Love. F. Durbridge
Murder with Love. Vechel Howard
Murder with Love. Garland Lord
Murder with Love. Dell Shannon
Murder—with Love. J. T. Story
Murder with Magic. R. St. Clair
Murder with Malice. M. Underwood
Murder with Menaces. V. Hansen
Murder with Minarets. C. Forsyte
Murder with Mirrors. A. Christie
Murder with Mushrooms. G. Ashe
Murder with Music. G. Riddell
Murder with Orange Blossoms. R. Darby
Murder with Pictures. G. H. Coxe
Murder with Relish. C. L. Taylor
Murder with Roses. A. McElfresh
Murder with Southern Hospitality. L. Ford
Murder with Variety. W. Arthur
Murder with Your Malted. Jerome Barry
Murder Within Murder. F. Lockridge
Murder Without Alibis. S. McPhellamy
Murder Without Clues. J. L. Bonney
Murder Without Clues. E. Pierson
Murder Without Crime. B. Healey
Murder Without Crime. J. Lee Thompson
Murder Without Icing. E. Lathen
Murder Without Makeup. E. Benjamin
Murder Without Malice. R. Plomley
Murder Without Malice. A. Spiller
Murder Without Men. T. B. Morris
Murder Without Morals. M. M. Marshall
Murder Without Motive. M. Carrel
Murder Without Motive. R. L. Goldman
Murder Without Mourners. Sutherland Scott
Murder Without Mystery. J. Playfair
Murder Without Regret. E. L. Cushing
Murder Without Regret. R. Trevor
Murder Without Risk. H. Adams
Murder Without Tears. L. Lupton
Murder Without Weapons. A. B. Cunningham
Murder Without Weapons. Means Davis
Murder Won't Out. P. Hobson
Murder Won't Wait. C. J. Daly
Murder Won't Wait. R. S. O'Connor
Murder Wore Green. R. P. Koehler
Murder Yet to Come. I. B. Myers
Murdered Alive! W. Braun
Murdered But Not Dead. Anne Austin
Murdered Cliche. J. Samuel
Murdered Man's Derby. E. A. St. Clair
Murdered Manservant. C. F. Gregg
Murdered Mathematician. H. S. Keeler
Murdered Millionaire. E. Queen
Murdered: One by One. F. Beeding
Murdered Sleep. G. Braddon
Murderer. J. Bounden
Murderer. R. A. K. Heath
Murderer. W. Morton
Murderer. A. Shaffer
Murderer. G. Simenon
Murderer Among Us. Carter Brown
Murderer at Large. W. A. Ballinger
Murderer at Large. D. Henderson
Murderer at Large. S. Horler
Murderer in the House. K. Clugston
Murderer in This House. R. King
Murderer Invisible. P. Wylie
Murderer Is a Fox. E. Queen
Murderer of New Orleans. W. Ward
Murderer of Sleep. M. Kennedy
Murderer Returns. E. D. Torgerson
Murderer Vine. S. Rifkin
Murderer Who Wanted More. B. Kendrick
Murderers. F. Brown
Murderers Are Silent. R. Clarke
Murderer's Bluff. F. Duncan
Murderer's Bride. H. Desmond
Murderer's Challenge. H. Footner
Murderer's Choice. A. M. Wells
Murderers Don't Smile. John Morgan
Murderer's Fen. A. Garve
Murderer's Holiday. D. H. Clarke
Murderers' Houses. Jennie Melville
Murderer's Island. Y. Tregarron
Murderer's Luck. H. Holt
Murderers Make Mistakes. F. W. Crofts
Murderer's Mansion. Irene Shaw
Murderer's Maze. R. Glover
Murderer's Maze. John Marsh
Murderers' Medicine. A. Train
Murderers Meet. Gwyn Evans
Murderer's Mistake. E. C. R. Lorac
Murderer's Moon. R. Dana
Murderer's Moon. R. Goyne
Murderer's Moon. G. Morgan
Murderers of Monty. R. Hull
Murderer's Row. R. Batchelor
Murderer's Row. D. Hamilton
Murderer's Stand-In. J. G. Brandon
Murderers Three. F. C. Tickner
Murderer's Trail. J. J. Farjeon
Murderer's Vanity. H. Footner
Murderer's Wench. P. Hoyt
Murdering Kind. Gwendoline Butler
Murdering Mr. Velfrage. Roy Vickers
Murderous Journey. E. McGirr
Murderous Suspense. G. M. Barnes
Murderous Welcome. J. Irwin
Murder's a Swine. N. Lombard

Murder's a Waiting Game. Anthony Gilbert
Murder's Always Final. Neill Graham
Murders Anonymous. E. Ferrars
Murders at Crossby. E. P. Frankland
Murders at Hibiscus Key. V. Siller
Murders at Highbridge. R. Slingsby
Murders at Impasse Louvain. Richard Gray Grayson
Murders at Loon Lake. K. Whipple
Murders at Moon Dance. A. B. Guthrie
Murders at Scandal House. P. Hunt
Murders at the Crab Apple Cafe. G. Manners
Murders at the Lakes. G. L. Jennings
Murders at the Manor. C. Ryland
Murders at Turbot Towers. S. J. Peskett
Murder's Burning. S. H. Courtier
Murders by Moonlight. A. Hyde
Murder's Coming. D. C. Cameron
Murder's End. R. Kelston
Murders for Sale. A. Weston
Murder's for the Birds. J. Beeley
Murders Form Fours. David Hume
Murders in Lovers' Lane. J. G. Dunton
Murders in Praed Street. J. Rhode
Murders in Sequence. M. Propper
Murders in Silk. M. Teagle
Murders in Surrey Wood. John Arnold
Murders in the Dispensary. J. Carr
Murders in the Mortuary. Austin Stone
Murders in the Rue Morgue. R. Brome
Murders in Volume 2. E. Daly
Murders I've Seen. P. Mechem
Murder's Just for Cops. L. Marshall
Murder's Little Helper. G. Bagby
Murder's Little Helper. Garland Lord
Murder's Little Sister. P. Branch
Murder's Money. G. A. Ralston
Murders Near Mapleton. B. Flynn
Murder's No Accident. A. S. Fleischman
Murder's No Accident. F. Orpet
Murder's No Picnic. E. L. Cushing
Murder's No Picnic. P. Hambledon
Murder's No Picnic. P. Muat
Murder's Not an Odd Job. R. Dennis
Murders of Richard III. Elizabeth Peters
Murders on Fox Island. M. P. Hood
Murders on the Square. T. George
Murder's Out of Season. L. Marshall
Murder's Rock. D. Reid
Murder's Shield. R. Sapir
Murder's So Permanent. E. Howie
Murder's Web. Dorothy Dunn
Murders While You Wait. Claude Hunter
Murdoch Legacy. Irma Walker
Murdock's Acid Test. G. H. Coxe
Muriel Wins Through. G. Thorne
Murillo Mystery. A. Eadie
Murillo Mystery. B. Poynter
Murmansk Assignment. J. Pattinson
Murmur of Mutiny. M. Pugh
Murmuring Willow. Rona Randall
Murmurs in the Rue Morgue. M. Cumberland
Murphy Gang. Roland Daniel
Murphy's Game. M. Tarmey
Murphy's Master, and other stories. J. Payn
Murray Hill Mystery. Nicholas Carter
Murray of the Scots Greys. L. Clarke
Murray, the Detective. Old Sleuth
Muscle Beach Party. Elsie Lee
Muscle Boy. B. Clifton
Muse Theatre Murder. T. A. Plummer
Museum Murder. J. T. MacIntyre
Museum Mystery. A. Soutar
Museum Piece No. 13. R. King
Mushalong. G. Goodchild
Mushroom Cave. R. Rosenblum
Mushrooms on Toast. Laurence Kirk
Music for Chameleons. T. Capote
Music from the Past. K. Cameron
Music Gallery Murder. R. Francis Foster
Music Master. Dorothy Fletcher
Music of Aquarius. Canella Lewis
Music Room. W. E. D. Ross
Music Tells All. E. R. Punshon
Music to Murder By. V. Hinkle
Music to Murder By. D. Pownall
Music When Sweet Voices Die. C. Q. Yarbro
Musical Comedy Crime. Anthony Gilbert
Mussolini Murder Plot. B. Newman
Muster of the Vultures. G. Fairlie
Mustering of the Hawks. J. Harris
Mutable Many. R. Barr
Mutation Mink. P. Traill
Mutatis Mutandis. D. Campton
Mute Witness. R. L. Pike
Muted Murder. S. Sinclair
Mutilators. M. Casey
Mutilators. B. Heatter
Mutiny. F. R. Bechdolt
Mutton Dressed As Lamb, and Live. J. M. Walsh
Muzzle Blast. B. Rossi
Muzzled Ox. C. Stanton
My Adventure in the Flying Scotsman. E. Phillpotts
My Atlantic Bride. H. Russell
My Aunt Agatha. M. Brenner
My Bad Boy. M. Neville
My Body. R. Dietrich

My Bones Will Keep. G. Mitchell
My Bonny Lies Under the Sea. R. Alan
My Brother, Cain. V. Thiessen
My Brother Michael. Mary Stewart
My Brother, the Druggist. Marvin Kaye
My Brother's Executioner. J. Laffin
My Brother's Killer. D. M. Devine
My Brother's Killer. J. Potts
My Brother's Killer. J. York
My Brother's Wife. Harry Davis
My Business Is Murder. H. Kane
My Caravaggio Style. D. L. Moore
My Child and I. F. Warden
My Coat Is Travel-Stained. F. Gamble
My Cousin Caroline's Wedding. H. Wood
My Cousin Cynthia, and others. P. C. De Crespigny
My Cousin Death. M. McMullen
My Cousin Rachel. D. Du Maurier
My Cousin Rachel. Diana Morgan
My Darlin' Evangeline. H. Kane
My Darling Is Deadpan. Carter Brown
My Darling's Ransom. R. Dowling
My Dead Body. G. Bagby
My Dead Wife. W. Worley
My Deadly Angel. J. Chelton
My Dear Heart. K. Lindsay
My Dear Miss Emma. P. Allardyce
My Dearest Elizabeth. A. Maybury
My Enemy Came Nigh. R. T. Bickers
My Enemy—My Wife. A. Haden
My Enemy's Friend. H. Osborne
My Face Beneath the Stone. J. Crecy
My Fair Lady. Georgius
My Father Sleeps. G. Mitchell
My First Crime. G. Mace
My Flesh Is Sweet. D. Keene
My Foe Outstretch'd Beneath the Tree. V. C. Clinton-Baddeley
My Fourteen Cases. Anonymous
My Friend Charles. F. Durbridge
My Friend Judas. P. Barrington
My Friend Maigret. G. Simenon
My Friend Pasquale and other stories. J. S. Tait
My Friend the Murderer and other mysteries and adventures. A. C. Doyle
My Friend Tony. W. Johnston
My Giddy Aunt. R. Cooney
My God How the Money Rolls In. J. Ripley
My Grand Enemy. J. Stubbs
My Grave Is for the Living. S. Connor
My Guess Was Murder. G. Cobden
My Gun, Her Body. J. Bogar
My Gun Is Quick. M. Spillane
My Heart and Stephanie. R. W. Kauffman
My Heart Went Dead. A. McElfresh
My Husband's First Love. H. Wood
My Indian Queen. G. Boothby
My Invisible Partner. T. S. Denison
My Japanese Prince. A. C. Gunter
My Killer Doesn't Understand Me. T. P. Mulkeen
My Kind of Game. A. Rome
My Kingdom for a Hearse. C. Rice
My Lady Bountiful. F. M. White
My Lady Caprice. J. Farnol
My Lady Cinderella. A. M. Williamson
My Lady Dangerous. S. Horler
My Lady Evil. P. J. Cooper
My Lady Mischief. J. L. Roberts
My Lady of the Yellow Domino. A. W. Marchmont
My Lady of Whims. F. Warden
My Lady Ruby and John Basileon, Chief of Police. G. F. Monkshood
My Lady Vamp. G. W. Gough
My Lady's Bath. C. N. Boyle
My Lady's Diamonds. A. Sergeant
My Lady's Garter. J. Futrelle
My Lady's Money. W. Collins
My Late Wives. Carter Dickson
My Laugh Comes Last. J. H. Chase
My Life Is Done. Sara Woods
My Lodger's Legacy. R. W. Hume
My Lord Duke. E. W. Hornung
M'Lord, I Am Not Guilty. F. S. Wees
My Lord Murderer. E. Mansfield
My Lord of Wrybourne. J. Farnol
My Lord the Felon. H. Hill
My Lost Self. A. W. Marchmont
My Love Has a Secret. A. Maybury
My Love Is Stone. C. Massie
My Love Is Violent. T. B. Dewey
My Love Johnny. M. McEvoy
My Love Noel. H. Nisbet
My Love Wears Black. O. R. Cohen
My Lovely Executioner. P. Rabe
My Masters. R. E. Salwey
My Mermaid Murmurs Murder. Carter Brown
My Miscellania. W. Collins
My Mother Was Hanged. E. S. Willards
My Mysterious Clients. H. Scribner
My Name Is Black! J. Nazel
My Name Is Celia. R. Kruger
My Name Is Clary Brown. C. Keppel
My Name Is Death. C. Birkin
My Name Is Death. L. Egan
My Name Is Legion. R. Zelazny
My Name Is Love. J. MacLaren-Ross
My Name Is Michael Sibley. J. Bingham

My Name Is Morgan. W. Woolfolk
My Name is Norval. T. D. White
My Neighbor's Wife. D. M. Disney
My Official Wife. R. H. Savage
My Old Man's Badge. F. Findley
My Own Murderer. R. Hull
My Pal, the Killer. C. Warwick
My Particular Murder. D. Sharp
My Path Belated. N. Ames
My Peril in a Pullman Car and other tales. A. Griffiths
My Poll and My Partner. T. P. Prest
My Private Hangman. N. Herries
My Rubies Are Blood Red. J. C. Crawley
My Search for Ruth. A. Clarke
My Shadow. P. Malloch
My Sister Erica. J. Blackmore
My Sister, Good Night. G. McDonell
My Sister, My Friend. Katherine Blake
My Sister Ophelia. A. Kosner
My Sister Sophie. J. Edgar
My Sister's Confession and other stories. M. E. Braddon
My Son, the Druggist. Marvin Kaye
My Son, the Murderer. P. Quentin
My Soul to Keep. E. Davis
My Strangest Case. G. Boothby
My Tattered Loving. G. R. Preedy
My Terrible Twin. F. Whishaw
My Time or Yours. W. D. Blake
My Tom-Boy Girl. C. E. Blaney
My Treasure, My Love. Lynna Cooper
My True Love Lies. L. G. Offord
My Turn Next. Winston Graham
My Turn Now. Janet Green
My Turn to Die. K. Royce
My Two Wives and other stories. G. R. Sims
My Undiscovered Crimes. F. Wicks
My Weird Wooing. T. V. Foote
My Wife Melissa. F. Durbridge
My Wife's Lover. J. Courage
My Word You Should Have Seen Us. J. Ripley
Mycroft Murder Case. A. Marsden
Myer for Hire. L. S. Taube
Mynns' Mystery. G. M. Fenn
Myopic Mermaid. Carter Brown
Mysteries. W. LeQueux
Mysteries and Adventures. A. C. Doyle
Mysteries and Miseries of New Orleans. N. Buntline
Mysteries and Miseries of New York. N. Buntline
Mysteries Elucidated. A. M. Mackenzie
Mysteries for Radio. W. Weathers
Mysteries of a Great City. W. LeQueux
Mysteries of Ann. Alice Brown
Mysteries of Black Valley. A. Mallory
Mysteries of Blair House. R. O. Eastman
Mysteries of Chicago. Anonymous
Mysteries of Crime, as Shown in Remarkable Capital Crimes. Anonymous
Mysteries of Ferney Castle. G. Lambe
Mysteries of Florence. G. Lippard
Mysteries of Heron Dyke. T. W. Speight
Mysteries of London. G. W. M. Reynolds
Mysteries of Modern London. G. R. Sims
Mysteries of Myra. C. H. Bullivant
Mysteries of Nashua. Anonymous
Mysteries of New Orleans. Anonymous
Mysteries of New York. Old Sleuth
Mysteries of Oakendale Abbey. Anonymous
Mysteries of Paris. E. Sue
Mysteries of Ryeburn Manor. J. Laurence
Mysteries of the Castle. M. P. Andrews
Mysteries of the Castle. J. B. White
Mysteries of the City. J. M'Levy
Mysteries of the Court of London. G. W. M. Reynolds
Mysteries of the Riviera. E. P. Oppenheim
Mysteries of Udolpho. A. Radcliffe
Mysterious Abduction. G. S. Goodman
Mysterious Affair at Styles. A. Christie
Mysterious Ambassador. L. Falk
Mysterious Aviator. N. Shute
Mysterious Beggar. A. A. Day
Mysterious Bohemian. A. M. Diehl
Mysterious Burglar. G. E. Walsh
Mysterious Cane of Dr. Chang. R. St. Clair
Mysterious Card. C. Moffett
Mysterious Case. K. F. Hill
Mysterious Castle. Nicholas Carter
Mysterious Cavern. Nicholas Carter
Mysterious Chinaman. J. S. Fletcher
Mysterious Chinese Mandrake, and other stories. I. D. Ekbergh
Mysterious Commission. M. Innes
Mysterious Crime at Burleigh Mansion. Anonymous
Mysterious Dagger. Anonymous
Mysterious Disappearance. L. Tracy
Mysterious Disappearance of a Bride. M. Danvers
Mysterious Disappearance of Helen St. Vincent. J. J. Flinn
Mysterious Disappearances. G. M. Winsor
Mysterious Dr. Oliver. J. B. Ellis
Mysterious Foe. Nicholas Carter
Mysterious Game. Nicholas Carter

Mysterious "Graft". Nicholas Carter
Mysterious Hand. A. J. Crandolph
Mysterious Inheritance. B. Marchant
Mysterious Journey. M. L. Tyrrell
Mysterious Juror. F. Du Boisgobey
Mysterious Madame. S. D'Erigny
Mysterious Mademoiselle. F. Grierson
Mysterious Mail Robbery. Nicholas Carter
Mysterious Marksman. Anonymous
Mysterious Marriage. E. Southworth
Mysterious Martin. T. Robbins
Mysterious Mickey Finn. Elliot Paul
Mysterious Millionaire. H. West
Mysterious Miss Cass. G. W. Appleton
Mysterious Miss Death. Gwyn Evans
Mysterious Miss Morrisot. V. Williams
Mysterious Missile. C. H. Snow
Mysterious Mr. Badman. W. F. Harvey
Mysterious Mr. Brent. G. Davison
Mysterious Mr. Frame. M. Merrick
Mysterious Mr. Garland. W. Martyn
Mysterious Mr. I. H. S. Keeler
Mysterious Mr. Jarvis. F. R. Giles
Mysterious Mr. Maynard. J. Hunter
Mysterious Mr. Miller. W. LeQueux
Mysterious Mr. Pickering. P. E. Curtiss
Mysterious Mr. Quin. A. Christie
Mysterious Mr. Reece. R. M. Graydon
Mysterious Mr. Rocco. J. Creasey
Mysterious Mr. Sabin. E. P. Oppenheim
Mysterious Mrs. Nutford. B. M. Clay
Mysterious Mrs. Wilkinson and other stories. W. E. Norris
Mysterious Monsieur Moray. Brian Stuart
Mysterious Murder. I. Crookenden
Mysterious Murder of Pearl Bryan. Anonymous
Mysterious Novice. S. Wilkinson
Mysterious Office. Jennette Lee
Mysterious Partner. A. Fielding
Mysterious Seal. W. C. Proby
Mysterious Stranger. C. H. Thorburn
Mysterious Suspect. J. Rhode
Mysterious Three. W. LeQueux
Mysterious Valley. G. W. Wicking
Mysterious Warning. Mrs. Parsons
Mysterious Way. J. Boland
Mysterious Waye. P. C. Wren
Mysterious Wife. Grove Wilson
Mysterious Yankee. Old Sleuth
Mysteriouser and Mysteriouser. G. Bagby
Mystery. Anonymous
Mystery. G. S. Crosby
Mystery. F. Lathom
Mystery. M. Paris
Mystery. S. E. White
Mystery. H. Wood
Mystery and Minette. H. Adams
Mystery and other stories. Annie Thomas
Mystery at a Country Inn. P. Owen
Mystery at Angel's End. J. Chancellor
Mystery at Arden Court. E. C. Holt
Mystery at Blackwater. D. Sutherland
Mystery at Butlin's. M. O'Nair
Mystery at Chillery. R. Francis Foster
Mystery at Crowstone. Colin Hope
Mystery at Folly Mill. J. Brooke
Mystery at Friar's Pardon. M. Porlock
Mystery at Furze Acres. D. Whitelaw
Mystery at Geneva. R. Macaulay
Mystery at Greenfingers. J. B. Priestley
Mystery at Greycombe Farm. J. Rhode
Mystery at Greystones. K. Lindsay
Mystery at Grimsdale. E. P. Frankland
Mystery at Hardacres. G. Morton
Mystery at Hermit's End. G. Morton
Mystery at Hidden Harbor. C. Fitzsimmons
Mystery at King's Grant. A. E. D.
Mystery at Lover's Cave. A. Berkeley
Mystery at Lynden Sands. J. J. Connington
Mystery at Manby House. J. Creasey
Mystery at Merrilees. M. Poole
Mystery at Moor Street. C. F. Gregg
Mystery at October House. Marjory Hall
Mystery at Olympia. J. Rhode
Mystery at Peak House. A. J. Rees
Mystery at Ramshackle House. H. Footner
Mystery at Spanish Hacienda. Jackson Gregory
Mystery at Stowe. V. Loder
Mystery at the Blue Villa. M. D. Post
Mystery at the Inn. J. H. Vahey
Mystery at the JHC Ranch. W. C. Tuttle
Mystery at the Rectory. A. Fielding
Mystery at Tudor Arches. L. Gribble
Mystery at Vellum. L. G. Horsefield
Mystery at Wadham Close. L. Souberge
Mystery Blues and other stories. P. Cheyney
Mystery Box. W. W. Sayer
Mystery Car. M. Gerard
Mystery Castle. Elsie Lee
Mystery Chain. L. G. Moberly
Mystery Crime Cases. Anonymous
Mystery Crime Cases. N. W. Firth
Mystery Cruise. K. Langmaid
Mystery Cruise. Taffrail
Mystery DeLuxe. R. King
Mystery Evans. B. Baker
Mystery Flier. E. T. Woodhall
Mystery Flight. John Davies

Mystery for Mary. V. Hanson
Mystery from the Air. J. Laurence
Mystery Gangster. G. Chester
Mystery Girl. C. Wells
Mystery Hand. B. Bolt
Mystery House. P. Hobson
Mystery House. K. Norris
Mystery House. J. M. Walsh
Mystery in Blue. G. E. Mallette
Mystery in Blue. W. Spence
Mystery in Glass. E. Kilvington
Mystery in Green. A. Vinton
Mystery in Hawaii. R. St. Clair
Mystery in Kensington Gore. M. Porlock
Mystery in Minchin Mews. R. Gar
Mystery in Red. F. Grierson
Mystery in Red. S. Williams
Mystery in St. James Square. G. Collins
Mystery in the Channel. F. W. Crofts
Mystery in the Drood Family. M. Saunders
Mystery in the English Channel. F. W. Crofts
Mystery in the Mist. C. Kingston
Mystery in the Ritsmore. W. A. Johnston
Mystery in the Snow. G. Darwent
Mystery in the Woodshed. Anthony Gilbert
Mystery in White. J. J. Farjeon
Mystery Island. E. H. Hurst
Mystery Island. F. Whishaw
Mystery Island. Palmer White
Mystery Keepers. M. Fox
Mystery Killer. H. Desmond
Mystery Lady. R. W. Chambers
Mystery Lamp. M. R. Rinehart
Mystery Maker. Seamark
Mystery Man. M. Ankrum
Mystery Man. S. Hocking
Mystery Man. J. M. Walsh
Mystery Man in the Tower. H. Chichester
Mystery Mandarin. J. W. Bobin
Mystery Manor. L. Gribble
Mystery Mansion. L. Archer
Mystery Mansion. Herman Landon
Mystery, Mayhem, and Murder! Jed Parish
Mystery Message. T. C. Bridges
Mystery Mile. M. Allingham
Mystery Militiaman. Ladbroke Blake
Mystery Mind. A. B. Reeve
Mystery Mission. S. Horler
Mystery Mission and other stories. S. Horler
Mystery Money. J. Laurence
Mystery Motive. M. Halliday
Mystery of a Bungalow. W. Chesney
Mystery of a Butcher's Shop. G. Mitchell
Mystery of a Diamond. F. H. Converse
Mystery of a Hansom Cab. F. Hume
Mystery of a Madstone. Anonymous
Mystery of a Madstone. K. F. Hill
Mystery of a Millionaire. M. J. Pemberton
Mystery of a Millionaire's Grave. G. Stables
Mystery of a Moonlight Tryst. I. D. Hardy
Mystery of a Motor Cab. F. Hume
Mystery of a Motor-Car. W. LeQueux
Mystery of a Shipyard. R. H. Savage
Mystery of a Studio and other stories. R. H. Fletcher
Mystery of a Turkish Bath. Rita
Mystery of a Wheelbarrow. W. H. Ferguson
Mystery of Achnaghoulash. Dave Smith
Mystery of Airedale Hall. B. Bolt
Mystery of Alfred Doubt. W. Hay
Mystery of Allan Grale. I. F. Mayo
Mystery of Allanwold. E. Van Loon
Mystery of Alton Grange. E. Everett-Green
Mystery of an Omnibus. F. Du Boisgobey
Mystery of Angelina Frood. R. A. Freeman
Mystery of Arrowhead Hill. L. W. Douglas
Mystery of Ashton Hall. B. Nitsua
Mystery of Avenue Road. A. Parsons
Mystery of Bar Harbor. Alsop Leffingwell
Mystery of Bernard Hanson. U. L. Silberrad
Mystery of Beacon Hill. L. G. Redmond-Howard
Mystery of Beaton Craig. Mark Allerton
Mystery of Beckers' Brook. A. Blair
Mystery of Belgrave Square. Curtis Yorke
Mystery of Belvoir Mansions. B. Bolt
Mystery of Bent Cove. F. D. Holmgren
Mystery of Black Pit. Anonymous
Mystery of Blackmoor Prison. J. Creasey
Mystery of Blencarrow. M. Oliphant
Mystery of Bloomsbury Crescent. Mrs. Lodge
Mystery of Bullen Point. R. C. Armour
Mystery of Burnleigh Manor. W. Livingston
Mystery of Captain Burnaby. A. S. McNalty
Mystery of Cedar Bluff. H. Weeks
Mystery of Cedar Valley. V. Henry
Mystery of Cell 13. G. H. Teed
Mystery of Central Park. N. Bly
Mystery of Choice. R. W. Chambers
Mystery of Clement Dunraven. J. Middlemass
Mystery of Cloomber. A. C. Doyle
Mystery of Clough Mills. Stuart Martin

Mystery of Colde Fell. C. M. Braeme
Mystery of Collingwood. Marilyn Ross
Mystery of "Crazy Canyon" Ranch. E. H. Ott
Mystery of Crooknose. L. W. Douglas
Mystery of Crowther Castle. G. W. H. Firmstone
Mystery of DS 24. T. Wallace
Mystery of Dagget's Bank. N. Ned
Mystery of Daria Kane. M. V. Hunt
Mystery of Dark Hollow. E. Southworth
Mystery of Dead Man's Heath. J. J. Farjeon
Mystery of Devil's Canyon. C. H. Snow
Mystery of Dr. Fu-Manchu. S. Rohmer
Mystery of Dudley Horne. F. Warden
Mystery of Echo Caverns. R. C. Payes
Mystery of Edwin Drood. C. Dickens
Mystery of Edwin Drood. L. Garfield
Mystery of Enid Belairs. D. Whitelaw
Mystery of Evangeline Fairfax. E. Kunst
Mystery of Evelin Delorme. A. B. Paine
Mystery of Fell Castle. A. Gask
Mystery of Fernridge Manor. R. Bodwell
Mystery of Fifty-Two. W. S. Masterman
Mystery of Flat 60. A. J. Sarl
Mystery of Flying V Ranch. R. E. Rochester
Mystery of Fourways. F. Warden
Mystery of Frances Farrington. E. Banks
Mystery of Fury Castle. Dan Ross
Mystery of Fury Castle. Marilyn Ross
Mystery of Fyfe House. V. Nielsen
Mystery of Glyn Castle. L. H. Brooks
Mystery of "Golden Lotus". L. Gerard
Mystery of Grange Drayton. E. Kerr
Mystery of Gruden's Gap. Mark Cross
Mystery of Grudge Mountain. A. P. Terhune
Mystery of Hanging Sword Alley. W. J. Bayfield
Mystery of Hartley House. C. S. Raymond
Mystery of Helmsley Grange. A. Askew
Mystery of High Eldersham. M. Burton
Mystery of Holly Tavern. L. Collis
Mystery of Horseshoe Island. F. W. Gumley
Mystery of Hotel Brichet. E. Chavette
Mystery of Hunting's End. M. G. Eberhart
Mystery of Jamaica Terrace. D. Donovan
Mystery of Jeanne Marie. H. E. Barlow
Mystery of Jessie Page, and other stories. H. Wood
Mystery of Joan Marryat. Mark Cross
Mystery of John Peppercorn. T. Gallon
Mystery of Judith. C. E. Pearce
Mystery of June 13. M. Severy
Mystery of Khufu's Tomb. T. Mundy
Mystery of Killard. R. Dowling
Mystery of King Cobra. D. Marfield
Mystery of King's Everard. C. Brandon
Mystery of Knickerbocker Towers. E. Thorne
Mystery of Kun-Ja-Muck Cave. G. F. Tibbetts
Mystery of Lady Chetwynd's Spectre. Anonymous
Mystery of Lady Chetwynd's Spectre. H. Lewis
Mystery of Lady Isobel. E. R. Punshon
Mystery of Ladyplace. C. Lys
Mystery of Landy Court. F. Hume
Mystery of Leighton Grange. M. E. Braddon
Mystery of Lincoln's Inn. R. Machray
Mystery of Lombardy Chambers. S. Westlaw
Mystery of Lostland Academy. A. M. Sholl
Mystery of Lucien Delorme. G. De Teramond
Mystery of Lynne Court. J. S. Fletcher
Mystery of Madeline Le Blanc. M. Ehrmann
Mystery of Mademoiselle. W. LeQueux
Mystery of Magdalen. Mrs. C. Kernahan
Mystery of Major Molineau, and Human Repentends. M. Clarke
Mystery of Mandeville Square. G. Campbell
Mystery of Mar Saba. J. H. Hunter
Mystery of Margaret. O. Read
Mystery of Martha's Vineyard. G. Dyer
Mystery of Martin Guerre. J. G. Sarasin
Mystery of Mary Anne and other stories. G. R. Sims
Mystery of Mary Hamilton. Roland Daniel
Mystery of Maybury Manor. Eric Wood
Mystery of Mayfair. J. S. Winter
Mystery of Me...? W. J. Elliott
Mystery of Mere Hall. Mrs. C. Kernahan
Mystery of Merlyn Mansions. W. Shute
Mystery of Metropolisville. E. Eggleston
Mystery of Milford Haven. Taffrail
Mystery of Mirbridge. J. Payn
Mystery of Miriam. J. W. Johnston
Mystery of Miss Motte. C. A. Mason
Mystery of Mr. Bernard Brown. E. P. Oppenheim
Mystery of Mr. Cross. C. Robbins
Mystery of Mr. E. Drood. O. C. Kerr
Mystery of Mr. Jessop. E. R. Punshon
Mystery of Mr. Mock. R. A. J. Walling
Mystery of Mr. X. S. Horler
Mystery of Mr. X. M. Porlock

Mystery of Mrs. Blencarrow. M. Oliphant
Mystery of Mitcham Common. Gwyn Evans
Mystery of Moat Farm. J. Hunter
Mystery of Monkswood. Mrs. Lodge
Mystery of M. Felix. B. L. Farjeon
Mystery of Monte Carlo. W. M. Graydon
Mystery of Moor Manor. F. W. Irwin
Mystery of Mortimer Strange. A. W. Marchmont
Mystery of Mostyn Manor. A. W. A'Beckett
Mystery of Mouldy Manor. T. Westgate
Mystery of Murray Davenport. R. N. Stephens
Mystery of Myrtle Cottage. O. Crawfurd
Mystery of Nelson's Coat. E. M. Keate
Mystery of New Orleans. W. M. H. Holcombe
Mystery of New York Bay. Old Sleuth
Mystery of Newton Ferry. L. Meynell
Mystery of Nine. W. LeQueux
Mystery of Norman's Court. J. Chancellor
Mystery of North Fortune. George Douglas
Mystery of Number Five. F. J. Whaley
Mystery of No. 47. J. S. Clouston
Mystery of No. 1. S. Horler
Mystery of No. 7 Bitton Court. P. Quiroule
Mystery of No. 13. H. B. Mathers
Mystery of No. 13 Cavendish Square. P. Quiroule
Mystery of Oldham. L. Bidston
Mystery of One Night. Old Sleuth
Mystery of Orchard House. J. Coggin
Mystery of Orcival. E. Gaboriau
Mystery of Orleton Manor. R. Jewell
Mystery of Paul Chadwick. J. W. Postgate
Mystery of Pauline's Lady. M. V. Woodgate
Mystery of Philip Bennion's Death. R. Marsh
Mystery of Pine Point. K. Norris
Mystery of Rapallo. Courtenay Pollock
Mystery of Redmarsh Farm. A. Marshall
Mystery of Renille Castle. L. H. Shorey
Mystery of Roaring Meg. B. L. Farjeon
Mystery of Rodney's Cove. E. S. Brooks
Mystery of Roger Bullock. T. Gallon
Mystery of St. Dunstans. T. Wright
Mystery of St. James' Park. J. E. Bloundelle-Burton
Mystery of St. Martin's Copse. Beatrix Hughes
Mystery of St. Michael's. G. Thorne
Mystery of St. Rule's. E. F. Heddle
Mystery of Saligo Bay. M. Pemberton
Mystery of Sett. J. Cowdroy
Mystery of Sherwood Towers. G. Verner
Mystery of Squadron X. W. Tyrer
Mystery of Stephen Claverton & Co. H. Knight
Mystery of Suicide Place. A. M. Miller
Mystery of Sun Dial Court. M. Wickes
Mystery of Sunny Fowt. P. Lee
Mystery of Swordfish Reef. A. W. Upfield
Mystery of Tara Heston. J. L. Rickard
Mystery of the Abandoned Cottage. W. M. Graydon
Mystery of the Abbe Montrose. S. Elvestad
Mystery of the African Expedition. R. Hardinge
Mystery of the African Farm. R. Hardinge
Mystery of the African Mine. R. Hardinge
Mystery of the "Agony". J. W. Bobin
Mystery of the Albanian Avenger. W. W. Sayer
Mystery of the American Envoy. J. Hunter
Mystery of the Amorous Music Master. G. Woden
Mystery of the Arab Agent. W. Jardine
Mystery of the Ashes. A. Wynne
Mystery of the Aztec Chain. John Norman
Mystery of the Baghdad Chest. A. Christie
Mystery of the Bankrupt Estate. A. Parsons
Mystery of the Barranca. H. Whitaker
Mystery of the Barren Lands. R. Cullum
Mystery of the Black Dagger. P. Elliott
Mystery of the Black Gate. B. G. Quin
Mystery of the Black Tower. J. Palmer
Mystery of the Blackmailed Baronet. H. E. Hill
Mystery of the Blitzed Tower. A. Parsons
Mystery of the Blue Geranium, and Other Tuesday Club Murders. A. Christie
Mystery of the Blue Inns. E. Anstey
Mystery of the Blue Train. A. Christie
Mystery of the Body on the Cliff. R. Hardinge
Mystery of the Bombed Hotel. A. Skene
Mystery of the Bombed Monastery. A. Parsons
Mystery of the Bonanza Trail. F. J. Arkins
Mystery of the Boule Cabinet. B. E. Stevenson
Mystery of the Cairo Express. A. Parsons
Mystery of the Campagna, and A Shadow on a Wave. Von Degan
Mystery of the Cape Cod Players. P. A. Taylor

560 / Mystery of the Cape Cod Tavern **Title Index**

M

Mystery of the Cape Cod Tavern. P. A. Taylor
Mystery of the Cashiered Officer. G. H. Teed
Mystery of the Castle. M. S. Boyd
Mystery of the Centre-Forward. P. Gill
Mystery of the Championship Belt. A. Steffens Hardy
Mystery of the Clasped Hands. G. Boothby
Mystery of the Clock. A. Murray
Mystery of the Closed Car. K. Sproul
Mystery of the Colored Circles. L. W. Badgett
Mystery of the Common. J. Blyth
Mystery of the Condemned Cottage. G. Chester
Mystery of the Confiscated Ship. G. Chester
Mystery of the Corbin Necklace. H. K. Webster
Mystery of the Corded Box. Mark Cross
Mystery of the Crashed Air Liner. G. Chester
Mystery of the Creek. J. J. Farjeon
Mystery of the Creeping Man. F. S. Wees
Mystery of the Crested Falcon. J. Noy
Mystery of the Crime in Cabin 66. A. Christie
Mystery of the Crimson Blind. F. M. White
Mystery of the Crooked Gift. A. Parsons
Mystery of the Crystal Skull. George M. White
Mystery of the "David M". D. W. MacArthur
Mystery of the Dead Man's Wallet. J. G. Brandon
Mystery of the Dead Police. M. Porlock
Mystery of the Demobilized Soldier. G. Chester
Mystery of the Derelict. J. G. Rowe
Mystery of the Deserted Camp. J. Drummond
Mystery of the Devil Mask. R. Hardinge
Mystery of the Docks. W. M. Graydon
Mystery of the Double Burglary. G. Chester
Mystery of the Dover Road. W. M. Graydon
Mystery of the Downs. J. R. Watson
Mystery of the East Wind. D. Marfield
Mystery of the Elms. S. W. Judge
Mystery of the Engraved Skull. S. Hope
Mystery of the Evil Eye. A. Wynne
Mystery of the Fast Mail. B. D. Adsit
Mystery of the Fiddling Cracksman. H. S. Keeler
Mystery of the Fifth Tulip. D. Deane
Mystery of the Film City. G. H. Teed
Mystery of the Five Guilty Men. J. Drummond
Mystery of the Flaming Hut. L. Best
Mystery of the Folded Paper. H. Footner
Mystery of the Forbidden Territory. R. Hardinge
Mystery of the Four Abreast. C. R. Cooper
Mystery of the Four Fingers. F. M. White
Mystery of the Four Rooms. H. H. C. Gibbons
Mystery of the Free Frenchmen. A. Parsons
Mystery of the French Milliner. B. Thomson
Mystery of the Frightened Lady. E. Wallace
Mystery of the Furlined Cloak. C. E. Pearce
Mystery of the German Prisoner. M. Frazer
Mystery of the Girl in Blue. F. Perry
Mystery of the Girl in Green. A. Parsons
Mystery of the Glass Bullet. B. Atkey
Mystery of the Golconda. W. N. Vaile
Mystery of the Gold Box. V. Williams
Mystery of the Golden Angel. F. Grierson
Mystery of the Golden Chalice. W. M. Graydon
Mystery of the Golden Wings. Rosa Lambert
Mystery of the Greek Exile. G. Chester
Mystery of the Green Bottle. J. G. Brandon
Mystery of the Green Car. A. Weissl
Mystery of the Green Caterpillars. J. M. Walsh
Mystery of the Green Garnet Murder. P. De Waal
Mystery of the Green Heart. M. Pemberton
Mystery of the Green Ray. W. LeQueux
Mystery of the Gregory Kotovsky. J. Pattinson
Mystery of the Grey Car. J. W. Bobin
Mystery of the Hasty Arrow. A. K. Green
Mystery of the Hated Man. J. M. Flagg
Mystery of the Haunted Square. J. Drummond
Mystery of the Heart. O. Binns
Mystery of the Hidden Room. M. Harvey
Mystery of the Hope Diamond. H. L. Gates
Mystery of the Horse with the Wrong Harness. O. L. Miller
Mystery of the House of Commons. F. Hope

Mystery of the Human Bookcase. W. Morton
Mystery of the Hundred Chests. A. Murray
Mystery of the Hush-Hush Factory. G. Chester
Mystery of the Hushing Pool. J. S. Fletcher
Mystery of the Hypnotic Room. Simon
Mystery of the Indian Relic. A. Parsons
Mystery of the Inn by the Shore. F. Warden
Mystery of the Ironworks. D. Lenton
Mystery of the Isle of Fortune. R. C. Armour
Mystery of the Italian Ruins. D. Long
Mystery of the Kidnapped Munition Worker. G. Chester
Mystery of the Kneeling Woman. M. Dalton
Mystery of the Living Shadow. W. W. Sayer
Mystery of the Locked Door. E. Baird
Mystery of the Locked Room. L. Rose
Mystery of the Locks. E. W. Howe
Mystery of the Lodge. M. D. Chellis
Mystery of the London Banker. J. S. Fletcher
Mystery of the Lorry Driver. P. Urquhart
Mystery of the Lost Battle-Ship. W. W. Sayer
Mystery of the Lost Dauphin. E. P. Bazan
Mystery of the Lost Legionnaire. M. Osborne
Mystery of the Lost Loot. H. King
Mystery of the Lotus Queen. H. H. Ross
Mystery of the Louvre. A. Bernede
Mystery of the Luminous Ray. Arthur Russell
Mystery of the Lyons Mail. F. A. Edwards
Mystery of the Mad Millionaires. W. Tyrer
Mystery of the Man from Rio. G. H. Teed
Mystery of the Mandarin's Idol. R. M. Graydon
Mystery of the Mansion Fire. H. H. C. Gibbons
Mystery of the Marbletons. M. Mackin
Mystery of the Marchers. W. Edwards
Mystery of the Marshes. G. Prout
Mystery of the Mason's Arms. A. Parsons
Mystery of the Middle Temple. R. Machray
Mystery of the Miniature. R. K. Edwards
Mystery of the Missing Angler. W. Tyrer
Mystery of the Missing Aviator. W. W. Sayer
Mystery of the Missing Constable. A. Blair
Mystery of the Missing Corpses. G. Elliott
Mystery of the Missing Doctor. C. Brisbane
Mystery of the Missing Envoy. P. Quiroule
Mystery of the Missing Formula. M. Dorrell
Mystery of the Missing Journalist. W. J. Bayfield
Mystery of the Missing Refugee. H. Scott
Mystery of the Moat. A. Sergeant
Mystery of the Moat House. D. Vane
Mystery of the Monkey-Gland Cocktail. R. East
Mystery of the Montauk Mills. E. L. Coolidge
Mystery of the Monument. A. Blair
Mystery of the Moving Island. Elinor Chamberlain
Mystery of the Mud Flats. M. Drake
Mystery of the Murdered Blonde. J. G. Brandon
Mystery of the Murdered Chef. R. Hardinge
Mystery of the Murdered Ice Cream Man. J. G. Brandon
Mystery of the Murdered Sentry. J. G. Brandon
Mystery of the Myrtles. E. Jepson
Mystery of the New Tenant. J. Hunter
Mystery of the Old Age Pensioner. G. H. Teed
Mystery of the Old Curiosity Shop. G. Chester
Mystery of the One-Day Alibi. A. Parsons
Mystery of the "Opal". R. S. Holland
Mystery of the Open Window. Anthony Gilbert
Mystery of the Outlawed Black. R. Hardinge
Mystery of the Painted Nude. W. Gore
Mystery of the Papyrus. G. B. Vale
Mystery of the Patrician Club. A. D. Vandam
Mystery of the Peacock's Eye. B. Flynn
Mystery of the Phantom Billionaire. M. J. De Lauer
Mystery of the Phantom Blackmailer. G. Verner
Mystery of the Platinum Nugget! W. W. Sayer
Mystery of the "Polarlys". G. Simenon
Mystery of the Pot-Bank. W. J. Bayfield
Mystery of the Purple Cloak. E. W. Terris
Mystery of the Rabbit's Paw. S. Jepson

Mystery of the Rajah's Jewels. P. Urquhart
Mystery of the Rajah's Son. C. Brisbane
Mystery of the Ravenspurs. F. M. White
Mystery of the Raymond Mortgage. F. S. Fitzgerald
Mystery of the Red Chateau. J. Hunter
Mystery of the Red Cockatoo. A. Parsons
Mystery of the Red Flame. G. Barton
Mystery of the Red-Haired Valet. G. Davison
Mystery of the Red Suitcase. L. M. Day
Mystery of the Red Tower. C. Brisbane
Mystery of the Red Triangle. W. C. Tuttle
Mystery of the Reunion Dinner. R. Hardinge
Mystery of the Rio Star. W. Tyrer
Mystery of the Royal Mail. B. L. Farjeon
Mystery of the Rue de Babylone. J. N. Raphael
Mystery of the Rue Soly. H. Balzac
Mystery of the S. S. Timor. G. Grantham
Mystery of the Sabotaged Jet. J. Drummond
Mystery of the Sandal-Wood Box. M. C. Barnard
Mystery of the Scented Death. Roy Vickers
Mystery of the Sea. B. Stoker
Mystery of the Sea Horse. L. Falk
Mystery of the Sealed Room. V. Andrews
Mystery of the Seaside Hotel. W. J. Bayfield
Mystery of the Second Shot. J. R. Gillies
Mystery of the Seine. G. H. Teed
Mystery of the Seven. W. Usher
Mystery of the 7 Bad Men. H. L. Gates
Mystery of the Seven Cafes. S. Horler
Mystery of the Shadow. F. Hume
Mystery of the Shadowed Footballer. M. Frazer
Mystery of the Shot P.C. G. N. Philips
Mystery of the Silver Dagger. R. Parrish
Mystery of the Silver Run. B. Marchant
Mystery of the Singing Walls. W. A. Stowell
Mystery of the Skating Rink. H. D. Dearden
Mystery of the Skeleton Key. B. Capes
Mystery of the Sleeping Car Express, and other stories. F. W. Crofts
Mystery of the Smiling Doll. H. Holt
Mystery of the Smoking Gun. C. J. Daly
Mystery of the Star Sapphire. E. Fraser
Mystery of the Stolen Despatches. A. Parsons
Mystery of the Stolen Hats. B. Graeme
Mystery of the Stolen Plans. M. Coles
Mystery of the Street Musician. J. G. Brandon
Mystery of the Suez Canal. C. H. Hillcoat
Mystery of the Summer-House. H. G. Hutchinson
Mystery of the Sunken Road. R. C. Armour
Mystery of the Swamp. W. M. Graydon
Mystery of the Swanley Viaduct. G. N. Philips
Mystery of the Swindler's Stooge. W. Tyrer
Mystery of the Sycamore. C. Wells
Mystery of the Tailor's Dummy. R. Sonin
Mystery of the Tarn. C. Wells
Mystery of the Thames. F. Warden
Mystery of the Third Gable. L. Barbee
Mystery of the Third Parrot. M. Dana
Mystery of the Thirteenth Chest. P. Urquhart
Mystery of the 13th Floor. L. Thayer
Mystery of the Thousand Peaks. A. Murray
Mystery of the Three Acrobats. J. G. Brandon
Mystery of the Three B Syndicate. E. Begbie
Mystery of the Three City's. J. G. Brandon
Mystery of the Three Demobbed Men. W. Tyrer
Mystery of the Three Fingers. M. Leighton
Mystery of the Tower Room. L. Despard
Mystery of the Tramp Steamer. C. Brisbane
Mystery of the Tumbling V. D. T. Lindsay
Mystery of the Turkish Agreement. W. W. Sayer
Mystery of the Twin Rubies. A. Livingston
Mystery of the Two-Faced Man. F. Grierson
Mystery of the 250,000 Rupees. A. Parsons
Mystery of the Underground Factory. G. Chester
Mystery of the Unicorn. W. Magnay
Mystery of the Uninvited Guest. W. Shute
Mystery of the Unknown Victim. W. Jardine
Mystery of the Vanished Trainer. J. Hunter

Title Index

Mystery of the Vanishing Aerodrome. P. Conde
Mystery of the Walled Garden. A. Salcroft
Mystery of the White Knight. C. MacLeod
Mystery of the Whitehall Bomb. A. Parsons
Mystery of the Woman in Red. Anthony Gilbert
Mystery of the Woman Overboard. W. Tyrer
Mystery of the Yellow Room. G. Leroux
Mystery of Theyne Manor. W. J. Passingham
Mystery of 31, New Inn. R. A. Freeman
Mystery of Tumbling Reef. B. Grimshaw
Mystery of Tumult Rock. C. P. Hauck
Mystery of Tunnel 51. A. Wilson
Mystery of Uncle Ballard. H. D. Stacpoole
Mystery of Vaucluse. J. H. Wallis
Mystery of Victor Grayson. R. Groves
Mystery of Villa Aurelia. B. E. Stevenson
Mystery of Villa Sineste. W. Livingston
Mystery of Vincent Dane. J. L. Rickard
Mystery of White Fell Gill. H. McKay
Mystery of Witch-Face Mountain. C. E. Craddock
Mystery of Wo-Sing. A. G. Hales
Mystery of Wolverston Grange. W. R. Sunman
Mystery of Woodcroft. Anonymous
Mystery of Woodleigh Grange. Anonymous
Mystery of X04. Jack Lewis
Mystery of X20. J. G. Brandon
Mystery on Happy Bones. K. Robeson
Mystery on Southampton Water. F. W. Crofts
Mystery on the Broads. G. H. Teed
Mystery on the Centre Court. H. Willett
Mystery on the Clyde. W. M. Duncan
Mystery on the Moor. J. J. Farjeon
Mystery on the Moors. B. Michaels
Mystery on the Queen Mary. B. Graeme
Mystery on the River. B. O'Farrell
Mystery on the Snow. K. Robeson
Mystery Plane. J. Bolton
Mystery Play. J. C. Van Itallie
Mystery Puzzle Book. L. Wren
Mystery Puzzles. A. Ripley
Mystery Queen. F. Hume
Mystery Reef. H. Bindloss
Mystery Road. E. P. Oppenheim
Mystery Still. F. Du Boisgobey
Mystery Stories. S. Ellin
Mystery Story. D. Pirie
Mystery Street. L. Noel
Mystery Tipster. F. Johnston
Mystery Tour. D. Rutherford
Mystery Under the Sea. K. Robeson
Mystery Underground. J. J. Farjeon
Mystery Villa. E. R. Punshon
Mystery Week-End. P. Wilde
Mystery Woman. J. U. Giesy
Mystery Woman. A. MacGowan
Mystic Diagram. Nicholas Carter
Mystic Events. F. Lathom
Mystic Manor. H. G. Weston
Mystic Mullah. K. Robeson
Mystic Number Seven. Annabel Gray
Mystic Romances of the Blue and Grey. A. C. Branscomb
Mystic Serpent. S. De Havilland
Mystic Voices. R. Pater
Mystics. K. Thurston
Myth Is Murder. Shane Martin
Mythmaker. S. Gainham

N or M? A. Christie
N3 Conspiracy. Nick Carter
Nabob and Knave. Nicholas Carter
Nabob's Jewel. C. A. Alington
Nabob's Widow. Elsie Lee
Nadine. G. Bocca
Nail of Suspicion. F. Crisp
Nails. R. L. Hill
Nairobi Nightcap. D. Fearon
Naked and Alone. Michael Lawrence
Naked and the Damned. R. Shafer
Naked and the Innocent. W. Ard
Naked and the Lost. F. M. Davis
Naked Angel. J. Webb
Naked Bishop. M. J. Sagola
Naked Blade. P. Saxon
Naked Canvas. Warwick Scott
Naked City. C. Einstein
Naked City. M. Wald
Naked Country. M. East
Naked Crusader. F. Archer
Naked Ebony. D. Cushman
Naked Edge. M. Ehrlich
Naked Eye. Henrietta Martin
Naked Face. S. Sheldon
Naked Fear. J. Farr
Naked Five. V. France
Naked Foot. H. Kaner
Naked from a Well. W. A. Ballinger
Naked Fury. D. Keene

Naked Hours. Wenzell Brown
Naked Hunter. W. Woolfolk
Naked in the Dark. G. Paul
Naked in the Night. J. Cleary
Naked in the Streets. R. Johnson
Naked Island. B. Heatter
Naked Jungle. H. Whittington
Naked Kiss. S. Fuller
Naked Lady. M. Corrigan
Naked Land. H. Innes
Naked Light. J. Moffatt
Naked Mistress. W. Deptula
Naked Morning. R. V. Cassill
Naked Murder. F. Erskine
Naked Murderer. E. Piper
Naked Nemesis. K. Conway
Naked Nuns. Colin Watson
Naked Runner. F. Clifford
Naked She Died. D. Tracy
Naked Skier. C. Short
Naked Spur. A. Ullman
Naked Storm. S. Eisner
Naked Sun. I. Asimov
Naked Sun. T. Willis
Naked Tide. Roderic Hastings
Naked to My Enemy. H. Jobson
Naked to My Pride. H. Rigsby
Naked to My Grave. H. Carmichael
Naked Villainy. C. G. Hodges
Naked Villainy. J. Davey
Naked When We Die. T. Martin
Nakia. L. Hays
Name for Evil. A. Lyttle
Name Is Archer. J. R. Macdonald
Name Is Chambers. H. Kane
Name Is Jordan. H. Q. Masur
Name Is Judas. R. Gaines
Name Is Malone. C. Rice
Name Is Smith. Eric North
Name My Own. C. Holicker
Name of Action. G. Greene
Name of the Game. D. Cory
Name of the Game Is Death. D. J. Marlowe
Name of the Game Is Death. C. Richardson
Name of the Game is Murder. E. Asinof
Name the Woman. A. M. Williamson
Name Your Poison. H. Reilly
Nameless Coffin. Gwendoline Butler
Nameless Crime. W. S. Masterman
Nameless Dread. J. K. Stafford
Nameless Five. J. Skene
Nameless Man. F. Du Boisgobey
Nameless Man. N. S. Lincoln
Nameless One. R. Temperley
Nameless Ones. L. Egan
Nameless Ones. R. T. M. Scott
Nameless Ones. L. Vardre
Nameless Order. Dargon
Nameless Road. S. Harvester
Nameless Stranger and What Happened to Flaunce. B. Reynolds
Nameless Thing. M. D. Post
Name's Death, Remember Me? S. Forbes
Name's Maguire. J. Himmel
Nancy Lee, Mill Lass. H. E. Inman
Nancy Manoeuvres. C. Gleig
Nancy, the Daring. K. Kimbrough
Nanny. E. Piper
Nap on Nighthawk. S. Horler
Napalm Bugle. E. Lacy
Naples, or Die! H. Chesham
Napoleon of the Press. M. Leighton
Napoleon Ring. A. Lowing
Napoleon Smith. W. J. Arkell
NARC. R. Hawkes
Narc. S. L. Stebel
Narcissus in the Way. G. V. McFadden
Narcissus Murders. XV8
Narracong Riddle. A. Derleth
Narrow Cell. Dale Clark
Narrow Escape. Annie Thomas
Narrow Exit. P. Henissart
Narrow Gauge to Murder. Carolyn Thomas
Narrow House. H. Fernee
Narrow Road. Robin Moore
Narrow Search. A. Garve
Narrowing Circle. H. Hill
Narrowing Circle. J. Symons
Narrowing Lust. G. Baxter
Narrowing Lust. H. Kane
Nasty Cropper. G. F. Underhill
Nasty Name Murders. R. Howes
Nasty Piece of Work. R. Croft-Cooke
Nat Foster, the Boston Detective. H. Rockwood
Nat Wedgewood, Jockey. J. Fairfax-Blakeborough
Natalie Limited. P. Trent
Natasha. C. W. Thayer
Nation Within. F. Fytton
Nation's Missing Guest. H. Footner
Nation's Peril. Nicholas Carter
Native Superstition. H. C. McNeile
Natural Causes. N. Cecil
Natural Causes. T. Gallagher
Natural Enemies. W. Adler
Nature of a Crime. J. Conrad
Nature's Nobility. J. Newall
Naughty But Dead. G. G. Fickling
Naughty Girls. Arthur Wise
Naughty Maid of Mitcham. D. Donovan
Naval Adventuress. P. Trent

Naval Detective's Chase. Anonymous
Naval Detective's Chase. N. Buntline
Navona 1000. M. Arrighi
Navy Colt. F. Gruber
Navy in Action. Taffrail
Navy Murders. W. Chambers
Navy Spy Murders. G. F. Eliot
Nazi Assassins. D. Cory
Nazi Hunter. B. Shaw
Nazi Overcoat. R. Lebherz
Nazi Shadows. E. L. Fleming
Nazi Speedway Plot. E. T. Woodhall
Nearest and Dearest. E. Southworth
Nearing Storm. D. Donnelly
Nearness of Evil. C. Mills
Neat Little Corpse. Max Murray
'Neath the Southern Cross. K. Lindsay
Nebulon Horror. H. B. Cave
Nebuly Coat. J. M. Falkner
Necessary Action. P. Wahloo
Necessary Corpse. R. C. Woodthorpe
Necessary Doubt. Colin Wilson
Necessary End. V. Gielgud
Necessary End. S. Harper
Necessary Evil. K. Roos
Neck and Neck. L. Bruce
Neck in a Noose. E. Ferrars
Neck of Sinners. H. Spencer
Necklace and Calabash. R. Van Gulik
Necklace of Death. H. Holt
Necklace of Parmona. L. T. Meade
Necklace of Skulls. I. Drummond
Necktie for Norman. J. L. Morrissey
Necromancer. L. Flammenberg
Necropolis. B. Copper
Ned Bachman, the New Orleans Detective. Alan Dale
Need a Body Tell? B. Cobb
Needful Journey. Winifred Duke
Needle. Hal Clement
Needle. H. N. Field
Needle. Francis King
Needle in a Haystack. G. Joseph
Needle That Wouldn't Hold Still. Hampton Stone
Needles. W. Deverell
Needle's Eye. Edward Lee
Needle's Kiss. Seamark
Needles of Death. P. Edwards
Needy Nine. Nicholas Carter
Nefarious Quest. H. Janson
Negative in Blue. Carter Brown
Negative Man. R. C. Galwey
Negative of a Nude. C. E. Fritch
Negative Value. J. Boland
Negatives. P. Everett
Neglected Clue. I. Ostrander
Neglected Fire. H. Horn
Negotiator. Clayton Matthews
Negotiator. R. M. Rogers
Negro. G. Simenon
Negrohead. R. Bridges
Neighbor. L. Koenig
Neighbors. M. Allwright
Neighbors. G. Simenon
Neil Nelson, the Veteran Detective. H. Rockwood
Neila Sen and My Casual Death. J. H. Connelly
Neither a Candle Nor a Pitchfork. J. Porter
Neither Do I Condemn Thee. A. Soutar
Neither Five Nor Three. Helen MacInnes
Neither Had I Rest. N. Cromarty
Neither Man Nor Dog. G. Kersh
Neither the Sea Nor the Sand. G. Honeycombe
Nell. S. Nichols
Nell Alone. Jennie Melville
Nella Waits. M. Millhiser
Nellie, the Obvious. K. Kimbrough
Nellie Was a Lady. J. Kirkpatrick
Nelly Jocelyn, Widow. J. Middlemass
Nelson Lord—One of Our Agents. G. Windsor
Nelson's Blood. G. Kent
Nemesis. A. Christie
Nemesis. J. M. Cobban
Nemesis. P. Davis
Nemesis at Raynham Parva. J. J. Connington
Nemesis Club. W. W. Sayer
Nemesis Club. Jenny Savage
Nemesis Wife. C. L. Evans
Nemesis Wore Nylons. Carter Brown
Nemo. T. Douglas
Nemo, the Shadow Detective. F. L. Broughton
Neon Graveyard. G. Baxt
Neon Haystack. J. M. Ullman
Neon Jungle. J. D. MacDonald
Neon Madman. J. Harvey
Neon Preacher. R. Chambers
Neon Rainbow. C. Terrot
Neopolitan Streak. T. Holme
Neptune. N. Gerson
Neptune's Son. R. S. Holland
Nerve. D. Francis
Nerve Beat. J. B. O'Sullivan
Nerve Centre. H. Janson
Nerve of Foley, and other railroad stories. F. H. Spearman

Nervestorm. M. Sharland
Nervous Miss Miles. M. Short
Nesbit's Compact. P. Trent
Nest-Egg for the Baron. Anthony Morton
Nest of Fear. H. Ellson
Nest of Rats. J. Wainwright
Nest of Spies. Geoffrey Davison
Nest of Spies. P. Souvestre
Nest of Traitors. G. Ashe
Nest of Vipers. T. Claymore
Nest of Vipers. Wallace Crawford
Nest of Vipers. G. Mitchell
Nest of Vultures. Robert MacLeod
Net. J. Pudney
Net. E. Ronns
Net Around Joan Ingilby. A. Fielding
Net of Cobwebs. E. S. Holding
Nether Millstone. F. M. White
Nets of Fate. O. Binns
Nets to Catch the Wind. D. Hitchens
Netta. F. M. White
Nettle. E. Wooll
Nettle Shade. J. Turner
Network. Godfrey Smith
Network. Roderic Wilkinson
Network of Crime. Nicholas Carter
Network of Fear. A. Yudkoff
Neutron Beam Murder. T. J. King
Neutron Two Is Critical. L. Dunning
Nevada Alibi. Dan Morgan
Nevada Detective. Anonymous
Nevada Gunslinger. V. Coffman
Never Had a Dull Moment. P. Cheyney
Never Again. Francis King
Never Ask a Policeman. D. J. Olivy
Never Be Caught. J. McKimmey
Never Bet Your Life. G. H. Coxe
Never by Chance. Sylvia Tate
Never Call It Loving. D. Eden
Never Come Back. J. Mair
Never Contract. D. Gerrity
Never Cross a Vampire. S. M. Kaminsky
Never Die Alone. D. Goines
Never Die in Honolulu. I. Hamilton
Ne'er-Do-Well. D. Yates
Never-Fail Blake. A. Stringer
Never-Fail Detective. H. Holmes
Never Fight a Lady. S. Truss
Never Fire First. J. Dorrance
Never Forget, Never Forgive. C. Fox
Never Give a Millionaire an Even Break. H. Kane
Never Go Dark. E. Bonett
Never Had a Chance. R. Farran
Never Had a Spanner on Her. J. Leasor
Never in Vain. J. L. Hardy
Never Kill a Client. B. Halliday
Never Kill a Cop! M. Colton
Never Kill a Cop. L. Costigan
Never Kill a Cop. H. Searls
Never Kill a Cop. J. B. West
Never Kill for Sport. J. L. Richard
Never Leave My Bed. J. T. Rogers
Never Live Twice. D. J. Marlowe
Never Look Back. J. Aeby
Never Look Back. H. Carter
Never Look Back. M. G. Eberhart
Never Mind the Lady. D. Garth
Never Mix Business with Pleasure. B. Graeme
Never Need an Enemy. A. M. Stein
Never Pick Up Hitchhikers. Ellis Peters
Never Put Off Till Tomorrow What You Can Kill Today. J. Godey
Never Say Dead. E. Kennedy
Never Say Die. E. Foote-Smith
Never Say Die. M. Malmer
Never Say Die. M. K. Ozaki
Never Say Die. I. S. Shriber
Never Say Live! David Hume
Never Say No to a Killer. J. Gant
Never Shake a Skeleton. A. Flett
Never Shoot a Lady. E. Hale
Never Smile at Children. E. T. French
Never Step on a Rainbow. W. Wolfe
Never Summer Mystery. T. Perry
Never Take Candy from a Stranger. R. Garis
Never to Die. Alice Brennan
Never Trust a Dame. C. Wheatley
Never Trust a Woman. Raymond Marshall
Never Turn Your Back. A. Capelli
Never Turn Your Back. M. Scherf
Never Wake a Dead Man. B. Bird
Never Walk Alone. R. King
Never-Was Girl. Carter Brown
Never Wed an Old Man. H. Caswell
Nevermore Affair. K. Wilhelm
Nevlo. K. Robeson
New Adventures of Ellery Queen. E. Queen
New Andromeda. C. Dawe
New Arabian Nights. R. L. Stevenson
New Bodies for Old. M. Renard
New Breed. L. Costigan
New Centurions. J. Wambaugh
New Chronicles of Don Q. K. Prichard
New Departure. K. Connor
New Detective Stories. G. Campbell
New England Gothic. A. J. Allen
New Exploits of Nick Carter. Nicholas Carter
New Face in Hell. R. Busby

New Gun Runners. Neil Gordon
New Idol. G. Leroux
New Jack Sheppard. E. A. Treeton
New Jersey Showdown. R. Mallory
New Kind of Killer. Jennie Melville
New Kind of Killer, an Old Kind of Death. Jennie Melville
New Leaf, and other stories. J. Ritchie
New Lease of Death. R. Rendell
New Lease of Life. G. Simenon
New Lease on Life. G. Simenon
New Made Grave. H. Footner
New Magdalen. W. Collins
New Man in Lowuni. J. Fores
New Master. A. Golsworthy
New Mexico Connection. C. Wilcox
New Mistress. G. M. Fenn
New Mrs. Aldrich. V. Stuart
New Monk. R. S.
New Moon. Taffrail
New Order. M. Gerard
New Orleans Holocaust. P. McCurtin
New Orleans Knockout. D. Pendleton
New Othello. I. D. Hardy
New People at the Hollies. Josephine Bell
New Race Diplomatist. J. B. Waterbury
New Rivers Calling. J. B. Hendryx
New Serpent in Eden. Nicholas Carter
New Shining White Murder. D. Launay
New Shoe. A. W. Upfield
New Sonia Wayward. M. Innes
New Tenant. E. P. Oppenheim
New Terror. G. Leroux
New Vigilantes. J. D. Horan
New Year's Eve in Lan-Fang. R. Van Gulik
New York by Night. Grace M. White
New York Connection. Robin Moore
New York Dance. D. E. Westlake
New York Detective. Old Sleuth
New York Necromancy. M. Macao
New York, New York. S. Kahn
New York One. Lawrence Levine
Newgate. T. P. Prest
Newhaven-Dieppe. G. Simenon
Newman Factor. J. S. Prager
News Caper. R. Jansson
News of Murder. A. Lejeune
News of Paul Temple. F. Durbridge
News Reel. R. J. Casey
News Travels by Night. B. Graeme
Newsdeath. R. Connolly
Newshound's Nemesis. R. Kirby
Newspaper Girl. A. M. Williamson
Newspaper Seller's Secret. W. Edwards
Next Door. F. Hume
Next Door to Danger. C. MacLeod
Next Door to Death. B. Cobb
Next Door to Murder. L. Cargill
Next Man. M. Z. Lewin
Next of Kin. G. Goodchild
Next o'Kin. W. M. Graydon
Next One to Die. V. Gunn
Next, Please. J. M. Walsh
Next Saturday in Milan. W. Tute
Next Stop—the Morgue. B. Winter
Next Time I'll Pay My Own Fare. R. V. Beste
Next Time, You'll Wake Up Dead. Philip Evans
Next to Die. J. Godey
Next to Die. G. Verner
Next-to-Last Train Ride. C. Dennis
Next Victim. Donald Stuart
Nic Barker I.D.B. D. Brechin
Nic Revel. G. M. Fenn
Nice and Easy. David Miles
Nice Bloke. C. Cookson
Nice Class of People. A. La Bern
Nice Cup of Tea. Anthony Gilbert
Nice Day for a Funeral. H. Howard
Nice Day for a Murder. V. Gunn
Nice Day for Murder. F. Murray
Nice Derangement of Epitaphs. Ellis Peters
Nice Enough to Murder. E. S. Russell
Nice Fillies Finish Last. B. Halliday
Nice Friendly Town. H. Calvin
Nice Girl Like You. R. Wormser
Nice Girl's Story. Rosemary Harris
Nice Guy Like Me. E. Cannon
Nice Guys Don't Win. S. Mitchell
Nice Guys Finish Dead. Albert Conroy
Nice Guys Finish Last. R. Kyle
Nice Lady. M. Hayman
Nice Little Killing. Anthony Gilbert
Nice Murderer. D. Delman
Nice Neighborhood. E. Bahr
Nice People Don't Kill. F. W. Bronson
Nice People Murder. M. E. Bradley
Nice People Poison. M. H. Bradley
Nice Place to Die. M. Culpan
Nice Quiet Girl. Philip Daniels
Nice Way to Die. H. Janson
Nice Way to Die. M. Warner
Nice Young Man. W. L. Harter
Nicest Corpse. John Morgan
Nicholas Goade, Detective. E. P. Oppenheim
Nicholas Lattermole's Case. C. Barry
Nicholas Snatch. P. Malloch
Nichovev Plot. Nick Carter

Nick Carter and the Green Goods Men. Nicholas Carter
Nick Carter and the Red Button. Nicholas Carter
Nick Carter, Detective. Nicholas Carter
Nick Carter Down East. Nicholas Carter
Nick Carter's Auto Trail. Nicholas Carter
Nick Carter's Chance Clue. Nicholas Carter
Nick Carter's Chinese Puzzle. Nicholas Carter
Nick Carter's Cipher. Nicholas Carter
Nick Carter's Clever Protege. Nicholas Carter
Nick Carter's Clever Ruse. Nicholas Carter
Nick Carter's Close Call. Nicholas Carter
Nick Carter's Close Finish. Nicholas Carter
Nick Carter's Convict Client. Nicholas Carter
Nick Carter's Counterplot. Nicholas Carter
Nick Carter's Death Warrant. Nicholas Carter
Nick Carter's Double Catch. Nicholas Carter
Nick Carter's Egyptian Clew. Nicholas Carter
Nick Carter's Fall. Nicholas Carter
Nick Carter's Girl Detective. Nicholas Carter
Nick Carter's Intuition. Nicholas Carter
Nick Carter's Last Card. Nicholas Carter
Nick Carter's Masterpiece. Nicholas Carter
Nick Carter's Menace. Nicholas Carter
Nick Carter's New Assistant. Nicholas Carter
Nick Carter's Persistence. Nicholas Carter
Nick Carter's Promise. Nicholas Carter
Nick Carter's Retainer. Nicholas Carter
Nick Carter's Roundup. Nicholas Carter
Nick Carter's Star Pupils. Nicholas Carter
Nick Carter's Subtle Foe. Nicholas Carter
Nick Carter's Swim to Victory. Nicholas Carter
Nick Carter's Treasure Chest Case. Nicholas Carter
Nick Carter's Wildest Chase. Nicholas Carter
Nick of the Woods. T. Taggart
Nick of Time. W. T. Hickman
Nick the Click. G. K. Wilkinson
Nick Westerman, Detective. A. L. Yates
Nickel Jackpot. J. J. Lamb
Nickel Ride. M. T. Kaufman
Nicky Nimble. Anonymous
Nicola. D. Daniels
Nicola. A. E. Lindop
Nicolette of the Quarter. V. MacClure
Niece of Abraham Pein. J. H. Wallis
Nig-Nog. E. Wallace
Nigel Fortescue. W. Westall
Night-Action! S. M. Parkman
Night After Night. S. Thurman
Night After the Wedding. The Gordons
Night Air Is Dangerous. Sutherland Scott
Night and Fog. A. Gask
Night and Fog. K. Netzen
Night & Green Ginger. D. Lockwood
Night and Morning. Old Sleuth
Night and No Moon. J. Odlum
Night and the City. G. Kersh
Night and the Judgement. L. Butler
Night Assassin. M. B. Dix
Night at Club Bagdad. O. F. Jerome
Night at Hogwallow. T. Strauss
Night at Krumlin Castle. Frank King
Night at Lost End. G. A. Chamberlain
Night at Sea Abbey. V. Coffman
Night at the Mocking Widow. Carter Dickson
Night at the Vulcan. N. Marsh
Night Attack. L. Crosby
Night Beat. Arthur MacLean
Night Before Dying. R. M. Coates
Night Before Murder. S. Fisher
Night Before the Wedding. The Gordons
Night Boat. T. Trent
Night Boat from Puerto Vedra. Donald MacKenzie
Night Boat to Paris. R. Jessup
Night Call. P. Merriman
Night Callers. F. Crisp
Night Child. C. De Blasis
Night Chills. D. R. Koontz
Night Club. P. Cheyney
Night Club. G. Simenon
Night-Club Crime. A. Skene
Night Club Lady. A. Abbot
Night Club Murder. J. G. Brandon
Night Club Murder. Roland Daniel
Night Club Murder. J. A. Jordan
Night Club Mystery. E. Jordan
Night Club Mystery. G. H. Teed
Night Coach. "Capstan"
Night Comer. Jack Wilson
Night-Comers. E. Ambler
Night Cover. M. Z. Lewin
Night Crossing. K. Kolb

Title Index

Nightmare in July / 563

Night Cry. W. L. Stuart
Night Darkens the Streets. A. La Bern
Night Drop. F. C. Davis
Night Encounter. Anthony Gilbert
Night Exercise. J. Rhode
Night Express Murder. L. A. Knight
Night Extra. W. P. McGivern
Night Falls at Bitterhill. P. Warren
Night Falls on the City. S. Gainham
Night Falls Too Soon. F. Chimenti
Night Flight to Zurich. C. F. Gregg
Night Flower. W. C. Butler
Night for Evil. Jack Lewis
Night for Screaming. H. Whittington
Night for Treason. J. Jakes
Night Freight. J. M. Yates
Night Freight Murders. Robert Fleming
Night Frost. B. Copper
Night Ghouls. R. Chetwynd-Hayes
Night Has a Thousand Eyes. G. Hopley
Night Has Another Voice. G. Colizzi
Night Has Eyes. E. Backhouse
Night Has Eyes. A. Kennington
Night Has Red Eyes. J. Millson
Night Hath Eyes. Andrea Hill
Night Hawk. D. Cory
Night Hawk. J. R. Holden
Night Hawk. E. Jepson
Night Hawk. A. Stringer
Night Hunt. M. Rostov
Night Hunters. J. Crecy
Night Hunters. J. Miles
Night I Caught the Sante Fe Chief. E. Thorpe
Night I Died. W. Irish
Night in George Square. S. Fraser
Night in Glengyle. J. Ferguson
Night in Havana. R. Sylvester
Night in October. M. Callard
Night in Which All Cats Are Gray. W. S. New
Night Intruder. D. Noel
Night Is a Child. R. Llewellyn
Night Is a Time for Listening. E. West
Night Is a Time to Die. J. Wainwright
Night Is for Screaming. Robert Turner
Night Is for Violence. D. Bateson
Night Is My Enemy. F. Carmichael
Night Journey. Winston Graham
Night Judgment at Sinos. J. Higgins
Night Jump—Cuba. P. Runyon
Night Lady. W. C. Gault
Night Letter. P. Spike
Night Lights. M. Pemberton
Night Lords. N. Freeling
Night Mail. Percy Fitzgerald
Night Mail. H. F. Wood
Night Man. A. Ullman
Night Marchers. J. Shelynn
Night Moves. A. Sharp
Night Must Fall. W. Drummond
Night Must Fall. Emlyn Williams
Night My Enemy. A. Maybury
Night Never Ends. F. Lorenz
Night of Camp David. F. Knebel
Night of Clear Choice. D. M. Disney
Night of Crime. A. Livingston
Night of Dread. J. Creasey
Night of Errors. M. Innes
Night of Evil. Genevieve St. John
Night of Fear. M. Dalton
Night of Fear. N. MacKenzie
Night of Four Hundred Rabbits. Elizabeth Peters
Night of Glass. P. Purser
Night of Horror. C. Buchanan
Night of Horror. A. Soutar
Night of January 16. A. Rand
Night of Love. B. E. M. Ward
Night of May Third. A. M. Wells
Night of Murder. C. Rushton
Night of Mystery. J. C. Ellis
Night of Peril. H. Bleackley
Night of Reckoning. F. Barrett
Night of Reckoning. S. Horler
Night of Reckoning. P. Ordway
Night of Reckoning. J. S. Strange
Night of Secrets. S. Warwick
Night of Secrets. J. Wetherell
Night of Shadows. F. Lockridge
Night of Terror. Joy Brown
Night of Terror. R. Desmond
Night of Terror. R. H. Wilkinson
Night of the Assassin. Don Smith
Night of the Assassins. B. Rossi
Night of the Avenger. Nick Carter
Night of the Black Horror. V. Norwood
Night of the Black Tower. Michael Sinclair
Night of the Bonfire. J. Blackmore
Night of the Bowstring. D. B. Olsen
Night of the Candles. Patricia Maxwell
Night of the Crime. H. Desmond
Night of the Crabs. G. N. Smith
Night of the Crisis. J. Ingersol
Night of the Darkest Moon. J. Peart
Night of the Dead. Dana Ross
Night of the Eagles. R. Collin
Night of the Enchantress. K. Troy
Night of the Fair. J. Baker
Night of the Fog. Anthony Gilbert
Night of the Fourth. J. Roffey
Night of the Fox. J. Gannold
Night of the Full Moon. J. N. Chance
Night of the Funeral. H. C. Davis
Night of the Garter Murder. R. Howes
Night of the Generals. H. H. Kirst
Night of the Good Children. M. Carleton
Night of the Griffin. E. Giles
Night of the Hawk. R. Raine
Night of the Hellebore. J. Reddoch
Night of the Horns. D. Sanderson
Night of the Hunter. D. Grubb
Night of the Jabberwock. F. Brown
Night of the Jackals. Ralph Hayes
Night of the Juggler. W. P. McGivern
Night of the Kill. Breni James
Night of the Letter. D. Eden
Night of the Living Dead. J. Russo
Night of the Long Shadows. H. St. Thomas
Night of the Moonrose. M. Lynch
Night of the Party. M. Cronin
Night of the Phantom. Marilyn Ross
Night of the Phoenix. N. De Mille
Night of the Picaroon. J. Cassells
Night of the Rape. L. White
Night of the Reaper. V. M. Grayland
Night of the Rose. H. Castillou
Night of the Ruby. L. Conway
Night of the Savage. G. Beare
Night of the Scorpion. S. O'Brien
Night of the Scorpion. L. Robin
Night of the Settlement. J. N. Chance
Night of the Shadow. M. Grant
Night of the Shooting Star. D. Vipond
Night of the Short Knives. B. Wilkinson
Night of the Sphinx. T. Leighton
Night of the Storm. J. Dallas
Night of the Storm. A. Gask
Night of the Storm. Magali
Night of the Stranger. J. Blackmore
Night of the 3rd Ult. H. F. Wood
Night of the Thirteenth. S. Warwick
Night of the Tiger. D. C. Cooke
Night of the Tiger. M. Kistler
Night of the Toads. Michael Collins
Night of the Tribolites. P. Leslie
Night of the Twelfth. M. Gilbert
Night of the 12th-13th. A. Steeman
Night of the 23rd. L. Jackson
Night of the Visitor. R. Willock
Night of the Watchman. J. Creasey
Night of the Wedding. C. N. Williamson
Night of the Wolf. W. H. Baker
Night of the Wolf. J. Kersey
Night of the World. F. H. Rose
Night of Vengeance. A. W. Sherring
Night of Violence. P. Barrington
Night of Violence. L. Charbonneau
Night of Wenceslas. L. Davidson
Night of Wrath. Y. Smith
Night on Penwith. F. B. Clark
Night on the Bare Mountain. J. D. White
Night on the Devil's Pathway. C. M. Russell
Night on the Island. M. M. Kaye
Night on the Killer Reef. A. MacVicar
Night on the Pathway. C. M. Russell
Night Operator. H. Packard
Night over Fitch's Pond. C. Jarrett
Night over Mexico. T. Downing
Night over the Wood. H. Addis
Night Passage to Kano. M. K. Robertson
Night Patrol. Griff
Night People. J. Finney
Night Pieces. T. Burke
Night Pillow. H. C. Rae
Night Raider. M. Barry
Night Raiders. A. Skene
Night Ride and other journeys. C. Beaumont
Night Riders. J. Cullum
Night Riders. N. Tranter
Night Run. Elizabeth Fenwick
Night Run from Java. G. Black
Night Safe Mystery. L. Carlton
Night Scenes in New York. T. Pastor
Night Scream. Evelyn Harris
Night Screams. B. Pronzini
Night Search. J. Mangione
Night Seekers. K. Royce
Night Shade. D. Daniels
Night Shadow. D. Daniels
Night Shadows. Colin Robertson
Night Shadows. Mary Sellers
Night Shift. R. Blaker
Night Squad. D. Goodis
Night Stalker. J. Rice
Night Stands at the Door. Katherine Blake
Night Stop. E. Trevor
Night Strangler. J. Rice
Night Surprise. F. Warden
Night Tennis. A. Davis-Goff
Night the Fog Came Down. J. Bude
Night, the Woman. S. Ransome
Night They Killed Joss Varran. G. Bellairs
Night They Stole Manhattan. L. Orde
Night Thorn. I. Gordon
Night Tide. G. Carpenter
Night Tide. J. R. Wilmot
Night Train. K. Millar
Night Train to Mombasa. J. Farrington
Night Train to Paris. M. Coles
Night Trains. P. H. Fine
Night Trains. Barbara Wood
Night Trap. Colin Robertson
Night Vision. Frank King
Night Visitor and other stories. A. Bennett
Night Waking. K. Snow
Night Walk. E. Daly
Night Walker. D. Hamilton
Night Walker. S. Stuart
Night Was Dark. J. Reach
Night Was Made for Murder. W. Cotton
Night Was Made for Murder. B. Winter
Night Was Our Friend. M. Pertwee
Night Watch. L. Fletcher
Night Watch. H. McCutcheon
Night Watch. J. Olsen
Night Watch. T. Walsh
Night-Watchman's Friend. M. Fitt
Night We Get Rich. W. Newton
Night Wheeler. Carter Brown
Night Whispers. C. Veley
Night Wind at Northwiding. F. Hurd
Night Winds. B. Cleeve
Night Wind's Promise. V. Vanardy
Night Wings. M. Gerard
Night Without Darkness. K. Orvis
Night Without End. F. Duncan
Night Without End. S. MacIvers
Night Without End. Alistair MacLean
Night Without Sleep. E. Moll
Night Without Stars. Winston Graham
Night-World. R. Bloch
Nightbeat. William Camp
Nightborn. L. Grex
Nightcap. M. Marcin
Nightcap and Plume. G. R. Preedy
Nightclimber. J. M. White
Nightclub Mystery. H. Clevely
Nightcomers. M. Hastings
Nightdive. C. D. Peel
Nightfall. J. Crosby
Nightfall. D. Daniels
Nightfall. D. Goodis
Nightfall. B. Myers
Nightfighter Spy. M. McKenna
Nightgleams. J. Thatcher
Nighthawk. W. M. Duncan
Nighthawk Mops Up. S. Horler
Nighthawk of the Northwest. S. A. White
Nighthawk Strikes to Kill. S. Horler
Nighthawk Swears Vengeance. S. Horler
Nighthawk the Mountain Detective. Anonymous
Nighthawks! J. G. Brandon
Nightingale. E. Pace
Nightingale at Noon. M. Summerton
Nightingales Never Sing. J. Courage
Nightlight. M. Bardos
Nightlights. B. Goldie
Nightly Deadshade. John Aiken
Nightly She Sings. E. Olmstead
Nightmare. E. S. Aarons
Nightmare. A. Blaisdell
Nightmare. L. Brock
Nightmare. G. Endore
Nightmare. R. H. Greenan
Nightmare. L. Greth
Nightmare. W. Irish
Nightmare. A. La Bern
Nightmare. J. L. Latham
Nightmare. G. Mygatt
Nightmare. R. Owen
Nightmare. C. Woolrich
Nightmare Abbey. T. L. Peacock
Nightmare Abbey. W. E. D. Ross
Nightmare Alley. W. L. Gresham
Nightmare and Dawn. M. Aldanov
Nightmare at Dawn. J. Philips
Nightmare at Mountain Aerie. F. Hurd
Nightmare at Noon. S. Sterling
Nightmare at Riverview. Angela Gray
Nightmare Baby. L. Du Breuil
Nightmare Candidate. K. Stewart
Nightmare Castle. W. Martyn
Nightmare Chase. E. Berckman
Nightmare Chessboard. T. B. Morris
Nightmare Chrysalis. R. Gatenby
Nightmare Conspiracy. Ralph Hayes
Nightmare Cottage. G. M. Wilson
Nightmare Cruise. Wade Miller
Nightmare Dance. M. Lynch
Nightmare Ends. F. Cowen
Nightmare Express. I. Haiblum
Nightmare Factor. T. N. Scortia
Nightmare Farm. Jack Mann
Nightmare Fiesta. D. Martyn
Nightmare for Dr. Morelle. E. Dudley
Nightmare Hall. A. L. McMurdie
Nightmare Honeymoon. R. Foley
Nightmare House. R. Foley
Nightmare House. B. Gray
Nightmare House. E. B. Martin
Nightmare in Algeria. J. Rosenberger
Nightmare in Colour. R. H. Greenan
Nightmare in Copenhagen. M. Albrand
Nightmare in Dublin. P. Loraine
Nightmare in Eden. M. Asher
Nightmare in July. C. Coleman

Nightmare in Manhattan. T. Walsh
Nightmare in Naples. J. Stagg
Nightmare in New York. D. Pendleton
Nightmare in Pewter. J. DeWeese
Nightmare in Pink. J. D. MacDonald
Nightmare in Rust. P. Audemars
Nightmare Incident. S. Brydon
Nightmare Island. Ralph Hayes
Nightmare Kick. Jon Stevens
Nightmare Machine. J. N. Datesh
Nightmare of Eyes. D. Rico
Nightmare of Murder. Mildred Davis
Nightmare on the Nile. C. Leader
Nightmare Street. H. Ellson
Nightmare Street. M. Tabor
Nightmare Town. D. Hammett
Nightmares. R. Bloch
Nightmares and Geezenstacks. F. Brown
Nightmare's End. J. James
Nightmare's Morning. M. Lynch
Nightmare's Nest. J. Arliss
Nightrunners. Michael Collins
Night's Black Agent. J. Bingham
Night's Candles. A. Hocking
Night's Cloak. E. R. Punshon
Night's Dark Secret. J. Shearing
Night's Evil. M. McShane
Night's Moves. O. Blakeston
Nights of the Long Knives. H. H. Kirst
Nights of the Round Table. Margery Lawrence
Nights with an Old Lag. W. J. Wintle
Nights with Sasquatch. J. Cotter
Nightshade. G. M. Allen
Nightshade. T. Collins
Nightshade. I. Foster
Nightshade. H. Imbert-Terry
Nightshade. J. N. Makris
Nightshade. Derek Marlowe
Nightshade. J. H. Robinson
Nightshade & Damnations. G. Kersh
Nightshade Ring. L. Hardy
Nightspawn. J. Banville
Nighttime Guy. T. Kenrick
Nightwalker. T. Tessier
Nightwalkers. B. Cross
Nightwalkers. James Norman
Nightwatchmen. B. Hannah
Nightwebs. C. Woolrich
Nightwind. S. Allis
Nightwing. M. C. Smith
Nightwitch Devil. K. Robeson
Nightwork. Irwin Shaw
Nihilist's Vengeance. E. C. Derby
Nikki. S. Friedman
Nile Green. A. Hocking
Nile Green. D. Jordan
Nimble Dollar, with other stories. C. M. Thompson
Nimble Ike, the Detective. Old Sleuth
Nimble Ike, the Trick Ventriloquist. Old Sleuth
Nimble Ike's Mystery. Old Sleuth
Nimble Ike's Romance. Old Sleuth
Nimrod. J. Midgley
Nimrod Affair. J. Fairlawn
Nina's Peril. A. M. Miller
Nine Against New York. Albert Leffingwell
Nine—and Death Makes Ten. Carter Dickson
Nine Bears. E. Wallace
Nine Bells. K. Davies
Nine Buck's Row. T. E. Huff
Nine Club. T. Clare
Nine Coaches Waiting. G. Bolton
Nine Coaches Waiting. Mary Stewart
Nine Commandments. J. Blackmore
Nine Cuts. B. Flynn
9 Dark Hours. L. G. Offord
Nine Days. E. C. Vivian
Nine Days' Blunder. W. G. Elliott
Nine Days' Murder. A. MacKinnon
Nine Days' Panic. R. Davis
Nine Doctors and a Madman. E. M. Curtiss
Nine Dragon Man. D. De Reszke
9:45. Owen Davis
Nine Green Bottles. J. Cowdroy
9 Had No Alibi. M. Silverman
Nine Holiday Adventures of Mr. P. J. Davenant in the Year 1915. F. S. Hamilton
Nine Horrors and a Dream. J. P. Brennan
911. T. Chastain
Nine Lives. M. Channing
Nine Lives Are Not Enough. J. Odlum
Nine Lives of Alphonse. J. L. Johnson
Nine Lives to Pompeii. W. Melton
Nine Men of Soho. J. MacLaren-Ross
Nine Men's Morrice. W. H. Pollock
Nine Mile Walk. H. Kemelman
Nine More Lives. Michael Morgan
Nine Nicks. J. Farndale
Nine O'Clock Curtains. J. M. Hickman
Nine O'Clock Shadow. J. T. Story
Nine O'Clock Tide. M. G. Eberhart
Nine of Hearts. B. L. Farjeon
Nine of Hearts. E. C. Mayne
Nine Pine Street. J. Colton
Nine Pointed Star. C. W. Sykes
Nine Points of the Law. H. Booth
Nine Points of the Law. W. S. Jackson

Nine Seven Juliet. L. Lafore
Nine Singing Apes. H. Hawton
Nine-Spoked Wheel. J. R. L. Anderson
Nine Strings to Your Bow. M. Walsh
Nine Tailors. D. L. Sayers
9009. J. Hopper
Nine Till Six. Aimee Stuart
9 Times Dead. D. Bogard
Nine Times Nine. H. H. Holmes
Nine Unknown. T. Mundy
Nine Waxed Faces. F. Beeding
Nine Wrong Answers. J. D. Carr
19. Roger Hall
Nineteen Impressions. J. D. Beresford
19 Red Roses. T. Nielsen
Nineteen Stories. G. Greene
Nineteen Thousand Pounds. B. Delannoy
Nineteenth Century Miracle. Z. Z.
Nineteenth Hole Mystery. H. Adams
Ninety Days to Nine-O. P. Shatte
98.4. C. Hodder-Williams
95 File. J. E. Martin
90 Gramercy Park. P. Dalton
Ninety in the Shade. A. R. Weekes
99 44/100% Dead. M. Franklin
99, Dark Street. F. W. Robinson
Ninety-Second Tiger. M. Gilbert
Ninja. E. Van Lustbader
Ninja's Revenge. P. Anthony
Ninon. M. Peterson
Ninth Candle. F. Ford
Ninth Car. A. R. Rooth
Ninth Circle. H. Steele
9th Directive. Adam Hall
Ninth Earl. J. Farnol
Ninth Earl of Whitby. N. Bell
Ninth Enemy. F. Vivian
Ninth Floor. K. O'Neil
Ninth Guest. G. Bristow
Ninth Guest. Owen Davis
Ninth Hour. B. Benson
Ninth Life. F. I. S. Eden
Ninth Life. E. Ferrars
Ninth Life. Jack Mann
Ninth Man. John Lee
Ninth Marquess. J. Cleary
Ninth Plague. D. T. Lindsay
Ninth Tentacle. M. Rippon
Ninth Week. Irene Alexander
Nipped in the Bud. S. Palmer
Nipponese Nightmare. J. Rosenberger
Nirvana Can Also Mean Death. H. Kane
Nirvana Contracts. J. P. Wohl
Nita's Place. H. Whittington
Nitroglycerine League. I. Stark
Nitty-Gritty Affair. G. Cross
Nixon Recession Caper. R. Maloney
No Alibi. B. Cobb
No Alibi. J. York
No Alibi for Murder. A. Parsons
No Angel. Morton Cooper
No Angels for Me. W. Ard
No Answer from a Corpse. R. Stahl
No Apparent Motive. E. C. Williams
No Bail for Dalton. M. Borgenicht
No Bail for the Judge. H. Cecil
No Beast So Fierce. E. Bunker
No Beast So Fierce. C. Rushton
No Better Fiend. E. McGirr
No Birds Sang. J. B. Hilton
No Blonde Is an Island. Carter Brown
No Body She Knows. Carter Brown
No Bones About It. Joan Fleming
No Bones About It. R. S. Wallis
No Bouquets for Brandon. V. Warren
No Business Being a Cop. J. L. O'Donnell
No Business for a Lady. J. L. Rubel
No Business of Mine. Raymond Marshall
No Case for the Crown. D. McLachlin
No Case for the Police. V. C. Clinton-Baddeley
No Castle of Dreams. M. McEvoy
No Cause for Dying. K. Evans
No Cause to Kill. D. Ramsay
No Certain Life. R. Neely
No Chance in Hell. N. Quarry
No Charge for Framing. D. Sanderson
No Charge for the Poison. B. Cobb
No Choice. E. B. D'Auvergne
No Choice for Sergeant Cluff. G. North
"No Clue!" J. Hay
No Clues. M. Leinster
No Clues for Dexter. B. Graeme
No Coffin for the Corpse. C. Rawson
No Coffins in China. C. Edwards
No Come-Back from Connie. D. Glinto
No Corpus Delecti. B. Bohnstedt
No Country for Old Men. A. Schwartz
No Coupons for a Shroud. N. Morland
No Crest for the Wicked. G. Morgan
No Crime for a Lady. Z. Popkin
No Crime Is Perfect. H. E. Wheeler
No Crime Like the Present. A. Gaines
No Crime Like the Present. M. Hervey
No Crime More Cruel. M. Halliday
No Crime So Great. Elliot Bailey
No Curtains for Cora. Gavin Holt
No Dame Wants to Die. M. Clinten
No Darker Crime. J. Creasey
No Diamonds for a Doll. P. Cagney
No Dice! A. Bocca
No Dignity in Death. R. Lockridge

No Doors, No Windows. H. Ellison
No Doubts After Friday. I. Waltmore
No Down Payment. J. McPartland
No Drums at Midnight. J. Troy
No Dust in the Attic. Anthony Gilbert
No Duty on a Corpse. Max Murray
No Earth for Foxes. M. O'Brine
No Easy Way Out. Robert Mason
No End of a Rogue. F. A. Clement
No End to Danger. M. Halliday
No End to Fear. H. Hossent
No Entry. M. Coles
No Epitaph for Mr. Zarke. C. I. D. Smith
No Escape. Josephine Bell
No Escape. E. Ellison
No Escape. C. B. Kelland
No Escape. M. Richmond
No Escape. R. R. Ryan
No Escape from Murder. N. MacKenzie
No Escape from Murder. P. Manton
No Evil Angel. E. Linington
No Excuse for Murder. M. Hervey
No Exit. G. Goodchild
No Exit. Winston Graham
No Exit. A. E. Redmond
No Face for a Killer. H. Spencer
No Face in the Mirror. R. Copeland
No Face to Murder. E. Howie
No Fatherland. H. H. Kirst
No Fear or Favour. H. Cecil
No Flowers by Request. S. Palmer
No Flowers for the General. B. Copper
No Flowers in Brazlov. F. Usher
No Flowers on My Grave. R. Magowan
No Footprints in the Bush. A. W. Upfield
No Friendly Drop. Henry Wade
No Fury. F. Beeding
No Future Fair Lady. Carter Brown
No Future for Luana. A. Derleth
No Gentle Lady. R. Buxton
No Gold When You Go. Peter Chambers
No Good from a Corpse. L. Brackett
No Grave for a Lady. J. Bonett
No Grave for March. M. E. Chaber
No Greater Love. W. LeQueux
No Guest at the Villa. D. Martyn
No Halo for Hedy. Carter Brown
No Halo for Me. J. Manor
No Haloes for Hoods. Craig Cooper
No Haloes in Hell. W. Wright
No Hands on the Clock. G. Homes
No Harm Intended. E. S. Holding
No Harp for My Angel. Carter Brown
No Head for Her Pillow. S. S. Taylor
No Hero. J. P. Marquand
No Hero. Desmond Martin
No Hiding Place. R. Foley
No Hiding Place. E. Lanham
No Higher Mountain. A. Armstrong
No Holiday for Crime. Dell Shannon
No Holiday for Death. L. Thayer
"No Honour—." Colin Hope
No Honour Amongst Spies. H. T. Rothwell
No House Limit. S. Fisher
No Hurry to Kill. N. Deane
No Judges' Rules. D. MacDonald
No Kisses from the Kremlin. H. T. Rothwell
No Known Grave. E. Berckman
No Land Without Liberty. J. G. Sarasin
No Last Words. B. Cobb
No Law Against Angels. Carter Brown
No Law in Illyria. T. S. Strachan
No Less Renowned. G. Hackforth-Jones
No Letters from the Grave. B. Copper
No Life for a Loser. P. A. Foxall
No Light Came On. Alice Campbell
No Lilies. H. Holt
No Limit. A. Applin
No Limit for Charlie. W. A. Harbinson
No Little Enemy. O. W. Bayer
No Looking Back. G. Greenaway
No Love for Paradise. J. Canon
No Love in a Bullet. E. Kennedy
No Love Lost. M. Allingham
No Love Lost. Robert Reeves
No Luck for a Lady. F. Mahannah
No Man for Murder. M. Ellis
No Man Pursues. H. S. Davis
No Man's Hand. J. L. Bonney
No Man's Hand. H. C. McNeile
No Man's Land. L. J. Vance
No Man's Laughter. K. Laing
No Man's Money. H. M. Rideout
No Man's Street. B. Nichols
No Man's Woman. A. Boyd
No Man's World. M. Caidin
No Marks for Trying. S. Allan
No Mask for Murder. A. Garve
No Match for Murder. J. F. Webb
No Match for the Law. O. Mills
No Mean Tartar. L. F. Hay
No Medal If I Die. J. Ward
No Medals for Murder. H. Holt
No Medals for the Major. M. Yorke
No Medicine for Murder. Jeanne Wilson
No Mercy for Margaret. B. Cobb
No Mercy in the Sky. J. Fores
No Moon Tonight. J. Courage
No Moonlight. P. H. Powell
No More a Brother. T. Newman
No More a Corpse. L. Brent

No More A-Roving. S. Troy
No More Ancestors. L. Robinson
No More Dying Then. R. Rendell
No More Love. M. Hervey
No More Monday Mornings. C. P. Crow
No More Murders. M. Lang
No More Witnesses. R. Warthen
No Mortgage on a Coffin. D. Glinto
No Motive for Murder. W. E. Johns
No Mourners Present. F. G. Presnell
No Mourning for the Matador. D. Ames
No Mourning in the Family. R. Philmore
No Murder. H. C. Bailey
No Murder of Mine. Alice Campbell
No Name. W. Collins
No Names on Their Graves. Geoffrey Davison
No Need for Violence. J. Burrows
No Need to Die. G. Ashe
No Need to Fear. A. McAllister
No News on Monday. R. Clapperton
No Next of Kin. D. M. Disney
No! No! the Woman! N. Klein
No Obelisk for Emily. S. H. Courtier
No One Knows My Name. Joyce Harrington
No One to Worry Us. T. S.
No Opera at the Op'ry House. T. J. Kelly
No Orchids for Miss Blandish. J. H. Chase
No Ordinary Cheyney. P. Cheyney
No Other Hunger. F. Mullally
No Other Killer. J. Corbett
No Other Tiger. A. E. W. Mason
No Other Victim. C. Franklin
No Other Way. L. Tracy
No Outlet. A. M. Chase
No Paradise. K. Royce
No Past Is Dead. J. J. Connington
No Patent on Murder. A. Takagi
No Peace for Archer. H. Clevely
No Peace for the Living. M. Hervey
No Peace for the Wicked. Peter Chambers
No Peace for the Wicked. E. Ferrars
No Percentage in Death. R. Angel
No Place for a Dame. M. Clinten
No Place for a Tickle. R. Cooper
No Place for Me. S. Morelli
No Place for Murder. G. H. Coxe
No Place for Strangers. W. H. Baker
No Place for the Young. E. Warman
No Place Like Home. J. B. Olesker
No Place to Be a Cop. F. Nolan
No Place to Hide. E. Lindall
No Place to Hide. C. Runyon
No Place to Live. E. Ronns
No Pockets in a Shroud. H. McCoy
No Pockets in Shrouds. L. Revell
No Profit in Dying. O. Beeby
No Proof. L. L. Lynch
No Proud Chivalry. M. Procter
No Quarter for a Star. Dulcie Gray
No Quarter Given. B. Rossi
No Question of Murder. P. Curtis
No Questions Asked. O. Bleeck
No Questions Asked. A. W. Frost
No Questions Asked. F. Rydell
No Questions Asked. E. Sherry
No Reason for Murder. E. Radford
No Red Herrings. Mary Scott
No Refuge. J. Boland
No Regrets for Clara. H. Janson
No Rehearsals for Murder. E. Ferrars
No Reprieve. H. Desmond
No Return Ticket. M. Russell
No-Risk Operation. J. Pattinson
No Room at the Morgue. A. Bocca
No Room for Joanna. Elizabeth Ford
No Ruined Castles. J. McGovern
No Safe Road. B. Munslow
No Sainted City. S. Bunce
No Sale. M. Cronin
No Sale for Haloes. Anthony Graham
No Scars to See. I. See
No Second Stroke. C. Rushton
No Second Wind. A. B. Guthrie
No Sentiment. A. Dick
No Sentiment in Murder. M. Cumberland
No Shame for the Devil. B. Cobb
No Sign of Life. M. Delving
No Sign of Murder. W. Reed
No, Sir Jeremy. A. Weymouth
No Sky. N. Balchin
No Sleep at All. James Warren
No Sleep for Elsa. T. C. H. Jacobs
No Sleep for Macall. G. Fairlie
No Slightest Whisper. D. Evans
No Smoke No Flame. Q. Downes
No Snow at Latching. M. Home
No Space for Murder. N. Brent
No Stockings. A. S. Roche
No Such Word. R. Pertwee
No Surrender. M. Albrand
No Sweet Aspersion. Y. Pickering
No Target for Bowman. H. Howard
No Tears Are Shed. Stratford Davis
No Tears at the Funeral. H. Arre
No Tears for Hilda. A. Garve
No Tears for Shirley Minton. K. Lowe
No Tears for Teddy. Surrey Smith
No Tears for the Dead. P. Audemars
No Tears for the Dead. S. Deane
No Tears for the Dead. R. Foley

No Tears from the Widow. Carter Brown
No Tears Shed. A. B. Caldwell
No Thanks for the Shroud. J. P. Carstairs
No Thanks to the Duke. A. Dunnett
No Thoroughfare. D. Egerton
No Through Road. B. Hector
No Through Road. M. Russell
No Time at All. C. Einstein
No Time for Corpses. R. Carni
No Time for Crime. C. M. Russell
No Time for Death. P. Capon
No Time for Terror. P. MacDonald
No Time to Die. R. Pape
No Time to Kill. J. Bonett
No Time to Kill. G. H. Coxe
No Time to Laugh. J. Norwood
No Time to Live. W. H. Baker
No Time to Live. L. T. Maxim
No Time to Play. K. Hewitt
No Traveller Returns. D. Ames
No Traveller Returns. A. Dean
No Trespassing. D. Tracy
No Trial—No Error. Colin Robertson
No Turning Back. W. F. Morris
No Turning Back. L. Robin
No Useless Coffin. R. Watkins
No Vacation for Maigret. G. Simenon
No Vacation from Murder. E. Lemarchand
No Villain Need Be. E. Linington
No Vindication. Mrs. C. Kernahan
No Walls of Jasper. J. Cannan
No Way Back from Prague. P. Brent
No Way Home. G. R. Preedy
No Way Out. O. Davis
No Way Out. W. McNeilly
No Way Out. B. Musto
No Way Out. R. O. Saber
No Way Out. A. Thornton
No Way to Treat a Lady. H. Longbaugh
No Weeds for the Widow. M. M. Raison
No Will to Die. W. Ellis
No Wind of Blame. G. Heyer
No Wings on a Cop. C. F. Adams
No Witness! C. Fitzsimmons
No Wooden Overcoat. J. P. Carstairs
No Wreath from Manuela. A. MacKinnon
No Wreaths for the Duchess. F. Grierson
Noah's Ark Murders. A. Douglas
Noble Blood. J. Hawthorne
Noble Error. M. L. Tyrrell
Noble Forger. C. C. Bergius
Noble Lord. E. Southworth
Noble Pirate. R. Foxall
Noble Profession. P. Boulle
Nobleman's Wife. H. Wood
Noblest Experiment in the Galaxy. L. Trimble
Nobody. L. J. Vance
Nobody Answered the Bell. R. Davies
Nobody Died for Honnie. D. Bogard
Nobody Heard the Shot. D. B. Chidsey
Nobody Is Safe. M. Cumberland
Nobody Knew They Were There. E. Hunter
Nobody Lives Forever. W. R. Burnett
Nobody Lives Forever. Peter Chambers
Nobody Loves a Dead Man. M. M. Raison
Nobody Loves a Loser. H. Kane
Nobody Needs a Corpse. M. Cronin
Nobody on the Road. G. Rose
Nobody Shoots Forever. S. A. Curtis
Nobody Stops Me. Eric North
Nobody Wins. G. P. Kenneally
Nobody Wore Black. D. Ames
Nobody's Daughter. C. Augusta
Nobody's Fortune. E. Yates
Nobody's Home. M. Short
Nobody's Man. E. P. Oppenheim
Nobody's Perfect. Douglas Clark
Nobody's Perfect. D. E. Westlake
Nobody's Sorry He Got Killed. A. D. Goldstein
Nobody's Vineyard. H. C. Bailey
Nobody's Widow. G. Warden
Nocturnal Assassin. I. Crookenden
Nodding Canaries. G. Mitchell
Nodding Towers. Sam Hill
Noise in the Night. S. Jepson
Nomads of the Night. G. Leroux
Non-Murder. J. Ingersol
None But the Lethal Heart. Carter Brown
None Dare Call It Treason. C. Gavin
None of Maigret's Business. G. Simenon
None of My Business. D. Sharp
None of Us Cared for Kate. J. Haythorne
None Shall Know. M. Albrand
None Shall Sleep Tonight. H. McCutcheon
None So Blind. M. A. Wilson
Nonsense Novels. S. Leacock
Noon Balloon to Rangoon. J. Haase
Noon Jury. Mark Ross
Noonday and Night. G. Mitchell
Noonday Devil. U. Curtiss
Noonday Devils. W. Martyn
Nooriabad File. G. Watson
Noose. P. MacDonald
Noose for a Lady. H. Carmichael
Noose for a Lady. G. Verner
Noose for Her. E. Crispin
Noose Is Drawn. W. A. Barber
Noose of Emeralds. B. Winter
Noose of Red Beads. T. J. King

Noose of Sin. F. Carco
Nor All Your Tears. L. Charbonneau
Nor Evil Dreams. Rosemary Harris
Nor Iron Bars. S. Dannett
Nor Spell Nor Charm. Alicen White
Nora's Love Test. M. C. Hay
Norgil: More Tales of Prestidigitection. M. Grant
Norgil the Magician. M. Grant
Norine's Revenge, and Sir Noel's Heir. M. A. Fleming
Norma Danton. Anonymous
Norroy, Diplomatic Agent. G. Bronson-Howard
Norslag. Michael Sinclair
North. J. B. Hendryx
North Beach Girl. J. Trinian
North Beat. J. Wood
North Cape. J. Poyer
North for Danger. Colin Robertson
North from Rome. Helen MacInnes
North from Singapore. M. Nabarro
North from Thursday. J. Cleary
North Kill. J. Wood
North of Bushman's Rock. G. Harding
"North of 55." A. Murray
North of the Law. S. A. White
North of the Stars. C. Stoddard
North of Welfare. W. Krasner
North Sea Hijack. Jack Davies
North Sea Mistress. K. Blickle
North Sea Mystery. H. Edmonds
North Sea Patrol. G. E. Rochester
North Shore Mystery. H. Fletcher
North Slope. Michael Parker
North Star. H. Innes
North Star Crusade. W. Katz
North to Rabaul. Christopher Wood
North Walk Mystery. W. N. Harben
Northern Mission. J. Wood
Northing Tramp. E. Wallace
Norths Meet Murder. F. Lockridge
Northward the Coast. E. Lindall
Northwater. C. Crowe
Northwest! H. Bindloss
Northwest Contract. L. Derrick
Northwest Law. S. A. White
Northwest Patrol. S. A. White
Northwest Trouble. C. Stoddard
Norval, the Detective. Old Sleuth
Norwich Victims. F. Beeding
Norwood Mystery. J. K. Blades
Nose for It. A. M. Stein
Nose on My Face. L. Payne
Nostradamus Traitor. J. Gardner
Not a Bad Man. J. Miglis
Not a Bad Show. F. Beeding
Not a Clue. A. De Mirjian
Not a Dog's Chance. W. R. Hutton
Not a Leg to Stand On. M. Burton
Not a Nice Murder! E. Wilmot
Not a Penny More, Not a Penny Less. J. Archer
Not After Midnight. D. Du Maurier
Not Comin' Home to You. P. Kavanagh
Not Dead Enough. Clay Henry
Not Dead Yet. D. Banko
Not Expected to Live. M. Cumberland
Not for a Curse. K. Kramer
Not for Export. M. Coles
Not for Sale. K. Gordon
Not Guilty. Anonymous
Not Guilty. W. E. Norris
Not Guilty. W. Phillips
Not Guilty, My Lord. H. Desmond
Not Herbert. H. I. Young
Not I, Said the Sparrow. R. Lockridge
Not I, Said the Vixen. B. S. Ballinger
Not in the Book. A. Watkyn
Not in the Contract. N. W. Hooke
Not in the Newspapers. John Gloag
Not in the Script. J. Bonett
Not in Utter Nakedness. D. Ames
Not Killed, Just Dead. D. Ambler
Not Long to Live. Mark Cross
Not Me, Inspector. H. Reilly
"Not Mentioned..." A. Soutar
Not My Murder. John Marsh
Not Negotiable. M. Coles
Not Nice People. N. Clevely
Not on the Records. Nicholas Carter
Not One of Us. J. Thomson
Not Our House. W. W. Prior
Not Proven. A. Askew
Not Proven. J. Dering
Not Proven. B. Graeme
Not Proven. P. Traill
Not Proven Castle. A. Wood
Not Quite Dead Enough. R. Stout
Not Quite So Black. D. G. Waring
Not Ready to Die. J. Monmouth
Not Safe to Be Free. J. H. Chase
Not Single Spies. D. Betteridge
Not Sleeping, Just Dead. C. Alverson
Not So Evil As Eve. J. Creighton
Not So Quickly. K. Fitzgerald
Not Sufficient Evidence. J. L. Rickard
Not the Glory. P. Boulle
Not to Be Opened. L. Osbourne
Not to Be Taken. A. Berkeley
Not to the Swift. H. Gibbs
Not to the Swift. L. Harrison

Not Too Narrow—Not Too Deep. R. Sale
Not Wanted. F. Hume
Not Wanted on Voyage. N. Spain
Not with a Bang. C. Pincher
Not with My Neck. T. Van Dycke
Not Wooed, But Won. J. Payn
Notch on the Knife. W. Haggard
Notched Hairpin. H. F. Heard
Note of Enchantment. E. H. Clements
Notebooks. S. Picard
Notebooks of Raymond Chandler and English Summer. R. Chandler
Notes of an Itinerant Policeman. J. Flynt
Nothing Bared. Johnny Morgan
Nothing But a Man. J. Thompson
Nothing But Blood. P. C. Smith
Nothing But Foxes. Roy Lewis
Nothing But the Night. J. Blackburn
Nothing But the Night. J. Yaffe
Nothing But the Truth. P. Orum
Nothing But the Truth. J. Rhode
Nothing Can Rescue Me. E. Daly
Nothing for Nothing. N. Easton
Nothing Happens to Children in Beverly Hills. Vi Wolfson
Nothing Hid. A. Marshall
Nothing in Her Way. C. Williams
Nothing Irredeemable. D. G. Waring
Nothing Is for Free. W. Newton
Nothing Is the Number When You Die. Joan Fleming
Nothing Last Forever. R. Thorp
Nothing Like Blood. L. Bruce
Nothing Man. J. Thompson
Nothing Matters. H. B. Tree
Nothing More Than Murder. J. Thompson
Nothing Personal. Peter Chambers
Nothing Personal. S. Wishman
Nothing to Declare. M. Coles
Nothing to Declare. R. Mann
Nothing to Hide. M. Perelli
Nothing to Hide. D. Spade
Nothing to Lose. R. Charles
Nothing to Lose But My Life. L. Trimble
Nothing to Pretend. E. Thorne
Nothing to Report. R. McLaughlin
Nothing Venture. P. Wentworth
Nothing's Certain But Death. M. K. Wren
Notice to Quit. J. Quince
Notorious. D. Keene
Notorious Landlady. I. Shulman
Notorious Miss Lisle. B. Reynolds
Notorious Miss Walters. S. Kyle
Notorious Sophie Lang. F. I. Anderson
Notting Hill Murder. C. Ryland
Notting Hill Mystery. C. Felix
Noughts and Crosses. E. Woodward
November. G. Simenon
November Joe, the Detective of the Woods. H. Prichard
November Man. B. Freemantle
November Man. B. Granger
November 9th at Kersea. A. Swift
November Reef. R. Maugham
November Wind. P. Geddes
Now and for Never. H. A. Hoare
Now and on Earth. J. Thompson
Now Dead Is Any Man. P. Audemars
Now, Gentlemen, Please. H. Fernee
Now I Lay Me Down to Die. E. Tebbetts-Taylor
Now Is the Time. L. Katcher
Now It's My Turn. M. E. Chaber
Now Like to Die. H. Brinton
Now Lying Dead. O. Norton
Now Lying Dead. P. H. Powell
Now or Never. M. Coles
Now Seek My Bones. S. H. Courtier
Now Try the Morgue. T. D. Smith
Now We Are Free. K. David
Now Will You Try for Murder? H. Olesker
Now You See It-Him-Them. G. DeWeese
Nowhere? A. M. Stein
Nowhere Man. Ritchie Perry
Nowhere Place. J. Lymington
Nowhere to Go. D. MacKenzie
Nowhere Weapon. Nick Carter
Nuclear Letters. G. Lancaster
Nude in Mink. S. Rohmer
Nude in Nevada. T. B. Dewey
Nude on the Rocks. Clay Henry
Nude on Thin Ice. G. Brewer
Nude on Thin Ice. C. Williams
Nude Was Framed. R. Drayton
Nude—with a View. Carter Brown
Nudist Murder. T. Stevenson
Nugget. R. Potts
Number. A. P. Carter
Number 18. C. M. Wills
Number 87. H. Hext
Number Fifteen. D. Whitelaw
No. 9 Belmont Square. M. Erskine
Number Nineteen. J. J. Farjeon
No. 19. E. Jepson
No. 19 State Street. D. G. Adee
No. 99. A. Griffiths
Number Nought. S. Truss
Number One. R. Masson
"No. 101." Wymond Carey
Number 1-2-3. F. Gerard
Number One with a Bullet. E. Jesmer
Number One's Last Crime. M. E. Cooke

Number Seven Queer Street. Margery Lawrence
No. 7, Saville Square. W. LeQueux
No. 17. J. J. Farjeon
Number Seventeen. L. Tracy
Number 70, Berlin. W. LeQueux
Number Seventy-Three. S. Kyle
Number Six. E. Wallace
Number 13. F. M. White
No. 13, Rue du Bon Diable. Arthur Sherburne Hardy
No. 13 Rue Marlot. R. De Pont-Jest
No. 13 Toroni. J. Regis
No. 13 Washington Square. L. Scott
"No. 3." L. K. Vincent
No. 3 the Square. F. Warden
Number to Call Is... R. Thompson
Number Two, North Steps. J. Dering
Numbered Account. A. Bridge
Numbers for Lovers. A. J. Fitzgerald
Numbers Man. D. J. Gerrity
Nun in the Closet. D. Gilman
Nun in the Cupboard. D. Gilman
Nun's Castle. Jennie Melville
Nuns of the Desert. E. DeActon
Nuplex Red. Simon Quinn
Nurse. A. Askew
Nurse Alice in Love. T. Charles
Nurse at Brooding Mansion. P. Warren
Nurse at Danger Mansion. D. Daniels
Nurse Elisia. G. M. Fenn
Nurse Lester's First Case. A. M. Griffin
Nurse on Nightmare Island. L. Eby
Nurse Revel's Mistake. F. Warden
Nurse Stacey Comes Aboard. Rona Randall
Nurse to Dives. T. Trent
Nursemaid Who Disappeared. P. MacDonald
Nursery Rhyme Murders. G. Verner
Nursery Tea and Poison. A. Morice
Nursing Home. A. Applin
Nursing Home Crime. C. Brisbane
Nursing-Home Murder. N. Marsh
Nut-Browne Mayd. G. Warden
Nut Case. P. Conway
Nylon Nightmare. Clayton Matthews
Nylon Pirates. N. Monsarrat
Nymph at Bay. E. P. Frankland
Nymph in the Night. H. Janson
Nymph to the Slaughter. Carter Brown
Nympho Named Silvia. H. Janson

O As in Omen. L. Treat
O Charitable Death. R. C. Payes
O Clouds Unfold. P. Capon
O.D. at Sweet Claude's. M. Gattzden
O Huge Angel. H. Baer
O.P.E.C. Project. R. Vacha
O Sweet McTavish. C. Brooks
Oak and Iron. J. B. Hendryx
Oakdale Affair. E. R. Burroughs
Oaks of Bashan. R. P. Pond
Oasis. J. Creasey
Oasis. P. Meredith
Oasis Nine. V. Canning
Oasis of Fear. K. Evans
Oasis of Tears. M. Richmond
Oath of Fear. W. J. Bayfield
Oath of Vengeance. J. K. Stafford
Obeah Murders. H. Footner
Obelisk Conspiracy. G. Marton
Obelists at Sea. C. D. King
Obelists en Route. C. D. King
Obelists Fly High. C. D. King
Obi. Anonymous
Obit Deferred. L. Trimble
Obit Delayed. H. Nielsen
Obituary Club. H. Pentecost
Object of Jealousy. A. Rutledge
Object of the Exercise. P. Ordway
Obligation. R. Neely
Obligations of Hercule. P. Audemars
Obliging Corpse. J. Courage
Obliging Husband. F. Barrett
Oblivion Tapes. T. Murari
Oblivious Host. M. Myers
Oblong Circle. H. P. Rednour
Obole of Paradise. Agnes Miller
Obols for Charon. S. Harvester
Obsequies at Oxford. E. Crispin
Observer Corps Mystery. R. Hardinge
Obsession. Alec Coppel
Obsession. S. Mitchell
Obsession. M. Tripp
Obsession. E. White
Obsession for Two. John Bentley
Obsession to Kill. M. Shane
Obsessions. T. Gurr
Obsessions. L. St. Clair
Obstinate Captain Samson. Gavin Douglas
Obstinate Girl. E. Jepson
Obstinate Murderer. E. S. Holding
Obstinate Virgin. S. Murray
Obvious Solution. C. F. Gregg
Occidental Sketches. B. C. Truman
Occupying Power. Evelyn Anthony
Ocean Knight. F. Du Boisgobey
Ocean of Fire. A. J. Griffin

Ocean Prize. J. Pattinson
Ocean Road. Jack Bennett
Ocean Secret. G. Boothby
Ocean Sleuth. M. Drake
Ocean Tragedy. W. C. Russell
Ocean's 11. G. C. Johnson
Octagon Crystal. P. Foley
Octagon House. G. Knevels
Octagon House. P. A. Taylor
Octangle. E. N. Sachs
October Cabaret. E. Quest
October Circle. R. Littell
October Day. F. Griffin
October Heat. G. De Marco
October House. K. C. Strahan
October Men. John Mills
October Men. A. Price
October Plot. C. Egleton
October Witch. Alanna Knight
Octopus of Crime. B. House
Octopus of Paris. G. Leroux
Octopus' Shadow. M. Carrel
Octopussy. I. Fleming
Octopussy and the Living Daylights. I. Fleming
Octoroon. M. E. Braddon
Odd—But Even So. P. C. Wren
Odd Flamingo. N. Bawden
Odd Issues. S. S. Sprigge
Odd Job. P. Flower
Odd Job Man. N. J. Crisp
Odd Job No. 101, and other future crimes and intrigues. R. Goulart
Odd Man In. L. A. G. Strong
Odd Man In. M. C. Tutt
Odd Man Out. F. L. Green
Odd Man Pays. D. L. Teilhet
Odd One Out. L. D. Stranger
Odd Pairs. L. Housman
Odd Trick. A. M. Meadows
Odd Woman Out. George Douglas
Odd Woman Out. S. Fox
Odd Woman Out. J. L. Linklater
Oddest of Courtships. J. W. De Forrest
Oddities of Short-Hand. J. B. Carey
Odds Against. D. Francis
Odds Against Her. A. Wood
Odds Against Linda. S. Ward
Odds Against Tomorrow. W. P. McGivern
Odds End. T. Wynne-Jones
Odds On. J. Lange
Odds on Bluefeather. L. Meynell
Odds on Death. C. Drummond
Odds on Gold. W. Hughes
Odds on Miss Seeton. H. Carvic
Odds on Murder. J. Dolph
Odds on Murder. M. Levien
Odds on the Hot Seat. J. Philips
Odds Run Out. H. Waugh
Oddways. H. Adams
Odean Theatre Mystery. D. Whitelaw
Odessa File. F. Forsyth
Odious Ones. J. Sohl
Odor of Bitter Almonds. J. G. Edwards
Odor of Violets. B. Kendrick
Odour of Decay. M. Jenson
Of All the Bloody Cheek. F. McAuliffe
Of Good and Evil. E. K. Gann
Of Hidden Depths. A. Windsor-Richards
Of High Degree. C. Gibbon
Of High Descent. G. M. Fenn
Of Ladies Dead. A. Hasluck
Of Love and Danger. J. MacLaren-Ross
Of Love and Intrigue. V. Coffman
Of Malicious Intent. L. Meynell
Of Masks and Minds. F. E. Smith
Of Mice and Murder. B. Whitaker
Of Midnight Honor. J. G. Vermandel
Of Missing Persons. D. Goodis
Of Royal Blood. W. LeQueux
Of Singular Purpose. Roy Lewis
Of Six Suspects. D. Newton
Of Tender Sin. D. Goodis
Of the Deepest Dye. C. Larking
Of This Death. V. Campbell
Of Unsound Mind. H. Carmichael
Of Wind and Fire. J. Blackmore
Ofanu. G. Forve
Off Duty. A. Coburn
Off-Islanders. H. Benchley
Off Lands End. W. Reid
Off Shore. Taffrail
Off the Beaten Track. F. St Mars
Off the Track. H. Juta
Off the Track in London. G. R. Sims
Off to the Wilds. G. M. Fenn
Off with Her Head! G. D. H. Cole
Off with His Head. N. Marsh
Off with His Head. J. L. Morrissey
Offense Against the Persons. H. Gilbert
Offer of Marriage. Lynna Cooper
Offering. James Reid
Office Scandal. F. A. Edwards
Office Secret. W. LeQueux
Officer! H. Footner
Officer and a Gentleman? and other stories. G. Thorne
Officer Factory. H. H. Kirst
Officer from Special Branch. T. Lilley
Officer 666. B. Currie
Officer, That's Your Man. P. G. Larbalestier

Title Index
Once upon a Crime / 567

Official Chaperon. N. S. Lincoln
Official Secret. A. Duncan
Offshore! S. Coulter
Ogden Enigma. G. Snyder
Ogilvie, Tallant & Moon. C. Q. Yarbro
Ogre. M. Ronson
Oh, Bury Me. Not. M. K. Wren
"Oh, Joshua!" Taffrail
Oh, Murderer Mine. N. Davis
Oh, No, You Don't. H. Carstairs
Oh! Where Are Bloody Mary's Earrings? R. Player
Oh, Wicked Wanda. F. Mullally
O'Houlihan's Jest. R. O'Grady
Oil Bastards. P. McCutchan
Oil by Murder. J. Paul
Oil Heist. W. A. Harbinson
Oil Slick. R. Sapir
Oil Strike. J. Wingate
Oil Under the Window. N. Berrow
Okewood of the Secret Service. D. Valentine
Oklahoma Firefight. L. Derrick
Oklahoma Punk. L. D. Estleman
Oktoberfest. F. De Felitta
Old Acquaintance. N. Guild
Old Admiral Death. R. Bridges
Old Age of Lecoq, the Detective. F. Du Boisgobey
Old Age of Monsieur Lecoq. F. Du Boisgobey
Old Anthony's Secret. W. J. Shaw
Old Bailey Mystery. A. Blair
Old Bank. W. Westall
Old Battle Ax. E. S. Holding
Old Blazer's Hero. D. C. Murray
Old Bones. H. Petersen
Old Bull Inn of Silver Street, Edmonton. Thomas Lee
Old Corcoran's Money. R. Dowling
Old Dark House. J. B. Priestley
Old Detective's Pupil. Anonymous
Old Detective's Pupil. Nicholas Carter
Old Die Young. R. Lockridge
Old Ebbie. F. A. M. Webster
Old Ebbie Returns. F. A. M. Webster
Old Electricity, the Lightning Detective. Anonymous
Old Electricity, the Lightning Detective. Old Sleuth
Old English Baron. Clara Reeve
Old English Peep Show. P. Dickinson
Old Evil House. L. F. Brooks
Old Factory. W. Westall
Old-Fashioned Christmas. A. Dick
Old-Fashioned Murder. M. McIntire
Old Fires and Profitable Ghosts. A. T. Quiller-Couch
Old Fox. W. Fennerton
Old Friend. V. Siller
Old Friends. Andrew Lang
Old Ghosts Never Die. M. Warner
Old Gibbet. E. Thornton
Old Goat. E. Greenwood
Old Gold Road. Ian Mitchell
Old Goriot. H. Balzac
Old Granstock. J. Easton
Old Gumber's Mill. E. J. Kyle
Old Hall, New Hall. M. Innes
Old Harry Hawks. Anonymous
Old House at Sandwich. J. Hatton
Old House at the Corner. F. Warden
Old House by the Sea. S. E. Phipps
Old House of Fear. R. Kirk
Old House of West Street. T. P. Prest
Old Ironsides Among the Italian Brigands. Old Sleuth
Old Isaacs from the Bowery. C. E. Blaney
Old Jew Mystery. H. Adams
Old Judge Priest. I. S. Cobb
Old King Cole. S. P. B. Mais
Old King Cole. E. Shanks
Old Lady Dies. Anthony Gilbert
Old Lattimer's Legacy. J. S. Fletcher
Old Lover's Ghost. L. Ford
Old Madhouse. W. F. De Morgan
Old Maid's Vengeance. F. Powell
Old Man Dies. G. Blundell
Old Man Dies. G. Simenon
Old Man Goriot. H. Balzac
Old Man in the Corner. B. Orczy
Old Man in the Corner Unravels the Mystery of the Fulton Gardens Mystery, and The Moorland Tragedy. B. Orczy
Old Man in the Corner Unravels the Mystery of the Pearl Necklace, and The Tragedy in Bishop's Road. B. Orczy
Old Man in the Corner Unravels the Mystery of the Russian Prince, and of Dog's Tooth Cliff. B. Orczy
Old Man in the Corner Unravels the Mystery of the White Carnation, and The Montmartre Hat. B. Orczy
Old Man Mystery. J. J. Farjeon
Old Man of the Moors. W. Jardine
Old Man Tutt. A. Train
Old Manor. C. F. Gregg
Old Manor Crime. W. Martyn
Old Manor House. Charlotte Smith
Old Man's Money. J. Reach
Old Masters. W. Haggard
Old Mill. P. W. Wilson

Old Mill Mystery. A. W. Marchmont
Old Miser's Mystery. Old Sleuth
Old Miser's Ward. Old Sleuth
Old Mr. Davenant's Money. F. Powell
Old Mrs. Camelot. E. Bonett
Old Mrs. Fitzgerald. A. Hocking
Old Mrs. Ommanney Is Dead. M. Erskine
Old Mrs. Warren. F. Wolseley
Old Murders Never Die. N. Carlson
Old Must Die. A. Gaines
Old Myddelton's Money. M. C. Hay
Old Offenders and a Few Old Scores. E. W. Hornung
Old Patch's Medley. M. Bowen
Old Phenomenal. Anonymous
Old Puritan, the Old Time Detective. Anonymous
Old Quartz, the Nevada Detective. E. T. Sawyer
Old Reliable. P. G. Wodehouse
Old Rogue's Tragedy. Rita
Old Rowley. M. M. Bodkin
Old Sinners Never Die. D. S. Davis
Old Sins Have Long Shadows. J. L. Rickard
Old Sleuth, the Avenger. Old Sleuth
Old Sleuth, the Detective. Old Sleuth
Old Sleuth, the Protean Detective. Anonymous
Old Sleuth to the Rescue. Old Sleuth
Old Sleuth's Greatest Case. Old Sleuth
Old Sleuth's Triumph. Old Sleuth
Old Sleuth's Winning Hand. Old Sleuth
Old Sleuth's Wonderful Revelation. Old Sleuth
Old Specie, the Treasury Detective. M. Manly
Old Specie, the Treasury Detective. A. Robertson
Old Stone House and other stories. A. K. Green
Old Stonewall, the Colorado Detective. J. R. Taylor
Old Stonewall, the "Shadower". Anonymous
Old Students Never Die. I. T. Ross
Old Terrible. Old Sleuth
Old Terrible, the Iron Arm Detective. Anonymous
Old Tollgate Mystery. W. J. Bayfield
Old Trade of Killing. J. Harris
Old Transform, the Secret Special Detective. Anonymous
Old Ugly Face. T. Mundy
Oldest Confession. R. Condon
Oldest Profession. B. Sarto
Oldest Road. D. G. Waring
Olga Knaresbrook, Detective. H. Campbell
Olga, the Disillusioned. K. Kimbrough
Olga's Crime. F. Barrett
Olive Varcoe. F. Barrett
Oliver Goldfinch. Emerson Bennett
Oliver Quendon's First Case. Cowdray Browne
Olivia. Gwendoline Butler
Olivia's Story. A. Winter
Olmec Head. D. Westheimer
Olura. G. Household
Olympic Mission. P. Ferguson
Olympic Sleeper. T. Barling
Om. T. Mundy
Omar, Fats and Trixie. J. Reese
Omega Assignment. David Lewis
Omega Document. J. A. MacKenzie
Omega Factor. J. Gerson
Omega-Minus. T. Allbeury
Omega Operation. N. Conway
Omega Terror. Nick Carter
Omega Threat. M. Washburn
Omen. M. Eyre
Omerta. P. McCurtin
Ominous Star. R. Foley
Omit Flowers. S. Palmer
Omit Flowers, Please. A. Gaines
Omni Strain. C. Patton
Omnibus Mystery. F. Du Boisgobey
Omnipotent Avenger. Old Sleuth
On a Blind Trail. J. K. Stafford
On a Crimson Trail. Nicholas Carter
On a False Charge. S. W. Hopkins
On a Fated Night. D. Malm
On a Field of Black. G. Tomlinson
On a Million-Dollar Trail. Nicholas Carter
On a Still Night. C. D. Peel
On Appeal. P. Dewdney
On Circumstantial Evidence. F. Marryat
On Compassionate Leave. L. Jackson
On Dangerous Ground. E. S. Drewry
On Death's Trail. Dick Stewart
On Desperate Seas. J. Pattinson
On Fortune's Wheel. R. M. Wells
On Government Service. F. A. M. Webster
On Hazardous Duty. David St. John
On Helle's Wave. H. Imber
On Her Majesty's Secret Service. Anonymous
On Her Majesty's Secret Service. I. Fleming
On Her Majesty's Service. A. Upward
On Ice. R. G. Dean
On Land and Sea. G. Simenon
On Murder's Skirts. T. Adler

On Schedule. E. L. Long
On Secret Service. R. Arnold
On Secret Service. J. Mowbray
On Secret Service. W. N. Taft
On Swan River. H. Footner
On Target. J. O. Mayo
On the Bed of the Ocean. E. S. Brooks
On the Borderland. F. B. Austin
On the Bridge at Midnight. Bruce Brandon
On the Brink. D. Batchelor
On the Brink. M. Endfield
On the Brink of a Chasm. L. T. Meade
On the Brink of Ruin. O. Spicer
On the Danger Line. G. Simenon
On the Danger List. M. Cumberland
On the Day of the Shooting. C. Franklin
On the Dead Run. W. B. Murphy
On the Double. Roger Fuller
On the Edge. R. Doliner
On the Edge of the Sea. F. L. Green
On the 8th Day. L. E. Okun
On the 11:40 Down. H. King
On the Embankment. R. Dowling
On the Eve of Triumph. Nicholas Carter
On the Fringe. T. W. Speight
On the Highest Hill. H. M. Stephenson
On the Hook. R. Powell
On the Inside. F. F. Kelly
On the Instructions of My Government. P. Salinger
On the Jury. R. Marsh
On the Jury. W. Phillips
On the Lightship. H. K. Viele
On the Line and Danger Signal. B. Hemyng
On the Make. J. D. MacDonald
On the Midnight Beat. J. G. Brandon
On the Night Express! H. H. C. Gibbons
On the Night Express. F. M. White
On the Night in Question. C. M. Wills
"On the Night of the 18th..." L. Meynell
On the Night of the Fire. F. L. Green
On the Night of the 14th. Mark Cross
On the Night of the Ninth. R. Trevor
On the Night of the Seventh Moon. V. Holt
On the Prime Minister's Account. O. Hogstrand
On the Rack. W. C. Hudson
On the Ragged Edge. Nicholas Carter
On the Rank. B. Hemyng
On the Right Wrists. A. Livingston
On the Rim of the Arctic. J. B. Hendryx
On the Road. B. Hemyng
On the Run. E. M. Bowen
On the Run. M. Constanduros
On the Run. Roland Daniel
On the Run. Angus Hall
On the Run. J. D. MacDonald
On the Scent. Anonymous
On the Secret Service of His Majesty, the Queen. S. Weinstein
On the Shady Side. F. Swinnerton
On the Shores of Night. A. Mans
On the Spot. E. Wallace
On the Stretch. J. Welcome
On the Stroke of Midnight. M. O. Rolfe
On the Stroke of Nine. A. Parsons
On the Track of Death. D. Rutherford
On the Trail of "Big Finger." S. Campbell
On the Way Out. John Williams
On the Wing. Old Sleuth
On the Wing of Occasions. J. C. Harris
On the Wings of Truth. J. B. Boydstun
On the Yard. M. Braly
On Their Track. Old Sleuth
On Ticket of Leave. S. Blake
On Ticket of Leave. J. G. Brandon
On Trial. E. L. Reizenstein
On Trial. D. Torbett
On Trial for His Life. Anonymous
On Trial for His Life. O. Harper
On Trust. T. Cobb
On Winding Waters. W. M. Graydon
Once a Copper. W. Terry
Once a Crime. E. Price
Once a Spy. R. Footman
Once a Thief. Z. Marko
Once a Widow. Lee Roberts
Once a Year Man. M. Tripp
Once Acquitted. A. R. Long
Once, and Then the Funeral. B. J. Farmer
Once Bit, Twice Hit. H. C. McNeile
Once Bitten, and What Ensued. G. M. Winsor
Once for All. M. Hillary
"Once I Was Blind." Andrew Stewart
Once in a Lifetime. J. Mayo
Once in a Red Moon. J. T. Rogers
Once in Tiger Bay. J. M. Walsh
Once More the Saint. L. Charteris
Once Off Guard. J. H. Wallis
Once over Deadly. F. Gruber
Once over Deadly. E. McNamara
Once Too Often. W. Chambers
Once Too Often. Mark Cross
Once Too Often. R. Lait
Once Too Often. F. Warden
Once upon a Christmas Time. G. R. Sims
Once upon a Crime. Mark Cross
Once upon a Crime. Michael Hall

O

Once upon a Crime. M. Kerrigan
Once upon a Crime. C. Monig
Once upon a Crime. R. Selman
Once upon a Friday. P. Moore
Once upon a Midnight. J. Reach
Once upon a Nightmare. Lynn Williams
Once upon a Private Eye. P. Quinn
Once upon a Time. E. Phillpotts
Once upon a Tombstone. E. Salter
Once You Stop, You're Dead. E. K. Goldthwaite
Ondine. C. Kozloff
One. D. Karp
I-A Stranger. A. Guirdham
One Across, Two Down. R. Rendell
One Against the Earth. D. Mainwaring
One Against the Odds. N. Fagan
One Alone. V. Siller
One Among None. R. Stratton
One Angel Less. H. W. Roden
One Angry Man. N. Daniels
One-Armed Murder. R. Gallagher
One Away. A. Prior
One Between. F. Cowen
One Black Summer. B. Jefferis
One Blonde Died. L. Edgley
One Bright Day. E. S. Miller
One Bright Summer Morning. J. H. Chase
One by One. Linda Lee
One by One. F. Nichols
One by One They Disappeared. M. Dalton
One Clear Call. F. N. Greene
One Corpse Missing. Z. H. Ross
One Corpse Too Many. Ellis Peters
One Cried Murder. S. H. Courtier
One Cried Murder. Jean Leslie
One Crime Too Many. J. Guil
One Dark Night. P. Bennetts
One Dead Debutante. H. Gould
One Deadly Dawn. H. Whittington
One Deadly Summer. S. Japrisot
One Death in the Red. E. Mazzaro
One Dip Dead. A. M. Stein
One-Dollar Rip-Off. R. Dennis
One Down. A. Bodelsen
One Down and Two to Slay. H. Brinton
"One Dreadful Night." R. S. L. Harding
One Drop of Blood. Anne Austin
One Enchanted Evening. M. Richmond
One Endless Hour. D. J. Marlowe
One Evening I Shall Return. Anne-Mariel
One-Eyed King. E. Fadiman
One-Eyed Knave. Ganpat
One-Faced Girl. C. Armstrong
One Fair Enemy. C. Dawe
One False Move. R. Drayton
One False Move. K. Roos
One Fearful Yellow Eye. J. D. MacDonald
One Fifty Three Oakland Street. D. Highland
One Fine Day. Elizabeth Ford
One Fine Day. M. Richmond
One Foot in the Grave. M. Cumberland
One Foot in the Grave. P. Dickinson
One Foot in the Grave. D. Grubb
One for My Dame. J. Webb
One for My Money. E. Chaze
One for Sleep. F. Bonham
One for the Book. Neill Graham
One for the Death House. J. M. Flynn
One for the Devil. E. Leroux
One for the Road. J. Beckett
One for the Road. F. Brown
One for the Road. P. Conway
One for the Road. R. Dietrich
One for the Road. B. Grant
One for the Road. W. J. White
144 Piccadilly. S. Fuller
One from Five. J. W. Lee
One Girl in a Million. L. Tracy
One Glorious Spring. M. Richmond
One Good Death Deserves Another. Ritchie Perry
One Good Turn. N. Easton
One Got Away. H. Whittington
One Grave Too Many. R. Goulart
One Half of the World. J. Barlow
One Hand Clapping. J. Kell
One Helluva Blow. G. Werner
One Horrible Night. E. Hayford
One Horse Race. T. H. Stone
One Hour to Kill. G. H. Coxe
100 Mysteries for Arm-Chair Detectives. J. C. Cannell
$106,000 Blood Money. D. Hammett
100 Kilo Club. S. Gandolfi
100 Megaton Kill. Ralph Hayes
$100,000 Kiss. Nicholas Carter
£100,000 Insurance Swindle. W. W. Sayer
£100,000 Versus Ghosts. R. Jocelyn
100,000 Welcomes. M. Kenyon
One Is a Lonely Number. B. Elliott
One Is One. A. Dick
One Is One. M. Tripp
One Jump Ahead. A. Armstrong
One Jump Ahead. R. Chapman
One Just Man. James Mills
One Kind and Another. B. Pain
One Last Chance. L. Noel
One Last Mad Embrace. J. T. Story
One Last Time. M. Carrel
One Life Between. A. M. Meadows

One Life, One Love. M. E. Braddon
One Lonely Night. M. Spillane
One Louisburg Square. W. E. D. Ross
One Love Is Too Many for an Agent. J. Mirkarimi
One Mad Night. J. Reach
One Maid's Mischief. G. M. Fenn
One Man in His Time. H. Janson
One Man in the World. J. Barlow
One-Man Jury. S. Ransome
One Man Must Die. A. B. Cunningham
One Man Saw Them Die. A. Webb
One Man Show. M. Innes
One Man Too Many. V. Coffman
One Man's Awe. V. Carrington
One Man's Crime. L. W. Brent
One Man's Death. S. Truss
One Man's Enemies. S. Truss
One Man's Meat. W. H. L. Crauford
One Man's Meat. Colin Watson
One Man's Muddle. E. B. Quinn
One Man's Murder. D. Delman
One Man's Poison. C. Fitzsimmons
One Man's Poison. S. Fox
One Man's Secret. Stratford Davis
One Man's Secret. A. Mills
One Man's War. B. Bavin
One Man's Wars. G. Hackforth-Jones
One Man's Woman. K. Hewitt
One Million Carats. L. D. Klausner
$1,000,000 in Corpses. E. Ronns
One Million Francs. A. Fredericks
£1,000,000 Film Murder. Donald Stuart
£1,000,000 Plot. A. Skene
£1,000,000. W. J. Elliott
One Minus One. R. D. MacDougall
One-Minute Murder. J. G. Brandon
One Minute Past Eight. G. H. Coxe
One Minute to Eternity. R. Weverka
One Monday We Killed Them All. J. D. MacDonald
One More Bridge to Cross. A. Hale
One More Nice White Body. D. Glinto
One More River. Laurence Kirk
One More Time. M. Avallone
One More Time. Jay Bell
One More Unfortunate. E. Lustgarten
One Murder Too Many. G. H. Coxe
One Murder Too Many. F. C. Davis
One Murder Too Many. E. Lanham
One Murder Too Many. J. C. Lenehan
One Murdered, Two Dead. M. Propper
One Must Survive. R. Charles
One Night in Styria. D. Howarth
One Night Mystery. Old Sleuth
One Night of Fear. A. Crane
One Night of Murder. H. Boyd
One Night of Terror. M. Carleton
One Night Stand. C. Bolt
One Night Stand. W. B. Murphy
One Night to Kill. C. Franklin
One Night with Nora. B. Halliday
One Night's Mystery. M. A. Fleming
119 Great Porter Square. B. L. Farjeon
One Object in Life. Nicholas Carter
One O'Clock. M. G. Lewis
One O'Clock at the Gotham. R. Foley
One of God's Dilemmas. A. Upward
One of Marlborough's Captains. M. Gerard
One of My Sons. A. K. Green
One of Our Agents Is Missing. David St. John
One of Our Dinosaurs Is Missing. D. Forrest
One of Our Grandmothers. E. C. Mayne
One of Our H-Bombs Is Missing. F. H. Brennan
One of Seven. R. Hardinge
One of the Bevans. R. Jocelyn
One of the Eleven. W. Tyrer
One of the Family. J. Payn
One of the Flying Squad. W. M. Graydon
One of the Guilty. W. L. George
One of the Ones. J. C. Snaith
One of These Seven. C. Logan
One of Those Things. P. Cheyney
One of Those Ways. M. B. Lowndes
One of Three. C. S. Raymond
One of Us. C. Emery
One of Us Is a Murderer. A. Le May
One of Us Must Die. A. Clarke
One of Us Works for Them. J. D. Hunter
One-Off Job. A. Willsdon
One-One-One. G. Hackforth-Jones
One Page Missing. A. Soutar
One Remained Seated. J. Slate
One Rose Less. P. Flower
One Sane Man. F. Beeding
One Shall Be Taken. A. Hocking
One Shipwreck Too Many. Nicholas Carter
One Shot. R. P. Greenfield
One Shot for Sadie. M. Brody
One Step from Murder. L. Meynell
One Step Too Far. Nicholas Carter
One Sunny Day. Joan Alexander
One Sword Less. C. D. Peel
One Tear for My Grave. M. Roscoe
One That Got Away. H. McCloy
One Thing Constant. V. B. Harris
One Thing Needful, and Cut by the County. M. E. Braddon
1001 Afternoons in New York. B. Hecht

One Thrilling Night. N. Berrow
One Thrilling Night. M. K. Douglas
One-Time Champ. Duff Johnson
One to Jump. George Douglas
One to Play. H. Adams
One Too Many. T. Kendrick
One Touch of Blood. S. S. Baker
One Touch of Murder. H. Fraser
One Traveller Returns. D. C. Murray
One Tropic Night. E. C. Vivian
One, Two, Buckle My Shoe. A. Christie
1-2-3 Murders. F. Gerard
One-Way Cemetery. M. Hinxman
One Way Only. L. A. Knight
One Way or Another. L. Sciascia
One Way Out. G. H. Coxe
One Way Out. G. Simenon
One Way Street. P. H. Irving
One Way Street. D. Keller
One Way Street. N. Marino
One-Way Ticket. B. Hitchens
One-Way Ticket. H. Howard
One-Way Ticket. H. Luger
One Way Ticket. A. Thackeray
One Way to Venice. J. A. Hodge
One-Way Trail. R. Cullum
One-Way Trip. R. Angel
One Who Kills. R. Cullum
One Who Passed By. T. Cobb
One Who Saw. H. Hill
One Wife's Ways. G. F. Fox
One Wonderful Night. L. Tracy
One Wreath with Love. J. Roffman
O'Neil McDarragh. Anonymous
O'Neil McDarragh, the Detective. T. Pastor
Onion Field. J. Wambaugh
Onlooker. Sheila Bishop
Only a Bullet. J. K. Stafford
Only a Clod. M. E. Braddon
Only a Flirt. R. Jocelyn
Only a Girl's Heart. E. Southworth
Only a Headless Nail. Dick Stewart
Only a Horse Dealer. R. Jocelyn
Only a Love Song. M. Richmond
Only a Love Story. R. Jocelyn
Only a Matter of Time. V. C. Clinton-Baddeley
Only a Photograph. Old Sleuth
Only a Shadow. D. C. Murray
Only a Woman. M. E. Braddon
Only at Sunset. D. Martyn
Only Children. David Fletcher
Only Couples Need Apply. D. M. Disney
Only Gentlemen Can Play. H. McLeave
Only Girl in the Game. J. D. MacDonald
Only Good Body's a Dead One. T. Kenrick
Only Good German. T. Allbeury
Only Good Secretary. J. Potts
Only Half the Doctor Died. Frank King
Only Her Hairdresser Knew... C. Carpenter
Only in New England. T. Roscoe
Only Mugs Die Young. Griff
Only Mugs Work. W. Greenwood
Only Security. Jessica Mann
Only Seven Were Hanged. Stuart Martin
Only Some Had Guns. R. Parker
Only Son. J. W. Bobin
Only the Good. Mary Collins
Only the Guilty. A. M. Stein
Only the Hyenas Laughed. Robin Moore
Only the Losers Win. G. M. Barnes
Only the Rich Die Young. H. Pentecost
Only the Ruthless Can Play. Jonathan Burke
Only the Unafraid. R. Kirkbridge
Only the Very Rich. Carter Brown
Only Three Died. P. H. Powell
Only with a Bargepole. J. Porter
Only Witness. E. J. Goodman
Onyxx. T. Chiu
Oonah. G. Payne
Opal-Eyed Fan. A. Norton
Opal Heart. M. Leighton
Opal Legacy. F. Kent
Opal Murder Case. B. Symons
Opal Pendant. E. Barr
Opal Pin. J. R. Gillies
Opal Serpent. F. Hume
Opal Street. J. Wetherell
Open City. H. Miller
Open Contract. F. Scarpetta
Open Day at the Manor. Elizabeth Ford
Open Door. E. A. Walcott
Open Door. F. M. White
Open Foe. A. Sergeant
Open House. M. Innes
Open Mouth. M. Urquhart
Open Prison. Lady A. Scott
Open Question. J. De Mille
Open Roadsteads. E. L. Long
Open Season. D. Osborn
Open Season. B. Thielen
Open Secret. T. Cobb
"Open, Sesame!" B. Reynolds
Open Shadow. B. Solomon
Open Verdict. M. E. Braddon
Open Verdict. F. L. Cary
Open Verdict. R. Cooper
Open Verdict. R. Keverne

Title Index

Open Verdict. W. LeQueux
Open Verdict. J. Rhode
Open Window. J. Fuller
Open Your Hand and Close Your Eyes. P. Bair
Opener of the Way. R. Bloch
Opening Door. H. Reilly
Opening Night. N. Marsh
Opera House Murders. D. Billany
Opera Murders. K. Williams
Operation Afrika. C. Whiting
Operation Alcestis. M. Rennert
Operation: Alpha Death. N. Conway
Operation Apricot. C. A. Haddad
Operation Artemis. Douglas Scott
Operation Atlantis. M. G. Braun
Operation Backlash. L. McManus
Operation Ballerina. Selwyn
Operation Barbarossa. B. Newman
Operation Breakthrough. D. J. Marlowe
Operation Burning Candle. Blyden Jackson
Operation Calpurnia. M. Rennert
Operation Carlo. J. Pendower
Operation Caroline. C. H. Gibbs-Smith
Operation Castanets. D. Martyn
Operation Catcher. S. Jackman
Operation Caucasian Fox. C. Whiting
Operation Che Guevara. Nick Carter
Operation Checkmate. D. J. Marlowe
Operation Cicero. L. C. Moyzisch
Operation Cleansweep. D. Graham
Operation Cobra. A. Bodelsen
Operation Cocaine. Don Romano
Operation Conquest. B. Gray
Operation Countdown. D. Streib
Operation Counterpunch. D. J. Marlowe
Operation Cuttlefish. D. R. Mounce
Operation Damascus. J. Levy
Operation Dancing Dog. J. M. Fox
Operation—Deadline. M. Dines
Operation Deathmaker. D. J. Marlowe
Operation Deep Six. K. Stanton
Operation Delta. A. McCall
Operation Diamond. "Capstan"
Operation Doctors. R. Roth
Operation Dragnet. E. P. Thorne
Operation Drumfire. D. J. Marlowe
Operation Endless Hour. D. J. Marlowe
Operation: Evangeline. C. W. Burleson
Operation Fireball. D. J. Marlowe
Operation Fireball. Sea Lion
Operation Flashpoint. D. J. Marlowe
Operation Fox Hunt. C. Whiting
Operation Godiva. L. Miller
Operation Goldkill. B. Cassiday
Operation Halter. Frank King
Operation Hammerlock. D. J. Marlowe
Operation Hercules. J. Scotter
Operation Hijack. Don Romano
Operation Hit Man. Don Romano
Operation Homicide. E. Adams
Operation Honeymoon. Frank King
Operation Hong Kong. P. McCurtin
Operation Ice Cap. James Dark
Operation Il Duce. C. Whiting
Operation Intrigue. W. Hermann
Operation Iscariot. B. Marshall
Operation Jealousy. M. G. Braun
Operation K. N. Daniels
Operation Kill Ike. C. Whiting
Operation—Kill or Be Killed. M. Dines
Operation Kuwait. H. Arvay
Operation Loan Shark. Don Romano
Operation "M.O." Taffrail
Operation Malacca. J. Poyer
Operation Manhunt. M. Coles
Operation Megali. M. Dekobra
Operation Mermaid. K. Stanton
Operation Midas. E. Ogilvie
Operation Mind-Murder. J. Rosenberger
Operation Moon Rocket. Nick Carter
Operation Mora. Christopher King
Operation—Murder. L. White
Operation N. N. Daniels
Operation Nazi-U.S.A. J. Gilman
Operation New York. G. De Villiers
Operation Nightfall. J. Miles
Operation Nightmare. G. Fredrics
Operation Nuke. M. Caidin
Operation Octopus. James Dark
Operation Overkill. H. Gantzer
Operation Overkill. D. J. Marlowe
Operation Overkill. J. Rosenberger
Operation Patch. J. Lucarotti
Operation Pax. M. Innes
Operation: Perfidia. L. Jordan
Operation Piracy. P. Somers
Operation Porno. Don Romano
Operation Prophet. R. B. Asprey
Operation Red Carpet. J. Boland
Operation Royal Family. G. Null
Operation S-L. N. Daniels
Operation Scorpio. D. Mariner
Operation Scuba. James Dark
Operation Sea Monster. K. Stanton
Operation Sky Drop. D. Brennan
Operation Snake. Nick Carter
Operation Snatch. John Marsh
Operation Stalag. C. Whiting
Operation Starvation. Nick Carter
Operation Steal. J. W. R. Morrison
Operation Steelfish. K. Stanton

Operation Stranglehold. D. J. Marlowe
Operation: Super Ms. A. Offutt
Operation Superman. H. Hawton
Operation T. N. Daniels
Operation Terror. The Gordons
Operation Thunderbolt. J. Rosenberger
Operation Tibet. P. Mondol
Operation—To Kill a Man. M. Dines
Operation Tokyo. T. Middleton
Operation Trigeminal. J. Bedford
Operation Urgent. Sutherland Scott
Operation VC. N. Daniels
Operation V.I.P. George Fisher
Operation Vengeance. R. Crane
Operation Weatherkill. P. Edwards
Operation Werewolf. C. Whiting
Operation Whiplash. D. J. Marlowe
Operation: World War Three. J. Milton
Operator. D. Honig
Operator. D. E. Westlake
Operator. C. Williams
Operator from Chicago. Duff Johnson
Operator No. 19. G. Goodchild
Operator X. Mark Ross
Operators. A. Prior
Ophelia. F. Stevenson
Ophelia, the Anxious. K. Kimbrough
Opium Clipper. E. L. Long
Opium Flower. D. Cushman
Opium Murders. P. Baron
Opium Smugglers of Frisco. O. Harper
Opium Strategem. H. Downs
Opperman Case. John Bentley
Opportunist. S. Youd
Opportunity. A. Soutar
Opposite Sex. M. Turni
Opposite the Jail. M. A. Denison
Or Be He Dead. J. Byrom
...Or Be He Dead. H. Carmichael
Or by Default. G. Vaizey
Or Give Me Death! E. Spencer
—Or Murder for Free. D. L. Potter
Or Was He Pushed? R. Lockridge
Oracle of Maddox Street. L. T. Meade
Orange Air. R. Doliner
Orange Axe. B. Flynn
Orange Blossoms. J. Shearing
Orange Divan. V. Williams
Orange Girl. B. Hemyng
Orange Necktie. P. Fry
Orange Ray. N. G. Kiddy
Orange-Tree Mystery. J. Rowland
Orange Wednesday. Leslie Thomas
Orange-Yellow Diamond. J. S. Fletcher
Orator. E. Wallace
Orchard Close. A. Askew
Orchard of Tears. S. Rohmer
Orchid Limousine. W. Braun
Orchids for Mother. A. Latham
Orchids to Murder. H. Footner
Orchids with Murder. T. B. Morris
Ordeal. D. Collins
Ordeal. Roger Fuller
Ordeal. The Gordons
Ordeal by Fire. A. Upward
Ordeal by Innocence. A. Christie
Ordeal by Moonlight. H. Kaner
Ordeal of Alick Hillersdon. W. M. Graydon
Ordeal of Ann Curtis. A. Askew
Ordeal of Major Grigsby. J. Sherlock
Ordeal of Mark Bannister. H. Leyford
Ordeal of Mrs. Snow. P. Quentin
Order a Coffin. T. McCoy
Order of Battle. I. Melchoir
Order of Death. B. Bearshaw
Order of Death. H. Fleetwood
Order of the Octopus. S. Horler
Ordered South. A. M. Williamson
Orders to Kill. D. Downes
Orders to Kill. C. Whiting
Ordinary Accident. T. Amberley
Ordinary Day. H. Brinton
Ordinary Lunacy. Jessica Anderson
Ordinary Man. M. Arrighi
Organ Speaks. E. C. R. Lorac
Organization. D. Anthony
Organization A. D. Brent
Organization. O. Demaris
Organizer. D. MacDonald
Orient Express. G. Greene
Orient Express. P. Remy
Origin of Evil. E. Queen
Origin of the Crabs. G. N. Smith
Original Carcase. G. Bagby
Original Penny Christmas Readings. G. M. Fenn
Orion Line. N. Luard
Orion, the Gold Beater. S. Cobb
Orion Was Rising. R. Palmer
Orloff Diamond. G. H. Teed
Ormerod's Landing. Leslie Thomas
Ormond. C. B. Brown
Orphan Ann. H. C. Bailey
Orphan-Monger. S. Paternoster
Orphan of Mars. J. Cannan
Orphan of the Rhine. E. Sleath
Orphan of the Shadows. P. Minton
Orphans of Brandenburg. H. Edmonds
'Orrible Murder. B. Trice
Orville College. H. Wood
Osage Bow. W. C. MacDonald

Oscar. Old Sleuth
Oscar Betrand. M. E. Braddon
Oscar Montague—Paranoiac. G. L. Walton
Oscar Mooney's Head. W. E. Huntsberry
Oshawa Project. P. Nolan
Osiris Died in Autumn. L. Langley
Osrick. R. Sickelmore
Ossian's Ride. F. Hoyle
Ossington Mystery. H. Richards
Ostenders. G. Simenon
Osterman Weekend. R. Ludlum
Ostrekoff Jewels. E. P. Oppenheim
Ostrich Man. A. Soutar
Oswald Gray. H. Wood
Otan Plot. B. Newman
Othello's Occupation. L. A. G. Strong
Other. T. Tryon
Other Ann Fletcher. S. Jaffe
Other Body in Grant's Tomb. R. Starnes
Other Brother. S. Claudia
Other Brown. A. Luehrmann
Other Bullet. N. B. Mavity
Other Cathy. N. Buckingham
Other Child. M. Chittenden
Other Cousin. D. Farrell
Other End. R. E. Roberts
Other Folks' Money. W. B. M. Ferguson
Other Gods. E. C. Vivian
Other Half. C. F. Coe
Other Half of the Orange. J. M. Scott
Other House. Henry James
Other House. C. Massie
Other Island. E. H. Clements
Other Juliet. A. Maybury
Other Man. F. Durbridge
Other Man. A. MacVicar
Other Man. E. Wallace
Other Man's Danger. M. March
Other Maritha. C. Leonard
Other Men's Lives. J. Chapman
Other Men's Shoes. A. Soutar
Other Miss Evans. E. Kyle
Other Mr. North. L. Beresford
Other Mother. J. Blackmore
Other One. C. Turney
Other Passenger. J. K. Cross
Other Paths to Glory. A. Price
Other People's Business. S. Pim
Other People's Money. E. Gaboriau
Other Person. F. Hume
Other Romilly. E. P. Oppenheim
Other Room. J. Blackmore
Other Shore of Time. P. DePolnay
Other Side of Midnight. S. Sheldon
Other Side of Summer. V. Maxwell
Other Side of the Door. L. Chamberlain
Other Side of the Door. H. Howard
Other Side of the Tunnel. C. Kendall
Other Side of the Wall. H. C. McNeile
Other Side of the Wall. S. Truss
Other Side of the World. A. Hale
Other Sins Only Speak. H. Kane
Other Than Natural Causes. Mark Cross
Other Three. B. Bolt
Other Woman. O. R. Cohen
Other Woman. R. Foley
Other World. K. Robeson
Others. G. Simenon
Otis Dunn: Manhunter. N. Richards
Otley. M. Waddell
Otley Forever. M. Waddell
Otley Pursued. M. Waddell
Otley Victorious. M. Waddell
Ottawa Allegation. P. Geddes
Ouija Board. T. Lester
Ould Flynn. E. L. Long
Our Admirable Betty. J. Farnol
Our Adversary. M. E. Braddon
Our Agent in Rome Is Missing. Nick Carter
Our Doom Is Gone. R. Harrison
Our First Murder. T. Chanslor
Our Island. Anonymous
Our Jubilee Is Death. L. Bruce
Our Lady of Darkness. B. Capes
Our Lady of Pain. J. Blackburn
Our Lady's Inn. J. S. Clouston
Our Man Flint. J. Pearl
Our Man in Camelot. A. Price
Our Man in Havana. G. Greene
Our Man in Morton Episcopi. D. Lees
Our Member Mr. Muttlebury. J. S. Clouston
Our Missile's Missing. Robin Moore
Our Mother's House. Julian Gloag
Our Mysterious Passenger, and other stories. R. H. Savage
Our Second Murder. T. Chanslor
Our Share of Love. W. E. D. Ross
Our Spacecraft Is Missing! P. Richards
Our Very Best People. C. S. Raymond
Our Widow. F. Warden
Out. Max Austin
Out. P. Rey
Out Brief Candle. J. Rosenberg
Out, Brief Candle! L. Thayer
Out by the River. L. Peters
Out, Damned Tot! N. Spain
Out for a Killing. J. W. Vandercook
Out for Kicks. W. Shaw
Out for the Kill. Anthony Gilbert
Out for Vengeance. Nicholas Carter

Out from Shanghai. S. M. Parkman
Out from the Night. A. M. Meadows
Out Goes She. R. Stout
Out Is Death. P. Rabe
Out of a Dark Sky. S. Horler
Out of Asia Alive. M. Derby
Out of Bounds. A. Watkyn
Out of Chaos. R. M. Wells
Out of Circulation. A. Bell
Out of Control. B. Kendrick
Out of Control. G. G. Liddy
Out of Crime's Depths. Nicholas Carter
Out of Death's Shadow. Nicholas Carter
Out of Evil. Richard Fisher
Out of Evil. Ganpat
Out of Evil. D. G. Waring
Out of Focus. Peter Townend
Out of His Head. T. B. Aldrich
Out of It All. C. Saxby
Out of Order. P. A. Taylor
Out of Prison. M. A. Denison
Out of Reach of the Law. J. W. Bobin
Out of Satan's Grip. C. Frisbie
Out of Season. M. Kenyon
Out of Shape. L. Greenbaum
Out of the Ashes. F. Grierson
Out of the Ashes. E. W. Mumford
Out of the Blue. F. Archer
Out of the Blue. H. C. McNeile
Out of the Dark. U. Curtiss
Out of the Dark. G. F. Gibbs
Out of the Dark. G. Knevels
Out of the Dark. Seamark
Out of the Darkness. C. J. Dutton
Out of the Deep. H. Wood
Out of the Depths. L. Holton
Out of the Desert. A. Dare
Out of the Dog House. Charles North
Out of the Dusk. B. Flynn
Out of the East. W. M. Hills
Out of the Fire. H. Howard
Out of the Foam. J. E. Cooke
Out of the Fog. J. C. Lincoln
Out of the Fog. Clarissa Ross
Out of the Fog. F. A. Symonds
Out of the Frying Pan. C. N. Boyle
Out of the Jaws of Death. P. Barrett
Out of the Labyrinth. L. L. Lynch
Out of the Mouths of Graves. R. Bloch
Out of the Net. A. Clare
Out of the Night. M. Andrau
Out of the Night. E. B. James
Out of the Night. B. Reynolds
Out of the Night. Dan Ross
Out of the Night. R. O. Saber
Out of the Night. M. White
Out of the Past. P. Wentworth
Out of the Past. M. Carr
Out of the Past. F. Hutchinson
Out of the Running. A. Askew
Out of the Shadow. A. Glanville
Out of the Shadows. H. Curties
Out of the Shadows. M. Halliday
Out of the Storm. R. Braddon
Out of the Underworld. I. Stark
Out of the War? M. B. Lowndes
Out of the Whirlwind. W. T. Walsh
Out of This World. M. Cumberland
Out of This World. J. Pendower
Out of Time. R. Crane
Out of Time. C. Franklin
Out of Wild Hills. C. Campbell
Out on Bail. R. L. Goldman
Out There. D. Donovan
Out to Win. J. A. Jordan
Out Went the Taper. R. C. Ashby
Out with the Tide. Nicholas Carter
Outbreak. Lionel Black
Outbreak! R. DeMaria
Outbreak. M. Ruuth
Outcast. M. E. Braddon
Outcast. H. Janson
Outcasts. A. Murray
Outcrop. Colin Cooper
Outer Gate. O. R. Cohen
Outer Ring. A. E. Lindop
Outerworld. I. Haiblum
Outfit. R. Stark
Outlaw. D. Hennessey
Outlaw and Lawmaker. C. Praed
Outlaw Empire. W. C. Tuttle
Outlaw Island. A. R. Hilliard
Outlaw Jess. A. Askew
Outlawed Guns. N. W. Firth
"Outlaws". Clarke Little
Outlaw's Bride. H. M. Jones
Outlaw's Oath. E. C. Derby
Outlaws of Halfaday Creek. J. B. Hendryx
Outlaws of the Blue. Nicholas Carter
Outlaws of Yugo-Slavia. W. W. Sayer
Outpost of Eternity. H. Arvonen
Outrage. M. Tarmey
Outrage in Manchukuo. V. Gielgud
Outrage on Gallows Hill. G. Bellairs
Outrageous Fortune. Elizabeth Ford
Outrageous Fortune. P. Wentworth
Outrageous Lady Caroline. Rachelle Edwards
Outrun the Constable. S. Jepson
Outrun the Dark. C. Bartholomew
Outside In. M. Z. Lewin
Outside Job. A. Brede

Outside the Law. J. Barnes
Outside the Law. A. Crawford
Outside the Law. W. Dale
Outside the Law. H. Leyford
Outside the Law. P. Loraine
Outside the Law. M. McGrath
Outsider. L. Cameron
Outsider. I. Cleaton
Outsider. M. K. Douglas
Outsider. J. Letherby
Outsider. H. Smart
Outsider in Amsterdam. J. Van De Wetering
Outsiders. A. E. Martin
Outsider's Year. F. Warden
Outward Walls. John Burke
Outwitted. O. Bland
Outwitted. R. Marsh
Outwitted at Last. S. A. Gardner
Oval Table. J. J. Farjeon
Oven. G. Thorne
Over and Above. J. E. Gurdon
Over and Done With. E. H. Clements
Over Her Dead Body. R. S. Prather
Over My Dead Body. R. Angel
Over My Dead Body. F. Mayfair
Over My Dead Body. S. Mitchell
Over My Dead Body. M. Risco
Over My Dead Body. R. Stout
Over My Dead Body. P. Williams
Over My Shoulder. Margery Lawrence
Over My Shoulder. I. Valdes
Over the Border. R. Barr
Over the Border. H. Whitaker
Over the Edge. S. Kemp
Over the Edge. David Miles
Over the Edge. L. Treat
Over the Edge. D. Westheimer
Over the Edge of the World. Nicholas Carter
Over the Garden Wall. C. Carnac
Over the High Side. N. Freeling
Over the Hills. J. Farnol
Over the Hump. E. S. Gardner
Over the Line. Alec Coppel
Over the Sea to Death. G. Moffat
Over the Top. D. Newton
Over the Tunnel. A. Rives
Over the Wall. T. D. Smith
Over Thin Ice. Mark Cross
Overboard. G. F. Worts
Overdose of Death. A. Christie
Overdrive. Mike Curtis
Overdrive. M. Gilbert
Overdue. F. Clifford
Overdue for Death. Z. H. Ross
Overflowing Rain. R. Stohlman
Overkill. N. Daniels
Overkill. W. Garner
Overkill. J. Lange
Overload. D. Cory
Overload of Hope. J. Fores
Overlook House. W. Payne
Overlooked. B. Hawker
Overlord. O. Demaris
Overlord of the Damned. G. Stockbridge
Overlords. N. Sligh
Overlords. W. Woolfolk
Overnight. R. Goyne
Overture in Venice. H. Rowan
Overture to Death. H. Desmond
Overture to Death. N. Marsh
Overture to Trouble. S. Maddock
Owl. J. Gray
Owl. Frank King
Owl and the Pussycat. O. Cameron
Owl Flies Home. B. Rodney
Owl Hoots. B. Rodney
Owl in the Cellar. M. Scherf
Owl Is Abroad. R. Bridges
Owl Meets the Devil. B. Rodney
Owl of Darkness. M. Afford
Owl Sang Three Times. V. Kelsey
Owl Taxi. H. Footner
Owlers. M. Mayhew
Owls Don't Blink. A. A. Fair
Owl's Warning. Herman Landon
Owner Lies Dead. T. Perry
Ownley Inn. J. C. Lincoln
Ox. J. Brothers
Oxford Gambit. J. Hone
Oxford Murders. A. Broome
Oxford Mystery. G. D. H. Cole
Oxford Tragedy. J. C. Masterman
Oyster-Bed Mystery. A. Murray
Ozmar the Mystic. E. Hulme-Beaman

P.A. to Murder. A. Tack
P As in Police. L. Treat
P.C. Richardson's First Case. B. Thomson
P.J., the Secret Service Boy. F. S. Hamilton
P. Moran, Operative. P. Wilde
P.O. Detective. B. D. Adsit
P.P.C. N. S. Lincoln
P's Progress. F. O'Rourke
P.S. Your Cat Is Dead. J. Kirkwood

P.S. Your Shrink Is Dead. J. Reisman
Pace. L. Allan
Pace Grows Hotter. B. Sarto
Pace That Kills. W. Fuller
Pace That Kills. Kevin O'Hara
Pace That Kills. E. Saltus
Pacific Blue. C. Dawe
Pacific Cavalcade. V. Coffman
Pacific North-West. D. Enefer
Pacific Pearl. M. Cronin
Pack Bay. W. Martin
Pack of Lies. G. Ashe
Package Deal. E. Hely
Package Holiday Spy Case. D. Betteridge
Package Included Murder. J. Porter
Package to Spain. M. Polland
Packard Case. W. Merrick
Packed for Murder. J. Blackburn
Packet of Death. H. Metcalfe
Packet of Trouble. F. U. Ashford
Pact. J. A. Brown
Pact. C. Connolly
Pact with Satan. L. Holton
Pact with the Devil. H. Desmond
Padded Cell. P. Conway
Padded Door. B. Flynn
Paddington Mystery. J. Rhode
Padgate Mystery. E. C. Reed
Padrone. Don Smith
Paduan Conspiracy. M. Walton
Pagan. W. F. Morris
Pagan Joe. T. A. Plummer
Pagan Madonna. H. MacGrath
Pagan Pagoda. M. Mundy
Pagans. A. Soutar
Pagan's Cup. F. Hume
Page Mr. Pomeroy. E. Jordan
Page Mr. Tutt. A. Train
Pageant, and other stories. E. H. W. Meyerstein
Pageant of Murder. G. Mitchell
Paging Blackshirt. R. Graeme
Paging the Saint. L. Charteris
Pagoda. J. A. Phillips
Pagoda Mystery. Maurice Worth
Paid. M. Dana
Paid in Full. R. Bay
Paid in Full. M. Cronin
Paid in Full. E. Ellison
Paid in Full. J. Goodwin
Paid in Full. L. Meynell
Paid in His Own Coin. E. J. Goodman
Paid Out. J. P. Bessell
Paid Piper. C. S. Forester
Paid with Death. Nicholas Carter
Paignton Honour. A. Askew
Painful Predicament of Sherlock Holmes. W. Gillette
Painswick Line. H. Cecil
Paint Me a Million. D. L. Goodrich
Paint-Stained Flannels. P. Fry
Paint the Town Black. David Alexander
Painted Angel. G. R. Preedy
Painted Dagger. J. Drummond
Painted Death. D. Enefer
Painted Death. P. Quiroule
Painted Dog. V. Gunn
Painted Doll Affair. A. MacVicar
Painted Face. J. Stubbs
Painted Faces. Colin Robertson
Painted for the Kill. L. Cores
Painted Honeymoon. S. H. Webb
Painted Lady. J. Boland
Painted Mask. M. Erskine
Painted Monster. A. Rowe
Painted on a Donkey Cart. J. Bogar
Painted Window. Lady A. Scott
Painted Woman. F. A. Kummer
Painted Woods. N. Henshaw
Painter of Flowers. H. Fleetwood
Painter of Parma. S. Cobb
Pair of Knaves. M. Cronin
Pair of Knaves and A Few Trumps. M. D. Flattery
Pakistani Agent. P. Robinson
Palace. D. G. Compton
Palace and Prison. F. H. Rose
Palace of Chance. Old Spicer
Palace of Love. J. Vance
Palace of Spies. H. Compton
Palace of Terror. E. J. Murray
Paladin. B. Garfield
Palais de Danse Tragedy. G. Chester
Pale Ape. M. P. Shiel
Pale Betrayer. D. S. Davis
Pale Blue Nightgown. L. Golding
Pale Door. Lee Roberts
Pale Ghost at Graves End. L. Richards
Pale Grey for Guilt. J. D. MacDonald
Pale Hand of Danger. M. Lynch
Pale Horse. A. Christie
Pale Moon Rising. M. O'Brine
Pale Pink House. F. Y. McHugh
Palermo Affair. C. Forbes
Palermo Ambush. C. Forbes
Palgrave Mummy. F. M. Pettee
Palindrome. P. Conway
Paliser Case. E. Saltus
Pall for a Painter. E. C. R. Lorac
Pallard the Punter. E. Wallace
Palludia. A. Burr
Palm for Mrs. Pollifax. D. Gilman

Title Index

Palm Springs. T. Ardies
Palmprint. J. Barnett
Palomino Blonde. T. Allbeury
Palzer Experiment. A. Murray
Pamela and Her Lion Man. M. Peterson
Pamela's Honeymoon. R. Jocelyn
Pamela's Palace. A. J. Fitzgerald
Pamplona Affair. Nick Carter
Panama Paradox. M. Wolfe
Panama Plot. A. B. Reeve
Panama Portrait. S. Ellin
Panama Power Play. L. Derrick
Panama Red. S. Diamond
Panda One Investigates. P. N. Walker
Panda One on Duty. P. N. Walker
Pandemic. T. Ardies
Pandora. P. Kaufman
Pandora. A. B. Reeve
Pandora Feature. I. Baker
Pandora Man. K. Newcomb
Pandora's Box. T. Chastain
Pandora's Box. R. Dundee
Pandora's Box. S. McKenna
Panelled Room. R. S. Holland
Panic! J. Creasey
Panic. H. McCloy
Panic! B. Pronzini
Panic Button. T. Beattie
Panic in Box C. J. D. Carr
Panic in Needle Park. James Mills
Panic in Paradise. A. Amos
Panic in Philly. D. Pendleton
Panic in Pursuit. S. Dewes
Panic in the Night. J. Stagg
Panic in the Solomons. K. M. Stevens
Panic on Page One. L. Stewart
Panic Party. A. Berkeley
Panic-Stricken. M. A. Wilson
Panic Walks Alone. W. L. Rivera
Panther Face. E. Woodward
Panther Jones for President. Stanley Johnson
Panther's Moon. V. Canning
Pantomime Girl. A. Applin
Pantoufle. Fredrick Jackson
Papa. A. M. Williamson
Papa La-Bas. J. D. Carr
Papa Pontivy and the Maginot Murder. B. Newman
Papa San Files. H. Henn
Paper Albatross. R. Croft-Cooke
Paper Bag. J. Rhode
Paper Bullet. O. Carney
Paper Chain. F. L. Cary
Paper Chase. H. Balfour
Paper Chase. O. W. Bayer
Paper Chase. L. Egan
Paper Chase. R. Esser
Paper-Chase. A. Fielding
Paper Chase. J. Kennedy
Paper Chase. M. Saxton
Paper Chase. J. Symons
Paper Chase. R. Watkins
Paper-Chase Mystery. A. Fielding
Paper Circle. B. Fischer
Paper Coffin. L. Lamensdurf
Paper Doll. J. Lennox
Paper Dolls. L. P. Davies
Paper Ghost. E. Lindall
Paper Mistress. D. Malm
Paper Money. Z. Stone
Paper Palace. R. Harling
Paper Pistol Contract. P. Atlee
Paper Prison. P. C. Wren
Paper Salvage Crime. G. Chester
Paper Thunderbolt. M. Innes
Paper Tomb. S. Donati
Paperback Thriller. Lynn Meyer
Paperbag. Richard Russell
Paperchase Murder. H. Seymour
Papers Mean Peril. Noel Lee
Papers of Andrew Melmoth. H. S. Davies
Papersnake. L. Meynell
Papyrus Murder. T. B. Morris
Parachute Murder. L. Mitchell
Parade of Cockeyed Creatures. G. Baxt
Parade of the Empty Boots. C. A. Seltzer
Paradigm Red. Harold King
Paradine Case. R. Hichens
"Paradise" Coal-Boat, and other tales. C. J. C. Hyne
Paradise Conspiracy. G. Tracey
Paradise County. R. Sparkia
Paradise Court. J. S. Fletcher
Paradise for Two. M. Richmond
Paradise Formula. A. Dipper
Paradise Garden. G. F. Gibbs
Paradise Gun. J. Flagg
Paradise Island. J. Caywood
Paradise Men. S. Harvester
Paradise Mystery. J. S. Fletcher
Paradise of Fools. D. Vane
Paradise Party. E. Hunter
Paradise Road. D. S. Milton
Paradise Smith. R. Johnston
Paradise Spells Danger. G. B. Mair
Paradise Trap. R. Crane
Paradiso. A. Prior
Paradoxes of Mr. Pond. G. K. Chesterton
Paragon. E. Trevor
Parajacker. J. Jack
Parallax View. L. Singer

Parasite. O. Demaris
Parasites. T. E. Wilson
Parcel of Fortune. E. H. Clements
Parcel of Their Fortunes. B. N. Byfield
Parcel Post Murder. B. Herbert
Parcels for Inspector West. J. Creasey
Parchment Key. S. Hopkins
Pardon My Blood. P. Whelton
Pardon My Body. D. Bogard
Pardon My Gun. Keith Campbell
Pardon My Gun. J. P. Carstairs
Pardon My Return. P. Leslie
Paris Agent. A. Mills
Paris Bit. I. Marder
Paris Drop. A. Furst
Paris in September. E. Randolph
Paris One. James Brady
Paris Trap. J. Hone
Parisian Adventure. L. H. Brenning
Parisian Detective. F. Du Boisgobey
Parisian Love. L. H. Brenning
Parisian Nights. R. Goyne
Parisian Pigeon Drop. J. P. Radford
Park. D. Gold
Park Avenue Executioner. David Wilson
Park Avenue Murder! Nicholas Carter
Park Avenue Tramp. F. Flora
Park Lane Mystery. J. Hatton
Park Lane Mystery. L. Tracy
Park Mystery. H. L. Phillips
Parker Case. J. Courage
Parker Pyne Investigates. A. Christie
Parkwater. H. Wood
Parliament of Owls. P. Buchanan
Parlor Games. R. Marasco
Parole. J. Ehrlich
Parrish for the Defense. H. Waugh
Parrot Faced Man. C. R. Gull
Parrot Man. R. Middlemiss
Parson o' Dumford. G. M. Fenn
Parson Thring's Secret. A. W. Marchmont
Parson's House. E. Cadell
Part for a Poisoner. E. C. R. Lorac
Part for a Policeman. J. Creasey
Part of Virtue. Roy Lewis
Part 35. J. N. Iannuzzi
Parted by Fate. L. J. Libbey
Parted on Her Wedding Morn. L. Price
Parting Breath. C. Aird
Partisan. M. Urquhart
Partisans Die Alone. R. Wilkes-Hunter
Partners. W. Harrington
Partners in Crime. A. Christie
Partners in Crime. H. King
Partners in Peril. Nicholas Carter
Partners of the Night. L. Scott
Partridge Kite. Michael Nicholson
Party. D. Telford
Party at No. 5. Shelley Smith
Party at the Penthouse. A. M. Chase
Party Every Night. F. Lorenz
Party for Lawty. M. Sarsfield
Party for the Shooting. L. Revell
Party Games. H. H. Kirst
Party Girl. M. Albert
Party in Dolly Creek. C. Blackstock
Party Man. C. B. Kelland
Party of Eight. L. Meynell
Party of the Year. J. Crosby
Party to Murder. O. Chase
Party to Murder. R. Verron
Party to Murder. L. White
Party Was the Pay-Off. E. S. Holding
Pas de Deux. O. Beer
Pasang Run. E. Trevor
Pascali's Island. B. Unsworth
Pascal's Mill. B. A. Williams
Pascoe's Ghost. R. Hill
Pasha's Web. H. Bradshaw
Pasquinado. J. S. Fletcher
Pass. R. G. Hubler
Pass Along, Madam! A. Webb
Pass Beyond Kashmir. B. Mather
Pass Key to Murder. B. Reed
Pass the Aspirin. C. L. Pancoast
Pass the Body. C. S. Sprigg
Pass the Gravy. A. A. Fair
Passage. B. Nicolaysen
Passage by Night. H. Marlowe
Passage in Park Lane. J. D. Rowley
Passage of Arms. E. Ambler
Passage Through Bohemia. F. Warden
Passage to Danger. E. Lanham
Passage to Jamaica. C. Jauniere
Passage to Samoa. D. Keene
Passage to Terror. E. Ronns
Passage to Violence. S. Kennedy
Passages from the Diary of a Late Physician. S. Warren
Passenger. F. Durbridge
Passenger. Elizabeth Fenwick
Passenger from Calais. A. Griffiths
Passenger from Scotland Yard. H. F. Wood
Passenger List. O. L. Rosmanith
Passenger on the U. C. Aveline
Passenger to Folkestone. J. S. Fletcher
Passenger to Frankfurt. A. Christie
Passenger to Nowhere. Anthony Gilbert
Passengers for Painted Rock. W. C. Tuttle
Passerman's Hollow. Jane Stuart
Passers-By. A. Partridge

Passing Advantage. M. McGarrity
Passing of Charles Lanson. L. Tracy
Passing of Evil. M. McShane
Passing of Gloria Munday. J. Garforth
Passing of Mr. Quinn. G. R. McRae
Passing of Night. J. F. Bradley
Passing of Third Floor Back. C. Houghton
Passing of Tony Blount. S. M. Parkman
Passing Show. R. H. Savage
Passing Strange. C. Aird
Passing Strange. R. Sale
Passing Stranger. M. Cody
Passing Stranger. L. Hoffman
Passing Time. M. Butor
Passion. R. Manvell
Passion and the Pity. E. Trevor
Passion Flower Puzzle. D. Rico
Passion Lighting the World. M. Dekobra
Passion Murders. D. Keene
Passion of Gabrielle. M. S. Boylan
Passion of New Eve. Angela Carter
Passion of the Beast. J. Lamarre
Passion of the President. J. Haslette
Passion Pact. H. Janson
Passion Pulls the Trigger. A. Wallace
Passion the Plaything. R. M. Gilchrist
Passionate. Carter Brown
Passionate Adventure. F. Stayton
Passionate Atonement. M. Richmond
Passionate City. I. S. Black
Passionate City. J. L. Rickard
Passionate Invaders. J. Clare
Passionate Land. G. Wagner
Passionate Pagan. Carter Brown
Passionate Particles. M. Peterson
Passionate Playmate. H. Janson
Passionate Quest. E. P. Oppenheim
Passionate Strangers. G. Wagner
Passionate Trail. A. Hillgarth
Passionate Victims. Lange Lewis
Passionate Waif. H. Janson
Passionate Youth. E. C. Reed
Passionless Quest. C. Cannell
Passions of Medora Graeme. Elsie Lee
Passion's Aftermath. J. M. Foster
Passion's Victim. H. Duval
Passive Crime, and other stories. The Duchess
Passover Commando. I. R. Cohen
Passport. R. Bagot
Passport. E. Voute
Passport for a Pilgrim. J. Leasor
Passport for a Renegade. K. Bennett
Passport in Suspense. J. Leasor
Passport into Fear. W. H. Baker
Passport Invisible. G. C. Shedd
Passport to Danger. J. Paull
Passport to Danger. M. Richmond
Passport to Danger. J. Stagg
Passport to Death. B. Home
Passport to Murder. E. Allen
Passport to Murder. Neill Graham
Passport to Oblivion. J. Leasor
Passport to Oblivion. Babs Lee
Passport to Panic. E. Reed
Passport to Paradise. C. Houghton
Passport to Peril. J. Leasor
Passport to Peril. S. Marlowe
Passport to Peril. Robert Parker
Passport to Terror. M. Daniels
Passport to Treason. M. O'Brine
Passports to Murder. P. Hambledon
Password. D. Kim
Past All Dishonor. J. M. Cain
Past Dies Hard. D. W. MacArthur
Past Finding Out. D. E. L. Patch
Past Master of Crime. D. J. MacKenzie
Past Praying For. Sara Woods
Past Tense. I. Lambot
Past Won't Die. M. Malmer
Pastime. A. Fowles
Pastourel. F. Soulie
Pat. T. Cobb
Pat o' Nine Tales. M. M. Bodkin
Patched-Up Affair. F. Warden
Patchwork Girl. L. Niven
Patchwork Man. D. Harper
Patchwork of Death. P. Nichols
Patchwork Palace. M. L. Tyrrell
Paternoster Ruby. C. E. Walk
Path of a Hundred Deaths. C. R. Gull
Path of a Star. A. Applin
Path of Fear. W. M. Graydon
Path of Ghosts. Robert MacLeod
Path of Ivory. W. R. Foran
Path of Lies. A. Askew
Path of the Spendthrift. Nicholas Carter
Path of Virtue. G. Warden
Path to Glory. S. Styles
Path to the Bridge. Brian Cooper
Pathless Trail. A. O. Friel
Paths of the Dead. H. Nisbet
Pathway of Adventure. R. Tyrrell
Pathway to Fame. P. Trent
Patience of Maigret. G. Simenon
Patience Pettigrew's Perplexities. C. Augusta
Patient. A. Christie
Patient. G. Simenon
Patient in Room 18. M. G. Eberhart
Patient Is the Hunter. R. Wilkes-Hunter
Paton Street Case. J. Bingham

Patricia, the Beautiful. K. Kimbrough
Patrick Butler for the Defense. J. D. Carr
Patriot. C. Durbin
Patriot. R. Seth
Patriot. A. E. Walter
Patriot for Hire. A. Sinclair
Patriot Game. J. De St. Jorre
Patriotic Murders. A. Christie
Patriots. J. Barlow
Patriots. June Drummond
Patriots. F. Whishaw
Patriot's Dream. B. Michaels
Patrol to Zaruse. J. Robb
Patron Saint and other stories. C. R. Gull
Patsy Prize. R. Cooper
Pattern. M. G. Eberhart
Pattern for Destruction. P. W. Fairman
Pattern for Murder. D. Knight
Pattern for Murder. I. S. Shriber
Pattern for Murder. E. Warman
Pattern for Panic. R. S. Prather
Pattern for Perfidy. John Bentley
Pattern in Beads. D. M. Bumpus
Pattern in Black and Red. F. Keene
Pattern in Poison-Ivy. G. Bowman
Pattern in Yellow. K. Hewitt
Pattern Is Murder. Jean Marsh
Pattern of Chalk. Dennis Miles
Pattern of Chance. G. Gardiner
Pattern of Conquest. K. Thompson
Pattern of Death. P. George
Pattern of Guilt. Gavin Holt
Pattern of Murder. M. G. Eberhart
Pattern of Murder. M. Symons
Pattern of Rape. H. Janson
Pattern of Violence. R. Busby
Patty's Partner. J. Middlemass
Paul Beck, Detective. M. M. Bodkin
Paul Beck, the Rule of Thumb Detective. M. M. Bodkin
Paul Burdon. W. Magnay
Paul Campenhaye, Specialist in Criminology. J. S. Fletcher
Paul Clifford. E. G. Bulwer-Lytton
Paul Clifford. T. P. Prest
Paul Deverell. Anonymous
Paul Ferroll. Anonymous
Paul Jones's Alias. D. C. Murray
Paul Pry's Poison Pen. E. Baird
Paul Quentin. F. M. White
Paul Richards—Detective. D. Dallas
Paul Temple and the Front Page Men. F. Durbridge
Paul Temple and the Harkdale Robbery. F. Durbridge
Paul Temple and the Kelby Affair. F. Durbridge
Paul Temple Intervenes. F. Durbridge
Paul, the Sage. F. M. White
Paul Vargas, a Mystery, and other tales. F. J. Fargus
Paula. D. Kingery
Paulette. K. Lindsay
Pauline. J. Hawthorne
Pauline—A Mystery. Nicholas Carter
Pauline's Lady. M. V. Woodgate
Paul's Apartment. V. Siller
Paulton Plot. H. Adams
Pauper of Park Lane. W. LeQueux
Pavement Artist Mystery. W. Jardine
Pavilion. Hilda Lawrence
Pavilion at Monkshood. A. Maybury
Pavilion by the Lake. A. J. Rees
Pavilion of Honour. G. R. Preedy
Pavilion on the Links. R. L. Stevenson
Paw in the Bottle. Raymond Marshall
Pawn. L. A. Knight
Pawn. F. Nichols
Pawn. N. P. Sutherland
Pawn in Jeopardy. E. Gresham
Pawn in Jeopardy. S. Rattray
Pawn in the Game. J. L. Hardy
Pawn of Evil. A. Leech
Pawn to King's Cross. E. Mazzaro
Pawned. F. Packard
Pawnee Tom. Old Sleuth
Pawns. D. L. Soderberg
Pawns and Kings. Seamark
Pawns Count. E. P. Oppenheim
Pawns of Fate. P. E. Bowers
Pawns of Fear. J. Manor
Pawns of Murder. W. Woodrow
Pawnshop Murder. J. G. Brandon
Paxton Plot. C. G. Mitford
Pay As You Die. R. Crawford
Pay-Day. H. Osborne
Pay-Grab Murders. P. Chester
Pay-Off. Joe Barry
Pay Off. J. C. Barton
Pay Off. Neill Graham
Pay Off. K. Laing
Pay Off. A. W. Sherring
Pay-Off for a Dumb Dame. F. Duggan
Pay-Off in Blood. B. Halliday
Pay-Off in Calcutta. R. Collier
Pay on the Way Out. J. Murphy
Pay Out. P. Elliott
Pay the Devil. Harry Patterson
Pay to Bearer. M. S. Jones
Paydirt. L. Durie

Paying Guest. P. Assinder
Paying Guest. L. A. Knight
Paying the Price. Nicholas Carter
Payment Deferred. J. Dell
Payment Deferred. C. S. Forester
Payment Down. J. H. Vahey
Payment for Silence. A. Rivers
Payment in Full. J. W. Bobin
Payment Suspended! J. W. Bobin
Payoff. H. Howard
Payoff. N. Karta
Payoff. J. Mack
Payoff. Mike Phillips
Payoff. Don Smith
Payoff. A. Veraldi
Payoff for Paula. J. Bogar
Payoff for the Banker. F. Lockridge
Payoff in Black. W. G. Schofield
Payoff in Switzerland. Robert MacLeod
Payoff on Fever Street. J. Wolf
Payola. D. Keene
Payroll. D. Bickerton
Payroll of Fate. W. C. Tuttle
Pazenger Problem. J. Plain
Peace Among the Pelicans. G. C. Foster
Peace and Peter Lamont. N. Harman
Peace Bridge. W. A. Low
Peacemaker. J. Remenham
Peacemaker. P. Trent
Peacock Fan. H. S. Keeler
Peacock Feather Murders. Carter Dickson
Peacock House and other mysteries. E. Phillpotts
Peacock Is a Bird of Prey. R. Foley
Peacock of Jewels. F. Hume
Peacock's Feather. S. Esmond
Peak House. A. J. Rees
Peak Performance. I. Baker
Peal of Ordnance. J. Lodwick
Peanut Butter & Jelly Is Not for Kids. B. Kelly
Pear-Tree. W. Hewlett
Pearl and Plain. A. Griffin
Pearl Choker. K. East
Pearl-Headed Pin. D. Durham
Pearl Island. H. C. Rowland
Pearl Necklace. A. Applin
Pearl of Blood. K. Netzen
Pearl of Great Price. A. Askew
Pearl of Oyster Island. H. Davie-Martin
Pearl Thief. B. Ruck
Pearls and Perjury. H. H. Lewis
Pearls Are a Nuisance. R. Chandler
Pearls Before Swine. M. Allingham
Pearls of Desire. A. J. Small
Pearls of Doom. G. H. Teed
Pearls of Pilolu. Alys Brown
Peccadilloes. F. Keene
Peccavi. E. W. Hornung
Peccavi. C. Massie
Peck of Salt. K. Royce
Peddler. D. Ring
Peddler. H. C. Rowland
Pedestal. G. Lanning
Pedigree. G. Simenon
Pedigree in Pawn. A. H. Veysey
Pedigreed Murder Case. J. S. Fletcher
Pedlar's Acre. T. P. Prest
Peel Rocke—Black Sheep. H. H. Ross
Peeping Tom Murders. J. Baynes
Peer and His Plunder. P. Hill
Peer and the Woman. E. P. Oppenheim
Peerage in Peril. R. E. Salwey
Peggy, the Concerned. K. Kimbrough
Peggy's Dilemma. T. Cobb
Peking Connection. Don Smith
Peking Dimension. N. Calmer
Peking Dossier. Nick Carter
Peking Duck. R. L. Simon
Peking Incident. G. Atcheson
Peking Man is Missing. C. Taschjian
Peking Payoff. I. Stewart
Peking Plot. Ralph Hayes
Peking Switch. J. J. Marsh
Peking/The Tulip Affair. Nick Carter
Pekoe Reef. F. Knight
Pel and the Faceless Corpse. M. Hebden
Pel Under Pressure. M. Hebden
Pelham. E. Bulwer-Lytton
Pelham Affair. L. Tracy
Pelham Murder Case. Monte Barrett
Pelican Island. A. D. Divine
Pelican Strikes Back. R. Arnold
Pelota Murder. J. Daymont
Peloton, Detective. H. A. Cartledge
Pembroke Mason Affair. G. Barton
Pemex Chart. Nick Carter
Pen-Friend. A. Wykes
Pen Is Deadlier. F. Carmichael
Penal Settlement. C. C. Lewis
Penalty Is Death! V. G. Kennedy
Penalty of Fate. M. E. Braddon
Penance of Brother Alaric. B. Graeme
Penance Was Death. L. B. McNamara
Pencarnan. J. Rigg
Pencil Points to Murder. W. A. Barber
Pending Investigation. R. McLaughlin
Pendragon. M. Howe
Pendulum. J. Christopher
Pendulum. R. Eastman
Penelope. E. V. Cunningham

Penelope of the Polyantha. E. Wallace
Penelope, the Damp Detective. W. C. Anderson
Penelope's Daughter. Dair Alexander
Penelve. R. H. Thomas
Pengard Awake. R. Straus
Penguin Island Murders. M. MacElwain
Penguin Pool Murder. S. Palmer
Penhallow. G. Heyer
Penknife in My Heart. N. Blake
Penman's Progress. S. Brydon
Penmarric. S. Howatch
Pennhaven. H. York
Pennies for His Eyes. W. M. Duncan
Pennies from Hell. David Alexander
Pennies on Her Eyes. M. L. Roby
Penniless Millionaire. D. C. Murray
Pennington Case. R. H. Wilkinson
Penny for the Guy. J. Roffman
Penny Murders. Lionel Black
Penny to Spend. Edward Brown
Penny Whipp. C. Massie
Pennycross Murders. M. Procter
Pennygreen Street. A. La Bern
Pennyworth of Murder. G. Meyrick
Penrose Mystery. R. A. Freeman
Pentagon. H. Searls
Pentagon Case. V. J. Fox
Pentallion. V. Blake
Penthouse. A. S. Roche
Penthouse Conspirators. C. Pincher
Penthouse Killings. H. Brown
Penthouse Murders. R. P. Holden
Penthouse Mystery. E. Queen
Penthouse Passout. Carter Brown
Penthouse Preview. M. Brody
People Against Nancy Preston. J. A. Moroso
People Against O'Hara. E. Lipsky
People Apart. L. T. Shortell
People Ask Death. G. Dyer
People Exchange. R. F. Baylus
People from the Sea. V. Johnston
People in Cages. H. Ashton
People in Glass House. June Drummond
People in Glass Houses. J. Ridgway
People Like Us. F. Vosper
People of Darkness. T. Hillerman
People of the Night. V. Russell
People of the River. E. Wallace
People on the Hill. V. Johnston
People vs. Withers and Malone. S. Palmer
People Will Talk. E. C. R. Lorac
People's Man. E. P. Oppenheim
Peplow's Paper-Chase. T. Gallon
Pepper-Pot Problem. O. Cecil
Perchance of Death. E. Linington
Perchance to Kill. S. W. Edgar
Perchance to Kill. C. Franklin
Perdida. F. W. Pangborn
Perdita's End. P. Tabori
Perdition Express. B. Lang
Pere Goriot. H. Balzac
Peregrination 22. P. Purser
Peregrine House. J. Flores
Peregrine's Progress. J. Farnol
Perennial Boarder. P. A. Taylor
Perfect Alibi. J. Laurence
Perfect Alibi. A. A. Milne
Perfect Alibi. C. S. Sprigg
Perfect Assignment. J. Moffatt
Perfect Carrier. Sheila Ross
Perfect Corpse. L. R. Wright
Perfect Crime. H. Kane
Perfect Crime. E. Queen
Perfect Crime, or Two. H. Monteilhet
Perfect Criminal. G. Furnivall
Perfect Demon! Allen Carter
Perfect Fool. F. Warden
Perfect Frame. W. Ard
Perfect Frame. John Morgan
Perfect Murder. J. Atholl
Perfect Murder. S. Devi
Perfect Murder. H. R. F. Keating
Perfect Murder Case. C. Bush
Perfect Pigeon. R. Wormser
Perfect Plot. G. Canary
Perfect Round. H. Adams
Perfect Score. R. E. Cummins
Perfect Thief. R. J. Bass
Perfect Treasure. J. Payn
Perfect Victim. J. McKimmey
Perfect Weapon. B. Michelson
Perfect Wife. J. Pendower
Perfectionist. L. Kauffmann
Perfidious Lydia. F. Barrett
Perfume of the Lady in Black. G. Leroux
Perfumed Lure. M. St. Dennis
Perfumes of Arabia. E. Dewar
Perhaps a Little Danger. E. H. Clements
Perhaps I Look Simple. R. B. Amos
Perhaps the Prodigal. J. Courage
Perhaps to Kill. H. C. Davis
Peril. S. Horler
Peril. L. Osbourne
Peril Ahead. J. Creasey
Peril at Cranbury Hall. J. Rhode
Peril at Dune's Edge. D. Quick
Peril at End House. A. Christie
Peril at End House. A. Ridley
Peril at Journey's End. Norman Lee
Peril at Midnight. Elaine Hamilton

Title Index

Peril at Polvellyn. M. McEvoy
Peril at Stone House. J. Corby
Peril at the Spy Nest. A. M. Chase
Peril in Darkness. H. Willett
Peril in Provence. R. Hugill
Peril in the Pyrenees. J. J. Farjeon
Peril Is My Pay. S. Marlowe
Peril Island. P. Brebner
Peril of Barnabas Collins. Marilyn Ross
Peril of Helen Marklove and other stories. W. LeQueux
Peril of Oliver Sargent. E. J. Bliss
Peril of Richard Pardon. B. L. Farjeon
Peril of the Course. M. K. Douglas
Peril of the Prince! E. S. Brooks
Peril of the Prince. H. Hill
Perilous Adventure. M. Richmond
Perilous Assignment. M. Marlowe
Perilous Country. J. Creasey
Perilous Crossways. J. S. Fletcher
Perilous Discovery. G. Johnston
Perilous Elopement. J. L. Rickard
Perilous Errand. M. Sutherland
Perilous Hazard. Mark Cross
Perilous Holiday. Don Smith
Perilous Love. M. Turner
Perilous Parole. Nicholas Carter
Perilous Passage. A. Mayse
Perilous Passage. B. Nicolaysen
Perilous Passport. E. Allen
Perilous Quest. J. Ames
Perilous Quest. T. A. Niccolls
Perilous Secret. D. Peacock
Perilous Sky. D. Rutherford
Perilous Transactions of Mr. Collin. F. Heller
Perilous Voyage. D. Quentin
Perilous Voyage. R. St. Clair
Perilous Waters. J. Blackmore
Perilous Waters. E. Nepean
Perilous Way. M. Cumberland
Perils in Persia. J. Bolton
Perils of Josephine. Ernest Hamilton
Perils of Pekin. W. M. Graydon
Perils of Petrograd. W. M. Graydon
Perils of the Red Box. H. Hill
Perimeter Fence. A. Crockett
Period of Evil. M. Halliday
Period Stuff. D. Yates
Peripheral Spy. B. Peterson
Periscope Red. R. Rohmer
Perish by the Sword. Poul Anderson
Perishable Goods. D. Yates
Perjured Alibi. W. S. Masterman
Permanent Eclipse. M. Maurice
Permanent Wave. Virginia Sullivan
Perpetrators. Anthony Gray
Perrin Murder Case. G. Morton
Perrine. D. Daniels
Perris of the Cherry Trees. J. S. Fletcher
Persecuted. F. Whishaw
Persecutor. I. Hamilton
Persian Cat. J. Flagg
Persian Death-Trap. J. Christian
Persian Price. Evelyn Anthony
Persian Ransom. Evelyn Anthony
Persian Tassel. O. S. Cornelius
Person Called "Z". J. J. Farjeon
Person of Some Importance. L. Osbourne
Person Shouldn't Die Like That. A. D. Goldstein
Personal Adventures of a Detective. A. Carmichael
Personal Appearance of a Lioness. V. Tracy
Persons Unknown. P. MacDonald
Persons Unknown. G. Moffat
Persons Unknown. H. Sutcliffe
Persons Unknown. L. Thayer
"Persons Unknown." V. Tracy
Persuaders #1. F. E. Smith
Persuaders #3. F. E. Smith
Persuaders #2. F. E. Smith
Persuaders Again! F. E. Smith
Persuaders at Large. F. E. Smith
Perturbing Spirit. J. Caird
Peruvian Contracts. F. Fowlkes
Peruvian Nightmare. M. Barry
Peruvian Printout. A. Haig
Perverted Village. A. Soutar
Pest. A. P. Terhune
Pester Finger. H. B. M. Watson
Petals on the Wind. V. C. Andrews
Peter Cornish's Revenge. H. C. McNeile
Peter Cotterell's Treasure. R. S. Holland
Peter Darington. Douglas V. Duff
Peter Grayleigh Flies High. Colin Robertson
Peter Gunn. H. Kane
Peter Hyde, M.P. P. Trent
Peter in Peril. V. Bridges
Peter Intervenes. E. Jepson
Peter Krimsov. L. S. Taube
Peter Ruff. E. P. Oppenheim
Peter Ruff and the Double-Four. E. P. Oppenheim
Peter Rugg, the Missing Man. W. Austin
Peter the Brazen. G. F. Worts
Peter's Pence. J. Cleary
Peter's Profession. C. L. Reid

Petersburg-Cannes Express. H. Koning
Petrella at Q. M. Gilbert
Petrodollar Takeover. P. Tanous
Petrograd Consignment. O. Sela
Petronov Plan. J. Pattinson
Petrovka 38. J. Semyonov
Petticoat Lane. G. Goodchild
Petticoat Lane Murders. V. Gunn
Pew Group. A. Oliver
Phantasmagoria. Anonymous
Phantasms. W. Gerrare
Phantom. J. Sylvester
Phantom Airman. R. Walker
Phantom Alibi. H. Leverage
Phantom and Barnabas Collins. Marilyn Ross
Phantom Army. M. Pemberton
Phantom at Lost Lake. D. Lyons
Phantom Bat. R. C. Elliott
Phantom Bells. R. St. Clair
Phantom Bride. L. Ames
Phantom Bride. M. M. Brown
Phantom Bus. R. St. Clair
Phantom Canoe. W. B. Mowery
Phantom Car. F. M. White
Phantom Circus. A. Spiller
Phantom City. K. Robeson
Phantom Clue. G. Leroux
Phantom Conspiracy. M. Barak
Phantom Cottage. V. Johnston
Phantom Death, and other stories. W. C. Russell
Phantom Detective Cases. N. W. Firth
"Phantom Dirigible." R. St. Clair
Phantom Empire. R. M. Sears
Phantom-Fighter. Seabury Quinn
Phantom Fingers. J. J. Farjeon
Phantom Fingers. L. Mearson
Phantom Flame of Wind House. K. Kimbrough
Phantom Fleet. Sea Lion
Phantom Footballer. F. W. Gumley
Phantom Fortune. M. E. Braddon
Phantom Fortune. K. C. Groom
Phantom Forward. S. Horler
Phantom Gondola. M. Dekobra
Phantom Greyhound. F. W. Gumley
Phantom Gunman. N. Morland
Phantom Holiday. M. Russell
Phantom Hollow. W. Verner
Phantom in the House. A. Soutar
Phantom in the Rainbow. S. La Master
Phantom in the Wings. Michael Elder
Phantom Island. R. Walker
Phantom Killer. Colin Hope
Phantom Killer. H. Taylor
Phantom Lady. Carter Brown
Phantom Lady. W. Irish
Phantom Leg. F. Du Boisgobey
Phantom Light. E. Price
Phantom Lover. A. Eadie
Phantom Lover. E. Mansfield
Phantom Manor. Marilyn Ross
Phantom Millionaire. M. E. Longman
Phantom Miner. R. St. Clair
Phantom Murderer. B. G. Quin
Phantom Musketeer. C. Brandon
Phantom of Belle Acres. Marilyn Ross
Phantom of Dark Harbor. Clarissa Ross
Phantom of Fog Island. Marilyn Ross
Phantom of Fonthill Park. K. R. Vernon
Phantom of Forty-Second Street. M. M. Raison
Phantom of Glencourt. Clarissa Ross
Phantom of Meadow Creek. Old Sleuth
Phantom of the Creek. G. H. Teed
Phantom of the Films. A. Eadie
Phantom of the High School. A. C. Martens
Phantom of the Mill. L. Bidston
Phantom of the Opera. G. Leroux
Phantom of the Pacific. W. W. Sayer
Phantom of the Sacred Well. P. Leonard
Phantom of the Snow. Marilyn Ross
Phantom of the Swamp. Marilyn Ross
Phantom of the Temple. R. Van Gulik
Phantom of the Thirteenth Floor. Marilyn Ross
Phantom Passenger. Mansfield Scott
Phantom Pilot. P. Conde
Phantom 'Plane. A. O. Pollard
Phantom President. G. F. Worts
Phantom Raider. R. Trevor
Phantom Railway. A. Wood
Phantom Reflection. A. Ashton
Phantom Room. E. E. Mande
Phantom Scarlet. W. Mills
Phantom Slayer. D. Steele
Phantom Spy. M. Brand
Phantom Spy. F. Russell
Phantom Stockman. G. Boothby
"Phantom Tiger." R. St. Clair
Phantom Torpedo-Boats. A. Upward
Phantom Tourer. G. Collins
Phantom Train. D. Timins
Phantom Violin. J. Renaud
Phantom Wedding. Marilyn Ross
Phantom Wedding. E. Southworth
Phantom Wife. M. V. Victor
Phantom Wires. A. Stringer
Phantom Wreck. Old Sleuth
Phantoms of a Physician. Alan Miller

Phantoms of the Cloister. I. H.
Phantoms over Potsdam. R. Vacha
Pharaoh with His Waggons and other stories. R. Croft-Cooke
Pharaoh's Crown. F. H. Rose
Pharaoh's Ghost. K. Robeson
Pharaoh's Turquoise. A. M. Judd
Pharos, the Egyptian. G. Boothby
Phase of Darkness. Robin Moore
Phil and Me. M. Woodhouse
Phil Conway. A. C. Gunter
Phil Scott, the Indian Detective. J. R. Taylor
Philadelphia Blow-Up. M. Barry
Philadelphia Murder Story. L. Ford
Philanthropic Burglar. Rita
Phileas Fox, Attorney. A. T. Sadlier
Philip Bennion's Death. R. Marsh
Philip Derby, Reporter. W. J. Abbot
Philip Henson M.D. George Hastings
Philip Mordant's Ward. Marianne Kent
Philip, the Draftsman. F. X. J. Coleman
Philipp Steele of the Royal Northwest Mounted Police. J. O. Curwood
Phillida. T. Cobb
Phillip and the Flappers. D. Newton
Phillip in Particular. D. Newton
Philly. Dan Greenburg
Philo Gubb, Correspondence School Detective. E. P. Butler
Philomel Foundation. J. Gollin
Philopena. H. K. Webster
Philosopher's Hemlock. M. Cranston
Philosopher's Murder Case. J. R. Crawford
Philosopher's Stone. Colin Watson
Philosophy of the Marquise. M. B. Lowndes
Phoebe, the Miller's Daughter. T. P. Prest
Phoenix. A. Aricha
Phoenix. L. P. Bachmann
Phoenix Assault. J. Kerrigan
Phoenix Formula. T. Leighton
Phoenix from the Ashes. H. Monteilhet
Phoenix from the Gutter. P. Motte
Phoenix in Castile. J. G. Sarasin
Phoenix in the Blood. Harry Patterson
Phoenix Inferno. M. Barry
Phoenix Man. J. Sherman
Phoenix No More. E. Gage
Phoenix Reaction. L. Phillips
Phoenix Sings. D. Cory
Phone Booth Mystery. J. Ironside
Phone Call. J. Messmann
Phone Calls. L. O'Donnell
Phone for a Hearse. B. Carson
Phoney Hitman. J. R. Pici
Phonies. W. B. M. Ferguson
Phonographic Mystery. L. Madreyhijo
Photo Finish. J. Bruce
Photo Finish. Howard Mason
Photo Game. Jack Lang
Photocrimes. M. Horton
Photogenic Soprano. D. Halliday
Photographer. P. Boulle
Photographer's Evidence. Nicholas Carter
Photographs Have Been Sent to Your Wife. P. Loraine
Phreak-Out! Carter Brown
Phryne. M. Dekobra
Phyllis. E. V. Cunningham
Phyllis, the Cautious. K. Kimbrough
Physical Attraction. H. Janson
Physician, Heal Thyself! E. Phillpotts
Physician's Fare. C. G. Learoyd
Pianist Shoots First. G. Fairlie
Piano Box Mystery. Nicholas Carter
Picaroon. E. Dudley
Picaroon and the Burglar Tools. H. Landon
Picaroon Collects. J. Cassells
Picaroon Does Justice. Herman Landon
Picaroon Gets the Run-Around. J. Cassells
Picaroon Goes West. J. Cassells
Picaroon in Pursuit. Herman Landon
Picaroon: Knight Errant. Herman Landon
Picaroon Laughs Last. J. Cassells
Picaroon Resumes Practice. Herman Landon
Picaroons. G. Burgess
Piccadilly Ghost. E. Spencer
Piccadilly Jim. P. G. Wodehouse
Piccadilly Murder. A. Berkeley
Piccadilly Puzzle. F. Hume
Pick and Run. J. Farrimond
Pick Up. J. B. O'Sullivan
Pick-Up on Noon Street. R. Chandler
Pick Up Sticks. E. Lathen
Pick Up the Pieces. J. F. Straker
Pick Your Victim. P. McGerr
Picked Up. A. Applin
Pickled Poodles. Larry Harris
Pickup. Raymond Marshall
Pickup Alley. E. Ronns
Picture Frame. L. Lamb
Picture Her Missing. Lynn Williams
Picture Him Dead. F. A. Clement
Picture Miss Seeton. H. Carvic
Picture of Death. K. Giles
Picture of Death. D. La Pointe
Picture of Death. E. C. R. Lorac

Picture of Death. R. Simons
Picture of Guilt. M. Innes
Picture of Innocence. H. Fleetwood
Picture of Millie. P. M. Hubbard
Picture of Murder. S. Curtis
Picture of the Victim. J. S. Strange
Pictures in a Mirror. W. M. Thomas
Pictures in the Dark. Ian Stuart
Pictures on the Wall. J. Breckenridge Ellis
Pictures of Death. K. Robeson
Pidgin Island. H. MacGrath
Piece by Piece. J. K. Stafford
Piece of Action. E. Cannon
Piece of Resistance. C. Egleton
Piece of Something. Harry Reed
Piece of the Moon. Robert Lambert
Piece of the Moon Is Missing. J. L. Johnson
Pieces of a Hero. W. Overgard
Pieces of Modesty. P. O'Donnell
Pieces of the Game. L. Gifford
Pied Piper. R. Paier
Pied Piper of Helfenstein. E. V. McCarthy
Piedouche, a French Detective. F. Du Boisgobey
Pierce the Gloom. M. Clare
Pierce with a Pin. K. Hopkins
Pierced Ear Murders. T. A. Plummer
Pierhead 627. D. Enefer
Pig in a Poke. L. Thayer
Pig Is Fat. L. M. Maynard
Pig-Tail Murder. F. Durbridge
Pig That Got Up and Slowly Walked Away. J. Ripley
Pigeon Among the Cats. Josephine Bell
Pigeon Blood Rubies. M. M. Bodkin
Pigeon House. V. Williams
Pigeon Loft Crime. J. G. Brandon
Pigeon Parade. Maz
Pigeon Project. Irving Wallace
Pigeon Wins. E. Woodward
Pigeon's Blood. M. Pereira
Pigs Have Wings. P. G. Wodehouse
Pigskin Bag. B. Fischer
Pilate Plot. Martin Page
Pilditch Puzzle. W. Morton
Pilebuck. J. Hawkins
Pilgrim at the Gate. D. Cory
Pilgrim Came Late. M. Purcell
Pilgrim Come Home. C. Rodda
Pilgrim of Desire. V. Black
Pilgrim on the Island. D. Cory
Pilgrim's End. L. B. McNamara
Pilgrims Meet Murder. Dexter Muir
Pilgrim's Rest. P. Wentworth
Pillar of Fire. M. Clare
Pillar of Light. L. Tracy
Pillars of Hell. R. Chester
Pillars of Salt. A. Mills
Pillory. B. Fleming
Pilot Error. B. Knox
Pilot's Graveyard. P. Conde
Pimlico Plot. M. McMullen
Pimp for the Dead. R. Dennis
Pimpernel 60. P. Kinsley
Pin Men. R. East
Pin to See the Peepshow. F. T. Jesse
Pinball Murders. T. B. Black
Pinch of Poison. F. Lockridge
Pinch of Snuff. R. Hill
Pinch of Snuff. M. Underwood
Pinchbeck Masterpiece. P. Cleife
Pincher Martin, O.D. Taffrail
Pinday and the "White Slaver". B. Sarto
Pinecastle. I. Manchester
Pinehurst. J. Rhode
Pink and the Brown. H. Atkinson
Pink Camellia. L. Bergstrom
Pink Carrara. Harris Evans
Pink Castle. C. Vincent
Pink Film. J. Bogar
Pink Panther. M. Albert
Pink Panther Strikes Again. F. Waldman
Pink Ribbon, As Told to the Police. O. Blakeston
Pink Shop. F. Hume
Pink Silk Alibi. B. Sanders
Pink String and Sealing Wax. R. Pertwee
Pink Umbrella. F. Crane
Pink Umbrella Murder. F. Crane
Pinkerton Ferret. C. Morris
Pinnacle of Ice. J. Raven
Pinned Man. G. Griswold
Pins and Needles. E. Greenwood
Pint of Murder. A. Craig
Pioneer. H. Bindloss
Pious Agent. L. Braine
Pipe Dream. P. Ferguson
Pipe Dream. J. Symons
Pipe Dream Finesse. D. Da Cruz
Pipeline to Death. A. Eichler
Piper of Arristoun. B. Goldie
Piper on the Mountain. Ellis Peters
Piperock Tales. W. C. Tuttle
Pipes Are Calling. Carter Brown
Pipes of Margaree. J. Aeby
Piping a Detective. Anonymous
"Piping Times." J. Farnol
Pippin's Journal. R. O'Grady
Piracies, Ltd. Bok

Piraeus Plot. H. Arvay
Pirate Airship. J. Noy
Pirate Love. M. Richmond
Pirate of Pittsburgh. H. E. O. Whitman
Pirate of the Pacific. K. Robeson
Pirates. Taffrail
Pirate's Ghost. K. Robeson
Pirate's Gold. D. Whitelaw
Pirates of the Air Way. R. C. Armour
Pirates of the Main. Stuart Martin
Pirate's Pack. J. G. Sarasin
Pirate's Purchase. B. A. Williams
Pirate's Retreat. Lieut. Carlton
Pirdale Island. A. O. Pollard
Pistol at My Head. A. Nuttall
Pistol for Miss Preedy. H. C. Davis
Pistols and Pedagogues. F. Evans
Pistols for Two. A. M. Stein
Pistols with Coffee. W. Du Bois
Pit. F. Merrilees
Pit and the Pendulum. L. Sheridan
Pit in the Garden. L. Meynell
Pit of Death. Breton Lee
Pit-Prop Syndicate. F. W. Crofts
Pit Town Coronet. C. J. Wills
Pitfall. F. L. Cary
Pitfall. J. J. Dratler
Pitfall. P. Ritchie
Pitfall. W. Magnay
Pitfall in August. H. Roman
Pitiful Rebellion. M. Peterson
Pitiless As Death. Anonymous
Pity for Pamela. M. Fitt
Pity Him Afterwards. D. E. Westlake
Pity It Wasn't George. J. F. Straker
Pity My Love. D. Winston
Pity My Simplicity. C. Massie
Pity the Honest. E. Lacy
Pity Us All. J. Reese
Place at Whitten. T. Keneally
Place Called Purgatory. J. Shelynn
Place Called Skull. J. N. Chance
Place for a Poisoner. E. C. R. Lorac
Place for Murder. E. Lathen
Place for the Wicked. E. Trevor
Place in the Country. S. Gainham
Place Like Hessberg. C. Fleet
Place of Devils. Lucinda Baker
Place of Execution. A. Curry
Place of Execution. M. Vinter
Place of Judgment. B. Levy
Place of Mischief. E. E. Cameron
Place of Mists. Robert MacLeod
Place of Sapphires. F. E. Randall
Place of Shadows. K. Booton
Place of Stones. C. Heaven
Place of the Dawn. Gordon Taylor
Place of the Dragons. W. LeQueux
Place on Dark Island. G. Corren
Place to Hide. Clifford King
Place to Stand. A. Bridge
Place with Two Faces. Josephine Mann
Plague Court Murders. Carter Dickson
Plague Makers. J. Pattinson
Plague of Demons. G. Ashe
Plague of Dragons. J. M. Brett
Plague of Sailors. B. Callison
Plague of Silence. J. Creasey
Plague of Spies. M. Kurland
Plague of Violence. H. Pentecost
Plague on Both Your Causes. J. Brunner
Plague on Both Your Houses. M. Ashton
Plague over London. T. Craig
Plague Panic. S. G. Hedges
Plague Spot. B. Tutton
Plaid Shroud. Marc Miller
Plain Case of Murder. L. Thayer
Plain Man. J. Symons
Plain Miss Cray. F. Warden
Plain Murder. C. S. Forester
Plain Unvarnished Murder. K. Klein
Plains of Silence. A. Askew
Plan for Escape. A. Bioy-Casares
Plan 79. C. F. Maxwell
Plan XVI. G. D. Browne
Planetary Journeys and Earthly Sketches. G. Raffalovich
Planetoid 127 and The Sweizer Pump. E. Wallace
Planned Coincidence. B. Mortlock
Plant Me Now. M. Hagen
Plant Poppies on My Grave. A. Kent
Plantation Inn. Patricia Maxwell
Plantation Murder. C. N. Govan
Planter. H. Whitaker
Plaster Saints. F. A. Kummer
Plaster Sinners. Colin Watson
Plastic Kind of Death. T. D. Carroll
Plastic Magicians. P. Leslie
Plastic Man. D. J. Gerrity
Plastic Nightmare. R. Neely
Plate of Ladies. G. Fraser
Plate of Red Herrings. R. Lockridge
Platinum Ass. A. Storey
Platinum Bullet. R. L. Graves
Platinum Cat. M. Burton
Platinum High School. I. Shulman
Platinum Jag. A. Storey
Platinum Smugglers. R. C. Armour
Play for Keeps. H. Whittington
Play for Millions. Nicholas Carter
Play for Murder. N. Deane

Play It Casual. H. Janson
Play It Cool. J. Gerstine
Play It Hard. G. Brewer
Play It Solo. Neill Graham
Play It to a Bust. Dave Greenberg
Play Like You're Dead. W. Masterson
Play Misty for Me. P. J. Gillette
Play Now—Kill Later! Carter Brown
Play or Pay. H. Smart
Play the Roman Fool and Die. Richard Grayson
Play with Death. C. Franklin
Play with Fire. E. Percy
Play with Matches. F. Ford
Playback. R. Chandler
Playback. The Gordons
Playboy. P. W. Fairman
Played the Hard Way. Griff
Played to a Finish. Nicholas Carter
Player. W. Downing
Player and the Guest. G. F. Newman
Player on the Other Side. E. Queen
Players. W. Magnay
Players and the Game. J. Symons
Players' Boy Is Dead. L. Tourney
Players in a Dark Game. S. Coulter
Playgirl. H. Janson
Playgirl Wanted. Roy Vickers
Playing a Bold Game. Nicholas Carter
Playing a Lone Hand. Nicholas Carter
Playing for a Fortune. Nicholas Carter
Playing for Time. R. Rand
Playing the Knave. F. Warden
Playing the Mischief. J. W. De Forrest
Playing with Fire. G. Sampson
Plaything of Fate. Nicholas Carter
Plaza Mystery. Maurice Worth
Plea for Justice. Nicholas Carter
Pleasant Dreams—Nightmares. R. Bloch
Pleasant Grove Murders. J. H. Vance
Pleasant Rogue. L. Keith
Pleasantries of Old Quong. T. Burke
Please Kill My Cousin. G. Fairlie
Please Omit Funeral. H. Dolson
Please Pass the Guilt. R. Stout
Pleasure Buyers. A. S. Roche
Pleasure Cruise Murder. W. Jardine
Pleasure Cruise Mystery. R. Forsythe
Pleasure Dome. E. Kyle
Pleasure-Dome. D. Madden
Pleasure Girl. B. Sarto
Pleasure House. P. Tabori
Pleasure Island. F. R. Adams
Pleasure of Your Death. M. Farhi
Pleasure Principle. P. McCurtin
Pleasure Seekers. H. V. Dixon
Pleasure's Daughter. Marilyn Ross
Pledge. F. Duerrenmatt
Pledged to the Dead. E. M. Poate
Plender. T. Lewis
Plenty Under the Counter. K. Hewitt
Plot. E. Hostovsky
Plot. K. P. Kelley
Plot. E. Piper
Plot. Irving Wallace
Plot Against a Widow. R. C. Ashby
Plot Against Roger Rider. J. Symons
Plot and Counterplot. Anonymous
Plot and Counterplot. Old Sleuth
Plot Counter-Plot. A. Clarke
Plot for a Warship. Nicholas Carter
Plot for an Empire. Nicholas Carter
Plot for Millions. S. Campbell
Plot for Murder. F. Brown
Plot for the Fourth Reich. Nick Carter
Plot in Private Life, and other tales. W. Collins
Plot It Yourself. R. Stout
Plot-Maker. W. Hewlett
Plot of the Yellow Emperor. A. Parsons
Plot That Failed. Nicholas Carter
Plot to Kill the President. J. Pearl
Plot Uncovered. Nicholas Carter
Plot Within a Plot. Nicholas Carter
Plots and Counterplots. L. M. Alcott
Plotters. A. Caillou
Plotters. R. Hardwick
Plotters. T. W. Speight
Plotters of Paris. E. Mitchell
Plotters of Peking. C. Dawe
Plucked. H. Smart
Plucky Bob. Old Sleuth
Plucky Girl. Old Sleuth
Plugged Nickel. P. Sherwood
Plume of Smoke. E. Morris
Plumley Inheritance. C. Bush
Plunder. B. Appel
Plunder. P. Meriton
Plunder. A. S. Roche
Plunder. F. F. Van De Water
Plunder Bar. S. M. Parkman
Plunder for the Picaroon. J. Cassells
Plunder of the Sun. D. Dodge
Plunder Pit. K. Snowden
Plunder Ship. H. Hill
Plunder Squad. R. Stark
Plunderers. F. Coen
Plunderers. E. Lefevre
Plunderers. E. P. Oppenheim
Plunderers. Morley Roberts
Plunge. C. Brogan
Plunge into Crime. Nicholas Carter

Title Index

Plunge into Peril. W. Spann
"Plunger." H. Smart
Plush and Guilt. J. Foss
Plush-Lined Coffin. Carter Brown
Plutonium. V. Mayhew
Plutonium Heist. W. M. Green
Poached Peerage. W. Magnay
Poacher. P. Baron
Poacher. B. McNaughton
Poacher's Bag. Douglas Clark
Poacher's Wife. C. Carew
Pocket Full of Clues. J. R. Langham
Pocket Full of Dead. J. Wyllie
Pocket Full of Rye. A. Christie
Pocket Hercules. E. Jepson
Pocketful of Clues. J. R. Langham
Pocock & Pitt. E. Baker
Pod, Bender & Co. G. A. England
Poe Must Die. M. Olden
Poe Papers. N. L. Zaroulis
Poellenberg Inheritance. Evelyn Anthony
Poet and the Lunatics. G. K. Chesterton
Poetic Justice. A. Cross
Poets and Murder. R. Van Gulik
Poinciana. P. A. Whitney
Poindexter Crashes the Fifth Column. G. C. Foster
Point Blank. P. Rosenberg
Point Blank. R. Stark
Point of a Gun. A. MacKenzie
Point of a Thousand Spears. L. P. Greene
Point of Death. N. Dun
Point of Death. I. Lambot
Point of Honour. A. Scholefield
Point of Lost Souls. J. J. Toombs
Point of Murder. M. Yorke
Point of No Escape. M. Colton
Point of Peril. E. Ronns
Point of Reference. Richard Russell
Point of Violence. Lois Duncan
Pointed Tower. V. Thompson
Pointer to a Crime. A. Fielding
Pointers to Crime. Nicholas Carter
Pointing Finger. M. Richmond
Pointing Finger. Rita
Pointing Man. M. Douie
Points and Lines. S. Matsumoto
Poirot and the Regatta Mystery. A. Christie
Poirot Investigates. A. Christie
Poirot Knows the Murderer. A. Christie
Poirot Lends a Hand. A. Christie
Poirot Loses a Client. A. Christie
Poirot on Holiday. A. Christie
Poirot's Early Cases. A. Christie
Poison. A. Askew
Poison. L. Thayer
Poison and the Root. R. Savage
Poison at Plessis. M. Dekobra
Poison Case Number 10. L. Cornell
Poison Chasers. H. Calvin
Poison Cocktail Murders. C. B. Molyneaux
Poison Cross Mystery. I. H. Irwin
Poison Cupboard. John Burke
Poison Dealer. G. Ohnet
Poison Death. Glint Green
Poison Duel. P. Dingwall
Poison Eye. M. S. Buchanan
Poison Flower. D. Daniels
Poison Fly Murder. H. Rutland
Poison for One. J. Rhode
Poison for One. E. Wilmot
Poison for Teacher. N. Spain
Poison for the Toff. J. Creasey
Poison from a Wealthy Widow. P. Haggard
Poison Gang. D. Steele
Poison Gas Robberies. J. Creasey
Poison in a Garden Suburb. G. D. H. Cole
Poison in Jest. J. D. Carr
Poison in Kensington. C. Kingston
Poison in Paradise. A. Hocking
Poison in Pimlico. Elbur Ford
Poison in Play. N. Spain
Poison in Public. C. Barry
Poison in the Blood. P. Dolan
Poison in the Garden Suburb. G. D. H. Cole
Poison in the Parish. M. Kennedy
Poison in the Pen. P. Wentworth
Poison in the Shade. E. Benfield
Poison Is a Bitter Brew. A. Hocking
Poison Is Queen. J. L. Morrissey
Poison Island. A. T. Quiller-Couch
Poison Island. K. Robeson
Poison Ivy. Carter Brown
Poison Ivy. P. Cheyney
Poison Ivy. J. P. Heggy
Poison Jasmine. C. B. Clason
Poison League. J. B. Harris-Burland
Poison Lockspur. C. W. Sanders
Poison of Asps. F. Marryat
Poison of Poppies. G. Brodie
Poison on the Menu. F. Ramsdale
Poison Oracle. P. Dickinson
Poison Parsley. A. Clarke
Poison Party. M. Brucker
Poison Pen. H. Desmond
Poison Pen. R. Llewellyn
Poison-Pen at Pyford. D. Fisher
Poison People. W. Haggard
Poison Plague. W. Levinrew
Poison, Poker and Pistols. E. M. Stone

Poison Pool. G. Collins
Poison Ring. M. Y. Halidom
Poison Shadows. W. LeQueux
Poison Speaks Softly. D. P. Clark
Poison Summer. J. L. Hensley
Poison Trail. A. Armstrong
Poison Tree. S. Stern
Poison Unknown. M. Dalman
Poison Unknown. C. J. Dutton
Poison War. Ladbroke Black
Poison Weed. M. Richmond
Poisoned Anemones. U. Sanford
Poisoned Arrow. Lieut. Carlton
Poisoned Arrows. J. Middlemass
Poisoned Chalice. A. Hocking
Poisoned Chocolates Case. A. Berkeley
Poisoned Fang. K. Bruce
Poisoned Glass. S. J. Stutley
Poisoned Goblet. A. Gask
Poisoned Letter. Anonymous
Poisoned Orchard. U. Curtiss
Poisoned Paradise. R. W. Service
Poisoned Pen. O. Binns
Poisoned Pen. A. B. Reeve
Poisoned Relations. G. Simenon
Poisoned Sleep. B. Graeme
Poisoned Stream. H. Habe
Poisoned Web. A. Clarke
Poisoner. G. Verner
Poisoners. D. Hamilton
Poisoners. G. R. Preedy
Poisoner's Base. B. Cobb
Poisoner's Mistake. B. Cobb
Poisonous Angel. Griff
Poisonous Relations. J. Cannan
Poisons of Exili. Nicholas Carter
Poisons Unknown. F. Kane
Poker Jim, Gentleman and other tales and sketches. G. F. Lydston
Poker King. M. Manly
Polar Treasure. K. Robeson
Poldrate Street. Garnett Weston
Pole Reaction. J. Bruce
Pole Star Secret. J. Rosenberger
Polferry Mystery. P. MacDonald
Polferry Riddle. P. MacDonald
Police at the Funeral. M. Allingham
Police Blotter. R. L. Pike
Police Chief. J. Ball
Police Detective Stories. L. Dexter
Police Murders. P. H. Powell
Police Patrol: 2000 A.D. M. Reynolds
Police Sergeant C21. R. Barnett
Police Station Mystery. R. Hardinge
Police Your Planet. E. Van Lhin
Policeboat Mystery. A. Blair
Policeman at the Door. C. Carnac
Policeman Flynn. E. Flower
Policeman in Armour. R. Penny
Policeman's Dread. J. Creasey
Policeman's Evidence. R. Penny
Policeman's Holiday. R. Penny
Policeman's Lot. E. Linington
Policeman's Lot. Henry Wade
Policeman's Nightmare. M. Cumberland
Policeman's Progress. B. Picton
Policeman's Triumph. P. Manton
Policemen in the Precinct. E. C. R. Lorac
Policy for Murder. J. Popplewell
Polite Pirate. "Capstan"
Political Plotter. Dick Stewart
Politician. V. Torrio
Politics Is Murder. E. Lanham
Polkadot Murder. F. Crane
Polluted City. G. Thorne
Polly Put the Kettle On. Joan Fleming
Polly, the Worried. K. Kimbrough
Polmarran Tower. C. Massey
Polo Ground Mystery. R. Forsythe
Pomeroy Abbey. H. Wood
Pomeroy, Deceased. G. Bellairs
Pomfret Mystery. A. D. Vinton
Pompeii Scroll. J. La Tourrette
Pompeii Splendor. J. La Tourrette
Ponson Case. F. W. Crofts
Pontifex, Son & Thorndyke. R. A. Freeman
Pontius Pilate Papers. W. Kiefer
Pool. M. R. Rinehart
Pool of Death. K. Patrick
Pool of Flame. L. J. Vance
Pool of Tears. J. Wainwright
Poor Dear Esme. A. M. Burrage
Poor Devils. D. Ely
Poor Harriet. Elizabeth Fenwick
Poor Man's Shilling. K. M. Knight
Poor Millie. T. Baird
Poor Miss Finch. W. Collins
Poor Old Lady's Dead. J. S. Scott
Poor, Poor Ophelia. C. Weston
Poor, Poor Yorick. F. C. Davis
Poor Prisoner's Defense. R. Sheldon
Poor Quail. D. Skirrow
Poor Roger Is Dead. M. Lynch
Pop Goes the Queen. B. Wade
Pope of Greenwich Village. Vincent Patrick
Poppies of Death. P. Edwards
Pop. 1280. J. Thompson
Porcelain Fish. H. R. Campbell
Porcelain Fish Mystery. H. R. Campbell
Porcelain Mask. J. J. Chichester

Porkchoppers. Ross Thomas
Pornbroker. Carter Brown
Porro Palaver. A. Broome
Porson's Flying Service. G. E. Rochester
Port Afrique. B. V. Dryer
Port Allington Stories and others. R. E. Vernede
Port Angelique. R. Jessup
Port Arthur Chicken. T. Chiu
Port of Call. W. Reyburn
Port of Destination. E. L. Long
Port of Little Ships. A. Wood
Port of London Murders. Josephine Bell
Port of Lost Cargoes. M. Hastings
Port of Missing Men. Meredith Nicholson
Port of No Return. P. M. Irvine
Port of No Return. R. M. Sears
Port of Seven Strangers. K. M. Knight
Port Orient. D. Cushman
Portals. E. A. Mann
Portcullis Room. V. Williams
Porterfield Legacy. C. Stephens
Portland Place Mystery. C. Kingston
Portland Place Mystery. E. D. Pierson
Portly Peregrine. P. Traill
Portrait in a Dusty Frame. M. Hebden
Portrait in Black. I. Goff
Portrait in Black. R. Vincent
Portrait in Smoke. B. S. Ballinger
Portrait Invisible. J. Gollomb
Portrait of a Beautiful Harlot. H. Howard
Portrait of a Beautiful Woman. C. Massie
Portrait of a Dead Heiress. T. B. Dewey
Portrait of a Dead Lady. M. A. Taylor
Portrait of a Judge and other stories. H. Cecil
Portrait of a Killer. C. D. E. Francis
Portrait of a Man with Red Hair. H. Walpole
Portrait of a Mobster. H. Grey
Portrait of a Murderer. A. Meredith
Portrait of a Scoundrel. E. Phillpotts
Portrait of a Spy. T. Thurston
Portrait of a Victim. R. E. McDowell
Portrait of a Witch. D. Daniels
Portrait of Alison. F. Durbridge
Portrait of Barbara. R. Squire
Portrait of Death. W. Bannister
Portrait of Doubt. R. Abbey
Portrait of Emma. L. Cheatham
Portrait of Evil. Jennifer Hale
Portrait of Fear. M. Richardson
Portrait of Fear. F. Usher
Portrait of Jirjohn Cobb. H. S. Keeler
Portrait of Love. Lynna Cooper
Portrait of Love. J. De Secary
Portrait of Murder. R. Bloomfield
Portrait of Rene. Harry Davis
Portrait of Sarah. V. Black
Portrait of Susan. G. Davies
Portrait of Terror. P. Minton
Portrait of the Accused. F. A. Symonds
Portrait of the Artist As a Dead Man. F. Bonnamy
Portraits of the Past. K. Cameron
Portrush Mystery. G. L. Curry
Portuguese Defection. G. DeVilliers
Portuguese Diamonds. G. Horne
Portuguese Escape. A. Bridge
Portuguese Fragment. O. Sela
Portuguese Silver. C. N. Buck
Poseidon's Shadow. A. P. Kobryn
Possess and Conquer. Wenzell Brown
Possess Me Not. F. Nichols
Possess the Land. Alan White
Possessed. D. Daniels
Possessed. C. Farr
Possessed. W. Gombrowicz
Possessed. F. Hurd
Possessed. C. Moffett
Possessed. G. F. Scott
Possessed. C. Turney
Possession. L. P. Davies
Possession. C. Fremlin
Possession of Elizabeth Calder. Melissa Napier
Possession of Joel Delaney. R. Stewart
Possession of Tracy Corbin. D. Daniels
Post After Post-Mortem. E. C. R. Lorac
Post-Mark Homicide. A. A. Marcus
Post Mortem. H. Carmichael
Post-Mortem. G. Collins
Post Mortem. G. Cullingford
Post-Mortem. M. Moiseiwitsch
Post-Mortem Evidence. S. Fowler
Post Office Burglars of the Shawangunk Mountains. L. A. Newcome
Post Office Case. D. M. Disney
Post Office Detective. Anonymous
Post-Office Detective. G. W. Goode
Post Road. W. D. Steele
Postage Stamp Murder. G. C. Bestor
Posted for Murder. V. Rath
Postern of Fate. A. Christie
Posthumous Papers. R. Barnard
Postman Always Rings Twice. J. M. Cain
Postman's Daughter, and other tales. H. Herman
Postman's Knock. J. F. Straker
Postmark Murder. M. G. Eberhart

Postmark Murder / 575

P

Postmaster of Market Deignton. E. P. Oppenheim
Postmaster's Daughter. L. Tracy
Postscript for Malpas. P. Pearson
Postscript to a Dead Letter. D. MacKenzie
Postscript to a Death. M. Cumberland
Postscript to Murder. P. Winn
Postscript to Nightmare. D. Hitchens
Postscript to Penelope. S. Gilruth
Postscript to Poison. D. Bowers
Pot of Trouble. D. Tracy
Pot Shot. L. Stallworth
Potentate. W. Fennerton
Potman Spoke Sooth. D. Fulk
Potomac Conspiracy. D. L. Levy
Potsdam Murder Plot. D. Betteridge
Potting Shed. G. Greene
Poulter's Passage. P. McCutchan
Pound of Flesh. B. Delannoy
Pour a Swindle Through a Loophole. D. Von Elsner
Pour the Hemlock. A. J. Russell
Powder Barrel. W. Haggard
Powder Train. W. Tute
Powdered Proof. M. S. Buchanan
Power. W. Harrington
Power. F. M. Robinson
Power. R. M. Stern
Power and the Glory. G. Greene
Power Barons. D. Streib
Power Bug. G. Osborne
Power Cube Affair. J. T. Phillifent
Power Eaters. D. Davenport
Power Failure. James Preston
Power Gods. B. Clifton
Power-House. B. Appel
Power-House. J. Buchan
Power House. W. Haggard
Power Kill. C. Runyon
Power Killers. J. Philips
Power of a Villain. Warren Miller
Power of Gold. C. Meyer
Power of the Borgias. W. LeQueux
Power of the Bug. I. Drummond
Power of the Unknown. A. Edgar
Power of Woman. A. C. Gunter
Power on the Scent. H. Clandon
Power Play. T. J. Culver
Power Play. The Gordons
Power Play. L. Johns
Power Play. R. Sapir
Power Plays. C. Wilcox
Power Sellers. P. Hall
Power to Kill. R. Hichens
Power Without Glory. M. C. Hutton
Powers and Maxine. C. N. Williamson
Powers of Darkness. D. Miall
Powers of Darkness. F. M. White
Powers of Lismara. P. Tierney
Powers of Mischief. W. Magnay
Powers That Prey. J. Flynt
Practice Makes Murder. B. Bearshaw
Practice to Deceive. G. Bradshaw
Practice to Deceive. E. Linington
Practise to Deceive. R. Lockridge
Praed Street Dossier. A. Derleth
Praed Street Papers. A. Derleth
Praetorius Point. N. Pierce
Prairie Detective. Anonymous
Prairie Detective. L. P. Richardson
Prairie Flowers. J. B. Hendryx
Prairie Gold. H. Bindloss
Prairie Patrol. H. Bindloss
Prairie Peril. C. Stoddard
Pray for a Brave Heart. Helen MacInnes
Pray for a Miracle. A. Amos
Pray for the Dawn. E. Harding
Pray Silence. M. Coles
Pray to the Hustler's God. J. Donahue
Prayer for the Dying. J. Higgins
Prayer for the Guilty. P. A. Foxall
Praying Mantis. Edgar Johnson
Praying Mantis. H. Monteilhet
Praying Mantises. H. Monteilhet
Praying Monkey. Gavin Holt
Preach No More. R. Lockridge
Preacher of the Lord. A. Askew
Preaching Jim. D. Donovan
Precious Company. J. Budd
Precious Porcelain. N. Bell
Precipice. F. Warden
Predator. R. Braddon
Predator. D. Pitts
Predator. A. York
Predators. D. Streib
Preface to a Killing. N. Ashe
Prelude for War. L. Charteris
Prelude to a Certain Midnight. G. Kersh
Prelude to a Killing. N. Ashe
Prelude to Blue Mountains. A. Hyder
Prelude to Crime. J. J. Farjeon
Prelude to Darkness. M. Naismith
Prelude to Horror. W. B. M. Ferguson
Prelude to Murder. G. C. Bestor
Prelude to Murder. Anthony Gilbert
Prelude to Murder. N. Leslie
Prelude to Murder. S. Noel
Prelude to Passion. H. Luger
Prelude to Peril. J. Sohl
Prelude to Peril. S. Toye
Prelude to Terror. Helen MacInnes

Prelude to Trouble. John Bentley
Premature Burial. M. H. Danne
Premedicated Murder. Douglas Clark
Premeditated Murder. P. Cheyney
Premier. G. Simenon
Premiere at Willow Run. Michelle Collins
Premier's Daughter. A. Askew
Preparatory School Murder. R. Macnaughtan
Prepare for Action. J. Creasey
Prescription for Death. Desmond Martin
Prescription for Murder. H. Lees
Prescription for Murder. S. Miles
Prescription: Murder. D. M. Disney
Prescription: Murder. W. Link
Presence. M. Eyre
Presence in a Empty Room. V. Johnston
Presence in the House. M. Lovell
Presenting Inspector Flagg. J. Cassells
Presenting the Dreamer. W. M. Duncan
President Fu Manchu. S. Rohmer
President Has Been Kidnapped! P. Richards
President Is Dead. P. Alexandre
President Is Missing. H. A. Milton
President Kettle. C. J. C. Hyne
President Plan. D. Meiring
President Vanishes. Anonymous
Presidential Emergency. W. Stovall
Presidential Plot. Stanley Johnson
President's Agent. J. Hilton
President's Doctor. W. Woolfolk
President's Grass Is Missing. P. Breen-Bond
President's Mistress. Patrick Anderson
President's Mystery Story. F. D. Roosevelt
President's Plane Is Missing. R. J. Serling
President's Ransom. H. Gantzer
President's Team. E. Meade
Press Agent for Murder. M. Ryerson
Press of Suspects. A. Garve
Pressing Peril. Nicholas Carter
Pressure. C. F. Coe
Pressure-Gauge Murder. F. W. B. Von Linsingen
Pressure Man. Roderic Wilkinson
Pressure Point. L. Agniel
Preston Jayne. Old Sleuth
Presumed Dead. J. Larteguy
Presumed Dead. P. Urquhart
Presumed Dead. D. Whitelaw
Presumption of Stanley Hay, M.P. N. Cay
Pretender. C. Hosken
Prettiest Girl I Ever Killed. C. Runyon
Pretty Boy. W. Cunningham
Pretty Boy Dead. J. Hansen
Pretty Enough to Kill. A. McAllister
Pretty Fanny's Way. R. M. Gilchrist
Pretty Jailer. F. Du Boisgobey
Pretty Lady. M. Babson
Pretty Maids All in a Row. F. Pollini
Pretty Miss Murder. W. T. Ballard
Pretty Miss Smith. F. Warden
Pretty Ones. D. Eden
Pretty Pass. D. Footman
Pretty Pink Shroud. E. Ferrars
Pretty Poison. S. Geller
Pretty Sinister. F. Beeding
Pretty Stenographer Mystery. Nicholas Carter
Prettybelle. Jean Arnold
Preventive Man. G. V. McFadden
Previous Lady. J. La Tourrette
Previously Reported Missing—Now? G. Chester
Prey! G. Beare
Prey by Dawn. H. Kane
Prey by Night. Malcolm Douglas
Prey for a Newshawk. H. Janson
Prey for Me. T. B. Dewey
Prey for the Dreamer. W. M. Duncan
Prey for the Nightingale. H. McCutcheon
Prey for the Picaroon. J. Cassells
Prey of the Eagle. P. G. Leonard
Prey of the Falcon. R. Charles
Prey of the Strongest. Morley Roberts
Preying Mantis. N. Rutledge
Preying Streets. Ledru Baker
Price. D. Chacko
Price. A. Hornblow
Price. F. Lynde
Price. G. F. Newman
Price of a Secret. Nicholas Carter
Price of a Secret. T. W. Speight
Price of a Soul. P. Trent
Price of Admiralty. M. B. Lowndes
Price of Admiralty. S. Stone
Price of an Impulse. J. P. Bessell
Price of an Orphan. P. Carlon
Price of Death. F. Usher
Price of Delusion. W. Magnay
Price of Diamonds. G. Kelly
Price of Exile. W. J. Makin
Price of Freedom. A. W. Marchmont
Price of Love. A. Applin
Price of Murder. J. D. MacDonald
Price of Pity. C. R. Gull
Price of Power. W. LeQueux
Price of Protection. Warren Miller
Price of Silence. M. Dalton

Price of Silence. S. Kyle
Price of Silence. F. Warden
Price of Silence. M. C. Weiner
Price of Treachery. Nicholas Carter
Price Tag for Murder. S. Dean
Price Was High. G. Hackforth-Jones
Pricking Thumb. H. C. Branson
Pride of Dolphins. M. Hebden
Pride of Healers. R. Hirschhorn
Pride of Heroes. P. Dickinson
Pride of Life. W. Magnay
Pride of Overmoor. E. Woodward
Pride of Pigs. J. Wainwright
Pride of Place. W. P. McGivern
Pride of Race. B. L. Farjeon
Pride of the Paddock. H. Smart
Pride of the Peacock. V. Holt
Pride of the Ring. B. Bolt
Pride of the Stable. E. J. Murray
Pride of the Trevallions. C. Salisbury
Pride of Women. K. Platt
Prideful Woman. H. G. Hutchinson
Priest of Piccadilly. A. Applin
Priestess of the Damned. V. Coffman
Priests of the Abomination. I. Drummond
Priest's Secret. E. Finn
Priest's Secret. W. M. Graydon
Priest's Secret. A. Maxwell
Prillilgirl. C. Wells
Prim Windows. J. Chancellor
Prima Donna's Husband. F. Du Boisgobey
Prime Cut. M. Roote
Prime Minister and Mrs. Grantham. C. Dawe
Prime Minster Is Dead. H. Simpson
Prime Minister's Boat Is Missing. J. Dyson
Prime Minster's Pencil. C. Waye
Prime Minister's Pyjamas. F. Evelyn
Prime Minster's Secret. W. Holt-White
Prime Time Corpse. J. Babbin
Primeval and other stories. M. Bannerjee
Primitives. S. B. Hough
Primrose. A. Mills
Primula. G. R. Preedy
Primus. B. Street
Prince and the Perjurer. A. Hillgarth
Prince and the Undertaker, and What They Undertook. Riccardo Stephens
Prince Cinderella. G. Alexander
Prince for Inspector West. J. Creasey
Prince in Petrograd. E. Jepson
Prince in the Garret. A. C. Gunter
Prince Karl. M. Gerard
Prince Karl. A. C. Gunter
Prince of Balkistan. A. Upward
Prince of Blackmail. C. Bishop
Prince of Darkness. B. Michaels
Prince of Darkness. E. Southworth
Prince of Darkness. F. Warden
Prince of Fraud. E. T. Sawyer
Prince of Good Fellows. R. Barr
Prince of India. L. Clarke
Prince of Liars. Nicholas Carter
Prince of Lovers. W. Magnay
Prince of Mischance. T. Gallon
Prince of Paradise. F. Gerard
Prince of Plunder. S. Horler
Prince of Poisoners. Ladbroke Black
Prince of Rogues. Nicholas Carter
Prince of Romance. R. Pertwee
Prince of Sinners. E. P. Oppenheim
Prince of Spies. G. Davison
Prince of Swindlers. G. Boothby
Prince of the Blood. J. Payn
Prince of the Captivity. J. Buchan
Prince of the Palais Royal. M. Pemberton
Prince of Thieves. J. J. Lynx
Prince of Trouble. Colin Hope
Prince of Turf Crooks. F. Johnston
Prince of Ventriloquists. Old Sleuth
Prince or Clown. M. Dekobra
Prince Punnie. A. W. Marchmont
Prince Saroni's Wife. J. Hawthorne
Prince Schamyl's Wooing. R. H. Savage
Prince Zaleski. M. P. Shiel
Princely Detective. Anonymous
Princely Quartet. J. Budd
Prince's Darling. G. R. Preedy
Prince's Diamond. E. Hulme-Beaman
Princes of Peele. W. Westall
Princess After Dark. S. Horler
Princess and the Pilot. N. Sheraton
Princess Brinda. M. Dekobra
Princess Galva. D. Whitelaw
Princess in Mufti. H. T. Johnson
Princess Kate. L. Tracy
Princess Maritza. P. Brebner
Princess Mary's Locked Book. A. M. Williamson
Princess Mazaroff. J. Hatton
Princess of Alaska. R. H. Savage
Princess of Copper. A. C. Gunter
Princess of Crime. Nicholas Carter
Princess of Happy Chance. T. Gallon
Princess of Jutedom. C. Gibbon
Princess of Paradise. Stuart Martin
Princess of Paris. A. C. Gunter
Princess of Persia. J. D. White
Princess of the Purple Palace. W. M. Graydon
Princess' Own. Roland Daniel

Title Index

"Princess Proxy." J. R. Warren
Princess Stakes Murder. K. Platt
Princess Zara. R. Beeckman
Printer's Devil. Bill Barclay
Printer's Devil. C. Dane
Printer's Error. G. Mitchell
Prinvest-London. V. Gielgud
Prior Betrothal. Elsie Lee
Priority for Death. P. Vane
Priority Murder. L. Ford
Priory of St. Bernard. N. Harley
Priory of St. Clair. S. Wilkinson
Priscilla Darling. Maz
Priscilla to the Rescue. T. Cobb
Prison. G. Simenon
Prison at Obregon. B. Adkins
Prison Breakers. R. H. Poole
Prison Breakers. E. Wallace
Prison Feud. James Preston
Prison Girl. Wenzell Brown
Prison House. D. F. Gardiner
Prison Murder. R. Dark
Prison of Ice. D. Axton
Prison Princess. A. Griffiths
Prisoner. P. Boileau
Prisoner. Roland Daniel
Prisoner. T. M. Disch
Prisoner. M. Gerard
Prisoner. D. McDaniel
Prisoner. D. St. Michaels
Prisoner at the Bar. J. Ashford
Prisoner Born. C. Aveline
Prisoner Go Free. D. Lee
Prisoner in the Hold. A. Parsons
Prisoner in the Mask. D. Wheatley
Prisoner in the Opal. A. E. W. Mason
Prisoner in the Skull. C. Dye
Prisoner in the Square. D. Quentin
Prisoner #3. H. Stine
Prisoner #2. D. McDaniel
Prisoner of Ellis Island. W. M. Graydon
Prisoner of Evil. D. Tower
Prisoner of Fire. E. Cooper
Prisoner of Garve. S. Shulman
Prisoner of Ingecliff. J. Bellamy
Prisoner of Lemnos. C. Gayet
Prisoner of Lost Island. J. Hunter
Prisoner of Love. H. Monteilhet
Prisoner of Love. M. Richmond
Prisoner of Malville Hall. D. Daniels
Prisoner of Ornith Farm. F. Powell
Prisoner of the Buddha. R. C. Armour
Prisoner of the Chateau. G. H. Teed
Prisoner of the Devil. Michael Hardwick
Prisoner of the Garret. B. Reynolds
Prisoner of the Kremlin. A. Murray
Prisoner of the Manor. R. Abbey
Prisoner of the Manor. R. Hardinge
Prisoner of the Mountains. W. M. Graydon
Prisoner of the Past. D. Noel
Prisoner of the Priory. C. Goodall
Prisoner of the Pyramid. F. Gerard
Prisoner of War. Grace M. White
Prisoner Pleads "Not Guilty". L. Thayer
Prisoners. M. Cholmondeley
Prisoner's Base. C. Fremlin
Prisoner's Base. E. Gresham
Prisoner's Base. R. Stout
Prisoner's Friend. A. Garve
Prisoner's Friend. G. Goodchild
Prisoners in the Wall. G. Radcliffe
Prisoners of Devil's Claw. E. H. Hawkins
Prisoners of Fear. M. Broughton
Prisoners of Peru. Gwyn Evans
Prisoners of the Desert. S. Blake
Prisoner's Plea. H. Waugh
Prisoner's Secret. J. K. Leys
Prisoner's Tale. G. F. Newman
Prissy. C. Hanley
Private and Confidential. P. Trent
Private Anger, and Flight and Pursuit. F. O'Rourke
Private Carter's Crime. J. Creasey
Private Death. M. Urquhart
Private Detective. A. Forrester
Private Detective. R. Machray
Private Detective. J. D. Shea
Private Detective No. 39. J. W. Postgate
Private Enquiry. C. H. Ross
Private Enterprise, and other stories. R. Standish
Private Eye. C. F. Adams
Private Eye. D. Dudley
Private Eyeful. H. Kane
Private Face of Murder. J. Bonett
Private I. J. Sangster
Private Inquiries. Dorothy Johnson
Private Investigation. K. Alexander
Private Killing. J. Benet
Private Lies. M. K. Cooper
Private Life. P. Selver
Private Life of Jack the Ripper. Richard Gordon
Private Life of Sherlock Holmes. M. Hardwick
Private Line. S. Maddock
Private Party. W. Ard
Private Pavilion. J. G. Edwards
Private Practice of Michael Shayne. B. Halliday
Private Practices. L. Wolfe
Private Report. K. Roberts
Private Sector. J. Hone
Private Sector. J. Millar
Private Undertaking. H. T. Teilhet
Private Vendetta. Roderick Grant
Private Vendetta. Bradshaw Jones
Private View. M. Innes
Private Wire to Washington. H. MacGrath
Private Worlds. S. Gainham
Private Wound. N. Blake
Privateer Captain. Waters
Privateers. H. B. M. Watson
Privateer's Defiance. B. Wayde
Privateersman's Legacy. F. Du Boisgobey
Privilege. John Burke
Privileged Character. J. Laborde
Prize of Gold. M. Catto
Prize of Traitors. D. Vallance
Prizewinner. F. Mullally
Pro. B. Hamilton
Pro-Am Murders. P. Cake
Probability Broach. L. N. Smith
Probability Factor. W. Kempley
Probation. M. L. Storer
Probationer! E. Price
Problem at Pollensa Bay and Christmas Adventure. A. Christie
Problem by Rail. E. C. Vivian
Problem Club. B. Pain
Problem for Superintendent Flagg. J. Cassells
Problem for the Dreamer. W. M. Duncan
Problem in Angels. L. Holton
Problem in Ciphers. "Capstan"
Problem in Ciphers. H. Hardinge
Problem Island. D. E. R. Sinclair
Problem of Cell 13. J. Futrelle
Problem of the Derby Favorite. J. W. Bobin
Problem of the Green Capsule. J. D. Carr
Problem of the Purple Maculas. J. C. Iraldi
Problem of the Wire Cage. J. D. Carr
Procane Chronicle. O. Bleeck
Proceed at Will. B. Wilkinson
Proceed to Judgement. Sara Woods
Proceed with Caution. J. Rhode
Procession of the Damned. W. Tucker
Procession of Two. R. Philmore
Procession—to Prison. D. Henderson
Prochain Episode. H. Aquin
Procrastination of Sergeant Cluff. G. North
Prodigal, and other stories. A. Soutar
Prodigal Soldier. F. H. Rose
Prodigals and Sons. J. Ayscough
Prodigals of Monte Carlo. E. P. Oppenheim
Prodigal's Portion. C. C. Lowis
Prodigal's Progress. F. Barrett
Prodigy. M. J. Livingston
Produce the Body. R. Goyne
Professional. J. D. Buchanan
Porfessional Guest. W. Garrett
Professional Jealousy. C. F. Gregg
Professional Prince. E. Jepson
Professional Thieves and the Detective. A. Pinkerton
Professionals. J. Harris
Professor. Roland Daniel
Professor. J. Lynn
Professor. Alan Thomas
Professor Aylmer's Experiment. A. J. Anderson
Professor Dies. J. Rowland
Professor Knits a Shroud. W. Van Arsdale
Professor on the Case. J. Futrelle
Prof. Slagg of London. D. E. Marvin
Professor's Christmas Party, and A Student of the Obvious. H. C. McNeile
Professor's Mystery. W. S. Hastings
Professor's Poison. Neil Gordon
Profile in Gilt. J. C. Nolan
Profile of a Murder. R. King
Profit for the Picaroon. J. Cassells
Profiteers. E. P. Oppenheim
Profligate. A. Hornblow
Progeny of the Adder. L. H. Whitten
Programme for a Puppet. Roland Perry
Programmed for Death. L. Gribble
Programmed Man. W. D. Blankenship
Programmer. Bruce Jackson
Progress of a Crime. J. Symons
Progress of Rachel. A. Sergeant
Progress of Romance Through Times, Countries, and Manners. Clara Reeve
Project Web. Barbara Rogers
Project X. Colin Robertson
Projects Section. T. Lilley
Prologue to Murder. M. B. Dix
Prologue to the Gallows. P. McGuire
Prom Concert Murders. A. Wood
Prometheus Operation. M. Elder
Prominent Among the Mourners. Carolyn Thomas
Promise. J. B. Hendryx
Promise for Death. J. Messmann
Promise for Tomorrow. E. Woodward
Promise of Diamonds. G. Ashe
Promise of Murder. M. G. Eberhart
Promise of the Phoenix. F. Gerard
Promise to Keep. L. A. Sunagel
Promise to Kill. P. Marlowe
Promised Land. R. B. Parker
Promise(s) of Marriage. E. Gaboriau
Promotion Tour. T. Harknett
Proof, Counter Proof. E. R. Punshon
Proof of the Poison. F. L. Cary
Proof of the Pudding. P. A. Taylor
Proof Positive. John Drummond
Proper Age for Love. C. Jauniere
Proper Carve-Up. M. Cronin
Property in Cyprus. Robert MacLeod
Property of a Gentleman. C. Gaskin
Prophecy of Duncannon. W. C. Green
Prophet of Fire. J. Creasey
Prophetess. J. Kidde
Prophetic Warning. Anonymous
Prophet's Mantle. F. Bland
Propsy. J. B. Douglas
Prose Romances of Edgar A. Poe. E. A. Poe
Prosecutor. B. Botein
Prosecutor. James Mills
Prosecutor. P. R. Van Zyl
Prospect's Dead. A. Tack
Protagonists. J. Barlow
Protection for a Lady. M. Delaney
Protection for a Lady. J. T. Story
Protector. M. Braly
Protector. Larry Harris
Protector Conclusion. J. Burmeister
Protectors. W. Haggard
Protectors. R. Miall
Protectors. W. Pine
Protege. C. Armstrong
Protege. M. MacPherson
Proteus. M. L. West
Proteus Pact. G. St. George
Protocol for a Kidnapping. O. Bleeck
Proud Adversary. Howard Mason
Proud Citadel. T. Charles
Prove It, Mr. Tolefree. R. A. J. Walling
Provenance. F. McDonald
Provenance House. E. St. Clair
Provenance of Death. K. Giles
Proverbial Murder Case. W. Sutherland
Providence Hall. C. Rodda
Province Puzzle. V. McConnor
Provincetown. B. Hirschfield
Provincial Crime. Lionel Black
Provincial Papers. J. Hatton
Proving Flight. D. Beaty
Provo Link. D. Hayward
Prowl Cop. G. Jones
Prowl No More, Lady. James Warren
Prowler. F. Rickett
Prowler in the Night. J. Matcha
Prowling Terror. C. T. Stoneham
Prudence Be Damned. M. McMullen
Pruneface. C. Gould
Prussian Blue. A. Hocking
Prynter's Devil. J. Wainwright
Psalm Stone. F. M. White
Psi Hunt. M. Kurland
Psychedelic Spy. T. A. Waters
Psychiatric Murders. M. S. Michel
Psychiatrist Says Murder. L. Freeman
Psychic. M. Franklin
Psychic Detective: The Unicorn. H. W. Holtzer
Psycho. R. Bloch
Psycho. P. Moore
Psycho in Focus. L. Smith
Psychopath Plague. S. G. Spruill
Psychotron Plot. J. Rosenberger
Pub Crawler. M. Procter
Pub on the Pool. A. D. Divine
Public Defender. G. Goodchild
Public Enemies. A. Bracey
Public Enemy. H. Clevely
Public Enemy. K. Glasmon
Public Enemy—No. l. B. Graeme
Public Ghost Number One. A. Soutar
Public Mischief. S. Maddock
Public Murders. B. Granger
Public School Murder. R. C. Woodthorpe
Publicity for Anne. A. M. Williamson
Publicity for Murder. E. Messenger
Publish and Perish. F. M. Nevins
Puck of Crooks' Hill. San Antonio
Pulitzer Prize Murders. D. Heyward
Pull the House Down. M. L. Tyrrell
Pulled Down. P. Paul
Pulling Strings. P. Conway
Pulling the Strings. F. E. Penny
Pulpit in the Grill Room. E. P. Oppenheim
Pulse of Danger. J. Cleary
Puma. U. Miehe
Puma Quest. Michael Hastings
Punch and Judy Murders. Carter Dickson
Punch and Judy Murders. G. Hart
Punch with Care. P. A. Taylor
Punctual Rage. C. Black
Punish Me with Kisses. W. Bayer
Punish the Sinners. J. R. Saul
Punitive Action. J. Robb
Punt Murder. A. Griffin
Puppet-Masters. W. Garner
Puppet on a Chain. Alistair MacLean
Puppets of Chance. R. P. Koehler
Puppets of Fate. S. Jepson
Puppets of Father Bouvard. W. M. Duncan
Puppet's Part. D. Carew

Purchase Price. R. Cullum
Pure As the Lily. C. Cookson
Pure Poison. H. Waugh
Pure Sweet Hell. Malcolm Douglas
Purgatory Street. R. McDougald
Puritan. Colin Watson
Puritan's Wife. M. Pemberton
Purity League. Alan Williams
Purloined Letter. R. Brome
Purloined Prince. Edgar Turner
Purloined Prince. Ian Wallace
Purloining Tiny. J. F. Bardin
Purple Aces. R. J. Hogan
Purple and the Gold. D. Daniels
Purple Ball. F. Packard
Purple Claw. H. Horn
Purple Dragon. K. Robeson
Purple Dressing Gown. P. Fry
Purple Fern. F. Hume
Purple Jacaranda. Nancy Graham
Purple Legion. G. F. Eliot
Purple Limited. H. Leverage
Purple Love. M. Gerard
Purple Mask. L. J. Miln
Purple Mist. G. E. Locke
Purple Onion Mystery. H. Ashbrook
Purple Parrot. C. B. Clason
Purple Pearl. A. Pryde
Purple Place for Dying. J. D. MacDonald
Purple Plague. D. Steele
Purple Pony Murders. S. E. Porcelain
Purple Rock. A. MacVicar
Purple Shadow. E. Snell
Purple Shadows. A. V. Bartram
Purple Sheba. K. Hayles
Purple Shells. R. L. Goldman
Purple Sickle Murders. F. W. Crofts
Purple-6. H. Brinton
Purple Spot. Nicholas Carter
Purple Stain. J. M. Walsh
Purple Threat. D. Dayle
Purple Trident. C. Whitton
Purple Twilight. P. Groom
Purple Zombie. K. Robeson
Purse Which Was Found and other stories. R. Marsh
Purser's Mate. E. L. Long
Pursue the Wind. L. Richards
Pursued. A. Mills
Pursued by the Law. J. M. Cobban
Pursuer. L. Golding
Pursuing Shadow. J. Laurence
Pursuit. L. G. Blochman
Pursuit. R. L. Fish
Pursuit. M. McLaren
Pursuit. R. Pertwee
Pursuit. F. Saville
Pursuit. A. Soutar
Pursuit. R. Unekis
Pursuit in Peru. C. L. Leonard
Pursuit of a Parcel. P. Wentworth
Pursuit of Agent M. D. Copp
Pursuit of Mr. Faviel. R. E. Vernede
Pursuit of the House Boat. J. K. Bangs
Pursuit Till Morning. A. Wykes
Pursuit to Algeria. Arthur MacLean
Push-Button Spy. L. James
Pushbutton Butterfly. K. Platt
Pusher. E. McBain
Pussy Cat, Pussy Cat. I. Taylor
Put Back the Clock. M. Richmond
Put on the Spot. J. Lait
Put Out That Light. R. C. Woodthorpe
Put Out That Star. H. Carmichael
Put Out the Light. H. Desmond
Put Out the Light. R. Foley
Put Out the Light. S. Truss
Put Out the Light. Ethel L. White
Put Yourself in Her Place. M. Leighton
Puzzle. L. Thayer
Puzzle for Fiends. P. Quentin
Puzzle for Fools. P. Quentin
Puzzle for Inspector West. J. Creasey
Puzzle for Pilgrims. P. Quentin
Puzzle for Players. P. Quentin
Puzzle for Puppets. P. Quentin
Puzzle for Wantons. P. Quentin
Puzzle in Paint. Kootz
Puzzle in Paisley. E. Gresham
Puzzle in Parchment. E. Gresham
Puzzle in Parquet. E. Gresham
Puzzle in Patchwork. E. Gresham
Puzzle in Pearls. G. Ashe
Puzzle in Petticoats. Kootz
Puzzle in Pewter. R. Grey
Puzzle in Poison. A. Berkeley
Puzzle in Porcelain. R. Grey
Puzzle in Pyrotechnics. J. Rowland
Puzzle Lock. R. A. Freeman
Puzzle of the Blue Banderilla. S. Palmer
Puzzle of the Briar Pipe. S. Palmer
Puzzle of the Five Pistols and other stories. Nicholas Carter
Puzzle of the Happy Hooligan. S. Palmer
Puzzle of the Pepper Tree. S. Palmer
Puzzle of the Red Stallion. S. Palmer
Puzzle of the Silver Persian. S. Palmer
Puzzled Policeman. G. Woden
Puzzling Shadow. Old Sleuth
Pyramid of Death. N. MacKenzie
Pyramid of Lead. B. Atkey
Pyramids of Snow. E. Metcalfe

Pyrrha. P. Grayson
Python Project. V. Canning
Pyx. J. Buell

Q & A. E. Torres
Q As in Quicksand. L. Treat
QBI: Queen's Bureau of Investigation. E. Queen
Q Document. J. H. Roberts
Q.E.D. L. Brock
Q.E.D. L. Thayer
QED: Queen's Experiments in Detection. E. Queen
QEII Is Missing. H. Harrison
"Q" Squad. G. Verner
Q's Mystery Stories. A. T. Quiller-Couch
Q33. G. Goodchild
Q33—Spy Catcher. G. Goodchild
Quadraphone Homicide. J. Weisman
Quaker City. G. Lippard
Quaking Widow. R. Colby
Qualified Adventurer. S. Jepson
Quality Bill's Girl. C. W. Tyler
Quality of Mercy. R. Carson
Qualtrough. Angus Hall
Quarantine. N. Hasluck
Quark Maneuver. M. Jahn
Quarrel. C. Houghton
Quarrel with Murder. M. Halliday
Quarrelling Room. J. B. Watney
Quarry. F. Duerrenmatt
Quarry. J. A. Moroso
Quarry. R. L. Pike
Quarry House. J. Ware
Quarter of Eight. W. B. Gibson
Quarter to Four. W. W. Cook
Quartet. E. Phillpotts
Quartet of Three. M. Tripp
Quartz Eye. H. K. Webster
Quayle of the Yard. P. Trent
Quayle's First Case. P. Trent
Que Viva Guevera. G. De Villiers
Quebec Connection. L. Derrick
Quebec Plot. L. Heaps
Queen Against Owen. A. Upward
Queen and the Corpse. Max Murray
Queen and the Gypsy. C. Heaven
Queen Anne's Gate Mystery. R. Arkwright
Queen City Murder Case. W. Bogart
Queen Dies First. I. Lambot
Queen from Mars. R. St. Clair
Queen in Danger. S. Rattray
Queen Is Dead. G. Kezer
Queen of a Day. J. S. Fletcher
Queen of America. R. H. Greenan
Queen of Blackmailers. M. O. Rolfe
Queen of Bohemia. J. Hatton
Queen of Chance. Dick Stewart
Queen of Clubs. H. Footner
Queen of Coins. Stephanie Hall
Queen of Crookdom. M. Welford
Queen of Crooks. Detective Dunn
Queen of Crook's Harem. B. Sarto
Queen of Diamonds. Nicholas Carter
Queen of Hearts. W. Collins
Queen of Hearts. L. Paige
Queen of Knaves and other stories. Nicholas Carter
Queen of My Heart. M. Richmond
Queen of Night. H. Hill
Queen of Spades. H. C. Bailey
Queen of Spades. M. McEvoy
Queen of Spades. T. J. Morrison
Queen of Spies. T. Coulson
Queen of the Black Hand. H. C. Davidson
Queen of the Gangsters. J. Fairfax-Blakeborough
Queen of the Highway. Old Sleuth
Queen of the Jesters. M. Pemberton
Queen of the Looking Glass. A. L. McAllister
Queen of the Meadow. C. Gibbon
Queen of the Mirage. K. Lindsay
Queen of the Night. K. Perkins
Queen of the Outlaw's Camp. Anonymous
Queen of the Riffs. Operator 1384
Queen of the Secret Seven. Anonymous
Queen of the Secret Seven. O. Harper
Queen of the Stage. F. M. White
Queen of the Underworld. J. W. Booth
Queen of the White Slaves. Grace M. White
Queen of the World. George Weston
Queen Sends for Mrs. Chadwick. David Sanders
Queen Street. M. Gant
Queen Sweetheart. A. M. Williamson
Queen Victoria's Revenge. H. Harrison
Queen Wasp. J. Middlemass
Queenie. W. F. Fauley
Queenie's Terrible Secret. A. M. Miller
Queen's Advocate. A. W. Marchmont
Queen's Bush. W. M. Brown
Queen's Desire. H. Nisbet
Queen's Error. H. Curties
Queen's Evidence. E. Kyle
Queen's Falcon. E. E. Blau
Queens Full. E. Queen

Queen's Gate Mystery. H. Adams
Queen's Gate Mystery. H. Curties
Queen's Grace. N. Tranter
Queen's Hall Murder. A. Broome
Queen's Hand. B. Reynolds
Queen's Harbour. Elizabeth Ford
Queens Have Died Young and Fair. Clementine Hunter
Queen's Justice. Edwin Arnold
Queen's Mate. M. Gerard
Queen's Pawn. V. Canning
Queen's Ransom. T. Dresden
Queen's Revenge. S. Cobb
Queen's Scarf. D. C. Murray
Queen's Scarlet. G. M. Fenn
Queen's Treasure. C. Ashdown
Queer Affair. G. Boothby
Queer Bag of Bodies. A. Webb
Queer Face. G. Verner
Queer Fish. J. Boland
Queer Folk Next Door. G. Woden
Queer Kind of Death. G. Baxt
Queer Looking Box, and other stories. M. Hervey
Queer Mr. Quell. W. J. Makin
Queer Partners. S. Murray
Queer Race. W. Westall
Queer Sisters. S. Harragan
Queer Things at Queechy. P. Gurney
Queerest Man Alive, and other stories. G. H. Hepworth
Quella. G. N. Farmer
Quest. N. De Mille
Quest. N. A. Temple-Ellis
Quest for Alexis. N. Buckingham
Quest for Superintendent Flagg. J. Cassells
Quest for the Bogeyman. F. Lockridge
Quest for the Picaroon. J. Cassells
Quest of Douglas Holms. H. E. Inman
Quest of El Dorado. A. Askew
Quest of Geoffrey Darrell. A. Sergeant
Quest of John Clare. Sea Lion
Quest of Julian Day. D. Wheatley
Quest of Juror 19. David Davidson
Quest of Krang. C. Van Horn
Quest of Mr. Sandyman. Neill Graham
Quest of Nigel Rex. G. Goodchild
Quest of Qui. K. Robeson
Quest of the Crooked. H. Maxwell
Quest of the Emerald. M. Seville
Quest of "The Lost Hope". Nicholas Carter
Quest of the Sacred Slipper. S. Rohmer
Quest of the Seeker. J. T. Elton
Quest of the Spider. K. Robeson
Quest of the "Stormalong". D. W. MacArthur
Quest of the Vanishing Star. R. Ladline
Quest of the Yellow Pearl. P. C. MacFarlane
Quest of Youth. J. Farnol
Quest of Youth. J. G. Sarasin
Quest Sinister. S. P. B. Mais
Quest to Kill. R. Severn
Questing Hound. G. Hackforth-Jones
Questing Man. M. Home
Question. M. Peterson
? Crime. R. B. Whorf
Question of Character. J. Hougron
Question of Coercion. G. Norham
Question of Degree. Roy Lewis
Question of Evidence. Old Spicer
Question of Guilt. Magali
Question of Identity. H. C. McNeile
Question of Identity. J. Thomson
Question of Inheritance. Josephine Bell
Question of Judgment. P. B. Young
Question of Loyalty. N. Freeling
Question of Max. A. Cross
Question of Mud. H. C. McNeile
Question of Murder. Anthony Gilbert
Question of Negligence. H. McLeave
Question of Policy. B. Wayde
Question of Proof. N. Blake
Question of Queens. M. Innes
Question of Taste. F. Bamford
Question of Time. H. Carmichael
Question of Time. Nicholas Carter
Question of Time. F. Duncan
Question of Time. H. McCloy
Questionable Shape. M. Cumberland
Questor Tapes. D. C. Fontana
Quests of Paul Beck. M. M. Bodkin
Quere Here for Murder. M. Babson
Quere Here for Murder. N. MacKenzie
Queue Up to Listen. A. Spiller
Quick and the Dead. P. Bennetts
Quick and the Dead. Griff
Quick and the Dead. E. Queen
Quick and the Dead. V. Starrett
Quick and the Wed. G. Bowman
Quick Brown Fox. W. R. Burnett
Quick Curtain. A. Melville
Quick Red Fox. J. D. MacDonald
Quick Tempo. N. Easton
Quickie Mysteries. A. Badger
Quickly Dead. B. Cobb
Quickness of the Hand. J. Mayo
Quicksand. Elliott Arnold
Quicksand. W. Greatorex
Quicksand. M. Land

Title Index

Quicksands of London. C. H. Bullivant
Quicksilver. Roland Daniel
Quicksilver. R. Graves
Quicksilver. N. Hartley
Quicksilver Pool. P. A. Whitney
Quickthorn. Lanora Miller
Quid Est. E. Mariner-Scarritt
Quidnunc County. R. M. Stern
Quiet American. G. Greene
Quiet As a Nun. Antonia Fraser
Quiet City. Mark Ross
Quiet Fear. M. Halliday
Quiet Game of Bambu. R. Gouze
Quiet Horror. S. Ellin
Quiet Killer. D. MacKenzie
Quiet Mrs. Fleming. R. Pryce
Quiet Murder. V. R. Muzzey
Quiet Ones. B. Graeme
Quiet Passion. L. Hoffman
Quiet Place in the Country. Henry Clement
Quiet River. P. M. Hubbard
Quiet River. J. D. White
Quiet Room in Hell. B. Copper
Quiet Sound of Fear. L. Paxton
Quiet Terror. W. Wall
Quiet Under the Sun. K. Fitzgerald
Quiet Violence. D. M. Disney
Quiet Waits the Grave. H. Janson
Quiet War. J. Browning
Quiet Woman. H. Carmichael
Quietly She Lies. E. M. D. Hawthorn
Quiller Memorandum. Adam Hall
Quincunx Case. W. D. Pitman
Quincy, M. E. T. Racina
Quincy, M. E. #2. T. Racina
Quinn. N. Scanlon
Quinn and the Desert Oil. N. Scanlon
Quinneys'. H. A. Vachell
Quinney's Adventures. H. A. Vachell
Quin's Hide. M. Summerton
Quinta Affair. N. Grey
Quintain. R. E. Harrington
Quintana Inheritance. E. Tokson
Quinton Clyde, Private Investigator. T. McCoy
Quintus Oakes. C. R. Jackson
Quirindi. K. R. Butler
Quislings over Paris. M. Cumberland
Quite by Accident. K. Booton
Quite Like Old Days. V. Bridges
Quittance in Full. T. W. Speight
Quixote of Magdalen. Mrs. C. Kernahan
Quonsett. J. F. Murphy
Quoth the Raven. B. Fischer

R Document. Irving Wallace
R. Holmes & Co. J. K. Bangs
R.I.P. P. MacDonald
R.I.S.C. R. C. Frazer
R in the Month. N. Spain
R.O.F. Murders. H. Varley
R.S.V.P. Murder. M. G. Eberhart
Ra-Ta-Plan—! D. Ogburn
Rabbi's Wife. D. Benedictus
Rabbitfoot. A. W. Grahame
Rabbit's Paw. S. Jepson
Rabble of Rebels. G. Ashe
Rabble's Curse. C. A. Fought
Race Against the Sun. D. Rutherford
Race for a Fortune. R. S. Holland
Race for a Wife. H. Smart
Race for Life. A. F. Pinkerton
Race for Life. J. Remy
Race for Life. F. Whishaw
Race for Life and other tales. Anonymous
Race for Millions. D. C. Murray
Race for Ten Thousand. Nicholas Carter
Race Gang. E. Woodward
Race of Death. Nick Carter
Race of Life. G. Boothby
Race Toward Death. N. MacKenzie
Race Track Crooks. N. Ridley
Race Track Gamble. Nicholas Carter
Race with Death. Dick Stewart
Race with Ruin. H. Hill
Race with the Sun. G. Church
Race with the Sun. L. T. Meade
Racecourse Tragedy. N. Gould
Rachel. S. Nichols
Rachel Dyer. J. Neal
Rachel, the Possessed. K. Kimbrough
Rachel Weeping. Shelley Smith
Racing Axes. James Preston
Racing Crazy. Duff Johnson
Racing Ramp. A. J. Sarl
Racing Rubber. H. Smart
Racing Yacht Mystery. B. Graeme
Racket. B. Cormack
Racket Busters, Incorporated. H. H. Lee
Racketeers. R. Sharp
Racketeers of the Turf. Carlton Ross
Racketeer's Will. W. P. Vickery
Rackets Incorporated. Griff
Racoon Lake Mystery. N. M. Hopkins
Radar Target. G. Vaughan
Radcliffe Case. John Bentley
Radford Shone. H. Hill

Radiance. A. Maybury
Radiation Hit. L. Derrick
Radingham Mystery. Roy Vickers
Radio Blackmail. L. G. Redmond-Howard
Radio Crook. R. Hardinge
Radio Detective. A. B. Reeve
Radio Mystery. J. Mowbray
Radio Studio Murder. C. Wells
Radioactive Camel Affair. P. Leslie
Radium Profiteer. G. N. Philips
Radium Terrors. A. Dorrington
Radkin Revenge. W. D. Roberts
Radnitz. J. Nathenson
Rafferty. B. S. Ballinger
Rafferty. L. White
Rafferty and the Gold Dust Twins. Lillian Roberts
Raffles. David Fletcher
Raffles. E. W. Hornung
Raffles After Dark. B. Perowne
Raffles and the Key Man. B. Perowne
Raffles' Crime in Gibraltar. B. Perowne
Raffles in Pursuit. B. Perowne
Raffles of the Albany. B. Perowne
Raffles of the M.C.C. B. Perowne
Raffles Revisited. B. Perowne
Raffles, the Amateur Cracksman. E. W. Hornung
Raffles Under Sentence. B. Perowne
Raffles vs. Sexton Blake. B. Perowne
Raft of Swords. D. Kyle
Rag and a Bone. H. Waugh
Rag Bag Clan. R. Barth
Rag Pickers. H. V. Dixon
Rage. R. Bachman
Rage. P. Friedman
Rage. J. Ramsay
Rage. L. V. Roper
Rage at Sea. F. Lorenz
Rage in Babylon. S. Mitchell
Rage in Harlem. C. Himes
Rage of Angels. S. Sheldon
Rage of Desire. Clayton Matthews
Rage to Die. R. Jessup
Rage to Kill. B. E. Lovell
Ragged Edge. J. Karney
Ragged Edge. J. T. MacIntyre
Ragged Robin Murders. G. Morton
Raging Waters. D. Daniels
Ragland. J. Van Orsdell
Rags. A. Applin
Rahab Link. J. A. MacKenzie
Raid. W. E. Johns
Raid. J. B. O'Sullivan
Raid on the Bremerton. I. Eachus
Raid on the Mint. F. Putnam
Raid on the Villa Joyosa. R. Hopkins
Raid over England. N. Leslie
Raiders Moon. A. Knox
Raiders of the Southern Seas. T. Wallace
Raiders Passed! J. Hunter
Rail-Road Forger and the Detectives. A. Pinkerton
Railroad Murder Case. R. M. Laurenson
Railway Detective. Anonymous
Railway Detective. H. Rockwood
Railway Hotel Murder. A. Compton-Rickett
Railway Tragedy. F. Du Boisgobey
Rain Before Seven. J. August
Rain Before Seven. M. Brandel
Rain Before Seven. P. Buckley
Rain Islands. J. Wood
Rain of Death. J. D. Kennedy
Rain of Terror. Malcolm Douglas
Rain on the Roof. G. Goodchild
Rain on the Roof. K. Lipky
Rain with Violence. Dell Shannon
Rainbird Pattern. V. Canning
Rainbow. W. H. Harding
Rainbow Affair. D. McDaniel
Rainbow Coloured Hearse. K. Bird
Rainbow Coloured Shroud. J. Hedges
Rainbow Conspiracy. D. Lees
Rainbow Deaths. J. Churchward
Rainbow Feather. F. Hume
Rainbow Glass. A. Dwyer-Joyce
Rainbow Gold. D. C. Murray
Rainbow Island. M. Caywood
Rainbow Island. L. Tracy
Rainbow Man. T. Pollock
Rainbow Mystery. W. LeQueux
Rainbow Nights, and other stories. A. Soutar
Rainbow Puzzle. E. C. Vivian
Rainbow/Seagreen Case. P. K. Palmer
Rainbow's End. J. M. Cain
Rainbow's End. Ellis Peters
Rainbrother. C. Edwards
Raise the Dark Gambler. Mary Sellers
Raise the Titanic! C. Cussler
Rajah of Dah. G. M. Fenn
Rajah of Ghanapore. H. E. Hill
Rajah's Casket. Douglas Christie
Rajah's Fortress. W. M. Graydon
Rajah's Revenge. A. Murray
Rajah's Ruby. L. Barbee
Rajah's Ruby. Nicholas Carter
Rajah's Sapphire. M. P. Shiel
Rajah's Second Wife. H. Hill
Rakehell. A. Rundle
Raking for the Moon. M. G. Lowe
Rale McCoy. M. J. J. McKeown

Rally to Kill. B. Knox
Rally to the Death. D. Rutherford
Ralph. N. Crabb
Ralph Norbreck's Trust. W. Westall
Ralph Ryder of Brent. F. Warden
Ralph the Bailiff and other tales. M. E. Braddon
Ralph Wildhawk. Anonymous
Ram Dass. C. Felix
Ramona. M. Risco
Rampage. B. Haning
Ramsden. T. Mundy
Ramsden Case. D. Chandler
Ramsey, the Detective. Old Sleuth
Ramshackle House. H. Footner
Ramshackle Inn. G. Batson
Randolph Mason, Corrector of Destinies. M. D. Post
Randolph Mason: The Clients. M. D. Post
Randolph Mason: The Strange Schemes. M. D. Post
Random Army. M. Polland
Random Factor. L. J. LaRosa
Random Killer. H. Pentecost
Random Track. Austin Ferguson
Random Track to Peking. Austin Ferguson
Randy Inheritance. J. N. Chance
Raneslough. M. Heath
Range Justice. R. Wilkes-Hunter
Ranger of the Susquehannock. R. W. Kauffman
Ranger of the Tomb. Wilhelmina Johnson
Ranger of the Tomb. T. P. Prest
Rank Outsider. J. Fairfax-Blakeborough
Ransom. J. Cleary
Ransom. C. F. Coe
Ransom. L. Crawford
Ransom. C. Hume
Ransom! J. Messmann
Ransom! A. S. Roche
Ransom. R. K. Smith
Ransom. P. Wheeler
Ransom Castle. M. Farnsworth
Ransom Commando. James Grant
Ransom for a Nude. Lionel Black
Ransom for London. J. S. Fletcher
Ransom for the First Lady. D. Thurlow
Ransom of the Angel. D. Dodge
Ransom Racket. L. Thayer
Ransom Run. M. Dibner
Ransom Town. P. Alding
Ransomed Madonna. L. White
Rape. L. Trevor
Rape of a Quiet Town. D. Lees
Rape of a Town. N. Daniels
Rape of Berlin. W. H. Baker
Rape of Europe. G. Sager
Rape of Sun Lee Fong. M. Macao
Rape of the Nicollet Mall Mannequin. Steve Hall
Rape of Venice. D. Wheatley
Raper. J. McCready
Raphael, M.D. Augustus Muir
Raphael "Resurrection". T. Newman
Rapid Fire. J. Butler
Rapidan. Jackson Gregory
Rapist. S. A. Krasney
Rapist. M. Kenyon
Rapist. D. Logan
Rapt in Glory. E. Silberstang
Rapture Beyond. K. N. Burt
Rare Adventure. B. Fergusson
Rare Coin Score. R. Stark
Rascal of Quality. Nicholas Carter
Rascals and Co. Nicholas Carter
Rascal's Nerve. M. O. Rolfe
Rash Conclusions. G. W. Appleton
Rashevski Ikon. J. Pattinson
Rasp. P. MacDonald
Raspberry Jam. C. Wells
Raspberry Reich. M. Mankowitz
Raspberry Tart Affair. F. Halliday
Rasprava. E. J. Harrison
Rasputin the Rascal Monk. W. LeQueux
Rasputinism in London. W. LeQueux
Rat. P. Bottome
Rat Alley. H. Robison
Rat Began to Gnaw the Rope. C. W. Grafton
Rat in a Trap. M. Vinter
Rat Pack. S. Stevens
Rat Race. A. Bester
Rat Race. D. Francis
Rat Report. C. Fitzgibbon
Rat Trap. W. LeQueux
Rat Trap. Craig Thomas
Rather a Common Sort of Crime. J. Porter
Rather a Vicious Gentleman. F. McAuliffe
Rather Cool for Mayhem. L. G. Blochman
Rather Like. J. Castier
Ratman's Notebooks. S. Gilbert
Rats. A. Christie
Rats. J. Herbert
Rats' Castle. R. Bridges
Rattle His Bones. J. Shore
Rattler. J. Cassells
Rattlers. J. Gilmore
Rattlesnake. H. Pink
Rattlesnake. K. Tynan
Rattling of Old Bones. Jonathan Ross
Ravaged. S. Friedman
Ravagers. D. Hamilton

Rave for a Roughneck. H. Janson
Raven. M. E. Cooke
Raven. B. Goldie
Raven. E. Sudak
Raven After Dark. D. MacKenzie
Raven and the Dove. K. Kinder
Raven and the Kamikaze. D. MacKenzie
Raven and the Paperhangers. D. MacKenzie
Raven and the Phantom. Clarissa Ross
Raven and the Ratcatcher. D. MacKenzie
Raven Feathers His Nest. Clarissa Ross
Raven in Flight. D. MacKenzie
Raven Is a Blood Red Bird. D. M. Marlowe
Raven Never More. G. Marton
Raven Settles a Score. D. MacKenzie
Raven Wings. Anne Edwards
Ravenburn. Laura Black
Ravencroft Mystery. W. H. L. Crauford
Ravendon. J. Blackmore
Ravenelle Riddle. E. B. Black
Ravenhurst. Marilyn Ross
Ravenkill. P. Warren
Raven's Beak. H. C. Nisbet
Raven's Causeway. C. Hodge
Raven's Eye. E. Bond
Raven's Feathers. D. Carey
Raven's Forge. Jennie Melville
Ravenscroft. D. Eden
Ravenscroft Affair. C. R. Gull
Ravenscroft Horror. C. R. Gull
Ravensdale Mystery. G. E. Locke
Ravensdene Court. J. S. Fletcher
Ravensgate. D. Rowan
Ravensgill. W. Mayne
Ravenshaw of Rietholine. B. Mitford
Ravensley Manor. Cecily Clark
Ravensmount. M. McEvoy
Ravensnest. C. Farr
Ravensridge. Jennifer Hale
Ravenswood. E. W. Gilliam
Ravenswood. J. L. Roberts
Ravenswood Hall. Angela Gray
Ravenswood Mystery. J. S. Fletcher
Raventree. S. Sloan
Ravine. K. Young
Raving Monarchist. J. Rathbone
Ravishing Idiot. C. Exbrayat
Ravishing of Lady Mary Ware. D. Wheatley
Raw Deal for Dames. M. Hampton
Raw Edge. B. Appel
Raw Gold. J. B. Hendryx
Raw Material. G. B. Savi
Raw Summer. J. Blackmore
Rawdon Murder Case. J. H. Acott
Rawhide Vixen. Tod Conrad
Rawson of the Mounted. E. Dorrance
Raxl, Voodoo Priestess. D. Daniels
Ray of Doom. W. S. Sykes
Raya. Frank King
Rayner Case. R. Wray
Rayner-Slade Amalgamation. J. S. Fletcher
Ray's Adventure. Old Sleuth
Rays of Darkness. L. Bamburg
Re-Enter Arnholt. G. Latta
Re-Enter Dr. Fu Manchu. S. Rohmer
Re-Enter Fu Manchu. S. Rohmer
Re-Enter Sir John. C. Dane
Reach for the Shadows. A. Dwyer-Joyce
Reach of Fear. D. L. Mathews
Reaching Hand. A. MacKenzie
Reader Is Warned. Carter Dickson
Ready for Death. H. J. Hultman
Ready for the Tiger. Sam Ross
Ready or Not. I. S. Shriber
Ready Revenge. C. Arley
Ready to Burn. C. J. Daly
Ready to Die. J. Frederics
Real Connection. E. Taillet
Real Cool Cat. J. Weil
Real Cool Killers. C. Himes
Real Detective. G. Dilnot
Real Endings. D. Duris
Real Estate Skeleton Caper. W. J. Jones
Real Gold. G. M. Fenn
Real Gone Goose. G. Bagby
Real Gone Guy. F. Kane
Real Inspector Hound. T. Stoppard
Real Killing. W. Keegan
Real Killing. J. Pattinson
Real Life. A. R. Weekes
Real Mrs. Daybrook. F. Warden
Real Serendipitous Kill. Hampton Stone
Real Thing. A. Philips
Realist. H. Flowerdew
Realization of Justus Moran. F. Carrel
Reap the Whirlwind. M. L. Roby
Reap What You Sow. M. Allwood
Reaper. G. Fairlie
Reaping. Bernard Taylor
Reaping the Whirlwind. Anonymous
Reaping the Whirlwind. Nicholas Carter
Rear Car. E. E. Rose
Rear View Mirror. C. B. Cooney
Reardon. R. L. Pike
Reason for Loving. A. Furness
Reason for Madness. T. S. Drachman
Reason for Murder. A. Hocking
Reason for Murder. J. Usher
Reason for Violence. D. Doubtfire
Reason to Kill. E. Zaremba
Reason Why. M. B. Lowndes

Reasonable Doubt. Edgar Smith
Reasonable Doubt. J. S. Strange
Reasonable Man. R. Busby
Rebecca. D. Du Maurier
Rebecca of the Snatch Racket. B. Sarto
Rebecca, the Mysterious. K. Kimbrough
Rebecca's Pride. D. N. Douglass
Rebel Chief. H. Nisbet
Rebel Heart. A. Maybury
Rebel Lady. K. Lindsay
Rebel Wife. Rona Randall
Rebel Woman. H. Whittington
Rebellion. W. A. Ballinger
Rebellion. N. Harman
Rebellion. S. P. B. Mais
Rebellion of Lee McGuire. C. B. Davis
Reborn. L. Simon
Rebound. J. Mayo
Recall. T. P. Walker
Recalled by the Double-Four. E. P. Oppenheim
Recalled to Life. G. Allen
Receipt for Murder. Gwendoline Butler
Receivers. B. Osborne
Reception at High Tower. D. Ward
Recess. H. Grisewood
Recess. Sophia Lee
Recipe for a Crime. R. Denham
Recipe for Diamonds. C. J. C. Hyne
Recipe for Homicide. L. G. Blochman
Recipe for Murder. J. Ashford
Recipe for Murder. A. Ridley
Recipe for Rubber. R. Stock
Reckless. R. Angel
Reckless Angel. M. B. Lowndes
Reckless Coulson. Jack Mann
Reckless Lady. Vera Brown
Reckless Lady. R. Foley
Reckless Masquerade. Rachelle Edwards
Reckoning. H. Atkinson
Reckoning in Ice. J. R. L. Anderson
Reclining Figure. H. Kurnitz
Reclining Figure. Marco Page
Reclining Nude. Maurice Watson
Recluse of Fifth Avenue. W. Martyn
Recoil. K. C. Groom
Recoil. B. Garfield
Recoil. J. L. Hardy
Recoil. B. How
Recoil. J. Thompson
Recoiling Vengeance. F. Barrett
Recollections of a Country Doctor. J. K. Spender
Recollections of a Detective. Waters
Recollections of a Detective-Police-Officer. Waters
Recollections of a Glasgow Detective Officer. T. P. MacNaught
Recollections of a Physician. W. H. Hillyard
Recollections of a Policeman. Waters
Recollections of a Relieving Officer. E. P. Rowsell
Recollections of a Sheriff's Officer. Waters
Recollections of an Irish Police Magistrate and Other Reminiscences of the South of Ireland. H. R. Addison
Reconnaissance. G. Gardiner
Reconnoitre Krellig II. J. J. Deegan
Record No. 33. I. C. Clarke
Record of Jeffrye Cranfield. G. C. Keech
Record of the Case. W. M. Graydon
Records of Vincent Trill of the Detective Service. D. Donovan
Recover or Kill. L. Butler
Recovery. S. L. Thompson
Rector. V. Gay
Rectory Governess. F. Hume
Recurrent Melody. R. Pinget
Recycled Souls. I. Ross
Red Account. V. Gielgud
Red Aces. E. Wallace
Red Alert. P. Bryant
Red Alert. Harold King
Red Altars. J. G. Brandon
Red Anger. G. Household
Red Bamboo. E. P. Thorne
Red Band. F. Du Boisgobey
Red Beard. P. Costello
Red Bicycle. F. Hume
Red Bishop. Howard Mason
Red Boomerang. J. G. Brandon
Red Boulders Mystery. P. Sebastian
Red Box. R. Stout
Red Box Clue. J. B. Ellis
Red Boxes. P. Northman
Red Bridal. W. Westall
Red Bull. R. Stout
Red Button. Will Irwin
Red Camarilla. E. J. Harrison
Red Camelia. F. Du Boisgobey
Red Canyon Mystery. W. B. Lawson
Red Carnation. Augustus Muir
Red Carnation. B. E. Stevenson
Red Carnation. P. A. Whitney
Red Carpet for the Shah. P. Ritner
Red Castle. H. C. Bailey
Red Castle Mystery. H. C. Bailey
Red Castle Women. M. Widdemer
Red Cavalier. G. E. Locke
Red Cecil, the Detective. Old Sleuth

Red Chancellor. W. Magnay
Red Chindvit Conspiracy. H. W. Holzer
Red Christmas. P. Ruell
Red Claws. M. Richmond
Red Club. H. R. Taunton
Red Coats Galloping. J. Welcome
Red Cobra. H. S. Banner
Red Cobra. F. Grierson
Red Colonel. G. Edgar
Red Colonel. G. Seton
Red Court Farm. H. Wood
Red Crescent. A. Murray
Red Cripple. C. Bradley
Red Dagger. J. Corbett
Red Dancer of Moscow. H. L. Gates
Red Danger. P. Wentworth
Red Darkness. A. B. Sherlock
Red Darkness. G. F. Worts
Red Dawning. M. Richmond
Red Death. G. Collins
Red Derelict. B. Mitford
Red Desert. H. Edmonds
Red Devil of the Air Police. J. Noy
Red Diamonds. J. H. McCarthy
Red Dice. Norman Lucas
Red Dog. J. D. Buchanan
Red Domino. W. W. Sayer
Red Dragon. W. Curtis
Red Dwarf. F. A. Symonds
Red Dwarf. M. Thynne
Red Eagle. Gavin Holt
Red Emerald. J. R. Scott
Red Emeralds. S. Gluck
Red Ending. H. Hervey
Red Escapade. R. Bax
Red Exit. J. Pattinson
Red Eye for the Baron. Anthony Morton
Red Eyes of Kali. T. C. H. Jacobs
Red Farm Mystery. J. Corbett
Red Fate. E. Forbes
Red Fathom. R. E. Alter
Red Falcons. A. Dempsey
Red File for Callan. J. Mitchell
Red Flame of Erinpura. J. Mundy
Red Flower Kill. W. J. Sheldon
Red Flowers of Death. C. Rudd
Red Flows the Barada. D. Weir
Red for Danger! E. Price
Red for Murder. H. Kemp
Red Fox. G. Seymour
Red Gardenias. Jonathan Latimer
Red Gate. R. Burke
Red Geranium. V. Siller
Red Glen. C. Campbell
Red Glove. Douglas Grant
Red God of Tragedy. Nicholas Carter
Red Gold. M. Leighton
Red Greed. Marion Roberts
Red, Green and Amber. P. Traill
Red Guard. Nick Carter
Red Hair. S. Kyle
Red-Haired Alibi. W. Collison
Red-Haired Death. S. Horler
Red-Haired Girl. C. Wells
Red Hand. S. Cobb
Red-Handed. L. Thayer
Red-Handed They Came. A. Wood
Red Harvest. D. Hammett
Red Hat. W. LeQueux
Red Hazard. A. O. Pollard
Red Head Herring. B. Healey
Red Head of the Red Sea. W. J. Makin
Red-Headed Dames and Murder. Roland Daniel
Red-Headed Man. F. Hume
Red-Headed Sinner. Jonathan Craig
Red Heart of the Incas. Jack Lewis
Red Hen Conspiracy. K. Benton
Red Heroin. W. Curtis
Red Herring. E. Acheson
Red Herring. W. Tucker
Red Herring Murder. P. D. Westbrook
Red Herrings. C. J. C. Hyne
Red Herrings Ltd. Laurence Kirk
Red Hill Tragedy. E. Southworth
Red Horse Caper. L. V. Roper
Red Horseman. K. Laing
Red, Hot and Deadly. M. Clinten
Red Hot and Morgue Bound. M. Brody
Red Hot Dollar and other stories from "The Black Cat". H. D. Umbstaetter
Red Hot Ice. F. Kane
Red-Hot Murder. S. Levinson
Red Hotel. H. Hervey
Red House. G. A. Chamberlain
Red House. Mrs. Hungerford
Red House. Derek Lambert
Red House. E. Nesbit
Red House Mystery. Mrs. Hungerford
Red House Mystery. A. A. Milne
Red House Mystery. R. Sergel
Red House on Rowan Street. R. Doubleday
Red Ice. J. Dallas
Red Idol. L. P. Greene
Red in the Morning. D. Yates
Red Invader. H. Edmonds
Red Is for Killing. G. Bagby
Red Is for Murder. Martin Meyers
Red Is for Murder. P. A. Whitney
Red Is for Shrouds. M. A. Taylor
Red Jaguar. N. McFather
Red Jaguar. J. Manor

Title Index

Red January. W. Chamberlain
Red Joker. Michael Nicholson
Red Judas. D. Newton
Red Kite Clue. O. F. Jerome
Red Kill. G. Richards
Red Knight. J. N. Chance
Red Lacquer Case. H. R. Jorgensen
Red Lacquer Case. P. Wentworth
Red Lady. K. N. Burt
Red Lady. A. Wynne
Red Lamp. M. R. Rinehart
Red League. Nicholas Carter
Red Ledger. F. Packard
Red Light. N. MacKenzie
Red Light Red. A. Radnor
Red-Light Will, the River Detective. Anonymous
Red Lights. G. Simenon
Red Lilac. L. Gorell
Red Lion. D. Tower
Red Lodge. V. Bridges
Red Lottery Ticket. F. Du Boisgobey
Red Mammon. D. Learmonth
Red Mark, and other stories. J. Russell
Red Mask. W. J. Makin
Red Masquerade. L. J. Vance
Red Mass. V. Williams
Red Menace. M. Grant
Red Mill Mystery. Detective Dunn
Red Mirage. P. Trent
Red Mirror Mystery. Gret Lane
Red Mist. J. Borgen
Red Money. F. Hume
Red Moon. J. B. Harris-Burland
Red Moon. K. Robeson
Red Morn. M. Pemberton
Red Mountain. W. W. Sayer
Red Mountain, Limited. E. A. Clancy
Red Mouse. W. H. Osborne
Red Murchison. Roland Daniel
Red Murder File. C. Dixon
Red Net. T. C. H. Jacobs
Red Nights of Paris. M. F. Goron
Red on Wight. D. Winsor
Red Owl. W. Gillette
Red Painted Box. M. Leighton
Red Paper. C. C. Hotchkiss
Red Paste Murders. A. Gask
Red Pavilion. M. Summerton
Red Pavilion. R. Van Gulik
Red Pawns. G. Griswold
Red Plague. Nicholas Carter
Red Plague in Bolivia. M. Macao
Red Poppies. E. Morrison
Red Queen Club. A. Broome
Red Radio. R. L. Hadfield
Red Rafferty. H. B. Kaye
Red Rain Mystery. H. Hill
Red Raincoat. H. Bourne
Red Rajah. F. Whittaker
Red Rat's Daughter. G. Boothby
Red Rays. Nick Carter
Red Rebellion. Nick Carter
Red—Red—Red. A. Kent
Red, Red Rose. M. McEvoy
Red Redmaynes. E. Phillpotts
Red Revenge. C. E. Pearce
Red Revenge. G. A. Ralston
Red Rhapsody. C. Fitzsimmons
Red Riding Hood. E. Jordan
Red Right Hand. J. T. Rogers
Red Rivington. W. Westall
Red Road. S. Harvester
Red Rods. Dale Clark
Red Room. W. LeQueux
Red Rope. F. Gerard
Red Rose for Annabel. Agnes Russell
Red Rose for Maria. D. Downes
Red Ruth. L. T. Meade
Red Sap. J. Easton
Red Saunders Bites the Dust. P. Renwick
Red Scar. A. Wynne
Red Scarf. G. Brewer
Red Scorpion. C. Buchanan
Red Sea Spy. W. J. Makin
Red Seal. M. Gerard
Red Seal. N. S. Lincoln
Red Shadow. P. Wentworth
Red Signal. Nicholas Carter
Red Skull. F. Hume
Red Skull. K. Robeson
Red Sky. V. James
Red Sky at Night. H. McCutcheon
Red Sky in the Morning. R. Johnston
Red Slayer. E. Leslie
Red Snow. O. Lange
Red Snow. K. Robeson
Red Snow at Darjeeling. L. G. Blochman
Red Spider. E. S. Brooks
Red Spider. K. Robeson
Red Spider Web. B. Newman
Red Spinner. E. Snell
Red Square. A. Wood
Red Stain. A. Abdullah
Red Stain. S. Campbell
Red Stain. V. Loder
Red Stain. W. Magnay
Red Staircase. Gwendoline Butler
Red Stands for Danger. R. Trevor
Red Star Mystery. C. Barry
Red Star of Night. W. A. MacKenzie

Red Stefan. P. Wentworth
Red Stilleto. A. Skene
Red Stockings. P. Fry
Red Stranger. Netley Lucas
Red Streak. P. Trent
Red Sun of Nippon. H. O. Yardley
Red Symbol. J. Ironside
Red Tape Murders. G. Verner
Red Tassel. D. Dodge
Red Terrors. K. Robeson
Red Threads. R. Stout
Red Thumb Mark. R. A. Freeman
Red Tiger. J. Carr
Red Token. O. Binns
Red Tower. L. V. Stevens
Red Triangle. Nicholas Carter
Red Triangle. Arthur Morrison
Red Turrets of Orne. C. Connell
Red Van. A. St. Aubyn
Red Van Mystery. G. Chester
Red Vulture. F. Sleath
Red War. J. Philips
Red Warning. V. Markham
Red Widow. W. LeQueux
Red Widow Murders. Carter Dickson
Red Wind. R. Chandler
Red Window. F. Hume
Red Wine of Rapture. Margaret Worth
Red-Winged Angel. A. MacKinnon
Redbeard. L. A. Knight
Redbird Affair. L. V. Stevens
Redcap. P. McCutchan
Redding Straik. R. Aitken
Reddy Brant, His Adventures. W. C. Tuttle
Redeemed. C. R. B.
Redeemer. H. Fleetwood
Redemption Factor. W. E. Chambers
Redemption of Grace Milroy. C. Dawe
Redemption of Richard. Marguerite Bryant
Redemption Range. Gavin Holt
Redfern's Miracle. E. Trevor
Redfingers. W. M. Duncan
Redhead. W. L. Andersch
Redhead. J. Creasey
Redhead for Danger. Arthur MacLean
Redhead for Free. K. T. McCall
Redhead for Mike Shayne. B. Halliday
Redhead from Chicago. L. Royer
Redhead from Sun Dog. W. C. Tuttle
Redheads Are Poison. B. Winter
Redheads Cool Fast. B. Winter
Redheads Die Young. B. Diamond
Redman Cave Murder. E. Barker
Redmaynes. G. E. Locke
Redolmo Affair. Nick Carter
Redoubtable Dexter. G. Hackforth-Jones
Reduction of Staff. F. J. Whaley
Redundancy Pay. J. R. L. Anderson
Reeds in the Wind. C. Gleig
Reef of Gold. M. H. Hervey
Reef Pearlers. S. M. Parkman
Reefer Boy. H. Ellson
Reel of Death. R. Simons
Reference to Death. L. R. Davis
Reflection of Evil. J. Roffman
Reflex. D. Francis
Reflex Action. C. Fitzsimmons
Reformation of Royce Remington. W. M. Graydon
Reformatory Girls. N. Tyre
Regan. I. K. Martin
Regan and the Bent Stripper. J. Balham
Regan and the Deal of a Century. I. K. Martin
Regan and the High Rollers. J. Balham
Regan and the Human Pipeline. J. Balham
Regan and the Lebanese Shipment. J. Balham
Regan and the Manhattan File. I. K. Martin
Regan and the Snout Who Cried Wolf. J. Balham
Regan and the Venetian Virgin. J. Balham
Regarding Sherlock Holmes. A. Derleth
Regatta Mystery. A. Christie
Regency Rake. Michael Hardwick
Regency Revenge. Michael Hardwick
Regency Royal. Michael Hardwick
Regensburg Legacy. J. Bickham
Regent Street Raid. J. G. Brandon
Regent's Candlesticks. J. Kyle
Reginald Vernon. W. H. Hillyard
Regis Arms Caper. R. H. Spencer
Regular Fraud. R. Jocelyn
Rehabilitated Man. Eric Lambert
Rehearsal for Death. G. Batson
Rehearsal for Death. Theodora Benson
Rehearsal for Murder. F. Bunce
Rehearsal for the Funeral. E. Colter
Reich Four. Nick Carter
Reign of Terror. H. Desmond
Reimann Curse. J. Deweese
Reincarnation in Venice. M. Ehrlich
Reincarnation of Peter Proud. M. Ehrlich
Reinhard Action. H. Eisenberg
Reins of Chance. C. R. Gull
Reivaulx Abbey. N. Davison
Rejected Bride. E. Southworth
Rejuvenation of Mrs. Semaphore. H. Godfrey
Rejuvenators. H. Miller

Rekill. I. K. Martin
Relative Murder. A. Hocking
Relative Stranger. A. Stevenson
Relative to Death. S. Forbes
Relative to Murder. E. Warman
Relative to Poison. E. C. R. Lorac
Relative Values. H. C. McNeile
Release the Lions. R. Croft-Cooke
Release the Prisoner. A. Wood
Released for Death. Henry Wade
Relentless. B. Garfield
Relentless Current. M. E. Charlesworth
Relentless Storm. C. Lorrimer
Religious Body. C. Aird
Reluctant Assassin. J. Dark
Reluctant Assassin. J. Godey
Reluctant Assassin. A. Reynaud-Fourton
Reluctant Bride. C. Laffeaty
Reluctant Cloak and Dagger Man. Ernest Paul
Reluctant Duchess. M. Richmond
Reluctant Executioner. John Marsh
Reluctant Gunman. W. H. Baker
Reluctant Hangman and other stories of crime. G. Allen
Reluctant Heiress. G. H. Coxe
Reluctant Heiress. A. Laine
Reluctant Hostess. H. Janson
Reluctant Hussy. R. Burke
Reluctant Lover. G. Ferrand
Reluctant Medium. L. Vardre
Reluctant Murderer. Bernice Carey
Reluctant Paragon. S. Farrant
Reluctant Prodigal. H. L. V. Fletcher
Reluctant Puritan. K. A. Shoesmith
Reluctant Rebel. M. Richmond
Reluctant Sleeper. J. Wainwright
Reluctant Sleuth. F. Crane
Reluctant Spy. J. Blackburn
Reluctant Spy. T. D. Calnan
Reluctant Spy. J. Laflin
Reluctant Spy. H. Wood-Hill
Reluctant Transgressor. M. Kane
Remains to Be Seen. M. Butterworth
Remains to Be Seen. M. Cumberland
Remains to Be Seen. H. Lindsay
Remarkable Adventures of Christopher Poe. R. C. Brown
Remarkable Case of Burglary. H. R. F. Keating
Remarkable Feat. Old Sleuth
Remarkable "Shadow". Old Sleuth
Rembrandt Decisions. A. V. Badgley
Rembrandt Murder. H. J. Forman
Rembrandt Panel. O. Banks
Remember! J. G. Sarasin
Remember Maybelle? Carter Brown
Remember That Face. F. Findley
Remember the Shadows. D. Duncan
Remember the Summer We Lived at the Pad. A. Lamb
Remember with Tears. H. Arvonen
Remembered Anger. M. Albrand
Remembered Death. A. Christie
Remembering Louise. Anna Gilbert
Remembrance of Miranda. M. Ingate
Remind Me to Forget. C. B. Dawson
Remington Set. J. Charlton
Reminiscences of a Great French Detective. Anonymous
Reminiscences of a Rogue. F. Martyn
Reminiscences of Chief-Inspector Littlechild. J. G. Littlechild
Reminiscences of Solar Pons. A. Derleth
Remittance-Woman. A. Abdullah
Remote Control. H. Carmichael
Remote Control. Clyde North
Remote Journey. L. Handley
Removals Ltd. Trill
Remove the Bodies. E. Ferrars
Remover. Roland Daniel
Remover Returns. Roland Daniel
Removers. D. Hamilton
Remus Code. S. Englander
Rena. B. Gayle
Render unto Caesar. K. Lindsay
Rendezvous. Evelyn Anthony
Rendezvous at Live Oaks. E. W. Strother
Rendezvous in Amsterdam. E. Randolph
Rendezvous in Austria. W. E. D. Ross
Rendezvous in Black. C. Woolrich
Rendezvous in Peking. Anne-Mariel
Rendezvous in Rio. G. Fallon
Rendezvous in Rio. Vince Howard
Rendezvous in Tripoli. C. Gayet
Rendezvous in Vienna. J. Ellis
Rendezvous of Mysteries. K. S. Nakagawa
Rendezvous on an Island. T. Claymore
Rendezvous with a Dead Man. Nicholas Carter
Rendezvous with Danger. J. Corbett
Rendezvous with Danger. M. Pemberton
Rendezvous with Danger. Lynn Williams
Rendezvous with Death. John Bentley
Rendezvous with Death. J. Corbett
Rendezvous with Death. J. Paull
Rendezvous with Fear. N. Davis
Rendezvous with Fear. A. Worboys
Rendezvous with the Past. K. M. Knight
Renegade Cop. Jonathan Craig
Renegade from Russia. H. C. Davis
Renegade Sheriff. W. C. Tuttle

Reno Rendezvous. L. Ford
Renshaw Fanning's Quest. B. Mitford
Renshaw Strike. Ian Stuart
Repaid in Like Coin. Nicholas Carter
Reparation. O. Williams
Repeat Performance. W. O'Farrell
Repeat the Instructions. R. V. Beste
Repent at Leisure. P. Conway
Repent at Leisure. R. Foley
Reply Paid. H. F. Heard
Report for a Corpse. H. Kane
Report from Argyll. A. MacKinnon
Report from Group 17. R. C. O'Brien
Report to the Commissioner. James Mills
Reporter. J. Stearn
Reporter. E. Wallace
Reporter Detective. D. J. MacKenzie
Reporter's Triumph. S. Campbell
Reporting Murder. D. Maggs
Reprieve of Roger Maine. G. McDonell
Reprisal. Arthur Gordon
Reprisal. W. P. McGivern
Reprisal. E. Vance
Reprise. C. Rayner
Reputation for a Song. E. Grierson
Requiem at Rogano. S. Knight
Requiem for a Blonde. K. Roos
Requiem for a Chaser. J. Conway
Requiem for a Cop. V. B. Miller
Requiem for a Crown. R. Vacha
Requiem for a Dream. H. Selby
Requiem for a Loser. J. Wainwright
Requiem for a Murder. S. Clausse
Requiem for a Rat. J. Godwin
Requiem for a Redhead. A. Bocca
Requiem for a Redhead. L. Hardy
Requiem for a Redhead. L. Kent
Requiem for a Schoolgirl. I. T. Ross
Requiem for Charles. H. Carmichael
Requiem for Redheads. W. H. Baker
Requiem for Robert. M. Fitt
Requiem for Rogues. David Hume
Requiem for Two Sisters. J. Turner
Requiem in Utopia. R. Starnes
Requiem of Sharks. P. Buchanan
Rescue from the Rose. J. B. Hilton
Rescuing Rupert. G. Thorne
Reservation for Murder. J. Wright
Reservations for Death. B. Kendrick
Reserve Two for Murder. J. Randall
Resident. W. Tute
Resident Magistrate. B. Marnan
Resisting Arrest. Steven Phillips
Resolute Jack. Old Sleuth
Resolved to Be Rich. E. H. Cooper
Resort. S. Stein
Resort to War. G. Revelli
Resources of Mycroft Holmes. C. Andrews
Respectable Miss Parkington-Smith. P. Allardyce
Respectable Woman. David Fletcher
Rest Hollow Mystery. R. N. Porter
Rest in Agony. I. Jorgensen
Rest Is Silence. P. Barrington
Rest Is Silence. V. Coffman
Rest Must Die. R. Foster
Rest You Merry. C. MacLeod
Restless Corpse. A. Pruitt
Restless Hands. B. Fischer
Restless Quiet. D. O'Connor
Results of a Duel. F. Du Boisgobey
Results of an Accident. T. C. H. Jacobs
Resurrection Day. K. Robeson
Resurrection Game. J. Midgley
Resurrection Man. T. Walsh
Resurrection Murder Case. S. H. Page
Resurrection of His Grace. C. Rae-Brown
Retake. Richard Hubbard
Retaliation. H. Flowerdew
Retaliators. D. Hamilton
Retired from the Yard. A. Parsons
Retreat from Oblivion. D. Goodis
Retreat into Night. R. Glendinning
Retribution. D. Essex
Retribution. C. R. Gull
Retribution. T. P. Prest
Retribution. E. Southworth
Return. Evelyn Anthony
Return. D. Winston
Return a Gain for Murder. R. Verron
Return from the Ashes. H. Monteilhet
Return from the Dead. M. Burton
Return from Vorkuta. David St. John
Return Load. D. Rutherford
Return Match. E. Cadell
Return of A. J. Raffles. G. Greene
Return of a Traitor. T. B. Morris
Return of Anthony Trent. W. Martyn
Return of Arsene Lupin. M. Leblanc
Return of Blackshirt. B. Graeme
Return of Blue Mask. Anthony Morton
Return of Blue Pete. L. Allan
Return of Bulldog Drummond. H. C. McNeile
Return of Cardannesley. G. Ellinger
Return of Clubfoot. V. Williams
Return of Colonel Pho. Ronald Simpson
Return of Dick Barton. Anonymous
Return of Dr. Fu-Manchu. S. Rohmer
Return of Frank Clamart. H. C. Rowland
Return of Frass. J. Chancellor
Return of George Washington. L. Brent

Return of Grey Shadow. G. E. Rochester
Return of Henry Prince. C. F. Gregg
Return of Hercules, Esq. Gwyn Evans
Return of Jack the Ripper. Mark Andrews
Return of Jennifer. H. Upshaw
Return of Jenny Weaver. M. Turnbull
Return of Mick Cardby. David Hume
Return of Mr. Benjamin. M. Short
Return of Mr. Budd. G. Verner
Return of Moriarty. J. Gardner
Return of Nighthawk. S. Horler
Return of Picklock Holes. R. C. Lehman
Return of Raffles. B. Perowne
Return of Sanders of the River. F. Gerard
Return of Sherlock Holmes. A. C. Doyle
Return of Solar Pons. A. Derleth
Return of Sumuru. S. Rohmer
Return of the Assassin. A. Tack
Return of the Black Gang. G. Fairlie
Return of the Ceteosaurus, and other tales. P. Radcliffe
Return of the Continental Op. D. Hammett
Return of the Cornish Soldier. Michael Barrett
Return of the Hood. M. Spillane
Return of the Howling. G. Brandner
Return of the Living Dead. J. Russo
Return of the Night Wind. V. Vanardy
Return of the Opium Wars. M. Macao
Return of the Pink Panther. F. Waldman
Return of the Royalist. K. A. Shoesmith
Return of the Shadow. W. B. Gibson
Return of the Shadow. M. Grant
Return of the Vagabond. G. M. Cohan
Return of Van Weik. C. Evelyn
Return of Wu Fang. Roland Daniel
Return of Yesterday. K. Ingram
Return They Must. John Marsh
Return to Adventure. N. Deane
Return to Aylforth. A. Eliot
Return to Ballyrock. A. Furness
Return to Clerycastle. M. Heath
Return to Cottington. F. Bamford
Return to Darkness. W. D. Roberts
Return to Death Valley. J. N. Chance
Return to Foxdale. L. Dartey
Return to Glenshael. M. Elgin
Return to Gravesend. M. Eyre
Return to Hawkeston Hall. L. Whitaker
Return to Love. J. Blackmore
Return to Murder. M. A. Taylor
Return to Octavia. D. Macomber
Return to Terror. M. Albrand
Return to Terror. T. Charles
Return to Terror. F. Hurt
Return to the Alcazar. E. Kyle
Return to the River. K. Hewitt
Return to the Scene. Q. Patrick
Return to Tiger Bay. J. M. Walsh
Return to Vienna. N. Buckingham
Return to Vikki. J. Tomerlin
Return to Violence. W. Spann
Reuben Foreman, the Village Blacksmith. D. Dale
Reunion. W. Kuhns
Reunion. Richard Russell
Reunion for Death. Martin Meyers
Reunion in Florida. T. Claymore
Reunion in Renfrew. W. E. D. Ross
Reunion with Murder. T. Fuller
Revealed by Lightning. I. Stark
Revelations of a Detective. A. Forrester
Revelations of a Lady Detective. Anonymous
Revelations of a Police Court Interpreter. J. Jacobsen
Revelations of a Private Detective. A. Forrester
Revelations of a Sly Parrot. John Bennett
Revelations of Inspector Morgan. O. Crawfurd
Revelations of the Secret Service. W. LeQueux
Revellers. L. Tracy
Revenge! R. Barr
Revenge. H. Brenton
Revenge. J. Cartwright
Revenge. J. Ehrlich
Revenge. N. Hynd
Revenge. Joseph Warren
Revenge at Indy. L. Kenyon
Revenge at Nightfall. Elliot Bailey
Revenge Can Wait. Irene Alexander
Revenge in "The Convent". C. B. Boyd
Revenge Incorporated. Dennis Phillips
Revenge of Annie Charlie. A. Fry
Revenge of Fantomas. M. Allain
Revenge of Gilbert Strange. W. Wood
Revenge of Moriarty. J. Gardner
Revenge of Taurus. R. Lory
Revenge of the Generals. Nick Carter
Revenge of Valerie. H. Nisbet
Revenge with a Vengeance. C. L. Reid
Revengeful Turk. I. Crookenden
Revenger. J. Messmann
Revenue Detective. Anonymous
Revenue Detective. Police Captain James
Rev. Captain Kettle. C. J. C. Hyne
Reverend Gentleman. J. M. Cobban

Rev. Miles Latimer. L. Gardiner
Reverend Randolph and the Avenging Angel. C. M. Smith
Reverend Randolph and the Fall from Grace, Inc. C. M. Smith
Reverend Randolph and the Holy Terror. C. M. Smith
Reverend Randolph and the Wages of Sin. C. M. Smith
Reverse Negative. A. Jute
Reverse the Charges. B. Flynn
Revised Proof. P. Conway
Revolt. G. B. Lissenden
Revolt in the Desert. J. Robb
Revolt from Bondage. H. D. Dearden
Revolt of Abbe Lee. J. McBrien
Revolt of Beatrix. F. Whishaw
Revolution Island. J. Fane
Revolution Script. B. Moore
Revolutionist. E. Garth
Revue Girl. A. Applin
Reward. Michael Barrett
Reward for a Defector. M. Underwood
Reward for the Baron. Anthony Morton
Reward for Treason. T. C. H. Jacobs
Reward Game. G. Hammond
Rex Mundi. G. Sims
Rexworth Mystery. S. Cummings
Rhapsody in Fear. J. N. Chance
Rhea. R. De Pont-Jest
Rheingold Route. A. Maling
Rhine Replica. M. Albrand
Rhinemann Exchange. R. Ludlum
Rhino for Rosamund. D. Fearon
Rhino in the Kitchen. D. W. MacArthur
Rhino Ritz. K. Abbott
Rhodesia. Nick Carter
Rhododendron Man. J. A. Tyson
Ribbon for My Repute. A. Sewart
Ribs of Death. Joan Aiken
Rich and Dangerous Game. L. White
Rich and the Damned. R. Himmel
Rich Die Hard. B. Nichols
Rich Get It All. F. Huston
Rich, Hip and Deadly. H. Paul
Rich Is the Treasure. M. Procter
Rich Man. G. Simenon
Rich Man, Dead Man. H. Waugh
Rich Man, Murder. H. Waugh
Rich Man, Poor Man. M. Foster
Rich Man's Wife. D. Donovan
Rich People. Morton Cooper
Rich to Die. B. Tutton
Rich Uncle. C. Keith
Rich Way to Die. K. Evans
Richard. Marguerite Bryant
Richard Arbour. J. Payn
Richard Parker. T. P. Prest
Richardson Goes Abroad. B. Thomson
Richardson Scores Again. B. Thomson
Richardson Solves a Dartmoor Mystery. B. Thomson
Richardson's Second Case. B. Thomson
Richest Corpse in Show Business. Dan Morgan
Richest Girl in the World. V. Coffman
Richest Man. E. Shanks
Richlands. A. S. Turnbull
Richmond. Anonymous
Rick. D. G. Falk
Rickerby's Folly. T. Gallon
Ricksha Clue. G. Ellinger
Rickshaw Bend. H. Arvonen
Ricochet. B. Copper
Ricochet. J. F. Straker
Riddle. D. Sherman
Riddle, and other stories. W. De La Mare
Riddle Me This. M. Roscoe
Riddle Me This! D. N. Rubin
Riddle of a Lady. Anthony Gilbert
Riddle of Big Ben. A. Parsons
Riddle of Crocodile Creek. W. M. Graydon
Riddle of Crooked Creek. J. W. Booth
Riddle of Cubicle 7. A. Parsons
Riddle of Dead Man's Mine. M. Frazer
Riddle of Dead Man's Pit. R. C. Armour
Riddle of Double Island. M. Corrigan
Riddle of Five Needle Creek. A. Blair
Riddle of Garth. Augustus Muir
Riddle of Helena. C. Houghton
Riddle of Identities. Nicholas Carter
Riddle of John Rowe. Winston Graham
Riddle of Loch Lemman. A. O. Pollard
Riddle of Nap's Hollow. L. A. Knight
Riddle of Rainbow Mountain. J. A. Rennie
Riddle of Riverdale. J. W. Bobin
Riddle of Samson. A. Garve
Riddle of the Amber Room. H. E. Hill
Riddle of the Amber Ship. M. E. Hanshew
Riddle of the Black Racketeers. J. Hunter
Riddle of the Blazing Bungalow. S. Blakesley
Riddle of the Body on the Road. E. S. Brooks
Riddle of the Book-Mark. W. J. Lomax
Riddle of the Burmese Curse. A. Parsons
Riddle of the Cambrian Venus. D. W. F. Hardie
Riddle of the Captured Quisling. A. Parsons
Riddle of the Cloisters. E. Burton

Title Index

Riddle of the Crooked Gambler. R. Hardinge
Riddle of the Dead. L. Bamburg
Riddle of the Dead Cats. A. Blackmon
Riddle of the Dead Man's Bay. J. G. Brandon
Riddle of the Disguised Greek. A. Parsons
Riddle of the Eighth Guest. B. Wheeler
Riddle of the Emeralds. P. C. De Crespigny
Riddle of the Escaped P.O.W. A. Parsons
Riddle of the Evil Eye. P. Quiroule
Riddle of the Film Star's Jewels. L. Jackson
Riddle of the Florentine Folio. E. S. Liddon
Riddle of the Forest. B. Tozer
Riddle of the French Alibi. W. Tyrer
Riddle of the Frozen Flame. M. E. Hanshew
Riddle of the Gambling Den. A. Parsons
Riddle of the Garage. H. H. C. Gibbons
Riddle of the Gas Meter. G. Chester
Riddle of the Golden Fingers. E. J. Murray
Riddle of the Great Art Exhibition. R. C. Armour
Riddle of the Greek Financier. J. G. Brandon
Riddle of the Green Cylinder. W. Jardine
Riddle of the Highwayman's Stone. R. Hardinge
Riddle of the Indian Alibi. A. Parsons
Riddle of the Invisible Menace. R. Hardinge
Riddle of the Italian Prisoner. J. Hunter
Riddle of the Keys. J. A. Kolbe
Riddle of the Kidnapped Pensioner. G. Chester
Riddle of the Lascar's Head. L. H. Brooks
Riddle of the Leather Bottle. J. Drummond
Riddle of the Lost Emigrant. R. C. Armour
Riddle of the Lost Ship. J. Hunter
Riddle of the Marsh. J. Blyth
Riddle of the Million Pound Bet. W. J. Bayfield
Riddle of the Missing Fire Watcher. G. Chester
Riddle of the Mummy Case. J. Drummond
Riddle of the Murdered Fisherman. G. Chester
Riddle of the Mysterious Light. M. E. Hanshew
Riddle of the Night. T. W. Hanshew
Riddle of the Night Garage. G. Chester
Riddle of the Phantom Plague. G. Verner
Riddle of the Prince's Stooge. A. Parsons
Riddle of the Purple Emperor. T. W. Hanshew
Riddle of the Rail. F. M. White
Riddle of the Rajah's Curios. A. Parsons
Riddle of the Ranch. W. Jardine
Riddle of the Ravens. L. Gribble
Riddle of the Receiver's Hoard. J. Drummond
Riddle of the Red Devil Costume. T. J. Saunders
Riddle of the Red Dragon. Gwyn Evans
Riddle of the Registry Office. H. H. C. Gibbons
Riddle of the Ring. W. LeQueux
Riddle of the River. J. Wear-Gifford
Riddle of the Roost. L. Brock
Riddle of the Rose. W. B. M. Ferguson
Riddle of the Rovers. A. B. Maurice
Riddle of the Ruins. L. Jackson
Riddle of the Runaway Cat. H. H. C. Gibbons
Riddle of the Russian Bride. A. Parsons
Riddle of the Russian Gold. G. H. Teed
Riddle of the Russian Princess. E. S. Liddon
Riddle of the Sands. E. Childers
Riddle of the Sealed Room. R. Hardinge
Riddle of the Smiling Man. J. Hunter
Riddle of the Spanish Circus. M. Corrigan
Riddle of the Spinning Wheel. M. E. Hanshew
Riddle of the Straits. H. Edmonds
Riddle of the Sunken Garden. Donald Stuart
Riddle of the Three Marked Men. G. N. Philips
Riddle of the Traveling Skull. H. S. Keeler
Riddle of the Turkish Baths. Gwyn Evans
Riddle of the Ugly Face. P. Quiroule
Riddle of the Uncensored Letter. J. Hunter
Riddle of the West End Hairdresser. H. H. C. Gibbons
Riddle of the Winged Death. H. P. Hanshew
Riddle of the Workman Squire. L. Jackson
Riddle of the Yellow Zuri. H. S. Keeler
Riddle of the Yukon. L. C. Douthwaite
Riddle of the Three-Way Creek. R. Cullum
Riddle of Wraye. J. Laurence
Riddle Ring. Justin McCarthy
Riddles of Hildegarde Withers. S. Palmer
Riddles Read. D. Donovan
Ride a Dead Horse. B. Edmunds
Ride a High Horse. R. S. Prather
Ride a Paper Tiger. W. Ash
Ride a Tiger. A. Booth
Ride a Tiger. D. Orgill
Ride a Tiger. A. A. Randall
Ride a White Dolphin. A. Maybury
Ride for a Fall. V. Gielgud
Ride on a Tiger. Dulcie Gray
Ride out the Storm. John Harris
Ride the Dark Moors. H. Stephenson
Ride the Dark Storm. N. Jones
Ride the Gold Mare. O. Demaris
Ride the Golden Tiger. Jonathan Black
Ride the Man Down. R. Dolphin
Ride the Nightmare. F. Dudley
Ride the Nightmare. R. Matheson
Ride the Pink Horse. D. B. Hughes
Ride the Roller Coaster. Carter Brown
Ride West of the Law. R. Wilkes-Hunter
Ride with Terror. Charles Henry
Rider in the Sky. L. A. Knight
Rider of Waroona. G. Firth Scott
Riders of the Sands. W. W. Sayer
Ridgway Woman. R. Neely
Rififi in New York. A. Le Breton
Rifled Gold. W. C. Tuttle
Rig. R. Wilcox
Rigdale Puzzle. C. Kingston
Rigging the Evidence. C. Carnac
Right and Wrong. B. Z. Spencer
Right for Murder. L. White
Right for Trouble. N. Easton
Right Hand Opposite. R. M. Stern
Right Honourable Corpse. Max Murray
Right Kind of House. A. C. Martens
Right Murder. C. Rice
Right of Reply. J. Harris
Right to Die. J. R. Davis
Right to Die. R. Stout
Right to Kill. R. R. Ryan
Right Turn for Murder. R. Verron
Right You Are, Mr. Moto. J. P. Marquand
Righted Wrong. E. Yates
Righteous Abel. J. Remenham
Rights of Mallaroche. C. N. Boyle
Rigoletto Murder. Angus Hall
Rigoville Match. D. Walker
Riley of the Special Branch. L. Gribble
Rim-Fire, Detective. C. Ballew
Rim of Terror. H. T. Teilhet
Rim of the Pit. Hake Talbot
Rim Rider. W. C. Tuttle
Rim-World Legacy. F. A. Javor
Rimers of Eldritch. L. Wilson
Rimfire Murders. Frank O'Brian
Rimualdo. W. H. Ireland
Rinaldi Rinaldini, Captain of Banditti. C. A. Vulpius
Ring-a-Ding-Ding. F. Kane
Ring-a-Ding Girl. D. Rico
Ring-a-Ding UFO's. R. Tralins
Ring and the Lamp. W. Rollins
Ring and Walk In. M. Borgenicht
Ring Around a Rogue. J. M. Flynn
Ring Around a Murder. G. Bagby
Ring Around Rosa. W. C. Gault
Ring Around Rosa. J. C. McMullen
Ring Around Rosy. Gordon Davis
Ring for a Noose. Anthony Gilbert
Ring for Luck. J. Pudney
Ring in Meiji. W. Butler
Ring o' Bells. G. R. Sims
Ring of Darkness. K. Ostrander
Ring of Dust. Nicholas Carter
Ring of Eyes. H. Footner
Ring of Fear. A. McCaffrey
Ring of Fire. B. Gavin
Ring of Innocent. B. Flynn
Ring of Iron. T. Stark
Ring of Kerry. J. Griffin
Ring of Liars. J. N. Chance
Ring of Mischief. M. Summerton
Ring of Rascals. Nicholas Carter
Ring of Roses. J. Blackburn
Ring of Roses. C. Brand
Ring of Rubies. L. T. Meade
Ring of Truth. G. H. Coxe
Ring the Bell at Zero. H. L. Nelson
Ring the Bell, Sister! L. Bell
Ring the Bell Softly. P. Bennetts
Ring Twice for Murder. A. Spiller
Ring Up Nighthawk. S. Horler
Ringed with Fire. Alice Campbell
Ringer. Dell Shannon
Ringer. E. Wallace
Ringer Returns. E. Wallace
Ringing Sands. O. Binns
Ringleader. L. Dunne
Ringnecker. S. H. Courtier
Rings on Her Finger. Laurence Kirk
Rio Casino Intrigue. V. W. Mason
Rio d'Oro. N. Tranter
Rio Rustlers. J. Dorrance
Riot Act. Will Greene
Riot Act. R. Philmore
Riot '71. L. Peters
Rip-Off. Carter Brown
Rip-Off! B. J. Hurwood
Rip-Off. W. C. Ulsh
Ripe for Development. John Gloag
Ripe for Rapture. H. Janson
Ripe Fruit. J. McPartland
Ripley Under Ground. P. Highsmith
Ripley's Game. P. Highsmith
Ripoff. A. Maling
Ripper. Mike Newton
Ripper. M. Procter
Ripper File. Elwyn Jones
Ripper Murders. M. Procter
Ripper Returns. A. Skene
Ripping Yarns. M. Palin
Ripple of Murders. J. Wainwright
Ripple on the Water. D. M. Low
Rippling Ruby. J. S. Fletcher
Rise and Fall of Legs Diamond. O. H. Gaylord
Rise at Dawn. N. Fisher
Rise of Ruderick Clowd. J. Flynt
Rise with the Wind. A. C. Marin
Risifi's Daughter. A. K. Green
Rising of the Lark. S. Styles
Rising of the Moon. G. Mitchell
Rising Sea. M. Hastings
Rising Star. D. C. Murray
Rising Storm. D. Wheatley
Rising Sun. H. L. V. Fletcher
Rising Suns. John Gloag
Risk. L. Earl
Risk. D. Francis
Risk All for Love. M. Richmond
Risky! L. Della
Risky Game. H. Bindloss
Risky Way to Kill. R. Lockridge
Rissole Mystery. S. Fowler
Rita Makes a Killing. E. Ellison
Rita Takes a Ride. N. Perrelli
Rite of Expiation. D. Riley
Rite of Passage. G. Landers
Rite of the Damned. L. Osborne
Rites for a Killer. J. M. Fox
Ritherton's Grange. S. De Havilland
Ritter Double-Cross. F. Nolan
Ritter's Gold. F. N. Hawkins
Ritual in the Dark. Colin Wilson
Ritz. T. McNally
Rival Claimants. E. P. Palmer
Rival Detectives. L. L. Lynch
Rival Detectives. H. Rockwood
Rival Lovers. Anonymous
Rival Lovers. O. Bradbury
Rival Millionaires. L. Fitzhamon
Rival Stables. M. K. Douglas
Rivals. T. P. Prest
Rivard House. F. E. Lambirth
River and the Rose. S. Abbott
River Detective and the Wharf Rat's Game. Old Sleuth
River Gang. Roland Daniel
River Gets Wider. R. L. Gordon
River Girl. C. Williams
River Grown Deep. M. Pereira
River House. Mrs. Mary Armat
River House Mystery. G. Verner
River House Mystery. S. Warwick
River in the Dark. M. Latham
River Is Cold. D. Rimel
River Men. G. Verner
River Mystery. A. J. Rees
River of Diamonds. T. Craig
River of Diamonds. G. Jenkins
River of Fate. Michael Hastings
River of Fear. Leslie T. White
River of Ice. K. Robeson
River of Life. J. Latey
River of Marriage. A. Furness
River of No Return. L. T. White
River of Pearls. R. De Pont-Jest
River of Stars. E. Wallace
River of Unrest. B. Mitford
River Passage. E. L. Long
River Pirate. C. F. Coe
River Rising. J. North
River Secrets. B. Hemyng
River Syndicate. C. E. Carryl
River Tragedy. Old Sleuth
River Will Hide Me. A. Wood
Rivera Collection. B. Adkins
Rivergate House. E. Grandower
Riverport Mail. O. Wright
Rivers to Cross. G. Goodchild
Rivers to Cross. R. Pertwee
Riverside Club Murder. A. Skene
Riverside Mystery. J. G. Brandon
Riverside 90. D. Enefer
Riverside Villas Murder. K. Amis
Riverslea. G. Norway
Riverton Wagers. H. Collinson Owen
Rivertown. J. L. Roberts
Rivertown Risk. J. L. Hensley
Riverwood. J. Corby
Riverwood. M. Lynch
Riviera Love Story. S. Jepson
Riviera Nights. B. Sarto
Riviera Showdown. H. Janson
Roach & Co., Pirates, and other stories. H. Fuller

Road. V. Siller
Road and the Star. B. Mather
Road Back. B. M. Scott
Road Back. S. Warwick
Road Block. H. Waugh
Road End. W. Morrison
Road Floozie. D. Glinto
Road from Chilanga. D. W. MacArthur
Road Home. G. Vaizey
Road House. W. Hackett
Road House Murder. A. Skene
Road House Murders. R. P. Koehler
Road Through the Wall. S. Jackson
Road to Bagdad. G. F. Gibbs
Road to Ballarat. K. Lindsay
Road to Canossa. J. Wood
Road to Desperation. M. H. Bradley
Road to El Saida. Paul Townend
Road to Folly. L. Ford
Road to Fortune. F. A. Kummer
Road to Gandolfo. M. Shepherd
Road to Glenfairlie. D. Garth
Road to Hell. Everatt Jackson
Road to Hell. H. Monteilhet
Road to London. D. S. Foster
Road to Marrakesh. G. Goodchild
Road to Midnight. M. Lynch
Road to Murder. V. Gunn
Road to Rhuine. S. Troy
Road to Romance. A. Soutar
Road to Ruin. Anonymous
Road to the Coast. J. Harris
Road to the Moon. W. C. Tuttle
Road to the Snail. W. P. McGivern
Road Winds Back. P. Conway
Roadblock. M. Borgenicht
Roadhouse Girl. D. Reid
Roadhouse Mystery. J. G. Brandon
Roadknight. R. M. Gilchrist
Road's End. Albert Conroy
Roads of Destiny. O. Henry
Roadside Night. E. N. Nistler
Roag's Syndicate. George Davis
Roanleigh. G. Mockler
Roar Devil. K. Robeson
Rob the Lady. Jonathan Burke
Robber Countess. S. Cobb
Robber King. P. Tyrell
Robberies Co., Ltd. N. Lloyd
Robbery at Portage Bend. T. Lund
Robbery at Rudwick House. V. L. Whitechurch
Robbery Blue. R. Busby
Robbery of the Orphans. F. Du Boisgobey
Robbery Under Arms. R. Boldrewood
Robbery with Violence. J. Rhode
Robe of Lucifer. F. M. White
Robert Ainsleigh. M. E. Braddon
Robert Ashton's Wedding Day, and other stories. H. Wood
Robert Macaire. Anonymous
Robert the Devil. G. Warden
Roberta Died. G. M. Wilson
Robespierre Serial. N. Luard
Robin and the 7 Hoods. J. Pearl
Robin Grey. C. Gibbon
Robin Hood Caper. F. Carmichael
Robin Hoodwinker, V.C. G. Davison
Robin Redbreast in a Cage. Myrtle Johnston
Robineau Look. K. M. Knight
Robineau Murders. K. M. Knight
Robinson. M. Spark
Robinson Factor. J. M. White
Robot Detective. M. Billett
Robthorne Mystery. J. Rhode
Rochemer Hag. L. W. King
Rock. H. Ellson
Rock! C. Stratton
Rock Ahead. E. Yates
Rock Baby. M. Woodhouse
Rock Harvest. H. C. Rae
Rock in the Baltic. R. Barr
Rock of Ages. F. H. Rose
Rock of Diamond. J. Quartermain
Rock of Justice. H. M. Richardson
Rock Rude. E. Stewart
Rockabilly. H. Ellison
Rockabye Contract. P. Atlee
Rocket for the Toff. J. Creasey
Rocket to the Morgue. H. H. Holmes
Rockets—Operation Manhattan. H. Edmonds
Rockfire. C. Dillon
Rocking Chair. F. Y. McHugh
Rockingham Diamond. H. Collinson Owen
Rocklitz. G. R. Preedy
Rocks and Romance. F. B. Johnson
Rocks and Ruin. H. J. Calin
Rocksburg Railroad Murders. K. C. Constantine
Rocky Libido in San Francisco. L. Folder
Rocky Mountain. Duff Johnson
Rocky Rhodes. W. C. Tuttle
Rococo Coffin. Richard Brown
Rod of Anger. D. Nabarro
Rod of Justice. A. Askew
Rod of the Snake. V. Short
Rodeo Murder Mystery. H. Pink
Roderick of Kildare. S. Cobb
Rodriguez Affair. J. Pattinson
Rogano. S. Knight

Roger Bennion's Double. H. Adams
Roger Quinney. P. H. Irving
Roger Sheringham and the Vane Mystery. A. Berkeley
Roger Sinclair's Treasure. N. Worth
Rogue. T. W. H. Crosland
Rogue. W. E. Norris
Rogue Aunt. J. N. Chance
Rogue by Compulsion. V. Bridges
Rogue Cop. W. P. McGivern
Rogue Cop. G. F. Newman
Rogue Diamond. J. B. Lynne
Rogue Eagle. J. McClure
Rogue Haven. B. Home
Rogue Hercules. D. Pitts
Rogue in Ambush. H. Hill
Rogue in Love. T. Gallon
Rogue Male. G. Household
Rogue of Afganistan. W. M. Graydon
Rogue of Quality. Nicholas Carter
Rogue of Rye. W. W. Dixon
Rogue Ransome—Manhunter. Dan Morgan
Rogue Ransome—Racket Buster. Dan Morgan
Rogue Ransome—Triggerman. Dan Morgan
Rogue Royal. Gwyn Evans
Rogue Running. M. Procter
Rogue with a Past. R. Wesley
Rogue Worth Trapping. Nicholas Carter
Rogues. R. H. Sherard
Rogues and Company. I. A. R. Wylie
Rogues and Diamonds. S. Jepson
Rogues and Vagabonds. G. R. Sims
Rogue's Badge. C. N. Buck
Rogue's Castle. S. Stanley
Rogue's Coat. T. Du Bois
Rogue's Conscience. D. C. Murray
Rogues Fall Out. H. Adams
Rogues Fall Out. F. Warden
Rogue's Gambit. A. Caillou
Rogue's Harbour. J. T. Story
Rogue's Harvest. N. Cromarty
Rogue's Haven. R. Bridges
Rogue's Heiress. J. Gallon
Rogue's Holiday. M. March
Rogues in Arcady. W. Magnay
Rogues in Clover. P. Wilde
Rogues in the Forest. C. T. Stonehan
Rogues' Island. B. Perowne
Rogue's Life. W. Collins
Rogues Ltd. C. R. Gull
Rogue's Luck. A. Wright
Rogues' March. G. Dilnot
Rogues' March. E. W. Hornung
ROgues' March. M. Turnbull
Rogue's Murder. W. Ard
Rogues' Nest. R. South
Rogues of Fortune. J. J. Chichester
Rogues of Ransom. G. H. Teed
Rogues of Society, and The Doctor of Duddlestone. G. F. Underhill
Rogues of the Desert. W. M. Graydon
Rogues of the North. A. M. Treynor
Rogues' Paradise. E. Pugh
Rogue's Progress. E. Oliver
Rogues Rampant. G. Ashe
Rogue's Ransom. G. Ashe
Rogue's Reach. Nicholas Carter
Rogues' Republic. G. H. Teed
Rogues' Syndicate. F. Froest
Rogue's Tragedy. B. Capes
Rokewood Tragedy. M. Pinkerton
Roland Yorke. H. Wood
Roles and Relations. D. Sarmiento
Roll Film Mystery. M. Poole
Roll, Jordan, Roll. D. P. Clark
Roll-Top Desk Mystery. C. Wells
Rollercoaster. B. Wohl
Rollicking Rogue. J. McCulley
Rolling Heads. A. M. Stein
Rolling Stone. J. Hartley
Rolling Stone. P. Wentworth
Rolling Stones. O. Henry
Rollo of Normandy. S. Cobb
Roman Adventure. M. MacKintosh
Roman Collar Detective. G. Johnson
Roman Gold. Michael Lewis
Roman Hat Mystery. E. Queen
Roman Magic. H. Fleetwood
Roman Mystery. R. Bagot
Roman Ring. C. P. Bracken
Roman Way. G. V. McFadden
Romance at Hillyard House. K. Norris
Romance at Random. H. B. M. Watson
Romance Comes to Scotland Yard. H. Black
Romance in Crimson. O. R. Cohen
Romance in the First Degree. O. R. Cohen
Romance of a Common Life. Waters
Romance of a Coward. M. Dekobra
Romance of a Madhouse. A. M. Meadows
Romance of a Maid of Honour. R. Marsh
Romance of a Million Dollars. E. Dejeans
Romance of a Pretty Girl. R. De Pont-Jest
Romance of a Queen. W. Chesney
Romance of a Salvation Army Girl. Old Sleuth
Romance of a Spy. E.7.
Romance of an Alter Ego. L. Bryce
Romance of Elaine. A. B. Reeve
Romance of Hellerism. A. S. Gifford
Romance of Lilies. C. H. Montague
Romance of Nikko Cheyne. R. Pertwee

Romance of Poisons. R. Cromie
Romance of Politics. A. Upward
Romance of the Castle. J. Elson
Romance of the Forest. A. Radcliffe
Romance of the Ruby. G. Campbell
Romance of the Woods. F. Whishaw
Romance on the Rhine. Elsie Lee
Romances of Crime. J. M'Levy
Romances of Mayfair. Anonymous
Romances of the Law. R. E. Francillon
Romances of the Road. Thormanby
Romanesque. R. McInerny
Romanoff Jewells. M. Grant
Romanov Ransom. A. A. Thompson
Romanov Succession. B. Garfield
Romantic Assignment. Elsie Lee
Romantic Journey. N. Buckingham
Romantic Road. G. Rawlence
Romantic Stories of the Legal Profession. R. E. Francillon
Romany Curse. S. Somers
Rome Express. Ruth Alexander
Rome Express. A. Griffiths
Romelle. W. R. Burnett
Rommany. F. Hurd
Rommel Plot. J. Tarrant
Rommel's Gold. Maggie Davis
Ronald o' the Moors. G. E. Locke
Ronald Standish. H. C. McNeile
Roof. Maurice Walker
Roof. D. Whitelaw
Rook Takes Knight. S. Palmer
Rookery. H. C. Rae
Rookery Detective. Anonymous
Rookies. C. Parker
Rook's Gambit. S. Rattray
Rook's Nest. G. W. Appleton
Rooksmiths. S. Truss
Rookwood. W. H. Ainsworth
Room at the Bottom. J. L. Potter
Room at the Hotel Ambre. A. Armstrong
Room Beneath the Stairs. K. St. Clair
Room, Board and Death. Marc Miller
Room Five. H. Drummond
Room for a Body. Josephine Bell
Room for a Ghost. Winifred Duke
Room for Murder. T. B. Dewey
Room for Murder. D. M. Disney
Room 14. M. Annesley
Room in Quiver Court. J. Cassells
Room in the Tower. J. Blackmore
Room in the Tower and other stories. E. F. Benson
Room Nineteen. F. Warden
Room Number 6. J. J. Farjeon
Room Number 3 and other stories. A. K. Green
Room of Mirrors. Nicholas Carter
Room of Mirrors. H. Flowerdew
Room of Secrets. C. Farr
Room of Secrets. W. LeQueux
Room Opposite, and other tales of mystery and imagination. F. M. Mayor
Room Service. Alan Williams
Room 13. E. Wallace
Room 37. H. Howard
Room to Die In. E. Queen
Room to Swing. E. Lacy
Room 12a. A. Marsh
Room Under the Stairs. Herman Landon
Room Upstairs. Mildred Davis
Room Upstairs. M. Dickens
Room with Dark Mirrors. V. Johnston
Room with No Escape. A. Barber
Room with the Iron Shutters. A. Wynne
Room with the Tassels. C. Wells
Room Without a Key. W. E. D. Ross
Rooming House. B. Roueche
Roommate. J. Wein
Rooms at Mrs. Oliver's. K. Kellow
Rooney. C. Cookson
Root and Branch. N. Tranter
Root of All Evil. J. S. Fletcher
Root of All Evil. F. Marryat
Root of All Evil. Dell Shannon
Root of All Evil. I. Stark
Root of Evil. J. Cross
Root of Evil. E. K. Goldthwaite
Root of His Evil. W. Ard
Root of His Evil. J. M. Cain
Rooted Sorrow. P. M. Hubbard
Roots of Fury. I. Shulman
Rope. P. Hamilton
Rope. A. Hitchcock
Rope Began to Hang the Butcher. C. W. Grafton
Rope Broke. D. Barr
Rope by Arrangement. H. Clandon
Rope-Dancer. V. Marchetti
Rope Enough. J. S. Strange
Rope Fodder. D. Thomas
Rope for a Convict. R. C. Woodthorpe
Rope for a Lady. B. Sarto
Rope for an Ape. D. Chambers
Rope for Breakfast. A. Spiller
Rope for Christmas. F. Griffin
Rope for General Dietz. J. Rossiter
Rope for the Baron. Anthony Morton
Rope for the Hanging. N. Morland
Rope for the Judge. H. Hawton
Rope of Sand. F. Bonnamy
Rope of Sand. C. Franklin

Title Index

Rope of Sand. P. Traill
Rope of Slender Threads. Nicholas Carter
Rope over Jezebel. R. Harrison
Rope to Spare. P. MacDonald
Rope Waits. L. Dean
Rope Which Hangs. G. Fairlie
Rope's End. P. Hamilton
Rope's End—Rogue's End. E. C. R. Lorac
Rosa at Ten O'Clock. M. Denevi
Rosalie. T. P. Prest
Rosalie Du Pont. Emerson Bennett
Rosaline Woodbridge. H. M. JOnes
Rosamunda. Marjory Hall
Rosaria. M. K. Robertson
Rosario Murder Case. Roland Daniel
Rosario, the Female Monk. M. G. Lewis
Rosary Murders. W. X. Kienzle
Rose and the Key. J. S. Le Fanu
Rose Bath Riddle. A. M. Rud
Rose Brocade. P. C. De Crespigny
Rose Can Kill. J. Ingersol
Rose for Ana Maria. F. Yerby
Rose from the Dead. P. Ernst
Rose in Darkness. C. Brand
Rose Lodge. H. Wood
Rose Medallion. James Grant
Rose of Algiers. C. H. Bullivant
Rose of Allandale. G. Stables
Rose of Blenheim. M. Gerard
Rose of Death. W. S. Masterson
Rose of Kantara. A. Richardson
Rose of Life. M. E. Braddon
Rose of Tibet. L. Davidson
Rose Petal Murders. C. G. Givens
Rose, Rose, Where Are You? R. Ellerbeck
Rose Seymour. N. Buntline
Rose Window. S. Blanc
Roseanna. M. Sjowall
Rosebud. J. Hemingway
Rosecrest Cell. V. Caspary
Roseheath. K. Troy
Rosemary for Death. Dexter Muir
Rosemary for Remembrance. S. Nichols
Rosemary's Baby. I. Levine
Rosery Folk. G. M. Fenn
Roses from a Haunted Garden. J. F. Webb
Rose's Last Summer. M. Millar
Rosevean. I. Bromige
Rosewell Heritage. M. F. Ford
Roshanara of the Seven Cities. W. R. Foran
Ross Forgery. W. H. Hallahan
Rossano. G. Lett
Rossi Killings. M. Stall
Rostron Outfit. Dan Morgan
Rostron Outfit in Chicago. Dan Morgan
Rostron Outfit in Mexico. Dan Morgan
Rostron Outfit in Rio. Dan Morgan
Rostron Outfit in Texas. Dan Morgan
Rostron Outfit—Undercover Agents. Dan Morgan
Rosy Pastor. N. Fitzgerald
Rothby. Marilyn Ross
Rothhaven. W. E. D. Ross
Rothschild Conversion. P. Buckman
Rotten Apples. E. P. Green
Rotten Deal. Demouzon
Rotten with Honour. Derek Robinson
Rotterdam Delivery. E. A. O'Neill
Rotunda. R. R. Siegrist
Rouge. H. McFall
Rough Air. E. Haycox
Rough Company. D. Hamilton
Rough Cut. L. Lambert
Rough Cut. A. McCullough
Rough Deal. W. Winward
Rough Going. G. Goodchild
Rough Justice. M. E. Braddon
Rough on Rats. W. Francis
Rough Passage. Gavin Douglas
Rough Passage. C. Hackforth-Jones
Rough Passage. A. Wright
Rough Seas to Sunrise. J. Ames
Rough Shoot. G. Household
Rough Trade. L. Rand
Roughneck. J. Thompson
Roumanian Envoy. G. N. Philips
Round Dozen. E. Cadell
Round Robin. G. W. Bain
Round Table Murders. P. Baron
Round Table Murders. Adrian Reynolds
Round the Block. Anonymous
Round the Clock at Volari's. W. R. Burnett
Round the Fire Stories. A. C. Doyle
Round the Red Lamp. A. C. Doyle
Round the World for a Quarter. Nicholas Carter
Round Trip. D. Tracy
Round Trip in the Year 2000. W. W. Cook
Round Trip to Nowhere. J. T. MacCargo
Roundabout. M. Allwright
Roundhead Retreat. John Sanders
Rouse the Demon. C. Weston
Rout of the Oliver Samuelsons. H. C. McNeile
Route of the Red Gold. D. J. Marlowe
Routine Investigation. H. Howard
Roving Hearts. K. Prichard
Rowforest. A. Weekes
Rowforest Plot. A. Weekes
Rowleston. B. Riefe

Rox Hall Illuminated. P. Paul
Roxy by Proxy. H. Janson
Roy of Roy's Court. W. Westall
Royal Abduction. A. W. Upfield
Royal Affair and other stories. G. Boothby
Royal Alliance. C. Dawe
Royal Bed for a Corpse. Max Murray
Royal Bluejacket. F. T. Jane
Royal Box. F. P. Keyes
Royal Chase. C. Buckley
Royal Exchange. J. M. Cobban
Royal Exchange. H. M. Raleigh
Royal Flush Murders. G. Verner
Royal Heritage. R. Pertwee
Royal Hoax. F. Whishaw
Royal Indiscretion. R. Marsh
Royal Ishmael. Winifred Duke
Royal Outlaw. S. Cobb
Royal Prisoner. P. Souvestre
Royal Rascal. A. Griffiths
Royal Special, and other stories. E. Burton
Royal Street. F. Swann
Royal Thief. Nicholas Carter
Royal Twins. T. P. Prest
Royal Wrong. F. M. White
Royce of the Royal Mounted. Ames Moore
Royston Affair. D. M. Devine
Rub-a-Dub-Dub. R. L. Fish
Rub-Out Specialty. Griff
Rubbed Out. R. Barnett
Rubber Band. R. Stout
Rubber Mask. F. L. Stickney
Rubber Smugglers. G. H. Teed
Rubber Stamp, and A Matter of Voice. H. C. McNeile
Rubberface. G. Stanley
Rubberneck. B. Shannon
Rubbish. S. Barrett
Rube Burrows League. M. Manly
Rubies, Emeralds and Diamonds. B. Chetwynd
Rubies of Rajmar. E. Eastwick
Ruby. F. Lorenz
Ruby. J. Siegal
Ruby. K. Stewart
Ruby Beyond Price. G. Campbell
Ruby Cup. L. K. Vincent
Ruby Heart of Kishgar. A. W. Marchmont
Ruby Maclaine. J. Roeburt
Ruby of a Thousand Dreams. Roland Daniel
Ruby Pin. Nicholas Carter
Ruby Sword. B. Mitford
Rude Awakening. H. Brinton
Rude Justice. L. Austen-Leigh
Rudolph and Adelaide. M. A. Marchant
Rue Bargain. R. M. Gilchrist
Rue the Day. M. Alan
Rue the Reservoir. Annabelle Melville
Rufin's Legacy. W. Gerrare
Rugged Way. E. W. Elkington
Ruin. E. S. West
Ruined Map. K. Abe
Ruins of Avondale Priory. I. Kelly
Ruled by Radio. R. L. Hadfield
Ruled off the Turf. Grace M. White
Rules Don't Apply. R. Hamilton
Rules of the Game. S. Morrow
Ruling Passion. R. Hill
Ruling the Planets. M. E. Burton
Ruling Vice. P. Trent
Rum Alley. A. O. Pollard
Rum and Coca-Cola Murders. Wenzell Brown
Rum Row Murders. C. R. Jones
Rum Week. N. Tranter
Rumble. H. Ellison
Rumble Murders. M. Deal
Rumble on the Docks. F. Paley
Rumor Hath It. C. Hale
Rumour at Nightfall. G. Greene
Rumpole. J. Mortimer
Rumpole of the Bailey. J. Mortimer
Rumpole's Return. J. Mortimer
Run. M. Shedd
Run! P. Wentworth
Run a Golden Mile. C. Joyce
Run Away to Murder. J. York
Run, Brother, Run! T. Brandt
Run by Night. H. Innes
Run, Chico, Run. Wenzell Brown
Run Corpse, Run. G. Pember-Hiller
Run Down. Robert Garrett
Run Far, Run Fast. L. A. Goldstone
Run, Fool, Run. F. Gruber
Run for Blood. G. Warren
Run for Cover. J. Welcome
Run for Doom. H. Kane
Run for Lover. H. Janson
Run for the Money. Dale Clark
Run for the Money. R. Colby
Run for Your Death. H. Hossent
Run for Your Life. B. Fischer
Run for Your Life. R. Foley
Run for Your Life! S. Noel
Run for Your Life! M. Stark
Run for Your Money. G. Nyland
Run for Your Money. H. Seymour
Run from Death. J. P. Duff
Run from the Hunter. K. Grantland
Run from the River. L. Barth

Run from the Sheep. E. Capit
Run If You Can. O. Dudley
Run If You're Guilty. J. McKimmey
Run in Diamonds. A. Saxon
Run, Killer, Run. N. Deemster
Run, Killer, Run. W. C. Gault
Run, Killer, Run. L. White
Run Lethal. R. Stark
Run Like a Thief. M. Niall
Run Man Run. C. Himes
Run, Mann, Run! J. Keenan
Run, Mongoose. B. Wilkinson
Run, Robber, Run. R. A. Anderson
Run...Run...Run. F. Taubes
Run Scared. M. G. Eberhart
Run, Shadow, Run. H. B. Cave
Run, Spy, Run. Nick Carter
Run, Thief, Run. F. Gruber
Run to Death. P. Quentin
Run to Earth. M. E. Braddon
Run to Earth. Nicholas Carter
Run to Earth. P. Grayson
Run to Evil. L. Egan
Run to Ground. R. Jocelyn
Run to Morning. J. Graham
Run Tough, Run Hard. C. Bingham
Run, Traitor, Run. R. Pierce
Run When I Say Go. H. Waugh
Run While You Can. W. Woolfolk
Run with the Fox. Craig Cooper
Run with the Hare. K. Abbey
Run with the Killer. J. Armour
Run with the Weasel. R. Wilkes-Hunter
Runagate. C. C. Lowis
Runagates Club. J. Buchan
Runaround. V. Warren
Runaway. M. Halliday
Runaway. N. Holland
Runaway. Richard Hubbard
Runaway. Old Sleuth
Runaway. J. Peter
Runaway. C. Stratton
Runaway Bag. A. P. Terhune
Runaway Black. R. Marsten
Runaway Corpse. James Warren
Runaway from Love. Rona Randall
Runaway Home! K. Booton
Runaway Match. H. Wood
Runaway Pigeon. L. Edgley
Runaway Wife. S. O'Donnell
Rundown. J. Magnuson
Rung In. A. Wright
Runner Is Red. J. B. Kovalsky
Runner Stumbles. M. Stitt
Running. R. Shaw
Running Amok. G. M. Fenn
Running Blind. D. Bagley
Running Deep. R. Petrie
Running Dog. D. De Lillo
Running Down a Double. Anonymous
Running Duck. P. Harcourt
Running Fight. E. P. Oppenheim
Running Killer. W. J. Elliott
Running Lions. J. D. White
Running Man. B. Benson
Running Man. L. Dietz
Running Man. Anthony Ferguson
Running Man. W. A. Harbinson
Running Nun. B. Flynn
Running of Beasts. B. Pronzini
Running Sand. Jonathan Wade
Running Scared. J. Burmeister
Running Scared. Craig Cooper
Running Scared. Gregory McDonald
Running Scared. B. McKnight
Running Scared. J. Mathewson
Running Special. F. Packard
Running Spy. J. Milton
Running Target. S. Frazee
Running the Blockade. W. H. Thomes
Running the Gauntlet. E. Yates
Running Thursday. P. Hastings
Running Tide. J. R. Gould
Running Water. A. E. W. Mason
Running Woman. P. Carlon
Runway to Death. C. M. Filgate
Runway Zero-Eight. J. Castle
Rupert Godwin. M. E. Braddon
Rupert Hall. H. Wood
Ruse of the Vanished Women. V. Gielgud
Rush Hour Crime. A. Skene
Rush on the Ultimate. H. R. F. Keating
Russian Coward. F. Whishaw
Russian Hi-Jack. N. Shore
Russian Hide-and-Seek. K. Amis
Russian Intelligence. M. Moorcock
Russian Interpreter. M. Frayn
Russian Judas. F. Whishaw
Russian Roulette. T. Ardies
Russian Roulette. A. Bloomfield
Russian Roulette. R. Freeborn
Russian Roulette. J. Mitchell
Russian Roulette. B. Picton
Rust of Murder. J. March
Rustle of Spring. K. Lindsay
Rustlers' Roost. W. C. Tuttle
Rustling End. D. G. Browne
Ruth. V. Caspary
Ruth Anstey. J. Middlemass
Ruth of the U.S.A. E. Balmer
Ruth, the Unsuspecting. K. Kimbrough
Rutherford. E. Fawcett

Ruthless. Raymond Marshall
Rutland Mystery. C. F. Gregg
Rx for Murder. J. Layhew
Ryan Affair. D. MacDonald
Ryan Girl. E. Goulding
Ryan's Rule. E. Leonard
Ryecroft Verdict. D. Whitelaw
Ryerson Mystery. P. Phelps
Rynox. P. MacDonald
Rynox Murder Mystery. P. MacDonald
Rynox Mystery. P. MacDonald

S.O.S. S. Horler
S—Portrait of a Spy. I. Adams
S.P.Q.R. P. H. Bonner
S.P.Y.S. T. R. Joyce
SS-GB. L. Deighton
S.S. Murder. Q. Patrick
S.S. Mystery. L. A. Knight
"S-S-S-Sh!" K. Carmel
Saba's Treasure. D. M. Douglass
Sabath Quest. I. Foster
Sabbath Slayer. B. Heygate
Saberlegs. E. Pace
Sabine. N. Freeling
Sable in the Rain. W. E. D. Ross
Sable Lorcha. H. Hazeltine
Sable Messenger. F. Vivian
Sable Night. A. Roy
Sables Spell Trouble. S. Mitchell
Sabotage. C. F. Adams
Sabotage. J. Creasey
Sabotage. R. C. Elliott
Sabotage. O. John
Sabotage at Sea. John Davies
Sabotage Broadcast. H. Innes
Sabotage Murder Mystery. M. Allingham
Sabotage Unlimited. P. Groom
Saboteurs. June Drummond
Saboteurs. J. W. Mason
Sabre Squadron. S. Raven
Sabre-Tooth. P. O'Donnell
Sabres on the Sand. G. Household
Sack of Monte Carlo. W. Frith
Sackcloth and Broadcloth. J. Middlemass
Sacked City. G. R. Preedy
Sacrament of Death. S. Esmond
Sacred City. W. W. Sayer
Sacred Crescents. W. Westall
Sacred Eye. J. Creasey
Sacred Herb. F. Hume
Sacred Shaft. J. Weatherhead
Sacrifice. C. H. Merrett
Sacrifice. F. E. Penny
Sacrifice. G. Simenon
Sacrifice. H. Sutton
Sacrifice. P. Trent
Sacrifice & Co. Winifred Graham
Sacrificial Pawn. F. Ryck
Sad Adventurers. M. Rutledge
Sad and Savage Dying. P. Audemars
Sad and Tender Flesh. S. D. Frances
Sad Cypress. A. Christie
Sad-Eyed Seductress. Carter Brown
Sad Road to the Sea. G. Kersh
Sad Song Singing. T. B. Dewey
Sad Sontag Plays His Hunch. W. C. Tuttle
Sad, Sudden Death of My Fair Lady. S. Forbes
Sad Variety. N. Blake
Sad Wind from the Sea. Harry Patterson
Saddle a Killer. N. Wylie
Saddle and Sabre. H. Smart
Saddled with Murder. S. Miles
Saddleroom Murder. N. K. McKechnie
Sadie, Don't Cry Now. H. Janson
Sadie Shapiro in Miami. R. K. Smith
Sadie Socks the Saboteurs. C. George
Sadie Swings the Blues. B. Shannon
Sadie When She Died. E. McBain
Sadist. E. T. Hamill
Safari. E. Rhodes
Safari for Spies. Nick Carter
Safari with Fear! R. Hardinge
Safari with Fear. J. York
Safe Behind Bars. Andrew Hall
Safe Conduct. J. England
Safe Custody. D. Yates
Safe House. J. Cleary
Safe Job. D. Vallance
Safe Number Sixty-Nine. J. S. Fletcher
Safe Place. A. Rider
Safe Road. K. N. Burt
Safe Secret. H. Carmichael
Safer Dead. J. H. Chase
Safer Than Life. R. R. Petersunne
Safety First Murders. E. Radford
Safety Last. G. Goodchild
Safety Last. J. Gray
Safety Pin. J. S. Fletcher
Saffron Robe. J. Browning
Saffron Summer. M. Summerton
Saffron's War. F. E. Smith
Saga of a Scoundrel. P. Barrington
Saga of Halfaday Creek. J. B. Hendryx
Saga of the Cliffs. E. L. Long

Sagas of the Mounted Police. W. B. Mowery
Sahara Road. S. Harvester
Sahara Strike. D. J. Cleary
Sahara Survival. Burt Cole
Said Dr. Spendlove. Hilda Lewis
Said the Spider to the Fly. R. Hugill
Said the Spider to the Fly. R. Shattuck
Said with Flowers. A. Nash
Saigon. Nick Carter
Saigon Singer. V. W. Mason
Sail a Crooked Ship. N. Benchley
Sail into Silence. D. Marble
Sailcloth Shroud. C. Williams
Sailor and the Widow. E. L. Long
Sailor and the Widow. Seafarer
Sailor, Take Warning. K. Roos
Sailor, Take Warning. R. Sale
Sailor's Bride. G. Boothby
Sailor's Luck. B. Heatter
Sailor's Rendezvous. G. Simenon
Saint Abroad. L. Charteris
Saint: Ace of Knaves. L. Charteris
Saint and Cynic. A. Simmons
Saint and Mr. Teal. L. Charteris
Saint and the Fiction Makers. L. Charteris
Saint and the Hapsburg Necklace. L. Charteris
Saint and the Last Hero. L. Charteris
Saint and the People Importers. L. Charteris
Saint and the Sizzling Saboteur. L. Charteris
Saint and the Templar Treasure. L. Charteris
Saint Around the World. L. Charteris
Saint at a Thieves' Picnic. L. Charteris
Saint at Large. L. Charteris
St. Bernard's Priory. N. Harley
Saint Bids Diamonds. L. Charteris
Saint Bodolph's Priory. T. J. H. Curties
Saint Catherine's Wheel. J. Griffin
Saint Cleans Up. L. Charteris
Saint Closes the Case. L. Charteris
St. Cloud Affair. B. Baskerville
St. Cuthbert's Tower. F. Warden
Saint Errant. L. Charteris
Saint-Fiacre Affair. G. Simenon
St. George Manor. R. M. Sears
Saint Goes On. L. Charteris
Saint Goes West. L. Charteris
Saint in Action. L. Charteris
Saint in England. L. Charteris
Saint in Europe. L. Charteris
Saint in Miami. L. Charteris
Saint in Mufti. C. Dawe
Saint in New York. L. Charteris
Saint in Pursuit. L. Charteris
Saint in the Sun. L. Charteris
Saint in Trouble. L. Charteris
Saint Intervenes. L. Charteris
St. Ives. O. Bleeck
St. Ives Murders. R. Wincor
St. Louis Showdown. D. Pendleton
Saint Maker. L. Holton
Saint-Malo Mystery. J. Maske
St. Martin's Eve. H. Wood
Saint Meets His Match. L. Charteris
Saint Meets the Tiger. L. Charteris
Saint of the Speedway. R. Cullum
Saint on Guard. L. Charteris
Saint on TV. L. Charteris
Saint on the Spanish Main. L. Charteris
Saint Overboard. L. Charteris
St. Peter's Finger. G. Mitchell
St. Peter's Plot. D. Lambert
Saint Plays with Fire. L. Charteris
Saint Returns. L. Charteris
Saint Sees It Through. L. Charteris
Saint Steps In. L. Charteris
Saint—The Brighter Buccaneer. L. Charteris
Saint—The Happy Highwayman. L. Charteris
Saint to the Rescue. L. Charteris
Saint: Two in One. L. Charteris
St. Valentine's Day Massacre. B. O'Hara
Saint vs. Scotland Yard. L. Charteris
Saint—Wanted for Murder. L. Charteris
Saints Are Sinister. B. Flynn
Saint's Getaway. L. Charteris
Saintsbury Affair. R. Doubleday
Saladin! A. Osmond
Salamander. M. L. West
Salamander Sword. L. Wilkinson
Salazar Grant. E. L. Withers
Salekov Kill. G. Richards
Salesman of Death. C. Leader
Salisbury Manuscript. W. M. Green
Sally. E. V. Cunningham
Sally. W. B. M. Ferguson
Sally of Scotland Yard. L. Gribble
Sally of the Underworld. Roland Daniel
Sally's in the Alley. N. Davis
Salome Syndrome. A. Sewart
Salt and Pepper. Alex Austin
Salt Cat Bank. A. Sax
Salt for the Tiger. W. C. Tuttle
Salt Is Leaving. J. B. Priestley
Salt Mine. D. Lippincott
Salt of the Earth. F. M. White

Salter's Folly. A. Marsden
Saltmarsh Murders. G. Mitchell
Salute Blue Mask. Anthony Morton
Salute for the Baron. Anthony Morton
Salute from a Dead Man. Donald MacKenzie
Salute Inspector Flagg. J. Cassells
Salute Mr. Sandyman. Neill Graham
Salute the Dreamer. W. M. Duncan
Salute the Picaroon. J. Cassells
Salute the Toff. J. Creasey
Salute to Bazarada and other stories. S. Rohmer
Salute to Blackshirt. R. Graeme
Salute to Murder. Neill Graham
Salute to Murder. R. P. Koehler
Salute to the Gods. Malcolm Campbell
Salute to Tomorrow. J. Nicholas
Salvage. H. Smart
Salvage Job. Robert MacLeod
Salvage of the Sea. W. M. Graydon
Salvage Pirates. G. Chester
Salvation. A. Askew
Salvation of Pisco Gabar and other stories. G. Household
Salvator. P. Gibbon
Salvatore. P. Tabori
Salving of a Derelict. M. Drake
Salzberg Affair. J. D. White
Salzburg Connection. Helen MacInnes
Sam Benedict: Cast the First Stone. Elsie Lee
Sam Casanova. M. Catto
SAM 7. R. Cox
Samain. M. E. Atkins
Samantha. J. Carew
Samantha. E. V. Cunningham
Samantha. D. Eden
Samara. N. Lewis
Samarai Affair. A. Behrend
Samaritan. P. Johnson
Same Difference. H. Janson
Same Lie Twice. R. Goulart
Sammy. D. Enefer
Samson. E. C. Vivian
Samson Strike. T. Williamson
Samson's Surrender. T. Lloyd
Samuel Boyd of Catchpole Square. B. L. Farjeon
Samuel Lyle, Criminologist. A. Crabb
San Diego Siege. D. Pendleton
San Francisco Vendetta. R. Mallory
Sanctuary. W. Faulkner
Sanctuary Club. L. T. Meade
Sanctuary Island. Robert (G.) Curtis
Sanctuary Isle. B. Knox
Sand and Satin. S. Rohmer
Sand Dollar. G. Sims
Sand Dollars. R. Terrall
Sand Pit. H. Jobson
Sand Rose. M. Summerton
Sand Trap. Ian Stuart
Sandal Wood Slipper. Nicholas Carter
Sandalwood Fan. K. W. Eyre
Sandalwood Fan. T. McMorrow
Sandbaggers. I. Mackintosh
Sandbar Sinister. P. A. Taylor
Sandcastle Murders. E. St. Clair
Sandcatcher. S. Jackman
Sandcliff Mystery. Scott Graham
Sanders. E. Wallace
Sanders of the River. E. Wallace
Sanderson: Master Rogue. J. J. Chichester
Sanderson's Diamond Loot. J. J. Chichester
Sandi, the King Maker. E. Wallace
Sandlappers. A. Rutherford
Sandler Inquiry. N. Hynd
Sandling Case. L. Tracy
Sandman. R. Ward
Sandover Goes Gay. D. Lee
Sandra Rifkin's Jewels. R. Doliner
Sands of Fear. Augustus Muir
Sands of Khali. M. Hastings
Sands of Lilliput. S. Dembo
Sands of Oro. B. Grimshaw
Sands of the Desert. P. Meredith
Sands of Windee. A. W. Upfield
Sands Street. W. Bogart
Sandwiches Are Not My Business. B. Kelly
Sandycroft Mystery. T. W. Speight
Sanfield Scandal. R. Keverne
Sant of the Secret Service. W. LeQueux
Santa Ana Wind. S. Ashton
Santa Claus Bank Robbery. A. C. Greene
Santa Dolores Stage. W. C. Tuttle
Santa Klaus Murder. M. D. Hay
Santa Maria. J. Fox
Santa Maria. Seafarer
Santos, Border Detective. W. B. Bannerman
Sappers and Miners. G. M. Fenn
Sapphire. E. G. Cousins
Sapphire. A. E. W. Mason
Sapphire Conference. P. Graaf
Sapphire Cross. G. M. Fenn
Sapphire King, and other stories. R. Dowling
Sapphire Ring. C. Granville
Sapphires on Wednesday. M. Gair
Saraband for a Smuggler. S. Brydon
Saracen Gardens. M. K. Simmons

Title Index

Saracen Shadow. Shane Martin
Sarah Brown, Detective. Anonymous
Sarah Brown, Detective. K. F. Hill
Sarah Mandrake. M. Wadelton
Saranoff Murder. M. L. Luther
Saratoga Lady. F. Y. McHugh
Saratoga Longshot. S. Dobyns
Saratoga Mantrap. D. St. Clare
Sardia. C. L. Daniels
Sargasso. E. Corley
Sargasso Ogre. K. Robeson
Sargasso People. Wade Miller
Sargasso Secret. K. Stanton
Sarita, the Carlist. A. W. Marchmont
Sark Street Chapel Murder. T. Cobb
Sarnia. H. Ford
Sarsen Place. Gwendoline Butler
Sarton Kell. K. Mallory
Sartoroe. J. A. Maitland
Satan Black. K. Robeson
Satan Bug. I. Stuart
Satan Buys a Wreath. M. Storm
Satan Comes Across. B. Barlay
Satan Has Six Fingers. V. Kelsey
Satan in High Heels. N. Chandler
Satan in Malibu. F. Cannon
Satan Is a Woman. G. Brewer
Satan Is Blonde. B. Sarto
Satan Ltd. Gwyn Evans
Satan, My Love. H. P. Holden
Stan Ring. Mike Newton
Satan Sampler. V. Canning
Satan Stone. Ralph Hayes
Satan Strike. J. Rosenberger
Satan Takes the Helm. C. Clements
Satan Touch. K. Royce
Satan Trap. Nick Carter
Satan Was a Man. E. H. Bierstadt
Satanic Power. V. Van Der Elst
Satanic Sex. A. J. Fitzgerald
Satanist. D. Wheatley
Satan's Acres. S. Wagner
Satan's Angel. S. Fisher
Satan's Apt Pupil. Nicholas Carter
Satan's Bay. Michael Hastings
Satan's Child. P. Saxon
Satan's Children. G. Simenon
Satan's Coach. F. Du Boisgobey
Satan's Coast. Elsie Lee
Satan's Daughters. O. Peters
Satan's Island. Marilyn Ross
Satan's Manor. Mark Andrews
Satan's Mistress. B. Graeme
Satan's Rock. Marilyn Ross
Satan's Sabbath. D. Pendleton
Satan's Sabbath. P. Valdez
Satan's Satellite. G. Davison
Satan's Seal. P. Rose
Satan's Secret. B. Stacey
Satan's Seed. J. Sherman
Satan's Sister. T. Angelo
Satan's Sister. R. J. Jensen
Satan's Snowdrop. G. N. Smith
Satan's Spring. S. Nichols
Satan's Sunset. S. Hufford
Satan's Widow. H. Whittington
Satellite Slaughter. L. Derrick
Saturday Epic. H. C. Rae
Saturday Games. B. Meggs
Saturday Night Knife and Gun Club. B. P. Reiter
Saturday Night Massacre. J. Armour
Saturday Night Town. H. Whittington
Saturday of Glory. D. Serafin
Saturday Out. L. Meynell
Saturday the Rabbi Went Hungry. H. Kemelman
Saturn over the Water. J. B. Priestley
Saturn Stone. L. Osborne
Satyr. J. McKimmey
Satyr Mask. Augustus Muir
Sausalito. S. Dodson
Savage. P. Boorstin
Savage. N. Clad
Savage Affair. V. Scott
Savage Breast. Manning Long
Savage Breast. J. Trinian
Savage Bride. C. Woolrich
Savage Chase. F. Lorenz
Savage City. A. J. Merak
Savage Day. J. Higgins
Savage Encounter. G. Goodchild
Savage Fire. D. Pendleton
Savage Freedom. Roderick Grant
Savage Game. J. Trevor
Savage Gentleman. P. Wylie
Savage Height. J. Trevor
Savage Holiday. R. Wright
Savage Interlude. D. Cushman
Savage Night. J. Thompson
Savage Oaks. J. Ellis
Savage Ransom. E. Lippincott
Savage Salome. Carter Brown
Savage Sequel. H. Janson
Savage Siren. H. Zore
Savage Sisters. Carter Brown
Savage Slaughter. B. Rossi
Savage Snow. W. Holt
Savage Squeeze. Arthur MacLean
Savage Streets. W. P. McGivern
Savage Streets. F. C. Miller
Savage Triangle. L. Royer

Savage Venture. W. A. Ballinger
Savage Way to Die. A. Shenton
Savage Women. Mike Curtis
Savaged. V. Burgoyne
Savannah. N. Faulkner
Savannah Purchase. J. A. Hodge
Savant's Vendetta. R. A. Freeman
Savaran and the Great Sand. D. Newton
Savarin's Shadow. R. Goyne
Save a Lady. W. Collison
Save a Rope. H. C. Bailey
Save Me from My Friends. E. F. Knight
Save the Witness. P. McGerr
Save Them for Violence. J. M. Fox
Save Your Pity. M. Hervey
Save Your Tears. Rick Madison
Saved at the Scaffold. A. F. Pinkerton
Saved by a Ruse. Nicholas Carter
Saved from the Harem. F. Du Boisgobey
Saverstall. J. Vicary
Savinelli. J. C. Molony
Saving a Rope. H. C. Bailey
Saving Clause. H. C. McNeile
Saving Face. P. Boulle
Saving of Christian Sergison. E. A. Treeton
Saving the Queen. W. F. Buckley
Saviour. H. Miller
Sawdust Angel. G. Bowman
Sawn Off. G. M. Fenn
Sawney Bean, the Man Eater of Midlothian. T. P. Prest
Saxon Ashe...Secret Agent. S. Ashe
Saxon's Ghost. S. Fisher
Say Au R'voir But Not Goodbye. M. P. Shiel
Say It with Bullets. R. Powell
Say It with Candy. H. Janson
Say It with Flowers. G. C. Foster
Say It with Flowers. G. Mitchell
Say It with Homicide. B. Diamond
Say It with Murder. Neill Graham
Say It with Murder. E. Ronns
Say It with Violence. D. Eames
Say No to Death. D. Cusack
Say Yes to Murder. W. T. Ballard
Sayle Case. T. Freeman-Hilton
Scales of Chance. H. Curties
Scales of Justice. B. Delannoy
Scales of Justice. G. L. Knapp
Scales of Justice. N. Marsh
Scales of Justice. F. M. White
Scallywag. G. Allen
Scalpel. H. McCoy
Scalps. M. Leinster
Scamp. V. Markham
Scamp Hunter. Dick Stewart
Scamp's Law. P. A. Foxall
Scandal. F. Nichols
Scandal at High Chimneys. J. D. Carr
Scandal at School. G. D. H. Cole
Scandal at Scotland Yard. B. Cobb
Scandal at the Home Office. F. A. Clement
Scandal Has Two Faces. M. E. Campbell
Scandal in Eden. G. Rogers
Scandal in the Chancery. Diplomat
Scandal-Monger. W. LeQueux
Scandal of Father Brown. G. K. Chesterton
Scandal on the Sand. J. Trinian
Scandal Point. J. Patrick
Scandal Street. W. H. Baker
Scandalize My Name. Fiona Sinclair
Scandalous Affair. Clarissa Ross
Scanner Darkly. P. K. Dick
Scapegoat. D. Du Maurier
Scapegoat. P. Orum
Scapegoat Dances. M. Benney
Scapegoats for Murder. A. Wilson
Scar. D. Vane
Scar of Crime. J. Corey
Scar on a Corpse. L. Paradise
Scar 77. G. Seton
Scarab. D. Creed
Scarab Clue. H. H. Ross
Scarab Murder Case. S. S. Van Dine
Scarabaeus. C. Lanza
Scarborough Hall. B. Upchurch
Scarborough House. S. A. Salvato
Scarborough Romance. F. Warden
Scarbrow. G. Bettany
Scare the Gentle Citizen. I. Crawford
Scarecrow. A. Fielding
Scarecrow. E. K. Goldthwaite
Scarecrow Creeps. J. Tobias
Scarecrow House. J. Hines
Scarecrow Murders. F. A. Kummer
Scarecrow Rides. R. Thordike
Scared Nymph. A. Applin
Scared Stiff. P. J. Rainier
Scared to Death. G. Bagby
Scared to Death. R. Foley
Scared to Death. A. Morice
Scarf. R. Bloch
Scarf. F. Durbridge
Scarf of Passion. R. Bloch
Scarf on the Scarecrow. M. J. Freeman
Scarface. A. Trail
Scarfaced Killer. B. Rossi
Scarhaven Keep. J. S. Fletcher

Scent of Violets

Scarlatti Inheritance. R. Ludlum
Scarlet Bat. F. Hume
Scarlet Bee. Tanjong
Scarlet Bikini. G. Croudace
Scarlet Blossoms. M. Peterson
Scarlet Button. Anthony Gilbert
Scarlet Car. R. H. Davis
Scarlet Circle. J. Stagge
Scarlet Cloak. P. Fry
Scarlet Clue. S. Hocking
Scarlet Cord. L. W. Sullivan
Scarlet Death. Roger Randall
Scarlet Fan. H. L. Gates
Scarlet Feather. H. Adams
Scarlet Feather. F. Gruber
Scarlet Feather. H. Townley
Scarlet Flower. T. Rourke
Scarlet Flush. Carter Brown
Scarlet Fortune. H. Herman
Scarlet Fountains. G. Milner
Scarlet Fox. E. H. Ball
Scarlet Gargoyle. T. F. Elstow
Scarlet Handkerchief. Le Jemlys
Scarlet Imperial. D. B. Hughes
Scarlet Imposter. D. Wheatley
Scarlet Iris. V. Thompson
Scarlet Lady. A. St. Aubyn
Scarlet Letters. E. Queen
Scarlet Lily. N. Brent
Scarlet Livery. Rupert Grayson
Scarlet Macaw. G. E. Locke
Scarlet Mask. W. E. Groves
Scarlet Mask. C. Rodda
Scarlet Messenger. H. Holt
Scarlet Night. D. S. Davis
Scarlet Runner. C. N. Williamson
Scarlet Ruse. J. D. MacDonald
Scarlet Saint. M. Sarne
Scarlet Scarab. L. C. Douthwaite
Scarlet Scarab. F. H. Mabley
Scarlet Scissors. B. Fischer
Scarlet Scourge. J. McCulley
Scarlet Scourge. Harrington Strong
Scarlet Seal. D. Donovan
Scarlet Shadow. W. Spence
"Scarlet Ship." R. C. Finney
Scarlet Sign. W. LeQueux
Scarlet Sin. A. Askew
Scarlet Sin. F. Marryat
Scarlet Sinners. D. Donovan
Scarlet Slippers. J. M. Fox
Scarlet Spade. E. K. Goldthwaite
Scarlet Spot. Dick Stewart
Scarlet Squadron. G. E. Rochester
Scarlet Starlet. D. Warren
Scarlet Surf at Makaha. P. Morgan
Scarlet Tanager. J. A. Tyson
Scarlet Thread. D. Downes
Scarlet Thread. M. P. Hood
Scarlet Thumb. J. March
Scarlet Thumb Print. G. Morton
Scarlet Tower. J. M. English
Scarlet Town. A. Askew
Scarlet Venus. C. Green
Scarlet Widow. R. Rioti
Scarlet Widow. B. Sanders
Scarlet X. H. Wickham
Scarlett Gets the Kidnapper. S. Horler
Scarlett Murder. W. Martyn
Scarlett—Special Branch. S. Horler
Scarred Chin. W. Payne
Scarred Hand. E. H. Robinson
Scarred Jungle. H. Footner
Scarred Man. Philip Daniels
Scarred Man. B. Heatter
Scarred Wrists. V. M. Steele
Scars of Dracula. Angus Hall
Scarthroat. Roland Daniel
Scarweather. A. Rolls
Scattered Death. I. Somerville
Scattergood Baines. C. B. Kelland
Scattergood Pulls the Strings. C. B. Kelland
Scattergood Returns. C. B. Kelland
Scavenger Kill. Ralph Hayes
Scavengers. B. Knox
Scavengers. Allan Nixon
Scavengers. D. O'Callaghan
Scavengers at War. C. Leader
Scenario for Murder. Dana Wilson
Send of the Sea. G. Jenkins
Scene Changing. E. Candy
Scene for Death. N. Hoult
Scene in the Ice-Blue Eyes. P. Winner
Scene of the Crime. J. Creasey
Scenes from the Show. G. R. Sims
Scenes of Crime. L. Egan
Scent from Heaven. H. Janson
Scent of Danger. E. Kyle
Scent of Danger. D. MacKenzie
Scent of Death. Morley Roberts
Scent of Fear. S. Dean
Scent of Fear. M. Yorke
Scent of Lilacs. Carolyn Wilson
Scent of Mayhem. R. T. Bickers
Scent of Mystery. K. Roos
Scent of New-Mown Hay. J. Blackburn
Scent of Roses. H. Bourne
Scent of Roses. G. Ferrand
Scent of Sandalwood. C. Colemen
Scent of the Rose. M. Peterson
Scent of Violets. R. Fabian

Scent of White Poppies. J. Christopher
Scented Danger. F. Cowen
Scented Death. A. Drummond
Scented Flesh. R. O. Saber
Schack Job. H. Kane
Schade. D. Thurlow
Schamyl, the Sultan, Warrior and Prophet of the Caucasus. T. P. Prest
Scheherazade. F. Warden
Scheme for One. A. Roberts
Schemer. W. E. Groves
Schemers. R. Fenisong
Schirmer Inheritance. E. Ambler
School for Liars. O. Norton
School for Murder. H. Carmichael
School for Murder. D. Scanlon
School for Scoundrels. A. Bracey
School on Lone Island. B. E. M. Ward
School on 103rd Street. R. S. Jefferson
Schoolboys Three. W. P. Kelly
Schooled to Kill. Dell Shannon
Schoolgirl Murder Case. Colin Wilson
Schoolmaster. W. J. Burley
Schoolmaster's Daughters. D. Eden
Schooner "Sybil". E. L. Long
Schroeder's Game. A. Maling
Schulsinger Affair. R. Temple
Schultz Money. M. Gair
Schwartz. D. C. Murray
Science Traps the Criminal. J. W. Booth
Scientific Forger. Nicholas Carter
Scientific Sprague. F. Lynde
Scientists. E. Lipsky
Scipio. T. Gates
Scissors Cut Paper. G. Fairlie
Scobie in September. B. Craig
Scoop. L. Meynell
Scorch. N. Williams
Score. R. Stark
Score for Superintendent Flagg. J. Cassells
Score for the Toff. J. Creasey
Score of Arms. R. Meade
Scornful Corpse. M. Kennedy
Scornful Man. Muriel Harris
Scorpio. S. Lawson
Scorpio. M. Roote
Scorpio 5. W. Harrington
Scorpio Letters. V. Canning
Scorpion. D. Carey
Scorpion. Mildred Davis
Scorpion. C. Hill
Scorpion. W. Penmare
Scorpion. E. A. Vizetelly
Scorpion Menace. L. Falk
Scorpion of Chateau Laverria. M. M. Fletcher
Scorpion Reef. C. Williams
Scorpion Sanction. G. Pape
Scorpion Signal. Adam Hall
Scorpion Summer. E. B. Selig
Scorpion Trap. A. Handley
Scorpion's Nest. J. Angus
Scorpion's Nest. H. McCutcheon
Scorpion's Suicide. F. Dale
Scorpion's Tale. W. Haggard
Scorpion's Trail. T. C. H. Jacobs
Scotch on the Rocks. D. Hurd
Scotland Expects. J. S. Clouston
Scotland Yard Alibi. D. Betteridge
Scotland Yard Can Wait! D. Frome
Scotland Yard: Department of Queer Complaints. Carter Dickson
Scotland Yard Experiences. G. H. Greenham
Scotland Yard Takes a Holiday. L. Allan
Scots Wha Ha'e. J. S. Clouston
Scott-Dunlap Ring. G. La Fountaine
Scottish Chieftains. H. M. Jones
Scoundrel. M. Aldanov
Scoundrel Mark. F. Dilnot
Scoundrel or Saint? G. Warden
Scoundrels & Co. C. Kernahan
Scoundrels Rampant. Nicholas Carter
Scourge. T. L. Dunne
Scourge of Damascus. S. Cobb
Scourge of the Desert. Operator 1384
Scourge of the Wizard. Nicholas Carter
Scourged by Fear. Nicholas Carter
Scout Grey—Detective. R. L. Bellamy
Scouts, Spies and Heroes of the Great Civil War. L. P. Brockett
Scouts, Spies and Detectives of the Great Civil War. L. P. Brockett
Scrambled Yeggs. O. R. Cohen
Scrambled Yeggs. D. Knight
Scrap-Metal Mystery. W. Tyrer
Scrap of Black Lace. Nicholas Carter
Scrap of Paper. H. C. McNeile
Scratch a Lover. J. G. Vermandel
Scratch a Thief. Z. Marko
Scratch a Thief. J. Trinian
Scratch on the Dark. B. Copper
Scratch on the Surface. T. Harknett
Scratch One. J. Lange
Scratchproof. M. Maguire
Scream. D. Launay
Scream and Scream Again. P. Saxon
Scream at Midnight. J. P. Brennan
Scream at Midnight. T. A. Plummer
Scream Away. Andrea Harris
Scream Bloody Murder. R. Telfair

Scream for Sarah. V. Heley
Scream in a Cave. E. Denby
Scream in Soho. J. G. Brandon
Scream in the Dark. N. Ridley
Scream in the Night. Monte Barrett
Scream in the Night. H. Desmond
Scream in the Sky. N. McCallum
Scream in the Storm. C. Farr
Scream of Murder. G. Ashe
Scream of the Doll. S. K. Wilson
Scream of the Dove. R. Charles
Scream on the Storm. C. Farr
Scream Street. Mike Brett
Screaming Bride. H. T. Teilhet
Screaming Cargo. J. M. Flynn
Screaming Dead Balloons. P. McCutchan
Screaming Fog. J. N. Chance
Screaming Gull. A. MacVicar
Screaming Mimi. F. Brown
Screaming Orchid. D. Enefer
Screaming Portrait. F. L. Fraser
Screaming Rabbit. H. Carmichael
Screaming Skull and other stories. S. Horler
Screams from a Penny Dreadful. Joan Fleming
Screen for Murder. A. Jeffers
Screen for Murder. E. C. R. Lorac
Screen Test. B. St. George
Screened. F. Wolseley
Screw Loose. Edward Lewis
Screwball King Murder. K. Platt
Scrimshaw Millions. L. Thayer
Scrope. F. B. Perkins
Scruples. T. Cobb
Sculptor's Daughter. F. Du Boisgobey
Scum in the Pot. W. A. Miller
Scutari. M. Zarubica
Scylla. Malden Grange Bishop
Sea Angel. K. Robeson
Sea Case. G. Volk
Sea Change. E. H. Clements
Sea Cliff. M. T. Hinkemeyer
Sea Could Tell. A. M. Williamson
Sea Dust. E. L. Long
Sea Fever. A. Trew
Sea Fog. J. S. Fletcher
Sea Fox. Nicholas Carter
Sea Fury. J. Pattinson
Sea Gate. J. Carey
Sea Gold. J. Remenham
Sea Gold. I. Slater
Sea Gull. J. D'Astor
Sea House. M. Summerton
Sea Jade. P. A. Whitney
Sea King's Daughter. B. Michaels
Sea Lavender. R. Gover
Sea Loot. A. D. Divine
Sea Magician. K. Robeson
Sea Monks. A. Garve
Sea Mystery. F. W. Crofts
Sea of Death. H. H. Ross
Sea of Fortune. R. Jocelyn
Sea of Troubles. Sea Lion
Sea Raiders. A. B. Sherlock
Sea Range. E. L. Long
Sea Scamps. H. C. Rowland
Sea Scrape. James Dark
Sea Shall Not Have Them. J. Harris
Sea Shroud. S. Gluck
Sea, Spray and Spindrift. Taffrail
Sea Spy. E. K. Chatterton
Sea Stalk. R. Kytle
Sea Tigers. P. Saxon
Sea Tower. K. Ostrander
Sea Trap. Nick Carter
Sea Treasure. E. Barr
Sea Trial. F. DeFelitta
Sea Troll. S. Blanc
Sea Urchin. A. Q. Roby
Sea Vengeance. R. Charles
Sea Vermin. K. Henshaw
Sea Whispers. W. W. Jacobs
Sea Wind. M. P. Dobner
Sea Wolves. M. Pemberton
Sea Wrack. R. Hitchcock
Seacliffe. J. W. De Forrest
Seacliffe. E. Noone
Seafire. B. Knox
Seaford's Snake. B. Mitford
Seagull Crag. E. Welles
Seagull Said Murder. M. Neville
Seajet Spies. N. Rich
Seal of Confession. H. A. Bulley
Seal of Death. Nicholas Carter
Seal of Silence. Nicholas Carter
Seal of Silence. A. F. Conder
Sealed Book. A. Livingstone
Sealed by a Kiss. J. Middlemass
Sealed Door. Nicholas Carter
Sealed Envelope. B. Bolt
Sealed Envelope. Lady A. Scott
Sealed Fountain. R. Roleine
Sealed Lips. S. Campbell
Sealed Lips. F. Du Boisgobey
Sealed Lips. M. Leighton
Sealed Lips. V. Yorke
Sealed Messenger. F. Hume
Sealed Orders. A. E. Carey
Sealed Orders. Nicholas Carter
Sealed Orders. R. Gover
Sealed Orders. E. J. Lysaght

Sealed Room Murder. M. Crombie
Sealed-Room Murder. R. Penny
Sealed Trunk. H. K. Webster
Sealed Valley. H. Footner
Sealed Verdict. L. L. Lynch
Sealed Verdict. L. Shapiro
Sealed with a Loving Kill. R. Ormerod
Sealed with Blood. S. Jason
Sealer. J. Wood
Seals. P. Dickinson
Seamew Abbey. F. Warden
Seance. M. McShane
Seance for Susan. L. B. Clark
Seance for the Dead. F. Hurd
Seance for Two. M. McShane
Seance on a Wet Afternoon. M. McShane
Search. M. Land
Search. R. Weverka
Search and Destroy. I. R. Blacker
Search and Destroy. J. P. Cody
Search and Destroy. Robin Moore
Search by Night. V. Lucas
Search for a Dead Nympho. P. W. Fairman
Search for a Missing Lady. Neill Graham
Search for a Motive. Dick Stewart
Search for a Scientist. C. L. Leonard
Search for a Secret. G. A. Henty
Search for a Sultan. M. Coles
Search for Basil Lyndhurst. R. N. Carey
Search for Bruno Heidler. S. Marlowe
Search for Elizabeth Brandt. W. Harrington
Search for Geoffrey Goring. David Wilson
Search for Joseph Tully. W. H. Hallahan
Search for Maggie Hare. E. Byrd
Search for Miss Sylvester. W. V. Cook
Search for My Great-Uncle's Head. P. Coffin
Search for Rita. Barry Cole
Search for Sergeant Baxter. B. Cobb
Search for Tabitha Carr. R. M. Stern
Search for the Blue Sedan. Gavin Douglas
Search for Tomorrow. E. Lindall
Search for Willie. W. D. Roberts
Search for X-Y-Z. H. S. Keeler
Search in the Dark. A. MacKenzie
Search in the Shadows. P. Warren
Search Me. C. Sodaro
Search Party. G. A. Birmingham
Search the Dark Woods. M. Land
Search the Lady. H. Duval
Search Through the Mist. L. V. Stevens
Search Warrant. J. Pattinson
Search Will Find It Out. B. Harraden
Searchers. John Foster
Searchers of the Dead. Kenneth O'Hara
Searching Spectre. S. Claudia
Searchlight on Hambledon. J. Dellbridge
Seared Hand. J. G. Rowe
Sea's Fool. F. Knight
Seaside Cafe Crime. W. Jardine
Seaside Comedy. I. Jerrold
Seaside Crime. W. Jardine
Seaside Mystery. C. B. Booth
Season for Death. A. Roudybush
Season for Murder. H. L. Nelson
Season for Violence. T. B. Dewey
Season of Assassins. G. Wagner
Season of Danger. R. Gatenby
Season of Desire. A. W. Lyons
Season of Doubt. J. Cleary
Season of Evil. Elsie Lee
Season of Evil. S. Morrow
Season of Nerves. J. Mayo
Season of Snows and Sins. P. Moyes
Season of the Falcon. C. Darby
Season of the Machete. J. Patterson
Season of the Skylark. J. T. Story
Season of the Stranger. S. Becker
Season to Be Deadly. R. Hardwick
Seasons of God. Edythe Latham
Seat of the Scornful. J. D. Carr
Seaview Manor. E. Grandower
Seaward for the Foe. H. Hill
Seaway Tombstone. K. Klein
Seawaymen. J. Wingate
Seawife. J. M. Scott
Seawitch. Alistair MacLean
Sebastian Strome. J. Hawthorne
Seclusion Room. F. Neuman
Second Baffle Book. L. Wren
Second Baronet. L. Tracy
Second Best. C. Stanton
Second Bounce. M. Cronin
Second Bout with the Mildew Gang. S. Fowler
Second Bullet. R. O. Chipperfield
Second Bullet. C. J. Dutton
Second Bullet. L. Thayer
Second Bureau. C. R. Dumas
Second Burial. A. M. Stein
Second Case of Mr. Paul Savoy. Jackson Gregory
Second Chance. P. Trent
Second Chance. E. Trevor
Second Chance. M. Woodrow
Second Class Passenger and other stories. P. Gibbon
Second Confession. R. Stout
Second Count. S. Pearson
Second Cousin Removed. S. Troy
Second Cousin Twice Removed. M. Pereira

Title Index

Second Curtain. Roy Fuller
Second Dandy Chater. T. Gallon
Second Deadly Sin. Lawrence Sanders
Second Death of Ramon Mercader. J. Semprun
Second Elopement. H. Flowerdew
Second Floor Mystery. E. D. Biggers
Second Front—First Spy. B. Newman
Second Guess. W. C. Brown
Second Guest. H. Beresford
Second-Hand Death. E. E. Sumner
Second-Hand Nude. B. Fischer
Second-Hand Tomb. R. J. White
Second House. Jan Alexander
Second-in-Command. G. Hackforth-Jones
Second in the Field. T. Cobb
Second Key. M. B. Lowndes
Second Knife. H. J. Gill
Second Lady. Irving Wallace
Second Lady Cameron. F. Thomson
Second Latchkey. C. N. Williamson
Second Life of Cecily Pride. C. Dalton
Second Longest Night. S. Marlowe
Second Love. T. W. Speight
Second Maigret Omnibus. G. Simenon
Second Mally Lee. E. Kyle
Second Man. E. Grierson
Second Mr. Carstairs. Nicholas Carter
Second Mrs. Locke. J. Cassells
Second Mrs. Lynton. W. Collison
Second Mrs. Savenage. H. W. Legett
Second Officer. Taffrail
Second Oldest Profession. W. Pinkham
Second Only to Murder. S. Box
Second Opinion. R. S. Thorn
Second Plan. C. G. Hope
Second Red Dragon. C. V. Bark
Second Romance. Elsie Lee
Second Saint Omnibus. L. Charteris
Second Seal. D. Wheatley
Second Season. Elsie Lee
Second Secret. E. Noone
Second Shot. A. Berkeley
Second Shot. L. Thayer
Second Sickle. U. Curtiss
Second Sight. C. Bartholomew
Second Sight. D. Williams
Second Storey Sinner. M. Brody
Second Storm. M. Sutherland
Second String. H. Janson
Second Stroke. F. Leslie
Second Tablet. C. E. Simon
Second Thoughts. M. Le Bas
Second Thursday. Elspeth Taylor
Second Tigress. Ganpat
Second Vanetti Affair. M. Lovell
Second Vespers. R. McInerny
Second Victory. M. L. West
Second Wager. H. R. Taunton
Seconds. D. Ely
Seconds and Thirds. E. L. Long
Secrecy. Eliza Fenwick
Secrecy at Sandhurst. C. Barry
Secrecy Essential. V. Bridges
Secrecy Street. M. Crossley
Secret. L. De Breuil
Secret. E. P. Oppenheim
Secret Adventure. O. Binns
Secret Adversary. A. Christie
Secret Agent. J. Conrad
Secret Agent. S. Horler
Secret Agent: Ashton-Kirk. J. T. MacIntyre
Secret Agent in Africa. Rupert Grayson
Secret Agent in Port Arthur. W. O. Greener
Secret Agent Number One. F. Frost
Secret Agent X-9. D. Hammett
Secret Agent X-9: Book Two. D. Hammett
Secret Agents of Brazil. Nicholas Carter
Secret Arena. E. Trevor
Secret at Jester Moor. R. Roleine
Secret at Midwinter End. M. E. Wakefield
Secret at Ravenswood. C. Farr
Secret at Sixty-Six Fathoms. S. Hope
Secret at the Abbey. A. Andre
Secret Attic. F. R. Adams
Secret Avengers. J. A. K. Curtis
Secret Barrier. C. Kingston
Secret Betrothal. D. Essex
Secret Beyond the Door. R. King
Secret Brotherhood. J. G. Brandon
Secret Brotherhood. H. Campbell
Secret Cargo. S. Esmond
Secret Cargo. J. S. Fletcher
Secret Ceremony. W. Hughes
Secret Chamber at Chad. E. Everett-Green
Secret Citadel. M. Heath
Secret Command. J. Hawkins
Secret Compact. J. B. Williams
Secret Dancer. N. Berrow
Secret Door. R. St. Clair
Secret Door. D. Vane
Secret Dragnet. B. Sanders
Secret Emerald Mines. G. H. Teed
Secret Enemy. E. O'Duffy
Secret Enemy. M. K. Robertson
Secret Enterprise. Basil Carey
Secret Errand. N. Deane
Secret Fear. A. E. W. Mason
Secret Fear. W. O'Farrell
Secret Fear. R. Underwood
Secret Files of Solar Pons. B. Copper
Secret Foe. G. Warden
Secret Formula. W. LeQueux
Secret Formula. A. Peters
Secret Formula. A. O. Pollard
Secret Fortune. M. E. Cooke
Secret Front. P. Gallico
Secret Gold. A. M. Williamson
Secret Guest Mystery. M. Welford
Secret Hand. Roland Daniel
Secret Hand. C. G. L. Du Cann
Secret Hand. S. Horler
Secret Hand. D. Valentine
Secret Harbour. S. A. White
Secret Heart. E. Shenkin
Secret History of Today. A. Upward
Secret: Hong Kong. F. M. Davis
Secret Hour. M. Richmond
Secret House. E. Wallace
Secret House of Death. R. Rendell
Secret in Seven Fathoms. M. Frazer
Secret in the Hill. B. Capes
Secret in the Sky. K. Robeson
Secret Information. R. Hichens
Secret Inheritance. B. L. Farjeon
Secret Inquest. A. Blair
Secret Inquiry. B. Cobb
Secret Isaac. J. Charyn
Secret Island. J. Fores
Secret Journal of Charles Dunbar. J. Maconechy
Secret Journey. R. Kirkbridge
Secret Judges. F. Grierson
Secret Kingdom. F. Richardson
Secret Life of Algernon Pendleton. R. H. Greenan
Secret Life of Mr. Beauty. G. Kay
Secret Life of the Ex-Tsaritza. W. LeQueux
Secret List of Heinrich Roehm. M. Barak
Secret Listeners. L. Goldman
Secret Listeners of the East. D. G. Mukerji
Secret Lover. E. Nepean
Secret Lovers. C. McCarry
Secret Loving Shadows. M. E. Atkins
Secret Marriage. A. W. Barrett
Secret Masters. G. Kersh
Secret Meeting. J. Rhode
Secret Melody. P. Minton
Secret Menace. Wilfred Barclay
Secret Millionaire. H. H. C. Gibbons
Secret Ministry. D. Cory
Secret Mission. F. S. Smythe
Secret Mission: Angola. Don Smith
Secret Mission: Athens. Don Smith
Secret Mission: Cairo. Don Smith
Secret Mission: Corsica. Don Smith
Secret Mission: Istanbul. Don Smith
Secret Mission: Morocco. Don Smith
Secret Mission: Munich. Don Smith
Secret Mission: North Korea. Don Smith
Secret Mission of Colonel Death. J. Rapier
Secret Mission: Peking. Don Smith
Secret Mission: Prague. Don Smith
Secret Mission: The Kremlin Plot. Don Smith
Secret Mission: Tibet. Don Smith
Secret Mission to Bangkok. V. W. Mason
Secret Mountains. J. Appleby
Secret Murder. G. Ashe
Secret Oath. Anonymous
Secret of a Letter. G. Warden
Secret of Ashton Manor House. E. Kerr
Secret of Awen Castle. F. Hurd
Secret of Ayanora. Basil Carey
Secret of Barnabas Collins. Marilyn Ross
Secret of Baron's Folly. H. M. Webster
Secret of Belledonne Room 16. A. DeVries
Secret of Benjamin Square. J. Plum
Secret of Berry Pomeroy. F. Whishaw
Secret of Bogey House. H. Adams
Secret of Canfield House. F. Hurd
Secret of Capri. W. Jardine
Secret of Castle Ferrara. C. Farr
Secret of Castle Voxzel. A. O. Pollard
Secret of Chateau Kendall. S. Richard
Secret of Chateau Laval. S. Marvin
Secret of Chauville. D. Whitelaw
Secret of Chimneys. A. Christie
Secret of Devil's Cave. Jennifer Hale
Secret of Draker's Folly. A. Murray
Secret of Dresden Farm. Genevieve St. John
Secret of Elizabeth. V. Caspary
Secret of Enoch Seal. J. B. Harris-Burland
Secret of Father Brown. G. K. Chesterton
Secret of Ferrars. R. Matheson
Secret of Fire 5. J. Olsen
Secret of Frontellac. F. K. Scribner
Secret of Gaunt House. F. H. Dimmock
Secret of Giltman Hall. J. Cheyney
Secret of Gnome Head. B. Strong
Secret of Graytowers. E. Randolph
Secret of Greylands. A. Haynes
Secret of Harbor House. Claudette Nicole
Secret of Haverly House. C. Bauman
Secret of Hayworth Hall. F. Hurd
Secret of Hedges Hall. Lynn Williams
Secret of High Eldersham. M. Burton
Secret of Holm Peel and other strange stories. S. Rohmer
Secret of Kensington Manor. Genevieve St. John
Secret of Killer Mountain Inn. K. Brooks
Secret of Kyriels. E. Nesbit
Secret of Lonesome Cove. S. H. Adams
Secret of Lucifer's Island. M. Lynch
Secret of Lynndale. F. Warden
Secret of MI6. L. Smith
Secret of Mallet Castle. Clarissa Ross
Secret of Marly Stones. D. Kamm
Secret of Matchams. N. Burnaby
Secret of Maxshelling. E. Everett-Green
Secret of Mirror House. Patrica Maxwell
Secret of Mohawk Pond. N. S. Lincoln
Secret of Monk's House. Rachelle Edwards
Secret of Moor House. Donald Stuart
Secret of Musterton House. G. Granby
Secret of Oil Creek. A. Parsons
Secret of Providence Lodge. R. E. Salwey
Secret of Quarry House. C. Lorrimer
Secret of Room No. 13. C. E. Pearce
Secret of Saint Florel. J. Berwick
Secret of Sam Barlow. A. J. Fenady
Secret of Saraband. M. Floyd
Secret of Saramount. L. Cheatham
Secret of Sarek. M. Leblanc
Secret of Scotland Yard. A. E. Bayly
Secret of Sea-Dream House. A. P. Terhune
Secret of Secrets. J. S. Fletcher
Secret of Seven. Donald Stuart
Secret of Seven Oaks. J. Coulson
Secret of Sheen. J. Laurence
Secret of Shower Tree. V. Coffman
Secret of Simon Cornell. H. Howard
Secret of Sir George Hartley. A. M. Diehl
Secret of Skye. A. S. Swan
Secret of Stark Island. Colin Desmond
Secret of Stillwater Mere. G. Chester
Secret of Strangeways. Joyce Bentley
Secret of Superintendent Manning. B. Cobb
Secret of Sylvia. Lee Borden
Secret of Tangles. L. Gribble
Secret of Tarn-End House. C. Randell
Secret of the African Settler. R. Hardinge
Secret of the African Trader. R. Hardinge
Secret of the Armamanets King. P. Quiroule
Secret of the Ashes. A. Ornstien
Secret of the Balkan Heiress. C. Brisbane
Secret of the Baltic. T. C. Bridges
Secret of the Barbican. J. S. Fletcher
Secret of the Bayou. F. Davenport
Secret of the Black Mere. Anonymous
Secret of the Black Wallet. W. W. Sayer
Secret of the Blue Macaw. I. L. Forrester
Secret of the Blue Vase. H. Tuite
Secret of the Bucket Shop. G. Jones
Secret of the Bungalow. R. J. Casey
Secret of the Burma Road. A. Parsons
Secret of the Carpathians. H. H. C. Gibbons
Secret of the Cask. R. C. Armour
Secret of the Castle Ruins. A. Parsons
Secret of the Cavern. Mrs. Burke
Secret of the Cellar. W. Edwards
Secret of the Chateau. C. Farr
Secret of the Chateau Leval. S. Richard
Secret of the Chinese Jar. F. Hume
Secret of the Circle. P. Quiroule
Secret of the Coconut Groves. G. H. Teed
Secret of the Cove. H. L. Deakin
Secret of the Creek. V. Bridges
Secret of the Dark Room. R. J. Casey
Secret of the Dead. L. T. Meade
Secret of the Dead. I. Stark
Secret of the Dead Convict. M. B. Dix
Secret of the Dead Man. P. Urquhart
Secret of the Demolition Worker. J. Hunter
Secret of the Dental Surgeon. R. Hardinge
Secret of the Desert. R. Hardinge
Secret of the Diamond. E. D. Pierson
Secret of the Diamonds. C. W. Greatorex
Secret of the Doubting Saint. L. Holton
Secret of the Downs. W. S. Masterman
Secret of the Evacuee. P. Marchant
Secret of the Everglades. B. Marchant
Secret of the Farm. G. Chester
Secret of the Fated Family. R. Hardinge
Secret of the Flames. W. M. Graydon
Secret of the Flames. R. Rodd
Secret of the Frozen North. W. W. Sayer
Secret of the Garden. A. Gask
Secret of the Ghostly Shroud. N. Buckingham
Secret of the Glacier. W. Jardine
Secret of the Glacier. A. Murray
Secret of the Glen. C. Brisbane
Secret of the Gold Locket. R. C. Armour
Secret of the Golden Horse. A. Parsons
Secret of the Grange. Mark Cross
Secret of the Grave. J. Hunter

Secret of the Graveyard. J. Addiscombe
Secret of the Green Lagoon. A. Murray
Secret of the Hills. W. Garrett
Secret of the Hold. J. Hunter
Secret of the Hulk. A. Murray
Secret of the Hulk. Donald Stuart
Secret of the Hunger Desert. A. Murray
Secret of the Identification Parade. W. Edwards
Secret of the Indian Lawyer. A. Parsons
Secret of the Jungle. R. Hardinge
Secret of the Jungle. G. Rees
Secret of the Lagoon. R. C. Armour
Secret of the Lake House. J. Rhode
Secret of the Lebombo. B. Mitford
Secret of the Little Flea. B. Munslow
Secret of the Little Gods. K. H. Taylor
Secret of the Living Skeleton. J. Drummond
Secret of the Loch. C. Brisbane
Secret of the Locket. E. St. Clair
Secret of the Man Who Died. R. Hardinge
Secret of the Mansions. W. J. Bayfield
Secret of the Marble Mantle. Nicholas Carter
Secret of the Marionettes. E. D. Pierson
Secret of the Marsh. O. Warner
Secret of the Marshbanks. K. Norris
Secret of the Marshes. M. Richmond
Secret of the Mere. D. Peacock
Secret of the Mere. J. J. Wray
Secret of the Midway Plaza. A. E. Dramond
Secret of the Mine. A. Steffens Hardy
Secret of the Missing Checks. H. Rockwood
Secret of the Moat. H. Desmond
Secret of the Monastery. S. G. Shaw
Secret of the Moor. M. Gerard
Secret of the Moor Cottage. H. R. Cromarsh
Secret of the Morgue. F. G. Eberhard
Secret of the Moroccan Bazaar. A. Parsons
Secret of the Night. G. Leroux
Secret of the Oblong Chest. W. W. Sayer
Secret of the Old Lighthouse. J. G. Rowe
Secret of the Pale Lover. Clarissa Ross
Secret of the Past. W. M. Graydon
Secret of the President's Daughter. G. H. Teed
Secret of the Priory. S. O. Bryan
Secret of the Priory. M. Richmond
Secret of the Raft. H. Townley
Secret of the Red Mountain. W. W. Sayer
Secret of the River. Dora Russell
Secret of the Roman Temple. A. Parsons
Secret of the Russian Refugees. W. M. Graydon
Secret of the Safe. A. Edgar
Secret of the Sale Room. R. Hardinge
Secret of the Saltings. V. Bridges
Secret of the Sanatorium. C. Brisbane
Secret of the Sandbanks. J. Plain
Secret of the Sandhills. A. Gask
Secret of the Sandhills. F. Marlowe
Secret of the Sands. W. Tyrer
Secret of the Sands. M. F. White
Secret of the Sapphire Ring. M. V. Woodgate
Secret of the Scarlet Bomber. P. Conde
Secret of the Screen. S. Fowler
Secret of the Sea. W. Allison
Secret of the Sea. C. M. Parsons
Secret of the Sea. T. W. Speight
Secret of the Sealed Room. Donald Stuart
Secret of the Second Door. R. Colby
Secret of the Seven Sisters. John Marsh
Secret of the Seven Spiders. G. Stanley
Secret of the Sheba. R. Hardinge
Secret of the Siding. J. Brooke
Secret of the Siegfried Line. M. B. Dix
Secret of the Silver Car. W. Martyn
Secret of the Six Black Dots. W. W. Sayer
Secret of the Sixty Steps. J. Drummond
Secret of the Smuggler's Cove. R. Hardinge
Secret of the Snows. G. Chester
Secret of the Snows. H. H. C. Gibbons
Secret of the Snows. J. Plain
Secret of the Snows. W. Tyrer
Secret of the Spa. C. L. Leonard
Secret of the Spectre's Nest. W. E. Groves
Secret of the Sphinx. H. Carew
Secret of the Square. W. LeQueux
Secret of the Stage. N. Ridley
Secret of the Stargazer's Club. Jack Carew
Secret of the Steps. G. Chester
Secret of the Storm County. Grace M. White
Secret of the Strong Room. G. H. Teed
Secret of the Sudan. W. Jardine
Secret of the Suez Canal. G. Rees
Secret of the Sunken Ships. G. Chester
Secret of the Surgery. J. W. Bobin
Secret of the Surgery. W. Jardine
Secret of the Swamp. G. Bettany
Secret of the Swinging Room. E. M. Robinson

Secret of the Ten Bales. A. Parsons
Secret of the Thieves' Kitchen. G. H. Teed
Secret of the Tomb. W. J. Bayfield
Secret of the Tong. A. Edgar
Secret of the Tower. Anthony Hope
Secret of the Two Blackmailed Men. W. M. Graydon
Secret of the Vampire Actress. W. M. Graydon
Secret of the Vault. G. Verner
Secret of the Veld. R. Hardinge
Secret of the Villa Como. S. Marvin
Secret of the Vineyard. M. Heath
Secret of the Weeping Monk. B. McMikle
Secret of the White Thug. R. Francis Foster
Secret of the Willows. Elna Stone
Secret of the Woods. P. Quiroule
Secret of the Zodiac. J. Sterne
Secret of Thirty-Seven Hardy Street. R. J. Casey
Secret of Thirty Years! W. W. Sayer
Secret of Thurlston Towers. L. H. Brooks
Secret of Torre Island. R. C. Armour
Secret of Trescobell. J. Hocking
Secret of Tso Feng. L. C. Douthwaite
Secret of Villa Vanesta. E. Glen
Secret of Wardale Court and other stories. Andree Hope
Secret of Weir House. F. Cowen
Secret of Wold Hall. E. Everett-Green
Secret of Wyvern Towers. T. W. Speight
Secret Orchards. Michael Burt
Secret Pact. A. O. Pollard
Secret Panel. Nicholas Carter
Secret Panel. A. S. Swan
Secret Paper. W. Wood
Secret Passage. F. Hume
Secret Pathway. A. Askew
Secret Pearls. O. Binns
Secret People. H. H. C. Gibbons
Secret Pilot. G. E. Rochester
Secret Place. J. P. Barter
Secret Police. John Lang
Secret Power. T. C. H. Jacobs
Secret Power. V. Van Der Elst
Secret Quest. G. M. Fenn
Secret Road. J. Ferguson
Secret Room of Morgate House. E. Grandower
Secret Sceptre. F. Gerard
Secret Sea-Plane. G. Thorne
Secret Search. E. R. Punshon
Secret Sentence. V. Baum
Secret Servant. G. Lyall
Secret Servant. B. Newman
Secret Service. C. T. Brady
Secret Service. A. Forrester
Secret Service. W. Gillette
Secret Service. W. LeQueux
Secret Service. P. Sebastian
Secret Service Girl. Roland Daniel
Secret Service Girl. J. M. Walsh
Secret Service Man. G. Dilnot
Secret Service Man. S. Horler
Secret Service Mystery. H. Pink
Secret Service Operator 13. R. W. Chambers
Secret Service Ship. C. E. Averill
Secret Service Smith. R. T. M. Scott
Secret Service Submarine. G. Thorne
Secret Service Woman. H. De Halsalle
Secret Services. G. Frankau
Secret Session. H. Janson
Secret Shame of the Kaiser. W. LeQueux
Secret Ship. E. K. Chatterton
Secret Sin. W. LeQueux
Secret Singing. Roy Lewis
Secret Sinners. B. McKnight
Secret Sister. A. Applin
Secret Six. F. Marion
Secret Society. D. Onyeama
Secret Soldier. J. Quigley
Secret Spring. P. Benoit
Secret Squadron in Germany. G. E. Rochester
Secret Square. E. Jepson
Secret Super-Charger. P. Gill
Secret Suspicion. M. O. Rolfe
Secret Syndicate. R. C. Frazer
Secret Syndicate. F. Whishaw
Secret Telephone. W. LeQueux
Secret Temple. C. Brisbane
Secret Tent. E. Addyman
Secret Terror. F. Hird
Secret That Was Kept. E. Robins
Secret Thread. E. Vance
Secret Toll. P. Thorne
Secret Tomb. M. Leblanc
Secret Tontine. R. M. Gilchrist
Secret Traffic. B. Tozer
Secret Trail. A. Armstrong
Secret Tunnel. R. C. Finney
Secret Understanding. Merle Miller
Secret Valley. Elliot Bailey
Secret Vanguard. M. Innes
Secret Vendetta. A. O. Pollard
Secret Voice. H. Desmond
Secret Voyage. Basil Carey
Secret War. N. Daniels
Secret War. D. Wheatley

Secret Way. J. S. Fletcher
Secret Ways. Alistair MacLean
Secret Ways. A. Soutar
Secret Weapon. F. Beeding
Secret Weapon. B. Newman
Secret Weapons. J. M. Walsh
Secret Witness. G. F. Gibbs
Secret Woman. V. Holt
Secretary. Anonymous
Secretary of Frivolous Affairs. M. Futrelle
Secretary of State for Death. H. Carstairs
Secrets. F. L. Bailey
Secrets. B. Hirschfeld
Secrets. J. R. Lowell
Secrets. S. Wagner
Secrets Can Be Fatal. M. Heath
Secrets Can't Be Kept. E. R. Punshon
Secrets for Sale. C. L. Leonard
Secrets for Sale. J. H. Vahey
Secrets of a Dark Plot in New York Society. A. S. Manly
Secrets of a Private Enquiry Office. Mrs. G. Corbett
Secrets of a Private Enquiry Office. J. Peddie
Secrets of Cromwell Crossing. D. Winston
Secrets of Dr. Taverner. D. Fortune
Secrets of Hillyard House. K. Norris
Secrets of Monte Carlo. W. LeQueux
Secrets of Potsdam. W. LeQueux
Secrets of Sedbury Manor. Marilyn Ross
Secrets of the Coast. S. Cobb
Secrets of the Courts of Europe. A. Upward
Secrets of the Dead-Letter Office. B. Hemyng
Secrets of the Foreign Office. W. LeQueux
Secrets of the Police. Grace M. White
Secrets of the River. B. Hemyng
Secrets of the Turf. B. Hemyng
Secrets of the White Tsar. W. LeQueux
Section 558. J. Hawthorne
Security Risk. G. Hackforth-Jones
Security Risk. T. C. H. Jacobs
Security Secrets Sold Here. B. Cobb
Sedan Murder Mystery. J. Wallace
Sedona. J. Farmer
Seduce and Destroy. J. Eastwood
Seducer. F. Flora
Seduction of a Tall Man. R. Gadney
Seductress. Carter Brown
Sedulous Ape. D. Batchelor
See How They Run. W. M. Green
See How They Run. A. Kennington
See How They Run. D. M. Mankiewicz
See It Again, Sam. Carter Brown
See Naples and Die. John Davies
See Naples and Die. J. Nathenson
See No Evil. W. Hughes
See No Evil. F. McDermid
See Nothing—Say Nothing. P. Carlon
See Rome and Die. L. Revell
See the Kid Run. B. Ottum
See the Living Crocodiles. C. V. Bark
See the Red Blood Run. N. N. Peebles
"See the Woman." D. Barnes
See Them Die. E. McBain
See Who's Dying. S. H. Courtier
See You at the Morgue. L. G. Blochman
Seed of Doubt. D. Keene
Seed of Empire. F. M. White
Seed of Envy. J. Remenham
Seed of Evil. P. Crawford
Seed of the Falcon. C. Darby
Seed of Violence. Williams Forrest
Seed Was Kind. D. Macardle
Seedbreakers. P. V. Timlett
Seeds of Destruction. J. Knowler
Seeds of Destruction. R. V. Beste
Seeds of Destruction. J. Griffin
Seeds of Destruction. D. Nabarro
Seeds of Doom. Ralph Hayes
Seeds of Hate. H. Carmichael
Seeds of Murder. V. W. Mason
Seeds of Murder. J. York
Seeds of Suspicion. J. McGreevey
Seeds of Suspicion. J. Roffman
Seeds of Violence. M. Sharman
Seeing. W. P. McGivern
Seeing Double. E. Ferrars
Seeing Eye. Josephine Bell
Seeing Is Believing. Carter Dickson
Seeing Life. E. P. Oppenheim
Seeing Red. T. Du Bois
Seek and Destroy. Ray Owen
Seek and Destroy. M. K. Robertson
Seek, Strike and Destroy. K. Stanton
Seeker to the Dead. A. M. Burrage
Seen and the Unseen. R. Marsh
Seen Dimly Before Dawn. N. Balchin
Seen in the Shadow. F. Hume
Seeress. G. B. Lissenden
Seersucker Whipsaw. Ross Thomas
Seidlitz and the Super-Spy. Carter Brown
Seine Fishers. J. Wood
Seine Mystery. C. Moffett
Seize a Passing Stranger. C. Joyce
Seizing of Singapore. I. Stewart
Selected Plays. Lady Gregory

Title Index

Self-Appointed Saint. A. E. Lindop
Self-Convicted. H. Wood
Self-Doomed. J. L. Farjeon
Self-Made. E. Southworth
Self-Made Thief. H. Footner
Self-Made Widow. P. Race
Self-Portrait of Murder. F. Bonnamy
Self-Raised. E. Southworth
Selicombe Murder. N. Islay
Sellers of Death. W. W. Sayer
Selling's Murder! A. Tack
Sellout. D. Jewell
Selmin of Selmingfold. B. Mitford
Selminster Murders. C. Ryland
Selsey Gold. H. C. Davis
Semi-Society. F. Richardson
Seminar in Evil. D. Winston
Semonov Impulse. J. Meldrum
Semper Inheritance. C. Carfax
Sempinski Affair. W. S. Kuniczak
Senator's Nude. B. Goode
Senator's Plot. Nicholas Carter
Senator's Ransom. K. Bernstein
Send Another Coffin. J. Grecco
Send Another Coffin. F. G. Presnell
Send Another Hearse. H. Q. Masur
Send Danger. M. Sutherland
Send for Angel. G. Montrose
Send for Mr. Robinson. J. M. White
Send for Paul Temple. F. Durbridge
Send for Paul Temple Again! F. Durbridge
Send for the Saint. L. Charteris
Send Him Victorious. D. Hurd
Send Inspector West. J. Creasey
Send No Flowers. Gavin Holt
Send No More Roses. E. Ambler
Send-Off. R. Hiscock
Send-Off. C. Leach
Send Superintendent West. J. Creasey
Sending. G. Household
Seneca, U.S.A. J. Roeburt
Senor Saint. L. Charteris
Sensation at Blue Harbour. J. L. Rickard
Sensational Case. F. Warden
Sensational Tales. S. Clarke
Sensational Trance. F. Dawson
Sense of Danger. E. Cannon
Sense of Guilt. G. Simenon
Sense of Reality. G. Greene
Sense of Survival. K. Casey
Sensitive Encounter. Canella Lewis
Sensualists. B. Hecht
Sent to His Account. E. Dillon
Sentence Deferred. A. Derleth
Sentence for Sin. H. Janson
Sentence of Death. J. York
Sentence of Life. Julian Gloag
Sentence of the Court. H. Hill
Sentence of the Court. F. M. White
Sentence of the Judge. H. E. Barlow
Sentence of the Six-Gun. A. M. Rud
Sentence Suspended. C. Joyce
Sentenced! S. Gibney
Sentenced to Death. R. Machray
Sentenced to Life. M. A. Hamilton
Sentiment, and other stories. V. O'Sullivan
Sentimental Crook. A. Wilson
Sentimental Kill. R. Clapperton
Sentimental Season. T. Cobb
Sentimental Series. G. Warden
Sentimental Spy. A. C. Ley
Sentimental Warrior. E. Jepson
Sentinel. J. Konvitz
Sentinel Point. N. Dorer
Sentries. E. McBain
Sentry-Box Murder. N. Gayle
September Can Be Dangerous in Edinburgh. B. Craig
September Comes In. F. M. McGuire
September September. S. Foote
September Story. R. Inchbald
Septimus and the Danedyke Mystery. Stephen Chance
Septimus and the Minister Ghost. Stephen Chance
Septimus and the Minister Ghost Mystery. Stephen Chance
Septimus and the Spy Ring. Stephen Chance
Septimus and the Stone of Offering. Stephen Chance
Sequel to Opposite the Jail. M. A. Denison
Sequel to Yesterday. P. A. Foxall
Sequin Syndicate. O. Hesky
Sequins Lost Their Lustre. S. Harvester
Serbian Assignment. Andrew Moore
Serena. J. Aeby
Serena. J. Fitzpatrick
Serenade. J. M. Cain
Serenade for a Shylock. A. Zeiger
Serenade for Murder. A. Wood
Serenade to the Hangman. M. Dekobra
Sergeant and the Queen. R. Crane
Sergeant Cluff and the Day of Reckoning. G. North
Sergeant Cluff and the Madmen. G. North
Sergeant Cluff and the Price of Pity. G. North
Sergeant Cluff Goes Fishing. G. North
Sergeant Cluff Rings True. G. North

Sergeant Cluff Stands Firm. G. North
Sgt. Corbin's War. R. Crane
Sergeant Cork's Casebook. A. Swinson
Sergeant Cork's Second Casebook. A. Swinson
Sergeant Death. D. G. Browne
Sergeant Death. F. P. Grady
Sergeant Death. J. Mayo
Sergeant Gray's Crime. J. Hunter
Sgt. Hawk. P. Clay
Sergeant Lancey Carries On. L. P. Greene
Sergeant Lancey Reports. L. P. Greene
Sergeant Lancey Tells the Tale. L. P. Greene
Sergeant Michael Cassidy, R. E. H. C. McNeile
Sergeant Ritchie's Conscience. F. Branston
Sergeant Ross in Disguise. B. Cobb
Sergeant Sir Peter. E. Wallace
Sergeant Verity and the Blood Royal. F. Selwyn
Sergeant Verity and the Cracksman. F. Selwyn
Sergeant Verity and the Imperial Diamond. F. Selwyn
Sergeant Verity and the Swell Mob. F. Selwyn
Sergeant Verity Presents His Compliments. F. Selwyn
Sergeant Von. Anonymous
Serious Investigation. L. Egan
Serle's Secret. F. Warden
Sern Charter. F. Ryck
Serpent-Headed Stick. J. Hawk
Serpent Heart. M. A. Taylor
Serpent in the Shadows. A. Barron
Serpent of Lilith. M. Villiers
Serpent Sleeping. E. Weismuller
Serpent Stirs. Richard Grant
Serpent Under It. E. Taylor
Serpentine Murder. L. Gribble
Serpent's Egg. D. Duncan
Serpent's Fang. Brian Stuart
Serpent's Smile. O. Hesky
Serpent's Tooth. S. Nichols
Serpent's Tooth. Sara Woods
Servant of Death. J. H. Wallis
Servant of Satan. L. Berard
Servant of the King. A. Griffin
Servants of the Goddess. H. Campbell
Servants of the Skull. B. House
Servant's Problem. V. P. Johns
Service of All the Dead. C. Dexter
Set. Gwen Davis
Set a Spy. M. McKenna
Set a Thief. E. E. Paramore
Set a Thief. L. Thayer
Set a Trap. E. G. Love
Set of Flats. A. Griffiths
Set of Rogues. F. Barrett
Set of Six. J. Conrad
Set to Partners. G. Warden
Set-Up. J. K. Baxter
Set-Up. R. Carni
Set-Up. L. Corradi
Set-Up. M. Franklin
Set-Up. E. G. Love
Set-Up. B. E. Miller
Set-Up. Robin Moore
Set Up for Danger. Rick Madison
Set-Up for Murder. P. Cheyney
Seth Bond. Old Sleuth
Seth Papers. F. Lauria
Settled Out of Court. H. Cecil
Settled Out of Court. R. A. Knox
Settler or Slaver. A. Murray
Settling of Accounts. C. G. Hart
Setup for Murder. L. A. Olmsted
Seven. J. D. MacDonald
Seven Against Greece. Nick Carter
Seven Agate Devils. K. Robeson
Seven Black Chessmen. J. Huntingdon
Seven Bloodhounds. M. Richmond
Seven Blue Diamonds. C. B. Stilson
Seven Chose Murder. Roy Vickers
Seven Clues. G. Verner
Seven Clues in Search of a Crime. B. Graeme
Seven Conundrums. E. P. Oppenheim
Seven Dawns to Death. B. Gray
Seven Day Soldiers. T. Kenrick
Seven Days Before Dying. H. Nielsen
Seven Days for Hanging. J. M. Spender
Seven Days from Midnight. Rona Randall
Seven Days' Hard. S. M. Parkman
Seven Days in a Pullman Car. A. Towner
Seven Days in May. F. Knebel
Seven Day's Mystery. F. R. Burton
Seven Days' Secret. J. S. Fletcher
Seven Days to a Killing. C. Egleton
Seven Days to Death. N. MacKenzie
Seven Days to Death. J. J. Marric
Seven Days to Disaster. Jonas Flagg
Seven Days to Never. F. Frank
Seven Dead. J. J. Farjeon
Seven Deadly Sisters. P. McGerr
Seven Dials Mystery. A. Christie
Seven Died. G. Homes
711—Officer Needs Help. W. Masterson
Seven Elms Mystery. H. B. Harris
Seven File. W. P. McGivern

Seven Footprints to Satan. A. Merritt
Seven Games in October. Charles Brady
Seven Gates to Nowhere. T. Willis
Seven Green Stones. P. Wentworth
Seven Guests of Fear. I. Barry
Seven Hells. C. Brooks
Seven Keys to Baldpate. E. D. Biggers
Seven Keys to Baldpate. G. M. Cohan
Seven Lamps. G. Verner
Seven Lean Years. C. Fremlin
Seven Lies South. W. P. McGivern
Seven Looked On. B. Malim
Seven Men. T. Roscoe
Seven Men Are Murdered. R. Wallace
Seven Minutes Past Midnight. W. Winward
7 Murders. R. H. May
7 Must Die. J. W. Bellah
Seven Nights at the Resort. D. Enefer
Seven of Hearts. M. Leblanc
Seven of Swords. R. E. Harrington
Seven-Per-Cent Solution. N. Meyer
Seven Pillars to Hell. H. Marlowe
Seven Red-Headed Men. H. Marlowe
Seven Red Herrings. E. P. Thorne
Seven Saints. G. Stanley
Seven Schemers. Nicholas Carter
Seven Screens. G. Dickson
Seven Seas Murders. V. W. Mason
Seven Seats to the Moon. C. Armstrong
Seven Secrets. W. LeQueux
Seven Shadows. G. Stanley
Seven Sins. S. Rohmer
Seven Sirens. Carter Brown
Seven Sisters. W. T. Ballard
Seven Sisters. R. Chapman
Seven Sisters. J. Lilly
Seven Slayers. P. Cain
Seven Sleepers. F. Beeding
Seven Sleepers. E. Ferrars
Seven Sons. A. Simon
Seven Sons of Mammon. G. A. Sala
Seven Stabs. J. Cameron
Seven Stars. V. Bridges
Seven Steps East. B. Benson
Seven Suspects. M. Innes
Seven Suspects. F. Ryerson
Seven Tears for Apollo. P. A. Whitney
7:30 Victoria. P. McGuire
Seven Thunders. R. Croft-Cooke
Seven Thunders. M. M. Lawrence
Seven Tickets to Singapore. Ared White
Seven Times Seven. J. Creasey
Seven to Die. H. Long
7 to 12. A. K. Green
Seven-Ups. R. Posner
Seven Votes for Death. P. Bannister
Seven Were Suspect. R. Goyne
Seven Were Suspect. K. M. Knight
Seven Were Veiled. K. M. Knight
Seven Who Waited. A. Derleth
Seven Women. Winifred Duke
Seven Year Friend. D. Huxley
Seven Year Secret. F. Hurt
Seven Years Dead. S. Truss
17 and Black. J. Waer
17 Ben Gurion. J. Hoffenberg
Seventeen Cards. E. C. Vivian
Seventeen Moments of Spring. J. Semenov
Seventeen Thieves of El-Kabil. T. Mundy
Seventeen Widows of Sans Souci. C. Armstrong
17th Letter. D. C. Disney
Seventeenth Stair. P. Paul
Seventh. R. Stark
Seventh All Hallows' Eve. R. Jensen
Seventh Chasm. O. Gard
Seventh Entanglement. E. Leslie
Seventh Fury. J. Castle
Seventh Game. D. Kowet
Seventh Hexagram. I. McLachlan
Seventh Juror. F. Didelot
Seventh Man. Wilson Barclay
Seventh Man. J. Scotland
Seventh Mask. H. Slesar
Seventh Mourner. D. Gardiner
Seventh Passenger. P. Capon
Seventh Passenger. A. MacGowan
Seventh Postcard. H. Flowerdew
Seventh Power. James Mills
Seventh Sense. H. R. Thompson
Seventh Shot. H. Coverdale
Seventh Sign. B. Flynn
Seventh Sinner. Elizabeth Peters
Seventh Station. R. McInerny
Seventh Vial. F. Sleath
Seventh Wife of Prince Hasson. M. Dekobra
Seventy Fathom Treasure. A. D. Divine
Seventy North—70°N. Taffrail
71 Hours. M. Mason
77, Park Lane. W. Hackett
77 Rue Paradis. G. Brewer
77 Sunset Strip. R. Huggins
77 Willow Road. H. D. Irvine
77th Day. H. Possendorf
70 Sutton Place. J. Di Mona
70,000 Witnesses. C. Fitzsimmons
Severed Hand. F. Du Boisgobey
Severed Hand. E. Lecale
Severed Hand. M. Serao
Severed Key. H. Nielsen
Severence. T. Cobb

Severing Line. S. Cardiff
Severith Style. D. Honig
Severn Affair. G. Warden
Sevier Secrets. D. Daniels
Seward's Folly. G. Lancaster
Sex Angle. H. Janson
Sex Castle. E. Lacy
Sex Clinic. Carter Brown
Sex Life. B. Cook
Sex Marks the Spot. S. Browning
Sex Trap. Carter Brown
Sex Trap. Bill Turner
Sex War. S. Merwin, Jr.
Sexless Spy. T. Hoyle
Sexton Blake and the Demon God. J. Garforth
Sexton Blake in Silesia. W. M. Graydon
Sexton Blake—Special Constable. J. W. Bobin
Sexton Blake's Vow. A. Steffens Hardy
Sexton Woman. R. Neely
Sexy Vixen. H. Janson
Shabby Eagles. B. Gaston
Shack-Up. A. Curry
Shackled. M. Crossley
Shackleton Called Sheila. D. Mariner
Shade Against the Sun. F. Greenland
Shade of Darkness. M. Torrie
Shade of Time. D. Duncan
Shades and Shadows. L. Churchill
Shades of Evil. S. Wagner
Shades of Gray. M. Denning
Shades of Greene. G. Greene
Shades of Peril. M. Cordell
Shadow. H. Bedford-Jones
Shadow. W. B. Gibson
Shadow. V. Kelly
Shadow. M. Level
Shadow. P. Mason
Shadow. A. Stringer
Shadow. Donald Stuart
Shadow. P. Urquhart
Shadow Acres. F. Y. McHugh
Shadow Agent. W. Martyn
Shadow, and other stories. J. Farnol
Shadow and the Blot. N. D. Lobell
Shadow and the Fear. J. Corby
Shadow and the Stone. L. Meynell
Shadow and the Web. Mary Allerton
Shadow at Dunston Hall. E. Desmond
Shadow Before. L. P. Davies
Shadow Before. W. Rollins
Shadow Behind. F. Warwick
Shadow Behind the Throne. O. Harper
Shadow Between. R. Pattison
Shadow Beware. M. Grant
Shadow Box. V. Coffman
Shadow Buttress. S. Styles
Shadow Called Janet. J. N. Chance
Shadow Crook. A. De Brune
Shadow Crook. G. H. Teed
Shadow Crusade. W. Mills
Shadow—Destination Moon. M. Grant
Shadow Detective. Old Sleuth
Shadow 81. L. Nahum
Shadow Falls. C. Lorrimer
Shadow Falls. G. Simenon
Shadow for a Lady. J. L. Linklater
Shadow from the Bogue. Clement Wood
Shadow from the Past. F. S. Gabbert
Shadow Game. D. Kamm
Shadow Game. M. Underwood
Shadow Glen. D. Daniels
Shadow—Go Mad! M. Grant
Shadow Guest. H. Waugh
Shadow Guests. Joan Aiken
Shadow Hall. J. P. Seabrooke
Shadow Hill. Joyce Wilson
Shadow in the Corner. M. E. Braddon
Shadow in the Courtyard. G. Simenon
Shadow in the House. S. Gluck
Shadow in the House. M. March
Shadow in the Sea. O. John
Shadow in the Sun. L. Meynell
Shadow in the Wild. W. Masterson
Shadow Knows. Diane Johnson
Shadow Laughs! M. Grant
Shadow Man. J. Goodwin
Shadow Mansion. Wilma Forrest
Shadow Men. D. Richberg
Shadow Men. G. Verner
Shadow of a Broken Man. G. Chesbro
Shadow of a Cat. P. Nottingham
Shadow of a Crime. H. Caine
Shadow of a Crime. J. Rhode
Shadow of a Crime. Mrs. G. Sheldon
Shadow of a Dead Man. T. W. Hanshew
Shadow of a Doubt. H. Judd
Shadow of a Gun. Martin Thomas
Shadow of a Hair. D. C. Meade
Shadow of a Hawk. M. Carrel
Shadow of a Killer. Allan Chose
Shadow of a Killer. W. Mole
Shadow of a Lady. H. Roth
Shadow of a Life. J. L. Hornibrook
Shadow of a Man. D. Daniels
Shadow of a Man. D. M. Disney
Shadow of a Man. E. W. Hornung
Shadow of a Past Love. W. D. Roberts
Shadow of a Rope. E. W. Hornung
Shadow of a Sin. H. Zore
Shadow of a Spy. A. MacKenzie

Shadow of a Stranger. A. Maybury
Shadow of a Tiger. Michael Collins
Shadow of a Vendetta. A. C. Gunter
Shadow of a Witch. P. Minton
Shadow of a Witch. M. Paradise
Shadow of an Alibi. J. Rhode
Shadow of an Assassin. I. Stark
Shadow of an Unknown Woman. D. Winston
Shadow of Ashlydyat. H. Wood
Shadow of Chu-Sheng. E. Thomas
Shadow of Death. G. Ashe
Shadow of Dr. Ferrari. E. P. Thorne
Shadow of Doctor Syn. R. Thorndike
Shadow of Doom. J. Creasey
Shadow of Doubt. A. S. Roche
Shadow of Egypt. H. H. Ross
Shadow of Evil. M. Black
Shadow of Evil. L. Blanchet
Shadow of Evil. C. Dawe
Shadow of Evil. D. Donovan
Shadow of Evil. C. J. Dutton
Shadow of Evil. D. Romaine
Shadow of Fear. R. C. Payes
Shadow of Fear. B. Spicer
Shadow of Fu Manchu. S. Rohmer
Shadow of Gilsland. M. Gerard
Shadow of Guilt. R. Bloomfield
Shadow of Guilt. Old Spicer
Shadow of Guilt. P. Quentin
Shadow of Hampton Mead. E. Van Loon
Shadow of Himself. M. Delving
Shadow of His Crime. J. W. Bobin
Shadow of John Wallace. L. Clarkson
Shadow of Larose. A. Gask
Shadow of Li Tong Su. C. Bishop
Shadow of Madness. H. Pentecost
Shadow of Malreward. J. B. Harris-Burland
Shadow of Monte Carlo and other stories. C. Kingston
Shadow of Murder. C. Blackstock
Shadow of Murder. M. F. Ford
Shadow of Murder. P. Laing
Shadow of My Brother. D. Grubb
Shadow of Peril. A. I. Zhdanov
Shadow of Polperro. F. Cowen
Shadow of Quong Lung. C. J. S. Doyle
Shadow of Ravenscliffe. J. S. Fletcher
Shadow of Salvador. J. Haslette
Shadow of Shame. Austyn Granville
Shadow of Sheila Ann. P. Wissmann
Shadow of Suspicion. W. A. Miles
Shadow of Tarleton Manor. B. M. Clay
Shadow of the Bars. E. D. Pierson
Shadow of the Bear. H. Hill
Shadow of the Caravan. S. O'Brien
Shadow of the Cliff. N. Kennedy
Shadow of the Cliff. C. E. Mallandaine
Shadow of the Cobra. D. Dalheath
Shadow of the Condor. J. Grady
Shadow of the Czar. J. R. Carling
Shadow of the Dragon. A. Kuller
Shadow of the Four. Mark Cross
Shadow of the Gallows. M. Richmond
Shadow of the Guillotine. G. E. Rochester
Shadow of the House. J. Lindsay
Shadow of the Hunter. C. Kerr
Shadow of the Killer. J. N. Chance
Shadow of the Knife. K. R. McKay
Shadow of the Leopard. M. Hartmann
Shadow of the Lynx. V. Holt
Shadow of the Mafia. L. Malley
Shadow of the Monsoon. W. Manchester
Shadow of the Needle. L. A. Sunagel
Shadow of the Palms. J. Law
Shadow of the Past. M. Richmond
Shadow of the Pyramid. R. Ritchie
Shadow of the Red Barn. P. Lindsay
Shadow of the Rock. G. Hackforth-Jones
Shadow of the Rope. I. Stark
Shadow of the Sun. S. Wagner
Shadow of the Tamaracks. Sara North
Shadow of the Truth. H. Arvonen
Shadow of the Volcano. D. Rowan
Shadow of the Wolf. R. A. Freeman
Shadow of the Wolf. Donald James
Shadow of the Yemen. B. Bolt
Shadow of Theale. F. Cowen
Shadow of Thirteen. J. J. Farjeon
Shadow of Time. C. Landon
Shadow of Tyburn Tree. D. Wheatley
Shadow of Wrong. C. Gibbon
Shadow on Capricorn. Clarissa Ross
Shadow on Mercer Mountain. D. Winston
Shadow on Mockways. M. Bowen
Shadow on Spanish Swamp. Genevieve St. John
Shadow on the Cliff. M. Burton
Shadow on the Course. B. Strong
Shadow on the Downs. R. C. Woodthorpe
Shadow on the Glass. C. J. Dutton
Shadow on the Hearth. F. Halsey
Shadow on the House. A. W. Barrett
Shadow on the House. F. Ford
Shadow on the House. M. Hansom
Shadow on the House. F. Stevenson
Shadow on the House. E. C. Vivian
Shadow on the Left. Augustus Muir
Shadow on the Moon. L. Churchill
Shadow on the Purple. Anonymous
Shadow on the Sea. M. Pemberton

Shadow on the Steppe. M. Billett
Shadow on the Threshold. M. C. Hay
Shadow on the Wall. H. C. Bailey
Shadow on the Wall. M. E. Coleridge
Shadow on the Wall. M. Dalton
Shadow on the Water. H. Ainsworth
Shadow on the Wind. A. Lowing
Shadow on the Window. G. Bagby
Shadow over Denby. Marilyn Ross
Shadow over Elveron. M. J. Kingsley
Shadow over Emerald Castle. Marilyn Ross
Shadow over Europe. N. Leslie
Shadow over Fairholme. S. Kyle
Shadow over Grove House. M. L. Roby
Shadow over Heldon Hall. N. Herbert
Shadow over Mount Sharon. F. Y. McHugh
Shadow over Pleasant Heath. K. Kimbrough
Shadow over Seventh Heaven. J. Arliss
Shadow over the Garden. C. Ross
Shadow Passes. E. Phillpotts
Shadow Passes. Y. Pickering
Shadow People. K. Laing
Shadow Play. C. Phillips
Shadow Play. L. Powell
Shadow Play. M. Werlin
Shadow Shooter. W. C. Tuttle
Shadow Show. P. Flower
Shadow Spy. N. Luard
Shadow Strikes. M. Grant
Shadow Syndicate. C. Hosken
Shadow That Caught Fire. H. Jobson
Shadow the Baron. Anthony Morton
Shadow Wife. D. Eden
Shadow Witness. F. L. Cary
Shadowbox. S. Noyes
Shadowboxer. N. Behn
Shadowboxer. M. A. Calde
Shadowed! H. Belloc
Shadowed. M. Cumberland
Shadowed by a Detective. V. Champlin
Shadowed by Danger. D. Mai
Shadowed by the C.I.D. T. A. Plummer
Shadowed by Three. L. L. Lynch
Shadowed by 2. Old Sleuth
Shadowed from Europe. Hawkshaw
Shadowed Lives. A. Applin
Shadowed Lives. W. M. Graydon
Shadowed Love. F. M. White
Shadowed Place. V. Scannell
Shadowed Millions. M. Grant
Shadowed Porch. E. Moor
Shadowed Round the World. J. K. Stafford
Shadowed Spring. C. Salisbury
Shadowed Staircase. P. Warren
Shadowed to Europe. Le Jemlys
Shadowed to His Doom. Old Sleuth
Shadowed Victory. A. Stringer
Shadowers. D. Hamilton
Shadowland. Elaine Evans
Shadowless Men. Bradshaw Jones
Shadows. Jan Alexander
Shadows. Winifred Duke
Shadows. F. Ryerson
Shadows. Will Scott
Shadows. J. Sherman
Shadows Across the Bayou. S. L. Anderson
Shadows and Dark Places. M. Lovell
Shadows at Noon. M. M. Goldsmith
Shadows at Noon. K. Hess
Shadows Before. D. Bowers
Shadows by the Sea. J. J. Farjeon
Shadows Don't Bleed. W. Wright
Shadows from the Past. D. Daniels
Shadows from the Thames. E. Noble
Shadows in a Hidden Land. S. Harvester
Shadows in Succession. E. K. Lobaugh
Shadows in the Fire. Eva Dane
Shadows in the Moonlight. Elizabeth Peters
Shadows in the Night. J. Reach
Shadows in the Sun. J. Edgar
Shadows in Umbria. J. La Tourrette
Shadows of a City Care Forgotten. Moses Williams
Shadows of Amanda. H. S. Nuelle
Shadows of Castle Fosse. J. Tattersall
Shadows of Death. James Lewis
Shadows of Evil. G. La Spina
Shadows of Fear. K. Hess
Shadows of Fieldcrest Manor. C. Stephens
Shadows of Life. C. Meyer
Shadows of One Another. T. R. Cox
Shadows of Passion. P. Gallagher
Shadows of Reddoch's Landing. Melissa Lee
Shadows of the Heart. F. Hurd
Shadows of the House. M. E. Atkins
Shadows of the Past. K. Cameron
Shadows of the Past. M. Craig
Shadows of the Past. G. Ferrand
Shadows of Tomorrow. D. Daniels
Shadows of Violence. K. Evans
Shadows on a Wall. C. E. Israel
Shadows on Abu Simbel. T. B. Morris
Shadows on the Bay. Rebecca Holland
Shadows on the Hill. M. Carleton
Shadows on the Landing. G. M. Wilson
Shadows on the Moon. K. Cameron
Shadows on the Moon. N. Fairweather
Shadows on the Moon. D. Houston
Shadows on the River. A. MacKenzie
Shadows on the Sand. G. Greenaway

Title Index

Shadows on the Sand. Rona Randall
Shadows on the Sceptered Isle. J. A. Stang
Shadows on the Tor. S. Brand
Shadows on the Wall. M. Reisner
Shadows on the Water. Dorothy Fletcher
Shadows over Seascape. Lynn Williams
Shadows over Silver Sands. M. Pemberton
Shadow's Revenge. M. Grant
Shadow's Shadow. M. Grant
Shadow's Shadow. L. Ragsdale
Shadows Sometimes Scream. L. Della
Shadows Tonight. A. Seifert
Shadows Waiting. A. Eliot
Shadowy Thing. H. B. Drake
Shadowy Third. Marco Page
Shady Doings. V. P. Johns
Shady Lady. C. F. Adams
Shady Lady. Carter Brown
Shady Place to Die. John Savage
Shaft. E. Tidyman
Shaft Among the Jews. E. Tidyman
Shaft Has a Ball. E. Tidyman
Shaft's Big Score. E. Tidyman
Shaft's Carnival of Killers. E. Tidyman
Shaggy Dog and other murders. F. Brown
Shaggy Dog and other stories. F. Brown
Shah-Mak. Alan Williams
Shake a Crooked Town. D. J. Marlowe
Shake Hands for Ever. R. Rendell
Shake Hands for Ever. E. Woodward
Shake Him Till He Rattles. M. Brady
Shake-Up. H. Edmiston
Shake-Up. Breni James
Shakedown. R. Ellington
Shakedown. B. Kerr
Shakedown. J. Kwitney
Shakedown. J. Mack
Shakedown. J. Nazel
Shakedown. Roney Scott
Shakedown for Murder. E. Lacy
Shakedown Hotel. E. J. Fredericks
Shakedown Kid. N. Singer
Shakedown Strip. L. Malley
Shaken Down. A. MacGowan
Shaken Leaf. D. Cory
Shakeout. K. Follett
Shakespeare Curse. J. Boland
Shakespeare Murders. Neil Gordon
Shakespeare Murders. A. R. Long
Shaking Shadow. Elizabeth Stuart
Shaking Spear. B. Flynn
Shall Do No Murder. H. Alexander
Shall We Joint the Ladies? J. M. Barrie
Shall We Send Flowers? P. Lauben
Shall We Tell the President? J. Archer
Shallow Grave. J. Quinn
Shallow Grave. J. S. Scott
Shallow Runs the River. Emma Moore
Sham Detective. Anonymous
Shaman. F. Coffey
Shamballah. J. F. Rossmann
Shambhala Strike. J. Rosenberger
Shame. R. Himmel
Shame Dance, and other stories. W. D. Steele
Shame of Arizona. W. C. Tuttle
Shame of Silence. M. Leighton
Snamelady. J. Mayo
Shameless. J. M. Cain
Shamrock Smash. J. Rosenberger
Shamus. R. Giles
Shamus. J. Mack
Shamus, Your Slip Is Showing. Carter Brown
Shandon Hall. J. L. Rickard
Shanghai. W. Marshall
Shanghai. B. J. Sussman
Shanghai Bund Murders. V. W. Mason
Shanghai Flame. A. S. Fleischman
Shanghai Honeymoon. M. Dekobra
Shanghai Incident. S. Dodge
Shanghai Jezebel. M. Corrigan
Shanghai Jim. F. Packard
Shanghai Lily. M. S. Jones
Shanghai Nights. T. Ile
Shankill Road Contract. P. Atlee
Shannon. P. Gallagher
Shannon Terror. T. Du Bois
Shannondale. E. Southworth
Shannonese Hustle. F. Bandy
Shanty Shed. H. Footner
Shape of a Stain. E. Ferrars
Shape of Danger. A. Kielland
Shape of Fear. L. B. Long
Shape of Fear. H. Pentecost
Shape of Illustion. W. E. Barrett
Shape of Murder. J. F. Straker
Shapes of Sleep. J. B. Priestley
Shapes That Creep. M. Bonner
Shard's Rock. D. Justin
Share and Share Alike. R. W. Kauffman
Sharendal. M. Carr
Shares in Murder. J. L. Waten
Sharing Her Crime. M. A. Fleming
Shark Among Herrings. G. Milner
Shark Bait Affair. J. Arliss
Shark Fighter. N. Brady
Shark Hunters. W. A. Ballinger
Shark River. R. Powell
Sharkbait. Richard Butler
Sharks of Society. B. Hemyng

Sharkskin Book. H. S. Keeler
Sharky's Machine. W. Diehl
Sharp Edge. R. Himmel
Sharp Edge. W. Wright
Sharp Night's Work. J. F. Fitts
Sharp Practice. J. Farris
Sharp Quillet. B. Flynn
Sharp Rise in Crime. J. Creasey
Sharper's Downfall. Nicholas Carter
Sharpshooter. J. Reese
Shatter. J. Farris
Shattered. K. R. Dwyer
Shattered. P. Trent
Shattered Affair. B. Palmer
Shattered Halo. A. McElfresh
Shattered Hopes. Roland Daniel
Shattered Raven. E. D. Hoch
Shattered Sheel. James Preston
Shayne Case. W. B. M. Ferguson
Shayne Dame. S. Harragan
She Ain't Got No Body. J. T. Story
She Asked for Adventure. A. Applin
She Asked for It. E. Berckman
She Asked for Murder. E. Sherry
She Ate Her Cake. B. Treynor
She Came Back. P. Wentworth
She Came by Night. J. Pendower
She Could Take Care. S. Truss
She Deserved to Die. F. Griffin
She Didn't Like Dying. N. Morland
She Died a Lady. Carter Dickson
She Died Because... K. Hopkins
She Died Dancing. K. Roos
She Died Downtown. B. Carson
She Died Laughing. L. Gribble
She Died, of Course. T. Warriner
She Died on the Stairway. K. Rhoades
She Died Without Lights. N. Mathews
She Died Young. A. Kennington
She Drew the Bolt. E. Elton
She Faded into Air. Ethel L. White
She Fell Among Actors. James Warren
She Fell Among Thieves. Gretchen Travis
She Fell Among Thieves. D. Yates
She Gave Me Hell and... D. Glinto
She Got What She Asked For. J. Ronald
She Had a Little Knife. J. L. Linklater
She Had It Coming—. Griff
She Had My Number. M. Delaney
She Had to Have Gas. R. Penny
She Kept on Dying. G. M. Wilson
She Left a Silver Slipper. F. Stevens
She Let Him Continue. S. Geller
She Married Raffles. B. Perowne
She, Me, and Murder. Robert Martin
She Means Trouble. Spike Gordon
She Met Murder. H. Desmond
She Modelled Her Coffin. D. Launay
She Never Grew Old. Garland Lord
She Never Reached the Top. E. K. Lobaugh
She Paid 'Em Off. Griff
She Painted Her Face. D. Yates
She Posed for Death. Russell Gordon
She Ruled with a Rod. B. Sarto
She Saw the Murderer. E. M. Crawford
She Screamed Blue Murder. K. Secrist
She Sees Things. G. M. Wilson
She Sent Her Mother to the Scaffold. W. Tyrer
She Shall Die. Anthony Gilbert
She Shall Have Murder. D. Ames
She Shark. J. Farr
She Should Have Cried on Monday. E. S. Russell
She Sleeps to Conquer. H. Janson
She Sure Slipped. M. Perelli
She, the Accused. M. Moiseiwitsch
She Vamped a Strangler. H. Duval
She Vanished in the Dawn. Anthony Gilbert
She Walked in Fear. Roy Vickers
She Walks Alone. H. McCloy
She Walks in Shadow. L. Paige
She Wanted a Guy. R. Rand
She Was His Secretary. A. Demerest
She Was My Beloved. K. Lindsay
She Was No Angel. B. E. M. Ward
She Was No Lady. A. Bocca
She Was Only the Sheriff's Daughter. S. Forbes
She Who Sleeps. S. Rohmer
She Who Was Helena Cass. L. Rising
She Who Will Not—. E. C. Vivian
She Woke to Darkness. B. Halliday
She Wore Pink Gloves. M. Dekobra
She Wouldn't Say Who. D. Ames
Shear the Black Sheep. D. Dodge
Shears of Destiny. Winifred Duke
Shears of Destiny. L. Scott
Shearwater. M. Jahn
Shed a Bitter Tear. H. F. S. Moore
"Shed No Tears." Don Martin
Sheep and the Wolves. G. Burnett
Sheep in Wolf's Clothing. C. Debans
Sheep May Safely Graze. S. Harvester
Sheep's Clothing. A. Lee
Sheep's Clothing. L. J. Vance
Sheer Bluff. Jonn Collins
Sheer Silk. W. J. Elliott
Sheets in the Wind. R. Cullum
Sheikh Bill. A. M. Williamson
Sheikh Stuff. H. M. Raleigh

Sheikh Touch, and other stories. B. Reynolds
Sheikh's Son. A. Murray
Sheik's Capture. Old Sleuth
Sheilah McLeod. G. Boothby
She'll Be Dead by Morning. D. Chambers
Shell Game. R. Powell
She'll Hate Me Tomorrow. R. Deming
She'll Love You Dead. C. Franklin
Shell of Death. N. Blake
Shell Scott Sampler. R. S. Prather
Shell Scott's Seven Slaughters. R. S. Prather
Shelter. L. Meynell
Sheltered. J. Leach
Sheltered Garden. S. Pim
Sheltering Night. S. Fisher
Shelton Conspiracy. R. Foley
Shem's Demise. M. Underwood
Shen's Pigtail, and Other Cues of Anglo-China Life. Mr. M—
Shepherd File. C. V. Bark
Shepherd's Crook. E. C. R. Lorac
Sherbourne's Folly. N. Barry
Sheridan Road Mystery. P. Thorne
Sheriff of Angel Gulch. C. E. Blaney
Sheriff of Dyke Hole. R. Cullum
Sheriff of Purgatory. Jim Morris
Sheriff of Wasco. C. R. Jackson
Sheriff Olson. M. G. Shute
Sheriff's Deputy. G. V. McFadden
Sherlock Holmes. C. George
Sherlock Holmes. W. Gillette
Sherlock Holmes. T. J. Kelly
Sherlock Holmes and the Arthritic Clergyman. V. Andrews
Sherlock Holmes and the Curse of the Sign of Four. D. Rosa
Sherlock Holmes and the Drood Mystery. E. L. Pearson
Sherlock Holmes and the Golden Bird. F. Thomas
Sherlock Holmes and the Sacred Sword. F. Thomas
Sherlock Holmes at Oxford. N. Utechin
Sherlock Holmes in Dallas. E. Aubrey
Sherlock Holmes in New York. D. R. Benson
Sherlock Holmes in Tibet. R. Wincor
Sherlock Holmes Versus Arsene Lupin. M. Leblanc
Sherlock Holmes vs. Dracula. L. D. Estleman
Sherlock Holmes vs. Jack the Ripper. E. Queen
Sherlock Holmes's War of the Worlds. M. W. Wellman
Sherri. John Benton
Sheryl. Ralph Hayes
She's a Cop, Ain't She? I. King
She's Fooling Thee! J. Middlemass
She's No Lady. J. Grecco
Shetland Plan. Taffrail
Shibumi. Trevanian
Shield and Sword. V. Kozhevnikov
Shield for Murder. W. P. McGivern
Shield of His Honor. R. H. Savage
Shield of Love. B. L. Farjeon
Shield of Silence. E. Balmer
Shield of the Law. W. M. Graydon
Shield Project. D. R. Mounce
Shift of Guilt. J. Bude
Shilling for Candles. J. Tey
Shills Can't Cash Chips. A. A. Fair
Shining Days. F. Ross
Shining Head. J. Madeley
Shining Mischief. B. Levy
Shining Trail. O. Binns
Shining Trap. D. Enefer
Ship Ashore. S. M. Parkman
Ship of Death. J. Creasey
Ship of Death. R. Sapir
Ship of Hate. R. Danton
Ship of Secrets. V. Loder
Ship of Spies. G. Sinstadt
Ship of the Damned. J. Hilton
Ship That Died of Shame, and other stories. N. Monsarrat
Ship to Shore Murder. T. Noice
Shipkiller. Justin Scott
Ships Aflame! J. Toussaint-Samat
Shipwrecked. G. Greene
Shipwrecked Detective. W. M. Graydon
Shipwrecked Schoolship. John Marsh
Shipyard Menace. J. Stamper
Shirley. E. V. Cunningham
Shirt Front. C. Blackstock
Shivering Bough. N. Burke
Shivering Mountain. P. Somers
Shivering Sands. V. Holt
Shoal Water. D. Yates
Shock! B. Clemens
Shock! V. Markham
Shock Corridor. M. Avallone
Shock Tactics. J. Bruce
Shock to Society. F. Warden
Shock Treatment. J. H. Chase
Shock Treatment. W. Van Atta
Shock-Wave. B. Copper
Shock Wave. D. S. Davis
Shocking Pink Hat. F. Crane
Shocking Secret. H. Roth

Shockwave. R. Cawley
Shockwave. D. Cory
Shoe Fits. R. Ladline
Shoes for My Love. Jean Leslie
Shoes That Had Walked Twice. J. Toussaint-Samat
Shoestring. P. Ableman
Shoestring's Finest Hour. P. Ableman
Sholto Budd. M. Cobb
Shoot. D. Fairbairn
Shoot! B. Newman
Shoot. E. Trevor
Shoot a Sitting Duck. David Alexander
Shoot at the Moon. W. F. Temple
Shoot If You Must. R. Powell
Shoot It. P. Tyner
Shoot It Again. E. Lacy
Shoot It Again, Sam. M. Avallone
Shoot Me Dacent. A. M. Stein
Shoot-Out. D. Enefer
Shoot the Moon. J. Page
Shoot the Piano Player. D. Goodis
Shoot the Scene. E. Queen
Shoot the Works. R. Ellington
Shoot the Works. B. Halliday
Shoot to Kill. J. Dekker
Shoot to Kill. B. Halliday
Shoot to Kill. Wade Miller
Shoot to Live. Griff
Shoot When Ready. W. H. Baker
Shoot Your Enemies. Richard Grant
Shooter Man. T. Barling
Shooting Gallery. H. C. Rae
Shooting Made Easy. K. Howard
Shooting of Dan McGrew. M. Kenyon
Shooting of Sergius Leroy. Roland Daniel
Shooting of the Green. J. Poyer
Shooting Script. G. Lyall
Shooting Star. R. Bloch
Shop at Sly Corner. E. Percy
Shop-Girl. C. N. Williamson
Shop in Loch Street. J. Wood
Shop on Threnody Street. M. F. Shura
Shop Window Murders. V. Loder
Shoplifter. R. H. R. Smithies
Shore House Mystery. Jean Marsh
Shorecliff. Marilyn Ross
Short and Sweet. T. Taggart
Short Bier. F. Kane
Short Cases of Inspector Maigret. G. Simenon
Short Circuit. H. Miller
Short Circuit. L. Oriol
Short Cut. D. Blunt
Short End of the Stick, and other stories. I. Shulman
Short Life. T. B. Allen
Short List. R. Philmore
Short Madness. A. Manning
Short Night. R. Kirkbridge
Short Night. Russell Turner
Short of Murder. P. Ernst
Short of Murder. T. T. Ness
Short Reaction. J. Gale
Short Shrift. Manning Long
Short-Term Wife. H. Janson
Short Time to Life. Mervyn Jones
Short Time to Live. G. Moffat
Short Walk to the Stars. Eric Lambert
Short Wave. J. Bruce
Short Weekend. T. S. Strachan
Shortest Night. G. B. Stern
Shortly Before Midnight... E. Nisot
Shorty Bill. H. C. McNeile
Shot. S. Creed
Shot at Dawn. J. Rhode
Shot at Dawn. G. M. Wilson
Shot at Night. T. A. Plummer
Shot from Above. J. K. Stafford
Shot from the Dark. Philip Chambers
Shot from the Door. C. Barry
Shot in Question. M. Gilbert
Shot in the Dark. H. Agg
Shot in the Dark. G. Fairlie
Shot in the Dark. L. Ford
Shot in the Dark. H. Kurnitz
Shot in the Dark. R. Powell
Shot in the Dark. F. Usher
Shot in the Night. B. Bolt
Shot in the Pulpit. S. M. Woodward
Shot in the Woods. O. Binns
Shot of Murder. J. Iams
Shot on Location. H. Nielsen
Shot on the Downs. V. L. Whitechurch
Shot-Silk. W. J. Elliott
Shot Silk. M. Maguire
Shot That Killed Graeme Andrews. H. L. Deakin
Shotgun. E. McBain
Shotgun. W. Wingate
Shotgun Gold. W. C. Tuttle
Should a Corpse Tell? G. Dugdale
Should Auld Acquaintance. D. M. Disney
Should She Have Left Him? W. C. Hudson
Should She Have Spoken? A. Forbes
Show Business. B. Ford
Show Girl. M. Pemberton
Show House—Sold. R. Thorndike
Show Me a Hero. P. Alexander
Show Must Go On. G. Verner
Show No Mercy. L. Hardy
Show of Force. C. D. Taylor

Show of Violence. Sara Woods
Show Red for Danger. R. Lockridge
Show-Up. C. E. Erbstein
Showbiz Wipeout. L. Derrick
Showboat Mystery. A. W. Clark
Showdown. R. Carni
Showdown. R. Caulfield
Showdown in Sydney. D. Reid
Showman's Daughter. Scott Graham
Shown on the Screen. Nicholas Carter
Shred of Evidence. R. C. Sherriff
Shrew Is Dead. Shelley Smith
Shrewsdale Exit. J. Buell
Shrewtzer Castle. Anonymous
Shriek in the Midnight Tower. K. Kimbrough
Shriek of Tyres. A. J. Rees
Shrieking Pit. A. J. Rees
Shrine of Kali. H. E. Hill
Shrinking. A. Lelchuk
Shriveling Murders. Zorro
Shroud for a Lady. E. Daly
Shroud for a Nightingale. P. D. James
Shroud for Grandmama. D. Ashe
Shroud for Jesso. P. Rabe
Shroud for Mr. Bundy. J. M. Fox
Shroud for My Sugar. Carter Brown
Shroud for Rowena. V. Rath
Shroud for Shylock. S. Ransome
Shroud for Unlac. S. H. Courtier
Shroud 9. Robert Turner
Shroud of Canvas. I. Lambot
Shroud of Darkness. E. C. R. Lorac
Shroud of Fog. W. D. Roberts
Shroud of Silence. N. Buckingham
Shroud of Snow. A. Mills
Shroud off Her Back. S. Ransome
Shroud Society. R. Crawford
Shrouded Death. H. C. Bailey
Shrouded Tower. T. Charles
Shrouded Walls. S. Howatch
Shrouded Way. J. Caird
Shrouded Woman. M. L. Bolton
Shrunken Head. R. L. Fish
Shuddering Castle. W. F. Fauley
Shuddering Fair One. P. J. Cooper
Shudders. A. Abbot
Shudders. L. E. Austin
Shulamite. A. Askew
Shut out the Sun. L. Alroy
Shuttered House. K. Roche
Shuttered Room. C. A. Snerman
Shuttered Room. J. Withers
Shuttle of Hate. R. Harrison
Shy Plutocrat. E. P. Oppenheim
Shylock Holmes: His Posthumous Memoirs. J. K. Bangs
Shylock of the River. F. Hume
Shyster Lawyer. L. F. Schmitt
Si-Fan Mysteries. S. Rohmer
Siamese Cat. J. Dekker
Siamese Cat. H. M. Rideout
Siamese Coup Affair. S. Weintraub
Siamese Twin Mystery. E. Queen
Siberian Road. S. Harvester
Sibling. E. Trevor
Sibyl Sue Blue. R. G. Brown
Sibylla. J. H. Robinson
Sic Transit Gloria. M. Kennedy
Sicilian Affair. M. MacKintosh
Sicilian Defense. J. N. Iannuzzi
Sicilian Heritage. J. Higgins
Sicilian Mysteries. J. A. K. Curtis
Sicilian Romance. A. Radcliffe
Sicilian Slaughter. Jim Peterson
Sicilian Specialist. N. Lewis
Sicily Street. R. Masson
Sick Fox. P. Brodeur
Sick Heart River. J. Buchan
Sick to Death. Douglas Clark
Sickle Murders. Trill
Sickly Flame. E. Gresham
Sickness of the Soul. H. E. Fuller
Sidartha. K. Behenna
Side-Effect. R. Hawkey
Sideshow Girl. J. Clayford
Sideshow Girl. S. Harragan
Sidewalk Caesar. D. Honig
Sidewalk Floozie. B. Sarto
Sidney Yorke's Friend. E. A. Bennett
Siege. P. Cave
Siege. V. B. Miller
Siege of Buckingham Palace. W. Nelson
Siege of Hampton Mall. B. Robertson
Siege of Scotland Yard. L. G. Redmond-Howard
Siege of Superport. J. B. Olesker
Siegfried Spy. B. Newman
Sigh for a Drum-Beat. P. Doncaster
Sight of Death. J. York
Sight Unseen. A. E. Lindop
Sight Unseen, and The Confession. M. R. Rinehart
Sign at Six. S. E. White
Sign in the Sky. A. Edgar
Sign of Arnim. W. Seton
Sign of Blood. P. Street
Sign of Evil. A. Wynne
Sign of Fear. A. Derleth
Sign of Seven. G. Stanley
Sign of Silence. W. LeQueux
Sign of the Black Feather. H. E. Hill

Sign of the Blue Dragon. J. Aeby
Sign of the Blue Triangle. S. Hope
Sign of the Burning Ship. L. A. Cunningham
Sign of the Cobra. Nick Carter
Sign of the Coin. Nicholas Carter
Sign of the Crescent. Dick Stewart
Sign of the Crossed Knives. Nicholas Carter
Sign of the Dagger. Nicholas Carter
Sign of the Dagger. H. O. Cooke
Sign of the Dagger. J. L. Jacolliot
Sign of the Death Circle. C. H. Snow
Sign of the Flying Fox. J. Grieg
Sign of the Four. A. C. Doyle
Sign of the Four. W. Spence
Sign of the Glove. C. Dawe
Sign of the Golden Goose. R. Danton
Sign of the Grinning Dragon. M. Grimshaw
Sign of the Knotted String. H. Harper
Sign of the Mute Medusa. Ian Wallace
Sign of the Nine. F. Grierson
Sign of the Prayer Shawl. Nick Carter
Sign of the Ram. M. Ferguson
Sign of the Saracen. Gwyn Evans
Sign of the Scorpion. B. Abbott
Sign of the Scorpion. E. Snell
Sign of the Serpent. J. Goodwin
Sign of the Serpent. W. M. Graydon
Sign of the Seven Sins. W. LeQueux
Sign of the Skull. J. A. Dunn
Sign of the Snake. D. Vane
Sign of the Spider. E. L. MacKeag
Sign of the Spider. B. Mitford
Sign of the Stranger. W. LeQueux
Sign of the Swan. M. Baillie-Saunders
Sign of the Thunderbird. R. Montana
Sign of the Tiger. O. Williams
Sign of the Triangle. J. Hocking
Sign on for Tokyo. A. Haig
Signal. Roland Daniel
Signal for Danger. T. Harnan
Signal for Death. J. Rhode
Signal for Invasion. H. Adams
Signal Thirty-Two. M. Kantor
Signals. D. Deutschman
Signature. B. Goldie
Signature to a Crime. O. L. Rosmanith
Signed in Yellow. E. H. Loban
Signet Active. T. Page
Signet of Death. L. Grey
Signing Off. J. T. MacIntyre
Signora. P. Andreae
Signora. E. D. Lyon
Signors of the Night. M. Pemberton
Signpost to Fear. M. Drin
Signpost to Murder. M. Doyle
Signpost to Murder. D. Folliott
Silas Sharp, the Silent Detective. Anonymous
Silecroft Case. J. C. Lenehan
Silence. Richard Hubbard
Silence. S. Kyle
Silence! A. Soutar
Silence After Dinner. C. Witting
Silence at Salerno. F. Steegmuller
Silence for the Murderer. F. W. Crofts
Silence in Court. P. Wentworth
Silence in Crete. E. Ayrton
Silence Is Deadly. L. Biggle
Silence Is Golden. Elsie Lee
Silence Observed. M. Innes
Silence of a Purple Shirt. R. C. Woodthorpe
Silence of Birds. M. Ashton
Silence of Dr. Duveen. M. Leighton
Silence of Herondale. Joan Aiken
Silence of Jeremy Langton. H. H. Ross
Silence of Mrs. Harrold. S. M. Gardenhire
Silence of the Night. R. Ormerod
Silence over Sinai. A. Awin
Silence So Deadly. C. Dekker
Silence Under Threat. B. Cobb
Silence with Voices. C. Carfax
Silenced. L. T. Meade
Silenced Witnesses. N. C. Rosenthal
Silencers. D. Hamilton
Silent Accuser. A. Soutar
Silent Are the Dead. G. H. Coxe
Silent Barrier. G. Templeton
Silent Barrier. L. Tracy
Silent Battle. G. F. Gibbs
Silent Battle. A. M. Williamson
Silent Bell. Elaine Hamilton
Silent Bullet. P. Elliott
Silent Bullet. A. B. Reeve
Silent Clue. M. Leighton
Silent Conquest. M. Gerard
Silent Cousin. Elizabeth Fenwick
Silent Cracksman. J. J. Chichester
Silent Cry. H. Jobson
Silent Dead. A. Gask
Silent Death. M. Grant
Silent Death. H. Leyford
Silent Dust. B. Fischer
Silent Enemy. K. Netzen
Silent Five. T. M. Longstreth
Silent Force. Harry Goddard
Silent Four. T. A. Plummer
Silent Gate. T. Hopkins
Silent Guardian. Nicholas Carter

Title Index

Silent Guests. A. E. Forrest
Silent Halls of Ashenden. D. Daniels
Silent Hostage. S. Gainham
Silent House. J. G. Brandon
Silent House. N. Deane
Silent House. F. Hume
Silent House. L. Tracy
Silent House in Pimlico. F. Hume
Silent Jury. Gwyn Evans
Silent Kind of War. J. Laflin
Silent Knife. J. D. Powell
Silent Liars. M. Underwood
Silent Loom. P. Inman
Silent Man. J. M. Walsh
Silent Men. C. Bidmead
Silent Menace. A. Skene
Silent Mountain. G. Bettany
Silent Murders. Neil Gordon
Silent Murders. Ernest Paul
Silent, My Love. C. Randell
Silent One. O. Cameron
Silent Partner. A. Bodelsen
Silent Partner. L. Brackett
Silent Partner. Nicholas Carter
Silent Partner. K. M. Knight
Silent Partner. Augustus Muir
Silent Passenger. G. W. Appleton
Silent Passenger. Nicholas Carter
Silent Place. R. C. Payes
Silent Pool. F. Cowen
Silent Pool. P. Wentworth
Silent Pursuit. D. J. Harrington
Silent Reach. O. White
Silent Room. F. Chimenti
Silent Salesman. M. Z. Lewin
Silent Scream. Michael Collins
Silent Scream. Jane Lake
Silent Seducers. R. Arana
Silent Seven. M. Grant
Silent Shore. J. E. Bloundelle-Burton
Silent Shot. C. H. Snow
Silent Signal. F. Hume
Silent, Silken Shadows. P. Dalton
Silent Siren. T. Sterling
Silent Sisters. Margaret Archer
Silent Six. Seamark
Silent Slain. C. Pilgrim
Silent Slayer. G. Verner
Silent Speaker. R. Stout
Silent Stranger. H. G. Harper
Silent Street. G. Barnett
Silent Syndicate. L. Bidston
Silent Terror. L. C. Douthwaite
Silent Terror. T. C. H. Jacobs
Silent Thunder. R. C. Barnes
Silent Thunder. Rona Randall
Silent Voice. S. Claudia
Silent Voyage. J. Pattinson
Silent Walls. M. L. Roby
Silent Watcher. F. Stevenson
Silent Watchers. I. D. Hardy
Silent Watchers. Dora Russell
Silent Witness. G. H. Coxe
Silent Witness. J. Dering
Silent Witness. H. Desmond
Silent Witness. M. F. Ford
Silent Witness. R. A. Freeman
Silent Witness. J. Hunter
Silent Witness. M. D. Post
Silent Witness. J. Walworth
Silent Witness. E. Yates
Silent Witness. M. Yorke
Silent Witnesses. J. S. Strange
Silent Women. M. P. Hood
Silent World of Nicholas Quinn. C. Dexter
Silhouette. E. Trevor
Silhouette Symbol. P. Quiroule
Silinski, Master Criminal. E. Wallace
"Silk!" W. J. Elliott
Silk and Cordite. D. Spade
Silk Purse. J. Tickell
Silk Road. S. Harvester
Silk Rope. G. Mountford
Silk Scarf Murders. J. Addiscombe
Silk Stocking Murders. A. Berkeley
Silk Stocking Murders. G. Chester
Silken Baroness. P. Atlee
Silken Baroness Contract. P. Atlee
Silken Net. Rachelle Edwards
Silken Nightmare. Carter Brown
Silken Shroud. J. Sandys
Silken Snare. H. Janson
Silken Threads. G. Afterem
Silken Web. M. Lynch
Silky. L. Rosten
Silky Ones Sting. Richard Grant
Silsby. S. Nichols
Silver and Death. R. Simons
Silver Arrow. A. Wynne
Silver Arrow Murder. T. Stevenson
Silver Bag. T. Cobb
Silver Bar Mystery. W. C. Tuttle
Silver Basilisk. S. Warwick
Silver Bears. P. E. Erdman
Silver Blade. C. E. Walk
Silver Buckshot. W. C. Tuttle
Silver Bugle. G. McDonell
Silver Bullet. F. Hume
Silver Bullet. P. H. Hunter
Silver Bullet Gang. J. Miles
Silver Butterfly. W. Woodrow

Silver Canyon. G. M. Fenn
Silver Castle. E. Quest
Silver Chest. Herman Landon
Silver Circle. A. Skene
Silver Cobweb. B. Benson
Silver Cord. G. A. Chamberlain
Silver Cord. R. Shambrook
Silver Death. G. F. Gibbs
Silver Death. M. Hervey
Silver Doll. B. Treynor
Silver Dolphin. V. Johnston
Silver Eagle. W. R. Burnett
Silver Falcon. Evelyn Anthony
Silver Fang. G. F. Worts
Silver Forest. B. A. Williams
Silver Fox. R. Hansard
Silver Goblet. R. Foxall
Silver Grass. G. Croudace
Silver Greyhound. B. Newman
Silver Greyhound. J. M. Walsh
Silver Hair Clue. Nicholas Carter
Silver Haze. J. Ruyle
Silver Horseshoe. G. Verner
Silver Jackass. C. K. Boston
Silver Key. Griff
Silver Key. E. Wallace
Silver King. A. W. Barrett
Silver King. H. A. Jones
Silver King Mystery. I. Greig
Silver King's Vengeance, and other stories. H. Herman
Silver Ladies. M. Erskine
Silver Lady. J. Facos
Silver Leopard. Z. Cass
Silver Leopard. W. S. Masterman
Silver Leopard. H. Reilly
Silver Medallion. P. Brebner
Silver Mirror. M. V. Woodgate
Silver Mistress. P. O'Donnell
Silver Panther. W. J. Elliott
Silver Peril. J. Rutledge
Silver Phantom Murder. Brian Stuart
Silver Pin. A. W. Barrett
Silver Pineapple. E. Kyle
Silver Poppy. A. Stringer
Silver Puma. A. Riefe
Silver Sandals. C. H. Stagg
Silver Scale Mystery. A. Wynne
Silver Shadow. L. Noel
Silver Shamrock. H. Curties
Silver Shroud. D. Creekmore
Silver Sickle Case. L. Brock
Silver Slave. G. Stanley
Silver Spade. L. Revell
Silver Spoon. A. Griffiths
Silver Stair. M. Leighton
Silver Strand. H. Hall
Silver Streak. J. C. Rogers
Silver Street. E. R. Johnson
Silver Street Killer. E. R. Johnson
Silver Tom, the Detective. Anonymous
Silver Tombstone. F. Gruber
Silver Tombstone Mystery. F. Gruber
Silver Trail. G. Templeton
Silver Unicorn. J. Blackmore
Silver Urn. F. Daingerfield
Silver Venus. H. McElroy
Silver-Voiced Murder. G. Morton
Silver Wood. D. Rowan
Silvered Cage. H. Blayn
Silverface. H. Long
Silverface Surrenders. H. Long
Silverhill. P. A. Whitney
Silvermead. J. Middlemass
Silverskull. P. Edwards
Simba Bwana. D. W. MacArthur
Simon. J. S. Clouston
Simon Lash, Detective. F. Gruber
Simon Lash, Private Detective. F. Gruber
Simon of Hangletree. A. J. Rees
Simon Takes "the Rap". T. A. Plummer
Simon Wheeler, Detective. M. Twain
Simple Art of Murder. R. Chandler
Simple Case of Ill-Will. E. Berckman
Simple Case of Susan. J. Futrelle
Simple Justice. T. B. Morris
Simple Life. N. Balchin
Simple Pass On. J. Cannan
Simple Peter Cradd. E. P. Oppenheim
Simple Way of Poison. L. Ford
Simple Way of Poison. A. Hocking
Simpson of Snells. W. Hewlett
Simultaneous Equations. L. Halley
Simultaneous Man. Ralph Blum
Sin. A. Applin
Sin. R. Vaughan
Sin and Johnny Inch. J. F. Straker
Sin and Sand. H. H. Ross
Sin and the Sinners. F. E. Smith
Sin and the Woman. D. Vane
Sin File. S. Ransome
Sin for Me. G. Brewer
Sin Has No Future. J. Cello
Sin in Their Blood. E. Lacy
Sin in Time. J. Conway
Sin Is a Redhead. S. Harragan
Sin Is Her Mantle. J. Cello
Sin Mark. M. P. Hood
Sin of Angels. A. M. Wells
Sin of David. M. Cumberland
Sin of Hong Kong. M. Corrigan
Sin of Joost Avelingh. M. Maartens

Sin of Laban Routh. A. Sergeant
Sin of Olga Zassoulich. F. Barrett
Sin of Preaching Jim. D. Donovan
Sin of Sacrifice. L. G. Redmond-Howard
Sin of Silence. O. Binns
Sin of Sister Betty. P. Cartrell
Sin of the Duchess. H. Townley
Sin Sniper. H. Garner
Sin Street. B. Bristow
Sin That Was His. F. Packard
Since There's No Help. A. Kennington
Sinews of War. E. Phillpotts
Sinful Stones. P. Dickinson
Sinful Woman. J. M. Cain
Sinfully Rich. H. Footner
Sinfully Yours. Carter Brown
Sing a Dark Song. W. D. Roberts
Sing a Song of Cyanide. N. Morland
Sing a Song of Homicide. J. R. Langham
Sing a Song of Murder. P. Drax
Sing a Song of Murder. R. P. Koehler
Sing a Song of Murder. J. R. Langham
Sing a Song of Murder. J. Michaels
Sing a Song of Murder. A. Spiller
Sing, Clubman, Sing! Kevin O'Hara
Sing Me a Moon. C. Darby
Sing Me a Murder. H. Nielsen
Sing Out, Sweet Homicide. J. Roeburt
Sing Sing Nights. H. S. Keeler
Sing Softly, Stranger. G. Greenaway
Sing Witch, Sing Death. R. Gellis
Singapore. W. Bogart
Singapore Downbeat. M. Corrigan
Singapore Exile Murders. V. W. Mason
Singapore Kate. Roland Daniel
Singapore Set-Up. J. Dekker
Singapore Wink. Ross Thomas
Singing Bone. R. A. Freeman
Singing Cave. J. Appleby
Singing Clock. V. Perdue
Singing Corpse. B. Dougall
Singing Diamonds. H. McCloy
Singing Ghost. R. St. Clair
Singing Harp. E. St. Clair
Singing Head. Janice Elliott
Singing Head. F. Hume
Singing in the Shrouds. N. Marsh
Singing Kid. W. C. Tuttle
Singing Lizard. J. Knowler
Singing Masons. F. Vivian
Singing Millionaire. M. Pereira
Singing River. W. C. Tuttle
Singing Room. N. Berrow
Singing Sands. J. Tey
Singing Shadows. D. Eden
Singing Soul. A. J. Foxall
Singing Spider. A. MacVicar
Singing Swans. A. Manners
Singing Sword. P. G. Larbalester
Singing Widow. V. P. Johns
Singing Wind. Jennifer Wade
Single Clue. Old Sleuth
Single File. N. Fruchter
Single Hair. H. Adams
Single Monstrous Act. K. Benton
Single Pilgrim. N. Lewis
Single Ticket to Death. G. Bellairs
Single to Hong Kong. K. Boyce
Single Track. Douglas Grant
Singled Out. S. Whitney
Singleton's Mill. Sinclair Buchan
Singular Case of the Multiple Dead. M. McShane
Singular Conspiracy. B. Perowne
Singular Crime. H. Nisbet
Singular Fury. H. L. Oleck
Singular Sinner. C. R. Harker
Sinister Abbey. Elsie Lee
Sinister Alibi. C. Wallace
Sinister Assignment. R. Fenisong
Sinister Cargo. M. Black
Sinister Cargo. S. H. Page
Sinister Castle. Gwyn Evans
Sinister Charade. D. Mariner
Sinister Civility. W. Croyland
Sinister Craft. R. Ladline
Sinister Crag. N. Gayle
Sinister Creek. J. Rowland
Sinister Eden. B. Cotterell
Sinister Encounter. J. Brooke
Sinister Errand. P. Cheyney
Sinister Garden. Marilyn Ross
Sinister Gardens. W. D. Roberts
Sinister History of Ambrose Hinkle. T. McMorrow
Sinister House. C. G. Booth
Sinister House. L. C. Douthwaite
Sinister House. C. Farr
Sinister House. L. Hall
Sinister House. T. Taggart
Sinister House. G. Verner
Sinister Inn. J. J. Farjeon
Sinister Island. Wadsworth Camp
Sinister Island. A. Wood
Sinister Isle of Love. E. Morley
Sinister Lady. D. M. Disney
Sinister Legacy. D. Martyn
Sinister Light. Frank King
Sinister Light. Ethel L. White
Sinister Love. L. Ames
Sinister Lovely. N. Karta
Sinister Madonna. W. Jackson

596 / Sinister Madonna — Title Index

Sinister Madonna. S. Rohmer
Sinister Man. E. Wallace
Sinister Mark. L. Thayer
Sinister Melody. F. Cowen
Sinister Moonlight. Colin Robertson
Sinister Murders. P. Cheyney
Sinister Playhouse. R. Armstrong
Sinister Quest. T. C. H. Jacobs
Sinister River. J. Soutar
Sinister Sanctuary. E. P. Thorne
Sinister Scourge. B. House
Sinister Secret. F. Gerard
Sinister Secret. A. Nettleton
Sinister Secret. A. O. Pollard
Sinister Service. W. E. Johns
Sinister Shadow. S. Hocking
Sinister Shadow. H. Holt
Sinister Shelter. C. L. Leonard
Sinister Sister. M. Brody
Sinister Smith. H. Atkins
Sinister Stars. J. Pattinson
Sinister Station. R. St. Clair
Sinister Stone. D. Winston
Sinister Stones. A. W. Upfield
Sinister Strangers. C. B. Kelland
Sinister Street. R. Burke
Sinister Street. S. Horler
Sinister Talent. J. Pendower
Sinister Valley. G. Stanley
Sinister Voice. Genevieve St. John
Sinister Warning. M. S. Michel
Sinister Widow. R. Armstrong
Sinister Widow Again. R. Armstrong
Sinister Widow at Sea. R. Armstrong
Sinister Widow Comes Back. R. Armstrong
Sinister Widow Down Under. R. Armstrong
Sinister Widow Returns. R. Armstrong
Sinister Wooing. B. Sarto
Sink Me the Ship. Sea Lion
Sinkiang Executive. Adam Hall
Sinless. M. H. Yardley
Sinless Crime. G. Fleming
Sinner. D. Linton
Sinner Take All. Wade Miller
Sinner Takes All. A. Bocca
Sinner Takes All. M. Corrigan
Sinner Takes All. D. Holt
Sinner Takes All. R. Watkins
Sinner, You Slay Me! Carter Brown
Sinners. E. S. Aarons
Sinners. Carter Brown
Sinners. D. Torbett
Sinners and Shrouds. Jonathan Latimer
Sinners Beware. E. P. Oppenheim
Sinners' Castle. A. Wood
Sinners Go Secretly. A. Wynne
Sinners in Clover. S. Toye
Sinners Never Die. A. E. Martin
Sinner's Shroud. T. Angelo
Sinners' Syndicate. C. Stanton
Sinnings of Seraphine. Mrs. C. Kernahan
Sino-Variant. A. Ind
Sin's Half Mile. D. Linton
Sins of Billy Serene. W. Ard
Sins of Rachel Ellis. P. Caveney
Sins of Severac Bablon. S. Rohmer
Sins of Society. C. Raleigh
Sins of Sumuru. S. Rohmer
Sins of the City. W. LeQueux
Sins of the Father. J. Blackburn
Sins of the Father. Lawrence Block
Sins of the Fathers. A. Applin
Sins of the Fathers. C. Houghton
Sins of the Fathers. R. Rendell
Sins of the Fathers. T. Walton
Sins of the Past. H. S. Nuelle
Sir Adam Disappeared. E. P. Oppenheim
Sir Anthony. A. Sergeant
Sir Anthony's Secret. A. Sergeant
Sir Christopher Leighton. M. L. Storer
Sir Devil. S. Styles
Sir Gregory's Silence. A. W. Marchmont
Sir Hector. R. Machray
Sir Hector's Watch. C. Granville
Sir Hilton's Sin. G. M. Fenn
Sir Jaffray's Wife. A. W. Marchmont
Sir Jasper's Tenant. M. E. Braddon
Sir John Dering. J. Farnol
Sir John Magill's Last Journey. F. W. Crofts
Sir Julian's Crime. F. Warden
Sir Morecambe's Marriage. F. Warden
Sir Penywern's Wife. F. Warden
Sir Peter's Arm. M. Cobb
Sir Ralph's Secret. J. M. Cobban
Sir Richard Penniless. C. Edwards
Sir Theodore's Guest and other stories. G. Allen
Sir Vincent's Patient. H. Hill
Sir, You Bastard. G. F. Newman
Sirdar's Oath. B. Mitford
Sire. L. Allan
Siren. T. A. Trollope
Siren and the Centaur. Conrad Phillips
Siren in Satin. D. Walshe
Siren in the Night. L. Ford
Siren on the Skids. M. Brody
Siren Signs Off. Carter Brown
Siren Song. D. Beaty
Siren Stars. R. Carrigan
Sirocco. A. Betteridge
Sister at Sea. Rona Randall

Sister Disciple. W. LeQueux
Sister, Don't Hate Me. H. Janson
Sister of Cain. Mary Collins
Sister Satan. G. Dilnot
Sister Simon's Murder Case. M. A. Hubbard
Sister Sinister. B. Diamond
Sister Susie—Spinster. A. Applin
Sister Theatre. G. Vaizey
Sisterhood. B. Black
Sisters at War. L. Robin
Sisters of Sorrow. A. Vandergriff
Sister's Sacrifice. G. Fleming
Sit-In. G. Anderson
Sittaford Mystery. A. Christie
Sitting Duck. M. Carr
Sitting Emperor. E. N. Willett
Sitting Target. H. Henderson
Sitting Up Dead. A. M. Stein
Situation, Grave! H. Janson
Situation Vacant. M. Burton
Situations Vacant. Norman Lucas
Six Bars at Seven. Mollie Kaye
Six Black Camels. E. Lanham
Six Came to Dinner. Roy Vickers
Six Cent Sam's. J. Hawthorne
Six Curtains for Stroganova. C. Brahms
Six-Day Week. A. Gardner
Six Days of the Condor. J. Grady
Six Days to Death. P. Alding
Six Dead Men. A. Steeman
Six Deadly Dames. F. Nebel
Six Feet of Dynamite. B. Gray
Six Foot Deep. H. Luger
Six Foot of Rope. H. R. Taunton
Six for the Toff. J. Creasey
Six Golden Angels. M. Brand
Six Graves to Munich. M. Cleri
Six Green Bottles. A. Hocking
Six Gun Empire. R. Wilkes-Hunter
Six-Gun Judgment. E. Z. Frank
Six-Hour Mystery. A. Marsden
Six Iron Spiders. P. A. Taylor
Six-Letter Word for Death. T. R. Frierson
Six Lines. N. A. Temple-Ellis
Six Lives and a Book. C. Houghton
Six Men. E. Radford
Six Men Died. G. Verner
Six-Mile Face. H. Gibbs
Six Minute Sketches. L. J. Huber
Six Minutes Past Twelve. Gavin Holt
Six Murders in the Suburbs. Roy Vickers
Six Nights of Mystery. W. Irish
Six Nuns and a Shotgun. Colin Watson
Six of One. P. Traill
Six Other Days. A. Meisels
Six Proud Walkers. F. Beeding
Six Queer Things. C. S. Sprigg
Six Ropes for Glory. J. G. Sarasin
Six Rubies. J. M. Forman
Six Seconds of Darkness. O. R. Cohen
Six Seconds to Kill. B. Halliday
Six Sign-Post Murder. C. Robbins
Six Silver Handles. G. Homes
633 Squadron. F. E. Smith
633 Squadron, Operation Rhine Maiden. F. E. Smith
Six Times Death. W. Irish
Six to Kill. B. Gray
6 to 10. J. Garden
Six Under Suspicion. C. Kingston
Six Weeks. L. Saunders
Six Weeks South of Texas. L. T. White
Six Were Present. E. R. Punshon
Six Were to Die. J. Ronald
Six Who Ran. M. E. Chaber
Sixes and Sevens. O. Henry
Sixpenny Dame. E. K. Goldthwaite
16 Beans. H. S. Keeler
Sixteen Bells. G. Hackforth-Jones
Sixteenth Stair. E. C. R. Lorac
Sixth Column. P. Fleming
Sixth Commandment. Howel Evans
Sixth Commandment. Lawrence Sanders
Sixth Commandment. C. Wells
Sixth Director. D. Newton
Sixth Directorate. J. Hone
Sixth Family. P. Diapoulos
"Sixth Key." R. St. Clair
Sixth of October. R. Hichens
Sixth Raid. P. Enefer
Sixth Seal. M. Wesley
Sixth Sense. R. Stewart
Sixth Sense Is Death. J. Garforth
Sixth Victim. W. M. Graydon
Sixty Days to Live. D. Wheatley
Sixty-Fifth Tape. F. Ross
Sixty-First Second. O. Johnson
64 Thousand Murder. V. Gunn
60 Hours of Darkness. A. Sederberg
69 Babylon Park. H. Whittington
Sixty-Nine Diamonds. J. Lord
Skater's Waltz. E. Kyle
Skein Well Tangled. J. K. Stafford
Skeleton. I. Crookenden
Skeleton at the Feast. C. Wells
Skeleton at the Villa Wolkonsky. C. Pincher
Skeleton Clew. Dick Stewart
Skeleton Closet of Jules de Grandin. Seabury Quinn

Skeleton Coast Contract. P. Atlee
Skeleton Finger. H. Hill
Skeleton in Concrete. J. E. Barry
Skeleton in Every House. Waters
Skeleton in the Clock. Carter Dickson
Skeleton in the Closet. A. B. Cunningham
Skeleton in the Closet. E. Southworth
Skeleton in the Cupboard. H. Hawton
Skeleton Island. G. Mitchell
Skeleton Key. B. Capes
Skeleton Key. R. Dowling
Skeleton Key. L. G. Offord
Skeleton Key. D. Winston
Skeleton Out of the Cupboard. V. Williams
Skeleton Staff. E. Ferrars
Skeleton Talks. F. G. Eberhard
Skeleton Walks! F. Metcalfe
Skeletons. G. Swarthout
Skeletons and Cupboards. R. Arnold
Skeleton's Clutch. T. P. Prest
Skeleton's Holiday. L. Ashley
Skeletons in the Cupboard. K. Fowler
Sketches of Gotham. I. Swift
Ski Lift to Love. H. Murray
Skin and Bone. E. Greenwood
Skin Dealer. M. Tripp
Skin Deep. P. Dickinson
Skin Deep. J. Gautier
Skin Deep. S. Hufford
Skin Deep. D. Wiles
Skin for Skin. Winifred Duke
Skin for Skin. D. Rutherford
Skin Game. F. Bonham
Skin o' My Tooth. B. Orczy
Skin Trap. W. Mole
Skinflick. J. Hansen
Skinman. M. Tarmey
Skinner. H. C. Rae
Skinnerball!! in Pursuit of Them. D. Joseph
Skirmish. C. Egleton
Skirts Bring Me Sorrow. H. Janson
Skirts of the Dead Night. W. W. Seward
Skuldoggery. F. Flora
Skulduggery. W. Marshall
Skull. J. Buffer
Skull. B. J. McOwen
Skull Beneath the Eaves. H. Best
Skull Mountain. D. Hawkins
Skull of Kanaima. V. Norwood
Skull of the Marquis de Sade and other stories. R. Bloch
Skull of the Waltzing Clown. H. S. Keeler
Skull Still Bone. J. Wyllie
Skullduggery on Halfaday Creek. J. B. Hendryx
Sky Bandits. G. E. Rochester
Sky Block. S. Frazee
Sky-Blue Life. M. Moiseiwitsch
Sky Divers. L. Cameron
Sky Fever, and other stories. W. E. Johns
Sky High. M. Gilbert
Sky High. W. E. Johns
Sky High. F. Ryerson
Sky-High Terror. R. Trevor
Sky Is Overcast. A. Booth
Sky-Jacked. S. Morgan
Sky Kill. D. Da Cruz
Sky Riders. L. Cameron
Sky-Rocket. M. Fitt
Sky Steward. K. Attiwill
Sky Walker. K. Robeson
Sky Wolves. G. Radcliffe
Skyborne Sapper. H. Chesham
Skye Cameron. P. A. Whitney
Skye Manor. J. Blair
Skyfire. T. Page
Skyhigh Betrayers. L. Derrick
Skyjacked. D. Harper
Skylark Mission. I. MacAlister
Skyline Message. Nicholas Carter
Skyprobe. P. McCutchan
Skyraiders. A. Marks
Skyriders. T. Wallace
Skyrocket Steele. R. Goulart
Sky's the Limit. R. Ladline
Sky's the Limit. E. Woodward
Skyscraper Murder. S. Spewack
Skytip. E. Reed
Skytrap. G. Harding
Skyway Vampire. P. Conde
Slab Happy. R. S. Prather
Slack Tide. G. H. Coxe
Slack Water. A. D. Divine
Sladd's Evil. P. McCutchan
Slade of the Yard. R. Essex
Slade, Range Detective. G. Tuttle
Slade Scores Again. R. Essex
Slag. D. McGibney
"Slag." J. T. MacIntyre
Slam the Big Door. J. D. MacDonald
Slander. A. S. Roche
Slander of Witches. R. Gehman
Slander Villa. C. Kingston
Slane's Long Shots. E. P. Oppenheim
Slant Eye. Roland Daniel
Slashed Portrait. J. Hines
Slasher. Max Collins
Slasher. Michael Collins

Title Index

Slasher. O. Demaris
Slasher. H. Desmond
Slasher. E. T. Hamill
Slate Landscape. J. Turner
Slaughter. Henry Clement
Slaughter Horse. M. Maguire
Slaughter in Satin. A. Bocca
Slaughter in Satin. Carter Brown
Slaughter in September. S. Jason
Slaughter in the Sun. S. Christie
Slaughter Run. A. Kilgore
Slaughter Street. L. Falstein
Slaughtered Lovelies. D. Stanford
Slaughterhouse. F. Scarpetta
Slaughter's Big Rip-Off. A. Kane
Slave. E. Amadi
Slave Bangle. G. Leroux
Slave Brain. D. Reid
Slave Junk. F. Packard
Slave Market of Mucar. L. Falk
Slave of Circumstances. E. D. Pierson
Slave of Crime. Nicholas Carter
Slave of Silence. F. M. White
Slave of the Mill. O. Harper
Slave Safari. R. Sapir
Slave Trade. H. Gold
Slavemaster. Nick Carter
Slaver. D. Reid
Slavers. R. Telfair
Slaver's Secret. P. Quiroule
Slaves of Ijax. J. R. Fearn
Slaves of Ishtar. Richard Grant
Slaves of Paris. E. Gaboriau
Slaves of Sumuru. S. Rohmer
Slaves of the Lamp. G. Bronson-Howard
Slay Me a Sinner. P. Audemars
Slay Me Suddenly. Antony Brown
Slay-Ride. D. Francis
Slay Ride. F. Kane
Slay Ride for a Lady. H. Whittington
Slay-Ride for Cutie. H. Janson
Slay the Loose Ladies. P. Quentin
Slay the Murderer. H. Holman
Slay Time. P. Muller
Slayboys. P. Kirk
Slayer. Roland Daniel
Slayer and the Slain. H. McCloy
Slayer of Souls. T. S. King
Slayground. R. Stark
Slaying in September. I. MacKintosh
Slaying of Julian Summers. Richard Williams
Slaying on the 16th Floor. Arthur MacLean
Slaying Squad. Robert Mason
Sledgehammer. W. Wager
Sleep. J. Creasey
Sleep and His Brother. P. Dickinson
Sleep, and the City Trembles. J. Garforth
Sleep Before Evening. D. Olson
Sleep for the Wicked. H. Howard
Sleep If You Dare. G. Usher
Sleep in a Ditch. M. Birmingham
Sleep in the Woods. D. Eden
Sleep Is Deep. H. L. Nelson
Sleep Is for the Rich. D. MacKenzie
Sleep Long, My Love. H. Waugh
Sleep Long, My Lovely. B. Winter
Sleep, My Love. Robert Martin
Sleep, My Love. Elizabeth Norman
Sleep My Love. L. Q. Ross
Sleep, My Pretty One. H. Howard
Sleep No More. M. Erskine
Sleep No More. F. Ryerson
Sleep No More. G. Sims
Sleep No More. S. S. Taylor
Sleep of Reason. C. P. Snow
Sleep of Spies. P. Harcourt
Sleep of the Unjust. L. Meynell
Sleep off the Highway. P. J. Sherman
Sleep-Walkers. D. Karp
Sleep Well, Christine. Alice Brennan
Sleep with Nightmares. D. C. Cooke
Sleep with Slander. D. Hitchens
Sleep with Strangers. D. Hitchens
Sleep with the Devil. D. Keene
Sleep Without Dreams. H. Kane
Sleep Without Morning. R. Foley
Sleeper. J. Browning
Sleeper. Eric Clark
Sleeper. B. Crowther
Sleeper. M. Hughes
Sleeper. H. Roth
Sleeper Agent. I. Melchior
Sleeper Wakes. G. F. Gibbs
Sleepers. D. Thurlow
Sleepers Can Kill. S. Jay
Sleepers East. F. Nebel
Sleeping Bacchus. H. S. Saunders
Sleeping Beauty. P. Boileau
Sleeping Beauty. R. Macdonald
Sleeping Beauty Murders. L. O'Donnell
Sleeping Bomb. J. Moffatt
Sleeping Bride. D. Eden
Sleeping Car Murders. S. Japrisot
Sleeping Cat. I. Ostrander
Sleeping Cop. I. Ostrander
Sleeping Cupid. E. G. Whitney
Sleeping Death. G. D. H. Cole
Sleeping Dogs. E. Ferrars
Sleeping Dogs. F. Ross

Sleeping Dogs. C. Wells
Sleeping Dogs Laugh. H. C. Danby
Sleeping Dogs Lie. Julian Gloag
Sleeping Dogs Lying. Kenneth O'Hara
Sleeping Draught. H. Adams
Sleeping Draught. C. E. Simon
Sleeping Girls Don't Lie. Hansjorg Martin
Sleeping House Party. Elisabeth Lambert
Sleeping Island. F. Vivian
Sleeping Life. R. Rendell
Sleeping Memory. E. P. Oppenheim
Sleeping Mountain. J. Harris
Sleeping Murder. A. Christie
Sleeping Partner. Winston Graham
Sleeping Salamander. C. Carfax
Sleeping Sphinx. J. D. Carr
Sleeping Tiger. D. M. Devine
Sleeping Tiger. M. Moiseiwitsch
Sleeping Witness. M. V. Heberden
Sleepless Eye. Warren Miller
Sleepless Lunch. J. Vaizey
Sleepless Man. Gwyn Evans
Sleepless Men. E. Nisot
Sleepwalker. H. McCloy
Sleepy Death. G. Ashe
Sleepy-Eyed Blonde. J. Monmouth
Sleeve of Night. P. Traill
Sleight of Hand. C. Carpenter
Slender Chance. D. O'Connor
Slender Clue. L. L. Lynch
Slender Margin. B. Francis
Slender Thread. P. J. Merrill
Slender Thread. S. Silliphant
Sleuth. A. Shaffer
Sleuth and the Liar. J. Sherwood
Sleuth Hound. G. Leroux
Sleuth o' the World. R. Rodd
Sleuth of St. James's Square. M. D. Post
Slice of Death. B. McKnight
Slice of Hell. M. Roscoe
Slice of the Cake. W. Newton
Slick and the Dead. A. Bocca
Slick and the Dead. P. Cleife
Slick Detective Yarns. Anonymous
Slick-Fingered Kate. Roland Daniel
Slick Revenge. J. Nazel
Sliding Death. K. Bruce
Sliding Scale of Life. J. M'Levy
Slight Case of Murder. H. Desmond
Slight Case of Murder. D. Runyon
Slight Mourning. C. Aird
Slightly Bitter Taste. H. Carmichael
Slightly Disjointed Affair. I. L. Dunn
Slightly Imperfect. Ann Chester
Slightly Scarlet. Percy Heath
Slime Beast. G. N. Smith
Sling and the Arrow. S. Engstrand
Slings and Arrows. C. Dawe
Slings and Arrows and other tales. F. J. Fargus
Slingshot. S. Jackman
Slinky Jane. C. Cookson
Slip-Carriage Mystery. L. Brock
Slip Coach. C. Baines
Slip of a Girl. S. Warwick
Slipperdown Chant. J. Rigg
Slippery Ann. H. C. Bailey
Slippery As Sin. P. Souvestre
Slippery Dick. H. Adams
Slippery Hitch. Gerald Butler
Slippery Staircase. E. C. R. Lorac
Slippery Step. R. Foley
Slips Sees Red. P. Boyd
Slit My Throat, Gently. Michael Brett
Sloan Square Scandal and other stories. Annie Thomas
Sloane Square Mystery. H. Adams
Slocombe Dies. L. A. G. Strong
Sloth and Heathen Folly. E. L. Robinson
Slow. John Gloag
Slow Burn. J. Ehrlich
Slow Burner. W. Haggard
Slow Death at Geneva. Diplomat
Slow Down the World. J. Ashford
Slow Gallows. W. Masterson
Slow Poison. P. Barrington
Slow Poison. J. Rowland
Slow Vengeance. J. Bude
Slowly, Slowly in the Wind. P. Highsmith
Slowly the Poison. June Drummond
Slug It Slay. E. Lanham
Slugger. P. Malloch
Sly As a Serpent. M. Halliday
Slyboots. P. Flower
Slype. R. Thorndike
Smack Man. N. De Mille
Small and Deadly. John Marsh
Small Back Room. N. Balchin
Small Change. Carnaby Brown
Small Gust of Wind. T. Magnuson
Small Hotel. Edward Morris
Small Hours of the Morning. M. Yorke
Small-Part Lady, and other stories. G. R. Sims
Small Tawny Cat. V. Coffman
Small Time Crooks. K. Howard
Small Town Corpse. Clarence Hunt
Small-Town D.A. P. Traver
Small Town in Germany J. Le Carre
Small Town Murder. B. W. Jefferson
Small Venom. W. Mole

Small War Made to Order. N. Lewis
Small Wilderness. M. Summerton
Small World of Murder. E. Ferrars
Smallbone Deceased. M. Gilbert
Smaller Penny. C. Barry
Smart-Aleck Kill. R. Chandler
Smart Bombs. P. Kirk
Smart Girls Don't Talk. H. Janson
Smart Guy. W. MacHarg
Smart Money Doesn't Sing or Dance. J. M. Glazner
Smartest Grave. R. J. White
Smash a Glass Image. K. Bird
Smash and Grab. V. McCall
Smash and Grab. C. Robbins
Smasher. T. Powell
Smashers. H. Paul
Smashers. D. E. Westlake
Smear Job. J. Mitchell
Smell of Evil. C. Birkin
Smell of Fear. R. Chandler
Smell of Fear. S. Dean
Smell of Fraud. G. Hogg
Smell of Garbage. V. Castang
Smell of Money. M. Head
Smell of Money. W. Newton
Smell of Murder. S. S. Van Dine
Smell of Peardrops. J. P. Carstairs
Smell of Smoke. M. Burton
Smell of Trouble. L. Trimble
Smile and Be a Villain. H. Jobson
Smile and Murder. F. A. Symonds
Smile of Cheng Su. E. P. Thorne
Smile of the Stranger. Joan Aiken
Smile on the Face of the Tiger. D. Hurd
Smiler Bunn Brigade. B. Atkey
Smiler Bunn, Byewayman. B. Atkey
Smiler Bunn, Crook. B. Atkey
Smiler Bunn, Gentleman-Adventurer. B. Atkey
Smiler Bunn, Gentleman-Crook. B. Atkey
Smiler Bunn, Manhunter. B. Atkey
Smiler with the Knife. N. Blake
Smiley's People. J. Le Carre
Smiling Corpse. Anonymous
Smiling Corpse. H. Bailey
Smiling Death. F. Grierson
Smiling Dogs. K. Robeson
Smiling Mask. Frank King
Smiling Medusa. Jean Muir
Smiling Spider. L. Halliday
Smiling the Boy Fell Dead. M. Delving
Smiling Tiger. L. G. Offord
Smiling Willie and the Tiger. J. Harris
Smith & Jones. N. Monsarrat
Smith Conspiracy. R. Neely
Smith of the Secret Service. R. T. M. Scott
Smith Slayer. "Burmar"
Smithfield Bargain. Rachelle Edwards
Smithfield Slayer. E. Bruton
Smith's Dream. C. K. Stead
Smith's Odyssey. G. D. Hooker
Smog. J. Creasey
Smoke-Filled Boudoir. Lawrence Williams
Smoke Screen. C. Hale
Smoke Screen. L. Saunders
Smoke-Screen. D. Walshe
Smokers of Hashish. N. Berrow
Smokes of Spring. A. M. Burrage
Smokescreen. D. Francis
Smoking Leg and other stories. J. Metcalfe
Smoking Mirror. H. McCloy
Smoky Cell. Robert (G.) Curtis
Smoldering Sea. U. S. Andersen
Smooth Justice. M. Underwood
Smooth Killing. W. H. L. Crauford
Smooth Runs the Water. M. Hill
Smooth Silence. M. Billett
Smouldering Fire. M. Clare
Smouldering Fire. G. Franklin
Smouldering Fuse. F. French
Smuggled Atom Bomb. P. Wylie
Smuggled Masterpiece. E. Jepson
Smuggled Sin. S. Harragan
Smuggler of King's Cove. S. Cobb
Smugglers. N. Gerson
Smugglers. F. Goldsmith
Smuggler's Ally. B. Wayde
Smugglers at Odds. J. K. Stafford
Smuggler's Bride. R. Laker
Smuggler's Buoy. A. O. Pollard
Smuggler's Fate. E. C. Derby
Smuggler's Gate. M. K. Simmons
Smuggler's Ghost. H. Wood
Smuggler's Haunt. K. A. Shoesmith
Smugglers' Moon. Colin Robertson
Smugglers' Moon. C. Springer
Smuggler's Moon. S. Thorpe
Smuggler's Pay for Firebrace. Seafarer
Smuggler's Secret. F. Barrett
Snaggletooth. S. Jepson
Snags and Shallows. C. C. Lewis
Snail-Watcher and other stories. P. Highsmith
Snake. J. Crosby
Snake. J. Godey
Snake. J. McClure
Snake. M. Spillane
Snake and the Arrow. M. Hastings
Snake Doctor. C. Garrison

Snake Doctor and other stories. I. S. Cobb
Snake Face. Roland Daniel
Snake Flag Conspiracy. Nick Carter
Snake Harvest. F. J. Thornton
Snake Hips. B. Sarto
Snake in the Grass. Anthony Gilbert
Snake in the Grass. J. Wellard
Snake Is Living Yet. S. Gilruth
Snake of Luvercy. M. Renard
Snake on 99. S. Farrar
Snake on the Grave. G. Beare
Snake Walk. Johnny Dark
Snake Water. Alan Williams
Snakes and Ladders. A. Broome
Snakes Have Fangs. D. Lee
Snakes of St. Cyr. W. O'Farrell
Snake's Pass. B. Stoker
Snake's Picnic. T. Herd
Snap. Jacqueline Wilson
Snap and Jenny. Old Sleuth
Snap Judgment. Anthony Stuart
Snapdragon. Margery Lawrence
Snapdragon Murders. B. Healey
Snappy Vendetta. H. H. Lee
Snapshot Chap. B. Lebhar
Snapshot Mystery. B. Bolt
Snare. J. A. Brown
Snare. N. Calef
Snare. L. Robin
Snare and the Game. Nicholas Carter
Snare Andalucian. A. M. Stein
Snare for Sinners. R. Fenisong
Snare for Witches. Elinor Chamberlain
Snare of Circumstance. E. E. Buckley
Snare of the Fowler. C. R. Gull
Snare of the Hunter. Helen MacInnes
Snark Was a Boojum. R. Shattuck
Snarl of the Beast. C. J. Daly
Snarl of the Lynx. R. Charles
Snarled Identities. Nicholas Carter
Snatch. R. Airth
Snatch. G. Ashe
Snatch. H. R. Daniels
Snatch. R. L. Goldman
Snatch. B. Graeme
Snatch. L. Mantz
Snatch. V. Markham
Snatch. B. Pronzini
Snatch. D. Scanlon
Snatch! R. Taylor
Snatch an Eye. H. Kane
Snatch Game. J. G. Brandon
Snatch of Music. L. Peters
Snatch the Lady. Craig Cooper
Snatched. G. Mcdonald
Snatched Dame. W. J. Elliott
Snatchers. L. White
Sneaks. E. P. Green
Sneaky People. T. Berger
Sneeze on a Monday. P. Tabori
Sneeze on Monday. S. Carver
Snide Man. Roland Daniel
Snipe Hunt. A. Dean
Sniper. N. De Mille
Sniper. P. Malloch
Sniper. H. Pentecost
Sniper. M. Stratford
Sniper. Richard Williams
Sniper. B. Wynne
Sniper Jackson. F. Sleath
Sniper Murders. Richard Grand
Snipe's Spinster. J. Nuttall
Sno' Haven. Lee Miller
Snow Along the Border. R. H. Sawkins
Snow Among the Stars. A. K. George
Snow Blind. A. M. Treynor
Snow Falcon. Ganpat
Snow Falcon. Craig Thomas
Snow Fury. R. C. Holden
Snow Heroine. M. Gerard
Snow in Essex. J. Clappen
Snow in June. J. Blackmore
Snow in Paradise. R. H. Sawkins
Snow in the Desert. A. Soutar
Snow Job. M. Gair
Snow Leopard. S. Miller
Snow on High Ground. R. H. Sawkins
Snow on the Ben. I. Stuart
Snow Rattlers. S. Rifkin
Snow Shadow. A. Norton
Snow Tiger. D. Bagley
Snow Upon the Desert. J. R. Warren
"Snow" Vogue. D. Glinto
Snow Was Black. G. Simenon
Snow-White Murder. L. Ford
Snowball. T. Allbeury
Snowbird. O. Binns
Snowbird. Larry Levine
Snowbound. P. Bronzini
Snowboys. F. Webb
Snowdon Labyrinth. T. Barling
Snowdrift. J. B. Hendryx
Snowfall and Other Chilling Events. E. Walter
Snowfire. P. A. Whitney
Snowflake and Shaky. C. Gould
Snowline. B. Mather
Snowman. N. Bogner
Snowman. A. Maling
Snowman Cometh. D. Reid
Snows of Offenburg. A. Andre
Snows of Yesterday. B. De Forrest
Snowstone. J. M. Scott
So Bad a Death. J. Wright
So Blue Marble. D. B. Hughes
So Bright a Lady. M. Turner
So Cold, My Bed. S. S. Taylor
So Cold the Night. R. L. Yorck
So Dark a Heritage. F. B. Long
So Dark a Shadow. F. Hurt
So Dark the Mirror. J. Blackmore
So Dead My Love! H. Whittington
So Dead My Lovely. D. Keene
So Dead, So Sweet. D. Linton
So Dead the Rose. M. E. Chaber
So Deadly the Web. Ray Owen
So Deadly Fair. Gertrude Warden
So Deadly My Love. S. Ransome
So Deadly, Sinner! Carter Brown
So Dear, So Deadly. L. Du Breuil
So Death Came. C. Ryland
So Deep Suspicion. Elizabeth Ford
So Dies the Dreamer. U. Curtiss
So Difficult to Die. J. Matheson
So Disdained. N. Shute
So Evil My Love. J. Shearing
So Fair, So Evil. P. Connolly
So Help Me God. Felix Jackson
So Hurt and Humiliated and other stories. Francis King
So I Killed Her. L. O. Mosley
So I'm a Heel. M. Heller
So It Goes On. H. Willett
So Late, Monsieur Calone. A. Page
So Like a Woman. G. M. Fenn
So Little Time. S. M. Combes
So Long As You Both Shall Live. E. McBain
So Long at the Fair. A. Thorne
So Long at the Fair. J. G. Vermandel
So Long, Sucker. M. Clinten
So Lovely She Lies. Carter Brown
So Lovely to Kill. Harrison Wade
So Lush, So Deadly. B. Halliday
So Many Dangers. T. B. Morris
So Many Doors. O. M. Hall
So Many Doors. A. Hocking
So Many Doors. L. Meynell
So Many Doors. E. R. Punshon
So Many Steps to Death. A. Christie
So Move the Body. Carter Brown
So Much Blood. Simon Brett
So Much Blood. B. Fischer
So Much Blood. Z. Popkin
So Much for Gennaro. J. Palmer
So Much in the Dark. J. Bude
So Near and Yet. C. Farr
So Near to Love. K. Lindsay
So Nude, So Dead. H. Hunter
So Pale, So Cold, So Fair. C. Birkin
So Pretty a Problem. F. Duncan
So Quiet a Death. N. Morland
So Rich, So Dead. G. Brewer
So Rich, So Lovely, and So Dead. H. Q. Masur
So Sad, So Fresh. B. Hamilton
So Sharp the Razor. B. Graeme
So Sits the Turtle. P. Traill
So Slender the Thread. C. Dixon
So Soon Done For. B. H. Babson
So Soon to Die. J. York
So Speed We. G. V. McFadden
So Sweet, So Deadly. D. Rico
So Sweet, So Wicked. S. Rand
So the Lady Died. E. Hale
So Thin Is the Veil. D. E. Bordeaux
So This Is Love! E. Woodward
So What Happens to Me? J. H. Chase
So What Killed the Vampire? Carter Brown
So Wicked My Love. B. Fischer
So Young a Body. F. Bunce
So Young, So Cold, So Fair. J. Creasey
So Young, So Wicked. Jonathan Craig
So Young to Burn. J. Creasey
So Young to Die. G. Tree
Sob-Sister Cries Murder. Carter Brown
Sober As a Judge. H. Cecil
Soccer League Scandal. W. D. Maydwell
Social Buccaneer. F. S. Isham
Social Evil. P. Grayson
Social Gangster. A. B. Reeve
Social Kaleidoscope. G. R. Sims
Social Sinner. R. Bacon
Social Sinners. H. Smart
Social Storming. W. Martyn
Socialism of Lady Jim. F. Warden
Society Detective. Anonymous
Society Detective. O. Maitland
Society Editor. H. C. Beck
Society Intrigues I Have Known. W. LeQueux
Society Jezebel. F. M. White
Society Marriage. A. Askew
Society of Fear. H. Arvay
Society of Nobles. I. Tattersall
Society of the Dispossessed. R. Foxall
Society of the Spiders. Roland Daniel
Society Scare. F. Warden
Society's Prodigal. P. Crowe
Sock-It-to-Em Murders. R. Deming
Soeur Angele and the Bell Ringer's Niece. H. Catalan
Soeur Angele and the Embarrassed Ladies. H. Catalan
Soeur Angele and the Ghosts of Chambord. H. Catalan
Soft Arms of Death. R. Hayward
Soft As Silk. M. C. McDougall
Soft at the Centre. E. Warman
Soft Breeze from Hell. H. Miller
Soft Cargo. H. Janson
Soft Centre. J. H. Chase
Soft-Footed Moor. K. Royce
Soft Guy. V. Hill
Soft in the Middle. M. Storey
Soft Sell. J. Bruce
Soft Talkers. M. Millar
Soft Targets. D. Ing
Soft Touch. J. D. MacDonald
Softcover Kill. T. Harknett
Softly As I Kill You. C. Neutzel
Softly Dust the Corpse. S. H. Courtier
Softly in the Night. M. E. Chaber
Softly, Softly. Elwyn Jones
Softly, Softly Casebook. A. Yarrow
Softly Treads Danger. M. McEvoy
Soho Cafe Crime. W. W. Sayer
Soho Jungle. D. Bateson
Soho Racket. G. Dickson
Soho Spiv. B. Sarto
Soho Spy. Colin Robertson
Solander Box Mystery. L. A. Knight
Solange Stories. F. T. Jesse
Soldato! Al Conroy
Solden's Women. Bill Turner
Soldier and a Gentleman. J. M. Cobban
Soldier from the Wars Returning. J. Tickell
Soldier of the Legion. O. Binns
Soldier of the Legion. C. N. Williamson
Soldier Who Came Back. G. Chester
Soldier's Love. A. W. Barrett
Soldiers' Revolt. H. H. Kirst
Sole Agent. K. Benton
Sole Condition. V. Caudwell
Sole Survivor. L. Falstein
Sole Survivor. G. Hackforth-Jones
Sole Survivor. Gavin Holt
Sole Survivor and The Kynsard Affair. Roy Vickers
Solemn High Murder. B. N. Byfield
Solent Intrigue. M. Easton
Solid Gold Buddha. W. H. Canaway
Solitaire Man. B. C. Spewack
Solitary Child. N. Bawden
Solitary Farm. F. Hume
Solitary House. E. R. Punshon
Solitary Man. J. Winchester
Solitary Witness. R. Collier
Solitude Island. J. Brophy
Solitude Limited. J. H. Vahey
Solo. J. Higgins
Solo Blues. P. Harcourt
Solo for No Voices. W. Paddon
Solo for Several Players. B. Jefferis
Solomon Isaacs. B. L. Farjeon
Solomon's Seal. H. Innes
Solomon's Story. W. J. Shaw
Solomon's Vineyard. Jonathan Latimer
Solstice Cipher. B. H. Boyer
Solstice Man. D. Quinn
Solution of a Mystery. J. S. Fletcher
Solve-a-Crime. A. C. Gordon
Solved in Thirty-Six Hours! H. H. C. Gibbons
Solved Mysteries. J. M'Govan
Solver of Mysteries and other stories. R. H. Todd
Solving a Mystery. D. Miall
Solving the Unsolvable. H. Mee
Somber Memory. V. Siller
Some Avenger, Rise! L. Egan
Some Beasts No More. K. Giles
Some Beckoning Wraith. P. Warren
Some Buried Caesar. R. Stout
Some Call It Perjury. L. Du Breuil
Some Cases of Sherwood Lang, Detective. C. D. Warren
Some Crime Stories. C. Windust
Some Dame. N. Karta
Some Dames Are Deadly. Jonathan Latimer
Some Dames Die Young. D. Foster
Some Dames Don't. P. Muller
Some Dames Don't. M. Perelli
Some Dames Play Rough. S. Mitchell
Some Day I'll Kill You. D. Chambers
Some Die Eloquent. C. Aird
Some Die Hard. Stephen Brett
Some Die Hard. N. Quarry
Some Die in Their Beds. M. L. Roby
Some Die Running. N. Daniels
Some Die Slow. W. Herber
Some Die Young. J. P. Duff
Some Die Young. J. Kilgore
Some Died Laughing! R. Dolphin
Some Further Adventures of Mr. P. J. Davenant. F. S. Hamilton
Some Geese Lay Golden Eggs. B. Graeme
Some Get It. B. Shannon
Some Kind of Grace. R. Jenkins
Some Kind of Hero. J. Kirkwood
Some Lie and Some Die. R. Rendell
Some Like 'Em Shot. F. Malina
Some Like It Cool. R. Kyle

Some Like It Hot. S. Marshall
Some Like It Tough. J. Karney
Some Look Better Dead. H. Janson
Some Men and Women. M. B. Lowndes
Some Mischief Still. J. E. Hasty
Some Must Die. G. Brewer
Some Must Die. L. Moody
Some Must Watch. B. Cobb
Some Must Watch. S. Ransome
Some Must Watch. Ethel L. White
Some Names Are Dangerous. M. Latham
Some of Your Blood. T. Sturgeon
Some Other Place, the Right Place. D. Harington
Some Persons Unknown. E. W. Hornung
Some Persons Unknown. R. Trevor
Some Plain—Some Coloured. J. J. Bell
Some Poisoned by Their Wives. S. Forbes
Some Put Their Trust in Chariots. A. Grey
Some Queer Stories. Anonymous
Some Rats Have Two Legs. Griff
Some Rise by Sin. C. Houghton
Some Rogues and Daphne. R. Tremayne
Some Run Crooked. J. B. Hilton
Some Slips Don't Show. A. A. Fair
Some Take a Lover. P. Traill
Some Tommies. M. Dekobra
Some Try Murder. R. P. Koehler
Some Unconventional People. B. Jebb
Some Unknown Hand. Elaine Hamilton
Some Unknown Person. S. Scoppettone
Some Village Borgia. S. H. Courtier
Some Women Won't Wait. A. A. Fair
Somebody at the Door. R. Postgate
Somebody Has to Lose. Peter Chambers
Somebody Just Grabbed Annie. C. Dennis
Somebody Killed Kelvin. H. Clevely
Somebody Killed Milner. G. P. Willis
Somebody Knew. M. Montgomery
Somebody Knows. J. Van Druten
Somebody on the Phone. W. Irish
Somebody Owes Me Money. D. E. Westlake
Somebody Shot the Captain. G. Pahlow
Somebody Wants Me Dead. Richard Williams
Somebody's Crooked. S. Toler
Somebody's Done For. D. Goodis
Somebody's Sister. D. Marlowe
Somebody's Story. H. Conway
Somebody's Walking Over My Grave. R. Arthur
Someday I'll Kill You. H. Desmond
Someone and Felicia Warwick. Raymond Mason
Someone at the Door. Dorothy Christie
Someone Else's War. J. Burmeister
Someone Falling. D. Ambler
Someone from the Past. M. Bennett
Someone Has to Take the Fall. W. Newton
Someone Is Bleeding. R. Matheson
Someone Is Killing the Great Chiefs of Europe. N. Lyons
Someone Is Watching. P. Field
Someone Killed Her Husband. C. B. Phillips
Someone Like You. R. Dahl
Someone Lying, Someone Dying. Jonathan Burke
Someone Must Die. M. Cumberland
Someone Waiting. K. Troy
Someone Waiting. E. Williams
Someone Walked over My Grave. J. B. O'Sullivan
Someone Will Die Tonight in the Caribbean. R. Puissesseau
Someone's Death. C. Larson
Someone's Sleeping in My Bed. J. Gonzales
Someone's Stolen Nellie Grey. Ira Walker
Somerset Murder Case. B. Flynn
Somerville Case. J. Corbett
Something About Midnight. D. B. Olsen
Something Between. M. Cockrell
Something Blue. C. Armstrong
Something Burning. N. Daniels
Something Doing. V. Vanardy
Something Evil. A. Hoffe
Something Evil. D. Quick
Something for Nothing. H. V. Dixon
Something for Nothing. J. T. Story
Something for the Birds. A. Dean
Something for the Birds. T. S. Drachman
Something in the Air. J. A. Graham
Something in the City. F. Warden
Something in the Heart. J. Lodwick
Something in the Shadows. V. Packer
Something Nasty in the Woodshed. K. Bonfiglioli
Something Nasty in the Woodshed. Anthony Gilbert
Something Occurred. B. L. Farjeon
Something of the Night. M. McMullen
Something of Value. J. Pattinson
Something on the Stairs. S. Maddock
Something or Nothing. J. W. Conway
Something Rich. J. Butler
Something to Hide. M. Burton
Something to Hide. P. MacDonald
Something to Hide. N. Monsarrat
Something to Hide. L. Sands
Something to His Advantage. W. F. Morris

Something to Kill About. D. Reid
Something Up a Sleeve. R. Lockridge
Something Wicked. H. McCutcheon
Something Wicked. C. Runyon
Something Worth Fighting For. R. Gadney
Something Wrong. E. Linington
Something Wrong. E. Nesbit
Something Wrong at Chillery. R. Francis Foster
Something's Afoot. James McDonald
Something's Happened to Kate. G. Holden
Sometime Wife. Carter Brown
Sometimes Life's Funny. J. J. Farjeon
Somewhere a Voice Is Calling. J. Lodwick
Somewhere in England. R. Gadney
Somewhere in Hamburg. M. Skinner
Somewhere in Sark. A. Philips
Somewhere in the House. E. Daly
Somewhere in the Night. Bill Barclay
Somewhere in This City. M. Procter
Somewhere in This House. R. King
Somewhere off Borneo. W. B. M. Ferguson
Somewhere Quiet. G. Norham
Somewhere Within This House. J. F. Webb
Somnambulist and the Detective. A. Pinkerton
Son. G. Simenon
Son-in-Law Syndicate. F. Marlowe
Son of Blackshirt. B. Graeme
Son of Desolation. M. Y. Halidom
Son of Flynn. E. L. Long
Son of His Father. R. Cullum
Son of Ishmael. L. T. Meade
Son of Mars. A. Griffiths
Son of Nightingales. M. Hathaway
Son of Sam. J. Breslin
Son of Sherlock Holmes. B. Preiss
Son of the Flying Tiger. M. Macao
Son of the Gods. Mrs. Lodge
Son of the Immortals. L. Tracy
Son of the Typhoon. James Bennett
Son of the Werewolf. G. N. Smith
Son of Three Fathers. G. Leroux
Son of Wallingford. G. R. Chester
Son of Wu Fang. Roland Daniel
Song for a Prince. R. Foxall
Song for a Siren. V. B. Harris
Song for the Angels. F. L. Green
Song of Corpus Juris. J. L. Hensley
Song of Doom. V. Markham
Song of India. M. Richardson
Song of Sixpence. F. A. Kummer
Song of the Dawn. K. Lindsay
Song of the Flea. G. Kersh
Song of the Scorpions. P. Tabori
Sonntag. Michael Sinclair
Sonny. T. J. Williams
Sonora Mutation. A. J. Elias
Sons and Fathers. H. S. Edwards
Sons and the Daughters. P. Gallagher
Sons of Belial. W. Westall
Sons of Fire. M. E. Braddon
Sons of Nippon. Bryan Peters
Sons of Satan. J. Creasey
Sons of Satan. W. LeQueux
Sons of Seven. C. B. Dignan
Sons of the Legion. G. E. Rochester
Sons of the Morning. J. Cassells
Sons of the Mounted Police. T. M. Longstreth
Sons of the Pioneers. J. Givens
Sons of the Wolf. B. Michaels
Sontag of Sundown. W. C. Tuttle
Sookey. D. Newton
Sooper's Cases. N. Morland
Sophisticates. G. Atherton
Sophy Bunce. T. Cobb
Sorcerer of the Castle. F. Stevenson
Sorcerers. David St. John
Sorcerers. D. Winslow
Sorcerer's Broth. R. Garland
Sorcerer's Chessman. M. Hansom
Sorcerer's House. G. Verner
Sorcerers of Set. Martin Thomas
Sorcerer's Shaft. F. Gerard
Sorceress. A. Destefano
Sorceress of the Strand. L. T. Meade
Sore Temptation. J. K. Leys
Sorrow for Angels. H. Arvonen
Sorrow of a Secret. M. C. Hay
Sorry, Chief. W. Johnston
Sorry State. M. Kenyon
Sorry Wrong Number. M. Simpson
Sorry, Wrong Number. A. Ullman
Sorry Wrong Number, and The Hitchhiker. L. Fletcher
Sorry You've Been Shot. A. Bocca
Sorry You've Been Troubled. P. Cheyney
Sort of Madness. E. B. Ronald
Sort of Traitors. N. Balchin
Sorting Van Murder. Mander Ross
Soukour Deadline. A. Trew
Soul Destroyers. Nicholas Carter
Soul Eater. Robert Alexander
Soul Hit. C. Haas
Soul Laid Bare. J. K. Egerton
Soul of a Man. D. Vane
Soul of a Shop Girl. C. E. Pearce
Soul of Croesus. G. Villiers-Stuart
Soul of Phyllis Fabian. Mrs. C. Kernahan
Soul of the Sword. R. Bridges
Soul Scar. A. B. Reeve

Souls Adrift. A. Askew
Souls in Bondage. P. Gibbon
Souls in Hell. John O'Neill
Souls on Fire. L. Tracy
Sound Alibi. M. Edwin
Sound an Alarm. G. Holden
Sound Machine. E. Snell
Sound of a Voice. L. Gardiner
Sound of Dying Roses. J. De Pre
Sound of Footsteps. L. Ford
Sound of Hasty Footsteps. B. La Force
Sound of Insects. Mildred Davis
Sound of Lightning. J. Cleary
Sound of Midnight. C. L. Grant
Sound of Murder. J. Bonett
Sound of Murder. W. Fairchild
Sound of Murder. K. Fearing
Sound of Murder. R. Stout
Sound of Murder. Martin Thomas
Sound of Rain. P. Muse
Sound of Revelry. O. R. Cohen
Sound of Rowlocks. W. D. Steele
Sound of the Sea. R. Abbey
Sound of the Weir. M. Ingate
Sound of Water. M. S. Gerry
Sound of Winter. F. L. Green
Sounder of Swine. P. Buchanan
Soundless Scream. M. Butterworth
Soundless Years. M. Home
Sour Apple Tree. J. Blackburn
Sour Cream with Everything. J. Porter
Sour Grapes. H. Bindloss
Sour Lemon Score. R. Stark
Source of Death. H. Windsor
Source of Fear. B. S. Ballinger
Sourdough Gold. J. B. Hendryx
South by Java Head. Alistair MacLean
South Coast Mystery. J. Drummond
South Coast Mystery. H. H. C. Gibbons
South Coast of Danger. V. Connolly
South Foreland Murder. J. S. Fletcher
South of Heaven. J. Thompson
South of Hell's Gates. Richard Butler
South of the Line. G. Volk
South of the Sun. Wade Miller
South Pacific Affair. E. Lacy
South Pole Terror. K. Robeson
South Sea Bubble. R. Pertwee
South Sea Gold. C. Rodda
South Sea Sarah, and Murder in Paradise. B. Grimshaw
Southarn Folly. P. Allardyce
Southern Daughter. D. Keene
Southern Electric Murder. F. J. Whaley
Southern Fires. J. G. Sarasin
Southern Moon. J. Parkhurst
Souvenir. P. Carlon
Souvenir from Qam. M. Connelly
Souvenir of Monique. M. Z. Bradley
Sovereign Solution. M. M. McNamara
Soviet Marriage. P. Trent
Sow the Wind. D. M. Disney
Soyuz Affair. S. Coulter
Space Bean. J. Robb
Space for Hire. W. F. Nolan
Spacehawk, Inc. R. Goulart
Spades at Midnight. S. Maddock
Spahis. M. McCracken
Spandau Quid. O. Fleming
Spandau Warrent. Allan Morgan
Spaniard. P. Pettit
Spaniard in the Works. J. Lennon
Spaniard's Gift. E. Welles
Spaniard's House. Robin Temple
Spaniard's Leap. H. Davie-Martin
Spaniard's Thumb. N. Berrow
Spanish Blood. R. Chandler
Spanish Cape Mystery. E. Queen
Spanish Chapel. D. Daniels
Spanish Connection. Nick Carter
Spanish Cove. L. A. Knight
Spanish Crown Affair. C. Conte
Spanish Death. E. R. G. R. Evans
Spanish Duet. F. Clifford
Spanish Galleon. N. Tranter
Spanish Hawk. J. Pattinson
Spanish Heels. D. Whitelaw
Spanish House. H. Bourne
Spanish Interlude. Margery Lawrence
Spanish Lady. M. Cronin
Spanish Lady. A. Fredericks
Spanish Prisoner. P. C. De Crespigny
Spanish Prisoner. F. Gruber
Spanish Prisoner. F. Tilden
Spanish Season. B. Oldsey
Spanish Steps. G. Goodchild
Spanish Steps. P. McGuire
Spanking Girls. Carter Brown
Spanner. T. Chastain
Spare the Vanquished. M. F. Page
Spare Time for Murder. J. Gale
Spargo. J. D. Scott
Sparkling Cyanide. A. Christie
Sparrows of Paris. M. Pei
Sparta Medallion. H. L. Lawrence
Spawn. R. Holles
Spawn of Satan. C. Birkin
Spawn of the Desert. W. C. Tuttle
Spawn of the Hawk. P. Conde
Spayde Conspiracy. J. Pattinson
Speak for the Dead. R. Burns
Speak Ill of the Dead. Peter Chambers

Speak Ill of the Dead. Richard Williams
Speak Justly of the Dead. E. C. R. Lorac
Speak No Evil. M. G. Eberhart
Speak No Evil of the Dead. M. L. Roby
Speak of the Devil. E. S. Holding
Speak Softly to the Dead. D. Bogard
Speak to Me of Love. D. Eden
Speaker. G. Ashe
Speaking Eye. Clark Smith
Speaking of Murder. A. Roos
Speaking of Murder. V. Van Urk
Speaking Stones. S. Cardiff
Spear. J. Herbert
Spear Gun Murders. B. Kendrick
Spearhead. F. M. Davis
Spearhead Death. M. Procter
Special Agent. Roland Daniel
Special Agent. N. Gerson
Special Agent. J. R. McCarthy
Special Branch: In at the Kill. J. Eyers
Special Collection. T. Allbeury
Special Delivery. V. Gielgud
Special Delivery. J. Pattinson
Special Detective: Ashton-Kirk. J. T. MacIntyre
Special Duty. P. N. Walker
Special Edition—Murder. A. Kent
Special Murders. A. Douglas
Special Orders for Commander Leigh. R. H. Savage
Special Providence. M. A. Hamilton
Special Relationship. W. Clark
Specialist. Jasper Smith
Specialist in Crime. G. G. Bolton
Specialists. Lawrence Block
Specialty of the House. S. Ellin
Specimen Case. E. Bramah
Speck of the Motley. F. Hume
Speckled Swan. Dexter Muir
Spectacle. R. Kruger
Spectacles of Mr. Cagliostro. H. S. Keeler
Specter of the Dunes. K. Ostrander
Spectral Bride. J. Shearing
Spectral Evidence. R. Hare
Spectral Mist. C. Ross
Spectre. R. Weverka
Spectre Bullet. T. Mack
Spectre Chief. F. Legge
Spectre Gold. H. Hill
Spectre in Brown. H. Adams
Spectre Lover. E. Southworth
Spectre Mother. Anonymous
Spectre of Dolphin Cove. K. Kimbrough
Spectre of Lanmere Abbey. S. Wilkinson
Spectre of the Camera. J. Hawthorne
Spectre of the Forest. J. McHenry
Spectre of the Turret. I. Crookenden
Spectre's Secret. S. Cobb
Sped Arrow. V. Watkinson
Speech Day Murder. F. Dobbs
Speed King. J. Addiscombe
Speed Queens. B. Bogar
Speedo! M. Urquhart
Speedwell. T. Claymore
Speedy Death. G. Mitchell
Speight Street Angle. O. Norton
Spell of Choti. Anita Allen
Spell of Sarnia. B. Reynolds
Spell of the Antilles. L. Robin
Spell of the Devil. F. E. Penny
Spell of the Snow. C. G. Mitford
Spellbound. F. Beeding
Spellbound. C. Vincent
Spells of Evil. P. Boileau
Spence and the Holiday Murders. M. Allen
Spence at the Blue Bazaar. M. Allen
Spence in Petal Park. M. Allen
Spencer Blair, G-Man. Roland Daniel
Spencer's Bag. W. M. Green
Spend Game. J. Gash
Spend the Night. Grant Lane
Sphinx. F. Converse
Sphinx. R. Cook
Sphinx's Lawyer. F. Danby
Spice Route Contract. P. Atlee
Spicy Lady. J. A. Daley
Spider. Elliot Bailey
Spider. R. Brome
Spider. F. Hume
Spider. F. Oursler
Spider. G. Oursler
Spider and the Fly. Graham Lord
Spider and the Fly. R. A. J. Walling
Spider at the Elvira. L. Dundas
Spider Ballet. A. G. Wilson
Spider Flies Again. J. R. Holden
Spider Game. G. Courtis
Spider Girls. D. Walshe
Spider House. V. W. Mason
Spider in the Cup. J. Shearing
Spider in the Morning. D. Hart-Davis
Spider in the Web. N. Brent
Spider Island. T. Taggart
Spider Joe. F. Johnston
Spider Lily. B. Fischer
Spider Man. T. A. Plummer
Spider Never Falls. Winifred Graham
Spider of Soho. S. Cranbrook
Spider of Truxillo. R. H. Savage
Spider on the Belly. W. Rabon

Spider Orchid. C. Fremlin
Spider Run Alive. B. Munslow
Spider Spinning. P. Troubetzkoy
Spider Stone. E. E. Cameron
Spider Strikes. M. Innes
Spider Strikes! R. T. M. Scott
Spider Underground. K. Royce
Spider Woman. J. Goodwin
Spider's. Richard Lewis
Spider's Debt. J. McCulley
Spider's Den. J. McCulley
Spider's Den. Harrington Strong
Spider's Eye. W. LeQueux
Spider's Fury. J. McCulley
Spiders in the Night. B. Edmunds
Spider's Parlor. Nicholas Carter
Spider's Parlour. P. Wynnton
Spider's Touch. V. Williams
Spider's Web. R. Brome
Spider's Web. A. Christie
Spider's Web. Roland Daniel
Spider's Web. Winifred Duke
Spiders' Web. S. Harvester
Spider's Web. R. W. Kauffman
Spider's Web. J. Nazel
Spider's Web. S. Rathbone
Spider's Web. Mansfield Scott
Spiderweb. R. Bloch
Spiderweb. Alice Campbell
Spiderweb. J. E. Persico
Spiderweb Clues. P. Thorne
Spies. T. Von Harbou
Spies. S. C. S. Stone
Spies Abounding. M. Annesley
Spies Abroad. Anonymous
Spies Against Them. C. R. Dumas
Spies Along the Severn. S. Maddock
Spies and Rebels. Operator 1384
Spies Are Abroad. J. M. Walsh
Spies Die at Dawn. H. Hossent
Spies from the Skies. J. M. Walsh
Spies Go Running. O. Quinn
Spies Have No Friends. H. Hossent
Spies in Action. M. Annesley
Spies in Amber. A. Armstrong
Spies in Ambush. J. H. Vahey
Spies in Concert. R. Stephenson
Spies in Pursuit. J. M. Walsh
Spies in Spain. J. M. Walsh
Spies in the Web. M. Annesley
Spies, Inc. J. D. Hunter
Spies Left! D. Betteridge
Spies Ltd. G. H. Teed
Spies Never Return. J. M. Walsh
Spies of Good Intent. G. Veraldi
Spies of Peace. W. Martyn
Spies of Peenemunde. D. Betteridge
Spies of the Kaiser. W. LeQueux
Spies of the Secret Police. J. G. Rowe
Spies of the Wight. H. Hill
Spies on the Roof. O. Quinn
Spies over France. James Stewart
Spies' Vendetta. J. M. Walsh
Spies Within. M. Annesley
Spike. A. De Borchgrave
Spiked Heel. R. Marsten
Spiked Lion. B. Flynn
Spill the Jackpot! A. A. Fair
Spin a Coin for Murder. V. B. Hoyt
Spin a Dark Web. A. Barron
Spin a Dark Web. M. Clare
Spin Me a Shadow. V. Black
Spin of the Coin. E. R. Punshon
Spin the Glass Web. M. Ehrlich
Spin the Web Tight. D. Lyon
Spin Your Crime. J. Carol
Spin Your Web, Lady! R. Lockridge
Spinach Jade. James Bennett
Spindrift. P. A. Whitney
Spine. H. Imber
Spinner of Death. Nicholas Carter
Spinners of Life. V. Thompson
Spinning Target. J. Nazel
Spinsters. John Williams
Spinsters in Jeopardy. N. Marsh
Spinster's Secret. Anthony Gilbert
Spiral. Robert Garrett
Spiral Path. Richard Grayson
Spiral Staircase. F. A. Leslie
Spiral Staircase. Ethel L. White
Spiral Web. J. M. Wallmann
Spirit and the Bride. H. J. Kaplan
Spirit Murder Mystery. R. Forsythe
Spirit of Brynmaster Oaks. A. J. Griffin
Spirit of Cove Island. R. M. Sears
Spirit-of-Iron. H. Steele
Spirit of Melissa Norgate. E. E. Mande
Spirit of the Castle. W. C. Proby
Spirit of Turrettville. Anonymous
Spirit Smugglers. G. H. Teed
Spiritualists and the Detectives. A. Pinkerton
Spitting Image. M. Avallone
Spiv's Mistake. J. Hunter
Splash of Red. A. MacKenzie
Splendid Adventure of Hannibal Tod. E. Jepson
Splendid Blackguard. R. Pocock
Splendid Coward. H. Townley
Splendid Crime. G. Goodchild
Splendid Exile. L. P. Greene
Splendid Imposter. F. Whishaw

Splendid Love. H. S. Cooper
Splendid Outcast. G. F. Gibbs
Splendid Sin. G. Allen
Splendor and the Dust. H. Gibbs
Splendour Falls. K. Lindsay
Splinter of Glass. J. Creasey
Splinter of Ice. B. Marriner
Splintered Man. M. E. Chaber
Splintered Sunglasses Affair. P. Leslie
Splinters of Fear. N. W. Erickson
Split. G. F. Newman
Split. R. Stark
Split Bamboo. L. Phillips
Split Down the Middle. David Miles
Split on Red. W. Hughes
Split Peas. H. Hill
Split Scene. F. Mullally
Spoil! E. G. Perrault
Spoil of the Desert. H. H. Hill
Spoiler of Men. R. Marsh
Spoilers. D. Bagley
Spoilers and the Spoils. Nicholas Carter
Spoils of Ararat. R. Katz
Spoils of Chance. Nicholas Carter
Spoilt Girl. F. Warden
Spoilt Kill. M. Kelly
Spoletta Story. J. D. White
Spoofs. R. B. Glaenzer
Spook Hole. K. Robeson
Spook Legion. K. Robeson
Spook Who Sat by the Door. S. Greenlee
Spooks. R. J. Sherman
Spooks Alive. L. Rose
Spooks and Spasms. J. Tobias
Spooks Sometimes Sing. J. Courage
Spooky Hollow. C. Wells
Spooky Junction. J. F. Stone
Spooky Riders. W. C. Tuttle
Spooky Tavern. J. Tobias
Spoonful of Luger. R. Ormerod
Sport for Inspector West. J. Creasey
Sport for the Baron. Anthony Morton
Sport of Chance. T. W. Speight
Sport of Fate. L. Clarke
Sport of Fate. R. Dowling
Sport of Fate. Old Spicer
Sport of Kings. A. S. Roche
Sport of the Gods. Grove Wilson
Sporting Chance. A. Askew
Sporting Deacon. C. E. Blaney
Sporting Offer. F. Warden
Sporting Proposition. J. Aldridge
Sports Freak. S. OCork
Sportsman-Detective. Mansfield Scott
Spot Marked X. B. Gray
Spot of Bother. V. Sylvaine
Spot of Murder and other stories. P. Cheyney
Spot the Lady. L. Powell
Spotlight. J. Korotkin
Spotlight. P. Wentworth
Spotlight on a Simple Case. Roberts Morgan
Spotlight on Murder. F. A. Symonds
Spotlight on Murder. Martin Thomas
Spotlight on Murder. J. Wellard
Spotted Hemlock. G. Mitchell
Spotted Men. K. Robeson
Spotted Soldiers. C. E. Dibb
Spread of Sail. J. D. White
Spreewald Collection. D. MacKenzie
Sprengler Cache. M. Stall
Sprig of Sea Lavender. J. R. L. Anderson
Spriggs the Cracksman. H. Hill
Spring Came Late. G. Greenaway
Spring Comes to the Crescent. Elizabeth Ford
Spring Cruise. L. A. Knight
Spring Darkness. J. Metcalfe
Spring Fire. V. Packer
Spring Harrowing. P. A. Taylor
Spring of Malice. J. Harris
Spring of the Tiger. V. Holt
Spring of Violence. Dell Shannon
Spring Term. B. Hamilton
Springboard. J. Fores
Springers. B. Mather
Springs of Violence. E. Lindall
Spun Silk. W. J. Elliott
Spur of Danger. C. C. Hotchkiss
Spurious Note Maker. J. K. Stafford
Spurs of Troodos. W. H. Murray
Spy. J. F. Cooper
Spy. N. Garbo
Spy. S. Horler
Spy. B. Newman
Spy. P. Thomas
Spy. T. Von Harbou
Spy Against the Reich. M. Annesley
Spy and Die. Martin Meyers
Spy and the Thief. E. D. Hoch
Spy at Angkor Wat. B. S. Ballinger
Spy at Evening. Donald James
Spy at No. 10. B. Newman
Spy at the Villa Miranda. Elsie Lee
Spy Business. J. Pendower
Spy Castle. Nick Carter
Spy Catchers. N. MacNeil
Spy Catchers. B. Newman
Spy Company. A. C. Gunter
Spy Concerto. C. Merlin
Spy Converted. P. Boulle

Spy Corner. M. Annesley
Spy-Counter Spy. M. Annesley
Spy-Counter Spy. D. Betteridge
Spy Flyers. W. E. Johns
Spy for a Spy. B. Mather
Spy for Churchill. R. Vacha
Spy for England. Martin Kent
Spy for Germany. E. Gimpel
Spy for Mr. Crook. Anthony Gilbert
Spy for Napoleon. Rachelle Edwards
Spy for Sale. L. Payne
Spy from Spain. J. G. Brandon
Spy from the Grave. James Dark
Spy Game. M. Lovell
Spy Game. J. McNeil
Spy Gang. P. Sebastian
Spy Ghost. N. Daniels
Spy Hunt. N. Daniels
Spy Hunter. W. LeQueux
Spy Hunters. J. Bolton
Spy-In. R. Deming
Spy in Amber. M. Malgamukar
Spy in Bangkok. B. S. Ballinger
Spy in Black. J. S. Clouston
Spy in Black. C. Weston
Spy in Camera. Richard Grayson
Spy in Chancery. K. Benton
Spy in Damascus. N. Vange
Spy in Khaki. M. McKenna
Spy in the Brown Derby. B. Newman
Spy in the Family. A. Waugh
Spy in the Hand. Henry Talbot
Spy in the Java Sea. B. S. Ballinger
Spy in the Jungle. B. S. Ballinger
Spy in the Navy. D. Lenton
Spy in the Nude. R. Seth
Spy in the Ointment. D. E. Westlake
Spy in the Room. D. Clift
Spy in the Tunnel. John Morgan
Spy in the Vodka. Ross Thomas
Spy in White Gloves. J. Laflin
Spy Is a Dirty Word. R. Temple
Spy Is Forever. R. P. French
Spy Island. M. Annesley
Spy Kill. L. W. Blanco
Spy Meets Spy. C. V. Frost
Spy Net. Ared White
Spy Now, Pay Later. N. Rich
Spy No. 13. R. W. Chambers
Spy of Osawatomie. M. E. Jackson
Spy on Approval. R. Child
Spy on Riverside Drive. C. Rauch
Spy or Die. B. Graham
Spy Paramount. E. P. Oppenheim
Spy Puppets. Geoffrey Davison
Spy Story. L. Deighton
Spy Trap. B. Graham
Spy 222. R. Dark
Spy Was Born. M. McKenna
Spy Who Came Home to Die. J. Weil
Spy Who Came in from the Cold. J. Le Carre
Spy Who Came in from the Copa. Dagmar
Spy Who Didn't. J. Laflin
Spy Who Died in Bed. G. Wolfenden
Spy Who Died of Boredom. G. Mikes
Spy Who Died Twice. M. Bar-Zohar
Spy Who Got Off at Las Vegas. D. Savage
Spy Who Hated Fudge. R. L. Hershatter
Spy Who Hated Licorice. R. L. Hershatter
Spy Who Loved America. J. Laflin
Spy Who Loved Me. I. Fleming
Spy Who Sat and Saited. R. W. Campbell
Spy Who Spoke Porpoise. P. Wylie
Spy Who Swopped Shoes. Geoffrey Davison
Spy Who Was Three Feet Tall. P. Rabe
Spy Who Wasn't Exchanged. A. Tack
Spy with a Cold Nose. R. Galton
Spy with the Blue Kazoo. Dagmar
Spy with the Scar. J. Rowland
Spying at the Fountain of Youth. W. Butler
Spying Blind. James Dark
Spying Blind. M. McKenna
Spylight. J. Leasor
Spylight. W. Taylor
Spymaster. D. Freed
Spymaster. P. Freund
Spymaster. E. P. Oppenheim
Spyrocket. W. Taylor
Spy's Wife. R. Hill
Spyship. T. Keene
Squaberry Canyon. A. Rutherford
Squadron Without a Number. G. E. Rochester
Square Circle. J. P. Judge
Square Dance. L. Wainwright
Square Deal. G. Goodchild
Square Emerald. F. Johns
Square Emerald. E. Wallace
Square in the Middle. W. C. Gault
Square Mark. Grace M. White
Square of Many Colours. J. Blackmore
Square One. H. Janson
Square Peg. G. Malcolm-Smith
Squaring the Triangle, and other stories. H. Kaner
Squaw Point. R. H. Shimer
Squeaker. E. Wallace
Squeaking Golbin. K. Robeson
Squealer. Johnny Dark
Squealer. G. Verner

Squealer. E. Wallace
Squealer's Secret. Donald Stuart
Squeeze. G. Brewer
Squeeze. D. Craig
Squeeze Play. J. McKimmey
Squeeze Play. T. H. Stone
Squid. K. Horan
Squire Errant. R. Foxall
Squire of Death. R. Lockridge
Squire of Kilderman. F. Burdon
Squire of Landrewn. G. V. Vosper
Squire Trevlyn's Heir. H. Wood
Squire's Fatal Will. M. Danvers
Squire's Heir. E. Everett-Green
Squire's Legacy. M. C. Hay
Stab in the Back. H. Adams
Stab in the Back. C. Drummond
Stab in the Dark. J. Rayter
Stab in the Dark. L. Trimble
Stable Mystery, and other stories. N. Gould
Stables Crime. M. Osborne
Stables to £1,000,000. Gordon Holt
Stacey. W. Sherman
Stacked Deck. F. Kane
Staffordshire Assassins. C. Stokes
Staffordshire Knot. J. Ruegg
Stag Party. W. Krasner
Stage Door. A. Applin
Stage Door Crime. G. Chester
Stage Door Fright. Dulcie Gray
Stage Door Murder. S. Bate
Stage-Struck. A. Applin
Stage Struck. S. Gray
Stages of Terror. B. Kingsley
Stain. F. Halsey
Stain of Suspicion. C. Williams
Stain on the Snow. G. Simenon
Stained Glass. W. F. Buckley
Stainless Steel Rat. H. Harrison
Stainless Steel Rat Saves the World. H. Harrison
Stainless Steel Rat Wants You. H. Harrison
Stainless Steel Rat's Revenge. H. Harrison
Stainless Steel Wreath. J. Hedges
Staircase 4. H. Reilly
Staircase of Surprise. F. A. Mathews
Stairs Lead Nowhere. H. Swiggett
Stairs of Sand. E. D. Pierson
Stairway. U. Curtiss
Stairway to an Empty Room. D. Hitchens
Stairway to Death. B. Fischer
Stairway to Murder. A. Kent
Stairway to Murder. O. Mills
Stairway to Murder. F. Usher
Stairway to Nowhere. H. Ellson
Stake in the Game. E. Berckman
Stake Out. Ken Blake
Stalag Mites. L. Grex
Stalemate. E. Berckman
Stalk a Long Shadow. R. Severn
Stalk the Hunter. M. A. Wilson
Stalk the Killer. Steve Davis
Stalk to Kill. R. Adam
Stalked by Fear. L. Robin
Stalker. B. Pronzini
Stalkers. P. Ketchum
Stalkers of the Sea. K. Stanton
Stalking. T. Seligson
Stalking Blind. S. Ashley
Stalking Horse. V. Gielgud
Stalking Horse. A. Rothberg
Stalking Lamb. M. Babson
Stalking Man. W. Tucker
Stalking of Adrian Lawford. Roderick Grant
Stalking Stranger. Colin Robertson
Stalking Terror. V. Coffman
Stamboul Intrigue. R. Charles
Stamboul Train. G. Greene
Stamp Me Mortal. J. Lodwick
Stamped for Death. E. McDowell
Stamped for Murder. B. Benson
Stampede. L. Sieveking
Stampeders. J. B. Hendryx
Stand and Deliver. G. Warden
Stand By! Taffrail
Stand By for Danger. P. Manton
Stand By—London Calling. H. S. Keeler
Stand By to Shoot. E. Cannon
Stand In. B. Kingsley
Stand-In. E. Piper
Stand-In for Danger. K. Hewitt
Stand-In for Danger. R. Rayner
Stand-In for Death. M. Echard
Stand-In for Murder. L. Gribble
Stand-In for Murder. A. C. MacLean
Stand-In for Murder. D. Reid
Stand Up and Die. R. Lockridge
Stand Up and Fight. David Hume
Standard-Bearers. K. Mayo
Standing into Danger. J. Griffin
Standish Gaunt Case. I. Patterson
Standish Place. I. Holland
Stanhope Gate Mystery. R. Machray
Stanhope of Chester. P. Andreae
Stanton Wins. E. M. Ingram
Star Above Paris. J. G. Sarasin
Star Crossed. M. Mead
Star-Crossed Love. Elsie Lee

Star-Crossed Lover. Carter Brown
Star Detective. D. Essex
Star Driver. L. Correy
Star Dust. J. Ronald
Star Fire. I. Swann
Star-Gazers. G. M. Fenn
Star House. R. Newell
Star in a Mist. A. Stringer
Star Is Falling. M. Richmond
Star King. J. Vance
Star Light, Star Bright. S. Ellin
Star of Danger. Elsie Lee
Star of Death. M. Gillen
Star of Earth. O. R. Cohen
Star of Evil. L. Noel
Star of Hollywood. E. Stilgebauer
Star of Ill-Omen. D. Wheatley
Star of Midnight. A. S. Roche
Star of Persia. R. Adams
Star of the East. C. E. Pearce
Star of the Goddess. M. Clare
Star Ruby Contract. P. Atlee
Star Spangled Contract. J. Garrison
Star Stalker. R. Bloch
Star Trap. Simon Brett
Star Trap. R. Colby
Star Well. A. Panshin
Star Witness. Rick Madison
Star Witness. J. Wood
Starbuck. Bryan Peters
Starcrossed Road. M. Farnsworth
Starett. A. V. Deutsch
Starfish Affair. J. N. Chance
Stargate. S. Robinett
Staring Eyes! T. A. Plummer
Stark Docket. S. Dave
Stark Inheritance. E. Kyle
Stark Island. Lynna Cooper
Stark Murder. L. Thayer
Stark Naked. L. R. Bourne
Starlet for a Penny. W. A. Ballinger
Starlight Motel Incident. J. Weisman
Starling Street. D. Palmtag
Starmaker. H. Denker
Starr Bedford Dies. R. Garnett
Starrbelow. C. Thompson
Starry-Eyed Chipmonk. S. M. Schley
Starry Eyed Murder. T. A. Plummer
Stars and Stripes. M. Dekobra
Stars Are Dark. P. Cheyney
Stars Cannot Tell. A. Maybury
Stars for the Toff. J. Creasey
Stars Give Warning. Brenda Conrad
"Stars I'd Give—." A. Soutar
Stars in the Heather. O. Wynd
Stars in the Water. J. Appleby
Stars of Evil. D. E. Stitt
Stars Scream Murder. A. B. Reeve
Stars Spell Death. J. Stagge
Starsky and Hutch. M. Franklin
Starstruck. E. Tidyman
Start Screaming Murder. T. Powell
Starting Gun. G. Bagby
Startling and Thrilling Narrative of the Dark and Terrible Deeds of Henry Medison, and His Associate and Accomplice, Miss Ella Stevens, Who Was Executed by the Vigilance Committee of San Francisco, on the 20th September Last. S. Drury
Startling Crimes and Notorious Criminals. D. Donovan
Startling Discovery. Old Sleuth
Starved. A. Thompson
Starvel Hollow Tragedy. F. W. Crofts
Stash Spots a Murder. R. Peters
State Department Cat. M. Plum
State Department Murders. E. Ronns
State of Emergency. J. Robb
State of Emergency. Sheila Ross
State of Fear. D. Reid
State of Grace. R. Tine
State of Seige. E. Ambler
State Puppet. Dorothy Bennett
State Secrets. W. B. Home-Gall
State Torch. J. G. Sarasin
State Trooper. N. B. Gerson
State vs. Elinor Norton. M. R. Rinehart
State vs. Elna Jepson. N. B. Mavity
State Visit. C. Egleton
Stateline. J. Van Der Zee
Stately Home Murder. C. Aird
Stately Homicide. G. Milner
Stateroom Opposite. A. H. Veysey
Statesman's Game. J. Aldridge
Station in the Delta. J. Cassidy
Station Master's Secret. A. Murray
Station Wagon in Spain. F. P. Keyes
Station Wagon Murder. M. Propper
Station X. G. M. Winsor
Statue. E. Phillpotts
Statue and the Lady. S. M. Wick
Status 1SQ. R. Herst
Stay Dead, Sweetheart. R. Drayton
Stay of Execution. H. Desmond
Stay of Execution. M. Gilbert
Stay of Execution. L. Halliday
Stay of Execution. E. C. Williams
Stay Out of Menchis. B. Sarto
Stay Until Tomorrow. A. Maybury
Steadfast Heart. M. Richmond
Steady, Boys, Steady. J. Mitchell

Steal Big. P. Mann
Steal Big. L. White
Stealing Lillian. T. Kenrick
Stealthy Death. M. Richmond
Stealthy Steve, the Six-Eyed Sleuth. N. Newkirk
Stealthy Terror. J. Ferguson
Steam Pig. J. McClure
Steamboatmen. C. J. C. Hyne
Stedman Gang. Roland Daniel
Steel Balloon. H. McLeave
"Steel" Callaghan. M. Chesney
Steel Casket and other stories. Nicholas Carter
Steel Crown. F. Hume
Steel Face. Gwyn Evans
Steel Garrotte. J. Ingersol
Steel Hit. R. Stark
Steel Mask. M. Carrel
Steel Mirror. D. Hamilton
Steel Necklace. F. Du Boisgobey
Steel Noose. A. Drake
Steel Palace. H. Pentecost
Steel Shutters. Gavin Holt
Steel Spring. P. Wahloo
Steel Trap. A. Sugar
Steele Bey's Revenge. T. Lund
Steeley Flies Again. W. E. Johns
Steeltown Strangler. H. S. Keeler
Steelyard Blues. Timothy Harris
Steep Steps. K. Ingram
Stella Buys a Shroud. M. Storm
Stella Nash. Ganpat
Stella Shall Die. H. Desmond
Stench of Poppies. I. Drummond
Step Aside to Death. S. Maddock
Step by Step. C. Collins
Step in the Dark. F. Cowen
Step in the Dark. K. Eyre
Step in the Dark. E. Lemarchand
Step in the Dark. Ethel L. White
Step in the House. R. Ramsay
Step into Murder. S. Curtis
Step into Quicksand. L. Treat
Step into Terror. Marilyn Ross
Step Lightly, Lady. Margery Lawrence
Step on the Stair. A. K. Green
Step Softly on My Grave. M. A. Hubbard
Step Stoftly, Sweetheart. Rod Callahan
Step Up, Sucker. Gene Ross
Stepfather. C. Jay
Stepford Wives. I. Levin
Stephen Vale. P. Trent
Stepmother's House. C. Bramwell
Stepping Blindfold. T. W. Speight
Steps Going Down. J. T. MacIntyre
Steps in Mystery. T. R. Morden
Steps in the Dark. M. Black
Steps in the Dark. M. Cumberland
Steps to Murder. R. King
Steps to Murder. R. P. Koehler
Steps to Nowhere. C. Leonard
Stereopticon. S. R. Lucas
Sterling Standard. G. Brandner
Stern Chase. G. Hackforth-Jones
Sterne of the Secret Service. J. A. Jordan
Stettin Secret. J. S. Thayer
Steve. G. Goodchild
Steve Bentley's Calypso Caper. R. Dietrich
Stevedore Mystery. B. North
Steward. E. Wallace
Stewardess Strangler. R. Gallagher
Stick at Nothing. A. Wood
Stick 'Em Up! F. Ryerson
Stick or Bust. R. Drayton
Sticking Place. Jessica Mann
Sticking Point. K. Jackson
Sticks and Stones. M. L. Dodge
Stiff As a Broad. G. G. Fickling
Stiff Silk. S. Milne
Stiff Upper Lip. P. Israel
Stiffs Can't Squeal. Griff
Stiffs Don't Vote. G. Homes
Stiffsons, and other stories. H. Jenkins
Stigma. Williams Forrest
Stigma for Valor. Williams Forrest
Stiletto. B. Rossi
Stiletto Signature. J. Messmann
Still and Woven Blue. R. Stookey
Still As the Grave. M. L. Roby
Still Dead. R. A. Knox
Still No Answer. L. Thayer
Still of Night. L. Powell
Still the World Is Young. K. Hewitt
Still They Smile. P. Conway
Still Water. K. N. Burt
Still Waters. Dorothy Fletcher
Still Waters. E. C. R. Lorac
Still Waters. F. F. Van De Water
Stillwater Tragedy. T. B. Aldrich
Stillwell Murder. M. T. Dawson
Sting. W. LeQueux
Sting. R. Weverka
Sting of Death. Jessica Mann
Sting of Death. P. D. Westbrook
Sting of the Adder. Nicholas Carter
Sting of the Honeybee. F. Parrish
Stingaree. E. W. Hornung
Stinagree Murders. W. S. Pleasants
Stinger. N. Gottlieb

Stink of Murder. W. Spann
Stinson's Reef. C. J. C. Hyne
"Stir." G. Ingram
"Stir" Crazy. B. Shannon
Stir of Echoes. R. Matheson
"Stir" Train. G. Ingram
Stirring Adventures. F. A. M. Webster
Stirrup Cup. J. A. Tyson
Stitch in Time. E. Lathen
Stitch in Time. A. Pearson
Stoat. L. Brock
Stockade. W. C. Tuttle
Stockbroker's Wife, and other sensational tales. B. Hemyng
Stockholders in Death. K. Robeson
Stoenberg Affair. R. A. Goodwin
Stoke Silver Case. L. Brock
Stolen Bacillus, and other incidents. H. G. Wells
Stolen Boat-Train. D. G. Browne
Stolen Brain. Nicholas Carter
Stolen Bride. E. Klein
Stolen Budget. J. S. Fletcher
Stolen Car. E. J. Rath
Stolen Cellini. Alan Thomas
Stolen Cipher. Sea Lion
Stolen Crown. J. W. Bobin
Stolen Death. L. Grex
Stolen Fiddle. W. H. Mayson
Stolen Formula Mystery. M. E. Cooke
Stolen Gold. J. Chancellor
Stolen Goods. C. B. Kelland
Stolen Heiress. C. Merrick
Stolen Home Secretary. L. Gribble
Stolen Honeymoon. M. Leighton
Stolen Husband. R. D. Andrews
Stolen Identity. Nicholas Carter
Stolen Idols. E. P. Oppenheim
Stolen Jewels. Old Spicer
Stolen Laces. J. W. Postgate
Stolen Laces. D. Simmons
Stolen Lady. A. Askew
Stolen Letter. C. Morris
Stolen Liberty Bonds. N. Ridley
Stolen Life. W. M. Bodkin
Stolen Like Magic Away. P. Audemars
Stolen Man. Mrs. C. Kernahan
Stolen Mask. W. Collins
Stolen Millionaire. S. Truss
Stolen Name. Nicholas Carter
Stolen Necklace. Roland Daniel
Stolen Nugget of Gold. N. Ridley
Stolen or Strayed. D. Collins
Stolen Partnership Papers. J. W. Bobin
Stolen Pay Train. Nicholas Carter
Stolen Pay Train and other stories. Nicholas Carter
Stolen Pearl. G. Warden
Stolen Peer. G. Boothby
Stolen Plans. R. Gar
Stolen Race. N. Gould
Stolen Race Horse. Nicholas Carter
Stolen Scar. Gret Lane
Stolen Signet. F. M. Smith
Stolen Singer. M. Bellinger
Stolen Souls. W. LeQueux
Stolen Squadron. C. L. Leonard
Stolen Statesman. L. Gribble
Stolen Statesman. W. LeQueux
Stolen Strychnine. B. Cobb
Stolen Submarine. R. Bacon
Stolen Submarine. S. Hope
Stolen Sweets. W. LeQueux
Stolen Test-Tube. W. Jardine
Stolen Virtue. C. Kingston
Stolen White Elephant. M. Twain
Stolen Will. W. S. Hayward
Stolen Will. M. Pinkerton
Stolen Woman. Wade Miller
Stomping Ground. Denis Hamill
Stone. Anthea Frazer
Stone. N. Tranter
Stone Around Her Neck. B. McKnight
Stone Baby. B. Healey
Stone Blunts Scissors. G. Fairlie
Stone Bull. P. A. Whitney
Stone Carnation. N. A. Hintze
Stone Cold Blonde. Adam Knight
Stone Cold Dead. R. Ellington
Stone Cold Dead. H. Garner
Stone Cold Dead in the Market. C. Landon
Stone-Cold Dead in the Market Affair. P. Leslie
Stone-Cold Dead in the Market Affair. J. Oram
Stone Dead. C. Ashton
Stone Dead. P. Laing
Stone Dead. San Antonio
Stone Dead. F. A. Symonds
Stone Dormitory. J. Turner
Stone Dragon and Other Tragic Romances. R. M. Gilchrist
Stone for His Head. B. Cobb
Stone House. D. Daniels
Stone Killer. J. Gardner
Stone Killer. F. Scarpetta
Stone Leopard. C. Forbes
Stone Maiden. W. Johnston
Stone Maiden. A. Manners
Stone Man. R. Robeson
Stone of Blood. J. Coulson
Stone Offering. Stephen Chance

Stone Roses. S. Gainham
Stone Walls. C. Heath
Stoned Cold Soldier. C. Dennis
Stonehaven. E. St. Clair
Stones of Enchantment. W. Martyn
Stones of Khor. D. Whitelaw
Stones of Satan. R. Wallace
Stones of Stavros. R. Ramsey
Stones of Strendleigh. G. Killoran
Stonewall Steevens Investigates. M. G. Kiddy
Stoneware Monkey. R. A. Freeman
Stool Pigeon. Roland Daniel
Stool Pigeon. L. Malley
Stop at Nothing. J. Welcome
Stop-at-Nothing Man. Roland Daniel
Stop at the Red Light. A. A. Fair
Stop on the Green Light! M. Barrington
Stop-Over Danger. V. Warren
Stop Press. M. Innes
Stop, Press! E. Spencer
Stop Press—Homicide! R. Dolphin
Stop Press in Scarlet. M. Brody
Stop Press Murder. G. Ramsey
Stop Press—Murder! P. Stirling
Stop That Man. C. Franklin
Stop That Man! R. Ladline
Stop Thief! G. C. Jenks
Stop Thief! C. Moore
Stop This Man! P. Rabe
Stopover for Murder. F. Mahannah
Stopover for Murder. T. H. Stone
Stopover: Tokyo. J. P. Marquand
Stopped Clock. J. T. Rogers
Store of Wrath. S. Truss
Store up the Anger. W. Ebersohn
Storefront Lawyers. A. L. Conroy
Stories and Reminiscences. Anonymous
Stories and Sketches. J. Payn
Stories Cops Only Tell Each Other. G. Radano
Stories from Scotland Yard. M. Moser
Stories from the Diary of a Doctor. L. T. Meade
Stories from the Note-Book of a Detective. D. Donovan
Stories in Black and White. G. R. Sims
Stories in Grey. B. Pain
Stories in the Dark. B. Pain
Stories of a World Renown Detective. Anonymous
Stories of Crime and Murder. C. K. Razdan
Stories of Darkness and Dread. J. P. Brennan
Stories of Donald Shoubridge. D. Shoubridge
Stories of East and West. H. D. Stacpoole
Stories of Fear. J. McLaren
Stories of Mystery and Horror. E. C. Gaskell
Stories of Ray Bradbury. R. Bradbury
Stories of the Broadmoor Patient, and the Poor Clerk. F. Wicks
Stories of the Railroad. J. A. Hill
Stories of the Railway. V. L. Whitechurch
Stories of the Seen and the Unseen. M. Oliphant
Stories of Three Burglars. F. R. Stockton
Stories of Today and Yesterday. P. C. De Crespigny
Stories Weird and Wonderful. H. Nisbet
Storm. H. L. V. Fletcher
Storm. Gavin Holt
Storm Against the Wall. L. Meynell
Storm and the Silence. D. Walker
Storm-Bound. J. G. Sarasin
Storm Breaks. A. Gask
Storm Canvas. E. L. Long
Storm Castle. Jan Anderson
Storm Center. B. E. Stevenson
Storm Centre. B. Musto
Storm Cloud over Vienna. O. L. Rosmanith
Storm Driven. A. Applin
Storm Evil. J. Robb
Storm Fear. C. Seeley
Storm Front. P. Finch
Storm Gang. Richard Grant
Storm Girl. J. C. Lincoln
Storm House. F. Hurd
Storm in a Sanctuary. K. Ingram
Storm in an Inkpot. C. Franklin
Storm in Harbour. G. Hackforth-Jones
Storm in the Family. J. Blackmore
Storm in the Mountains. N. Buckingham
Storm in the Sand. T. B. Morris
Storm Is Rising. G. Dyer
Storm Island. K. Follett
Storm Knight. F. E. Smith
Storm Lady. J. H. Vahey
Storm Maiden. K. Lindsay
Storm Music. D. Yates
Storm of Spears. A. C. Marin
Storm of Wrath. A. Dwyer-Joyce
Storm over Bitterhill. P. Warren
Storm over Fox Hill. G. Addison
Storm over Hollywood. J. Reach
Storm over Ibiza. R. Roleine
Storm over Paris. S. Noel

Title Index

Storm over Rockall. W. H. Baker
Storm over Roseheath. K. Troy
Storm over Windmere. C. Alcott
Storm Signals. R. H. Savage
Storm South. P. McCutchan
Storm Squad. P. Leslie
Storm Tarn. P. Troubetzkoy
Storm Tide. A. MacVicar
Storm Tossed. M. S. Jones
Storm Warning. J. Higgins
Storm Wind Rising. J. Rouverol
Storm Witch. E. Barr
Storm-Wrack. H. Hill
Stormberg Jewel Case. K. M. Sheahan
Stormcliff. M. T. Walworth
Stormhaven. Jennifer Hale
Stormlight. J. N. Chance
Storm's End. Rebecca James
Stormtide. B. Knox
Stormy Night. C. Hale
Stormy Paradise. K. Lindsay
Storrington Papers. D. Eden
Story Behind the Verdict. F. Danby
Story of a Dark Crime. Hawkshaw
Story of a Dead Woman. J. Kirkpatrick
Story of a Great Sin. M. Leighton
Story of a Killer. D. Spade
Story of a Sin. H. B. Mathers
Story of Antony Grace. G. M. Fenn
Story of Barbara. M. E. Braddon
Story of Charles Strange. H. Wood
Story of Clovelly's Wife. W. J. Newton
Story of Dorothy Grape, and other tales. H. Wood
Story of Dorothy Stanfield. O. Micheaux
Story of Ivy. M. B. Lowndes
Story of Joan Courage. R. Rodd
Story of Leland Gay. A. R. Weekes
Story of Professor X. J. Budd
Story of Rachel. R. Abbey
Story of the Fast Mail. C. Thornton
Story of the Foss River Ranch. R. Cullum
Story of the Phantom. L. Falk
Story of the Stage. C. R. Gull
Story Teller. G. Buhet
Story-Teller. P. Highsmith
Story That Could Not Be Told. M. Albrand
Story to Tell. P. Fleming
Story Without a Name. A. Stringer
Stout Cortez. G. Goodchild
Stowaway. R. Johnston
Stowaway. A. Mills
Stowaway. G. Simenon
Stowaway. L. Tracy
Stowaway Girl. L. Tracy
Stowaway of the S. S. Wanderer. A. Parsons
Stowmarket Mystery. L. Tracy
Straight. S. Knickmeyer
Straight Ahead for Danger. W. M. Duncan
Straight and Crooked. M. McShane
Straight Clue. Old Sleuth
Straight Crooks. H. Fielding
Straight Furrow. Constance Rutherford
Straight Man. K. Nelson
Straight-Out Detective. Old Sleuth
Straight Road. G. Radcliffe
Straight Shooting. W. C. Tuttle
Straight Time. E. Bunker
"Straight to the Mark." Old Sleuth
Straight-Up Girl. D. Glinto
Stranded. E. R. Beach
Stranded in Arcady. F. Lynde
Strands of Red...Hair! Glint Green
Strange Adventures of a Magistrate. T. R. Threlfall
Strange Adventures of Bromley Barnes. G. Barton
Strange Adventures of Handel Archimedes. C. W. Sykes
Strange Adventures of Miss Brown. R. Buchanan
Strange Adventures of Mr. Collin. F. Heller
Strange Adventures of Mr. Middleton. W. A. Curtis
Strange Adventures of Richard Conway Bowen. C. R. Benstead
Strange Affair. B. Toms
Strange Affair at Greylands. Mark Cross
Strange Affair of the Shot Gun Sniper. W. Tyrer
Strange Affair of the Widow's Diamonds. H. Clevely
Strange Affection. G. Des Cars
Strange Bargain. H. Whittington
Strange Bedfellow. E. Berckman
Strange Blue Yawl. L. Fletcher
Strange Boarders. G. Batson
Strange Boarders of Palace Crescent. E. P. Oppenheim
Strange Capers. A. Meeker
Strange Caravan. Margery Lawrence
Strange Career of Bishop Sterling. S. Endicott
Strange Cargo. M. Richmond
Strange Case. Anonymous
Strange Case for Dr. Rolland. J. Judson
Strange Case of Cavendish. R. Parrish
Strange Case of Deacon Brodie. F. Bramble
Strange Case of Dr. Bruno. F. E. Daniel
Strange Case of Dr. Earle. F. W. Crofts
Strange Case of Dr. Jekyll and Mr. Hyde. R. L. Stevenson
Strange Case of Edgar Heriot. F. Grierson
Strange Case of Eleanor Cuyler. K. Crosby
Strange Case of Habberton's Mile. W. J. Bayfield
Strange Case of Harriet Hall. M. Dalton
Strange Case of Henry Toplass and Capt. Shiers. J. W. Postgate
Strange Case of John R. Graham. V. Kutchin
Strange Case of Lucile Clery. J. Shearing
Strange Case of Mary Page. F. Lewis
Strange Case of Mr. Henry Marchmont. J. S. Fletcher
Strange Case of Mr. Jocelyn Thew. E. P. Oppenheim
Strange Case of Mr. Pelham. A. Armstrong
Strange Case of Mortimer Fenley. L. Tracy
Strange Case of Pamela Wilson. Mark Cross
Strange Case of Peter the Lett. G. Simenon
Strange Case of Sir Merton Quest. A. Soutar
Strange Case of the Antlered Man. E. S. Brooks
Strange Case of the Footman's Crime. G. Chester
Strange Case of Vincent Hume. D. Miall
Strange Case of Vintrix Polbarton. I. Marshall
Strange Case of William Cook. R. Keverne
Strange Cases of Dr. Stanchon. J. D. Bacon
Strange Cases of Magistrate Pao. L. Comber
Strange Cases of Mason Brant. N. M. Hopkins
Strange Citadel. R. Spain
Strange Clients. S. DeHavilland
Strange Clues. J. M'Govan
Strange Code of Justice. R. K. Isley
Strange Conflict. D. Wheatley
Strange Corner. Mildred Davis
Strange Corpse on Murder Mile. D. Boyle
Strange Countess. E. Wallace
Strange Crime in Bermuda. E. S. Holding
Strange Crimes. W. Westall
Strange Death of a Doctor. L. Landon
Strange Death of Manny Square. A. B. Cunningham
Strange Death of Martin Green. D. Frome
Strange Delilah. B. B.
Strange Destiny. C. Dawe
Strange Disappearance. A. K. Green
Strange Disappearance of Eugene Comstocks. M. R. Hatch
Strange Disappearance of John Haversham. I. D. Hardy
Strange Disappearance of Lady Delia. L. Tracy
Strange Disappearance of Mary Young. M. Propper
Strange Doctor and other mystic stories. V. Van Der Elst
Strange Doings on Halfaday Creek. J. B. Hendryx
Strange Enchantment. B. L. Farjeon
Strange Enchantment. P. Webling
Strange Ending. E. R. Punshon
Strange Experiences of Mr. Verschoyle. T. W. Speight
Strange Experiment. Valentine
Strange Face of Murder. W. A. Ballinger
Strange Fate. R. S. L. Harding
Strange Fellowship of Maxwell Gale. W. Bouchier
Strange Flaw. H. S. Wilcox
Strange Fortune. J. Salt
Strange Fugitive. M. Callaghan
Strange Happening. N. MacKenzie
Strange Harmony. A. Carr
Strange Heritage. M. A. Clune
Strange Heritage. L. Harper
Strange Heritage. T. Uphill
Strange Holiday. E. Gill
Strange Honeymoon. O. R. Cohen
Strange Infatuation. L. Harrison
Strange Inheritance. G. Simenon
Strange Inheritance. P. Trent
Strange Instrument. N. Rennie
Strange Journeys. B. Hemyng
Strange Land. H. Innes
Strange Landing. L. Meynell
Strange Legacy. A. Barron
Strange Legacy. L. Bergstrom
Strange Legacy. E. M. Williams
Strange Legacy of Aunt Bettina. L. Crail
Strange Little Snakes. J. Turner
Strange Lovers. J. Trinian
Strange Mansion. T. Rook
Strange Manuscript Found in a Copper Cylinder. J. De Mille
Strange Message. Dora Russell
Strange Money. Mark Ross
Strange Motives. R. Goyne
Strange Murder of Hatton, K. C. H. Adams
Strange Murders at Greystones. E. N. Wright
Strange Nocturne. Andrea Hill
Strange Occupation. J. A. Park
Strange Occurrences. Leopold Davis
Strange Paradise. D. Daniels
Strange Partner. D. Lee
Strange Partners. G. Wintle
Strange Place for Murder. C. Barroll
Strange Prisoner. M. Home
Strange Pursuit. N. R. De Mexico
Strange Pursuit. P. Wynnton
Strange Quartet. K. Rhodes
Strange Relations. Jerome Barry
Strange Rendezvous. H. D. Dearden
Strange Report. John Burke
Strange Return. A. B. Cunningham
Strange Ritual. H. Janson
Strange Romance. B. Herbert
Strange Salvation. K. Hewitt
Strange Sanctuary. E. Butler
Strange Schemes of Randolph Mason. M. D. Post
Strange Secrets. V. Coffman
Strange Sin. C. Kernahan
Strange Sisters. F. Flora
Strange Smell of Murder. L. Dundas
Strange Stories. G. Allen
Strange Stories from a Chinese Studio. H. A. Giles
Strange Stories of a Detective. Anonymous
Strange Stories of a Detective. Waters
Strange Stories of Strange People. O. Dale
Strange Story. E. Bulwer-Lytton
Strange Story. Hilda Lewis
Strange Story in the Falconer Papers. U. L. Silberrad
Strange Story of Linda Lee. D. Wheatley
Strange Sylvester Affair. L. Thayer
Strange Tales of a Nihilist. W. LeQueux
Strange Tangle. Alice King
Strange Visitor. H. Elsna
Strange Way Home. R. Easterling
Strange Welcome. F. A. Chittenden
Strange Will. H. S. Keeler
Strange Witness. D. Keene
Strange Witness. B. Symons
Strange Wooing. C. Gibbon
Strange Wooing. R. Marsh
Strange Wooing of Mary Bowler. R. Marsh
Strange World. M. E. Braddon
Strange Young Man. L. Gerard
Strangely She Died. N. Morland
Stranger. L. Barbee
Stranger. C. Dumas
Stranger. B. Forbes
Stranger Among Friends. E. Lindall
Stranger and Afraid. E. Ferrars
Stranger and Afraid. M. Hardt
Stranger at Christmas. A. MacVicar
Stranger at Home. G. Sanders
Stranger at Midnight. Coriola
Stranger at My Door. M. Kistler
Stranger at Pembroke. A. Eliot
Stranger at Plantation Inn. P. Maxwell
Stranger at the Gate. J. Edgar
Stranger at the Gates. Evelyn Anthony
Stranger at the Wedding. F. Lynch
Stranger at Wildings. M. Brent
Stranger Beware. Rick Madison
Stranger by Night. M. Lynn
Stranger by the Lake. Beatrice Parker
Stranger Called the Blues. S. Coulter
Stranger Came Back. C. Franklin
Stranger City Caper. R. H. Spencer
Stranger in a Dark Land. J. Wellsley
Stranger in Galah. Michael Barrett
Stranger in Her House. H. Arvonen
Stranger in His Grave. Dorothy Bennett
Stranger in My Arms. E. Raskin
Stranger in My Grave. M. Millar
Stranger in My Midst. V. Ross
Stranger in the Dark. H. Nielsen
Stranger in the House. A. Caballero
Stranger in the House. S. Mayfield
Stranger in the Land. M. Pereira
Stranger in the Night. P. S. McCoy
Stranger in These Parts. E. F. Boyd
Stranger in Town. R. Bloomfield
Stranger in Town. B. Halliday
Stranger in Town. J. Reach
Stranger in Town. J. D. White
Stranger Is Watching. M. H. Clark
Stranger on the Cliff. Josephine Bell
Stranger on the Highway. H. R. Hays
Stranger Than Fiction. C. Dawe
Stranger Than Fiction. H. Desmond
Stranger Than Truth. V. Caspary
Stranger Threatens. L. Dartey
Stranger to Herself. B. Williams
Stranger to Himself. J. Hansen
Stranger to Myself. S. Shubin
Stranger to Town. L. P. Davies
Stranger, Tread Light. Jean Muir
Stranger with My Face. P. McGerr
Stranger Within the Gates. C. N. Boyle
Strangers Among the Dead. G. Bellairs
Strangers and Afraid. T. Sterling

Strangers and Afraid / 603

S

Strangers and Pilgrims. M. E. Braddon
Strangers at Collins House. Marilyn Ross
Strangers from the Sea. A. MacVicar
Stranger's Gate. E. P. Oppenheim
Strangers in Comapny. J. A. Hodge
Strangers in Flight. M. G. Eberhart
Strangers in 7-A. F. Farrington
Strangers in the House. G. Simenon
Strangers in the Night. Genevieve St. John
Strangers in the Sun. M. Sheppard
Strangers Meeting. Winston Graham
Stranger's Meeting. R. Savage
Strangers of the Glen. H. M. Jones
Strangers on a Train. P. Highsmith
Strangers on Friday. H. Whittington
Strangers on the Moor. S. Thorpe
Strangest Grand National. F. Johnston
Strangle Hold! Al Conroy
Strangle Hold. M. McMullen
Strangled Witness. L. Ford
Stranglehold. H. Arvay
Stranglehold. H. Carmichael
Stranglehold. D. Cory
Stranglehold. J. Creighton
Stranglehold. A. Hocking
Stranglehold. G. C. Knapp
Stranglehold. D. T. Lindsay
Stranglehold. B. Reynolds
Strangler. D. Black
Strangler. H. Desmond
Strangler. L. Marshall
Strangler. T. A. Plummer
Strangler. E. C. Reed
Strangler. San Antonio
Strangler. Hampton Stone
Strangler. M. Thynne
Strangler. T. J. Williams
Strangler Fig. J. S. Strange
strangler Who Couldn't Let Go. Hampton Stone
Strangler's Holiday. K. Steel
Strangler's Moon. C. Leader
Stranglers of Bombay. Stuart James
Strangler's Serenade. W. Irish
Strasbourg Legacy. W. Craig
Strasburg Collection. E. L. McGinnis
Stratford Affair. P. Hastings
Straus. A. Bodelsen
Strausser Transfer. Don Smith
Straw Donkey Case. A. S. Fleischman
Straw Man. D. M. Disney
Straw Virgin. A. Barker
Strawberry Blonde Jungle. Carter Brown
Strawberry Marten. P. G. Winslow
Straws in the Wind. C. Dawe
Straws in the Wind. P. C. De Crespigny
Straws in the Wind. W. C. Tuttle
Strawstack. D. C. Disney
Strawstack Murders. D. C. Disney
Stray Bullet. D. Franklin
Streak of Light. R. Lockridge
Streaked-Blond Slave. Carter Brown
Streaked Peril. Nicholas Carter
Streaked with Crimson. C. J. Dutton
Streaker Murders. P. Dorian
Stream Sinister. K. M. Knight
Streamlined Dragon. L. C. Goldsmith
Streamlined Murder. P. MacTyre
Street. D. Lindquist
Street Cops. W. Klasne
Street 8. D. Fairbairn
Street Games. Eddie Stone
Street of Fear. J. Fast
Street of Fortune. M. L. Tyrrell
Street of Grass. P. Audemars
Street of No Return. D. Goodis
Street of Painted Lips. M. Dekobra
Street of Strange Faces. L. J. Vance
Street of the Crying Woman. G. Homes
Street of the Five Moons. Elizabeth Peters
Street of the Leopard. N. Morland
Street of the Lost. D. Goodis
Street of the Serpent. F. Beeding
Street of the Singing Fountain. Rona Randall
Street of the Small Steps. R. Willock
Street Paved with Water. Robin Temple
Street Paved with Water. A. Wood
Street Players. D. Goines
Street Singer. J. T. MacIntyre
Street That Died. W. Reyburn
Streetcar to Hell. J. Dekker
Streets of Blood. P. Rawls
Streets of Death. Dell Shannon
Streets of Shadow. L. McFarlane
Strelsen Castle Mystery. H. Pink
Strength of the Weak. Dick Stewart
Stretelli Case and other mystery stories. E. Wallace
Strethcairn. C. A. Collins
Stretton Case. H. Howard
Stretton Darknesse Mystery. M. Dalton
Stretton Street Affair. W. LeQueux
Stricken. M. J. Bosse
Strictly a Loser. E. Sherry
Strictly Business. O. Henry
Strictly for Cash. J. H. Chase
Strictly for Felony. Carter Brown
Strictly Illegal. M. Clinten
Strictly Legitimate. M. Cronin

Strictly Private. Therese Benson
Strictly Private Business. M. Cronin
Striding Folly. D. L. Sayers
Strike Deep. A. North
Strike for a Kingdom. M. Gallie
Strike for Death. J. Creasey
Strike for Freedom. Nicholas Carter
Strike Force 7. I. MacAlister
Strike Force Terror. Nick Carter
Strike North. W. H. Baker
Strike of Millions. E. T. Sawyer
Strike Out Where Not Applicable. N. Freeling
Strike Terror. H. Steirman
Strike Zone. Richard Curtis
Strikeback! R. Crane
Strikefast. R. Charles
Striker Portfolio. Adam Hall
Strikers, Communists, Tramps and Detectives. A. Pinkerton
Striking Force. Douglas Christie
String Glove Mystery. H. R. Campbell
String of Pearls. T. P. Prest
Strip Death Naked. N. Longmate
Strip for Murder. R. S. Prather
Strip for Violence. E. Lacy
Strip Jack Naked. W. Garner
Strip Tease. J. Bruce
Strip Tease Angel. D. Linton
Strip-Tease Macabre. L. Gribble
Strip-Tease Murders. G. R. Lee
Strip Without Tease. Carter Brown
Stripe for a Stripe. J. Sandys
Striped Majesty. Reginald Campbell
Striped Suitcase. C. Carnac
Stripped for Murder. R. Blake
Stripped for Murder. B. Fischer
Stripped to Kill. R. Drayton
Stripper. Carter Brown
Stripper, You've Sinned. Carter Brown
Striptease. G. Simenon
Striptease for Murder. P. Denver
Striptease for Murder. B. Laster
Strode Venturer. H. Innes
Stroke of a Knife. Burnham F. Mason
Stroke of Death. Josephine Bell
Stroke of Light. J. L. Hardy
Stroke of One. R. A. J. Walling
Stroke of Policy. Nicholas Carter
Stroke of Seven. R. Wade
Stroke Sinister and other stories. S. Horler
Strolling Players. A. Dwyer-Joyce
Strong Arm. R. Barr
Strong-Arm. B. Copper
Strong As Death. F. Adams
Strong Dose of Poison. H. Desmond
Strong Man. H. R. F. Keating
Strong Man's Way. C. H. Bullivant
Strong Poison. D. L. Sayers
Strong Right Arm. P. Trent
Strong Room. R. A. J. Walling
Strong Room of the Sutro. E. L. Long
Strongarm. D. J. Marlowe
Strongbox. H. Swiggett
Stronger Hand. J. Goodwin
Stronghold. S. Ellin
Stroud Case. E. C. Williams
Struck Dead. Anonymous
Struck Down. J. G. Rowe
Struck Down. H. Sherry
Struggle. Gavin Douglas
Struggle to Win. Old Sleuth
Struggle with Destiny. Nicholas Carter
Strumpet's Fool. F. Griffin
Strychnine for One. T. A. Plummer
Strychnine Tonic, and A Dose of Cyanide. G. D. H. Cole
Stryker. William Crawford
Stryker. C. Scarborough
Stuart Legacy. R. Kerr
Stuart Strain. W. D. Roberts
Stubble. Winifred Duke
Stubb's Run. P. L. Sandberg
Stud Game. D. Anthony
Studd. A. Cullen
Studdingly Stables Mystery. B. Strong
Student Body. N. Fitzgerald
Student Body. M. R. Hodgkin
Student Fraternity Murder. M. Propper
Studies in Black and Red. J. Forster
Studio Crime. G. Chester
Studio Crime. I. Jerrold
Studio Model. B. Delannoy
Studio Murder Mystery. L. Edgley
Studio Mystery. R. C. Armour
Studio Mystery. F. Aubrey
Studio One Murder. W. A. Ballinger
Study in Scarlet. A. C. Doyle
Study in Suspense. A. Soutar
Study in Terror. E. Queen
Study of Death. F. Leslie
Stuff to Give the Troops. J. MacLaren-Ross
Stuffed Man. J. B. O'Sullivan
Stuffed Men. A. M. Rud
Stuffed Swan. J. Appleby
Stumble on the Threshold. J. Payn
Stumbling. D. E. Smalley
Stunt Man. P. Brodeur
Sturgeon's West. T. Sturgeon
Sturgis Wager. E. Morette

Sturmer. I. F. Romer
Stuttering Death. L. Como
Stylist. G. Cullingford
Styx Complex. Russell Rhodes
Sub. Taffrail
Sub Killers. San Antonio
Sub Rosa. C. T. Murray
Sub-Zero! R. W. Walker
Subaltern, the Policeman, and the Little Girl. B. Fforde
Subject—Murder. C. Witting
Subject of Harry Egypt. D. Broun
Subjugated Beast. R. R. Ryan
Submarine at Bay. A. Mars
Submarine Flotilla. G. Hackforth-Jones
Submarine Girl. Edgar Turner
Submarine Mystery. K. Robeson
Submarine Signalled...Murder! A. R. Bosworth
Submarine Trail. Nicholas Carter
Submariner. E. Stephens
Subscription to Murder. M. V. Heberden
Substitute Bride. Lynna Cooper
Substitute Millionaire. H. Footner
Substitute Prisoner. M. Marcin
Subterranean Club. L. Geoghegan
Subtle Adversary. C. Scofield
Subtle Minotaur. A. Alderson
Subtle Trail. J. Gollomb
Suburban Saraband. R. Harrison
Suburban Vendetta. J. K. Leys
Subway in the Sky. B. Birch
Subway Murder. M. S. Buchanan
Subway Mystery. B. Bolt
Subways Are for Killing. W. B. Murphy
Successful Alibi. M. E. Cooke
Successful "Shadow". Old Sleuth
Such a Gorgeous Kid Like Me. H. Farrell
Such a Nice Client. Josephine Bell
Such a Nice Family. June Drummond
Such an Enmity. R. Pertwee
Such Bitter Business. Elbur Ford
Such Bright Disguises. B. Flynn
Such Friends Are Dangerous. W. Tyrer
Such Is Death. L. Bruce
Such Men Are Dangerous. B. Diamond
Such Men Are Dangerous. P. Kavanagh
Such Men Are Dangerous. Martin Thomas
Such Natural Deaths. L. Anson
Such Nice People. S. Scoppettone
Such Nice People. Mary Scott
Such Power Is Dangerous. D. Wheatley
Such Stuff As Screams Are Made Of. R. Bloch
Such Women Are Dangerous. J. Webb
Sucker Bait. R. O. Saber
"Sucker for a Red-Head." M. Storm
Sucker Money. R. H. Rohde
Sucker Punch. Duff Johnson
Sucker Punch. Raymond Marshall
Sucker Trap. M. Kane
Sucking Pit. G. N. Smith
Sudden Darkness. E. McCrae
Sudden Death! A. Bocca
Sudden Death. F. W. Crofts
Sudden Death. D. Delman
Sudden Death. B. C. Skottowe
Sudden Death. L. Thayer
Sudden Death at Scotland Yard. G. Begbie
Sudden Death of the M.F.H. E. Weldon
Sudden Fear. E. Sherry
Sudden Lady. M. G. Lowe
Sudden Silence. C. Fitzsimmons
Sudden Squall. J. C. Nolan
Sudden Storm. V. Siller
Sudden Vengeance. E. Crispin
Suddenly a Corpse. H. Q. Masur
Suddenly a Shroud. M. Kerrigan
Suddenly a Widow. G. H. Coxe
Suddenly at His Residence. C. Brand
Suddenly at Home. F. Durbridge
Suddenly, at Singapore. G. Black
Suddenly at the Priory. J. Williams
Suddenly by Shotgun. N. Daniels
Suddenly by Violence. Carter Brown
Suddenly He Knew. W. Vinn
Suddenly in Paris. A. Roudybush
Suddenly, in the Air. Karen Campbell
Suddenly, in Vienna. H. McCutcheon
Suddenly It's Murder. J. T. Story
Suddenly It's Sin. H. Janson
Suddenly One Night. K. Roos
Suddenly White Gardening. E. Lemarchand
Suddenly You're Dead. W. Wright
Sue for Mercy. V. Heley
Suez Patrol. J. R. Holden
Suez Side Ace. J. R. Holden
Suffer a Sea Change. C. De Blasis
Suffer a Witch. N. Fitzgerald
Suffer a Witch. R. Foley
Suffer a Witch to Die. E. Davis
Suffer! Little Children. P. Van Greenaway
Suffer the Children. J. R. Saul
Sufficient Rope. C. F. Gregg
Sugar. G. Brewer
Sugar and Vice. H. Janson
Sugar Cuts the Corners. L. Marshall
Sugar for the Lady. L. Marshall
Sugar Man's Dead. J. Franklin
Sugar on the Carpet. L. Marshall
Sugar on the Cuff. L. Marshall

Title Index

Sugar on the Kill. L. Marshall
Sugar on the Loose. L. Marshall
Sugar on the Prowl. L. Marshall
Sugar on the Target. L. Marshall
Sugar Shannon. Adam Knight
Sugar, You're a Scoop! M. Brody
Sugarplum Staircase. R. English
Suicide Academy. Daniel Stern
Suicide Alibi. J. Rowland
Suicide and Murder. E. Jones-Evans
Suicide Can Be Murder. Roland Daniel
Suicide Circle. W. J. Elliott
Suicide Clause. H. Carmichael
Suicide Club. R. Brome
Suicide Club. R. L. Stevenson
Suicide Excepted. C. Hare
Suicide Fleet. H. Desmond
Suicide House. E. Snell
Suicide in San Juan. S. Jason
Suicide Passage. A. A. Randall
Suicide Seat. Nick Carter
Suicide Spies. M. Annesley
Suicide Squad. Richard Curtis
Suicide Squad. R. Goyne
Suitable for Framing. M. Holbrook
Suitable for Framing. J. A. Phillips
Suitcase Full of Money. W. C. Thompson
Sullen Sky Mystery. H. C. Bailey
Sullivan. H. C. Rae
Sultana. H. C. Rowland
Sultan's Daughter. D. Wheatley
Sultan's Pearls. Nicholas Carter
Sultan's Skull. W. K. Smith
Sultry Avenger. H. Janson
Sulu Sea Murders. V. W. Mason
Sumatra Seven Zero. O. Wynd
Summer Adventure. Alan Thomas
Summer Assassin. Jennie Melville
Summer at Raven's Roost. E. Grandower
Summer Book. M. Pemberton
Summer Camp Mystery. N. Blake
Summer Concerto. G. Ferrand
Summer Fires. B. Reiss
Summer for Witches. M. Lynch
Summer Girl. C. Crane
Summer Holiday. G. Simenon
Summer House. D. Daniels
Summer in Rome. P. H. Bonner
Summer Lightning. G. F. Hummel
Summer Moon. G. Goodchild
Summer of Deceit. L. Robin
Summer of Evil. H. Arvonen
Summer of Fear. S. Marvin
Summer of Sighs. P. Gallagher
Summer of the Dragon. Elizabeth Peters
Summer of the Fire Ship. N. Faulkner
Summer of the Red Wolf. M. L. West
Summer Scandal. E. Kyle
Summer School Mystery. Josephine Bell
Summer Shock. Thorne Lee
Summer Showers. H. Arthur
Summer Soldier. N. Guild
Summer Solstice. M. T. Hinkemeyer
Summer Stranger. G. Wagner
Summer Street. H. Ellson
Summer Sunday. D. Eden
Summer Velvet. F. Y. McHugh
Summerhaven. L. Masterton
Summerhouse. P. Wentworth
Summer's Cloud. J. Tattersall
Summer's Day. I. Jerrold
Summer's Lease. C. Larner
Summerstorm. A. Cleaver
Summit. S. Marlowe
Summit Chase. R. Sapir
Summit House Mystery. L. Dougall
Summit Kill. Clark Howard
Summoned to Darkness. A. Sheridan
Summoning. J. Pintoro
Summons. A. E. W. Mason
Summons from Baghdad. A. MacKinnon
Summons to Adventure. A. Pelham
Sumuru. S. Rohmer
Sun Chemist. L. Davidson
Sun Dance Murders. P. McCurtin
Sun Dog Loot. W. C. Tuttle
Sun God. R. C. Armour
Sun in the Hunter's Eyes. M. Derby
Sun Is a Witness. A. M. Stein
Sun Virgin. R. Charles
Sunburned Corpse. Adam Knight
Sunburst. D. Cory
Sunday. G. Simenon
Sunday Best. B. Rubens
Sunday Evening. M. Lynn
Sunday Fix. J. Nazel
Sunday Hangman. J. McClure
Sunday Pigeon Murders. C. Rice
Sunday the Rabbi Stayed Home. H. Kemelman
Sunday Woman. C. Frutteo
Sunflower. M. Sharp
Sundial. S. Jackson
Sundial. F. M. White
Sundial Clue. B. Bolt
Sundial Drug Mystery. J. Ronald
Sundiver. D. Brin
Sundown Gun. P. Owen
Sundry Fell Designs. O. Mills
Sunk Island. J. B. Harris-Burland
Sunk Without Trace. D. Devine
Sunk Without Trace. S. M. Parkman
Sunken Sailor. P. Moyes

Sunlight and Gloom. G. Fleming
Sunlit Ambush. M. Derby
Sunningdale Mystery. A. Christie
Sunny Draper. C. Phillips
Sunny Stories, and some shady ones. J. Payn
Sunrise. P. Way
Sunset at Sheba. J. Harris
Sunset Express. F. Marlowe
Sunset Gang. W. Adler
Sunset Hour. M. Summerton
Sunset over Soho. G. Mitchell
Sunset People. H. Kastle
Sunset Strip. J. Reach
Sunshine and Snow. H. Smart
Sunshine Corpse. Max Murray
Sunshine Killers. G. Tippette
Sunstrike. P. McCutchan
Sup with the Devil. S. Troy
Super. J. Cornwell
Super-Barbarians. C. Dawe
Super-Celeste. P. Way
Super-Cinema Murder. L. A. Knight
Super Fly. P. Fenty
Super-Gangster. F. G. Eberhard
Super Man Chu. S. M. Sullivan
Super Spy. Carter Brown
Super Spy. W. Holt-White
Superdoll. L. August
Superdude. John Craig
Supergun Mission. L. Derrick
Superintendent Slade Investigations. L. Gribble
Superintendent Wakley's Mistake. G. D. H. Cole
Superintendent Wilson's Holiday. G. D. H. Cole
Superintendent's Room. J. Ashford
Superkill. J. Tiger
Supermind. Mark Phillips
Supernatural Clue. S. Campbell
Supernatural Solution. M. Parry
Supersonic. Basil Jackson
Superstar Murder. J. P. Hudson
Supplanter. P. Trent
Suppressed Evidence. V. Yorke
Suppressed Sensations. Anonymous
Suppression. W. Hallatt
Surabaya. Grant Holmes
Surakarta. W. MacHarg
Sure Thing. R. S. Prather
Surf Queen. Stuart Martin
Surfeit of Lampreys. N. Marsh
Surfeit of Sun. Sean Graham
Surfeit of Suspects. G. Bellairs
Surfside Caper. L. Trimble
Surfside 6. J. M. Flynn
Surgeon. Alan Thomas
Surgeon of Gaster Fell. A. C. Doyle
Surgeons Adrift. E. L. Long
Surinam Affair. J. Rosenberger
Surly Sullen Bell. R. Kirk
Surprise for the Four. Mark Cross
Surprise of His Life. Old Sleuth
Surprise Party Murder. E. V. Brewster
Surprise! Surprise! A. Christie
Surprise, Surprise. M. McCloy
Surprises of an Empty Hotel. A. C. Gunter
Surprising Experiences of Mr. Shuttlebury Cobb. R. A. Freeman
Surprising Husband. R. Marsh
Surprising Sanctuary. L. Cargill
Surregar's Raft. P. Kenley
Surrendered. R. Rand
Surrey Cat. A. Sinclair
Surrey Wood Mystery. J. Arnold
Surrounded. B. Coffey
Survival of the Fittest. E. Sherry
Survival Run. R. Hoskins
Survival Zero. M. Spillane
Survivor. M. Brandel
Survivor. J. Herbert
Survivor. T. Keneally
Survivor. E. P. Oppenheim
Survivor. J. Q.
Survivor. Sydney Smith
Survivor of Darkness. V. Coffman
Survivor of Darkness. D. Daniels
Survivors. Anne Edwards
Survivors. H. Innes
Survivors. G. Simenon
Survivor's Secret. J. G. Brandon
Susan Turnbull. A. C. Gunter
Susanna, Don't You Cry! M. Plum
Susannah Screaming. C. Weston
Susannah, the Righteous. K. Kimbrough
Susie and the F.B.I. R. St. Clair
Susie Comes to Soho. B. Sarto
Suspect. G. Fairlie
Suspect. B. M. Gill
Suspect. H. L. Nelson
Suspect. E. Percy
Suspect. Gertrude Walker
Suspect Scientist. L. Meynell
Suspected. G. Dilnot
Suspected. F. P. Rathbun
Suspected. L. Stratenus
Suspected Four. W. D. Roberts
Suspected Governess. Anonymous
Suspected Six. H. Scott
Suspects All. Marco Page

Suspects—Nine. E. R. Punshon
Suspense. B. Graeme
Suspense. G. Hughes
Suspense. K. Lindsay
Suspense. H. S. Merriman
Suspense. I. Ostrander
Suspense. R. M. Stern
Suspension of Mercy. P. Highsmith
Suspicion. P. Brebner
Suspicion. M. Hervey
Suspicion. E. J. Landon
Suspicion. V. Loder
Suspicion. C. Lys
Suspicion. F. Riddell
Suspicion. Lee Roberts
Suspicion. R. Timperley
Suspicion Aroused. D. Donovan
Suspicion in Triplicate. B. Cobb
Suspicion Was Aroused. A. Brock
Suspicions. B. Betcherman
Suspicious Characters. D. L. Sayers
Suspicious Circumstances. P. Quentin
Suspicious Company. M. Richmond
Sussex Cuckoo. B. Flynn
Sussex Downs Murder. J. Bude
Sutherland's Law. L. Galloway
Sutter House. E. Orford
Sutter's Sands. M. C. Donahue
Sutton Papers. S. Jepson
Sutton Place Murders. R. G. Dean
Suva Harbour Mystery. F. Arthur
Suvarov Adventure. D. Kyle
Svengali Plot. T. Hoyle
Swag. C. F. Coe
Swag. E. Leonard
Swallow Them Up. J. F. Straker
Swallowed Up. W. Woodrow
Swamp Fever. B. Sarto
Swamp Fire. D. Kingery
Swamp Kill. Whit Harrison
Swamp Man. D. Goines
Swamp of Cardelli. T. Craig
Swamp Rats. L. Falk
Swamp Sanctuary. B. McKnight
Swamp Sister. R. E. Alter
Swampers. H. Nisbet
Swamps of Death. Hawkshaw
Swan Dive. K. Korman
Swan Island Murders. V. Lincoln
Swan River Story. P. Hastings
Swan Sang Once. M. Carleton
Swan Song. E. Crispin
Swan Song. H. Robertson
Swan-Song Betrayed. Josephine Bell
Swan Song for a Siren. Carter Brown
Swan Song for a Thrush. G. Joseph
Swann. D. Sherman
Swansong for a Rare Bird. A. Draper
Swap. W. Wager
Swarthmoor Tragedy. E. P. Frankland
Swashbuckler, and other tales. B. Reynolds
Swastika. R. Kail
Swastika Hunt. D. Cory
Swastika Rises. C. Short
Sway of Sin. Nicholas Carter
Swaying Corpse. R. Platt
Swaying Pillars. E. Ferrars
Swaying Rock. A. J. Rees
Sweat of Fear. R. C. Dennis
Sweeney. I. K. Martin
Sweeney Todd. A. Rosser
Sweeney Todd, the Demon Barber of Fleet Street. H. C. Wheeler
Sweeper. G. Paulsen
Sweeps. B. Granger
Sweepstake Murders. J. J. Connington
Sweepstake Winner. E. Jepson
Sweet Adelaide. J. Symons
Sweet and Deadly. V. Chute
Sweet and Deadly. M. Corrigan
Sweet and Deadly. D. Duncan
Sweet and Deadly. P. MacDonald
Sweet and Deadly. F. Olbrich
Sweet and Low. E. Lathen
Sweet and Low. N. Perrelli
Sweet and Low-Down. J. Waer
Sweet Bait of Money. F. Cox
Sweet Blond Trap. W. C. Gault
Sweet Charlie. H. Kane
Sweet Cheat. H. Crooker
Sweet Cyanide. C. Noone
Sweet Danger. M. Allingham
Sweet Deadly Passion. V. Hawthorne
Sweet Death. F. Hurt
Sweet Dreams. R. Sapir
Sweet Enemy. Robin Temple
Sweet Epitaph. M. Lynn
Sweet Evil. C. Platt
Sweet Evil. J. D. White
Sweet Hostage. N. Benchley
Sweet Inisfail. R. Dowling
Sweet Is Revenge. J. F. Molloy
Sweet Is the Rose. H. D. Irvine
Sweet Jael. S. Farrant
Sweet Justice. Colin Robertson
Sweet Lady Death. P. Malloch
Sweet Mace. G. M. Fenn
Sweet Money Girl. B. Appel
Sweet Murder. M. S. Michel
Sweet Nelly. M. Callard
Sweet Night for Murder. M. Neville

Sweet Poison. Douglas Clark
Sweet Poison. M. Fitt
Sweet Poison. T. C. H. Jacobs
Sweet Poison. R. Penny
Sweet Racket. John Gloag
Sweet Reason. R. M. Littell
Sweet Revenge. S. Gilruth
Sweet Revenge. T. Racina
Sweet Revenge. J. C. Shaffer
Sweet Ride. R. S. Prather
Sweet Shame of Fury. S. D. Frances
Sweet Sinner. H. Nisbet
Sweet Sister Seduced. S. B. Hough
Sweet Smelling Death. V. Gunn
Sweet, Sweet Summer. J. Gaskell
Sweet Talk. H. Janson
Sweet Water. M. Cronin
Sweet Wild Wench. W. C. Gault
Sweet William Is Dead. L. O'Brien
Sweetbriar in Town, and other tales. D. C. Murray
Sweetcrab. M. Summerton
Sweeter for His Going. S. Truss
Sweeter Than Honey. A. Applin
Sweetheart. S. Swanton
Sweetheart and Wife. Anonymous
Sweetheart Deal. R. Rosenblum
Sweetheart, Here's Your Grave! H. Janson
Sweetheart of the Razors. P. Cheyney
Sweetheart Submarine. G. Thorne
Sweetheart, Sweetheart. Bernard Taylor
Sweetheart, This Is Homicide. Carter Brown
Sweetheart with a Wreath. M. Storm
Sweethearts and Wives. G. Hackforth-Jones
Sweetie, Hold Me Tight. H. Janson
Sweetman Curve. G. Masterton
Sweets and Sinners. A. Griffin
Swell Garrick. J. Spencer
Swell-Looking Babe. J. Thompson
Swell Night for Murder! G. Brandon
Swift Hand of Vengeance. Clifton Yorke
Swift Solution. F. J. Whaley
Swift Summer. John Burke
Swift to Its Close. S. Troy
Swifter Than a Weaver's Shuttle. J. W. Gambier
Swiftly to Evil. B. Arthur
Swimming Frog. C. Brooks
Swimming Pool. M. R. Rinehart
Swimming Pool Murder. J. Bolton
Swindler Named Zefano. C. H. Guenter
Swing Away, Climber. G. Carr
Swing, Brother, Swing. N. Marsh
Swing High, Sweet Murder. S. H. Courtier
Swing It, Death. Gavin Holt
Swing Low, Sweet Death. R. T. Campbell
Swing Low, Sweet Harriet. G. Baxt
Swing Low, Swing Dead. F. Gruber
Swing Music Murder. Harlan Reed
Swing, Swing Together. P. Lovesey
Swinger Who Swung by the Neck. Hampton Stone
Swingers. Carter Brown
Swinging Corpse. D. Linton
Swinging Death. B. Flynn
Swinging Murder. Lionel Black
Swinging Shutter. C. Fraser-Simson
Swinging Virgin. D. Rico
Swirling Waters. M. Rittenberg
Swiss Account. L. Waller
Swiss Arrangement. W. Fairchild
Swiss Conspiracy. M. Stanley
Swiss Deal. H. Arvay
Swiss Legacy. A. A. Thompson
Swiss Secret. J. Messmann
Swiss Shot. Michael Bradley
Switch. M. Jahn
Switch. E. Leonard
Switch. P. Ridgeway
Switch #2. M. Jahn
Switch Bitch. R. Dahl
Switched Out. R. Lait
Switchblade. P. Rawls
Switcheroo. E. McDowell
Swooning Venus. A. Marsden
Sword and Dragon. B. Pocock
Sword and the Net. W. Stuart
Sword and the Scales. H. McLeave
Sword for the Baron. Anthony Morton
Sword in the Air. A. C. Gunter
Sword in the Pool. D. Marfield
Sword of Allah. C. L. Clifford
Sword of Allah. M. Olden
Sword of Damocles. A. K. Green
Sword of Fate. H. Herman
Sword of Fate. D. Wheatley
Sword of Fortune. B. Bolt
Sword of Ganelon. R. Parker
Sword of Genghis Khan. James Dark
Sword of Harlequin. J. K. Keith
Sword of Honour. D. Beaty
Sword of Justice. F. Duncan
Sword of Monsieur Blackshirt. D. Graeme
Sword of Peace. A. Askew
Sword of Silk. M. Carrel
Sword of Vengeance. G. Chester
Sword-Points of Love. M. Peterson
Sword Swallower. R. Goulart
Sword to the Resue. P. D. Curtis
Swordlight. A. Rundle
Swordsman of Fortune. L. P. Greene
Swordsman of Warsaw. T. Pastor
Sworn to Silence. A. M. Miller
Sybaritic Death. A. Roudybush
Sybil Brotherton. E. Southworth
Sybil Cipher. J. M. Simmel
Sybil, Trapper of Men. M. Barbour
Sydney for Sin. M. Corrigan
Sylvanian Adventure. F. Wheeler
Sylvester Sound, the Somnambulist. H. Cockton
Sylvia. E. V. Cunningham
Sylvia Arden. O. Crawfurd
Sylvia in Flowerland. L. Gardiner
Sylvia's Chauffeur. L. Tracy
Symbol of the Cat. Neill Graham
Symbol of Vengeance. D. Mariner
Symphony in Murder. A. R. Long
Symphony in Two Time. A. Irving
Syncopated Love. W. J. Makin
Syndic. C. M. Kornbluth
Syndicate. P. McCurtin
Syndicate. A. Masters
Syndicate Girl. F. Kane
Syndicate Murders. W. R. Randall
Syndicate of Death. F. Foden
Syndicate of Death. H. E. Wheeler
Syndicate of Evil. W. R. D. McLaughlin
Syndicate of Rascals. Nicholas Carter
Syndicate of Sinners. G. Warden
Syndicate That Failed. A. Goldberg
Syndicate Wife. H. Messick
Syndrome Equation. J. Rolt
Synonym for Murder. R. Clarke
Synthetic Gentleman. Channing Pollock
Synthetic Philanthropist. J. H. Wallis
System. H. Calvin
System's Hand. M. T. Jones

T As in Trapped. L. Treat
T. Racksole and Daughter. A. Bennett
TNT for Two. J. Byron
Tabitha. A. Ridley
Table. Robert (G.) Curtis
Table D'Hote. Douglas Clark
Table Near the Band, and other stories. A. A. Milne
Tabloid Murders. Clement Wood
Tachi Tree. L. O'Donnell
Taffin. J. M. Mallet
Taffin's First Law. L. Mallet
Tag Murders. C. J. Daly
Tagget. I. A. Greenfield
Tail Job. H. Kane
Tail of Gold. D. Hennessey
Tail of the "Dozing Cat." E. Messenger
Tail Spin Morgan. T. Wallace
Tail Sting. H. Janson
Tailspin Sammy. A. W. Clark
Tailwind to Danger. C. H. Wallace
Taint of Innocence. M. Childs
Taint of Plague. Bradshaw Jones
Tainted Gold. P. Trent
Tainted Gold. H. N. Williams
Tainted Money. A. Manning
Tainted Power. C. J. Daly
Tainted Token. K. M. Knight
Tainted Turf. D. Learmonth
Take a Body. M. Halliday
Take a Dark Journey. M. Erskine
Take a Murder, Darling. R. S. Prather
Take a Pair of Private Eyes. J. T. McIntosh
Take a Step to Murder. D. Keene
Take All You Can Get. S. Fisher
Take Any City. G. Joseph
Take-Away Girl. G. Tracey
Take Away the Lady. Gavin Holt
Take Care. N. Bond
Take Death for a Lover. W. H. Baker
Take Death for a Lover. A. Berry
Take Heed of Loving Me. H. Elsna
Take It and Like It. S. Morelli
Take It Crooked. F. Beeding
Take It Easy. M. Perelli
Take It on the Lam. R. Drayton
Take Me Alive. B. Tutton
Take Me As I Am. W. H. Fielding
Take Me Home. F. Flora
Take Me to My Friend. H. D. Jordan
Take Murder... J. Wainwright
Take My Drum to England. D. Cory
Take My Face. P. Held
Take My Life. Winston Graham
Take-Off. W. Ash
Take One Ambassador. A. Broinowski
Take One for Murder. M. E. Chaber
Take Only As Directed. J. Byrom
Take-Over. V. B. Miller
Take Over, Angel. B. Sarto
Take-Over Man. J. Wainwright
Take the Money and Die. W. Williams
Take the War to Washington. P. Van Greenaway
Take Thee a Sharp Knife. R. T. Campbell
Take This Gun. R. Wilkes-Hunter
Take This Life. S. Bunce
Take This My Heart. K. Lindsay
Take This—Sweetie. H. Janson
Take Two at Bedtime. M. Allingham
Take Two Popes. H. Calvin
Take Up the Bodies. K. T. Knoblock
Take What's Coming. B. Sarto
Take Your Last Look. Matt Brady
Taken at the Flood. G. Bonner
Taken at the Flood. M. E. Braddon
Taken at the Flood. A. Christie
Taken at the Flood. B. Newman
Taken by Assault. Morley Roberts
Taken by Force. K. Stellier
Taken for Dollars. Spike Gordon
Takeoff. C. M. Kornbluth
Takeover. D. Thurlow
Takeover. R. Wormser
Takeover Bid. S. Gainham
Takers. M. Ehrlich
Takers. H. J. Taub
Taking Care of Mrs. Carroll. P. Monette
Taking Gary Feldman. S. Cohen
Taking Life Easy. Kevin O'Hara
Taking of Pelham One Two Three. J. Godey
Talatala. G. Simenon
Talbott Agreement. R. M. Garvin
Tale for Midnight. F. Prokosch
Tale of a Physician. A. J. Davis
Tale of Fleur. E. C. Vivian
Tale of Mystery. Anonymous
Tale of Pimlico. Gavin Douglas
Tale of Sin, and other tales. H. Wood
Tale of the Lazy Dog. Alan Williams
Tale of the Town. George Hastings
Tale of Twenty-Five Hours. B. Matthews
Tale of Two Clocks. J. H. Schmitz
Tale of Two Murders. H. C. Asterley
Tale of Two Murders. E. Ferrars
Tale of Two Thieves. G. Beardmore
Tale Untold. E. Morrison
Talent for Dying. J. A. Potter
Talent for Murder. J. L. Benton
Talent for Murder. J. Wainwright
Talent for Murder. A. M. Wells
Talent for Violence. W. Manson
Talented Mr. Ripley. P. Highsmith
Tales. E. A. Poe
Tales and Stories. M. W. Shelley
Tales by a Female Detective. A. Forrester
Tales for the Marines. R. Blatchford
Tales from a Rolltop Desk. C. Morley
Tales from Two Pockets. K. Capek
Tales in a Jugular Vein. R. Bloch
Tales in Eccentric Life. W. A. Hammond
Tales in Prose and Verse. T. E. Heath
Tales in Prose and Verse. D. C. Murray
Tales of a Cruel Country. G. Cumberland
Tales of a Government Official. A. Griffiths
Tales of Adventure. R. H. Savage
Tales of Adventurers. G. Household
Tales of an Antiquary. Anonymous
Tales of Chinatown. S. Rohmer
Tales of East and West. S. Rohmer
Tales of Fantasy and Fact. B. Matthews
Tales of Hate. Winifred Duke
Tales of Heroism and Records of Strange and Wonderful Adventures. Anonymous
Tales of Intrigue and Revenge. S. McKenna
Tales of Love and Death. R. Aickman
Tales of Love and Hate. C. H. Crichton
Tales of Mynheer Amayat. H. D. Stacpoole
Tales of Mystery and Crime. W. Wallace
Tales of Mystery and Horror. M. Level
Tales of Mystery and Horror. C. D. Pamely
Tales of Mystery and Revenge. N. Langley
Tales of Mystery and Romance. F. Moorhouse
Tales of Romance and Mystery. H. Rockwood
Tales of Secret Egypt. S. Rohmer
Tales of Suspense. W. Collins
Tales of Terror. D. Donovan
Tales of Terror. E. Sudak
Tales of Terror and Mystery. A. C. Doyle
Tales of Terror and the Supernatural. W. Collins
Tales of the Black Widowers. I. Asimov
Tales of the Cliffs. W. H. Bracewell
Tales of the Coast Guard. L. Warneford
Tales of the Coastguard and other stories. Anonymous
Tales of the Mounted Police. W. B. Mowery
Tales of the Mysterious and Macabre. A. Blackwood
Tales of the R.I.C. Anonymous
Tales of the Rock. M. Anderson
Tales of the Scientific Crime Club. R. Cummings
Tales of the Strong Room. F. Denison
Tales of the Tenements. E. Phillpotts
Tales of the Uneasy. V. Hunt
Tales of the Unexpected. R. Dahl
Tales of the Weird and West Countree. M. St. Germain
Tales of the Wild and Wonderful. Anonymous
Tales of Today. G. R. Sims

Title Index

Tales of Two Continents. R. Barr
Tales out of Court. F. T. Hill
Tales Told to the Magistrate. R. E. Corder
Talika, the Geisha Girl. Nicholas Carter
Talisman. C. Crowe
Talisman. J. Godey
Talk of the Devil. F. Baker
Talk of the Town. J. Payn
Talk of the Town. C. Williams
Talk to Me About England. P. Ferris
Talkative Policeman. R. Penny
"Talkie" Murder Mystery. W. Shute
Talking Clock. F. Gruber
Talking Clues. R. C. Finney
Talking of Murder. L. N. Morgan
Talking Skull and other selected short stories grave and gay. G. H. R. Young
Talking Sparrow Murders. D. L. Teilhet
Talking Turkey. K. A. Saddler
Tall, Balding, Thirty-Five. A. Firth
Tall, Dark and Dead. K. Jaediker
Tall, Dark and Deadly. H. Q. Masur
Tall Dark Man. A. Chamberlain
Tall, Dark Stranger. J. Wellsley
Tall Dolores. M. Avallone
Tall Headlines. A. E. Lindop
Tall House Mystery. A. Fielding
Tall Man. Gavin Douglas
Tall Man. John Ross
Tall Man Walking. K. Wolffe
Tall Pines in Paddington. C. Edwards
Tall Timber. G. Goodchild
Tallant for Disaster. A. York
Tallant for Trouble. A. York
Tallants of Barton. J. Hatton
Talleyrand Maxim. J. S. Fletcher
Tallyman. B. Knox
Tallyman's Fate. L. Jackson
Talon. J. Coltrane
Talons of the Hawk. J. Hines
Tamara. M. L. Dodge
Tamarind. F. Hurd
Tamarind Seed. Evelyn Anthony
Tamer. N. Fokker
Tamer of Men. O. Binns
Taming of Carney Wilde. B. Spicer
Taming of Nancy. G. Goodchild
Taming of Neville Ibbetson. W. M. Graydon
Taming of Sydney Marsham. H. C. McNeile
Taming the Furies. P. A. Foxall
Tan and Sandy Silence. J. D. MacDonald
Tanagra Affair. P. Kenny
Tancredi. L. Cameron
Tandem Rush. F. V. Huber
Tandra. Robert Mason
Tang Murders. C. Cruickshank
Tangent Factor. Lawrence Sanders
Tangent Objective. Lawrence Sanders
Tangier. W. Bayer
Tangier Assignment. C. Rougvie
Tangle. W. S. Masterman
Tangle. H. L. Phillips
Tangle. H. A. Wrenn
Tangle of Terror. E. J. Murray
Tangled Case. Nicholas Carter
Tangled Cord. F. Lockridge
Tangled Destinies. D. Donovan
Tangled Evidence. P. C. De Crespigny
Tangled Flags. A. C. Gunter
Tangled in Crime. Nicholas Carter
Tangled Lives. T. W. Speight
Tangled Marriage. C. Dawe
Tangled Miracle. H. Herne
Tangled Skein. Nicholas Carter
Tangled Skein. A. D. Fonblanque
Tangled Threads. Nicholas Carter
Tangled Trails. W. M. Raine
Tangled Web. M. Andrau
Tangled Web. N. Blake
Tangled Web. J. D. Levick
Tangled Web. L. G. Moberly
Tangled Web. J. Moffatt
Tangled Web. L. A. Sunagel
Tangled Web. G. Vaizey
Tangles Unravelled. E. K. Johnson
Tanglewood Murder. L. Kallen
Tanglewood Mystery. C. E. Pearce
Tango. C. Rodda
Tango Briefing. Adam Hall
Tango November. J. Howlett
Tania. T. Lester
Tank of Sacred Eels. I. Drummond
Tanker. R. Kruger
Tannahill Tangle. C. Wells
Tanner's Tiger. Lawrence Block
Tanner's Twelve Swingers. Lawrence Block
Tap on the Shoulder. M. Dupree
Tapestry Odyssey. P. Conway
Tapestry of Death. D. M. Bowick
Tapestry of Fear. M. Pemberton
Tapestry of Terror. M. Ruuth
Tapestry Room Murder. C. Wells
Tapestry Triangle. T. P. Kelley
Tapping on the Wall. H. Hull
Taps, Colonel Roberts. H. Gibbs
Tarakian. L. Peters
Tarantula Strike. Nick Carter
Target. W. W. Haines
Target Amin. J. Konrad

Target Capricorn. Agnes Russell
Target: Charity Ross. J. Bickham
Target Criminal. P. N. Walker
Target Doomsday Island. Nick Carter
Target Five. C. Forbes
Target for Conquest. B. Gray
Target for Malice. Barbara Cooper
Target for Murder. G. E. Giles
Target for Terror. M. Hershman
Target for Terror. T. C. H. Jacobs
Target for Target. S. A. Martinez
Target for Their Dark Desire. Carter Brown
Target for Tonight. R. Telfair
Target in Taffeta. B. Benson
Target Is H. L. Derrick
Target Manhattan. D. Mallory
Target Manhattan. D. Pitts
Target Mayflower. R. Hirschhorn
Target: Mike Shayne. B. Halliday
Target Plutex. P. Bryers
Target Practice. N. Meyer
Target Risk. J. Wingate
Target: The Men They Were Once. S. Masters
Target Westminster. B. M. Gull
Tarn House. R. Brock
Tarnham Connection. W. Tute
Tarnished Angel. H. Pentecost
Tarnished Gold. W. Mills
Tarnished Love. Gerry Travis
Tarnished Woman. V. Thompson
Tarot Cards in Thessaly. H. Latouche
Tarot Murders. M. Warner
Tarot Spell. W. D. Roberts
Tarot's Tower. Jennie Melville
Tarry and Be Hanged. Sara Woods
Tashkent Crisis. W. Craig
Task Demolition. R. Wilkes-Hunter
Task of Destruction. Michael Barrett
Taskmaster. Harold King
Taste for Blood. J. B. West
Taste for Brilliants. N. Clad
Taste for Cognac. B. Halliday
Taste for Death. P. O'Donnell
Taste for Honey. H. F. Heard
Taste for Murder. H. F. Heard
Taste for Violence. B. Halliday
Taste of Ashes. H. Browne
Taste of Blood. D. Batchelor
Taste of Blood. Ralph Hayes
Taste of Brass. R. D. Locke
Taste of Conspiracy. C. Egerton-Thomas
Taste of Death. Richard Grayson
Taste of Death. F. McGrew
Taste of Fears. M. Millar
Taste of Fears. Sara Woods
Taste of Murder. J. Cannan
Taste of Murder. I. Lambot
Taste of Poison. R. Ullmann
Taste of Power. W. J. Burley
Taste of Proof. B. Knox
Taste of Sangria. C. Keith
Taste of Sin. G. Brewer
Taste of Terror. M. Albrand
Taste of Treasure. G. Ashe
Taste of Vengeance. L. R. Davis
Tatterley. T. Gallon
Tattershall Castle. B. Gilbert
Tattoo Mystery. W. LeQueux
Tattooed Arm. I. Ostrander
Tattooed Man. T. C. H. Jacobs
Tattooed Triangle. J. G. Brandon
Tattooed Wrist. Old Spicer
Tau Cross Mystery. J. J. Connington
Taurus Trip. T. B. Dewey
Tavern. G. M. Cohan
Tavern and the Arrows. A. Carlyle
Tavern Wench. S. Farrant
Taverns in Terrazzo. M. J. Ragosta
Tavistocks. A. Griffin
Tawny Menace. B. Sanders
Taxed to Death. R. Simons
Taxi-Cab Murder. J. G. Brandon
Taxi Man's Quest. G. Chester
Taxicab Riddle. Nicholas Carter
Tea and Arsenic. C. Sodaro
Tea and Trickery. N. B. Chute
Tea at Four. R. H. Wilkinson
Tea at the Abbey. C. E. Vulliamy
Tea on Sunday. Lettice Cooper
Tea-Shop in Limehouse. T. Burke
Tea Time Tragedy. M. Beckett
Tea Tray Murders. C. Bush
Teach You a Lesson. J. Hollis
Teach Yourself Treachery. Jonathan Burke
Teacher Goes Abroad. E. Randolph
Teacher's Blood. I. T. Ross
Teak Forest. P. Ordway
Team of Crooks. A. Steffens Hardy
Tear in the Silk. L. O'Flaherty
Tears Are for Angels. P. Connolly
Tears for Jessie Hewitt. E. Sherry
Tears for the Bride. Robert Martin
Tears in Paradise. J. Blackmore
Tears of Angels. H. Curties
Tears of Autumn. C. McCarry
Tears of Blood. M. Carrel
Tears of Hate. G. Thorne
Tease. G. Brewer
Tease. R. H. R. Smithies
Teaser Set to Kill. M. Brody

Technicians of Death. T. Williamson
Technique for Treachery. S. Truss
Teddington Tragedy. D. H. Landels
Teddy Bear. G. Simenon
Teddy-Boy Mystery. J. Drummond
Teen-Age Jungle. H. Whittington
Teen-Age Mafia. Wenzell Brown
Teen-Age Mobster. B. Appel
Teen-Age Terror. Wenzell Brown
Teeth for the Brigadier. M. Hamilton
Teeth of the Dragon. M. Grant
Teeth of the Tiger. M. Leblanc
Tejera Secrets. M. Orr
Telefair. C. Rice
Telefon. W. Wager
Telegram from Le Touquet. J. Bude
Telegraph Clue. I. Stark
Telegraph Secrets. B. Hemyng
Telekiller. John Warwick
Telemann Touch. W. Haggard
Telephone Call. J. Rhode
Telephone Girl. A. Askew
Television Murders. W. A. Ballinger
Television Mystery. R. St. Clair
Television Plays. K. Parker
Tell Death to Wait. A. Boutell
Tell Her It's Murder. H. Reilly
Tell It to the Birds. J. H. Chase
Tell It to the Dead. L. Vardre
Tell Me Now, and Again. R. Llewellyn
Tell No Tales. G. Day
Tell No Tales. G. Limnelius
Tell-Tale Clock Mystery. J. Carmack
Tell-Tale Murder. P. Weathers
Tell-Tale Photographs. Nicholas Carter
Tell-Tale Tart. P. Duncan
Tell-Tale Watch. G. Hocker
Tell Them Nothing. H. Ellson
Tell Them What's-Her-Name Called. Mildred Davis
Tell You What I'll Do. H. Cecil
Telling of Murder. D. Rutherford
Telling the Truth. W. Hewlett
Telltale Print. C. B. Booth
Telltale Tattoo. J. Sharp
Telltale Telegram. H. Burnham
Telzey Toy. J. H. Schmitz
Tempania Mystery. J. M. Walsh
Temperamental Journey. P. Groom
Tempering Steel. S. Jepson
Tempest at Dawn. M. Richmond
Tempest at Summer's End. J. Thatcher
Tempest Driven. R. Dowling
Tempest in a Tea-Cup. W. Shand
Tempest Weaves a Shroud. W. Shand
Tempestuous Petticoat. M. A. Gibbs
Tempestuous Wooer. G. T. Ockley
Temple at Ilumquh. J. Laflin
Temple Dogs. R. L. Duncan
Temple Dogs Guard My Fate. D. Sinclair
Temple Falls. A. MacVicar
Temple, K. C. E. K. Webb
Temple Murder. H. M. Richardson
Temple of Darkness. Marilyn Ross
Temple of Dawn. Colin Robertson
Temple of Death. F. Du Boisgobey
Temple of Death. E. Mitchell
Temple of Fear. Nick Carter
Temple of Slumber. Neill Graham
Temple of the Dead. V. Norwood
Temple of the Flaming God. D. T. Lindsay
Temple of Vice. Nicholas Carter
Temple Tower. H. C. McNeile
Temple Tree. D. Beaty
Temple's Trial. E. Everett-Green
Templeton Case. V. L. Whitechurch
Templeton Memoirs. D. Daniels
Tempt a Tigress. Carter Brown
Tempt Me Not. A. Weymouth
Temptation in a Private Zoo. A. Dekker
Temptation of Adam. H. Gruber
Temptation of Father Anthony. G. Horton
Temptation of Gideon Holt. Mrs. C. Kernahan
Temptation of Mary Gordon. S. Horler
Temptation of Selma. C. Dawe
Temptation of Tavernake. E. P. Oppenheim
Temptation to Steal. N. B. Gerson
Temptations of Hercule. P. Audemars
Temptations of Valerie. H. Whittington
Tempter. A. Bloomfield
Tempting Anne Brayton. A. Applin
Tempting of Paul Chester. A. Askew
Tempting of Tavernake. E. P. Oppenheim
Temptress. Carter Brown
Temptress. W. LeQueux
Temptress. S. Shulman
Temptress on Trial. J. Laffin
Ten Against Nura. Michael Barrett
Ten Black Pearls. C. F. Gregg
Ten Commandments. G. R. Sims
Ten Crowded Hours. C. A. Alington
Ten Dangerous Hours. G. B. Jenkins
Ten Day Mystery. Old Sleuth
Ten Days Before the Wedding. L. Barbee
Ten Day's Leave. W. M. Graydon
Ten Days, Mr. Cain. B. Freeborn
Ten Days to Oblivion. M. Cooney
Ten Days Wonder. E. Queen
Ten Faces of Cornell Woolrich. C. Woolrich
Ten Fathoms Deep. J. Templeton

Ten Grand Story. B. Carson
Ten Grand Tallulah and Temptation.
 Carter Brown
Ten Green Brothers. A. MacVicar
Ten Holy Horrors. F. Beeding
Ten Hours. H. S. Keeler
Ten Jewels. P. Wynnton
Ten Little Indians. A. Christie
Ten Little Niggers. A. Christie
Ten Million. M. Hellinger
Ten Million Dollar Cinch. J. Pattinson
Ten Million Dollar Girl. C. Miron
Ten Minute Alibi. A. Armstrong
Ten Minutes on a June Morning. F. Clifford
Ten Peacocks. A. Wood
Ten Per Cent of Your Life. S. Winchester
Ten Plus One. E. McBain
Ten Seconds to Hell. L. P. Bachmann
Ten Seconds to Zero. K. Stanton
Ten Star Clues. E. R. Punshon
Ten Steps to the Gallows. J. Wainwright
Ten Teacups. Carter Dickson
Ten Thirteen. C. Edwards
10:30 from Marseilles. S. Japrisot
Ten-Thirty on a Summer Night. M. Duras
Ten-Thirty Sharp. H. Gibbs
$10,000 Reward. C. B. Booth
Ten Thousand Passports to Hell. H. P. Lees
£10,000 Trophy Race. P. Gill
Ten Thousand Several Doors. M. Craig
Ten Times Dynamite. Nick Carter
Ten-Tola Bars. B. Wohl
Ten Trails to Tyburn. B. Graeme
Ten True Secret Service Stories. D. B. Shaw
10.12 Express. W. E. Grogan
Ten Were Missing. M. Allingham
Ten Words of Poison. B. Perowne
Ten Years After. J. W. Bobin
Ten Years Among the Mail Bags. J. Holbrook
Tenacity. G. Cottar
Tenant. John Gill
Tenant. R. Topor
Tenant for Death. C. Hare
Tenant for the Tomb. Anthony Gilbert
Tenant of Chesdene Manor. A. C. Ley
Tenant of No. 13. L. Jackson
Tenant of the Grange. M. Gerard
Tenants of Malory. J. S. Le Fanu
Tendency to Corrupt. R. Barker
Tender Conspiracy. Eric Lambert
Tender Is the Knife. Joan Shepherd
Tender Killer. S. B. Hough
Tender Leaves. Robert Mason
Tender Poisoner. J. Bingham
Tender to Danger. E. Reed
Tender to Moonlight. E. Reed
Tenderfoot. L. Allan
Tennessee Smash. D. Pendleton
Tennessee Tess. C. E. Blaney
Tennis Club Mystery. J. Reach
Tennis Murders. T. L. Welch
Tennyson Code. R. Cooper
Tension. H. Janson
Tension. J. Wainwright
Tentacles. D. Lyon
Tenth Commandment. V. Bridges
Tenth Commandment. Lawrence Sanders
Tenth Leper. F. Didelot
Tenth Life. R. Lockridge
Tenth Point. T. Walsh
Tenth Session. R. Quilty
Tenth Victim. R. Sheckley
Tenth Year of the Ship. N. Lewis
Tents of Shame. E. C. Reed
Tents of Shem. G. Allen
Terence O'Rourke, Gentleman Adventurer. L. J. Vance
Teresa of Watling Street. A. Bennett
Term of Silence. H. Halsey
Term of Terror. P. Flower
Term of Trial. J. Barlow
Terminal Connection. Robin Moore
Terminal Three. H. Miller
Termination Order. P. Friedman
Terminators. D. Hamilton
Terminators. B. Mather
Terms of Surrender. L. Tracy
Terrace Suicide Mystery. L. Gribble
Terracotta Palace. A. Maybury
Terrarium. J. Head
Terrible Baron, and other stories. B. Reynolds
Terrible Crime. E. G. Jones
Terrible Door. G. Sims
Terrible Family. F. Warden
Terrible Hand. L. F. Hay
Terrible Hobby of Sir Joseph Londe, Bt. E. P. Oppenheim
Terrible Inheritance. G. Allen
Terrible Island. B. Grimshaw
Terrible Legacy. G. W. Appleton
Terrible Night. P. Cheyney
Terrible Ones. Nick Carter
Terrible People. E. Wallace
Terrible Performance. J. Bergner
Terrible Pictures. B. Healey
Terrible Secret. G. Fleming
Terrible Secret. M. A. Fleming

Terrible Thing Has Happened to Miss Dupont. P. Hobson
Terrible Thirteen. Nicholas Carter
Terrible Threat. Nicholas Carter
Terrible Time to Die. T. Scaduto
Terrible Tuesday. D. Pendleton
Terrible Youth. Old Sleuth
Terrible Wild Flowers. G. Kersh
Terrified Heart. A. Grace
Terrified Society. H. T. Teilhet
Terrified Target. A. Grace
Terriford Mystery. M. B. Lowndes
Territorial Rights. M. Spark
Terror. R. Bloch
Terror. J. Creasey
Terror. E. Wallace
Terror. R. Wilkinson
Terror Alliance. J. D. Hunter
Terror at Black Oaks. J. Reach
Terror at Bramble Tor. Jean Carew
Terror at Dark Harbor. Clarissa Ross
Terror at Dearcliff House. G. Davies
Terror at Deepcliff. D. Nile
Terror at Golden Sands. R. Roleine
Terror at Nelson Woods. S. Richard
Terror at Octagon House. A. Coffman
Terror at Seacliff Pines. F. Hurd
Terror at Staups House. Frank King
Terror at Tansey Hill. S. Roberts
Terror at Tree Tops. A. Parsons
Terror by Day. G. Ashe
Terror by Night. R. D. Bunnell
Terror by Night. R. Chetwynd-Hayes
Terror by Night. J. M. Cobban
Terror by Night. L. Crosby
Terror by Night. P. W. Fairman
Terror by Night. A. W. Gough
Terror by Night. C. R. Gull
Terror by Night. N. Klein
Terror by Night. P. Luck
Terror by Night. M. Richmond
Terror by Twilight. K. M. Knight
Terror Catches Up. H. Kaner
Terror Chronicle. B. Sang
Terror Comes Creeping. Carter Brown
Terror Comes to London. C. Bishop
Terror Comes to Twelvetrees. S. Horler
Terror Factor. E. Wuorio
Terror for the Toff. J. Creasey
Terror-Go-Round. J. Moffatt
Terror in Exton. Molly Nelson
Terror in Room 201. T. Mitcheltree
Terror in Taormina. A. Hesse
Terror in Taos. L. Derrick
Terror in the Bay. I. F. Turek
Terror in the Fog. N. Berrow
Terror in the Navy. K. Robeson
Terror in the Night. S. Blayne
Terror in the Night. Old Sleuth
Terror in the Night and other stories. R. Bloch
Terror in the Sun. M. Avallone
Terror in the Sun. R. Glendinning
Terror in the Sunlight. A. McAllister
Terror in the Thames. A. D. Divine
Terror in the Town. E. Ronns
Terror in Times Square. A. Handley
Terror in Tokyo. N. Perrelli
Terror Is My Trade. S. Marlowe
Terror Island. R. C. Armour
Terror Island. M. E. Longman
Terror Keep. E. Wallace
Terror Loch. W. McNeilly
Terror Love. N. Norman
Terror Lurks in Darkness. D. Hitchens
Terror Manor. M. E. Edward
Terror of Frankenstein. D. F. Glut
Terror of Gold-Digger Creek. G. H. Teed
Terror of Lonely Tor. Donald Stuart
Terror of Stormcastle. A. Leech
Terror of Tangier. G. H. Teed
Terror of the Air. W. LeQueux
Terror of the Handless Corpse. W. Dale
Terror of the Moat House. L. C. Douthwaite
Terror of the Pacific. J. G. Brandon
Terror of the Shape. C. Jude
Terror of the Tenements. A. Skene
Terror of the Tongs. J. Sangster
Terror of Thunder Creek. S. Hope
Terror of Tongues. Roy Vickers
Terror of Torlands. T. C. H. Jacobs
Terror of Toynham Hall. H. K. McDonnell
Terror of Tregarwith. J. Sylvester
Terror on Broadway. David Alexander
Terror on Compass Lake. T. Davis
Terror on Duncan Island. C. Farr
Terror on Halfaday Creek. J. B. Hendryx
Terror on the Docks. M. Franklin
Terror on the Island. J. Ferguson
Terror on Tip-Toe. S. Horler
Terror over London. G. F. Fox
Terror Package. R. Chavis
Terror Rides the West Wind. Rick Madison
Terror Ship. C. Edwards
Terror Squad. R. Sapir
Terror Stalks Abroad. M. Richmond
Terror Stalks by Night. N. W. Firth
Terror Syndicate. D. Seaman
Terror Touches Me. S. Forbes
Terror Tournament. J. M. Flynn
Terror Tower. F. W. Irwin

Terror Tower. C. Rushton
Terror Tower. G. Verner
Terror Trade. M. Lester
Terror Trap. J. Creasey
Terror Trap. W. D. Roberts
Terror Truckers. S. Jason
Terror Walks by Night. H. Desmond
Terror Walks Tonight. J. Kirkpatrick
Terror Wave. H. S. Banner
Terror Wears a Feathered Cloak. T. W. Crawford
Terror Wears a Smile. L. Grex
Terrorist. R. Moss
Terrorists. N. De Mille
Terrorists. M. Sjowall
Terrorizers. D. Hamilton
Terrors and other stories. A. Marshall
Terror's Cradle. D. Kyle
Terrors of the Earth. S. Forbes
Terry of Tangistan. Douglas Christie
Test. M. M. Bodkin
Test Case. B. D. Ashe
Test Match Murder. D. Batchelor
Test Match Murder. A. Tack
Test Match Mystery. H. Pink
Test of Anarchy. E. C. Derby
Test of Courage. Nicholas Carter
Test of Love. E. Southworth
Testament. D. Morrell
Testament of Cairo, 1898. R. Maugham
Testament of Caspar Schultz. M. Fallon
Testament of Death. Norman Lucas
Testament of Evil. Bradshaw Jones
Testament of John Hastings. A. C. Fox-Davies
Tester. W. Palmer
Testament to Violence. P. A. Foxall
Testimony by Silence. D. M. Disney
Testing of Olive Vaughn. P. Brebner
Testing of Tony. M. Cumberland
Testkill. T. Dexter
Tether's End. M. Allingham
Tetramachus Collection. P. Van Rjndt
Teville Obsession. C. Stafford
Texan. J. B. Hendryx
Texas Bank Murders. Christopher Culley
Texas by the Tail. J. Thompson
Texas Gold. J. Reese
Texas Storm. D. Pendleton
Texas Wind. J. M. Reasoner
Text for Murder. P. Fielding
Thameside Gold. M. Welford
Thaneworth House. K. Kimbrough
Thank You, Mr. Conquest. B. Gray
Thank You, Mr. Moto. J. P. Marquand
Thank You, Mr. Pendlebury. A. Webb
Thanks for the Apple. K. Hewitt
Thanks for the Felony. L. Grex
Thanks to Dr. Molly. S. Fairway
Thanks to Murder. J. Krumgold
Thanks to the Saint. L. Charteris
That Affair at Elizabeth. B. E. Stevenson
That Affair at Portstead Manor. G. E. Locke
That Affair at St. Peter's. E. A. Brown
That Affair at the Cedars. L. Thayer
That Affair Next Door. A. K. Green
That American Girl. S. Warwick
That Awful Mess on Via Merulana. C. E. Gadda
That Brain Again. H. Janson
That Bullet Hole Has a History! H. C. McNeile
That Charming Crook. Frank King
That Cold Day in the Park. R. Miles
That Dame Sal. D. Linton
That Dark Inn. S. Nichols
That Darn Cat. The Gordons
That Dinner at Bardolph's. R. A. J. Walling
That Evening in Shanghai. P. Thorne
That Fatal Feeling. E. Kennedy
That Fatal Night. M. Richmond
That Fatal Touch. M. L. Roby
That Fatal Tree. V. Day
That Feeds on Men. I. Wilson
That Fellow MacArthur. S. Jepson
That Fiddler Fellow. H. G. Hutchinson
That Followed After. J. G. Lockhart
That French Girl. J. Hilton
That Frenchman! A. C. Gunter
That Gay Nineties Murder. F. Daingerfield
That Girl from Istanbul. M. G. Braun
That Girl in the Alley. M. Kelly
That Glover Woman. H. Ellson
That He May Die. G. Braddon
That Mainwaring Affair. A. M. Barbour
That Man Bolt. P. Crowcraft
That Man Gull. Anthony Stuart
That Man Returns. G. Fairlie
That Nairobi Affair. B. Leslie-Melville
That Night. J. Blackmore
That Night at Nine. D. R. Sperduti
That Night It Rained. H. Waugh
That Old Gang of Mine. Leslie Thomas
That Room in Camden Town. Griff
That Royle Girl. E. Balmer
That Strange Sylvester Affair. L. Thayer
That Summer at Bacclesea. Elizabeth Ford
That Summer's Earthquake. M. Bennett

Title Index

That Villain, Romeo! J. F. Molloy
That Was No Lady. Keith Campbell
That Was Yesterday. M. Home
That Washington Affair. J. Hay
That We Might Live. Alan Thomas
That Which Is Crooked. D. M. Disney
That Which Is Crooked. Warren Hill
That Which Is Hidden. R. Hichens
That Wilmslow Girl! J. Oakley
That Winslow Woman. R. Pell
That Yew Tree's Shade. C. Hare
That's All I Need. D. Spade
That's Her Problem. M. Hampton
That's Mark Avery. M. L. Tyrrell
That's No Way to Die. L. Kelley
That's Piracy, My Pet. Carter Brown
That's the House, There. L. Singer
That's the Spirit. M. V. Heberden
That's the Way the Money Goes. S. Miller
That's Where the Cat's At, Baby. B. B. Johnson
That's Your Man, Inspector! D. Frome
Theatre Crime. F. Andreas
Theatre of Life. G. R. Sims
Theban Mysteries. A. Cross
Theft in Kind. M. Summerton
Theft of Magna Carta. J. Creasey
Theft of the Crown Jewels. E. Jepson
Theft of the Iron Dogs. E. C. R. Lorac
Thefts of Nick Velvet. E. D. Hoch
Their Dusty Hands. M. Carleton
Their Flowers Were Always Black. P. Hastings
Their Great Adventure. W. M. Graydon
Their Man in the White House. T. Ardies
Their Nearest and Dearest. Bernice Carey
Their Rainbow Had Black Edges. Gerald Butler
Their Wife. D. Walshe
Thelma. V. Caspary
Theme Is Murder. M. A. De Ford
Theme Is Murder. Gavin Holt
Then Came Bronson. W. Johnston
Then Came the Police. C. M. Wills
Then Came Two Women. C. Armstrong
Then Came Violence. J. Ball
Then There Were Three. G. Homes
Theodora. K. Lindsay
Theodosia. J. A. Bartlett
Therapy in Dynamite. V. B. Miller
There Ain't No Justice. J. Curtis
There Are Dead Men in Manhattan. J. Roeburt
There Are Giants. E. Woodward
There Are More Ways of Killing... M. Fitt
There Are Thirteen. F. Beeding
There Are Worse Jungles. N. Tranter
There Came Both Mist and Snow. M. Innes
There Could Be Trouble. B. Carson
There Goes Davy Cohen. W. Owen
There Goes Death. G. Ashe
There Goes His Ghost. J. Atholl
There Goes Shorty Higgins. J. Karney
There Goes the Bride. W. Maner
There Has Been a Murder. H. Holt
There Is a Death, Elizabeth. Gerald Butler
There Is a Destiny. R. J. Burge
There Is a Green Hill. Robert Mason
There Is a Serpent in Eden. R. Bloch
There Is a Tide... A. Christie
There is a Tide—. E. Wooll
There Is No Justice. R. B. Dominic
There Is No Opgu. A. Wood
There Is No Return. A. Blackmon
There Is No Silence. M. Dolinsky
There Is No Yesterday. K. Lindsay
There Is One S.O.S. J. B. O'Sullivan
There Is Something About a Dame. M. Avallone
There Lies Your Love. Jennie Melville
There Must Be Some Mistake. M. Babson
There Must Be Victims. M. Cumberland
There None Embrace. F. Shroyer
There Sits Death. P. McGuire
There Was a Crooked Man. D. Keene
There Was a Crooked Man. K. Roos
There Was a Crooked Man. C. Witting
There Was a Crooked Man. G. W. Yates
There Was a Door. T. Mundy
There Was a Little Man. C. Conrad
There Was a Witness. E. Salter
There Was an Old Man. E. Phillpotts
There Was an Old Woman. E. Davis
There Was an Old Woman. E. Phillpotts
There Was an Old Woman. E. Queen
There Was No Island. L. Handley
There Was No Moon. F. Hay
There Were No Asper Ladies. E. Ascher
There Were No Windows. N. Hoult
Thereby Hangs a Corpse. M. Mullen
Thereby Hangs a Tale. G. M. Fenn
Therefore I Killed Him. H. Jobson
There's a Hippie on the Highway. J. H. Chase
There's a Reason for Everything. E. R. Punshon
There's Always a Dame. B. Sarto
There's Always a Murder. K. Parker
There's Always a Payoff. R. P. Hansen
There's Always a Price Tag. J. H. Chase
There's Always Time to Die. O. R. Cohen
There's Always Tomorrow. A. Meredith
There's Been Murder Done. K. T. Knoblock
There's Danger, Miss Minden! A. Jackson
There's Death in the Churchyard. W. Gore
There's Death in the Cup. A. Hocking
There's Money in Murder. G. Barnett
There's No One in the Village. O. Rees
There's Trouble Brewing. N. Blake
Theresa. T. P. Prest
Thermal Thursday. D. Pendleton
These Arrows Point to Death. W. O'Farrell
These Cliffs Are Dangerous. L. March
These Haunted Streets. John Burke
These Lonely, These Dead. R. Colby
These Lonely Victories. E. West
These Names Make Clues. E. C. R. Lorac
These Men and Women. S. Horler
These Small Glories. J. Cleary
These Tigers' Hearts. J. Land
These Unlucky Deeds. R. M. Stern
These Within. L. K. Vincent
Theseus Code. M. Hammond
Thespian Detective and other theatrical stories. B. Delannoy
Theta Syndrome. E. Trevor
They All Bleed Red. R. Sted
They All Came Back. J. Courage
They All Ran Away. E. Ronns
They Being Dead Yet Speak. C. Massie
They Blocked the Suez Canal. A. D. Divine
They Buried a Man. Mildred Davis
They Burn for Me. B. Sarto
They Call It Murder. Peter Chambers
They Call It Murder. Tom Hart
They Call It Murder. B. Mantelow
They Call Him Death. David Hume
They Called Him Nighthawk. S. Horler
They Came by Night. B. Lyndon
They Came by Night. S. Truss
They Came to Baghdad. A. Christie
They Came to Kill. M. Scherf
They Came to London. P. Tabori
They Can Only Hang You Once. D. Hammett
They Can Only Kill You Once. D. Brennan
They Can't All Be Guilty. M. V. Heberden
They Can't Hang Caroline. Roy Vickers
They Can't Hang Me! J. Mallett
They Can't Hang Me! J. Ronald
They Carry a Torch. J. Blackmore
They Couldn't Go Wrong. R. Armstrong
They Cracked Her Glass Slipper. Gerald Butler
They Deal in Death. R. Terrall
They Died in the Spring. J. Pullein-Thompson
They Died Laughing. A. Green
They Do It with Mirrors. A. Christie
They Do It with Mirrors. J. C. Conaway
They Don't Always Hang Murderers. B. Herbert
They Don't Dance Much. James Ross
They Don't Live Long. J. Cello
They Don't Make Them Like That Any More. J. Leasor
They Drive by Night. J. Curtis
They Found a Way Back. N. Sheraton
They Found Atlantis. D. Wheatley
They Found Each Other. G. Fairlie
They Found Him Dead. G. Heyer
They Hadn't a Clue. Q. Downes
They Hang Them in Gibraltar. B. Perowne
They Hunted a Fox. Alice Campbell
They Journey by Night. D. Ames
They Kidnapped Stanley Matthews. L. Gribble
They Kill by Night. K. Medusa
They Killed a Spy. M. Hastings
They Liked Entwhistle. R. A. J. Walling
They Lived with Death. H. Desmond
They Love Not Poison. Sara Woods
They Met at Mrs. Bloxom's. H. Norwood
They Never Came Back. B. Flynn
They Never Came Back. David Hume
They Never Came Back. E. P. Thorne
They Never Looked Inside. M. Gilbert
They Never Say When. P. Cheyney
They Rang Up the Police. J. Cannan
They Rubbed Him Out. J. L. Cora
They Sailed on a Friday. T. C. Paynter
They Say I'm Bad. B. Shannon
They See in Darkness. Ethel L. White
They Shoot Horses, Don't They? H. McCoy
They Stand Accused. G. Braddon
They Stay for Death. Sara Woods
They Stole a Ship. C. H. Barker
They Stuck at Nothing. R. Ladline
They Talked of Poison. M. Evermay
They Tell No Tales. M. Coles
They Tell No Tales. A. Spiller
They Tell No Tales. L. Thayer
They Thought He Was Dead. S. Horler
They Used Dark Forces. D. Wheatley
They Used to Play on Grass. Gordon M. Williams
They Vanish at Night. Frank King
They Voted Me to Die. J. Laffin
They Waited for the Night. V. Dale
They Walk in Darkness. G. Verner
They Want Me Dead. P. Bannon
They Wanted Him Dead! L. Eyles
They Watched by Night. J. Rhode
They Went Thataway. D. A. Brown
They Were Seven. E. Phillpotts
They Wetted His Head. H. Fernee
They Who Sin. J. Roeburt
They Won't Believe Me. G. McDonell
They Won't Lie Down. M. Annesley
They Wouldn't Be Chessman. A. E. W. Mason
They'll Never Find Out. F. Duncan
They're Coming to Kill You, Jane. K. Carr
They're Going to Kill Me. K. M. Knight
They're Not Home Yet. F. Rydell
They've Got Me Again. D. Linton
They've Killed Anne. M. Olden
They've Shot the President's Daughter. E. Stewart
Thick Blue Sweater. P. Fry
Thickening Light. G. Ferrand
Thicker Than Water. M. Halliday
Thicker Than Water. J. Payn
Thicker Than Water. M. Polland
Thicker Than Water. J. Sandys
Thicker Than Water. W. C. Tuttle
Thicket. P. Gallagher
Thief. R. Croft-Cooke
Thief. M. L. Tyrrell
Thief by Night. D. Peacock
Thief in the Night. Nicholas Carter
Thief in the Night. E. W. Hornung
Thief in the Night. P. Manton
Thief in the Night. E. Wallace
Thief in the Night. T. Walsh
Thief Is an Ugly Word. P. Gallico
Thief of Clubs. G. Johns
Thief of Hearts. Rachelle Edwards
Thief of Time. J. Wainwright
Thief or Two. Sara Woods
Thief Taker. J. Sturrock
Thief Who Came to Dinner. T. L. Smith
Thief Who Couldn't Sleep. Lawrence Block
Thief Who Painted Sunlight. O. Bleeck
Thief Who Was Robbed. Nicholas Carter
Thieves. Aix
Thieves' Carnival. J. Anouilh
Thieves Fall Out. C. Kay
Thieves' Highway. Ruth Grayson
Thieves' Hole. D. Howarth
Thieves' Honour. S. Gluck
Thieves' Justice. A. Marsden
Thieves' Kitchen. J. N. Chance
Thieves Like Us. R. E. Alter
Thieves Like Us. E. Anderson
Thieves Market. A. I. Bezzerides
Thieves' Nights. H. S. Keeler
Thieves of Alexandria. J. Hunter
Thieves of Enchantment. P. Audemars
Thieves' Picnic. L. Charteris
Thieves' Wit. H. Footner
Thieving Fingers. F. Du Boisgobey
Thin Air. H. Browne
Thin Air. W. Marshall
Thin Air. J. Pudney
Thin Air. G. E. Simpson
Thin Edge of Mania. M. Macklin
Thin Edge of Violence. W. O'Farrell
Thin Ice. M. Richmond
Thin Line. E. Atiyah
Thin Line. R. Doliner
Thin Man. D. Hammett
Thin Red Line. A. Griffiths
Thin-Spun Thread. A. Hocking
Thing at the Door. H. Slesar
Thing at Their Heels. H. Hext
Thing in the Brook. P. Storme
Thing in the Night. K. Virden
Thing in the Road. T. M. White
Thing in the Woods. Harper Williams
Thing That Happens to You. E. Berckman
Thing That Made Love. D. V. Reed
Thing to Love. G. Household
Things As They Are. W. Godwin
Things Happen. R. Glover
Things Men Do. Raymond Marshall
Things That Are Caesar's. R. W. Kauffman
Things That No One Tells. E. C. Mayne
Things That Women Do. F. Warden
Think Fast, Mr. Moto. J. P. Marquand
Think Inc. A. Diment
Think of a Number. A. Bodelsen
Think of Death. R. Lockridge
Thinking Machine. J. Futrelle
Thinking Machine Affair. Joel Bernard
Thinking Machine on the Case. J. Futrelle
Third Alibi. M. Dalman
Third Angle. S. Lamont
Third Arm. K. Royce
Third Assassin. H. C. Davis
Third Attempt. H. E. Wheeler
Third Baffle Book. L. Wren
Third Bullet. Carter Dickson
Third Bullet and other stories. J. D. Carr
Third Case of Mr. Paul Savoy. Jackson Gregory
Third Child. A. Nichols
Third Crime Lucky. Anthony Gilbert
Third Day. J. Hayes

Third Degree. Joe Barry
Third Degree. M. B. Dix
Third Degree. C. Franklin
Third Degree. A. Hornblow
Third Degree. C. R. Jackson
Third Diamond. J. B. Ellis
Third Ear. C. Siodmak
Third Encounter. Sara Woods
Third Eye. E. Leroux
Third Eye. Ethel L. White
Third Figure. C. Wilcox
Third Force. H. Matheson
Third Force. D. Sinclair
Third Girl. A. Christie
Third Half. Mildred Davis
Third Horseman. J. B. O'Sullivan
Third Hour. G. Household
Third Identity. R. Gatenby
Third Key. H. H. C. Gibbons
Third Key. G. Verner
Third Kiss. H. Flowerdew
Third Man. J. G. Bethune
Third Man and The Fallen Idol. G. Greene
Third Messenger. P. Wynnton
Third Miracle. L. Tracy
Third Mistake. A. W. Barrett
Third Murderer. C. J. Daly
Third on a Seesaw. N. MacNeil
Third Owl. R. J. Casey
Third Party Risk. N. Bentley
Third Party Risk. G. Cullingford
Third Policeman. Flann O'Brien
Third Possibility. S. Jepson
Third Robin Featherstone. L. C. Douthwaite
Third Round. H. C. McNeile
Third Seat Back. K. Sunderland
Third Shadow. D. Nile
Third Shot. F. W. Irwin
Third Side of the Coin. F. Clifford
Third Skin. J. Bingham
Third Spectre. W. E. D. Ross
Third Statue. Shane Martin
Third Time Unlucky. Mark Cross
Third Time Unlucky! L. Meynell
Third Time Unlucky. T. B. Morris
Third Tower. A. Abbott
Third Truth. M. Bar-Zohar
Third Twin. Clay Henry
Third Victim. J. J. Farjeon
Third Victim. Donald Stuart
Third Victim. C. Wilcox
Third Visitor. G. Anstruther
Third Volume. F. Hume
Third Warning. Augustus Muir
Third Wife. J. Himes
Third Woman. J. De Pre
Thirst. G. N. Smith
Thirsty Evil. P. M. Hubbard
Thirsty Evil. G. Verner
Thirteen. F. B. Austin
Thirteen. H. Balzac
13. P. Loraine
Thirteen at Dinner. A. Christie
13 Castle Walk. D. Bodeen
13 Clues for Miss Marple. A. Christie
Thirteen Days. I. Jefferies
13 for Luck! A. Christie
13 French Street. G. Brewer
Thirteen Guests. J. J. Farjeon
Thirteen in a Fog. B. Graeme
Thirteen Men. T. Thayer
Thirteen Moons. M. L. Tyrrell
Thirteen O'Clock. E. Bond
Thirteen Problems. A. Christie
Thirteen Stannergate. G. M. Wilson
Thirteen Steps. W. Chambers
13 Steps to Lime Street. D. Enefer
Thirteen Towers. C. Caldwell
Thirteen Ways Home. E. Nesbit
13 Thirteenth Street. N. S. Lincoln
Thirteen Toy Pistols. E. E. Halleran
Thirteen Trumpeters. L. Meynell
13 West Street. L. Brackett
13 White Tulips. F. Crane
Thirteen Winston Street. J. Wetherell
Thirteenth Bed in the Ballroom. E. H. Fonseca
Thirteenth Brydain. M. Moule
Thirteenth Chair. B. Veiller
13th Chime. T. C. H. Jacobs
13th Code. W. Jardine
Thirteenth Day. C. George
13th Doll. A. Loring
Thirteenth Floor. J. F. W. Hannay
Thirteenth Guest. F. Hume
Thirteenth Guest. A. Trail
13th Hour. S. Horler
Thirteenth Hour. John Lee
Thirteenth House. C. Barry
Thirteenth Juror. F. T. Hill
Thirteenth Letter. N. S. Lincoln
Thirteenth Lover. R. Clarke
13th Lover. M. Dekobra
13th Man. M. T. Bloom
Thirteenth Man. Mrs. C. Kernahan
13th Mummy. G. Radcliffe
13th Murder. F. G. Eberhard
13th Spy. Nick Carter
Thirteenth Treasure. Charlotte Hunt
Thirteenth Trick. R. Braddon
Thirty Days. H. Wales

Thirty Days Hath July. Alice Brennan
Thirty Days Hath September. P. Capon
30 Days Hath September. D. C. Disney
Thirty Days Hath September. O. John
Thirty Days to Live. P. Conway
Thirty Days to Live. Anthony Gilbert
30° North 165° East. P. J. Stam
.38. W. Ard
.38 Automatic. E. C. Vivian
Thirty-Eighth Floor. Clifford Irving
Thirty Famous Chinese Stories. W. I-Ting
Thirty-First Bullfinch. H. Reilly
Thirty-First Floor. P. Wahloo
Thirty-First of February. J. Symons
Thirty-Four East. Alfred Coppel
"30" Manhattan East. H. Waugh
Thirty-Nine Steps. J. Buchan
Thirty-Ninth Victim. P. Griffiths
Thirty Pieces of Silver. A. Soutar
Thirty-Second Floor. E. Dudowicz
Thirty Seconds over New York. R. Buchard
36 Hours. C. K. Hittleman
.32 Calibre. D. McGibney
Thirty Years After. W. M. Graydon
This Ancient Evil. D. Daniels
This Animal Is Dangerous. Reginald Campbell
This Animal Must Die. F. Scarpetta
This Band of Spirits. Nick Carter
This Body Must Die. A. Sergeant
This Business of Bumfog. M. Donne
This Chequered Floor. P. Bamford
This City Is Ours. D. Pitts
This Creeping Evil. Sea Lion
This Crowded Earth & Ladies' Day. R. Bloch
This Dame Dies Soon. H. Janson
This Dame Spells Death. C. Wheatley
This Dark Desire. J. Conway
This Dark Monarchy. F. Leary
This Darkening Universe. L. Biggle
This Day's Madness. D. G. Waring
This Deadly Dark. L. Wilson
This Deadly Grief. P. Power
This Death Was Murder. M. Evermay
This Delicate Murder. H. Clandon
This Doll Is Dangerous. Frank King
This Downhill Path. A. Clarke
This Drakotny—. P. McCutchan
This Evil Village. Marilyn Ross
This Fatal Writ. Sara Woods
This Fearful Paradise. J. Ames
This Fell Sergeant. D. Garner
This Frightened Lady. Marilyn Ross
This Fortress. M. Coles
This Game of Murder. R. Deming
This Ghost Business. A. W. Clark
This Girl for Hire. G. G. Fickling
This Gun for Gloria. B. Mara
This Gun for Hire. G. Greene
This Gun for Justice. V. J. Santiago
This Hood for Hire. H. Janson
This House Is Burning. Mona Williams
This House Is Haunted. R. Bridges
This House to Let. W. LeQueux
This Inward Horror. J. R. Warren
This Is Death Calling. J. Sandys
This Is Dynamite. Richard Grant
This Is for Keeps. G. Joseph
This Is for Real. J. H. Chase
This Is Harry Flynn. J. Jost
This Is It. H. Ellson
This Is It, Michael Shayne. B. Halliday
This Is Jezebel. D. Cory
This Is Mr. Fortune. H. C. Bailey
This Is Murder. W. Ard
This—Is Murder! C. Fitzsimmons
This Is Murder. C. J. Kenny
This Is Murder. P. Muller
This Is Murder, Lady! N. W. Firth
This Is Murder, Mr. Herbert and other stories. D. Keene
This Is Murder, Mr. Jones. T. Fuller
This Is My Murder. M. B. Dix
This Is My. R. Deming
This Is the Castle. N. Freeling
This Is the House. Shelley Smith
This Is What Happened. T. Claymore
This Is Your Life. B. Newman
This Kill Is Mine. D. Evans
This Land Turns Evil Slowly. M. L. Roby
This Little Angel Went to Hell. P. Fenton
This Little Measure. Sara Woods
This Little World. D. C. Murray
This Man Belongs to Me. M. Richmond
This Man Dawson. H. E. Helseth
This Man Did I Kill? M. Halliday
This Man I Love. W. E. D. Ross
This Man Is a Spy. D. L. David
This Man Is a Stranger. H. B. Kaye
This Man Is Dangerous. P. Cheyney
This Man Is Death. A. Capelli
This Man Is Mine. K. Lindsay
This Man Must Die! W. A. Ballinger
This Man's Doom. L. Thayer
This Man's Wife. G. M. Fenn
This Mortal Coil. L. Allen
This Mortal Coil. J. R. Warren
This Murder Comes to Mind. R. Ormerod
This Murderous Shaft. H. J. Hultman
This New Corn. D. G. Waring

This One Night. D. Robins
This Other Eden. E. V. Knox
This Outward Angel. Alanna Knight
This Passionate Land. H. Janeway
This Path Is Dangerous. F. J. Whaley
"This Road Is Dangerous!" H. D. Dearden
This Road Is Dangerous. M. Richmond
This Rough Magic. Mary Stewart
This Shrouded Night. Dana Ross
This Side Murder. J. Bonett
This Side of Hell. R. Charles
This Side of Terror. D. Bateson
This Side of the Sky. J. Barlow
This Side Up. H. Luger
This Son of Vulcan. W. Besant
This Spy Must Die. P. Saxon
This Story of Yours. J. Hopkins
This Suitcase Is Going to Explode. T. Ardies
This Sweet Sickness. P. Highsmith
This Tangled Web. E. O. Allen
This Time Forever. A. J. Merak
This Traitor, Death. D. Cory
This Troublesome World. L. T. Meade
This Undesirable Residence. M. Burton
This Unnecessary Murder. F. S. Wees
This Was a Woman. H. Zore
This Was No Accident. J. A. Saxon
This Water Laps Gently. M. Ingate
This Way for a Shroud. J. H. Chase
This Way for Hell. S. Morelli
This Way for Hell. Gene Ross
This Way Out. J. Ronald
This Way Out. A. M. Shoil
This Way to Evil. H. P. Lees
This Will Kill You. Jerome Barry
This Witch. W. Tucker
This Woman Is Dangerous. Mark Ross
This Woman Is Death. S. D. Frances
This Woman Is Death. H. Janson
This Woman Is Death. M. Storm
This Woman Is Wanted. Roland Daniel
This Woman Is Wanted. G. Goodchild
This Woman to This Man. C. N. Williamson
This Woman Wanted. R. Foley
This Won't Hurt You. N. Fitzgerald
This World Is Wide Enough. G. Greenfield
This Year—Next Year. Lionel Brown
This Year's Death. J. Godey
This Yellow Slave. L. Durie
This'll Kill You. Peter Chambers
This'll Kill You. M. Randolph
This'll Slay You. A. Payne
Thistle Sifters. C. R. Burke
Thomas Berryman Number. J. Patterson
Thomas Crown Affair. E. L. Heyman
Thomas Document. H. Gantzer
Thomas Shelton's Ghost. J. Brocke
Thompson the Detective. J. L. Hempstead
Thompson's Progress. C. J. C. Hyne
Thor Option. M. Benassi
Thorn in the Dust. P. Audemars
Thorne in the Flesh. R. Petrie
Thorne House. J. Ware
Thorne Theatre Mystery. Joshua Willard
Thornley Colton, Blind Detective. C. H. Stagg
Thornley Colton, Blind Reader of Hearts. C. H. Stagg
Those on the List. A. Parsons
Those Other Days. E. P. Oppenheim
Those Seven Alibis. C. G. Booth
Those Subtle Weeds. J. A. Lordahl
Those That Have Eyes. P. Conway
Those Westerton Girls. F. Warden
Those Who Have Come Back. P. C. MacFarlane
Those Who Prey Together Slay Together. D. Von Elsner
Those Who Return. M. Level
Those Who Smiled, and other stories. P. Gibbon
Those Who Walk Away. P. Highsmith
Those Who Walk in Darkness. G. C. Shedd
Thou Art the Man. M. E. Braddon
Thou Shalt Not Kill. B. Heygate
"Thou Shalt Not Kill." M. B. Lowndes
Thou Shell of Death. N. Blake
Thou Shouldst Be Living. J. Byrom
Though I Know She Lies. Sara Woods
Thoughtless Yes. H. H. Gardener
Thousand and One Afternoons in Chicago. B. Hecht
Thousand and Second Night. F. Heller
Thousand Coffins Affair. M. Avallone
Thousand Doors. A. Rothberg
Thousand Faces of Night. Harry Patterson
Thousand Francs Reward. E. Gaboriau
Thousand Hands. Bruce Norman
Thousand-Headed Man. K. Robeson
Thousand Secrets. J. Selborne
Thousand Witnesses. G. Beardmore
Thousandth Case. G. Dilnot
Thousandth Woman. E. W. Hornung
Thread of Evidence. B. Picton
Thread of Proof. H. Hill
Threads of Gold. L. V. Stevens
Threads of Intrigue. Lynn Williams
Threads of Love. E. Randolph
Threat of Dragons. L. R. Davis
Threat of the Cloven Hand. Richard Grant
Threat Warning Red. A. Fox

Title Index

Threatening Eye. Colin Robertson
Three. F. Hume
Three Act Tragedy. A. Christie
Three Against Fate. M. A. Hamilton
Three Alibis. J. F. W. Hannay
Three Amateurs. Michael Lewis
Three Among Mountains. H. Slater
Three at the Angel. M. Procter
Three at Wolfe's Door. R. Stout
Three Bad Girls. S. Harragan
Three Bad Nights. B. Buckingham
Three Beans. M. Coles
Three Beds in Manhattan. G. Simenon
Three Black Bags. M. P. Angellotti
Three Black Dots. O. Binns
Three Blind Mice. V. Bridges
Three Blind Mice. A. Christie
3 Blind Mice. A. Seifert
Three Blind Mice. J. Wood
Three Blue Anchors. O. Binns
Three Boy Detectives. Old Sleuth
Three Brass Balls. G. R. Sims
Three Brass Elephants. Herman Landon
Three Bright Pebbles. L. Ford
Three Brothers. J. Pickersgill
Three Candles for the Dark. Rosemary Harris
Three Cheers for Treason! Robert Mason
Three Coffins. J. D. Carr
Three Colonels. P. Cosgrave
Three-Coloured Pencil. S. P. B. Mais
Three-Cornered Cover. G. Marton
Three-Cornered Murder. Jean Leslie
Three-Cornered Wound. G. Dyer
Three Corners to Nowhere. M. Caidin
Three Corpse Trick. M. Burton
Three Couriers. C. MacKenzie
Three Cousins Die. J. Rhode
Three Cries of Terror. A. Ashton
Three Crimes. M. Burton
Three Crows. J. Hunter
Three Daggers. C. F. Gregg
Three Dates with Death. V. Gunn
Three Daughters of Night. D. Vane
Three Day Alliance. H. R. Simpson
Three Day Pass—to Kill. J. W. Burke
3-Day Terror. V. Packer
Three Days in Hong Kong. F. Crane
Three Days of the Condor. J. Grady
Three Days' Terror. J. S. Fletcher
Three Days Terror. P. Manton
Three Days to Live. R. Charles
Three Dead. D. Magarshack
Three Dead Men. P. McGuire
Three Dead, One Hurt. S. Mackenzie
Three Die at Midnight. J. Hunter
Three Die at Midnight. P. Meriton
Three Died Beside the Marble Pool. C. M. Chapin
Three Died for Morson. C. Ryland
Three Died That Night. Gret Lane
3 Died Variously. G. E. Giles
Three Doors to Darkness. W. Palmer
Three Doors to Death. R. Stout
Three Dots and a Dash. T. Taggart
Three Down Vulnerable. Z. H. Ross
Three Envelopes. H. Drummond
Three Exploits of M. Parent. J. Lermina
Three Faces East. A. P. Kelly
Three Faces of Death. J. Weisman
Three Fair Philanthropists. A. M. Muzzy
Three Fears. J. Stagge
Three Finger Marks. Old Spicer
Three Fingered Death. G. M. Wilson
Three Fingers in the Door. F. Metcalfe
Three Fishers. F. Beeding
Three for a Killing. D. Leach
Three for Adventure. M. Halliday
Three for the Chair. R. Stout
Three for the Gallows. E. McDowell
Three for the Money. W. T. Ballard
Three for the Money. Joe Barry
Three for the Money. J. McConnaughey
Three Freaks. T. Robbins
Three Frightened Men. B. Gray
Three Gentlemen from New Caledonia. R. D. Hemingway
3 Girls and a Killer. H. D. Spatz
Three Glass Eyes. W. LeQueux
Three Gnomes. W. Verner
Three Gold Crowns. K. Robeson
Three Graces. P. Hobson
Three Green Bottles. D. Devine
Three Ha-Pence to the Angel. Charles Harris
Three Hostages. J. Buchan
Three Hours to Hang. A. MacKenzie
330 Park. S. Cohen
Three Hundred Grand. J. Pattinson
361. D. E. Westlake
Three Hunting Horns. M. Fitt
Three Imposters. A. Machen
Three in a Cell. R. Croft-Cooke
Three Inquisitive People. D. Wheatley
Three Jolly Vagabonds. J. Budd
Three Judges. H. Maxwell
Three Just Men. E. Wallace
Three Keys. F. Ormond
Three Keys to Murder. M. Holloway
Three Knaves. S. L. Greenleaf
Three Knaves. E. Phillpotts
Three Knots. W. LeQueux

Three Knots. R. Parker
Three Layers of Guilt. J. Ashford
Three Lepers' Heads. P. Quiroule
Three Letters to Pan. J. Blackmore
Three Lights Went Out. R. G. Dean
Three Little Tramps. Old Sleuth
Three Lost Ladies. H. R. Campbell
Three Lovers and One Lass. A. M. Meadows
Three Masked Men. J. N. Pentelow
Three Masks of Death. J. N. Chance
3 Megaton Gamble. D. Terman
Three Men and a God, and other stories. N. Newham-Davis
Three Men and a Maid. Robert Fraser
Three Men Die. S. G. Millin
Three Men for the Job. D. Ambler
Three Men in a Plane. C. Winchester
Three Men Murdered. A. A. Archer
Three Men Out. R. Stout
$3 Million Turn-Over. Richard Curtis
Three Millions! W. T. Adams
Three Minus Two. D. MacKenzie
Three Minutes to Midnight. Mildred Davis
Three Motives for Murder. R. Winsor
Three Must Die! D. Gregory
Three Mysteries. T. Douglas
Three Names for Murder. H. R. Campbell
Three Nights. E. Hostovsky
Three Oak Mystery. E. Wallace
Three of a Kind. J. M. Cain
Three of a Kind, and The Haunting of Jack Burnham. H. C. McNeile
Three of Clubs. V. Williams
Three of Diamonds. K. M. Knight
Three of Hearts. J. M. Cain
Three on the Road. S. Ryder
Three People's Secret. G. M. Fenn
Three-Pipe Problem. J. Symons
Three Plays. E. De Filippo
Three Plays. J. Mortimer
Three Plots for Asey Mayo. P. A. Taylor
Three Point Murder. R. C. Finney
Three Potato, Four. W. Greatorex
Three Prize Plays. N. Holland
Three Problems for Solar Pons. A. Derleth
3 Professional Ladies. G. F. Newman
Three Quick and Five Dead. G. Mitchell
Three R's. Ganpat
Three Rainbows. K. Hewitt
Three Recruits, and the Girls They Left Behind Them. J. Hatton
Three Roads to Millar
Three Roads to a Star. D. Garth
"Three Rounds Rapid—." R. Hardinge
Three Saw the Murder. H. L. Blair
Three Sentinels. G. Household
3-7-9 Murder. G. Morton
Three Sevens. P. P. Sheehan
Three Short Biers. J. Starr
Three Short Men. F. Vivian
Three Shots. O. Gray
Three Silent Men. E. P. Thorne
Three Silver Birches. R. M. Sears
Three Sisters Flew Home. M. Fitt
Three Sisters of Briarwick. K. Kimbrough
Three Sisters of No End House. N. Farnsworth
Three Slips to a Noose. Fiona Sinclair
Three Spies for Glory. M. McKenna
Three Steps to Hell. V. Warren
Three Steps to Murder. N. MacKenzie
Three Strangers. M. Dalman
Three Strangers. G. Joseph
Three Straw Men. A. Derleth
Three Strings. N. S. Lincoln
Three Sundays to Live. Roland Daniel
Three Taps. R. A. Knox
Three Taps at Twelve. A. Saunders
Three Taps on a Wall. L. Barbee
Three Thirds of a Ghost. T. Fuller
3-13 Murders. T. B. Black
Three Thousand Dollars. A. K. Green
Three Tiers of Fantasy. N. Berrow
Three-Time Losers. G. Bagby
Three Times a Victim. F. L. Wallace
Three Times Dead. M. E. Braddon
Three to Be Read. P. Wylie
Three to Make Murder. Victor Patrick
Three-Toed Pussy. W. J. Burley
Three Trails. W. M. Graydon
Three Trials of Manirema. J. J. Veiga
Three Verdicts. F. I. Katzenberger
Three-Way Split. G. Brewer
Three Wayward Girls. F. Warden
Three Went In. N. A. Temple-Ellis
Three Were to Die. F. C. Ticknor
Three Who Died. A. Derleth
Three Who Paid. Donald Stuart
Three Widows. Bernice Carey
Three—with Blood. A. M. Stein
Three Witnesses. S. Fowler
Three Witnesses. R. Stout
Three Wives. Alex Fraser
Three Women. W. Reyburn
Three Women in Black. H. Reilly
Three Women in the House. E. Thompson
Three Wooden Overcoats. H. Clevely
Three Worlds of Johnny Handsome. J. Godey
Three Yards of Cord. C. Brooks
Three Years After. N. Buntline

Threefold Cord. F. Vivian
Threefold Disappearance. Nicholas Carter
Threefold Threat. D. Miall
Threepence to Marble Arch. P. McGuire
Threepersons Hunt. B. Garfield
Three's a Crowd. D. M. Disney
Three's a Shroud. R. S. Prather
Threescore Years. P. Capon
Threshing Floor. J. S. Fletcher
Threshold. S. Coulter
Threshold of Fear. A. J. Rees
Thrice Captive. A. Griffiths
Thrice Judas. F. Grierson
Thrice Past the Post. H. Smart
Thrice Upon a Killing Spree. P. Quinn
Thrifty Abe. Old Sleuth
Thrill. B. Petty
Thrill a Minute with Jack Albany. J. Godey
Thrill Kids. V. Packer
Thrill Killers. R. Novak
Thrill Machine. I. Hamilton
Thriller. Ted Hart
Thriller of the Year. Glyn Jones
Thrilling Adventures of a New York Detective. Anonymous
Thrilling Detective Stories. T. P. MacNaught
Thrilling Mystery. Old Sleuth
Thrilling Stories. Anonymous
Thrilling Stories of the Railway. V. L. Whitechurch
Throbbing Dark. F. Arthur
Throne of Bayonets. K. Fitzgerald
Throne of Peril. C. M. Hincks
Throne of Satan. James Dark
Through a Glass Darkly. Anonymous
Through a Glass Darkly. T. Blakemore
Through a Glass Darkly. V. Gielgud
Through a Glass, Darkly. H. McCloy
Through a Glass Darkly. E. Phillpotts
Through a Glass Darkly. B. Symons
Through Another Gate. R. Bridges
Through Another Gate. G. Vaizey
Through Devil's Gate. D. P. Neeley
Through Fire and Water. R. C. Armour
Through Folly's Mill. A. Askew
Through the Bamboo Curtain. M. Urquhart
Through the Cellar Wall. Nicholas Carter
Through the Dark and Hairy Wood. S. Herron
Through the Dark Curtain. P. Saxon
Through the Eyes of the Judge. B. Graeme
Through the Lens. M. Massey
Through the Night. F. Ryerson
Through the Wall. C. Moffett
Through the Wall. K. Sully
Through the Wall. P. Wentworth
Through War to Peace. Benjamin F. Mason
Throw. A. Bloomfield
Throw Back the Little Ones. P. Colombo
Thug Executive. J. N. Chance
Thugs and Bottles. San Antonio
Thumb-Mark. Warren Hill
Thumb Stroke. F. Du Boisgobey
Thunder Above. A. J. Wallis
Thunder Ahead. Malcolm Campbell
Thunder at Dawn. H. Gibbs
Thunder at Noon. Harry Patterson
Thunder Dragon Gate. T. Mundy
Thunder Heights. P. A. Whitney
Thunder in Europe. J. Creasey
Thunder in the Air. L. Barbee
Thunder in the Kirk. A. Marlowe
Thunder Island. J. Hunter
Thunder Island. L. Johns
Thunder Island. G. Volk
Thunder-Maker. J. Creasey
Thunder on the Roses. M. Peyrou
Thunder on Sunday. Karen Campbell
Thunder on the Right. Mary Stewart
Thunder over South Parish. A. J. Allen
Thunder over the Reefs. P. Minton
Thunder Rock. Anita Allen
Thunderball. I. Fleming
Thunderbird. D. Garth
Thunderbird Range. W. C. Tuttle
Thunderbolt. J. G. Sarasin
Thunderbolt and Lightfoot. J. Millard
Thunderbolt Collects. J. McCulley
Thunderbolt's Jest. J. McCulley
Thunderstrike in Syria. Nick Carter
Thurb Revolution. A. Panshin
Thurman Lucas. H. E. Read
Thursday at Dawn. W. J. Luddecke
Thursday Island. M. Keck
Thursday the Rabbi Walked Out. H. Kemelman
Thursday Turkey Murders. J. McGreevey
Thursday Turkey Murders. C. Rice
Thursday Woman. M. Davidson
Thursday's Blade. F. C. Davis
Thursday's Folly. J. Philips
Thurtell's Crime: The Story of a Strange Tragedy. D. Donovan
Thus Far. J. C. Snaith
Thy Arm Alone. J. Slate
Thy First Begotten. N. Bell
Thy Guilt Is Great. C. I. D. Smith
Tiara. Anthony Mann
Tiberius Smith. H. Pendexter
Tic-Tac. D. Learmonth

Tick of Death. P. Lovesey
Tick of the Clock. H. Asbury
Tick...Tick...Tick. P. Rock
Tickencote Treasure. W. LeQueux
Ticker-Tape Murder. M. Propper
Ticket. C. Stratton
Ticket for Death. E. M. Bowen
Ticket of Leave. G. Simenon
Ticket-of-Leave Girl. A. M. Meadows
Ticket-of-Leave Man. C. H. Bullivant
Ticket-of-Leave Man. Tom Taylor
Ticket-of-Leave Man. H. C. Williams
Ticket San Diego. A. Bocca
Ticket to Buffalo. A. Dean
Ticket to Eternity. G. Shayne
Ticket to Hell. H. Whittington
Ticket to Oblivion. Robert Parker
Ticket to Ride. Ritchie Perry
Tickets for Death. B. Halliday
Ticking Clock. F. Lockridge
Ticking Heart. D. B. Olsen
Ticking Terror Murders. D. L. Teilhet
Tickletoby. H. Wayne
Tidal Wave. G. Simenon
Tide Can't Wait. L. Trimble
Tide of Death. J. M. Hickman
Tide of Fortune. M. Gerard
Tide Race. H. Gilbert
Tide Rip. Robin Temple
Tide Waits for No Man. H. La Garde
Tide Watchers. S. M. Parkman
Tideless Sea. G. Volk
Tidemill. D. Daniels
Tides of Tremannion. K. A. Shoesmith
Tidewrack. N. Tranter
Tidings of Joy. G. Goodchild
Tidy Death. N. Lombard
Tie and Trick. H. Smart
Tied for Murder. C. Fitzsimmons
Tied up in Tinsel. N. Marsh
Tiffany Caper. J. Purtell
Tiger Among Us. L. Brackett
Tiger at Bay. B. Picton
Tiger by the Tail. J. H. Chase
Tiger by the Tail. L. Goldman
Tiger Claws. F. Packard
Tiger Dawn. S. Jepson
Tiger from the Shadows. Bradshaw Jones
Tiger-Heart. J. G. Sarasin
Tiger Hill. Ardath Wise
Tiger House. R. St. Clair
Tiger in Red Weather. J. Wyllie
Tiger in the Bed. M. Catto
Tiger in the Night. R. Kyle
Tiger in the Night. J. M. Walsh
Tiger in the North. S. Harvester
Tiger in the Smoke. M. Allingham
Tiger in the Streets. L. Malley
Tiger Kittens. A. Zuckerman
Tiger Lily. G. Dilnot
Tiger Lily. G. M. Fenn
Tiger Lily. C. N. Williamson
Tiger Mark. P. Graham
Tiger Milk. D. Garth
Tiger of Baragunga. J. I. Emery
Tiger of Canton. G. H. Teed
Tiger of Cloud River. R. Cullum
Tiger of Karan. D. Lenton
Tiger of Mayfair. H. Holt
Tiger on My Back. Gordons
Tiger Reef. M. Hastings
Tiger River. A. O. Friel
Tiger Snake. H. S. Keeler
Tiger Sniffs the Rose. H. G. Carlisle
Tiger Standish. S. Horler
Tiger Standish Comes Back. S. Horler
Tiger Standish Does His Stuff. S. Horler
Tiger Standish Has a Party. S. Horler
Tiger Standish Steps on It. S. Horler
Tiger Standish Takes the Field. S. Horler
Tiger Street. E. Trevor
Tiger Strikes Again. C. M. Wills
Tiger Ten. W. D. Blankenship
Tiger, Tiger. G. Goodchild
Tiger Tooth. E. Woodward
Tigerman of Terrahpur. F. Lecale
Tigers Are Hungry. C. Early
Tiger's Back. J. W. Mason
Tiger's Claw. W. Braun
Tiger's Claw. A. P. Terhune
Tiger's Claws. Colin Robertson
Tiger's Coat. E. Dejeans
Tiger's Cub. E. Phillpotts
Tiger's Cub. G. Seton
Tigers Fight Alone. F. Duncan
Tigers Have Claws. B. Graeme
Tiger's Head Mystery. E. T. Sawyer
Tiger's Necklace. R. St. Clair
Tiger's Wife. Wade Miller
Tight Circle. J. F. Straker
Tight Corner. B. Copper
Tight Corner. A. W. Marchmont
Tight Corner. Sam Ross
Tight Rope. A. L. Burks
Tight Sqeeze. W. Fuller
Tightening of the Coils. Old Spicer
Tightening String. A. Bridge
Tightrope. James Grant
Tightrope. J. Legaret
Tightrope for Three. M. Babson
Tightrope Men. D. Bagley

Tightrope Minor. T. Topor
Tightrope Walker. D. Gilman
Tigress. J. Bogar
Tigress. Carter Brown
Tigress. M. Derby
Tigress. H. Janson
Tigress of Brazil. B. Sarto
Tigress of the Evening. Anne-Mariel
'Til Death. E. McBain
'Til Death Do Us Part. A. Hynd
Tiled House Mystery. W. M. Duncan
Till Death Do Us Part. J. D. Carr
Till Death Do Us Part. L. Trimble
Till Doomsday. Robin Temple
Till It Hurts. N. Quarry
Till Life Us Do Part. E. Petersen
Till Murder Do Us Part. W. H. L. Craufurd
Till the Clock Stops. J. J. Bell
Till the Dying Day. A. Watkins
Tillinger Codicil. T. Beattie
Tilsit Inheritance. C. Gaskin
Tilted Moon. B. Perowne
Tim Frazer Again. F. Durbridge
Tim Frazer Gets the Message. F. Durbridge
Timbalier. C. W. Coleman
Timber Beasts. C. Stoddard
Timber Line. W. E. Murphy
Timber Wolf. J. Templeton
Timberjack. D. Cushman
Time After Time. K. Alexander
Time and the Torture. N. Sligh
Time at Tarragon. J. Tattersall
Time Bargains. T. W. Speight
Time Before This. N. Monsarrat
Time Bomb. J. D. Atwater
Time Bomb. H. Howard
Time Bomb. W. Tucker
Time Clock of Death. Nick Carter
Time Dissolver. J. Sohl
Time Enough to Die. P. Rabe
Time for a Murder. G. Coverack
Time for Caution. P. Cheyney
Time for Crime. P. C. Williams
Time for Killing. J. Rowland
Time for Murder. P. O. McGuire
Time for Murder. H. P. Martin
Time for Murder. R. O. Saber
Time for Murder. J. Stagg
Time for Passion. H. Rigsby
Time for Payment. H. H. Kirst
Time for Pirates. G. Black
Time for Scandal. H. H. Kirst
Time for Sleeping. J. Moffatt
Time for Survival. P. McCutchan
Time for Tea. J. Coates
Time for Treason. P. Deane
Time for Treason. O. Hesky
Time for Truth. H. H. Kirst
Time for Vengeance. G. Osborne
Time for Violence. A. Goddard
Time in the End. F. M. McGuire
Time Is an Ambush. F. Clifford
Time Is an Enemy. S. J. Baker
Time Limit. R. Sheckley
Time Lock. C. E. Walk
Time, Murderer, Please. C. Dyer
Time of Assassins. R. Batchelor
Time of Day. F. Durbridge
Time of Dreaming. J. Edgar
Time of Illusion. R. Roleine
Time of Killing. W. Hardy
Time of Madness. R. Early
Time of Night. R. Swazee
Time of Predators. J. Gores
Time of Reckoning. W. Wager
Time of Temptation. P. Audemars
Time of Terror. H. Pentecost
Time of Terror. L. White
Time of the Burning Mask. D. Rowan
Time of the Crime. Donald Stuart
Time of the Fire. M. Brandel
Time Off for Death. G. Braddon
Time Off for Murder. Z. Popkin
Time Out. D. Ely
Time Remembered, Time Lost. Rona Randall
Time Right Deadly. S. Gainham
Time Running Out. K. Booton
Time Running Out. R. Crane
Time Terror. K. Robeson
Time to Change Hats. M. Bennett
Time to Die. George Douglas
Time to Die. Hilda Lawrence
Time to Embrace. Lili Palmer
Time to Hate. S. Truss
Time to Kill. C. Barling
Time to Kill. Alec Brown
Time to Kill. L. Darbon
Time to Kill. G. Household
Time to Kill. M. Lynch
Time to Kill. Diana Morgan
Time to Kill. R. Ormerod
Time to Kill. W. Reed
Time to Kill. Colin Robertson
Time to Kill. T. Spain
Time to Kill. J. M. Walsh
Time to Kill. G. Ward
Time to Kill. J. Weeks
Time to Kill...A Time to Die. J. Pearl
Time to Murder and Create. Lawrence Block

Time to Prey. F. Kane
Time to Prey. F. Keinzley
Time to Retreat. Brian Cooper
Time to Run. S. Waldron
Time Too Soon. E. Lindall
Time-Torn Man. H. Hosegood
Time Trap Gambit. L. Maddock
Time-Worn Town. J. S. Fletcher
Timeless Serpent. Roger Fuller
Timeless Sleep. R. C. Galway
Timelock. D. Cory
Time's Hour Glass. A. E. Carey
Time's Revenges. D. C. Murray
Times Square Connection. F. Scarpetta
Timetable for the General. B. Frizell
Timetable Murder. R. Denbie
Timid Tycoon. R. C. Frazer
Timothy Twill's Secret. F. J. Proctor
Tin Bath Murder. M. G. Hugi
Tin Cowrie Dass. H. M. Rideout
Tin God of Twisted River. W. C. Tuttle
Tin Hats. F. MacIsaac
Tin Soldier. E. Cannon
Tin Tree. J. Quince
Tin Trumpets at Dawn. J. Appleby
Tincture of Murder. Sutherland Scott
Tinker, Tailor, Soldier, Spy... J. Le Carre
Tinker's Kitchen. A. R. L. Gardner
Tinker's Lone Hand. A. Murray
Tinker's Pride. N. Tranter
Tinkletop's Crime and other tales. G. R. Sims
Tinkling Symbol. P. A. Taylor
Tinman. T. Gallon
Tinsley's Bones. P. Wilde
Tinted Vapours. J. M. Cobban
Tiny Carteret. H. C. McNeile
Tiny Diamond. C. M. Russell
Tiny Luttrell. E. W. Hornung
Tip and Run. W. Tait
Tip Off. A. W. Sherring
"Tipster." Roland Daniel
Tipster. G. Verner
Tiptoe thro' a Graveyard. M. Storm
Tirana Assignment. C. Portway
Tired Spy. D. Stone
Tisket, a Casket. J. L. Linklater
Titanic Hotel Mystery. J. Hawk
Tithe the War Mystery. G. Chester
Title Is Murder. H. L. Nelson
Titled Counterfeiter. Anonymous
Titled Counterfeiter. Nicholas Carter
Titty's Dead. P. Hobson
To a Blindfold Lady. J. Purtell
To Any Lengths. G. Simenon
To Be a Hero. J. McCague
To Be Hanged. B. Hamilton
To Bed at Noon. V. Gielgud
To Bed at Noon. J. Shearing
To Borrow Trouble. N. Borgenicht
To Burgundy and Back. D. M. Low
To Cache a Millionaire. M. Scherf
To Catch a Crooked Girl. P. W. Fairman
To Catch a King. H. Patterson
To Catch a Rainbow. E. Thompson
To Catch a Rat. W. Harris
To Catch a Shadow. Bradshaw Jones
To Catch a Spy. A. A. Randall
To Catch a Spy. B. Sanders
To Catch a Spy. C. Scott
To Catch a Thief. M. Burton
To Catch a Thief. D. Dodge
To Catch a Thief. Daphne Sanders
To Catch a Thief. L. Thayer
To Catch a Viper. J. Wyllie
To Cease upon the Midnight. A. Hocking
To Comfort the Signora. E. G. Cousins
To Defeat the Ends of Justice. H. Compton
To Die a Little. C. Carfax
To Die a Little. H. Jobson
To Die Elsewhere. T. Wilden
To Die for a Golden Leaf. R. P. Hilldrup
To Die in California. N. Thornburg
To Die or Not to Die. H. Kane
To Dream of Evil. L. Hoffman
To Dusty Death. H. McCutcheon
To Dwell in Shadows. N. G. Smith
To Effect an Arrest. H. Steele
To Fear a Painted Devil. R. Rendell
To Find a Killer. L. White
To Guard the Right. H. Zachary
To Hang a Witch. P. Wissmann
To Have and to Hold. Macdonald Newton
To Have and to Hold. M. Richmond
To Have and to Kill. Robert Martin
To Hell for Half-a-Crown. J. Cross
To Hell in a Basket. I. R. Blacker
To Hell Together. H. V. Dixon
To Hell with the Law. E. Martin
To Hide a Rogue. T. Walsh
To Keep or Kill. W. Tucker
To Kill a Call Girl. P. A. Foxall
To Kill a Cat. W. J. Burley
To Kill a Cat. R. Pertwee
To Kill a Coconut. P. Moyes
To Kill a Cop. R. Daley
To Kill a Corpse. E. Ascher
To Kill a Dead Man. C. W. Runyon
To Kill a Hero. John Morgan
To Kill a House. S. Roberts

Title Index

To Kill a Jogger. J. Messmann
To Kill a Judge. G. Ogan
To Kill a Killer. K. Hunt
To Kill a Snowman. C. Miron
To Kill a Witch. Alice Brennan
To Kill a Witch. B. Knox
To Kill Again. R. Stout
To Kill or Die. J. York
To Kill or to Die. J. York
To Kill the Pope. K. Wlaschin
To Kiss, or Kill. D. Keene
To Know Is to Die. C. H. Guenter
To Let, Furnished. Josephine Bell
To Live and Die in Dixie. T. Roscoe
To Live Forever. J. Vance
To Live in Danger. B. Magee
To Love a Dark Stranger. V. Coffman
To Love a Stranger. L. A. Olmsted
To Love a Stranger. B. Paul
To Love Again. A. Furness
To Love Again. D. Noel
To Love and Be Wise. J. Tey
To Love and to Perish. E. Dudley
To Love and Yet to Die. S. D. Frances
To Make You Mine. M. Richmond
To Make an Underworld. Joan Fleming
To Market, to Market. A. Richards
To Meet Mr. Stanley. Dorothy Johnson
To Meet the Law. F. A. M. Webster
To Nick a Good Body. Barry Norman
To Play the Devil. Angus Hall
To Protect the Guilty. J. Ashford
To Ravish Rani. N. McGuyer
To Reach a Dream. N. C. Heard
To Ripen or to Kill. Marjorie Robertson
To Run a Little Faster. J. Gardner
To Save His Life. K. Roos
To See a Stranger. M. Lynn
To See Ourselves. G. C. Pollock
To Seek Where Shadows Are. M. Benedict
To Set Her Free. G. M. Robins
To Shadow Our Love. L. Ames
To Slay the Dreamer. A. Cordell
To Sleep No More. R. Angel
To Spite Her Face. H. Dolson
To Stalk a Killer. C. Gayet
To Study a Long Silence. V. C. Clinton-Baddeley
To the Adventurous. E. Nesbit
To the Bitter End. M. E. Braddon
To the Bitter End. J. M. Simmel
To the Castle. Janice Bennett
To the Castle. D. Malm
To the Dark Tower. M. S. Gross
To the Dark Tower. Francis King
To the Dark Tower. L. B. Long
To the Dark Tower Came. K. O. Jones
To the Devil—a Daughter. D. Wheatley
To the Eagle's Nest. J. Di Mona
To the Ends of the Earth. Nicholas Carter
To the Gallows I Must Go. T. S. Matthews
To the Honor of the Fleet. R. H. Pilpel
To the Minute and Scarlet and Black. A. K. Green
To the Tombaugh Station. W. Tucker
To the Tune of Murder. H. M. Ballard
"To This End." B. Malim
To This Favour. S. Gilruth
To Venus in Five Seconds. F. T. Jane
To Wake the Dead. J. D. Carr
To Walk the Night. J. Land
To Walk the Night. J. Mangione
To Walk the Night. W. Sloan
To What Dread End. M. V. Heberden
To Win and to Lose. K. Netzen
To Win the Love He Sought. E. P. Oppenheim
To Windward. H. C. Rowland
Toast Is Death! F. W. Gumley
Toast to a Corpse. David Hume
Toast to Tomorrow. M. Coles
Toasted Blonde. C. Reeve
Tobacco Auction Murders. Robert Turner
Tobey's First Case. C. L. Burnham
Toby Jug Murders. H. A. Wrenn
Toby Scuffell. P. Capon
Toby Shed. Taffrail
Tocsin. A. Askew
Todd Dossier. C. Young
Todmanhawe Grange. J. S. Fletcher
Toff. J. Creasey
Toff Among the Millions. J. Creasey
Toff and Old Harry. J. Creasey
Toff and the Crooked Copper. J. Creasey
Toff and the Curate. J. Creasey
Toff and the Dead Man's Finger. W. V. Butler
Toff and the Deadly Parson. J. Creasey
Toff and the Deep Blue Sea. J. Creasey
Toff and the Fallen Angels. J. Creasey
Toff snd the Golden Boy. J. Creasey
Toff and the Great Illusion. J. Creasey
Toff and the Kidnapped Child. J. Creasey
Toff and the Lady. J. Creasey
Toff and the Runaway Bride. J. Creasey
Toff and the Sleepy Cowboy. J. Creasey
Toff and the Spider. J. Creasey
Toff and the Stolen Tresses. J. Creasey
Toff and the Teds. J. Creasey
Toff and the Terrified Tax Man. J. Creasey

Toff and the Trip-Trip-Triplets. J. Creasey
Toff at Butlin's. J. Creasey
Toff at the Fair. J. Creasey
Toff Breaks In. J. Creasey
Toff Down Under. J. Creasey
Toff Goes Gay. J. Creasey
Toff Goes On. J. Creasey
Toff Goes to Market. J. Creasey
Toff in New York. J. Creasey
Toff in Town. J. Creasey
Toff in Wax. J. Creasey
Toff Is Back. J. Creasey
Toff on Board. J. Creasey
Toff on Fire. J. Creasey
Toff on Ice. J. Creasey
Toff on the Farm. J. Creasey
Toff on the Trail. J. Creasey
Toff Proceeds. J. Creasey
Toff Steps Out. J. Creasey
Toff Takes Shares. J. Creasey
Together Brothers. J. Robinson
Togo Commando. H. Arvay
Toilers of Babylon. B. L. Farjeon
Toilers of the Thames. B. Hemyng
Toils of Silence. H. S. Cooper
Token. L. Tracy
Token. G. Verner
Token of Evil. E. Grayson
Tokyo Doll. J. McPartland
Tokyo Escapade. S. Walker
Tokyo Intrigue. W. Bender
Tokyo Purple. L. Derrick
Told at Monte Carlo. A. M. Williamson
Told by Twilight. Douglas Stewart
Told in the East. T. Mundy
Told in the Marketplace. F. B. Austin
Told in the Rockies. A. M. Barbour
Told in the Twilight. H. Wood
Toledano. George Davis
Toledo Dagger. R. Brennan
Toledo Sword. M. L. Tyrrell
Toll. M. L. Fowler
Toll for the Brave. Harry Patterson
Toll-House Murder. A. Wynne
Toll the Bell for Murder. G. Bellairs
Tolliver Case. R. A. J. Walling
Toltec Cup. Anonymous
Tom and Jerry. Anonymous
Tom and Jerry. T. Pastor
Tom Brown's Body. G. Mitchell
Tom Chester's Sweetheart. J. Hatton
Tom Dawson. F. Warden
Tom Fox. Anonymous
Tom Gerrard. L. Becke
Tom Harris. S. Themerson
Tom Ossington's Ghost. R. Marsh
Tom Rocket. A. Fonblanque
Tom Sawyer, Detective, and other stories. M. Twain
Tom, the Young Explorer. Old Sleuth
Tom Tiddler's Island. J. J. Connington
Tomb for Mr. Lee. R. Wilkes-Hunter
Tomb of the Twelfth Iman. R. Bulliet
Tomb of T'Sin. E. Wallace
Tomb with a View. N. Robbins
Tomb with a View. L. Sieveking
Tomboy. H. Ellson
Tombs of Blue Ice. R. Faust
Tombstone for a Troubleshooter. W. C. MacDonald
Tombstone Treasure. F. Hume
Tombstones Are Free to Quitters. B. Sarto
Tommy Weston, Adventuress. W. Sheridan
Tomorrow a Stranger. E. M. Williams
Tomorrow and a Day. H. Janson
Tomorrow and Yesterday. N. Sligh
Tomorrow Country. Jack Wilson
Tomorrow File. Lawrence Sanders
Tomorrow Is Murder. Carter Brown
Tomorrow Plus X. W. Tucker
Tomorrow Trap. M. Borgenicht
Tomorrow We Die. K. Lindsay
Tomorrow We'll Be Sober. M. Cranston
Tomorrow Will Be Monday. M. Marlette
Tomorrow's Another Day. W. R. Burnett
Tomorrow's Ghost. A. Price
Tomorrow's Harvest. M. Richmond
Tomorrow's Horizon. G. E. Meagher
Tomorrow's Silence. N. Goller
Tomorrow's Treason. P. Harcourt
Tomorrow's Yesterday. B. Graeme
Tong. Bok
Tong Men and a Million. E. Kinsburn
Tongking! D. Cushman
Tongue of Treason. R. Crane
Tongue-Tied Canary. N. Bentley
Toni Diamonds. G. Latta
Tonight and Tomorrow. S. Troy
Tonight in Sacarra. Michael Barrett
Tonight Is for Death. Gavin Holt
Tonight They Die to Mendelssohn. F. Gordon
"Tontine Bell." E. Kyle
Tontine Treasure. H. M. Webster
Tony Rome. A. Rome
Too Beautiful to Die. M. Carroll
Too Black for Heaven. D. Keene
Too Busy to Die. H. W. Roden
Too Clever by Half. L. Meynell

Too Close for Comfort. M. Carr
Too Curious. E. J. Goodman
Too Dangerous to Be Free. J. H. Chase
Too Dangerous to Live. David Hume
Too Dead to Run. J. Manor
Too Dead to Talk. A. E. Jones
Too Fast We Live. R. Glendinning
Too French and Too Deadly. H. Kane
Too Friendly, Too Dead. B. Halliday
Too Good to Be True. M. Halliday
Too Good to Be True. J. F. Hutton
Too Hard to Handle. D. Nabarro
Too Hot for Hawaii. T. B. Dewey
Too Hot for Hell. K. Vining
Too Hot to Handle. I. Fleming
Too Hot to Handle. F. G. Presnell
Too Hot to Handle. S. Sterling
Too Hot to Hold. D. Keene
Too Hot to Kill. S. Sterling
Too Innocent to Kill. D. M. Disney
Too Late. S. Dixon
Too Late for Death. D. Linton
Too Late for Mourning. R. Foster
Too Late for Tears. H. Carmichael
Too Late for Tears. P. Henneker
Too Late for Tears. R. Huggins
Too Late for the Funeral. R. Ormerod
Too Late to Mend. T. Rainham
Too Late to Shout. R. Drayton
Too Late to Talk. Nicholas Carter
Too Late! Too Late! The Maiden Cried. Joan Fleming
Too Like the Dead. D. Chambers
Too Like the Lightning. D. Chambers
Too Lively to Live. A. Damer
Too Long Endured. L. Thayer
Too Lovely to Live. R. Fenisong
Too Many Boats. C. L. Clifford
Too Many Bones. R. S. Wallis
Too Many Bottles. E. S. Holding
Too Many Candles. M. Eatock
Too Many Chiefs. S. Marlowe
Too Many Clients. R. Stout
Too Many Clues. C. Henderson
Too Many Cooks. R. Stout
Too Many Cousins. D. G. Browne
Too Many Crooks. R. S. Prather
Too Many Crooks. E. J. Rath
Too Many Crooks. I. Trent
Too Many Crooks Spoil the Caper. F. Norman
Too Many Doctors. H. Roth
Too Many Doors. L. Crosby
Too Many Enemies. W. Haggard
Too Many Ghosts. P. Gallico
Too Many Innocents. O. Beeby
Too Many Magicians. Randall Garrett
Too Many Murderers. G. Childerness
Too Many Murderers. G. Compton
Too Many Murderers. M. L. Stokes
Too Many Sinners. S. Stark
Too Many Suspects. J. Rhode
Too Many Women. M. K. Ozaki
Too Many Women. R. Stout
Too Many Yesterdays. D. Linton
Too Many Yesterdays. K. Rogers
Too Married. A. Applin
Too-Mini Murders. P. Morgan
Too Much Ambition. E. Ellison
Too Much for Mr. Jellipot. S. Fowler
Too Much of Water. B. Hamilton
Too Much Poison. A. Rowe
Too Old to Die. Gretchen Travis
Too Rich to Die. H. V. Dixon
Too Rich to Live. S. Morgan
Too Sharp by Half. B. Hemyng
Too Small for His Shoes. L. Payne
Too Smart to Live. E. Ellison
Too Soon for Daisies. W. Dinner
Too Soon to Die. H. Janson
Too Soon to Die. Henry Wade
Too Strange a Hand. D. Quick
Too Sweet to Die. R. Goulart
Too Tough for Death. D. Steel
Too Tough to Die. G. Bruce
Too Tough to Die. R. Gadhart
Too Tough to Die. F. Gruber
Too Tough to Live. Griff
Too Young to Die. R. O. Saber
Too Young to Die. L. White
Tooth and Nail. Nicholas Carter
Tooth and the Nail. B. S. Ballinger
Tooth Merchant. C. L. Sulzberger
Top Assignment. G. H. Coxe
Top Bloody Secret. S. Hyland
Top Boot. M. Kennedy
Top Dog. F. Hume
Top Floor Back. G. Radcliffe
Top-Floor Killing. W. A. Roberts
Top Landing. P. Brebner
Top of the Heap. A. A. Fair
Top Secret. J. Bruce
Top Secret. L. Halliday
Top Secret Kill. J. P. Cody
Top Secret No. 1. W. Jardine
Top Spot for Danger. R. Bentinck
Top Steal. A. Tack
Top Storey Murder. A. Berkeley
Top Ten. H. Janson
Topaz. L. Uris
Topaz for My Lady Fair. J. J. Toombs
Toper's End. G. D. H. Cole

Topkapi. E. Ambler
Topless Dancer Hangup. P. Morgan
Topless Tulip Caper. C. Harrison
Topology of a Phantom City. A. Robbe-Grillet
Topsy and Evil. G. Baxt
Torch. G. Wright
Torch Bearers. B. V. Dryer
Torch for a Dark Journey. L. Shapiro
Torch Murder. C. R. Jones
Torhaven Mystery. J. B. Harris-Burland
Torment for Trixy. H. Janson
Torment Was a Redhead. Richard Williams
Torment Was a Woman. B. Carons
Tormented. D. Daniels
Tormented. F. E. Smith
Tormented. C. Weston
Tormenter. B. Swift
Tormentors. G. Bellairs
Torn Curtain. R. Wormser
Torn Letter. E. Balmer
Torn-Out Page. Dora Russell
Torquemada Principle. J. Morgulas
Torquemada Puzzle Book. Torquemada
Torrid Temptress. H. Janson
Torrington Square Mystery. M. L. Eades
Tortoiseshell Cat. N. Royde-Smith
Tortuous Trails. H. Footner
Torture Chamber and other stories. V. Van Der Elst
Torture Contract. F. Scarpetta
Torture Island. L. R. G. Hart
Torture Machine. D. Dayle
Torture Machine. P. Tabori
Torture Trust. B. House
Tortured Angel. D. Garth
Tortured Boy. H. C. Davis
Tortured Heart. E. Southworth
Tortured Love. H. Duval
Tortured Path. K. F. Crossen
Torturer. P. Saxon
Torturer's Horse. R. Inman
Torvick Affair. M. Sariola
Toss of a Coin. Nicholas Carter
Toss of a Penny. Nicholas Carter
Total Eclipse. J. Brunner
Totem. Blyden Jackson
Totem. D. Morrell
Touch a French Pom-Pom. J. P. Carstairs
Touch and Go. L. Della
Touch and Go. J. Middlemass
Touch and Go. E. C. Vivian
Touch and Go. P. Wentworth
Touch Not the Cat. Mary Stewart
Touch of Chill. Joan Aiken
Touch of Danger. James Jones
Touch of Darkness. J. Crowe
Touch of Death. J. Creasey
Touch of Death. C. Williams
Touch of Drama. G. Cullingford
Touch of Evil. L. Colby
Touch of Evil. Arthur MacLean
Touch of Evil. W. Masterson
Touch of Fear. Dorothy Christie
Touch of Fear. J. Ware
Touch of Jonah. L. Holton
Touch of Judas. L. Wilkinson
Touch of Malice. J. Wainwright
Touch of Murder. J. B. Cearley
Touch of Myrrh. Charlotte Hunt
Touch of Purple. E. Trevor
Touch of Red. W. Fennerton
Touch of Stagefright. J. Davey
Touch of Terror. S. Farrant
Touch of the Child, and other stories. T. Gallon
Touch of the Nettle. J. M. Scott
Touch of the Sun. H. B. Kaye
Touch of the Witch. J. Wetherell
Touch of Thunder. Brian Cooper
Touch Pitch. L. Peck
Touch the Lion's Paw. Derek Lambert
Touchdown. M. Russell
Touchfeather. J. Sangster
Touchfeather, Too. J. Sangster
Touching Evil. N. S. Rosen
Touchstone. E. Bradford
Tough and the Tender. A. MacLeod
Tough and the Toughs. J. Creasey
Tough Company. C. Dawe
Tough Cop. J. Roeburt
Tough Die Hard. Robert Martin
Tough for You, Hazel. D. Foster
Tough Get Going. G. Bagby
Tough Ghosts. W. J. Elliott
Tough Guys. M. Spillane
Tough Justice. San Antonio
Tough Luck L.A. Murray Sinclair
Tough on the Wops. B. Toler
Tough One to Lose. T. Kenrick
Tough Spot for Cupid and other stories. P. Cheyney
Tough Tontine. A. Sewart
Tough Town. J. Karney
Toughs Afloat. M. Hervey
Toughs Ashore. M. Hervey
Tour. D. Ely
Tour de Force. C. Brand
Tour de Force. P. Cleife
Tour of Terror. J. W. Bobin
Touring Company Crime. A. Steffens Hardy
Tourist Trap. Ted Stratton

Tournament. J. Q.
Tournament of Shadows. N. Carnac
Tournelles Plot. H. Drummond
Towards Tomorrow. J. Blackmore
Towards Zero. A. Christie
Towards Zero. G. Verner
Tower. P. M. Hubbard
Tower. S. Lansdell
Tower. R. M. Stern
Tower Abbey. I. Holland
Tower Hill Mystery. A. W. Barrett
Tower in the Sea. J. Thatcher
Tower Mystery. P. McGuire
Tower of Babel. M. L. West
Tower of Darkness. H. Hawton
Tower of Evil. J. Rhode
Tower of Hate. F. Shroyer
Tower of Kilraven. C. Crowe
Tower of Malecombe. J. D'Astor
Tower of Monte Rado. Sheila Ross
Tower of Strength. Nicholas Carter
Tower of Terror. J. I. Lawrence
Tower of the Crow. D. Polk
Tower of the Dark Light. E. E. Mande
Tower Park. E. De Vincent
Tower Room. D. Daniels
Tower Room. M. L. Ruby
Tower Room. D. Spicer
Tower Room. J. Trevelyan
Tower Room Mystery. R. St. Clair
Towers of Fear. C. Farr
Towers of Love. S. Birmingham
Towers of Silence. David St. John
Towers of Terror. D. Dayle
Towers of Urbandine. G. C. Carr
Town Cried Murder. L. Ford
Town Hall Crime. A. Blair
Town Is Full of Rumors. R. Wilson
Town Lady and Country Lass. F. Warden
Town of Masks. D. S. Davis
Town of Shadows. J. Drummond
Town Parole. Alex Hamilton
Town That Saw No Evil. Harry Kantor
Town That Went Sick. S. Truss
Town Without Pity. M. Gregor
Townsend Murder Mystery. O. R. Cohen
Toy. K. Booton
Toy Lamb. B. Flynn
Toying with Fate. Nicholas Carter
Toyland. Mark Smith
Toys of Death. G. D. H. Cole
Toys of Desperation. A. Crockett
Traced and Tracked. J. M'Govan
Traced Through a Dream. C. Courteney
Tracer of Lost Persons. R. W. Chambers
Traces of Brillhart. H. Brean
Traces of Merrilee. H. Brean
Tracey. S. Nichols
Track of Midnight. G. F. Scott
Track of the Beast. Ralph Hayes
Track of the Slayer. B. Strong
Tracked Across the Atlantic. Nicholas Carter
Tracked Across the Seas. Wilfred Barclay
Tracked and Taken. D. Donovan
Tracked by a Female Detective. Old Sleuth
Tracked by a Pin. R. Hackstaff
Tracked by a Tattoo. F. Hume
Tracked by a Woman. "Goldey"
Tracked by a Woman. Old Sleuth
Tracked by Fate. F. Hume
Tracked by the Ogpu. E. Jepson
Tracked by Wireless. W. LeQueux
Tracked Down. L. Edgley
Tracked Down. H. Hill
Tracked on a Wheel. Old Sleuth
Tracked Out. A. W. A'Beckett
Tracked to Death. M. Redwing
Tracked to Doom. D. Donovan
Tracked to His Doom. J. K. Stafford
Tracked to the West. N. Ridley
Tracker of Skull Island. Michael Hastings
Tracker Tracked. G. Furnivall
Tracker Tracked. B. Wayde
Tracking of K.K. D. Grey
Tracking Trantor. G. Chater
Trackless Death. A. Livingston
Trackless Thing. J. Atholl
Tracks in the Snow. G. R. Benson
Trade-Off. V. B. Miller
Trade-Off. G. F. Newman
Trade Wind. M. M. Kaye
Trade Winds over Kokio. L. C. Raef
Trademark of a Traitor. K. M. Knight
Trader Brook. K. Hayles
Trader Random. O. Binns
Trader's Daughter. W. M. Graydon
Trader's License. J. England
Trading with Bodies. Griff
Traditions. Anonymous
Traditions of London. Waters
Trafalgar Square. Gavin Holt
Trafalgar Square Mystery. C. Brisbane
Traffic in Souls. E. H. Ball
Traffic with Evil. A. Johns
Traficante. F. Hilaire
Tragedies of Mr. Pip. E. Jepson
Tragedies of Oak Hurst. B. Marean
Tragedy After Tea. C. Ashton

Tragedy and Strategy. Old Sleuth
Tragedy at Beechcroft. A. Fielding
Tragedy at Blue Aloes. M. Richmond
Tragedy at Cumberland Park. Arthur Russell
Tragedy at Draythorpe. L. Grex
Tragedy at Freyne. Anthony Gilbert
Tragedy at Law. C. Hare
Tragedy at Ravensthorpe. J. J. Connington
Tragedy at the Beach Club. W. A. Johnston
Tragedy at the Thirteenth Hole. M. Burton
Tragedy at the Unicorn. J. Rhode
Tragedy at Twelvetrees. A. J. Rees
Tragedy at Wembley. C. F. Gregg
Tragedy in a Brick Box. J. Budd
Tragedy in Blue. M. Bramhall
Tragedy in E Flat. L. Gribble
Tragedy in Pewsey Chart. H. Willett
Tragedy in the Dark. Elaine Hamilton
Tragedy in the Hollow. F. W. Crofts
Tragedy in the Rue de la Paix. A. Belot
Tragedy in Turquoise. L. Trimble
Tragedy Indeed. A. Belot
Tragedy Near Tring. J. K. Ryland
Tragedy of a Flirtation. H. B. Vogel
Tragedy of an Indiscretion. J. W. Brodie-Innes
Tragedy of Andrea. E. P. Oppenheim
Tragedy of Ascot Mills. S. Campbell
Tragedy of Brinkwater. M. L. Moodey
Tragedy of Captain Harrison. R. C. J.
Tragedy of Featherstone. B. L. Farjeon
Tragedy of Ida Noble. W. C. Russell
Tragedy of Redmount. M. E. Holmes
Tragedy of the Bromleigh's. R. Hardinge
Tragedy of the Chinese Mine. I. Greig
Tragedy of the Great Emerald. W. Chesney
Tragedy of the Silver Moon. A. Gask
Tragedy of the West End Actress. J. G. Brandon
Tragedy of Windyridge. R. Hardinge
Tragedy of X. B. Ross
Tragedy of Y. B. Ross
Tragedy of Z. B. Ross
Tragedy on a Trooper. J. Strange
Tragedy on the Line. J. Rhode
Tragic Case of John Renold. H. Allan
Tragic Case of the Station Master's Legacy. J. Drummond
Tragic Curtain. S. H. Page
Tragic Lesson. J. H. Vahey
Tragic Mystery. J. Hawthorne
Tragic Mystery. Old Sleuth
Tragic Quest. F. W. Irwin
Tragic Quest. Old Sleuth
Tragic Target. M. V. Heberden
Trail from Devil's Country. A. M. Treynor
Trail of a Human Tiger. Nicholas Carter
Trail of a Tramp. N. Quarry
Trail of Adventure. O. Binns
Trail of Blood. J. Potter
Trail of Blood. C. Rushton
Trail of Death. W. M. Graydon
Trail of Deceit. W. C. Tuttle
Trail of Doom. R. C. Armour
Trail of Fear. A. Armstrong
Trail of Fu Manchu. S. Rohmer
Trail of Raider No. 1. S. Blakesley
Trail of the Axe. G. Cullum
Trail of the Barrow. Anonymous
Trail of the Barrow. J. Mooney
Trail of the Beast. A. Abdullah
Trail of the Black King. A. Armstrong
Trail of the Catspaw. Nicholas Carter
Trail of the Cloven Hoof. A. Eadie
Trail of the Dead. B. F. Robinson
Trail of the Dope Chief. J. Hunter
Trail of the Fingerprints. Nicholas Carter
Trail of the Ghosts. N. Thurley
Trail of the Hunted. R. Wilkes-Hunter
Trail of the Lonely River. H. Edmonds
Trail of the Lotto. A. Armstrong
Trail of the Missing Scientist. A. Parsons
Trail of the Old Lag. W. J. Bayfield
Trail of the Ruby. W. Proudfoot
Trail of the Serpent. M. E. Braddon
Trail of the Serpent. T. E. B. Clarke
Trail of the Serpent. E. Southworth
Trail of the Serpent. C. Worth
Trail of the Shadow. H. Bedford-Jones
Trail of the Shadow. S. M. Parkman
Trail of the Skull. Gavin Holt
Trail of the Squid. H. Wickham
Trail of the Tiger. R. C. Armour
Trail of the White Knight. B. Graeme
Trail of the White Turban. C. Brisbane
Trail of the Yoshiga. Nicholas Carter
Trail to Death. R. Wallace
Trail to Kingdom Come. W. C. Tuttle
Trail to the End. J. K. Stafford
Trail to Treason. C. Dixon
Trail Under the Sea. R. H. Poole
Trailer Mystery. R. St. Clair
Trailer Park. J. Vaughn
Trailing Death. G. Begbie
Trailing of the Picaroon. Herman Landon

Train. G. Simenon
Train a Fast Gun. R. Wilkes-Hunter
Train from Katanga. Wilbur Smith
Train Wreck! J. Jack
Trainer's Secret. A. Steffens Hardy
Trains That Met in the Blizzard. R. P. Woodward
Traitor. L. Allan
Traitor! W. H. Baker
Traitor. L. Divomlikoff
Traitor. S. Horler
Traitor. G. Sheen
Traitor. H. Wouk
Traitor and Loyalist. A. R. Weekes
Traitor and Spy. A. Steffens Hardy
Traitor Betrayed. O. Mills
Traitor Blitz. J. M. Simmel
Traitor Dragoon. W. M. Graydon
Traitor for a Cause. G. Markstein
Traitor Game. D. McLeish
Traitor in London. F. Hume
Traitor in the Fleet. E. L. MacKeag
Traitor Mask. F. A. Smith
Traitor Spy. T. C. H. Jacobs
Traitor Unmasked. G. Davison
Traitor Within. Alicen White
Traitors. P. Chester
Traitors. E. P. Oppenheim
Traitor's Bridge. N. Sligh
Traitor's Crime. R. Jeffries
Traitor's Cross. F. Grierson
Traitor's Doom. J. Creasey
Traitor's Exit. J. Gardner
Traitor's Gate. C. Gavin
Traitors' Gate. S. Harvester
Traitor's Gate. G. Osborne
Traitor's Gate. E. Wallace
Traitor's Gate. D. Wheatley
Traitor's Gate and other stories. G. M. Fenn
Traitor's Harvest. M. Richmond
Traitor's Island. F. Hay
Traitor's Island. J. Pendower
Traitor's Market. G. Dickson
Traitor's Mask. D. Noel
Traitor's Mountain. S. Styles
Traitor's Pass. D. Duff
Traitor's Purse. M. Allingham
Traitor's Road. D. Daniels
Traitor's Rock. G. E. Rochester
Traitor's Tide. R. Goyne
Traitor's Way. B. Hamilton
Traitor's Wife. D. Montross
Traitor's Wooing. H. Hill
Tramp. E. Wallace
Trample an Empire. W. Mole
Tramplers. J. Manor
Tramp's Evidence. E. C. Vivian
Trance. J. Fielding
Trans-Siberian Express. W. Adler
Transactions of Lord Louis Lewis. R. Pertwee
Transactions of Oliver Prince. R. E. Forbes
Transatlantic Ghost. D. Gardiner
Transatlantic Puzzle. M. O. Rolfe
Transatlantic Trouble. L. Grex
Trascendental Murder. J. Langton
Transformation. J. Fielding
Transformation of Timothy. T. Cobb
Transformation Scene. C. Houghton
Transgressing the Law. F. Whittaker
Transgressor. F. Thompson
Transgressors. J. Thompson
Transient Guest, and Other Episodes. E. Saltus
Transister Girls. Paul Daniels
Transit of the Red Dragon, and other tales. E. Phillpotts
Transome Murder Mystery. P. Luck
Transparent Traitor. F. Gerard
Transplant. J. Weatherhead
Transport Murders. J. G. Brandon
Transvection Machine. E. D. Hoch
Trap. Jenifer Beckett
Trap. D. Billany
Trap. M. Brenner
Trap. John Burke
Trap. J. L. Cotte
Trap. D. Donovan
Trap. M. Foster
Trap. T. Hubert
Trap. George E. Jones
Trap. E. Jordan
Trap. N. Karta
Trap. Mrs. C. Kernahan
Trap. J. Knowler
Trap. D. Winston
Trap for a Lonely Man. Robert Thomas
Trap for a Redhead. S. Palmer
Trap for Bellamy. P. Cheyney
Trap for Cinderella. S. Japrisot
Trap for Fools. J. Pendower
Trap for Lovers. J. Blackmore
Trap in the Tunnel. G. Ellinger
Trap #6. S. Ransome
Trap of Fate. I. D. Hardy
Trap of Tangled Wire. Nicholas Carter
Trap Spider. K. Royce
Trap the Baron. Anthony Morton
Trapdoor. D. Bloodworth
Trapeze. M. Catto

Trapped. R. Hayward
Trapped. J. Hougron
Trapped. H. Innes
Trapped. L. Mantz
Trapped. M. L. Roby
Trapped by a Female Detective. Old Sleuth
Trapped by a Woman. Nicholas Carter
Trapped in His Own Net. Nicholas Carter
Trapped Ones. L. Charbonneau
Trapper of Rat River. C. Stoddard
Trapper's Victim. C. Brisbane
Trapping the Moonshiners. Old Sleuth
Trappings Are Gorgeous. H. D. Dearden
Traps. F. Duerrenmatt
Traps Need Fresh Bait. A. A. Fair
Trash Stealer. J. Potts
Travel the Hard Way. M. Hervey
Traveling Butcher. Alice Campbell
Traveling Corpse. K. Steel
Traveling Horseman. N. Luard
Traveling Skull. H. S. Keeler
Traveller Returns. P. Wentworth
Travelling Deadman. J. Varnam
Travelling Executioners. B. Newman
Travels with a Duchess. M. Gallie
Travels with My Aunt. G. Greene
Travers, a Mystery Story. R. B. Siddall
Traverse of the Gods. B. Langley
Trawl Adrift. E. L. Long
Treacherous Border. N. Thurley
Treacherous Mission. D. Noel
Treacherous Road. S. Harvester
Treachery. K. Lindsay
Treachery. L. S. Stanhope
Treachery at Guadamonte. D. Martyn
Treachery in Trieste. C. L. Leonard
Treachery in Type. Josephine Bell
Treachery Trade. E. Cannon
Tread Gently, Death. R. P. Koehler
Tread Lightly, Angel. F. C. Davis
Tread Softly. B. Flynn
Tread Softly. P. Malloch
Tread Softly. F. Rickett
Tread Softly in This Place. B. Cleeve
Tread Softly, Nurse Scott. Marilyn Ross
Tread Warily. Hilary Mason
Tread Warily at Midnight. M. Carr
Treason at Home. Mrs. Greenough
Treason by Truth. W. H. Baker
Treason-Felony. J. Hill
Treason in My Breast. Anthony Gilbert
Treason in the Egg. L. A. G. Strong
Treason Line. D. Torr
Treason Remembered. W. H. Baker
Treason Under Seal. W. V. Cook
Treasure. A. E. Hotchner
Treasure. Larry Levine
Treasure at Greyladies. H. Leyford
Treasure by Degrees. D. Williams
Treasure Chest. M. L. Roby
Treasure for Treasure. Justin Scott
Treasure House of Martin Hews. E. P. Oppenheim
Treasure Hunt. T. Pace
Treasure Hunters. W. H. Baker
Treasure Nets. G. Fairlie
Treasure of Big Waters. R. Cullum
Treasure of Captain Scarlett. A. Sergeant
Treasure of Caricar. R. W. Hinds
Treasure of Christophe. O. Binns
Treasure of Israel. W. LeQueux
Treasure of Sainte-Foy. MacDonald Harris
Treasure of Scarland. M. B. Dix
Treasure of Seacliff Manor. Y. Norman
Treasure of the Cosa Nostra. J. Ridgway
Treasure of the Manchus. R. C. Armour
Treasure of the Sun. H. McCutcheon
Treasure of Wycliffe House. J. Judson
Treasure on Camise. Alan Graham
Treasure on Earth. Laurence Kirk
Treasure on the Broads. W. G. Elliott
Treasure Royal. W. Garrett
Treasure Trail. R. Pertwee
Treasure Train. A. B. Reeve
Treasure Up in Smoke. D. Williams
Treasury Alarm. J. Davey
Treasury-Officer's Wooing. C. C. Lewis
Treasury's Millions. B. Wayde
Treble Chance Murder. V. Gunn
Treble Cross. H. Howard
Tree Frog. M. Woodhouse
Tree of Evil. R. Morrison
Tree of Heaven. E. Raymond
Treen and Wild Horses. P. F. Gaye
Tregaron's Daughter. M. Brent
Tregarthen. G. Norway
Tregarthen's Wife. F. M. White
Tregear's Treasure. J. Remenham
Trek East. T. Mundy
Trek or Treat. E. St. Clair
Trelawny. I. Holland
Trelawny's Fell. I. Holland
Tremayne Case. Alan Thomas
Tremayne's Wife. Charlotte Hunt
Trembling Earth. F. Clifford
Trembling Earth Contract. P. Atlee
Trembling Flame. L. J. Vance
Trembling Hills. P. A. Whitney
Trembling Thread. C. Franklin
Tremendous Event. M. Leblanc

Tremlett Diamonds. A. St. Aubyn
Tremlow Murder Case. R. Dark
Tremolo. E. Borneman
Tremor of Forgery. P. Highsmith
Tremor of Intent. A. Burgess
Tremor Violet. D. Lippincott
Tremorra Towers. H. York
Trench's Wives. Anonymous
Trenfell Castle. H. Moray
Trent Fights Again. W. Martyn
Trent Intervenes. E. C. Bentley
Trent of the Lone Hand. W. Martyn
Trent Trail. W. Martyn
Trent's Last Case. E. C. Bentley
Trent's Own Case. E. C. Bentley
Trespass. A. Askew
Trespass. F. Knebel
Trespass. N. Tranter
Trespass in the Sun. J. Pudney
Trespassers. A. Coburn
Trespassers Will Die. M. Seuffert
Trevayne. J. Ryder
Trevena's Daughter. B. Davis
Treveryan. A. Du Maurier
Trevlyn Hold. H. Wood
Trevor Case. N. S. Lincoln
Trewinnot of Guy's. Mrs. C. Kernahan
Triad. M. Leader
Triad. H. K. Marks
Triad Conspiracy. A. M. MacKay
Triad Imperative. Dwight Martin
Triad 21. H. Arvay
Trial. W. Harrington
Trial. D. M. Mankiewicz
Trial and Error. A. Berkeley
Trial and Terror. L. Treat
Trial and Triumph. Anonymous
Trial at Bannock. J. Bier
Trial by Ambush. L. Ford
Trial by Desire. K. G. Ballard
Trial by Fury. C. Rice
Trial by Love. M. Cambards
Trial by Murder. E. S. Holding
Trial by Murder. G. Hoster
Trial by Ordeal. O. Mills
Trial by Perjury. J. Creighton
Trial by Slander. T. Macrae
Trial by Terror. P. Gallico
Trial by Terror. R. Lockridge
Trial by Water. H. Footner
Trial by Wilderness. T. M. Longstreth
Trial from Ambush. L. Ford
Trial of Adolph Hitler. P. Van Rjndt
Trial of Alvin Boaker. J. Reywall
Trial of Bebe Donge. G. Simenon
Trial of Billy Jack. H. Liebling
Trial of Callista Blake. E. Pangborn
Trial of Gideon, and Countess Almara's Murder. J. Hawthorne
Trial of Gregor Kaska. F. Andreas
Trial of John and Henry Norton. R. Puccetti
Trial of Lizzie Borden and other radio plays. D. Henderson
Trial of Lobo Icheka. D. Creed
Trial of Mary Dugan. B. Veiller
Trial of Mary Dugan. W. A. Wolff
Trial of Parson Finch. S. Gibney
Trial of Scotland Yard. Stuart Martin
Trial of Soren Qvist. Janet Lewis
Trial of the Golden Girl. R. Dolphin
Trial of Vincent Doon. W. Oursler
Trial of Vivienne Ware. K. M. Ellis
Trial Run. D. Francis
Triall Case. L. Durie
Trials and Tribulations of Aaron Amsted. K. A. Lapatine
Trials of a City Detective. Anonymous
Trials of Commander McTurk. C. J. C. Hyne
Trials of Love. H. M. Jones
Trials of O'Brien. R. L. Fish
Trials of Rumpole. J. Mortimer
Trials of the Phideas. E. L. Long
Triangle. M. Leighton
Triangle Has Four Sides. P. Barrington
Triangle Man. G. F. Gibbs
Triangle Murder. R. Batchelor
Triangle of Death. Jon Hart
Triangle of Fear. J. N. Chance
Triangle of Terror. Gwyn Evans
Triangle of the Grey Wolf. J. Addiscombe
Tribal Town. H. Munro
Tribunal. P. Bair
Tribute to Satan. J. B. Dayne
Trick of Diamonds. A. Auswaks
Trick of Time. F. Hume
Trick or Treat. D. M. Disney
Trick Thirteen. T. Reese
Trick, Trial and Triumph. A. Cheviot
Tricked and Trapped. I. Stark
Tricks and Triumphs. Old Sleuth
Tricks of the Trade. R. L. Fish
Trickshot. Randolph Harris
Tried for Her Life. E. Southworth
Tried for His Life. Anonymous
Tried for His Life. B. Hemyng
Trieste. D. Cory
Trificante Treasure. D. Winston
Trifles. S. Glaspell
Trigger Finger. C. R. Cooper
Trigger Lady. P. Swan

Trigger Man. R. Posner
Trigger Mortis. F. Kane
Trigger of Conscience. R. O. Chipperfield
Trigger Points. M. Mayer
Triggerman. B. Rossi
Triggerman! G. Usher
Triggers Are Trumps. W. J. Elliott
Trilogy in Jeopardy. H. Kane
Trimmed Lamp. O. Henry
Trinity. R. Bridges
Trinity Implosion. Robin Moore
Trinity in Violence. H. Kane
Trio for Blunt Instruments. R. Stout
Trip to Eternity. G. Monro
Trip Trap. J. Rathbone
Triple. K. Follett
Triple Bite. B. Flynn
Triple Crime. Nicholas Carter
Triple Cross. Joe Barry
Triple Cross. Nicholas Carter
Triple Cross. J. Roeburt
Triple Cross. J. K. Stafford
Triple Cross Murders. A. R. Long
Triple Death. C. Carnac
Triple Exposure. Peter Townend
Triple Identity. Nicholas Carter
Triple Jeopardy. R. Stout
Triple Knavery. Nicholas Carter
Triple Knock. Nicholas Carter
Triple Mirror. J. Gautier
Triple Mirror. L. James
Triple Murder. Colin Hughes
Triple Murder. C. Wells
Triple Mystery. A. Luehrmann
Triple Quest. E. R. Punshon
Triple Scar. E. A. Barron
Triple Slay. Adam Knight
Triple Terror. H. Kane
Triple Threat. K. Roos
Triple Zero. A. Whitney
Tripleship Cracksman. N. Adam
Tripoli Documents. H. Kane
Triptych. R. G. Jones
Tripwire. B. Garfield
Triton Ultimatum. L. Delaney
Triumph. C. F. Coe
Triumph for Inspector West. J. Creasey
Triumph of Elaine. A. B. Reeve
Triumph of Evil. P. Kavanagh
Triumph of Hilary Blackland. B. Mitford
Triumph of Inspector Maigret. G. Simenon
Triumph of John Kars. R. Cullum
Triumph of McLean. G. Goodchild
Triumph of Manhood. M. Leighton
Triumph of Tinker. E. Jepson
Triumphal Chariot. P. H. Irving
Triumphant Defeat. B. Christianson
Triumphant Prodigal. W. Martyn
Triumphs of Eugene Valmont. R. Barr
Triumphs of Fabian Field: Criminologist. D. Donovan
Triumverate. H. Baldwin Taylor
Trixy. Mrs. G. Sheldon
Trocadero. L. Waller
Trodmore Turf Mystery. F. Johnston
Troika. D. Gurr
Troika. S. Harvester
Troika. D. Montross
Trojan Cow. G. Tippette
Trojan Gold. S. Cudahy
Trojan Hearse. R. S. Prather
Trojan Horse. H. Innes
Trooper MacLean. C. Stoddard
Trooper O'Neill. G. Goodchild
Tropic Moon. G. Simenon
Tropical Deathpact. Nick Carter
Trot. D. Ely
Trotter. B. Fforde
Trouble! B. Graeme
Trouble A-Brewing. J. Bude
Trouble Aboard. T. Muir
Trouble Ahead. E. Gunton
Trouble at Glaye. B. Reynolds
Trouble at Hanard. V. Beynon-Harris
Trouble at Harrison High. J. Farris
Trouble at Moon Dance. A. B. Guthrie
Trouble at Number Seven. G. Bullett
Trouble at Pinelands. E. M. Poate
Trouble at Saxby's. J. Creasey
Trouble at the Inn. Roland Daniel
Trouble at the JHC. W. C. Tuttle
Trouble at the Top. C. B. Flood
Trouble at Turkey Hill. K. M. Knight
Trouble at Wrekin Farm. Josephine Bell
Trouble Buster. N. W. Firth
Trouble Calling. A. Bocca
Trouble Comes Double. R. P. Hansen
Trouble Follows Me. K. Millar
Trouble in Burma. V. W. Mason
Trouble in College. F. J. Whaley
Trouble in Hunter Ward. Josephine Bell
Trouble in Paradise. Nick Carter
Trouble in Paradise. R. L. Fish
Trouble in the Air. K. Kay
Trouble in the Bank. H. C. Davis
Trouble in Thor. J. Valentine
Trouble in Tokyo. J. Bruce
Trouble in Triplicate. R. Stout
Trouble in West Two. K. Fitzgerald
Trouble Is a Dame. Carter Brown
Trouble Is My Business. R. Chandler

Trouble Is My Name. R. Dolphin
Trouble Is My Name. S. Marlowe
Trouble Makers. C. Fremlin
Trouble Man. J. D. Black
Trouble on the Frontier. Douglas Christie
Trouble on the Thames. V. Bridges
Trouble on Tuesday. S. Carver
Trouble Rides Tall. H. Whittington
Trouble Trailer. W. C. Tuttle
Trouble Trip. W. H. Canaway
Trouble with Ava. S. Friedman
Trouble with Crime. J. Noel
Trouble with Fidelity. G. Malcolm-Smith
Trouble with Guns. J. Noel
Trouble with Harry. J. T. Story
Trouble with Murder. R. Bax
Trouble with Penelope. B. Healey
Trouble with Product X. Joan Aiken
Trouble with Ruth. R. Rayner
Trouble with Series Three. M. Kenyon
Trouble with Tycoons. H. B. Taylor
Trouble with Women. J. P. Heggy
Troublecross. Jessica Mann
Troubled Deaths. R. Jeffries
Troubled Harvest. E. Woodward
Troubled Heritage. M. Richmond
Troubled House. K. Booton
Troubled Journey. R. Lockridge
Troubled Midnight. R. Garland
Troubled Minds. Stratford Davis
Troubled Night. R. Drayton
Troubled Star. J. August
Troubled Tranton. W. E. Norris
Troubled Waters. H. Hill
Troublemaker. J. Hansen
Troublemaker. J. Potts
Troubles of Colonel Marwood. A. C. Fox-Davies
Troubles of Doctor Cortland. S. Friedman
Troubleshooter. D. Dodge
Troupe of Star-Crossed Killers. T. Journet
Trout in the Milk. H. Holman
Trout in the Milk. M. Underwood
Trout Inn Mystery. W. Greenleaves
Trout Inn Tragedy. W. Greenleaves
Truce of the Bear. H. C. McNeile
Truckful of Gold. S. J. L. Zake
True. I. Blair
True Adventures of the Secret Service. C. E. Russell
True Blue, the Detective. Old Sleuth
True Confessions. J. G. Dunne
True Detective Stories. A. L. Drummond
True Detective Stories. M. Moser
True Detective Stories from the Archives of the Pinkertons. C. Moffett
True Son of the Beast! Carter Brown
True Stories of Celebrated Crimes. G. Barton
True Tales of the D.C.I. K. Detzer
Truly Remarkable Life of the Beautiful Helen Jewett. Anonymous
Trump Card. D. Vane
Trumpets of November. W. S. Thurston
Trunch. D. Durrant
Trunk Call. J. J. Farjeon
Trunk Call Mystery. J. J. Farjeon
Trunk Call to Murder. E. Radford
Trunk Crime. E. Percy
Trunk Crime Number Three. W. Tyrer
Trust a Woman? H. Foley
Trust McLean. G. Goodchild
Trust-Money. W. Westall
Trust No One at All. A. McAllister
Trust the Police. P. Elliott
Trust the Saint. L. Charteris
Trust Them and Die. Jeffry Scott
Trusted Like the Fox. Raymond Marshall
Trusted Like the Fox. Sara Woods
Trusted Rogue. Nicholas Carter
Trusting Victim. D. Lyon
Trusty Servant. G. V. McFadden
Truth About Belle Gunness. L. De La Torre
Truth About Claire Veryan. S. Truss
Truth About Lord Tench. Donald Stuart
Truth About My Father. P. Martens
Truth About Peter Harley. James Mills
Truth About the Case. M. F. Goron
Truth About Unicorns. B. J. Reynolds
Truth Came Out. E. R. Punshon
Truth Comes Limping. J. J. Connington
Truth Game. D. Hurd
Truth of the Matter. J. Lutz
Truth or Dare. Jacqueline Wilson
Truth Will Out. Charlotte Francis
Truth with Her Boots On. H. Cecil
Truxton Cipher. H. Gruppe
Try Anything Once. A. A. Fair
Try Anything Once. J. Pendower
Try Anything Twice. P. Cheyney
Try This One for Size. J. H. Chase
Try to Find a Dead Man. M. Ashton
Trying Patient. J. Payn
Tryst for a Tragedy. E. C. R. Lorac
Tryst with Terror. W. Winthrop
Tsing-Boum. N. Freeling
Tube. P. Boileau
Tucker's People. I. Wolfert
Tudor Garden Mystery. G. Verner

Tudor Murder. E. Hyde
Tuesday Blade. B. Ottum
Tuesday Club Murders. A. Christie
Tuesday the Rabbi Saw Red. H. Kemelman
Tule Marsh Murder. N. B. Mavity
Tule Witch. J. Toombs
Tulip Tree. H. Rigsby
Tumbled House. Winston Graham
Tumbleweed. J. Van De Wetering
Tumbling River Range. W. C. Tuttle
Tumult and the Shouting. H. Gibbs
Tumult in San Benito. John Arnold
Tumult in the North. G. R. Preedy
Tumulto. B. Williams
Tuna Is Not for Eating. B. Kelly
Tundra Trail. C. Stoddard
Tune in on Terror. J. Tobias
Tune in Tonight. R. Clark
Tune to a Corpse. P. Drax
Tuned for Murder. K. Robeson
Tunnel. A. Bristowe
Tunnel. R. Byrne
Tunnel. H. Friedman
Tunnel. B. Kendrick
Tunnel from Calais. A. D. Divine
Tunnel Mystery. J. C. Lenehan
Tunnel Mystery and Its Solution. A. W. A'Beckett
Tunnel of Darkness. R. N. Winstead
Tunnel Terror. K. Robeson
Tunnel 13. M. M. Raison
Tunnel to Doom. R. W. Hinds
Tunnel War. J. Poyer
Turbo. D. Rutherford
Turbulence. C. Hodder-Williams
Turbulent Duchess. P. Brebner
Turbulent Messiters. Elizabeth Ford
Turbulent Tales. R. Sabatini
Turf and Veldt. D. J. Belgrave
Turf Bandits. E. Woodward
Turf Conspiracy. N. Gould
Turf Crook. F. Johnston
Turf Mystery. J. Fairfax-Blakeborough
Turf Racketeers. F. Johnston
Turkey-Track Rampage. B. Haning
Turkish Bloodbath. Nick Carter
Turkish Mafia Conspiracy. Ralph Hayes
Turkish Spy. Charles Cooper
Turkish White. M. Arrighi
Turmoil at Brede. S. Truss
Turmoil in Zion. G. Bellairs
Turn Back from Death. H. Desmond
Turn Blue, You Murderers. Michael Brett
Turn Killer. B. Lecomber
Turn Left for Danger. B. Gray
Turn Left for Murder. S. Marlowe
Turn Left or Be Killed. N. Ashbaugh
Turn of a Card. Nicholas Carter
Turn of a Wheel. A. Rowe
Turn of the Screw. Henry James
Turn of the Table. J. Stagge
Turn of the Tide. F. M. White
Turn on the Heat. A. A. Fair
Turn the Light Out As You Go. E. Lustgarten
Turn-Up. A. Sewart
Turn up a Stone. A. Cade
Turncoat. Nick Carter
Turncoat. H. G. Evart
Turncoat. G. Langelaan
Turncoat. J. Lynn
Turning. Justin Scott
Turning Point. H. Clevely
Turning Sword. S. Bayne
Turning Sword. G. V. McFadden
Turning Wheel. D. Donovan
Turnpike House. F. Hume
Turns of Time. P. Audemars
Turnstile of Night. W. Allison
Turnstile of Night. A. M. Williamson
Turquoise Clues. A. Cecil
Turquoise Hazard. A. B. Caldwell
Turquoise Lament. J. D. MacDonald
Turquoise Mask. P. A. Whitney
Turquoise Shop. F. Crane
Turquoise Spike. F. Archer
Turquoise Talisman. S. Wagner
Turquoise Trail. W. C. Tuttle
Turquoise/Yellow Case. P. K. Palmer
Turret Room. C. Armstrong
Tuscany Madonna. M. Canfield
Tut, Tut! Mr. Tutt. A. Train
Tutt and Mr. Tutt. A. Train
Tutt for Tutt. A. Train
Twana. A. Du Camp
Tweak the Devil's Nose. R. Deming
Tweedledum and Tweedledee. Alec Coppel
Tween Snow and Fire. B. Mitford
Twelfth Crime. S. Cross
Twelfth Mile. E. G. Perrault
Twelfth Night Murders. C. Ryland
Twelfth of August. W. R. Morris
12th of Never. D. Heyes
Twelve Apostles. G. Verner
Twelve Chinamen and a Woman. J. H. Chase
Twelve Chinks and a Woman. J. H. Chase
Twelve Deaths of Christmas. M. Babson
Twelve Disguises. F. Beeding
Twelve Girls in the Garden. Shane Martin
Twelve Horses and the Hangman's Noose. G. Mitchell
Twelve Hours to Destiny. M. K. Robertson

Twelve in a Grave. Nicholas Carter
Twelve Maidens. S. Farrar
Twelve Midnight Street. R. Davis
12 Must Die. Zorro
Twelve on Endurance. Michael Hastings
Twelve Steps at Miramar. M. Reisner
Twelve Tales. G. Allen
Twelve Tales of Suspense and the Supernatural. D. Grubb
12:30 from Croydon. F. W. Crofts
Twelve Tin Boxes. Nicholas Carter
Twelve to Dine. E. Nisot
Twelve Trains to Babylon. A. Connable
12:20 P.M. W. G. Beymer
Twelve Wise Men. Nicholas Carter
Twentieth Day of January. T. Allbeury
20th of July. H. H. Kirst
Twenty East of Greenwich. J. Lodwick
2835 Mayfair. R. Richardson
Twenty-Fifth Hour. C. V. Gheorghiu
Twenty-Fifth Hour. M. Kelly
Twenty-First Burr. V. Lauriston
Twenty-First Century Sub. F. Herbert
Twenty-Five Sanitary Inspectors. R. East
Twenty-Four Hours. L. T. Meade
24 Hours to Kill. J. McKimmey
24th Horse. H. Pentecost
24th Level. K. Benton
Twenty Miles to Terror. Eddie Stone
Twenty Minutes to Kill. A. M. Chase
29 Herriott Street. J. Hutton
Twenty-One Clues. J. J. Connington
Twenty-One Stories. G. Greene
Twenty Per Cent. T. Macrae
Twenty Plus Two. F. Gruber
27th Ride. A. D. Welton
Twenty-Six Clues. I. Ostrander
26 Three-Minute Mysteries. N. Morland
Twenty-Third Man. G. Mitchell
Twenty-Third Web. R. Himmel
Twenty-Thousand Thieves. Eric Lambert
22 Brothers. D. Sage
22 Fires. J. Agel
Twenty-Two Windows. Roland Daniel
Twenty Years of Hate. Donald Stuart
Twentymen. P. Purser
Twice a Victim. C. Joyce
Twice American. E. M. Ingram
Twice As Dead. D. Spade
Twice Broken. M. Peterson
Twice Checked. Graham Hastings
Twice Dead. J. Bude
Twice Dead. E. M. Channon
Twice Dead. L. D. Names
Twice Dead. J. Rhode
Twice Dead. Colin Robertson
Twice Dead. Marilyn Ross
Twice Lost. P. Paul
Twice Murdered. C. H. Snow
Twice Murdered Man. N. Toye
Twice Retired. R. Lockridge
Twice Round the Clock. B. Houston
Twice So Fair. N. Tyre
Twice Ten Thousand Miles. F. Lynch
Twice Times Murder. R. Sonin
Twice-Told Tales. N. Hawthorne
Twice Tried. W. LeQueux
Twice Upon a Crime. P. Quinn
Twice Wronged! J. W. Bobin
Twickenham Peerage. R. Marsh
Twig Is Bent. E. Thompson
Twilight at Dawn. Max Murray
Twilight at Monticello. W. H. Peden
Twilight at the Elms. D. Daniels
Twilight for Taurus. M. Lynch
Twilight Forest. C. Hamilton
Twilight of Death. L. Langley
Twilight of the Generals. H. H. Kirst
Twilight People. R. Batchelor
Twilight Return. J. Kimbro
Twilight Strangler. C. Miron
Twilight Walk. A. B. Shiffrin
Twilight Web. W. E. D. Ross
Twillford Mystery. G. F. Scott
Twin Athletes. Old Sleuth
Twin Detectives. K. F. Hill
Twin Detectives "Which Wins". Anonymous
Twin Killing. G. Bagby
Twin Mystery. Nicholas Carter
Twin Serpents. R. S. Thorn
Twin Sisters. R. Marsh
Twin Tales. A. Stringer
Twin Tragedy. M. Carr
Twin Ventriloquists. Old Sleuth
Twinkle, Twinkle, Little Spy. L. Deighton
Twinkleface, the Merry Elf. M. Peterson
Twins. Bari Wood
Twins Murder Case. H. G. Hutchinson
Twins of Suffering Creek. R. Cullum
Twist and other stories. J. J. Farjeon
Twist for Two. H. Janson
Twist in the Silk. Z. Cass
Twist in the Trail. W. J. Bayfield
Twist of a Stick. G. Peters
Twist of Fate. J. De Secary
Twist of Hate. C. Joyce
Twist of Sand. G. Jenkins
Twist of the Knife. V. Canning
Twist of the Rope. J. Bude
Twist of Yarn. E. Lookabee
Twist the Knife Slowly. K. Clugston

Twisted Cameo. K. Kimbrough
Twisted Cross. A. Pinchot
Twisted Evidence. M. B. Dix
Twisted Face. F. A. Kummer
Twisted Face Defends His Title. G. Davison
Twisted Face Strikes Again. G. Davison
Twisted Face, the Avenger. G. Davison
Twisted Foot. H. M. Rideout
Twisted Grin. A. Salcroft
Twisted Key. R. Willock
Twisted Mirror. Leonard Lee
Twisted Nerve. Peter Evans
Twisted Ones. V. Packer
Twisted People. J. Philips
Twisted Tales. L. H. Fox
Twisted Tales. Christopher Ward
Twisted Thing. M. Spillane
Twisted Thread. J. Moffat
Twisted Tongues. Jonathan Burke
Twisted Trails. W. C. Tuttle
Twisted Tree. L. Benedict
Twisted Wire. R. Falkirk
Twister. E. Wallace
Twisters. V. Hansen
Twister's Double. C. Davy
Twittering Bird Mystery. H. C. Bailey
'Twixt Devil and Deep Sea. A. M. Williamson
'Twixt Sword and Glove. A. C. Gunter
'Twixt the Lights. W. W. Fenn
Two. C. Trieschman
Two After Malic. L. Peters
Two Against Scotland Yard. D. Frome
Two and Two Make Five. T. E. B. Clarke
Two and Two Make Five. B. Graeme
Two and Two Make Twenty-Two. G. Bristow
Two Apaches of Paris. A. Askew
Two Aunts and a Grandmother. T. B. Morris
Two Black Pearls. M. Leighton
Two Bottles of Relish. R. Plomley
Two Bullets for Briggs. D. MacDonald
Two by Day and One by Night. V. Bell
Two by Tricks. E. Yates
Two Clues. E. S. Gardner
Two Conspirators. Old Sleuth
Two Conspirators. M. O. Rolfe
Two Crosses. W. J. Newton
Two Dames Too Many. M. Perelli
Two Days, Two Nights. P. O. Sundman
Two Dead. V. Loder
Two Dead Charwomen. N. Morland
Two Dead Men. J. Anker
Two Deaths for a Penny. N. Burnaby
Two Deaths Must Die. R. Himmel
Two Destinies. W. Collins
Two Died at Three. C. F. Gregg
Two Died in Singapore. J. Sherwood
Two Ends in the Town. J. Bude
Two-Face. E. Dudley
Two-Faced. B. Graeme
Two-Faced Death. R. Jeffries
Two-Faced Man. V. Vanardy
Two Faced Murder. Jean Leslie
Two Faces of Death. W. Wright
Two Faces of Fear. J. Wellsley
Two Faces of January. P. Highsmith
Two Faces of Love. D. Noel
Two Faces of Murder. G. Batson
Two Faces of Nemesis. A. Melville-Ross
Two False Moves. J. Middlemass
Two Feet from Heaven. P. C. Wren
Two-Five to Mardon. K. Field
Two Flights Up. M. R. Rinehart
Two-Fold Inheritance. G. Boothby
Two for a Pair. D. Walshe
Two for Inspector West. J. Creasey
Two for Tanner. Lawrence Block
Two for the Grave. R. B. Houston
Two for the Money. M. Halliday
Two for the Price of One. T. Kenrick
Two Forces. E. W. Elkington
Two Gay Sleuths. H. K. Kaye
Two Girls and a Saint. G. Warden
Two Goodwins. R. M. Gilchrist
Two Graphs. J. Rhode
Two Gun Hedgehopper. T. Wallace
Two-Gun Sue. Douglas Grant
Two Guns for Hire. N. MacNeil
Two Heads Are Better. Elliott Lewis
Tow Hearts Apart. F. Lee
Two Hot to Handle. E. Lacy
Two Hours to Doom. P. Bryant
Two Houses on the Cliff. M. V. Woodgate
£250 Marriage Case. J. G. Brandon
Two Hundred Rule. H. Hamilton
200% Rule. E. A. Pollitz
Two Hundred Pounds Reward, and other tales. J. Payn
Two If by Sea. R. Bax
Two Imposters. P. Audemars
Two in a Tangle. W. LeQueux
Two in Shadow. J. Blackmore
Two in the Bush. G. Bagby
Two in the Bush. G. Blumberg
Two in the Dark. G. G. Magnus
Two Kinds of Murder. D. MacDonald
Two Kings. G. Johnston
Two Kisses. H. Smart
Two Knaves and a Queen. F. Barrett
Two Knocks for Death. W. Jackson

2 L.O. W. S. Masterman
Two Ladies in Verona. Lionel Black
Two Lads and a Lass, and other stories. F. Warden
Two Legacies. Mrs. C. Kernahan
Two Little Children and How They Grew. D. M. Disney
Two Little Rich Girls. M. G. Eberhart
Two Little Ships. E. L. Long
Two Lives in Parenthesis. George Long
Two Living and One Dead. S. Christiansen
Two Lovers Too Many. Joan Fleming
Two Lucky People. T. Kenrick
Two Magics. Henry James
Two Meet Trouble. M. Halliday
Two Men from Kimberley. H. B. Baker
Two Men from the East. T. A. Plummer
Two Men in Twenty. M. Procter
Two Men Missing. G. Ashe
Two Million. H. B. Vogel
$2,000,000 Blueprint. C. Miron
Two Minute Warning. G. La Fountaine
Two Mrs. Camerons. W. Carter
Two Mrs. Carrolls. H. Arvonen
Two Mrs. Carrolls. M. Vale
Two Mrs. Farrells. John Marsh
Two Moods of a Man. H. G. Hutchinson
Two Much! D. E. Westlake
Two Must Die. H. Kane
Two Must Die. Colin Robertson
Two Mysteries. G. H. Teed
Two Names for Death. E. P. Fenwick
Two O'Clock Courage. G. Burgess
209 Thriller Road. Sam North
Two of Diamonds. L. Brock
Two on the Trail. H. Footner
Two Pardons. H. S. Vince
Two Pinches of Snuff. W. Westall
Two Plus Two. Nicholas Carter
Two Plus Two. A. Cochran
Two Plus Two Equals Minus Seven. J. F. Adams
Two Red Capsules. D. T. Lindsay
Two Sets to Murder. L. Peters
Two Shadows for Death. J. Wolf
Two Shadows Pass. Clifford King
Two Shots. P. Luck
Two Sisters. E. Southworth
Two Smart Dames. Gene Ross
2 Spruce Lane. Gretchen Travis
Two-Star Pigeon. M. Wolfe
Two Stolen Idols. F. Packard
Two Strange Adventures. K. Cornwallis
Two Strange Ladies. H. S. Keeler
Two Strange Men. J. S. Clouston
Two Strokes of the Bell. C. H. Montague
Two Tales of the Occult. M. Eliade
Two-Thirds of a Ghost. H. McCloy
Two Thousand Maniacs! H. G. Lewis
Two Thrillers. A. Christie
Two Tickets Puzzle. J. J. Connington
Two Tickets to Destruction. G. S. Foster
Two Tickets to Tangier. V. W. Mason
Two-Timing Blonde. Carter Brown
Two to Slay. H. Brinton
Two to Tangle. F. Kane
Two Undertakers. F. Beeding
Two Villains in One. Nicholas Carter
Two-Way Frame. T. Harknett
Two-Way Mirror. D. Launay
Two-Way Witness. F. Franklin
Two Ways to Die. L. Thayer
Two Ways to Murder. E. Radford
Two Weeks Before Murder. W. Metcalfe
Two Weeks to Find a Killer. C. Davis
Two White Elephants. A. H. Veysey
Two Who Talked. Frank King
Two with a Gun. P. Malloch
Two Women. M. Pemberton
Two Women in Black. J. W. Postgate
Two Wonderful Detectives. Old Sleuth
Two Worlds of Peggy Scott. D. Daniels
Twopence for a Rat's Tail. S. M. Lott
Twopenny Box. J. N. Chance
Two's Company. M. Kennedy
Twospot. B. Pronzini
Tycoon and the Tigress. W. R. Cox
Tycoon of Crime. R. Wallace
Tycoon's Death-Bed. G. Bellairs
Tyger at Bay. A. Riefe
Tyger by the Tail. A. Riefe
Tyger! Tyger! R. C. K. Ginn
Tyler Mystery. P. Temple
Typed for a Corpse. A. Pruitt
Typewritten Letter. R. H. Sherard
Typhoon. J. W. McConaughy
Typhoon Shipments. K. Klose
Typhoon's Secret. S. N. Sheridan
Tyrants of Today. C. L. Johnstone
Tyree Legend. W. Kelley
Tyson Murder Case. T. J. O'Connell

U-Boat in the Hebrides. A. D. Divine
U.N. Affair. S. Jason
U-700. J. Follett
Ubiquitous Yank. Old Sleuth
Ugly Customer. C. F. Gregg

U

Ugly Face of Love and other stories. G. Kersh
Ugly Man. Anonymous
Ugly Woman. M. Cameron
Ugly Woman. W. O'Farrell
Uist Project. J. Wood
Ukridge. P. G. Wodehouse
Ullman Code. R. Bernhard
Ulsterman. A. Lane
Ultimate. J. Lund
Ultimate Act. L. P. Bachmann
Ultimate Client. M. Avallone
Ultimate Conclusion. A. C. Fox-Davies
Ultimate Code. Nick Carter
Ultimate Game. J. W. Cummings
Ultimate Island. L. Sieveking
Ultimate Solution. E. Norden
Ultimatum. P. Bonnecarrere
Ultimatum. B. Meyer
Ultimatum. R. Rohmer
Ultimatum. A. Trew
Ultimatum: PU-94. U. Dan
Ultraviolet Widow. F. Crane
Umbrella-Maker's Daughter. J. Caird
Umbrella Murder. C. Wells
Umgasi Diamonds. E. De Caire
Un Mystere. H. Greville
Unaccepted Death. H. Gilson
Unaccountable Crook. Nicholas Carter
Unafraid. Gerald Butler
Unafraid. E. M. Ingram
Unaltered Cat. A. Lewin
Unappointed Rounds. D. M. Disney
Unbarred Door. C. H. Bullivant
Unbecoming Habits. T. Heald
Unbegotten. J. Creasey
Unbidden. R. Chetwynd-Hayes
Unbidden Guests. Dick Stewart
Unbriefed Mission. L. Bridgemont
Uncanny. W. Louder
Uncanny Adventures. E. Ascher
Uncanny Stories. May Sinclair
Uncas Island Murders. F. W. Bronson
Uncertain Agent. S. Donald
Uncertain Death. Anthony Gilbert
Uncertain Glory. H. Meadow
Uncertain Judgement. G. Mitcham
Uncertain Quest. E. Messenger
Uncertain Sound. Roy Lewis
Uncertain Treasure. D. Lee
Uncertain Trumpets. B. McGregor
Uncertain Voyage. D. Gilman
Uncharted. S. M. Parkman
Uncharted Island. S. M. Parkman
Uncharted Seas. D. Wheatley
Unclaimed Daughter. Anonymous
Unclaimed Letter. A. M. Sholl
Unclaimed Million. H. Maxwell
Uncle Abner, Master of Mysteries. M. D. Post
Uncle from India. E. D. Pierson
Uncle Harry. T. Job
Uncle James's Golf Match. H. C. McNeile
Uncle Joe's Legacy and other stories. G. Boothby
Uncle Oscar's Niece. G. Goodchild
Uncle Paul. C. Fremlin
Uncle Sagamore and His Girls. C. Williams
Uncle Sam, Detective. W. A. Dupuy
Uncle Sam's Bad Boys. B. D. Adsit
Uncle Silas. J. S. Le Fanu
Uncle Simon. M. Stacpoole
Uncle William and other stories. D. G. Browne
Uncle Xavier. D. H. Landels
Unclean. G. Des Cars
Uncle's Advice. W. Hewlett
Uncle's Crime. J. H. Robinson
Uncoffin'd Clay. G. Mitchell
Uncollected Cases of Solar Pons. B. Copper
Uncollected Wodehouse. P. G. Wodehouse
Uncommitted Man. R. E. Pickering
Uncommon Cold. E. H. Clements
Uncommon Danger. E. Ambler
Uncommon Market. H. Janson
Uncomplaining Corpses. B. Halliday
Unconfessed. M. H. Bradley
Unconfessed. Maxwell Gray
Unconquerable. Helen MacInnes
Unconscious Crime. N. T. Oliver
Unconscious Witness. R. A. Freeman
Uncounted Hour. W. Allen
Uncover Agent. H. Janson
Uncreated Man. A. Fryers
Uncrowned Prince. J. J. Farrington
Uncut Diamonds. D. Brechin
Undaunted. J. Harris
Undefeated. J. Thompson
Under a Ban. Mrs. Lodge
Under a Black Veil. Nicholas Carter
Under a Cloud. J. K. Ludlum
Under a Cloud. V. Siller
Under a Cloud. T. W. Speight
Under a Mask. J. K. Leys
Under a Mask. J. B. Williams
Under a Strange Mask. F. Barrett
Under a Veil. Old Sleuth
Under Cover. W. Martyn
Under Cover. R. C. Megrue
Under Cover Man. J. Wilstach

Under Cover of Night. R. M. Gilchrist
Under Cover of Night. M. L. Stokes
Under Dog and other stories. A. Christie
Under Dogs. H. Footner
Under Egyptian Skies. S. Rathbone
Under False Colors. Nicholas Carter
Under False Pretenses. A. Sergeant
Under Fate's Wheel. L. L. Lynch
Under Fire. R. Parker
Under Gemini. R. Pilcher
Under Groove. A. Stringer
Under His Thumb. Anonymous
Under His Thumb. D. J. MacKenzie
Under Lock and Key. T. W. Speight
Under London. V. Gielgud
Under Love's Rule. M. E. Braddon
Under Masks. H. F. Wood
Under Observation. Douglas Christie
Under One Roof. J. Payn
Under Orion. J. Law
Under Police Observation. G. Chester
Under Police Protection. J. G. Brandon
Under Pressure. F. Herbert
Under Proof. J. Cannan
Under St. Paul's. R. Dowling
Under Seal of the Confessional. Mrs. C. Kernahan
Under Sealed Orders. G. Allen
Under Sealed Orders. J. G. Brandon
Under Sealed Orders. H. A. Cody
Under-Secretary. W. LeQueux
Under Sentence. Mary Cross
Under Sentence of Death. Old Sleuth
Under Suspicion. H. W. Leggett
Under Suspicion. A. MacVicar
Under Suspicion. A. Sergeant
Under Suspicion. R. Trevor
Under the Black Eagle. A. W. Marchmont
Under the Broad Arrow. M. Leighton
Under the Cherry Tree. P. Traill
Under the Dragon Throne. L. T. Meade
Under the Eagle's Wing. G. H. Teed
Under the Eye of Night. R. E. Mills
Under the Fourth—? P. Luck
Under the Goad. C. A. Brandreth
Under the Golden Bough. G. F. Gibbs
Under the Great Seal. J. Hatton
Under the Influence. C. Kerr
Under the Lens. F. B. Austin
Under the Long Barrow. C. Haddon
Under the Quiet Water. F. S. Wees
Under the Red Flag. M. E. Braddon
Under the Red Flag. M. J. Pemberton
Under the Red Star. M. Gerard
Under the Rose. H. Wood
Under the Shadow. H. L. Jones
Under the Skin. Dorothea Bennett
Under the Spell of the Orient. C. E. Perry
Under the Sunset. B. Stoker
Under the Surface. J. K. Stafford
Under the Tiger's Claws. Nicholas Carter
Under the Wall. Nick Carter
Under the Will, and other tales. M. C. Hay
Under the Willows. E. Van Loon
Under Three Flags. B. L. Taylor
Under Twelve Stars. H. S. Keeler
Under Two Skies. E. W. Hornung
Under Western Eyes. J. Conrad
Under-World. L. Osbourne
Undercover Agent. E. Ellison
Undercover Cat. The Gordons
Undercover Cat Prowls Again. The Gordons
Undercover Cutie. M. Brody
Undercover Girl. Roland Daniel
Undercover Man. H. H. Kirst
Undercover Woman. H. Herzog
Undercurrent. J. Bogar
Undercurrent. M. Boggon
Undercurrent. B. Jefferis
Undercurrent. B. Pronzini
Underdog. W. R. Burnett
Underground. J. S. Dutton
Underground. J. J. Farjeon
Underground. J. Hallums
Underground. J. K. Leys
Underground. J. Raskin
Underground. C. Stratton
Underground Cities Contract. P. Atlee
Underground Connection. P. Niesewand
Underground Man. R. Macdonald
Underground Men. M. Carrel
Underground Mystery. R. H. Sherard
Underground Syndicate. A. M. Williamson
Underhandover. Kenneth O'Hara
Underkill. B. Crowther
Understrike. J. Gardner
Understudy. D. H. Landels
Understudy to Murder. Dulcie Gray
Undertaker. J. Quinn
Undertaker Dies. Garnett Weston
Undertaker Wind. W. Masterson
Undertaker's Field. H. Compton
Undertow. D. Cory
Underwood Mystery. C. J. Dutton
Underworld. I. Wolfert
Underworld Nights. C. Raven
Underworld of Zello. J. J. Deegan
Undesirable Company. F. Ryck
Undetective. B. Graeme
Undine. P. B. Young

Undiplomatic Exit. J. Sherwood
Undisclosed Client. E. Wallace
Undiscovered Crimes. Waters
Undivided Light. C. Massie
Undoing of Mrs. Cransby. H. C. McNeile
Undoubted Deed. J. Davey
Undressed to Kill. P. Cheyney
Undying Serpent. T. B. Morris
Une Tenebreuse Affaire. H. D. Balzac
Unearthly. D. Daniels
Uneasy Alibi. N. Karta
Uneasy Freehold. D. Macardle
Uneasy Is the Grave. J. S. Strange
Uneasy Lies the Dead. M. E. Chaber
Uneasy Lies the Head. W. L. Rohde
Uneasy Money. M. Tannock
Uneasy Street. B. Chetwynd
Uneasy Street. S. Coburn
Uneasy Street. Wade Miller
Uneasy Street. A. S. Roche
Uneasy Sun. M. Butterworth
Uneasy Terms. P. Cheyney
Uneasy Virtue. Reginald Campbell
Uneasy Virtue. Dana Wilson
Uneasy Years. L. Noel
Unending Track. J. Farrimond
Unequal Match. Rachelle Edwards
Unexpected. F. Hume
Unexpected Adventure. T. F. W. Hickey
Unexpected Angel. J. B. Watney
Unexpected Corpse. E. L. Cushing
Unexpected Daughter. P. Trent
Unexpected Death. Dell Shannon
Unexpected Guest. A. Christie
Unexpected Legacy. E. R. Punshon
Unexpected Mrs. Pollifax. D. Gilman
Unexpected Move. S. Campbell
Unexpected Night. E. Daly
Unexploded Man. Leslie Watkins
Unfair Exchange. M. Babson
Unfair Fare Affair. P. Leslie
Unfair Lady. G. Fairlie
Unfeeling Sky. P. Saxon
Unfinished Business. M. Cronin
Unfinished Business. C. Lucas
Unfinished Clue. G. Heyer
Unfinished Crime. E. S. Holding
Unfinished Crime. H. McCloy
Unfinished Letter. Nicholas Carter
Unfinished Murder. E. W. Lyon
Unfit to Plead. J. Dellbridge
Unfolding Years. A. Gask
Unforbidden Sin. Roy Vickers
Unforeseen. D. Macardle
Unforeseen. J. C. Snaith
Unforgetting Heart. Margery Lawrence
Unforgivable Sin. A. Applin
Unforgiven. Maynah Lewis
Unforgiving Moment. F. Cowen
Unforgiving Wind. J. Harris
Unforgotten. L. Conway
Unforgotten. D. Winston
Unfortunate Murderer. R. Hull
Unfortunate Replacement. M. Jahn
Unfortunate Rogue. Warren Miller
Unfriendly Persuasion. W. A. Ballinger
Ungilded Lily. Morton Cooper
Unguarded. D. Daniels
Unguarded Hour. A. W. Marchmont
Unguarded Hour. D. Vane
Unguarded Moment. H. A. Wrenn
Unhallowed Murder. S. Nash
Unhandsome Corpse. S. Campion
Unhappy Hooligan. S. Palmer
Unhappy Hophead. Spike Gordon
Unhappy Lady and other stories. P. Cheyney
Unhappy New Year. C. C. Estes
Unhappy Parting. Elsie Lee
Unhappy Rendezvous. A. Nash
Unhappy Returns. E. Lemarchand
Unhappy Ship. E. L. Long
Unheeded Warning. Dick Stewart
Unholy Child. C. Breslin
Unholy Crusade. D. Wheatley
Unholy Dying. R. T. Campbell
Unholy Flame. O. L. Rosmanith
Unholy Matrimony. Winifred Graham
Unholy Sanctuary. M. Higgins
Unholy Spell. C. Vincent
Unholy Terror. George Douglas
Unholy Three. T. Robbins
Unholy Trio. H. Kane
Unholy Trio. J. Ronald
Unholy Wife. J. Roeburt
Unholy Wish, and other stories. H. Wood
Unholy Writ. D. Williams
Unhurrying Chase. M. Markey
Unicorn. C. Goodall
Unicorn Caper. J. W. Lampp
Unicorn Group. L. R. Bobker
Unicorn Murders. Carter Dickson
Unidentified Woman. M. G. Eberhart
Uniformed Killers. R. Wallace
Uninvited. F. A. Chittenden
Uninvited. D. Macardle
Uninvited Corpse. P. Whelton
Uninvited Ghost. L. Rose
Uninvited Guest. G. H. Coxe
Uninvited Guests. J. J. Farjeon
Union Bust. R. Sapir
Union Down. S. Campbell

Title Index

Unique Hamlet. V. Starrett
Unity Penfold. M. Tabor
Universe Against Her. J. H. Schmitz
Unjust Jury. Winifred Duke
Unjustly Branded. R. H. Poole
Unkindly Cup. H. McElroy
Unkindness of Ravens. T. B. Reagan
Unknown. J. Barclay
Unknown. E. Southworth
Unknown Agent. M. Annesley
Unknown Assailant. P. Hamilton
Unknown Blond. L. L. Brookman
Unknown Countess. Emerson Bennett
Unknown Enemy. Gret Lane
Unknown Foe. J. K. Stafford
Unknown Goddess. A. Philips
Unknown Hand. M. Peterson
Unknown Man #89. E. Leonard
Unknown Man, Seen in Profile. Kenneth O'Hara
Unknown Menace. Donald Stuart
Unknown Mission. N. Deane
Unknown Murderer. H. Liggett
Unknown Path. Lady A. Scott
Unknown Quantity. M. G. Eberhart
Unknown Quantity. W. E. Johns
Unknown Quest. Ralph Scott
Unknown River. J. M. Scott
Unknown Seven. H. Coverdale
Unknown Skyjacker. S. N. Rampal
Unknown Terror. H. Holt
Unknown Tomorrow. W. LeQueux
Unknown Warrior. J. Leasor
Unknown Woman. L. Hoffman
Unlamented. D. Daniels
Unlatched Door. L. Thayer
Unlawful. C. Turner
Unlawful Justice. John Gloag
Unlawful Occasions. H. Cecil
Unlawful Occasions. P. Wentworth
Unleashed Will. Christopher Clark
"Unless a Child Is Born—." B. Heygate
Unlighted House. J. Hay
Unloved. D. Birkley
Unloved Wife. E. Southworth
Unlucky Break. O. Mills
Unlucky Dip. Margaret Henry
Unlucky for Some. A. Behrend
Unlucky Number. E. Phillpotts
Unmasked at Last. H. Hill
Unnamed. W. LeQueux
Unnatural Break. T. Girtin
Unnatural Causes. H. Hawton
Unnatural Causes. P. D. James
Unnatural Death. M. Richmond
Unnatural Death. D. L. Sayers
Unnatural Deeds. E. Nisot
Unnatural Selection. J. Ranbern
Unneutral Murder. H. Footner
Unofficial Executor. H. R. F. Moulton
Unofficial Spy. A. O. Pollard
Unorthodox Corpse. Carter Brown
Unpardonable Crime. D. B. Miller
Unpardonable Sin. A. D. Vinton
Unpleasantness at the Bellona Club. D. L. Sayers
Unpossessed. W. H. Fielding
Unprofessional Spy. M. Underwood
Unprotected. I. Barry
Unpublishable Memoirs. A. S. W. Rosenbach
Unquenchable Flame. A. J. Rees
Unquiet Corpse. W. Sloan
Unquiet Grave. J. S. Strange
Unquiet Night. P. Carlon
Unquiet Night. M. Cronin
Unquiet Sleep. W. Haggard
Unraveled Knots. B. Orczy
Unravish'd Bride. J. Hope-Simpson
Unreasonable Doubt. E. Ferrars
Unrelenting. C. W. Dodge
Unrepentant. C. Phillips
Unrepentant Sinners. L. Royer
Unrequited Affection. H. Balzac
Unruly Son. R. Barnard
Unscheduled Flight. H. Atkinson
Unscrupulous Mr. Callaghan. P. Cheyney
Unseen! A. P. Terhune
Unseen. Ethel L. White
Unseen Assassin. H. Janson
Unseen Barrier. M. Gerard
Unseen Ear. N. S. Lincoln
Unseen Enemy. C. Landon
Unseen Foes. Nicholas Carter
Unseen Hand. L. L. Lynch
Unseen Hand. C. H. New
Unseen Hand. I. Stark
Unseen Hand. Valentine
Unseen Hands. R. O. Chipperfield
Unseen Torment. K. Kimbrough
Unseen Witness. B. Bolt
Unsheltered. D. Ward
Unsolved. B. Graeme
Unsolved Mysteries. V. Tweedale
Unsought Adventure. H. A. Kennedy
Unspeakable. S. Ransome
Unspeakable Turk. G. Horton
Unspoken Word. M. Gerard
Unsuccessful Man. T. Nielsen
Unsuitable Job for a Woman. P. D. James
Unsung Road. S. Harvester
Unsuspected. C. Armstrong

Unsuspected. R. Brome
Unsuspected Chasm. M. Innes
Unsuspected Evil. D. M. Disney
Unsuspecting Victim. J. F. Drexler
Untamed. V. Norwood
Untaxed Whiskey. B. Wayde
Untidy Murder. F. Lockridge
Until Death. S. Somers
Until She Dies. W. Wright
Until She Was Dead. R. Hull
Until Temptation Do Us Part. Carter Brown
Until the Day She Dies. J. MacLaren-Ross
Until They Are Dead. John Lloyd
Until You Are Dead. H. Kane
Untimely Death. C. Hare
Untimely Frost. E. G. Cousins
Untimely Guest. M. Babson
Untimely Ripped. M. McShane
Untimely Slain. J. Gray
Unto Death Utterly. M. Cumberland
Unto the Third Generation. M. P. Shiel
Untold Tale. L. K. Vincent
Untouchable Juli. J. Aldridge
Unwanted Child. P. Conway
Unwanted Corpse. M. Burton
Unwanted Witness. George Douglas
Unwashed Gods. E. C. Vivian
Unwelcome Corpse. B. Frost
Unwelcome Rapture. M. Richmond
Unwelcome Visitor. A. Corliss
Unwilling Adventurer. John Gloag
Unwilling Angel. Alan Stuart
Unwilling Bride. F. Hume
Unwilling Guest. E. Ellison
Unwilling Rebel. M. Lynch
Unwilling to Wed. M. Richmond
Unwise Virgin. Mrs. C. Kernahan
Up a Winding Stair. H. V. Dixon
Up Against It. C. Vanardy
Up and Coming Man. F. Branston
Up for Grabs. A. A. Fair
Up from the Grave. D. Craig
Up Jumped the Devil. C. F. Adams
Up, McLean! G. Goodchild
Up North. T. Lund
Up North. J. H. Vahey
Up the Gardon Path. M. Burton
Up the Garden Path. J. Rhode
Up the Ladder of Gold. E. P. Oppenheim
Up This Crooked Way. H. Holman
Up Tight. John Allen
Up-Tight Blonde. Carter Brown
Up to Her Neck. J. N. Chance
Up to No Good. A. M. Stein
Up to the Hilt. A. Rowe
Upfold Farm Mystery. A. Fielding
Upfold Witch. Josephine Bell
Upland Mystery. M. R. Hatch
Upmarket Affair. T. Harknett
Upper Case. M. Merrick
Upside Down Murders. H. Austin
Upside Down Tree. H. Kruger
Upstairs. J. L. Rickard
Upstairs and Downstairs. C. Carnac
Upstairs and Downstairs. R. S. Thorn
Upstairs, Downstairs. C. Carnac
Upstart. P. P. Read
Uranian Jewel Case. R. Dark
Uranium Murders. J. E. Barry
Urban District Lover. J. T. Story
Urbane Guerilla. Stanley Johnson
Urgent Action. N. Forde
Urgent Delivery. N. Forde
Urgent Enquiry. N. Forde
Urgent Hangman. P. Cheyney
Urgent Private Affairs. H. F. Moulton
Urgent Trip. N. Forde
Urgent Wedding. N. Forde
Urn Burial. P. Ruell
Ursala, the Proud. K. Kimbrough
Ursula Lenorme. T. W. Speight
Ursula Vanet. A. Mills
Us or Them War. W. Garner
Used in Evidence. P. Froud
Utmost Ebb. R. Harrison
Utopia Affair. D. McDaniel
Utter Death. J. Hymers
Uttermost Farthing. R. A. Freeman
Uttermost Farthing. M. B. Lowndes

V As in Victim. L. Treat
V.C. D. C. Murray
"V" for Vengeance. D. Wheatley
V for Vitality. H. Janson
V.I.P. W. L. Rohde
V.I.P. E. Trevor
V-J Day. A. Fields
V-Mann Papers. C. Cruickshank
V Plan. G. Seton
V2 Expert. A. J. Evans
V2 Virus. E. Cannon
Vaaldorf Diamond. Eva Dane
Vacancy. P. Mann
Vacancy with Corpse. M. Burton
Vacant Possession. M. Butcher

Vacant Throne. D. Hanna
Vacation with Fear. J. T. Story
Vagabond Nights. H. S. Keeler
Vagabond Sonata. L. Geoghegan
Vagabond Vamp. H. Janson
Vagabond's Honor. E. D. Pierson
Vagrant Bride. Mrs. C. Kernahan
Vagrant Duke. G. F. Gibbs
Vagrant Wife. F. Warden
Vaia's Lord. J. Middlemass
Vail's Gate. J. Cabot
Vain Ambitions. R. Gaines
Vain Escape. E. C. Vivian
Vain Pride. C. Kingston
Vain Sacrifice. Nicholas Carter
Vaivaisukko's Bride. D. Scott-Moncrieff
Val Strange. D. C. Murray
Valago Crest. J. A. Bartlett
Valazy Family and other narratives. Waters
Valcour Meets Murder. R. King
Valdez Is Coming. E. Leonard
Valentine Estate. S. Ellin
Valentine Vaughan Omnibus. R. T. Hopkins
Valentine Victim. D. McLeish
Valerie. S. Nichols
Valhalla. George Long
Valhalla Exchange. H. Patterson
Valiant Jester. M. Edwin
Valiant View. T. Mundy
Valkyrie Mandate. R. Vaughan
Vallency Tradition. G. Merrick
Vallette Heritage. L. Bronte
Valley. Clifford Irving
Valley and the Shadow. W. H. Boore
Valley of Achor. P. C. De Crespigny
Valley of Bells. D. Whitelaw
Valley of Creeping Men. R. Crawley
Valley of Death. W. R. Hutton
Valley of Death. S. Jason
Valley of Death. Paul Ross
Valley of Doom. M. Richmond
Valley of Fear. J. Creasey
Valley of Fear. A. C. Doyle
Valley of Fear. R. Gar
Valley of Fear. F. A. Symonds
Valley of Ghosts. J. Tobias
Valley of Ghosts. E. Wallace
Valley of Green Shadows. L. A. Knight
Valley of Hanoi. H. Blacker
Valley of Headstrong Men. J. S. Fletcher
Valley of Lies. G. Goodchild
Valley of Lost Gold. G. Bettany
Valley of Night. J. Farnol
Valley of No Escape. James Preston
Valley of No Return. C. Virmonne
Valley of Poppies. J. Hatton
Valley of Shadows. D. Lyons
Valley of Silence. C. Randell
Valley of Skulls. O. Sackville
Valley of Smugglers. A. W. Upfield
Valley of Suspicion. F. Riddell
Valley of Suspicion. W. C. Tuttle
Valley of Terror. Donald Stuart
Valley of the Assassins. I. MacAlister
Valley of the Damned. V. Norwood
Valley of the Ravens. N. Buckingham
Valley of the Shadow. W. LeQueux
Valley of the Shadow. H. C. McNeile
Valley of the Shadow. M. Richmond
Valley of the Shadows. D. Daniels
Valley of the Shadows. Diane Stevens
Valley of Twisted Trails. W. C. Tuttle
Valley of Vanishing Herds. W. C. Tuttle
Valley of Vultures. P. Edwards
Valley Vixen. B. A. Williams
Valparaiso. F. R. E. Nicolas
Valrose Mystery. W. LeQueux
Valse Caprice. Gavin Holt
Valse Macabre. K. M. Knight
Value for Murder. Craig Cooper
Vamp Till Ready. T. Rieman
Vampire. R. Hodder
Vampire. S. Horler
Vampire. J. Sherman
Vampire Abroad. M. Dalman
Vampire Affair. D. McDaniel
Vampire, and sixteen other stories. L. H. Fox
Vampire Bat. R. St. Clair
Vampire Cameo. D. Nile
Vampire Chase. Stephen Brett
Vampire City. T. S. King
Vampire Contessa. Marilyn Ross
Vampire Curse. D. Winston
Vampire in the Shadows. M. Lovell
Vampire Man. G. Verner
Vampire Murders. R. Wallace
Vampire of N'Gobi. R. Cullum
Vampire of the Andes. H. Carew
Vampire of the Skies. J. Corbett
Vampire Tapes. A. Randolphe
Vampires and the Witch. L. Falk
Vampire's Moon. P. Saxon
Vampires of Finistere. P. Saxon
Vampires of the China Coast. Bok
Vampires of Vengeance. J. A. Kolbe
Vampires Overhead. A. Hyder
Vampire's Trail. Nicholas Carter
Vampyre of Moura. V. Coffman
Van Alstine Case. Nicholas Carter
Van Beck Will. H. W. Jessup

Van Dreisen Affair. H. Roth
Van Dylk Diamonds. A. Applin
Van Dyne Collection. M. D. Scott
Van Langeren Girl. Brian Cooper
Van Norton Murders. C. R. Jones
Van Peltz Diamonds. Anonymous
Van Rhyne Heritage. L. Bronte
Van Roon. J. C. Snaith
Van Suyden Sapphires. Charles Carey
Van, the Government Detective. H. P. Halsey
Vancenza. M. Robinson
Vandals. W. Hildick
Vandekkers. R. Thorndike
Vanderlyn's Adventure. M. B. Lowndes
Vandersley. Edward Brown
Vandor Mystery. C. F. Gregg
Vanessa. K. Martin
Vanish in an Instant. M. Millar
Vanished. M. Carleton
Vanished. F. Knebel
Vanished. B. Pronzini
Vanished Emperor. P. Andreae
Vanished Guest. O. Binns
Vanished Messenger. E. P. Oppenheim
Vanished Million. W. W. Sayer
Vanished Prospector. T. Lund
Vanished Squadron. J. R. Holden
Vanished Stamps Mystery. M. Poole
Vanished Vice-Counsel. M. Annesley
Vanished Yacht. E. H. Burrage
Vanisher. K. Robeson
Vanishing Act. M. Butterworth
Vanishing Bride. Magali
Vanishing Celebrities. A. Alington
Vanishing Cheques. B. Capes
Vanishing Clue. H. K. McDonnell
Vanishing Corpse. Anthony Gilbert
Vanishing Corpse. E. Queen
Vanishing Death. W. M. Graydon
Vanishing Death. N. Vane
Vanishing Diamond. G. Campbell
Vanishing Diary. J. Rhode
Vanishing Emerald. Nicholas Carter
Vanishing Goddess. P. S. McCoy
Vanishing Gold Truck. H. S. Keeler
Vanishing Hand. E. L. Wilson
Vanishing Heiress. Nicholas Carter
Vanishing Idol. G. F. Gibbs
Vanishing Ladies. R. Marsten
Vanishing Man. R. A. Freeman
Vanishing Men. R. W. Child
Vanishing Men. W. B. M. Ferguson
Vanishing Men. G. M. Winsor
Vanishing Murderer. C. J. Dutton
Vanishing of Betty Varian. C. Wells
Vanishing of Ira Bouck. J. St. David
Vanishing of Tera. F. Hume
Vanishing Point. Coningsby Dawson
Vanishing Point. P. Flower
Vanishing Point. P. Wentworth
Vanishing Professor. F. MacIsaac
Vanishing Senator. J. Philips
Vanishing Shadows. J. Maconechy
Vanishing Smuggler. S. Chalmers
Vanishing Trick. H. Carmichael
Vanishing Vixen. R. B. Sparkia
Vanishing Yacht. E. Anstey
Vanity Box. A. M. Williamson
Vanity Case. C. Wells
Vanity Dies Hard. R. Rendell
Vanity Row. W. R. Burnett
Vanity's Daughter. H. Smart
Vantage Hall. C. Gluyas
Vantage Point. K. Rogers
Vantage Striker. H. Simpson
Vantine Diamonds. Seamark
Varanoff Tradition. O. Panbourne
Vardy. J. Harris
Variation on a Theme of Murder. C. G. Jarvie
Variety. R. Connell
Variety Jack. Old Sleuth
Variety of Weapons. R. King
Varney the Vampire. T. P. Prest
Vase Mystery. V. Loder
Vasiliko Affair. M. Culpan
Vasty Deep. S. C. Cumberland
Vatchman Switch. P. Kinsley
Vatican Cellars. A. Gide
Vatican Swindle. A. Gide
Vatican Target. B. Schiff
Vatican Vendetta. Nick Carter
Vault of Doom. A. Skene
Vaults of Blackarden Castle. A. Gask
Vavel, the Wonderful Treasure Seeker. Old Sleuth
Veetols. Anthony Graham
Vegas. M. Franklin
Vegas Trap. Hal Kantor
Vegas Vampire. J. Sherman
Vegas Vendetta. D. Pendleton
Vegetable Duck. J. Rhode
Veil of Death. R. Simons
Veil of Islam. L. Noel
Veil of Silence. A. Seilaz
Veil of Treachery. D. Daniels
Veil Withdrawn. B. J. Maddux
"Veiled Beauty." Old Sleuth
Veiled Hand. F. Wicks
Veiled Isis. Michael Hastings
Veiled Lady. L. Falk

Veiled Lady. H. Sealis
Vailed Lady. F. Warden
Veiled Lady and The Mystery of the Baghdad Chest. A. Christie
Veiled Man. W. LeQueux
Veiled Murder. Alice Campbell
Veiled Picture. E. J. Lysaght
Veiled Prisoner. G. Leroux
Veiled Vampire. A. Eadie
Veiled Woman. A. Abdullah
Veils of Death. N. Vane
Veils of Fear. G. Mark
Vein of Violence. W. C. Gault
Veins of Compassion. P. Audemars
Veldt Official. B. Mitford
Veldt Vendetta. B. Mitford
Vellum. B. Goldie
Velvet Ape. D. C. Holmes
Velvet Black. R. W. Child
Velvet Claw. A. Dorrington
Velvet Fleece. L. Eby
Velvet Hammer. D. Franklin
Velvet Hand. H. Footner
Velvet Hand. H. Reilly
Velvet Johnnie and other stories. P. Cheyney
Velvet Jungle. D. J. Chiodo
Velvet Lawn. C. Felix
Velvet Mask and other stories. L. Gribble
Velvet Shadows. A. Norton
Velvet Target. G. Holden
Velvet Trap. J. Blackmore
Velvet Vixen. Carter Brown
Velvet Well. J. Gearon
Venables. G. Wagner
Vendetta. J. Boland
Vendetta. H. Carmichael
Vendetta. L. Durbin
Vendetta. J. Gilmore
Vendetta. J. L. Haas
Vendetta. P. McCurtin
Vendetta. N. Quarry
Vendetta! Richard Williams
Vendetta Castle. S. Marino
Vendetta Con Brio. B. De Bilio
Vendetta Contract. J. Messmann
Vendetta for the Saint. L. Charteris
Vendetta in Spain. D. Wheatley
Veneered Scamp. J. Middlemass
Venetian Affair. Helen MacInnes
Venetian Bird. M. Canning
Venetian Blind. W. Haggard
Venetian Blonde. A. S. Fleischman
Venetian Charade. H. York
Venetian Key. A. Upward
Venetian Mask. Colin Robertson
Venetian Portrait. C. Virmonne
Venetian Secret. E. Bond
Venetian Swimmer Mystery. S. G. Hedges
Venetian Vendetta. S. Jason
Venetians. M. E. Braddon
Vengeance. A. Murray
Vengeance. B. Tozer
Vengeance Business. Jim Ryan
Vengeance Due. J. Sandys
Vengeance in the Air. Colin Hope
Vengeance in the Sun. M. Pemberton
Vengeance Is Also Mine. W. Palmer
Vengeance Is Mine. D. Dane
Vengeance Is Mine. Ralph Hayes
Vengeance Is Mine. M. Leighton
Vengeance Is Mine. R. Marlowe
Vengeance Is Mine. J. Middlemass
Vengeance Is Mine. Mark Richards
Vengeance Is Mine! M. Spillane
Vengeance Is Ours. P. Saxon
Vengeance Man. M. Coles
Vengeance Man. D. J. Marlowe
Vengeance of ? J. Wallace
Vengeance of Blue Pete. L. Allan
Vengeance of Five. H. K. McDonnell
Vengeance of Flynn. E. L. Long
Vengeance of Henry Jarroman. Roy Vickers
Vengeance of Hurricane Williams. Gordon Young
Vengeance of Kali. I. Marshall
Vengeance of Larose. A. Gask
Vengeance of Li-Sin. N. Vane
Vengeance of Mrs. Dangers. S. Kyle
Vengeance of Monsieur Blackshirt. D. Graeme
Vengeance of Mortimer Daly. M. Locke
Vengeance of Mynheer Van Lok and other stories. H. D. Stacpoole
Vengeance of Science. J. Dalmaine
Vengeance of Sheevra. O. Williams
Vengeance of the Cat Goddess. J. Stephens
Vengeance of the Golden Hawk. J. Rosenberger
Vengeance of the Ivory Skull. M. Harvey
Vengeance of the Tong. Ben Rogers
Vengeance of Three. W. M. Graydon
Vengeance of Valdone. B. Ferm
Vengeance Pulls the Trigger. S. M. Schley
Vengeance Run. R. Rostand
Vengeance Street. R. Bloomfield
Vengeance Under Law. F. Castle
Vengeance with a Twist and other stories. P. Cheyney

Vengeful Sinner. H. Whittington
Vengeful Virgin. G. Brewer
Venice of the Black Sea. H. Robertson
Venice Plot. R. Rudorff
Venice Preserve Me. J. Appleby
Venice Train. G. Simenon
Venner Crime. J. Rhode
Venom. Johnny Dark
Venom. A. Scholefield
Venom Business. J. Lange
Venom House. A. W. Upfield
Venom in Eden. M. Boniface
Venom in the Cup. G. Joseph
Venom of the Cobra. R. Charles
Ventilated Head. A. Nuttall
Ventriloquist. E. Belasyse
Ventriloquist Detective. Old Sleuth
Venture. J. Cummings
Venture. R. N. Grisewood
Venturers All. L. Gorell
Venturous Lady. G. H. Coxe
Venus Afflicted. F. Mullally
Venus Besieged. E. C. Reed
Venus Death. B. Benson
Venus Died at Dawn. L. H. Hart
Venus Disarmed. J. Dole
Venus Fly-Trap. J. Wainwright
Venus in Plastic. J. Mitchell
Venus Makes Three. H. Janson
Venus on Wheels. M. Dekobra
Venus Probe. David St. John
Venus Trap. J. M. Ullman
Venus Unarmed. Carter Brown
Venus Unarmed. L. Treat
Venus with Pistol. G. Lyall
Vera Gerard Case. J. C. Cooke
Verboten. S. Esmond
Verdict. A. Christie
Verdict. J. B. Lynne
Verdict. L. Martin
Verdict Afterwards. D. Ensor
Verdict in Question. S. Jepson
Verdict of Twelve. R. Postgate
Verdict of You All. Henry Wade
Verdict Suspended. H. Nielsen
Verdict Without Jury. A. Webb
Vermilion. N. Aldyne
Verner's Pride. H. Wood
Veron Mystery. H. C. Bailey
Verona's Father. D. C. Murray
Veronica Died Monday. G. Trotta
Veronica'S Room. I. Levin
Veronique. V. Coffman
Verrall Street Affair. M. E. Cooke
Versus Inspector Maigret. G. Simenon
Versus the Baron. Anthony Morton
Versus the C.I.A. G. De Villiers
Vertigo. P. Boileau
Very Big Bang. P. McCutchan
Very Black Deed. W. Manson
Very Breath of Hell. G. Beare
Very Cagey Lady. J. Elbert
Very Cold for May. W. P. McGivern
Very Dead of Winter. S. Nichols
Very Deadly Game. V. B. Miller
Very Dry with a Twist. D. Banko
Very Fall of the Sun. S. Hazo
Very First Lady. S. Dunleavy
Very Good Hater. R. Hill
Very Long Odds and A Strange Finish. C. Rae-Brown
Very Ordinary Murder. A. Sewart
Very Private Island. Z. Z. Smith
Very Private Secretary. B. Reynolds
Very Queer Business, and other stories. W. Westall
Very Quiet Murder. F. Crane
Very Quiet Place. A. Garve
Very Rough Diamond. F. Warden
Very Special Agent. G. Napier
Very Thin Line. M. Borgenicht
Very Welcome Death. D. L. Mathews
Very Wicked. Clifton Adams
Very Wicked. N. Hudson
Very Young Couple. B. L. Farjeon
Vesey Inheritance. Gwendoline Butler
Vesper Bells. B. H. Hyatt
Vesper Service Murders. V. W. Mason
Vespucci Papers. B. Healey
Vessel May Carry Explosives. S. Harvester
Vestibule Limited Mystery. M. Manly
Vestibule Limited Mystery. A. Robertson
Vestry Murder. T. A. Plummer
Vet It Was That Died. M. Silverman
Veterans. Eric Lambert
Via Berlin. C. Marriott
Viaduct Murder. R. A. Knox
Vial of Death. Nicholas Carter
Vial with the White Powder. J. B. Williams
Vibart Affair. G. M. Fenn
Vicar. J. Hatton
Vicar in Hell. A. Melville
Vicar of Moura. V. Coffman
Vicar's Experiments. A. Rolls
Vicar's People. G. M. Fenn
Vicar's Secret. C. E. Jeffery
Vice and Its Victim. T. P. Prest
Vice City. B. Sarto
Vice Cop. R. Deming
Vice Cop. M. Reed

Title Index

Vice Czar Murders. F. Charles
Vice Isn't Private. B. Cleeve
Vice Merchants. R. McCary
Vice Net. M. Carey
Vice Squad. H. Spencer
Vice Squad. J. Van Raalte
Vice Squad. L. T. White
Vice Squad Cop. M. Carey
Vice Town. E. Willie
Vice Trap. E. Gilbert
Vice Volcano. B. Sarto
Viceroy's Protege. G. Boothby
Vicious Breed. B. Sarto
Vicious Circle. A. Evans
Vicious Circle. Manning Long
Vicious Circles. Anthony Stuart
Vicious Circuit. C. G. Jarvie
Vicious Circuit. J. Langdon
Vicious Pattern. M. V. Heberden
Vicious Virtuoso. L. Lombard
Vicky Van. C. Wells
Victim. Josephine Bell
Victim! Carter Brown
Victim. W. Drummond
Victim. T. Journet
Victim. D. Winston
Victim Died Twice. H. Liggett
Victim for Hire. P. Morales
Victim Must Be Found. A. Hocking
Victim Needs a Nurse. J. Redfern
Victim of Black Magic. G. H. Teed
Victim of Circumstances. Nicholas Carter
Victim of Circumstances. M. Underwood
Victim of Deceit. Nicholas Carter
Victim of Fashion. H. M. Jones
Victim of His Clothes. H. Fielding
Victim of Love. N. Buckingham
Victim of Rape. Eddie Stone
Victim of the Aurora. T. Keneally
Victim of the Combine. G. Chester
Victim of the Crooked Hypnotist. J. Hunter
Victim of the Cult. W. Jardine
Victim of the Devil's Bowl. R. Hardinge
Victim of the Gang. G. H. Teed
Victim of the Girl Spy. M. B. Dix
Victim of the Occult. I. Stark
Victim of the Red Mask. S. Hope
Victim of the Secret Service. J. G. Brandon
Victim of the Thieves' Den. J. G. Brandon
Victim of the Waterway. G. N. Philips
Victim of Villainy. F. L. Broughton
Victim Unknown. D. Reid
Victim Was Important. J. Rayter
Victims. P. Boileau
Victims. T. Gift
Victims. B. M. Gill
Victims. James Grant
Victims. E. McCabe
Victims. A. Maimane
Victims. J. Pearl
Victims. J. Rossiter
Victim's Niece. B. Hector
Victims of Circumstance. P. Conway
Victims of Devil's Alley. P. Urquhart
Victims of the Devil's Triangle. D. Sawn
Victims of Villainy. Andrew Murray
Victims Unknown. R. Clapperton
Victor. D. Kirby
Victor and Vanquished. M. C. Hay
Victor Maury, the French Detective. G. Reynolds
Victor Versus Verhasst. D. Kirby
Victoria. R. Gadney
Victoria Grandolet. H. Bellamann
Victoria Pruitt Comes to Town. R. G. Cochran
Victoria Winters. Marilyn Ross
Victorian Album. E. Berckman
Victorian Crown. E. Noone
Victoria's House. F. Carmichael
Victorine. F. P. Keyes
Victors. J. Harris
Victor's Spoils. I. Stark
Victory Murders. F. Johns
Victory Song. H. Adams
Vidocq of New York. C. Fulton
Vidocq, the Police Spy. Vidocq
Vienna Elephant. E. Leather
Vienna Pursuit. A. Goddard
Vienna Summer. N. Buckingham
Viennese Love. H. Bettauer
View from Chickweed's Window. J. Vance
View from Daniel Pike. B. Knox
View from the Terrace. L. Meynell
View of the Mountain. G. Greenaway
View to a Death. Kenneth O'Hara
Viewless Winds. M. C. Morgan
Vigorous Daunt, Billionaire. A. Pratt
Viking Feast Mystery. L. A. Knight
Viking Process. N. Hartley
Viking's Skull. J. R. Carling
Villa Aurelia. B. E. Stevenson
Villa Caprice. Irene Alexander
Villa Fountains. V. Coffman
Villa Jane. J. Laing
Villa Mimosa. J. Tickell
Villa Mystery. H. Flowerdew
Villa Nova. C. Selden
Villa of Shadows. C. Farr

Villa of the Scorpions. E. Follett
Villa on the Shore. M. Butterworth
Villa Petroff. D. Whitelaw
Villa Rossignol. M. L. Storer
Village Affairs. R. Armfelt
Village Afraid. M. Burton
Village Blacksmith. D. Dale
Village Called Death. P. Motte
Village East. R. Chambers
Village Gentleman, and The Attorney at Law. A. Duncombe
Village Mystery. Mrs. C. Kernahan
Village Mystery. Benjamin F. Mason
Village Never Knew. B. Goldie
Village of Fear. F. Cowen
Village of Fear. M. Jenson
Village of Fear. Donald Stuart
Village of Rogues. J. Sturrock
Village of Stars. P. Stanton
Village Policeman. I. Niall
Village Pub Murders. F. Krull
Village Scandal. H. M. Jones
Village Tale. N. Kennedy
Village Temptress. F. Whishaw
Villain and the Virgin. J. H. Chase
Villain of the Piece. Graham Fisher
Villainous Company. R. Fenisong
Villainous Saltpetre. C. Witting
Villainous Scheme. Nicholas Carter
Villains. C. Keppel
Villains. J. Rossiter
Villains Galore. G. Bell
Villain's Tale. G. F. Newman
Villain's Work. Dick Stewart
Villainy. G. Bettany
Villainy at Vespers. J. Cockin
Villiers Touch. B. Garfield
Vindicator. J. J. Dalton
Vindicator. E. P. Oppenheim
Vinegar—and Cream. H. T. W. Bousfield
Vines of Yarrabee. D. Eden
Vineyard Chapel. D. Daniels
Vintage Murder. N. Marsh
Vintage So Evil. M. Vinter
Vintage Stuff. A. Brede
Violante. G. R. Preedy
Viola's Dilemma. T. S. King
Violated One. J. Hanley
Violator. H. Kane
Violator. John Warwick
Violence. C. Woolrich
Violence in Paradise. D. Buttenshaw
Violence in Quiet Places. J. T. Story
Violence in Velvet. M. Avallone
Violence Is Golden. B. Halliday
Violence Is Golden. C. H. Thames
Violence Is My Business. S. Marlowe
Violence of Hate. H. P. Lees
Violent Air. C. Renn
Violent Breed. S. A. Curtis
Violent Brink. A. Beevor
Violent Brothers. E. Bruton
Violent City. J. Hawkins
Violent Dark. L. Gribble
Violent Dawn. C. Rudd
Violent Death. Roy Lewis
Violent Death. W. Sproule
Violent Death of a Bitter Englishman. B. Cleeve
Violent End. V. Kathrens
Violent Ends. G. Simenon
Violent Enemy. H. Marlowe
Violent Flame. F. T. Jane
Violent Holiday. R. Wilkes-Hunter
Violent Hours. F. Castle
Violent Hours. P. Saxon
Violent Hours. R. Walsh
Violent Keepsake. L. Grex
Violent Lady. M. E. Knerr
Violent Night. Whit Harrison
Violent Night. R. Jackson
Violent Ones. Howard Hunt
Violent Ones. P. Saxon
Violent Saturday. W. L. Heath
Violent Security. G. Burnett
Violent World of Hugh Greene. Colin Wilson
Violent World of Michael Shayne. B. Halliday
Violet Forster's Lover. R. Marsh
Viper. H. Footner
Viper. L. Pryor
Viper in Her Bosom. P. Muller
Viper of Luxor. G. Seton
Viper Three. W. Wager
Viper's Bite. J. D. Fitz
Viper's Brood. B. Sarto
Viper's Game. R. Rostand
Viper's Sting. H. Desmond
Viper's Vengeance. R. Trevor
Viper's Vengeance. B. E. M. Ward
Virgin Cay. B. Heatter
Virgin Collector. D. Ambler
Virgin Fortress. M. Pemberton
Virgin Heiresses. E. Queen
Virgin Huntress. E. S. Holding
Virgin in Flames. S. Rohmer
Virgin Kills. R. Whitfield
Virgin Luck. L. Meynell
Virgin Widow. A. Matthey
Virginia. C. Dawe
Virginia. K. Lindsay

Virginia and Magdalene. E. Southworth
Virginia Box and the "Unsatisfied". J. Moffatt
Virginia's Quest. M. Caywood
Virginia's Quest. J. Templeton
Virginia's Thing. H. Woodfin
Virgins Die Lonely. N. Perrelli
Virgin's Vendetta. N. Perrelli
Virility Factor. H. Kane
Virtues of Hell. P. Boulle
Virtuous Vamp. J. S. Clouston
Virus X. S. Horler
Visa for Violence. M. Risco
Visa to Death. E. Lacy
Visa to Limbo. W. Haggard
Viscount Lacklands. A. Griffiths
Visibility Nil. P. Conde
Visibility Nil. M. Elgin
Visible and Invisible. E. F. Benson
Vision. D. R. Koontz
Vision of Beauty. J. Hatton
Vision of Murder. J. M. Brillant
Vision of the Foam. J. MacEnery
Vision Sinister. N. Karta
Visions of Esmares. Elna Stone
Visions of Heydrich. P. Everett
Visit from a Broad. H. Janson
Visitation. R. Amare
Visiting Villain. C. Wells
Visitor. J. Cunningham
Visitor. Anthony Gilbert
Visitor. Maureen Lee
Visitor. C. Randau
Visitor. K. White
Visitors for Venning. C. Ryland
Vital Statistics. T. Chastain
Vitriol Thrower. F. Du Boisgobey
Viva McHugh. J. Flynn
Vivanti. S. Horler
Vivanti Returns. S. Horler
Vivero Letter. D. Bagley
Vivia. E. Southworth
Vivian Morgan's First Case. F. Curtis
Vivienne—Gently Where She Lay. A. Hunter
Vivier of Vivier, Longman & Company, Bankers. W. C. Hudson
Vixen. M. E. Braddon
Vixen. Carter Brown
Vixen. L. Fitzhamon
Vixen 03. C. Cussler
Vodka on Ice. H. McLeave
Voice. Anthony Gilbert
Voice at Johnnywater. B. M. Bower
Voice from the Cell. A. MacKenzie
Voice from the Dark. E. Phillpotts
Voice from the Dead. B. Copper
Voice from the Grave. D. M. Disney
Voice from the Grave. Clarissa Ross
Voice from the Grave. Clifton Yorke
Voice from the Living. M. Lovell
Voice from the Night. C. E. Sterrey
Voice from the Past. Nicholas Carter
Voice from the Void. W. LeQueux
Voice from Yesterday. F. Crisp
Voice in the Closet. Herman Landon
Voice in the Dark. C. Lorrimer
Voice in the Darkness. P. Bennetts
Voice in the Fog. H. MacGrath
Voice Like Velvet. D. H. Landels
Voice of Air. E. Berckman
Voice of Armageddon. D. Lippincott
Voice of Bethia. T. Cobb
Voice of Murder. M. Erskine
Voice of the Charmer. L. T. Meade
Voice of the City. O. Henry
Voice of the Corpse. Max Murray
Voice of the Crab. G. Halls
Voice of the Dolls. D. Eden
Voice of the House. M. Erskine
Voice of the Lobster. R. J. Casey
Voice of the Murderer. G. Walsh
Voice of the Night. B. Coffey
Voice of the Peacock. E. Salter
Voice of the Seven Sparrows. H. S. Keeler
Voice of Vice. R. Angel
Voice on the Telephone. Mildred Davis
Voice on the Wind. D. Daniels
Voice on the Wire. E. H. Ball
Voice out of Darkness. U. Curtiss
Voices out of Time. Deborah Lewis
Voiceless Ones. J. Creasey
Voiceless Victims. G. Thorne
Voices. G. J. Brenn
Voices from the Bottom of the World. T. M. Walker
Voices in an Empty House. Joan Aiken
Voices in an Empty Room. P. Loraine
Voices in the Fog. K. Cameron
Voices in the Wind. E. V. Allen
Voices Long Hushed. B. A. Pauley
Voices of Doom. B. Copper
Voices of Terror. C. Virmonne
Voices of the Storm. J. Sandys
Volcano. K. Hayles
Volcano Island. A. Wood
Volcanoes Above Us. N. Lewis
Volcanoes of San Domingo. Adam Hall
Voluptuaries. B. E. Ullman
Von Eyssen Deception. R. Hirschhorn
Von Stahmer Jigsaw. P. Lovegrove

622 / Voodoo — Title Index

Voodoo. J. Esteven
Voodoo Death. M. Grant
Voodoo Die. R. Sapir
Voodoo Drum. P. Saxon
Voodoo Drums. V. Leigh
Voodoo Drums. E. Wilmot
Voodoo Goat. A. Gaines
Voodoo Island. G. H. Teed
Voodoo Murders. M. Avallone
Voodoo Violence. H. Janson
Voodoo'd. K. Perkins
Vorovich Affair. S. L. Stebel
Vortex. J. Cleary
Vortex. F. Whishaw
Vote Against Poison. J. Sherwood
Vote for Death. N. Longmate
Vote for Murder. Richard Martin
Vote for the Toff. J. Creasey
Vote for Violence. G. Johns
Vote to Kill. D. Hurd
Vote X for Treason. B. Cleeve
Vow. P. Trent
Vow of Love. F. Y. McHugh
Vow of Vengeance. A. Carlyle
Voyage Home. Alan Graham
Voyage into Nowhere. J. Wood
Voyage into Peril. Seatarer
Voyage into Violence. F. Lockridge
Voyage of Death. M. Cruz
Voyage of Fear. R. Hardinge
Voyage of the "San Marcos". M. Hastings
Voyage of the Secret Duchess. F. Hurd
Voyage with Murder. J. York
Voyeur. A. Robbe-Grillet
Vrouw Grobelaar and Her Leading Cases. P. Gibbon
Vrouw Grobelaar's Leading Cases. P. Gibbon
Vulcan Bulletins. S. Gulliver
Vulcan Disaster. Nick Carter
Vulcan's Hammer. D. Da Cruz
Vulnerable. D. Collins
Vulture. J. Carrick
Vulture. C. Heath
Vulture. G. Scott-Heron
Vulture. Harold Ward
Vulture in the Sun. J. Bingham
Vulture Is a Patient Bird. J. H. Chase
"Vulture" Strikes. Harold Ward
Vultures Gather. A. Hocking
Vultures in the Sky. T. Downing
Vultures in the Smoke. P. A. Foxall
Vultures, Ltd. B. Gray
Vultures of Desolate Island. G. E. Rochester
Vultures of Erin. N. J. Dunn
Vultures of the Dark. R. E. Enright
Vultures of the Sky. P. Conde
Vultures of the White Death. R. J. Hogan
Vulture's Prey. T. De Saix
Vye Murder. I. Wray
Vyvyans. Andree Hope

W.H.O.R.E. Carter Brown
W.I.L. One to Curtis. P. Loraine
WO7. M. Drake
W.l. P. McGuire
W Plan. G. Seton
Waddington Cipher. W. A. Johnston
Wade House. F. Hurd
Wade Inheritance. L. V. Brown
Wager. Ladbroke Black
Wager. R. L. Fish
Wager, and The House at Fernwood. F. Oursler
Wager for Love. Rachelle Edwards
Wages of Fear. G. Arnaud
Wages of Peril. J. Bechdolt
Wages of Rascality. Nicholas Carter
Wages of Sin. M. E. Braddon
Wages of Sin. E. Yates
Wages of Zen. James Melville
Wagoner's Halt Mystery. M. Poole
Waif of the River. J. Farnol
Waifs and Strays. O. Henry
Waifs of Circumstance. L. Tracy
Waikiki Widow. J. Sheridan
Wail for the Corpses. L. Treat
Wailing Frail. R. S. Prather
Wailing Rock Murders. C. Orr
Wailing Woman. D. Shattuck
Wait. E. Berckman
Wait for Death. G. Ashe
Wait for Death. J. Veitch
Wait for It, Pal. A. Bocca
Wait for Me, Wendy. J. Marie
Wait for the Corpse. Max Murray
Wait for the Dawn. M. Albrand
Wait for the Wake. M. Carr
Wait for the Wedding. C. Fremlin
Wait for What Will Come. B. Michaels
Wait, Just You Wait. E. Berckman
Wait Long, Wait Still. M. M. Thomas
Wait Until Dark. F. Knott
Wait Until Midnight. V. Pittinger
Wait Until the Evening. H. Bennett
Waiting. Mary Napier

Waiting Darkness. W. D. Roberts
Waiting Eyes. E. Bond
Waiting for a Tiger. B. Healey
Waiting for Caroline. A. McAllister
Waiting for Nothing. T. Kromer
Waiting for Oliver. S. Troy
Waiting for the News. L. Litwak
Waiting for the Police and other stories. J. J. Farjeon
Waiting for Thursday. H. Jobson
Waiting for Willa. D. Eden
Waiting Game. M. Powell
Waiting Game. P. Wayland
Waiting in the Shadows. Marilyn Ross
Waiting Race. E. Yates
Waiting Room Mystery. A. Blair
Waiting Sands. S. Howatch
Waiting to Hear from William. B. H. Deal
Wake All the Dead. S. Kilpatrick
Wake for a Lady. H. W. Roden
Wake for Mourning. Shane Martin
Wake in Fright. K. Cook
Wake of a Lawyer. A. Holmes
Wake of the Icarus. N. Benchley
Wake of the Setting Sun. W. A. Stowell
Wake the Sleeping Wolf. R. Foley
Wake the Sleeping Wolf. T. McCoy
Wake Up and Scream. M. K. Ozaki
Wake Up Dead. W. Wall
Wake Up Screaming! A. Kent
Wake Up to Murder. D. Keene
Wake Up with a Stranger. F. Flora
Wakefield Witches. D. Winston
Walbury Case. A. Hilliers
Walde-Warren. Emerson Bennett
Waldo. L. Kauffmann
Walk a Black Wind. Michael Collins
Walk a Crooked Mile. R. Deming
Walk a Crooked Mile. R. P. Hansen
Walk a Crooked Mile. J. Philips
Walk a Crooked Mile. S. Truss
Walk a Tightrope. J. Ellis
Walk Around the Square. D. Winston
Walk at a Steady Pace. N. Fisher
Walk at Night. D. Craig
Walk-In. V. Scott
Walk in Dead Man's Wood. J. S. Scott
Walk In, Death. P. Malloch
Walk in Fear. W. H. Baker
Walk in Fear. W. T. Ballard
Walk in Shadow. J. Fast
Walk in the Dark. C. Phillips
Walk in the Dark. J. Roffman
Walk in the Jungle. G. Canary
Walk in the Paradise Garden. A. Maybury
Walk in the Shadows. R. Dolphin
Walk into Darkness. J. Ellis
Walk into Murder. P. Helm
Walk into My Parlour. D. Eden
Walk into My Parlour. A. Hocking
Walk into My Parlour. Rona Randall
Walk into Yesterday. Mildred Davis
Walk of the Devil. M. Kane
Walk on the Blind Side. J. T. MacCargo
Walk out on Death. C. Armstrong
Walk Softly. W. Sproule
Walk Softly in Fear. M. Butterworth
Walk Softly, Men Praying. O. Wynd
Walk Softly, Walk Deadly. L. Bergman
Walk Softly Witch! Carter Brown
Walk Softly, Witch. Carter Brown
Walk the Bloody Boulevard. A. A. Marcus
Walk the Dark Bridge. W. O'Farrell
Walk the Dark Streets. W. Krasner
Walk the Night Unseen. Lucinda Baker
Walk to the River. W. Hoffman
Walk to Your Grave. N. M. Newland
Walk with Care. P. Wentworth
Walk with Evil. R. Wilder
Walk with Me into Darkness. J. McKelvey
Walker in Shadows. B. Michaels
Walker of the Secret Service. M. D. Post
Walking Corpse. G. D. H. Cole
Walking Dead. P. Dickinson
Walking Dead. M. Hervey
Walking Dead Man. H. Pentecost
Walking Shadow. L. G. Offord
Walking Shadow. J. Pattinson
Walking Shadow. J. M. Walsh
Walking Shadows. M. Gelien
Walking Stick. Winston Graham
Walking Tall. D. Warren
Walking Tall: Part 2. Webster Carey
Walking the Dusk. L. J. Webb
Walking Trip. H. Buckmaster
Walking Wind. F. M. Proud
Walking Wounded. J. Laffin
Walking Wounded. R. S. Stokes
Wall. M. R. Rinehart
Wall in the Long Dark Night. O. Wynd
Wall of Eyes. M. Millar
Wall of Jeopardy. W. Spann
Wall of Masks. B. Coffey
Wall of Men. W. Rollins
Wall Street and the Woods. W. J. Flagg
Wall Street Haul. Anonymous
Wall Street Haul. Nicholas Carter
Wall Street Murders. D. M. Hoffecker
Wall Street Swindlers. J. Sharp
Wall Street Wonder. D. J. MacKenzie
Wallace at Bay. A. Wilson

Wallace Intervenes. A. Wilson
Wallace of the Secret Service. A. Wilson
Walled Parrot. J. Weston
Wallingford. E. C. Savidge
Wallingford and Blackie Daw. G. R. Chester
Wallingford in His Prime. G. R. Chester
Walls Are High. J. Van Raalte
Walls Came Tumbling Down. B. H. Deal
Walls Came Tumbling Down. J. Eisinger
Walls of Silence. D. Hawkins
Walnut Door. J. Hersey
Walt Wheeler, the Scout Detective. H. Rockwood
Walter Duerell. Anonymous
Walter Syndrome. R. Neely
Walter's Word. J. Payn
Walther P.38. J. Wainwright
Walton Mystery. L. Reynolds
Waltz Across Texas. M. Crawford
Waltz in Scarlet. Muriel Bradley
Waltz into Darkness. W. Irish
Waltz of Death. P. B. Maxon
Waltz of My Heart. M. Richmond
Wandering Dogies. W. C. Tuttle
Wandering Knife. M. R. Rinehart
Wandering Romanoff. B. Kennedy
Wandering Spirit. Anonymous
Wandering Widows. E. Ferrars
Wanderings of Asaf. Afghan
Want to Stay Alive? J. H. Chase
Wanted! C. Dawe
Wanted! D. Donovan
Wanted. W. M. Graydon
Wanted: A Clew. Nicholas Carter
Wanted: A Fool. P. E. Curtiss
Wanted: A Murderess. M. Holbrook
Wanted at His Office. Leonard Cooper
Wanted by the Gestapo. A. O. Pollard
Wanted by the Police. O. Harper
Wanted by Two Clients. Nicholas Carter
Wanted: Danny Fontaine. W. Ard
Wanted: Dead Men. M. E. Chaber
Wanted: Dead or Alive. M. Hervey
Wanted Dead or Alive! M. Leinster
Wanted for Killing. J. Welcome
Wanted for Murder. L. Charteris
Wanted for Murder. R. Gilmour
Wanted for Murder. H. Holt
Wanted for Murder. N. Rutledge
Wanted for Questioning. Mark Cross
Wanted for Questioning. W. McNeilly
Wanted Man. H. Cecil
Wanted—One Body! R. Dyer
Wanted: Someone Innocent. M. Allingham
Wanting Factor. G. DeWeese
Wanton. Carter Brown
Wanton City. O. M. Hall
Wanton for Murder. H. Klinger
Wanton Fury. J. A. Broom
Wanton Princess. D. Wheatley
Wanton Venus. M. Leblanc
Wantons Die Hard. L. Gribble
Wapping Butt. L. Blake
War Against Charity Ross. J. Bickham
War Against the Mafia. D. Pendleton
War Cache. D. Newton
War Dog Stirs. H. Hastings
War from the Clouds. Nick Carter
War Game. A. Price
War in the Gates. L. A. B. Cooke
War Maker. A. Hillgarth
War of Brains. Nicholas Carter
War of Nerves. P. Brickhill
War of Nerves. Robert Graham
War of Nerves. R. Starko
War of the Dons. P. Rabe
War of the Running Fox. B. Langley
War Runners. W. McNeilly
War Story. G. McGill
War Terror. A. B. Reeve
Ward of Navarre. M. Gerard
Warden of the North. L. C. Douthwaite
Wardour Street Mystery. R. Dark
Ware Case. G. Pleydell
'Ware Danger. G. Ashe
'Ware Wolf. E. L. Forester
Warehouse Murder. Davies
Warlock. J. M. Flynn
Warlock. M. Olden
Warlock. W. Tucker
Warlock's Daughter. Angela Gray
Warlock's Woman. J. De Pre
Warlords. B. Langley
Warm and Golden War. N. Luard
Warmaster. P. McCutchan
Warn That Man! V. Sylvaine
Warn the Baron. Anthony Morton
Warned Off. J. Fairfax-Blakeborough
Warned Off. N. Gould
Warned Off! J. Hunter
Warned Off. R. S. Sievier
Warning Bell. S. Ransome
Warning Bell. Grace M. White
Warning Shot. W. Masterson
Warning to Critics. A. Melville
Warped in the Making. H. Ashton-Wolfe
Warrant for a Wanton. M. Gillian
Warrant for Arrest. F. Didelot
Warrant for X. P. MacDonald
Warrant No. 113. E. Gaboriau
Warrielaw Jewel. W. Peck

Title Index

Warring Sky. P. Saxon
Warrior's Playtime. G. Hackforth-Jones
Wars Within Wars. Sheila Ross
Warsaw Document. Adam Hall
Warwick. M. T. Walworth
Wary Transgressor. Raymond Marshall
Was Ever Woman in This Humor Wooed? C. Gibbon
Was He Guilty? E. A. Dupuy
Was He Severe? H. Wood
Was It a Ghost? Anonymous
Was It Montelli? L. Cargill
Was It Murder? F. Du Boisgobey
Was It Murder? G. Trevor
Was It Murder? J. H. Waring
Was Murder Done? S. Fowler
Was She Justified? F. Barrett
Was She Poison? D. Linton
Was She Worth It? M. Leighton
Was the Mayor Murdered? T. A. Plummer
Was This Murder? B. Stoner
Washermen. Peter Hill
Washington IOU. D. Pendleton
Washington Legation Murders. V. W. Mason
Washington Never Slept Here. L. Greth
Washington Payoff. Gordon Davis
Washington Square Enigma. H. S. Keeler
Washington Whispers Murder. L. Ford
Washington Woman. D. Varnado
Wasp. J. Cleft-Addams
Wasp. U. Curtiss
Wasp in the Web. R. B. Amos
Wasp's Nest. A. Matthews
Waste Lands. C. Dawe
Wasted Crime. D. C. Murray
Wasted Fires. H. Nisbet
Wasted Pride. P. Nottingham
Wastrel Goes West. J. Street
Watch Across the Channel. M. McKenna
Watch Below. Taffrail
Watch Dog. A. Hornblow
Watch It, Dr. Adrian
Watch McLean. G. Goodchild
Watch Mr. Moh. J. Cowdroy
Watch of Evil. P. Le Bailly
Watch on the Bridge. D. Garth
Watch on the Wall. H. Burnett
Watch Sinister. M. Blizard
Watch the Wall, My Darling. J. A. Hodge
Watch Your Step. G. M. Savage
Watchdogs of Abaddon. I. Melchior
Watched Out. E. A. Clancy
Watcher. D. Hitchens
Watcher. K. N. Smith
Watcher. G. Verner
Watcher. C. Wilcox
Watcher and other weird stories. J. S. Le Fanu
Watcher at the Door. G. H. Hall
Watcher by the Threshold. J. Buchan
Watcher in the Dark. D. Daniels
Watcher in the Shadows. G. Household
Watcher in the Wood. M. G. Kiddy
Watcher on the Shore. I. Lambot
Watchers. A. E. W. Mason
Watchers. W. D. Roberts
Watchers. V. Siller
Watchers in the Hills. W. R. Foran
Watchers of the Dark. L. Biggle
Watchers of the Plains. R. Cullum
Watches of the Night. G. R. Sims
Watchful at Night. J. Fast
Watching Brief. J. Pattinson
Watching Eye. Alicen White
Watchmaker. G. Simenon
Watchmaker of Everton. G. Simenon
Watchman. D. Grubb
Watchman's Stone. Rona Randall
Water for the Fire. J. Fores
Water Horse. Genevieve Scott
Water on the Brain. C. MacKenzie
Water Trail. J. Stark
Water Weed. Alice Campbell
Water Witch. R. Thorndike
Waterfront. F. Findley
Waterfront Cop. W. P. McGivern
Watering Places of Good Peace. G. Jenkins
Waterloo. F. E. Smith
Waterman. Eric Lambert
Watermead Affair. R. Barr
Waters of Centarus. R. G. Brown
Waters of Death. I. A. Greenfield
Waters of Madness. W. A. Ballinger
Waters of Sadness. J. Cassells
Waters of the North. L. C. Douthwaite
Watershed. N. Tranter
Watersplash. P. Wentworth
Watertown Mystery. H. Rockwood
Waterview Manor. E. Welles
Watson's Choice. G. Mitchell
Watson's Revenge. M. Mallett
Wave Hangs Dark. A. Dipper
Wave. Christopher Hyde
Wave of Fatalities. M. Delving
Waves Behind the Boat. Francis King
Wax. Ethel L. White
Wax Apple. T. Coe
Wax Flowers for Gloria. P. Flower
Waxwork. P. Lovesey
Waxworks Murder. J. D. Carr
Waxworks Spies. H. C. Davis

'Way Loft. E. L. Long
Way Back. J. Mitchell
Way Beyond. J. Farnol
Way of a Maid. C. Dawe
Way of a Wanton. R. S. Prather
Way of an Eagle. D. Potter
Way of Deception. L. Beresford
Way of Escape. C. Stanton
Way of Sinners. M. Leighton
Way of the Cardines. S. P. Hyatt
Way of the Four. Mark Cross
Way of the North. J. B. Hendryx
Way of the Strong. R. Cullum
Way of the Tamarisk. V. Maxwell
Way of the Weasel. J. Mowbray
Way of the Wicked. Nicholas Carter
Way of the Wicked. W. Woolfolk
Way of the World. W. T. Adams
Way of the World. D. C. Murray
Way of These Women. E. P. Oppenheim
Way Out. B. Graeme
Way Out Wanton. H. Janson
Way Some People Die. J. R. Macdonald
Way the Cookie Crumbles. J. H. Chase
Way Through the Wood. N. Balchin
Way to Adventure, and two other stories. J. G. Dunbar
Way to Dusty Death. Alistair MacLean
Way to Go, Doll Baby! W. R. Cox
Way to Gold. W. D. Steele
Way to Nowhere. M. McShane
Way to the Old Sailor's Home. T. Baird
Way to Win. W. LeQueux
Way We Die Now. M. Z. Lewin
Way We Love. S. Friedman
Waylaid by Wireless. E. Balmer
Waylaid in Boston. Elliot Paul
Wayland of the Guides. B. Bolt
Wayland 13. F. Shroyer
Ways and Means. H. Cecil
Ways of Death. Hans C. Owen
Ways of Men. H. Flowerdew
Ways of the Hour. J. F. Cooper
Ways of the Millionaire. O. Crawford
Ways That Are Wary. L. De Bra
Wayward. Carter Brown
Wayward Angel. V. Chute
Wayward Blonde. M. Corrigan
Wayward Blonde. J. Creighton
Wayward Girl. B. Reynolds
Wayward Girl's Fate. Hawkshaw
Wayward Heart. J. MacKenzie
Wayward Madonna. V. Black
Wayward Nymph. C. H. Barker
Wayward Season. V. S. Gunn
Wayward Wahine. Carter Brown
Wayward Widow. W. C. Gault
Wayward Woman. A. Griffiths
We All Killed Grandma. F. Brown
We Always Treat Women Too Well. R. Queneau
We Are for the Dark. D. Eden
We Died in Bond Street. J. Ward
We Don't Want to Lose You. V. Bridges
We Have Always Lived in the Castle. S. Jackson
We Have Always Lived in the Castle. H. C. Wheeler
We Haven't Seen Her Lately. E. Ferrars
We Must Have a Trial. M. Leek
We Must Kill Toni. I. S. Black
We Never Die in the Winter. A. Manning
We Saw Him Die. A. M. Stein
We Shall See. E. Wallace
We Shot an Arrow. G. Goodchild
We, the Accused. E. Raymond
We the Condemned. N. Karta
We, the Condemned. J. Robb
We, the Killers. Michael Brett
We the Unworthy. J. Courage
We Walk with Death. H. Desmond
We Who Survived. S. Noel
We Will Meet Again. J. Hawkins
Weak and the Strong. A. Kent
Weak-Eyed Bat. M. Millar
Weak-Kneed Rogue. Nicholas Carter
Weaker Vessel. D. C. Murray
Wealth Seeker. M. Grant
Weapon. J. Howell
Weapon Heavy. E. Reese
Weapon of Night. Nicholas Carter
Weapons of Mystery. J. Hocking
Wear the Butcher's Medal. J. Brunner
Weasel Hunt. J. K. McDougall
Weather of My Fate. P. Conway
Weather War. L. Leokum
Weathercock. E. H. Clements
Weatherel Affair. J. W. De Forrest
Weatherman Guy. J. Burmeister
Weave a Rope of Sand. E. Trevor
Weave a Wicked Web. P. Kruger
Weaver Webb. Old Sleuth
Weavers. A. Askew
Weavers and Weft, and other tales. M. E. Braddon
Weaving the Web. Nicholas Carter
Weaving the Web. H. Mee
Web. Rolf Bennett
Web. H. Brooke
Web. C. Gibson-Jarvie
Web. F. T. Hill
Web. S. Horler

Web. F. A. Kummer
Web. M. Mallay
Web. F. Urquhart
Web in Childhood. Winifred Duke
Web of Allyngrood. F. Chimenti
Web of Deceit. C. A. Smith
Web of Deception. F. Chimenti
Web of Destiny. Seamark
Web of Enchantment. M. Richmond
Web of Evil. Joselyn Chadwick
Web of Evil. L. Emerick
Web of Fate. T. W. Speight
Web of Fear. L. Linares
Web of Fear. M. Reisner
Web of Guilt. J. DeWeese
Web of Hate. L. Thayer
Web of Horror. C. Farr
Web of Love. W. E. D. Ross
Web of Murder. Seamark
Web of Murder. J. Troy
Web of Murder. J. Westerham
Web of Murder. H. Whittington
Web of Obsession. Andrea Hill
Web of Peril. D. Daniels
Web of Salvage. B. Callison
Web of Shadows. E. Backhouse
Web of Silence. J. Wainwright
Web of Spies. Nick Carter
Web of the Spider. H. B. M. Watson
Web of Wan Li. L. Beresford
Web to Catch a Spider. C. Joyce
Webs in the Way. G. M. Fenn
Wed for Wealth. A. Wood
Wedded But Not a Wife. F. Warden
Wedderburn's Will. T. Cobb
Wedding Bargain. A. S. Turnbull
Wedding-Chest Mystery. A. Fielding
Wedding Day. C. N. Williamson
Wedding Eve Murder. B. M. Dix
Wedding Guest Sat on a Stone. R. Shattuck
Wedding Journey. M. Eatock
Wedding March Murder. Monte Barrett
Wedding Night Murder. C. Bush
Wedding Ring. H. M. Jones
Wednesday at Noon. J. Corbett
Wednesday Midnight. P. S. McCoy
Wednesday the Rabbi Got Wet. H. Kemelman
Wednesday the Tenth. G. Allen
Wednesday's Wrath. D. Pendleton
Weed. C. L. Cooper
Weed. J. Pattinson
Weeds. H. Imbert-Terry
Weeds of Hate. O. Binns
Week by the Sea. Elizabeth Ford
Week-End at Green Trees. M. Meynell
Week-End at Thrackley. A. Melville
Week-End Crime Book. J. M. Walsh
Week-End Murder. N. Brady
Week-End Murders. A. A. Archer
Week-End with Death. Hilary Gray
Week-Ends for Harry. H. Holland
Week of Love. J. Leasor
Week of Passion. Edward Jenkins
Week of Suspense. G. Greenaway
Week of Suspense. A. MacKenzie
Week of the Succubus. T. R. Austin
Week to Kill. D. Delman
Weekend at the Villa. D. G. Quintano
Weekend Girls. Jonathan Burke
Weekend in Baghdad. R. Wadham
Weekend Mystery. R. A. Simon
Weekend of Shadows. H. Atkinson
Weekend of Terror. J. L. Purvis
Weekend to Danger. T. Vail
Weekend to Kill. H. Atkinson
Weekend to Kill. Ian Stuart
Weekend with Death. P. Wentworth
Weekend with Maxwell. E. G. Cousins
Weep for a Blonde. B. Halliday
Weep for a Wanton. L. Treat
Weep for Her. Sara Woods
Weep for Me. J. D. MacDonald
Weep for Willow Green. P. Kruger
Weep No More, Lady. R. Cocking
Weep No More My Brother. S. Watson
Weep Not Fair Lady. John Evans
Weeping and the Laughter. V. Caspary
Weeping Ash. Joan Aiken
Weeping Lady. J. L. Roberts
Weeping Tower. C. Randell
Weeping Willow Murders. C. Koonce
Weighed in the Balance. Nicholas Carter
Weight of Evidence. R. Ormerod
Weight of the Crown. F. M. White
Weight of the Evidence. M. Innes
Weighted Scales. B. Musto
Weir Boyd Mystery. S. G. Hedges
Weird Adventures of the Shadow. M. Grant
Weird Courtship. Old Sleuth
Weird Gift. G. Ohnet
Weird Idol of Penang Towers. G. Wells
Weird Legacies. M. Ashley
Weird Legacy. F. Johnston
Weird of Deadly Hollow. B. Mitford
Weird o' It. M. P. Shiel
Weird Picture. J. R. Carling
Weird Sea Mystery. Old Sleuth
Weird Sisters. R. Dowling
Weird Treasure. Nicholas Carter
Weird Wedlock. R. M. Gilchrist
Weird World of Wes Beattie. J. N. Harris

624 / Weirdown Experiment — Title Index

Weirdown Experiment. W. Hildick
Welcome Back to Wayland. F. Shroyer
Welcome, Danger! J. Reach
Welcome Danger. Robert Simpson
Welcome Death. G. Daniel
Welcome for a Hero. Robin Perry
Welcome Home! H. Adams
Welcome Home, Lily Glow. Clay Henry
Welcome, My Dear, to Belfry House. S. Forbes
Welcome, Proud Lady. June Drummond
Welcome Sundays. N. Keifetz
Welcome to the Grave. M. McMullen
Welcome to Xanadu. N. Benchley
Welded Lives. G. Ingram
Welding the Chain. Dick Stewart
Welfleet Mystery. Mrs. G. Sheldon
Well-Born Corpse. E. Benjamin
Well Caught. A. Armstrong
Well Caught, McLean! G. Goodchild
Well-Dressed for Murder. Laverne Rice
Well-Dressed Skeleton. B. Williams
Well-Furnished Life. E. McCrae
Well, I'll Be Hanged! Kevin O'Hara
Well-Known Face. Josephine Bell
Well Now, My Pretty—. J. H. Chase
Well-Told Lie. C. Hobhouse
Wellington's. M. Olden
Wellspring. E. H. Hawkins
Wench Is Dead. F. Brown
Wench Is Dead. R. Fenisong
Wench Is Wicked. Carter Brown
Wentworth Hall. A. O'Neill-Barna
Wentworth Mystery. W. Phillips
We're All Guilty. J. Reach
Were Death Denied. D. Yates
Were He a Stranger. M. Craig
Were They Justified? A. Philips
Werewolf. C. L. Swem
Werewolf Among Us. D. Koontz
Werewolf by Moonlight. G. N. Smith
Werewolf of Elphinstone. R. C. Armour
Werewolf of Paris. G. Endore
Werewolf Trace. J. Gardner
Werewolf Walks Tonight. M. Avallone
Wes Hardin's Gun. J. Reese
West End. J. G. Brandon
West End Horror. N. Meyer
West Highland Spirits. C. J. C. Hyne
West of Aztec Pass. W. C. Tuttle
West of Jerusalem. G. De Villiers
West of Rio Grande. T. Craig
West of the Moon. A. Burr
West Pier. P. Hamilton
West Point Lieutenant. Old Sleuth
West Shore Mystery. Old Sleuth
West Side Jungle. J. Ridgway
Westbound Murder. C. S. Wallace
Western Express Robbery. N. Ridley
Western Ferret. I. Stark
Westerner. L. Allan
Westgate Mystery. Darby St. John
Westhorpe Mystery. I. D. Hardy
Westlade Murders. T. A. Plummer
Westlakes. T. Cobb
Westland Case. Jonathan Latimer
Westminster Disaster. F. Hoyle
Westminster Mystery. Elaine Hamilton
Westminster One. T. Willis
Weston of the North-West Mounted Police. T. Lund
Weston of the Royal North-West Mounted Police. T. Lund
Westwood Mystery. C. J. Dutton
Westwood Mystery. A. Fielding
Wetback. W. O'Farrell
Wettermark. E. Chaze
We've Been Waiting for You. E. Thornbury
Wexford. J. Ellis
Whadda We Do Now, Butch? S. Talmy
Wharf Sinister. A. Grace
What a Body! A. Green
What a Tangled Web. A. Hocking
What Are the Bugles Blowing For? N. Freeling
What Are Your Angels Now? P. Groom
What Became of Alex Bretherton? P. Harris
What Became of Eugene Ridgewood? P. James
What Become of Mr. Desmond. C. N. Boyle
What Beckoning Ghost. D. G. Browne
What Befell a Bristol Trader. J. Johnson
What Can You Lose? R. B. Saxe
What Changed Charley Farthing. M. Hebden
What Crime Is It? D. Gardiner
What Dark Secret. D. Dudley
What Did Hattie See? K. Roos
What Did I Do Tomorrow? L. P. Davies
What Do I Care? D. Linton
What Dread Hand. C. Brand
What Dread Hand. E. Gill
What Else Could I Do? T. Claymore
What Ever Happened to Baby Jane? H. Farrell
What Fools Men Are! S. Murray
What Fools Women Are! D. Vane
What Gentleman Strangles a Lady? R. G. Dean
What Happened at Andals? John Arnold
What Happened at Hazelwood. M. Innes

What Happened Is This. B. Von Hutten
What Happened to Forester. E. P. Oppenheim
What Happened to Hammond? H. Blayn
What Happened to Mary? R. C. Brown
What Hast Thou Done? J. F. Molloy
What Have They Done to You, Ben? B. Reade
What He Cost Her. J. Payn
What He Least Expected. Holworthy Hall
What Immortal Hand. J. Curtis
What Is This Mystery? M. E. Braddon
What Is Your Verdict. T. J. R. Sennocke
What Lies Beneath. B. Swift
What Mrs. McGillicuddy Saw! A. Christie
What News of Kitty? D. Quentin
What Next? Winifred Graham
What Next? J. T. Patterson
What Night Will Bring. H. Bailey
What—No Body? Mary Archer
What—No Witnesses? Mary Archer
What Now My Love. F. Salas
What of Terry Conniston? B. Garfield
What Old Father Thames Said. C. Nelson
What Price Doubloons? Frank King
What Price Murder. C. F. Adams
What Price Murder? M. Grable
What Price Paradise? A. Hillgarth
What Really Happened. B. Halliday
What Really Happened. M. B. Lowndes
What Rhymes with Murder? J. Iams
What Rough Beast. J. Trench
What Say the Jury? C. M. Wills
What Shall I Cry. A. Binkley
What Shall It Profit? H. E. Inman
What She Ought to Be. F. Warden
What Should a Man Do? H. G. Hutchinson
What Should You Know of Dying. T. Wells
What Stranger Cause? F. Bamford
What the Doctor Ordered. V. Bridges
What the Peeper Saw. J. Gratus
What Thinkest Thou, Simon? Winifred Graham
What to Do Until the Undertaker Comes. T. Wells
What Was It? and other stories. Fitz-James O'Brien
What Will the World Say? C. Gibbon
What Would You Have Done? L. Tracy
Whatever Dies. P. Woodruff
Whatever Goes Up. B. Millhauser
Whatever Happened to Aunt Alice? U. Curtiss
Whatever Happened to Ruby? W. Owen
What's at the End? L. Beresford
What's Become of Anna? T. Tucker
What's Become of Screwloose? and other stories. R. Goulart
What's Better Than Money? J. H. Chase
What's Bred in the Bone. G. Allen
What's Funny About Murder. Craig Cooper
What's Happening? J. N. Iannuzzi
What's in a Name? A. Spiller
What's in the Dark? E. Queen
What's Past Is Prologue. M. McKenna
What's the Matter with Helen? R. Deming
What's with You? D. Ambler
What's Wrong at Pyford? D. Fisher
What's Ya Problem? H. Zore
Whatsoever a Man Soweth. W. LeQueux
Whatsoever Things Are True. S. Harvester
Wheat and Tares. P. Trent
Wheat Killing. P. Tanous
Wheatstack. J. S. Fletcher
Wheel. Alan White
Wheel Fortune. Karen Campbell
Wheel Is Fixed. J. M. Fox
Wheel o'Fortune. L. Tracy
Wheel of Circumstance. D. W. Spurgeon
Wheel of Death. R. T. M. Scott
Wheel of Fate. P. Saint-Lambert
Wheel of Fire. J. Middlemass
Wheel of Fortune. Karen Campbell
Wheel Spins. Ethel L. White
Wheel That Turned. K. M. Knight
Wheelchair Corpse. W. Levinrew
Wheeler, Dealer! Carter Brown
Wheeler Fortune. Carter Brown
Wheeling Light. F. Hume
Wheels. J. Spenser
Wheels Beneath. G. Kelton
Wheels in the Forest. J. N. Chance
Wheels of Anarchy. M. Pemberton
Wheels Within Wheels. H. Mee
Wheels Within Wheels. C. Wells
When a Man Yields. Nicholas Carter
When a Rogue's in Power. Nicholas Carter
When All Is Staked. Nicholas Carter
When Ape Is King. O. Wynd
When Beggars Choose. K. N. Burt
When Brave Men Tremble. Nicholas Carter
When Carruthers Laughed. H. C. McNeile
When Clews Are Hidden. Nicholas Carter
When Cold Steel Clashed. C. Frisbie
When Conscience Sleeps. W. J. Bayfield
When Crook Meets Crook. A. Spiller
When Dames Get Tough. H. Janson
When Danger Threatens. Mark Cross
When Danger Threatens. Sea Lion
When Dead Men Tell Tales. J. Goodwin
When Death Walks. J. Corbett

When Destruction Threatens. Nicholas Carter
When Dorinda Dances. B. Halliday
When Duty Calls. M. I. Burke
When Eight Bells Toll. Alistair MacLean
When Emmalyn Remembers. E. Marlow
When Fell the Night. E. Queen
"When First We Practise." W. Cheame
When Fools Endanger Us. R. Ladline
When Footsteps Echo. B. Copper
When Greek Meets Greek. J. Hatton
When Greek Meets Greek. P. Trent
When Honors Fall. Nicholas Carter
What I Grow Rich. Joan Fleming
When I Say Goodbye, I'm Clary Brown. C. Keppel
When I Was Czar. A. W. Marchmont
When in Greece. E. Lathen
When in Rome. N. Marsh
When It Was Dark. G. Thorne
When Jealousy Spurs. Nicholas Carter
When Johnny Died. C. Rougvie
When Last I Died. G. Mitchell
When Last Seen... M. J. Herrick
When London Sleeps. H. T. Johnson
When Love Called. A. W. Marchmont
When Love Was Not Enough. Clifford Mason
When Michael Calls. J. Farris
When My Ship Comes Home. C. Massie
When Necessity Drives. Nicholas Carter
When No Man Pursueth. M. B. Lowndes
When No Man Pursueth. D. Sharp
When One Door Shuts. M. Pereira
When Only the Bougainvillea Blooms. I. Charles
When Passions Rule. F. Hart
When Rogues Conspire. Nicholas Carter
When Rogues Fall Out. R. A. Freeman
When Rogues Fall Out. J. Hatton
When Satan Ruled. C. R. Gull
When Scholars Fall. T. Robinson
When Shadows Fall. N. C. Heard
When Shall I Sleep Again? N. W. Firth
When She Wakes. L. O'Brien
When She Was Bad. W. Ard
When Spy Meets Spy. R. Walker
When Strangers Came. J. Raven
When Strangers Meet. R. Bloomfield
When the Bough Breaks. S. Rosenberg
When the Case Was Opened. J. Bude
When the Cat's Away. G. Bullett
When the Century Blooms. J. Wetherell
When the Clews Point Wrong. Dick Stewart
When the Devil Drives. F. Warden
When the Devil Was Sick. C. Carnac
When the Devil Was Sick. Charles Ross
When the Empire Crashed. A. W. Marchmont
When the Gallows Is High. P. Hastings
When the Gangs Came to London. E. Wallace
When the Gods Laughed. P. Audemars
When the Gunmen Came. J. Hunter
When the Heart Is Young. A. M. Meadows
When the Jury Disagreed! J. Hunter
When the Moon Died. R. Savage
When the Police Failed. R. Ladline
When the Quarry Turns. I. Stark
When the Rainbow Is Pale. G. Joseph
When the Sea Gives Up Its Dead. Mrs. G. Corbett
When the Sun Goes Down. C. Blackstock
When the Trap Was Sprung. Nicholas Carter
When the Wicked Man... J. F. W. Hannay
When the Wicked Man. G. Thorne
When the Wicked Prosper. Nicholas Carter
When the Wind Blows. C. Hare
When the Wind Cries. Claudette Nicole
When the Witch Is Dead. M. L. Roby
When the World Was Younger. M. E. Braddon
When They Kill Your Wife. J. Crowe
When Thief Meets Thief. H. S. Keeler
When Thieves Fall Out. Mark Cross
When Thieves Fall Out. S. A. Curtis
When Thieves Fall Out. J. K. Stafford
When Thieves Fall Out. B. Thomson
When Threads Get Tangled. J. K. Stafford
When Three Makes Two. H. Carstairs
When Tragedy Grins. Grace M. White
When Trails Cross. J. K. Stafford
When Trails Were New. T. Mundy
When Tutt Meets Tutt. A. Train
When Victims Meet. H. Roman
Where All the Girls Are Sweeter. Richard Butler
Where Angel Treads. G. Montrose
Where Angels Fear... B. Hemyng
Where Are the Children? M. H. Clark
Where Are You Going? A. Applin
Where Dead Men Walk. H. Leverage
Where Did Charity Go? Carter Brown
Where Did the Girls Go? M. Cousin
Where Eagles Dare. Alistair MacLean
Where Every Prospect Pleases. R. Halket
Where Evil Waits. M. Lynch
Where Helen Lies. R. Foley
Where Ignorance Is Bliss. R. Greene
Where Is Barbara Prentice? M. Burton
Where Is Bianca. E. Queen
Where Is Evie Alton? H. Bourne
Where Is Holly Carleton? S. Marvin

Title Index

Where Is Jane? Lynn Williams
Where Is Janice Gantry? J. D. MacDonald
Where Is Jenny Now? F. S. Wees
Where Is Jenny Willet? W. H. L. Crauford
Where Is Nancy Bostwick? R. Foley
Where Is She Now? L. Meynell
Where Is the Withered Man? N. Deane
Where Murder Waits. Gordon Davis
Where No Fire Burns. M. Garratt
Where No Flags Fly. F. Ayer, Jr.
Where Nothing Ever Happens. L. Shippey
Where Peril Beckons. Nicholas Carter
Where Satan Dwells. F. Stevenson
Where Secrecy Begins. J. C. Nolan
Where Shadows Lie. M. Lynch
Where Shadows Linger. J. S. May
Where Some Men Are Men. G. F. Worts
Where Terror Stalked. C. Birkin
Where the Clue Leads. I. Stark
Where the Dark Streets Go. D. S. Davis
Where the Desert Ends. W. LeQueux
Where the East Wind Blows. A. Mair
Where the Fresh Grass Grows. Brian Cooper
Where the Heart Is. A. Hale
Where the Jungle Ends. Ken Blake
Where the Lost Aprils Are. E. Ogilvie
Where the Pavement Ends. J. Russell
Where the River Bends. J. M. Scott
Where the Shoe Pinches. L. T. Meade
Where the Snow Was Red. H. Pentecost
Where the Spies Are. J. Leasor
Where the Trail Ended. W. M. Graydon
Where There Are Vultures. A. Heckstall-Smith
"Where There Is a Will..." A. Griffin
Where There Was Smoke. B. Flynn
Where There's a Head. L. Gorell
Where There's a Will. Anne Burton
Where There's a Will. K. Chase
Where There's a Will. R. S. Hastings
Where There's a Will. Ellis Peters
Where There's a Will. M. R. Rinehart
Where There's a Will. R. Stout
Where There's Smoke. C. B. Kelland
Where There's Smoke. E. McBain
Where There's Smoke. S. Sterling
Where Vultures Reign. Laurie Davis
Where Was Trail Murdered? T. A. Plummer
Where You Throw Blood. B. Sarto
Whereabouts Unknown. B. Reynolds
Where's Emily. C. Wells
Where's Mr. Chumley? S. Truss
Where's Zenobia? F. Du Boisgobey
Wherever Lynn Goes. Beatrice Parker
Which Doctor? E. Candy
Which I Never. L. A. G. Strong
Which—Innocent or Guilty? E. S. Clem
Which Mrs. Bennett? A. Littlefield
Which Mrs. Torr? Maude Parker
Which of Them? P. Black
Which of Us Is Safe? M. Cumberland
Which One? R. A. Bennet
Which the Justice, Which the Thief. W. Harrington
Which Way Came Death? F. Wolseley
Which Way to Die? E. Queen
Whiff of Death. I. Asimov
Whiff of Money. J. H. Chase
While Guy Was in France. T. Cobb
While London Sleeps. R. Dowling
While Love Lay Sleeping. R. Neely
While Murder Waits. B. Cassiday
While Murder Waits. J. Esteven
While of Sound Mind. S. McKenna
While She Sleeps. Ethel L. White
While Still We Live. Helen MacInnes
While the Bells Rang. C. L. Clifford
While the City Sleeps. C. Einstein
While the Coffin Waited. J. Sheridan
While the Fetters Were Forged. Nicholas Carter
While the Patient Slept. M. G. Eberhart
While the Wind Howled. A. Gaines
While There Is Life. W. Markall
Whilst the Crowd Roared. S. Horler
Whim to Kill. Dell Shannon
Whims. Wanderer
Whims of Fate. C. Jauniere
Whip. S. E. Mason
Whip. R. Parker
Whip and the Tongue. H. L. V. Fletcher
Whip Hand. V. Canning
Whip Hand. R. Crawford
Whip Hand. D. Francis
Whip Hand. I. Gordon
Whip Hand. W. F. Sanders
Whip of the Will. Mrs. C. Kernahan
Whip-Poor-Will Mystery. H. Footner
Whiplash. H. Janson
Whiplash. R. W. Taylor
Whipping Boy. S. Holmes
Whipping Boy. P. Orum
Whipping Boys. G. Cullingford
Whipping Girl. R. Rodd
Whips of Time. N. Giles
Whirl of a Bird. G. Peters
Whirligig. R. L. Fish
Whirligig of Time. L. Biggle
Whirligig of Time. D. De Jong
Whirligigs. O. Henry
Whirling Death. Nicholas Carter

Whirlpool. J. L. Henderson
Whirlpool. D. Lamson
Whirlpool. V. Morton
Whirlpools. J. P. McGinty
Whirlwind. J. Creasey
Whirlwind Beneath the Sea. K. Stanton
Whiskered Footman. E. Jepson
Whiskers and Soda. F. Richardson
Whiskey Drips. J. J. Brooks
Whisky Johnny. C. McManus
Whisper Can Kill. G. Sherry
Whisper Down the Moon. C. Darby
Whisper Her Name. Howard Hunt
Whisper His Sin. V. Packer
Whisper If You Dare! A. MacKenzie
Whisper in a Lonely Place. G. Sinstadt
Whisper in the Dark. K. Troy
Whisper in the Darkness. T. E. Huff
Whisper in the Dust. Stephanie Hall
Whisper in the Forest. N. Ames
Whisper in the Glen. P. M. Hubbard
Whisper in the Gloom. N. Blake
Whisper Murder! V. Kelsey
Whisper Murder Softly. P. Bannon
Whisper of Danger. Clarissa Ross
Whisper of Darkness. M. Lynn
Whisper of Death. V. Hanson
Whisper of Death. V. Siller
Whisper of Evil. R. Gatenby
Whisper of Fear. C. Randell
Whisper of Fear. Elna Stone
Whisper of Heather. L. Benedict
Whisper of Shadows. J. L. H. Whitney
Whsiper of the Axe. R. Condon
Whisper on the Stair. L. Mearson
Whisper Town. J. Philips
Whisperer. W. M. Duncan
Whisperer. Mrs. C. Kernahan
Whisperer. J. M. Walsh
Whispering Buddha. J. C. Cowles
Whispering Cat Mystery. J. Kains
Whispering Caverns. A. Winter
Whispering Chorus. P. Sheehan
Whispering Corpse. W. P. McGivern
Whispering Cracksman. B. Perowne
Whispering Cup. M. Seeley
Whispering Dead. A. Ganachilly
Whispering Death. D. Carney
Whispering Death. J. Pattinson
Whispering Death. J. Spencer
Whispering Ear. C. B. Clason
Whispering Gables. S. Abbott
Whispering Galleries. B. Goldie
Whispering Gallery. W. E. D. Ross
Whispering Ghost. S. Chalmers
Whispering Hill. M. Albrand
Whispering House. M. Erskine
Whispering Island. N. McFather
Whispering Knights. G. Mitchell
Whispering Lane. F. Hume
Whispering Leaves. D. Collett
Whispering Lodge. S. Murray
Whispering Man. W. M. Duncan
Whispering Man. H. Holt
Whispering Man. H. K. Webster
Whispering Master. F. Gruber
Whispering Money. Richard Bennett
Whispering Pines. R. C. Schimmel
Whispering Riders. W. B. Bannerman
Whispering Runes. Doris Shannon
Whispering Shadows. Herman Landon
Whispering Steel. J. Nicholas
Whispering Tongues. Laurence Kirk
Whispering Wall. P. Carlon
Whispering Walls. W. Spence
Whispering Willows. C. Osborne
Whispering Window. C. Fitzsimmons
Whispering Windows. T. Burke
Whispering Wires. H. Leverage
Whispering Wires. K. L. McLaurin
Whispering Woman. K. Verner
Whispers. D. R. Koontz
Whispers. Louis Dodge
Whispers from the Dark Side of Tomorrow. O. Peters
Whispers in the Dark. S. Hacker
Whispers in the Dark. J. M. Walsh
Whispers in the Night. Clarissa Ross
Whispers in the Night. W. E. D. Ross
Whispers in the Sun. M. Greig
Whispers in the Wind. Marsha Alexander
Whispers in the Wind. R. Wissman
Whispers of the Flesh. F. Flora
Whistle and I'll Come. P. McCutchan
Whistle at My Window. H. Arvonen
Whistle for the Crows. D. Eden
Whistle in the Wind. D. Daniels
Whistle Me over the Water. W. Leighton
Whistle of Doom. B. Ludwig
Whistle of Fate. R. Marsh
Whistle Past the Graveyard. R. Deming
Whistle Up the Devil. Derek Smith
Whistler's Lane. Anthea Fraser
Whistling Hangman. B. Kendrick
Whistling in the Dark. H. K. Carpenter
Whistling in the Dark. L. Gross
Whistling Key. V. Gunn
Whistling Legs. R. McDougald
Whistling Legs. M. Foster
Whistling Sands. E. Dudley
Whistling Shadow. M. Seeley
Whistling Wires. P. Groom

White Alley. C. Wells
White Angel. J. Corbett
White Arab. E. P. Thorne
White Arrow. A. Wynne
White August. J. Boland
White Badger. G. Talbot
White Bikini. Carter Brown
White Bird, and other stories. W. J. Newton
White Blackbird. H. Douglas
White Bride. F. M. White
White Cad Cross-Up. W. F. Nolan
White Camel. L. Allan
White Camellia. F. Grierson
White Camellias. A. T. Brooks
White Castello. M. McEvoy
White Cat. G. Burgess
White Chalet. L. Cross
White Cipher. H. Leverage
White Circle. C. J. Daly
White Cockatoo. M. G. Eberhart
White Cottage Mystery. M. Allingham
White Countess. F. Warden
White Cowl. F. H. Harrison
White Crash Helmet. P. Fry
White Crow. P. MacDonald
White Crown and other stories. H. D. Ward
White Cruiser. N. Buntline
White Crusaders. A. W. Halse
White Dacoit. B. Mather
White Death. W. M. Graydon
White Death. R. Sheckley
White Desert. C. R. Cooper
White Dominoes. F. M. Pettee
White Dress. M. G. Eberhart
White Eagle. Roland Daniel
White Face. E. Wallace
White-Faced Man. Gavin Holt
White Falcon. J. McVean
White Feather Mystery. M. Williamson
White Feathers. G. I. Cervus
White Fires Burning. C. Dillon
White for a Shroud. D. C. Cameron
White for Danger. David Stevens
White Friar. Donald Stuart
White Gas. R. Keverne
White Gauntlet. P. Brebner
White Ghost of Fenwick Hall. A. Wharton
White Girls Eastward. T. Craig
White Glove. W. LeQueux
White Glove. F. M. White
White Gold. O. Binns
White Gold. M. D. Orr
White Hand and a Black Thumb. H. Spicer
White Hand and the Black. B. Mitford
White Hand Murder Mystery. M. E. Campbell
White Hand of Athene. J. Thorne
White Hands of Justice. O. Binns
White Hell. D. Tracy
White Hen. P. Traill
White Horse Inn. G. Simenon
White Horse to Banbury Cross. R. Llewellyn
White Horsemen. C. Stanton
White House. M. E. Braddon
White Island. N. Lansdale
White Jade. Jan Alexander
White Jade. W. D. Roberts
White Jade Fox. A. Norton
White Khan. C. Dillon
White King of Africa. W. M. Graydon
White Lady. E. Kyle
White Lady of Khaminavatka. R. H. Savage
White Leaves of Death. P. Audemars
White Lie. G. R. Beardmore
White Lie. W. LeQueux
White Lie and No Glory. D. Mariner
White Lie Assignment. P. Driscoll
White Lie Company, and The Woman with the Green Eyes. A. Soutar
White Lie the Dead. P. Loraine
White Line Fever. C. S. Cotelo
White Man's Chance. J. McCulley
White Man's Justice: Black Man's Grief. D. Goines
White Man's Prestige. E. Leslie
White Man's Stride. L. P. Greene
White Mask. J. M. Walsh
White Mazurka. B. Boyer
White Menace. J. Rhode
White Menace. Colin Robertson
White Mercenary. P. Saxon
White Mice. R. H. Davis
White Midnight. C. Risku
White Moll. F. Packard
White Motley. M. Pemberton
White Negro. A. Mills
White Nigger. F. A. M. Webster
White Night. F. Rosaire
White Night, Red Dawn. F. Nolan
White Owl. E. Snell
White Panthers. D. Vane
White Pavilion. V. Johnston
White Peacock. M. L. Roby
White Peril. G. Bartram
White Peril. S. Westlaw
White Phantom. M. E. Braddon
White Phantom. W. Braun
White Phantom. J. Hunter
White Pierrot. P. Barrington

White Poppy. H. Osborne
White Prior. F. Hume
White Priory Murders. Carter Dickson
White Python. V. Canning
White Raiment. C. H. Bullivant
White Refugees. R. C. Armour
White Rider. L. Charteris
White Rook. J. B. Harris-Burland
White Rook. H. M. Kahler
White Room. L. P. Davies
White Rose. Alanna Knight
White Rose Mystery. G. Biss
White Rose of Memphis. W. C. Falkner
White Sapphire. L. F. Hartman
White Satin. J. L. Rickard
White Savage. A. W. Upfield
White Shield. B. Mitford
White Shroud. R. Nicholas
White Sin. A. Wood
White Siren. S. Maddock
White Snake. A. Mills
White South. H. Innes
White Stacks. W. Hewlett
White Streak. S. Gluck
White Trails over London. R. Wilkes-Hunter
White Taureg. Operator 1384
White Vampire. A. M. Judd
White Velvet. R. Rohmer
White Violets. E. Crandall
White Virgin. G. M. Fenn
White Walls. M. Pemberton
White Widows. S. Merwin Jr.
White Wig. G. Verner
White Witch. F. Warden
White Witch of Mayfair. George Griffith
White Witch of the Matabele. J. Whishaw
White Witch of the South Seas. D. Wheatley
White Witch's Warning. Anonymous
White Wizard. N. Buntline
White Wolverine Contract. P. Atlee
Whitebird Murders. T. B. Black
Whitechapel Murder. F. Allen
Whitechapel Murders. A. F. Pinkerton
Whitechapel Mystery. N. T. Oliver
Whiteoakes Murder. J. Laurence
Whiteout! D. Kyle
Whitewater. B. Knox
Whither Do You Wander? J. Tickell
Whither Thou Goest. W. LeQueux
Whitney Case. John Bentley
Whitton's Folly. Pamela Hill
Who? P. Baron
Who? A. Budrys
Who? E. Kent
Who? A. W. Marchmont
Who? A. J. Palermo
Who Are You, Linda Condrick? P. Carlon
Who Benefits? L. Thayer
Who Called Diamonds? G. Brodie
Who Calls the Tune. N. Bawden
Who Closed the Casement? T. Cobb
Who Cries for a Loser? Ray Owen
Who Cut the Colonel's Throat. W. L. Hay
Who Dares? Loring Brent
Who Dialled 999? C. F. Gregg
Who Did It. Anonymous
Who Did It? N. Gould
Who Died at the Grange? M. Halliday
Who Died Last. F. Du Boisgobey
Who Dies? S. P. B. Mais
Who Dies for Me? S. H. Courtier
Who Dies Next? H. J. Wurr
Who Dies There? J. P. Duff
Who Dies There? H. Kane
Who Do Women?... M. Corrigan
Who Else But She? S. Fowler
Who Evil Thinks. R. Glendinning
Who Fired the Factory? T. A. Plummer
Who Giveth This Woman? W. LeQueux
Who Goes Hang? S. Hyland
Who Goes Home? R. Curle
Who Goes Next? J. Wainwright
Who Goes There? B. K. Benson
Who Goes There? L. Paxton
Who Goes There? D. Vane
Who Has Wilma Lathrop. D. Keene
Who He? A. Bestor
Who Is Elissa Sheldon? D. Montross
Who Is Guilty? P. Woolf
Who Is John Noman? C. H. Beckett
Who Is Lewis Pinder? L. P. Davies
Who Is Mary Stark? L. Kropp
Who Is Melody? P. Drew
Who Is My Enemy? Barbara Cooper
Who Is My Neighbor? N. Balchin
Who Is Nemo. R. Douglas
Who Is Simon Warwick? P. Moyes
Who Is Teddy Villanova? T. Berger
Who Is the Ace? N. Anthony
Who Is the Heir? M. Collins
Who Is the Man? J. S. Tait
Who Is the Next? H. K. Webster
Who Is This Girl? H. T. Miller
Who Is This Man? A. MacGowan
Who Keeps the Keys? F. Leslie
Who Kill to Live. H. Harris
Who Killed Agatha Christie? T. Gates
Who Killed Alfred Snow? J. S. Fletcher
Who Killed Amanda? G. Monro
Who Killed Ann Gage? R. St. Clair

Who Killed Aunt Caroline? G. Richards
Who Killed Aunt Maggie? Medora Field
Who Killed Beau Sparrow? Roger Fuller
Who Killed Brother Treasurer? C. M. Wills
Who Killed Caldwell? C. Wells
Who Killed Carson? H. H. C. Gibbons
Who Killed Cavelotti? A. Newell
Who Killed Charmian Karslake? A. Haynes
Who Killed Chloe? M. Allingham
Who Killed Cock Robin? H. Hext
Who Killed Coralie? The Aresbys
Who Killed Diana? H. Hext
Who Killed Dick Whittington? E. Radford
Who Killed Dr. Sex? Carter Brown
Who Killed Enoch Powell? Arthur Wise
Who Killed Frankie Leash? M. Echard
Who Killed Gatton? E. C. Vivian
Who Killed Gerald Cruden? Alan Graham
Who Killed Gregory? Eugene Jones
Who Killed Henry Wickenstrom. Mark Cross
Who Killed Honeybee? Craig Cooper
Who Killed Jefferson Broome? M. Keynes
Who Killed Lady Poynder? R. Marsh
Who Killed Lord Brixham? G. De Jeans
Who Killed Lord Henry Rollestone? J. Daye
Who Killed Lord Luxmore? M. Leighton
Who Killed Madcap Millicent? Roger Fuller
Who Killed Me? J. Allan
Who Killed Mr. Fisk. J. Brooke
Who Killed Mr. Garland's Mistress. R. Forrest
Who Killed My Wife? R. Goyne
Who Killed Netta Maul? F. Arthur
Who Killed Oliver Cromwell? L. Gribble
Who Killed Peter Trueman? Anonymous
Who Killed Pretty Becky Low? A. B. Cunningham
Who Killed Rebecca? M. Halliday
Who Killed Robert Prentice? D. Wheatley
Who Killed Robin Cockland? P. Luck
Who Killed Roger Whitely? B. Allerton
Who Killed Rosa Gray? F. Usher
Who Killed Santa Claus. T. Feely
Who Killed Stella Pomeroy? B. Thomson
Who Killed Stephen Tennant? T. S. King
Who Killed Sweet Sue? H. Kane
Who Killed the Chauffeur? G. V. Vosper
Who Killed the Count? B. Delane
Who Killed the Crooner? R. Trevor
Who Killed the Curate? J. Coggin
Who Killed the Doctor? M. Burton
Who Killed the Doctors? A. Peters
Who Killed the Husband? H. Footner
Who Killed the Pie Man? P. Lore
Who Killed the Snowman? J. Browner
Who Killed Trainer Lincoln? A. Steffens Hardy
Who Killed Uncle? H. Javits
Who Killed Utopia? Paul Walker
Who Killed William Drew? Harrington Strong
Who Killed You, Cindy Castle? K. Carr
Who Knows? I. A. Greenfield
Who Knows Julie Gordon? K. Booton
Who Lies Bleeding? H. Carstairs
Who Lies Here? Ellis Peters
Who Lies There? P. Johnson
Who Maimed Spurto? J. Fairfax-Blakeborough
Who Murdered Reynard? S. Fowler
Who Murdered Westaway? G. Comley
Who Needs Enemies? E. Kent
Who Needs Forever? E. I. English
Who Opened the Door? T. Cobb
Who Owned the Jewels? M. V. Victor
Who Pays the Piper? P. Wentworth
Who Plays with Sin. A. Spiller
Who Poisoned Hetty Duncan? and other detective stories. D. Donovan
Who Put It There? Mary Scott
Who Rides a Tiger. D. M. Disney
Who Rides a Tiger? Colin Robertson
Who Rides on a Tiger. M. B. Lowndes
Who Rides the Tiger. B. Myers
Who Said Murder. M. Halliday
Who Saw Her Die? P. Moyes
Who Saw Her Die? M. Warner
Who Saw Him Die? M. Halliday
Who Saw Maggie Brown? K. Roos
Who Says a Corpse Has to Be Dull. D. Von Elsner
Who Says Murder? P. King
Who Screamed? J. Courage
Who Shall Be Victor? E. A. Dupuy
Who Shall Condemn? J. C. Shannon
Who Shall Hang? M. Magill
Who Shot the Bull? B. Knox
Who Shot the Spy? Anonymous
Who Should Have Died? M. Silverman
Who Spies, Who Kills? E. Queen
Who Spoke Last? J. V. Turner
Who Steals My Name. James Fraser
Who Steals My Name. G. Richards
Who Stole Sassi Manoon? D. E. Westlake
Who Strikes by Night. Richard Grant
Who Sups with the Devil? P. McCartney
Who the Heck Is Sylvia. J. Porter
Who Told Clutha. H. Munro

Who Told the Belle? N. Perrelli
Who Took Tobi Rinaldi? G. Mcdonald
Who Walk in Fear. N. Bell
Who Walks by Moonlight? M. McEvoy
Who Was Clare Jallu? P. Boileau
Who Was Ellen Smith? K. Ayling
Who Was He? P. Little
Who Was He? M. V. Victor
Who Was Lady Thurne? F. Warden
Who Was the Jester? G. Ashe
Who Was the Killer? J. Corbett
Who Was the Killer? N. Wray
Who Was the Lady I Saw You With. N. Krasna
Who Was This Woman?, Two Photographs, and The King of Hearts. H. C. McNeile
Who Were You With Last Night? F. Raphael
Who Will Watch the Watchers. E. Fadiman
Who Wins. M. A. Fleming
Who Would A-Murdering Go? Walter Blake
Who'd Shoot a Genius? S. M. Schley
Who'd Want to Kill Old George. R. Upton
Whodunit? A. Radnor
Whole Hog. M. Kenyon
Whole Truth. J. Ehrlichman
Who'll Buy My Evil? A. Caillou
Whom God Hath Joined. F. Hume
Whom Gods Destroy. Clifton Adams
Whom Nobody Owns. A. Spiller
Whom the Gods Destroy. A. G. Bennett
Whom the Gods Would Destroy. Nicholas Carter
Whore-Mother. S. Herron
Whoreson. D. Goines
Who's Afraid? E. S. Holding
Who's Been Sitting in My Chair? C. Armstrong
Who's Been Sleeping in My Grave? Janet Hart
Who's Calling? H. McCloy
Who's for Dying. M. MacQuade
Who's Got the Bastard Pope? P. A. Fulford
Who's Guilty? L. J. Huber
Who's in Charge Here? H. H. Kirst
Who's Next? J. Allan
Who's on First? J. Allan
Who's on First. W. F. Buckley
Who's on First? J. Sharkey
Who's Sorry Now? D. Linton
Who's the Guy? A. J. Evans
Who's the Murderer? E. Sleath
Who's the Target? M. Carr
Whose Body? D. L. Sayers
Whose Corpse? S. Ransome
Whose Hand? V. Loder
Whose Hand? W. G. Willis
Whose Head? W. E. Huntsberry
Whose Little Girl Are You? D. Craig
Whose Millions? Joseph Montague
Whose the Hand? Diana Forbes
Whose Was the Crime? G. Warden
Whose Was the Hand? W. J. Bayfield
Whose Was the Hand? M. E. Braddon
Whose Was the Hand? J. E. Muddock
Whose Wife? C. H. Bullivant
Whoso Findeth a Wife. W. LeQueux
Whosoever Loveth. W. LeQueux
Why? E. D. Bartlett
Why Be Lonely? M. B. Lowndes
Why Call It Homicide? R. Kirby
Why Did He Do It? B. Capes
Why Did She Die? J. Coggin
Why Did Trethewy Die? R. A. J. Walling
Why Didn't They Ask Evans? A. Christie
Why It Happened. M. B. Lowndes
Why Jane Matcham Disappeared. M. Carane
Why Kill a Butler? P. H. Powell
Why Kill Johnny? H. Carmichael
Why Murder? N. Deane
Why Murder? J. Philips
Why Murder Mrs. Hope? J. Courage
Why Murder the Judge? C. S. Hammock
Why Not? George Scott
Why Pick on Me? Raymond Marshall
Why Pick on Me? P. Muller
Why Pick on Pickles? M. Durham
Why She Cries, I Do Not Know. W. Masterson
Why She Left Him. F. Warden
Why Shoot a Butler? G. Heyer
Why Should Sylvia? H. Janson
Why Slug a Postman? S. Truss
Why So Dead? E. Queen
Why Someone Had to Die. J. Roffman
Why Squeal on Me? Max Gordon
Why They Married. M. B. Lowndes
Wicked. A. Applin
Wicked Angel. T. Caldwell
Wicked As the Devil. M. Halliday
Wicked Designs. L. O'Donnell
Wicked Flee. A. Hocking
Wicked Girl. M. C. Hay
Wicked Guardian. Elsie Lee
Wicked Lord. R. Foxall
Wicked Marquis. E. P. Oppenheim
Wicked Pack of Cards. Rosemary Harris
Wicked Pack of Cards. H. R. Williamson
Wicked Saint. E. Bruton
Wicked Shall Flourish. H. Desmond
Wicked Streets. Wenzell Brown

Title Index

Wings of Fear / 627

Wicked Uncle. P. Wentworth
Wicked Way to Die. J. Sturrock
Wicked Woman. Anne Austin
Wicked World. A. M. Meadows
Wicked Wynsleys. Alanna Knight
Wickedest Man. J. Millard
Wicker Man. Robin Hardy
Wide Arch. D. Stivens
Wide Boy! M. Hervey
Wide Boys Never Work. R. Westerby
Wide Girl. M. Hervey
Wide Open Door. T. E. B. Clarke
Wide Sargasso Sea. J. Rhys
Widening Stain. W. B. Johnson
Wider Sea of Love. F. E. Smith
Widow. C. Blackstock
Widow. N. Freeling
Widow. Francis King
Widow. G. Simenon
Widow and the Cavalier. R. Armstrong
Widow and the Web. Robert Martin
Widow Barony. W. R. Burnett
Widow Bewitched. Carter Brown
Widow Cherry. B. L. Farjeon
Widow from Spain. J. Pendower
Widow Gay. A. A. Marcus
Widow Had a Gun. G. H. Coxe
Widow in White. E. Bond
Widow in White. F. A. Chittenden
Widow Lerouge. E. Gaboriau
Widow Maker. F. Diamond
Widow-Makers. M. Blankfort
Widow Mortimer. T. P. Prest
Widow of Bath. M. Bennett
Widow of Ratchets. O. Brookes
Widow of Zanzibar. R. Anthony
Widow Watchers. F. Archer
Widow with the Pink Gloves. M. Dekobra
Widow Wondered Why. W. J. Coughlin
Widow Wore Red. R. Wormser
Widow Wore White. C. P. Cleary
Widower. V. Siller
Widower. G. Simenon
Widower's Wife. T. Charles
Widowmaker. M. Fagyas
Widowmaster. L. Bergson
Widows' Blackmail. R. Fenisong
Widows Can Be Dangerous. N. Leslie
Widow's Cruise. N. Blake
Widow's Escort. B. De Bilio
Widow's Might. M. Dekobra
Widow's Mite. E. S. Holding
Widow's Necklace. E. Davies
Widows of Broome. A. W. Upfield
Widows of the Magistrate. K. West
Widows of Westwood. Marilyn Ross
Widows Ought to Weep. D. B. Olsen
Widow's Peak. J. Nicholas
Widow's Pique. B. Treynor
Widow's Plight. R. Fenisong
Widow's Son. E. Southworth
Widow's Walk. Anonymous
Widow's Walk. M. Bishop
Widow's Walk. S. Nichols
Widow's Walk. C. Rabou
Widow's Walk. M. Yates
Widow's War. Alan Williams
Widows Wear Weeds. A. A. Fair
Widow's Web. U. Curtiss
Widows Won't Wait. D. Hitchens
Wieland. C. B. Brown
Wife at Sea. G. Simenon
Wife by Purchase. P. Trent
Wife He Never Saw. M. Marcin
Wife in the Dark. H. Desmond
Wife in Toledo. J. Budd
Wife Next Door. R. V. Cassill
Wife of Baal. M. Dalton
Wife of Elias. E. Phillpotts
Wife of Ronald Sheldon. P. Quentin
Wife of the Red-Haired Man. B. S. Ballinger
Wife or Death. E. Queen
Wife or No Wife? and A Close Shave. T. W. Speight
Wife-Smuggler. M. Tripp
Wife Who Died Twice. E. Bohle
Wife Who Disappeared. B. Flynn
Wife Who Ran Away. T. Mascott
Wife Whom God Forgot. C. H. Bullivant
Wife's Dream. T. P. Prest
Wife's Honor. E. A. Young
Wife's Victory. E. Southworth
Wigwam and Cabin. W. G. Simms
Wilberforce Legacy. Josephine Bell
Wilby Conspiracy. P. Driscoll
Wild. G. Brewer
Wild Abyss. John Gunn
Wild and Weird. G. Campbell
Wild Apple Orchard. D. Lee
Wild Beauty. D. Donovan
Wild Bird. H. Footner
Wild Card. R. Hawkey
Wild Cat. Laura Black
Wild-Cat Scheme. E. M. Keate
Wild-Catters. C. J. C. Hyne
Wild Cry of Love. B. Paul
Wild Darrie. D. C. Murray
Wild Dreams. Michael Sinclair
Wild Duck Murders. T. Du Bois
Wild Flame. Winifred Duke
Wild Georgie. J. Middlemass

Wild Girl. H. Janson
Wild Girl. D. Keene
Wild Goose Chase. F. C. Wynne
Wild Grapes. B. Jefferis
Wild Grow the Lilies. Christy Brown
Wild Horse Valley. W. C. Tuttle
Wild Hunt. J. Tattersall
Wild Is My Heart. T. Thomas
Wild Island. Antonia Fraser
Wild Justice. G. A. Birmingham
Wild Justice. F. Clifford
Wild Justice. T. B. Morris
Wild Justice. J. Pattinson
Wild Justice. Wilbur Smith
Wild Lonesome. H. Whittington
Wild Man of Cape Cod. F. MacIsaac
Wild Midnight Falls. M. E. Chaber
Wild Night. R. Foley
Wild Onion. Loren Carroll
Wild Party. J. McPartland
Wild Pitch. A. B. Guthrie
Wild Reckoning. M. Richmond
Wild Secret. M. Clare
Wild Sheba. A. Askew
Wild Sound of Murder. D. De Villiers
Wild Summer. Jack Wilson
Wild to Possess. G. Brewer
Wild Town. J. Thompson
Wild Track. Alex Hamilton
Wild Trip. M. Arrighi
Wild Turkey. R. L. Simon
Wild Violets. R. B. Field
Wild Wave. K. Hess
Wild Week-End. T. C. H. Jacobs
Wild Winds. M. Unsworth
Wild Wooing. F. Warden
Wildcat. D. Ambler
Wildcat. Carter Brown
Wildcat. S. Gluck
Wildcatters. Bryan Cooper
Wilde Alliance. I. Mackintosh
Wilder Curse. K. Robeson
Wilderness. T. B. Clegg
Wilderness. R. Donaldson
Wilderness. R. B. Parker
Wilderness Inn. J. L. Roberts
Wilderness Patrol. H. Bindloss
Wilderness Patrol. C. Stoddard
Wilderness Road. A. Davidson
Wilders Walk Away. H. Brean
Wildfire. Nicholas Carter
Wildfire. J. Foxx
Wildfire at Midnight. Mary Stewart
Wildfire Love. J. Blackmore
Wildwater Terrace. R. E. Salwey
Wiles of the Wicked. W. LeQueux
Wiles of Wilhelmina. F. Warden
Wilful and Premeditated. F. W. Crofts
Wilful Lady. J. Sturrock
Wilful-Missing. D. G. Waring
Wilful Murder. J. York
Wilful Susie. A. Applin
Wilful Ward. F. Warden
Wilful Way. H. Compton
Will. R. M. Stern
Will and the Deed. D. Ogburn
Will and the Deed. Ellis Peters
Will and the Way. B. Capes
Will and the Willful. M. Webb
Will Anyone Who Saw the Accident... J. Ashford
Will He Betray Her? H. Wood
Will in the Way. M. Burton
Will-o'-the-Wisp. P. Wentworth
Will of the Tribe. A. W. Upfield
Will on the Watch. Ernest H. Robinson
Will-Power. H. Janson
Will to Die. F. Anderson
Will to Kill. R. Bloch
Will to Kill. G. Brodie
Will to Survive. E. Salter
Will You Walk a Little Faster. R. Braddon
Willard. S. Gilbert
Willard and His Bowling Trophies. R. Brautigan
Willfreud Curse. S. F. Griffin
William Allair. H. Wood
William Conrad. P. Boulle
William Cook—Antique Dealer. R. Keverne
William Jordan Junior. J. C. Snaith
Willing to Die. J. S. Le Fanu
Willing Transgressor, and other stories. A. G. Plympton
Willing Witness. B. Cobb
Willough Haven. G. Killoran
Willoughby Affair. G. W. Appleton
Willoughby Manor. J. Wetherell
Willow Grove. J. A. Bartlett
Willow Herb. Rona Randall
Willow Pattern. R. Van Gulik
Willow Pattern War. W. H. Canaway
Willow Pond. M. K. Simmons
Willow Weep. D. Daniels
Willowbrake. R. M. Gilchrist
Willowford Woods. R. M. Gilchrist
Wills of Jane Kanwhistle. S. Fowler
Willy Velvet, Homicide Detective. R. L. Wimberly
Wilson and Some Others. G. D. H. Cole
Wilson Calling. G. D. H. Cole

Wilson's Gold. G. Tippette
Wilson's Luck. G. Tippette
Wilt Thou Have This Woman? J. M. Cobban
Wilton's Silence. P. Trent
Wily Widow. A. Bouvier
Wimbledon Common Trap. J. Hunter
Win, Place and Die! L. Lariar
Win Some, Lose Some. B. Halliday
Wind and the Rain. J. M. Simmel
Wind and the Waterfall. R. Gathorne-Hardy
Wind at Winter's End. Deborah Lewis
Wind Blows Death. C. Hare
Wind Chill Factor. T. Gifford
Wind-Chime Legacy. A. W. Mykel
Wind from Nowhere. O. Micheaux
Wind in His Fists. K. Murphy
Wind in Our Hands. M. Duston
Wind in the Cypress. R. M. Sears
Wind in the East. A. Burr
Wind in the East. H. Edmonds
Wind in the Snottygobble Tree. J. T. Story
Wind of Death. G. Black
Wind of Death. M. Wilson
Wind of Desire. K. Lindsay
Wind off the Sea. D. Beaty
Wind over the Citadel. L. Ames
Wind over the Citadel. W. E. D. Ross
Wind Tunnel. D. Buckingham
Wind-Up Doll. Carter Brown
Wind Was Cold. H. Clevely
Wind Without Rain. G. McDonell
Windblow Mystery. E. Gellibrand
Windfall. Andrea Harris
Windfall. A. Leslie
Windfall. M. Pflaum
Windfall Harvest. M. Edwin
Windfellow. C. Edwards
Winding Road. C. Dawe
Winding Sheet. R. Cassilis
Winding Stair. J. A. Hodge
Winding Stair. A. E. W. Mason
Winding Way. J. S. Fletcher
Windmill Mystery. J. J. Farjeon
Window. K. Ingram
Window. J. Reach
Window at the White Cat. M. R. Rinehart
Window Episode. E. Geller
Window Hack. R. Standish
Window in Chungking. S. H. Courtier
Window in the Dark. E. Kilvington
Window in the Dark. F. O'Rourke
Window on the Seine. F. Y. McHugh
Window on the Square. P. A. Whitney
Window over the Way. G. Simenon
Window with the Sleeping Nude. R. L. Bellem
Windows. H. B. Gilmour
Windows Facing West. V. MacFadyen
Wind's End. H. Asquith
Winds of April. I. D. Baharav
Winds of Evil. A. W. Upfield
Winds of Fear. J. Ames
Winds of Fortune. J. Farnol
Winds of Midnight. J. Blackburn
Winds of Night. K. Troy
Winds of Terror. P. H. Howell
Winds of the Old Days. B. Aswad
Winds of the World. T. Mundy
Winds of Time. H. Gibbs
Winds of Wakefield. T. R. Bernard
Windscreen Weepers and other stories of horror and suspense. Joan Aiken
Windswept Farm. W. Hewlett
Windward Passage. Mark Brewer
Windy Side of the Law. Sara Woods
Wine in a Venetian Goblet. J. McConnell
Wine of the Generals. R. P. Jones
Wine of Vengeance. J. Wellsley
Wine of Violence. N. S. Boardman
Wine of Violence. L. Egan
Wine of War. E. G. Cousins
Wine Room Murder. S. Vestal
Wine with Veronica. A. Redwood
Wine, Women...and Death. W. Deptula
Wine, Women, and Murder. Desmond Martin
Wine, Women and Murder. J. Roeburt
Wines of Cyprien. D. Daniels
Wingarden. Elsie Lee
Winged Danger. A. Foxe
Winged Death. J. R. Holden
Winged Murderer. F. MacIsaac
Winged Mystery. A. W. Upfield
Winged Victory. N. Leslie
Winged Witnesses. H. Robertson
Wingrave Case. P. Luck
Wings Above the Claypan. A. W. Upfield
Wings Above the Diamantina. A. W. Upfield
Wings Behind Bars. P. Trent
Wings of Adventure. A. Whitehouse
Wings of Chance. M. Leinster
Wings of Darkness. P. Audemars
Wings of Darkness. E. Milburn
Wings of Death. M. Boniface
Wings of Desire. M. Dekobra
Wings of Destiny. W. F. Moore
Wings of Destiny. George Weston
Wings of Destiny. Christopher Wilson
Wings of Doom. G. E. Rochester
Wings of Fear. M. G. Eberhart

Wings of Love. C. R. Gull
Wings of Love. P. Trent
Wings of Madness. J. Philips
Wings of Mystery. W. Gavine
Wings of Peace. J. Creasey
Wings of Revolution. J. R. Holden
Wings of Romance. W. E. Johns
Wings of the Black Death. G. Stockbridge
Wings of Tomorrow. P. Traill
Wings of Victory. F. M. White
Wings of the Falcon. B. Michaels
Wings over Africa. D. T. Lindsay
Wings over Panama. G. Church
Wings over the Amazon. D. T. Lindsay
Wings over the Atlantic. A. D. Divine
Wings Without Freedom. J. G. Sarasin
Winifred. D. M. Disney
Wink. K. Bennett
Winking at the Brim. G. Mitchell
Winner Take All. G. Fairlie
Winner Take All. J. McKimmey
Winner Takes All. R. Douglas
Winners. J. Mitchell
Winner's Circle. J. Hayes
Winner's Share. R. Beardwood
Winnifred's Way. A. Griffith
Winning a Princess. Old Sleuth
Winning Clue. J. Hay
Winning of Winifred. L. Tracy
Winning Through. A. Applin
Winning Through. J. Templeton
Winning Trick. N. Brand
Winnowing Winds. A. Marlowe
Winny Darling. E. Southworth
Winsome Lass. K. Lindsay
Winston Affair. H. Fast
Winston Churchill Murder. K. Netzen
Winston of the Prairie. H. Bindloss
Winter. G. Horne
Winter After This Summer. S. Ellin
Winter and the White Witch. B. Gaston
Winter at Blackfoot. C. Gayet
Winter Bride. C. Salisbury
Winter in a Dark Land. M. Lynch
Winter Keeper. J. Crecy
Winter Kill. S. Fisher
Winter Killing. F. Irwin
Winter Kills. R. Condon
Winter Landscape. N. Brand
Winter Murder Case. S. S. Van Dine
Winter of Discontent. G. Frankau
Winter of Fear. S. Tempest
Winter of Madness. D. Walker
Winter of the Fox. J. Roffman
Winter of the Wildcat. B. Gaston
Winter Quarry. P. Henissart
Winter Reckoning. N. M. Kennedy
Winter Spy. P. Henissart
Winter Stalk. J. L. Stowe
Winter Wears a Shroud. R. Chapman
Winter Wheat. E. Woodward
Wintermute. C. Brookhouse
Winter's Tale. Robert Hardy
Wintershade. E. Evans
Winterton Hotel Mystery. J. Corbett
Winterwood. D. Eden
Winton Street Mystery. H. Carstairs
Wipe-Out! D. J. Cleary
Wipeout. J. Tiger
Wire Devils. F. Packard
Wire Tappers. A. Stringer
Wired for Scandal. F. L. Wallace
Wireless Call. Mrs. C. Kernahan
Wiretap! C. Einstein
Wisdom of Father Brown. G. K. Chesterton
Wise and Foolish Virgin. G. Warden
Wise Fool. S. Jepson
Wise Fool. E. C. Reed
Wise Man of Welby. N. Worth
Wise Thrush. F. Hutchinson
Wise Virgin. G. Goodchild
Wise Virgin. M. McGrath
Wiseguys. V. Teresa
Wish Me Dead. D. West
Wish You Were Dead. R. Chapman
Wish You Were Dead. H. McCloy
Wishful Think. B. Newman
Wishing Smith. C. J. C. Hyne
Wisteria Cottage. R. M. Coates
Wistful Wanton. P. Muller
Witch. B. Michaels
Witch. B. St. James
Witch Alone. M. Higgins
Witch at the Funeral. F. Hurt
Witch Door. E. Ogilvie
Witch Finder, the Evil at Monteine. B. Ball
Witch from the Sea. P. Carr
Witch Haven. L. Churchill
Witch Hill Murder. P. G. Winslow
Witch House. E. Walton
Witch Hunt. S. Harvester
Witch-Hunt! D. Reid
Witch Man. M. B. Houston
Witch Miss Seeton. H. Carvic
Witch of Bralhaven. Marilyn Ross
Witch of Chelsea. O. Hartley
Witch of Goblin's Acres. W. E. D. Ross
Witch of Manhattan. Old Sleuth
Witch of Murray Hill. Stephanie Hall
Witch of Nun. F. Newton
Witch of the Hills. F. Warden
Witch of the Lowtide. J. D. Carr
Witch of Wykham. M. Carr
Witch or Wife. S. Rathbone
Witch Temple. Alan Graham
Witch Tree. L. B. Long
Witch Wood. C. Hale
Witchcraft for Panda One. P. N. Walker
Witchcraft Murder. J. Ingersol
Witchdance in Bavaria. Robert MacLeod
Witcheries of Craig Isuff. W. F. Williams
Witches. Carter Brown
Witches. P. Curtis
Witches' Cove. Marilyn Ross
Witches' Holiday. M. Lynch
Witches' Ladder. L. Osborne
Witches' Moon. J. Verner
Witches of All Saints. J. Tattersall
Witches of Brimstone Hill. H. Arvonen
Witches of Notting Hill. W. A. Ballinger
Witches of Omen. A. Leech
Witches of Turnstone Bay. A. Burns
Witches of Windlake. M. Lynch
Witches' Pond. F. Hurd
Witches' Pond. S. Wells
Witches' Sabbath. P. Allardyce
Witchfinder. M. Hilliard
Witching. F. Ravenswood
Witching Hill. E. W. Hornung
Witching Hour. Rona Randall
Witching Hour. F. Stevenson
Witching Hour. Augustus Thomas
Witching Night. C. S. Cody
Witchrock. B. Knox
Witch's Brew. N. Faulkner
Witch's Castle. D. Daniels
Witch's Cauldron. E. Phillpotts
Witch's Crossing. F. Stevenson
Witch's Doing. A. Dick
Witch's Hammer. C. Farr
Witch's House. C. Armstrong
Witch's Island. D. Daniels
Witch's Mark. June R. Lewis
Witch's Moon. G. Jackson
Witch's Song. M. Lynch
Witch's Suckling. G. Hall
Witch's Tower Mystery. J. Kains
Witch's Web. D. Spicer
Witchstone. V. Graham
Witchwater. G. M. Wilson
With a Bare Bodkin. C. Hare
With a Madman Behind Me. T. Powell
With a Strange Device. E. F. Russell
With a Vengeance. G. Di Pego
With a Vengeance. Dell Shannon
With a View to Matrimony, and other stories. J. Blyth
With All John's Love. M. B. Lowndes
With Bated Breath. Alice Campbell
With Blood and Kisses. R. Shattuck
With Bullet and Steel. J. K. Stafford
With Cause Enough? S. Fowler
With Chains of Brass. I. Stark
With Clipped Wings. M. S. Boyd
With Cossack and Convict. W. M. Graydon
With Criminal Instinct. R. Hardinge
With Dead Bodies. J. Cadman
With Edged Tools. H. S. Merriman
With Extreme Prejudice. B. Mather
With Fate Conspire. Y. MacManus
With Fondest Thoughts. C. Blackstock
With Gauge and Swallow, Attorneys. A. Tourgee
With Hoops of Steel. F. F. Kelly
With Intent. L. Henderson
With Intent to Deceive. M. Coles
With Intent to Destroy. K. Rogers
With Intent to Kill. B. Cobb
With Intent to Kill. G. H. Coxe
With Intent to Kill. Dell Shannon
With Intent to Kill. E. C. Vivian
With Links of Steel. Nicholas Carter
With Love from Rachel. S. Murray
With Murder for Some. H. C. Huston
With Murder in Mind. E. Ferrars
With Murder in Mind. J. Roffman
With My Friends. B. Matthews
With My Knives I Know I'm Good. J. Rathbone
With My Little Eye. D. Durrant
With My Little Eye. Roy Fuller
With No Crying. C. Fremlin
With One Stone. R. Lockridge
With Option to Die. R. Lockridge
With Shackles of Fire. Nicholas Carter
With Sirens Screaming. Ernest Booth
With Soul So Dead. G. Mason
With the Unhanged. R. Dowling
With This Ring. M. G. Eberhart
With Time Running Out. L. W. Robinson
With What Motive? T. C. H. Jacobs
Withdraw Thy Foot. F. R. Sumner
Withdrawing Room. C. MacLeod
Withered Garland. H. Gibbs
Withered Man. N. Deane
Withered Murder. A. Shaffer
Withering Fire. M. Bowen
Within an Inch of His Life. E. Gaboriau
Within Four Walls. E. Baulsir
Within Fourteen Days. W. M. Graydon
Within Sound of the Weir. T. S. Hake
Within the Bubble. J. Shearing
Within the Labyrinth. N. Lewis
Within the Law. M. Dana
Within the Law. B. Veiller
Within the Maze. H. Wood
Within the Precincts of the Prison. A. Lunn
Within the Vault. L. Thayer
Within This Circle. G. Beaumont
Within This House. F. Crisp
Within Twenty-Four Hours. H. Leyford
Without a Clue. Nicholas Carter
Without a Grave. P. Nottingham
Without a Name. Dick Stewart
Without a Trace. S. Ransome
Without a Warrant. H. Brooks
Without Clues. J. Helm
Without Gloves. J. B. Hendryx
Without Issue. H. Cresswell
Without Judge or Jury. R. Rodd
Without Justification. J. L. Rickard
Without Lawful Authority. M. Coles
Without Love or Licence. H. Smart
Without Malice. B. Graeme
Without Mercy. J. J. Dratler
Without Mercy. J. Goodwin
Without Motive. Winston Graham
Without Motive. Colin Robertson
Without Music. G. Fox
Without Orders. M. Albrand
Without the Law. H. F. Moulton
Without the Option. A. Hocking
Without Trace. C. Goodall
Without Trace. W. LeQueux
Without Trumpet or Drum. John Sanders
Without Warning. W. H. Baker
Without Witness. A. Armstrong
Witness. R. G. Toepfer
Witness. D. Uhnak
Witness at Large. M. G. Eberhart
Witness at the Window. C. Barry
Witness Before the Fact. E. Ferrars
Witness Box. V. Karsland
Witness for the Crown. Richard Gordon
Witness for the Defence. A. E. W. Mason
Witness for the Prosecution. A. Christie
Witness in Peril. M. Marlette
Witness in Support. J. H. Vahey
Witness My Death. Roy Lewis
Witness of the Sun. H. S. Williams
Witness on the Roof. A. Haynes
Witness This Woman. G. F. Fox
Witness to Murder. E. Harrison
Witness to the Crime. J. Hunter
Witness to the Deed. G. M. Fenn
Witness to Treason. M. J. Ragosta
Witness Tree. H. C. Wire
Witnesses. A. Holden
Witnesses. G. Simenon
Witnesses and the Watchmaker. G. Simenon
Wits' End. W. Spence
Wives to Burn. L. G. Blochman
Wizard Detective. Old Sleuth
Wizard of Berner's Abbey. M. Hansom
Wizard of Death. R. Forrest
Wizard of the Cue. Nicholas Carter
Wizard Tramp. Old Sleuth
Wizard's Aunt. J. Laing
Wizard's Daughter. B. Michaels
Wizard's Spyglass. E. Kinsburn
Wobble to Death. P. Lovesey
Wohldorf Shipment. P. O'Hara
Wolf. H. Holt
Wolf at the Door. F. Warden
Wolf by the Ears. Roy Lewis
Wolf Cop. R. Jessup
Wolf Creek Valley. W. C. Tuttle
Wolf Hollow Bubbles. D. H. Keller
Wolf Howls "Murder". M. L. Stokes
Wolf Hunt. M. Elder
Wolf Hunt. C. Whiting
Wolf in Man's Clothing. M. G. Eberhart
Wolf in Sheep's Clothing. J. K. Leys
Wolf in the Clouds. R. Faust
Wolf in the Fold. V. Loder
Wolf Man. A. Machard
Wolf Mountain. P. L. Sandberg
Wolf-Net. Winifred Graham
Wolf of Corsica. W. J. Elliott
Wolf of the Evenings. Winifred Graham
Wolf Pack. R. Cullum
Wolf Pack of Lobo Butte. W. C. Tuttle
Wolf Shows His Teeth. B. Sarto
Wolf Swept Down. R. Ladline
Wolf That Follows. H. Clevely
Wolf to the Slaughter. R. Rendell
Wolf Tone. L. Goldman
Wolf Tracks. D. Case
Wolf Troubleth Not. B. M. Scott
Wolf Within. Nicholas Carter
Wolf! Wolf! Josephine Bell
Wolf Woman. A. Stringer
Wolfen. W. Strieber
Wolfe's Cloister. B. Plagemann
Wolf's Claw. H. Holt
Wolf's Crag. D. Whitelaw
Wolfsbane. Craig Thomas
Wolftrap. E. Bercovici
Wolves and the Lamb. J. S. Fletcher
Wolves and the Lamb. A. Soutar
Wolves Come Down from the Mountain. M. Strong

Title Index

Wolves of Chaos. H. MacGrath
Wolves of Craywood. Jan Alexander
Wolves of New York. A. W. Aiken
Wolves of the Night. S. Horler
Wolves of the Sea. G. Leroux
Wolves of Washington. Anonymous
Woman Accused. D. Durham
Woman Accused. J. Templeton
Woman Against the World. George Griffith
Woman Against Woman. M. A. Holmes
Woman Always Knows. A. Cleft-Addams
Woman Always Wins. C. H. Bullivant
Woman and Her Master. J. F. Smith
Woman and the Prowler. S. Friedman
Woman and the Wheel. T. B. Morris
Woman Aroused. E. Lacy
Woman at Bay. Nicholas Carter
Woman at Bay. G. H. Coxe
Woman at Dead Oaks. J. Kirkpatrick
Woman at Iron Crag. A. S. Adcock
Woman at Kensington. W. LeQueux
Woman at Risk. M. Tripp
Woman Ayisha. T. Mundy
Woman Bars the Way. M. Leighton
Woman Cain. R. Richmond
Woman Delia. P. Piper
Woman Dominant. E. C. Vivian
Woman from A.U.N.T. B. Negulesco
Woman from Outside. H. Footner
Woman from the East. E. Wallace
Woman He Chose. J. H. Wallis
Woman Hunt. F. Ryck
Woman in Armour. D. C. Murray
Woman in Bed. M. Tripp
Woman in Black. H. Adams
Woman in Black. E. C. Bentley
Woman in Black. Nicholas Carter
Woman in Black. J. Ford
Woman in Black. M. Y. Halidom
Woman in Black. M. Heath
Woman in Black. W. Spence
Woman in Exchange. H. Buck
Woman in Grey. A. M. Williamson
Woman in Marble. C. Dekker
Woman in Mauve. G. MacMillan
Woman in 919. J. P. Seabrooke
Woman in Number Five. L. Meynell
Woman in Purple Pajamas. W. Kent
Woman in Question. J. R. Scott
Woman in Red. S. Campbell
Woman in Red. Anthony Gilbert
Woman in Red. R. St. Clair
Woman in Silk and Shadow. D. Daniels
Woman in the Alcove. A. K. Green
Woman in the Car. R. Marsh
Woman in the Case. Mark Allerton
Woman in the Case. C. R. Gull
Woman in the Case. H. Malot
Woman in the Case. F. P. Rathburne
Woman in the Case. N. Thurley
Woman in the Case. Bessie Turner
Woman in the Dark. D. Hammett
Woman in the Dark. F. W. Robinson
Woman in the Maze. M. Dobner
Woman in the Mirror. Winston Graham
Woman in the Picture. J. August
Woman in the Sea. Shelley Smith
Woman in the Shadow. L. J. Vance
Woman in the Wardrobe. P. Antony
Woman in the Way. W. LeQueux
Woman in the Window. J. H. Wallis
Woman in the Woods. C. Blackstock
Woman in White. W. Collins
Woman in Whitehall. R. Walker
Woman Intervenes. R. Barr
Woman Is Dead. R. King
Woman Missing and other stories. H. Nielsen
Woman Named Anne. H. Cecil
Woman Named Smith. M. C. Oemler
Woman of Action. P. Trent
Woman of Business. A. Griffiths
Woman of Cairo. J. Flagg
Woman of Character. Julian Gloag
Woman of Danger. N. W. Firth
Woman of Death. G. Boothby
Woman of Death. Old Sleuth
Woman of Destiny. S. Maddock
Woman of Evil. Nicholas Carter
Woman of Kronstadt. M. Pemberton
Woman of Mystery. Nicholas Carter
Woman of Mystery. A. K. Green
Woman of Mystery. M. Leblanc
Woman of Mystery. G. Ohnet
Woman of Nerve. N. T. Oliver
Woman of Nerve. R. M. Wells
Woman of Paris. G. Des Cars
Woman of Saigon. P. Saxon
Woman of Shanghai. M. L. Berges
Woman of Sorek. A. Gould
Woman of Steel. Nicholas Carter
Woman of Straw. C. Arley
Woman of the Grey House. G. Simenon
Woman of the Iron Bracelets. F. Barrett
Woman of Valor. A. Topol
Woman on Her Own. J. Blackmore
Woman on the Place. H. Whittington
Woman on the Roof. M. G. Eberhart
Woman on the Roof. H. Nielsen
Woman on the Spot. J. Hunter
Woman out of Nowhere. L. Hoffman
Woman Pays. S. Warwick

Woman Possessed. C. Randell
Woman Question. D. Malm
Woman Racket. G. Lawrence
Woman Spy. H. De Halsalle
Woman Stealer. Harry Mills
Woman Tempted Him. W. Westall
Woman, the Man, and the Monster. C. Dawe
Woman, the Mystery. H. Herman
Woman: The Sphinx. F. Hume
Woman Under the Mountain. R. McDougald
Woman Who Dared. L. L. Lynch
Woman Who Dared. A. M. Williamson
Woman Who Held On. F. Hume
Woman Who Knew. M. Pemberton
Woman Who Saved the World. W. Holt-White
Woman Who Stole Everything and other stories. A. Bennett
Woman Who Tempted. G. Warden
Woman Who Understood. Mrs. C. Kernahan
Woman Who Waited. T. C. H. Jacobs
Woman Who Was. P. Boileau
Woman Who Was No More. P. Boileau
Woman Who Was Not. A. Applin
Woman Who Would Not Die. C. B. Bauman
Woman Wins. R. Barr
Woman Wins. C. H. Bullivant
Woman Wins. R. Machray
Woman with a Gun. G. H. Coxe
Woman with a "Record". L. Jackson
Woman with a Secret. R. Ferguson
Woman with Claws. Williams Forrest
Woman with One Hand, and Mr. Ely's Engagement. R. Marsh
Woman with the Diamonds. F. Warden
Woman with the Portuguese Basket. E. Wuorio
Woman with the Yellow Eyes. C. Dawe
Woman with the Yellow Hair and Other Modern Mysteries. Anonymous
Woman with Two Smiles. M. Leblanc
Woman Without a Name. L. M. Janifer
Woman Without a Name. G. Lenotre
Woman Worth Winning. G. M. Fenn
Womanhunt. M. Derby
Woman's Burden. F. Hume
Woman's Calvary. J. Middlemass
Woman's Courage. F. Wicks
Woman's Debt. W. LeQueux
Woman's Devotion. J. W. Postgate
Woman's Eyes. G. Weill
Woman's Face. F. Warden
Woman's Fate. E. Southworth
Woman's Footprint. E. R. Punshon
Woman's Friend. M. Storm
Woman's Hand. Nicholas Carter
Woman's Hand. J. R. Coryell
Woman's Honor. E. P. Green
Woman's Honor. E. A. Young
Woman's House. H. L. V. Fletcher
Woman's Prerogative. G. B. Lissenden
Woman's Ransom. F. W. Robinson
Woman's Revenge. M. Pemberton
Woman's Story. F. Warden
Woman's Tragedy. L. L. Lynch
Woman's Vengeance. M. A. Holmes
Woman's Vengeance. J. Payn
Woman's View. H. Flowerdew
Woman's World. A. Askew
Women Are Like That. T. C. H. Jacobs
Women Are Like That. E. Woodward
Women Are Skin Deep. F. Whelton
Women at Belguardo. M. Erskine
Women—Dope—and Murder. Roland Daniel
Women Hate Till Death. H. Janson
Women in the Case. L. Tracy
Women in White. J. Reach
Women Like to Know. Kevin O'Hara
Women of London. B. Hemyng
Women of Morning. A. Sewart
Women of Paris. B. Hemyng
Women of Peasenhall. R. J. White
Women Swore Revenge. I. H. Irwin
Women to Love. S. Drago
Women Who Wait. E. Bissell
Women's Battalion. W. A. Ballinger
Won by Magic. Nicholas Carter
Wonder Jack. Old Sleuth
Wonderful Career of Ebenezer Lobb. A. Upward
Wonderful Detective. Old Sleuth
Wonderful Scheme. H. S. Keeler
Wonderful Scheme of Mr. Christopher Thorne. H. S. Keeler
Wondering Moon. George Weston
Wood and the Trees. M. Elgin
Woodchuck Hunt. U. Becher
Woodchuck Jerry. Old Sleuth
Woodchuck Jerry, the Country Detective. Old Sleuth
Woodcutter Operation. K. Royce
Wooden Hand. F. Hume
Wooden Indian. C. Wells
Wooden Overcoat. P. Branch
Wooden Spectacles. H. S. Keeler
Wooden Wolf. John Kelly
Woodley Lane Ghost and other stories. M. V. Dahlgren
Wooing of a Fairy. G. Warden
Wooing of Esther Gray. L. Tracy
Wooing of Grey Eyes, and other stories. Riccardo Stephens
Wooing of Martha. C. G. Mitford

Woolf Sarason, Special Agent. M. Moiseiwitsch
Woolen Monkey. G. Goodchild
Word and the Will. J. Payn
Word for Word and Letter for Letter. A. J. D. Biddle
Word in Her Ear. P. Conway
Word of Honour. H. C. McNeile
Word of Six Letters. H. Adams
Word of the Sorceress. B. Mitford
Words for Murder Perhaps. E. Candy
Words Have Wings. N. Berrow
Work for the Hangman. B. Graeme
Work of Darkness. J. Karney
Work of Her Hands. A. Askew
Workers All. P. Trent
Works in Darkness. J. B. Harris-Burland
Working for the Man. R. Dennis
Working Man Detective. D. J. MacKenzie
Works of the Late Edgar Allan Poe. E. A. Poe
World Championship Mystery. W. J. Passingham
World Grabbers. P. W. Fairman
World in My Pocket. J. H. Chase
World Masters. George Griffith
World of Crime. M. F. Goron
World of Sin. H. T. Johnson
World of Tim Frazer. F. Durbridge
World of Violence. Colin Wilson
World Outside. H. MacGrath
World Rapers. B. von Block
World-Shakers. D. Reid
World Stood Still. W. Holt-White
World, the Flesh, and the Devil. M. E. Braddon
World Under Snow. D. K. Broster
World Without Dreams. R. Garland
World Without End. Winifred Graham
Worldbreaker. J. Milton
Worldy Goods. A. Soutar
World's a Stage. K. Kellow
World's Blackmail. L. Cleeve
World's End. J. Conaway
World's Fair Goblin. K. Robeson
World's Fair Murders. J. Ashenhurst
World's Finger. T. W. Hanshew
World's Great Snare. E. P. Oppenheim
Worm of Death. N. Blake
Worms Must Wait. J. Wainwright
Worse and More of It. N. E. Henshaw
Worse Than a Crime. F. Crane
Worse Than Death. L. Lamb
Worse Than Murder. E. Berckman
Worse Than Murder. D. Duncan
Worst Case on Record. Nicholas Carter
Worst Enemy. G. Hackforth-Jones
Worst Man in the World. S. Horler
Worst Man in the World. F. Richardson
Worst Squadron in France. G. E. Rochester
Worst Way to Die. B. Rossi
Worsted Viper. G. Mitchell
Wotan Warhead. J. Follett
Wotan's Wedge. F. Gerard
Would You Kill Him? G. P. Lathrop
Wound and the Scar. V. Scannell
Wound of Love. R. V. Cassill
Wounded and the Slain. D. Goodis
Wounded Heart. K. Ross
Wounds of Treason. M. Vinter
Woven Web. P. Audemars
Wrack. M. Drake
Wraith. P. MacDonald
Wraith of Olverstone. F. Warden
Wraiths and Changelings. G. Mitchell
Wraithwood. L. Churchill
Wrap It Up. A. Dean
Wrath of Fu Manchu and other stories. S. Rohmer
Wrath of Garde. J. La Plante
Wrath of God. J. Graham
Wrath of the Lion. Harry Patterson
Wrath to Come. E. P. Oppenheim
Wraxton Marne. R. Ray
Wreath for a Dead Angel. H. Kimberley
Wreath for a Lady. M. Baroni
Wreath for a Redhead. Carter Brown
Wreath for a Redhead. Peter Chambers
Wreath for a Redhead. B. Moore
Wreath for a Spy. R. Tashkent
Wreath for America. R. Raine
Wreath for Jenny's Grave. Charlotte Hunt
Wreath for Miss Wong. C. Leader
Wreath for Rebecca. Carter Brown
Wreath for Rivera. N. Marsh
Wreath for the Bride. M. Lang
Wreath for the Lady. H. Holt
Wreath from Bangkok. C. Leader
Wreath of Bones. J. N. Chance
Wreath of Camellias. G. B. Mair
Wreath of Cherry Blossom. C. Leader
Wreath of Lords and Ladies. James Fraser
Wreath of Orchids. M. Shoebridge
Wreath of Poppies. C. Leader
Wreath of Roses. J. Blackburn
Wreath of Water-Lilies. P. Flower
Wreck. P. J. Cooper
Wreck of the Chinook. L. Tracy
Wreck of the Grey Cat. Winston Graham
Wreck of the Mary Deare. H. Innes

Wreck of the Redwing. B. Grimshaw
Wrecked in Port. E. Yates
Wrecker. Ruth Alexander
Wrecker. A. Ridley
Wrecker. R. L. Stevenson
Wreckers. F. Lynde
Wreckers Must Breathe. H. Innes
Wrecking Crew. D. Hamilton
Wrecking of Offshore Five. R. Johnston
Wrecking Ray. G. E. C. Webster
Wrenfield Mystery. G. Woden
Wrestler on the Shore. L. Lurgan
Wrist Mark. J. S. Fletcher
Write It Murder. H. Arre
Write Me a Murder. Amanda Carter
Write Me a Murder. F. Knott
Write Murder Down. R. Lockridge
Write-Off. P. Malloch
Write Off the Redhead. M. Brody
Write on Both Sides of the Paper. M. Kelly
Writing on the Wall. H. Adams
Written in Blood. Nicholas Carter
Written in Cypher. E. Gaboriau
Written in Dust. M. Burton
Written in Red. C. H. Montague
Wrong Body. Anthony Gilbert
Wrong Body. V. A. Van Sickle
Wrong Box. G. Napier
Wrong Box. R. L. Stevenson
Wrong Case. J. Crumley
Wrong House. C. F. Gregg
Wrong Letter. W. S. Masterman
Wrong Man. H. C. Bailey
Wrong Man in the Mirror. P. Loraine
Wrong Mr. Chamberlain and other stories. P. Herring
Wrong Move. A. Burr
Wrong Road. A. Griffiths
Wrong Murder. C. Rice
Wrong Murder Mystery. C. Barry
Wrong Murderer. H. Clevely
Wrong Number. P. Luck
Wrong Ones. J. McKimmey
Wrong Road. A. Griffiths
Wrong Road by Hook or Crook. A. Griffiths
Wrong Saturday. E. Thompson
Wrong Side of the Sky. G. Lyall
Wrong Slant of Red. H. L. Skalland
Wrong Target. John Wolfe
Wrong That Was Done. John Marsh
Wrong That Was Done. F. W. Robinson
Wrong Turning. T. E. B. Clarke
Wrong Venus. C. Williams
Wrong Verdict. W. S. Masterman
Wrong Verdict. A. O. Pollard
Wrong Way Down. E. Daly
Wrong Way to Die. E. Messenger
Wrong Wife. A. S. Roche
Wrongdoer. A. Upward
Wrongly Condemned. B. Harte
Wrychester Paradise. J. S. Fletcher
Wu Fang. Roland Daniel
Wu Fang's Revenge. Roland Daniel
Wulfheim. M. Furey
Wyatt's Hurricane. D. Bagley
Wych Stone. M. McEvoy
Wycherly Woman. R. Macdonald
Wychford Poisoning Case. A. Berkeley
Wychwood. N. St. John
Wycliffe and the Pea-Green Boat. W. J. Burley
Wycliffe and the Scapegoat. W. J. Burley
Wycliffe and the Schoolgirls. W. J. Burley
Wycliffe in Paul's Court. W. J. Burley
Wycliffe-Pepin Case. A. Fane
Wye Valley Mystery. Essex Smith
Wylder's Hand. J. S. Le Fanu
Wyllard's Weird. M. E. Braddon
Wyndham's Pal. H. Bindloss
Wyndham's Partner. H. Bindloss
Wyndspelle. A. Vandergriff
Wyndspelle's Child. A. Vandergriff
Wynnum. D. Hennessey
Wyoming Tragedy. W. B. M. Ferguson
Wyss Pursuit. Adam Hamilton
Wyvern Mystery. J. S. Le Fanu

X. E. Sudak
X Esquire. L. Charteris
X14. G. Lennox
X. Jones. H. S. Keeler
X. Jones of Scotland Yard. H. S. Keeler
X Marks the Spot. Muriel Stafford
X Marks the Spot. M. Butterworth
X Marks the Spot. L. Thayer
X-On. R. M. Hunt
X-Rated Corpse. M. Avallone
X-Ray Menace. M. Herscholt
X-Ray Murders. M. S. Michel
X-Ray Solution. K. Voldeng
X v. Rex. M. Porlock
XX—A Fatal Clue. Anonymous
XYY Man. K. Royce
XYZ. A. K. Green

Xander Pursuit. Adam Hamilton
Xavier Affair. R. L. Fish
Xelucha and Others. M. P. Shiel
X's Page. N. Miller

Y. Cheung, Business Detective. H. S. Keeler
Yacht of Mystery. W. M. Graydon
Yakuza. L. Schrader
Yang Meridian. J. Leasor
Yangtze Run. P. O'Hara
Yank. A. Sugar
Yank in Fleet Street. R. McLoughlin
Yankee Lawyer—The Autobiography of Ephraim Tutt. A. Train
Yankee Napoleon. J. F. Macpherson
Yankee Poodle. C. H. Gibbs-Smith
Yankey Rue, the Ex-Pugilist Detective. Old Sleuth
Yaroslav Incident. D. Mariner
Yard Lengths. D. Shoubridge
Yashar Pursuit. Adam Hamilton
Yasmin. A. Lowing
Yatton Murders. L. Galletley
Yawning Lion. M. Warrick
Yazoo Mystery. I. Craddock
Year and a Day. G. Thorne
Year As a Lion. E. Roman
Year of August. M. Saxton
Year of Living Dangerously. C. J. Koch
Year of Miracle. F. Hume
Year of the Ape. L. Chang
Year of the Boar. L. Chang
Year of the Dragon. L. Chang
Year of the Dragon. B. Copper
Year of the Golden Ape. C. Forbes
Year of the Horse. L. Chang
Year of the Rat. L. Chang
Year of the Rat. M. Zarubica
Year of the Rooster. M. K. Simmons
Year of the Snake. L. Chang
Year of the Tiger. L. Chang
Year of the Tiger. M. Fallon
Years Between. P. Trent
Years of the Hungry Tiger. J. G. Davis
Yell Bloody Murder. J. Shallit
Yell Ruddy Murder. J. Shallit
Yellerlegs. L. C. Douthwaite
Yellow Angels. H. E. Helseth
Yellow Arrow Murders. W. W. Mason
Yellow Badge. J. Middlemass
Yellow Beetle. A. B. Sherlock
Yellow Brand. Nicholas Carter
Yellow Brick Road. E. Cadell
Yellow Bungalow Mystery. L. Gribble
Yellow Card Mystery. P. G. Larbalestier
Yellow Cat. H. C. Gibbons
Yellow Cat. C. Knight
Yellow Circle. P. Foley
Yellow Circle. C. E. Walk
Yellow Claw. S. Rohmer
Yellow Claws of Wong. E. H. Robinson
Yellow Cloud. K. Robeson
Yellow Corsair. James Bennett
Yellow Crayon. E. P. Oppenheim
Yellow Crystal. A. Wynne
Yellow Danger. M. P. Shiel
Yellow Death. U. Key
Yellow Devil. Roland Daniel
Yellow Devil. J. J. Farjeon
Yellow Diamond. G. F. Gibbs
Yellow Diamond. A. Sergeant
Yellow Disc Murder. Nicholas Carter
Yellow Disc Murders. T. A. Plummer
Yellow Document. M. Allain
Yellow-Dog Contract. Ross Thomas
Yellow Door. D. Whitelaw
Yellow Dove. G. F. Gibbs
Yellow Dragon. A. Mills
Yellow Dusk. B. Bedwell
Yellow Face. W. M. Graydon
Yellow Face. F. M. White
Yellow Fangs. T. F. Elstow
Yellow Fetish. T. W. Pierson
Yellow Fiend. Mrs. Alexander
Yellow Fiend. W. J. Elliott
Yellow Flag. I. S. Black
Yellow Flag. E. Yates
Yellow Gods. J. G. Brandon
Yellow Gold of Tiryns. H. Osborne
Yellow Hand. A. Upward
Yellow Hearse. F. Mahannah
Yellow Hibiscus. J. Templeton
Yellow Hoard. K. Robeson
Yellow Holly. F. Hume
Yellow House. E. P. Oppenheim
Yellow Hunchback. F. Hume
Yellow Is for Fear and other stories. D. Eden
Yellow Jacket. E. Snell
Yellow Journalist. M. Michelson
Yellow Label. Nicholas Carter
Yellow Letter. W. A. Johnston
"Yellow—Like Gold!" Douglas Christie
Yellow Magic. E. Thomas
Yellow Man. C. Dawe
Yellow Mask. J. G. Brandon

Yellow Mask. W. Collins
Yellow Men and Gold. G. Morris
Yellow Mistletoe. W. S. Masterman
Yellow Munro. G. Fairlie
Yellow Music Kill. W. J. Sheldon
Yellow Overcoat. S. Acre
Yellow Paint War. W. C. Taylor
Yellow Peril. G. Hackforth-Jones
Yellow Peril. M. P. Shiel
Yellow Phantom. L. Cargill
Yellow Rat. F. Grierson
Yellow Ribbon. W. LeQueux
Yellow Robe Murders. Melville Burt
Yellow Robed Wago. Marion Roberts
Yellow Rock. D. Footman
Yellow Room. M. R. Rinehart
Yellow Room. G. Shipway
Yellow Satchel. F. Whishaw
Yellow Scourge. C. Steele
Yellow Seven. E. Snell
Yellow Shadows. S. Rohmer
Yellow Shadows of Death. R. Wallace
Yellow Shop. F. MacIsaac
Yellow Skull. G. H. Teed
Yellow Snake. R. Wallace
Yellow Spider. J. C. Beecham
Yellow Stockings. D. W. MacArthur
Yellow Strangler. Colin Robertson
Yellow Streak. V. Williams
Yellow Stub. E. Lynn
Yellow Taxi. J. Stagge
Yellow Terror. R. Harding
Yellow Ticket. V. Morton
Yellow Tiger! G. H. Teed
Yellow Triangle. Margery Lawrence
Yellow Trousers. P. Fry
Yellow Turban. C. Jay
Yellow Typhoon. H. MacGrath
Yellow Vengeance. P. Urquhart
Yellow Villa. S. Blanc
Yellow Violet. F. Crane
Yellow Viper. S. Fairway
Yellow Wagon. C. Edwards
Yellow Will Out! Warren Hill
Yellow Wolf. T. S. King
Yellow Yoke. A. Askew
Yellowfish. J. Keeble
Yellowleaf. Sacha Gregory
Yellowstones. G. Goodchild
Yellowthread Street. W. Marshall
Yermakov Transfer. Derek Lambert
Yes, Inspector McLean. G. Goodchild
Yesterday Is Dead. B. Barnes
Yesterday Walkers. S. Harvester
Yesterday's Bones. S. Tower
Yesterday's Child. Barbara Wood
Yesterday's Enemy. W. Haggard
Yesterday's Enemy. M. Moiseiwitsch
Yesterday's Evil. L. B. Clark
Yesterday's Evil. D. Daniels
Yesterday's Love. J. L. Rickard
Yesterday's Man. J. Midgley
Yesterday's Murder. C. Rice
Yesterday's Murder. J. York
Yesterday's Poison. Ruth Grayson
Yesterday's Spy. L. Deighton
Yesteryear Phantom. W. E. D. Ross
Yet She Must Die. H. McCutcheon
Yet She Must Die. Stella Phillips
Yet She Must Die. Sara Woods
Yetta the Magnificent. J. F. Macpherson
Yield to the Night. Joan Henry
Yield to the Night. J. Karney
Yo-Ho, and a Bottle of Rum! H. M. Stephenson
Yoga Mist. E. P. Thorne
Yogi Shrouds Yolanda and Poison Ivy. Carter Brown
Yokohama Hood. J. R. Fernandes
Yolan. J. Tickell
Yolan of the Plains. J. Tickell
Yonder. M. B. Houston
Yonder Grow the Daisies. W. Lipman
Yoris. R. Ingham
Yorkshire Moorland Murder. J. S. Fletcher
Yoshar the Soldier. W. Harrington
You and Me. A. Plater
You Asked for It. I. Fleming
You Belong to Me. Sam Ross
You Bet Your Life. S. M. Kaminsky
You Can Always Blame the Rain. M. Fredman
You Can Always Duck. P. Cheyney
You Can Call It a Day. P. Cheyney
You Can Deal Me In. W. Newton
You Can Help Me. M. Birmingham
You Can Keep the Corpse. Colin Robertson
You Can Only Die Once. J. Beedle
You Can Run So Far. M. Barnes
You Can Say That Again. J. H. Chase
You Can't Believe Your Eyes. Joan Fleming
You Can't Call It Murder. Neill Graham
You Can't Call It Murder. D. Ramsay
You Can't Catch Me. L. Lariar
You Can't Die Here. S. Coburn
You Can't Die Laughing. A. A. Fair
You Can't Die Tomorrow. L. Gribble
You Can't Do Business with Murder. D. Von Elsner
You Can't Escape. L. M. Janifer

Title Index

You Can't Gag the Dead. M. Propper
You Can't Get Away by Running. W. Chambers
You Can't Get Away with Murder! A. Spiller
You Can't Hit a Woman and other stories. P. Cheyney
You Can't Ignore Murder. R. Teague
You Can't Keep the Change. P. Cheyney
You Can't Kill a Corpse. L. Trimble
You Can't Kill Shadows. R. Goyne
You Can't Kill the Dead. E. Bowen-Rowlands
You Can't Live Forever. H. Q. Masur
You Can't See Around Corners. J. Cleary
You Can't Stop Me. W. Ard
You Can't Trust Duchesses and other stories. P. Cheyney
You Could Die Laughing, and The Swingers. J. Adams
You Did It. E. K. Goldthwaite
You Die in Valpaso. B. Sarto
You Die Next, Jill Baby! K. Carr
You Die Today. B. Kendrick
You Don't Die Twice. R. Angel
You Don't Need an Enemy. R. M. Stern
You Don't Say! H. Luger
You Find Him—I'll Fix Him. Raymond Marshall
You Flash Bastard. G. F. Newman
You Gotta Be Rough. M. Fiaschetti
You Have Yourself a Deal. J. H. Chase
You Kill Me. J. D. MacDonald
You Kill Me! P. Muller
You Know the Way It Is. A. E. Jones
You Leave Me Cold! S. Rogers
You Live Once. J. D. MacDonald
You Murdered Me. R. Tarne
You Must Never Go Back. B. Cleeve
You Never Know with Women. J. H. Chase
You Never Learn. M. Cronin
You Nice Bastard. G. F. Newman
You Only Die Once. H. B. Kaye
You Only Hang Once. H. W. Roden
You Only Live Twice. I. Fleming
You Only Live Until You Die. S. Weinstein
You Pay for Pity. W. Mole
You Pay the Price. Griff
You Pay Your Money. M. Cronin
You Play the Black and the Red Comes Up. R. Hallas
You Remember the Case. T. Claymore
You Shall Know Them. Vercors
You Slay Me. D. Spade
You Stand Accused. D. Hughston
You Take the Rap. Spike Gordon
You Talk Too Much. B. Shannon
You, the Jury. J. M. Liebeler
You, the Jury. J. Reach
You Too Can Have a Body. F. Robinson
"You Took Me...Keep Me." D. Glinto
You Want to Die, Johnny? G. Black
You Will Die Today! R. I. Wakefield
You Will Like It Here. N. Dorer
You Won't Let Me Finish. Joan Fleming
You Won't Need a Coat. E. Messenger
You'd Be Surprised. P. Cheyney
You'll Be Better Off Dead. M. Storm
You'll Be Sorry! S. Rogers
You'll Be the Death of Me. M. Lynch
You'll Catch Your Death. David Hume
You'll Die, Darling. M. Grove
You'll Die Laughing. Craig Cooper
You'll Die Laughing. B. Elliott
You'll Die Laughing. M. Grove
You'll Die Laughing. J. Tobias
You'll Die Next! H. Whittington
You'll Die Now! R. Drennen
You'll Die Today. M. Grove
You'll Die Tomorrow. M. Grove
You'll Die Tonight. M. Grove
You'll Die When You Hear This. M. Grove
You'll Die Yesterday. M. Grove
You'll End Up Dead. L. H. Hart
You'll Fry Tomorrow. M. V. Heberden
You'll Get Yours. T. Wills
You'll Hang, My Love. F. Swann
You'll Have to Talk. D. Steel
You'll Like My Mother. N. A. Hintze
You'll Never Get Me. S. Morelli
You'll Never Get to Heaven. S. Mitchell
You'll Never See Me Again. W. Irish
You'll Never Take Me. R. D. Mead
You'll Play This My Way. D. Spade
Young Accused. A. Furness
Young Alladin. Old Sleuth
Young and Deadly. J. Carrick
Young and Fair. N. R. Nash
Young and Violent. V. Packer
Young and Wild. Morton Cooper
Young Ann. Elizabeth Ford
Young Archduchess. W. LeQueux
Young Beck. M. M. Bodkin
Young Blood. E. W. Hornung
Young Blood. F. Lynde
Young Buffalo. C. E. Blaney
Young Buffalo in New York. C. E. Blaney
Young Can Die Protesting. T. Wells
Young Cardinaud. G. Simenon
Young Chauncey. Old Sleuth
Young Chevalier. D. W. MacArthur

Young Dash. Old Sleuth
Young Detective. R. Abbott
Young Dillinger. S. Stuart
Young Don't Cry. R. Jessup
Young Engineer. Old Sleuth
Young Eve and Old Adam. T. Gallon
Young Flynn. E. L. Long
Young Gingers. Old Sleuth
Young Girl's Bondage. J. R. Wilmot
Young Girl's Life. B. L. Farjeon
Young Harold. Old Sleuth
Young Ladies' Room. Elizabeth Ford
Young Lord Folliot. N. H. Romanes
Young Love. J. G. Brandon
Young Lucifer. C. Blackstock
Young Magician. Old Sleuth
Young Man from Lima. J. Blackburn
Young Man, I Think You're Dying. Joan Fleming
Young Man in Question. J. L. Rickard
Young Man on a Bicycle. V. Canning
Young Man with a Scythe. A. Kennington
Young Men May Die. D. Craig
Young Mr. Gibbs. J. L. Rickard
Young Mrs. Barter's Repentence. D. C. Murray
Young Mrs. Caudle. G. R. Sims
Young Mrs. Henniker. J. L. Rickard
Young Prey. H. Waugh
Young Savages. E. Hunter
Young Sleuth's Victory. A. Kutch
Young Vanish. F. Everton
Young Vigilance. Old Sleuth
Young Villain with Wings. R. Kruger
Young Wallingford. G. R. Chester
Young Widow. E. E. Cameron
Young Wife's Trial. F. Warden
Young Wolves. H. Janson
Younger Venus. N. Royde-Smith
Youngest Miss Brown. F. Warden
Youngest Soldier of the Grand Armee. F. Du Boisgobey
Your Casket Awaits, Madame. M. Lynch
Your Daughter Will Die! J. P. Cody
Your Day in the Barrel. P. Furst
Your Deal, My Lovely. P. Cheyney
Your Friendly Neighborhood Death Pedlar. J. Sangster
Your Golden Jugular. W. Squerent
Your Loving Victim. P. McGerr
Your Money and Your Life. G. Milner
Your Money and Your Wife. Ritchie Perry
Your Move, Delaney! B. Singer
Your Neck in a Noose. E. Ferrars
Your Number Is Up. A. Mills
Your Red Wagon. E. Anderson
Your Secret Friend. M. Torrie
Your Secret Is in a Well. Elaine Turner
Your Shot, Darling! L. Bergquist
Your Time Is Up. E. F. Hornung
Your Turn, Mr. Moto. J. P. Marquand
You're a Long Time Dead. R. Clapperton
You're Best Alone. P. Curtis
You're Better Off Dead. Peter Chambers
You're Dead, My Lovely. Gene Ross
You're Dead Without Money. J. H. Chase
You're Fairly Welcome. J. Ditton
You're Hired: You're Dead. K. Carr
You're in the Racket, Too. J. Curtis
You're Lonely When You're Dead. J. H. Chase
You're My Man! C. C. Waddell
You're Never Too Old to Die. A. D. Goldstein
You're No Lady. Spike Gordon
You're Welcome to Ulster! M. Gallie
You're Wrong, Delaney. B. Singer
Yours Truly, Angus MacIvor. N. Harman
Yours Truly, Jack the Ripper. R. Bloch
Youth at Bay. L. Vincent
Youth Hostel Murders. G. Carr
Youth Hostel Mystery. L. Dowsett
Youth Without Glory. B. Von Hutten
Youthful Imposter. G. W. M. Reynolds
You've Bet Your Life. G. Ashe
You've Got Him Cold. T. B. Dewey
You've Got It Coming. J. H. Chase
You've Had Your Chance. J. Cairo
Yu-Chi Stone. E. Snell
Yu-Malu, the Dragon Princess. T. Leslie
Yu'an Hee See Laughs. S. Rohmer
Yukon Gold. W. D. Blankenship
Yukon Kid. J. B. Hendryx
Yunnan Terminus. R. Neebel
Yvonne, the Confident. K. Kimbrough

Z Cars. T. K. Martin
Z Cars Again. A. Prior
"Z" Case. Roland Daniel
Z Document. Nick Carter
Z Effect. M. Laurens
Z for Zaborra. E. Wuorio
"Z" Murders. J. J. Farjeon
Z Papers. G. S. Simmons
"Z" Ray. E. Snell
Z-Sting. I. Wallace
Z Warning. D. Oran

Zadda Street Affair. W. Jackson
Zadig. Voltaire
Zadok's Treasure. M. Arnold
Zahara. M. T. Walworth
Zaharan Pursuit. Adam Hamilton
Zakari's Skull. Michael Barrett
Zakhov Mission. A. Gulyashki
Zalea. R. C. Garland
Zaleski's Percentage. D. MacKenzie
Zambesi Break. T. Beattie
Zambra the Detective. H. Hill
Zantelli. Old Sleuth
Zanzibar Intrigue. V. W. Mason
Zap Day. J. Lindblad
Zastrozzi. P. B. Shelley
Zebra-Striped Hearse. R. Macdonald
Zelda. Carter Brown
Zeluco. J. Moore
Zemba. M. Grant
Zembya Expedition. J. Rosenberger
Zen There Was Murder. H. R. F. Keating
Zenia: Spy in Togoland. C. Cameron
Zenobie Capitaine. F. Du Boisgobey
Zeph and other stories. G. R. Sims
Zeppelin Destroyer. W. LeQueux
Zeppelin's Passenger. E. P. Oppenheim
Zero Always Wins. P. Gascoigne
Zero at the Bone. E. Ferrars
Zero Cool. J. Lange
Zero Factor. W. O. Johnson
Zero Hour. L. C. Douthwaite
Zero Hour. Colin Robertson
Zero in the Gate. S. Farrar
Zero Minus Nine. E. P. Thorne
Zero 08:00. B. Gaston
Zero Take All. H. Janson
Zero the 14th. H. Clevely
Zero Trap. P. Harcourt
Zhukov Briefing. A. Trew
Zia. P. Wynnton
Zig-Zag Man. J. C. Goodwin
Zig-Zag the Clown. F. Du Boisgobey
Zig Zag...to Armageddon. T. Foster
Ziggurat. R. Katz
Zilov Bombs. D. G. Barron
Zinger. L. Davidov
Zinsser Implant. L. Kamarck
Zinzin Road. F. Knebel
Zion Road. S. Harvester
Zitlaw the Cruel. S. Wilkinson
Zodiac. D. Lees
Zodiac Killer. J. Weissman
Zofloya. C. Dacre
Zola's Thirteen. G. Morton
Zolar's Astrological Murder Mysteries. Zolar
Zolotov Affair. R. H. Rimmer
Zombie. E. Lecale
Zombie. D. Lynn
Zombie. R. St. Clair
Zone of Fire. H. Hill
Zone Zero. J. Robb
Zoo Gang. P. Gallico
Zoo Murder. F. Grierson
Zoo Murders. J. Farr
Zoo Ship. G. Volk
Zoom! Peter Townend
Zoot-Suit Murders. T. Sanchez
Zurich/AZ 900. M. Albrand
Zuss Imperative. P. Cleife
Zylgrahoff. J. C. Shannon

Settings Index

Settings Index

ABYSSINIA. SEE: ETHIOPIA.

ACADEMIA (ACAD. SCHOOL SETTINGS AT ALL LEVELS)
Aird, C. Parting Breath
Anderson, R. Cover Her with Roses
Anthony, D. Midnight Lady and the Mourning Man
Asimov, I. Death Dealers
August, J. Troubled Star
Bagby, G. Corpse with the Purple Thighs
Barry, C. Secrecy at Sandhurst
Bell, Josephine. Summer School Mystery
Bidwell, M. Death and His Brother
Blackstock, C. Melon in the Cornfield
Blake, N. Morning After Death
  Question of Proof
Boyd, M. Murder in the Stacks
Bramhall, M. Murder Is Contagious
Bronson, F. W. Bulldog Has the Key
Broome, A. Cambridge Murders
  Oxford Murders
Bruce, L. Death at St. Asprey's School
Brucker, M. Death in the Dormitory
Bullett, G. Judgment in Suspense
Burley, W. J. Taste of Power
Burton, M. Murder in the Coalhole
  Murder out of School
Bush, C. Case of the Dead Shepherd
Caird, J. Murder Scholastic
Campbell, M. E. Scandal Has Two Faces
Candy, E. Words for Murder Perhaps
Carr, J. D. Dead Man's Knock
Cassill, R. V. Dormitory Women
Chater, L. Course in Murder
Christie, A. Cat Among the Pigeons
  They Do It with Mirrors
Clark, Douglas. Golden Rain
Clinton-Baddeley, V. C. Death's Bright Dart
Clutton-Brock, A. Murder at Liberty Hall
Cohen, O. R. May Day Mystery
Cole, G. D. H. Knife in the Dark
  Off with Her Head!
  Scandal at School
Collins, R. Case of the Philosopher's Ring
Compton, G. Disguise for a Dead Gentleman
Constantine, K. C. Blank Page
Coxe, K. B. Murder Most Foul
Crispin, E. Case of the Gilded Fly
  Love Lies Bleeding
Cross, A. Poetic Justice
  Theban Mysteries
Dalmas, H. Exit Screaming
Dane, J. Y. Murder Cum Laude
Davidson, T. L. Murder in the Laboratory
Davis, D. S. Shock Wave
Davis, Mildred. Tell Them What's-Her-Name Called
Davis, S. Death in Seven Hours
Devine, D. M. Death Is My Bridegroom
  Devil at Your Elbow
DeWeese, G. Wanting Factor
DeWeese, J. Web of Guilt
Dillon, E. Death in the Quadrangle
Dwight, O. Close His Eyes
Ellis, V. Death Comes Like a Thief
Eustis, H. Horizontal Man
Evans, F. Pistols and Pedagogues
Fairway, S. Long Tunnel
Farrar, S. Murder Goes to School
Farrer, K. Gownsman's Gallows
Fenwick, E. Long Way Down
Fenwick, E. P. Murder in Haste
Fiske, D. Academic Murder
Foote-Smith, E. Gentle Albatross
Ford, L. By the Watchman's Clock
Freeman, K. Gown and Shroud
Fuller, T. Harvard Has a Homicide
Gilbert, M. Night of the Twelfth
Gill, B. M. Death Drop
Gilla, E. N. Cap and Gown for a Shroud
Graaf, P. Sapphire Conference
Graham, J. A. Involvement of Arnold Wechsler
Gray, J. Untimely Slain
Greenbaum, L. Out of Shape
Gresham, E. Puzzle in Parchment
Hardy, W. Lady Killer
Harrison, William. In a Wild Sanctuary
Hawton, H. Murder by Mathematics
Heddle, E. F. Mystery of St. Rule's
Hill, R. Advancement of Learning
Hobson, P. Titty's Dead
Hodgkin, M. R. Student Body
Holland, I. Grenelle
Hollis, J. Teach You a Lesson
Holman, C. Death Like Thunder
Holton, L. Corner of Paradise
Hopkins, K. Campus Corpse
Hoppe, J. Lesson Is Murder
Hoster, G. Goodbye, Dear Elizabeth
Hubbard, M. A. Murder Takes the Veil
Hughes, B. Murder in the Zoo
Hull, H. Tapping on the Wall
Iams, J. Corpse of the Old School
Ince, D. In Those Dark Woods

Innes, M. Death at the President's Lodging
  Old Hall, New Hall
  Weight of the Evidence
Irving, A. Bitter Ending
James, P. D. Shroud for a Nightingale
Johnson, W. B. Widening Stain
Johnston, W. Innocent Murderers
Karp, D. One
Keech, S. Ciphered
Kelly, M. Dead Man's Riddle
Kemelman, H. Tuesday the Rabbi Saw Red
Kennington, A. Bagful of Bones
Kenyon, M. Whole Hog
Koehler, R. P. Case of the Dead Cadet
Kyd, T. Blood Is a Beggar
Laing, P. Lady Is Dead
Landels, D. H. Headmaster
Lang, B. Crockett on the Loose
Langley, L. Dead Center
Langton, J. Memorial Hall Murder
La Roche, K. A. Dear Dead Professor
Lathen, E. Come to Dust
Lathrop, G. P. In the Distance
Lawrence, A. Dean's Death
Le Carre, J. Murder of Quality
Lemarchand, E. Death of an Old Girl
Leslie, Jean. One Cried Murder
  Two Faced Murder
Levin, I. Kiss Before Dying
Lewis, Lange. Juliet Dies Twice
  Murder Among Friends
Lewis, R. Error of Judgment
Lilly, J. False Face
Lockridge, F. Drill Is Death
Lockridge, R. Twice Retired
Long, A. R. Death Looks Down
  Shakespeare Murders
Longmate, N. Head for Death
McCloy, H. Man in the Moonlight
  Through a Glass Darkly
Macdonald, R. Chill
MacDuff, D. Murder Strikes Three
McGrew, F. Taste of Death
MacKay, A. Death Is Academic
MacLeod, C. Luck Runs Out
  Rest You Merry
Macnaughtan, R. Preparatory School Murders
Magoon, C. I Smell the Devil
Mainwaring, M. Murder at Midyears
Mais, S. P. B. Who Dies?
Maner, W. Die of a Rose
Mann, Jessica. Captive Audience
  Only Security
Manton, P. Greyvale School Mystery
Marin, A. C. Storm of Spears
Martens, A. C. Phantom of the High School
Masterman, J. C. Oxford Tragedy
Melville, J. New Kind of Killer, an Old Kind of Death
Miles, Dennis. Pattern of Chalk
Millar, K. Dark Tunnel
Miller, J. Murder of a Professor
Mitchell, G. Laurels Are Poison
  Spotted Hemlock
Mitchell, R. E. Design for November
Morice, A. Murder in Outline
Morrah, D. Mummy Case
Nash, S. Dead of a Counterplot
Nicholas, R. White Shroud
Olsen, D. B. Enrollment Cancelled
Onions, O. In Accordance with the Evidence
Owen, H. C. Ways of Death
Parker, R. B. Godwulf Manuscript
Patrick, Q. Death and the Maiden
  Death Goes to School
  Murder at Cambridge
Pearson, A. Murder by Degrees
Peden, W. H. Twilight at Monticello
Peters, Ellis. Black Is the Colour of My True Love's Heart
Philips, J. Nightmare at Dawn
Pilgrim, C. Silent Slain
Post, M. Candidate for Murder
Propper, M. Student Fraternity Murder
Queen, E. Campus Murders
  Devil's Cook
Rath, V. Ferryman, Take Him Across!
Rees, D. Cambridge Murders
Rennert, M. Circle of Death
  Operation Alcestis
Robinson, R. Landscape with Dead Dons
Robinson, T. When Scholars Fall
Ross, I. T. Murder out of School
  Requiem for a Schoolgirl
  Teacher's Blood
Ruark, E. B. Campus Killings
Saber, R. O. Black Dark Murders
St. Clair, R. High School Mystery
Savage, R. Murder Goes to School
Shepherd, E. Murder in a Nunnery
Sholl, A. M. Mystery of Lostland Academy
Simmons, A. Death on the Campus
Smithies, R. H. R. Academic Question
Spain, N. Death Before Wicket
  Poison for Teacher
Spencer, P. Full Term
Sproul, K. Death and the Professors

Steel, K. Murder Goes to College
Stein, A. M. Case of the Absent-Minded Professor
Strange, M. Midnight
Sutton, H. Sacrifice
Symons, J. Paper Chase
Taylor, Edith. Serpent Under It
Tey, J. Miss Pym Disposes
Thomas, C. Prominent Among the Mourners
Trevor, G. Murder at School
Varnam, J. Traveling Deadman
Vulliamy, C. E. Don Among the Dead Men
Wakefield, R. I. You Will Die Today!
Wallace, F. Front Man
Wallis, J. H. Mystery of Vaucluse
Waugh, H. Last Seen Wearing
Wees, F. S. Mystery of the Creeping Man
Wells, Carolyn. Mystery Girl
Whaley, F. J. Reduction of Staff
  Trouble in College
Whitechurch, V. L. Murder at the College
Williams, D. Treasure by Degrees
Williams, G. M. Silk Rope
Wolseley, F. Which Way Came Death?
Woodbury, D. O. both titles
Woodfin, H. Virginia's Thing
Woodthorpe, R. C. Public School Murder
Yorke, M. Cast for Death

AFGHANISTAN (AFGHAN.)
Block, Lawrence. Here Comes a Hero
Bolt, B. Wayland of the Guides
Caillou, A. Afghan Assault
Harvester, S. Silk Road
Osborne, H. White Poppy

AFRICA (AFR. SEE ALSO: AFRICA, EAST; AFRICA, NORTH; AFRICA, WEST; INDIVIDUAL COUNTRIES)
Aarons, E. S. Assignment—Black Gold
  Assignment—Golden Girl
  Assignment—Silver Scorpion
  Assignment—Star Stealers
Allen, E. Death on Delivery
Ambler, E. Dirty Story
Armour, T. Blood Tells
Atlee, P. Skeleton Coast Contract
Bagley, D. Flyaway
Beaty, D. Excellency
Bernier, J. M. Mission to Burundi
Bickham, J. Regensburg Legacy
Black, Lionel. Chance to Die
Block, Lawrence. Me Tanner, You Jane
Boothby, G. Sailor's Bride
Brett, J. M. Plague of Dragons
Butler, K. R. Desert of Salt
Butler, W. Mr. Three
Carstairs, J. P. Concrete Kimono
Carter, Nick. Six Bloody Summer Days
Charles, R. This Side of Hell
Cleary, D. J. Sahara Strike
Cole, B. Sahara Survival
Corrigan, M. Danger's Green Eyes
Cory, D. Height of Day
Crawley, R. both titles
Creasey, J. Mountain of the Blind
Cullen, A. Studd
Curtis, Robert. Green Pack
Dembo, S. Sands of Lilliput
Dryer, B. Port Afrique
Evans, P. Breach of Fate
Falk, L. at least 9 titles
Farmer, P. J. Adventure of the Peerless Peer
Farrington, J. Night Train to Mombasa
Fearon, D. Rhino for Rosamund
Ferrars, E. Swaying Pillars
Forrester, L. Diamond Beach
Gerard, F. Justice of Sanders
  Law of the River
  Return of Sanders of the River
Gibbs, G. F. Yellow Diamond
Goodchild, G. Last Secret
Grant, M. Shadow's Revenge
Grant, Richard. Legacy of Danger
Grayson, Rupert. Secret Agent in Africa
Gwynne, P. N. Firmly by the Tail
Hall, Adam. Tango Briefing
Halliday, M. Death out of Darkness
Harris, J. Old Trade of Killing
Hartmann, M. Days of Thunder
  Leap for the Sun
Harvester, S. Sahara Road
Hayes, Ralph. Nightmare Conspiracy
Huxley, E. Merry Hippo
  Murder on Safari
Jackson, C. J. Kicked to Death by a Camel
Jason, S. Blood Vengeance
Jenkins, G. Bridge of Magpies
Johnston, W. Missed It by That Much
Jordan, D. Black Account
Jude, C. Terror of the Shape
Kolarz, H. Kalahari

636 / Africa, East

Leonard, C. L. Expert in Murder
Leslie, P. Radioactive Camel Affair
Lindsay, D. T. Wings over Africa
Lyall, G. Wrong Side of the Sky
MacLeod, R. Drum of Power
MacPherson, M. Protege
Macao, M. Kak-Abdullah Conspiracy
Mair, G. B. Miss Turquoise
Mason, A. Losers Keepers
Mason, A. E. W. Winding Stair
Meade, R. Lost Fraulein
Merrick, W. No One of That Name
Mills, A. Black Royalty
Milne, S. Beware the Lurking Scorpion
Mitford, B. many titles
Moore, Robin. Only the Hyenas Laughed
   Phase of Darkness
Mundy, T. Ivory Trail
Neebel, R. Halo Solution
Norwood, E. both titles
Parkes, R. Fourth Monkey
Percy, D. C. Hidden Valley
Rabe, P. Spy Who Was Three Feet Tall
Raymond, P. Matter of Assassination
Richardson, M. Daughter of the Sacred
   Mountain
Robeson, K. Land of Long Juju
   Munitions Master
Sanders, Lawrence. Tangent Factor
   Tangent Objective
Sangster, J. Touchfeather, Too
Sapir, R. Slave Safari
   Summit Chase
Shannon, C. Fatal Footsteps
Sheraton, N. African Terror
Simenon, G. Tropic Moon
Simpson, H. R. Assignment for a Mercenary
Smith, David. Leo Conversion
Snell, E. Red Spinner
Southon, A. E. Laughing Ghosts
Telfair, R. Slavers
Tippette, G. Mercenaries
Tokson, E. Desert Captive
Townend, Paul. Road to El Saida
Wallace, E. 6 titles
Webster, F. A. M. Black Shadow
Wheatley, D. Secret War
Wingate, W. Bloodbath
Zeno. Grab

AFRICA, EAST (AFR., E. SEE ALSO: AFRICA; AFRICA, NORTH; AFRICA, WEST; INDIVIDUAL COUNTRIES)

Drummond, I. Frog in the Moonflower
Hayes, Ralph. Taste of Blood
Huxley, E. Death of an Aryan
MacLeod, R. Lake of Fury
Pitts, D. Rogue Hercules

AFRICA, NORTH (AFR., N. SEE ALSO: AFRICA; AFRICA, EAST; AFRICA, WEST; INDIVIDUAL COUNTRIES)

Bridges, A. Lighthearted Quest
Canning, V. Golden Salamander
Foss, J. Flesh and Blood
Home, M. House of Shade
Maybury, A. Midnight Dancers
Rabe, P. Box
Weston, Garnett. Hidden Portal
Wheatley, D. Sword of Fate
William, P. Affair at Abu Mina
Williams, Alan. Barbouze
Wolf, J. Death Rides a Camel

AFRICA, WEST (AFR., W. SEE ALSO: AFRICA; AFRICA, EAST; AFRICA, NORTH; INDIVIDUAL COUNTRIES)

Best, H. both titles
Broome, A. 9 titles
Cameron, C. Zenia: Spy in Togoland
Ferguson, A. Running Man
Greene, G. Heart of the Matter
Head, M. Cabinda Affair
Huxley, E. Murder at Government House
Hyne, C. J. C. Kate Meredith, Financier
McCutchan, P. Bluebolt One
Meredith, P. Crocodile Man
Robinson, L. W. General Goes Too Far
Tabori, G. Good One
Weston, C. Danju Gig
Wyllie, J. all 7 Dr. Quarshie titles

AIRCRAFT (AIR.)

Bonnell, J. F. Death Flies West
Campbell, Karen. Suddenly in the Air
Corley, E. Air Force One
Dent, L. Dead at the Take-Off
Didelot, F. Many Ways of Death
Ferguson, Austin. Jet Stream
Field, T. Five
Harper, D. Hijacked
King, C. D. Obelists Fly High
LeQueux, W. Terror of the Air
Page, S. H. Murder Flies the Atlantic
Teilhet, D. L. Death Flies High

ALABAMA (ALA. SEE ALSO: SOUTH)

Connolly, P. So Fair, So Evil
Deal, B. H. Walls Came Tumbling Down
Grantland, K. Run from the Hunter
Howell, P. H. Winds of Terror
Knight, K. M. Robineau Look
Manly, M. Rube Burrows League
Mason, S. E. Crimson Feather
   House That Hate Built
   Murder Rents a Room
Thompson, R. Number to Call Is...
Williams, C. Long Saturday Night

ALASKA

Boyd, E. M. all 3 titles
De Laguna, F. Fog on the Mountain
Head, H. S. Death Below Zero
Hendryx, J. B. Connie Morgan in Alaska
Laforest, S. Intruder
MacLean, Alistair. Athabasca
Robeson, K. Mountain Monster
Rosenberger, J. Alaska Conspiracy
Shimer, R. H. Squaw Point
Simmons, D. Let the Bastards Freeze in the Dark

ALBANIA (ALB. SEE ALSO: BALKANS)

Daniels, N. Overkill
Driscoll, P. White Lie Assignment
Fallon, M. Keys of Hell
Gilman, D. Unexpected Mrs. Pollifax
Kinsley, P. Pimpernel 60
Martin, I. K. Rekill
Rosenberger, J. Albanian Connection
Wellard, J. Action of the Tiger

ALBUQUERQUE (ALBUQ. SEE ALSO: NEW MEXICO; SANTE FE; SOUTHWEST)

Curtiss, U. Danger: Hospital Zone
   Don't Open the Door
   Menace Within
   Poisoned Orchard

ALGERIA (SEE ALSO: ALGIERS; AFRICA, NORTH)

Appleby, J. Singing Cave
Creasey, J. Hounds of Vengeance
Lee, John. Assignment in Algeria
MacLean, Arthur. Pursuit to Algeria
Rosenberger, J. Nightmare in Algeria
Sellers, C. Algerian Incident
Vance, J. H. Man in the Cage
Whittington, H. Guerrilla Girls
Williams, Alan. Long Run South

ALGIERS (SEE ALSO: ALGERIA; AFRICA, NORTH)

Aarons, E. S. Assignment—Madeleine
Gluck, S. Red Emeralds
Stead, P. J. In the Street of the Angel
Stokes, D. Captive in the Night

AMSTERDAM (AMST. SEE ALSO: HOLLAND)

Carter, Nick. Amsterdam
Freeling, N. Criminal Conversation
   Long Silence
   Love in Amsterdam
   Over the High Side
Glaskin, G. M. Man Who Didn't Count
Grimsey, L. Amsterdam Connection
Helm, P. Death Has a Thousand Entrances
MacLean, Alistair. Puppet on a Chain
Miglis, J. Masterwork
Miller, S. Snow Leopard
Mills, W. Shadow Crusade
Randolph, E. Rendezvous in Amsterdam
Ross, Angus. Amsterdam Diversion
Van de Wetering, J. 6 titles
Winsor, D. Death Convention

ANDORRA

Ames, D. Murder, Maestro, Please
Appleby, J. Secret Mountains
MacKintosh, M. King and Two Queens

ANGOLA (SEE ALSO: AFRICA)

Smith, Don. Secret Mission: Angola
Walker, Martin. Mercenary Calling

ANTARCTIC (SEE ALSO: ARCTIC)

Griffin, J. Antarctic Convergence
Innes, H. White South
Keneally, T. Victim of the Aurora
Robeson, K. South Pole Terror
Wheatley, D. Man Who Missed the War

ANTWERP (SEE ALSO: BRUSSELS; BELGIUM)

Flynn, B. League of Matthias
MacKintosh, I. Slaying in September
Riefe, A. Tyger by the Tail
Roberts, K. Center of the Web

ARABIA. SEE: SAUDI ARABIA.

ARCTIC (SEE ALSO: ANTARCTIC)

Adams, F. R. Long Night
Carter, Nick. Ice Bomb Zero
Dark, J. Operation Ice Cap
Edwards, P. Ice Goddess
Gosling, P. Zero Trap
Harris, J. Unforgiving Wind
Johnson, J. L. Piece of the Moon Is Missing
MacLean, Alistair. Bear Island
   Ice Station Zebra
Perrault, E. G. Spoil!
Robeson, K. Devil Ghengis
   Lost Giant
   Polar Treasure
Rosenberger, J. Operation Mind-Murder
   Pole Star Secret

ARGENTINA (ARG. SEE ALSO: BUENOS AIRES; SOUTH AMERICA)

Barrett, Michael. Reward
Benton, K. Red Hen Conspiracy
Carter, Nick. Plot for the Fourth Reich
Cory, D. Johnny Goes South
Creighton, J. A. House of Fury
Galwey, R. C. Assignment Argentina
Greene, G. Honorary Consul
Hayes, R. King's Ransom
Kiefer, W. Kidnappers
Timins, D. Extra Passenger
Wheatley, D. Gateway to Hell
Wood, C. Death on the Pampas

ARIZONA (ARIZ. SEE ALSO: PHOENIX; TUCSON; SOUTHWEST)

Adams, C. F. Private Eye
Austin, H. Death Has Seven Faces
Baker, Lucinda. Place of Devils
Blankenship, W. D. Helix File
Branwell, C. Cousin to Terror
Brown, F. One for the Dead
Bunnell, R. Terror by Night
Chavis, R. Terror Package
Clifford, F. Overdue
Clifton, B. Let Him Go Hang
Creasey, J. Foothills of Fear
Creighton, J. Not So Evil As Eve
Dobbins, P. H. Death in the Dunes
Eyre, M. Absence
Foley, R. Sleep Without Morning
Ford, P. L. Great K & A Train Robbery
Fuller, R. Fear in a Desert Town
Garfield, B. Relentless
   What of Terry Conniston?
Gluck, S. Wildcat
Gordon, M. Little Man Who Wasn't There
Gordons. Captive
   Make Haste to Live
   Ordeal
Harper, R. Death to the Dancing Masters
Hillerman, T. Blessing Way
   Listening Woman
Ives, J. Fear in a Handful of Dust
Kantor, Harry. Town That Saw No Evil
Killoran, G. Willough Haven
Knight, C. Affair of the Painted Desert
Kuttner, H. Man Drowning
La Tourrette, J. Madonna Creek Witch
Leinster, M. Scalps
McCurtin, P. Sun Dance Murders
MacDonald, W. C. Action of Arcanum
Millhiser, M. Michael's Wife
Moore, L. Cold Waters
Myers, B. Evil Ever After
O'Hanlon, J. D. Murder at Horsethief
Olsen, D. B. Cat Wears a Mask
Page, J. Shoot the Moon
Pendleton, D. Arizona Ambush
Peters, Elizabeth. Summer of the Dragon
Prather, R. S. Cockeyed Corpse
Robeson, K. Red Skull
   Stone Man
Rollins, W. Midnight Treasure
Roper, L. V. Death—As in Matador
Rossiter, J. Murder Makers
Rowan, D. Time of the Burning Mask
St. John, G. Death in the Desert
Savage, E. Shady Place to Die
Scherf, M. Banker's Bones
Simenon, G. Maigret and the Coroner
Siodmak, C. Donovan's Brain
Smith, M. C. Nightwing
Spicer, B. Long Green
Stratton, C. Rock!
Thomas, Augustus. Arizona
Tracy, D. Pot of Trouble
Trimble, L. Fit to Kill
   Love Me and Die
Webb, J. Make My Bed Soon

ARKANSAS (ARK. SEE ALSO: SOUTH)

Cooper, Monte. Death Near the River
McPartland, J. I'll See You In Hell
Morris, Jim. Sheriff of Purgatory
Murray, M. M. Arkansas Ranger
Robeson, K. Crimson Serpent

Settings Index

ATHENS (SEE ALSO: GREECE; BALKANS; CRETE; MACEDONIA)
Appleby, J. Captive City
Doody, M. Aristotle Detective
Fenton, E. Double Darkness
Ferrand, G. Encounter in Athens
Fitzgerald, K. Dangerous to Lean Out
Greene, H. FSO-1
Highsmith, P. Two Faces of January
Kenny, P. Tanagra Affair
Lowden. D. Boudapesti 3
Marlowe, D. J. Raven Is a Blood Red Bird
Roberts, J. Judas Sheep
Smith, Don. Secret Mission: Athens
Stein, A. M. Body Search
   I Fear the Greeks
Tute, W. Matter of Diplomacy

ATLANTA (SEE ALSO: GEORGIA; SOUTH)
Anthony, Elizabeth. Ballet of Fear
Dennis, R. probably all 12 JH titles
Diehl, W. Sharkey's Machine
Dunne, T. L. Scourge
Holden, G. Don't Go in Alone
   Down a Dark Alley
Hopkins, L. C. Candle
Keifetz, N. Welcome Sundays
Logue, J. Follow the Leader
Moore, H. F. S. Shed a Bitter Tear
Moore, R. A. both titles
Pendleton, D. Dixie Convoy
Sibley, C. Malignant Heart

AUSTRALIA (SEE ALSO: MELBOURNE; SYDNEY; SOLOMON ISLANDS; TASMANIA)
Adams, F. Australian Life
Ainsworth, P. Devil's Hole
Ashe, G. Taste of Treasure
Atlee, P. Kiwi Contract
B. and R. Helen Elwood, the Female Detective
Backhouse, E. Mists Came Down
   Web of Shadows
Barnard, R. Death of an Old Goat
Boldrewood, R. Robbery Under Arms
Boothby, G. Bushigrams
   Love Made Manifest
   Race of Life
   Sheilah McLeod
Boucher, B. Megawind Connection
Brown, C. Lover, Don't Come Back!
Carlon, P. Forty Pieces of Alloy
Carter, Nick. Day of the Dingo
   Executioners
Clapperton, R. No News on Monday
   Sentimental Kill
Cleary, J. Just Let Me Be
   Justin Bayard
Corrigan, M. Big Squeeze
Courtier, S. H. at least 19 titles
Creasey, J. Toff Down Under
Daniels, N. Operation T
Davis, Helen. "For So Little"
De Fraga, G. Murder by Wash of Light
De Weese, G. Charles Fort Never Mentioned Wombats
Donovan, D. Out There
Dorrington, A. Children of the Cloven Hoof
Eden, D. Afternoon for Lizards
Elliott, P. Silent Bullet
Flower, P. at least 12 titles
Francis, D. In the Frame
Garve, A. Boomerang
Gask, A. 7 titles
Gould, N. Who Did It?
Hamilton, I. Man with the Brown Paper Face
Hennessey, D. Australian Bush Track
   Caves of Shend
Hobart, R. Blood on the Lake
   Dangerous Cargoes
Hume, F. Madame Midas
Innes, H. Golden Soak
Jefferis, B. One Black Summer
Jones, P. Johnny Lost
Keneally, T. Place at Whitten Survivor
Lang, John. Botany Bay
Lindall, E. Killers of Karawala
Little, C. Great Black Kanba
Lloyd, V. Don't Tie Me Down
Lord, Gabrielle. Fortress
McCutchan, P. All-Purpose Bodies
McDaniel, D. Utopia Affair
MacKenzie, N. Three Steps to Murder
McShane, M. Ill Met by a Fish Shop on George Street
Mace, H. And Death Came Too
Madden, E. S. Craig's Spur
Martin, A. E. Bridal Bed Murders
   Curious Crime
   Sinners Never Die
Martin, L. W. Murder on Mount Capita
Morgan, P. Deadly Group Down Under
   Girl in the Telltale Bikini
Morton, A. Sport for the Baron
Murray, M. Right Honourable Corpse
Neville, M. at least 10 titles
North, E. Nobody Stops Me
Nottingham, P. Wasted Pride
Peters, G. Mark of a Buoy
   Twist of a Stick
Pratt, A. Great "Push" Experiment
Preston, James. Axes of Hate
   Shattered Steel
Punshon, E. Earth's Great Lord
Renwick, P. Black Hogan Strikes Again
   Leatherface Lonergan Stakes a Claim
Richards, P. Our Spacecraft Is Missing!
Robertson, Andrew. The Kidnapped Squatter
Robertson, M. To Ripen or to Kill
Rothwell, U. Death on the Run
St. Thomas, H. Night of the Long Shadows
Salter, E. There Was a Witness
   Will to Survive
Smith, Spenser. Dead Don't Matter
Stutley, S. J. Poisoned Glass
Thomes, W. H. Belle of Australia
   Bushrangers
   Gold-Hunters' Adventures
Thompson, E. Find a Crooked Sixpence
   Hunter in the Dark
   To Catch a Rainbow
   Twig Is Bent
Thynne, R. Boffin's Find
Upfield, A. W. all 33 titles
W., W. Detective's Album
Walker, T. Felonry of New South Wales
Wallace, J. Invasion
   Millionaire Gangster
Watkins, A. Till the Dying Day
White, O. Silent Reach
Whitman, C. Death out of Focus
Wicking, G. W. Bales of Trouble
   Glory Box Mystery
Winn, P. Dead Innocent
   Fact X
   Postscript to Murder
Wood, Christopher. Dead Center
Workman, J. Contrabandits
Wright, A. Rogue's Luck
   Rung In

AUSTRIA (SEE ALSO: VIENNA)
Albrand, M. Call from Austria
Ambler, E. Uncommon Danger
Beeding, F. Nine Waxed Faces
Blake, K. Night Stands at the Door
Carnac, C. Crossed Skis
Carr, G. Corpse in the Crevasse
   Lewker in Tirol
Chance, J. N. Involvement in Austria
Christopher, J. Caves of Night
Coles, M. Basle Express
Cory, D. Dead Man Falling
De Villiers, G. Countess and the Spy
Dratler, J. J. Ducks in Thunder
Elliot, P. Danube Covenant
Fitt, M. Murder Mars the Tour
Gale, A. Angel Among Witches
Gilbert, M. After the Fine Weather
Goddard, A. Vienna Pursuit
Greene, H. "Mozart" Leaves at Nine
Groner, A. Lady in Blue
   Man with the Black Cord
Halliday, L. Smiling Spider
Hardt, M. Stranger and Afraid
Hely, E. Long Shot
MacInnes, H. Above Suspicion
   Horizon
   Prelude to Terror
   Salzburg Connection
Magee, B. To Live in Danger
Meade, R. Danube Runs Red
Minton, P. Hand of the Imposter
Moore, Dorinne. Legacy of Emeralds
Neumann, R. Inquest
Patterson, H. Valhalla Exchange
Peters, Ellis. Horn of Roland
   House of Green Turf
   Will and the Deed
Pollard, A. O. Sinister Secret
Roberts, J. L. Dornstein Ikon
Ross, Marilyn. Marta
Ross, W. E. D. Forbidden Castle
Rowan, H. Snowfall
Salter, E. Once Upon a Tombstone
Stern, R. M. Kessler Legacy
   Merry Go Round
Stewart, M. Airs Above the Ground
Von Doderer, H. Every Man a Murderer
Wingate, J. Avalanche
Yates, D. at least 6 titles
Yorke, M. Silent Witness

AZORES
Wheatley, D. They Found Atlantis

BAGHDAD (SEE ALSO: MIDDLE EAST; MESOPOTAMIA)
Christie, A. They Came to Baghdad
Greenlee, S. Baghdad Blues
Griffith, Glyn. Fire over Baghdad
MacKinnon, A. Assignment in Iraq
   Red-Winged Angel
Wadham, R. Weekend in Baghdad

BAHAMAS (SEE ALSO: NASSAU; WEST INDIES; CARIBBEAN)
Bagley, D. Bahamas Crisis
Carmichael, F. Double in Diamonds
Carter, Nick. Target Doomsday Island
   Trouble in Paradise
Chandler, B. Coral Kill
Cheyney, P. Dark Bahama
Dark, J. Come Die with Me
Derrick, L. Deepsea Shootout
Du Bois, W. Case of the Frightened Fish
Fleming, I. Thunderball
Ford, L. Bahamas Murder Case
Halliday, D. Dolly and the Doctor-Bird
Heatter, B. Naked Island
King, T. J. Noose of Red Beads
MacDonald, J. D. Man of Affairs
Perry, Ritchie. Holiday with a Vengeance
Q., J. Tournament

BALI (SEE ALSO: INDONESIA; BORNEO; DJAKARTA; JAVA; NEW GUINEA; SUMATRA)
Conyn, C. Bali Ballet Murder
Fleischman, A. S. Danger in Paradise

BALKANS (SEE ALSO: ALBANIA; BULGARIA; GREECE; RUMANIA; MACEDONIA; TURKEY; YUGOSLAVIA)
Ambler, E. Judgment on Deltchev
Atlee, B. Black Feather
Betteridge, D. Balkan Spy
Dodge, D. Lights of Skaro
Farjeon, J. J. Black Castle
Haggard, W. Old Masters
Holt, Gavin. Irina
Linnell, G. Black Ghost of the Highway
Meynell, L. Dark Square
   His Aunt Came Late
Oppenheim, E. P. Stranger's Gate
Peters, L. Cry Vengeance
Pollard, A. O. Fifth Freedom
Poyer, J. Balkan Assignment
Reed, E. Maras Affair
Robeson, K. King Maker
Sherwood, J. Mr. Blessington's Plot
Tokson, E. Cavender's Balkan Quest
Weir, D. Balkan Saga
Williams, D. Agent from the West

BALTIMORE (BALT. SEE ALSO: MARYLAND)
Baylus, R. F. Midsummer Night's Murder
Bortner, N. S. both titles
Daly, C. J. Amateur Murderer
Ford, L. Girl from the Mimosa Club
   Trial by Ambush
Gelb, A. L. Janissary
Grossbach, R. ...And Justice for All
Harris, Colver. Going to St. Ives
Pendleton, D. Friday's Feast
Strange, J. S. For the Hangman
Warren, C. M. Deadhead
Williams, J. B. Dead Yet Living

BANGKOK (SEE ALSO: THAILAND; FAR EAST)
Aarons, E. S. Assignment—Bangkok
Blackstock, C. When the Sun Goes Down
Campbell, Reginald. Bangkok Murders
Corrigan, M. Menace in Siam
Hall, Adam. 9th Directive
Mason, V. W. Secret Mission to Bangkok
Morse, E. Emerald Buddha
Templeton, J. Yellow Hibiscus
Williamson, T. Technicans of Death

BARBADOS (SEE ALSO: WEST INDIES, CARIBBEAN)
Coxe, G. H. Man Who Died Twice
   Moment of Violence
   Uninvited Guest
Fish, R. L. Green Hell Treasure
Mole, W. Goodbye Is Not Worthwhile
Morgan, M. Darkness at Bromley Hall

BEIRUT (SEE ALSO: LEBANON; MIDDLE EAST)
Alan, R. Beirut Pipeline
Black, I. S. Journey to a Safe Place
Bradley, Michael. Blood Bargain
Carter, Nick. Turncoat
Daniels, N. Operation N
Mannin, E. Mission to Beirut
Stagg, J. Assignment in Beirut

BELFAST (SEE ALSO: IRELAND; DUBLIN)
De Villiers, G. Belfast Connection
Green, F. L. Mist on the Waters
   Odd Man Out
Seymour, G. Harry's Game

B

B

BELGIAN CONGO (Bel. Cong. See also: Africa)
Caillou, A. Congo War Cry
Canning, V. Black Flamingo
Greene, G. Burnt-Out Case
Head, M. Congo Venus
  Devil in the Bush
Iams, J. Body Missed the Boat
Kiefer, W. Lingala Code
Lejeune, A. Glint of Spears
Maggio, J. Company Man
Martyn, W. Stones of Enchantment
Wallace, C. H. Crashlanding in the Congo

BELGIUM (Belg. See also: Antwerp; Brussels)
Carter, Nick. Race of Death
Coles, M. Not Negotiable
Kirk, L. Embassy Madonna
Kyle, E. Love Is for the Living
Wheatley, D. Desperate Measures
White, Alan. Long Drop

BELGRADE (See also: Yugoslavia; Balkans; Macedonia)
Bleeck, O. Protocol for a Kidnapping

BELIZE (See also: South America)
Coxe, G. H. Inside Man
  With Intent to Kill

BERLIN (East and West. See also: Germany; Frankfurt; Hamburg; Munich)
Bahr, J. Holes in the Wall
Baker, W. H. Rape of Berlin
Ballinger, B. S. Lopsided Man
Black, C. Death's Head
Brand, M. Phantom Spy
Caine, J. Cold Room
Carter, Nick. Berlin
  Under the Wall
Chaber, M. E. No Grave for March
  So Dead the Rose
  Splintered Man
Coles, M. Green Hazard
  Not for Export
Davison, Geoffrey. Berlin Spy Trap
De Villiers, G. Checkpoint Charlie
Ferguson, J. Stealthy Terror
Fitt, M. Bulls Like Death
Gainham, S. Cold Dark Night
Hall, Adam. Berlin Memorandum
Hughes, W. Inside Out
Jones, R. P. Man Who Killed Hitler
Joseph, M. Berlin at Midnight
Kaye, M. M. Death Walked in Berlin
Kerrigan, J. Phoenix Assault
Kirst, H. H. Twilight of the Generals
Lee, John. Thirteenth Hour
Lindquist, D. Berlin Tunnel 21
McGill, G. War Story
McGovern, J. Berlin Couriers
Marlowe, D. Dandy in Aspic
Marlowe, S. Drum Beat—Berlin
  Valkyrie Encounter
Miehe, U. Dead One in Berlin
Revelli, G. Amanda in Berlin
Richards, D. Double Game
Saxon, P. Last Days of Berlin
Scholefield, A. Berlin Blind
Simmel, J. M. Sybil Cipher
Thayer, C. W. Checkpoint
Tiger, J. Superkill
Trembath, H. Murder in Berlin
Tucker, D. Blaze of Riot
Underwood, M. Unprofessional Spy
West, E. These Lonely Victories
Winnington, A. Berlin Epitaph
Winward, W. Seven Minutes Past Midnight
Wiseman, T. Day Before Sunrise

BERMUDA
Ames, J. Fearful Paradise
Burnham, D. Last Act in Bermuda
De Blasis, C. Suffer a Sea Change
Denbie, R. Death Cruises South
Ford, F. Play with Matches
Garth, D. Bermuda Calling
Holding, E. S. Strange Crime in Bermuda
King, C. D. Bermuda Burial
Mason, V. W. Castle Island Case
  Gracious Lily Affair
Patrick, Q. Return to the Scene
Sharp, W. Murder in Bermuda
Siller, V. Bermuda Murder
  Last Resort
Thayer, L. Prisoner Pleads "Not Guilty"

BOLIVIA (See also: South America)
Atlee, P. Irish Beauty Contract
Carter, Nick. Operation Che Guevara
Cleary, J. Mask of the Andes
Dodge, D. Red Tassel
Macao, M. Red Plague in Bolivia

Sage, D. Moon Was Red

BOMBAY (See also: India; Calcutta; New Delhi)
Chettur, S. K. Bombay Murder
James, S. Stranglers of Bombay
Keating, H. R. F. Inspector Ghote Plays a Joker
Olbrich, F. all 3 titles

BORNEO (See also: Indonesia; Malaysia; Bali; Djakarta; Java; New Guinea; Sumatra)
Beecham, J. C. both titles
Black, G. You Want to Die, Johnny?
Cushman, D. Jewel of the Java Sea
Kyle, D. Green River High
MacLeod, R. Isle of Dragons
Snell, E. Crimson Butterfly
  Yu-Chi Stone
Wilkes-Hunter, R. Borneo Patrol

BOSTON (See also: Massachusetts; Cape Cod; New England)
Aldyne, N. Vermilion
Bailey, F. L. Secrets
Banks, O. Rembrandt Panel
Barry, M. Boston Avenger
Behn, N. Big Stick-Up at Brink's!
Benjoya, M. Final Judgment
Benton, J. L. Art Treasure Murders
Brown, G. Murder on Beacon Hill
Burgess, G. Two O'Clock Courage
Capeto, I. Few Drops of Murder
Carleton, M. Cry Wolf
  Vanished
Carter, Nick. Revenge of the Generals
  Snake Flag Conspiracy
Casey, R. Jesus Man
Cheatham, L. Portrait of Emma
Coburn, A. both titles
Coffman, V. Mistress Devon
Cook, R. Coma
Cotton, W. Night Was Made for Murder
Coxe, G. H. 27 titles
Curtiss, U. Second Sickle
Davey, J. Treasury Alarm
Dean, E. Murder Is a Collector's Item
  Murder Is a Serious Business
Derrick, L. Bloody Boston
Fenwick, E. P. Two Names for Death
Fitzsimmons, C. Crimson Ice
Forbes, S. Buried in So Sweet a Place
Fuller, T. Harvard Has a Homicide
  Reunion with Murder
  Three Thirds of a Ghost
Gillette, W. Astounding Crime on Torrington Road
Gillmore, R. Opal Pin
Goldberg, M. Anatomy Lesson
Goldthwaite, E. K. Root of Evil
Green, T. J. Flowered Box
Greenan, R. H. Bric-a-Brac Man
  Heart of Gold
  It Happened in Boston
  Queen of America
Gresham, E. Lucifer Was Tall
Harvey, M. R. P. Berkeley Street Mystery
Heatter, B. Golden Stag
Heyman, E. L. Thomas Crown Affair
Higgins, G. V. 5 titles
Hirschhorn, R. Pride of Healers
Holt, W. Savage Snow
Hudson, J. Case of Need
Irwin, I. H. Body Rolled Downstairs
  Many Murders
  Murder Masquerade
  Poison Cross Mystery
Jones, C. R. Rum Row Murders
Kimbrough, K. Kathrine, the Returned
Knight, K. M. They're Going to Kill Me
Langton, J. Memorial Hall Murder
Levon, F. Manx Cat
Lorimer, G. False Gods
McCloy, H. Burn This
  Question of Time
  Sleepwalker
McCurtin, P. Boston Bust-Out
McDonald, G. Confess Fletch
  Flynn
MacLeod, C. Family Vault
  Withdrawing Room
Malcolm-Smith, G. Lady Finger
Martin, W. Pack Bay
Martyn, W. Bathurst Complex
Masiello, J. Family Trouble
Merwin, Sam, Jr. Knife in My Back
Meyer, L. Paperback Thriller
Montague, C. H. Written in Red
Morton, A. Branch for the Baron
Ness, T. T. Short of Murder
Nile, D. Terror at Deepcliff
Parker, R. B. God Save the Child
  Godwulf Manuscript
  Looking for Rachel Wallace
  Mortal Stakes
Paul, Elliot. Waylaid in Boston
Pendleton, D. Boston Blitz
Quick, D. Fifth Dagger

Reid, J. Offering
Rich, W. Brain-Waves and Death
Robinson, J. H. Boston Conspiracy
Rockwood, H. Clarice Dyke, the Female Detective
  Donald Dyke, the Yankee Detective
  Harry Pinkurten, the King of Detectives
  Nat Foster, the Boston Detective
Romano, D. Banacek
Ross, Clarissa. Gemini in Darkness
Ross, W. E. D. One Louisberg Square
St. John, N. Medici Ring
Scarlett, R. all 5 titles
Schofield, W. G. Payoff in Black
Scott, Mansfield. Behind Red Curtains
Severy, M. Darrow Enigma
Skehan, E. M. Bullet for Georgie
Smith, A. T. Death in the Cards
Stackelberg, G. Double Agent
Steers, H. Death Will Find Me
Storm, M. Cry, Tiger!
Taylor, M. I. Man Who Awoke
Tilton, A. Beginning with a Bash
Waitt, I. Death a la King
Wells, T. at least 8 titles
Wolk, G. 400 Brattle Street

BRAZIL (See also: Rio De Janeiro; South America)
Aarons, E. S. Assignment—Amazon Queen
Alexander, Jan. Bishop's Palace
Anthony, P. Amazon Slaughter
Benton, K. 24th Level
Brewer, G. Appointment in Hell
Caillou, A. Assault on Kolchak
Cameron, L. Girl with the Dynamite Bangs
Canning, V. Man from the Turkish Slave
Carter, N. Amazon
  Ten Times Dynamite
Charles, R. Three Days to Live
Fish, R. L. Brazilian Slay Ride
  Bridge That Went Nowhere
  Isle of the Snakes
  Shrunken Head
  Trouble in Paradise
Footner, H. Scarred Jungle
Gregor, P. Jump into the Sun
Hastings, Michael. Snake and the Arrow
Higgins, J. Last Place God Made
Kirk, L. Farm at Sante Fe
Leonard, C. L. Fourth Funeral
Leslie, P. Diving Dames Affair
Lindsay, D. T. Wings over the Amazon
McCutchan, P. Screaming Dead Balloons
Middlemiss, R. Parrot Man
Mills, A. Gentleman of Rio
Murphy, W. B. Timber Line
Neilan, S. Braganza Pursuit
Pattinson, J. Petronov Plan
Perry, Ritchie. Fall Guy
  One Good Death Deserves Another
Robeson, K. Death Green
Rosenberger, J. Mato Grosso Horror
Sarto, B. Tigress of Brazil
Sherman, D. King Jaguar
Spinelli, M. Assignment Without Glory
Thackeray, K. Counterflood

BRITISH GUIANA. See: Guyana.

BRITISH HONDURAS. See: Belize.

BRUSSELS (Brus. See also: Antwerp; Belgium)
Albrand, M. Meet Me Tonight
Baker, W. H. Brussels Dossier
Bickers, R. Scent of Mayhem
Fennerton, W. Jensen Scenario
Gainham, S. Takeover Bid
Lambert, R. Monsieur Faux-Pas

BUCHAREST (Buch. See also: Rumania; Balkans)
Household, G. Lives and Times of Bernardo Brown
Mason, V. W. Bucharest Ballerina Murders
Williams, V. Fox Prowls

BUDAPEST (Buda. See also: Hungary)
Aarons, E. S. Assignment—Budapest
Carter, Nick. Devil's Cockpit
  Ebony Cross
Fagyas, M. Fifth Woman
Frank, P. Affair of State
Gallico, P. Trial by Terror
Gielgud, V. Death in Budapest
Mason, V. W. Budapest Parade Murders
Melville, Alan. Danube Flows Red
Parker, Robert. Headquarters Budapest
Pickering, R. E. Himself Again
Rosenberger, J. Budapest Action
Sjowall, M. Man Who Went Up in Smoke
Tickell, J. Yolan of the Plains

Settings Index

BUENOS AIRES (BUEN. A. SEE ALSO: ARGENTINA; SOUTH AMERICA)

Bruce, J.   Live Wire
Cumberland, M.   Which of Us Is Safe?
Denevi, M.   Rosa at Ten O'Clock
Desmond, H.   Doorway to Death
Heberden, M. V.   Engaged to Murder
Leonard, C. L.   Sinister Shelter
McCurtin, P.   Deadliest Game
Pollard, A. O.   Deal in Death
Puig, M.   Buenos Aires Affair
Romsey, P.   Lidless Eye
Sage, D.   22 Brothers

BULGARIA (BULG. SEE ALSO: BALKANS; MACEDONIA)

Braddon, G.   Death Rings No Bell
Gilman, D.   Elusive Mrs. Pollifax
Grey, A.   Bulgarian Exchange
Gulyashki, A.   Zakhov Mission
Haddad, C. A.   Academic Factor
Hossent, H.   Fear Business
Littell, R.   October Circle
Orvis, K.   Night Without Darkness
Thompson, A. A.   Message from Absalom

BURMA (SEE ALSO: FAR EAST)

Atlee, P.   Star Ruby Contract
Blankenship, W. D.   Tiger Ten
Carr, R.   Love in Burma
    Red Tiger
Carter, Nick.   List
Cooper, Brian.   Van Langeren Girl
Derby, M.   Echo of a Bomb
Douie, M.   Pointing Man
Eggar, A.   Hatanee
Harvester, S.   Dragon Road
Johnston, G. H.   Death Takes Small Bites
Lowis, C. C.   District Bungalow
    Four Blind Mice
MacLeod, R.   Cave of Bats
Macao, M.   Rape of Sun Lee Fong
Marlowe, G.   Burma Battle
Mason, V. W.   Trouble in Burma
Mitton, G. E.   Green Moth
Mundy, M.   Pagan Pagoda
Roberts, M.   Mask for Crime
Savi, G. B.   Last Lap
Wynd, O.   Sumatra Seven Zero

CAIRO (SEE ALSO: EGYPT; AFRICA, NORTH)

Brewer, G.   Appointment in Cairo
Burke, L. J.   Cairo Counterplot
Caillou, A.   Alien Virus
Carter, Nick.   Cairo Mafia
Evans, K.   Oasis of Fear
Flagg, J.   Woman of Cairo
Flett, A.   Never Shake a Skeleton
Heckstall-Smith, A.   Man with Yellow Shoes
Hedges, S. G.   Diamond Duel
Hocking, A.   All My Pretty Chickens
    Nile Green
Hone, J.   Private Sector
Kay, C.   Thieves Fall Out
King, F.   Raya
MacGrath, H.   Carpet from Baghdad
Manchester, W.   Beard the Lion
Martyn, W.   Cairo Crisis
Mason, V. W.   Cairo Garter Murders
O'Brine, M.   Corpse to Cairo
Rhodes, K.   It Happened in Cairo
Robeson, K.   Pharaoh's Ghost
Sheraton, N.   Cairo Ring
Smith, Don.   Secret Mission: Cairo
Thorne, E. P.   Chinese Poker
Tute, W.   Cairo Sleeper

CALCUTTA (SEE ALSO: BOMBAY; NEW DELHI; INDIA)

Baker, W. H.   Angry Night
Carter, Nick.   Night of the Avenger
Collier, R.   Pay-Off in Calcutta
Rushton, J.   No Beast So Fierce
Sinclair, Fredric.   Drop One, Carry Four
Tokson, E.   Appointment in Calcutta

CALIFORNIA (CALIF. SEE ALSO: LOS ANGELES; SAN DIEGO; SAN FRANCISCO; WEST)

Adams, F. R.   King's Crew
Adleman, R. H.   Annie Deane
Ainsworth, E.   Death Cues the Pageant
Alexander, Irene.   Revenge Can Wait
Alexander, Jan.   House at Rose Point
    House of Fools
Alexander, K.   Private Investigation
Alexander, M.   Birthmark of Fear
Allen, Anita.   False Face of Death
Alverson, C.   Not Sleeping, Just Dead
Ames, L.   House of Haddon
    Hungry Sea
Anderson, W. C.   Penelope, the Damp Detective
Anonymous.   Running Down a Double

Anthony, D.   Organization
    Stud Game
Arden, W.   Deal in Violence
Ardies, T.   Palm Springs
Armstrong, C.   8 titles
Arthur, R.   Somebody's Walking over My Grave
Ashby, K.   Climb a Dark Cliff
    Crown Valley
Ashe, G.   Rabble of Rebels
Ashton, S.   Santa Ana Wind
Babcock, D. V.   Hannah Says Foul Play
Baker, M.   Hilltop Murder
Ball, J.   Cool Cottontail
Ballard, W. T.   Murder Can't Stop
Barker, P.   Carver
Barmby, C.   James Cope
Barns, G. M.   Deadly Summer
Barry, J. E.   Uranium Murders
Bauman, C.   Secret of Haverly House
Bechdolt, F. R.   Mutiny
Benet, J.   Private Killing
Bennett, R. A.   Which One?
Biggers, E. D.   Chinese Parrot
    Keeper of the Keys
Birkley, D.   both titles
Bishop, G.   Apparition
Blankenship, W. D.   Programmed Man
Bloomfield, R.   5 titles
Blunt, D.   Dead Giveaway
Bocca, G.   Fourth Horseman
Bonner, G.   Taken at the Flood
Bonner, M.   Last Twist of the Knife
Booth, C. G.   Gold Bullets
    Murder at High Tide
    Sinister House
Boucher, A.   Case of the Seven Sneezes
Bradley, Muriel.   at least 4 titles
Braly, M.   On the Yard
Braun, R. A.   Murder, Four Miles High
Brisco, P.   Horror at Gull House
Brodeur, P.   Stunt Man
Brown, Carter.   at least 47 titles
Buchanan, J. D.   Red Dog
Burks, A. L.   Tight Rope
Burnett, W. R.   Cool Man
    Dark Hazard
    High Sierra
Cain, J. M.   Double Indemnity
    Mildred Pierce
    Past All Dishonor
    Postman Always Rings Twice
Caine, H. T.   Carpenter, Detective
Cake, P.   Pro-Am Murders
Cameron, E. E.   Curse of the Casa Del Monte
    House on the Beach
Cameron, O.   Catch a Tiger
    Fire Trap
    Silent One
Camp, William.   Jacobs Park Killings
    Night Beat
Cardiff, S.   Speaking Stones
Carey, Bernice.   all 8 titles
Carrel, M.   Case of the Innocent Witness
Carter, N.   Red Rebellion
Cassels, L.   Bad Investment
Castle, F.   Dead and Kicking
    Lovely and Lethal
Causey, J. O.   Frenzy
    Killer Take All!
Chaber, M. E.   Hangman's Harvest
Chalmers, S.   Affair of the Gallows Tree
Chambers, P.   probably all 18 titles
Chambers, W.   Bring Me Another Murder
    Dead Men Leave No Fingerprints
    Once Too Often
Chandler, R.   5 titles
Charteris, L.   Saint to the Rescue
Chase, J. H.   at least 16 titles
Chase, K.   Where There's a Will
Chaytor, L.   Course in Murder
Chester, P.   Murder Forestalled
Cheyney, P.   Dames Don't Care
Child, N.   Murder Comes Home
Church, G.   Race with the Sun
Chute, V.   both titles
Clark, Dale.   Death Wore Fins
    Narrow Cell
    Red Rods
    Run for the Money
Clarke, R.   Murderers Are Silent
Clason, C. B.   Murder Gone Minoan
    Poison Jasmine
Claudia, S.   Madness at the Castle
Clement, H.   Any Old Port in a Storm
    By Dawn's Early Light
Clifton, B.   Murder Specialist
Coffey, B.   Voice of the Night
Colby, L.   Touch of Evil
Collins, Mary.   Dog Eat Dog
    Only the Good
Colter, E.   Gull Cove Murders
Conrad, B.   Endangered
Conroy, Albert.   Mr. Lucky
Cooper, P. J.   Inheritance Restaurant
Correll, A. B.   Murder Is an Art
Coulter, H. G.   Death Comes to Casanova
Cousins, E. G.   Weekend with Maxwell
Cox, I. E.   Murder Among Friends
Craig, M.   Were He a Stranger

California / 639

Crane, F.   Black Cypress
Crane, R.   Tongue of Treason
Crawford, L.   Ransom
Creasey, J.   Blight
Crowe, J.   all 6 titles
Cullen, J.   Don't Get Caught
Currier, J. L.   Cargo of Fear
Da Cruz, D.   Double Kill
Daemer, W.   Case of the Lonely Lovers
Daniels, D.   Beaumont Tradition
    Castle Morvant
    Vineyard Chapel
Daniels, N.   Rape of a Town
Davies, Melissa.   Face of Chalk
Davis, Gwen.   Aristocrats
Davis, L. R.   Threat of Dragons
Davis, N.   Sally's in the Alley
Dean, Dudley.   Lila My Lovely
Deming, R.   Anything But Saintly
    Death of a Pusher
Dennis, R. C.   both titles
De Puy, E. S.   Hospital Homicides
    Long Knife
Deutschman, D.   Signals
Dewey, T. B.   Can a Mermaid Kill?
    Girl in a Punchbowl
    Girl with the Sweet Plump Knees
    Go, Honeylou
Dixon, H. V.   6 titles
Dodson, S.   Sausalito
Dowdell, D. K.   Hawk over Hollyhedge Manor
Dudley, O.   all 3 titles
Duncan, D.   Madrone Tree
    Shade of Time
Dundee, R.   Inferno
Dunning, J.   Looking for Ginger North
Durrant, T.   Marble Forest
Du Soe, R. C.   Devil Thumbs a Ride
Dyer, G.   Three-Cornered Wound
Eberhart, M. G.   Escape the Night
Eby, L.   Velvet Fleece
Echard, M.   Before I Wake
    Who Killed Frankie Leash?
Edgley, L.   Fear No More
Eldredge, B.   both titles
Ellis, J. B.   Mysterious Dr. Oliver
Ellis, V.   Death Comes Like a Thief
Engstrand, S.   More Deaths Than One
    Sling and the Arrow
Ericson, L.   Deadly Advice
Evans, John.   If You Have Tears
Fair, A. A.   24 titles
Falk, L.   Mystery of the Sea Horse
Farr, C.   House of Secrets
    Sinister House
Farr, J.   Lady and the Snake
Farrar, H.   Murder Goes to School
Farrell, H.   Such a Gorgeous Kid Like Me
Fay, D.   Black Pearl of Passion
Femling, J.   Backyard
Fickling, G. G.   5 titles
Field, P.   Someone Is Watching
Finney, J.   House of Numbers
    Night People
Fisher, S.   Take All You Can Get
Fitzgerald, A. J.   Pamela's Place
Fitzsimmons, C.   One Man's Poison
    Tied for Murder
Fleischman, A. S.   Venetian Blonde
Flynn, J. M.   7 titles
Fogelson, G.   Jewel: Undercover Cop
Foley, R.   This Woman Wanted
Forbes, J. D.   Murder in Full View
Fox, J. M.   Wheel Is Fixed
Foxx, J.   Wildfire
Franklin, K.   Murder at Shirttail Flats
Fray, A.   And Kill Once More
Freeman, K. W.   Murder Sets the Pace
Gardiner, D.   Transatlantic Ghost
Gardner, E. S.   at least 15 titles
Garvin, R. M.   FORTEC Conspiracy
Gates, H. L.   Death Counts Five
Gault, W. C.   Bad Samaritan
    Cana Diversion
    County Kill
    Wayward Widow
George, P.   Cool Murder
Gooney, W. M.   Moment of Truth
Goldman, L.   Fall Guy for Murder
    Tiger by the Tail
Goldman, R. L.   Hartwell Case
Goldstein, A. D.   Nobody's Sorry He Got Killed
    You're Never Too Old to Die
Gordons.   Big Frame
    Case of the Talking Bug
    Operation Terror
Goulart, R.   5 titles
Gregory, J.   Emerald Murder Trap
    House of the Opal
Gregory, Stephan.   Frame Up
Gruber, F.   Silver Tombstone
    Twilight Man
Hall, O. M.   Murder City
    So Many Doors
Hammett, D.   Dain Curse
    Red Harvest
Hamill, P.   Limbo
Hankins, A. P.   Cole of Spyglass Mountain

C

Hansen, J. Fadeout
    Man Everybody Was Afraid Of
    Skinflick
    Troublemaker
Hansen, R. P. 6 titles
Harrington, R. E. Seven of Swords
Harris, A. Baroni
Hastings, B. Demon Within
Hasty, J. E. Angel with Dirty Wings
Hawthorne, J. Golden Fleece
Hayes, R. Hungarian Game
Hayward, R. Trapped
Head, M. Smell of Money
Heard, H. F. Reply Paid
Heath, E. Murder of a Mystery Writer
Heath, M. 6 titles
Heller, M. So I'm a Heel
Himmel, R. Two Deaths Must Die
Hitchens, B. End of the Line
    Grudge
    Man Who Followed Women
Hitchens, D. 11 titles
Holden, A. Girl on the Beach
Holland, M. Fallen Angel
Homes, G. 8 titles
Houser, L. Lake of Fire
Houston, D. Shadows on the Moon
Houston, J. D. Continental Drift
Howard, Clark. Hunters
    Killings
    Mark the Sparrow
Howard, J. A. Murder in Mind
Hubler, R. Chase
Hurd, F. Nightmare at Mountain Aerie
Hutter, A. D. Death Mechanic
Jackson, O. T. Dark Love, Dark Magic
Jason, S. Valley of Death
Johnson, Diane. Shadow Knows
Johnston, R. Mourning Trees
Johnston, W. And Loving It.
Kane, F. Esprit de Corpse
Katcher, L. Now Is the Time
Kaufman, D. Pandora
Keene, D. Dead in Bed
    Take a Step to Murder
Kelston, R. Murder's End
Kent, F. House at Canterbury
Kinsburn, E. Wizard's Spyglass
Kirby, D. Death at My Heels
Kirsch, J. Bad Moon Rising
Knight, C. 15 titles
Koontz, D. R. Vision
Lacy, E. Napalm Bugle
Lamb, J. J. Chinese Straight
Lambert, R. Piece of the Moon
Lambirth, F. E. Rivard House
La Pointe, D. Flames over the Castle
Larsen, G. D. Kilbourne Connection
Larson, C. Matthew's Hand
Lawson, W. B. Dalton Boys in California
Lee, T. Monster of Lazy Hook
Leitfred, R. B. Corpse That Spoke
    Death Cancels the Evidence
Leslie, Jean. 6 titles
Lewellen, T. C. Billikin Courier
Libby, A. F. Long Fast Ride
Lipke, K. Rain on the Roof
Lipsky, E. Devil's Daughter
Little, C. Blackout
Lord, J. Sixty-Nine Diamonds
Lynds, D. Crossfire
Lyon, D. 7 titles
Lyons, A. Killing Floor
McAllister, A. L. House of Vengeance
McCall, J. J. Downbeat on a Debutante
McCurtin, P. Vendetta
McDaniel, D. Dagger Affair
McDermid, F. See No Evil
McDonald, G. Confess Fletch
Macdonald, J. R. Find a Victim
    Name Is Archer
MacDonald, P. Guest in the House
Macdonald, R. 11 titles
MacDonald, W. C. Gloved Saskia
McDowell, G. Reprieve of Roger Maine
McDonell, M. Althea
MacGowan, A. Who Is This Man?
MacKenzie, D. Kyle Contract
MacKenzie, J. A. Rahab Link
McKimmey, J. Run If You're Guilty
    Squeeze Play
    Winner Take All
MacLean, Alistair. Goodbye California
MacLeod, Ruth. Mendocino Menace
MacManus, Y. With Fate Conspire
MacNeil, N. Death Ride
    Spy Catchers
McPartland, J. Big Red's Daughter
    Face of Evil
    Last Night
    Ripe Fruit
Mahannah, F. Broken Angel
    Golden Goose
    Stopover for Murder
    Yellow Hearse
Mainwaring, D. One Against the Earth
Makris, J. N. Nightshade
Mankiewicz, D. M. Trial
Mannon, M. M. all 3 titles
Manor, J. all 4 titles
Marble, D. Sail into Silence
Marfield, D. Ghost on the Balcony

Marin, A. C. Storm of Spears
Marks, H. K. Triad
Marlowe, D. J. Operation Drumfire
Marshall, R. Sucker Punch
Mascott, T. Wife Who Ran Away
Mason, G. With Soul So Dead
Mason, R. Someone and Felicia Warwick
Masterton, W. 11 titles
Matheson, R. Stir of Echoes
Matthews, C. Dive into Death
Mavity, N. B. 5 titles
Mayfair, F. Over My Dead Body
Melchior, I. Marcus Device
Millar, K. Three Roads
Millar, M. 6 titles
Miller, Marc. Death at the Easel
Miller, Wade. Girl from Midnight
    Kiss Her Goodbye
    Kitten with a Whip
Millhauser, B. Whatever Goes Up
Morella, J. Ince Affair
Morgan, P. Death Car Surfside
Morrow, S. Rules of the Game
Morrow, W. C. Blood-Money
Murphy, M. Dangerous Legacy
Makagawa, K. S. Rendezvous of Mysteries
Nash, A. all 4 titles
Neely, R. 5 titles
Nelson, H. Island of Escape
Nielsen, H. 6 titles
Nielsen, V. both titles
Norris, K. Mystery House
    Secret of the Marshbanks
O'Brien, S. Night of the Scorpion
    Shadow of the Caravan
Obstfeld, R. Dead-End Option
O'Connor, R. S. Murder Won't Wait
O'Farrell, W. Golden Key
    Gypsy, Go Home
Offord, L. G. Glass Mask
    Smiling Tiger
O'Hanlon, J. D. Murder at 300 to 1
Olsen, D. B. 12 titles
O'Malley, P. Affair of John Donne
    Affair of Jolie Madame
    Affair of the Blue Pig
    Affair of the Bumbling Briton
O'Rourke, F. Private Anger, and Flight
    and Pursuit
    P's Progress
Packard, F. From Now On
Pagano, J. Condemned
Page, M. Reclining Nude
Palmer, P. K. Turquoise/Yellow Case
Palmer, S. Omit Flowers
    Puzzle of the Pepper Tree
    Unhappy Hooligan
Pendleton, D. Battle Mask
    Terrible Tuesday
Perdue, V. Alarum and Excursion
Pilpel, R. H. High Anxiety
Platt, K. Princess Stakes Murder
    Pushbutton Butterfly
Porter, R. N. Rest Hollow Mystery
Potter, J. A. Talent for Dying
Prather, R. S. Ride a High Horse
    Slap Happy
Priestley, J. B. Doomsday Men
Pronzini, B. 5 titles
Queen, E. Madman Theory
    Room to Die In
Quentin, P. Puzzle for Fiends
Race, P. Killer Take All
Radcliffe, J. Blackwood
Ranier, P. J. Scared Stiff
Rath, V. 7 titles
Rayter, J. Asking for Trouble
Reese, J. Looters
Reeves, Robert. Cellini Smith, Detective
Renn, J. Violent Air
Rico, D. Daisy Dilemma
    Nightmare of Eyes
Rigsby, H. As a Man Falls
    Calliope Reef
    Kill and Tell
Ritchie, R. W. Deep Furrows
Roberts, W. D. at least 5 titles
Robeson, K. 5 titles
Robinson, David. Confession of Andrew
    Clare
Rosenthal, N. C. Silenced Witnesses
Ross, Clarissa. Spectral Mist
Ross, Gene. Lady, Throw Me a Curve
    Two Smart Dames
Ross, Paul. Dynamite Monster Boogie Concert
    Hitchhike Killer
    Valley of Death
Ryder, S. Three on the Road
Ryerson, F. Seven Suspects
Sadler, M. Circle of Fire
St. John, G. Invisible Trap
Salas, F. What Now My Love
Sanders, G. Crime on My Hands
Sapir, R. Dr. Quake
Savage, M. Coach Draws Near
Saxby, C. Death Joins the Woman's Club
    Death Wore Roses
    Out of It All
Saxon, J. A. Half-Past Mortem
Scarpetta, F. Torture Contract
Scott, Thurston. Cure It with Honey

Sears, R. M. Golden Sentinels
    Grangerfjord Monks
    Heir of Grangerfjord Castle
Shattuck, R. Half-Haunted Saloon
    Wedding Guest Sat on a Stone
Sheldon, W. J. Man Who Paid His Way
Sherman, P. J. Sleep off the Highway
Shippey, L. Girl Who Wanted Experience
    Where Nothing Ever Happens
Shriber, I. S. Last Straw
Simmons, M. K. Cameron Hill
    Diamonds of Alcazar
Simpson, C. H. Life in the Mines
Snyder, Z. K. Heirs of Darkness
Stadley, P. Autumn of a Hunter
Stanton, K. Seek, Strike and Destroy
Steele, C. Yellow Scourge
Stein, A. M. We Saw Him Die
Stein, S. Resort
Stevenson, F. Dark Odyssey
    Ides of November
    Shadow on the House
Stone, A. L. Julie
Strahan, K. C. Hobgoblin Murder
Swanton, S. Sweetheart
Taylor, S. W. Man with My Face
Teilhet, D. L. Big Runaround
    Broken Face Murders
Telfer, D. Guilty Ones
Terhune, A. P. Black Gold
    Grudge Mountain
Thayer, L. 9 titles
Thomas, Ross. Chinaman's Chance
Thompson, A. L. Love, the Sorcerer
Thompson, J. Nothing Man
Thornburg, N. Cutter and Bone
    To Die in California
Toombs, J. Fog Maiden
Trask, K. Dead Men Do Tell
Trimble, L. Cargo for the Styx
    Date for Murder
    Nothing to Lose But My Life
    Surfside Caper
Trott, S. Housewife and the Assassin
Tucker, W. Dove
Turney, C. Other One
Usher, J. both titles
Vance, J. H. Fox Valley Murders
    Pleasant Grove Murders
Vernier, P. California Factor
Von Elsner, F. Pour a Swindle Through a
    Loophole
    Who Says a Corpse Has to Be Dull
Waddell, E. L. Murder at Drake's
    Anchorage
Wade, A. Isle of Peril
Wade, B. Pop Goes the Queen
Walker, Irma. Lucifer Wine
Waters, T. A. Lost Victim
Way, I. S. House on Sky High Road
Wayland, P. Counterstroke
Webb, D. Damned Lovely
Wells, S. Footsteps in the Air
    Murder Is Not Enough
    Witches' Pond
Werlin, M. Shadow Play
Werner, G. One Helluva Blow
Westheimer, D. Going Public
Weston, Garnett. Dead Men Are Dangerous
    Murder in Haste
White, L. Death Takes the Bus
Whittington, H. Doomsday Affair
    One Deadly Dawn
Wilcox, C. Third Figure
    Watcher
Williams, B. Borderline Case
Williams, M. This House Is Burning
Wilmer, D. Dead Fall
Winston, D. Death Watch
Winter, B. Night Was Made for Murder
Wissmann, R. Desert of Darkness
Wolf, J. Two Shadows for Death
Wormser, R. Invader
    Nice Girl Like You
Worth, C. Trail of the Serpent
Zane, L. Brenda

CAMBODIA (CAMB. SEE ALSO: FAR EAST)
Ballinger, B. S. Spy at Angkor Wat
Carter, Nick. Cambodia
Casey, R. J. Cambodian Quest
    Four Faces of Siva
St. John, David. Festival for Spies
Sandberg, B. Brass Diamonds

CANADA (CAN. SEE ALSO: MONTREAL; OTTAWA; TORONTO; WINNIPEG; VANCOUVER)
Allan, L. at least 18 titles
Anderson, A. Affair at Timber Lake
Apple, A. E. Mr. Chang of Scotland Yard
Arvonen, H. at least 6 titles
Bagley, D. Landslide
Bailey, Eric. Cradle's Revenge
Baird, T. Way to the Old Sailor's Home
Bettany, G. Silent Mountain
    Villainy
Bindloss, H. Harden's Escape
Binns, O. Clancy of the Mounted Police
    Lady of the North Star

Settings Index

Blankenship, W. D. Yukon Gold
Bonnamy, F. Man in the Mist
Boyd, A. No Man's Woman
Boyd, H. One Night of Murder
Brillant, J. M. Vision of Murder
Brown, Carter. Seven Sirens
Buchan, J. Sick Heart River
Cade, P. Death Slams the Door
Carleton, S. LaChance Mine Mystery
Carter, Nick. High Yield in Death
Cassells, J. Picaroon Goes West
Castle, J. Flight into Danger
Clare, J. Passionate Invaders
Cocking, R. Die with Me, Lady
    Weep No More, Lady
Cody, H. A. Long Patrol
Connor, R. Corporal Cameron
Craig, A. Pint of Murder
Craig, John. If You Want to See Your
    Wife Again
    In Council Rooms Apart
Cresswell, M. Murder in a Road Gang
Cullum, R. at least 4 titles
Curwood, J. O. Philipp Steele of the
    Northwest Mounted Police
Cushing, E. L. Blood on My Rug
Dallas, J. Night of the Storm
Daniels, D. Jade Green
Dawson, C. Murder Point
Dean, A. Encounter with Evil
De Mar, P. Gnome Mine Mystery
Dennis, R. MacTaggart's War
Derrick, L. Mankill Sport
    Quebec Connection
Disney, D. C. 17th Letter
Dorrance, E. Get Your Man
Dorrance, J. Long Arm of the Mounted
    Never Fire First
Douthwaite, L. C. Ghost Trail
    Murder Goes West
    Warden of the North
    Waters of the North
Farr, C. at least 5 titles
Footner, H. Shanty Sled
    Tortous Trails
    Woman from Outside
Forrest, A. E. Silent Guests
Fry, A. Revenge of Annie Charlie
Garner, H. all 3 titles
Gaunt, M. B. Leases of Death
Goodchild, G. Ace High
    Man Who Wasn't
    Square Deal
    Trooper O'Neill
Hagen, M. A. Dig Me Later
Hamilton, D. Interlopers
    Ravagers
    Terrorizers
Harris, J. N. Weird World of Wes Beattie
Henderson, J. Copperhead
Hendryx, J. B. most of the 58 titles
Hill, H. Spectre Gold
Herron, S. Miro
Hyde, C. Wave
Innes, H. Atlantic Fury
    Land God Gave to Cain
Jardin, R. Devil's Mansion
Jason, S. Death Race
John, O. Disinformer
Johnson, L. Heads for Death
    Murder Began Yesterday
Johnston, Madeleine. Death Casts a Lure
Keirstad, B. S. Brownsville Murders
Kelland, C. B. Case of the Nameless
    Corpse
Kendall, R. S. both titles
Kennedy, M. Escape to Quebec
Knox, A. Raider's Moon
Kyle, D. Raft of Swords
Lee, Thomas. Old Bull Inn of Silver
    Street, Edmonton
Lewis, R. Fenokee Project
Lincoln, V. Swan Island Murders
Lindblad, J. Zap Day
Longstreth, T. M. Murder at Belle Butte
    Sons of the Mounted Police
Lovell, M. Guardian Spectre
    Hand over Mind
    Imitation Thieves
    Presence in the Family
Lund, T. Murder of Dave Brandon
    Robbery at Portage Bend
    Weston of the Royal North-West
    Mounted Police
McClean, J. S. Aerie
McKechnie, N. K. Saddleroom Murder
McLeish, D. both titles
Marlowe, G. Espionage!
Martin, I. K. Billions
Martyn, W. Death by the Lake
Marvin, S. Chateau in the Shadows
Millar, M. Air That Kills
    Fire Will Freeze
    Weak-Eyed Bat
Moore, B. Royce of the Royal Mounted
Mounce, D. Shield Project
Mowery, W. B. all 3 titles
Newton, D. Double Crossed
Nicole, Claudette. House at Hawk's End
North, J. River Rising
O'Donnell, L. Death Schuss
O'Grady, R. Bleak November

Osborne, L. Keys of Hell
Packard, F. Hidden Door
    Sin That Was His
Prichard, H. November Joe, the Detective
    of the Woods
Reilly, H. Compartment K
Richard, S. Terror at Nelson Woods
Ridley, N., Jr. Stolen Nugget of Gold
Robeson, K. 7 titles
Roper, G. G. Death on an Island
Ross, Marilyn. at least 8 titles
Scott, J. M. Unknown River
Shannon, D. Lodestar Legacy
Shelley, S. Bowmanville Break
Smiley, V. Cove of Fear
Smith, F. A. Dragon's Breath
Stark, R. Blackbird
Stead, R. J. C. both titles
Steele, H. all 3 titles
Stoddard, C. Trooper MacLean
Switzer, R. I Was Going Anyway
Templeton, G. both titles
Templeton, J. Dead or Alive
Terman, D. Free Flight
Thayer, N. Still No Answer
Thurley, N. Murder Strikes North
Treynor, A. M. Snow Blind
Vanardy, V. Up Against It
Van de Water, F. F. Havoc
Vermandel, J. G. Scratch a Lover
Vipond, D. Night of the Shooting Star
Walker, D. Black Dougal
    Mallabec
Wees, F. S. M'Lord, I Am Not Guilty
Weston, Garnett. Legacy of Fear
    Murder on Shadow Island
Wheatley, D. Strange Story of Linda Lee
White, S. A. Morgan of the Mounted
    Nighthawk of the Northwest
    Northwest Law
Whitney, J. L. H. Whisper of Shadows
Williams, V. Dead Man Manor
Wynne-Jones, T. Odd's End
Yates, B. Dead in the Water

CANARY ISLANDS (Can. Is. See also: SPAIN; MADRID; MAJORCA)
Atlee, P. Silken Baroness
Harding, R. Appointment in Tenerife
Walsh, J. M. Danger Zone

CAPE COD (See also: BOSTON; MASSACHUSETTS; NEW ENGLAND)
Abbot, A. Creeps
Arnold, M. Cape Cod Caper
Barroll, C. Strange Place for Murder
Benson, B. Burning Fuse
Bramhall, M. Button, Button
    Murder Is an Evil Business
Buck, C. N. Portuguese Silver
Cameron, E. E. Place of Mischief
Carpenter, C. Sleight of Hand
Clark, M. H. Where Are the Children?
Dickens, M. Room Upstairs
Farnsworth, M. Dark Wood
Farr, C. House of Treachery
Fitzsimmons, C. Death Rings a Bell
Forbes, S. Welcome, My Dear, to Belfry
    House
Gresham, E. Puzzle in Paisley
Irwin, I. H. all 5 titles
Johnston, V. Phantom Cottage
Kingsley, B. Black Angel
Knight, K. M. 14 titles
Lincoln, J. C. Out of the Fog
    Ownley Inn
MacIsaac, F. Wild Man of Cape Cod
McMullen, M. Dangerous Funeral
Mead, R. Moses Bottle
Murphy, J. F. Quonsett
Ostrander, I. Island of Intrigue
    McCarty, Incog.
Parker, R. B. Promised Land
Phillips, Carey. Cape Cod Caper
Reilly, H. Double Man
Ross, Marilyn. Dark Stars over Seacrest
Rossi, B. Muzzle Blast
Shay, F. Murder on Cape Cod
Simmons, M. K. Captain's House
Stratton, R. Decorated Corpse
Taylor, P. A. 23 titles
Welles, E. Captain's Walk
Yates, M. Widow's Walk

CAPE TOWN (See also: SOUTH AFRICA; JOHANNESBURG; TRANSVAAL)
Creasey, J. Call the Toff
Drummond, June. Welcome, Proud Lady
Richmond, M. Masked Terror
Scobie, A. Cape Town Affair

CARACAS (See also: VENEZUELA; SOUTH AMERICA)
Carter, Nick. Agent Counter Agent
Coxe, G. H. One Minute Past Eight

CARIBBEAN (Carib. See also: WEST INDIES; INDIVIDUAL WEST INDIES COUNTRIES)
Arnold, S. J. Creole
Atlee, P. Fer-de-Lance Contract
    Rockabye Contract
Bagley, D. Wyatt's Hurricane
Bell, Josephine. Wilberforce Legacy
Bingley, D. E. Caribbean Crisis
Black, I. S. Caribbean Strip
Blochman, L. G. Blow-Down
Boothby, G. Kidnapped President
Boylan, M. S. Passion of Gabrielle
Bretonne, A. M. Dark Talisman
Caidin, M. Three Corners to Nowhere
Calmer, N. Avima Affair
Canning, V. Delivery of Furies
Carr, A. H. Z. Finding Maubee
Carter, Nick. Death Message: Oil 74-2
    Doctor Death
    War from the Clouds
Chaber, M. E. Gallows Garden
Chambers, W. Dry Tortugas
Charteris, L. Saint on the Spanish Main
Christie, A. Caribbean Mystery
Clifford, F. Hunting-Ground
Coffman, V. Curse of the Island Pool
    Enemy of Love
    Isle of the Undead
Conroy, Albert. Looters
Cotler, G. Mission in Black
Coxe, G. H. Barotique Mystery
    Woman with a Gun
Cronin, M. Caribbean Kidnap
Daniels, D. Island of Evil
    Raxl, Voodoo Princess
    Strange Paradise
Darby, R. Death Boards the Lazy Lady
Dickinson, P. Walking Dead
Douglass, D. M. all 3 titles
Eberhart, M. G. House of Storm
Farr, C. Dark Citadel
    Heiress to Corsair Keep
    Mansion Malevolent
    Mansion of Menace
Fenisong, R. Ill Wind
Flagg, J. Paradise Gun
Fleming, I. Doctor No
Flynn, J. Viva McHugh
Forbes, S. Last Will and Testament of
    Constance Cobble
Fuller, W. Brad Dolan's Blonde Cargo
Garth, D. Thunderbird
Gilford, C. B. Dead Man Out
Graves, R. L. Black Gold of Malverde
Halliday, B. Violence Is Golden
Hamilton, D. Intimidators
    Mona Intercept
Heatter, B. Devlin's Triangle
Herzog, A. Aries Rising
Holding, E. S. Speak of the Devil
Holland, I. Kilgaren
Jamieson, L. both titles
Johnston, R. Red Sky in the Morning
Kains, J. Curse of the Golden Skull
Kauffman, R. W. Money to Burn
Key, S. A. Mark of Cain
Lyall, G. Shooting Script
McCloy, H. Goblin Market
Mansfield, P. H. Final Exposure
Marlowe, D. J. Route of the Red Gold
Marlowe, H. Passage by Night
Marquand, J. P. Last Laugh, Mr. Moto
Mersereau, J. Corpse Came Ashore
Moore, Robin. Caribbean Caper
Mounce, D. R. Operation Cuttlefish
Moyes, P. Angel Death
    To Kill a Coconut
Muir, T. Death in Soundings
Mulholland, P. H. Calypso Murders
O'Donnell, L. Tachi Tree
Orgill, D. Ride a Tiger
Orr, M. Tejera Secrets
Plantz, D. Marked for Death
Prather, R. S. Dead Man's Walk
Puissesseuo, R. Someone Will Die Tonight
    in the Caribbean
Queen, E. Killer Touch
Reid, D. Caribbean Crisis
Rhys, J. Wide Sargasso Sea
Richards, P. President Has Been Kidnapped
Robeson, K. Dagger in the Sky
    Mystery on Happy Bones
Robison, H. Rat Alley
Rosenberger, J. Caribbean Caper
    Satan Strike
Runyon, C. Color Him Dead
    To Kill a Dead Man
Sale, R. Not Too Narrow—Not Too Deep
Sandberg, P. L. King's Point
Sanders, P. Hat of Authority
Sapir, R. Voodoo Die
Saxby, C. Even Bishops Die
Sheckley, R. Calibre .50
Stanton, K. Cold Blue Death
Stribling, T. S. Clues of the Caribbees
Sugar, A. Enforcer
Tattersall, J. Damnation Reef
Tiger, J. Wipeout
Van Hearn, J. Don't Betray Me

Walker, M. Code Name: Rapier
Weeks, J. Limbo Touch
Wells, T. Hark, Hark, the Watchdogs Bark
Westlake, D. E. I Gave at the Office
 Who Stole Sassi Manoon?
Wetherell, J. Maiden of Glory Island
Winthrop, W. Island of the Accursed
Woodhouse, M. Phil and Me

CASABLANCA (Casa. See also: Morocco; Africa, North; Tangier)

Carter, Nick. Casbah Killers
 Safari for Spies
Leopold, C. Casablack
Ross, Clarissa. Casablanca Intrigue

CENTRAL AMERICA (Cent. Am. See also: Individual Countries)

Ash, W. Ride a Paper Tiger
Brand, N. Death in the Forest
Carter, Nick. Tropical Deathpact
Chantler, D. T. Capablanca Opening
Church, G. Bombs Burst Once
Coles, M. Dangerous by Nature
Franklin, C. Trembling Thread
Harris, Roger. L.S.D. Dossier
Hastings, Michael. Death Across the Tamagash
Hilton, J. President's Agent
Hough, S. B. Mission in Guemo
Keene, D. Flight by Night
Kilgore, A. Killer Genesis
 Slaughter Run
Koehler, R. P. Blue Parakeet Murders
 Salute to Murder
Levey, R. A. Dictators Die Hard
MacKenzie, D. Night Boat from Puerto Vedra
Marin, A. C. Rise with the Wind
Owen, Richard. Nightmare
Robeson, K. Golden Peril
 Man of Bronze
Ronns, E. Passage to Terror
Tolman, H. Hero by Proxy

CEYLON (Cey.)

Aarons, E. S. Assignment—Ceylon
Beaty, D. Temple Tree
Christie, S. Crash and Carry
Creighton, J. A. Mask of Evil
Harvester, S. Moonstone Jungle
Sela, O. Portuguese Fragment
Wheatley, D. Dangerous Inheritance

CHANNEL ISLANDS (Chan. Is. See also: England)

Bonfiglioli, K. Something Nasty in the Woodshed
Conway, J. D. Island of Fear
Ferguson, J. Death Comes to Perigord
Graham, J. Game of Heroes
La Garde, H. Tide Waits for No Man
Le Huray, C. P. Death for a Holiday
Patterson, J. M. Doubly Dead
Robinson, Derek. Kramer's War
Troy, S. Waiting for Oliver
Vane, P. Here Is the Evidence
Volk, G. Cliffs of Sark

CHARLESTON (See also: West Virginia; South Carolina; South)

Carr, J. D. Dark of the Moon
Ford, L. Road to Folly
Hayward, R. Soft Arms of Death
Long, L. B. House of the Deadly Nightshade
Macomber, D. Clearing in the Fog
Mitchell, I. Asylum
O'Farrell, W. Causeway to the Past
Ross, A. B. Murder Cure

CHICAGO (Chi. See also: Illinois; Midwest)

Acre, S. Yellow Overcoat
Anderson, G. Sit-In
Anonymous. Mysteries of Chicago
Ashenhurst, J. World's Fair Murders
Ballinger, B. S. Body Beautiful
 Body in the Bed
 Portrait in Smoke
Balmer, E. Achievements of Luther Trant
 Breath of Scandal
 Dragons Drive You
 Keeban
Barry, Joe. Fall Guy
 Third Degree
 Triple Cross
Barry, M. Chicago Slaughter
Baynes, J. Meet Morocco Jones in the Case of the Syndicate Hoods
Belanger, C. Five Man War
Benson, O. G. Cain's Woman
Blake, E. Jade Green Cats
Bloch, R. American Gothic
Bonnamy, F. Death by Appointment
Booth, C. B. Mr. Clackworthy
Brown, F. 8 titles
Brunner, B. Face of Night
Bryson, L. Gloved Hand
Burnett, W. R. Little Caesar
 Silver Eagle
Burroughs, E. R. Efficiency Expert
 Girl from Farris's
Capelli, A. Chicago Payoff
Carroll, C. Chicago
Carroll, Leslie. Blackmailer and the Blonde
Carroll, Loren. Wild Onion
Cashman, J. Gentleman from Chicago
Caspary, V. Evvie
Charteris, L. Call for the Saint
Christian, K. Death and Bitters
Clark, E. C. Fatal Element
Clason, C. B. Dragon's Cave
 Fifth Tumbler
 Man from Tibet
 Purple Parrot
Cook, B. Sex Life
Cormack, B. Racket
Corne, M. E. Death at a Masquerade
 Magnet for Murder
Corrigan, M. Dumb As They Come
Crump, P. Burn, Killer, Burn
Crunden, A. B. Chicago Winter's Tale
D'Amato, B. Hands of Healing Murder
Derrick, L. Computer Kill
Dewey, T. B. 10 titles
Donohue, H. E. F. Higher Animals
Eagle, J. Hoodlums
Eberhart, M. G. 6 titles
Edwards, J. G. 6 titles
Elliott, W. J. Snatched Dame
Evans, F. Pistols and Pedagogues
Evans, John. Halo for Satan
 Halo in Blood
 Halo in Brass
Fairman, P. W. Glass Ladder
 Search for a Dead Nympho
Forbes, S. Sad, Sudden Death of My Fair Lady
Fox, G. R. Fangs of the Serpent
Fredericks, E. J. Shakedown Hotel
Freeman, M. J. Case of the Blind Mouse
 Scarf on the Scarecrow
Garfield, B. Death Sentence
Gillian, M. Warrant for a Wanton
Glasmon, K. Public Enemy
Gordons. Case File: FBI
 FBI Story
Granger, B. Public Murders
Grant, M. Gangdom's Doom
Greeley, A. Death in April
Greenburg, D. Philly
Greenlee, S. Spook Who Sat by the Door
Gross, M. S. To the Dark Tower
Gruber, F. Gold Gap
 Leather Duke
 Navy Colt
 Scarlet Feather
Haas, J. L. Vendetta
Harris, L. M. Pickled Poodles
Harrison, William. In a Wild Sanctuary
Hawkins, O. Chicago Hustle
Hecht, B. Thousand and One Afternoons in Chicago
Herber, W. Death Paints a Portrait
 King-Sized Murder
Himmel, R. Beyond Desire
 I Have Gloria Kirby
 Rich and the Damned
 Twenty-Third Web
Hodges, C. G. Murder by the Pack
 Naked Villainy
Hoyne, T. T. Intrigue on the Upper Level
James, F. Killer in the Kitchen
Janson, H. Affairs of Paula
 Chicago Chick
 Nice Way to Die
Jerome, O. F. Murder at Avalon Arms
 Red Kite Clue
Johnson, E. R. Cardinalli Contract
Johnson, M. C. Damned Trifles
Kaminsky, S. M. You Bet Your Life
Keeler, H. S. at least 16 titles
Keene, D. at least 5 titles
King, S. Between Murders
Klasne, W. Street Cops
Knebel, F. Convention
Lait, J. Put on the Spot
Latimer, Jonathan. Headed for a Hearse
 Lady in the Morgue
 Sinners and Shrouds
Laurence, R. Fast Buck
Le Jemlys. Lawyer Manton of Chicago
Levin, M. Compulsion
Lloyd, W. Bergen Worth
Lore, P. Looking Glass Murders
 Murder Behind Closed Doors
Lorimer, G. Acquittal
Lynch, L. Against Odds
 Sealed Verdict
MacDonald, J. D. One Fearful Yellow Eye
McGivern, W. P. But Death Runs Faster
 Heaven Ran Last
 Very Cold for May
McGraw, L. Hatchett
MacHarg, W. Blind Man's Eyes
 Indian Drum
Maling, A. Bent Man
 Go-Between
Marshall, S. Some Like It Hot
Mazzarro, E. Bootleg Angel
 Chicago Dateline
 One Death in the Red
Merwin, B. Girl and the Bill
Morgan, Dean. Roston Outfit in Chicago
Nielsen, H. Gold Coast Nocturne
O'Donnell, S. Runaway Wife
Olesker, J. B. No Place Like Home
Ozaki, M. K. at least 6 titles
Parrish, R. Case and the Girl
Paulsen, G. Sweeper
Payne, W. Scarred Chin
Pendleton, D. Chicago Wipeout
Perdue, V. Singing Clock
Peters, Bill. Blondes Die Young
Pinkerton, A. F. Dyke Darrel, the Railroad Detective
 Jim Cummings
 Marked for Life
 Saved at the Scaffold
Plum, M. Killing of Judge MacFarlane
 Murder at the World's Fair
Postgate, J. W. Private Detective No. 39
Pruitt, A. both titles
Raymond, C. S. Men on the Dead Man's Chest
Razio, R. Blondie Beg Your Bullet
Rea, M. P. Compare These Dead!
 Curtain for Crime
 Death of an Angel
Rice, C. 10 titles
Richberg, D. Shadow Men
Robeson, K. Sky Walker
Roeburt, J. Al Capone
 Mobster
Ronald, J. Murder for Cash
Rosenberger, J. Death Merchant
Ross, Sam. He Ran All the Way
Russell, C. M. Case of the Topaz Flower
 Dreadful Reckoning
Saber, R. O. at least 8 titles
Sapir, R. Union Bust
Sarto, B. Chicago Dames
Scarpetta, F. Mafia Wipe-Out
Scotland, J. Seventh Man
Shura, M. F. Shop on Threnody Street
Smalley, D. E. Stumbling
Smith, C. M. all 4 titles
Smith, Mark. Death of the Detective
Smith, T. L. Thief Who Came to Dinner
Spencer, R. H. Regis Arms Caper
Starrett, V. 5 titles
Storm, M. Chicago Terror
Straus, R. Pengard Awake
Strobel, M. Ice Before Killing
Targ, W. Case of Mr. Cassidy
Thayer, J. S. Hess Cross
Thomas, Ross. Porkchoppers
Thorne, P. Murder in the Fog
 Sheridan Road Mystery
 Spiderweb Clues
Tiger, J. Death Hits the Jackpot
Torrio, V. all 4 titles
Ullman, J. M. Good Night, Irene
 Lady on Fire
 Venus Trap
Van Sickle, V. A. Wrong Body
Vedder, J. K. Last Doorbell
Vinton, A. Mystery in Green
Wagoner, D. Man in the Middle
Wallace, E. On the Spot
Waller, L. "K"
Warren, V. Runaround
Watkins, M. Chicago
Webster, H. K. Sealed Trunk
Weisman, J. Three Faces of Death
Welton, A. D. 27th Ride
Weverka, R. Sting
Whitney, P. A. Red Is for Murder
Wight, N. Death in the Inner Office
Williams, K. both titles

CHILE (See also: South America)

Boothby, G. In Strange Company
Carter, Nick. Inca Death Squad
Dodge, D. Long Escape
 Plunder of the Sun
Fielding, J. Trance
Ganachilly, A. Whispering Death
Hudson, C. Final Act
Robeson, K. Man Who Shook the Earth
Schwartz, A. No Country for Old Men

CHINA (See also: Peking; Shanghai; Formosa; Hong Kong; Mongolia; Far East)

Aarons, E. S. Assignment—Manchurian Doll
Abdullah, A. Remittance-Woman
Ames, J. B. Emerald Buddha
Anne-Mariel. Rendezvous in Peking
Appel, B. Four Roads to Death
Ballinger, B. S. Chinese Mask
Barker, A. Dragon in Spring
Black, G. Dragon for Christmas
Boothby, G. Doctor Nikola
Brent, M. Moonraker's Bride

Settings Index

Caillou, A. Assault on Ming
Carter, Nick. Defector
   14 Seconds to Hell
   Operation Starvation
   Red Guard
Cleary, J. High Road to China
Collins, G. Chinese Red
Comber, L. Strange Cases of Magistrate Pao
Cordell, A. Bright Cantonese
Creasey, J. Death in the Rising Sun
Crossen, K. F. Tortured Death
Derby, M. Echo of a Bomb
Ellinger, G. Ricksha Clue
Garvin, R. M. Talbott Agreement
George, P. Commander-1
Gibbs, G. F. Vanishing Idol
Gluck, S. Thieves' Honour
Harknett, T. Crown: Bamboo Shoot-Out
Harvester, S. Shadows in a Hidden Land
Hebden, M. Killer for the Chairman
Hume, F. Mandarin's Fan
Johnson, S. Doomsday Deposit
Jones, Jack. Journey into Death
Keck, M. Behind the Devil Screen
Kennedy, J. R. Chairman
Lenton, D. Blue Mandarin
Macao, M. Return of the Opium Wars
Mathews, F. A. Staircase of Surprise
Meagher, G. E. Tomorrow's Horizon
Mills, A. Escapade
Mosher, J. S. Liar Dice
Nabarro, G. North from Singapore
Neebel, R. Yunnan Terminus
Norman, James. all 3 titles
Packard, F. Dragon's Jaw
Pentecost, H. Chinese Nightmare
Phillips, L. Split Bamboo
St. John, David. Mongol Mask
Sapir, R. Assassins Playoff
   Chinese Puzzle
Sheldon, W. J. Yellow Music Kill
Simon, R. L. Peking Duck
Sinclair, D. Temple Dogs Guard My Fate
Skoggard, D. China Hand
Starrett, V. Laughing Buddha
Sullivan, S. M. Super Man Chu
Taylor, Thoeodore. Body Trade
Teed, G. H. Murder in Manchuria
   Tiger of Canton
Teilhet, H. T. Assassins
Thomey, T. Flight to Takla-Ma
Thorne, E. P. Smith of Cheng Su
Van Gulik, R. all 18 titles
Varney, G. Bungalow of Dead Birds
Wallace, E. Tomb of T'sin
Wees, F. S. Last Concubine
West, K. House That Chak Built
Wheatley, D. Island Where Time Stands Still
Yardley, H. O. Crows Are Black Everywhere

CHURCH

Birmingham, G. A. Hymn Tune Mystery
Byfield, B. N. Solemn High Murder
Gilbert, M. Close Quarters
Heald, T. Unbecoming Habits
Howie, E. No Face to Murder
Hughes, Babette. Murder in Church
Nash, S. Unhallowed Murder

CINCINNATI (CIN. SEE ALSO: OHIO; CLEVELAND; COLUMBUS; MIDWEST)

Clark, M. B. Model Corpse
Gilla, E. N. Cap and Gown for a Shroud
McCombs, R. L. F. Clue in Two Flats
Reston, J. Knock at Midnight
Valin, J. both titles

CLEVELAND (CLEVE. SEE ALSO: OHIO; CINCINNATI; COLUMBUS; MIDWEST)

Ballenger, D. Blood for Breakfast
Dye, W. H. Devil's Cameo
Eastman, R. Pendulum
Foster, R. Laughing Buddha Murders
Harrington, W. Trial
Livingston, M. J. Prodigy
MacDougall, J. K. Weasel Hunt
Martin, Robert. Key to the Morgue
   Sleep, My Love
Pendleton, D. Cleveland Pipeline
Rabe, P. Bring Me Another Corpse
Shriber, I. S. Invitation to Murder
   Pattern for Murder
Tidyman, E. Line of Duty

COLOMBIA (COLOM. SEE ALSO: SOUTH AMERICA)

Browne, G. A. Green Ice
Carter, Nick. Plot for the Fourth Reich
Stein, A. M. Only the Guilty

COLORADO (COLO. SEE ALSO: DENVER; WEST)

Adler, W. Natural Enemies
Brandt, T. Run, Brother, Run!
Brett, Stephen. Some Die Hard
Burns, R. Farnsworth Score
Carter, Nick. Human Time Bomb
Clason, C. B. Blind Drifts
Dean, E. Murder a Mile High
Derrick, L. Radiation Hit
Dramann, J. Last Victim
Dunning, J. Holland Suggestions
Edmunds, B. Beware the Crimson Cord!
Faust, R. Wolf in the Clouds
Gardiner, D. Lion in Wait
Guinn, W. Death Lies Deep
Halliday, B. Murder Wears a Mummer's Mask
Hamilton, D. Steel Mirror
Hawkins, E. H. Wellspring
Hill, A. H. Murder on the Mountain
Kimbrough, K. Unseen Torment
Kruger, P. Bronze Claws
   Cold Ones
   If the Shroud Fits
   Weave a Wicked Web
Kunst, E. Mystery of Evangeline Fairfax
Loban, E. H. Calloused Eye
MacDonald, E. House at Gray Eagle
McGerr, P. Catch Me If You Can
Mechem, P. both titles
Murphy, T. Aspen Incident
Nelson, H. L. 9 titles
Parker, M. Which Mrs. Torr
Parrish, R. Strange Case of Cavendish
Pearl, J. Time to Kill...A Time to Die
Pendleton, D. Colorado Kill-Zone
Perry, T. both titles
Rodell, V. Free-Lance Murder
Sandberg, P. L. Wolf Mountain
Saxby, C. Death in the Sun
Schier, N. Death Goes Skiing
   Death on the Slopes
   Murder by the Book
Stevens, Diane. Labyrinth
Taylor, J. R. Old Stonewall, the Colorado Detective
Thomas, C. Narrow Gauge to Murder
Tracy, L. Terms of Surrender
Vaile, W. N. Mystery of the Golconda
Walker, Irma. Murder in 25 Words or Less
White, L. Operation—Murder
Whitney, P. Domino

COLUMBUS (SEE ALSO: OHIO; CINCINNATI; CLEVELAND; MIDWEST)

McGrew, F. Taste of Death
Martin, Robert. Catch a Killer

CONGO. SEE: BELGIAN CONGO.

CONNECTICUT (CONN. SEE ALSO: NEW ENGLAND)

Acheson, E. Red Herring
Aiken, R. Ghost Hunters
Armstrong, C. Unsuspected
Armstrong, M. Murder in Stained Glass
Avery, R. Murder a Day!
Balmer, E. Five Fatal Words
Barber, W. A. Pencil Points to Murder
Barker, E. Cobra Candlestick
Blayne, S. Terror in the Night
Blizard, M. Conspiracy of Silence
   Late, Lamented Lady
Booton, K. Andrew's Wife
Boyers, B. White Mazurka
Brennan, J. P. Chronicles of Lucius Leffing
Bronson, F. W. Bulldog Has the Key
   Uncas Island Murders
Brown, Carter. Murderer Among Us
   Sex Clinic
Burke, R. Here Lies the Body
Caldwell, T. Late Clara Beame
Caspary, V. Bedelia
Cassiday, B. Corpse in the Picture Window
   Floater
Chambers, D. Some Day I'll Kill You
Coffin, C. Dogwatch
Collins, Michael. Nightrunners
Cores, L. Let's Kill George
Correy, L. Star Driver
Coxe, G. H. 7 titles
Crosby, L. Midsummer Night's Murder
   Too Many Doors
Curtiss, U. 6 titles
Dalton, P. Silent, Silken Shadows
Daly, E. Evidence of Things Seen
Daniels, D. House of Stolen Memories
   Lady of the Shadows
Davis, J. R. Right to Die
Davis, L. R. Reference to Death
   Taste of Vengeance
Davis, T. Murder on Alternate Tuesdays
Dean, R. G. Murder by Marriage
   What Gentleman Strangles a Lady?
Dempsey, A. Red Falcons
Derrick, L. Animal Game
Disney, D. C. Death in the Back Seat
   30 Days Hath September
Disney, D. M. 27 titles
Dolson, H. all 4 titles
Drew, M. A. Diabolist
Du Bois, T. 5 titles
Du Bois, W. Case of the Haunted Brides
Duff, B. Ask No Questions
Dutton, C. J. Clutching Hand
Eberhart, M. G. Murder in Waiting
Eichler, A. Moment for Murder
Eyre, M. Presence
Fenisong, R. Jenny Kissed Me
Fenwick, E. Poor Harriet
Fischer, B. Bleeding Scissors
Foley, R. 7 titles
Footner, H. Murder Runs in the Family
   Whip-Poor-Will Mystery
Forbes, S. Bury Me in Gold Lame
Forrest, R. 5 titles
Gartland, H. Globe Hollow Mystery
Gatenby, R. Nightmare Chrysalis
Gerson, N. Special Agent
   State Trooper
Giles, G. E. Target for Murder
Goldthwaite, E. K. Scarecrow
Goulart, R. Ghosting
Grandower, E. Seaview Manor
Green, A. K. Chief Legatee
Hatch, M. R. P. Bank Tragedy
Hawk, J. House of Sudden Sleep
Hayes, J. Third Day
Heberden, M. V. That's the Spirit
   Tragic Target
   Vicious Pattern
Highland, D. Death Is a Dark Man
Hill, K. both titles
Hintze, N. Listen, Please Listen
Holland, R. Danger on Cue
Howarth, C. M. Eyes in the Night
Hunt, P. Murder Among the Nudists
   Murder for Breakfast
James, Rebecca. House Is Dark
Johns, V. P. Shady Doings
Kains, J. Witch's Tower Mystery
Kendrick, B. Odor of Violets
King, C. D. Arrogant Alibi
Knight, K. M. Rendezvous with the Past
Landon, H. Hands Unseen
Lanham, E. Death in the Wind
   Death of a Corinthian
   Six Black Camels
Lathen, E. Place for Murder
Lauferty, L. Hungry House
Leonard, C. L. Stolen Squadron
Letton, J. Incident at Hendon
Levin, I. Deathtrap
Lincoln, N. S. Secret of Mohawk Pond
Linzee, D. Death in Connecticut
Lippincott, D. Savage Ransom
Livingston, A. Trackless Death
Lockridge, F. Golden Man
Lockridge, R. Murder in False-Face
Lord, G. She Never Grew Old
Ludlum, R. Matlock Paper
Lynch, M. Creighton's Castle
McCloy, H. Changeling Conspiracy
   Long Body
MacFadyen, V. Bittern Point
McGerr, P. For Richer, for Poorer
McHugh, F. Y. Bluethorne
McMullen, M. Country Kind of Death
   Welcome to the Grave
Mace, M. Headlong for Murder
Mack, C. K. Chameleon Variant
Mario, Q. Death Drops Delilah
Marlowe, S. Translation
Maxwell, H. K. Girl in a Mask
Murphy, W. B. Leonardo's Law
Owen, P. Mystery of a Country Inn
Penfield, C. both titles
Pentecost, H. 6 titles
Philips, J. 7 titles
Queen, E. Inspector Queen's Own Case
Randolph, M. Breathe No More
Rathbone, R. A. Death in the Drawing Room
Reilly, H. 6 titles
Richard, S. Ashley Hall
Robeson, K. Red Moon
Rogers, J. T. Red Right Hand
Ronns, E. Catspaw Ordeal
   Gift of Death
Roos, K. Grave Danger
Ross, Clarissa. Glimpse into Terror
Rowe, A. Up to the Hilt
St. John, G. Secret of Kensington Manor
Saunders, L. Devil's Den
Seabrooke, J. P. Four Knocks on the Door
   Shadow Hall
Shane, S. Diamonds in the Dumpling
Siller, V. Complete Stranger
   Hell with Elaine
Simenon, G. Man on the Bench in the Barn
Simpson, H. R. Rendezvous Off Newport
Smithies, R. H. R. Shoplifter
Steel, K. Imposter
   Judas, Incorporated
Stevens, F. She Left a Silver Slipper
Steward, D. Acupuncture Murders
Strange, J. S. Black Hawthorn
   Clue of the Second Murder
   Night of Reckoning
Sutton, H. Sacrifice

Taylor, H. B. Duplicate Triumverate
Thayer, L. 5 titles
Tracy, D. Death Calling—Collect
Tryon, T. Other
Tyler, E. Murder on the Bluff
Vance, L. J. No Man's Land
Walker, H. Case of the Missing Gardener
Wallis, J. H. Mystery of Vaucluse
Walton, G. L. Oscar Montague—Paranoic
Waugh, H. at least 14 titles
Wells, Carolyn. 8 titles
Wells, T. How to Kill a Man
Weston, George. Wondering Moon
Whitney, P. A. Spindrift
Wickham, H. Clue of the Primrose Petal
Wilde, P. 5 titles
Wood, S. Murder of a Novelist
Woods, Stockton. Laughing Man

COPENHAGEN (COPEN. SEE ALSO: DENMARK; GREENLAND; SCANDINAVIA)
Albrand, M. Nightmare in Copenhagen
Anker, J. Two Dead Men
Ardman, H. Endgame
Bodelsen, A. One Down
  Think of a Number
Heller, F. Emperor's Old Clothes
Kyle, E. Mirror Dance
MacLeod, Robert. Dragonship
Nielsen, H. Stranger in the Dark
Nielsen, T. Gallowsbird's Song
Oram, J. Copenhagen Affair

CORSICA (CORS. SEE ALSO: FRANCE; MARSEILLES; NICE; PARIS; MEDITERRANEAN ISLAND)
Anonymous. Columbia
Atkey, P. Juniper Rock
Deane, S. No Tears for the Dead
Grant, James. Island of Gold
Hammond, L. Life to Lose
Joseph, G. Needle in a Haystack
Newman, B. Death to the Spy
Philips, A. Girl Out in Corsica
Smith, Don. Corsican Takeover
  Secret Mission: Corsica
Welcome, J. Wanted for Killing

CRETE (SEE ALSO: GREECE; ATHENS; MEDITERRANEAN ISLAND)
Ayrton, E. Cretan
Hay, F. There Was No Moon
Highsmith, P. Two Faces of January
Palmer, J. Cretan Cipher
Stewart, M. Moon-Spinners
Yorke, M. Mortal Remains

CUBA (SEE ALSO: HAVANA; WEST INDIES; CARIBBEAN)
Booth, C. G. Kings Die Hard
Buchanan, J. D. Professional
Doliner, R. Orange Air
Dolph, J. Dead Angel
Duncan, Lee. Fidel Castro Assassinated
Fuller, W. Tight Squeeze
Kent, A. Corpse to Cuba
Lewis, N. Small War Made to Order
Mason, V. W. Yellow Arrow Murders
Mayer, E. E. Cobra Team
Null, G. Cuban Expedition
Richards, C. Gentle Assassin
Rosenberger, J. Castro File
Runyon, P. Night Jump—Cuba
Sanderson, D. No Charge for Framing
Walsh, P. E. Murder in Baracoa
Whittington, H. Rebel Woman
Willets, G. Anita, the Cuban Spy
Yates, M. T. Death Sends a Cable

CYPRUS (SEE ALSO: MEDITERRANEAN ISLAND)
Appleby, John. Bad Summer
Blackstock, C. Mr. Christopoulos
Everitt, B. Cold Front
Gage, W. W. Appointment with Dishonor
Grant, Roderick. Private Vendetta
Haggard, W. Protectors
Hocking, A. Night's Candles
  So Many Doors
Kaye, M. M. Death Walked in Cyprus
MacLeod, R. Property in Cyprus
Mather, B. With Extreme Prejudice
Nicole, Claudette. Mistress of Orion Hall
Summerton, M. Ghost Flowers
Wills, C. M. Clue of the Golden Ear-Ring

CZECHOSLOVAKIA (CZECH. SEE ALSO: PRAGUE)
Block, Lawrence. Cancelled Czech
Copp, D. Pursuit of Agent M
Davidson, L. Night of Wenceslas
Desmond, H. Hand of Vengeance
MacInnes, H. Snare of the Hunter

MacLean, Alistair. Last Frontier
Paterson, N. Man on a Tight Rope
Rushton, C. Bloody with Spurring
Sinclair, O. Bitter Sweet Summer
Skvorecky, J. Mournful Demeanour of Lieutenant Boruvka
Stein, A. M. Finger

DALLAS (SEE ALSO: TEXAS; HOUSTON; SAN ANTONIO; SOUTHWEST)
Aubrey, E. Sherlock Holmes in Dallas
Crane, F. Flying Red Horse
Estes, C. C. Eavesdropping on Death
  Moon Gate
Head, L. Terrarium
Sanders, W. F. Whip Hand

DAMASCUS (SEE ALSO: SYRIA; MIDDLE EAST)
Arvay, H. Damascus Countdown
Kaplan, H. Damascus Cover
Leasor, J. Passport for a Pilgrim
Levy, Joseph. Operation Damascus
Vange, N. Spy in Damascus

DELAWARE (DELA. SEE ALSO: SOUTH)
Howard, H. Sleep for the Wicked
Poe, E. A., Jr. House Party Murders
White, L. Night of the Rape

DENMARK (DEN. SEE ALSO: COPENHAGEN; GREENLAND; SCANDINAVIA)
Bodelsen, A. all titles
Eden, D. Shadow Wife
Elvestad, S. Case of Robert Robertson
Orum, P. Nothing But the Truth
  Whipping Boy
Rosenhayn, P. Joe Jenkins' Case Book
Rosenkrantz, P. Man in the Basement

DENVER (SEE ALSO: COLORADO; WEST)
Burns, R. Alvarez Journal
  Angle of Attack
  Speak for the Dead
Downing, W. all 3 titles
Flynn, J. Bannerman
Karr, L. Housesitter
Kimbrough, K. Twisted Cameo

DETROIT (DET. SEE ALSO: MICHIGAN; MIDWEST)
Barry, M. Detroit Massacre
Estleman, L. D. Motor City Blue
Goines, D. Dopefiend
Howes, R. Night of the Garter Murder
Jackson, J. A. both titles
Kienzle, W. X. both titles
Lang, B. Crockett on the Loose
Lathen, E. Murder Makes the Wheels Go Round
Leonard, E. 5 titles
Litwak, L. Waiting for the News
Pendleton, D. Detroit Deathwatch
Q, J. Bunnies
Rossi, B. Mafia Death Watch
Santiago, V. J. Dead End Delivery
Smith, V. E. Jones Men
Weisman, J. Evidence
  Heroin Triple Cross
  Starlight Motel Incident

DISTRICT OF COLUMBIA. SEE: WASHINGTON D.C.

DJAKARTA (SEE ALSO: INDONESIA; BALI; BORNEO; JAVA; NEW GUINEA; SUMATRA)
Carter, Nick. Judas Spy
  Time Clock of Death

DOMINICAN REPUBLIC (DOM. REP. SEE ALSO: WEST INDIES; CARIBBEAN)
Siller, V. Road

DUBLIN (DUB. SEE ALSO: IRELAND; BELFAST)
Dillon, E. Death in the Quadrangle
Gill, B. McGarr at the Dublin Horse Show
Loraine, P. Dublin Nightmare
Perrin, R. Jewels
Queneau, R. We Always Treat Women Too Well
Redmond, L. Death Is So Kind
Stein, A. M. Shoot Me Dacent
White, W. J. One for the Road
Wilkinson, B. Run, Mongoose

DUTCH WEST INDIES. SEE: INDONESIA.

DUTCH GUIANA. SEE: SURINAM.

ECUADOR (ECUA. SEE ALSO: SOUTH AMERICA)
Edwards, P. Valley of Vultures
Wallace, C. H. Tailwind to Danger

EDINBURGH (EDIN. SEE ALSO: SCOTLAND; GLASGOW; HEBRIDES)
Bramble, F. Strange Case of Deacon Brodie
Brett, Simon. So Much Blood
Granger, B. November Man
Hely, E. Mark of Displeasure
Kelly, M. Dead Man's Riddle
Kirk, R. Lord of the Hollow Dark
M'Govan, J. all 7 titles
McKelway, S. C. Edinburgh Caper
M'Levy, J. Curiosities of Crime in Edinburgh
  Sliding Scale of Life
Mann, Jessica. Charitable End
Mitchell, G. My Bones Will Keep
Munro, H. Brain Robbers
Piper, P. Death in the Canongate
Ross, Angus. Edinburgh Exercise
Ross, Marilyn. Curse of Black Charlie
Stephens, R. Cruciform Mark

EGYPT (SEE ALSO: CAIRO; AFRICA, NORTH)
Aarons, E. S. Assignment—The Cairo Dancers
Alter, R. E. Thieves Like Us
Boothby, G. Pharos, the Egyptian
Christie, A. Death Comes As the End
  Death on the Nile
  Murder on the Nile
Cook, R. Sphinx
Cooper, C. Turkish Spy
El Hakim, T. Maze of Justice
Elsworthy, A. L. Death Glides In
Follett, K. Key to Rebecca
Griffiths, A. Bid for Empire
Harvester, S. Breastplate for Aaron
Hastings, M. Veiled Isis
Holden, J. R. Spider Flies Again
  Suez Patrol
  Suez Side Ace
Hymers, J. Utter Death
Lange, J. Easy Go
  Last Tomb
Leader, C. Nightmare on the Nile
Leasor, J. Never Had a Spanner on Her
Leighton, T. Night of the Sphinx
McKinley, F. B. Death Sails the Nile
Mann, Jack. Egyptian Nights
Mundy, T. Mystery of Khufu's Tomb
Munslow, B. No Safe Road
Pape, G. Scorpion Sanction
Parsons, A. Death by the Nile
Peters, Elizabeth. Crocodile on the Sandbank
  Jackal's Head
Rathborne, S. Masked in Mystery
Rees, G. Secret of the Suez Canal
Rohmer, S. 6 titles
Sackville, O. Curse of Amen-Tah
Sinclair, F. Drop One, Carry Four
Stevenson, F. House at Luxor
Sugar, A. Aswan Assignment
Taylor, P. W. Murder in the Suez Canal
Teed, G. H. Bottom of Suez
Walsh, J. M. King's Messenger
Weigall, A. King Who Preferred Midnight
Wheatley, D. Quest of Julian Day
  Sultan's Daughter
Wood, Barbara. Hounds and Jackals
Wynne, F. E. Mediterranean Mystery
Zorro. Gray Creatures

ENGLAND (ENG. HERE IS A SELECTION OF BOOKS WITH ENGLISH SETTINGS BY NON-BRITISH AUTHORS. SEE ALSO: NEXT ENTRY; CHANNEL ISLANDS; ISLE OF MAN)
Alexander, Joan. One Summer Day
Allison, W. Alias Richard Power
  Turnstile of Night
Ambler, E. Hunters
Andrews, C. Affair of the Malacca Stick
Asher, M. Black Wind
Astley, J. Fall of Midas
Atwater, J. D. Time Bomb
Austin, Alex. Salt and Pepper
Avallone, M. London, Bloody London
  One More Time
B. and R. Helen Ashwood, the Female Detective
Balmer, E. Waylaid by Wireless
Banner, M. Q37
Barry, M. Sherbourne's Folly
Baxt, G. Affair at Royalties
Bennett, E. D. Gower Court Manor
Bennett, Janice. Haunted

Settings Index

England

Berckman, E. Heir of Starvelings
    Long Arm of the Prince
    Nightmare Chase
    Victorian Album
Bernard, R. Death Takes a Sabbatical
Bernard, T. Moonshadow Mansion
Biggers, E. D. Agony Column
Black, E. B. Ravenelle Riddle
Blaker, R. Jefferson Secret
Bleeck, O. Highbinders
Bonner, G. Castlecourt Diamond Case
Boutell, A. Death Brings a Storke
    Tell Death to Wait
Boyer, B. H. Solstice Cipher
Boyer, R. L. Giant Rat of Sumatra
Bradley, M. H. Hanging Matter
Bradshaw, H. Pasha's Web
Brandner, G. London
Bristowe, A. Tunnel
Brookes, O. Widow of Ratchets
Brooks, A. T. White Camellias
Brown, Carter. at least 6 titles
Buchanan, P. Sounder of Swine
Buck, P. Death in the Castle
Buckley, W. F. Saving the Queen!
Burt, M. Granville Crypt Murders
Burton, Anthony. Coventry Option
Campbell, H. R. 5 titles
Campbell, Ramsey. Doll Who Ate His Mother
Carmichael, F. Night Is My Enemy
Carr, J. D. at least 29 titles
Carter, Nick. 5 titles
Cashman, J. Cook General
    Kid Glove Charlie
Caspary, V. Husband
Chapman, H. W. Limmerston Hall
Charles, I. Grenencourt
Cheyney, J. Secret of Giltham Hall
Chimenti, F. Web of Allyngrood
Clark, Cecily. Ravensley Manor
Clark, G. Baroness of Bow Street
    Dulcie Blight
Claudia, S. Clock and Bell
Cleaver, A. Summerstorm
Clift, D. Spy in the House
Coffman, V. 6 titles
Collins, F. Case of the Philosopher's Ring
Cooke, M. B. Clutch of Circumstance
Coppel, Alfred. Dragon
Crane, F. Applegreen Hat
Crawford, P. Seed of Evil
Crichton, M. Great Train Robbery
Crossen, K. F. Big Dive
Cunningham, E. V. Assassin Who Gave Up His Gun
Curle, R. Who Goes Home?
Dall, J. Death of a Revolutionist
Damer, A. Too Lively to Live
Daniels, N. Magnetic Man
Darby, C. at least 14 titles
Davidson, T. L. Murder in the Laboratory
Davis, B. Trevena's Daughter
Davis, Mildred. Third Half
Davis, R. H. In the Fog
De La Torre, L. Detections of Dr. Sam: Johnson
    Dr. Sam: Johnson, Detector
    Elizabeth Is Missing
Delving, M. 6 titles
Derleth, A. 11 titles
Devon, N. House of Illusion
Dibdin, M. Last Sherlock Holmes Story
Dickson, Carr. Bowstring Murders
Dickson, Carter. 21 titles
Dircks, J. H. Dr. Thorndyke's Dilemma
Disch, T. M. Prisoners
Dobyns, S. Man of Little Evils
Donaldson, N. Goodbye, Dr. Thorndyke
Drago, F. Devil's Church
Eastvale, M. As the Sparks Fly
Edwards, Anne. Survivors
Eliot, A. Return to Aylforth
Ellis, E. S. Eye of the Sun
Estleman, L. D. Dr. Jekyl and Mr. Holmes
    Sherlock Holmes vs. Dracula
Evans, C. L. Nemesis Wife
Exbrayat, C. Ravishing Idiot
Eyre, K. W. Monk's Court
Farmer, J. Sedona
Farmer, P. Legend of Piper's Hole
Fish, R. L. Gross Carriage of Justice
    Incredible Schlock Homes
    Memoirs of Schlock Homes
    Murder League
Flores, J. Hawkshead
Folliott, D. Signpost to Murder
Footner, H. Anybody's Pearls
Fox, G. F. Terror over London
Franklin, M. 5th of November
Fraser, F. L. Screaming Portrait
Frome, D. 14 titles
Gallico, P. Too Many Ghosts
Galton, R. Spy with a Cold Nose
Garfield, B. Paladin
Garrett, Randall. Too Many Magicians
Gayle, N. Death Follows a Formula
    Sinister Crag
Gellis, R. Sing Witch, Sing Death
Gluck, S. Great London Mystery
Gollomb, J. Girl in the Fog

Grant, M. Shadow Beware
Greenleaf, S. G. Three Knaves
Grey, N. Foxglove Summer
Grove, M. You'll Die Laughing
Hall, G. Silver Strand
Hall, R. L. Exit Sherlock Holmes
    King Edward Plot
Halliday, F. Case of Indelicate Champagne
Hardy, L. Requiem for a Redhead
Hargrave, L. Clara Reeve
Harris, Marilyn. Bledding Sorrow
Hart, C. G. Settling of Accounts
Hartenfels, J. Doctor Death
Haughey, T. B. all 4 titles
Heard, H. F. Notched Hairpin
    Taste for Honey
Heberden, M. V. To What Dread End
Heller, F. London Adventures of Mr. Collin
Hershman, M. Target for Terror
Hesky, O. Life Sentence
Higgins, M. Changeling
    Unholy Sanctuary
    Witch Alone
Highsmith, P. Story-Teller
Hodel, M. P. Enter the Lion
Holland, I. De Maury Papers
Holzer, H. Psychic Detective: The Unicorn
Howatch, S. at least 5 titles
Hubell, N. Adventures of Creighton Holmes
Huber, B. Death and the Dowager
Huff, T. E. Meet a Dark Stranger
    Nine Bucks Row
Hufford, S. Trial of Innocence
Hunt, Charlotte. Gemini Revenged
    Gilded Sarcophagus
    Lotus Vellum
Hurd, F. Curse of the Moors
    Rommany
    Secret of Awen Castle
Hynd, N. False Flags
Ind, A. Sino-Variant
Janifer, L. M. Woman Without a Name
Johnston, V. Hour Before Midnight
Jorgensen, H. Red Lacquer Case
Kauffman, R. W. Beg Pardon, Sir!
Kent, E. Who?
Kilpatrick, S. Wake All the Dead
Kimbrough, K. Joanne, the Unpredictable
    Shadow over Pleasant Heath
King, Alison. Dreamer, Lost in Terror
    Marcia, the Innocent
King, L. W. Rochemer Hag
Kingsbury, M. Beware the Fog
Klein, E. Blackmailer
Kummer, F. A. Green God
    Web
Kurland, M. Infernal Device
Kyd, T. Cover His Face
Laker, R. Smuggler's Bride
Landon, H. 5 titles
Lange, J. Venom Business
Latham, L. Identity Crisis
La Tourrette, J. Previous Lady
Laumer, K. Afrit Affair
    Gold Bomb
Lewis, Canella. Sensitive Encounter
Lindley, E. Brackenroyd Inheritance
    Devil in Crystal
Litzinger, B. Watch It, Dr. Adrian
Livingston, W. Mystery of Burnleigh Manor
Lomas, G. R. Hostages
Lord, J. Bannerman Case
Luhrs, V. Longbow Murder
McCloy, H. Further Side of Fear
McDaniel, D. Rainbow Affair
MacKay, A. M. Triad Conspiracy
McKnight, C. Gravetide
McMullen, M. Pimlico Plot
    Something of the Night
Madden, A. W. Amberley Diamonds
Maling, A. Rheingold Route
Mann, P. Steal Big
Markham, V. 6 titles
Marlow, E. Falconridge
    Lady at Lyon House
    Master of Phoenix Hall
    Midnight at Mallyncourt
Martin, K. Vanessa
Meyer, N. West End Horror
Michaels, B. Sons of the Wolf
    Wait for What Will Come
    Wizard's Daughter
Miller, Lanora. Quickthorn
Mitchelson, A. Earthquake Machine
    Hellbirds
Moffett, C. Bishop's Purse
Mooney, J. Trail of the Barrow
Moore, Robin. London Switch
Morton, D. Province of Darkness
Murray, P. Free Agent
Nelson, C. M. Barren Harvest
Nichols, S. House of Rancour
    Silsby
Noone, E. Daughter of Darkness
Norman, Elizabeth. Castle Cloud
    If the Reaper Ride
O'Grady, L. Artist's Daughter

O'Grady, R. Pippin's Journal
O'Neill, A. High Bid for Murder
Oram, J. Stone-Cold Dead in the Market Affair
Palmer, S. Adventure of the Marked Man
    Puzzle of the Silver Persian
Parker, Beatrice. Betrayal at Blackcrest
    Come to Castlemoor
Patrick, Q. Cottage Sinister
    Death Goes to School
    Murder at Cambridge
Payes, R. C. Bride of Fury
    Devil's Court
Pearlman, G. Adventures of Sherlock Holmes' Smarter Brother
Pearson, E. L. Sherlock Holmes and the Drood Mystery
Pendleton, D. Assault on Soho
Peters, Elizabeth. Camelot Caper
    Murders of Richard III
Pinkerton, A. F. Whitechapel Murders
Piper, E. Stand-In
Plum, J. Secret of Benjamin Square
Polk, D. House on the Black Moor
Post, M. D. Bradmoor Mystery
    Sleuth of St. James's Square
Poyer, J. Tunnel War
Pritchett, A. Karamour
    Legacy of Evil
    Malpas Legacy
    Mill Reef Hall
Queen, E. Study in Terror
Ragosta, M. King John's Treasure
Randell, C. Curse of Deepwater
    Mallory Grange
    Whisper of Fear
Ratcliffe, S. Castle Captive
Revell, L. Party for the Shooting
Rice, Louise. By Whose Hand?
Richmond, D. Dunkirk Directive
Rider, A. Safe Place
Rigg, J. Slipperdown Chant
Roberts, J. L. Castlereagh
    Jade Vendetta
    Ravenswood
Robeson, K. Sea Magician
Roby, M. L. Broken Key
    Marsh House
    Pennies on Her Eyes
    Still As the Grave
Roffey, J. Hostile Witness
Romaine, D. Shadow of Evil
Root, G. T. Bird in the Hand
Ross, Dana. Demon of the Darkness
    This Shrouded Night
Ross, Marilyn. at least 6 titles
Roth, H. Shadow of a Lady
Rowan, D. Silver Wood
Ruben, W. S. Murder: Love Story
Rubens, B. Sunday Best
Ryck, F. Loaded Gun
Saberhagen, F. Holmes-Dracula File
St. Clair, K. Room Beneath the Stairs
St. John, N. both titles
Sebastian, M. both titles
Shepherd, E. both titles
Sherman, R. Jigsaw
Shoebridge, M. Ranleigh Court
Shulman, S. Bride of Devil's Leap
    Castlecliff
    Daughters of Astaroth
Siegel, B. Adventures of Richard O'Boy
Simenon, G. Maigret's Revolver
Sladek, J. Black Aura
    Invisible Green
Souvestre, P. Slippery As Sin
Stafford, C. Honour of Ravensholme
    House by Exmoor
Stanford, A. Mission in Sparrow Brush Lane
Stang, J. A. Shadows on the Sceptered Isle
Stephenson, M. House on Wrath Moor
Stevenson, F. Kilmeny in the Dark Wood
Stokes, M. L. Case of the Judas Spoon
Straub, P. Julia
Swiggett, H. Strongbox
Taylor, G. E. Death of Jason Darby
Teilhet, D. L. Odd Man Pays
Thierry, J. Adventure of the Eleven Cuff-Buttons
Thomas, F. both titles
Tidyman, E. Goodbye, Mr. Shaft
Tourney, L. Players' Boy Is Dead
Trevelyan, J. Greythorne
Vance, L. J. Bandbox
    Black Bag
    Red Masquerade
Villiers, M. Serpent of Lilith
Wagner, S. Cove in Darkness
Wakefield, M. E. Secret at Midwinter End
Wallace, C. H. Highflight to Hell
Watkins, R. H. Master of Revels
Waugh, H. Shadow Guest
Wellman, M. W. Sherlock Holmes' War of the Worlds
West, E. Night Is a Time for Listening
White, Alicen. Evil That Walks Invisible
Whitney, P. A. Hunter's Green
Willock, R. Night of the Visitor
Wilson, M. Wind of Death
Withers, J. Echo in a Dark Room

Wood, Barbara. Curse This House
Woodbridge, H. H. Dig: Two Heads Wanted
Woodley, R. Deadly Encounter
York, E. Medea Legend
York, H. Malverne Manor
    Tremorra Towers
Zochert, D. Murder in the Hellfire Club

E

ENGLAND (ENG. HERE IS A REPRESENTATIVE LISTING OF BRITISH AUTHORS WHO PRINCIPALLY USE ENGLISH SETTINGS. SEE ALSO: PREVIOUS ENTRY; CHANNEL ISLANDS; ISLE OF MAN)

Abbey, Ruth
A'Beckett, A. W.
Adams, H.
Adams, S.
Addiscombe, J.
Adye, J.
Aiken, Joan
Ainsworth, H.
Aird, C.
Alais, E. W.
Alan, M.
Alding, P.
Alexander, John
Alexander, Ruth
Alington, C.A.
Allan, S.
Allardyce, P.
Allen, A.
Allen, G.
Allen, M.
Allerton, Mark
Allingham, M.
Amberley, R.
Ames, D.
Anderson, J. R. L.
Andover, H.
Anson, L.
Appleton, G. W.
Applin, A.
Armour, R. C.
Armstrong, A.
Armstrong, R.
Arnold, J.
Arnold, R.
Ashe, G.
Ashford, J.
Ashton, C.
Askew, A.
Atkey, B.
Austen-Leigh, L.
Austwick, J.
Babson, M.
Bailey, Elliott
Bailey, H. C.
Baker, I.
Balfour, H.
Balham, J.
Ball, B.
Ballinger, W. A.
Bamburg, L.
Barclay, B.
Barling, C.
Barnard, R.
Barnett, G.
Barnett, J.
Baron, P.
Barrett, F.
Barrington, P.
Barry, C.
Bawden, N.
Baxter, G.
Bayfield, W. J.
Beckett, M.
Begbie, G.
Bell, Josephine
Bell, V.
Bellairs, G.
Belloc, H.
Bennett, A.
Bennetts, P.
Bentley, E. C.
Bentley, J.
Berkeley, A.
Bessell, J. P.
Bidston, L.
Bingham, J.
Black, Ladbroke
Black, Lionel
Blackburn, J.
Blackmore, J.
Blair, A.
Blake, N.
Bobin, J. W.
Bodkin, M. M.
Boland, J.
Bolt, B.
Bolton, J.
Bouchier, W.
Bowers, D.
Boyle, C. N.
Bracey, A.
Braddon, M. E.
Brady, N.
Bramah, E.
Branch, P.
Brand, C.
Brandon, C.
Brandon, G.

Brandon, J.
Branston, F.
Brebner, P.
Brent, N.
Brett, S.
Bridges, R.
Bridges, V.
Brinton, H.
Brisbane, C.
Brock, A.
Brock, L.
Brooks, C.
Brooks, E. S.
Brooks, L. H.
Brown, A. C.
Browne, D. G.
Bruce, L.
Bruton, E.
Bryce, C.
Bude, J.
Bullivant, C. H.
Bulwer-Lytton, E.
Burke, J.
Burke, T.
Burley, W. J.
Burnaby, N.
Burnett, G.
Burt, M.
Burton, Miles
Busby, R.
Bush, C.
Butler, Ragan
Cadell, E.
Campbell, R. T.
Cannan, J.
Capes, B.
Cargill, L.
Carmichael, H.
Carnac, C.
Carr, J.
Carter, Y.
Carvic, H.
Cassells, J.
Cecil, H.
Chance, J. N.
Chance, Stephen
Chancellor, J.
Channon, E. M.
Chapman, R.
Chester, G.
Chesterton, G. K.
Cheyney, P.
Chittenden, F. A.
Christie, A.
Clandon, H.
Clark, Douglas
Clement, F. A.
Clevely, H.
Clinton-Baddeley, V. C.
Clouston, J. S.
Cobb, B.
Cobb, T.
Cockin, J.
Coggin, J.
Cole, G. D. H.
Collins, G.
Collins, W.
Connington, J. J.
Conrad, C.
Cooke, M. E.
Cookson, C.
Coram, C.
Corbett, Mrs.
Corbett, J.
Courage, J.
Cowdroy, J.
Cowen, F.
Craufurd, W. H. L.
Crawford, R.
Creasey, J.
Crispin, E.
Crombie, H.
Cromwell, A. G. E.
Cronin, M.
Cross, L.
Cross, Mark
Cullingford, G.
Culpan, M.
Curties, H.
Dalman, M.
Dalton, M.
Dane, C.
Daniel, R.
Dark, R.
Darlington, W. A.
Davies, L. P.
Davis, George
Davis, H. C.
Davis, M.
Davison, G.
Dawe, C.
Deane, D.
Deane, N.
De Crespigny, P. C.
Delannoy, B.
Desmond, H.
Despard, L.
Dickens, C.
Dickson, Grierson
Dignam, C. B.
Dilnot, G.
Dix, M. B.

Dolphin, R.
Donavan, J.
Donovan, D.
Douglas, George
Doyle, A. C.
Drax, P.
Drummond, C.
Drummond, J.
Dudley, E.
Duke, W.
Du Maurier, D.
Duncan, F.
Duncan, W. M.
Durbridge, F.
Durham, H.
Durham, M.
East, R.
Easton, N.
Eden, D.
Edgar, A.
Edgar, J.
Edwards, W.
Egleton, C.
Emerson, D.
Ephesian
Erskine, M.
Esmond, H.
Evans, G.
Everton, F.
Eyles, L.
Fairlie, G
Falkirk, R.
Farjeon, B. L.
Farjeon, J. J.
Farmer, B. J.
Farnol, J.
Farrar, S.
Farrer, K.
Ferrars, E.
Field, K.
Field, Moira
Fielding, A.
Fitt, M.
Fleming, Joan
Fletcher, David
Fletcher, J. S.
Fletcher, R. J.
Flynn, B.
Foster, R. Francis
Fowler, S.
Fox-Davies, A. C.
Foxall, R.
Francis, B.
Frankau, G.
Franklin, C.
Fraser, A.
Fraser, James
Frazer, M.
Fredman, M.
Freeman, R. A.
Fremlin, C.
Froest, F.
Fuller, R.
Furnivall, G.
Gale, J.
Gallon, T.
Gammon, D. J.
Garrett, W.
Garve, A.
Gask, A.
Gerard, F.
Gerard, M.
Gibbons, H. H. C.
Gielgud, V.
Gilbert, A.
Gilbert, M.
Giles, K.
Gloag, John
Goodchild, G.
Goodman, J.
Goodwin, J.
Gore, W.
Gorell, L.
Goyne, R.
Graaf, P.
Graeme, B.
Graham, Neill
Graham, Winifred
Grant, Richard
Gray, B.
Gray, D.
Graydon, W. M.
Green, Glint
Gregg, C. F.
Grex, L.
Gribble, L.
Grierson, E.
Grierson, F.
Griffith, G.
Gunn, V.
Haggard, W.
Hale, E.
Halliday, M.
Hamilton, B.
Hamilton, E.
Hamilton, F. S.
Hardinge, R.
Hardy, A. S.
Hare, C.
Hare, R.
Harris, Rosemary
Harris-Burland, J. B.

Harrison, R.
Hart, I. R. G.
Hastings, Macdonald
Hastings, P.
Hawton, H.
Haynes, A.
Heald, T.
Herman, H.
Hext, H.
Heyer, G.
Hichens, R.
Hill, H.
Hill, H. E.
Hill, R.
Hilton, J. B.
Hobson, H.
Hobson, P.
Hocking, A.
Hodder-Williams, C.
Hollingsworth, L.
Holmes, G.
Holt, Gavin
Holt, H.
Holt, V.
Hope, C.
Hope, S.
Horler, S.
Hornung, E. W.
Hubbard, P. M.
Hull, R.
Hume, D.
Hume, F.
Hunt, K.
Hunter, A.
Hunter, J.
Hurt, F.
Hutchinson, H.
Hyland, S.
Hyne, C. J. C.
Hythe, G.
Innes, M.
Ironside, J.
Islay, N.
Jackson, L.
Jackson, M.
Jacobs, T. C. H.
James, P. D.
Jardine, W.
Jeffries, R.
Jenkins, H.
Jepson, E.
Jepson, S.
Jobson, H.
Johnson, Z.
Jones, B.
Jones, E.
Keate, E. M.
Kelly, M.
Kemp, H.
Kennedy, M.
Kernahan, C.
Kernahan, Mrs. C.
Keverne, R.
Kiddy, M. G.
King, Frank
Kingston, C.
Knight, L. A.
Kyle, S.
Ladline, R.
Laing, K.
Lane, B.
Larbalestier, P.
Launay, D.
Laurence, J.
Leaderman, G.
Le Fanu, J. S.
Leighton, M. C.
Lemarchand, E.
Lenehan, J. C.
Le Queux, W.
Lester, F.
Lester, V.
Lewis, J.
Lewis, Michael
Lewis, Roy
Lewis, T.
Ley, A. C.
Leyton, P.
Limnelius, G.
Llewellyn, R.
Locke, G. E.
Loder, V.
Lorac, E. C. R.
Lovesey, P.
Lowndes, M. B.
Lucas, N.
Luck, P.
Lustgarten, E.
Lynn, M.
MacDonald, P.
McGirr, E.
McGuire, P.
MacKenzie, A.
MacKenzie, D.
MacKenzie, N.
Mackenzie, S.
McLean, A. C.
MacLean, Arthur
McLeave, H.
MacLeod, H. C.
McNeilly, W.
McShane, M.

Maddock, S.
Magee, M.
Magnay, W.
Maguire, M.
Makin, W. J.
Malloch, P.
Mann, Jack
Manton, P.
March, J.
March, M.
Marlowe, F.
Marlowe, P.
Marric, J. J.
Marsden, A.
Marsh, Jean
Marsh, John
Marsh, Richard
Marshall, I.
Marshall, L.
Martin, A. R.
Martin, Richard
Martyn, W.
Masterman, W. S.
Maybury, A.
Mayhew, M.
Meade, L. T.
Meadows, C.
Melville, Alan
Melville, J.
Meriton, P.
Meynell, L.
Mills, O.
Millward, E. J.
Milne, A. A.
Mitchell, G.
Moore, A.
Morice, A.
Morland, N.
Morris, T. B.
Morrison, A.
Morrissey, J. L.
Mortimer, J.
Morton, A.
Morton, G.
Moyes, P.
Muir, Dexter
Murray, A.
Murray, E. J.
Newman, B.
Newman, G. F.
Nichols, B.
Norman, F.
Norsworthy, G.
North, G.
O'Duffy, E.
O'Hare, Kenneth
O'Hara, Kevin
Oppenheim, E. P.
Orde-Powlett, N.
Osborne, M.
Parsons, A.
Payn, J.
Payne, L.
Perowne, B.
Pertwee, R.
Peters, Ellis
Peterson, M.
Petrie, R.
Philips, G. N.
Phillips, C.
Phillips, H. L.
Phillpotts, E.
Philmore, R.
Picton, B.
Plummer, T. A.
Pollard, A. O.
Poole, M.
Porter, J.
Postgate, R.
Powell, P. H.
Price, A.
Priestley, J. B.
Proctor, M.
Proudfoot, W.
Punshon, E. R.
Quin, B. G.
Quiroule, P.
Radford, E.
Randall, R.
Redmond-Howard, L. G.
Rees, A. J.
Reeve, Christopher
Reid, D.
Remenham, J.
Rendall, R.
Rhode, J.
Robbins, C.
Robertson, C.
Rodd, R.
Roffman, J.
Rogers, B.
Rolls, A.
Ronald, J.
Ross, Jonathan
Rowland, J.
Royce, K.
Ruegg, J.
Rushton, C.
Ryan, R. R.
Ryland, C.
Sanders, B.
Sandys, J.

Sayers, D. L.
Scott, J. S.
Scott, Sutherland
Scott, Will
Seamark
Sennocke, T. J. R.
Sergeant, A.
Shand, W.
Sharp, D.
Sheahan, K. M.
Shearing, J.
Sheldon, R.
Shore, P. R.
Silverman, M. R.
Simon
Simons, R.
Sims, G.
Sims, G. R.
Slate, J.
Smith, H. M.
Smith, Shelley
Snaith, J. C.
Sonin, R.
Soutar, A.
Southworth, L.
Spain, N.
Spiller, A.
Sprigg, C. S.
Stand, M.
Stanners, H. H.
Stone, Austin
Stone, S.
Story, J. T.
Straker, J. F.
Street, J.
Strong, B.
Strong, L. A. G.
Stuart, D.
Swinson, A.
Sykes, W. S.
Symonds, F. A.
Symons, B.
Symons, J.
Symons, M.
Tack, A.
Tattersall, J.
Temple-Ellis, N. A.
Terris, E. W.
Tey, J.
Thomas, A.
Thomson, B.
Thorndike, R.
Thorne, G.
Thynne, M.
Toye, S.
Trench, J.
Trent, P.
Trevor, R.
Troy, K.
Troy, S.
Truss, S.
Turner, Bill
Turner, J.
Turner, J. V.
Tyrer, W.
Underwood, M.
Upward, A.
Urquhart, P.
Usher, F.
Usher, G.
Vahey, J. H.
Valentine, D.
Vane, D.
Vane, N.
Van Greenaway, P.
Verner, G.
Verron, M.
Vickers, R.
Vincent, K.
Vivian, E. C.
Vivian, F.
Volk, G.
Vosper, G. V.
Vulliamy, C. E.
Waddell, M.
Wade, H.
Wainwright, J.
Wakefield, H. R.
Walker, P. N.
Walker, R.
Wallace, C.
Wallace, E.
Walling, R. A. J.
Walsh, J. M.
Ward, J.
Warden, F.
Warden, G.
Warner, D.
Warner, M.
Warren, J.
Warren, J. R.
Warriner, T.
Waters
Watson, C.
Watson, H. B. M.
Waye, C.
Webb, A.
Webster, F. A. M.
Welford, M.
Wentworth, P.
Weymouth, A.
Whaley, F. J.

E

Wheeler, H. E.
White, E. L.
White, F. M.
White, R. J.
Whitechurch, V. L.
Whitelaw, D.
Willett, H.
Williamson, Audrey
Willis, T.
Willock, C.
Wills, C. M.
Wilson, Colin
Wilson, G. M.
Wilson, Gregory
Wilson, P. W.
Wise, Arthur
Witting, C.
Wodehouse, P. G.
Woden, G.
Wood, A.
Wood, E.
Wood, Mrs. H.
Woods, S.
Woodthorpe, R. C.
Worth, M.
Wright, J.
Wynne, A.
Wynnton, P.
Yates, D.
York, J.
Yorke, M.

ETHIOPIA (Ethio. See also: Africa, North)
Aarons, W. B. Assignment Sheba
Atlee, P. Judah Lion Contract
Carter, Nick. Z Document
Trench, J. Beyond the Atlas

FAR EAST (See also: Individual Countries)
Aarons, E. S. Assignment—Helene
Aarons, E. S. Assignment—Sulu Sea
Agniel, L. D. Pressure Point
Ambler, E. Night-Comers
  Passage of Arms
Ballinger, B. S. Spy in the Java Sea
Binns, O. Red Token
Black, G. Bitter Tea
  Night Run from Java
Bloodworth, D. Any Number Can Play
Bok. Dragons to Slay
  Vampires of the China Coast
Boothby, G. Beautiful White Devil
Butler, R. Fingernail Beach
Carter, Nick. Vulcan Disaster
Cushman, D. Opium Flower
  Port Orient
Dark, J. Bamboo Bomb
Davis, F. M. Kiss the Tiger
Derby, M. Out of Asia Alive
Driscoll, P. Pangolin
Duncan, R. L. Temple Dogs
Edwards, P. Laughing Death
Footman, R. Once a Spy
Givens, J. Friend in the Police
Glemser, B. Grand Opening
Gluck, S. Dragon in Harness
Gordons. Menace
Harvester, S. Bamboo Screen
  Tiger in the North
Hayes, Ralph. Death Makers Conspiracy
Haythorne, J. None of Us Cared for Kate
Hervey, H. Black Parrot
Horn, H. Murder at Linpara
Horton, G. Edge of Hazard
Hurd, D. Smile on the Face of the Tiger
Laing, A. Dr. Scarlett
McLaughlin, W. R. D. Syndicate of Evil
Mair, G. B. Girl from Peking
Marquand, J. P. No Hero
Mason, V. W. Sulu Sea Murders
Mills, A. Blue Spider
  Intrigue Island
Packard, F. 5 titles
Patterson, H. Sad Wind from the Sea
Phillips, J. A. Pagoda
Proud, F. M. Golden Triangle
Robeson, K. Flaming Falcons
  Thousand-Headed Man
Snell, E. Yellow Seven
Stacpoole, H. D. House of Crimson Shadows
Stone, S. C. S. Dragon's Eye
  Spies
Thayer, J. S. Earhart Betrayal
Thorne, E. P. Black Sunset
  House of the Fragrant Lotus
Vivian, E. C. Forbidden Door
Walsh, J. M. Face Value
  Island Alert
Woodman, M. Medusa Kiss

FIJI (See also: South Pacific)
Arthur, F. all 4 Spearpoint titles
Stuart, I. Dark Crusader
Vandercook, J. W. Murder in Fiji

FINLAND (Fin. See also: Helsinki; Scandinavia)
Grayson, Rupert. Escape with Gun Cotton
Lyall, G. Most Dangerous Game
Risku, C. White Midnight
Vicary, J. Ice Maiden
Wuorio, E. L. Midsummer Lokki

FLORENCE (See also: Italy; Milan; Naples; Rome; Sardinia; Sicily; Venice)
Fletcher, Dorothy. Music Master
Gault, M. Face of Death
Gilbert, M. Etruscan Net
Griffin, J. Florentine Madonna
Lippard, G. Ladye Annabel
Lorrimer, C. Voice in the Dark
Stein, A. M. One Dip Dead
Thomas, H. W. Long Shadow

FLORIDA (Fla. See also: Jacksonville; Miami; Tampa; South)
Adams, E. L. Gambler's Throw
Alter, R. E. Carny Kill
  Swamp Sister
Ard, W. All I Can Get
Beatty, E. Jupiter Missile Mystery
Benedict, L. Fatal Flower
Biggers, E. D. Love Insurance
Bowen, N. Hear No Evil
Brace, T. Murder Goes in a Trailer
  Murder Goes to the Dogs
Braly, M. Master
Breen, R. Adam's Child
Brent, R. L. Liquidator
Brewer, G. at least 12 titles
Brody, M. Teaser Set to Kill
Brown, Carter. Death of a Doll
Caidin, M. Maryjane Tonight at Angels Twelve
Caillou, A. Swamp War
Carrier, W. Bay of the Damned
Carter, Nick. 5 titles
Chambers, W. Bright Star of Danger
  In Savage Surrender
Chase, J. Mark of the Red Diamond
Chase, J. H. 6 titles
Chelton, J. My Deadly Angel
Churchill, L. Shades and Shadows
Claymore, T. Reunion in Florida
Colby, R. Make Mine Vengeance
  Quaking Widow
Conroy, Al. Strangle Hold!
Cooper, C. R. Action in Diamonds
Coxe, G. H. Never Bet Your Life
Crabb, N. Ralph
Crane, F. Murder on the Purple Water
Daly, C. J. Hidden Hand
Davis, Gordon. Ring Around Rosy
Dean, R. G. Layoff
Dent, L. Lady Afraid
Derrick, L. Cryogenic Nightmare
  Demented Empire
De Witt, J. Murder on Shark Island
Dietrich, R. Be My Victim
  One for the Road
Donohue, M. Sutter's Sands
Du Bois, T. Rogue's Coat
Duncan, L. Point of Violence
Eberhart, M. G. Another Man's Murder
  Unidentified Woman
  White Dress
Evans, E. Shadowland
Feegel, J. R. Death Sails the Bay
Fickling, G. G. Bombshell
Floyd, M. Secret of Saraband
Flynn, J. M. Surfside 6
Foley, R. Wild Night
Foster, R. Bier for a Chaser
Freemantle, B. Charlie Muffin's Uncle Sam
Fuller, W. Back Country
  Girl in the Frame
  Goat Island
  Pace That Kills
Glendinning, R. Terror in the Sun
  Who Evil Thinks
Green, A. What a Body!
Green, E. P. Sneaks
Gunter, A. C. Don Belasco of Key West
Hale, C. He's Late This Morning
  Murder in Tow
Hale, Jennifer. Beyond the Dark
  House of Strangers
  House on Key Diablo
  Stormhaven
Halliday, B. 6 titles
Harrington, W. Scorpio 5
Heatter, B. Scarred Man
Hillgarth, A. Change for Heaven
Himmel, R. I'll Find You
Hirschfeld, B. Key West
Holden, L. Hide-Out
Holley, H. Blood on the Beach
Houston, M. B. Yonder
Hurst, E. H. Mystery Island
Johnson, J. L. Nine Lives of Alphonse
Johnston, V. White Pavilion
Jordan, L. Operation: Perfidia
Kane, H. My Darlin' Evangeline

Kauffmann, L. Waldo
Keene, D. Brimstone Bed
  Homicidal Lady
  Hunt the Killer
  Wake Up to Murder
Kelley, L. That's No Way to Die
Kendrick, B. 5 titles
Kerr, B. Damned If He Does
  Shakedown
King, R. Case of the Redoubled Cross
  Faces of Danger
  Malice in Wonderland
Kingsley, R. Blind Chance
Knight, K. M. Silent Partner
Knotts, R. And the Deep Blue Sea
Lariar, L. Day I Died
Latimer, Jonathan. Dead Don't Care
Law, J. Shadow of the Palms
Lewis, Jack. Night for Evil
Lockridge, F. Murder by the Book
Lockridge, R. Death by Association
  Troubled Journey
Lordahl, J. A. Those Subtle Weeds
Lutz, J. Buyer Beware
Lynch, M. Silken Web
McBain, E. Goldilocks
  Sentries
MacDonald, J. D. 18 titles
McDowell, M. Cold Moon over Babylon
Mackenzie-Lamb, E. Labyrinth
McKnight, B. 9 titles
MacLean, Alistair. Fear Is the Key
McLendon, J. Deathwork
McMahon, T. P. Jink
Maling, A. Loophole
Manson, W. Deadly Game
Marchant, B. Secret of the Everglades
Marlowe, D. J. Name of the Game Is Death
  Never Live Twice
  Operation Whiplash
Martin, A. Kastle Krags
Mayfield, S. Lonely Terror
Merle, R. Day of the Dolphin
Messmann, J. Bullet for the Bride
Metcalfe, W. Two Weeks Before Murder
Morgan, S. Too Rich to Live
Murphy, J. Long Reconnaissance
Murray, W. Sunshine Corpse
Muse, P. Eight Candles Glowing
Nelson, Mildred. Island
Norton, A. Opal-Eyed Fan
Pace, T. all 3 titles
Packard, F. Four Stragglers
Palmtag, D. Starling Street
Payne, P. This'll Slay You
Pendleton, D. Thermal Thursday
Pope, E. Colcorton
Powell, R. And Hope to Die
  Shark River
  Shell Game
  Shot in the Dark
Ransome, S. 11 titles
Rea, M. P. Blackout at Rehearsal
  Death Walks the Dry Tortugas
Reilly, H. Lament for the Bride
Richards, W. Dead Man's Tide
Roche, A. S. In the Money
  Pleasure Buyers
Rohde, W. L. Uneasy Lies the Head
Rohmer, S. Moon Is Red
Rome, A. My Kind of Game
Ronns, E. Dark Destiny
  I Can't Stop Running
Sax, A. Salt Cat Bank
Shedd, G. C. Lady of Mystery House
Siller, V. Lonely Breeze
  Mood for Murder
Singer, N. Diamond Stud
Somers, S. Romany Curse
Spillane, M. By-Pass Control
Springer, C. Smuggler's Moon
Sproul, K. Mystery of the Closed Car
Stanford, D. Bargain in Blood
Sterling, S. Dead Right
Stone, Elna. Dark Masquerade
Strange, J. S. Strangler Fig
Terhune, A. P. Secret of Sea-Dream House
Thames, C. H. Violence Is Golden
Thayer, F. Five Bullets
  Jaws of Death
Thomas, D. Gulf Coast Run
Thompson, W. C. Suitcase Full of Money
Toole, W. Death in Deep Shadows
Tracy, D. Corpse Can Sure Louse Up a Weekend!
  Flats Fixed—Among Other Things
  Fun and Deadly Games
  Hated One
Tralins, R. Ring-a-Ding UFOs
Walker, Irma. Murdoch Legacy
Watson, S. Weep No More My Brother
Webb, J. F. Craigshaw Curse
Welles, E. Spaniard's Gift
White, L. Death at Sea
  Flight into Terror
  Lament for a Virgin
Whitney, P. A. Poinciana
Whittington, H. at least 5 titles
Williams, C. All the Way
  Go Home, Stranger
  Man on the Run
  Talk of the Town

Settings Index

Winston, D. Trificante Treasure
Worts, G. F. Red Darkness
Yarnell, D. Mantrap

FORMOSA (SEE ALSO: FAR EAST; CHINA)
Marlowe, D. J. Operation Checkmate
Quigley, J. Secret Soldier

FRANCE (FR. MONACO IS INCLUDED HERE. SEE ALSO: MARSEILLES; NICE; PARIS; CORSICA)
Aarons, E. S. Girl on the Run
A'Beckett, A. W. Hard Luck
Abro, B. July 14 Assassination
Aiken, Joan. Smile of the Stranger
Albert, M. Gargoyle Conspiracy
    Pink Panther
Albrand, M. Day in Monte Carlo
    None Shall Know
Allain, M. at least 4 of 5 titles
Allbeury, T. Lantern Network
Allen, Warner. Death Fungus
Ambler, E. Epitaph for a Spy
    Kind of Anger
Ames, D. Corpse Diplomatique
Ames, J. Dark Carnival
Anderson, J. Storm Castle
Annesley, M. Agent Intervenes
Anonymous. Titled Counterfeiter
Anthony, Evelyn. Occupying Power
Arley, C. Dead Man's Bay
    Ready Revenge
Ashe, G. Death from Below
    Elope to Death
    Rogue's Ransom
    Wait for Death
Audemars, P. most titles
Aufricht-Ruda, H. Case for the Defendant
Aveline, C. all titles
Bair, P. Gypsum Flower
Baker, W. H. Traitor
Ballard, K. G. Gauge of Deception
Bark, C. V. See the Living Crocodiles
Barker, A. Big Fix
Barker, C. H. Devil's Brood
Barr, R. Triumphs of Eugene Valmont
Barrett, J. Monte Carlo Stories
Baskerville, B. St. Cloud Affair
Beare, G. Snake on the Grave
Beeding, F. 6 titles
Bell, Josephine. House Above the River
Bellairs, G. 10 titles
Belot, A. Flower of Crime
    Men Are What Women Make Them
Bentley, J. Mr. Marlow Chooses Wine
Bentley, N. Third Party Risk
Berckman, E. Lament for Four Brides
    Voice of Air
Beresford, J. D. Decoy
Beresford, L. What's at the End?
Bernanos, G. Crime
Bernede, A. both titles
Berry, J. Don't Betray Me
Beste, R. V. Faith Has No Country
Blackstock, C. Gallant
Bocca, G. Nadine
Boileau, P. most if not all titles
Boissiere, A. both titles
Boothby, G. Woman of Death
Bordeaux, H. House That Died
Boulle, P. Noble Profession
Boyle, K. Frenchman Must Die
Bradley, Michael. Corsican Cross
Brahms, C. Casino for Sale
Bramson, K. Case of Dr. Morel
Braun, M. G. Opeation Jealousy
Brennan, R. Toledo Dagger
Brewer, G. Mediterranean Caper
Bridge, A. Emergency in the Pyrenees
Bright, A. Golden Earnest
Brown, H. J. Duffy
Browne, E. Murder by Appointment
Buckingham, N. Storm in the Mountains
Burke, R. Frightened Pigeon
Bush, C. Case of the Climbing Rat
Butler, Gerald. Choice of Two Women
Butterworth, M. Soundless Scream
Calef, N. Frantic
Calvin, H. It's Different Abroad
Campbell, A. Juggernaut
    Keep Away from Water
Canfield, M. Tuscany Madonna
Canler, M. Autobiography of a French Detective
Canning, V. Castle Minerva
    Limbo Line
    Melting Man
    Scorpio Letters
Carfax, C. Sleeping Salamander
Carr, G. Ice-Axe Murders
Carr, J. D. Captain Cut-Throat
    Emperor's Snuff Box
Carstairs, J. P. Gardenias Bruise Easily
Carter, Nick. Gallagher Plot
    Man Who Sold Death
Catalan, H. all 3 titles
Chadwick, C. Moving House of Foscaldo
Charles, R. Flight of the Raven

Chase, J. H. Not Safe to Be Free
    You Have Yourself a Deal
Cheyney, P. Dark Interlude
    I'll Say She Does!
Christie, A. Murder on the Links
    Mystery of the Blue Train
Claretie, J. Crime of the Boulevard
Coffman, V. at least 6 titles
Coles, M. Crime in Concrete
    Death of an Ambassador
    Night Train to Paris
    Three Beans
Connell, V. Monte Carlo Mission
Conte, M. Cassie
Cooper, P. J. My Lady Evil
Coppee, F. Guilty Man
Coppel, Alec. Moment to Moment
Courage, J. Affair Ravel
Cousin, M. Where Did the Girls Go?
Creasey, J. Toff and the Deep Blue Sea
Crofts, F. W. Cask
Crosby, J. Affair of Strangers
Cross, B. Nightwalkers
Cross, J. Grave of Heroes
Cumberland, M. at least 31 titles
Dard, F. Man of the Avenue
Davis, B. Fourth Day of Fear
Davis, D. S. God Speed the Night
De Bremont, A. Black Opal
Deighton, L. Yesterday's Spy
De Jean, G. Who Killed Lord Brixham?
Dekobra, M. Operation Magali
D'Erigny, S. Mysterious Madame S
Des Cars, G. Brute
Desmond, H. Turn Back from Death
De Teramond, G. Mystery of Lucien Delorme
Detzer, K. Broken Three
Dewhurst, E. After the Ball
Didelot, F. Seventh Juror
Diplomat. Scandal in the Chancery
Dodge, D. To Catch a Thief
Downes, D. Orders to Kill
Du Boisgobey, F. most of the 67 titles
Dumas, C. R. Second Bureau
Du Maurier, D. Scapegoat
Eberhart, M. G. White Cockatoo
Edwards, Alexander. Last of Sheila
Edwards, G. Mystery of the Lyons Mail
Egerton, T. Design for an Accident
Eliot, A. Shadows Waiting
Ellerbeck, R. Rose...Rose...Where Are You?
Fairlie, G. Double the Bluff
    Scissors Cut Paper
Farjeon, J. J. Sinister Inn
Farrere, C. House of the Secret
Faust, R. Tombs of Blue Ice
Fear, W. H. Killers
Ferm, B. Vengeance of Valdone
Ferrars, E. Hunt the Tortoise
Fickling, G. G. Honey on Her Tail
Flagg, J. Murder in Monaco
Fleming, I. Casino Royale
Forbes, C. Stone Leopard
Forsyte, C. Diving Death
France, V. Naked Five
Franklin, C. Fear Runs Softly
    Trembling Thread
Franklin, S. Malcontents
Freeling, N. 8 titles
Freyer, F. Black, Black Hearse
Frith, W. Sack of Monte Carlo
Frost, F. Secret Agent Number One
Fry, P. Thick Blue Sweater
    Yellow Trousers
Gaboriau, E. most if not all 16 titles
Gaite, F. Brief Candles
    Come and Go
    Family Matter
Gallico, P. Zoo Gang
Gardner, J. Liquidator
Garrett, R. Murder and Magic
Garth, D. Tortured Angel
Gaston, B. Death Dealers
Gates, H. L. House of Murder
Gavin, C. None Dare Call It Treason
Geddes, P. Hangman
Gibbs, G. F. Splendid Outcast
Gilbert, A. Passenger to Nowhere
Gilbert, H. Hotels with Empty Rooms
Gill, E. Crime Coast
Gill, J. Kiki
Glen, E. Secret of Villa Vanestra
Goldie, B. Green Tabloids
Goodchild, G. Monster of Grammont
Gordon, R. Chaperone
Gouze, R. Quiet Game of Bambu
Graeme, B. La Belle Laurine
Graeme, D. Inn of the Thirteen Swords
    Monsieur Blackshirt
    Sword of Monsieur Blackshirt
    Vengeance of Monsieur Blackshirt
Graham, Winston. Night Without Stars
Gray, B. House of the Lost
Greville, H. Un Mystere
Gribble, L. She Died Laughing
Grierson, F. Mysterious Mademoiselle
Griffiths, A. Rome Express
Guil, J. Once Crime Too Many
Gunter, A. C. City of Mystery
    That Frenchman

Haines, W. W. Target
Hallatt, W. Suppression
Halliday, M. Go Ahead with Murder
    Murder Week-End
Hambledon, P. Murder's No Picnic
Hamilton, E. Casino Mystery
Hardy, A. S. both titles
Harris, J. Spring of Malice
Harris, MacDonald. Treasure of Sainte-Foy
Hastings, P. Field of the Forty Footsteps
Healey, B. Death in Three Masks
    Waiting for a Tiger
Heatter, B. Mutilators
Heaven, C. Place of Stones
Hebden, M. Death Set to Music
    Pel and the Faceless Corpse
    Pel Under Pressure
Heckstall-Smith, A. Where There Are Vultures
Highsmith, P. Boy Who Followed Ripley
    Ripley Under Ground
    Ripley's Game
Hill, C. Jackdaw
Hitchcock, R. Sea Wrack
Holt, V. King of the Castle
Horler, S. Checkmate
    Evil Chateau
    Grim Game
    Princess After Dark
Hougron, J. Question of Character
Hugill, R. Peril in Provence
Hume, D. Bring 'Em Back Dead!
Hunter, A. Honfleur Decision
Hynd, N. Revenge
Imber, H. House of the Apricots
Irving-James, T. Dinner After Death
Jacobs, T. C. H. 8 titles
Jacquemard-Senecal. both titles
James, Maryl. Brandy on the Rocks
Japrisot, S. Lady in the Car with Glasses and a Gun
    One Deadly Summer
    10:30 from Marseilles
    Trap for Cinderella
Jarvie, C. G. Vicious Circuit
Jepson, S. Fear in the Wind
Jessup, R. Deadly Duo
    Night Boat to Paris
Johns, W. E. No Motive for Murder
Jones, B. Layers of Deceit
    Testament of Evil
Kassak, F. Come Kill with Me
Kelly, M. Twenty-Fifth Hour
Kent, S. Lions at the Kill
Kenyon, L. Challenge at Le Mans
    Countdown at Monaco
Kimbro, J. Twilight Return
Kingston, C. Infallible System
    Shadow of Monte Carlo and other stories
Kirst, H. H. Hero in the Tower
Koehler, R. P. Puppets of Chance
Laborde, J. Dominici Affair
    Privileged Character
Lacy, E. Sex Castle
Lambert, R. Crime in Quarantine
    Mediterranean Murder
Lange, J. Scratch One
Leblanc, M. most or all 23 titles
Lees, D. Zodiac
Lem, S. Chain of Chance
LeQueux, W. Court of Honour
Leroux, G. most of the 29 titles
Leslie, P. Hell for Tomorrow
Level, M. Shadow
Levy, B. Missing Matisse
    Shining Mischief
Lewis, Canella. Music of Aquarius
Leyford, H. Murder Man
Lister, S. Delorme in Deep Water
Locke, W. J. Joyous Adventures of Aristide Pujol
Lodwick, J. First Steps Inside the Zoo
Loraine, P. Day of the Arrow
Lowndes, M. B. Chink in the Armor
    Uttermost Farthing
Luard, N. Orion Line
Luddecke, W. J. Thursday at Dawn
Lyall, G. Midnight Plus One
Macardle, D. Dark Enchantment
McCloy, H. Smoking Mirror
McConnor, V. Provence Puzzle
McCutcheon, H. Black Attendant
McHale, T. Alinsky's Diamond
MacInnes, Helen. Agent in Place
    Assignment in Brittany
MacKenzie, D. Knife Edge
    Postscript to a Dead Letter
    Raven and the Paperhangers
MacLean, Alistair. Caravan to Vaccares
    Way to Dusty Death
MacLeod, Robert. Cargo Risk
Malm, D. To the Castle
Manceron, G. Deadlier Sex
Markham, V. Song of Doom
Marlowe, S. Search for Bruno Heidler
Marsh, N. Spinsters in Jeopardy
Marsland, A. Cache-Cache
Martin, Shane. Saracen Shadow
Marton, G. Obelisk Conspiracy

Marvin, S. Summer of Fear
Maske, J. Cherbourg Mystery
    Saint-Malo Mystery
Mason, A. E. W. 5 titles
Mason, Howard. Proud Adversary
Massey, R. Crime in the Boulevard Raspail
Maybury, A. I Am Gabriella!
    Moonlit Door
Mayo, J. Hammerhead
Meadow, H. Uncertain Glory
Mercer, I. Man Gets into His Tomb
Messer, M. Mouse Trap
Minton, P. Orphan of the Shadows
    Secret Melody
Monsarrat, N. Castle Garac
Monteilhet, H. Andromache
    Return from the Ashes
    Road to Hell
Moore, I. Chateau Sinister
Morton, A. Baron in France
Morton, P. Destiny's Child
Mountjoy, H. Minister of Police
Munro, J. Man Who Sold Death
Murray, M. Breakfast with a Corpse
    Good Luck to the Corpse
    King and the Corpse
Murray, W. H. Dark Rose the Phoenix
Newman, B. Maginot Line Murder
Nisot, E. Shortly After Midnight
Noel, S. Prelude to Murder
O'Brien, H. V. Four-and-Twenty Blackbirds
O'Brine, M. Pale Moon Rising
O'Farrell, W. Grow Young and Die
    Snakes of St. Cyr
Offutt, A. Operation: Super Ms.
Ohnet, G. Great Marl-Pit
    Woman of Mystery
Old Sleuth. Giant Detective in France
Oppenheim, E. P. 21 titles
Orczy, B. Castles in the Air
    Man in Gray
Orgill, D. Days of Darkness
    Jasius Pursuit
Orvis, K. Into a Dark Mirror
Osborn, C. J. French Decision
Palmer, B. Blind Man's Mark
    Flesh and Blood
Parker, Robert. Ticket to Oblivion
Paul, B. Seventeenth Stair
Peck, L. Tough Pitch
Pell, F. Hangman's Hill
Pendleton, D. Continental Contract
Pendower, J. Widow from Spain
Penmare, W. Man Who Could Stop War
Pertwee, R. Such an Enmity
Pollitz, E. A. Forty-First Thief
Pons, M. Mademoiselle B.
Post, M. D. Monsieur Jonquelle, Prefect of Police
Praviel, A. Murder of Monsieur Fualdes
Price, A. '44 Vintage
    Other Paths to Glory
Radford, E. Death at the Chateau Noir
Radford, J. P. All of Our Aircraft Are Missing
Renard, M. all 4 titles
Renaud, J. J. Phantom Violin
Revelli, G. Commander Amanda Nightingale
Reynaud-Fourton, A. Reluctant Assassin
Reynolds, B. Whereabouts Unknown
Reynolds, Q. Man Who Wouldn't Talk
Richards, Ross. Murder on the Monte
Richardson, A. Rose of Kantara
Rippon, M. all 4 titles
Rives, A. Incident
Roche, R. M. Clermont
Rochester, G. E. Worst Squadron in France
Rohmer, E. S. Bianca in Black
Ross, Marilyn. Sinister Garden
Rostand, R. D'Artagnan Signature
Roudybush, A. Gastronomic Murder
Rowland, H. C. Sultana
Rushton, C. Devil's Power
Russell, C. E. Adventures of the D.C.I.
Rutherford, D. Black Leather Murders
Ryck, F. Sacrificial Pawn
    Undesirable Company
    Woman Hunt
St. John, David. Diabolus
    On Hazardous Duty
Saltmarsh, M. Clouded Moon
San Antonio. Crooks' Hill
    Hatchet Man
    Tough Justice
Sanders, B. To Catch a Spy
Sanders, J. Firework for Oliver
Sarasin, J. G. Fleur de Lys
    Mystery of Martin Guerre
Sarto, B. Death by the Seine
    Riviera Nights
Saul, J. R. Birds of Prey
Scarpetta, F. Body Count
    Die, Killer, Die
    Stone Killer
Scholefield, A. Point of Honour
Scott, Ralph. Unknown Quest
Scott, Jeremy. Angels in Your Beer
Scribner, F. K. Secret of Frontellac
Service, R. W. House of Fear

Seton, G. V Plan
    W Plan
Shearing, J. Forget-Me-Not
    Lady and the Arsenic
Shulman, S. Lady of Arlac
Sieveking, L. Room with a View
Simenon, G. most titles set in Paris or elsewhere in France
Simmel, J. M. Wind and the Rain
Simpson, H. R. Three Day Alliance
Smith, Don. Man Who Played Thief
    Payoff
Souvestre, P. Fantomas
    Nest of Spies
Sparroy, H. Leper's Bell
Steeman, A. Night of the 12th-13th
Stein, A. M. Moonmilk and Murder
    Rolling Heads
    Snare Andalucian
Stephenson, R. Festival Death
Stevenson, A. French Inheritance
Stevenson, B. E. Destroyer
    Kingmakers
    Villa Aurelia
Stewart, M. Madam, Will You Talk?
    Nine Coaches Waiting
    Thunder on the Right
Strong, M. Danger Feeds My Fear
Stuart, John. Ashes to Ashes
Summerton, M. Nightingale at Noon
Tarrant, J. Rommel Plot
Tattersall, I. Society of Nobles
Teed, G. H. Mystery of the Seine
Teilhet, H. T. Double Agent
    Private Undertaking
Terrall, R. Madam Is Dead
Thomas, Craig. Wolfsbane
Thomas, Leslie. Ormerod's Landing
Thurston, T. Portrait of a Spy
Tomerlin, J. Comeback
Tom-Gallon, N. Monsieur Zero
Toussaint-Samat, J. both titles
Travers, H. Madame Aubrey Dines with Death
Usher, F. Stairway to Murder
Vance, E. Reprisal
Vance, L. J. Alias the Lone Wolf
Vestal, S. Wine Room Murder
Vignant, J. F. Alpine Affair
Walker, Mark. Cassis...Resort to Vengeance
Wallis, R. S. Blood from a Stone
Warden, G. Nut-Browne Mayd
Warriner, T. Death's Dateless Night
Waters. Experiences of a French Detective Officer
Way, P. Super-Celeste
Weil, B. Dossier IX
Welcome, J. Hell Is Where You Find It
    Run for Cover
Wellsley, J. Wine of Vengeance
West, E. Man Running
Weyman, S. J. Man in Black
Wharton, E. Two of Diamonds
Wheatley, D. 6 titles
Whitelaw, D. League of St. Louis
Wilden, T. To Die Elsewhere
Wilkinson, B. Proceed at Will
Williams, C. Wrong Venus
Williams, V. Mannequin
    Pigeon House
    Red Mass
Williamson, C. N. Berry Goes to Monte Carlo
Wills, C. M. Colonel's Foxhound
Wilson, G. M. Do Not Sleep
Woods, K. Murder in a Walled Town
Yates, D. Gale Warning
    Red in the Morning
    She Fell Among Thieves
Young, M. Chateau in Brittany

FRANKFURT (Frank. See also: Germany; Berlin; Hamburg; Munich)
Malcolm, J. Discourse with Shadows
Monteilhet, H. Murder at the Frankfurt Book Fair

FRENCH ANTILLES (Fr. Ant. See also: West Indies; Caribbean)
Ambler, E. Doctor Frigo
Myers, B. Nightfall

FUTURE (Here listed are books explicitly set at a time later than that of writing. Year and place of setting given where identified. See also: Past)
Agnew, S. Canfield Decision (1983, Wash. D.C.)
Alexander, P. Show Me a Hero (ca.1990, Eng.)
Allen, R. Captain Gardner of the International Police
Anderson, I. F. Cypher 8
Arch, E. L. both titles
Arlen, M. Hell! Said the Duchess
Asimov, I. Caves of Steel
    Naked Sun

Ball, J. First Team
Barrow, D. Zilov Bombs
Baylus, R. F. People Exchange (2086, NYC)
Bear, D. Keeping Time (1999, NYC)
Belloc, H. But Soft—We Are Observed (1979, Eng.)
Biggle, L. all 5 titles
Brin, D. Sundiver (2200s)
Chamberlain, W. Red January (1969, U.S.)
Christian, J. Five Gates to Armageddon (1985, Jerus.)
Clark, Curt. Anarchaos
Condon, R. Entwining (1984, Wash. D.C.)
Cook, W. W. Round Trip to the Year 2000 (2000, U.S.)
Corley, E. Jesus Factor (U.S.)
Craig, D. Alias Man (1970s, Eng.)
    Contact Lost (1970s, Eng.)
    Message Ends (1970s, Eng.)
Cussler, C. Vixen 03 (1988, U.S.)
D'Agneau, M. Eeny Meeny Miny Mole
Daventry, L. Man of Double Deed (2090)
Deegan, J. J. Beyond the Fourth Door
Donne, M. Claret, Sandwiches and Sin (1979, Afr.)
Dunleavy, S. Very First Lady (1985, Wash. D.C.)
Egleton, C. Judas Mandate (Eng.)
    Last Post for a Partisan (Eng.)
    Piece of Resistance (Eng.)
Evans, E. E. Man of Many Minds
Fast, J. Mortal Gods (2226)
Finlay, I. Azanian Assignment (1981, S. Afr.)
Forbes, C. Year of the Golden Ape (1977, S.F.)
Fowler, S. Adventure of the Blue Room (1990, Eng.)
Freiwalds, J. Famine Plot (1980)
Gardner, J. Golgotha
Goulart, R. Odd Job No. 101
    Sword Swallower
    What's Become of Screwloose?
Gray, C. Murder in Millenium VI
Green, M. Delphi Calculus
Hawkey, R. Wild Card (U.S.)
Heard, H. F. Doppelgangers (1997)
Herbert, F. Dragon in the Sea (2000s)
Hoch, E. D. Fellowship of the Hand (2000s)
    Frankenstein Factory (2000s)
    Transvection Machine (2000s)
Hogan, J. P. Inherit the Stars
Hoyne, T. T. Intrigue on the Upper Level (Chi.)
Hughes, G. Green Fire
Hurd, D. Send Him Victorious (1975, Eng.)
Ing, D. Soft Targets (1980-1)
Javor, F. A. Rim-World Legacy
Johnson, S. God Bless America (1976, U.S.)
Keeler, H. S. Box from Japan (1942, Chi.)
Killough, L. Doppelganger Gambit
Koontz, D. R. Night Chills (1977, Maine)
Kurland, M. Psi Hunt (U.S.)
Kytle, R. Fire and Ice
Leinster, M. Doctor to the Stars
Lippincott, D. E Pluribus Bang! (Wash. D.C.)
Long, F. B. John Carstairs, Space Detective
Lord, Graham. God and All His Angels (Eng.)
McCarry, C. Better Angels (1990s, U.S.)
Maddock, L. all 4 titles (2400s)
Maine, C. E. Count-Down
Marriott, H. P. F. Iron Detective of Germany
Matthews, Clyde. Ides of March Conspiracy (1980s, NYC, Wash. D.C.)
Merwin, S., Jr. Killer to Come
Moore, C. L. Doomsday Morning
Morris, Jim. Sheriff of Purgatory (1996, Ark.)
Nelson, W. Siege of Buckingham Palace (ca.1985, Eng.)
Niven, L. Long Arm of Gil Hamilton (2124)
    Patchwork Girl
Noel, S. I Killed Stalin (1959)
Nolan, W. F. Space for Hire
Oppenheim, E. P. Wrath to Come (1950, Fr.)
Pape, G. Scorpion Sanction (Egypt)
Pearson, P. Postscript for Malpas (1985, Scot.)
Phillips, M. Brain Twister
    Impossibles (1972, NYC)
    Supermind (1973)
Pratt, F. Double Jeopardy
Reynolds, M. Police Patrol: 2000 A.D.
Ritner, P. Red Carpet for the Shah
Robens, H. Hambro's Itch
Robinett, S. Stargate
Schmitz, J. H. all 5 titles
Smith, L. N. Probability Broach (1987)
Sohl, J. Altered Ego (2000s)

Spruill, S. G. Psychopath Plague
Stapp, R. More Perfect Union (1981, U.S.)
Stein, B. Croesus Conspiracy (1982-4)
Topol, A. Fourth of July War (1983, Iran)
Tyson, J. A. Scarlet Tanager (1930, Wash. D.C.)
Vance, J. 5 titles
Van Lhin, E. Police Your Planet
Verron, R. Day of the Dust (Eng.)
Wallace, Ian. Croyd
    Deathstar Voyage (space)
    Door to Enigma
    Heller's Leap
    Purloined Prince
    Sign of the Mute Medusa
Way, P. Super-Celeste
Wesley, M. Sixth Seal (Eng.)
Wheatley, D. Black August (Eng.)

GENEVA (SEE ALSO: SWITZERLAND; ZURICH)

Beeding, F. Little White Hag
    Seven Sleepers
Carr, J. D. In Spite of Thunder
Carter, Nick. Nowhere Weapon
Carvic, H. Miss Seeton Sings
Diplomat. Slow Death at Geneva
Macauley, R. Mystery at Geneva
Moyes, P. Death on the Agenda
Nisot, E. False Witness
    Hazardous Holiday
    Twelve to Dine
    Unnatural Deeds
Oldfeld, P. Death of a Diplomat
Torr, D. Treason Line
Upton, R. Golden Fleecing
Walker, M. Code Name: Judas

GEORGIA (GA. SEE ALSO: ATLANTA; SOUTH)

Alexander, Jan. Moon Garden
Balmer, E. Golden Hoard
Brent, R. L. Cocaine Connection
Brewer, G. Backwoods Teaser
Brooks, H. Without a Warrant
Carr, J. B. Man with Bated Breath
Daniels, D. Night Shadow
    Unearthly
Daniels, H. R. Girl in 304
Derrick, L. Divine Death
Dougall, L. Earthly Purgatory
Field, Medora. both titles
Fitz, J. D. Graven Image
Gordon, Arthur. Reprisal
Gray, Angela. Nightmare at Riverview
Hopkins, L. C. Black Buck
Jessup, R. Cry Passion
MacDonald, J. D. Crossroads
Matschat, C. H. Murder in Okefenokee
Nicole, Claudette. Circle of Secrets
Parkhurst, J. Southern Moon
Ross, Marilyn. Long Night of Fear
Siegel, D. How Still My Love
Upchurch, B. Scarborough Hall
Walsh, P. E. KKK
Wellard, J. Snake in the Grass
Whitney, P. A. Lost Island
Williams, B. A. Pirate's Purchase

GERMANY (GER. BOTH EAST AND WEST GERMANY ARE INCLUDED HERE. SEE ALSO: FRANKFURT; HAMBURG; MUNICH; BERLIN)

Abdullah, A. Man on Horseback
Albrand, M. Door Fell Shut
    Linden Affair
    Rhine Replica
Allain, M. Yellow Document
Andreas, F. all 4 titles
Angellotti, M. P. Three Black Bags
Annesley, M. Spy Against the Reich
Anonymous. Shrewtzer Castle
Ashe, S. I Am Saxon Ashe
Bachmann, L. P. Lorelei
    Phoenix
Ballard, K. G. Gauge of Deception
Beech, W. Article 92: Murder-Rape
Beeding, F. Not a Bad Show
Behn, N. Shadowboxer
Berckman, E. Evil of Time
    Strange Bedfellow
Bernard, J. Burning Fuse
Betteridge, D. Dictator's Destiny
    Escape of General Gerard
    Potsdam Murder Plot
Beymer, W. G. Middle of Midnight
Blackburn, J. Ring of Roses
Blagowidow, G. Last Train from Berlin
Brunner, J. Wear the Butcher's Medal
Buckley, W. F. Stained Glass
Burke, J. W. Three Day Pass—to Kill
Butler, Gwendoline. Brides of Friedberg
Cargill, L. Lady Was Elusive
Carr, J. D. Castle Skull
Carter, N. Bright Blue Death
    Korean Tiger
    Reich Four

Chance, J. N. Killer Reaction
Charteris, L. Getaway
Chase, J. H. Whiff of Money
Cleri, M. Six Graves to Munich
Coles, M. Drink to Yesterday
    No Entry
    Now or Never
    Pray Silence
Cory, D. Pilgrim on the Island
Craig, W. Strasbourg Legacy
Cross, J. Dark Road
Davidson, L. Making Good Again
Day, W. B. Man from M.O.D.
Delamare, G. Midnight King
Di Mona, J. To the Eagle's Nest
Duncan, A. Official Secret
Fallon, M. Testament of Caspar Schultz
Fanger, H. Life for a Life
Farr, C. Castle on the Rhine
Ferguson, J. Terror on the Island
Firth, A. Tall, Balding, Thirty-Five
Fischer, E. Berlin Indictment
Ford, Hilary. Bella on the Roof
Forsyth, F. Odessa File
Fox, J. M. Cheese from a Mousetrap
Frank, L. Cause of the Crime
Freeling, N. Dresden Green
    Gadget
Fuller, S. Dead Pigeon on Beethoven Street
Gaite, F. Far Traveler
Gardiner, W. J. Man on the Left
Gibbs, G. F. Golden Bough
    Silver Death
    Yellow Dove
Glendinning, R. Mission to Murder
Goodchild, G. Q33
Gordon, Alex. Cipher
Gray, B. Six Feet of Dynamite
Grayson, R. Thieves' Highway
Gregor, M. Town Without Pity
Hall, Adam. Striker Portfolio
Hall, Michael. Once Upon a Crime
Harrington, W. Search for Elizabeth Brandt
Hawthorne, J. Professor's Sister
Hebden, M. Mask of Violence
Hedges, J. Gold Plated Hearse
Higgins, J. Day of Judgement
    Eagle Has Landed
Hittleman, C. K. 36 hours
Hogan, R. J. Aces of the White Death
    Bat Staffel
    Vultures of the White Death
Holt, Gavin. Dark Street
Hunter, J. D. Expendable Spy
    One of Us Works for Them
Innes, H. Air Bridge
Jacques, N. Dr. Mabuse, Master of Mystery
Johnson, J. L. Handful of Dominoes
Jones, V. Monument of Terror
Kail, R. Swastika
Kastner, E. Missing Miniature
Kennedy, J. D. Rain of Death
Kenrick, T. 81st Site
Keystone, O. Major Crime
Kielland, A. Dangerous Honeymoon
King, Frank. Crooks' Cross
Kirst, H. H. most of the 13 titles
Latimer, J. Border of Darkness
Lee, Elsie. Dark Moon, Lost Lady
    Romance on the Rhine
    Sinister Abbey
LeQueux, W. Behind the German Lines
    More Secrets of Potsdam
McCormick, J. Last Seen Alive
McGarrity, M. Passing Advantage
McKenna, M. Nightfighter Spy
Mackenzie, A. M. Dusseldorf
MacKenzie, D. Double Exposure
MacLean, Alistair. Where Eagles Dare
Mans, A. On the Shores of Night
Marchmont, A. W. Dash for a Throne
Marlowe, S. Trouble Is My Name
Martin, H. Sleeping Girls Don't Lie
Mason, Howard. Red Bishop
Melchior, I. Haigerloch Project
    Order of Battle
Miehe, U. Puma
Moore, Dorinne. Caverns of Falkenhorst
Morgulas, J. Torquemada Principle
Nolan, F. Mittenwald Syndicate
    Ritter Double-Cross
Parsons, Mrs. Castle of Wolfenbach
    Mysterious Warning
Persico, J. E. Spiderweb
Peters, Elizabeth. Borrower of the Night
Pinkham, W. Second Oldest Profession
Preedy, G. R. Painted Angel
Rabe, P. Shroud for Jesso
Ramsey, E. Kummersdorf Connection
Raven, S. Sabre Squadron
Robertson, Charles. Elijah Conspiracy
Robinson, B. F. Trail of the Dead
Rochester, G. E. Return of Grey Shadow
    Secret Squadron in Germany
Rohmer, S. Day the World Ended
Rosenkrantz, P. Magistrate's Own Case
Rostov, M. Eroica
    Night Hunt

Rushton, C. Murder in Bavaria
    No Second Stroke
Saffron, R. Demon Device
St. George, G. Proteus Pact
Saltmarsh, M. Indigo Death
Sela, O. Exchange of Eagles
Semenov, J. Himmler Ploy
Seton, G. Red Colonel
    W Plan
Seymour, G. Contract
Shapiro, L. Sealed Verdict
Shaw, B. Nazi Hunter
Sherwood, J. Disappearance of Dr. Bruderstein
Short, C. Black Room
    Dark Lantern
Simmel, J. M. Cain '67
    Dear Fatherland
    Love Is Just a Word
Sinclair, Michael. Sonntag
Sinstadt, G. Fidelio Score
Siodmak, C. Third Ear
Smith, R. A. Fox Trap
Storm, J. Dark Emerald
Tarrant, J. Clauberg Trigger
Teilhet, D. L. Talking Sparrow Murders
Thomas, Leslie. Orange Wednesday
Thomas, P. Code Name: Rubble
    Spy
Thomas, Ross. Cold War Swap
    Eighth Dwarf
Thompson, S. L. Recovery
Tiger, J. Code Name: Little Ivan
Tobias, K. Lady in the Lightning
Vance, E. Escape
Wager, W. Time of Reckoning
Watson, H. B. M. Alise of Astra
Weill, G. Fuhrer Seed
Wheatley, D. Faked Passports
    Scarlet Imposter
    Second Seal
    They Used Dark Forces
White, Alan. Long Night's Walk
Williams, V. Crouching Beast
Willis, T. Lions of Judah
Wilson, A. Wallace Intervenes
Wormser, R. Torn Curtain

GIBRALTAR (GIB.)

Berrow, N. Terror in the Fog
Betteridge, D. Gibraltar Conspiracy
Biggers, E. D. Inside the Lines
Horler, S. Bullet for the Countess
McCutchan, P. Gibraltar Road
Newman, B. Death Under Gibraltar
Perowne, B. Gibraltar Prisoner
    Raffles' Crime in Gibraltar

GLASGOW (SEE ALSO: SCOTLAND; EDINBURGH; HEBRIDES)

Boyd, E. Dark Number
Devine, D. M. My Brother's Killer
Knox, B. 11 titles
McIlvanney, W. Laidlaw
MacNaught, T. P. Recollections of a Glasgow Detective Officer
Malloch, P. Break-Through
    11.20 Glasgow Central
    Lady of No Compassion
Miller, H. Mourning Brooch
Munro, H. Clutha Plays a Hunch
    Who Told Clutha
Rae, H. C. Marksman
Ross, Marilyn. Phantom of the Snow
Swan, A. S. Maclure Mystery

GREECE (SEE ALSO: ATHENS; BALKANS; CRETE; MACEDONIA)

Aiken, Joan. Butterfly Picnic
    Last Movement
Appleby, J. Aphrodite Means Death
Arundale, J. Bread and Olives
Ballinger, B. S. Beacon in the Night
Bell, Josephine. Catalyst
Bennett, Janice. House of Athena
Black, I. S. Man on the Bridge
Blake, P. Escape to Athena
Brunner, J. Good Men Do Nothing
Bryon, C. Foreign Matter
Carter, Nick. Assassin—Code Name Vulture
    Liquidator
    Seven Against Greece
    Ultimate Code
Cole, G. D. H. Greek Tragedy
Davis, D. S. Enemy and Brother
Davis, H. C. Perhaps to Kill
Dickinson, P. Lizard in the Cup
Divomlikoff, L. Traitor
Filgate, C. M. Runway to Death
Fisher, N. Rise at Dawn
Forbes, C. Heights of Zervos
Francis, E. Elena
Goshgàrian, G. Atlantis Fire
Gruber, F. Greek Affair
Hawkins, F. N. Ritter's Gold
Higgins, J. Night Judgment at Sinos
Hodge, J. A. Strangers in Company
Horton, G. Monk's Treasure

Innes, H.   Levkas Man
Jason, S.   Grecian Bloodbath
Jones, James.   Touch of Danger
Katcher, L.   Blind Cave
Lathen, E.   When in Greece
Loraine, P.   Dead Men of Sestos
MacInnes, H.   Decision at Delphi
   Double Image
McManus, L.   Operation Backlash
Markham, R.   Colonel Sun
Martin, Shane.   Myth Is Murder
Maybury, B.   Walk in the Paradise Garden
Michaels, B.   Sea King's Daughter
Mitchell, J.   Death and Bright Water
Morley, E.   Sinister Isle of Love
Muir, Jean.   Smiling Medusa
Osborne, H.   Arcadian Affair
Patterson, H.   Dark Side of the Island
Pendower, J.   Traitor's Island
Phillifent, J. T.   Corfu Affair
Rosenblum, R.   Cover Stories
Ross, Marilyn.   Night of the Phantom
Sheen, G.   Assignment Greece
Stallworth, L.   Pot Shot
Stewart, M.   My Brother Michael
   This Rough Magic
Streib, D.   Deadly Crusader
Wheatley, D.   Dangerous Inheritance
   Mayhem in Greece
Whitney, P. A.   Seven Tears for Apollo
Wilk, M.   Eliminate the Middle Man
Wilson, I.   Empty Tigers
Worboys, A.   Lion of Delos
Yorke, M.   Grave Matters

GREENLAND (GREEN. SEE ALSO: DENMARK; COPENHAGEN; SCANDINAVIA)
Axton, D.   Prison of Ice
Higgins, J.   East of Desolation
Kyle, D.   In Deep
MacLean, Alistair.   Night Without End
Raven, J.   Pinnacle of Ice
Scott, J. M.   Snowstone

GUATEMALA (GUAT. SEE ALSO: CENTRAL AMERICA)
Amos, A.   Pray for a Miracle
Clifford, F.   Amigo, Amigo
Daniels, D.   Maya Temple
Graves, R. L.   Quicksilver
Hill, R. L.   Evil That Men Do
Knight, K. M.   Bells for the Dead
Leonard, P. G.   Phantom of the Sacred Well
McLarty, N.   Chain of Death

GUIANA (SEE ALSO: GUYANA; SURINAM; SOUTH AMERICA)
Coxe, G. H.   Assignment in Guiana

GUYANA (SEE ALSO: GUIANA; SURINAM; SOUTH AMERICA)
Aarons, W. B.   Assignment Tiger Devil
Capon, P.   Amongst Those Missing
Coxe, G. H.   Man on a Rope

HAITI (SEE ALSO: WEST INDIES; CARIBBEAN)
Ballinger, W. A.   Drums of the Dark Gods
Binns, O.   Treasure of Christophe
Carter, Nick.   Black Death
   Terrible Ones
Daniels, D.   Dark Island
Davison, J.   Devil's Horsemen
Graeme, D.   Drums Beat Red
Greene, G.   Comedians
Hogan, R. J.   Flight from the Grave
McCurtin, P.   Battle Pay
Marlowe, D.   Nightshade
Phillips, J. A.   Deadly Mermaid
Roscoe, T.   Murder on the Way!
Ross, Marilyn.   Haiti Circle
Smith, Don.   Haitian Vendetta
Teed, G. H.   Voodoo Island
Thorne, E. P.   Assignment Haiti
   Caribbean Affair
Wheatley, D.   Strange Conflict

HAMBURG (HAMB. SEE ALSO: GERMANY; BERLIN; FRANKFURT; MUNICH)
Baker, W. H.   It Happened in Hamburg
McDougall, M. C.   Chase the Snowman
Ross, A.   Hamburg Switch
Skinner, M.   Somewhere in Hamburg

HANOI (SEE ALSO: VIET NAM; SAIGON; FAR EAST)
Blacker, I. R.   Search and Destroy
Carter, Nick.   Asian Mantrap
   Hanoi

HAVANA (SEE ALSO: CUBA; WEST INDIES; CARIBBEAN)
Barry, M.   Havana Hit
Carter, Nick.   Death Mission: Havana
Coxe, G. H.   Murder in Havana
   Woman at Bay
Cutler, R.   Gates of Sagittarius
Darby, R.   Death Conducts a Tour
Davis, Gordon.   I Came to Kill
Dudley, F.   Havana Hotel Murders
Greene, G.   Our Man in Havana
Gross, S.   Havana X
Guenter, C. H.   Dead Drop in Havana
Sanger, J.   Case of the Missing Corpse
Spewack, S.   Murder in the Gilded Cage
Sylvester, R.   Big Boodle
Wade, R.   Knave of Eagles

HAWAII (HAW. PRINCIPALLY HONOLULU SETTINGS)
Aresbys.   Mark of the Dead
   Murder at Red Pass
Avallone, M.   Hawaii Five-O
   Terror in the Sun
Bickerton, D.   King of the Sea
Biggers, E. D.   Black Camel
   House Without a Key
Bingham, C.   It Happened in Hawaii
Carter, Nick.   Doomsday Formula
   Hawaii
Cassiday, B.   Girl in the Trunk
Castle, F.   Hawaiian Eye
Coffman, V.   Chinese Door
   House of Sandalwood
Corrigan, M.   Honolulu Snatch
Crane, R.   Paradise Trap
Davis, Mildred.   Strange Corner
Deptula, W.   both titles
Dewey, T. B.   Too Hot for Hawaii
Dudley, D.   What Dark Secret
Eyre, K. W.   Sandalwood Fan
Fair, A. A.   Some Women Won't Wait
Farr, C.   Island of Evil
Ford, L.   Honolulu Story
Hamilton, D.   Betrayers
Hamilton, I.   Never Die in Honolulu
Harris, H.   Angry Battalion
Hintzi, N.   Aloha Means Goodbye
Huntsberry, W. E.   both titles
Knebel, F.   Dave Sulkin Cares!
Knight, C.   Affair of the Ginger Lei
   Affair of the Splintered Heart
Laflin, J.   Silent Kind of War
Long, Max.   all 3 titles
Marquand, J. P.   Think Fast, Mr. Moto
Morgan, P.   Hang Dead Hawaiian Style
   Scarlet Surf at Makaha
Morrison, R.   Tree of Evil
Nash, N. R.   East Wind, Rain
Pendleton, D.   Hawaiian Hellground
Prather, R. S.   Dance with the Dead
St. Clair, R.   Mystery in Hawaii
Schuler, F.   Pearl Harbor Cover-Up
Sheridan, J.   Kahuna Killer
   Mamo Murders
   Waikiki Widow
Steven, E. E.   Kat and Copy-Cat
Teilhet, D. L.   Feather Cloak Murders
Vandercook, J. W.   Murder in Hawaii
Von Elsner, D.   Countdown for a Spy
   How to Succeed at Murder Without Really Trying
   Those Who Prey Together Slay Together
Walker, Irma.   Maunaloa Curse
Webb, J. F.   Is This Coffin Taken?
   Somewhere Within This House
Whittington, H.   Brass Monkey
Wylie, P.   Spy Who Spoke Porpoise
Yates, M. T.   Murder by the Yard

HEBRIDES (SEE ALSO: SCOTLAND; EDINBURGH; GLASGOW)
Barr, R.   Dark Island
Black, G.   Big Wind for Summer
Bridge, A.   Dangerous Islands
Campbell, Karen.   Thunder on Sunday
Devine, A. D.   U-Boat in the Hebrides
Dickinson, P.   Seals
Ferrars, E.   Wandering Widows
Hebden, M.   Dark Side of the Island
Kirk, R.   Old House of Fear
Knox, B.   Devilweed
MacVicar, A.   Killings on Kersivay
Pugh, M.   Last Place Left
Ross, Marilyn.   Loch Sinister
Roy, A.   All Evil Shed Away

HELSINKI (SEE ALSO: FINLAND; SCANDINAVIA)
Fleming, Joan.   You Won't Let Me Finish
Sariola, M.   both titles

HISTORICAL SETTINGS. SEE: PAST.

HOLLAND (HOLL. SEE ALSO: AMSTERDAM)
Aarons, E. S.   Assignment—Lowlands
Albrand, M.   No Surrender
Arley, C.   Matter of Opportunity
Ashe, S.   Saxon Ashe...Secret Agent
Brent, N.   No Space for Murder
Canning, V.   House of the Seven Flies
Clive, J.   Last Liberator
Freeling, N.   Because of the Cats
   Double Barrel
   Gun Before Butter
   Strike Out Where Not Applicable
Jones, T.   Dutch Treat
McCarthy, M.   Cannibals and Missionaries
Maartens, J.   Sin of Joost Avelingh
Mandel, P.   Black Ship
Marlowe, A.   Thunder in the Kirk
Moyes, P.   Death and the Dutch Uncle
Perry, Ritchie.   Dutch Courage
Scott, Annjeanette.   Count of Van Rheeden Castle
Simenon, G.   Crime in Holland

HONG KONG (H. KONG. SEE ALSO: CHINA; SHANGHAI; PEKING; FORMOSA; FAR EAST)
Ames, J.   Perilous Quest
Atlee, P.   Kowloon Contract
Black, G.   Eyes Around Me
Brown, Carter.   Bird in a Guilt-Edged Frame
   Chinese Donavan
   Hong Kong Caper
Brown, Wenzell.   Hong Kong Aftermath
Carter, Nick.   Defector
   Dragon Flame
   Peking/The Tulip Affair
Chaber, M. E.   Jade for a Lady
   Man in the Middle
Cooke, D. C.   14th Agent
Corrigan, M.   Sin of Hong Kong
Crane, F.   Three Days in Hong Kong
Crowcraft, P.   That Man Bolt
Daniels, D.   Affair in Hong Kong
   House of the Seven Courts
Daniels, N.   Baron of Hong Kong
Dark, J.   Assignment Hong Kong
Davis, F. M.   Secret: Hong Kong
Davis, J. G.   Years of the Hungry Tiger
Dodge, D.   Hooligan
Drake, F.   Double Identity
Freemantle, B.   Inscrutable Charlie Muffin
Gerson, N. B.   All That Glitters
Hall, Adam.   Mandarin Cypher
Harcourt, P.   Agents of Influence
Harding, R. S. L.   Demon of Hong Kong
Le Carre, J.   Honourable Schoolboy
McCurtin, P.   Operation Hong Kong
McLachlan, I.   Seventh Hexagram
Manson, W.   Chinese Conundrum
Marshall, W.   5 titles
Mason, V. W.   Hong Kong Airbase Murders
Matthews, Clayton.   Hong Kong
Maybury, A.   Jeweled Daughter
Mills, A.   Stowaway
Milton, J.   Death Makers
Morton, A.   Baron and the Chinese Puzzle
O'Callaghan, D.   Scavengers
Peters, Bryan.   Hong Kong Kill
Ross, Clarissa.   Jade Princess
Sela, O.   Bengali Inheritance
Sheldon, W. J.   House of Happy Mayhem
Stewart, I.   Peking Payoff
Wheatley, D.   Bill for the Use of a Body

HONOLULU. SEE: HAWAII.

HOSPITAL (HOSP.)
Bayne-Powell, I.   Death Enters the Ward
Bell, Josephine.   Murder in Hospital
   No Escape
   Trouble in Hunter Ward
   Wolf! Wolf!
Binder, O. O.   Hospital Horror
Brand, C.   Green for Danger
Bryan, M.   Intent to Kill
Calderwood, C.   Bonesetter's Brawl
Candy, E.   Which Doctor?
Clark, M. H.   Cradle Will Fall
Cook, R.   Coma
Curtiss, E. M.   Nine Doctors and a Madman
Curtiss, U.   Danger: Hospital Zone
Davis, M.   Hospital Murders
   Murder Without Weapons
De Puy, E. S.   Hospital Homicides
   Long Knife
Eberhart, M. G.   From This Dark Stairway
   Glass Slipper
   Patient in Room 18
Edwards, J. G.   all 8 titles
Eyles, A. W.   Murder in Hospital
Fast, J.   Bright Face of Danger
Fitz, J. D.   Viper's Bite
Francis, B.   Death on the Roof
Gill, B. M.   Victims
Green, Gerald.   Hostage Heart
Greene, J. E.   Madmen Die Alone
Holding, E. S.   Miasma
Horvitz, L.   Compton Effect
Hubbard, M. A.   Murder at St. Dennis
Kerr, J.   Emergency Room
Lees, H.   Death in the Doll's House
   Prescription for Murder
Leonard, G.   Beyond Control

Little, C. Black Corridors
   Black Stocking
   Black Thumb
McClintock, A. Case of the Three Broken Necks
McCully, W. Doctors Beware!
McEvoy, H. Jones, A., Finds the Body
Marsh, N. Nursing-Home Murder
Neuman, F. Seclusion Room
Perry, F. Mystery of the Girl in Blue
Perry, J. D. Murder Walks the Corridors
Reiter, B. P. Saturday Night Knife and Gun Club
Ross, A. B. Murder Cure
Royce, K. Woodcutter Operation
Sapir, R. Murder Ward
Scott, Sutherland. Murder in the Mobile Unit
Sinclair, Fiona. Dead of a Physician
Sobel, I. P. Dr. Monte Cristo
Trevor, E. Theta Syndrome
Truax, R. Accident Ward Mystery
Wakefield, R. I. Death the Sure Physician
Ward, R. Sandman
Williamson, B. G. Death Stalks the Ward

HOUSTON (SEE ALSO: TEXAS; DALLAS; SAN ANTONIO; SOUTHWEST)
Dale, J. A. Long Distance
Donahue, J. Confessor
   Lady Loved Too Well
   Pray to the Hustlers' God
Goldman, L. Judd for the Defense #2
Holmes, A. Wake of a Lawyer
Moore, Robin. Search and Destroy
Saunders, L. Smoke Screen
Wolfe, J. Drilling for Death

HUNGARY (HUNG. SEE ALSO: BUDAPEST)
Blackstock, C. Knock at Midnight
Bridge, A. Tightening String
De Villiers, G. Countess and the Spy
Fagyas, M. Widowmaker
Luard, N. Warm and Golden War
Newton, D. Red Judas
Parker, Robert. Passport to Peril
Roby, M. L. Hidden Book
Vance, L. J. Woman in the Shadow
Wheatley, D. Traitor's Gate
Williams, V. Three of Clubs

ICELAND (ICE.)
Bagley, D. Running Blind
Dobner, M. P. Sea Wind
MacLeod, Robert. Incident in Iceland
Marlowe, S. Danger Is My Line

IDAHO (IDA. SEE ALSO: WEST)
Easton, L. Driven Flesh
Lane, G. Stolen Scar
Offord, L. G. Clues to Burn
Robeson, K. Glass Mountain
Shaw, R. Running

ILLINOIS (ILL. SEE ALSO: CHICAGO; MIDWEST)
Balmer, E. Shield of Silence
Barry, Joe. Pay-Off
Browne, H. Taste of Ashes
Casey, R. J. Third Owl
Cook, E. Forbidden Tower
Crane, F. Golden Box
Cromie, A. Lucky to Be Alive?
Curtis, W. A. Strange Adventures of Mr. Middleton
Davis, D. S. Shock Wave
Dewey, T. B. Deadline
   Handle with Fear
   Hue and Cry
Eatock, M. Haunted Heirloom
Eberhart, M. G. Danger in the Dark
   Fair Warning
Foote-Smith, E. Never Say Die
Grandower, E. Secret Room of Morgate House
Hanley, E. Guilty As Charged
Howard, J. A. Bullet-Proof Martyr
Johnson, R. Lady in Dread
Jorgenson, N. Circle of Vengeance
Keeler, H. S. Chameleon
Kenyon, M. Whole Hog
Lobaugh, E. K. I Am Afraid
   She Never Reached the Top
Lore, P. Who Killed the Pie Man?
MacDonald, J. D. Death Trap
McInerny, R. all 5 RD titles
Neidig, W. J. Fire Flingers
Pendleton, D. Monday's Mob
Plum, M. Dead Man's Secret
Potts, J. Go, Lovely Rose
Rice, C. Eight Faces at Three
Roberts, D. Beginning of a Crime
Rosenberger, J. Death Trap
Runyon, C. Black Moth
Scott, Denis. Beckoning Shadow

Spencer, R. H. Abu Wahab Caper
   Stranger City Caper
Stokes, M. L. Wolf Howls Murder
Tucker, W. Chinese Doll
   Dove
   To Keep or Kill
Unekis, R. Chase
Vale, R. M. House on Rainbow Leap
Van Atta, W. Good Place to Work and Die
   Hatchet Man
   Shock Treatment
Wallis, J. H. Woman He Chose
Warren, V. Brandon Returns
Webster, H. K. Who Is the Next?
Whitehead, J. House on the Hill
Wilder, T. Eighth Day

INDIA (SEE ALSO: BOMBAY; CALCUTTA; NEW DELHI; INDIAN OCEAN)
Abdullah, A. Red Stain
Aiken, Joan. Lightning Tree
Angus, J. Scorpion's Nest
Arnold, Edwin. Queen's Justice
Blochman, L. G. Bengal Fire
   Bombay Mail
   Red Snow at Darjeeling
   Wives to Burn
Breem, W. Leopard and the Cliff
Bruce, K. Fakir's Curse
   Sliding Death
Campbell, H. Secret Brotherhood
Carter, Nick. Double Identity
Casberg, M. A. Death Stalks the Punjab
Channing, M. King Cobra
   Nine Lives
Cooke, D. C. c/o American Embassy
Cooper, Brian. Mission for Betty Smith
   Touch of Thunder
   Van Langeren Girl
Cox, E. C. all 3 titles
Creasey, J. Wings of Peace
Dellbridge, J. Moles of Death
Drummond, I. Necklace of Skulls
Easton, R. Ferrol Bond
Edwards, P. Holocaust Auction
Eliade, M. Two Tales of the Occult
Emery, J. I. Tiger of Baragunga
Ferguson, J. Secret Road
Fforde, B. Trotter
Fisher, Richard. Indian Police
Griffiths, A. Before the British Raj
Kaye, M. M. Death Walked in Kashmir
Keating, H. R. F. 10 titles
Marlow, E. Danger in Dahlkari
Marlowe, S. Killers Are My Meat
Mason, A. E. W. Sapphire
Mather, B. 5 titles
Morton, A. Baron Goes East
Mukerji, D. G. Secret Listeners of the East
Mundy, T. at least 12 titles
Parsons, A. No Alibi for Murder
Penny, F. E. Malabar Magician
   Pulling the Strings
   Spell of the Devil
Peters, Ellis. Death to the Landlords!
Richardson, M. Song of India
Roadarmel, P. Kaligarh Fault
Rosenberger, J. Hell in Hindu Land
Ross, Clarissa. Kashmiri Passions
St. John, David. Towers of Silence
Selwyn, F. Sergeant Verity and the Imperial Diamond
Seton, G. K Code Plan
Shannon, D. Black Scorpion
Snyder, C. M. Flaw in the Sapphire
Soutar, A. Chosen of the Gods
Taylor, P. W. Murder in the Taj Mahal
Thorne, B. Bengali Spider Plan
   Death Rust
   Ganges Mud
Vance, L. J. Bronze Bell
Wheatley, D. Rape of Venice
Wilson, A. Crimson Dacoit
   Devil's Cocktail
   Mystery of Tunnel 51
Woodruff, P. Call the Next Witness

INDIAN OCEAN (IND. O. SEE ALSO: INDIA; BOMBAY; CALCUTTA; CEYLON; NEW DELHI)
Chase, P. Betrayal in Eden
Francis, B. Death on the Atoll
Innes, H. Strode Venturer
Poyer, J. Operation Malacca

INDIANA (IND. SEE ALSO: INDIANAPOLIS; MIDWEST)
Adler, T. On Murder's Skirts
Bonnamy, F. Rope of Sand
Brown, F. Dead Ringer
Cameron, K. at least 6 titles
Carkeet, D. Double Negative
Daniels, D. House on Circus Hill
De Weese, J. Hour of the Cat
Endore, G. Detour at Night
Hays, H. R. Stranger on the Highway
Hensley, J. L. all 8 titles
Kingsley, M. J. Shadow over Elveron

Lewin, M. Z. Enemies Within
Lowe, K. Haze of Evil
McElfresh, A. Keep Back the Dark
Meredith, M. House of a Thousand Candles
Rickett, F. both titles
Russell, A. J. Devalino Caper
Saber, R. O. Deadly Lover
Sapir, R. Power Play
Stratton, Thomas. Mind-Twisters Affair

INDIANAPOLIS (SEE ALSO: INDIANA; MIDWEST)
Hayes, J. Desperate Hours
Kenyon, M. Revenge at Indy
Lewin, M. Z. 5 titles
Stark, R. Rare Coin Score

INDONESIA (INDON. SEE ALSO: DJAKARTA; BALI; BORNEO; JAVA; NEW GUINEA; SUMATRA)
Atlee, P. Ill Wind Contract
   Makassar Strait Contract
Carey, B. Dangerous Isles
Daniels, J. R. Firegold
Derby, M. Sunlit Ambush
East, M. McCreary Moves In
Harvester, S. Golden Fear
Holnes, G. Surabaya
McCurtin, P. Guns of Palembang
Stacpoole, H. D. Tales of Mynheer Amayat

IOWA (IA. SEE ALSO: MIDWEST)
Atwater, M. M. Crime in Corn-Weather
Boyd, C. B. Revenge in "The Convent"
Brown, Carter. Silken Nightmare
Collins, Max. Bait Money
   Blood Money
   Broker's Wife
Deming, R. What's the Matter with Helen?
Gruber, F. Fourth Letter
Howard, H. Room 37
Hultman, H. J. This Murderous Shaft
Jeffery, R. Mine
Lafore, L. Nine Seven Juliet
Millhiser, M. Nella Waits
Plum, M. Susanna, Don't You Cry!
Rice, C. Thursday Turkey Murders
Schmitt, L. F. Shyster Lawyer

IRAN (SEE ALSO: TEHERAN; MIDDLE EAST)
Aarons, E. S. Assignment—Moon Girl
Adams, R. Star of Persia
Brackett, L. Silent Partner
Bulliet, R. Tomb of the Twelfth Imam
Copeland, W. Five Hours from Isfahan
De Villiers, G. Versus the C.I.A.
Epstein, E. J. Cartel
Flagg, J. Persian Cat
Harvester, S. Unsung Road
Jason, S. Appointment in Iran
Landon, C. Flag in the City
Rider, W. W. Dyed for Death
Sheckley, R. White Death
Somerville-Large, P. Couch of Earth
Topol, A. Fourth of July War

IRELAND (IRE. BOTH IRELAND AND NORTHERN IRELAND INCLUDED HERE. SEE ALSO: BELFAST; DUBLIN)
Addison, H. R. Recollections of an Irish Police Magistrate
Atlee, P. Shankill Road Contract
Banville, J. Birchwood
Birmingham, G. A. Fidgets
   Lost Lawyer
   Search Party
Blake, N. Private Wound
Brandon, B. Cliffs of Night
Brewster, D. Heart's Grown Brutal
Brydon, S. Guns over the Border
Caswell, H. Never Wed an Old Man
Christopher, J. Little People
Clancy, A. Blind Plot
Cleeve, B. Death of a Painted Lady
   Death of a Wicked Servant
   Vote X for Treason
Clifford, F. Wild Justice
Coffman, V. Beckoning
   Cliffs of Dread
Connor, R. I Am Death
Cooper, Lynna. Hour of the Harp
Cowen, F. Curse of the Clodaghs
Crofts, F. W. Sir John Magill's Last Journey
Crowe, C. Abbeygate
   Tower of Kilraven
Curry, G. L. Portrush Mystery
Curtis, Robert. Irish Police Officer
Daniels, D. Cormac Legend
   Mirror of Shadows
Denning, M. Beyond the Prize
De St. Jorre, J. Patriot Game
Dillon, E. Death at Crane's Court
   Sent to His Account
Douglas, Aleck. Murder Hole Road
Driscoll, P. In Connection with Kilshaw

Du Bois, T. Cavalier's Corpse
  Shannon Terror
Dunn, N. J. Vultures of Erin
Dunne, L. Ringleader
Dwyer-Joyce, A. Moonlit Way
  Rainbow Glass
  Reach for the Shadows
Eden, D. Whistle for the Crows
Fitzgerald, A. J. Blackthorn
Fletcher, J. S. Golden Spur
Foley, L. both titles
Forbes, S. Terror Touches Me
Ford, Hilary. Castle Malindine
Forrest, Wilma. Last Hope House
Fry, P. Bright Green Waistcoat
Gallie, M. You're Welcome to Ulster!
Garve, A. House of Spiders
Gaskin, C. Edge of Glass
Gilford, C. B. Crooked Shamrock
Gill, B. McGarr and the Politician's Wife
  McGarr on the Cliffs of Moher
Gray, B. Conquest in Ireland
Griffin, J. Ring of Kerry
Guinness, K. D. Fisherman's End
Harris, Andrea. Irish Affair
Heath, M. 5 titles
Henry, Michael. Murder in the Old Jail
Herron, S. Hound and the Fox and the Harper
  Through the Dark and Hairy Wood
  Whore-Mother
Higgins, J. Savage Day
Jones, K. O. To the Dark Tower Came
Keating, H. R. F. Dog It Was That Died
Kent, N. Hint of Murder
Kenyon, M. May You Die in Ireland
  100,000 Welcomes
  Rapist
  Shooting of Dan McGrew
La Tourrette, J. Joseph Stone
McCaffrey, A. Kitternan Legacy
McCullough, E. M. Five Devils of Kilmainham
McGinley, P. Bogmail
McMullen, M. My Cousin Death
Meade, L. T. Home of Silence
Morgan, C. Devil's Cavern
Nichols, S. Serpent's Tooth
Nicole, Claudette. Cliffs of Death
  Dark Whispers
  Haunting of Drumroe
O'Brien, F. Third Policeman
O'Flaherty, L. Informer
O'Grady, R. O'Houlihan's Jest
O'Neill, D. Life Has No Price
Ostrander, K. Ghosts of Ballyduff
  Sea Tower
O'Sullivan, J. B. Blacklash
  Cold Chisel
  There Is an S.O.S.
Patterson, H. Cry of the Hunter
Paul, B. Curse of Halewood
Phillifent, J. T. Mad Scientist Affair
Pim, S. Common or Garden Crime
Polk, D. Tower of the Crow
Polland, M. Little Spot of Bother
  Thicker Than Water
Powell, M. Waiting Game
Poyer, J. Shooting of the Green
Randell, C. Black Candle
Reid, D. Beat on an Orange Drum
Richardson, M. Candle in the Wind
Roby, M. L. House at Kilgallen
Rodney, B. Owl Flies Home
Rosenberger, J. Shamrock Smash
Seaman, D. Bomb That Could Lip-Read
Spain, P. Blood Scenario
Stevenson, F. Curse of the Concullens
Thum, M. Abbey Court
Tierney, P. Powers of Lismara
Welles, E. Fahnsworth Manor
White, T. D. My Name Is Norval
Wylie, N. both titles

ISLE OF MAN (See also: England; Channel Islands)
Bellairs, G. 5 titles
Estey, D. Lost Tale
Fraser, Anthea. Island in Waiting

ISRAEL (Isr. See also: Jerusalem; Tel Aviv; Middle East)
Arnold, M. Zadok's Treasure
Baker, I. Justice for Judas
Bax, R. Death Beneath Jerusalem
Carter, Nick. Assignment: Israel
Falkirk, R. Twisted Wire
Gordon, N. Jerusalem Diamond
Haddad, C. A. Bloody September
  Moroccan
  Operation Apricot
Haggard, W. Visa to Limbo
Harvester, S. Zion Road
Hesky, O. Different Night
Hoffenberg, J. 17 Ben Gurion
Hunter, J. H. Banners of Blood
Jason, S. Sealed with Blood
Johnson, J. L. Code Name Sebastian
Kemelman, H. Monday the Rabbi Took Off
Klinger, H. Lust for Murder
Latham, A. Orchids for Mother
Leonard, E. Hunted
Meisels, A. Six Other Days
O'Neill, A. Da Vinci Road
Rogers, B. Doomsday Scroll
Sachar, H. M. Man on the Camel
Sapir, R. Last Temple
Singer, S. M. For Dying You Always Have Time
Tucker, W. This Witch

ISTANBUL (Istan. See also: Turkey; Middle East; Balkans)
Ambler, E. Light of Day
Carter, Nick. Istanbul
Fleming, Joan. When I Grow Rich
Forsyte, C. Diplomatic Death
Hayes, Ralph. Turkish Mafia Conspiracy
Hughes, D. T. Istanbul Elopement
Ross, Clarissa. Istanbul Nights
Smith, Don. Secret Mission: Istanbul
Stein, A. M. Deadly Delight
Walsh, J. M. Death at His Elbow
Wheatley, D. Eunuch of Stamboul
Whitney, P. A. Black Amber

ITALY (It. See also: Florence; Milan; Naples; Rome; Sardinia; Sicily; Venice)
Aarons, E. S. Assignment—Lili Lamaris
  Assignment—Palermo
  Assignment—Sorrento Siren
Albrand, M. After Midnight
  Without Orders
Ambler, E. Send No More Roses
Anthony, Evelyn. Malaspiga Exit
Arpino, G. Crime of Honor
Ashe, G. Life for a Death
Baker, W. H. Night of the Wolf
Baskerville, B. By Whose Hand?
Beeding, F. Black Arrows
  Six Proud Walkers
Bennett, Dorothy. Curious Were Killed
Black, Lionel. Two Ladies in Verona
Boothby, G. Farewell Nikola
Brande, D. Most Beautiful Lady
Brown, Carter. Seidlitz and the Super-Spy
Bryan, J. Contessa Came Too
Butterworth, M. Villa on the Shore
Cameron, L. Amphorae Pirates
Canning, V. Castle Minerva
Carter, Nick. Mark of Cosa Nostra
Cassiday, B. Operation Goldkill
Chaber, M. E. Lonely Walk
Cleary, J. Peter's Pence
Cleeve, B. You Must Never Go Back
Coffman, V. Demon Tower
Coles, M. Man in the Green Hat
Cory, D. Intrigue
Cowen, F. Hounds of Carvello
Crookenden, I. Horrible Revenge
Dalton, M. Wife of Baal
Daniels, D. Magic Ring
Dark, J. Spy from the Grave
Davis, S. His Father's Ghost
Deane, N. Double for Murder
De Bilio, B. Vendetta Con Brio
De Villiers, G. West of Jerusalem
Donovan, D. Scarlet Seal
Downes, D. Red Rose for Maria
Duane, A. Hadrian Ransom
Du Maurier, D. Flight of the Falcon
Fenisong, R. Schemers
Ferrars, E. Alibi for a Witch
Fisher, N. Walk at a Steady Pace
Fitzgerald, N. Imagine a Man
Flagg, J. Dear, Deadly Beloved
  Lady and the Cheetah
Fletcher, Dorothy. Late Contessa
Follett, E. Villa of the Scorpions
Forbes, H. Detective in Italy
Forgione, L. Men of Silence
Fruttero, C. Sunday Woman
Gilbert, M. Death in Captivity
Gill, B. McGarr and the Sienese Conspiracy
Greene, H. Flags at Doney
Gruber, F. Etruscan Bull
Gunn, V. All Change for Murder
Haggard, W. Hard Sell
Halidom, M. Y. Poison Ring
Halliday, L. Devil's Door
Harling, R. Endless Colonnade
Harris, Rosemary. Double Snare
Hathaway, N. Silence of Nightingales
Highsmith, P. Talented Mr. Ripley
Holt, Gavin. Sole Survivor
Hotchner, A. E. Dangerous American
Howlett, J. Christmas Spy
Hume, F. Creature of the Night
Hummel, G. F. Summer Lightning
Innes, H. Angry Mountain
  Lonely Skier
Irwin, W. Julius Caesar Murder Case
Jay, W. Fear in Borzano
John, O. Thirty Days Hath September
Johnston, V. Etruscan Smile
Knight, K. M. Invitation to Vengeance
Lathom, F. Italian Mysteries
La Tourrette, J. Pompeii Scrolls
  Shadows in Umbria
Lee, Elsie. Clouds over Vellanti
Lee, John. Lago
Lem, S. Chain of Chance
Leonard, C. L. Treachery in Trieste
Leslie, P. Splintered Sunglasses Affair
Livingston, W. Mystery of Villa Sinestre
Lombardi, C. Lighting Seven Candles
Loraine, P. Angel of Death
  Mafia Kiss
Lynch, F. Stranger at the Wedding
McEvoy, M. Calabrian Summer
McGinnis, E. L. Strasburg Collection
MacGrath, H. Cellini Plaque
MacInnes, H. North from Rome
MacPherson, M. Protege
Maddock, S. Conspirators in Capri
Marshall, R. Mission to Siena
  Wary Transgressor
Marvin, S. Secret of the Villa Como
Masterson, W. Hunter of the Blood
Mather, B. Geth Straker
Maxwell, V. Way of the Tamarisk
Mayo, J. Let Sleeping Girls Lie
Meade, E. Murder Squad
Melton, W. Nine Lives to Pompeii
Meredith, K. L. Golden Chalice
Michaels, B. Wings of the Falcon
Mills, Hugh. In Pursuit of Evil
Mitchell, G. Twenty-Third Man
Moore, Dorinne. Masquerade at Monfalcone
Moore, Robin. Italian Connection
Morgan, R. Golden Hoard
Moyes, P. Dead Men Don't Ski
Newman, B. Mussolini Murder Plot
Nixon, Alan. Item 7
North, J. Legend of the Thirteenth Pilgrim
O'Brine, M. Mills
Old Sleuth. Giant Detective Among the Italian Brigands
  Old Ironsides Among the Italian Brigands
Oppenheim, E. P. Daughter of the Marionis
Orgill, D. Astrid Factor
  Death Bringers
Paradise, M. Face of an Angel
Pendower, J. Operation Carlo
  Sinister Talent
Pollack, C. Mystery of Rapallo
Price, A. October Men
Prokosch, F. Tale for Midnight
Quinn, Simon. Human Factor
Quinnell, A. J. Man on Fire
Radcliffe, A. Italian Mysteries of Udolpho
Radcliffe, M. A. Manfrone
Ragosta, M. J. Taverna in Terrazzo
Raven, S. Brother Cain
Ridgway, J. Treasure of the Cosa Nostra
Rosenblum, R. Good Thief
Ross, W. E. D. Dark Villa of Capri
Rutherford, D. 5 titles
Sawkins, R. H. Snow in Paradise
Sciascia, L. One Way or Another
Seymour, G. Red Fox
Slater, N. Falcon
Smith, Don. Padrone
Snell, E. Blue Murder
Snelling, L. Heresy
Somers, J. Brethren of the Axe
Steegmuller, F. Silence at Salerno
Stein, A. M. Lend Me Your Ears
Stern, R. M. Bright Road to Fear
Stevenson, A. Coil of Serpents
Stone, D. Tired Spy
Strutton, B. Glut of Virgins
Summerton, M. Dark and Secret Place
Taylor, M. A. Appointment in Verona
Thompson, V. Scarlet Iris
Toye, N. Twice Murdered Man
Van Rjndt, P. Tetramachus Collection
Waller, L. Coast of Fear
Watson, C. Black Jack
West, M. L. Big Story
  Salamander
Williams, V. Courier to Marrakesh
Williamson, T. Connector
Withers, E. L. Heir Apparent
Young, G. Code-Name Caruso

JACKSONVILLE (Jack. See also: Florida; Miami; Tampa; South)
Humes, L. R. Bridge to Nowhere
Levison, E. all 3 titles

JAKARTA. See: Djakarta.

JAMAICA (Jam. See also: West Indies; Caribbean)
Ashe, R. Hurricane Wake
Carter, Nick. Jamaican Exchange
Chadwick, J. Web of Evil
Dark, J. Operation Scuba
Eberhart, M. G. Enemy in the House
Elman, R. Breadfruit Lotteries

Settings Index

Heath, M. Castlereagh
Lange, J. Grave Descend
Morris, John. all 3 titles
Murray, M. Neat Little Corpse
Rohmer, S. Virgin in Flames
Ryder, J. Cry of the Halidon
Scott, V. Kreutzman Formula
Shearing, J. Golden Violet
Terrall, R. Sand Dollars
Tidyman, E. Shaft's Carnival of Killers

JAPAN (Jap. See also: Tokyo; Far East)

Barry, L. Sudden Silence
Bellah, J. W. Brass Gong Tree
Blood, A. Jade Rabbit
Browne, Courtney. Ancient Pond
Cade, Robin. Fear Dealers
Carter, Nick. Day of the Dingo
  Sign of the Prayer Shawl
Daniels, Paul. Transister Girls
Duncan, R. L. Day the Sun Fell
  Fire Storm
Fernandes, J. R. Yokohama Hood
Fleming, I. You Only Live Twice
French, R. R. Spy Is Forever
Harvester, S. Copper Butterfly
King, Francis. Custom House
Knapp, G. C. Stranglehold
McMahon, T. P. Mayday
Matsumoto, S. Points and Lines
Melville, J. Chrysanthemum Chain
  Wages of Zen
Nichols, L. Key to Midnight
Norman, E. Kill Me in Atami
  Kill Me in Yokohama
Queen, E. Guess Who's Coming to Kill You?
Rampo, Edogawa. Japanese Tales of Mystery and Imagination
Rance, J. Bullet Train
Roberts, J. H. February Plan
Rosenberger, J. Nipponese Nightmare
Royce, K. Bustillo
Seward, J. Assignment: Find Cherry
  Cave of the Chinese Skeletons
  Eurasian Virgins
Takagi, A. both titles
Thayer, L. Two Ways to Die
Wheatley, D. Bill for the Use of a Body
Whitney, P. A. Moonflower
Wynd, O. Walk Softly, Men Praying

JAVA (See also: Indonesia; Bali, Borneo; Djakarta; New Guinea; Sumatra)

Carter, Nick. Time Clock of Death

JERUSALEM (Jerus. See also: Israel; Tel Aviv; Middle East)

Blackburn, J. Flame and the Wind
Carter, Nick. Jerusalem File
Christian, J. Five Gates to Armageddon
Christie, Agatha. Appointment with Death
Dixon, R. Going to Jerusalem
Littell, B. Dolorosa Deal
Mandino, O. Christ Commission

JOHANNESBURG (Johan. See also: South Africa; Cape Town; Transvaal)

Monig, C. Once Upon a Crime

KANSAS (Kan. See also: Midwest)

Adleman, R. H. Bloody Benders
Blankenship, W. D. Leavenworth Irregulars
Booth, C. B. Amateur Detectives
Chase, J. H. No Orchids for Miss Blandish
Conway, J. W. Something or Nothing
Forbes, S. Grieve for the Past
  If Two of Them Are Dead
Kingsley-Smith, T. Forsaken
Mechem, K. Frame for Murder
Reese, J. Weapon Heavy
Ruse, P. Alumni Murders

KANSAS CITY (Kan. City. See also: Missouri; St. Louis; Midwest)

Eliot, G. F. Federal Bullets
Head, M. Accomplice
Johnson, E. R. Judas
Roscoe, M. Death Is a Round Black Ball
  One Tear for My Grave
  Riddle Me This

KENTUCKY (Ky. See also: Louisville; South)

Buchanan, P. Murder of Crows
Buck, C. N. Mountain Justice
Clark, D. P. Poison Speaks Softly
  Roll, Jordan, Roll
Cobb, I. S. Judge Priest Turns Detective

Crane, F. Daffodil Blonde
  Death in Lilac Time
Cunningham, A. B. 19 titles
Daingerfield, F. That Gay Nineties Murder
Damien, C. Appleshaw
Daniels, D. Lanier Riddle
Echard, M. I Met Murder on the Way
Halliday, B. Taste for Violence
Hayes, J. Winner's Circle
Hill, D. C. Deadly Messiah
Kingsley, M. J. Black Man, White Man
Leonard, E. Moonshine War
Lyons, A. W. Murder at Prospect, Kentucky
McDowell, R. E. Hound's Tooth
Morrell, D. First Blood
Nicole, Claudette. Bloodroots Manor
Nolan, J. C. Sudden Squall
Parmer, C. Murder at the Kentucky Derby
Thayer, G. Dark Rider
Thompson, F. Transgressor
Walker, Ira. Someone's Stolen Nellie Grey

KENYA (See also: Africa, East)

Farrington, J. Hand
Fearon, D. Nairobi Nightcap
Hayes, Ralph. Scavenger Kill
Jacks, O. Autumn Heroes
Kaye, M. M. Later Than You Think
Leslie, N. Death Comes to Kenya
Leslie-Melville, B. That Nairobi Affair
Peverett, A. Death Stalks in Kenya
Stoneham, C. T. Kenya Mystery

KOREA (Kor. Both north and south Korea included here. See also: Far East)

Carter, Nick. Korean Tiger
Crane, R. Sergeant and the Queen
  Sgt. Corbin's War
  Strikeback!
Forrest, Williams. Stigma
Harvester, S. Troika
Rosenberger, J. Operation Thunderbolt
Sheldon, W. J. Gold Bait
Smith, Don. Secret Mission: North Korea
Stokes, M. L. Under Cover of Night
Stroup, W. Mark of Pak San Ri

KUWAIT (Kuw. See also: Middle East)

Arvay, H. Operation Kuwait

LAOS (See also: Far East)

Ballinger, B. S. Spy in the Jungle

LAS VEGAS (Las Veg. See also: Nevada; Reno; West)

Andersen, I. Big Night
Ard, W. Mr. Trouble
Ballard, W. T. Dealing Out Death
  Murder Las Vegas Style
  Pretty Miss Murder
  Seven Sisters
Barry, M. Desert Stalker
Cameron, L. File on a Missing Redhead
Carter, Nick. Eight Card Stud
  Mind Poisoners
Cox, W. R. Murder in Vegas
Derrick, L. Blood on the Strip
Duff, J. P. Dangerous to Know
Einstein, C. Blackjack Hijack
Fair, A. A. Spill the Jackpot!
Foley, R. Call It Accident
Foster, R. Blonde and Beautiful
Franklin, M. Vegas
Frazer, R. C. Mark Kilby and the Secret Syndicate
Goldthwaite, E. K. Cut for Partners
Gruber, F. Honest Dealer
Herries, N. My Private Hangman
Howard, V. Murder with Love
Joey. Joey Collects
Lamb, J. J. Nickel Straight
MacDonald, J. D. Only Girl in the Game
Moore, Arthur. Las Vegas
Paul, Elliot. Black and the Red
Pendleton, D. Vegas Vendetta
Prather, R. S. Find This Woman
Reese, J. Omar, Fats and Trixie
Renek, M. Las Vegas Strip
Rice, J. Night Stalker
Rossi, B. Las Vegas Vengeance
Scherf, M. If You Want a Murder Well Done
  To Cache a Millionaire
Sederberg, A. 60 Hours of Darkness
Thomas, C. Cactus Shroud
Tucker, W. Procession of the Damned
Waer, J. Murder in Las Vegas
Williams, B. Stranger to Herself

LEBANON (Leb. See also: Beirut; Middle East)

Atiyah, E. Donkey from the Mountains
  Lebanon Paradise
Cleary, J. Season of Doubt
Griswold, G. Red Pawns
Jay, C. Arms for Adonis
Katcha, V. Don't Look Down
Keller, B. Baghdad Defections
McCurtin, P. Spoils of War
Osborne, H. Pay-Day
Stewart, M. Gabriel Hounds
Tyndall, J. Death in Lebanon

LEIPZIG (Leip. See also: Germany)

Clifford, F. Naked Runner
White, J. D. Leipzig Affair

LIBYA (See also: Africa, North)

Edwards, P. Fist of Fatima
Graham, J. Bloody Passage
Smith, Don. Libyan Contract

LIMA (See also: Peru; South America)

Levey, R. A. Murder in Lima

LISBON (See also: Portugal; Madeira)

Benton, K. Sole Agent
Brennan, F. H. Memo to a Firing Squad
Caillou, A. Assault on Loveless
Fish, R. L. Hochmann Miniatures
Footner, H. Unneutral Murder
Gifford, T. Man from Lisbon
MacKenzie, D. Spreewald Collection
Patterson, H. To Catch a King
Prokosch, F. Conspirators
Rich, K. Lucifer Mask
Robeson, K. Hate Genius
Telfair, R. Target for Tonight

LITHUANIA (Lith.)

Annesley, M. Spies in the Web

LONG ISLAND (L.I. See also: New York; New York City; Rochester)

Adams, S. H. Flying Death
Albrand, M. Taste of Terror
Alexander, Irene. Ninth Life
Aronson, H. Establishment of Innocence
Ashbrook, H. Most Immoral Murder
  Murder Makes Murder
  Murder of Steven Kester
Austin, H. Drink the Green Water
Barrett, Monte. Pelham Murder Case
Barry, Jerome. Strange Relations
Bentley, J. Call Off the Corpse
Bentley, J. Duane of the FBI
Bogart, W. Murder Is Forgetful
Bonnell, J. F. Death over Sunday
Bonney, J. L. Death by Dynamite
Booth, C. B. House of Rogues
  Seaside Mystery
  Telltale Plot
Box, E. Death Likes It Hot
Brewster, E. V. Surprise Party Murder
Bruce, G. Claim of the Fleshless Corpse
Burke, R. Murder on High Heels
Cameron, D. C. Grave Without Grass
Carrington, E. S. Crimson Goddess
Chamberlain, G. A. In Defense of Mrs. Maxon
Charteris, L. Lady on a Train
Chase, A. M. Peril at the Spy Nest
Chichester, J. J. House of the Moving Room
Clancy, E. A. Fast Money
Clarkson, L. Shadow of John Wallace
Cobb, I. S. Murder Day by Day
Coleman, C. Nightmare in July
Crane, C. Summer Girl
Crosby, L. Night Attack
Curle, R. Corruption
Dane, J. Y. Cabana Murders
Darby, R. Beauty Sleep
Davey, J. Touch of Stagefright
Davis, Mildred. Invisible Border
Debretti, H. Before I Wake
De Forrest, B. Snows of Yesterday
Delman, D. Nice Murderers
  One Man's Murder
De Pre, J. Die, Jessica, Die
Eberhart, M. G. Nine O'Clock Tide
  Witness at Large
Ehrlich, J. Drowning
Farrington, F. Little Game
Fenisong, R. Wench Is Dead
Fischer, B. Silent Dust
Fitzsimmons, C. Manville Murders
  Mystery at Hidden Harbor
  No Witness!
Foster, I. Moorwood Legacy
Frost, L. Murder at Large
Gibson, W. B. Grove of Doom
Glidden, M. W. both titles
Goldthwaite, E. K. Sixpenny Dame
Green, E. P. Rotten Apples

Griffin, A. J. Ocean of Fire
   Spirit of Brynmaster Oaks
Hawthorne, V. Diary of Evil
   Sweet Deadly Passion
Heyward, D. Pulitzer Prize Murders
Hildick, W. Vandals
Hinkemeyer, M. T. Dark Below
Hobhouse, A. Hangover Murders
Holding, E. S. 5 titles
Hopkins, L. both titles
Hubbard, Regina. Curse of Nightwind
Hubbard, Richard. Daughter of Despair
Isaacs, S. Compromising Positions
Johns, A. Traffic with Evil
Johnston, V. Light in the Swamp
   People from the Sea
   Silver Dolphin
Johnston, W. Tragedy at the Beach Club
Jones, C. R. Van Norton Murders
Jones, E. Who Killed Gregory?
Jordan, E. Devil and the Deep Blue Sea
   Life of the Party
Kane, H. Frenzy of Evil
Kelsey, V. Bride Dined Alone
King, S. If I Die Before I Wake
Klein, N. Terror by Night
Lacy, E. Devil for the Witch
Laflin, J. Spy Who Didn't
Lariar, L. Win, Place and Die!
Lathen, E. Stitch in Time
Lauferty, L. Crimson Thread
Liddon, E. S. Riddle of the Russian
   Princess
Lilly, J. Death in B-Minor
Linakis, S. Killing Ground
Livingston, A. Double Cross
   Night of Crime
Loring, A. 13th Doll
Lottman, E. Hemlock Tree
McCloy, H. Change of Heart
   Deadly Truth
McGivern, W. P. Savage Streets
McGurk, S. Big Dig
McRoyd, A. Death in Costume
Malmar, M. Never Say Die
Martyn, W. Return of Anthony Trent
Mason, V. W. Seeds of Murder
Mayfield, S. Stranger in the House
Ostrander, I. Tattooed Arm
Palmer, S. Miss Withers Regrets
Parker, M. Death Do Us Part
   Intriguer
Pentecost, H. Die After Dark
   Homicidal Horse
Philips, J. Death Delivers a Postcard
Popkin, Z. So Much Blood
Potts, J. Death of a Stray Cat
Puzo, M. Godfather
Queen, E. Egyptian Cross Mystery
Quick, D. Something Evil
Raison, M. M. No Weeds for the Widow
Reeve, A. B. Adventuress
   Stars Scream Murder
Ridgway, J. Hardly a Man Is Now Alive
Roberts, W. A. Haunting Hand
Robeson, K. Cartoon Crimes
   Dr. Time
Ronns, E. Say It with Murder
Ross, Clarissa. Drifthaven
Roueche, B. Fago
   Feral
Rud, A. M. Rose Bath Riddle
   Stuffed Men
Ryerson, F. Borgia Blade
Schley, S. M. Dream Sinister
Scott, Denis. Murder Makes a Villain
Scott, L. Living Dead Man
Seabrooke, J. P. Green Bag
Shane, S. Lady in Danger
Sloane, W. To Walk the Night
Smith, L. D. Corpse with the Listening
   Ear
   Death Is Thy Neighbor
   Follow This Fair Corpse
Smith, W. K. Sultan's Skull
Steel, K. Crooked Shadow
Stevenson, F. Bianca
Stokes, M. L. Dying Room
Stone, Hampton. Strangler Who Couldn't
   Let Go
Strange, J. S. Picture of the Victim
Teta, J. Clock at Ravenswood
Thayer, L. Alias Dr. Ely
   Man's Enemies
   Persons Unknown
   That Affair at the Cedars
Todd, P. Blood All Over
Tyson, J. A. Rhododendron Man
Vanardy, V. Lady of the Night Wind
Watkins, R. H. Air Murders
   Half a Clew
Watson, Clarissa. Bishop in the Back
   Seat
Webb, L. J. Walking the Dusk
Wells, Carolyn. 11 titles
Westlake, D. E. Bank Shot
Wheelock, D. Murder at Montauk
White, L. 5 titles
Whitney, P. A. Golden Unicorn
Williams, V. Clock Ticks On
   Masks Off at Midnight
Willoughby, J. Crimsoned Millions

Worts, G. F. Blue Lacquer Box

LOS ANGELES (L.A. SEE ALSO: CALIFORNIA; SAN DIEGO; SAN FRANCISCO; WEST)

Adams, C. F. Decoy
   What Price Murder
Allen, E. C. Laguna Contracts
Ames, C. Gorgonzola, Won't You Please
   Come Home?
Andersen, U. S. Hard and Fast
Andrews, C. Butterfly Murder
Armour, J. Killer's Category
Armstrong, C. 6 titles
Ashton, A. Phantom Reflection
Babcock, D. V. Gorgeous Ghoul
   Homicide for Hannah
Baker, L. Cheaters
Ball, J. 5 titles
Ballard, W. T. Say Yes to Murder
   Walk in Fear
Ballinger, B. S. Heir Hunters
   Law
   Not I, Said the Vixen
Banks, R. E. both titles
Bannister, W. Portrait of Death
Barkley, D. Freeway
Barnes, D. all 3 titles
Barry, M. Los Angeles Holocaust
Baxt, G. Neon Graveyard
Baynes, J. Peeping Tom Murders
Berckman, E. She Asked for It
Bergman, A. Hollywood and Le Vine
Bergquist, L. Your Shot, Darling!
Beynon, J. Cypress Man
Bishop, M. G. Scylla
Black, J. D. Trouble Man
Bloch, R. Night-World
Blodgett, M. Captain Blood
Booth, C. G. Cat and the Clock
Booth, E. With Sirens Screaming
Boston, C. K. Silver Jackass
Boucher, A. Case of the Baker Street
   Irregulars
   Case of the Crumpled Knave
   Case of the Solid Key
Boyer, C. Mosaic Earring
Boyers, B. Murder by Proxy
Brackett, L. No Good from a Corpse
Braham, H. Call Me Deadly
Braun, W. Murder in Hollywood
Brent, L. W. One Man's Crime
Brown, Carter. at least 32 titles
Brown, F. His Name Was Death
   Murderers
   Wench Is Dead
Burnett, W. R. Nobody Lives Forever
   Romelle
Byers, C. A. Inverness Murder
Cain, P. Fast One
Cameron, L. Outsider
Campbell, R. W. Killer of Kings
Carmichael, F. Pen Is Deadlier
Carr, K. Don't Bet on Living, Alice
Carrel, M. Emerald Heart
Carson, R. Golden Years Caper
   Quality of Mercy
Caspary, V. Weeping and the Laughter
Castle, F. Violent Hours
Chaber, M. E. Day It Rained Diamonds
   Flaming Man
   Softly in the Night
Chandler, R. High Window
   Killer in the Rain
   Little Sister
   Long Goodbye
Charbonneau, L. And Hope to Die
Chase, J. H. Eve
   What's Better Than Money?
Child, N. Diamond Ransom Murders
Childs, T. Cold Turkey
Clad, N. Taste for Brilliants
Clarke, R. Synonym for Murder
Clason, C. B. Green Shiver
   Whispering Ear
Cochran, A. Two Plus Two
Coffey, B. Surrounded
Cohen, O. R. at least 6 titles
Colby, R. 5 titles
Collins, Mary. Death Warmed Over
Collins, Michael. Slasher
Colter, E. Cheer for the Dead
Colton, M. Double Take
Cope, H. Death Stalks the Fleet
Copper, B. most if not all 30 of the
   Mike Faraday books
Cox, W. R. Tycoon and the Tigress
Crain, W. W. Psycho Squad
Crawford, O. Execution
Creighton, J. Half Interest in Murder
Crooker, H. Hollywood Murder Mystery
Cunningham, E. V. 5 titles
Curtis, W. Red Dragon
Dana, R. Death Was the Echo
Daniels, D. Larrabee Heiress
Daniels, N. Arrest and Trial
   Missing Witness
   One Angry Man
Davidson, M. Thursday Woman
Dejeans, E. Double House
Dekker, C. Woman in Marble

Dekobra, M. Hangman Never Waits
   Lady Is a Vamp
   Madonna in Hollywood
Demaris, O. 5 titles
Deming, R. at least 7 titles
Derrick, L. Showbiz Wipeout
   Target Is H
Dewey, T. B. 7 titles
Dexter, B. I'll Sing You the Death of
   Bill Brown
Dickinson, W. Dead Man Talks Too Much
Disney, D. C. Golden Swan Murder
Dodge, D. Shear the Black Sheep
Dooley, R. Flashback
Dratler, J. J. Judas Kiss
   Pitfall
Duff, J. P. Run from Death
   Some Die Young
   Who Dies There?
Duke, W. Fair Prey
Dunne, J. G. True Confessions
Eachus, I. Raid on the Bremerton
Eby, L. Blood Runs Cold
   Death Begs the Question
   Hell Hath No Fury
Echard, M. Stand-In for Death
Edgley, L. Angry Heart
   Dirty Business
   Judas Goat
Edingtons. Monk's Hood Murders
   Murder to Music
   Studio Murder Mystery
Egan, L. all 20 titles
Eichler, A. Election by Murder
Endore, G. Methinks the Lady—
Evans, K. L. Feast for Spiders
Fair, A. A. Beware the Curves
Farr, J. Deadly Combo
Farrell, H. What Ever Happened to Baby
   Jane?
Fast, J. Inner Circle
Fenady, A. J. both titles
Fickling, G. G. Girl on the Prowl
   Naughty But Dead
Fielding, J. Transformation
Fisher, S. Big Dream
   Giveaway
   I Wake Up Screaming
   Image of Hell
Fitzsimmons, C. Evil Men Do
Fleming, Robert. Night Freight Murders
Flowers, C. It Never Rains in Los Angeles
Ford, L. Devil's Stronghold
Foster, R. Invisible Man Murders
Fox, J. M. 10 titles
Francis, W. Bury Me Not
   Rough on Rats
Franklin, M. at least 8 titles
Fray, A. Built for Trouble
   Dame's the Game
   Dice Spelled Murder
Frazer, R. C. Hollywood Hoax
Fritch, C. E. Negative of a Nude
Galloway, D. Lamaar Ransom—Private Eye
Gardner, E. S. about 83 titles
Gault, W. C. 16 titles
Gibbons, C. Murder in Hollywood
Gifford, T. Hollywood Gothic
Gless, E. G. Murder at Tall Tip
Goines, D. Inner City Hoodlum
Goldman, R. L. Murder of Harvey Blake
Goodis, D. Of Missing Persons
Gordon, R. Dead Level
Gordons. 5 titles
Graham, Anthony. Death Business
Gray, B. Conquest in California
Grayson, Rupert. Gun Cotton in Hollywood
Grote, W. Cain's Girl Friend
Grove, M. You'll Die, Darling
   You'll Die Today
   You'll Die When You Hear This
Gruber, F. 7 titles
Hallas, R. You Play the Black and the
   Red Comes Up
Hansen, J. Death Claims
Harrington, R. E. Quintain
Harris, N. In the Shadows
Harris, Timothy. Good Night and Goodbye
   Heat Wave
Haycox, E. Rough Air
Hays, L. Harry-O #2
Heath, E. Death Takes a Dive
Hecht, B. I Hate Actors!
Heinecke, H. J. And the Winds Blew
Heyman, E. L. Dead Heat on a Merry-Go-
   Round
Heyes, D. Kiss-Off
Hitchens, B. F.O.B. Murder
   One-Way Ticket
Hitchens, D. Fools Gold
   Sleep with Slander
   Stairway to an Empty Room
Hoffenberg, J. Desperate Adversaries
Hoffman, L. Fear Among the Shadows
Holland, M. Glass Heart
Holmes, H. H. both titles
Holton, L. 9 titles
Howard, J. A. Die on Easy Street
Huggins, R. all 4 titles
Hughes, B. Murder in Church

Settings Index

Hughes, D. B. Bamboo Blonde
    Davidian Report
    In a Lonely Place
Hunt, H. Lovers Are Losers
Hunt, M. V. Mystery of Daria Kane
Huston, F. Rich Get It All
Hutton, J. F. Too Good to Be True
Ingersol, J. Rose Can Kill
Irvine, R. R. Freeze Frame
    Horizontal Hold
    Jump Cut
Israel, P. Hush Money
Jahn, M. Switch
Jason, S. Hollywood Assassin
Jerome, O. Five Assassins
Johnson, B. B. Death of a Blue-Eyed Soul Brother
    Mother of the Year
Johnson, E. R. God Keepers
Johnston, V. House Above Hollywood
Johnston, W. Banyon
Jones, G. E. Trap
Judd, H. Shadow of a Doubt
Kaminsky, S. M. Bullet for a Star
    Howard Hughes Affair
    Murder on the Yellow Brick Road
    Never Cross a Vampire
Kane, A. Slaughter's Big Rip-Off
Kane, F. About Face
    Bare Trap
    Dead Rite
    Mourning After
Kane, H. Peter Gunn
Kastle, H. Sunset People
Keene, D. at least 6 titles
Kelland, C. B. Murder Makes an Entrance
Kerr, J. Emergency Room
Knight, C. Affair of the Corpse Escort
    Affair of the Fainting Butler
Knight, D. both titles
Koehler, R. P. Murder Expert
    Murder in the Green Sedan
    Steps to Murder
Kolb, K. Couch Traip
Koontz, D. R. Whispers
La Fountaine, G. Two Minute Warning
Land, M. Quicksand
Langham, J. R. both titles
Lariar, L. He Died Laughing
Larson, C. Muir's Blood
    Someone's Death
Laumer, K. Deadfall
Lawrence, A. both titles
Lawson, S. Scorpio
Lee, Edward. both titles
Leslie, Jean. Hair of the Dog
Lewis, Lange. Birthday Murder
    Juliet Dies Twice
    Meat for Murder
    Murder Among Friends
Lewis, Margo. Concept for Murder
Linington, E. all 10 titles
Linklater, J. L. at least 6 titles
Locke, R. D. Taste of Brass
Loraine, P. Ask the Rattlesnake
Ludwig, J. Little Boy Lost
Luther, M. L. both titles
Lyons, A. 3 titles
MacCargo, J. T. Faces of Murder
McCoy, H. They Shoot Horses, Don't They?
McDermid, F. Ghost Wanted
Macdonald, R. Moving Target
Macdonald, J. R. Meet Me at the Morgue
    Way Some People Die
Macdonald, R. Barbarous Coast
    Ferguson Affair
    Instant Enemy
McDonnell, G. Intruder from the Sea
    My Sister, Good Night
McGivern, W. P. Reprisal
MacKenzie, J. A. Omega Document
McManis, J. A. Hooded Asp
McMurdie, A. L. Nightmare Hall
MacNeil, N. Two Guns for Hire
McPartland, J. Wild Party
Mann, E. A. Portals
Marble, M. S. both titles
Marlowe, D. J. Operation Deathmaker
Martin, A. L. Crimson Frame
    Death on a Ferris Wheel
    Fear Comes Calling
Martinez, J. Jigsaw John
Martinez, S. A. Target for Terror
Martyn, W. Chromium Cat
Matcha, J. Prowler in the Night
Matheson, R. Ride the Nightmare
    Someone Is Bleeding
Mayo, N. Benefit
Meggs, B. Saturday Games
Melchior, I. Watchdogs of Abaddon
Meyer, N. Target Practice
Millar, M. Beast in View
    Stranger in My Grave
Millard, O. Missing Person
Miller, Wade. Big Guy
    Tiger's Wife
Millington, F. Crime Across the Way
Mitchell, S. Lonely Shroud
Moore, P. Death Drives the Lead Car
Morgan, John. Death to Comrade X
Morgan, M. Decoy
    Nine More Lives

Morgan, P. Too Mini Murders
Murray, W. Killing Touch
Myers, P. B. Hollywood Murder
Neely, R. No Certain Life
Newland, N. M. Walk to Your Grave
Newman, B. Spy in the Brown Derby
Nielsen, H. Borrow the Night
    Woman on the Roof
Nixon, Allan. Goodnight, Garrity
Nolan, W. F. Death Is for Losers
    White Cad Cross-Up
Nuetzel, C. both titles
Obstfeld, R. Goulden Fleece
O'Callaghan, M. Death Is Forever
Odlum, J. Mirabilis Diamond
O'Hanlon, J. D. As Good As Murdered
    Murder at Malibu
Olsen, D. B. at least 6 titles
Palmer, L. Cat-Eye
Palmer, S. Cold Poison
    Puzzle of the Happy Hooligan
    Rook Takes Knight
Patrick, A. Beyond the Law
Paul, Elliot. Black Gardenia
Peeples, S. A. Man Who Died Twice
Pendleton, D. Death Squad
Perdue, V. Case of the Foster Father
    Case of the Grieving Monkey
    He Fell Down Dead
Peters, B. Big H
Platt, K. 5 titles
Prather, R. S. 27 titles
Presnell, F. G. Too Hot to Handle
Preston, J. Heil! Hollywood
Pryor, L. Viper
Queen, E. 5 titles
Quentin, P. Suspicious Circumstances
Rabe, P. It's My Funeral
    Stop This Man!
    War of the Dons
Race, P. Self-Made Widow
Racina, T. Sweet Revenge
Raison, M. M. Murder in a Lighter Vein
    Nobody Loves a Dead Man
Rawson, T. I Want to Live!
Reach, J. Storm over Hollywood
    Sunset Strip
Reese, J. Pity Us All
Reeves, Robert. No Love Lost
Rice, C. April Robin Murders
Rico, D. Passion Flower Puzzle
Rider, S. Misplaced Corpse
Rifkin, S. McQuaid
Robeson, K. Seven Agate Devils
Rock, P. Hickey and Boggs
Rolfe, E. Glass Room
Rosaire, F. White Night
Rosmanith, O. L. Signature to a Crime
Ross, Marilyn. Behind the Purple Veil
Ross, Paul. Freebie and the Bean
Ross, S. Hang-Up
Rovin, J. both titles
Rubel, J. L. No Business for a Lady
Rubin, R. Annulment
Ryerson, F. Shadows
Sadler, M. Here to Die
Sale, R. Benefit Performance
    Lazarus #7
    Passing Strange
Sanchez, T. Zoot-Suit Murders
Sanders, G. Stranger at Home
Santiago, V. J. Detour to a Funeral
Sapir, R. Brain Drain
Saul, O. Dark Side of Love
Saxby, C. Death over Hollywood
    Murder at the Mike
Saxon, J. A. Liability Limited
Saxon, V. Hollywood Hitman
Scarpetta, F. Death to the Mafia
Scott, R. Shakedown
Shagan, S. City of Angels
Shannon, D. all 31 titles
Simon, R. L. both titles
Sinclair, M. Tough Luck L.A.
Smith, P. C. Nothing But Blood
Sohl, J. Odious Ones
Solomon, B. Gone Man
    Open Shadow
Spain, J. all 3 titles
Stadley, P. Black Leather Barbarians
Stanley, J. Bogart 48
Stanley, R. Hippy Cult Murders
Starr, Jimmy. all 3 titles
Stewart, L. Panic on Page One
Stewart, S. Big Rip-Off
Stilgebauer, E. Star of Hollywood
Stratford, M. Sniper
Stratton, C. Dead on Arrival
    Hostages
    Runaway
Sutton, J. Cassady
Taylor, A. F. How I Made a Million Dollars
Taylor, F. House of the Hunter
Taylor, S. S. all 3 titles
Tebbetts-Taylor, E. Now I Lay Me Down to Die
Thayer, L. Guilty!
Thomey, T. And Dream of Evil
    Killer in White
Thompson, G. Murder Mystery
Thorp, R. Nothing Lasts Forever

Tralins, R. Dragnet '67
Trask, M. Murder in Brief
Trevor, L. all 3 titles
Treynor, B. all 3 titles
Trinian, J. House of Evil
Truesdell, J. Be Still, My Love
Vasquez, R. Giant Killer
Verner, G. Con Man
Von Elsner, D. Don't Just Stand There, Do Someone
Vowell, D. both titles
Wager, W. Blue Moon
Walker, T. P. Recall
Wallace, F. L. both titles
Wallace, R. Death Under Contract
Wambaugh, J. Black Marble
    New Centurions
Warren, D. Case of Rape
    Scarlet Starlet
Webb, J. 9 titles
Weisman, J. Quadraphone Homicide
Westheimer, D. Avila Gold
Weston, C. Poor, Poor Ophelia
    Rouse the Demon
    Susannah Screaming
Weston, Garnett. Undertaker Dies
Weverka, R. Griff
Wheatley, D. Such Power Is Dangerous
White, L. T. Me, Detective
Whitfield, R. Death in a Bowl
Whittington, H. Don't Speak to Strange Girls
Wiles, D. Death Flight
Wilk, M. Moving Picture Boys
Williams, B. Make a Killing
    Stranger to Herself
    Well-Dressed Skeleton
Williams, B. A. End to Mirth
Williamson, A. M. Black Sleeves
Wilmer, D. Memo for Murder
Wilson, Dana. Make with the Brains, Pierre
Wolfson, V. Nothing Happens to Children in Beverly Hills
Wormser, R. Hanging Heiress
Young, C. Todd Dossier

LOUISIANA (La. See also: NEW ORLEANS; SOUTH)

Arkham, C. Deadly Friendship
Barron, A. Serpent in the Shadows
Bellamann, H. Victoria Grandolet
Camp, W. Sinister Island
Carter, A. S. Adopted Face
Cockrell, F. Dark Waters
Conaway, J. World's End
Crane, F. Buttercup Case
Crawford, R. A. Image of Evil
Crecy, J. Night Hunters
Crosby, J. Dear Judgment
Daingerfield, F. Ghost House
Daniels, D. at least 5 titles
Davenport, F. Secret of the Bayou
Eberhart, M. G. With This Ring
Effinger, G. A. Felicia
Eyre, M. Return to Gravesend
Fitzgerald, A. J. House of Tragedy
Fleming, Jane. Hawthorn Wood
Fletcher, M. M. Scorpion of Chateau Laverria
Footner, H. Trial by Water
Hall, G. Blue Taper
Hayworth, E. Evil at Bayou Laforche
Heath, M. Calderwood
    Legend of Blackhurst
    Marshwood
Herber, W. Live Bait for Murder
Hitchens, D. In a House Unknown
Hubbard, M. A. Murder Takes the Veil
Hurd, F. House of Shadows
Kane, F. Poison Unknown
Keene, D. Big Kiss-Off
    Bring Him Back Dead
    Notorious
Kimbrough, K. Shriek in the Midnight Tower
Knoblock, K. T. Murder in the Mind
    Take Up the Bodies
Kruger, P. Message from Marise
Long, A. R. It's Death, My Darling!
    Murder Goes Mad
MacIvers, S. Cry of the Wind
    Night Without End
Martin, Carl. Delta Deputies
Matschat, C. H. Murder at the Black Crook
Maxwell, P. Bewitching Grace
    Dark Masquerade
    Plantation Inn
    Stranger at Plantation Inn
Milburn, E. Wings of Darkness
Nicole, Claudette. When the Wind Cries
Nicole, Claudia. Moonwater
Nottingham, P. Hatred's Web
Reddoch, J. Night of the Hellebore
Robeson, K. Quest of the Spider
Ronns, E. Death Is My Shadow
Ross, Sam. Tight Corner
Rydell, F. Annalisa
St. John, G. Shadow on Spanish Swamp
Sellars, M. House on Black Bayou

Tracy, D. Look Down on Her Dying
  Naked She Died
Weston, H. G. House of False Faces
Wood, C. Shadow from the Bogue

LOUISVILLE (SEE ALSO: KENTUCKY; SOUTH)
Colby, R. Captain Must Die
McDowell, E. Bloodline to Murder
  In at the Kill
  Stamped for Death
  Three for the Gallows
Revell, L. No Pockets in Shrouds
Sellers, M. Raise the Dark Gambler

MACEDONIA (MACED. SEE ALSO: BALKANS; BULGARIA; GREECE; YUGOSLAVIA)
Allen, T. Jade Elephants

MACAO (SEE ALSO: CHINA; FAR EAST; SHANGHAI; PEKING; FORMOSA)
Black, G. Golden Cockatrice
Carter, Nick. Macao
Fleischman, A. S. Look Behind You, Lady
Hardy, L. Nightshade Ring
Harknett, T. Crown: Macao Mayhem

MADEIRA (SEE ALSO: PORTUGAL; LISBON)
Farnsworth, R. M. Castle That Whispered
Ferrars, E. Skeleton Staff
  Witness Before the Fact
White, Alicen. Watching Eye

MADISON (SEE ALSO: WISCONSIN; MIDWEST)
Derleth, A. Death by Design
  Narracong Riddle

MADRID (SEE ALSO: SPAIN; CANARY ISLANDS; MAJORCA)
Bagby, G. Body in the Basket
Carter, Nick. Code Name: Werewolf
Cory, D. Hammerhead
Fletcher, Dorothy. Meeting in Madrid
Lee, John. Caught in the Act
Marlowe, S. Drum Beat—Madrid
Naughton, E. Case in Madrid
Roos, A. Few Days in Madrid
Strachan, T. S. Short Weekend

MAINE (SEE ALSO: NEW ENGLAND)
Abbott, A. Third Tower
Abbott, S. Whispering Gables
Angus, S. Arson and Old Lace
Barber, W. A. Drawn Conclusion
Bishop, M. Widow's Walk
Blizard, M. Men in Her Death
Bonnamy, F. Blood and Thirsty
Bradley, M. H. Nice People Murder
Brean, H. Clock Strikes Thirteen
Burleigh, D. Q. Kristiana Killers
Combes, S. M. Caly
Cooper, Lynna. Stark Island
Daly, E. Deadly Nightshade
Daniels, D. at least 12 titles
Dean, R. G. Affair at Lover's Leap
De Blasis, C. Night Child
Dibner, M. Ransom Run
Disney, D. M. Voice from the Grave
Eldridge, G. D. Millbank Case
Ellis, J. Walk a Tightrope
Esteven, J. While Murder Waits
Fairman, P. W. That Girl
Farr, C. at least 7 titles
Fitzpatrick, J. Serena
Gerry, M. S. Sound of Water
Gibson, W. Crime over Casco
Gilman, D. Tightrope Walker
Gordon, E. Freer's Cove
Hatch, M. R. P. Strange Disappearance of Eugene Comstocks
Holland, R. S. Minot's Folly
  Mystery of the "Opal"
Holt, H. J. Midnight at Mears House
Hood, M. P. all 6 titles
Hopkins, N. M. Racoon Lake Mystery
Howe, F. Legacy of Lanshore
Hufford, S. Cove's End
Johnston, V. Presence in an Empty Room
Kimbrough, K. Augusta, the First
  Jane, the Courageous
  Margaret, the Faithful
Koontz, D. R. Night Chills
Kyle, R. Nice Guys Finish Last
Laing, A. Cadaver of Gideon Wyck
Landon, H. Gray Magic
  Owl's Warning
Leffingwell, A. Mystery of Bar Harbor
Letton, J. Cragsmoor
Livingston, A. Magic for Murder
McCurtin, P. Cosa Nostra
Martyn, W. Murder Island
Mayor, D. It's an Ill Wind
Meservey, R. Masquerade into Madness

Nebel, F. Fifty Roads to Town
Nichols, S. Widow's Walk
Nicole, Claudette. Dark Mill
Nightingale, U. Bitters Wood
Noone, E. Seacliffe
Norwood, H. Death Down East
Ogilvie, E. Bellwood
  Dancer in Yellow
  Dreaming Summer
Orford, E. Maze
Orr, C. Wailing Rock Murders
Osborne, D. Fog Island
Packard, F. Miracle Man
Parker, R. B. Wilderness
Patterson, A. M. Heaviest Pipe
Phillips, J. Hermit's End
Potts, J. Troublemaker
Pronzini, B. Games
Revell, L. Silver Spade
Rinehart, M. R. Yellow Room
Roberts, W. D. Invitation to Evil
Robeson, K. Squeaking Goblin
Ronns, E. Million Dollar Murder
  Murder Money
Ross, Clarissa. Corridors of Fear
  Durrell Towers
  Out of the Fog
Ross, Dana. Figure in the Shadows
  Lodge Sinister
Ross, Marilyn. at least 33 titles
Ross, W. E. D. Twilight Web
Rowe, A. Fatal Purchase
  Little Dog Barked
Sanborn, R. B. Murder on the Aphrodite
Scott, A. Falcon's Island
Sloane, W. Edge of Running Water
Stein, A. M. Coffin Country
  Nose for It
Stuart, E. Shaking Shadow
Swann, F. Brass Key
Thayer, L. Accident, Manslaughter or Murder?
Turnbull, M. Return of Jenny Weaver
Van de Wetering, J. Maine Massacre
Warren, P. Ghost at Ravenkill Manor
  Ravenkill
Webb, J. F. Carnavaron's Castle
Wells, Carolyn. Murder on Parade
  Vanishing of Betty Varian
Westbrook, P. D. Infra Blood
  Red Herring Murder
Williams, B. A. Dreadful Night
  Mischief
  Pascal's Mill
  Silver Forest
Young, E. A. Luke Darby

MAJORCA (MAJ. SEE ALSO: SPAIN; MADRID; CANARY ISLANDS)
Angus, W. Murder in Mallorca
Asher, Miriam. Nightmare in Eden
Ashford, J. Double Run
Bryan, M. Murder in Majorca
Canning, V. Manasco Road
Carr, G. Holiday with Murder
Crosby, J. Nightfall
Dodson, S. Majorca
Gale, A. Harvest of Terror
Gilruth, S. Drown Her Remembrance
Hintze, N. Cry Witch
Jeffries, R. 5 titles
MacLeod, R. All Other Perils
Mercer, I. Mission to Majorca
Tabori, P. Murder in Majorca

MALAYA. SEE: MALAYSIA.

MALAYSIA (MAL. MALAYA INCLUDED HERE. SEE ALSO: FAR EAST)
Aarons, E. S. Assignment—White Rajah
Black, G. Time for Pirates
Carter, Nick. Cobra Kill
Derby, M. Big Water
  Malayan Rose
  Tigress
Fleischman, A. S. Malay Woman
Harvester, S. Yesterday Walkers
Lilley, T. Projects Section
Maugham, W. S. Ah King
Meade, D. C. Death over Her Shoulder
  Fatal Shadows
Packard, F. Gold Skull Murders
Sheen, G. Malayan Story
Sherlock, J. Ordeal of Major Grigsby
Thorne, E. P. Jungle Hut
Yorke, S. Agency House, Malaya

MALI (SEE ALSO: AFRICA, WEST)
Capstan. Inkosi-Carver Investigates

MALLORCA. SEE: MAJORCA.

MALTA (SEE ALSO: MEDITERRANEAN ISLAND)
Bagley, D. Freedom Trap

Butler, Gwendoline. Coffin in Malta
Butterworth, M. Vanishing Act
Cass, Z. Island of the Seven Hills
Galway, R. C. Assignment Malta
Hedges, S. G. Malta Mystery
Howard, R. Secret of Simon Cornell
Lindsay, K. Suspense
MacLeod, R. Killing in Malta
Maddock, S. Gentlemen of the Night
Mullally, F. Malta Conspiracy

MANILA (SEE ALSO: PHILIPPINES; FAR EAST)
Chamberlain, Elinor. Appointment in Manila
Coxe, G. H. Dangerous Legacy
Kennedy, J. Paper Chase
Knight, C. Affair of the Circus Queen
Langdon, J. Vicious Circuit
Orbison, K. Key to the Case
Teed, G. H. Five in Fear

MARSEILLES (MARS. SEE ALSO: FRANCE; NICE; PARIS; CORSICA)
Caillou, A. Marseilles
Lefevre, C. Murder in Marseilles
Leonard, C. L. Search for a Scientist
Malo, V. G. Murder on the Mistral
Moore, Robin. French Connection II
Pereira, M. Singing Millionaire
Smith, Don. Marseilles Enforcer
Thomas, Louis. Good Children Don't Kill

MARYLAND (MD. SEE ALSO: BALTIMORE)
Bellah, J. W. Bones of Napoleon
Blizard, M. Dark Corner
Brode, R. Clue of the Curious Cat
Broun, D. Egypt's Choice
Cain, J. M. Galatea
  Magician's Wife
Coffin, C. Mare's Nest
Coffin, G. Forgotten Fleet Mystery
Creighton, J. Inn of Evil
Daiger, K. S. both titles
Daniels, D. Blackthorn
  Emerald Hill
  Lily Pond
Disney, D. C. Balcony
  Strawstack
Du Breuil, L. Legend of Molly Moor
Fletcher, L. Strange Blue Yawl
Footner, H. Dark Ships
  Island of Fear
  Ramshackle House
Ford, L. 6 titles
Frome, D. Strange Death of Martin Green
Gaines, A. While the Wind Howled
Hamilton, D. Night Walker
Hart, F. N. Hide in the Dark
Hayes, W. E. all 3 titles
Johnson, M. W. Let's Go Play at the Adams'
Kingsbury, M. Island of Fog
Kummer, F. A. Scarecrow Murders
  Twisted Face
Lincoln, N. S. Fifth Latchkey
  Thirteenth Letter
Longstreet, S. Crime
McGerr, P. Murder Is Absurd
Michaels, B. Prince of Darkness
  Walker in Shadows
Norton, A. Snow Shadow
  White Jade Fox
Ostrander, K. Foxfire Cove
Padget, M. House of Strangers
Peters, Elizabeth. Love Talker
Revell, L. Bus Station Murders
Rice, C. Telefair
Robins, R. Murder at Bayside
Ronns, E. Point of Peril
St. Clair, D. Lady's Not for Living
St. John, G. Night of Evil
Sapir, R. Murder Ward
Sterling, S. Big Ear
Sutphen, V. T. In Jeopardy
Tracy, D. Big X
  How Sleeps the Beast
  Round Trip
Truscott, L. K. Dress Gray
Welles, E. Waterview Manor
White, L. Crimshaw Memorandum
  Marilyn K
Winston, D. Adventuress
  Love of Lucifer

MASSACHUSETTS (MASS. SEE ALSO: BOSTON; CAPE COD; NEW ENGLAND)
Angus, D. Death on Jerusalem Road
August, J. Advance Agent
Baker, C. Gay Head Conspiracy
Benson, B. all titles
Blake, N. Morning After Death
Bramhall, M. Tragedy in Blue
Brean, H. Hardly a Man Is Now Alive
Bretonne, A. M. Gallows Stands in Salem
Buchanan, P. Parliament of Owls
Byfield, B. N. Harder Thing Than Triumph

Settings Index

Cameron, D. C.   Murder's Coming
Cardiff, S.   Fool's Apple
Carey, C.   Checkhov Proposal
Carleton, M.   Swan Sang Once
Carr, J. B.   Death Whispers
Chamberlain, Elinor.   Snare for Witches
Clugston, K.   Murderer in the House
Coburn, A.   Trespassers
Coxe, G. H.   Eye Witness
Curtiss, P. E.   Gay Conspirators
Curtiss, U.   Deadly Climate
   Iron Cobweb
   Noonday Devil
   So Dies the Dreamer
Dalmas, H.   Fowler Formula
Dana, M.   Lake Mystery
Daniels, D.   Two Worlds of Peggy Scott
Daniels, H. R.   Accused
   House on Greenapple Road
Decker, D.   Devil's Punchbowl
Dessart, G.   Man Died Here
Disney, D. M.   Enduring Old Charms
Dyer, G.   Adriana
Eberhart, M. G.   Wolf in Man's Clothing
Farnsworth, M.   Evil That Waited
Fast, J.   Watchful at Night
Forbes, S.   Terrors of the Earth
Foster, I.   Sabath Quest
Fried, B.   Concerto in the Key of Death
Fuller, T.   Keep Cool, Mr. Jones
Futrelle, M.   Secretary of Frivolous
   Affairs
Graham, J. A.   Arthur
Green, A. K.   Doctor Izard
   XYZ
Hagerty, H. J.   Jasmine Trail
Harris, L.   Don't Be   No Hero
Hart, S.   Martha's Vineyard Affair
Highsmith, P.   Deep Water
Jordan, E.   Trap
Kains, J.   Devil Mask Mystery
Kallen, L.   Tanglewood Murder
Kemelman, H.   6 titles
Kimbrough, K.   Rebecca, the Mysterious
Knight, K. M.   Terror by Twilight
Langton, J.   Dark Nantucket Noon
   Transcendental Murder
Leonard, A. B.   Judson Murder Case
Leslie, W.   Love or Whatever It Is
Lifson, D. S.   Headless Victory
Littlefield, A.   Which Mrs. Bennett
Long, L. B.   Legacy of Evil
Lovesmith, J.   Legacy of Fear
Lowndes, M. B.   Lizzie Borden
Lynch, M.   Where Shadows Lie
McCloy, H.   Imposter
McDonald, G.   Running Scared
McFarlane, L.   Murder Tree
McHugh, F. Y.   Shadow over Mount Sharon
MacLeod, C.   Luck Runs Out
   Rest You Merry
Malcolm-Smith, G.   Come Out, Come Out
Marsten, R.   Even the Wicked
Mason, V. W.   Vesper Service Murders
Norris, K.   Black Flamingo
O'Brien, L.   Sweet William Is Dead
Pendleton, D.   Savage Fire
   War Against the Mafia
Pentecost, H.   Deadly Friend
Pidgin, C. F.   Chronicles of Quincy Adams
   Sawyer, Detective
   Hidden Man
Popkin, Z.   Murder in the Mist
Quick, D.   Doctor Looks at Murder
Randall, F. E.   Haldane Station
Randall, W.   Deadly the Daring
Rennert, M.   3 titles
Reybold, M.   Inspector's Opinion
Ritter, M.   Caroline, Caroline
Robeson, K.   Hex
   Nightwitch Devil
Ronns, E.   Terror in the Town
Roof, K. M.   Murder on the Salem Road
Ross, Clarissa.   at least 6 titles
Ross, Dan.   Cliffhaven
Ross, Marilyn.   Don't Look Behind You
Russell, E. S.   Nice Enough to Murder
   She Should Have Cried on Monday
Rydell, F.   If She Should Die
   No Questions Asked
St. Clair, E.   Sandcastle Murders
Saul, J. R.   Comes the Blind Fury
Sax, A.   Death in the Colony
Saxton, M.   Danger Road
Scribner, H.   My Mysterious Clients
Shattuck, R.   Snark Was a Boojum
Sherman, D.   Riddle
Smith, R. N.   Death Be Nimble
Stagge, J.   8 titles
Stephan, L.   Murder R.F.D.
Stevenson, F.   Dark Encounter
   Witch's Crossing
Strange, J. S.   Unquiet Grave
Stratton, R.   One Among None
Sumner, C. R.   Withdraw Thy Foot
Tilton, A.   7 titles
Trevelyan, J.   Landsend Terror
Vandergriff, A.   Bell Tower of Wyndspelle
   Wyndspelle
   Wyndspelle's Child
Van Hazinga, C.   House on Gannet's Point
Wagner, E.   Case of Bottled Murder

Wallis, R. S.   No Bones About It
Waters, T. A.   In the Halls of Evil
Waugh, H.   Last Seen Wearing—
Wells, Carolyn.   7 titles
Wells, T.   Creature Was Stirring
   Have Mercy Upon Us
Wernick, S.   Blood Tide
Wheeler, K.   Easy Come
Wickware, F.   Dangerous Ground
Williams, S.   Mystery in Red
Winsor, R.   Always Lock Your Bedroom Door
   Corpse That Walked
Zaroulis, N. L.   Poe Papers

MEDICAL SETTINGS. See: HOSPITAL.

MEDITERRANEAN ISLAND (Med. Is. See ALSO: CORSICA; CRETE; CYPRUS; MAJORCA; SARDINIA; SICILY)
Ames, D.   Lucky Jane
Birmingham, G. A.   Island Mystery
Brand, C.   Tour de Force
Fitt, M.   Late Uncle Max
Howard, L.   Invitation to Paradise

MELBOURNE (Melb. See Also: AUSTRALIA; SYDNEY; SOLOMON ISLANDS; TASMANIA)
Afford, M.   Blood on His Hands!
Gray, D.   Murder in Melbourne
Hume, F.   Mystery of a Hansom Cab
North, E.   Name Is Smith
Preston, James.   Racing Axes
Stutley, S. J.   Melbourne Mystery
Westlaw, S.   Mystery of Lombardy Chambers

MEMPHIS (See Also: TENNESSEE; NASHVILLE; SOUTH)
Dana, R.   Death of a Millionaire
Falkner, W. C.   White Rose of Memphis
Foote, S.   September September
Wells, Charlie.   Last Kill

MESOPOTAMIA (Mesop. See Also: TURKEY; MIDDLE EAST)
Christie, A.   Murder in Mesopotamia

MEXICO (Mex. See Also: MEXICO CITY)
Aarons, E. S.   Come Back My Love
Adkins, B.   all 3 titles
Ames, R.   Dangerous One
Angus, S.   Dead to Rites
Ardies, T.   Their Man in the White House
Atlee, P.   Death Bird Contract
Bagley, D.   Vivero Letter
Bedford-Jones, H.   Shadow
Blackburn, J.   Young Man from Lima
Blanc, S.   Green Stone
   Rose Window
   Yellow Villa
Buchan, Stuart.   Fleeced
Buckingham, B.   both titles
Burleson, C. W.   Mexican Affair
Caillou, A.   Death Charge
Cain, J. M.   Serenade
Carter, Nick.   5 titles
Chadwick, C.   Cactus
Chambers, W.   Action at World's End
   You Can't Get Away by Running
Charbonneau, L.   Lair
Chase, K.   Killer Be Killed
Chute, V.   Wayward Angel
Coffey, B.   Wall of Masks
Cohen, A. A.   Acts of Theft
Content, N.   Hideaway
Crane, F.   Ultraviolet Widow
Crawford, William.   Chinese Connection
Cronin, M.   Sweet Water
Currier, J. L.   Cargo of Fear
Curtiss, U.   In Cold Pursuit
Darby, R.   If This Be Murder
Davis, N.   Mouse in the Mountain
Deptula, W.   Naked Mistress
Derrick, L.   Baja Bandidos
   Mexican Brown
Dewey, T. B.   Golden Hooligan
Downing, T.   Case of the Unconquered Sisters
Downing, T.   7 titles
Duff, J. P.   Run from Death
Elias, A. J.   Sonora Mutation
Ellson, H.   Killer's Kiss
Falk, L.   Slave Market of Mucar
Faust, R.   Death Fires
Fickling, G. G.   Dig a Dead Doll
Flynn, J.   It's Murder, McHugh
Flynn, J. M.   Danger Zone
   Screaming Cargo
Fuentes, C.   Hydra Head
Gerard, F.   Prisoner of the Pyramid
Gilman, D.   Unexpected Mrs. Pollifax
Graham, J.   Wrath of God
Grayson, Rupert.   Gun Cotton in Mexico
Grew, W.   Murder Has Many Faces
Hamilton, D.   Menacers
   Retaliators

Hanson, J. W.   Brother Berserk
Harrison, H.   Montezuma's Revenge
Hartshorne.   Mexican Assassin
Heath, P.   Assassins for Tomorrow
Hedges, J.   Mexican Mourning
Hines, J.   Talons of the Hawk
   Third Wife
Homes, G.   Street of the Crying Woman
Howard, H.   Routine Investigation
Howard, V.   Murder on Her Mind
Hume, F.   Harlequin Opal
Keener, J.   Borderline
Kelly, B.   Tuna Is Not for Eating
Kirk, L.   Cuernavaca Question
Knight, C.   Affair of the Black Sombrero
Knight, K. M.   7 titles
Knye, C.   House That Fear Built
Koehler, R. P.   Hooded Vulture Murders
Lacy, E.   Moment of Untruth
Lange, O.   Incident at La Junta
Leonard, P. G.   Prey of the Eagle
Levine, Larry.   Treasure
MacDonald, J. D.   Damned
   Dress Her in Indigo
   Empty Trap
MacLean, Arthur.   Mission to Mexico
MacLean, J.   Deadfall
MacNeil, N.   Mexican Slay Ride
Madsen, A.   Borderlines
Maling, A.   Decoy
Markson, D.   Going Down
Marlowe, D. J.   Operation Hammerlock
Marlowe, S.   Cawthorn Journals
Masterson, W.   Dark Fantastic
   Last One Kills
Millar, M.   Ask for Me Tomorrow
Miller, W.   5 titles
Morgan, Dean.   Rostron Outfit in Mexico
Muir, Jean.   Stranger, Tread Light
Murray, C.   Day of the Dead
Nash, C.   Murder Is My Shadow
North, J.   High Valley
Oliver, L.   Mexican Adventure
O'Rourke, F.   High Dive
Paradis, V. A.   Cocaine Caper
Patterson, H.   Thunder at Noon
Pendleton, D.   Acapulco Rampage
Peters, Elizabeth.   Night of Four Hundred
   Rabbits
Phillips, J.   House of Darkness
Phillips, J. A.   Suitable for Framing
Prather, R. S.   Darling, It's Death
Queen, E.   Kiss and Kill
   Last Score
Quentin, P.   Follower
   Run to Death
Rabe, P.   Time Enough to Die
Rayter, J.   Stab in the Dark
Rilla, W.   Dispensable Man
Robeson, K.   Hell Below
Rosenberger, J.   Mexican Hit
Rowan, D.   Shadow of the Volcano
Russell, C. M.   Ill Met in Mexico
Salas, F.   What Now My Love
Scarpetta, F.   Icepick in the Spine
Shepherd, John.   Lights, Camera, Murder
Stark, R.   Damsel
Stein, A. M.   8 titles
Travis, Gerry.   Big Bite
Twist, P.   Gilded Hideaway
Warren, G.   Laughing Widow
Westheimer, D.   Olmec Head
Weverka, R.   One Minute to Eternity
Wheatley, D.   Unholy Crusade
Whitaker, H.   Mystery of the Barranca
White, L.   Mexico Run
Whitlach, J.   Gannon's Line
Williams, B.   Tumulto
   Well-Dressed Skeleton
Winston, D.   Castle of Closing Doors
Woolrich, C.   Savage Bride

MEXICO CITY (Mex. City. See Also: MEXICO)
Barry, M.   Killing Run
Brown, Carter.   Murder Wears a Mantilla
Cheyney, P.   Don't Get Me Wrong
Eberhart, M. G.   Wings of Fear
Gatenby, R.   Whisper of Evil
Highsmith, P.   Game for the Living
Lucas, C.   Unfinished Business
Millar, M.   Listening Walls
Morales, V.   Victim for Hire
Palmer, S.   Puzzle of the Blue Banderilla
Prather, R. S.   Pattern for Panic
Quentin, P.   Puzzle for Pilgrims
Trimble, L.   Dead and the Deadly
   Till Death Do Us Part
Waer, J.   17 and Black
Weintraub, S.   Mexican Slay Ride
Wilson, David.   Park Avenue Executioner

MIAMI (See Also: FLORIDA; JACKSONVILLE; TAMPA; SOUTH)
Banko, D.   Very Dead with a Twist
Barry, M.   Miami Marauder
Brace, T.   Murder Goes Fishing
Brown, Carter.   Graves, I Dig!
Chaber, M. E.   Bonded Dead

660 / Michigan

Chambers, D. Case of Caroline Animus
    Darling, This Is Death
Charteris, L. Saint in Miami
Colby, R. Kim
    Murder Mistress
Conners, T. Combat Zone—Miami
Deane, J. Moon over Miami
Ellin, S. Bind
    Star Light, Star Bright
Ernst, P. Lady, Get Your Gun
Fisher, D. E. Last Flying Tiger
Foster, R. Too Late for Mourning
Frazer, R. C. Mark Kilby and the Miami Mob
Fuller, W. Brad Dolan's Miami Manhunt
Halliday, B. at least 47 titles
Heyman, E. L. Miami Undercover
Kastle, H. Miami Golden Boy
Keene, D. Miami 59
Kendrick, B. Eleven of Diamonds
King, R. Murder Masks Miami
King, T. J. Noose of Red Beads
La France, M. Miami Murder-Go-Round
Macklin, M. Thin Edge of Mania
Malina, F. Some Like 'Em Shot
Pendleton, D. Miami Massacre
Robeson, K. Red Snow
Rome, A. Lady in Cement
    Miami Mayhem
Russell, C. M. Murder Steps In
Sapir, R. Kill or Cure
Sarto, B. Miami for Murder
Scarpetta, F. Mafia Massacre
Schley, S. M. Dr. Toby Finds Murder
Smith, R. K. Sadie Shapiro in Miami
Terhune, A. P. Black Caesar's Clan

MICHIGAN (Mich. See also: Detroit; Midwest)
Armstrong, A. Case of the Weird Sisters
Bramhall, M. Murder Is Contagious
Brennan, A. Brooding House
    Devil Take All
    Fear No Evil
Brucker, M. Poison Party
Byfield, B. N. Forever Wilt Thou Die
Cameron, D. C. White for a Shroud
Cloutier, H. Murder, Absolutely Murder
Coffin, P. Search for My Great Uncle's Head
Dodge, M. L. Sticks and Stones
Goff, G. Black Bag
Green, C. Scarlet Venus
Greenbaum, L. Out of Shape
Hale, C. 10 titles
Hall, F. H. In the Lamb White Days
Harrington, J. No One Knows My Name
Henry, C. Welcome Home, Lily Glow
Howes, R. Case of the Copy-Hook Killing
    Death Dupes a Lady
    Death Rides a Hobby
Kent, F. Opal Legacy
Lang, B. Brand of Fear
    Perdition Express
Loban, E. H. Signed in Yellow
MacVeigh, S. Corpse and the Three Ex-Husbands
Magoon, C. I Smell the Devil
Marlett, M. Escape While I Can
Martin, Robert. Echoing Shore
Mead, S. How to Succeed at Business Spying by Trying
Millar, K. Dark Tunnel
Millar, M. Vanish in an Instant
Nielsen, H. Crime Is Murder
Osborn, D. Open Season
Plum, M. Murder at the Hunting Club
Porter, M. E. Mercy of the Court
Prentis, J. H. Case of Doctor Horace
Roberts, W. D. Murder at Grand Bay
Robeson, K. Devil's Playground
    Monsters
Shriber, I. S. Murder Well Done
Smith, Mark. Toyland
Spike, P. Night Letter
Toombs, J. J. Point of Lost Souls
Traver, R. Anatomy of a Murder
    Small-Town D.A.
Valentine, J. Trouble in Thor
Welles, P. Angels in the Snow

MICRONESIA
Kluge, P. F. Day That I Die

MIDDLE EAST (Mid. East. See also: Individual Countries)
Aarons, E. S. Assignment—Afghan Dragon
    Assignment—Karachi
    Assignment—Zoraya
Aarons, W. B. Assignment 13th Princess
Aldridge, J. Mockery in Arms
Ambler, E. Levanter
Aricha, A. Phoenix
Arvay, H. Piraeus Plot
    Stranglehold
Atlee, P. Spice Route Contract
Awin, M. Silence over Sinai
Bagley, D. Spoilers
Ballinger, B. S. Source of Fear
Barrett, Michael. Ten Against Nura
Beare, G. Bee Sting Deal
    Bloody Sun at Noon
    Very Breath of Hell
Bennett, K. Devil's Current
Benton, K. Craig and the Midas Touch
Black, Lionel. Arafat Is Next!
Boothby, G. Bid for Freedom
Caillou, A. Assault on Fellawi
    Dead Sea Submarine
    Who'll Buy My Evil?
Canning, V. His Bones Are Coral
Carter, Nick. Green Wolf Connection
Charles, R. Clash of Hawks
Chase, P. Deadly Crusade
Childs, M. Taint of Innocence
Christian, J. Persian Death-Trap
Connell, C. Most Delicious Evil
Connelly, M. Souvenir from Qam
Coppel, Alfred. Thirty-Four East
Cronin, M. Marksman
Da Cruz, D. Captive City
    Landfall Finesse
Davidson, L. Long Way from Shiloh
De Mille, N. By the Waters of Babylon
Dickinson, Peter. Poison Oracle
Edwards, Samuel. Exploiters
Evans, Jonathan. Misfire
Fairbairn, D. Street 8
Garbo, N. Cabal
Garner, W. Andra Fiasco
Gibbs, G. F. Road to Bagdad
Gilbert, M. Ninety-Second Tiger
Green, W. M. Man Who Called Himself Devlin
Groner, A. Mene Tekel
Gruber, F. Bridge of Sand
Guenter, C. H. Dead in Aqaba
Haggard, W. Median Line
    Powder Barrel
Hamilton, Adam. Yashar Pursuit
Harvester, S. Assassins Road
Harwood, R. Genoa Ferry
Heller, P. Thousand and Second Night
Household, G. Arabesque
    Doom's Caravan
John, O. Dead on Time
Johnston, R. Black Camels of Qashran
Kalb, M. In the National Interest
Kane, H. Tripoli Documents
Laflin, J. Temple at Ilumquh
Lane, K. Gambit
Lee, Elsie. Drifting Sands
Lyall, G. Judas Country
MacAlister, I. Driscoll's Diamonds
MacLean, R. Baited Blonde
MacLeod, R. Place of Mists
Mason, C. Hostage
Mason, Robert. More News from Middle East
Maugham, R. Man with Two Shadows
Melville-Ross, A. Blindfold
Moore, Robin. Dubai
Moss, W. S. Bats with Baby Faces
Mundy, T. Jimgrim and Allah's Peace
    King in Check
O'Connor, D. Slender Chance
Operator 1384. Jackals of the Secret Service
Pace, E. Saberlegs
Peters, Elizabeth. Dead Sea Cipher
Ponthier, F. Assignment Basra
Pugh, M. Murmur of Destiny
Rathbone, J. With My Knives I Know I'm Good
Roberts, D. Journey from Baghdad
Roberts, T. A. Heart of a Dog
Rohmer, S. Egyptian Nights
    Mask of Fu Manchu
Rosenberger, J. Psychotron Plot
    Vengeance of the Golden Hawk
Rowe, J. Aswan Solution
St. Clair, L. Fortune in Death
Sandys, J. Stripe for a Stripe
Schiff, B. Vatican Target
Sheckley, R. Time Limit
Sherwood, J. Undiplomatic Exit
Sigel, E. Kermanshah Transfer
Spouse, M. Hammerword Technique
Starnes, R. Flypaper War
Thorne, E. P. They Never Come Back
Tiger, J. Doomdate
Topol, A. Woman of Valor
Tripp, M. Kilo Forty
Tyndall, J. Death in the Jordan
West, M. L. Tower of Babel
Williamson, T. Doomsday Contract
Winston, P. Assignment in Bahrein

MIDDLE WEST. See: Midwest.

MIDWAY ISLAND (Midway Is.)
Yates, M. T. Midway to Murder

MIDWEST (See also: The Twelve Individual States)
August, J. Troubled Star
Austin, Anne. Avenging Parrot
    Murder Backstairs
    Murdered But Not Dead
    One Drop of Blood
Bloch, R. Terror
Blochman, L. G. Clues for Dr. Coffee
    Diagnosis: Homicide
    Recipe for Homicide
Bloomfield, R. Stranger in Town
Booth, C. B. Kidnapping Syndicate
Borgenicht, M. Don't Look Back
Boyd, M. Murder in the Stacks
Braun, L. J. all 3 titles
Burnett, W. R. Asphalt Jungle
    Little Man, Big World
Cooper, J. L. Grasshopper Summer
Corrigan, M. I Like Danger
Coughlin, W. J. Stalking Man
Davis, D. S. Judas Cat
    Town of Masks
Dean, R. G. Murder in Mink
    Murder Through the Looking Glass
Deming, R. Tweak the Devil's Nose
De Weese, J. Nightmare in Pewter
Dorian, P. Streaker Murders
Dwight, O. Close His Eyes
Eberhart, M. G. Pattern
Fonseca, E. H. Thirteenth Bed in the Ballroom
Foote-Smith, E. Gentle Albatross
Gatenby, R. Aim to Kill
    Hanged for a Sheep
Givins, C. G. Rose Petal Murders
Goldman, R. L. Death Plays Solitaire
    Murder Behind the Mike
    Murder Without Motive
    Snatch
Gruber, F. Laughing Fox
Hanson, V. Death Walks the Post
Heffernan, D. Murder at Sunset Gables
Hickok, F. Eye for an Eye
Howie, E. Cry Murder
    Murder for Two
Hubbard, M. A. Sister Simon's Murder Case
    Step Softly on My Grave
Hultman, H. J. Death at Windward Hill
    Find the Woman
Johnson, E. R. Mongo's Back in Town
Livingston, A. In Cold Blood
Lowe, K. Catalyst
    No Tears for Shirley Minton
MacDonald, J. D. You Live Once
McKimmey, J. Cornered!
    Perfect Victim
Marino, N. both titles
Mills, R. Leading Lady
Monahan, J. Big Stan
Montgomery, I. Golden Dress
Moseley, L. Dead of Summer
Murphy, M. Borrowed Alibi
Post, M. Candidate for Murder
Potter, D. Way of an Eagle
Potts, J. Lightning Strikes Twice
Rimel, D. W. Curse of Cain
Roberts, Lee. Case of the Missing Lovers
    Pale Door
Rogers, S. You Leave Me Cold!
    You'll Be Sorry!
Roueche, B. Black Weather
Russell, C. M. 10 titles
Rutledge, N. Beware the Hoot Owl
    Preying Mantis
    Wanted for Murder
Scott, M. S. Crime Hound
Seifert, A. Shadows Tonight
Sohl, J. Prelude to Peril
Spillane, M. Long Wait
Stark, R. Butcher's Moon
    Slayground
Stein, A. M. Case of the Absent-Minded Professor
Thomas, C. Prominent Among the Mourners
Tucker, W. Man in My Grave
    Red Herring
Wallace, F. Front Man
Wallis, R. S. Cold Bed in the Clay
    Too Many Bones
Webster, H. K. Butterfly
Wormser, R. Late Mrs. Five

MILAN (See also: Italy; Florence; Naples; Rome; Sardinia; Sicily; Venice)
Ambler, E. Cause for Alarm
Carter, Nick. Massacre in Milan
Creasey, J. Prince for Inspector West
Scerbanenco, G. Duca and the Milan Murders
Tute, W. Next Saturday in Milan

MILWAUKEE (Milw. See also: Wisconsin; Madison; Midwest)
Brown, F. Here Comes a Candle
Duhart, W. H. Deadly Pay-Off
Gault, W. C. Bloody Bokhara
Thornburg, N. Knockover

Settings Index

MINNEAPOLIS (Mpls. See also: Minnesota; Midwest)
Anonymous. Bob Younger's Fate
Brennan, D. Badge of Honor
Gifford, T. Cavanaugh Quest
Hall, Steve. Rape of the Nicollet Mall
    Mannequin
Loomis, N. Murder Goes to Press
Odlum, J. Nine Lives Are Not Enough
Seeley, M. Whistling Shadow

MINNESOTA (Minn. See also: Minneapolis; Midwest)
Arctander, J. W. Guilty?
Bestor, G. C. Prelude to Murder
Brennan, D. Insurrection!
    Lay-Over Town
Claire, M. Drowning Wire
Greene, J. E. Laughing Loon
Hinkemeyer, M. T. Fields of Eden
    Summer Solstice
Hopkins, A. T. Have a Lovely Funeral
Kelsey, V. Whisper Murder!
Kruger, P. Weep for Willow Green
Mead, R. D. You'll Never Take Me
O'Malley, P. Affair of Swan Lake
O'Meara, W. Minnesota Gothic
Seeley, M. Beckoning Door
    Chuckling Fingers
    Crying Sisters
    Listening House
    Whispering Cup
Stanley, S. Rogue's Castle
Walker, Gertrude. So Deadly Fair
Wallis, R. S. Forget My Fate
Watson, L. In a Dark Time
Wolffe, K. Death's Long Shadow

MISSISSIPPI (Miss. See also: South)
Barrett, Monte. Murder at Belle Camille
Boles, P. D. Mississippi Run
Bristow, G. Two and Two Make Twenty-Two
Buchanan, P. Requiem of Sharks
Chaze, E. Wettermark
Daniels, D. House of Many Doors
Eliot, A. Stranger at Pembroke
Faulkner, W. all 3 titles
Foote, S. Follow Me Down
Ford, L. Murder with Southern Hospitality
Hays, S. B. Go Down, Death
Holloway, E. H. Cobweb House
Judson, W. Kilman's Landing
Kimbrough, K. Thanesworth House
Murfi, L. Magnolia Curse
Pauley, B. A. Voices Long Hushed
Pearson, A. Murder by Degrees
Rosenberg, S. When the Bough Breaks
Sellars, M. Cry of the Cat
Vance, W. Homicide Lost
Weill, G. Bonnet Man
Whitten, L. H. Moon of the Wolf
Zumwalt, E. Masquerade of Evil

MISSOURI (Mo. See also: Kansas City; St. Louis; Midwest)
Allen, E. V. Voices in the Wind
Bannon, P. Whisper Murder Softly
Cassiday, B. Buried Motive
Cleary, J. Vortex
Dawson, C. B. Remind Me to Forget
Dent, L. Lady in Peril
Ginty, E. B. Missouri Legend
Gruber, F. Hungry Dog
Howie, E. No Face to Murder
Lutz, J. Bonegrinder
    Truth of the Matter
Moor, E. Shadowed Porch
Randolph, V. Camp-Meeting Murders
Robeson, K. Evil Gnome
Rosenberger, J. Armageddon, USA!
Roueche, B. Last Enemy
Seifert, A. Deeds Ill Done
    3 Blind Mice
Smith, M. A. Legacy of the Lake

MONACO. See: France.

MONGOLIA (See also: China; Russia)
Dark, J. Sword of Genghis Khan
Edwards, P. Needles of Death
Harvester, S. Nameless Road
Oliver, L. Mongolian Interlude

MONTANA (Mont. See also: West)
Adams, C. F. Shady Lady
Berthold, M. P. Local Call
Bradley, Muriel. Murder in Montana
Cameron, O. Butcher's Wife
Cleary, J. Sound of Lightning
Crecy, J. Winter Keeper
Grady, J. Shadow of the Condor
Guthrie, A. B. Genuine Article
    No Second Wind
    Wild Pitch

Hufford, S. Delicate Deceit
Millard, J. Thunderbolt and Lightfoot
Paul, Elliot. Fracas in the Foothills
Rinehart, M. R. State vs. Elinor Norton
Sapir, R. Last War Dance
Scherf, M. 8 titles
Siller, V. Somber Memory
    Under a Cloud
Simpson, C. H. Life in the Far West
Stout, R. Death of a Dude
Zochert, D. Another Weeping Woman

MONTE CARLO. See: France.

MONTREAL (Montr. See also: Canada; Ottawa; Toronto; Vancouver; Winnipeg)
Apple, A. E. Mr. Chang's Crime Ray
Atlee, P. Canadian Bomber Contract
Block, Lawrence. Tanner's Tiger
Brett, Martin. Darker Traffic
    Dum-Dum for the President
    Hot Freeze
Bryan, M. Intent to Kill
Buell, J. Four Days
    Pyx
Curtis, Richard. Death in the Crease
Hardin, P. Frightened Dove
McFarlane, L. Streets of Shadow
Malloch, P. Hardiman's Landing
Marcott, J. Hard to Kill
Moore, B. Revolution Script
Orvis, K. Damned and Destroyed
Pape, G. Chain Reaction
Pendleton, D. Canadian Crisis
Power, P. both titles
Torgerson, E. D. Murderer Returns
Trevanian. Main
Vermandel, J. G. 5 titles
Wayland, P. Double Defector

MOROCCO (Mor. See also: Casablanca; Tangier; Africa, North)
Binns, O. Three Black Dots
Brothers, W. P. Morocco Episode
Byfield, B. N. Parcel of Their Fortunes
Coriola. Intrigue in Morocco
Daniels, D. Affair in Marakesh
Drummond, I. Tank of Sacred Eels
Eliot, A. Incident at Villa Rahmana
Goodchild, G. Road to Marrakesh
Gordons. Tiger on My Back
Gray, D. For Richer for Richer
Innes, H. Strange Land
Jason, S. Blood Debt
Leader, C. Murder in Marrakech
Leonard, C. L. Fanatic of Fez
McConnell, M. Clinton Is Assigned
Sands, M. Maroc 7
Seton, G. Colonel Grant's Tomorrow
Sherry, J. Loring Affair
Smith, Don. Secret Mission: Morocco
Williamson, S. Glory Trap
Winston, P. Doomsday Vendetta

MOSCOW (See also: Russia; Mongolia)
Arvay, H. Moscow Intercept
Barling, T. Olympic Sleeper
Bruce, J. Flash Point
Chambers, P. Moscow Manhunt
Carter, Nick. Moscow
    13th Spy
Chaber, M. E. So Dead the Rose
    Wild Midnight Falls
Datesh, J. N. Moscow Tape
Flannery, S. Kremlin Conspiracy
Francis, D. Trial Run
Frayn, M. Russian Interpreter
Garve, A. Murder in Moscow
Grant, D. Moscow 500
Grant, M. Romanoff Jewels
Hall, Adam. Scorpion Signal
Harvester, S. Moscow Road
Kaplan, H. Chopin Express
Lippincott, D. Salt Mine
Littell, R. Mother Russia
Litvinoff, E. His Master's Voice
Mair, G. B. Death's Foot Forward
Mefford, W. H. Games of 80
Murphy, W. B. Dangerous Games
Newman, B. Moscow Murder
Ovalov, L. S. Comrade Spy
Patterson, J. Jericho Commandment
Redgate, J. Last Decathlon
Redwood, A. Deadline Moscow
Robeson, K. Red Spider
Ross, Clarissa. Moscow Mists
Salisbury, J. Moscow Gold
Semyonov, J. Petrovka 38
Shub, J. L. Moscow by Nightmare
Smith, Don. Secret Mission: The Kremlin
    Plot
Tack, A. Spy Who Wasn't Exchanged
Thayer, C. W. Moscow Interlude
Tiger, J. Countertrap
Vacha, R. Moscow 1980
Wood, A. Red Square

MOZAMBIQUE (Mozam. See also: Africa, East)
Carter, Nick. N3 Conspiracy
Driscoll, P. Barboza Credentials
Scobie, A. Murder a la Mozambique
Wilson, David. Murder in Mozambique

MUNICH (See also: Germany; Berlin; Frankfurt; Hamburg)
Daniels, N. Hunt Club
Dowdell, D. K. House in Munich
Horstman, T. Kessler Alliance
Huch, R. Deruga Trial
Kirst, H. H. Time for Payment
    Time for Scandal
    Time for Truth
MacLeod, R. Witchdance in Bavaria
Mullally, F. Munich Involvement
Smith, Don. Secret Mission: Munich
Ulrich, M. Bank Robbery

NAMIBIA. See: South West Africa.

NAPLES (See also: Italy; Florence; Milan; Rome; Sardinia; Sicily; Venice)
Anonymous. Cavern of Horrors
Baker, L. Preying Streets
Crookenden, I. Mysterious Murder
Curtiss, E. M. Dead Dogs Bite
Davies, J. See Naples and Die
Holme, T. Neopolitan Streak
Maddock, S. Gentlemen of the Night
Marshall, R. You Find Him—I'll Fix Him
Nathenson, J. See Naples and Die
Rabe, P. House in Naples
Stagg, J. Nightmare in Naples
Veraldi, A. Payoff
Wheatley, D. Rising Storm

NASHVILLE (Nashv. See also: Tennessee; Memphis; South)
Kaye, M. Grand Old Opry Murders
Patterson, J. Thomas Berryman Number
Pendleton, D. Tennessee Smash

NASSAU (See also: Bahamas; West Indies; Caribbean)
Dietrich, R. My Body
Lange, J. Drug of Choice
McCulley, W. Blood on Nassau's Moon

NEBRASKA (Neb. See also: Midwest)
Barnes, R. C. Silent Thunder
Eberhart, M. S. Mystery of Hunting's End
Fleet, C. Place Like Hessberg
Kempley, W. Probability Factor
Portnoy, H. N. Hot Rain
Stark, R. Jugger
Travis, Gretchen. Too Old to Die

NEPAL
Carr, G. Corpse at Camp Two
Carter, Nick. Katmandu Contract
    Operation Snake
Court, K. But Don't Go Alone
Davidson, P. Katmandu Affair
Hart-Davis, D. Heights of Rimring
Leigh, S. Dark Labyrinth

NETHERLANDS. See: Holland.

NEVADA (Nev. See also: Las Vegas; Reno; West)
Adams, C. F. Crooking Finger
    Sabotage
Brent, L. Who Dares?
Chaber, M. E. Born to Be Hanged
Chase, J. H. One Bright Summer Morning
Cox, W. R. Death on Location
Daniels, N. Lady for Sale
Dewey, T. B. Nude in Nevada
Dodge, D. Bullets for the Bridegroom
Eberhart, M. G. El Rancho Rio
Fitzgerald, A. J. Devil's Gate
Heath, M. Secrets Can Be Fatal
Homes, G. Build My Gallows High
Johnston, V. Howling in the Woods
Kane, F. Due or Die
McKimmey, J. Man with the Gloved Hand
Marlowe, D. J. Four for the Money
Morgan, Dean. Four Guns to Carson City
    Nevada Alibi
Olden, M. They've Killed Anna
Queen, E. And on the Eighth Day
Ralston, G. Chain Reaction
    Murder's Money
Roberts, W. D. Search for Willie
Ross, Z. H. Three Down Vulnerable
Strahan, K. C. Desert Lake Mystery
    Desert Moon Mystery
Taylor, M. A. Red Is for Shrouds
    Return to Murder

Trevor, E. Night Stop
Van der Zee, J. Stateline
Wire, H. C. Marked Man

NEW DELHI (SEE ALSO: INDIA; BOMBAY; CALCUTTA)
Bahadur, K. P. Murder in the Delhi Mail
Carter, Nick. Sign of the Cobra
Peters, Ellis. Mourning Raga

NEW ENGLAND (NEW. ENG. SEE ALSO: THE SIX INDIVIDUAL STATES)
Adams, S. H. Secret of Lonesome Cove
Aldrich, T. B. Stillwater Tragedy
Allan, Dina. Melody of Murder
Allen, A. J. New England Gothic
Bagby, G. Corpse Candle
Benedict, L. Lucifer Cult
Bernard, R. Deadly Meeting
Blair, H. L. Three Saw the Murder
Blake, E. Death Down East
Borneman, E. Tremolo
Bramhall, M. Murder Solves a Problem
Bronson, F. W. Nice People Don't Kill
Bronte, L. 6 titles
Brown, Carter. Terror Comes Creeping
Brown, D. F. Grimm Death
Carleton, M. Bride Regrets
Carmichael, F. Exit the Body
Chambers, W. E. Death Toll
Chase, A. M. Danger in the Dark
Chipperfield, R. O. Trigger of Conscience
Clauson, C. Jaws of Circumstance
Converse, F. Into the Void
Converse, F. H. Mystery of a Diamond
Corby, J. Farewell to the Castle
Crabb, A. Ghosts
Crandall, E. White Violets
Crowe, C. Northwater
Daly, C. J. Man in the Shadows
Daly, E. Unexpected Night
Daniels, D. Voices on the Wind
de Vincent, E. Tower Park
De Weese, J. Reimann Curse
Disney, D. M. 8 titles
Dodge, L. Midsummer Madness
Du Bois, T. 5 titles
Dutton, C. J. 5 titles
Eberhart, M. G. Jury of One
Ellery, J. Family Affairs
Esteven, J. By Night at Dinsmore
  Door of Death
Eustis, H. Horizontal Man
Fenisong, R. Villainous Company
Fenwick, E. Goodbye, Aunt Elva
Findley, F. Counterfeit Corpse
Fischer, B. Girl Between
  Kill to Fit
Foley, R. Back Door to Death
  Bones of Contention
  Put out the Light
Forbes, S. Business of Bodies
  Encounter Darkness
  Relative to Death
Ford, F. Ninth Candle
Foster, M. Humdrum House
Foster, W. B. From Six to Six
Fredericks, J. Everybody's Ready to Die
Fuller, A. both titles
Grant, C. L. Hour of the Oxrun Dead
  Last Call of Mourning
Greenan, R. Secret Life of Algernon Pendleton
Gresham, E. Prisoner's Base
Hayes, J. Long Dark Night
Head, A. Everybody Adored Cara
Heath, E. A. Affair at Tideways
Hirschhorn, R. Target Mayflower
Holbrook, M. Wanted: A Murderess
Holding, E. S. Widow's Mite
Holland, I. Trelawny
Jackson, G. Witch's Moon
Jansen, L. M. Bride of the Shadows
Jordan, E. Page Mr. Pomeroy
Kamarck, L. Bellringer
King, R. Lethal Lady
Koehler, R. P. Doctor's Murder Case
Lathen, E. Pick Up Sticks
Lawrence, Hilda. Blood upon the Snow
  Time to Die
Livingston, A. Monk of Hambledon
Lynch, M. at least 6 titles
McHenry, J. Spectre of the Forest
Mainwaring, M. Murder at Midyears
Malan, E. Cobwebs and Clues
Mayor, D. Last Call for Lissa
Monette, P. Taking Care of Mrs. Carroll
Noone, E. Dark Cypress
Ogilvie, E. Face of Innocence
Owen, H. C. Ways of Death
Patrick, Q. Grindle Nightmare
Payne, W. Overlook House
Pentecost, H. Around Dark Corners
  Day the Children Vanished
  Murder As Usual
Petersen, H. D.A.'s Daughter
Philips, J. Murder Arranged
Pilgrim, C. Silent Slain
Porcelain, S. E. Crimson Cat Murders

Potts, J. Little Lie
Queen, E. 6 titles
Randall, F. E. Place of Sapphires
Reagan, T. B. Caper
Reilly, H. Murder on Angler's Island
  Thirty-First Bullfinch
Reisner, M. Four Witnesses
  Hunted
Rinehart, M. R. Wall
Roberts, W. D. Key Witness
Rogers, K. Vantage Point
Ronns, E. Net
Roos, K. Requiem for a Blonde
Roscoe, T. Only in New England
Ross, F. Sleeping Dogs
Rowe, A. Curiosity Killed the Cat
Rowland, H. C. Peddler
Russell, E. S. Fortunate Island
Rutledge, N. Easy to Murder
Rydell, F. They're Not Home Yet
Selig, E. B. Mariner's End
Serrester, L. Frog Murders
Smith, F. S. House and the Tower
Snodgrass, G. M. Crestwood Traps
Sproul, K. Death and the Professor
Stagge, J. Scarlet Circle
Steeves, H. R. Good Night, Sheriff
Stein, A. M. Chill Factor
Stone, G. Z. Dear Deadly Cara
Storm, M. Edge of Danger
Talbot, H. Rim of the Pit
Thielen, B. Open Season
Thompson, J. Kill-Off
Tyler, C. W. both titles
Van de Water, F. F. Alibi
Walton, E. Witch House
Warren, P. Apprentice to Terror
Wells, Carolyn. Anybody But Anne
  Mystery Girl
  Tannahill Tangle
  Where's Emily?
Whipple, K. Fires at Fitch's Folly
  Murders at Loon Lake
Whitney, P. A. Sea Jade
Wilkinson, R. H. Mad Murder
Williams, V. Clue of the Rising Moon
Winston, D. Emerald Station
Winter, A. Whispering Caverns
Woodbury, D. O. both titles

NEW GUINEA (SEE ALSO: INDONESIA; DJAKARTA; BALI; BORNEO; JAVA; SUMATRA)
Binns, O. By Papuan Waters
Halls, G. Voice of the Crab
Harvester, S. Paradise Men
Hastings, M. Satan's Bay
Innes, H. Solomon's Seal
Jay, C. Beat Not the Bones
Jay, G. M. Feast of the Dead
MacAlister, I. Skylark Mission
McCarthy, D. Fate of O'Loughlin
McCurtin, P. Body Count
Muir, Denis. Death Defies the Doctor
South, M. Curse of the Sightless Fish
Vandercook, J. W. Murder in New Guinea
Wallace, T. Mystery of DS 24
  Skyriders

NEW HAMPSHIRE (N.H. SEE ALSO: NEW ENGLAND)
Aldrich, T. B. Out of His Head
Avallone, M. Man from AVON
Badgley, A. V. Rembrandt Decision
Black, Lawrence. Case of the Pornographic Photos
Borgenicht, M. Extreme Remedies
Douglas, L. W. Mystery of Crooknose
Fredericks, J. Emergency Exit
Green, A. They Died Laughing
Gresham, E. Puzzle in Parchment
Hatch, M. R. P. Missing Man
Heatter, B. Act of Violence
Hurd, F. Secret of Canfield House
Landon, H. Forbidden Door
Lathen, E. Come to Dust
Lathrop, G. P. In the Distance
Leonard, C. Other Maritha
Letton, J. Haunting of Cliffside
  Jenny and I
McIntire, J. Old-Fashioned Murder
McNab, O. Horror Story
Orr, C. Dartmouth Murders
Ottolengui, R. Conflict of Evidence
Palmer, R. Orion Was Rising
Parsons, C. M. Secret of the Sea
Samson, J. Auctioneer
Stewart, E. Rock Rude
Stewart, R. Sixth Sense
Wallis, J. H. Niece of Abraham Pein
Whitney, P. A. Silverhill
Williams, T. Followed Man

NEW JERSEY (N.J. SEE ALSO: NEWARK)
Ames, R. Awake and Die
  Devil Drives
Ard, W. No Angels for Me
Arden, W. Dark Power
Bahr, E. J. Help, Please

Balmer, E. Torn Letter
Beck, H. C. Death by Clue
Block, Lawrence. Specialists
Bonner, G. Girl at Central
Booton, K. Runaway Home!
Bradley, J. If Hate Could Kill
Callahan, C. Ace of Death
Cameron, L. Barca
  Tancredi
Chamberlain, G. A. Red House
Clark, M. H. Cradle Will Fall
Cunningham, E. V. Alice
Davis, L. R. Barren Heritage
  Evidence Unseen
Gates, N. Hush Hush Johnson
Gilmore, C. C. Atlantic City Proof
Goldsmith, N. Atlantic City Murder Mystery
Goodis, D. Burglar
Gottlieb, N. Stinger
Grant, M. Shadow Strikes
Gunther, M. Epidemic 9
Haaf, B. T. Crystal Pawns
Halleran, E. E. Thirteen Toy Pistols
Hanson, V. Mystery for Mary
Heberden, M. V. Drinks on the Victim
  Murder Goes Astray
Hobart, D. B. Clue of the Leather Noose
Holt, A. Bier for a Hussy
Howie, E. Murder at Stone House
Hunvald, H. Masterpiece of Nice Mr. Breen
Iams, J. Girl Meets Body
Kane, H. Crumpled Cup
  Run for Doom
Keith, C. Hiding Place
  Missing, Presumed Dead
Knebel, F. Trespass
Kozloff, C. Ondine
Lathen, E. Murder to Go
Leonard, C. L. Secret of the Spa
Levinrew, W. Murder on the Palisades
Little, C. Black Gloves
  Black-Headed Pins
  Black Piano
McMullen, M. Man with Fifty Complaints
Mallory, R. New Jersey Showdown
Martyn, W. Scarlett Murder
Meredith, D. W. Christmas Card Murders
Moroso, J. A. Listening Man
Murphy, W. B. Atlantic City
  Bay City Blast
Napier, M. Possession of Elizabeth Calder
Noel, S. Few Die Well
Noone, E. Second Secret
North, H. Expressway
O'Donnell, L. Babes in the Woods
Packer, V. Something in the Shadows
Pendleton, D. Jersey Guns
Pentecost, H. Steel Palace
Pettit, M. Axmann Agenda
Pratt, F. Cunning Mulatto
Propper, M. Ticker-Tape Murder
Queen, E. Halfway House
Quinn, Seabury. Devil's Bride
Reagan, T. B. Inside-Out Heist
Riley, D. Rite of Expiation
Robeson, K. Giggling Ghosts
  Midas Man
Ronns, E. Corpse Hangs High
  Decoy
Rosten, L. King Silky!
Rothberg, A. Stalking Horse
Ryan, S. Death Never Sleeps
Sadler, M. Mirror Image
Sapir, R. Created: The Destroyer
  Mafia Fix
Scarpetta, F. Kill!
Scherf, M. Corpse Grows a Beard
Scoppettone, S. Some Unknown Person
Shane, S. Baby in the Ash Can
Simmons, M. K. Gypsy Grove
Smith, Edgar. Reasonable Doubt
Spain, T. Time to Kill
Stark, R. Deadly Edge
  Man with the Getaway Face
Stevens, S. Dead City
Stevenson, B. E. That Affair at Elizabeth
Stratton, Ted. Tourist Trap
Swem, C. L. Werewolf
Teague, R. You Can't Ignore Murder
Terhune, A. P. Blundell's Last Guest
  Letters of Marque
  Loot!
  Unseen!
Thayer, L. 8 titles
Turnbull, M. Coast Road Murder
Wahl, A. H. Handsome, But Dead
Wallmann, J. M. both titles
Wells, Carolyn. All at Sea
  Clue
  Maxwell Mystery
  Umbrella Murder
Westlake, D. E. Jimmy the Kid
Whitney, P. A. Winter People
Wise, W. Amazon Factor
Wolff, W. A. Murder at Endor
Wylie, P. Murderer Invisible
Yates, G. W. Body That Wasn't Uncle
Zawadsky, P. Demon of Raven's Cliff

Settings Index

NEW MEXICO (N. Mex. See also: ALBEQUERQUE; SANTE FE; SOUTHWEST)

Aeby, J. Serena
Ames, D. Murder Begins at Home
Ames, N. Whisper in the Forest
Armstrong, M. Blue Santo Murder Mystery
Boniface, M. Wings of Death
Bowen, J. Man Without a Head
Brown, F. Far Cry
Castle, F. Murder in Red
Crane, F. Amethyst Spectacles
   Horror on the Ruby X
   Polkadot Murder
   Turquoise Shop
Crawford, William. Stryker
Curtiss, U. Forbidden Garden
   Hours to Kill
Derrick, L. Terror in Taos
Eberhart, M. G. Chiffon Scarf
Farnsworth, M. Companion to Evil
   Cross for Tomorrow
Faust, R. Burning Sky
Hamilton, D. Assignment: Murder
   Silencers
Head, L. Crystal Clear Case
Hillerman, T. Dance Hall of the Dead
   People of Darkness
Kelland, C. B. Death Keeps a Secret
King, Harold. Paradigm Red
Knight, C. Death of a Big Shot
Koehler, R. P. Here Come the Dead
   Road House Murders
   Sing a Song of Murder
   Some Try Murder
Lange, O. Red Snow
Lipsky, E. Lincoln McKeever
Masterson, W. Undertaker Wind
Mosler, B. Y. Horror at the Hacienda
Noyes, S. Shadowbox
O'Malley, P. Affair of the Red Mosaic
O'Rourke, F. Man Who Found His Way
Pendleton, D. Wednesday's Wrath
Reilly, H. Day She Died
Rifkin, S. Snow Rattlers
Robeson, K. Glass Man
Ronns, E. Don't Cry, Beloved
Ryan, F. C. Murder on the Ranch
Spicer, B. Act of Anger
   Kellogg Junction
Stern, R. M. Death in the Snow
   Murder in the Walls
   You Don't Need an Enemy
Stowe, J. L. Winter Stalk
Swarthout, G. Skeletons
Thomas, C. Hearse Horse Snickered
Trimble, L. Tragedy in Turquoise
Whittington, H. Ticket to Hell
Williamson, A. Secret Gold
Winston, D. Devil's Daughter
   Secrets of Cromwell Crossing
Withers, E. L. Salazar Grant

NEW ORLEANS (New Or. See also: LOUISIANA; SOUTH)

Anonymous. Mysteries of New Orleans
Atlee, P. Green Wound
Bedford-Jones, H. Mardi-Gras Mystery
Bristow, G. Gutenberg Murders
   Invisible Host
   Mardi-Gras Murders
Buntline, N. Mysteries and Miseries of New Orleans
Carr, J. D. Deadly Hall
   Ghosts' High Noon
   Papa La-Bas
Chaber, M. E. Hearse of Another Color
Claymore, T. Appointment in New Orleans
   Dead Men Don't Answer
Conaway, J. Big Easy
Conroy, Al. Murder Mission!
Coulson, J. Fear Stalks the Bayou
Coxe, G. H. One Way Back
Craddock, I. Yazoo Mystery
Crane, F. Indigo Necklace
Dale, Alan. Ned Bachman, the New Orleans Detective
Daniels, D. Dark Stage
   Ghost Song
Derrick, L. Mardi Gras Massacre
Dorsett, D. Dueling Oaks
Du Breuil, L. Mirror Image
Eberhart, M. G. Bayou Road
Ellis, J. Wexford
Fair, A. A. Owls Don't Blink
Feibleman, P. S. Charlie Boy
Fleming, Rudd. Cradled in Murder
Gibson, W. B. Mask of Mephisto
Halliday, B. Michael Shayne's Long Chance
   Murder and the Married Virgin
Hancock, H. I. Detective Johnson of New Orleans
Harris, T. Black Sunday
Hines, J. Legend of Witchwynd
Holcombe, W. H. Mystery of New Orleans
Holden, G. Deadlier Than the Male
Irish, W. Waltz into Darkness
Kains, J. Whispering Death
Knoblock, K. T. There's Been Murder Done
Lobaugh, E. K. Shadows in Succession
Locke, D. House of Two Wives
Long, A. R. Murder by Scripture
Long, L. B. Crucible of Evil
   Lemoyne Heritage
McCurtin, P. New Orleans Holocaust
MacDonald, J. D. Murder for the Bride
Morrow, S. Insiders
Ogan, G. Murder in the Wind
   To Kill a Judge
Otis, G. H. Bourbon Street
Pendleton, D. New Orleans Knockout
Perkins, K. Voodoo'd
Pinkerton, M. Woman's Revenge
Potter, J. L. Kill, Sweet Charity, Kill
Richards, C. Marble Jungle
Stone, E. M. both titles
Thayer, L. Guilt Edged
Treat, L. D As in Dead
Vanderveer, S. Death for the Lady
Ward, W. Murderer of New Orleans
Wells, Charlie. Let the Night Cry
Wills, G. At Button's

NEW YORK CITY (NYC. See also: NEW YORK; LONG ISLAND; ROCHESTER)

Aarons, E. S. 5 titles
Abbey, K. Beyond the Dark
   Run with the Hare
Abbot, A. 7 titles
Abbot, W. J. Philip Derby, Reporter
Abdullah, A. Bungalow on the Roof
Abrahams, R. D. Death in 1-2-3
Adams, F. U. both titles
Aiken, A. W. all 4 titles
Aiken, J. Voices in an Empty Room
Albrand, M. Final Encore
   Manhattan North
Alden, W. Lost Million
Alexander, David. 14 titles
Allan, D. at least 4 titles
Allan, F. both titles
Allan, H. Tragic Case of John Renold
Allan, L. Five for One
   Jungle Crime
   Man on the Twenty-Fourth Floor
   Masked Stranger
Andress, L. Caper
Andrews, Mark. Bomb Squad
   Return of Jack the Ripper
Andrews, P. Cop Story
Anonymous. Dark Masquerade
   Man from the West
   Mysterious Marksman
   Smiling Corpse
Anthony, Evelyn. Assassin
   Rendezvous
Appel, B. Brain Guy
   Dark Stain
   Life and Death of a Tough Guy
Archer, R. both titles
Ard, W. 9 titles
Arden, W. Deadly Legacy
Arleo, J. Grand Street Collector
Armstrong, C. Lay On, MacDuff!
Arnold, E. Quicksand
Arrighi, M. Death Collection
   Freak-Out
   Hatchet Man
Arthur, B. Swiftly to Evil
Asbury, H. both titles
Ashbrook, H. Murder Comes Back
   Murder of Cecily Thane
   Purple Onion Mystery
Ashe, J. D. Shroud for Grandmama
Ashe, G. Man Who Stayed Alive
   No Need to Die
Asimov, I. Murder at the ABA
Asinof, E. Name of the Game Is Murder
Austin, Anne. Black Pigeon
Austin, H. Drink the Green Water
Avallone, M. at least 21 titles
Avery, A. A. Anything for a Quiet Life
Avery, R. Murder on the Downbeat
Axelrod, G. Blackmailer
Babbin, J. Prime Time Corpse
Bacon, J. D. Medusa's Head
Bacon, P. Inward Eye
Bagby, G. 42 titles
Baker, R. Conspiracy
Baker, S. S. both titles
Ball, E. H. all 3 titles
Ball, J. Killing in the Market
Ballard, P. D. Brothers in Blood
   Death Brokers
Ballinger, B. S. 6 titles
Banks, E. Mystery of Frances Farrington
Barber, M. Britz of Headquarters
Barber, W. A. Deed Is Drawn
   Drawback to Murder
   Murder Draws a Line
   Noose Is Drawn
Barbour, A. M. That Mainwaring Affair
Bardin, J. F. all 4 titles
Barker, A. Apollo Legacy
Barlay, B. Satan Comes Across
Barnes, D. Outside the Law
Barrett, Monte. Murder Off Stage
   Wedding March Murder
Barron, J. High Cost of Murder
Barry, Jerome. 6 titles
Barry, Joe. Homicide Hotel
Barry, M. Harlem Showdown
   Night Raider
Barth, R. Rag Bag Clan
Basinsky, E. Big Steal
Baxt, G. 5 titles
Bayard, F. Death and Lilacs
Bayer, O. W. Eye for an Eye
Baylus, R. F. People Exchange
Bayne, S. Turning Sword
Bear, D. Keeping Time
Bechdolt, J. Wages of Peril
Beeckman, R. Last Woman
Bell, A. Out of Circulation
Benedict, G. Case of the Deadly Drops
Benjamin, Edla. Murder Without Makeup
Bennett, Jay. Catacombs
Bensen, D. R. Sherlock Holmes in New York
Benson, T. Death Wears a Mask
   Strictly Private
Benton, J. Marji and the Kidnap Plot
Benton, J. L. Talent for Murder
Berger, T. Who Is Teddy Villanova?
Bergman, A. Big Kiss-Off of 1944
Bergman, L. Walk Softly, Walk Deadly
Bernhard, R. S. Girls in 5J
Betcherman, M. Suspicions
Bierstadt, E. H. Satan Was a Man
Bird, B. Death in Four Colors
   Downbeat for a Dirge
Blake, W. D. My Time or Yours
Blaney, C. E. Child Slaves of New York
   Young Buffalo in New York
Blankfort, M. Widow-Makers
Blayne, S. Gay Ghastly Holiday
Blazer, J. S. Deal Me Out
Bleeck, O. Procane Chronicle
Bliss, A. Camden Ruby Murder
Bliss, T. Broadway Butterfly Murders
Blizard, M. Watch Sinister
Blochman, L. G. See You at the Morgue
Block, C. B. Art for Keeps
Block, Lawrence. 8 titles
Block, Libbie. Bedeviled
Blood, M. both titles
Bloom, M. T. 13th Man
Bly, N. Mystery of Central Park
Bogard, D. Pardon My Body
Bogart, W. Hell on Friday
   Murder Man
Bohle, E. Wife Who Died Twice
Bond, E. Evil in the House
Bonner, G. Black Eagle Mystery
Bonney, J. L. Murder Without Clues
Booth, C. B. Deceiver's Door
Booth, L. F. both titles
Borgenicht, M. Ring and Walk In
Bosse, M. J. Incident at Naha
Botein, B. Prosecutor
Bourjaily, V. Game Men Play
Boutelle, C. Artificial Fate
   Beyond the End
Bowen, R. S. both titles
Box, E. Death in the Fifth Position
Boyd, F. Flesh Peddlers
   Johnny Staccato
Brace, T. Murder Goes to the World's Fair
Bradley, M. H. Murder in Room 700
Brady, C. T. Corner in Coffee
Brand, M. Six Golden Angels
Brandel, M. Rain Before Seven
Brean, H. Darker the Night
   Matter of Fact
   Traces of Brillhart
Brenn, G. J. Voices
Breslin, J. .44
Brett, Michael. all 10 titles
Brett, Michael. Diamond Kill
Brett, Mike. both titles
Brewer, J. Get Dumm!
Bronson-Howard, G. Birds of Prey
   Black Book
   Enemy to Society
Brothers, J. Ox
Broun, D. Counterweight
   Subject of Harry Egypt
Brown, Carter. at least 9 titles
Brown, F. Murder Can Be Fun
Brown, H. Penthouse Killings
Brown, J. Night of Terror
Brown, J. E. Incident at 125th Street
Brown, Wenzell. at least 8 titles
Browner, J. Death of a Punk
Bruce, G. both titles
Brussel, J. A. Just Murder, Darling
Bryant, Matt. Cue for Murder
Bryce, L. Romance of an Alter Ego
Buck, C. N. Alias Red Ryan
   Marked Men
Buntline, N. Mysteries and Miseries of New York
Buranelli, P. Big Nick
   News Reel Murder
Burgess, G. Find the Woman
   Ladies in Boxes
Burke, J. F. all titles
Burke, R. 5 titles
Burne, G. Murder to Music
Burnham, H. Murder of Lalla Lee
Byfield, B. N. Solemn High Murder
Caldwell, A. B. No Tears Shed
   Turquoise Hazard

664 / New York City

Calin, H. J.   Rocks and Ruin
Cameron, D. C.   And So He Had to Die
   Death at Her Elbow
   Dig Another Grave
Cameron, L.   Block Busters
Campbell, S.   Below the Dead-Line
Cannon, C.   both titles
Cardiff, S.   Inner Steps
Carey, M.   Vice Squad Cop
Carpenter, C.   Deadhead
   Games Murderers Play
   Only Her Hairdresser Knew
Carpenter, H. K.   Whistling in the Dark
Carpenter, M.   Experiment Perilous
Carter, M.   Call Me Killer!
Carter, Nicholas.   Death Has Green Eyes
   Empire of Crime
   Park Avenue Murder!
Carter, Nick.   5 titles
Caspary, V.   Laura
   Murder in the Stork Club
Cassiday, B.   While Murder Waits
Cavanagh, A.   Children Are Gone
Chalmers, S.   House of Two Green Eyes
Chamberlain, G. A.   Great Van Suttart Mystery
Chambers, D.   Frightened Man
   Last Secret
   She'll Be Dead by Morning
   Too Like the Lightning
Chambers, R.   all 3 titles
Chambers, R. W.   Tracer of Last Persons
Champlin, V.   Shadowed by a Detective
Chandler, D.   Glass Totem
Chanslor, T.   both titles
Charteris, L.   Call for the Saint
   Saint in New York
   Saint on Guard
Charyn, J.   Blue Eyes
   Education of Patrick Silver
   Marilyn the Wild
   Secret Isaac
Chase, A. M.   Party at the Penthouse
   Twenty Minutes to Kill
Chase, J.   Green Jade Necklace
Chase, J. H.   Try This One for Size
   Twelve Chinks and a Woman
Chastain, T.   High Voltage
   911
   Pandora's Box
   Vital Statistics
Cheatham, L.   Marriage Pact
Chesbro, G.   Affair of Sorcerers
   City of Whispering Stone
   Shadow of a Broken Man
Chester, Ann.   Slightly Imperfect
Chevigny, P.   Criminal Mischief
Chichester, J. J.   Bigamist
   Sanderson: Master Rogue
   Silent Cracksman
Child, R. W.   Vanishing Men
Chiu, T.   Port Arthur Chicken
Christian, N.   both titles
Clancy, E. A.   Watched Out
Clark, M. H.   Stranger Is Watching
Clarke, D. H.   Murderer's Holiday
Clauson, C.   Gloyne Murder
Cochran, R. G.   Victoria Pruitt Comes to Town
Coe, T.   Don't Lie to Me
   Jade in Aries
   Kinds of Love, Kinds of Death
   Murder Among Children
Coffey, B.   Face of Fear
Cohane, M. E.   Murder One!
Cohen, O. R.   Danger in Paradise
   Don't Ever Love Me
   Love Has No Alibi
   Sound of Revelry
Cohen, S.   330 Park
Cohler, D. K.   Gamemaker
Colburn, L.   Death in a Small World
Colby, R.   Secret of the Second Door
Collins, H.   Cut Me In
Collins, J. H.   Great Taxi-Cab Mystery
Collins, Michael.   6 titles
Collison, W.   6 titles
Coltrane, J.   Talon
Conant, P.   Dr. Gatskill's Blue Shoes
Condon, F.   Dancing Doll
Condon, R.   Death of a Politician
Connable, A.   Twelve Trains to Babylon
Connell, E.   I Had to Kill Her
Cook, T. H.   both titles
Cooke, J. C.   Vera Gerard Case
Coombs, M.   Moment of Need
Corcoran, W.   Dark Waters
Corder, E.   Bite
Cores, L.   Corpse de Ballet
   Misty Curtain
   Painted for the Kill
Cornell, L.   Poison Case Number 10
Coverdale, H.   both titles
Cowan, S.   Bitter Justice
Cox, W. R.   Death Comes Early
Coxe, G. H.   Fashioned for Murder
   Fifth Key
Craig, Jonathan.   at least 10 titles
Crane, F.   Cinnamon Murder
   Pink Umbrella
Cranston, C.   Murder on Fifth Avenue

Crawford, J. R.   Philosopher's Murder Case
Creasey, J.   Murder, London-New York
   Toff in New York
Creed, W.   Death Wears a Green Hat
Crockett, L.   Gentlemen with Lugers
Crooker, H.   Crime in Washington Mews
Crosby, J.   Party of the Year
Crosby, K.   Strange Case of Eleanor Cuyler
Cross, A.   In the Last Analysis
   Poetic Justice
   Theban Mysteries
Crossen, K. F.   Case of the Curious Heel
   Case of the Phantom Fingerprints
Crozier, A. O.   Magnet
Csida, J.   Crime Is of the Essence
Cudahy, S.   Trojan Gold
Cullen, C.   Deadly Chase
Cunningham, E. V.   7 titles
Cunningham, R.   Ceremony in the Lincoln Tunnel
Currie, B.   Officer 666
Curtiss, P. E.   Wanted: A Fool
Da Cruz, D.   Fire Kill
Daley, J. A.   Spicy Lady
Daley, R.   To Kill a Cop
Dallas, R.   Master Hand
Dalton, P.   90 Gramercy Park
Daly, C. J.   8 titles
Daly, E.   9 titles
Dana, F.   Murder at the New York World's Fair
Dana, M.   Master Mind
   Mystery of the Third Parrot
   Within the Law
Dane, J. Y.   Christmas Tree Murders
   Grasp at Straws
   Murder Cum Laude
Daniels, C. L.   Bronze Buddha
Daniels, D.   Summer House
   Veil of Treachery
Daniels, N.   Captive
   Deadly Game
   Mausoleum Key
Darby, R.   Murder with Orange Blossoms
Davies, F.   Cross of Gold Affair
Davies, G.   Portrait of Susan
Davis, D. S.   8 titles
Davis, E.   There Was an Old Woman
Davis, F. C.   11 titles
Davis, Mildred.   Room Upstairs
   Sound of Insects
Day, L.   both titles
Dean, A.   Snipe Hunt
Dean, G.   Case of Marie Corwin
   Case of the Fifth Key
Dean, R. G.   Murder of Convenience
   Murder on Margin
   On Ice
   Sutton Place Murders
Dean, S.   all 9 titles
De Andrea, W. L.   Killed in the Ratings
   Lunatic Fringe
Deane, J.   Great Pretender
Dejeans, E.   Moreton Mystery
   Romance of a Million Dollars
Dekker, J.   Manhunt in Manhattan
De Laguna, F.   Arrow Points to Nowhere
Delancey, R.   Murder Below Wall Street
De Lillo, D.   Running Dog
Dell, A.   Johnny on the Spot
Demarest, A.   Murder on Every Floor
Demarest, P. G.   House on Washington Place
De Mexico, N. R.   Madman on a Drum
De Mille, N.   at least 5 titles
De Mirjian, A.   Not a Clue
Denbow, W.   Chandler
De Pre, J.   Aquarius, My Evil Third Woman
Derrick, L.   Countdown to Terror
   Hijacking Manhattan
De Steiguer, W.   Jewels for a Shroud
Deutsch, A. V.   Starett
De Villiers, G.   Operation New York
Dexter, L.   Case of the Brooklyn Mobsters
Diamond, F.   Murder in Five Columns
   Murder Rides a Rocket
   Widow Maker
Dickenson, F.   Kill 'Em with Kindness
Dines, M.   Abrams and Jones, Homicide
Dixon, S.   Too Late
Doe, J.   Eye-Witness
Doherty, E. J.   Broadway Murders
Doliner, R.   On the Edge
Dolph, J.   all 5 titles
Dooley, H. H.   Last Rights
Dougall, B.   I Don't Scare Easy
Drake, D.   all 3 titles
Drennen, R.   Murder Beat
Droge, E. F.   Honor Legion
   In the Highest Tradition
Du Bois, T.   Death Tears a Comic Strip
   High Tension
   Late Bride
Du Bois, W.   Case of the Deadly Diaries
Dudowicz, E.   Thirty-Second Floor
Duff, B.   Central Park Murder
Eastman, E.   Mouse with Red Eyes
Eastman, R. O.   Mysteries of Blair House

Eberhard, F. G.   Microbe Murders
   13th Murder
Eberhardt, W. F.   both titles
Eberhart, M. G.   6 titles
Edgar, K.   I Hate You to Death
Edwards, Stafford.   Money Order Murder
Egerton, J. K.   Soul Laid Bare
Ehrlich, M.   Spin the Glass Web
Eichler, A.   5 titles
Einstein, C.   Bloody Spur
   Naked City
Eisinger, J.   Walls Came Tumbling Down
Elbert, J.   Very Cagey Lady
Elias, A. J.   Bowman Test
Elias, D.   Gory Details
Ellin, S.   Dreadful Summit
   Eighth Circle
   Mirror, Mirror on the Wall
Ellington, R.   Exit for a Dame
   Just Killing Time
   Shoot the Works
Elliott, W. J.   Dope Devils
Ellson, H.   Duke
   I'll Fix You
   Tomboy
Ely, D.   Seconds
Endicott, J. S.   Crime Inc.
Endicott, S.   Mayor Harding of New York
Enefer, D.   Dark Kiss
   Deadly Quiet
   Long Chance
England, G. A.   Greater Crime
English, A.   Edge of Violence
English, R.   Sugarplum Staircase
Enright, R. E.   both titles
Erickson, N. W.   Splinters of Fear
Ericson, W.   Fallen Angel
Ernst, P.   Bronze Mermaid
   Hangman's Hat
Erskine, F.   Naked Murder
Ethan, J. B.   all 3 titles
Fairlie, G.   No Sleep for Macall
Fairman, P. W.   To Catch a Crooked Girl
Falk, L.   Golden Circle
Falkner, L.   Murder Off Broadway
Falstein, L.   both titles
Farrington, F.   Strangers in 7A
Fast, J.   Model for Murder
   Street of Fear
   Walk in Shadow
Fauley, W. F.   Queenie
Faur, M. P.   Friendly Place to Die
Fearing, K.   Big Clock
   Generous Heart
   Loneliest Girl in the World
Fenisong, R.   16 titles
Fenwick, E. P.   Murder in Haste
Ferguson, W. B. M.   Escape to Eternity
   Shayne Case
Ferm, B.   Edge of Beauty
Ferris, W.   Across 110th
Fetta, E. L.   Murder in Style
   Murder on the Face of It
Fiaschetti, M.   You Gotta Be Rough
Fickling, G. G.   Blood and Honey
Field, T.   Killer's Carnival
Fielding, H.   Equal Partners
   Straight Out
Fields, A.   V-J Day
Findley, F.   Man in the Middle
   Murder Makes Me Mad
   My Old Man's Badge
   Waterfront
Finley, G.   Death Strikes Out
Finley, S.   Case of the Black Sheep
Firth, N. W.   Manhattan Bombshell
Fischer, B.   7 titles
Fish, R. L.   Trials of O'Brien
Fisher, D. E.   Crisis
Fisher, Rudolph.   Conjure Man Dies
Fisher, S.   Winter Kill
Fitzpatrick, J.   Dreamwalker
Fitzsimmons, C.   Girl in the Cage
   Moving Finger
   Whispering Widow
Fleetwood, H.   Order of Death
Fleming, E.   Murder Takes a Honeymoon
Flora, F.   Park Avenue Tramp
Flynn, W. J.   Barrel Mystery
Foley, P.   Yellow Circle
Foley, R.   13 titles
Footner, H.   23 titles
Ford, B.   Show Business
Forman, H. J.   both titles
Forrest, D.   Great Dinosaur Robbery
Forrester, I. L.   Dangerous Inheritance
Foster, M.   Crooked
   Whistling Man
Foster, R.   Girl from Easy Street
Foster, Robert Frederick.   Cab No. 44
Fowler, K.   All the Skeletons in All the Closets
Fox, D.   Ethel Opens the Door
   Handwriting on the Wall
   Man Who Convicted Himself
Frank, W.   Chalk Face
Franklin, Edgar.   In and Out
Franklin, Eugene.   all 3 titles
Franklin, S.   Chickens in the Airshaft
Frazer, A.   Fall of Marty Moon

Frazer, R. C. Mark Kilby Solves a Murder
    Mark Kilby Stands Alone
    Mark Kilby Takes a Risk
Fredericks, A. Film of Fear
    Little Fortune
Freeman, L. Case on Cloud Nine
    Psychiatrist Says Murder
Friedman, H. Tunnel
Friedman, R. Insurrection of Hippolytus Brandenburg
Frost, B. Corpse Died Twice
    Corpse Said No
    Unwelcome Corpse
Fuller, R. Eve of Judgment
    Ordeal
Fuller, S. Dark Page
Fulton, C. Vidocq of New York
Futrelle, J. Diamond Master
    Simple Case of Susan
Futrelle, M. Lieutenant What's-His-Name
Gage, N. Bones of Contention
Gallagher, G. I Found Him Dead
Gallagher, R. Doomsday Committee
    One-Armed Murderer
    Stewardess Strangler
Gallant, G. S. Living Image
Gallico, P. Hand of Mary Constable
Galway, R. C. Assignment New York
Gant, M. Queen Street
Gard, O. Seventh Chasm
Gardiner, D. What Crime Is It?
Garrity. Dragon Hunt
Gartland, H. House of Cards
Gatenby, R. Evil Is As Evil Does
Gates, H. L. Scarlet Fan
Gattzden, M. O.D. at Sweet Claude's
Gayle, N. Death in the Glass
Geller, M. Corpse for a Candidate
    Disco Deathbeat
    Mayhem on the Coney Beat
George, D. R. Death Meets the Deadline
George, T. both titles
Gerrity, D. J. Numbers Man
    Plastic Man
Gibbs, A. Murder Between Drinks
Gibson, W. Mother Goose
    Quarter of Eight
    Voodoo Death
Giles, R. Shamus
Gillespie, R. Crossword Mystery
Gillmore, R. Alster Case
    Ebony Bed Murder
Glick, C. Laughing Buddha
Gluck, S. 8 titles
Godey, J. 6 titles
Gold, D. Park
Goldman, W. Marathon Man
Goldsmith, G. Murder on His Mind
Goldstein, A. D. Person Shouldn't Die Like That
Goldthwaite, E. K. Marble Forest
Gollomb, J. Curtain of Storm
    Portrait Invisible
    Subtle Trail
Goodis, D. Nightfall
Goodman, G. Killing in the Market
Goodrich, D. L. Paint Me a Million
Gordon, H. Dead on Arrival
Gordon, I. Burden of Guilt
Gould, H. One Dead Debutante
Grace, A. Wharf Sinister
Grafton, S. Most Dangerous Game
Graham, J. A. Aldeburg Cezanne
    Something in the Air
Grandower, E. Rivergate House
Grant, M. 24 titles
Grayson, Rupert. Gun Cotton—Adventure Nine
Green, A. K. 9 titles
Green, W. M. See How They Run
Greenan, R. H. Nightmare
Greenberg, D. Love Kills
Gregory, F. L. Cipher of Death
Gresham, E. Pawn in Jeopardy
Grew, W. Doubles in Death
Grey, H. Portrait of a Mobster
Greig, M. Fire in His Hand
Griff. Brooklyn Moll Shoots Bedmate
    Demon Barber of Broadway
    Vice Queens on Broadway
Griswold, G. Checkmate by the Colonel
Gropper, M. H. Is No One Innocent?
Grove, M. You'll Die Tonight
Grove, W. Man Who Said No
Gruber, F. 6 titles
Gunter, A. C. Dr. Burton's Success
Haggard, P. all 4 titles
Hall, G. Witch's Suckling
Hall, G. H. End Is Known
Hallahan, W. H. Catch Me, Kill Me
    Dead of Winter
    Search for Joseph Tully
Halliday, B. Armed...Dangerous...
    She Woke to Darkness
Halliday, F. Chocolate Mousse Murders
Halpern, J. Jade Unicorn
Hamill, D. Stomping Ground
Hamill, E. T. Child Killer
    Sadist
    Slasher
Hamill, P. Deadly Piece
Hammett, D. Thin Man

Hammock, C. S. Why Murder the Judge?
Handley, A. Kiss Your Elbow
Hannon, E. Doors
Harben, W. N. Caruthers Affair
Hardwick, R. Hawk
Harrington, J. all 3 titles
Harris, C. A. Con Man
Harris, Colver. Hide and Go Seek
Harris, L. M. Protector
Harrison, Bruce. A-100
Harrison, C. both titles
Harvey, M. Clue of the Clock
    Dragon of Lung Wang
    House of Seclusion
    Mystery of the Hidden Room
Hastings, George. Philip Henson M.D.
Hastings, W. S. Man in the Brown Derby
Hawkes, R. Kill for It
    NARC
Hawthorne, J. 5 titles
Hazard, F. Hex Murder
Healy, E. P. both titles
Heard, H. F. Murder by Reflection
Hebach, J. Murder of Bishop Conrad
Heberden, M. V. 10 titles
Hecht, B. Count Bruga
    Florentine Dagger
    1001 Afternoons in New York
Heffernan, W. Broderick
Heller, L. Murder in Makeup
Henriquez, R. A. Four Way Proof
Hershman, M. Guilty Witness
Hervey, M. Brooklyn Angel
Herzog, D. Undercover Woman
Higginson, H. W. Murder by the Arch
Highsmith, P. Blunderer
    Dog's Ransom
Himes, C. all 10 titles
Hirschberg, C. Florentine Finish
Hitchcock, A. Rope
Hitchens, D. Baxter Letters
Hjortsberg, W. Falling Angel
Hoch, E. D. Shattered Raven
Hochstein, P. Fatal Fetish
Hodgkin, M. R. Dead Indeed
Hoffecker, D. M. Wall Street Murders
Hogarth, E. Goose Is Cooked
Holbrook, M. Suitable for Framing
Holden, R. P. Penthouse Murders
Holland, I. Marchington Inheritance
    Moncrieff
Honig, D. Seventh Style
Horan, J. D. New Vigilantes
Hornblow, A. Argyle Case
    Profligate
Horvitz, L. Compton Effect
Howard, H. at least 19 titles
Howe, J. M. Accessory for Murder
Hudiberg, E. Killer's Game
Hudson, W. C. J. P. Dunbar
    Jack Gordon, Knight Errant, Gotham 1883
    Man with a Thumb
Hughes, D. B. 5 titles
Hughes, R. Ladies' Man
Hull, H. Close Her Pale Blue Eyes
Hunter, E. Big Fix
    Matter of Conviction
Hurley, G. Have You Seen This Man?
Hurwood, B. J. Rip-Off!
Hutton, W. R. Broadway Racket
Hynd, N. Sandler Inquiry
Iams, J. Death Draws the Line
    Into Thin Air
Iannuzzi, J. N. Part 35
Irish, W. Deadline at Dawn
    Phantom Lady
Irwin, T. D. Collusion
Irwin, W. House of Mystery
    Red Button
Jacks, J. Murder on the Wild Side
Jackson, B. Operation Burning Candle
Jackson, Felix. So Help Me God
Jackson, G. Court of Shadows
Jaediker, K. Tall, Dark and Dead
Jaffe, M. Death Goes to a Party
Jaffe, R. Other Anne Fletcher
Jahn, M. Killer on the Heights
    Quark Maneuver
James, Robert. Death Wears Pink Shoes
Janifer, L. M. Final Fear
    You Can't Escape
Jarvis, F. G. Murder at the Met
Jason, S. 24 titles
Jeffers, H. P. Adventure of the Stalwart Companions
Jenkins, W. Man Who Feared
Jenks, G. C. Stop Thief!
Jerome, O. F. Corpse Awaits
    Murder As Usual
Jessup, H. W. Van Beck Will
Jessup, R. Lowdown
Joey. Hit #29
Johns, F. Square Emerald
Johns, V. P. Murder by the Day
    Servant's Problem
Johnson, K. Blue Sunshine
Johnson, O. Max Fargus
    Sixty-First Second
Johnson, Sandy. CUPPI

Johnston, V. Face in the Shadows
    People on the Hill
    Stone Maiden
Johnston, W. 5 titles
Johnston, W. Barney
    Get Smart!
    Marriage Cage
Jones, C. R. King Murder
    Torch Murder
Jones, I. Clue of the Hungry Corpse
Jordan, E. After the Verdict
    Night Club Mystery
Judson, W. Alice and Me
Kahn, S. New York, N.Y.
Kamarck, L. Dinosaur
    Zinsser Implant
Kane, F. 20 titles
Kane, H. 33 titles
Kantor, Hal. Blown Away
Kantor, M. Signal Thirty-Two
Kaplan, A. Killing for Charity
Karney, J. at least 7 titles
Kastle, H. Death Squad
Kastle, H. D. Countdown to Murder
    Hot Prowl
Kauffman, R. W. Share and Share Alike
    Spider's Web
Kaufman, W. I Hate Blondes
Kaye, M. 5 titles
Keene, D. Bye, Baby Bunting
    Mrs. Homicide
    Too Hot to Hold
Keith, C. Diamond-Studded Typewriter
Kelland, C. B. Great Mail Robbery
    Stolen Goods
    Where There's Smoke
Keller, H. A. Death Sits In
Kendrick, B. 10 titles
Kennedy, M. It Began in New York
Kenrick, T. Chicago Girl
    Nighttime Guy
Kent, E. House Opposite
Keystone, O. Arsenic for the Teacher
Kidde, J. Prophetess
Kieran, J. Come Murder Me
King, F. Down and Dirty
    Night Vision
King, I. She's a Cop, Ain't She?
King, O. B. Five Million in Cash
King, R. Crime of Violence
    Holiday Homicide
    Murder by the Clock
Kingsley, S. Detective Story
Kirkwood, J. P.S. Your Cat Is Dead
Klainer, J. A. Judas Gene
Klein, N. No! No! the Woman!
Klinger, H. Essence of Murder
    Murder Off Broadway
    Wanton for Murder
Knight, Adam. I'll Kill You Next!
    Murder for Madame
    Stone Cold Blonde
    Triple Slay
Knight, K. M. Exit a Star
Koenig, L. Neighbor
Kootz, both titles
Kramer, K. Kiss Me Quick
Krasney, S. A. Death Cries in the Street
    Design for Dying
    Homicide Call
    Homicide West
Krone, C. Blood Wrath
Krumgold, J. Thanks to Murder
Kurnitz, H. Invasion of Privacy
Kuttner, P. Man Who Lost Everything
Kwitney, J. Shakedown
Kyle, R. Blackmail, Inc.
    Model for Murder
    Some Like It Cool
Lacy, E. at least 11 titles
Laflin, J. Spy Who Loved America
Lait, J. Beast of the City
    Gangster Girl
Lake, P. A. Leffert's Disease
Lamb, A. Greenhouse
Landon, H. 9 titles
Lanham, E. Monkey on a Chain
    No Hiding Place
    Politics Is Murder
    Slug It Slay
Lantry, M. Assignment New York
Lariar, L. Death Is Confidential
    Friday for Death
    Girl with the Frightened Eyes
    Man with the Lumpy Nose
Larkin, R. T. Godmother
Larosa, L. J. Random Factor
Lathen, E. 6 titles
Lawrence, J. I. Tower of Terror
Lawrence, Michael. Naked and Alone
Lawrence, S. Daughters of Music
Lawson, W. B. Jesse James at Coney Island
    Jesse James in New York
Lebhar, B. Black Eye Snapshot
Le Breton, A. Rififi in New York
Lee, Babs. Measured for Murder
    Model Is Murdered
Lee, G. R. G-String Murders
Lee, Linda. One by One

N

Lee, Norma. Beautiful Gunner
    Broadway Jungle
    Lover—Say It with Mink!
Lees, H. Dark Device
Leffingwell, A. Nine Against New York
Leinster, M. Murder Will Out
Leonard, F. Box 100
Leonard, G. Beyond Control
Leverage, H. Whispering Wires
Levine, Lawrence. New York One
Levinrew, W. Murder from the Grave
Levon, F. Much Ado About Murder
Lewis, Arthur Henry. Apaches of New York
    Boss, and How He Came to Rule New York
    Confessions of a Detective
Lewis, I. both titles
Lieberman, H. City of the Dead
Lipsky, E. Kiss of Death
    Murder One
Lipsyte, M. Hot Type
Little, C. Black Coat
    Black Curl
    Black House
    Black Shrouds
Livingston, A. Light Fingered Ladies
Lloyd, N. Robberies Co., Ltd.
Lobell, N. D. Shadow and the Blot
Lockridge, F. 30 titles
Lockridge, R. 13 titles
Logan, C. One of These Seven
Long, Manning. Dull Thud
    False Alarm
    Savage Breast
Longbaugh, H. No Way to Treat a Lady
Longo, L. Family on Vendetta Street
Lord, G. Murder's Little Helper
Loring, A. Mark of Satan
Luehrmann, A. Curious Case of Marie Dupont
    Other Brown
Lutz, J. Jericho Man
Lynch, L. Danger Line
    Lost Witness
Lynds, D. Charlie Chan Returns
Lynn, J. Professor
Lyon, W. Criminal Court
Lyons, D. Flower of Evil
McBain, E. Guns
McCloy, H. 8 titles
McCretton, M. Beauty Can Kill
McCully, W. Death Rides Tandem
McCurtin, P. 6 titles
MacDonald, J. D. Nightmare in Pink
MacDonald, P. Dark Wheel
McDougald, R. Blushing Monkey
    Deaths of Lora Karen
    Whistling Legs
McDowell, M. Gilded Needles
McFarlane, A. E. Behind the Bolted Door?
McGerr, P. Death in a Million Living Rooms
    Follow, As the Night
    Seven Deadly Sisters
McGirr, E. Murderous Journey
McGivern, W. P. 5 titles
MacGrath, H. Drums of Jeopardy
    Green Stone
    World Outside
McGurk, S. Grand Central Murders
MacHarg, W. Affairs of O'Malley
MacInnes, H. Neither Five Nor Three
McIntyre, J. T. In the Dead of Night
    Museum Murder
MacIsaac, F. Don't Let Him Burn!
    Hole in the Wall
    Vanishing Professor
McKenzie, D. J. Wall Street Wonder
McLaughlin, R. Nothing to Report
    Pending Investigation
McMorrow, T. both titles
McMullen, M. But Nellie Was So Nice
    Doom Campaign
    Prudence Be Damned
    Strangle Hold
McRoyd, A. Double Shadow Murders
    Golden Goose Murders
MacVeigh, S. Grand Central Murder
Maas, P. Made in America
Macao, M. New York Necromancy
Madderom, G. Jewels That Got Away
Malcolm-Smith, G. Square Peg
Malina, P. Murder over Broadway
Maling, A. Koberg Link
Malley, L. Stool Pigeon
Mallory, D. Target Manhattan
Mallory, R. Harlem Hit
Mancini, A. Minnie Santangelo and the Evil Eye
    Minnie Santangelo's Mortal Sin
Mandeville, C. Last Days of New York
Manly, A. S. Secrets of a Dark Plot in New York Society
Manly, M. Old Specie, the Treasury Detective
Mann, P. Dog Day Afternoon
Manners, D. X. Dead to the World
Manson, W. Duke
Marasco, R. Burnt Offerings
Marcus, A. A. Make Way for Murder

Marfield, D. Man with a Paper Skull
    Mystery of King Cobra
    Mystery of the East Wind
    Sword in the Pool
Mario, Q. Murder in the Opera House
    Murder Meets Mephisto
Markson, D. Epitaph for a Dead Beat
    Epitaph for a Tramp
Marlowe, D. J. 6 titles
Marlowe, S. Catch the Brass Ring
    Model for Murder
    Turn Left for Murder
Marsten, R. Big Man
    Runaway Black
Martin, I. K. Regan and the Manhattan File
Martin, W. Anthony Trent, Master Criminal
    Recluse of Fifth Avenue
    Triumphant Prodigal
Mason, Clifford. When Love Was Not Enough
Massey, M. Through the Lens
Masur, H. Q. all 12 titles
Mathewson, Joseph. Alicia's Trump
Matthews, B. Last Meeting
Matthews, Clyde. Ides of March Conspiracy
Maurice, A. B. Riddle of the Rovers
Mearson, L. all 3 titles
Merrick, Mark. Great Travers Case
Merrick, Mollie. Upper Case
Merritt, A. Seven Footprints to Satan
Merwin, S., Jr. Death in the Sunday Supplement
    Matter of Policy
    Message from a Corpse
    Murder in Miniatures
Messmann, J. Jogger's Moon
    Promise for Death
    Revenger
    Stiletto Signature
Meyers, M. Kiss and Kill
Meyers, Manny. Last Mystery of Edgar Allan Poe
Michaels, A. Diamonds
Michel, M. Psychiatric Murders
    Sweet Murder
    X-Ray Murders
Miller, A. Colfax Book-Plate
Miller, B. E. Set-Up
Miller, F. C. Savage Street
Miller, V. Fernanda
Miller, V. B. all 9 titles
Mills, James. One Just Man
    Panic in Needle Park
    Prosecutor
    Seventh Power
Minick, M. Kung Fu Avengers
Minton, P. Dark of Memory
Mitchell, D. L. In Times Square
Mitchell, L. Parachute Murder
Mitchell, W. Goldfish Murders
Monsky, M. Looking Out for #1
Montague, J. Whose Millions?
Moore, H. F. S. Death at 7:10
Moore, Robin. Set-Up
Morette, E. Sturgis Wager
Morgan, Dean. Murder on Coney Island
Morgan, W. L. Ice Man
Morley, C. Haunted Bookshop
Moroso, J. A. People Against Nancy Preston
Morrow, S. Dancing with a Tiger
Morton, G. Perrin Murder Case
Morton, W. Murderer
    Mystery of the Human Bookcase
Mulkeen, T. P. both titles
Mullen, C. Thereby Hangs a Corpse
Mumford, E. W. Out of the Ashes
Murphy, W. B. 7 titles
Napier, B. Dear Hungarian Friend
Neely, R. Death to My Beloved
    Madness of the Heart
    Walter Syndrome
    While Love Lay Sleeping
Newell, A. Who Killed Cavelotti?
Newman, G. F. Guvnor
Niall, M. Run Like a Thief
Nichols, F. Angel Face
    Loner
Nickolay, M. Brother and Sister
Nicolai, C. Killer Is Loose
Nicolet, C. C. Death of a Bridge Expert
Nile, D. Evil Men Do
Nisot, E. Sleepless Men
Noel, S. Empire of Evil
Norden, C. Ultimate Solution
Novak, R. all 3 titles
Nyland, G. Mr. South Burned His Mouth
Oakroyd, S. Maybe He's Dead
Odlum, J. Morgue Is Always Open
O'Donnell, L. 11 titles
O'Farrell, W. 6 titles
O'Hanlon, J. D. Murder at Coney Island
O'Higgins, H. J. Adventures of Detective Barney
    Detective Duff Unravels It
Old Sleuth. at least 6 titles
Olden, M. Gossip
    Informant
    Poe Must Die

Olesker, H. all 3 titles
Oppenheim, E. P. Other Romilly
Orde, L. Night They Stole Manhattan
Ormond, F. Three Keys
Osborne, W. H. all 5 titles
Osbourne, L. Peril
Ostrander, I. 7 titles
Ostrander, K. Image Seller
Ottolengui, R. Artist in Crime
    Crime of the Century
    Final Proof
Ottum, B. both titles
Oursler, W. Departure Delayed
    Folio on Florence White
    Trial of Vincent Doon
Packard, F. 11 titles
Packer, V. Young and Violent
Padgett, L. Day He Died
Page, M. Fast Company
    Shadowy Third
Page, S. Legend in Blue Steel
Page, S. H. Fool's Gold
    Sinister Cargo
    Tragic Curtain
Pahlow, G. Somebody Shot the Captain
Palmer, P. Murder from Heaven
Palmer, S. 8 titles
Panbourne, O. Varanoff Tradition
Paradise, V. Girl Died Laughing
Paris, M. Mystery
Parke, F. G. First Night Murder
Parker, M. Along Came a Spider
Pastor, T. Night Scenes in New York
Patrick, D. Danger Next Door
    Death for Dear Clara
Patrick, V. Pope of Greenwich Village
Patterson, I. Standish Gaunt Case
Paul, B. Fourth Wall
Pearl, J. Lepke
    Victims
Peckham, R. Murder in Strange Houses
Peebles, N. N. both titles
Pendleton, D. Command Strike
    Nightmare in New York
    Satan's Sabbath
Pentecost, H. 31 titles
Percy, C. Death Is Skin Deep
Perrin, F. V. Don
Perry, W. Home in the Dark
    Kremlin Watcher
    Murder at the U.N.
Peters, E. both titles
Philips, J. 13 titles
Phillips, C. B. Someone Killed Her Husband
Phillips, D. G. Master Rogue
Phillips, J. A. Case of the Shivering Chorus Girls
Phillips, M. Impossibles
Phillips, Steven. Resisting Arrest
Picano, F. Lure
Pierce, N. Messenger from Munich
Pike, R. L. Mute Witness
    Police Blotter
    Quarry
Piper, E. Innocent
    Motive
    Naked Murderer
    Nanny
Pitman, W. D. Quincunx Case
Pitts, D. This City Is Ours
Platt, K. Dead As They Come
Platt, R. Swaying Corpse
Poate, E. M. Behind Locked Doors
    Doctor Bentiron: Detective
Popkin, Z. Death of Innocence
    Death Wears a White Gardenia
    No Crime for a Lady
    Time Off for Murder
Porcelain, S. E. Purple Pony Murders
Posner, R. Mafia Man
    Seven-Ups
Post, M. D. Corrector of Destinies
Potts, J. 6 titles
Poynter, B. Murder on 47th Street
    Murillo Mystery
Procter, A. Murder in Manhattan
Prosper, J. Gold-Killer
Purtell, J. Tiffany Caper
Quarry, N. 6 titles
Queen, E. 26 titles
Quentin, P. 7 titles
Quinn, J. all 3 titles
Raison, M. M. Phantom of Forty-Second Street
Ralston, G. A. Deadly, Deadly Art
Ramsay, D. Descent into the Dark
    Little Murder Music
Randall, B. Fan
Randall, W. R. Crystal Eye
Ransome, S. Death Checks In
Rathbone, C. K. both titles
Rathbone, S. Miss Pauline of New York
Rauch, C. Spy on Riverside Drive
Rawlings, F. Lisping Man
Rawls, P. Streets of Blood
Rawson, C. Death from a Top Hat
    Footprints on the Ceiling
    Great Merlini

Settings Index

New York City

Reach, J. Late Last Night
    Danger—Girls Working!
Reed, W. Motive for Murder
    Time to Kill
Reeve, A. B. 17 titles
Reeves, Robert. Dead and Done For
Reilly, H. 15 titles
Reiss, B. Summer Fires
Reno, M. R. Final Proof
Rice, C. Having Wonderful Crime
    Sunday Pigeon Murders
Richards, A. To Market, to Market
Richards, C. Death of an Angel
Riddell, G. Murder with Music
Riddell, J. John Riddell Murder Case
Ridgway, J. Adam's Fall
Riefe, A. Conspirators
    Lady Killers
Rieman, T. Vamp Till Ready
Riess, C. High Stakes
Rifkin, S. Ladyfingers
    McQuaid in August
Rigsby, H. Clash of Shadows
Robbins, T. Master of Murder
Roberts, W. A. Mind Reader
    Top-Floor Killer
Robertson, Alexander. Irish Monte Cristo's Search
    Old Specie, the Treasury Detective
Robeson, K. 32 titles
Robins, E. Secret That Was Kept
Robinson, E. H. Scarred Hand
Roche, A. S. at least 13 titles
Rockwood, H. Harry Sharpe, the New York Detective
    Neil Nelson, the Veteran Detective
Roeburt, J. 8 titles
Rogers, J. T. Once in a Red Moon
Rohde, R. H. Hunted Down
Rohde, W. L. Heel
Rohmer, S. 5 titles
Ronald, J. She Got What She Asked For
Ronns, E. Art Studio Murders
    Death in a Lighthouse
Roos, K. 13 titles
Root, P. Devil on the Stairs
Roote, M. Badge 373
Rosen, V. Gun in His Hand
Rosenbaum, R. Murder at Elaine's
Rosenberg, P. Contact on Cherry Street
    Point Blank
Rosenberger, J. Blueprint Invisibility
    Manhattan Wipeout
    Operation Overkill
Ross, Albert. If I Knew What I Was Doing
Ross, B. Drury Lane's Last Case
    Tragedy of X
    Tragedy of Y
Ross, Donald. Murder C.O.D.
Ross, I. T. all 5 titles
Rossi, B. Head Crusher
    Triggerman
Rosten, L. Silky!
Roth, H. Button, Button
    Crimson in the Purple
    Mask of Glass
    Sleeper
Rowe, A. Deadly Intent
    Too Much Poison
Rowland, H. C. Return of Frank Clamart
Rutledge, N. Cry Murder
    Emily Will Know
Sachs, E. N. Octangle
Sadlier, A. T. Phileas Fox, Attorney
Sagola, M. J. both titles
St. Dennis, M. both titles
Saks, E. E. Innocents on Broadway
Salter, M. Cat's-Paw
Sanborn, B. X. Doom-Maker
Sanders, D. To Catch a Thief
Sanders, Lawrence. Anderson Tapes
    First Deadly Sin
    Second Deadly Sin
    Tenth Commandment
Sandroff, R. Fighting Back
Sann, P. Dead Heat
Santiago, V. J. Eye for an Eye
Sapir, R. Bressio
    Mugger Blood
Sarto, B. Bowery Birdie
    Manhattan Terrors
Saunders, C. C. Design for Treachery
Saunders, L. Columnist Murder
Savage, R. H. Checked Through, Missing Trunk No. 17580
Scaduto, A. Terrible Time to Die
Scarborough, C. Stryker
Scarpetta, F. Times Square Connection
Scherf, M. 5 titles
Schisgall, O. Devil's Daughter
Schley, S. M. Who'd Shoot a Genius?
Schoenfeld, H. Let Them Eat Bullets
Scott, J. Treasure for Treasure
Scott, L. 5 titles
Scott, Mansfield. Black Circle
Scott, R. T. M. 8 titles
Scott-Heron, G. Vulture
Seabrooke, J. P. Woman in 919
Sellars, E. K. Murder a la Mode
Selman, R. Once Upon a Crime

Shane, S. Lady in a Million
    Lady in Lilac
Shannon, J. Devil's Passkey
Sharkey, J. Both titles
Sharp, W. Murder of the Honest Broker
Shaw, J. T. Blood on the Curb
Shay, F. Charming Murder
Sheehan, P. P. House with a Bad Name
Sheldon, S. Naked Face
Shenkin, E. Brownstone Gothic
Sher, J. Cold Companion
Sheridan, J. Chinese Chop
Sherry, E. Backfire
    Girl Missing
    No Questions Asked
    Strictly a Loser
Short, C. Big Cat
Siddall, R. B. Travers
Sideman, A. Murder on Both Sides
Siegel, J. Ruby
Silberstang, E. Losers, Weepers
Siller, V. It Had to Be You
    Paul's Apartment
    Watchers
Simenon, G. Maigret in New York's Underworld
Simon, L. Irving Solution
Simon, R. A. Weekend Mystery
Slesar, H. Enter Murderers
    Grey Flannel Shroud
    Thing at the Door
Smith, Dennis. Glitter and Ash
Smith, F. Broadcast Murders
Smith, J. C. S. Jacoby's First Case
Smith, K. N. Watcher
Smith, L. D. Girl Hunt
Smith, Martin. Canto for a Gypsy
Smith, W. K. Bowery Murder
Smith, Y. Banana Murders
Smithies, R. H. R. Academic Question
Snell, D. Lights, Camera...Murder
Snow, K. Night Waking
Snow, W. Golden Nightmare
Somerville, C. Artist in Crime
Somerville, I. Scattered Death
Spatz, H. D. Death on the Nose
Spewack, S. Skyscraper Murder
Spillane, M. 17 titles
Sproul, K. Birthday Murder
Squerent, W. Your Golden Jugular
Stade, G. Confessions of a Lady Killer
Stagg, C. H. Silver Sandals
    Thornley Colton, Blind Detective
Stanley, F. G. Murder Leaves a Ring
Stanley, O. Legal Fire
Stark, M. Run for Your Life!
Stark, R. Black Ice Score
    Hunter
Stark, S. Too Many Sinners
Sted, R. They All Bleed Red
Steel, K. 5 titles
Steele, C. Invisible Empire
    March of the Flame Marauders
    Masked Invasion
Steele, J. House of Iron Men
Stein, A. M. Lock and Key
    Pistols for Two
Stephens, R. N. Mystery of Murray Davenport
Sterling, S. 17 titles
Sterling, T. House Without a Door
Stevens, S. Go Down Dead
    Rat Pack
Stevenson, B. E. 5 titles
Stewart, E. Heads
Stewart, F. M. Mephisto Waltz
Stewart, R. Apparition
    Possession of Joel Delaney
    Sixth Sense
Stinson, H. Fingerprints
Stockbridge, G. City Destroyer
    City of Flaming Shadows
    Death and the Spider
    Wings of the Black Death
Stockwell, G. Candy Killings
    Embarrassed Murderer
Stokes, M. L. Case of the President's Heads
    Lady Lost Her Head
Stone, Hampton. 17 titles
Stout, R. 44 titles
Stovall, W. Minus Pool
Stowell, W. A. Marston Murder Case
    Mystery of the Singing Walls
Strange, J. S. 10 titles
Streiber, W. Wolfen
Stringer, A. at least 7 titles
Strong, Harrington. Brand of Silence
Stuart, Anthony. Force Play
Stuart, W. L. Dead Lie Still
Sudak, E. Icepick in Ollie Birk
Sugar, A. Kill City
Taylor, Matt. Famous McGarry Stories
Teagle, M. both titles
Telfair, R. Corpse That Talked
Templeton, C. Kidnapping of the President
Terrall, R. They Deal in Death
Thatcher, J. Nightgleams
Thayer, L. 12 titles
Thayer, T. Illustrious Corpse
Thomas, A. E. Double Cross

Thomas, E. Death Rides the Dragon
    Yellow Magic
Thomas, Jim. Cross Purposes
Thompson, J. Child of Rage
Thompson, V. Green Ray
Thurman, S. "Mad Dog" Coll
Tidyman, E. Shaft
    Shaft Among the Jews
Toepfer, R. G. Endplay
Topor, T. Bloodstar
Torbett, D. Kick-In
    On Trial
Torgerson, E. D. Cold Finger Curse
Torres, E. Carlito's Way
    Q & A
Towne, S. Death Out of Thin Air
Tracy, L. Bartlett Mystery
    House of Peril
Tracy, V. Moment After
    Personal Appearance of a Lioness
Train, A. at least 10 titles
Traubel, H. Metropolitan Opera Murders
Travis, Gretchen. She Fell Among Thieves
Treat, L. 5 titles
Tree, G. Case Against Butterfly
    Case Against Myself
Trotta, G. Veronica Died Monday
Turnbull, M. Rogues' March
Uhnak, D. 5 titles
Ullman, A. Sorry, Wrong Number
Vanardy, V. 5 titles
Van Atta, W. Adam Sleep
Vance, L. J. at least 11 titles
Van de Water, F. F. Hidden Ways
    Plunder
Van Dine, S. S. 11 titles
Van Lustbader, E. Ninja
Van Urk, V. both titles
Veiller, B. Bait for a Tiger
    Trial of Mary Dugan
Veley, C. Night Whispers
Venning, M. Jethro Hammer
    Murder Through the Looking Glass
Violett, E. Double Take
Waddell, C. C. Juror No. 17
    Midnight to High Noon
Walk, C. E. Time Lock
Walker, Gerald. Cruising
Wallace, A. Passion Pulls the Trigger
Wallace, R. 11 titles
Wallis, J. H. 5 titles
Walsh, P. E. Murder Room
Walsh, T. 8 titles
Ward, E. Five for Bridge
Ward, Harold. "Vulture" Strikes
Ward, R. Sandman
Warren, P. Nurse at Brooding Mansion
Warren, V. Brandon in New York
    By Fair Means or Foul
Watson, Clarissa. Fourth Stage of Gainsborough Brown
Waugh, H. 6 titles
Webster, H. K. Ghost Girl
    Whispering Man
Weil, J. Real Cool Cat
Weill, G. Woman's Eyes
Wein, J. Roommate
Wein, L. Mayhem in Manhattan
Weiner, H. Crime on the Cuff
Weir, H. C. Miss Madelyn Mack, Detective
Wellard, J. Moment in Time
Wells, A. M. Murderer's Choice
    Sin of Angels
    Talent for Murder
Wells, Carolyn. 23 titles
West, J. B. Bullets Are My Business
    Eye for an Eye
    Never Kill a Cop
    Taste for Blood
Westlake, D. E. 11 titles
Wheelock, D. Dead Giveaway
White, G. M. Fast Life in New York
    New York by Night
White, L. 8 titles
White, M. Out of the Night
White, S. E. Sign at Six
Whitney, P. A. Quicksilver Pool
    Window on the Square
Whitney, S. Singled Out
Wilcox, C. McCloud
Williams, Alan. Room Service
Williams, Alexander. Death over Newark
    Murder in the WPA
Williams, Henry. How to Murder Your Wife
Williams, H. S. Witness of the Sun
Williams, J. B. Leaves from the Notebook of a New York Detective
Williams, S. In the Tenth Moon
Williamson, C. N. Lord John in New York
Wills, T. You'll Get Yours
Wilmot, J. P. all 3 titles
Wilson, David. Corpse Maker
    Killing
Wilson, M. A. Footsteps Behind Her
    Stalk the Hunter
Winchester, J. Solitary Man
Wishman, S. Nothing Personal
Wohl, J. P. Nirvana Contracts
Wolff, W. A. Manhattan Night
    Trial of Mary Dugan
Wolfson, P. J. Bodies Are Dust
Wolk, G. Man Who Dealt in Blood

668 / New York State

Wood, B.   Killing Gift
Wood, W.   Secret Paper
Woodrow, W.   Burned Evidence
   Pawns of Murder
Woodward, H.   both titles
Woolfolk, W.   Naked Hunter
   Run While You Can
Woolrich, C.   Black Angel
   Bride Wore Black
Wormser, R.   Communist's Corpse
   Man with the Wax Face
Worth, C.   Corpse That Knew Everybody
Worts, G. E.   Dangerous Young Man
Wright, R.   Disappearance of Kimball Webb
Wright, W.   Blonde Target
Wylie, P.   Savage Gentleman
Xantippe.   Death Catches Up with Mr. Kluck
Yaffe, J.   Nothing But the Night
Yates, G. W.   There Was a Crooked Man
Yates, M.   Death Casts a Vote
Yates, P.   Death Comes to Dinner
   Death in the Hands of Talent
   Dress Circle Murders
Yorck, R. L.   So Cold the Night
Young, R. E.   Murder at Mansons
Yudkoff, A.   Circumstances Beyond Control
Zeiger, A.   Serenade for a Shylock
Zore, H.   Alibi off Broadway

NEW YORK STATE (N.Y. SEE ALSO: LONG ISLAND; NEW YORK CITY; ROCHESTER)

Alcott, C.   Dungeons of Crowley Hall
Alexander, Jan.   Second House
Allen, E. O.   Hounds of the Moon
Alverson, C.   Fighting Back
Ard, W.   Like Ice She Was
Armstrong, C.   Black-Eyed Stranger
   Innocent Flower
Avallone, M.   Fallen Angel
Bacheller, I. A.   House of the Three Ganders
Bagby, G.   Ring Around a Murder
Ballard, K. G.   Bar Sinister
Barrington, M.   Stop on the Green Light!
Beam, M.   Murder in a Shell
Benchley, N.   Catch a Falling Spy
Bennett, Jay.   Death Is a Silent Room
Biggers, E. D.   Seven Keys to Baldpate
Blochman, L. G.   Rather Cool for Mayhem
Blumberg, J.   Hit Woman
Bond, E.   Clouded Mirror
Booton, K.   Troubled House
Borgenicht, M.   Margin for Doubt
   Tomorrow Trap
Brand, M.   Granduca
Branson, H. C.   Case of the Giant Killer
   Fearful Passage
Broun, D.   From 9 O'Clock to Jamaica Bay
Brown, Carter.   Had I But Groaned
Browne, H.   Thin Air
Bunn, T.   Closet Bones
Camp, Wadsworth.   Gray Mask
Campbell, J.   Homing
Carr, J. D.   Panic in Box C
Carter, Nick.   Weapon of Night
Cartrell, P.   Sin of Sister Betty
Chadwick, C.   Cactus
Chambers, D.   Death Against Venus
Chambers, R. W.   Flaming Jewel
Chichester, J. J.   King of Diamonds
   Rogues of Fortune
Chimenti, F.   Silent Room
Chipperfield, R. O.   Above Suspicion
   Man in the Jury Box
   Unseen Hand
Coe, T.   Wax Apple
Collins, Michael.   Walk a Black Wind
Collins, Michelle.   both titles
Collison, W.   Red-Haired Alibi
Corby, J.   As Deadly Does
Corren, G.   Place on Dark Island
Coxe, G. H.   Groom Lay Dead
Craig, Jonathan.   So Young, So Wicked
Crane, C.   Girls Are Missing
Cross, A.   James Joyce Murder
Crow, C. P.   No More Monday Mornings
Cushman, C. F.   I Wanted to Murder
Dalton, P.   Darkening Willows
Daly, E.   Death and Letters
   Night Walk
Daniels, D.   at least 16 titles
Davis, D. S.   Black Sheep, White Lamb
Davis, T.   Terror on Compass Lake
Deal, B. H.   Waiting to Hear from William
Dean, A.   14 titles
Dean, D.   Murder on Stilts
DeAndrea, W. L.   Hog Murders
Debrett, H.   Lonely Way to Die
Delman, D.   Sudden Death
Deming, R.   Hit and Run
Dickson, Carter.   Graveyard to Let
Disney, D. M.   Hospitality of the House
Dobner, M.   Gingerbread House
   Heather
Dobyns, S.   Saratoga Longshot
Dougall, B.   Singing Corpse
Drachman, T. S.   Reason for Madness

DuBois, T.   Armed with a New Terror
   Devil and Destiny
   Fowl Play
   Seeing Red
Duncombe, F.   Death of a Spinster
Dunn, J. A.   Death Gamble
Dutton, C. J.   Crooked Cross
   Out of the Darkness
Eberhard, F. G.   Super-Gangster
Eberhart, M. G.   Another Woman's House
   Danger Money
   Unknown Quantity
Ehrlich, J.   Cry, Baby
   Slow Burn
Einstein, C.   No Time at All
Eliot, A.   Dark Beneath the Pines
Ellin, S.   Stronghold
Ellis, K. M.   Dolores Divine, Guilty or Innocent?
England, G. A.   Alibi
Fagan, N.   both titles
Farris, J.   Captors
Fenisong, R.   Snare for Sinners
Fenwick, E.   Passenger
   Silent Cousin
Ferguson, W. B. M.   Black Company
   Riddle of the Rose
Ferm, B.   False Idols
Fischer, B.   8 titles
Fish, R. L.   Handy Death
Fisher, S.   Night Before Murder
Fitzsimmons, C.   Bainbridge Murder
Fleming, I.   Spy Who Loved Me
Fletcher, Dorothy.   Brand Inheritance
Foley, R.   Ape in Velvet
   Man in Shadow
Footner, H.   House with the Blue Door
Foster, M.   Trap
Fox, D.   Doom Dealer
Fox, G. F.   One Wife's Ways
   Witness This Woman
Freytag, J.   Amber Palace
Frost, W. A.   Marworth Mystery
Fuller, T.   This Is Murder, Mr. Jones
Gatenby, R.   Deadly Relations
   Season of Danger
Gearon, J.   Velvet Well
Gibbs, G. F.   Triangle Man
Gilbert, N. R.   Affair at Pine Court
Giles, G. E.   3 Died Variously
Gill, J.   Dead of Summer
Gillespie, R.   Little Sally Does It Again
Gluck, S.   Blind Fury
Godey, J.   Gun and Mr. Smith
Goldsmith, M. M.   Double Jeopardy
Goldthwaite, E. K.   Don't Mention My Name
Grady, F. P.   Sergeant Death
Green, A. K.   9 titles
Gresham, E.   Puzzle in Parquet
Grey, D.   Tracking of K.K.
Gruber, F.   Talking Clock
Hall, Stephanie.   Whisper in the Dark
Harding, W. H.   Rainbow
Harper, R.   Hanged Men
Hart, F. N.   Bellamy Trial
Hayes, Ralph.   Deadly Prey
Heberden, M. V.   Lobster Pick Murder
   They Can't All Be Guilty
Helm, J.   both titles
Highland, R.   153 Oakland Street
Highsmith, P.   Glass Cell
   This Sweet Sickness
Hilliard, J.   Morgan's Castle
Hirsch, L.   Murder Steals the Show
Hirschfeld, B.   Secrets
Hoch, E. D.   City of Brass
Holding, E. S.   Unfinished Crime
   Virgin Huntress
Holland, I.   Counterpoint
   Tower Abbey
Holland, R.   Hunter
Howie, E.   Murder for Christmas
Hudson, W. C.   Dugdale Millions
Hunt, P.   Murders at Scandal House
Hunter, E.   Every Little Crook and Nanny
Irving, A.   Deadline
Jackson, B.   Programmer
Jackson, C. R.   Quintus Oakes
Jagoda, R.   Friend in Deed
James, Rebecca.   Storm's End
Jeffers, A.   Screen for Murder
Johnson, B. B.   Bad Day for a Black Brother
Johnson, P.   Hung Until Dead
Johnston, V.   Along a Dark Path
Johnston, W.   Waddington Cipher
Jones, Jennifer.   all 3 titles
Kallen, L.   Introducing C. B. Greenfield
Kane, H.   Two Must Die
Kauffman, R. W.   Miss Frances Baird, Detective
Kelland, C. B.   Lady and the Giant
Kelley, L. P.   Deadlocked!
Kelley, W.   Tyree Legend
Kent, W.   Woman in Purple Pajamas
King, C. D.   Careless Corpse
King, R.   8 titles
Kinney, T.   Devil Take the Foremost
Klein, N.   Destroying Angel
Knevels, G.   By Candle-Light
   Diamond Rose Mystery
Knight, Adam.   Knife at My Back

Kyle, R.   Kill Now, Pay Later
Lacy, E.   Pity the Honest
Land, J.   To Walk the Night
Lane, J.   Kill Me Tonight
   Murder Menagerie
   Murder Spoils Everything
Langley, L.   Osiris Died in Autumn
Lariar, L.   Death Paints the Picture
Lathen, E.   Banking on Death
   Sweet and Low
Lathrop, G. P.   Would You Kill Him?
Latimer, Joanthan.   Murder in the Madhouse
Lawrence, Hilda.   Death of a Doll
Liebeler, J. M.   You, the Jury
Lilly, J.   Death Thumbs a Ride
   Seven Sisters
Livingston, A.   Guilty Accuser
   On the Right Wrists
Lockridge, F.   Murder Out of Turn
   Pinch of Poison
   Tangled Cord
   Ticking Clock
Lockridge, R.   21 titles
Long, Manning.   Bury the Hatchet
   Vicious Circle
Low, G.   Invitation to Kill
Ludlum, R.   Osterman Weekend
Lupton, L.   Murder Without Tears
Lynch, J.   Face to Face
McCloy, H.   Mr. Splitfoot
   Through a Glass, Darkly
McCully, W.   Doctors Beware!
McCutcheon, G. B.   Daughter of Anderson Crow
MacDonald, H. C.   Death Walks Softly
MacDonald, J. D.   All These Condemned
   Judge Me Not
MacGrath, H.   Blue Rajah Murder
McKnight, C.   House in the Shadows
McMahon, T. P.   Hubschmann Effect
McNamara, E.   Once over Deadly
MacNeil, N.   Hot Dam
Macrea, T.   all 3 titles
MacVeigh, S.   Murder Under Construction
Mace, M.   Motto for Murder
Madsen, D.   Black Plume
Mallory, A.   Apperson's Folly
   Black Valley Murders
   House of Carson
   Mysteries of Black Valley
Maloney, R.   Nixon Recession Caper
Manners, D. X.   Memory of a Scream
Manson, W.   Man Called Black
   Talent for Violence
Marasco, R.   Parlor Games
Marfield, D.   Mandarin's Sapphire
Marlowe, D. J.   Shake a Crooked Town
Martyn, W.   Last Scourge
Melville, Annabelle.   Rue the Reservoir
Miller, Merle.   Secret Understanding
Miller, V.   Hide the Children
Moorhouse, H.   Gauntlet of Alceste
   Golden Scarab
Morland, C.   Legacy of Winterwyck
Moroso, J. A.   Quarry
Morton, W.   Little Lady Lost
   Masquerade
Mosley, L. O.   So I Killed Her
Mullen, C.   Good Place for Murder
Myers, I. B.   Give Me Death
Mygatt, G.   Nightmare
Napier, M.   Child of Satan
Nichols, A.   Third Child
Nichols, F.   Be Silent, Love
Nicholson, M.   Siege of the Seven Suitors
Nicolson, J. U.   Fingers of Fear
Nile, D.   Mistress of Farrondale
Noone, E.   Heirloom of Tragedy
OCork, S.   Sports Freak
Ogburn, D.   Will and the Deed
Olmsted, H. J.   Hot Diary
Olsen, D. B.   Devious Design
Orvis, K.   Disinherited
Ostrander, I.   6 titles
Packer, V.   Alone at Night
   Girl on the Best Seller List
Padgett, L.   Brass Ring
Page, S. H.   Resurrection Murder Case
Patrick, Q.   Death and the Maiden
Patterson, I.   Eppworth Case
Pember-Hiller, G.   Run Corpse, Run
Pentecost, H.   Deadly Trip
   Honeymoon with Death
Philips, J.   Murder Clear, Track Fast
Phillips, R. R.   Death Smiles
Plagemann, B.   Boxwood Maze
Poate, E. M.   Murder on the Brain
Powell, F.   House on the Hudson
Pronzini, B.   Running of Beasts
Queen, E.   Copper Frame
   Finishing Stroke
   House of Brass
Quentin, P.   Man in the Net
Quintano, D.   Weekend at the Villa
Randall, F. E.   Hedgerow
Randolph, M.   Grim Grow the Lilacs
Ransome, S.   Shroud for Shylock
Rauch, C.   Landlady
Rawson, C.   Headless Lady
   No Coffin for the Corpse
Reagan, T. B.   Blood Money

Settings Index

Reed, D. V.   I Thought I'd Die
Reed, W.   Marked for Murder
  No Sign of Murder
Reeve, A. B.   Film Mystery
  Mystery Mind
Reilly, H.   5 titles
Rice, Laverne.   Well-Dressed for Murder
Ridgway, J.   People in Glass House
Rigsby, H.   Tulip Tree
Rinehart, M. R.   Bat
  Swimming Pool
Roberts, Lee.   Death of a Ladies' Man
  Suspicion
Robeson, K.   6 titles
Ronns, E.   They All Ran Away
Roos, K.   Cry in the Night
Rosenblum, R.   Sweetheart Deal
Ross, B.   Tragedy of Z
Ross, Marilyn.   Face in the Shadows
Rossi, B.   Blood Oath
Roth, H.   Content Assignment
Sadler, M.   Falling Man
St. Clare, D.   Saratoga Mantrap
St. John, G.   Dark Watch
  Secret of Dresden Farm
  Sinister Voice
Salvato, S. A.   Briarcliff Manor
Sanders, Lawrence.   Sixth Commandment
Sanders, M. K.   Bride Laughed Once
Sapir, R.   Murder's Shield
Scherf, M.   Green Plaid Pants
Schubert, J. D.   Keep
Scott, Dana.   Five Fatal Letters
Scott, Milton.   Dear, Dead Harry
Seabrooke, J. P.   Eyewitness
Seeley, C.   Storm Fear
Shaw, J. T.   It Happened at the Lake
Sherburne, J.   Death's Pale Horse
Sherry, E.   Tears for Jessie Hewitt
Shriber, I. S.   Dark Arbor
  Family Affair
  Head over Heels in Murder
Siller, V.   Curtain Between
  Old Friend
  Widower
Simmons, M. K.   Willow Pond
Sinclair, R. B.   It Couldn't Be Murder
Singer, L.   That's the House, There
Smith, Garret.   I Did It!
Smith, T. L.   Devil and Webster Daniels
Smithies, R. H. R.   Disposing Mind
Spillane, M.   Twisted Thing
Stanford, D.   Slaughtered Lovelies
Stark, R.   Green Eagle Score
  Seventh
Starr, Jonathan.   Grapevine
Steel, K.   Ambush House
  Murder in G-Sharp
Stein, A. M.   Cradle and the Grave
Stern, R. M.   Cry Havoc
  These Unlucky Deeds
Stevenson, B. E.   House Next Door
Stout, R.   Double for Death
  Hand in the Glove
  Some Buried Caesar
Strange, J. S.   Murder on the Ten-Yard Line
Strobel, M.   Kiss and Kill
Sutton, E.   Dead Fingers
Swiggett, H.   Corpse in the Derby Hat
Taylor, Edith.   Serpent Under It
Taylor, H. B.   Trouble with Tycoons
Terhune, A. P.   Amateur Inn
Thayer, L.   5 titles
Thompson, V.   Mr. Guelpa
Tibbetts, G. F.   Mystery of Kun-Ja-Muck Cave
Tomerlin, J.   Return to Vikki
Travis, Gretchen.   Cottage
Treat, L.   7 titles
Turnbull, A. S.   Wedding Bargain
Van Arsdale, W.   Professor Knits a Shroud
Vance, L. J.   Bandbox
Van Deusen, D.   Garden Club Murders
Van de Water, F. F.   Eye of Lucifer
  Still Waters
Van Dine, S. S.   Winter Murder Case
Van Raalte, J.   Walls Are High
Venning, M.   Man Who Slept All Day
Wade, H.   So Lovely to Kill
Wallace, R.   Murder Stalks a Billion
Walsh, T.   Action of the Tiger
  Face of the Enemy
  Tenth Point
Warwick, C.   My Pal, the Killer
Waters, T. A.   Blackwood Cult
Waugh, H.   Madam Will Not Dine Tonight
Webb, J. F.   No Match for Murder
Webster, H. K.   Alleged Great-Aunt
Wells, Carolyn.   16 titles
Westlake, D. E.   Killy
Westminster, N.   Moon in Shadow
Weston, H. G.   Mystic Manor
Wetherell, J.   Her Stepfather's House
Wharton, E.   White Ghost of Fenwick Hall
White, L.   House Next Door
Whitney, P. A.   Stone Bull
  Thunder Heights
Widdemer, M.   Red Castle Women
Wilkins, W. A.   Cleverdale Mystery
Willard, J.   Thorne Theatre Mystery
Williams, D.   Second Sight

Winsor, R.   Three Motives for Murder
Wood, C.   Tabloid Murders
Wright, M.   Murder on Polopel
Wylie, P.   Corpses at Indian Stones

NEW ZEALAND (N.Z.)
Bagley, D.   Snow Tiger
Cooper, Barbara.   Drown Him Deep
  Target for Malice
Eden, D.   Bride by Candlelight
  Cat's Prey
  Lamb to the Slaughter
Graeme-Holder, W.   Decker
Jay, S.   both titles
Keinzley, F.   Time to Prey
Mantell, L.   all 3 titles
Marsh, N.   Colour Scheme
  Died in the Wool
  Photo-Finish
  Vintage Murder
Messenger, E.   at least 5 titles
Murray, F.   Invitation to Danger
Salter, E.   Death in a Mist
Sandford, K.   Dead Reckoning
Scott, Gavin.   Hot Pursuit
Stephenson, R.   Body in My Arms
Subond, V.   House over Hell Valley

NEWARK (See also: NEW JERSEY)
Holden, L.   Dead Wrong
Levinrew, W.   For Sale—Murder
Paul, G.   Little Killer
Toma, D.   Airport Affair

NICARAGUA (Nic. See also: CENTRAL AMERICA)
Carter, Nick.   Ice Trap Terror

NICE (See also: FRANCE; MARSEILLES; PARIS; CORSICA)
Kenrick, T.   Only Good Body's a Dead One
Leslie, P.   Finger in the Sky Affair

NIGERIA (Nig. See also: AFRICA, WEST)
Klop, T.   Harmattan

NORTH CAROLINA (N.C. See also: SOUTH)
Brent, R. L.   Invitation to a Strangling
Buchanan, C.   Black Cloak Murders
Burt, K. N.   Red Lady
Cook, M. B.   In Hot Blood
Cooney, C. B.   Rear-View Mirror
Daniels, D.   Woman in Silk and Shadows
Forbes, S.   Go to Thy Death Bed
Haas, B.   Daisy Canfield
Hardy, W.   Little Sin
Hay, J.   Winning Clue
Kimbrough, K.   Spectre of Dolphin Cove
Kosner, A.   My Sister Ophelia
Lockridge, R.   Death in a Sunny Place
MacGrath, H.   Green Stone
MacKay, A.   Death Is Academic
Maner, W.   Image Killer
Moore, H. F. S.   Murder Goes Rolling Along
Ogburn, D.   Death on the Mountain
Poate, E. M.   Trouble at Pinelands
Polsky, T.   Cudgel
Ross, James.   They Don't Dance Much
Talbot, H.   Hangman's Handyman
Winston, D.   Gallows Way
Zachary, H.   To Guard the Right

NORTH DAKOTA (N. Dak. See also: MIDWEST)
Beeching, J.   Dakota Project
O'Malley, P.   Affair of Chief Strongheart
Scherf, M.   Don't Wake Me Up While I'm Driving
Stark, R.   Score

NORTHWEST (N.W. See also: OREGON; WASHINGTON)
Hinds, R. W.   Tunnel to Doom
Keeble, J.   Yellowfish
Lake, J.   Silent Scream
Saul, J. R.   Cry for the Strangers
Sellers, M.   Night Shadows

NORWAY (Nor. See also: OSLO; SCANDINAVIA)
Barnard, R.   Death in a Cold Climate
Bingham, J.   Night's Black Agent
Carr, G.   Lewker in Norway
Christiansen, S.   Two Living and One Dead
Crecy, J.   Evil Among Us
Elvestad, S.   Man Who Plundered the City
Francis, D.   Slay-Ride
Hamilton, D.   Terminators
Innes, H.   Blue Ice
Kielland, A.   Live Dangerously

Lewis, David.   Andromeda Assignment
Lie, J.   Devil's Birthday
Lyall, G.   Blame the Dead
Maitland, J. A.   Sartoroe
Perry, Ritchie.   Your Money and Your Wife
Purser, P.   Peregrination 22
Robeson, K.   Haunted Ocean
Viller, F.   Black Tortoise
Whitney, P. A.   Listen for the Whisperer

OCEAN. See: SHIP.

OHIO (See also: CINCINNATI; CLEVELAND; COLUMBUS; MIDWEST)
Anthony, D.   Midnight Lady and Mourning Man
Arden, W.   Goliath Scheme
Bandy, E.   Blackstock Affair
Brackett, L.   Eye for an Eye
  Tiger Among Us
Brennan, L. A.   Death at Flood Tide
Burtis, T.   Flying Blood
Cain, J. M.   Rainbow's End
Campbell, M. E.   Scandal Has Two Faces
Carrel, M.   Tears of Blood
Chaber, M. E.   As Old As Cain
Chacko, D.   both titles
Chamberlain, A.   Tall Dark Man
Churchill, L.   Death Rides a Black Steed
Clark, W. A.   Girl on the Volkswagen Floor
Corne, M. E.   Death at the Manor
Crowell, W.   Murder in Mocking Valley
Cullinan, T.   Eighth Sacrament
Dominic, R. B.   Attending Physician
  Murder Out of Commission
Elliott, B.   One Is a Lonely Number
Hardin, P.   Hidden Grave
Harrington, W.   Which the Justice, Which the Thief
Hintze, N.   You'll Not Like My Mother
Hultman, H. J.   Murder on Route 40
Iams, J.   Corpse of the Old School
Johnson, B. B.   That's Where the Cats At, Baby
Johnson, G.   both titles
King, R.   Diagnosis: Murder
Lacy, E.   Room to Swing
Lanning, G.   Pedestal
McConnaughey, J.   Three for the Money
MacDougall, J. K.   Death and the Maiden
McGrew, F.   Murder by Mail
Marlett, M.   Devil Builds a Chapel
Martin, J. E.   95 File
Martin, Robert.   5 titles
Miles, J.   Blackmailer
Morse, F. V.   Black Eagles Are Flying
Olson, D.   If I Don't Tell
Presnell, F. G.   No Mourners Present
  Send Another Coffin
Roberts, Lee.   If the Shoe Fits
  Once a Widow
Robeson, K.   Nevlo
Shriber, I. S.   As Long As I Live
  Body for Bill
Stevenson, L. L.   Big Game
Stokes, M. L.   Iron Tiger

OKLAHOMA (Okla. See also: OKLAHOMA CITY; SOUTHWEST)
Allen, T. B.   Short Life
Anderson, E.   Thieves Like Us
Cole, D.   Murder at the White Tulip
Cornell, L.   Murder Case Number 33
Cunningham, W.   Pretty Boy
Derrick, L.   Oklahoma Firefight
Elder, M.   Wolf Hunt
Jackson, K.   both titles
Knickmeyer, S.   both titles
Miles, J.   Dally with a Deadly Doll
  Night Hunters
Moore, Robin.   Big Paddle
Reagan, T. B.   Bank Job
Robeson, K.   Derrick Devil
Rossi, B.   Scarfaced Killer
Williams, C.   Big Bite
Wright, M.   Army Post Murders

OKLAHOMA CITY (Okla. City. See also: OKLAHOMA; SOUTHWEST)
Thiessen, V.   My Brother, Cain

OPERA. See: THEATRE.

OREGON (Oreg. See also: PORTLAND; NORTHWEST)
Barry, I.   House of Deadly Night
Brautigan, R.   Hawkline Monster
Brennan, A.   Castle Mirage
Byron, J.   TNT for Two
Cooper, P. J.   Moonblood
  Shuddering Fair One
Cunningham, C.   Demons of Highpoint House
Derrick, L.   High Disaster
Echard, M.   If This Be Treason
Farr, C.   House on the Cliffs

Heath, M. Return to Clerycastle
Kennedy, N. Village Tale
Lee, T. Summer Shock
Meyers, A. Murder Ends the Song
Mitcheltree, T. Terror in Room 201
Nicole, Claudette. Haunted Heart
Offord, L. G. Walking Shadow
Olsen, D. B. Cats Have Tall Shadows
Strahan, K. C. Footprints
   Meriweather Mystery
   October House
Trimble, L. Give Up the Body
Wren, M. K. all 4 titles

ORIENT. SEE: FAR EAST; INDIVIDUAL COUNTRIES.

OSLO (SEE ALSO: NORWAY; SCANDINAVIA)
Nielsen, H. False Witness
Roberts, R. Crayfish Club

OTTAWA (SEE ALSO: CANADA; MONTREAL; TORONTO; VANCOUVER; WINNIPEG)
Champagne, P. Fair Affair
Rohmer, R. Ultimatum

PAKISTAN (PAK.)
Hubbard, P. M. Custom of the Country
Jay, C. Yellow Turban
Leasor, J. Passport to Peril
McLeave, H. Borderline Case
Mundy, M. Death Is a Tiger

PALESTINE. SEE: ISRAEL.

PANAMA (PAN. SEE ALSO: CENTRAL AMERICA)
Amos, A. Fatal Harvest
   Panic in Paradise
Chambers, W. Navy Murders
Coxe, G. H. Candid Imposter
   Death at the Isthmus
Derrick, L. Panama Power Play
Knight, K. M. Death Came Dancing
   Tainted Token
   Trademark of a Traitor
Rosenberger, J. Kronos Plot
Thomas, E. Shadow of Chu-Seng
Wolfe, M. Panama Paradox
Yarborough, C. Condor Conspiracy

PARAGUAY (PARAG. SEE ALSO: SOUTH AMERICA)
Lieberman, H. Climate of Hell

PARIS (SEE ALSO: FRANCE; NICE; MARSEILLES)
Abdullah, A. Trail of the Beast
Adams, I. End Game in Paris
Albrand, M. Mask of Alexander
   Remembered Anger
Allan, J. Who's Next?
Andrews, C. Affair of the Syrian Dagger
Annesley, M. Spy-Counter Spy
Anthony, Evelyn. Return
Appleton, G. W. Frozen Hearts
Armstrong, A. Spies in Amber
Ash, W. Take-Off
Aveline, C. Passenger on the U
Bachmann, L. P. Ultimate Act
Barak, M. Enigma
Baron, S. End of the Line
Behr, E. Getting Even
Black, E. B. Crime of the Chromium Bowl
Blackmore, J. Angel's Tear
Boileau, P. Living and the Dead
Boland, J. Counterpol in Paris
Boulle, P. Photographer
Bove, E. Murder of Suzy Pommier
Bowick, D. M. Tapestry of Death
Brady, J. Paris One
Brenning, L. H. 5 titles
Brickhill, P. Deadline
Bunker, J. Diamond Cut Diamond
Butterworth, M. Black Look
Campbell, A. Click of the Gate
   Desire to Kill
   No Light Came On
   Spiderweb
Campden, J. Hundredth Acre
Carco, F. Noose of Sin
Carr, J. D. Corpse in the Waxworks
   Four False Weapons
   It Walks by Night
Carter, Nick. Jewel of Doom
   Nowhere Weapon
   Operation Starvation
Catalan, H. Soeur Angele and the Embarrassed Ladies
Catto, M. Sam Casanova
Cheyney, P. You'd Be Surprised
Clement, H. Darling Lili
Coen, F. Plunderers

Coffman, V. Masque by Gaslight
   Small Tawny Cat
   Veronique
Cole, K. S. I'm Afraid I'll Live
Cory, D. This Traitor, Death
Crane, F. Murder in Blue Street
Creasey, J. Toff Goes Gay
Cumberland, M. at least 21 titles
Daniels, N. Spy Ghost
Deighton, L. Expensive Place to Die
Dekobra, M. Prince or Clown
Demouzon. Mouche
De Pont-Jest, R. Case of Dr. Plemon
Dickson, Carter. Unicorn Murders
Didelot, F. 5 titles
Dorland, M. Double-Cross Circuit
Du Boisgobey, F. many/most of the 67 titles
Edwards, Anne. Miklos Alexandrovitch Is Missing
Egleton, C. Seven Days to a Killing
Ellin, S. House of Cards
Ely, D. Trot
Endore, G. Werewolf of Paris
Fairlie, G. Stone Blunts Scissors
Fisher, N. Last Assignment
Fishter, J. F. Ambassador of Death
Fleming, Joan. Good and the Bad
   Hell's Belle
Flynn, J. M. Warlock
Fowler, S. Who Murdered Reynard?
Fox, J. M. Dark Crusade
Frances, S. D. Sad and Tender Flesh
Fredericks, A. Blue Lights
   One Million Francs
Fry, P. Brown Suede Jacket
   Long Overcoat
Fytton, F. Nation Within
Gascar, P. Lambs of Fire
Goldberg, M. Karamanov Equations
Goron, M. F. both titles
Graeme, B. Cherchez la Femme
   Lady in Black
   Man from Michigan
Graeme, R. Blackshirt Finds Trouble
Grant, M. Zemba
Gray, B. Big Brain
Grayson, Richard. Monterant Affair
   Murders at Impasse Louvain
Green, Gerald. Faking It
Greenfield, I. A. High Terror
Greenwood, E. French Farce
Grierson, E. 6 titles
Groc, L. Bus That Vanished
Haedrich, M. Crack in the Mirror
Harcourt, P. At High Risk
Harrison, M. Exploits of Chevalier Dupin
Head, M. Accomplice
   Murder at the Flea Club
Hebden, M. Eyewitness
Hely, E. Dominant Third
Hemyng, B. Women of Paris
Herber, W. Almost Dead
Hodges, A. Body in the Car
   Embassy Murder
Hunt, H. Violent Ones
Israel, P. French Kiss
   Stiff Upper Lip
Jacobs, T. C. H. Target for Terror
Japrisot, S. Goodbye, Friend
Jepson, S. Noise in the Night
Johnston, Gunnar. Two Kings
Johnston, V. House on the Left Bank
   Room with Dark Mirrors
Joyce, T. R. S.P.Y.S.
Kane, F. Maid in Paris
Kessel, J. Bernan Affair
Knight, Adam. Girl Running
Kotzwinkle, W. Fata Morgana
Lacroix, J. P. Innocent Gunman
Lacy, E. Go for the Body
Law, J. Gemini Trip
Legaret, J. Tightrope
Lenton, D. Crooks of Paris
Leroux, G. Kiss That Killed
Levene, P. Ambrose in Paris
Lucas, N. Red Stranger
Lyons, N. Champagne Blues
McConnor, V. French Doll
MacGrath, H. Wolves of Chaos
MacKenzie, N. Fear Stalks the City
Maas, E. Lady at Bay
Machard, R. Wolf Man
Malm, D. On a Fated Night
Malo, V. G. And Why Not?
Mara, B. French for Murder
   This Gun for Gloria
Marder, I. Paris Bit
Marlowe, S. Drum Beat—Dominique
Marshall, B. Accounting
Merrick, W. Packard Case
Millar, R. Half a Corpse
Mills, A. Apache Girl
   Cafe in Montparnasse
   Paris Agent
Miln, L. J. Purple Mask
Mitchell, E. Plotters of Paris
Moffett, C. Master Mind
   Seine Mystery
   Through the Wall
Monteilhet, H. Prisoner of Love
Mooney, J. Millionaire's Folly

Muir, A. Red Carnation
Nason, L. H. Contact Mercury
Netzen, K. To Win and to Lose
Newman, B. Otan Plot
Noel, S. Storm over Paris
Noro, F. Do No Evil
Ohnet, G. Poison Dealer
Oppenheim, E. P. Seeing Life
Owen, H. C. Adventures of Antoine
Paul, Elliot. Hugger-Mugger in the Louvre
   Mayhem in B-Flat
   Murder on the Left Bank
   Mysterious Mickey Finn
Perowne, B. Singular Conspiracy
Peters, L. Tarakian
Porter, J. Chinks in the Curtain
Powell, L. Black Casket
Poynter, B. Disappearance of Mary Amber
Randolph, E. Paris in September
Raphael, J. N. Mystery of the Rue de Babylone
Reynolds, G. Victor Maury, the French Detective
Richmond, M. Evening in Paris
Robinson, E. M. Secret of the Swinging Room
Rollins, W. Ring and the Lamp
Ronald, E. B. Sort of Madness
Ross, W. E. D. Forbidden Castle
Roudybush, A. Death of a Moral Person
   Female of the Species
   House of the Cat
   Suddenly in Paris
Rowland, H. C. Closing Net
Rutherford, D. Comes the Blind Fury
   Creeping Flesh
St. Clair, L. Emerald Trap
St. James, B. April Thirtieth
Saint-Laurent, C. Cautious Maiden
San Antonio. From A to Z
   Stone Dead
   Strangler
   Thugs and Bottles
Saxe, R. B. Ghost Does a Richard III
Service, R. W. Master of the Microbe
Seton, G. K Code Plan
Shepherd, Joan. both titles
Sherard, R. H. Ghost's Revenge
Simenon, G. about 62 Maigret volumes, plus many non-series titles
Sinclair, Michael. How to Steal a Million
Sneddon, R. W. Monsieur X
Souvestre, P. Exploits of Juve
   Limb of Satan
   Messengers of Evil
   Royal Prisoner
Steeman, A. Six Dead Men
Steward, B. Evermore
Strange, J. S. Catch the Gold Ring
Stubbs, J. Painted Face
Sue, E. Mysteries of Paris
Tabori, P. Perdita's End
Teilhet, D. L. Murder in the Air
Thompson, V. Pointed Tower
Thomson, B. Richardson Goes Abroad
Torr, D. Diplomatic Cover
Travers, H. Madame Aubry and the Police
Treat, L. Venus Unarmed
Vail, L. Murder! Murder!
Vance, L. J. Lone Wolf
Vexin, N. Murder in Montmartre
Vidocq. Memoirs of Vidocq
Wallace, Irving. Plot
Waller, L. Trocadero
Ward, D. House in Paris
Westlake, D. E. Castle in the Air
Weston, George. Wings of Destiny
Wheatley, D. Desperate Measures
   Prisoner in the Mask
   "V" for Vengeance
Wheeler, P. And the Bullets Were Made of Lead
Wickham, H. Boncouer Affair
   Trail of the Squid
Wilkinson, B. Night of the Short Knives
Wood, H. F. Englishman of the Rue Cain
Young, G. Devil's Passport

PAST (HERE LISTED ARE BOOKS EXPLICITLY SET AT A TIME DISTINCTLY EARLIER THAN THE TIME OF WRITING. YEAR AND PLACE OF SETTING ARE GIVEN WHERE IDENTIFIED. SEE ALSO: FUTURE)
Abbey, R. Girl from the Sea (Eng.)
   Prisoner of the Manor (Eng.)
Abbott, S. Castle of Evil (1953, Rum.)
   River and the Rose (1860s, south)
Aiken, Joan. Castle Barebane (1800s, Scot.)
   Lightning Tree (1700s, Eng.)
   Smile of the Stranger (1790s, Fr.)
Ainsworth, P. Devil's Hole (1877, Australia)
Aldanov, M. Key (1917, Russ.)
Alexander, Jan. Darkwater (1860s, south)
Allbeury, T. Lantern Network (WWII, Fr.)
Allen, E. O. Hounds of the Moon (1940s, N.Y.)

Settings Index

Amis, K. Riverside Villas Murder (1930s, Eng.)
Anderson, J. Affair of the Blood-Stained Egg Cosy (1930s, Eng.)
Andrews, Mark. Return of Jack the Ripper (1888, NYC)
Archer, Margaret. Gull Yard (1840, Eng.)
Arvonen, H. Sorrow for Angels (1890, Can.)
Ashton, A. Phantom Reflection (1935, L.A.)
Astley, J. Fall of Midas (ca.1900, Eng.)
Bair, P. Gypsum Flower (1944, Fr.)
Baird, T. Way to the Old Sailor's Home (1939, Can.)
Baker, Lucinda. Place of Devils (1879, Ariz.)
    Walk the Night Unseen (ca.1900, S.F.)
Baker, W. H. Night of the Wolf (1945, It.)
    Rape of Berlin (1945, Berlin)
    Strike North (1941, ship)
    Traitor! (1942, Fr.)
Bamford, F. Return of Cottington (1768, Eng.)
Banville, J. Birchwood (1800s, Ire.)
Barak, M. Enigma (1944, Paris)
Barrett, Max. House Across the Park (1800s, Eng.)
Barton, J. Forest of Death (WWII)
    Kill Hitler (WWII)
    Lightning Strikes (WWII)
Barwick, J. Hangman's Crusade (1941, Europe)
Becher, U. Woodchuck Hunt (1938, Switz.)
Becker, S. Covenant with Death (1923, S.W.)
Beech, W. Article 92: Murder, Rape (1946, Ger.)
Behn, N. Shadowboxer (1944, Ger.)
Bellamy, J. Prisoner of Ingecliff (1700s, Eng.)
Bennett, H. Wait Until Evening (WWII, Va.)
Bennetts, P. Footsteps in the Fog (1800s, Eng.)
    Ring the Bell Softly (1865, Eng.)
    Voice in the Darkness (1870, Eng.)
Bensen, D. R. Sherlock Holmes in New York (1901, NYC)
Benson, B. K. Who Goes There? (ca.1860, U.S.)
Bentley, P. House of Moreys (1809, Eng.)
Berckman, E. Long Arm of the Prince (ca.1600, Eng.)
Bergman, A. Big Kiss-Off of 1944 (1944, NYC)
    Hollywood and LeVine (1947, L.A.)
Beste, R. V. Faith Has No Country (WWII, Fr.)
Bishop, M. Killraven (Scot.)
    Widow's Walk (1870s, Maine)
Black, C. Death's Head (1945, Berlin)
Black, Laura. Castle Raven (1800s, Scot.)
    Glendraco (1860, Scot.)
    Wild Cat (1862, Scot.)
Blackburn, J. Flame and the Wind (ca.30 A.D., Jerus.)
Blackstock, C. Factor's Wife (1816, Scot.)
    Knock at Midnight (1938, Hung.)
    Shirt Front (1936, Eng.)
Blagowidow, G. Last Train from Berlin (WWII, Ger.)
Blake, P. Escape to Athens (1945, Greece)
Blake, V. Dark Guardian (Eng.)
Blake, W. D. My Time or Yours (1846, NYC)
Bloch, R. American Gothic (1893, Chi.)
Boles, P. D. Limner (1870, Va.)
    Mississippi Run (1800s, Miss.)
Bond, E. Evil in the House (1860s, NYC)
Boulle, P. Noble Profession (WWII, Fr.)
Boyer, B. H. Solstice Cipher (1944, Eng.)
Boyer, R. L. Giant Rat of Sumatra (1893, Eng.)
Brady, L. Love Tap (1972, Wash. D.C.)
Bramble, F. Strange Case of Deacon Brodie (1788, Edin.)
Brautigan, R. Dreaming of Babylon (1942, S.F.)
    Hawkline Monster (1902, Oreg.)
Breem, W. Leopard and the Cliff (1919, India)
Brent, M. Capricorn Stone (ca.1900, Eng.)
    Kirkby's Changeling (1900, Eng.)
    Tregaron's Daughter (ca.1900, Venice)
Brink, C. Bellini Look (1929, Venice)
Bristowe, A. Tunnel (1900, Eng.)
Bronte, L. Gathering at Greystone (1812, New Eng.)
    Greystone Tavern (1776, New Eng.)
Brophy, J. Day They Robbed the Bank of England (1900, Eng.)
Bryant, W. Blue Russell (1899, West)

Buckingham, N. House Called Edenhythe (Eng.)
    Jade Dragon (1800s, Port.)
    Vienna Summer (1897, Vienna)
Buckley, W. F. Saving the Queen (1940s, Eng.)
    Stained Glass (1950, Ger.)
Burke, John. Black Charade (ca.1890, Eng.)
    Devil's Footsteps (1888, Eng.)
    Ladygrove (ca.1890, Eng.)
Burton, Anthony. Coventry Option
Butler, Gwendoline. Brides of Friedberg (1800s, Ger.)
    Coffin for Pandora (1800s, Eng.)
    Red Staircase (1917, Russ.)
    Vesey Inheritance (1800s, Eng.)
Butler, Ragan. Captain Nash and the Honour of England (ca.1770, Eng.)
    Captain Nash and the Wroth Inheritance (1771, Eng.)
Cain, J. M. Past All Dishonor (1860s, Calif.)
Caine, J. Heathcliff (1800s, Eng.)
Cameron, K. Curse of Whispering Hills (1860s, Ind.)
    Evil at Whispering Hills (Ind.)
    Shadows on the Moon (Ind.)
Campbell, P. Cedarhaven (1859, Wash.)
Campbell, R. W. Circus Couronne (1914, Switz.)
Carr, J. D. Bride of Newgate (1815, Eng.)
    Captain Cut-Throat (1805, Fr.)
    Deadly Hall (1927, New Or.)
    Demoniacs (1757, Eng.)
    Devil in Velvet (1675, Eng.)
    Fire, Burn! (1829, Eng.)
    Ghosts' High Noon (1912, New Or.)
    Hungry Goblin (1869, Eng.)
    Most Secret (1815, Eng.)
    Murder of Sir Edmund Godfrey (1815, Eng.)
    Papa La-Bas (1858, New Or.)
    Scandal at High Chimneys (1865, Eng.)
    Witch of the Low Tide (1907, Eng.)
Carr, P. Lion Triumphant (1500s, Eng.)
    Miracle at St. Bruno's (1500s, Eng.)
    Witch from the Sea (1500s, Eng.)
Carroll, R. Disappearance (1957-67, Europe)
Cashman, J. Cook General (1870s, Eng.)
    Gentleman from Chicago (1800s, Chi.)
    Kid Glove Charlie (1870s, Eng.)
Chalmers, S. Crime in Car 13 (1913, U.S.)
Chamberlain, Elinor. Snare for Witches (1663, Mass.)
Chamberlain, L. Other Side of the Door (1865, S.F.)
Chambers, R. W. Secret Service Operator 13 (1862, U.S.)
Chapman, H. W. Limmerston Hall (1800s, Eng.)
Charles, I. Grenencourt (Eng.)
Charteris, L. Catch the Saint (1930s, Phil., Eng.)
    Saint and the Hapsburg Necklace (ca.1940, Vienna)
Cheatham, L. Marriage Pact (1830, NYC)
    Portrait of Emma (1700s, Boston)
    Secret of Saramount (ca.1900, South)
Chevalier, H. For Us the Living (1929-41, S.F.)
Chevalier, P. Grudge (WWII, Eng.)
Cheyney, J. Secret of Giltham Hall (1600s, Eng.)
Chimenti, F. Silent Room (1910, N.Y.)
Chittenden, M. Face in the Mirror
Christie, A. Death Comes As the End (2000 B.C., Egypt)
Clark, Cecily. Ravensley Manor (1800s, Eng.)
Clark, G. Baroness of Bow Street (ca.1810, Eng.)
    Dulcie Bligh (ca.1810, Eng.)
Clark, L. Murder of the Prime Minister (1812, Eng.)
Clarke, A. Lady in Black (1882, Eng.)
Cleary, J. High Road to China (1920s, China)
Clement, H. Darling Lili (WWI, Paris)
Clements, A. Mistress of the Moor (1909, Scot.)
Clive, J. Last Liberator (1963, Holl.)
Coen, F. Plunderers (WWII, Paris)
Coffman, V. Dark Gondola (1790s, Venice)
    Dark Palazzo (1797, Venice)
    Demon Tower (It.)
    Gaynor Women (1880s, Va.)
    House on the Moat (1810, Eng.)
    Hyde Place (ca.1900, S.F.)
    Marsanne (ca.1820, Eng.)
    Mist at Darkness (1821, Eng.)
    Mistress Devon (ca.1850, Boston)
    Moura (1815, Fr.)
    Vampyre of Moura (1821, Fr.)
    Veronique (1790, Paris)
Coles, M. Drink to Yesterday (1917, Ger.)

Comber, L. Strange Cases of Magistrate Pao (ca.1100, China)
Connell, C. Meet Me at Philippi (ca.50 B.C., Rome)
    Most Delicious Poison (ca.50 B.C., Mid. East)
Connor, K. New Departure (1800s)
Conot, R. E. Ministers of Vengeance (1920s, S.F.)
Conway, L. Abbot's House (Eng.)
Cooper, Brian. Genesis 38 (1903, Eng.)
Cooper, Lynna. Hour of the Harp (1800s, Ire.)
Cooper, P. J. My Lady Evil (ca.1815, Fr.)
Copeland, W. Five Hours from Isfahan (1943, Iran)
Coppee, F. Guilty Man (1866, Fr.)
Copper, B. Dossier of Solar Pons (1920s, Eng.)
    Further Adventures of Solar Pons (Eng.)
    Necropolis (1800s, Eng.)
    Secret Files of Solar Pons (Eng.)
    Uncollected Cases of Solar Pons (Eng.)
Creasey, J. Masters of Bow Street (1739-1829, Eng.)
Crichton, M. Great Train Robbery (1855, Eng.)
Crofts, F. W. Cask (1910-12, Fr.)
Crookenden, I. Horrible Revenge (1500s, It.)
Crunden, A. B. Chicago Winter's Tale (WWI, Chi.)
Cunningham, C. Demons of Highpoint House (1910, Oreg.)
Curties, T. J. H. Saint Botolph's Priory (ca.1640, Eng.)
Cutler, R. Gates of Sagittarius (1939, Havana)
Dacre, C. Zofloya (1400s)
Daingerfield, F. That Gay Nineties Murder (1890, Ky.)
Daley, J. A. Spicy Lady (1968, NYC)
Dalton, P. Darkening Willows (ca.1910, N.Y.)
Daniels, D. Attic Rope (La.)
    Bell (1892, Maine)
    Blackthorn (1903, Md.)
    Child of Darkness (1911, N.Y.)
    Circle of Guilt (ca.1910, S.F.)
    Cliffside Castle (1890, N.Y.)
    Conover's Folly (1890, Maine)
    Dance in Darkness (1890, N.Y.)
    Dark Stage (1892, New Or.)
    Darkhaven (1890, N.Y.)
    Guardian of Willow House (1915, N.Y.)
    House of Many Doors (Miss.)
    House of Stolen Memories (1800s, Conn.)
    House on Crocus Hill (1895, Ind.)
    In the Shadows (N.Y.)
    Journey into Terror (ca.1860, S.C.)
    Lady of the Shadow (Conn.)
    Lanier Riddle (1890, Ky.)
    Leland Legacy (1890, N.Y.)
    Man from Yesterday (ca.1900, N.Y.)
    Marble Leaf (N.Y.)
    Marriott Hall (1880, Maine)
    Mistress of Falcon Hill (1867, La.)
    Mostly by Moonlight (1871, Maine)
    Night Shadow (1895, Ga.)
    Poison Flower (1895, Vt.)
    Possessed (1890, Maine)
    Shadow of a Man (1890, La.)
    Shadows from the Past (1890, N.Y.)
    Silent Halls of Ashenden (N.Y.)
    Summer House (ca.1900, NYC)
    Templeton Memoirs (1890, N.Y.)
    Tidemill (1895, Va.)
    Tormented (1883, La.)
    Unearthly (1880, Ga.)
    Vineyard Chapel (1918, Calif.)
    Voices on the Wind (1895, New Eng.)
    Web of Peril (N.Y.)
    Whistle in the Wind (1885, La.)
Darby, C. Falcon and the Moon (1886, Eng.)
    Falcon for a Witch (ca.1910, Eng.)
    Falcon Rising (1818, Eng.)
    Falcon Sunset (1916, Eng.)
    Falcon Tree (1841, Eng.)
    Falcon's Claw (1399, Eng.)
    Flaunting Moon (1644, Eng.)
    King's Falcon (1644, Eng.)
Davenport, F. Secret of the Bayou (La.)
DeAndrea, W. L. Lunatic Fringe (1896, NYC)
De Blasis, C. Night Child (1865, Maine)
Deighton, L. SS-GB (1941, Eng.)
Dekobra, M. Diamond Queen (1900, Trans.)
De La Torre, L. Detections of Dr. Sam: Johnson (ca.1770, Eng.)
    Dr. Sam: Johnson, Detector (ca.1770, Eng.)
    Elizabeth Is Missing (1753, Eng.)
    Heir of Douglas (1700s, Scot.)

672 / Past

Settings Index

Demarest, P. G. House on Washington Place (1860s, NYC)
De Marco, G. October Heat (1934, S.F.)
Deming, R. What's the Matter with Helen? (1933, Ia.)
Dennis, R. MacTaggart's War (1940, Can.)
De Pre, J. Die, Jessica, Die (1910, L.I.)
    Sound of Dying Roses (1871, Va.)
    Third Woman (1912, NYC)
Derleth, A. Adventure of the Orient Express (1930s, Europe)
    Adventure of the Unique Dickensians (1930s, Eng.)
    Casebook of Solar Pons (1930s, Eng.)
    Chronicles of Solar Pons (1930s, Eng.)
    In re Sherlock Holmes (1930s, Eng.)
    Memoirs of Solar Pons (1930s, Eng.)
    Mr. Fairlie's Final Journey (1930s, Eng.)
    Praed Street Dossier (1930s, Eng.)
    Praed Street Papers (1930s, Eng.)
    Reminiscences of Solar Pons (1930s, Eng.)
    Return of Solar Pons (1930s, Eng.)
    Three Problems for Solar Pons (1930s, Eng.)
Dibdin, M. Last Sherlock Holmes Story (1888, Eng.)
Dickson, Carter. Fear Is the Same (1795, Eng.)
Disney, D. M. At Some Forgotten Door (1886, Conn.)
    That Which Is Crooked (1898-1946, Conn.)
Ditton, J. Copley's Hunch (WWII)
Doliner, R. Thin Line (1963, Viet Nam)
Donaldson, N. Goodbye, Dr. Thorndyke (1943, Eng.)
Donovan, D. Scarlet Seal (ca.1500, It.)
Doody, M. Aristotle Detective (332 B.C., Athens)
Doran, J. In the Depths of the First Degree (1862, Va.)
Dorsetts, D. Dueling Oaks (New Or.)
Downes, D. Scarlet Thread (WWII)
Drummond, June. Slowly the Poison (1911, S. Afr.)
Du Breuil, L. Legend of Molly Moor (Md.)
Dudley, E. Picaroon (1700s, Eng.)
Du Maurier, D. Jamaica Inn (ca.1815, Eng.)
Eastvale, M. As the Sparks Fly (1800s, Eng.)
Eberhart, M. G. Bayou Road (1863, New Or.)
    Casa Madrone (1906, S.F.)
    Family Fortune (ca.1860, W. Va.)
Eden, B. Bella (1800s, Eng.)
    Samantha (1800s, Eng.)
    Sleep in the Woods (1800s, Eng.)
Eden, M. Murder of Lawrence of Arabia (1930s, Saud. Arab.)
Edgar, J. Dancer's Daughter (Eng.)
Edwards, H. All Night at Mr. Stanyhursts (1783, Eng.)
Edwards, R. Captain's Lady (Eng.)
Egleton, C. October Plot (WWII, Eng.)
Elder, M. Prometheus Operation (1945, U.S.)
Ellis, J. Wexford (1852, New Or.)
Elsna, H. Cast a Long Shadow (1905, Eng.)
    Cherished Ones (ca.1910, Eng.)
Emerick, L. Web of Evil (1887, Pa.)
Emerson, D. Murder in the Family (1840, Eng.)
Endore, G. Werewolf of Paris (1871, Paris)
Epstein, E. J. Cartel (1953, Iran)
Esmond, H. Darsham's Folly (Eng.)
    Eye Stones (1800s, Eng.)
Estey, D. Lost Tale (WWII, Isle of Man)
Estleman, L. D. Dr. Jekyll and Mr. Holmes (1890s, Eng.)
    Sherlock Holmes vs. Dracula (1890, Eng.)
Eyre, M. Girl in the Tiffany Dress (1810, Pitt.)
Fagyas, M. Devil's Lieutenant (1909, Vienna)
Fairbairn, R. Devil Kinsmere (1670 Eng.)
Falkirk, R. all titles in Blackstone series (1820s, Eng.)
Fantoni, B. Mike Dime (1948, Phil.)
Farmer, J. Sedona (1838, Eng.)
Farmer, P. J. Adventure of the Peerless Peer (1916, Afr.)
Farnol, J. all Shrig titles (ca.1815-1820, Eng.)
Farnsworth, M. Evil That Waited (1904, Mass.)
Farrant, S. Lady of Rogan's Tower (Eng.)
    Reluctant Paragon (1800s, Eng.)
    Touch of Terror (1860s, Eng.)
Ferrand, G. House of Glass (Venice)
Fields, A. V-J Day (1945, NYC)
Fleming, H. K. Day They Kidnapped Queen Victoria (1867, Eng.)
Fleming, Jane. Hawthorn Wood (La.)

Fleming, Joan. Every Inch a Lady (1950s, Eng.)
    Screams from a Penny Dreadful (1800s, Eng.)
    Too Late! Too Late! the Maiden Cried. (1800s, Eng.)
Flores, J. Hawkshead (1800s, Eng.)
Flynn, J. Bannerman (1916, Denver)
Follett, J. Churchill's Gold (1941, ship)
    U-700 (1941)
Follett, K. Key to Rebecca (1942, Egypt)
    Storm Island (WWII)
Foote, S. September September (1957, Memphis)
Forbes, C. Heights of Zervos (1941, Greece)
Forbes, S. Buried in So Sweet a Place (1918, Boston)
    Deadly Kind of Lonely (1934, Tex.)
    Go to Thy Death Bed (1891, N.C.)
    If Two of Them Are Dead (1930s, Kan.)
    Sad, Sudden Death of My Fair Lady (1933, Chi.)
    She Was Only the Sheriff's Daughter (1940s, Tex.)
Ford, Hilary. Bride for Bedivere (1800s, Eng.)
    Castle Malindine (1860s, Ire.)
Forrest, Wilma. Anne of Destiny House (Scot.)
    Last Hope House (1855, Ire.)
Forsyte, C. Decoding of Edwin Drood
Fox, G. F. Terror over London (Eng.)
Foxall, R. Amorous Rogue (ca.1750, Eng.)
    Dark Forest (1807, Eng.)
    Little Ferret (1807, Eng.)
    Noble Pirate (ca.1750, Eng.)
    Silver Goblet (1808, Eng.)
    Society of the Dispossessed (ca.1750, Eng.)
Foxx, J. Freebooty (1863, S.F.)
Frankland, E. P. Murders at Crossby (900s, Eng.)
Freytag, J. Amber Palace (N.Y.)
Fytton, F. Nation Within (ca.1960, Paris)
Gadda, C. E. That Awful Mess on the Via Merulana (1927, Rome)
Gainham, S. Mythmaker (1946, Vienna)
    Stone Roses (1948, Prague)
Galloway, D. Lamaar Ransom—Private Eye (WWII, L.A.)
Garbo, N. Cabal (1967, Mid. East)
Garfield, B. Paladin (WWII, Eng.)
    Romanov Succession (1941, Europe)
    Tripwire (1880s, West)
Gast, K. P. Dil Dies Hard (1915, Wash.)
Gavin, C. None Dare Call It Treason (1941, Fr.)
Gellis, R. Sing Witch, Sing Death (ca.1900, Eng.)
Gibbs, M. A. Amateur Governess (1897, Eng.)
Gilbert, Anna. Family Likeness (1800s, Eng.)
    Flowers for Lilian (1800s, Eng.)
    Images of Rose (1883, Eng.)
    Look of Innocence (ca.1890, Eng.)
Gilbert, M. Death in Captivity (WWII, It.)
Gilmore, C. C. Atlantic City Proof (ca.1928, N.J.)
Godfrey, E. Case of the Cold Murderer (1969, Toronto)
Gordon, R. Private Life of Jack the Ripper (1888, Eng.)
Gores, J. Hammett (1928, S.F.)
Grace, A. Wharf Sinister (ca.1860, NYC)
Graeme, B. Cherchez la Femme (1800s, Paris)
    Lady in Black (1800s, Paris)
Graeme, D. Inn of the Thirteen Swords (ca.1600, Fr.)
    Monsieur Blackshirt (ca.1600, Fr.)
    Sword of Monsieur Blackshirt (ca.1600, Fr.)
    Vengeance of Monsieur Blackshirt (ca.1600, Fr.)
Graham, J. Wrath of God (1922, Mex.)
Graham, W. Wreck of the Grey Cat (1898, Eng.)
Grandower, E. Blackbourne Hall (ca.1910, NYC)
    Rivergate House (1800s, NYC)
    Secret Room of Morgate House (1896, Ill.)
Grant, D. Emerald Decision (1940, Eng.)
Gray, Angela. Lattimore Arch (1895, Wash. D.C.)
    Nightmare at Riverview (1885, Ga.)
Grayson, Richard. Monterant Affair (ca.1900, Paris)
    Murders at Impasse Louvain (ca.1900, Paris)
Green, F. L. Odd Man Out (1920s, Belfast)
Greene, H. Flags at Doney (1956, It.)
Grey, H. Portrait of a Mobster (1920s, NYC)
Grierson, E. Massingham Affair (1890s, Eng.)

Grossbach, R. Cheap Detective (1940, S.F.)
H., I. Phantoms of the Cloister (1420, Eng.)
Haines, W. W. Target (1944, Fr.)
Hall, R. L. Exit Sherlock Holmes (1906, Eng.)
    King Edward Plot (1906, Eng.)
Hamilton, M. A. Special Providence (1917, Eng.)
Hanley, E. Guilty As Charged (1930s, Ill.)
Harding, W. H. Rainbow (1925, N.Y.)
Hardwick, M. Prisoner of the Devil (1895, Eng.)
    Regency Rake (ca.1820, Eng.)
    Regency Revenge (ca.1820, Eng.)
    Regency Royal (ca.1820, Eng.)
Hargrave, L. Clara Reeve (1800s, Eng.)
Harrington, W. Search for Elizabeth Brandt (1938-45, Ger.)
Harris, J. Covenant with Death (WWI)
    Sunset at Sheba (1914, S. Afr.)
Harrison, M. Exploits of Chevalier Dupin (1800s, Paris)
    I, Sherlock Holmes (1881-91, Eng.)
Hastings, P. Act of Darkness (1890s, Eng.)
    Conservatory (1871, Eng.)
    Field of the Forty Footsteps (1790s, Fr.)
Hayes, L. Challoners of Bristol (1811, R.I.)
    Harlequin House (1869, S.C.)
Head, M. Accomplice (1934, Paris; 1935, Kan. City)
Heard, H. F. Black Fox (1870s)
Heath, M. House of the Strange Women (1800s, Calif.)
Heaven, C. Castle of Eagles (1847, Vienna)
    Fires of Glenlochy (1700s, Scot.)
Heffernan, W. Broderick (1920s, NYC)
Higgins, J. Day of Judgement (1963, Ger.)
    Eagle Has Landed (1943, Ger.)
    Last Place God Made (1930s, Brazil)
Hill, P. Devil of Aske (1700s, Eng.)
Hilton, J. B. Dead-Nettle (1904, Eng.)
    Gamekeeper's Gallows (1877, Eng.)
    Rescue from the Rose (1911, Eng.)
    Some Run Crooked (1958, Eng.)
Hirschfeld, B. Bonnie and Clyde (1932, U.S.)
Hirschhorn, R. Target Mayflower (1944, New Eng.)
Hitchcock, R. Attack the Lusitania! (1915)
    Sea Wrack (1940, Fr.)
Hodel, M. P. Enter the Lion (1875, Eng.)
Hodge, J. A. Here Comes a Candle (1812, Mass.)
    Maulever Hall (Eng.)
    Winding Stair (1806, Port.)
Holt, V. Lord of the Far Island (ca.1900, Eng.)
    Secret Woman (1800s, Eng.)
Horler, S. Blanco Case (1876, Eng.)
    Man of Evil (1600s, Eng.)
Hubell, N. Adventures of Creighton Holmes (1930s, Eng.)
Huff, T. E. Nine Bucks Row (ca.1890, Eng.)
Huffman, L. House Behind the Mint (1870s, S.F.)
Hunter, J. D. Expendable Spy (1945, Ger.)
Hunter, S. Master Sniper (WWII)
Hurd, F. Curse of the Moors (Eng.)
    House on Russian Hill (1800s, S.F.)
    Secret of Awen Castle (Eng.)
Hylton, S. Caprice
Ireland, W. H. Gondez the Monk (1200s)
Irwin, W. Julius Caesar Murder Case (ca.50 B.C., It.)
Jackman, S. Operation Catcher (1944, Yem.)
Jackson, Eileen. Autumn Lace (1800s, Wales)
James, Donald. Shadow of the Wolf (1941, Eng.)
Janeway, H. This Passionate Land (1850s, South)
Jeffers, H. P. Adventure of the Stalwart Companions (1880, NYC)
Johnston, V. House on the Left Bank (1870, Paris)
    Masquerade in Venice (1880, Venice)
    Silver Dolphin (1840s, L.I.)
Johnston, W. Banyon (1937, L.A.)
Jones, K. O. To the Dark Tower Came (1840s, Ire.)
Jones, R. P. Man Who Killed Hitler (WWII, Berlin)
Jones, T. Dutch Treat (1940, Holl.)
Kail, R. Swastika (WWII, Ger.)

Settings Index   Past / 673

Kaminsky, S. M. Bullet for a Star (1940, L.A.)
    Howard Hughes Affair (1942, L.A.)
    Murder on the Yellow Brick Road (ca. 1940, L.A.)
    Never Cross a Vampire (1942, L.A.)
    You Bet Your Life (ca.1940, Chi.)
Kantor, Hal. Blown Away (1915-1948, NYC)
Kavanaugh, C. Bride of Lenore (1891, Va.)
Keane, C. Crossing (1945, ship)
Keating, H. R. F. Murder of the Maharajah (1930, India)
    Remarkable Case of Burglary (1871, Eng.)
Kelland, C. B. Dangerous Angel (1870s, S.F.)
    Lady and the Giant (1869, N.Y.)
Kelly, M. That Girl in the Alley (1936, Eng.)
Keneally, T. Victim of the Aurora (1910, Antarctic)
Kennedy, W. Legs (1920s, U.S.)
Keppel, C. Madam, You Must Die (1798, Eng.)
    When I Say Goodbye (1700s, Eng.)
Ker, A. Adeline Saint Julian (1632)
    Edric the Forester (1066)
Kerr, R. Stuart Legacy (1800s, Scot.)
Kerrigan, J. Phoenix Assault (1945, Berlin)
Kessel, J. Bernan Affair (1921, Paris)
Kiefer, W. Lingala Code (1960s, Bel. Congo)
Kimbrough, K. Augusta, the First (1742, Maine)
    Dorothy, the Terrified (1863, South)
    Jane, the Courageous (1771, Maine)
    Joanne, the Unpredictable (1834, Eng.)
    Kathrine, the Returned (1900, Boston)
    Marcia, the Innocent (1845, Eng.)
    Margaret, the Faithful (1783, Maine)
    Rebecca, the Mysterious (1822, Mass.)
    Thanesworth House (1800s, Miss.)
Kinder, K. Raven and the Dove (1876, Eng.)
King, F. Raya (1942, Cairo)
King, H. Four Days (1953, U.S.)
King, L. W. Rochemer Hag (1800s, Eng.)
Kingsley, B. Black Angel (1933, Cape Cod)
Kingsley-Smith, T. Forsaken (1930s, Kan.)
Kirsch, J. Bad Moon Rising (1960s, Calif.)
Kirst, H. H. Hero in the Tower (1940, Fr.)
    Night of the Generals (1942-56, Ger.)
    Nights of the Long Knives (1933-9, Ger.)
    Twilight of the Generals (1938, Berlin)
Knight, S. Requiem at Rogano (1902, Eng.)
Knox, A. Raider's Moon (ca.1790, Can.)
Koning, H. Petersburg-Cannes Express (1900, train)
Kotzwinkle, W. Fata Morgana (1861, Paris)
Kurland, M. Infernal Device (ca.1890)
Kyle, D. Black Camelot (1944)
Laker, R. Smuggler's Bride (1809, Eng.)
La Fountaine, G. Scott-Dunlap Ring (1870s, U.S.)
Laine, A. Reluctant Heiress (ca.1820, Eng.)
Lambe, G. Mysteries of Ferney Castle (1600s, Eng.)
Langley, B. Traverse of the Gods (1944, Switz.)
Lathom, F. Unknown (ca.1530, Eng.)
Laumer, K. Deadfall (1948, L.A.)
Leasor, J. Unknown Warrior (WWII)
Lee, Elsie. Silence Is Golden (1860s, Eng.)
Lee, John. Lago (WWII, It.)
    Ninth Man (1942, Wash. D.C.)
    Thirteenth Hour (1944, Berlin)
Leighton, T. Night of the Sphinx (1936, Egypt)
Leonard, P. G. Phantom of the Sacred Well (1879, Guat.)
Leopold, C. Casablack (1942, Casa.)
Levi, P. Head in the Soup (1972, Eng.)
Ley, A. C. At Dark of Moon (1804, Eng.)
    Letters for a Spy (ca.1800, Eng.)
    Tenant of Chesdene Manor (ca.1820, Eng.)
Lincoln, N. S. Lost Despatch (1865, Wash. D.C.)
Lindley, E. Brackenroyd Inheritance (1800s, Eng.)
Linzee, D. Death in Connecticut (1971, Conn.)
Lipsky, E. Devil's Daughter (1880s, S.F.)
    Lincoln McKeever (1890s, N. Mex.)
Litvinoff, E. Blood on the Snow (ca. 1920, Russ.)
Litwak, L. Waiting for the News (1939-43, Det.)

Long, H. Golden Cat
Lovesey, P. all Sgt. Cribb titles (ca. 1880, Eng.)
Lowndes, M. B. Lizzie Borden (1890s, Mass.)
Ludlum, R. Rhinemann Exchange (WWII)
    Scarlatti Inheritance (1918-1944)
Luhrs, V. Longbow Murder (1100s, Eng.)
Lynch, F. Dangerous Magic (ca.1910, Scot.)
Lynch, M. Blacktower (1900, New Eng.)
    Creighton's Castle (1920s, Conn.)
    Night of the Moonrose (1892, U.S.)
    Road to Midnight (1888, U.S.)
    Where Evil Waits (1782, New Eng.)
    Witches' Holiday (ca.1900, U.S.)
Lynx, J. J. Prince of Thieves (ca.1900, Eng.)
Lyons, D. Flower of Evil (NYC)
Lyons, E. Haunting of Abbotsgarth (1900, Eng.)
MacAlister, I. Skylark Mission (1941, New Guinea)
McCarry, C. Secret Lovers (1960, Europe)
McCarthy, M. Cannibals and Missionaries (1975, Holl.)
McCloy, H. Smoking Mirror (1940, Fr.)
MacDonald, E. House at Gray Eagle (1904, Colo.)
McDowell, M. Gilded Needles (1882, NYC)
McEvoy, M. Calabrian Summer (WWII, It.)
    Peril at Polvellyn (1800s, Eng.)
McFadden, G. V. Preventive Man (1829, Eng.)
    Turning Sword (ca.1815, Eng.)
McGill, G. War Story (WWII, Berlin)
McHugh, F. Y. Blackthorne (ca.1910, Conn.)
McIvers, S. Cry of the Wind (1800s, La.)
    Night Without End (ca.1870, La.)
McKnight, C. Gravetide (1800s, Eng.)
MacLean, Alistair. Breakheart Pass (1870s, West)
    Force 10 to Navarone (WWII, Yugos.)
    Guns of Navarone (WWII, Turk.)
McQuinn, D. E. Targets (1969, Saigon)
Maass, E. Lady at Bay (1672, Paris)
Maass, J. Gouffe Case (1889, Paris)
Madden, A. W. Amberley Diamonds (1800s, Eng.)
Madsen, D. Black Plume (1835-52, N.Y.)
Malcolm, J. Discourse with Shadows (1945, Frank.)
Mandel, P. Black Ship
Mandino, O. Christ Commission (36 A.D., Jerus.)
Manners, A. Singing Swans (1800s, Scot.)
    Stone Maiden (ca.1905, Scot.)
Margolin, P. Heartstone (1960, U.S.)
Mariner, D. Chatham Rats (WWII)
Markham, V. Scamp (ca.1720, Eng.)
Markstein, G. Cooler (1944, Eng.)
Marlow, E. Danger at Dahlkari (1800s, India)
    Falconridge (1800s, Eng.)
    Lady at Lyon House (1800s, Eng.)
    Master of Phoenix Hall (1888, Eng.)
    Midnight at Mallyncourt (1800s, Eng.)
Marlowe, S. Valkyrie Encounter (1944, Berlin)
Marshall, B. Accounting (1933, Eng.)
Martin, A. E. Sinners Never Die (1895, Australia)
Martin, H. Sleeping Girls Don't Lie (1951, Ger.)
Massey, C. Bride of Invercoe (1800s, Scot.)
    Polmarram Tower (1830, Eng.)
Mathieson, T. Devil and Ben Franklin (1734, Phil.)
    Great "Detectives"
Maxwell, P. Secret of Mirror House (ca.1870, South)
Mayhew, M. Master of Aysgarth (1832, Eng.)
    Owlers (1700s, Eng.)
Mazzaro, E. Bootleg Angel (1920s, Chi.)
    One Death in the Red (1920s, Chi.)
Melchior, I. Haigerloch Project (1945, Ger.)
    Order of Battle (WWII, Ger.)
    Sleeper Agent (WWII, Europe)
Melville, J. Raven's Forge (1800s, Eng.)
Meyer, N. Seven-Per-Cent Solution (ca.1890)
    West End Horror (ca.1890, Eng.)
Meyers, Manny. Last Mystery of Edgar Allan Poe (1846-7, NYC)
Michaels, B. Wings of the Falcon (1860, It.)
    Wizard's Daughter (1857, Eng.)
Milburn, E. Wings of Darkness (ca.1860, La.)
Miln, L. J. Purple Mask (1803, Paris)
Mitchelson, A. Earthquake Machine (1906, Eng.)
    Hellbirds (ca.1905, Eng.)
Moore, Robin. Big Paddle (1933, Okla.)
Morella, J. Ince Affair (1924, Calif.)

Morgulas, J. Torquemada Principle (1938, Ger.)
Morland, C. Legacy of Winterwyck (1842, N.Y.)
Morley, G. T. Deeds of Darkness (1500s)
Morrison, A. Hole in the Wall (1800s, Eng.)
Morton, P. Province of Darkness (1800s, Eng.)
Mountjoy, H. Minister of Police (1700s, Fr.)
Murphy, D. J. Fatal Revenge (1670)
Nash, N. R. East Wind, Rain (1941, Haw.)
Neely, R. Walter Syndrome (1938, NYC)
Neilan, S. Air of Glory
    Braganza Pursuit (1800s, Brazil)
Neilson, M. Bride of Alderburn
    Dark Path
Netzen, K. To Win and to Lose (1940, Paris)
    all series books (WWII)
Nichols, S. House of Rancour (1800s, Eng.)
    Rachel (ca.1770, Pa.)
    Serpent's Tooth (1845, Ire.)
    Silsby (1600s, Eng.)
Nile, D. Evil Men Do (NYC)
    Mistress of Farrondale (ca.1880, N.Y.)
    Terror at Deepcliff (Boston)
Nolan, F. Mittenwald Syndicate (1945, Ger.)
    Oshawa Project (ca.1946)
    White Nights, Red Dawn (1915, Russ.)
Noone, E. Corridor of Whispers (1800s, Pa.)
    Dark Cypress (New Eng.)
    Daughter of Darkness (1890s, Eng.)
    Heirloom of Tragedy (N.Y.)
    Seacliffe (Maine)
    Second Secret (1860s, N.J.)
    Victorian Crown (ca.1870, W. Va.)
Norman, Elizabeth. Castle Cloud (1850, Eng.)
    If the Reaper Ride (ca.1850, Eng.)
Norton, A. Opal-Eyed Fan (ca.1850, Fla.)
O'Brien, S. Shadow of the Caravan (1862, Calif.)
O'Brine, M. Pale Moon Rising (1942, Fr.)
O'Grady, L. Artist's Daughter (1800s, Eng.)
Olden, M. Poe Must Die (1840, NYC)
Orczy, B. Man in Gray (ca.1810, Eng.)
O'Rourke, F. Man Who Found His Way (1927, N. Mex.)
Ostrander, K. Image Seller (1800s, NYC)
O'Toole, G. J. A. Cosgrove Report (1868, Wash. D.C.)
Palmer, J. Haunted Cavern (ca.1450, Scot.)
    Mystery of the Black Tower (1300s)
Palmer, S. Adventure of the Marked Man (1890s, Eng.)
Parker, Beatrice. Come to Castlemoor (1800s, Eng.)
Parkhurst, J. Southern Moon (1800s, Ga.)
Patterson, H. To Catch a King (1940, Lisbon)
    Valhalla Exchange (1944, Austria)
Pauley, B. A. Voices Long Hushed (1880s, Miss.)
Payes, R. C. Bride of Fury (ca.1890, Eng.)
    Devil's Court (1720, Eng.)
Pearlman, G. Adventures of Sherlock Holmes' Smarter Brother (1891, Eng.)
Pearson, D. Loom of Tancred (1800s, Eng.)
Pearson, E. L. Sherlock Holmes and the Drood Mystery (1914, Eng.)
Peeples, S. A. Man Who Died Twice (1922, L.A.)
Perowne, B. Raffles of the Albany (ca.1900, Eng.)
    Raffles of the M.C.C. (ca.1905, Eng.)
Perrin, R. Jewels (1907, Dublin)
Perry, A. Callander Square (ca.1882, Eng.)
    Cater Street Hangman (1881, Eng.)
Perry, Robin. Welcome to a Hero (1962, Wash. D.C.)
Persico, J. E. Spiderweb (ca.1946, Ger.)
Peters, Elizabeth. Crocodile on the Sandbank (1880, Egypt)
Peters, Ellis. Monk's Hood (1100s, Eng.)
    One Corpse Too Many (1138, Eng.)
Petrie, G. Branch Bearers (ca.1860, Eng.)
Phillips, J. Greenwood (ca.1865, South)
Pilpel, R. H. To the Honor of the Fleet (1912, ship)
Piper, P. Margot Leck (1880s, Eng.)
Player, R. Month of the Mangled Models (1800s, Eng.)
Plum, J. Secret of Benjamin Square (1800s, Eng.)
Ponthier, F. Assignment Basra (1940s, Mid. East)

P

Post, M. D. Methods of Uncle Abner (ca.1850, Va.)
    Silent Witness (ca.1850, Va.)
    Uncle Abner, Master of Mysteries (ca.1850, Va.)
Potter, J. Death in the Forest
    Trail of Blood (1536, Eng.)
Poyer, J. Tunnel War (1911, Eng.)
Praviel, A. Murder of Monsieur Fualdes (1817, Fr.)
Preedy, G. R. Painted Angel (1809-11, Ger.)
Price, A. '44 Vintage (1944, Fr.)
Pritchett, A. Karamour (Eng.)
    Legacy (1800s, Eng.)
    Malpas Legacy (1800s, Eng.)
    Mill Reef Hall (Eng.)
Prokosch, F. Tale for Midnight (1500s, It.)
Queen, E. And on the Eighth Day (1943, Nev.)
    Study in Terror (1888, Eng.)
Radcliffe, A. Castles of Athlin and Dunbayne (Middle Ages, Scot.)
    Mysteries of Udolpho (1600s, It.)
    Sicilian Romance (1580, Sic.)
Rae, H. C. Rookery (ca.1850, Eng.)
Rafferty, S. S. Fatal Flourishes (ca. 1750, U.S.)
Ragosta, M. J. Lorena Veiled (ca.1905, Pa.)
Rauch, C. Spy on Riverside Drive (1943, NYC)
Raynes, J. Legacy of the Wolf (1857, Scot.)
Reese, J. Weapon Heavy (1800s, Kan.)
Reynolds, G. Victor Maury, the French Detective (1807, Paris)
Rhys, J. Wide Sargasso Sea (1830s, Carib.)
Richards, C. Death of an Angel (1890s, NYC)
    Marble Jungle (1890s, New Or.)
Richards, D. Double Game (1939, Berlin)
Richmond, D. Dunkirk Directive (WWII, Eng.)
Riefe, B. Auldearn House (1930s, Scot.)
Rigg, J. Pencarnan (1920, Wales)
    Slipperdown Chant (ca.1910, Eng.)
Roberts, J. L. Castlereagh (1819, Eng.)
    Jade Vendetta (1890s, Eng.)
    Ravenswood (1800s, Eng.)
    Wilderness Inn (1795, West)
Roberts, W. D. Radkin Revenge (1862, Calif.)
    Search for Willie (ca.1900, Nev.)
    Stuart Strain (1850, Calif.)
    White Jade (1885, Calif.)
Robinson, Derek. Eldorado Network (1941, Eng.)
Rockwood, H. Walt Wheeler, the Scout Detective (1862, Va.)
Roeburt, J. Al Capone (1919-29, Chi.)
    Mobster (1929, Chi.)
    Sing Out, Sweet Homicide (1925, NYC)
Roof, K. M. Murder on the Salem Road (ca.1850, Mass.)
Roosevelt, J. Family Matter (1943, U.S.)
Roscoe, T. To Live and Die in Dixie (1902, Va.)
Rose, G. Bright Adventure (ca.1905, S. Am.)
    Clear Road to Archangel (1917, Russ.)
Rosen, V. Gun in His Hand (1931, NYC)
Ross, Clarissa. Face in the Pond (1870, Scot.)
    Istanbul Nights (1861, Istan.)
    Kashmiri Passions (1856, India)
    Moscow Mists (Moscow)
Ross, Dana. Demon of the Darkness (1889, Eng.)
    Figure in the Shadows (1894, Maine)
    Raven and the Phantom (1800s, Phil.)
Ross, Marilyn. Curse of Black Charlie (1775, Edin.)
    Dark Towers of Fog Island (1877, Can.)
    Death's Dark Music (1919, Scot.)
    Ghost and the Garret (1837, Eng.)
    Ghost Ship of Fog Island (ca.1900, Can.)
    Mask of Evil (1853, Va.)
    Mistress of Moorwood Manor (1879, Eng.)
    Phantom Manor (1881, Eng.)
    Phantom of Fog Island (1870, Can.)
    Phantom of the Snow (1854, Glasgow)
    Pleasure's Daughter (ca.1670, Eng.)
    Satan's Rock (1900, Can.)
    Temple of Darkness (1665, Eng.)
    Vampire Contessa (1880s, Eng.)
Ross, W. E. D. Twilight Web (1892, Maine)
    Whispering Gallery (1884, Va.)
Rostov, M. Night Hunt (1962, Ger.)
Royde-Smith, N. Altar-Piece (ca.1910, Eng.)
Russell, A. Larksong at Dawn (Scot.)
Russell, W. C. Tragedy of Ida Noble (1838, ship)
Saberhagen, F. Holmes-Dracula File (1897, Eng.)

Sachar, H. M. Man on the Camel (ca.1972, Isr.)
Saffron, R. Demon Device (1917, Ger.)
St. Clair, L. Obsessions (1918-58, U.S.)
St. George, G. Proteus Pact (WWII, Ger.)
St. James, B. April Thirtieth (ca.1800, Paris)
St. John, N. Guinevere's Gift (ca.1905, Eng.)
    Medici Ring (1874, Boston)
    Wychwood (1800s, Eng.)
Salisbury, C. Dark Inheritance (ca.1850, Eng.)
Salvato, S. A. Briarcliff Manor (ca. 1850, N.Y.)
Sanchez, T. Zoot-Suit Murders (1943, L.A.)
Sanders, J. Cromwell's Cavalier (1650s, Eng.)
    Firework for Oliver (1654, Fr.)
    Hat of Authority (1656, Carib.)
    Roundhead Retreat (1600s)
    Without Trumpet or Drum (1600s)
Sarasin, J. G. Fleur de Lys (1600s, Fr.)
    Mystery of Martin Guerre (1500s, Fr.)
Scherf, M. Don't Wake Me While I'm Driving (1920s, N. Dak.)
Schnurr, W. Johnny Death (1933-4, U.S.)
Scholefield, A. Alpha Raid (WWI)
Schubert, J. D. Keep (1880s, N.Y.)
Schuler, F. Pearl Harbor Cover-Up (1941, Haw.)
Scoppettone, S. Some Unknown Person (1906-1977, N.J.)
Scott, Douglas. Gift of Artemis (WWII)
Seaman, D. Chase Royal (1800s, Eng.)
Sebastian, M. Bow Street Brangle (ca.1820, Eng.)
    Bow Street Gentleman (ca.1820, Eng.)
Sela, O. Exchange of Eagles (1940, Ger.)
    Petrograd Consignment (1919, Russ.)
Sellars, M. House on Black Bayou (1700s, La.)
Selwyn, F. Cracksman on Velvet (1800s, Eng.)
    Sergeant Verity and the Blood Royal (1860, Pa.)
    Sergeant Verity and the Imperial Diamond (1800s, India)
    Sergeant Verity and the Swell Mob (ca.1860, Eng.)
    Sergeant Verity Presents His Compliments (1860, Eng.)
Semenov, J. Himmler Ploy (WWII, Ger.)
Shaffer, E. A. Major Washington (1754, Va.)
Shearing, J. Airing in a Closed Carriage (1889, Eng.)
    Aunt Beardie (1794, Eng.)
    Blanche Fury (1848-50, Eng.)
    Fetch (1870, Eng.)
    For Her to See (1800s, Eng.)
    Forget-Me-Not (1800s, Fr.)
    Golden Violet (1860, Jam.)
    Lady and the Arsenic (1869, Fr.)
    Laura Sarelle (1700s, Eng.)
    Mignonette
    Moss Rose (1800s, Eng.)
Sheldon, R. Harsh Evidence (1874, Eng.)
Shelley, S. Bowmanville Break (1943, Can.)
    Francine (1944, Sp.)
Shenkin, E. Brownstone Gothic (1871, NYC)
    Midsummer's Nightmare (1923, U.S.)
Sheppard, S. Four Hundred (1872, Eng.)
Sherburne, J. Death's Pale Horse (1880s, N.Y.)
Sheridan, A. M. Summoned to Darkness (1891, Venice)
Sherridane, D. Heart of a Gangster (1920s, S.F.)
Shimer, R. H. Cricket Cage (1886, Seattle)
Shoebridge, M. Ranleigh Court (1800s, Eng.)
Short, C. Black Room (1892, Ger.)
Shreve, S. R. Children of Power (1954, Wash. D.C.)
Shulman, S. Bride of Devil's Leap (1800s, Eng.)
    Lady of Arlac (1892, Fr.)
Siegel, B. Adventures of Richard O'Boy (1850s, Eng.)
Simmel, J. M. Sybil Cipher (1950s, Berlin)
Simpson, G. E. Fair Warning (WWII)
Sinclair, A. Facts in the Case of E. A. Poe (1811, U.S.)
Singer, N. Shakedown Kid (1930s, U.S.)
Skoggard, B. China Hand (ca.1948, China)
Smith, Catherine. Barozzi (1500s, Venice)
Smith, Shelley. Afternoon to Kill (ca. 1910, Eng.)
Spike, P. Night Letter (1940, Mich.)
Squire, R. Portrait of Barbara (1891, Eng.)
Stafford, C. Honour of Ravensholme (1800s, Eng.)
    Moira (Scot.)

Stanford, A. Mission in Sparrow Brush Lane (1943, Eng.)
Stanley, J. Bogart 48 (1948, L.A.)
Stanley, S. Rogue's Castle (Minn.)
Stephenson, M. House on Wath Moor (1800s, Eng.)
Stevens, R. T. Flight from Bucharest (1918, Europe)
Stevenson, F. Curse of the Concullens (1865, Ire.)
    Dark Odyssey (ca.1845, Calif.)
    Ides of November (1950s, Calif.)
    Kilmeny in the Dark Wood (1800s, Eng.)
    Shadow on the House (1905, Calif.)
    Witch's Crossing (1870, Mass.)
Stevermer, C. J. Death of a Borgia (ca.1400, Rome)
Steward, B. Evermore (1889, Paris)
    Lincoln Diddle (1860s, U.S.)
Stone, Elna. Visions of Esmaree (1930s, South)
Stubbs, J. Case of Kitty Ogilvie (1700s, Scot.)
    Dear Laura (1890s, Eng.)
    Golden Crucible (1906, S.F.)
    My Grand Enemy (1750s, Eng.)
    Painted Face (1902, Paris)
Sturrock, J. Conspiracy of Poisons (ca.1800, Eng.)
    Village of Rogues (ca.1800, Eng.)
    Wicked Way to Die (ca.1800, Eng.)
    Wilful Lady (1802, Eng.)
Sussman, B. J. Shanghai (1945, Shanghai)
Swinson, A. Sergeant Cork's Casebook (ca.1890, Eng.)
    Sergeant Cork's Second Casebook (ca.1890, Eng.)
Symons, J. Blackheath Poisonings (1890s, Eng.)
    Bland Beginning (1924, Eng.)
    Sweet Adelaide (1880s, Eng.)
Tarrant, J. Clauberg Trigger (1945, Ger.)
    Rommel Plot (WWII, Fr.)
Taschdjian, C. Peking Man Is Missing (1940s, Peking)
Tattersall, J. Chanter's Chase (ca.1800, Eng.)
    Damnation Reef (ca.1890, Carib.)
    Dark at Noon (Wales)
    Lady Ingram's Retreat (1808, Eng.)
    Midsummer Masque (ca.1810, Eng.)
    Wild Hunt (1809, Eng.)
    Witches of All Saints (1811, Eng.)
Taylor, G. E. Death of Jason Darby (1778, Eng.)
Tempest, S. Winter of Fear (1872, Eng.)
Thatcher, J. Nightgleams (ca.1900, NYC)
Thayer, J. S. Earhart Betrayal (1946, Far East)
    Hess Cross (1942, Chi.)
    Stettin Secret (1947, Pol.)
Thomas, Craig. Wolfsbane (1963, Fr.)
Thomas, F. Sherlock Holmes and the Golden Bird (1890, Eng.)
    Sherlock Holmes and the Sacred Sword (1890, Eng.)
Thomas, Leslie. Ormerod's Landing (1940, Fr.)
Thomas, Ross. Eighth Dwarf (1946, Ger.)
Thompson, E. To Catch a Rainbow (1868, Australia)
Thomsen, F. Second Lady Cameron (1800s, Scot.)
Thorndike, R. Amazing Quest of Doctor Syn (1780, Eng.)
    Courageous Exploits of Doctor Syn (ca.1780, Eng.)
    Doctor Syn (ca.1780, Eng.)
    Doctor Syn on the High Seas (ca.1780, ship)
    Doctor Syn Returns (ca.1780, Eng.)
    Further Adventures of Doctor Syn (ca.1780, Eng.)
    Shadow of Doctor Syn (ca.1780, Eng.)
Thornton, F. J. Snake Harvest (1898, Phil.)
Thum, M. Abbey Court (1800s, Ire.)
    Fernwood (1860s, Va.)
Thurman, S. "Mad Dog" Coll (1932, NYC)
Thynne, R. Boffin's Find (1850s, Australia)
Tippette, G. Bank Robber (1800s, West)
    Wilson's Gold (1800s, West)
    Wilson's Luck (1800s, West)
Tokson, E. Cavender's Balkan Quest (ca.1914, Balkans)
Tomlinson, G. On a Field of Black (1875, Pa.)
Torrio, V. Bootlegger (1920s, Chi.)
    Executioner (1920s, Chi.)
Tourney, L. Players' Boy Is Dead (1601, Eng.)
Tozer, B. Riddle of the Forest (1890s, Eng.)
Tracy, D. Editor (1932, U.S.)
Trevelyan, J. Greythorne (1800s, Eng.)
Truscott, L. K. Dress Gray (1960s, Md.)
Tryon, T. Other (1930s, Conn.)
Tucker, J. Blaze of Riot (1933, Berlin)

Settings Index

Turnbull, A. S. Wedding Bargain (1935, N.Y.)
Turpin, A. Little Medicine Bottle (1930s)
Tyler, W. T. Man Who Lost the War (1945-7, Europe)
Tynan, K. Agatha (1926, Eng.)
Unsworth, B. Idol Hunter (1908, Turk.)
Unsworth, M. Wild Winds (1800s, Scot.)
Vale, R. M. House on Rainbow Leap (1865, Ill.)
Vandergriff, A. Bell Tower of Wyndspelle (ca.1770, Mass.)
   Wyndspelle (ca.1770, Mass.)
   Wyndspelle's Child (1815, Mass.)
Van Gulik, R. all 18 titles (600s, China)
Vaughan, M. Discretion of Dominick Ayres (1896, Eng.)
Vaughan, R. Valkyrie Mandate (1963, Saigon)
Villiers, M. Serpent of Lilith (ca.1860, Eng.)
Vincent, C. Garden of Satan (1892, U.S.)
Vosper, G. V. Squire of Landrewn (1838, Eng.)
Wagner, G. Season of Assassins (1940s)
Walk, C. E. Paternoster Ruby (1892, U.S.)
Walker, P. Women in Whitehall (1917, Eng.)
Wallace, E. Devil Man (1875, Eng.)
Warren, P. Castle of Dreams (ca.1860, U.S.)
Watson, C. In a Dark Time (1973, Minn.)
Webb, J. F. Somewhere Within This House (1887, Haw.)
Weissman, J. Zodiac Killer (1960s, S.F.)
Wellman, M. W. Sherlock Holmes's War of the Worlds (1902, Eng.)
Westlake, D. E. Gangway! (1874, S.F.)
Weston, H. G. House of False Faces (1860s, La.)
   Mystic Manor (1890, N.Y.)
Weyman, S. J. Man in Black (1637, Fr.)
Wheatley, D. Code Word—Golden Fleece (1939, Pol.)
   Come into My Parlour (1941, Russ.)
   Dark Secret of Josephine (1793-4, W.I.)
   Desperate Measures (1814-5, Belg., Paris)
   Evil in a Mask (1806-9, Russ., Port.)
   Gateway to Hell (1953, Arg.)
   Irish Witch (1812-4, U.S., Ire.)
   Launching of Roger Brook (1783-7, Fr., Eng.)
   Man Who Killed the King (1793-4, Fr.)
   Prisoner in the Mask (1890s, Paris)
   Rape of Venice (1796-8, India, Venice)
   Ravishing of Lady Mary Ware (1809-12, Port., Russ.)
   Rising Storm (1789-92, Naples, Fr.)
   Second Seal (1914, Vienna, Eng.)
   Shadow of Tyburn Tree (1787-9, Scand., Russ.)
   Sultan's Daughter (1798-9, Egypt, Fr.)
   They Used Dark Forces (1943, Ger.)
   Traitor's Gate (1942, Hung.)
   Vendetta in Spain (1906, Sp.)
   Wanton Princess (1800-05)
White, Alan. Long Drop (WWII, Belg.)
   Long Hand of Death (WWII)
   Long Night's Walk (WWII, Ger.)
White, R. J. Smartest Grave (1901, Eng.)
   Women of Peasenhall (1902, Eng.)
Whitney, P. A. Quicksilver Pool (ca.1806, NYC)
   Sea Jade (1870s, New Eng.)
   Trembling Hills (1906, S.F.)
   Window on the Square (1870s, NYC)
Wilder, T. Eighth Day (ca.1900, Ill.)
Willis, T. Lions of Judah (1939, Ger.)
Wilson, P. W. Black Tarn (1909, Eng.)
   Bride's Castle (1893, Eng.)
   Old Mill (1912, Eng.)
Winston, D. Adventuress (ca.1900, Md.)
   Gallows Way (1858, N.C.)
   Haversham Legacy (1860s, Wash. D.C.)
Winward, W. Hammerstrike (1942, Eng.)
   Seven Minutes Past Midnight (1945, Berlin)
Wiseman, T. Day Before Sunrise (1945, Berlin)
   Game of Secrets (1947, Wash. D.C.)
Withers, E. L. Heir Apparent (1941, It.)
Wood, Barbara. Curse This House (1800s, Eng.)
   Night Trains (WWII, Pol.)
Wood, H. H. Dig: Two Heads Wanted (1847, Eng.)
Woolrich, C. Doom Stone (1757-1941, U.S.)
York, E. Medea Legend (Eng.)
York, H. Malverne Manor (1800s, Eng.)
   Tremorra Towers (1870, Eng.)
   Venetian Charade (1881, Venice)
Zaroulis, N. L. Poe Papers (1890s, Mass.)
Zochert, D. Murder in the Hellfire Club (1775, Eng.)

PEKING (SEE ALSO: CHINA; SHANGHAI; FORMOSA; HONG KONG; FAR EAST; MONGOLIA)

Aarons, E. S. Assignment—Peking
Becker, S. Last Mandarin
Bennett, James. Spinach Jade
Carter, Nick. Peking/The Tulip Affair
Daniels, N. Baron's Mission to Peking
Drake, F. Appointment in Peking
Marquand, J. P. Thank You, Mr. Moto
Smith, Don. Peking Connection
   Secret Mission: Peking
Taschdjian, C. Peking Man Is Missing

PENNSYLVANIA (PA. SEE ALSO: PHILADELPHIA; PITTSBURGH)

Aswad, B. Winds of the Old Days
Black, R. J. Killing of the Golden Goose
Booton, K. Quite by Accident
   Time Running Out
   Toy
Brown, C. B. Wieland
Buranelli, P. Happy Nightmare
Caldwell, A. B. Death Rattle
Carr, J. D. Poison in Jest
Chamberlain, G. A. Night at Lost End
Chase, J. Behind the Purple Mask
   Golden Imp
Clark, W. C. Murder Goes to Bank Night
Colbron, G. I. Club Car Mystery
Constantine, K. C. all 4 titles
Davies, L. Terror at Dearcliff House
Davis, F. C. Deep Lay the Dead
   Graveyard Never Closes
   Let the Skeletons Rattle
Dyer, G. Storm Is Rising
Emerick, L. Web of Evil
Eppley, L. Murder in the Cellar
Gibbs, G. F. Castle Rock Mystery
   Out of the Dark
Green, A. K. House in the Mist
Hall, G. Juliet Room
Hart, C. G. Flee from the Past
Highsmith, P. Cry of the Owl
Holland, R. S. How Murder Speaks
Hultman, H. J. Ready for Death
Hunter, J. D. Spies, Inc.
Keith, C. Crayfish Dinner
   Rich Uncle
Kelland, C. B. Mark of Treachery
Knotts, R. Meeting by Moonlight
Koontz, D. R. After the Last Race
Laing, P. If I Should Murder
Letton, J. Allegra's Child
Leverage, H. Phantom Alibi
Lippincott, N. Murder at Glen Athol
Long, A. R. Corpse at the Quill Club
   Once Acquitted
McGivern, W. P. Pride of Place
MacNeil, N. Third on a Seesaw
Martin, H. R. House on the Marsh
Massey, M. Left Hand Left
Mayo, K. Mounted Justice
Michaels, B. House of Many Shadows
Myers, I. B. Murder Yet to Come
Nichols, S. Rachel
   Sunless Day
   That Dark Inn
Noone, E. 5 titles
Plagemann, B. Wolfe's Cloister
Popkin, Z. Dead Man's Gift
Powell, R. Don't Catch Me
Propper, M. Station Wagon Murder
Ragosta, M. J. Lorena Veiled
Ransome, S. 7 titles
Reilly, H. Doll's Trunk Murder
Reisner, M. House of Cobwebs
Rowe, J. N. Judas Squad
St. Clair, E. Provenance House
   Singing Harp
Seidman, R. J. Bucks County Idyll
Shallit, J. Yell Bloody Murder
Spatz, H. D. Murder with Long Hair
Steele, C. Army of the Dead
Stein, A. M. Nowhere?
Stilson, C. B. Seven Blue Diamonds
Stone, A. American Pep
Strange, J. S. Make My Bed Soon
Tomlinson, G. On a Field of Black
Turnbull, P. Madame Judas
Weber, R. Grave-Maker's House
Whitney, P. A. Snowfire
Yates, P. Curtain Call for Murder

PERSIA. SEE: IRAN.

PERU (SEE ALSO: SOUTH AMERICA)

Barry, M. Peruvian Nightmare
Benton, K. Craig and the Jaguar
Carter, Nick. Red Rays
Hale, M. Empire on Arumac
Hebden, M. Portrait in a Dusty Frame
Leonard, C. L. Pursuit in Peru
Leroux, G. Bride of the Sun
Myers, M. R. Journey to Cuzco

Stein, A. M. Up to No Good

PHILADELPHIA (PHIL. SEE ALSO: PENNSYLVANIA; PITTSBURGH)

Barry, M. Philadelphia Blow-Up
Biddle, A. J. D. Word for Word and Letter for Letter
Blum, R. Simultaneous Man
Booton, K. Who Knows Julie Gordon?
Brown, C. B. Arthur Mervyn
   Ormond
Carr, J. D. Burning Court
Charteris, L. Catch the Saint
Chase, J. Blue Shadow Mystery
Conroy, Al. Death Grip
Fantoni, B. Mike Dime
Fitzmaurice, E. Circumstantial Evidence
Ford, L. Philadelphia Murder Story
Ford, M. F. Shadow of Murder
Goodis, D. Fire in the Flesh
Hallahan, W. H. Keeper of the Children
Holland, R. S. House of Delusion
   Panelled Room
Krasney, S. A. Mania for Blondes
   Morals Squad
Kyd, T. Blood Is a Beggar
   Blood of Vintage
   Blood on the Bosom Divine
Lewis, Arthur H. Copper Beeches
Lippard, G. Quaker City
Long, A. R. Death Looks Down
   Symphony in Murder
   Triple Cross Murders
McGivern, W. P. Big Heat
   Shield for Murder
McMullen, M. Death by Bequest
   Funny, Jonas, You Don't Look Dead
Marchant, W. Firebird
Mathieson, T. Devil and Ben Franklin
O'Neil, K. Death Strikes at Heron House
   Mooney Moves Around
   Ninth Floor: Middle City Tower
Pendleton, D. Panic in Philly
Powell, R. False Colors
Propper, M. 12 titles
Ronns, E. Gang Rumble
Ross, Dana. Raven and the Phantom
Savidge, E. C. Wallingford
Selwyn, F. Sergeant Verity and the Blood Royal
Shallit, J. Billion Dollar Body
   Kiss the Killer
   Lady, Don't Die on My Doorstep
Spicer, B. 5 titles
Thornton, F. J. Snake Harvest
Williams, S. Aconite Murders
   Murder of Miss Betty Sloan
Witley, A. F. Dangerously Blonde

PHILIPPINES (PHILIP. SEE ALSO: MANILA; FAR EAST)

Del Mar, D. Blood Pearls of Sulu
Kenyon, M. Sorry State
Mason, V. W. Fort Terror Murders

PHOENIX (SEE ALSO: ARIZONA; TUCSON; SOUTHWEST)

Barry, M. Phoenix Inferno
Brown, F. Five-Day Nightmare
Gage, E. Phoenix No More
Hughes, D. B. Expendable Man
Maling, A. Schroeder's Game
Wohl, J. P. Blind Trust Kills

PITTSBURGH (PITT. SEE ALSO: PENNSYLVANIA; PHILADELPHIA)

Creed, W. Death Comes Grinning
Dwyer, D. Legacy of Terror
Eyre, E. Girl in the Tiffany Dress
Rinehart, M. R. Case of Jennie Brice
Stone, E. C. Fear Rides the Fog
Whitfield, R. Green Ice

POLAND (POL. SEE ALSO: WARSAW)

Annesley, M. Vanished Vice-Counsel
Conway, P. Escape to Danger
Iams, J. Shot of Murder
MacInnes, H. While Still We Live
Marchmont, A. W. In the Cause of Freedom
Marshall, B. Month of the Falling Leaves
Nasielski, A. Ace of Spades
Thayer, J. S. Stettin Secret
Wheatley, D. Code Word—Golden Fleece
Wilkinson, R. H. Zittaw the Cruel
Wood, Barbara. Night Trains

PORTLAND (SEE ALSO: OREGON; NORTHWEST)

Trimble, L. Blondes Are Skin Deep
Williams, W. Take the Money and Die

PORTUGAL (PORT. SEE ALSO: LISBON; MADEIRA)

Bridge, A. Malady in Madeira
   Portuguese Escape

Buckingham, N.   Jade Dragon
Charteris, L.   Saint in Pursuit
De Villiers, G.   Portuguese Defection
Fleming, Joan.   Death of a Sardine
Grey, N.   Dark Sun, Pale Shadows
Hodge, J. A.   Winding Stair
Holton, L.   Deliver Us from Wolves
Knight, L. A.   Pawn
Lee, Babs.   Passport to Oblivion
Lee, Elsie.   Satan's Coast
MacLeod, Robert.   Burial in Portugal
   Salvage Job
Pemberton, M.   Guilty Secret
Souza, E.   Blue Rum
Spencer, E.   Death of Captain Shand
Walker, D.   Diamonds for Moscow
Walker, Martin.   Infiltrator
Wheatley, D.   Evil in a Mask
   Ravishing of Lady Mary Ware

PORTUGUESE EAST AFRICA. SEE: MOZAMBIQUE.

PORTUGUESE WEST AFRICA. SEE: ANGOLA.

PRAGUE (SEE ALSO: CZECHOSLOVAKIA)
Chase, J. H.   Have This One on Me
Cleeve, B.   Exit from Prague
Crecy, J.   My Face Beneath the Stone
Drummond, I.   Diamonds of Loreta
Gainham, S.   Stone Roses
George, J.   Kill Dog
Heym, S.   Hostages
Hostovsky, E.   Missing
Skvorecky, J.   Miss Silver's Past
Smith, Don.   Secret Mission: Prague
Wheatley, D.   Curtain of Fear

PUERTO RICO (P. Rico. SEE ALSO: SAN JUAN; WEST INDIES; CARIBBEAN)
Carter, Nick.   Filthy Five
Dane, Mark.   Felicia
Gayle, N.   Murder at 28:10
   Sentry-Box Murder
Ingersol, J.   Game Called Murder
Ives, J.   Marchand Woman
Jason, S.   Suicide in San Juan
Knight, Adam.   Sunburned Corpse
Lathen, E.   Longer the Thread
Nessen, R.   First Lady
Pendleton, D.   Caribbean Kill
Sheppard, M.   Strangers in the Sun
Stark, R.   Dame
Telfair, R.   Good Luck, Sucker

RAILWAY. SEE: TRAIN.

RELIGIOUS SETTINGS. SEE: CHURCH.

RENO (SEE ALSO: NEVADA; LAS VEGAS; WEST)
Cain, J. M.   Jealous Woman
   Sinful Woman
Evans, D.   No Slightest Whisper
Ford, L.   Reno Rendezvous
Hamilton, D.   Removers
Homes, G.   No Hands on the Clock
Land, M.   Dream Buyers
Quentin, P.   Puzzle for Wantons
Ross, John.   Devil's Gate Road
Ross, Z. H.   One Corpse Missing
Torrey, R.   42 Days for Murder

RHODE ISLAND (R.I. SEE ALSO: NEW ENGLAND)
Bond, E.   Waiting Eyes
Disney, D. M.   Did She Fall or Was She Pushed?
Dutton, C. J.   Shadow on the Glass
Eliot, G. F.   Navy Spy Murders
Footner, H.   Easy to Kill
Ford, L.   Invitation to Murder
Hayes, L.   Challoners of Bristol
Lamb, A.   Greystones
Lambert, G. B.   Murder in Newport

RHODESIA (Rhod. SEE ALSO: AFRICA)
Ballinger, W. A.   Call It Rhodesia
Butler, K. R.   Fall of Rock
Carter, Nick.   Rhodesia
Creasey, J.   Sleep
Early, R.   Time of Madness
Gilman, D.   Mrs. Pollifax on Safari
Hartmann, M.   Game for Vultures
Langley, B.   War of the Running Fox
McCurtin, P.   Massacre at Umtali
MacKenzie, N.   Strange Happening
MacKinnon, C. K.   Lost Hyena
Rothwell, H. T.   No Honour Amongst Spies

RICHMOND (SEE ALSO: VIRGINIA; SOUTH)
Edwards, Anne.   Child of Night

RIO DE JANEIRO (Rio de J. SEE ALSO: BRAZIL; SOUTH AMERICA)
Bernstein, K.   Senator's Ransom
Caillou, A.   Terror in Rio
Carter, Nick.   Carnival for Killing
   Checkmate in Rio
Chaber, M. E.   Six Who Ran
Fallon, G.   Rendezvous in Rio
Fish, R. L.   Always Kill a Stranger
   Diamond Bubble
   Fugitive
   Xavier Affair
Harvey, M.   Vengeance of the Ivory Skull
Howard, V.   Rendezvous in Rio
Kelsey, V.   Owl Sang Three Times
   Satan Has Six Fingers
Mason, V. W.   Rio Casino Intrigue
Morgan, Dean.   Roston Outfit in Rio
Pierson, E.   Good Neighbor Murder
Seymour, H.   In the Still of the Night

ROCHESTER (Roch. SEE ALSO: NEW YORK; LONG ISLAND; NEW YORK CITY)
Dean, A.   Deadly Contact

ROMANIA. SEE: RUMANIA.

ROME (SEE ALSO: ITALY; FLORENCE; MILAN; NAPLES; SARDINIA; SICILY; VENICE)
Airth, R.   Snatch
Arrighi, M.   Navona 1000
Bagot, R.   Roman Mystery
Ballinger, W. A.   Starlet for a Penny
Bentley, J.   Macedonian Mixup
Benton, K.   Spy in Chancery
Bonner, P. H.   S.P.Q.R.
Bracken, C. P.   Roman Ring
Calvin, R.   Italian Gadget
Carter, Nick.   Massacre in Milan
   Our Agent in Rome Is Missing
Close, R.   Boheme Connection
Collin, R. O.   Imbroglio
Colombo, P.   Throw Back the Little Ones
Connell, C.   Meet Me at Philippi
Daniels, M.   Passport to Terror
Durston, P. E. H.   Mortissimo
Fleetwood, H.   Foreign Affairs
   Girl Who Passed for Normal
   Roman Magic
Gadda, C. E.   That Awful Mess on Via Merulana
Gardner, A.   Six-Day Week
Goodchild, G.   Spanish Steps
Habe, H.   Poisoned Stream
Hanna, D.   Vacant Throne
Heller, F.   Mr. Collin Is Ruined
Howard, H.   Secret of Simon Cornell
Jason, S.   Instant Dead
Jones, D.   Month of the Pearl
Lester, T.   Episode in Rome
Linzee, D.   Discretion
Lorac, E. C. R.   Murder on a Monument
McGivern, W. P.   Margin of Terror
McGuire, P.   Spanish Steps
McInerny, R.   Romanesque
MacKintosh, J.   Roman Adventure
Marcus, C.   Mark Castle—Cable Address: Rome
Marlowe, S.   Peril Is My Pay
Marsh, N.   When in Rome
Maybury, A.   Terracotta Palace
Morley, E.   Intrigue in Rome
Murray, W.   Mouth of the Wolf
O'Brine, M.   Killers Must Eat
Peters, Elizabeth.   Seventh Sinner
   Street of the Five Moons
Pierce, R.   Run, Traitor, Run
Revell, L.   See Rome and Die
Rosenberger, J.   Massacre in Rome
Rostand, R.   Killing in Rome
Rothstein, R.   Hand of Fatima
Rotsstein, A. N.   Judgment in St. Peter's
Stein, A. M.   Sitting Up Dead
Stevermer, C. J.   Death of a Borgia
Stuart, Anthony.   Vicious Circles
Tine, Robert.   State of Grace
Wlaschin, K.   To Kill the Pope
Wolk, G.   Leopold Contract

RUMANIA (Rum. SEE ALSO: BUCHAREST; BALKANS)
Aarons, E. S.   Assignment—Mara Tirana
Abbott, S.   Castle of Evil
Gheorghiu, C. V.   Immortals of the Mountain
McDaniel, D.   Vampire Affair
Nile, D.   Vampire Cameo
Ross, R.   Falls the Shadow
Sandulescu, J.   Carpathian Caper
Saxon, P.   Vampire's Moon
Stoker, B.   Dracula
Stuart, Anthony.   That Man Gull

RUSSIA (Russ. SEE ALSO: MOSCOW; MONGOLIA)
Aarons, E. S.   Assignment—Suicide
Adler, W.   Trans-Siberian Express
Aldanov, M.   Key
Allbeury, T.   Man with the President's Mind
Bax, R.   Came the Dawn
   Red Escapade
Behn, N.   Kremlin Letter
Bernstein, K.   Intercept
Block, Lawrence.   Tanner's Twelve Swingers
Burgess, A.   Tremor of Intent
Butler, Gwendoline.   Red Staircase
Campbell, G.   Wild and Weird
Charles, R.   Arctic Assignment
Clark, Eric.   Black Gambit
Coles, M.   Alias Uncle Hugo
Creasey, J.   Prophet of Fire
Daniels, N.   Spy Hunt
De Halsalle, H.   Woman Spy
Dostoevski, F. M.   Brothers Karamazov
   Crime and Punishment
Drummond, A.   Scented Death
Edelman, M.   Call on Kuprin
Edmonds, H.   Trail of the Lonely River
Ferguson, A.   Random Track to Peking
Freemantle, B.   Face Me When You Walk Away
Garfield, B.   Kolchak's Gold
Garve, A.   Ashes of Loda
Grayson, Rupert.   Gun Cotton Goes to Russia
Hall, Adam.   Sinkiang Executive
Harvester, S.   Red Road
Hope, C. G.   Second Plan
John, H.   Carnellian Circle
John, O.   Beam of Black Light
   Shadow in the Sea
Kaledin, V. K.   Flash D 13
Kiddy, M. G.   Devil's Dagger
Kyle, D.   Cage of Ice
Laflin, J.   Reluctant Spy
Lambert, D.   Yermakov Transfer
Lawrence, Hadley.   Intruder
LeQueux, W.   Strange Tales of a Nihilist
Le Voleur.   By Order of the Brotherhood
   In the Tsar's Dominions
Litvinoff, E.   Blood on the Snow
McCutchan, P.   Man from Moscow
   Moscow Coach
MacKenzie, N.   In Great Danger
McLeave, H.   Double Exposure
Marlowe, S.   Death Is My Comrade
Morton, V.   Yellow Ticket
Nolan, F.   White Nights, Red Dawn
Old Sleuth.   American Detective in Russia
Osborne, G.   Traitor's Gate
Porter, J.   Neither a Candle Nor a Pitchfork
   Package Included Murder
   Sour Cream with Everything
Richmond, M.   Red Claws
Robeson, K.   Fortress of Solitude
Rose, G.   Clear Road to Archangel
Rosenberger, J.   Fatal Formula
Rosenblum, R.   Mushroom Cave
Ruse, G. A.   Houndstooth
Ryck, F.   Green Light, Red Catch
Sangster, J.   Foreign Exchange
Saxon, P.   This Spy Must Die
Scott, R. T. M.   Mad Monk
Sela, O.   Petrograd Assignment
Seton, G.   Eye for an Eye
Smith, Carmichael.   Atomsk
Stohlman, R.   Overflowing Rain
Thomas, Craig.   Snow Falcon
Tucker, W.   Warlock
Van Rjndt, P.   Blueprint
Wallace, E.   Book of All Power
Wees, F. S.   Country of the Strangers
Wentworth, P.   Red Stephan
Wheatley, D.   5 titles
White, E. L.   Elephant Never Forgets
Williams, Alan.   Gentleman Traitor

SAIGON (SEE ALSO: VIET NAM; HANOI; FAR EAST)
Carter, Nick.   Saigon
Chase, J. H.   Lotus for Miss Quon
Kasper, R. C.   Love Spy, Love
Leader, C.   Cargo to Saigon
McQuinn, D. E.   Targets
Magnuson, T.   Small Gust of Wind
Mason, V. W.   Saigon Singer
Saxon, P.   Woman of Saigon
Vaughan, R.   Valkyrie Mandate

ST. LOUIS (SEE ALSO: MISSOURI; KANSAS CITY; MIDWEST)
Beach, E. R.   Joshua Humble
Bent, S.   Buchanan of "The Press"
Dean, R. G.   Murder Makes a Merry Widow
Dunn, D.   Murder's Web
Franklin, M.   Justice Has No Sword
Lawson, W. B.   Frank James in St. Louis
Pendleton, D.   St. Louis Showdown
Sapir, R.   Sweet Dreams
Scarpetta, F.   Slaughterhouse

Settings Index

Smith, T. L. Money War

SALT LAKE CITY (SEE ALSO: UTAH; WEST)
Maling, A. Lucky Devil

SAN ANTONIO (SEE ALSO: TEXAS; DALLAS; HOUSTON; SOUTHWEST)
Davis, J. F. Chinese Label
Marlowe, D. J. Operation Counterpunch
North, S. Jasmine for My Grave

SAN DIEGO (SEE ALSO: CALIFORNIA; LOS ANGELES; SAN FRANCISCO; WEST)
Adams, C. F. Black Door
    Contraband
Douglas, B. Bloody Precinct
Fleischman, A. S. Straw Donkey Case
Hays, L. Harry-O
Masterson, W. Slow Gallows
Miller, Wade. 8 titles
Pendleton, D. San Diego Siege
Stowell, W. A. Wake of the Setting Sun
Wells, S. Death Is My Name

SAN FRANCISCO (S.F. SEE ALSO: CALIFORNIA; LOS ANGELES; SAN DIEGO; WEST)
Adams, C. F. Up Jumped the Devil
Aiken, E. Love and I
Alexander, Jan. Jade Figurine
Alexander, K. Time After Time
Alverson, C. Goodey's Last Stand
Anderson, Poul. all 3 TY titles
Archer, F. Malabang Pearl
    Turquoise Spike
    Widow Watchers
Aresbys. Who Killed Coralie?
Atherton, G. Avalanche
Baker, Lucinda. Walk the Night Unseen
Barry, R. Bay Prowler
Bartholomew, C. Second Sight
Bedford-Jones, H. Shadow
Bennett, Dorothy. Murder Unleashed
Bezzerides, A. I. Thieves Market
Biggers, E. D. Behind That Curtain
    Fifty Candles
Blair, M. Final Ring
Booth, C. G. Those Seven Alibis
Booth, E. Broken Window
Bosse, M. F. Man Who Loved Zoos
Boucher, A. Case of the Seven of Calvary
Boyle, J. Boston Blackie
Braly, M. Shake Him Till He Rattles
Brautigan, R. Dreaming of Babylon
    Willard and His Bowling Trophies
Bretnor, R. Killing in Swords
Brykczynski, T. Caged
Burnham, H. Telltale Telegram
Capelli, A. Frisco Hi-Jack
Carter, Nick. Mind Poisoners
Chamberlain, Esther. Coast of Chance
Chamberlain, L. Other Side of the Door
Chambers, W. Dog Eat Dog
    Thirteen Steps
Charleston, W. Hero Rat
Chevalier, R. For Us the Living
Cheyney, P. Can Ladies Kill?
Coffman, V. Fear of Heights
    High Terrace
    Hyde Place
Cohen, I. R. Passover Commando
Cohen, S. Diane Game
Collins, Mary. Dead Center
    Fog Comes
    Sister of Cain
Conot, R. E. Ministers of Vengeance
Cooke, G. M. Man Behind the Mask
Crane, F. 6 titles
Daniels, D. Circle of Guilt
    Juniper Hill
Davis, K. Dark Side
    Forza Trap
De Bra, L. Ways That Are Wary
De Marco, G. October Heat
Dixon, H. V. Killer in Silk
Dodge, A. M. Eye of the Peacock
Dodge, D. Death and Taxes
    It Ain't Hay
Dong, E. Heart Beat
Doyle, C. W. Shadow of Quong Lung
Drury, Rev. S. Startling and Thrilling Narrative
Duncan, D. Bramble Bush
Dyer, G. Catalyst Club
    Five Fragments
    Long Death
    People Ask Death
Eberhart, M. G. Casa Madrone
Edwards, Alexander. Black Bird
Emery, G. Front for Murder
Eshleman, J. M. both titles
Eyre, K. W. Chinese Box
    Sandalwood Fan
Fair, A. A. Some Slips Don't Show
    Top of the Heap
Falk, L. Hydra Monster

Fessier, M. Fully Dressed and in His Right Mind
Fickling, G. G. Stiff As a Broad
Finnegan, R. Bandaged Nude
    Many a Monster
Fisher, S. Hell-Black Night
    Saxon's Ghost
Fitzsimmons, C. Sudden Silence
Flynn, J. Blood on Frisco Bay
    Body for McHugh
    Five Faces of Murder
    McHugh
Flynn, J. M. Ring Around a Rogue
Folder, L. Rocky Libido in San Francisco
Forbes, C. Year of the Golden Ape
Ford, L. Siren in the Night
Foxx, J. Freebooty
Fraser, E. Emerald Necklace
    Mystery of the Star Sapphire
Freytag, J. Mercenary
Gann, E. K. Of Good and Evil
Gardner, E. S. Case of the Backward Mule
    Case of the Substitute Face
    Murder up My Sleeve
Garlington, P. Aces & Eights
Gates, H. L. Laughing Peril
    Murder in the Fog
Gillette, P. Chinese Godfather
Gilmer, J. L. both titles
Girard, B. Cool Jade
Gold, H. Slave Trade
Goldsmith, G. Layout for a Corpse
Goodis, D. Dark Passage
Gores, J. 6 titles
Gosling, P. Running Duck
Grant, M. Green Eyes
Greenleaf, S. both titles
Greenwald, N. Lady Cat
Gregory, J. Case for Mr. Paul Savoy
    Ladyfingers
Grossbach, R. Cheap Detective
Gunn, J. Deadlier Than the Male
Hamilton, I. Twilight Forest
Hammett, D. 8 titles
Hardin, J. Amateur Hour
Harper, O. Opium Smugglers of Frisco
Held, P. Take My Face
Helmore, N. Affair at Quala
Holzer, H. W. Red Chindvit Conspiracy
House, B. Curse of the Mandarin's Fan
Huffman, L. House Behind the Mint
Hurd, F. House on Russian Hill
Hurlbut, E. H. Lanagan, Amateur Detective
James, B. both titles
Kains, J. Green Lama Mystery
    Laughing Dragon Mystery
Kane, F. Guilt-Edged Frame
    Line-Up
Keating, H. Murder by Death
Kelland, C. B. Dangerous Angel
Keneally, G. P. Nobody Wins
Kenrick, T. Tough One to Lose
Kinlay, A. Killers Cannot Live
Kinsburn, E. Tong Men and a Million
Kuttner, H. Murder of a Wife
    Murder of Ann Avery
    Murder of Eleanor Pope
Lang, H. Corpse on the Hearth
Lee, Elsie. Sam Benedict
Leitfred, R. H. Man Who Was Murdered Twice
Leslie, Jean. Shoes for My Love
Loraine, P. Voices in an Empty Room
Loughead, F. H. Man Who Was Guilty
Lovell, B. E. both titles
McDonald, G. Who Took Toby Rinaldi?
MacGowan, A. Million Dollar Suitcase
    Mystery Woman
    Seventh Passenger
    Shaken Down
McKimmey, J. Blue Mascara Tears
MacLean, Alistair. Golden Gate
Mair, G. B. Jade Cat
Mallory, R. San Francisco Vendetta
Marko, Z. Scratch a Thief
Marlowe, D. Somebody's Sister
Mavity, N. P. Man Who Didn't Mind Hanging
Maylon, B. J. Corpse with Knee Action
Merrick, Mollie. Mysterious Mr. Frame
Mersereau, J. Murder Loves Company
Miller, Marc. Plaid Shroud
    Room, Board and Death
Minton, P. Fog Hides the Fury
Montandon, P. Intruders
Morgan, W. Enforcer
Morrow, S. Murder May Follow
Muller, M. Edwin of the Iron Shoes
Neely, R. Sexton Woman
Nelson, H. L. Copper Lady
    Dead Giveaway
    Fountain of Death
    Title Is Murder
Nelson, Mildred. Dark Stone
Nicholson, S. Yellow Journalist
Nicolai, C. Murder in the Fine Arts
Offord, L. G. Murder on Russian Hill
    My True Love Lies
    9 Dark Hours
    Skeleton Key
Oleck, H. L. Singular Fury

Olsen, D. B. Clue in the Clay
Orpet, F. Murder's No Accident
Palmer, S. Hildegarde Withers Makes the Scene
Park, O. Chinatown Connection
Pendleton, D. California Hit
Pike, R. L. Bank Job
    Deadline 2 A.M.
    Gremlin's Grampa
    Reardon
Pronzini, B. Labyrinth
    Vanished
    Twospot
Queen, E. Four Johns
Quentin, P. Puzzle for Puppets
Quinn, T. Great Bridge Conspiracy
Raison, M. M. Gay Mortician
Rath, V. 6 titles
Rayter, J. Victim Was Important
Reed, I. Last Days of Louisiana Red
Rigsby, H. Murder for the Holidays
Ring, D. Peddler
Rivera, W. L. Panic Walks Alone
Roan, T. Dragon Strikes Back
Roberts, W. D. Jaubert Ring
Robeson, K. Death Machine
Rock, P. Dirty Harry
Rogers, J. C. Foul Play
Roscoe, M. Slice of Hell
Ryan, J. both titles
Ryerson, F. Fear of Fear
St. Clair, M. Daddy's Gone a'Hunting
St. Martin, T. Jill
Santiago, V. J. Kill or Be Killed
Sapir, R. Holy Terror
Scortia, T. N. Nightmare Factor
Sherridane, D. Heart of a Gangster
Silver, R. Bogus Lover
Simpson, Robert. Welcome Danger
Sims, G. Hunters Point
Stacpoole, H. D. Mystery of Uncle Ballard
Stanley, J. Dark Side
Stewart, A. Devil's Toy
Strahan, K. C. Death Traps
Stubbs, J. Golden Crucible
Swaim, L. Killing
Taylor, S. W. Grinning Gismo
Teilhet, D. L. Crimson Hair Murders
    Ticking Terror Murders
Thayer, L. 5 titles
Thompson, P. Ironside
Thompson, L. S. Death Stops the Show
Thoreau, D. City at Bay
Trimble, L. Design for Dying
Trinian, J. North Beach Girl
    Scratch a Thief
Upton, R. Who'd Want to Kill Old George?
Valley, M. Magnum Force
Vance, J. View from Chickweed's Window
Van der Zee, J. Blood Brotherhood
Van Dycke, T. Not with My Neck
Walcott, E. A. both titles
Wallace, R. Yellow Shadows of Death
Wambaugh, J. Choirboys
Ward, S. Odds Against Linda
Weissman, J. Zodiac Killer
Westlake, D. E. Gangway!
Whitney, P. A. Trembling Hills
Wick, C. Faceless Man
Wilcox, C. 11 titles
Wiley, H. Copper Mask
    Jade
    Manchu Blood
    Murder by the Dozen
Williams, B. Conflict of Interest
    Matter of Confidence
Williams, C. Nothing in Her Way
Wilson, L. This Deadly Dark
Worley, W. My Dead Wife
Yarbro, C. Q. Music When Sweet Voices Die
Zackel, F. both titles

SAN JUAN (SEE ALSO: PUERTO RICO; WEST INDIES; CARIBBEAN)
O'Donnell, L. Murder Under the Sun

SANTE FE (SEE ALSO: NEW MEXICO; ALBEQUERQUE; SOUTHWEST)
Farnsworth, M. Great Stone Heart
Hughes, D. B. Blackbirder
    Ride the Pink Horse
McKnight, B. Downwind
Morgan, Dean. Assignment to Sante Fe
Reilly, H. Follow Me
Schier, N. Demon of the Opera
Whitney, P. A. Turquoise Mask

SARDINIA (SARD. SEE ALSO: ITALY; FLORENCE; MILAN; NAPLES; ROME; SICILY; VENICE)
Miller, Wade. Mad Baxter
Townend, Peter. Zoom!

SAUDI ARABIA (Saud. Arab. See also: MIDDLE EAST)
Carter, Nick. Arab Plague
Dewar, E. Perfumes of Arabia
Durie, L. This Yellow Slave
Eden, M. Murder of Lawrence of Arabia
Gerard, F. Prince of Paradise
Hastings, Michael. Sands of Khali
Innes, H. Doomed Oasis
MacAlister, I. Valley of the Assassins
Marlowe, H. Seven Pillars to Hell
Marlowe, S. Manhunt Is My Mission
San Antonio. Knights of Arabia
Turner, E. Your Secret Is in a Well

SCANDINAVIA (Scand. See also: INDIVIDUAL COUNTRIES)
Bagley, D. Tightrope Men
Wheatley, D. Shadow of Tyburn Tree
York, A. Co-Ordinator

SCHOOL. See: ACADEMIA.

SCOTLAND (Scot. See also: EDINBURGH; GLASGOW; HEBRIDES)
Aiken, Joan. Castle Barebane
Anthony, Elizabeth. Dramatic Murder
Barrett, C. F. Douglas Castle
Bishop, M. Killraven
Black, G. Cold Jungle
Black, Laura. Castle Raven
   Glendraco
   Wild Cat
Blackstock, C. Factor's Wife
   Shadow of Murder
Bland, J. Death in Waiting
Blickle, K. North Sea Mistress
Buchan, J. 5 titles
Buckingham, N. Call of Glengarron
Caird, J. all 5 titles
Campbell, C. Murder up the Glen
Campbell, H. R. Murder Set to Music
Carr, J. D. Case of the Constant Suicides
Chalmers, S. Blood on the Heather
   Greater Punishment
Cleaton, I. Outsider
Clements, A. Christabel's Room
   Highland Fire
   Mistress of the Moor
Clements, E. H. High Tension
   Perhaps a Little Danger
Corrigan, M. Riddle of Double Island
Courage, J. Nightingales Never Sing
Craig, B. Scobie in September
Creasey, J. Flood
Crofts, F. W. Groote Park Murder
Crowe, C. Talisman
Davies, E. Widow's Necklace
Davies, L. P. Assignment Abacus
De La Torre, L. Heir of Douglas
Devine, D. M. Doctors Also Die
   Fifth Cord
   His Own Appointed Day
   Illegal Tender
Dick, A. MacAlister Looks On
Dipper, A. Golden Virgin
Dorer, N. You Will Like It Here
Dorien, R. House of Dread
Duff, D. Loch Spy
Duncan, W. M. Murder of a Cop
Dunnett, A. No Thanks to the Duke
Elgin, M. Return to Glenshael
   Visibility Nil
Ferguson, J. Dark Geraldine
   Night in Glengyle
Ferrars, E. In at the Kill
Fletcher, J. S. Copper Box
Forrest, Wilma. Anne of Destiny House
Foster, John. Searchers
Fraser, Antonia. Wild Island
Frost, K. Death Registers at the Eagle Arms
Galwey, G. V. Murder on Leave
Gardiner, D. Seventh Mourner
Gardiner, G. At the House of Dree
Garrett, W. Secret of the Hills
Gaston, B. Death Crag
   Deep Green Death
   Drifting Death
Gordon, E. Birdwatcher
Gordon, N. Factory on the Cliff
Grant, Roderick. Stalking of Adrian Lawford
Gray, B. Conquest in Scotland
Halliday, D. Dolly and the Singing Bird
Hamilton, D. Devastators
Hamilton, H. At Night to Die
Hammond, G. Reward Game
Hastings, MacDonald. Cork on the Water
Hayes, L. Dark Legend
Heaven, C. Fires of Glenlochy
Hill, L. Daggers Drawn
Hill, P. Whitton's Folly
Honeycombe, G. Neither the Sea Nor the Sand
Howarth, D. Thieves' Hole
Howatch, S. Waiting Sands
Hubbard, P. M. Causeway
   Graveyard
   Whisper in the Glen
Huff, A. P. Key to Hawthorn Heath
Hull, R. Last First
Hunter, A. Gently North-West
   Gently with Love
Hutchinson, H. Lost Golfer
Innes, H. Sabotage Broadcast
Innes, M. Lament for a Maker
Jamison, A. Lairds of Turriff Hall
Johnston, V. Deveron Hall
Jones, H. M. Scottish Chieftains
Kelly, M. Write on Both Sides of the Paper
Kerr, R. Stuart Legacy
Knight, Alanna. Lament for Lost Lovers
   Legend of the Loch
   October Witch
   White Rose
Knox, B. 17 titles
Knox, R. A. Double Cross Purposes
   Still Dead
Kyle, E. Mally Lee
Lechmere, D. In Deadly Peril
Lee, Elsie. Mansion of the Golden Windows
Leslie, M. Cavanaugh Keep
Lewis, Deborah. Lady in the Tapestry
   Voices Out of Time
Lewis, R. Of Singular Purpose
Lillie, H. Listening Silence
Lyell, W. D. House in Queen Anne Square
Lynch, F. Dangerous Magic
MacArthur, D. W. Landfall
   Mystery of the "David M"
McCloy, H. One That Got Away
MacClure, V. House of Dearth
McCutchan, P. Coach North
McCutcheon, H. Killer's Moon
   Red Sky at Night
MacKinnon, A. Cormorant's Isle
   Dead on Departure
   House of Darkness
   Map of Mistrust
MacKintosh, M. Double Dealers
MacLeod, A. all 3 titles
McNeilly, W. Case of the Stag at Bay
McShane, M. Night's Evil
MacVicar, A. at least 16 titles
Mair, A. Douglas Affair
Mair, G. B. Live, Love, and Cry
Malcolm, M. Headless Beings
Malloch, P. Fugitive's Road
   Walk In, Death
Manners, A. Singing Swans
   Stone Maiden
Manton, P. Murder in the Highlands
Marsh, John. Operation Snatch
Marshall, Edison. Death Bell
Massey, G. Bride of Invercoe
Maybury, A. Dark Star
Mitchell, G. Winking at the Brim
Moffat, G. Miss Pink at the Edge of the World
   Over the Sea to Death
Morris, E. Five Fowlers
Muir, A. Blue Bonnet
   Satyr Mask
   Shadow on the Left
   Third Warning
Muir, T. Death on the Loch
   Death Under Virgo
Munro, H. Clue for Clutha
Ogilvie, E. Devil in Tartan
Ostrander, K. Doom of Glendour
Parker, Richard. Gingerbread Man
Pearson, P. Postscript for Malpas
Peck, W. Warrielaw Jewel
Peters, Elizabeth. Legend on Green Velvet
Rae, H. C. Few Small Bones
   Saturday Epic
   Shooting Gallery
   Skinner
Randall, R. Watchman's Stone
Randell, C. Weeping Tower
Raynes, J. Legacy of the Wolf
Richmond, M. Traitor's Harvest
Riefe, B. Auldearn House
Rochester, G. E. Dead Man's Gold
Ross, Clarissa. Face in the Pond
Ross, Dan. Castle on the Cliff
Ross, Marilyn. Cauldron of Evil
   Cellars of the Dead
   Death's Dark Music
   Waiting in the Shadows
Roy, A. Curtained Sleep
   Devil in the Darkness
Ruell, P. Castle of the Demon
Russell, A. Larksong at Dawn
Saxon, P. Satan's Child
Sayers, D. L. Five Red Herrings
Scott, Annjeanette. Castle for the Left Hand
Shulman, S. Prisoner of Garve
Sinclair, Michael. Dollar Covenant
Smith, Clark. Speaking Eye
Stafford, C. Moira
Stand, M. Death Came with Darkness
Stern, R. M. I Hide, We Seek
   Manuscript for Murder
Stevenson, A. Mask of Treason
Stevenson, D. E. Crooked Adam
Stevenson, T. Murder at the Bar
Stuart, V. Darnley's Bride
Stubbs, J. Case of Kitty Ogilvie
Taffrail. Shetland Plan
Tain, I. Cherrycake Death
Tavis, A. Duke's Day
Thomes, Martin. Laird of Evil
Urquhart, M. Grey Man
Vicary, J. Castle at Glencarris
Walker, D. Ash
   Winter of Madness
Walsh, M. Man in Brown
Warrick, W. Bandit Trust
   Yawning Lion
West, M. L. Summer of the Red Wolf
Wheatley, D. Malinsay Massacre
Whitelaw, D. Horror on the Loch
Wilkinson, R. Big Still
Williams, V. Portcullis Room
Willock, R. I, Victoria Strange
Wurr, H. J. all 3 titles
Wynne, A. Loving Cup
   Murder in Thin Air
   Murder of a Lady

SEA. See: SHIP.

SEATTLE (See also: WASHINGTON; NORTHWEST)
Arre, H. Golden Shroud
Brock, S. Just Around the Coroner
Curtis, W. Red Heroin
Derrick, L. Northwest Contract
Edwards, Alexander. McQ
Hoyt, R. Decoys
Iles, B. Murder in Mink
Kelsey, V. Fear Came First
Pendleton, D. Firebase Seattle
Reed, Harlan. Swing Music Murder
Rice, J. Night Strangler
Ross, Z. H. Overdue for Death
Shimer, R. H. Cricket Cage
Silliphant, S. Slender Thread
Warden, M. Dead Ringer
Warren, V. Invitation to Kill

SENEGAL (Sen. See also: AFRICA, WEST)
O'Neil, K. Death at Dakar

SHANGHAI (See also: CHINA; PEKING; FORMOSA; HONG KONG; FAR EAST; MONGOLIA)
Booth, C. G. General Died at Dawn
Corrigan, M. Shanghai Jezebel
Dekobra, M. Honeymoon in Shanghai
Dodge, S. Shanghai Incident
Fleischman, A. S. Murder's No Accident
   Shanghai Flame
Ile, T. Shanghai Nights
Marshall, W. Shanghai
Mason, V. W. Shanghai Bund Murders
Morland, N. Concrete Maze
   Sing a Song of Cyanide
Smith, Don. China Coaster
Sussman, B. J. Shanghai
Thorne, P. That Evening in Shanghai

SHIP
Aarons, E. S. Sinners
Adams, C. F. And Sudden Death
Adams, E. L. Death Charter
   Murder in the Hurricane
Addis, H. Dark Voyage
Allen, Will. Contraband Cruises
Allison, W. Secret of the Sea
Anderson, J. R. L. Death in the North Sea
Antill, E. Murder in Mid-Atlantic
Ard, W. Babe in the Woods
   Girl for Danny
Arliss, J. Shark Bait Affair
Armstrong, R. Sinister Widow at Sea
Austin, H. Lilies for Madame
Avallone, M. Assassins Don't Die in Bed
Babson, M. Murder Sails at Midnight
Baker, F. Cartwright Is Dead, Sir!
Baker, W. H. Strike North
Barry, C. Death of a First Mate
Bax, R. Red Escapade
Beach, E. L. Cold Is the Sea
Benchley, N. Sail a Crooked Ship
Bentley, J. Mr. Marlow Takes to Rye
Berckman, E. Hovering Darkness
Blake, N. Widow's Cruise
Blanc, S. Sea Troll
Blochman, L. G. Midnight Sailing
Boothby, G. Ocean Secret
Bosworth, A. R. Full Crash Dive
Brandon, J. Mr. Pennington Comes Through
   Murder on the High Seas
Brean, H. Traces of Merrilee
Brewer, M. Windward Passage
Bunce, F. So Young a Body
Burton, Miles. Murder in Absence

Settings Index

Cable, B. Double Scoop
Cameron, O. Owl and the Pussycat
Carr, J. D. Blind Barber
Carter, Nick. Sea Trap
Chambers, D. Blonde Died First
Charles, E. F. Death Crosses the Line
Charles, R. Scream of the Dove
Charteris, L. Saint Overboard
Childers, E. Riddle of the Sands
Clements, C. Hell Ship to Kuma
    Satan Takes the Helm
Cobb, B. Corpse at Casablanca
Cole, G. D. H. Greek Tragedy
Collins, D. Ordeal
Collins, G. Channel Million
Connell, R. Murder at Sea
Coxe, G. H. Inland Passage
Cranston, C. Murder Maritime
Creasey, J. Toff on Board
Crofts, F. W. Enemy Unseen
    Loss of the Jane Vosper
Danton, R. Ship of Hate
Dearden, R. L. Care of the Commander
Derrick, L. Deepsea Shootout
Dickson, Carter. Nine—and Death Makes Ten
Divine, A. D. Terror in the Thames
Dodge, D. Angel's Ransom
Douglas, Gavin. Rough Passage
Douglass, D. M. Many Brave Hearts
Drago, F. Cruise with Death
Drax, P. High Seas Murder
Du Bois, T. Face of Hate
Eberhart, M. G. Five Passengers from Lisbon
Edgar, J. Honduras Double Cross
Ellis, W. Knife Edge
Emery, S. At Nine Bells
Filer, T. Man on Watch
Finney, J. Assault on a Queen
Fish, R. L. Rub-a-Dub-Dub
Fitzsimmons, C. This—Is Murder!
Flagg, J. Death and the Naked Lady
Fletcher, L. Girl in Cabin B54
Follett, J. Churchill's Gold
Footner, H. Dangerous Cargo
Forbes, S. Name's Death, Remember Me?
Forsythe, R. Pleasure Cruise Mystery
Garve, A. Hero for Leanda
Gibbs, G. F. Foul Weather
Gielgud, V. Necessary End
Gill, E. Crime de Luxe
Gilruth, S. Corpse for Charybdis
Gould, S. Murder of the Admiral
Graeme, B. Hate Ship
    Mystery on the Queen Mary
    Racing Yacht Mystery
Green, W. M. Avery's Fortune
Groom, P. Temperamental Journey
Gruppe, H. Truxton Cipher
Hagen, M. A. Murder—But Natch
Hamilton, B. Too Much of Water
Hannay, J. F. W. Gin and Ginger
Harper, Olive. Caught in Mid-Ocean
Harper, R. J. Dragonhead Deal
Harris, Colver. Murder in Amber
Harrison, H. QEII Is Missing
Hawk, J. Mid-Ocean Tragedy
Hebden, M. Pride of Dolphins
Hilton, J. Ship of the Damned
Hocking, A. Mediterranean Murder
Holding, E. S. Lady Killer
Holton, L. Touch of Jonah
Howes, R. Callao Clue
    Death on the Bridge
    Nasty Name Murders
Hufford, S. Midnight Sailing
Hunter, J. White Phantom
Innes, H. Maddon's Rock
    Mary Deare
James, Robert. Board Stiff
Jenkins, G. Grue of Ice
Johnston, R. Angry Ocean
    Stowaway
Johnston, W. Sorry, Chief
Joseph, A. Logan
Kane, F. Conspirators
    Crime of Their Life
Keane, C. Crossing
    Heir
Keene, D. Passage to Samoa
Keinzley, F. Cottage at Chapelyard
Keyes, M. Dead Parrot
King, C. D. Obelists at Sea
King, R. 5 titles
Knight, Adam. Sunburned Corpse
Knight, C. Affair of the Scarlet Crab
Knight, Maxwell. Crime Cargo
Kytle, R. Last Voyage
Lanham, E. One Murder Too Many
    Passage to Danger
Laumer, K. Drowned Queen
Leroux, G. Floating Prison
Little, C. Grey Mist Murders
Lockridge, F. Voyage into Violence
Lockridge, R. Inspector's Holiday
Loder, V. Ship of Secrets
Lorenz, F. Rage at Sea
McCloy, H. She Walks Alone
McCutchan, P. Redcap
McGerr, P. Save the Witness
MacIsaac, F. Death Rides the Deep

MacKinnon, A. No Wreath from Manuela
MacLean, Alistair. Golden Rendezvous
    South by Java Head
    When Eight Bells Toll
Mainwaring, M. Murder in Pastiche
Marsh, N. Clutch of Constables
    Swinging in the Shrouds
Martin, Shane. Wake for Mourning
Martyn, W. Murder Walks the Deck
Maxwell, V. Way of the Tamarisk
Miller, Wade. Nightmare Cruise
Morton, A. Baron on Board
Murray, M. No Duty on a Corpse
Nash, S. Death over Deep Water
Nelson, M. Crusoe Test
Neville, M. Hateful Voyage
Ockley, G. T. Devil on Board
O'Neill, E. A. Rotterdam Delivery
Oppenheim, E. P. Bird of Paradise
    Strange Case of Mr. Jocelyn Thew
Packard, F. Devil's Mantle
Palmer, J. Above and Below
Patrick, Q. S.S. Murder
Pattinson, J. Contact Mr. Delgado
    Mystery of the Gregory Kotovsky
Patton, D. K. Murder on the Pacific
Pilpel, R. H. To the Honor of the Fleet
Pleasants, W. S. Stingaree Murders
Price, W. Death Is a Stowaway
Quentin, D. Perilous Voyage
Radcliffe, G. In the Grip of the Brute
Reed, Harlan. Case of the Crawling Cockroach
Rhodes, K. Crime on a Cruise
Riesenberg, F. Left-Handed Passenger
Rinehart, M. R. After-House
Robeson, K. Mystery Under the Sea
    Red Terrors
    Sargasso Ogre
Rosenberger, J. Iron Swastika Plot
Ross, H. H. Mystery of the Lotus Queen
Ross, W. E. D. Fogbound
Roth, H. Too Many Doctors
Russell, W. C. Tragedy of Ida Noble
Sale, R. Death at Sea
Salisbury, C. Dolphin Summer
Sapir, R. Ship of Death
Saxby, C. Death Cuts the Film
Scott, Justin. Shipkiller
Scott, Mansfield. Phantom Passenger
Sears, R. M. Port of No Return
Shaw, F. H. Atlantic Murder
Shaw, J. T. Derelict
Shore, V. B. Murder on the Glass Floor
Simons, R. Murder First Class
Slater, I. Sea Gold
Smith, Wilbur. Eye of the Tiger
Snow, C. P. Death Under Sail
Spicer, B. Taming of Carney Wilde
Stahl, R. Death Stalks "The Wild Goose"
Stanley, M. B. Alscott Experiment
Stanton, K. Operation Sea Monster
Starrett, V. Murder on "B" Deck
Stein, A. M. Kill Is a Four-Letter Word
Stephenson, H. M. Yo-Ho, and a Bottle of Rum!
Stone, A. L. Decks Ran Red
Streib, S. Predators
Taylor, P. W. Murder in the Flagship
Teed, G. H. Killer Aboard
    Murder Ship
Thayer, L. Dead Reckoning
    Last Trump
    Lightning Strikes Twice
Thorndike, R. Doctor Syn on the High Seas
Trask, K. Murder Incidental
Trew, A. Antonov Project
Trott, N. Monkey Boat
Vance, L. J. Lone Wolf's Last Prowl
    Lone Wolf's Son
    Sheep's Clothing
Webb, F. Caviar Cruise
Wells, Carolyn. Bronze Hand
Wells, S. Murder Is Not Enough
Wheatley, D. Murder off Miami
    Uncharted Seas
White, L. Rich and Dangerous Game
Whitfield, R. Virgin Kills
Whitman, H. E. O. Pirate of Pittsburgh
Wilkinson, K. Murder on the High Seas
Williams, C. Aground
    Dead Calm
Williams, V. Fog
Wilson, M. A. Panic-Stricken
Wilson, S. Greatest Crime
Wood, J. Friday Run
    Lisa Bastian
Worts, G. F. Silver Fang
Wynd, O. Death the Red Flower
Yates, M. T. Hush-Hush Murders
York, A. Captivator
    Fascinator
York, J. Voyage with Murder

SIAM. SEE: THAILAND.

SICILY (SIC. SEE ALSO: ITALY; FLORENCE; MILAN; NAPLES; ROME; SARDINIA; VENICE)

Anonymous. Avenger
Bishop, S. Onlooker
Brydon, S. Manhunt in Sicily
Charteris, L. Vendetta for the Saint
Clifford, F. Another Way of Dying
Crookenden, I. Fatal Secrets
Curtis, J. A. K. Sicilian Mysteries
Gielgud, V. To Bed at Noon
Higgins, J. In the Hour Before Midnight
Howlett, J. Tango November
Larkin, R. T. Honor Thy Godmother
McEvoy, M. Castle Doom
MacKintosh, M. Sicilian Affair
Marchmont, A. W. My Lost Self
Montague, E. Demon of Sicily
Moore, J. Zeluco
Peterson, Jim. Sicilian Slaughter
Radcliffe, A. Sicilian Romance
Rossmann, J. Mind-Masters
Sciascia, L. Equal Danger
    Man's Blessing
Sinclair, Fiona. Meddle with the Mafia
Urquhart, M. Bitter Lemon Mob

SIERRA LEONE (SEE ALSO: AFRICA, WEST)

Daniels, N. Operation S-L

SINGAPORE (SING. SEE ALSO: FAR EAST)

Aarons, E. S. Assignment—Nuclear Nude
Black, G. Suddenly, at Singapore...
Bogart, W. Singapore
Corrigan, M. Singapore Downbeat
Crisp, P. A. In the Shadow of the Dragon
Dekker, J. Singapore Set-Up
Derby, M. Five Nights in Singapore
    Ghost Blonde
    Sun in the Hunter's Eyes
Foxx, J. Jade Figurine
Kirk, L. Man on the Raffles Verandah
Mason, V. W. Singapore Exile Murders
Murray, M. Doctor and the Corpse
Nicholas, J. Asbestos Mask
Pitt, R. Month of the Evil Moon
Sherwood, J. Two Died in Singapore
Stewart, I. Seizing of Singapore
Thomas, Ross. Singapore Wink

SOLOMON ISLANDS (SOL. IS. SEE ALSO: AUSTRALIA; SOUTH PACIFIC)

Frazer, M. Four Jealous Men
Stevens, K. M. Panic in the Solomons

SOUTH (SEE ALSO: THE 14 INDIVIDUAL STATES)

Abbott, S. River and the Rose
Alexander, David. Bloodstain
Alexander, Jan. Darkwater
Allerton, Mary. Shadow and the Web
Arnold, J. Prettybelle
Blackmon, A. both titles
Burton, C. D. Long Goodnight
Cheatham, L. Secret of Saramount
Cohen, O. R. May Day Mystery
Daingerfield, F. Linden Walk Tragedy
Deasy, M. Coriola Affair
Ellis, M. No Man for Murder
Garrison, C. Snake Doctor
Givens, C. G. Jig-Time Murders
Gonzales, J. Follow That Hearse!
Greene, W. Death in the Deep South
Greer, B. Halloween
Hardwick, R. Plotters
    Season to Be Deadly
Hawkins, D. Headsman's Holiday
    In Memory of Murder
    Walls of Silence
Hay, J. Bellamy Case
Hilldrup, R. P. To Die for a Golden Leaf
Hines, J. Slashed Portrait
Holden, G. Killer Loose!
    Something's Happened to Kate
    Sound an Alarm
    Velvet Target
Janeway, H. This Passionate Land
Jensen, R. J. House That Samael Built
Johnson, E. R. Cage Five Is Going to Break
Jones, M. Cry in Absence
Keene, F. Pattern in Black and Red
Kimbrough, K. Dorothy, the Terrified
Lawrence, H. Pavilion
McCarthy, D. Killing at the Big Tree
Macomber, D. Return to Octavia
Maxwell, P. Secret of Mirror House
Morrow, S. Moonlighters
Ogburn, D. Ra-Ta-Plan—!
Packer, V. 3-Day Terror
Phillips, J. Greenwood
Rifkin, S. Dispensable Man
Rilla, W. Dispensable Man
Rock, P. Tick...Tick...Tick
Sapir, R. Chained Reaction
Short, C. Blue-Eyed Boy

Stacy, O. Murder at Cypress Hall
Stone, Elna. Secret of the Willows
    Visions of Esmaree
Taylor, J. R. Macon Moore, the Southern Detective
Terrall, R. Killer Is Loose Among Us
Thomas, Ross. Fools in Town Are on Our Side
Trehearne, E. Storm at Midnight
Van Deusen, D. Murder Bicarb
Walk, C. E. Silver Blade
Warden, L. Murder on Wheels
White, L. Death of a City
Williams, C. Big City Girl

SOUTH AFRICA (S. AFR. SEE ALSO: CAPE TOWN; JOHANNESBURG; TRANSVAAL)

Anthony, N. Diamond Racket
Ashe, G. Promise of Diamonds
Avallone, M. Blazing Affair
Burmeister, J. Running Scared
Christie, A. Man in the Brown Suit
Crosbie, J. Gun Runners
Deane, N. Look at Murder
    Murder Ahead
Desmond, H. Lady, Where Are You?
    Murder Strikes at Dawn
    Silent Witness
Dodge, D. Troubleshooter
Driscoll, P. Wilby Conspiracy
Drummond, June. Farewell Party
    Saboteurs
    Slowly the Poison
E., W. T. I.D.B.
Ebersohn. W. Lonely Place to Die
Finlay, I. Azanian Assignment
Francis, D. Smokescreen
Frost, W. A. Man Between
Gardiner, G. Pattern of Chance
Gates, N. Decoy in Diamonds
Glanville, E. Fair Colonist
Godfrey, P. Death Under the Table
Goff, O. Eye of the Peacock
Gray, D. Baby Face
Grayson, Rupert. Gun Cotton, Secret Agent
Greene, L. P. at least 16 titles
Harris, P. Letters of Discredit
Hartmann, M. Shadow of the Leopard
Hickman, H. Bachelor Party
Hornblow, A. Mask
Jason, S. African Contract
Jenkins, G. River of Diamonds
Leroux, E. One for the Devil
    Third Eye
McClure, J. 7 titles
MacKenzie, N. Dark Night
    Death Holds His Court
Meynell, L. Danger Round the Corner
Milne, S. False Witness
Mitford, B. Veldt Official
    Veldt Vendetta
Niesewand, P. Member of the Club
Peter, J. Runaway
Rosenberger, J. Invasion of the Clones
Sampson, V. Murder of Paul Rougier
Sheldon, L. V. I.D.B. in South Africa
Taube, L. S. Diamond Boomerang
Taylor, P. W. Murder in the Game Reserve
Vahey, J. H. Mr. Nemesis
Van Rensburg, H. Man with Two Ties
Van Wijk, J. L. Iselane
Van Zyl, P. R. Prosecutor
Von Linsingen, F. W. B. Pressure-Gauge Murder
Wheatley, D. Fabulous Valley
Whishaw, F. Diamond of Evil
Whitney, P. A. Blue Fire
York, J. Safari with Fear

SOUTH AMERICA (S. AM. SEE ALSO: INDIVIDUAL COUNTRIES)

Atlee, P. Black Venus Contract
Bagley, D. High Citadel
Bandolier, S. Murder Manana
Barrett, Michael. Last Flowers
Berrow, N. Claws of the Cougar
Boorstin, P. Savage
Caillou, A. Plotters
Chambers, W. Coast of Intrigue
Clifford, F. Act of Mercy
Cory, D. Johnny Goes West
Dundas, L. all 3 titles
Faust, R. Long Count
Fox, C. Sweet Bait of Money
Hall, Adam. Volcanoes of San Domingo
Harwood, R. Guilt Merchants
Holbrook, M. Crime Wind
Household, G. Three Sentinels
Laflin, J. Spy in White Gloves
Le May, A. One of Us Is a Murderer
Luceno, J. Head Hunters
Marlowe, S. Murder Is My Dish
Marquand, J. P. It's Loaded, Mr. Bauer
Mills, A. Pursued
Oppenheim, E. P. Man and His Kingdom

Ordway, P. Teak Forest
Packer, B. J. Caro
Pattinson, J. Last Stronghold
Pendleton, T. Hodak
Pollard, A. O. Death Game
Q., J. Survivor
Reed, E. Passport to Panic
Robeson, K. Blood Countess
    Dust of Death
    Freckled Shark
    Spook Hole
Rose, G. Bright Adventure
Rossiter, J. Deadly Green
Salkeld, M. Missing from the Shelf
Sangster, J. Your Friendly Neighborhood Death Dealer
Sickelmore, R. Osrick
Tiger, J. Mission Impossible
Tracy, L. Terms of Surrender
Trevor, J. Savage Game
Wahloo, P. Assignment
Wheatley, D. Star of Ill-Omen
Woodhouse, M. Moon Hill
Woolrich, C. Black Alibi

SOUTH CAROLINA (S.C. SEE ALSO: CHARLESTON; SOUTH)

Ball, J. In the Heat of the Night
Blackwood, S. Lamontane
Clark, P. Dark River
Cohen, O. R. Gray Dusk
Daniels, D. Journey into Terror
Disney, D. C. Hangman's Tree
Dunn, J. A. House on Doubloon Inlet
Govan, C. N. Plantation Murder
Guild, N. Old Acquaintance
Hayes, L. Harlequin House
Head, A. Always in August
Holland, I. Darcourt
Holman, H. all 5 titles
Hunt, Clarence. Small Town Corpse
Jefferson, B. W. Small Town Murder
Joseph, A. Killers at Sea
King, R. Duenna to a Murder
Marlowe, D. J. Vengeance Man
Nightingale, U. Dawn Comes Soon
Piper, E. Plot

SOUTH DAKOTA (S. DAK. SEE ALSO: MIDWEST)

Hubbard, M. A. Murder at St. Dennis

SOUTH PACIFIC (S. PAC. SEE ALSO: INDIVIDUAL ISLANDS OR COUNTRIES)

Adams, H. By Order of the Five
Binns, O. Secret Pearls
Boothby, G. Lady of the Island
Brown, Carter. No Blonde Is an Island
Carey, Basil. Dead Man's Shadow
Cotler, G. Bottletop Affair
Dana, R. Murder in Paradise
Forsythe, R. Murder on Paradise Island
Gluck, S. Deeper Scar
Grimshaw, B. Mystery of Tumbling Reef
    South Sea Sarah
Hastings, Michael. Green Silence
Innes, M. Appleby on Ararat
McGuire, P. Burial Service
Nisbet, H. Children of Hermes
Peel, C. D. Nightdive
Pentecost, H. Brass Chills
Robeson, K. Deadly Dwarf
    Fantastic Island
Rostand, R. Viper's Game
Sackville, M. Island of Ghosts
    McLoon of the South Seas
Walsh, J. M. Girl of the Islands
Wheatley, D. White Witch of the South Seas
Wickham, H. Scarlet X
Williams, V. Return of Clubfoot
Young, G. Vengeance of Hurricane Williams

SOUTH WEST AFRICA (S. W. AFRICA)

Carter, J. Diamond Mercenaries
Jenkins, G. Twist of Sand
Stander, S. Flight from the Hunter

SOUTHWEST (S.W. SEE ALSO: 4 INDIVIDUAL STATES)

Abbey, E. Monkey Wrench Gang
Anderson, R. Cover Her with Roses
Ashe, G. Long Search
Becker, S. Covenant with Death
Braly, M. Felony Tank
Chase, J. H. Come Easy—Go Easy
Cooper, W. Death Has a Thousand Doors
Creasey, J. Drought
Curtiss, U. Out of the Dark
Dessart, G. Cry for the Lost
Dobbins, P. H. Death Trap
Dunning, L. Keller's Bomb
Garfield, B. Hit
Goldsmith, M. M. Detour

Hamilton, D. Ambushers
    Death of a Citizen
    Intriguers
Hays, L. Nakia
Jason, S. Slaughter in September
Jones, R. P. Heisters
Keene, D. If the Coffin Fits
Locke, D. Drawstring
MacDonald, J. D. Purple Place for Dying
MacNeil, N. Death Takes an Option
Matthews, C. Nylon Nightmare
Neider, C. Authentic Death of Hendry Jones
Niall, M. Bad Day at Black Rock
Nielsen, H. Detour
Pronzini, B. Panic!
Ripley, C. Murder Walks Alone
St. Clair, E. A. Murder Unplanned
Stein, A. M. Sun Is a Witness
Taylor, R. W. Doomsday Square
Thorpe, E. Night I Caught the Sante Fe Chief
Walsh, R. Violent Hours
Weiss, M. L. Death Hitches a Ride
West, D. Wish Me Dead
Wormser, R. Drive East on 66

SOVIET UNION. SEE: RUSSIA.

SPAIN (SP. SEE ALSO: MADRID; CANARY ISLANDS; MAJORCA)

Ames, D. Landscape with Corpse
    Man in the Tricorn Hat
    Man with Three Chins
    No Mourning for the Matador
Arliss, J. Lady Killer Affair
Atkey, P. Blue Water Murder
Ballard, K. G. Bar Sinister
    Coast of Fear
Barclay, J. Unknown
Barker, A. If Anything Should Happen to Me
Beeding, F. Four Armourers
    Hell Let Loose
    Hidden Kingdom
    Mr. Bobadil
Berrow, N. It Howls at Night
Beste, R. V. Next Time I'll Pay My Own Way
Bird, K. Mozart Fiddle
Bonett, J. Better Dead
    No Time to Kill
    Private Face of Murder
    This Side Murder
Bridge, A. Episode at Toledo
Brown, Antony. Slay Me Suddenly
Bruce, L. Death on the Black Sands
Burmeister, J. Someone Else's War
Carter, Nick. 5 titles
Charteris, L. Thieves' Picnic
Cleife, P. Pinchbeck Masterpiece
Clifford, F. Green Fields of Eden
    Spanish Duet
    Third Side of the Coin
Coles, M. Knife for the Juggler
Cordell, A. To Slay the Dreamer
Corrigan, M. Riddle of the Spanish Circus
Cory, D. 8 titles
Creasey, J. Mists of Fear
Deane, N. Death in the Spanish Sun
De Mille, J. Castle in Spain
Denby, E. Mrs. W's Last Sandwich
Dines, M. Operation—Kill or Be Killed
Dixon, J. E. Killers in the Sun
Dodge, D. Carambola
Douglas, M. Prey by Night
    Pure Sweet Hell
Duras, M. Ten-Thirty on a Summer Night
Eden, D. Marriage Chest
Egerton, C. Hour of Truth
Ellery, J. Death on the Circuit
Farjeon, J. J. Peril in the Pyrenees
Farr, C. Web of Horror
Fernandez, A. Castle of Lugas
Fitzgerald, K. Quiet Under the Sun
Frances, S. D. To Love and Yet to Die
Fry, P. Paint-Stained Flannels
Galway, R. C. Assignment Andalusia
Goldston, R. C. Catafalque
Graham, J. Khufra Run
Gray, B. Calamity Conquest
Gruber, F. Spanish Prisoner
Haggard, W. Scorpion's Tail
Halliday, D. Dolly and the Cookie Bird
Harper, S. Necessary Evil
Harrison, E. Fatal Hour
Hebden, M. Errant Knights
Henaghan, J. Azor!
Hocking, A. Mediterranean Murder
Hopkins, R. Raid on the Villa Joyosa
Hossent, H. Memory of Treason
Household, G. Olura
Jacobs, T. C. H. Deadly Race
    Woman Who Waited
Johnston, V. I Came to a Castle
Keyes, F. P. Station Wagon in Spain
Lange, J. Odds On
    Zero Cool
Lansdale, N. White Island

Settings Index

Leonard, C. Steps to Murder
Lodwick, J. Somewhere a Voice Is Calling
Luard, Nicholas. Robespierre Serial
McCutcheon, H. Treasure of the Sun
McEvoy, M. Queen of Spades
McGerr, E. Funeral Was in Spain
McGivern, W. P. Caper of the Golden Bull
    Bulls
    Choice of Assassins
McGuire, P. O. Fiesta for Murder
MacInnes, H. Message from Malaga
MacKenzie, D. Raven in Flight
MacKintosh, M. Appointment in Andalusia
Marlowe, D. J. Operation Stranglehold
Marlowe, S. Jeopardy Is My Job
Marshall, J. Follow a Shadow
Martyn, D. Sinister Legacy
Messmann, J. Inheritors
Mundy, M. Death Cries Ole
Murphy, J. El Greco Puzzle
    Pay on the Way Out
Norman, B. Matter of Mandrake
Oldsey, B. Spanish Season
Ordway, P. Night of Reckoning
Pendower, J. Anxious Lady
Perowne, B. Tilted Moon
Polland, R. Package to Spain
Prichard, K. Chronicles of Don Q
    Don Q's Love Story
    New Chronicles of Don Q
Rathbone, J. Bloody Marvelous
    Carnival!
    Raving Monarchist
Reade, B. Ibeza Syndicate
Revelli, G. Amanda in Spain
Rhodes, Russell. Herod Conspiracy
Richmond, H. Passport to Danger
Rising, L. She Who Was Helena Cass
Roos, K. Scent of Mystery
    Suddenly One Night
Ross, Angus. Ampurias Exchange
    Burgos Contract
Rossiter, J. Golden Virgin
    Rope for General Dietz
St. John, David. Return from Vorkuta
Sanderson, D. Cry Wolfram
Saxon, A. Run in Diamonds
Shelley, S. Francine
Smith, Don. Death Stalk in Spain
Spicer, B. Burned Man
    Day of the Dead
Stark, J. Greek Virgin
Stein, A. M. Snare Andalucian
Symons, J. Plot Against Roger Rider
Tarmey, M. Outrage
Tilden, F. Spanish Prisoner
Townend, Peter. Out of Focus
Vizetelly, E. A. Scorpion
Wahloo, P. Lorry
Wallace, B. E. Man Who Could Not Swim
Walsh, J. M. Spies in Spain
Weil, J. Spy Who Came Home to Die
West, E. Man Running
Wheatley, D. Golden Spaniard
    Vendetta in Spain
Worboys, A. Every Man a King
Yates, G. W. Body That Came by Post

SRI LANKA. SEE: CEYLON.

STOCKHOLM (STOCK. SEE ALSO: SWEDEN; SCANDINAVIA)
Donnel, C. P. Murder-Go-Round
Eden, D. Waiting for Willa
Lang, M. Death Awaits Thee
Regis, J. Copper House
Sjowall, M. 6 titles

SUDAN (SEE ALSO: AFRICA)
Farjeon, J. J. Dangerous Beauty
McCarry, C. Miernik Dossier

SUMATRA (SUM. SEE ALSO: INDONESIA; DJAKARTA; BALI; BORNEO; JAVA; NEW GUINEA)
Aarons, E. S. Assignment—Sumatra
Cleary, J. Long Pursuit

SURINAM (SURI. SEE ALSO: SOUTH AMERICA)
Coxe, G. H. Double Identity
Newell, R. Star House
Rosenberger, J. Surinam Affair

SWEDEN (SWED. SEE ALSO: STOCKHOLM; SCANDINAVIA)
Aarons, E. S. Assignment—Black Viking
Carter, Nick. Bright Blue Death
Coffman, V. Looking-Glass
Craig, P. Gate of Ivory, Gate of Horn
Hamilton, D. Wrecking Crew
Hogstrand, O. all 3 titles
Hubert, T. Trap
Katz, R. Ziggurat
Lang, M. No More Murders
    Wreath for the Bride

Regis, J. No. 13 Toroni
Sjowall, M. Cop Killer
    Murder at the Savoy
    Roseanna
Starnes, R. Requiem in Utopia
Sundman, P. O. Two Days, Two Nights
Walter, H. Bullet for Charles
White, E. L. Step in the Dark

SWITZERLAND (SWITZ. SEE ALSO: GENEVA; ZURICH)
Albrand, M. Hunted Woman
Ames, D. Crime Out of Mind
Arnold, Elliott. Code of Conduct
Becher, U. Woodchuck Hunt
Bennett, Dorothea. Under the Skin
Bordeaux, H. Murder Party
Brewer, G. Devil in Davos
Bridge, A. Numbered Account
Campbell, R. W. Circus Couronne
Canning, V. Panther's Moon
Carling, J. R. Weird Picture
Carr, G. Murder on the Matterhorn
Carter, Nick. Counterfeit Agent
    Eyes of the Tiger
Cartwright, J. Horse of Darius
Cleeve, B. Assignment to Vengeance
Dark, J. Sea Scrape
Drummond, June. Cable-Car
Duerrenmatt, F. Judge and His Hangman
    Pledge
Edwards, Anne. Haunted Summer
    Survivors
Erdman, P. Billion Dollar Sure Thing
Fairchild, W. Swiss Arrangement
Fleming, I. On Her Majesty's Secret Service
Fletcher, L. ...And Presumed Dead
Flynn, J. Five Faces of Murder
Gair, M. Snow Job
Gilman, D. Palm for Mrs. Pollifax
Greene, H. Cancelled Accounts
Griswold, G. Pinned Man
Guild, N. Lost and Found Man
Haggard, W. Visa to Limbo
Hossent, H. No End to Fear
Kavanaugh, C. Deception
Knight, K. M. High Rendezvous
Lakin, R. Angel Take Care
Langley, B. Traverse of the Gods
Lunn, P. Evil in High Places
McCrae, E. House of the Whispering Winds
MacInnes, H. Pray for a Brave Heart
MacLeod, Robert. Pay-Off in Switzerland
Mair, G. B. Kisses from Satan
Marlowe, A. Winnowing Winds
Marlowe, S. Francesca Summit
Marvin, S. Chalet Bougy-Villars
Masterson, W. Man on a Nylon String
Maxfield, H. S. Legacy of a Spy
Meynell, L. Die by the Book
Minton, P. Engraved in Evil
Moyes, P. Season of Snows and Sins
Pearson, D. A. G. Goldon Stone
Penmare, W. Scorpion
Plain, J. Secret of the Snows
Quest, E. Silver Castle
Rey, P. Out
Reynolds, B. Accessory After the Fact
    Affair at the Chateau
Scott, J. M. Other Half of the Orange
Sherwood, J. Limericks of Lachasse
Snell, E. Murder in Switzerland
Stand, M. Death Came in Lucerne
Stanley, M. Swiss Conspiracy
Stein, A. M. Alp Murder
Summerton, M. Ring of Mischief
Townend, Paul. Died O' Wednesday
    Man on the End of the Rope
Trevanian. Eiger Sanction
Walker, D. Devil's Plunge
Waller, L. Swiss Account
White, Ared. Spy Net
Williams, Alan. Shah-Mak
Wood, S. Death in Lord Byron's Room

SYDNEY (SYD. SEE ALSO: AUSTRALIA; MELBOURNE; SOLOMON ISLANDS; TASMANIA)
Beeby, O. all 4 titles
Berrow, N. Eleventh Plague
Brown, Carter. Coffin Bird
Cleary, J. Helga's Web
Cook, K. Bloodhouse
Flower, P. Crisscross
Galway, R. C. Assignment Sydney
Gardiner, H. Murder in Haste
Godwin, J. Requiem for a Rat
Hamilton, I. Persecutor
    Thrill Machine
Mann, L. Murder in Sydney
Martin, A. E. Death in the Limelight
Neville, M. Murder and Poor Jenny
    Murder in Rockwater
    My Bad Boy
Reid, S. Showdown in Sydney
Sherlock, A. B. Yellow Beetle
Singer, B. Don't Slip, Delaney

SYRIA (SYR. SEE ALSO: DAMASCUS; MIDDLE EAST)
Bayne, S. Agent Extraordinary
Carter, Nick. Thunderstrike in Syria
Household, G. High Place
Imber, H. House of the Apricots

TAHITI (SEE ALSO: SOUTH PACIFIC)
Atlee, P. Paper Pistol Contract
Bestor, G. C. Postage Stamp Murder
Gardner, A. Assignment in Tahiti
Vance, J. H. Deadly Isles

TAIWAN. SEE: FORMOSA.

TAMPA (SEE ALSO: FLORIDA; JACKSONVILLE; MIAMI; SOUTH)
Powell, T. 5 titles
Whittington, H. Humming Box

TANGANYIKA (TANG. SEE ALSO: TANZANIA; AFRICA; ZANZIBAR)
Scholey, J. Dead Past

TANGIER (SEE ALSO: MOROCCO; CASABLANCA; AFRICA, NORTH)
Ames, D. They Journey by Night
Baker, W. H. Guardians
Bayer, W. Tangier
Carstairs, J. P. No Wooden Overcoat
    Smell of Peardrops
Carter, Nick. Omega Terror
Crane, F. Coral Princess Murders
Dickson, Carter. Behind the Crimson Blind
Fry, P. Grey Sombrero
Gilruth, S. Snake Is Living Yet
Luard, N. Dirty Area
McCutcheon, H. Yet She Must Die
Mason, V. W. Deadly Orbit Mission
    Two Tickets to Tangier
Rougvie, C. Tangier Assignment
Seymour, H. Intrigue in Tangier
Summers, K. Design for Death
Teilhet, H. T. Terror in Tangier
Verner, G. Faceless Ones
Wallace, E. Man from Morocco
Wilkinson, L. Appointment in Tangier

TANZANIA (TANZ. SEE ALSO: TANGANYIKA; ZANZIBAR; AFRICA)
Blair, J. Danger at Olduvai
Rhodes, Richard. Last Safari

TASMANIA (TAS. SEE ALSO: AUSTRALIA; SYDNEY; MELBOURNE; SOLOMON ISLANDS)
Bridges, H. House of Storms
Butler, R. South of Hell's Gates
Mace, H. Murder Among Those Present
Parker, Richard. Boy on a Chain

TEHERAN (SEE ALSO: IRAN; MIDDLE EAST)
Mayo, J. Once in a Lifetime
Pace, E. Nightingale

TEL AVIV (SEE ALSO: ISRAEL; JERUSALEM; MIDDLE EAST)
Hesky, O. Sequin Syndicate
    Serpent's Smile
    Time for Treason

TENNESSEE (TENN. SEE ALSO: MEMPHIS; NASHVILLE; SOUTH)
Alexander, Jan. Devil's Dance
Bourgeau, A. Lonely Way to Die
Bradley, M. H. Murder in the Family
Cameron, K. 5 titles
Carey, Webster. Walking Tall
Carmack, J. Tell-Tale Clock Mystery
Clark, D. P. Just for the Bride
Farris, J. Sharp Practice
Ford, L. Burn Forever
Heath, W. L. Violent Saturday
Kendrick, B. Out of Control
Morris, W. R. Twelfth of August
Seifert, S. Death Stops at the Old Stone Inn
Warren, R. P. Meet Me in the Green Glen
Whitney, P. A. Glass Flame
Wingate, W. Shotgun

TEXAS (TEX. SEE ALSO: DALLAS; HOUSTON; SAN ANTONIO; SOUTHWEST)
Allan, F. K. Death in Gentle Grove
Amos, A. Borderline Murder
Austin, Anne. Wicked Woman
Baker, A. both titles
Bannerman, W. B. Santos, Border Detective

682 / Thailand

Barron, A. Bride of Menace
　　Dark Vengeance
　　Murder Is a Gentle Kiss
　　Strange Legacy
Barry, J. E. Skeleton in Concrete
Bell, J. One More Time
Boniface, M. Murder As an Ornament
　　Venom in Eden
Cameron, E. both titles
Carlton, M. Hot Oil
Charteris, L. Saint on Guard
Chase, A. M. Murder of a Missing Man
Clifford, C. L. While the Bells Rang
Cohen, B. Coliseum
Crawford, M. Waltz Across Texas
Cunningham, A. B. Death of a Bullionaire
Dean, R. G. Murder Most Opportune
Derrick, L. Supergun Mission
Downing, T. Death Under the Moonflower
　　Last Trumpet
　　Murder on Tour
Ellis, J. S. Heart of Oak Detective
Estes, C. C. Unhappy New Year
Forbes, S. Deadly Kind of Lonely
　　She Was Only the Sheriff's Daughter
　　Some Poisoned by Their Wives
Freeman, M. J. Murder of a Midget
Gatenby, R. Season of Danger
Greene, A. C. Santa Claus Bank Robbery
Halliday, B. Murder Is My Business
Hannay, J. F. W. Thirteenth Floor
Holden, R. P. Death on the Border
Hopkins, K. Campus Corpse
Howard, J. A. Murder Takes a Wife
Hughes, D. B. Candy Kid
Kistler, M. Night of the Tiger
La Fountaine, G. Flashpoint
Lane, J. Like a Man
Lee, G. R. Mother Finds a Body
Levinson, S. both titles
Lingo, A. E. Murder in Texas
McLendon, J. Eddie Macon's Run
Mandelkau, J. Leo Wyoming Caper
Maxwell, R. Minus Man
Morgan, Dean. Rostron Outfit to Texas
Newcomb, K. Pandora Man
O'Farrell, W. Wetback
O'Malley, F. Best Go First
Parker, M. Death Makes a Deal
Pendleton, D. Texas Storm
Perkins, K. Moccasin Murders
Putnam, G. P. Hot Oil
Reasoner, J. M. Texas Wind
Reeves, Ruth. Lament for a Lonesome Corpse
Roberts, Lee. Judas Journey
Roos, K. One False Move
Sapir, R. Final Death
Stein, A. M. Blood on the Stars
Stein, P. Grand Scam
Thompson, J. Killer Inside Me
　　Texas by the Tail
Ullman, A. Naked Spur
Wallace, R. Uniformed Killers
Werry, R. R. Hammer Me Home
White, J. M. Game of Troy
Woody, W. Mistress of Horror House

THAILAND (Thai. See also: Bangkok; Far East)
Aarons, E. S. Assignment—Cong Hai Kill
Ballinger, B. S. Spy in Bangkok
Black, G. Wind of Death
De Villiers, G. Death on the River Kwai
Harvester, S. Battle Road
　　Dragon Road
Mills, James. Truth About Peter Harley
Sheldon, W. J. Red Flower Kill

THEATRE
Anthony, Elizabeth. Ballet of Death
　　Ballet of Fear
Baker, R. M. Death Stops the Rehearsal
Brand, C. Death of Jezebel
Brandon, J. G. Murder on the Stage
Brett, Simon. Comedian Dies
　　So Much Blood
　　Star Trap
Bromley, G. Midsummer Night's Crime
Bude, J. Death Steals the Show
Colburn, L. Death of a Prima Donna
Collins, Michelle. Premiere at Willow Run
Crispin, E. Case of the Gilded Fly
　　Swan Song
Crozier, J. Murder in Public
Daniels, D. Castle Morvant
Davis, K. Forza Trap
Dayle, D. Death in the Theatre
Fletcher, David. Don't Whistle "MacBeth"
Francis, B. Death in Act IV
Holland, R. Danger on Cue
Holt, Gavin. Death Takes the Stage
　　No Curtains for Cora
Jarvis, F. G. Murder at the Met
Keating, H. R. F. Death of a Fat God
Lang, M. Death Awaits Thee
Lee, G. R. G-String Murders
Lockridge, R. Old Die Young
Loraine, P. Exit with Intent

MacDonald, P. Crime Conductor
McDuff, E. M. Murder in the Theatre
Mario, Q. Murder in the Opera House
Marsh, N. Opening Night
　　Vintage Murder
Melville, J. Raven's Forge
Mitchell, G. Death at the Opera
Morice, A. Death in the Round
　　Murder in Mimicry
　　Murder in Outline
Munro, H. Brain Robbers
Paul, B. Fourth Wall
Peters, Ellis. Funeral of Figaro
Plummer, T. A. Muse Theatre Murder
Roos, K. Made Up to Kill
Schier, N. Demon of the Opera
Stewart, A. Devil's Toy
Traubel, H. Metropolitan Opera Murders
Verner, G. Show Must Go On
Williamson, Audrey. both titles
Wilmot, J. R. Death in the Stalls
Yarbro, C. Q. Music When Sweet Voices Die

TIBET (Tib.)
Carter, Nick. Red Guard
Channing, M. White Pythom
Cleary, J. Pulse of Danger
Cory, D. Johnny Goes East
Davidson, L. Rose of Tibet
Easton, R. Dog-Face
　　Red Sap
Edwards, P. Deadly Cyborgs
Evarts, H. G. Turncoat
Fallon, M. Year of the Tiger
Harvester, S. Chinese Hammer
MacKenzie, N. Seven Days to Death
Mason, V. W. Himalayan Assignment
Mather, B. Break in the Line
Mondol, P. Operation Tibet
Mundy, T. Old Ugly Face
　　Ramsden
　　Thunder Dragon Gate
Murray, W. H. Five Frontiers
Pelham, A. Fortress of Ashes
Robeson, K. Meteor Menace
Smith, Don. Secret Mission: Tibet
Wincor, R. Sherlock Holmes in Tibet

TOKYO (See also: Japan; Far East)
Aarons, E. S. Assignment—Tokyo
Bender, W., Jr. Tokyo Intrigue
Bruce, J. Hot Line
Carter, Nick. Temple of Fear
Corrigan, M. Lady from Tokyo
Crane, R. Operation Vengeance
　　Time Running Out
Dark, J. Assignment Tokyo
Derrick, L. Tokyo Purple
De Villiers, G. Hostage in Tokyo
Duncan, R. L. Dragons at the Gate
Goble, N. Condition Green: Tokyo
Kenrick, D. Death in a Tokyo Family
McPartland, J. Affair in Tokyo
　　Danger for Breakfast
　　Tokyo Doll
Marquand, J. P. Stopover: Tokyo
Middleton, T. Operation Tokyo
Miller, L. Operation Godiva
Norman, E. 5 titles
Perrelli, N. Terror in Tokyo
St. John, David. One of Our Agents Is Missing
St. Moore, A. Angel Face Tatters the Kimono
Sheldon, W. J. Blue Kimono Kill
Walker, S. Tokyo Escapade

TORONTO (See also: Canada; Montreal; Ottawa; Vancouver; Winnipeg)
Case, D. Wolf Tracks
Godfrey, E. Case of the Cold Murderer
Malloch, P. Cop-Lover
Millar, M. Devil Loves Me
　　Iron Gates
　　Wall of Eyes
Reeves, J. Murder by Microphone
Ross, H. Fleur de Lys Affair
Watson, P. Alter Ego
Wees, F. S. Faceless Enemy
　　Where Is Jenny Now?
Wright, R. B. Final Things

TRAIN
Adler, W. Trans-Siberian Express
Alexander, Ruth. Rome Express
Burton, Miles. Death in the Tunnel
Carter, Nick. Butcher of Belgrade
Chalmers, S. Crime in Car 13
Christie, A. Murder on the Orient Express
　　Mystery of the Blue Train
Coolidge, E. L. Mountain Limited
Davis, T. Full Fare for a Corpse
Denbie, R. Death on the Limited
Dent, L. Lady to Kill
Downing, T. Lazy Lawrence Murders
　　Vultures in the Sky

Fisher, Laine. Fare Prey
Forbes, C. Avalanche Express
Gordons. Campaign Train
Greene, G. Stamboul Train
Hagen, M. A. Plant Me Now
Highsmith, P. Strangers on a Train
Japrisot, S. 10:30 from Marseilles
King, C. D. Obelists en Route
Koning, H. Petersburg-Cannes Express
Lambert, D. Yermakov Transfer
MacLean, Alistair. Breakheart Pass
MacVeigh, S. Streamlined Murder
Nebel, F. Sleepers East

TRANSVAAL (Trans. See also: South Africa; Cape Town; Johannesburg)
Dekobra, M. Diamond Queen

TRINIDAD (Trin. See also: West Indies; Caribbean)
Brown, Wenzell. Rum and Coca-Cola Murders
Coxe, G. H. One Hour to Kill
Underwood, M. Arm of the Law
Vandercook, J. W. Murder in Trinidad

TUNISIA (Tun. See also: Africa, North)
Benton, K. Craig and the Tunisian Tangle
Davis, Maggie. Rommel's Gold
Evans, K. Shadows of Violence
Henissart, P. Narrow Exit
Jacobs, T. C. H. Target for Terror
Jepson, S. Death Gong
McCutchan, P. Sladd's Evil
Pendower, J. Mission in Tunis
Summerton, M. Sand Rose

TURKEY (Turk. See also: Istanbul; Middle East; Balkans)
Aarons, E. S. Assignment—Ankara
Angus, S. Death of a Hittite
Arnold, M. Exit Actors, Dying
Atlee, P. Underground Cities Contract
Bartram, G. Aelian Fragment
　　Fair Game
Carter, Nick. Strike Force Terror
　　Turkish Bloodbath
Davison, Geoffrey. Chessboard Spies
Drummond, I. Stench of Poppies
Farrere, C. Man Who Killed
Fleming, Joan. Nothing Is the Number When You Die
Forsyte, C. Murder with Minarets
Garve, A. Ascent of D-13
Gilman, D. Amazing Mrs. Pollifax
Katz, R. Spoils of Ararat
Luther, R. Intermind
MacLean, Alistair. Guns of Navarone
Mason, V. W. Dardanelles Derelict
Moyzisch, I. C. Operation Cicero
Munro, J. Innocent Bystanders
Rathbone, J. Diamonds Bid
　　Hand Out
　　Kill Cure
　　Trip Trap
Roudybush, A. Sybaritic Death
Saltmarsh, M. Highly Inflammable
Settle, M. L. Blood Tie
Unsworth, W. Idol Hunter
Westall, W. Sacred Crescents
Wood, C. Death in Ankara

TUCSON (See also: Arizona; Phoenix; Southwest)
Brown, F. Lenient Beast
Creighton, J. Evil Is the Night
Homes, G. Hill of the Terrified Monk
Nielsen, H. Killer in the Street
Reid, D. Death Waits in Tucson

UGANDA (See also: Africa)
Hayes, R. Track of the Beast
Watkins, L. Killing of Idi Amin
Zake, S. J. L. Truckful of Gold

UNITED STATES (U.S. Here is a selection of titles by non-U.S. authors which use non-specific or varying U.S. settings. See also: each of the fifty states; Washington, D.C.; Puerto Rico; Virgin Islands)
Allbeury, T. Man with the President's Mind
Brennan, R. Man Who Walked Like a Dancer
Bryant, P. Two Hours to Doom
Cheyney, P. Don't Get Me Wrong
　　Poison Ivy
Como, L. both titles
Cooper, Craig. at least 5 titles
Coughlin, W. J. Destruction Committee
Curtis, Robert. Smoky Cell
Drummond, I. Power of the Bug
Elias, D. Cause of the Screaming

Settings Index

Elliott, W. J. Bren Hardy, Tough Dame
   Tough Ghosts
Fleming, I. Diamonds Are Forever
   Live and Let Die
Francis, D. Blood Sport
Gardner, J. Understrike
"G-Man". all 4 titles
James, Max. Death Is Where You Meet It
Jepson, E. Grinning Avenger
Johnson, Duff. Chiseller
Kane, M. Sucker Trap
Kennedy, E. all 5 titles
Kirby, D. Carnival of Death
   Death Man
Lewis, T. Boldt
McCutchan, P. Dead Line
Marshall, R. Blondes' Requiem
   Hit and Run
   Lady, Here's Your Wreath
Martyn, W. Death Fear
   Men Without Faces
Mitchell, S. most if not all 15 titles
Morelli, S. Take It and Like It
Morton, A. Affair for the Baron
Muller, P. Danger—Dame at Work
   Hasty Heiress
   Lady Is Lethal
   Slay Time
O'Sullivan, J. B. Don't Hang Me Too High
   I Die Possessed
Pulman, J. Fixation
Quartermain, J. Rock of Diamond
Smith, T. D. Now Try the Morgue
Steward, P. Gaboreau the Terrible
Sutherland, W. Death Rides the Air Line
Tate, R. Emperor on Ice
Tracy, L. No Other Way
Ward, Harold. Blood of a Buddha
   Vulture
Warren, V. Farewell by Death
Wheatley, D. Irish Witch
   Strange Story of Linda Lee
Whitelaw, D. Murder in Motley

UNIVERSITY. See: ACADEMIA.

URUGUAY (URUG. SEE ALSO: SOUTH AMERICA)
Daniels, N. License to Kill

U.S.S.R. SEE: RUSSIA.

UTAH (SEE ALSO: SALT LAKE CITY; WEST)
Bellamy, J. Mistress of Ghosthaven
Conroy, Al. Soldato!
George, P. Final Steal
Mailer, N. Executioner's Song
Mayer, R. Execution
Pollock, T. Rainbow Man
Robeson, K. Mad Mesa
Shattuck, R. Said the Spider to the Fly
Snyder, G. Ogden Enigma

VANCOUVER (VAN. SEE ALSO: CANADA; MONTREAL; OTTAWA; TORONTO; WINNIPEG)
Ardies, T. Kosygin Is Coming
Atlee, P. White Wolverine Contract
Bonner, M. Shapes That Creep
Deverell, W. Needles
Layhew, J. Rx for Murder

VENEZUELA (VENEZ. SEE ALSO: CARACAS; SOUTH AMERICA)
Braun, M. G. Apostles of Violence
De Villiers, G. Que Viva Guevara
East, R. Pearl Choker
Halliday, B. Caught Dead
Mason, V. W. Maracaibo Mission
Owen, Richard. Eye of the Gods

VENICE (SEE ALSO: ITALY; FLORENCE; MILAN; NAPLES; ROME; SARDINIA; SICILY)
Aarons, E. S. Assignment—The Girl in the Gondola
Albrand, M. Mask of Alexander
Anne-Mariel. Murder in Venice
Brent, M. Tregaron's Daughter
Brink, C. Bellini Look
Canning, V. Venetian Bird
Carter, Nick. Mission to Vengeance
Coffman, V. Dark Gondola
   Dark Palazzo
Ehrlich, M. Reincarnation in Venice
Ferrand, G. House of Glass
Flagg, J. Death's Lovely Mask
Healey, B. Stone Baby
   Vespucci Papers
Hedges, S. G. Venetian Summer Mystery
Highsmith, P. Those Who Walk Away
Hill, R. Another Death in Venice
Hodge, J. A. One Way to Venice
Jacobs, T. C. H. Secret Power
Jason, S. Venetian Vendetta
Johnston, V. Masquerade in Venice
MacInnes, H. Venetian Affair
Marshall, R. Mission to Venice
Pendower, J. Trap for Fools
Poynter, B. Disappearance of Mary Amber
Robertson, C. Clash of Steel
Rowan, H. Overture in Venice
Rudorff, R. Venice Plot
Sheckley, R. Game of X
Sheridan, A. M. Summoned to Darkness
Smith, Caroline. Barozzi
Spark, M. Territorial Rights
Stein, A. M. Cheating Butler
Sterling, T. Evil of the Day
   Silent Siren
Vesey, A. H. Clock and the Key
Wallace, Irving. Pigeon Project
Wheatley, D. Rape of Venice
York, H. Venetian Charade

VERMONT (VT. SEE ALSO: NEW ENGLAND)
Abbey, K. And Let the Coffin Pass
Ashbrook, H. Murder of Sigurd Sharon
Barber, W. A. Murder Enters the Picture
Brandon, W. Dangerous Dead
Brean, H. Wilders Walk Away
Brookhouse, C. Wintermute
Cardiff, S. Severing Line
Carpenter, A. Cat Got Your Tongue?
Chapin, C. Three Died Beside the Marble Pool
Colburn, L. Death Through the Mill
Cornish, C. Dead of Winter
Daniels, C. J. Poison Flower
   Yesterday's Evil
Dutton, C. J. House by the Road
Emery, S. House That Whispered
Farnsworth, M. Menace of Marble Hill
Foley, R. Girl on a High Wire
Fought, C. A. Rabble's Curse
Garland, I. Abandon Hope
Gordon, E. Freebody Heiress
Hansen, R. P. Back to the Wall
   Mark Three for Murder
Harris, Rosemary. Three Candles for the Dark
Hastings, D. G. Death at the Depot
Holder, W. Case of the Dead Divorcee
Judd, M. Murder Is a Best Seller
McAllister, A. Look over Your Shoulder
McHale, T. Lady from Boston
Markham, V. Dead Are Prowling
Merrill, P. J. Slender Thread
Morella, J. Dark Memories
Packer, V. Come Destroy Me
Pelley, W. D. Blue Lamp
Pentecost, H. Where the Snow Was Red
Philips, J. Laughter Trap
   Murder in Marble
   Thursday's Folly
Pronzini, B. Night Screams
Richard, L. Intruder at Maison Benedict
Rohde, W. L. High Red for Dead
Rossi, B. Killing Machine
Strange, J. S. Reasonable Doubt
Taschdjian, C. Classified Death
Thielen, B. Charm of Finches
Wayland, P. Waiting Game
Wells, Carolyn. Killer
   Room with the Tassels
   Spooky Hollow
Westbrook, P. D. It Boils Down to Murder
   Sting of Death
Whitaker, L. Return to Hawkeston Hall
Winston, D. Lotteries

VIENNA (SEE ALSO: AUSTRIA)
Andersch, A. Redhead
Bettauer, H. Viennese Love
Buckingham, N. Return to Vienna
   Vienna Summer
Callas, T. City of Kites
Charteris, L. Saint and the Hapsburg Necklace
Colbron, G. I. Joe Muller, Detective
Daniels, N. Some Die Running
Duke, M. Bormann Receipt
Ellis, Julie. Rendezvous in Vienna
Fagyas, M. Devil's Lieutenant
Fletcher, Dorothy. Farewell to Vienna
Gainham, S. Mythmaker
   Time Right Deadly
Greene, G. Third Man
Hall, G. M. Watcher at the Door
Heaven, C. Castle of Eagles
Leather, E. Vienna Elephant
Lewis, F. J. Climax
Lorac, E. C. R. Murder in Vienna
McCutcheon, H. Suddenly, in Vienna
Maddock, S. Doorway to Danger
Marlowe, S. Passport to Peril
Milton, J. Baron Sinister
Oppenheim, E. P. Last Train Out
Page, A. So Late, Monsieur Calone
Pickering, R. E. Himself Again
Rosmanith, O. L. Storm Clouds over Vienna
Rothberg, A. Great Waltz
Simmel, J. M. Caesar Code
Storm, J. Bitter Rubies
Vance, L. J. Dead Ride Hard
Vreeland, F. Dishonored
Weissl, A. Mystery of the Green Car
Wheatley, D. Second Seal
Wuorio, E. L. Woman with the Portuguese Basket

VIET NAM (SEE ALSO: HANOI; SAIGON; FAR EAST)
Anne-Mariel. Tigress of the Evening
Baker, W. H. Judas Diary
Cassidy, J. Station in the Delta
Collingwood, C. Defector
Crowther, J. Firebase
Daniels, N. Operation VC
Doliner, R. Thin Line
Elegant, R. S. Kind of Treason
Harvester, S. Battle Road
Honig, L. For Your Eyes Only
Kempley, W. Invaders
Rivers, G. Five Fingers
Rohan, D. Browning Touch
Ross, W. Bamboo Terror
Whittington, H. Burden's Mission
Williams, Alan. Tale of the Lazy Dog
Wolfe, M. Chinese Fire Drill
   Man on a String
   Two-Star Pigeon

VIRGIN ISLANDS (VIR. IS.)
Barbour, R. H. Death in the Virgins
Charles, I. When Only the Bougainvillia Blooms
Davis, Mildred. Scorpion
Dietrich, R. Steve Bentley's Calypso Caper
Ellington, R. Stone Cold Dead
Farrer, H. G. How Evil the Word
Jevons, M. Murder at the Margin
Johns, V. P. Hush, Gabriel!
Morrow, S. Season of Evil
Riefe, A. Tyger at Bay
Scarpetta, F. Kill Them All
Stein, A. M. Home and Murder
Whitney, P. A. Columbella

VIRGINIA (VA. SEE ALSO: RICHMOND; SOUTH)
Aarons, E. S. Assignment—Treason
Acheson, E. Murder to Hounds
Andrews, V. C. Flowers in the Attic
Anthony, D. Blood on a Harvest Moon
Atkins, T. Blue Man
Barton, G. Ambassador's Trunk
Bennett, H. Wait Until Evening
Berliner, R. Manhood Ceremony
Boles, P. D. Limner
Carr, J. D. Dead Man's Knock
Claudia, M. Master of Foxhallow
Coffman, V. Gaynor Women
Cohen, O. R. Romance in Crimson
Colby, R. Lament for Julie
Daniels, D. Curse of Mallory Hall
   Illusion at Haven's Edge
   Nightfall
   Tidemill
Dean, R. G. Case of Joshua Locke
Demijohn, T. Black Alice
De Pre, J. Sound of Dying Roses
Devine, S. both titles
Disney, D. M. 5 titles
Doran, J. In the Depths of the First Degree
Eberhart, M. G. Hunt with the Hounds
Ford, L. False to Any Man
   Town Cried Murder
Fredericks, A. Mark of the Rat
Gaines, A. Old Must Die
   Voodoo Goat
Grey, R. both titles
Hale, Jennifer. Ravensridge
Hay, J. "No Clue!"
Henle, T. Death Files for Congress
Hintze, N. Stone Carnation
Hoffman, W. Walk to the River
Holland, I. Grenelle
James, L. Triple Mirror
Johns, V. P. Singing Widow
Kavanaugh, C. Bride of Lenore
Kevern, B. Dark Eden
Koehler, R. P. Tread Gently, Death
Laing, P. Brief Case of Murder
Lee, Elsie. Winegarden
Leonard, C. L. Deadline for Destruction
Lincoln, N. S. Meredith Mystery
   Moving Finger
Long, Manning. Short Shrift
McCloy, H. Slayer and the Slain
McDonald, G. Fletch's Fortune
McNamara, L. B. Pilgrim's End
Mack, E. Death of a Portrait
Maner, W. Die of a Rose
Marsten, R. Murder in the Navy
Michaels, B. Patriot's Dream
   Witch
Ostrander, K. Specter of the Dunes
Packer, V. Whisper His Sin
Peden, W. H. Twilight at Monticello

Peters, Elizabeth. Devil-May-Care
Post, M. D. Methods of Uncle Abner
   Silent Witness
   Uncle Abner, Master of Mysteries
Revell, L. Kindest Use a Knife
Robeson, K. Devil on the Moon
Rockwood, H. Walt Wheeler, the Scout Detective
Ronns, E. State Department Murders
Roscoe, T. To Live and Die in Dixie
Ross, Clarissa. Ghosts of Grantmeer
Ross, Marilyn. Mask of Evil
Ross, W. E. D. Dark Is My Shadow
   Whispering Gallery
   Whispers in the Night
Rossi, B. No Quarter Given
Sapir, R. Death Check
Scott, J. R. Woman in Question
Shaffer, E. A. Major Washington
Siller, V. Echo of a Bomb
Stapleton, D. Corpse and Robbers
Thomas, E. Dancing Death
Thum, M. Fernwood
Walk, C. E. Yellow Circle
Webster, J. Four-Pools Mystery
Whipple, K. Killings in Carter Cave

WALES

Ashby, R. C. Death on Tiptoe
   Out Went the Taper
Bailey, H. C. Mr. Fortune Finds a Pig
Blaisdell, A. Nightmare
Boore, W. H. both titles
Brand, C. Cat and Mouse
Burley, W. J. Three-Toed Pussy
Carnac, C. Impact of Evidence
Carr, G. 6 titles
Chance, S. Septimus and the Stone of Offering
Clements, E. H. Other Island
Cory, D. Circe Complex
Cowan, G. K. both titles
Creasey, J. Toff at Butlin's
Daniel, G. Welcome Death
Delving, M. Die Like a Man
Devine, A. D. Admiral's Million
Dudley, E. To Love and to Perish
Elson, J. Romance of the Castle
Eyerly, J. Leonardo Touch
Farjeon, J. J. Greenmask
Fletcher, H. L. V. Miss Agatha
Gallie, M. Strike for a Kingdom
Goyne, R. Missing Minx
Graham, Alan. Who Killed Gerald Cruden?
Graham, Winston. Woman in the Mirror
Gray, B. Leave It to Conquest
Gunn, V. Death on Shivering Sands
Hardie, D. W. F. Riddle of the Cambrian Venus
Harris-Burland, J. B. Disc
Healey, B. Blanket of the Dark
Hill, Peter. Enthusiast
Howard, Linden. Foxglove Country
Hubbard, P. M. Dancing Man
Hunter, A. Gently to the Summit
Hurst, H. S. Dark Is My Destiny
Jackson, Eileen. Autumn Lace
James, Hallam. Fair Isle Jumper Mystery
John, O. Sabotage
Kamm, D. Secret of Manly Stones
Lewis, N. Every Man's Brother
Lewis, Roy. Distant Banner
   Witness My Death
Lovell, M. Ghost of Megan
McGirr, E. Entry of Death
Markham, V. Death in the Dusk
Melville, J. Nun's Castle
Millward, E. E. Copper Bottle
Moffat, G. Persons Unknown
Niall, I. Village Policeman
Norton, O. Corpse-Bird Cries
O'Hara, K. Searchers of the Dead
Peters, Ellis. City of Gold and Shadows
Rees, A. J. Brink
Remenham, J. Righteous Abel
Richardson, S. Green Cape
Rigg, J. Pencarran
Rutland, H. Bleeding Hooks
Sanford, U. Poisoned Anemones
Stafford, C. Teville Obsession
Tattersall, J. Dark at Noon
Thomas, Murray. Buzzards Pick the Bones
Troy, S. Swift to Its Close
Vahey, J. H. Storm Lady
Verner, G. Dene of the Secret Service
Wellsley, J. Castle on the Mountain
Williams, Raymond. Volunteers

WARSAW (SEE ALSO: POLAND)

Annesley, M. Room 14
Hall, Adam. Warsaw Document
Simpson, Ronald. End of a Diplomat
Tripp, M. Wife-Smuggler

WASHINGTON D.C. (WASH. D.C.)

Adler, W. Casanova Embrace
Agnew, S. Canfield Decision
Alner, J. Z. Capital Murder
Anderson, Patrick. President's Mistress
Anonymous. President Vanishes
Archer, J. Shall We Tell the President?
Avallone, M. Missing!
Barton, G. Pembroke Mason Affair
   Strange Adventures of Bromley Barnes
Bartram, G. White Peril
Bass, M. R. Force Red
Bayer, O. W. Brutal Question
Black, C. Asterisk Destiny
Blacker, I. R. Kilroy Gambit
Blake, R. Stripped for Murder
Bonnamy, F. Dead Reckoning
   King Is Dead on Queen Street
   Portrait of the Artist As a Dead Man
Borgenicht, M. Corpse in Diplomacy
Box, E. Death Before Bedtime
Brady, L. Love Tap
Cain, J. M. Institute
Calde, M. A. Shadowboxer
Calmer, N. Avima Affair
Carroll, J. Madonna Red
Carter, Nick. 5 titles
Cody, J. P. Search and Destroy
   Top Secret Kill
Coffin, G. Murder in the Senate
Condon, R. Entwining
Da Cruz, D. Vulcan's Hammer
Davey, J. Undoubted Deed
Davis, D. S. Old Sinners Never Die
Davis, Gordon. Counterfeit Kill
   House Dick
Dean, R. G. Body Was Quite Cold
   Case of Joshua Locke
Deane, P. Time for Treason
Derrick, L. Capitol Hell
Dietrich, R. 7 titles
Diplomat. 5 titles
Disney, D. C. Explosion
Dominic, R. B. 5 titles
Donnel, C. P. Murder-Go-Round
Dunleavy, S. Very First Lady
Eberhart, M. G. Man Next Door
Ehrlichman, J. both titles
Footner, H. Nation's Missing Guest
Ford, L. 8 titles
Futrelle, J. Elusive Isabel
Gaines, A. Omit Flowers, Please
Garbo, N. Confrontation
Garland, R. C. Zalea
Gerould, G. H. Midsummer Mystery
Godey, J. Talisman
Goode, B. Senator's Nude
Goodrum, C. A. both titles
Gordons. Power Play
Grady, J. Six Days of the Condor
Gray, Angela. Lattimore Arch
Green, A. K. Filigree Ball
Halliday, B. Violent World of Michael Shayne
Hamilton, D. Murderer's Row
Harrington, R. E. Death of a Patriot
Hart, F. N. Crooked Lane
Hay, J. Melwood Mystery
   That Washington Affair
   Unlighted House
Henkin, H. Crisscross
Hermann, W. Operation Intrigue
Huston, H. C. both titles
James, L. Caliph Intrigue
   Capital Hill Affair
Jason, S. Corporate Caper
Johnson, S. Panther Jones for President
Johnston, W. Get Smart Once Again!
Kamarck, L. Informed Sources
Karp, D. Brotherhood of Velvet
Kelly, J. Diplomatic Incident
Knebel, F. Dark Horse
   Seven Days in May
Knowland, H. Madame Baltimore
Kummer, F. A. Death at Eight Bells
   Design for Murder
Kurland, M. Last President
Lambert, D. Red House
Larkin, R. T. For Godmother and Country
Latham, A. Orchids for Mother
Lee, John. Ninth Man
Leonard, C. L. Secrets for Sale
Levy, D. L. Potomac Conspiracy
Lincoln, N. S. 16 titles
Lippincott, R. E Pluribus Bang!
Ludlum, R. Chancellor Manuscript
McCall, A. Holocaust
McCarthy, J. R. Special Agent
McGerr, P. Is There a Traitor in the House?
   Legacy of Danger
   Pick Your Victim
McGhee, E. Last Caesar
MacInnes, H. I and My True Love
McLeish, R. Man Who Wasn't There
Mace, M. Blondes Don't Cry
Manson, W. Very Black Deed
Marlowe, S. Homicide Is My Game
   Mecca for Murder
   Violence Is My Business
Mason, V. W. Washington Legation Murders
Matthews, Clyde. Ides of March Conspiracy
Meyer, L. both titles
Michaels, B. Ammie, Come Home
Moore, Robin. Chinese Ultimatum
Morice, A. Murder in Mimicry
Morris, C. Stolen Letter
Moyes, P. Black Widower
Nessen, R. First Lady
O'Brien, R. C. Report from Group 17
Oran, D. Z Warning
O'Toole, G. Cosgrove Report
Patrick, K. Death Is a Tory
Pendleton, D. Washington IOU
Perrett, G. Executive Privilege
Perry, Robin. Welcome for a Hero
Philips, P. At Bay
Picard, S. Notebooks
Pierson, E. Defense Rests
Plum, M. Murder of a Redhaired Man
   State Department Cat
Powell, R. All Over But the Shooting
   Lay That Pistol Down
   Shoot If You Must
Pronzini, B. Acts of Mercy
Revell, L. Men with Three Eyes
Rinehart, M. R. Man in Lower Ten
Robeson, K. Blood Ring
   Merchants of Disaster
   Smiling Dogs
Robinson, L. W. Assassin
Rogers, J. T. Stopped Clock
Rogers, R. M. Negotiator
Ross, L. Q. Adventure in Washington
Roudybush, A. Before the Ball Was Over
   Capital Crime
   Sybaritic Death
Russell, A. J. Pour the Hemlock
Salinger, P. On the Instructions of My Government
Santiago, V. J. This Gun for Justice
Sapir, R. Head Men
Scherf, M. Dead: Senate Office Building
Scott, J. R. Cab of the Sleeping Horse
   Man in Evening Clothes
   Red Emeralds
Serling, R. J. President's Plane Is Missing
Shreve, S. R. Children of Power
Siller, V. Good Night, Ladies
   One Alone
Smith, Martin. Analog Bullet
Spore, K. Death of a Scavenger
Starnes, R. And When She Was Bad She Was Murdered
   Another Mug for the Bier
   Other Body in Grant's Tomb
Steele, C. Blood Reign of the Dictator
   Legions of the Death Master
Stein, A. M. Death Takes a Paying Guest
Stewart, E. They've Shot the President's Daughter
Swerdlow, J. Code Z
Taylor, W. Admiral's a Spy
Teilhet, D. L. Fear Makers
Thomas, Ross. Backup Men
   Cast a Yellow Shadow
   Money Harvest
Thornburg, E. We've Been Waiting for You
Truman, M. Murder in the White House
Tully, A. Brahmin Arrangement
Tyson, J. A. Scarlet Tanager
Ullman, B. E. Voluptuaries
Van Orsdell, J. Ragland
Von Elsner, D. Ace of Spies
Wallace, Irving. R Document
Wallace, R. Green Glare Murders
Wallis, J. H. Capitol City Mystery
Wayland, P. Double Defector
West, J. B. Cobra Venom
White, L. House on K Street
Whitehurst, B. Death on Capitol Hill
Whitten, L. H. Progeny of the Adder
Wilhelm, K. City of Cain
Wilkinson, B. Last Clear Chance
Winston, D. Haversham Legacy
Woolfolk, W. President's Doctor
Yardley, H. O. Blonde Countess
   Red Sun of Nippon

WASHINGTON STATE (WASH. SEE ALSO: SEATTLE; NORTHWEST)

Adams, L. Z. Mirror Murder
Ashe, G. Death in the Trees
Ball, J. Police Chief
Barns, G. M. Murder Walks the Stairs
   Only the Losers Win
Barry, I. Darkness at Mantia
Brandner, G. Aardvark Affair
Brock, S. all 4 titles
Campbell, P. Cedarhaven
Chittenden, M. Findlay's Landing
Delmonico, A. Eyrie of an Eagle
Farr, F. Elephant Valley
Gaines, A. No Crime Like the Present
Gast, K. P. Dil Dies Hard
Gillis, J. Killers of Starfish
Hawkins, J. Violent City
Herbrand, J. Dangerous House
Hyde, C. Wave
Jones, N. Case of the Hanging Lady
   Ride the Dark Storm
Kendall, K. Death Rides the Storm
Kevern, B. Darkness Falling
   Key
Lamson, D. Whirlpool
Leffland, E. Mrs. Munck

Settings Index

Marion, E. Keys to the House
Montgomery, I. Death Won a Prize
Moore, E. Shallow Runs the River
Paul, C. Child Is Missing
St. John, Darby. Westgate Mystery
Sears, R. M. Spirit of Cove Island
Stewart, J. Before It's Too Late
Trimble, L. 5 titles
Wetherell, J. Cottage at Avalanche

WEST (See also: Individual States)
Allen, G. Jaws of Death
Ames, N. My Path Belated
Anthony, W. Men of Mystery
Barbour, A. M. At the Time Appointed
Bonnamy, F. Death on a Dude Ranch
Bowman, J. House of Hate
Bryant, W. Blue Russell
Cooper, C. R. Mystery of the Four Abreast
Craig, M. Cranes of Ibycus
Crumley, J. Last Good Kiss
   Wrong Case
Dewey, T. B. My Love Is Violent
Eberhart, M. G. Man Missing
Fine, P. H. Night Trains
Frazee, S. Sky Block
Gardiner, D. Drink for Mr. Cherry
Garfield, B. Tripwire
Gibbs, G. F. Hunted
Grant, M. Shadow—Destination Moon
Green, A. K. Mayor's Wife
Guthrie, A. B. Murders at Moon Dance
Gutteridge, L. Killer Pine
Hale, C. Ghost River
Hawkins, W. E. Cowled Menace
Haycox, E. Murder on the Frontier
Humphreys, R. Hunch
Isely, R. K. Strange Code of Justice
Kay, K. Trouble in the Air
Lynch, L. Mountain Mystery
Lynde, F. Grafters
McKimmey, J. Long Ride
MacLean, Alistair. Breakheart Pass
Mantle, B. In the House of Another
Millhiser, M. Willing Hostage
Overholser, S. Molly and the Confidence Men
Packard, F. Wire Devils
Peel, C. D. Flameout
Powell, R. Say It with Bullets
Reed, J. D. Free Fall
Reese, J. Sharpshooter
   Texas Gold
   Weapon Heavy
   Wes Hardin's Gun
Roberts, J. L. Wilderness Inn
Robeson, K. Tunnel Terror
Sanders, C. W. Murder Trail
Snow, C. H. Bonanza Murder Case
   Highgrade Murder
   Lakeside Murder
   Sign of the Death Circle
Spilken, A. Burning Moon
Stevens, Diane. Valley of the Shadows
Taylor, J. R. Gipsy Blair, the Western Detective
Teilhet, H. T. Rim of Terror
Tuttle, W. C. most of the 82 titles
Worts, G. F. Laughing Girl

WEST INDIES (W.I. See also: Individual Countries; Caribbean)
Anderson, J. R. L. Death in the Caribbean
Desmond, H. Edge of Horror
East, R. Twenty-Five Sanitary Inspectors
Footner, H. Obeah Murders
Gaskin, C. Fiona
Grace, A. Hawksbill Manor
Grove, M. You'll Die Tomorrow
Gulliver, H. Kill with Style
Haggard, W. Telemann Touch
Heberden, M. V. Murder Follows Desmond Shannon
Pattinson, J. Angry Island
Root, P. Evil Became Them
Smith, Shelley. This Is the House
Wheatley, D. Dark Secret of Josephine
York, A. Tallant for Disaster
   Tallant for Trouble

WEST VIRGINIA (W. Va. See also: Charleston; South)
Anthony, D. Blood on a Harvest Moon
Ashley, S. Stalking Blind
Bird, B. Hawk Watch
   Never Wake a Dead Man
Clark, P. Flight into Darkness
Davis, D. S. Clay Hand
Eberhart, M. G. Family Fortune
Evans, E. Wintershade
Fitz, J. D. Devon Maze
Grubb, D. Watchman
Noone, E. Victorian Crown
Stout, R. Too Many Cooks

WINNIPEG (See also: Canada; Montreal; Ottawa; Toronto; Vancouver)
Silver, A. Good Time Charlie's Back in Town Again

WISCONSIN (Wis. See also: Madison; Milwaukee; Midwest)
Allis, S. Nightwind
Brock, R. Tarn House
Canyon, C. Junior League Murders
Clason, C. B. Death Angel
Collins, Max. Slasher
Coulson, J. Stone of Blood
Delmonico, A. Chateau Chaumond
Derleth, A. 9 titles
Eberhart, M. G. Hangman's Whip
Fonseca, E. H. Affair at the Grotto
   Death Below the Dam
Hanson, V. Casual Slaughters
Kruger, P. Finish Line
Kutchin, V. Strange Case of John R. Graham
Landers, G. Hunting Shack
Lord, G. Murder, Plain and Fancy
Nonweiler, A. Murder on the Pike
O'Finn, T. Happy Holiday!
Ozaki, M. K. Inquest
   Wake Up and Scream
Rice, C. Trial by Fury
Russell, C. M. I Heard the Death Bell
Stratton, Thomas. Invisibility Affair
Von Elsner, D. You Can't Do Business with Murder
Wells, Carolyn. Deep-Lake Mystery

WYOMING (Wyo. See also: West)
Avallone, M. Lust Is No Lady
Baird, T. Poor Millie
Davis, T. Full Fare for a Corpse
Eby, L. Case of the Malevolent Twin
Ferguson, W. B. M. Wyoming Tragedy
Ford, L. Old Lover's Ghost
Friedman, P. Rage
Gallagher, R. Murder by Gemini
Gibbs, G. F. Anything Can Happen
Kelland, C. B. Sinister Strangers
Lynch, L. Woman's Tragedy
Morrell, D. Totem
Parker, M. Murder in Jackson Hole
Robeson, K. Green Eagle
Seeley, M. Eleven Came Back
Stout, R. Mountain Cat

YEMEN (Yem. See also: Middle East)
Harvester, S. Treacherous Road
Jackman, S. Operation Catcher

YUGOSLAVIA (Yugos. See also: Belgrade; Balkans; Macedonia)
Brett, Martin. Flee from Terror
Canning, V. Forest of Eyes
Carter, N. Hour of the Wolf
   Turncoat
Gainham, S. Silent Hostage
Gray, B. Follow the Lady
Hossent, H. Run for Your Death
Leonard, C. Hostage in Illyria
Leonard, C. L. Treachery in Trieste
MacLean, Alistair. Force 10 from Navarone
Marlowe, S. Drum Beat—Marianne
Rothberg, A. Thousand Doors
Sayer, W. W. Outlaws of Yugo-Slavia
Smith, Don. Dalmatian Tapes
   Perilous Holiday
Stein, A. M. Never Need an Enemy
Stout, R. Black Mountain
Symons, J. Man Who Lost His Wife
Travis, Gretchen. Holiday of Fear
Woodhouse, M. Rock Baby

ZAIRE. See: Belgian Congo.

ZAMBIA (See also: Africa)
Gilman, D. Mrs. Pollifax on Safari

ZANZIBAR (Zanz. See also: Tanzania; Tanganyika; Africa)
Aarons, W. B. Assignment Tyrant's Bride
Kaye, M. M. House of Shade
Mason, V. W. Zanzibar Intrigue

ZIMBABWE. See: Rhodesia.

ZURICH (See also: Switzerland; Geneva)
Albrand, M. Zurich/AZ900
Rooth, A. R. Ninth Car
Willock, R. Street of the Small Steps

Series Index

Series Index

Abbot, John; B. Whitaker
Abbott, Pat and Jean; F. Crane
Abbott, Samuel G.; J. R. Langham
Abner, Uncle; M. D. Post
"Ace," The; S. Horler
Acton, Kit (Marsden); M. Bramhall
Adam 12; M. Stratford,
    C. Stratton
Adams, Insp.; L. Hollingsworth
Adams, Adelaide; A. Blackmon
Adams, Anthony; T. Brace
Adams, Bradley; M. Dekobra
Adams, Donald O'Keefe; D. Sage
Adams, Hilda; M. R. Rinehart
Adjusters, The; P. Winston
Adkins, Harry; R. Foxall
Adrano, Johnny; Michael Bradley
Adrian, Insp. Christopher; M. R. Silverman
Ainsworth, Martin; M. Underwood
Albany, Jack; J. Godey
Allain, Insp.; B. Graeme
Allan, Rocky; V. Rath
Allard, Nick; B. Barclay,
    Roger Harris
Allen, Peter; L. Anson
Alleyn, Roderick; N. Marsh
Allison, John; R. Meade
Allport, Det. Insp.; F. Everton
Aloha, Johnny; D. Keene
Alvarez, Insp.; R. Jeffries
Amberdon, Telzey; J. Schmitz
Ambers, Marilyn; E. St. Clair
Ames, Martin; A. Eichler
Ames, Sid; H. W. Roden
Ames, William; L. Freeman
Amsterdam, Johnny; Michael Lawrence
Anders, Insp./Supt.; H. Jobson
Anderson, Ben; G. Compton
Anderson, Christine; M. Mace
Anderson, Everett; K. S. Daiger
Anderson, Sgt. Pepper; L. Trevor
Anderson, Insp. Tom; L. Southworth
Angele, Soeur; H. Catalan
Anhalt, Mici; L. O'Donnell
Annesley, George; F. Everton
Annie, Polack; J. Lait
Anstruther, Bill; J. Nicholas
Anstruther, Colin; J. Plain
Anthony, Wade; Eric Heath
Anthropol Detective Agency; L. Trimble
Antonio, San; San Antonio
Antony, Mark; C. Curzon
Appleby, John; M. Innes
Appleby, Pecos; R. P. Koehler
April, Johnny; M. Roscoe
Aragon, Tom; M. Millar
Arbuthnot, Montrose; N. A. Temple-Ellis
Archer, Lew; John Macdonald,
    John Ross Macdonald,
    Ross Macdonald
Archer, Matt; Clay Henry
Archer, Maxwell; H. Clevely
Archer, Oceola; Joseph Baker Carr
Argee, Trigger; J. Schmitz
Argyle, Albert; J. T. Story
Aristo Autos; J. Leasor
Ark, Simon; E. D. Hoch
Armitage, Bryan; B. Cobb
Armstrong, Inspector; A. White
Arnholt; G. Latta
Arnold, Insp.; Miles Burton
Arrest and Trial; N. Daniels
Arrow, Frank; W. Deptula
Arrow, Sgt. Steve; L. Mantell
Artifex, Simon; R. Keverne
Asch, Jacob; Arthur Lyons
Ash, Andrew; F. Grierson
Ashe, Saxon; Saxon Ashe
Ashe, Steve; J. A. Howard
Asher, Tim; H. J. Hultman
Ashley, Robert Lee; Chester K. Steele
Ashton, Simon; E. Antill
Assassin, The; P. McCurtin
Aswell, Peter; Wenzell Brown
Attar; Robert Graham
Atwell, Sgt. Nick; M. Underwood
Aubrey, Madame; H. Travers
Audley, David; A. Price
Austen, William; A. Hocking
Austin, Steve; M. Caiden
Autos, Aristo; J. Leasor
Avenger, The; K. Robeson
Avengers, The; N. Daniels,
    J. Garforth,
    K. Laumer,
    P. MacNee
Avengers, The New; J. Carter,
    J. Cartwright,
    P. Cave,
    W. Harris
Aveyard, William; James Fraser
Aylwin, Jerome; A. Curry

Bailey, Hilary Dunsany III; H. Bailey
Bailey, Hilea; H. Bailey
Bailey, Stuart; R. Huggins
Bain, Joe; J. H. Vance
Bain, Joshua; J. A. MacKenzie
Baines, Scattergood; C. B. Kelland
Baird, Frances; R. W. Kauffman
Baker, Insp./Supt.; O. Mills
Baker, Charles A.; H. C. Huston
Baker, Larry; Carter Brown
Baker, Paul; B. Norman
Baley, Elijah; I. Asimov
Ballard, Greg; D. Sinclair
Balzic, Mario; K. C. Constantine
Banacek; D. Romano
Banion, Dan; R. Finnegan
Banner, Rex; Robert Chapman
Bannerman; J. Flynn
Banning, Bill; H. Easton
Bannion, Burns; E. Norman
Bannister, Guy; M. Crossley
Barcello, Lee; S. Ransome
Barclay, George; Ernest Paul
Baretta; A. Patrick,
    T. Racina
Barlach, Hans; F. Duerrenmatt
Barlow, Supt. Charles; Elwyn Jones
Barlowe, Insp.; C. I. D. Smith
Barnaby, Capt.; L. T. White
Barnard, Insp.; T. C. H. Jacobs
Barne, Richard; E. G. Cousins
Barnes, Berkeley; Eugene Franklin
Barnes, Bromley; G. Barton
Barnes, John; R. Ottolengui
Barnett, Cory; B. E. Miller
Barney, Al; J. H. Chase
Baron, The; A. Morton
Baron, Bruce; N. Daniels
Baron, Hugo; Michael Brett
Barrie, Dennis; A. Reynolds
Barrin, John; Gret Lane
Barron, Peter and Janet; R. Darby
Barrow, Jake; N. Quarry
Barrows, Winston; M. L. Eades
Barry, Insp.; A. Rowe
Barry, Alun; Kenneth O'Hara
Barth, Kay; N. Schier
Bartlett, Nell; D. Elias
Bartley, John; C. J. Dutton
Barton, Dick; M. Dorrell,
    L. Pryce,
    A. Radnor
Bascombe, Carver; K. Davis
Basil, Insp.; P. Hebson
Bass, Insp.; S. Truss
Bass, Stanley; D. Anthony
Bassett, Insp. George; C. Ryland
Bassett, Justin; R. Stratton
Bastian, Lt. Andy; M. Wormser
Bastion, Prof. Luther; Gavin Holt
Bastion, William; R. Harrison
Bathurst, Anthony; B. Flynn
Bathurst, Neil; L. L. Lynch
Batman; W. Lyon
Battle, Supt.; A. Christie
Batts, Singer; T. B. Dewey
Bawtry, Sam; D. Enefer
Baxter, Tory; M. Blair
Baynes, Dr.; V. Bell
Beagle, Lutie and Amanda; T. Chanslor
Beagle, Otis; C. K. Boston,
    F. Gruber
Beale, Edward; R. Penny
Beaumont, Henry; M. E. Atkins
Beck, Insp.; C. Ryland
Beck, Lucy; P. Conway
Beck, Martin; M. Sjowall
Beck, Paul; M. M. Bodkin
Beckett, Lee; J. Crowe
Bede, Simon; B. N. Byfield
Beef, Sgt.; L. Bruce
Beeke, William; E. S. Brooks
Belcourt, Robert; C. Rougvie
Beldrum, Archibald; L. F. Hay
Bell; E. R. Punshon
Bell, Garnett; C. H. Bullivant
Bellamy, Harker; S. Horler
Bellamy, John; T. C. H. Jacobs
Bellecroix, Stephen; D. Craig
Belot, Frederic; C. Aveline
Ben the Tramp; J. J. Farjeon
Benasque, Mike; A. Caillou
Bencolin, Henri; J. D. Carr
Bendilow, Supt. Edmund; Carleton Wallace
Benedict, Jerry; E. Ronns
Benedict, Sam; H. L. Oleck,
    Brad Williams
Benjamin, Paul; B. Garfield
Bennett; Elliott Lewis
Bennett, Jim; Robert Martin
Bennion, Roger; H. Adams
Bent, John; H. C. Branson
Bentiron, Dr.; E. M. Poate
Bentley, Steve; R. Dietrich
Beresford, Tommy & Tuppence; A. Christie
Berkley, George Stanhope; L. Meynell
Bernard, Paul; S. Gluck
Besserley, General; E. P. Oppenheim
Best, Petunia; B. Chetwynd
Beverley, Jim; A. Marsden
Bey, Nur; J. Rathbone
Bignon, Orestes; F. Didelot
Birdseye, Miriam; N. Spain
Birge, Sam; W. Krasner
Birkett, Sam; L. Payne
Birtley, Mr.; C. A. Alington

Bishop, Adrienne; J. Ellery
Bishop, Hugo; S. Rattray
Bishop, Robin; G. Homes
Bishop, Shauna; J. J. Montague
Black, Supt.; J. N. Chance
Black; W. Manson
Black; J. Nazel
Black, Capt.; M. Pemberton
Black, Jonathan; R. Garnett
Black John; J. B. Hendryx
Black Pearl; W. D. Roberts
Black Widowers; I. Asimov
Blackburn, Jeffery; M. Afford
Blackgrove, Tim; I. MacKintosh
Blackwood, Riley; V. Starrett
Blackshirt; B. Graeme,
    R. Graeme
Blackshirt, Lord; B. Graeme
Blackshirt, Monsieur; D. Graeme
Blackstone, Edmund; R. Falkirk
Blade, Jud; K. Jackson
Blaine, Larry; L. R. Davis
Blair, Margot; K. M. Knight
Blair, Nigel; L. F. Hay
Blair, Major Peter; J. R. L. Anderson
Blaise, Modesty; P. O'Donnell
Blake, Arab & Andy; Richard Powell
Blake, Jana; J. C. Conaway
Blake, Jonathan; J. N. Chance
Blake, Red; Edward Lee
Blake, Sexton; D. Ames,
    R. C. Armour,
    W. Arthur,
    J. Ascott,
    W. H. Baker,
    W. A. Ballinger,
    W. J. Bayer,
    L. Bidston,
    Ladbroke Black,
    A. Blair,
    S. Blake,
    S. Blakesley,
    J. W. Bobin,
    G. Bowman,
    J. G. Brandon,
    T. C. Bridges,
    C. Brisbane,
    E. S. Brooks,
    L. H. Brooks,
    Jonathan Burke,
    Lewis Carlton,
    Philip Chambers,
    Gilbert Chester,
    S. Christie,
    H. Clevely,
    J. Creasey,
    G. Dilnot,
    M. B. Dix,
    Rex Dolphin,
    L. C. Douthwaite,
    S. Drew,
    J. Drummond,
    A. Edgar,
    W. Edwards,
    R. C. Elliott,
    L. Essex,
    Gwyn Evans,
    F. D. Fawcett,
    R. Francis Foster,
    M. Frazer,
    C. Vernon Frost,
    J. Garforth,
    C. Gates,
    H. H. C. Gibbons,
    N. Goddard,
    R. Goyne,
    B. Gray,
    R. M. Graydon,
    W. M. Graydon,
    V. J. Hanson,
    R. Hardinge,
    A. S. Hardy,
    Edwin Harrison,
    Harry Egbert Hill,
    C. M. Hincks,
    W. B. Home-Gall,
    S. Hood,
    S. Hope,
    D. H. Hyde,
    L. Jackson,
    W. Jardine,
    G. Johns,
    J. G. Jones,
    A. Kent,
    Hilary King,
    A. Kirby,
    Jack Lewis,
    D. Long,
    Arthur MacLean,
    W. McNeilly,
    A. Maxwell,
    M. Mead,
    P. Meriton,
    O. Merland,
    H. C. Miln,
    Andrew Murray,
    Edgar Joyce Murray,
    M. Osborne,
    A. Parsons,
    W. J. Passingham,
    J. N. Pentelow,
    B. Perowne,

G. N. Philips,
M. Poole,
R. H. Poole,
J. Purley,
P. Quiroule,
G. Rees,
Desmond Reid,
W. Reynolds,
Ross Richards,
P. Saxon,
W. W. Sayer,
H. Scott,
Stanley Gordon Shaw,
W. Shute,
A. Skene,
J. Stagg,
J. Stamper,
W. E. Stanton-Hope,
J. T. Story,
D. Stuart,
G. Sydney,
J. Sylvester,
F. A. Symonds,
G. H. Teed,
Martin Thomas,
H. Townley,
W. Tyrer,
P. Urquhart,
G. Verner,
W. P. Vickery,
T. C. Wignall,
Richard Williams
Bland, Insp.; J. Symons
Blatchington, Everard; G. D. H. Cole
Blayne, Sebastian; S. Blayne
Blaze, Joe; R. Novak
Blessingay, Insp.; G. J. Barrett
Blessington, Charles; J. Sherwood
Bligh, Dulcie; G. Clark
Blinkwell, Prof.; S. Fowler
Bliss, Insp.; J. Remenham
Bliss, Jim; Christopher Booth
Bliss, Vicky; Elizabeth Peters
Blixen, Nils-Frederik; C. Larson
Blood, Mark; A. Morgan
Bloom, John Isidore; E. Warman
Blow, Dr. William; K. Hopkins
Blue, Sibyl Sue; R. G. Brown
Blunt, Mortimer; M. Cranston
Blunt, Sandy; P. Yates
Bodyguard, The; R. Reinsmith
Bognor, Simon; T. Heald
Bolan, Mack; D. Pendleton,
    Jim Peterson
Bolland, Henry; H. Andover
Bolt, Dave; Richard Curtis
Bolt, John; R. Hawkes
Bonaparte, Napoleon; A. W. Upfield
Bond, Christopher; W. Martyn
Bond, Israel; S. Weinstein
Bond, James; Ian Fleming,
    R. Markham,
    Christopher Wood
Bondurant, Victor; J. G. Edwards
Bonner, Dol; R. Stout
Boone, Jefferson; J. Messmann
Booth, Silas; J. L. Linklater
Bordelon, Johnny; M. Ogan
Borden, Steve; B. Dougall
Borges, Insp.; J. & E. Bonett
Borham, John; G. Brown
Bounty, Peter; T. Downing
Bourne, Insp.; R. C. Finney
Bourne, "Daddy"; G. V. Galwey
Bowman, Supt.; J. Burrows
Bowman, Glenn; Hartley Howard
Boyd, Danny; Carter Brown
Boyd, Felix; S. Campbell
Boyd, Nile; G. Jackson
Boyne, Jerry; A. MacGowan
Bracken, Donald; J. S. Blazer
Bradbury, Insp.; N. Longmate
Brade, Capt. Courtney; K. Wolffe
Brade, Simon; H. R. Campbell
Bradfield, Peter; C. Witting
Bradley, Supt.; Colin Robertson
Bradley, Adela Beatrice Lestrange;
    G. Mitchell
Bradley, Ben; W. G. Forbes
Bradley, Bill; G. Tree
Bradley, Luke; H. Pentecost
Bradley, Rupert "Brad"; E. B. Ronald
Bradshaw, Noah; Madeleine Johnston
Brady, Franklin; A. McRoyd
Bragg, John; Henry Wade
Brain, Big; G. Brandner
Brain, Colonel; H. Cecil
Bramley, Insp.; A. Broome
Brand, Jake; R. L. Brent
Brand, Mark; J. J. Connington
Brandeis, Kyle; W. Ash
Brandon, Anthony; Bryan Peters
Brandon, Mark; V. Warren
Brandstetter, Dave; J. Hansen
Brannigan, Supt.; Andrew MacKenzie
Branscombe, Geoffrey; H. Matheson
Branson, Al; R. P. Koehler
Brant, Mason; N. M. Hopkins
Bray, Insp. Bernard; C. S. Sprigg
Breck, Adam; K. Orvis
Bredder, Joseph; L. Holton
Bredon, Miles; R. A. Knox

Breed, Barr; B. S. Ballinger
Breen, Jim; J. Karney
Breeze, Benedict; I. Bayne
Brendel, Ernst; J. C. Masterman
Brennan, Michael; F. Zackel
Brent, Carey; M. W. Glidden
Brent, Dudley; D. Marfield
Brent, Jimmy; H. Kemp
Brentford, Insp.; S. B. Hough
Brett, Alan; Robert Garrett
Brett, Brian; C. Monig
Brett, Chester; Gwyn Evans
Brett, Chico; Kevin O'Hara
Brett, Dixon; T. Stanleyan King
Brett, Mike; Keith Campbell
Brett, Reginald; L. Tracy
Brewer, William; H. McElroy
Brews, Insp.; V. Loder
Brewster, Amy; S. Merwin, Jr.
Briconi; B. Baskerville
Briercliffe, Ronald; F. Beeding
Brierly, Herman; W. Levinrew
Briganti, Robert; P. McCurtin
Briggs; R. L. Fish
Briggs, Tommy; D. MacDonald
Bright, Rosie; Judge Ruegg
Brindle, Max; A. S. Fleischman
Briscoe, Sam; P. Hamill
Britain, William; J. Courage
Brock, Insp. David; R. J. White
Brock, John; D. Skirrow
Brogan, Cole; J. Poyer
Bronson, Richard; P. Rawls
Brook, Roger; D. Wheatley
Brooke, Clay; H. Crooker
Brooks, Mike; H. T. Rothwell
Broom, Herbert; F. Hurt
Brown, Father; G. K. Chesterton
Brown, Angel; G. Montrose
Brown, Benvenuto; E. Gill
Brown, Forsythia; R. C. Payes
Brown, Deputy Sheriff Jake; D. Cameron
Brown, Jane & Dagobert; D. Ames
Brown, Vee; C. J. Daly
Browne, Freddie; M. Poole
Bruce, James; R. Johnston
Brunel, Jacques; C. Gavin
Bryant, John; Richard Grayson
Bryce, Emily & Henry; M. Scherf
Bryden, Avis; E. Phillpotts
Buck, Insp.; A. Marsden
Buckby, Lionel; John Gloag
Buckle, Ebenezer; N. Brady
Budd, Robert; G. Verner
Buell, Martin; M. Scherf
Bull, George; M. Kennedy
Bull, Homer; L. Lariar
Bullion, Simon; M. B. Dix
Bullock, Helen; B. N. Byfield
Bunce, Dr. Nathaniel; E. M. Curtiss
Bunker, Terry; Paul Ross
Bunn, Smiler; B. Atkey
Burford, Insp. Archie; V. MacClure
Burgess, Insp. Jim; C. Franklin
Burke, Insp./Supt. Curtis; R. Trevor
Burke, Eleanora; V. Perdue
Burke, Jerry; Asa Baker
Burke, Shamus; H. M. Webster
Burke's Law; R. Fuller
Burmann, Cheviot; B. Cobb
Burnell, John; F. Vivian
Burnivel, Insp.; E. Candy
Burr, Jason; D. Kent
Burr, Thad; Anonymous
Burrell, Jacob; G. Boothby
Burrill, William; Adam Gordon MacLeod
Burton, Insp.; G. E. Locke
Burton, Major Dick; M. Beckett
Butcher, The; S. Jason
Butler; P. Kirk
Butler, Morgan; D. Anthony
Butler, Patrick; J. D. Carr
Button, Harry; J. Barbette
Byrne, Insp.; E. C. Vivian
Byrnes, Insp.; J. Hawthorne

Cable, Brevet; B. Callison
Cabot, Philip; R. McDougald
Cadee, Don; S. Dean
Cadfael, Brother; Ellis Peters
Cadman, Insp.; C. Rushton
Cage, B. F.; P. Israel
Cage, Huntington; A. Riefe
Cain; B. Freeborn
Cain, Cabot; A. Caillou
Cainsforth, Duncan; J. Maske
Cairn, Donald; V. Loder
Caldwell, Prof.; M. K. Ozaki
Cale, Martyn; P. Long
Caliban; P. Warren
Callaghan, Slim; P. Cheyney
Callaghan, "Steel"; M. Chesney
Callahan, Brock; W. C. Gault
Callan, David; J. Mitchell
Cam, Insp.; J. Cockin
Camberwell, Ronald; J. S. Fletcher
Camellion, Richard; J. Rosenberger
Cameron, Janice; J. Sheridan
Cameron, Paul; W. Wright

Campbell, Humphrey; G. Homes
Campbell, Pat; E. Colter
Campbell, Susan; P. Heneker
Campenhaye, Paul; J. S. Fletcher
Campion, Albert; Margery Allingham,
    Youngman Carter
Cane, David; J. Courage
Cannon; P. Denver,
    D. Enefer,
    R. Gallagher
Cannon, Curt; Curt Cannon
Cannon, Dave; M. Delving
Canuck, Johnny; J. Moffatt
Capricorn, Supt. Merlin; P. G. Winslow
Carberry, Jane; B. Symons
Carbo; J. Quartermain
Cardby, Mick; David Hume
Cardiff, Insp./Supt.; D. Gray
Cardigan, Burgess (Buzz); D. Rico
Cardigan, Peter; Monte Barrett
Cardinal, Insp. James; M. Walton
Carding, Hugh; G. Collins
Cardolini, Frank; D. J. Gerrity
Carlisle, Kenneth; Carolyn Wells
Carlito; E. Torres
Carmichael, Justine; K. Chase
Carmichael, Michael; P. Durst
Carnaby; P. N. Walker
Carner, Mary; Z. Popkin
Carolus, Lucian; E. Ascher
Carpenter, Chips; G. Eldredge
Carr, Dan; Willard K. Smith
Carradine, Steve; M. K. Robertson
Carrados, Max; E. Bramah
Carrick, Webb; B. Knox
Carrington, Derek; B. Netton
Carrington, F. T.; J. S. Clouston
Carroll, David; O. R. Cohen
Carroll, Jimmy; H. McCutcheon
Carruthers; R. L. Fish
Carruthers, John; E. C. Cox
Caspian, Dr. Alexander; John Burke
Carson, Don; A. Pruitt
Carstairs; N. Davis
Carstairs, "Apples"; S. Myles
Carstairs, Brett; S. Horler
Carter; E. R. Punshon
Carter, Jack; T. Lewis
Carter, Nick; Nicholas Carter,
    Nick Carter
Carter, Ralph; T. Lilley
Carter, Steve; A. R. Long
Carter, Tony; David Hume
Cartwright, Bill; P. Morgan
Carvel, Kelly; N. Daniels
Carver, Rex; V. Canning
Caryll, Victor; G. Fairlie
Casey, Flash; P. Ayres,
    S. Bristol,
    G. H. Coxe
Cass, Jeff; R. Severn
Castang, Henri; N. Freeling
Castle, Darby; Jan Michaels
Castle, Peter; G. Davison
Castleman, Marc; R. Kutak
Castleton, James; C. A. Alington
Cauldron, Insp.; S. Fowler
Caution, Lemmy; P. Cheyney
Cavender, Alec; E. Tokson
Cawthorne, Supt.; R. Silverwood
Cellini, Dr. Emmanuel; M. Halliday
Chace, Insp.; V. Loder
Chadwick, John; G. Cobden
Chalice, Harry; Donald MacKenzie
Challis, Bart; W. F. Nolan
Challis, Prof. Ronald; Shane Martin
Chambers, Peter; H. Kane
Chambrun, Pierre; H. Pentecost
Chameleon; J. La Plante
Champnell, Augustus; Richard Marsh
Chan, Charlie; E. D. Biggers,
    D. Lynds
Chan, David; C. Leader
Chance, John Newton; J. N. Chance
Chandos; D. Yates
Chane, Alexander; Ralph Hayes
Chang, Mr.; A. E. Apple
Chantecoq; A. Bernede
Chaos, Jacob; Shelley Smith
Chard, Peter; G. Verner
Chard, Simon; B. Malim
Charles, Mrs.; M. Warner
Charleston, Sheriff Chick; A. B. Guthrie,
    Jr.
Charlesworth, Insp.; C. Brand
Charlesworth, Sgt.; J. S. Fletcher
Charlesworth, James; J. Sandys
Charlie's Angels; M. Franklin
Charlton, Insp.; C. Witting
Chase; N. Daniels
Chatham, Erik; R. Neebel
Chavasse, Paul; M. Fallon
Cheri-Bibi; G. Leroux
Cherrington, Richard; G. Daniel,
    D. Rees
Cheyney, Colonel; P. Cosgrave
Chill; J. Sherman
Chillders, Dr. Russell V.; J. Sherman
Chipstead, "Bunny"; S. Horler
Chisholm, Paul; A. W. Eyles
Chitterwick, Ambrose; A. Berkeley
Chopper Cop; Paul Ross

Christie, Bob; James Preston
Christopher, Bob; R. R. Irvine
Christopher, James; Curtis Steele
Chucky, Insp.; C. Brand
Church, Johnny; V. Howard
Circle, Secret; G. Null
Cirret, Antoine; E. Hely
Clackworthy, Amos; Christopher B. Booth
Clamart, Frank; H. C. Rowland
Clancy, Lt.; R. L. Pike
Clancy, Peter; L. Thayer
Clane, Terry; E. S. Gardner
Clapp, Lt. Austin; Wade Miller
Claremont, Clarice; C. Cranston
Clark, Clark Clark; S. S. Baker
Clarke, Horace; I. Lewis
Clarkson-Parry, James; B. G. Quin
Claw, Tut; V. A. Paradis
Clay, Cutty; H. MacGrath
Clay, Lucien; R. Gore-Browne
Clay, Stephen; S. E. Porcelain
Claymore, Tod; T. Claymore
Clayton, Jack; S. Gluck
Clayton, Jeff; W. Ward
Cleek, Hamilton; H. P. Hanshew,
    M. E. Hanshew,
    T. W. Hanshew
Clerihew, Mr.; Warner Allen,
    E. C. Bentley
Cleveland, John; S. Fowler
Clifford, Bob; Leroy Scott
Clift, Cornelius; E. Heath
Clinton, Hortense; M. Hagen
Clouseau, Insp.; F. Waldman
Clown, Crimson; J. McCulley
Club, Catalyst; G. Dyer
Clubfoot; D. Valentine,
    V. Williams
Cluer, Dan; W. B. M. Ferguson
Cluff, Sgt. Caleb; G. North
Clume, Asaph; R. L. Goldman
Clunk, Joshua; H. C. Bailey
Cluthra; H. Munro
Clymping, Viscount; V. Gielgud
Cobb, Ira; R. Winsor
Cockrill, Insp.; C. Brand
Cody; D. Brierley
Coffee, Dr.; L. G. Blochman
Coffin, Sgt./Insp. John; Gwendoline But-
    ler
Colby, Al; D. Dodge
Cole, Harlan; J. Donahue
Cole, Schyler; Frederick C. Davis
Collier, Hugh; M. Dalton
Collin, Mr.; F. Heller
Collins; B. Hitchens
Collins, Barnabas; Marilyn Ross
Collins, Lizzie; E. L. Long
Colt, Thatcher; A. Abbot
Colton, Thornley; C. H. Stagg
Columbo; H. Clement,
    L. Hays,
    A. Lawrence
Colwyn, David; A. J. Rees
Cominsec, Agent of; Ralph Hayes
Commandos, Israeli; A. Sugar
Conacher, Steve; Adam Knight
Condon; D. Jordan
Condor, The; J. Grady
Condor, Bart; W. Wright
Conley, Sgt. Chuck; J. M. Fox
Conlin, Capt./Insp.; Clement Wood
Connell, Dan; J. Foxx
Connell, David; J. Weatherhead
Connor, Doc; J. Dolph
Conquest, Norman; B. Gray
Conrad, Clive; Frank King
Conroy, Insp. Thomas; H. Asbury
Considine, Steve; R. P. Wilmot
Constantine, Dr.; M. Thynne
Continental Op; D. Hammett
Conway, Brian Dinsmore; Simon Stone
Conway, Rupert; E. Leather
Cool, Bertha; A. A. Fair
Cop, Chopper; Paul Ross
Coppersmith; R. J. Griffin
Coquenil, Paul; C. Moffett
Corbin, Ben; R. Crane
Cord, Talos; Robert MacLeod
Cordry, Jason; J. D. O'Hanlon
Corey, Lee; T. Williamson
Cork, Sgt.; A. Swinson
Cork, Montague; MacDonald Hastings
Cornelius, Jerry; M. Moorcock
Cornell, Dr. Alexander; M. Scott Michel,
    Milton Scott
Cornford, Insp.; M. Kennedy
Cornish, Katherine (Kay); Virginia Hanson
Corridon, Martin "Brick Top"; R. Marshall
Corrigan, "Biff"; W. Morton
Corrigan, Mark; M. Corrigan
Corrigan, Tim; E. Queen
Cory, Dr. Patrick; C. Siodmak
Costaine, Tony; N. MacNeil
Cotten, Neal; Sam S. Taylor
Cotterell, Martin; J. Trench
Cotton, Gunston; Rupert Grayson
Coulson, Rex; J. Mann
Courtenay, Det. Insp.; N. Berrow
Courtney, Maggie; A. Pearson
Coyle; J. Philips
Crader, Carl; E. D. Hoch

Craft, Sebald; I. Patterson
Crag, Osborne; S. Elvestad
Cragg, Sam; F. Gruber
Craggs, John; C. A. Alington
Craig, Prof.; Babette Hughes
Craig, Sgt.; I. Jefferies
Craig, John; J. Munro
Craig, Peter; K. Benton
Craig, Steve; B. Winter
Craig, Tom; V. Van Urk
Craine, Paul; E. P. Healy
Cramer, Insp.; R. Stout
Crammond, Roger; T. Muir
Crane, Bill; Jonathan Latimer
Crane, Lionel; D. Stuart
Crane, Paul; Wade Curtis
Cranfurd, Liane; S. Gilruth
Cranley, Nick; F. Kane
Cranmer, Steve; S. Knickmeyer
Cranston, Lamont; W. B. Gibson,
    M. Grant
Crawford; D. Cushman
Crawford, Thea; Jessica Mann
Creevy, Winston; J. Lord
Creighton, Peter; A. Livingston
Crewe; John R. Watson
Crewe; V. Vanardy
Cribb, Sgt.; P. Lovesey
Crichton, Tessa; A. Morice
Criddle, Adrian; B. Strong
Crispin, John; R. Foxall
Crockett, Fred; B. Lang
Crole, Simon; R. H. Leitfred
Crombie, Sam; G. H. Coxe
Cromwell, Bill "Ironsides"; V. Gunn
Crook, Arthur; Anthony Gilbert
Crosley, Lee; R. Tralins
Crow, Insp.; R. Lewis
Crow, Anderson; G. B. McCutcheon
Crow, Martin; G. Norsworthy
Crowder, George; H. Pentecost
Crown, John; T. Harknett
Croyd; I. Wallace
Cullinan, Timothy; O. Martin
Cummings, Insp.; Paul McGuire
Cunningham, "Brains"; E. P. Thorne
Curfew, Max; J. Brunner
Curtis, Hugh; P. Somers
Curtis, Lyle; E. L. Fetta
Curwen, Insp. Peter; R. Vickers
Curzon, Amanda; F. Usher
Cutting, Samuel; P. D. Westbrook
Cyber, Adam; P. Heath

Dack, Capt.; P. Meriton
Dain, Stephen; R. Sheckley
Dakkers, Sam; Mike Brett
Dakota; G. A. Ralston
Dale, Insp. James; J. C. Cooper
Dale, Jimmie; F. Packard
Dale, Martin; H. Landon
Dalgliesh, Adam; P. D. James
Dalton Boys, The; W. B. Lawson
Dalziel, Andrew; Reginald Hill
Dancer, April; M. Avallone,
    S. Latter,
    P. Leslie
Dane, Bartholomew; Rex Dark
Dane, Timothy; W. Ard
Dangerfield, Maxine; C. Franklin
Daniels, Supt.; G. Baxter
Daniels, Charmian; J. Melville
Daniels, Webster; Terrence Lore Smith
Danning, David; D. Von Elsner
Darby, Parrish; The Aresby's
Darcy, Lord; R. Garrett
Dare, Susan; M. G. Eberhart
Dark Shadows; Marilyn Ross
Darling, Kiss; J. Yardley
Darren, Graham; A. Lenton
Darroch, Mike; J. MacKinnon
Darrow, Percy; S. E. White
Darzek, Jan; L. Biggle
Davenant, P. J.; F. S. Hamilton
Davie, Dr.; V. C. Clinton-Baddeley
Davies, Bill; Sara Elizabeth Mason
Davies, John; Margot Bennett
Davis, John George; J. Ripley
Davison, Gilbert; R. J. Fletcher
Dawlish, Patrick; G. Ashe
Dawson, Chief Insp.; B. Copplestone
Dax, Saturnin; M. Cumberland
Day, Julian; D. Wheatley
de Gier, Detective; J. Van de Wetering
de Goede, Demosthenes H.; J. Lermina
de Grandin, Jules; Seabury Quinn
de la Bath, Hubert Bonisseur; J. Bruce
de Lancey, Marka; B. Frost
de Richleau, Duke; D. Wheatley
de Rohan, Raoul; D. Graeme
de Silva, Jose; R. L. Fish
Deacon, William; H. Brean
Dean, Garry; P. Whelton
Dean, Paul; B. Francis
Deane, Robert; J. W. Vandercook
Death, Dr.; Zorro
Death Merchant, The; J. Rosenberger
Death Squad; F. Colter

Decker, Bill; L. Treat
Decker, Paul; A. I. Albert
Decker, Paul; G. Hackforth-Jones
Decker, Tyger (Tygrus Gerald); A. Riefe
Dee, Judge; R. Van Gulik
Dee, Mr.; D. Cory
Deene, Carolus; L. Bruce
Defenders, The; R. Fuller
DeHavilland, Mr.; J. N. Chance
Delaney; B. Singer
Delaney, Al; T. B. Black
Delaney, Edward X.; Lawrence Sanders
Delaney, Joe; F. Archer
Delaroy, "Steeley"; W. E. Johns
Delphond, Stanley; F. Halliday
Dene, Dorcas; George R. Sims
Dene, Michael; G. Verner
Dene, Trevor; V. Williams
Denning, Ned; M. Sebastian
Denton, Micky; F. Kane
Department of Dead Ends; R. Vickers
Derben, Insp. Frank; P. A. Foxall
Desouza, Frank; F. Olbrich
d'Espinal, Harcourt; B. Healey
Destroyer, The; R. Sapir,
    W. B. Murphy
Deutsch, Richard; J. Christian
Deventer, Piet; J. R. L. Anderson
Devereaux, Johnny; J. Roeburt
Deville, Rufus; J. Noy
Devlin, Brock; Scott Mitchell
Devlin, Timothy; B. Heatter
Devore, Dennis; Dorothy Bennett
DeWitt, Manny; P. Rabe
Dexter, Charles; J. Fredman
di Ganzarello, Alessandro; I. Drummond
Di Gris, Jim; H. Harrison
Diavolo, Don; S. Towne
Dice, Commander Allan; Peter Hill
Dickerson, Joseph; E. K. Goldthwaite
Diego, Lt.; V. Kelsey
Digburn, Howard; B. Sanders
Digby, Insp.; I. Wray
Digby, Athelstan; W. F. Harvey
Dilke, Matthew; L. Gutteridge
DiMarco, Jeff; D. M. Disney
Dingle, James; G. Osborne
Disher; Will Scott
Dixon, George; R. Edwards,
    T. Willis
Dixon, Sgt. Joe; R. Wormser
Doan; N. Davis
Dobbs, John; R. B. Saxe
Dodds, Septimus; Sutherland Scott
Docker, Insp.; H. Pink
Doight, Henry; B. Symons
Dolan, Brad; W. Fuller
Dollanganger, Cathy; V. C. Andrews
Dollanganger, Chris; V. C. Andrews
Dolling, Ursula; J. S. Clouston
Donahue, Lorna; Katharine Hill
Donan, Gil; M. P. Hood
Donavan, Paul; Carter Brown
Doner, Dan (DeeDee); F. Shay
Donnegan, Lt. Peter; D. Quick
Donovan; L. Parker
Donovan; J. Philips
Donovan, Dick; Dick Donovan
Doome, Sheridan; S. Fisher,
    S. Gould
Dormouse, The; Frank King
Dortmunder, John; D. E. Westlake
Douglas, Brian; John Lee
Dowling, Father Roger; R. McInerny
Downey, Corporal; J. B. Hendryx
Downs, Insp.; V. Sampson
Doyle, Patrick Michael; A. Newell
Doyne, Dennis; C. Baines
Draco, Pete; Richard Foster
Dragnet; R. Deming,
    D. Knight,
    R. Tralins,
    D. Vowell
Dragoon, Ransom; F. Diamond
Drake, Desmond; Sea-Lion
Drake, Dexter; E. Barker
Drake, Earl; Dan J. Marlowe
Drake, Simon; M. Maguire
Drake, Simon; H. Nielsen
Drake, Stephen; C. Wilcox
Drake, Steve; R. Ellington
Dreamer, The; W. M. Duncan
Drew, Adam; Virginia Hanson
Drew, James; W. Garrett
Drew, Sgt. Ronnie; F. Vivian
Drewer, Timothy; Hilary Landon
Drewry, Chief Insp.; N. Burnaby
Drex, Quentin; Gwyn Evans
Drexel, Michael; G. Usher
Driffield, Sir Clinton; J. J. Connington
Driscoll, Stuff; R. King
Drum, Chester; S. Marlowe
Drummond, Bulldog; G. Fairlie,
    H. C. McNeile,
    H. Reymond
Drury, Insp. Dennis; W. S. Sykes
Drury, Dynamite; L. P. Greene
Drury, Frank; P. Marlowe
Dryden, Ben; M. Hartmann
Du Cas, Insp.; H. Imbert-Terry
Duane, Stephen; J. L. Benton
Ducane; J. Bingham

Duff, MacDougal; C. Armstrong
Duffy, Insp./Supt.; N. Fitzgerald
Duggan, Bud; M. Geller
Duker, Casson; W. Mole
Duluth, Peter; P. Quentin
Dundas, Michael; V. Rath
Dundee, James F. "Bonnie"; Anne Austin
Dunjer. I. Haiblum
Dunn, Jim; H. L. Nelson
Dupin, C. Auguste; M. Harrison, E. A. Poe
Dupuy, M.; Anthony Gilbert
Durell, Sam; E. S. Aarons, W. B. Aarons
Durkin, Dan; A. M. Chase
Durkin, James; A. Stringer
Dust, Joe; P. Graaf
DuVivien, Johnny; N. Spain
Dyke, Toby; E. (X.) Ferrars
Dynes, Lathom; H. Robertson

Eady, Quentin; E. P. Thorne
Eagle, John; P. Edwards
East, Floyd; C. Rushton
East, Mark; Hilda Lawrence
Easy, John; R. Goulart
Eddie, Crying; Donald MacKenzie
Eddison, Bob; M. Delving
Edwards, Jane Amanda; Charlotte Murray Russell
Egerton, Scott; Anthony Gilbert
Egg, Montague; D. L. Sayers
Egypt, Harry; D. Broun
87th Precinct; E. McBain
Eisenberg, Aaron; P. Chase
Eldon, Bill; E. S. Gardner
Eliot, Charlotte; E. M. Filgate
Elizabeth; F. Kilpatrick
Elk, Insp.; E. Wallace
Ellis, Tony; R. P. Koehler
Ellison (Pitt), Charlotte; A. Perry
Elton, Fox; Ared White
Elver, Horace Augustus; G. Dilnot
Emerson, Amelia Peabody; Elizabeth Peters
Emery, Val; G. Dilnot
Emory, Jason; Kootz
Emp, Insp. H.; S. Horler
Enforcer, The; A. Sugar
England, Anthony; W. J. Elliott
Entwhistle, Ebbie; F. A. M. Webster
Erridge, Matt; A. M. Stein
Essex, Steve; S. Waldron
Evans, Insp.; W. J. Makin
Evans, Educated; E. Wallace
Evans, Homer; Elliot Paul
Evans, Michael; B. Graham
Everhard, Donald; P. Steward
Ewart, Edgar; A. E. Walter
Executioner, The; D. Pendleton, Jim Peterson
Expediter, The; P. Edwards

Face, Twisted; G. Davison
Faide, Major; H. Wade
Fair, Prosper; B. Atkey
Fairbanks, Hank; E. Dean
Fairfield, Peggy; E. S. Liddon
Fairr, Melville; M. Venning
Falcon; J. Crozier
Falcon, Supt.; D. Yates
Falcon, The; D. Drake
Falkenstein, Jesse; L. Egan
Fane, Martin & Richard; M. Halliday
Fang, Wu; Roland Daniel
Fanks, Octavius; F. Hume
Fannin, Harry; D. Markson
Fanshaw, Jim; H. Poole
Fansler, Kate; A. Cross
Fantomas; M. Allain, P. Souvestre
Faraday, Mike; B. Copper
Farrant, Harry; Lord Gorell
Farrant, Michael; P. G. Larbalestier
Farrel, John; B. Hitchens
Farrel, Mike; Carter Brown
Farrell, Bruno; E. Mazzaro
Farrow, Marcus Aurelius; Angus Ross
Faulkner, Reggie; E. Snell
Fedora, Johnny; D. Cory
Fell, Gideon; J. D. Carr
Fellows, Fred; H. Waugh
Felse Family; E. Pargeter, Ellis Peters
Feltham, Peter; B. Mather
Felton, Ray; John Marsh
Fen, Gervase; E. Crispin
Fenby, Insp.; R. Hull
Fenn, Christopher; M. L. Stokes
Fennell, Geoff; E. P. Thorne
Fenner, Dave; J. H. Chase
Fenner, Jack; G. H. Coxe
Fenner, Maxwell; L. F. Booth
Fenton, Horace Spurgeon; J. T. Story
Fenton, Lawrie; M. Annesley
Fenwick, Sgt.; R. Batchelor

Ferenc, Dr.; Richard Savage
Ferguson, Detective; N. S. Lincoln
Ferron, Les; D. Keene
Feston, Bernard; K. Fitzgerald
Fielding, Henry Arthur; D. Sharp
Fillinger, Insp.; Paul McGuire
Finch, Insp.; J. Thomson
Finch, Martyn; P. Cleife
Finch, Septimus; M. Erskine
Finnegan, John; N. Forrest
Finney, Mary; M. Head
Firebrace, Capt.; Seafarer
Firth, Ian; Ludovic Peters
Fitzgerald, Homer; Charlotte Murray Russell
Flack, Jeremy; J. Maske
Flagg, Insp.; J. Cassells, W. M. Duncan
Flagg, Conan; M. K. Wren
Flagg, Steven; W. B. Day
Flagg, Webster; V. P. Johns
Flamm, Greg; I. Wilson
Flatchley, John; J. McCulley
Flecheux, Robert; Demouzon
Fleck, Peter; R. Clapperton
Flecker, James; Josephine Pullein-Thompson
Fleming, Insp.; J. Cameron
Fleming, Roger; S. Harvester
Fletcher, I. M.; G. McDonald
Fletcher, Johnny; F. Gruber
Fletcher, Stephen; G. Davison
Flick, Robert; J. Ehrlich
Flicker, Gil; E. J. Millward
Flique, Anatole; C. G. Booth
Flower, Insp.; Moira Field
Flute, Adam; D. Launay
Flynn, Capt.; E. L. Long
Flynn, Xavier; J. Braine
Folly, Supt.; J. York
Fontaine, Danny; W. Ard
Force, Check; Ralph Hayes
Ford, Alan; Carolyn Wells
Ford, Brad; Hank Hobson
Fordingham, Brian; S. Horler
Forge, Barney; R. Starnes
Forrester, Michael; F. S. Wees
Fortescue, John; C. Brandon
Fortune, Chester; T. H. Stone
Fortune, Dan; Michael Collins
Fortune, Hannibal; L. Maddock
Fortune, Reggie; H. C. Bailey
Fortune, Temple; T. C. H. Jacobs
Fosse, Guy; E. Cannon
Four Just Men; S. Waldron
Fowler, Dan; G. F. Eliot
Fowler, Grant; P. Richards
Fowler, Timothy; C. Harris
Fox, Paul; D. Mounce
Fox, Tecumseh; R. Stout
Foy, Supt. Francis; Lionel Black
Frame, Reynold; M. Evermay
Frampton, Andrew; T. A. Plummer
Frankenstein; D. F. Glut, M. W. Shelley
Franklin, Margo; J. Jenkins
Frant, Arabella; D. Fearon
Fraser, Alan; H. Desmond
Fraser, Geoffrey; Elliot Bailey
Fraser, James; J. Wood
Frass; J. Chancellor
Frayne, Ambrose and Dominique; J. T. McIntosh
Frazer, Tim; F. Durbridge
Frederickson, Robert; G. Chesbro
Freeman, John; J. Ironside
Freeman, Jub; L. Treat
Freer, Virginia; E. Ferrars
French, Bill; C. Hale
French, Joseph; F. W. Crofts
Frend, Max; B. Chetwynd
Frere, Royston; W. J. Elliott
Frost, Insp.; H. Maynard Smith
Frost, Gerald; S. Horler
Frost, Hank; A. Kilgore
Frost, Henry; Josephine Bell
Fry, Pete; P. Fry
Fu Manchu; S. Rohmer
Furling, Richard; F. Grierson
Furneaux, Insp.; G. Holmes, L. Tracy
Furnival, Insp.; A. Haynes
Furnival, Matthew; S. Phillips
Fusil, Insp.; P. Alding
Fyles, Sgt./Insp.; R. Cullum

G-8; R. J. Hogan
Gaden, Supt.; P. H. Powell
Gail, John; S. D. Frances
Gail and Mitch; Gordons
Gaines, Vicky; F. Diamond
Galbreath, D. A. Carey; W. McCully
Gale, Simon; P. Verner
Gall, Joe; P. Atlee, J. A. Phillips
Gallagher, Gale; G. Gallagher
Galt; J. Gollomb

Galt, Jason; M. Lovell
Galt, Oliver; V. France
Gamadge, Henry; E. Daly
Gane, Paul; M. Woodman
Gannon, Mike; D. Ballenger
Gantian, Colonel; C. Dawe
Gantt, Barney; J. S. Strange
Garde, Vance; J. La Plante
Garden, Ben; T. Pace
Garfield, Grant; C. Franklin
Garfin, Mike; Martin Brett
Garnett, Insp.; R. Philmore
Garnett, David; C. Egleton
Garrett, Colin; G. Brandner
Garrison, Roger; J. Rovin
Garrison, Victor; D. Kirby
Garrity, Tony; Allan Nixon
Garstang; R. A. J. Walling
Garth, Insp.; H. Blayn, M. Karta
Garton, Joe; G. Hackforth-Jones
Garth; W. Camp
Gates, Ben; R. Kyle
Gates, Carol; L. Colburn
Gaunt, Jonathan; Robert MacLeod
Gaunt, Michael; G. Braddon
Gautier, Insp.; Richard Grayson
Gaylord, Supt.; W. M. Duncan
Gently, Insp./Supt.; A. Hunter
George, Edwin; C. A. Goodrum
Gerson, Keith; J. Vance
Gethryn, Anthony; P. MacDonald
Ghent, Insp.; B. Francis
Ghost, The; R. B. Saxe
Ghote, Ganesh; H. R. F. Keating
Gibbon, Insp.; Barbara Cooper
Gibson, Christopher; I. Montgomery
Gibson, Glen; J. Bentley
Gibson, Jeremiah X. "Gibby"; Hampton Stone
Gideon, George; W. V. Butler, J. Creasey, J. J. Marric
Gidleigh, Insp.; S. Truss
Gifford, Adam; A. Lejeune
Gilette, Jenny; E. Gresham, R. Grey
Gill, Eve; S. Jepson
Gilles, M.; J. Decrest
Gilliant, Supt.; J. Wainwright
Gilly, Mr.; W. M. Duncan
Gilmartin, Supt. Lawrence; C. Barry
Gimblet, Mr.; Mrs. C. Bryce
Girl from H.A.R.D.; J. Moffatt
Girl from U.N.C.L.E.; M. Avallone, S. Latter, P. Leslie
Girland, Mark; J. H. Chase
Glendower, Tobias; M. Arnold
Glenne, Al; M. G. Braun
Gloom, Insp.; Frank King
Glover, Insp.; M. Evermay
Glover, Insp.; L. Lamb
Glover, Derek; S. C. Mason
Godbold, Insp.; B. Bolt
Goddin, Haggai; O. John
Godfrey, Jim; B. E. Stevenson
Godwin, Cynthia; G. Beare
Gold, Marty; M. Kaye
Gold, Lt. Max; O. R. Cohen
Golden, Sammy; Jack Webb
Good, Carl; R. O. Saber
Good, Simon; George Davis
Goodey, Joe; C. Alverson
Goodwin, Archie; R. Stout
Gordon, Alison; W. Wager
Gordon, Ben; I. T. Ross
Gordon, Chet; K. Millar
Gordon, Insp. Hugh; S. Gilruth
Gore, Colonel; L. Brock
Gorham, Insp.; J. Cowdroy
Gorse, Ernest Ralph; P. Hamilton
Goss, Nathaniel; C. Willock
Goulburn, Richard; J. S. Fletcher
Gould, Bart; J. Hilton, J. Milton
Gould, Harry; R. Obstfeld
Grady, Lt. Bill; I. S. Shriber
Graham, Angel; Richard Russell
Graham, Kate; J. Arliss
Graham, Peter; B. Thomson
Graham, Richard; J. Welcome
Grainger, Supt. Paul; F. Sinclair
Gramport, Insp.; G. Barnett
Granby, Colonel; F. Beeding
Grandison, Capt.; B. Bolt
Grant, Alan; G. Daviot, J. Tey
Grant, Casey; D. Rico
Grant, David; G. B. Mair
Grant, Douglas; F. N. Millar
Grant, Duncan; G. Seton
Grant, Harry; B. Freeborn
Grant, Laurie; M. MacKintosh
Grant, Michael; Roland Daniel
Grant, Patrick; M. Yorke
Grant, Victor; B. Ethan
Granville, Clive; M. McKenna
Graves, Insp.; W. J. Makin
Gray, Insp.; P. Piper
Gray, Lt.; E. Lanham
Gray, Colin; M. Channing

Gray, Linda; D. Cory
Gray, Michael; H. Kuttner
Graydon, Kendal; H. E. Wheeler
Grayle, Barnaby; W. W. Sayer
Grayleigh, Peter: Colin Robertson
Great Merlini, The; C. Rawson
Greaves, Emma; Lionel Black
Green, Gregory George Gordon; J. Mann
Green, Horatio; B. Nichols
Green, Jeff; C. Keith
Greene, "Tubby"; R. Goyne
Greenfield, C. B.; L. Kallen
Greenleaf, Mr.; H. O. Yardley
Greensleeves; W. M. Duncan
Greenway, Lt. Claude; L. S. Thompson
Greer, James; N. Gayle
Gregg, Avery; R. P. Koehler
Gregory, Dan; L. Jamieson
Gregory, Scott; R. Stratton
Grey, Colwin; A. J. Rees
Grey, Roman; Martin Smith
Grey, Scout; R. L. Bellamy
Grey Shadow; G. E. Robinson
Griddle, L. F. "Scoop"; T. Polsky
Grierson, Insp.; H. J. Wurr
Grigson, Denzil; A. Broome
Grijpstra, Detective; J. Van de Wetering
Grofield, Alan; R. Stark
Grogan, Insp.; M. Neville
Groode, Mr.; G. Griswold
Gross, Sam; J. P. Wohl
Grundt, Adolph; D. Valentine,
 V. Williams
Gryce, Ebenezer; A. K. Green
Guardians, The; P. Saxon
Guelpa, Mr.; V. Thompson
Guinness, Ray; N. Guild
Gull, Vladimir; Anthony Stuart
Gulliver, Insp.; G. Burnett
Gunning, Ed; W. J. Elliott
Guttman, Max; A. D. Goldstein
Guy, Brian; J. Ridgway

Haham, David; C. A. Haddad
Haig, Alec; A. Haig
Haig, "Digger"; S. H. Courtier
Haig, Leo; C. Harrison
Hailey, Eustace; A. Wynne
Hale, Jim; R. Knotts
Hale, Max; G. H. Coxe
Hale, Max; K. Sandford
Hales, Ann; M. Ingate
Hall, Satan; C. J. Daly
Hall, "Tubby"; P. Hambledon
Hallan, Insp.; George Douglas
Halley, Sid; D. Francis
Halliday, David; H. Baldwin Taylor
Halliday, Willie; M. Fredman
Halstead, Arthur; W. E. Hayes
Hambledon, Rupert; J. Dellbridge
Hambledon, Tommy; M. Coles
Hamilton, Anthony; F. Frost
Hamilton, Gil; L. Niven
Hammer, Mike; M. Spillane
Hanaud, Insp.; A. E. W. Mason
Hand, Christopher; S. H. Page
Handyman, The; J. Messmann
Hanlon, George; E. E. Evans
Hanlon, Red; Mollie Merrick
Hannasyde, Supt.; G. Heyer
Hannay, Richard; J. Buchan
Hannegan, Edge; B. E. Lovell
Hanvey, Jim; O. R. Cohen
Harald, Simon; J. Welcome
Hardin, Bart; David Alexander
Hardin, Mark; L. Derrick
Harding, Prof.; H. H. Stanners
Harding, Derek; M. Worth
Hardman, Jim; Ralph Dennis
Hardy, Bren; W. J. Elliott
Hardy, Patrick; Martin Meyers
Harker, Hawthorne Albert; M. Olden
Harkness, William; M. Warrick
Harland, John; R. Foley
Harlequin, George; M. L. West
Harley, John; A. Tack
Harley, Paul; S. Rohmer
Harman, Mike; J. M. Walsh
Harmas, Steve; J. H. Chase
Harpe, Angela; James D. Lawrence
Harper, Bill; P. Ernst
Harper, Stephen; Walter C. Brown
Harragan, Steve; S. Harragan
Harrigan; P. O'Malley
Harrington Convent; E. Shepherd
Harris, Albie; A. Dean
Harris, Jim and Kate; T. MacRae
Harris, Leonard; R. Keverne
Harris, Paul; G. Black
Harris, Sam; M. Cronin
Harrison, Clay; Clifton Robins
Harrow, Insp.; Shipley Adams
Harry-O; L. Hays
Hart, Stephen; J. Barton
Hartley, Hashknife; W. C. Tuttle
Hartley, Roger; G. Ellinger
Harty, Cass; J. Y. Dane
Harvard, Bingham; V. Vanardy

Harvard, Paul; C. H. Gibbs-Smith
Harvester, Steve; J. M. Fox
Harvey; D. Hurd
Haskell, Insp.; W. Sutherland
Hastings, Bill and Coco; L. G. Offord
Hastings, Frank; B. Pronzini,
 C. Wilcox
Hastings, Jefferson; J. Hay
Hastings, Jimmy; C. G. Givens
Haswell, Jimmie; H. Adams
Hatch, Cyrus; Frederick C. Davis
Hatfield, Prof. Paul; S. Rogers
Havilland, Antony; V. Gielgud
Havoc, Johnny; J. Jakes
Hawaii Five-O; M. Avallone,
 H. Harris
Hawk, Michael; D. Streib
Hawke, Dixon; Anonymous
 J. Creasey
Hawkehurst, Valentine; M. E. Braddon
Hawkes, A. B. C.; Ephesian
Hawkins, Tony; H. Harrison
Hawks, Joaquin; B. S. Ballinger
Hayes, Father; P. Leslie
Hayes, Julia; D. S. Davis
Hayes, Lee; E. Lacy
Hazard, Bill; P. Marlowe
Hazard, Eric; L. Crosby
Hazell, James; P. B. Yuill
Hazelrigg, Insp.; M. Gilbert
Head, Insp.; E. C. Vivian
Headcorn, Insp.; A. Campbell
Headhunters, The; J. Weisman
Headley, Insp.; T. B. Morris
Heald, Max; H. Hossent
Hearne, Bunjy; T. Craig
Hedley, Paul; B. Healey
Heffernan (or Hefferman), Hooky;
 L. Meynell
Heimrich, Merton; F. & R. Lockridge,
 R. Lockridge,
 R. & F. Lockridge
Heldar, Sally & Johnny; H. Hamilton
Hellier, James; M. Cronin
Helm, Ben; B. Fischer
Helm, Matt; D. Hamilton
Hemingway, Clarence E.; J. Maske
Hemlock, Jonathan; Trevanian
Hemmingway, Insp.; G. Heyer
Hemyock, Maurice; D. G. Browne
Henderson, Insp.; C. Barling,
 P. Barrington
Henry, George Herbert; J. Sharkey
Henry, Gil; C. W. Grafton
Henry, Rush; Joe Barry
Hepburn, Maurice; Lord Gorell
Hero, Alexander; P. Gallico
Hero, Pepperoni; B. Kelly
Heron, Felix; G. Verner
Heron, Patrick; C. Brogan
Herring, Timothy; M. Torrie
Herrivell, Richard; J. Bentley
Hetherege, Millicent; R. Bernard
Hewes-Bradford, Barrington; A. Hamilton
Hewitt, Jefferson; J. Reese
Hewitt, Martin; Arthur Morrison
Heysen, Pete; I. Hamilton
Higgins, Cuthbert; C. F. Gregg
Higgins, Matthew; Means Davis
Highway; Garnett Weston
Hill, Asmun; H. Hawton
Hill, Dave; B. Adkins
Hillary, Charles; F. McGrew
Hiller, Gregory; Jack Laflin
Hiscock, Insp.; Jeremy Potter
Hite, Quinny; R. Burke
Hitman, The; K. Ross
Hobbs, Sgt.; Michael Lewis
Hodson, Mr.; Margaret Bidwell
Hoeffler; P. O'Malley
Hogg, Miss; A. Lee
Holderly Hall; K. Cameron
Holliday, Felix; Arthur E. Jones
Holliday, Hiram; P. Gallico
Holly, Insp.; R. Postgate
Holman, Rick; Carter Brown
Holmes, Sherlock; V. Andrews,
 R. L. Boyer,
 D. R. Bensen,
 J. D. Carr,
 M. Dibdin,
 Adrian Conan Doyle,
 Arthur Conan Doyle,
 L. D. Estleman,
 W. Gillette,
 G. Gravatt,
 R. L. Hall,
 Michael Hardwick,
 M. Harrison,
 M. P. Hodel,
 J. C. Iraldi,
 M. Jaffee,
 H. P. Jeffers,
 T. J. Kelly,
 M. Kurland,
 F. A. Leslie,
 N. Meyer,
 A. Mitchelson,
 Roberts Morgan,
 S. Palmer,
 G. Pearlman,
 E. L. Pearson,

 E. Queen,
 D. Rosa,
 F. Saberhagen,
 V. Starrett,
 A. M. Stokes,
 F. Thomas,
 N. Utechin,
 M. W. Wellman,
 R. Wincor
Holmes, William; C. V. Bark
Holton, Paul; Charlotte Hunt
Homes, Schlock; R. L. Fish
Honegger, George; J. S. Strange
Honeybath, Charles; M. Innes
Hood, Adam; N. Rich
Hood, Charles; J. Mayo
Hood, Mark; James Dark
Hook, Insp.; Gret Lane
Hook, Sam; H. T. Teilhet,
 M. Tolman
Hopkins, Sgt.; V. Sampson
Hopkins, John; Roland Daniel
Hopton, Insp.; J. C. Woodiwiss
Horne, Charles; W. Tucker
Horne, Harry; J. Gonzales
Hornsley, Michael; E. Salter
Horwitz, Lt. Jacob; D. Delman
Horton; L. Butler
Houghton, Bill; M. Culpan
Houston, Sam; E. S. De Puy
Howard, Anthony; H. McCutcheon
Howden, John; W. Mills
Howe, Larry; Eugene Franklin
Hoyland, Mr.; P. C. Williams
Hubbard, Mike; M. Seuffert
Huff, Percy Aloysius; C. Edwards
Hughes, Elwyn; D. W. F. Hardie
Hughes, Matt; Aylwin Lee Martin
Hughes, Nora; L. R. Davis
Hugo, John; A. Green
Huish, Martin; S. Horler
Hume, Hampton; B. Bird
Hume, Laurie; W. M. Duncan
Hunt, Elsie Mae; A. M. Stein
Hunt, Frederick; Lillian Day
Hunt, Lucius; J. Wellard
Hunter, The; Ralph Hayes
Hunter, Adam; N. Conway
Hunter, Ed & Am; F. Brown
Hunter, Max; W. T. Ballard
Hunter, Pete; A. A. Marcus
Hunter, Philip; M. Procter
Hunter, Tony; R. G. Dean
Hunters, The; P. Tabori
Huntington, Colin; G. Condon
Huuygens, Kek; R. L. Fish
Hyde, Barney; N. Brent
Hyde, John George Norman; J. Boland
Hyer, Hank; K. Steel

I Spy; J. Tiger
Iceman; J. Nazel
Ike, Nimble; Old Sleuth
Illusionist, The; J. P. Radford
Inch, Johnny; J. F. Straker
Ingram, John; C. Williams
Inquisitor, The; Simon Quinn
Invaders, The; Rafe Bernard,
 K. Laumer,
 P. Leslie
Irish, Jeremiah; N. Child
Ironside; J. Thompson
Irving, Paul; L. Grex
Irving, Rip; O. Mills
Iskirlak, Nuri; Joan Fleming
Israeli Commandos; A. Sugar
It Takes a Thief; G. Brewer

J, Anna; P. Swan
Jacara; V. Norwood
Jack the Juggler; Old Sleuth
Jacks, Wilton; J. H. Wallis
Jackson, Insp. John Jay "Jailbird";
 D. T. Lindsay
Jackson, Juliet; M. Turnbull
Jackson, Kane; W. Arden
Jackson, William; W. B. Murphy
Jagedinski, Anna; P. Swan
Jagger, Mick; W. Garner
James, Insp.; R. Bax
James, Harry; K. Giles
James, Jesse; W. B. Lawson
James, Mike; Denis Scott
Janson, Hank; H. Janson
Jardino, Robbie; N. Singer
Jason; J. N. Chance
Jason, Alex; A. Sugar
Jaxon, Wood; M. S. Michel
Jazine, Earl; E. D. Hoch
Jeffrey, Arthur; H. K. Webster
Jellipot, Mr.; S. Fowler
Jenkins, Joe; P. Rosenhayn
Jensen, Lt. Christopher; L. Langley
Jensen, Peter; P. Wahloo
Jeremy, John; Jeffrey Montague

Jericho, John; H. Pentecost
Jerningham, Peter; I. B. Meyers
Joey; Joey
Johnson, Insp.; D. Batchelor
Johnson, Coffin Ed; C. Himes
Johnson, Johnson; D. Halliday
Johnson, Dr. Sam; L. de la Torre
Johnson, Steve; H. L. Nelson
Jolivet, Insp.; J. Shepherd
Jones, Barnabas; M. L. Stokes
Jones, Cleopatra; R. Goulart
Jones, Glyn; G. Osborne
Jones, Grave Digger; C. Himes
Jones, Jason; K. F. Crossen
Jones, Jupiter; T. Fuller
Jones, Morocco; J. Baynes
Jones, Russell; M. Mundy
Jones, Zachary; H. Steirman
Jordan; L. Butler
Jordan, Dan; Harlan Reed
Jordan, Jack; William Du Bois
Jordan, Marc; R. M. Laurenson
Jordan, Scott; H. Q. Masur
Joyce, Michael; L. Cornell
Judd for the Defense; L. Goldman
Judd, George; E. Bruton
Justice, Peter; F. Duncan
Justus, Jake & Helene; C. Rice

Kane, Insp.; R. Scarlett
Kane, Adam; W. R. Burnett
Kane, Andy; Carter Brown
Kane, Sugar; L. Marshall
Kane, Tom; D. Jordan
Karlov, Vladimer; Ralph Hayes
Karns, Joe; G. De Weese
Kate, Lady; Anonymous
Kauffman, Insp. Max; T. Chastain
Kavanagh, Knock-Out; B. Stuart
Kay, Bromley; J. M. Walsh
Kearney, Daniel, Associates; J. Gores
Keate, Sarah; M. G. Eberhart
Keats, Colin; V. B. Shore
Keeble, Magnus; A. Wood
Keefe, Michael; Michael Wolfe
Keegan; B. Ball
Keen, Franklyn; H. Long
Keen, Gregory; L. Hardy
Keene, Arnold; Eric Wood
Keene, Max; R. O. Saber
Keene, Oliver; J. M. Walsh
Keith, Harrison; Nicholas Carter
Keith, John; N. Daniels
Kellaway, Bill; Gwyn Evans
Keller; N. De Mille
Keller, Konstantin; H. H. Kirst
Kellerway, Detective; W. H. L. Crauford
Kelling, Sarah; C. MacLeod
Kellog, Casey; P. Meriton
Kells, Michael; P. Cheyney
Kelly, Lt.; H. Roth
Kelly, Aloysius; B. Worsley-Gough
Kelly, Homer; J. Langton
Kelly, Joe; R. Avery
Kelly, Joseph; L. Ford
Kelly, Samuel Moses; J. F. Burke
Kendall, Insp.; J. J. Farjeon
Kendrick, Don; A. MacKinnon
Kennedy, Bill; L. Charteris
Kennedy, Craig; A. B. Reeve
Kenny, Mike; E. Dillon
Kent, Addison; H. Moorhouse
Kent, Brice; G. E. Giles
Kent, Christopher; J. Boswell
Kenton, Malcolm; S. Harvester
Kenworthy, Supt. Simon; John Buxton Hilton
Kenyatta; Al C. Clark
Kenyon, Sidney; N. J. Crisp
Kerr, Constable; P. Alding
Kerrigan, Lt.; J. Harrington
Kerrigan, Peter; N. Gordon
Kerry, Daniel "Red"; S. Rohmer
Kerry, Don; J. Ashford
Ker(r)wood, Charles Douglas; Allan Duncan
Kettle, Owen; C. J. C. Hyne
Kettle, Sebastian; J. D. White
Keyne, Skelton; C. Wood
Kham, Chin Kwang; Richard Foster
Khan, Asaf; Afghan
Kharduni; A. Soutar
Kidd, Randy; Dagmar
Kidnadze, Gyp; K. Vincent
Kilby, Insp.; J. C. Lenehan
Kilby, Mark; R. C. Frazer
Kilgerrin, Paul; Charles L. Leonard
Killain, Johnny; Dan J. Marlowe
Killers, The; K. Netzen
Killinger, Jedediah, III; P. K. Palmer
Killy, Francis Xavier; Simon Quinn
Kilpi, Osmo; M. Sariola
Kincaid, Rogan; H. Talbot
Kincaid, Tom; W. R. Cox
King, Frank; Frank King
King, Jason; P. Miall
King, Mike; Graham Fisher
King, Reefe; A. Barker
King, Sam; R. E. Banks
King, Wylie; L. Saunders

Kirby, Grant; C. Richards
Kirby, Jacqueline; Elizabeth Peters
Kirby, William; S. Horler
Kirk, Ashton; J. T. MacIntyre
Kirk, General Charles; J. Blackburn
Kline, John; P. Martin
Knickman, Insp.; A. Eichler
Knight, Clarence; Frank King
Knightly, Charles; S. Horler
Knollis, Gordon; F. Vivian
Knowles, Colin; R. East
Knowles, Randy; H. Holzer
Knox, Jonathan; R. E. McDowell
Koa, Komako; Max Long
Koesler, Father Bob; W. X. Kienzle
Kojak; Abby Mann,
    V. B. Miller
Kolchak, Carl; J. Rice
Kollin, Lars; O. Hogstrand
Koregorvsky; A. Wood
Koval, Stash; R. Peters
Koyala; J. C. Beecham
Kozminski, Abraham; Q. Downes
Krag, Asbjorn; S. Elvestad
Krahmer, Lt. Ben; S. A. Krasney
Krales, Josh; H. Gould
Kramer, Lt.; J. McClure
Kramer, Phil; P. Kruger
Kreutzemark, Prof.; F. Beeding
Krim, Major; D. Marfield
Krim, Harvey; E. V. Cunningham
Krug, Al; C. Weston
Kruger, Herbie; J. Gardner
Kusak, Handsome; C. Rice
Kyd, Thomas; Timothy Harris
Kyle, Insp.; R. Vickers
Kyle, Tim; Robin Moore

La Bas, Papa; I. Reed
Lacaita, Nigel; W. A. MacKenzie
Lacy, A. Lincoln; M. Strobel
Laidman, Insp. Martin; S. Seaton
Laing, Patrick; P. Laing
Laird, Andrew; R. MacLeod
Lam, Donald; A. A. Fair
Lamb, Insp. Ernest; P. Wentworth
Lamb, Sgt. Johnny; J. Donavan
Lambert, Valerie; J. Allan
Lancey, Sgt.; L. P. Greene
Land, Marty; David Alexander
Landon, Geoffrey; G. Sinstadt
Landon, Harvey; J. Pattinson
Lane, Drury; B. Ross
Lane, Jimmy; F. Ryerson
Lane, Lorimer; Carolyn Wells
Lane, Paul; F. & R. Lockridge
Langham, Insp. Neville; R. Daniel
Langley, Bill; P. Meriton
Langley, Tom; J. Monmouth
Langry, Jimmy; Francis Leslie
Lanson, Mike; J. H. Bond
Lanyard, Michael; L. J. Vance
Largo, Lou; W. Ard
Larkin, Jim; M. Russell
Larose, Gilbert; A. Gask
Larren, Simon; R. Charles
Larrimore, Tracy; J. Paull
Larson, Abe; S. A. Krasney
Lash, Simon; F. Gruber
Latham, Grace; L. Ford
Latimer, Charles; E. Ambler
Latimer, Charles & James; F. Gaite
Lavender, Jimmie; V. Starrett
Layton, Anne & David; Marion Roberts
Le Breton, Miles; J. Esteven
Leaphorn, Joe; T. Hillerman
Leather, Danny; D. Lawrence
Leathermouth; C. Dawe
Lecain, Insp.; F. Didelot
Lecoq, Monsieur; E. Gaboriau
Lee, Sgt./Insp. Brian "Bonny"; George Douglas
Lee, Gerry; K. Hopkins
Lee, Gypsy Rose; G. R. Lee
Lee, Judith; Richard Marsh
Lee, Norma "Nicky"; Norma Lee
Lee, Quong; T. Burke
Leffing, Lucius; J. P. Brennan
Left, Richard; C. Forsyte
LeGrande, Richard; I. R. Blacker
Leigh, Simon; R. Temple
Leighton, Shirley; P. Ernst
Leith, Gwynn; V. B. Shore
Leithen, Edward; J. Buchan
Leland, Joseph; R. Thorp
Leland, Quinn; Franklin M. Davis
Lennox, Insp./Supt.; J. Wainwright
Lennox, Bill; W. T. Ballard
Lennox, Bill; John Shepherd
Leric, Det. Insp.; R. Busby
Leroy, J. R. "Rick"; B. Perowne
Leslie, Supt.; W. M. Duncan
Lessinger; R. Essex
Lester, Edward; E. Levison
Lester, "Tiger"; D. Betteridge
Levert, M.; J. Toussaint-Samat
Levin, Roger; A. Furst

LeVine, Jack; A. Bergman
Levy, Lt.; E. S. Holding
Lewis, Gregory; D. Frome
Lewis, Jenny & Hunter; E. Gresham, R. Grey
Lewker, Abercrombie; G. Carr, S. Styles
Li-Sin; N. Vane
Liberator, The; N. Deane
Lincoln, John Abraham; D. Dodge
Lincoln, Matt; E. Garth
Lindon, Insp.; C. Whitman
Lindsay, Ralph; Ben Benson
Linge, Malko; G. De Villiers
Link, Barry; Vigilant
Linley; A. E. Martin
Lintott, Insp. John; J. Stubbs
Liquidator, The; R. L. Brent
Lissendale, Gerald; S. Horler
Little, Jim; Maude Parker
Littlejohn, Thomas; G. Bellairs
Llorca, Juan; D. Ames
Lloyd, Sheriff Bill; W. Reed
Locke, Jeremy; M. Challis
Locke, Kim; K. F. Crossen, C. Richards
Locken, Mike; R. Rostand
Logan; A. Joseph
Logan, Mike; Henry Holt
Logan, Richard; H. McCutcheon
Lone Wolf, The; M. Barry
Lone Wolf, The; L. J. Vance
Lonergan, Leatherface; P. Renwick
Long, Chester; C. Carpenter
Long, Sgt. Jerry; J. M. Fox
Long, Lydford; H. Carstairs
Lonto, Tony; E. R. Johnson
Loomis, Clay; Leonard Sanders
Lord, Michael; C. Daly King
Louis, Ben; E. S. Russell
Love, Jason; J. Leasor
Love, Pharoah; G. Baxt
Lovejoy; J. Gash
Lovel, Jack; O. J. Currington
Lovick, Insp.; G. M. Wilson
Low, Ambrose; H. Cecil
Lowe, Trevor; G. Verner
Luccan, Rory; N. Morland
Lucias, Ben; R. Howes
Luck, Simon; John Marsh
Luckraft, Insp.; A. J. Reese
Ludlow, Adam; S. Nash
Lumb, Tommy; L. Cross
Lumsden, Archie; M. Saltmarsh
Lund, Eric; R. S. Wallis
Lundberg, Nels; L. Saunders
Lupin, Arsene; M. Leblanc
Luther, Frank; E. Lanham
Lydney, George; S. Fox
Lyle, Insp.; J. Wainwright
Lyle, Samuel; A. Crabb
Lynch, Bertram; J. W. Vandercook
Lynx; Vigilant
Lyon, Insp.; P. Winn
Lyons, Pauline; Elizabeth Anthony
Lyson, Charles; E. P. Oppenheim

McAdden, Ric; C. Leader
MacAllister, Ross; C. Coram
McAlpin, Insp. William; R. H. R. Smithies
McAlpine, Philip; A. Diment
MacArthur, Ian; S. Jepson
McBain, Vicky; Colin Robertson
McBride, Rex; C. F. Adams
McCaig, Insp./Supt.; H. C. Rae
McCale, Duke; Gerald Brown
McCall, Andrew; M. Carrel
McCall, Bert; N. MacNeil
McCall, Mike; C. Leader
McCall, Mike; E. Queen
MacCallum, Duncan; A. MacKinnon
McCarthy, Patrick Aloysius; G. Brandon, J. G. Brandon
McCarty, Timothy; I. Ostrander
McCloud; C. Wilcox, David Wilson
McClue, Ferris; H. Wickham
McCorkle; Ross Thomas
McCoy, Johnny; J. Wolfe
McCoy, Ross; S. Gluck
MacCray, Philip; O. F. Jerome
McCunn, Duncan; J. Buchan
MacDonald, Insp.; E. C. R. Lorac
MacDonald, Lynn; K. C. Strahan
McDumont, Insp. Walter; H. Garner
MacFarlane, Rev. P. J.; A. MacVicar
McGarr, Insp.; B. Gill
McGee, Travis; John D. MacDonald
McGinty, Slade; J. Pendower
M'Govan, James; J. M'Govan
McGrath, Peter; Michael Brett
McGregor; H. Kane
M'Guire, Insp.; G. Coverack, J. Russell Warren
McGurk, Gail; D. Marfield
McHugh; Jay Flynn
MacInnes, Kevin; F. Bandy
McIntyre, Mac; M. E. Corne

MacKay, Insp.; E. L. Cushing
McKay, Ellis; L. A. G. Strong
McKay, Robin; John Morris
McKechnie; B. Hitchens
McKee, Insp. Christopher; H. Reilly
McKeene, Deville; R. Walker
McKellar, Ross; N. N. Peebles
McKeller, Insp.; H. McCutcheon
McKelvie, Graydon; M. Harvey
McKenzie, Shane; R. Magowan
McKinnon, Todd; L. G. Offord
Maclain, Duncan; B. Kendrick
McLean, Insp.; G. Goodchild
McLean, Anne "Davvie" Davenport;
    Margaret Tayler Yates
Maclean, Gregor; R. Copeland
MacLean, Roy; B. Gaston
MacLeod, Neil; Allan Campbell McLean
McLintock, Bruce; A. MacVicar
MacLurg, Marcus; R. Petrie
McMurdo, Andy; N. Morland
MacNab, Francis; J. Ferguson
MacNeill, Supt.; W. M. Duncan
McNeill, Anne & Jeffrey; T. Du Bois
Macomber, Elisha; K. M. Knight
McQuaid, Damian; S. Rifkin
Macrae, Hawk; A. Barker
Macready, Sheriff; H. Holman
Macsporran, Insp.; L. Hill
MacTavish, Alonzo; P. Cheyney
McTavish, O. Swete; C. Brooks
MacVeigh, Andy & Sue; S. MacVeigh
MacWhorter, Angus; H. S. Keeler
MacWilliams, Eve; M. Blizard
M-Squad; D. Saunders
Maasten, Nicholas; O. Sela
Macall, Johnny; G. Fairlie
Macauley, Mr.; R. Thorndyke
Macauley, Mike; N. Marino
Mace, Insp.; R. Keverne
Madden, David; D. M. Disney
Madden, Joseph; V. J. Santiago
Madero, Jose Manuel; G. Homes
Madigan, Lt.; E. Lanham
Madigan, Cash; B. Cassiday
Mado, George; W. Tute
Magellan, Philip; P. McCurtin,
    F. Scarpetta
Magic, Mark; Anthony P. Morris
Magill, Moss; Dorothy Gardiner
Maguire, Joe; J. P. Radford
Maguire, Johnny; R. Himmel
Mahon, Ambrose; S. H. Courtier
Mahoun, Nicky; Clark Smith
Maidment, Richard; M. Cronin
Maitland, Antony; S. Woods
Maitland, George; M. Severy
Maitland, Jim; H. C. McNeile
Major, The; John Ross
Major, Aubrey St. John; L. P. Greene
Malcolm, Mr.; G. Fairlie
Malcolm, James "Solo"; N. Graham
Malcolm, Richard; J. Grady
Malins, Tommy; M. B. Dix
Mallaby, James; Bruce Norman
Mallard, Insp./Supt. "Duck"; A. Spiller
Mallett, Insp.; C. Hare
Mallett, Supt.; M. Fitt
Mallett, Dan; F. Parrish
Mallett, William; D. Orgill
Mallin, David; R. Ormerod
Mallory; C. Stoddard
Mallory, Capt.; Alistair MacLean
Mallory, Sgt.; T. J. R. Sennocke
Mallory, Vic; J. H. Chase
Malloy, Chance; L. Dent
Malone, Jim; T. C. H. Jacobs
Malone, John J.; L. M. Harris,
    C. Rice
Malone, Kenneth; M. Phillips
Malone, Scobie; J. Cleary
Malone, Steven; N. Morland
Man from U.N.C.L.E.; M. Avallone,
    Joel Bernard,
    J. Hunter Holly,
    P. Leslie,
    D. McDaniel,
    J. Oram,
    J. T. Phillifent,
    Thomas Stratton,
    H. Whittington
Manchenil, Bolivar; D. M. Douglass
Manciple, Prof. Gideon; K. Hopkins
Mandarin, Dr. Rance; Zorro
Mandell-Essington, Francis; J. S. Clouston
Manderton, Insp.; V. Williams
Mandrake, Prof.; J. & E. Bonett
Mandrell, Augustus; F. McAuliffe
Manfred, Judge; A. R. Hilliard
Mann, Tiger; M. Spillane
Mannering, John; A. Morton
Mannering, Randolph; S. Paternoster
Manners, Harley; C. J. Dutton
Manners, Silas; J. Moffatt
Manning, Supt.; B. Cobb
Manning, Johnny; M. Dines
Mannix; M. Avallone,
    J. T. MacCargo
Mansel, Jonah; D. Yates

Manson, Doctor; E. Radford
Manton, Simon; M. Underwood
Mappin, Amos Lee; H. Footner
March, Colonel; J. D. Carr,
    C. Dickson
March, Erik; G. G. Fickling
March, Justin; S. Horler
March, Milo; M. E. Chaber
March, Septimus; L. Bamburg
Margetson, Sgt./Insp./Supt.; E. M. Keate
Maria, Black; J. Slate
Markham; Lawrence Block
Marks, Jonathan; G. M. Barnes
Marksman, The; P. McCurtin,
    F. Scarpetta
Marle, Jeff; J. D. Carr
Marley, Lawrence; J. Walker
Malone, Johnny; F. Ferguson
Marlow, Supt. "Cissie"; G. Dickson
Marlow, Dick; J. Bentley
Marlow, Peter; J. Hone
Marlow, Sam; A. J. Fenady
Marlowe, Greg; Greg Marlowe
Marlowe, Philip; R. Chandler
Marne, John; W. Keenan
Marple, Jane; A. Christie
Marquis, Sir Henry; M. D. Post
Marrell, Peter; Stanley Hopkins, Jr.
Marryat, Stephen; M. Leek
Marsden, Insp. Christopher; E. Backhouse
Marsden, Eric; Anthony Graham
Marsh, Emma; E. Dean
Marsh, John; J. N. Chance
Marsh, Kate; Gret Lane
Marshall, Sgt./Insp.; B. Newman
Marshall, George; C. Barling,
    P. Barrington
Marshall, John; M. Denning
Marshall, John & Suzy; J. M. Fox
Marshall, Megan; Michelle Collins
Marshall, Nick; M. Mitcham
Marsham, Peter; L. Cross
Martin, Insp.; R. Amberley
Martin, Anthony; W. Francis
Martin, Ben; J. Messmann
Martin, Insp. Clancy; Wallace Jackson
Martin, Supt. Donald; M. Bardsley
Martin, Emil; M. A. Taylor
Martin, George; F. Beeding
Martin, John; Colin Robertson
Martin, Ray; R. Reinsmith
Martin, Tavy; D. Winsor
Martin, William; K. Stanton
Martineau, Insp.; M. Procter
Martini, David; R. Raine
Martinson, Arthur; C. Fitzsimmons
Martinson, John; H. Clevely
Martiny, Paul; W. Haggard
Marvin, Dr. Joan; L. Eyles
Marvin, Pete; B. Edmunds
Mason, Chief Insp.; R. Armstrong
Mason, Paul; C. Leader
Mason, Perry; E. S. Gardner,
    W. McCleery
Mason, Randolph; M. D. Post
Massey, Richard; V. Siller
Master, Murder; J. Rosenberger
Masters, Carl; L. L. Lynch
Masters, Supt. George; Douglas Clark
Masters, J. C. K. "Jiggers"; A. Rud
Masuto, Sgt. Masao; E. V. Cunningham
Mata, Hoani; V. M. Grayland
Mather, Robert; B. Graeme
Matson, Gunnar; Breni James
Matthews, Freye; J. Palmer
Matthews, James; W. Oursler
Max, Gaston; S. Rohmer
Mayberry, Noel; G. Tree
Mayhew, Stephen; D. B. Olsen
Maynard, Garrett; H. Swiggett
Mayo, Asey; Phoebe Atwood Taylor
Mead, Selena; P. McGerr
Meatyard, Chief Constable George;
    S. Horler
Medford, Insp.; H. Roth
Medford, Joe; J. Starr
Meldrum, "Tiny"; A. Glanville
Melrose, John; W. Mills
Mendoza, Julian; J. Ronald
Mendoza, Luis; D. Shannon
Menendez, Insp.; S. Blanc
Mensing, Loren; F. M. Nevins
Mercenary, The; A. Kilgore
Mercer, Penny & Vincent; H. Clandon
Meredith, Insp.; J. Bude
Meredith, Lt.; D. Ramsay
Meredith, John; F. Gerard
Merlini, Great; C. Rawson
Merlotti, Nick; J. Deane
Merriman, Mike; Jonathan Burke
Merrion, Desmond; Miles Burton
Merrivale, Henry; J. D. Carr,
    C. Dickson
Mersey, Supt.; F. A. Clement
Meynell, David; I. Baker
Micklem, Don; R. Marshall
Migglewade, Montague; E. Hale
Mildmay, Geoffrey; B. Wilkinson
Miles, Don; L. Kenyon
Miller, Alan; P. Hunt
Miller, Doc; H. Peterson
Miller, James; M. B. Dix

Miller, Nick; Harry Patterson
Millington, Earl of; G. Hackforth-Jones
Mills; M. O'Brine
Millwall, Insp.; J. Sandys
Milton, Arthur; L. Henderson
Mind-Masters; I. Ross,
    J. F. Rossmann
Minter, Supt.; E. Wallace
Miro; S. Herron
Mission Impossible; J. Tiger,
    M. Walker
Mitchell, Insp.; N. S. Lincoln
Mitchell, Sgt./Lt. Charley; W. A. Wolff
Mitchell, Peter; G. W. Cooke
Mitchell, Robert Leroy; R. Ottolengui
Mitchell, Scott; J. Harvey
Mitchell, Steven; Josephine Bell
Mitchell, William; H. A. Wrenn
Mod Squad; R. Deming,
    William Johnston
Moh, Li; J. Cowdroy
Mohune, Peter; P. Groom
Mondo; A. Destefano
Mongo; G. Chesbro
Monk, Richard; M. Underwood
Montero, Insp.; S. Nash
Montgomery, Kirke; A. Mallory
Montigny, Pierre; E. D. Torgerson
Moody, Hank; R. Chambers
Moody, Nathaniel; E. C. Lester
Moon, Manville; R. Deming
Mooney, Supt.; D. Magarshack
Mooney, Jerry; K. O'Neil
Moore, Toussaint M.; E. Lacy
Moran, Jigger; J. Roeburt
Morck, Insp. Jonas; P. Orum
Moreau, Birge; V. Vanardy
Morelle, Dr.; E. Dudley
Moreno, Pedro; P. Morales
Moreton, Commander; D. Boyle
Morgan, Connie; J. B. Hendryx
Morgan, David; R. Owen
Morgan, Elwyn; S. Farrar
Morgan, Glyn; Rosa Lambert
Morgan, Gutsy; Duff Johnson
Morganthau, Molly; G. Bonner
Moriarty, Prof.; J. Gardner
Morini, Johnny; Al Conroy
Mornington, Anthony; M. B. Dix
Morrison, Dan; J. Shallit
Morrison, Nigel; N. Fisher
Morro, Nick; P. Buranelli
Morse, Insp.; C. Dexter
Mortdecai, Charlie; K. Bonfiglioli
Morthoe, Julian; P. M. Wilson
Moss, Phil; B. Knox
Mosson, Major; L. Cargill
Most Deadly Game, The; R. Gallagher
Mostyn, Colonel; M. Hebden
Moto, Mr.; J. P. Marquand
Mott, Daisy Jane; Jennifer Jones
Muffin, Charlie; B. Freemantle
Muir, George; F. Grierson
Mulcahaney, Norah; L. O'Donnell
Mulcahy, Eugene; J. Street
Muldoon, Hart; J. Flagg
Muldrew, Gordon; L. Allan
Mulheisen, Sgt.; J. A. Jackson
Muller, "Dusty"; A. Glanville
Muller, Joe; G. I. Colbron,
    A. Groner
Muller, Paul; Paul Muller
Mulligan, Tim; A. M. Stein
Mundy, Al; G. Brewer
Munro, Peter; I. S. Black
Murder Master; J. Rosenberger
Murdoch, Bruce; N. Deane
Murdock, Kent, G. H. Coxe
Murdock, Rachel & Jennifer; D. B. Olsen
Murgatroyd, William; W. H. Osborne
Murmur, Heron; S. Harvester
Murray, Bill; A. Colin
Mustard, Buddy; Roland Daniel
Mycroft, Mr.; H. F. Heard
Myrl, Dora; M. M. Bodkin

Nash, Aubrey; T. Davis
Nash, Capt. George; Ragan Butler
Nash, Monty; R. Telfair
Nelson, Ed; F. Norman
Nelson, Capt. Gridley; R. Fenisong
Nevers, Billy; J. M. Glazner
New Avengers; J Carter,
    J. Cartwright,
    P. Cave,
    W. Harris
Newberry, Millicent; Jennette Lee
Newsom, Insp.; F. Stewart
Nicholls, Insp. Trevor; G. Peters
Nicholson; M. Kelly
Nicholson, Nick; R. Barr
Nicolson, Lloyd; P. Wayland
Nicolson, Supt. Mark; R. Charles
Nighthawk; S. Horler
Nightingale, Amanda; G. Revelli
Nightingale, Insp. Brett; M. Kelly
Nikola, Dr.; G. Boothby
Noble, Branders; A. Richard Martin

Noble, Stewart; M. MacKintosh
Nolan, Frank; Max Collins
Nolan, John; C. Nicolai
Noon, Ed; M. Avallone
Norgil; M. Grant
Norrington, Jennifer; I. Drummond
Norris, Mrs.; D. S. Davis
Norroy, Yorke; G. Bronson-Howard
Norse, Rae; J. Esteven
North, Mr. & Mrs.; F. & R. Lockridge
North, Edward; Colin Robertson
North, Hugh; Van Wyck Mason
North, Nora; M. Duke
North, Pam & Jerry; F. & R. Lockridge
Northeast, Guy; J. Cannan
Norton, Dave; P. Malloch

Oakes, Blackford; W. F. Buckley
Oakes, Boysie; J. Gardner
Oakes, Quintus; C. R. Jackson
Oath, Hamish; D. Durrant
O'Breen, Fergus; A. Boucher
O'Brien, Patrick; I. H. Irwin
O'Brien, Sarah; M. Marlett
O'Connor, Lefty; B. Shannon
O'Day, Chauncey; A. Gaines
O'Day, Double; Gwyn Evans
O'Dell, Barry; R. O. Chipperfield
Odell, Philip; L. Powell
Odom, Hiram; W. Boniface
O'Hannay, James; C. Rushton
O'Hara, Terence; P. Costello
O'Kelly, Michael the; M. O'Brine
Okewood, Desmond; D. Valentine
Old Man in the Corner; B. Orczy
Old Sleuth; Anonymous,
    Old Sleuth
O'Leary, Lance; M. G. Eberhart
O'Malley, Supt.; M. Kenyon
O'Malley, Brian; Roland Daniel
O'Malley, Shaun; Gene Ross
O'Mara, Shaun; P. Cheyney
O'Neill, Jim; D. M. Disney
Op, Continental; D. Hammett
Opara, Christie; D. Uhnak
Operator 5; Curtis Steele
Ord, Insp.; Austen Allen
Orient, Dr. Owen; F. Lauria
Ormiston, Colonel; J. M. Walsh
Ormsberry, Van Dusen; J. S. Strange
O'Rourke, Terence; L. J. Vance
Ortiz, Johnny; R. M. Stern
O'Shaunnessey; Jessica Ryan
Otani, Supt. Tetsuo; James Melville
Otis, Miss; B. Sarto
Otley, Gerald; M. Waddell
Owen, Bobby; E. R. Punshon
Owen, Dr. Hillis; A. M. Welles
Ozmar; E. Hulme-Beaman

Pace, Quentin; R. Denbie
Packard, James; R. C. Galway
Padillo; Ross Thomas
Padre, The; R. Goyne
Palfrey, Dr.; J. Creasey
Palmer, Harry; L. Deighton
Pancho, Don; B. Buckingham
Paola and George; G. Sampson
Paradise, Mike; J. Canon
Pardoe, Chief Insp.; D. Bowers
Parew, Thibault; G. Eldredge
Paris, Charles; Simon Brett
Paris, Wade; Ben Benson
Parker, Insp.; J. Austwick
Parker; R. Stark
Parnell, Tim; Don Smith
Parr, Deputy; F. I. Anderson
Parrott, Liz; Manning Long
Parry, Franklin; R. Keverne
Parry, Insp. Lane; M. Sarsfield
Pascal, Lt.; H. Pentecost
Paternoster, Colonel; R. Inchbald
Paterson, Ross; K. Field
Patras, Commissaire; F. Grierson
Patten, Roger; A. A. Randall
Pauton, Colin; P. Purser
Pavlov, Gregory (Grischa); Jessica Ryan
Payne, Detective; Old Sleuth
Payne, Madeline; L. L. Lynch
Payne, Sham; K. Secrist
Peace, Commander Geoffrey; G. Jenkins
Peacemaker, The; A. Hamilton
Peachy, St. George; R. Starnes
Peacock, Percy; P. Fitzsimmons
Pearson, Supt. Andrew; E. Shepherd
Pearson, Insp. Jack; Roland Daniel
Peck, Judge Ephraim; A. Derleth
Pedley, Ben; S. Sterling
Peiffer, Insp. Harry; W. Marshall
Pel, Insp. Clovis; M. Hebden
Pelazoni, Lexey Jane; L. Head
Pellew, Gregory; V. Gielgud
Pemberty, Dick; P. Conde
Pendlebury, Mr.; A. Webb
Penetrator, The; L. Derrick

Penk, Insp.; W. Gore
Pennington, Arthur Stukeley; G. Brandon,
    J. G. Brandon
Pennington, Peter; E. Snell
Pennoyer, Miles; Margery Lawrence
Penny, Mr.; M. Moiseiwitsch
Penny, Alice; A. Bliss
Penny, Archibald; Wallace Jackson
Pennyfeather, A.; D. B. Olsen
Pepper, Supt.; Frank A. Smith
Perfect, Johnny; J. Noel
Perkins, Bruce; J. Lilly
Perkins, Douglas; M. Babson
Perkins, R. I.; R. Garnett
Perks, Matilda; R. C. Woodthorpe
Perrin, Christopher; C. Waye
Pete, Blue; L. Allan
Peters, Anna; J. Law
Peters, Casey; H. F. S. Moore
Peters, Toby; S. Kaminsky
Petersen, Brian; J. P. Cody
Petrella, Patrick; M. Gilbert
Petrie, Amos; J. V. Turner
Pettengill, Insp.; A. Rowe
Pettigrew, Francis; C. Hare
Phantom, The; L. Falk
Phantom Detective, The; Robert Wallace
Phantom, Gray; Herman Landon
Phelan, Lt.; M. K. Ozaki
Phelan, Johnny; J. P. Duff
Phelan, Sam; T. Kyd
Phelps, Chet; G. Childerness
Phenwick Women; K. Kimbrough
Phibes, Dr.; W. Goldstein
Philis; Ritchie Perry
Philpotts, Freddy; A. B. Caldwell
Phin, Thackeray; J. Sladek
Phoenix, Joe; A. W. Aiken,
    Anonymous
Pibble, James; P. Dickinson
Picaroon, The; J. Cassells
Picaroon, The; Herman Landon
Pilgrim, Mr.; D. Cory
Pilgrim, The; M. Cronin
Pilgrim, Black; G. Stanley
Pinaud, Monsieur; P. Audemars
Pinch, Dearborn V.; E. P. Green
Pincus, Silky; L. Rosten
Pine, Paul; H. Browne,
    J. Evans
Pink, Melinda; G. Moffat
Pink, Norman; M. McShane
Pinkerton, Evan; D. Frome
Piper, John; H. Carmichael
Piper, "Peter"; A. R. Long
Piper, Peter; N. B. Mavity
Piron, Jim; E. McGirr
Pitt, Insp.; J. F. Straker
Pitt, Dirk; C. Cussler
Pitt, Insp. Thomas; A. Perry
Placard, Nicholas; Demouzon
Place, Thackeray; K. Williams
Plante, Guy; J. Palmer
Pleydell, Bertram; D. Yates
Plotkin, Sylvia; G. Baxt
Plummer, Jeff; D. Lees
Plush, Paul; O. Keystone
Poe, Edgar Allan; D. Madsen,
    M. Olden,
    A. Sinclair,
    B. Steward
Poggioli, Henry; T. S. Stribling
Pointer, Insp.; A. Fielding
Poirot, Hercule; A. Christie
Policewoman; L. Trevor
Pollard, Insp./Supt. Tom; E. Lemarchand
Pollifax, Emily; D. Gilman
Pons, L. Rees; C. D. King
Pons, Solar; B. Copper,
    A. Derleth
Ponsonby, Peter; Jean Leslie
Ponting, Bob; B. Bolt
Pontivy, Papa; B. Newman
Poole, Insp.; Henry Wade
Port, Daniel; P. Rabe
Posse, Insp.; A. Alington
Post, Dr. Anthony; A. Irving
Potter, Brock; A. Maling
Potter, Hiram; R. Foley
Powell, Richard; A. Fowles
Power, William; H. Clandon
Powers, Johnny; J. Rayter
Powledge, Lt.; M. P. Rea
Poynings, Roger; Michael Burt
Precinct, 87th; E. McBain
Preed, Mr.; Ladbroke Black
Prentice, John; Sea-Lion
Prentis, Insp.; E. Backhouse
Prentiss, Agatha Welch; V. P. Johns
Prescot, Julian; Julian Prescot
Preston, Johnny; P. Chester
Preston, Mark; Peter Chambers
Price, Jimmy "Wiggly"; J. J. Chichester
Price, Ronald; J. Cannan
Pride, Duncan; A. Frazer
Pride, Jeff; J. Heneghan,
    A. O'Neill
Pride, Nassim; R. Petrie
Priest, Judge; I. S. Cobb
Priestley, Dr. Lancelot; J. Rhode
Prike, Leonidas; L. G. Blochman

Primrose, John; L. Ford
Prince, Henry; C. F. Gregg
Pringle, Romney; C. Ashdown
Prisoner, The; T. M. Disch,
    H. Stine
Private Eye; B. Pronzini
Probyn, Julia; A. Bridge
Professionals, The; Ken Blake
Protection Ltd.; N. Harman
Prouse, Dalton; J. McCulley
Prye, Paul; M. Millar
Puma, Joe; W. C. Gault,
    R. Scott
Purbright, Insp.; C. Watson
Purdue, Chance; R. H. Spencer
Pusser, Sheriff Buford; Webster Carey,
    W. R. Morris
Pym, Henry; W. J. Burley
Pym, Nicholas; J. Sanders
Pym, Mrs. Palmyra; N. Morland
Pyne, Parker; A. Christie

Q, Don; K. Prichard
Q33; G. Goodchild
Quade, Oliver; F. Gruber
Quaile, Insp.; J. M. Walsh
Quan, Samuel; G. Begbie
Quane, Crispin; E. Kilvington
Quantrill, Insp. Douglas; S. Radley
Quarles, Christopher; P. Brebner
Quarles, Francis; J. Symons
Quarry; Max Collins
Quarshie, Dr.; J. Wyllie
Quartz, Dr.; Nicholas Carter
Quayle, Everard Peter; P. Cheyney
Quayle, Hilary; M. Kaye
Quayle, Kit; J. Aldridge
Quayle, Peter; P. Trent
Quayne, Maxwell; F. A. Symonds
Queen, Ellery; E. Queen
Queen, Richard; E. Queen
Queen's Investigator; M. Cooney
Quentin, Peter; R. Quest
Quero, Mercedes; G. E. Locke
Quest, Philip; Peter Townend
Quest, Philip; N. Vane
Quill, Insp.; C. Brahms
Quill, Supt.; L. Lamb
Quiller; Adam Hall
Quin, Harley; A. Christie
Quin, Sebastian; S. Horler
Quince, Dion; P. Cake,
    T. L. Welch
Quincy; T. Racina
Quinn; H. Carmichael
Quinn; N. Scanlon
Quinn, Rupert; Alan Williams
Quinney, Joe; H. A. Vachell
Quint, Peter; H. Austin
Quintain, Richard; W. H. Baker,
    W. A. Ballinger
Quinto, Gimiendo Hernandez; James Norman
Quirke, Adam; V. Gribdan
Quist, Gregory; W. C. MacDonald
Quist, Julian; H. Pentecost
Qwilleran, Jim; L. J. Braun

Race, Colonel; A. Christie
Race, Blue Jean Billy; C. W. Tyler
Radcliff; R. Mallory
Radnitz, Herman; J. H. Chase
Raeburn, Mark; M. Gair
Raffles, A. J.; David Fletcher,
    G. Greene,
    E. W. Hornung,
    B. Perowne
Rainey, Jim; P. McCurtin
Ramsay, Andrea Reid; C. H. Matschat
Ramsay, David; C. H. Matschat
Ramsay, Steve; C. H. Wallace
Ramsdale, Lucy; H. Dolson
Ramsey, Hec; D. Owen
Randall, D. C.; The Gordons
Randall, Mark; C. Eland
Randolph, Rev. C. P. "Con"; C. M. Smith
Raneleigh, Arthur; M. L. Luther
Rankin, Tommy; M. Propper
Ransome, Rogue; Dean Morgan
Ransome, Steve; S. Ransome
Rant, Stephen; H. E. Wheeler
Rason, Insp. George; D. Durham,
    R. Vickers
Rason, Det. Insp. J.; D. Durham,
    S. Kyle,
    R. Vickers
Ratlin, Sgt.; J. Roffman
Ravel, Claude; B. Jones
Raven, John; D. MacKenzie
Raven, Richard; J. Griffin
Ravenhill, Anthony; R. Francis Foster
Raymond, Sgt.; N. Longmate
Razio, Rick; R. Razio
Razoni, Ed; W. B. Murphy
Read, Anthony; S. Toye
Reamer, Donald; W. M. Duncan

Reardon, Lt. Jim; R. L. Pike
Rector, Pete; V. Siller
Reddman, Joe; W. Downing
Reed, Sgt.; C. Drummond
Reed, Lal; C. Wood
Reeder, J. G.; E. Wallace
Reeder, Paul; Robert C. Dennis
Rees, Idewald; B. Mather
Regan, Jack; J. Balham,
    I. K. Martin
Regan, Insp. Michael; E. Hale
Regina; Dagmar
Register, Mark; Arthur Douglas
Rehm, Jimmy; W. Herber
Reid, Andrea; C. H. Matschat
Reilly, Harry; G. Corbin
Remington, J. A.; R. Ladline
Remover, The; Roland Daniel
Remsen; D. Montrose
Renard, Hercule; P. Audemars
Rennert, Hugh; T. Downing
Revel, Michael; N. Berrow
Revenger, The; J. Messmann
Rex, Nigel; G. Goodchild
Reynolds, Insp.; Elaine Hamilton
Reynolds, Maxine; M. Grove
Rezaire, Jimmie; A. Armstrong
Rhoden, Steve; Ira Walker,
    Irma Walker
Rhodenbarr, Bernie; L. Block
Rhodes, James; D. Gober
Rhymer, Arnold; U. Key
Riam, George; D. O. Woodbury
Rice, Bill; M. Stand
Rice, Miles Standish; B. Kendrick
Richards, Paul; D. Dallas
Richardson, P. C.; B. Thomson
Richmond, Frank; Anthony Graham
Rickman, Colonel; J. M. White
Rickman, Roy; D. Craig
Ridgway, Martin; P. Helm
Ridley, Nat; N. Ridley, Jr.
Riggs, Bingo; C. Rice
Riley, Pete; P. Quinn
Rillington, Anthony; N. Orde-Powlett
Rim-Fire; C. Ballew
Ringer, The; E. Wallace
Ringrose, John; E. Phillpotts
Ringway, Stephen; S. M. Lott
Ringwood, Richard; K. Farrer
Ripley, Charles; J. Wainwright
Ripley, John; The Gordons
Ripley, Tom; P. Highsmith
Rivers, Ed; T. Powell
Rivers, Julian; C. Carnac
Rizzi, Capt.; T. Sterling
Roath, Sheila; D. Craig
Robak, Donald; J. L. Hensley
Roberts, George; M. Symons
Roberts, Randy; Carter Brown
Robins, Constable; M. Stand
Rock, Johnny; B. Rossi
Rockford Files; M. Jahn
Rockwell, Chris; D. Linzee
Rockwell, Rocky; J. Iams
Roden, Jess; A. B. Cunningham
Rodway, Insp.; J. K. Ryland
Roersch, Sgt. Edmund; H. Kastle
Rogers, Bull; A. Brede
Rogers, Huntoon; C. Knight
Rogers, John; Jonathan Ross
Rogers, Pogy; Z. H. Ross
Roharik, Larry; J. M. Eshleman
Roi, Leo; P. Lore
Rolfe, Helga; J. H. Chase
Rolfe, Simon; J. L. Bonney
Rolfe, Zack; J. J. Lamb
Rollison, Richard; W. V. Butler,
    J. Creasey
Rome, Tony; A. Rome
Rook, Howie; S. Palmer
Roper, Max; K. Platt
Roper, Piers; K. Follett
Roque, Konrad; G. Morton
Rosher, Alf; J. S. Scott
Ross, Supt.; J. J. Connington
Ross, Charity; J. Bickham
Ross, Insp. Gordon; Lord Gorell
Ross, Martin; A. Allyson
Ross, Mike; K. Carr
Ross, Paul; P. Heneker
Rostetter, Tommy; A. Campbell
Roston Outfit; Dean Morgan
Roth, Max; H. Arvay
Rouletabille, Joseph; G. Leroux
Rourke, Peter; D. C. Cooke
Rourke, Timothy; J. Wolf
Rowlands, Bill; Norman Lucas
Royce, Rupert; J. Aldridge
Rudd, Insp.; J. Thomson
Rudd, Hugh; H. C. Davis
Rudd, Matt; R. Deming
Ruff, Peter; E. P. Oppenheim
Rumpole; J. Mortimer
Rusby, Myles; V. Markham
Rushton, Grant; G. H. Teed
Russell, Alan; N. Fitzgerald
Russell, Charles; W. Haggard
Russell, Franklin; R. M. Baker
Rutherford, Jumbo; N. Leslie
Ryan, Lt.; M. Scherf
Ryan, Bill; M. Morgan

Ryan, Charlie; J. C. Lenehan
Ryan, Frank; E. Leonard
Ryan, Jim; P. Ernst
Ryan, Sean; B. Cleeve
Ryder, Dick; H. B. M. Watson
Rye, Bill; J. Spain
Ryker; N. De Mille,
    E. T. Hamill
Ryvet, Insp.; C. Carnac

Saber, Insp. Joel; Gavin Holt
Saber, Sarah; D. Linzee
Sabin, Mr.; E. P. Oppenheim
Sader, Jim; D. Hitchens
Safford, Ben; R. B. Dominic
Sage, Malcolm; H. Jenkins
Saint, The; L. Charteris
St. Amand, Jean Henri; D. L. Teilhet
St. Cyr, Claudine; Ian Wallace
St. George, Philip; M. Avallone
St. Ives, Philip; O. Bleeck
St. Vincent, Britt; I. Ross;
    J. F. Rossmann
Salisbury, Arthur; R. Crawford
Sallis, Oscar; F. Usher
Sallust, Gregory; D. Wheatley
Salmond, Andrew; L. Dundas
Samson, Capt.; Gavin Douglas
Samson, Albert; Michael Z. Lewin
Samson, John; M. Tripp
San Antonio; San Antonio
Sand, Robert; M. Olden
Sanders, Commissioner; F. Gerard,
    E. Wallace
Sanderson, Insp.; David Hume
Sanderson, Maxwell; J. J. Chichester
Sanderson, Phil; L. Grex
Sands, Insp.; M. Millar
Sands, Jim; R. J. Casey
Sandyman, Mr.; N. Graham
Sanford, Joe; F. M. Proud
Santangelo, Minnie; A. Mancini
Santos; W. B. Bannerman
Sarel, Richard; J. Bryan
Sargeant, Peter; E. Box
Sark, Mortimer; J. Hawk
Sasha; A. Wood
Saturday, Johnny; L. Goldman
Saumarez, John; C. Dane
Saunders, Insp.; V. M. Steele
Saunders, Jeff; M. Bar-Zohar
Savage, Doc; K. Robeson
Savage, John; J. Trevor
Savage, Mark; M. Eden
Savage, Matt; Craig Cooper
Savage, Myra; M. McShane
Savage, Rampion; James Turner
Savage, Steve; David Lewis
Saville, Bill; Roland Daniel
Savoy, Paul; J. Gregory
Sawyer, Quincy Adams; C. F. Pidgin
Saxe, Christopher; S. Shane
Saxon, Ludovic; J. Cassells
Scant, Jerry; L. A. Knight
Scarf, Paul; Raymond Boyd
Scarfe, Det. Sgt.; J. Goodwin
Scarlett, Doctor; A. Laing
Scarlett, John; B. Bolt
Scarlett, Peter; S. Horler
Schaefer, William; D. Estow
Schmidt, Insp.; G. Bagby
Schofield, Pete; T. B. Dewey
Scipio, Danny; T. Gates
Scott, John; S. Picard
Scott, Philip; Hartley Howard
Scott, Shell; D. Knight,
    R. S. Prather
Scott, Spider; K. Royce
Scotter, Mr.; T. Warriner
Scudamore, Laura; R. Armstrong
Scudder, Matt; L. Block
Search; R. Weverka
Seary, Major Hutton; John Ross
Sebastian; J. L. Bickham
Second Bureau; C. R. Dumas
Secret Agent; W. H. Baker,
    W. A. Ballinger,
    P. Leslie,
    W. McNeilly
Secret Agent X-9; D. Hammett
Secret Circle; G. Null
Seeton, Miss; H. Carvic
Segrove, James; D. Durham,
    R. Vickers
Seidlitz, Mavis; Carter Brown
Selbon, Paul & Peter; J. McCulley
Selby, Doug; E. S. Gardner
Selby, Pete; Jonathan Craig
Seldon, Dick; W. S. Masterman
Semlake, Insp.; J. Varnam
Seng-Chu; E. Thomas
Sergeant, Jock; D. DaCruz
Sessions, Frank; H. Waugh
Seton, Mike; T. C. H. Jacobs
Severance, Grace; M. Scherf
Severn, Insp.; G. Bromley
Severson, Knute; T. Wells
Sevrel, Insp.; C. Worth

Shadow, The; W. B. Gibson,
    M. Grant
Shadowers, The; D. Fox
Shadows, Dark; Marilyn Ross
Shaft, John; E. Tidyman
Shand, Dale; D. Enefer
Shandy, Prof. Peter; C. MacLeod
Shane, Insp.; S. Truss
Shane, Peter; F. Bonnamy
Shanley, Joseph; Jack Webb
Shannon, Supt.; C. Ryland
Shannon, Clinton; Lee Roberts
Shannon, Desmond; M. V. Heberden
Shannon, John J.; C. F. Adams
Shannon, Michael; G. Bowman
Shannon, Patrick; J. Quinn
Shapiro, Nathan; F. & R. Lockridge,
    R. Lockridge
Shard, Simon; P. McCutchan
Shark, Tiger; K. Stanton
Sharpe, Morrison; L. Cargill
Sharpshooter, The; B. Rossi
Shaw, Esmonde; P. McCutchan
Shaw, Paul; M. Sadler
Shayne, Michael; B. Halliday
Shearer, Frank; R. Crawford
Shelley, Insp.; John Rowland
Sheridan, David; C. Davy
Sheridan, Jim; V. Torrio
Sheringham, Roger; Anthony Berkeley
Sherman, Phil; Don Smith
Sherwood, Insp.; J. Bude
Shields, Jefferson; P. Carlon
Shimoni, Tami; O. Hesky
Shirley, Patrick C.; O. Mills
Shock, Ben; P. Buchanan
Shoestring, Eddie; P. Ableman
Sholto, Sam; D. Hart-Davis
Shomar, Shomri; H. Klinger
Shore, Jemima; Antonio Fraser
Shrig, Jasper; J. Farnol
Sidel, Isaac; J. Charyn
Silber; Gunnar Johnson
Silence, John; A. Blackwood
Silk, Dorian; S. Harvester
Silk, Lou; J. H. Chase
Silk, Steve; J. B. O'Sullivan
Silver, Insp.; Henry Holt
Silver, Maud; P. Wentworth
Silvestri, Guy; M. Rennert
Simmons, Bernard; F. & R. Lockridge,
    R. Lockridge
Simon, Benjamin; G. Dean
Simon, Grant; H. Pentecost
Simpson; R. L. Fish
Simpson, Arthur Abdel; E. Ambler
Sims, Det. Insp.; F. Grierson
Sinclair, Alec; D. W. MacArthur
Sinclair, Arthur; W. S. Masterman
Skane, Insp.; D. Marfield
Skarratt, Insp.; J. S. Fletcher
Skrene, Vincent; F. Richardson
Slade; D. Bagley
Slade, Anthony; L. Gribble
Slade, Geoffrey; F. Lester
Slade, John; R. Essex
Slade, Nicholas; R. C. Woodthorpe
Slane, Insp.; S. Maddock
Slaughter; H. Clement,
    A. Kane
Sleuth, Satan; M. Avallone
Sloan, Insp. C. D.; C. Aird
Slone, Maggie; Elizabeth M. Stone
Smaile, Oliver; J. Adye
Small, David; H. Kemelman
Smarles, Insp. Joshua; M. Urquhart
Smart, Maxwell; William Johnston
Smiley, George; J. Le Carre
Smith, Captain; The Edingtons
Smith, Inspector; S. Troy
Smith, Aurelius; R. T. M. Scott
Smith, Beau; Z. H. Ross
Smith, Cellini; Robert Reeves
Smith, Daye; F. Usher
Smith, John; H. Pentecost
Smith, John; M. Plum
Smith, John; J. Sangster
Smith, Kim; J. Boland
Smith, Lancelot Carolus; N. Berrow
Smith, Nayland; S. Rohmer
Smith, Necessary; K. F. Crossen
Smith, Supt. Owen; J. Barnett
Smith, T. B.; E. Wallace
Smyth, Millard; E. M. Boyd
Sneed, Insp. Terry; G. F. Newman
Snow, John; R. H. Sawkins
Soldon, Sgt. Louis; B. Turner
Solo, Napoleon; M. Avallone,
    Joel Bernard,
    J. Hunter Holly,
    P. Leslie,
    D. McDaniel,
    J. Oram,
    J. T. Phillifent,
    Thomas Stratton,
    H. Whittington
Spade, Danny; D. Ambler
Spade, Richard; B. B. Johnson
Spade, Sam; D. Hammett
Spalding, Eric; W. C. Harvey
Spanner, J. T.; T. Chastain
Sparrow, Charlie; T. Ardies

Speare, Luke; Frederick C. Davis
Spearpoint, Insp.; F. Arthur
Spears, Simon; V. Gielgud
Special Operation Executive; J. H. Crisp
Special Squad; D. Franklin
Specialist, The; E. Lecale
Speed, Martin; G. Elliott,
  M. G. Hugi,
  John Norman
Speed, Maxwell; R. Starnes
Speer, Giff; D. Tracy
Spence, Supt. Ben; M. Allen
Spence, Philip; J. Jenkins
Spencer, John; Lou Smith
Spencer, Tony; O. Beeby
Spenser; Robert B. Parker
Spicer, Robert; M. Danvers
Spider, The; J. McCulley
Spider, The; R. T. M. Scott,
  G. Stockbridge
Spinnet, Phineas; A. Soutar
Spotted Moon, Charlie; C. Q. Yarbro
Spratt, Sgt.; George Douglas
Spring, Penelope; M. Arnold
Spring, Terry; J. Kains
Springfield, Mr.; J. Sandys
Squad, Ms.; M. Endfield
Stallard, Vincent; G. Beare
Standish, John; K. Netzen
Standish, Ronald; H. C. McNeile
Standish, Tiger; S. Horler
Stannard, Rand; R. L. Hershatter
Stanton, Hugh; R. Vickers
Star, Black; J. McCulley
Stark, John; T. Harknett
Starr, Jason; P. Heath
Starsky & Hutch; M. Franklin
Starte, Roger & Kate; Eric Williams
Stash; R. Peters
Staunton, Insp. Robert; Peter Hill
Staveley; Clifton Robbins
Steel, Alan; Colin Robertson
Steel, Raeburn; C. Brooks
Steele, Argus; Babs Lee
Steele, Jim; D. Chambers
Steele, Insp. Malcome; Mansfield Scott
Steele, Rocky; John B. West
Steevens, Stonewall; M. G. Kiddy
Stenton, Jack; T. Dexter
Stevens, Insp.; B. Graeme
Stevens, Dave; K. A. Saddler
Stevens, Gavin; W. Faulkner
Stewart, Allan; V. Siller
Steytler, Det. Sgt.; S. Milne
Stockwell, "Spider"; J. R. Holden
Stoddart, Insp.; A. Haynes
Stole, Sebastian; C. Wogan
Stone, Curt; J. Seward
Stone, Fleming; Carolyn Wells
Stone, J. Rockingham; R. Armstrong
Stone, "Rolling"; K. Laing
Stone, Shep; J. Jacks
Stoner, Harry; J. Valin
Stoner, Mark; R. Hayes
Storey, Rosika; H. Footner
Storm, Insp.; J. M. Walsh
Storm, Christopher; W. A. Barber
Straight, Ricky; G. Morgan
Strang, Jim; G. Dilnot
Strang, John & Sally; H. Brinton
Strange, James; E.B. Quinn
Strange, Jeff; A. Gaines
Strange, Violet; A. K. Green
Strange Report; John Burke
Strangely, Peter; E. B. Black
Strangeways, Nigel; N. Blake
Stratton, Mark; R. T. Bickers
Straussman; G. Davison
Streeter, Joe; J. F. Burke
Strickland, Insp.; G. Dilnot
Strickland, Jack; H. Balfour
Striker, Jason; P. Anthony
Strong, Mike; P. Cagney
Strong, Philip; W. Oursler
Strong, Robert; Colin Robertson
Stryker, Colin; William Crawford
Stryker, John; D. Barnes
Stuart, David; J. K. MacDougall
Stuart, Scott; G. Coffin
Stubbs, John; R. T. Campbell
Sturrock, Jeremy; Jeremy Sturrock
Styles, Peter; J. Philips
Sullivan, Bob; F. Mullally
Sultan, Wm. (Sultan's Harem); H. Austin
Summers, "Doc"; F. Marlowe
Summers, Steve; J. Manor
Sumuru; S. Rohmer
Sutherland, Chief of Police; F. Eberhard
Swain, Ape; D. Da Cruz
Swan; R. Philmore
Sweetwater, Caleb; A. K. Green
Swift, Leighton; C. R. Jones
Swinton, Insp.; P. Flower
Swinton, Insp.; I. Greig
Switch; M. Jahn
Sydenham; D. Seaman
Syn, Dr.; R. Thorndyke

Tabor, Chester C.; M. Cruz
Taffin; L. Mallet
Taggart; Ralph Hayes
Taine, Roger; G. Household
Talbot, Clem; T. P. Mulkeen
Tallant, Col. Munro; A. York
Tallis, Roger; J. Rossiter
Tamara; E. Ambler
Tancred, Dr. Benjamin; G. D. H. Cole
Tandy, Michael "Napper"; N. Shepherd
Tangent, Peter: Lawrence Sanders
Tanner, Evan; L. Block
Tanner, John; S. Greenleaf
Tarleton, Dr. Frank; A. Upward
Tarleton, John; F. F. Van de Water
Taylor, Pete; R. D. Abrahams
Teal, Insp. Claude Eustace; L. Charteris
Teed, Russell; D. Montrose
Telefair, Kitty; F. Stevenson
Tellford, Jeff; D. Fisher
Tempest, Ashley; A. C. Fox-Davies
Tempest, Bill; W. Shand
Templar, Simon; L. Charteris
Temple, Evelyn; Lord Gorell
Temple, Paul; F. Durbridge,
  Paul Temple
Templeton, Paul; R. Goyne
Terhune, Theodore I.; B. Graeme
Tern, Bill; B. E. Wallace
Terrel, Timothy; S. Maddock
Terrell, Frank; J. H. Chase
Terrence, Michael & "Terry"; G. Brandon
Thackeray, Constable; P. Lovesey
Thane, Colin; B. Knox
Thatcher family; P. Yates
Thatcher, John Putnam; E. Lathen
Theobald, Kate; Lionel Black
Then Came Bronson: William Johnston,
  C. Stratton
Thew, Insp.; D. G. Browne
Thomas, Ethel; C. Fitzsimmons
Thompson, Chief Insp.; Peter Drax
Thompson, Jake; Evelyn Cameron
Thompson, Mike; J. Paull
Thompson, Pat; R. G. Dean
Thorndyke, John; J. H. Dirckx,
  N. Donaldson,
  R. A. Freeman
Thorne, Tommy; Charles H. Snow
Thunderbolt, The; J. McCulley
Thursby, Roger; H. Cecil
Thursday, Max; Wade Miller
Tibbett, Henry & Emmy; P. Moyes
Tibbs, Virgil; J. Ball
Tierney, James; J. A. Moroso
Tiger Shark; K. Stanton
Tintagel, Lord & Lady; F. Draco
Titterton, Adrian; Edward Brown
Tobin, Insp.; Dorothy B. Hughes
Tobin, Matthew; A. Caillou
Tobin, Mitchell; T. Coe
Toby, Quentin; S. M. Schley
Todd, Insp.; J. Halstead
Todd, Fraser; H. L. Jones
Todd, Irving; P. Conde
Todd, Jerry; M. J. Freeman
Toff, The; W. V. Butler,
  J. Creasey
Tolefree, Philip; R. A. J. Walling
Tompkins, Tommy; F. Branston
Tonelli, Pietro; Alexander Williams
Tong, Harry; E. Burgess
Tope, Insp.; Ben Ames Williams
Tope, Edward; H. C. Davis
Toplitt, Kingsley; G. Stockwell
Torrent, Andrew; L. Cores
Torreyton, Dick; E. F. Charles
Torry, Derek; J. Gardner
Touchfeather, Katy; J. Sangster
Tower, Hugo; V. France
Townsend, Schuyler; F. Gordon
Townshend, Mr.; J. M. Cobban
Tracy, Dick; C. Gould,
  William Johnston
Tracy, John; T. Wallace
Tracy, Noel; Alex Fraser
Tracy, Philip "Spike"; H. Ashbrook
Traherne, Sydney; M. St. Dennis
Train, Rick; B. Fischer
Trant, Timothy; Q. Patrick,
  P. Quentin
Travers, Insp.; P. Barrington
Travers, Ludovic; C. Bush
Treadgold, Insp.; A. Weymouth
Treadgold, Mr.; V. Williams
Treasure, Mark; D. Williams
Tredennick, Angeline; R. B. Sanborn
Trees, Peter; John Q.
Trelawney; A. Melville-Ross
Trelawny, Edward; A. R. Long
Trelawny, John; G. Goodchild
Treloar, Septimus; Stephen Chance
Tremaine, Mordecai Euripides; F. Duncan
Tremayne, Charles; N. MacKenzie
Trent, Anthony; W. Martyn
Trent, Gregory; A. Seifert
Trent, Maria; H. Kane
Trent, Philip; E. C. Bentley
Trenton, Garaway; J. P. Carstairs
Trenton, Hilda; D. Lyon
Trenton, Richard; Anne Burton
Trevor, Carole; J. Philips

Treynor, Jimmy; A. Livingston
Trothe, Edmund; R. Llewellyn
Trotter, Tuddleton; H. S. Keeler
Troy, David; Alan Gardner
Troy, Jeff & Haila; K. Roos
Tuck, Richard; Lange Lewis
Tucker, Charity; P. Buchanan
Tucker, Coleridge, III; I. Drummond
Tucker, Mike; B. Coffey
Tudor, Mark; A. Nash
Tuke, Harvey; D. G. Browne
Tully, Jasper; D. S. Davis
Tumbler, Hector; S. Crabtree
Tupper, Amy; Josephine Bell
Turnbull, Roger; J. Tyndall
Tutt, Ephraim; A. Train
Twins, Avenging; J. McCulley
Twombley, Jabez; Sidney Williams
Twotoes, Tommy; David Alexander
Tyler, Dennis; Diplomat
Tyler, Jeff; J. L. Potter
Tyler, Julia; L. Revell
Tyson, Henry; F. A. Kummer

U.N.C.L.E., Girl from: M. Avallone,
  S. Latter,
  P. Leslie
U.N.C.L.E., Man from: M. Avallone,
  Joel Bernard,
  J. Hunter Holly,
  P. Leslie,
  D. McDaniel,
  J. Oram,
  J. T. Phillifent,
  Thomas Stratton,
  H. Whittington
Urban, Robert; C. H. Guenter
Urizar, Miguel; H. McCloy
Ursula, Sister; H. H. Holmes
Usher, Ambrose; J. Davey

V, Monsieur; A. Upward
Vachell, Supt.; E. Huxley
Valcour, Lt.; Rufus King
Valeshoff; E. Ambler
Vallance, Bill; W. Proudfoot
Vallon, Johnny; P. Cheyney
Van der Valk, Insp.; N. Freeling
Van der Valk, Arlette; N. Freeling
Van Dusen, S. F. X.; J. Futrelle
Van Kill, Hendrik; S. Bayne
Van Larsen, Max; G. Baxt
Van Loan, Richard Curtis; Robert Wallace
Vance, Philo; W. Butterfield,
  J. Riddell,
  S. S. Van Dine
Vane, Sydney; N. Islay
Vaness, Richard; M. Black
Vanessa, Sarah; J. Storm
Vanner, Rick; M. V. Heberden
Varallo, Vic; L. Egan
Varney, Chick; Jerome Barry
Velvet, Nick; E. D. Hoch
Venable, Tessie; H. Holley
Venables, Charles; C. St. John Sprigg
Venn, Sgt.; L. Brock
Venneker, Paul; P. Geddes
Vereker, Anthony; R. Forsythe
Verity, Mr.; P. Antony
Verity, Sgt. William; F. Selwyn
Vernet, Van; L. L. Lynch
Vernon, Larry; D. Bateson
Verrell, Anthony; B. Graeme
Verrell, Richard; B. Graeme
Veseloffsky, Baron; S. Horler
Vickary, Grant; R. Hobart
Vigilante, The; V. J. Santiago
Villiers, Anthony; A. Panshin
Villiers, Francis; B. Rodney
Vine, Gil; S. Sterling
Vivanti, Paul; S. Horler
von Kaz, Baron; D. L. Teilhet
von Kopf, Olga; H. De Halsalle
Vorobeitchik, Wenceslas; A. Steeman
Voss, Abelard; D. C. Cameron
Vulture, The; Harold Ward

Wace, Fadiman; Roger Simons
Wade; G. Bristow
Wager, Gabriel; R. Burns
Wainwright, James; B. Mather
Wake, Insp.; C. Kingston
Walk, Insp. John; R. Daniel
Wallace, Leonard; Alexander Wilson
Wallace, Michael; Roland Daniel
Wallingford, James Rufus; George Randolph Chester
Wallion, Maurice; J. Regis
Walsh, Lt. Marty; O. R. Cohen
Ward, Peter; David St. John
Ward, Watson; B. Delannoy

Ware, Anthony; S. Wells
Ware, Drexel; C. Andrews
Waring, Scarsdale; T. Stanleyan King
Warlock, Mike; P. Haggard
Warren, James; James Warren
Warrender, Elizabeth; G. D. H. Cole
Warrington-Reeve, Claude; Josephine Bell
Warwick, John; J. McCulley
Watchman, Sam; B. Garfield
Waterlow, Roger; C. MacKenzie
Watson, Mr.; Dorothy Gardiner
Wayne, Morgan; M. Blood
Wayne, Rodney; A. G. E. Cromwell
Wayne, Steve; T. Harknett
Wayward, Carl; L. Treat
Weaver, Nicky; N. Weaver
Weaver, T. S.; D. Keith
Webb, John & Anne; F. G. Presnell
Webley; L. Maddock
Webster, Dallas; D. Stanford
Webster, Danile; R. Sale
Weigand, Bill; F. & R. Lockridge
Welch, Agatha; V. P. Johns
Wells, Prof.; F. Grierson
Wells, Clifford; N. S. Bortner
Welpton, Sam; J. A. Saxon
Wentworth, Lyon; R. Forrest
Wentworth, Richard; R. T. M. Scott, G. Stockbridge
Wesley, Sheridan; H. Waugh
West, Ambrose; P. Levene
West, Henry Highland; J. Nazel
West, Honey; G. G. Fickling
West, Janine; E. Welles
West, Roger; J. Creasey
Westborough, Theocritus Lucius; C. B. Clason
Westlake, Hugh; J. Stagge
Weston, Mrs. Caywood; E. Thomas
Weston, Dick; T. Lund
Weston, Geoffrey; T. B. Haughey
Weston, James; James Warren
Weston, Tommy; W. Sheridan
Wexford, Insp.; R. Rendell
Wharton, Sam; D. Buckingham
Wheat, Whitney; J. Lane
Wheeler, Al; Carter Brown
Whelan, Dick; Laurence Dwight Smith
Whispering Hills; K. Cameron
White, Al; G. Holden
White, George; M. M. Mannon
White, Lace; Jeannette Covert Nolan
White, Col. Peregrine; B. Spicer
Whitfield, Bob; R. A. Moore
Whitney, Whit; D. Dodge
Wick, Christer; Maria Lang
Widgeon, Insp.; Alan Thomas
Widowers, Black; I. Asimov
Wield, Insp.; Glint Green
Wigan, James; B. J. Farmer
Wiggin, Gramps; E. S. Gardner
Wilde, Carney; B. Spicer
Wilde, Jonas; A. York
Wilkins, Insp.; F. Beeding
Wilkins, Insp.; Murray Thomas
Willard, Nell; M. Lynch
Williams, Chief Insp.; H. Clevely
Williams, George; J. Di Mona
Williams, Paul; H. C. McDonald
Williams, Race; C. J. Daly
Williams, Remo; R. Sapir, W. B. Murphy
Willing, Basil; H. McCloy
Willis, George; W. Hughes
Willum, Persis; Clarissa Watson
Wilson, Dick; K. Sproul
Wilson, Supt. Henry; G. D. H. Cole
Wimble, "One Week"; H. Burnham
Wimsey, Lord Peter; D. L. Sayers
Wine, Moses; Roger L. Simon
Winkley, Mr.; H. Rutland
Winkman, Jake; D. Von Elsner
Winston, Peter; J. Laflin, P. Winston
Winter, Insp./Supt. William; Gwendoline Butler
Winters, Matt; I. Oellrichs
Wintino, Dave; E. Lacy
Wintringham, David; Josephine Bell
Wise, Justus; A. W. Barrett
Wise, Pennington; Carolyn Wells
Witherall, Leonidas; A. Tilton
Withers, Hildegarde; S. Palmer
Woar, Hazlitt; G. W. Yates
Wolfe, Nero; R. Stout
Wolfram, Hugo; R. Graves
Woodfield, Will; E. Foote-Smith
Woodhead, Alister; E. H. Clements
Woods, Insp.; D. E. Muir
Woodward, James Rowland, VII; J. S. Blazer
Woolfe, Miss; Winifred Graham
Woolrich, Tony; M. M. Raison
Wortenheimer, Silas; D. Learmonth
Wragge, Arnold "Tiger"; P. Capon
Wraithlea, Commander; P. Walker Taylor
Wrayne, Daphne; Mark Cross
Wren, Insp.; N. A. Temple-Ellis
Wright, David; J. F. Straker
Wright, Eddie; C. Mullen
Wu, Lily; J. Sheridan
Wulff, Burt; M. Barry

Wycliffe, Charles; W. J. Burley
Wyndham Saga; S. Nichols
Wynnton, Robert; S. Horler

X, Secret Agent; B. House

Yamamura, Trygve; P. Anderson
Yard, John; Ralph Hayes
Yardley, John; R. Garnett
Yates, Susan; E. L. Fetta
Yedder, Ira; E. Bond
Yeoman, Giles; M. Woodhouse
Ygrec, Insp. Maurice; M. Rippon
York, Insp.; M. Durham
York, Supt. Richard; A. Williamson
York, Sherrett; Gavin Holt
Young, Bernard; Eric Wood
Young, Wilson; G. Tippette

Z, Department; J. Creasey
Zambra, Sebastian; Headon Hill
Zane, Martin; L. Trimble
Zane, Thornton; M. Massey
Zimmerman, Lt. Al; T. George
Zondi, Sgt.; J. McClure
Zordan, Anna; J. Eastwood

Series Character Chronology

Series Character Chronology

Year	Character	Type	Country	Book Type	Number of Books	Author
1878	Ebenezer Gryce	police	A	hb	13	A. K. Green
1878	James M'Govan	police	B	hb	7	J. M'Govan
1887	Insp. Byrnes	police	A	hb	5	J. Hawthorne
1887	Sherlock Holmes[1]	private	B	hb	9	A. C. Doyle
1888	Dick Donovan	police	B	hb	15	D. Donovan
1889	Nick Carter	private	A	pb	100s	Nicholas Carter
1891	Old Sleuth	private	A	pb	(8)	Old Sleuth
1891	Robert Spicer	private	B	pb	(6)	M. Danvers
1895	Capt. Owen Kettle		B	hb	(14)	C. J. C. Hyne
1895	Dr. Nikola	criminal	B	hb	5	G. Boothby
1898	Paul Beck	private	B	hb	6	M. M. Bodkin
1898	Jesse James	criminal	A	pb	(6)	W. B. Lawson
1899	Harrison Keith	private	A	pb	51	Nicholas Carter
1899	Francis Mandell-Essington		B	hb	7	J. S. Clouston
1899	A. J. Raffles	criminal	B	hb	17+	E. W. Hornung / B. Perowne / D. Fletcher / G. Greene
1903	Jim Godfrey	amateur	B	hb	6	B. Stevenson
1906	Felix Boyd	private	A	pb	6	Scott Campbell
1906	Augustus S. F. X. Van Dusen	private	A	hb	6	J. Futrelle
1907	Arsene Lupin	criminal	F	hb	16	M. Leblanc
1907	Joseph Rouletabille	amateur	F	hb	5	G. Leroux
1907	Ashley Tempest	private	B	hb	(5)	A. C. Fox-Davies
1907	Dr. John Thorndyke	private	B	hb	30	R. Austin Freeman / N. Donaldson / J. H. Dirckx
1908	Four Just Men	adventurer	B	hb	5	E. Wallace
1908	J. Rufus Wallingford	criminal	A	hb	5	G. R. Chester
1909	Insp. Furneaux	police	B	hb	(15)	G. Holmes / L. Tracy
1909	Fleming Stone	private	A	hb	61	Carolyn Wells
1910	Jeff Clayton	private	A	pb	29	W. Ward
1910	Hamilton Cleek	police	B	hb	12	T. W. Hanshew / M. E. Hanshew / H. P. Hanshew
1910	Insp. Hanaud	police	B	hb	6	A. E. W. Mason
1911	Father Brown	amateur	B	hb	6	G. K. Chesterton
1911	Commissioner Sanders	police	B	hb	15	E. Wallace / F. Gerard
1912	Smiler Bunn	criminal	B	hb	9	B. Atkey
1912	Richard Duvall	private	A	hb	5	A. Fredericks
1912	Craig Kennedy	private	A	hb	26	A. B. Reeve
1912	Edward Leithen	private	B	hb	7	J. Buchan
1912	Judge Priest	amateur	A	hb	7	I. S. Cobb
1913	Dr. Fu Manchu	criminal	B	hb	16	S. Rohmer
1913	Sgt. Jasper Shrig	police	B	hb	(11)	J. Farnol
1914	Michael Lanyard	criminal	A	hb	8	L. J. Vance
1915	Sexton Blake	private	B	pb	100s	various hands
1915	P. J. Davenant	amateur	B	hb	6	F. S. Hamilton
1915	Fantomas	criminal	B	hb	13	P. Souvestre / M. Allain
1915	Richard Hannay	amateur	B	hb	6	J. Buchan
1915	Dr. Syn	criminal	B	hb	7	R. Thorndyke
(1916)	Insp. Mitchell	police	A	hb	(10)	N. S. Lincoln
1916	Connie Morgan		A	hb	(8)	J. B. Hendryx
1917	Jimmie Dale	adventurer	A	hb	5	F. Packard
1917	Timothy McCarty	amateur	A	hb	5	I. Ostrander
1918	Dr. Adolph Grundt	spy	B	hb	7	D. Valentine / V. Williams
1918	Anthony Trent	criminal	B	hb	25	W. Martyn
1919	Peter Clancy	amateur	A	hb	60	L. Thayer
1919	Pennington Wise	private	A	hb	8	Carolyn Wells
1920	Bulldog Drummond	adventurer	B	hb	18	H. C. McNeile / G. Fairlie / H. Reymond
1920	Reggie Fortune	police	B	hb	22	H. C. Bailey
1920	Hercule Poirot	private	B	hb	41	A. Christie
1921	John Bartley	private	A	hb	8	C. J. Dutton
1921	Blue Pete		B	hb	20	L. Allan
1921	Gunston Cotton	spy	B	hb	14	Rupert Grayson
1921	Paul Harvey	private	B	hb	5	S. Rohmer
1921	Francis McNab	private	B	hb	6	J. Ferguson
1921	Jonah Mansel		B	hb	12	D. Yates
1921	Ephraim Tutt	private	A	hb	14	A. Train
1921	Cuthbert Vanardy	adventurer	A	hb	5	Herman Landon
1922	Tommy & Tuppence Beresford	amateur	B	hb	5	Agatha Christie
1922	Jerry Boyne		A	hb	5	A. MacGowan
1922	Cheri-Bibi	adventurer	F	hb	5	G. Leroux
1922	Insp. J. Rason	police	B	hb	(17)	D. Durham / S. Kyle / R. Vickers
1923	Jim Hanvey		A	hb	6	O. R. Cohen
1923	Insp. Luckraft	police	B	hb	7	A. J. Rees
1923	Aurelius Smith	spy	A	hb	7	R. T. M. Scott
1923	Supt. Henry Wilson	police	B	hb	25	G. D. H. Cole
1923	Lord Peter Wimsey	amateur	B	hb	15	D. L. Sayers
1924	Insp. Joseph French	police	B	hb	32	F. W. Crofts
1924	Colonel Anthony Gethryn	amateur	B	hb	12	P. MacDonald
1924	Colonel Wyckham Gore	amateur	B	hb	7	L. Brock
1924	Jimmie Haswell	private	B	hb	9	H. Adams
1924	Jimgrim	spy	B	hb	13	T. Mundy
1924	Aubrey Major		B	hb	(19)	L. P. Greene
1924	Insp. Pointer	police	B	hb	23	A. Fielding
1924	Insp. George Rason	police	B	hb	(9)	D. Durham / R. Vickers
1924	Anthony Ravenhill	amateur	B	hb	(7)	R. F. Foster
1924	J. G. Reeder	police	B	hb	5	E. Wallace
1924	Insp. Sims	police	B	hb	13	F. Grierson

Year	Character	Type	Country	Book Type	Number of Books	Author
1925	Charlie Chan	police	A	hb	7	E. D. Biggers D. Lynds
1925	Peter Creighton	private	A	hb	5	A. Livingston
1925	Sgt. Elk	police	B	hb	5	E. Wallace
1925	Supt. Laurence Gilmartin	police	B	hb	(15)	C. Barry
1925	Dr. Eustace Hailey	amateur	B	hb	28	A. Wynne
(1925)	Hashknife Hartley		A	hb	(20)	W. C. Tuttle
1925	Dr. Lancelot Priestley	amateur	B	hb	72	J. Rhode
1925	Roger Sheringham	amateur	B	hb	10	A. Berkeley
1925	Madame Rosika Storey	amateur	A	hb	8	H. Footner
1925	Richard Verrell	criminal	B	hb	30	B. Graeme R. Graeme
1925	Paul Vivanti	criminal	B	hb	6	S. Horler
1926	Supt. Battle	police	B	hb	5	Agatha Christie
1926	Ben	amateur	B	hb	8	J. J. Farjeon
1926	Corp. Downey	police	A	hb	(9)	J. B. Hendryx
1926	Gilbert Larose	police	B	hb	28	A. Gask
1926	Nat Ridley	private	A	pb	15	N. Ridley, Jr.
1926	Mortimer Sark	amateur	B	hb	5	J. Hawk
1926	Sir Arthur Sinclair	police	B	hb	(26)	W. S. Masterman
1926	Ludovic Travers	amateur	B	hb	63	C. Bush
1926	Philo Vance	amateur	A	hb	12	S. S. Van Dine
1927	Anthony Bathurst	amateur	B	hb	53	B. Flynn
1927	Miles Bredon	amateur	B	hb	5	R. Knox
1927	Chandos	adventurer	B	hb	10	D. Yates
1927	Martin Dale	criminal	B	hb	9	Herman Landon
1927	Sgt. Trevor Dene	police	B	hb	5	V. Williams
1927	Sir Clinton Driffield	police	B	hb	17	J. J. Connington
1927	Scott Egerton	amateur	B	hb	10	Anthony Gilbert
1927	Philip MacCray		A	hb	5	O. F. Jerome
1927	Jimmie Rezaire	private	B	hb	5	Anthony Armstrong
1927	Race Williams	private	A	hb	7	C. J. Daly
1928	Prof. Luther Bastion	amateur	B	hb	(17)	Gavin Holt
1928	Colonel Alistair Granby	spy	B	hb	17	F. Beeding
1928	Insp. Cuthbert Higgins	police	B	hb	35	C. F. Gregg
1928	Sgt. Patrick Aloysius McCarthy	police	B	hb	(54)	J. G. Brandon
1928	Lynn MacDonald	private	A	hb	7	K. C. Strahan
1928	Bill Saville		B	hb	(6)	Roland Daniel
1928	Insp. Shane	police	B	hb	6	S. Truss
1928	Maud Silver	private	B	hb	32	P. Wentworth
1928	Simon Templar	adventurer	B	hb	49+	L. Charteris
1928	Sir Leonard Wallace	spy	B	hb	(8)	Alexander Wilson
1929	Insp. Napoleon Bonaparte	police	B	hb	29	A. W. Upfield
1929	Dame Beatrice Bradley	amateur	B	hb	58+	Gladys Mitchell
1929	Albert Campion	amateur	B	hb	26	M. Allingham Y. Carter
1929	Insp. Carter & Sgt. Bell	police	B	hb	5	E. R. Punshon
1929	Insp. Hugh Collier	police	B	hb	(13)	M. Dalton
1929	Continental Op	private	A	hb	10	D. Hammett
1929	Insp. Frost	police	B	hb	7	H. M. Smith
1929	Insp. Alan Grant	police	B	hb	6	G. Daviot J. Tey
1929	Colonel Duncan Grant	spy	B	hb	7	G. Seton
1929	Sarah Keate	amateur	A	hb	7	M. Eberhart
1929	Insp. McLean	police	B	hb	55	G. Goodchild
1929	Harley Manners	amateur	B	hb	6	C. Dutton
1929	Peter Piper	amateur	A	hb	5	N. B. Mavity
1929	Insp. John Poole	police	B	hb	8	Henry Wade
1929	Ellery Queen	amateur	A	hb	45	E. Queen
1929	Tommy Rankin	police	A	hb	14	M. Propper
1929	Maxwell Sanderson	criminal	A	hb	5	J. J. Chichester
1929	Jim Sands	amateur	A	hb	5	R. J. Casey
1929	Insp. Silver	police	B	hb	(15)	Henry Holt
1929	Supt. Anthony Slade	police	B	hb	(33)	L. Gribble
1929	Jimmy Traynor	private	A	hb	5	A. Livingston
1929	Lt. Valcour	police	A	hb	11	Rufus King
1929	Anthony Vereker		B	hb	6	R. Forsythe
1929	Insp. Williams	police	B	hb	(5)	H. Clevely
1930	Henri Bencolin	police	A	hb	6	J. D. Carr
1930	Hugh Carding	private	B	hb	7	G. Collins
1930	Joshua Clunk	private	B	hb	12	H. C. Bailey
1930	Thatcher Colt	police	A	hb	8	A. Abbot
1930	James F. Dundee	police	A	hb	5	Anne Austin
1930	Prof. Henry Fielding	amateur	B	hb	(9)	D. Sharp
1930	Commissioner Denzil Grigson	police	B	hb	(7)	A. Broome
1930	Insp. Kane	police	A	hb	5	R. Scarlett
1930	Insp. Christopher McKee	police	A	hb	31	H. Reilly
1930	Amos Lee Mappin	amateur	A	hb	10	H. Footner
1930	Jeff Marle	amateur	A	hb	6	J. D. Carr
1930	Jane Marple	amateur	B	hb	16	Agatha Christie
1930	Kate Marsh	amateur	B	hb	8	G. Lane
1930	Desmond Merrion	amateur	B	hb	61	M. Burton
1930	Capt. Hugh North	spy	A	hb	25	V. W. Mason
1930	Evan Pinkerton	amateur	A	hb	12	D. Frome
1930	Sebastian Quin		B	hb	5	S. Horler
1930	Insp. Reynolds	police	B	hb	(8)	Elaine Hamilton
(1930)	Jerry Scant	amateur	B	hb	(5)	L. A. Knight
1930	Insp. Skane	police	B	hb	5	D. Marfield
1930	Ronald Standish	private	B	hb	5	H. C. McNeile
1930	Insp. John Swinton	police	B	hb	5	I. Greig
1930	Philip Tracy	amateur	B	hb	7	H. Ashbrook
1930	Dennis Tyler	police	A	hb	7	Diplomat
1930	Daphne Wrayne	private	B	hb	47	Valentine Mark Cross
1931	Black John		A	hb	(18)	J. B. Hendryx
1931	Ronald Camberwell	private	B	hb	11	J. S. Fletcher
1931	Major Peter Castle	spy	B	hb	(6)	Gilderoy Davison
1931	Asaph Clume	private	A	hb	6	R. L. Goldman

Year	Character	Type	Country	Book Type	Number of Books	Author
1931	Lamont Cranston	adventurer	A	pb	45	Maxwell Grant / W. B. Gibson
1931	Insp. Cummings	police	B	hb	5	P. McGuire
1931	Colonel Peter Gantian	spy	B	hb	11	C. Dawe
1931	Clay Harrison	private	B	hb	5	Clifton Robbins
1931	Paul Irving		B	hb	(6)	L. Grex
1931	Insp. Wilton Jacks	police	A	hb	6	J. H. Wallis
1931	Mr. Jellipot	private	B	hb	(10)	S. Fowler
1931	Insp. MacDonald	police	B	hb	46	E. C. R. Lorac
1931	Asey Mayo	amateur	A	hb	24	P. A. Taylor
1931	Li Moh	amateur	B	hb	6	J. Cowdroy
1931	Gordon Muldrew	police	B	hb	(6)	Luke Allan
1931	Peter Shane	amateur	B	hb	(6)	Gilderoy Davison
1931	Insp. Stevens	police	B	hb	13	B. Graeme
1931	Twisted Face	criminal	B	hb	(8)	Gilderoy Davison
1931	Insp. John Walk	police	B	hb	(5)	Roland Daniel
1931	Hildegarde Withers	amateur	A	hb	17	S. Palmer
1932	Insp. Barnard	police	B	hb	(14)	T. C. H. Jacobs
1932	Harker Bellamy		B	hb	11	S. Horler
1932	Insp. Archie Burford	police	B	hb	6	V. MacClure
1932	Mick Cardby	private	B	hb	(27)	David Hume
1932	Gordon Craigie (Dept. Z)	spy	B	hb	29	J. Creasey
1932	Insp. Fillinger	police	B	hb	6	P. McGuire
(1932)	Insp. Andy Frampton	police	B	hb	(48)	T. A. Plummer
1932	Christopher Hand	private	A	hb	5	S. H. Page
1932	Lessinger	criminal	B	hb	7	R. Essex
1932	Insp. Jules Maigret	police	F	hb	73+	G. Simenon
1932	Amos Petrie	police	B	hb	7	J. V. Turner
1932	John Slade	police	B	hb	5	R. Essex
1932	Tiger Standish	spy	B	hb	12	S. Horler
1932	Philip Tolefree	private	B	hb	22	R. A. J. Walling
1933	Supt. Edmund Bendilow	police	B	hb	(5)	Carlton Wallace
1933	Christopher Bond	private	B	hb	9	W. Martyn
1933	Supt. Robert Budd	police	B	hb	(24)	G. Verner
1933	Major Dick Burton		B	hb	6	M. Beckett
1933	Rex Coulson	adventurer	B	hb	6	Jack Mann
1933	Duke de Richleau	spy	B	hb	11	D. Wheatley
1933	Dr. Gideon Fell	amateur	A	hb	27	J. D. Carr
1933	Trevor Lowe	amateur	B	hb	(14)	G. Verner
1933	Perry Mason	private	A	hb	85	E. S. Gardner
(1933)	Colonel Ormiston	spy	B	hb	(11)	J. M. Walsh
1933	Constable Owen	police	B	hb	35	E. R. Punshon
1933	Arthur Stukely Pennington	amateur	B	hb	(29)	J. G. Brandon / G. Brandon
1933	Dr. L. Rees Pons	amateur	A	hb	5	C. D. King
1933	Hugh Rennert	police	A	hb	6	T. Downing
1933	P. C. Richardson	police	B	hb	8	B. Thomson
1933	Charlie Ryan		B	hb	5	J. C. Lenehan
1933	Phineas Spinnet	private	B	hb	(21)	A. Soutar
1933	Timothy Terrel	spy	B	hb	(18)	S. Maddock
1934	Insp. Roderick Alleyn	police	B	hb	31+	N. Marsh
1934	Major Jack Atherley	amateur	B	hb	(8)	C. Ashton
1934	Sgt. Geoffrey Boscobell	police	B	hb	13	C. M. Wills
1934	Insp. Head	police	B	hb	(12)	E. C. Vivian
1934	Richard Herrivell	amateur	B	hb	9	John Bentley
1934	Grace Latham and/or John Primrose	amateur	A	hb	16	L. Ford
1934	Insp. Michael Lord	police	A	hb	5	C. D. King
1934	Sir Henry Merrivale	amateur	A	hb	24	Carter Dickson / J. D. Carr
1934	Judge Ephraim Peck	amateur	A	hb	10	A. Derleth
1934	Capt. Ryan		B	hb	(11)	E. L. Long
1934	Gregory Sallust	spy	B	hb	11	D. Wheatley
1934	Mr. Swan	amateur	B	hb	5	R. Philmore
1934	Paul Templeton	private	B	hb	13	R. Goyne
1934	Insp. Treadgold	police	B	hb	7	A. Weymouth
1934	Nero Wolfe	private	A	hb	47	R. Stout
1935	Sheriff Rocky Allan	police	A	hb	6	V. Rath
1935	Insp. Victor Bonderant	police	A	hb	7	J. G. Edwards
1935	Freddie Brown	amateur	B	hb	(8)	M. Poole
1935	Mr. De Havilland		B	hb	(12)	J. N. Chance
1935	Jane Amanda Edwards	amateur	A	hb	12	C. M. Russell
1935	Laurie Fenton	spy	B	hb	(14)	M. Annesley
1935	Lt. Bill French	police	A	hb	12	C. Hale
1935	James Greer	amateur	A	hb	5	N. Gayle
(1935)	Dixon Hawke	private	B	pb	20	anonymous
1935	Sgt. Hemingway	police	B	hb	8	G. Heyer
1935	Percy Huff	amateur	B	hb	(5)	C. Edwards
1935	Henry Hyer	private	A	hb	9	K. Steel
1935	Elisha Macomber	amateur	A	hb	16	K. M. Knight
1935	Insp. Meredith	police	B	hb	(26)	J. Bude
1935	Mr. Moto	spy	A	hb	6	J. P. Marquand
1935	Kent Murdock	amateur	A	hb	23	G. H. Coxe
1935	Peter O'Brien		A	hb	5	I. H. Irwin
1935	Double O'Day		B	hb	(6)	Gwyn Evans
1935	Mrs. Palmyra Pym	police	B	hb	24	N. Morland
1935	Lt. Peter Quint	police	A	hb	5	H. Austin
1935	Grant Rushton		B	hb	(5)	G. H. Teed
1935	Doc Savage	adventurer	A	pb	102	K. Robeson
1935	Insp. Schmidt	police	A	hb	47+	G. Bagby
1935	Insp. Shelley	police	B	hb	(17)	J. Rowland
1935	Nigel Strangeways	private	B	hb	16	N. Blake
1936	Sir John Appleby	police	B	hb	31+	M. Innes
1936	Insp. Edward Beale	police	B	hb	8	R. Penny
1936	Sgt. William Beef	police	B	hb	8	L. Bruce
1936	Roger Bennion	amateur	B	hb	27	H. Adams
1936	Robin Bishop	amateur	A	hb	5	G. Homes
1936	Simon Brade	amateur	A	hb	(7)	Harriette Campbell
1936	Insp. Cheviot Burmann	police	B	hb	(42)	B. Cobb
1936	David Cane	amateur	B	hb	(6)	J. Courage
1936	Lemmy Caution	police	B	hb	12	P. Cheyney
(1936)	Clive Conrad	private	B	hb	(21)	Frank King
1936	Arthur Crook	private	B	hb	51	Anthony Gilbert
1936	Bartholomew Dane	private	B	hb	(7)	Rex Dark
1936	Dr. Septimus Dodds	private	B	hb	(11)	Sutherland Scott
1936	Peter Duluth	amateur	A	hb	8	P. Quentin

Year	Character	Type	Country	Book Type	Number of Books	Author
1936	Barney Gantt	amateur	A	hb	8	J. S. Strange
1936	Insp. Gidleigh	police	B	hb	24	S. Truss
1936	Gregory George Gordon Green	private	B	hb	8	Jack Mann
1936	Jupiter Jones	amateur	A	hb	5	T. Fuller
1936	Anne & Jeffrey McNeill	amateur	A	hb	19	T. Du Bois
1936	Sir John Meredith	police	B	hb	17	F. Gerard
1936	Dick Pemberty	spy	B	hb	(9)	P. Conde
(1936)	"Rem" Remington		B	hb	6	R. Ladline
1936	Insp. Ryvet	police	B	hb	6	C. Carnac
1936	Irving Todd		B	hb	(6)	P. Conde
(1936)	Insp. Wake	police	B	hb	(6)	C. Kingston
1936	Theocritus Lucius Westborough	amateur	A	hb	10	C. B. Clason
1936	Dr. Hugh Westlake	amateur	A	hb	9	J. Stagge
1936	Tony Woolrich	amateur	A	hb	5	M. M. Raison
1937	Maxwell Archer	adventurer	B	hb	(7)	H. Clevely
1937	Insp. Harry Charlton	police	B	hb	11	C. Witting
1937	Jason Cordry	amateur	A	hb	5	J. O'Hanlon
1937	Gerald Frost	adventurer	B	hb	7	S. Horler
1937	Insp. Headcorn	police	B	hb	5	Alice Campbell
1937	Peter Justice	adventurer	B	hb	(5)	F. Duncan
1937	Oliver "O.K." Keene	spy	B	hb	(12)	J. M. Walsh
1937	Sgt. Johnny Lamb	police	B	hb	5	J. Donavan
1937	Capt. Ben Lucias	police	A	hb	6	R. Howes
1937	Capt. Duncan Maclain	private	A	hb	14	B. Kendrick
1937	Insp. John Mallett	police	B	hb	6	C. Hare
1937	John Mannering	criminal	B	hb	47	Anthony Morton
1937	Insp. Steven Mitchell	police	B	hb	12	Josephine Bell
1937	Mr. Pendlebury	amateur	B	hb	(9)	A. Webb
1937	Huntoon Rogers	amateur	A	hb	18	C. Knight
1937	Doug Selby	police	A	hb	9	E. S. Gardner
1937	Lt. Timothy Trant	police	A	hb	8	Q. Patrick / P. Quentin
1937	Dr. David Wintringham	amateur	B	hb	13	Josephine Bell
1937	Leonidas Witherall	amateur	A	hb	8	A. Tilton
1938	Sgt. Peter Bradfield	police	B	hb	9	C. Witting
1938	Slim Callaghan	private	B	hb	10	P. Cheyney
1938	Humphrey Campbell	private	A	hb	5	G. Homes
1938	Mary Carner	private	A	hb	5	Z. Popkin
1938	Sgt. Paul Dean	police	B	hb	(5)	B. Francis
1938	Michael Dundas	amateur	A	hb	8	V. Rath
1938	Insp. Septimus Finch	police	B	hb	21+	M. Erskine
1938	Cyrus Hatch	amateur	A	hb	8	F. C. Davis
1938	Tony Hunter	private	A	hb	10	R. G. Dean
1938	Supt. Mallet	police	B	hb	(18)	M. Fitt
1938	Lt. Stephen Mayhew	police	A	hb	7	D. B. Olsen
1938	The Great Merlini	amateur	A	hb	5	C. Rawson
1938	Peter Mohune	spy	B	hb	(5)	P. Groom
1938	Insp. George Muir	police	B	hb	15	F. Grierson
1938	Richard Rollison	adventurer	B	hb	61	J. Creasey / W. V. Butler
1938	Insp. Joel Saber	police	B	hb	(6)	Gavin Holt
1938	Paul Temple	amateur	B	hb	11	F. Durbridge / P. Temple
1938	Basil Willing	amateur	A	hb	13+	H. McCloy
(1939)	Insp. William Austen	police	B	hb	(29)	Anne Hocking
1939	Peter & Janet Barron	amateur	A	hb	5	R. Darby
1939	Luke Bradley	police	A	hb	5	H. Pentecost
(1939)	Insp. Cadman	police	B	hb	(5)	C. Rushton
1939	Tod Claymore		B	hb	6	T. Claymore
1939	Insp. Bill Cromwell	police	B	hb	43	V. Gunn
1939	Patrick Dawlish	spy	B	hb	50	G. Ashe
1939	Homer Evans	amateur	A	hb	9	Elliot Paul
1939	Jack Fenner		A	hb	5	G. H. Coxe
1939	Peter Grayleigh	adventurer	B	hb	14	Colin Robertson
1939	Supt. Gordon Knollis	police	B	hb	(11)	F. Vivian
1939	Donald Lam	private	A	hb	29	A. A. Fair
1939	John J. Malone	private	A	hb	14	C. Rice
1939	Dick Marlowe	private	A	hb	(8)	John Bentley
1939	Philip Marlowe	private	A	hb	7	R. Chandler
1939	Bruce Murdoch	spy	B	hb	6	N. Deane
1939	Rachel & Jennifer Murdock	amateur	A	hb	13	D. B. Olsen
1939	Fergus O'Breen	private	A	hb	6	A. Boucher
1939	Papa Pontivy	spy	B	hb	(16)	B. Newman
1939	Sheriff Jess Roden	police	A	hb	21	A. B. Cunningham
1939	Desmond Shannon	private	A	hb	17	M. V. Heberden
1939	Mike Shayne	private	A	hb	69	B. Halliday
1939	Jim Steele	amateur	A	hb	7	D. Chambers
1939	Matt Winters	amateur	A	hb	(7)	I. Oellrichs
1939	Alister Woodhead	spy	B	hb	13	E. H. Clements
1940	Jane Carberry		B	hb	(5)	B. Symons
1940	Saturnin Dax	police	B	hb	(34)	M. Cumberland
1940	Toby Dyke	amateur	B	hb	5	E. X. Ferrars
1940	Earl of Millington		B	hb	(5)	G. Hackforth-Jones
1940	Supt. Roger Ellerdine	police	B	hb	(10)	C. M. Wills
1940	Johnny Fletcher & Sam Cragg	amateur	A	hb	14	F. Gruber
1940	Henry Gamadge	amateur	A	hb	16	E. Daly
1940	Capt. Bill Grady	police	A	hb	8	I. S. Shriber
1940	Tommy Hambledon	spy	B	hb	26	M. Coles
1940	Elsie May Hunt & Tim Mulligan	amateur	A	hb	18	A. M. Stein
1940	Rex McBride	private	A	hb	6	C. F. Adams
1940	Pam & Jerry North	amateur	A	hb	26	F. Lockridge
1940	"Peter" Piper		A	hb	(6)	A. R. Long
1940	Christopher Storm	amateur	A	hb	7	W. A. Barber
1940	Edward Trelawny	amateur	A	hb	(6)	A. R. Long
1940	Haila & Jeff Troy	amateur	A	hb	9	K. Roos
1940	Harvey Tuke	police	B	hb	7	D. Browne
1941	Pat & Jean Abbott	amateur	A	hb	(25)	F. Crane
1941	John Bent	private	A	hb	7	H. C. Branson
1941	Mike Brett	spy	B	hb	6	Keith Campbell
1941	Insp. Cockrill	police	B	hb	7	C. Brand
1941	Quinny Hite	private	A	hb	5	R. Burke
1941	"Tiger" Lester	spy	B	hb	(12)	D. Betteridge

Series Character Chronology

Year	Character	Type	Country	Book Type	Number of Books	Author
1941	Insp. Thomas Little-john	police	B	hb	57+	G. Bellairs
1941	Buddy Mustard	private	B	hb	(14)	Roland Daniel
1941	Liz Parrott	amateur	A	hb	(6)	Manning Long
1941	Theodore I. Terhune	amateur	B	hb	8	B. Graeme
1942	Jack "Flash" Casey	amateur	A	hb	7	G. H. Coxe
1942	Roger Fleming		B	hb	(7)	S. Harvester
1942	Paul Kilgerrin	private	A	hb	11	C. B. Leonard
1942	Insp. Gridley Nelson	police	A	hb	13	R. Fenisong
1942	Dr. Stanislaus Alexander Palfrey	spy	B	hb	33	J. Creasey
1942	Marshal Ben Pedley	police	A	hb	9	S. Sterling
1942	Francis Pettigrew	private	B	hb	5	C. Hare
1942	Lt. Richard Tuck	police	A	hb	5	Lange Lewis
1942	Insp. Roger West	police	B	hb	42	J. Creasey
1943	Martin Ames	amateur	A	hb	(6)	A. Eichler
1943	Supt. John Bellamy	police	B	hb	(7)	T. C. H. Jacobs
1943	Arab & Andy Blake	amateur	A	hb	5	R. Powell
1943	Rush Henry		A	hb	(5)	Joe Barry
1943	Insp. Carl Knickman	police	A	hb	(6)	A. Eichler
1943	Lydford Long	amateur	B	hb	13	H. Carstairs
(1943)	Mallory	police	A	hb	(7)	C. Stoddard
1943	John Marshall	private	B	hb	13	J. M. Fox
1943	Dr. Morelle	amateur	B	hb	15	E. Dudley
1943	Jim O'Neill	police	A	hb	5	D. M. Disney
1944	Kit Acton	amateur	A	hb	5	M. Bramhall
1944	Maria Black	amateur	B	hb	5	J. Slate
1944	Steve Carter		A	hb	(7)	A. R. Long
1944	Garry Dean	amateur	A	hb	6	P. Whelton
1944	Gervase Fen	amateur	B	hb	11	E. Crispin
1944	Insp. Grogan	police	B	hb	(19)	M. Neville
1944	Abbie Harris	amateur	A	hb	6	A. Dean
1944	Dr. Harry Manson	police	B	hb	(35)	E. Radford
1944	Mordecai Tremaine		B	hb	(6)	F. Duncan
1945	Sgt. Peter Bradfield	police	B	hb	5	C. Witting
(1945)	Insp. Alan Frazer	police	B	hb	(33)	H. Desmond
1945	Jub Freeman	police	A	hb	10	L. Treat
1945	Ben Helm	private	A	hb	6	B. Fischer
1945	Asmun Hill		B	hb	(5)	H. Hawton
1945	Patrick Laing	amateur	A	hb	6	P. Laing
1945	Jenny Gilette (Lewis) & Hunter Lewis	amateur	A	hb	6	R. Grey
1945	Sir Abercrombie Lewker	amateur	B	hb	17	S. Styles / Glyn Carr
1945	The Padre	amateur	B	hb	5	R. Goyne
1945	Prof. A. Pennyfeather	amateur	A	hb	6	D. B. Olsen
1945	Solar Pons	private	A	hb	16	A. Derleth / B. Copper
1945	Insp. Julian Rivers	police	B	hb	15	C. Carnac
1945	Steve Silk	private	B	hb	(14)	J. B. O'Sullivan
1945	Prof. John Stubbs	amateur	B	hb	7	R. T. Campbell
1945	Mitch Taylor	police	A	hb	7	L. Treat
1945	Insp. York	police	B	hb	(5)	M. Durham
1946	Supt. Andrew Ash	police	B	hb	13	F. Grierson
1946	Insp. William Bastion	police	B	hb	(5)	R. Harrison
1946	Lt. Austin Clapp	police	A	hb	7	Wade Miller
1946	Major Brains Cunningham	spy	B	hb	(15)	E. P. Thorne
1946	Jeff DiMarco	amateur	A	hb	8	D. M. Disney
1946	Johnny DuVivien		B	hb	5	N. Spain
1946	Insp. Flagg	police	B	hb	(33)	J. Cassells / W. M. Duncan
1946	Grant Garfield	private	B	hb	(20)	C. Franklin
1946	Insp. Merton Heimrich	police	A	hb	25	F. Lockridge / R. Lockridge
(1946)	Insp. "Duck" Mallard	police	B	hb	(17)	A. Spiller
1946	John Prentice		B	hb	(5)	Sea-Lion
1946	Insp. Michael Regan	police	B	hb	5	E. Hale
1946	Dick Tracy	police	A	pb	7	C. Gould / W. Johnston
1947	Silas Booth	private	A	hb	(6)	J. L. Linklater
1947	Roger Brook	spy	B	hb	12	D. Wheatley
1947	Peter Chambers	private	A	hb	34	H. Kane
1947	Insp. Garth	police	B	hb	6	H. Blayn / N. Karta
1947	Mike Hammer	private	A	hb	11	M. Spillane
1947	Insp. Hazelrigg	police	B	hb	8	M. Gilbert
1947	Ed & Am Hunter	amateur	A	hb	7	F. Brown
1947	Capt. Steve Johnson	police	A	hb	5	H. L. Nelson
1947	Scott Jordan	private	A	hb	11	H. Q. Masur
1947	Johnny Liddell	private	A	hb	31	Frank Kane
1947	Mac	private	A	hb	17	T. B. Dewey
1947	Supt. Arthur Manning	police	B	hb	(7)	B. Cobb
1947	Insp. Dick Mason	police	B	hb	9	R. Armstrong
(1947)	Miss Otis		B	pb	(18)	B. Sarto
1947	Insp. Lancelot Carolus Smith	police	B	hb	5	N. Berrow
1947	Max Thursday	private	A	hb	6	Wade Miller
1947	Julia Tyler	amateur	A	hb	7	L. Revell
1947	Gil Vine	private	A	hb	8	S. Sterling
1948	Jane & Dagobert Brown	amateur	B	hb	12	D. Ames
1948	Reverend Martin Buell	amateur	A	hb	7	M. Scherf
1948	Doc Connor	amateur	A	hb	5	J. Dolph
1948	Mark Corrigan	spy	B	hb	30	M. Corrigan
1948	Roger Crammond		B	hb	8	T. Muir
1948	Insp. Peter Curwen	police	B	hb	(7)	R. Vickers
1948	Steve Drake	private	A	hb	5	R. Ellington
1948	Jeremiah X. Gibson	police	A	hb	18	Hampton Stone
1948	Eve Gill	amateur	B	hb	6	S. Jepson
1948	Insp. Andy McMurdo	police	B	hb	(8)	N. Morland
1948	Philip Odell		B	hb	(5)	Lester Powell
1948	Supt. Sandyman	police	B	hb	(7)	Neill Graham
1949	Lew Archer	private	A	hb	19	J. Macdonald / J. R. Macdonald / R. Macdonald
1949	Dr. Douglas Baynes	amateur	B	hb	6	V. Bell
1949	Miriam Birdseye	amateur	B	hb	5	N. Spain

Year	Character	Type	Country	Book Type	Number of Books	Author
1949	Charles Blessington	spy	B	hb	(5)	J. Sherwood
1949	Judge Dee	police	B	hb	18	R. van Gulik
1949	Jim Dunn	private	A	hb	8	H. L. Nelson
1949	Temple Fortune	private	B	hb	(20)	T. C. H. Jacobs
1949	Carney Wilde	private	A	hb	7	B. Spicer
1950	George Dixon	police	B	hb	6	T. Willis Rex Edwards
1950	Insp. Ambrose Mahon	police	B	hb	(7)	S. H. Courtier
1950	Lefty O'Connor		B	pb	(5)	B. Shannon
1950	Insp. Ronald Price	police	B	hb	5	J. Cannan
1950	John Ripley	police	A	hb	5	Gordons
1950	Shell Scott	private	A	pb	37	R. S. Prather
1950	John Cornelius Franklin Scotter	private	B	hb	7	T. Warriner
1950	Luke Speare & Schuyler Cole	private	A	hb	6	F. C. Davis
1950	Sumuru	criminal	A	pb	5	S. Rohmer
1951	Rex Banner	amateur	B	hb	(7)	Robert Chapman
1951	Jim Bennett	private	A	hb	(12)	Robert Martin
1951	Hugo Bishop	amateur	B	hb	6	S. Rattray
1951	Glenn Bowman	private	B	hb	(38)	H. Howard
1951	Chico Brett	private	B	hb	16	Kevin O'Hara
1951	Steve Conacher	private	A	hb	8	Adam Knight
1951	Montague Cork	amateur	B	hb	5	Macdonald Hastings
1951	Timothy Dane	private	A	hb	9	W. Ard
1951	Simon Drake	private	B	hb	6	H. Nielsen
1951	Insp. George Felse (and family)	police	B	hb	13+	E. Pargeter Ellis Peters
1951	Carl Good	private	A	pb	(5)	R. O. Saber
1951	Insp. Hugh Gordon	police	B	hb	7	S. Gilruth
1951	Vicky McBain	private	B	hb	8	Colin Robertson
1951	Johnny Maguire	private	A	pb	6	R. Himmel
1951	Insp. George Marshall	police	B	hb	(12)	P. Barrington C. Barling
1951	Michael the O'Kelly		B	hb	7	M. O'Brine
1951	Capt. Wade Paris	police	A	hb	10	Ben Benson
1951	Lt. Romano	police	B	hb	9	David Alexander
1951	Laura Scudamore	criminal	B	hb	6	R. Armstrong
1952	Hooky Heffer(m)an	private	B	hb	15+	L. Meynell
1952	Milo March	private	A	hb	21	M. E. Chaber
1952	John Piper	private	B	hb	(37)	H. Carmichael
1952	Father Shanley	amateur	A	hb	9	J. Webb
1952	Insp. Smith	police	B	hb	(10)	S. Troy
1953	James Bond	spy	B	hb	17	I. Fleming R. Markham Christopher Wood
1953	Mark Brandon	private	B	hb	7	V. Warren
1953	Insp. Patrick Duffy	police	B	hb	9	N. Fitzgerald
1953	Johnny Fedora	spy	B	hb	(16)	D. Cory
1953	Barney Hyde	private	B	hb	9	N. Brent
1953	Ralph Lindsey	police	A	hb	7	Ben Benson
1953	Johnny Macall	private	B	hb	6	G. Fairlie
1953	Richard Maidment		B	hb	(6)	M. Cronin
1953	William Mitchell		B	hb	5	H. A. Wrenn
1953	Hart Muldoon		A	pb	5	J. Flagg
1953	Ed Noon	private	A	hb	30+	M. Avallone
1953	Joe Puma	private	A	pb	8	R. Scott W. C. Gault
1953	Gregory Quist	private	A	hb	8	W. C. MacDonald
1954	Don Cadee	private	A	hb	9	S. Dean
1954	Steve Craig	private	B	hb	(9)	B. Winter
1954	Brad Dolan	adventurer	A	pb	6	W. Fuller
1954	Gil Donan		A	hb	5	M. P. Hood
1954	Horatio Green	amateur	B	hb	5	B. Nichols
1954	Bart Hardin	amateur	A	hb	8	David Alexander
1954	Insp. Simon Manton	police	B	hb	(13)	M. Underwood
1954	Insp. Harry Martineau	police	B	hb	(14)	M. Procter
1954	Lt. Pascal	police	A	hb	6	H. Pentecost
1954	Insp. Pitt	police	B	hb	(7)	J. F. Straker
1954	Rampion Savage	amateur	B	hb	12	James Turner
1954	Ludovic Saxon	adventurer	B	hb	(21)	J. Cassells
1954	John & Sally Strang	amateur	B	hb	(6)	H. Brinton
1954	Larry Vernon		B	hb	(6)	D. Bateson
1955	Insp. William Baker	police	B	hb	(8)	O. Mills
1955	Brock Callahan	private	A	hb	9	W. C. Gault
1955	John Chadwick	private	B	hb	7	G. Cobden
1955	Carolus Deene	amateur	B	hb	23	L. Bruce
1955	Chester Drum	private	A	pb	20	S. Marlowe R. S. Prather
1955	Sam Durell	spy	A	pb	46	E. S. Aarons W. B. Aarons
1955	Insp. George Gently	police	B	hb	26+	A. Hunter
1955	Commander George Gideon	police	B	hb	23	J. J. Marric W. V. Butler J. Creasey
1955	Miss Hogg	private	B	hb	9	A. Lee
1955	Sugar Kane	private	B	hb	29	L. Marshall
(1955)	Malcolm Kenton		B	hb	(5)	S. Harvester
1955	Solo Malcolm	private	B	hb	(37)	Neill Graham
1955	Hiram Potter	amateur	A	hb	11	Rae Foley
(1955)	San Antonio	police	F	hb	(8)	San Antonio
1955	Mavis Seidlitz	private	B	pb	(12)+	Carter Brown
1955	Pete Selby	police	A	pb	10	Jonathan Craig
1956	Steve Carella (87th Precinct)	police	A	pb	34+	E. McBain
1956	Quentin Eady	amateur	B	hb	(6)	E. P. Thorne
1956	Michael Grant		B	hb	(7)	Roland Daniel
1956	Morocco Jones	private	A	pb	5	Jack Baynes
1956	Daniel Port	private	A	pb	5	P. Rabe
1956	Julia Probyn	spy	B	hb	7	A. Bridge
1956	Nathan Shapiro	police	A	hb	12	F. Lockridge R. Lockridge
1956	Dave Smith	amateur	B	hb	(13)	F. Usher
1956	Ambrose Usher	amateur	B	hb	5+	J. Davey
(1956)	Al Wheeler	police	B	pb	(49)+	Carter Brown
1957	Bill Banning	private	B	hb	8	Nat Easton
1957	Steve Bentley	amateur	A	pb	9	R. Dietrich
1957	Insp. Bradbury	police	B	hb	5	N. Longmate

Year	Character	Type	Country	Book Type	Number of Books	Author
(1957)	Supt. Bradley	police	B	hb	(11)	Colin Robertson
1957	Prof. Ronald Challis	amateur	B	hb	5	Shane Martin
1957	Insp. John Coffin	police	B	hb	13+	Gwendoline Butler
1957	Brad Ford	private	B	hb	5	H. Hobson
1957	Pete Fry	private	B	hb	15	P. Fry
1957	Insp. "Digger" Haig	police	B	hb	(6)	S. H. Courtier
1957	Grave-Digger Jones & Coffin Ed Johnson	police	A	pb	8	C. Himes
1957	Insp. Lovick	police	B	hb	(15)	G. M. Wilson
1957	Mark Raeburn	private	B	hb	6	M. Gair
1957	Pete Schofield	private	A	pb	9	T. B. Dewey
1957	Colin Thane & Bill Moss	police	B	hb	16+	B. Knox
1957	Honey West	private	A	pb	11	G. G. Fickling
1958	Burns Bannion	private	A	pb	7	Earl Norman
1958	Jake Barrow	private	A	pb	6	N. Quarry
(1958)	Danny Boyd	private	B	pb	(29)+	Carter Brown
(1958)	Marc Brody	amateur	B	pb	(22)	M. Brody
1958	Tony Costaine & Bert McCall	private	A	pb	7	N. MacNeil
1958	Hubert Bonnisseur de la Bath	spy	F	hb	(17)	Jean Bruce
1958	Matt Erridge	amateur	A	hb	19+	A. M. Stein
1958	Ben Gates	private	A	pb	5	R. Kyle
1958	Richard Graham	amateur	B	pb	5	J. Welcome
1958	Jeff Green	private	A	hb	5	C. Keith
1958	Max Heald	spy	B	hb	6	H. Hossent
1958	Gen. Charles Kirk	spy	B	hb	(8)	J. Blackburn
1958	Insp. Gregory Pellew	police	B	hb	11	V. Gielgud
1958	M. Pinaud	police	B	hb	23+	P. Audemars
1958	Julian Prescot	private	B	hb	9	J. Prescot
1958	Insp. Purbright	police	B	hb	10+	Colin Watson
1958	Colonel Charles Russell	spy	B	hb	19+	W. Haggard
1958	Supt. Swinton	police	B	hb	(7)	P. Flower
1958	Garaway Trenton		B	hb	7	J. P. Carstairs
1959	Colonel Richard Barne		B	hb	(6)	E. G. Cousins
1959	Father Joseph Bredder	amateur	A	hb	11+	L. Holton
1959	Chief Fred Fellows	police	A	hb	11	H. Waugh
1959	Mark Kilby	private	B	pb	6	R. C. Frazer
1959	Johnny Killain	private	A	pb	5	D. J. Marlowe
1959	Lou Largo	private	A	pb	6	W. Ard
1959	McHugh	spy	A	pb	5	J. Flynn
1959	Monty Nash	spy	A	pb	5	R. Telfair
1959	Ed Rivers		A	pb	5	T. Powell
1959	Rocky Steele	private	A	pb	6	J. B. West
1959	Insp. Henry Tibbett	police	B	hb	15+	P. Moyes
1959	Insp. Fadiman Wace	police	B	hb	16	R. Simons
1960	Insp. Herbert Broom	police	B	hb	(6)	F. Hurt
1960	Sgt. Caleb Cluff	police	B	hb	11	G. North
1960	Insp. Paul Grainger	police	B	hb	5	Fiona Sinclair
1960	Matt Helm	spy	A	pb	18+	D. Hamilton
1960	Lt. Luis Mendoza	police	A	hb	31+	Dell Shannon
1960	Commander Esmonde Shaw	spy	B	hb	15+	P. McCutchan
1960	Dorian Silk	spy	B	hb	(12)	S. Harvester
1960	Giff Speer	police	A	pb	9	D. Tracy
1961	Supt. Bradley	police	B	pb	6	Colin Robertson
1961	Stephen Dain	police	A	pb	5	R. Sheckley
1961	David Danning	private	A	hb	8	D. von Elsner
1961	Jesse Falkenstein	private	A	hb	10+	L. Egan
1961	Adam Flute	private	B	hb	6	D. Launay
1961	Paul Harris	amateur	B	hb	13+	G. Black
1961	Hoeffler & Harrigan	spy	A	pb	7	P. O'Malley
1961	Rick Holman	private	B	pb	(37)+	Carter Brown
1961	Mark Preston	private	B	hb	24+	Peter Chambers
1961	Dale Shand	private	B	hb	(11)+	D. Enefer
1961	George Smiley	spy	B	hb	7+	J. LeCarre
1961	John Putnam Thatcher	amateur	A	hb	17+	Emma Lathen
1961	Vic Varallo	police	A	hb	11+	L. Egan
1962	Pierre Chambrun	amateur	A	hb	15+	H. Pentecost
1962	Paul Chavasse	spy	B	hb	6	M. Fallon
1962	Supt. Adam Dalgliesh	police	B	hb	7+	P. D. James
1962	Charmian Daniels	police	B	hb	(7)	Jennie Melville
1962	Capt. Jose da Silva	police	A	hb	10	R. L. Fish
1962	Earl Drake	criminal	A	pb	12	D. J. Marlowe
1962	Ian Firth	private	B	hb	(6)	Ludovic Peters
1962	Mr. Holmes	spy	B	hb	7	C. V. Bark
1962	Adam Ludlow	amateur	B	hb	5	S. Nash
(1962)	Slade McGinty	private	B	hb	(5)	J. Pendower
1962	Antony Maitland	private	B	hb	31+	Sara Woods
1962	Nameless ("Harry Palmer" in films)	spy	B	hb	7+	L. Deighton
1962	Parker	criminal	A	pb	16	R. Stark
1962	Claude Ravel	spy	B	hb	(9)	Bradshaw Jones
1962	Bernard Simmons	police	A	hb	7	F. Lockridge R. Lockridge
1962	Insp. Joshua Smarles	police	B	hb	8	M. Urquhard
1962	Insp. Van der Valk	police	B	hb	10	N. Freeling
1962	Steve Wayne	private	B	hb	(9)	T. Harknett
1963	Larry Baker	amateur	B	hb	(6)+	Carter Brown
1963	Lt. Lee Barcello	police	A	hb	6	S. Ransome
1963	Jan Darzek		A	hb	5+	L. Biggle
1963	Hubert de la Bath		F	pb	(15)	J. Bruce
1963	Brock Devlin	private	B	hb	(12)	Scott Mitchell
(1963)	Supt. Frank Drury	police	B	hb	(5)	P. Marlowe
1963	Joe Gall	spy	A	pb	23	J. A. Phillips P. Atlee
1963	Bart Gould	spy	A	pb	8	Joseph Hilton J. Milton
1963	David Grant	spy	B	hb	10	G. Mair
1963	Insp. George Judd	police	B	hb	5	E. Bruton
1963	Simon Larren	spy	B	hb	(10)+	R. Charles
1963	Insp. Marcus MacLurg	police	B	hb	(5)	R. Petrie
1963	James Packard	spy	B	hb	12	R. C. Galway
1963	Supt. Donald Reamer	police	B	hb	13	W. M. Duncan
1964	Insp. Salvador Borges	police	B	hb	5	J. Bonett
1964	Webb Carrick	police	B	hb	11+	B. Knox

Year	Character	Type	Country	Book Type	Number of Books	Author
1964	Jimmy Carroll		B	hb	(5)	H. McCutcheon
1964	Nick Carter	spy	A	pb	143+	Nick Carter
1964	Bart Condor	private	B	hb	(6)	W. Wright
1964	Talos Cord	spy	B	hb	6	Robert MacLeod
1964	Insp. Wilfred Dover	police	B	hb	10+	J. Porter
1964	Kate Fansler	amateur	A	hb	5+	A. Cross
1964	Insp. Ganesh Ghote	police	B	hb	11+	H. R. F. Keating
1964	Alan Grofield	criminal	A	pb	7	R. Stark
1964	Gregory Hiller	spy	A	pb	5	J. Laflin
1964	Charles Hood	spy	B	hb	(6)	J. Mayo
1964	John Keith	spy	A	pb	8	N. Daniels
1964	Dr. Jason Love	spy	B	hb	8+	J. Leasor
1964	Travis McGee	adventurer	A	pb	18+	John D. MacDonald
1964	Sgt. Ivor Maddox	police	A	hb	10+	E. Linington
1964	Insp. Trevor Nicholls	police	B	hb	7	G. Peters
1964	Boysie Oakes	spy	B	hb	9	J. Gardner
1964	Nicholas Pym		B	hb	5	John Sanders
1964	Richard Quintain	spy	B	pb	(16)	W. A. Ballinger W. H. Baker
1964	Bill Rice		B	hb	(8)	M. Stand
1964	Rabbi David Small	amateur	A	hb	7+	H. Kemelman
1964	Curt Stone		A	hb	5	J. Seward
1964	Peter Styles	amateur	A	hb	16+	J. Philips
1964	Insp. Reg Wexford	police	B	hb	11+	R. Rendell
1965	Modesty Blaise	spy	B	hb	12+	P. O'Donnell
1965	Dr. Emmanuel Cellini	amateur	B	hb	11	Michael Halliday
1965	John Gail	spy	B	hb	(5)	S. Frances
1965	Joaquin Hawks	spy	A	pb	5	B. S. Ballinger
1965	Paul Hedley	amateur	B	hb	6	B. Healey
(1965)	Mark Hood	spy	B	pb	(13)	James Dark
1965	Insp. Bill Houghton	police	B	hb	5	M. Culpan
1965	Insp. Harry James	police	B	hb	9	K. Giles
1965	John Jericho	amateur	A	hb	6	H. Pentecost
1965	Quiller	spy	B	hb	9+	Adam Hall
1965	Kelly Robinson & Alexander Scott	spy	A	pb	7	J. Tiger
1965	Maxwell Smart	spy	A	pb	9	W. Johnston
1965	Napoleon Solo	spy	A	pb	22	various hands
1965	Virgil Tibbs	police	A	hb	6+	J. Ball
1965	Dick Van Loan	adventurer	A	pb	22	R. Wallace
1965	Peter Ward	spy	A	pb	10	D. St. John
(1966)	Jonathan Blake		B	hb	(33)+	J. N. Chance
1966	Mike Brooks	spy	B	hb	5	H. T. Rothwell
1966	James Christopher	spy	A	pb	11	Curtis Steele
1966	Barnabas Collins	amateur	A	pb	32	Marilyn Ross
1966	Tim Corrigan	police	A	hb	6	E. Queen
1966	Jules de Grandin	private	A	hb	7	Seabury Quinn
1966	Mike Faraday	private	B	hb	30+	B. Copper
1966	Haggai Godin	spy	B	hb	6	O. John
1966	Insp. Hallan	police	B	hb	(11)+	George Douglas
1966	Timothy Herring	amateur	B	hb	6	M. Torrie
1966	Phil Kramer	private	A	hb	5	P. Kruger
1966	Pete McGrath	private	A	pb	10	Michael Brett
1966	Jim Piron	private	B	hb	9	E. McGirr
1966	Emily Polifax	amateur	A	hb	5	D. Gilman
(1966)	Supt. Charles Ripley	police	B	hb	(6)+	J. Wainwright
1966	Secret Agent X	spy	A	pb	8	B. House
1966	Knute Severson	police	A	hb	15	Tobias Wells
1966	Insp. Christopher Dennis Sloan	police	B	hb	9+	C. Aird
1966	Evan Tanner	spy	A	pb	7	Lawrence Block
1966	Mitch Tobin	amateur	A	hb	5	T. Coe
1966	Jonas Wilde	spy	B	hb	9	A. York
1966	Giles Yoeman	spy	B	hb	5	M. Woodhouse
1967	Martin Beck	police	S	hb	10	M. Sjowall
1967	Dave Cannon	amateur	A	hb	5	M. Delving
1967	Carnaby		B	hb	(10)+	P. N. Walker
1967	Dr. Davie	amateur	B	hb	5	V. C. Clinton-Baddeley
1967	Supt. Folly	police	B	hb	6	J. York
1967	Dan Fortune	private	A	hb	10+	Michael Collins
1967	Insp. Matthew Furnival	police	B	hb	(5)	Stella Phillips
1967	Insp. Robert Fusil	police	B	hb	11+	P. Alding
1967	Dr. Paul Holton	amateur	A	pb	6	Charlotte Hunt
1967	Paul Muller	private	B	hb	15	P. Muller
1967	Insp. Tom Pollard	police	B	hb	11+	E. Lemarchand
1967	Sgt. Bob Reed	police	B	hb	5	C. Drummond
1967	San Antonio	police	F	pb	10	San Antonio
1968	Insp. Anders	police	B	hb	13	H. Jobson
1968	Insp. William Aveyard	police	B	hb	9+	James Fraser
1968	Sam Bawtry		B	hb	(9)+	D. Enefer
1968	Tommy Briggs		B	hb	6	D. MacDonald
1968	Angel Brown		B	hb	13	G. Montrose
1968	James Dingle & Glyn Jones		B	hb	(5)	G. Osborne
1968	James Hellier		B	hb	(6)	M. Cronin
1968	Kane Jackson	private	A	hb	5	W. Arden
1968	Johnson Johnson	amateur	B	hb	5+	D. Halliday
1968	Insp. Simon Kenworthy	police	B	hb	6+	J. B. Hilton
1968	Supt. James Pibble	police	B	hb	6+	P. Dickinson
1968	Pete Riley	private	B	hb	(5)	P. Quinn
1968	Insp. George Rogers	police	B	hb	8+	Jonathan Ross
1968	Ben Safford	amateur	A	hb	6+	R. B. Dominic
1968	Mark Savage	spy	B	hb	5	M. Eden
1968	Matt Savage		B	hb	(6)	Craig Cooper
1968	Miss Emily Seeton	amateur	B	hb	5	H. Carvic
1968	Phil Sherman	spy	A	pb	21	Don Smith
1968	Supt. Charles Wycliffe	police	B	hb	9+	W. J. Burley
1969	Steve Austin	spy	A	hb	5	M. Caidin
1969	Mack Bolan	adventurer	A	pb	38+	D. Pendleton Jim Peterson
1969	Cabot Caine	adventurer	A	pb	5	A. Caillou
1969	Bill Cartwright	spy	A	pb	10	P. Morgan
1969	Peter Craig	spy	B	hb	6+	Kenneth Benton
1969	Insp. Crow	police	B	hb	8	Roy Lewis
1969	Paul Decker		B	hb	6	G. Hackforth-Jones

Year	Character	Type	Country	Book Type	Number of Books	Author
1969	G-8	spy	A	pb	8	R. J. Hogan
1969	Lt. Frank Hastings	police	A	hb	11+	C. Wilcox
1969	Insp. George Masters	police	B	hb	13+	Douglas Clark
1969	Jennifer Norrington, Alessandro Di Ganzarello, Coleridge Tucker	adventurer	B	hb	9+	Ivor Drummond
1969	Philip St. Ives	private	A	hb	5+	O. Bleeck
1969	Kate Theobald		B	hb	(6)	Lionel Black
1969	Richard Wentworth	adventurer	A	pb	11	R. T. M. Scott / G. Stockbridge
1960	Dr. David Audley	spy	B	hb	9+	A. Price
1970	Dave Brandstetter	private	A	hb	5+	J. Hansen
1970	Butcher	police	A	pb	29+	S. Jason
1970	Sgt. Cribb	police	B	hb	8+	P. Lovesey
1970	Tessa Crichton	amateur	B	hb	14+	A. Morice
1970	Supt. Andrew Dalziel	police	B	hb	6+	Reginald Hill
1970	Marcus Aurelius Farrow	spy	B	hb	13+	Angus Ross
1970	Jonathan Gaunt	police	B	hb	6+	Robert MacLeod
1970	Patrick Grant	amateur	B	hb	6	M. Yorke
1970	Malko Linge	spy	F	pb	15	G. de Villiers
1970	Sgt. Robert Mather	police	B	hb	9+	B. Graeme
1970	Constance Morrison-Burke	amateur	B	hb	5+	J. Porter
1970	Max Roper	private	A	hb	7+	K. Platt
1970	Spider Scott	criminal	B	hb	5	K. Royce
1970	John Shaft	private	A	hb	7	E. Tidyman
1970	Tiger Shark	spy	A	pb	11	K. Stanton
1970	Richard Abraham Spade	adventurer	A	pb	5	B. B. Johnson
1971	Insp. Finch	police	B	hb	7+	J. Thomson
1971	Lt. Kramer	police	B	hb	6+	J. McClure
1971	"Nameless"	private	A	hb	7+	B. Pronzini
1971	Julian Quist	amateur	A	hb	10+	H. Pentecost
1971	Donald Robak	private	A	hb	5+	J. L. Hensley
1971	Albert Samson	private	A	hb	5+	M. Z. Lewin
1971	Kitty Telfair	amateur	A	pb	6	F. Stevenson
1971	Matthew Tobin	adventurer	A	pb	7	A. Caillou
1971	Remo Williams	police	A	pb	41+	R. Sapir / W. B. Murphy
1972	Lee Beckett	private	A	hb	6+	J. Crowe
1972	Dick Benson	adventurer	A	pb	36	K. Robeson
1972	Edmund Blackstone	police	B	hb	6	R. Falkirk
1972	Richard Camellion	spy	A	pb	42+	J. Rosenberger
1972	Lt. Jacob Horowitz	police	A	hb	5+	D. Delman
1972	Johnny Morini	adventurer	A	pb	5	Al Conroy
1972	Philis	spy	B	hb	10+	Ritchie Perry
1973	Supt. Charles Barlow	police	B	hb	6+	Elwyn Jones
1973	Major Peter Blair	police	B	hb	7+	J. R. L. Anderson
1973	Simon Bognor	police	B	hb	5+	T. Heald
1973	John Bolt	police	A	pb	9	R. Hawkes
1973	Jefferson Boone	adventurer	A	hb	6	J. Messmann
1973	Dakota	private	A	pb	5	G. Ralston
1973	John Eagle	spy	A	pb	14	Paul Edwards
1973	Mark Hardin	adventurer	A	pb	39+	L. Derrick
1973	Alex Jason	adventurer	A	pb	5	A. Sugar
1973	Deputy Marshal Sam McCloud	police	A	pb	6	C. Wilcox / David Wilson
1973	Mace	adventurer	A	pb	8	L. Chang / C. K. Fong
1973	Philip Magellan	adventurer	A	pb	22	F. Scarpetta / P. McCurtin
1973	Ben Martin	adventurer	A	pb	6	J. Messmann
1973	Norah Mulcahaney	police	A	pb	5+	L. O'Donnell
1973	Melinda Pink	amateur	B	hb	5+	G. Moffat
1973	Jeff Pride		A	pb	5+	A. O'Neill / J. Heneghan
1973	Ed Razoni & William Jackson	police	A	pb	6	W. B. Murphy
1973	Johnny Rock	adventurer	A	pb	16	B. Rossi
1973	John Stark	adventurer	B	pb	12	J. Hedges
1973	Burt Wulff	adventurer	A	pb	14	M. Barry
1974	Insp. Alvarez	police	B	hb	5+	R. Jeffries
1974	Jacob Ashe	private	A	hb	5+	A. Lyons
1974	Jake Brand	adventurer	A	pb	5	R. L. Brent
1974	Henri Castang	police	B	hb	5+	N. Freeling
1974	Jim Hardman	private	A	pb	12	Ralph Dennis
1974	Francis Xavier Killy	spy	A	pb	6	Simon Quinn
1974	Lt. Kojak	police	A	pb	9	V. B. Miller
(1974)	Insp. Lennox	police	B	hb	(6)+	J. Wainwright
1974	David Mallin	private	B	hb	(13)+	R. Ormerod
1974	John Raven	police	B	hb	7+	D. MacKenzie
1974	Mike Ross	private	A	pb	7	K. Carr
1974	Sgt. Joe Ryker	police	A	pb	8	N. DeMille / E. T. Hamill
1974	Britt St. Vincent		A	pb	5	J. F. Rossmann / I. Ross
1974	Supt. Simon Shard	police	B	hb	5+	P. McCutchan
1974	Spenser	private	A	hb	6+	Robert B. Parker
1974	Taggart	spy	A	pb	6	R. Hayes
1974	Sgt. William Verity	police	B	hb	5+	F. Selwyn
1974	Henry Highland West		A	pb	7	J. Nazel
1975	Huntington Cage	private	A	hb	6	A. Riefe
1975	Supt. Merlin Capricorn	police	B	hb	5+	P. G. Winslow
1975	Alexander Chane	adventurer	A	pb	5	R. Hayes
1975	Grijpstra & DeGier	police	A	hb	7+	J. Van de Wetering
1975	Patrick Hardy		A	pb	5	Martin Meyers
1975	Turlock Loams	private	A	hb	9	J. Ruyle
1975	Joseph Madden	adventurer	A	pb	6	V. J. Santiago
1975	Dr. Quarshie	amateur	A	hb	7+	J. Wyllie
1975	Charles Paris	amateur	B	hb	6+	Simon Brett
1975	Insp. Harry Peiffer	police	B	hb	5+	W. Marshall
1975	Jack Regan	police	B	hb	10+	I. R. Martin / J. Balham
1975	Max Roth	spy	B	pb	(9)+	H. Arvay
1975	John Yard	adventurer	A	pb	5	R. Hayes
1976	Jim Rainey	adventurer	A	pb	9	P. McCurtin
1976	Richard Raven		B	hb	10+	J. Griffin

Year	Character	Type	Country	Book Type	Number of Books	Author
1976	Starsky & Hutch	police	A	pb	8	M. Franklin
1976	Janine West	amateur	A	pb	5	E. Welles
1977	Charlie's Angels	private	A	pb	5	M. Franklin
1977	Father Roger Dowling	amateur	A	hb	5+	R. McInerny
1977	Toby Peters	private	A	hb	5+	S. M. Kaminsky
1978	Tory Baxter	amateur	A	pb	8	M. Blair
1978	Dr. Russell V. Childers	private	A	pb	7+	J. Sherman
1978	Maxine Reynolds	amateur	A	pb	7	M. Grove
1978	Terry Spring	amateur	A	pb	6	J. Kains

[1] Many later authors used this character for novels, as well as for plays, usually adapted from Doyle's stories; these later volumes are not included in this count. See the Series Index.

JUL 2 4 1987